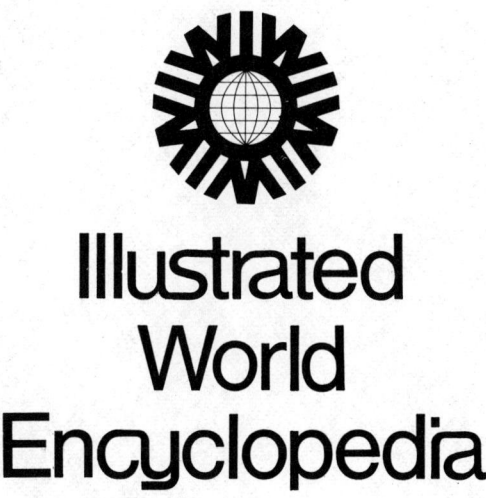

Illustrated
World
Encyclopedia

Illustrated World Encyclopedia

ONE VOLUME EDITION

Bobley Publishing Corp.

WOODBURY, NEW YORK

editorial staff

EDWARD BOBLEY   *Editorial Director Emeritus*

ROGER BOBLEY   *Editor-in-Chief*

NEAL LEVIN   *Director of Art and Production*

DORIS MILLSPAUGH   *Associate Editor*

ELAINE VIDERS   *Editorial Assistant*

WILLIAM S. KONECKY   *Production Adviser*

A Few Facts About Format

All entries in this encyclopedia are arranged alphabetically. Headings are set in bold-face type, and those for certain of the more important, longer, or often-looked-for entries (such as those for states and countries) are larger than the others. Cross-references appear in capital letters. The guide word at the top outside corner of each left-hand page indicates the first entry that begins on that page; the guide word at the top outside corner of each right-hand page indicates the last entry that starts on that page. At the back of the book are a pronunciation guide to difficult proper nouns found throughout the encyclopedia, and an eight-page atlas section containing political maps of the world.

preface

Over the course of nearly a quarter century now, millions of Americans have consulted the pages of *Illustrated World Encyclopedia* to answer the questions that continually arise during the normal course of events at school, at work, and in the home of every enlightened family. How old was Abraham Lincoln when he died? Who was Ajax the Greater? Are tigers larger than lions? What is a liberal? Who fought whom in World War I? How many Popes have been named Paul? On what date did Neil Armstrong first step onto the moon? Exactly how are fossils formed? . . . These are just a tiny fraction of the thousands upon thousands of intriguing subjects covered in this reference work.

Until now, however, *Illustrated World Encyclopedia* was, like most fine encyclopedias, available only in large, multi-volume editions. But, by eliminating all but the best and most important illustrations and by making certain other changes in format, this remarkable one-volume edition was made possible. In fact, for the very first time, virtually the entire encyclopedic content of a well-known, 6,720-page, 21-volume encyclopedia has been re-published in a single 1,600-page volume.

The great advantages and conveniences of being able to obtain from a single volume what previously had been housed in twenty-one, are quite obvious: the very affordable price . . . the extraordinary portability . . . the great reduction in required shelf space . . . the elimination of having to search for the appropriate volume. Yet, practically all the factual reference material you and your family will ever need can be found between the covers of this carefully cross-referenced one-volume compilation of over 7,300 articles on 15,000 subjects.

Illustrated with 2,000 pictures, photographs, diagrams, drawings, tables, charts, and spot maps, the encyclopedia also contains an alphabetical pronunciation guide that lists 4,650 names used in the text that the reader may have difficulty in pronouncing correctly, and that instantly and easily indicates the correct pronunciation for those who don't know how to use diacritical marks. And, there's even an eight-page atlas – a graphic presentation of the entire world in maps.

This wonderful new one-volume edition of *Illustrated World Encyclopedia* is indeed proof that a substantial encyclopedia need no longer warrant the huge investment usually associated with such an all-encompassing reference work. We believe it will prove to be a significant contribution to reference book publishing, and will serve the American public well.

The Editors
and Publishers

contributors and consultants

CHARLES J. ADAMEC
Chairman, Department of Classics
Knox College

ERNEST K. AKAMINE
Plant Physiologist
University of Hawaii

JOHN G. ALBRIGHT
Professor and Head (Ret.),
Department of Physics
University of Rhode Island

DAVID A. BAERREIS
Professor of Anthropology
University of Wisconsin

ROBERT L. BAILEY
Professor of Poultry Husbandry
A & T College, North Carolina

Col. RUSSELL J. BALDWIN, U.S.A.
Ret.
Former Chief of Engineering Division
Ordnance Procurement Center

ROBERT BALZER
President
Balzer's, Los Angeles

Capt. R. S. BARNABY, U.S.N. Ret.
Chief, Aeronautics Section
Franklin Institute, Philadelphia

Dom WILFRID BAYNE
The Priory, Portsmouth, R.I.

NICHOLAS BELA
Water Polo Coach
New York Athletic Club

ARTHUR C. BERDAHL
Chairman, Department of Music
Fresno State College

E. L. BOWSHER
Superintendent of Schools
Toledo Board of Education

WALTER C. BURKHART
Professor of Bacteriology
University of Georgia

MALCOLM E. CAMPBELL
Dean, School of Textiles
North Carolina State College

RICHARD LEE CAYLOR
Professor of Biology
Delta State College

PAUL JONES CHAPMAN
Head, Division of Entomology
New York State
Agriculture Experiment Station
Cornell University

LOUIS S. CHASE, M.D.
Assistant Professor of Psychiatry
Tufts Medical School

TEMA SHULTS CLARE
Assistant Professor of Botany
University of Southern California

JOHN D. CLARK
Foote Mineral Company
Philadelphia

WILLIAM E. COLE
Head, Department of Sociology
University of Tennessee

GEORGE ARTHUR CRABB, Jr.
Supervisor, Michigan Hydrological
Research Station
U.S. Department of Agriculture

EDWARD B. DANSON
Assistant Professor of Anthropology
University of Arizona

BERNARD DAVIS
Director, National Philatelic Museum
Philadelphia

DAVID L. DEJARNETTE
Archaeological Museum,
Mound State Monument, Alabama

Baron ROBERT De NEXON
President,
Chanel International, Paris

SIGISMOND deR. DIETTRICH
Head, Department of Geography
University of Florida

Capt. JAMES B. DONNELLY, U.S.N.
Ret.
Research Institute
Temple University

ELLSWORTH C. DOUGHERTY, M.D.
Lecturer in Physiology
University of California

WILLIAM E. EKMAN
Professor of Mathematics
and Astronomy
University of South Dakota

WILLARD H. ELLER
Professor and Chairman,
Department of Physics
University of Hawaii

JOHN B. ENTRIKIN
Head, Department of Chemistry
Centenary College

MARSHALL W. FISHWICK
Associate Professor of American
Studies
Washington and Lee University

The Rev. PATRICK J. FLYNN, C.S.P.
Paulist Information Center
New York City

JOHN MILTON FOGG, Jr.
Professor of Botany and
Vice-President
University of Pennsylvania

LAWRENCE FREEMAN
Professor of Business
Communication
University of Oklahoma

PERCIVAL GOODMAN
Architect

R. A. GRAY
Secretary of State, Florida

ROBERT S. GRIFFIN
Professor of English
University of Nevada

FOSTER E. GROSSNICKLE
Professor of Mathematics
New Jersey State Teachers College

Gen. ALFRED M. GRUENTHER,
U.S.A. Ret.
President, American Red Cross

CHESTER HALE
The Chester Hale School of Ballet

DONALD J. HART
Dean, School of Business
Administration
University of Idaho

JAMES J. HAYES
Director of General Education,
Professor of English
Oklahoma City University

LORETTA E. HEIDGERKEN, R.N.
Professor of Nursing Education
The Catholic University of America

FRANCES HEINTZ
Assistant Professor of
Home Economics
Wayne University

LOREN R. HEIPLE
Head, Department of Civil
Engineering
University of Arkansas

JOSEPH R. HENDERSON
Chairman, Division of Social Science
Union College

PAUL HENLE
Professor and Chairman
Department of Philosophy
University of Michigan

JOHN G. HERNDON
Professor of Public Finance
Haverford College

CARLETON P. HODGE
Foreign Service Institute

JOSEPH W. HOLLEY
Assistant Chancellor
University System of Georgia

W. HAVRE HOLLINS
Director, Printing and Journalism
*Alabama Agricultural
and Mechanical College*

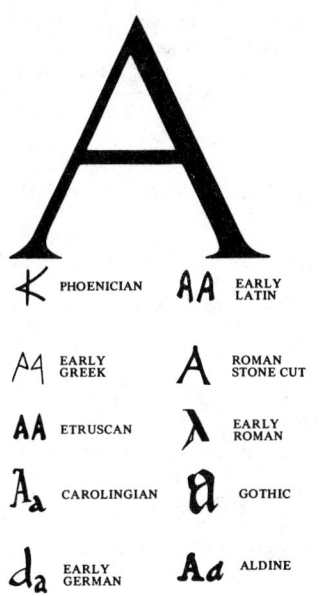

𐤊 PHOENICIAN	**AA** EARLY LATIN		
A4 EARLY GREEK	**A** ROMAN STONE CUT		
AA ETRUSCAN	**λ** EARLY ROMAN		
A𝑎 CAROLINGIAN	**𝕒** GOTHIC		
𝑑𝑎 EARLY GERMAN	**A𝑎** ALDINE		

A𝑎 RENAISSANCE

A or a

A or a is the first letter of the English alphabet. Our first bit of "learning" is our ABC's, so it might be said that the first thing we learn is the letter A. Originally this letter, like most other letters, was a picture. When men first invented writing, more than five thousand years ago, they wrote their words in pictures instead of letters. The letter A may have started as a picture of an eagle.

An alphabet of letters and not pictures was used by the ancient Phoenicians, more than a thousand years before Jesus was born. In their language the word for ox was *aleph* and it was represented by a letter that looks like this: ≮ . A few hundred years later the Greeks began to use the Phoenician alphabet, but they turned the letters around and that made the letter A look more like the way it looks today.

Our capital A came to us from the Romans. The small a, and the small *a* that is used in handwriting, were developed later. They are easier for handwriting because a writer does not have to lift his pen from the paper to make separate lines, as he would for the capital A.

Originally, the letter A was pronounced as in *far* or *father*—what we call the "broad a," or "Italian a." It is very fitting that this should be the first letter in our alphabet, for it is as natural a sound as a human being can make. It is the sound that comes out when we simply open our mouths and make a sound. To make any other sound we have to change the position of the mouth or lips or tongue. In most European languages, the letter A is most often pronounced as in *father*, and British people pronounce it that way far more often than Americans do.

In our English language, the letter A can be pronounced in several different ways. We call it the "long a" in a word like *blade* and the "short a" in a word like *man*. Still another A sound is heard in the word *fall* or *water*. In *fare*, the *a*

has a sound very much like that of *e* in *there*. In *alone* it is much more of an "uh" sound. In *was* and many other words it is not pronounced the same by all speakers of English and some pronounce it as "u." In *war* it is often pronounced as though it were "o."

Aa

Almost anywhere you look on a map of Europe, you are likely to see a river called "the Aa." There are forty rivers in Europe with this name. Most of them are small, and none is very important. They got their name from the old language spoken by the Germanic peoples thousands of years ago, in which the sound "aa" (like the sound you use for a sheep's baa, but without the *b*) meant "flowing water." Near two rivers named Aa, both of them in Latvia (a part of Russia then, and now ruled by Soviet Russia), there were battles between German and Russian armies in 1917, during World War I.

Aachen

Aachen is an important city in West Germany. It has a population of about 242,000, which makes it a little bigger than New Haven, Connecticut, and there are many factories there, but mostly Aachen is important because of the part it has played in history. The ancient Romans built the first town there. The great emperor Charlemagne was born there. Beginning more than a thousand years ago, and for hundreds of years after that (until the year 1531), the coronations of the emperors of the Holy Roman Empire (the great realm of the German states in Europe) were held in the chapel of Aachen's famous castle. Much of this castle, and of the beautiful cathedral beside it, was destroyed in World War II, when Aachen was severely damaged by bombs.

The French call the city Aix-la-Chapelle (which means "springs at the chapel") because there are fine springs there and because of the famous chapel. For a few years, from 1801 to 1814, the city belonged to France. The treaties ending two wars were signed here, and there is a separate article about them.

AACHEN. Population, 242,000. Location, North Rhine-Westphalia province, West Germany.

aardvark

The aardvark is an animal that lives in South Africa and lives by eating ants. It is also called an *anteater;* but the Dutch-speaking settlers of South Africa called it aardvark (which in Dutch means "earth pig") because it looks like a small, ugly pig, though its ears and tail are longer than a pig's. The aardvark's long snout can be poked deep into anthills, and its long tongue is so sticky that the ants stick to it and very few escape. In South Africa the aardvark is considered good to eat and is hunted for its meat.

aardwolf

The aardwolf is a small animal, about the size of a fox, which is found in South Africa. Its name means "earth wolf," and it burrows in the ground. The

aardwolf is related to the African hyena, and like the hyena it is a very timid animal. It hides during the day but ventures out at night in search of food. It eats other small animals and white ants. It is called also *maned jackal* and *earth wolf*.

Aaron

Aaron was the first High Priest of the Jews, and this was so important that for more than a thousand years no one could be a Jewish priest unless he was descended from Aaron. Yet Aaron, like many important men, had earlier made great mistakes and later repented.

As you can read in the Bible, in the Book of Exodus, Aaron was the older brother of Moses, the hero who led the Jewish people out of Egypt where they had been slaves. Moses' speech was slow and hard to understand, so God gave Aaron the task of speaking for him. When Moses went up to the top of Mt. Sinai to receive instructions from God, Aaron made a golden calf and let the people worship it, in defiance of the Ten Commandments. God punished Aaron and the people, but Aaron repented and in time he was forgiven. He married Elisheba, and his son Eleazar became High Priest after him. The mountain on which Aaron died became known as the Mount of Aaron. It is now called Mount Hor.

Aaron belonged to the tribe of Levi, and because of this the descendants of the tribe had special duties and privileges in the Jewish religion. There is a separate article about the LEVITES.

Like other members of his people, Aaron usually carried a staff, which in old times was called a "rod." God had Aaron do several miracles by touching things with this staff, or rod. The name "Aaron's rod" is now given to several flowers, especially a kind of goldenrod, and to some ornaments used in buildings.

abacus

The abacus is the earliest "adding machine" known to history. It has been used for thousands of years, especially in oriental countries, and it is still much used in China, Japan, and other countries. The colored beads strung on wires on the side of a baby's play pen are an abacus, and nearly everyone has seen one though very few know what it is.

There are several forms of abacus. The one shown in the picture is a Chinese abacus, which they call a *swanpan* or reckoning-board. The beads above the middle bar are called *quints* and count 5 each when pushed down to the bar; the beads below count 1 each when pushed up to the bar. Each wire strung with beads is called a *column* because it represents one column of figures. Suppose the operator of an abacus wants to record the number 7; in the extreme right-hand column he pushes down one upper bead and pushes up two of the lower beads. In the second column from the right these would count 70; in the third column, 700; and so on. The operator actually does the arithmetic in his head, step by step, and records it on the abacus as he goes along, just as we do with pencil and paper (and in fact abacuses

were used in prehistoric times, before men could write), but it is faster with an abacus than with pencil and paper.

Abadan

Abadan is a city on Abadan Island in southwest Iran. It is the oil refining center of the Anglo-Iranian Oil Company. In 1951 Iran nationalized all oil-producing properties in the country; that is, the Iranian government took possession of them. The British population, including all the engineers and technicians of the refineries, withdrew and left virtually the entire city idle. Iran did not have enough trained men to keep the refineries going. In 1954 Iran made an agreement with Anglo-Iranian and seven other foreign oil companies, and the refineries were reopened. Abadan's population is 270,726.

abalone

The abalone is a shellfish that lives in warm, shallow ocean waters. It is found in great quantities along the shores of California and other Pacific states, where it is very popular as food. Unlike oysters and clams, but like the snail, the abalone has only one shell, but this shell is large (several inches long) and very useful, since the inside is "mother-of-pearl" from which buttons and jewelry are made, and the uncut shell may be used as an ashtray, bowl, or ornament. The abalone is often called *ear-shell* or *sea-ears*.

"Abalone hunting" is a popular beach sport with Californians. The hunter puts on artificial webbed feet and dives deep among the rocks, where he cuts the abalone loose from the rocks with a sharp knife; the abalone "steak" is then cooked outdoors. Usually it is first pounded, which makes it more tender. The dried flesh of the abalone is considered fine food in the Far East.

Abbas and the Abbassides

Abbas was a wealthy merchant of Mecca, in Arabia, and uncle of Mohammed. At first he was against Mohammed, but later he was converted to Mohammed's religion and was one of its chief apostles after Mohammed's death. Abbas was born about 566 and died in 652. The Abbassides, or Abbassids, were a family of Mohammedan rulers of the Saracen empire, from the year 750 to 1258, because they were related to Abbas and Mohammed. Abbassid caliphs (rulers) fostered the arts and sciences, and the splendor of their courts, especially those of Harunal-Rashid (786–809), and Al-Mamun (813–833), stands out against the crude courts of the European sovereigns of the time.

Abbey, Edwin Austin

Edwin Austin Abbey was one of the principal American painters of the last hundred years. He was born in Philadelphia in 1852. Every year thousands of persons visit the Boston Public Library to see his most famous work, "The Quest of the Holy Grail," a huge painting in 15 sections. He is one of three

Americans who have been commissioned to paint the coronation of an English king—"the crowning of Edward VII" in 1901. He died in 1911.

abbey

An abbey is the home, including all the grounds and buildings, of a community of men or women who have devoted themselves to a religious life, not as priests or ministers but as monks or nuns. The head of such a community is called an *abbot* if a man, or an *abbess* if a woman. The abbey usually includes a building built around a large courtyard called a cloister. In this building the monks or nuns have their tiny rooms, called cells, in which they live, study, work, and pray. There is also a church or chapel in which religious services are held. Westminster Abbey in London, the famous church where the kings and queens of England are crowned, used to be part of such a religious community.

Other religious faiths have abbeys, but the most famous ones are Christian.

In the Roman Catholic Church, the abbey is sometimes a monastery or convent whose director, the abbot or abbess, is responsible directly to the Pope and not to an intermediary bishop. The first such abbey was founded by St. Benedict, about the year 529, and within a thousand years of that time there were nearly 1,000 abbeys in Europe and other Christian countries. The number has steadily diminished since, so that in 1950 there were not two hundred in the world.

The abbey had its own farmlands (worked wholly or partly by the community); buildings that included church, library, infirmary, kitchens, laundries, workshops, dormitories for the community and guests (the abbey was the hotel of medieval Europe); and a cemetery. Throughout the Dark Ages, Christianity, scholarship and art were pre-

British Railways

ABBEYS

The abbey of this cathedral in Wales once owned thousands of acres of land. Drawing at right shows what is inside the walls. The big building, with the nave, choir, and tower, is the cathedral. Each cellarium is a storeroom. The monks have little cells, or rooms, in which they live. In the chapel they worship and pray. The refectory is a large dining hall. The abbot has a private apartment and offices. The open space in the center is surrounded by cloisters, or covered walks. See picture below.

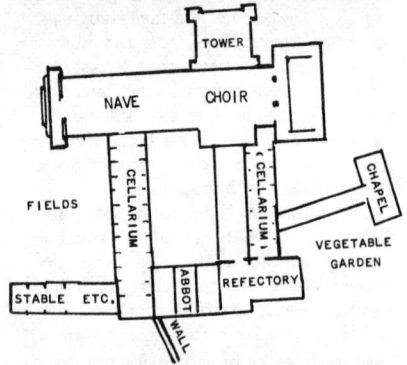

Spanish Tourist Bureau

British Railways

The city of Bath in southwestern England is the site of Bath Abbey. Construction of the abbey was begun at the end of the 15th century.

served only in the abbeys, chiefly Benedictine. The Cluniac, Cistercian and Carthusian Orders, in France, Burgundy, and Britain, also established many abbeys. The abbots became equal to the most powerful noblemen.

Many famous churches, such as Westminster Abbey, were once part of abbeys, and estates such as Newstead Abbey, home of Lord Byron, were abbatial dwellings.

Read also CONVENT and MONASTERY.

Abbey Theatre

The Abbey Theatre was a theater in Dublin, Ireland. Though there was constant bickering over its policies, it had great influence on modern drama. The Abbey Theatre produced regional, poetic and literary plays by William Butler Yeats, J. M. Synge, Lady Gregory, Lennox Robinson, Lord Dunsany, Paul Vincent Carroll, Padraic Colum, Sean O'Casey and others, and developed such actors as Dudley Digges, William and Frank Fay, Sara Allgood, Whitford Kane, Orson Wells, J. M. Kerrigan, and Barry Fitzgerald. The theater was destroyed by fire in 1951.

Abbott, Sir John

Sir John Joseph Caldwell Abbott was made prime minister of Canada in 1891. He was born in St. Andrews, Quebec, in 1821 and studied at McGill University, where he was dean of the Law School for ten years. He was considered an authority on commercial law. He died in 1893.

abbreviation

Abbreviation is the shortening of a word to save space and time in writing it. The proper distinction between an abbreviation and a contraction is that an abbreviation should be pronounced as though it were the whole word, for example: *Mr.*; a contraction should be pronounced as spelled, for example *can't.* Many abbreviations have come to be used as nouns or other parts of speech, for example G.I., UNRRA, CBS. It is still considered less than proper to pronounce other abbreviations as spelled, for example *Mass.* for Massachusetts or *Pa.* ("PA") for Pennsylvania. An ab-

breviation should be followed by a period, though some prefer to omit the period when the first and last letters of the abbreviation are respectively the same as those of the full word (as *Mr*).

Titles such as Doctor, Professor, General, etc., should not be abbreviated unless the person's given name or initials are used: For example, "Dear Doctor Jones"; "Dr. John Jones"; Professor Smith"; "Prof. J. G. Smith."

A.B.C. Powers

Argentina, Brazil and Chile, three of the largest South American countries, are usually called the "A.B.C. Powers" when they act together in any international matter. Each is an independent country, of course, and there is no actual political connection between them. In 1914 the three countries were asked to act together in settling a dispute between the United States and Mexico, and they were first called the A.B.C. Powers at that time.

Abd-el-Kader

Abd-el-Kader was an Arab leader in Algeria. He fought against both Turkish and French control of North Africa. He was born in 1807 and became a hero to his people before he was twenty-five years old. Between 1832 and 1847 he fought many battles against the French, but finally he was captured and imprisoned in France. He was released by Napoleon III in 1852 and thereafter made his home in Damascus, where he died in 1883. The name has various spellings, such as *Abd-el-Kadir* and *Abdu-l-Kadir*.

Abd-el-Krim

In North Africa, where for many years most of the people were under the control of European countries, Abd-el-Krim was a leader of his people, the Riffs, and other natives of Morocco. He was born in 1880, led his first revolution in 1920, and was successful until 1925, when French and Spanish armies combined to defeat him. In 1926 he surrendered and was exiled to Réunion, an island in the Indian Ocean owned by France, but in 1947 he escaped and began again to work for North African independence. He retired from active work in 1952 and died in 1963.

abdication

A king is said to abdicate when he signs a paper by which he agrees that he will not be, and will not try to be, king any longer. A king may do this for any number of reasons; some kings have done it because they wanted to devote their lives to religious service, some because they felt they had failed as rulers and wanted their people to have a better king. In the most famous case of our times, Edward VIII of England abdicated (and became the Duke of Windsor) because he could not keep his throne and also marry the woman he wanted to. Nearly always, however, kings abdicate only because they are forced to. In former centuries no man could remain king very long unless the nobles of his country wanted him, and in our age a majority of the whole population must want him.

Abdications have been very numerous in this century. Emperor William II of Germany abdicated after his country lost

World War I; King Alfonso XIII of Spain had to abdicate in 1931 because his people wanted a republic. Often a king abdicates in favor of his son, as did King Carol of Rumania in 1940, King Leopold of Belgium in 1951, and King Farouk of Egypt in 1952. In 1948 a queen, Wilhelmina of the Netherlands, abdicated so that her daughter Juliana could become queen; Wilhelmina did not have to abdicate, because the people of the Netherlands loved her, but being a king or queen is a very hard job, and Queen Wilhelmina, who was old and tired, thought her daughter would be better for the people. There are separate articles on all these kings and queens.

Outstanding abdications of ancient times were those of the Roman dictator Sulla (79 B.C.) and the Roman Emperor Diocletian (A.D. 305). Several popes have abdicated, among them Benedict IX (1048), Celestine V (1294), and Gregory XII (1415). Nearly all abdications have been involuntary, but some rulers have abdicated to become religious recluses, as did the Holy Roman Emperor Charles V in 1558. Napoleon abdicated twice, first in 1814, after which he was exiled to Elba, and the second time in 1815, after his defeat at Waterloo.

abdomen

The abdomen is the front section of the body, between the chest and the hips; it is the part we usually call "the stomach," but actually it includes much more than the stomach. In medical terms, it is the area from the *thorax,* or chest, to the *pelvis,* or place where the body joins the legs. The muscles of the abdomen are thick and heavy, forming a sort of wall to protect the "abdominal cavity" within which lie the liver, kidneys, stomach, bladder, spleen, intestines, and gall bladder. These are described in separate articles and in the article on the HUMAN BODY.

Other animals that, like men, have backbones—they are called *vertebrate* animals—have abdomens like the human one. In creatures of other kinds, the area where the food is digested is called the abdomen. An octopus, for example, has an abdomen in one of its eight tentacles (which we usually call "arms"). So has the starfish. The abdomen of an ant is its large rear section, behind the section on which its legs grow.

Abdominal pain, often called "stomach ache," can be caused by a disorder in any one of the organs located there, or may originate from a troubled chest condition that is relayed by the nervous system. Pain that increases with pressure on the abdomen is often a sign of inflammation of one of the internal tissues. A sudden, very sharp pain that subsides almost immediately may indicate the rupture of an infected organ. Both of these symptoms can lead to very serious consequences unless a physician is consulted at once. The common types of abdominal disturbance—cramps, nausea, "gas pains," and vomiting—may be due to indigestion or to a more serious disorder, such as appendicitis, ulcers, or an obstruction within the digestive tract. It is therefore unwise and may be dangerous to apply self-treatment by the use of

enemas, laxatives, or hot compresses. See also the articles on APPENDICITIS and STOMACH.

Abdul-Hamid

Abdul-Hamid was the name of two sultans of Turkey, both of whom engaged in costly wars with Russia. **Abdul-Hamid I,** who was born in 1725 and died in 1789, became sultan in 1774. Turkey had already lost an important possession, the Crimean Peninsula, in a war against Russia, France, and Great Britain. Abdul-Hamid I wanted to win back what had been lost, so he began the losing war of 1781–91. **Abdul-Hamid II,** who was born in 1842 and died in 1918, was sultan 1876–1909. He lost large territories in a war with Russia in 1877–78. He was notoriously cruel and was charged with responsibility for Turkish massacres in Armenia in the early 1890's. The YOUNG TURKS deposed him in 1909; there is a separate article about them.

Abel

Adam and Eve, the first man and woman, had Cain as their first son and Abel as their second son. Abel was a shepherd. He was also the first man ever to be murdered. In the Bible, chapter 4 of the Book of Genesis, it is told that Abel's offering of lambs pleased the Lord more than Cain's offering of garden produce, and Cain killed Abel in jealous anger.

Abelard

One of the favorite romantic stories of all time is that of Heloise and Abelard. Peter (or, in French, *Pierre*) Abelard was a real person, born in France in the year 1079, nearly 900 years ago. He was a scholar and a schoolteacher, and he fell in love with Heloise when she was his pupil. The uncle of Heloise, named Fulbert, was canon, or head, of the Cathedral of Notre Dame in Paris, a man of great influence; and he did not approve of Abelard. After Abelard and Heloise were secretly married, Fulbert hired a gang of cutthroats to attack Abelard and mutilate him. Thinking himself unfit to remain the husband of Heloise, Abelard retired to the monastery of St. Denis and became a monk. Heloise also sought a religious life, becoming an abbess. They wrote beautiful letters to each other for the rest of their lives, and their names have since been used as an example of love and devotion. Abelard lived on till 1142 and continued to study and write on philosophy. He and Heloise are buried together in Paris.

Abercrombie, James

James Abercrombie (also spelled Abercromby) was a British general in Canada during the French and Indian War. He tried to capture Ticonderoga, but was defeated with great losses by General Montcalm on July 8, 1758. He was succeeded by Jeffrey Amherst in September, and in 1759 he returned to England, where as a Member of Parliament he voted for the anti-American laws that led to the Revolutionary War. He was born in 1706 and died in 1781.

Aberdeen

Aberdeen is the third-largest city in Scotland. It has a population of almost 182,000, making it a little smaller than Austin, Texas. It is an important harbor, located on the North Sea at the mouth of the River Dee. There are fine granite quarries in that section, and Aberdeen is sometimes called "the Granite City" because of its many buildings made of white granite, including famous St. Machar Cathedral. There are also iron foundries, and large herring and salmon fisheries. Aberdeen is the capital of Aberdeen (or Aberdeenshire) County.

ABERDEEN, SCOTLAND. Population 182,000. See SCOTLAND.

Aberdeen, South Dakota, pop. 26,966, is a rail center. **Aberdeen, Washington,** pop. 18,028, is a port city where the Chehalis and Wishkah rivers meet. **Aberdeen, Maryland,** pop. 13,064, is a residential town near Aberdeen Proving Grounds.

Aberdeen Proving Grounds, a U.S. Army installation, is in Hartford County, Maryland, on the west coast of Chesapeake Bay. A post was established there in 1919, and it became the site of the Army's Ordnance School in 1940. The Army uses Aberdeen for the development and testing of new weapons and vehicles, and for training ordnance specialists. It is 18 miles long and 6 miles wide, and it contains four permanent buildings and about 300 temporary structures added during World War II.

aberration

Aberration of light is what seems to be a change in the position of an object, caused not because the object is moving but because the observer is moving. In astronomy, the stars seem not to be in their true position in the heavens, because the earth moves in its orbit during the time it takes light to come from a star to the earth. The effect is that a star seems to move forward with the earth. The rotation of the earth on its axis and the effect of the velocity of light on telescopic observation also contribute to the aberration. This was first explained and accurately measured by an English astronomer, James Bradley, in 1727. Using a star in the constellation Draco, he observed that in March, when the earth is traveling in the direction of the line joining the star to the sun, a telescope must be tilted toward the south to see the star; in September, when the earth is traveling away from this line, the telescope must be tilted toward the north.

In optics, aberration refers to faulty focusing of light. *Spherical aberration* occurs in curved lenses and mirrors, because rays from their centers and rays near their outside edges do not focus at the same point. Unless correction is made by altering the curvature, a fuzzy image results. *Chromatic aberration,* found in lenses but not in mirrors, occurs when a beam of light is dispersed and appears as various colors. This is because different colors have different wave lengths, and so have different angles of refraction. The aberration is corrected by the use of more than one lens. See also ACHROMATISM.

Abidjan

Abidjan is a city in Africa with a population of 247,000. It is the capital of the IVORY COAST, a former French colony, now an independent nation.

Abigail

The story of Abigail is told in the Bible, in the book 1 Samuel, chapter 25. She was a beautiful widow whom David married. David met her when he was pursuing her first husband, Nabal, a wealthy farmer, who had defied him. Abigail delayed David and his party by feeding them, and so protected her husband from David's vengeance. Later, when Nabal died, David sent for Abigail and married her. Because Abigail had called herself David's "handmaid," Beaumont and Fletcher chose the name Abigail for a lady's maid in their play *The Scornful Lady,* and since then a maid has occasionally been called an abigail.

abolitionists

Ever since slavery has been practiced on earth, there have been people who opposed it as a wicked practice and wanted to abolish it. In the United States, in the period from about 1830 until the Civil War ended slavery, those who worked and spoke most vigorously against slavery were called abolitionists. Some were of the North, some of the South. They held meetings, published booklets, made speeches on street corners, and formed political parties to fight slavery. William Lloyd Garrison was one of the most active abolitionists in his writing and speaking; John Brown went even farther and tried to free the slaves by force. The abolitionists were much persecuted. Slave-owners opposed them, of course, and hired ruffians to attack them; but there were many others, who had no strong feelings of their own about slavery, who were violently opposed to abolitionism because they feared it might lead to war. They threw stones at abolitionist speakers, broke up their printing presses, and burned their pamphlets. Eventually the question of slavery did lead to war, and after the Civil War ended there was no further need for an abolitionist movement.

The anti-slavery movement in Amer-

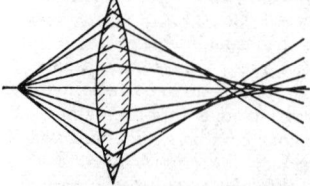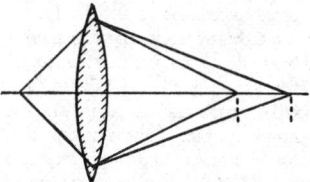

ABERRATION (optical). The diagram on the left shows spherical aberration. Rays passing through the lens at different points focus at different points. At the right, chromatic aberration. Violet rays, being shorter than red rays, will focus at a point before the red rays. A perfect image in either case depends on the rays' focusing at the same point.

ica began publicly when a Society for the Abolition of Slavery was formed in Philadelphia in 1775, with Benjamin Franklin as president and Benjamin Rush as secretary. A New York Manumission Society was formed in 1785 with John Jay as president. Dozens of similar societies were formed in the first half of the 19th century. They agitated for anti-slavery legislation, preached, lectured, and published tracts and papers. *The Appeal*, a newspaper published by Benjamin Lundy in St. Clairsville, Ohio, was the first anti-slavery publication (1816); most famous was *The Liberator*, begun by William Lloyd Garrison in 1831. The Quakers at all times were active supporters of the movement, and many clergymen of other sects, notably Charles G. Finney, preached abolitionism as an essential of Christianity. The abolitionists formed the UNDERGROUND RAILWAY, about which there is a separate article. See also the articles on Harriet Beecher STOWE, and FREESOIL party.

Aboukir

Aboukir is a village in Egypt and also the name of a bay below the village, where the great river Nile meets the Mediterranean Sea. Here the great British naval hero, Horatio Nelson, defeated a French fleet in 1798 and prevented Napoleon from gaining control of all North Africa for France. This was the famous Battle of the Nile. The present population of Aboukir, sometimes spelled Abukir or Abu Qir, is about 2,000. See NAPOLEONIC WARS and NELSON.

Abraham

Abraham is called "the father of the Jews." It was to him, as told in the Bible (Book of Genesis), that God first revealed Himself and made the covenant (that is, the agreement, or promise) by which the Jews were to become God's chosen people. The Lord also promised the land of Canaan to the descendants of a son of Abraham and his wife Sarah.

The story of Abraham is told in Genesis, chapters 11 to 25. His name originally was Abram, and he was married to Sarai. With Abram's father, Terah, they set out from a great city of ancient times, called Ur of the Chaldees, for the land of Canaan, but stopped at the city of Haran, where Terah died. At the age of 75, on command of God, Abram went into the land of Canaan. He was obviously then a man of great wealth, with hundreds of servants. Abram was the first man to whom God appeared; God had spoken but had not appeared to Adam and to Noah. God promised Abram children, and Abram did have a son named Ishmael, but Sarai was not Ishmael's mother. God then promised Abram a son of whom Sarai would be the mother, and at this time God changed Abram's name to Abraham, meaning "father of much people," and Sarai's name to Sarah, meaning "princess" and "mother of kings." Sarah gave birth to a son, named Isaac, when she was ninety years old and Abraham was ninety-nine.

God then tempted Abraham, com-

manding him to offer the life of his son Isaac as a sacrifice. Abraham took Isaac to the altar, and prepared to kill him in sacrifice, but an angel appeared and told Abraham to spare his son. Abraham found a ram and sacrificed it instead.

After Sarah's death Abraham took another wife, Keturah or Cetura. They had six sons. Various Arab tribes are said to have been descended from these sons and Ishmael; the Israelites were descended from Isaac.

Abraham died at the age of 175. The Bible tells of many other adventures of Abraham. His time was probably about four thousand years ago.

Abraham, Plains of

Just outside the city of Quebec, in Canada, on the top of a hill with steep sides, is a high level field called the Plains of Abraham. Here, in 1759, the English general James Wolfe defeated the French general, the Marquis de Montcalm, in a battle that decided the last of the French and Indian Wars. The result was important to North Americans, because if the battle had gone the other way the language and background of a majority of our people might have been French instead of English. In 1948 the Plains of Abraham became a Canadian National Park, and visitors to Quebec should see it. See FRENCH AND INDIAN WARS.

abrasives

Abrasives are materials used to abrade, which means to rub off. Grinding and polishing are done with abrasives. Grindstones used to sharpen axes, sandpaper used to make wood smooth, scouring powders, steel wool, silver polish, the side of a match box, and even rubber erasers, all contain abrasives.

There are many abrasive materials. Some are very hard, some are much softer. Diamond is the hardest of all, and many diamonds that are not good enough to use in jewelry are used as abrasives. Other abrasives are silicon carbide, a manufactured abrasive; corundum, which includes rubies and sapphires; emery, garnet, sandstone, flint, pumice, and rouge. These are crushed and put through sieves that separate the finer and the coarser grains. The grains may then be mixed with a paste or soap; or baked with clay, as a brick is, to make a grinding wheel; or stuck onto a sheet of paper or cloth with glue, as sandpaper is.

A person who needs an abrasive decides which to use by considering the work it is expected to do. He may select a hard or soft, coarse or fine-grained abrasive to suit this use. Coarse grains are used where a lot of material is to be ground away. Fine grains are used for polishing.

ABRASIVE PROCESS

In grinding, each abrasive grain acts as a chisel, removing a small chip from the surface it passes over. The size of the grain determines the size of the scratch left on the surface; the marks left by very fine grains can be seen only under a microscope, and the surface will seem entirely smooth to the eye. It is not known whether some buffing and polishing operations actually grind the surface or smear it (hammer or smooth it down);

some dull surfaces are smoother by profilometer tests than highly polished surfaces.

Metallic abrasives, in the form of shot and grit, are often used in blasting operations, as in shot-peening springs and other metal parts: They are hurled against the metal surface with such force as to hammer it. Sand-blasting is a similar process.

Sharpening a big lumber saw with an abrasive wheel. It is called "gumming" the saw. The top saw must be sharpened once each day, the bottom saw four times a day.

Carborundum Company

PROPERTIES OF ABRASIVES

Hardness is important, since for example only diamond dust is hard enough to polish a diamond, but an abrasive can be too hard for some soft material such as aluminum. In many cases the abrasive is not so hard as the material it cuts. The abrasive must be brittle enough to break down when dull and expose a new sharp grain to the work. Resistance to heat is important, since the friction of grinding produces high temperatures.

See also HARDNESS, and articles on the several abrasives named above.

Absalom

Absalom was the third son of King David; his story, as told in the Bible (II Samuel), is a great example of the love of a father for his son. Absalom was far from being a good son or a good man. He murdered his brother Amnon. He led a revolt to throw his father off the throne and make himself the king instead. But when David's armies defeated the rebels, and Absalom was killed in the battle, David wept, and cried, "O my son Absalom, my son, my son Absalom! would God I had died for thee, O Absalom, my son, my son!"

Absalom had very long hair. When he had lost the battle he tried to run away, riding a mule; but his hair caught in the branches of a tree and he was stopped long enough for his pursuers to catch up with him. Though David had asked that

the youth be spared, one of David's generals killed him, knowing he would only threaten his father again if he lived.

absenteeism

The word "absenteeism" has two principal meanings.

In the original sense, an absentee is a person who receives his income from one country or place, but lives and spends it in another country or place. In ancient Rome and in powerful countries ever since, noblemen and other rich men have owned vast estates in colonial or subject countries but have lived in the capitals of their own countries. For hundreds of years this caused dissatisfaction in Ireland; as early as 1380, the Irish presented a petition on absenteeism to the English Parliament, and in 1634 the Irish Parliament passed a law fining members of the Irish nobility who lived in England or anywhere else except Ireland. Recently, the word absenteeism has been applied also to the owning (principally through large corporations) of important businesses such as chain stores by those who do not live in the community they serve.

Industrial absenteeism has become costly in mass production, since an assembly line does not operate well unless everyone who has a job to do is there. During World War II, this became a serious problem in the United States. Absenteeism is greatest when there is a labor shortage, with jobs plentiful and wages high. Workers often stay away from work for rest or pleasure. Race tracks in the United States were closed for a period during World War II because of absenteeism from work of so many who attended them. Absenteeism is greater among women than among men, because they are more likely to be affected by home responsibilities. Some industries have set up emergency nursing services for employees who have illness at home, and recreations at their plants, to reduce the amount of absenteeism.

absinthe

Absinthe is a highly intoxicating and dangerous drink. It affects the nerve centers and can produce hallucinations or mental derangement. The importation and sale of absinthe is illegal in the United States, France, Switzerland (where it originated), and other countries. Absinthe is made by steeping wormwood leaves in alcohol, together with anise, angelica, dittany, and other roots and herbs; it is green in color, with a licorice flavor, and its alcoholic content may exceed 70%.

absolute zero

The absence of all heat, however little, is called absolute zero. Of course, everyone is familiar with "zero weather" and knows it is very cold, but there is still a great deal of heat in the air. Otherwise it could not become even colder and fall "below zero." Absolute zero is the stage at which it could not become any colder. On the Fahrenheit thermometer that most of us use, this would be more than 459 degrees below zero! On the centigrade thermometer more often used in science, it is more than 273 degrees

below zero. (The exact figures are: —459.72° F.; —273.16° C.)

As long as there is any heat at all, there is some motion of the tiny molecules that make up all matter. Absolute zero is the point at which all motion ceases. Such coldness can only be imagined; it could never be proved, because the presence of someone near enough to observe it would provide enough heat to raise the temperature. Read also the articles on MOLECULE and TEMPERATURE.

absolution

In the Roman Catholic Church, a priest may give absolution, or forgiveness of sins, after a person has confessed his sins with true sorrow. The words of Christ are used as authority (from John 20:23 in the Bible): "Whose sins you shall forgive, they are forgiven them; and whose sins you shall retain, they are retained." Protestants have generally held absolution not necessary to receiving God's grace.

absorption

When one kind of matter changes its nature and becomes part of another kind of matter, it is said to be absorbed, and the process is called *absorption*. The body absorbs food, or at least absorbs the nourishing part of it; a piece of bread or a dish of spinach actually becomes flesh and blood and bone, this being called *digestive absorption*. A plant absorbs water, and minerals dissolved in water, through its roots; it absorbs carbon dioxide, a gas that is part of the air, through its leaves. These processes are more fully described in the articles on DIGESTION and METABOLISM and PHOTOSYNTHESIS.

A different kind of absorption occurs when wet hands are dried on a towel. The water on the hands is absorbed, or soaked in, by the fibers of which the towel is made, but it does not change its nature. From the towel the water is once again absorbed, this time into the air by the process known as EVAPORATION.

Even light can be absorbed, as is explained in the article on LIGHT, and it is this kind of absorption that makes us see colors. If a material will absorb every color except blue, for instance, then when light shines on it the other colors will be absorbed and the blue will be reflected back into our eyes, becoming the only color we can see. A material that absorbs almost no light looks white to us; a material that absorbs nearly all the light that strikes it looks black.

Heat offers a good example of absorption. When any two things touch, the one that is colder will absorb heat from the one that is warmer—and will keep on absorbing heat until the two things have the same temperature. It does not matter whether it is a solid, a liquid or a gas (the air is a gas) that does the touching. When a pan is put on a fire it absorbs heat from the fire and becomes hot. Any food in the pan then absorbs heat from the pan and "cooks."

A striking example is found in the way ice cream freezes in an old-fashioned ice-cream freezer. At first, the ice cream is a

liquid. It is put into a container surrounded by ice. Salt is put on the ice, forming a salt solution which is colder than ice. Heat from the ice cream is absorbed by the walls of the container which were made cold by the salt solution. This loss of heat results in the ice cream's cooling and hardening. Part of the heat comes from the air around the freezer, but much of the heat comes from the liquid "ice cream" inside the container. In fact, this liquid loses so much heat that it becomes cold enough to freeze, and turns into solid ice cream.

Abu-Bekr

Abu-Bekr, or Abu Bakr, was the first Mohammedan caliph or king and head of the religion. He was born in the year 573 and died in 634. He was Mohammed's only companion when Mohammed fled from his enemies, which was called the Hegira, and became Mohammed's principal apostle. His name, meaning "father of the virgin," was given him when his daughter Ayesha became Mohammed's wife. After Mohammed's death in 632, Abu-Bekr spread the Mohammedan faith over Arabia. He lived so simply that at his death he owned only one robe, one camel, and one Ethiopian slave.

Abydos

Two ancient cities were named Abydos, but the one we remember best was on the Asiatic side of the Dardanelles strait, the narrow body of water between Greece and Asia Minor. Across this strait, which was then called the Hellespont, Leander swam every night (in the story of HERO AND LEANDER), from Abydos to Sestos. It was also at this Abydos that Xerxes built a bridge of boats to carry his army across the water.

The other Abydos was in Egypt, and archaeologists have discovered in its ruins many ancient writings, ornaments, and buildings from times hundreds of years before the birth of Christ.

abyss

The word *abyss* has several meanings. It means "the bottomless pit," because in the Greek language it actually meant "without a bottom." But it is also used to describe the bottom of the ocean where the water is more than a mile deep. At this depth hardly anything is the same as it is in shallower waters.

No plants grow on the ocean bottom at such depths, and there is no light at all, because the rays of the sun cannot reach farther than a few hundred feet through the water.

Until very recently, scientists in their bathyspheres could not go so far down, but they could still let down traps and bring up abyssal fish, such as anglers, for study. These are quite different from fish that swim near the surface. Many of them have no eyes (with no light, they do not need them). The mouths and teeth of these fish are very large, as they have to be to gather in enough food, for there are no schools of small fish and no sea plants for them to feed on. The water

is icy cold. The pressure is tremendous, because of the weight of all the water above. A single quart of water weighs almost two pounds; even a small fish has several tons of water resting on it. Such pressure would immediately kill a fish accustomed to shallower water. Because they are so strangely unlike the fish we know, abyssal fish seem hideously ugly to us.

ABYSSAL FISH (See ABYSS)

1. The angler fish, an abyssal fish, is one of the ugliest and strangest of all creatures. It is a big fish, 3 to 5 feet long, and it lives by killing and eating other fish. Its spine grows out of its nose to form a sort of fishing hook that attracts other fish. Its beard is believed to glow in the black waters of the deep sea.

2. Another kind of angler fish, with a feathery "fishhook" growth on its head.

3. This is another kind of big angler fish. The bony rod sticking out from it is not so much like a fishhook, but when another fish bites at it the angler fish gobbles it up.

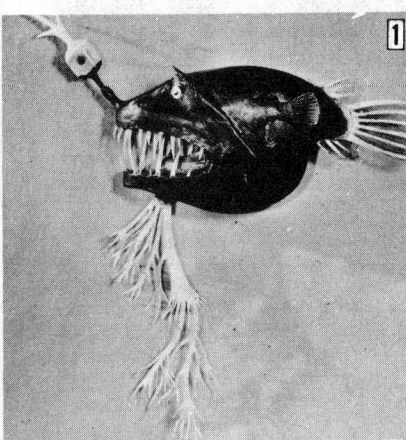

Abyssinia, a former name for Ethiopia. See ETHIOPIA.

acacia

The acacia is a small tree or a shrub that grows wild in tropical countries and is raised in greenhouses farther north because of its beautiful flowers. The wood of some acacia trees makes fine furniture; the sap of some acacias is very sweet-smelling and is used in making perfumes, and besides gives us "gum arabic," the sticky substance that makes gum drops "chewy" and is also used in making some glues.

academic freedom

Academic freedom is freedom in teaching. It is a teacher's right to express to his students his knowledge and beliefs without control by any government. Many of those who believe in academic freedom say it should include the teacher's freedom from control of his private life; that he should never lose his teaching position because of his opinions, his membership in a particular political party, or his personal habits.

Scientists throughout the ages have said that learning cannot advance as it should if a scholar can be persecuted for treason (opposition to the government) or heresy (opposition to the accepted religion). The great Greek philosopher Socrates and the Italian scientist Galileo were only two of many who have been persecuted for expressing ideas that were far ahead of their times. However, even the most liberal thinkers have usually admitted that authorities must forbid the teaching of ideas or habits that are dangerous to the public or damaging to the students—just as freedom of speech depends on preventing libel and dishonest advertising.

From about 200 years ago until the 1920s there was almost complete academic freedom in the principal countries of Europe and in the United States. When the Bill of Rights was added to the United States Constitution in 1789 the writers of the amendments were not worried enough about academic freedom to mention it. Then after World War I dictatorships arose in several big European countries—Italy, Germany, and Russia—and academic freedom in those countries was wholly destroyed. Not even scientific facts could be taught if they did not conform to the propaganda that the government was using. A teacher could be imprisoned or even put to death for failure to teach the government's "line."

In the United States there was almost complete academic freedom until the 1940s. In 1925, a Tennessee science teacher named John T. Scopes was fined for teaching the theory of evolution, but there were almost no other cases of the same kind. However, after World War II many teachers lost their positions, or were threatened with loss of them, because they were or had previously been Communists. Since then the question of academic freedom has been a subject of argument.

academy

The first academy was a grove of trees, used as a public park, in the city of Athens in ancient Greece. It was named more than 2,300 years ago for a great Greek warrior, Academus, one of the athletes who used the park.

The Greek philosopher Plato, the wisest man of his time, used to stroll in this grove with his pupils, teaching them. Because of this, they called Plato and his followers "the Academy," and ever since that time the word has been used to mean a school or other institution of learning, or a group of learned men who form an association for study. When a boy goes away to school, he is likely to go to a military academy, and in this case "academy" means "high school." Officers of the United States armed services are trained at one of the country's "service academies" such as the United States Military Academy at West Point, and here "academy" means "college." A great writer, or artist, or architect, or geographer, may be elected to an "Academy," and in this case the word means a society, or club. This kind of academy is always a society of very distinguished men, and it is an honor to be elected to one.

The most famous of these academies is the French Academy. It is more than 300 years old, having been founded in 1636, and it can never have more than forty members, who are called the "forty Immortals." These men of the French Academy have decided for hundreds of years what is proper in speaking and writing the French language, and they have helped many sciences to advance. Other countries have distinguished academies too. In the United States there is the American Academy of Arts and Letters, which never has more than fifty members. It never became as well known in this country as the French Academy is in France and throughout the world.

The first application of the term to a society of learned men was in 1582, when the Accademia della Crusca was founded in Italy "to enhance the purity of the Italian language."

Academy Awards

Academy Awards are prizes given each year for the best performances and other work contributing to motion pictures, by the Academy of Motion Picture Arts and Sciences, an organization in Hollywood, California, founded in 1927. The Academy has other purposes, for example, "to represent to the public the point of view of the creators of films, to promote the art and science of films, and to focus public attention on the best in motion pictures"; but it is best known for its Academy Awards.

The active membership in 1975 was a little more than 3,500. The Academy has the following branches: actors, art directors, cinematographers, directors, executives, film editors, musicians, producers, public relations, short subjects, sound, writers. Each branch is represented on the 26-member Board of Governors.

Candidates for Academy Awards are nominated by the producers. About twenty-five awards are made each year, for best motion picture, best actor and actress in leading and supporting roles, best direction, screen writing, music, art direction, costume design, editing, sound recording, photography, etc. Awards are made for technical advances, special awards are sometimes given for contributions that do not fit any particular classification, and the Irving Thalberg Memorial Award may be given for outstanding contributions over a period of years.

The board of governors of the Academy elects the prize-winners, and every year they present the prizes during a

televised ceremony at some large theater. The television broadcast of this affair pays most of the Academy's expenses. Each prize is a little statue with the figure of a man on top of it. One of the first actresses who won one of these statues nicknamed the little man "Oscar," and the name has stuck. Ever since, winning an Academy Award has been known as "winning an Oscar."

Acadia

The part of Canada that is now Nova Scotia and Prince Edward Island, and also a part of the province of New Brunswick and the state of Maine in the United States, was once called Acadia and belonged to France. That was more than 200 years ago. About 12,000 French people had come over, just as the Pilgrims had come to Massachusetts and had made homes for themselves there.

Then in 1755, during the French and Indian Wars between England and France, the English won possession of Acadia. They insisted that everyone in Acadia become subjects of the British king, instead of the French king, and about seven thousand Acadians—more than half of them—refused to do it. So the English governors made these French people move from Acadia to parts of what is now the United States. The poet Henry Wadsworth Longfellow wrote one of his finest poems, called "Evangeline," about these unhappy thousands who had to leave their homes and move hundreds of miles away. His poem is about a girl named Evangeline, and the young man she was to marry, named Gabriel. Gabriel was one of those sent away. Evangeline followed him, hoping to find him. She went to Louisiana, where many of the Acadians had gone, but could not find him there; then she went all the way to Michigan looking for him, and finally to Philadelphia. There she found him, but both were very old and he was dying.

Many Louisiana descendants of the Acadians who went there are called "Cajuns" (which is just a mispronunciation of "Acadians").

There is an Acadian National Park in the northernmost part of Maine.

acanthus

The acanthus is a small, flowering herb, also known as *bear's-breech.* Its name is from the Greek word *akantha,* meaning a thorn; it is not a thorny plant, but its leaves and often its flowers end in sharp points. The beautiful form of the acanthus has for thousands of years been used as a design in architecture, especially on a Corinthian column.

Acapulco

Acapulco is a city in southwest Mexico, a seaport on a bay of the Pacific Ocean. Its harbor has been called the best on the American Pacific coast. For more than 250 years from the date of its founding (which was in the year 1550) Acapulco was the principal Pacific seaport of Spanish America. The city is surrounded by granite cliffs, which reflect the sunlight and increase the summer heat, but a tunnel has been cut through the rocks so that the cooler sea breezes can reach the city.

On one of the cliffs overlooking the city is the castle of San Diego, which was once a fortress that defended it.

Acapulco is one of Mexico's most popular resorts during its season (January to May), with luxury hotels, two long beaches, deep-sea fishing, and hunting in the nearby mountains. It was somewhat damaged by an earthquake in 1957. The population is about 200,000.

accent

The word accent has several meanings, but mostly it applies to stress or emphasis given to a particular syllable in a word or to particular words in a sentence. In the English language, there is no such thing as a word of two or more syllables in which none is accented.

Accent is either *pitch accent* (for example the rising inflection ending a question) or *stress accent* (accomplished by a greater expulsion of breath in uttering the accented syllable). Different degrees of loudness are referred to as primary stress, secondary stress, tertiary stress. Without accented syllables there could be no poetry: See the article on METER.

In a second sense, an accent is a diacritical mark, a symbol placed over or under a letter to show how it is pronounced, and if it is stressed. The Greeks used three such accents, the acute (´), grave (`), and circumflex (^); these accents are used in modern French and other languages. The acute, which signified a raising of the voice in Greek, is used in Spanish and sometimes in English to show a stressed syllable.

In a third sense, an accent is a peculiarity of speech that characterizes the speaker as belonging to a particular linguistic group: for example, one is said to have "a foreign accent." All men (barring deformity) are physically capable of uttering the same sounds; but they are usually trained in childhood to utter only those of their own language and can seldom, in adult life, master others without special instruction. Neither of the English *th* sounds (of *this* and *thing*) can readily be spoken by people from other countries, nor can most Chinese differentiate between the *r* and *l* sounds; but likewise the English native can seldom master the German *ach,* the rolled *r,* or the French *u.* Teachers of speech can often help a person remove a "heavy" foreign accent by correcting his pronunciation of only a few sounds, as they have demonstrated in teaching acceptable American speech to foreign actors and actresses imported to Hollywood. Almost any group more or less isolated in a section of a country, as the southern U.S., will within a few generations develop a characteristic "accent." See also MUSIC.

accidents

An accident is something that happens unexpectedly to hurt a person. If you hit somebody and he hits you back and hurts you, that is not an accident because you should have expected it. But if you climb on a rickety chair to reach something, and the chair lets you fall and hurt yourself, that is called an accident because you did not expect it—at least, it is supposed that if you had expected to fall you would not have climbed on the chair.

In the United States alone, nearly 102,500 persons are killed in accidents every year, and for every one person who dies in an accident there are about 100 who are hurt in accidents but do not die. This means there must be nearly ten million Americans who are hurt in accidents every year. The biggest group of those who are killed, about 46,000, die in automobile accidents of one kind or another, and the second-largest group, about 25,500, die as a result of accidents at home. Floods, hurricanes, earthquakes, and other acts of nature are not classed as accidents.

Youngsters should stay away from excavations, docks, empty houses, abandoned mines, and railroad property.

Drownings are the third largest cause of accidental death in very young children. All children should learn how to swim and do so with a buddy—and only in supervised areas.

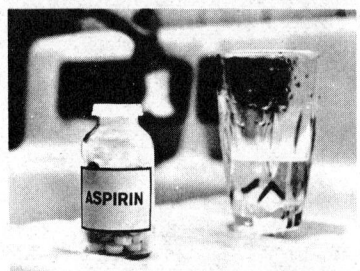

Every year 400 children under 5 years of age die from accidental poisonings. One of the major causes is aspirin. Taken in large doses, it can be fatal.

Long ago, many people believed that accidents were the will of God and could not be prevented. Since then they have learned that most accidents happen because someone is careless and nearly all accidents could be prevented. Yet during World War II more Americans were hurt by accidents in the United States than in battle overseas.

An organization called the National Safety Council, with headquarters in Chicago, spends all its time trying to

teach people how to be more careful and avoid accidents. Big factories, automobile companies, and many others who are interested in preventing accidents at work and on the road, spend millions of dollars every year to prevent accidents. When a worker in a factory is hurt, the factory produces less and makes less money. Automobile accidents and home accidents, too, keep people away from work and cost the whole country money.

See also the article on INSURANCE.

accordion

The accordion is a musical instrument that is popular throughout the world. It is made of a bellows between two boxlike ends and has a number of metal reeds (flat, flexible pieces of metal) that vibrate to sound different notes when air blows across them. Opening or closing the bellows creates the flow of air. The player has a keyboard, like a piano keyboard, that he plays with his right hand to sound the notes, and a number of buttons that he operates with his left hand to make chords. Because of its keyboard, the instrument is often called a *piano accordion*. For many years accordions had no keyboards, only the buttons. There are still small accordions, and similar instruments called *concertinas*, that have only buttons.

Bruno

A modern piano accordion.

The accordion is a new instrument, as musical instruments go; it is less than 150 years old. For fifty years or more it was manufactured chiefly in Paris, France, and was considered little more than a toy. It has become a very complex instrument—the largest accordions have as many as 120 buttons and up to 50 keys—and an accordion player can give a concert all by himself.

accounting

An accountant goes over the bookkeeping records of a business to find out how much the business is actually worth, and how much money it is making, and (very often) how it could make more money. His profession is called *accountancy,* or, more often, *accounting.* The first step in accounting is bookkeeping (and there is a separate article on

BOOKKEEPING in a later section), but accounting only begins there. The bookkeeper sets down the figures that show how much money a business has taken in and how much it has spent, but the accountant tells what the figures mean.

Very few people realize how big a part the accountant has played in the growth of the United States. Until about 100 years ago, accounting was not a very important or very well developed profession. This means it is a very young profession, considering that there have been doctors for thousands of years and lawyers for almost as long. Then, as businesses grew bigger and bigger, and government laws grew more and more complex, the need for accounting grew. The general public would not invest in a big business unless it had a system for proving that their money was being spent wisely. Accountants provided this system. A big business with dozens of branches and thousands of employees would be in a constant mess if it were not for accounting systems to show exactly how its money was being spent and with what success, and accountants worked out the system for that too. Alfred P. Sloan, for many years head of General Motors Corporation, one of the biggest businesses in the world, once said that good accounting is the backbone of successful business.

Accounting is a profession, which means that the person who practices it must have special education. An accountant must know much more than bookkeeping. He must know the principles of analyzing bookkeeping records —that is, taking every separate item and discovering exactly what it means. He must know a great deal of law as it applies to businesses, especially tax laws and laws relating to an employer's duty to his employees. Many accountants have their own offices and work for several different companies, going from one to the other to examine and analyze their books; this is called public accounting and the accountant who practices it must know a great deal about the actual operation of many different kinds of business, and must pass an examination that makes him a Certified Public Accountant.

FINANCIAL STATEMENTS

The accountant shows the result of business operations by what is called a balance sheet. A balance sheet is divided into two parts. In one part is shown everything a company owns, whether in money or in things that are worth money. These are its assets. In the other part of the balance sheet, the accountant sets down everything the company owes, or must eventually be prepared to pay. These are the company's liabilities. The difference between the assets and the liabilities is the company's net worth. This balance sheet, or financial statement, shows a company's net worth on some particular date that is the end of an accounting period. If between one accounting period and another a company's net worth grows, then during that period the company has made money; if its net worth becomes less, the company has lost money or has paid out its profits.

It is not possible to tell what a company is worth merely from how much cash and other assets it has. That is one of the important things accounting has taught business over the course of the years. Suppose a publisher of magazines sells a million subscriptions for $3.00 each and takes in $3,000,000, which he has in cash in the bank. It might seem that he has an income of $3,000,000 from this, but the accountant shows that it is not so; in fact, the $3,000,000 goes on the publisher's balance sheet as a liability, not as an asset, even though it is cash in the bank. That money belongs to the subscribers until the publisher has finished sending them their magazines. Every time he sends each subscriber one issue of the magazine, the accountant takes $\frac{1}{12}$ of the $3,000,000, or $250,000, and shows it as income. The rest still is owed to the subscribers. Such money is called deferred income, and cash that is actually on hand but must be held for a particular purpose is called a reserve.

Again, suppose a man buys a truck and goes into the trucking business. The truck cost him $4,000. At the end of the year, he has taken in $10,000 from his charges for trucking, and has spent only $5,000, which makes it seem that he has a $5,000 profit. But the accountant knows that in four years the truck will wear out and he will have to buy another one. So the accountant takes off one-fourth of the $4,000 he spent for the truck, and reduces his profit by $1,000. That is called depreciation.

The basic principles of accounting are quite simple, but the businesses it serves have become so complex that years of study are required to learn the profession well. A young man who wants to be an accountant, after studying in college, usually works in the offices of an experienced accountant as a "junior." He does not make a high salary as a junior, but he keeps on learning until he can himself become a Certified Public Accountant and open his own office. Many accountants specialize, just as doctors do, on one or more particular phases of accounting, spending must of their time as cost accountants or as consultants in some business or profession.

AUDITING

Every accountant is an auditor. In one sense, however, auditing is a special branch of accounting. The auditor examines the accounts of a company to make sure they are correct. This is important in government organizations from the mighty Federal Government of the United States down to the tiniest town, because taxpayers want to be sure their money is being spent honestly and intelligently. It is important in businesses, because the stockholders, who are the real owners, turn the control over to just a few persons—directors and officers— and they too want to know that their investment is being protected.

When an accountant makes a careful audit, he investigates everything personally. If the company's records show that it has a million dollars worth of merchandise on hand to be sold, the accountant goes and looks at it. If the

company's books show that certain persons owe it money, the accountant "verifies" these accounts—that is, he gets in touch with the persons concerned and finds out from them that they really do owe the money. Years ago, before accounting was developed to its present state, it was not unusual for investors in a business to be cheated by the managers of the business. Today that has been stopped, due to accounting.

COST ACCOUNTING

The cost accountant analyzes the money a company is spending so that he knows exactly how much it costs the company to perform every operation of its business. For example, if the company is manufacturing chewing gum, he will tell them not only that each piece of chewing gum cost them, say, one-fifth of a cent; but exactly how much every operation that goes into the making of the chewing gum costs, down to hundredths or thousandths of a penny. Manufacturers in particular want to know this, so they will know how much to charge for their products to give them a fair profit. In addition, the cost accountant is often able to point out savings that will allow them to increase their profits and reduce their selling price to the public. The fact that Americans can buy so much good merchandise at such low prices is in many cases due to savings that have been pointed out by accountants. In some unusual cases, an accountant has saved a manufacturer money by raising the level of a workman's bench a few inches so that the workman would not have to stoop so low to get to his work, and would not become so tired and work less well toward the end of the day; or by spacing machines differently to make them more convenient; or by showing that the cost of shipping raw materials to the factory would make it worthwhile to build another factory closer to where the materials are; or in many other ways.

TAX ACCOUNTING

Taxes have become so many and so large that every business has to consider taxes before it makes any plans. There may be as many as a dozen tax forms to fill out, all of them complicated, and all of them required on a certain date, and the accountant must know about all of them. There may be reasons why a company should wait a year before adding a new building or new machine to its properties, or an equally good reason why the company should do it immediately, solely because of the way the decision will affect the taxes it pays.

Then, there are individuals who are not really in business at all but are bewildered by the complications of tax forms and who go to accountants to get help in making out their income taxes. Tax accountants very often save their clients more money in reduced taxes than they charge in fees.

In many aspects of tax accounting, the accountant is engaged in work resembling a lawyer's work. There are special tax courts, and many accountants argue cases before these courts just as lawyers do.

These are usually cases in which the government has demanded a tax higher than the taxpayer thinks he should pay, and the accountant's job is to prove to the court that the taxpayer is right.

The accounting profession generally disapproves of specialization, but many businesses have become so complicated that a specialized knowledge of the client's business is essential to good accounting.

In all large enterprises, original entries have come to be made by accounting machines instead of by hand. Accountants increasingly must be familiar with such machines. Designers of the machines must have both accounting and engineering knowledge. (See CALCULATING MACHINE.)

In public accounting, some knowledge of law is necessary. Nearly all CPAs are products of full college courses in schools of business administration, or the equivalent in extension courses available at many universities.

Accra

Accra, or Akkra, is the capital of Ghana, in Africa. It became the capital of the Gold Coast (the British territory that later became Ghana) in 1876, growing up around three forts built during the 1600s by French, Dutch and English slave traders and gold miners. Then it became a center for deep-sea fishing, fish-canning, and the shipping of cocoa and gold. In 1951 the official population of Accra was 135,456, but it increased greatly in size after it became the capital of Ghana, and its population was about 665,000 in 1973.

Aceldama

After Judas had betrayed Jesus, as told in the New Testament (in the 27th chapter of the Gospel of Matthew), he repented. He gave back the 30 pieces of silver that he had been paid, and he hanged himself. The 30 pieces of silver were used to buy a field that belonged to a potter (a maker of pottery) and Judas was buried there. In the first chapter of the Book of Acts, this field, which we usually call the Potter's Field, is given the name of Aceldama, which means "the field of blood."

acetate

Acetates are chemicals that are made by using acetic acid. Cellulose acetate, especially in the form of photographic film and a thermoplastic molding compound, has come to be called simply "acetate," as have certain products made from it, such as all-plastic phonograph records (though most such records are now made of a vinyl resin). Some other important acetates are: lead acetate (known also as sugar of lead because of its sweetish taste); verdigris, an acetate of copper used in paints and dyeing, and seen often as a green substance that forms on bronze statues, etc.; iron acetate, used in the treatment of anemia; and sodium acetate. Amyl acetate (known as banana oil because its smell resembles that of bananas, due to a similarity in chemical content), ethyl acetate, and benzyl acetate have fragrant odors and are used in perfumes and flavors.

acetic acid

Acetic acid is an acid occurring in fruits and oils. Diluted with water, it has been known from early times as vinegar. It has such large-scale industrial application (as in rayon yarns, plastics, artificial leathers) that it is probably the most important organic acid.

acetylene

Acetylene is the name of a gas that is very important in many ways. You cannot see acetylene, but when it is mixed with oxygen, the life-giving gas that makes up much of the air, the mixture burns with one of the hottest and brightest flames known. It is so hot that it will melt steel and cut through even the walls of a safe. It is often used in welding—that is, joining two pieces of metal by melting the edges of both and letting them harden together—but electric welding is now more often used. (See the article on WELDING.) The flame of this burning mixture, called oxyacetylene gas, is so bright that users of it usually wear dark goggles: these also protect their eyes against flying sparks. Acetylene is also used in the making of synthetic (artificial) rubber.

Acetylene was first prepared and identified in 1832, but was not commercially important until the discovery in 1892 of a cheap method of making calcium carbide. It became important as a lighting fuel, including use in the headlamps of bicycles and early automobiles, in which water was permitted to drop on calcium carbide. In the acetylene torch now in wide use, acetylene from one tank and oxygen from another are fed under pressure into a mixing chamber, preheated, and ignited at the nozzle of the torch. The resulting flame, exceeding 6000° F., will cut cleanly through steel and is used in demolition of steel structures.

Achaea

Achaea, or Achaia, was a region of about 750 square miles in ancient Greece, on the northern part of the peninsula called the Peloponnesus, including most of the coastline of the Gulfs of Calydon and Corinth. It is known to have existed as a state more than 2,500 years ago (about 700 B.C. to 146 B.C.). It was conquered by the Romans and became the Roman province of Achaea.

The Achaeans were one of the four main branches of the Greek people, and they ruled southern Greece from about 1400 B.C. to 1200 B.C. The great Greek poet Homer often used the name Achaean for all the Greek people of those ancient times.

Achates

Achates, in Greek legend, was the faithful friend and companion of Aeneas. He was called "fidus Achates" (faithful Achates), a phrase still used to describe a devoted follower.

Achilles

Achilles is a character in one of the greatest stories of all time, a story that may be more than 3,000 years old and was told by the great poet Homer hundreds of years before the birth of Christ, and by hundreds of writers since. It is

the story of how the Greeks went to war against the city of Troy.

The greatest of the Greek warriors was Achilles. No one could beat him; he even chased the Trojan champion, Hector, around the walls of Troy. One reason no one could beat Achilles was that he could not be hurt by swords or arrows or spears in any part of his body except one—his heel. But that one vulnerable (which means "woundable") spot finally caused his death.

When Achilles was still a tiny baby, his mother Thetis had a vision that he would be killed in battle. Now, in those days there was a belief that the waters of the river Styx had magic powers that would make anyone safe from death. So Thetis took the tiny Achilles and dipped him in the river Styx. When she dipped him in, she held him by one of his heels, and the waters of the river did not touch that spot. So during the Trojan wars, the vision Thetis had seen finally came true. An arrow struck Achilles in the heel, in his one vulnerable spot, and killed him. Ever since, the weakest point of any person has been called his "Achilles' heel."

Achilles died when an arrow hit his heel.

Achilles' tendon

The Achilles' tendon is a cord, or tendon, in the body. It stretches from the middle of the back of the leg to the heel, and gets its name from the story of Achilles, which you can read about just above this. The Achilles' tendon is very strong, and almost as hard as if it were bone. It is of great importance to our walking, because to walk comfortably we must bend the foot with each step.

acids

The acids we know best are liquids that have a sour taste or a burning effect. In chemistry, acids can be either solids, liquids, or gases, and have many uses. They conduct electricity, and they combine with other chemicals to form useful products.

The liquid acids that we know have some water in them. Some are quite mild, and outside of their sour taste they are either useful or at least harmless to our bodies. Vinegar is water and acetic acid. We digest food because there is hydrochloric acid in our stomachs that dissolves it. It is the citric acid in lemons, grapefruit, and related fruit, that gives them their pleasant sour taste. The lactic acid in milk causes it to curdle and it is useful because it makes cheese. But

hydrofluoric acid is so strong that it will burn a hole in glass, as you can read in the article on ETCHING, and if you dropped some sulfuric acid on your skin, it would burn you as badly as fire.

If one of these burning acids should touch your skin, the way to neutralize it is to put an alkali on the burned place. There is a separate article on ALKALIS, which include such common household things as soda. In chemical laboratories, there is usually a pan of soda water around, and if a chemist is touched by an acid, he quickly plunges his hand into this soda water, which stops the acid from burning him. This must be done immediately, because the acid burns very fast.

An interesting experiment can be conducted with litmus paper, which is used in chemistry. Litmus paper comes in two colors, red and blue. If an acid touches blue litmus paper, the paper turns red; if an alkali touches red litmus paper, the paper turns blue. So, if you dip a piece of blue litmus paper into even such a mild acid as orange juice, it will turn red; if you dip a piece of red litmus paper into a glass of plain soda water, it will turn blue. Chemists use this paper to tell quickly whether a chemical is acid or alkali.

Acids are of great industrial importance in metallurgy, chemical analysis, the manufacture of plastics, and nearly every other field employing chemistry.

In chemistry, alkalis are called *bases*. An acid will react with a base (or alkali) to form a salt. According to the ionization theory of Arrhenius, the properties of acids are due to the presence in their solutions of hydrogen ions (H^+), the plus sign indicating that the ion has positive electric charge.

There are strong and weak acids, the strong acids having a higher concentration of hydrogen atoms; sulfuric acid and nitric acid are strong, while citric acid, carbonic acid and acetic acid are weak acids. Organic acids, usually characterized by the carboxyl group—COOH, are not so strong as many inorganic acids, such as hydrochloric and nitric acid. Important organic acids are acetic acid, citric acid, lactic acid (present in sour milk), oxalic acid, and tartaric acid. Acids can be prepared in several ways, one method being to dissolve an anhydride in water; it is typical that the anhydride does not show acid properties until it is dissolved in water.

Acids can dissolve many metals and other substances not dissolved by pure water. Hydrochloric acid will dissolve iron, zinc, aluminum, and many other metals. Nitric acid will dissolve copper, which is not dissolved by hydrochloric acid. A mixture of hydrochloric and nitric acids is used to dissolve gold, platinum and other precious metals that are not soluble in either acid alone. (This mixture was known to alchemists as *aqua regia*, "royal water," since it would dissolve the "noble" metals.) Oxalic acid is used to dissolve rust while leaving the metal untouched. The chemical analysis of nearly any metal, ore or other mineral product is accomplished by dissolving the product in an acid. Nitric and sulfuric

acids are used in huge amounts in the preparation of plastics, laquers, synthetic textiles, and explosives. Sulfuric acid is also used for pickling steel and in the production of phosphate fertilizers; it is perhaps the most important acid industrially.

acne

Acne is the name of a very unpleasant but usually harmless disease—the breaking out of many pimples and blackheads on the face. This most often happens to boys and girls between the ages of 10 or 12 and 19 or 20. The cause of acne is not definitely known, and any number of different things may cause it, including the changes that take place in the body in the process of growing up. Persons with large pores in their skins are more likely to have it than persons with very closely grained skin in which the pores are small.

Doctors advise the following to those who have acne: The first rule is to keep the face very clean. When the attack is bad, the face should be washed with very hot water which causes the pores to open and makes it easier for the blackheads to come out. Some doctors advise squeezing out the worst blackheads and opening the pimples with a sterilized needle, then squeezing the pus out of them. It is important also to keep clean with frequent baths, to get plenty of sunlight and fresh air, to avoid constipation, and not to eat too many oily or starchy foods. Advertised remedies for acne should be avoided unless they are advised by a doctor, and of course it is best to consult the doctor anyway.

In medicine, this kind of acne is called *acne vulgaris*. There is a form of acne that occurs less often, called *acne rosacea*, in which the symptoms are a red and swollen nose and unusual redness of the face.

Acoma

Acoma is an Indian pueblo about sixty miles west of Albuquerque, New Mexico. The pueblo has been occupied for at least a thousand years and is, with Oraibi, one of the oldest in the United States. It was first visited by the Spaniards under Francisco Coronado in 1540. Its position on an isolated sandstone mesa 394 feet high, a defensive site accessible only by a road cut like a spiral staircase in the rock, has earned it the name of Sky Pueblo. The present reservation includes 234,085 acres, and has a population of 1,920. The Acoma Indians are known for their pottery-making.

Aconcagua

Mount Aconcagua is the highest mountain peak in the Western Hemisphere. It is in the great Andes chain of mountains that runs all the way down through South America. Aconcagua is in the part of the Andes that lies in Argentina, in the southern part of South America. It is more than 23,000 feet high—nearly four and one-half miles. The highest peak in North America, Mount McKinley in Alaska, is 20,300 feet high, but though Mount Aconcagua is the highest mountain in our hemisphere, it is far from being the highest mountain in the world. Mount Everest is more

than a mile higher, and there are more than 200 peaks in the big mountain ranges lying around India that are higher than Aconcagua. Mountain climbers reached the peak of Aconcagua in 1897, and others have climbed it since. It is an extinct volcano.

aconite

Aconite is the name of a group of perennial flowering herbs also known as monkshood, wolfsbane, blueweed, or friar's cap. The leaves or roots of some kinds of aconite yield a strong narcotic drug (also called aconite) that is used in some medicines to reduce fever.

acotyledon

Acotyledonous plants, in botany, are primitive plants that lack the cotyledons, or primary leaves, present in seed plants, and that reproduce by means of spores. The group is known as *Cryptogamia* and includes horsetails and ferns; clubmosses, mosses, and liverworts; and mushrooms, molds, and seaweeds.

acoustics

The word acoustics means the whole science of sound—what causes it, how it travels, and its effects. But there is another article on SOUND, and here we will consider acoustics only as most people use the word: to mean the "listening qualities" of a theater, an auditorium, a room, and so on. In a theater with "good acoustics" a word spoken from the stage can be heard as clearly in the last row as in the first. In a theater with "bad acoustics" the sound may be too soft to hear by the time it reaches the last row; or music may make such echoes that it makes the ears ring; or in any number of ways the sound may be unpleasant.

WHAT IS SOUND?

To understand the principles of acoustics, you must first know something about what sound is and how it travels. Sound begins with a vibration, or shaking; in the case of the sound of a voice, it begins with a vibration in the throat. This shakes the air, causing waves to go out through the air. When these waves strike the ear of a listener, his eardrum makes understandable sounds of them.

As the sound waves move through the air, if they strike something that will not vibrate the sound will suddenly stop going forward. Something soft like a rug, or heavy velvet draperies, will stop a sound; they are said to "absorb" it. But when the sound waves strike a surface that will vibrate, the sound is bounced back as a new set of sound waves. An echo is an example of a sound that strikes a surface that bounces it back. In a small room, a noise sounds much louder than it does in a large hall, or out of doors, because the four walls, the floor and the ceiling all bounce the sound back—unless they have been "soundproofed" by being covered with a material that absorbs sound. A surface that vibrates and bounces back the sound is said to "reflect" sound.

A simple illustration will show the workings of these principles. Any toy noisemaker will do for the experiment. Sound it in the bathroom with the door closed, and the noise will be very great; the bathroom floor and walls are hard and sound-reflecting, and even the bathroom fixtures help to reflect the sound. Open the bathroom door and do it again, and it will not sound so loud. Then take it into a large room, and the sound will be still softer.

HOW THE ACOUSTICS EXPERT WORKS

Giving a theater, hall or other room good acoustics is a difficult scientific problem. First, the acoustics expert will want to know exactly what kind of sound is to be used in the room. If he wants the hall to be suitable for piano concerts, he will find out exactly how long it takes the sound of a piano's notes to reach the farthest corner of the hall, and how long it takes that sound to bounce back. He will then choose wall coverings, and sometimes coverings for the ceiling and floor as well, that will bounce back the sound at the right rate of speed to make the piano seem at its very best in all parts of the hall at the same time. If the hall is to be used for a large orchestra, he does the same thing with the sound of the orchestra at full strength. If it is to be used for speakers, or actors, he tests it for keeping the sound clear at the back of the hall even though the speaker uses only a normal tone of voice. It is possible to arrange the acoustics of a large auditorium so that a whisper at one end of the room can be heard clearly at the other end—even several hundred feet away. If the hall is just being built, the problem is one on which the architect and acoustics engineers will work together to plan the shape of the walls and height of the ceiling.

An echo is heard if the reflection of a sound wave reaches the ear $\frac{1}{15}$th of a second or more after the direct sound wave; a reverberation results if two or more reflections reach the ear at intervals of less than $\frac{1}{15}$th second. The dimensions of a room and the nature of its interior surfaces determine the intensity of sound; the smaller the room, the greater the intensity; the harder the interior surface, the greater the intensity. Sound is absorbed, or deadened, by soft surfaces such as rugs, hangings, and cork ceilings, and the clothing of the audience. Concave surfaces concentrate sound waves and are used in theaters when it is desirable to reflect sounds toward an audience. Convex surfaces carry sound waves for long distances if not dispersed, which makes possible the speaking tube and produces unusual effects when words spoken at one end of an arch or vault can be heard clearly at the other end but not by a person a few feet from the speaker.

The demands of motion-picture theaters, radio transmission, and sound recording, have made acoustical engineering an important profession.

Acre

Acre, which is also called St. Jean d'Acre, is a city and seaport in Israel, on the Mediterranean Sea. Its present population is about 33,000. Many years ago, when this part of the world was called Palestine, Acre was the most important city of the CRUSADES, which were wars fought by Christians and Mohammedans for control of the Holy Land. The Crusaders captured Acre in the year 1104, lost it in 1187, and recaptured it in 1191 after a long siege. It was ruled by the Knights of St. John, a religious order of soldiers. In 1291 the Mohammedans recaptured it, and this was the

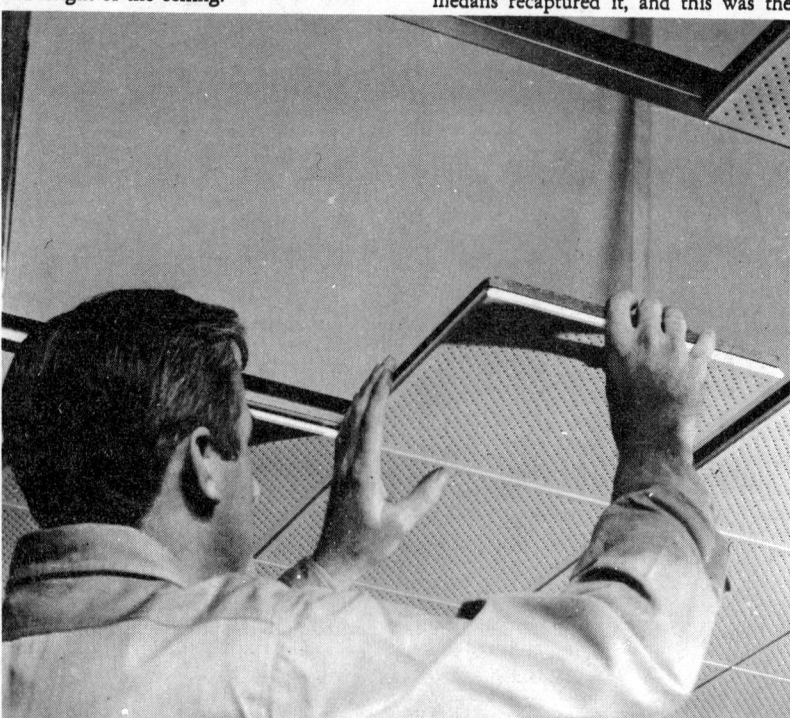

Johns-Manville

Good planning can make a noisy room much quieter. The acoustic ceiling this man is putting up will absorb a great deal of the clattering noise made by typewriters in the office. Those square blocks are made of metal with a lot of little holes, and they are filled with a sound-absorbent pad of mineral wool. You cannot see the pad inside, but when sound hits the holes in the metal it bounces into the pad. The pad absorbs the noise and softens it.

end of the Crusades. In more ancient history, Acre was controlled by Egyptians, Assyrians, and Romans, before the Mohammedan Arabs captured it in 638. In 1517 Acre became part of the Turkish empire. Napoleon Bonaparte attacked Acre in 1799 but the Turks, aided by British ships, forced him to withdraw. Other battles were fought at Acre in World War I, when the British captured it from the Turks in 1918, and in 1948, during the fighting between Israel and the Arabs.

There is also a large territory called Acre in west Brazil. It has 59,139 square miles and a population of 215,500. The forests of this territory contain much wild rubber and some gold and tin.

acrobat

Acrobats are men and women who turn handsprings and somersaults, throw each other around, jump, and do other tricks requiring strength and skill. They perform in circuses, on the stage, and on television shows. Years of practice and good teamwork are needed to make a fine acrobat. The tricks done by acrobats are called *acrobatics*.

The chief kinds of acrobat are:

TUMBLERS and LEAPERS. They turn handsprings and somersaults (but all acrobats can do that very well). The tumblers and leapers also train themselves to jump in the air, turn one or more somersaults in midair, and land either on their feet or on their backs. It would seem that when they land on their backs they would be hurt, but they are not because they land at exactly the right point and are rolling as they do so, so that no part of the body hits the floor or the ground too hard.

BALANCERS. These are the acrobats who build themselves into formations with perhaps one of them (called the "understander") standing on the stage; two more acrobats standing on his shoulders; and maybe three more acrobats standing on their shoulders. It might seem that men must be very strong to do this, especially the one who holds up all the others, but this kind of acrobatics can be done without great strength. Of course, all acrobats are strong, but skill and training mean much more.

TRAMPOLINE JUMPERS. A trampoline is a sheet of heavy cloth, usually canvas, fastened to a wooden frame by dozens of short, very strong elastic cords. When an acrobat jumps on it, he bounces back, high into the air. Some of the funniest of all acrobatic acts are done by trampoline jumpers, who can make themselves bounce into the air in all kinds of funny positions—on their backs, with their arms and legs stuck out in crazy directions, and in other funny postures. Though a trampoline jumper may sometimes make himself seem clumsy, he really is a very skillful performer who always intends to do exactly what he is doing.

Other acrobats are called aerialists, including the trapeze artists who work high in the air; tightrope walkers who walk on wires, or ride bicycles across them, or do other tricks of balancing; and various acrobats who do their tricks

on horses, highstands, or even in the water. These are usually not called acrobats, and more can be read about them in the article CIRCUS.

There have been acrobats since the very earliest times, thousands of years ago. A great deal of science goes into their training. This science was improved through the centuries until it reached its peak during the last century. There were many circuses then, in Europe and America, and the vaudeville show, a show made up of several different acts, was especially popular in the United States. When the movies came along, about fifty years ago, both circuses and vaudeville shows became less popular. Before, there had been jobs for thousands of acrobats; since then, there have been opportunities for far fewer. The coming of television has given them new opportunities. The Japanese and the Italians have developed many great acrobats.

Acrobats have been popular for thousands of years. This high-wire act is performed out-of-doors.

acropolis

In ancient Greece, where nearly every city was at war with nearly every other city at one time or another, each city would have a walled-in section. This would usually be the highest part of town, and was called an acropolis, in Greek meaning "top of the city." Because the acropolis was the safest part of town, the finest buildings would be built there.

The most famous and most beautiful acropolis was the one at Athens. It was built some 2,500 years ago, and is now in ruins, but even the ruins are beautiful. The finest building was the Parthenon, a temple to the goddess Athena. Many consider it the most beautiful building of all time. It was so well built that much of it still stands. In Nashville, Tennessee, there is a reproduction of this famous building.

ACTH

ACTH, or *adrenocorticotrophic hormone* (of which ACTH are the initials), is a hormone produced by the pituitary gland located at the base of the brain. It is one of the so-called "wonder drugs," used in the treatment

of rheumatoid arthritis, bronchial asthma, rheumatic fever, and many other disorders arising from severe inflammation, acute allergy, or shock. ACTH does not act directly on these ailments but stimulates the adrenal glands to release another hormone, cortisone, which is a key factor in body resistance to disease and injury. ACTH is prepared commercially from animal glands. Treatment does not provide a permanent cure, but often suppresses severe and crippling pain. To be effective, ACTH or cortisone must be taken continuously.

Other conditions that have responded favorably to treatment by these drugs are: inflammations of the heart, kidneys, lungs, eyes; allergic edema (excess fluid in the tissues); breathing allergies; severe cases of hay fever and eczema; ulcerative colitis; physiologic shock resulting from burns, wounds, or acute infections. ACTH and cortisone aggravate certain diseases, such as diabetes and tuberculosis and some mental disorders, and are generally ineffective against diseases caused by invading bacteria.

actinic rays

Some rays, such as rays of light, can produce actual changes in what they touch. These are called actinic rays. The most common example is found in photography. The film is coated with a chemical that changes when light strikes it; when the light striking it is reflected from a person or object, the film becomes a picture of that person or object. This is an actinic effect.

actors and actresses, see the article THEATER.

act of God

An act of God, in law, is an occurrence beyond the influence or control of man and of a character that could not have been prevented by foresight, prudence, or care. A person who is unable to perform a contract by reason of such an occurrence is not liable for his failure to perform. A disaster such as a hurricane, earthquake, fire or flood has invariably been held to be an act of God; illness, crippling accident, a strike by employees and similar factors have often been held to be foreseeable. Wartime hazards such as enemy action or governmental restrictions are usually classed as acts of God. Many contracts include a *force-majeure* clause, a provision releasing a party from liability for failure to perform due to circumstances beyond his control.

Acts

Acts of the Apostles is the fifth book of the New Testament. It was written in Greek, about the year 80 to 90, and most authorities believe it was written by St. Luke. who wrote the Gospel of Luke, though it was not received into the New Testament until later. The book describes the spread of Christianity from Jerusalem to Rome, especially by Paul, whose conversion to Christianity after a vision on the road to Damascus is described in chapter 9.

Adam and Eve

The story of Adam and Eve comes from the Bible. Adam was the first man,

and Eve was the first woman. The first chapter of the Book of Genesis, known as "The Story of Creation," tells how God made the heavens and earth in six days. On the sixth of these days He made Adam, the first man. In the following chapters, it tells that Adam was made out of the dust of the ground, before God made him come to life; and how God then caused Adam to fall asleep, and took out one of his ribs, and made Eve from this rib. (Nevertheless, men and women have the same number of ribs.)

Adam and Eve lived in a beautiful land called the Garden of Eden. It was full of fine fruit trees, and God told them they might eat the fruit of any tree but one. This was the Tree of Knowledge, and whoever ate the fruit of the Tree of Knowledge would become like gods, and know the difference between right and wrong. There was a serpent in the garden, and he said to Eve, "Why not eat the fruit of the Tree of Knowledge? You will not die, and you will become wise." So Eve picked the fruit of the tree and ate some, and gave it to Adam and he ate some. Before this, they had worn no clothes and were not ashamed; but now they thought it was wrong and put clothes on. God saw this, and knew they had eaten the forbidden fruit. (In most stories, this fruit is supposed to be an apple; but the Bible does not actually say what kind of fruit it is.)

God punished Adam and Eve by making them leave the Garden of Eden, and he punished the serpent by saying it would have to "go on its belly" always. Adam and Eve left the Garden of Eden, but lived a long time after that. They had two sons, Cain and Abel, about whom there are separate stories in this encyclopedia; and another son named Seth, and various other sons and daughters. Adam lived to be 930 years old, which seems remarkable now but was not unusual for the men named in the Book of Genesis; the oldest of these men, Methuselah, lived to be 969 years old.

Adam, Robert and James

Robert Adam was one of the greatest British architects. It is said that he "changed the face of London"; and many of the finest old houses in the big American cities, such as New York, Boston, and Philadelphia, are based on the style he set. Though he did his best work nearly two hundred years ago, it still influences our ideas of good taste in buildings and furniture.

Though most of his work was done in London, Robert Adam was born in Edinburgh, Scotland, in 1728. His brother James Adam, who was also a noted architect, but never as famous as Robert, was born there two years later. Robert Adam went to Italy when he was twenty-six years old, and learned a great deal from the ruins of the buildings of ancient Rome, in its "classic" period that dated back to the time of Christ. When he returned to London, he put into practice the many ideas he had formed in Italy. He was the first English architect to use stucco, the first to build a series of

houses in one block so that they look like one imposing building, and the first architect to design the interiors and the furniture of the houses he built. Robert Adam died in 1792 and James Adam, who was two years younger, died two years later, in 1794.

Adam's apple

The Adam's apple is a projection at the front of the throat, especially of males, formed by the cartilage of the larynx, organ of the voice. The Adam's apple is so called from the forbidden fruit (apple), humorously supposed to have stuck in the throat of Adam.

Adam's Peak

Adam's Peak is a mountain in Ceylon, 7,360 ft. high, site of a shrine for Moslem, Hindu and Buddhist pilgrims. It is named for a hollow five feet deep at the summit, attributed by Moslems to Adam standing on one foot for 1,000 years as penance after his expulsion from the Garden of Eden. The Hindus attribute the footprint to Siva and the Buddhists to Buddha.

Adams

The name Adams has been borne by many prominent Americans. Foremost among them is the family that gave this country two of its earliest presidents, John Adams and John Quincy Adams, and another of its greatest and earliest patriots, Samuel Adams (who was a cousin of John Adams); there are separate articles about these men in the following pages.

Abigail Adams was the wife of John Adams, the founder of this great family. She was the first American First Lady (wife of a president) to live in the White House, which was opened in 1800 while John Adams was still president. She was also the first American woman to have both a husband and a son who became president, but she did not live to see her son president because she died in 1818, and John Quincy Adams was elected president in 1824. Her maiden name was Abigail Smith and she was born in 1744. There are several biographies of Abigail Adams, some of them for children.

Charles Francis Adams was a son of John Quincy Adams. He was born in 1807 and died in 1886. He became a lawyer, studying under Daniel Webster, but instead of practicing law he served in the legislature of Massachusetts, ran for vice-president in 1848 but was defeated, and then served in Congress. During the Civil War he was American minister to Great Britain (a position as important then as that of ambassador is now). This first Charles Francis Adams had three sons who became famous. One of them, also named **Charles Francis Adams**, was a general in the Union Army in the Civil War and at one time was president of the Union Pacific Railroad. His brother **Henry Brooks Adams** was a professor and writer whose autobiography, named *The Education of Henry Adams,* is considered one of the greatest American books. He was born in 1838 and died in 1918. The third and youngest brother, **Brooks Adams,** who was born in 1848 and died in 1927, wrote many books of

history. Almost all members of this famous Adams family wrote a great deal, both books and letters, and there are many books about them.

In our own century, another **Charles Francis Adams** (born in 1866) served as Secretary of the Navy under President Herbert Hoover, from 1929 to 1933. The first Charles Francis Adams was his grandfather, so of course President John Adams was his great-great-grandfather. This Charles Francis Adams also won one of the yacht races for the AMERICA'S CUP, about which there is a separate article. He died in 1956.

The names of some other prominent Americans who were named Adams, but were not related to the family of President John Adams, are:

Franklin Pierce Adams, better known as F.P.A. (the name under which his best-known writing was done), who edited a daily column called "The Conning Tower" in a famous newspaper, the *New York World,* and also became known to millions by being a member of the panel on a famous radio quiz show, "Information Please." Many of those who became America's best writers had their first writings published, when they were quite young, in "The Conning Tower." F.P.A. was born in Chicago in 1881 and died in New York in 1960.

James Truslow Adams was a writer of history, and won the Pulitzer Prize in 1921 for his book *The Founding of New England.* He was born in Brooklyn in 1878 and died in 1949.

Maude Adams was one of the best loved American actresses, especially in the role of Peter Pan, which she was the first to play in the United States. She was born in Salt Lake City, Utah, in 1872, and her real name was Kiskadden, but she used a different name (her mother's maiden name) on the stage, as so many actresses and actors do. She died in 1953.

John Adams

No man ever did more to make his native land strong and independent than John Adams, who became the second president of the United States. When John Adams was born, on October 19, 1735, the American states were merely colonies under the rule of the King of England, and no one had dreamed of a nation called the United States. Then the dream was born, and after many struggles and hardships it came true. John Adams played an important part every step of the way. As a young man, he predicted freedom for his country. He was at the first Continental Congress, met to unite the colonies. He helped to write the Declaration of Independence and was one of its signers. Having helped to make the United States possible, he served it first as vice-president — the first man to hold that office — and then as president.

John Adams lived ninety years, the longest life among all presidents of the United States. Late in this long life, he found that his great work had been forgotten by many of the people; he was jeered at by crowds and cursed in newspapers. Sad and bitter, he retired to his farm in Massachusetts to live his life out. But in later years he found himself again

Harvard University

loved and respected by the American people, and he died a contented man.

HIS EARLY YEARS

John Adams was born at Braintree Massachusetts, a farming community about twenty miles south of Boston. The Adams family was descended from a Puritan who had come to Massachusetts from England 100 years before that. John Adams' father was a farmer, who made a good living and had gone to college at Harvard; the Adams family were members of the Congregational Church, as were most of the people in that region. In later years, John Adams changed to the Unitarian Church.

As a boy and later as a man, John Adams was small; but he was strong, for boyhood on a farm means hard work and develops a sturdy body. Young John was serious, too, and a good student. He graduated from Harvard when he was 20 years old, taught school for a year at Worcester, Massachusetts, studied law, and in 1758, when he was 23 years old, became a lawyer at Braintree. He was quite successful as a lawyer. When he was 29 years old, he married a girl from nearby Weymouth, Massachusetts, Abigail Smith, who was to become famous as a fitting wife for a great president. In 1768, when he was 33 years old, he moved with his wife and baby son, John Quincy Adams, to the big city of Boston, to practice law there.

THE START OF A GREAT CAREER

While he was still a twenty-year-old school teacher, John Adams had made a remarkable prophecy. America was then an unimportant outpost of a great empire ruled by England. But Adams said, "Mighty states and kingdoms change. A few people came over into this new world for conscience' sake; this apparently trivial incident may transfer the great seat of empire to America. Our people will, in another century, become more numerous than in England itself. The united force of Europe will not be able to subdue us." At the end of the century that he spoke of, the population of the United States was more than double that of England, and not long after it was the most powerful nation on earth.

Then in 1765, while John Adams was still living in Braintree, the English Parliament passed the "Stamp Act." There is a separate article about the Stamp Act in this encylopedia; briefly, it required that anyone using any sheet of paper as a legal document should buy a stamp to put on the paper, and the price of the stamp went to the British government. This was a tax that Americans would have to pay but from which they would get no benefits—one of the great complaints that led to the American Revolution.

The colonies throughout America argued angrily against the Stamp Act. In Massachusetts John Adams was one of those selected to argue against it before the British Governor in Boston. Addressing the Governor and his Council, Adams declared boldly that the Stamp Act was void, because Parliament had no right to make such a law. It required courage to do this, but Adams was noted for his bravery.

The Boston of 1768, when John Adams took up his profession there, was a city of excited people, most of them unfriendly toward everything British. At one time it seemed that Adams' courage would hurt his popularity with these people. In 1770 the "Boston Massacre" occurred, when a small body of British soldiers led by a Captain Preston fired on a crowd of Bostonians, killing three of them and wounding five more. But Captain Preston had not ordered them to fire, and when he was brought to trial John Adams defended him, and persuaded the jury that Captain Preston was "not guilty." Adams thought his political career was ruined at that point, but he found it was not so. The people respected him just as much—perhaps more —for the courage he had shown. Four years later, in 1774, when the first Continental Congress of the American colonies met in Philadelphia, John Adams was one of the men chosen to represent Massachusetts. It was from this Continental Congress, and the bold decisions it was to make, that the United States of America eventually came into being.

THE STRUGGLE FOR LIBERTY

Eleven of the American colonies sent delegates to the first Continental Congress. They had little idea of full independence for the United States. Most of them wanted only to persuade the King of England to treat them fairly, so that once more they could live happily as British colonies. A few fiery patriots like Patrick Henry of Virginia wanted full independence. John Adams was on their side; he believed that if the British did not change their treatment of the American colonies, the colonies should declare their independence and if necessary go to war to win it.

Little was done at the first Continental Congress, but when the second Continental Congress met in 1775, the spirit was different. Now most of the delegates were willing to take risks in order to have independence. John Adams was there again as a delegate from Massachusetts. Of course he was again on the side that favored independence, and he

was on the committee that was formed to prepare a Declaration of Independence. This famous declaration was adopted on July 4, 1776, and John Adams was one of the signers.

The Revolutionary War had begun, and the new United States needed help from some powerful European nation. Again John Adams was called upon. Taking along his eleven-year-old son, John Quincy Adams, he went to France and helped Benjamin Franklin to enlist the aid of the French government, which meant so much to the colonies in their fight. Countries at war need a great deal of money, too, and Adams persuaded first the French government and then the Dutch government to lend money to the United States, two million dollars each. Finally, in 1783, John Adams was one of the three Americans (the other two being Benjamin Franklin and John Jay) who arranged the Treaty of Paris, by which the United States was recognized as a new independent nation.

HOW HE BECAME PRESIDENT

In 1788, when the people of the United States went to the polls for the first time to choose a president, the manner in which a president was elected was not the same as it is today. Today, each voter votes for a president and a vice-president, two different men. In those days, the vote was cast for one man only, to be president. The person who got the most votes became president; the person who got next to the most votes became vice-president. It was natural that George Washington, the greatest national hero, should be elected president. John Adams got the biggest vote next to Washington's, and was elected the first vice-president of the United States.

At this time, Adams was fifty-three years old. He was a courteous man in his speech, and very polished in his manner. But he was irritable, and was also called "imperious"—that is, he liked to have his own way, and thought his opinion was better than anyone else's. This did not win him a great many friends, though he was admired for his courage and ability.

Washington remained president for two terms, and both times Adams was vice-president. In 1797, when Washington decided he did not want a third term, John Adams got the most votes and was elected president, and Thomas Jefferson got next to the most votes and was elected vice-president.

As president, John Adams had a stormy time. It was a difficult period, and tempers were running high. The French Revolution was under way, and all the kings of Europe were afraid for their crowns, fearing that the revolution would spread to their countries. In the United States, there was argument as to whether the rich people only, or all the people, rich and poor alike, should rule the country. The most tactful of presidents would have had trouble keeping everyone satisfied. John Adams, with his habit of being outspoken and courageous in the face of possible unpopularity, was sure to make enemies—and he did.

Adams had never approved of the French Revolution. He thought it went too far, especially when the revolutionists there killed the French king and queen. The American government, he believed, should have titles of nobility, such as were used in European countries, and it should have a senate made up of "the aristocracy"—that is, the families that were richest and most prominent. This idea was unpopular with the majority of Americans, and Adams was accused even of favoring the establishment of a king in the United States, though this was not so.

Then came the "XYZ Affair." The revolutionary government of France was doing a great many things that seemed unfriendly to the United States. American ships were being captured on the high seas by French privateers (that is, pirates acting with the consent of their government), and the French government would not stop them.

Some private representatives of the French government proposed that the United States should pay a large amount of money, perhaps $250,000, to have the attacks stopped. The French representatives who made this proposal refused to sign their names, and used only initials; that is why they were called X, Y and Z, and the whole thing was called the XYZ Affair. The American people were greatly angered by this. Their slogan was, "Millions for defense, but not one cent for tribute." Many of them wanted to go to war against France if necessary. But President Adams was unwilling to risk another war. All this happened in 1797 and 1798, the first year that Adams was president, and it made him very unpopular.

The Alien and Sedition Acts also hurt his popularity. Under these laws, passed by Congress, foreign-born persons, or those who criticized the government, could be arrested and punished. This violated rights that had been guaranteed to the people by the Constitution. The Alien and Sedition Laws were so hated by Americans that they did not last very long, but people did not soon forget that Adams had been in favor of them.

Thomas Jefferson, who liked the most republican form of government, with no king and no nobility, and who opposed the Alien and Sedition Laws, became the country's most popular man. When John Adams ran for re-election as president in 1800, Jefferson beat him easily. After his defeat Adams left Washington for his home in Braintree, (now called Quincy) Massachusetts. Adams was so upset by the election results that he did not even remain for Jefferson's inauguration.

Adams was now retired from active political office, but he closely followed national events. The bitterness and unhappiness that the public had felt toward him while he was President were gone. His advice and opinions were printed and read throughout the country. The American people appreciated his efforts, his integrity, and his loyalty.

With the passing of time, John Adams and Thomas Jefferson resumed their friendship; today their letters are of great historical interest. They contain com-

The Bettmann Archive, Inc.

Before becoming President, John Adams served as an American diplomat abroad. This picture depicts Adams' introduction to King George III of England. Adams was sent to negotiate a peace settlement with Great Britain.

ments on history, government, religion, and philosophy.

Adams followed the successful political career of his son, John Quincy Adams, with great pride. John Quincy Adams became the sixth President of the United States while his father was still alive.

John Adams died on July 4, 1826, exactly fifty years after the signing of the Declaration of Independence. According to popular belief, his last words were, "Thomas Jefferson still survives." Unknown to Adams, Jefferson had died a few hours earlier in his home in Virginia.

The great leaders of the American Revolution—George Washington, Benjamin Franklin, Patrick Henry, Samuel Adams, John Hancock, and Thomas Jefferson—were now part of history. Adams was the last of these men to die. He had been among the first to enter the fight for his country's independence.

John Quincy Adams

John Quincy Adams was the sixth president of the United States, elected in 1824 and serving from 1825 to 1829. He was the son of President John Adams, the only case in which the son of a president has become president. He is also the only former president who returned, after his term of office, as a congressman in the House of Representatives (Andrew Johnson, after having been president, served as a senator). Though John Quincy Adams was recognized as a superior man and a most valuable man to his country, his accomplishments were not spectacular, and the one principally worth remembering—the Monroe Doctrine—bears another man's name.

HIS EARLY YEARS

There was no other boyhood in American history like that of John Quincy Adams; there could not have been, for no other boy ever had the opportunity to be present in person at such an eventful period in the birth of a nation. He was born in the family home at Braintree, in Massachusetts, on July 11, 1767, while his father, John Adams, was still no more than a successful Massachusetts lawyer. Like his father before him, he was a serious and studious child, but even more so.

When John Quincy Adams was only 11 years old, his father was sent to France as representative of the American colonies, which were engaged in the Revolutionary War for their independence; and John Adams took his 11-year-old son with him. In France, the young John Quincy Adams went to school for two years and learned French, which was to be of value to him in his later work as an American diplomat. Then his father went as American representative to Holland, and again the boy went along, attended school in Amsterdam, and became familiar with the Dutch language. When John Quincy Adams was 14, he accompanied the American minister to Russia, Francis Dana, as his secretary and acquired still more knowledge of the world, its peoples, and its languages. After a return to America, he made still another trip to France with his father, when he was 17. Then he entered Harvard College, and graduated in 1787, when he was 20. After college he studied law and could have been a lawyer, but he preferred politics.

The political genius of John Quincy Adams became apparent when he was still

a very young man. The burning issue of the years shortly after 1789 was the French Revolution which had broken out in 1789, and the question of the day was, what should be the attitude of America? John Quincy Adams, without signing his own name, wrote two series of articles for the Boston newspapers. They were so well done that many readers thought his father, the wise and experienced John Adams, had written them. George Washington, as president, considered this young man one of the country's most valuable diplomats, and kept him engaged from 1794 to 1801 as the United States minister in Holland, England, and Prussia. During this period, in 1797, John Quincy Adams married Miss Louisa Johnson, the daughter of the American consul in London.

Nevertheless, as John Quincy Adams approached his fortieth year, he decided that his political career was finished. He accepted a position as a professor at Harvard, and was satisfied to spend the rest of his life there.

Museum of Fine Arts, Boston

HOW HE BECAME PRESIDENT

The year was 1809; James Madison was president of the United States; and it was a troublous time for the world. Napoleon, with his fearsome French army, off and on was at war with the world. The British, his chief enemy, fought back with their powerful navy, capturing any ships at sea that were trading with France or its allies; and often this included American ships. President Madison was having a hard time keeping the country at peace, when some of the most influential American men were pressing him to go to war against England rather than let the country's shipping be swept off the seas. In this unpleasant situation, President Madison would not let one of the country's best diplomats go to waste, in a teaching job. He persuaded John Quincy Adams to re-enter public service and become minister to Russia; and Adams, to whom politics was a first love, left Harvard and accepted the appointment. From that time until his death, he was uninterruptedly in public life.

War finally came, the War of 1812, and it was fought and finished. In 1817, James Monroe became president and called John Quincy Adams back from abroad to become Secretary of State. He served in that position throughout the two terms, eight years, of James Monroe's presidency, and it was toward the end of this period, in 1823, that the Monroe Doctrine was pronounced.

The French Revolution was now over. The kings of Europe again felt safe on their thrones. They began to give thought to the smaller revolutions that had succeeded while they were engaged with France—the revolutions that had made the Spanish-speaking countries of South America independent republics. Why, thought the kings, should we not now send our armies across the seas to reconquer these weak countries of South America and bring them again under European control?

That was the time when John Quincy Adams proposed an American statement that this country would not permit any European power to interfere with the independence of any country in our part of the world. President Monroe stated it in a speech, and it became a policy of the United States that has never been changed or weakened. Since the United States became strong enough to fight any number of foreign enemies, if necessary, the Monroe Doctrine has seemed a simple thing to enforce; but in 1823 the United States was not a strong country, and it took great courage and boldness to defy the powerful nations of Europe.

HIS ELECTION AS PRESIDENT

The presidential election of 1824 was one of the closest the United States ever had. No one got a majority. Andrew Jackson, who later would be elected president twice, got 99 votes in the electoral college; that was the most. John Quincy Adams was second with 84 votes. William H. Crawford of Virginia had 41, and Henry Clay, the great Kentucky senator, had 37. Since no one had more than half the votes, the House of Representatives had the right to decide the presidency—the same system that would be used today if no candidate for president had a majority (more than half) of the votes in the electoral college.

When it came to a vote in the House of Representatives, Henry Clay had enough influence to make his supporters vote for John Quincy Adams, and Adams was elected president over Jackson. When he took office, Adams appointed Clay to be Secretary of State, and there was some talk of a "deal." But actually there had been no arrangement between Adams and Clay. The two men had served together in negotiations in Europe, and Clay had reason to support Adams rather than Andrew Jackson, who was his bitter political opponent. Just as Clay liked Adams enough to elect him president, Adams liked Clay enough to make him Secretary of State.

Very little happened while John Quincy Adams was president. There was peace in Europe, which meant that the United States was not drawn into the arguments of foreign nations. The Erie Canal was opened, and the first railroads were built, and both contributed to the improvement in transportation that was eventually to mean so much in making the country big and prosperous. Slavery was occasionally an issue, and Adams (true to his New England background and sentiments) was always on the side of those who opposed the extension or encouragement of slavery. Meanwhile, the following of Andrew Jackson, which had been the largest in the United States in the 1824 elections, even though it was not a full majority, became larger and larger until, in 1828, when the next elections were held, Jackson won easily and Adams lost.

John Quincy Adams was not disturbed. He had served well during his life, and he was satisfied to go back to his home in Quincy, Massachusetts, and live quietly. He was a scholar, an excellent writer of both prose and poetry, and a fine speaker. He had nothing to fear of the future.

THE CROWNING OF A GREAT CAREER

So John Quincy Adams went back to his home, rich and famous and admired, and did not dream that he would ever again be a public figure. Then, two years later, his community asked him to be a candidate for Congress. He accepted. He was elected by a big majority, and from then until the end of his life—seventeen more years—he served in the House of Representatives, always speaking for the wise and honorable course in government. He did not live to be 90 years old, as his father had, but he lived to be 81, and they called him "The Old Man Eloquent." He died as he would have wanted to, from a stroke while he was actively serving in Congress, on February 23, 1848. His last words were, "This is the last of earth. I am content."

Adams, Samuel

It is sure that no one did more to make the United States a free and independent nation than did Samuel Adams of Boston, one of the great founding fathers. It may be that no one else did so much. Samuel Adams wanted the revolution more than anyone else. He stirred up the spirits and tempers of Americans when otherwise they might have been content to make a bad peace with the English king. He started some of the dramatic events, like the Boston Tea Party, that "stirred men's souls." He faced danger and dared the fates time after time. From the success of the revolution he gained far less in fame and fortune than any of the others who approached him in stature. Yet he did not seem to care.

A cousin of John Adams, the second president, but a few years older, Samuel Adams was born in Boston in 1722. Like his cousin John, he went to Harvard. Also like his cousin John, he had independent ideas when he was quite young; at the age of 21, he proposed the question, "Is it not lawful to resist the king if you cannot otherwise preserve your country?"

Samuel Adams was in business, but he did not make money; in fact, he lost what little money he had. He was more interested in opposing the harsh acts of the English king and Parliament, which were then trying to collect unfair taxes from the American colonies, not yet a separate nation.

When in 1765 the Stamp Act was

passed by Parliament, forcing Americans to buy a tax stamp, and put it on every piece of paper used in legal transactions, Samuel Adams opposed it vigorously. The British did not like that, but they were trying to keep the Americans peaceful, and General Thomas Gage, who commanded all the British soldiers in this country, called Samuel Adams to him and said, "You should make your peace with the king." Adams, who was a Puritan and very strict in his religion and behavior, answered, "I have made my peace with the King of kings. I will not abandon the cause of my country."

In 1774 a Continental Congress was called in Philadelphia, with representatives of eleven of the American colonies present. Samuel Adams was a delegate from Massachusetts, and he was one of the few (that included Patrick Henry of Virginia) who were in favor of full independence for America. In fact, he had already been talking about full independence for five years. In a speech at the Continental Congress, he said, "If only one of a thousand could live and keep his liberty, and the other nine hundred and ninety-nine had to die, I would still favor it. One free man must enjoy more happiness than a thousand slaves."

General Gage did not forget that Samuel Adams had defied him. He sent the British troops out of Boston on April 18, 1775, because he had heard that Samuel Adams and John Hancock were staying in Lexington, Massachusetts, and he wanted to capture them. Paul Revere's famous ride was chiefly to warn Adams and Hancock that the British soldiers were coming to get them. Of course, what happened was that a battle began at Concord and it started the Revolutionary War. But Paul Revere had succeeded in warning the two patriots and they escaped. Later, when General Gage was still trying to make peace with the colonies and bring them back under the rule of the British king, he offered a pardon to everyone except Samuel Adams and John Hancock, whom he called "arch traitors."

When the Revolutionary War was won, Samuel Adams returned to Boston. He served as governor of Massachusetts, 1794 to 1797, but he never held any national office that might reward him for the good work he had done. He lived and died a poor, hard-working man, but with the satisfaction of knowing he had succeeded in helping a great country to gets its start. Samuel Adams died at the age of 81, in 1803.

Addams, Jane

Jane Addams was a woman who spent all her life trying to help people who were not as fortunate as she was, who did not have comfortable houses to live in and warm clothes to wear when it was cold, or enough food to eat. She was born over a hundred years ago, in 1860, and she died in 1935, when she was 75 years old. She never married. Because of the work she did, Jane Addams became famous throughout the world, and the place in Chicago where she helped the poor people, a place called Hull House, became famous too. Very few men or women have done as much

to help people to better, happier, lives as Jane Addams did. In 1931 she was given the Nobel Peace Prize, because of other work she had done to bring peace to the world.

When Jane Addams was a little girl, most working men in factories did not make enough money to support themselves and families decently. Jane was born a rich girl, but she suffered when she saw how much worse other people lived. Her original home was in Cedarville, Illinois, near Chicago. When she had grown up and graduated from school (Rockford College) she went to Chicago and with a friend, Miss Ellen Starr, rented a building in Chicago that had been built by a man named Hull. In this building she and Miss Starr, and other people who wanted to help the poor, taught the poor people how to take care of their children better, eat better, clothe themselves better, and even earn more money. At the same time, Miss Addams and her helpers at Hull House were working to keep the employers of these people from paying them too little and working them too hard. Working conditions in the United States are now far better than they used to be, and much better than they are on any other continent, and much of the credit for this improvement must be given to Jane Addams.

addax

The addax is a kind of antelope, known for its long, twisted horns. It is about three feet high at the shoulder; weighs up to 500 lbs; has a mane on its neck; and has horns 3 to 4 feet long, and spiraling. Its color is white but in front it is usually reddish brown. It is found in North Africa and Arabia.

adder

The name adder is used for several different kinds of snake, usually for poisonous snakes that are properly called vipers. For example, the moccasin is often called a *water adder,* and the copperhead is often called a *red adder.* Perhaps the best-known snake that is called an adder is a viper found in Africa, called the *puff adder.* Its name comes from the fact that it puffs up its body like a big balloon. It is very poisonous, but will attack only if it is bothered by someone.

Other poisonous types include the Old World hooded cobras; the blue adder (*crait*) and the banded adder (*rajsamp*) of India; the death adders of Australia; and ten species of vipers found in Eurasia and Africa. Nonpoisonous types include the hog-nosed snakes of North America that spread the hood when alarmed, much as do the poisonous hooded cobras.

Addis Ababa

Addis Ababa is the capital city of the empire of Ethiopia, in east Africa. The name means "new flower." Situated in the midst of high mountains, it is quite a big city in which unpaved streets and thatch-roofed mud huts present a startling contrast to the numerous modern buildings that have been constructed in recent years. Addis Ababa is the cultural center of Ethiopia. The city has nine movie theaters and

four daily newspapers (one English, one French, and two in Amharic, the official native language). The newspapers are all government controlled. Most of the colleges and technical schools of the country are located in Addis Ababa, including the new Haile Selassie I University, to which the emperor donated a palace that is now part of the campus. Other architectural landmarks are the St. George Cathedral, St. Mary's Church, the imperial palace, many attractive new government buildings, and Africa Hall, an impressive modern structure which is the headquarters of the United Nations Economic Commission for Africa.

There are only a few small industries in Addis Ababa, but the city is important as a distribution center for the products of the whole country. Roads connect the city to the provinces, and a railroad connects it with the seaport of Djibouti in the Territory of the Afars and Issas (formerly French Somaliland). A few miles south of the city there is an international airport.

ADDIS ABABA. Population 912,000. Capital and largest city of Ethiopia. Founded 1887 by Emperor Menelik; became capital in 1889.

Addison, Joseph

Joseph Addison was an English writer who lived about 250 years ago. He became famous for his essays (short compositions in which the author expresses his personal opinion), and also because he was one of the first men to publish a magazine. Addison was born in 1672. His father was a very prominent clergyman. After attending Oxford (which he entered at the age of 15), Addison became a friend of several men who were powerful in English politics, and during most of his life he held some government job that permitted him to live comfortably. From 1708 until he died in 1719, Addison was a Member of Parliament.

Addison

Though he wrote some poetry and two plays, Addison was best known for his essays in *The Tatler* and *The Spectator,* which were called newspapers but were more like today's magazines. *The Tatler* was published by Richard Steele, a friend of Addison's; it was issued three times a week, in London. *The Spectator* was published by Addison and Steele together and was issued daily. The best of Addison's essays were signed with the name of an imaginary character, Sir Roger de Coverly, whom Steele invented to represent a typical, conservative English gentleman. Addison is buried in Westminster Abbey.

address

Forms of address are proper ways of addressing letters or other written communications, especially to persons having titles of rank or official position. Traditionally there are two forms, one for use by "equals" of the person addressed, the other for use by that person's "inferiors"; such social distinctions are seldom made now. There is no case in which the saluta-

Addis Ababa has many new and modern buildings. This is the headquarters of the New State Bank of Ethiopia.

Ethiopian Airlines

tion "Sir:" to a man or "Madam:" to a woman can be incorrect, even to those of imperial rank; in the U.S. "Dear Sir:" and "Dear Madam:" are equally acceptable. Such forms as "May it please Your Majesty:" to a king or queen, and "Your Grace:" or "My Lord Duke:" to a duke, and dozens of similar forms, have passed from actual use. In formal correspondence with a high-ranking clergyman, "Reverend Sir:" and "Reverend Madam:" remain proper. The address to a man, formerly "John Doe, Esq.," has become uniformly "Mr. John Doe," except as an occasional courtesy to a member of the legal profession. See ABBREVIATIONS for additional information. Specific forms of address are:

President or Vice President. *Address:* The President, The White House, Washington, D.C. *Salutation:* Sir; Mr. President; or Dear Mr. President. Same for the Vice President, but the address is Senate Office Building.

Royalty. *Address:* His (or Her) Majesty King (or Queen) ——; followed by the name of the capital of the country. *Salutation:* Sir (or Madam). The princes or princesses, His or Her Royal Highness Prince (or Princess) ——; followed by the exact address. Same salutation as for king or queen.

Nobility. *Address:* The Earl (Countess, Marquess, Duke) of ——; for lesser titles, Lord ——; followed by the exact address. *Salutation:* Sir (or Madam); My dear Duke (Marquess, etc.); My dear Lord ——.

Clergy. Always use "The Reverend (or Rev.) John Doe," with or without Mr. or Dr.; "The Rev. Mr. Doe" if the first name or initials are not included; never "Reverend" without "the" or "The Reverend Doe" with first name or initials. The Pope is addressed as His Holiness, the Pope, State of Vatican City, Italy, and the salutation is "Your Holiness." A cardinal is addressed as His Eminence, John, Cardinal Doe, followed by the address, and the salutation is "Your Eminence." In the Roman Catholic Church a bishop or archbishop is "The Most Reverend ——," and a monsignor is "The Very Reverend ——"; in Protestant churches a bishop or archbishop is "The Right Reverend ——." The salutation is "Most Reverend (Very Reverend, Right Reverend) Sir"; to a lesser clergyman, it may be "Dear Doctor (or Mr.) ——."

Military. The exact rank should be given in the address: Maj. Gen. John Doe. The higher rank is used in the salutation: Dear General Doe. Warrant officers and noncommissioned officers are addressed as Mr.

Governmental. In the U.S. any legislator, cabinet officer, diplomatic officer, administrator, governor or other state official, or mayor may be addressed as "The Hon. John Doe (or Mr. Doe)" and the salutation may be "Sir," "Dear Sir," "Dear Mr. Ambassador," "Dear Senator Doe," or "Dear Mr. Doe." A Congressman or legislator is addressed only as "Mr." Similar officers of foreign countries should be addressed as "His Excellency, the French Ambassador," etc., and the salutation is "Your Excellency."

Judges. A chief justice should be addressed: The Chief Justice, Supreme Court of the U.S. (or a state); followed by the name of the capital. The salutation may be "Sir:" or "Mr. Chief Justice." Any other jurist with the title of justice should be addressed "Mr. Justice John Doe," and the salutation is "Sir:" or "Mr. Justice Doe." A judge with any other title should be addressed "The Hon. Judge John Doe," the salutation being "Dear Sir:" or "Dear Judge Doe."

Ade, George

George Ade was an American newspaperman and playright, famous as a humorist. He was born in Indiana in 1866 and attended Purdue University. As a newspaperman in Chicago he wrote short articles in which he used the latest slang, and these were a great success when published in a book called *Fables in Slang* in 1900. His plays were very successful. He died in 1944.

Adelaide

Adelaide is the name of the capital city of South Australia, one of the seven states into which Australia is divided. Though its population figures (35,032) make it seem small, Adelaide is really a big and important city. Also it is one of the most modern cities in the world. About nine out of ten of Adelaide's people live in the suburbs. The total population is more than 808,000. There are many factories, banks and insurance

companies, schools and colleges, and churches. Seven miles away is Port Adelaide, through which the goods of the big state of South Australia are shipped out and goods that it buys are brought in. Port Adelaide was where the first settlers of South Australia landed in 1836. They began to build Adelaide a year after, in 1837. A few years later, important copper deposits were found nearby, and soon afterward Adelaide became one of the big wheat-selling cities of the world. Since then it has become more of a business center. The river Torrens flows through Adelaide, to Port Adelaide and the sea. It has been dammed to make a beautiful lake in Adelaide.

ADELAIDE, SOUTH AUSTRALIA. Population, with suburbs, 808,600 (1973). Capital of South Australia, fourth-largest city in Australia. Founded 1837, incorporated 1840.

Adelie Coast

The Adelie Coast is an area of 150,000 square miles in Antarctica, near the Indian Ocean. It was discovered by Dumont D'Urville in 1840 and was claimed by France. Later, from 1911 to 1914, it was explored by Sir Douglas Mawson and an Australasian expedition. The area contains many glaciers and may have the strongest winds in the world.

Aden

Aden is the former name of a large territory on the southern coast of Arabia. It is now an independent country called the People's Democratic Republic of Yemen, covering about 112,000 square miles or about the size of Arizona. The capital of the old territory of Aden was the small fishing port called Aden. It is now the capital of the Republic. The port became an important trade center after the British captured it in 1839, because the increased use of steamships and the opening of the Suez Canal in 1869 brought increased traffic to the city. The British extended their control over the area by making treaties with local rulers. In return for England's promise to protect the territory against enemies, the British were given the right to guide the rulers in foreign affairs.

In 1959, the British agreed to grant independence to Aden by 1968. Before that date, however, local Arabs who resented the presence of the British began to terrorize the British and those who sided with them. In 1967, England began removing its troops from the area. Later in the year it granted independence to the entire territory.

The inhabitants of the area are mostly Arabs, with some Indians, Pakistanis, and Somalis. The most common spoken language is Arabic, but nearly everyone understands English. Most of the people are Moslems.

The climate is extremely hot, with summer temperatures about 130°F. or higher. There is less than 3 inches of rain per year. The coast is mostly desert, and agriculture is confined to the mountainous areas a few miles inland.

ADEN. (People's Democratic Republic of Yemen.) Area, 112,000 square miles. Population (1971 estimate) 1,470,000. Capitals, Aden and Medina as-Shaab. Languages, Arabic, English and others. Religion, Moslem. Monetary Unit, Dinar.

Adenauer, Konrad

Konrad Adenauer was an anti-Nazi German, opposed to Hitler before World War II, who became the leading statesman of West Germany after the war. He had been lord mayor of the city of Cologne from 1917 to 1933, and founded Cologne University in 1925. During the war the Nazis kept him in concentration camps, the big prison camps where they kept political enemies.

Adenauer was born in 1876, so he was almost seventy years old when World War II ended in 1945. The Allied Occupation Forces released him and made him again mayor of Cologne. Adenauer was a founder of the Christian Democratic Union party in West Germany and helped to draft the constitution of the Federal Republic of Germany (West Germany). In 1949 he became the first chancellor (head of the government) in West Germany, and he was re-elected in 1953, 1957, and 1961. He retired October 15, 1963. Adenauer did much to restore friendship with the United States. He died on April 19, 1967.

adenoids

Between the nose and the throat there are some tiny organs of the body called "lymph glands" which are useful in keeping the body healthy as long as they are healthy themselves, but which often swell up until they nearly block the throat. When this happens, the condition is called adenoids.

Adenoids is a disease of children. It seldom happens to adults. When a child does have adenoids, it may cause earache or eye trouble; and especially it interferes with the breathing because of the way the passage in the throat is narrowed. A child with adenoids has trouble breathing through his nose, and constant breathing through the mouth is not good. Also, adenoids can cause a great deal of snoring, coughing or sneezing, and difficulty in speaking clearly.

Adenoids should almost always be removed. It is a simple operation, and within a few days both the operation and the adenoids are forgotten and the child feels much better.

One kind of adhesive is paper paste, which is made in tanks like this. It is powder at first, and then water is added to turn the powder into paste. It has to be heated, and almost cooked, before the right amount of adhesive quality, or stickiness, will develop. After this man has mixed the paste until it is absolutely smooth, it will be put into large barrels and shipped to other factories where it is put in smaller jars. Millions of tons of paste a year are used in the United States.

adhesives

Adhesives stick things together. Glue is an adhesive; so is paste, and so is the gum on the sticky side of a postage stamp. There are different names usually used for different kinds of adhesives, depending on what they are made of: *paste* is made of starch, such as flour; *glue* is made of animal products, for example the bones of animals; *mucilage* is made from gummy parts of plants; and *cement* is a solid substance, ranging from powdered stone to rubber and many plastics, that can be dissolved or made soft with a liquid. In the case of nearly all adhesives, the liquid dries in the air and the solid part of the adhesive is left to keep the two things joined together.

Nearly everything is porous, meaning that there are tiny holes in it. While an adhesive is in its liquid or wet form, it can flow into those tiny holes. When it dries out, there are still parts of the adhesive in the tiny holes. This holds them tightly, just as the roots of a tree are held tightly in the earth. If the adhesive is clinging in this way to two different things that are close together, it holds them together and makes it hard to pull them apart.

Even a material that is not porous, for example glass or china, can be held by an adhesive if its surface is rough. The adhesive will flow under the jagged little points that cause the rough surface, and will form a sort of hook there, making it hard to pull away the adhesive (or anything sticking to it).

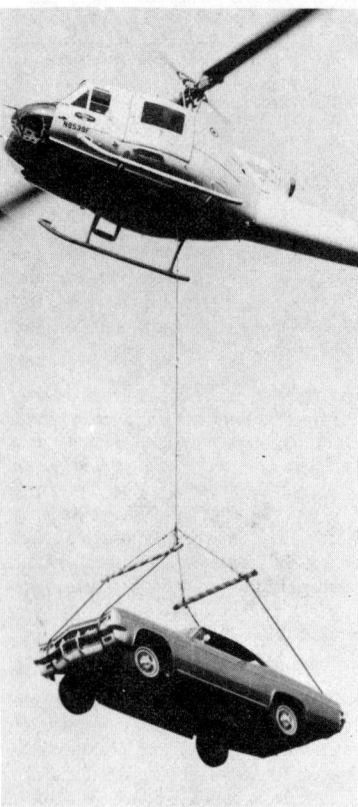

3M Co.

A super-strong adhesive is used to suspend a 2-ton car from a helicopter. One square inch of adhesive, a thousandth of an inch thick, connects the line with the rig supporting the car.

HB Fuller Co.

Hot melt adhesive, often used in bookbinding, has to be melted before it is applied; then it dries very swiftly.

These are simple ways in which adhesives work. There are other, more complicated ways. Sometimes an adhesive will actually dissolve the surface of the material it is put on, and when the surface dries the adhesive is part of it. Some adhesives are called "heat sealing"—make them hot enough and they become sticky, but after they cool they are hard and no longer sticky.

Hundreds of different kinds of adhesives are used. Paste is the cheapest, but it is seldom used except for paper, because it will not hold heavy things together. Artists use rubber cement, which is rubber dissolved in a liquid like gasoline; the advantage of rubber cement is that it does not wrinkle paper, and it can be rubbed off paper without leaving a trace, when it is no longer wanted for its adhesive effect. Plastic cements are most often used for mending broken dishes, and for making pieces of wood stick together, as on a chair or table. The invention of cellulose tape opened a large and useful new field for adhesives. The cellulose tape sold as "Scotch tape" and under other trade names is very unusual because the sticky side will stick to almost anything except the smooth side of cellulose tape. That permits the tape to be wound in rolls and handled very easily.

The principle that causes adhesives to join things together is called *adhesion*. You can read more about it in the article on COHESION.

Adirondacks

In the northeast section of New York State are the Adirondack Mountains, the oldest mountains in the United States. They are part of the Appalachian chain that arose about 225 million years ago, before the age of dinosaurs. The Adirondacks are about 155 million years older than the Rocky Mountains. When the center of the earth cooled many millions of years ago, the earth's crust shrank and wrinkled, forming mountain ranges in many places. Fossil evidence shows that the Adirondacks were among the mountains that pushed up at a time when the only forms of life on land were a few kinds of primitive plants and animals. There were no birds, no mammals, and no flowering plants. About a million years ago or less, a great glacier, or river of ice, moved slowly southward, scraping the Adirondacks as it passed; it cut deep dents that now form many beautiful lakes and make that section of New York State a favorite summer resort. The glacier de-

posited sand and huge boulders along the way, making rocky and sandy slopes in many places.

adjective

A word is called an adjective when it is used to make a noun (that is, the name of a thing) mean more than it would all by itself. If you look out the window and say, "There are men in the garden," anyone who hears you gets a certain idea of what you see. If you said, "There are three men in the garden," he would get a better idea. If you say, "There are three tall young men in the garden," he gets a still better idea. *Three, tall,* and *young* are all adjectives. They are said to "modify" the word *men,* which is a noun, because they give a clearer picture of what the noun means.

A part of speech is a kind of word that has a particular duty when you say it or write it. Noun is a part of speech; the duty of a noun is to tell what a thing is. Verb is a part of speech; the duty of a verb is to tell what something does. Adjective is a part of speech; the duty of an adjective is to tell what a thing is like. An adjective is used to modify a noun, which is, to describe it, to tell how it is different from other things that might be thought of when that particular noun is used.

Sometimes a noun does not mean anything at all unless there is an adjective to describe it or limit it. If you say, "It is a day," it means nothing. If you say, "It is a cold day," the adjective *cold* gives your words meaning.

THE KINDS OF ADJECTIVE

An adjective is said to be *attributive* when it comes before the noun it modifies. If you speak of "a sweet apple," *sweet* is an attributive adjective modifying the noun *apple.* An adjective is said to be *predicative* when it comes after the noun it modifies. If you say, "The apple is sweet," *sweet* is a predicative adjective modifying the noun *apple.*

A predicative adjective can be used only after the verb *to be* in one of its forms (am, is, are, was, were, been); or a word that might be replaced by a form of the verb to be, for example *seem* or *become;* or after a verb that expresses one of our senses: *feel, look, sound, taste, smell.* You can say, He is healthy, He looks healthy, He seems healthy. Or, The cloth feels smooth, The apple tastes sweet, The music sounds good, The perfume smells good. *Healthy* and *smooth* and *sweet* and *good* are predicative adjectives.

In the English language, adjectives often appear in other kinds of sentence, different from these, because a word or words that would make it clear that they are adjectives have been dropped out—being "understood," as it is said—because the sentence is perfectly clear without them. Sometimes it is a certain noun that is dropped, as in the sentence, for instance, "The blind read with their fingers." If you put the word "people" after blind, you can see that blind is an adjective. In cases like this, the adjective is always preceded by the word *the,* and its use is called *substantive.* This is only one of many technical terms in grammar. You do not have to know them all to recognize adjectives and use them properly.

When an attributive phrase includes a word that is not regularly an adjective the phrase is hyphenated (a *cast-iron* stove); when the phrase is predicative, the hyphen is not used (The stove is cast iron).

COMPARISON OF ADJECTIVES

Often it is desirable for an adjective to show not only what a noun is like, but also to show how it compares with other things of the same kind. Two automobiles may both be fast, but one will go one hundred miles an hour and the other will go only eighty miles an hour. We can use an adjective to show which is which.

When we show this kind of difference between exactly two persons, things, or groups, the word *more* can be used, or *-er* can be added to the adjective, as by saying of the automobile that goes one hundred miles an hour, "It is faster than the other." With short adjectives such as *fast, -er* is added. With long adjectives, the word *more* is used because it is easier to say: "Men are stronger than women; John is more athletic than William." This is called the *comparative degree.*

When we compare three or more persons, things, or groups, *-est* is added to short adjectives, and the word *most* is used before long adjectives. This is called the *superlative degree.* "There are three boys, and John is the tallest; but as between the two others, William is taller." "Men are usually heavier than women, but whales are the heaviest animals alive."

Read also the article PART OF SPEECH.

adjutant bird

There is a very big, funny bird called the adjutant, or adjutant bird. It is related to the stork and is found in India, some of the islands near India, and parts of Africa. It may be six or seven feet high, with long legs, a heavy body, and a long bill. It is a dark gray color on its top and wings, and white below. It has a pouch in its neck that it puffs out with air when it flies. The adjutant feeds on small animals and also on carrion—the bodies of dead animals. Feathers from its tail and wings were much used, years ago, in making fans and in decorating women's hats; they are called marabou because they look like feathers of the real marabou, which is a different bird. The adjutant bird got its name from being seen so often strutting around parade grounds of the British army in India. The Indian government protects the adjutant, for its function in disposing of carrion and destroying reptiles.

Adler, Alfred

Alfred Adler was an Austrian psychiatrist, or doctor specializing in mental disorders. He was the first man to use the term *inferiority complex.* Adler was born in 1870. For some years he was a follower of the more famous Austrian psychiatrist Sigmund Freud, but he disagreed with Freud in some matters and broke away to express his own ideas of "Individual Psychology." Adler had great influence on many ideas of child psychology that are now used in schools. He died in 1937.

N.Y. Zoological Society

This adjutant bird is taller than most men.

Adler, Felix

Felix Adler was the founder of the system of education and religion known as Ethical Culture. He was born in Germany about one hundred years ago (in 1851) but was brought to the United States when he was only six years old. After graduating from Columbia University in New York City and then teaching social and political ethics. He founded the New York Society for Ethical Culture. In 1902 he became a professor at Columbia University, teaching social and political ethics. He died in 1933, but the Ethical Culture movement that he founded still has several schools in New York. See the article on ETHICAL CULTURE.

admiral

Admiral is the title of the highest-ranking officers of a navy. Usually an admiral commands a fleet of big ships or has an equally important duty in the offices of the navy. Since navies have had their own aviation branches, there have also been "flying admirals" who are in charge of air operations.

All navies have at least three grades of admiral. When an admiral makes his headquarters on a ship in a fleet at sea, the ship is called the flagship of the fleet and it flies the admiral's personal flag, with a number of stars that show the admiral's rank. The ranks and stars are: Admiral (or "full admiral"), 4 stars; Vice Admiral, 3 stars; Rear Admiral, 2 stars. In the United States Navy there is also a lower grade of rear admiral, with one star. This rank was formerly called commodore. When two or more admirals are in the same place, the highest-

ranking flies a blue flag and the others fly red flags.

Most navies now have a five-star rank, to which different titles are given: Admiral of the Fleet in Britain, General Admiral in Russia, and Fleet Admiral in the United States. Congress established the rank of Fleet Admiral in 1945, and in 1946 the title was given to four men: W. D. Leahy, E. J. King, C. W. Nimitz, and W. F. Halsey. An admiral of any rank is addressed simply as "Admiral" when you speak to him.

The word admiral came to us from the Arabs, in whose language *amir-al* means commander, or chief, of the——. The first full admiral in the United States Navy was David G. Farragut, for whom Congress created the rank in 1866. George Dewey, the American naval hero in the Spanish-American War, was given a special title, Admiral of the Navy, which no one else has held.

Admiralty

In the United States, the navy is under the control of the Department of the Navy, which is part of the Department of Defense. There is a Secretary of the Navy who is in charge of the Department of the Navy, and he is usually a man who is not a naval officer; and there is a Chief of Naval Operations who is a naval officer and who advises the Secretary of the Navy.

In Great Britain, the department of the government that does the same thing is called the Admiralty. The head of the department is appointed by the Prime Minister, and usually he is not a naval officer. He is called the First Lord of the Admiralty. Winston Churchill was First Lord of the Admiralty during World War I and again during World War II, until he became the Prime Minister. Most of the other members are high-ranking naval officers. The members, who are called lords commissioners, are the First Sea Lord and Chief of Naval Staff; the Second Sea Lord and Chief of Naval Personnel; the Third Sea Lord and Controller of the Navy; the Fourth Sea Lord and Chief of Supplies and Transport; the Fifth Sea Lord and Deputy Chief of Naval Staff (air); the Vice Chief of Naval Staff; the Assistant Chief of Naval Staff; the Parliamentary and Financial Secretary; the Civil Lord; and the Permanent Secretary. The First Lord and the Civil Lord are members of Parliament and resign automatically if the Prime Minister resigns.

Admiralty Islands

Admiralty Island is the name of an island that belongs to the United States, and lies off the coast of Alaska; the Admiralty Islands are a group of small islands in the South Pacific Ocean, thousands of miles away, and they are governed by Australia.

The United States possession, Admiralty Island, is about 90 miles long and about 35 miles wide; its northern tip is only a few miles from the city of Juneau. The island is mountainous, with its highest point 4,639 feet above sea level, or almost a mile. There are many pine trees on Admiralty Island, and they are valuable as timber, while the waters surrounding the island are fine fishing grounds.

The Admiralty Islands in the South Pacific, like so many of the islands in that part of the world, are old volcanoes of which just the tips stick out of the ocean. Coconut trees grow there, and the natives dive for pearls in the clear waters around the islands. In World War II, the Japanese captured the Admiralty Islands and based some airplanes there, but the United States recaptured them in 1944, and they were returned to the control of Australia. See the article on the BISMARCK ARCHIPELAGO.

adobe

Adobe houses are found all through Mexico and the Southwest of the United States, western Texas, Arizona, New Mexico, and parts of southern California. The word adobe simply means sun-dried clay in the Spanish language. It has been used for thousands of years in North Africa, and the Spanish learned how to make bricks of clay from the Mohammedan invaders who conquered Spain for a period of a few hundred years, back in the Middle Ages. The Spaniards brought the word to America, and also the best method of making the clay bricks, when they came over four hundred and more years ago.

The adobe bricks are made by wetting clay, mixing it with straw or hay, and packing it into wood frames that make it into the shape of a brick. These frames are put out in the sun, where they dry. After the bricks dry, they are used for building a house. Adobe houses are usually only one story high. They are very comfortable, cool inside in the summer and warm in winter, and also fireproof. Because they are made of clay, which is little more than mud, you might think that they would wash away in a heavy rain, but they do not. An adobe house usually lasts 100 years or more, and some are known to have lasted as long as 300 years.

See also the article BRICK.

adolescence

Adolescence is the period in which a boy or girl is changing from a child into a man or woman. A boy or girl in this stage of development is said to be *adolescent,* and is called *an adolescent.* There is no definite age at which adolescence begins, and none at which it ends. Some boys and girls become adolescent when they are 10 or 11 years old (or even younger); with some, adolescence does not even begin until they are 14 or 15. Some are out of adolescence by the time they are 18 or 19, while with some it lasts into the twenty-fifth year. However, almost any 16- or 17-year-old is fairly sure to be adolescent.

Some of the signs of adolescence are physical. A boy grows hair on his upper lip and around his chin, and needs to shave; he also grows hair in his pubic region, around his sex organs. His voice begins to change to a deeper level, but is likely to "break" without his being able to control it. In a girl, the physical signs are the beginnings of menstruation, a discharge of blood at regular intervals, which eventually will probably become once each month; she also may begin to grow hair in the pubic region, and her breasts may grow larger and occasionally feel sore.

Changes in tastes and habits are also likely to come during this period. Boys begin to be more interested in girls, and girls in boys. Both boys and girls will have a tendency to take everything too seriously, to feel self-conscious and ashamed whenever they seem to do anything wrong or awkward; to become very particular about the way they dress and what they say and what other people do and say—especially the other people that they love and feel responsible for, like their parents and other members of the family. It is not unusual for an adolescent to feel ashamed of his parents, home, and abilities, in a period like this.

There is no "cure" for adolescence. Everyone has to go through it. The wise adolescent will try to understand what is happening to him, and laugh as others do at the unnecessary worries and fears that are likely to bother him at this time, but that will be forgotten in later years.

Adonis

Adonis was a character in Greek mythology, the stories the ancient Greeks told about their gods and goddesses. Adonis was a very handsome young man. He was so handsome that the most beautiful goddess of all, Aphrodite (whom the Romans called Venus), fell in love with him. Adonis loved to hunt; Aphrodite, who knew it was dangerous, begged him not to. But he hunted anyway, and was killed by a wild boar. As the Greeks believed, this meant that Adonis had to spend the rest of time in the "underworld," which was their version of hell. But Aphrodite persuaded the other gods to let Adonis come up to earth for six months out of every year. She changed his blood into a flower, which we call the anemone, and which blooms every spring. According to the story, when the anemone blooms, it means that Adonis is leaving the underworld and coming to earth to be with Aphrodite. When the cold weather comes again, he must go back to the underworld. Shakespeare wrote a poem about Venus and Adonis.

adoption

Adoption is a legal process that creates the relationship of parent and child between persons who were not actually parent and child. Once the child is adopted, he is no longer legally related to his real parents but only to his adopted parents. For example, if an adopted parent dies intestate (without leaving a will), the adopted child inherits his share of the property; but in such a case the adopted child would not inherit anything from his actual parents.

Among the ancient Hebrews and Egyptians, and in ancient Rome (two thousand years ago or more), adoption was permitted. In the English common law, on which United States law is based, adoption was unknown. Therefore legal adoption did not exist in the United States until the states passed laws permitting it, and there are many differences between the laws of the different states. Some state laws require that the parent be considerably older than the child, but some laws make no mention of age and it

would be legally possible for the "child" to be older than the parent. In some states a child above a certain age, such as twelve, cannot be adopted without his consent. In most states, if the parents of the child are married both must consent to the adoption, but if they are not married only the mother's consent is required. In all states, a child may not be adopted without the consent of a court, and the courts usually require a thorough examination of the child and a thorough investigation of the adopting parents before it will permit the adoption.

Usually the court requires that the child be mentally and physically normal and prefers to have the child be of the same race, religious background and general appearance as the adopting parents. The parents must be happily married, respectable, and financially able to bring up the child comfortably. Most of the Church organizations in the United States have branches that arrange for adoptions, and there are other organizations that do the same, in addition to the official adoption agencies of states and cities. Nevertheless, there are so many parents who want to adopt children that there are not enough children to satisfy all of them and for years there has been a "black market" in babies, in which parents pay fees running into the thousands of dollars to "brokers" who arrange for them to adopt babies.

Psychologists have made a thorough study of the problems of the adopted child, who may often feel that he is different from other children who live with their actual parents. Some parents hesitate to tell a child that he was adopted, but today most parents consider it better to tell the child as soon as he is able to understand what "adopted" means, and to reassure the child by explaining that they selected him because they wanted him, while actual parents have no power of selection over children born to them naturally.

adrenal glands

The adrenal glands, also called the suprarenal glands, are organs of the body that lie just above the kidneys. (*Adrenal* means "on the kidneys"; *suprarenal* means "above the kidneys.") There is a separate article on GLANDS and what they do. The adrenals are in the group called ductless glands.

There are two adrenal glands. Each has two parts, an inner section called the *medulla* and an outer section called the *cortex*. The medulla produces a hormone called adrenalin, or epinephrine. When you are threatened with danger, or when your brain tells you that you simply must have more strength to do something necessary, the adrenal glands pour out more adrenalin and this flows through the blood to the heart and makes the heart beat faster and the strength increase. Also it is adrenalin that makes you blush when you are embarrassed and that makes your hair stand on end when you are angry or afraid.

The cortex manufactures many hormones; twenty-eight of them are known. Some of these hormones are considered necessary to life. The best known is cortisone and it is used as a drug in the treatment of some diseases.

It was once thought that a person could not live without his adrenal glands, but since Cortisone became available in 1949 many persons have lived after their adrenals stopped working, by being treated with Cortisone and other hormones that are normally produced by the adrenals.

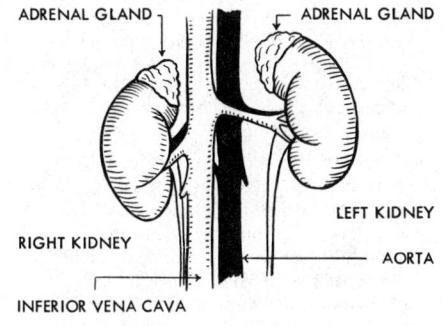

ADRENAL GLAND — ADRENAL GLAND

RIGHT KIDNEY

LEFT KIDNEY

AORTA

INFERIOR VENA CAVA

Here you can see how the adrenal glands are placed directly at the top of the kidneys.

Adrian

Adrian was the name of six Popes of the Roman Catholic Church. One of them, Adrian IV, whose name originally was Nicholas Breakspear, was the only Englishman who ever became Pope.

Adrianople

Adrianople is our name for a city in Turkey in Europe. The Turkish name for the city is Edirne. The city was built more than 1,800 years ago, in the year 125, and was named Adrianapolis for the Roman emperor Hadrian. Many battles have been fought for Adrianople, and in early times it was captured by barbarians who were attacking Rome, by Christian Crusaders, and by Turks. The Turks captured it in the year 1360 and made it their capital in 1366. It grew to a population of 100,000, which was very large for those times.

Then in 1453 the Turks captured Constantinople (now called Istanbul), which became the Turkish capital. Adrianople has never been very important since, and its population is now 316,425. Cloths and leather goods are manufactured in Adrianople. It is famous for the beautiful mosque (Mohammedan church) of Sultan Selim II, built about four hundred years ago.

Adriatic Sea

The Adriatic Sea is a large body of water, the part of the Mediterranean Sea that runs up between Italy and the coast of Yugoslavia. Many of the principal Italian cities that are famous for their seagoing peoples, such as Venice, are on the Adriatic Sea. So is the city of Trieste, which for many years has been the chief Mediterranean seaport for Central European countries, and after World War II caused trouble between Yugoslavia and Italy. On the Adriatic Sea are many fine harbors, beautiful beaches that are summer resorts for the people of Italy and for visitors to Italy, and a world of cities, buildings, and ruins where one can look into the history of thousands of years ago, when the Roman Empire, on Italy, ruled the world.

The Adriatic is about 500 miles long and 58 to 140 miles wide. It is 4,035 deep at its deepest point. Other important cities on the Adriatic are Ancona, Bari and Brindisi on the Italian side, Fiume, Split and Dubrovnik on the Yugoslavian side, and Durres in Albania.

adult

An adult is a person who has reached maturity in bodily growth, mental development, or age—in other words, who is "grown up." Physiologically, the person must have achieved full growth and strength, and the age may vary with sex, race, and culture (see the article on ADOLESCENCE). Laws usually set the age at twenty-one and the effect is that the person attains to certain rights, such as voting, legal right to make contracts, etc. The age at which a person is considered adult has varied greatly among different peoples. In the United States, where the definition of an adult is made by the states, there has been much agitation since World War II to lower the age to 18 and some states have done so.

Aduwa or Adowa

Aduwa is a town in Ethiopia. It is quite small, with a population of only about 5,000, but it is famous for battles in two wars between Italy and Ethiopia. In 1896 Italy was trying to conquer Ethiopia and make it an Italian colony, and 15,000 Italian troops attacked Aduwa. Against them the Ethiopian emperor Menelik II had an army that had very few modern weapons, many of his men having only spears while the Italians had rifles and artillery; but there were so many Ethiopians that they surrounded the Italians and killed most of them. Italy then gave up the war against Ethiopia; but in 1935 Italy attacked again and this time they won the battle of Aduwa easily and conquered all of Ethiopia. However, after World War II Italy was forced to give Ethiopia back to its rightful government.

Advent

The word *advent* means "coming." It is often used to mean the coming of Christ as the savior of the world. In Christian churches, the season of the Advent has been observed for well over one thousand years; it lasts four weeks, beginning with the Sunday that is nearest to Saint Andrew's Day, which is November 30, and lasting until Christmas.

Adventists

Adventists are members of Christian churches in which it is believed that Jesus Christ will again come to earth in person. The Bible says Christ will come again, so this is a part of the belief of every Christian church, but the Adventists have special beliefs as to the time and manner of his coming. There have been several churches of Adventists. The largest in the United States is the Seventh-Day Adventists, who observe the Sabbath on Saturday instead of Sunday. The original Sabbath was Saturday. The first Adventist Church was

founded in Washington, New Hampshire by William Miller, who predicted that the second coming of Christ would occur between 1843 and 1844. Other Adventist groups are the Church of God (Adventist); Life and Advent Union; Church of God (Oregon, Illinois); and the Primitive Advent Christian Church.

adverb

A word is called an adverb when it is used to tell how something is done, or where it is done, or when. An adverb is one of the parts of speech. A part of speech is a kind of word that has a particular duty when you say it or write it.

If you say, "The choir sings," you tell what the choir does. If you say, "The choir sings clearly," you tell how the choir does it. The word *clearly* is an adverb that tells how. In the sentence "I saw John yesterday," *yesterday* is an adverb that tells when; in, "I see him there," *there* is an adverb that tells where.

When a word adds to the meaning of another word, it is said to *modify* it; in the sentence "The choir sings clearly," *clearly* adds to the meaning of *sings*. In this case, the adverb *clearly* modifies the verb *sings*. An adverb may modify a verb, or an adjective, or another adverb. If you say, "It is a very clear day," *very* is an adverb that modifies the adjective *clear*. If you say, "The choir sings very clearly," the adverb *very* modifies another adverb, *clearly*.

In the English language, most adverbs end with *-ly*. In fact, you can form an adverb from almost any adjective by adding *-ly* to the adjective, as in the case of *clear* and *clearly*. However, there are many adverbs that do not end in *-ly*. The word *there*, used above, is an example.

COMPARISON OF ADVERBS

Often it is desirable for an adverb to show not only how something is done, but also to show how it compares with the way other things are done. Two men may both write well, but one may write better than the other. The word *better* is an adverb that shows how the two men compare in the way they write.

Adverbs are compared in the same way as adjectives (see ADJECTIVE). When there are exactly two ways of doing things to be compared, the form of the adverb is said to be *comparative*, and it is formed by adding *-er* to a short adverb, or using the word *more* before a longer adverb. "John came sooner than I did"—*sooner* is the comparative form of *soon*. "John sang more clearly than I did"—*more clearly* is the comparative form of *clearly*.

When there are three or more ways of doing something and you want to compare them, you use the *superlative* form of the adverb, which is formed by adding *-est* to short adverbs, or using the word *most* before longer adverbs. "They all ran fast, but John ran fastest"—*fastest* is the superlative form of *fast*. "They all sang clearly, but John sang most clearly"—*most clearly* is the superlative form of *clearly*.

POSITION OF ADVERBS

In the English language, the meaning of a sentence often depends on syntax (how the words are arranged).

Usually an adverb should come before an adjective, an adverb or a phrase that it modifies and should come after a verb, though there are some exceptions. The adverb *only* is often used incorrectly. For example, the sentence "He only bathes on Saturdays" might mean that on Saturdays he does not eat, walk, etc., but only bathes; "He bathes only on Saturdays" or "on Saturdays only" makes the meaning clear. Good American writers are careful about their use of *only,* while good English writers usually consider the position unimportant. There is a famous sentence, "She told me that she loved me," in which the word *only* before each of the seven words produces a different meaning.

See also the article PART OF SPEECH.

advertising

Advertising is telling other people that you have something you want to sell to them. When we say today that a person advertises, we mean he is paying someone else to publish (that is, "to make public") the information that he has something to sell.

There are many ways in which this information may be made public. The different ways are called *media* by advertising men. These may be printed announcements ("ads") in newspapers and magazines; or spoken announcements ("commercials") on radio and television broadcasts; or displays, such as billboards, electric signs, and posters; or direct mail, which means mailing a letter to the person you want to sell to; or souvenirs, such as matchbooks or calendars with the advertiser's name on them; and many other media all the way up to skywriting.

Advertising is a big business in the United States. In a typical year in the 1960s, American businessmen spent more than 11-billion dollars advertising the things they had for sale. The biggest share of this—more than a third—was spent for "space" in newspapers. Another third of the 11-billion dollars was shared about equally by television and direct mail. This means that each of these media received about 15% of all the money that was spent. Magazines and radio accounted for about 15%. The rest of the advertising money was split up among the many other media.

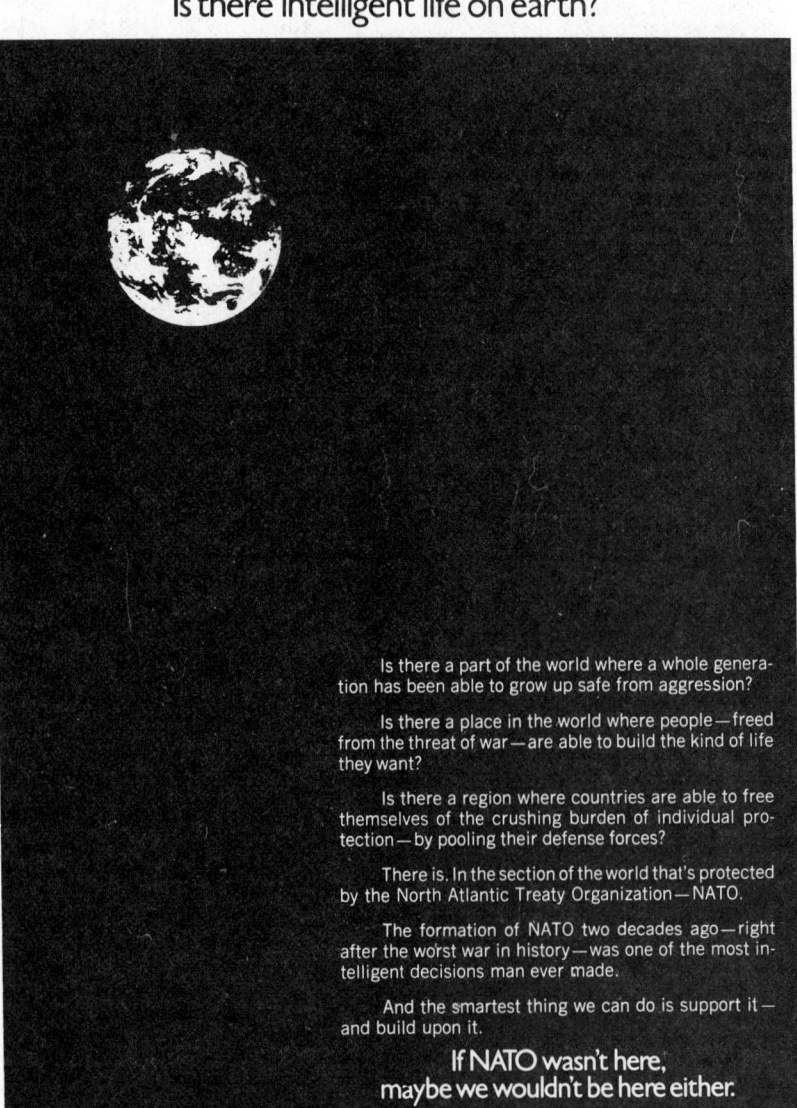

Is there intelligent life on earth?

Is there a part of the world where a whole generation has been able to grow up safe from aggression?

Is there a place in the world where people—freed from the threat of war—are able to build the kind of life they want?

Is there a region where countries are able to free themselves of the crushing burden of individual protection—by pooling their defense forces?

There is. In the section of the world that's protected by the North Atlantic Treaty Organization—NATO.

The formation of NATO two decades ago—right after the worst war in history—was one of the most intelligent decisions man ever made.

And the smartest thing we can do is support it—and build upon it.

If NATO wasn't here, maybe we wouldn't be here either.

J. W. Thompson/Atlantic Council

This advertisement was prepared for an agency concerned with educating people about the "free world" (the nations which are not run by dictators).

Advertising is also an art. The best authors and artists combine their skills to write and illustrate the ads. The finest actors appear in commercials on television and radio. It may be a good joke to groan when a commercial comes on, and to skip over advertising pages, but very few persons fail to notice them. The best brains go into making them attractive and interesting.

Advertising is also a career. Nearly 500,000 people in the United States make their living from advertising. Nearly every manufacturer or store has an advertising department. There are hundreds of *advertising agencies,* companies whose business is helping other companies to advertise the things they have to sell. Advertising agencies have offices all over the country—all over the world, for that matter. Newspapers, magazines, broadcasting networks and stations, all employ large staffs of men and women in their advertising departments. Advertising work has the reputation of being interesting and giving a bright and ambitious person a chance to make a great deal of money. A large number of boys and girls look forward to advertising as the work they will do when they are out of school.

HOW ADVERTISING BEGAN

It is usual to say that a flower "advertises" to the bees and butterflies, by dressing itself up in bright colors; and that a bird "advertises" when it sings a love song to its mate; and that a man "advertises" every time he makes his wishes known. But that is not the kind of advertising we are talking about here.

It was not really advertising when, in the old days, a peddler used to drive his cart through the streets of a town and shout "Apples for sale!" or whatever words would let the townsfolk know what he had in the cart and was offering for sale. But when a merchant in the Orient would bring his camel caravan to a town, and would spread out his pottery and silks and rugs in the market place, and then would hire someone with strong legs and a loud voice to go through all the streets and shout "Abdul the Merchant has arrived at the market place with rugs, silks, spices and other fine things from China!"—that was true advertising, because he was paying someone else to make public the news of what he had for sale.

For many years, even for centuries, that was the chief kind of advertising— the "crier" in the streets. Storekeepers did hang signs out in front of their stores, just as they do today, so that passers-by would know where to buy things. Of course, hundreds of years ago most of the people could not read, so the shoemaker would hang out a big shoe, and the baker a picture of a loaf of bread, and so on; and some of those signs have lasted right down to the present day, for example the barber's pole.

Modern advertising began when printing was invented, about 500 years ago. The first English printer, William Caxton, printed a poster advertising pies; that was in the year 1480, twelve years before America was discovered by Chris-

topher Columbus. It wasn't long before someone thought of publishing a newspaper, and it wasn't long after that that someone else thought of advertising in a newspaper; it was done in Germany as early as 1591, and in England in 1625. Since that time, or for more than 300 years, nearly every newspaper has published paid advertisements. But until quite a short time ago, these were not much more than printed notices, all looking alike as do classified advertisements in today's newspapers. And in England the advertisements almost always covered the front page of the newspaper The news began farther back.

The kind of advertising we see today was born and grew entirely in the United States. It was an American invention; and it remains an American specialty.

The first ad in America appeared in the Boston News Letter, a newspaper published in Boston, Massachusetts, in 1704. It was a plain notice, just like the ones in England and European countries. For about 150 years American advertising stayed that way. Then it began to change. Ads began to have clever pictures and forceful "copy," written in such a way that people would want to come and buy.

Much of the credit for bringing about this change belongs to the advertising agency. The first agency was opened in 1840, in Philadelphia; others came along in the following years, and by the 1870s there were several. Here for the first time were men whose *only* interest was advertising—planning it, buying it, selling it, and making it pay. In many ways our lives would be much different today if it were not for the revolution in advertising brought about by the advertising agencies.

HOW AN ADVERTISING AGENCY WORKS

An advertising agency is a company, often a very big one, where everyone is an expert on something connected with advertising. There is the layout man, who knows how to fit printing type and pictures together for the greatest "eye appeal." There is the media man, who knows how many people read each magazine, and what kind of people they are, and what kind of merchandise can be sold to them. There is the television man, who knows how to produce a show or a commercial; and the copywriter, who knows how to describe the product well and make people want to buy it; and the "account executive," whose job is to plan the advertising of a particular product or "account." These are only a few examples. There are literally dozens of

other specialized jobs in an advertising agency.

The advertising agency's customer is called a *client*. The client is the company that has the product for sale. The agency prepares the advertising, but the client does not pay more than he would have paid if he had gone to the trouble and expense of preparing the advertising himself. Whatever the advertising costs, the agency gets 15% of it—but this is paid by the magazine, newspaper, broadcasting company or any of the other media that carries the advertising. The money the client spends for this kind of advertising is called "commissionable" because the agency receives a commission on it. There are some kinds of advertising that are not commissionable; for example, when the agency prepares letters and circulars to go out by mail. In such cases the client pays a fee to the agency for its work, and this is called a "service charge."

Advertising agency business is big business, because so much money is spent on advertising. There are more than 300 companies in the United States with a budget for advertising of more than a million dollars a year. On every million dollars, the advertising agency gets commissions of $150,000.

WHO REALLY PAYS FOR ADVERTISING

Many people have grumbled about the billions of dollars that are spent for advertising. "It comes right out of the customers' pockets," they complain. "If the manufacturers didn't spend all that money for advertising, they could sell us the goods that much cheaper."

But could they? It is no accident that people in the United States, where most of the advertising of the world is done, also have most of the desirable goods in the world—automobiles, electric refrigerators and washing machines, good clothes and good food, and all kinds of conveniences in their homes. The United States is a country of mass production. When products are made in great quantities, they cost less and more people can afford to buy them. Manufacturers could not count on selling so many if they could not advertise and let the public know about the product they have for sale. Therefore they would not make so many, and the price of everything would have to go up.

You also hear people complain of the advertisements themselves, especially the commercials on television and radio. "They spoil the show," these people will complain. But if it were not for the com-

An American advertisement of 1858.

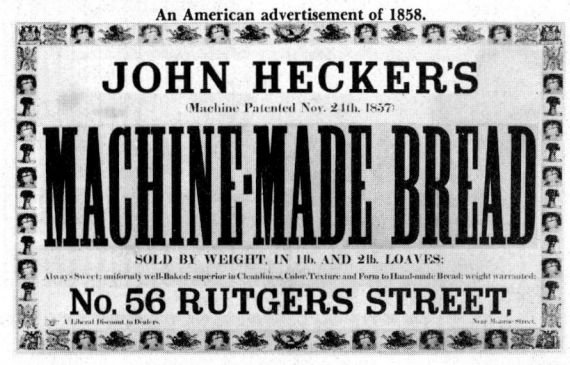

EASTMAN INVENTS A PRETTY STRONG GLUE

It's not special photography. It's special glue. We call it Eastman 910® Adhesive. It glues almost anything to almost anything. Without mixing, without solvents, without heating, and without a lot of waiting.

It's the kind of new product you develop when you have hundreds of people doing nothing but developing new products. (Like many progressive companies, over half our sales come from products that weren't even around ten years ago.) Philco-Ford uses Eastman 910 to bond aluminum to aluminum. Cessna uses it to bond rubber to acrylic plastic. Bendix uses it to bond steel to brass. One of our tennis-playing product managers used it to repair a flapping rubber sole—putting the sneak back in his sneakers. A false-toothed friend of ours used it to glue a tooth chip to his chipped tooth. And finally, we know a taxidermist who uses it to keep his friends from falling apart at the seams.

We make Eastman 910 Adhesive, and a lot of other good things, at Eastman Chemical Products, Inc. in Kingsport, Tennessee. Where we've found some down-to-earth answers to a lot of up-in-the-air questions.

Eastman Chemicals / Kodak

Fred Wittner Co./Eastman Chemical

This eye-catching advertisement, in which a piano is shown glued to the ceiling, was prepared by a modern creative advertising agency for a glue manufacturer.

mercials, no one could afford to put on the shows themselves. It is the advertiser who pays for them. It is also the advertiser that pays for the newspaper and magazine you read. Every newspaper and magazine is sold to you for less than it actually costs. A magazine that you buy for 50 cents may cost the publisher 65 or 70 cents. The publisher sells his magazine at a loss because he wants more circulation—more readers. The greater his circulation, the more he can charge the advertisers. The buyer of the magazine benefits from this.

KEEPING ADVERTISING HONEST

Most advertisers have always been honest, but there have always been some who want to deceive the public. Dishonest advertisers try to make false claims for their products. This could weaken the faith of the public in all kinds of advertising, and everyone would suffer.

Today there are many things that act to prevent an advertiser from being dishonest.

The Federal Trade Commission, called the FTC, is a branch of the United States Government. It checks on the claims made by advertisers. If an advertiser makes claims that are not true, the Federal Trade Commission sues him and forces him to stop. The Department of Health, operating under a law passed by Congress, called the Pure Food and Drug Act, examines foods and medicines to make sure they are as good as their labels say they are. Dishonest claims for patent medicines have become a thing of the past. The selling of products that are poisonous or harmful is rapidly being stopped.

The Better Business Bureaus are private organizations, but like the Federal Trade Commission they expose dishonesty in business and advertising and make it difficult or impossible for a company to fool the public in its advertising.

Honest publishers do not accept advertising unless the manufacturer is substantial and can be depended on, and unless the advertising itself is trustworthy. A would-be dishonest advertiser would have a hard time getting anybody to sell him the advertising space or time nowadays.

There were never many dishonest advertisers, but it takes only a few to hurt all. The advertising business has grown a great deal since the advertisements themselves became more dependable.

HOW AN AD IS MADE

You see an ad in a magazine. How did it happen to be there—that exact ad, in that magazine, on that date?

Here is the way, step by step.

Our story will begin when a manufacturer appoints an advertising agency to handle his advertising for him. Let us suppose that this particular manufacturer makes a brand of soap for washing dishes, doing the laundry, and other kitchen purposes.

First, the account executive of the advertising agency studies the product. He compares it with every other kind of kitchen soap. He will probably send samples to a laboratory, to have it tested by scientists. From the laboratory, he will probably find out what this soap has that makes it different from, and perhaps better than, other soaps.

Next, the account executive wants to know what kind of soap American women want in their kitchens. He may send out a large crew of men and women to go from one house to another and ask the women questions. From the results of this "survey" the agency will make out a list of what is most appealing in a soap.

Suppose they find out that American housewives like soapsuds with fine, small bubbles. And suppose, by coincidence, their client's soap (the laboratory said) happens to make these small, fine bubbles. That will be a "selling point" worth advertising.

The third step is to find the best way to advertise this selling point. They may choose some catchy name, like "pearls,"

or "beads," to describe the suds made by their soap. Or they may decide to use a certain kind of picture that will surely attract the attention of these women. Or they may decide to pay some famous person to "endorse" the soap, because experience has shown that the name and picture of a famous person will usually attract attention to an ad.

Once they have decided, the production department will take over. The production men will find the best writers, the best artists, the best layout men. They will plan ads that are very appealing in words and appearance.

The next step is to select the media. Suppose the survey has shown that this particular kind of soapsuds appeals most to women whose husbands earn about $5,000 a year and live in medium-sized towns. The media expert will look for any magazine and newspaper that is read by women whose husbands earn about $5,000 and live in medium-sized towns. He will not spend the advertiser's money on magazines and newspapers that sell chiefly to richer women or to poorer women, or in bigger cities, or in smaller towns.

At this point the media department of the agency will present to the client a "schedule." This will be a list of the newspapers and magazines in which the agency thinks the ad ought to appear, with the dates on which the agency thinks the ad should run, and with the price of each ad.

The cost of an ad depends partly on the circulation—number of readers—of the publication. It depends partly on the quality of this circulation. A publication whose readers are rich can charge more than a publication whose readers are poor. Publications with rich readers are called "class" media. Their readers buy more, because they can afford to.

The advertising business is so well organized that all kinds of information are available to every agency and advertiser. An organization known as the Audit Bureau of Circulations (called the "ABC") makes sure that no publication claims a higher circulation than it actually has. Many of the publications themselves make surveys to find out how much money their readers have, and how they spend it. There are independent organizations that make surveys of the same kind. Every magazine and newspaper guarantees that each issue will sell a certain number of copies, or more, and if fewer copies are sold, it has to give some of the advertiser's money back.

The cost of advertising in a newspaper or magazine depends on how much space the ad occupies. The page is always considered to be divided into columns, and each column is measured by the "agate line" or "line." There are fourteen lines to the inch. Each line costs so much, depending on the circulation. If an advertiser takes "a fourteen-line ad," it means his ad is one inch deep and one column wide, and if the price is one dollar per line, he pays fourteen dollars for it.

Advertising in big magazines and newspapers is expensive. The space for a full-page, black-and-white advertisement in a large newspaper will cost an advertiser about $5,000, in addition to

the thousands of dollars he spends preparing the advertisement itself. Advertising in magazines, such as *Fortune*, costs a good deal more. A monthly magazine charges more than a weekly magazine or a daily paper with the same circulation, because the monthly magazine stays around the house longer before the next issue comes, and there is more chance that someone will see the ad. Most magazines are read by the whole family, so when a publication has a circulation of, for example, 3,000,000 copies, they actually have as many as 12,000,000 or 15,000,000 readers. These figures help them to persuade agencies to buy their advertising space instead of space in other magazines and newspapers.

When the schedule, scientifically prepared, has been presented by the agency to the client, the client's advertising manager may make a change or two, here or there, then he signs the schedule. The agency makes out an order to the publication in which the ad is to appear. The agency's production department makes sure that the type is set for the ad, and the art work done, and everything delivered to the publication for its "closing date," which may be from six weeks to three months before the advertisement is actually in the hands of readers. Now there remains only to wait until the ad appears.

CHOOSING A RADIO OR TV SHOW

It may be that women who prefer this kind of soap don't read magazines very much, but do spend a lot of time watching television or listening to the radio. In this case, the agency will probably advise the advertiser to try a radio or television program.

Again, the agency will have all kinds of figures at its disposal. It will know what hours are the best if one wants to reach these particular women, and what kind of show appeals to them best. This may be a play, it may be a comedian, and it may be a quiz, but whatever the survey shows, that is the kind of program this particular client will want to sponsor.

Television is very expensive advertising. Some programs cost four or five million dollars for a single year. But this is not what interests an advertiser most. The advertiser wants to know how many persons will actually see or hear his ad, and how much it costs him for each one. If the advertiser spends a million dollars, and one hundred million persons see his show, it costs him one cent per person to reach them with his advertising. If he can spend two million dollars and reach 500 million people, it costs him less than half a cent a person. This will mean he has spent his advertising money more wisely, even though in actual cash he spent a million dollars more.

DECIDING WHAT TO ADVERTISE

There are many different media for advertising. All have their appeals, because different advertisers have different purposes in advertising.

If a company makes a great many different products, it may want to advertise its company name, rather than any of the products it makes. Its purpose is to persuade people that it is an honest, reliable company, and that any time they see its name on any kind of product, they can feel safe. When a company advertises its own name, instead of the name of one of its products, the advertising is called "institutional advertising."

More often, a company will want to advertise the particular name or trademark it puts on a brand of soap, or canned peas, or chewing gum, or whatever else it makes. In that case, it advertises the name of that particular product. This is called "product advertising."

Another advertiser may want its customers to remember it at all times, not merely from time to time. A taxicab company, for example, may want its name and telephone number to be handy whenever a person anywhere wants a taxi. A company like that might advertise with calendars to hang on the wall, or desk pads, or matches. It would not be likely to advertise in a newspaper, because a person would probably not be looking at a newspaper at exactly the time that he is thinking about calling a taxi.

A company may make machinery and sell to other manufacturers, not to the general public. This kind of company would advertise in trade journals—magazines that are published only for people in a certain line of work. The advertiser would pick a trade journal read by the manufacturers who are most likely to be customers for his machines.

The advertising business has become so huge that you could name almost anything a person might want to advertise, and any way he might want to advertise it, and there would be a well-known place and way for him to do it.

ADVERTISING STATISTICS

Until the 20th century, most advertising was local (chiefly in newspapers). Annual expenditures in the U.S. did not exceed $200,000,000. These grew rapidly when magazine circulation well into the millions, then radio and later television made it possible to reach national audiences. With the development of advertising as a big business, large advertising expenditures were considered necessary to business success and represented from 0.5% to 28% of the cost of nearly every trademarked product. In the 1960s the advertising industry employed nearly 500,000 persons. Annual expenditures for media were $2,000,000,000 in 1940, $5,700,000,000 in 1950, and $16,545,000,000 in 1969 when more than 16,000 companies were listed as national advertisers, and more than 300 had annual advertising budgets exceeding $1,000,000. The 1969 budgets were spent as follows:

Network Television . . .
                $1 billion 700 million
Magazines . . . .
                1 billion 200 million
Local Television . . . . .
                1 billion 100 million
Outdoor . . . . 233 million
Newspapers . . . . 97 million
Network Radio . . . . . 50 million

    Total . . . . . . $4 billion 380 million

In addition to this vast sum, 11 billion 620 million dollars were spent on advertising in other media such as farm publications, direct mail, trade journals, and truck advertising. The total spent in all media was therefore 16 billion dollars.

In 1970, the industries doing the greatest amount of national advertising in newspapers and in magazines were the automotive and food industries, respectively. The industries doing the greatest amount of advertising on television were the food and toiletries industries, respectively.

ADVERTISING AGENCIES

In 1803, James Hardie of New York announced his profession as "writing petitions, memorials, letters, advertisements, etc." In 1840, Volney B. Palmer of Philadelphia opened an advertising agency, which bought space from newspapers and resold it, at a profit, to advertisers. Similar agencies were opened by J. Walter Thompson in Chicago (1868) and N. W. Ayer in Philadelphia (1869). Both survived and in the 1950s Thompson was the largest advertising agency and Ayer one of the largest. In the early 1900s there were an estimated 200 advertising agencies in the U.S. In 1970 there were more than 5,750, with about 100,000 employees, more than half of whom were employed by the seventy largest agencies. These agencies earned about 10 billion dollars and had payrolls in excess of 785 million dollars. But the field is growing, and there is a great need for new people.

SPACE RATES

All publications charge by the *agate line*. The *milline* rate is the cost per line per million of circulation; if a publication has 1,000,000 circulation and charges $2.00 per line, its milline rate also is $2.00. The rate varies also with position and color: the back cover of a magazine costs more than any other position, and a four-color ad costs about 20% more than a one-color ad. In a run-of-the-press (ROP) ad, the publication may place the ad where it pleases. Typical 1970 rates for full-page, black-and-white ads in U.S. publications were:

PUBLICATION	PAGE RATE
Time	23,400
Sports Illustrated	13,640
Scientific American	5,200
Ladies' Home Journal	28,600
Better Homes & Gardens	33,775
Ebony	7,044
National Geographic	24,100
Reader's Digest	48,475

Each publication issues a *rate card* at intervals, giving its basic rates (always with discounts ranging from 1% to 9% for quantity purchases) and its closing dates (date on which the copy or plate for the ad must be delivered, which is two to ten weeks before publication date in magazines and one to five days for newspapers). Newspapers have national rates and local rates; a local advertiser may pay 50% less than a national advertiser.

RADIO AND TV RATES

Broadcasting stations and networks sell time, usually in units of 15 minutes, 30 minutes, and one hour, but also *spots* of 10 seconds to one minute. The advertiser, called a *sponsor*, pays the cost of the program except on spot purchases. The rate is based on the anticipated audience; it is highest in the early evening hours.

Various *rating methods* are used to estimate the number of persons who listen to any particular radio program or watch any particular television program; the earliest method, the Hooper rating, used telephone

calls to ascertain what program a particular household is listening to; the Nielsen method selects certain households and places mechanical devices on their radio or TV sets to register what programs they hear; other services use a combination of these and other sampling techniques.

A sponsor is usually required to contract for a series of broadcasts in units of 13 weeks, to use a program that is acceptable to the station or network, and to devote no more than three minutes of time to commercials for each half hour of show time.

Some radio broadcasts have been heard by more than 45,000,000 persons, and some television programs have been seen by more than 60,000,000. Typical 1949 rates for radio time exceeded $1,000 per hour for a single station in New York City and $10,000 per hour for coast-to-coast networks; these have remained the same as television reduced radio audiences. Television rates in 1970 were about $3,600 per hour for a single station in New York City and $10,700 per hour for a network. Some 39-week television shows, including time and program, cost the sponsor more than $5,000,000. Since 1953, the tendency has been for two or more sponsors to divide the cost of an expensive show.

ADVERTISING DEPARTMENTS

Every large advertiser maintains its own advertising department, even though in some cases the work of this department duplicates that of the agency. Advertising departments employ about 300,000 persons, ten times as many as advertising agencies. They prepare and buy most local advertising and nearly all advertising by counter displays, direct mail, giveaways, and displays.

About 15% of all those employed in the advertising business, or nearly 50,000 persons, are engaged in testing the effectiveness of different kinds of advertising.

RESTRICTIONS ON ADVERTISING

Dishonest advertising was general until the 20th century. Unfounded claims by advertisers have been discouraged by activities of the Federal Trade Commission, the Department of Health (operating under the Pure Food and Drug Act), and Better Business Bureaus. Most publishers and broadcasters refuse advertising from unreliable firms. A few publications do not accept liquor advertising, and liquor advertising by radio or television is forbidden by both Federal and state laws, though wines and beers may be so advertised. Any advertising matter in a publication must be clearly labeled "advertisement," though some smaller publications run *reading notices* (editorial matter published to reciprocate for paid space bought by the advertiser).

aedes

The aedes mosquito is a kind of mosquito that lives in very hot countries. It carries the parasites, or tiny germs, that cause the diseases yellow fever and dengue fever. Yellow fever was one of the great dangers of tropical America until a group of doctors in the United States Army, headed by Walter Reed, discovered and proved (in 1901) that the aedes spreads the disease by biting a person who already has it and then depositing the virus in the next person it bites. The disease was then brought under control by destroying the aedes eggs or larvae (young mosquitoes) before they could grow. The building of the Panama Canal was delayed by yellow fever among the workers and the canal was completed only after the aedes mosquitoes in Panama were destroyed.

A.E.F., the initials of the American Expeditionary Forces, which went to Europe from the United States to fight in World War I. See separate article.

Aegean Civilization

Nearly five thousand years ago, one of the earliest civilizations in the history of mankind grew up on the island of Crete, on the Peloponnesus (which is a peninsula of Greece), and on some other islands in the Aegean Sea. The people who created this civilization were in the Bronze Age; that is, they had discovered how to use the softer metals but had not yet learned to use iron.

Probably the principal center of this civilization was the city of Cnossus, on Crete. Another was the city of Mycenae, on the Peloponnesus. For this reason, the age is sometimes called the Cretan-Mycenaean Civilization, and more often it is called the Minoan Civilization after Minos, a king of Crete about whom there are legends in Greek mythology. The period of the Aegean Civilization is often divided into three periods: the Early Minoan, from about 2700 to 2000 B.C.; the Middle Minoan, from 2000 to 1600 B.C.; and the Late Minoan, from 1600 to about 1400 B.C., when foreign invaders (who probably had iron weapons) conquered the people of the Aegean region and destroyed their cities. These invaders may have been the earliest Greeks to reach that region.

The people of the Aegean region built beautiful palaces and created fine works of art. They also developed a knowledge of writing, perhaps as early as the ancient Egyptians did. They knew the ancient Egyptians and ancient Babylonians and probably traded with them.

Aegean Sea

The Aegean Sea is a part of the Mediterranean Sea that runs up between the countries of Greece and Turkey. It is dotted with hundreds of islands, which are called the Aegean Archipelago, or simply the *Archipelago*. (An archipelago is a group of islands.) Here was born one of the earliest great civilizations of man—see the article on the AEGEAN CIVILIZATION.

In all parts of the region of the Aegean Sea, the climate is pleasant and mild and the water is clear and beautiful. On many of the islands, there is fine land for farming. These islands have been much fought over, through the ages and right up to recent times. Almost all of them now belong to Greece.

The Aegean Sea is about 400 miles by 200 miles. Its islands, which are of volcanic origin, include Euboea, the Cyclades, the Sporades, and the Dodecanese. Aegean seaports include the Piraeus, Salon-

ika, Volos, and Kavalla, in Greece, and Izmir or Smyrna, in Turkey. The seacoast is indented with many bays and gulfs.

aeolian harp

An aeolian harp is a musical instrument, made of strings stretched over a wooden frame. The strings are not plucked, as they are on most stringed instruments of this kind. Instead, the player blows air across them or between them, and the air makes the strings vibrate and produce music. (See the article on SOUND to understand how this happens.) Serious musicians seldom play the aeolian harp, considering it more of a toy than a musical instrument. It was given its name because Aeolus was god of the winds in Greek mythology.

aerial photography

Aerial photography is the branch of photography devoted to taking photographs from aircraft. Photographs have been taken from aircraft (balloons, and later airplanes) for more than 100 years—the first were taken about 1860—but during World War II it was greatly developed as a means of making maps for military use. Many inaccuracies in previous maps were corrected, especially those of the Pacific theater of war.

An aerial map is made by assembling a series of pictures into a *mosaic:* a group of matched photographs that have been reduced or enlarged to a single scale. It is usually constructed with reference to a system of ground control points established by a ground survey, and is then called a *controlled mosaic.* The making of aerial maps is known as *photogrammetry*.

Aerial photographs are also used to record enemy troop movements and fortifications in warfare, and to provide data for geological, agricultural and forestry surveys.

Aerial photographs are made with high-speed cameras equipped with lenses of long focal length—3 to 100 inches. For low altitudes, high-speed panchromatic film with yellow or red filters is used; for high altitudes, infrared film is used. The length of film ranges from 20 inches to 100 feet. Exposures are made by holding the camera with its optical axis either at a true vertical or slightly oblique. Vertical photographs are utilized in mosaics; oblique ones for identification purposes.

aerodynamics is the study of how air and other gases move and why they behave as they do; it is very important in understanding why an airplane flies. It will be explained in the article on FLIGHT.

aerolite

An aerolite is a stone meteorite, a stony mass that has fallen to earth after wandering through space. Most aerolites look like rocks found on earth. Nearly all the known elements have been identified in them. Usually the interior consists of small round particles, called *chondri*, that are different from any chondri in the earth's rocks.

aeronautics, see FLIGHT and NAVIGATION.

aerosol

An aerosol is air or some other gas that contains a great many very fine droplets of a liquid or particles of a solid. Fog or mist is an aerosol of a liquid (water) in air, and smoke is an aerosol of solids in air. "Aerosol bombs" are often used as sprays, especially for insecticides. A liquid insecticide is mixed with a compressed gas, and when the gas is released through a valve the liquid is sprayed in fine droplets. Spraying liquids through a small nozzle produces the same effect. Today, aerosols are discouraged. Scientists have theorized that the aerosols may be destroying the ozone layer. This is the part of the atmosphere which protects us from the sun's ultraviolet rays.

Aeschines

Aeschines was a great orator of ancient Athens, in Greece, more than two thousand years ago. Next to Demosthenes, he was considered the greatest orator of his time. In those times political power came from ability to speak to the people and win their support. King Philip of Macedon was trying to combine the Greek states under his rule, and Aeschines supported him while Demosthenes was his greatest enemy. The people sided with Demosthenes and finally Aeschines had to leave Athens. He died in exile on the island of Rhodes, near Greece.

Aeschines was born in 389 B.C., of a poor and unimportant family. He had been a soldier, a clerk, and an actor before his gift for public speaking and writing made him important. He died in 314 B.C., seventy-five years old.

Aeschylus

Aeschylus was a writer of plays, one of the greatest of all time, who lived 2,400 years ago in the city of Athens, in ancient Greece. It was Aeschylus who invented the tragedy, a sad play in which the hero is usually doomed to die.

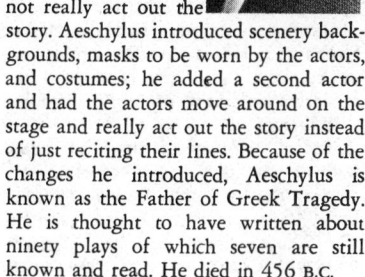

Aeschylus was born in 525 B.C. Before his time, a serious Greek play would have a big chorus, of perhaps fifty persons, and just one actor. The actor and the chorus talked to each other but did not really act out the story. Aeschylus introduced scenery backgrounds, masks to be worn by the actors, and costumes; he added a second actor and had the actors move around on the stage and really act out the story instead of just reciting their lines. Because of the changes he introduced, Aeschylus is known as the Father of Greek Tragedy. He is thought to have written about ninety plays of which seven are still known and read. He died in 456 B.C.

The seven known plays are: *Prometheus Bound; The Seven Against Thebes; The Persians; Agamemnon; The Choëphori; Eumenides;* and *The Suppliants.*

Aesculapius

In the stories of the ancient Greeks, Aesculapius was a great physician or healer. Later they called him the god of medicine, and built a temple to him. The priests of this temple were called Asclepiads and they were the doctors of ancient Greece and Rome.

There are many stories about Aesculapius, and in some of them it is said that he could bring the dead back to life. One unusual thing about the temples of Aesculapius was that the priests raised snakes in them, and each snake was supposed to hold the spirit of a god.

Aesop

Aesop was a writer who lived 2,600 years ago in ancient Greece. His stories, called *fables,* were so clever and amusing that they are still read today. A fable is a story with a "moral"—that is, a lesson that can be learned from it. Although Aesop was really writing about the foolish things that people do, the characters in his stories are always animals—foxes, crows, frogs, and so on—who talk and behave like human beings.

Aesop lived on Samos, a Greek island in the Aegean Sea. He is said to have been a slave who was freed by his master. The exact time or reason for his death is not known, but some writers of history say that he angered a mob of people in the Greek city of Delphi and they threw him over a cliff.

Afghan hound

The Afghan hound is long-legged and slender, like other hounds, but in other ways it does not look a bit like any other kind of dog. It has such long, thick hair on its chest and legs that it almost seems to be wearing fur leggings and chest protector. Its ears are so long they hang down all the way to its shoulder. The tail is unusual, too. The Afghan hound's tail is quite short, and it curls high up over the dog's back like the top of a question-mark, ending in a thin little point.

In Afghanistan, from which country Afghan hounds come, the dogs are used to hunt leopards and gazelles because they can run so fast, even over land where there are many rocks and high bushes. Afghan hounds are very good jumpers.

Many people keep Afghans as pets, and they are very gentle, quiet dogs, but they are too large for a city apartment and they need a great deal of care as well as plenty of space for exercise. Their long, silky hair has to be brushed frequently, to keep it from getting tangled and dirty.

The Afghan hound's color can be white, gray, black, tan, or brown. An Afghan hound usually is about 2½ feet high at the shoulder and weighs about 50 pounds.

Afghan Hound Club of America

Afghanistan

Afghanistan is a small country in southwestern Asia, about halfway around the world from the United States. It is wedged in among the countries of Iran, Pakistan, and the U.S.S.R., and has no outlet to the sea. It is about the size of Texas, having an area of 250,966 square miles, and about 17 million people live there, which is about one and a half as many as there are in Texas.

THE PEOPLE WHO LIVE THERE

Most of the people of Afghanistan follow the Mohammedan religion, but they belong to several different tribes who came from different places and speak different languages. Through the ages one conquering army after another passed through Afghanistan and always some of the soldiers have stayed there, and married, and formed new tribes.

More of the people belong to the Durani tribe than to any other. The Durani say they are descended from the Jews who were slaves of King Nebuchadnezzar in Babylon, thousands of years ago, as told in the Book of Daniel in the Bible. They call themselves Beni-Israel, which means "sons of Israel." But actually the Durani came to Afghanistan from Persia (the country now called Iran), and they speak a Persian language called Pushtu, which is the official language of the country.

Another big tribe, the Pathans, came originally from India, and still another, the Ghilzais, were once Turks. With the Durani, these tribes make up about half the people of Afghanistan, and together they are called Afghans. (The "-istan" in the name means "held by," so Afghanistan means "land held by the Afghans.")

Among the smaller tribes, there are the Hazars, who once were Mongol people and were brought to Afghanistan by the cruel conqueror Genghis Khan. These are the Kaffirs, who once were Greeks, and whose name means "unbelievers"—that is, people who are not Mohammedans. There are the Tafirs, who may have been the earliest of all the people to live in Afghanistan.

Although this country is made up of different cultures, the people follow similar lifestyles. For example to all Afghans, the family is very important and includes several generations. The oldest male is the ruler in his particular household.

Most Afghan men wear long cotton shirts over full white pants. On their heads, they place a skullcap covered by a turban. Women also wear pants that are black in color. Over their pants, they wear a long loose dress tied by a sash. Often, a woman will tie a cotton scarf around her head. In the past when a woman would leave her home, she would cover herself from head to toe with a long veil called a burka. Only by peering through a lacy part in the burka could she even see. Now the custom of wearing such a veil is dying out. Today only the older women still wear burkas.

Most Afghan men are farmers and depend on their own farm to meet all of their family's needs. While the men work in the fields, the women manage the home. The village mosque, an Islam church, is the center of religious and social activity especially for the men. For even though the country is changing, the women lead relatively secluded lives.

The children first learn to read and write from the Mohammedan priest. He teaches them from the Koran, the Holy Book or Bible of their religion. It is only since 1931 that Afghanistan has had a law requiring all children to go to school.

HOW THE PEOPLE LIVE

Most of the people of Afghanistan are either farmers or shepherds. They are quite poor. The average Afghan makes only about as much money in a year as the average American makes in a week.

The farmers live in houses in villages. They have to work very hard, because there is no modern farm machinery and there is not enough rainfall to make the land very fertile. The farmers raise enough food for their families. Their biggest crop is wheat. They also raise cotton, tobacco, sugar beets, and other plants and vegetables, which they sell. The women are famous for weaving rugs and making handmade jewelry, and the children used to help, working all day from the time they were five or six years old. Now they go to school, but they still work during other hours.

About one-fourth the people are nomads ("wanderers"). They live in tents and move from place to place. Many of these nomads are the shepherds. Among the sheep they raise is the karakul, from which is made a black, curly fur that is used for women's fur coats.

There are several big cities, and Kabul, the capital of the country, has a population of 307,000, with a university, and a college of arts. But only one family out of twelve lives in a city. (In the United States, more than half the people live in cities.) It is only the people in the cities who ever see books or newspapers, but somehow any important news soon spreads all over the country, through the chiefs of the tribes.

Though Afghanistan has laws that apply to all the people, the farmers in the villages and the nomads wandering through the country are ruled in most matters by the chiefs of their tribes.

There isn't much "fun," as the American would think of fun, for either grown-ups or children. No television, no movies; and radio broadcasts are for the few people in the cities, because the farmers and shepherds don't have radio sets. But children love to hear the village "story-teller" read or tell stories, often playing on a stringed instrument like a guitar as he does so.

WHAT KIND OF PLACE IT IS

Most of the people of Afghanistan live in the central part of the country, on level plains with rivers running through them and high mountains rising on all sides. Some of these mountains, the Hindu Kush range on the eastern border, are among the highest in the world.

On the plains, where the farming is done, there is a "rainy season" from December to April, but even during this season there is very little rain. At other times there is no rain at all and the temperature often goes as high as 120°, which is higher than it ever gets in the United States, except in desert regions like Death Valley. The farmers have to depend on the melting snows running down from the mountains in three important rivers, the Amu Darya, the Kabul, and the Helmand. From these the farmers get water for their fields.

On the slopes of the mountains, the shepherds tend their flocks of sheep. Here it is sometimes very hot, often 100°, as it is in the valleys, and sometimes it is very cold, 12° below zero—both hotter and colder than it ever is in most parts of the United States.

The people might be rich if they could make use of the valuable minerals in these mountains. It is believed that there are iron, gold, copper, and other metals, and oil, too, in the southern part of the country. But the Afghans lack two things needed for mining. They do not have the machinery and they do not have the transportation. There are no railroads at all in Afghanistan. There are some roads, from the capital city of Kabul to the other cities, but there are very few automobiles. Most of the traveling is done by caravans of camels, or riding a camel or on horseback.

There are many animals, both wild and tame. The tame ones include the Afghan hound, about which you can read in the article just before this one. One of the unusual wild animals is the jerboa, a little jumping rat with long hind legs; it looks like a tiny kangaroo. Many of the wild animals seen in zoos are native to Afghanistan—tigers, leopards, bears, and others.

HOW THE PEOPLE ARE GOVERNED

Afghanistan is a constitutional monarchy, which means that it has a king, a parliament that makes the laws, and a written constitution that protects the rights of the people. A new constitution, adopted in 1964, places limits on the power of the shah.

Mohammed Zahir Shah ("shah" means king) became king in 1933 and has done much to make the country more modern, by building roads and factories and schools.

All citizens who are 20 years old or more may vote. They elect members of the National Assembly, one of the two branches of the parliament. The other branch, the House of Elders, has 84 members, one-third of whom are appointed by the Shah.

Afghanistan is divided into provinces. There are ten provinces, and each has a governor appointed by the parliament.

Every man from 22 to 42 years old must serve in the army. There are only 90,000 men in the army, but the others can be called if they are needed. The air force, while small, is being modernized with new jet fighters and bombers and new bases to handle the biggest jet airliners.

AFGHANISTAN IN THE PAST

For thousands of years, Afghanistan has been used as a battleground. Some armies have come to conquer the country itself. Others have passed through on their way to fight other countries. One reason for this is the Khyber Pass.

The Khyber Pass is a fairly low and level gap in the giant Hindu Kush mountains, whose highest peaks are almost five miles high. That has made the Khyber Pass the only way to reach India from the west.

Alexander the Great, the king who almost conquered the world more than 2,000 years ago, marched his armies through Afghanistan, and he was only one of the great conquerors who have ruled the land. The Mongols led by Genghis Khan did so much damage, burning villages and towns and killing the people, that Afghanistan did not recover for hundreds of years. Its people became wild and warlike. Raiding parties of fierce Afghans used to ride through the Khyber Pass and swoop down on the British settlements in India, killing and robbing. Finally the British, in 1878, sent armies into Afghanistan. There were several bloody battles, but the British won them and took charge of Afghanistan's affairs.

Afghanistan became fully independent again in 1907. A few years after World War I, a very modern king named Amanullah came to the throne. He was too modern for the people, who did not want to change their old way of living. They made King Amanullah abdicate. After him came Nadir Shah, who had been a great warrior. He became king in 1931 but was assassinated two years later because he was just as modern as Amanullah was. The present king, Mohammed Zahir Shah, is Nadir Shah's son. He is a modern ruler too, but the people have finally come to like modern ways and he has not had trouble with them.

Today, Afghanistan lives at peace with its neighbors and is respected as a country that is rapidly improving itself. In 1946 it joined the United Nations. The United States has lent it some money ($362,900,000 as of 1969) to use for improvements such as irrigation of the farms and machines for the factories. One measure of advancement is that thirty years ago four out of five Afghans could not read or write; today four out of five can read and write.

AFGHANISTAN—SUMMARY

Area. 253,256 sq. mi.
Population. 17,000,000 (1973 estimate). About 50% Afghans, including Pathans (of

Indian origin), Duranis (Persian), and Ghilzai (Turkish); remainder Hazars (Mongoloid), Kaffirs (Greek), and Tafirs, believed by some to be the original inhabitants.

Language. Persian and Pashto or Pushtu (the official language), both of the Hindu-Iranian group and written in Arabic characters.

Religion. Mohammedan, with freedom of religion.

Principal Cities. Capital, Kabul (pop. 456,000. Others: Mazar-i-Sharif (40,000), in the north; Herat (62,000), in the west; Khandahar (121,000), in the south; Jalabad (44,000), in the east; Ghazni (25,000), in the central area.

Government. Constitutional monarchy (constitution of 1964). Mohammed Zahir Shah became king in 1933. Parliament of two houses; the lower house, called the House of the People, has 215 members elected by the people for a 4-year term; the upper house, or House of Elders, has 84 members, one-third of whom are appointed by the king, the other two-thirds are elected. Citizens over the age of 20 may vote. Women voted for the first time in 1965. The country is divided into 29 provinces each of which is divided into districts and sub-districts. Each province has a governor who is assisted by a council of elected members.

Education. Compulsory through sixth grade. Both elementary and higher education free. Boys and girls have separate schools.

Currency. The monetary unit is the afghani, worth about 2⅖ U. S. cents (1970).

Flag. Three bars, black, red (in center), green. In red bar, two ears of wheat around a mosque.

Commerce. Industrial development small but growing; self-sustaining agriculture. Per capita income, about $82. Exports (about $59,000,000 per year in 1962-63) chiefly grain, other farm produce, and furs (see (KARAKUL). Imports (in balance with exports) chiefly machinery and textiles.

Transportation. No railroads; one navigable river. About 10,700 miles of highways connecting chief cities and to Pakistan via Khyber Pass. Two airlines. Other transportation chiefly by camel and pony.

Topography. Average elevation, 4,000 ft., with central plateau bordered by high mountains (Hindu-Kush system, highest elevation 25,250 ft.), and desert in south. Four river systems are the Amu Darya (the only navigable river), the Hari Rud, the Helmand, and the Kabul. There are few lakes.

Natural Resources. Abundant, but undeveloped, deposits of coal, minerals, and probably petroleum. About 2% of total area under cultivation, mostly requiring irrigation.

Climate. Dry continental climate, cold in winter, hot in summer, except in Jalalabad basin (subtropical). Annual rainfall, 10 in. on central plateau.

Africa

Africa is a continent, the second-largest of the big masses of land that make up the earth. Only Asia is larger. Africa has 11,500,000 square miles; North America has about 9,300,000 square miles including Canada, the United States, and Mexico.

About 391,000,000 people live in Africa. This is more than live in North America, though in Africa as in North America there are big regions of mountains and deserts where few people live.

Africa is shaped somewhat like a pear, with the wide part "on top"—that is, in the north. This is the part closest to the Americas. By jet planes, many parts of Africa can be reached from America or Europe in a few hours, but weeks are required to reach other parts because there are very few good roads, railroads, or airports.

For hundreds of years Africa was called "the Dark Continent." No one in Europe and America knew much about it. It had not been explored, the way America was, until less than 100 years ago. In the last hundred years much has been learned about Africa and its people.

Some parts of Africa are as modern and up-to-date as the United States, but millions of square miles are still wild jungle and desert.

THE COUNTRIES OF AFRICA

Like other continents, Africa has a number of different countries and territories under different governments. Until after World War II most of these territories were controlled by European countries, but they preferred to be independent and one by one they have broken away.

France, Great Britain and Belgium, which had the largest African colonies, had decided by about 1955 to grant independence to any territory that wanted it and that seemed capable of self-government.

All the new nations immediately joined the United Nations and with so many votes they soon became a powerful influence in the U.N. Assembly, especially in questions involving racial rights, for most of these new nations have large black majorities.

Most of the former colonies changed to independence peacefully. (An exception was Zaire, once known as the Belgian Congo and the Democratic Republic of Congo. Zaire fought hard for independence.) But political difficulties arose in most of the countries after they had been independent for a few years. By 1966 governments had been overthrown by force in ten of the new countries and there were even more cases in which a revolution was attempted but failed.

Usually the countries' armed forces took over the government by a "coup" (coup d'etat, a French phrase for a change of government in which one group of leaders replaces another, often with little or no bloodshed, without involving the people who are governed).

There were successful coups in Algeria, 1965; Republic of the Congo, 1963; Zaire, (formerly Belgian Congo) 1965; Central African Republic, 1966; Dahomey, 1963, and again in 1965; Ghana, 1966; Nigeria, 1966; Togo, 1963; Upper Volta, 1966; Zanzibar, 1964 (before it became part of Tanzania).

There are several reasons why the new African nations were so unstable (changeable) politically.

When European countries set up their African colonies, they captured territories without considering the people who lived in them. Often the people belonged to different tribes who spoke different languages and distrusted one another. Each tribe wanted to control the country.

The new countries were given independence on condition that they have democratic governments with constitutions to guarantee the freedom of the people. The first elections gave power to the men who had led the struggle for independence. Often these men promptly made themselves dictators, suppressing free speech, and opposition political parties, and free elections. They spent money to glorify themselves and to put up buildings and displays that might have made the country look great but did not help the people. And all members of the government demanded bribes before they would do anything.

Communist countries, especially China, tried to control the new countries and were opposed by the big European countries and the United States, so in many of the new governments there were two groups, each receiving money and advice from one foreign country or another, and so forced to oppose each other.

In all coups it was the country's Army that took over control, since a national army is usually the only powerful organization outside the government.

THE TERRITORIES

Only Portugal and Spain retained most of their territories in Africa after the trend to independence began. Portugal's territories were Angola, Cabinda, Portuguese Guinea, and Mozambique. They are now independent countries. Spain retained Spanish Sahara, Ifni (now part of Morocco), and Spanish Guinea (now Equatorial Guinea, independent since 1968). France retained only French Somaliland (now French Territory of the Afars and the Issas) and until 1975, the Comoro Islands, a group of islands off southeast Africa.

The Republic of South Africa kept control of South-West Africa, although this had long been the subject of dispute between South Africa and the United Nations.

Great Britain kept Mauritius, St. Helena, and Seychelles.

THE PEOPLES

The earliest peoples of North Africa were related to the Arabs, Jews, and others who spoke languages called Semitic. Along the western part of the Mediterranean coast, the largest group of these people were the Berbers; along the eastern part, they were the Egyptians. The descendants of these earliest North Africans still live there, but their ancestors married so many of the Arabs and Turks and other races that invaded their countries that today they are a mixture of several bloods.

Nearly all of these North Africans follow the Mohammedan religion. They speak languages that are much like Arabic, because that is the language in which the Koran, the Mohammedan Holy Book, is written. In the western part of North Africa, the men wear turbans on their heads, and long flowing robes, just as the Arabs do. Some of them live in big cities and follow the ways of Europeans and Americans. Others are nomads, or wandering tribes, who move from one place to another to do their farming or to raise sheep and cattle. Still others are farmers who live on their own farms or work for big landowners. Most of the Egyptians are farmers, but there are big, modern cities, especially Cairo and Alexandria.

The Ethiopians are a Semitic people too, but they are chiefly Christians. They are very dark-skinned, and many of them still paint their faces and wear little more than loincloths, as many Negroes of Africa do, but it is a mistake to call Ethiopians Negroes, or to call Negroes Ethiopians, though the mistake is often

made. They are of different origins.

Except for the northern edges of the vast African continent, nearly all the natives are of the Negro race. These will be described next.

THE NEGRO PEOPLES

The section that runs across Africa from the Nile to the Atlantic Ocean was once all called the Sudan, which means the African Negro Land. The Negroes who live in this territory are called the Sudanese. They were the most advanced of the original Negroes of Africa, and at one time they had big empires of their own. They adopted the religion of the invading Arabs years ago, and the Arab costume.

Negroes related to the Sudanese live throughout Africa, all the way down to the Cape of Good Hope at the southern tip. They are called Bantus. But neither the Sudanese nor the Bantus are all alike. They are of many tribes, religions, and customs. Some are nearly giants in size; among the Watusi, for example, the men are often seven feet or more tall. Some tribes are of average size, like Europeans.

Nearly all of the African Negroes are good farmers, and hardworking people. There are many things that only the women do, however. It is not considered a man's work to do anything but hunt for the family's meat. Many African Negroes love meat, and they eat all kinds. By some of the tribes, snakes, crocodile meat and monkey meat are considered delicious.

The women make pots and pans out of a plant called the bottle gourd, and their system of making them is very unusual. While the gourd is growing, they tie strings around it wherever they want it to stay slim and narrow, and it will grow only where it is not tied. The cord makes little necks here and there, wherever it is tied, and then when the big gourd is ripe, the women take it off the vine and put it in the sun to dry. When it is completely dry and hard, it is painted and decorated. It is called a calabash, and it is used for pots and pans, or water jugs, or sometimes for drums.

Some gourds make a fine booming noise when they are beaten with the hands, and that is the sound of jungle drums that can be heard for miles across the wild sections of Africa. The natives have drumbeats that mean very definite things. There is one kind of beat, for instance, that might mean, "We have just seen a caravan of white men approaching across the desert." Another kind of beat might mean, "There's a herd of elephants stampeding to the south." Each kind of beat means something different, and in a very short space of time, news travels for hundreds of miles. One tribe starts it, the next picks it up, and the next, and the next, until all the native tribes for miles and miles know the story.

In most of the settlements, the natives live in little, round, grass-thatched huts. They drive poles into the ground in a circle, and pull the tops together in a point. Then they weave straw in and out between the poles, or pack the spaces with mud, to form walls and a roof. Sometimes they build separate roofs, by

PRINCIPAL NATIONS AND TERRITORIES OF AFRICA

NAME AND DATE OF INDEPENDENCE	CAPITAL CITY	REMARKS
1. Algeria, 1962	Algiers	
2. Angola, 1975	Luanda	Formerly a province of Portugal
3. Arab Republic of Egypt	Cairo	Formerly United Arab Republic
4. Botswana, 1966	Gaborone	Formerly Bechuanaland
5. Burundi, 1962	Bujumbura	A kingdom; formerly part of Ruanda-Urundi
6. Cabinda	Luanda	Really part of Angola, though located north of it and separated from it
7. Cameroon, 1961	Yaounde	Formerly the French Cameroons, plus the southern part of the British Cameroons
8. Central African Republic, 1960	Bangui	Formerly part of French Equatorial Africa
9. Chad, Republic of, 1960	N'Djamena	Formerly part of French Equatorial Africa
10. Dahomey, 1960	Porto-Novo and Cotonou	Formerly part of French West Africa
11. Equatorial Guinea, 1968	Malabo	Formerly Spanish Guinea, a Spanish province
12. Ethiopia, 1896	Addis Ababa	
13. French Territory of the Afars and the Issas	Djibouti	Formerly French Somaliland
14. Gabon Republic, 1960	Libreville	Formerly part of French West Africa
15. Gambia, The, 1965	Banjul	Former British colony and protectorate
16. Ghana, 1957	Accra	Formerly the Gold Coast plus British Togoland
17. Guinea, 1958	Conakry	Formerly part of French West Africa
18. Guinea-Bissau, 1974	Bissau	Formerly Portuguese Guinea (a colonial possession)
19. Ifni	Sidi Ifni	Former province of Spain, now part of Morocco
20. Ivory Coast, 1960	Abidjan	Formerly part of French West Africa
21. Kenya, 1963	Nairobi	Formerly a British colony and protectorate
22. Lesotho, 1966	Maseru	Formerly Basutoland
23. Liberia, 1847	Monrovia	Africa's oldest republic
24. Libya, 1951	Tripoli	Ruled by Turkey from 1551 to 1911, then by Italy until after World War II
25. Malagasy Republic, 1960	Tananarive	Formerly Madagascar
26. Malawi, 1964	Lilongwe	Formerly Nyasaland

making a second ring of poles outside the first, and setting a roof on top of the outside ring, so that the roof isn't attached to the house walls at all, but just forms a sort of shed over the house. In some parts of Africa the natives build their house on long poles, like stilts, or high up between the trunks of trees, and climb to them on ladders. This protects them against crawling insects and snakes, and against wild animals.

SOME NATIVE CUSTOMS

The African Negroes have many customs that people in Europe and America are not used to seeing. For example, they have very fancy hair styles. Sometimes their hair is wound up on sticks into such long, complicated shapes that they cannot lie down flat at night. They rest the back of their necks on a wooden block, to hold their hair off the ground, so that the carefully twisted sticks of stiffly arranged hair will not be messed up.

The Sara tribe of Chad pierce the upper and lower lips of young girls and insert a small wooden disk into the openings. Over a period of years, larger and larger disks are used, until the lips are stretched to an enormous size. Some of the older women wear disks as big as dinner plates. The custom may have started centuries ago to make the women unattractive to the slave-traders. Sara girls today prefer smaller disks, but even with these, eating and talking are very difficult. When John Ringling brought some of the Sara women to America to travel with his circus, he called them "Ubangis", but this is not correct—there is no tribe known as Ubangis.

The people of some tribes make scratches on their skin, and keep them from healing until great scars develop all over the body. Each tribe has its own patterns for scars, and a native can tell what tribe a stranger belongs to by the shape of the scars scratched into his skin.

One of the customs that nearly all tribes have is the great ceremonial dance on the evening before a hunt. For this they dress up in fancy costumes, and dance to the rhythm of their drums, while they pray to the gods of the hunt to send plenty of game to shoot the next day when the hunters go out.

The most elaborate costumes are worn by the witch doctors who, in addition to their magical duties, serve as religious leaders, medical men, judges in disputes, and counselors in family affairs. The

PRINCIPAL NATIONS AND TERRITORIES OF AFRICA

NAME AND DATE OF INDEPENDENCE	CAPITAL CITY	REMARKS
27. Mali, 1960	Bamako	Formerly the Sudanese Republic
28. Mauritania, 1960	Nouakchott	Formerly part of French West Africa
29. Morocco, 1956	Rabat	Formerly a French protectorate with Spanish rule in the north
30. Mozambique, 1975	Lourenco Marques	Formerly under Portuguese rule since 1505
31. Niger, 1960	Niamey	Formerly part of French West Africa
32. Nigeria, 1960	Lagos	Formerly a British colony and protectorate
33. Republic of the Congo, 1960	Brazzaville	Formerly the French Middle Congo
34. Republic of South Africa, 1910	Cape Town (legislative) Pretoria (administrative)	Formerly the Union of South Africa
35. Rhodesia, 1965	Salisbury	Formerly Southern Rhodesia
36. Rwanda, 1962	Kigali	Formerly part of Ruanda-Urundi
37. Sao Tome and Principe, 1975	Sao Tome	Two islands off the West coast of Africa, formerly under Portuguese rule
38. Senegal, 1960	Dakar	Formerly part of French West Africa
39. Sierra Leone, 1971	Freetown	Former British colony and protectorate
40. Somalia, 1960	Mogadishu	Formerly British and Italian Somaliland
41. South-West Africa, or Nambia, 1968	Windhoek	Formerly part of the Republic of South Africa
42. Spanish Sahara	Aiun	Province of Spain
43. Sudan, 1956	Khartoum	Formerly the Anglo-Egyptian Sudan
44. Swaziland, 1968	Mbabane	Former British Colony
45. Tanzania, 1964	Dar es Salaam	Formerly Tanganyika and Zanzibar
46. Togo, 1960	Lome	Formerly French Togoland
47. Tunisia, 1956	Tunis	Former French protectorate
48. Uganda, 1963	Kampala	Former British protectorate
49. Upper Volta, 1960	Ouagadougou	Former French territory
50. Zaire, 1960	Kinshasa	Formerly the Belgian Congo, then the Democratic Republic of the Congo
51. Zambia, 1964	Lusaka	Formerly Northern Rhodesia

witch doctor is very important to the tribe's welfare. Christian missionaries have been in Africa for years, but many tribes live in regions that are hard to reach, and they still worship the same spirits and gods their ancestors did.

THE RECORD OF SLAVERY

Slavery in various forms has been practiced for thousands of years, and until very recent times was considered a normal part of life. Ancient historical records show that it was customary to make slaves of convicted criminals, prisoners of war, and persons who could not pay their debts. Early civilizations found the system profitable: Greek temples, Egyptian pyramids, Roman roads and aqueducts were all built with slave labor. African kingdoms were no different; they slave-traded for many centuries before any Europeans arrived on their shores. In those times and places, however, a slave could advance himself by hard work and eventually buy his freedom; he could inherit goods; he might even marry into the master's family and acquire wealth and position. Slaves were usually well treated, and cruelty was forbidden by law. When European traders found that huge fortunes could be made in the slave market, slavery became their biggest business. They encouraged tribes to raid the villages of other tribes and kidnap everyone they could carry off; the victims were chained together, crowded into dirty, leaky ships, and transported to Europe and the Americas to be sold as slaves. The story of the slave trade and its cruelties is a disgraceful blot on the history of the western world. There is a separate article on SLAVERY.

THE PRIMITIVE PEOPLES

In the central parts of Africa there are some very primitive tribes of people who have not accepted civilization and live much as their ancestors did for many thousands of years.

There is one group called the Pygmies. These are very small people. They live in the dense jungle sections of the Congo basin. Pygmy men are no taller than a 12-year-old child in the United States—about four and a half feet tall. They are very shy, and will hide when strangers come near, but they are very brave hunters and hunt the elephant. For hunting as well as for protection, they have poison-tipped arrows. Many Pygmies are nomadic; that is, they never stay long in one place, but build temporary shelters in trees to protect themselves from floods and wild animals. They hunt for their meat, and gather wild berries, fruits, and grains to eat, moving to new territory when the supply runs low. They have always lived in this carefree way, but in recent years many of the Pygmies have settled in small villages and practice simple agriculture. They are peaceful people if no one bothers them, and they never start trouble with other tribes. They speak a form of the Bantu language, but cannot read or write. They have no schools or churches.

Another interesting tribe in South Africa are the Bushmen, who live in and around the Kalahari Desert in much the same manner as their ancestors did. Like their ancestors, Bushmen have a great talent for painting men and animals on cave walls and on rock shelters. Wherever they have roamed, they have left colorful paintings of hunts, fights, and dances. Bushmen are small, slender people with both Negroid and Mongoloid features. Like the Pygmies, Bushmen live in temporary camps, moving on when food is scarce. They own only what they can carry, sharing possessions with the group. The Bushmen arrived in southern Africa long before the taller, "true" Negroes did. Between the 12th and 15th centuries, however, Bantu-speaking Negroes migrated south and eventually outnumbered the Bushmen. The language of the Bushmen contains clicking sounds, as does that of the Hottentots, a related group of people who are a similar physical type, but slightly taller. Hottentot women have an accumulation of fat below the waist in back. Great numbers of Hottentots were killed by conquering Bantu tribes or died of disease. Their main foods are milk, wild fruits and nuts, and whatever meat they can get by hunting. They raise cattle for trading purposes. Both Bushmen and Hottentots have a great number of folk tales and songs that were passed down from their ancestors.

WHAT AFRICA IS LIKE

The equator runs through the middle of Africa. Here it is always hot, and there is much rain, so that every kind of plant grows so fast and so big that you can hardly control it. This is the famous jungle. The leaves are so thick that the sun never reaches the ground except when a tree falls over. Monkeys and snakes and insects by the millions live in the jungles. Millions of men live there too, even though the climate is not very healthful and the danger from animals and insects is very great.

In the northern part of Africa is the Sahara Desert, the biggest desert in the world. It covers an area of more than three million square miles, so it is bigger than the entire United States. Parts of the desert are vast stretches of level sand. Other parts are mostly rock and gravel. In the Sahara it seldom rains, though occasionally the rain comes down in torrents. There are few places where there is enough water for plants to grow. In parts of the Sahara it gets as hot as 120 degrees. No place in the United States is ever that hot except Death Valley, a desert in California.

But though it is so hot during the day, nights on the Sahara are always cold. You would need a thick blanket

every night. That is because the air is so dry there is nothing to hold the heat once the sun has gone down, and the sand cools rapidly after dark.

Apart from the Sahara, the northern part of Africa is very much like the southern part of France and Spain. It is warm and fertile along the coast, but dry where it joins the Sahara.

Think of almost any kind of weather, or just about any kind of climate you have ever heard of—there is some part of Africa that has it. There is warm or cold weather, dry or rainy weather. There are deserts, mountains, wide stretches of grassy plains, big rivers with fertile valleys, jungles where you would have to cut a path for yourself to get anywhere because the plants are so thick, big lakes and waterfalls (one of which, Victoria Falls, is as big and beautiful as Niagara.)

Farther to the south, Africa is in the temperate zone, as the United States is. The climate is quite pleasant. In the southeast section, there are mountains with peaks that are so high there is snow on them all year around. These are Mt. Kilimanjaro, 19,565 feet high, and Mt. Kenya, 17,040 feet high. These mountains are in a section with many rivers and lakes. Lake Victoria, which was named for Queen Victoria of England, is especially famous, and it is very beautiful. It is on the borders of Kenya, Tanzania, and Uganda.

In the plains of South Africa there is plenty of rainfall for rich and productive farming. The winters never get very cold, and even in the very coolest sections there is very little snow.

Throughout Africa there are millions of wild animals. There is a separate article on this; see HUNTING. Besides elephants and lions, there are enormous herds of zebras running wild; gorillas live in the jungles (though no one is permitted to hunt them now); and there are thousands of smaller varieties of ape, and many monkeys. The crocodile, rhinoceros, hippopotamus, and wild boar all live in Africa. There are herds of giraffes and many kinds of deer, many different snakes, and birds with beautiful plumage. Wild beasts live in Africa just as they have for hundreds of thousands of years.

THE RICHNESS OF AFRICA

The natives lived in Africa for tens of thousands of years without knowing or caring that they had one of the richest continents on earth. But the countries of Europe knew it—though even they did not know how much wealth was hidden in the mountains and mining lands of Africa. Anyway, the European nations managed to split up most of Africa among themselves, often with such quarrels that they almost led to warfare. Once the native peoples of Africa got their land back, the development of their rich resources became their chief problem.

Most of the world's diamonds come from Africa. Zaire and the Republic of South Africa lead in diamond production. Also, over half of the world's supply of gold comes from Africa. The Republic of South Africa is a major gold producer.

Experts believe that Africa has the world's largest copper deposits. Copper is mined in Zaire and Zambia, where huge copper deposits can be found. In 1952, great iron mines were opened for the first time in Liberia. Other important minerals found include tin, lead, zinc, and bauxite.

But the most valuable property Africa holds was not even thought about until very recent years. It is uranium, from which atomic energy is obtained. The Congo and other parts of the central African region may turn out to be the place from which most of the world's uranium is obtained.

Africa could easily feed much of the world, if its fertile lands could be farmed and its other lands cleared and irrigated as land in the United States has been. For many years North Africa has produced wheat and cotton and other valuable crops for Europe, but the greatest part of Africa is still undeveloped. Some fine and beautiful woods, mahogany and ebony and others, come from Africa.

Electric power is unknown in most parts of Africa, but there are rivers that could supply enough electricity to run factories and supply big cities beyond anything Europe has. The power in African rivers had never been used, except for a few places on the Nile and in South Africa, until the last twenty years or so. Since then, the rivers have been developed rapidly.

THE EXPLORATION OF AFRICA

For thousands of years no part of Africa was known except North Africa. There, the Egyptians had the earliest civilization known to modern man. The people of Carthage (which is now Tunisia) fought for years against the powerful Romans, whom they almost defeated with their great generals Hamilcar and Hannibal. (There are separate articles about HAMILCAR and HANNIBAL.) Ethiopia, in northeast Africa, was a civilized country hundreds of years before the time of Christ, and some of the Negro peoples—especially the Hausa—had thriving cities. But the rest of Africa was not known at all.

Then the great explorers, especially those from Portugal, began to sail from Europe to India and China, to bring back silks and spices and other fine things that Europe did not have. Their voyages took them southward around Africa. As much as seven hundred years ago they had sailed down the west coast of Africa and they built little towns near harbors where they could stop to rest and take on fresh water and food. Bartholomew Diaz sailed all the way to the Cape of Good Hope in the year 1488. Vasco da Gama sailed all the way around Africa a few years later. Dutch, British and French sailors followed him.

It was only a few years after Columbus discovered America that Europeans began taking African slaves to the New World; the first were landed in Haiti in 1510. The slave trade continued for three hundred years. But the slavers landed only on the coast. The Dutch started their Cape Colony in 1652, and the first British colony dates from 1807,

but these too stayed near the coast. The rest of Africa remained "the Dark Continent," unknown and unexplored.

A Scottish missionary, Dr. David Livingstone, was the first white man to learn much about the unexplored part of Africa. He went where no man had ever gone before. Among his discoveries was the Victoria Falls. One of the most interesting stories of Africa is how Dr. Livingstone became sick somewhere in the unexplored interior and was thought to be lost. James Gordon Bennett, a famous New York newspaper publisher, sent a reporter named Henry Morton Stanley to find him, and Stanley not only found Dr. Livingstone but became the greatest of all African explorers. There are special stories about these famous men and their adventures in Africa.

There was still to be much trouble in Africa. The British and the Boers (descendants of the first Dutch settlers in South Africa) fought the Boer War; the Italians twice went to war to gain control of Ethiopia; the Germans under Hitler threatened war if they could not get back Tanganyika and the other African colonies they had lost in World War I. Men will probably continue to quarrel over Africa for a long time. But it is no longer the unknown continent. As surely as America was developed and became great, so, some day, will Africa.

EUROPEANS IN AFRICA

Since the Dutch and British first started colonies in Africa, things have changed a great deal. From just a few handfuls of people from England and Holland, many settlements have grown up and become great modern cities. In fact, if you were to walk through the streets of any large African city, you would see modern and western looking streets.

British Information Service
Native African sculpture.

In the Republic of South Africa alone there are more than 3,000,000 people of European descent. Rhodesia and Kenya have a large European population. Also, in east and in south Africa, there are about a half a million Indians living.

RACIAL TURMOIL

For years, especially since World War II, the native and white races have clashed in parts of Africa. After years of being exploited for their country's wealth, the natives began to rebel against the white settlers. Unfortunately, the

A modern city in Africa resembles cities of the United States.

farming methods are often primitive, and laborers suffer generally from sleeping sickness or other debilitating diseases. Nevertheless, Africa is the world's most important supplier of a number of materials. Egyptian cotton, West African palm oil and cocoa, East African sisal, tobacco from Southern Rhodesia, coffee and timber from the Congo and Liberian rubber are all important agriculture exports. South Africa supplies most of the world's diamonds and much of its gold.

The Congo, Zambia and Morocco produce most of the world's cobalt, and the Congo is believed to be the free world's most important source of uranium. Manganese, copper, tin, chrome, vanadium and asbestos are other mineral exports. There is large industrial development only in the Republic of South Africa.

Transportation. Africa has about 45,000 miles of railways, the fewest of any continent. Most of these are concentrated in the Republic of South Africa and in North Africa, leaving vast regions without railroads. Inland waterways, including the Nile, Congo, Niger, Senegal, and Volta, and the great lakes of east central Africa, carry most of the traffic for large areas. Modern highways are rare.

white man had always treated the natives as an inferior race who could be nothing but laborers or servants. In the Republic of South Africa, the system of separation of races (called *apartheid*, which means "apartness' or, as it is called in the United States, "segregation") causes constant trouble. In 1965 the relatively few British people who controlled Rhodesia declared the country independent rather than give voting rights to the natives.

In spite of these difficulties, Africa is an active force in the modern world. A rich continent of many different people and customs, it faces many challenges.

This new mosque is in the city of Kano, in Nigeria, where there are many Mohammedans. They go to a mosque as Christians go a church.

Despite the great changes in Africa, this native still lives as his ancestors did.

AFRICA—SUMMARY

Area. About 11,500,000 sq. mi., the second-largest continent.

Population. About 330,000,000.

Religion. Predominantly Islam in the north, native religion or Roman Catholic in central Africa, and Protestant in the south.

Languages. In North Africa the main language is Arabic, but Berber is also important. South of the Sahara Desert hundreds of different languages are spoken. One Bantu tongue, Kiswahili, is widely used for trade in East Africa. In the Republic of South Africa, English and Afrikaans are both official languages.

Commerce. The average annual income per person throughout the continent is probably less than $50. For nearly all the people, the main source of livelihood is agriculture. South of the Sahara, soil erosion is common,

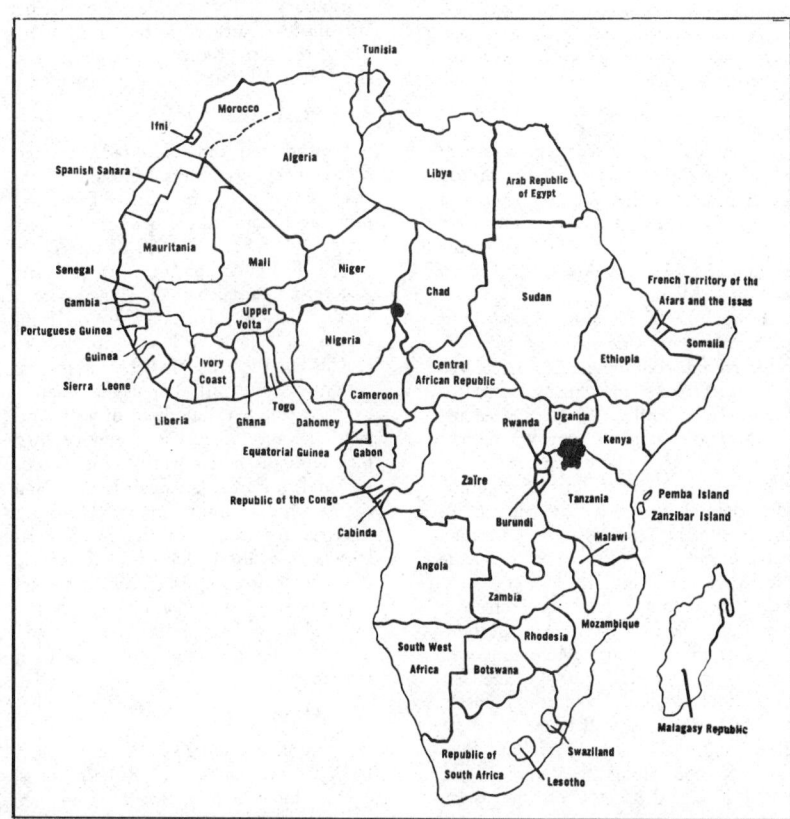

Africa's smooth coasts afford few natural harbors. Camel caravans are still used in the Sahara, and human bearers in equatorial regions, but there is increasing use of motor vehicles specially designed to cross the desert or plains.

Topography. Aside from the Atlas mountains in the northwest corner of Africa, some fertile land along the Mediterranean, and the Nile valley, northern Africa is dominated by the vast Sahara desert, 3,000,000 sq. mi. of arid and semi-arid rocky plateau and sand. South of the Sahara are grasslands merging into the equatorial rain forest that stretches from the west coast across the Gulf of Guinea and into the Congo basin. South and east of the Congo, Africa is almost all plateau, 3,000 ft. and more above sea level. The important mountains lie in this region—the Abyssinian plateau, source of the Blue Nile, in Ethiopia; twin ranges in east and central Africa, divided by the Great Rift valley; and the Drakensberg, or Dragon mountains, in the eastern Republic of South Africa. The highest peaks are in the Kenya plateau east of the Great Rift—Mt. Kilimanjaro (19,565 ft.) and Mt. Kenya (17,040 ft.). This also is the area of great lakes—Victoria, Tanganyika, Nyasa, Chad, Rudolf, Edward, and Albert. The Zambezi river, Africa's fourth-longest, cuts across this eastern spine of mountains, and near its headwaters are the Victoria Falls, highest in the world. To the south and west are the interior *veld* or plateau of South Africa and the Kalahari desert.

Natural Resources. (See also *Commerce,* above.) Great iron-ore deposits in Liberia were tapped for the first time in 1952. Coal resources in South Africa and Southern Rhodesia promise commercial yields for many years ahead. Oil deposits in the Sahara were drilled by France and began to produce in commercial quantities in 1957. There is some production of oil in Egypt. Africa's potential of hydro-electric power is the largest in the world; see DAMS.

Climate. Africa's climate has wide variations. The Sahara receives an annual rainfall ranging from 5 inches to none at all, and the temperature reaches 120 degrees in the summer. West Africa and the Congo basin receive more than 80 inches of rain a year. The upland plateaus, even in west Africa, have temperate climates. South Africa lies in the temperate zone, with mild weather and rare snowfalls in the winter.

African campaign

During World War II it was very important to both sides to have control of Africa, and especially North Africa along the Mediterranean Sea. For three years the warring countries, especially Britain and Germany, fought for control of North Africa.

It was one of the most seesaw fights in history. First one side and then the other would seem to win a complete victory, and chase the enemy back for hundreds of miles. Then the enemy would make a stand somewhere, prepare a campaign of its own, and pretty soon it would seem to be winning. United States troops saw their first fighting in North Africa; so did Australian troops, who were very important in the North African campaign, as were Canadian troops. Some great generals won their reputations in North African fighting, including Marshal Montgomery of the British, Marshal Rommel of the Germans, and General Eisenhower himself.

When World War II began, in 1939, Italy controlled Libya, stretching hundreds of miles along the Mediterranean, and Eritrea and Ethiopia on the eastern side of Africa. The British had forces in Egypt and also on the Red Sea.

Italy was not then in the war. When Italy did enter the war, in May, 1940, fighting between the British and the Italians began. In this fighting, the British were soon successful. Their commander was Sir Archibald Wavell. The Italians did not have enough tanks to match the British. More than 300,000 Italians surrendered.

Then Marshal Rommel and his famous German Afrika Korps entered the fighting. Early in 1941 Rommel attacked in Libya and drove the British back to the border of Egypt. Sir Claude Auchinleck became the British general in command, and in the fall of 1941 he attacked, drove the Germans back, and captured many of them. In the spring of 1942, again Rommel scored a great victory, almost capturing Alexandria; the British finally stopped the German advance at the village of El Alamein, which was to become famous for that reason. The British changed generals again, Sir Harold Alexander becoming the commander and Sir Bernard Montgomery taking over the British Eighth Army.

The United States had sent General Eisenhower to England to take command of American forces there and to prepare the great "Operation Torch," at its time the most ambitious landing operation known. In the fall of 1942, the expedition sailed from Britain and the United States—more than eight hundred ships, nearly 300,000 British and American troops. On October 23, 1942, Montgomery started a great attack from Egypt in the east; on November 8, the American and British forces landed in the western part of North Africa. Rommel was caught between the two forces. Montgomery drove him nearly 1,500 miles to the west, and there the Americans attacked. For a while, the Germans still made a battle of it, but on May 13, 1943, the last of them surrendered and the North African Campaign was over.

Afrikaans

More than three hundred years ago Dutch-speaking settlers from the Netherlands first went to South Africa, and more and more followed until the largest group of Europeans in South Africa were of Dutch origin. Just as the American language developed from English, so did Afrikaans develop from Dutch, and it is still very much like Dutch, but there are distinct differences, partly because all languages change over the course of hundreds of years and partly because settlers in a new country pick up many native words—the Americans did from the American Indians, and the Dutch did from the native Africans.

Afrikaans is one of the two official languages of the Union of South Africa, the other being English. From it we get such words as *boss, spoor,* and *trek.* About two million people speak Afrikaans and more than ten thousand books have been written in it.

Afton

Afton is a stream in Ayrshire, Scotland. It is the subject of Robert Burns' poem, "Flow Gently, Sweet Afton."

Agadir

Agadir is a seaport on the west coast of Morocco, in North Africa. Its population in 1961 was 30,111. Agadir is remembered because of the "Agadir incident" of 1911, which seemed likely to start World War I three years before it actually started in 1914. At that time Morocco was ruled by France. The German government, saying that its business interests in Morocco were not properly protected, sent a small warship, the *Panther,* to Agadir. France and Great Britain considered this a threat of war, so the Germans recalled the *Panther* and the crisis was temporarily ended.

Aga Khan

Aga Khan is the title of the leader of the Ismaili sect, a large group of Mohammedans, who live mostly in Pakistan with some large groups in East Africa. The title means "lord chief."

The most famous Aga Khan was Aga Khan III, whose full name was Aga Sultan Sir Mohammed Shah. He was born in 1877 and died, at the age of eighty, in 1957. As a young man he did a great deal to make his people more modern, prosperous, and healthy; for example, he persuaded them to be vaccinated against smallpox by letting them see him be vaccinated. He lived much of his life in England and in Europe. He was a very rich man and his stable of racing horses was one of the greatest ever assembled; after his death it was managed by his son, Aly Khan, who died in 1960. In 1936, when the Aga Khan had been their leader for fifty years, his people gave him his weight in gold, and ten years later they gave him his weight in diamonds; he weighed about 246 pounds. He gave all the money back to the people to use for education. The Aga Khan was a great friend to England and used his influence to persuade India to support the Allies in World War I.

When the old Aga Khan died, he named his grandson, Karim, a 20-year-old son of Prince Aly who had been a student at Harvard College in the United States, to be the new leader, Aga Khan IV.

Agamemnon

Agamemnon was king of Mycenae in ancient Greece. He was the commander-in-chief of the Greek forces throughout the TROJAN WARS, about which there is a separate article, and he is one of the leading characters in Homer's great poem, the *Iliad.* While Agamemnon was away commanding the Greek armies, his wife Clytemnestra fell in love with Aegisthus, a Greek prince. When Agamemnon returned from the Trojan War, Clytemnestra and her lover murdered him.

Later, Agamemnon's son, Orestes, avenged the murder by killing both Clytemnestra and Aegisthus.

agar-agar or agar

Agar-agar is a gummy or gelatin-like substance that is made from a red seaweed. When it is dissolved in water it swells up to great size, and because of this it is used as a laxative, because bulk helps in digestion of food. Agar-

agar is also used in cooking, especially in China and other Oriental countries, and in laboratory experiments it is used as a base in which to grow bacteria.

Agassiz, Louis

Jean Louis Agassiz was a great naturalist who lived about a hundred years ago. He made many important discoveries about glaciers and about prehistoric fishes and other animals, which he studied by means of their fossils. Agassiz was born in Switzerland, in 1807, and in 1846 he settled in the United States and became a professor at Harvard University. He died in 1873.

The **Agassiz Museum** (of natural history) at Harvard is named for Louis Agassiz, and there are three mountains called **Mt. Agassiz** in his honor, one in Utah, one in Arizona, and one in New Hampshire; but more important than these is **Lake Agassiz.** This lake no longer exists, but in prehistoric times it covered a vast area of the present states of Minnesota and North Dakota and the province of Manitoba. It was about 700 miles long and 250 miles wide. It lasted for about a thousand years but most of it gradually drained into Hudson Bay, leaving numerous small lakes. The rest of the former lake bed is rich wheat-growing land.

Alexander Agassiz, son of Louis Agassiz, also became a great naturalist and contributed much to the knowledge of the oceans and of mining. He was born in 1835 and died in 1910.

agate

Agate is a hard stone, a kind of quartz, that is formed in streaks or layers of different colors. It is translucent, which means that the light shines through it, and it is very hard and can be polished to a shining surface. The finest agate is made into settings for rings and pins and brooches and is classed as a semiprecious stone.

There is no limit to the number of different patterns formed by the many colors in agate, but the principal kinds are called *banded agate,* which has wavy layers of different colors; *clouded agate,* which has patches of color; and *moss agate,* also called Mocha stone, which has dark marks that look like moss or ferns. In some pieces of agate the layers of color form rings that look like an eye, and people in Oriental countries sometimes used to cut this into the shape of an eye and wear it on a chain around the neck, calling it "the evil eye"; they thought it would drive away evil spirits that might attack them.

There is a great deal of agate in the world, and as a stone it is not very expensive. That is the reason children's marbles can be made out of it.

Agate is deposited from water in cavities in rocks, different-colored layers being deposited as conditions change. As many as 17,050 bands to the inch have been counted. Sometimes the alternate bands consist of chalcedony and opal.

Agate occurs most importantly in Uruguay, Brazil, Czechoslovakia, and India. In the United States it is found in Oregon, Washington, Wyoming, Montana, California, and the Lake Superior district. Agate occurs naturally in all colors, but most of the highly colored agate used for commercial purposes has been chemically colored. Idar-Oberstein, Germany, and Providence, Rhode Island, are the chief cutting, polishing and staining centers.

agave

Agave is a plant that grows in very dry regions of America. It will even grow in deserts. Many people call it the century plant, because of an old legend that it blooms only once in a hundred years. Though there is no truth in this, the agave does not bloom every year as most plants do; nor does it bloom at any regular time. When it does bloom, a stem or spike shoots up from the center of the stiff, spiny leaves at the base. This spike may grow to a height of twenty feet or even more within a few weeks, and the flower is on top of it.

Some kinds of agave are used in Mexico to make liquors called pulque and mescal. Rope is made out of the stringy fibers of the leaves. These fibers rank second to cotton in commercial importance in the U.S. Among these are *henequen,* or *Yucatan sisal; sisal;* and *istle.*

The common American variety of agave, called the American aloe or century plant, blooms when it is ten or more years old; it then dies, and new plants develop from suckers at its base.

age: for the ages in world history, see ARCHAEOLOGY and GEOLOGY; for the age of man, see LIFE EXPECTANCY and GROWTH.

agent

An agent is a person who acts for another person, who is called the *principal.* The powers and duties of an agent are defined by law in most places. An authorized act of an agent is just as effective as though the principal himself had performed it. The agent's authority is only what the principal has given him, but if the agent exceeds this authority and the person with whom he deals might reasonably believe that the agent has the authority he claims, then the principal is bound by the agent's act. For example, a company is bound by promises made by its salesmen if the promises are reasonable enough for a customer to accept them. The principal can make the agent pay for the cost of the agent's unauthorized acts, but the principal himself is responsible to a person who trusted in the agent's authority.

An agent may be known by various names in different businesses: *attorney, broker, commissioner,* etc. The principal is often called a *client.* Salesmen in various fields are often called agents, but usually they are not agents in the legal sense. For example, a salesman of life insurance is often called an "insurance agent," but in life insurance the word agent properly means a person who is the only authorized representative of the company in a particular territory and can employ salesmen, issue policies, accept payments, and maintain records, as though his office were part of the company's office. Other forms of insurance are sold through *brokers,* who have no authority to act for the insurance companies.

Persons in theatrical and creative arts are usually represented by agents who bargain for them in obtaining employment and fixing their pay. *Theatrical agents* have existed for at least one hundred years and became large business enterprises with the growth of salaries paid to actors, writers and directors in motion pictures, radio, and television. The theatrical agent's fee is 10% of the client's earnings. *Booking agents* are theatrical agents but sometimes serve as representatives of the employer (theater, nightclub, etc.) as well as of the performer ("talent"). *Musicians' agents* perform the same service but often charge higher fees, 15% or more. *Literary agents* sell authors' manuscripts to publishers, for a fee of 10%. *Artists' agents* usually receive 33⅓%. *Advertising agencies* are described under ADVERTISING.

ageratum

Ageratum is a name for about thirty herbs and shrubs of the daisy family. They are grown and sold for border plantings. The two most popular varieties bloom throughout the summer and the flowers do not appear to grow old. The plant grows 1 to 2 feet high and has heart-shaped leaves and clusters of small blue flowers.

Agincourt

Agincourt is a tiny village in the north of France. Only 114 people live there. But the name is well remembered in history because of a great battle that was fought there more than five hundred years ago, in the year 1415. This battle took place in a war between England and France, which was part of a long series of wars, the Hundred Years' War.

Before the Battle of Agincourt, the best fighters had been knights wearing heavy armor, mounted on horses that also were protected by armor, and fighting with swords and lances and battle-axes. When the Battle of Agincourt was fought, the French army still depended on knights. But the English army, under King Henry V, had developed a new weapon. It was the longbow, of the type that Robin Hood used, and it had been made so strong, and the archers in the English army had been trained so well, that they could shoot an arrow hard enough to pierce the steel armor of the knights. The longbowmen did not need to wear armor, because they could shoot the knights down before the knights could get close enough to attack them with their swords and lances. This was a double advantage, because a man can get around much faster when he is not weighted down with heavy armor. The English longbowmen won the fight so easily, and killed so many of their French enemy, that no country ever again tried to win a war with armored knights. The Battle of Agincourt, for that reason, was called the "death of knighthood." Shakespeare wrote about it in his play *Henry V.*

Agnes, St.

Saint Agnes was a Christian martyr who lived nearly 1,700 years ago, from about 287 to 303. She was beheaded during the persecution of Christians by the Roman emperor Diocletian. She was of a noble Roman family, and her great beauty had tempted a man named Sempronius, from whose brutality she was saved by a miracle. He was struck blind, but recovered his sight through her prayers. Her feast day is January 21. Saint Agnes' Eve was once believed to be a night when a young girl might see her future husband in a dream.

Agnew, Spiro T.

Spiro Theodore Agnew was elected Vice President of the United States in 1968 when Richard M. Nixon was elected President. Nixon and Agnew had run on the Republican Party ticket against Democrats Hubert Humphrey (for president) and Edmund Muskie (for vice-president).

Spiro Agnew was born in 1918, the son of a Greek immigrant father and a Virginia-born mother. He attended public school in Baltimore, Maryland and later studied chemistry at Johns Hopkins University for three years. After interrupting his college education to serve in the Army during World War II, he obtained a law degree from the University of Baltimore Law School in 1947. Unfortunately, he did poorly at law and had to take a job as a supermarket manager in order to support his wife whom he married in 1942. When he entered politics in 1960, he lost the race for a judgeship in Baltimore County but was elected County Executive two years later. In 1967, he became Governor of Maryland. He served in this capacity until 1969 when he became the 39th Vice-President of the United States under Richard M. Nixon. Charges of tax evasion on payments made to Mr. Agnew by Maryland contractors resulted in his resignation on October 10, 1973. He pleaded "no contest" to the charges and was sentenced to three years probation and a $10,000 fine. Spiro T. Agnew was the first Vice-President to resign under duress (pressure).

agnostic

An agnostic is a person who is not religious and does not believe in God, but neither does he say there is no God. He simply says he does not know whether God exists or not. In fact, the word agnostic is taken from Greek words that mean "not knowing." The agnostic is different from the atheist. The atheist says he is sure there is no God. The word agnostic was first used by Thomas Huxley, a great English scientist, in 1869. Many Americans have been agnostics, but many more—in fact, nearly everyone—believes in God and is a member of some religion.

agouti

The agouti is a small animal, about the size of a hare or rabbit (two feet long), that lives in the forests of the West Indies islands and parts of South America. Its flesh is white and tender and it once was the chief food of the Indians on the islands. The agouti is a rodent, or gnawing animal. Its hind legs are longer than its front legs, and it has strong claws. It sits erect on its haunches while eating, holding food in its forepaws, and sits the same way when looking or listening. Its color is usually brown.

Agra

Agra is a big city in India. It is important as a manufacturing center and it contains many beautiful buildings and Agra University, but chiefly it is famous because the Taj Mahal is there. The TAJ MAHAL, about which there is a separate article, is the finest monument ever built. From the year 1526 until 1658, Agra was the capital of the Mogul empire, which included not only India but much of the continent of Asia. In 1973 the population of Agra was about 508,700.

agriculture

American Airlines

The word agriculture means "taking care of the 'fields"—in other words, what we are used to thinking of as farming. And, in fact, agriculture and farming mean just about the same thing. But usually we would say "agriculture" when we mean the entire work and science of using the earth to produce food and other plants that are valuable to us; and we would use the word "farming" to mean some particular branch of this, for example dairy farming, or chicken farming.

Many different sciences go to make up the whole work of agriculture. Many different sciences have helped in making agriculture the respected and profitable work it is today.

This has not always been so. Farming used to be laborious, poorly paid work. A farmer had to work hard in his fields all day long, just to raise enough food for his own family. Usually his wife had to help, and had no time for comfortable living; his children had to help, and had no time to get good educations. Today the young man or woman of a family in the field of agriculture will go to one of the hundreds of agricultural colleges and universities in the United States and will learn to make the family's farm even better in the future.

In this encyclopedia there are separate articles on DAIRY FARMING and CATTLE FARMING and FARM MACHINERY and other branches of agriculture.

HOW AGRICULTURE HAS CHANGED

There have been farmers as long as there has been history and for tens of thousands of years before that. Agriculture is probably the oldest work done by man. In the Bible, the first man born on earth—Cain, the son of Adam and Eve—was "a tiller of the soil," in other words a farmer. Through most of these thousands of years, nearly everyone had to be a farmer because a farmer could not raise much more food than was needed to feed him and his family. Even in the days of the American Revolution, less than two hundred years ago, eight out of every ten Americans were farmers. Today, only one American out of twenty lives on a farm. But that one American working on a farm today can raise twice as much food as eight farmers could in those days.

But if you could have spent even a day with one of those ancient farmers, and could compare it with what you would see today on a modern farm of the United States with its bags of scientifically created seed, and its tractors to prepare the soil for planting, and its seeders to plant the seed at mathematically proper spots, and its other machines to cultivate the soil and kill the pests that destroy crops, and reap the crop when it is grown and transport it to the barn and then to the market, you would think you were in two different worlds—and so you would be. It took man a long time to learn how to raise his food in the ground.

First, man had to learn that plants would give him food. Then he learned that the plants would grow better if the soil around them were loosened, and he would hack away at the soil with tools that he had made by chipping off pieces of stone until a piece with sharp edges for digging would remain. One season it would not rain, and the plants would die, and from this he learned that plants need water, so in dry seasons he would carry water from a nearby pond or stream and throw it on the soil. He learned that plants grow from seeds, and that freed him to move to places where plants were not already growing, because he could take the seed with him, and plant it, and make his food grow where it had not grown before. Even later than this, he learned that some plants that were dry and hard and not worth eating could be made into good food if they were made hot enough for long enough, and out of this new knowledge came the art of cooking. Bit by bit, slowly at first but with ever-increasing rapidity, he added to this earliest knowledge until agriculture became what it is today.

THE CROPS WE RAISE

Nearly ninety-five out of every hundred acres used for growing plants in agriculture in the United States are used to grow food. Some of this food is for us to eat. Some of it is to feed livestock, which will eventually become meat or will give milk or will lay eggs.

The other five acres are used for crops

like cotton, from which our clothes are made; or tobacco, or trees for fruit and nuts, or for other plants besides vegetables.

Almost none of these crops is anything like the crops that our prehistoric ancestors raised. In their day, most plants grew wild on earth. For example the biggest crop of our western world, wheat, was simply tall wild grasses waving on the hillsides. The ancient Egyptians, probably at least ten thousand years ago, discovered that the kernels of wheat would make bread. They noticed which plants would grow best and saved the seeds from those plants and gradually improved the quality of the wheat they grew. The Chinese, and other Orientals, did the same thing with rice. The American Indians did the same thing with maize, the plant that we call corn. In the course of hundreds of years, the food plants that came to be raised were almost entirely different from the original plant that had been eaten by the earliest men. We are still doing the same things, but now the experiments are made by scientists in laboratories, and they take years instead of hundreds of years.

The same kind of development has spread different plants all over the world when once they grew in only a few parts of the world. There was a time when no one outside of Asia had ever heard of oranges. But explorers, visiting Asia, ate the oranges and liked them, and took the seeds back home to be planted. Today more oranges are grown in California and Florida than anywhere else in the world, and they are better oranges—bigger, sweeter, juicier—but they never grew in this country until the seeds were brought in from abroad.

America has made its gift of new food plants to the world. Corn was mentioned above. Potatoes were not known before America was discovered, but the plants were taken to Europe and became so much better known over there that we call one of these native American plants by the name of another country—Irish potatoes—because the Irish people raised so many of them at one time. In Mexico and South America, there was a plant that was completely strange to anyone who had never been there before. We now call this plant the tomato. It was so unusual that it took many years to persuade people from other countries that it was even safe to eat. Men not only learned how to improve the plants they knew, they learned also to create new plants.

Scientists learned that plants mate and have offspring very much as animals do. A male plant and a female plant are both needed to produce a seed from which a new plant will grow. This suggested taking one kind of male plant and another kind of female plant and trying to produce new foods that would combine the qualities of two other foods. Luther Burbank, an American who made a lifelong study of this, created many new plants. He created new, better-tasting fruits by mixing the pollens of two different plants (a process called cross-pollination) and his creations included such things as the honeydew melon

and the grapefruit we see most often on our table today. The same kind of work produced string beans without strings (and most people today have forgotten the time when string beans had such strong, tough and unpleasant strings in them that you could hardly bite through them), and oranges that give much more juice than other oranges, a development that led to the habit of drinking orange juice for breakfast today. Before then, oranges did not have enough juice to make it worthwhile to squeeze them.

The science of chemistry was a great help to agriculture. Farmers would discover that certain insects were ruining their plants. The insects would eat the leaves, or bore into the vegetables or fruits, or even attack the roots and keep the plants from growing. There were poisons that would kill the insects, but those same poisons might kill the plants —or else make the fruit of those plants poisonous to the people who ate them. The problem was to find chemicals that would kill insects without hurting the plant. Chemists have discovered liquids that you can spray or powders that you can dust on many plants that will keep the insects from eating them but will not keep the plants from growing and will not be dangerous to people who eat the vegetables or fruits. Not all the problems have been solved, so the work goes on and every year new ways are found to combat the pests and the diseases of our food plants and so to make the crops bigger and healthier.

THE TOOLS MEN FARM WITH

Plants must have minerals from the soil if they are to grow. They take in these minerals through their roots. But the minerals must be dissolved in water before the plants can take them in. Water does not flow easily through soil that is hard and caked, any more than it can flow through a brick, which was originally the same kind of earth but has been pressed and baked until it is dry and solid. Therefore, to make plants grow best, the farmer must loosen the soil and make it soft and crumbly.

It was told above how man learned to loosen the soil by breaking it up with crude pieces of stones sharpened to cutting points. Not too long after that, man learned to make the rake and hoe, implements with which he could cut into the soil and loosen it without bending over or kneeling. When he learned to tame and domesticate animals, man invented the plow, a heavy tool that would turn over and loosen more of the soil, and that could be pulled with the strength of a horse or an ox. All these implements go back to prehistoric times. All of them remained almost unchanged until not much more than 100 years ago.

A man with a hand tool, such as a hoe, could hardly loosen the soil in an acre in a full day's work. And a man with a plow, and a strong animal to pull it, could do several acres. But even that was not enough of an advancement. To do that well, a man had to work hard every day from sunrise to sunset. No free man was willing to do that if he could help it. So the rule of life was that countries went to war, captured slaves from other countries, and set the slaves to

work in their fields. For thousands of years, farming was done by slaves or by men who were little better than slaves. Captured slaves did the farming in ancient Rome. Men called serfs, who were about the same as slaves, did the farming in Europe from the time that Rome fell until modern times. In the United States, the entire wealth of the southern states was based on its Negro slaves that worked in the cotton fields, until the Civil War ended slavery. Slaves cannot advance a science because they have no reason to care whether the science advances or not. Agriculture became a respectable occupation and a scientific study when it became the work of free men and not slaves.

Nat'l. Film Board of Canada

This big combine, harvesting wheat in Saskatchewan, Canada, does as much work in one day as twenty men used to do in a week.

The first farm machinery was not advanced enough to change the old order of things. An Englishman, Jethro Tull, invented a "drill" (a machine for planting seed) more than two hundred years ago, but men still had to loosen the soil by hoeing all day, and then had to reap the crop by hand. When Eli Whitney invented the cotton gin, a machine for separating the usable fluffy fibers of the cotton plant from its unusable pod, he greatly stimulated the raising of cotton because it was now much easier to convert it to a usable condition, for making thread and after that cloth, but this did not actually advance the science of agriculture. Cotton still had to be cultivated and raised by the old-fashioned way.

The first great advancement was when Cyrus McCormick invented the reaper in 1831. This machine was designed for cutting grain, and even the first crude machine would cut as much grain in a day as five men had been able to cut before. The biggest thing the reaper did, however, was to show people that many of the old jobs of farming could be done by machine when formerly they had been done by hand. It was an easy step from there to the cultivators, the harrows, the haying machines, and all the other farm machinery that followed in quick succession. The coming of the

Motor Age brought the tractor, which could do the work of twenty or thirty horses. Soon the giant "cats" were dragging over the acreage of the United States machines that could do everything that man had ever done, do it fifty or a hundred times as fast, and do it better. The farmer who once would have had to struggle to feed his own family could now almost literally "feed the world."

By the 1950s, the problem in the United States was not how to get enough food for the people but what to do with all the food that was left over after the people had been well-fed. For thousands of years, periods of famine in China and India and even in Europe could cause millions to die of starvation. As the twentieth century entered its second half, the means were there for feeding all these millions, and the only problem—how to get it to them—was the job not of agriculture but of transportation and international money relations.

THE SOIL IN WHICH THINGS GROW

Plants grow by a very complex process. The leaves, which are above the ground, take in some of the nourishment that the plant needs by absorbing sunlight and turning it into chemicals. The roots, which are below the ground, soak up minerals dissolved in water, these minerals coming from the soil in which the roots grow.

In the picture below, a team of oxen pulls a modern farm machine, in Arkansas.

U.S. Dept. of Agriculture Photo

A plant never runs out of sunlight, but the soil does run out of chemicals. When this happens, healthy plants will no longer grow in it. There must be a waiting period in which the soil can enrich itself with more minerals of the kind the plant needs.

So long ago that history does not go back so far, men learned that they must let the ground rest between crops. The ancient Egyptians, nearly ten thousand years ago, let a field "lie fallow" every few years, which meant that they planted nothing in it or else planted a crop (such as alfalfa or another hay) that could grow without taking any important minerals out of the soil, and in fact would cause the soil to acquire new minerals to replenish the ones it had lost. Not long after that, farmers learned that various fertilizers (which were then generally called manure) would supply minerals to the soil and make it grow better plants.

Finally, scientists began to apply their knowledge of chemistry to the problem and to analyze the soil to see what chemicals and minerals it needed and did not have. These missing chemicals and min-

The man at the left does not have new equipment but tries to use the most modern farm practices. The Department of Agriculture helps by telling him what he needs to keep his soil in good condition, and how to practice crop rotation for the best possible harvests each year. If he had more modern equipment, he could do even better.

erals, especially nitrates, carbon, iron, and others, they could feed to the soil so that the soil in turn could feed them into the roots of the plants.

One of the ways of preventing the soil from wearing out, and one that has been known for thousands of years but is still practiced, is called crop rotation. First a certain field is used to raise a crop that takes from the soil some of the minerals but not all. Then a crop is raised that does not take those same minerals, but does use the ones that were left from the year before, and that restores to the soil the minerals that were taken out by the previous crop. These missing minerals are restored because they are in the roots and stems of the plants that die, and rot, and become part of the soil. Rotation means "turning around," and the rotation of crops is a changing from one crop to another, then going back to the first one, so that the whole process goes around as though in a circle.

The farmer learned all these things, and he bought the best seed and the best fertilizer, and he worked very hard, and he still found his farm becoming less and less valuable. The reason, very often, was "erosion," which means "wearing away"; in spite of everything he did, the topsoil, which is the most important soil, was wearing or washing away from his farm.

The topsoil is the layer of soft, black earth that lies on top of the harder, poor level of clay or packed sand that is called subsoil. The topsoil is rich in the stuff that life is made of. It is the level of soil that is soaked when it rains. Through this topsoil worms and insects burrow, both loosening it while they live and enriching it when they die. Just because it is on top, the topsoil is most likely to wash away in a heavy rain or blow away when it is dry and the winds are high, leaving for the farmer only the barren subsoil in which he cannot grow anything of value.

The problem of soil erosion became so severe that even in the rich United States, not more than thirty years ago, many farmers were unable to make a decent living because their soil was no good. It was one of the great problems of the country. The problem has now been solved to a very large extent. One

way has been to cut level fields or terraces into hilly country, so that when the water pours down from the hills it will stay on the level terraces and soak in instead of washing the soil down into streams, and from there into rivers, and from there into the ocean, where it is lost forever. Ditches are dug to trap topsoil that would otherwise be washed into the streams, and good supplies of water make it possible to keep the soil damp enough so that it will not blow like dust into a high wind.

Consulate General of Colombia
Corn harvesting in Colombia.

Sugar cane harvesting in Australia.
Australian News & Information Bureau

41

Strip planting does two things to preserve farmland. It provides a constant ground cover crop, in strips that hold back the water in the soil; and also it gives farmers a simple way of changing crops from year to year so that the soil never wears out.

U.S. Dept. of Agriculture

Standard Oil Company of New Jersey   *U.S. Dept. of Agriculture*

This stretch of level land between Kansas City and Lawrence, Kansas, is beautiful to see from an airplane. The patterns formed by the different shades of green make it look like a great artist's arrangement of colors.

To get full use of the rain that falls in a dry section, everyone must cooperate. The Department of Agriculture Soil Conservation Section helps farmers save valuable rainfall. Water in one farmer's land will soak into the soil and seep through to the next field.

THE PROBLEM OF WATER

No matter how well the soil is cared for, with crop rotation and good fertilizers and protection against soil erosion, it still must have water or plants will not grow. Land without water is desert. Land with water is fertile. Even the Sahara Desert would be a rich farming country if enough water could be supplied to it.

Many parts of the world do not have enough rainfall during the year to grow the food the people need. Where there is plenty of rain, the climate is likely to be tropical and too hot for men's comfort or health. Even where there is normally water enough for farming, a dry year, or drought, will come along now and then. This used to cause famine in big countries like China and India, where at best many people hardly have enough to eat.

Where nature does not supply enough water for farming, the problem can often be solved by irrigation. This is the bringing of water to farmlands from rivers or wells nearby. The oldest way of irrigating land is to dig ditches or trenches to carry water from a river or stream. They were doing this thousands of years ago in Egypt. The great rice fields of China and other countries in the Orient are formed by irrigation.

There are other ways of irrigating fields. Sometimes big pipes are laid on the ground, with holes punched in them every few inches. Water is pumped through the pipes, and as it flows through it sprays out of the holes and waters the fields. Another way is to drive a tank truck between the rows of plants, spraying them much as trucks sprinkle city streets—or the way you would water a garden with a watering can, except on a much larger scale.

Many things we love to eat depend on a large supply of water. Tomatoes and oranges and lemons must be juicy to be good, and this means there has to be plenty of water for the plants to suck

up. The government is constantly building dams and aqueducts to store the water of rivers and carry it to the farms when it is needed.

Agriculture, Department of

The Department of Agriculture is one of the main divisions of the United States Government. Agriculture, or farming, is one of the most important parts of American life, and the purpose of the Department of Agriculture is to help the farmer in every way. It was established about a hundred years ago, in 1862, the eighth United States Department to be formed. The head of it is the Secretary of Agriculture, one of the government's most important officials and a member of the President's cabinet.

A total of 98,694 people work for the Department of Agriculture. There are 84,301 full-time workers and 13,390 part-time workers in the United States, 487 people in United States territories and possessions, and 516 in foreign countries to keep us up to date on what other governments are doing for farmers.

The Department of Agriculture is divided into fifteen big sections. One section takes care of preparing "literature," or booklets, to teach farmers all that is known about farming, and to help the farmers' wives. Some of these booklets tell mothers how to care for their babies and children, and give instructions and recipes for cooking, canning, and preserving, and tell how to plan nourishing, well-balanced meals for the family. Other booklets explain the best and most modern methods of bee-keeping, poultry-farming, cattle-raising, and nearly every other kind of farming. There are booklets to explain how leather is made out of animal hides, and how skins of wild animals are made into fur. There is a Department of Agriculture booklet to tell how to do almost everything that is done around a home or on a farm, even how to knit and crochet. Many of these booklets cost only 5 cents or 10 cents apiece.

The Forest Service is part of the Department of Agriculture. It has scientists who check constantly for plant diseases that might attack our trees. It plants trees to replace those that are cut for timber, so we will not run out of wood.

Another division of the Department of Agriculture lends money to farmers, so that they can improve their farms, or form cooperative organizations for the purpose of improving soil conservation and water development systems. This is the Farmers Home Administration.

The Commodity Credits Corporation pays money to farmers each year to make sure they get enough money for the things they grow. If the market price is too low, the Commodity Credits Corporation pays the difference necessary to make up what seems a fair price. This is called a subsidy.

The Agricultural Research Administration, another branch of the main department, makes scientific studies of all farming methods.

The Department also provides crop

reports and meat-inspection service. It seeks to eradicate plant and animal pests and diseases. It administers the school-lunch program.

agrimony

Agrimony is a name used for a group of herbs of the rose family. They are sometimes grown in herb gardens and their sweet-smelling leaves are used in making a kind of tea used as a medicine and tonic. A yellow vegetable dye is taken from the roots of one kind.

Agrimony grows 1 to 5 feet high, in small clumps. It bears small, yellow, five-petaled flowers, usually in July and August.

Agua

Agua is an inactive volcano about 12,300 feet high in Guatemala. Its name, which in Spanish means water, stems from an unexplained flood in 1541 that swept down the mountain after three days of rain and earthquakes, completely destroying the town of Santiago do los Caballeros de Guatemala, which was then the capital, now called Ciudad Vieja. More than 1,000 persons were killed. The survivors founded a new city, Antigua, which was the capital until 1776.

ague

Ague is a name applied to various forms of malarial fever, especially to *shaking ague,* whose symptoms include extremes of chills and fever, and heavy sweating. Such fevers occur chiefly in hot, damp climates; but the deaths of King James I of England and of the British ruler Oliver Cromwell were once supposed to have been caused by ague contracted in London. See MALARIA.

Aguinaldo, Emilio

Emilio Aguinaldo became a leader of his people in the Philippine Islands when he was quite a young man. He was born in 1869, on the largest island of the Philippines, Luzon. At that time the Philippine Islands were colonies of Spain. When patriotic Filipinos revolted against Spanish rule, Aguinaldo joined them. He was then 25 years old. The Spanish put down the revolution, and they exiled Aguinaldo.

In 1898, the United States went to war against Spain, in the Spanish-American War. The Philippine Islands revolted again. Aguinaldo went back to help lead the revolt, and was made a general. He fought bravely with the United States troops.

The United States won the war easily. Spain was forced to give up its control over Cuba and the Philippine Islands. The United States thought Cuba was now ready to govern itself, and Cuba became an independent country. But the United States Government thought that the Philippine people were not quite ready to govern themselves. General Aguinaldo disagreed. So in June 1898 he set up an independent Philippine government and became its first president. He formed an army and began to fight to chase the Americans out of the islands. The United States won that fight, too, and in 1901 captured General Aguinaldo. He said he believed he had been wrong, and he took an oath of allegiance to the United States.

The Philippine people still admired and respected General Aguinaldo, but he did not appear very much in public life. More than thirty years later, he did become a candidate for president of the Philippine Islands, but he was defeated by President Manuel Quezon. However, when the Japanese went to war against the United States in World War II and occupied the Philippine Islands, he let them make him head of the controlled Philippine government they set up there, although he did say he disapproved of their attack on Pearl Harbor. The Filipinos, who were fighting so bravely against the Japanese, considered this treason on the part of their old leader, but because he had been such a great patriot long ago they did not take any steps to punish him. He died in 1964.

Agulhas

Cape Agulhas is the most southerly point of Africa, about 50 miles southeast of the Cape of Good Hope. It is in West Cape Province, Republic of South Africa. It is named for its saw-edged reefs (in Portuguese *agulhas* means needles).

Ahithophel

Ahithophel, whose name is also spelled Achitophel, was an adviser to King David, in the Bible. When David's son Absalom rebelled against his father, Ahithophel joined Absalom and commanded Absalom's forces. Absalom lost, and Ahithophel went home, "put his household in order, and hanged himself." The story is told in 2 Samuel, chapters 15 to 17.

Ahmedabad

Ahmedabad, or Ahmadabad, is an important city in Gujarat state, India. It is a manufacturing center, especially for cotton mills, and is a seat of the Gujarat sect of Jainism. The Juma Masjid or Great Mosque of Ahmedabad, built in the 15th century, is one of the most beautiful in the East. In 1973 the population of Ahmedabad was about 2,210,200.

Ahriman

Ahriman is the god of darkness and evil in ZOROASTRIANISM, a religion about which there is a separate article. He and the whole unclean kingdom of the *devas,* or evil spirits, oppose Ormuzd (or Ahura Mazdah), the god of light, in the world process; but after a period of 12,000 years, Ahriman will be defeated by the good forces.

ai

Ai is a name for the three-toed sloth, which lives hanging upside down from branches of trees. It is 3 to 4 feet long, weighs up to 60 pounds, and has powerful claws and enduring strength in its long arms, which protect it against snakes. Although it cannot stand, and walks with difficulty, it travels along branches gracefully and quickly. However, it seldom moves except to find food, and then very slowly (about 30 feet per minute). It is the best climber among mammals and its hind feet have a power of grasping that no other mammal possesses. It is called *ai* from its cry. See the article SLOTH.

Aida

Aida is a grand opera by Giuseppe Verdi, a great Italian composer. The story of Aida is set in Egypt, because Verdi wrote it for the khedive (that is, the king) of Egypt, to be performed at the opening of the Cairo Opera House in 1869. Actually it was not performed until two years after that, in 1871. It was a great success from the start. Aida is still performed in the United States many times each year by both large and small opera companies.

THE STORY OF THE OPERA

Aida is the name of a princess of Ethiopia. She has been captured by the Egyptian army and is now the slave of Amneris, daughter of the king of Egypt. Aida is in love with Rhadames, even though he led the Egyptian army that defeated Ethiopia and captured her. The Princess Amneris is in love with Rhadames too, and is very jealous of Rhadames because he loves Aida and not her. Because of her jealousy, she has Rhadames accused of betraying his country. He is not guilty, but they condemn him to death anyway. They bury him alive in a large tomb. Aida, because she loves him, has hidden herself in the tomb and is buried alive with him. The opera ends with them waiting together to die, while Amneris mourns for Rhadames, sorry for what she has done.

This opera has some very beautiful music that is often played and sung in concerts. In the first act there is a famous aria, *Celeste Aida,* which was one of the great tenor Enrico Caruso's most famous solos. In the second act, there is a great triumphal march of the Egyptian armies returning victorious from Ethiopia. There is also a magnificent ballet. The costumes and scenery recall the times of ancient Egypt in the days of the Pharaohs.

Aiken

Aiken is a city in South Carolina. It is the location of a large plant of the Atomic Energy Commission. For many years Aiken has been a fashionable winter resort. Its population in 1970 was 13,436.

Aiken, Conrad

Conrad Potter Aiken was an American poet and novelist. He was born in Savannah, Georgia in 1889 but moved to Massachusetts in 1900. In 1911, he graduated from Harvard University. Aiken won the Pulitzer Prize for poetry in 1930 for his *Selected Poems.* His poetry has a musical quality. He died in 1973.

ailanthus

The ailanthus is a tree that is native to Asia, and is thought to have been brought to America from England in the early 19th century. It is also called the "Tree of Heaven." Because it is a very strong plant that is not affected by dust, smoke, or insects, and can take root and grow in places where other trees would die, it is often planted along city streets to provide shade. Its leaves sometimes grow to be two or more feet long, and the tree can grow to be 60 feet high. It bears clusters of small greenish flowers. The flowers of the male tree have a very disagreeable odor.

Ainu

The people we call the Japanese have not always lived in Japan. They invaded the Japanese Islands from Asia, about a thousand years ago and perhaps even longer ago than that. At that time there were already people living in Japan, and some of their descendants are still there. They are called the Ainus. They belong to the Caucasian race, as Europeans and Americans do. They are short, like the Japanese, but their skin is quite white. About 15,000 people in their settlements are identified as Ainu, but at the most, only 300 pure-blooded Ainus are left. Their religion teaches that bears are messengers from their supreme god; bears were killed in a "sending back" ritual in which their spirits carried Ainu prayers back to the god. Bear sacrifice is now outlawed. Also forbidden now is the ancient custom of tattooing moustaches on the faces of young girls. The older Ainu people try to preserve their vanishing culture, but the young ones prefer the modern Japanese ways. Many young Ainu people attend Japanese schools and eventually marry full-blooded Japanese husbands or wives. Races of people related to the Ainus live in Siberia and on the Russian island of Sakhalin, but the largest settlement of true Ainus is on the Japanese island of Hokkaido.

air

Air is a mixture of gases, mostly nitrogen and oxygen, containing small amounts of water vapor and solid particles. Surrounding the earth and known as the atmosphere, the air is our main source of oxygen.

About 78% of air is nitrogen; about 21% is oxygen. The rest consists of small amounts of argon, carbon dioxide, neon, helium, methane, krypton, hydrogen, nitrous oxide, ozone, sulfur dioxide, and ammonia. Pollen, bacteria, dust, and other solid particles are also present.

Much of the fascinating story of air is told in the article on ATMOSPHERE. Some other interesting facts will be found in the article on AIR COMPRESSION. Here the air will be considered only as a gas.

The air we breathe in is not the same as the air we breathe out. Our bodies take some of the oxygen from the air, combine it with carbon (an important element of which our bodies are made) and breathe out a combination of carbon and oxygen called carbon dioxide (which is, technically, a chemical *compound*), in addition to the nitrogen and other gases that our bodies do not use. The air that we inhale, if it is pure and fresh, contains about 21% oxygen and well under 1% carbon dioxide. The air that we exhale contains about 14% oxygen and 5% carbon dioxide. Much of this carbon dioxide that people and animals breathe out is removed from the air by green plants which need carbon dioxide to live. Most plants also require nitrogen, which they obtain from the soil in which they grow.

Air has weight. Although gases do not weigh much, the air reaches so far up into the sky that the weight of it puts a pressure of nearly 15 pounds on every square inch of the earth. That explains why you can suck things up through a straw. When you suck the air out of the straw, the weight of air pressing down on your drink or other liquid forces it into the empty straw and so into your mouth.

The oxygen in the air is what makes it possible for things to burn. If you put a burning piece of paper on a saucer and cover it with an upside-down glass, it will almost immediately go out. That is because it soon burns up the oxygen that is in the air inside the glass, and then there is no more oxygen.

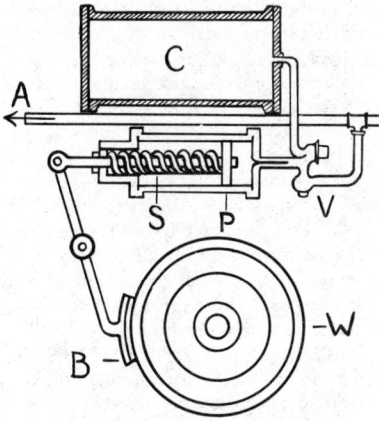

Bendix-Westinghouse

AIR BRAKE. An air compressor keeps the tank ("C") full of compressed air. The tube ("A") is also full of compressed air, and this compressed air keeps a valve ("V") shut so that air cannot get from the tank to the piston ("P"). The spring ("S") pushes the piston far back in the cylinder, so that the brake ("B") does not press against the wheel ("W"), and the wheels can turn. The tube "A" runs from the locomotive along all the cars. To apply the brakes, the engineer lets air escape from this tube. Now the valve can open. This lets air from the compressor press against the piston. Since the air pressure is much stronger than the spring, the piston is pushed forward, the brake presses against the wheel, and the train stops. The safety in this arrangement is that if the tube "A" should ever break or open (as, for instance, if two cars come apart), the valves will automatically open and apply the brakes.

Air is a very fine insulating material, because it is a poor conductor of heat. This fact makes it harder to get a room warm, because the air will not carry the heat from a fire or stove. But the same fact makes it possible to seal heat or coldness out of a room or refrigerator or other place by having two panes of glass or metal with dead air in between them. On a hot day, the room inside will be cooler because the heat cannot get in; on a cold day the room will stay warmer because the heat inside cannot get out.

airbrake

An airbrake is a brake that uses the power of compressed air to stop a wheel from turning. There is a separate article on BRAKES that explains how a clamp or "shoe" grips a turning wheel and makes it stop turning. In a light automobile, or on a bicycle, a man has enough strength to work a brake. When you take a truck or bus weighing dozens of tons, or a train weighing many hundreds of tons, the strength of a man is not enough. The tremendous power of compressed air, which is explained in the article on AIR COMPRESSION, is needed.

Back in the last century, about a hundred years ago, the brakes on trains worked slowly and not very well. They depended on man power. On each railroad car, there was a big wheel on top, which turned a long screw reaching down to the wheels, where long rods joined it with a block of iron or wood that was the brake shoe. There was a railroad employee called a brakeman on each car. When the engineer wanted to stop the train, he blew a signal on his whistle. Each brakeman would then turn the wheel to apply the brakes and stop the train. This took so long that many trains were wrecked because they could not stop in time, and many people were killed. Another trouble with these hand brakes was that the different brakemen turned their wheels at different times, so that one of the cars would slow down quicker or faster than others, and passengers inside would be bumped even when the train did stop smoothly.

An American inventor named George Westinghouse thought he could solve this problem by using the power of compressed air to apply all the brakes on the train at the same time, and much better than men could do it. He went to work on the problem, and in the year 1869 he had developed an airbrake that would stop a train. There were still many things wrong with his first invention, and it took many years before it was perfected, but it made railroad travel smooth and comfortable, and airbrakes based on George Westinghouse's invention (with many improvements that have been added since) are used today not only on trains but on every heavy vehicle that needs to stop quickly and safely when its driver wants it to.

The Westinghouse airbrake began with an air compressor. You can read in the article on AIR COMPRESSION how much power a small stream of compressed air can exert. The air compressor in a railroad train, or bus, or truck, or streetcar, is driven by the same power that drives the wheels forward. It stores up tanks full of compressed air, to be ready for use when they are needed. A line, which is a thin pipe, leads this compressed air to the brakes. The air pressure applies the brakes with far greater power than human strength could exert.

EARLY TROUBLES WITH AIRBRAKES

With the first airbrakes, when the engineer wanted to stop the train he opened a valve that let compressed air from the tank force a brake shoe against the rim of each wheel. This would prevent the wheel from turning. When the engineer wanted to start the train again he would close the valve. With the air pressure removed, the wheels could turn freely again. The trouble was that if the air pressure fell too low, or the line broke, the brakes could not be applied and there would be danger of accidents.

So a few years later—in 1872—Westinghouse replaced his first airbrake with an automatic one. In the automatic airbrake, the normal condition of the brake is "on," so that the train cannot move. The engineer has to open his valve and apply air pressure to take the brakes *off*. If anything goes wrong, the brakes must automatically stop the train.

THE DEAD MAN'S PEDAL

The "dead man's pedal" was one of the big changes that were made in the original Westinghouse airbrake. There were some bad wrecks because the engineer of the train would faint or even die, and be unable to apply the brakes. Then the train would keep going at full speed, crash into something, and cause a lot of damage. When an airbrake is used with the dead man's pedal, if the engineer relaxes and takes his foot off the pedal for any reason, the brakes go on and the train stops automatically. This same device has been used on subway trains and on streetcars.

The airbrakes on big trucks and buses work on the same principle as those on trains, but they do not use the dead man's pedal and the brakes are worked by two small brake shoes that are placed inside the rim of a brake drum in each wheel, and that press this rim outward against the wheel when they want to stop it. The driver of a bus or truck has a brake pedal at his right foot, very much like those in automobiles. When he steps even lightly on this brake pedal, it brings the enormous power of compressed air to bear on the brakes, and even a giant twenty-ton trailer truck stops quickly.

CONSTRUCTION AND OPERATION

An air compressor operated by the driving wheels builds up air pressure in a main storage tank in the locomotive; this pressure is about 50 to 100 lbs. per sq. in. A line of pipe, joined by flexible hose between cars, delivers this compressed air to an auxiliary tank in each car. The auxiliary tanks are regulated by valves having triple outlets—to the tank, the air line, and the brake cylinder. The normal condition of the brake is *on* under pressure from the car tank. A counter-pressure from the main line is necessary to take the brake *off*. Thus, if the air line breaks, as when a car becomes detached from a train, the brakes are applied automatically.

Air brakes have been perfected to the point where they can halt a 150-car freight train in four seconds. In 1921 they were adapted to trucks and buses. Electropneumatic brakes rather than air brakes are standard on all American subways.

air brush

An air brush is like an atomizer with which perfume is sprayed, or a spray gun with which houses and automobiles and other things are painted. It is not like a brush at all. It is more like a pistol, except that the operator works it by pressing down a lever instead of by pulling a trigger. A stream of air is brought to it from compressed air in a tank. The air brush is attached to a little can full of paint. The air sprays the paint out through a nozzle. If just a little bit of air is let through the nozzle, the paint comes out in a fine spray; this creates a light color like the blush on the cheeks of a little girl's doll (which was painted with an air brush, as all dolls are). If a lot of air is let into the air brush, a solid thin stream of paint comes out, such as to make the eyebrows on the doll.

The animated cartoons in colors, that you see in the movies, were all colored with air brushes. That is how they get

such beautiful shadings of color. Working with an air brush is not easy, but it is possible to study it and learn to do it very well, as thousands of people have done. Then it is possible to make very attractive pictures with the air brush.

air compression

Air is a gas, which is a substance—exactly as a piece of iron is a substance, except that a gas is so much thinner. Air is so thin that you can press it into a smaller space, exactly as you can a sponge. All of the air in an average-sized room could be compressed to occupy no more space than a bread box. In fact, air can be compressed, if cooled enough, so that it becomes a liquid. But take away the pressure that has forced the air into such a small space and it wants to fly back to its original size, exactly as a sponge does. It puts forth so much force in trying to return to its original size that this force can be put to use to drive many machines and serve many useful purposes.

When a rubber balloon is blown up, the air has to fit itself into a smaller space and become compressed. The more it is compressed, the more power it exerts in trying to get out of that rubber balloon. Blow long enough and this power will be so much that it will break the rubber balloon with a loud pop. Yet there are not more than a few pounds of pressure in that rubber balloon. You can imagine how much force air can apply when so much air is forced into a tank or other space that it exerts hundreds of pounds of pressure in its effort to get out. It can drive many machines and do many jobs that a man is not strong enough to do.

The compression of air is accomplished by quite a simple device. Any pump for a bicycle tire is an example of it. There is a "cylinder"—the round, hollow tube of the bicycle pump. There is a piston, the wadding that moves up and down in the tube when it is worked by a rod and handle attached to it. There are two valves. One valve opens into the small tube that leads to the bicycle tire. The other valve opens on the outside air. When you press the piston down, it closes the valve that leads to the outside air and opens the valve that leads to the tire. The piston forces all the air that is in the cylinder into the bicycle tire. At this point, you pull the handle back and move the piston to the top of the cylinder again. This closes the valve that leads to the tire, and at the same time opens the valve that leads to the outside air. Air rushes in from the outside and fills the cylinder again. Now you press down again; you again close the valve to the outside and open the valve to the tire, and you press more air into the tire. As you pump away at the handle, it takes more and more of your strength to move that piston down. That is because the compressed air that is already in the tire is pressing back on the piston with almost as much strength as you have to press the handle down. If you keep on long enough, either the tire will burst from the force of the compressed air inside it, or the power of that air will be so great that you will no longer have the strength to push the piston down.

An air compressor for use in factories

and in other big ways works on the same principles as the bicycle pump, but it is run by an electric motor or gasoline engine that can exert more strength than a person can and so can force more compressed air into a tank. Once the tank is full of air under high pressure, it can be used for many purposes.

The many tools that are operated or driven by compressed air include: rock drills, which can bore deep holes in the hardest rock; spray guns, which spray paint on wood or metal much faster and much more evenly than anybody can paint with a brush; rivet guns, which fasten big pieces of metal together with rivets (short, thick, round-headed nails); and giant hammers used in factories to hammer heavy pieces of metal into any desired shape. While the tool is being used, the compressor keeps working all the time to keep the tank full of compressed air. A strong rubber hose carries the compressed air from the tank to the handle of the tool. By pressing a little trigger or button in the handle, the operator opens a little valve that lets air into the tool. Compressed air tools are much more powerful than hand tools.

Another purpose of compressing air is to supply it faster to an apparatus requiring atmospheric oxygen, as in the jet turbine used in jet airplanes. Here the compressor is in the form of a turbine that rotates at about 18,000 revolutions per minute. The jet turbine was developed from the supercharger, a fuel-and-air compressor used in gasoline airplane engines at high altitudes where the air is rarefied and its oxygen content low. A similar application is the injector of a diesel engine, which forces air and fuel into the cylinder.

The temperature of a gas is determined by the average speed of its molecules. When a gas is expanded by putting it in a larger container than it was originally in, the molecules are slowed down because they use up energy in pushing each other apart. However, when a gas is compressed, its molecules are pushed together by outside pressure, and this "push" speeds them up, raising the temperature. This is why powerful compressors must be cooled.

air conditioning

Anything that is done to make the air cleaner or more comfortable is air conditioning. Even a window or a stove is an air-conditioning device. But today when people speak of air conditioning they usually mean air cooling.

In this article, we will speak of air conditioning mostly in the sense of the cooling of air. The heating of air will be left for the article on HEATING. But the air-conditioning machine that brings cool air into a house or store or theater, to reduce the discomfort of the summer's heat, also filters the air, to clean it of dust and other impurities; it dries the air, removing some of the moisture or water that makes the hot outside air so uncomfortable; and it freshens the air by taking out of the room the stale used air.

AIR CONDITIONING IS IMPORTANT

It is very nice to be cool in the summer time, but that is not the biggest job done by air conditioning. Air conditioning is important in many other ways.

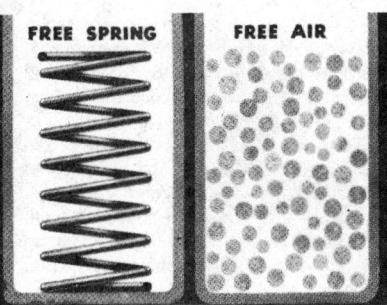 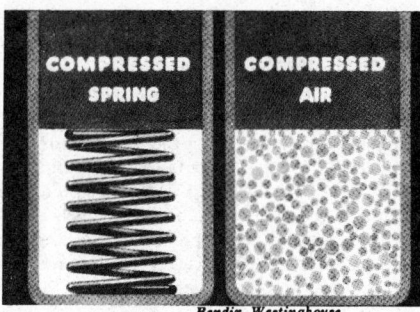

Bendix Westinghouse

These diagrams show how air compressors work. At the left is a picture of two cylinders. In one is a spring, in the other air. If you put a round, tight disc in each and press down, as in the picture at the right, you compress them. Let go, and pressure pops them out.

It is important in manufacturing. Some factories make parts out of metal, and they must fit very tightly. Metal becomes larger when it is hot and smaller when it is cold. This is the process of EXPANSION AND CONTRACTION, about which there is a separate article. Factories cannot make metal parts to exactly the size they want them if they must make them in hot factories and then send them out into colder temperatures where they will shrink down to a smaller size. This is only one of hundreds of examples of ways in which air conditioning has helped factories.

Air conditioning is important to business. Motion picture theaters used to have very bad business in the summertime, because it was so hot and uncomfortable inside. Stores used to sell less merchandise in the summertime, because people did not want to go into a hot store to buy. Now the theaters and the stores are air-conditioned, and many people go in just because it is cooler inside than outside.

Air conditioning is important in offices. People do not work as well when they are hot and uncomfortable as when they are cool and comfortable. By air-conditioning their offices, many companies have made money in the long run because their employees work better. Many new buildings in New York, Chicago, and other big cities are now being built with no windows that open. Instead they have glass walls that let in enough light but keep out dust, dirt, and street noises. The fresh air is supplied by an air-conditioning system that runs pipes, called ducts, to every office. The air-conditioning system sucks in fresh air from the outside, cleans and dries and cools it, and then pumps it into the offices. At the same time, it sucks out all the stale air. Some of these air-conditioning systems also heat the offices in the winter by pumping in warm air instead of cold.

Air conditioning is important in other ways. People who suffer from hay fever often have air conditioning because it filters out from the air all the dust and pollen that make them sneeze.

WHY HOT WEATHER IS UNCOMFORTABLE

When you wash a dish but don't dry it with a towel, it will soon dry itself in the air. The moisture on that dish will evaporate. That means it will be sucked up by the air. The air has room in it for a great deal of moisture, which is water in such tiny drops that they cannot be seen. Every human being must get rid of some of the waste matter in his body by perspiring. When he perspires, moisture comes out of the pores in his skin and lies there. He usually does not feel it, because the air soaks it up, just as it soaks up the water from that dish. All evaporation causes coolness, and the evaporation of perspiration keeps our bodies cool.

But the air can hold only so much moisture. When it already has as much moisture in it as it can hold, it is said to be saturated and it will take in no more. The dish would not dry. The perspiration would not evaporate and cool our bodies. It lies on the skin, wet and clammy. This often happens in very hot weather.

When the air is saturated with moisture, we say the weather is "sticky" or "muggy." We say, "The humidity is terrible," meaning that the air is very humid, or full of moisture. That is a case in which air conditioning is helpful. One of its jobs is to take the extra moisture out of the air. Then when the air reaches us inside it can again take on more moisture and it soaks up the perspiration. We no longer drip and feel uncomfortable.

HOW AIR CONDITIONING WORKS

There are different kinds of air conditioner. The big ones that are put into theaters and stores and office buildings and hotels are hidden away in the basement, and all you see are the grills out of which the conditioned air comes. But you will also often see the "room air conditioner," the window box that fits into the window and serves only one room, usually in a house.

A room air conditioner looks like a long metal box about 12 to 15 inches high and anywhere from 24 to 30 inches wide—the width of the window. It is made to rest on the window sill with part of it inside the room and the rest of it opening into the outside air.

Air from the outside is drawn into the box by a powerful fan. It passes through a filter that removes dust, dirt, and pollen. The filter is a flat, square metal frame holding a woolly sort of material. Dust and dirt cannot pass through this filter. Only clean air gets through.

The clean air is then blown over a group of little copper pipes called a cooling coil. The pipes are cold, so they chill or cool the air. Cold air cannot hold as much moisture as warm air, so the moisture in the warm air turns to drops of water which drip down through the cooling coil to the back of the box, where they are carried away by a pipe. A fan called an exhaust blower then blows this moisture out into the outside air. The exhaust blower also sucks stale air out of the room through an opening in the front of the box. While this is going on, the clean cool air passes from the cooling coil to another opening in the front of the box and out into the room.

The basic principle of the air-conditioning machine is this: The more space a substance occupies, the more heat it will hold. The method of compressing a gas into a smaller space was explained in the article on AIR COMPRESSION. When a gas is compressed into a smaller space, it gives off heat. This heat flows into the container in which the gas is held, and the container becomes hot, just as a pan becomes hot when it is put over a fire. When a gas is allowed to expand into a larger space, it absorbs heat from the outside. This heat is taken first from the container in which the gas is held, and the container becomes cold. So in an air-cooling machine, a gas is first compressed and the heat it gives off is blown into the outside air; then the compressed gas is allowed to flow into pipes called a *cooling coil,* and to expand and create coldness there, and air is blown over the cold pipes and into the room.

Most air-conditioners use a gas called *freon,* because it is so easy to change from a liquid, or compressed state, to a gas, or expanded state. Freon is a liquid at temperatures under 35° Fahrenheit, but at 35° it will boil, or turn into gas.

When the switch of a room air-conditioner is turned on, the compressor begins to work. It compresses the freon gas. Some of the heat produced in this process is sent into the outside air. Some remains in the freon gas.

The warm freon now moves through a pipe to a condensing coil. This is simply a metal box in which the pipe goes around and around in spiral turns. In larger air conditioners the condensing coil is cooled by cold water, which flows in and out of the box. In a room air conditioner, the coil is cooled by a stream of cold air from an electric fan called an exhaust blower. The warm freon gas condenses or becomes liquid when it strikes the cold copper tubes of the condensing coil. This liquid freon is then carried by a pipe to the cooling coil, where it again begins to vaporize and turn to gas, and the whole process starts all over again.

A room unit may range from ⅓ ton for a small room to ¾ or 1 ton for a large room or combination of rooms. A ton of cooling capacity is equivalent to melting a ton of ice, or removing 288,000 British Thermal Units, in a 24-hour period; about one horsepower compressor capacity, using about 1,000 watts of electricity, is needed per ton.

INDUSTRIAL AND BUSINESS USES

The first commercial air-conditioning machine was patented by a brewer, Robert Portner, and installed in a brewery in Alexandria, Va., in 1880; its object was to filter and (by baking) dehumidify the air, to remove and to inhibit the growth of airborne microörganisms that would corrupt brewer's yeast. In 1902, Willis Carrier developed the first "modern" air-conditioning machine for a printer in Brooklyn, N.Y., to prevent gain or loss of moisture from affecting

the size or flatness of paper and to overcome other problems in printing.

Air conditioning for personal comfort was first installed in the lobby and public rooms of the Blackstone Hotel in Chicago, Ill., in 1921. The first department-store installation was in the J. L. Hudson Co. in Detroit, Mich., in 1924. During the 1920s motion-picture theaters throughout the U.S. installed air conditioning; before the end of the 1930s its use in theaters and auditoriums, restaurants, and other public places, was nearly 100%. During and after World War II, new office buildings and hotels were generally air-conditioned throughout. The largest such installation was in the Pentagon Building in Washington, D.C. In 1958, air-conditioning a large new office building added $1,000,000 or more to the cost of construction; in a building of the size of the Empire State Building it would be nearly $5,000,000. To air-condition an existing structure cost 25% to 40% more, and the use of large expanses of glass, as in the United Nations Building, added about 15% to the cost, despite the use of special glass that filters out the hottest rays. Operation of a large installation may cost from $4,000 to $10,000 per month.

A temperature of 74° F. and relative humidity of 50% are considered a comfortable combination; higher temperatures are comfortable if humidity drops proportionately, and air movement of 15 to 25 ft. per minute increases comfort.

HEAT PUMP

The *heat pump* or reverse-cycle procedure uses the heat of the condensing coil to heat the house in winter and the coldness of the refrigeration coil to cool it in summer; air may be blown over either coil and into the house. So long as the outside temperature is not below 45° F., a heat pump can draw enough heat from the air to keep a house comfortable. In colder climates, a warm-water well or other underground source of heat is required.

In office buildings and hotels, where space is too valuable to expend on ducts to carry conditioned air, pipes carry compressed air and hot or chilled water to each room. The occupant of the room can control its temperature by letting the air blow over coils through which the water runs.

OTHER METHODS

A central air-conditioning system for a large open space, such as a theater or lobby, is frequently based on one of the oldest systems, developed by Willis Carrier, who discovered in 1902 that air will lose moisture when passed through a spray of chilled water and gain moisture when the water is hot. Ice is often used instead of cold water. Mechanical refrigeration, however, is suitable for most purposes. One of the most economical systems uses low-pressure steam to chill water. Water is sprayed into a vacuum chamber, where it vaporizes, absorbing heat from liquid water outside. The water vapor in the chamber is then absorbed by a salt solution. This method does not require moving parts and is often used

where the vibration of machinery would be objectionable.

There are some standard legends in the history of early air conditioning: that a Roman emperor, Heliogabalus, had his slaves carry snow from the mountains to relieve his summers; and that the caliph Mahdi of Baghdad, A.D. 755, had a building with double walls, between which he packed snow. It is probable, however, that except for ventilation there was no real air conditioning before the late 19th century.

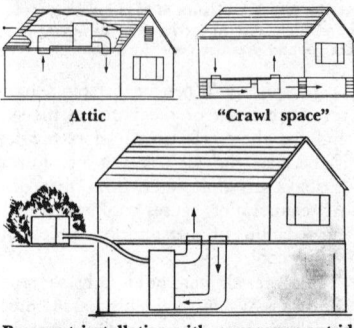

Attic   "Crawl space"

Basement installation with compressor outside

Utility room
and attic
installation
Chrysler Airtemp

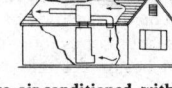

Many new houses are air-conditioned with air-cooled units (requiring no plumbing).

aircraft carrier

An aircraft carrier is a warship capable of landing and launching planes, and equipped to service these planes and their crews. The planes take off from and land on a floating runway, or flight deck, that causes the ship to be called a "flattop." It is this flight deck that makes the ship an aircraft carrier. The United States Navy was the pioneer in the creation of the aircraft carrier. The first time an airplane ever took off from a warship was on November 14, 1910, when a plane of the United States Navy took off from a platform on the bow of the cruiser *Birmingham*. On January 18, 1911, the battleship *Pennsylvania* built on its stern a platform so large that it was able not only to launch a plane but also to land one. In 1922, the United States built its first warship exclusively for the purpose of carrying and flying aircraft —the first real aircraft carrier, in basic design not much different from the aircraft carriers of today. It was the United States Ship *Langley*.

Before the end of World War II the aircraft carrier had become the first-line ship of every navy, for both offensive and defensive purposes. The Navy had been reorganized around the carrier. By 1957 the battleship, which for more than five hundred years had been the most important warship, had ceased to be used at all.

THE CLASSES OF AIRCRAFT CARRIER

In 1958, aircraft carriers in the United States Navy were divided into "classes," depending on size and purpose. The navies of other countries have similar carriers, but the United States has more than any other country. The classes of U.S. carriers are described by letters:

CVA, "attack carriers," the largest class, including the "supercarriers" such as the *Saratoga* and *Forrestal* and previous large carriers such as *Midway* and *Franklin Delano Roosevelt*. Displacement is about 60,000 tons and the flight deck about 900 by 113 feet and 60 to 70 feet above the water.

CVS, "anti-submarine carriers," such as the *Antietam*, with flight decks up to 880 ft. and displacement of 25,000 or more tons.

CVL, 600-foot flight decks and 10,-000 to 15,000 tons displacement.

CVE, "escort carriers," called "jeep" carriers, about 580-foot flight deck and 8,000 tons.

CVHA, "assault helicopter carriers," even smaller than the CVEs, about 7,000 tons.

CVAA, "antiaircraft carriers," small but of varying sizes.

There were also CVHE, "escort helicopter carriers," and CVU, "utility carriers," all "in mothballs" (not in active service, but available).

The big carriers can carry large planes for offensive as well as defensive purposes.

The smaller carriers, the CVLs and the CVEs, are used mostly in submarine hunting and patrol. They can carry about 50 single-engine planes, whereas the bigger carriers, the CVAs and CVSs, can carry about 90 single-engine planes.

In the middle of any of these aircraft carriers, along the right side is a structure called the *island*, where the smokestacks are, and from where the ship is steered. In every other way, except for its flat top where the planes land and take off, the carrier is like any other ship.

FLIGHT OPERATIONS

Before a flight all the planes that are going to fly are spotted (arranged or parked) on the back half of the flight deck. They are brought up from the hangar deck, where they have been stored (and repaired when necessary). This hangar deck is one story below the flight deck, down in the hull, and is a little smaller than the flight deck. The carrier has three very large elevators, one toward the front of the deck, one to the rear, and one (called the deck-edge elevator) on the left side in the middle, to bring them up. If there are jets, they are spotted in front.

The pilots are "briefed"—told what to do on the flight—in "ready rooms" located just below the hangar deck. When the call comes over their loudspeaker from the bridge, "Pilots, man your planes!" they run up to the flight deck and get into their planes. On a signal they all start their engines together, and a short time later the carrier turns into the wind and adjusts her speed so that there will be 30 knots of wind blowing down the deck. (If the wind is 20 knots, the carrier goes 10 knots.) The jets are catapulted off first, and then others are catapulted off until the remaining parked planes occupy only half the deck. Then they can take off under their own power.

There are two catapults, one on each side of the front of the ship. Jets have to be catapulted because they cannot

The U.S. Navy's huge carrier *Enterprise* is powered by atomic energy. The ship, which was launched in 1961, is 1,123 feet long, can carry seven aircraft squadrons, and has a total crew and air group of more than 4,500 men. The *Enterprise* has a canted deck, which slants outward to give the effect of two separate runways. As a result, separate planes can take off and land at the same time, and there is less danger that wings of big bombers will hit the island.

accelerate fast enough to get flying speed.

THE PLANES IN ACTION

While the planes are on their mission, the carrier watches them on its radar scopes and keeps in constant contact with them by radio. It directs them to the enemy planes, which can also be seen on the screen, and directs them back to the carrier when they are ready to return. This is done in CIC, the Combat Information Center, a room in the center of the ship, where all the radar scopes are.

When the planes come back from their mission they circle over the carrier in formation, breaking off from the formation one by one to land in turn. In the final approach to the landing they fly a 180° (half a circle) left turn at a level altitude just a little above the flight deck. When about 500 feet from the ship they begin to see the L.S.O. (landing signal officer), who stands in the back left corner of the ship. He has two paddles, one in each hand, with which he signals to the pilot, telling him whether he is too low or high, or too slow or fast; whether to come on in and land, or to go around and try again. When the planes are landing at night, the L.S.O. wears fluorescent clothing—clothing that gleams in the dark—so the pilots can always see him.

Every plane has a tail hook that the pilot can lower from the cockpit. This hook, when it lands on the deck, will catch one of nine arresting (stopping) wires, which are one-inch cables stretched across the deck about 8 inches above it.

As soon as the plane catches onto a wire, men called *hookmen* run out from the side of the ship, take the wire out of the hook, and make sure that the hook goes back up into the plane.

If a pilot forgets to put his hook down—and he does sometimes forget, since a pilot more often lands on land

than on a carrier—he is given a wave-off—that is, he is told to go around and try again, and this time to get the hook down. When this happens it is a custom for him to buy the L.S.O. and his hookspotter "geedunks"—carrier talk for ice cream cones.

If a plane misses all nine wires, which are set up over about half of the deck, there is a barrier of more wires strung across the deck at the middle of the ship to stop him. This barrier is made of cables like the arresting wires. They are strung across the deck, 4 to 8 feet above the deck, and can be lowered. After his plane is stopped, the pilot taxis forward over the lowered barrier, to get out of the way of the other planes. Finally, when all the planes have landed, the deck is respotted, the planes are pulled back with tractors to the rear again, and all is ready for the next flight.

Always following a carrier is a destroyer, to pick up aviators who for some reason miss the carrier and land in the water. Too, there is usually a helicopter that hovers near, to help the destroyer.

FLUSH-DECK CARRIERS

Since World War II all new carriers have been designed with a *canted deck*— a flight deck with one section that sticks out at an angle. This permits some planes to land at the same time that others are taking off. (See picture above.)

Before the canted deck was developed, there was a plan to build "flush-deck" carriers on which there would be only a small island that could be lowered into the ship. Then a giant bomber with its big wingspread could land without danger that its wings would hit the island. The no-island idea was abandoned because the canted deck makes it unnecessary.

Since the flight deck is a lot smaller than the runway at an airport, there is never much margin for error and mis-

takes are very dangerous. But most carrier pilots feel that it is not much more difficult to land on a carrier than it is to drive a car into a garage.

The carrier is usually guarded by cruisers and destroyers, and also by its own guns and planes. Four large carriers of the U.S. Navy have been sunk, but after the Battle of Midway in June, 1942, the Navy perfected the carriers' defenses so well that no more large carriers were lost for the rest of World War II, although some were slightly damaged.

AS A CITY

A carrier is a city in itself. It has a crew of 3,000 men, consisting of sailors, aviators, and plane crews. Of course, it has room to sleep and feed them. It carries enough fuel and gasoline for the ship and the planes to stay at sea for months at a time. It also supplies the destroyer with all its needs. Carriers have movies, soda fountains, shoeshine shops, tailors, every kind of store, and even basketball courts on the hangar deck, which can be used when the planes aren't parked there. The latest carriers are designed with escalators to take the men up and down the various levels of the ship.

The machine and repair shops are factories in themselves, with complete facilities for repair and maintenance of planes.

CARRIERS IN THE ATOMIC AGE

Since World War II, the United States has relied for defense chiefly on huge bombing planes carrying nuclear bombs, so that the country can retaliate if an enemy attacks. Part of this plan has been to maintain a ring of airbases in foreign countries. Super-carriers, able to carry heavy bombers, can act as floating airbases in case these land bases are taken away by the foreign countries or are destroyed by the enemy. Except for the submarine, the aircraft carrier is the only naval vessel that can be expected to play a major part in a future big war.

aircraft engine, see AIRPLANE ENGINE.

Airedale

The Airedale is one of the most popular dogs among American and English people. It is the largest of the terriers. In appearance it is wiry-haired, with a heavy tan body that has dark markings on it. Its tail is always cut short or docked. Its ears are never cut, but it is bred to have short ears.

It is one of the best fighting dogs known, and has been used in big-game hunting in Africa, India, Canada, and the United States, and in police work in Germany and Great Britain. During World Wars I and II it was used to carry messages, even though this meant crossing the battlefronts where firing was going on. When some dogs might have been scared and run away, the Airedale was so faithful that it kept on going until it delivered the message.

The Airedale was first bred in Great Britain, and got its name because it was used for hunting small game in the valley of the River Aire. This was less than

100 years ago. It is a very affectionate dog and is a fine pet even for small children. The Airedale is about 22 inches high at the shoulder, and weighs between 40 and 70 pounds.

Harham Kennels

An Airedale terrier is about two feet tall.

Air Force, U.S.

The Air Force is one of the three armed forces that have the duty of defending the United States against any enemy that might attack. The other two armed forces are the Army and the Navy. The Air Force is the youngest of the three. Through World War II it was a branch of the Army and was called the Army Air Corps or Army Air Forces. On September 18, 1947, the Air Force became independent. Because air power is absolutely necessary in modern warfare, many people consider the Air Force the most important branch of the defenses of the United States.

There are four ways in which the Air Force must be prepared to defend the United States and fight for the country in time of war.

1. If the enemy sends bombing planes to attack the United States or any of its possessions or bases, the job of the Air Force is to fight them in the air and destroy them or chase them off. For this it uses "fighter planes," especially of the type called interceptors, and guided missiles including "anti-missile missiles."

2. In time of war the Air Force must bomb enemy territory, to destroy the factories in which they make war materials, and the bases from which they might attack the United States, and sometimes for the purpose called retaliation—that is, to punish the enemy for its attacks on the United States. For these purposes the Air Force uses bombing planes of various types, and guided and ballistic missiles. This is called *strategic* air warfare.

3. When United States soldiers are fighting in the field, or when an amphibious attack is made, the Air Force has the job of supporting the ground forces. To do this, is must first win "control of the skies" where the fighting is going on, by engaging the enemy air forces in battle. Then it can provide an "air umbrella" for friendly ground forces, protecting them while at the same time it attacks enemy troops, fortified positions, and supplies. For these purposes the Air Force uses fighters and light bombers. This is called *tactical* air warfare.

4. The Air Force transports both men and supplies for the Army and other serv-

ices. For this it has huge fleets of transport planes. The Air Force also has planes for reconnaissance (observation of enemy positions), for scouting, for aerial photography, for refueling other planes in midflight, for training, and for other purposes that are different from actual fighting.

For the carrying out of these duties, the U.S. Air Force had, as of December 31, 1965, approximately 831,759 men.

ORGANIZATION OF THE AIR FORCE

The Department of the Air Force is one of the three branches of the Department of Defense, along with the Army and Navy. Its head is the Secretary of the Air Force, a civilian, appointed by the President. The highest-ranking Air Force officer is the Chief of Staff, with rank of general; he is a member of the Joint Chiefs of Staff. Other officers, noncommissioned officers, and enlisted men have the same grades and pay as in the Army (see ARMY, U.S.).

In the U.S. Air Force there are sixteen Major Commands, each with its own specialized duties. Among the chief ones are:

Strategic Air Command (SAC). 239,-000 men in 1965. Charged with strategic air warfare.

Tactical Air Command (TAC). 75,-000 men in 1965. Charged with tactical air warfare.

Air Defense Command (ADC). 110,-000 men in 1965. Charged with the operation of aircraft as required for the defense of the United States. ADC is the air branch of NORAD (North American Air Defense Command), which includes the other armed services and various governmental and civilian organizations. (See NORAD).

Other Major Commands include the Air Training Command, Air Force Systems Command, and Air University (not for cadets, but for advanced training of present officers, in six schools).

THE PLANES OF THE AIR FORCE

The Air Force, as of 1965, had 15,000 aircraft. These included fighter (tactical) aircraft, and troop transport and cargo planes to support the Army; global airlift aircraft, including "flying hospitals," to serve all the Armed Forces; strategic aircraft to attack distant targets; tankers; air defense interceptors; reconnaissance aircraft; weather planes; search and rescue aircraft; helicopters; trainers; and "airborne radar platforms," such as the early warning aircraft.

Principal strategic aircraft are:

B-52—This intercontinental range heavy bomber can fly faster than 650 miles per hour at very low altitudes or above 50,000 feet. With missiles launched from the air plus the weapons carried in its bomb bays, the B-52 can hit several targets hundreds of miles apart on one mission.

B-58 "Hustler"—The fastest aircraft in the Strategic Air Command in 1965 was this delta-winged jet bomber.

KC-135—An aerial tanker to refuel jet aircraft in the air at greater speed and high altitude.

FB-111—A new aircraft designed to fly twice as fast as the B-52 and have approxi-

mately the same range, scheduled for 1968.

SR-71—In 1966 the SR-71 was in the testing phase of development. The SR-71 is a long-range, manned supersonic strategic military reconnaissance aircraft, which employs the most advanced observation equipment in the world. The SR-71 can fly at more than 2,000 miles per hour at an altitude of more than 80,000 feet, and can cover with its reconnaissance "eyes" an area of 60,000 square miles in 1 hour.

Principal tactical aircraft are:

F-105 "Thunderchief"—This is an all-weather tactical fighter which can fly faster than 1,400 miles per hour at altitudes above 55,000 feet. It can carry many types of weapon, including rockets, air-to-air missiles, 20mm cannon, and conventional bombs.

F-4C "Phantom"—This is a multi-purpose tactical aircraft that flies more than twice the speed of sound. It reaches altitudes greater than 90,000 feet and it has a range of more than 1,500 miles. It can carry nuclear weapons as well as a great variety of missiles, rockets, and conventional bombs.

Aircraft used by the Tactical Air Command also include troop and cargo transports and assault aircraft. One of these is:

C-130 "Hercules"—Manufactured by Lockheed Aircraft Corporation, it is powered by four turboprop jet engines. Possessing a long range, high speed capability, the C-130 is the backbone of Tactical Air Command's airlift strength.

Principal Airlift Aircraft are:

C-141 "Starlifter," the first jet aircraft designed for the particular needs of Military Airlift Command (MAC). It came into operation in 1965 and can carry 63,000 pounds nonstop across the Atlantic at more than 500 miles per hour, or from the West Coast to Hawaii. Used to transport equipment to Vietnam and on the return flight as a "flying hospital ward." As a troop carrier it airlifts up to 154 combat troops, 123 paratroops or 80 litter patients.

C-130E "Hercules," a late-model prop-jet aircraft with a cruising speed of 320 miles per hour. It will airlift 92 combat troops or 64 paratroops for airdrop, or can carry up to 74 litter patients for aeromedical evacuation.

C-5A—The world's largest jet transport aircraft; powered by four fan-jet engines, able to take off and land on relatively short runways with a mammoth load of cargo, for instance sixteen three-quarter-ton trucks, or fourteen supersonic jet fighters, or thirty jeeps.

Convair Photo

The F-102 delta-winged, supersonic jet interceptor streaks over an Air Force base in California. It is designed to fly in any kind of weather.

60 YEARS OF AIR FORCE PLANES
1. Wright Biplane of 1909.
2. Airplane of U.S. Army Signal Corps, 1916.
3. Boeing low-wing bomber, the YIB-9 of 1931. One of the first modern designs.

4. B-17G, Flying Fortress of World War II.
5. KC-97, post-World War II refueling plane.
6. B-47B, jet bomber of 1954.
7. F-4C of 1965, tactical fighter.
8. FB-111, supersonic bomber of 1968.

ways been able to get as many recruits as it needs without having to draft them. In fact, the recruiting officers often have to discourage young men and women who are in too much of a hurry to get into the Air Force. "Finish your education," they say, "then fly." A good education is especially important in the Air Force, because so many duties of the airman fall into scientific fields.

For the young person who wants a good career, however, the Air Force offers exceptional opportunities. There are more than forty "career fields" in all, Air Force positions in which the airman gets training that will be of value to him should he leave the Air Force and return to civilian life. A few of these are: Communications (radio, etc.); metal-working; mechanic on internal-combustion and other engines; parachute repair; rocket propulsion; teaching; administration; meteorology. There are many others. All Air Force people can take correspondence courses from the United States Armed Forces Institute, which is at Madison, Wisconsin.

Male applicants for enlistment in the Air Force must be between 17 and 27 years old, and female applicants must be between 18 and 27 years of age. Applicants must be in good physical condition and of good moral character. They must pass aptitude and mental tests administered by the USAF Recruiting Service.

PILOT TRAINING

Aviation cadets in training to be pilots first take a pre-flight course that lasts three months. Then they receive about six months of flying training. When a cadet has soloed, he has more to learn, in classroom work, about the scientific phases of flying. After this, there are five months more of flying training and three months of advanced training. The process takes at least fourteen months. Only when he has completed it satisfactorily does the cadet receive his "wings."

During training, the cadet gets his living and a monthly allowance of $109.20, plus a free $10,000 life insurance policy. When he finishes he is commissioned as a second lieutenant.

AIRCRAFT OBSERVER TRAINING

The aviation cadet in training as an aircraft observor finishes a pre-flight course lasting three months, then has primary training lasting thirty weeks (about seven months). The further training is different for different kinds of work, but all successful candidates receive their commissions after fourteen months of training. Some of them become crew members of planes, for example navigators; some become ground officers in engineering, electronic, or other fields; some specialize in photography, meteorology, and so on.

WOMEN IN THE AIR FORCE

Women can be full members of the Air Force. They are known as the WAF ("Women in the Air Force"). They take their basic training at San Antonio, Texas, then a large number of them go to Air Force Technical Schools.

The WAF have many different occupations. Some of the career fields open to women are: communications, photog-

WINGS, GROUPS, AND SQUADRONS

Whether the purpose of the operation is strategic or tactical, the Air Force assigns its planes to the job in units that are known as wings, groups, and squadrons.

A wing is the basic unit. It is made up of a number or group of planes, the men who fly them, the men who service and supply them, and all the other men who do work that is necessary to keep the planes flying.

Suppose there are forty-five medium bombers at an Air Force base. The actual crews who man these bombers number about 275 men; they are the men who are in the planes when they take off on a mission. Behind them are 492 other men who service the planes, supply them with fuel, load them with bombs, guide them to their targets and keep in radio contact with them, and do other work connected with the flying and operation of the planes. Behind all these are 1,783 more men who must maintain and supply the airbase, run the medical units, do the "paper work" of keeping records and issuing orders, and perform numerous other duties. Altogether, these 3,000 men make a "wing."

Each wing is composed of a combat group, three supporting groups, and a headquarters unit. The combat group is the striking force. This is the outfit that flies the planes. In peacetime, a group has three squadrons; in wartime, it has four. A squadron is simply a number of planes commanded by the ranking officer in one of its planes. When planes can be refueled in the air, there may be another squadron, the refueling squadron. Such a squadron has about 20 planes.

At some bases in the Strategic Air Command, the bomber squadrons are combined with missile squadrons to form a Strategic Aerospace Wing. SAC missile wings usually consist of three or four missile squadrons. A Minuteman squadron has 50 missiles in underground launch silos. At the end of 1965 the Air Force had 54 Titan II ICBMs (Intercontinental Ballistic Missiles) and nearly 1,000 Minuteman I and II ICBMs.

THE MEN AND WOMEN IN THE AIR FORCE

The people in the United States Air Force are not all flying men, but all have important jobs, and the Air Force has al-

K-C-135 jet tanker refuels B-52 Stratofortress.

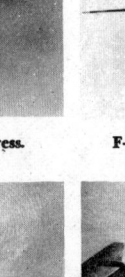

F-101B Voodoo supersonic jet interceptor.

B-58 Hustler, first supersonic bomber.

F-104 Starfighter supersonic jet fighter.

raphy, computer systems, medical and dental, and administration.

In 1965, the WAF numbered about 5,000 women, including 750 officers. To maintain this strength, about 2,000 enlisted women and 125 woman officers are recruited each year.

HISTORY OF THE AIR FORCE

The use of air power in the United States began on August 1, 1907, when the United States Army set up an "aeronautical division" consisting of one officer and two enlisted men to study the "flying machine," but it took more than forty years for this to become the United States Air Force that exists today.

At first, airplanes were considered useful only for observing where the shells fired by the artillery were falling, so that the aim could be corrected. Then airplanes were thought to be useful for scouting out enemy positions. When World War I came along in 1914, the European countries found that aviation was a real fighting arm of the military services, and the United States ordered several thousand planes, but not all of them were delivered before the end of the war. Colonel William ("Billy") Mitchell was in charge of the planes used by the United States Army in World War I, but he had little to work with.

After World War I, the Army and Navy both experimented with airships, especially dirigibles, but there were many accidents. Mitchell, now a General, insisted that air power would decide all future wars, and that airplanes would destroy battleships. Although he proved this in actual tests, most of the higher-ranking officers in both the Army and Navy disagreed with him and he was forced to retire. Not until years later was it known that he had been right all the time, and that the United States could have been far ahead of other countries, instead of far behind them, if it had taken his advice.

During the 1930s, Italy and Germany especially showed how important air power would be in the next war. The Air Force, which was then the Army Air Corps, designed and tested some of the finest fighting planes in the world, but Congress had not given it enough money to build up a good fighting force. Not until France fell before the German armies in 1940, in the first year of World War II, and President Franklin D. Roosevelt called upon the United States to arm the free world, did the Air Force receive the go-ahead it needed. When President Roosevelt said United States industry must produce 50,000 planes a year—more than any other country had ever produced—most people said it was impossible; but before World War II ended, that production rate had been almost doubled.

Under General Henry H. Arnold, the Army Air Forces during World War II became the greatest in the world, though it was much weaker at the start of the war than the Government was able to admit. Though the air forces had 275,000 enlisted men and 23,000 officers, and 12,000 planes on Pearl Harbor Day in 1941, most of the planes were old and the enemy and allied countries alike had greater air power than the United States. In rapid succession the United States proved that planes could be built faster than anyone had ever supposed, that modern science could make it possible to bomb the enemy around the clock (in daylight as well as at night), and that a war could be decided by destruction of the enemy from the air. The final proof of American leadership came when the atomic bomb was developed and its use against Japan ended the war in a matter of weeks and may have saved several hundred thousand American lives that would have been lost if it had been necessary to invade Japan.

During World War II, the Army Air Force dropped nearly three million tons of bombs on the enemy and destroyed more than fifteen thousand enemy planes. The air forces grew to almost two and a half million men and eighty thousand planes.

All during World War II there had been argument about making the Air Force a separate branch of the armed services. When the war was over, this was done. The Air Force became a separate Department on September 18, 1947,

on equal terms with the Army and Navy, under the Secretary of Defense.

When the fighting broke out in Korea in 1950, the Air Force took on wartime duties as an independent branch of the armed services. It controlled the sky over Korea throughout the fighting. The most widely followed air action during this fighting was the battles between U.S. Air Force Sabrejets and Russian-built MiGs. The Sabrejets downed 800 MiGs while losing only 58 planes.

In the fighting in Vietnam, the Air Force continued to play an active role. At the end of 1965, there were 22,000 Air Force members in Vietnam. Their missions included support for ground troops, airlift and air rescue operations, and the bombing of military targets and enemy supply lines.

See also AIRPOWER, GUIDED MISSILE.

Air Force Academy

The United States Air Force Academy is a college for the education of future Air Force officers, similar to the Military Academy at West Point and the Naval Academy at Annapolis. The Air Force Academy occupies a site of 1,750 acres about six miles north of Colorado Springs, Colorado. Before this site was chosen, in 1954, a selection committee considered four hundred different locations in twenty-two states.

Although the permanent Academy buildings were not ready for use until 1958, the Academy actually opened in July, 1955, in temporary quarters at Lowry Air Force Base near Denver, Colorado. There were 305 cadets in the opening class. Full enrollment for the Academy was set at 2,500. The cost of building the Academy was set at $126,000,000. The design of the buildings has been considered too modern or unconventional by many critics, including the noted architect Frank Lloyd Wright.

STUDIES AND DEGREES

The course of studies at the Air Force Academy is devoted about half to special subjects connected with aviation or military science and about half to more usual college subjects such as English, history, philosophy, geography, psychology, law, economics, government, etc. At the Military Academy such subjects account for only 38% of the course, and at the Naval Academy only 24%. A graduate of the Air Force Academy receives the degree of Bachelor of Science and is commissioned a second lieutenant. In most cases entrance is by competitive examination among those nominated. Each member of Congress may make ten nominations and others are made by the President, the Vice President, and the Secretary of the Air Force.

Even with full enrollment the Air Force Academy was not planned to supply more than half of the officers needed, the others coming from R.O.T.C., Officer Training School, and the Airman Education and Commissioning program.

See the article on COLORADO for pictures.

air gun

An air gun is any weapon that uses the force of compressed air, instead of an explosive, to shoot a bullet, pellet, or other projectile. Modern air guns look

Below: What goes on inside a BB gun. All the different parts are numbered. First you drop a number of BBs through the hole in the front of the *muzzle* (21). You have the gun pointed upward, so they will fall through the *barrel* (19) to the *shot follower* (17) and into the *magazine* (15). The magazine in a gun is the place where bullets are kept for use as needed. This BB gun need not be loaded every time. It will continue to fire as long as there are BBs in the magazine. One BB at a time will drop into the *firing chamber* (13).

Now you pull back the *handhold* (16). This forces back two *cocking levers* (8) and (14). These move a *cocking arm* (7) that is attached to the *trigger* (3) by a *safety bar* (4). At the same time they move a *piston* (10) that compresses the *spring* (9) and later compresses air in the *chamber* (11). The cocking arm forces back a *plunger* (5) and hooks it over the top of a *sear* (2). The *stock* (1) is placed against the shoulder; the gun is aimed by lining up the *sights* (20) and (6); and the trigger is pulled. This releases the spring, which flies forward and pushes the compressed air through a small hole in the *air tube* (12), and forces the BB out through the *shooting barrel* (18).

Daisy Manufacturing Co.

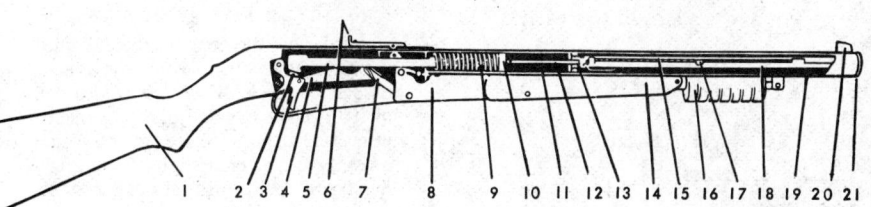

I   2 3 4 5 6 7   8   9 10 11 12 13 14 15 16 17 18 19 20 21

Washington, Philadelphia, and New York for the U.S. Post Office; this service was extended to Chicago in 1919 and to San Francisco in 1920. Until 1924 the mail planes flew only by day, transferring their pouches to trains at night.

By the Carey Act of 1925, Congress authorized the carrying of airmail by private airlines. Payments made under this Act helped greatly to advance the aviation industry in the United States. By 1976, the U.S. Post Office sent about 51 billion airmail letters each year. The cost of sending an airmail letter in the United States was originally 24 cents; since 1928 it has ranged from 5 to 17 cents an ounce. In 1958, the price became 7 cents. By 1976, it had risen to 17 cents. The cost of sending airmail overseas depends upon the distance it is sent.

like firearms, but the principle of the air gun is an old one, going back to the blowguns of savage tribes in Africa, South America, and Malaya. The most popular modern air gun is the air rifle or "BB gun"; but air pistols are popular for target-shooting and also for self-protection, especially in states where it is not legal to keep a regular pistol. Air guns, though dangerous, seldom kill anything larger than small game.

BLOWGUN. The blowgun is a long reed or hollowed rod, sometimes as long as seven feet. A slender dart is put in one end. The user closes his lips over the other end and blows suddenly and violently. The momentary compression of air behind the dart sends it out with great speed.

AIR RIFLE. As with the blowgun, the basic principle is the momentary compression of air. A spring, released by a trigger, forces air through a small hole directly behind a piece of metal shot, which is a small pellet of lead or brass. The momentary or sudden compression of the air builds up enough force to send the shot for distances of 150 to 300 feet. Often the shot used is size "BB," which is about $^{18}/_{100}$ths of an inch in diameter (written .18"); that is, five BBs in a row would measure almost an inch. An air rifle can drive a BB with enough force to kill small game or penetrate an inch of wood at close range. Boys' air rifles use somewhat smaller shot. The most powerful air rifles take .22 caliber bullets or even larger, but air rifles have never proved to be useful in warfare. They are popular for target practice. See the illustration on the preceding page for explanation of the air rifle's mechanism.

FRANKLIN PISTOL. The Franklin pistol propels shot of .177" to .22" caliber with enough force to kill small game. It does not use a spring for momentary compression of air. Instead it has a reservoir or chamber of compressed air, with a pump for maintaining the air pressure. When the trigger is pulled, air is released from the chamber to the barrel.

On the same principle are various pistols and rifles that are classed as air guns but do not actually use compressed air, using instead another gas such as carbon dioxide. A cartridge of the gas, highly compressed, is mounted on the gun.

airlift

An airlift is the use of airplanes to transport all necessary food and supplies to an entire large group, such as an army or the people of a city. The most famous airlift was from April 1, 1948, to September 30, 1949, when United States and British cargo planes supplied West Berlin, the Allied part of Berlin, Germany, with both food and fuel. About two million people live in West Berlin. Altogether the planes carried 2,343,315 tons of food and fuel (chiefly coal) to West Berlin. At the peak, a plane landed in Berlin every three minutes and six thousand tons were landed every day.

Although the United States, Britain and France controlled the western part of Berlin, the entire city lies within East Germany, controlled by Soviet Russia. The airlift became necessary when Russia refused to let freight be moved into West Berlin by railroad or truck. This blockade was probably begun because Russia was angered by the Marshall Plan and later by the use of new currency, the westmark, in West Berlin. Russia gave up the blockade finally because the airlift was so successful that the blockade had little effect. See the article on BERLIN.

There are frequent nonmilitary or peacetime uses of an airlift to supply groups marooned by heavy snows, when roads and rail lines are closed; and often there are airlifts planned in advance, for example to supply mountain-climbing parties. In these cases the supplies are dropped by parachute.

air mail

One of the earliest uses of aviation was to carry mail. A letter can now be carried to almost anywhere in the world by regular airmail and reaches its destination from one day to several weeks earlier than it could if it were carried by land or ship. Since the late 1930s, nearly all important mail that must travel several hundred miles or more has been sent by airmail.

Mail was first carried by air in 1870, when the French capital, Paris, was besieged by German troops and the French used balloons to send messages out of the city. Airmail as a regular postal service originated in the United States. In 1918, U.S. Army planes carried mail between

airplane

The airplane is the most widely used of all aircraft. Except for some use of helicopters and very rare use of balloons and blimps, airplanes do all the work of military, commercial and private aviation.

Nearly all airplanes are designed to be land-based: that is, to land on a flying field or perhaps the deck of an aircraft carrier. A relatively small number of planes are made to land on water. These are called *seaplanes;* or, if they can land either on water or on land, they are called *amphibians.* They differ from land-based airplanes only in their landing gear, as explained below.

In 1971 it was estimated that there were about 350,000 airplanes in the world, about 135,000 of them in the United States and about 85,000 of them in the Soviet Union. Billions of dollars are spent each year for the manufacture of new airplanes. About half this amount is spent by the United States on the production of new military aircraft.

Airplanes vary in size from the small private plane with a wingspread of less than 20 feet and powered by an engine of 100 horsepower or even less, to the giant bombers with wingspread of more than 200 feet and jet powerplants producing more than 60,000 horsepower. But the basic principles of all airplanes are the same. They fly because of the lift they derive from their wings, as explained in the article FLIGHT; their basic parts are the engine, or powerplant; the fuselage or body; the wings, tail, controls, and landing gear.

AIRPLANE ENGINES

Two types of airplane engine are used: the reciprocating or conventional engine, which is an internal-combustion engine that works on the same principle as an automobile engine; and the jet engine. These are described in the articles on the INTERNAL COMBUSTION ENGINE and on the JET ENGINE.

Since 1951 all important military planes have used jet engines, and since 1953 there has been increasing use of jet engines in the larger transport planes or airliners. But the conventional gasoline-burning engine is used on all small planes.

Airplane engines deliver much more power per pound than automobile engines. An airplane engine must deliver at least one horsepower, and usually more, for each pound it weighs. Automobile engines can supply at the most one-third of one horsepower per pound.

Normally an automobile hardly ever uses more than 25 to 35 percent of its full horsepower. An airplane needs its full horsepower for takeoffs and climbs, and normally cruises at 65 percent of its power capacity. The biggest problem in building airplane engines is finding metals that are strong enough to stand the high heat and pressure (especially in the case of the jet engines) and which at the same time are light enough. Various alloys of aluminum, nickel, chromium, and steel are most commonly used in constructing airplane engines.

THE FUSELAGE

The body, or fuselage, is usually long and narrow—to provide less resistance to the wind. It may be large, so that many passengers may be carried inside, as in an airliner, or small, so that only a pilot is carried, as in a fighter plane. The pilots' seats are usually placed on the top side and toward the front, so that the pilot may see better. Cargo when carried also goes in the fuselage.

Long ago, in the early days of flying, the fuselage was merely a framework of wood with cloth stretched over it. Metals had not been developed that were light enough, especially since the engines of those days were not very powerful. But for 30 years and more, fuselages have been made all of metal, usually some alloy of aluminum.

Usually there is only one fuselage but the U. S. Air Force F-82 of 1953 had two fuselages, and the C-119 had a fuselage that split into two booms as it neared the tail.

THE WINGS

A very important part of the airplane is the wing, for the air blowing over the wings produces the lift by which the plane rises or flies. At the outer ends of the wings are the *ailerons,* by which the pilot keeps the plane level, banks it, or rolls it. Also located on the wings are the *flaps.* By using them the pilot can make the plane climb or glide more steeply.

The wings often contain the gas tanks. Wings are usually attached at about the middle of the fuselage, except in small planes and flying boats with high wings they are farther forward.

There is usually only one wing on each side, attached near the bottom of the fuselage, where it will not interfere with the pilot's view. Every plane with one wing on each side is called a monoplane.

The engines for multi-engine planes are located on the forward edge of the wings or just beneath them. If a plane has only a single engine it is located at the front end of the fuselage. Those with rear propellers are *pushers.* Engines may be all jet, all conventional or propeller engines, or a combination of the two.

THE TAIL

Another necessary part of the airplane is the empennage or tail section. This is attached to the back of the fuselage and is composed of two parts. The part that stands upright is called the *fin.* Hinged to the back of the fin is the *rudder.* It steers the plane to either side. The fixed horizontal part is called the *horizontal stabilizer.* It helps the wings and ailerons keep the plane level. Hinged to the back of the horizontal stabilizer is the *elevator,* which steers the airplane up and down.

THE LANDING GEAR

There are two types of landing gear: conventional, with which the plane sits in a three-point attitude on the ground with tail down; and tricycle, with which the airplane rests in a level position. By 1953, all planes being manufactured, except for a few small types, were of the tricycle type. This arrangement enables the pilot to see better while taxiing, since the plane is level.

Most landing gears are also retractable. That is, they can be drawn up into the fuselage while the plane is airborne, so as to reduce drag and thus gain higher speeds. (In 1949, the British Navy began experimenting with planes without landing gear, since without the additional weight greater performance could be obtained. They landed them on rubber mats on carriers, and catapulted them for take-off.)

The seaplane differs from the land

plane in landing gear. The bottom of the seaplane's fuselage is shaped like a boat's hull so it can land and take off from water. Some seaplanes, instead of having hulls, have one or two pontoons attached to the bottom of the fuselage.

The amphibian is a plane that may use either land or water to take off or land. It usually has a hull with wheels attached on the outside or inside of it, and the pilot may lower the wheels if he wants to come down on land.

AIRPLANE MANUFACTURE

Airplanes are manufactured, much the same as automobiles are, on a mass production basis. They are constructed of lightweight metals. Joints are riveted instead of being welded, because that gives them greater strength. From drawing board to the first test flight sometimes takes a long time; for the Air Force's B-52 it was eight years.

DEVELOPMENT OF THE AIRPLANE

The airplane grew out of experiments with the GLIDER, about which there is a separate article. Men who had experimented with gliders long before the year 1900 knew that the airplane was theoretically possible, but there was no engine efficient enough to supply the proper proportion of high horsepower and low weight. Airplanes first became practical when the gasoline engine was developed in the 1890s, and nearly every advancement since has been made possible by the development of more powerful engines. The known principles of aerodynamics plus the gasoline engine were combined by the brothers Orville Wright and Wilbur Wright in the first attested airplane flight, of 59 seconds, at Kitty Hawk, North Carolina, on December 17, 1903.

The Wright brothers' plane and other early planes were *biplanes,* having a tier of two wings. By 1925 aerodynamic testing had proved that the second wing was unnecessary and the *monoplane* soon replaced the biplane. The most famous early monoplane was the *Spirit of St. Louis,* in which Charles A. Lindbergh made the first solo nonstop flight across the Atlantic in 1927.

Multi-engined planes were made as early as 1910, when the Wright brothers mounted two engines on a plane to increase power (and increase the payload) and also for safety purposes, to permit the plane to continue in flight if one engine failed. A German plane designed in 1929, the DO-X, was able to triple the size of the largest plane then existing by using six engines, but the extra engines did not increase the payload enough to justify the additional cost. The first plane designed as a commercial passenger plane, the Ford Tri-motor of 1926, had three engines, one at the nose and one on each wing. By 1932, two-engined planes had been found to be more efficient, and by the end of the 1930s, the largest planes had been more or less standardized with four engines; there has been no change from this general pattern except for some six- and eight-motor planes and except that the U.S. Air Force's B-36 bomber of 1947 had six conventional engines plus four jet engines. Horsepower increased in fifty years from

The United States Air Force's C-133 Cargomaster.

U.S. Air Force

The Boeing Company

The huge Boeing 747, shown here in production, can comfortably accommodate more than 360 passengers.

The FB-111 is a jet bomber used by the United States Strategic Air Command. It carries either nuclear or non-nuclear weapons, and can fly faster than twice the speed of sound. (Sound travels about 1 mile every five seconds.)

U.S. Air Force

the 12 h.p. of the Wright brothers' 1903 engine to more than 4,000 h.p. in the largest 1953 engines; but by that time jet engines were delivering the equivalent of 16,000 h.p. (10,000 lbs. thrust).

Speed increased regularly on a similarly rapid scale. The Wright brothers' 1903 speed of 30 miles per hour became more than 300 m.p.h. for many 1953 airliners, more than 500 m.p.h. for the fastest gasoline-powered military planes, and supersonic speeds, often more than 1,000 m.p.h., for the fastest jet planes. By 1958 the fastest planes were designed for twice and three times the speed of sound. The increase in speed was due to improvements in nearly every aspect of airplane design and manufacture. Greater knowledge of aerodynamics, derived chiefly from wind-tunnel tests, led to better streamlining to reduce air resistance, improved wing design to increase lift, and improved propellers that produced stronger thrust. Gradual increase in the airplane's "ceiling"—the highest altitude at which it can fly—helped make greater speeds possible, for at such heights air resistance is less. For passenger comfort at altitudes of 10,000 to 30,000 feet, the *pressurized cabin* was developed, tightly sealed and with inside pressure built up to nearly that of sea level, by an air compressor. For still higher altitudes, aviators wear pressurized suits. Metallurgists developed metals that would withstand greater heat, making possible superchargers and jet engines, and also providing the strength required to withstand the stresses at supersonic speeds. Far more powerful fuels were developed. (See AVIATION and AIR FORCE, U.S.).

air plant

Any plant that obtains all its food from air and sunlight alone is called an air plant, or *epiphyte*. Air plants need no soil, taking all their moisture from the atmosphere. They are found chiefly in tropical regions where the air is very humid, but they grow also in colder climates. Air plants often fasten themselves to other plants, but they are not parasites. They take nothing from the "host" plant on which they grow, merely using it (or sometimes a rock) for support. Most air plants have no roots but some have air-roots that absorb moisture from the air or from water that lies in hollows on the host plant or rock.

There are many different kinds of air plants. They include varieties of ferns, mosses, lichens, algae, bromiliads, and a few orchids. Some South American air orchids grow at altitudes of 2,000 to 7,000 feet. The Mexican Cattleya orchid grows on rocks and low trees, about eight feet above the ground, facing north or on the north side of a hill. Other types grow in the shade on river banks or in deep, damp woods.

The name *air plant* is sometimes applied to a plant that is also called *life plant* or *floppers*. Its flowers are greenish or yellowish-white with purple tints on the outside, and it has reddish petals.

air pocket

An airplane flying through the air will often hit a "bump," or air pocket. These bumps are sometimes frightening

to inexperienced travelers, but they are not dangerous. An air pocket is a current of air that causes the plane to rise or fall very suddenly, sometimes only a few feet, sometimes fifty feet or more.

Hot air rises because it is lighter than cool air. When the ground below the plane is very hot, the warm air from the ground will rise, which causes the cool air to rush downward and carry the plane down with it. Also, moving air tends to follow the earth's surface. As a plane approaches a mountain it may hit a rising current that will bump it upward, and as it passes the top of a mountain it is likely to hit a descending current of air and to bump downward with this current. Descending currents of air, causing air pockets, will also be found near thunderstorms, because warm air will be rising.

airport

An airport is a place built for the takeoff and landing of airplanes and for all the services needed by those who use airplanes or work in aviation. A modern airport must have all of the following:

1. The airfield itself: Runways on which the planes land and take off; taxiways leading from the runways to the hangars and buildings; a control tower; beacon, warning lights, runway lights, etc.

2. All the equipment needed by skilled men who guide and inform the pilots, such as radio, radar, weather and map rooms, etc., and offices for the men and equipment.

3. Hangars and machine shops for repairs.

4. Freight depots and, except for some military airports, passenger terminals.

Even for a fair-sized city, several square miles are needed for an airport; a very big city usually requires about ten square miles, for otherwise the runways cannot be made long enough for the largest transcontinental and overseas planes. Largest of all must be the military airfields on which heavy bombers can land.

The modern airport came into being about 1935, but no airport built before World War II is large enough for the big transport planes and increased passenger traffic of the 1970s. Nearly every big city in the world has built a new airport or has rebuilt its previous airport since World War II. In most cases it was necessary to build a new airport in a new location, farther from the city, because the space required (several thousand acres) either is not available close to a city or is too expensive.

In 1960, there were about 6,881 airports in the United States, divided about as follows (approximate figures): municipal airports, 2,500; commercial, 1,750; limited use (private but with public not prohibited), 1,375; military, 375; private, 500.

Airports are divided by the Civil Aeronautics Administration into seven classes, as follows:

CLASS OF AIRPORT	LENGTH OF RUNWAYS
Personal and secondary	1500–3000 ft.
Feeder	3000–3500 ft.
Trunkline	3500–4200 ft.
Express	4200–5000 ft.
Continental	5000–5900 ft.
Intercontinental	5900–7000 ft.
Intercontinental express	7000–8400 ft.

On military airports serving jet bombers, far longer runways are needed—more than 10,000 feet. New York's Kennedy Airport has runways 9,500 feet long.

The above runway lengths are for sealevel airports; at higher altitudes they must be longer.

THE RUNWAYS

First of all, strong runways are needed. Most modern planes are too heavy to land in grass fields, as their wheels would sink into the ground and upset them. The biggest transport and military planes weigh 100,000 pounds or more—equal to about forty automobiles —so the runways must be stronger even than highways.

Normally the length of a runway is about 6,000 feet, though they may be as short as 4,000 feet or as long as 10,000 feet. The width is usually about 200 feet, though at military fields they are about 300 feet wide so that small planes can land on either side. This way, a group of planes can land or take off more quickly.

Planes could land on shorter runways; the extra length is for safety. Pilots say: "The first third (of the runway) is to land on, the second third to taxi on, and the last third is life insurance." Planes can usually take off and land in one-third to one-half of a 6,000-foot runway. Jet planes require somewhat more space, since they accelerate and decelerate more slowly. Most multi-engine planes have reversible propellers (propellers that can be made to push the plane backwards and so help it to stop) and also brakes on the wheels, so they can land in even shorter space.

Planes always land and take off into the wind, for reasons explained in the article on PILOTING; so at any airport there are as many runways, usually five, as there are directions from which the wind is likely to blow. Runways are numbered by the first two digits of their magnetic compass heading. A runway that is on a course of 320 magnetic would be called 32, and the number is painted at the end of the runway. Also, the length of the runway is painted on it and is shown by means of a white painted bar for each 1,000 feet, big enough so that the pilot can read it from the air. Other marks are painted at the one-third and two-third distances. For planes without radios a tetrahedron (△) which may be moved by the wind or mechanically, or a wind sock, tells the direction of the wind.

At the large fields there are always several fire trucks, a crane, and an ambulance for use in case the pilot has an accident while he is landing or taking off. If the plane catches fire, or if anyone has been hurt in the crash, help is right there waiting.

To get to the runway from the hangars, parking areas, or passenger terminal, there is a taxiway, which is just like a driveway for a car.

THE TOWER

Every large field has a central tower in which one or more men direct the traffic of planes at the field. When a pilot wishes to taxi from his parking place, he calls the tower on his radio, and the tower tells him which runway to use, the one that is most nearly in line with the direction of the wind. The man in the tower also tells him the altimeter setting—the barometric pressure at the moment. (See the BAROMETER article.) The altimeter is the instrument for telling how high he is above sea level. He sets the current barometric pressure, and if the airport is 100 feet above sea level, since he is on the airport, his altimeter, when set correctly, will also tell him that. When the pilot gets to the starting end of the runway, after he has warmed up the plane and checked to see that everything about the plane is working right, he asks the tower for permission to take off, and if no one else is landing or taking off, the tower tells him to go ahead.

The procedure is just reversed for landing. The pilot calls when he is about ten minutes away from the airport. Landing planes have priority, since they are usually low on fuel when returning. The tower gives the pilot instructions on his radio where and when to land. The men in the tower also have a gun that shoots colored lights, by which they can give more instructions to the pilot.

Planes without radios or at least without receivers usually don't land at crowded airports, because it is too hard for them to get directions.

HELPS TO LANDING

At night the runways are lit up with a row of white lights on each side, except that the sidelights for some hundreds of feet at each end of the runway are amber, or yellow, so that pilots will know they are coming to the end. There are four red lights across each end, and the taxiways have blue lights. Only the runway in use is lighted, and the control tower tells the pilot by radio the direction from which he should approach this runway. Planes without radio learn the proper direction from the "sock," which is lighted at night.

Airports also have blind-landing devices that guide the pilot from some position over or near the airport to the end of the runway when he is unable to see it because of bad weather. Several such devices are used. One is GCA, Ground Control Approach, in which men in a truck located about halfway down on the side of the runway use radar to guide or "talk" the pilot down; another is ILS, Instrument Landing System, which is a series of radios that transmit signals to an instrument in the plane by which the pilot can guide himself down. By 1958, both the U.S. Air Force and the principal airlines had dropped both these methods for RAPCON, Radar Approach Control, which by radar gives the pilot a "view" of how he is approaching the field.

"OPERATIONS"

In addition there is at every airport a place which is most commonly called "operations." This provides information on three things: weather, navigation, and clearance.

At the weather desk a pilot can find out the weather where he is going, and all along the way. He then can tell whether he will have to direct his plane

by instruments, or whether he can do it by merely watching the ground.

At the navigation table he figures out the compass heading to fly, allowing for any wind present, and also the time it will take him. Thus he knows whether he will have enough fuel, since he already knows how much the plane uses per hour.

Finally there is the clearance desk. This is operated by the Civil Aeronautics Administration, or CAA, the branch of the United States government that operates the *airways* (described in the article AIR TRANSPORTATION).

The pilot must "file a clearance," that is, he must fill out a form giving his destination, route, and other details of the flight he plans, if he is going to use IFR, Instrument Flight Rules. This means he will be flying in the clouds without looking at the ground, relying on his instruments to tell him where he is and whether he is on his correct course. When the CAA "clears" his flight—gives him permission to go ahead—it keeps a record of the flight and will not permit another flight on the same course at the same time, so that two planes will not bump into each other.

During the first twenty years of commercial aviation it was considered unnecessary for a pilot to clear a flight on which he would fly VFR, Visual Flight Rules, meaning that he would be able to see the ground and the surrounding air at all times. Then a series of midair collisions forced the entire question to be reëxamined. But experienced pilots have always made it a practice to file their flight plans anyway, even for VFR flights. One advantage is that the flight plan gives the expected time of arrival, and if a plane is an hour or more overdue the CAA begins to look for it.

THE HANGARS

Large airports also have hangars, or large garages, where planes may be stored and repaired. There are also parking spaces outside of the hangars, either concrete or asphalt, where planes may be tied down, since small planes are easily blown by the wind.

THE TERMINAL

Passenger airports have in addition a building called a terminal, where passengers buy tickets, check their baggage, and get on and off the planes. Restaurants and stores are often found there, just as they are in railroad stations. There is usually a post office for the government. There are also places to handle air cargo or freight.

At military fields there are places for the officers and men to live and eat, plus recreational facilities.

SEA AIRPORTS

Water airports, or "sea ports," are the same as land airports except that the runways are the water, which is marked out by buoys. There are also concrete ramps on which a plane may taxi out of the water if it is an amphibian (a plane that has wheels as well as a hull or float), or if the plane is made so that wheels can be attached to it while it is still in the water, so that

it may be towed out. Most seaplanes are made this way. In addition, a small boat patrols the water runways, taking away logs and other debris that would punch holes in a hull or pontoon and make the seaplane sink.

SOME AIRPORT RULES

Civilian planes are forbidden to land at military airports unless they are in some kind of trouble, lost, almost out of gas, or having engine trouble, and can't make it to a civilian field, or if they have special permission beforehand from the commanding officer of the field. Military planes, however, can land at any airport that is large enough, and at any military airport.

A private plane is charged a fee for landing at an airport, much as a private automobile is charged at a garage. The fee may range from a few dollars to $50 or more, depending on the size of the airport and the size of the plane.

Information a pilot may need about airports, such as field elevation, radio frequencies, location, and so on, can be found in charts put out by the government.

See also AIR TRANSPORTATION.

airpower

A nation's airpower is its total strength in aviation, which it can use to wage war. Airpower was not important in warfare until the 1930s, but then it became clear that airpower would control every future war.

Three things make up a nation's airpower: 1, the number of actual warplanes it has; 2, its transport planes, including those owned by airlines; 3, its production capacity, which includes factories, raw materials, skilled labor and technicians such as engineers. The third was most important in World War II, when Germany had great strength in the air at the start but the United States had superior production capacity and so could overtake Germany. However, the atomic bomb and other nuclear weapons make many experts believe that in any future war a nation's production capacity may be destroyed before it can be used.

AIR WARFARE

In air warfare, a nation uses its airpower in three ways. The first way is called *strategic*. It is the use of bombing planes to destroy the enemy's factories and cities, and his supplies of food, weapons, and ammunition, so that soon he cannot continue fighting. The second way is called *tactical*. That is the use of planes to win a particular battle by destroying the enemy's troops and supplies in the field, by dropping paratroopers, etc. The third way is called *ancillary*, or helping. It is the use of aircraft for transportation of supplies and men, and for observation and photography. In sea warfare, airpower is used for the same purposes.

Throughout World War II it was proved that overwhelming superiority in the air was the deciding factor in any battle and in the war itself. Early in the war Germany defeated France by tactical air warfare, since the French Army without air support was helpless before German forces supported by aircraft. Germany then attempted to conquer Britain by

strategic air warfare, but this failed because German bombers were not able to get through British fighter planes. After gaining air superiority, the United States and Britain rendered Germany helpless by strategic air warfare (constant bombings of Germany's industrial cities) but the final invasions of Germany were made possible by air superiority in tactical air warfare. With the coming of the atomic bomb, strategic air warfare defeated Japan with two bombs dropped in 1945. Sea warfare in World War II was almost entirely a matter of airpower, battles being fought by carrier-based planes far from the battle fleets.

After World War II the United States decided to rely on strategic air warfare and air defense as a protection against future wars—to discourage an enemy attack by the ability to destroy the enemy in an answering attack, and at the same time to make the home air defense strong enough to stop attacking planes. Most experts believed, however, that an enemy attack cannot be stopped and that the threat of retaliation is the only real defense. (See GUIDED MISSILE, ROCKET.)

ORGANIZATION OF AIR FORCES

When it became clear, in the 1930s, that airpower would control future wars, several nations made their air forces independent branches of their armed services. The Royal Air Forces of Great Britain and Canada were among the first. Germany set up its separate air force, the *Luftwaffe*. The United States, however, kept its air forces as a branch of the Army until after World War II, establishing the U.S. Air Force as an independent service in 1947. All countries have kept separate air establishments in their navies.

Military authorities still disagree on the best way to organize the fighting air forces of a country. Some believe that tactical air forces should be controlled by the Army, naval air forces by the Navy, and strategic air forces by the separate Air Force. Their argument is that the commander of an army in the field is handicapped if he must ask an Air Force commander for air support, instead of being able to control it himself.

HISTORY OF AIRPOWER

In World War I there were not enough warplanes and they were not powerful enough to have much effect. Nevertheless, at the end of the war in 1918 many officers were convinced that airpower would become as important as it has actually become. In the United States an Army officer, Brig. Gen. William Mitchell, tried so desperately to convince his superiors of the coming importance of airpower that he was court-martialed for insubordination and was forced out of the Army. An Italian officer, Gen. Giulio Douhet, had more success. In 1924 he wrote a book, *The Command of the Air*, that convinced Italian and later German leaders that airpower would win the next war. The importance of airpower was first tested in the Spanish Civil War of 1936–1939, when Germany and Italy on one side and Russia on the other helped Spanish forces for the purpose of testing their own aircraft and other weapons. The effectiveness of airpower

in Spain forecast the part it was to play in World War II.

See also AIR FORCE.

airship, see AVIATION and BALLOON.

airsickness

Airsickness is temporary discomfort sometimes felt by travelers in airplanes, due to the motion of the aircraft up, down, or sideways, and sometimes due to high speed and rapid acceleration. These may disturb the internal organs of the body because of inertia (natural resistance to a change of position). A sufferer from airsickness may feel nausea, dizziness, or weakness. Airsickness is about the same as seasickness.

Altitude sickness is not the same as airsickness; it is a form of *anoxia* (lack of oxygen) and is caused by high altitudes, usually 15,000 feet or more. The symptoms may be headache, fatigue, nervousness, or weakness. Pressurized cabins almost always prevent altitude sickness.

air transportation and airways

Air transportation is the carrying of paying passengers and freight in aircraft. Commercial air transportation began in the United States in 1927. During the 1930s it became a large business and after World War II it rapidly became the principal form of long-distance passenger transportation; in 1954 it passed railroads in carrying passengers on trips of 200 miles or more, and in 1957 it passed steamships in carrying overseas passengers. Air freight remained a small and specialized branch of air transportation.

Throughout the world air transportation grew at a similarly rapid rate, and in some parts of the world, especially in Africa and Asia where there are few railroads, it became even more important. By the middle 1960s, United States airlines were carrying more than 75,000,000 passengers a year, including about 5,000,-000 overseas passengers. The airlines flew about 40 billion passenger miles compared to about 20 billion passenger miles for railroads. There were about 20,000 scheduled landings and takeoffs each day. Within the United States about 1,850 airliners were used, and international lines operated about 900 airliners.

Except for a few "taxi services" using helicopters on short runs, nearly all air transportation is by airplane. There are three principal types of airplane in use: 1, two-engine and four-engine planes, propeller-driven by "regular" (reciprocating) gasoline engines, and carrying 30 to 90 passengers, the smaller one being used for relatively short distances between cities that do not have the largest airport facilities; 2, the turbo-propeller plane driven by a gas turbine, as in the Vickers Viscount plane, used chiefly for moderate distances less than transatlantic; and 3, turbo-jet, introduced as early as 1953 in the British Comet plane and gradually being put into use at the end of the 1950s, in giant planes designed for 100 or more passengers. Speeds ranged from 300 to 400 miles per hour in the propeller-driven planes and more than 550 miles per hour in the jet planes. The cost per plane ranged from about $500,000 for a two-motor plane such as the Douglas DC-3 to about $2,000,000 for the largest propeller-driven planes such as the Douglas DC-7 used in transcontinental and overseas flights. The first big jet-powered airliner built in the United States, the Boeing 707, cost $15,000,000 and even in production quantities planes of similar size cost more than $4,000,000. In a test flight a jet airliner flew coast to coast (Seattle to Baltimore) in 3 hours 48 minutes. Even with earlier aircraft, the saving in time over railroad or ship travel was 90% or more, except that on relatively short flights the time required to and from the airport, usually about two hours in all, reduced the time advantage of air travel.

AIRWAYS AND REGULATION

In the United States, commercial air transport is subject to regulations made by the Civil Aeronautics Board (CAB), an independent agency of the U.S. government. These regulations are administered by the Civil Aeronautics Administration (CAA), a bureau of the U.S. Department of Commerce.

The CAB establishes safety standards for the operating condition of aircraft, licenses of pilots, proper flying weather, etc. It issues permits to airlines to fly in the United States and it coöperates with foreign authorities to regulate international air transportation. It controls rates and maintains the Federal airways system.

lisions impossible, but modern conditions have produced unexpected problems, as explained later in this article.

The CAA aids all private and commercial aviation. By the middle 1950s it had built up a nationwide network of 300 range stations, 500 position markers, 2,000 beacons, 400 communication stations, and 23 large Airway Traffic Control centers. There were weather-forecast stations at about 275 airports, receiving data from the U.S. Weather Bureau. (The principal airlines use this service but also maintain their own weather offices.) There were about 75,000 miles of low- and medium-frequency radio ranges along the airways and about 60,000 miles using very high frequency (VHF), which was rapidly taking the place of the others.

The CAA equips and operates all control towers, control centers, and Interstate Airway Communications (INSAC) stations.

See also the article AIRPORT.

INTERNATIONAL AIR TRANSPORTATION

An international treaty governing air transportation was made at Paris, France, in 1919. It is called the Paris Convention. In spite of several attempts it has not been replaced by a new treaty. The United States is not a party to the Paris Convention but has adopted its main provisions, including the doctrine that each nation controls the sky over its own territory. Another provision is that in international flights an airline is not liable for more than about $8,000 for the death or injury of any passenger.

In 1947 the International Civil Avia-

John F. Kennedy International Airport in Jamaica, New York (a suburb of New York City).

An airway is an approved flying route from one place to another. It is ten miles wide and is equipped with beacons, radio-range stations and other aids to night or blind flying, and traffic control centers at the chief cities or airports. The airways are considered to be divided into traffic levels, and aircraft flying east or north must fly at odd-numbered altitudes such as 3,000 feet, 7,000 feet, or 15,000 feet (above sea level), etc., while aircraft flying west or south use the even-numbered altitudes such as 4,000 feet, 16,000 feet, etc. Theoretically this makes head-on col-

tion Organization was founded by the United Nations, and through its efforts nearly all nations coöperate in safety and traffic-control methods, but this organization has no power to enforce any regulations.

TRAFFIC AND SAFETY PROBLEMS

Scheduled airliners make more than 97% of their scheduled flights. The death and injury record of the airlines is almost as good as that of railroads, and insurance companies charge the same rates for life and accident insurance on

airliners and railroads. On the average, fatality rates (deaths in air travel) are about 0.6 per 100 million passenger miles, compared to 0.1 for railroads. In international travel the airline rate is 0.1. The rate is 2.5 for passenger automobiles.

Nevertheless the air traffic problem has become almost as great as the problem of automobile traffic. There are three reasons. First is the increased number of planes in the air. At times during the day a much-traveled course, for example between New York City and Washington, D.C., is used by one hundred or more planes every hour; they are less than a minute's flying time apart. The second reason is the increased speed of planes. In that single minute or less a plane travels several miles and a slight miscalculation of wind or position can bring together two planes that are supposed to be ten miles or more apart. Third, military planes are not subject to CAA rules; their flights are often secret, for security reasons; and they are mostly jets, traveling at such speeds that even on a clear day they may not be seen in time to avoid a collision. An increasing number of collisions during the 1950's led to constant study of the problem of keeping the airways safe. Also, there is now strict security at all airports because of the hijacking of airplanes by terrorists.

Increased traffic has also created problems in meeting time schedules. An airliner often arrives at its destination on time but must then circle the airfield for thirty minutes or more before its turn to land comes.

FIRST-CLASS AND AIR-COACH TRAVEL

The airline passenger has a choice between first-class travel and air-coach (or tourist) travel. First-class travel is much more expensive. It is often a bit faster, but seldom more than a few minutes—perhaps as much as an hour on long trips. The difference is that in first-class travel there are fewer seats in the plane, and the passenger has more leg room (which may be important to big men but seldom to women and children); the first-class service includes meals served free if the traveling time is the same as a regular mealtime; and the first-class planes often take off and land at hours that are considered more convenient. There are a few other differences.

On overseas flights, first-class and tourist passengers travel in different sections of the same plane and there is almost no difference except that the first-class section provides more room per passenger. In 1958 a new service was put into effect, the "economy" class, with rates even lower than the tourist class and little difference in accommodations.

SCHEDULED AND NONSCHEDULED LINES

First-class service is offered only by the scheduled airlines. Tourist or air-coach service is offered by both the scheduled and nonscheduled airlines. The difference between these two types of airline is just what their names say. The CAA (Civil Aeronautics Administration) authorizes the scheduled airlines to land and take off at certain airports, to fly certain routes, and to have prearranged regular schedules for taking off, just like a railroad's.

The nonscheduled airlines, or nonskeds, as they are called, are not allowed to provide regular service. They must wait until they have a planeload of passengers for a particular destination and then take off. Nonskeds usually operate between places that are fairly far apart; for instance, from coast to coast, with one stop in the middle, or the length of a coast, as from New York to Miami.

Some people believe that the nonskeds are not as safe as the scheduled airlines. This is only partially true and only then as to some of the smaller nonskeds. The larger and wealthier nonskeds are in some cases even larger than the smallest of the scheduled airlines. The CAA requires all airlines, scheduled or nonscheduled, to maintain certain minimum standards as to the pilot qualifications, plane maintenance or repair, the load the plane may carry, and the weather conditions under which they may fly. But the airlines with large amounts of capital go far beyond these standards set by the CAA, because it helps them to give better service and maintain a better safety record. For financial reasons the smaller airlines—mostly nonskeds—are sometimes not able to go so far. They must, of course, comply with the minimum standards.

First-class airline rates in the 1950s average 6 to 8 cents per mile in domestic travel and 15 cents in overseas travel. These were only slightly higher than railroad and steamship rates.

RESERVATIONS

For all air travel, unlike railroad travel, the rule is that the passenger must make a reservation in advance. However a passenger can almost always get a seat at the last minute if he is at the airport. It is necessary to make reservations a little further in advance for tourist flights than for first-class flights.

Passengers are allowed 40 to 60 pounds of personal baggage free; on international flights the allowance is 66 pounds first class and 44 pounds tourist. Any excess baggage must be paid for at the rate of ½ of 1 per cent of the fare per pound, thus making it very expensive to carry excess baggage.

AIR FREIGHT

Freight, express and airmail are carried by both airliners and cargo planes. The largest use of air freight is in hauling goods that are perishable and would be harmed by a long railroad or truck haul. Some businesses have candy, fresh flowers, seafood, and some kinds of fruit regularly delivered by air. Air freight is widely used in emergencies to transport various articles needed quickly.

CHARTER SERVICE

One further service that is available in air transportation is the charter plane. Just as one would charter a bus, a plane may be chartered. Both private companies and the scheduled and nonscheduled airlines provide this service.

Aisne

Aisne is the name of a department (which is like a large county) in northeast France, near the border of Belgium. It is also the name of a river, 175 miles long, that runs through this county. Several great battles have been fought along this river, including one in 58 B.C. when Julius Caesar defeated the Gauls. During World War I, in April 1917 French forces made a great attack along the Aisne but failed; there were 118,000 casualties. In May 1918 the Germans made their last great attack on the Aisne. They got across the river and almost reached Paris. Troops from the United States and Canada, as well as from the other Allies, finally drove them back. A few months later the Germans admitted defeat and the armistice was signed.

AISNE. Area, 2,868 square miles. Population, 526,346. Capital, Laon, population 25,623.

Ajax

In Homer's famous story of the TROJAN WARS (about which there is a separate article), there were two Greek warriors named Ajax. One, "Ajax the Greater," was second only to Achilles as a warrior. When Achilles died, Ajax wanted his armor; but it was given instead to Ulysses and Ajax killed himself. The other Ajax, "Ajax the Less," was second only to Achilles as a swift runner. This Ajax offended the gods and they killed him with lightning.

Akbar

Akbar, or Jelaled-din Mohammed, was one of the great emperors of Hindustan or India. He was born in 1542 and died in 1605. The name Akbar means "the Great" in Arabic. Akbar enlarged his original realm, Delhi, combining it with numerous small states. He built roads, introduced a relatively modern system of taxation, and standardized weights and measures; and he encouraged the arts and sciences, especially literature. Akbar was Mohammedan but was tolerant of other religions and established schools for both Hindus and Moslems. He was descended from Tamerlane.

Akron

Akron is a city in northern Ohio. It is called "the rubber capital of the world" because so many of the biggest rubber manufacturers have their factories and headquarters there. In early days, the Indians' freight route ran through the site of Akron and it was a station on the old Indian Portage Path.

AKRON, OHIO. Population 275,425; urban area, 553,371 (1970 census). County seat of Summit County. On the Little Cuyahoga River. Settled 1807.

Alabama

Alabama is a state in the "deep south" of the United States. Its nickname is "the Cotton State," and at one time almost everybody in Alabama lived on the cotton crop. Now other crops are just as important to Alabama as cotton is, and manufacturing is more important than agriculture.

The name Alabama came from an Indian word, perhaps from a tribe of Indians, the Alabamas, in whose language the word alabama meant farmer; but this is not surely known.

About 7,000 square miles in central Alabama, around Birmingham, the state's largest city, hold the richest iron and coal deposits in the South. Birmingham ranks third in the United States in steel production (behind Pittsburgh and Chicago). Another great industrial development, built more recently, is along the Tennessee River in the northern part. The southern part of Alabama is a rich farming section. During the 1960s Alabama produced about $5,373,000,000 worth of mined and manufactured goods each year and about $749,600,000 in agricultural products.

Alabama's biggest industries, next to steel, are textiles (cloth, yarn, and clothing, principally of cotton but including plastics such as rayon), and chemicals. The chief agricultural product next to cotton comes from the trees, which are cut for lumber, papermaking, and other purposes.

In population, Alabama ranks 21st in the United States, with three and a half million people living there. In area it ranks 28th, having 50,708 square miles. It became a state in 1819, and was the 22nd state admitted to the United States. The capital is Montgomery.

THE PEOPLE OF ALABAMA

In Alabama there are about two million white people and about one million Negroes.

Most of the two million white people of Alabama were born there, as were their parents and grandparents. Alabama was one of the Confederate States that fought against the Union, or North, in the Civil War of 1861–65, and the capital of Alabama, Montgomery, for a short time was capital of the Confederacy. Southern feeling is still very strong among the white people of Alabama; the Confederate flag is often seen displayed and there are many monuments to soldiers who died in the Confederate armies.

Most of the million Negroes work on farms or are laborers in factories. For many years the Negroes were very poor. They lived in one-room cabins in the country, and in the cities they lived in small, shabby houses called shanties. They did not usually have bathrooms or running water or electric lights. Since World War II the Negroes have earned more money and they now live much better than they did before, but they are still poorer than most of the white people.

The churches are very important in the social life of people in Alabama. Nearly everyone goes to Sunday School and to church, and especially in the smaller towns people have their clubs and parties and picnics through their churches.

WHAT THE STATE IS LIKE

The southern, the central and the northern parts of Alabama are quite different.

The southern part is the "Black Belt" section. At the very southern end, of course, Alabama has a seacoast—a very short one, where long, deep, Mobile Bay runs north from the Gulf of Mexico to the city of Mobile, second-biggest city in the state. Near the seacoast there is sandy soil, as there usually is near the ocean; and there are forests of pecan and other

The governor's mansion in Montgomery, built in 1900, is one of the capital city's show places.

Alabama Bureau of Publicity and Information

trees; and there are swamps and marshes where many alligators live. A few miles above this region begins a "belt" of rich, black topsoil, twenty to fifty miles or more wide. This beltlike strip of land winds northward to the central part of the state. It is the blackness of its soil that gave it the name "Black Belt." Once it was considered one of the finest cotton-raising places on earth. But the farmers used to have such bad years when the cotton crop failed, or when cotton prices fell too low, that they now raise peanuts and vegetables and other crops, as well as cotton, and they are much better off.

The central part of the state is called the "Coal Mountain" section. Driving through this part, one is likely to see coal miners with axes on their shoulders and lamps on the fronts of their caps. There is much iron ore in those mountains and other valuable minerals.

The northern part of Alabama is the "Tennessee Valley" section. The Tennessee River enters Alabama in the northeast corner, flows all the way across the state, and in the northwest corner flows back into the state of Tennessee.

Northern Alabama is very beautiful. The river flows through the Cumberland Plateau (a plateau is a region that is high, like a mountain, but level, like a plain). On both sides of the river, as it flows through the state, hills and mountains rise. Many "mountaineers" live in these hills, as they do in the mountains of Kentucky and Tennessee and several other Southern states.

Less than a lifetime ago, northern Alabama was nothing more than farming country, and much of it was not even much good for farming. Too much of the good soil had washed away. Then, in 1933, the Tennessee Valley Authority of

the United States Government began to develop the river. Beginning at a part of the river called Muscle Shoals, which was a long section of rapids where the water flowed so fast and the river was so rocky that no boat could get through, the "TVA" built three great dams—Wilson Dam, Wheeler Dam, and Guntersville Dam. These dams made big lakes where before there had been only the river. Water flowing over the dams turned great generators, producing electricity to run factories and bring electric light and power to cities and farms in several states. The dams also put an end to the terrible floods that for many years had damaged towns and farms along the Tennessee River. After all this was done, northern Alabama began to be as busy and prosperous as the rest of the state.

Many an independent nation could envy the state of Alabama. It is said that the most important things a country can have are fertile farmlands, so it can raise its own food; and forests, for wood; and coal and iron mines, to feed its factories; and rivers that can be dammed to produce electricity and navigated to transport goods; and a seacoast so that it can trade with other countries. Alabama has them all.

The climate, though it often gets uncomfortably hot in the summer, is ideal for farming and cattle-raising.

Besides the Tennessee River in the north, Alabama has several big rivers in the south. Among these are the Coosa, Alabama, Cahaba, Tombigbee, Black Warrior and Tallapoosa Rivers—all but one of them Indian names. The Alabama and Tombigbee run together and form the Mobile River, which flows into Mobile Bay.

Railroads and highways reach nearly

every part of the state.

GOVERNMENT

Alabama, like most states, is governed by a Governor, a Senate, and a Legislature or House of Representatives. The Governor and members of both legislative houses are elected for four-year terms. The Senate is limited to 35 members, the Legislature to 106 members, and they meet every two years for a sixty-day term. They meet in the capital, Montgomery. Judges are elected and serve six-year terms. There are 67 counties in the state.

EDUCATION

Everyone has to go to school between the ages of seven and sixteen at least. There are about four thousand public schools in Alabama. About 826,000 students are enrolled in the public elementary and high schools. Nearly half the students go to big consolidated schools, to which they are taken by school buses.

Alabama is one of the states that have resisted integration of races in the schools (white and black children attending the same school). Today blacks and whites are integrated. See the article on EDUCATION.

Among Alabama's institutions of higher learning, some are free state institutions, while others receive financial aid from the state. Among the principal ones are:

University of Alabama, at University. Enrollment, 12,039 in 1971, both men and women. The medical and dental colleges are in Birmingham.

Alabama College, at Montevallo. Enrollment, 2,400 in 1971, both men and women.

Alabama Agricultural and Mechanical College (for blacks), at Normal. Enrollment 2,184 in 1971.

Tuskegee Institute, at Tuskegee, the world's first and most famous college for Negroes, is partly supported by the state. Enrollment 3,001 in 1971. There is a separate article about TUSKEGEE in a later volume.

Among the principal private colleges are Howard College and Birmingham-Southern college, both at Birmingham. There are State Teachers Colleges at Florence, at Jacksonville, at Livingston, and at Troy.

ALABAMA IN THE PAST

When the Spanish explorer Hernando De Soto first entered what is now Alabama, in the year 1540, it was a land of the Creek and the Choctaw Indians, and De Soto had to fight and win a bloody battle from them before he could cross the state. The battle was fought in what is now Clarke County, and it is said that 11,000 Indians were killed and only 82 of De Soto's Spanish soldiers. An earlier Spanish explorer, Pánfilo de Narváez, had passed through Alabama in 1528. For more than a hundred years after De Soto's time Alabama was inhabited only by Indians. The English and French as well as the Spanish claimed it. From 1699 to 1763, the French held Alabama as part of the Louisiana Territory, and at one time Mobile was the

capital of Louisiana. After 1763 northern Alabama was British, being part of Georgia until 1798 and then part of Mississippi; and southern Alabama was part of Florida and belonged to Spain. In the early 1800s the southern part was acquired by the United States and Alabama with its present boundaries became a state in 1819. Most of the Indians had moved west of the Mississippi River, but the white settlers still had bloody encounters with the Creek Indians until they were moved out in 1836.

By this time Alabama was an important cotton-raising state and the "Black Belt" had many big plantations whose rich owners lived in fine mansions and owned hundred of slaves. Although only a small number of Alabama's people owned slaves, the slave-owners had great power.

When Abraham Lincoln was elected President in 1860, and it appeared that the slaves would be set free, Alabama was one of the southern states that took the lead in seceding from the United States. Alabama seceded on January 11, 1861, the fourth state to do so. The first Confederate capital was Montgomery (until July, 1861, when Richmond, Virginia, was made the capital). During the Civil War Alabama contributed 122,000 men to the Confederate armies, and 35,-000 of them were killed or wounded.

Alabama's cities and farms were badly hurt by Union armies in the Civil War, and after the war Alabama was very poor. "Carpetbaggers" controlled the state government and robbed it of millions. Gradually, the original citizens of the state got control of it back. Alabama was always considered part of the "solid South," meaning that it never voted for anyone but a Democratic candidate for office; but in 1948 it voted for the "Dixiecrat" candidate instead of for President Harry Truman. In 1952 it voted Democratic again.

PLACES TO SEE IN ALABAMA

William B. Bankhead National Forest, 560,604 acres, in the northwest, about 30 miles from Decatur, west of U.S. Route 31. Beautiful forests, where deer roam through the underbrush; a favorite vacation spot for campers and hikers; hundreds of hunters come to the annual deer hunt every November; Natural Bridge is one of the principal scenic attractions.

Talladega National Forest, 200,000 acres, with two divisions in central and eastern Alabama, one on U.S. Route 82 about 45 miles from Selma; the other on U.S. Route 241, near Anniston. Robinson Creek Falls is an outstanding attraction.

Conecuh National Forest, 339,573 acres along the Florida border, on U.S. Route 29; has a large recreational area with a 50-acre lake and picnic grounds.

Cheaha State Park, 2,679 acres, near Anniston, on U.S. Route 241. Contains Cheaha Mountain, the highest point in the state.

De Soto State Park, 4,650 acres, near Mentone, in the northeast, east of U.S. Route 11. Contains many beautiful cascades and waterfalls; famous De Soto Falls, 120-foot waterfall, is outstanding.

Azalea Trail, in Mobile, in the southwest, on U.S. Route 90; a 17-mile road along which magnificent flowers bloom every spring.

Mardi Gras, in Mobile, a colorful celebration on each Shrove Tuesday (the day before Lent). It has been held for the last 250 years.

Boll Weevil Monument, in Enterprise, on U.S. Route 84. Perhaps the only monument in the world erected to an insect. When the boll weevil destroyed the entire cotton crop about 55 years ago, the farmers were forced to plant peanuts, which became such a successful industry that the people erected the Boll Weevil Monument in appreciation.

Mound State Monument, 12 miles from Tuscaloosa, in west central Alabama, east of U.S. Route 11. Made up of 34 Indian mounds, which cover 300 acres; once used by Indians as temples, houses, and community meeting places.

Statue of Vulcan, the Roman god of fire, in Birmingham, on top of Red Mountain. It is 53 ft. high, weighs 60 tons, and stands on a tower 127 feet high; it can be seen by people all over the city.

Ginko Tree, in Selma, in central Alabama, on U.S. Route 80. A rare tree from China that grows through the roof of a cotton warehouse.

Saltpeter Cave, near Scottsboro, in the northeast, on U.S. Route 72. Once a cave-dwelling for Indians; later a temporary courtroom of Jackson County while the first courthouse was being built; Confederate soldiers mined the saltpeter and used it for gunpowder during the Civil War.

The First White House of the Confederacy, in Montgomery, on U.S. Route 80. The home of Jefferson Davis, where he was sworn in as first President of the Confederacy; now a museum with many interesting Civil War relics.

Talladega, in the northeast, on U.S. Route 241. One of the oldest white settlements in the state; near the place where Andrew Jackson fought the Battle of Horseshoe Creek, and defeated the Creek Indians.

Ivy Green, in Tuscumbia, in the northwest, on U.S. Route 72; the birthplace of Helen Keller.

ALABAMA — SUMMARY

Area. 50,708 sq. mi. (28th in U.S.) Greatest length, 330 miles; width, 200 miles. Coastline (on Gulf of Mexico) 53 miles.

Population. 3,539,000 (1973 est.); (21st in U.S.): 2,528,983 white, 908,247 black, 6,935 other races. 58.4% of population in cities. Per capita income $3,724 (1973).

Religion. Predominantly Protestant: Baptist, Methodist, Presbyterian, Episcopal. About 10% Roman Catholic.

General information. Admitted to U.S. Dec. 19, 1819, the 22nd state. *State motto*, We dare defend our rights. *State flower*, Camellia (1959); *tree*, yellow pine or Southern pine; *bird*, yellowhammer. *State song*, "Alabama."

Principal cities (see separate articles): *Capital*, Montgomery (pop. 257,816), in central area. *Largest*, Birmingham (558,099), in central area; Mobile (257,816), in the south; Gadsden (67,706), in the northeast.

Transportation. 5,316 miles of railroads. Navigable rivers: Alabama, Tombigbee, Mobile, Tennessee, Black Warrior.

Commerce. *Agriculture:* chief crops cotton (about 800,000 bales per year), tobacco, corn, rice, sugarcane, peanuts; also truck-farming and fruit-growing. 211,361 farms; 20,500,000 acres, 8,500,000 acres under cultivation. Value of agricultural products (year), $749,600,000. *Industry:* leading products cotton goods, textiles (factories in about 60 cities); iron and steel; lumber products including wood pulp, paper, furniture, railroad ties, fence posts; chemicals, cars, machinery, coke. Annual value of mined and manufactured products, about $5,373,000,000. *Hydroelectric power:* 1,299,000 kilowatts per year (4th in U.S.).

Climate. Temperate; mean temperature in north 60° F., in south 67° F. Annual rainfall, 52 inches; occasional snow in north.

Natural resources. Rich deposits of coal, iron, limestone, sandstone, clay. Extensive forests of oak, hickory, pine, cedar, elm. Fur-bearing animals (fox, mink, rabbit, racoon).

Alabama Claims

During the Civil War, 1861–65, the North (Union) had a large navy; the South (Confederacy) had no warships. The Confederacy bought thirteen warships from Great Britain, the chief one being named the *Alabama,* and the British permitted these ships to leave British ports and attack Union ships at sea. The *Alabama,* under Captain Raphael Semmes, cruised 22 months without ever entering a Confederate port and sank or captured 68 Union ships, until on June 19, 1864, at the port of Cherbourg, France, it was attacked and sunk by the U.S.S. *Kearsage* under Captain John A. Winslow.

After the war the United States claimed damages from Great Britain for its losses, and these were known as the "Alabama Claims." Ambassadors from Italy, Switzerland, Brazil, Great Britain, and the United States (represented by Charles Francis Adams) met in Geneva, Switzerland, in 1871 to settle the dispute and they awarded to the United States $15,500,000, which Great Britain paid.

alabaster

Alabaster is a kind of stone, like marble in appearance but softer. It is used for statues, vases, and other sculpture. There are two kinds of alabaster. One, a variety of gypsum, is white or delicately shaded, semi-translucent, and with a pearly luster. This is the softer alabaster. It is found chiefly in Italy, but some comes from Spain, England, and elsewhere. The other, harder kind, called *Oriental alabaster* or *onyx marble,* is deposited as stalagmites in caves. This alabaster was used in sculpture by the ancient Greeks and Romans. It is a calcium carbonate mineral and is found in Italy and in other countries on the Mediterranean Sea.

Alamo

The Alamo is an old fort in San Antonio, Texas, that was built originally as a Spanish mission, or church, and became the scene of a famous battle. It was built in 1718 by Franciscan priests and was called the Mission of San Antonie de Valero. In 1836, American settlers in Texas were trying to win independence from Mexico, to which Texas belonged at the time. The Mexican General Santa Anna, with an army of more than 3,000 men, was sent to attack the Alamo. A little group of 180 Texas soldiers under Colonel William B. Travis were caught inside the fort. They fought bravely for ten days. When all but a few of the Americans had been killed, those who survived offered to surrender if their lives would be spared. Santa Anna agreed to the condition, but broke his promise and killed them all. Among them were Davy Crockett and James Bowie. The Alamo fell on March 6, 1836. After that the battle cry of Texans fighting for independence was "Remember the Alamo!"

Aland Islands

The Aland Islands are a group of about 6500 islands at the entrance of the Gulf of Bothnia, between Sweden and Finland. They are a department (county) of Finland, but they once belonged to Sweden and most of the people are of Swedish descent. The Alands are important because their many harbors are almost never frozen over. Ice-free harbors are highly advantageous during wartime, and there are not many of them in that part of the world. Finland, Sweden and Russia all wanted the Alands and in 1921 the League of Nations awarded them to Finland but gave the islanders self-government. After World War II, both Finland and Russia agreed never to fortify the harbors.

Only about 80 of the islands are inhabited. Farming and fishing are the chief occupations. The group is named for the largest island, Aland, which is about 285 square miles in area. The name means "land of streams."

ALAND ISLANDS. Area, 1,450 kilometers. Population, 22,787. Capital, Mariehamn, population 9,500.

Alaric

Alaric was a name borne by two kings of the Visigoths, a savage Teutonic (German) people, about 1,500 years ago when the Roman Empire still ruled most of the civilized world and the Germans, whom the Romans called barbarians, fought them constantly.

Alaric I was born about 376. He invaded the Roman Empire several times but was driven out each time by the Roman general, Stilicho. In the year 408, when Stilicho was dead, Alaric surrounded the walled city of Rome and threatened to starve the people to death unless they paid him a ransom. He withdrew after the city paid him. In the year 410 his victorious army entered Rome and his soldiers robbed it for six days. However, he forbade his men to harm women or destroy religious buildings. A few months later he died.

Alaric II became king of the Visigoths in 484. He ruled over all of Spain and part of southern France. The wealth of his lands excited the jealousy of Clovis, king of the Franks, a German people who ruled much of France. Clovis killed Alaric II in a battle at Vouillé, France, in 507, and completely defeated the Visigoth army.

Alaska

Alaska is the northernmost state of the United States, and until the admission of Hawaii in 1959 it was the newest. It is the largest state in area, 2½ times as big as Texas and one-fifth as large as all the rest of the states combined. Alaska was a territory of the United States (not wholly self-governing) until 1958, when an Act of Congress (passed June 30, 1958) approved the admission of Alaska as the forty-ninth state.

Alaska is a peninsula at the extreme northwest of the continent of North America. Its area is 586,400 square miles, and in this vast area there are no more people than in a city the size of Akron, Dayton, or El Paso. Its total population in 1976 was about 325,000 (which included members of the armed services), and it ranks last among the states. Because Alaska contains vast regions that have not been fully explored or settled, it has been given the nickname of The Last Frontier.

The ALEUTIAN ISLANDS, about which there is a separate article, are part of Alaska. With these islands included,

The Alamo can still be seen in San Antonio, Texas. It was built in 1718 by Franciscan (Catholic) priests and was called the Mission of San Antonio de Valero.

San Antonio Chamber of Commerce

An aerial view of Nome, Alaska located on the Seward Penninsula of the Bering Sea. Today it is a barren and desolate village used chiefly as a military base and trade center for western Alaska.

Alaska stretches about 2,000 miles from one end to the other. It is nearly 1,500 miles from Seattle, the nearest big city of the continental United States, to central Alaska. By land it is about 3,000 miles, as far as it is coast-to-coast from New York to California. Alaska's only boundary is with Canada, so it is necessary to cross foreign territory to get there by land. The Alaska Highway, built for military purposes during World War II, makes it possible to drive automobiles and trucks to Alaska. Travel to Alaska by boat from the Pacific Coast states takes two or three days and by air, of course, only a few hours.

Alaska became especially important to the defense of the United States in World War II and has remained important. Japan could easily have bombed United States cities from bases in Alaska or on the Aleutian Islands. At the western tip of Alaska, across a narrow stretch of water called the Bering Strait, only fifty miles wide in some places, lies Siberia, which belongs to Russia. Land invasion of America is possible over the Bering Strait and through Alaska. In fact, it is thought that the American Indians first came to America, thousands of years ago, by crossing from Asia when the strait was frozen over in the winter.

There are many exciting stories about Alaska, because about 1900 there was a big "gold rush" that caused thousands of adventurers, both good men and desperate men, to seek their fortunes there. They lived a rough and often lawless frontier life. The poet Robert W. Service wrote some of his most popular poems, and Jack London wrote some of his best stories, about the gold-rush days in Alaska.

THE PEOPLE OF ALASKA

The people who lived in Alaska earliest were some tribes of American Indians, and also Eskimos and Aleuts, who are related to American Indians. These still live there. They trap bears and otters and foxes and other animals, for their furs and meat; and they fish in the rivers and in the seas around Alaska. These natives do very little farming, and many of them eat nothing but meat and fish, as their ancestors did. There are about ten thousand Eskimos in Alaska, and about ten thousand members of other Indian tribes. Many of these have adopted the white men's ways, live in the cities or near them, and work in the fishing or canning industries of southern Alaska.

The white people in Alaska, somewhat more than 236,700 of them, nearly all came to Alaska from the United States, and some from Canada. There are about fifteen thousand who came from Norway and other Scandinavian countries, and there are a few thousand whose ancestors were Russians and went to Alaska when it belonged to Russia.

These white Alaskans live chiefly in the southern and western parts, where the cities and towns are. Nearly half of them live in or near the cities or towns. Life there is very much as it is in any part of the United States.

There is not much farming in Alaska. One reason is that most of the year it is too cold for crops to grow; but the chief reason is that Alaska does not need to grow much food, having such a small population to support. There are only about 15,000 acres used as farmland in the entire state, and only about 7,500 acres actually produce crops. But where crops are grown, the land yields more per acre than most land in the continental United States.

Most of the people of Alaska work in the three big industries: fishing and canning (especially salmon); cutting of timber from the huge forests; and mining the rich deposits of lead, tin, and precious metals such as gold. The fur trade is also important, especially in seal skins. There is almost no manufacturing.

The cost of living is very high in Alaska. In the capital, Juneau, and other parts of the Panhandle section, which is nearest the continental United States, it is 20% to 25% higher than in Seattle; in cities farther north it ranges from 40% to 50% higher.

WHAT THE LAND IS LIKE

Alaska is not nearly as cold as you might suppose. In the southern and western parts, where most of the people live, it seldom goes below freezing. Neither is Alaska ever very warm in summer. The average temperature in summer is only 56 degrees; in winter it is about 32 degrees. In the central and northern parts of Alaska the winter temperature is usually below zero, and the coldest parts may go to 76° below.

There are two big mountain ranges in Alaska. In the southern part there is the Alaska Range, which includes Mount McKinley, the highest mountain in North America (20,320 feet high). Across the northern part of Alaska is the Brooks Range. Here the highest peaks are less than 10,000 feet high.

The big Yukon River runs through central Alaska and empties into the Bering Sea at the west. It is very long— about 2,100 miles—and deep, so that steamboats and smaller boats can travel almost its entire length. The Yukon is very important in carrying the products of the mines and forests to the sea, where they can be shipped to the United States and other countries.

Alaska can be divided into three regions. *Arctic Alaska* runs from the northern coast on the Arctic Ocean to the Brooks Range, a distance of about 150 miles. This is a low, treeless region, sometimes called the Alaskan tundra. It is very cold in winter and very few people live there. *Interior Alaska* is chiefly the valley of the Yukon River, between the mountain ranges. It has huge areas of swampy, mosquito-infested lowland with scattered groups of small trees. It is cold in winter but very hot and humid in summer. The *Pacific Slope,* which lies along the Pacific Ocean in the south and southeast of Alaska, is hilly and has many streams and waterfalls. Here the climate is temperate and there is good farmland. Hundreds of islands, some quite large such as Kodiak and the big Aleutian islands, lie off the coast of the Pacific Slope. From the mountains above the Pacific Slope some of the world's biggest glaciers descend to the sea. Alaska has 18,000 square miles of glaciers.

Two other sections are: The *Alaskan Peninsula,* a small peninsula at the southwest, with many small volcanoes called fumaroles; and the *Panhandle,* a thin strip of land along the western coast of Canada. This section includes the capital, Juneau, and the Alexander Archipelago, a group of more than a hundred small islands.

There are very few railroads and highways in Alaska. In the winter, much traveling is done by dogsled as it was long ago, but in modern times the people do most of their traveling by airplane.

GOVERNMENT AND EDUCATION

Like most states, Alaska has a governor and two legislative or lawmaking houses, a Senate with sixteen members and a House of Representatives with twenty-four members. While Alaska was a Territory its governor was appointed by the President of the United States and its courts were part of the Federal Court system, but now they are elected by the people. The capital is Juneau.

In Alaska, as in all parts of the United States, education is free and everyone must attend school. There is one small but modern university, the University of Alaska, which is near the city of Fairbanks. In 1971 its enrollment was 2,039 men and women.

THE CITIES OF ALASKA

Alaska's cities are small compared with the chief cities of other states, but they have more big-city facilities such as stores and restaurants because unlike American towns of the same size they are not close to some much bigger city. Following are the chief cities of Alaska. The population figures have all been taken from the 1970 census.

Anchorage, population 124,542, including suburbs. The largest city in Alaska, a seaport, and a fishing and canning center, on Cook Inlet, an arm of the Gulf of Alaska, in the south of Alaska.

Towering over every other mountain in North America, Mount McKinley stands 20,320 feet high in McKinley National Park, Alaska.

Alaska Airlines

Juneau, population 13,556, capital of Alaska and its third-largest city. It is on the narrow strip of land that runs along the sea to the south of the Alaskan peninsula.

Fairbanks, population 45,864, the largest inland city, in the central part of Alaska.

Nome, population 5,749, the largest town in western Alaska. It is on Seward peninsula, the part of Alaska that comes closest to Siberia.

Sitka, population 6,109, on Baranoff Island, near Juneau. Sitka was the capital of Alaska until 1912.

Kodiak, population 9,409, Alaska's oldest city, on Kodiak Island south of Alaska, Headquarters of 17th Naval District; fishing and hunting (kodiak bear).

ALASKA IN THE PAST

Captain Vitus Bering, the great Danish navigator, discovered Alaska more than two hundred years ago (in 1741). He was sailing for Russia, not for his native Denmark, and Russia claimed the territory and in 1784 established fur-

Alaska Airlines

Eskimo mother at Nome carries her baby in her parka, which is made extra roomy for that purpose.

Alaska Airlines

An Eskimo woman making mukluks (moccasin-like boots) in Alaska.

trading posts there. For many years, Alaska was called "Russian America." In those days, there were hundreds of thousands of sea otters on the Alaskan coasts, and the fur of sea otter is by many considered the finest in the world, even finer than sable and mink. The Russians were cruel to the natives and very unwise in their business. They killed so many of the sea otters that they almost wiped them out, and this valuable fur has been lost to the world ever since, except in very small quantities.

In 1867 the United States bought Alaska from Russia for $7,200,000. The purchase was made by William H. Seward, who was Secretary of State then,

and Alaska was so far away and so undeveloped that the American people thought he had spent the government's money foolishly. They called Alaska "Seward's Folly." But when gold was discovered in the Yukon in 1897, thousands of Americans passed through Alaska to get there; and they discovered more gold in Alaska than in the Yukon. This, the discovery of other mineral wealth, and the defensive importance of Alaska, made Seward's "folly" prove to be one of the best buys any country ever made.

Admission of Alaska as a state was proposed many times from 1946 on, but usually Congress coupled it with admission of Hawaii, to which many Senators were opposed. In 1954 the House of Representatives passed a bill admitting both Alaska and Hawaii, but the Senate did not. In 1958 the House voted to admit Alaska, without mention of Hawaii, and on June 30 the Senate also passed the bill. President Eisenhower promptly signed it.

PLACES TO SEE IN ALASKA

Tongass National Forest, 16,500,000 acres, on the southeast coast. Visitors spend their vacations there camping, canoeing, skating, and hiking.

Chugach National Forest, 5,000,000 acres, near Prince William Sound in the south; a vacation spot.

Mount McKinley National Park, 3,030 square miles, in central Alaska, 123 miles from Fairbanks. Second in size to Yellowstone National Park in the United States.

Glacier Bay National Monument, 1,820 square miles, near Juneau. Made up of vast and magnificent glaciers, which can be seen from a plane or boat.

Child's Glacier, in the northeast, near Copper River. A magnificent ice cliff, 200 to 300 feet high, about as high as the Capitol Building in Washington.

Sitka National Monument, 57 acres, in southeast Alaska. Contains an Indian stockade 150 years old.

Kasaan National Monument, 28 acres, on Prince of Wales Island. Contains the ruins of the former Haida Indian Village; one can see totem poles, Indian grave houses, and monuments that are very old.

Katmai National Monument, 1,700 square miles, in the southwest. Contains the famous Valley of Ten Thousand Smokes, filled with volcanoes from which pour great columns of white vapor.

Chief Shakes' Community House, on Wrangell Island, in the southeast. Contains a fascinating collection of household tools and works of art of the Tlingit Indians.

Yukon Trail, in central Alaska, the famous path taken by the miners in the gold rush almost sixty years ago.

White Pass and Chilkoot Pass, near Skagway, in the southeast. Dangerous mountain trails taken by the miners into the Yukon Territory.

Richardson Highway, a beautiful highway between Valdez and Fairbanks, along which can be seen the deserted towns known as "ghost towns," once filled with miners seeking gold.

Metlakatla, on an island in the southeast. A coöperative Indian village, where everything is owned by the people, including the great sawmill, and their canning and boat-building industries.

Ward's Cove, near Ketchikan, in the southeast. An excellent place for hunting bear and deer.

Mitkof Island, about 100 miles from Juneau. Mink- and fox-raising.

ALASKA—SUMMARY

Area. 566,432 sq. miles.
Population. (1970 census) 302,173.
General information. Capital, Juneau. Motto, North to the Future. Flower, forget-me-not. Bird, Willow Ptarmigan. Song, "Alaska's Flag." Admitted to the Union, 1958. Official abbreviation, Alas., or AK.

Alaska Highway

The Alaska Highway is a long road built to connect the United States, Canada, and Alaska. At one time it was called the "Alcan" highway. It starts at Dawson Creek, British Columbia, a town about 500 miles north of the United States border, it passes through Whitehorse, capital of the Yukon Territory of Canada, and it ends in Fairbanks, Alaska, a distance of 1,527 miles.

The highway was built in 1942, during World War II, to supply American soldiers in Alaska. Seven regiments of United States Army Engineers, and more than 6,000 civilians, built the road in six months.

The Alaska Highway is kept open all year, but travelers should carry blankets or sleeping robes if they drive over it in the very cold weather. The surface is paved in some parts and gravel or clay in others. On the way is a 2,130-foot suspension bridge over the Peace River.

Alaska Highway

Albania

Albania is a small country in Europe, not much larger in area than Maryland, which is one of the smallest states of the United States. Albania's population is about two and a half million people, which is about a million less than Maryland has. In 1946 Albania got a Communist government and after that no one could find out much about what goes on there, but no one ever did know much about what went on in Albania. It is one of the oldest countries of Europe, yet is one of the most mysterious.

Albania lies on the eastern shore of the Adriatic Sea, just across the narrow waters from the Italian peninsula and Rome. Two thousand years ago, Albania was called Illyria. It was a prosperous colony of the Roman Empire, which was then the center of the civilized world.

Albanian Mission to the U.N.
These women are soldiers in the Albanian Army.

Yet today Albania is a poor, backward land.

One reason, perhaps, is the high mountains that hem Albania in from its neighbors. Another reason may be that so many different conquerors have come to Albania to kill and oppress the people.

THE PEOPLE OF ALBANIA

Many of the people who live in Albania today are descended from the ancient Illyrians who lived there before written history began. They speak a language brought down through the ages from that ancient people. Other Albanian people came there, long ago, from Greece, which is Albania's neighbor on the south. The Turks, and Slavic people from different parts of what is now Yugoslavia, and Italians, have all ruled Albania at one time or another, and some of them have stayed there.

Most of the Albanians are poor, and they make their livings in the two oldest kinds of work known to man: farming, and tending cattle and sheep. Albania has some good farmland, but there is hardly enough of it, and besides the Albanians do not have modern farm machinery and do not use the best methods of farming. Sometimes they cannot raise as much food as they need.

Nearly three out of four Albanians follow the Mohammedan religion. The Turks, who conquered the country five hundred years ago and ruled it until 1912, brought Mohammedanism with them. The people who are not Mohammedans are Christians, belonging to either the Greek Orthodox Church or the Roman Catholic Church. Since Albania has had a Communist government, which is opposed to all these religions, Albanian Mohammedans and Christians alike have had trouble keeping in touch with the heads of their churches in other countries.

The people of Albania dress in the eastern fashion, very much as the Turks did thirty and more years ago, before European customs of dress were introduced there.

According to law, education through grammar school is required and is free, but this law is often broken and it is possible that as many as half of the people cannot read and write.

WHAT THE LAND IS LIKE

Along the Adriatic Sea, Albania has level land that has plenty of rainfall and is good for farming. Behind this the mountains rise steeply, and the Alpine section in northern Albania has peaks nearly 10,000 feet high. The climate is warm in the south, as it is in southern Italy, and temperate in the north, except in the mountains, which are very cold in the winter.

Every few miles, a river springs from the mountains and flows through Albania to the sea. The principal rivers are the Drin in the north, the Shkumbi in central Albania, and the Vijosë in the south.

The natural resource that has proved most valuable to Albania so far is oil. The best oilfields are in the low mountains in the south. The oil is carried by pipelines to the seaport of Vlona. In one way this oil has not been too lucky for Albania, because in 1939 Italy, which did not have enough oil of its own, started a war against Albania to get it.

Albania has some coal mines, and the mountains are believed to hold large amounts of valuable minerals, but so far they have not been mined. Albania has neither the machines for mining nor the railroads or roads to carry the minerals away. There are few automobiles. Official travel between Albania and other Communist countries came to be chiefly by airplane after 1948 when Yugoslavia became unfriendly with Soviet Russia. In the dispute between Communist China and Soviet Russia for leadership of the Communist world, Albania sided with the Chinese Communists. In 1961, Russia broke off all relations with Albania.

THE GOVERNMENT OF ALBANIA

When World War II ended, Communists were in control of Albania and set up a dictatorship of the type known as a "People's Republic." In this form of government there is a parliament, and members of it are elected by the people, but the actual control is in the hands of a presidium, or executive board, which is composed of top-ranking members of the Communist Party. Members of this presidium are not elected by the people; in effect, they appoint themselves. Members of the parliament vote the way the presidium tells them to vote. The people have no real voice in their own government and there is no personal liberty as it is known in the United States.

The capital of Albania is Tirana. See the article on TIRANA.

ALBANIA IN THE PAST

Albania has been ruled by one foreign country after another for more than two thousand years. Except for brief periods it was never really independent until the year 1912.

The Roman Empire made Albania (then called Illyria) a colony about 100 years before the time of Christ. When Rome fell to German invaders in the 5th century, Albania fell with it. After that, for about a thousand years, the Slavs of Europe and the East Roman emperor in Byzantium would occasionally fight over Albania, and one after the other would control it. Finally, in 1444, the Turks invaded Albania. A great Albanian hero named George Castriota, who was called "Scanderbeg," fought them bravely for twenty-five years, but they finally conquered. In the centuries that followed the Albanians adopted the Turkish ways that they still have, but from time to time they still fought for independence. Turkey finally became so weak that this had to be granted in 1912.

After World War I, a leader named Ahmed Zogu rose to power, and in 1928 he made himself King Zog. He is remembered in America partly because his queen, whom he married in 1938, was half American. In 1939, when Italy invaded and then annexed Albania, Zog had to flee with his wife and baby son, who was only two days old.

In World War II, while Albania was occupied by Italians and then by Germans, Albanian "partisans" fought them under the command of Enver Hoxha. He was a Communist and was supported by Soviet Russia. After the war it was easy for him to set up a Communist government. Diplomatic relations with the Soviet Union were broken in 1971 because Albania has Stalinist and pro-Chinese attitudes.

ALBANIA—SUMMARY

Area. 11,101 sq. mi. Greatest length about 210 miles, width about 50 miles. Coastline about 150 miles on Adriatic Sea. Population, 2,350,000 (1976 estimate); 99.8% native Albanian.

Language. Albanian (an Indo-European language); Gheg dialect in the north, Tosk dialect in the south.

Religion. Principally (70%) Moslem; 19% Orthodox Christian, 11% Roman Catholic.

General Information. Flag, red with black double-headed eagle. Monetary unit, the lek, worth about 20 cents (U.S.).

Principal cities. Tirana (population 170,-000), the capital; Shkoder or Scutari (49,830); Korca or Koritsa (45,000); Durres or Durazzo (53,160).

Description. Most of country mountainous (spurs of the Dinaric Alps) with altitudes of 3,000 ft. or higher; lowlands along the Adriatic coast.

Climate. Mild along seacoast; extremes of temperature inland: average in summer 78° F., in winter 45° F. Rainfall, inland, 80 to 100 inches a year.

Natural resources. Petroleum, rock salt, bitumen, copper, chromite, iron, lignite, coal; extensive forests. About 15% of land can be farmed; uplands contain much pasturage.

Transportation. Railways: 125 miles. Roads: 2,000 miles. Rivers: only the Bujuna is navigable.

Commerce. Industrial development is slight but increasing. Agriculture occupies most of the population. Corn is the chief crop; other crops are wheat, rye, oats, barley, tobacco, cotton, sugar beets, olives, citrus fruit. Limited exports of wool, hides, fur, cheese, petroleum, bitumen, copper, chromite, bauxite.

Government. Constitution of 1946. A legislature of one chamber, represented by a cabinet of 13 ministers headed by a premier and 3 vice-premiers. Actual control is by the heads of the Albanian Workers Party National Liberation Movement (Communist Party), with no opposition party or candidates permitted.

Education. Free education compulsory for ages 7 to 14. About 3,500 elementary and secondary schools, with enrollment about 168,-000. Enrollment in colleges in 1971: 15,000. Illiteracy is high.

Military. Army of 30,000, first trained by the U.S.S.R., later reputed to use arms supplied by Communist China.

Albany

Albany is the capital of the state of New York. It is on the west bank of the Hudson River, about 145 miles from New York City. Albany was first settled by Dutch people in 1624, only a few years after the Pilgrims landed in Massachusetts. It was called Beverwyck until 1664, when the English took it from the Dutch and named it Albany, which was an ancient name for Scotland.

Albany is a trading and manufacturing center. In colonial days many Indians brought furs to Albany to trade for cloth, knives, and other things they needed. Albany is a seaport, because seagoing ships can sail up the Hudson all the way to Albany. The Erie Canal was originally built (in 1817) to carry freight from Albany on the Hudson across New York to the west.

The capitol, the building from which the state of New York is governed, is on the side of a steep hill, almost at the top. It is built of granite and has spires at its corners but no dome as many capitols do. It was finished in 1898.

ALBANY, NEW YORK. Population, 285,-618 (1970 census). Capital, New York State. County seat, Albany County. On the Hudson River. Settled 1624. Chartered 1686, the oldest chartered city in the U.S.; became the state capital in 1797.

Albany Congress

The Albany Congress, also called the Albany Convention, was a meeting of American colonies held in Albany, New York, in June, 1754, before the United States became independent.

New York, Massachusetts, Connecticut, New Hampshire, Rhode Island, Pennsylvania and Maryland sent representatives. The reason for meeting was that the Indians had been attacking farms and villages, and the colonies could fight the Indians better together than singly. Benjamin Franklin was the representative from Pennsylvania. He said there should be a colonial union, a government of all the colonies, that would protect the colonists from attack by Indians, collect taxes, and have its own army and navy. Franklin's plan was not approved by the colonies, nor by the British government that ruled the colonies. Still the Albany Congress was important, because many ideas in the Constitution of the United States were taken from Benjamin Franklin's plan.

albatross

The albatross is a large bird that lives mostly in the ocean regions, below the Equator, but is also found in the North Pacific. Most albatrosses are white with dark patches on their backs, but some are brown with white heads. The albatross may be as much as 4 feet long and has the greatest wingspread of all birds (12 feet from tip to tip). It spends most of its time flying over its ocean home. It comes to land only to mate and to lay a single egg in a clearing on sandy soil or on a rocky ledge. The courtship of albatrosses is like a square dance, with much bowing.

The albatross feeds on the surface of the ocean, where it catches fish, and tiny shellfish that float on top of the water. Its beak, about 4 inches long, has a sharp hook on the end. The albatross is a very greedy eater, and when it is full it has trouble getting into the air again. It skitters awkwardly over the surface of the water for several hundred yards before it can take off.

The albatross likes to follow ships. It can glide and soar for hours and hardly ever beat its wings. In the days when ships had sails, the sailors thought it was bad luck to kill an albatross. The English poet Coleridge wrote about this superstition in a famous ballad called *The Rime of the Ancient Mariner*.

Albéniz, Isaac

Isaac Manuel Francisco Albéniz was a Spanish composer and pianist, called the father of modern Spanish music. He was born in 1860. He is best known for two piano suites, *Iberia* and *España*, but he also wrote operas, songs, and compositions for orchestra. He is noted for his use of Spanish rhythms and folklike melodies. Albéniz died in 1909.

Albert, King of the Belgians

King Albert is a great hero to the people of Belgium, because he had the courage to defy the powerful German army in World War I. King Albert, who was born in 1875, was only 39 years old and had been king of Belgium only five years when World War I broke out in 1914. Because they could reach France easier by going across Belgium, the Germans broke their word and sent their armies into neutral Belgium. King Albert knew Belgium had no chance against

Germany, but he knew that honorably the Belgians had to fight, and they did. King Albert stayed with his soldiers all through the war, even though almost all of Belgium had been conquered. His wife, Queen Elizabeth, went to work in a soldiers' hospital, where she scrubbed floors and bandaged wounded soldiers.

As a boy, King Albert had studied engineering, being especially interested in ships and airplanes. He died in 1934 when he fell while mountain-climbing, a sport he loved. He was 59 years old.

Albert, Prince

Prince Albert was the husband of Queen Victoria of England. He was called the prince consort, the word *consort* meaning a husband or wife.

Victoria and Albert had a real love match. Victoria had become queen when she was only eighteen and a year later she met Albert, who was a prince in a little German kingdom called Saxe-Coburg-Gotha. He was her first cousin. She fell in love with him and he with her. When they were married, each of them was only twenty years old. This was in the year 1840.

He was a tall, handsome young man, with reddish hair and a reddish mustache. A long coat that he made popular is still called a "Prince Albert."

Prince Albert was a devoted husband and a very wise adviser to the queen. The English people liked him very much. He and Queen Victoria had nine children. But in 1861, Prince Albert suddenly died. He had been born in 1819, so he was only 42 years old. Queen Victoria was heartbroken then, and she lived for forty years more and always mourned for Prince Albert. She had many monuments built in his memory. The chief one is the Albert Memorial in London. It is a big statue of the prince, seated, below a spire 175 feet high. It is decorated with very fancy sculpture.

Alberta

Alberta is one of the provinces of Canada. It is in the western part, and the Canadian Rockies run through it, so it is known as "Fifty Switzerlands in One" because of the many high mountains and lofty peaks. Its beautiful scenery has made it a popular place for people to go on their vacations. Alberta ranks fourth in size among the Canadian provinces, having 255,285 square miles, which is slightly smaller than the state of Texas. In population Alberta also ranks fourth in Canada, with nearly one and a half million inhabitants. The province was named after Princess Louise Caroline Alberta, a daughter of Queen Victoria of England. It became a province in 1905. The capital is Edmonton.

THE PEOPLE OF ALBERTA

The people of Alberta originally came from many different countries to seek their fortune in the vast, rich country of Canada. More than half the Albertans came from Great Britain. Others came from European countries, especially Austria, Russia, and the Scandinavian countries. A smaller number were French Canadians from the eastern part of Canada; these still speak French and observe many French customs. There are some Indians, who live on reservations. Two hundred years ago the Indians were the only people living in Alberta.

The first settlers of Alberta were cattle ranchers. Raising cattle is still a leading industry, but many more Albertans are now farmers and raise millions of bushels of wheat, oats, and barley. They also raise sugar beets and potatoes, in the southern part of the province. In the northern part, like the Indians who lived there before them, they trap such fur-bearing animals as squirrel, beaver, and fox; they cut timber in the great Albertan forests; and they work the rich coal mines of the Rockies, producing more coal than any other province.

Oil is one of the most important industries of Alberta, which has rich oil-fields and large refineries.

More than half the people of Alberta live in the country. The rest live in the cities, Edmonton and Calgary and others. They work in meat-packing plants, flour mills, dairies, and refineries. Others have jobs in canneries and beet-sugar factories in and near Raymond.

Once, when Alberta had a very small population, the people could not support a lot of different churches. They joined with people in other western provinces and formed the United Church of Canada. This is the largest church of Alberta, but there are Anglican, Roman Catholic, Presbyterian and Baptist churches.

WHAT ALBERTA IS LIKE

A visitor to Alberta will find that various parts of the province look quite different. In the north are the great forests, which extend over more than half of Alberta. From these forests logs are shipped to sawmills on the Peace River and the Athabaska River. In the northeast is Lake Athabaska, the largest of Alberta's many lakes. Part of the lake is in the neighboring province of Saskatchewan.

The central part of Alberta is mostly farm land where the people raise grain and cattle. In the center of this section is Edmonton, the capital and largest city of the province. It is a busy manufacturing center with petroleum-refining plants, paper mills, flour mills, and meat-packing plants.

The southern part of Alberta is prairie, with excellent grazing land on which cattle can be raised. In the southwest are the magnificent Canadian Rockies with their valuable coal deposits and their beautiful national parks.

The people of Alberta live in a pleasant climate, particularly in the summer. The average temperature then is about 60 degrees. In the winter it is much colder and in the north the temperature can drop to 20 degrees below zero.

There are railroads throughout most of Alberta, but in the north the rivers are the chief means of transportation. A highway links Edmonton with the Alaska Highway in British Columbia.

THE GOVERNMENT OF ALBERTA

The head of the government of Alberta is a lieutenant-governor, who represents the British Queen. He is appointed by the Canadian government. The province is actually run by a Prime Minister. He is appointed by a legislature, which is elected by the people. The Prime Minister has a cabinet, just as the President of the United States has. He stays in office as long as he can keep the confidence of the majority of the legislature. The legislature is elected for a five-year term. Judges are appointed by the Canadian government in Ottawa, and hold office until age 75. The provincial government is in the capital, Edmonton.

Everyone has to go to school between the ages of 6 and 16, and there are many fine grammar schools and high schools all through the province. The Universities of Alberta, Calgary, and Lethbridge provide higher education.

CHIEF CITIES OF ALBERTA

The leading cities of Alberta, with population figures, are:

Edmonton, population 442,365 (1974), the capital and largest city, a manufacturing center, in the central part of the province.

Calgary, population 433,389 (1974), second-largest city, a manufacturing center, in the southern part of the province.

Lethbridge, population 43,612 (1974), third-largest city, cannery center, in the southern part of the province.

Medicine Hat, population 27,430 (1974), fifth-largest city, center for pottery-making, in the southern part of the province.

ALBERTA IN THE PAST

When the first white traders from Quebec came to Alberta in 1751, in search of furs, they found various Indian tribes living in the country. Explorers and trappers were the only white men for many years in that territory.

Gradually trading posts were set up by men like Peter Pond and Alexander Mackenzie, and by the Hudson's Bay Company and the North West Company, who were bitter rivals. By 1821 the Hudson's Bay Company was the most powerful fur-trading company in the territory.

In 1870 Canada paid the Hudson's Bay Company and the British for some of their rights in Alberta and made it one of the Northwest Territories. The Northwest Mounted Police were making this region safe for settlers, and more and more people came into the territory. More came after the Canadian Pacific Railway was finished in 1883. In 1905 Alberta became a province. Discoveries of important oil and natural gas fields have added to Alberta's prosperity.

An aerial view of the city of Edmonton, Alberta's capital and largest city.

PLACES TO SEE IN ALBERTA

Jasper National Park, 4,200 square miles, in the Canadian Rocky Mountains, western Alberta, 200 miles north of Banff, on Highway 16. Jasper, one of Canada's largest parks, has magnificent ice fields, deep canyons, and towering peaks. Snake Indian Falls, Miette Hot Springs, and Punch Bowl Falls are particular attractions.

Banff National Park, 2,585 square miles, in the Canadian Rocky Mountains, in western Alberta, on State Highway 1. A beautiful vacation spot, with high peaks, ice fields, lakes, and green valleys.

Watertown Lakes National Park, together with Glacier National Park across the southern border in Montana, form the International Peace Park, 204 square miles, on U.S. Route 89. Noted for its beautiful mountains, trails, waterfalls, and lakes.

Buffalo National Park, 197 square miles, in eastern Alberta. This park, established in 1908, became a part of Wood Buffalo National Park in 1922.

Elk Island National Park, 75 square miles, in central Alberta, 25 miles from Edmonton, on State Highway 16. Buffaloes, elks, deer, and moose, under protection; a large recreation area for tourists.

Nemiskan National Park, 8 square miles, in southern Alberta, near Lethbridge, on State Highway 4. An area set aside for the protection of a herd of pronghorn antelopes.

Wood Buffalo National Park, 17,300 square miles, in northern Alberta and the Northwest Territories. A large preserve of forests and open plains, where buffaloes, bears, beavers, moose and waterfowl live.

Banff, a popular winter and summer resort in the Banff National Park. Attracts mountain climbers and skiers.

Lake Louise, in the "Lakes in the Clouds" region of the Banff National Park. A famous tourist resort; the very beautiful blue lake reflects the snowy mountains, cliffs, forests, and sky.

ALBERTA—SUMMARY

Area. 255,285 sq. mi. (4th in Canada).

Population. 1,714,000 (1974 estimate); 40% in cities. 60% of British descent, 5% French, 30% other European, 2% American Indian.

Religion. About 75% Protestant: United Church, Anglican, Presbyterian, Baptist. About 19% Roman Catholic.

General information. Formed as province Sept. 1, 1905. *Coat of arms,* the cross of St. George at the top, a view of the Albertan mountains and fields in the middle, and a field of wheat at the bottom. *Flag,* this coat of arms on the flag of Canada. *Flower,* wild rose. *Official abbreviation,* Alta.

Government. Lieutenant-governor appointed by Canadian government. Premier and cabinet chosen by the majority party in the provincial legislature. Legislature, one house with 75 members elected for maximum terms of five years. Judges appointed by Canadian government serve until age 75. All citizens 18 or older may vote.

Transportation. About 6,900 miles of railroads, 86,800 miles of motor roads (6,300 paved). Navigable waterways, the Peace, Athabaska and Saskatchewan Rivers.

Commerce. *Agriculture:* chief crops wheat, barley oats (annual grain production more than 465,000,000 bushels); also sugar beets, potatoes. Beef and dairy cattle second only to grains in importance. *Industry:* leading crops coal (more than 9,000,000 short tons annually); crude oil (about 536,000,000 barrels annually); natural gas, salt, lumber, fresh-water fish, furs, refined petroleum products, meat products, flour.

Albertus Magnus, St.

Albertus Magnus was a great philosopher in the Roman Catholic Church. He was born about 1193. He was the teacher of St. Thomas Aquinas, who was often called the greatest Catholic philosopher. Albertus Magnus (a title meaning "the Great" in Latin) wrote twenty-one volumes on many branches of knowledge—theology, philosophy, natural history, physics, and astronomy. He was given the title *Doctor Universalis* (doctor of all knowledge). He was a priest and for a short time was a bishop, but most of his life he taught in European universities. In 1931 he was canonized as a saint. He died in 1280.

Albigenses

The Albigenses, also called the Albigensians or the Cathari, were a religious group who became very numerous in the south of France in the 11th to 13th centuries. Their name came from the city of Albi, France. The Albigenses opposed the Catholic clergy and believed only the spiritual world is important. Because they disagreed with many Church teachings they were condemned as heretics. In the early 1200s Pope Innocent III sent a crusade against the Albigenses and thousands were killed on both sides before peace was made in 1229. The Church won and the Albigensian movement died out.

albino

Living things—plants and animals —normally contain certain pigments, or coloring matter. One of these pigments is *melanin,* which gives a dark color to people's skin, hair, and eyes; and there are many other pigments. When a living thing does not have the pigments that are natural to its kind, it is called an *albino.* The condition of being an albino is called *albinism,* and it is not a disease because it seldom does any harm, except to give the person or plant a whitish look. Albinism is hereditary.

Human albinos have hair that is nearly white and as a rule is soft and silky, and skin that is very fair and is often rough and scaly. Their eyes are somewhat pink, because of the blood showing through, and they can usually not bear strong light —because it is the coloring that protects our eyes from too much light. Negroes have a lot of melanin in their skins, and blonds have very little. When a person stays in the sunshine a great deal, his skin stores a lot of melanin and he becomes darker. It is said that he is "tanned."

There are many albinos among animals, for example, white mice, white rabbits, white crows, and the sacred white elephant of Siam.

Albion

Albion is another name for England. It is what the ancient Greeks and Romans called the entire island of Britain. To them, the word meant "white" and it is sometimes said that Britain got this name because of the great cliffs of chalk along the English Channel, especially near Dover, but is doubtful if that is the reason. Scotland was often called Alban, or Albany. Napoleon called England "perfidious Albion" (treacherous Albion) and its enemies sometimes use that phrase even today.

Albright, Jacob

Jacob Albright was a clergyman and the founder of the Evangelical Church. He was born near Pottstown, Pennsylvania, in 1759. In 1803 he became a Methodist minister but he disagreed with some of its teachings. After his death in 1808 some of his followers formed the Evangelical Association, and in 1946 this Church joined with the United Brethren of Christ to form the present Evangelical United Brethren Church. Albright Col-

lege in Reading, Pennsylvania, is named for Jacob Albright.

albumin

Albumin is a sticky substance that is found in living things. The white of an egg is almost pure albumin (but here it is spelled albumen). There is albumin in the blood, and when you cut yourself the albumin helps make the blood clot (become hard and dry). Albumin is also present in vegetables and in milk as well as in eggs. Although albumin dissolves in water, it coagulates (becomes solid) when it is heated.

Because of its stickiness, albumin is used in making paste. Albumin in dry powder form will keep for a long time without spoiling. In liquid form it spoils rapidly. There is a small amount of sulfur in albumen; it gives rotten eggs their bad odor, and it causes silver forks and spoons to turn black from eggs.

Serum albumin, taken from the blood, is injected into the blood to combat shock. Albumen, or egg white, is used as an antidote for many poisons because it forms a coating around them.

Albuquerque

Albuquerque is the biggest city in New Mexico. It is on the banks of the Rio Grande river, and it is a very beautiful place, with wide streets and gleaming white buildings. Many people go there during the winter because it is always warm and sunny. It is about 5,000 feet above sea level and the air is so dry that even on the hottest days it is comfortable.

Spanish people settled Albuquerque first, in 1706; the name Albuquerque is Spanish. Mexico is only about 200 miles away, and there are many Mexicans in the city. They wear gay, bright-colored shirts and bandannas. There are usually cowboys around, too, because there are many large ranches outside of Albuquerque. The Pueblo Indian Reservation is nearby. Albuquerque is the seat of the University of New Mexico.

Though its population of 243,751 does not seem large in comparison with eastern cities, Albuquerque is the main shopping center for people who live on ranches and in smaller towns for miles around.

ALBUQUERQUE, NEW MEXICO. Population, 309,681 including suburbs (1970 census). Situated on the Rio Grande. Settled 1706.

Albuquerque, Affonso d'

Affonso d'Albuquerque was a Portuguese governor in the East Indies. He was born about 1453, and at the age of fifty, in 1503, he was sent to Malabar to take charge for the Portuguese government. He conquered Goa (in India) for his country, and later extended Portuguese control to Ceylon, the Sunda Isles, the peninsula of Malacca, and the island of Ormuz. The natives in these places loved him so well that after his death they prayed for his help in protecting them from cruel governments that came later. In folk songs and stories he is sometimes called "Albuquerque the Great" and "the Portuguese Mars." He died in 1515.

Alcaeus

Alcaeus was a Greek poet who lived about 2,500 years ago, 620 to 570 B.C. He came from a noble family and was born on the island of Lesbos. His poems dealt with love, war, and patriotism. Some show a hatred of tyranny. He is believed to have originated a poetry form called the Alcaic, later used by the poetess Sappho and the Latin poet Horace. In English, the only important poet to use this form was Swinburne.

Alcatraz

Alcatraz is a prison-island in San Francisco Bay, easily seen from San Francisco, California. From 1933 to 1962, it was used by the United States government to imprison dangerous criminals. The twelve-acre island is almost impossible to escape since it is surrounded by swirling water and jagged rocks. First fortified by the Spanish, Alcatraz was a United States military prison from 1859 to 1933. The island, known as "The Rock," was abandoned in 1962.

alcazar

An alcazar is simply a castle, in the Arabic language. We think of an alcazar as a castle or palace in Spain, built in the years (before Columbus discovered America) when Spain was under the control of Mohammedans. The ALHAMBRA, about which there is a separate article, is the most famous of the alcazars.

alchemy

Thousands of years ago, when very little was known about the science of chemistry, there were men in ancient Egypt who believed there was a wonderful material called the "philosopher's stone" that could change common metals like iron or lead into gold. They believed also that this philosopher's stone, or some other chemical, could make men live forever without ever becoming old.

These men were called alchemists, and the experiments they performed in trying to find the philosopher's stone were called alchemy. Their work was useful only because it led to the science of chemistry and because the alchemists discovered some useful medicines.

The Egyptians passed their knowledge on to the ancient Greeks. The Greeks passed it on to the Arabs who lived in Palestine, Arabia, north Africa, and Spain. Men in Europe got their knowledge of alchemy from the Arabs. In western Europe during the Middle Ages, the ignorant common people usually looked upon alchemists with fear and thought they were magicians or wizards.

alcohol

Alcohol is a thin, colorless liquid that looks like water. It is used in medicine, in chemical products, in foods, and in drinks. It can be made from wheat, corn, potatoes, sugar beets, most starchy vegetables, and fruits. However, most alcohol is made from grain—such as corn, rye, and wheat—by the chemical process known as fermentation. (There is a separate article about FERMENTATION.) In the United States, a great deal of alcohol is made from petroleum, about as much as is made from grain.

Whiskey, brandy and wines are called alcoholic beverages. Beer and ale also contain alcohol, but in smaller amounts. It is the alcohol in alcoholic beverages that makes a person drunk (unable to control himself normally) if he drinks too much. This condition is also called intoxication. There is a disease called alcoholism, or dipsomania ("thirst craziness"), in which a person is unable to control his desire for alcoholic drinks.

When a person's temperature rises much above normal because of a fever, alcohol is often sponged on the skin. The reason for this is that alcohol dries very quickly. As it dries it carries heat away with it.

Alcohol is very useful as an antiseptic —that is, to kill germs.

Alcohol will not freeze even in the coldest weather known to man. Water will freeze at 32 degrees (Fahrenheit), while alcohol at 286 degrees below zero will only thicken slightly. For this reason it is sometimes used as an antifreeze in automobiles.

Alcohol is used as a solvent, because fats, oils, and some dry solids will dissolve in it. Drugs known as tinctures— for example, tincture of iodine—are dissolved in alcohol. Pure iodine is a dry, purplish-black solid. Alcohol is also an excellent fuel. It burns with a clean blue flame that leaves little or no soot. In an alcohol burner, a cotton wick, like a thick cord, soaks up alcohol from a container and burns just as the wick of a candle does. Alcohol is also an excellent fuel for automobiles and is mixed with gasoline in countries where gasoline is very expensive.

Chemically, alcohol is a carbohydrate composed of hydrogen, carbon, and oxygen, plus the hydroxyl group OH. The principal forms of alcohol are ethyl alcohol, or ethanol, which is usually called grain alcohol and occurs in alcoholic beverages; and methyl alcohol, or methanol, usually called wood alcohol, which is used in rubbing alcohol but causes sickness or even death if drunk.

Alcott, Louisa May

Louisa May Alcott was the author of Little Women, the most popular book for girls that has ever been written (nearly three million copies of it have been sold since it was published in 1868). Miss Alcott, whose family came from Connecticut, and who happened to be born in Germantown, Pennsylvania—a suburb of Philadelphia—while her father was working as a teacher there, lived most of her life in Concord, Massachusetts. This city was then the home of Ralph Waldo Emerson and other great American writers.

Miss Alcott started to write when she was only a girl, and she usually wrote about people she actually knew. Little Women was a story about herself and her three sisters, as well as of their friends and neighbors in nearby towns in Massachusetts. Her other famous books were Little Men, An Old-fashioned Girl, Eight Cousins, and Jo's Boys (a sequel to Little Women).

She was born in 1832, and Little Women was published in 1868. She did some

teaching, was the editor of a magazine for children, and wrote some stories and articles that were not for children. She died in 1888. Her father, Amos Bronson Alcott, was a famous teacher, born in 1799; he lived as long as his daughter did, dying in 1888. He was one of those who supported the BROOK FARM experiment, about which there is a separate article in this encyclopedia.

Alcuin

Alcuin was a learned priest who was born in England more than 1,200 years ago, in the city of York. He is best remembered as an educator. When he was a young man, schools and education had almost completely vanished from Europe, which was torn by wars and lawlessness. Alcuin met Charlemagne, the great emperor of the German territories (now France and Germany) in the year 781. Charlemagne persuaded him to live in France and organize schools and systems of education, and this was Alcuin's chief work for the rest of his life. Alcuin was born in 735 and died in 804.

Alden, John

John Alden was a young man (twenty-one years old) who sailed with the Pilgrims from England to Plymouth, Massachusetts in 1620, on the ship *Mayflower.* He was not really one of the "Pilgrim fathers," because he was hired to make the trip as a skilled worker and did not come because of his religious convictions; but he stayed in Massachusetts, became an important citizen, and married Priscilla Mullens, daughter of one of the Pilgrims.

John and Priscilla had eleven children, and it has been estimated that more than one million Americans are descended from John and Priscilla Alden.

The poet Longfellow was one of the descendants of John and Priscilla and wrote a famous poem, "The Courtship of Miles Standish," about them. In the poem, Captain Miles Standish, a more important member of the colony, asks John Alden to go to Priscilla and ask her if she would marry him (that is, if she would marry Miles Standish). But Priscilla liked John Alden, who was a younger and more handsome man, and she said to him, "Speak for yourself, John." When Captain Standish heard about this, he persuaded John Alden to marry Priscilla.

John Alden was born in 1598 and died in 1687.

alder

The alder is a tree that grows best in moist or swampy soil. It is found in North America, Great Britain and northern Asia. The alder grows 30 to 60 feet high. It is a beautiful tree with dark green leaves and bark that is almost black. The wood is sometimes used for furniture, and makes an excellent charcoal for gunpowder. When men need to use a wood that will not rot or weaken under water, they usually choose alder wood. The supports of most of the houses that are built over the canals in Amsterdam are alder wood poles that have been under water for many years. The bark of the alder is used in tanning leather and is also used by fishermen to dye their nets. The alder is also called *Alnus,* which is part of its scientific name. The red alder and the European black alder are the principal types.

Alderney

Alderney is a small island between France and England. It belongs to England, though it is much nearer to France. Alderney is one of four islands in a group called the Channel Islands (because they are in the English Channel). This little island is only one mile wide, and less than four miles long, but about 1,686 people live on it. It is very pretty, with beautiful green fields and pastures everywhere. The houses are small and neat looking, and many of them are hundreds of years old. It is famous for its cows, which give very rich milk. Alderney cows are small and are very pretty. They are usually brown and white.

See the article on CATTLE.

Aldershot

Aldershot is a small city in England, in Hampshire county, only about 25 miles north of the English Channel. It is a name that comes up in books occasionally because for many years the British army had a big camp there, where the soldiers lived when the country was not engaged in war. This camp is now one of the principal camps in England for the training of the British army.

ALDERSHOT, ENGLAND. Population, about 39,500 (1973). Military training center.

Aldrich, Nelson and Winthrop

Nelson Wilmarth Aldrich was a United States financier and Senator. He was born in Rhode Island, in 1841, and served that state in Congress as a Representative (1879–81) and Senator (1881–1911). Through his interests in banking, manufacturing, and public utilities he was a spokesman for big business. He died in 1915. His daughter Abby married John D. Rockfeller Jr. His son Winthrop Williams Aldrich, born in 1885, was a prominent lawyer, was president and later chairman of the Chase National Bank in New York City, and in 1953 was appointed Ambassador to Great Britain, serving through 1956. He died in 1973.

Aldrich, Thomas Bailey

Thomas Bailey Aldrich, who lived from 1836 to 1907, wrote many books of prose and poetry, but he remains best known for a book called *The Story of a Bad Boy.* Millions of American children  have read this book. It is really the story of Aldrich's own boyhood, which was spent mostly in Portsmouth, New Hampshire. In the book, he called the town Rivermouth and himself Tom Bailey. In many ways Tom Bailey would remind you of Tom Sawyer. He was not really a bad boy, he was mischievous.

Aldrich worked on several newspapers and magazines and was the editor of *The Atlantic Monthly,* a very famous magazine. Other books of his that young readers still find interesting are *Marjorie Daw* and *Too Many Pets.*

ale

Ale is a kind of beer. In England it is the general name for beer. In the United States it means beer brewed in a special way, with a different kind of yeast. It sometimes contains more alcohol than beer does.

Alemán, Miguel

Miguel Alemán y Valdes, a Mexican statesman and lawyer, was President of Mexico from 1946 to 1952. He was born in 1902, of Spanish and Indian ancestry. His father, also named Miguel Alemán, was a village storekeeper who led a small revolt against the Mexican dictator Porfirio Diaz from 1904 to 1911. His son Miguel Alemán as a lawyer was a defender of labor and labor unions. He was a judge, governor of the state of Veracruz, and a cabinet minister before he was elected president. The Communists supported him for president but learned that he was a liberal, not a Communist, and turned against him. After his term as president, Aleman returned to the practice of law in Mexico City and became Director of the Tourist Department.

Alencon

Alencon is a city in northwest France. It is famous for the beautiful lace, known as *point d' Alençon,* that has been made there for centuries. Alençon has a fine Gothic cathedral that was built in the 15th to 18th centuries. The city suffered some damage from bombs in World War II. The population in 1973 was about 33,388.

Aleutians and Aleuts

The Aleutians are a long chain of islands that begin at the western tip of Alaska and reach into the Pacific Ocean for a thousand miles. There are more than a hundred islands in the Aleutians.

The people who live on these islands are called Aleuts. They are a kind of American Indian, related to the Eskimos. They are short and sturdy and have dark skin and black hair. The Aleuts are fishermen, and they also trap blue fox, seal and sea otter for their valuable fur.

There are no trees on any of the Aleutian Islands. The ground is very rocky and very little plant life grows on it. On some of the Aleutians there are volcanoes that are still smoking and may blow up again some day.

Vitus Bering, a Danish explorer sailing for Russia, discovered the Aleutian Islands in 1741. He also was the first to reach Alaska. When the Russian Government learned how rich the islands were in fur-bearing animals, it sent traders to the Aleutians. These traders forced the Aleuts to work like slaves and were very brutal, killing many Aleuts.

In 1867 the United States bought Alaska and the Aleutian Islands from Russia. New American laws made it easier for the Aleuts to live and go about their fishing and hunting. Most of the time Americans paid little attention to the Aleutian Islands, but when Japan became warlike the United States government woke up to the fact that the Aleutians are very close to Japan. The United States Navy built a naval base at Dutch Harbor, which is on an Aleutian island called Unalaska.

In 1942 the Japanese bombed Dutch Harbor and occupied Kiska and Attu, two Aleutian islands. At that time there were about 4,000 Aleuts living on the small islands. They were all taken to safer islands near the Alaskan coast. American sailors and soldiers landed on Attu and fought a bloody battle with the Japanese. After 19 days of fighting in the cold and fog, the Japanese forces were wiped out. Soon they abondoned Kiska. After the war the Aleuts were moved back to their islands.

ALEUTIAN ISLANDS. Area, about 6,500 square miles. Population, about 8,057. Government, part of Alaska. Total, about 140 islands, chiefly: 5 Aleut or Near Islands (largest are Attu and Agattu); about 30 very small Andreanov Islands; about 31 Fox Islands (largest are Unalaska, Unimak, Umnak, and Akutan); about 15 Rat Islands (largest are Rat, Kiska, and Amchitka).

alewife

The alewife is a fish like the shad and herring, that lives in the ocean but swims up rivers to lay its eggs. At exactly the same time every year, millions of alewives used to swim up the rivers of Maine and Nova Scotia. The Indians and early settlers there could drop in a net any place and scoop out a whole netful of fish. Since the rivers have become unclean, there are not nearly so many alewives today, but they are still an important food fish.

Alexander

There have been many kings, emperors and Popes named Alexander. The most famous was ALEXANDER THE GREAT, about whom there is a separate article following this one.

POPE ALEXANDER

Eight Popes have taken the name Alexander. All but two were Italians; Alexander V was Greek and Alexander VI was a member of the Borgia family of Spain; see the article on the BORGIAS. The Popes named Alexander were:

NAME	BORN	DIED	REIGN
Alexander I	Not known		106–116
Alexander II	Not known	1073	1061–1073
Alexander III	Not known	1181	1159–1181
Alexander IV	Not known	1261	1254–1261
Alexander V	Not known	1410	1409–1410
Alexander VI	1431	1503	1492–1503
Alexander VII	1599	1667	1655–1667
Alexander VIII	1610	1691	1689–1691

ALEXANDER, CZAR OF RUSSIA

Until the Russian Revolution of 1917, Russia was ruled by emperors, called czars or tsars (a form of the word Caesar), who supposedly had absolute power over the life and death of everyone in the country. Three czars were named Alexander. All were members of the Romanoff family.

Alexander I was born in 1777, became czar in 1801, and died in 1825. He was a handsome and pleasant young man and was about as democratic in feeling as a czar could be in those times. He lived in the period of the NAPOLEONIC WARS, about which there is a separate article; first he fought Napoleon, then in 1807 made friends with Napoleon, but had to fight again when Napoleon invaded Russia in 1812. He was one of the powerful European monarchs who controlled Europe after Napoleon was beaten in 1814. Officially, he died in 1825; but some believe he actually retired to a religious life.

Alexander II, his grandson, born in 1818, became czar in 1855. In 1861 he freed the serfs, the Russian farmers who were little better than slaves. He was assassinated in 1881.

Alexander III, his son, was born in 1845, became czar in 1881, and died in 1894. Perhaps because of his father's assassination, he was very undemocratic and there was little freedom in Russia during his reign. However, there was much improvement in education and in industry and the Trans-Siberian Railroad was built during his reign.

See the article on RUSSIA.

ALEXANDER, KING OF YUGOSLAVIA

Serbia, the small European country that became part of Yugoslavia after World War I, had two kings named Alexander and both were assassinated. Alexander of Serbia, born in 1876, was king from 1893 to 1903; he was killed by Serbians who wanted the Karageorgevich family to become kings. Alexander I, first king of Yugoslavia, was a Karageorgevich. He was born in 1888, became king in 1921, and was assassinated while visiting in France in 1934, by Croats, another Yugoslavian people who did not want to be ruled by a Serbian.

Alexander Archipelago

The Alexander Archipelago is a group of more than one hundred islands off the coast of the Alaska Panhandle. The islands are mountainous. Among them are Chicagof, Admiralty, Baranof and Prince of Wales Islands. Tlingit Indians inhabit the islands. Fishing is their chief occupation.

Alexander the Great

Of all the kings of history who have tried to conquer the whole world, Alexander the Great was the earliest and he may have come closest to it. This was more than 2,300 years ago. Alexander, who was born in 356 B.C. and died in 323 B.C., became the king of Macedonia, a small country north of Greece, in 336 B.C. when he was only 20 years old. Before Alexander died he made Macedonia the most powerful country on earth.

The father of Alexander was King Philip of Macedonia. Philip was a great warrior and wise statesman. When Alexander became king, his father Philip had already established the control of Macedonia over the several Greek states. Greece was the center of learning then, and Alexander studied as a boy under the great Greek philospher Aristotle.

There are many legends about Alexander the Great, and this should be expected. When he lived, the gods of the ancient Greek mythology were still thought to have been real gods, and many stories were made up to make it appear that Alexander's great victories were caused by the blessings of the gods and not by his own skill. One story says that when he was only a boy he tamed and rode the famous horse Bucephalus that no one else could ride.

There had been a prophecy that the rider of this horse would be a great king of Macedonia.

Then there was the old legend of the Gordian knot. Whoever could untangle the Gordian knot was supposed to be the next ruler of all of Asia, and Alexander cut it through with his sword.

Like a great many successful rulers and generals, Alexander was able to be very severe when he thought he had to be, and this was true even when he was a young king not more than 21 years old. He had been fighting the "barbarians" (as they were later called)— the Germanic tribes who occupied parts of Europe to the north of Macedonia. The Greek cities heard that he was dead, and one of them, Thebes, revolted. Alexander took his army back to Thebes, destroyed the entire city, and either killed or made slaves of nearly everyone who lived there. This was harsh treatment, but it made all the rest of Greece afraid to revolt against him.

Then Alexander led his well-trained army into Persia, where he conquered the great king of Persia, Darius, and made himself the ruler of that country. He next conquered Egypt, then one of the centers of the civilized world, and founded the city of Alexandria. His next goal was Asia, and he marched his armies through Afghanistan and into India, and conquered India. There was no other general who was as good. In most of Alexander's great victories the enemy had larger armies than he had, but he outsmarted the enemy commanders. He might even have gone on to conquer all of Asia, if he had lived long enough. But a fever overtook him, and he died when he was not quite 33 years old, at the city of Babylon in Persia.

The greatness of Alexander is partly in the way he spread education and culture to the countries he conquered. The Greeks were the great thinkers, the great architects, and the great builders. Wherever Alexander went he left colonies that transplanted the beauty and knowledge of the Greek cities to places hundreds or thousands of miles away. Many scholars believe that Alexander the Great speeded up the civilization of the world by several hundred years.

Alexander, Harold

Harold Rupert Leofric George Alexander was a British military leader of World War II. He was born in Ireland in 1891 and served on the Western Front in World War I. In 1940 he commanded the evacuation of 300,000 British troops from the French port of Dunkirk. In 1942, he was appointed commander in chief of all British forces in the Middle East and in 1943 he became deputy commander in chief of Allied forces in North Africa, under General Eisenhower. He was promoted to the rank of field marshal in 1944 and was supreme Allied commander in the Mediterranean theater of operations during the final six months of the war in Europe. In 1946 be became Governor General of Canada and in 1952 British Minister of Defense. He was made Viscount Alexander of Tunis in 1946 and Earl of Errigal in 1952. He died in July, 1969.

Alexandria

Alexandria is a city in Egypt. In ancient times it was one of the great cities of the world; then it was destroyed, and rebuilt, and it became one of the great cities of the modern world, with a population of more than two million. Alexandria is a great seaport on the Mediterranean Sea near the mouth of the Nile River. The modern city was built near the ruins of the ancient city.

THE ANCIENT CITY

Alexander the Great, conqueror of nearly all the civilized world, had Alexandria built in 332 B.C. to replace Tyre as a seaport. It was one of ten or more cities Alexander named for himself. The city was built with straight streets lined with trees. From the center of the city one broad avenue ran north and south and another broad avenue ran east and west. The main buildings were of marble. They had graceful columns and beautiful sculpture.

A great lighthouse was built on an island in the harbor of Alexandria. The island was called Pharos and the lighthouse became known as the Pharos. It stood 300 feet high and was known as one of the Seven Wonders of the World. A long causeway (a strip of land that serves as a bridge) was built to connect the island of Pharos with the mainland. The causeway held back the sea and made an inner harbor.

Alexandria was a great center of trade, but it also was for several hundred years the greatest center of knowledge. The library at Alexandria was the largest in the world. It contained all the knowledge then known to man. There were more than 700,000 books in the library and they were written in all the important languages. (The books were actually rolls of papyrus, which was the "paper" of those times.) The great library of Alexandria was destroyed by an army of Mohammedan Arabs in the year 640 A.D., nearly a thousand years after Alexandria was first built. There is an old story that the Arab commander had the library burned because, he said, "The Koran (the Mohammedan Holy Book) contains all the true knowledge of the world, so the library is not needed." This story is no longer believed. It was told by enemies of the Arabs, to make it appear they were barbarians. Actually the Arabs encouraged literature.

Alexandria was the capital of Egypt from the time it was completed, in the Greek and then Roman empires, until it was destroyed by the Arabs. It was the capital of the Egyptian queen Cleopatra. Today the site of the ancient city is only a mass of broken stone and ruins.

THE MODERN CITY

The modern city of Alexandria is a busy seaport built near the ruins of the ancient city. A mixture of many types of Mediterranean people scurry about their business in the warm sunshine. Ships from all over the world enter the fine harbor.

In World War II Alexandria became important because it controlled the approach to the Suez Canal. The German Marshal Rommel and his famed Afrika Corps tried desperately to seize Alexandria. Once they almost succeeded, but they were finally beaten back after a great battle against the British at El Alamein, a town a few miles west of Alexandria. This was in October 1942. The Germans never threatened Alexandria again.

Alexandria, Virginia

Alexandria, Virginia, is a residential suburb of Washington, D.C. Its population in 1970 was 110,938 but it is growing rapidly. Mount Vernon, the estate of George Washington, is nearby.

alexandrite

Alexandrite is a semiprecious stone used in jewelry. It is often considered the birthstone for June, along with the pearl and moonstone. It is found in various parts of the world, including Mexico, and is usually in the form of smooth pebbles left on the ground by streams of water. Alexandrite looks like colored glass that is one color in daylight and another color under electric light—it may be blue with red lights in the daytime and lavender with blue lights under the electric lights. Alexandrite is sometimes called *cat's-eye*.

alfalfa

Alfalfa is a plant somewhat like clover, green and sweet-smelling, with small flowers of yellow, blue, or purple, when it blooms. Many farmers plant alfalfa to give their fields a rest from growing vegetables, because the alfalfa will help to nourish the field and also makes wonderful hay to feed to cattle. In fact, the word alfalfa means "the best fodder." It is cut when it is about three feet high. Alfalfa is also called *lucerne* or *medick*.

Alfonso, King of Spain

There have been many Spanish kings named Alfonso, which is a popular name in Spain, but the one remembered best today is Alfonso XIII, who was the last king of Spain. One remarkable thing about Alfonso XIII is that he became king the minute he was born (which was in the year 1886) because his father had died before he was born. Alfonso was a brave and clever man who was very well liked by those who knew him, but he was not a good ruler. He turned the government over to a dictator, General Primo de Rivera, but the people were very poor and did not have enough jobs or enough to eat, and there were many secret revolutionary groups that plotted against the king. In April, 1931, Alfonso saw that he could no longer be king, and he abdicated and left the country. Spain became a republic. He died in 1951. Read also the article on SPAIN.

Alfred the Great

Alfred the Great was a wise, brave king in England about a thousand years ago. He defended his people against terrible enemies and brought peace and order to his country, Wessex, in the southern part of the island of Great Britain. (There were several kings in England then.) Alfred's people were called the West Saxons.

Alfred was born about 849 and became king in 871. The Danes invaded his country soon after that, but he drove them out. A few years later they came back and this time they beat Alfred's army and the king had to hide in a swamp.

King Alfred did not give up. He wandered among his people in disguise. Slowly he gathered his scattered army together again. Once he stayed at the home of an old woman who told him to watch some cakes she was baking. When he fell asleep before the fire and let the cakes burn, the old woman, not knowing he was the king, scolded him and called him a good-for-nothing. But finally Alfred gathered his army together and defeated the Danes in a great battle.

King Alfred the Great.

Alfred set up a good government, passed wise laws, and brought peace and order to his country. In those days most of the people could not read or write, and the few who could write used only the Latin language. Alfred brought teachers and learned men from all parts of his country and from other lands in Europe, to write books and teach the people. King Alfred helped to write the books. Instead of Latin he used the language of the people, Anglo-Saxon, which came to be the English language we speak today. He established Christianity, which the people had been mixing with their old pagan religion. He built new fortresses and rebuilt cities. He built England's first navy.

In 892 the Danes attacked again and after fighting them for four long years Alfred defeated them again. He died in 899, when he was about 50 years old.

algae

Algae are special kinds of plants that grow in water. There are about fifteen thousand different kinds of algae. The green scum on the surface of a pond is a form of algae. Most of the many kinds of seaweed are algae. Some seaweeds grow to a length of 200 feet. Seaweed has been called the grass of the ocean. Without algae there would be no fish, just as there would be no animal life on land if there were no plants for animals to eat. Algae have no roots, stems or leaves. Some float freely on or near the surface of the water, because their pods are filled with air. They must float in order to get the sunlight that they need to grow on.

Most algae are green, but some are other colors. The Red Sea gets its name from the red algae that grow there. In many parts of the world people have found uses for seaweed. The Japanese eat certain kinds and also use it to fertilize their crops. From some seaweeds iodine and other medicines are made. Some forms of algae contain a substance that is put in ice cream to make it smooth.

algebra

Algebra is a way of figuring, just as arithmetic is. Both algebra and arithmetic are branches of the science of mathematics. Algebra is the branch of mathematics that is studied next after arithmetic. It begins as a kind of shorthand. For example, the simple job of adding 4 and 2 together can be expressed like this:

$$\frac{\begin{array}{r} 4 \\ 2 \end{array}}{6}$$

—or like this:

$$4 + 2 = 6$$

—or like this:

Four + Two = Six

In algebra it could be written:

$$F + T = S$$

—using the first letters of the words to stand for the numbers.

EQUATIONS

Such a statement, $F + T = S$, is called an equation. An equation is a statement that two things are equal. There are many rules governing equations. By the use of these rules it is often possible to do two important things: Discover unknown numbers that appear in equations with known numbers; and make calculations with big numbers just as easy as calculations with small numbers.

The basic rules governing equations include the following:

1. If a quantity added to one side is instead subtracted from the other side, the equation is still correct. If

$$F + T = S$$
then $F = S - T$
and $T = S - F$

An unknown number is often found by the use of this rule in the following manner. If it is known that F is 4 and S is 6, but it is not known what T stands for, and the equation is

$$F + T = S$$
then $4 + T = 6$
and $T = 6 - 4$
so $T = 2$

2. If each side is multiplied by the same factor (number) the equation is still correct. If

$$F + T = S$$
then $2F + 2T = 2S$

(In algebra the multiplication sign is not used when two symbols are placed side by side; $F \times T$ is written FT and $2 \times T$ is written 2T.)

and also

$$132,486F + 132,486T = 132,486S$$

Likewise, if each side is divided by the same quantity, the equation remains correct. This is usually written in the form of a fraction:

$$F + T = S$$

therefore $\dfrac{F + T}{2} = \dfrac{S}{2}$

Calculations of large numbers are often simplified by this rule. A letter such as N can be allowed to stand for the number 132,486. The equation then becomes simply $NF + NT = NS$. It is never necessary to multiply or divide large numbers until the final step of the calculations.

3. If the same quantity is added to both sides or is subtracted from both sides, the equation remains correct:

$$F + T = S$$
therefore $F + T + N = S + N$
and $F + T - N = S - N$

This rule permits *cancellation*, which simplifies many calculations. If given the last two equations shown above, for example, one would simply cancel the N from each side.

NOTATION

In algebra it is customary to use certain symbols, or marks, and certain letters to represent quantities and operations. Seldom would the letters F, T and S actually be used as they are in the examples given above. Usually the early letters of the alphabet, *a, b, c,* etc., are used to stand for *constants,* fixed or known numbers, and the late letters, *x, y, z,* to stand for *variables,* quantities that may have various values or that are unknown. The letter *n* is used to mean "any given (or known) number." In standard algebraic notation, or system of mathematical shorthand, the following are other customs:

Quantities to be multiplied are written side by side if they are not all numerals (for example, 2*a* means $2 \times a$ and *ab* means $a \times b$) but the multiplication sign, $\times$, is used when numerals are to be multiplied (2×2 cannot be written 22, which as usual means twenty-two).

Parentheses show operations to be performed first; $2(a + b)$ means that *a* and *b* should first be added together and then multiplied by 2.

POWERS

A *power* of a number is the product, or result, you get when you multiply the number by itself, one or more times. It is expressed by an *exponent,* a small number written after and higher than the number. Thus, 3^2 (when you read it aloud, you say "three squared") means 3×3, or 9; and 2^5 means $2 \times 2 \times 2 \times 2 \times 2$, or 32 (it is read "two to the fifth power").

ROOTS

A *root* is the opposite of a power. It is a number that must be multiplied by itself to produce a given number. It is written with a *radical sign,* as $\sqrt[3]{64}$ (read "the cube root of 64"); the answer here is 4, since 4^3 ($4 \times 4 \times 4$) is 64. When the sign is used without a little number, it means *square root,* as $\sqrt{25} = 5$.

SERIES

A *series* is a group of numbers related by some rule. In an *arithmetic* series, such as 1, 4, 7, 10 . . . , a constant number (here, 3) is added to each term to give the next. In a *geometric* series, such as 1, 2, 4, 8 . . . , each term is multiplied by a constant number (here, 2) to produce the next. Series often provide the best way to find out the value of important unknown numbers in physics and other sciences.

Alger, Horatio

Horatio Alger, Junior, was an American writer who wrote at least a hundred books for boys. Millions of copies of his books were sold, during his life and long after his death. All of them were books about boys who started life in humble circumstances, perhaps as orphans or as poor boys, but who worked hard and were honest and eventually became very successful. The critics did not think Horatio Alger's books were good, but the American people loved them.

Alger was born in Revere, Massachusetts, a suburb of Boston, in 1834. He became a minister in the Unitarian Church, then moved to New York City and did some work helping the poor boys who sold newspapers, worked as shoeshine boys, and did other things that hardly paid them enough to live on. Many of his books were written about boys who found themselves in just those circumstances. His titles were catchy, like *Luck and Pluck,* or *Sink or Swim,* or *Ragged Dick.*

Alger's recipe for success did not work so well with himself. In spite of the millions of copies his books sold, he never made much money out of them and he died poor in the year 1899.

Algeria

Algeria is a large country in North Africa, across the Mediterranean Sea from France and Spain. Its coast on the Mediterranean Sea is the famous Barbary Coast, where Mohammedan pirates used to attack ships and capture Christians to be held for ransom or sold as slaves.

Algeria became an independent nation in 1962, after more than 100 years of being governed by France. During this period there were many rebellions by Algerian patriots who wanted their country to be independent, and after World War II this grew into full-fledged warfare. The French people finally decided it was better to make Algeria independent than to lose so many lives fighting.

In area Algeria is about four times as big as France, but its population of over 17,000,000 is small because so much of the country is part of the Sahara Desert.

WHO LIVES IN ALGERIA

People of many different races and origins live in Algeria. Those who have been there longest are the Berbers (and it is from them that the name "Barbary Coast" came); they speak their own language, a very old one, but it has been mixed with other languages, especially Arabic. There are many Arabs living in Algeria. Many of the Arabs are nomads ("wanderers") who have no permanent homes but live in tents. There are probably more than three million Berbers and more than three million Arabs in Algeria.

The other people of Algeria include many Negroes, who long ago were brought from the heart of Africa and sold as slaves, but who have been free ever since the French came to control the country. There used to be about a million Europeans, mostly French, Spanish, and Italian; many Jews, who went to Algeria hundreds of years ago; and Turks, who once conquered the country. Many of these different peoples have married one another. Since Algeria became independent, most of the French people, called *colons*, have left, and many of the Jews have moved to Israel.

Most of the people of Algeria follow the Mohammedan religion.

HOW THE PEOPLE LIVE

Most of the people of Algeria earn their living by farming in the fertile valleys and plains along the northern coast. This section is called the Tell ("hill") and was famous for its rich soil as long ago as Roman times. The native farmers were very poor until the French introduced modern machinery and methods. Today, Algerian farmers grow large quantities of wheat and other grain, olives, figs, and many fruits, including grapes, from which they make wine.

The farms of the *colons* and the factories formerly owned by the French, have been nationalized (put under state control).

Most of the villages of the natives are on the slopes or mountainsides. The Berbers work at farming and cultivating fruit trees; the Arabs raise livestock, the other important occupation next to farming. The greatest possession of the Arabs is their sheep, but their horses and mules are also noted for their excellence.

In the cities, the modern Algerian— whether native or foreign — lives and dresses like the people who live in cities in the United States. Some of the Mohammedans still wear their native dress, and a few of the women wear veils over the lower part of their faces.

Education has grown slowly in Algeria. The Mohammedans did not like to send their children to French schools. Now most of the children go to school. Among the Arab nomads, schooling is very difficult because they do not stay in one place very long. Children often are taught only by traveling teachers who stay a few weeks.

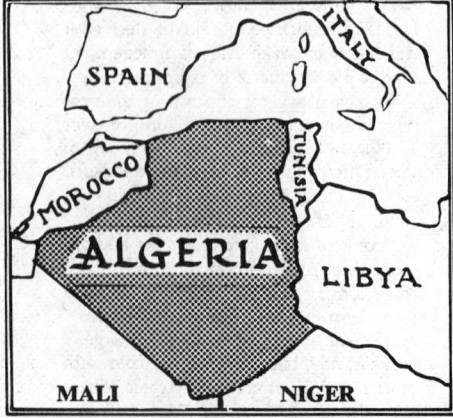

WHAT KIND OF PLACE IT IS

Algeria is a mountainous country, crossed by the high Atlas Mountains which divide Algeria from the Sahara

Desert in the south. On the mountain slopes cedar and oak trees grow, sometimes to gigantic size. Until the country was built up, the people were not able to make use of the wood of these trees because they had no good roads or railroads to carry the timber to the cities. Now roads and railroads have been built and lumber is a flourishing industry.

Most of the rivers in the mountains are not very useful. The most important is the Chéliff, which is about 400 miles long and empties into the Mediterranean. In the rainy season, which is from October to March, it becomes swollen and dangerous as it rushes down from the mountains. In the center of Algeria there used to be many marshes, but the government has drained them and turned them into prosperous farmland.

In the south is the desert, uninhabited and barren, except for spots, called *oases,* where there is water. Some of these oases are natural springs, but many have been made by irrigation. In these areas there is farming. Oil has been found in parts of the Sahara and is being developed by the government with French assistance.

Algeria's climate varies a great deal. People living in the north have a comfortably warm climate like that of Florida. In the desert, south of the mountains, it is very hot. In the mountains it is cool in summer, with severe winters.

Every year, from May to September, there are great wind storms called siroccos. The hot wind from the desert blows across the country, filling the air with fine sand. But Algeria has, on the whole, a healthful climate.

HOW THE PEOPLE ARE GOVERNED

Algeria is a republic but has never been a true democracy, governed by a majority vote of the people. The first president was Ahmed Ben Bella, one of the leaders of the National Liberation Front (F.L.N.), which led the fight for Algerian independence. Ben Bella established a socialist government and allowed no opposition either to himself or to the F.L.N. Ben Bella's socialist policies, such as nationalizing farms and factories, proved disastrous and the country went heavily into debt. Much money was also wasted on projects designed for "show" and not to help the people. In 1965, the Algerian Army ousted Ben Bella and took power. An Army leader, Colonel Houari Boumediene, became the president.

THE CITIES OF ALGERIA

Algeria is divided into three departments, or states, each having the same name as the biggest city in it.

ALGIERS. The city of Algiers is the capital of Algeria. There is a separate article about it.

ORAN. This is a big city, with a population of 327,493 (in 1973), on the Mediterranean Sea. The French navy has a big naval base here (the base being also called Mers-el-Kebir, which is the name of the district next to Oran). When the Germans occupied France during World War II, the British fleet in the Mediterranean sailed up to this naval base and destroyed most of the French warships in it, so that the Germans could not get them. In 1942 Allied troops under General

Eisenhower landed at Oran and captured it easily.

CONSTANTINE. This is the largest inland city of Algeria. It has a population of 243,558.

Another large city in the Constantine department is BôNE, a city of 164,844 population. It is a seaport on the Mediterranean.

These men are musicians who play their tambourines in the streets of the city.

ALGERIA IN THE PAST

There have been people living in Algeria for many thousands of years, but during most of this period it has been a colony of some other country. It was a thriving colony of ancient Rome for about 500 years. The Romans called the colony Numidia and the Berber people Numidians.

St. Augustine, one of the greatest figures in the history of the Christian church, was the bishop of Hippo, an ancient city that was near the present site of Bône.

From about the year 440 on, Algeria was conquered many times. First the Germans came. Then came Mohammedan invaders, the Arabs and later the Turks. Ever since, Algeria has been a Mohammedan country. About 1700 it became an independent country with a king whose title was dey. Under the deys Algeria became a home for pirates.

In 1836, a French consul in Algiers insulted the dey, whose name was Hussein. The dey became angry and hit the consul. France used this as an excuse to go to war and make Algeria a French colony. By 1850, all of northern Algeria had been conquered but fighting went on. The Sahara regions were not brought under French control until 1909. The Arab rebel leader Abd-el-Kader led uprisings of Algerians against France in the period before 1850.

Algerians admit that French rule caused the country to advance very rapidly in agriculture, roadbuilding and railroads, the treatment and prevention of disease, and education. But the Algerians wanted full independence. The French government tried to appease them by making Algeria a full member of Metropolitan France (as though it were a part of France in Europe), but in 1954 Algerian rebels began a war for independence.

This war lasted for almost nine years. Every year it became worse. French troops

The workers in this photograph are working for the Algerian Government in promoting a new rural development project. The farmers work on a rotation basis and are paid in foodstuffs.

won battles but could not win a decisive victory. Many were killed and atrocities were committed by both sides.

When Charles de Gaulle came to power in France in 1958, he promised peace in Algeria by letting the Algerian people choose how they wished to be governed. Most Frenchmen approved of this policy, because the war was costly in money and lives, but an underground group, called the O.A.S., led by *colons* and some French Army generals, plotted to keep Algeria part of France—if necessary by overthrowing de Gaulle.

Trans-World Airlines

At Djemila, a few miles from Constantine, stand the ruins of the Arch of Caracalla. Caracalla was a Roman emperor, about 200 A.D., when Algeria belonged to Rome.

From 1958 to 1962 the war continued while de Gaulle tried to negotiate a settlement with Algerian leaders. The O.A.S. rebellion failed and in 1962 the people of Algeria voted overwhelmingly for independence. Algeria became an independent nation on July 3, 1962. In 1965 the government was overthrown by a junta (army).

ALGERIA. Area, 919,591 square miles Population (1975) 17,000,000. Languages, French, Arabic, Berber, and others. Religion, chiefly Mohammedan. Government, republic. Monetary unit, dinar, worth about 20½ cents (U.S.).

Algiers

The capital and largest city of Algeria, with a population of more than 943,000, is Algiers. It is an important seaport on the Mediterranean Sea. Part of Algiers is a very modern French city. The other part is a native quarter, called the Casbah, in which the people are nearly all Mohammedans of Arabic and Berber ancestry, dressing in the native fashion that their people have followed for hundreds of years, and following Mohammedan customs. Algiers is more than a thousand years old. It was once the capital of Mohammedan rulers of northern Africa. Thousands of soldiers of the United States Army visited Algiers or were stationed there.

ALGIERS, ALGERIA. Population with suburbs, 943,000 (1975 estimate). Capital of Algeria. On the Mediterranean Sea.

Algonquin Indians

The Indians of North America belonged to many different small nations or tribes. Each tribe spoke a different language, but in some cases there were anywhere from a dozen to a hundred different tribes whose languages were much alike. Scientists call these a "language group" or "family." The largest of these is the Algonquin (or Algonquian) family of tribes.

The Algonquin Indians lived mostly in the northeastern part of America. Their territory stretched from the Atlantic coast westward to the Mississippi River, southward as far as Tennessee and Virginia, and northward as far as Hudson Bay in what is now Canada. A few Algonquin

tribes, such as the Arapaho and Cheyenne, lived on the plains. Another tribe, called the Blackfoot, lived as far west as the Rocky Mountains.

The first Indians met by the white settlers from Holland, France and England were Algonquins. There were about one hundred of these Algonquin tribes. They were always at war with one another. They would make raids to get scalps, which were pieces of skin with hair on them, cut from the heads of enemies whom they had killed. The more scalps a warrior brought back with him from a raid on another tribe, the more he was admired.

Many of the Algonquin tribes were friendly to the white settlers when they first arrived, but they were soon at war with the colonists because the white men wanted the Indians' land for farming. In these wars the whites were just as cruel as the Indians. Both sides burned villages and killed women and children. In the French and Indian Wars, when England fought to control the New World, the Algonquins fought on the French side. But in the end the British destroyed most of the New England Algonquin tribes. Others were gradually pushed back into the forest by the whites and driven toward the west. Very often only a few Indians were left out of a tribe of several hundred. On their westward journeys they had to pass through the territory of unfriendly Indians who attacked and killed many of them.

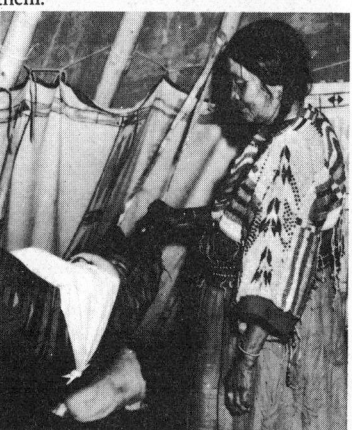

U.S. Indian Service, photo by Morrow

A Blackfoot woman rocking a baby in her tepee on the Blackfoot Reservation in Montana.

Some of the most famous Indians in the early history of the United States were Algonquin. Massasoit, chief of the Wampanoags in New England, welcomed the Pilgrims when they landed at Plymouth. He taught them how to raise corn and signed a peace treaty with them. He never broke this treaty, even though the Pilgrims sometimes were cruel and unfair to his people. Another famous Algonquin was Pocahontas, who saved the life of Captain John Smith, leader of the first English settlement at Jamestown, Virginia, when he was captured by the Powhatan Indians. Later she married one of the English settlers, John Rolfe.

HOW THE ALGONQUINS LIVED

The Algonquin tribes lived in houses called wigwams, made of poles covered with elm-tree bark. In winter the poles were covered with mats woven out of cat-

tail stalks, because these were warmer than bark. The floor was earth that had been stamped down with the feet. A fire was built in the middle of the floor and smoke escaped through a small hole in the roof. Raised platforms around the sides were used for sleeping and sitting.

The clothing worn by both men and women was usually made from deerskins. They wore soft shoes of deerskin called moccasins. The men usually wore only a breechcloth during the summer.

The women raised corn, squash, and beans, in small forest clearings. The men were forest hunters, and deer supplied most of their meat as well as fine skins for clothing. They made jugs and pots out of clay and knew how to make strong thread and twine from the inner bark of such trees as the swamp ash and linden. Until the white man came they knew nothing about metal, and made knives, needles and tools out of animal bones and stone. Their weapons were bows and arrows, knives, and battle axes called tomahawks. The arrowheads, knives and ax heads were made of stone. One of the best things made by the Algonquins was the birch-bark canoe, a boat that was strong enough to carry three people yet light enough to be carried by one man. It was made of a framework of light strong wood tied tightly together and covered with birch-bark. Using a canoe, the Algonquin Indian could travel swiftly and silently for long distances.

Their medicine men knew a great deal about healing herbs and roots, and many of the white settlers called upon them for help when they were ill.

Algonquin Indian women had their own beauty aids. They used bear fat to keep their hair glossy, and wore their hair long, since this was considered beautiful. They put fish oil and eagle fat on their faces to keep the skin soft. Sometimes they mixed red color into the fat to give color to the face, just as women do today when they put rouge on their faces. The men took even greater care of their hair than the women. They dressed it with bear fat every day and even mixed soot into it to make it look blacker than it was. They shaved their heads except for a ridge of hair in the middle of the head from front to back and often tied all sorts of ornaments like bits of shell and stone into it. They also painted pictures of animals and birds on their bodies and carried bags of paint about with them as part of their toilet kit. Both men and women liked to wear an embroidered band of skin around the head. In this they often stuck a row of feathers, but the big feathered headdress so often seen on Indians in the movies was not worn by Algonquin Indians but mostly by the Sioux, a tribe of the western plains.

Each tribe had a chief who was the leader in peace and war, but serious problems were discussed by a kind of mass meeting of all the people of the tribe. This meeting was often called a powwow, a word now used in the English language also. At the powwow a big fire was built and everybody sat around it and ate food. Some sang sacred songs and offered prayers. There was much pounding of drums, shaking of rattles, singing, and dancing. In between the singing and dancing there was a discussion of the problem. This might go on for days until a decision was made.

Algonquin tribes living along the Atlantic coast were the Abnaki, Algonkin, Delaware, Mahican, Massachusetts, Micmac, Narraganset, Neskapi, Pequot, Powhatan, and Wampanoag tribes. Algonquin tribes living around the Great Lakes were the Cree, Illinois, Kickapoo, Menomini, Miami, Ojibway, Ottawa, Potawatomi, Sauk and Fox, and Shawnee.

Alhambra

The Alhambra is a palace in Granada, a city in the south of Spain. It was built when the Moors and other people of the Mohammedan religion had conquered Spain and ruled there. The Alhambra was built mostly by Christians who had been made slaves by the Mohammedan rulers. It took more than one hundred years to build the Alhambra. It is such a big place that it covers thirty-five acres, which is as much as sixteen or seventeen city blocks.

The Alhambra is not one building, but many. There are several palaces, and a strong fortress that looks like a castle, with high towers and walls. The palaces are finished in bright colors; even the roofs of the palaces are painted red and blue and brown and gold. There are windows made of wood carved to look like lace; the floors and some of the walls and ceilings are of marble and painted tiles arranged in patterns and pictures. The wooden parts of the walls and ceilings are painted white and gold. There are many marble columns and archways. Some of the palaces are built in the shape of a square, with a garden in the center. In the gardens there are pools with live goldfish, carved fountains, and bright flowers.

In 1492, the same year that Columbus sailed on his voyage to discover America, the Spanish people drove the Moors out of their country. In the fighting they destroyed much of the Alhambra. Three hundred years later a king of Spain, Ferdinand VII, had the Alhambra rebuilt and restored. The writer Washington Irving wrote a book about the Alhambra.

Alien and Sedition Laws

The Alien and Sedition Acts were laws passed by the Congress of the United States in 1798, when the nation was only a few years old. The Alien Laws gave the President the right to send a foreigner out of the United States if war occurred. To become a citizen, a foreigner had to live in America 14 years. The Sedition Laws allowed the government to put a person in jail if he criticized the government.

Spanish Tourist Office
The Court of the Lions is perhaps the most admired portion of the Alhambra. The lions may be seen around the fountain. The windows and arches look like lacework.

All of these laws took away rights that the people felt the Constitution of the United States had given them. They hated the laws so much that they would not re-elect John Adams, who was President when the laws were passed. Two states of the United States, Virginia and Kentucky, passed resolutions that the laws were unconstitutional. None of these laws was used very much, and they ended in 1801.

alimentary canal

The alimentary canal is the entire pathway through the body along which food travels from the time it is swallowed to the time the unused part of it leaves the body as waste. It is a series of big and little pipes, all connected together to form one tube about 30 feet long. It begins at the mouth and goes down through the neck and chest into the belly; there it winds around through the intestines and ends in a small opening at the back of the body called the anus.

The entire alimentary canal is lined with a thin, moist skin called mucous membrane, like the lining of the mouth.

The digestion of food takes place in the different parts of the alimentary canal. After food is chewed and swallowed it passes through the pharynx, a tube about 4½ inches long, and down into the esophagus, another tube about 9 inches long that connects with the stomach. The stomach is a pear-shaped bag about 11 inches long and 4 inches wide. In the walls of the stomach there are glands, or tiny sacs, that pour out liquids called digestive juices. These help break down the food. In the stomach the food is only partially digested. It passes into the small intestine, a long narrow tube about 23 feet long, which takes up most of the belly or abdomen. It is in this long, winding tube that the digestion of food is completed.

What remains of the food now passes on to the colon, or large intestine, which is a bigger but shorter tube than the small intestine. The last eight inches of the colon is called the rectum. The waste matter of the body is stored here until it is forced out of the anus.

alimony

Alimony is money paid by a husband for the support of a former wife, from whom he is divorced or legally separated by a court order. Alimony is decided by the judge in the divorce or separation trial. Money paid by private agreement is not correctly called alimony; it must be ordered by a judge in court. Any amount that a man pays for the support of children is not part of the alimony payment. Not all divorced wives receive alimony. In many cases they do not ask the judge to award them alimony; sometimes the judge will decide that the wife has enough income and property of her own; and alimony is not awarded if the wife is at fault in the divorce action and the husband brought the suit against her.

Sometimes a judge will order *temporary alimony* during the time when the divorce suit is being prepared. This is also called *alimony pendente lite,* which is Latin for "alimony while waiting for the written (decree)." All alimony ends when a divorced wife marries again.

alkali

Alkalis are chemicals that are used in making many different products. An alkali is also called a *base*. It may be in the form of a liquid, a gas, or a solid. When bases are combined with acids, the acids are neutralized and salts are formed which can be dissolved easily in water.

The lye or caustic soda that is used to clear sluggish drains of grease in kitchens and bathrooms is an alkali, called sodium hydroxide by chemists. It can burn holes in such things as leather, wood, cloth, and human flesh. It is a deadly poison if swallowed by mistake. (To stop the burning action on the skin, the place touched should be thoroughly rinsed with water and then treated by the application of a weak acid, such as vinegar or lemon juice.) Lye is also used in the manufacture of paper, aluminum, glass, and soap (which is a mixture of lye with fat or oil).

There are also weak alkalis, such as washing soda and baking soda, or bicarbonate of soda. When a strong acid touches the skin its burning action can be stopped by a solution of a weak soda.

Farmers sometimes have trouble getting crops to grow in soil that has too much alkali in it. Such soil must be flooded with water and then drained, to remove the excess alkali.

alkaloid

Alkaloids are a group of chemicals that are usually made from plants and are used in drugs. Some of the best known of these alkaloids are morphine, opium, quinine, cocaine and nicotine.

Opium is a drug made from a flower, the poppy. Poppies from which opium can be made grow mostly in eastern Asia. Opium, and drugs such as morphine that are made from opium, are used as pain killers, but are very dangerous.

Quinine is a medicine made from the bark of the cinchona tree, which grows in Peru and in parts of southeastern Asia. It is used as a cure for malaria, a fever that attacks people in the southern part of the United States and in the tropical parts of Africa, South America, and Asia.

Cocaine is a pain killer made from the leaves of the coca plant of western South America. It is very dangerous, just as are the drugs made from opium. Cocaine was once used by dentists, but novocaine, a substitute for it, is now used instead.

Nicotine is made from the leaves of the tobacco plant. It is very poisonous, but the amount of nicotine in smoking tobacco is too small to be poisonous. Nicotine is often mixed with water and other liquids and sprayed on plants, to kill insects that destroy crops.

There are several cases, besides that of novocaine, in which artificial drugs have been made to replace the ones made from plants. One example is atabrine, which is often used instead of quinine to prevent or control malaria.

Allah

Allah is the name given to God in the Mohammedan religion. Like the Christians and Jews, the Mohammedans believe in only one God. They say this in the following way: "There is but one God and his name is Allah." The word Allah comes from two Arabic words, *al ilah,* which mean "the God."

All-American

The name All-American is given to an athlete who has been chosen as the best at his position in his particular sport. The first well-known All-American teams were football teams. They were picked by a man named Walter Camp, every year beginning in 1889 until he died in 1925. He had played football himself and at one time was the coach at Yale University. Today magazines and newspapers and sportscasters all over the country choose All-American teams and there is no "official" All-American team.

All-American teams are chosen in many sports, football, basketball, baseball, lacrosse, soccer, and others.

All-American Canal

The All-American Canal is the longest irrigation canal in the United States. It was built by the U.S. Bureau of Reclamation in the years between 1934 and 1940, as part of the Boulder Canyon project. It is 80 miles long and carries water from the Colorado River above Yuma, Arizona, to the Imperial Valley in California.

Alleghenies

The Allegheny Mountains, or Alleghenies, are a small range in the eastern part of the United States. This range is the central section of the bigger mountain range known as the Appalachians. The Alleghenies stretch between the Catskill Mountains in New York and the Blue Ridge Mountains in Virginia and the Carolinas. The highest peak is the Peak of Otter, in Virginia. It is 4,000 feet high at its summit.

Many millions of years ago, before there were people living on the earth, there was a flat plain where the Alleghenies are today. On that plain were a great many plants. No such plants grow today. Some of them were like ferns but as big as trees. They made a huge, extremely thick mat that gradually became packed down, and grew harder and harder until it eventually turned into coal. Later, when the earth's crust wrinkled because it was cooling inside, mountains were pushed up, with the coal deep inside them. Miners dig both hard and soft coal out of these mountains today, in Pennsylvania and West Virginia. There are also rich deposits of iron, oil, natural gas, and clay.

The Allegheny range is 500 miles long. It includes the highest points in Pennsylvania (Mt. Davis, 3,213 feet) and West Virginia (Spruce Knob, 4,860 feet).

Allegheny River

The Allegheny River rises in north Pennsylvania and joins the Monongahela River at Pittsburgh to form the Ohio River. It is 325 miles long. The Allegheny is navigable for small craft for about 200 miles above Pittsburgh, and it was an important commercial route before the railroads were built.

allegory

An allegory is a story in which a character represents an idea as well as a person. This can also be done in other forms of art, for example, painting and dancing. Father Time may appear as a character in a story or in a picture, an old man with a long gray beard, to represent the idea that everyone grows old. In dancing, a character named Death may appear as a skeleton to represent the idea that everyone must die.

The allegory that is best known in English literature is *Pilgrim's Progress* by John Bunyan. In this book, the hero is a man named Christian, but the idea is the fact that man is always looking for goodness. The other characters stand for ideas in the same way.

Another famous old English allegory is the story of Everyman. Some of the fables of Aesop and other writers may be thought of as allegories if you consider the animals to stand for ideas, for example, the fox standing for cleverness, the bee for thrift, and the owl for wisdom. The mythology of the ancient Greeks and Romans was allegorical, with the god Mars representing war, Venus love, and so on.

Allen, Ethan

Ethan Allen was an American hero in the Revolutionary War. He was the leader of the "Green Mountain Boys" from Vermont, and he is remembered as Vermont's greatest man of his time, but he was not born there. Vermont was not a state (or separate colony) then, and very few people lived there. Ethan Allen was born in Litchfield, Connecticut, on January 10, 1738, nearly forty years before the Revolutionary War began. He fought for the British in the French and Indian Wars, just as George Washington did. After this fighting, when the Governor of New Hampshire offered good farmlands "across the Green Mountains" to some of the soldiers, Ethan Allen was one of those who went there and built himself a home in what is now Vermont. These settlers, though they called themselves the Green Mountain "Boys," were really men.

As leader of these Green Mountain Boys, Ethan Allen rebelled against British rule before the Declaration of Independence was signed. On May 10, 1775, he and his Green Mountain Boys, with the help of Benedict Arnold and some soldiers from Connecticut, attacked Fort Ticonderoga in New York State, held by the British, and captured it. Ethan Allen's words in that attack have become famous. "Surrender," he shouted, "in the name of Jehovah and the Continental Congress!"

The Continental Congress sent Allen to Canada, to see if he could persuade the Canadians to join the Revolution. On his second trip to Canada he was captured by the British. They put iron shackles on his hands and feet and threw him into the hold of a ship. He was kept there for five weeks before the ship sailed. As soon as the ship left Quebec, the captain released Allen from his dungeon until they reached England. The British knew Ethan Allen was too valuable to kill. They sent him back to America and exchanged him for a British colonel who had been captured by the Americans.

The Continental Congress greeted Ethan Allen with the greatest honor, and Vermont made him a major general. After the Revolutionary War was won, he spent his time as a delegate to the Continental Congress, trying to persuade them

to recognize Vermont as a state. He died in 1789, when he was 52 years old, thinking he had failed; but two years later Vermont became a state.

Allen, Florence

Florence Allen was the first woman to be a judge of the United States Circuit Court of Appeals, to which she was appointed in 1934. She was born in 1884, in Salt Lake City, Utah. After a brief period as a music editor and lecturer, she practiced law in Cleveland, Ohio. From 1922 to 1934 she was a judge of the Supreme Court of Ohio. In 1934, she was appointed to the United States Circuit Court of Appeals. She died in 1966.

Allen, Fred

Fred Allen was the stage name of John Florence Sullivan, a radio and television comedian who was born in Cambridge, Massachusetts in 1894, and died in 1956. He began his theatrical career as a juggler in vaudeville. Later he went on to musical comedy and motion pictures. His first radio appearance was in 1932, and for many years he and his wife, Portland Hoffa, starred in radio. He was considered one of the greatest natural wits and most original thinkers in the theatrical world.

Allenby, Lord

Edmund Henry Hynman Allenby was a British military leader in World War I. He was born in 1861 and joined the British army in 1882. He served in African colonial wars and in the Boer War (1899–1902) as cavalry commander, and for the first three years of World War I he served in France. In 1917 he became commander in chief of the Egyptian Expeditionary Force fighting the Turks in Egypt and Palestine. He conducted a brilliant campaign and with the aid of a young officer, T. E. Lawrence, won the support of Arabs and others who were then ruled by Turkey. After Turkey's surrender in 1918 Allenby was promoted to field marshal. In 1919 he was made Viscount Allenby of Megiddo and Felixstowe. He died in 1936.

Allentown

Allentown is a city in eastern Pennsylvania. It is on the Lehigh River. There are coal and iron mines and many large steel mills in the surrounding region, and in Allentown there are factories that make steel products and also cement, textiles, and electrical parts. Muhlenberg College is in Allentown. The city of Bethlehem, with a population of 72,686 in 1970, is only three miles away.

During the Revolutionary War the Liberty Bell was hidden in Allentown when the British threatened to take Philadelphia. The Zion Reformed Church. where the bell was hidden, still stands.

ALLENTOWN, PENNSYLVANIA. Population (1970 census) 109,527. County seat of Lehigh County. Founded about 1752.

allergy

An allergy is an unusual sensitivity to a substance that is normally harmless. A person who has an allergy to a certain substance will develop symptoms of illness when he comes in contact with it. When the substance is removed, the symptoms disappear. People may have allergies to foods, drugs and other chemicals, dusts and pollens, fabrics and furs, bacteria, light rays, temperature changes, air pressure, and many other things. Emotional strain, or unconscious fears, or extreme dislikes, may produce symptoms of sickness.

Examples of allergic diseases are hay fever, asthma, eczema and other skin ailments, and a number of stomach or digestive disorders. It has been estimated that about 10% of all the people in the United States have at least one allergy.

No one knows exactly what causes allergies, and it is only recently that people became aware that they existed. It is often very difficult to determine precisely what substance (called the *allergen*) is causing the unpleasant reaction. The tests are usually made by a dermatologist, or skin specialist. He puts a number of patches on the patient's skin, each patch containing a small amount of some substance known to be an allergen. When the patches are removed the skin beneath will be irritated and inflamed if the patient is allergic to the substance in the patch. But there are so many possible allergens that the tests may take a long time.

Various drugs have been developed to help people who suffer from allergies.

KINDS OF ALLERGEN

There are in general five different kinds of allergens, or things that cause an allergic reaction:

Airborne substances—pollens (especially ragweed, sagebrush, goosefoot), dusts, fungi, animal emanations, tobacco and train smoke, vapors, perfumes, cosmetics, and various strong odors.

Foods—wheat, eggs, milk, fish, pork, strawberries, nuts, chocolate.

Contact substances—plants (poisonivy, poison oak), flowers, chemicals, fabrics, dyestuffs, rubber, furs, leather, jewelry, cosmetics, animal hairs, feathers.

Drugs—aspirin, quinine, barbiturates, sulfa drugs, penicillin.

Infectious agents—bacteria, viruses, and various parasites.

Allies

In World War I, when the fighting broke out in 1914, Great Britain, France and Russia fought together against Germany and Austria-Hungary (which was then a large, powerful nation in central Europe). Great Britain, France and Russia were called "the Allies," and Germany and Austria-Hungary were called "the Central Powers."

The name Allies became popular, and when World War II began in 1939 it was again applied to Great Britain and France. The United States, when it joined the war during World War I, was known as one of the Allies, and again in World War II when Russia and later the United States went in, they were said to have "joined the Allies."

alligator

The alligator is the largest reptile of the United States. The alligator looks like a big lizard, but it is not a lizard. It is related to the crocodiles, but has a broader snout and a bigger tail. It spends most of its time swimming or sunning itself on the shore. A fully-grown male alligator may be as much as 15 to 19 feet long and may weigh up to 600 pounds, but most of them are smaller—up to 10 feet long for males, and 7 or 8 feet for females. This includes the tail. An alligator's tail is about as long as his body.

Alligators live in freshwater streams in the southern United States from North Carolina to Texas, and also in China. Once they were thought to live to be 100 years old, but actually 30 to 50 years is closer to it. The alligator is one of the few reptiles that has a voice. It can roar or bellow loudly.

Female alligators build nests of leaves and other material that they scrape up along the shore. They lay about 30 eggs, 2 to 3 inches long. The young alligators are 8 to 10 inches long when they hatch, and grow about a foot a year at first, then more slowly. Young alligators are often captured as "pets," but this is very foolish. They seldom live in captivity, and if they do they soon become dangerous.

An alligator eats other animals. It captures them, drowns them in the water, then swallows them. Alligators are timid and seldom attack men, but if they do they are dangerous. They often swing their big, strong tails in fighting. Alligator skin makes very fine leather, but because they are in danger of becoming extinct, American alligators are now protected by laws against killing them.

New York Zoological Society

The alligator looks like a big lizard.

alligator pear, another name for the avocado. See AVOCADO.

alliteration

Alliteration is the use of two or more words that begin with the same letter or sound, such as "tried and true," "safe and sound," "hale and hearty," or "in the merry month of May."

A thousand years ago, poets who wrote in the Old English language used alliteration instead of rhyme. In the article on ANGLO-SAXON there is an example of this. A poet today often uses both rhyme and alliteration, but alliteration is used more in humorous poetry than in serious poetry.

alloy

An alloy is a metal made by melting two or more pure metals in a very hot furnace and mixing them together. When they cool and harden, they form a new metal. This is an alloy. Other alloys are made by mixing a melted metal with

small amounts of a chemical that is not a metal.

There are so many alloys made by man today that it would take a very thick book to list all of them. Usually an alloy is better for some special use than a pure metal would be. One of the first alloys made by man was bronze, a mixture of copper and tin. Thousands of years ago, long before man discovered iron, bronze was used for knives, swords, shields, and tools. Ancient man had found that copper was too soft for knives and other cutting tools. Then he learned that by adding a little tin to copper he could make a metal that was harder than either tin or copper. Brass is another alloy made with copper. It is made by adding zinc to the copper and is much harder than either of these metals.

Some of the strongest alloys are amalgams, which are mixtures of mercury with other metals. These alloys are made without melting either metal.

Steel is one of the most important alloys in common use. It is made by melting iron and adding small amounts of pure carbon while the iron is still a hot liquid. Carbon is not a metal. Coal and charcoal —wood that has been burned black—are examples of carbon. Pure iron is a fairly soft metal. With enough carbon added, it becomes very hard. Stainless steel is made by mixing the metals chrome and nickel with the hot melted steel. These metals will not rust, so the entire alloy will not rust.

Very few pure metals are used by modern man. Even the silver dimes, quarters, and half dollars we use have a little copper added to them to make them harder. Pure silver is a very soft metal and would wear out very quickly. Not all alloys are intended to make a harder or stronger metal. Sometimes a softer metal is needed. Solder is an alloy of tin and lead. It is useful because it melts at a very low temperature.

Scientists called metallurgists work constantly to develop new and better alloys. Some of the best known have special "trade names" given to them by their inventors. See the articles on METALS and on the different metals such as IRON, COPPER, and so on. New alloys are being created all the time.

All Saints' Day

All Saints' Day is a religious holiday. On this day, Catholics honor all the blessed persons who have died and reached heaven. The holiday falls on November 1 each year. All Saints' Day used to be called All Hallows' Day ("Hallow" means bless). The night before was called All Hallows' Eve. Now we call this night Hallowe'en.

All Souls' Day

All Soul's Day is celebrated the day after All Saints' Day. On All Souls' Day, Catholics pray for those who have died. Their prayers are to help those who have died to enter heaven. On All Souls' Day, special services are held in the churches. Some people also observe the day by putting flowers on the graves of those who have died.

allspice

Allspice is the berry of a tree that grows on the island of Jamaica, in the West Indies. Another name for the berry is *Jamaica pepper*. Allspice gets its name because it is supposed to combine the flavor of several other spices, such as cinnamon, clove, and nutmeg. The berries must be picked before they become ripe. If they ripen on the tree they will become spoiled and bitter. After the berries are picked they are dried in the sun. Usually the berries are then ground to make a powder that can easily be sprinkled on food that is being cooked to flavor it. An oil made from the berries is used in perfumes. The wood of the tree is used in canes and umbrella handles.

Allston, Washington

Washington Allston was one of the finest American painters of portraits and other pictures, about a hundred and fifty years ago. He was born in the little town of Waccamaw, South Carolina, in 1779. After going to college at Harvard, he studied art in London, Paris, and Rome. He was a close friend of Samuel Taylor Coleridge, the English poet; Washington Irving, the American writer; and other great men of his time. His portraits and his paintings of scenes from the Bible may be seen in many art galleries, especially in London and Boston. They called him "the American Titian" because he used rich colors as the artist Titian did. One of Washington Allston's pupils was Samuel F. B. Morse, inventor of the telegraph. Allston died at Cambridge, Massachusetts, in 1843, when he was 64 years old.

Alma-Ata

Alma-Ata is a city in the Soviet Union. It is the capital of the Kazakh Soviet Socialist Republic. Alma-Ata used to be called Vernyi. Its population in 1972 was about 735,000.

almanac

An almanac is a book published once each year to give many useful facts and to be a complete calendar for the coming year. An almanac usually tells for each day of the year what time the sun will rise and when it will set, how full the moon will be, and at what times the tide will be high and low. Some almanacs also try to predict the weather in advance, but this cannot be done scientifically so far in advance.

The first almanac was probably made in ancient Egypt, thousands of years ago. The Nile River overflowed its banks every year, and the Egyptian people wanted to know about when this would happen. The priests studied the movements of the stars and the moon. They knew that so many full moons would have to appear after one flood before the next one came. The priests then told the people when to expect the next flood.

Almanacs became popular in Europe during the Middle Ages, about six or seven hundred years ago. There were almanacs that pretended to foretell wars, the death of kings, earthquakes, and fires.

One of the earliest and most famous American almanacs was begun in 1732 by Benjamin Franklin. He called it *Poor Richard's Almanack*. Poor Richard was a name that Franklin used for himself. Franklin not only gave the usual kind of almanac information; he also included many witty sayings. *The Old Farmers' Al-*

manac, started in 1766, is still read by many farmers in New England. Some almanacs published by large newspapers and by book publishers are filled with records of the events of past years and are actually small encyclopedias.

almond

The almond is a tree that grows in warm climates. It is related to the peach tree. The almond tree has light-pink blossoms and fruit that looks like peaches but is not eaten. Inside each fruit is a shell, and inside the shell is a nut, called an almond.

When the fruit of the almond tree ripens, it becomes leathery and hard and peels away from the nut. There are two kinds of almond. One is sweet and the other is bitter. The bitter almond is like the nut inside a peach pit. It should not be eaten. Many almonds are grown in the warm valleys of California.

aloe

Aloe is the name of a plant that grows best in tropical countries, where it is very hot. African natives use the fibers of the leaves to weave nets. The plant is best known as the source of a drug called *aloes*. This drug is contained in the juice of the aloe leaves. It has a very bitter taste. It is used in medicine to help in cleaning out the stomach. In South America some people use the dried stems of the aloe as tinder to start fires. The leaves of the aloe have sharp, spiny points. The aloe plant grows to be as much as 10 feet high. It belongs to the lily family. The aloe was brought to South America and Mexico by the Spaniards, hundreds of years ago.

Netherland West Indies Tourist Committee

The aloe is a small plant that can be grown in a flowerpot . Its leaves are crushed and the juice used to make medicine.

Aloysius, Saint

Saint Aloysius was born in Italy in 1568. His name originally was Luigi Gonzaga. He became a Jesuit priest and devoted his life to the care of the sick. He died in Rome during a plague in 1591. He was canonized as a saint by the Roman Catholic Church in 1726 and is the patron saint of boys and young men.

alpaca

The alpaca is an animal that lives in the Andes Mountains of South America. It is related to the llama, the guanaco, and the vicuña, which also live in South America. All these animals are members of the camel family, but do not have humps, nor are they as large as camels. The alpaca looks very much like a sheep with a long neck. It is usually brown but may also be grayish, white, black, or a mixture of these colors. It is a valuable animal because of its long, wooly hair. This hair is used in the weaving of fine woolen cloth.

The Indians of Bolivia and Peru keep herds of alpacas. The animals graze on pastures high in the Andes Mountains. Some alpacas live 15,000 feet above sea level. The Indians weave colorful blankets of alpaca hair. The alpaca is sheared once a year, and the wool is mostly sent to England and America. The alpaca, unlike the llama, is never used as a beast of burden.

alphabet

An alphabet is a system of using certain marks, which we call "letters," to stand for particular sounds. There are many different alphabets in the world today, and it has taken thousands of years to develop them. The English alphabet of twenty-six letters is also called the "Roman alphabet," because we got it from the ancient Romans, who had gotten it from the Greeks. We call it *alphabet* because the first two letters of the Greek alphabet were called *alpha* and *beta*—in other words, calling it the alphabet then was exactly the same as calling it the ABC's today.

The simplest way of putting an idea down on paper is to draw a picture, and that is how men first began to write, six thousand years ago or more. Our alphabet has come to us gradually from picture-writing of this sort. The picture-writing from which our alphabet is descended was done in ancient Egypt; it was called hieroglyphic writing. Picture-writing was able to express ideas as well as objects. For example, a little picture of a man could represent the word "man," but a picture of a man lying on the ground with a spear in him would represent the idea "death." The Chinese and even the American Indians developed methods of writing in pictures. But there was not much that could be said this way, and it would have taken hundreds of thousands of pictures to express everything—many more than a person could hope to learn in a lifetime.

Out of the early picture-writing came the use of pictures to stand for syllables. Suppose a picture of a pole or stake in the ground were used to represent the word "pole," and a picture of a lamp burning to represent the word "light." Putting the two together, you would have pole-light, which could mean polite—an idea that could never be expressed by a picture. Using pictures in this way to represent sounds instead of things, men were able to increase the usefulness of their writing by many times. The Chinese still use this kind of writing in syllables. The trouble is that there are so many different syllables, it takes a scholar years to learn them all. In the Chinese language there are more

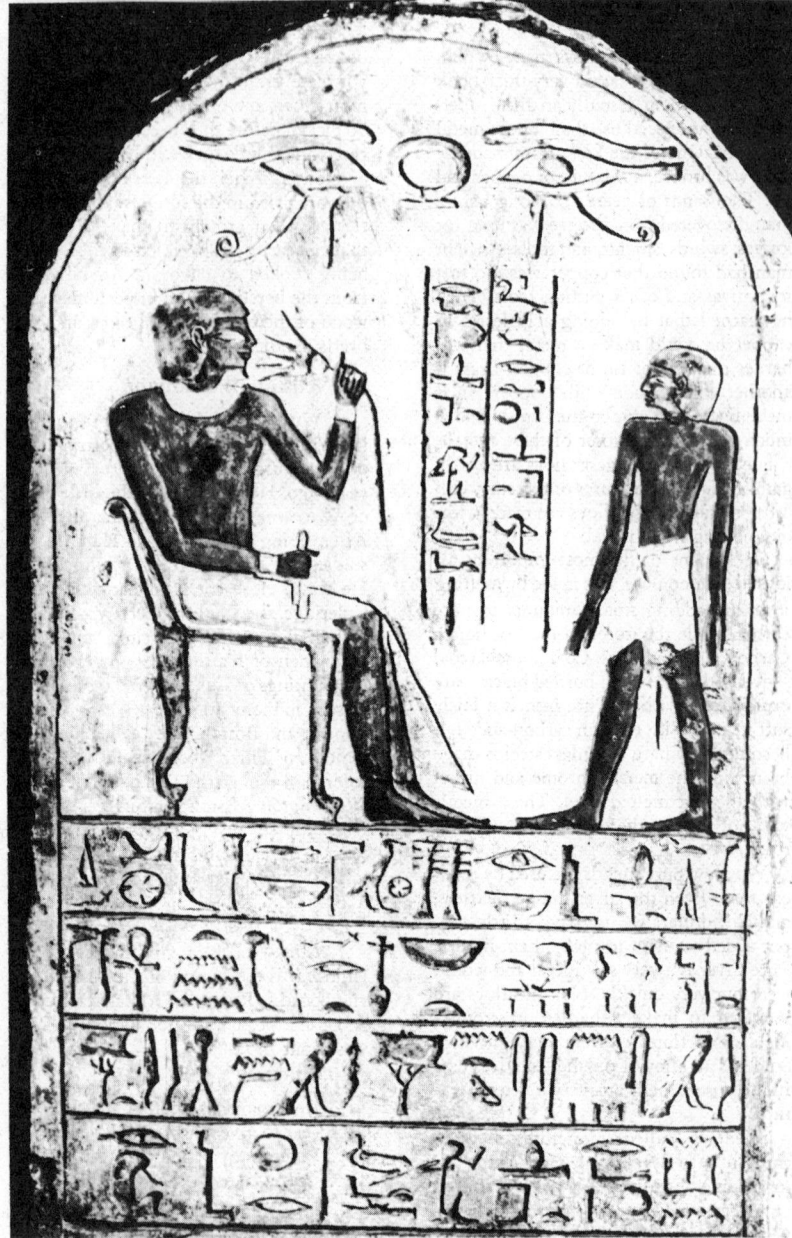

Ephron Gallery—Margot L. Wolf

The Egyptian alphabet was written in pictures instead of letters. This is a stele, a slab of stone used as a tombstone. It was made for the grave of a king. The eyes at the top are supposed to keep away evil spirits. The picture letters are called hieroglyphics, and the two lines going up and down tell what the king did while he was alive. The man at the left is the king, eating; the figure at the right is his son. Below is a prayer that asks the Egyptian god Osiris to keep the king comfortable. The tombstone tells that this king died about 3,500 years ago. Much of the English alphabet grew out of the Egyptian alphabet.

than fifty thousand and most of these are being used even today. A Chinese student does not master the writing of his language until he is beyond the age at which an American student may have graduated from college—say, twenty-five years old. In comparison with his thousands of characters, the American schoolboy has to learn only twenty-six letters.

Therefore the next step in the development of the alphabet was to have a symbol, or letter, for each sound that was used in the language being spoken. There are many more sounds that a human being can use than we have in our alphabet, and the alphabets used for other languages have in them certain letters that we do not need in writing the English language. But also we have some letters that they do not need. No alphabet needs more than thirty or forty letters. A child can master these in a year or two.

Writing with letters instead of with pictures is more than five thousand years old. Just as we got our alphabet from the Greeks, they got theirs from the Semitic peoples—the Phoenicians and the Jews and other ancient peoples who spoke Semitic languages. But, like most Oriental peoples, they wrote from right to left. When the Greeks took their alphabet, they changed the direction of writing and wrote from left to right as we do today. In doing this, they turned the letters around. The exact form of our capital letters was developed chiefly by the ancient Romans. Our small letters, and our handwriting, were developed because with them it is possible to write faster.

The English alphabet, like other alphabets that are used throughout the world, is very far from perfect. There are many people who are anxious to change it so

that it will be easier to tell how a word should be pronounced. Nevertheless, the modern alphabet is one of the greatest works of the human mind and has been at least as responsible as anything else man has done for the growth of civilization.

Alps

The Alps are a great chain of mountains in southern Europe. Parts of six European countries are in this great mountain range. The Alps run north from the Mediterranean coast and form the boundary between France and Italy. Then they turn east and run through most of Switzerland and through parts of northern Italy, southern Germany, and Austria. From here they turn south into northern Yugoslavia to the coast of the Adriatic Sea. In all they extend 680 miles and cover an area of 80,000 square miles.

Several million people live in the valleys and on the lower slopes of the mountains. Above 8,000 feet, the snow and ice never melt. There are more than four hundred high mountain peaks in the Alps; many of them are over 10,000 feet high. The highest peak is Mont Blanc in France; it is 15,781 feet above sea level.

Flocks of sheep graze high in the rocky stretches of the Swiss Alps.   *Swiss National Tourist Office*

GROUPS AND RANGES

The Alps are divided into three main groups and in each group there are seven or more distinct ranges. The Western Alps are in France and Italy; the Central Alps in Switzerland, north Italy, and south Germany; and the Eastern Alps in Austria, Yugoslavia, and Albania. Famous ranges include the Ligurian Alps on the coast of northwest Italy; the Maritime Alps between France and Italy, overlooking the Riviera; the Bernese Alps in south central Switzerland; the Allgau Alps and Bavarian Alps between Bavaria (southern Germany) and the Tyrol, which is an alpine district of Austria and Italy; the Dolomites in north Italy; the Dinaric Alps on the west coast of Yugoslavia; and many others.

Famous passes include the Brenner Pass, where a railroad with twenty-two tunnels connects Innsbruck, Austria, with Bolzano, Italy; the Simplon between Switzerland and Italy, with the longest tunnel ever built (12⅓ miles); and the Great St. Bernard pass between Switzerland and Italy, with its refuge where Augustinian monks train St. Bernard dogs to rescue lost travelers.

There are many other passes, through which there are either railroads or highways or both; and there are dozens of long valleys through which roads and railroads carry travelers to nearly every part of the Alpine region except the mountain peaks themselves.

Mountain peaks that are known best by their German names are Jungfrau, Matterhorn, Finsteraarhorn, Grossglockner, Dufourspitze and Wildspitze. Some of the French names, besides Mont Blanc, are Grand Combin, Barre des Écrins, and Montgenèvre. Gran Paradiso, Marmolada and Bernina are Italian names.

There are many high pastures in the mountains below the snow-line. At the beginning of every summer the farmers drive their herds of cows up the moun-

tains to these high pastures. There the cows graze during the warm summer months, while the farmers live in little stone huts on the mountain slopes. Toward the end of summer the farmers cut hay. The hay is needed to feed the cows during the long winter months. When the summer is over the farmers drive the cows back down the mountain to the valley farms.

Swiss cheese is made from the milk of cows that graze in the high Alpine pastures. The milk chocolate made with the milk of these cows is famous throughout the world.

VACATIONS IN THE ALPS

Summer or winter, there are always tourists and visitors in the Alps. Many people come to see the beauties of the mountains. In the summer, the snow-capped peaks are mirrored in beautiful blue lakes. The scenery is beautiful, the climate is good, and there is mountain-climbing in summer and winter sports in winter, skiing, skating, and bobsled-racing. Almost all the people who live in the Alps are expert skiers. They start skiing on the snow-covered slopes when they are young children.

In the spring, the snow that covers the slopes of the Alps begins to melt. Three great European rivers get their start in this way. From the Alps, the Rhine flows north to the North Sea, the Rhone flows south to the Mediterranean, and the Po flows east to the Adriatic. Alpine streams also help to make the Danube River one of the largest in Europe.

LAKES AND GLACIERS

There are many lakes, both large and small, in the Alps, some of them several thousand feet above sea level. Among the large ones are Lakes Geneva, Lucerne, Zurich, Constance, Brienz, Thun, Lugano, Como, Garda, and Maggiore. On nearly every lake there are resort towns and cities. The most popular resorts include Chamonix, Zermatt, Interlaken, St. Mor-

itz and Davos in Switzerland; Sankt Anton, Innsbruck, Kitzbühel, Salzburg and Bad Gastein in Austria; Garmisch-Partenkirchen and Berchtesgaden in south Germany; and Cortina d'Ampezzo and Bolzano in Italy.

There are more than 1,200 glaciers in the Alps, most of them (nearly 500 each) in Switzerland and Austria. The glaciers form from snow at or near the mountain peaks and descend for distances as great as 16 miles. The largest is the Aletsch, in the Bernese Alps. The most popular with tourists is the Mer de Glace (which means "sea of ice" in French), on Mont Blanc. The glaciers cover 1,600 square miles.

ALPINE ANIMALS

Many kinds of animals used to live in the Alps. There were large numbers of bison, elk, wolves, and wild boars. They have disappeared. A few harmless brown bears and foxes live in the lower forests of the mountains. Mountain climbers sometimes see chamois in the high Alps. The chamois is a small antelope; it is one of the most sure-footed animals in the world. Because it has suction cups on its feet, it can cling to a small pinnacle of rock, or jump from rock to rock, without losing its footing.

See also the articles AVALANCHE, GLACIER, and MOUNTAINS.

Alsace-Lorraine

Alsace-Lorraine is a territory in Europe, between France and Germany. It is on the Rhine River and in a mountainous country that is rich in coal and iron, so it is a valuable territory to own and France and Germany have fought over it for hundreds of years. First one has owned it, then the other. Today it is part of France. When it is German territory, its German name is Elsass-Lothringen.

The people of Alsace-Lorraine are partly French and partly German, and partly a combination of the two; many of them prefer to call themselves simply Alsatians. Most of them are farmers, clothmakers, or miners.

Originally, Alsace was one province and Lorraine was another, to the north of Alsace. The biggest city of Alsace is Strasbourg, which is famous for its fine geese (from which *pâté de foie gras* is made, meaning "paste of fat goose," a food that is used as an appetizer and sandwich spread). Strasbourg is a large manufacturing city. The capital of Lorraine is Metz and the biggest city is Nancy.

The Germans had Alsace-Lorraine most of the time until about two hundred years ago, when it became French. The people became accustomed to speaking the French language. During the French Revolution, in 1792, the national anthem of France—La Marseillaise—was written in Strasbourg.

Then in 1871 the Germans won a big war from France, the Franco-Prussian War. They took Alsace-Lorraine away, and they decreed that German was the official language and the children could no longer learn French in the schools. Sad stories were published in France and other countries about how unhappy the Alsatians were when they had to give up French and become Germans.

In World War I, the French beat Germany and got Alsace-Lorraine back. In World War II, while the Germans were winning, they claimed Alsace-Lorraine again for a few years, but since they lost the war at the end the territory became French again. It is now divided into three departments (that is, counties) of France —Moselle, Haut-Rhin, and Bas-Rhin. A map made after World War II may not even have Alsace-Lorraine on it. Alsace-Lorraine has 5,607 square miles and the population in 1973 was about 3,686,850.

Altai Mountains

The Altai Mountains are a long range of mountains in central Asia. They belong to Russia and form part of the border separating southern Siberia from northern Mongolia. In some parts of the range the mountains rise to almost 15,000 feet above sea level, but for the most part they are below 10,000 feet. There are many beautiful lakes in the Altai, and three great Siberian rivers begin as streams in these mountains. The rivers are the Obi, Irtysh, and Yenisei.

Most of the people who live in these mountains are Mongols or Kalmucks. They are herdsmen, miners, and forest workers. The miners dig for gold, silver, and lead. Much lumber is cut in the dense forests in the Altai Mountains. In the for-

ests there are deer and rabbits, but also there are many bears and wolves.

The ancient Chinese called the Altai the "Golden Mountains," because they knew there was much precious metal in the ground there.

altar

An altar is a bench or stand used in religious services. Usually an altar is used for the making of a sacrifice, or presenting of a gift, to God or to some object or being that is thought to be a god, as in primitive religions. Christians have used the altar for taking communion, burning candles as a form of worship, or kneeling in prayer. Most persons consider that an altar, though it is a stand of about the size and shape of a table, should be solid and should not have legs as a table does. Altars have often been beautifully carved and decorated.

Altdorf

Altdorf is a town in central Switzerland, the capital of the canton of Uri. It was there, according to legend, that William Tell shot an apple from his son's head and saved his life. A nearby village, Burglen, is said to have been Tell's birthplace. Altdorf contains the oldest Capuchin monastery in Switzerland. The population in 1973 was about 7,500.

alternating current

Electric current for household use comes from a generator in a powerhouse. Some generators produce current that always flows the same way. For example, when an electric light is burning the current is always flowing in through one wire and out the other. Electric current that does not change its direction is called direct current. Other generators produce current that flows first through one of the wires, then through the other wire. It changes its direction in this way 120 times every second. Current that so changes its direction is called alternating current.

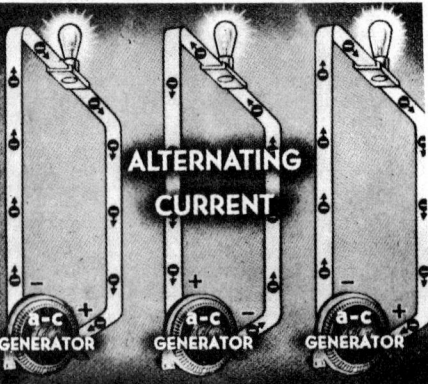

General Electric

Electric current from an alternating-current, or A-C, generator changes direction 120 times every second. This is about the time it takes to switch on a light. But since electricity travels about 186,000 miles per second, you never notice the change. The electricity goes into the wire from the side of the generator that is marked (−), lights the lamp, and returns into the side marked (+). The (−) side is called "negative" and the (+) side is called "positive."

When the current has flowed once in one direction and once in the other direction, it is said to have completed a cycle. If it changes direction 120 times in a second, it has completed 60 cycles.

Most of the electric current used in the United States is 60-cycle alternating current. The abbreviation of alternating current is A.C., and for direct current is D.C. See also the article GENERATOR.

altimeter

An altimeter is an instrument used in an airplane to tell the pilot how high above sea level he is flying.

The altimeter used in most airplanes is a kind of barometer. This is an instrument used to measure air pressure. The article on AIR tells how the weight of the air presses down on the ground, so that at sea level the pressure of the air is more than fourteen pounds on every square inch of the earth. The higher you go into the air, the lower the air pressure is. An altimeter uses this air pressure to show how high the plane is.

But the altimeter does not show how high the plane is above the ground. A plane might be flying at an altitude of 15,000 feet, but it would be only a thousand feet or so above the ground if the land in that district happened to be 14,000 feet above sea level.

The pilot adjusts his altimeter to the actual sea-level pressure before leaving the airport and then corrects it in flight by new information given to him by radio. He flies high enough to be above any mountain he may pass on his course. The barometer altimeter is correct within about 300 feet.

The *radio altimeter* works on the principle of radar, sending electrical impulses to the surface and measuring the time required for them to bounce back. It is very accurate (within 15 feet) over water but it is not reliable over land. Big planes usually have both kinds of altimeter.

Altiplano

The Altiplano is a large plateau, a high, level region, in Bolivia, extending to Argentina and Peru. It is about 12,000 feet above sea level and is about 500 miles long in the north-south direction and 40 to 60 miles wide in the east-west direction. Three-fourths of the people of Bolivia live in the Altiplano region. Its mineral deposits are Bolivia's greatest source of wealth. The plateau is cold, barren, and windswept. Lakes Titicaca and Poopó are on the Altiplano.

Altoona

Altoona is a city in central Pennsylvania, at the foot of the Allegheny Mountains and near a rich bituminous coal-mining region. It is also a manufacturing city for textiles, electrical and metal products, and automobile parts. The largest railroad manufacturing and repair shops in the world, those of the Pennsylvania Railroad, were Altoona's largest industry for many years but after 1957 they were closed. Just outside Altoona is the scenic Horseshoe Bend of the railroad. Altoona was settled about 1768. The population in 1970 was 62,900.

alumina

Alumina is a mineral composed of aluminum and oxygen. It is usually found in an ore called bauxite, but alumina when it is almost pure and crystalline is corundum, which in its finest form is a

precious stone—sapphire or ruby—and in less beautiful forms is found in such abrasives as emery. Alumina is also called *aluminum oxide*. It has many uses in manufacturing and chemistry. In the form of a white powder, it is used in producing aluminum.

aluminum

Aluminum is a metal of a silvery gray color. It is an element, which means that it is not made by combining other substances. Aluminum is useful in many ways. It is much lighter than most other metals. It never rusts. Being soft, it is easily hammered, rolled or pressed into any desired shape. Aluminum is lighter than copper and is almost as good for conducting electricity. This makes it useful as electric wire and parts of electric machines. It can be rolled into sheets thinner than tissue paper, called *foil*, which are used to wrap things that would be spoiled by dirt or water. It is one of the best conductors of heat, which makes it good for pots and pans. It combines well to make alloys. Thousands of products are made of aluminum.

HOW ALUMINUM WAS FOUND

Although there is more aluminum in the earth than any other metal, it was not discovered until copper, iron, tin, and other metals had been known for thousands of years. One reason for this is that such metals as copper and iron are much easier to separate from ore or rocks in which they occur. Not until man had learned a great deal about chemistry was he able to discover how to separate metallic aluminum from the rocks, clay and earth in which it is found.

Even then the chemical method of separating aluminum from its ores was so expensive that a pound of aluminum cost more than a pound of gold or silver. It was not until man learned how to make use of electricity that a cheap way of making aluminum was discovered.

In 1825 Hans Christian Oerstad, a chemist who lived in Denmark, made a tiny amount of pure aluminum by heating certain chemicals together. Nobody paid much attention to Oerstad's discovery. Several years later a German chemist named Friedrich Wöhler repeated Oersted's experiment in a slightly different form and obtained another very tiny amount of aluminum.

A chemist in France, Henri Sainte-Claire Deville, became interested in the new metal. In 1852 he improved on Wöhler's work. He produced a pound of aluminum for $545 (today a pound costs about 25 cents).

Napoleon III, the French Emperor, heard about the marvelous light metal. He offered Sainte-Claire Deville a big reward if he could produce aluminum more cheaply and in larger amounts. The emperor wanted aluminum for his armies. Sainte-Claire Deville managed to bring the cost of aluminum down from $545 a pound in 1852 to $17 in 1856, but this was not cheap enough.

THE HALL PROCESS

Some years later a young American named Charles Martin Hall, 22 years old, began trying to find a cheap way of making aluminum. He experimented with it

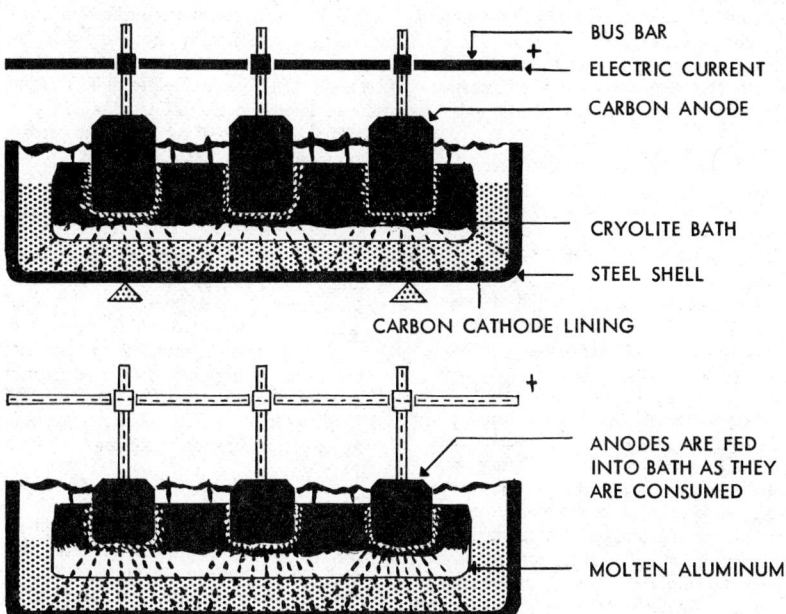

This is the "Hall Electrolytic Cell" in which aluminum is made. Look first at the diagram on top. There is a tank, lined with carbon. In this tank there is a liquid, or "bath," of a chemical called cryolite in which alumina, also called aluminum oxide (a compound of aluminum and oxygen), has been dissolved, much as sugar is dissolved in coffee to sweeten it. Electric current flows through a heavy metal bar (called a *bus bar*) and into blocks of carbon hanging from it. These blocks of carbon act as *anodes* (meaning they have a positive charge of electricity), and the lining of the tank acts as a *cathode*, a pole having a negative charge of electricity, which attracts the electricity from the anodes and causes it to flow through the cryolite bath. The electricity, flowing through, separates the aluminum from the oxygen by electrolysis. The aluminum settles on the bottom of the tank in molten (melted) form, as shown in the diagram at the bottom. The process wears away the carbon anodes, but the bus bar lowers them gradually into the cryolite bath as they become smaller.

during his senior year at Oberlin College in Ohio. After graduation he continued his experiments in the family woodshed. Hall's idea was to mix alumina, a white powder known to chemists as aluminum oxide, with some liquid and then pass an electric current through the mixture to separate the pure aluminum from the oxygen.

Hall finally discovered that if he melted a rock called cryolite in a very hot furnace he could make alumina melt and mix completely with this liquid rock. When he passed an electric current through this mixture the alumina separated into pure aluminum and oxygen. February 23, 1886, was the happiest day of Hall's life. On that day he discovered a cheap way to make aluminum in large quantities.

Strangely enough, another young man, a French youth named Paul Louis Toussaint Héroult, who like Hall was only 22 years old, discovered how to make aluminum by exactly the same method and only a few months later. Héroult made his discovery in France and neither of the two young men knew anything about the other's work.

The discoveries of Hall and Héroult brought the price of aluminum down to $8 a pound. By 1914 the cost was 34¢ a pound, and in 1950 the price had dropped to 18¢ a pound.

HOW ALUMINUM IS MINED

The ore from which aluminum is obtained today is called bauxite. It is an earthy-looking material and may be as hard as rock or as soft as clay. It may be pink, tan, yellow, red, white, or any combination of these colors. Bauxite is found in many different parts of the world. Most bauxite used in America comes from the island of Jamaica, in the West Indies; or from Dutch Guiana and British Guiana, in South America; or from Arkansas.

In some places the bauxite mine is underground, but usually open-pit mining is used. In open-pit mining, giant power shovels and other powerful earth-moving machinery remove bushes and trees and then dig away a layer of gravel and dirt. After that the bauxite is scooped out of the earth. It is a mixture of lumps and fine material when it is first removed from the mine. Crushing machines break up the big lumps. The bauxite is then dried in ovens called kilns, to drive off moisture. Then it is shipped by train or ship to the factory at which it will be refined or purified.

HOW ALUMINUM IS MADE

Most metals are made directly from their ores, and then purified. Bauxite must first be purified to separate the alumina from the iron and other impurities in the ore before the metal can be made.

Bauxite is refined by the Bayer process, invented by Karl Bayer, a chemist who lived in Austria. In this process, the crushed, washed and dried bauxite from the mines is further crushed and ground into powder. It is then mixed with certain chemicals, put into tanks called digesters, and strained through filters. The impurities that remain behind in the filters are called "red mud." What passes through the filters is *sodium aluminate* and is poured into giant tanks, each as high as a six-story building.

As the liquid in the tanks cools, fine white crystals of *aluminum hydroxide* settle to the bottom of the tanks. Aluminum

hydroxide is aluminum oxide chemically combined with water. The aluminum hydroxide is heated until it is white-hot, in slowly turning giant kilns, to drive off the water. The result is the snowy white powder called aluminum oxide or alumina.

THE ELECTROLYTIC PROCESS

Now the process of changing the white powder into the silvery-gray metal begins. The alumina is taken to electrolytic cells. These are rectangular steel tanks lined with carbon. Coal and charcoal are good examples of carbon, but these are not quite as pure as the carbon used in electrolytic cells. Inside the tank is a bath of melted cryolite. Big blocks of carbon attached to metal rods hang down from above into the cryolite. Electricity passes down the metal rods. It runs through the blocks of carbon and the cryolite to the thick carbon lining of the tank. Alumina is fed into the tank and mixes with the cryolite. Pure melted aluminum separates from the alumina and lies at the bottom of the tank, while the oxygen escapes into the air. The strong electric current that passes from the carbon blocks to the carbon lining of the tank produces tremendous heat, so that the cryolite and the aluminum at the bottom of the tank remain in a liquid form.

From time to time, melted aluminum in the tank is ladled out with a long-handled dipper and poured into the hollow molds called "pigs," where it cools and hardens. The aluminum is now ready for use by industry and can be made into all the shapes that are needed.

A tremendous amount of electricity is consumed in refining aluminum. Large aluminum smelting plants must be located on rivers where dams make inexpensive electrical power available.

A small amount of aluminum is produced at Boliden, Sweden, from another mineral that contains alumina, called *andalusite*. Several experiments have been made in the hope of obtaining aluminum from other minerals.

A mixture of powdered aluminum and powdered iron oxide is known as *thermite*; when it is ignited, the temperature rises to as much as 3000° C. (5432° F.). This heat is used in welding, and to thaw ice jams.

alyssum

Alyssum is the name of a group of herbs of the mustard family, also known as *madwort*. It is grown in rock gardens and as a border plant. In Greek, alyssum means madness, and the plant was once thought to prevent hydrophobia. The common *sweet alyssum*, a low, fragrant plant with white blossoms, is closely related to this group.

Alyssum grows ½ to 2 feet high and bears small yellow or white flowers.

Amalekites

The Amalekites were an ancient tribe who lived in Biblical times. They were fierce warriors who made their home in the desert south of Israel. The Amalekites were enemies of the Jews. They attacked the Jews that Moses had led across the Red Sea, and killed many of them. The Bible tells us of other times when the Amalekites attacked the Jews in Israel.

But a prophet named Balaam predicted that the Amalekites would be destroyed, and they were, first by King Saul of Israel, and twenty years later by the Jews under David. The few Amalekites who escaped were later wiped out. An Arabian poet writes, "The race of Amlach (the Amalekites) has disappeared and there is left of it neither mean man nor mighty."

amalgam

Amalgam is the name given to a mixture of mercury and any other metal. Mercury is the only metal that is a cool liquid, instead of a solid. It mixes very easily with other metals, except iron and platinum. The best-known amalgam is mercury and silver, used by dentists to fill cavities. Other amalgams are important in many manufacturing processes.

amalgamation

When two or more groups join together, they are said to amalgamate. Business firms often amalgamate because it costs less to run one big company than several smaller ones. General Motors Corporation is an amalgamation. Chevrolet, Oldsmobile, Buick and Cadillac automobiles used to be made by different companies. They joined together to form a new large company.

General Foods is an amalgamation of several smaller food companies. There is often amalgamation in labor unions too. The Amalgamated Clothing Workers Union is formed from what were once several smaller unions.

Amana Society

The Amana Society is the name given to a group of seven villages in central Iowa. It is a communal society, which means that all members of the community share in the profits of the work in which they all engage. It was developed in 1855 by members of the Community of True Inspiration, who had fled from religious persecution in Germany. In 1932 it became a coöperative corporation. The society has about 1,400 members.

amanita

Amanita is the name of a group of mushrooms of the agaric family. Among the amanita mushrooms are two that are dangerously poisonous, the *death cup* and the *fly agaric*. There are also a few edible varieties of amanita, such as *Caesar's mushroom*. The fly agaric contains a large quantity of the poisonous alkaloid *muscarine*, and it is consumed in Siberia and parts of northeast Asia for its intoxicating effect. Its use is habit-forming. It makes the user see or imagine things that are not really there, become dizzy, do and say things he does not realize he is doing or saying, and finally lose consciousness.

amaranth

Amaranth is the common name for a number of herbs that are grown for their colorful foliage and some for their flowers. The most common of these are also known as *love-lies-bleeding* or *tasselflower*, which has crimson flower spikes; and *Joseph's-coat*, named for its many-colored leaves. They grow as high as 3 to 6 feet. The group also includes such annoying weeds as pigweed and tumbleweed. In ancient times the amaranth was used in memorial decoration. In poetry it is often a symbol of immortality.

Amarillo, Texas

Amarillo, Texas, is the marketing and shopping center for 26 counties in the Panhandle region. It is also an important oil- and helium-producing center. The city was settled in 1887. The population of Amarillo was 127,010 in the census of 1970.

amaryllis

Amaryllis is the name of a large group of flowering tropical plants. Some are kept as house plants in the house, and some grow in lawns and parks. With the exception of the belladonna lily, most of the cultivated forms of amaryllis are hybrids, or combinations of two or more different kinds. The amaryllis family also includes the narcissus and the daffodil, as well as such important fiber plants as sisal and certain kinds of hemp. The plants grow 1½ to 2 feet high and have rose-colored, fragrant, lilylike blossoms. The roots are bulbs.

amateur

In sports, an amateur is a person who earns no money from his participation or skill in athletic contests or exhibitions. Until about forty years ago there was a very sharp distinction between the amateur and the professional. The amateur was considered a gentleman, and the professional (who was usually a teacher, coach, or paid contestant) was not. Most of the distinction has vanished, but Olympic matches are still open only to amateurs, as are intercollegiate and interscholastic sports. A person who has once received pay for playing can never again be an amateur; in 1914 the famous Indian athlete, Jim Thorpe, was required to give up the prizes he had won in an Olympic competition because he had once received payment for playing baseball.

There are various organizations in the United States that make the rules to determine what constitutes an amateur in different kinds of competitions. The most important of these are the Intercollegiate Amateur Athletic Association, the Amateur Athletic Union, the U. S. Golf Association, the U. S. Lawn Tennis Association, and the American Olympic Committee.

Until the 1940s a person lost amateur standing if he accepted payment for endorsing sporting goods, working for a manufacturer of sporting goods, writing regularly about his sport, or earning money in any way that he would be able to do only because of his prominence in the sporting field. Some of these restrictions have been lifted, but teaching or playing the sport for money is still forbidden to the amateur. In many cases the associations and the athletes have conspired to get around these rules with large payments for expenses in traveling and living away from home, and with prizes that can be sold and converted into cash.

Amati

The finest violins ever made were made hundreds of years ago in the Italian city of Cremona. No one has ever found

a way to make violins better, or even as good. The first great violin-maker in Cremona was named Andrea Amati. He was born about the year 1530 and died in 1611. His sons Antonio and Geronimo were also great violin-makers, and Andrea's grandson Nicolo was the finest violin-maker of the family. He was also a teacher of Antonio Stradivari, by many considered the greatest violin-maker who ever lived, and of Andrea Guarnieri. Amati violins still sell for thousands of dollars each. The Amati family also made cellos, violas, and bass violins.

Amazon

The Amazon is a river in South America, one of the greatest rivers in the world. It is about 3,900 miles long. The Nile in Africa, and the Missouri and Mississippi rivers together, in the United States, are slightly longer than the Amazon. The Amazon, however, has more water in it than any other river in the world. It flows from the Andes Mountains, in Peru, all the way across Brazil to the Atlantic Ocean. Along the way, seventeen other large rivers empty into the Amazon. At its Atlantic mouth, the Amazon is 150 miles wide. Ocean liners can go 1,000 miles upstream, and for smaller ships the main stream is navigable to the foothills of the Andes.

Through most of its length, the Amazon runs through some of the wildest jungles on the face of the earth. In these jungles there are still wild tribes of Indians. The jungles of the Amazon are called rain forests. It is always very damp and hot there. Most of the Indian villages are near the banks of the great river itself. The Indians who live in the jungle wear very little clothing, and their homes are crude, thatched shelters. They travel mostly by river in dugout canoes. It is almost impossible to travel far in the dense jungle. The Indians use big knives to cut their way through the undergrowth.

The Amazon is teeming with life. Big and little fish of all kinds swim in its waters. The jungles are noisy with the cries of animals and birds. The Indians are fishers and hunters. Life is full of danger for them. They must be careful when they go fishing because there are many crocodiles in the Amazon. There are fierce jaguars and cougars in the jungle. There is danger from other Indians, too. Some of them used to be cannibals and headhunters. In the headhunting tribes, a warrior was judged by the number of heads he had taken. These Indians shrank the heads and kept them.

Many strange animals live in the Amazon jungle. The capybara is the largest rodent in the world. The coati is related to the raccoon, but has a longer nose. The tapir is a hoofed animal about the size of a large dog. The sloth spends its life hanging upside down from a jungle tree. The armadillo has a hard shell and looks like a baby tank. Anteaters use their long, sticky tongues to gather their food. Many kinds of monkeys swing through the jungle trees. Colorful birds fly through the air. There are parrots and macaws and toucans. The Indians use blowguns to catch animals and birds. Some of the darts shot from the blowguns are poison-tipped.

For hundreds of miles, the Amazon is 3 to 5 miles wide. Near the ocean it is so wide you cannot see across it. It is 100 to 200 feet deep. So that all its water will not flow into the ocean and be wasted, ditches like the one shown in this picture lead the water away to irrigate the country near by and make it good for farming. The map shows the network of rivers that form the Amazon. They drain an area almost as big as the entire United States, nearly 3,000,000 square miles.

The Amazon region produces tapioca from the cassava tree that grows in the jungle, mahogany for furniture, indigo for dyes, sarsaparilla for flavoring, and quinine, a drug used to combat malaria. Much coffee is grown in the Amazon basin.

The first person to navigate the full length of the Amazon was the Spanish explorer Francisco de Orellana, in 1540 and 1541.

Amazons

The early Greek story-tellers told of a nation of women warriors called Amazons. These legendary women were supposed to have lived in a country on the Mediterranean Sea. They did not permit any men in their nation. The Amazons were strong and swift. They fought in battle against the men of other nations. Once each year the Amazons visited another country. The men in this country became the fathers of the Amazon children. The boy children were not kept by the Amazons. Some stories say they were put to death; others, that they were sent back to their fathers. The girl children were brought up and trained to become Amazons themselves.

ambassador

Representing one country in its dealings with other countries is called diplomacy, and a person who does this is called a diplomat. (See DIPLOMACY.) An ambassador is the highest ranking diplomat.

An ambassador from the United States represents the President of the United States. The head of a foreign country is supposed to treat him as though he were the President of the United States. Actually, however, an ambassador simply follows the instructions of the department of his country that has the duty of conducting affairs with other countries. In the United States, this is the Department of State and the head of it is the Secretary of State. In most other countries, this department is called the foreign ministry and the head of it is called the foreign minister.

An ambassador lives in the capital of the country to which he is sent. The building in which he lives and has his offices is called the embassy. His full title is usually "envoy extraordinary and ambassador plenipotentiary." Envoy simply means that he is a person who was sent; the title "envoy extraordinary" does not have much meaning any more. But "plenipotentiary" means "full of power," and this means that the ambassador has the right to act for his country, for example, by signing a treaty to which the country must live up.

Supposedly an ambassador is sent only to the most important other countries with which a country must deal. To less important countries, it would send a lower-ranking diplomat called a minister. Today the United States sends ambassadors to most countries. Since 1955 the United States has had a special rank, Career Ambassador, for its principal diplomats. A Career Ambassador's rank is like that of a Fleet Admiral in the Navy, or a General of the Army.

amber

Amber is a dark yellow, stonelike material that is used to make beads, mouthpieces of smoking pipes, cigarette holders, and many carved ornaments. Most of the world's amber comes from coasts of Germany and Russia on the Baltic Sea. Millions of years ago certain kinds of pine trees grew along the shores of the Baltic Sea. From time to time these trees gave off a brownish yellow liquid, resin, which dripped down into the ground. After millions of years in the ground the resin turned into a sort of stone, which we now call amber.

The ancient Greeks and Romans used to make jewelry and ornaments out of amber. They discovered that if a piece of amber is rubbed hard on cloth, bits of wool, cotton, dust and other fine particles will cling to the amber for a time. The Greeks and Romans did not know that this was caused by static electricity, but their name for amber was *electrum* and it is from this word that the word electricity comes.

ambergris

Ambergris is a fatty, waxlike material. It is found floating on the surface of the waters of tropical seas. Sometimes it is washed up on the beaches of countries in the tropics, where it is warm all year. It can also be found in some whales that are caught. Ambergris is gray, yellowish, black, or a mixture of any of these colors, and has a very sweet pleasant smell. It is the result of a disease in the intestine of the sperm whale. The ambergris passes out of the body of the whale, along with other waste, but floats on the water because it is fatty. It has no particular shape or form and may weigh from half an ounce to as much as 100 pounds. It is tremendously valuable because it is very important in the manufacture of perfumes.

Amboina

Amboina is a small island in the East Indies, one of the group of islands known as the Moluccas. At various times it belonged to the Portuguese, the English, and for many years to the Dutch. Now it is part of the Republic of Indonesia. Once the Moluccas were called the Spice Islands, because of the many kinds of spice grown there. Clove and nutmeg are important crops of Amboina, as well as coconut trees. The climate of Amboina is tropical, hot and wet all year. The people are Malayans and Polynesians. In World War II Amboina was an important Allied Naval base but was captured by Japan in 1942.

AMBOINA. Area, 314 sq. mi. Population, 66,821. Capital, Amboina (pop. 17,334), naval base and airport.

ambulance

An ambulance is a large car for carrying sick or injured people to a hospital. It usually has a removable bed or stretcher in the back. Most hospitals and police and fire departments in cities maintain ambulances. Usually an ambulance has right of way over all other traffic except fire-fighting equipment. In most cities, a doctor always goes in an ambulance making an emergency call.

In many of the smaller communities, where there is not a local hospital large enough to have its own ambulance, the Volunteer Ambulance Corps is proving very helpful. This is a non-profit organization that trains and equips local people to operate an ambulance, administer first aid, and move the sick and injured correctly.

The first organized ambulance service is believed to have been started in France during the Napoleonic wars (shortly after the year 1800) by a French military surgeon, Dr. Dominique Jean Larrey. In World War II and later, as in Korea, ambulance service became greatly improved with the introduction of helicopter ambulance services.

ameba or amoeba

An ameba (also spelled *amoeba*) is a tiny animal. It is so small that it can be seen only through a microscope. In almost any drop of water from a river, swamp, or pond, seen through a microscope, there are several strange shapes that look like splotches of clear jelly with a few dark dots inside them. These jellylike splotches are amebas. They have no legs, feet, arms, or head.

When an ameba wants to move, it pushes a part of its body forward like a long foot and the rest of it flows into this foot. Then it does the same thing all over again and in this way it can move in any direction. The foot that the ameba pushes out is call a *pseudopod* (meaning "false foot") because it is not really a foot.

The ameba has no mouth. When it finds a tiny bit of food it pushes out pseudopods on both sides of the food. These slowly close around it until it is completely surrounded. The food is then drawn inside the ameba's body, where it is kept in a little pocket, called a *food vacuole,* until it is digested. The waste material that remains after the food is digested is kept in another little pocket or vacuole. After a time this vacuole rises to the surface of the body and explodes and sprays the waste outside.

The ameba has a dark spot inside its jelly called a nucleus. At times this splits in two and then there are two amebas, each with its own nucleus and vacuoles.

Plants and animals are made up of millions or billions of tiny parts called cells. An ameba has only one cell. There are many one-celled animals besides the ameba. However, ameba cells are different from those of plants, human beings, or the larger animals such as horses, cows, and dogs.

amendment

An amendment is a change made in a law. Most important, in the United States, are the amendments that have been made in the Constitution.

A proposed amendment to the Constitution must first be voted by a two-thirds majority in both the Senate and the House of Representatives. Then it must be ratified (approved) by the legislatures of three-quarters of the States.

The first ten amendments are called the BILL OF RIGHTS, about which there is a separate article. Most famous of these is the Fifth Amendment, which says that a person cannot be forced to testify against himself. A witness in a trial or hearing is said to "take the Fifth" when he refuses to answer a question because it might incriminate him.

Other famous amendments are the 18th (see PROHIBITION), the 19th (see SUFFRAGE), and the FIFTH and FOURTEENTH AMENDMENTS. See also the article CONSTITUTION.

America

One of the two chief patriotic hymns of the United States is named *America.* It is second only to *The Star-Spangled Banner,* which is the national anthem. *America* has the same tune as the British national anthem, *God Save the Queen* (or *King*). The words for *America* were written by a Boston minister named Sam-

uel Francis Smith, more than a hundred years ago, in 1832. He found the tune in a German songbook and did not know it was the tune for *God Save the King.* It is not considered necessary to stand up when *America* is played, but most Americans do.

American Expeditionary Forces

The American Expeditionary Forces, or A.E.F., was that part of the U.S. Army that served overseas in World War I; it included 2,086,000 men, of whom 1,390,000 were in combat service on the western front (France and Belgium), 256,000 were battle casualties, and about 50,000 were killed. It was commanded by General John J. Pershing. The first unit arrived in France in June 1917.

Both Pershing and Newton D. Baker, U.S. Secretary of War, insisted that the A.E.F. function as an independent army, but they permitted some units to be separated temporarily (March to July 1918) during a major German offensive. In May the 1st Division held back a German attack on the Somme; in June the 2nd Division repulsed a German attack at Château-Thierry and took the offensive at Belleau Wood; in July four U.S. divisions helped stop the German offensive in the Second Battle of the MARNE. The A.E.F. was organized as a separate army Aug. 10, 1918, fought at St. Mihiel, and was the major Allied force in the Meuse-Argonne campaign, a 47-day battle in which 1,200,000 U.S. troops were engaged and casualties were 120,000. After the Armistice (Nov. 11, 1918) part of the A.E.F. became the American Army of Occupation in Germany, with headquarters at Coblenz.

American Federation of Labor

The American Federation of Labor (called the A.F. of L. or the A.F.L.) was founded about seventy-five years ago, in 1881, as an association to which many different labor unions belong. A labor union is an organization of a group of workers who have the same kind of job. The two chief kinds of labor union are the *industrial union,* whose members usually work in factories, and the *craft union,* whose members practice a skilled trade such as plumbing or printing.

At first, all the unions that belonged to the A.F. of L. were craft unions. From 1936 until 1955 there was another large labor organization, the C.I.O. (CONGRESS OF INDUSTRIAL ORGANIZATIONS, about which there is a separate article), in which most of the unions were industrial unions. In 1955 the A.F. of L. and the C.I.O. joined to form a single organization, called "The American Federation of Labor and Congress of Industrial Organizations."

In this organization, every union is independent. It pays part of its dues each year to support the national organization, but it does not have to do everything the national organization wants to have done and it can withdraw from membership if it wants to.

Samuel Gompers, a founder of the A.F. of L., was its president from its founding in 1881 until he died in 1924. Then William Green was president until he died in 1952, and George Meany became

85

president in 1953. When the A.F. of L. was formed, working men had very few rights. By bargaining with employers, and often by strikes, the A.F. of L. did much to win higher pay and shorter working hours for American labor.

American Indians, a redskinned people who lived in North and South America before it was settled by white men from Europe. See the article on INDIANS, AMERICAN.

American Legion

The American Legion is the largest group of veterans in the United States. It was organized after World War I in Paris, France, by a small group of Americans who had fought in the war. In the next few years, more than a million other Americans joined the organization. The American Legion became very strong. It has groups called *posts* in cities and towns all over the United States. Each post is led by a commander, with other officers under him. There are state commanders and a national commander. After World War II, several million more veterans joined the American Legion. In 1972 the membership was 2,702,992 men in more than 16,000 posts.

The American Legion has become one of the strongest and most important organizations in the country. It was largely responsible for the creation of the United States Veterans Administration.

A member of the Legion is called a Legionnaire. He has a military-looking uniform. On his cap is embroidered the name of his post. If a Legionnaire is or has been an officer of the post, his rank is also embroidered on his cap. Legionnaires attend post meetings to discuss the business of the post and to pass laws for the post. At the meetings they sometimes pass resolutions that approve or disapprove of what other people are doing. Legionnaires also meet for social purposes. They have dances and entertainments. They organize bands and have military drills. In most towns, the American Legion sponsors a boy's baseball club. These clubs play games all over the country, and at the end of each season a tournament is held to pick the winning team.

The American Legion holds an annual convention. Delegates from all the posts meet in a different city each year. Prominent Americans make speeches to the delegates. The main business of each convention is the election of officers for the coming year. The new national commander and his staff are chosen by a vote of all the delegates. The final business of the convention is to choose a city where the next year's convention will be held.

Two parades are held at each convention. One is a formal military parade, with all the Legionnaires in uniform. The other parade is held by a Legion group called the Forty and Eight. The Forty and Eight is named after French boxcars that many of the soldiers rode in during World War I. These boxcars were made to carry forty men and eight horses. The members wear funny costumes and play pranks.

The American Legion publishes a monthly magazine that goes to all its members.

American Legion Photos

125,000 spectators turned out to watch the American Legion's Big Parade on Pennsylvania Avenue in Washington, D.C. (1966). More than 50,000 Legionnaires and their families attended the 48th American Legion National Convention.

Women related to Legionnaires may belong to the Women's Auxiliary, which has a million members.

American Revolution, the war in which the United States won its independence: see REVOLUTIONARY WAR.

Americas, the

Though "America" is often used to mean the United States, all the countries in the Western Hemisphere—including North and South America and the islands near them—are "the Americas." There are twenty-three independent countries in the Americas:

NORTH AMERICA	SOUTH AMERICA
Canada	Argentina
Mexico	Bolivia
United States	Brazil
	Chile
CENTRAL AMERICA	Colombia
Belize	Ecuador
Costa Rica	Paraguay
El Salvador	Peru
Guatemala	Uruguay
Honduras	Venezuela
Nicaragua	
Panama	

ISLANDS
Cuba
Dominican Republic
Haiti

These countries have not always been friendly with one another. Especially the Latin-American countries, where most of the people speak Spanish (in Brazil, Portuguese; in Haiti, French), have often been afraid of interference by the United States, which is so much bigger.

THE OAS

During this century the American countries have tried to coöperate in a series of Pan-American conferences and by founding the Pan-American Union in 1910. The Organization of American States, or OAS, founded in 1948, has taken action several times to settle disorders in American countries, and when Cuba was arming with nuclear weapons in 1962, or the Dominican Republic was torn by revolution in 1965, the countries of the OAS acted together for the protection of all of them.

See also the articles on PAN-AMERICANISM, the GOOD NEIGHBOR POLICY, and JAMES MONROE.

America's Cup

The America's Cup is a prize in international yacht racing. It is named for a yacht named *America,* which won a big yacht race held by England more than a hundred years ago. The *America* and other yachts that have held this cup since have been from the United States. Challengers have all been British except for two Canadian and three Australian challengers. Sir Thomas Lipton challenged several times for Britain but never won. Harold S. Vanderbilt won the last three races (1930, 1934, 1937) in which Class J yachts were used, 80 to 100 feet long. Since such a yacht costs more than a million dollars, in 1957 the rules were changed. Smaller yachts (called 12-meter yachts, with length no more than 44 feet at the water line) raced for the cup in 1958, 1962, 1964, 1967, 1970 and 1974. The U. S. won and retained the cup in all of those years.

Amerigo Vespucci, see the article on VESPUCCI, AMERIGO.

Ames, Iowa

Ames is a city in Iowa, the seat of Iowa State University of Science and Technology, which had an enrollment in Spring, 1971, of 18,000. Ames Laboratory, a major research and development installation of the Atomic Energy Com-

mission, is located there. The city was founded in 1865. It is on the Skunk River. The population in 1970 was 39,505.

amethyst

Amethyst is a semiprecious stone used in jewelry. It is a clear violet or purple in color and is a kind of quartz, a mineral that is found in great quantities all over the world. Many amethysts are found in the United States, in the region of Lake Superior, but the best amethysts for jewelry come from Scotland, Russia, India, and Ceylon.

The ancient Greeks believed that if a person drank wine from a cup carved out of amethyst, or if he dropped an amethyst in his cup, he would not become drunk, and that is where the amethyst got its name—from a Greek word that means "not intoxicating." The amethyst is the birthstone for February.

Amherst

Amherst is a town in the western part of Massachusetts. It was settled in 1703 and in 1759 it was named for Baron Jeffrey Amherst, Commander of British forces in America from 1758 to 1763. Amherst is the birthplace of the American poetess, Emily Dickinson. There are two colleges in Amherst—the University of Massachusetts, which in 1976 had an enrollment of 25,884, both men and women, and Amherst College, which in 1976 had an enrollment of 1,300 men and women. The population of Amherst in 1970 was 17,926.

Amherst College for men was opened in 1821 and was chartered in 1825 by the Congregational Church. In 1973 it became coeducational.

Amiens

Amiens is a city in northern France. In the oldest part of the city there are buildings that were put up hundreds of years ago. The seven hundred year old cathedral in Amiens is one of the most beautiful in all Europe. The people of Amiens manufacture fine velvet, silk, woolen and cotton cloth, and carpets. A famous treaty was signed at Amiens in 1802, to end one of the NAPOLEONIC WARS, about which there is a separate article.

Amiens was the scene of a great battle of World War I. This battle was won by the Allies. In World War II Amiens was occupied for four years by the Germans and more than half the town was destroyed by Allied bombs.

AMIENS, FRANCE. Population (1973) 122, 865. Capital of Somme department.

Amish

The Amish are members of a branch of the Mennonite Church. They began as a small group of Protestant Christians who left Germany in 1683, came to America, and settled in what is now Pennsylvania. The Amish do not believe in baptizing infants. They refuse to take oaths or to carry weapons. The rules of their faith are based on the Bible only and their aim is to live as much as possible as Christians did in the days of the Apostles. They live in small villages and towns of their own and are very successful, prosperous farmers. They wear strange, old-fashioned clothing without zippers. The men wear broadbrimmed hats and often have beards. The women wear very plain, long dresses and their hats look like the sun-bonnets women used to wear a hundred years ago. The Amish take their name from Jacob Amman, who was the leader of their group when they left Germany.

Ammon

Ammon was one of the chief gods of ancient Egypt, thousands of years ago. The Egyptians pictured many of their gods as having animal heads. Statues of Ammon usually show him with a human head. At one time Thebes was the capital city of the Egyptian kingdom. The people who lived in Thebes worshiped Ammon as the supreme god. They built a great temple to honor him. The early Greeks believed Ammon to be the same as Zeus, their chief god. The Romans thought he was Jupiter, their chief god.

ammonia

Ammonia is a gas that has many uses. It is used to make ice, in fertilizers for the soil, and in some explosives. What is called ammonia in the home is actually a little of the gas mixed with a lot of water. It is used as a cleaner because it dissolves fats and greases. Ammonia has a sharp, choking smell.

When ammonia is cooled and then compressed it turns into a liquid. This liquid is allowed to run through pipes into big refrigerators, such as those in butcher shops, and here it turns back into a gas and draws the heat out of the air around the pipes.

When mixed with nitric acid, ammonia forms a chemical called *ammonium nitrate*, which is used in explosives and also in fertilizers. Ammonia added to hydrochloric acid forms *ammonium chloride*, also called *sal ammoniac*, which is used in dry-cell batteries and in some medicines.

Ammonia got its name because the ancient Egyptians, thousands of years ago, found the white powder ammonium chloride near the temple of Ammon.

Ammunition

Anything that is put into a gun to make it fire a shot is called ammunition. Therefore ammunition includes both the bullet that is fired from a pistol and the gunpowder that sends it on its way. Ammunition may range all the way from the cartridge for a .22 rifle to the giant shell in an 18-inch gun of a battleship, which can send a mass of armor-piercing steel weighing more than a ton for a distance of twenty miles, or a ballistic missile with an atomic warhead that will travel thousands of miles and destroy a city.

But usually the word *munitions* is used to describe all kinds of explosives used in warfare (including ammunition), and the word *ammunition* is used to describe only what is used in firearms.

WHAT MAKES A GUN "FIRE A SHOT"?

A substance is said to "explode" when it suddenly tries to occupy more space than it is occupying at the time. Either it turns into a gas, usually by burning, or it changes chemically into another substance that requires more space, as in atomic fission.

When a substance explodes, it pushes out with great force in all directions. Suppose this happens inside a gun. In every direction but one, the explosion cannot push very far because the hard metal of the gun stops it. But in that one direction, the barrel of the gun is open. So the explosion pushes in that direction and sends the bullet through the barrel with great force. (The "kick" of a gun is caused by the force of the explosion pushing backward at the same time.)

All ammunition must include some explosive. There are substances that explode by burning and substances that explode by shock. Gunpowder was the first explosive used in ammunition. It burns very fast. In burning it turns to gas. The gas expands so rapidly that it can send a bullet or cannon ball on its way with great speed. Other explosives have been found that are more powerful than gunpowder. A chemical called fulminate of mercury is used in many cartridges; it explodes from shock—that is, when it is struck a sharp blow, as by the hammer of a revolver.

Usually two different explosives are used in any particular kind of ammunition. There will be a small amount of one explosive and a larger amount of another. When the first, small, charge explodes, it sets off the other.

HOW AMMUNITION HAS CHANGED

In the last hundred years ammunition has changed greatly. In the rifles used by America's pioneers, a person had to pour gunpowder down the barrel of a rifle, then pack it down with a long rod called a ramrod, and then drop a lead ball in after it. Then when he pulled the trigger, a steel part of the rifle would scratch against a piece of flint and make a spark. The spark would fire the gunpowder and make it explode. This was the flintlock musket or pistol. Cannons were fired in much the same way.

Next came the cartridge, as it is known today. The cartridge has a hollow

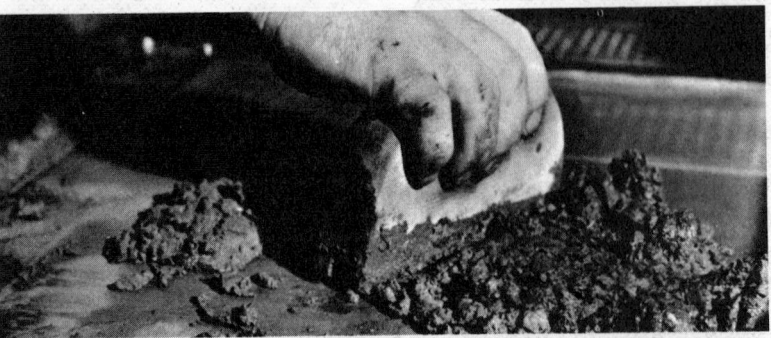

National Archives

When gunpowder is being prepared, it must be kept moist to prevent an accidental explosion.

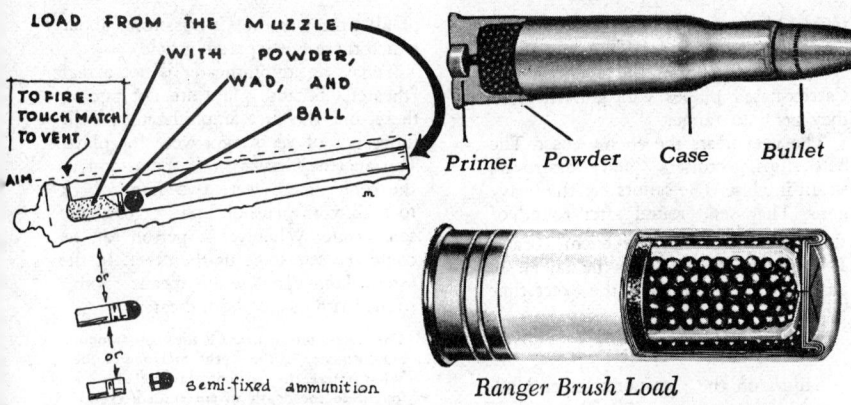

LOAD FROM THE MUZZLE WITH POWDER, WAD, AND BALL

TO FIRE: TOUCH MATCH TO VENT

AIM

Semi-fixed ammunition

Artillery Through the Ages

Primer   Powder   Case   Bullet

Ranger Brush Load

Western Winchester

The early cannon was loaded from the muzzle. It could fire an iron ball (as shown in the gun), a tubelike bullet (center), or a cylinder full of small balls (bottom).

Two kinds of ammunition are shown above. Top is a cartridge that shoots a single bullet. Bottom is a shotgun shell that discharges sprays of shot like small beads.

shell made of brass. Gunpowder is packed into this, and then a lead or steel bullet is pressed in. At the closed end of the brass shell is a *percussion cap* ("percussion" means "striking"). The percussion cap contains fulminate of mercury or some other substance that explodes from shock. Pulling the trigger of the gun makes the hammer strike the percussion cap. It explodes, which makes the gunpowder explode, and off flies the bullet. Shells used in shotguns are made the same way except that many small lead balls, called *shot,* are packed into a cardboard case with a charge of gunpowder and a percussion cap at the end.

Big cannons were soon using the same kind of ammunition as the pistol or rifle, but the "bullet" is called a *shell* and the explosives are contained in a *shellcase.* The shells used in artillery are so big that each contains a big charge of explosive that explodes when it strikes the target, causing much more damage than plain metal could.

MODERN AMMUNITION

The standard small-arms ammunition used by the U.S. Army is .30 caliber. It can be used in the standard (Garand M1) automatic rifle and also in some machineguns. It has a muzzle velocity (speed when leaving the rifle) of 2,700 feet per second. Ammunition for pistols and submachineguns is .45 caliber and for large machineguns is .50 caliber. The bullets are usually coated with a copper-zinc alloy that is harder than the lead bullet but soft enough to be cut by the rifling of the barrel. Some bullets are coated with steel under the alloy, to give them more penetrating power.

Hunting ammunition is similar but is seldom steel-coated. Shotgun ammunition has a paper shell with a brass cap. It is rated by its *gauge,* the weight of the lead shot in the shell: a 4-gauge shell has ¼ pound of shot, a 16-gauge shell $\frac{1}{16}$ pound, and so on. (Often lighter pellets are substituted in a shell of the same size.)

The types of artillery ammunition most used in warfare are *high explosive, armorpiercing,* and *white phosphorus.* The high-explosive shell is used against personnel and in antiaircraft artillery; it scatters bits of metal that serve as bullets. The armor-piercing shell is designed to explode after penetrating an enemy tank, the side or deck of a ship, or a fortifica-

tion. It has a sharp nose made of the hardest metal available. The white phosphorus shell is used as an incendiary agent and for making smoke screens.

A fuse inside the shell sets off its explosive charge at the proper time. Most artillery shells are fused to explode immediately on contact, but delayed-action fuses are used in armor-piercing shells and in some high-explosive shells used against enemy positions (so that they will bury themselves in the ground before exploding). The delayed-action fuse may be a slow-burning material or a series of fuses, each of which ignites the next. A newer type of fuse is the PROXIMITY FUSE, which electronically detonates the explosive when the shell is within a certain distance of its object. See also BALLISTICS, EXPLOSIVES, and ROCKET.

The latest development in ammunition is GUIDED MISSILES, about which there is a separate article.

amnesia

Amnesia is a kind of sickness in which a person cannot remember anything. A person with amnesia may be unable to remember his own name, or where he lives, or who his parents or his children are. Sometimes amnesia is caused by an injury to the brain. Sometimes it is caused by a kind of mental disturbance. Amnesia usually lasts only for a few hours or days, but it may last for years.

For many years, doctors did not know very much about amnesia or how to treat it. They have come to understand it well only since World War I. In some cases amnesia has been helped by hypnotism and in some cases by a drug, sodium pentathol. See also BRAIN.

amnesty

An amnesty is a kind of pardon given to an entire group of persons who have been accused or convicted of crimes. Kings used to grant amnesties, sometimes to hundreds or thousands of prisoners, to celebrate an occasion such as a royal marriage or the birth of a prince. There have been few amnesties in American history. The principal ones occurred because of the Civil War of 1861–65. In 1867 President Andrew Johnson granted a pardon to all who had fought for the Confederacy.

Amos

Amos was a prophet who wrote

one of the books of the Bible. His book is one of twelve books called "the minor prophets." Amos lived at a place called Tekoa, in the kingdom of Judah. In the Book of Amos, in the Old Testament, he wrote that he was a shepherd. He was unhappy because the people of Israel, who at this time were a different country from Judah, were turning away from God, and he prophesied that they would be conquered.

Ampère, André

André Marie Ampère was a French scientist who made important discoveries in the field of electricity. He was born in Lyons, in France, in 1775. It was Ampère who discovered the close connection between magnetism and electricity. In modern science the *ampere,* named in honor of this French scientist, is the unit by which the rate of flow of an electric current is measured. Ampère died in 1836.

amphibians

Amphibians are animals that usually live part of their lives by getting oxygen from water, as fish do, and another part of their lives breathing air as most of the land animals do. Frogs, toads, salamanders, newts and mudpuppies are amphibians. Most of them were born and lived part of their life in the water, and then came out on land.

Amphibians are vertebrates, which means they have backbones. They are cold-blooded animals, which means they are cold when their surroundings are cold and warm when they are in a warm place.

Amphibians are hatched from eggs. The mother lays the eggs in the water, leaves them, and never sees them again. In about a week, the egg hatches. What comes out is a tadpole or polliwog if it is going to grow into a frog or toad, and a creature very much like a tadpole if it is the young of one of the other amphibians. It has a round head and a long tail. The tadpole can live only in water. It breathes through gills, as a fish does, and swims by wiggling its tail. Not until it grows older will it develop lungs and be able to breathe air. Tadpoles lose their tails when they become frogs or toads, but the other amphibians do not.

All amphibians have smooth skins. The toad's skin is lumpy, but the bumps are underneath the skin and the surface of the skin itself is really smooth.

The salamander spends almost all of its time in the water. Its skin becomes very dry if it stays on land too long. The newt leaves the water when it is fully grown, and lives on land. At this time it is orange in color, with red spots on its back. After living on land for two or three years, the newt returns to live in water. It changes its color from orange to green. The red spots remain on its back. The mudpuppy lives all its life in the water, and even keeps its tadpole gills.

Newts and salamanders look very much like lizards, but are different in two important ways. Lizards have scaly skin. Lizards have claws on their toes; newts and salamanders do not.

Amphibians do not eat a great deal. Their favorite food is insects. They are very helpful to man because they eat many insect pests.

amphibious warfare

Amphibious warfare is combined sea and land fighting. It is the landing of troops on a coast held by the enemy. The navy, the army and the air force work together as a team in amphibious warfare.

The greatest amphibious operation of all time took place in World War II. This was the Allied invasion of the coast of Normandy in France, which was held by Germany. In June 5, 1944, the great amphibious battle began. There were four thousand ships in the Allied invasion fleet. More than two million sailors, soldiers and airmen took part in the invasion. A few hours after the landing began, there were 176,000 soldiers on the Normandy beaches along a sixty-mile front.

Amphibious warfare goes back to ancient times, but the coming of air warfare has changed it from its ancient pattern. Both air superiority and control of the sea are necessary to an amphibious landing, but if the invaders' air superiority is overwhelming they can destroy the defenders' naval power before the landing is attempted.

"ISLAND-HOPPING"

Amphibious warfare was very important in World War II. The Normandy landing was the most important, but there were many others, both in the European theater of war and in the Pacific. In the war against the Germans, successful landings were made in North Africa, Sicily, Italy and southern France. In the war against Japan, the warfare was almost entirely amphibious. Landings were made on one island after another. This became known as "island-hopping." Each island taken brought the battle closer and closer to Japan itself.

American forces made amphibious attacks on Guadalcanal in the Solomon Islands, on Kwajalein in the Marshalls, on Tarawa in the Gilbert Islands, on Iwo Jima in the Volcano Islands, on Leyte in the Philippines, and on Okinawa in the Ryukyu Islands close to Japan. The war in the Pacific ended soon after atomic bombs were dropped on Japan, but the Japanese islands would surely have been invaded if the war had not ended when it did. The invasion of Japan would have been the greatest amphibious warfare in history.

HOW IT IS DONE

Amphibious warfare requires trained men and many kinds of special equipment. Not just any soldiers and sailors take part in an invasion. There are special camps where men who will take part in an invasion are trained. At the same time, plans are being made for the actual invasion. Aerial pictures of the enemy coast are studied to find the strong points and weak points of the enemy defenses.

When all is ready the soldiers board transports, equipment is loaded on cargo ships, and the fleet sails, escorted by a naval task force that includes carriers and

several big-gun ships. If the invaders have bases near enough, land-based bombers are already bombing the enemy coast. Carrier-based planes will join them as they get into range.

The fleet nears the enemy coast. The battleships, cruisers and destroyers steam in close. The sailors fire the heavy guns. They send round after round of shells crashing onto the enemy beach. D-day is at hand. D-day is the day an invasion begins. H-hour is the exact time when the invasion starts.

THE LANDING

Sailors on the transports lower landing boats into the water. The soldiers climb down rope ladders and jump into the landing boats. Each boat holds about fifty soldiers. Other landing boats carry tanks, heavy guns, trucks, jeeps, ammunition, and many other supplies. The landing boats pull away from the transports and cargo ships. They circle around until they form a line of about twenty landing boats.

At a given signal, the line of landing boats heads for the beach. The beach has been bombarded from the air, but it is still strongly defended. The enemy opens fire on the incoming landing boats. The invading soldiers crouch low in the steel-sided boats. The first line of landing boats comes in to the beach. They come to a stop when the bottoms scrape along the sand. The front of each boat drops down into the water and the soldiers wade out. Each soldier carries his rifle high in the air to keep it dry. The soldiers reach the beach and drop down. They open fire on the enemy.

THE BEACHHEAD

Line after line of landing craft reaches the beach. Soon there are thousands of soldiers. Tanks and heavy guns are landed. The invaders slowly advance up the beach. Sometimes the soldiers wriggle forward on their stomachs. Sometimes they run for short distances in a zigzag line to avoid being hit. Sometimes the enemy fire is too strong and the soldiers have to dig trenches in the sand. The wounded are carried back to the landing boats, and the boats head back to the transports or to hospital ships.

Until the beach is won, the navy is in charge of the amphibious operation. Usually after two or three days the attacking forces have established themselves strongly in enemy territory. The amphibious part of the warfare has come to an end. The army generals take over command and the navy steams off.

amphitheater

An amphitheater is a place where some form of entertainment goes on in the center, and seats for the audience rise all around it. A stadium or a football "bowl" is an amphitheater. Usually an amphitheater is outdoors, but sometimes the same kind of seating arrangement indoors, as for basketball or hockey games, is also called an amphitheater. Some amphitheaters were constructed by nature, not built by man; these are places where steep hills rise in a circle, so that the audience can sit on the hillsides and look down on the entertainment in the center. The most famous amphitheater

of all time was the COLOSSEUM, about which there is a separate article.

Today, an amphitheater is not a real "theater," because plays are not put on there, but the first amphitheaters, built thousands of years ago, were for plays. The ancient Greeks built them, and in the center there were two stages, back to back, with plays on both stages at the same time. Wherever a person sat, he could see one stage or the other. In the Greek language, *amphi-* means "both," so the word meant "both theaters."

The Colosseum in Rome is the most famous amphitheater in the world, and one of the oldest. Here, in ancient days, gladiators fought to the death to entertain a crowd.

Italian State Tourist Office

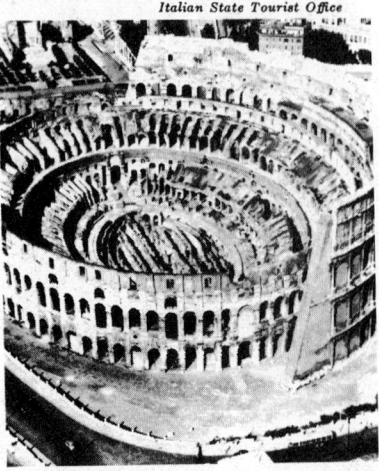

amplification

Amplification is a method of increasing a flow of electrons in an electromagnetic wave. It is used in radio and other sound transmission, such as phonographs and hearing aids, to increase the loudness of a sound. The first amplifier that was strong enough to make radio possible was the Audion tube perfected in 1912 by Lee DeForest. The transistor is a simpler and smaller device, but more limited in power. See ELECTRONICS.

amplitude

Amplitude is the difference between the highest and lowest points of a wave or motion—for example, the length of the stroke of a pendulum. Light waves are measured by the amplitude as well as by their *frequency* (the number of high and low points in a given distance and time). In radio, sounds would be heard as a constantly rising and falling sound if they were not modulated (regulated) by a process called *amplitude modulation*, or AM, which changes the amplification every time the amplitude changes. See also FREQUENCY and FREQUENCY MODULATION.

Amsterdam

Amsterdam is an important city in the Netherlands, the country in northwestern Europe where the Dutch people live. Amsterdam is the capital of the Netherlands, and the biggest and most important city. It is located on the North Sea Canal. This canal flows into the IJsselmeer (formerly called the Zuider Zee), which was a large, shallow inlet of the North Sea but has now been dammed and partly filled in to make farmland. Amsterdam is a major

seaport though it is more than twenty miles from the IJsselmeer.

Some of the largest banks in the world are in Amsterdam. It is famous for its diamond-cutting industry. Rough diamonds, which look like ordinary pebbles, are brought here to be cut and polished until they become the beautiful jewels we see in rings, bracelets, and other fine ornaments.

Amsterdam has many famous museums and art exhibitions. In the western part of the city, tourists and visitors go to see Rembrandt House, the home and studio of Rembrandt van Ryn, greatest of the Dutch painters, who lived 350 years ago. Here may also be found the City Museum and Ryks Museum, both of which contain many famous paintings. The tomb of Admiral de Ruyter, the great naval hero of the Netherlands, who died in 1676, is located in Amsterdam. The city was built on water and thus has a great number of canals on which barges and boats carry freight to and from all parts of the country. More than 350 bridges connect these islands. Almost 900,000 people live in Amsterdam.

AMSTERDAM. Population 852,479. 1,625,-000 including suburbs. Capital and largest city of the Netherlands.

Amsterdam is also the name of a city of about 25,524 people in the state of New York. It is famous for factories where fine rugs and carpets are made.

AMSTERDAM, NEW YORK. Population 25,524 (1970 census).

Amu Darya

The Amu Darya river is an important river of central Asia and is about 1,600 miles long. High in the Hindu Kush mountains of northeastern Afghanistan, the Amu Darya begins its flow. At this point, it is called the Panj River. From here, the river continues southwestward to form 600 miles of natural boundary between Afghanistan and the USSR. Once inside the USSR, the river proceeds on its course for more than 800 miles to end finally in the ARAL SEA.

Although only the last half of the river is deep enough to be navigable, the river's water is very valuable for irrigating the barren land along its course. As a result of irrigation, cotton, fruit, alfalfa, and other crops can be grown along the river. The river's ancient name was Oxus.

Amundsen, Roald E. G.

The first man to reach the South Pole was Roald Engelbregt Gravning Amundsen, a great explorer from Norway. Amundsen was born in Norway in 1872. His first trip to the Antarctic region was made when he was only 25 years old. He was making plans in 1909, when he was 37 years old, to reach the North Pole. Then he found that Robert Peary, an American admiral and explorer, had arrived there before him. Amund-

sen decided that he would be the first man to reach the South Pole. He arrived at the edge of the Antarctic continent in 1911 and set up a camp at a place called the Bay of Whales. From here he and his party traveled by dogsled. On December 14, 1911, they reached the South Pole.

In 1926 Amundsen and Lincoln Ellsworth, an American explorer, bought an airship called the *Norge* and flew from the islands of Spitsbergen across the North Pole to Alaska. That made Amundsen the first explorer to reach both the North and the South Poles. He was also the first man ever to take a ship through both the Northwest Passage from the Atlantic Ocean to the Pacific and the Northeast Passage from the Atlantic to the Arctic Ocean.

Amundsen lost his life heroically in 1928, attempting to rescue another explorer, Umberto Nobile of Italy, whose airship, the *Italia,* had crashed in the Arctic.

See also the articles ANTARCTICA and ARCTIC REGION.

Amur River

The Amur is a long river, 2,621 miles long, in southeastern Siberia, a part of Soviet Russia, in Asia. For much of its winding length it forms the border between China and Siberia. It empties into the Tatar Strait, a narrow channel between Siberia and the island of Sakhalin in the Pacific Ocean. River boats can travel up and down its whole length, ocean steamers can sail up the Amur 300 miles, but in winter it is closed by ice.

Anabasis

The anabasis was a famous march of an army of Greek soldiers nearly 2,400 years ago. In the Greek language the word means "the going up." The Greek army (usually called "the Ten Thousand," though actually there were more than 13,000 of them) found themselves in enemy territory and a thousand miles from home. They had gone into Persia, the greatest empire of that time, to help Cyrus, the king's brother, revolt against Artaxerxes, the king. Cyrus was killed on the first day of battle and the Greeks had no more reason to fight.

It was the winter of the year 400 B.C. The Greeks had almost no food or supplies. To get home they had to cross freezing mountains and fight off tribes that were warlike and unfriendly.

The story of how they did this makes one of the most famous of all books of history. It was written by Xenophon, who was the principal leader of the Greeks on their march. He wrote the book within a few years of the time the march was made. The book, like the march itself, is usually called the *Anabasis,* but also it is called *The Persian Expedition* or *The Persian Campaign.*

anaconda

The anaconda is a very large snake found in the jungles of northern Brazil, in South America. Its body is 6 to 8 inches thick and 12 to 24 feet long. Anacondas are probably the heaviest snakes in the world. In color they are grayish green, with large black dots scattered over their backs and pinkish streaks on their lower sides. A salmon-colored streak bordered with black runs from the corner of the mouth to the eye.

Anacondas are not poisonous, but they are very dangerous. The anaconda is carnivorous, or meat-eating. It kills its prey by wrapping a few coils of its body around the victim and crushing it to death. It spends most of its time in rivers and streams, where it kills ducks and small animals. When necessary it can climb trees. It belongs to the same family as the boa.

Am. Museum of Natural History
A big anaconda stretched out straight is longer than three beds, placed end to end.

Anacreon

Anacreon was a famous poet of ancient Greece. He was born nearly 2,500 years ago (563 B.C.) in Teos, a city on the west coast of Asia Minor, which is now part of Turkey. For a time Anacreon lived on the island of Samos, and later he lived in Athens. He wrote about the joy of living. When he died, about 478 B.C., he was 85 years old.

anagrams

An anagram is the letters of a word rearranged to form a different word or words—for example, CAT is an anagram of ACT. For thousands of years, people have been making anagrams just for the fun of it—in the same way that they work crossword puzzles for the fun of it. The best anagrams are the ones that turn some word into a phrase that describes it, as TELEGRAPH is turned into GREAT HELP. One strange anagram is ANGERED and ENRAGED, which use the same letters and mean the same thing.

THE GAME OF ANAGRAMS. Two or more persons can play an interesting game with *anagram tiles,* which are little squares of wood or cardboard with letters stamped on them. These can be bought in stores, or a homemade set can be made on heavy cardboard cut in ¾-inch squares. The number of tiles you should make for each letter are:

A	15	J	2	S	12
B	4	K	2	T	15
C	6	L	8	U	8
D	8	M	5	V	4
E	20	N	15	W	4
F	5	O	15	X	2
G	4	P	4	Y	5
H	10	Q	2	Z	2
I	12	R	15		

The letter is marked on one side only; the other side is blank. All tiles are turned face down and shuffled around so that no one can be sure what letter any of them is. Four tiles are turned face up and put in the center of the table.

Each player in turn draws one tile and turns it up. If he can use it, with other tiles that are already turned up in the center, to make a word of *three or more*

letters, he makes the word and puts it face up, in a row, in front of him. Then he can draw another tile and try to make another word. But if he cannot use the letter he draws, he puts it face up in the center to join the letters that are already there, and it is the next player's turn.

For example, the letters in the center are J, F, C, and T. If you pick up an A, you can make ACT, or CAT, or (even better) FACT. But if you drew an R you would not be able to make any word. You would put your R face up in the center and your turn would end.

You can *steal a word* from an opponent if you add at least one letter to it and rearrange the letters in any way. For instance, another player has in front of him the word MAN, which he made before when it was his turn. In your turn, you draw an E. You can add the E to his word, turn it into NAME, and take it for your own word. You could also use a letter or letters from the center to steal the word. You could not turn his MAN into MANE and take it, because you would not be rearranging his word.

The game ends when any player gets five words in front of him. This player wins the game.

There are many other ways to play anagrams. One kind of anagram game, called Scrabble, became very popular during the 1950s. Games of this kind are sold in stores.

Anaheim

Anaheim is a city in Southern California, near Los Angeles. Disneyland, one of the world's most famous amusement parks, was built there in 1956. Anaheim was founded by German immigrants in 1857. It is in a rich fruit-growing region and has aircraft and other factories. In 1965 a big-league baseball team, the California "Angels," built its stadium in Anaheim. Its population was 14,556 in 1950; by 1970 it had grown to 166,701.

anamorphism

Anamorphism is the distorting, or pulling out of shape, of a picture. An anamorphic picture looks unnatural from the front but natural when seen from an angle, for example from far to the side. An anamorphic mirror, or anamorphoscope, is a curved mirror such as those often seen in amusement parks; it can make a person look very tall or very squat. The *anamorphic lens* is used in motion pictures and is called by various trade names such as Cinemascope. It permits a wide picture to be photographed on a narrow film and then expanded to cover a wide screen. It was first demonstrated by Henri Chrétien of France in 1937 but was not adopted until 1952, when producers were suffering from the competition of television. See MOTION PICTURES.

Ananias

The earliest Christians, in the years shortly after Jesus was on earth, decided to share what they owned equally. Those that had houses or land sold them and gave the money to the apostles, or leaders of the new Christian church. Ananias and his wife, Sapphira, belonged to this little group of Christians. When Ananias and Sapphira sold their land, they pretended they were giving St. Peter, the leader of the apostles, all the money they received. They did not tell him that they had kept part of it. Peter knew they were lying, and scolded them. They fell down on the ground and died. Ever since then, the name Ananias has been used to mean a liar. The story of Ananias and Sapphira is told in the New Testament, in the 5th chapter of Acts, verses 1 to 11.

anarchism

Some people believe that all forms of government are unnecessary. They are called *anarchists,* and what they believe in is called *anarchism.* An anarchist says that government and rules do more harm than good. He believes that people will coöperate with each other and behave themselves without rules of any kind.

Anarchism is as old as history. The Stoics, a group of philosophers in ancient Greece, believed in a world without laws, schools, or any force on the individual. In 1793 the British writer William Godwin argued against all forms of government, and in the 1800s similar ideas were held by Pierre Proudhon of France and Prince Peter Kropotkin and Mikhail Bakunin of Russia.

When people live without any government it is called *anarchy.* Conditions close to anarchy often exist for short periods of time when a government has just been overthrown and a new government has not yet been established, or after a great catastrophe, such as a fire or earthquake.

anatomy

Anatomy is the scientific name for the study of the structure of living things, whether they are animals or plants. Anatomy covers how a living thing is made up, what its parts are, where they are located, and what their shape is. It has nothing to do with the way they work; that is part of *physiology.*

The anatomy of the human body is one of the most important things a doctor must know.

THE EARLIEST STUDIES

The study of anatomy goes back many hundreds of years. The early Egyptians probably knew a great deal about anatomy. Thousands of years ago they were able to prepare dead bodies and make mummies from them. In ancient Greece men knew something about the dissection of animals, the cutting up of bodies to learn how they are made. But the early Greek doctors knew very little about human anatomy.

One of the most famous Greek doctors was a man named Hippocrates, who lived about 2,500 years ago. He was the first one to write about anatomy and to treat it as a science. He made a skeleton of brass to show something about the bones of the body. A Greek philosopher named Aristotle also wrote about anatomy, although he admitted that he knew little about the parts of the human body.

The first really important name in anatomy is that of Erasistratus. He was a Greek doctor who lived about two hundred years after Hippocrates. Erasistratus was the first to dissect human bodies. He lived in Alexandria, Egypt, the great center of knowledge at that time. The Egyptian king gave Erasistratus permission to dissect the bodies of criminals. In this way Erasistratus was able to find out more about the human body than anyone who had lived before him. His writings are lost to us, but some of them have been mentioned in the writings of another man, named Galen, a Greek physician who lived almost two thousand years ago.

Galen moved to Rome, where he did much work in anatomy. The Romans had a law forbidding the use of dead bodies for dissection. Galen sometimes broke the law in secret, but most of his dissection was done on apes.

After Galen, nothing important was done in anatomy for several hundred years. Then, about 700 years ago, several Italian universities started courses in anatomy. But little progress was made until the 16th century. Then we come to a great name in the science of anatomy. The name is Andreas Vesalius.

HOW THE MODERN SCIENCE BEGAN

Vesalius was born in the year 1514, in the city of Brussels, now a part of Belgium. He began to study anatomy at the age of 14, while he was a student in France. After several years, Vesalius decided that he had learned all he could in France, and traveled to Italy. There he spent three years studying and dissecting bodies, and three more years in writing about his studies. The work of Vesalius is the foundation of modern anatomy. His drawings were very accurate and even today are accepted as excellent pictures of the parts of the human body. Vesalius died in 1564.

The invention of the microscope, in the 17th century, was a great help to the study of anatomy. It enabled scientists to study the cells of the human body. The invention of x-rays permitted examination without dissection. But even today scientists do not know all there is to be known about the human body.

WHO STUDIES ANATOMY

Anatomy is studied by students in medical school. They learn about the body from books, lectures, and pictures, and by dissecting bodies.

In many places and at many times it has been illegal to dissect bodies. This has made it difficult for students of anatomy. The law was often broken, however. There were men who were called "body-snatchers." These men stole bodies from cemeteries and sold the bodies to medical schools. Governments finally became convinced that anatomy is an important science and that dead bodies are needed for the study of anatomy. Today, some people wish to help mankind after they die and will their bodies to medical schools.

Anatomy is also studied by artists. They must know something about the parts of the human body so that they may be able to draw human figures accurately. The great Italian painter, Leonardo da Vinci, made many sketches of the bone and muscle structure of the body.

HOW ANATOMY IS STUDIED

The study of anatomy is divided into several sections. Each section is a study of a part of the human body. The main sections in the study of anatomy are as follows: 1, the bones of the body; 2, the muscles; 3, the brain and nervous system; 4, the heart and blood vessels; 5, the lungs

and other organs with which we breathe; 6, the digestive system.

You can find further, helpful information under HUMAN BODY.

ancestor worship

In some religions, people worship the spirits of those who have lived in the past, their ancestors. These ancestors may have been members of a family, of a tribe, or of a nation. This is called ancestor worship. It may be the worship of people as individuals, or of the whole group of those who have lived in the past.

There are usually three reasons why people worship their ancestors. The first reason is to honor them. The second is that they are afraid the ghosts of their ancestors may visit them. The third is the belief that those who have died can do something for the living members of the family or tribe.

Some form of ancestor worship is often found among primitive tribes, but even civilized people have practiced ancestor worship. The ancient Romans regarded their ancestors as protecting spirits. Each Roman household worshiped its ancestors daily.

Ancestor worship is still practiced in parts of Asia and Africa, particularly by the Chinese people, though the Communist government of China is rapidly stopping the practice there.

Anchorage

Anchorage is a city in central Alaska, the largest city in the state. It was founded in 1915 as the headquarters of the Alaska Railroad. Anchorage is in the central part of Alaska's southern coast and is a seaport on Cook Inlet. It is the site of a U.S. Army post and an airbase. Anchorage serves a wide area as a shopping center. Its population in the 1970 census was 124,542.

anchovy

An anchovy is a fish that is closely related to the herring. It is thin and is silvery in color. It has a long snout and a very large mouth. The anchovy lives in salt water and is very rarely found in fresh water. Fishermen catch anchovies in the Mediterranean Sea and along the Atlantic coast near Spain, Portugal, and France.

Most fishing for anchovy is done at night. The fish are attracted by lights on the boats and are hauled in by the thousands in nets. The fishermen clean and salt the fish.

Anchovies are good in salads, mixed with eggs, and as appetizers before dinner, but they have a very salty taste and one cannot eat too many at one time.

Andalusia

Andalusia is the name of the most southern part of Spain. Its area, 33,765 square miles, is about the same as South Carolina's but its population of 6,000,000 is more than twice that of South Carolina.

Andalusia is beautiful, with high mountains, many rivers, fertile plains, and a lovely seacoast. It is rich in minerals —copper, iron, zinc, tin, lead and silver are mined in the Andalusian mountains. It is famous for its cattle and horses. Seville, Cordova, Cadiz, Granada and other famous old cities are in Andalusia.

The farmers of Andalusia grow wheat, olives, oranges, chestnuts, and grapes. The grapes are used to make some of the most famous wines in the world, sherry, Amontillado and Málaga.

The name Andalusia comes from a Germanic people that lived there nearly fifteen hundred years ago. These people were the Vandals, but the V got lost somewhere.

Even earlier than that, the Phoenicians, the Greeks, the Carthaginians and the Romans, all of them from countries on the Mediterranean Sea, had colonies in Andalusia. From 711 to 1492 Andalusia was ruled by Moors, Mohammedans who came from Africa. They were among the most cultured and learned people of their time. The Moorish influence is still seen in the customs and language of the people who live in Andalusia.

The men of Andalusia are tall and handsome, and the women are among the most beautiful in Spain.

Spanish State Tourist Bureau
Andalusian styles in dress (above) have influenced those of Latin America. Andalusian architecture shows Moorish influence.

Andaman Islands

The Andaman Islands, in the Bay of Bengal, are part of India. In all they cover 2,508 square miles and have a population of 89,000. The original inhabitants were Negritos but only a few hundred remain. Most of the present inhabitants are from India, about half of them Hindus and half Mohammedans. Some are descended from prisoners at a prison camp that was maintained from 1858 to 1945 at Port Blair, the capital, on South Andaman Island. Port Blair is a town of about 12,000.

Andersen, Hans Christian

Hans Christian Andersen was a great writer of fairy tales. His life was like one of his own stories, with sadness and humor and a happy ending. He was born in the little town of Odense, in Denmark, over 165 years ago (in 1805). His father was a poor shoemaker. Hans was a homely boy. He was not bright at school,  and the other boys made fun of him. But he loved to read, and to listen to folk tales and songs, and he had an excellent memory.

Hans was only 11 years old when his father died. When he was 14 he set out for Copenhagen, the biggest city in Denmark, to make his fortune. There he was often hungry and homeless. He wanted to be an actor, and could not find a job acting. But he got a scholarship given by King Frederick VI of Denmark and was able to go back to school and to the University. Then he wrote travel books, plays, novels, and poetry. But his fairy tales, based on childhood memories, were what made him famous. His stories about "The Emperor's New Clothes" and "The Ugly Duckling" are probably the most famous.

When Hans Christian Andersen died, at the age of 70 (in 1875), he was honored and loved all over the world.

Anderson

There have been several famous Americans named Anderson.

Marion Anderson is outstanding among American singers. She was born in Philadelphia in 1908. Her first important concert was with the New York Philharmonic Orchestra in 1925, when she was only 17 years old. Since then she has sung in important cities and countries all over the world, and many critics have said she has the greatest voice of her times. Miss Anderson is a member of the Negro race and in 1954 she became the first member of her race to sing with the Metropolitan Opera Company in New York City.

Mary Antoinette Anderson was one of America's most famous actresses. She was born in Sacramento, California, in 1859, and made her stage debut in 1875. She had to retire in 1889, when she was at the peak of her fame, because of illness. She died in 1940.

Maxwell Anderson, a noted playwright, was born in Atlantic, Pennsylvania, in 1888. His first successful play, which he wrote with Laurence Stallings, was *What Price Glory?*, produced in 1924. His works include many other successful plays. He died in 1959.

Sherwood Anderson, who was born in Camden, Ohio, in 1876 and died in 1941, wrote many novels and short stories. His most successful book is *Winesburg, Ohio.* It is a collection of short stories.

Andersonville

Andersonville is a village in Georgia, with a population of only 274. A Confederate military prison there during the Civil War was one of the worst in history in its conditions of filth, hunger, lack of shelter, and disease. Its burial ground, in which are buried 13,741 Union soldiers who died there as prisoners of war, is a national cemetery. After the war Captain Henry Wirz, superintendent of the prison, was hanged. The novel *Andersonville,* by McKinlay Kantor, is one of many books about the prison.

Andes

The Andes are great mountains of South America. They run from the northern to the southern end of the continent, along its Pacific coast. The total length of the Andes chain of mountains is more than 4,000 miles. Most of Chile, Peru, Ecuador and Colombia, and parts of Argentina, Bolivia and Venezuela, are in the Andes.

The Andes are the second-highest range of mountains in the world. Only the Himalayas in Asia are higher. North America has a peak, Mount McKinley in Alaska, that is 20,300 feet high, but

seventeen peaks in the Andes are higher than that. The highest of them, Aconcagua, is about 23,000 feet high. (See the article on ACONCAGUA.) The highest lake in the world, Lake Titicaca, is in the Peruvian Andes. The Andes average 12,000 feet in height.

The Spanish explorer Francisco Pizarro and his men reached the Andes more than four hundred years ago. They found beautiful Indian cities but they destroyed most of them.

Most of the people who live in the Andes today are a mixture of Indian and Spanish. They are farmers, miners, and herders of sheep and other animals. Most of them are very poor. Their farms are high in the mountains. The Indians who live at the highest altitudes can endure the thin atmosphere because their lungs have 25% more air capacity than is normal for a human being.

The Andes run through tropical country, but for the most part the climate in the mountains is cool or cold. The high peaks are always covered with snow. It is very difficult to cross the Andes from east to west. Only two railroad lines cross the Andes, and parts of these lines run through long tunnels. Most of the people who cross the Andes must travel along narrow, winding footpaths. The travelers use narrow footbridges to cross deep ravines. Some of the bridges are nothing but swaying spans of rope.

The people either carry loads on their back or use pack animals. The Indians use the llama as a beast of burden. The llama is a member of the camel family. The mule also has become an important beast of burden in the Andes.

The Andes vary in width from forty miles to more than four hundred miles. They rise almost straight up, in many places, from the shores of the Pacific Ocean. The eastern slopes of the Andes are not as steep as the western. Because the eastern slopes catch more rain, many great South American rivers, including the Amazon, begin there.

There are still active volcanoes in the Andes. The best known is Cotopaxi, which is more than nineteen thousand feet high.

The Andes Mountains are rich in metals. There are great silver mines in Peru and Bolivia. Much copper and mercury, and some gold, are found in the mountains. Bolivia has some of the largest tin mines in the world.

RANGES AND PEAK

The highest range, between Argentina and Chile, includes Aconcagua and also Mounts Tupungato (21,490 feet) and Mercedario (21,885 feet). The Transandine Railway crosses this range at Socompa Pass (12,657 feet). Also in this range is the famous statue of the Christ of the Andes (see illustration).

The central Andes divide into two ranges in Peru and Bolivia, with high (12,000-foot) plateaus between. In Peru are several volcanoes, including Llullaillaco (22,015 feet) and Antofalla (21,100 feet). The Central Railroad, highest in the world, crosses this range. The highest peak is Huascarán (22,205 feet). The Bolivian range includes the volcanoes Illimaní (21,185 feet) and Illampú (21,275 feet) and also Lake Titicaca.

The north Andes include Chimborazo (21,577 feet) and Cotopaxi (19,344 feet) in Ecuador. Ranges and subranges run along the northern seacoast of South America into Venezuela.

Andorra

Andorra is a tiny country in Europe, between France and Spain. It is one of the two smallest countries in the world (the other being San Marino). All of Andorra covers less area than the city of Chicago. Only about eleven thousand people live in Andorra. Until recently Andorra was hardly known to the outside world, but now there is a large radio station there, one of the most powerful in all Europe. Tourists from other countries are welcomed.

THE PEOPLE WHO LIVE THERE

The people of Andorra are of Spanish ancestry and speak a dialect of the Spanish language. They also speak French and regular Spanish. The people live simply, farming their land or raising sheep. They are very proud of their ancient customs, which have changed very little in hundreds of years. Most of them belong to the Roman Catholic Church.

The Andorrans raise enough crops to feed themselves, and grow enough tobacco to sell some of it to other countries. They manufacture very little except paper for cigarettes, and some rough cloth. An Andorran earns very little actual money (only about thirty dollars a year), but there are almost no taxes and food and clothing are inexpensive. Strangely enough, though the people are poor, one out of every nine now owns an automobile.

Children are not required to go to school as in most modern countries, though there are free parish schools. Most of the people can neither read nor write. There is only one movie theater in the entire country. A favorite sport of the men is izard hunting. The izard is a small goatlike antelope that lives in the mountains. The people do not travel often, and marry among themselves, so that many of the families in Andorra are related. There are telephones in Andorra, but no long-distance lines, so they cannot call anyone outside their own country.

WHAT KIND OF A PLACE IT IS

All of Andorra is mountainous, with many small streams. People fish in the streams and hunt in the mountains. The summers are warm but never get too hot. Heavy snows begin to fall in early November, after which it is impossible to get out of Andorra into France. There are no railroads, and the one good road, which was built in 1934, is completely blocked up until spring.

HOW THE PEOPLE ARE GOVERNED

In the time of the great emperor Charlemagne, more than a thousand years ago, the Andorrans helped him fight the Moors, the Mohammedan people from North Africa who were trying to invade France. As a reward Charlemagne allowed the Andorrans to govern themselves. Today, as for more than six hundred years, the government of Andorra is supposed to be supervised by the French government and by the Bishop of Urgel in Spain, but they never really interfere with Andorra's government. Each year the Andorrans do send a small gift of money to the French government and to the bishop, quite as a matter of custom.

Andorra has a council of twenty-four men, who are elected every four years. Twice a year they meet, dressed in the same costumes that Andorrans wore hundreds of years ago. The government gets its money by selling postage stamps, automobile licenses, and electric power to light people's houses. Until 1933, only the heads of families could vote. At that time the law was changed so that all men could vote. However, in 1941 this system was abolished and the previous method of election restored. In 1970, women were given the right to vote. Andorra has no armed forces, and only 20 policemen plus a chief. Their "military" budget is $5 a year for ammunition used in ceremonies. Andorra has no diplomatic relations with other countries. A large part of the country's income is provided by the many tourists who visit Andorra.

ANDORRA. Area, 190 square miles. Population (1973 estimate), 19,500. Language, Catalan dialect of the Spanish language. Religion, Roman Catholic. Government, republic. Capital, Andorra la Vella (population 7,664). Monetary unit, none; French francs and Spanish pesetas used. Flag, three vertical bars, blue, yellow, red, with coat-of-arms on yellow.

André, John

Major John André of the British Army was hanged as a spy during the Revolutionary War. But though André had a fair trial, and his death was justified, George Washington himself called him "unfortunate," and the British made a hero of him and built a monument to his memory in Westminster Abbey.

André was connected with the treachery of the American general Benedict ARNOLD, about whom there is a separate article. Arnold gave the plans of the American fortress at West Point to Major André, who was caught with the plans in his boots. The three American soldiers who captured him took him to George Washington's headquarters at Tappan, in Rockland County, New York State, on the west bank of the Hudson River near West Point. André was tried by a board of American generals and sentenced to death.

John André was a British officer but came of a Swiss family and was educated in Geneva, Switzerland. He had great talent for painting and writing poetry. He was born in 1751, and was 29 years old when he was hanged on October 2, 1780.

Andrew, Saint

St. Andrew was the first disciple of Jesus, as told in the New Testament (Matthew 4:18 and John 1:40, and in many other parts of the Gospels). Andrew and his brother Simon, who is best known as St. Peter, were fishermen, whom Jesus told to leave their nets and become "fishers of men." They were born in the town of Bethsaida, in Galilee.

After the Crucifixion of Jesus, Andrew became an apostle (or missionary) and preached the gospel in several parts of Greece and in lands on the Black Sea, in what is now part of Russia. He is said to have been crucified about 60 or 70 A.D. at Patrae, in Greece, on a cross shaped like an X. He is the patron saint of Scotland, and the X-shaped "cross of St. Andrew" may be seen on the British flag. He is also the most venerated saint of the Russians, because he was the first man to preach in their territory.

Andrews, Roy Chapman

Roy Chapman Andrews, an explorer and student of animal life, was born in Beloit, Wisconsin, in 1884. In 1906 he formed a connection with the American Museum of Natural History in New York, for whom he made many expeditions on both sea and land. His most famous expeditions were to Asia, especially the Gobi Desert. Before he was 30 he was considered the leading authority on whales. Many of his books and articles are not written in technical language and are very popular. He retired in 1942 and died in 1960.

Andreyev, Leonid

Leonid Nikolayevich Andreyev was a Russian author, born in 1871. He wrote novels and plays that protested against the Russian government of the czars, but he did not like the Communist government either and lived in Finland after the revolution of 1917, until his death in 1919. His play *He Who Gets Slapped* was his most popular in the United States.

anemia

Anemia is a sickness caused by poor blood. (It is also spelled *anaemia*.) The blood of a person with anemia does not have enough red blood cells, or red corpuscles, or else it does not have enough iron in it. The red blood cells get their color because they contain iron. This iron is in a protein substance called *hemoglobin*, which helps the lungs to take in oxygen from the air.

A doctor takes a sample of a person's blood if he thinks that person has anemia. The doctor compares the color of the blood sample with a color chart. The color chart shows how red a healthy person's blood should be.

Some people with anemia are helped by eating foods that contain a lot of iron. Liver is usually the food that helps most. Eggs, oranges, prunes, green vegetables and red meat all contain iron and are good for a person with anemia.

Pernicious anemia, a dangerous condition that attacks the nervous system, is caused by a shortage of vitamins and other things needed to make red blood cells in the body. Injections of liver extract, vitamin B-12, and the folic acid vitamin will usually control it.

anemometer

An anemometer is a small device used by weather forecasters to measure the speed of the wind. There are many different kinds but the one most commonly used today was invented in 1846 by Dr. Thomas Romney Robinson in England.

The Robinson anemometer has an

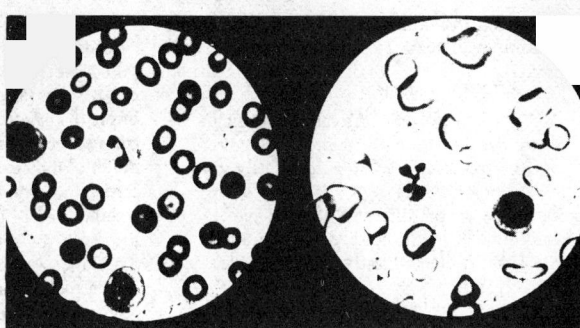

Abbot Laboratories

Anemia is detected by examination of blood under a microscope. The blood in the picture at the left is healthy; the red cells (smaller circles) have normal color. The picture at the right shows the blood of an anemic person.

upright rod with four arms sticking out from it. There is a little metal cup at the end of each arm. When the wind blows against this anemometer, the metal cups catch the wind and make the upright rod whirl around. Attached to the lower end of the rod is a meter with a round dial that looks like the speedometer of an automobile. The turning of the rod registers on the dial how fast the wind is blowing. Anemometers are also used in mines to test the strength of ventilating air currents and to test the flow of gas from natural gas wells.

anemone

There is a large group of wild, flowering plants called anemone, or windflower. The ones most often seen blossom in May, June, and July. The anemone grows to a height of about three feet. The flowers are large and may be blue, violet, pink, white, or yellow. One kind, the tall anemone, is also called the thimbleweed. In Greek mythology the anemone was supposed to have grown from the blood of Adonis. The name windflower came from a mistaken belief that the wind opened the blossoms.

anesthesia

Anesthesia is the loss of feeling, particularly the loss of a feeling of pain. *General anesthesia* is a deep sleep in which there is no feeling at all. *Local anesthesia* is the loss of feeling in only a part of the body.

Sometimes anesthesia is the result of disease. People who have paralyzed arms or legs often cannot feel anything in the paralyzed places.

Anesthetics, or drugs that produce anesthesia, are given for surgical operations. A *general anesthetic* puts the patient into a deep sleep; ether is a general anesthetic, breathed in through a mask that is put over the face. A *local anesthetic* is used to numb a part of the body; novocaine is a local anesthetic, injected under the skin with a needle, as a dentist does when he is going to pull a tooth.

HOW ANESTHETICS WORK

Pain is felt through the nervous system. There are tiny nerve endings in all parts of the body. When one of these is hurt, the nerve carries the message to the brain. A local anesthetic deadens the nerve endings, so there is no message of pain to deliver; a general anesthetic keeps the brain from feeling the message of pain even if it is delivered.

Freezing is a form of anesthesia. As a matter of fact, ice once was used as a local anesthetic.

All anesthetics that doctors use have

only a temporary effect. A doctor can make anesthesia last as long as he thinks necessary. A specialist in anesthesia is called an anesthesiologist.

HISTORY OF ANESTHETICS

Since ancient times, doctors have tried to do something about relieving pain during operations. Many kinds of drugs and medicines were tried. Almost all of them did as much harm as good. Some doctors used to get a patient drunk before an operation. Others have even knocked the patient out by beating him over the head with a club.

The first real use of anesthesia came during the years from 1842 to 1846. There are some arguments as to who were the first men to use anesthetics successfully. Three names stand out above the others. Dr. Crawford W. Long performed an operation in Georgia in 1842 and used ether as an anesthetic. Ether is still in wide use today. In 1844 a dentist, Dr. Horace Wells, inhaled a gas called nitrous oxide (laughing gas). Another dentist then pulled one of Dr. Wells's teeth. Dentists still use nitrous oxide as an anesthetic for pulling teeth. In 1846 another dentist, Dr. William T. G. Morton of Boston, used ether in several operations

Since that time, many anesthetics have been discovered and many improvements have been made in anesthesia. Among them are *spinal anesthesia,* which prevents any feeling from the waist down, and *nerve block,* which deadens a main nerve route to the brain. Both are given by injection and leave the patient fully conscious.

angel

The word *angel* once meant "messenger." An angel is a messenger from God. There are many passages in the Bible that tell of God's sending an angel to earth, to deliver a message or perform some act. St. Paul said (in the Bible) that there are different ranks among angels. In the Middle Ages it was believed that there were nine orders of angels: seraphs (highest), cherubs, thrones, dominions, virtues, powers, principalities, archangels, and angels (lowest). Three archangels are named in the Bible: Gabriel, Michael, and Raphael.

Angel Falls

The highest waterfall in the world, 3,212 feet high, is Angel Falls on Auyán-Tepuí (Devil's Mountain) in Venezuela. It is 20 times the height of Niagara Falls. The water flows from an underground river, drops 2,648 feet, hits a ledge, and then drops 564 feet more. An American gold-prospector, Jimmy Angel,

discovered the falls in 1935 while flying over in an airplane.

Angelico, Fra

Fra Giovanni Angelico, which meant Brother John the painter of angels, was one of Italy's great painters, about five hundred years ago. He was born about the year 1387, and his real name was Guido di Pietro. He became a brother in a Dominican monastery when he was 20 years old.

All the paintings of Fra Angelico are on religious subjects from the New Testament. Until his death in 1455, he spent most of his time decorating churches and other religious buildings with frescoes (a kind of painting done on the plaster surface of a wall). Every year thousands of people go to see his paintings in the convent of San Marco in Florence, Italy. Other great paintings by Fra Angelico may be seen in the Vatican, the Pope's palace in Rome. His best-known pictures are *The Flight into Egypt, The Last Judgment, The Coronation of the Virgin, The Annunciation,* and a group of frescoes (in the Vatican) on St. Stephen and St. Lawrence.

Fra Angelico was such a pious and humble man that when the Pope offered to make him Archbishop of Florence he refused, preferring to remain a simple monk.

angina pectoris

Angina pectoris is a kind of heart disease that usually affects only older people. It happens when the heart does not get enough oxygen. The person who has an attack of angina pectoris feels a sudden, very sharp pain in his chest, and has trouble breathing. A person who is likely to have an attack of angina pectoris is usually given drugs that make the blood vessels expand and carry more blood, and such a person must avoid physical exertion such as hard exercise or climbing stairs, and also excitement or overeating—anything that would make the heart try to beat faster.

Fear may cause angina pectoris and in any case makes the pain greater.

Angles and Anglo-Saxon

The Angles were a German people who moved into England about 1,500 years ago, in the 5th century A.D., and have lived there ever since. It is from them that England ("Angle-land") and the English language got their names. Two other German tribes, the Saxons and the Jutes, went to England at the same time. All these Germanic peoples were among the ancestors of the Englishmen of today.

The Angles were warriors and sailors. They must have been very good-looking people, because there is a story that when Pope Gregory saw some of them in Rome he exclaimed, "Not Angles, but angels!" Until the Angles, Saxons and Jutes invaded England, it had been a colony of the Roman Empire.

Within a few hundred years, most of the people in England were speaking a Germanic language that came to be called Anglo-Saxon, after the Angles and the Saxons. It is now usually called Old English. Many of the simple words we use today come from this Anglo-Saxon language.

The English people, and American descendants of them, have come to be called the Anglo-Saxon peoples, but this is not scientifically accurate. The present English and other British peoples come from several sources: the Celts, who lived in England even before the Romans came, and who are still found in Wales, Ireland, and parts of Scotland; the Romans; the Angles, Saxons, and Jutes; the Danes and other Scandinavian tribes; the French from Normandy; and many others who have gone to England to live in the course of the centuries. Americans are even more a mixture of different nationalities than this. But all who speak the English language owe part of it to the original Anglo-Saxons.

The Anglo-Saxon language was little written until the time of King ALFRED, about whom there is a separate article.

Anglican Communion

The Church of England and the Churches that have grown from it in foreign lands—the Protestant Episcopal Church in the United States, the Church of Ireland, and the Anglican Churches of Australia, South Africa, and other countries—are called the Anglican Communion (denomination). Their representatives meet every ten years at Lambeth, a district in London, England. At the Lambeth Conferences they decide on doctrines on which all agree. The Archbishop of Canterbury is unofficially the leader of the conference but the separate Churches are self-governing. However, all agree on the same basic faith, expressed in "the Thirty-nine Articles," and all use almost the same Book of Common Prayer.

Angola

Angola, also known as Portuguese West Africa, is a large Portuguese territory on the west African coast just below the equator. The capital is Luanda. The area is 481,351 square miles, twice the size of Texas. The population is 5,800,000 (1973).

Not many years ago, the Negroes of Angola were primitive tribesmen. They hunted and fished and farmed small plots of ground. Today they are becoming more and more civilized. Many of them read and write.

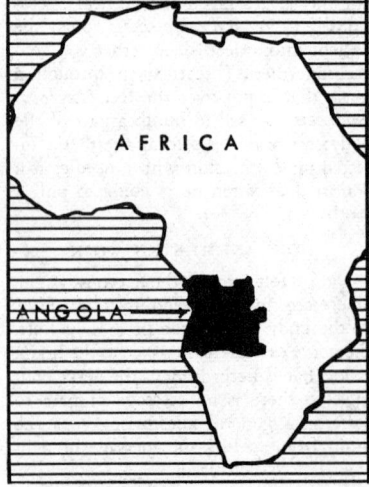

Principal crops are coffee, corn, sugar, palm-oil, and palm kernels. Angola also exports diamonds and iron ore.

Angola was discovered by a Portu-

guese explorer named Diogo Cam in 1484. The Portuguese were not always good rulers in Angola. They made slaves of the natives and did almost nothing to improve conditions in Angola. Today the Portuguese government treats the natives better. It has built state schools and has allowed the natives partly to govern themselves. But many of the people want complete independence, which Portugal has refused to grant. In 1961 the natives began guerrilla (or underground) warfare against the Portuguese. Although not a full-scale war, the fighting has continued and has spread to Mozambique and other Portuguese possessions in Africa. See CABINDA.

Angora cat

Angora cat is a term used to refer to any kind of cat that has long fur. The Angora cat is not a breed of cat. The breeds of cat include: the Abyssinian, the Burmese, the Domestic Shorthair, the Himalayan, the Manx, the Persian, the Rex, the Russian Blue, and the Siamese. Of these nine breeds, the Persian and the Himalayan are the only two breeds with long hair. Since the term Angora cat is misleading, it is no longer used by cat experts.

aniline

Aniline is a chemical oil. It was once the most important chemical in the making of dyes, and it is still used in dyes, medicines, and explosives. Pure aniline is a colorless oil, but when left exposed to air it turns brown. The first aniline dye was a purple or violet color. It is poisonous, particularly if it gets into the blood, and that is why it is not used as much as it once was. Some aniline is extracted from a plant called indigo, but mostly it is taken from coal tar. A German chemist was the first man to produce aniline, in 1826.

animal life

Animals are not only lions and tigers, bears and wolves, horses and cows, dogs and cats, and so on. The huge whales of the sea and the tiniest flies are animals, and there are those which can be seen only through a microscope. All living things are divided into only two main groups, known as *flora,* or plant life, and *fauna,* or animal life.

THE DIFFERENCE BETWEEN PLANTS AND ANIMALS

All living things must eat, and breathe, in order to live. It is by asking these questions: How does it eat? and how does it breathe? that we are able to tell the difference between plants and animals.

The biggest difference is that plants can make their own food out of air and water, aided by sunlight. Animals cannot. Therefore animals must get their food by eating plants, or by eating other animals that get their food by eating plants.

Plants "breathe in" a gas called *carbon dioxide* from the air and "breathe out" the gas called *oxygen.* Animals breathe in oxygen and breathe out carbon dioxide. Thus they help each other to live. That explains, too, why the air

is so pure and fresh in the country, where many plants are growing. The oxygen given off by the plants makes the air fresh.

Another difference between plants and animals is in the ability to feel things, and move about. A plant cannot say, "It is too hot here; I think I'll move over there," nor can it run away when it is being hurt. Most animals, even the simplest ones, can move toward what they want, and away from something dangerous or unpleasant.

There are times when it is hard to tell whether the living organism is a plant or an animal, and there are some that even the scientists cannot classify as one or the other. Perhaps the simplest way to put it is to say that some living things are partly plant and partly animal, not entirely either one.

HOW ANIMALS ARE CLASSIFIED

More than one million kinds of animals are known to exist, and undoubtedly there are more. Nearly two million other known kinds are extinct—that is, they once existed but none of their kind are left on earth. To study these animals and write about them understandably, scientists must classify them, sort them into groups that are alike in some ways. The science of classifying these animals is called taxonomy. Most taxonomists use the following classifications:

The *phylum* is the largest grouping. Each phylum includes a large number of animals that have the same general body plan, different from the body plans of other groups of animals. There are 18 to 25 different phyla.

Each phylum is divided into *classes*. Members of each class have features in common that other classes in the phylum do not have.

Each class is divided into *orders*, again according to features that its members share.

Each order is divided into *families*. Usually the members of a family are suited to some particular condition of living.

Each family is divided into *genera* (the plural of *genus*, or "kind"). Members of the same genus are much alike. They can often mate together (as lions and tigers sometimes do) but usually do not do so unless they are also members of the same species.

Each genus is divided into *species*. Members of the same species are alike in all important ways. They naturally mate together.

There are various subdivisions—subphyla, subclasses, and so on. Even the smallest classification, the species, can be divided into *varieties*, or *breeds*, for example the many breeds of dog, which mate freely with one another.

Man, for example, belongs to the phylum Chordata, consisting of all animals having a nerve cord along the back (and some other characteristics). He belongs to subphyla Vertebrata, consisting of animals having spinal columns. His class is Mammalia, animals who bring forth living young and nurse them. His order is Primates, largely because he has fingers and toes. His family is Hominidae; his genus is *Homo*, or man, and his species is *sapiens*, or intelligent. Scientifically, man is *Homo sapiens*, for all animals are named by genus and species. This is called the binomial (two-name) system.

A dog, like a man, belongs to the Chordata, Vertebrata, and Mammalia. But his order is Carnivora, or meat-eaters; his family is Canidae, or doglike animals; his genus is *Canis*, or dog; and his species is *familiaris*, or domestic. Its scientific name is *Canis familiaris*, domestic dog. Beyond that it has a breed, such as Airedale or collie.

HOW ANIMALS ARE FORMED

All living things, whether plants or animals, are made up of tiny particles called cells. There is a separate article about the CELL in this encyclopedia. Here we will pause only to explain that the cells that form animals are usually very small —it would take several thousand of them to measure an inch, so that they cannot be seen without a microscope—and that many millions or billions of them may be needed to make the body of a single animal.

The simplest of all animals may have only a single cell. Such animals are called *protozoans*. Most of them live in water, and some have shells, even though they are so small themselves. Many are *parasites*, which means they cannot live by themselves, but must live in the bodies of other animals, or in plants. The article on AMEBA, in another volume of this encyclopedia, tells how one of these onecelled animals lives. Some protozoans, small as they are, are very important as food for other animals; they are found in plankton, which is a mass of tiny plants and animals drifting in the sea. Plankton is the chief food of the gigantic whale, and human beings could eat plankton without harm.

Most animals, unlike the protozoans, are formed not only of many cells but of many different *kinds* of cell. Cells of the same kind form a particular kind of solid matter, or *tissue*, in an animal's body. For instance, in the human body the nerves are made of nerve tissue, which is formed of nerve cells; and in the same way different cells form the tissue of our muscles, bones, skin, and so on.

The cells in the body are constantly dying and being replaced by new cells that are made of the food eaten. For instance, one's skin flakes off in tiny particles, often so small they cannot be seen, while new skin grows underneath. Losing old cells and growing new ones is part of the process called "living."

HOW ANIMALS LIVE

Though they are different in so many millions of ways, there are some ways in which nearly all animals are the same.

They all need oxygen to live. Both air and water contain oxygen. Land animals breathe it in from the air. Sea and freshwater animals, such as the fish, breathe it in from the water. Some animals are called *amphibians*, which means "living both ways"; they begin life as waterbreathing animals, and then change into air-breathing animals. Frogs are examples of amphibians. When very young they live in the water and have gills, as fish do; at this stage of their lives they are called tadpoles. Then the gills change to lungs and the water-breathing tadpoles become air-breathing frogs. There is a separate article about AMPHIBIANS.

Another way in which all animals are alike is in the food they eat. All food for animals must contain the element called *carbon*. A substance containing carbon is called *organic matter*. It is because our food contains carbon that we can breathe out carbon dioxide, which the plants need for their life.

Of course, food containing carbon, which will keep animals alive, is found in many different forms. Animals that eat only meat are called *carnivorous* ("meat-eating"). Animals that eat only plants are called *herbivorous* ("plant-eating"). And animals that eat both kinds of food, as human beings do, are called *omnivorous* ("eating everything"). But in every case, the carbon in an animal's food comes from plants. Though carnivorous animals (such as lions) do not themselves eat plants, their food is the meat of animals (such as deer) that eat only plants.

All animals are alike, also, in having certain *senses*. Animal senses include: touch, smell, taste, hearing, and sight. Human beings have all five senses. Not every animal does. The only one of the five senses that every animal has, more or less, is the sense of touch, or feeling.

Different animals feel things in different ways. Human beings, for example, feel things through nerves that run from the skin to the brain. Some forms of animal life, such as insects, have special "feelers" through which they use their sense of touch.

Though some animals lack one or more of the five senses, the senses they do have may be much keener than man's. Some birds, for example, can see small objects on the ground when they are flying thousands of feet in the air. (It is not true, however, that a cat or any other animal can "see things in the dark"; it is possible to see only when there is some light). It is quite true, however, that dogs have a very keen sense of smell. Most animals can taste well enough to know what food is fit for them and what is not. And most animals also have a sense of hearing, which is actually the ability to feel vibrations in the air or water, though many animals cannot tell the difference between different kinds of sound, as we can.

All animals are born with certain *instincts*. An instinct causes an animal to behave in some particular way that is natural to it, without thinking about it. In fact, very few animals have the power to think, but all of them do certain things that keep them alive, and cause them to mate with others of their kind and produce more animals of the same kind. Instinct causes a hen to sit on her eggs, to keep them warm so they will hatch; it causes some birds to fly south in the winter; it causes some fish to swim hundreds and even thousands of miles to rivers where fish of that kind always go to lay their eggs.

There is a great deal of difference between intelligence and instinct. Intelligence is the ability to learn. Some members of the animal kingdom, besides men, have the ability to learn. Among the most intelligent are apes and monkeys, dogs and cats, elephants and horses, and a few birds such as crows, falcons (which can be trained to help men hunt), and lovebirds. But even the most intelligent animals cannot be compared to human be-

ings in intelligence, while their instinct sometimes permits them to do things a human being could never do.

WHERE ANIMALS LIVE

There is no part of the earth on which there is not some animal life. Some animals live at the north and south poles, where it is always frozen; some at the equator, where it is always hot. Some live in the depths of the ocean, and some on the peaks of the highest mountains.

The surroundings in which an animal lives are called its *environment*. When an animal has special qualities that help it to stay alive in some particular environment, and that other animals do not have, it is said to be *specialized*. Fishes and other forms of animal life that live deep down in the sea have bodies that will stand the weight of thousands of feet of water pressing down on them; this depth would kill any land animal. Some of them are made so that they do not need light to find their food or protect themselves against danger; others create their own light, having the power to glow in the dark. In the same way, polar bears are specialized; their thick fur protects them against the cold of the climate in which they live.

Human beings can be specialized, too. The dark skin of the African native helps him to endure the great heat and burning sunlight of the hot country in which he lives. Some South American Indians living high in the Andes mountains, where there is very little oxygen in the air, have lungs that are bigger than the lungs of other men, and this lets them take in more oxygen when they breathe.

DIFFERENT KINDS OF ANIMALS

It is easy to divide animals into some groups according to differences it does not take a scientist to see; for instance, the difference between land animals, which breathe air, and water-breathing animals, such as fish.

Most of the forms of animal life that are seen most often, and known best, can be divided into two big groups: those that have backbones, and those that do not. Animals that have backbones are called *vertebrates,* and animals that do not have backbones are called *invertebrates.*

ANIMALS WITH BACKBONES

The animals that have backbones are called "higher" forms of animal life. These include:

MAMMALS. Human beings are mammals, and so are all furry animals whose young are born alive and fed with milk from the mother's body until they are old enough to feed themselves. There are other ways in which all mammals are alike. They are warm-blooded animals, which means that the body itself keeps the blood warm; birds are also warm-blooded, but all fish, amphibians, and reptiles are cold-blooded, and the temperature of their blood depends on the temperature of the air or water around them.

Human beings are mammals that walk on two legs and are called *bipeds.* Nearly all the others walk on four legs, and are called *quadrupeds.* Most mammals are covered with fur, and all have more or less hair on their bodies, although men have the least of all. Whales, porpoises, and

dolphins, although they live in the ocean and swim about like fish, are mammals, have milk for their young, and must breathe air. Even when they sleep, they do not keep their noses under water for long. These strange mammals look much like fish. Another peculiar mammal is the platypus, or duckbill. This animal lays eggs, as a bird does, but is covered with fur. It nurses its young after they hatch, and there is no doubt that it is a mammal. These strange creatures, and also the echidnas, the only other egg-laying mammals, live in Australia and Tasmania.

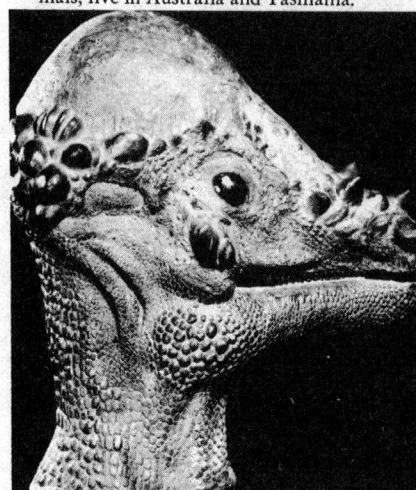

Am. Museum of Natural History
The pachycephalosaurus lived millions of years ago. It had a thick, domed skull. This is a scientifically constructed model of the way it looked when living.

REPTILES. Millions of years ago the earth was ruled by creatures called dinosaurs. They were reptiles, which means that they were cold-blooded and covered with scales. They laid eggs, from which their young were hatched. Some were bigger than the biggest trucks, sometimes really "as big as a house." Most of them ate plants, but some were meat-eaters and ate other dinosaurs. But eventually they were all dead, and they became extinct.

The reptiles that live today are like some of the extinct ones, except that none grows to be so large. The biggest are the crocodiles and alligators, which live on riverbanks in America, Africa, and Asia. Snakes, of all kinds, are reptiles. So are turtles, terrapins, and tortoises; lizards and iguanas; and the poisonous Gila monster, which is also a lizard, dwelling in the desert regions of North America.

BIRDS. Children today learn about birds by watching them in their natural homes, in the trees, or on the ground. They see how the birds build their nests, lay their eggs, and then feed the hungry little birds after they are hatched. Most of these birds are songbirds and perchers, and there are so many types that even to list them would require a whole book. Most of these familiar birds belong to such species as the thrushes, larks, swallows, woodpeckers, sparrows, warblers, wrens, swifts, owls, jays, crows, and ravens.

We can say of birds that they are all covered with feathers, and that they all lay eggs, but we cannot say that they all fly. In fact, the biggest bird of all, the African ostrich, cannot fly at all, but runs very fast on its two powerful legs. The rhea, of South America, and the casso-

wary, of Australia, are both wingless birds related to the ostrich. Another type is the emu, also of Australia. Then there are the penguins, diving and swimming birds of the Antarctic. They have wings, not to fly with but to use as paddles in the water. When they walk about on land, they look like little people dressed in frock coats, and are very comical.

Many species of birds *migrate,* which means that they travel from one distant place to another, twice a year. The migrations are usually from north to south, and from south to north, and sometimes cover thousands of miles. Ducks and geese spend the summer near the Arctic Circle, and during the fall they fly all the way to nesting grounds near the equator. Some of them stop along the way. Birds that make these semiannual flights are called *migratory birds,* or *birds of passage.* Not much is known about their reasons for migrating, nor how they find their way over such distances. Pigeons, when they are taken from their homes, usually try to find their way back, and generally do. This habit is further trained in the birds, and they become known as "homing" pigeons, and are used to carry messages back to a home base, when they are released at another faraway place.

FISH. Fish are water-breathing animals with backbones. They breathe through gills, and have scales. Most of them lay eggs (called *roe*) which grow into fish of the same kind. There are many thousands of different kinds of fish, perhaps as many as 50,000 different kinds, though not all of these have been found and classified by scientists. Some fish can live only in the fresh water of lakes and rivers, and some can live only in the salt water of the oceans and seas. Fish range in size from tiny tropical fish that are much less than an inch long to big sharks that are as much as fifty feet long. Some kinds of fish are the strangest-looking animals we know, but we have to remember that a thing looks "strange" only when we are not used to it. Some animals that we call fish, such as the jellyfish, are not really fish at all, because they do not have backbones. They will be described later in this article.

ANIMALS WITHOUT BACKBONES

The animals that do not have backbones, the invertebrates, outnumber the vertebrates many times. There are at least ten times as many kinds of animals without backbones. The ones we see most often are the insects.

INSECTS are so numerous that they are the largest single division of the animal world. They are the beetles, bees, ants, termites, grasshoppers, mantises, June bugs, flies, crickets, wasps and hornets, moths, butterflies, cockroaches, and countless others. They run, jump, walk, fly, swim, and burrow through the earth. They eat many things—plants, live animals, and dead animals. Some are parasites and must live on other plants or animals.

In many insects there is a change between birth and maturity, or growing-up, which is called *metamorphosis.* This includes two, and sometimes three, different stages, at which times the insect looks and acts as though it were not the same creature at all. When there is complete metamorphosis, with three stages, the in-

97 ANIMATED CARTOON

sect first hatches from an egg, in the form of a little worm, or grub. This is called the *larval* stage, and the little worm is called a *larva*. The larva eats and eats, and grows larger. Then it enters the *pupal* stage, at which time the insect sometimes spins a silky envelope, called a *cocoon,* all around itself. There it sleeps for a time, and then comes out, with wings and other changed features. There are several kinds of metamorphosis, with different kinds of stages, depending upon the insect.

CRUSTACEANS are animals that have their skeletons, or bones, on the outside of their bodies, as insects do. They are mostly water animals, such as lobsters, crabs, shrimps, and crayfish.

Spiders and scorpions look like insects but are not. Insects never have more than three pairs of legs, or six legs in all, while spiders have four pairs, or eight, and crabs and some other shellfish have five pairs, or ten. Some little "bugs," such as ticks, wood lice, sand fleas, and mites, which most people call insects, are really related to the spiders and crabs.

MOLLUSKS. A mollusk has a soft body, usually inside a hard shell. Snails are mollusks that live on land, and oysters, clams, scallops, and mussels are mollusks that live in the water. Some types can move about, carrying their shells with them; others, like the oysters, attach themselves to one spot, and lie with their shells opened, waiting for food to drift in. Then the shell closes. The squid and octopus are also mollusks, with "tentacles," or arms, attached to a large head. Each tentacle has rows of suction cups, so they can hold to a rock with one tentacle or more, using the others to seize and hold fish to be eaten. They swim backward by blowing out a jet of water, but they can also swim forward, although with much less speed, by waving their tentacles. When they are frightened they pour a black inky fluid into the surrounding water so that they cannot be seen by their enemies, and are sometimes called "inkfish." At one time, millions of years ago, the mollusks were the highest form of life.

CORALS are tiny little animals that live in colonies of millions and millions, in the ocean, usually near the shore. They have little shells, and when they die these shells harden. After thousands of years, the shells are piled so high that they rise above the surface of the water. Sometimes sand and earth pile up on top, and then plants start to grow and people come to live there. These are called coral islands, or atolls. When the coral deposits form a ring offshore it is called a coral reef, or barrier reef. Certain types of coral are of a beautiful reddish-pink color, and are used to make necklaces and other ornaments.

JELLYFISH are made of a jellylike substance, but are mostly water. They have no bones, or any rigid matter, and float in the water wherever the current takes them. Some are harmless blobs of jelly, but others, such as the Portuguese man-of-war, have poisonous stinging cells that they use to kill their prey, and this poison can be dangerous to human beings, although the type of jellyfish that stings bathers at the seashore is not likely to do more than cause some annoyance.

STARFISH and other related salt-water animals live on the floor of the ocean. Their tentacles, or arms, stick out from their bodies like the rays of a star, and they are full of holes through which the animal drinks in water. Like the corals and sponges, which are also animals, they seem to resemble plants.

WORMS are of many kinds, round and flat, long and short, thick and thin. Sometimes what we think is a worm is really the larva of an insect, as explained above. The best-known worms are the earthworms, the ones we think of as "fishing worms."

Many worms are parasites, and when they get into the bodies of animals they cause much harm. Among these is the tapeworm, which lives in the intestines of an animal. It is a flat worm, and it has a small head to which is attached a body made of segments, or connected parts. Other parasitic worms are the hookworm, various roundworms, and pinworm. Worms can get into the body through infected meat or fish, and that is why these foods are carefully inspected by the governments of most modern countries. When there is any doubt, the meat or fish must be well-cooked, as heat kills the worms and destroys their eggs.

Finally there are the protozoans, the creatures at the very bottom of the "ladder of life," which were described earlier in this article.

There are separate articles about all these forms of animal life, and about many of the different animals. Read also the article on ZOOLOGY.

animal worship

Animal worship is a form of religion in which animals are considered sacred or even thought to be gods. It has been known since earliest times. Usually it began in the belief that the souls of dead persons lived on in animals.

Many animals have been considered godlike or sacred in different places and at different times. In ancient Egypt the gods were thought to have animal heads. One god had a hawk head, another a jackal head, another a bull head, and so on. Most of the American Indian tribes believed in animal worship. Each tribe had a sacred animal, called a totem. The picture of the animal was usually painted on the tepee and clothing.

Animal worship is still practiced in many parts of the world. In India there are sacred cows. In parts of Asia white elephants are considered holy. Among some tribes of Africa the leopard and other animals are worshiped. Some Tlingit Indians of Alaska worship the crow.

animated cartoon

An animated cartoon is a series of individual drawings, each slightly different from the one before it, made on film and projected as a motion picture. However, there were animated cartoons before there were movies. More than a hundred years ago the same effect was produced with drawings on a wheel to be spun or on sheets to be flipped with the fingers. In 1906 a patent for a motion-picture animated cartoon was issued to J. Stuart Blackton. In the 1920s, short animated cartoons based on newspaper comic strips (Bud Fisher's "Mutt and Jeff" and Pat Sullivan's "Felix the Cat"), and Max Fleischer's "Out of the Inkwell" series combining cartoons with live-action photography, were popular in movie theaters.

In 1928 Walt Disney introduced the character "Mickey Mouse" in the first talking cartoon. Mickey Mouse became internationally popular. Disney also made the first animated cartoon in color, *The Three Little Pigs,* in 1935, and the first full-length feature picture in animated cartoons, *Snow White and the Seven Dwarfs,* in 1937. *Snow White* cost $1,500,000 and by 1966 had grossed $50,000,000.

Production of a full-length animated cartoon requires the services of about 150 artists for a year. There are 40,000 separate drawings to each 750 feet of film, 60 to 120 drawings to each five seconds depending on how fast the action is.

HOW AN ANIMATED CARTOON IS MADE

An animated cartoon starts with an idea for a story. An artist then draws many pictures to show the different places that will appear in the story. These pictures are tacked up on a board. At this point the story looks very much like a story as told in a comic book. The pictures tacked up on a board are called a *story board.* Several artists talk about what should be shown in each picture. They discuss the characters that will appear in each picture, and what the characters will do. They plan every movement that will be made by every character in the story.

The *background artists* then start to work. They draw a picture of each scene that will be shown in the story. All the details are shown in each background picture.

THE ANIMATOR'S JOB

For example, the action is to show a man walking up to a house, opening the door, and going inside.

The picture of the house is finished and given to a special artist. This artist is called an *animator.* He is the one who draws the pictures of the things that move. The animator works on a glass drawing board that has a light underneath it. He uses thin white paper so that the light will show through.

The animator draws his first picture of the man starting to walk up to the house. Next, he draws a picture of the man just after he has started his first step, with his foot a little farther forward. The next picture shows the man with his foot out still farther. Each picture is just a little different from the picture before it and the picture after it.

Each picture is placed on top of the ones done before. The light shining from underneath makes it possible for the animator to see the outline of each picture. This makes it easy for him to see how the motion is being shown. In the case we are describing, he can see each part of the steps the man is taking, as the man walks toward the house. Let us say it takes the man five seconds to reach the door of the house. That is, it will take the man five seconds as we watch him on the screen. For each second of the man's walk, the animator must draw twenty-four separate pictures. That makes 120 pictures altogether for the five-second walk. Twenty-four pictures for each second of action are necessary, because twenty-four frames of motion-picture film are projected on a screen each second.

Each picture the animator draws must be different from the picture before it and the picture after it by just the right amount. Otherwise the man will walk with a jerky motion.

THE INKER

When the animator is through with a series of pictures, he turns them over to another artist. This artist is called an *inker*. He traces each picture onto a transparent plastic sheet (cellophane). He then goes over the outline of each drawing with ink, a job called *inking in*. This drawing is called a *cel* (for cellophane). The cels are then given to an artist who paints in all the colors for each figure. This artist paints the man's face and hair and clothing and anything else that has to be colored. He paints the colors on the back of the cel, so that the black outline on the front of the cel still shows.

PHOTOGRAPHING

The cels and the background picture are sent to the *cameraman*. The background picture is placed in front of the camera and the first cel is put over the picture. The cameraman snaps this, making his first frame of motion-picture film. He then removes the first cel and places the second cel over the background picture. He snaps this and it becomes the photograph on the second frame of film. The cameraman continues, placing a new cel over the proper background picture for each frame of film he photographs. A cel placed over the background picture does not cover up any part of the background except that part that is behind the walking man. All the rest of the background picture shows through the clear cellophane.

ADDING THE SOUND

Not only do the figures in an animated cartoon move, they also talk and sing. The sound is recorded separately and added to the film. An animator must make the lips of a talking figure move so that it looks as though the figure were actually speaking. The animator has to know exactly how many drawings he must make for each word that is spoken. When Bugs Bunny says, "What's up, Doc?" the animator must make Bugs Bunny's mouth move in exactly the right way. If "What's up, Doc?" takes fourteen frames on the sound track alongside the pictures on motion-picture film, the animator must make fourteen drawings of Bugs Bunny saying "What's up, Doc?" The fourteen separate drawings must look the way Bugs Bunny's lips would look if they were saying this.

Motion pictures with puppet characters are often like animated cartoons in appearance but are not made the same way. See PUPPET.

Anjou

Anjou was a province, or county, in northwest France during the Middle Ages. Its capital was the city of Angers, which is now a large modern city with a population (in 1973) of 135,000. Count Geoffrey IV of Anjou, who lived from 1129 to 1151, married Matilda, an English princess, and their son became King Henry II of England. Geoffrey's nickname was Plantagenet, so Henry II and his descendants were called the Plantagenet or Angevin kings of England.

Ankara

Ankara is the capital of Turkey. It is in Anatolia, in the part of Turkey that is in Asia. Ankara is an old city, founded more than two thousand years ago (in 200 B.C.), but it has not been the capital of Turkey very long. It was made the capital in 1920 by Kemal Ataturk, the leader who made Turkey a republic. Before then, Istanbul was the capital. At that time Ankara was a very small city, but now it is a large one, with more than 2 million people living there. In 1929 the name was changed from Angora, its ancient name.

Ankara is a very modern city, with theaters, schools, libraries, and wide streets lined with shops and bright with electric lights.

For many years Ankara has been the center of a great wool industry. This wool, called mohair, is made from the long hair of the Angora goat. It will not "felt," or mat down, as other wools do. Rugs made of mohair are among the finest in the world.

ANKARA. Population (1973 estimate) 2,-208,800. Capital of Turkey.

Annam

Annam is one of three former states (Tonkin, Annam and Cochin China), located on the southeast coast of Asia, that make up the Viet Nam Republic. With an area of 57,840 square miles, it is about the same size as Iowa or North Carolina. About eight million people live there.

In ancient times, the people of Annam were ruled by the Chinese, but they finally drove out the Chinese and became independent. Less than a hundred years ago, the French marched in with an army and took control of the country. In World War II, the country was invaded and occupied by the Japanese. After the war the people of Annam made their country a republic, with the name of Viet Nam. But in July, 1954, when a truce was signed ending the fighting in the Indochina war, Viet Nam was divided into North and South Viet Nam. In 1956, fighting began again, this time between the Communist Viet Cong of South Viet Nam (aided by North Viet Nam) and South Viet Nam (aided by the United States). Peace was made in 1972, after millions of simple people and their beautiful land had suffered tremendous damage. See VIET NAM.

Annapolis

Annapolis is the capital of the state of Maryland. It is on a little peninsula, or arm of land, in the Severn River, and is almost like an island. Chesapeake Bay is less than two miles away. Annapolis is more than three hundred years old. It was settled about 1648 by English Puritans, and its first name was Providence. Later the name was changed to Anne Arundel Town, and then in 1694 to Annapolis, for Anne of England, who became Queen Anne (*polis*, in the Greek language, means "city," so Annapolis is "Anne's city").

Annapolis is the seat of the United State Naval Academy (which is often called Annapolis).

St. John's College is also at Annapolis. It is one of the oldest colleges in America, founded in 1789, and dates back even further, because it grew out of King William College, which was founded in 1696. St. John's became famous in the 1930s by using the reading of "great books" as a basis for education.

The state house in Annapolis dates back to 1772 and has seen many historic events. While the Continental Congress was meeting there, in 1783, George Washington appeared before it and handed back his commission as American commander-in-chief, since the Revolutionary War had been won.

ANNAPOLIS, MARYLAND. Population, 29,-592 (1970 census). Capital of Maryland and seat of U.S. Naval Academy.

Annapurna

On the third of June, 1950, two members of a French mountain-climbing expedition to the Himalaya Mountains, the highest in the world, climbed to the top of Annapurna. This is a mountain in the kingdom of Nepal, in Asia. It is 26,-500 feet above sea level. Annapurna was the highest peak that men had ever climbed, though since that time they have climbed even higher. (See the article on MT. EVEREST.)

These men were Maurice Herzog, leader of the group, and Louis Lachenal. The other members of the party were Lionel Terray, Gaston Rébuffat, Marcel Ichac (the cameraman), Jacques Oudot (the surgeon), Francis de Noyelle, Jean Couzy, and Marcel Schatz, all Frenchmen; and eight Sherpas (natives of Nepal, and professional mountaineers) led by a Sherpa named Ang-Tharkey.

Outside the chapel at the Naval Academy in Annapolis, midshipmen march in formation.

Photos Courtesy E. P. Dutton & Co., Inc.

To stand on the summit of Annapurna and hold up the French flag was a moment of great pride to Maurice Herzog. He was the first man to reach the top of Annapurna.

The extreme cold of the high altitude on Annapurna gave Maurice Herzog a bad case of frostbite. His hands were frozen so badly that he finally lost several fingers.

When the little group started back down the mountain, they had lots of trouble. Many of the men suffered frozen feet and hands, and Herzog lost his gloves, which is almost the worst thing that can happen. The party was caught in an avalanche (a big snow-slide) at one time. The doctor had to cut off most of Herzog's fingers and toes, because they had been frostbitten. Some of the men had to be carried most of the way. They were all brave men, and when they reached home they were given many honors.

Annapurna, in the Nepalese language, means "The Goddess of the Harvests."

Ann Arbor

Ann Arbor is a city in Michigan, on the Huron River 35 miles west of Detroit. The University of Michigan is at Ann Arbor and the city is also a manufacturing center for fine tools and instruments and a business center for the rich farming area around it. Ann Arbor was settled in 1824. The population in 1970 was 99,797.

Anne, St.

Saint Anne, according to tradition, was the mother of the Virgin Mary, though her name does not appear in the Bible. Her festival is celebrated on July 26.

Anne, Queen of England

Queen Anne was the last member of the Stuart family to reign over England. She was born in 1665 and died in 1714. At that time the United States were still colonies of England, so she was queen of America too. Anne was a small, fat, stupid woman. As a queen she did almost nothing except what her friends and ministers told her to do. Yet during her reign Britain became a great and important country and some of the greatest thinkers and scientists of all time, including Sir Isaac Newton, lived in England and did their best work.

When Anne was 18 years old (in 1683) she was married to Prince George of Denmark, but he did nothing to help her. Anne's father was King James II, and she sided against him when he became very unpopular in England. The king had to flee to France, and Anne's sister Mary became queen. (See the article on WILLIAM AND MARY.) Then in 1702, when she was 37 years old, Anne became queen.

During Anne's reign, Ireland was added to the kingdom that already included England, Scotland, and Wales. This was in 1707. Also, the War of the Spanish Succession was fought, to keep France and Spain from becoming one big country in Europe, and England won that. The great British military leader in this war was the Duke of Marlborough, an ancestor of Winston Churchill, the even greater British leader in World War II. The wife of the Duke of Marlborough, Sarah Jennings Churchill, was Queen Anne's closest friend; she called Anne "Mrs. Morley" and Anne called her "Mrs. Freeman." Sarah's influence helped make the Duke of Marlborough very rich and important. Later, Anne became unfriendly toward Sarah Churchill and liked a Mrs. Masham better, but the War of the Spanish Sucession was already won. In America, this was called "Queen Anne's War."

None of Queen Anne's children lived to reign over England. When she died, in 1714, the English crown passed to the first of the German kings of England, King George I.

annealing

Annealing is a way of making metal softer by heating it and then letting it cool very slowly. If metal is heated and then cooled very quickly, for instance by dipping it in water, it will be very hard but also very brittle—that is, it will break easily. Metal that has been annealed is soft but does not break as easily. It is possible to make metal as hard or as soft as is wished, by annealing it. The metal is heated, and allowed to cool slowly for a certain length of time; at this point it is cooled rapidly. The longer it cools slowly, the softer it becomes. Annealing can also be used on other materials, such as glass.

annual

Every kind of plant grows from a seed, but some plants will grow and blossom only one time, then will die and not grow again unless a new seed is planted. Such a plant is called an *annual*, because the word *annus*, in Latin, means "year." Plants that live for two years are called *biennials*, and plants that store enough food in their roots to grow again for several years are called *perennials*. Most annuals grow during a certain season, usually germinating (beginning to grow) in the spring and dying in the fall.

annual rings

When the trunk of a tree is sawed through, we can see that there are many rings, starting at the center, and growing outward in distinct circles to the outer bark. These rings are called "annual rings," because "annual" means "yearly" and usually one ring is formed for every year of the tree's life. By counting these rings we can tell how old the tree was, and by examining the width and regularity of separate rings, we can tell what has happened to the tree at any time—when it was sick, and when conditions of water and climate were good or bad. If insects ate up the leaves one year, or if there was a drought, *two* rings might be formed in one season. These are called "false rings," and it is easy for scientists to tell them from the others.

One important use of annual rings is in furniture manufacturing and carpentry. Wood, as it dries, "moves," or warps, in a direction away from the small rings, or center; so by looking at the rings, the carpenter knows better how to glue, or fasten, the pieces of wood together.

annuity

An annuity is an income paid to a person every year as long as he lives. Usually the same amount is paid each year. In former times annuities were often given as pensions or rewards by a king or government. Today they are a form of insurance sold by life insurance companies.

The *annuitant* (person who receives the income) may pay one lump sum payment and begin to receive income immediately or may make installment payments (called *deposits*) until some agreed age, such as 65, when the income begins. A *straight life annuity* pays the annuitant up to the time of his death, when all payment stops; the income depends on the annuitant's age, being about 7% of the amount deposited at the age of 60. An annuity *with installments certain* guarantees a certain number of payments, and a *cash refund* annuity guarantees a minimum return, payable to the annuitant's beneficiary if he dies before receiving it. Both yield less annual income than the straight life annuity.

By the tax laws passed in 1954, an annuitant pays no United States income tax on 4% of the cost of the annuity.

Annunciation

The Annunciation (which means "announcement") was the occasion when the angel Gabriel told the Virgin Mary that Jesus would be born, as told in the Bible, in the first chapter of Luke. Christian churches celebrate this on March 25 each year. See the picture on page 270.

anode, one of the "poles" through which electricity flows, is explained in the articles on ELECTRICITY and GENERATOR.

anointment

Anointment is the putting of oil on the body in a ceremony. The ancient Hebrews, and perhaps the Egyptians before them, poured a bit of spiced olive oil on the head of a new king in a ceremony like the coronation ceremony of more modern times. *Messiah,* or *Christ,* means "the anointed one," or king. Anointment is still part of the English coronation ceremony. Unction is a form of anointment, used in some churches in certain rites such as baptism and confirmation.

anopheles

The anopheles is a kind of mosquito that carries the disease malaria, a dangerous fever. The female feeds on the blood of men and animals, and after biting a diseased person may carry the germs of malaria and deposit them in the next person it bites. The male does not bite. See MALARIA.

Anschluss

Anschluss is a German word meaning "joining together." It is a word that was heard a great deal in the years before World War II. Germany and Austria were two separate countries then, as they are now, but Adolf Hitler, the German dictator, wanted to join them together as one country. His argument was that they spoke the same language and so should be united. Some of the Austrian people wanted to join with Germany, but not all of them. They would not vote for Anschluss. So Hitler sent the German armies into Austria, in 1938, and forced the Anschluss. It was about the same thing as if the United States sent its armies into Canada to make Canada become part of the United States, because the people speak the same language and the countries are next to each other. When World War II ended, Austria became a separate country again.

ant

Ants are called "social" insects. This means that they live together in groups and each ant has his own duties that help the entire group to stay alive. That is the way human beings live, but it is very unusual for animals to live that way. The ant and the bee are social insects.

Every ant is born with a definite job to do. That job never changes during the ant's lifetime. Some ants live to be several years old, which is a very long life for an insect.

THE QUEEN

Every colony of ants has its *queen,*

USDA Photo

which may live ten years or even more. If it were not for the queen, there would be no colony, because all the ants in a colony are the "children" of its queen. She founds the colony in the first place, and after the moment when she chooses the place where she wants to make her home, she spends her entire life laying eggs. She never leaves her home again, and when she finally dies the colony leaves the old home for good, setting up housekeeping with a new queen in a different spot.

The queen ant originally has wings, and she uses them just once. This is when she goes on her "nuptial flight." This is a house-hunting and mating flight, when she mates with male ants and chooses the place where the colony will live. Once she has chosen the spot she will not need wings again, so she rubs them off before she starts her life work of egg-laying.

LIFE IN THE ANT HILL

From the first group of eggs to hatch come the *workers,* and nursemaids who will take care of the fast-growing family of baby ants and of the eggs themselves before they hatch.

The workers provide the queen with food, and keep the passages of the ant home clean at all times. There will be many hatches of worker ants, but when it is time for the mating season the queen ant lays eggs that will hatch into future queen ants, and male ants which are not useful at any work.

The job of some of the ants is to build a well-ventilated, well-arranged home, and to make additions to it as the colony increases and needs larger quarters. An ant hill looks like an insignificant heap of sand, but inside it is cleverly divided into passages, food storage sections, ventilation tunnels, egg-hatching rooms, and queen's quarters. The builder ants are responsible for this home.

Other ants are the dairymen of the ant colony. Just as human beings keep cows for milk, there are ants who herd tiny insects called aphids and plant lice, for the sweet fluid that can be milked from them. They take good care of their herds, too, protecting them from other insects that might be dangerous to them, as a farmer would protect his cows from wolves. They even carry the smaller creatures to new plants or leaves, where the aphids or plant lice will find better "pasturage."

Still other ants in the colony are posted as guards. These are the policemen or soldier ants. If danger is likely from any direction, they run through the passages and warn others to be on the alert. Ants communicate with each other by means of their antennas, or feelers.

THE BODY OF THE ANT

Ants are found everywhere on the face of the earth, and they are easily recognized by their shape. All ants have a three-part body formation. The body has a head with feelers, or antennas, attached to it; a middle section called a *thorax,* to which six legs are attached; and a rear section, which is the ant's abdomen.

Some kinds of ants are only a fiftieth of an inch long when fully grown, while the largest kinds may be as much as a full inch in length. Experts believe that there are over two thousand different kinds, and at least two hundred kinds in America. Most familiar in the United States and Canada are the red and black ants that can be seen almost anywhere. Many ants have strong biting jaws, like small pincers, which may be used for self-defense. Ants also use their mouths to carry things.

DANGEROUS ANTS

Among the many interesting types of ants in the world are the "warrior" or "Amazon" ants. These ants go out on robbing expeditions and capture other ants' eggs, larvae, and food supply. They then take their loot home, tend the eggs and larvae carefully until the young ants appear, and make slaves of them for life. The warrior ants do nothing for themselves after that. They are fed, bathed, and protected by their slaves, and eventually become so soft and lazy that they are helpless if anything happens to the slaves. They cannot even keep themselves alive without help.

Another remarkable kind of ant is the African *driver ant.* This is probably the most dangerous and ferocious ant in the world. Driver ants travel in broad columns, devouring everything in their path. They are flesh-eaters, and will strip every speck of flesh from any bird or animal unfortunate enough to be caught in their path and unable to get out of the way. Even lions will run from them, and if a few succeed in swarming onto them and start biting, the animals run wildly to reach water, where they can drown their tormentors. In any land where the driver ants' columns travel, the natives get out of their way quickly.

The vast majority of ants, in spite of the two unpleasant types just mentioned, are hard-working, industrious insects, with a highly-organized community life, and a very efficient manner of dividing and sharing the work of the colony. Every ant must work, or the rest of the workers will get rid of him.

Termites are not ants, as many people suppose, though they look like ants. There is a separate article on TERMITES.

Antarctica

Antarctica is officially a continent, covering 5,000,000 to 6,000,000 square miles (almost twice as much as the smallest continent Australia) and extending 1,000 miles or more in every direction from the South Pole which is near the center of the continent. More than nine-tenths of the region is covered by ice all year. In most places the ice is 100 feet or more thick; in some places it is at least 1,800 feet thick.

Great sheets of ice extend from the land out into the ocean, often for 100 or more miles, in some places up to 800 or more miles. Until 1840 or later it was believed that Antarctica was only an ice sheet over the ocean, similar to the North Polar region. Even the great scientific studies made in the 1950s have not established how much of the region has a land base and it is not impossible that Antarctica is an island group instead of a continent, with permanent ice shelves between the islands. There are numerous permanent ice shelves along the coasts. The largest, the Ross Ice Shelf, has an area of about 150,000 square miles.

The climate of Antarctica is colder than that of any other part of the earth, the average temperature being below freezing in the summer and 70° below zero or colder in the winter. The year-round average is about 40 degrees lower than that of the Arctic Circle. Nevertheless, summer heat, changes in temperature, and winds cause huge sections of ice to break off and float out to sea as icebergs.

Antarctica is mountainous. It averages 7,000 feet above sea level, with over 50 peaks above 10,000 feet. The highest, in the Markham Mountains, are over 15,000 feet high. Winds sometimes exceed 200 miles per hour. The outer regions of Antarctica have heavy snowfall which cannot be measured accurately because it is hard to tell which snow has just fallen and which was blown from somewhere else. However, the interior of the continent (which means most of Antarctica) has no rain at all and only about three inches of snow a year. This is because the cold air does not hold much moisture.

Where the ice layer is absent, permanently or temporarily, mosses, lichens, and fungi and some coarse grasses grow. There are almost no bacteria; the average may be one per pint of snow, as compared to several billion per pint in temperate zones. Animal life is confined to birds—the penguin, skua, and some gulls such as the petrel—and to sea mammals such as the seal and sea lion. The surrounding waters are rich in whales, other sea mammals, hundreds of species of fish, and diatoms and other algae. Explorers have found fossils that indicate a former period, perhaps 300,000,000 years ago, in which the continent was warm and trees and flowering plants grew.

There is much dispute as to the value of Antarctica's resources. There is known to be some coal. Some geologists have placed high estimates on the mineral wealth, in such metals as platinum, gold, and uranium; others have not considered the mineral resources very valuable. Admiral Richard E. Byrd, one of the principal Antarctic explorers, proposed using

1. In 1913 the U.S.S. *Bear* sailed to the Bay of Whales in the Antarctic Ocean. It went to pick up the men of an expedition that had gone there before. The tame and friendly penguins look on with great curiosity.
2. Admiral Richard E. Byrd welcomes Admiral Richard Cruzen to Little America, in 1947. Airplanes have made travel in the Antarctic quicker and easier than it was when explorers could travel only by dog sled.
3. The American flag flies over the base camp in Little America. It is the middle of the Antarctic summer but the ground is always covered with snow and ice. Little America was the first United States base in Antarctica but better ones were found and in 1958 it was decided to abandon it.
4. From the South Pole all directions are north. In this map the course to the United States would be toward the upper right-hand corner.

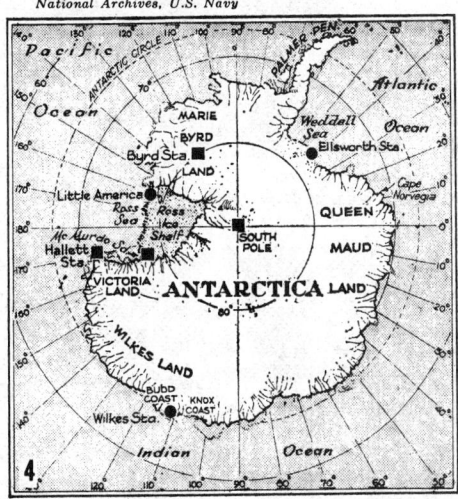

the region as a storage place for vast quantities of food for future use. Because of the cold and the absence of bacteria food lasts indefinitely there.

Chile, Norway, Australia, New Zealand, and Great Britain have claimed territory on the continent, on the basis of explorations. As late as 1955 the United States and Soviet Russia had made no claims but had indicated that they might make claims in the future.

History. Capt. James Cook, the British explorer, may have sighted Antarctica in 1774 and if so was the first navigator to do so. Russian claims are based on a voyage of F. von Bellinghausen in 1819, when he sailed into the Antarctic Circle and sighted land, which however is now known to have been an island off the Antarctic coast. In 1840 a U.S. Navy ship entered the waters now called the Amund-

sen Sea, on the northwest of Antarctica, and its commander, Charles Wilkes, identified the land as a continent. A British fleet under J. Clark Ross (for whom the Ross Sea and Ice Shelf are named) approached the western coast in 1841 and Ross agreed with Wilkes that Antarctica is a continent.

In the early 1900s explorers began a race to reach the South Pole. Roald Amundsen of Norway reached it first, in December, 1911. He was only a few weeks ahead of R. F. Scott of England, who lost his life on the return trip. Ernest Shackleton, who had been with Scott on an earlier trip in 1903, explored other parts of the continent in 1915. Sir Guy Wilkins of Great Britain was the first man to explore Antarctica by air and to fly over the South Pole (in 1928). Rich-

ard Evelyn Byrd of the U.S. Navy, who followed him by a few months, became the principal explorer of Antarctica. On January 6, 1929, Byrd set up a permanent base called Little America on the Ross Ice Shelf. He left his base standing at Little America and made return expeditions in 1933, 1939, 1946, and 1955. The United States continued the 1955 expedition through the International Geophysical Year of 1958, when teams of scientists from many different countries conducted exploration and research in Antarctica. Since then the pace of scientific activity has been stepped up even more. In 1960, for example, the United States spent $19,000,000 to maintain some 120 scientists there. By 1962 the number had increased to 200, and almost every kind of scientist was represented—biologists, physicists, geologists, glaciologists, meteorologists, cosmic-ray experts, and others.

The U.S. Antarctic Research Program is financed and coordinated by the National Science Foundation and administered by its Office of Antarctic Programs. The U.S. program is coordinated with that of other nations through the Committee on Polar Research of the National Academy of Sciences. Logistic support (supplies) is provided by the U.S. Navy and through cooperation with other countries.

ANTARCTICA. Uninhabited continent, 5,300,000 square miles. Location, surrounding South Pole.

anteater

There are several animals that live by eating ants. They have long, sticky tongues that they use to reach into ant hills. The ants stick to their tongues, and so are carried into their mouths. There are large anteaters, as much as 7 feet long, and smaller anteaters that may be only 2 feet long. Anteaters are found in Central America and in South America. Some animals in other parts of the world eat ants and are sometimes called anteaters. They include the aardvark of Africa and the pangolin of Africa and Asia.

Am. Museum of Natural History
The giant anteater has no teeth, but can fight with its heavy claws. A full-grown collie would look small beside it.

antelope

Antelopes are animals related to the deer and cow. There are many kinds of antelope, and they are found in nearly every part of the world, but mostly in Africa and Asia. They are cud-chewing animals and the males have horns on their heads. Antelopes can run very fast; the gazelle, a kind of antelope, can run 40 miles an hour or more. The biggest antelope is the eland, which is about 6 feet high. Antelopes eat grass and the leaves and bark of trees, as deer do. Some antelopes are hunted for their meat. Their

hides make good leather and their fur is popular for women's sport coats but does not last long. Antelopes are usually sand-colored or grayish brown on the back and cream or white on the belly.

antenna

An antenna is a feeler, occurring in pairs, on the heads of most insects, shellfish, and other animals. Some antennas are used for feeling, some for smelling, and others for seeing. They often look like hairs, but are actually part of the body of the creature on which they are found. Certain fish, such as catfish, have antennas called *barbels* under their chins.

Anthony, Saint

St. Anthony is one of the great saints of the early years of the Christian Church. He lived about three hundred years after the time of Jesus. St. Anthony founded the first Christian monastery, a community of holy men who lived apart from all other people, never married, and devoted their lives to prayer and thoughts of God.

St. Anthony was born about the year 251 in Egypt. His parents were very rich, but he gave away all his money to the poor and when he was 20 years old he went into the desert to pray and live entirely alone. Old stories tell how evil spirits tried to tempt St. Anthony to give up his holy life, and great artists have painted pictures showing the "Temptation of St. Anthony," but the demons failed to move him. When he was 30 years old he retired even further into the desert to be more alone with his own thoughts.

Other Christian holy men who admired St. Anthony came out into the desert to be near him. In the year 305 he was finally persuaded by these admirers to leave the desert and become their leader. After a few years he went away again, to live by himself in the desert near Thebes, an important city of ancient Egypt. He died in the year 350 or later, when he was about one hundred years old.

Anthony, Susan B.

Miss Susan Brownell Anthony was a woman born in the United States nearly a hundred and fifty years ago who spent all her life trying to change anything she thought was wrong. She came from New England, having been born in Adams, Massachusetts, in 1820. In her younger years, Negroes were slaves in the Southern states, and she fought against slavery. She was also a leader in the temperance movement, which opposed the drinking of whiskey and other alcoholic liquors, and in the women's suffrage movement, which was the effort to give women the right to vote, when only men had enjoyed this right before. She died in 1906.

anthrax

Anthrax is a deadly disease of animals, chiefly cows, sheep, horses and pigs. Sometimes, but not often, human beings get it. Anthrax is caused by a tiny germ known as the anthrax bacillus. The germ was first discovered by a German scientist named Robert Koch in 1876. A few years later, the great French scientist Louis Pasteur found a way to control the disease. He vaccinated cows and sheep to protect

them against anthrax. Before Pasteur's time, the disease often wiped out whole herds of animals. Today anthrax is a rare disease.

anthropology

Anthropology is the study of man—what he is like, and how he lives and behaves, and almost everything else about him. The name comes from the Greek words *anthropos,* meaning "man," and *logos,* meaning "study." Anthropology is one of the most important modern sciences, but less than a hundred years ago it was practically unknown.

Anthropologists study man in different ways. Some study the history of man, others study present-day man. Some anthropologists are interested in where man came from, others in where he lives now. Some anthropologists want to learn how man survived through the ages, others are interested in how man fits himself for life in the modern world.

THE WAYS OF STUDYING MAN

Anthropology is usually divided into three parts. The first part is the study of geography in relation to man. It is the study of how man lives in different parts of the world and in different climates. The second part of anthropology is the study of the races of mankind. This kind of anthropology compares the races to find differences and similarities between the different races of mankind. In this study the anthropologist is interested mostly in what men look like—the color of their skins, their height and weight and body structure, and the shapes of their heads, noses, and jaws. The third part of anthropology is the study of man's culture. This means how man uses his intelligence, and what his activities are. In this study, the anthropologist learns how man has built his home, what kind of clothing he wears, what tools he uses, and what arts and crafts he works at. This third part of anthropology also studies man's social life, his language, religion, marriage customs, and family life. It includes the study of how man governs himself.

Anthropologists study prehistoric man, ancient man, the modern savage, and civilized man. Anthropologists journey to all parts of the world to study man. They stay in small villages in India and China. They live with the Eskimos in Alaska, and with the jungle tribes in Africa. They study the people at work and at play. They learn something about the language, and listen to the stories the people tell. They listen to the songs and watch the dances and festivals.

There are specialists in each of the branches of anthropology and separate names for the branches in which they specialize: *Physical anthropology* is the study of man's body or physical equipment and how it affects his progress; this includes *biometry* and *anthropometry,* the science of measuring the body and comparing the measurements of different races and groups. *Ethnology* is the study of different peoples and cultures, or ways of life. *Sociology* is the study of human behavior in groups living together. *Linguistics* is the study and comparison of all the languages used by men in all times. *Archaeology* is the study of man through

the things he has made and used, such as tools, works of art, and building. *Applied anthropology* is the study of human behavior so as to predict how men will act in certain situations.

anti-aircraft defense

Anti-aircraft defense includes all the ways in which people and places are protected against attack by enemy airplanes. The main purpose of anti-aircraft defense is to knock enemy bombing planes out of the sky. This can be done in either of two ways. The first way is to have a strong air force that can battle the enemy planes in the sky and keep them from reaching their targets. The second way is to fire shells or other missiles into the air and destroy the enemy planes before they can do any damage.

Another defense is to remove the target to where the enemy cannot find it or underground to where he cannot reach it; or to hide it by camouflage. Even firefighting to reduce the damage done by bombs is a part of anti-aircraft defense.

THE USE OF RADAR

The whole system of anti-aircraft defense depends on knowing that the enemy planes are coming. This is done mostly by *radar*. A radar set sends out radio waves. The radio waves hit anything they come into contact with and are bounced back to the radar set. To a trained eye, these radio waves show the presence and location of a distant object, such as aircraft. A radar screen is like a television screen, except it does not show a clear picture or even the outline of an aircraft. The picture of an airplane on a radar screen is not identifiable as an airplane, but usually appears as a small point of light known as a radar blip.

ANTI-AIRCRAFT ARTILLERY

It is almost impossible to score a direct hit on a high-flying airplane. The shells fired from anti-aircraft guns are set to explode near the enemy aircraft. In this way the fragments or pieces of the exploded shells will hit the enemy aircraft. The newest type of anti-aircraft weapon is not a gun but a rocket. A rocket is fired from the ground and controlled in its flight by radio. It is called a *guided missile,* because the radio or radar guides it to its target—the enemy aircraft.

It is even harder to hit an enemy missile that flies into the stratosphere at a speed of several thousand miles an hour and then drops onto its target, but anti-aircraft defense includes "anti-missile missiles" to intercept and explode such

missiles in midair. (See GUIDED MISSILES and AIR FORCE.)

Anti-aircraft guns are placed all around a place that must be defended against air attack. They are grouped in *batteries.* A battery usually consists of four guns. As many as five hundred guns were fired at one time in defending cities during World War II. Enemy bombers were often forced to fly through a thick hail of exploding shells. The airmen in World War II used two nicknames for anti-aircraft fire. The first name, "flak," came from the German word for anti-aircraft. The second name, "ack-ack," came from the initials of anti-aircraft, and also the noise made by the firing of the guns.

OTHER ANTI-AIRCRAFT DEFENSES

There are other ways of defending against air attack. In World War II, cities were protected by *balloon barrages.* Hundreds of balloons were sent high into the air. From them hung cables thousands of feet long. Enemy aircraft sometimes flew against the thin steel cables and were destroyed.

Smoke screens were also used in anti-aircraft defense. Thousands of smoke pots were lighted around the place being defended, and the air soon became thick with smoke. Enemy pilots found it difficult to see the target through the smoke. Smoke screens are no longer so effective, since enemy planes carry radar and can "see" through a smoke screen (and also through fog).

Camouflage used to be another form of anti-aircraft defense. When something is camouflaged it is changed to look like something else. One form of camouflage is to paint a building in such a way that it looks like the country around it and cannot be distinguished from the air. Another form of camouflage uses nets with patches of cloth that look like leaves. These nets are often used to cover small buildings or artillery pieces. Camouflage, like smoke screens, is no longer so effective. Enemy planes using radar can easily penetrate through camouflage.

The defense of North America against air attack is entrusted to NORAD, (North American Air Defense) combining various armed services and government agencies in the United States and Canada.

antibiotics

Most diseases that attack the human body are caused by tiny living things called bacteria. Antibiotics are a group of medicines or drugs that help the body

fight and destroy harmful bacteria. (*Anti-*, meaning "against," and *biotic*, meaning "living," are words taken from the Greek language.)

Although they are used as medicines, antibiotics themselves are taken from living things—tiny forms of plant life found either in the soil or in mold. (Today, however, many antibiotics can be synthesized at a much lower cost.) Some molds are poisonous to human beings, but others are harmless and sometimes very useful. The green mold used in cheese belongs to a family of molds known as *Penicillium.* From one of these molds, *Penicillium notatum,* comes the wonderful antibiotic called penicillin.

Penicillin was the first of the antibiotics. It was accidentally discovered by Dr. Alexander Fleming of Scotland when he was working in the laboratory of St. Mary's Hospital in London, England, in 1928. Dr. Fleming was trying to kill some dangerous bacteria called *staphylococci.* One day he noticed that a glass dish in which he was growing some of these staphylococci had become covered with a green mold—and that at the same time the staphylococci had all died! After ten years of work, with the aid of other doctors, Dr. Fleming produced the drug we now call penicillin. During World War II it saved the lives of thousands of wounded men. There is a separate story about PENICILLIN.

Antibiotics do not kill bacteria, but stop their growth and prevent them from increasing. This gives the *leucocytes* in the blood a chance to destroy them. Leucocytes are tiny, round white cells that can be seen only through a microscope. They float in the blood and attack harmful bacteria in the blood. The human body also fights bacteria by making certain substances or chemicals called *antibodies* in the blood, and the antibodies kill bacteria. However, sometimes the bacteria increase so fast and there are so many of them that the body cannot kill them off fast enough and when this happens the sick person usually dies. By preventing the bacteria from increasing in number, antibiotics give the body a chance to create antibodies in time to destroy the bacteria of disease.

Many of the antibiotic drugs have *mycin* or *mycetin* in their names. This is because the fungus growths (one of which is mold) are called *mycetes* in technical medical language. The first of these drugs to be successful was streptomycin. This was discovered by Dr. Selman Waksman at the Agricultural Experiment Station of Rutgers University in New Brunswick, New Jersey. Dr. Waksman was born in Russia, but came to the United States as a youth and studied at Rutgers. He became interested in *actinomycetes,* a family of plants—so tiny they can be seen only through a microscope—that are found by the millions in the soil in almost any part of the country. Convinced that actinomycetes could kill some of the bacteria that cause disease in human beings, Dr. Waksman began experimenting in 1940 with the different kinds of plant life in this family. In 1943, Dr. Waksman and some of his assistants produced streptomycin from one of the actinomycetes. This drug attacked diseases against which penicillin did not work, for ex-

A radar screen aboard a guided missile carrier. *U.S. Navy*

ample tularemia, a dangerous fever that human beings get from rabbits; certain diseases of the bladder and kidneys; blood poisoning; and tuberculosis. Several diseases that used to kill people are no longer considered even dangerous, thanks to the antibiotics.

Scientists have been working ever since to discover new antibiotics, and they have discovered many. There are aureomycin, terramycin, and several others that can be used against diseases that penicillin and streptomycin do not stop. Also, some persons who are made sick by some of the antibiotics find that they can take others without bad effects.

When antibiotics are mixed into the feed given to chicks, calves, and little pigs, these animals grow much faster and larger than those that get the usual feed. Another use of antibiotics, especially aureomycin, is to delay the spoiling of foods. Spoilage is caused by bacteria. The antibiotic is injected into meat, fish and other perishable foods.

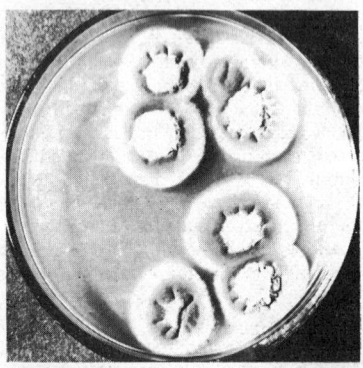
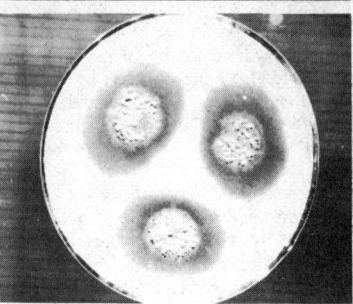

Schenley Laboratories, Inc.

Top. The white spots of mold in the dark rings will be made into penicillin.
Bottom. Penicillin in three spots on this plate made the bacteria stop growing.

Antichrist

The Bible speaks of a "beast" or evil spirit that is the enemy of Christ and tries to prevent him from coming to earth to help mankind. The Jewish scriptures written before the time of Jesus mentioned this evil being, and books written after the time of Jesus portrayed the Antichrist as one who would oppose the second coming of Christ, but whom Christ will defeat on the last day of the world. Enemies of the Christian Church, also, have often been called Antichrists. In our century, Adolf Hitler and Joseph Stalin were both sometimes called Antichrists. The number 666 is connected with Satan or the Antichrist in the Bible (in the last book of the New Testament, called the Revelation or Apocalypse, chapter 13, verse 18).

Antietam, Battle of

Antietam Creek, near the village of Sharpsburg, Maryland, was the scene of a famous battle in the Civil War, on September 17, 1862, between Northern troops under General G. B. McClellan and Southern troops commanded by General Robert E. Lee. McClellan had a far larger army but he was unable to drive back Lee's troops, who held their lines in this very bloody battle. On the following day, both sides maintained their positions without any more fighting. Finally, that evening, Lee quietly withdrew his troops and marched back into the state of Virginia. McClellan might have followed him immediately and continued the battle, but did not. The Battle of Antietam was Lee's first invasion of Northern territory and was a failure. McClellan had 75,000 men and lost 12,000. Lee had 52,000 and lost 14,000.

antifreeze

An antifreeze is a liquid that is added to water to keep it from freezing. When water freezes and turns to ice, it expands—takes up more space. The force of water expanding is so great that it will break the hardest metal. Water is used in automobile engines to keep them cool while they run, and if this water is allowed to freeze in the winter it can crack the iron block of the engine. That is why antifreezes are necessary.

Water freezes at 32° Fahrenheit; a typical antifreeze will not freeze until the temperature is 40° below zero. A mixture of 5 quarts of water and 4 quarts of antifreeze will prevent freezing at zero; 4 quarts of water and 5 quarts of antifreeze reduce this to 8° below zero.

Alcohol is a good antifreeze, but when the automobile is running it becomes hot and the alcohol boils away, so it must be replaced very often. Most people use antifreezes that do not boil away when the engine is running. There are several chemicals that do this. One of the most popular is called *ethylene glycol*, which is sold under various trade names such as Prestone and Zerex.

An instrument called the HYDROMETER, about which there is a separate article, is used in filling stations to test the liquid in the cooling system and find out the temperature at which it will freeze.

Antigua

Antigua is one of the Leeward Islands in the British West Indies. Its area is 108 square miles and its population is 63,000, mostly Negroes. Antigua was discovered by Columbus in 1493 and has been a British colony since 1632. In 1941 the United States built a naval base on its northeast coast.

Antilles

The Antilles are a large group of islands in the Caribbean Sea. The Greater Antilles include Cuba, Hispaniola (Haiti and the Dominican Republic), Jamaica, and Puerto Rico (U.S.). The Lesser Antilles include Barbados, the Windward Islands and the Leeward Islands (British); Trinidad and Tobago; Virgin Islands (U.S.); Curaçao (Dutch); and Margarita (Venezuelan). Together with the Bahamas they form the West Indies. Many of the islands were discovered between 1493 and 1503 by Columbus.

antimony

Antimony is a hard, silvery-white metal. Like iron, aluminum, and silver itself, antimony is an *element*. That is, it does not have to be made by mixing other metals together. Antimony is taken from an ore called *stibnite,* which is found in Europe and in Asia, chiefly in China and Japan. The principal use of antimony is in alloys (see the article on ALLOYS), in which it makes a metal like lead harder, and a metal like iron whiter. In some compounds antimony makes a red dye.

Antioch

Antioch is one of the oldest cities on earth. It is in southeast Turkey, 20 miles from the Mediterranean Sea. Antioch was founded about 300 B.C. In its early days it was a most magnificent city, with a population of about 300,000, and rivaled Rome in splendor and beauty. It was in Antioch that the followers of Jesus first came to be called Christians. Antioch is mentioned in the New Testament, in the Book of Acts. The city has been captured and partly destroyed by its enemies several times, and earthquakes nearly destroyed it in 1872, so very little remains of the ancient city except the ruins of some of the walls and aqueducts, which carried water into the city. Today there is only a small city of about 57,900 people where the ancient city stood.

anti-Semitism

Prejudice against Jews is called anti-Semitism, and a person who hates Jews is called an anti-Semite. These are not correct words, because the Semitic peoples include Arabs, who follow the Mohammedan religion, Syrians, who are Christians, and many others, as well as the Jews.

Prejudice against any particular people—whether because of their religion, their color, or their race—is contrary to the teaching of the Christian Church, and therefore a true Christian cannot be anti-Semitic, but nevertheless anti-Semitism has existed for many years and in many countries. This is chiefly because in most countries the Jews have been a small group living in the midst of a much larger group. A small group of this sort is called a *minority*. It is quite usual to find prejudice against minority groups. In former times anti-Semitism was displayed in the *ghetto*, or district in which Jews were forced to live, in European cities; the *pogrom*, or mob attack on Jews, encouraged by the government in Russia; and *genocide*, or murder of all Jews, in Germany.

Intelligent and educated people are not anti-Semitic, but a skillful and dishonest politician can often arouse great hatred of Jews among ignorant people.

antiseptic

An antiseptic is something that kills germs, or prevents their growth, and so prevents or stops an infection. Germs cause infection, just as they cause food to rot or become putrid. Iodine and hydrogen peroxide are well-known antiseptics. Alcohol, salt water, vinegar and many other household preparations are antiseptics.

A great English doctor, Lord Joseph Lister, was the father of antiseptic sur-

gery; that is, he was the first man to prevent infection after an operation by killing all the germs on his hands and instruments. He was sure that germs caused infection. About 1867, Lister performed the first antiseptic operation. He had all the surgical instruments boiled, he washed his hands, and he kept everything around the patient clean and germ-free. Before this, many patients died after operations. Today, a patient rarely dies from an infection after an operation. Surgery is now completely antiseptic.

In daily life, the best antiseptic is soap and water.

antitoxin

A *toxin* is a poison produced in the body by germs or bacteria that cause certain kinds of disease. An *antitoxin* is something that works against this kind of poison. Diphtheria, cholera, scarlet fever and tetanus (lockjaw) are among the diseases caused by toxins produced by germs.

The body manufactures substances to fight off these toxins and make them harmless. These substances are called antitoxins. Enough antitoxin is usually manufactured by the body, but when the disease is too strong other antitoxins must be injected into the body. The antitoxin comes from the blood of an animal that has been given the disease. The animal is ill for a short time and soon recovers. After recovery the animal's blood contains a large amount of antitoxin. The antitoxins taken from the blood of such an animal are used to help people who have that particular disease.

Diphtheria germs are injected into horses to obtain an antitoxin against diphtheria. A person inoculated with this antitoxin will seldom catch the disease.

A modern medical way of avoiding disease is to use a *toxin-antitoxin*. A mild toxin is injected into the body, which then starts to produce its own antitoxin.

Read also the article on IMMUNITY.

Anti-Trust Acts are laws passed by Congress to regulate certain kinds of big business. See the article on MONOPOLY.

Antony, Mark

Mark Antony was a statesman and general who ruled a part of the Roman Empire and fell in love with Cleopatra, Queen of Egypt, in one of the greatest love stories of history. All this happened about two thousand years ago. Mark Antony's name in Rome was Marcus Antonius. He was born about 83 B.C. and became an officer in the armies of Julius Caesar, Rome's greatest general, who became his friend. When Caesar was killed by several Roman senators, as told in the article on Julius CAESAR, Mark Antony made such a stirring speech at Caesar's funeral that the people of Rome became angry at the killers and they were forced to flee from the city.

After Caesar's death, Mark Antony became one of the three rulers of Rome, along with Octavian, Caesar's adopted son, and Emilius Lepidus, a Roman general. They divided the vast Roman Empire, which included North Africa, most of Europe, and parts of Asia. Each of them was called a *triumvir*, which means "one of three rulers," and their reign was called a *triumvirate*. Antony was given control of the empire in Asia and in Egypt, the greatest country of northern Africa. He went to Egypt, where he fell in love with Cleopatra, the young and beautiful queen of Egypt.

Octavian, who had the western part of the empire but wanted all of it, made war on Antony. He defeated Antony in a great sea battle near Actium in Greece, then invaded Egypt. Deserted by his own army, which went over to Octavian, Antony committed suicide by falling on his sword. He died in 30 B.C. Cleopatra then took her own life by letting a poisonous snake bite her.

Antwerp

Antwerp is a great city in Belgium. It is located on the Scheldt River, close to the North Sea, and has a population of about 914,790 people. Besides being the most important center of business in Belgium, Antwerp is also famous for its cathedral and art treasures. The great Cathedral of Notre Dame in Antwerp is one of the largest in Europe and has a spire 400 feet high. Inside the cathedral are some of the great paintings of such famous artists as Rubens, Van Dyck, and others. There are also many museums and art galleries.

Antwerp is a shipping center and is also the principal diamond-cutting and diamond-trading center of the world.

Antwerp is a very old city and has seen many wars. It has been partly destroyed many times, but each time its people have rebuilt it. When Napoleon, the great French general and emperor, conquered Antwerp in 1803, he found it completely deserted. The people had fled from their homes to escape from the French soldiers. In 1914, at the beginning of World War I, the Germans attacked Antwerp. There were great rings of forts to protect the city, but they were destroyed by German guns. Again many of the people fled, to the neighboring country of Holland, but they later came back to fight and win. In World War II Antwerp was again taken by the Germans and was freed by the victorious British and American troops.

ANTWERP, BELGIUM. Population (in 1973) 234,100; with suburbs, 914,800. On the Scheldt River, 60 miles from the North Sea.

Anzio

In January, 1944, during World War II, the United States Fifth Army and other Allied forces were fighting against the Germans in the southern part of Italy. They were trying to capture Rome, the capital of Italy. An American army corps (about forty thousand men) made an amphibious landing near Anzio, a small city of 6,000 people on the western coast of Italy, about 30 miles south of Rome. The Germans brought up strong forces and there was hard fighting until late in May, when the Americans broke through the German lines and helped to capture Rome on June 4.

Apache Indians

The Apaches are a tribe of North American Indians who live mostly in the southern parts of the states of New Mexico and Arizona in the United States and the states of Chihuahua and Coahuila in Mexico. At one time the Apaches were the fiercest and most savage warriors among the Indians of the Southwest. They were wonderful horsemen and wandered from place to place raiding their more peaceful neighbors and robbing them of their food, horses, and sheep. They not only fought and robbed their Indian neighbors, but they also fought against all white men.

The first white men the Apaches met were the Spanish explorers who conquered what we now call Mexico. It was from the Spanish that the Apaches first learned about horses. They stole the Spaniards' horses and learned to ride them and to fight on horseback. Later, when Mexico became an independent country, they attacked the Mexicans. When the territory that is now the states of New Mexico and Arizona became a part of the United States, the cavalry of the United States Army had to fight for years before the Apaches, who had been led by chiefs Geronimo, Cochise, and Victorio, surrendered in 1886.

Geronimo was the most famous of the Apache chiefs. He was one of the most skillful of all Indian fighters. Geronimo's family had been captured and sent as prisoners to St. Augustine, Florida, and he surrendered only when a messenger from the American General Nelson A. Miles told him that he would be allowed to live with his wife and children. But the change of climate was unsuited to the Indians, so they were sent to Fort Sill, Oklahoma, in the West. Here Geronimo died in 1909.

Although the Apaches were one tribe, they were divided into several bands. Today, several of these bands live peacefully on reservations in New Mexico and Arizona. There are more than 8,000 Apache Indians living on Arizona reservations and about 2,500 in New Mexico.

The name "apache" is also used in the French language for dangerous criminals in Paris, the capital and biggest city of France. It is pronounced in the French manner (uh-POSH) and means about the same as our words "hoodlum" or "gangster."

ape

Apes are the animals that look most like human beings. They are also called *anthropoid apes* (*anthropoid* means "like a man"). Apes have short, bent legs and very long arms. They are covered with hair, which may be black, brown, a reddish brown, or gray. Apes do not have tails as monkeys do. (There is a separate article on MONKEYS.)

An ape is like a man in other ways. It has 32 teeth, as a man does. It has a brain like a man's, too, but the brain is smaller. Some scientists believe that an ape can learn anything that a four-year-old child can learn; but apes never learn to talk. Apes sometimes walk upright as men do, but usually they walk on their feet and the knuckles of their hands.

There are no apes in the Americas (unless they are brought across the seas for use in zoos and shows). Apes come from Africa and Asia. There are four kinds of ape: GORILLA, CHIMPANZEE,

ORANG-UTAN, and GIBBON. There are separate articles about these apes.

Apennines

The Apennine Mountains are a long, narrow range in Italy. They run all the way from the northern part of Italy to the southern part, about 840 miles, covering 80% of the area of Italy. The highest peaks of the Apennines are in the south, where Mount Corno reaches 9,585 feet. In the central part the tallest peak is Mount Vettore, 8,126 feet, and in the north it is Mount Cimone, 7,126 feet. The beautiful, snowy-white stone known as Carrara marble, from which many famous statues have been made, comes from the central Apennines. Many roads and railroads cross the Apennines to connect the eastern and western parts of Italy.

The Apennines run the entire length of Italy, dividing it as though it were a spine down the back of the country.

aphid

The aphid, or *plant louse,* is an insect that feeds on the green parts of plants. It is so small that it often takes fifteen or twenty aphids in a row to measure an inch. The various kinds of aphid differ in color but are most often greenish. They are soft-bodied and sluggish. Some aphids have wings, others do not. Aphids suck the sap or juice of a plant with mouths that look like tubes. This destroys many farm crops and vegetables. Since aphids breed in tremendous numbers, they would destroy much more if there were not many insects that eat aphids. Great numbers of aphids are also eaten by birds. Farmers protect their crops against aphids by spraying plants with a poison called nicotine sulfate.

Some aphids give off a sweet liquid called honeydew, which ants like to lick off their backs. Many ants keep "herds" of aphids, and feed them, in order to get this honeydew, just as farmers keep cows to get milk. For this reason aphids are sometimes called "ant cows."

apocalypse

"Apocalypse" means a prophecy of what is to happen in the future. The last book in the New Testament is called "the Apocalypse," because it is a prophecy. Another name for it is "the Revelation of St. John," meaning that it tells of things that were made known to St.

John the Apostle in a vision. In this book of the Bible, St. John pictures war, hunger, disease, and death in the form of warriors riding horses, so they have been called "the Four Horsemen of the Apocalypse."

An apocalypse usually tells of how the world is to come to an end. There are other parts of the Bible that are called apocalyptic, because they prophesy things to come.

Apocrypha

The Apocrypha are "hidden" or "secret" books that are included in many Bibles but whose origin is not surely known. Usually fourteen books of Apocrypha are listed, though four of them are only additions to books that are in all Bibles, the books of Daniel and Esther. The Authorized ("King James") Bible contained all fourteen when it was published in 1611 but they are no longer included. Catholic Bibles include eleven of the fourteen.

These are the Apocrypha included in Catholic Bibles: Six additional chapters in the book of Esther. Three sections of the book of Daniel: Susanna and the Elders; Bel and the Dragon; and the Song of the Three Children. The book of Tobias or Tobit. The book of Judith. The Wisdom of Solomon. Ecclesiasticus, also called the Wisdom of Jesus (or Jeshua) the son of Sirach. The book of Baruch. Two books of Machabees or Maccabees.

The other three are: 1 Esdras (or Ezra), 2 Esdras, and the Prayer of Manasseh or Manasses.

Many other apocryphal books were written in the early centuries of the Christian Church.

Apollo

Apollo, or Phoebus Apollo, was one of the ancient Greek gods. He was the god of music, poetry, light, and healing. Apollo was the son of Zeus, the king of the ancient Greek gods, and was second in importance only to his father. His twin sister was Artemis, the moon goddess, called Diana by the ancient Romans. Apollo was considered the friend and adviser of mankind, and especially of young men.

Those who worshiped Apollo believed that if he became angry at somebody, that person would die. He was the bringer of light and the god of the sun. He was also the protector of flocks and herds of animals. Apollo was the father of Asclepius (the Roman Aesculapius), the god of healing and medicine. The wolf, deer, swan, raven and mouse were animals sacred to Apollo and under his special protection. Apollo was usually attended by the nine Muses, the goddesses who ruled over all the arts, such as music, poetry, and dancing.

Statues of Apollo usually show him as a young and beautiful man, wearing a laurel wreath on his head and carrying a lyre, an ancient stringed musical instrument like a harp. The most famous ancient Greek statue of Apollo is in the Belvedere, a part of the Vatican, or palace of the Pope, in Rome, Italy.

apoplexy

Apoplexy is a sudden attack of illness caused by a sudden bleeding in the brain, or sometimes by the clogging of a

blood vessel in the brain. It is often called a *stroke.* Apoplexy is often dangerous, but not always; and doctors can usually warn people against it and help them to prevent it. Children almost never have a stroke of this kind.

apostle

An apostle is a messenger—a person who is sent to carry a message. The men closest to Jesus were called *disciples,* which means "pupils" or "learners," but also, because he sent them out to carry the Christian religion to other countries, they were called apostles. The names of the original apostles were Peter, Andrew, John, Philip, two named James, Matthew, Bartholomew, Thomas, Thaddeus, and Simon. Judas, who had been one of the disciples but who betrayed Jesus, was replaced by Matthias. Paul, who became one of the greatest of the apostles, and Barnabas, who traveled with him, were also called apostles of Jesus. The book Acts of the Apostles, in the New Testament, tells about them.

Appalachian Mountains

The longest and biggest range of mountains in the eastern part of North America stretches from Canada to Alabama. It is called the Appalachian Mountains, and it is about 1,600 miles long. The Appalachians are made up of many smaller mountain ranges. In the northern part there are the White Mountains of New Hampshire and the Green Mountains of Vermont. To the south and west of these are the Catskill Mountains in New York; the Allegheny Mountains of Pennsylvania, Maryland, West Virginia, and Virginia; the Blue Ridge Mountains that stretch from Pennsylvania to Georgia; the Black Mountains of North Carolina, and the Unaka Mountains in Tennessee and North Carolina. The Great Smoky Mountains of Tennessee and North Carolina are also a part of the Appalachian chain, as are the Adirondacks in New York.

In the Appalachians there are many different kinds of minerals and ores, and some of them are very important, especially the coal mines of Pennsylvania and West Virginia.

The Appalachian Mountains are more than 225,000,000 years old. At one time a large part of the United States was a big shallow sea. Then, when the inside of the earth was cooling off, the surface ground crumpled and folded, and pushed the water back into what is now the Atlantic Ocean. When the inside of the earth cooled, it cooled a little at a time and the earth's crust wrinkled a little at a time.

Later, great rivers of ice called *glaciers* slipped slowly south. They dug big valleys and lakes here and there, and scraped off some surfaces and made them smoother, or less wrinkled, than they had been. In some places the glaciers dragged big rocks with them and left them along the way also.

None of the Appalachians are high enough to have snow on their peaks all year round, but some peaks reach heights over 6,000 feet. The highest is Mount Mitchell, in North Carolina, 6,684 feet, in the Black Mountains. Also in the Black Mountains is Balsam Cone, 6,645

feet. In the north, the highest peaks are Mount Washington in the White Mountains, with a height of 6,288 feet, and Mount Adams, also in the White Mountains, 5,798 feet.

The APPALACHIAN TRAIL is a footpath extending 2050 miles from Mt. Katahdin, Maine, to Mt. Oglethorpe, Ga., and traversing the crests of the Appalachian ranges. Its highest point is Clingman's Dome, 6,642 ft., in the Great Smoky Mountains. The trail is equipped with hostels for hikers. It was opened in 1921.

appendix

An appendix is something added. In the human body the appendix is a small tube that is joined at one end to the large intestine and closed at the other end. Its full name is the *vermiform* (wormshaped) *appendix*.

The appendix is totally unnecessary to the human body. The only thing it can do is cause trouble. If food gets into the appendix and stays there, the appendix becomes sore. This is the disease *appendicitis*. It may start simply as a stomach ache, followed by a fever.

Appendicitis often goes away in a short time, but sometimes an operation is necessary, an *appendectomy*, to remove the appendix. The danger is that an infected appendix will burst, scattering infection all through the *peritoneum*, the region in which the appendix is located. This leads to *peritonitis*, which is so dangerous that an appendectomy is usually worthwhile to avoid any chance of it. The operation is almost never dangerous if done in time.

When there are any symptoms that might indicate appendicitis, it is important to avoid laxatives and hot-water bottles or heating pads until a doctor has been called.

Appian Way

Ancient Rome, which was the biggest and most powerful country in the world more than two thousand years ago, had such wonderful roads that some of them still exist and are usable. Some historians think the great roads had much to do with making Rome so rich and powerful. The most famous of these roads was called the Appian Way. The building of it began about 312 B.C. It was paved with heavy blocks of stone, and was about 15 feet wide. At first it ran from Rome to Capua and by 244 B.C. it had been extended to Brindisium (now called Brindisi), making it about 350 miles long. It was named for the Roman governor Appius Claudius Caecus, who began it.

apple

The apple is the fruit of a tree that grows in countries that have a temperate climate, the kind of climate the United States and southern Canada have. No other fruit tree is as widely grown and as well known.

Most apple trees grow in orchards. They are usually spaced about 30 feet apart. The tree may grow as high as 40 feet. It bears beautiful white blossoms in the spring. Some apples ripen in late summer, some in early autumn, and some in late autumn.

There are thousands of different kinds of apple. Some of the best-known varieties are the Winesap, Baldwin, McIntosh, greening, Delicious, Northern Spy, and Jonathan. More people eat apples than any other fruit in the world.

Cider is apple juice, but often it is allowed to ferment and become vinegar.

The "forbidden fruit" that Adam and Eve ate in the Garden of Eden is usually pictured as an apple. Actually, the Bible does not say exactly what kind of fruit it was. Apples were often important in Greek mythology.

Appleseed, Johnny

Johnny Appleseed is the nickname of a man whose real name has been almost forgotten. He was John or Jonathan Chapman and he was born in Boston, Massachusetts, over two hundred years ago, in 1775. Nothing is known of him, after that, until he was 26 years old. Then he began to do the thing that gave him his famous name. He began to plant apple trees.

For almost fifty years, Johnny Appleseed walked and rode horseback through western Pennsylvania, Ohio, and Indiana. Everywhere he went he carried bags of apple seeds and planted them. Thousands of settlers came to know this strange, lonely man. Johnny Appleseed was a religious man, and he loved nature. He believed it was his duty to go up and down the land planting apple seeds. He looked like a scarecrow in his ragged clothing, but the children all learned to love him.

Some nights he spent at farmhouses, and told stories for his supper. Other times he camped out alone in the fields and woods. He did nearly all his traveling on foot.

No harm ever came to Johnny Appleseed in his lonely travels through the wilderness. The Indians knew him and treated him as a friend, and even the wild animals left him alone.

Appomattox Courthouse

Appomattox Courthouse is the name of a village in the state of Virginia, where, on April 9, 1865, General Robert E. Lee, the commanding general of the Confederate Armies, surrendered to General Ulysses S. Grant, commanding general of the Union Armies. The two generals met in a large farmhouse, the McLean house. Lee's surrender practically ended the Civil War, though one Confederate Army did not surrender till later. Appomattox Courthouse is now a national historical monument and is part of the city of Appomattox, whose population is 1,400 (1970) census.

apprenticeship

A boy who works in return for being taught a trade is called an *apprentice,* and is said to be serving his *apprenticeship*. This form of training started thousands of years ago and became very important in the Middle Ages. At that time everything was made either in a small shop or in the home of a skilled workman. The most highly skilled workmen were called *master craftsmen.* Each master craftsman had several apprentices working for him. The apprentices came to the master craftsman when they were boys of twelve or fourteen. They agreed to stay with the master craftsman for a period of seven years, during which he would teach them his trade.

The apprentices lived with the master craftsman and were fed by him, but did not receive any wages. They started out by doing errands and cleaning up around the shop. Little by little they learned the skills of the craft. At the end of seven years, an apprentice became a *journeyman*. After several years of work, a journeyman might become a master craftsman himself.

A journeyman might travel around, getting work where he could find it. The name "journeyman," however, does not come from the worker's travels. The name comes from the French word *jour,* meaning "day." The journeyman worked by the day.

The age of machinery has almost ended the need for apprentices in each trade or craft. There are still some apprentices, but very few.

Today, many young people learn a trade or skill in school or college.

apricot

The apricot is a fruit related to the peach and the plum. It grows on a tree that looks very much like a peach tree, but its blossoms are more like those of the plum tree. The skin of the apricot is not as fuzzy as that of the peach. It is also a little more orange in color than the peach. The fruit is rather stringy and is not quite as juicy as the peach or the plum.

The apricot is believed to have been first grown in China. Now it is grown in warm climates all over the world. The tree grows 20 to 30 feet high. It bears pink flowers in early spring, and the fruit becomes ripe in late summer or early autumn. Only about one-third of the apricots grown are eaten as fresh fruit. Most of the crop is dried or canned. Apricots are rich in iron and vitamin A.

April Fools' Day

April Fools' Day is the name given to the first day of April. It is also known as *All Fools' Day*. This is the day on which people like to play tricks and practical jokes on each other. The custom is very old, and nobody knows exactly how it started.

aptitude tests are tests given to find out what kind of job a person is best suited for. They are explained in the article on INTELLIGENCE TESTS.

aquamarine

Aquamarine is the name of a semi-precious stone. It gets its name from the Latin words *aqua,* meaning "water," and *marine,* meaning "sea." Therefore, the name aquamarine means it has the color of sea water, a bluish-green. Aquamarine is a form of mineral called beryl and is related to the emerald but is much less valuable. It is often used in rings and other kinds of jewelry, and is used as a birthstone for March. Some aquamarine is found in the United States, but the best stones come from South America and Asia.

aquaplaning

Aquaplaning is the name given to a water sport. In aquaplaning, one end

of a long rope is attached to a motorboat and the other end is attached to a flat board called an aquaplane. As the motorboat speeds along in the water, it pulls the aquaplane along behind it. The speed at which the aquaplane moves causes it to skim along the top of the water. A person riding an aquaplane holds on to a rope attached to the front of the board. Aquaplaning is a very thrilling sport. A beginner can have lots of fun just standing straight on the aquaplane as it goes along at about ten miles an hour. More experienced aquaplaners like more speed, and sometimes the motorboat goes as fast as fifty miles an hour, though this can be dangerous.

In aquaplaning, the main idea is to hang on and not be thrown no matter what happens. The driver of the motorboat will sometimes make sharp turns. When this happens, an inexperienced rider will fall off the aquaplane. Experienced aquaplaners learn how to keep their balance at all times. Some even do acrobatic tricks on the board. They stand on their heads, or stand for a time without holding on. Sometimes two people aquaplane together. One person sits on the other's shoulders, or even stands on them. The greatest trick in this sport is to ride an aquaplane up a wooden ramp in the water. When the aquaplane gets to the edge of the ramp, it sails several yards through the air before landing in the water again. Only skillful aquaplaners can do this trick and keep their balance.

One very popular form of aquaplaning is water-skiing. Instead of a board, a pair of skis are used. The skis are slightly larger than the kind used on snow. Water-skiing is more thrilling than aquaplaning because it is harder to ride two skis than one board. The trick is to keep the skis together. If they start to separate, the "skier" may wind up doing a split in the water.

aquarium

An aquarium is a place where fish, water animals and water plants are kept. A goldfish bowl or a home fish tank is an aquarium. There are bigger aquariums in many cities of the world. They are large buildings, very much like zoos, except that everything in them is a part of water life only. In the large aquariums the life in the huge water tanks is shown very much as it would be under natural conditions, in a lake or ocean.

Many people have tanks full of brilliant-colored tropical fish. People with large homes in the country sometimes have outdoor aquariums. These are usually small ponds in which fish, turtles and frogs are kept. Nearly all fish are kept in cold-water aquariums. A heated aquarium is necessary for tropical fish. Usually an electric light bulb or two will keep the water warm enough.

An aquarium must be open at the top. The opening must be large enough so that air can reach the water. The size of the opening depends largely on how many fish there are in an aquarium. The more fish, the larger the opening should be. Each fish in an aquarium needs a certain amount of oxygen. Some of this oxygen must get into the water from the air above it.

An aquarium should have clean sand at the bottom. Small stones or shells should also be at the bottom. These stones and shells can be arranged in any attractive way. Next, an aquarium needs water plants. The plants should have their roots deep in the sand at the bottom of the aquarium.

The fish for an aquarium should be carefully chosen. They should be the right size for the aquarium. The worst thing is to have fish that are too large for a tank, and do not have enough room to swim around. Only fish that get along well together should be placed in an aquarium.

The fish in an aquarium will get some of their food from the plants, but other food will have to be placed in the water for them. They should not be overfed.

An aquarium should be clean before fish are put in it. It must be thoroughly rinsed with clear water. Any trace of soap or disinfectant will be harmful to fish. Once fish have been put into the aquarium, it does not have to be cleaned. The plants in the aquarium will usually use up any of the waste matter from the fish. Sometimes small snails are put into an aquarium, because they help keep it clean. The snails are scavengers, which means they eat all the waste matter and bits of left-over food in the aquarium.

Occasionally the water in an aquarium will evaporate, and the water level will go down. When fresh water is put into an aquarium to raise the water level, it must be the same temperature as the water in the aquarium.

A table on which an aquarium is placed must be very sturdy, because water is very heavy.

aquatic plants are plants that grow in water. See the article on WATER PLANTS.

aqueduct

An aqueduct is a canal, a pipe, or a tube that is built to carry large quantities of water from one place to another. The name comes from the Latin words *aqua,* meaning "water," and *ductus,* meaning "canal." Most aqueducts bring water to people living in large cities.

The first aqueducts were built by the Greeks, more than 2,500 years ago. The Greeks dug canals and cut tunnels through the hills and rocks to bring water from the hills to their cities. One Greek aqueduct was a tunnel almost a mile long, cut through a hill. The tunnel was 8 feet wide and 8 feet high, and a stream of water 3 feet deep ran through it.

The most famous aqueduct-builders were the ancient Romans. They also dug canals and cut tunnels. But the Romans did something else that no one else had done. They built long stone bridges to help carry water to their cities.

The Roman water-carrying bridges often stretched for mile after mile across valleys and fields. These Roman aqueducts were marvels of engineering and architecture. They were built of stone and brick, and the water tube on top was large and usually lined with cement. The Romans could have built their aqueducts on top of solid walls, but people would not have been able to get through these walls. So the Roman aqueducts consisted of hundreds and even thousands of arches, one after the other. Some of the Roman aqueducts were built with one row of arches on top of another, and some even have three rows of arches. Today there are still ruins of ancient Roman aqueducts in Italy, France, Spain, and North Africa. A few Roman aqueducts are still in use.

Aqueducts bring water to many large modern cities. Water is brought to New York City through aqueducts. The Croton Aqueduct was finished in 1842. Since the Croton Aqueduct is able to bring 60 million gallons of water to New York City every day, it was natural for people to think that no more water would ever be needed. But New York grew and grew and grew. Today the people of New York often use twenty times as much water as the Croton Aqueduct, large as it is, can supply. New York's water is brought from as far as 100 miles away.

The people of Los Angeles need and use less than half the water needed by the people of New York City. The aqueduct bringing water to Los Angeles, however, is over twice as long as the longest New York City aqueduct. The water brought by aqueduct to Los Angeles comes from the Sierra Nevada Mountains, more than 230 miles away.

Modern aqueducts are not built above

Ruins of an ancient Roman aqueduct beside a country road in Italy.

ground as were the Roman bridge aqueducts. Most modern aqueducts are either tunnels drilled through rock or large pipes laid underground.

Aquinas, see THOMAS AQUINAS, SAINT.

Aquitaine

Aquitaine or Aquitania is the old name for a region in southwest France. The Aquitanians were a tribe of Gauls who lived there before the time of Christ; when Julius Caesar wrote that "all Gaul (France) is divided in three parts," one of these three parts was Aquitania. The region became part of France in 1137 when Eleanor of Aquitaine, the ruling duchess, married King Louis VII of France. She divorced Louis and in 1152 she married Henry II of England, so for many years the English kings claimed Aquitaine but never actually ruled it.

Arabia

Arabia is the largest peninsula in the world, a big body of land (a million square miles, more than a third as big as the United States) with water almost all around it. Arabia lies between the continents of Asia and Africa, but is considered part of Asia. Most of Arabia is a sandy desert, so not many people live there, considering how big it is. The population is about thirteen million, about that of Pennsylvania.

Nine different countries make up Arabia. The biggest, Saudi Arabia, occupies almost all the territory but also has most of the desert land. The other eight are Aden (Protectorate and Colony), Bahrein Islands, Kuwait, Oman and Masqat, Qatar, Trucial Coast, and Yemen. Iraq, Jordan, Israel, Lebanon, and Syria are sometimes considered part of the Arabian peninsula.

The importance of Arabia to the Western World is chiefly in its rich supplies of oil, which are drilled, refined and sold by American and British companies. To the hundreds of millions of Mohammedans in the world, Arabia is sacred because the Prophet Mohammed was born there, in the city of Mecca, to which every Mohammedan tries to make a pilgrimage at least once in his life.

THE PEOPLE OF ARABIA

The people of Arabia are almost all Arabs, the most ancient of the Semitic races, and one of the earliest civilized people. Their beginnings go far, far back in time. They belong to several different tribes, the most important being the Bedouins, who claim to be pure Arabian. The tribes speak various forms of the Arabic languages, some of which have mingled with the African language. Nearly all of them follow the Mohammedan religion. There are separate articles on the ARABS and ARABIC LANGUAGE.

In Arabia people live either in towns or villages or they are *nomads*—people who have no fixed homes, and travel around as shepherds and herdsmen. These nomads make up a large part of the population of Arabia, and are members of the Bedouin tribe. They live out-of-doors in tents, roving from one place to another. One reason they wander so much is because the terrible heat in sum-

mer forces them to search continually for water and grass for their animals. The raising of horses, camels, sheep and goats is their chief work. The Arabian horses they raise are famous for speed and beauty all over the world. The sheep and goats are milked by the women, while the men milk the camels. A large part of the milk is made into butter and cheese. The wool is spun by the women and woven into rugs or into the black tents used by the Bedouins. (See BEDOUIN.)

The Arabs who are not nomads live in the towns or villages, which always have walls of dried mud built around them. The houses are usually two stories high, with flat mud roofs and little windows. The largest and most important room in an Arabian house is called the "kahwah" or coffee room. Here the men congregate and the women rarely enter.

The clothes of an Arab are loose and of a light material suitable to the very hot climate. An Arab man wears a long cotton shirt, often with a leather belt around his waist, and sometimes a cloak over his shoulders. A handkerchief often covers his head, held in place by a band. In some parts of Arabia the men wear loose pantaloons, and turbans. The poor people, however, simply wear wide pieces of cloth around their hips and around their shoulders. Open sandals are worn by nearly everybody.

An Arabian woman wraps her whole figure, including her head, in a wide piece of cloth that trails behind. Underneath she wears pantaloons and a long shirt. The women rarely cover their faces with veils as women in other Eastern countries do. They are fond of jewelry and often wear bracelets and rings. An Arabian woman usually combs her hair in a long braid, which hangs down her back.

The food the Arabians eat is very simple: bread made into thin cakes, a few vegetables, boiled mutton or camel's flesh, dates, and fruit. Rice is considered a delicacy and is eaten only by the rich. Though tea is popular, coffee is the chief drink of the Arabs, who drink it without sugar or milk at all times of the day. It is always served to welcome a new guest. Unlike people in the United States, the Arabians eat only one meal a day, soon after sunset. They disapprove of overeating and they seldom drink wine.

The chief occupation of the people in the towns and villages is farming. They use very primitive methods, but they have learned how to irrigate the crops, which would otherwise die because of the very small amount of rain that falls. So much of the country is desert that the crops are only enough to feed the people. The large exceptions are dates and coffee, which grow in the southwestern part of Arabia. Around the city of Medina, the farmers grow more than a hundred varieties of dates. The waters along the coast swarm with many kinds of fish, including the shark, which the people eat, so that fishing is an important occupation.

The Arabs of Arabia are very backward in manufacturing, but they like commerce and trade. An Arab usually likes to carry some object with him that he can exchange or sell.

Some of the children learn reading and writing from their mothers at home, as well as history and poetry. They are also

taught politeness and self-control, for which Arab children are noted. The Arabians have few schools, and there is little education as it is known in the United States.

WHAT KIND OF PLACE IT IS

One-third of Arabia is covered by great deserts with high ridges of sand called dunes. These dunes are sometimes more than a day's journey in length, and the valleys of sand between the dunes take three or four hours to cross. However, there are some large, fertile valleys in Arabia, and here a large part of the population lives.

The climate of Arabia is one of the hottest and driest in the world. The temperature is often 110 to 120 degrees, hotter than it ever is in the United States. In some parts of the country hardly a shower falls during the year, but there are many oases in the deserts. An oasis is a watering spot, with a spring and usually with shade trees, where caravans of merchants or pilgrims can rest.

There are no forests in Arabia, but there are vast stretches of desert grass, which make admirable pasture land for the horses. The most familiar animal in Arabia is the camel, which can travel 20 to 25 miles a day and needs water only every third or fourth day.

Arabian Nights Entertainments

The *Arabian Nights Entertainments* is a famous collection of stories that were originally written in the Arabic language. The stories are all several hundred years old. Some were written in Persia, some in Egypt, some in Turkey, and some in India. The stories are sometimes called the *Thousand and One Nights,* or *The Thousand Nights and a Night.* The story is:

There was a great king who hated women, so he would marry a different woman each day and have her killed the next morning. His last queen was named Scheherazade. She avoided being killed by telling the king stories each night. She did not finish a story on the night she started it. The king would be so interested he would allow her to live until the next night so he could hear the end of the story.

In the *Arabian Nights* are stories about kings and beggars and thieves and magicians. All sort of wonderful adventures are described in these stories. People turn into animals, and animals into people. There are flying carpets and flying horses and castles in the sea. Some of the famous *Arabian Nights* stories are "Ali Baba and the Forty Thieves," "Sinbad the Sailor," and "Aladdin and His Wonderful Lamp."

Arabian Sea

The Arabian Sea is an arm of the Indian Ocean on the south coast of Asia, between India and Arabia. It is about 1,800 miles wide and covers about 900,000 square miles. In places it is 13,000 to 16,500 feet deep. The chief ports are Bombay and Cochin in India, Karachi in Pakistan, and Aden in Arabia.

Arab Federation

The Arab Federation was a union of the kingdoms of Iraq and Jordan. It was formed February 14, 1958, and lasted less than a year. King Feisal II of Iraq

and King Hussein of Jordan were cousins, members of the Hashemite family, and they joined their countries together with Feisal the head of the new Federation. But in August, there was a revolution in Iraq led by the Iraqi Army; Feisal was killed and Iraq declared itself a republic and withdrew from the Federation. Hussein proclaimed himself the head of the Federation but was not able to win the support of the Iraqi. British airborne troops were flown into Jordan to help Hussein prevent a revolution in his own country. See the articles on JORDAN and IRAQ.

Arabic language

Arabic is the spoken and written language of the Arabs. It is similar in sound to the Hebrew language, in which many books of the Bible were first written. Both these languages are called Semitic languages, because they came from the Semitic peoples who lived around the Mediterranean Sea several thousand years ago. There are twenty-eight letters in the Arabic alphabet. The language, like Hebrew, is written from right to left, instead of from left to right. The Arabic language is spoken and written by people in North Africa, including Egypt. It is also known to Mohammedans everywhere, because it is the language of the Koran, the Mohammedan Holy Book, which is written in classical Arabic. The spoken language of today is somewhat different. Many of the words in the English language were originally Arabic words. Among them are *algebra, alcohol,* and *magazine.*

Arab League

The Arab League was formed by the countries of Egypt, Iraq, Jordan, Lebanon, Saudi Arabia, Syria and Yemen. In March, 1945, these countries agreed to work together in business, education, and most particularly in their policies toward other countries. When the new state of Israel was formed in 1948, the Arab League members were not friendly and made war on it. The Israeli defeated the Arab League armies in a war that lasted nine months. The Arab League members made a treaty, or agreement, in April, 1950 (which went into effect in August, 1952) that if any member of the Arab League was attacked, all the other member nations would go to war with it; but when Israel invaded Egypt in 1957 no other country went to Egypt's aid. Libya, on the Mediterranean coast of North Africa, joined the Arab League soon after it became an independent nation in December, 1951. The Sudan, Morocco and Tunisia also joined the league in the 1950s. Kuwait became a member in 1961 and Algeria joined officially in 1962. See EGYPT.

Arabs

The Arabs are people who live in North Africa and in that part of southwest Asia near the Mediterranean Sea. The Arabs, like the Jews, are a Semitic people. This means they are descended from the Semitic tribes that inhabited the lands of the Old Testament. The Arabs form almost the entire population of Egypt, Arabia, Iraq, Syria, Lebanon, and Jordan, and a large part of the population of Libya, Tunis, Algeria, and Morocco. There are also many Arabs in what was

once Palestine and is now Israel. Altogether there are more than 50 million Arabs. Almost all Arabs are Moslems—followers of the Mohammedan religion. The Arabs belong to the Caucasian or white race, but most of them are a mixture of white, brown and black peoples.

In Biblical times the Arabs were nomads—they wandered over the desert. Most of the modern Arab people have settled down on farms and in cities, but there are still some wanderers. The wandering Arabs are called Bedouins. The Arab farmers and workers are called fellahs. The Arabs who are better off live in well-built homes and wear beautiful robes. All Arabs speak the Arabic language.

The camel is the Arab's favorite beast of burden. Jackasses are also used to carry things. The warriors of the desert tribes have always ridden spirited horses. The white Arabian horse is one of the swiftest and most beautiful in the world.

The desert tribes are composed of many related families. The head of each tribe is called the sheik. The desert Arabs live in tents that can easily be taken down and folded and carried to their next camp.

The Arabs once had a great empire. During the Middle Ages, this empire included all the places the Arabs live in today, and also parts of southern Europe. During the Middle Ages, the Arab empire and civilization were greater than those of western Europe. The Arabs introduced many important things to Europe. They brought gunpowder, the finest steel sword blades, the mariner's compass, and the manufacture of silk and cotton goods. They were the first to use writing paper. Arab writers and doctors and scientists were the most learned in the world. The Arab emperor was called the caliph. The Arab empire broke up over 500 years ago, and today little is left of its glory.

See also the section on "the people of Arabia" in the article ARABIA, and see BEDOUIN.

arachnid

The arachnids are a class of animals including the spiders, ticks and mites, scorpions, harvestmen (the "daddy-long-legs"), and some others. They are not insects. An arachnid has a two-part body, head and abdomen; four pairs of walking legs; and two pairs of appendages or "arms," front and rear, the front ones often being pincers. Though all existing arachnids are small, some extinct ones were nearly 10 feet long. Arachnids belong to a larger group, the *arthropods,* which include the crabs. See ANIMAL LIFE.

Aragon

Aragon is the name of a section in Spain. It is just across the Pyrenees Mountains from southern France. In former times Aragon was an independent kingdom.

More than a million people live in Aragon. Most of them live on farms in the country or in small towns. The farmers grow crops of wheat, rye, corn, and barley. They also keep large flocks of sheep and many pigs. The sheep are mostly a breed called merino. They give the finest wool in the world.

Aragon was part of the early Roman empire. Later it was ruled by Gothic tribes from Germany. They were conquered more than a thousand years ago by the Arabs. After a few hundred years of Arab rule, the people of Aragon formed their own kingdom. The kingdom of Aragon was joined with the kingdom of Castile, a neighboring part of Spain. Ferdinand and Isabella, who in 1492 gave Columbus the ships and money to reach the New World, were king and queen of Aragon and Castile. Soon after, Aragon became part of the kingdom of Spain. In the Spanish Civil War, fought in 1936 to 1939, the river Ebro, which flows through Aragon, was the scene of some of the heaviest fighting.

ARAGON. Area, 18,382 square miles. Population (1970) about 2,000,000. Location, northeast Spain. Chief city, Saragossa (population 479,845).

Aral Sea

The Aral Sea is a large body of water in Asia, in the territory of the Soviet Union about 175 miles east of the Caspian Sea. Its area of 24,635 square miles makes it the fourth largest inland sea in the world (after the Caspian Sea and Lakes Victoria and Superior). It is very shallow, 55 feet average depth. It has no outlet. Two large rivers, the Amu Darya and the Syr Darya, flow into it. The water is salty, but less so than ocean water.

Aramaic

Aramaic is a language that was spoken in Palestine and nearby countries for about 1,400 years, from about 700 B.C. to about 700 A.D. It is the language Jesus spoke. Originally it was the language of the Aramaeans, a Semitic people of North Arabia. When the Mohammedan religion spread it was replaced by Arabic.

Ararat

Ararat is the name of a mountain in eastern Turkey, near the borders between Turkey, Iran, and Armenia. The mountain has two peaks; one, 16,495 feet high, is the highest peak in Turkey, the other is 12,877 feet high. They are extinct volcanoes.

The Bible tells us that after the Flood, Noah landed his Ark on top of Mt. Ararat. The Armenians call Ararat *Masis Leusar,* which means "Mountain of the Ark." The Persians call the mountain *Koh-i-Nuh,* which means "Noah's Mountain." Long ago, people believed that no one was permitted to reach the top of Ararat. Since 1700, however, many mountain climbers have reached the top of Ararat.

Mt. Ararat is a beautiful sight with its snow-covered top. Most high mountains are parts of mountain ranges, but Ararat stands alone. This makes it look even higher than it really is. About a hundred years ago, Ararat erupted and caused a great earthquake. The eruption and earthquake destroyed many villages, and many people were killed.

arbitration

Arbitration is a way of settling arguments and disagreements between people. It is what happens when people agree to let somebody else settle an argument for them. The person who settles the argument is called an *arbitrator.* An arbitrator listens to both sides of an ar-

gument and then decides who is right and who is wrong. The arbitrator's decision is called an *award*.

Arbitration is often used to settle arguments and disputes between labor and management. "Labor" means the workers for a company, and "management" means the owners of the company, or the officers who run the company for the owners. Arguments between labor and management are usually over how much the workers shall be paid, how many hours a week they should work, and what holidays and vacations they will get. Some labor disputes are easily settled by arbitration. More often there is *mediation*, which is different because a mediator cannot make an award. He can only help the two sides to agree.

Lawsuits are often settled by arbitration. An organization called the American Arbitration Association will appoint arbitrators to settle arguments that would otherwise become lawsuits. The American Arbitration Association charges very little for this, sometimes only $25 or $50 when a lawsuit would cost hundreds of dollars or even more. Many states have laws to govern arbitration, making it easy for people to stay out of court. Many contracts nowadays say that any dispute will be settled by arbitration and not by a lawsuit.

International arbitration is the settling of disputes between countries. Two countries that cannot agree on something decide to let a third country act as the arbitrator. Since 1899 there has been an international court of arbitration. It is composed of a group of arbitrators from several different countries. Its permanent seat is at The Hague, the capital of the Netherlands. At present it is called the International Court of Justice and was set up under the Charter of the United Nations.

Arbor Day

Arbor Day is the name given to a day in spring when trees are planted. It is not a national holiday, but it is celebrated in most of the United States. In some states Arbor Day is in April, and in other states it is in May. On this day schoolchildren are taught about the beauty and usefulness of trees. The children join other groups and plant trees in places where there are few or none at all. The first Arbor Day was celebrated in the state of Nebraska, in 1872.

arbutus

There are several plants called arbutus. Some of them are trees and shrubs. They are grown in gardens because they are evergreens and because they have pretty pink or white flowers in the spring. Some arbutus plants grow 20 feet high or even higher, but most of them are small. One kind, called the *strawberry tree*, has a sweet fruit that is somewhat like the strawberry.

Trailing arbutus is a very low shrub that creeps along the ground. It is also called the *mayflower*. Its pink or white flowers are very beautiful.

Arcadia

Arcadia was the name of a state in ancient Greece, thousands of years ago. It was surrounded on all sides by mountains. This is one of the most beautiful parts in all of Greece. The people who lived in ancient Arcadia were mostly shepherds and hunters. They were a simple and happy people. They loved music and dancing and the beauties of nature. The Arcadians were hospitable to strangers and loved to entertain them. Many other ancient Greeks envied the simple life of the Arcadians. To live in Arcadia has always meant to live happily in a peaceful, beautiful land.

arch

When men first began to build big buildings, thousands of years ago, they discovered the arch. An arch is usually built of pieces of stone. It forms an opening or doorway, and at the same time is so strong that it will hold up a very heavy weight on top of it. Men in those days did not have giant steel girders to hold up their buildings, but they were still able to make high, strong buildings and long bridges by using arches.

If you take two pieces of cardboard and lean them against each other, they will both stand up, though either by itself would fall. Each presses against the other with a force that keeps the other from falling. At the same time, they form a covered opening.

The arch, too, uses the forces of different pieces of building material pressing against one another. Usually these pieces are cut to fit together in a curved shape. At the top is a piece called the *keystone*. When the weight of the building above presses down on the keystone, it makes every piece of stone in the arch press against the piece below it. The heavier the weight, the tighter the stones will fit together and the stronger the arch will be.

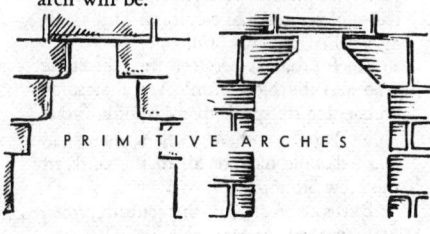

PRIMITIVE ARCHES

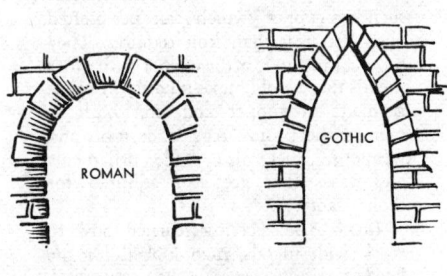

ROMAN

GOTHIC

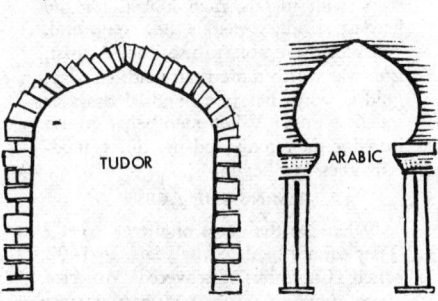

TUDOR

ARABIC

Take those two pieces of cardboard again, leaning against each other. If you were to put something on top of them, the bottom of each piece of cardboard would try to slide outward and the whole thing would fall down. The same is true of an arch. The pieces of stone at the bottom try to slide outward. The force with which they try to slide is called *thrust*. To stop them from sliding, a heavy pile of stone or other material is built beside the bottom of each side of the arch. This is called a *buttress*, or an *abutment*. Sometimes two arches are built beside each other. The bottom of one arch touches the bottom of the other. Each presses against the other with a force called *counterthrust* and keeps the other from sliding.

Arches have been built in many different shapes. The arch is still used in many buildings.

TRIUMPHAL ARCHES

Because arches are beautiful as well as strong, they have often been built as memorials, just as statues are. In ancient Rome, conquering generals who returned from the wars would parade with their armies and prisoners down avenues on which there would be a line of arches. The parade would march through these arches. An "arch of triumph" (that is, an arch to celebrate a victory) did not hold up any building. It was built all by itself, as a monument.

Nearly every triumphal arch is actually three arches. There is one large arch in the center, which must be large enough for the procession to pass through. (Two lanes of automobile traffic pass through the triumphal arch at Washington Square in New York City.) Then there are two smaller arches at the sides. Sometimes these are set sideways to the main arch, as in the picture on the facing page; sometimes they face in the same direction as the main arch, as though for "sidewalks" on each side of the "street" in the center.

The most famous of all ancient arches is the Arch of Constantine, built by Constantine, the first Christian emperor of Rome, who reigned from 306 to 337 A.D. This arch is still standing in Rome and is much better preserved than most of the ancient Roman structures there. See the article ROME for a picture of it.

Probably the most famous arch today is the *Arc de Triomphe de l'Etoile* (French, meaning "arch of triumph of the star") in Paris, France. It celebrates the great victories of Napoleon, the French general and emperor, and building of it began in 1806.

In New York City there is a triumphal arch in honor of George Washington (mentioned above). It forms the entrance to Washington Square at the foot of Fifth Avenue.

archaeology

Archaeology means "the knowledge, or study, of what is ancient." It is one of the sciences in which mankind is studied. An archaeologist studies men who lived many thousands of years ago. The earliest writings are less than ten thousand years old, but archaeologists can go back more than fifty times that far and tell something about the men who lived then.

This is done by digging up and studying the things made by these earliest men. Things made by men are called *artifacts.* An artifact is anything that was made by man and not by nature. The earliest artifacts were simply pieces of hard rock that men had chipped into the form of tools for cutting or digging, or to use as weapons to protect themselves against wild beasts. The arrowheads of the American Indians are examples of these. But artifacts from later ages might be very skillfully made tools, or magnificent works of art. Some artifacts that have been found by archaeologists are as much as 500,000 years old. In parts of the United States, they have found things made by men who lived 12,000 years ago or more.

The way any group of men lives, including all the things they make, and the way they get their food, and what they know, and how they worship, and their customs in marriage and government—in short, the way they behave—is called a *culture.* Archaeologists try to tell, from the relics they find, exactly what kind of culture they have discovered, and how long ago it was. The skill with which they can do this seems almost magical.

The things any group of men makes, and the way they make them, archaeologists call an *industry.* For example, some settlements of very ancient men are found to have made their tools by taking pieces of flint and chipping off flakes of the stone until they made a sharp edge that could be used as a knife. This was the only way they knew how to make cutting tools. Archaeologists would call this a "flake industry." Today, an industry is composed of many companies with big factories and the most scientific kind of machinery, manufacturing automobiles, or refining oil, printing books, or making any of the thousands of other products that seem necessary to our lives.

HOW HUMAN CULTURE HAS DEVELOPED

Archaeologists class the various cultures of mankind into certain periods or "ages," based on how far advanced or civilized the ancient men were. There are various ways of naming these ages, and different archaeologists prefer different ways, but the ones best known are these:

OLD STONE AGE. This is the earliest of the ages. Man had learned very little. He was a "food-gatherer"—he had not learned to cultivate the soil or to keep and train domestic animals such as cows and chickens. He moved from one place to another in search of food that grew wild, and he killed and ate animals. His tools were chipped from stone, or made from sticks and bones. He lived in the open, or in shelters made from boughs, or in caves. This age is also called the *Paleolithic* age.

NEW STONE AGE. Man next advanced to a stage in which he could stay in one place and grow plants he could eat for food. He learned to keep animals for milk and meat and leather and wool. He still made his tools by chipping them from stones, but he could do this much better than man could in the Old Stone Age, and some of the

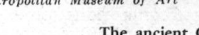
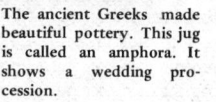

The ancient Greeks made beautiful pottery. This jug is called an amphora. It shows a wedding procession.

The oldest iron weapon ever discovered. It is about 3,500 years old.

axes and digging tools of the New Stone Age, with strong wooden handles and sharp flint heads, are beautifully made. Man also learned to form clay into the proper shape for jars and bowls, and to bake it into pottery. At the time that Christopher Columbus discovered America, most of the American Indians had a New Stone Age culture. This age is also called the *Neolithic* age. There was so much progress between the Old Stone Age and the New Stone Age that some archaeologists speak of a "Middle Stone Age" between them, when men had learned some but not all of the skills of the New Stone Age.

BRONZE AGE. In this culture, men first learned to use metals. The first metals they used were the softer metals, such as copper, which can be melted with less heat than iron requires. They soon learned to mix the copper with other metals that would make it harder. Bronze is made of copper and tin. With it, men of the Bronze Age made tools and weapons. They also made ornaments and vases that are still admired for their beauty.

IRON AGE. Having learned how to work with metals, men looked for the hardest, strongest metals they could find, and soon were able to use iron. At first, iron was worth more than gold. (Today, gold is worth nearly a hundred times as much as iron.) When men began to use iron for their tools and machines, modern times had begun.

TIMING THE AGES

What are the dates of these "Ages"? They cannot be dated by years. In 1492, when Columbus discovered America, three thousand years had passed since European civilization reached the Iron Age, yet the American Indians were still in the New Stone Age and halfway

around the world, in Australia, there were people who were still in the Old Stone Age.

We know when our own civilization developed. We call this the "Western" civilization, and it came to us from Europe. The "Eastern" or "Oriental" civilization of China and other countries in Asia developed separately. However, our own advanced culture actually began in parts of Asia and Africa. In the land that is now Iraq, in the Holy Land of Palestine (now Israel) and other countries on the eastern end of the Mediterranean Sea, and in Egypt in North Africa, men first began to use the language and the sciences from which our modern ones grew. This area is called "the cradle of civilization." Men lived in this area and their culture was in the Old Stone Age for 500,000 years or more. They entered the New Stone Age at least 10,000 years ago, which was about 8000 B.C. They were in the Bronze Age by 2500 B.C., and in the Iron Age by 1500 B.C.—that is, about four thousand years ago.

Men learn from one another. When one group of men meets another group that is more advanced, the backward group can advance much more rapidly. The American Indians did not have to go from the New Stone Age to the Bronze Age and then to the Iron Age by learning things gradually for thousands of years. By meeting the Europeans who were already far more advanced, the Indians went from the New Stone Age to the Iron Age and even to modern civilization in a matter of a few years.

Because different "Ages" have appeared at different times in different parts of the world, an archaeologist cannot simply look at an ancient tool or pottery bowl and say, "This was made

in the year 20,000 B.C." But there are ways in which archaeologists can tell how old an artifact is. Sometimes they can tell almost exactly how old it is. The latest way they have found to do this is by measuring the radioactivity of ancient remains of plant and animal life. A radioactive substance gives off rays of energy at a regular rate. By knowing how much radioactivity the substance had to begin with, and by measuring how much radioactivity it has left, scientists can tell exactly how old it is.

DIGGING INTO THE PAST

An archaeologist digs deep into the earth to find the record of men who lived in other ages. In hundreds or thousands of years, whole cities become covered with mud and dust and rubbish. This becomes packed down into hard soil or clay, and can even harden into stone. Often one house is built on another, or even a whole city on top of another that has been buried.

In the valley of the Tigris and Euphrates Rivers, in Iraq, many great mounds rise from the level ground. Archaeologists call these *tells* (meaning "hills"). Each was formed when some ancient mud house collapsed, another was built on it and collapsed, and so on, over a period of thousands of years. Some of the tells are more than 60 feet high and have twenty or more levels, on each of which old tools, pottery, and other household things may be dug out. Each level represents at least a hundred years, sometimes several hundred, and of course the lower the level, the older the relics—but the newest of them is 5,000 or more years old.

Archaeologists learn most from the remains of an ancient household. They call it a *kitchen midden*. The utensils tell how advanced the people were, and often there are bones to tell what fish or meat they ate.

It is hard work to be an archaeologist. Sometimes, when he thinks he is on the trail of something very breakable, he even digs with his fingers, for fear a shovel might break the precious object. An archaeologist goes to faraway places where it is bitter cold or where it is too hot for comfort, camps out, eats little except canned food, and works from early morning to late night. When he is at home, usually at a college or a museum, he studies hard to keep up with the latest discoveries. But the work is so fascinating that hundreds of men choose it as a career.

FAMOUS FINDS IN ARCHAEOLOGY

The science of archaeology began about five hundred years ago when many people found it profitable to dig up old marble statues and ornaments that had been made by the ancient Greeks and Romans, and sell them to rich noblemen. Most of these were found in Greece, Italy, and islands in the Mediterranean Sea, which had been the centers of civilization for more than two thousand years.

Men began to study these artistic relics, and found that they could learn from them about the ways of life of other men who had lived long ago. Because this is such an interesting study, scientists became interested in man-made things from prehistoric times, even if they were not beautiful pieces of art.

Egyptian State Tourist Administration
The final coffin covering the mummified remains of the ancient Egyptian King Tutankhamen. The King was locked away inside a series of cases, each portraying the King's likeness and composed of either wood or, in the case of the final coffin, gold.

Then, by accident, some farmers in Italy discovered that they were living on top of an ancient Roman city that had been buried for more than sixteen hundred years. The name of this city was Herculaneum. It and another city of ancient Rome, named Pompeii, were built beside a great volcano named Vesuvius. In the year 79, an eruption of Vesuvius poured out so much lava and dust that both Herculaneum and Pompeii were buried. In the year 1719, archaeologists began to dig to uncover them. After more than fifty years, they had uncovered two complete cities with fine houses, theaters, streets, temples, and everything else that showed exactly how people had lived in ancient Rome. (See the article POMPEII.)

At the end of that century, one of the greatest of all archaeological discoveries was made in Egypt. This was the finding of the ROSETTA STONE, about which there is a separate article. The Rosetta Stone was a sort of "billboard," used in the years before paper was made and when men had to carve their writings on stones or on tablets of clay. The Rosetta Stone had the same words in two different languages. One language was Greek, which the scientists already knew well. The other was ancient Egyptian, which they did not know. From the Rosetta Stone they learned to read ancient Egyptian. Ever since, archaeologists have been able to read whatever ancient Egyptian writing they have dug up, and this has helped them to learn much about the history of Egypt and the people who lived there thousands of years ago.

The Rosetta Stone was discovered in 1799. Many other discoveries were made during the next hundred years, but perhaps the most interesting was the Altamira caves, in the mountains of northern Spain. On the walls of these caves are paintings of bulls and other animals that were hunted by prehistoric men. These paintings were made by men

who lived as much as twenty thousand years ago, maybe even more, but they are so well done that many modern artists can admire them as much for their beauty as for their age. From paintings like these, archaeologists find out about the culture of that age.

Archaeology goes on constantly. Finds have been made on every continent and on many islands.

AMERICAN ARCHAEOLOGY

In many parts of the United States, archaeologists have found relics of people who lived thousands of years before Columbus discovered America. In fact, these relics have helped other scholars to decide when the people we call "American Indians" first came to the continent of North America from Asia, where their original home was, perhaps as many as 35,000 years ago, or more.

In Illinois, Ohio, Wisconsin, and other parts of the Midwest, and as far south as Alabama, there are relics of the MOUND BUILDERS, about whom there is a separate article. The Mound Builders built great mounds of earth and stone and used them for houses, and for churches, and for burial places for their dead. The "cliff dwellers" of the American Southwest left their "apartment houses" on the sides of cliffs in such good condition that you can walk into them and see how people lived three thousand years ago. The MAYANS and AZTECS in Central America, and the INCAS and other prehistoric men who came long before them in Peru and other parts of South America, are other ancient men of the Western Hemisphere about whom there are separate articles.

Read also the article on GEOLOGY.

Archangel

Archangel is the name of a large oblast, or province, in the northern part of Russia, and also the name of a large city, capital of the oblast. Archangel is so far north that it is very cold, and from late September until spring it is frozen and icebound. The province of Archangel includes Russian islands in the Arctic Sea. More than a million people live in the province. Those who live in the most northern part are the peoples called Lapps and Samoyeds. These people keep herds of reindeer, from which they get their food and clothing.

The city of Archangel is one of the great seaports of Russia. During World War II, most of the war materials sent by the United States to Russia were landed at Archangel.

ARCHANGEL. Population (1973 estimate) 1,100,000. Oblast (regional political division) of the U.S.S.R. Includes mainland section and Russian islands in the Arctic sea. Capital city, Archangel, population (1973 estimate) 300,000; major port on Dvina Gulf.

archery

Shooting a bow and arrow is called archery. Thousands of years before history was first written, men used the bow and arrow. (See BOW AND ARROW.) Today archery is mainly a sport, but it was important in hunting and in warfare until firearms were developed.

The American Indian was an expert archer before the coming of the Euro-

peans. Before the invention of gunpowder the fate of a nation could depend on how good its archers were. For two hundred years after the introduction of firearms, archery continued in warfare; for an archer could shoot several arrows in the time required to reload and fire a musket, while the range was almost the same, about 400 yards. The legend of William Tell's shooting an apple off his son's head, in Switzerland, and of Robin Hood's adventures in Sherwood Forest, show how good the archers were then. A mere handful of English "longbowmen" under King Richard the Lion-Hearted withstood the charge of an entire Saracen army, during the Crusades.

Today archery is one of the most popular sports, both in competition and in hunting, and is governed by rules and standards.

RULES FOR CONTESTS

In most camps, and in many schools, there is an archery contest, or tournament, at the end of the season. The rounds are like those in official competition. (A "round" is the word used to mean shooting a certain number of arrows at a certain distance.)

FIELD. The field for men is usually 100 yards long, with the targets at one end, and a fixed shooting line at the other, with other shooting lines marked 40, 50, 60 and 80 yards from the targets. Shooting lanes, one for each target, should be at least 15 to 20 feet wide.

TARGETS. The target used in national tournaments is handmade, of rye-straw, 50 inches in diameter, and about 5 or 6 inches thick. For practice, and general use, a straw butt is usually set up, by piling bales of straw together. The regulation target "face" is of paper or cloth. The center, or bull's-eye, is 9.6 inches in diameter, and the diameter of the entire scoring surface is 48 inches. Between the center and the circumference there are four circles, or bands, each 4.8 inches in width. The colors of the center and bands, and their values in scoring are as follows:

A hit in the GOLD	counts 9
" " " RED	" 7
" " " BLUE	" 5
" " " BLACK	" 3
" " " WHITE	" 1

SCORING. Scoring in archery is on the basis of points, rather than the number of hits. In a tournament, the archer (or team) scoring the highest number of points is the winner. If there is a tie, the archer wins who has the highest score at the longest range. If there is still a tie, the archer wins who has the highest score at the next longest distance, and so on. A record is kept of the score for each arrow, the number of hits, and then the total number of points. For instance, if six arrows were shot, and of the six, two were hits in the GOLD, one in the RED, one in the BLUE, and two in the WHITE, the score would be: 6-32, or 9 plus 9 plus 7 plus 5 plus 1 plus 1. When an arrow is on the dividing line of two colors, it is always given the higher value of the two. An arrow that passes through the target, or bounces off, is scored as 5 points.

JUNIOR EVENTS

Junior American Round for Boys and Girls
  30 arrows at 50 yards
  30 " " 40 "
  30 " " 30 "
Junior Columbia Round for Girls
  24 arrows at 40 yards
  24 " " 30 "
  24 " " 20 "
Junior Metropolitan Round for Boys and Girls
  30 arrows at 40 yards
  30 " " 30 "
  30 " " 20 "

The National Archery Association, with headquarters in Amherst, Massachusetts, makes the rules, keeps records, and publishes reports. There are many magazines and books devoted to archery.

Archimedes

Archimedes was a great mathematician and scientist who lived more than two thousand years ago. He was born in 287 B.C., and died in 212 B.C., in the ancient city-state of Syracuse on the island of Sicily. At that time Sicily was a Greek island, but now it is part of Italy.

Many stories are told about the way Archimedes made his great inventions and scientific discoveries. Perhaps it did not all happen exactly the way the stories say. Probably Archimedes, like every other great scientist, had to work long and hard to make his inventions and discoveries. But that does not matter, because the stories are interesting. Here are some of them:

Once the Romans tried to invade Syracuse from the sea. As their ships neared the coast, they suddenly burst into flame. Archimedes had set up mirrors on the coast of Syracuse to catch the sun's rays and reflect them against the Roman ships. The hot rays set the ships on fire.

Archimedes was a friend of King Hiero of Syracuse, and often solved problems for the king. Once the king suspected that a new crown was not made with pure gold. He asked Archimedes to find out if the crown was pure gold. Archimedes thought and thought about how he could find the answer. One day as he was bathing in one of the public baths in Syracuse, he suddenly thought of the answer. He jumped from the tub shouting, "Eureka, Eureka!" which means "I have found it, I have found it!" He was so excited he ran home without putting his clothes on. He had discovered the principle of *specific gravity,* that an object displaces its own volume in water. By measuring the water displaced by the crown against water displaced by pure gold weighing the same, he found that the crown was not pure gold.

An important invention of Archimedes was the water screw. This was used to pump water, or to raise it from one level to another. The water screw is really nothing but a large, long screw encased in a wooden pipe. When the handle on top of the screw is turned, the water is forced up into the pipe and finally flows from the top of it.

Archimedes was one of the first great mathematicians. Much of the work he did is important to us today. He learned how to measure circles, spheres, cylin-

ders and other figures. When he was an old man, Archimedes asked that a cylinder and a sphere be carved on his tombstone after he died.

The Romans conquered Syracuse in 212 B.C. During the battle Archimedes was sitting in the public square drawing mathematical figures in the dirt. The Roman general, Claudius Marcellus, had given orders that the soldiers were not to harm Archimedes. But a soldier seeing Archimedes did not know him, and killed him with his sword. The Roman general buried Archimedes with great honor and the sphere and the cylinder were carved on his tombstone.

architecture

An architect is a man who is in charge of everything connected with putting up a new building. He decides what the new building should look like when it is finished. He decides what materials should be used in making the new building—whether it should be made of wood, or brick, or stone, or anything else. He makes the plans that must be followed by the men who do the actual work of putting the building together. The architect's profession is called *architecture*.

The architect must be both an artist and a scientist. Planning the appearance of a building is called *design*. To make the building beautiful, the architect must be an artist, because beautiful buildings are works of art in the same way that beautiful pieces of sculpture are. The actual job of putting up the building is called *construction*. To plan the building so that it will be strong and long-lasting, the architect must know many scientific facts that it has taken men thousands of years to learn. Design and construction are two branches of architecture.

STYLES IN ARCHITECTURE

We often speak of a particular *style* of architecture.

For instance, we say a certain house is an example of "colonial architecture." That means it is the kind of house that Americans built during the time, two hundred years or so ago, when the states were British colonies and not yet the independent United States. Or we speak of "Roman architecture." That means the kind of buildings that were built when the Roman Empire was the most powerful nation on earth, about two thousand years ago.

Styles in architecture have changed much in the course of history.

First, men have learned to do things better. There was a time when the best way to make a building strong was to use heavy blocks of hard stone. There were no steel girders in those days. So architects of long ago designed their best buildings in marble or other hard stone, and architects today design their best buildings around steel. The outward appearance of the building changes because different materials are used. Before glass was invented, buildings looked different because they had no windows. Today, because glass is being made better and stronger every year, new buildings are likely to look almost

TWA

The Trans World Airlines terminal at Kennedy Airport in New York City was designed by American architect Eero Saarinen, who lived from 1910 to 1961.

as though they were solid walls of glass.

Another reason that styles change is that men's ideas of beauty change. Houses that were built seventy-five or a hundred years ago are called "Victorian" houses because that was the time when Queen Victoria was reigning in England. Victorian houses were quite fancy. They were considered very beautiful at the time, but people today consider them ugly because today people like their houses to be plain, and not to be decorated with all sorts of fancy curlicues and ornaments.

The cost of building has a lot to do with styles in architecture. Thousands of years ago, no one but kings and powerful noblemen could afford fine houses and buildings. There was little thought of the rights of human beings in those days. A powerful man would make slaves of men who were weaker, and of enemies he had conquered in warfare. The great structures of the past, such as the pyramids in Egypt and the great marble temples of Greece, could be built because thousands of slaves worked for many years, moving great blocks of stone, without being paid. In a modern democracy like the United States, that would be impossible. But science has progressed so much that even stronger buildings are made in a few months, with far fewer men, all of whom are well paid for their work; and poor men as well as rich men can have comfortable houses to live in and office buildings and factories to work in.

HOW ARCHITECTURE HAS CHANGED

Our entire civilization, in America and Europe, is called the *Western,* or *Occidental,* civilization. It grew out of the lands on the Mediterranean Sea, where civilization began thousands of years ago—Egypt, and Greece, and Italy (which was the seat of the Roman Empire). Architecture was a part of this civilization. So we call our styles in architecture *Western,* and they are different from the *Eastern,* or *Oriental,* architecture of China and India and other lands in Asia.

Styles in Western architecture changed as men learned more about engineering and other branches of science.

Here are some of the most important styles of architecture that have been developed in the thousands of years of our Western civilization:

EGYPTIAN ARCHITECTURE. When a building has a heavy roof, or any floor above the ground floor, a strong structure is needed. In the earliest buildings,

this was done by building a heavy wall, or a line of posts, and laying a flat piece across it. This flat piece is called a *beam,* or *lintel.*

The beam or lintel is still used in millions of houses and buildings. As used by the ancient Egyptians, it created buildings of great beauty, but thousands of slaves were needed to put the huge stone lintels weighing many tons on top of the posts. The slaves would build a hill of packed sand to the top of the posts; then they would slide the stone slabs up the sand hills and put them in place on the posts; and then they would clear away the sand, leaving the building.

The Egyptians decorated their buildings with beautiful pictures—scenes from daily life, flowers and animals, and words written in their "picture-writing," or *hieroglyphics.*

GREEK ARCHITECTURE. The buildings of ancient Greece, built nearly 2,500 years ago (about 450 B.C.) have never been surpassed for beauty. Like the Egyptians and other early builders, they used the post or column and the lintel. Their buildings were not as huge as those of the Egyptians, because they were built more by free men than by slaves. The finest examples of ancient Greek architecture are on the Acropolis at Athens. (There is a separate article on the ACROPOLIS.)

There is beauty in pictures; there is also beauty in lines. The Greek buildings were beautiful because the lines and forms of them were so graceful. This was especially true of the great columns that supported the buildings. The finest Greek buildings were made of beautiful white marble and decorated with some of the greatest sculpture of all time. (See the separate articles on COLUMN and the PARTHENON.)

ROMAN ARCHITECTURE. The Egyptians and Greeks had known about the arch, but had not used it in their finest buildings. The Romans used the arch as the basis of their architecture. A series of arches, each touching the next make a curved ceiling called a *vault.* A number of arches that meet at the same point on top, in a sort of upside-down bowl shape, make a *dome.* The vault and the dome, still seen in many great buildings, came to us from Roman architecture. The Romans also borrowed the columns of Greek architecture, and ornamented their buildings with sculpture in the Greek manner. The Pantheon, a great temple that can still be seen in the city of Rome, is an example of how the

Greek and Roman styles of architecture were combined.

BYZANTINE ARCHITECTURE. When Germanic invaders began to overrun Italy, which had been the seat of the Roman Empire, the capital city was changed to Constantinople, the city that is now called Istanbul. Before it was called Constantinople, this city had been named Byzantium. So the Roman Empire that was centered in Constantinople came to be called the Byzantine Empire, and its architecture is called Byzantine.

Because Constantinople was at the point where Europe meets Asia, in Byzantine architecture the Western architecture of Europe and the Eastern architecture of Asia were combined. Byzantine buildings used the vault and the dome even more than the Romans had, but decorated them in Eastern style. Inside and out, the buildings were decorated with fancy carvings that were far different from the plain lines that had made the Greek buildings so beautiful, and colorful mosaics—pictures made of bits of colored glass and tile—made portions of the floors and walls look like Oriental rugs. The Church of St. Sophia, in Istanbul, is the best example of this combining of two styles.

Thomas Jefferson Memorial Foundation
Monticello, the home of Thomas Jefferson in Virginia, is a fine type of American architecture. Jefferson designed it.

GOTHIC ARCHITECTURE. The great cathedrals of Europe, built in the Middle Ages (beginning about a thousand years ago), brought in a new style of architecture called Gothic. In Gothic architecture, many arches are used; but these arches rise to a sharp point, while the Roman arches had been shaped in the more regular curve of a circle. The reason for the pointed arch was that it allowed higher, straighter walls, and in these walls more windows could be placed to let in light. These windows became things of beauty with their pictures and designs in stained glass— the same idea as the mosaics of the Byzantine churches, but done in such a way as to let the light come through. But Gothic buildings were made of quiet gray stone, not the gleaming white marble of Greece and Rome; and the carved decorations were not always beautiful women and handsome men. Often they were hideous monsters called *gargoyles* or meaningless shapes of no real beauty. Still, there was great beauty in Gothic architecture.

RENAISSANCE ARCHITECTURE. The Renaissance was the "new birth of learning" that arrived in Europe about five hundred years ago. The Renaissance did

not bring any new ideas in architecture, but it encouraged study of the classical styles of Greece and Rome, and this made architectural design better.

MODERN ARCHITECTURE. Until fifty or seventy-five years ago, the only developments in architecture for hundreds of years had been in design. About two hundred years ago, Robert Adam designed the simple, plain-fronted city house that he first built in London, England, and that was copied in cities throughout Europe and America. In the same period was developed the American "colonial" house seen not only throughout New England but all over the country, and the "southern mansion" with its high wooden pillars or columns. Nearly all houses were the same in construction, with a strong foundation wall of stone or brick, beams (often the trunks of big trees) laid across these walls, and the house built on them. Space was found by building upward—always two or three stories, and often four or five stories.

Great public buildings were decorated lavishly, in styles called *baroque* and *rococo*. Houses came to have frills and ornaments all over them, and tiny spires and domes wherever the architect could find place for them. We call these decorations "gingerbread" now, and do not think they are very pretty.

A mosque (Mohammedan house of worship). It is in the Byzantine style.

The real modern age in architecture began about seventy-five years ago. Two things made it possible: the strength of concrete reinforced with steel, with which giant skyscrapers could be built; and the elevator, which allowed the skyscraper to be used conveniently.

With these developments, architects began to build the great skyscrapers, the office buildings and apartment houses and hotels, that we know today. They were still influenced by old ideas of design. The Woolworth Building, completed in 1913, is quite fancy. The big buildings of Rockefeller Center, by comparison, are very plain. Even newer buildings—the United Nations and Lever Brothers buildings in New York, for instance—are straight-sided, boxlike forms on which most of the outer surface is glass, not stone or brick as in older buildings.

Churches, too, have changed slowly in design. Nearly all of them have continued to follow the needs of older times, when high steeples were needed so that the townfolk could hear the bells ring. Today, with loudspeakers, the steeples are not needed, and modern architects recognize this. Some of the latest places of worship are low, graceful buildings far different from the severe ones of the past.

The houses in which people live are changing in the same way. Whenever possible, the architect builds the entire house on one floor, so there will be no stairs to climb. The "ranch house," which has only one story and rambles all over the property, has become a rather popular design.

GREAT ARCHITECTS AND BUILDINGS

Here is a list of some of the great architectural works of this century.

Radio City, New York, by a group of architects, including Reinhard and Hofmeister; Corbett, Harrison and MacMurray; and Hood and Fouilhoux.

Buildings at Cranbrook Academy, Birmingham, Michigan, by Eliel Saarinen.

Johnson's Wax Building in Racine, Wisconsin, and Guggenheim Museum, New York, by Frank Lloyd Wright, considered by many the greatest modern architect.

Philadelphia Savings Society Building, by Howe and Lescaze.

United Nations Secretariat Building, by Wallace K. Harrison and Associates, in New York.

Automotive factories in the Detroit area, by Albert Kahn.

Nebraska State Capitol, by Bertram Goodhue.

Buildings and Dams for the Tennessee Valley Authority, by Roland Wank.

New York Daily News Building, by Raymond Hood.

HOW AN ARCHITECT WORKS

Suppose you want to have a new house or a new building for a business. First you must buy or own the land. Then you go to an architect and tell him what kind of building you want, how much you want to spend, and what you are going to use it for. If it is to be a private house, the architect must know how big a family will live there; if it is to be an office building, he must know how many people will work there; and so on. You are now one of the architect's "clients."

First the architect will draw a picture, or sketch, of the way he thinks the building should look from the outside; and a "rough" design of how the rooms will be arranged inside, and how big each room will be. The architect will keep in mind not only the size of the lot but also the kind of land it is. He will plan one kind of construction for a hard or rocky base and another if he must build on soft ground that will settle under the weight of a heavy house. He will plan differently for hilly than for level ground. The materials he selects will depend on how much you want to spend; he cannot build you a marble mansion if you can only afford brick or wood.

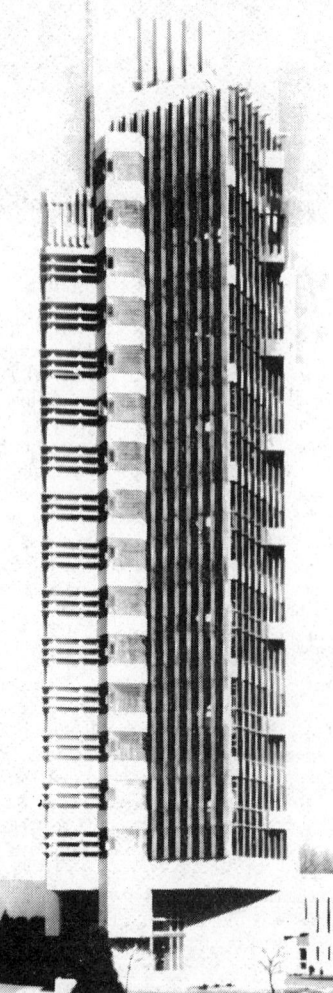

The Price Tower in Bartlesville, Oklahoma, designed by Frank Lloyd Wright and completed in 1958. It combines office and apartment space.

After the architect has carefully gone over his plans with you, and you have approved them, *working drawings* will be made by *draftsmen*, men or women skilled in mechanical drawing. Unless it is to be a very simple house, the architect will hire an engineer to work out the technical aspects. Every inch of the house will be planned exactly.

Now blueprints are made of the finished drawings, and are sent to several *contractors*. Each contractor sends the architect a *bid*, which is to say that he names a price for which he will do the actual work of putting up the building. The architect will remain in charge of the work, but the contractor will actually hire the workmen and buy all the materials. Usually he will have various *subcontractors* to do special jobs, such as plumbing. The *contract* will be given to the contractor that the architect thinks will do the best job, and if possible this will be the one who made the lowest bid.

For doing all this, the architect charges a fee based on the cost of the building. This fee is most often six per cent; that is, six dollars for every hundred dollars the building costs. For a $100,000 building, the fee would be $6,000. But on buildings that cost much

less, or when a great deal of special work is needed, the fee may be ten per cent or more.

An architect must know a great deal about everything connected with building. Like a doctor, lawyer, or other professional man, he must be specially educated for his profession in a college or school of architecture, and he must continue to study throughout his career, to keep up with the latest developments. In most states, he must pass an examination to become a licensed architect.

arclight

An arc is a curved line—a part of the side of a circle, like this: ⌒. An arclight is an electric light that is caused when a current of electricity leaps through the air in such a curved line.

The arclight is made of two pieces of carbon, each attached to an electric wire. With the pieces of carbon touching, electricity is allowed to flow through them. Then the pieces of carbon are pulled slightly apart. Little pieces of electricity, called *ions*, are left in the air between them. The electric current keeps on flowing after the carbon ends are pulled apart, but now it must leap through the air (helped by the ions) to get from one piece of carbon to the other. This creates tremendous heat—almost 3,500 degrees, which is hot enough to melt iron—and a very bright light.

Arclights are used in powerful searchlights, and for lighting motion pictures, and in other cases where very bright light is needed. Arclights are also used in treating people with sore muscles and aching backs. Sometimes other metals are used instead of carbon.

Arctic Ocean

The Arctic Ocean is the large body of water that surrounds the North Pole. It covers about 5,400,000 square miles —nearly twice the area of the United States The northern coasts of Europe, Asia and North America form the boundaries of the Arctic Ocean.

The main body of water lies in a basin and has an average depth of 4,200 feet. It is 14,350 feet deep at the North Pole. The greatest depth recorded is 17,850 feet. Smaller seas that form part of the Arctic Ocean are shallow. The Barents Sea, Kara Sea, Laptev Sea, East Siberian Sea and Chukchi Sea have an average depth of only 600 feet; but Beaufort Sea is part of the deep basin.

The ocean is stormy much of the time. Icepacks 7 to 10 feet thick cover much of its surface all year. However, the Arctic is never completely frozen over. There are small icebergs floating near most of the islands. The large icebergs form in the Greenland glaciers and are carried south by the outflowing currents.

There are many islands in the Arctic Ocean. Among those explored are the Canadian Arctic Archipelago, Wrangel Island, Herald Island, the New Siberian Islands, Severnaya Zemlya, Novaya, Zemlya, Franz Josep Land, and Spitsbergen. Few of them contain much life, but there are many fish, seals and walrus in the open waters. There used to be many whales, but most of these have been killed by whalers. Except for lost polar bears, only plankton (floating or weakly swimming vegetable or animal life) is found in the ice-covered waters.

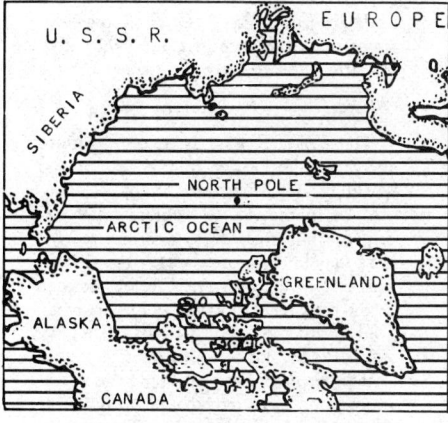

Much water flows from the Arctic into the Atlantic, especially around Greenland. This is because in the extremely low temperature there is slow evaporation and because the Arctic is fed by four major rivers, the Mackenzie, Lena, Yenesei, and Ob. The outflow forms the North Atlantic Drift and the East Greenland Current between Greenland and Norway, and the Labrador Current west of Greenland. The current within the Arctic itself flows in a circle.

Also because of the fresh-water inlets and slow evaporation the waters of the Arctic are less salty than those of any other ocean.

Until recently, most of the Arctic Ocean was never seen by man. Many ships attempted to cross the Arctic Ocean, but few of them got very far.

In 1926 the explorers Roald Amundsen and Lincoln Ellsworth flew over the Arctic and since then much has been learned by observation from the air and by aerial photography. Radar and an instrument called the fathometer, for measuring depths, have brought more information about the ocean floor. In 1954, Russian scientists discovered an Arctic Ocean Divide, an underwater ridge about 1½ miles high, between Greenland and the New Siberian Islands.

See the articles ARCTIC REGION and NORTH POLE.

Arctic Region

The Arctic Region is the most northern part of the world. It is that part of the earth that lies between the North Pole and the Arctic Circle. The Arctic Circle is an imaginary line drawn around the earth about 1,700 miles from the North Pole, or at about 70 degrees north latitude. Parts of Europe, Asia and North America are above the Arctic Circle, and therefore are part of the Arctic Region. Greenland lies almost entirely in the Arctic Region. Only its southern tip is below the Arctic Circle. The Arctic Ocean covers more than half the Arctic Region.

THE PEOPLE OF THE ARCTIC

People live only in the southern part of the Arctic Region, and only a few live there. Some Eskimos live in northern Alaska and Greenland. The Lapps, or Laplanders, live in the most northern parts of Norway, Sweden, Finland, and Russia. The Samoyeds live in the northern part of Russia and Western Siberia. The Chukchis live in the eastern part of Siberia.

Within the Arctic Circle no trees grow, nor wild plants and shrubs. The only plants that grow are mosses and lichens. They grow on what is called the *tundra*. This looks like a moss-covered plain or prairie. Two kinds of animal graze on the tundra. They are the reindeer and the musk ox. The reindeer is found mostly in the Lapp country, and the musk ox in eastern Siberia. The Laplanders keep herds of reindeer. They get their food and clothing from the reindeer, and even make their tents from reindeer hide. The musk ox are not domestic animals, but roam the tundra of eastern Siberia in herds. The Chukchis hunt the musk ox, and use the meat for food and the hide for clothing and shelter.

The Eskimos in Alaska and Greenland live near the seacoast. They hunt the seal, and catch fish in the Arctic Ocean. The Alaskan Eskimos also grow vegetables during the short Arctic summer.

In the Arctic there are two seasons— winter and summer. During the long winter months the sun never shines and it is dark all the time. In the winter the temperature stays far below zero and everything is completely frozen over. During the short summer the sun shines all day long. It even shines at midnight, so it is called the "midnight sun."

During the summer the southern lands in the Arctic Region are sometimes as warm as the United States is. Plants grow very fast and very large during the Arctic summer, because they have sunshine all the time. The Arctic people are active only during the summer. That is the time when they do their hunting and fishing, or move about with their herds. During the winter they do nothing but stay in their igloos and tents, and try to keep warm. They spend the winter days making clothing, eating and sleeping, and telling stories.

HOW THE ARCTIC WAS EXPLORED

Until a thousand years ago nothing was known of the Arctic Region. Then the Norsemen began exploring the region. Little by little, their boats went further and further into the Arctic Region. The first known voyage of exploration was led by the famous Norseman named Eric the Red. He and his men reached the coast of Greenland. Since then, many explorers have journeyed across the Arctic Circle. As the years went by, they drew closer and closer to the North Pole. (There is a separate article about the NORTH POLE.)

One of the best-known Arctic explorers was Henry Hudson, who first sailed into the waters of northern Canada in 1607. The great body of water called Hudson Bay is named after him.

During the 16th and 17th centuries, many explorers entered the region in search of a Northwest Passage to the Orient. Expeditions were led by Martin Frobisher (1576–78), John Davis (1585–87), William Barents (1594–96), Henry Hudson (1607–11), and William Baffin (1615–16). Later exploration was accomplished by Alexander Mackenzie and other fur traders in the

18th century. Many geographical features in the Arctic are named after these explorers. Exploration was stimulated by efforts to reach the NORTH POLE, first accomplished by Robert E. Peary in 1909. In 1937–38, six nations—Great Britain, Canada, Denmark, Norway, the Soviet Union, and the United States—sent scientists to investigate the Arctic. In 1937, Ivan Papinin and four fellow Russians landed by plane on an ice floe near the North Pole. They drifted for nine months and made valuable daily radio reports on meteorological and magnetic data.

Many Arctic explorers were lost and never heard from again. They either died because of the cold, or their ships were crushed in the Arctic ice.

ANIMALS OF THE ARCTIC

In the Arctic Region there are polar bears, which can live farther north than almost any other animal. Lone polar bears are often seen from airplanes, as the bears wander over the polar ice floes.

Seal and walrus swim in the Arctic waters, or flop about on the rocks and ice. The Arctic fox roams over most of the Arctic Region. It lives in snowbanks or burrows under the rocks. There are wolves, Arctic hares, birds called ptarmigans, and little mouselike animals called lemmings. The musk ox and reindeer, or caribou, graze on the Arctic tundra.

The Arctic fox, Arctic hare and ptarmigan have one thing in common. They all change their color during the year. In the winter their coats are white and blend with the ice and snow, and in the summer their coats are colored to blend with the green and the brown of the tundra. The feet of all Arctic animals are protected against the cold ice and snow. The fox, polar bear and rabbit have hair and fur on the pads of their feet. The ptarmigan has warm feathers on its feet. The fur and feathers on the feet of these animals not only help to keep their feet warm but also keep them from slipping on the ice.

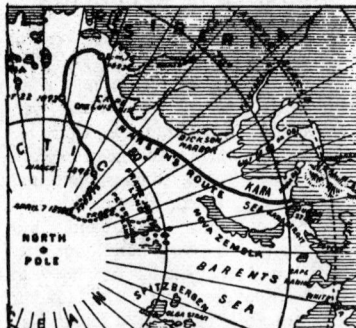

In 1895, Nansen's expedition from Norway by boat took two years, and did not quite reach the North Pole. Today a plane can fly the same distance in just a few hours.

The ptarmigan is the only bird that lives in the Arctic all the year around. It looks very much like a chicken. Other birds come to the Arctic in the summer to make their nests, lay eggs, and hatch their young. Some of these birds come from places far from the Arctic. The Arctic tern flies from far in the Southern Hemisphere, ten thousand miles away, to its Arctic summer home. In the summer, many of the Arctic islands and rocky coasts are full of nesting birds.

Among these summer bird residents are terns, plovers, gannets, snow owls, grebes, loons, and puffins. Most of these birds are fish-eaters. They circle over the water until they see fish, then they dive into the water to catch the fish.

IMPORTANCE OF THE ARCTIC

The Arctic Region is becoming more and more important to the rest of the world. Today, there are many weather stations in the Arctic Region. Here scientists study the Arctic weather, so that they may know more about what weather will be below the Arctic Circle. The men in the weather stations try to predict when cold weather is going to move from the Arctic to the lands south of it.

The airplane has also made the Arctic more important than it used to be. Now that men fly, they have found that crossing the Arctic is the shortest way from northern Europe and Asia to North America. In case of war, countries will have to protect themselves from attack by enemy aircraft flying over the Arctic. The United States and some other countries have air bases and anti-aircraft installations in the Arctic Region.

Scientists believe that the Arctic Region is rich in natural resources. Oil and coal and other minerals, including gold, have been found there. The Russians are believed to mine gold in eastern Siberia above the Arctic Circle.

Arden Forest

The Forest of Arden is in north Warwickshire, a county in England. It is now 17 miles long and 12 miles wide, but at one time it covered 5,000 square miles of central England. Some of the stories of Robin Hood, and Shakespeare's play *As You Like It*, are set in the Forest of Arden.

Luxembourg Consulate General
The small town of Clervaux is in the Ardennes section of Luxembourg. The Castle of Clervaux (in the foreground) was built during the days of feudalism in the 12th century. Behind it is the Benedictine Abbey constructed in 1910.

Ardennes

Ardennes is the name of a forest section in Europe. The forest covers part of Belgium, the Grand Duchy of Luxembourg, and a part of northern France. Most of the forest is hilly, and there are many ravines with small streams running through them. The Ardennes was the scene of much heavy fighting in both World War I and World War II. The Germans invaded France in 1914 and again in 1940 by attacking through the Ardennes. Part of the famous German attack known as the "Battle of the Bulge," in World War II, was in the Ardennes forest.

Argentina

Argentina is the second-biggest country in South America. It has about a million square miles, which means the United States is just about three times as big as Argentina (and so is Brazil, which is the biggest country in South America). Brazil also has a population three times as big as Argentina's. More than twenty million people live in Argentina. But Argentina is the richest country in South America. It sells more meat, corn, and wheat to foreign countries than any other country does. It is sometimes called "the market-basket of the world," because it produces so much food.

The name "Argentina" comes from the Latin word meaning silver, because the Spanish settlers, hundreds of years ago, found silver mines in the mountains there. However, the Argentines found that their rich soil was far more valuable than any silver or gold.

The country is also called the Argentine Republic (or simply "The Argentine"), and sometimes the United States of Argentina.

THE PEOPLE WHO LIVE THERE

Most of the people of Argentina are descended from settlers who came from Spain and Italy about one hundred years ago. They worked on farms and ranches, and some of them married the Indians who were already living there. Other

settlers came from France, England, and Germany. Today, most of the people are Argentine-born, and nearly all of them are members of the Roman Catholic Church. There are very few full-blooded Indians in Argentina. The language of Argentina is Spanish, but more of the people have Italian than Spanish ancestors.

The Argentines are hard-working and independent, and in many ways are like the people of the United States. They are very proud of their country and of its education, art, and music.

The famous *gaucho* is the cowboy who takes care of the great herds of cattle on the Argentine plains. He does not look at all like a cowboy in the United States. He wears a small round hat, baggy trousers, a wide belt, and a scarf around his neck, and often carries a *poncho*. The poncho is worn as a cape or used as a blanket. The gaucho is a wonderful horseman, and he is very proud of his skill.

Until twenty or thirty years ago, Argentine women were not allowed very much freedom. Housework was supposed to be their only interest. Today, women can vote and can take part in business and in the arts.

HOW THE PEOPLE LIVE

The early settlers of Argentina were given great stretches of land so they would be encouraged to cultivate the empty plains. These became large estates, which have remained in the same families. It has been said that about sixteen million acres of land are owned by only fifty families. Their beautiful homes, little villages of workers, and sweeping lands, are worth millions of dollars. The *caudillos*, or rich landowners, often travel and live in other countries, leaving their estates in the care of overseers.

Most of the small farmers do not own their land, and live very much as their ancestors did. Farm workers receive very low wages, and more and more of them have gone to work in the cities. Although farming is still the most important industry in the country, three out of five people now live in the large cities. They work in the great meat-packing plants, in flour mills, and in factories. There are also many Argentines who work the silver, gold, and copper mines in the Andes Mountains.

The average annual per capita income in Argentina is only about $199. This is higher than in any other South American country, but it is less than one-tenth the average per capita income in the U.S.

Argentina is very modern. There are free clinics and hospital service for poor people. There is also free care for mothers and their babies. The country has about 180 newspapers and many beautiful magazines. All over Argentina there are movie houses and music and art centers. More people have radios, telephones and automobiles than in any other South American country. There are also many railroads and highways. Living in Buenos Aires, the capital and biggest city of Argentina, is much like living in New York or Chicago or another of the biggest American cities.

Everyone has to go to school between the ages of 6 and 14. There are about fifteen thousand public schools and two thousand high schools. Argentina has several very modern universities. There are usually more girls than boys in the classes, which would be very unusual in any other country.

WHAT KIND OF PLACE IT IS

Argentina is about as far below the equator as the United States is above the equator. This makes the climate about the same but the seasons just the opposite of those in the United States. When it is summer in New York, it is winter in Buenos Aires.

In the northern part of Argentina is the Gran Chaco (which means "hunting ground"). It is a hot, damp region, with semitropical forests containing some of the world's most valuable trees. Wild animals such as the jaguar, puma and monkey are found in this area.

Also in the north is the Tucumán region, which is called Argentina's "garden spot." Most of the nation's sugar is grown there, as well as corn, tobacco, rice, and alfalfa. There are fine pastures where cattle graze.

Perhaps the best-known part of Argentina is the *pampas* (meaning "great plain"), in the central section. It is a warm, dry region called the world's richest grainlands, because corn and wheat grows so well there, and also flax, grapes, alfalfa, and sugar. In the eastern part of the pampas, the nation's finest cattle are raised.

The Andes Mountains, which run along the western border of Argentina, contain valuable mines. In the southern part of the moutains are some of the country's most beautiful lakes and snow-capped peaks. In the northwest is Mt. Aconcagua, 22,835 feet high.

The southern part of Argentina is the Patagonia region (meaning "big feet"). It is colder and much less fertile than the pampas. Sheep are raised there in large numbers and one of the most expensive furs in the world comes from a little Patagonian rodent, the chinchilla. Another rodent running wild in this region is the Patagonian hare, a kind of rabbit that may weigh as much as 30 pounds.

Off the southern tip of Argentina are a group of islands called Tierra del Fuego. These are warmer and more fertile than Patagonia. Visitors to this region may see many penguins on the rocky coast. Tierra del Fuego is cut off from Argentina by the Strait of Magellan, where its coast is swept by wild winds, fog, and huge waves. This has been called the loneliest coast in the world. Part of it is owned by Chile.

In Argentina, as in the United States, the climate is different in various sections. The northern part has a hot climate like that of Florida (except that when it is summer in Argentina, it is winter in Florida). In July, during the Argentine winter, the temperatures may drop to 30 degrees. The pampas around Buenos Aires also have a warm climate, and the winters are extremely mild. Flowers bloom in Buenos Aires most of the year, and in the past thirty-five years there has been only one snowfall. In Patagonia, in the south, it is colder and windier. In the winter months, the temperature can drop to 18 degrees.

Along the slopes of the Andes Mountains it is very dry, as it is in some western states in the United States.

1. Guards in front of important buildings in Buenos Aires, Argentina, wear elaborate uniforms with gold epaulettes on the shoulders. This guard is standing before the Casa Rosada, or Pink House. It is the President's house, like our White House.
2. This is a gaucho of the Argentine. A gaucho was originally a cowboy who was partly Spanish and partly Indian. Now all Argentine cowboys are called gauchos. They are noted for their skill at riding horses and roping cattle. The prairie is called the pampas there.

CHIEF CITIES IN ARGENTINA

The leading cities of Argentina, with 1973 populations are:

Buenos Aires, population 5,900,000, the capital, largest city in the country, and eighth-largest in the world. There is a separate article about BUENOS AIRES.

Rosario, population 751,000, the second-largest city, commercial center, in the northeastern part of Argentina.

Córdoba, population 846,000, the third-largest city, industrial center, in the northern part.

Avellaneda, population 329,626, the fourth-largest city, industrial center, in the northeastern part.

HOW THE PEOPLE ARE GOVERNED

Argentina is a constitutional republic, which means that it has a president, a legislature that makes laws, and a constitution that protects the rights of the people. The constitution of Argentina was modeled after that of the United States, with separate executive, legislative

and judicial branches.

The president is elected for a six-year term. There is also a vice-president, as in the United States. Freedom of religion is guaranteed by the constitution, but both president and vice-president must be members of the Roman Catholic Church. There is a legislature composed of two houses, a Senate and a Chamber of Deputies (like the House of Representatives). The members of both houses are elected by the people.

Argentina is divided into fourteen provinces and each one has its own governor and legislature, as do the states in the United States. Everyone who is 18 years old or more has to vote. Those who do not vote may be made to pay fines.

Every man from 20 to 45 years old must serve in the army for one year, or in the navy for two years.

ARGENTINA IN THE PAST

Spaniards were the first white men in Argentina. In 1516 Juan Diaz de Solis led a party up the Rio de la Plata but Indians killed him and most of his crew. In 1536, Pedro de Mendoza with 1,200 men and 100 horses founded Buenos Aires. Indians massacred this colony but by 1563 it was permanently established. Until 1776, Argentina was part of the Spanish colony of Peru; then until 1810 it was a separate Spanish colony. On May 25, 1810 (which is still celebrated as Argentine Independence Day), Argentina became self-governing but still recognized the Spanish King. In 1816, at a meeting called the Congress of Tucumán (an Argentine city), Argentina declared its independence as a republic.

Fighting continued, against Spanish forces, until 1821. The Argentine leader and national hero was General José de SAN MARTIN, about whom there is a separate article. San Martin helped the other great South American independence leaders, General Bernardo O'Higgins of Chile and Simón Bolívar, and they helped him.

The first officials of the new republic struggled against the caudillos, who wanted to be supreme rulers on their vast estates. In 1830 a dictator named Juan Manuel Rosas seized power and ruled like the worst dictators of modern times, with secret police, torture, and exile of his political enemies (20,000 of them). In 1852 Rosas was overthrown by a revolutionary army led by Justo José de Urquiza. A democratic constitution was adopted in 1853 and Argentina was more or less a democratic country until the time of World War II. Then the Argentine Army gradually got power, and by 1944 there was a new dictator, an Army colonel named Juan Domingo PERÓN, about whom there is a separate article.

Perón won the support of the laboring people. His supporters, called Peronistas, included a popular motion-picture actress, Eva Duarte, whom Perón married in 1944. Perón did not allow freedom of speech or opposition, but he actually had the support of the majority of the people through about 1953. Gradually the opposition forces became stronger. In 1955 Perón quarreled with the Roman Catholic Church, which excommunicated him. This cost him more of his supporters. In September 1955 a group of Army and Navy officers headed by General Eduardo Lonardi assumed power and exiled Perón. Gradually the government became democratic again. Freedom of the press was restored in 1956 and civil liberties were restored in 1957. In May, 1958, Arturo Frondizi was inaugurated as constitutional president. During his early years in office, he faced many economic, political and military crises. In 1962, after followers of Perón won the elections, the armed forces overthrew Frondizi and dissolved the Congress. In 1963 free elections were again held and a new president was elected, but Argentina continued to have economic and political problems.

ARGENTINA—SUMMARY

Area. 1,084,359 sq. mi. Greatest length, about 2,900 miles; greatest width, about 800 miles; coastline on Atlantic Ocean, about 1,615 miles.

Population. 23,983,000 (1973 estimate). 88% white (42% of Italian stock, 33% of Spanish stock); 10% mestizos (mixed white and Indian).

Language. Spanish, with many Italian words added, and some English words.

Religion. 93.6% Roman Catholic, 2% Protestant, 1.6% Jewish, remainder chiefly Indian religions.

General Information. *Flag:* blue, white and blue horizontal bars with a rising sun on the white bar. *National anthem:* Himno Nacional Argentino (1860).

Principal Cities. (Official 1973 estimates.) Buenos Aires (pop. 5,900,000); Rosario (pop. 751,000); Córdoba (pop. 846,000); Avellaneda (pop. 329,600); San Martin (pop. 269,514); Lanus (pop. 244,473); La Plata (pop. 406,000); Tucuman (pop. 290,000); Santa Fe (pop. 260,000); Vicente Lopez pop. 149,958).

Transportation. *Railroads,* 27,000 miles, state-owned and-operated; connections with Chilean, Bolivian, Paraguayan and Brazilian lines. *Merchant marine* (in 1973), 315 ships, total tonnage 1,196,817. *Highways,* 125,470 miles; about 2 million automobiles registered in 1973. *Water,* the Rio de la Plata river system to the north; sea-going ships go 358 miles up the Rio Paraná.

Government. Republic; constitution of 1853, revised in 1951 and again in 1958. Elective offices (all elected by direct vote) include President and Vice-President, who must be native-born Catholics; and Congress, a 47-member Senate and a 197-member Chamber of Deputies. Voting compulsory for men and women over 18. Provinces have their own congresses and courts.

Currency. The basic monetary unit is the peso, worth about ½ cent (U.S.).

Military. Compulsory 1-year service in army, or two years in navy, between ages of 20 and 45.

Commerce. Argentina exports more meat and meat derivatives, more corn, wheat, linseed oil, and quebracho than any other nation. Chief imports are machinery and vehicles, partially and wholly manufactured goods, iron, petroleum, chemicals. *Cattle industry:* (6th in world, behind India, U.S., Brazil, U.S.S.R, and China); 47,700,000 sheep (4th in world); 4,000,000 hogs; 7,250,000 horses. *Industry:* highly industrialized; food and textile products, machinery, and metal manufactures. *Exports and imports:* balanced, each about $1,250,000,000 (U.S.) per year.

Natural Resources. About 700,000 sq. mi. farmlands, including pampas 250,000 sq. mi.; ⅛ under cultivation. Some mineral resources, not fully exploited or even investigated. Production of crude oil in 1959 was 7,100,000 metric tons (40% of national requirements). Potential waterpower great but undeveloped.

Climate. Temperate in most of the country. Rainfall, 20 to 60 inches per year.

argon

Argon is the name of a gas that is a chemical element. It has no color or odor. The air is about one percent argon.

Argon is an *inert* gas. That means it will not join with other things to form chemical compounds, as oxygen joins with metal to form rust. Because argon is an inert gas it is used in electric light bulbs, for it does not combine or burn with the hot metal filament (wire).

Argonne Forest

The Argonne Forest is in Northeastern France. It is about 25 miles long and 10 miles wide and is very hilly, with the highest hills rising over 1,000 feet. In World War I the United States Army fought and won a great battle there. It was called the Battle of the Meuse-Argonne, because much of the fighting was along the Meuse River at the side of the forest. It was the last great battle of the war.

The battle began in the last week of September, 1918, and continued for more than a month. Slowly the Germans were pushed back and finally they were routed. More than one million Americans fought in the Argonne Forest, and 117,000 American soldiers were killed or wounded.

aristocracy

The word *aristocracy* is used today to mean people whose families have been rich and important for a long time, and a member of such a family is called an *aristocrat.* Originally, aristocracy meant "government by the best people." England used to be considered an aristocracy, because only the "upper classes" could be Members of Parliament, officers in the army, judges, or ministers of the churches.

Aristophanes

Aristophanes was the first great writer of comedies, or funny plays. He lived about 2,400 years ago in ancient Greece, when it was the only place where art and learning were advanced. Everyone went to the theater in ancient Greece, and Aristophanes used his plays to tell them what customs he thought were wrong or silly. He poked fun at politicians in his play *The Knights;* teased lawyers in *The Wasps* and writers in *The Frogs;* and pleaded for peace in *The Peace* and *Lysistrata.* Others were *The Clouds* and *The Birds.* He wrote his plays in poetry, and it was some of the best poetry ever written. Aristophanes was born about 448 B.C. and died about 385 B.C.

Aristotle

Hundreds of years before the time of Christ, wise men in Greece began to think about the reasons for everything that goes on in the world—why fire is hot and, water is wet, how plants and

animals grow, why men think and act as they do, and everything else they saw, felt, or thought. These men called themselves *philosophers,* which meant "lovers of knowledge." Aristotle, who was born in 384 B.C., was one of the greatest of these philosophers.

Aristotle was the son of a doctor in the court of the King of Macedon, one of the ancient Greek countries. When Aristotle was 17 years old he went to Athens and for 20 years he was a pupil of Plato, who was then greatest philosopher. Then for two years he taught the Macedonian prince who was to become Alexander the Great. After Alexander became king, Aristotle went back to Athens to teach young philosophers. He died in 322 B.C.

Aristotle's "school" of philosophy was called the *peripatetic school.* The word *peripatetic* is Greek for "walking about." Aristotle and his pupils did not sit in a classroom, but usually walked about out of doors while they talked.

Aristotle wrote several famous books. In his books on *Animals,* Aristotle invented a system for classifying living creatures, much as scientists do today. His book *Physics* discusses the elements, motion, astronomy, and God, among a variety of other topics of a scientific and general nature. In his book *Politics,* Aristotle writes about why people need government and what kind of government is best. The ideas of Aristotle were accepted as true for nearly 2,000 years after his death.

arithmetic

Arithmetic is a way of counting. It is used for counting or separating groups of things quickly.

A child learns some simple arithmetic before he goes to school. If a child has two cookies and you give him another one, then ask, "How many cookies have you now?" he will answer, "Three." He did not go back to the beginning and count one, two, three. He put two and one together and knew the total was three. That is addition, which is a branch of arithmetic. He did not know he was using arithmetic, but he was.

Addition is one of the short cuts for counting. Just as it saved the child the trouble of counting up to three, it saves others the trouble of counting up to twenty, or a thousand, or a million.

TIME AND MONEY

Everyone uses arithmetic every day, far more often than most people realize. Especially it is used in connection with *time* and *money.* We measure time by the clock and the calendar, and both require arithmetic. Our entire knowledge of money is based on arithmetic.

For example, a game is to begin at 2 o'clock and last three hours. Without realizing that he is using addition, one adds $2 + 3 = 5$ and knows the game will be over at 5 o'clock.

Or one buys drinks for himself and two friends and they cost 15 cents each. He puts down 50 cents, knowing he will get 5 cents change; he probably does not realize that he has mentally used both

multiplication, $3 \times 15 = 45$, and subtraction, $50 - 45 = 5$.

THE NUMBERS WE USE

Arithmetic is done with ten symbols that we call "numerals" or "figures" or "numbers." The symbols we use—1, 2, 3, 4, 5, 6, 7, 8, 9, and 0—are called Arabic numerals, because they came to us from the Arabs, who in turn learned them from the Hindus in India. There have been hundreds of different systems of numbering. The ancient Greeks and Romans simply used letters of the alphabet. A letter would mean one thing in a word and another thing as a number. For example, the Romans used V to mean 5, and the Greeks used it to mean 40. Arabic numerals have replaced these systems because they make arithmetic much easier.

In our system of numbers, we count everything by how many tens there are, plus any smaller amount that is less than ten. For example, 83 means eight tens and three more. We call this the *decimal system,* because in the Latin language the word *decem* means "ten." Probably, thousands of years ago, men came to count by tens because there are ten fingers to count with on the two hands.

This system of counting by tens (or by some such figure that is much more than one) is the basis of arithmetic. Thousands of years ago, under the systems that were used, only a scholar could master arithmetic. Today, a pupil in any school learns it in a few years. The illustration will give an idea of how much easier it makes counting.

Take a number as we write it:

$$4,312$$

The 2 at the right is in the "units" or "ones" column. It means that in this number there are two "ones."

The 1 next to it is in the "tens" column. This column shows how many tens there are in the number.

The 3 is in the "hundreds" column. Every figure in this column stands for ten tens.

The 4 is in the "thousands" column. Every figure in this column stands for one hundred tens.

And every additional column stands for ten times as many tens as does the column before it.

The article on NUMBERS tells more of their history and uses.

HOW MEMORY IS USED

With the decimal system, you can do the most complicated arithmetic possible as easily as you can figure in numbers that are all lower than ten. Take a case of adding:

$$4,312$$
$$5,473$$

Suppose we must add these numbers. We start in the "ones" column at the right: 3 and 2 are 5. Next, the "tens" column: 7 and 1 are 8. Next, the "hundreds" column: 4 and 3 are 7. Finally, the "thousands" column: 5 and 4 are 9. The result is:

$$4,312$$
$$5,473$$
$$9,785$$

We have added a figure in the thousands, but all we had to know was how to add figures lower than ten.

There are so few ways in which figures under ten can be used that all the combinations can be memorized within a few years of school work. Once we have memorized them, we are through with that job for life.

THE BRANCHES OF ARITHMETIC

The four ways of doing arithmetic are addition, subtraction, multiplication, and division.

Each of these ways has its special symbols and its special words. Many educators believe that some of the special words are not necessary, and that simpler words should be used, words that a student in school already knows from his everyday life.

ADDITION is a way of putting two or more groups together to form one bigger group, called the *sum.* Addition answers the question, "How many are there altogether?" It uses the symbol $+$ (called the "plus mark") and can be written like this:

$$3 + 2 = 5 \quad \text{or} \quad \begin{array}{r} 3 \\ +2 \\ \hline 5 \end{array} \quad \text{or} \quad \begin{array}{r} 3 \\ 2 \\ \hline 5 \end{array}$$

In any of the three cases, it could be read, "Three plus two equals five," or "three and two make five," or "three added to two makes five."

SUBTRACTION answers the question "How many will be left if I take one group away from a bigger group?" It uses the symbol $-$ (called the "minus sign"), and it is written like this (with its special words shown in the parentheses):

$$3 - 2 = 1 \quad \text{or} \quad \begin{array}{r} 3 \text{ (minuend)} \\ -2 \text{ (subtrahend)} \\ \hline 1 \text{ (difference)} \end{array}$$

This would be read, "Three minus two equals one." However, it is simpler and clearer to say, "Three, take away two, leaves one," and some teachers prefer that.

MULTIPLICATION is a shorter way of doing addition. Its symbol is $\times$. Instead of having to write out a long series of numbers like $8 + 8 + 8 + 8 + 8$, or putting them in a column that might stretch all over the page, you can simply write 6×8 ("Six eights," or "Six times eight"). A number that is to be increased by multiplication (in this example, 8) is a *multiplicand.* The number by which it is increased (in this example, 6) is a *multiplier.* The result of the multiplication is the *product.* It is more usual to call each number that figures in multiplication a *factor;* in 6×8, both 6 and 8 are factors.

DIVISION is the opposite of multiplication. By division you find out how many times one number can be contained in another (will "go into" the other). The symbol for division is $\div$. The number that is to be divided is the *dividend.* The number by which it is divided is the *divisor.* The result is the *quotient.* Division can be written like this:

$$48 \div 6 = 8$$
$$\text{or} \quad 6\overline{)48}^{\,8} \quad \text{or} \quad 6\,/\,48\,/\,8$$

Fractions and percentage are forms

of division. There are separate articles on FRACTIONS and PERCENTAGES.

See also ALGEBRA.

Arizona

Arizona is a state in the Southwest of the United States. Sometimes it is called the "Copper State," because the copper mines of Arizona are the finest in the country. And sometimes it is called "the Grand Canyon State," because in northwest Arizona the Colorado River flows between cliffs a mile high, known as the Grand Canyon. Arizona is a favorite place for vacations, because it is warm and sunny even in the winter. In the summer it is very hot, but it is more comfortable than most places farther north because there is very little humidity.

Arizona ranks sixth in size among the states, having 113,575 square miles. In population it ranks 33rd, with more than a million and a half people living there. It was admitted to the Union February 14, 1912, the 48th state. Its name comes from the Spanish, who called the region *arida zona*, meaning "dry belt," or a place with little water.

THE PEOPLE OF ARIZONA

Tribes of Indians lived in Arizona for thousands of years before the white men came. About 280 years ago, white settlers began coming from other parts of the United States and from Mexico, which was then known as New Spain. Today, three out of every five Arizonans come from English-speaking people. About one out of four is Spanish-American, and one out of nine is Indian. Most of the Indians belong to the Apache, Navaho, Hopi and Pima tribes. More full-blooded Indians live in Arizona than in any other state. The children of the Spanish-speaking families go to English-language schools, but they usually speak Spanish at home.

The Indian tribes in Arizona live on reservations. They have customs and ceremonies that are of great interest to visitors. The Navahos, one of the largest and best-known tribes, live in the northern part of the state, where they raise sheep and ponies. They are famous for the bright-colored blankets and baskets they weave, and for the silver jewelry they make by hand.

The Hopi Indians live in villages called pueblos, in the northern part of the state, and people can visit them. These pueblos are "apartment houses" built of sunbaked bricks, and are hundreds of years old. A Hopi village is usually built on top of a high mesa, which is a flat-topped hill made of rock, with very steep sides. In the past, this protected the Hopis from enemy attacks. Today they peacefully raise sheep and work on farms. They have many colorful ceremonies, including a famous snake dance.

The largest number of Arizonans are farmers. They grow grain and fruit in the fertile river valleys, or raise cattle on ranches. Others work in the rich copper, gold and silver mines. In the cities they work in factories and plants. They smelt copper, which is one of Arizona's leading industries, make butter and cheese, and are meat packers. An important industry in Arizona is making ice for railroad refrigerator cars.

The Roman Catholic church has the largest membership in Arizona. There are also many Mormons, Methodists, Presbyterians, and Baptists.

WHAT ARIZONA IS LIKE

Arizona is a strange and beautiful state, with many wonderful sights to see.

Most of the northern part of Arizona is the awe-inspiring Plateau Region. (A plateau is high, like a mountain, but level, like a plain.) Here one can see great volcanoes that no longer erupt, and lofty mountains with deep canyons cut in them by the mighty Colorado River, which runs across northwestern Arizona and then southward to form its boundary with California. There are separate articles about several famous features of northern Arizona: the GRAND CANYON, which people from all over the world come to see; the PAINTED DESERT with its many-colored rocks; and a strange forest, known as the PETRIFIED FOREST, where the ancient trees have turned to stone.

The large Plateau Region of northern Arizona is cut off from the rest of the state by a great stone ridge called the Mogollon Mesa. In central Arizona there is a mountain region, which runs from northwest to southeast. Here the miners work the rich copper, gold and silver mines. The highest point in the state is at Humphreys Peak, 12,655 feet high. However, there are also wide, fertile valleys in this region, where the farmers raise corn, wheat, and barley. They also raise some of the finest cotton, known as *Pima,* and grapefruits, strawberries, and melons. The soil is so dry that the farmers depend almost entirely on irrigation, and they have received great help in recent years from the large dams built by the United States government. Hoover Dam, in the northwest, is the highest dam in the world.

Some of the largest forests of yellow pine, juniper, and cedar in North America grow in this region.

The southwest of Arizona is beautiful desert country. Here the temperature sometimes rises to 120 degrees, but the air is so clear and dry that people can live there quite comfortably, though they have to be careful to stay out of the hot noonday sun. Many people go to this part of Arizona for their health.

In the desert grow some interesting plants that cannot be seen in other parts of the United States. The most famous is the large cactus, known as the giant saguaro, which has great prickly leaves pointing upward like huge arms. It sometimes grows as high as 50 feet and it can live for more than 200 years. Jackrabbits, horned toads and snakes live in the desert. One of the strangest desert animals is the Gila monster, which is a large, ugly lizard, colored orange and black, with a poisonous bite.

Arizona has one of the largest herds of buffalo (bison) in the United States, and the greatest number of mule deer. They live in the national parks, where they are protected from hunters. In the Arizona forests there are black and brown bear and mountain lions.

The climate of Arizona is generally dry and clear and very healthful. In most of the state the average temperature in summer is about 79 degrees, while in winter it is about 42 degrees. There is very little rainfall.

THE GOVERNMENT OF ARIZONA

In Arizona, as in most states, there is a Governor at the head of the government. The laws are made by a Legislature composed of two houses, a Senate and a House of Representatives. The Governor and members of both houses are elected to serve two-year terms. Judges are elected and serve six years. The capital is Phoenix.

There are about 418,000 pupils attending public elementary and high schools. State colleges and universities include:

University of Arizona, at Tucson. Enrollment, 24,726 in 1971.

Arizona State College, at Tempe. Enrollment, 23,476 in 1971.

The state maintains an agricultural school at Tucson and 2 junior colleges at Thatcher and Phoenix. The largest Indian school in the Southwest, at Phoenix, is also run by the government. It has an enrollment of more than 700.

CHIEF CITIES OF ARIZONA

The leading cities of Arizona, with 1970 census populations (or later estimates), are:

Phoenix, population 581,562, the state capital and largest city. There is a separate article about PHOENIX.

Tucson, population 262,933, the second-largest city, winter resort, in the southern part of the state. There is a separate article about TUCSON.

Mesa, population 62,853, fourth-largest city, in the heart of the farming region, in the south central part of the state.

Tempe, population 62,907, the third-largest city.

Yuma, population 29,007 the fifth-largest city.

ARIZONA IN THE PAST

Hundreds of years before any white men came to Arizona, it was occupied by a race of Indians, whose ruined cities and fortifications can still be seen throughout the state. About four hundred years ago, the first Spaniards entered the region of Arizona in search of precious metals. Later, Spanish missionaries came to what is now southern Arizona, converted many of the Indians to Christianity, and introduced new methods of farming to them. However, settling this part of the country was very slow because of the fierce resistance of the Apache Indians to white settlers.

For a long time, Arizona was a part of Mexico. After the Mexican War, fought between Mexico and the United States about one hundred years ago, Mexico let most of Arizona become part of the United States. Five years later, the United States bought the rest of Arizona from Mexico and made it part of the New Mexico territory. In 1863, Arizona was made a separate Territory

and in 1912 it became a state. During the 1950s its population grew faster (73.7%) than that of any other state except Nevada and Alaska.

PLACES TO SEE IN ARIZONA

Grand Canyon National Park, 645,-295 acres, in north central Arizona, 37 miles from Flagstaff, west of U.S. Route 89.

Canyon de Chelly National Monument, 83,840 acres, in the northeast, in the Navaho Indian Reservation, north of U.S. Route 66. Prehistoric Indian ruins built at the base of sheer red cliffs or in caves in canyon walls; modern Navaho Indian homes and farms.

Casa Grande National Monument, 472 acres, in south central Arizona, 2½ miles from Coolidge, west of U.S. Routes 80 and 89. Ruined adobe tower built by Indians who farmed the Gila Valley 600 years ago; only prehistoric building of its type still standing.

Chiricahua National Monument, 10,-694 acres, in the southeast, 70 miles from Douglas, west of U.S. Route 80. Wilderness of unusual rock shapes; layers of rock tell the story of nearly a billion years of the earth's history. (See picture on page 3564.)

Navajo National Monument, 360 acres, in the northeast, in the Navaho Indian Reservation, east of U.S. Route 89. Three of the largest of the known cliff dwellings—Betatakin, Keet Seel, and Inscription House.

Petrified Forest National Monument, 85,303 acres, in the northeast, 19 miles east of Holbrook, on U.S. Routes 260 and 66. An abundance of petrified trees in brilliant and varied colors; Indian ruins; part of the Painted Desert.

Pipe Spring National Monument, 40 acres, in the northwest, 13½ miles west of Fredonia, on U.S. Route 89. Historic fort and other structures built by the Mormons, 1867-70.

Saguaro National Monument, 54,971 acres, in the southeast, 20 miles east of Tucson, on U.S. Route 80. Cactus forest containing giant saguaro, found only in deserts of southern Arizona and northwestern New Mexico.

Organ Pipe Cactus National Monument, 328,161 acres, in the southwest, crossed by the Sonoyta-Rocky Point Highway. Rare desert plants found nowhere else in the United States.

Sunset Crater National Monument, 3,040 acres, in the north central part, 14 miles northeast of Flagstaff, east of U.S. Route 89. An extinct volcano, and large fields of cinders and lava; upper part of volcano colored as if by sunset glow.

Tonto National Monument, 1,120 acres, in central Arizona, 3 miles southeast of Roosevelt, north of U.S. Route 80. Well-preserved cliff dwellings occupied by Pueblo Indians six hundred years ago.

Tumacacori National Monument, 10 acres, in the south, 18 miles north of Nogales, on U.S. Route 89. Historic Spanish Catholic Mission building near site first visited by Father Kino, a Jesuit, in 1691.

Tuzigoot National Monument, 42 acres, in central Arizona, 2 miles east of Clarkdale, on U.S. Route 89. Some of the most interesting prehistoric pueblo ruins, lived in almost one thousand years ago.

Walnut Canyon National Monument, 1,641 acres in north central Arizona, 8 miles from Flagstaff, on U.S. Route 89. Cliff dwellings built by Pueblo Indians about eight hundred years ago.

Wupatki National Monument, 35,-813 acres, in north central Arizona, 28 miles northeast of Flagstaff, on U.S. Route 89. Red sandstone prehistoric pueblos built by ·a group of farming Indians.

Painted Desert, 366 miles long, in north central Arizona, Route 66. A region of plateaus, brilliantly colored red yellow, blue, and brown.

Tombstone, in the southeast, on U.S. Route 80. The most famous of the old mining towns, once noted for its violence and lawlessness.

A giant Saguaro cactus near Phoenix, Arizona. The flower of this cactus is Arizona's state flower.

ark

The story of Noah's ark is told in the Bible in the book of Genesis. God told Noah there would be a great flood and told him to build an ark, or ship, in which he and his family and living creatures of all kinds could be saved.

Noah built his ark of gopherwood. It was shaped like a big box, with several decks or floors and with a roof on top. It was about 400 to 450 feet long, 70 feet wide, and 50 feet high. The wood was covered with pitch or tar, so that it would not leak. Into this ark Noah took his wife, his three sons and their wives, and two each of all the living things he could find. The ark sailed safely during the flood and finally landed on Mount Ararat.

The word *ark* really means "chest," or "box." The Ark of the Covenant was a sacred chest in which the Israelites of Biblical times carried the written law that God had given to them to follow. The word *covenant* means "agreement," or "promise," and the Ark of the Covenant represented the agreement God had made with men, to protect them if they would obey His commandments.

In the wars between the Israelites and Philistines, about 3,000 years ago, the Philistines captured the Ark of the Covenant. It was finally restored to Jerusalem by King David, who was so happy he danced for joy.

Arkansas

Arkansas is one of the southern states of the United States. During the Civil War it was among the eleven states that seceded from the Union and formed the Confederate States of America. Once Arkansas was called "the Bear State," because so many hunters came there to shoot the wild bears living in the caves. Now it is known as "the Wonder State," because it is so rich in minerals.

The name "Arkansas" came from a tribe of Indians, known as the Quapaw, who lived there before the white men came. In their language Arkansas means "downstream people."

In area, Arkansas ranks 27th among the states, having 53,102 square miles, which is a little larger than New York State. In population it ranks 32nd, with almost two million people living there. It became a state in 1836, and was the 25th state admitted to the United States. The capital is Little Rock.

THE PEOPLE OF ARKANSAS

More than half the people of Arkansas are farmers. Around the fertile river plains, in the eastern and southern parts, they raise a great deal of fine cotton, and Arkansas is the third-largest cotton-raising state in the United States. The farmers also grow a great deal of corn and about a fifth of all the rice in the country. In the northwest, the people raise valuable beef and dairy cattle.

Many Arkansans also work in the rich mines. Arkansas has the best bauxite, the ore from which aluminum is made. Others cut timber in the great forests. Only about one person in five lives in a city. In the cities are plants that manufacture lumber and aluminum products, shoes, garments, furniture, and watches. There are also huge food-processing plants and many large oil refineries.

In the east of Arkansas, along the Mississippi River, many people live and work on big cotton plantations, like those in "the Deep South." In the southwestern part of the state there are large ranches, and the people of Arkansas are much like Texans and even talk the same way, with a slow drawl.

Perhaps the most interesting people are those who live in the Ozark Mountains, farther north, in the western part

of Arkansas. These people are a proud, independent group, whose ancestors were English and Scottish, and they have kept many of the customs they brought to America with them two hundred and more years ago. Their ballads, "mountain music" and round dances are famous. For many years they were often suspicious of strangers, but more and more tourists have visited the Ozarks.

The people of Arkansas belong to many different churches. The largest are the Baptist, Methodist, Church of Christ, and Presbyterian. About one person in every five is a Negro.

WHAT THE STATE IS LIKE

Below the Ozark Mountains is a broad fertile valley, known as the Arkansas River Valley. Strangely enough, it contains several high mountain peaks. Blue Mountain and Magazine Mountain, both about 2,900 feet, are the highest points in the state. These and other peaks to the south are part of the Ouachita Mountains. The people in this region mine the valuable coal and bauxite, and produce lumber and wood products on a large scale. This area has many gas wells and the only diamond deposits in the United States.

In the Ouachita Mountains there are many mineral and hot springs, which people visit for their health. The city of Hot Springs is one of the most popular health resorts in the United States.

The largest section of Arkansas, more than half the state, is the Mississippi River Valley. The Mississippi runs along the eastern boundary. This valley is extremely fertile for growing cotton, corn, rice, and sweet potatoes. The southeastern section has great moss-covered trees and swamps. Some of the largest forests are in the Mississippi River Valley, as are valuable oil fields.

The climate of Arkansas is quite mild. Though the temperature can go as high as 100 degrees in the summer, cool breezes from the Gulf of Mexico relieve the heat. There is very little snow in winter, and cold weather seldom lasts more than a few days. The average temperature in January is 41 degrees; in July it is about 80 degrees. One reason the farmers' crops grow so well is because Arkansas gets a great deal of rain.

The people have depended for a very long time on the river for transportation. The Mississippi, Arkansas, Red and Ouachita Rivers carry products to the market on large barges.

THE GOVERNMENT OF ARKANSAS

The government of Arkansas, like that of most states, is headed by a Governor and the laws are made by a Legislature composed of two houses, a Senate and a House of Representatives. The members of the House of Representatives are elected to serve two-year terms. The Governor and members of the Senate are elected to serve four-year terms. Judges are elected to serve eight years. In order to vote people must pay a poll tax.

There are about 460,000 students enrolled in public elementary and high schools. About half the school-children go to big consolidated schools, to which they are taken in school buses.

Among the principal state-operated colleges and universities are:

University of Arkansas at Fayetteville. Enrollment, 11,426 in 1971 (co-ed).

Arkansas Agricultural and Mechanical College, at Monticello. Enrollment, 1,587 in 1971.

Arkansas Agricultural, Mechanical, and Normal College at Pine Bluff. Enrollment, 3,305 in 1971 (co-ed).

Arkansas College at Batesville. Enrollment, 351 in 1971 (co-ed).

Arkansas Polytechnic College, at Russellville. Enrollment, 2,252 in 1971 (co-ed).

Arkansas State College at Jonesboro and Beebe. Enrollment, 3,001 in 1971 (co-ed).

CHIEF CITIES IN ARKANSAS

The leading cities of Arkansas, with populations from the 1970 census, are:

Little Rock, population 132,483, the state capital and largest city. There is a separate article about LITTLE ROCK.

North Little Rock, population 60,040, the third-largest city.

Fort Smith, population 62,802, the second-largest city, business center in west Arkansas.

Pine Bluff, population 57,389, the fourth-largest city, in central part of state.

Hot Springs, population 35,631, the fifth-largest city, famous health resort, in the western part of the state.

ARKANSAS IN THE PAST

Long before any white men came to Arkansas, the Quapaw and Osage Indians roamed through the region. However, about four hundred years ago, the Spaniards led by Hernando de Soto explored part of Arkansas. in search of treasures. French explorers, such as Marquette and Joliet, and La Salle, later explored the region further. The first permanent settlement was made by the French in 1686.

In 1803 the United States bought from France a large section of land, known as the *Louisiana Purchase,* which included the Arkansas territory. People from other parts of the country began to settle here. In those days cotton was the most valuable crop a farmer could raise, and many settlers, especially those from Tennessee and Kentucky, started plantations.

Although Arkansas was not very heavily populated, it became a separate Territory in 1819, and in 1836 it became a state.

The cotton-growing region was soon filled with big plantations, whose rich owners lived in fine mansions and owned hundreds of slaves to raise the cotton. Although only a small number of the people owned slaves, they were the richest and most powerful. When Abraham Lincoln became President in 1861, and it appeared that the slaves would be set free, Arkansas followed the example of other slave-holding states and seceded from the Union in May, 1861.

After the Civil War, the people were very poor in Arkansas as in other Southern states. The building of the railroads in the 1870s and 1880s brought to Arkansas many new settlers from Germany, Austria, Poland, and Italy. Gradually the state began to develop its mineral wealth and forests.

In 1957 Arkansas became a center of Southern resistance to the United States Supreme Court "segregation" decision (that Negro and white children must be allowed to attend the same schools.) The School Board admitted nine Negro students to a high school in the capital, Little Rock. The state's governor, Orval Faubus, called out state troops to prevent their attending, but President Eisenhower sent troops of the U.S. Army to enforce their attendance. Most of the Negro students finished the school year but in 1958 the people of Arkansas backed Faubus by

Little Rock Chamber of Commerce

The Old State House in Little Rock served as the state capitol until 1911. It is now a museum operated by the Arkansas History Commission.

electing him to another term as governor.

PLACES TO SEE IN ARKANSAS

Hot Springs National Park, 1,019 acres, in western Arkansas, on U.S. Route 70. Healthful mineral and hot springs; beautiful parks, gardens and lakes; magnificent view of four states from tower on top of Hot Springs Mountain.

Buffalo River State Park, 3,000 acres in the north between Yellville and Marshall, on State Highway 14. Overlooks Buffalo River from sheer rock cliffs; beautiful scenery with canyons, caves, and waterfalls; fishing is the chief attraction.

Calico Rock, on the White River, in the north, about 12 miles northwest of Melbourne, on State Highway 56. A bluff of limestone rock, whose high, smooth wall is variously colored with squares, stripes, spots, and angles.

Diamond Cave, in the northwest, 5 miles south of Jasper, on State Highway 7. No one has ever reached the end of this cave. Strangely shaped stalactites and stalagmites, which look like giant icicles, grow in the many beautiful chambers of the cave.

Big Hurricane Cavern, in the northwest, 7 miles south of Western Grove, on U.S. Route 65. So named because many years ago a violent storm hurled uprooted trees into the mouth of the cave; once noted for the bears and wildcats killed within its shelter; has fantastic formations, including an onyx parrot and a stone airplane.

Mammoth Spring, in the north, about 11 miles north of Hardy, on U.S. Route 63. One of the largest springs in North America; a torrent of cold, blue water rushes from it at the rate of 200 million gallons a day.

Old Arsenal, in Little Rock, on U.S. Highways 67-70-65. The birthplace of Douglas MacArthur.

Arkansas River

The Arkansas River is about 1,500 miles long. Its source is the Colorado and it winds through Kansas, Oklahoma, and Arkansas, where it joins the Mississippi. The principal cities on it are Wichita, Kansas; Tulsa, Oklahoma; and Little Rock, Arkansas. It is navigable by steamboats for about 650 miles except in the dry season, when it drops 20 feet. It also has frequent floods, but dams have been built and are being built to control them.

Arkwright, Sir Richard

Richard Arkwright was an English inventor. Nearly two hundred years ago he built the first cotton-spinning frame, a machine that made thread from soft, fluffy cotton. Though he was born poor and never had much education (because when he was born, in 1732, poor people could not often go to school), his invention finally made him very rich and famous. Also, it helped to make England

richer than any other country. Before Arkwright's invention of the cotton-spinning frame, about 1768, cotton thread was made by hand, very slowly, on a wooden spinning wheel.

In 1771 Arkwright set up the first cotton-spinning factory that had machinery driven by waterpower. Arkwright was honored for his invention in 1786 when the King of England made him a knight. He died in 1792.

Arlington Cemetery

Arlington National Cemetery is the best-known military cemetery in the United States. It covers 420 acres on the former estate of General Robert E. Lee (and of the Custis family, descendants of Mrs. George Washington) in the state of Virginia, just across the Potomac River from Washington, D. C. Over 150,000 American heroes lie buried in these grounds. Each grave, that of general as well as private, is marked by a simple white stone. Arlington became a military cemetery during the Civil War.

President John F. Kennedy is buried at Arlington; his grave is marked by a torch that burns continually. His brother, Senator Robert Kennedy, is also buried there.

The tomb of the Unknown Soldier stands in Arlington Cemetery. The Unknown Soldier was one of the thousands who were killed in World War I, and whose bodies could never be identified. In 1958 the bodies of an unidentified service man from World War II and from the Korean war were buried beside it. The tomb is a memorial to all unknown war dead. It is guarded night and day by a special honor guard. On the tomb are inscribed these words: "Here rests in honored glory a soldier known but to God."

armada

Armada is a Spanish word that means a great fleet of ships. Usually when people speak of "the Armada," they mean the great Spanish fleet of 1588. In that year the Spanish King Philip decided to invade and conquer England. He gathered together the greatest fleet in history, up to that time. The Armada consisted of 130 warships. It was manned by more than 8,000 sailors and the ships carried almost 2,500 cannon. On board the ships there were almost 20,000 soldiers.

The English gathered together 180 ships, not as large as the Spanish warships but faster and manned by better sailors. The English commanders were Lord Howard, Sir John Hawkins and Sir Francis Drake. They fought more skillfully than the Spaniards and finally caused panic among the Spaniards by taking eight ships, filling them with gunpowder, smearing them with tar, setting them on fire, and then letting them drift toward the Spanish fleet. The Armada ran, and if the English had not run out of gunpowder they might have destroyed the entire fleet.

The Spanish admiral ordered the Armada to sail around Scotland and Ireland. A great storm hit the Armada as it was passing between Scotland and the Orkney Islands. The shores of Scotland and Ireland became strewn with the wrecks of Spanish ships. In September and October, fifty-four broken and battered ships finally reached Spain. Only 9,000 men were left of almost 30,000 who had set out several months before.

armadillo

The armadillo is an animal that is related to the anteater. It lives in South America and Central America, and is sometimes found in Texas. Its length is 2 to 2½ feet plus a 12- to 15-inch tail. It weighs 12 to 15 pounds. Its body is covered by a shell much like that of a turtle. This horny shell-like covering is not one piece, but is made up of several overlapping bands. When attacked, the armadillo can roll itself into a ball and be protected by its shell. Also, it can burrow very quickly into the ground and it can run very fast.

The armadillo eats almost anything it can find. In addition to ants and other insects, it eats worms, grubs, small animals, snakes, roots, and leaves. The armadillo has a funny way of crossing a stream or river. It runs rapidly to the bank of the river and then jumps as far as it can. As it lands on the water, air gets caught under its shell and helps the armadillo to float on top of the water.

Am. Museum of Natural History

Armadillo meat is a tasty dish to many people in Central and South America.

Armageddon

Armageddon is the name of a place in Palestine (now a part of Israel) where many battles have been fought, and where Biblical predictions say the last battle of the world will be fought, just before the world comes to an end. It is a large, flat-topped hill in Galilee and Samaria.

Armenia

Armenia is a name that has long been used for a region in Asia, between the Black Sea and the Caspian Sea, where the people called Armenians have lived for thousands of years.

Today, about one-third of this region is the Armenian Soviet Socialist Republic, a part of the Soviet Union, and the rest is in northeast Turkey.

THE ARMENIAN PEOPLE

The Armenian people have their beginnings far back in ancient times. They have been scattered over many countries, but they have always managed to preserve their nationality and their religion. They speak the Armenian language and are members of the Armenian Church, which is an independent Christian church. There are about 3,500,000 Armenians. About 1,502,800 live in the Armenian

S.S.R., about 1,000,000 in other parts of the Soviet Union, and the rest in Turkey and other countries.

The Armenians who live in the country are quite dark, with straight black hair and often large noses. Though they are excellent farmers, they are poorly educated and very superstitious. The Armenians living in the towns and cities are quite different. They look more like the Persians (the people living in Iran), and in fact many of them are descended from Persians whom their forefathers married. They are very intelligent and make good businessmen and merchants, as were their ancestors in Roman times. Many Armenians have come to the United States and have become citizens.

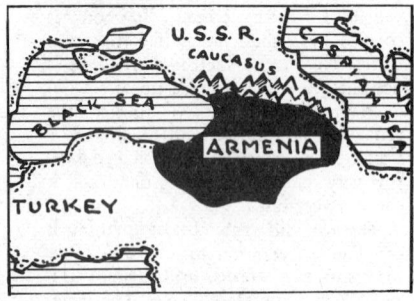

HOW THE PEOPLE LIVE

The majority of the Armenians are farmers. Under many harsh foreign rulers, the farmers were kept poor and ignorant of modern ways of farming. In the past forty years, with the introduction of better irrigation and new machinery, the Armenian farmer has been able to grow more and bigger crops. He raises cotton, grain, tobacco, and grapes and other fruits.

In the larger cities, such as Yerevan (or Erivan), the capital, and Leninakan, the people make cloth, furniture, and artificial rubber.

Once only the children of wealthy families went to school. In recent years more schools have been built, and the children go to them as they do in European and American countries. Once there were no colleges at all for the Armenians, and now there are ten, as well as trade schools. More than three out of four Armenians—all but the older people—can now read and write.

The Armenians like food more highly spiced than Americans do. Their favorite meat is lamb, prepared in various ways. A most popular food among them is called *madzoun*, which is like junket, or clabber.

One of the favorite games of the people is *tavli*, which is their word for backgammon. They also have colorful folk dances and songs, in which men, women and children all join at festivals.

WHAT KIND OF PLACE IT IS

Armenia is high, level country, partly surrounded by mountains that are rich in copper and lead. On the mountain slopes the shepherds tend their flocks of sheep. Mount Ararat is in the Turkish part. The winters are long and severe, and the summers are hot. The farmers get little rain, so they must use artificial irrigation. Although Armenia is quite civilized, such wild beasts as the tiger, bear and leopard still roam in the woods.

HOW THE PEOPLE ARE GOVERNED

The Armenian Soviet Socialist Republic is under Communist rule, which means that the people have no freedom of speech and have no real voice in electing their government. They vote for their governing body, or *soviet*, but they are told whom they must vote for. You can read more about this system of government in the article on the UNION OF SOVIET SOCIALIST REPUBLICS.

ARMENIA IN THE PAST

Many hundreds of years before Christ, Armenia was a powerful kingdom. About 2,300 years ago it was conquered by Alexander the Great, the king who almost ruled the world. After that, one powerful army after another invaded Armenia, and its people were divided up under different rulers, especially the Russians and the Turks.

About sixty years ago, the Armenians living under the Turks suffered from massacres that shocked the whole world. All through the summer of 1895, Armenian men, women and children were killed in great numbers by Turkish soldiers and mobs. The Turkish Sultan did nothing to stop the attacks. Whole villages were destroyed. The worst massacre of all took place in Constantinople, where more than four thousand Armenians were killed. Until World War I, these massacres occurred from time to time, and many Armenians fled to other countries.

At the end of World War I, Northern Armenia was made into a republic. Shortly afterward, it joined the Soviet Union.

ARMENIAN SOVIET SOCIALIST REPUBLIC Area, 11,580 square miles. Population 1,958,-000. Capital, Yerevan (Erivan), population 578,000. Language, Armenian. Religion, Christian. Government, Soviet republic in the U.S.S.R. Monetary unit, U.S.S.R. ruble.

Arminius

Arminius is a hero in the early history of the German people. Most of Europe was then a great wilderness covered with thick forests, and the German people were wild and uncivilized. The Romans in those days ruled most of the civilized world. They sent a big army into central Europe. Arminius gathered other German tribes around him and hid them in the wilderness. The great Roman army was taken completely by surprise and entirely destroyed. Varus, the Roman general, committed suicide in shame at his defeat. This was in the year 9. Arminius was later killed by some of his German enemies. He was born in 17 B.C. and killed in A.D. 21. The modern spelling of his name is Hermann.

armistice and Armistice Day

An armistice is an agreement to stop fighting in a war. It may apply to the whole war, or just to part of it. Sometimes opposing commanders agree to an armistice for a short period of time, to take care of their dead and wounded. After this type of armistice, the fighting begins again. A "cease-fire" is about the same thing. A general armistice stops fighting in an entire war.

When people speak of "the Armistice," they usually mean the one that ended the fighting in World War I.

The World War I armistice was signed in a railroad car near Compiègne, a town in northern France. Generals of the Allied and German armies met there. They agreed to stop fighting at 11 o'clock in the morning on November 11, 1918. The Germans admitted they had lost the war.

There had been a false rumor of an armistice on November 8. In history it is called the "false Armistice."

November 11 was called Armistice Day after 1918, with parades and a minute of silence at 11 A.M. to honor those who died in World War I. After World War II, Congress changed the name to "Veterans Day," to honor the dead of all the wars. In Europe V-E Day, May 8, 1945, when World War II ended in Europe, is a holiday. In the United States it is not.

armor

Armor is what a soldier wears or uses to protect himself in warfare. The use of armor goes back several thousand years. The earliest armor was a crude shield made of wood or leather. The ancient Chinese wore heavily padded suits in battle. More than four thousand years ago the Assyrians and Babylonians, who lived in what is now Iraq, Syria, and Lebanon, used body armor, shields, and helmets, made of leather and bronze. About 2,500 years ago the Etruscans, a people who lived in what is now Italy, wore metal breastplates, leg guards, and helmets. The soldiers of ancient Greece and Rome usually wore armor.

THE ARMOR WORN BY KNIGHTS

The greatest use of armor was seen during the Middle Ages. The Normans who conquered England in the year 1066 wore coats of linked chains. This chain armor was known as "mail."

The men who made armor were called armorers. They were among the most skilled craftsmen of the Middle Ages. They made gloves of chain mail, in addition to the coats and tunics. The helmets worn during this time were usually bowl-shaped and made of iron. Chain mail was rarely used after the 14th century. It was replaced by armor made of plates of metal. The first solid-plate metal armor was used to cover only the elbows, kneecaps, and other small parts of the body.

The knights of the 15th century wore complete suits of plate armor. From head to toe, they were completely encased in these metal suits. The suits were hinged at the shoulders, elbows, hips and knees. Otherwise the knight would not have been able to move around. Some of the suits were so heavy that the knights had to be lifted onto their horses. These knights wore helmets that completely covered their heads and faces. The helmets had visors in front through which the knight could see. The visors could also be raised. When a knight met a friendly knight, he raised his visor so the other knight could see who he was. Our custom of tipping our hats in greeting may have come from this.

The armor worn by the knights in the Middle Ages was often highly decorated. The skilled armorers engraved designs on the metal. The knights carried shields that were beautifully painted and decorated with their coats of arms. Even the horses wore armor. Usually a horse's armor protected his head, his neck, and the front of his body.

When firearms came to be used, in the 16th century, the use of armor began to decline. Bullets would go through the metal suits. The King of Sweden from 1611 until 1632, named Gustavus Adolphus, gave up wearing his armor, and kept only his metal helmet. His soldiers loyally followed him in discarding their armor. After that, armor was worn less and less by the armies of Europe.

MODERN ARMOR

Armor became useful again in World War I. The soldiers of all the armies wore metal helmets. These helmets were made of hardened steel, and were useful in protecting the soldier's head against injury from the fragments of bursting shells. The helmets used in World War II were better than those used in World War I. They were deeper and protected more of the head and back of the neck.

Some body armor was also used in World War II. Many American fliers wore "flak suits." These suits were really nothing more than vests and aprons. The vests and aprons had many pockets in them, into which small plates of metal were placed. These flak suits saved many fliers from injury. (The word *flak* comes from the German word for anti-aircraft artillery.)

Many experiments have been made with bullet-proof clothing. During the Korean War, the United States soldiers sometimes wore bullet-proof clothing. It was usually made of a lightweight plastic material, several layers in thickness. These bullet-proof articles of clothing could stop all but a direct hit.

The word "armor" is also used to describe tanks and cars that are protected by heavy metal plates. Today we speak of an *armored division*. This means a division of soldiers that has tanks and armored vehicles of many kinds. The tanks and armored vehicles are made of very strong steel. Armor plate is also used on warships. The sides, decks and turrets of a warship are strengthened by additional thicknesses of steel plate. In airplanes, the pilot's cockpit may be protected by armor plate. The armor plate in an airplane must be thin and light. An airplane would be slowed down if the weight of the armor were too great.

Armour, Philip

Philip Danforth Armour was a founder of the great meat-packing industry in the United States. He was born in 1832 and after the Civil War ended in 1865 he and his brother Herman Armour bought a grain business in Chicago and added a meat department. Philip Armour pioneered in developing refrigerated freight cars for the shipping of meat, and also in canning meat and in developing by-products such as drugs from cattle used for meat. He died in 1901.

Armstrong, Edwin

Edwin Howard Armstrong was an engineer, the inventor of FM radio and other important improvements in radio. He was born in New York City in 1890. In 1918 he developed the superheterodyne radio and in 1939 FM. In 1954 he committed suicide, in New York City; his reason for that is not known.

Armstrong, Louis

Louis Armstrong is considered by many to have been the greatest jazz trumpeter that ever lived. Music experts credit him, more than anyone else, with developing the Negro music of New Orleans into an art form that became famous all over the world.

He was born in New Orleans on July 4, 1900. Shortly afterward, his father deserted the family, and Louis grew up in extreme poverty. As a child, he helped support his mother, sister, and himself by singing on the streets for pennies, and by doing any other odd jobs he could get. When he was 13 he was sent to a boys' home, where he met Peter Davis, an instructor there, who taught him to play the bugle and the cornet. He joined the home's band, and played at funerals, picnics, and social gatherings. After 18 months at the boys' home, he left with the equivalent of a 5th-grade education, the only schooling he ever had. Working as a junkman and selling coal to support himself, he seized every opportunity to play in small, local bands. While he was with Fate Marable's band on the Mississippi river boat *Sidney,* one of the players taught him to read music. At the age of 22 he became second cornetist in "King" Oliver's famous jazz band in Chicago, and made his first recordings. The pianist in that band was Lilian Hardin, a trained musician, who gave him his first real musical education. They were married in 1924. She convinced him that, in order to make headway in music, it would be wise to leave the band, which he did. Later he joined the Fletcher Henderson orchestra at the Roseland Ballroom in New York. There he met many trained musicians, and was greatly educated and influenced by

them.

In 1925 he returned to Chicago, where he gave up the cornet for the trumpet, and began to make records under his own name. By 1929 he was world famous. In 1932 he made a tour of Europe, where, in London, a music magazine editor invented the name "Satchmo," a garbled version of his earlier nickname, "Satchelmouth." During the next 30 years he made many tours of Europe, the Far East, the Middle East, South America, and Africa, where he received large and enthusiastic receptions. He said he felt "at home" in Africa. No one, not even Armstrong himself, knew how many recordings he made, but the estimate is about 1,500, of which many are now rare collectors' items. He died in New York in July, 1971. In New Orleans, a jazz museum was built around the remains of the shack where he was born.

Armstrong, Neil

Neil Armstrong was the first man to set foot on the moon. He was born August 5, 1930 on his grandparents' farm near Wapakoneta, Ohio. As a teen-ager he had many interests, including music and Scouting, but his earliest and most important interest was in aviation. He began taking flying lessons at the age of fourteen and received his pilot's license on his sixteenth birthday.

In 1947 he entered Purdue University to study aeronautical engineering as a Naval Air Cadet. After two years there he was called to active duty and was sent to Pensacola, Florida for flight training, and from there to Korea, where he flew 78 combat missions. He was shot down once, and won three Air Medals. After the Korean conflict, he returned to Purdue and received his B.S. degree in 1955.

After spending the next seven years as a test pilot, Armstrong volunteered for America's astronaut program. As the command pilot of Gemini 8, Armstrong, with Air Force Major David Scott, performed the first manual space docking maneuver in history on March 13, 1966. On January 9, 1969, the National Aeronautics and Space Administration announced that Armstrong, Edwin E. Aldrin, Jr., and Michael Collins (all space-flight veterans) would be the crew for Apollo 11, which would land men on the moon. At

exactly 10:56 p.m., eastern daylight time, on July 20, 1969, Armstrong stepped onto the moon's surface and spoke these famous words: "That's one small step for a man, one giant leap for mankind."

army

An army is a group of armed and equipped men joined together to fight a war on land. In an army, the soldiers are organized under the leadership of

officers and commanders. The first armies were nothing more than all the men of a tribe fighting together under their chief. Then special men came to be chosen to be the soldiers in a nation. The first really organized armies were those in Egypt, more than 3,500 years ago. The early Egyptian armies were composed entirely of foot soldiers. These soldiers carried spears and bows and arrows. Not many years later the Assyrian and Babylonian armies had not only foot soldiers, but soldiers in horse-drawn chariots.

The early Greek city-states had armies that were well organized. Pehaps the greatest army of early times was led by ALEXANDER THE GREAT, about whom there is a separate article. His army conquered most of the civilized world of that time. The Romans, not long after the time of Alexander, had the best-organized of all ancient armies. The men were well-trained and led by excellent officers. The Roman armies were composed of smaller groups called legions. A legion was much like an army division today. The Roman legions were practically unbeatable. They were often outnumbered, but their training and organization were able to overcome the larger groups of the enemy. The Romans had the first army engineers, who built roads and bridges. The Romans also had the best organization for supplying food and equipment to their armies.

The Roman Empire finally grew weak and fell to the barbarians. The civilized world was plunged into the Dark Ages, and the art of military organization was forgotten for centuries. During those centuries, armies were mostly groups of peasants led by mounted knights. These armies had very little organization, and were often made up of soldiers who would fight for anyone who would pay them. They usually spent more time in robbing the people than in fighting a battle.

THE FIRST MODERN ARMIES

The first signs of modern military organization appeared in the 15th century. The Turks invaded Europe and took many young boys as prisoners. They trained these young captives as soldiers. These soldiers became known as the Janizaries. The Janizaries were the first real standing, or permanent, army of modern history.

During the 17th century, many nations in Europe began to have standing armies, trained and organized into regiments. The soldiers in each regiment were subject to rules and discipline. They began to wear regular uniforms. Each regiment was commanded by a noble with the rank of colonel. These nobles often knew little about fighting.

Frederick the Great, king of a German country called Prussia, in the 18th century, was one of the first commanders to train his army thoroughly. He made his small army the best in Europe. Napoleon, whom some consider the greatest of all army commanders, invented much of the system that is used in armies today. He had infantry, artillery and cavalry soldiers in each division. Two or more divisions formed a corps. Napoleon could give commands through an organized system of officers, heading corps, divisions, and regiments.

During the 19th century almost all of the European nations adopted universal military service. Every young man had to give a year or two of his life to military training and duty. Before this, most of the soldiers were volunteers. In the American Civil War, the draft was used by the United States for the first time. Every young man picked in the draft had to serve unless he was unfit for duty. The 19th century also saw the rise of the great German army. The Germans used railroads to transport the soldiers from one place to another. They were the first to have a general staff. This meant they had a group of high officers who made plans for battle. By World War I, all armies had general staffs.

For modern army methods see the next article, on the U.S. ARMY.

Army, U. S.

The United States Army is the organization of soldiers trained to defend the United States and fight its battles on land wherever the enemy may be. The United States Army was born on June 14, 1775 — long before there was any "United States." On that day General Washington took command of the militias, or local armies, of the American colonies. There has been a United States Army ever since.

The size of the Army has not always been the same. During wars, the Army grows in size, and during peacetime it shrinks. There were only about five hundred soldiers in the United States Army in 1789, when the first Congress met. There were more than eight million soldiers in the Army in 1945, at the end of World War II. Congress decides how many men will be in the Army at any one time.

VOLUNTEERS AND THE DRAFT

A *volunteer* is a person who goes to an Army Recruiting Station and says he wants to join the Army. When there are not enough volunteers to supply all the soldiers the country needs, Congress passes a law to *draft* men—that is, to make them join the Army. There were "wartime drafts" during the Civil War and during World War I. Just before the United States entered World War II, Congress passed the first "peacetime draft law." That was in 1940. When the United States entered World War II, in 1941, the peacetime draft had helped to make the Army big enough.

The crisis in Vietnam caused the Army to be increased to more than a million men without change in the peacetime draft law, which is: Men liable to the draft may volunteer and choose the branch of service they wish to enter; if they are drafted, they are placed as the Government wishes. All men from 18½ to 26 years of age can be drafted into the Army.

Men who volunteer and men who are drafted start Army life in the same way and undergo the same training.

WHAT HAPPENS WHEN A MAN ENTERS THE ARMY

All those who volunteer and all those who are drafted are given a complete medical examination. Only those who are physically fit are accepted for Army service. The Army sends these men to training camps somewhere in the United States. The young soldiers stay at their first camp for at least eight weeks. Here they receive what is called *basic training*. Each new soldier is given his Army clothing, and other articles he will need. The clothing issue includes five cotton summer uniforms and two woolen winter uniforms. Everything else he will wear in the Army is issued to him at this time. He gets shoes, underwear, socks, an overcoat, a blouse (jacket), towels, caps, work uniforms, a belt, a raincoat, and ties. He also receives two barrack bags to hold his clothing, a canteen for water, a mess kit for his food when he is in the field (in the Army *mess* means "food"), bedding, and a bedding roll and knapsack.

The new soldier lives in a barracks with many other new soldiers. He must keep his bed and belongings neat and clean. All the soldiers are responsible for keeping the barracks clean. They are inspected every day.

The new soldier spends his first few days at camp in getting used to his new surroundings. Wearing the uniform is the first step in making him feel like a soldier. He attends many lectures, and learns things about Army life. He is told about his duties, and his rights, in the Army. He learns about military law, and military courtesy and customs. He is taught how to keep himself clean and healthy. He is given shots to inoculate him against typhoid fever and lockjaw, and he is vaccinated against smallpox.

BASIC TRAINING

The new soldier is given basic infantry training during his first eight weeks in the Army. He learns how to drill and march in formation. He spends several hours each day on the drill field, learning how to keep in step and how to make military turns. He is given a rifle, and he learns how to take care of it. He is shown how to take the rifle apart and put it together again, and how to keep it clean. When he is thoroughly familiar with the rifle, he is taken to the firing range and given target practice. He also learns how to use the bayonet and the hand grenade. Later he is given training with mortars, machineguns, and bazookas. He is taught how to protect himself in case of chemical attack. He puts on a gas mask and goes through a room filled with tear gas.

During these first eight weeks, the soldier is also given physical training. For an hour or two each day he does all sorts of exercises. This helps to harden him and make him stronger. He continues to attend lectures. He learns more about military justice and law, and is also given information on what is going on in the world, and why it is necessary for him to be in the Army. He also learns one of the most important things in his Army career. This is the necessity for teamwork. The Army depends on teamwork. Every soldier must work together with every other soldier. Teamwork also depends on discipline. Every soldier must obey all the orders and commands that are given to him. With-

out discipline there could be no effective Army.

The new soldier also spends time in kitchen police (this is work done in the Army kitchen or mess hall), and other jobs that have to be done around an Army camp, such as cleaning up (called "policing"). Not all of his time is spent in work and training, however. Each evening he is allowed to relax and do whatever he wishes. He may go to a movie in the camp, write letters, read, watch television, or just chat with his buddies. He may also go to the PX (Post Exchange, a sort of store) and buy things, drink soda, eat ice cream and cake, or play games. The soldier may receive visitors, such as his family and friends, on Sunday afternoons.

At the end of eight weeks, the new soldier is usually sent to another camp for an additional eight weeks of training. At the new camp he will be trained in the branch of the Army to which he has been assigned. It may be the infantry, the artillery, the engineers, the signal corps, or one of the other branches of the Army. He is taught how to use and operate the special tools, equipment and weapons of his new branch.

At the end of his sixteen weeks of basic training, the soldier is usually sent to join a unit. The unit is the group with which he will identify himself. It may be a division in the infantry, a battery in the field artillery, or some other group.

Some soldiers are sent to schools where they may learn special skills, such as radio repair and operation, truck and auto mechanics, cooking, clerking and typing, radar operation, and many others.

All through the basic training period, the new soldier remains a private. He cannot be promoted until he is through with his training.

RANK IN THE ARMY

The Army is divided into two main groups, *officers* (also called *commissioned officers*) and *enlisted men*. In each group there are various ranks, or grades. Every time a man is promoted to a higher grade in his group he receives more pay. These are the grades:

ENLISTED MEN	OFFICERS
Sergeant Major (highest)	General of the Army (highest)
First Sergeant or Master Sergeant	General
Sergeant 1st Class	Lieutenant General
Staff Sergeant	Major General
Sergeant	Brigadier General
Corporal	Colonel
The above are called Noncommissioned Officers	Lieutenant Colonel
	Major
	Captain
Private 1st Class	First Lieutenant
Private (lowest)	Second Lieutenant (lowest)

Every officer ranks above every enlisted man. An enlisted man is required to treat an officer with respect, by saluting him and saying "Sir" when he speaks to him. Officers and enlisted men do not live or eat together, and are not supposed to go together socially. This is because experience has shown that an army loses fewer men in battle if there are no personal feelings between the officers, who command, and the enlisted men, who must obey the commands.

There is a special class called *warrant officers,* who rank between officers and enlisted men but are given the courtesies and privileges of officers. Warrant officers usually have special skills in technical duties, such as accounting, traffic management, and other jobs that are not connected with actual fighting. Of course, many officers and enlisted men also work at jobs like these.

An enlisted man can become an officer if he is chosen for an Officer Candidate School and passes all the tests. If he does pass, he will first receive a commission as a second lieutenant.

Women can have the same ranks in the Army as men. You can read about this in the separate article on WOMEN IN THE ARMED FORCES.

ARMY PAY

In 1941, an Army private was paid only $21 a month, but Congress voted several pay increases, and in 1973 a private was receiving $307.20 a month. As one advances in rank he receives more pay. A general receives a base pay of $2,263.50, and in addition receives allowances for food and quarters. An enlisted man who serves overseas receives additional pay for foreign service, and soldiers who engage in very dangerous duty receive extra pay. This includes parachute-jumping, for which an enlisted man receives an extra $55 a month, and an officer an extra $110 a month.

TIME IN THE ARMY

The Army day is divided differently from the civilian day. In the Army, A.M. and P.M. are not used. There is one 24-hour day. At 1 o'clock in the afternoon, the Army time is "1300 hours." At six-thirty in the evening it is "1830 hours." The Army indicates different times of the day by bugle calls. The bugle was formerly used to call men for different formations, and different activities. Today the bugle is not used in some places, but the name of the bugle call is still used to indicate a particular time. The most important bugle calls are *reveille,* when the soldiers have to get up; *mess call,* which comes three times a day to call the soldiers to their meals; *assembly,* which is the main call for the soldiers to fall into formation; *retreat,* when the day's work ends and the flag is lowered; and *taps,* when all Army activity ends and the lights go out. In many places, the bugle calls are now played on a phonograph record and broadcast over loudspeakers.

THE SALUTE AND OTHER RULES

One of the first thing a soldier learns in the Army is the salute, which is given by smartly raising the right hand, with the fingers straight out and together, to the right eyebrow. All enlisted men are required to salute officers, and junior officers are required to salute higher-ranking officers. The officer who is saluted must return the salute. Soldiers also salute when the flag passes by and when the national anthem is played.

When a soldier is carrying a rifle, he salutes in a different manner. "Present arms!" is an order for a formal salute:

He holds his rifle straight up and down in front of him. In the less formal *rifle salute* the rifle is still upright but at the soldier's side; he does this when he is standing guard. Guard duty is performed by all soldiers. A soldier on guard duty usually walks his post for two hours, and then rests for four hours. This schedule goes on for one whole day, with the soldier alternately standing guard for two hours and resting for four. Each day the guard is changed in a formal military ceremony known as the *guard mount.* The old guard hands over the duties of guarding the post to the new guard. As the new guard takes over, the old guard smartly marches away.

The guard is under the command of a different officer each day. The officer is called the officer of the day. He is the official representative of the commander of the post or camp. He is responsible to the commander for everything that happens in the camp during that day.

Every soldier in the Army is governed by the uniform code of military justice. This was once known as the *Articles of War.* Under the code, or the Articles of War, the soldier must obey all the rules and regulations that have been made for him. A company commander can give his men light punishment for small offenses. All serious cases are tried by what is called a *court-martial.* Several officers form a court-martial and listen to the cases brought before them. The court-martial has the power to punish all military crimes.

Every soldier is allowed thirty days leave each year. He is also sometimes given passes that allow him to go home for periods from one to three days. The passes depend on his good behavior and the custom of the camp to which he has been assigned.

BRANCHES OF THE ARMY

The United States Army is divided into what are called *Arms* and *Services.* The *Arms* are the fighting branches of the Army, and the *Services* are the ones that are mainly connected with supplying the fighting branches.

The Arms include infantry, artillery, and armor.

The Services are called *ancillary.* They include the chemical corps, the quartermaster corps, the finance department, the ordnance corps, the medical corps, the adjutant general's department, the corps of chaplains, the transportation corps, and the judge advocate general's department. The adjutant general's department is concerned with keeping the records of the Army. The judge advocate general's department is concerned with military law. The ordnance corps furnishes the guns and weapons. The corps of engineers and the signal corps are considered both Arms and Services. Some of their duties are fighting or being at the front lines, and others are concerned with servicing and supplying the front-line troops.

Each branch of the Army is divided into many types and sizes of units. Let's look at the infantry. The smallest group in the infantry is the *squad,* which consists of eight men, usually plus a sergeant, who leads it. Several squads make up a *platoon,* which is usually led by a

second lieutenant. Three rifle platoons and a weapons platoon make up a *company*. A weapons platoon has recoilless rifles and mortars. A company is commanded by a captain. It is considered the soldier's home, since he eats, sleeps, trains and fights with his company. There are about two hundred men in a company. Companies are identified by letters—such as Company A, Company B, Company C, etc. In Army slang, words are used for the initials: Company D is "Dog Company," Company F is "Fox Company."

Three rifle companies and a weapons company make up a *battalion*, which is usually commanded by a lieutenant colonel. Three battalions usually make up a *brigade*, commanded by a colonel. It is the basic fighting force of the Army. A brigade may be selected to do a particular job of fighting.

Three to five brigades usually make up a *division*. A division is commanded by a major general, and it is the smallest unit of the Army that is virtually an army in itself. This is so because it combines all of the Arms and many of the Services. In addition to the three infantry regiments, a division has a battalion of tanks, several battalions of field artillery, a battalion of engineers, a signal company, an intelligence company, and several other service units. There are also armored divisions, and airborne divisions, which have particular jobs in a war. There are about fifteen thousand men in each division. All the soldiers in a division wear the shoulder patch of that division.

An *army* is made up of several divisions and various Service groups. A lieutenant general is usually in command of an army, but during wartime an army may be commanded by a full general. During World War II, there were as many as a dozen different fighting armies in the United States Army. They were scattered over Europe and the Pacific. In peacetime, the United States is divided into five army areas. The headquarters of these five armies are at Fort Meade, Maryland; Fort McPherson, Georgia; Fort Sheridan, Illinois; Fort Sam Houston, Texas; and the Presidio, in San Francisco, California. There may also be one or more armies overseas. For example, after World War II the United States kept one occupation army in Germany, and another in Japan and other parts of the Far East.

WHAT A SOLDIER SHOULD KNOW

The United States Army has had a long and colorful history. It has been large and it has been small. It has fought wars all over the earth, and it has served its country in peacetime. Through it all, the Army has developed, become more efficient and more modern. In the old days a young soldier was often bullied and treated roughly; today, while he is thoroughly trained and disciplined, he is treated as a human being.

The main point of the Army training and the Army way of life is to make each soldier feel "that he is the best soldier, in the best platoon, in the best company, in the best regiment, in the best division, in the best army, in the best country in the world."

See also the articles on NATIONAL GUARD, UNITED STATES MILITARY ACADEMY, and the section on *Women's*

Army Corps in the article WOMEN IN THE ARMED FORCES.

Arnold, Benedict

Benedict Arnold was an American general in the Revolutionary War. He  is remembered as a brave and skillful soldier, but unfortunately he is also remembered as a traitor who betrayed his country and went over to the British side.

He was born in Norwich, Connecticut, in 1741, so he was only 34 years old when fighting broke out in 1775 between the American colonies and the British. He had been a druggist and bookseller in New Haven, and had sailed to the West Indies on a trading ship. Now he raised a company of soldiers and helped Ethan Allen to capture Fort Ticonderoga (see the article on ETHAN ALLEN). In 1776, when he was barely 35 years old, he was made a brigadier general, and he fought bravely for America in several battles.

Though he was so young, Arnold became angry when five other men were appointed to the rank of major general ahead of him. Even though he was made a major general soon after, he remained dissatisfied. He was put in command of American troops at Philadelphia, and while he was there he married a beautiful young woman who sympathized with the British. This may have had some effect on what he did later. Anyway, in 1780 when he was put in charge of the American fort at West Point, in New York (where the United States Military Academy now is), he decided to go over to the British side and gave the plans of the fort to the British Major John ANDRÉ, (about whom there is a separate article). André was caught, but Arnold escaped to England. The British, too, despised him as a traitor and he lived a very unhappy life in England until he died there, in 1804.

Arnold, Henry Harley

The first head of the United States Air Force (and the first person ever to  hold the rank of General of the Air Force) was General Henry Harley Arnold, whose nickname was "Hap" Arnold. General Arnold was born in Gladwyne, Pennsylvania in 1886, and was graduated from the United States Military Academy at West Point in 1907. As a lieutenant in the United States Army he was assigned to the work of experimenting with the airplane, which was then new and unproved. Throughout World War II he headed the Army Air Corps, and when the Air Force became a separate service in 1947 he was its first head. He died in 1950.

Arnold, Matthew and Thomas

Matthew Arnold was an English poet and writer and was the most respected critic of the works of other writers. He was born in 1822. His early poems, written in the years 1841 to 1845,

gave him a good reputation as a writer. He was professor of poetry at Oxford from 1857 to 1867. He wrote many essays and made several lecture tours, including two in the United States. His best-known poems include "Thyrsis" and "Rugby Chapel." He died in 1888.

Thomas Arnold, father of Matthew Arnold, was an English clergyman and for 14 years was headmaster at Rugby, a famous school for boys in England. The headmaster in the book *Tom Brown's School Days,* once very popular among boys, was based on Dr. Arnold. He was born in 1795 and died in 1842. His son's poem "Rugby Chapel" was written in memory of him.

Arpad

Arpad, who lived about a thousand years ago, was a national hero of Hungary. His father, Amos, was leader of the Magyar people who settled Hungary in the 9th century. Arpad was the first Magyar king of Hungary and greatly extended its possessions. He died in 907. It is not known when he was born.

arsenal

An arsenal is a factory or a storage place for war equipment such as guns, ammunition, and other supplies used by soldiers and sailors.

There are still several arsenals in the United States, owned by the government. Among them are the Rock Island Arsenal in Illinois, and the Springfield Arsenal in Massachusetts, which makes rifles used by the United States Army.

arsenic

Arsenic is a metal that is soft and brittle and can easily be pounded into a powder. It is an *element*—it is not made by mixing other metals together. It is bluish-gray in color and has a shiny surface that easily becomes dull and tarnished when exposed to the air. Arsenic is found in rocks and earth in many parts of the world, most often in the ores of iron, cobalt, and silver. There is little arsenic mined in North America.

When people speak of arsenic, they usually mean a deadly poison. Pure arsenic is not very poisonous, but mixed with other things it is one of the deadliest poisons known to man. It mixes easily with oxygen and with other metals. Arsenic poisons are used to kill insects (particularly those that destroy fruit), and as weed-killers. Arsenicals, medicines containing arsenic, were once important but most of them have been replaced by antibiotics.

arson

Arson is a crime—the unlawful burning of or setting fire to a building or any other kind of property. A person who accidentally sets fire to property is not committing arson. Those who commit arson may also be charged with murder, if anyone is burned to death in the fire. Arson may also be charged against a person who sets fire to his own property, if by setting the fire purposely he hoped to collect insurance.

art

When men copy the beauties of nature, or make beautiful things that they

invent themselves, and do so very skill-fully, it is called *art*.

The *fine arts* are painting, sculpture, architecture, poetry and other fine writing, music, drama (plays on the stage), and dancing. Other arts are known as the *useful,* or *decorative, arts;* these include pottery-making, dress-designing, weaving, and many others in which useful things can be made beautiful. Often the *graphic arts* are considered a separate branch. The graphic arts are printing, bookbinding, and other processes of making books and printed matter.

The love of beauty seems to be something that man is born with. More than fifteen thousand years ago, primitive and ignorant cavemen drew pictures on the walls of their caves, and some of them—for example, the paintings of bulls and bison and other animals on the walls of caves near Altamira, in Spain, and in other parts of Europe—are a match for many of the best modern paintings. More than two thousand years ago the ancient Greeks made statues that are at least as good as, and some believe better than, anything that has been done since.

There are separate stories on all the different kinds of art, PAINTING, and SCULPTURE, and MUSIC, and others.

COMMERCIAL ART

Thousands of men and women make a career of *commercial art*. This means that they prepare the illustrations and the other printed matter that is used in advertisements and in publications such as books, magazines, and newspapers. Commercial artists may be *illustrators,* and actually draw the pictures to illustrate books, articles, or advertising, but more often they do what is called *mechanical work:* lettering; designing *layouts* (the position of type and pictures on a printed sheet); and *paste-ups* or *mechanicals,* the final preparation of material that is to be photographed and printed.

Commercial art is closely related to the graphic arts. A commercial artist must know a great deal about printing, the reproduction of pictures in printed form, and photography. A commercial artist makes a good living but does not often become as famous as a "creative artist" such as a painter or sculptor does. There are many schools that train commercial artists.

Artaxerxes

Three kings of ancient Persia were named Artaxerxes. During their reigns the Persian Empire became the greatest on earth. **Artaxerxes I** lived from 465 B.C. to 425 B.C. He was the son of Xerxes, an even greater king. **Artaxerxes II** was king from 405 B.C. to 360 B.C. He ruled Persia at the height of its power. He was called the Great King and many other kings paid tribute to him. Cyrus the Younger, brother of Artaxerxes II, revolted against him in 401 B.C.; Artaxerxes defeated him at the Battle of Cunaxa, where Cyrus was killed. The Greek historian Xenophon told about this in a famous history, the *Anabasis*. **Artaxerxes III,** who lived from 360 B.C. to 338 B.C., was noted for cruelty and was poisoned by a servant.

arteries

The arteries are the tubes that carry blood from the heart to all parts of the body. (The tubes that carry blood back to the heart are called *veins*.)

The name artery comes from the Greek language, in which *arteria* means "an air-keeper." The Greeks, thousands of years ago, believed that the arteries carried the air one breathes in.

The arteries are round hollow tubes, much like macaroni or rubber tubing. The walls of an artery have three layers. The outer layer is elastic, as rubber is. The middle layer is a muscle. The inner layer is smooth and transparent.

When the heart beats it pumps blood into the arteries. The main artery leading from the heart is called the *aorta*. Blood flows from the aorta into many other arteries. The arteries branch off into smaller and smaller arteries as they carry the blood through the body.

The blue blood vessels seen under the surface of the skin are veins. The arteries are buried deeper inside the body. When a vein is cut, the blood usually flows out slowly. When an artery is cut, the blood gushes out in spurts.

Arteries, like other parts of the human body, may become diseased. Such diseases are almost always found in very old people. The most common form of arterial disease is called *arteriosclerosis.* This means "hardening of the arteries." The arteries lose their elasticity and are apt to break and crack.

See also the articles BLOOD, HEART, and HUMAN BODY.

artesian well

An artesian well brings water to the earth's surface from far below the ground. Since early times man has known that water could be found below the earth's surface, even where there were no streams or rivers, lakes or ponds. Man learned to dig holes, called *wells,* to reach the water underground. Most of these wells are shallow and are called *surface wells;* such wells are usually no more than 20 feet deep. An artesian well is usually at least 200 feet deep, and some are more than 2,000 feet deep.

An artesian well is made by drilling into the ground, often in the same way that oil wells are drilled. The hole made by the drill must strike a layer of spongy sandstone that runs underground from some higher (a hilly or mountainous) place far away, and that has soaked up water. The sandstone must lie between layers of hard rock that do not hold water. When the drill reaches the sandstone bearing water, the water will come up through the drilled hole. This happens because the water is under pressure. The pressure is built up because of the water running down from the higher ground.

The principle of the artesian well can be shown in a simple home experiment. Take a large funnel or rubber water bag and attach a rubber tube at the bottom. Fill the funnel or bag with water and hold the tube in a loop with the open end *above* the level of the funnel or bag. No water will run out. Then lower the open end of the tube

below the surface of the funnel or bag. The water will start to run out of the tube. This is because the water at the open end of the tube is trying to rise up to the level of the water in the funnel or bag.

arthritis

Arthritis is a disease that affects the joints of the body. The word means "inflammation of the joints."

Just as a machine needs oil to run well, the joints of the body need oil. The small amount of necessary oil comes oozing out of the ends of the bones and lines the sockets of such joints as the knee and the hip. Arthritis occurs because the joints become dry.

A person can get arthritis in two ways. He may be bruised, or suffer a broken bone, which allows air and infection to reach the joint. Or he may get arthritis in old age because the joints dry up. This type of arthritis is called rheumatism. Rheumatism can also come from exposure to damp weather, colds, infections and inflammations.

There are several treatments to ease the pain of arthritis, but so far there has been no cure that works in every case. The use of some drugs, such as *ACTH* and *cortisone,* has helped some people to recover from crippling arthritis, but aspirin works about as well. Doctors sometimes prescribe a combination of aspirin and hormones. See also the article on HORMONES.

Chester Arthur

Chester Alan Arthur was President of the United States from 1881 to 1885, the twenty-first man to be president. He had been elected vice-president in 1880; but President James Garfield was assassinated and died after serving for only a few months. That made Arthur president for almost a full term.

History has not made President Arthur a very famous man. The years when he

Gale Research Co.

was president are called "uneventful." But he was honest and capable, and some of his acts as president were more valuable to the United States, in the long run, than the acts of more famous presidents.

One thing that President Arthur did was to put the Civil Service into effect.

Before that, too many employees of the United States Government had been appointed for political reasons. The Civil Service brought in a system by which capable men could get jobs by passing examinations and keep them even if a new political party came into power. This made the government more efficient.

President Arthur was a Republican. He was a good-looking and charming man, very popular socially. His only enemies were dishonest politicians whom he would not help.

HIS EARLY YEARS

Chester Arthur was the first man born in Vermont to become president. (The only other one was Calvin Coolidge.) Arthur was born on October 5, 1830, in Fairfield, Vermont, a very small town in the northwest part of the state, about forty miles from the Canadian border. It was a farming community, and he was the son of the town's Baptist minister. He attended Union College in Schenectady, New York, studied law, and became a lawyer in New York City when he was 23 years old.

As a lawyer, Arthur was quite successful and also attracted some notice. Those were the years just before the Civil War. In the South, nearly four million Negroes were slaves; in the northern states, there was no slavery. Arthur succeeded in freeing a slave who had run away from a southern slave state to the free northern state of New York. It was an important case because there were many runaway slaves, and the Fugitive Slave Laws were bitterly argued.

When he was 29 years old, Arthur married Miss Ellen Lewis Herndon of Virginia. They had three children, but one died as a baby.

The Civil War broke out in 1861, and Chester Arthur joined the militia of New York State. He was promoted finally to the position of quartermaster general, which meant he was in charge of supplying the New York troops with uniforms, food, and other supplies.

HOW HE BECAME PRESIDENT

As a lawyer in New York, Arthur had been an active member of the Republican Party. After the war, he was given an appointment that was looked upon as a fine political reward. He was made Collector of the Port of New York. This means he was in charge of collecting the customs taxes on goods shipped into New York from foreign countries.

There was much dishonesty in government in those days, and when Rutherford B. Hayes became President of the United States in 1877 he cleaned out many dishonest employees. Arthur was not accused of dishonesty, but he was asked to resign nevertheless. He refused to resign, because that would seem to be admitting he had been dishonest. President Hayes forced him to give up the office anyway, but Arthur's reputation and his standing with the party remained good enough so that in the Republican convention of 1880 he received the nomination for vice-president.

Then came the assassination of President Garfield, and on September 19, 1881 Chester Alan Arthur became the president.

WHAT ARTHUR ACCOMPLISHED

The most long-lasting achievement of President Arthur's administration was the CIVIL SERVICE ACT, about which there is a separate article. He was not a strong president in some respects, because he did not control or influence many of the laws passed by Congress, and sometimes they passed important laws against his wishes or over his veto. But he dutifully executed the laws that Congress did pass.

President Arthur wanted to be re-elected, but the Republican Party would not renominate him in 1884. Instead, they nominated James G. Blaine, who lost the election to the Democratic candidate, Grover Cleveland. President Arthur lived less than two years after his term ended, dying on November 18, 1886. His wife had died in 1880, even before he was nominated for the vice-presidency.

Arthur, King

The story of King Arthur and his Knights of the Round Table has been told and retold for hundreds of years and is one of the great stories of all time. Many books have been written about King Arthur and his men, and several movies have pictured their great adventures. Most of the stories were made up, but some of them were based on things that actually happened.

There probably was a real King Arthur, who was king of a British people that lived in England more than 1,500 years ago and who led them in battles against the Anglo-Saxons who invaded England. This real King Arthur was a great hero, but not nearly as great as the King Arthur of the stories. In the Middle Ages the people loved to hear stories of great warriors, as told by troubadours and minstrels who traveled around telling stories and singing ballads. The troubadours and the people of about seven hundred years ago did not know how warriors fought or dressed for battle in the time of the real King Arthur. They told of Arthur and his knights as though they were knights of the Middle Ages, wearing the kind of armor that was worn many hundreds of years after Arthur actually lived.

THE STORY OF ARTHUR

According to the stories, Arthur was the son of a king called Uther Pendragon. When Arthur was born, his father gave him to a friendly knight to bring up as the knight's own son. The young Arthur grew up not knowing that he was the son of the king. When Arthur was a young man, his father, Uther Pendragon, died. The story tells that there was a sword in a stone. The rightful king would be the man who could pull the sword out of the stone. Many tried, but none could budge the sword from the stone. Finally Arthur quite easily pulled the sword from the stone. He was hailed as the new king.

The story of King Arthur goes on to tell how he won the fair Guinevere and made her his queen. It tells how he estab-

lished the Round Table, where he and his knights would eat and meet to decide questions of war. Many of the knights in the story of King Arthur are famous. Among the best known are Sir Lancelot, Sir Galahad, Sir Gawain, Sir Bedivere, and Sir Percivale. All these knights were brave, honest, courteous, and loyal. There were other knights who were evil men. One of them was Sir Modred, who finally wounded the king and caused his death. Merlin, the great magician, was King Arthur's counselor.

The stories of King Arthur and his Round Table have been made into plays, operas, and movies. This is a movie King Arthur.

20th-Century Fox

King Arthur lived and had a great castle in a place called Camelot. He and his knights often journeyed to far-off places to perform noble deeds and save people in distress.

The end of the story of King Arthur tells of his wounding at the hands of Sir Modred. The dying king was carried to a barge and set adrift on the water. As the barge drew farther and farther from land, a group of fairies took Arthur and disappeared with him. The story tells us that Arthur was taken to a wonderful fairyland called Avalon. Some people believed that some day Arthur would return to help England when it needed him.

All the stories of King Arthur together are called "the Arthurian legend." They can be read in many books. The classic collection of them is in Sir Thomas Malory's book *Morte d' Arthur,* published in 1469. The poet Tennyson told many of them in a series of poems called *Idylls of the King.*

artichoke

There are two different vegetables called artichoke. One is the *Globe artichoke,* and the other is the *Jerusalem artichoke.* They are both eaten, but in most other ways they are entirely different.

The Globe artichoke grows like a thistle, with long, prickly leaves, and white or purple flowers. The part that we eat is the thick, fleshy, leaflike scales of the bud, and the fleshy core of the bud, which is tender and sweet. It is usually prepared by boiling it in salted water until the outer leaves are soft. When it is served, the leaves are peeled off, dipped into

melted butter, or in mayonnaise or some other sauce, and eaten. It is native to southern Europe, but is widely cultivated in California.

Globe artichokes, about 4 inches long. The leaves are pulled off one by one.

Breck's, Boston

The Jerusalem artichoke, also known as *girasole*, is a sunflower that has an edible part growing underground, somewhat like Irish potatoes. It is cooked and eaten very much like a potato. A flour made from the Jerusalem artichoke can be made into noodles and spaghetti that contain no starch. These are very popular among people on certain kinds of diet. The Jerusalem artichoke is native to North America, and is widely cultivated in California and elsewhere.

article

The little words *the* and *a* (or *an*) are called *articles*. In the English language they are useful to show whether the speaker means some particular person or thing, or just any person or thing. If you say, "I saw a man yesterday," it might have been any of thousands or millions of men that you saw; you were not very definite about it, so the article *a* (or *an*) is called the *indefinite article*. If you say, "I saw a man I had seen the day before," it has to be one particular man, and for that reason *the* is called the *definite article*. The article *an* means the same thing as *a*, but is used when the next word begins with a vowel (*a, e, i, o,* or *u*), so that you say "an elephant" but "a lion." In many languages there are no articles; the Latin spoken in ancient Rome did not have articles, and the Russian language spoken today does not have articles. Articles are useful for making your meaning clearer when you say something, but they are often used when they are not really necessary.

Articles of Confederation

After the United States had won its independence in the Revolutionary War, until the Constitution was adopted in 1788, the thirteen original states worked together under an agreement called the Articles of Confederation. Twelve states had accepted the Articles as early as 1777, but the other state, Maryland, did not agree until March 1781. The Articles of Confederation did not work very well because in the Congress, where each state had one vote, no decision could be made unless the vote was unanimous. This gave every state "veto power."

artificial limbs

A limb such as a leg, arm or hand that has been amputated, cut off of the body, can usually be replaced with an artificial part that will do the same job and, often, do it just as well. The science of making artificial limbs is called *prosthetics*.

Until fifty or sixty years ago, a lost leg was replaced with a plain stick of wood or "peg leg," a missing hand with an unsightly hook, and an arm not at all. Present-day artificial legs are seldom noticeable and if there is any appreciable stump left from the natural leg the amputee (person who has lost a limb) can walk with only a slight limp if any and can dance or drive an automobile. Artificial arms can if necessary be controlled by shoulder muscles. The "wrist" of the artificial limb is often threaded, and the amputee screws on an imitation hand for show but replaces it with a special appliance, such as an arrangement of hooks and metal "fingers," for doing skilled tasks.

artificial respiration

Respiration is breathing. In certain kinds of accidents people stop breathing and will die very quickly unless they are helped to start again. The help that is given in these cases is called *artificial respiration*. It is a way of forcing air into the lungs of a person who is unable to breathe for himself.

The most frequent use of artificial respiration is in cases of drowning. Persons have been brought back to life after they have stopped breathing for several minutes. Some had to be worked on for hours.

A method called the *Schafer prone pressure method* was used for almost fifty years, from 1903 to 1951. It is a good method, but it forces into the lungs only the amount of air that a person breathes normally.

A Dane named Holger Nielsen invented a new method, called the *back pressure method*. It has been officially approved and used since 1951.

NEILSEN BACK-PRESSURE METHOD

1. *Position of the subject.* Place the subject face down, in prone position. Bend his elbows and place his hands one upon the other. Turn his face to one side, placing his cheek on hands.

2. *Position of the operator.* Kneel on one knee at the head of the subject, facing him. Place the knee at the side of subject's head, near his forearm. Place the other foot near the other elbow. If more comfortable, kneel on both knees, one on each side of the subject's head. Place your hands on the flat of the subject's back so that the heels lie just below a line running between the armpits. With the tips of the thumbs just touching, spread the fingers downward and outward.

3. *Compression phase.* Rock forward until the arms are approximately vertical and allow the weight of the upper body to exert slow, steady, even pressure downward upon the hands. This forces air out of the patient's lungs. Your elbows should be kept straight so pressure will be exerted directly downward on the subject's back.

4. *Position for expansion phase.* Release the pressure, avoiding a final thrust, and commence to rock slowly backward. Place your hands upon the subject's arms just above his elbows.

The Nielsen back pressure method forces huge gulps of air into the lungs. This makes it easier and quicker for a person to resume normal breathing again. The Nielsen method also helps in getting rid of water or gas in the lungs. To see how this method works, see the illustration on the preceding page.

THE MOUTH-TO-MOUTH METHOD

Some people have had good success by putting their mouths to the mouths of drowned persons and blowing air from their own lungs into the drowned persons' lungs, after any water in them has been forced out by the back pressure method.

This method is called "mouth-to-mouth rescue breathing." It has been approved by United States armed services, and the Red Cross has approved it for reviving children. The method, as described by the American Medical Association, is:
1. Clear victim's throat of water, mucus, food.
2. Tilt victim's head back to open the air passage.
3. Hold victim's jaw in jutting-out position.
4. Pinch victim's nostrils to prevent air leakage, unless victim is a small child.
5. Blow into victim's mouth (and nose, if victim is a small child) until you see the chest lift.
6. Listen to the victim breathe out while you breathe in.
7. Repeat about 12 times a minute for an adult, about 20 times a minute for a child.

MECHANICAL METHODS

Artificial respiration may also be given by mechanical means. The "iron lung" that is used to help people with infantile paralysis is a form of artificial respiration. The pulmotor is another type of mechanical artificial respiration. It is most often used by firemen to help people whose breathing has stopped because of suffocation or gas poisoning. A mask is placed over a person's nose and mouth and the pulmotor pumps air into the lungs through the mask, and then sucks the air out. See IRON LUNG.

artificial satellite

A satellite is a body in the heavens that revolves around a larger body, flying around and around it ceaselessly. The moon is a satellite of the earth. A manmade object that is caused to revolve around the earth in the same way is called an *artificial satellite*. The course in which it revolves is called its *orbit*.

Anything that flies around in a circle tries to fly off in a straight line. That is called *centrifugal force*. Any power that draws it back toward the center and keeps it from flying off is *centripetal force*. A weight can be spun around on the end of a string, but when the string is let go the weight will fly across the room because the centrifugal force supplied by its speed is still there and the centripetal force—the strength used to hold the string—is no longer there.

In the case of an artificial satellite, the centrifugal force is supplied by the great speed at which the artificial satellite is

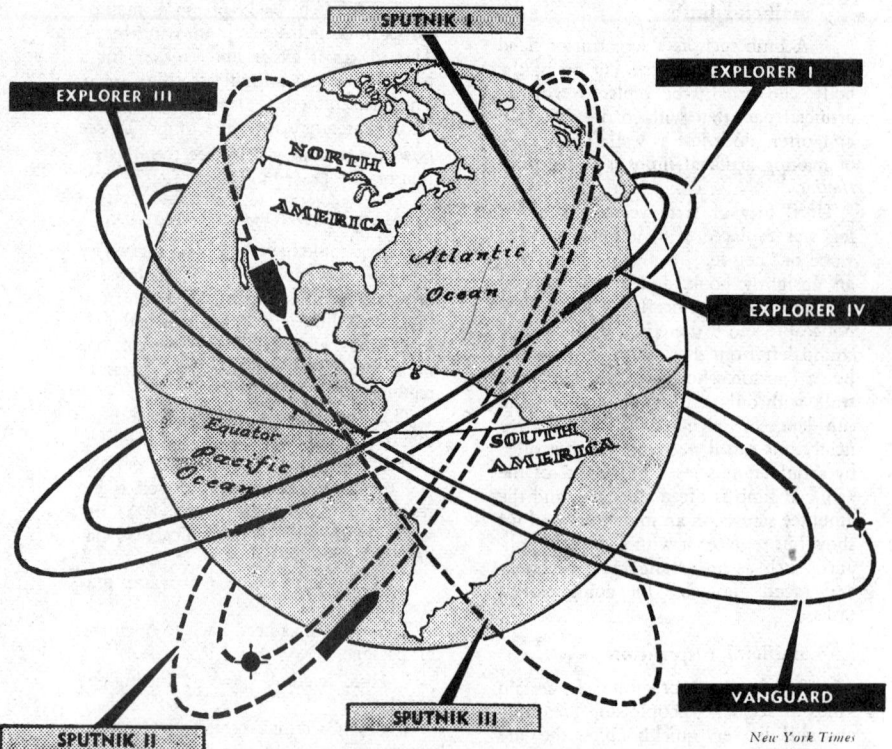

Orbits of the earliest artificial satellites. Since the earth is constantly spinning, the artificial satellite does not pass over the same parts of the earth in each revolution.

New York Times

made to travel. The centripetal force is supplied by the pull of the earth's gravity. The pull of gravity depends on the weight of the two bodies and how far apart they are. The centrifugal force depends on how fast the satellite is traveling. If the two forces exactly balance each other, the satellite will continue in its orbit almost forever. The moon is very heavy but also it is very far away and at its speed of 2,300 miles per hour it will revolve in its orbit for billions of years. An artificial satellite weighing several hundred pounds must travel about 1,650 miles per hour to stay in orbit a few hundred miles above the earth for a few months or years. At this short distance from the earth, the artificial satellite is gradually slowed down by bits of gas from the atmosphere and by meteors that strike it, and when it loses speed it falls to earth. In totally empty space it would fly on eternally at the same speed.

SATELLITES FOR SPACE TRAVEL

In all scientific plans for space travel—for example, to Mars, or Venus, or the moon—an artificial satellite or space station must first be placed in orbit about 1,075 miles from the earth at a speed of about 15,840 miles per hour. Fuel and supplies for the space ship can be loaded on such a satellite much more cheaply than they can be carried on a space ship that must escape entirely from the pull of the earth's gravity—a feat that requires a speed of more than 25,000 miles per hour. The space ship would need only to reach the artificial satellite, take on fuel and supplies, and proceed into space with much less power and speed than would be required to lift such a heavy load off the earth.

All artificial satellites and space ships must be driven by rockets (see the article ROCKET) and there must always be at least two big rockets—one or more to supply enough speed to escape the earth's gravity plus one or more others to point and propel the craft in the proper direction to enter an orbit. Smaller rockets are carried to change direction or to act as "brakes" when landing.

THE ORBIT

An artificial satellite does not usually revolve around the earth in a circle but in an ellipse, which is an oval or egg-shaped curve. That is how the earth travels around the sun each year. The satellite's farthest distance from the earth is called its *apogee* and its nearest distance its *perigee*.

But a circular orbit is possible; and if an artificial satellite can be put into a circular orbit at exactly the same speed at which the earth is turning, the artificial satellite will remain always over the same spot on earth. Since 1960, several artificial satellites have been placed in orbit by the United States to intercept and reflect back to earth television signals, so that the same television show can be seen in parts of the earth thousands of miles apart. The first TV satellites, called Echo (August 1960), Telstar, Relay, or Syncom, only partly accomplished this; but in 1965 the Early Bird satellite was put into circular orbit in one spot relative to earth.

THE SPACE RACE

For the International Geophysical Year (1957, continued through 1958) every country tried to advance man's knowledge of the earth. In 1955 President Eisenhower announced that the United States would contribute by launching artificial satellites. During the next ten years, the U.S. and Russia (the Soviet Union) both tried for new developments in artificial satellites. Except for television satellites Russia won every race.

On October 4, 1957, Russia put the first artificial satellite into orbit. It was called *Sputnik,* meaning "traveler." It weighed 184 pounds, reached an altitude of 560

miles, and circled the earth in about 1 hour 36 minutes. *Sputnik II,* weighing 1,120 pounds, was launched in November, 1957, carrying a dog named Laika, which was the first living thing to travel in space.

Sputnik I fell to earth in January, 1958, and in the same month the first successful U. S. satellite, *Explorer I,* was put into orbit. It weighed 30½ pounds and carried only instruments with which to radio back to earth information about the nature of outer space. It detected the Van Allen Radiation Belt and eventually fell back to earth on March 31, 1970, a little more than twelve years after its launching.

Russia's *Lunik II* was the first spaceship to land on the moon (September, 1959), and her *Lunik III* took the first pictures of the dark side of the moon (October, 1959). Neither craft carried men.

The first man to orbit the earth was a Russian, Yuri Gagarin, in April, 1961; the second was John Glenn, Jr. of the United States, in February, 1962. The first man to step outside a spacecraft in orbit and float alongside it was Russia's Aleksei Leonov, in March, 1965; the second was Edward White of the United States, in June, 1965.

On July 20, 1969, astronaut Neil Armstrong of the United States (about whom there is a separate article) a member of the *Apollo 11* team, became the first man to set foot on the moon.

artillery

The word "artillery" is used to describe the many kinds of large and heavy guns, or cannons, that are used in warfare. Artillery also means the branch of the army that uses these guns.

The first "artillery pieces," thousands of years ago, were battering rams and catapults. Battering rams were used to knock holes in the walls of a castle or a town. Catapults were used to sling huge stones over the walls.

The history of modern artillery began almost a thousand years ago, when the Chinese invented gunpowder. The first firearms were cannons. "Small arms"—pistols and muskets—came later. The Chinese and later the Hindus in India made crude cannons that fired pieces of rock. Artillery pieces were first used in Europe about five hundred years ago. They fired iron cannon balls. These cannons were small, clumsy, inaccurate, and difficult to move around. Sometimes they burst and killed more artillerymen than enemy soldiers.

Slowly but surely they became better, more powerful, and easier to handle. New kinds of ammunition were developed. One kind was called grapeshot. Instead of one large cannon ball, many small ones were fired at the same time. They scattered and covered a wider area and were very damaging against enemy troops. Later, cannon balls were made hollow and contained an explosive charge of powder. When these cannon balls hit, they exploded and scattered jagged pieces of metal. Modern artillery fires ammunition that looks much like the cartridge used in a rifle.

TRAJECTORY

The path taken by the shell from the gun to the target is called its *trajectory.* The trajectory of a shell may vary from almost a straight line to a very high

curve. To get a better idea of trajectory, let us look at a game of baseball. When a batter hits a line drive that hardly rises many feet above the ground, the ball is following a low trajectory. When a batter hits a towering fly to the outfield, the ball is following a high trajectory.

The higher the muzzle of the gun points into the sky, the higher will be the trajectory of the shell fired from it. A low trajectory is needed to get distance —to hit a target far away. A high trajectory is needed to hit a near-by target. A field-artillery piece called a *howitzer* fires shells of a very high trajectory. Howitzers are most often used to reach targets that lie on the other side of a high hill. A low-trajectory shell would crash into the hillside. A high-trajectory shell drops from above onto the target on the other side of the hill. Aiming artillery is a science. It requires education in mathematics and physics.

THE FIELD ARTILLERY

Artillery has been used in two main ways. Its first and greatest use has been to accompany the infantry, or foot soldiers, in the field of battle. This type of artillery is called field artillery.

The job of the field artillery is to support the infantry or other troops in the field. One way this is done is by knocking out fortified enemy positions. Another way is by a *barrage*. Suppose the infantry wants to work in some exposed place. The artillery keeps up a steady fire of shells that fall just beyond this place. The enemy cannot move through the line where the shells are falling, so they cannot attack the working troops. When its own troops want to attack, the field artillery supports them by *artillery preparation*. They bombard the place to be attacked, sometimes for several hours, to drive the enemy out of it. Then their own troops can move in.

The basic field artillery group is the *battery*. A battery is composed of at least four artillery pieces and the soldiers necessary to handle them. These artillerymen work together in perfect teamwork. They must be trained to move their guns quickly, set them up and get them ready for firing. When the guns are ready to be fired, each artilleryman has his special job. Some are far ahead of the lines where they can observe the target and direct the aiming of the gun. These observers also tell the gun crews how close the shells are falling on the target.

In modern warfare, some of the observers fly in light planes over the target to direct the fire from the guns. Other artillerymen work in the fire-direction center. Here they receive all information about the target—how far away it is, what direction it lies in, and how close the shells are falling. Radar is also used to locate a target. Much of the target information is now fed into a machine that automatically figures out how the gun should be fired. These machines can almost think, and they give highly accurate firing information to the gun crews. The gun crews take care of loading, firing and unloading the guns. Even the loading, firing and unloading are often done automatically. The gun crews just see that everything is in perfect working order.

Modern field artillery pieces can be moved very quickly from one place to another. Tanks are really a form of artillery that can go anywhere at any time. Other large guns are mounted on vehicles that are similar to tanks. These vehicles are called *mobile gun carriers*. Other and larger guns are pulled by tractors. The largest artillery pieces are mounted on railroad flatcars.

DEFENSE ARTILLERY

The second important use of artillery is to defend a country from attack from outside. *Coast artillery* defends against attack from the sea. These coast-artillery guns are embedded in great, solid fortresses. They are bigger and heavier than anything used in field artillery. *Anti-aircraft artillery* defends against bombing planes. The anti-aircraft artillery was originally part of the coast artillery in the United States Army. Today anti-aircraft artillery is much more like field artillery. Anti-aircraft batteries are set up wherever the fighting is being carried on and wherever it is necessary to defend targets from enemy air attacks. See the article on ANTI-AIRCRAFT DEFENSE.

NAVAL ARTILLERY

Some of the biggest and heaviest artillery is placed on warships. Naval guns are used in battles between warships at sea and also to support amphibious landings on enemy soil. At these times naval ships come close to shore and fire their big guns at the enemy targets inland.

The most modern forms of artillery fire ROCKETS and atomic shells similar to the ATOMIC BOMB. There are separate articles about these.

Aryan

Long ago, thousands of years before any history was written, there was probably some tribe of the Eurasian regions that spread out for thousands of miles into the lands that are now known as India and Europe. The language spoken by this tribe grew into the dozens of languages that are now known as English and French and German and Greek and Latin and Slavic and many others. These languages are usually called *Indo-European* (because they are spoken by people living between India and Europe), but formerly they were also called *Aryan*.

Now the word Aryan is applied to languages spoken by the Indo-European tribes that conquered India and Iran (Persia). In the old language of India, called Sanskrit, *Arya* means "The noble one, the lord," and the conquerors called themselves "lords" of the people.

The name *Aryan* does not apply to any particular race of people.

asbestos

Asbestos is the name given to a soft, rocklike mineral that is best known for being fireproof. Asbestos is mined in much the same way as coal and other minerals are. The largest asbestos mines are in Canada. Other mines are in Vermont and Arizona in the United States, in Russia, and in South Africa. Asbestos rock is very soft and can be picked apart by hand. It has strands, or fibers, that can be woven into cloth or pressed into cardboard sheets. Most asbestos is a grayish white in color, but some of it is green, brown or blue.

Canadian asbestos, called *chrysotile*, is the most valuable. It can stand heat of 5,000° Fahrenheit and its fibers are so fine that six miles of thread can be spun from a pound of chrysotile. Asbestos is not hurt by water and does not rot.

There are hundreds of uses for asbestos. Since ancient Roman times, thousands of years ago, it has been used for lampwicks. The asbestos wick soaks up oil; the oil burns but the wick itself does not, and therefore does not need to be replaced. Asbestos curtains are used in theaters so that a fire cannot spread from the stage to the audience. Asbestos clothing is worn by firefighters in some places. Men who work with very hot or fiery materials wear asbestos gloves. Asbestos mats are used in kitchens to place hot pots on. Another use is for automobile brake linings.

Asbestos is not only fireproof but is also a good insulating material. This means that it holds heat in and does not allow it to escape. Asbestos is used to insulate hot furnaces, boilers and pipes. It is packed between the inner and outer walls of a house, and placed under the roof, to keep the heat from escaping during the winter and to keep the heat out during the summer.

Asbury, Francis

Bishop Francis Asbury was founder of the Methodist Church in America. He was born in England, in 1745, and became a preacher when he was 16. In 1771 John Wesley, the first Methodist, sent him to America as a missionary. In America he preached 16,500 sermons and traveled 270,000 miles. He died in 1816.

Ascension

The Ascension was the rising of Jesus to heaven 40 days after his resurrection from the dead. It is told about in the gospels of Mark (16:19) and Luke (24:51). The place of the Ascension is thought to be Mount Olivet near Jerusalem. The feast of the Ascension is celebrated in most Christian churches 40 days after Easter.

Ascension Island

Ascension Island is a British possession in the middle of the South Atlantic Ocean. Its area is 34 square miles and it includes an extinct volcano 2,870 feet high. During World War II the United States secretly built an airfield on Ascension Island and used it as a refueling base for aircraft, and in 1956 it became a U.S. missile-launching base. The island was discovered on Ascension Day, 1501, by a Portuguese ship.

ash

The ash is the name of a tree that grows in North America, Europe, and Asia. There are at least fifty kinds of trees that bear the name ash. Some of them are related to the olive tree, and others to the lilac and jasmine. Ash trees grow best in dry soil. The North American ash grows to a height of 120 feet, but the European ash grows from 50 to 80 feet high. The ash tree bears tight little clusters of flowers that have no petals. The dark green leaves are

made up of several pairs of small narrow leaflets. The wood of the ash is very hard and has been used by man for centuries. Ash was often used in the manufacture of wheels and wagons. Today it is used for baseball bats, skis, and furniture.

Asheville

Asheville is a resort city in the Blue Ridge mountains in western North Carolina. It is also a manufacturing city for textiles and furniture. Asheville was named for John Ashe, an American general in the Revolutionary War. The population is 57,681 (1970 census). Novels of Thomas Wolfe are set in Asheville, where he lived.

Ash Wednesday

Ash Wednesday is the day on which Roman Catholics and members of some other Christian churches begin their Lenten fast. Lent is the period that comes just before Easter, and Ash Wednesday is about seven weeks before Easter. On that day a Catholic goes to church, kneels before the priest, and receives a smudge of ashes on his forehead. The priest places the ashes on each forehead in the form of a cross. As he does this the priest says, "Remember, man, that thou art dust and unto dust thou shalt return." The ashes are made by burning the palm leaves that were used on Palm Sunday the year before.

Asia

Asia is a continent; it is one of the seven big masses of land that make up the Earth. Asia is by far the biggest of the continents. Its 16,911,000 square miles make it five times as big as the United States. Actually it is much bigger than this. Europe, which is considered a separate continent, is really part of Asia, because Europe and Asia are not separated by oceans or seas as all other continents are. Some people consider Europe and Asia the same continent, and call it Eurasia. Considered this way, it has more than 20,000,000 square miles. The second-biggest continent, Africa, has about 11,500,000.

More than half of all the people on earth live in Asia. This means about 1,800,000,000 people, almost ten times as many as live in the United States.

Asia is on the other side of the world from the United States and Canada. It takes weeks to get there by boat and several days to fly.

Like other continents, Asia has a number of different countries and territories under different governments. There are separate articles about most of these countries and territories, but here they are, briefly:

THE FAR EAST

CHINA, the country with the biggest population on earth (more than eight hundred million), and a big area, too, larger than that of the United States.

KOREA, one of the most ancient countries of the world, but now divided into two sections, NORTH KOREA and SOUTH KOREA.

MONGOLIA, a big region in the central part of Asia. It is controlled by the U.S.S.R. Most of Mongolia is desert or mountains, and very few people live

there—fewer than a million.

TIBET, a country in the high mountains of central Asia that is actually a part of China but governed itself without much interference until the Chinese Communist government took over control in 1953.

THAILAND, or SIAM, a country of about the same size as Burma, both in area and in population.

BURMA, a smaller country in the southern part of Asia, beside India. It is almost as big as Texas in size and has more than twice as many people.

MALAYSIA, which includes the Malay peninsula (a narrow arm of land stretching into the sea) and some islands and parts of islands. See the articles on MALAYA and the MALAY PENINSULA and MALAY ARCHIPELAGO.

INDO-CHINA, which is four separate countries: North and South VIET NAM, CAMBODIA, and LAOS. This was formerly called "French Indo-China," because it was controlled by France. See also the articles ANNAM and FRENCH INDO-CHINA.

SIBERIA, the largest region in Asia, and several other territories that are part of the SOVIET UNION (Union of Soviet Socialist Republics, or U.S.S.R.). Siberia covers the entire northern part of Asia. Because it is so far north, most of it is quite cold and only about fifteen million people live there.

CENTRAL ASIA (MIDDLE EAST)

INDIA, the next-biggest country in population. Once the name "India" included other countries that are now independent, and all these countries together made an area so big that it was called "the Indian subcontinent."

PAKISTAN, which was formerly part of India. It was separated from India because most of the people who live in Pakistan are of the Mohammedan religion, while most of the people who live in India are of the Hindu religion.

NEPAL, a small kingdom north of India. It was formerly part of India.

BHUTAN, a small mountain kingdom formerly allied with and partly controlled by India.

AFGHANISTAN, a kingdom in the southwestern part of Asia, about the same size as Burma or Siam.

IRAN, the country known in ancient times as Persia, large in area but not able to support a big population because so much of it is desert.

IRAQ, which with Egypt was one of the first two civilized countries on earth, several thousand years ago. Iraq was formerly called Mesopotamia.

SOUTHWEST ASIA (NEAR EAST)

SAUDI ARABIA, a kingdom, which covers most of the big western part of Asia known as the Arabian peninsula. Even more than Iran, Saudi Arabia is desert land and its population is small.

YEMEN, a very small republic, about the size of the state of Missouri in both area and population, in the southern end of the Arabian peninsula.

PEOPLE'S DEMOCRATIC REPUBLIC OF SOUTHERN YEMEN, a small country formerly called Aden.

OMAN, a small country at the bottom

tip of the Arabian peninsula, ruled by a sultan (king).

JORDAN, a kingdom at the north of the Arabian peninsula, occupying part of the Holy Land. Its people are Arabs.

ISRAEL, the new republic founded by Jews in Palestine (the Holy Land), on the eastern coast of the Mediterranean Sea.

LEBANON, a small republic north of Israel, on the Mediterranean Sea.

SYRIA, An ancient country south of Turkey, on the Mediterranean Sea; now a republic. Unlike other peoples of Asia, most Syrians are Christian.

TURKEY, which occupies the part of Asia that reaches farthest to the west, known as Asia Minor. A small part of Turkey is also in Europe.

All these different countries make up the continent of Asia, and Asia includes other countries on the islands near the continent—CEYLON, off the southern tip of India; JAPAN, and the Republic of the PHILIPPINES (Philippine Islands), off the eastern coast; and the big islands of INDONESIA near the southeastern coast.

THE PEOPLE OF ASIA

In a region as vast as Asia, there are so many different peoples, customs, and languages that it would be hard to count them all. It is not possible to say that the people of Asia are "like this" or "like that," because what is true in one part of Asia may not be true in other parts. Still, it is possible to make a few statements that are true of nearly all of Asia:

Most of the people of Asia belong to the Mongoloid race. This is one of the three great races of mankind, the other two being *Caucasoid* and *Negroid*.

The Mongoloid people are a dark-skinned people. They are called the "yellow" people but actually their skin colors range from a yellowish color to a dark, reddish brown—the skin color of the American Indians, who are also a Mongoloid people.

The Mongoloid race is the most numerous in the world. But the Caucasoid, or "white," race has for hundreds of years controlled nearly all the wealth of the world. Within the last fifty years, the Mongoloid peoples have begun to seek a greater share of this wealth for themselves. So, although there are so many different types of Mongoloid peoples in Asia, and although they live in different countries and speak different languages and have fought bitterly among themselves for thousands of years, they are now coming to feel that they are all one people.

Besides this, the Mongoloid people of Asia (and of the many islands in the Pacific Ocean) feel themselves somehow allied with the Negroid, or "black," race of Africa, and also with the millions of Caucasoid people who live in Asia, but most of whom are somewhat darker-skinned than the European and American Caucasoids.

THE RELIGIONS OF ASIA

There are very few Christians in Asia. Missionaries have carried Christianity to many parts of the vast con-

tinent, especially in China, but the number of Christians is still small compared to the numbers who follow other religions.

The Mohammedan religion is the largest in the southwestern part of the continent. In Arabia and Asia Minor, in Afghanistan and in Pakistan, nearly everyone is a Mohammedan. More than a thousand years ago, the Mohammedans also spread their religion to other parts of southern Asia and the islands near it.

Most of the people of India follow the Hindu religion. There are several different branches of Hinduism. Some of them teach that all life, including animal life, is sacred.

The biggest religion of China and several of the other countries is Buddhism, based on the teachings of a man called Gautama Buddha who lived more than five hundred years before Jesus was born. Buddhists do not consider Buddha a god, but he was the founder of their religion.

Many other religions are practiced in Asia, just as there are many small churches and denominations in the United States. Some Asiatic peoples worship their ancestors, believing them to have become gods when they died. Shinto, the religion followed by many Japanese, recognizes other gods. Followers of the great Chinese philosopher Confucius are often considered as members of a religious sect, and their religion is called Confucianism. Taoism is another Asiatic religion based on the teaching of a wise man of the past.

HOW THE PEOPLE LIVE

Until very recently, life in Asia was of a kind that Americans would consider very backward. A few of the people—the princes, noblemen, and great merchants—were very rich, richer than anyone in America or Europe ever seems to be, with thousands of jewels and hundreds of servants and big palaces. All the rest of the people were very poor. They usually did not get quite enough to eat, and every now and then when the crops failed there would be a famine and millions of them would die. Disease killed millions more while they were children or young men and women. Very few of the people could read and write, and most of them lived in the poorest kind of huts, with no electricity or running water or cooking stoves. Nearly all of them were farmers. They worked hard from morning to night and were still poor. All this was true not only of some parts of Asia, but of nearly every part, from west to east, from north to south.

Asia is still far behind Europe and America, but conditions have been improving every year. More and more of the people are becoming educated. The methods of farming are becoming more modern. Ways of preventing disease are being taught to the people, and doctors and medicines and hospitals are saving those who do become sick. Asia still does not raise quite enough food for its huge population, and it may be some time before many of the people have bathrooms and refriger-

ators and automobiles, but they are improving their conditions every year.

Of course, it would be wrong to think that all of Asia is backward. There are many big cities with fine buildings and factories and universities. It is to the people outside the big cities that real civilization is now being introduced.

WHAT THE LAND IS LIKE

Asia is so big that it has nearly every climate and every kind of territory. The northern part reaches almost to the North Pole and is frozen nearly all year long. The southern part reaches almost to the equator—most of it is farther south than Florida—and so it is warm all the year long. The highest mountains in the world, the Himalayas, cover much of the central part of Asia. One of the biggest deserts in the world, the Gobi Desert, is in the eastern part. Millions of square miles of Siberia, in the north, are *tundra*—flat, mossy plains that are frozen most of the year. And, of course, parts of Asia are jungles where vegetation is thick, and other parts are wonderful fertile farmlands where rice and other grain is grown.

The Caspian Sea, the biggest inland sea in the world, is in the western part of Asia. Three tremendous lakes, named Aral, Balkhash, and Baikal, are in the central part; they compare in size with the Great Lakes of North America. At least a dozen of the world's greatest rivers are in Asia.

The mineral wealth of Asia is known to be very great, but it has not been developed enough for even a guess at its value. Iran is rich in oil. Siberia is believed to have the greatest gold reserves in the world. Many precious stones and rare minerals that are scarce everywhere else are plentiful in Asia.

THE PAST AND FUTURE OF ASIA

The people of Asia made an early start toward civilization, then allowed themselves to fall far behind Europe. About 1,500 years ago, when most of Europe was held by savage tribes, and when America was known only to the American Indians, the Chinese and Koreans and some of the Indians had developed advanced civilizations. Printing and paper and even gunpowder were known to the Asiatics long before the Europeans learned about them. But then for some reason the Asiatics stopped advancing while the Europeans kept on.

Beginning about four hundred years ago, the strong countries of Europe began to conquer parts of Asia and make possessions of them. During the period that followed, right up to the present century, the best parts of Asia fell under the control of Europeans. The British had India and Malaya and some smaller parts. The French had Indo-China. The Dutch had several of the big islands that are now Indonesia. Spain had the Philippine Islands. Several countries seized special rights in China—and these included one Asiatic country, Japan, which became a modern industrial power like the countries of Europe and America. Russia extended its control all across northern Asia to the Pacific Ocean.

In the 20th century nearly all the people of Asia have won their independence. but Asiatic people still distrust the white peoples, because they remember the years in which they had reason to.

British Information Service

In southern Asia much cotton is grown and there are big factories to spin thread and weave cloth. The factory shown is in Bombay, India. It has a day nursery to care for the children of the factory workers.

ASIA—SUMMARY

Area. About 16,900,200 sq. mi. (including offshore islands). Greatest length, 6,280 miles; greatest width, 5,270 miles. Coastline, about 45,000 miles.

Population. About 1,783,000,000. About 70% Mongoloid, chiefly in the east; about 30% Caucasoid, chiefly in the southwest. Malays and Polynesians on the eastern and southeastern islands. Some tribes of Negroid stock on the islands in the south. Eskimo peoples, resembling North American Indian stocks, in the extreme northeast. Small European groups in most areas.

Languages. Chiefly those of the Sino-Tibetan (Indo-Chinese), Mongolian, Turkic, Malayo-Polynesian, and Indo-Iranian (Indo-European) and Dravidian families.

Political Organization. 31 independent or semi-independent states and 18 territories with some degree of self-government. Numerous regions and tribes that remain distinct within modern political divisions.

Commerce. Agriculture is the principal occupation. *Principal crops:* grains, chiefly rice (the largest crop), wheat and millet; fats and oils (especially soybean, peanut, and copra); sugar cane, cotton, jute, and silk. *Principal industries:* cotton fabrics (Japan, China and India); jute in India; many manufactured goods in Japan and the U.S.S.R. *Mineral exports:* petroleum, tin, manganese, chromite, iron ore, tungsten, antimony.

Transportation. Railroads chiefly in India, Japan, China, U.S.S.R. and Pakistan (each more than 5,000 miles). River navigation chiefly on Yangtze and West Rivers in China, Irrawaddy in Burma, and some Siberian rivers except in winter.

Topography. In the north, lowlands cover west central Asia and most of Siberia. The central zone consists of high plateaus, some to 15,000 ft. in Tibet, enclosed by great mountain ranges. At the meeting point of India, Pakistan, Afghanistan and the U.S.S.R. is an elevated area called the Pamir, with valleys more than 11,000 ft. high and mountains still higher. From the Pamir, mountain ranges extend east and west, forming a back-

bone across the center of the continent. To the east lie the Himalayas, including the highest peaks of the world (Mt. Everest, K-2 and others). North of them is the great plateau of Tibet and, still farther northeast, the tableland of Han-hai, which includes the Gobi and Takla Makan deserts. From it a succession of ranges extend northeast. West of the Kamir are the Hindu Kush mountains. In the extreme south are plateaus in India and Arabia. Other mountain chains include the Ural, between Europe and Asia, and the Caucasus, between the Black and Caspian Seas. The main rivers of Siberia, the Ob (2,500 miles), Yenisei (2,300 miles), and Lena (2,645 miles), drain into the Arctic Ocean; the rivers of the east and southeast, including the Amur (2,700 miles), Yangtze (3,100 miles), Mekong (2,600 miles), Yellow or Hwang-ho (2,700 miles) and West or Si-kiang (1,250 miles), into the Pacific; in the southwest, the Salween (1,750 miles), Irrawaddy (1,250 miles), Brahmaputra (1,800 miles), Indus (1,900 miles), and Tigris and Euphrates (1,700 miles), drain into the Indian Ocean; in the central portion, the Amu Darya (1,560 miles), and Syr Darya (1,770 miles), flow into the Aral Sea. Some rivers disappear in desert sands.

Lakes include the Caspian Sea (152,000 sq. mi., the world's largest); Aral Sea (24,600 sq. mi., 4th largest); Baikal (12,000 sq. mi.); and Balkhash (6,670 sq. mi.).

Asia has two major forest areas, separated by the interior steppes and barren plateaus. In the north are the taiga (pine forests) and tundra (treeless plains)) of Siberia, and in the south are rain forests.

Natural Resources. Southeast Asia is the world leader in natural rubber, tin and tungsten, and is important in the production of manganese, chromite, mica and graphite. The oil deposits of the Near East and of Siberia may be the largest in the world. Siberia has rich forests and untold mineral wealth not yet used. Potential hydroelectric and atomic energy in immense quantities. About 10% of Asia is good farmland.

Climate. Generally the north and west regions are temperate and the south and east are influenced by the rainy season (monsoon). Almost half the continent has too little rainfall. Arctic conditions in north; see ARCTIC REGION.

Asia Minor

Asia Minor is a small peninsula at the extreme west of Asia. It is part of Turkey.

Most of Asia Minor is a plateau—high, like a mountain, but level, like a plain. This plateau forms the central part of the region. Mountains lie around it on all sides except the western side. Many streams and small rivers crisscross the plains.

There were famous ancient cities on the shores of Asia Minor, including Troy, Ephesus, and Smyrna. Many ancient wars were fought in this region. Asia Minor was included in the empire of Alexander the Great, in the Roman Empire, and in the Byzantine Empire. For nearly a thousand years it has been part of Turkey. The people who live in Asia Minor today are descended from

Turks, Greeks, Syrians, Armenians, Jews, and other peoples.

asp

Asp is a name that has been used for different kinds of poisonous snakes. The asp is mentioned in the Bible and in early Greek and Roman writings. It is hard to tell exactly what snake was meant by these early writers. They used the word "asp" whenever they wrote about any poisonous snakes. Cleopatra, an ancient queen of Egypt, killed herself by allowing an asp to bite her. The asp of Cleopatra was probably the Egyptian hooded cobra. This snake is 3 to 5 feet long and has a wide flat neck.

asparagus

Asparagus is a vegetable that is cultivated in many countries. When asparagus grows, green shoots or "spears" stick out of the ground and are cut off with a sharp knife when they are 6 to 8 inches long. After asparagus is planted, it must be allowed to grow for three years before it is cut. After that the bed will continue to yield new shoots for nine or ten years. If not cut, asparagus grows to be several feet high. Florists use the lacy, fernlike branches, which have pretty red berries on them, to decorate flower arrangements.

aspen

The aspen is a tree that belongs to the poplar family. It is sometimes called either "quaking aspen" or "trembling aspen." This is because the lightest breeze will cause the leaves of the aspen to dance and quiver. The leaves are shiny green and heart-shaped. In the fall, the leaves turn yellow. The grayish bark of the aspen is one of the main foods of the beaver. The wood is light and soft, and is used to make paper, boxes, and match sticks. The aspen grows in northern parts of the world. It is 20 to 40 feet high.

asphalt

Asphalt is a bitumen, as coal is. This means it is composed of decayed vegetable and plant life that existed millions of years ago. The decayed plant life was buried underground and slowly changed into thick crude oil. When exposed to air, it hardens into asphalt. Asphalt is also called *pitch* or *mineral pitch.*

Lake asphalt is found in great quantities on the island of Trinidad, at La Brea, California, in Venezuela, and on the shores of the Dead Sea. Blocks of hard asphalt are cut from the surface of an asphalt lake. The liquid asphalt oozes into the place where the blocks were cut, and soon hardens.

Asphalt is also found in petroleum. When petroleum is refined to get oil and gasoline, asphalt is also obtained.

There are many uses for asphalt. Its most important use is in paving roads and driveways. For this purpose, asphalt is melted and mixed with sand and fine gravel. The hot mixture is spread over a roadbed and smoothed out. A final coating of almost pure asphalt is melted and mixed with sand used as roofing material. It is spread on some roofs with fine gravel. Other roofs are covered with asphalt roofing

paper or asphalt shingles. One very fine kind of asphalt, called *Gilsonite,* or *uintaite,* can be molded like a plastic. Gilsonite is very hard and does not melt or soften as easily as most asphalt does. Plain asphalt will soften in the hot sun, at temperatures of about 100 degrees.

aspirin

Aspirin is the medicine that is most widely used to relieve pain and reduce fever. It is usually sold in the form of small white tablets. In 1953 about a hundred such tablets were sold for every man, woman and child in the United States alone. Most persons can take aspirin safely, but some people cannot. Overdoses are dangerous, especially to children. Aspirin was first prepared in 1853 by C. F. Gerhardt, a German chemist. It began to be made in the United States about 1900. Its name in chemistry is acetylsalicylic acid.

ass

The ass is an animal like the horse, and related to the horse; but it is smaller, and has big pointed ears and a tuft of hair at the end of its tail. An ass brays in a loud, unmusical voice. Its usual color is gray, sometimes streaked or striped with a darker shade. It is also known as a *donkey.* A male ass is called a *jackass* and a female is called a *jenny.* The burro, used as a pack animal in desert places, principally in Mexico and the Southwest of the United States, is a smaller breed of ass.

The ass may be 2½ to 4 feet high and weighs 300 to 1,000 pounds. It lives 30 to 40 years (longer than a horse). The ass is bred with the horse to produce the mule. The onager of western Asia and the kiang of Tibet are wild asses.

No animal has served man better than the ass. It is not nearly as stupid as people believe, and its "stubbornness" is well suited to hot, dry, desert places, where hurrying would only use up strength and increase thirst. The ass is very sure-footed in mountain places.

The Bible often mentions the ass. The Gospel of St. Matthew tells how Jesus rode into Jerusalem on an ass.

assassination

Assassination is the murder of an important person, such as a king or a president. Sometimes a ruler is killed by someone who thinks a change in government would be good for the country; sometimes a ruler is killed because one of his rivals wants to grab control of the country. It is called assassination in either case. Many kings have been assassinated. Four United States Presidents have been assassinated—Abraham Lincoln in 1865; James A. Garfield in 1881; William McKinley in 1901; and John F. Kennedy in 1963. After McKinley's death, the Secret Service was put in charge of guarding the President. Unsuccessful assassination attempts were made on Presidents Andrew Jackson, Theodore Roosevelt, Franklin D. Roosevelt, Harry Truman, Gerald Ford.

The first assassins were a group of Mohammedans who tried to kill all their political enemies. This group would select one man to do the killing, and would give him hasheesh, a kind of dope, to make him reckless. The word

assassin comes from *hasheesh*. The original Assassins lived in Persia and Syria about nine hundred years ago.

assaying

Assaying is the testing of an ore to see how much valuable metal can be taken out of it. The United States government will assay any ore to find out how much gold or silver it contains. Assaying can be done by heating the ore until the metal melts and runs out, or by putting the ore in chemicals that will dissolve the metals in it. The metals are then separated from the chemical. An *Assay Office* will issue an official report on how much metal there is in a particular ore; for instance, it will say, "This rock assays fourteen ounces [of gold] to the ton [of ore]."

Assumption

In the Christian religion, the Assumption is the taking to heaven of the body as well as the soul of the Virgin Mary. It is a dogma, or official belief, in the Roman Catholic Church that when Mary died her soul did not go to heaven alone but her entire body went with her soul. The Feast of the Assumption, celebrating this, is on August 15.

Belief in the Assumption is very old among Catholics, going back at least 1,500 years, but it was made a dogma very recently, by Pope Pius XII in 1950.

The Bible tells of others who were taken bodily to heaven: Jesus, both after the Crucifixion and after the Resurrection; the prophet Elijah; and probably Enoch, a grandson of Adam.

Assyria

Assyria was the name of a country that was great in ancient times. Long ago there was a city named Assur, or Ashur, on the banks of the Tigris River, in the land that is now Iraq. This city was built more than four thousand years ago. The people who lived there named the city after their chief god, Assur, and the people became known as Assyrians. For hundreds of years the Assyrians fought against neighboring tribes and added land to their small kingdom. Finally the kingdom of Assyria became rich and important. They built another city on the Tigris River, named Nineveh, that became one of the great cities of the world.

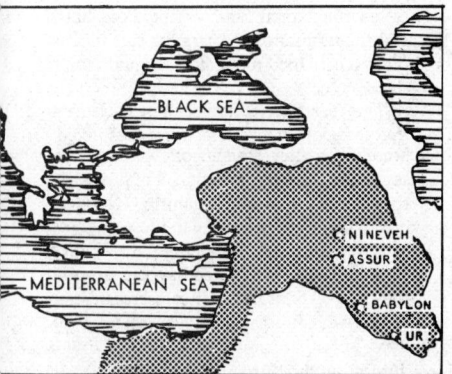

The people of Assyria were mostly farmers, but in the cities there were fine craftsmen who could do much better work with metals than could most people in those ancient times. The Assyrians were the first to use iron-tipped spears and arrows, and to make war chariots, and armor to protect themselves.

The Assyrians learned much from the people they conquered. From the Babylonians they learned how to tell time, and also improved their knowledge of writing. They also borrowed laws from the Babylonians. Although they were warlike, the Assyrians also loved beautiful things, and their cities were decorated with colorful art.

Great kings of Assyria included Sargon II (about 700 B.C.), Sennacherib, who came after him, and Ashur-Bani-Pal, who was king from 668 B.C. to 625 B.C. and who assembled a library of 30,000 books.

Like other ancient empires, Assyria was finally destroyed by its many enemies, and ceased to exist nearly 2,500 years ago, about 600 B.C.

Astaire, Fred

Fred Astaire is the stage name of a famous dancer and actor in the theater and motion pictures. His real name was Frederic Austerlitz and he was born in Omaha, Nebraska, in 1899. He and his sister, Adele Astaire, began to attend a ballet school when he was four and she was six. In 1916 they made a sensational success as a dancing team in vaudeville, then they appeared together in several musical comedies. In 1932 Adele Astaire married an English nobleman, Lord Charles Cavendish, and retired from the stage. Fred Astaire went on to a series of even greater successes in musical motion pictures, with Ginger Rogers, Rita Hayworth and others as his dancing partners. He is credited with creating the most popular form of theatrical dancing, a combination of ballroom dancing and tap dancing.

Astarte

Astarte was the chief goddess of several ancient peoples, including the Assyrians and Phoenicians. Her name is also spelled Ashtoreth and Ashtaroth. She was often pictured as a cow, or as a woman with a cow's head. The Greek goddess Aphrodite (whom the Romans called Venus) was based on Astarte. Astarte was goddess of the moon.

aster

Aster is the name of several varieties of flowers with blossoms whose rays spread out from the center. This gives them a sort of star shape, and that is how the flowers got their name, because in the Greek language *aster* means "star."

Asters range in color from white to several shades of pink and to some different shades of blue or purple. The plants range from small, leafy types to shrubs the size of a rosebush. Asters are found in temperate climates.

Asters belong to the COMPOSITE family of plants, about which there is a separate article. There are more than 600 different kinds of aster and most of them grow in the United States and other parts of North America. They are perennials (blooming from year to year without replanting) and may grow one to six feet high.

asteroid

Asteroids, also called *planetoids*, are heavenly bodies that are like planets

except they are much smaller. The first asteroid to be discovered was Ceres, in 1801. About 1,600 others have been recorded since then. Only one asteroid, Vesta, is ever bright enough to be seen with the naked eye.

When an unknown asteroid is discovered it is given a number, consisting of the year of discovery and two letters standing for the part of the month. Then, if it proves to be a new asteroid, it is given a permanent number, and the discoverer, if he cares to, may give it a name. Ceres is the largest asteroid, measuring 480 miles in diameter (compared to almost 8,000 miles for the Earth). It is believed that about 150 asteroids have diameters greater than 50 miles. The majority are very much smaller.

Asteroids occur in a variety of shapes, and the asteroid Eros most probably is shaped like a dumbbell.

See the article on the SOLAR SYSTEM.

asthma

Asthma is a disease that affects a person's breathing.

The disease tightens the branches of the windpipe leading from the throat to the lungs. Some asthma is caused by heart trouble or kidney trouble. Most often, however, the disease is caused by dust, flower and plant pollen, nearness to animal hair or fur, or chemicals in the air. Some people often get attacks when they are angry, irritated, or fearful.

Sometimes a person who has asthma may be free from attacks for long periods of time. Then suddenly an attack comes. There is no sure cure for asthma, but there are many ways of relieving it. Frequently a person with asthma finds relief by moving to a different climate. The best climate for asthmatics is usually a dry, warm climate. Relief can also be gotten by breathing in the fumes and vapors of certain medicines. Other medicines can be taken by mouth or by injection. See also ALLERGY.

astigmatism

Astigmatism is a kind of imperfect eyesight. A person with astigmatism cannot see everything clearly and sharply, and sometimes sees some things off to the side of where they actually are. Astigmatism is caused by a flat spot on part of the eyeball. The front of the eyeball should be perfectly rounded, like the surface of a ball. The eye of a person with astigmatism is not perfectly rounded, but is more like the surface of the bowl of a spoon. In a normal, perfectly rounded eye, all the rays of light from an object come to a point at the back of the eye. The flattening of the front of the eye prevents some of the rays of light from meeting at that point, and fuzziness results.

There is no way of getting rid of the flatness on the surface of the eye, so rounded glasses are used. The rounded surface of the lens acts to correct the flat part of the eyeball. With proper glasses, a person with astigmatism can see things as clearly and sharply as anyone can.   (Diagram on next page.)

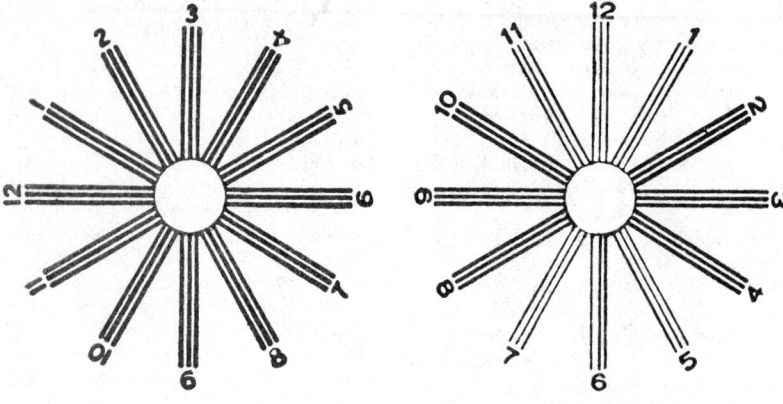

Better Vision Institute, Inc.

Astigmatism makes things seem lopsided or distorted. To test for it, parallel lines like these are used. The lines in the picture at the left are equally black, but a person with astigmatism may see them as shown at the right, and some may not be visible at all.

Astor

A boy from the town of Waldorf, in Germany, came to the United States in 1783, when he was 20 years old.

His name was John Jacob Astor. His father had been a butcher in Germany, but in the United States he went into the fur business and founded the American Fur Company, which controlled the sale of furs for more than twenty years. From this he made a great fortune, and he was wise enough to buy land on Manhattan Island, where much of the valuable real estate of New York City is now. John Jacob Astor's family became one of the most famous in the world. His sons and grandsons increased the fortune he had begun. John Jacob Astor's great-grandson, William Waldorf Astor, changed from American to British nationality and became Lord Astor (a viscount); he married Nancy Langhorne of Virginia, who became famous as Lady Astor, a member of the British Parliament. The descendants of John Jacob Astor still own more real estate in New York City than any other family.

Astrakhan

Astrakhan is a port on the Caspian Sea, at the mouth of the Volga River, in the Soviet Union. It is an important center for the export of fish and caviar. The population is 324,000. In former times—from about 1250 to 1554—Astrakhan was an important city in the vast empire of the Tatars, or Mongols. It declined in size after it was conquered by the Russians, then grew rapidly again after the 1870s, when great oilfields were developed at nearby Baku.

astrology

The first men who ever studied the stars in the heavens, thousands of years ago, believed that the stars were gods. They called themselves *astrologers*, which means "students of the stars," and they began a study called *astrology*.

According to astrologers, a person's entire life is controlled or influenced by the positions of the stars in the heavens at the moment he is born. By "casting a horoscope" (figuring out the appearance of the sky at the time of birth) the astrologer undertakes to tell what kind of person one is, what his future is, and what exact times are propitious (lucky) or unlucky for him. Astrologers also predict future political events. A French astrologer named Nostradamus, who lived about 400 years ago (1503 to 1566), made many predictions that seemed to come true in this century.

Kings and other famous men have had astrologers who advised them on everything they should do. Many American newspapers have daily advice to readers, based on astrology, and millions of books and magazines on astrology are still sold. But all men of science call astrology a superstition that sometimes is harmful, or expensive at least, to those who believe in it.

See also the article ZODIAC.

astronaut, a person who has traveled through space. See SPACE TRAVEL.

astronomy

Since the beginning of history men have gazed at the sky on clear nights to watch the countless stars and wonder how many there are, and what they are made of, and how far away they are, and many other things about them. The study of the stars is the oldest of all sciences. It is called *astronomy*.

For most of these thousands of years men did not know very much about the heavenly bodies in the skies, and much of what they believed was wrong. Some men of ancient times thought the stars were gods, and feared them. Others believed that the stars can affect human affairs, as explained in the article on ASTROLOGY.

Today, astronomy has become one of the most advanced of the sciences. Astronomers have exact knowledge of many things about the stars, and they are learning more all the time.

THE UNBELIEVABLE UNIVERSE

The Earth on which we live is just a tiny speck in a universe that is so vast that the mind cannot even imagine how big it is. Even the sun, which is more than a hundred times as big as the Earth, is no more than a tiny speck in the universe. All the stars we can see, and billions upon billions of stars that we cannot see, are suns too. The biggest stars are called giant stars and the littlest stars are called dwarf stars. Our sun is a star of only average size. Some of the giant stars are a million times as big as our sun. They look small in the heavens only because they are so far away.

Stars are so far away that here again we have something the human mind can hardly even imagine. The sun is 93,000,000 miles from the Earth. But the nearest star is about twenty-four trillion (24,000,000,000,000) miles away. That is the nearest. Most of the stars are so much farther away that to write down the distance we would have to fill almost a page with zeros.

Therefore astronomers use a different measure of distance. The speed of light is about 186,000 miles per second—nothing can travel faster than light. The distance to a star is measured in *light years*. A light year is the distance light, at its rate of 186,000 miles per second, will travel in a year. The distance is about six trillion miles. Even so, most of the stars are so far away that it takes their light thousands of years to reach us.

HOW ASTRONOMY HAS DEVELOPED

It may seem miraculous that astronomers have been able to measure this vast universe, to find out the distances of stars that are so far away, and even to tell what substances make up a particular star; but they have learned to do all these things.

The early watchers of the skies picked out groups of stars that seemed to be together in the sky, or that were arranged in shapes that were easy to remember. They called these groups of stars *constellations* and gave them names, naming them for the gods in their mythology, or for animals or characters in their favorite stories. We still use their ancient names for these constellations.

The ancient astronomers saw, too, that most of the stars seemed to move through the skies together, as though they were stuck into the sky as a jewel is embedded in metal. These they called the "fixed" stars. One of these stars never moved at all, but stayed in one place directly to the north; so this was called the North Star, or the Pole Star, and for thousands of years the star in this place has helped navigators to guide their ships at sea.

The early astronomers also noticed that five of the "stars" were not fixed. Sometimes they rose in one part of the sky, sometimes in another. These bodies they called *planets,* meaning "wanderers." Today we know that these planets are not stars at all. They are bodies similar to our Earth, and revolve around the sun. There are other planets, but only five can be seen with the naked eye. These are Mercury, Venus, Mars, Jupiter, and Saturn.

Our science of astronomy probably began with the Chaldeans, an ancient people who had a great kingdom in the land that is now Iraq, about 3,000 years ago. Egyptians, Chinese and other peoples knew much about the stars even earlier, probably more than 5,000 years ago, but the Chaldeans started what may

be called modern astronomy. A few hundred years later, in the 6th century B.C., the Greek philosophers led by Pythagoras worked out what we now know to be true: That the earth is ball-shaped and that it and the other planets revolve around the sun. This is the *heliocentric* theory, meaning "the sun in the center."

But the Greek philosopher Aristotle, who lived about 200 years later, believed in the *geocentric* theory, that is, that the earth is the center of the universe. An Egyptian scientist named Ptolemy, who lived about a hundred years after Jesus, adopted Aristotle's view and put it in a famous book on astronomy, the *Almagest.* The early Christian Church also adopted Aristotle's view and made it official. For more than a thousand years no one in Christian countries was allowed to dispute the geocentric theory.

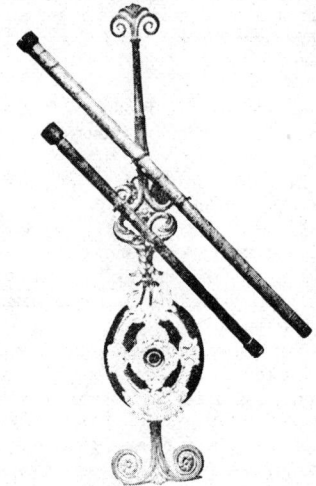

Yerkes Observatory
Galileo's telescope was the first used for studying the stars. Although it was very weak, it was the beginning of modern astronomy.

Then, about the year 1500, the great Polish astronomer Nicolaus Copernicus established the fact that the sun, not the earth, is the center of the *solar system* (the sun and its planets) and that the sun is simply one of the stars. Toward the end of the 1500s a Danish astronomer named Tycho Brahe built a fine observatory near Copenhagen, Denmark, and Brahe's assistant, Johannes Kepler, using this observatory, was able to prove that Copernicus was right.

THE TELESCOPE

Galileo, the great Italian scientist, was the first man to use a telescope for studying the stars. This was not much more than three hundred years ago. Galileo's telescope was very weak compared to modern ones, but it changed the study of astronomy immediately. He saw that the Milky Way is not merely a bright cloud of "stardust" but is in fact millions of stars. He proved there were other planets that had not been recognized before. Without the telescope, the eye can see about six thousand stars. The latest telescopes, such as the ones on Mount Wilson and Mount Palomar in California, bring billions of stars into sight.

As we watch the stars, they seem to be moving through the sky. But it is the Earth that is really moving.

Yerkes Observatory   *Mount Wilson Observatory*
The observatories in these two pictures don't look much like Galileo's small room. The Yerkes telescope (left) is forty inches across; the Mount Wilson telescope is a hundred inches. The lenses are made of the clearest glass that can be manufactured.

The Earth is always turning like a top. As it turns, half of it always faces the sun and has "daylight," while the other half is away from the sun and has darkness. There are always stars all around the world, but in the daylight the brightness of the sunshine keeps us from seeing them. So the stars seem to disappear in the daytime.

While it turns, the Earth is also traveling at a high rate of speed around the sun. It travels in a curve that is called its *orbit.*

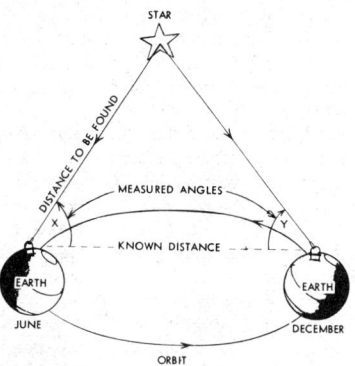

Measuring distance by triangulation.

Look at the sky some night and observe the positions of some stars. Then look two hours later. The stars will seem to have moved to the west. A month later, the stars will be even farther to the west, while in the eastern part of the sky there will be some stars we could not see before. That is because the Earth has moved to a different position. It takes the Earth a year to complete its orbit, so a year later the position of the stars will look exactly the same again.

Wherever you stand on Earth, you see one particular portion of the sky. Change to a different place and you will see a different part of the sky. In the United States and Canada, we are in the Northern Hemisphere. We do not see the same stars that are seen in Brazil or Argentina or other countries in the Southern Hemisphere, and they do not see the same stars that we do.

STUDYING THE STARS

Astronomers measure the distances of stars by a process called *triangulation.* When the Earth is at one end of its

orbit, they observe the star to see what angle it makes with the Earth. Then when the Earth is at the other end of its orbit they observe the star and take the angle again. They draw a triangle with the star at one point; the other two points are the points from which they observe the star. When one side and two angles of a triangle are known, it is possible to work out the length of the other sides.

The material of which a star is made can be learned by use of an instrument called the *spectroscope.* Every different substance, or element, gives off a different kind of light when it burns. The spectroscope catches the light from a star and breaks it up into the different wave lengths or colors. These tell what elements are to be found in the star.

Other instruments, besides the telescope and the spectroscope, that are important in astronomy are: The *photometer,* which measures the luminosity, or brightness of the light rays, of a heavenly body; the *bolometer,* which detects any change in the radiant energy, or force of the rays, coming from a heavenly body; and the *interferometer,* which shows when the size of a heavenly body changes (for many stars, composed of gases, sometimes have sudden and extreme changes in size). And the camera must be included, for it has been almost as important to astronomy as the telescope. Today, astronomers seldom study the stars by looking at them through a telescope, but instead study photographs made with the telescope.

BRANCHES OF ASTRONOMY

Modern astronomy has several branches. *Descriptive astronomy* is the putting together of all known facts to make a general description of the universe. *Astrometry* deals with the measurement of the positions, distances, sizes and motions of the heavenly bodies. *Practical astronomy* is the science of the instruments used in astronomy. *Gravitational astronomy,* also called *celestial mechanics,* is the study of the motions of heavenly bodies based on known principles of forces and movements. *Astrophysics,* the newest branch of astronomy, is the study of what the heavenly bodies are made of, their temperature, their atmospheres,

their radiation and brightness, and so on. All branches of astronomy are useful in the science of *cosmography*, the mapping of the universe, and in *cosmogony*, the study of how the universe came to exist and what its future is.

The Study Guide (in the last volume) lists many other articles on subjects related to astronomy. See also the articles TELESCOPE and SPECTROSCOPE.

Asunción

Asunción is the capital city of Paraguay, one of the countries of South America. Paraguay does not have any seacoast, but Asunción is on the great Paraguay River, on which ships can sail all the way to the Atlantic Ocean. More than 400,000 people live in Asunción, and in most ways it is a clean, modern city with fine streets and buildings. Ascunción is a very old city. It was built by the Spanish settlers of South America about 1537, more than four hundred years ago, and at first was their principal city in South America. The population in 1973 was about 438,-000.

Athabascan Indians

The Athabascan Indians are a group of American Indian tribes that once ranged all the way from the Arctic coast to Mexico and west to the Pacific Coast. They were not farmers, living on wild vegetable foods and fish. They used toboggans, snowshoes, birchbark boats, and cone-shaped tent houses. From other tribes they later learned agriculture, pottery-making, and basketry. The name is also spelled *Athapascan*.

The **Athabaska River** of Canada flows through the Athabascans' original territory. It is 765 miles long and it flows northward through Alberta to empty into **Lake Athabaska**, a long, narrow lake of 3,058 square miles, which lies between Alberta and Saskatchewan.

atheism

An atheist is a person who does not believe in God. He believes that man himself sets the standards for what is right and what is wrong. The word *atheism* comes from the Greek language; *a* means "not" and *theism* means "belief in God."

Athelstan

Athelstan, or Aethelstan, was the first king to take the title of King of Britain. He was the grandson of Alfred the Great and was born in the year 895. He won control of most of the island of Great Britain, but not all. Athelstan was the victor at the Battle of Brunenburgh, a famous battle. He died in 939.

Athenaeum

Athenaeum was the name given in ancient Greece to any temple to honor the goddess Athena (the goddess that the Romans called Minerva). Athena was the goddess of wisdom and knowledge, the arts and sciences. At one such temple, in Athens, poets and writers would meet together to talk and read their writings. The name became so closely associated with learning that a school or a literary club or magazine is often called Athenaeum.

Athens

Athens is the capital city of Greece. It is a modern, big city as the capitals of other European countries are, and more than two million people live in Athens and its suburbs. But Athens is also one of the most important cities of history. Thousands of years ago, when most of the men on earth were still ignorant savages, the learning and the science and the art of today had their start in Athens.

About five thousand years ago, men first built a city where Athens stands today. They built the city around a rocky hill about four hundred feet high. On this hill they built walled-in fortifications called an ACROPOLIS, about which there is a separate article. The people lived around the hill and farmed the land. If an enemy attacked, they could all go to the Acropolis for safety.

All cities in those ancient times passed under the rule of one king after another, fought and lost many wars, sometimes were conquered and ruled by neighboring peoples, and sometimes conquered the neighboring peoples and ruled them. For hundreds of years, Athens rose and fell in this way. But about three thousand years ago—not long after the year 1000 B.C. — the people of Athens began to develop a civilization greater than the world had known before.

The first step toward this was the Greek language as the Athenians used it. Athens was in a region of Greece called Attica and the form of Greek spoken in Athens is called Attic. No other language then had the words needed to write great books of science as well as great poetry and other literature. The poetry of Homer, written in this language, is still as great as any that has ever been written. In the hundreds of years that followed, the drama was born in the plays of Aeschylus, Sophocles, Euripides, Aristophanes, and others. Three of the greatest philosphers of all time, Socrates, Plato, and Aristotle, taught and wrote in this Greek language. Laws written in this language, by the great statesman Solon and others, gave Athens one of the earliest democratic governments. The Greek language is still used by scholars throughout the world.

Athens became a democracy in 508 B.C. The two hundred years that followed were the times of its greatest glory. During this period the sculptor Phidias and other Athenian sculptors built the magnificent buildings on the Acropolis and carved statues that are still models of beauty. The people elected their own leaders. Athens was a "city-state," which means that it was a city but also an independent country. There were many slaves, however.

In 338 B.C., Athens was conquered by King Philip of Macedon, a neighboring country in Greece. (Philip was the father of Alexander the Great, who conquered almost the entire civilized world.) After it fell under the rule of Macedon, Athens did not become big and independent again for more than two thousand years. The Romans ruled it, then a series of conquerors until the Turks made it part of Turkey about

four hundred years ago. Athens became just a small town.

In the year 1834, the entire country of Greece became independent again and Athens was made the capital. It began to grow and now is a great city again. It is the seat of the Greek Orthodox Church (also called the Orthodox Catholic Church), and the capital of the kingdom of Greece. About two-thirds of all the manufacturing in Greece is done in or near Athens.

The remains of many of the great buildings of ancient Athens, including the Acropolis, can still be seen there. During World War II, the Germans occupied Greece and captured Athens, but it was not damaged.

ATHENS, GREECE. Population about 863,000; with suburbs 2,100,000 (1973). Capital of Greece; seaport on Aegean Sea (through its suburb Piraeus).

athlete's foot

Athlete's foot is the name given to a type of itching infection that affects the feet. It is caused by a fungus which is often found in damp places such as shower-room and locker-room floors. The infection is called athlete's foot because athletes often get it in shower and locker rooms. Most modern locker rooms now have foot-baths that contain a chemical to kill the fungus.

The best way to avoid athlete's foot is to dry the feet thoroughly and use a foot powder. A mild case of athlete's foot causes the toes to itch and burn. In a severe case, blisters break out and the skin becomes white and moist and easily peels off, leaving raw spots. It often requires a doctor's care.

athletics

Physical sports and games are called *athletics*, and a person who engages in them is called an *athlete*. Most of our modern athletics are founded upon the skills that primitive man needed to survive. He had to run fast to escape from wild beasts. He had to leap for the low branches of trees, and jump over rocks and fallen trees in his path. He had to fight against wild animals and men. He learned to throw stones, and to use clubs.

The first contests were foot races, weightlifting, and wrestling.

Early civilizations used athletics as training for war. The Olympic Games, which began in Greece more than 2,500 years ago—about 700 B.C.—were the first organized athletics in which athletes competed for prizes.

PROFESSIONALS AND AMATEURS

Anyone who receives payment for being an athlete or for teaching others to be athletes is considered a "professional." An "amateur" is not allowed to accept payment; if he does so, even once in his life, he is considered a professional and may never again be classed as an amateur. Games played by professionals are usually called *sports* and games played by amateurs are usually called *athletics*, though they may be the same game.

GAMES AND CONTESTS

Athletics may be either *games* or *contests*. Games may be played by individuals or by teams. By far the largest group includes games of the "ball and goal" type,

which are played by two teams. In these games the object is to keep possession of the ball, carry it forward into the opponent's territory, and cross his goal. The official amateur games in this group include American Rugby (football), English Rugby, soccer, ice hockey and field hockey, shinny (in which sticks are used to carry the ball), lacrosse (in which a *crosse*, strung somewhat like a tennis racket, is used), polo, water polo, and basketball. Six-man football and touch football are also recognized as official games, and there are many minor games.

"Ball and tag" games are also team games, in which the object is to strike, or bat, the ball in such a way that a prescribed distance can be run before the opposing team can recover the ball and tag the runner. They include baseball, cricket, softball, and countless minor or unofficial games.

"Exchange ball" games are those known as *net games* and *wall games*. The object is to strike the ball in such a manner that it cannot be properly returned. This group includes tennis, table tennis or Ping-Pong, badminton, volley ball, handball, squash, jai-alai (pelota), and pallone (an Italian game like tennis). Here also there are hundreds of minor games.

CONTESTS

Contests include a wide variety of athletic events, such as running, jumping, swimming, boxing, wrestling, the throwing of various objects (such as the discus or javelin), weightlifting, climbing, hurdle races, and walking. This group includes everything from log-rolling contests to racing on snowshoes, and there are established records in every one.

The rules and definitions used in amateur games in the United States are usually those of the Amateur Athletic Union, or A.A.U.

There are separate articles on OLYMPIC GAMES, TRACK AND FIELD SPORTS, and the various games and contests.

Atlanta

Atlanta is the capital of the state of Georgia. It is the biggest city in the state and one of the biggest in the South. It was founded as the town of "Terminus," in 1837, four years after a settler called Hardy Ivy had built his cabin there on land that had formerly belonged to the Creek Indians. In 1845 the city was named Atlanta.

At that time north Georgia, where Atlanta is, was not nearly so important as the seacoast, where Savannah was the important city. But Atlanta grew faster than any other city in the South. During the Civil War it was a most important center for the Confederate forces. It was taken by General Sherman during the decisive Atlanta Campaign of 1864, and much of the city was burned, but the progressive Atlantans rebuilt it even faster than they had built it originally. When Georgia began to recover from the war, Atlanta was the most important city. It became the capital in 1868.

Atlanta today is a center of education, industry, and business. It is the home of the Georgia Institute of Technology (Georgia Tech), Emory and Oglethorpe Universities, Atlanta University and the

Atlanta University System (for Negroes), and many others. The Federal Penitentiary in Atlanta is known all over the world as a model institution of its kind. Coca-Cola originated in Atlanta and is made there.

Points of interest include the Archives Building, with its historical museum; the domed capitol, in which is the state library; the High Museum of Art; and the Cyclorama of the Battle of Atlanta. STONE MOUNTAIN (about which there is a separate article), with its gigantic carvings of Confederate heroes, is only fifteen miles from Atlanta.

ATLANTA, GEORGIA. Population 496,973 (1970 census). Capital and largest city in the state. Founded 1837.

Atlantic Charter

In the summer of 1940, the British were fighting all alone in World War II. France had been conquered by the Germans, and the United States had not yet entered the war. The United States wanted to help the British, but the American people wanted to be sure that the British would use this help to fight for the same goals that the United States was seeking.

In August, 1941, the President of the United States (Franklin D. Roosevelt) and the British Prime Minister (Winston Churchill) met on the U.S. heavy cruiser *Augusta* in the Atlantic Ocean near Newfoundland. On August 14 they issued a statement of what both countries stood for. It is called the Atlantic Charter.

In the Atlantic Charter the two countries said that they did not seek to win new territory in the war; that they wanted all people to have the right to choose their own countries and governments; that all countries should be helped to have prosperity and freedom; and that the use of force should be ended and all countries should work for peace. See the FOUR FREEDOMS, which stated briefly much that was said in the Atlantic Charter.

Atlantic City

Atlantic City is a famous resort on the coast of New Jersey. Millions of people go there every year to enjoy swimming from the fine beach and for other amusements. Atlantic City is warmer in winter and cooler in summer than the country around it, and draws many visitors from the cities of Philadelphia, 70 miles away, and New York, 130 miles away. Many national organizations have their conventions there in the big Convention Hall, which seats almost 50,000 people. In several piers built out over the water, there are theaters that offer a variety of shows.

A boardwalk stretches for over 7 miles along the beach, is 50 to 60 feet wide, and is lined with shops, restaurants, various amusements, and dozens of first-class hotels. One can be pushed down the boardwalk in picturesque rolling chairs, consisting of seats mounted on carriage wheels and wide enough for two or three persons. The sandy beach, known as Absecon Beach, is one of the finest in the world. In Atlantic City, "Miss America" is selected from beautiful young women representing all parts of the United States. In serving its many visitors, Atlantic

City has become one of the biggest cities in New Jersey. The population in 1970 was 47,859.

Atlantic Ocean

The Atlantic Ocean is the second-largest ocean in the world, covering about 31,830,000 square miles. Including bays, gulfs, and other inland seas, the area is more than 41,000,000 square miles. Only the Pacific Ocean is larger. The largest continent, Asia, has about 17,000,000 square miles. The Atlantic Ocean, particularly the North Atlantic, has borne more traffic than any other trade route in history.

A look at the map shows that the Atlantic is shaped like the letter "S." Its northern boundary is about the northernmost point of the British Isles. It bends toward the west, to the Grand Banks, where the ocean floor rises like a shelf off the coast of Newfoundland and where are found the most important fishing grounds in the world. The narrow part of the letter "S" is where Dakar, Africa, is only about 1,800 miles from the bulge of Brazil. Then the ocean widens once again to meet the Antarctic in the south. The average depth of the Atlantic Ocean is about two and a half miles.

The Atlantic Ocean connects with the Pacific through the Panama Canal and through "Drake's Passage" below South America; and with the Indian Ocean through the Mediterranean Sea, the Suez Canal, the Gulf of Suez, and the Red Sea.

TIDES AND CURRENTS

In the article on TIDES you can read that there are different numbers of tides per day in different bodies of water and even in the same body of water. The Atlantic is more regular than other oceans. Almost throughout its entire shoreline there are two high tides and two low tides daily.

The tides produce currents, which reverse their direction with the flow of the water. But there are other currents, not caused by the tides, which maintain a steady flow of water in one direction, like great rivers, flowing through the open sea as if there were banks on both sides. One such current is the *Gulf Stream*. It begins in the Gulf of Mexico, where the water is warm, and flows northeast along the coast of North America, except that it is separated from the coast by the "cold wall," which is a strip of cold water. The Gulf Stream is about a mile deep. It flows at an average speed of 3 to 4 miles per hour.

THE ATLANTIC DRIFT

When the Gulf Stream starts northward it has a surface temperature of 80 degrees—warm enough to swim in comfortably, even in the winter. As it proceeds farther north, and loses speed, the water becomes cooler, but it is still warmer than the surrounding waters. As the Gulf Stream nears the British Isles and the Scandinavian countries, it ceases to be a current and becomes a "drift" of water, called the North Atlantic Drift. Its effect upon the Scandinavian countries and British Isles is of tremendous importance. If it were not for the masses of warm water, raising the temperature

of the air, those countries would surely be as frozen as the Arctic.

THE ATLANTIC RIDGE

The floor of the ocean is not level. It consists of mountains and valleys, knolls and dales, just like the land surface. The only difference is that it is covered with water.

In the Atlantic is found the biggest undersea mountain range in the world, called the Atlantic Ridge. It begins near Iceland, and runs through the middle of the ocean as far south as the very tip of Africa. Then it turns east toward the Indian Ocean. Near the equator it is cut by a deep canyon, a "mountain pass," known as the Romanche Trench. Most parts of the ridge rise 5,000 to 10,000 feet above the sea bottom, and another mile or more of water covers most of the peaks. Some peaks rise out of the water, and these are islands. (Most sea islands are actually the peaks of underwater mountains.) Pico Island, in the Azores, is the highest point, rising 17,000 feet above the ocean floor, with 8,000 feet of its land above the water.

ATLANTIC DATA

The shape, or contour, of the floor of the Atlantic has been very well charted. The laying of the first transatlantic cables, between 1850 and 1865, revealed many facts, including the existence of the Atlantic Ridge. With the discovery of echo-sounding and the deepsea camera, the story of the underseas landscape could be completed. The deepest waters of the Atlantic (such ocean spots are called *deeps*, or *trenches*) are the Milwaukee Depth, near the Bahamas, found by the U.S.S. *Milwaukee* in 1939, which drops to 30,246 feet, and the Dolphin Deep, near Puerto Rico, which is 27,972 feet deep.

THE SMALLER SEAS

Smaller seas of the Atlantic are Hudson and Baffin Bays, the Caribbean Sea, and the Gulf of Mexico, in the west; the North Sea, Baltic Sea, Bay of Biscay, Mediterranean Sea, and Gulf of Guinea, in the east.

See also the articles on OCEAN and on the SARGASSO SEA.

Atlantis

There is a story thousands of years old about a "lost island" in the Atlantic Ocean. The story was told by the ancient Greeks, and had been handed down from father to son for many generations before the Greek philosopher Plato wrote a famous story about it, about 375 B.C.

The island of Atlantis, according to Plato's story, was really a series of islands. Imagine in the center a hill, surrounded by a ring of water; the ring of water surrounded by a circle of land, then another ring of water and one of land, until there were nine rings of water and nine of land. The islands had been created by Neptune, god of the sea, for Cleito, his beloved. From their children the king and people of Atlantis were descended.

The islands were very rich, and the people content. The city was built of black and red stone; the roofs of the

The Greek island of Thera may have been the main island in Atlantis.

© 1967 by The New York Times Company.
Reprinted by permission.

houses were of red copper and flashed in the sun; and there were two beautiful temples, one surrounded by a golden wall and the other with silver walls, golden pinnacles, and a roof of ivory.

In 1967, a city buried by a volcanic eruption in 1500 B.C., was found near Greece. Archeologists say this might be Atlantis.

Atlas

The Atlas Mountains stretch along the Mediterranean seacoast of North Africa for about 1,500 miles. They are high mountains and prevent Mediterranean rain clouds from reaching the Sahara Desert.

There are several ranges. Nearest the sea is the Maritime or Little Atlas range, about 400 miles long and with an average height of 5,000 feet. The Great Atlas range stretches 400 miles from Morocco to Algeria and averages 10,000 feet; it includes the peak called Debje Toubkal, 13,665 feet, the highest in the system.

An ancient Greek legend tells the story of the Titans, a race of giants who were the ancestors of the Greek gods and ruled the world until they were defeated in battle by the Greek gods. To prevent the Titans from ever trying to regain their power, they were punished in various ways. Atlas, one of the Titans, was made to hold the world on his shoulders. A book of maps is called an atlas because old maps made hundreds of years ago were decorated with a picture of Atlas holding the world on his shoulders.

atmosphere

Atmosphere is all the gas that surrounds a planet such as the earth. On the earth, the atmosphere is the gas we call air, which is necessary to life. On other planets the atmosphere might be other and deadly gases.

The earth's atmosphere is made up almost entirely of the gases nitrogen and oxygen, but there are many other gases that exist in it in very small quantities. About 78% of the atmosphere is nitrogen, about 21% is oxygen, and most of the other 1% is argon. But some of the gases that exist in tiny quantities are very

important. They include carbon dioxide, from which plants take the carbon they need for growth; ozone, a form of concentrated oxygen that is found chiefly in a layer called the *ozonosphere* or *ozone layer* about 10 to 36 miles above the earth's surface and helps keep the earth warm; and helium and hydrogen, which are very light and rise to the top of the atmosphere.

DENSITY OF THE ATMOSPHERE

The atmosphere is held to the earth by the power of gravity. Close to the surface, the air is very dense (thick). Its weight and its pressure are at their highest. Farther out, it becomes thinner, or less dense, until about 250 miles from the surface there is no air at all. This is the end of the atmosphere.

About 17,000 feet above the earth, the air is only half as dense as it is at sea level; when a person at that altitude breathes he takes in barely enough oxygen to stay alive. At about 34,000 feet (6½ miles) the air is only one-fourth as dense and will not support life. A cubic mile of air at sea level weighs 5,-600,000 tons—more than 11 billion pounds or 180 billion ounces—but data from artificial satellites show that 220 miles out a cubic mile of the atmosphere weighs only 2 ounces!

See the articles on AIR, BOILING POINT, ARTIFICIAL SATELLITE, and SOUND, for some effects of the density and pressure of the air.

LAYERS OF THE ATMOSPHERE

The atmosphere has two main layers. The layer closest to the earth is the *troposphere*. This layer goes up as much as 11 miles over the equator but only 5 miles over the North and South Poles; in the temperate zones (including the United States) it is 6 to 7 miles. Everything above is the *stratosphere*, reaching out to the *exosphere* (space beyond the atmosphere). Where the troposphere meets the stratosphere is called the *tropopause*.

The stratosphere has two important layers. In the ozonosphere, mentioned above, ozone absorbs ultraviolet and infrared rays from the sun's light rays. This creates a warm layer that slows down the cooling of the earth. Above the ozonosphere is the *ionosphere*, where the air is affected by electrical waves (See ION.) Radio carries for long distances because electromagnetic waves bounce back from the ionosphere. Regions or layers called D, E and F mark the end of the ozonosphere and the beginning and end of the ionosphere.

Within the troposphere, the temperature goes down rapidly at higher altitudes; that is why high mountains are always covered with snow. For every 300 feet of altitude the temperature goes down about 1° Fahrenheit; this is called the *lapse rate*. At the tropopause the temperature is 60° to 70° below zero. In the stratosphere the atmosphere stays at the same low temperature up to the levels (such as the ozonosphere) where it goes up to 300°, 400°, or even 1,000° *above* zero.

EXPLORATION OF THE ATMOSPHERE

The first man to explore the stratosphere was Auguste PICCARD, about whom there is a separate article. In 1931

he rose in a balloon to nearly ten miles and in 1932 he reached 54,120 feet, which is more than ten miles. Most knowledge of the atmosphere comes from unmanned balloons, and more recently from rockets and artificial satellites, which rise hundreds of miles carrying instruments that record conditions at different heights. Some information is automatically radioed back to earth and some is taken from the instruments when they fall back to earth.

CIRCULATION — EFFECT ON WINDS

At low levels the air is so tightly bound to the earth by gravity that even the rotation of the earth at 1,000 miles per hour does not move it. At high altitudes the rotation and motion of the earth, along with the light and heat rays from the sun, cause the atmosphere to circulate, or move around the earth, in a definite pattern. This pattern is:

1. A belt of low pressure or windless calms, called *doldrums,* near the equator.
2. *Trade winds,* just beyond the doldrums. They blow toward the doldrums, somewhat westward.
3. Two belts of calms, called the *horse latitudes,* beyond the trade winds (about 30° from the equator, the latitude in which Florida is).
4. Two regions where the prevailing (usual) winds are *westerlies,* in the middle temperate zones, for example the latitudes in which New York and London are in the north, or Buenos Aires in the south.
5. Regions around the poles where the winds travel at high speeds in large circles (*polar whirls*).

WATER IN THE AIR

Everywhere throughout the lower atmosphere there is some *humidity,* or water vapor, in the air. There may be a great deal of it or very little. In liquid form it is rain. In cold weather the water vapor, which is really water in the form of a gas, may change from a vapor form and then turn quickly into the shape of snowflakes. Sometimes this water vapor may turn into ice instead of snow. This frozen rain is called *hail.* Hail may be as small as peas or as large as hen's eggs.

There are times when the water vapor in the air floats slowly toward the ground in the form of very tiny droplets of water. This is called fog. The fog lies on the ground but may stretch upward for as much as a thousand feet or more. When the fog is very heavy it may prevent you from seeing more than five or ten feet ahead.

Clouds are another form of water vapor in the air. Like fog they are made up of tiny droplets of water, but they float high in the air instead of spreading out along the ground. They may float as high as 50,000 feet above the ground. Clouds are usually higher in the summer than in the winter. Some parts of the United States are cloudier than others. In most parts of America it is cloudy about half the time.

DUST IN THE AIR

There is always some dust in the atmosphere. At high levels over the ocean there is least dust. The most dust is found low over cities and is caused by the smoke from coal and oil fires used in heating and manufacturing. Volcanoes shoot tons of fine ash and dust into the air whenever they erupt or explode. This dust may float in the air at very high levels for years at a time. The wind blowing over fields where the earth has been turned over by plows will often lift fine bits of earth, sand, and tiny seeds high into the air. Some of this dust will settle down to earth very quickly but much of it will float in the air for as long as three years.

Water vapor in the air will condense or turn to liquid when it touches certain kinds of dust. Each tiny particle or bit of dust becomes the center of a droplet of water. When there are enough droplets they form fog, clouds, rain, or snow.

However, the amount of water vapor in the atmosphere is quite small. If all of it turned to rain at the same time, it would cover the earth with only about 1½ inches of rain in the summer and half that much in the winter.

The brilliant colors we sometimes see at sunrise and sunset are caused by dust. The dust scatters the rays of sunlight, changing them into bright colors. The sky's blue color is caused by vapor and dust. All the colors that we see are caused by light rays that have different wave lengths. Blue has very short waves. The dust in the atmosphere holds back the shorter waves of light from the sun but the long ones, which look red to us, are able to get through.

atoll

An atoll is a small island shaped like a ring or horseshoe, found in the warm waters of tropical seas. Inside the ring there is water, called a lagoon. The ring is made of the skeletons of millions upon millions of tiny sea creatures called coral. These creatures live together in huge colonies. They live where the water is less than 510 feet deep, because they need sunlight, which cannot reach very far into deep water.

Coral like to live in waters that are close to the shores of an island. After thousands of years the skeletons of dead coral form a rock wall like a ring around the island. Then suppose an earthquake causes the island to settle below the water. The coral ring remains, and is an atoll.

Dirt, pieces of wood, mud, and other rubbish are washed over the rough coral rock by the waves, and in time soil is formed over the rock. Seeds carried for miles by the ocean winds will drop on this soil and certain kinds of palm trees and other plants will grow on the atoll. Sometimes the waves will break off pieces of the top of the ring or wash away a large section of it so that the atoll has the shape of a horseshoe above the water. The water of the lagoon inside the ring is never very deep. There are many atolls in the South Pacific Ocean. See also the article on CORAL.

atom

Everything in the universe is composed of tiny particles called atoms. Atoms are so small that in the smallest grain of sand there are billions of atoms.

For thousands of years, men have written and guessed about the nature of tiny particles like these, but they did not have any real idea of what an atom is like. Thinking men in ancient Greece, including one named Democritus, 2,500 years ago, asked this question: What would happen if you should cut a piece of iron into smaller and still smaller pieces? You would finally get to a particle so small that you could not cut it further. They called this imaginary particle the atom, which in the Greek language meant "uncuttable." But they did not have any real idea of what an atom is like.

Then, about 150 years ago, an Englishman named John Dalton made a great step forward. In fact, he really started the science that has become modern chemistry. The ancient Greeks were on the right track, he said; all matter is composed of atoms, and there are different kinds of atoms, one kind for iron and another kind for gold and a different kind for each other chemical element. But all the atoms of one kind are exactly alike. All iron atoms are the same, all gold atoms are the same, and so on.

Because of this, chemists were able to find out how the weight of one atom compares with the weight of a different atom. It would be impossible to weigh a single atom, because it is too small— it takes billions of atoms to make an ounce. But we know now that hydrogen, which is a gas, has the lightest atom; that oxygen, the life-giving gas in the air, weighs about 16 times as much as hydrogen, and that iron weighs about 56 times as much. The "atomic weight" of every element is known.

THE ATOM IS NOT "UNCUTTABLE"

In the next great advance, about sixty years ago, chemists made the startling discovery that atoms are not "uncuttable" after all, and that the atom is not the smallest possible particle. Some elements, such as uranium and radium, break to pieces gradually by giving off rays; that is, they throw off some of the particles of their atoms. They continue to do this until they change into lead, which is a lighter element than uranium or radium.

Scientists were spurred on by this discovery. They began to study the atom in every way they could think of. By the time of World War II, they had found out much about the atom. Unhappily, the first great use of this new knowledge was the atomic bomb, which is used to destroy things; but they knew they were on their way to uses that would be of great benefit to mankind.

WHAT THE ATOM IS LIKE

A picture of the solar system usually shows the sun in the center and several planets, one of which is the Earth, revolving around it. Except for the fact that the atom is so small, and the sun and the planets so huge, the atom is much like the solar system.

Each atom has a center, called its *nucleus.* In this center are one or more particles called *protons.* A proton is a particle that has a positive electrical

THE ATOM

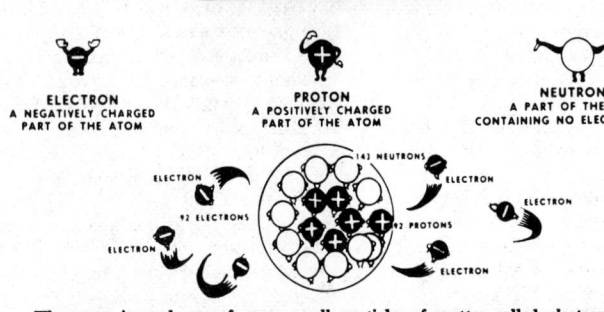

ELECTRON
A NEGATIVELY CHARGED
PART OF THE ATOM

PROTON
A POSITIVELY CHARGED
PART OF THE ATOM

NEUTRON
A PART OF THE ATOM
CONTAINING NO ELECTRIC CHARGE

The atom is made up of many small particles of matter called *electrons*, *protons*, and *neutrons*. The heaviest atom in nature is the uranium atom, which supplies atomic energy. This atom contains 92 electrons, with 92 protons and 143 to 146 neutrons in its nucleus. Electrons travel constantly in loops around the nucleus, much as planets travel around the sun.

charge.

Revolving around this center, or nucleus, are particles of negative electricity called *electrons*. An electron is very light. It takes 1,845 electrons to weigh as much as one proton.

As you can read in the article on ELECTRICITY, positive and negative electricity attract each other. You may have seen how this works with two magnets. Each magnet has a positive end and a negative end. Touch the positive end of one magnet to the negative end of another and they will cling together; but two negative ends, or two positive ends, will not stay together. The atom is held together because the protons are positive and the electrons are negative.

Every atom has exactly as many protons as electrons, so that the positive and the negative balance each other. The nucleus of the hydrogen atom has one proton, and therefore the hydrogen atom has one electron. All other atoms are heavier than hydrogen, having two or more protons in their nuclei. The "atomic number" of any element is the number of protons or electrons in each of its atoms. For example, the atomic number of hydrogen is 1. The atomic number of uranium is 92, because there are 92 protons and 92 electrons in the uranium atom.

There is still another particle that goes to make up the atom. This is called a *neutron*. A neutron weighs about the same as a proton, but it does not have any electrical charge at all, either positive or negative. Neutrons are found only in the nucleus of the atom, as protons are. Neutrons add to the weight of the atom.

Because of these neutrons, the same element may have atoms of different weights. Different atoms of the same element are called *isotopes*. Uranium, for example, has several isotopes. The uranium atom always has 92 protons in its nucleus, but one of its isotopes, called U-238, has 146 neutrons (146 neutrons + 92 protons = 238), while the isotope called U-235 has 143 neutrons in its nucleus (143 + 92 = 235). The atomic weight is about the same as the neutrons plus the protons; for example, the atomic weight of U-238 is about 238.

A *stable* element is composed of atoms that do not rapidly throw off their particles—their protons, neutrons, and electrons—in the form of rays. The lighter elements are usually stable. The heavier

elements are often *unstable*. They readily break down into different isotopes and even into different elements. This is explained in the articles on ATOMIC ENERGY and RADIOACTIVITY.

Hundreds of years ago there were men called *alchemists* who tried to change cheap metals, such as lead, into gold. They never succeeded, but today it is possible to change some elements into other elements by changing the number of protons, neutrons and electrons in them. To do this, we must knock out some of the particles, or add other particles. This is very hard to do, because the forces binding the particles together are very great. But as science progresses, it is being done more and more.

atomic bomb

An atomic weapon is one that makes use of the great explosive force produced when an atom releases any of the particles of which it is made. The first atomic bomb (also called an *atom bomb* or *A-bomb*) began an entirely new era in warfare and perhaps in the history of the human race.

During World War II, Germany was defeated largely by the dropping of huge bombs called "blockbusters". The largest blockbusters each contained as much as a ton, 2,000 pounds, of the powerful explosive TNT. Thousands of these bombs were dropped. It was expected that thousands would be dropped on Japan, against which the war continued.

Then on August 6, 1945, an American airplane dropped a single bomb on Hiroshima, Japan, a city of about 175,000 people. It was the first atomic bomb used in warfare. Though it was not even as large as a blockbuster, it was *twenty thousand* times as powerful. Unlike previous bombs, this one did not explode on the ground, but 1,500 feet above the city. The flash when it exploded could be seen for 200 miles. The explosion flattened buildings in nearly four square miles— several hundred city blocks—and it killed 70,000 people.

When Japan did not answer a United States demand for surrender, an American plane dropped a second atomic bomb, three days later, on the somewhat larger city of Nagasaki. Because Nagasaki is a hilly city, most of its people were sheltered from the blast, but even so 35,000 died and about 40,000 were injured. The next day, August 10, Japan asked for peace. Two bombs had won a war.

No atomic weapon has been used in war since then, but the United States and

the Soviet Union have since made atomic bombs that are hundreds or thousands of times more powerful than the atomic bombs that defeated Japan, and the HYDROGEN BOMB, about which there is a separate article, is many times more deadly than the atomic bomb.

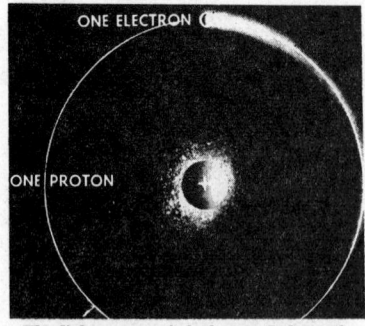

ONE ELECTRON

ONE PROTON

The lightest atom is hydrogen. It has only one electron and one proton, and no neutrons.

THE START OF THE ATOMIC BOMB

The article ATOM explains how the atom is formed, with protons and neutrons in its center, or *nucleus,* and electrons in a ring around the nucleus. Tiny though the atom is, these particles are held together by great power.

At the start of World War II it had been known for about 50 years that atoms could produce a great amount of energy if it could be released; that the potential energy in a single quart of water might destroy a city. The exact amount of potential energy was not known until the great scientist Albert Einstein worked out the following formula, which later became famous:

$$E = mc^2$$

The formula means that the energy, or power, produced is the mass (size and weight) of the atomic particle times the square of the speed of light. An atomic particle is unbelievably tiny but the speed of light is 186,300 and the square of the speed of light is 186,300 × 186,300, or 34,707,690,000. Even a tiny mass becomes considerable when multiplied by a figure like that.

The object was to "split" the atom, to "smash" it or break it apart so as to release some of the energy holding its particles together. When war seemed likely in 1939, a group of American scientists and also Einstein wrote to President Franklin D. Roosevelt and told him that the atomic bomb seemed possible. Roosevelt decided that it must be tried, even at great cost.

Later, when the United States was drawn into the war, the Canadian and British governments collaborated with the United States in the building of the atomic bomb.

Perfecting the atomic bomb cost two billion dollars. The work on it was the best-kept military secret in history.

THE MANHATTAN PROJECT

As the article on ATOMIC ENERGY explains, the success of the bomb depended on a "chain reaction" in the form of uranium called U-235. A chain reaction means that the splitting of one atom causes others to split, and those cause still others to split, and so on. The first problem was to get enough U-235, and

this required a large plant and plenty of electrical power.

Such a plant was set up at Oak Ridge, Tennessee. The job was given the code name "Manhattan Project," and General Leslie R. Groves was put in charge of it.

As soon as a small quantity of U-235 was obtained, the next step was to see if a chain reaction would actually take place. On the squash courts of the University of Chicago's athletic stadium the first atomic "pile" was set up. The test proved that a chain reaction did occur.

A large atomic pile was then built at Oak Ridge, and another plant was built at Hanford, Washington. Six years after Einstein wrote his letter, a bomb was completed.

THE TEST BOMB

On July 16, 1945, the first atomic bomb was tested far out on a desert in New Mexico. The bomb was dropped from a steel tower and the result was observed from shelters ten miles away. The War Department described it in these words:

"At the appointed time there was a blinding flash lighting up the whole area brighter than the brightest daylight. A mountain range three miles from the observation point stood out in bold relief. Then came a tremendous sustained roar and a heavy pressure wave which knocked down two men outside the control tower. Immediately thereafter, a huge multicolored surging cloud boiled up to an altitude of over 40,000 feet. Clouds in its path disappeared . . .

"The test was over, the project a success."

TRIGGERING THE BOMB

The test answered the last question: Would the bomb actually go off?

It is not a simple matter to "trigger" an atomic bomb. If there is enough pure U-235 in a mass to cause an explosion, it will explode "of itself." The only protection is to keep the mass of U-235 below a certain "critical" size. Scientists had to calculate this size—they could not experiment in a laboratory to find it out.

The bomb had to be made in two parts. Each part would be below the critical size, but the two parts when brought together would be above the critical size. So the "trigger" would be some mechanism to unite the two parts.

The reaction, once it starts, runs through the entire load in about one-millionth of a second. It explodes long before any but a small fraction of the material (about three-tenths of one per cent) is fissioned.

THE DECISION TO USE THE BOMB

President Harry S. Truman made the decision to drop an atomic bomb on a big Japanese city. His decision has been criticized in many countries including the United States, for he knew that tens of thousands of Japanese civilians would die, but if the bomb had not been used the war against Japan could not have been won without an amphibious invasion that would have cost several hundred thousand Allied and Japanese lives.

When World War II ended, there was a widespread belief that international treaties should be signed outlawing the bomb. But Soviet Russia refused to enter such a treaty and soon (in 1950 or before) had developed an atomic bomb of its own. Britain and Canada already had the atomic bomb, through partnership with the U.S., and France's scientists perfected one by 1957, [Communist] China by 1963.

No nation can be sure it has perfected a nuclear weapon until it has been tested. When a nation successfully tests a nuclear bomb, every other nation immediately knows about it, as will be explained below. Russia's first atomic bombs were tested in Siberia; the United States tested its biggest bombs near islands such as Bikini and Eniwetok in the Pacific Ocean; France used the Sahara Desert, and China used one of its own deserts.

In 1961 the U.S. and U.S.S.R. agreed not to test atomic bombs, except underground, so as to avoid the danger of radioactive fall-out.

NUCLEAR WEAPONS AND FALL-OUT

Both the atomic and the hydrogen bomb are called *nuclear weapons* because their power comes from the nucleus of the atom. Their principles are different but have the same result.

The atomic bomb uses *fission,* or splitting: one atom is split into two parts. The hydrogen bomb uses *fusion,* or welding together: two atoms are joined to make one.

For example, with fission an atom having 10 neutrons might be split into two atoms of 5 and 4 neutrons. With fusion, two atoms having 6 and 5 neutrons might be joined to make one atom having 10 neutrons. But in either case there would be one neutron left over and the release of that neutron is what supplies the desired energy.

A problem created by the testing of nuclear bombs is that each explosion releases much radioactive material that can be very harmful to man and also to all animals and plants. A Japanese fishing boat, despite many warnings, got too close to an American test in 1953 and the men aboard were so badly burned by the radioactivity in the air that some died or were injured for life.

The radioactive material floats over the earth as dust and finally falls to earth, for which reason it is called *fall-out.* Some scientists believe this fall-out is very dangerous, others say there is too little to be dangerous. Only time can prove which is right, but the danger caused many persons including leading scientists to urge that all tests be stopped. Russia proposed to the United States that they be stopped but President Eisenhower insisted that Russia first coöperate in a plan to prevent future atomic wars. In the meantime scientists worked to develop the "clean" nuclear weapon from which there is no radioactive fall-out.

HOW EXPLOSIONS ARE DETECTED

There are several different ways by which the explosion of a nuclear bomb can be detected thousands of miles away. The principal ones are:

1. By seismograph, which registers the shock to the earth, especially underground.
2. By "listening" devices, which detect the sound waves sent out by the explosion (unless it is underground).

3. By examining the upper atmosphere for radioactive debris, particles of atoms sent out by the explosion. At 6 to 8 miles above the earth these travel about 1,200 miles per day.
4. By sensitive instruments that will record on photographic film or by radio the special x-rays and light rays produced by an explosive.

In 1958 scientists representing all countries that had nuclear weapons worked out a plan for about 200 detection posts, scattered throughout the world so as to detect an explosion anywhere.

See HYDROGEN BOMB, RADIOACTIVITY, and ATOMIC ENERGY.

atomic energy

The particles that make up the tiny atom are held together with tremendous force. More than fifty years ago, scientists began to realize that if an atom could be "smashed"—that is, if the particles in it could be made to fly apart—the large amount of energy that had been holding them together might be released for a useful purpose—to run machines, supply heat, and so on.

The way to smash something is to bombard it with something else. In the case of the atom, this is not so easy.

NEUTRON BOMBARDMENT

Hitting the nucleus, or center, of an atom may be compared to firing a BB gun at a fly buzzing around somewhere in an acre of ground surrounded by chicken wire. The chance of hitting it is not great! But if a million BBs could be fired at a swarm of flies, some hits would surely be scored.

For bombarding the atom, scientists chose the neutron. There are some neutrons in the nuclei of most atoms. A neutron is heavy (for its size) and it has no electrical charge that might affect its direction. So scientists began to bombard atoms with streams of neutrons. Every now and then a neutron would hit the nucleus of an atom and would smash it, driving out one of its neutrons.

In 1933 an Italian scientist, Enrico Fermi, discovered that sometimes the nucleus is not smashed by the neutron but instead "captures" it. The neutron becomes part of the nucleus, thus creating a heavier atom. Bombarding uranium, which has the atomic number 92, Fermi produced a new element, *neptunium,* with an atomic number of 93.

Other experimenters joined in to learn what else happens in the neutron bombardment. They included O. Hahn and F. Strassman in Germany, and in Denmark Otto R. Frisch and Lise Meitner (who had fled from the Nazis in Austria). They discovered that neutron bombardment could split a uranium nucleus into two nearly equal parts.

Most of the uranium found in the earth has the atomic weight 238, but about seven uranium atoms in a thousand are lighter, with the atomic weight 235. This lighter atom is called U-235. It is fissionable (can be split) by neutron bombardment; and the effect of a hit on U-235 was found to be that it broke the nucleus into two parts, at the same time releasing a few free neutrons and giving effect to Einstein's formula $E = mc^2$.

In January, 1939, the Danish scientist Niels Bohr visited Princeton University and told Fermi, Einstein and other American scientists about these discoveries.

THE CHAIN REACTION

It was the release of the free neutrons that excited the scientists. So far there had been no real gain in smashing an atom; it took as much energy to smash the atom as the smashed atom released. But if smashing one atom would release neutrons to smash other atoms, which in turn would release neutrons to smash still other atoms, the "chain reaction" would generate enormous explosive force in a fraction of a second.

The first application of this newly found principle was in the building of the ATOMIC BOMB, which is the subject of the article before this one.

ATOMIC REACTORS

In developing the "A-bomb," the government built one plant at Hanford, Washington, whose purpose was to produce *plutonium*. Plutonium is an artificial element, number 94. It is fissionable, and so can be used in atomic bombs.

Plutonium is produced in what is called a *reactor*. This is a kind of tank, filled with U-235. The U-235 is fissioned at a slow rate so that it will not explode. The neutrons that do the fissioning are slowed down by *moderators*. These are bricks made of a substance, such as graphite, that will slow down the neutrons and help them to hit nearby atoms and split them. Rods of cadmium, boron or other material that will absorb neutrons are thrust into the mass of U-235, and the more rods are used, the slower the chain reaction will be.

The slow fissioning of U-235 produces not only plutonium but also several hundred other substances. During the war, these by-products were thrown away. After the war, the Atomic Energy Commission was set up to direct the work of the plants and to seek peacetime uses for atomic energy. The by-products began to be saved and analyzed. Many of them have turned out to have great value in medicine, industry, and agriculture.

RADIOACTIVE ISOTOPES

Isotopes are different forms of the same chemical element (as explained in the articles on the ATOM). Many of the heavier isotopes are radioactive. This makes them very valuable in medicine.

Radium has long been used in the treatment of cancer, but it is a very rare element and very expensive. Now radioactive substances that will do the same work as radium, and in most cases do it more safely, are available to hospitals and doctors at prices they can afford.

Another use of radioactive isotopes is as "tracers." For example, carbon 14 is radioactive, yet can be taken into an animal or plant body without harm. Because it is radioactive its course through the body can be traced, and it helps in the study of physiology.

POWER FROM ATOMS

The explosion of an atomic bomb generates heat comparable to the interior of the sun. Even the "slow burning" in a reactor produces so much heat that the tank must be cooled by special methods.

Any heat is a source of power, and atomic heat can be put to work in many ways, for example, to make steam for steam engines. The United States Navy was first to try atomic power in a submarine, the *Nautilus*. It proved to be so much better than any other source of power that the Navy proceeded to "lay down" (start building) a fleet of eight atomic-powered submarines and also atomic-powered warships of three other kinds: a carrier, the *Enterprise;* a guided-missile cruiser, the *Long Beach;* and a guided-missile destroyer.

In developing atomic energy for peaceful uses, the United States, Canada and Britain work together. In 1957 six European nations formed an alliance called EUR-ATOM to pool their atomic knowledge. They were France, Italy, West Germany, Belgium, the Netherlands, and Luxembourg.

The **Atomic Energy Commission,** created by Act of Congress in 1946, is a five-man board that decides what atomic energy in the United States can be used for peaceful purposes and what information must be kept secret.

Read also the articles on the ATOM, RADIOACTIVITY, and SUBMARINE.

atomizer

An atomizer is a device for spraying perfume or other liquids. The liquid is placed in a small bottle, and a small tube leads down into the liquid. This is joined to another tube with a nozzle at one end and a rubber bulb at the other end. When the rubber bulb is squeezed, a blast of air is forced across the upper opening of the glass tube in the liquid. A rapid stream of air over the top of a tube reduces the air pressure in the tube. This causes the air pressure in the bottle to force the liquid up through the tube and into the path of the blast of air. The air carries the liquid along and forces it through the narrow opening at the nozzle. This divides it into very small droplets so that it comes out as a fine spray or mist. It is not really separated into atoms, but it is said to be "atomized" because the bits of water in the spray are so small.

Attica

Attica is a region of Greece, the part that includes the capital, Athens. In ancient times Attica was one of the independent Greek countries. It was the center of Greek civilization about 2,000 B.C., then was conquered and was unimportant for about a thousand years, then became important again when Athens, after 700 B.C., became history's first center of great learning and art. The language, architecture and art of the Golden Age of Athens are often called Attic. The people of Attica were Ionians, one of the main branches of the Greek people. The modern region of Attica has 1,310 square miles and a population of 1,546,234.

Attila

Attila was king of the Huns, a wandering warlike people from Asia who invaded Europe about 1,500 years ago. He was the cruelest and most terrible conqueror of his times. He became king of the Huns in the year 434. He conquered most of eastern Europe, and in Greece he destroyed seventy cities, killing and robbing helpless people. At a place called Chalons, in France, Attila was defeated by Aetius, a Roman general, and Theodoric I, a German king, in the bloodiest battle of those times. The next year, 451, he was about to attack the great city of Rome, but the Pope, Leo I, persuaded him not to harm the city. Attila died in 453. He was such a cruel and terrible killer that many Christians called him the Scourge of God (that is, "God's whip").

Attlee, Clement

Clement Richard Atlee is the name of an English statesman, holder of many important offices in the British government including the highest office of all, prime minister. Attlee was born in London, in 1883. He attended Oxford University and became a lawyer. Then he became so interested in helping London's poor laboring people that he became a prominent member of the Labour Party.

During World War I, Attlee fought in the British Army and rose to the rank of major. After that war he served in Parliament and became leader of the Labour Party in 1935. During World War II he was a member of Winston Churchill's cabinet as deputy prime minister. He was prime minister from 1945 to 1951. In 1955, he was made an earl and a member of the House of Lords. Clement Attlee died on October 9, 1967.

Auchinleck, Claude

Sir Claude John Eyre Auchinleck was one of the principal British army commanders in World War II. He was born in 1884 and as a young man adopted military life as a career. In World War II he was not very successful. In 1940 he commanded an attack on Norway that failed, and in 1941 and 1942 he commanded British forces in North Africa that were pushed back into Egypt. In 1943 he was made commander in India and in 1946 he was promoted to field marshal, highest rank in the British Army.

The name Auchinleck is Scottish. It was the name of the family estate of the British author James Boswell, and was pronounced *affleck*.

Auckland

Auckland is the largest city and principal seaport in New Zealand. It is on North Island. The population in 1973 was 152,300 (with suburbs, 603,500).

Auckland was founded in 1841 and was the capital of New Zealand until 1865. It is on an isthmus, or narrow strip of land, only 6 miles wide, and there are harbors on both sides, but the great harbor is on the east side. Auckland is about 5,500 miles from San Francisco. It is the seat of Auckland University, and has large shipyards (for shipbuilding), the principal New Zealand naval base, and many factories.

auction

An auction is a method of selling any kind of property or possession, pub-

licly, to whoever offers to pay the highest price. Auction sales go back to ancient times. In nearly all states and countries they are governed by very strict laws.

The sale is conducted by an *auctioneer,* who must have a license. The sale must be advertised in advance and must be open to the public. Before the sale (usually a full day or more before) the property must be put on display so that it can be seen by those who may be interested in *bidding* (offering to buy it) at the sale.

At the auction, the auctioneer stands on a platform, called the *block.* Usually he has a desk or stand in front of him and he has a gavel, or small mallet, with which he can knock on the stand to get attention. The buyers sit or stand in front of the block. Each item to be sold is called a "lot," and the auctioneer may group several things in one lot to save time. As each lot comes up, the auctioneer describes it (and if it is small enough it is shown on the block); then the auctioneer asks for bids. Anybody in the room can make a bid, as long as it is higher than the previous bid. Usually a person bids simply by saying what he will pay, for example "Fifty dollars." A person can bid over and over again, raising his offer to outbid others, until the item is finally sold.

The auctioneer may turn down a first bid because he considers it too low, and he may turn down a later bid because it does not increase the previous bid by enough. For example, he does not have to accept a first bid of ten dollars on something that is obviously worth a hundred, and if fifty dollars is bid he may refuse a second bid of fifty-one dollars, insisting that the increase to at least sixty. But once the auctioneer has accepted two bids from different bidders, he cannot refuse to sell the item. It must be sold to the highest bidder.

After each bid, the auctioneer must wait a reasonable time to hear other bids. Often he says "Going," then after a few seconds he again says "Going," and if still there is no further bid he brings down his gavel hard and says "Sold!"—naming the person who made the highest bid. He is said to *knock down* the property to this bidder.

Other laws governing auctions are: A person who is not at the sale can leave a bid for the auctioneer to make for him, but the auctioneer will not make more than one bid for the same bidder on the same lot. The owner of the property being sold may bid for it himself (and if he buys it he is said to *bid it in*), or he may have the auctioneer bid it in for him. This is done to prevent property from being sold at too low a price. It is illegal to employ two bidders (called "shills") to bid against each other and run the price up. A bid at an auction is a verbal contract to buy and the auctioneer may sue a bidder who refuses to pay what he offered. The auctioneer's fee is a percentage of the selling price. It may be 10% or 20% on low-priced items but as little as 1% on valuable real estate.

Some things, such as tobacco, cotton, fruit, raw furs, livestock, objects of art, and many others, are usually sold at auction. In these sales most of the bidders are professionals. They make their bids by private signals they have agreed upon with the auctioneer. The auctioneer states these bids in a kind of singsong chant that the professionals can understand but that makes little sense to anyone who happens to wander in.

A red flag hanging outside a store, warehouse, or house is a sign that an auction sale is being held.

Auden, W. H.

Wystan Hugh Auden, a leading modern poet, was born in York, England in 1907. He moved permanently to the United States in 1939. Auden received the Pulitzer Prize in 1948 for his long poem, *The Age of Anxiety.* He died in 1973.

Audubon

John James Audubon was an American artist and scientist who studied birds. He was born in 1785 in Haiti, which was then a colony of France, and was educated in France. He came to the United States in 1804 and became tremendously interested in studying American birds. Audubon lived in Kentucky from 1808 to 1826 and made many drawings and paintings of the wild birds there. To make a living, he also painted portraits.

Audubon went to England in 1826 to find a publisher for his books about birds. The beauty of his pictures of American birds made his book, *Birds of America,* famous. Audubon returned to America in 1842 and lived in New York City until his death in 1851. In honor of Audubon, there are about 200 clubs called Audubon Societies that protect and study wildlife in America.

Augsburg

Augsburg is a city in Bavaria, which is the largest part of southern Germany. Though Augsburg is a big and important city, it is best remembered because of the "Augsburg Confession," which was made there more than four hundred years ago, in the year 1530. In that year Martin Luther, the man who started all Protestant churches, made a famous statement of his religious beliefs. The word *confession* means a statement of religious faith, besides its other meanings. Luther's statement is called the Augsburg Confession because it was made at Augsburg.

Augsburg started as a Roman colony in 14 B.C. This city has figured in history right up to World War II. It was bombed for five years (1940–45) as an important German industrial city.

AUGSBURG, GERMANY. Population (1971 estimate) 210,000. Commercial city, textile center of southern Germany. On the Lech River.

augur

In ancient Rome, people believed in many gods, and they believed these gods would give them secret signs to guide them. Sixteen men called the *augurs* were appointed to discover the wishes of the gods. Before sending an army into battle, passing a law, or making any other big decision, the government would call upon the augurs to decide whether it was a good or bad time. The augurs would then watch for a sign from the gods. For instance, if lightning flashed in the sky from left to right, it was a favorable sign and meant that the gods approved of what the government planned to do. If the lightning flashed from right to left, it was an unfavorable sign. Sometimes a sheep was sacrificed and its liver examined; the augurs were supposed to tell from this whether the time was good or bad.

Augusta

Augusta is the capital city of Maine. Its population in 1970 was 21,945. It is on the Kennebec River. As early as the year 1628, there was a trading post known as Cushnoc where Augusta now stands, and in 1754 Fort Western was built there and a settlement grew up. In 1831 it was made the capital of Maine, and in 1849 it was incorporated as a city. Augusta has abundant water and is a center for industries that need water, such as paper manufacturing and cotton goods. Near by is Hallowell, Maine, where famous granite is quarried, and the domed capitol building in Augusta is made of this gleaming white stone.

AUGUSTA, MAINE. Population 21,945 (1970 census). Capital of Maine, and county seat of Kennebec County. On the Kennebec River. Begun as a trading post in 1628.

Augusta is also the name of an important city in Georgia, on the Savannah River. Its population in 1970 was 59,864 and it is important in the cotton and textile businesses. Augusta is a popular vacation spot in the winter. President Dwight D. Eisenhower drew much attention to Augusta when it became his favorite place for rest and golf and a special house was built there for the Eisenhowers.

Augustine, Saint

St. Augustine was one of the great men in the Christian religion more than 1,500 years ago, when Christianity had not yet spread through the world. He was the Bishop of Hippo, which was then a big city in North Africa. His full name was Aurelius Augustinus, and he was born in the year 354. As a young man he was rich and lived a gay life in the city of Rome. Then he became a Christian and devoted the rest of his life to the Church. One book that he wrote, called *The Confessions of St. Augustine,* tells the story of his life and also tells what he believes in. It is one of the greatest books of all time. St. Augustine died in the year 430.

Augustus (Caesar)

Two thousand years ago, Rome was the greatest nation in the world. It had been a republic for hundreds of years. Augustus Caesar changed it to an empire and after 27 B.C. Rome was ruled by emperors.

Augustus was born in 63 B.C. His name was Octavian and he was the adopted son of Julius Caesar, the great

general and statesman who ruled Rome as dictator before Octavian. Julius Caesar was murdered, and control of Rome passed into the hands of three men—Mark Antony, Lepidus, and Octavian. Later Octavian fought and defeated Antony, made Lepidus resign, and became the ruler of Rome.

Octavian never wore a crown and never called himself king or emperor, but he had all the power of an emperor and acted like one. He was one of Rome's greatest leaders. He built many roads, set up a good postal system, built beautiful marble temples and palaces, and created a good police force and fire protection system in the city of Rome, the capital of the empire. He encouraged colonists to settle in the empty lands of the empire and established a fair and honest system of taxes. He helped artists and writers, including Horace, Virgil, Ovid, and Livy.

The Roman senate gave Octavian the title "Augustus," which means great or majestic, and named the eighth month of the year August in his honor. His family name was Caesar, so he has become known as Augustus Caesar. He died in the year 14 A.D.

auk

Auk is the name given to several different kinds of sea birds. They live in the northern ocean regions and get their food by diving below the surface of the water for fish and other sea life. An auk's body is much like that of a duck, but the auk has a shorter, thicker neck and a heavier beak. Its back is black and its breast is white. It has webbed feet that are set back close to the tail. Because of this the auk waddles around clumsily on land. The little auk, called *auklet* or *dovekie*, is about the size of a small pigeon. The razor-billed auk is about eighteen inches high. It gets its name because its beak is very sharp. There once was another kind of auk, called the great auk. No great auk have been seen alive for more than a hundred years. They were killed by greedy hunters for their soft, downy feathers. The great auks were about three feet high and looked something like penguins.

Auks live in the open sea during the winter months. They either float on top of the water or perch on icebergs. Sometimes they are found as far south as the New England coast of the United States. In the spring, the auks go north to the Arctic Circle, where they breed and lay their eggs on rocky ledges.

Auriol, Vincent

Vincent Auriol was President of France from 1947 to 1954. He was born in 1884 of a family of well-to-do farmers. He became a member of the Chamber of Deputies in the French Parliament in 1914, became one of the leaders of the Socialist Party, and served in several cabinets. Because he voted against giving power to the pro-German Pétain ("Vichy") government when France surrendered to Germany in 1940, during World War II, Auriol was put in jail. He was released after a few months and in 1943 he escaped from France and joined the Fighting French government

of Charles de Gaulle. He was the first President of the Fourth Republic formed in France after the war and in 1951 he made an official visit to the United States and Canada, the first French President to do so while in office.

aurora

The *aurora borealis* is a strange and beautiful display of lights that appear from time to time in the northern sky. They are seen most often during the months of March and October. The lights have many colors and shapes. Often they are brilliantly colored and look like enormous, brightly colored rainbows stretching from one end of the sky to the other in a great curve. The lights may be as little as ten miles or as much as five hundred miles high. In North America they may be seen from as far south as Mexico, but very seldom. As many as a hundred a year may be seen from northern Canada and Alaska.

The aurora of the southern skies is called the *aurora australis*. This southern aurora can be seen from the southern tip of South America, the southern parts of the continent of Australia, and from the Antarctic Continent.

Aurora was the Roman name for the goddess of the dawn in ancient mythology; in Greek mythology she was called Eos. *Aurora borealis* actually means "northern dawn," and it is often called the NORTHERN LIGHTS; *aurora australis* means "southern dawn."

Austen, Jane

Jane Austen was a writer of novels in England, about 150 years ago. Her novels are still read and enjoyed. Jane Austen was born in 1775 and was the daughter of a minister. She never married, but lived with her family in small English towns. Her books tell us much about the way the English people, especially the upper classes, lived in the English towns, and how people thought and acted in her time. She died in 1817. Her best-known novel is *Pride and Prejudice*.

Austerlitz

Austerlitz is the name of a small town of about 4,000 people in Czechoslovakia, 12 miles east of the large city of Brno. One of the great battles of history was fought there. In 1805 Napoleon, the French emperor, was at war against Austria and Russia. The decisive battle of that war was fought at Austerlitz on December 2. Napoleon's army of 80,000 men was slightly smaller than the combined Austrian and Russian armies, but Napoleon's men were better trained and organized and were able to inflict a severe defeat upon the enemies. Some of the Austrian and Russian soldiers tried to avoid being captured by crossing a frozen lake. Napoleon ordered his guns to fire on the lake. The cannon fire broke the ice on the lake, and many of the fleeing soldiers were drowned.

Austin

Austin is the capital of the state of Texas. It is on the Colorado River and is built on a group of hills. Austin was made the capital when Texas became an independent republic in 1839, and capital of the new state when Texas joined the United States in 1845. The city was named in honor of Stephen Fuller AUSTIN (see the next article). The University of Texas and several other colleges and state institutions are at Austin. The imposing capitol building, made of Texas marble, was built in 1885. It stands on a hill called Capitol Hill.

AUSTIN, TEXAS. Population 251,808 (1970 census). Capital of Texas. County seat of Travis County. On the Colorado River. Settled 1838.

Austin, Stephen Fuller

Stephen Fuller Austin was one of the great men of Texas in its early days. He was born in 1793 in Austinville, Virginia. His father, Moses Austin, went to Texas in 1821 to establish a colony there, but died the same year. Texas was then a part of Mexico. In 1822, Stephen Austin got permission from the Mexican government to settle a colony of several hundred American families in Texas, as his father had planned to do. In 1833 the American colonists sent Austin to Mexico City, capital of Mexico, to ask the Mexican government to allow Texas to have a separate state government of its own. The Mexicans refused and put Austin in prison for a year.

When he was released from prison and returned home he found the Texans in revolt against Mexico. For a time he was commander-in-chief of the Texas army that fought against Mexico. Later he was sent to the United States to get money and supplies for the Texas army.

In 1836, when Texas had become an independent country after defeating the Mexicans, he ran for the presidency of Texas but was beaten by Sam Houston. He became secretary of state under President Houston. Austin died in 1836.

Australia

Australia is the biggest island but the smallest continent on earth. It is about the same size as the United States —about three million square miles— but its thirteen million people are not as many as there are in New York City and its suburbs. The capital is Canberra.

Australia is sometimes called the land "Down Under" because it is on the other side of the earth from North America and northern Europe. From New York it takes about 20 hours to jet there and about three weeks to sail there by ocean liner.

The cities around the coast of Australia, and a few inland towns as well, are as up-to-date and modern as the cities of the United States. However, there are some sections of Australia where no white men live and where the land is wild and unsettled.

THE PEOPLE WHO LIVE THERE

Most of the people living in Australia are descended from British people who went there within the last hundred years. When the white settlers first arrived, they found a race called the Australoids, dark-skinned but quite different from the African Negro people. Their skins vary in color from pale chocolate tan to real black, and their hair is wavy or curly. Between 45,000 and 50,000 of those original Australians still live there. They are called Bushmen.

Some natives have learned to speak English and many of them have become very good farmers and sheep herders. In the far north of Australia there are still wild tribes of natives who live almost exactly as they did hundreds or even thousands of years ago. They wear no clothes, except when it is cold enough so that they need clothing for warmth. They make fires with sticks, and they hunt game with spears and boomerangs.

HOW THE PEOPLE LIVE

In spite of the primitive Bushmen, Australia is really quite advanced. Nearly half the people live in modern cities. Industry is well developed.

Outside of the cities there are many huge farms, which the Australians call "stations," where grain and other crops, sheep, hogs and cattle are raised. The Australian sheep industry is the most important in the country. Australia supplies nearly a third of all the wool used in the world, and more than 300,000 tons of lamb and mutton a year. Wheat is the biggest agricultural crop.

Fruit raising also became important when farmers found that transplanted fruit trees would grow well in Australian soil. Now they have big canning factories, and Australian canned fruits, and vegetables as well, can be found in every part of the world.

HOW THE PEOPLE ARE GOVERNED

Australia is the only continent that is all one country. It is a member of the British Commonwealth of Nations, which means it is an independent nation, and it is one of the most advanced countries of the world. Queen Elizabeth of England is also Queen of Australia. There is a governor general, who represents the British Crown (the Queen), and two houses in the legislature, which makes the laws.

There are six states in the Commonwealth of Australia, and two territories. The states are New South Wales, Victoria, Queensland, South Australia, Western Australia, and the island of Tasmania. The territories are Northern Territory and Australian Capital Territory, which is somewhat equivalent to the District of Columbia in the United States.

Each state has its own legislature, as the states of the United States do. The central government has charge of the post office and regulates the telephone and telegraph systems and of course the money system. Each state in Australia owns and operates the railway lines within its borders. This has caused some difficulty, because the gauge (width) of

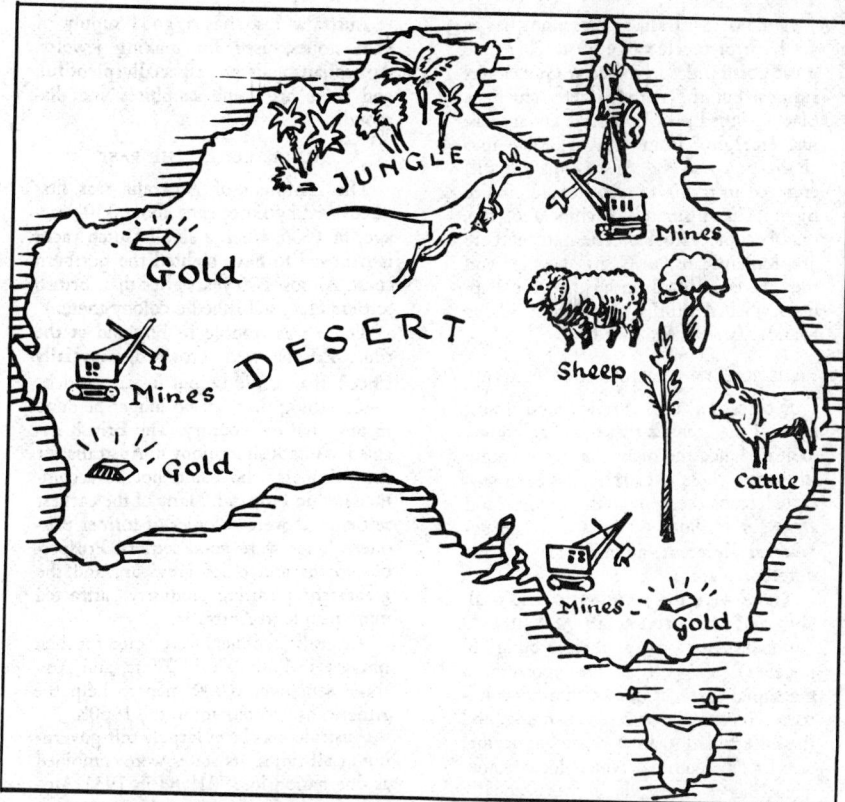

Australia is rich in natural resources but it is such a young country that they have not been entirely developed. Millions of dollars' worth of gold is taken each year from the gold mines. Copper, iron, silver, uranium and many other minerals come from other mines. Australia is the world's largest sheep-raising and wool producing country. Cattle and beef are also important products, as is wheat.

the tracks was different in different states, so that a train could not cross a state line and a traveler had to change railroad lines at state borders. This has been corrected for the most part.

All children must go to grammar school, and anyone who wants a good education can get one free at trade schools, agricultural colleges and universities.

In social security, the Australian government is even more advanced than the United States. There are pension funds for many different groups of people. There are pensions for the blind, the old, the unemployed, those with tuberculosis, and in some cases the families of former soldiers. Not only are these groups protected by pensions, but there is a cash bonus paid to the parents of every child born in the Commonwealth.

WHAT THE COUNTRY IS LIKE

The continent of Australia is nearly all smooth and level. This is because it is what geologists call "old" land. It has been worn down by millions of years of winds and rains, until the hills in most parts of the country are gentle, rolling slopes, somewhat like the hills of New England. There is, however, one large mountain range. It runs from north to south near the east coast and is called the Great Dividing Range. In the southern part, called the Australian Alps, that are high, rugged peaks.

Out in the Pacific Ocean, about sixty miles off the east coast of Australia, is a coral ridge, the GREAT BARRIER REEF, about which there is a separate article.

The climate of Australia in some

places is like that of the United States, but in other places it is much hotter and drier. About one-third of the continent is tropical. This is in the northern section, because Australia is in the southern hemisphere, and the northern part is nearest the equator. The central part of the continent is very dry and there is not enough rain to grow crops. It is called the Great Central Desert.

There are many rivers, but none of them is deep enough for large boats to travel on it. Even the smaller rivers usually flood the land around them every spring, when the heavy rains fall. In many places, the overflow of the streams is used to provide irrigation, and now there are many fertile fields where once there was just wasteland.

TERRITORIES AND POSSESSIONS

Australia governs several large regions, in addition to TASMANIA (which is a state), that are not on the continent. There are separate articles about most of these. They include:

PAPUA and NEW GUINEA, which together make up about half of the large island of New Guinea, only about 100 miles north of the mainland across Torres Strait.

The islands of the BISMARCK ARCHIPELAGO, including the ADMIRALTY ISLANDS. These, together with the Territory of New Guinea, Australia governs under a trusteeship of the United Nations.

The Australian Antarctic Territory, a vast region of about 2,500,000 square miles (almost as big as Australia itself) on the Antarctic continent. This possession is wholly undeveloped, as all of Antarctica is.

None of Australia's possessions has as yet been of much value to it. There are great possibilities in the New Guinea territories, but the natives there, chiefly a black-skinned people called Papuans, are just emerging from a savage state into civilization and the Australians are still engaged in trying to educate and civilize them. The Bismarck Archipelago, too, may become valuable. The natives there are Melanesians, a Negro people, and they were more advanced than the Papuans when Australia took control of the islands after World War I.

AUSTRALIAN ANIMALS AND PLANTS

Early settlers of Australia found almost none of the animals that they had known in other lands and many that were wholly strange to them. Australia had been separated from the rest of the earth's land areas for millions of years and had developed different animals (and many different plants).

There were the KANGAROO, the wallaby, and the KOALA, all MARSUPIALS (animals that carry their young in pouches), as well as the opossum, a marsupial that was known in other countries. The DINGO, or Australian dog, and the duck-billed PLATYPUS, an egg-laying, web-footed mammal which looks somewhat like a furry duck, were equally strange. Others were the ECHIDNA, or spiny anteater, and the WOMBAT, a large burrowing animal. (See the separate articles on these animals.) The birds were not so different, except for the EMU, a bird that is like an ostrich and cannot fly; the KOOKABURRA, or "laughing jackass," known for its strange cry; and the LYREBIRD, whose tail feathers stand up and look like a harp. There are more poisonous snakes in Australia than on any other continent.

Among the plants that were first found on Australia is the EUCALYPTUS, which like most Australian trees is an evergreen, and the ACACIA, which is the national flower of Australia.

Today there are plants and animals from all over the world in Australia. Settlers have imported them, and they have done well in the Australian climate.

Australia's big problem is rabbits. It began when an Englishman took a pair of rabbits to Australia as pets. The rabbits escaped and were never caught. That one pair of rabbits was the start of a tremendous rabbit population. Over a period of years, there were finally so many wild rabbits that they were eating and spoiling the farmers' crops. To keep them under control the Australians have built long fences and held annual rabbit hunts. There are so many rabbits in Australia that thousands of rabbit skins are exported every year.

VALUABLE THINGS IN AUSTRALIA

Two years after the 1849 "gold rush" when gold was discovered in California, the same thing happened in southern Australia. In 1851 the population of Port Phillip, where the city of Melbourne is today, increased from 50,000 to 250,000. Even today, gold mining is very important in Australia.

Australia also has large iron and coal deposits and a good supply of other necessary minerals.

Australia also has a good supply of gem stones, used for making jewelry. Australian opals are especially plentiful, and there are some sapphires and diamonds.

AUSTRALIA IN THE PAST

The continent of Australia was first discovered by Europeans about 350 years ago, in 1606, when a small Dutch yacht is believed to have sighted the northern coast. Almost 200 years after that, British settlers first established a colony there.

There was trouble in England at the time. Prisons were crowded, especially since a man could be put in jail for debt —something that can no longer be done in any civilized country. The British decided to establish a colony in Australia for the prisoners who could not be accommodated in England. Many of the earliest settlements were colonies of former prisoners. They were good settlers. Prosperous towns and cities grew up, and the great sheep-raising industry attracted more people to Australia.

Australia's soldiers were noted for their bravery in both World Wars, and Australia sent over 6,000 men to help the Americans in Vietnam in the 1960's.

Australia has been largely self-governing at all times. Its states were combined as one nation in 1901 and in 1931 Australia became fully independent as a member of the British Commonwealth of Nations. Australia has had one Socialist government and one Labor government but each time the more conservative Nationalist Party won the next elections.

AUSTRALIA—SUMMARY

Area. 2,974,581 sq. mi. Greatest length 2,400 miles (east-west); width, 2,000 miles (north-south).

Population. 12,560,000 (1973 estimate); chiefly British. About 50,000 Australian aborigines. Per capita income, $1,590.00 (1968 estimate).

Language. English.

Religion. 55% Protestant (chiefly Anglican), 25% Roman Catholic. Others 20%.

Principal Cities. (1973 estimates) Capital, Canberra (pop. 200,000); Sydney (Pop. 2,500,000); Melbourne (pop. 2,200,000); Brisbane (pop. 720,000); Adelaide (pop. 727,000); Perth (pop. 500,000); Hobart (pop. 120,000).

Government. Independent member of [British] Commonwealth of Nations; technically a kingdom with same sovereign as England, but crown is represented by a Governor General selected by Australian government. Federal parliament has two houses, Senate (60 members) and House of Representatives (124 members), elected by people, with universal suffrage. Government controlled by Prime Minister and cabinet (12 members) representing majority party in Parliament.

Currency. Monetary unit, Australian dollar, worth $1.12 (U.S.) (In 1966, Australia changed to the American decimal system.)

Military. Under the National Service Act of 1951, all men of 18 must have military training.

Commerce. Produces nearly 30% of the world's wool; annual lamb and mutton production about 325,000 tons. Second industry is wheat-raising, annual export about 124,000,000 bushels. Other exports are beef, minerals, sugar, barley, oats. Main imports: metals, machinery, textiles, paper, tobacco, oil, tea, rubber, silk. Complete factory system, equipped to produce locomotive supplies, airplanes, automobiles, electrical supplies, light machine tools, and steel.

Transportation. Extensive rail lines (35,000 miles of tracks), state-owned and operated, serving mainly coastal areas. Air transport to all areas. In 1973 there were 200,000 miles of hard-surface roads, and 350,000 miles of cleared or natural surface roads.

Topography. Comparatively level terrain. The Great Dividing Range extends down the entire east coast; at its southern tip are the Australian Alps (highest point, Mt. Kosciusko, 7,328 ft.). The Great Plateau covers more than half the continent on the west. East and west coastlines relatively unbroken, but north and south coasts deeply indented with the Great Australian Bight, a part of the Indian Ocean, on the south, and the Gulf of Carpenteria on the north. About 60 miles off the east coast the Great Barrier Reef extends 1,200 miles. Longest permanent river, the Murray River; main tributaries are the Darling and Murrumbridgee Rivers.

Climate. Northern third of the continent is tropical, rest is temperate. Central section is semidesert, with scant rainfall. Eastern coastal plains are temperate, with annual rainfall 20 to 50 inches. Climate of southeast coastal region, from Brisbane to Adelaide, resembles that of California. Climate of southwest corner is similar.

Natural Resources. Most important mineral is gold, with about $37,000,000 worth mined each year. Others: lead, zinc, copper, iron, silver, tungsten, rutile, uranium. Also gem stones, notably opals, and some sapphires and diamonds. Some lumber from forests in south, southeast, and southwest.

Austria

Austria is a country in central Europe. In size and population it compares with the state of Ohio, with about 32,000 square miles and about seven million people. Austria was once one of the richest and most powerful countries in Europe, and had a great empire, but it suffered much during World Wars I and II. Yet it remains important for its history, its magnificent capital, Vienna, and the high level of education and craftsmanship among its people. Much of Austria lies in the Alps, the great mountains of southern Europe.

THE PEOPLE WHO LIVE THERE

The people of Austria are almost entirely German, and speak the German language. They are mostly of the Roman Catholic religion. About a third of them live in cities (most of these in Vienna).

The people in each district of Austria have their own local costumes and customs and several different dialects are spoken. In some places the people are lively and gay; in other districts they are more quiet and serious. Some are tall and blonde, others are thin and dark.

The farmer in the Tyrol, which is a district in the Alps, usually wears coarse woolen clothes, and his wife wears a long dress covered by a clean apron. However, on Sundays and holidays she looks particularly colorful with a silk apron, a colored kerchief over her shoulders, and a stiff hat with gold braid and tassels, with long satin or velvet ribbons hanging down her back. In other districts the costume varies, but it is always bright and colorful.

Once Vienna, the capital, was said to be the happiest city on earth. It was called "the city of the waltz." But World War II and the years of military occupa-

tion that followed brought great hardships. Many beautiful buildings were destroyed and the people were very poor. By the 1960s, however, conditions had improved greatly.

HOW THE PEOPLE LIVE

About half the people in Austria are farmers. But the soil is poor and they cannot raise enough food to feed the country. Large quantities of it have to be bought from other countries. Many Austrians work in factories. Among the products are iron and steel, textiles, aluminum, and machine tools. These industries have been helped by American money and methods. Still, the average Austrian worker must support his family on about $65 a month.

Children have to go to school between the ages of 6 and 14, and almost everybody in Austria can read and write. Some of the world's most famous colleges are in Austria.

The Austrians have always loved music. The great composers Haydn and Mozart were Austrians, and Beethoven lived in Vienna much of his life. In most of the cities and towns, people have formed little orchestras. There are also small orchestras that play in wine gardens. The opera house in Vienna is famous, and in Salzburg every year there is a great music festival that brings people from all over the world.

The Austrians like winter sports, and the mountains are a fine place to go skiing, sledding, and ice skating.

WHAT KIND OF A PLACE IT IS

Next to the Swiss people, Austrians live in the most mountainous region in Europe. The Alps cover most of the country and attract many tourists. Although almost every kind of mineral has been found in the Alps, the Austrians mine only small amounts of the gold, silver, coal, and copper.

The great river in Austria is the Danube. People who love Johann Strauss's waltz, *The Beautiful Blue Danube,* are often disappointed to discover that it is not really blue, but a muddy green. It is the second-largest river in Europe, after the Volga, and it carries important freight within Austria and to other countries.

HOW THE PEOPLE ARE GOVERNED

Austria is a republic. It has a president and a parliament that makes the laws. The actual head of the government is the chancellor, who represents the majority party in parliament. (His position is the same as that of the prime minister in England.) The chancellor and his cabinet run the country while they are in office, but the parliament, which has 215 members, can change the chancellor and cabinet at any time.

IN THE PAST

Austria gets its name from *Oesterreich* (German for "Eastern Kingdom"), which it was first called some nine hundred years ago. For hundreds of years Austria was ruled by the HAPSBURG royal family, about which there is a separate article. Over the centuries large portions of land were given to Austria through royal marriages or through treaties, and the country came to be one of the most important monarchies in Europe. But most of the Austrian empire was always composed of people who were not really Austrians, who spoke different languages and had different customs and did not want to be ruled by Austria. When this is so, a country is not really strong. In 1866, when Austria and Prussia had a war to decide which would be most powerful among the German countries, Prussia defeated Austria in such a short time that the war is called the Seven Weeks' War. The next article, on AUSTRIA-HUNGARY, tells how the great Austrian empire fell apart. Austria lost its empire and became a small republic.

The Austrian republic was poor and the people were unhappy. Adolf Hitler became the dictator in Germany, and many Austrians thought that by joining Germany they could become prosperous and powerful again. A Fascist, or Nazi, party arose in Austria in the early 1930s. They fought bitter and bloody battles with those who opposed joining Germany. In 1934 they murdered Chancellor Englebert Dollfuss, the head of the Austrian government. Chancellor Kurt von Schuschnigg, who came after Dollfuss, was weak, and in 1938 Hitler marched his armies into Austria without much opposition and declared the country part of Germany. This was called the *Anschluss* (meaning "joining together" in German).

Austria spent the next seven years under Nazi rule and so was on the losing side in World War II. In 1945 the Allies captured Austria. The country and the capital, Vienna, were each divided into four zones, British, American, French, and Russian. The occupation of Austria continued for ten years. The Americans sent food and money to help the people, but the Russians took machinery and even whole factories, and almost anything that was movable, and moved it to Russia as war reparations. This made Austria poorer than ever. Finally in 1955 a peace treaty was signed. Austria became independent again and joined the United Nations.

AUSTRIA—SUMMARY

Area. 32,369 sq. mi. Greatest length 362 miles; width varies from 37.5 miles in the east to 162.5 miles in the west.

Population. 7,400,000 (1973 estimate), chiefly Austrian (German). The principal national minority (9.1%) is Polish.

Language. Principally German, spoken by 95.3% of the population. Others: Polish, Croatian, Slovenian, Hungarian, Czech.

Religion. Principally (89%) Roman Catholic, 6.2% Protestant, 0.2% Jewish. Freedom of worship is guaranteed.

Principal Cities. Vienna (pop. 1,641,000); Graz (pop. 251,900); Linz (pop. 205,700); Salzburg (pop. 122,100).

Government. Federal republic (1929 constitution). President elected by popular vote for a six-year term, represents the republic in foreign relations, has limited powers. Government controlled by a chancellor and cabinet chosen by a federal parliament. The parliament has two houses. There are 50 representatives chosen by provincial assemblies and 165 representatives elected by popular vote. Each serves for four years. All citizens more than 21 years old may vote.

Education. Compulsory between the ages of 6 and 14. About 7% of the population receive secondary education; about 2.5% receive university education.

Currency. Monetary unit, the Schilling, worth slightly less than 4 cents (U.S.).

Commerce. Chiefly industrial economy. Chief exports are lumber, iron and steel, and finished goods; main imports are food (18% of total) and coal.

Transportation. 3,773 miles of railroad and 55,000 miles of highway. Most important navigable river is the Danube.

Topography. About 73% of the land is covered by spurs of the eastern Alps. Mountain ranges run east and west, leveling in the north and northeast into the Danube River basin. In the east and southeast are forested foothills, merging with Hungarian plain. Principal rivers are the Danube, Inn, Enns, Drau, Ill, and Mur.

Natural Resources. About 20% of the land can be farmed; another 30% is suitable for grazing. Chief crops are grains, potatoes, sugar beets. Livestock raising and dairying produce 50% to 60% of farm income. Minerals include large deposits of high-grade iron ore in Styria, and lignite, magnesite, salt, talc, graphite, gypsum, copper, lead, and zinc. There are extensive spruce forests. Austria is rich in petroleum and in hydroelectric power potential (30 billion kilowatt-hours yearly).

Climate. In valleys, winter lasts 2 to 3 months. Mean annual temperature in the north is 46° F., with a range of 40°. Lowlands in the east and south are somewhat warmer. Average annual rainfall, 25 to 30 inches.

General Information. Flag, three horizontal bars, red, white and red.

Austria-Hungary

Today, Austria and Hungary are two separate countries, but until the end of World War I they were united in one big empire called Austria-Hungary, or the Austro-Hungarian Empire. This empire included large parts of what are now Czechoslovakia, Poland, Rumania, and Yugoslavia. The empire had an area of 261,241 square miles, bigger than any European country except Russia. The ruler of Austria-Hungary was the emperor of Austria and at the same time the king of Hungary. He was a member of the HAPSBURG family, about which there is a separate article. In World War I, Austria-Hungary was on the same side as Germany and was the enemy of the United States and the other Allies. After it lost the war, in 1918, Austria-Hungary was broken up into separate countries.

autograph

Anything written is an autograph, but the hobby of collecting autographs applies only to signatures or signed letters and other documents of famous persons. The value of the autograph depends upon the fame of the personage, the interest of the document, and the scarceness of that person's autographs. At one time autograph letters of Button Gwinnett, a signer of the Declaration of Independence, were unusually valuable because so few were available: one of his letters sold in 1928 for $51,000. But in 1945 another Gwinnett letter sold for $150. A signature alone almost never has any value.

Some collectors specialize. One collected 7,000 autographs of John Brown of Ossawatomie. The oldest autographs date from the early 8th century.

automation

Automation is the use of automatic machinery in manufacturing. Usually the word means a process in which the product is never touched by human hands until it is completed. In packaging and bottling, fully automatic machinery has been used since the 1920s. Similarly automatic machinery for more complex manufacturing became possible with the development of the electric eye, electronic computers, control tapes, and other devices of the kind. The word automation is new; it was first used in 1947 when a group of engineers at the Ford Motor Company, designing automatic machinery, were called the "Automation Department."

automaton

An automaton is a machine that is made to act like a person or animal and do some of the things they can do. For hundreds of years, men who are good at mechanics have enjoyed making automatons. Usually these have been so interesting that they could be exhibited in museums or other places and people would pay to see them work. Some automatons have been built to play musical instruments. Nearly two thousand years ago a book (by Hero of Alexandria) described a group of artificial birds that warbled in chorus. Some of the most famous automatons have been "chess players" that played games against human beings and usually beat them. (The "automatic chess player" was always just big enough so that a live person could be hidden inside to control the moves made by the automaton.) Some automatons have phonograph devices inside so that they can talk. In some books and movies there are automatons that are supposed to be able to think, but this is not really possible. The automaton can do only what its machinery is built to do. The word *robot* is also used for machines that do things automatically.

automobile

Automobile means "moving by itself." By an automobile is usually meant a vehicle that carries a few passengers over land, is driven by its owner, and is propelled (made to go) by an engine that burns gasoline. The present century has been called the automobile age and that is correct, at least for the United States. In the United States there are more than 61,430,594 passenger cars—more than one per family, and three times as many as in all other countries together—and there are 12,000,000 trucks, more than there are in the rest of the world. The automotive industry, the making of automobiles and trucks, is the largest in the United States and in the world.

In 1900, as the century began, workable automobiles had just been invented. In 1910 they were still rare and a curiosity. After World War I, in the early 1920s, more than half the American families still did not have cars.

INVENTION OF THE AUTOMOBILE

Before automobiles, the horse-drawn carriage was the means of private transportation. But horses could not go very

The automobile age brought with it this typical scene of the speeder and the "motorcycle cop"—in 1915. The automobile is a Packard touring car. Windshields had been invented but were optional accessories. The car would go 40 or more miles per hour but probably the driver had not been going so fast: The speed limit was 12.

fast—about nine miles an hour—and were a nuisance to keep, so for hundreds of years men had dreamed of "carriages that would go without horses."

The earliest automobiles were called horseless carriages. Some inventors tried electricity, some tried steam, and both steam and electric cars were made until the 1920s. But electric cars were slow, because they had to carry heavy storage batteries, and while steam cars were very good and very fast, the driver had to wait to "get up steam" before he could start. So the automobile, like the airplane, really became possible only when the "gas engine," or INTERNAL COMBUSTION ENGINE, was developed.

Two Germans made the first workable automobiles, about 1885. Their names were Gottlieb Daimler and Karl Benz. They did not work together, but each produced a "horseless carriage" using a gas engine. The first automobile manufactured for sale was the French *Panhard,* using Daimler's invention.

In the United States, a man named George B. Selden of Rochester, N.Y., got patents in 1895 on a crude version of the kind of automobile that is still in use. It had a gasoline engine. It had a *transmission,* a device that caused the engine, which ran at high speeds, to turn the rear wheels at a lower speed. The rear wheels pushed the car forward and the driver steered with a lever that controlled the front wheels. With a device called a *clutch,* the driver could connect or disconnect the engine and the transmission, depending on whether he wanted to go or stand still.

Even before Selden got his patent, Charles and Frank Duryea had made automobiles and Henry Ford was making one. Other great pioneers who made automobiles before the year 1900 were Ransom E. Olds, Alexander Winton, Elwood Haynes, Elmer Apperson, and several others. There were automobiles named for all these men, but only the name Olds has survived (in the Oldsmobile).

Within the ten years that followed, literally hundreds of new makes of automobile appeared on the market. The number of different makes became less and less every year. During the 1930s, the "depression years" when business

was so bad for everyone, all but the biggest had to go out of business.

HOW THE AUTOMOBILE DEVELOPED

The early automobiles had only one or two cylinders. They ran with a loud chug-chug that sounded much like a long series of small firecrackers going off. They had no windshields and, of course, no windows. To start them, you had to get in front and turn a crank. The tires were very poor in quality and you could seldom drive more than ten or fifteen miles without having a "puncture"—a hole in the tire that would let the air out. Then you would have to stop and change tires, which was a very hard job then because the tire had to be forced onto the wheel. The springs were stiff, shock absorbers had never been heard of, and the roads were bad, so passengers were bounced unmercifully as they rode along. Most cars had no headlights, but some used carbide gas lamps that burned with a dim, flickering light that made it very hard to drive at night. If an automobile could go 12 miles an hour, that was pretty good, and 25 miles an hour was breezing along at a great rate.

Here is how the familiar parts of an automobile were developed over the course of years:

ENGINE. The early one- and two-cylinder cars soon changed to four- or six-cylinder cars. Henry Ford built a six before he changed to the four-cylinder models (the "Model T," from 1908 to 1926, and the "Model A," from 1928 to 1931, that were the biggest-selling automobiles of their time). After a while, manufacturers came to think that the more cylinders, the better the car. The Packard "Twin-Six," a twelve-cylinder car, and several eight-cylinder cars, came out in the 1920s. In the 1930s, Cadillac made not only a twelve but a sixteen. Finally, manufacturers settled on six or eight cylinders, especially eight, as the best number to deliver power and not burn too much gasoline.

CLUTCH. There was not much change in the clutch for many years. The early clutch brought together a revolving disk connected with the motor and a disk connected with the driving wheels; while the

two disks touched, they would revolve together and the power from the motor would turn the driving wheels and make the car go. But gradually the disks would wear down and the car would need a new clutch. In the 1930s, Chrysler introduced a "fluid clutch" that used oil, which cannot wear down, and by the 1950s the power could be transmitted from the engine to driving wheels by automatic transmissions that required no separate clutch. By 1954 it was becoming unusual for an automobile to have a clutch.

TRANSMISSION. The transmission of every automobile, for more than thirty years, was a "gear box" in which there were different gears that would cause the car to go at different speeds. The lower the speed, the greater the power. Most cars had "three speeds forward and one reverse," which meant that the driver could choose whether to go forward at first or low speed, second or intermediate speed, or third or high speed. The driver chose his speed by moving a lever (the gear-shift lever). At first, this lever was outside the car, on the running board. Then it struck up from the floor next to the driver's seat. Then, about 1937, it was mounted on the steering wheel. After World War II, automatic transmissions (under such trade names as Hydromatic, Dynaflow, Fordomatic, and so on) began to replace the older types.

HORSEPOWER AND SPEED. Twenty horsepower was high for an engine of those days. Both speeds and horsepower increased gradually through the years. In the 1920s it was a fast car that would go 60 miles an hour—only the most expensive cars would. In the 1930s, most cars would go as high as 70 miles an hour, and expensive cars had 100 horsepower. By the 1960s the automobiles ranged from 100 and more horsepower for the cheapest cars to 250 or even 300 horsepower for the most expensive cars, and speeds ranged from 80 to 120 or more miles per hour.

TIRES. The early tires used high air pressure; the pressure inside them had to be 40 to 60 pounds to make them hard enough to carry the weight of the car. Being so hard, they did not give a very comfortable ride. In the early 1920s "balloon tires" came in. These were bigger and presented more rubber to the road, which made them skid less. They used less air pressure—only 25 to 30 pounds—and so were softer and made riding more comfortable. By the 1940s or even before, a puncture or any other tire failure had become very unusual. Until the 1950s every tire had to have an "inner tube" to hold the air, but in 1956 the tubeless tire was introduced.

BRAKES. At first, there were brakes only on the rear wheels of the car. To put on the brakes, the driver stepped on a pedal, and the faster the car was going the harder he had to step. In the 1920s, "four-wheel brakes" came in. There were brakes on front wheels as well as rear wheels, which made it easier to stop the car. In the 1930s, the use of hydraulic brakes increased the power of the brakes (see HYDRAULIC POWER). And in the 1950s came power brakes, which apply the power automatically when the brake pedal is pressed.

ACCESSORIES. Automobiles were once sold with no "accessories" at all—no windshield, no horn, no bumpers, no speedometer. To start the car you had to crank it. One by one, these devices were made standard equipment that came with the car. First the windshield was added. Then came the self-starter—a special motor that cranked the car—and by 1914 fine automobiles were advertising, "It starts from the seat!" The windshield wiper arrived about 1920, and at first the driver had to reach forward and move it when he wanted to wipe the rain off the windshield. Heaters arrived in the 1930s.

CHANGES IN AUTOMOBILE BODIES

The first automobiles were modeled after the buggies and carts that people were used to. Only a few of them even had canvas tops—after all, who would want to drive an automobile while it was raining? Here is how the bodies of automobiles developed:

TOURING CARS AND ROADSTERS. An automobile with both front and back seats was called a *touring car;* an automobile with only the front seat was called a *roadster.* The top was made of cloth, and on a nice day it could be put down, much as the top of a convertible goes down now, except that it took two men and a lot of time to do it. Along about 1920, automobiles that could advertise a "one-man top" had a great advantage; but their claims were only partly true, because it was still pretty hard for one man to handle the top all alone. If it rained, there were curtains made of cloth and celluloid or isinglass that could be pinned to the sides. Very sporty roadsters had "rumble seats"—back seats that opened up in the place where the "trunk" or baggage compartment is on modern cars. There was no top at all over rumble seats.

SEDANS AND COUPÉS. There were closed cars in the very early days of the automobile, but they were used only in cities and they were very expensive. The automobile engine of those days was not powerful enough to drive a heavy car very fast. Ninety-nine out of a hundred cars were "open" touring cars or roadsters. The sedan began to replace the touring car about 1925. A coupé was a closed car with one seat (the same word is still used, though there is almost always a small back seat in addition to the front seat). The sedan with only two doors was called a *coach.* By the 1930s, most automobiles were closed cars, as they still are.

CONVERTIBLES. Very expensive touring cars of the early years had side windows instead of curtains, and were called *phaetons;* very expensive roadsters with side windows were called *cabriolets* or *convertible coupés.* The tops had to be put up and down by hand; automatic tops did not arrive until almost 1940 and did not become standard until after World War II.

SIZE OF AUTOMOBILES. In the United States, the trend was always to bigger automobiles. Every effort was made to have the lowest-priced cars look as big as the most expensive ones. The *wheelbase* (distance from the center of the front wheel to the center of the rear wheel) gradually increased from 80 to 120 or more inches, and overall lengths from front to rear bumper went up to 16, 18 or more feet. The width increased from 5 or 6 feet on early cars to 8 feet on later ones, making unsafe the highways that had been built for narrow cars. In Europe, the trend was to smaller and less powerful automobiles, largely because gasoline there is scarcer and much more expensive (65 cents to $1 per gallon in 1958). Economy-minded Americans began to buy large quantities of foreign-built small cars in the 1950s, but still the demand for them did not exceed 10% to 15% (a maximum of about 300,000 imported small cars to 2,000,000 larger ones made in the United States).

AUTOMOBILE MANUFACTURING

Almost from the start, the manufacturing of automobiles introduced methods that had never been seen before. These methods have come to be called "mass production" and "assembly-line production." R. E. Olds and Henry Ford were the pioneers. They saw that automobiles could be made cheaper if they could be turned out in great quantities. Ford really saw his dream come true, with more than a million cars a year coming from his factories every year. See also the articles on MASS PRODUCTION and MOTOR VEHICLES.

automobile racing

The race is the oldest form of sport known to mankind, so it is not surprising that men began to race in automobiles almost as soon as they began to build them. The first automobile races were held at Narragansett, Rhode Island, before the year 1900, but automobiles would only go 10 or 12 miles an hour then, so the races were not very exciting. Race horses go more than twice that fast. However, by 1902 a man had gone faster than a mile a minute in an automobile (it was William K. Vanderbilt of New York, a very rich man who later built a fine automobile race track on Long Island).

The most famous racing driver of the early automobile years was named Barney Oldfield. Henry Ford's business of selling automobiles was not making money, so Ford decided to make a fast racing car and try to win prize money in races. He built the car, which he called "Number 999," and Barney Oldfield drove it for him and won several races.

In 1911 a group of automobile manufacturers built an automobile race track at Indianapolis, Indiana, so that new ideas for automobiles could be tested. The track was of hardwood, oval in shape and 2½ miles around. Since then, every year on Memorial Day (May 30), the biggest of all automobile races has been held on this track, which is now asphalt-covered. It is a 500-mile race. The average speed of the winning car has risen gradually, from 74½ miles per hour in 1911 to more than 139 miles per hour in 1961.

Smaller races were held at fair grounds all over the United States, on the same tracks that were used for horse races. These were called "dirt-track races," and they were very dan-

gerous. Since the 1930s, "stock-car races" have been more popular. These are also races on dirt tracks, but closed cars—sedans and coupés—are used. In the old dirt-track races, open cars were used. Many drivers were killed when their cars skidded and turned over. In closed cars they are much safer.

"Midget racers" were once very popular. These are tiny open cars, just barely big enough to hold the driver. Because they are so small, they seem to be going very fast even when the speed is only 40 to 60 miles an hour. Midget races, too, are very dangerous.

The most popular races now are in sport cars, which are low and small but very powerful. A sport car is suitable for private use as well as for racing. Usually sport cars compete in "drags," which are tests of acceleration and speed, one car at a time going over the "drag strip" to be timed.

Some drivers have preferred to race "against time" and not against other cars. The favorite place for trying to set speed records is Bonneville, Utah, on the hard "salt flats" near the Great Salt Lake. Another favorite place is the hard sandy beach at Daytona Beach, Florida. The driver gets a start, then races a mile and is timed; he turns around and races the mile in the other direction. This is so the wind cannot help him. The average time of the two runs is his record. John R. Cobb, in 1947, set a record of a little over 394 miles an hour, at Bonneville. Before that, Sir Malcolm Campbell, an Englishman, had held the record. Going in one direction, Cobb went faster than 400 miles an hour. Ab Jenkins holds most of the records for longer distances. He has averaged more than 190 miles per hour for 200 miles.

Automobile racing is a more popular sport in Europe than in America. The most famous track races there are held at Le Mans, a suburb of Paris, France. The most famous highway race is Italy's Mille Miglia, or thousand mile race.

autonomy

The word *autonomy* means "independence," and it is used in speaking of countries that have the right to govern themselves. However, in international politics today the word does not mean exactly that. A country is usually called autonomous when it is independent in some ways but is controlled by some other country in other ways. An example would be a country that makes its own laws and controls everything that happens in its own land, but has to follow the lead of some bigger country in its dealings with foreign nations.

Many parts of the Union of Soviet Socialist Republics (the U.S.S.R.) are called "autonomous." This is a special use of the word. It means that the countries elect their own officials for governing local affairs. In all other ways, they must obey the orders of the U.S.S.R. government in Moscow, Russia.

avalanche

When a tremendous mass of snow, ice, or loose rocks and earth slides down the side of a hill or mountain, it is called an avalanche. Anything tends to slide downhill, but usually snow or rocks will cling to a mountainside. When a mass of snow becomes too heavy, perhaps because of a big snowfall, or because the sun has melted a lower layer that was holding up the top layer, part of it may start sliding, which will carry all the rest along with it. Avalanches can be very dangerous. They can bury people, houses, and even whole villages. Avalanches sometimes go faster than 100 miles an hour, and the biggest ones have contained five million tons of snow. A loud noise, such as a rifle shot or even a man shouting, can start an avalanche. The sound waves make the snow or ice shake a little, which may be just enough to loosen it.

The worst places for avalanches are in the Alps, the big mountain chain in southern Europe (Switzerland, Austria, and Italy), and in Alaska. The biggest disaster ever caused by an avalanche was in the Alps in 1916, when nine thousand soldiers of the Austro-Hungarian Army were buried and died under tons of snow. There have been big avalanches of rocks breaking off the cliffs at Niagara Falls, and once (in 1935) six hundred tons broke off the Rock of Gibraltar and slid into the sea.

The Swiss Army is prepared to defend its country by starting avalanches to bury invaders. For this reason it has studied avalanches and has even taught its men to "ride" them—actually, to "swim" in the avalanche, using a kind of backstroke. In 1952 six men rode an avalanche safely down a 650-foot slope. Success depends on being on top of the avalanche at the start.

Ave Maria

In the Bible, in the Gospel of St. Luke, it is told how an angel of God appeared to Mary, greeting her, "Hail, Mary! the Lord is with thee: blessed art thou among women!" and telling her that Jesus would be born. In Latin, the words *Ave Maria* mean "Hail, Mary," and they begin one of the most beautiful prayers used in the Christian religion. The full prayer is: "Hail, Mary, full of grace, the Lord is with thee: blessed art thou among women. Blessed is the Fruit of thy womb, Jesus. Holy Mary, Mother of God, pray for us sinners, now and at the hour of our death. Amen." Great composers of music have set this beautiful prayer to music that is also beautiful, the two most famous being those of Schubert and Gounod.

aviary

An aviary is a large cage or building in which live birds are kept. The name aviary comes from the Latin word *avis*, which means, "bird." There have been aviaries since ancient times.

Most zoos have aviaries on their grounds. When the weather is warm enough the birds are put in outdoor cages. Otherwise they are kept in heated birdhouses. Only birds that will live together peacefully are put in the same aviary. Usually birds from the same part of the world are put in the same aviary.

A good aviary should have the kind of plants and trees in it that the birds are used to. Roosts and perches should be provided for the birds that need them. An indoor aviary should always be kept at the proper temperature for the birds that live there. The keeper of an aviary must know the various kinds of food that the birds eat, and provide it for them as often as they need it. The captive birds in an aviary will lay eggs and hatch them if they are well taken care of.

aviation

We use the word *aviation* to mean flying through the air by men, in the direction in which they want to go—just as a bird does. As long as men have looked up and seen birds in the air, they have dreamed of flying. But for thousands of years it was not much more than a dream. Only a few men ever thought it was really possible. Some even believed it was wrong to try, saying that God had reserved flight for the birds. It is not much more than fifty years since the dream really came true. But since then the progress has been so rapid that today there seems to be no limit to the future of flight by man.

The dream came true on December 17, 1903, when two brothers from Dayton, Ohio, named Orville and Wilbur Wright launched an airplane at Kitty Hawk, a beach on the coast of North Carolina. The plane, with Orville at the controls, flew only about a hundred feet and stayed in the air only twelve seconds, but it proved that man could build a machine that is heavier than air and still make it fly.

LEGENDS, FAILURES, AND THE BALLOON

The ancient Greeks had a story, thousands of years ago, about a man named Daedalus and his son Icarus. They were in prison on the island of Crete, in the Mediterranean Sea near Greece. Daedalus made a pair of wings for each of them so that they could fly home to Greece. He made the wings of feathers held together with wax, and he warned Icarus not to fly too near the sun; but Icarus disobeyed him, and the sun melted the wax. The wings fell apart and Icarus fell into the sea and was drowned. Daedalus got home safely.

That was only a story, of course. A man cannot fly with wings as a bird does; he is not strong enough. For hundreds of years men tried, and some of them who jumped off the sides of mountains or high buildings were injured or killed. One of the greatest men who ever lived, Leonardo da Vinci, who lived four hundred years ago, drew plans for three flying devices: a pair of stationary wings, for gliding; a pair of flapping wings; and a sort of helicopter. He was wrong about the first two, and he had enough sense not to try them, but he turned out to be right about the helicopter.

Just as men had taken the idea of wings from the birds, thousands of thinking men who had watched soap

bubbles lifted and carried by the air thought of devices that finally were realized in the balloon. The balloon became a reality a little less than three hundred years ago; its story is told in the article on BALLOON. But this still was not real aviation, even though balloonists were called aviators, because there was no way to make the balloon travel exactly where a man wanted it to. By the time the balloon had developed into the airship, which could be controlled, it was too late. The airplane had already outstripped it.

HOW MEN CAME TO FLY

More than a hundred years ago—fifty years before the Wright brothers—a group of Englishmen led by Sir George Cayley, whom the British people call "the father of aeronautics (flight)," had worked out the scientific principles of flight. They knew that wings were needed—not the flapping wings of a bird, but the broad surfaces of an airplane's wing. They made it possible to build gliders that worked (as you can read in the article on the GLIDER). But they ran into the same problem as the wing-flappers and the balloonists. There was no engine that would deliver the power needed for real aviation. A steam engine would do it, but steam engines were so heavy that all the power would be needed to lift the engine, and there was no sense in that.

In 1880, the great American inventor Thomas A. Edison was given $1,000 to study aviation, and he gave some thought to the helicopter, but he decided that it would take three or four horsepower—and where could such a powerful motor be found? (Big modern planes use more than twelve *thousand* horsepower.)

When the "gas engine" was developed to the point at which the automobile became possible, at the same time aviation became a reality. The pioneers were the Wright brothers and a man named Samuel Langley. Langley actually built workable flying machines before the Wrights did, but his first public test failed while the Wrights' succeeded, so they are best remembered. The aircraft carrier *Langley* honors the other great pioneer. His first plane and the Wrights' first plane can be seen in the Smithsonian Institution in Washington, D.C.

THE BARNSTORMING ERA

At first, airplanes were not good enough to have any real value, except as a curiosity. For ten years after the Wright brothers' flight of 1903, aviation was kept alive by men who were devoted to flying and who toured the country (called "barnstorming") to perform at circuses and fairs where people would pay to see them. These daredevils performed acrobatics with their planes, walked on the wings, made parachute jumps, and took customers for joyrides. Many were killed, but they served aviation well, because they kept up interest in it.

Military aviation began with World War I, and found the United States far behind the big European countries. The United States Army had started its air corps (which has become the Air Force) in 1907, and had ordered its first plane from the Wright brothers in 1908. Glenn Curtiss, another of the great aviation pioneers, had proved in 1910 that bombing planes could be used. But the French, English and Germans were all ahead of the United States. Americans received wonderful training when they formed a flying group that they called the Lafayette Escadrille (in honor of the French Marquis de Lafayette, who had helped the United States win its independence in the Revolutionary War), and fought for France against Germany.

The airplanes used in World War I would not go much more than 100 miles an hour. They fought each other with machine guns, which fired bullets through the propellers.

There was a question at this time if the airship or the airplane would become more important in aviation. The German Count Zeppelin had built huge cigar-shaped balloons that were driven forward by gasoline engines and that could be steered. Such an airship was called a *dirigible*, a word meaning "steerable." They were also called *zeppelins*. London was bombed by zeppelins long before bombing planes were used.

HOW AVIATION GREW

The world learned from World War I, which ended in 1918, how much could be done with aviation and how great its possibilities were. Every year aircraft was improved. Speed records toppled. Planes stayed in the air longer. They flew greater distances. They carried more passengers.

In the United States, an army officer named General William Mitchell, known as "Billy" Mitchell, saw how important aviation would be in future wars. He proved that bombs from an airplane could sink a battleship. He pleaded for government support of aviation. But higher-ranking officers would not believe him. They forced him to resign from the Army. It took years for the United States to catch up with other countries in plans for military planes.

But businessmen were not wholly blind to the possibilities of aviation. Commercial aviation really began in the United States when air mail was introduced in 1926. (Army planes had carried mail as early as 1918.) The first regularly scheduled passenger service was begun in 1926, between Salt Lake City, Utah, and Los Angeles, California. (Zeppelins had carried passengers in Germany as early as 1910). The first commercial airline in the United States, Pan American Airways, began operations in 1927. The first coast-to-coast service in the United States dates from 1929; but a passenger had to take a train from New York to Ohio, fly from Ohio to Oklahoma, take another train to New Mexico and fly from there to Los Angeles. The time, 48 hours, beat the railroads but still does not compare with the nonstop flights of the 1960s, made in less than seven hours.

The first flights across the Atlantic Ocean were made in 1919. First, a plane of the United States Navy, the NC-4, commanded by Albert C. Read, flew from New York to Newfoundland, to the Azores, and to Portugal in Europe. The same year two British fliers, John Alcock and A. W. Brown, flew from Newfoundland to Ireland, nonstop—the first nonstop flight across the Atlantic. Pan American Airways began commercial flying between the United States and South America in 1930.

The flight that did the most, by far, to make the world wake up to the possibilities of aviation was the nonstop flight made by Charles Lindbergh from New York to Paris, France, in 1927. It took him 33 hours, he covered 3,610 miles, and he flew all alone. Amelia Earhart was the first woman pilot to fly across the Atlantic, in 1932.

A group of four planes of the United States Army flew all around the world in 1924; it took them 175 days. In 1931 Wiley Post and Harold Gatty did it in eight days. In 1949 a United States Army B-50, commanded by James Gallagher, flew around the world nonstop, refueling four times. It took them 3 days, 22 hours, and 1 minute.

Major Charles E. Yeager, in 1947, became the first man to fly faster than the speed of sound. He did it in an experimental rocket plane, the Bell XS-1, and his top speed was more than 1,000 miles an hour. On October 11, 1961, Maj. Robert M. White, USAF, in the X-15 rocket plane over Edwards Air Force Base in California, established an unofficial altitude record of 215,000 feet.

By the end of World War II there was no doubt that aviation had become as important in modern life as the automobile fifty years before. There are more than 800,000 registered pilots in the United States, and more than 100,000 civil aircraft. Aviation has become one of the chief industries, employing about 650,000 people.

USES OF AVIATION

Besides its importance in warfare (which everyone hopes will never again be necessary), and its carrying of passengers and freight throughout the world, aviation is useful in many other ways.

Many of the great explorations, including the North Pole and the South Pole, have been carried out in airplanes. Aviation helps men to learn more about the world and to find new territories.

Mapmakers have found aerial photography cheaper and more accurate than older methods.

Farmers use airplanes to "dust" their fields with poisons, to kill insects that would ruin their crops. Farmers also are helped by rainmaking, which is done by scattering "dry ice" from airplanes and causing clouds to turn into rain.

Aviation, especially through the use of helicopters, can reach many places where there are no roads and railroads, and rescue sick or injured persons who otherwise would die.

Observation from airplanes can spot forest fires before they spread enough to become dangerous; direct traffic and prevent traffic jams; report on storms and give warnings to people living on shore and to ships at sea; and there are literally hundreds of other uses.

aviation medicine

Aviation medicine is the study of what happens to men who fly high in the air, higher than men have ever been before.

Above 10,000 feet, there is not quite enough oxygen in the air to keep a man as alert as he should be. At 18,000 feet up, a man can still breathe, with some difficulty, but he loses most of his strength. Above 20,000 feet there is so little oxygen that a person might lose consciousness. Therefore aviators at high altitudes wear oxygen masks, which feed extra oxygen to them.

The speeds of modern planes also bring up many questions. Does it hurt a man to fly at speeds greater than the speed of sound? Is he affected by how rapidly the speed of the plane is increased? Is his blood affected when he dives, perhaps at a speed of more than 1,000 miles an hour, from a very high altitude where there is very little air pressure to a much lower altitude where the air pressure is much greater?

Specialists in aviation medicine study all these problems and many others. They build special chambers where all the conditions are the same as they are miles above the earth. They study the effects on aviators. They decide what kind of special clothes an aviator should wear, what medicines will keep him awake and alert, and how much extra oxygen he will need.

The success of artificial satellites in 1957 and 1958 made possible further research. At first animals were sent up to test their reaction to space travel, but by 1961 U.S.S.R. and U.S. astronauts were making orbital and sub-orbital flights into space. See ARTIFICIAL SATELLITE.

Avignon

Avignon is a small city in the southeastern part of France on the Rhone River. It is a very ancient city and was part of the Roman Empire more than two thousand years ago. From 1309 to 1377 Avignon was the home of the Popes, the heads of the Roman Catholic Church. Tremendous walls, built at the command of the Popes more than five hundred years ago to protect Avignon from enemy armies, still stand and completely surround the city. At the northern end of the town there is a very high rock that rises steeply above the Rhone River. On the flat top of this rock stand the ancient Cathedral of Notre-Dame des Doms, built almost eight hundred years ago, and the Palace of the Popes, begun in 1316 and completed in 1370. The Palace was really a huge fortress, covering more than an acre. It is now owned by the city government. There is also a fine museum, full of statues and paintings and other works of art. Petrarch, one of Italy's greatest poets, lived and studied for the priesthood in Avignon nearly six hundred years ago. The people who live in Avignon today make soap and chemicals, silk, leather, flour, and wine.

AVIGNON, FRANCE. Population 64,581. Capital of Vaucluse department.

Avila Camacho

Manuel Avila Camacho was Presi-dent of Mexico from 1940 to 1946. He was born in 1897 and when he was a youth of 17 he joined the revolutionaries who were trying to replace the corrupt government Mexico then had. He supported President Cardenas and as president carried on Cardenas's liberal policies.

avocado

The avocado tree grows in Mexico, Cuba, the hot countries of Central America, and in southern California. Its fruit, which is also called avocado, looks like a huge pear, but is dark green in color. Another name for this fruit is *alligator pear,* probably because of its rough, warty skin. An avocado is four to seven inches long and has an unusually big pit inside. The flesh of the fruit is not sweet. It is very soft and yellow and has a mild, nutty flavor. It is eaten in salads.

Avon

Avon is the name of a small river in the south of England. It is famous only because William Shakespeare lived in a town called Stratford-on-Avon that is on the Avon River. Shakespeare is often called "the Bard of Avon."

axis

An axis is really a center line, or shaft, around which a solid body turns. The axis of the Earth is an imaginary line running from the North Pole to the South Pole, because the Earth rotates around that line. In 1936 the word got a strange new meaning. At that time, the European countries of Italy and Germany were controlled by dictators who were plotting to conquer all of Europe and many other parts of the world and divide it between them. The Italian dictator was named Benito Mussolini and the German dictator was named Adolf Hitler. When they became allies in 1936, they announced that a line between Rome, the capital of Italy, and Berlin, the capital of Germany, was now "the axis"—meaning the center of Europe. Because of this they came to be called "the Axis Powers," and this was soon shortened to "the Axis." Later in 1936, when Japan and Germany made a treaty, Japan was said to have joined the Axis. The Axis countries did start the war they had planned, which was World War II, but they lost it and the Axis came to an end.

axolotl

Axolotl is the Mexican name for the larval form of the tiger salamander. A salamander is an amphibian that looks like a lizard, but is not. Even though most axolotls live their entire lives in this immature state and never become adults, they are still able to reproduce. Like all amphibians, they lay their eggs in fresh water. The Mexican people consider axolotls very good to eat. They are about 11 inches long, with a finned tail, underdeveloped legs, and gills. Until 1865 it was thought that axolotls were a separate species, but in that year a few of them in a zoo tank lost their gills and changed into adults. It was the first time anyone knew that axolotls were really young tiger salamanders. There are separate articles on AMPHIBIAN, SALAMANDER, and LARVA.

Ayr

Ayr is the name of a county in Scotland, and also of a city, the capital of the county. The county is also called Ayrshire. It is best known because of the famous Ayrshire dairy cattle that were originally bred there, and also because the great poet Robert Burns came from there and was often called the Ayrshire poet, or the Ayrshire ploughman. Burns' birthplace, Alloway, is a suburb of the city of Ayr, and his poem *Tam o' Shanter* is said to have been written about an inn in Ayr. The city is a seaport, a manufacturing center, and a resort on the Firth of Clyde at the mouth of the Ayr River. The population of the city is 43,400. The county has 1,132 square miles and a population of 331,700.

azalea

Azalea is a name given to various flowering shrubs that are related to the rhododendron. They grow in many parts of North America. There are about 200 different kinds, but the two kinds most popular in the United States are the ones called *swamp honeysuckle* and *pinxter flower.*

An azalea may grow to be about 6 feet high. The leaves are long (about 4 inches) and pointed. The flowers are shaped like funnels and may be white, yellow, pink, or red. The azalea usually blooms in the late spring or early summer.

Azerbaijan

Azerbaijan is a region in Asia, along the southwest shore of the Caspian Sea. Part of it is in Iran and the rest is part of the Soviet Union, being one of the republics that make up the Union of Soviet Socialist Republics. The official name of the Soviet part is the Azerbaijan (or Azerbaizhan) Soviet Socialist Republic. Because it has rich oilfields, Azerbaijan is valuable to both the Soviet Union and Iran, and during and after World War II the Soviet Union tried to start a revolution in the Iranian part and to take over the whole territory, but the attempt failed.

Iranian Azerbaijan covers about 41,-000 square miles and has a population of about 3,200,000. It was once a separate province of Iran but now it is divided among three provinces. Most of the land is a stony plateau, a high, level region. The summers are hot and the winters are cold. There is very little rainfall except along the shore of the Caspian Sea. About half of the people are Kurds, an Asiatic people of the Mongol race, and they live as nomads, moving from place to place to find grazing land for the sheep they raise. The rest of the people are Iranians and most of them are farmers, growing grains, fruit, tobacco, and cotton. There is some mining of coal and salt, but the principal mineral wealth of the region, the oil, is not yet being taken from the ground in any quantity.

The Azerbaijan S.S.R. is slightly smaller in area (about 33,000 square miles) and larger in population (about 3,900,000). Here the great oil reserves, which are among the largest in the world, have been thoroughly developed. The

greatest oilfields are around the capital city, Baku, which is the fifth-largest in the Soviet Union (see BAKU). Of the other cities, Kirovabad, with a population of about 116,000, is the largest. There are many railroads and pipelines for the oil. The climate is about the same as in the Iranian part but there is more fertile land and it is better developed. Wheat, corn, tea, and olives are among the principal crops.

Throughout the Azerbaijan region, most of the people follow the Mohammedan religion. In the Iranian part the principal language is Iranian and in the Soviet part the languages are Turkish and Russian.

AZERBAIJAN IN THE PAST

In ancient times (800 or 900 years before Christ) Azerbaijan formed part of Armenia and was ruled by Armenian kings, but the people were not Armenians. Then the region was conquered by Romans, Arabs, Mongols, Turks, and finally Persians (Iranians). From 1825 to 1828 Russia and Persia fought for Azerbaijan and at the end of that war it was divided between them.

After World War I, the Russian part of Azerbaijan decided that it wanted to be an independent republic, and for a brief period in 1919 and 1920 it was independent, with an anti-Communist government. Soviet troops attacked, for the Baku oilfields were too important to Russia to risk losing them. There were several bloody battles and thousands of anti-Communists were killed. In 1920 a soviet government was established and in 1936 Azerbaijan became a separate soviet republic.

Azores

The Azores are a group of nine little islands in the Atlantic Ocean, about eight hundred miles west of Portugal. The largest island of the group is called St. Michael's and is about thirty-five miles long. The other islands are: Terceira, St. Mary's, Formigas, St. George, Graciosa, Fayal, Pico, Corvo, and Flores. The Azores have belonged to Portugal since the year 1432. The islands are really the tops of mountains that reach all the way down to the bottom of the ocean. Earthquakes have shaken the islands many times in the past, destroying whole towns.

In the Azores the temperature is rarely lower than 48 degrees or higher than 82 degrees. The soil is fertile and produces good crops of grain and fruits. Many of the people who live there are fishermen, and catch such fish as tunny, mullet, and bonito.

Most of the people in the Azores came originally from Portugal, but there are also many whose ancestors came from Flanders.

AZORES. Island group in Atlantic Ocean, belonging to Portugal. Area, 888 square miles. Population (in 1973) about 327,500. Chief city, Ponta Delgada.

Azov, Sea of

The Sea of Azov is a small branch of the Black Sea, roughly circular in shape and connected to the Black Sea by the narrow Kerch Strait. The Sea of Azov is about 200 miles long and 80 miles wide, covering about 14,000 square miles, but it is very shallow, only about 49 feet. The Don and Kuban Rivers flow into it. The entire sea is surrounded by territory of the Soviet Union. The principal cities on it are Rostov-on-Don, Taganrog, Zhdanov, and Kerch. There is fishing for sturgeon, pike, carp, and herring.

Aztecs

The Aztecs were a race of Indians who were rulers over Mexico more than six hundred years ago, before the first white men came from Europe. In the beginning the Aztecs were just a wandering tribe that came down into central Mexico from the north. They were cruel and savage warriors and soon conquered most of the Indian tribes around them. They founded the city of Tenochtitlan, where Mexico City, the capital of Mexico, stands today. From this great city they ruled many of the Indian peoples of Mexico.

The Aztecs worshipped the sun and the moon as gods, but the most important god of their religion was Huitzilopochtli, the god of war. They built huge stone pyramids with flat tops on which they set up great temples to Huitzilopochtli. On the altars inside these temples the Aztec priests sacrificed prisoners of war by killing them.

In spite of their warlike ways, the Aztecs were great builders and engineers. The king's palace in Tenochtitlan had hundreds of richly furnished rooms arranged around three great open squares. There were vast public gardens with tropical plants from the south of Mexico and wonderful artificial lakes and pools fed by aqueducts through which water traveled from miles away. The Aztecs had laws and courts of justice with judges and lawyers. Drunkenness and stealing were punished severely.

The Aztecs had a huge army. Their soldiers were armed with bows and arrows, spears, and huge clubs with two rows of razor-sharp stones set in the head.

The Aztec priests were able to read and write and had a kind of writing in which they used little pictures instead of letters. They also used certain symbols or pictures for numbers. The priests were the teachers of noblemen's children. The schools were large buildings attached to the temples. Here the children were taught history, picture writing, religion, and the laws of their nation. Girls were taught to spin cotton into thread, to make cloth, and to cook. Boys who were strong were taught how to be soldiers. The sons of skilled craftsmen were taught their trade by their fathers.

The Aztecs raised corn, tomatoes, beans, squash, and some other vegetables. The corn was ground into a coarse powder or meal with grinding stones, and was made into flat round cakes. The Aztecs made *chocolatl*, a

An Aztec calendar stone, or "Stone of the Sun." The Aztecs were skilled astronomers.

chocolate drink from cocoa beans, long before white men even knew about it. They also smoked tobacco in pipes. The Aztecs were skilled metal workers and made beautiful ornaments out of gold and silver.

In 1520 a small army of Spanish soldiers and explorers, led by Hernando Cortes, arrived in Mexico and defeated the Aztec army after fierce fighting. The Aztec king, Montezuma II, was killed by them, and Mexico became a part of the Spanish Empire with Cortes as governor.

See also the articles on CORTES and MONTEZUMA.

B

PHOENICIAN	EARLY LATIN
EARLY GREEK	ROMAN STONE CUT
ETRUSCAN	EARLY ROMAN
CAROLINGIAN	GOTHIC
EARLY GERMAN	ALDINE
RENAISSANCE	

B or b

The letter B is the second letter of the alphabet. It can be traced all the way back to the earliest writing known to man, in Egypt thousands of years ago. In the Hebrew language, in which much of the Bible was written, the letter was called *beth,* a word that meant "house." The ancient Greeks took this same letter and called it *beta.* The first letter of the Greek alphabet was called *alpha,* and the second letter *beta,* and from these we get our English word *alphabet.*

The ancient Hebrews made the symbol ۹ stand for the letter beth. The earliest Greek symbol for beta was ᐊ.

In some early languages, writing was read from right to left (and in some languages, such as Hebrew, it still is). But the Greeks changed and began to read from left to right, as we do today. When they made this change, they turned the letters around. The sign for beta then became ᗷ, which with slight changes came to us through the Romans.

In many German books, much fancier capital letters are used. The "German black-letter" capital B is 𝕭.

Read also the article ALPHABET.

Baal

More than three thousand years ago the country that is now Israel was called Canaan, and the people who lived there, the Canaanites, worshiped an imaginary god called Baal. They built idols, or statues, of this god, and bowed to them. The Jews settled in Canaan at that time, and though their religion told them to worship only the one God, Jehovah, some of them did as the Canaanites did and worshiped Baal. The prophet Elijah warned the people not to worship Baal, and many of those who did were punished. The story is told in the Bible, in the book named 1 Kings (in Catholic Bibles, 3 Kings).

Imaginary gods named Baal were worshiped for many hundreds of years in different parts of the world. Some of the ancient peoples of Ireland worshiped a god called Be 'al, and this may have been another version of the name Baal.

Babel

The story of the Tower of Babel is told in the Bible, in the first book, Genesis. The people of the world decided to build a tower so high it would reach heaven. All peoples then spoke the same language. God did not want the tower built and before it was finished He caused the people to start speaking in different languages so that no group or tribe could understand the others. The people then scattered to different parts of the earth and the tower was never finished.

The tower was a ziggurat, or temple, of the type built about 5,000 years ago. It was being built at a city called Babel, which was an early settlement at the place where later the great city of Babylon was built. Archaeologists who have dug into the buried ruins of Babel have learned that the tower may have been about 400 feet square at its base and as much as 600 feet high, which would make it the highest manmade structure of ancient times.

baboon

Baboons are the largest members of the monkey family, but they are smaller than the apes. Baboons are sometimes called "dog-faced" monkeys because they have long snouts, or muzzles. They are found in most parts of Africa where there are rocky hills, but most of them live in the mountains of South Africa. They live in troops of about 20 to more than 100, and climb around looking for birds' eggs, lizards, insects, and other little animals that they like to eat. Sometimes they raid farms and villages, as they also like to eat fruits and vegetables. Baboons have powerful jaws and sharp teeth and are such savage fighters that even lions fear to attack them. The average full-grown baboon is about two feet tall and weighs about fifty pounds.

There are several different kinds of baboon. The largest is the *chacma* which has a shaggy coat of grayish brown hair and white rings around its eyes. The *gelada* baboon has a mantle of dark hair on its neck and shoulders, and a "brush" at the tip of its tail. It makes its home in the rocky hills of Ethiopia. Another baboon, the *mandrill,* is a very startling creature. Its face has stripes of bright red, yellow, white, and blue, and there are

big scarlet patches around its short, stubby tail. The *Hamadryas* baboon has a mane of light grayish hair on its head, neck, and shoulders. The ancient Egyptians believed that these baboons were sacred animals.

Babylon and Babylonia

Babylonia was a land of ancient times where one of the earliest civilizations grew up. It takes its name from the city of Babylon, which was its capital for many years. Babylonia goes back in history almost five thousand years. From time to time for more than 1,500 years, from about 2000 B.C. to about 500 B.C., Babylonia was a great empire that ruled many neighboring lands including Palestine and even Egypt. At first Babylonia was a state in the southeastern corner of the country now called Iraq, where the great rivers Tigris and Euphrates flow close together.

About 3000 B.C., a people known as the Sumerians lived in this land. They raised crops of wheat and barley, and kept cattle, sheep, and goats. The Sumerians had an alphabet of wedge-shaped letters and wrote on soft clay tablets, which they baked hard in ovens. These clay tablets have been found in the ruins of the ancient Sumerian cities.

About 2800 B.C., a group of wandering tribes from the Arabian Desert south of the Sumerian cities settled on the plains of Babylonia. They built a city called Akkad between the Tigris and Euphrates Rivers. By about 2500 B.C., under King Sargon, they had conquered the Sumerians but adopted their civilization. The people of Akkad belonged to the family of peoples known as Semites. Jews and Arabs are examples of Semites.

A few hundred years after this, the Amorites, another tribe of Semites, came from the west and conquered Babylonia. One of the Amorite kings, named Hammurabi, who reigned about 2000 B.C., made a town named Babylon his capital. Babylon became one of the greatest cities of those ancient times. Its walls were 12 miles around and more than 100,000 people lived there. Hammurabi brought order, peace, and prosperity to Babylonia. He brought together all the laws of the older conquered races, added them to the Amorite laws, and had them carved on a great stone that archaeologists have found and read. Trade and commerce grew and ships carried cargoes of goods up and down the Tigris River. There were schools where boys learned to write and read and studied arithmetic.

There is much written about Babylon in the Bible. One of its kings, Nebuchadnezzar, about 2,500 years ago, built a palace with "hanging gardens" that were called one of the Seven Wonders of the World. At that time, too, the Babylonians conquered the Jews of Palestine and kept them as captives in Babylonia for nearly a hundred years. This is called the period of the Babylonian Captivity. It was during this period that the prophet Daniel was put into the lions' den.

Finally, in 537 B.C., the Persians conquered the Babylonians and their great nation came to an end. The city of Babylon was gradually destroyed by conquerors until by about 100 B.C. there was nothing left of it.

baby-sitting

Baby-sitting is one of the principal teen-age occupations in the United States. A baby-sitter is a part-time nurse who usually does no housework such as cooking for the child and often does not even put the child to bed; the baby-sitter is simply protection against dangers such as fire or sudden illness.

Teen-age baby-sitters and the parents who employ them are often breaking both state and Federal laws without being aware of it. In many states a baby-sitter under 18 legally requires "working papers." The law requires that money paid to baby-sitters be reported and "Social Security" taxes paid on it. If the baby-sitter is injured by an accident while at work, the employing parents are legally responsible.

SAFETY RULES FOR BABY-SITTERS

The National Safety Council proposes the following rules for baby-sitters:

Before the child's mother leaves—

Know what can be done to make her child feel certain that he is being protected. Be sure you know the answers to these questions.

1. Have the parents told the child they are leaving?
2. Does the child know your name?
3. Do you know the child's name and his nickname?
4. Have you the written time schedule for the child's play, meals, bath and sleep?
5. Where are the child's clothing, play equipment, bath articles and sleeping garments?
6. What undressing procedures are customarily followed?
7. Is the child to be bathed in the tub at bedtime?
8. How are sleeping garments and covers prepared for restful and safe sleep, and where is he to sleep?

Know how to control danger spots in and around the house. Ascertain the following:

1. Are the fires or the heating system under control?
2. How is the kitchen stove lighted? Turned off?
3. Where are the safe areas in which the child has been taught to play?
4. What safety reminders does the child most frequently need? For example:
   (a) Does he stay away from the stove? The hot water tank?
   (b) Does he stay away from electric cords?
   (c) Does he stay away from the sewing machine?
   (d) Does he stay away from the windows?
   (e) Does he stay away from the stairs?
5. Are medicines, cleaning agents, lye, etc., out of the child's reach?

Know what to do in case of an emergency.

1. At what telephone number can you reach the parents?
2. If they cannot be reached by telephone, whom should you call?
3. Where are the first-aid supplies?
   (a) How should you treat a slight burn?
   (b) How should you treat a slight cut?
   (c) How should you treat a slight scratch?
4. In case of fire, do you know the fire department telephone number?

Bacchus

Bacchus was one of the gods that the ancient Romans believed in more than two thousand years ago. He was the same as the god that the ancient Greeks called Dionysus. Bacchus, or Dionysus, was the god of grapes and wine. His father was the chief god, Zeus, and his mother was a human named Semele.

The ancient Greeks and Romans both held festivals in honor of Bacchus. The Greeks called their festivals Dionysia; the Romans called their Bacchanales. At these festivities the people drank wine, sang in groups, and danced. Usually they drank too much and became noisy and wild, so wild parties are still called "Bacchanalian." The Greeks also believed Dionysus was the god of the theater, and all their plays were performed in large outdoor theaters built in his honor.

Bach, Johann Sebastian

Johann Sebastian Bach was a great composer of music who lived in Germany more than 200 years ago. His music is still played and enjoyed by musicians and music lovers all over the world. Bach was born in 1685 in the city of Eisenach in Germany. He studied the violin with his father, who was also a musician, and learned to play the organ and the harpsichord, a musical instrument very much like the piano.

Bach had a large family—twenty children—but still found time to compose more music than almost any man who ever lived. He made his living by playing the organ in churches and by training and leading groups of church singers. He was considered the greatest organist of his time and the greatest composer of music for the organ. He wrote many hymns and much religious music, including *Mass in B Minor* and the *Passion According to St. Matthew*. The music he composed for the harpsichord is now played on the piano. The best-known is a group called "The Well-Tempered Clavier." Much of his work is *chamber music* written for very small orchestras or for groups of three or four musicians who played in a small room instead of a big concert hall. Bach died in 1750 in the city of Leipzig, Germany. He was blind in his last year.

Bach came from a musical family and several of his sons were important composers too. Karl Philipp Emanuel Bach, his most talented son, composed music that is still played. He was born in 1714 and died in 1788.

backgammon

Backgammon is a game for two players. It is the oldest game of which we have record. Equipment for playing it was found in an Egyptian tomb five thousand years ago. Egyptians and people who live in their part of the world are still the best players of it.

WHAT YOU NEED

To play backgammon you need a backgammon board and pieces, two dice cups with four dice, and a doubling cube. The backgammon board is shown in the picture on the next page. The long, narrow triangles, or *points*, are colored, one light and then one dark, and so on. Down the middle of the board runs a *bar*.

The pieces, or *stones*, are in two colors, fifteen of each. We will call them black and white, and name the players for those colors, although the actual stones are usually colored black and red, or red and white. The placing of the pieces on the board to begin a game is shown in the picture. Here the points are shown numbered, to make the game easier to follow.

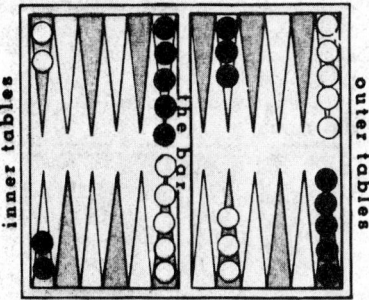

HOW YOU PLAY

You decide by agreement who is to use the white stones and who is to use the black; suppose *you* take the white men for this game. To decide first turn, you and your opponent each shake up one die in your dice cup and cast it. Your opponent, "Black," rolls a five and you roll a two. Having the higher number, he moves first, and for his first move he must use the numbers 5–2, which were thrown to decide first turn.

The moves consist in advancing stones from point to point, depending on the numbers on the dice. The direction in which White moves his pieces runs from Black's points 1 to 12, then from White's points 12 to 1. Black's direction is from White 1 to 12 then from Black 12 to 1. There is no limit to the number of stones of one color that may stand on one point. But stones of different colors may never stand on the same point.

The roll 5–2 is not a very good opening roll. Black plays it in the usual way, by moving one stone from W12 (your 12-point) to B8 (his 8-point), and another from W12 to B11. From now on we will indicate such moves as: W12–B8, W12–B11.

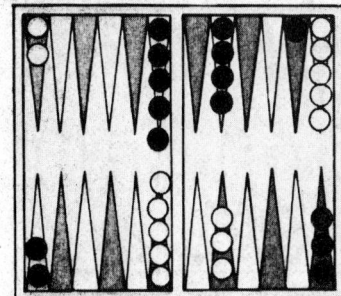

In this move, Black used the 5 on the dice for one stone and the 2 for another. If he had wished, he could have used both numbers for one stone, as by moving W12–B6.

What you are both trying to do is to get all your stones into your own inner or home table.

MAKING A POINT

It is now your turn. You shake both

your dice in your cup and roll 6–1. This is a "natural," a very good early roll because it *makes the bar.* Your 7-point is your *bar point.* You move B12–W7 and W8–W7. Making a point is putting two or more stones on it. That prevents any of your opponent's stones from landing on that point.

Now it is Black's turn. He shakes his two dice in his cup, casts them, and gets 3–2. With the 3 he *splits* his "runners," the two men in your home table, advancing one of them B1–B4. With the 2 he *covers* his stone on B11, by bringing down another stone from his *comfort station,* your 12-point.

Here is the position after Black makes this move:

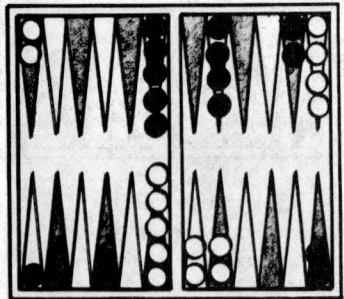

Your next roll is 2–2. In backgammon, *doublets* are taken twice over. That means you may move *four* twos, a total of 8 points. You could move four different stones 2 points each, or one stone 8 points; or in any other combination you like. You start by moving two from W6–W4.

The Black single stone on your 4-point is a *blot.* If an opponent's stone lands on a point occupied by a blot, the blot is *hit* and *sent to the bar.* So you pick up his stone on W4 and place it on the bar. Hitting his blots is a way of delaying the opponent, so as to get ahead in the race to bring the stones around. You hit W4 with two stones so as to *make the point* and prevent him from hitting back.

You still have two deuces to take. You decide to move the two stones from W7–W5. This opens your bar point, but makes your 5-point. It is a good exchange when you have sent one of his men to the bar. As a general rule, the best points to make are those in your home table.

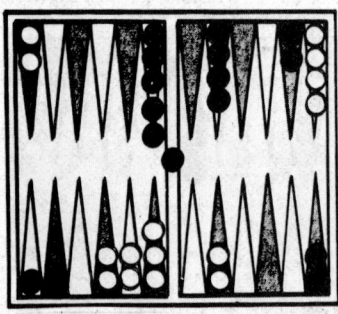

Black now rolls 5–4. Having a stone on the bar, he may not make a move until this stone *enters.* The bar is like an imaginary "zero" point just outside your home table, and must move from there to a higher point before any other move may be made. As you have ·*closed* your 5-point and 4-point, his roll of 5–4 does not let his stone enter. As he has *missed,* he picks up his dice without making a move. If he had rolled a 1, 2, or 3, he could have entered the stone on the bar.

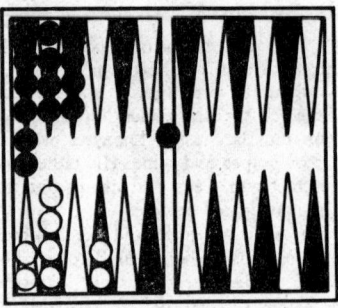

Now we will move to the last stage of the game. When a player has succeeded in moving all his stones into his own home table, he may *bear them off.* That is, every time he throws a number that is as high or higher than a number in his home table, he may remove a stone from that point—if he has a stone on that point. If you have stones only on your 1-, 2- and 4-points, and you throw a 4–1 or 5–1, you may bear off two stones, one from the 4-point and one from the 1-point. But if you throw a 3–1, you may bear off only one stone—from the 1-point —and move the stone from the 4-point down to the 1-point.

While you are bearing off, you may hit an opposing stone—or he may hit you, if he has a stone in your inner table or on the bar, and you leave a blot in your inner table that he can hit. If one of your stones is hit at this time, you must enter it and bring it all the way around into your home table before you can begin bearing off again.

The first player to bear off all his stones wins the game. If the opponent has not borne off any stones, the winner has a *gammon,* which counts double. If the opponent still has a stone in the winner's inner table, or on the bar, the game is a *backgammon,* and counts three times as much as a single game.

DOUBLING THE GAME

When you think you are ahead in the game, you may *double.* Now your opponent may either *drop,* in which case you win the game; or he may play on, in which case the game will count double for whoever wins it. A game may be doubled any number of times, but the only player who has the right to double is the player who did *not* double the last time.

Suppose a game has been doubled three times, and each double was accepted, and then one player wins a gammon. He wins 16 games! The first double made the game worth 2, the second double 4, the third double 8, and the gammon 16.

Backgammon is a game of skill, and a good player will almost always beat a poor player. There are many books that tell how to play backgammon well.

Bacon, Sir Francis

Francis Bacon was a statesman, writer, and philosopher or thinker who

lived in England about 350 years ago. He was "Sir Francis" because he was a knight, and he became also Baron Verulam and Viscount St. Albans. His writings on philosophy, natural science, and

literature are still read. He was born in 1561 and became important as an adviser to King James I and as Lord Chancellor, one of the highest positions in the government of England. He was accused of wrongfully accepting money to do favors for certain people, and pleaded guilty in court. He was put in prison for a short time and then retired to private life and spent the rest of his life writing. He died in 1626. Bacon is famous for his essays and for works in which he showed that the ideas of ancient scientists and philosophers were often wrong. Many people have believed that it was actually Bacon who wrote the works of William Shakespeare (see SHAKESPEARE).

Bacon, Nathaniel, see BACON'S REBELLION.

Bacon, Roger

Roger Bacon was a great scientist who lived in England about 650 years ago. He was born in the year 1214 and became a monk of the order of St. Francis, a society of men in the Roman Catholic Church who swear to be forever poor, to obey the head of the society, never to marry, and never to own anything. A member  of this society is called *friar,* which means "brother."

Bacon became a teacher at Oxford University. At that time men learned about science by reading books written by Aristotle and other great writers who had lived 1,500 years earlier in Greece. No one was allowed to question these ideas. Bacon said this method of learning science was all wrong. Like modern scientists, he believed that experiments should be performed to discover the truth. He also believed that science students should study mathematics. Bacon's ideas, which seem wise and right today, were considered crazy and dangerous in his own time, and he was put in prison. He spent almost 14 years there but probably was released before he died in 1294.

Bacon's Rebellion

In 1676, a hundred years before the American colonies rebelled against England, a man named Nathaniel Bacon led a rebellion of settlers against William Berkeley, the governor of Virginia, which was then a colony of England. The government of the colony had fallen into the hands of Berkeley and a few rich planters who owned huge plantations or farms on the broad plains near the seacoast of Virginia. When Indians began attacking the farmers in the west, Berkeley would not send any troops to protect the colonists. The people of the colony then asked Bacon to help them. Bacon gathered an army of volunteers and drove out the Indians. Because Bacon had raised an army without orders from the government of the colony, Berkeley declared him a rebel and a traitor. Bacon went to Jamestown, the main city of the colony, and forced Berkeley to make him an officer of the colony's volunteer army. As soon as Bacon left to fight the Indians, Berkeley again declared him a traitor and began gathering an army to attack him.

Bacon returned once more to Jamestown, captured the city, and drove Berkeley out. Soon after that, Bacon became sick and died; but Berkeley lost his position as governor when the king found out about his mad behavior. Nathaniel Bacon was born in 1647 and died in 1676.

bacteria

Bacteria are living plants that are so tiny that they cannot be seen without a microscope. One of them may be as small as 1/25,000th of an inch. Thousands of them could be put on the period at the end of this sentence. Seldom is a bacterium larger than 1/2,000th of an inch.

There are bacteria nearly everywhere—floating in the air, living in the soil, on furniture, on the page of this book, on our hands and in our bodies and so on. Sometimes bacteria are called *germs,* and sometimes they are called *microbes* (which means tiny bits of life). Bacteria do not have leaves and stems and roots as do most of the plants you can see. Each one is much like a very tiny bit of living jelly surrounded by a clear, thin covering called a membrane.

KINDS OF BACTERIA

There are more than 1,600 different kinds of bacteria. We hear mostly of bacteria that make us sick, and there are many of these; but most bacteria are not harmful at all, and some bacteria are so useful to mankind that we could not live without them.

Some of these useful bacteria make it possible for certain plants to use nitrogen, a gas in the air, without which the plants could not grow. Some bacteria cause milk to sour, so that cheese can be made of it. Others turn fruits or grain into alcohol, wine, cider, or vinegar. Other bacteria help people and other living things to digest food.

Some bacteria get their food by living on dead animals or plants. These are called *saprophytes* and are very useful bacteria because the dead animals and plants they destroy help to make the soil rich and fruitful. Bacteria that get their food by living on live animals or plants are called *parasites.* Most of these bacteria cause disease.

Some bacteria are shaped like short rods—in fact, the name *bacteria* comes from a word that means "rod-shaped." The first known bacteria were rod-shaped. Now the rod-shaped bacteria are called *bacilli;* spiral or corkscrew-shaped bacteria are called *spirilla* and *spirochetes;* and round or oval bacteria are called *cocci,* which means they look like seeds or grain.

Some bacteria must have air to live; these are called *aerobic.* Others die if they come in contact with air; these are called *anaerobic.* Sunlight kills almost all bacteria.

Bacteria increase their numbers very rapidly. They do not have seeds or lay eggs. Instead, each bacterium splits and separates into two bacteria. When it is warm, some bacteria divide every fifteen minutes. In less than one day, one bacterium can become more than a hundred million bacteria, if each one is able to divide itself. It is when bacteria multiply to such great numbers that they cause the condition called disease. Fortunately,

this can happen only occasionally. In the blood stream, for instance, the white corpuscles (the disease-fighting ones) catch and destroy most of the bacteria before they have a chance to split.

BACTERIOLOGY

Bacteriology is the study of bacteria to find out how to kill the harmful bacteria that cause disease and how to make use of the good bacteria. A bacteriologist is a person who studies bacteria. To do this, he uses a microscope. The science of bacteriology really began when the first microscope was invented, in 1663, by a Dutchman named Anton van Leeuwenhoek, whose hobby was grinding lenses that would make things look bigger.

When a doctor wishes to find out what it is that is making a person sick, he often thinks that it might be a certain type of bacteria. First he must find out exactly what kind of bacteria it is. He takes a little piece of glass called a *slide,* and smears on it the saliva, blood, pus from a sore, or whatever else he thinks may show the bacteria that are causing the sickness. This is called a *smear.* The smear is sent to a laboratory, where it is placed in colored chemicals called *stains.* The stains dye the bacteria so that they are easier to see under the microscope. Different bacteria come out in different colors, and this is one way of identifying them. When a particular kind of bacteria has been identified as causing a certain disease, scientists cause huge numbers of these bacteria to grow in a *culture* and then experiment with different drugs until they find one that will kill the bacteria but not hurt the sick person or animal.

Doctors had suspected for years that bacteria caused disease, but Louis Pasteur, a French chemist, was the first to prove it in 1862. A few years later, Robert Koch, a German doctor, learned how to grow bacteria when he wanted them, and how to prove whether or not they caused disease. There are separate articles about PASTEUR and KOCH.

Bacteriologists have discovered many ways to overcome disease by killing harmful bacteria.

Long ago they learned that by keeping things very clean they could do away with many diseases. Now doctors boil their instruments before using them, because bacteria cannot live in such heat. After an instrument has been boiled and all of the bacteria have been killed, it is said to be *sterile.* Bandages, cotton and other hospital equipment are all sterilized before they are used.

See also the articles on ANTITOXIN and VACCINATION.

Another job of bacteriologists is to discover ways to make useful bacteria do more good. By "planting" certain bacteria in the soil, they help the farmer to grow bigger and better vegetables and fruits. They also help industry, by discovering what kinds of useful bacteria make the best cheese, or vinegar, or other products.

Baden-Powell, Sir Robert

Robert Baden-Powell, a soldier of Great Britain, was the man who started

the Boy Scout movement. He was born in 1857 and served in the army of his country for almost 35 years, and was a lieutenant general when he retired in 1910. He was also a painter and sculptor, but his main interest was in training young people to become good citizens. Because of this interest Baden-Powell founded the Boy Scouts, in 1908. With his sister Agnes he began the Girl Scout movement at the same time. In Great Britain the Girl Scouts are called Girl Guides. Now there are Boy Scouts and Girl Scouts all over the world. The King of England made Baden-Powell a knight and later a baron, Lord Baden-Powell. He died in 1941.

badger

The badger is an animal related to the skunk, weasel, and mink. It is broad and flat, and about two feet long when full-grown. It has coarse gray or brown fur, upon which are white stripes and other marks. The badger lives in burrows, sleeps during the day, and hunts for food at night. It feeds on small animals, insects, birds, and honey. It is found in central and western North America, from Alaska to Mexico. The badger has powerful claws and it is one of the best of all diggers. It can dig so fast that it disappears underground very quickly when it is in danger. It can also dig smaller animals out of their burrows very easily.

The European badger, found throughout Europe and Asia, looks very much like its American cousin, but is larger. Badgers are fierce fighters. Long ago, hunters would surround the badger with dogs, which would kill it. This was called "badgering," and we sometimes hear the word used to express "teasing." That cruel sport is no longer practiced. Badgers are trapped for their valuable hair, which is used to make brushes. Some people consider badgers good to eat. The "Badger State" is Wisconsin.

Bad Lands

Bad Lands are a rocky, desertlike country where the rocks are worn away by the weather and the climate is so dry that plants cannot grow. There are occasional heavy rains that first wash all the soil off the rocky hills and then, by the process called *erosion* or eating away, wear down the rocks—usually into very strange shapes. The most famous Bad Lands are in South Dakota, near the Black Hills. They have been made a national park and attract many tourists.

badminton

Badminton is a game played with rackets that are somewhat like tennis rackets, except that they are longer and lighter. The racket is sometimes called a *battledore.* Also used is a *shuttlecock,* or "bird," a small half-ball made of cork, with about 15 feathers stuck around its flat side. Badminton is played on a court 44 feet long by 17 feet wide, with a net 5 feet high stretched across the middle of the court. There may be two players (singles) or four (doubles, or teams). For doubles, the court is widened to 20

feet. The object of the game is to "volley" the "bird" back and forth across the net. When a player fails to return it across the net, or hits it out of bounds, he loses the point. To "volley" you must hit the bird while it is in the air, before it touches the ground.

Scoring is as follows: You can score only when you are the *server*. The server begins each point by tossing the bird in the air and hitting it over the net. If the other side returns the bird, you must also return it (over the net and within bounds) and if you fail on a return, you lose the serve, but if the other side misses, you score one point. The first side to score 15 points wins the game. In women's and children's games, 11 points is usually a game.

Badminton is usually played outdoors, when it is not too windy, but it can also be played indoors. It is a very fast game, perhaps one of the fastest, because the bird makes many surprise dives and dips and does not go straight like a ball.

Badminton was introduced into England about 100 years ago by army officers who had seen it played in India, where it is called Poona. English people saw it played at Badminton House, the home of the Duke of Beaufort, and they called it the "Badminton game." In 1939 the first international matches, with teams from several countries, were played. The president of the International Badminton Federation, Sir George A. Thomas, offered a trophy, the "Thomas Cup," to the winning team.

Malaya, Thailand, and other parts of Southeast Asia, where the game has been played for many centuries, produce more good players than other countries. Malaya won the first official world championship, beating Denmark.

Battledore and **Shuttlecock** is a simpler game of the same kind. Paddles instead of rackets may be used.

Badoglio, Pietro

Pietro (Peter) Badoglio was an Italian army officer and, later, a statesman. He was born in 1871. He was a general in World War I and in 1926 was made a field marshal, the highest rank in the Italian Army. He commanded the Italian Army that invaded and conquered Ethiopia in 1935 and remained in command through the first few months that Italy fought in World War II, but Italy was doing so badly in the war that he retired. He had gotten along well with Mussolini's Fascist government of Italy, but in 1943, when Italy had obviously lost the war and Mussolini was thrown out, Badoglio was made premier, or head of the Italian government and he signed an armistice with the Allies. A new premier was elected in 1944 and Badoglio retired again. He died in 1956.

Baedeker, Karl

Karl Baedeker was a printer and publisher in Germany. He became famous about 100 years ago by publishing an excellent series of guidebooks for tourists. Baedeker published a separate guidebook for each country in Europe. From these books a traveler could learn all about such things as palaces, museums, libraries, art exhibits, castles,

schools, and other famous buildings, natural wonders, and places to eat and sleep, and how to travel, in any country he wanted to visit.

Baffin Bay and Island

Baffin Island, formerly called Baffin Land, is a large island of 183,810 square miles in the Arctic Sea, between northern Canada and Greenland. Baffin Island belongs to Canada. It is in a body of water called Baffin Bay. Both were discovered by the English explorer William Baffin, about 1616. The island is mostly ice-covered rock, although there are some grassy spots. The climate is very cold and severe, and for more than two hundred years the island was almost uninhabited, except for a few Eskimo villages. Today there are some trading posts, schools, and missions. The Royal Canadian Mounted Police have established posts there, and there is a hospital at Pangnirtung, which is the largest town on the island. About 3,000 people live on the island. Baffin Island is the world's fifth-largest (see ISLAND).

Baghdad or Bagdad

Baghdad, or Bagdad, is the capital of Iraq, the country that was once called Mesopotamia. The Tigris River runs through the city and so there are many bridges. Few cities on earth can boast of so colorful or historic a past as can Baghdad. The early trade route between Europe and Asia passed through Baghdad. It was a center of great riches, as well as learning, from the time of its founding about 1,200 years ago. Under the rule of the caliph (emperor) Harun-al-Rashid, during the ninth century (about 1,100 years ago), Baghdad was one of the most beautiful and important cities in the world, the center of Islam (the Mohammedan religion). Many stories in the *Arabian Nights* are set in Baghdad.

Baghdad has been attacked and occupied by many peoples—Mongols, Persians, and Turks. The British captured it during World War I, and in 1920 it became the capital of the new state of Iraq. Baghdad is a center for the manufacture of rugs, silks, perfumes, drugs, and ceramics. It has an airport and is connected by rail with many important cities such as Jerusalem, Basra, and Teheran.

BAGHDAD, IRAQ. Population, 1,745,328. Capital of Iraq. On the Tigris River.

Baghdad Pact

The Baghdad Pact is an international treaty made in November 1955, setting up the Middle East Treaty Organization. Five nations met in Baghdad and signed the treaty: Great Britain, Turkey, Pakistan, Iran, and Iraq. The actual purpose of the treaty was to resist any effort by the Soviet Union to control the territories of the nations that signed, and they agreed to fight together if necessary to prevent this. The United States did not sign the treaty but in 1958, when a revolution in Iraq made it seem possible that Iraq would withdraw from the treaty organization, the United States government announced that it would help all the treaty nations to defend themselves if necessary.

Baghdad Railway

The Baghdad Railway connects Europe with the principal cities and countries of the Near East. From Istanbul, in Turkey, branches run to points in Syria, Lebanon, Israel, Egypt, Iraq, Iran, and the U.S.S.R. When the railroad was first started, in 1896, by German engineers, there was a slogan in Germany, "Berlin to Baghdad!" This meant that Germany wanted to increase its business with the Near East. The British, French and Russians considered the Baghdad Railway a threat to their own trade, so Turkey stopped building it. The British finally completed the construction of the railroad in 1920.

bagpipe

The bagpipe is a musical instrument that is just what its name sounds like— a bag pipe, or pipes. The bag is made of leather, and you put it under your arm. Then you blow it up by blowing through a "blow pipe." Then you squeeze air out by pressing on the bag. The air blows through three musical pipes, called *drones*, that play one constant droning note, and another pipe, called the *chanter*, that plays the melody. The melody is produced by fingering the chanter. There are seven holes on the chanter for the fingers, and one behind for the thumb.

The bagpipe is the national instrument of Scotland, and the Scottish *pibroch*, or martial tune, is a very stirring sound when played by the "pipes." The Irish also have some claim to the bagpipe, and the French "musette" is a bagpipe with two chanters. The bagpipe is believed to be more than two thousand years old.

British Travel Association
Bagpiper of a Scottish military band.

Bahaism

Bahaism is a religion that was started in Persia (now called Iran) over one hundred years ago, in 1862. It was begun by a man named Murza Hussain Ali, who called himself Baha Ullah. The people of Persia did not like his teachings and sent him away. After he died, in 1892, his son, Abdul Baha, carried on his work and brought Bahaism to people

in America and Europe. The Bahaists believe that God has come to earth at different times, through many different men, whom they call prophets. Some of these prophets are Moses, Jesus, Mohammed, Buddha, and their founder, Baha Ullah. The Bahaists do not have any priests or ministers, as do the Christian religions. The headquarters of the Bahaists in the United States was established by Abdul Baha at Wilmette, Illinois, in 1912. There are about 6,000 Bahaists in the United States.

National Spiritual Assembly

The Bahai Temple in Wilmette, Illinois, is a fine example of Asian architecture in the Midwestern United States.

Bahamas, or Bahama Islands

The Bahamas is an independent nation in the West Indies. It is made up of about 700 islands which are located southeast of Florida, stretching along the east coast of Cuba, and reaching almost to Haiti. Most of the Bahama islands are small and uninhabited. About 186,000 people, most of whom are black, live there. The principal islands are New Providence, upon which is the capital city of Nassau; Andros; Grand Bahama; Crooked Island; the Biminis; Eleuthera; San Salvador; and Great and Little Abaco.

The islands were a British colony for about 300 years, headed by a governor appointed by the king or queen of England. In 1973, they became an independent member of the British Commonwealth, headed by a Prime Minister.

The Bahamans grow sisal, a kind of hemp from which ropes are made. Other products are salt, crayfish, cucumbers, tomatoes, and pulpwood. The people fish, and also catch large sea turtles, which are used for food. In World War II the United States leased land in the Bahamas from the British, and established naval bases and airfields there.

BAHAMAS. Independent nation of over 700 islands in the West Indies. Area, 4,403 sq. miles. Population (1976 estimate) 190,000. Capital, Nassau (population, 105,000).

Bahrain

Bahrain is an Arab Sheikdom consisting of eight islands in the Persian Gulf. The largest, Bahrain Island, is about 30 miles long and 10 miles wide, and lies about 15 miles off the coast of Arabia. The chief commercial center and capital city of Manama is on Bahrain Island. The islands have been inhabited since the Stone Age.

Bahrain's biggest industry is production of oil, which was discovered there in 1932. Boat building, weaving, and pottery making are traditional small industries. At one time, pearl-diving was an important activity. Some farming is made possible by piped artesian well water. Vegetables and dates are the most important crops.

Bahrain is an important trade center, with a fine port, an international airport, modern hotels, and many new, small businesses. From 1861 until 1971, when it announced its independence, Bahrain was a British protectorate.

BAHRAIN. Independent sheikdom comprised of eight islands in the Persian Gulf. Total area, 231 square miles. Population (1976 estimate) 225,000. Capital, Manama, population (1976 estimate) 80,000.

Baikal, or Baykal

Lake Baikal, in eastern Siberia, is the largest freshwater lake in Eurasia, and the deepest lake in the world. Its area is 12,162 square miles and its greatest depth is 6,364 feet. It is nearly 400 miles long, and 20 to 40 miles wide. It is also probably the oldest lake in the world; at the hottest time of the year its surface water never gets warmer than 66° F. From January until May it is covered with ice about four feet thick. In the summer it is crossed by large ships, but in the winter people and goods are transported by sled. The lake is full of fish, including sturgeon and very large salmon. Lake Baikal is of special interest to biologists because it contains many forms of animal life that are not found anywhere else in the world.

Bailey, Ann

Ann Bailey was a daring heroine of the American frontier two hundred years ago, in the days when the colonists were still battling Indians in the eastern part of America. She was born in Liverpool, England in 1742 and came to America when she was 19 years old to make her home in the western part of the colony of Virginia. The Shawnee Indians who lived there were afraid the white settlers were going to take their land from them, and they made war on the colonists.

Ann Bailey's husband was killed during a battle with the Shawnees, and after that she began to wear men's clothes and became a messenger, carrying important news through dangerous Indian territory from one white settlement to another. One day the Indians surrounded Fort Lee, at a place that has now become the city of Charleston, West Virginia. Ann slipped out of the fort at night and rode more than 100 miles on horseback through the wilderness to another fort to get more gunpowder for the colonists. She then rode back again through Indian territory and delivered the gunpowder to the defenders of Fort Lee, who were then able to defeat the Indians. Ann Bailey was 83 years old when she died in 1825.

bakelite

See the entry on PLASTICS.

baking powder

Baking powder is a white powder that is added to dough in certain kinds of baking. When this powder becomes

wet it releases gas bubbles, and these bubbles cause the dough to swell up, or "rise." Yeast is used instead of baking powder when bread is baked. Baking powder is used chiefly for cookies, biscuits, and cakes. The name of the gas released by baking powders is carbon dioxide.

Baking powder is a mixture of soda with other chemicals.

Baku

Baku is the capital of the Soviet Socialist Republic of Azerbaijan. About 1,060,000 people live there, which is about twice as many as live in Buffalo, N.Y. The city is fourth-largest in Russia. It is on the Caspian Sea and has a large modern harbor. It is connected by pipelines to the great oil fields of Batum. Baku is one of the largest centers of petroleum refining and shipping in the world, and the largest in Russia. The "Old City" is bowl-shaped and rises in terraces from the water. It is picturesque, with Moslem houses of worship, the ruins of an Arabian fort built a thousand years ago, the ancient palace of the khans (Mongol kings), and many other interesting buildings. The "New City" is a modern industrial center, in which there are several universities, theaters, and libraries. The people who work in the factories of Baku and the suburbs around it build machinery and ships and make cotton and wool cloth.

Balaam

Balaam, in the Bible, was a prophet called by the king of Moab to put a curse on the great hordes of Israelites who were flocking into the country of Moab. The king was afraid of such great crowds of strangers in his land. Balaam started out for Moab, riding on an ass. Suddenly an angel of the Lord appeared to the ass, and the ass was fearful and refused to move. Balaam could not see the angel, and he whipped the ass to make it go on. Instead of moving, the ass seemed to speak to Balaam. It was the voice of the angel, speaking through the mouth of the ass. Balaam was warned not to curse the Israelites, but to say only what the Lord commanded him to say, when the time came for him to speak. Balaam obeyed the angel, and when he finally spoke he did not curse the Israelites, but predicted that they would eventually become more powerful than the people of Moab, Edom, Amalek, and other neighboring tribes. His prediction came true.

Balaclava or Balaklava

Balaclava is a town on an arm of land called the Crimean peninsula, which sticks into the Black Sea, in Asia. It is part of the U.S.S.R. Today Balaclava is a resort town to which people go for the mild winter climate and the fine beach. Only a few thousand people live there all year round. About a hundred years ago—on October 25, 1854—in the Crimean War in which Britain, France and Turkey fought against Russia, there was a famous battle at Balaclava.

It was during the battle of Balaclava that the famous Charge of the Light Brigade took place. The Light Brigade was a cavalry unit. One of England's great poets, Alfred, Lord Tennyson, wrote a

poem about that charge; it says:

"Theirs not to make reply,
Theirs not to reason why,
Theirs but to do and die:
Into the valley of Death
Rode the six hundred."

A terrible mistake was made when the Light Brigade was ordered to advance into a valley completely surrounded by Russian cannons on the hillsides. More than 700 men started out (although the poem says 600) and only 195 came back. The attack was a useless waste of the lives of brave men.

balalaika

The balalaika is a stringed musical instrument like the guitar. It has three or more strings, a long neck, and a body in the shape of a triangle (three-cornered). The balalaika is played by plucking the strings with one hand while the fingers of the other hand press the strings against the neck. The strings are of gut, silk, or steel. There are some two-stringed balalaikas. Balalaikas are made in different sizes, whose tones range from soprano to bass. They are often played by groups that may include thirty or forty players. The balalaika was once the most popular instrument in Russia and it is associated with Russian folk music.

balance

A balance is a kind of scale that is used to weigh things. It is the most accurate kind of scale. It works like a seesaw with a pan at each end.

A balance has a metal *beam*, or *lever*, from which the pans hang. The beam rests on a very thin knife-edge on top of an upright rod. This knife-edge is called a *pivot*, or *fulcrum*.

HOW TO USE A BALANCE

Anything to be weighed on a balance scale is placed in one of the pans, then weights are placed in the other pan until the two pans are exactly level. (A pointer extending down from the fulcrum shows when they are level.) The weights are marked to show how much each weighs —a pound, an ounce, or even a small portion of an ounce. The total of the weights tells the weight of the object in the other pan. For very accurate weighing, for example by druggists making up prescriptions, the weights are carefully tested so that they will be exactly the same as weights kept by the National Bureau of Standards in Washington, D.C. Before anything is weighed, one should make sure that the balance scale is perfectly adjusted—that is, that the pans are level when both are empty. Usually there is a screw at the fulcrum with which the scale can be adjusted. In the most delicate kind of weighing, even dust on one of the pans can affect the accuracy. Scales for such weighing are usually kept in glass cases.

There is another way to test the accuracy of the weighing: Switch the object and the weights from one pan to the other. Unless the pans still balance (are level), the scale is inaccurate.

Many scales used in laboratories will weigh things accurately within a thousandth of an ounce.

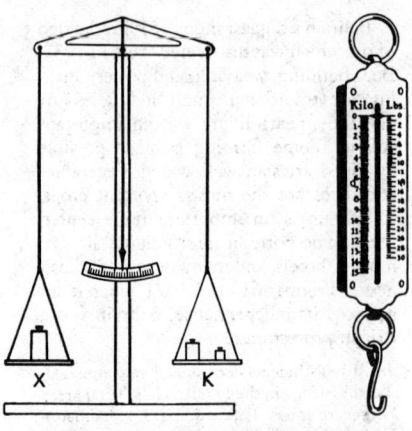

At the left is a balance scale. The object to be weighed is placed on side X. Standard weights are placed on side K. When the two sides are in perfect balance, the weight of the object on X can be told by adding up the total of standard weights on K. The scale on the right has a spring on the back. An object must weigh a pound to pull the bar down to the figure 1. This shows weight in pounds and kilograms.

The kind of balance we have just described is called a *lever*, or *equal-arm*, balance. This is because the arms of the lever from which the pans hang are of equal length. Such balances were the first scales. They were used by the Egyptians, thousands of years ago, to weigh things like wheat. The wheat would be placed in one large pan or basket and a stone in the other. The stone usually weighed about fourteen pounds. When the lever was balanced, it meant that there were fourteen pounds of wheat in the basket. In England people still count weight by stones. A person may weigh "ten stone"—that is, ten times fourteen pounds, or 140 pounds.

BEAM BALANCES

Some balances can weigh very heavy things like people or trucks. In such a balance the arms are not equal. There is a weight on the long arm of the lever. This weight can be moved back and forth on the lever. The short arm of the lever is connected to a large platform. For trucks, this platform may be as large as the floor of a large room. A weight on the long arm of a lever will balance a much heavier weight on the short arm. The farther out you place the weight on the long arm, the heavier the weight it will balance on the short arm. The weight on the lever is adjusted until the lever is perfectly level or horizontal. The lever looks somewhat like a ruler. It is marked to tell you how much weight there is on the platform. This kind of balance is often called a *beam balance*. A pound weight on the long arm of the lever may balance two hundred pounds or more on the platform. For outdoor use, or for use in different parts of a plant, there is a portable beam balance called a *steelyard*.

SPRING SCALES

There is another type of scale that is not really a balance. This is a spring scale. It is entirely different from the lever balance. It has a spring with a pointer at one end and a hook or pan at the other. If you wish to weigh something on the spring balance, you attach it to the hook or place it in the pan. This will stretch or compress the spring and pull the pointer along a dial. The dial is marked to tell you the weight of what you are weighing. Spring balances cannot be used to weigh very heavy things, and they are not very accurate because the spring gradually stretches, but they are useful for weighing letters, groceries, and other light things.

Balboa

Balboa is a town in the Panama Canal Zone. It is on the Pacific Ocean side of the canal, three miles from the city of Panama. In Balboa are the headquarters for the Canal Zone, the canal itself, and the Panama Railway. Almost all the people who live in Balboa are in the United States Army or employed by the United States Government. Balboa was named after the great explorer Vasco de Balboa. The population in the 1970 census was 2,568.

Balboa, Vasco Nuñez de

Vasco Nuñez de Balboa, a Spanish soldier and explorer, discovered the Pacific Ocean about four hundred and fifty years ago. Balboa was born about 1475. In 1501 he settled in Hispaniola, a large island belonging to Spain in the Caribbean Sea, where he tried unsuccessfully to become a farmer. He soon owed money to many people, and he could not pay them, so he decided to escape. He hid himself aboard a ship that sailed to the east coast of what is now called Panama, the narrow neck of land that connects North America to South America. When he arrived at Panama, Balboa took command of the expedition and made friends with all the Indian chiefs. From one of these chiefs he learned that there was a great sea beyond the mountains of Panama. With some friendly Indians as guides, Balboa led 190 soldiers and 1,000 Indians through the thick jungles of Panama. The expedition climbed to the top of the mountain range. From here Balboa could see the new and unknown ocean that no white man had ever seen before. This was on September 29, 1513. Then the king of Spain sent a new governor, Pedro Arias de Avila, to rule the new territory explored by Balboa. Avila became jealous of Balboa and put him in prison. Balboa was accused of being a traitor and was executed in 1517.

Balder

In the old Norse mythology, or religion, Balder was the god of light. He was the son of Odin and Frigga. His mother, like the mother of Achilles, wanted to protect Balder from harm. She made everyone promise not to hurt him—except the mistletoe plant. Finally, a dart made of mistletoe struck Balder and killed him.

Baldwin, Stanley

Stanley Baldwin was an important British statesman between World War I and World War II. He was born in 1867, and he grew up to be very rich, because his grandfather owned one of the largest iron and steel businesses in all of England. But Baldwin used his money to help his country. At one time, he gave more than half a million dollars

to the government when it was badly in debt.

Baldwin held many important positions in the British government. He was Prime Minister, the highest position in the English government, at three different times. While he was head of the government for the third time, he refused to let King Edward VIII marry an American woman named Wallis Warfield Simpson. Edward gave up his throne to marry Mrs. Simpson, and became the Duke of Windsor. Baldwin was the leader of the CONSERVATIVE PARTY, about which there is a separate article. He died in 1947.

Balearic Islands

The Balearic Islands are a group of islands in the Mediterranean Sea, off the east coast of Spain. The largest island is Majorca, or Mallorca, upon which is the town of Palma or Palma de Mallorca, the capital. Minorca and Iviza are the second- and third-largest, and there are several smaller islands. These islands have been known and inhabited for several thousand years. They have been invaded and ruled by the Carthaginians, the Romans, the Moors, and finally the Spanish. They are now a part of Spain. The Moors based a powerful fleet of pirate ships in the Balearic Islands, from which they raided towns along the Spanish coast, and attacked ships at sea. The climate of the islands is mild and balmy and many tourists and vacationists go there, particularly in the wintertime. The people of the Balearics are fine fishermen, and work small farms. They grow olives, fruits and grapes.

BALEARIC ISLANDS. Island group in Mediterranean Sea. Province of Spain. Area, 1,936 square miles. Population, 441,842. Capital, Palma (population 153,682).

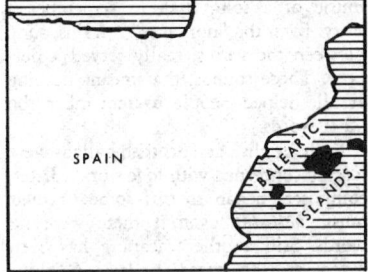

Balfe, Michael

Michael William Balfe was an Irish musician and composer. He was born in Dublin in 1808. His best-known work is the light opera *The Bohemian Girl*, in which is the popular song "I Dreamt I Dwelt in Marble Halls." It was first performed in 1843. Balfe died in 1870.

Balfour, Arthur James

Arthur Balfour was an important British statesman. He was born in 1848. During his lifetime he held many important positions in the British government. For five years he was the Prime Minister, which is the highest position. From 1916 to 1919, while the British were fighting in World War I, he was Foreign Secretary,

Ewing Galloway
The island of Mallorca in the Balearics has carefully terraced hillside farms.

which is like being Secretary of State in the United States government.

In 1917, Balfour published the famous Balfour Declaration. At that time, Great Britain controlled Palestine. But the Jewish people wanted to be independent and make Palestine a homeland for the Jews. The Balfour Declaration encouraged the Jewish people, because it said that Great Britain would support the building of a Jewish homeland. The later British governments did not live up to the Balfour Declaration but the Jews finally realized their ambition by founding the nation of Israel, in 1948. Balfour was made an earl because of his many services to his country, and became Lord Balfour. He died in 1930.

Bali

Bali is an important island of Indonesia, in the southern Pacific Ocean. It is one of the most beautiful places in the South Seas, and many people have gone there to enjoy the splendid scenery and to see the native dances and festivals. Bali is about the size of Delaware, two thousand square miles, and more than 2,196,000 people live there. They are of the Mongoloid race and follow the

Hindu religion. Most of them are farmers, and they raise important coffee, sugar and rice crops. Others work in the forests and cut down the valuable teakwood trees. Many of the people are very fine artists and sculptors. They make beautiful gold and silver jewelry, pottery, and cloth with wonderful designs.

Ewing Galloway
Balinese music is rhythmic but sounds strange to American ears. This musician is playing on a gamelang, a set of gongs that have ringing, bell-like tones.

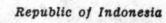
The Balinese woodcarvers are among the best in the world. Below is shown a small statue of the god Vishnu mounted for a journey. Every detail is perfect.

Republic of Indonesia

Republic of Indonesia
This Balinese girl is dressed in an ancient and elaborate dance costume. The headdress, neckpiece, and bracelet are made by village craftsmen.

Most of Bali is mountainous. There are two active volcanoes, one of which, Agung, is more than 10,000 feet high. But there are also fertile regions in the valleys and along the coast. Bali is pleasantly warm all year round, which is one reason it is such an attractive vacation spot. There are many roads on the island, but no railroads.

Bali was ruled by the Dutch for more than three hundred years. During World War II the island was occupied by the Japanese and after the war the people got their freedom from the Dutch and became part of Indonesia.

BALI, Area, 2,147 square miles. Population, about 2,196,000 (1973 estimate). Capital, Singarja (about 12,600).

Ewing Galloway
The old man is the master of ceremonies of a Balinese dance play. He is telling the story before the girls behind him perform the dance itself.

Balkans

The Balkans are a group of countries in a part of southeast Europe called the Balkan peninsula, between the Adriatic Sea and the Black Sea. All through history countries have fought to get control of the Balkans, because so much of the trade between Europe and Asia passes through them. So many wars have started in the Balkans that they have been called "the powder keg of Europe."

The Balkan peninsula is about 175,-000 square miles in size, which is not much larger than the state of California, but about 59,624,000 people live there—almost three times as many people as live in California. The countries of the Balkan peninsula are: Yugoslavia, Rumania, Bulgaria, Greece, Albania, and the part of Turkey that lies in Europe. There are separate articles about these countries.

The people of the Balkans are of several racial stocks and religions. The first people to settle in this part of Europe were the Albanians and the Greeks. Many other peoples followed—Slavs, Rumanians, Bulgarians, Turks, and others. They settled in different parts of the peninsula, and each group kept its own customs and beliefs. All of these groups wanted to be independent, and sometimes they fought other countries, sometimes they fought each other, for the right to govern themselves.

Most of the people are farmers. Many of them are poor, because much of the land is rocky and mountainous. Many of the people raise cattle, goats, and sheep. There is not much manufacturing.

BALKAN GEOGRAPHY

The Balkan peninsula is very mountainous, with many short rivers. The famous Danube River flows from central Europe through the Balkans and then empties into the Black Sea. The Balkan mountains stretch from Yugoslavia to the Black Sea, rising to about 7,800 feet in the central part. Many fierce battles have been fought in these mountains. Along the western border of the Balkans are the Dinaric Alps, which also have lofty peaks. These mountain ranges contain many valuable minerals, but most of them have not yet been mined. The people have neither the machines for mining, nor enough good railroads and roads to carry the minerals away. It gets very cold in the winter in the mountains, but in the southern part of the peninsula the climate is warm, as it is in southern Italy.

Five hundred years ago, the powerful Turks invaded the Balkan countries and gradually conquered them. The Balkan nations fought bravely, but they were not strong enough to drive out the Turks. For centuries afterward, the Turkish Empire controlled the Balkans. The Balkan people were unhappy and wanted to be free to rule themselves.

THE BALKAN WARS

By the beginning of this century, the Turks had become much less powerful. In 1911, the Turks and Italians went to war. The Balkan countries saw this as a good opportunity to drive the Turks out of Europe. Bulgaria, Greece, Serbia and Montenegro formed a secret alliance. (These last two countries are now part of Yugoslavia.) They declared war on Turkey in 1912, and the first Balkan War began. The four Balkan countries attacked the Turks at various points and defeated them.

Bigger European countries tried to get the Balkan nations and Turkey to sign a peace treaty, but Turkey refused, and so the fighting started again. Turkey was defeated in several more battles, and finally, in May, 1913, a peace treaty was signed. Turkey lost all its European possessions, except a small strip including Constantinople (the city that is now called Istanbul).

The Balkan countries then began to quarrel among themselves about who would get this land. Serbia was very bitter when Albania was declared an independent state by the European powers. Serbia wanted Albania because it was on the Adriatic Sea and Serbia needed seaports. When it could not get Albania, Serbia demanded a large part of the territory of Macedonia from Bulgaria. Bulgaria refused, and began to prepare for war. Serbia was joined by Greece, Rumania, and Montenegro. They demanded that Bulgaria share the lands it had gained in the first Balkan War. The Bulgarians didn't answer the demand, and instead attacked Serbia in June, 1913. This was the beginning of the second Balkan War.

The war lasted only one month. Bulgaria could not defend itself against four enemies, and had to surrender and give up territory to all of them. But this was not the end of trouble in the Balkans. More and more, the people were demanding a separate state for each nationality. Some of the Slavic people who were ruled by Austria-Hungary, an empire that was ended by World War I, demanded independence. They began to meet secretly in cities, and even broke out in riots. Europe became very nervous. In 1914, a Slav assassinated the Archduke Ferdinand of Austria in the streets of Sarajevo, while he was riding in his carriage. This incident caused the outbreak of World War I, in which almost all the European countries and later the United States were involved.

After World War I, the Allies formed the new country of Yugoslavia. It was made up of the former countries of Serbia and Montenegro, plus Bosnia, Herzegovina, and Dalmatia, which had been part of Austria-Hungary. In World War II, the Balkans again became the scene of much fighting. The Nazis invaded and finally occupied all of these countries. After the war, all the Balkan countries except Greece and Turkey came under the domination of Russia and set up communist governments.

ballad

A long time ago, people used to sing lively little tunes and dance to them. They called these songs *ballads*. During the Middle Ages, men known as troubadours used to make up verses about all manner of things—battles, weddings, shipwrecks, and tales of people's lives—and sing them, to entertain people. The troubadours' songs were so interesting that people found they would rather listen than dance, and after a while the word ballad no longer meant a dance, but a song that told a story.

In those days, when very few people could read and write, ballads were important as a means of remembering stories, and even actual history. It is much easier to remember the words and music of a song than to remember a story. Even the "nonsense" refrains, sung between the verses, really served a purpose. Those sounds, that meant nothing at all, helped people to remember the other words.

Early English and Scottish ballads were largely concerned with love stories. Later, composers began to call some of their music *ballades*, even if there were no words. Still another meaning has been given to the word ballad. A slow, dreamy, sentimental song is called a ballad in the field of popular music. When the famous songwriter Irving Berlin entered the United States Army in 1917 (for World War I) and was asked what he did for a living, he answered, "I write sentimental ballads."

ballast

Ballast is something heavy that is used to hold things down or keep them in place. It can be bags of sand, rocks, lead, and even water.

Ballast is very important in ships. If a ship is too light, the wind and waves make it bob around like a cork. So when it is not fully loaded, ballast is placed in its bottom. Balloons use ballast to give the balloonist more control. The ballast is usually bags of sand or water hanging over the side of the balloon. When the balloonist wants to rise higher, he drops some ballast. Racing cars use ballast. The engine at the front is so heavy that weight must be carried at the rear to keep

it down.

Submarines use water as ballast. When a submarine is about to dive under water, the sailors let seawater enter special tanks. This makes the submarine heavier, and it sinks in the same way a floating bottle sinks when it is filled with water. The water is pumped out when the submarine is about to rise. This makes it lighter and able to float to the surface.

Many ships that use oil as fuel (as most ships of the United States Navy and other navies do) are built so that sea water can be pumped into their oil tanks after the oil from those tanks has been used. During World War II, some destroyers that had empty oil tanks, and that were waiting to take on more fuel from oil tankers, sank while they were waiting, because they did not have enough ballast.

Rock ballast is used to weight down the wooden crossties on railroad tracks. If they were not weighted, a heavy train clanking along the tracks at high speed, and swaying from side to side, could shift the ties and move the tracks.

ball bearings are explained in the article on BEARINGS.

ballet

Ballet is a kind of dancing that tells a story—like a play without words. This form of dancing is usually performed on a stage, with scenery and costumes. Ballet is more than just dancing with the legs and feet. A ballet dancer's entire body moves gracefully to the music played by the orchestra. The movement of the arms, and even facial expressions, mean much in ballet. The music for a ballet is written to fit the dancing. Sometimes the music is written, and then the dance is made up to go with it. Sometimes the dance comes first and the music is written afterwards. The people who make up the dance are called "choreographers," and the people who make up the music are called "composers."

Dance steps are "written down," just as a writer puts his ideas on paper, or a painter paints a picture on paper, or a musician writes a tune on paper. This is called *dance notation*.

The first ballet that was like our ballet of today was performed about 350 years ago in France. It was called "The Comic Ballet of the Queen." It was a big success, and everyone liked it. Many people became interested in this new kind of dancing; but at first they called them "Masques." These were dress-up parties at which everyone wore a mask and costume. In these masques some of the dancers told stories. One famous masque was "Comus," written by the great English poet, John Milton.

Because ballet first became popular in France, most of the words we use in talking about ballet are in the French language. A famous composer named Jean Baptiste Lully, who lived in Paris, France, three hundred years ago, had the first school for ballet dancers and musicians, and another man, named Pierre Beauchamp, found there were five basic positions that had to be learned by ballet dancers. These five positions are still the most important parts of ballet, and every

ballet dancer must learn them and constantly practice them.

THE FIVE POSITIONS

If you were going to learn the positions you would start by standing next to a chair or table and holding on with one hand. This would take the place of the "barre," as it is called in a dancing school. (A real barre is a wooden rail fastened to the wall, just high enough to be held with one hand or both hands.) Now, while you are holding one hand on the barre (or on the back of the chair), raise the other arm out to your side. Then put your heels together, and turn your toes out so that your feet point away from each other. This is called the "turn-out," and is the *first position*. It is very important.

Second position. Now, while you are standing in first position, slide out the foot that is farthest away from the barre. If your whole leg is turned out from the hip, and not just your feet, this is not hard to do—that is, if the first position is right.

Third position. Now, from second position, slide the outside foot to the middle (instep) of the inside foot, trying to keep both feet at right angles with one another. Try to keep both feet turned out and both legs straight.

Fourth position. From the third position, slide your front foot out in front of you about as far as the length of your back foot, and let the *heel* of your front foot be in line with the *toes* of your back foot. (This is hard to do at first, but gets easier the more it is done.)

Fifth position. From the fourth position, slide your front foot back until it is alongside your back foot, with your heels and toes next to each other. Your knees are not supposed to bend at all. Now you are in fifth position, which is the position most often used in ballet dancing.

THE BALLERINA

The "ballerinas" are the girl dancers in a ballet company who take the important roles, or parts. The prima ballerina is the girl who dances the most important part. If the ballet happened to be a story about a girl named "Anna," the prima ballerina would be Anna. In other words, she is the heroine, or female "lead." Ballet masters (who teach the dancers their parts and steps) and directors of ballet companies and the "corps de ballet" of opera companies, select girls who show exceptional talent in dancing school, and who have acting ability, to become ballerinas. You must start young to be a ballerina, and you must study

very hard for many years before making any public appearance, except for school recitals. Even after you are a professional, you must keep on studying and taking lessons. You must study music and languages and art and acting. You must train like an athlete and study like an artist. A ballerina must practice every day except when she is sick.

BALLET SCHOOL

If you were going to study ballet dancing and were starting at ballet school, here is what you would do. When you got to school you would see a large room with a smooth wooden floor, and a piano in one corner, or perhaps a phonograph. Along the wall on one side there would be a rail like the one we mentioned before. This is the barre.

Before you started to dance you would change into your practice clothes. Girls studying ballet usually wear a special type of costume called a *leotard*, a one-piece garment that fits snugly from the shoulders to the thighs, but you do not absolutely have to have it. You can use any clothes that are easy to stretch and bend in. Then you would put on your ballet slippers. If you were an advanced pupil who had studied for a long time, you might put on a pair of slippers called *pointes*, with hard toes for dancing on the tips of your toes, but if you were not an advanced pupil you would only be learning to dance on "half-toe," like standing on tiptoe, and this is called *demi-pointe*.

When the class starts you will probably practice at the barre for about a half hour, doing the five positions and exercises to stretch and strengthen your legs. Here are a few of the principal exercises that are always used in ballet school. Some of them are to learn technique, which means the kind of movement you will use in actual dancing, so that very hard steps are made easy. The names are in French, but mean just what you are doing. For example, *bras* in French means "arm," and *porter* means "to carry," so the movement we call *port de bras* in ballet just means "carry the arms," and when we hear that term we know it means to move the arms around gracefully in different positions.

EXERCISES AT THE BARRE

After you have practiced the five positions, first with your right foot, and then with your left, your teacher will show you how to do the next exercises at the barre. There are *demi-plies* in different positions. *Demi* means half, and *plie* means bend, so it means "half-bend."

For instance, if you are in the first position, you bend your knees outward, so that you squat down a little, but only halfway. You keep your feet flat on the floor, and turned out. You go up and down slowly and gracefully. This is an important exercise, because most dance movements have it in them. Ballerinas use it to "warm up" before dancing. You would probably do some demi-plies in second, fourth and fifth positions. After doing the demi-plie, you would probably be shown how to do the *grand-plie*, which means "full bend." You start just like the demi-plie, but when you are as far as you can go, you let your heels come up from the floor a little, and go on down until you are almost squatting, then slowly rise again. In the second position your heels stay on the floor, but in the fourth and fifth positions they rise slightly as they do in the first position.

Next you might do the exercise called *battement tendu*. You stand in the fifth position, and you slide one foot out in front of you as far as it will go, without lifting the toe from the floor, but your leg stays in its turned-out position. You would do this movement with both your right and left foot, and then to the side, and then behind you. After each kick, you move your foot back to fifth position. Then you put the battement tendu and plie together, so that as you stretch your leg out you are standing straight up, but as you bring it back, you bend, or plie. You would practice this to the front, to the side, and to the back, first with one foot and then with the other.

Then there are arm exercises—the *port de bras* we mentioned before. There are many different kinds, some at the barre and some away from the barre.

When all the leg exercises and ports de bras are easy for you to do at the barre, you can do them away from the barre. Then you are more advanced, and can go on to other things. You can learn to do turns, and go spinning around. You can learn to rise up on your toes, or *pointes*. This begins with an exercise called *relevé*, and means rising up on your toes from second position without holding on to the barre, though at first you will have to hold on to the barre to keep your balance.

As you learn more and more you will soon know all of the hundreds of other ballet words that are spoken in French —and also the steps that they name.

KINDS OF BALLET

Ballet has changed very greatly since it began four hundred years ago, but some of the old ballets are occasionally seen in theaters today. Some of them had no real story, but were like acting out various ideas, such as a boy and girl making love, or jealousy, or other human actions and emotions. There were some characters that were used over and over in many ballets by different composers and writers. They were named Pierrot, Harlequin, Columbine, Pantalon, and others, and were taken from a kind of show they had a long time ago called *pantomime*. Many of the things that were started long ago are still in use today. Dancers no longer wear masks, but the kind of little skirt they used to wear is still worn today. It is called a *tutu*,

and there are two kinds, the *classic tutu*, a short skirt made of many layers of white cloth, and a *romantic tutu*, made the same way only longer. The classic tutu comes down to just above the knees, but the romantic tutu comes down to the ankles.

There are three kinds of ballet: *Classic Ballet*, where dancers wear the old costumes, and where the dancing is done on the toes (by the girls, but not the boys), with all of the classic positions; *Romantic Ballet*, which is almost like classic ballet, with some things extra; and *Modern Ballet*, in which the dancers wear whatever kind of clothes they need to make them look like what they are supposed to be in the story.

ballistics

Ballistics is the study of what happens to guns and ammunition when they are fired. People who study ballistics are called ballisticians or ballistics experts. They collect information from firing tests. In firing tests, a gun is fired, then examined. This information is used to make better guns and munitions, and to tell people how to shoot guns safely and more accurately.

POLICE BALLISTICS

Most police departments have ballistic laboratories. In these laboratories ballistics experts examine guns and ammunition that have been fired in crimes and have been brought in by the police as evidence. When a gun is fired, it leaves marks on the ammunition cartridge case and on the bullet. Each gun has its own peculiar mark. By examining the bullet through a microscope, ballistics experts can tell from what gun it was fired. If they know where the lead nose of the cartridge (or bullet) landed, and in what position it was found, they can also tell from where and how far away the gun was fired. Sometimes they can tell if the person who fired the gun was moving or standing still. This information is used to catch and convict persons who have committed crimes with firearms.

MILITARY BALLISTICS

The chief use of ballistics is in military warfare. Without a knowledge of ballistics it would be very difficult to aim and fire a rifle safely, drop a bomb on a target, or aim a rocket or an antiaircraft gun.

Ballistics has helped to develop many new military weapons, including the atom and hydrogen bombs, the atom-gun, rocket guns and guided missiles (some of which are called *ballistic missiles*; see GUIDED MISSILES).

The study of ballistics is divided into three parts: *interior, exterior* and *terminal* ballistics.

INTERIOR BALLISTICS

Interior ballistics is the study of what happens inside a gun when it is fired. A gun, like a revolver or rifle, is loaded by placing a cartridge containing an explosive in the gun barrel. (In all but the heaviest artillery, the cartridge or shell itself contains the explosive. See the article on AMMUNITION.)

When the trigger is pulled, the explosive (usually gun powder) is set on fire. The gases that are formed push the bullet out of the gun with great force. This force can be measured with a tool called a *crusher gauge*. The gauge is placed over a hole in the side of the gun barrel. When the gun is fired, the gases press against the side of the barrel and push down a cylinder of copper or lead in the pressure gauge. Ballistics experts can tell how much gas pressure there is in the barrel by measuring how far down the cylinder is pressed.

The pressure behind a bullet forces it out of the muzzle, or end of the barrel, with great speed. Some bullets leave a gun at 2,000 miles an hour. The speed with which a bullet leaves a gun is called the *muzzle velocity*. The muzzle velocity can be measured with a block of wood hanging from a string. This is called a *ballistic pendulum*. The bullet is fired into the wood block. By measuring how far the block swings back, and also weighing the block and the bullet, ballistics experts can find out the muzzle velocity.

As a bullet or shell flies through the air, it loses speed because of wind resistance. At best, its speed at the target is three-quarters of its muzzle velocity.

With such information, ballistics experts can tell how much powder to put in a cartridge, how heavy the bullet should be, and how wide and long the gun should be for it to fire accurately.

EXTERIOR BALLISTICS

Exterior ballistics studies the path of the bullet through the air. This path is called the *trajectory*. When the bullet leaves the gun, it meets air resistance. It is also acted on by gravity. This gives its path a peculiar shape. If there were no air resistance, the path would be a curve called a parabola. (See the diagram on page 530, which shows how a cannon ball is shot through the air.)

In firing a gun, you must take air and wind resistance into account. You must set the gun sights so that when you aim and fire the gun, the bullet will not be blown away from its target.

To find out how a bullet looks in flight, ballistics experts take pictures of it with special high-speed cameras. They can take 10,000 pictures a second.

TERMINAL BALLISTICS

When a bullet or bomb has hit a target, measurements are made to see how much of the target has been destroyed. Pictures are taken of the damage and the photographs are studied. These pictures help munitions manufacturers to design ammunition that will do the most damage.

Most ships and tanks are *armored*. That is, they are built of hard steel to resist the enemy's guns. The "rule of thumb" is that an armor-piercing shell will go through about as much armor as the caliber of the shell: a 4-inch shell will go through 4 inches of armor; a 16-inch shell will go through 16 inches of armor, and so on. There is an unending effort to make armor that cannot be pierced, and to make guns and shells that will overcome the newest and strongest armor.

balloons and airships

A balloon is a bag filled with gas to make it float in the air. It will float if the gas inside it is enough lighter than air. To float, the bag and the gas together must weigh less than a quantity of air that would occupy the same space.

The simplest example is the rubber toy balloon. If blown up with air, the toy balloon will not float. The rubber bag weighs more than air, and this plus the air inside makes the whole weight more than the weight of the air around it. The air-filled toy balloon will fall to the floor and stay there. But at parks and fairs, where balloons are filled with a very light gas, they will rise into the air and float away unless they are held down by a string or stick.

When a balloon is filled with a light gas, or with hot air (which is lighter than cool air), it will rise and will continue to rise as long as it is lighter than air. The higher the altitude, the thinner the air is and the less it weighs. Eventually the balloon reaches an altitude where it is no longer lighter than the air around it. Then it will rise no more. That is its "ceiling."

A balloon would rise even better if it could contain a vacuum—no air at all—instead of a light gas. But this cannot be done. The pressure of the gas inside is needed to make the bag bulge out and occupy its full space. With a vacuum inside the bag would collapse from the pressure of the air outside. (See the articles AIR, AIR COMPRESSION, and VACUUM.)

The principle of the balloon was discovered about 150 years ago. Men knew that smoke rises. Smoke is a kind of warm air. It rises in the heavier cool air around it. One day two brothers named Montgolfier, who lived in France, decided to find out if a bag filled with smoke would rise into the air.

They placed some burning charcoal near the opening of a large linen bag about 18 feet wide, and filled the bag with smoke. The bag began to rise into the air and reached a height of a mile and a half. The bag remained in the air for ten minutes. When the smoke began to cool, the bag slowly came down to the ground. This was in June, 1783.

In August, 1783, a French scientist named Jacques Charles discovered that air is 14 times heavier than hydrogen gas. He decided to fill a balloon with hydrogen instead of smoke. He took a large silk bag, which held so much hydrogen that it took him four days to fill it. Thousands of people gathered in Paris to watch the balloon rise. When the balloon was filled, it was released by cutting ropes attached to bags of sand that had held the balloon down.

Charles' balloon rose high into the air. Forty-five minutes later it landed in a field fifteen miles away. To the workers in the field, the balloon looked like a monster from another world. They were so frightened that they ran to the balloon and immediately tore it to pieces. They were afraid it might kill them.

A month later a sheep, a rooster and a duck were sent up in a basket attached to a balloon. (A basket or car attached to a balloon is called a gondola.) The animals were not hurt, so in October

1783 another Frenchman, François de Rozier, went up in the basket himself, the first man to do so. This time the balloon was filled with hot air, because hydrogen was still hard to get. The balloon was connected to the ground by long guide ropes to keep it from floating away. Such a balloon is called a *captive balloon*. Balloons not connected to the ground are called *free balloons*.

The gases most used in balloons are hydrogen, helium, and illuminating gas. Hydrogen is the lightest. Helium is scarce and very expensive, but it has one great advantage that hydrogen and illuminating gas do not have—it will not burn. Illuminating gas is cheap and is used in most free balloons.

Official Navy Photo

This U.S. Navy balloon will rise to a height of three miles. The men will check air and wind conditions aloft. They will bring back samples of upper air to be studied.

USES OF BALLOONS

Captive balloons were used for military observation as early as 1794, during the French Revolution. Captive balloons were also used during the American Civil War. Soldiers went up in their balloons and saw what the enemy was doing, then dropped messages to the ground. During World Wars I and II thousands of captive balloons were sent up over cities such as London. The balloons had wires and cables hanging from them. Enemy planes had to fly higher than the balloons or else get caught in the wires and cables. When they flew high, they could not aim their bombs so well. These balloons were called *barrage balloons*.

Free balloons were used during the French Revolution to drop small bombs. The balloons would be floated over enemy territory with a lighted fuse inside them, to explode the bombs when the balloon was over enemy territory. Sometimes the wind changed and the balloons were blown back and the bombs exploded over the people who sent them up.

Free balloons are much used by scientists to examine the air miles above the ground. These balloons go many miles into the air.

A free balloon always carries *ballast*, usually sandbags. When the men in a balloon want to rise higher they throw out some of the ballast. This makes the

balloon and its load lighten, and causes it to go higher. When the scientists want to come down they let some gas out of the balloon by pulling a cord connected to a valve on top of the balloon. The balloons are made of specially treated cotton cloth or silk. They are often more than 30 feet across. One famous balloon called the Explorer II measured 192 feet across. In 1935 two United States Army officers went up in the Explorer II and reached a height of almost 14 miles.

Balloon races are held every year in England and the United States. The purpose of these races is to see which balloon can stay up in the air the longest and travel the farthest distance.

Some balloons are sent high into the air without any men inside the gondola. These balloons are called *weather*, or *sounding*, balloons. They contain radio transmitters that send signals down to the ground, giving scientists information about the air above. Some balloons have gone more than 28 miles up. (The record for a manned balloon is 113,500 feet, or nearly 21½ miles.) When it reaches a certain height, a sounding balloon explodes and the instruments inside are carried gently to the ground by parachutes.

DIRIGIBLES

Less than a hundred years after the first successful balloons were made, men had made a kind of balloon that could be driven by an engine and steered. Such a balloon is called a dirigible, which means "able to be directed, or steered." A Frenchman named Henri Giffard made the first dirigible, in 1852, but most of the credit for the great dirigibles is due to a German, Count Ferdinand von Zeppelin, after the year 1900. In fact, dirigibles are often called *Zeppelins*. They are also called *airships*.

Zeppelin's airships were cigar-shaped, which makes it harder for the wind to blow them around. They were *rigid* airships, meaning that they had a metal framework inside the "bag," and they were divided into many airtight compartments, so that if the gas leaked out of one compartment the others would remain full and would keep the airship afloat. The first "bombers" were Zeppelins used by the Germans to drop bombs on London during World War I. Count von Zeppelin also began the first air transport. He had a passenger service among the big cities of Germany, and later—during the 1930s—these big airships carried passengers from Europe to North and South America. The United States Navy also used many dirigibles.

These great dirigibles were 700 to 800 feet long and held about 6,500,000 cubic feet of gas. They would go 70 to 100 miles per hour and had a range of 10,000 miles. A big one would carry about a hundred passengers. The Navy dirigibles could also carry four or five fighter planes. The dirigibles were driven by gasoline engines and propellers as on an airplane—as many as eight propellers on a big airship.

Unfortunately, there were many bad accidents in dirigibles, which cost many lives. The last of these was in 1937, when the German passenger airship *Hindenburg*, the biggest ever built, caught fire when it was landing at Lakehurst, New

Jersey. The fire was possible only because the *Hindenburg* used hydrogen gas instead of helium gas (which does not burn). The United States controls all the helium in the world and refused to help the warlike plans of the German government by selling them helium. Nevertheless, the big airships never became popular again, especially since airplanes were being made bigger and faster than ever.

BLIMPS

A smaller type of airship, that is still seen in the skies over some big cities, is the *semi-rigid* or *nonrigid* airship, usually called a *blimp*. It is much smaller than the big dirigibles—only 100 to 200 feet long, with perhaps 200,000 to 650,000 cubic feet of gas. The blimp does not have the metal framework of the rigid dirigibles, but it is cigar-shaped as they are. During World War II, blimps were very useful in spotting enemy submarines. In peacetime, they are used to carry advertising banners over big cities.

ballot

When a person votes in an election, he is said to *cast a ballot*. The ballot is a piece of paper on which are printed the names of all the *candidates*—that is, persons who want to be elected. The voter marks an X beside the name of each candidate he wants to vote for. Then he folds the paper so that no one else can see where he put his X's; this makes it a *secret ballot*. Finally he drops it through a slot into a *ballot box*. Later, all the ballots will be taken out of this box and the votes for each candidate will be counted, to find out who was elected.

Every state of the United States and all civilized countries must use some form of secret ballot. If they did not, people might be afraid to vote against some powerful politician, for fear he would find out and punish them later.

The written ballot we use is called the Australian ballot, because it was first used in Australia, about a hundred years ago (in 1856). The latest form of voting is the *voting machine*. Instead of marking an X, you pull down a little lever beside the candidate's name. A very efficient, completely automatic adding machine is built into the voting machine, and when you pull the lever it adds one vote to your candidate's total. This is faster and more accurate than marking and counting paper ballots. The voter stands behind a curtain, so the ballot is still secret.

Long ago, men voted by dropping little balls into the ballot box. A white ball meant "yes" and a black ball meant "no." The Italians called these *ballota*, which means "little balls," and that is where we got the word ballot. When a person wants to join a club and the members vote against him, he is said to be "blackballed."

See also the article on ELECTIONS.

Balmoral Castle

Balmoral Castle is a private palace of British kings and queens. It is in Scotland, and its name means "majestic dwelling" in the Gaelic language that once was spoken in the Scottish Highlands. The castle grounds are on the River Dee, about 50 miles west of the city of Aber-

deen, and cover 40,000 acres. Balmoral was bought for Queen Victoria in 1848 by Prince Albert, who was her consort (husband). Balmoral Castle may be visited by the public when the royal family is not there.

balsa

The balsa tree is sometimes called the corkwood tree. It grows in the forests near the equator in South America, especially in Ecuador. The wood is the lightest known wood. It is only about one-half as heavy as cork. That is why it is used in making airplanes. During World War II great quantities of balsa wood were used in aircraft construction. The wood is also used for making life preservers and floats. Model airplanes and boats are usually made of balsa wood because it is soft and easy to carve. The balsa tree grows faster than almost any other tree—about 10 feet a year. A full-grown tree is about 90 feet tall.

The book *Kon-Tiki* by Thor Heyerdahl tells the amazing story of a balsa wood raft that floated across the Pacific Ocean. Six scientists built this simple raft out of balsa logs 40 feet long. They started in Peru, on the west coast of South America, and let the ocean currents carry them in the raft more than 4,000 miles across the ocean, to an island called Puka Puka. They wanted to show that the Peruvians who lived hundreds of years ago could have made the voyage on similar craft. After more than three months in the ocean the huge balsa logs had absorbed some water but were still light enough to float easily.

balsam

Balsam is a sticky, white liquid that oozes out of blisters on the bark of fir trees. It is usually called *Canada balsam*, because it comes from the balsam fir tree that grows in Canada and also in the northeastern United States. Balsam is used in making some kinds of varnish. Because of its pleasant odor, often it is also used in soaps and perfumes. It is used to cement lenses together and to make permanent slides for a microscope because it makes the glass stick tightly but does not interfere with the light coming through the glass. A permanent microscope slide is made by placing the object to be viewed on one piece of glass, putting one drop of balsam on the object, then placing another piece of glass over it. A few days are allowed for drying.

The Canada balsam tree grows to 70 or 80 feet high. Its wood is light and not very valuable. It is also called the *Balm of Gilead fir*. Balm of Gilead is mentioned in the Bible; it was a fragrant resin used as an incense and to flavor medicines, and it was a kind of balsam but not the same as Canada balsam.

Balthazar was one of the Three Wise Men, or MAGI, about whom there is a separate article.

Baltic Sea

The Baltic Sea is a large body of water that is nearly surrounded by several countries of northern Europe—Denmark, Germany, Russia, Finland, Poland and Sweden. The sea is 163,050 square miles in size, which is larger than the state

of California. It is the shallowest of all the seas. At no point is it more than 180 feet deep. It has many sand banks and islands, and it is often swept by violent storms. All of this makes it very dangerous for ships. Despite this, the Baltic Sea is important to the trade and business of the countries around it.

The Baltic Sea is divided into several parts. The northern part is called the Gulf of Bothnia and is between Sweden and Finland. The eastern part includes the Gulf of Finland and the Gulf of Riga. The southern part has many shallow lagoons, called "haffs."

Two hundred and fifty rivers run into the Baltic, so it contains much less salt than the Atlantic Ocean. This makes the Baltic freeze more quickly, and ships cannot get through the ice in the northern parts during the winter and early spring. In 1809, a Russian army crossed the Gulf of Bothnia on the ice.

The Baltic Sea is filled with salmon, herring, and trout, and many people living on its shores are fishermen or work in large fisheries. Along the coast of Germany, people gather amber (see the article on AMBER).

Some of the most important Baltic ports are Copenhagen, Denmark; Helsinki, Finland; Stockholm, Sweden; and Kiel, Germany.

Baltic States. These are Lithuania, Latvia, and Estonia, all of which are parts of the Soviet Union. There are separate articles about them.

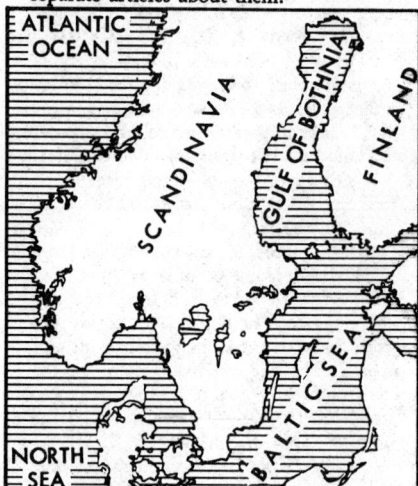

Baltimore

Baltimore is the largest city in the state of Maryland and the sixth-largest in the United States, with nearly a million people living there. It is situated at the mouth of the Patapsco River, near where the river flows into Chesapeake Bay. The harbor of Baltimore is one of the busiest and most important in the United States. Ships from all over the world carry cargoes to and from Baltimore.

Almost every kind of manufacturing is done in Baltimore, including shipbuilding, food processing, oyster packing, copper refining, and airplane manufacturing. The largest spice factory in the world is in Baltimore. The city is also famous for its many universities and its medical school.

An interesting sight in Baltimore is the rows and rows of houses that look

exactly alike. Each is built of red brick and has a small white stoop, or set of steps, in front of it. Druid Hill Park in Baltimore is one of the finest in the United States. There are many monuments (as in the illustration).

Baltimore is only 40 miles from Washington, D.C., and both cities are growing so fast that the space between is rapidly becoming citylike to form one of the greatest metropolitan areas in the United States. In 1958 a tunnel under the harbor was opened to carry automobile traffic on the main road from New York to Washington.

Baltimore was settled in 1729 and was named for the Lords Baltimore. In the War of 1812, Baltimore was bravely defended against a British attack. During the bombardment of Fort McHenry, near Baltimore, Francis Scott Key wrote the words of *The Star Spangled Banner,* the national anthem of the United States. The first railroad in the United States, the Baltimore & Ohio, was started in the city. The "Baltimore Clipper," a famous type of sailing vessel used more than a hundred years ago, was built in the Baltimore shipyards. The first telegraph line was from Baltimore to Washington.

BALTIMORE, MARYLAND. Population 905,-759 in the 1970 census. On the Patapsco River, 40 miles northeast of Washington, D.C. Settled 1729. Named for the Lords Baltimore.

Baltimore, Lords

George Calvert, Baron Baltimore, was an English nobleman who founded the state of Maryland. He was born about 1580 and died in 1632. He held many high positions in the government of England, and King James I rewarded him with a big part of the eastern coast of America, which then belonged to England. Lord Baltimore, who was a Roman Catholic, wanted to set up the colony as a place where Catholics could practice their religion in peace.  The colony was later named Maryland, in honor of a Catholic queen of England called Henrietta Maria. Lord Baltimore died before he could found the colony. His son Cecilius, the second Lord Baltimore, founded Maryland in 1632 but never went there. He sent his son, Charles Calvert, who later became the third Lord Baltimore, to govern the colony.

Baltimore oriole

The brightly colored plumage of the Baltimore oriole is a familiar sight in the United States east of the Rocky Mountains. The male is a beautiful orange and black, with white bars on its wings. The colors on the coat of arms of the Lords Baltimore are gold and sable, which are like orange and black. The oriole is about seven inches long.

The oriole's nest hangs from the branch of a tree, instead of resting on top of the branch as most other birds' nests do. The female builds the nest, while her mate spends his time singing. The nest is woven of straws, grass, strings and reeds that the bird gathers. It is shaped like an old-fashioned purse, with the opening at the top. Some birds occasionally build nests with a closed top, and make the opening on the side instead. Baltimore orioles are important to man because they kill many insects, but they eat fruit and are not welcome around orchards.

Baluchistan

Baluchistan, or Beluchistan, is a large region in southwest Asia, covering nearly 200,000 square miles and with more than a million people. It was once a separate country, but now most of it is part of Pakistan and the rest, not quite a third, is part of Iran. The Iranian part is the poorer part, mostly desert and with only about 454,000 inhabitants.

Most of the people of Baluchistan belong to a native stock called the Baluchis, after whom the country was named. They speak a language which is somewhat like Persian, and they believe in the Mohammedan religion. They are divided into many tribes. These people are strong, active, and tall, and most of them are nomads (wanderers).

Another group of people living in Baluchistan is the Brahuis. For a long time they were the leaders of the country. They are Mohammedans but speak a different language from the Baluchis. It is more like the Hindu language spoken in India.

HOW THE PEOPLE LIVE

Most of the people of Baluchistan are either shepherds or farmers. The nomads raise camels, sheep, and horses, but they do not raise much cattle because the pasture land is so poor. The farmers raise cotton, tobacco, and fruits that thrive in a hot climate. The people do some mining of coal, iron, and lead, but cannot take full advantage of the many rich minerals in their country because they lack machinery and good transportation. One product they manufacture is rough blankets, which are woven by men and women alike.

The chief food of the natives is milk and meat, which they prefer half cooked. They frequently live in black tents woven by the women. There are still slaves in Baluchistan, and some of the men have several wives. Children get hardly any education, except what they are taught at home by their parents.

Baluchistan is a mountainous country. The farmers struggle to keep the sandy soil irrigated, but their principal rivers, the Bolan and Nula, are small and have very little water except after a heavy rain. The climate varies greatly, with severely cold winters and very hot summers.

In ancient times Baluchistan was known as Gedrosia, and until 250 years ago the people were ruled by Hindu princes. Then the Brahuis took over the country, and the Khan (king) of Khelat was acknowledged as the leader of the people. More than a hundred years ago the British made an agreement with the Khan: They paid him a large sum of money every year, and he let them keep an army in his country. In 1947, when Pakistan became a separate country, most of Baluchistan became a part of it, but the British still maintain some forts there.

BALUCHISTAN. Area, 194,139 square miles. Population (1971) census), 1,854,996. In Iran, 60,000 square miles; 454,996 population. In Pakistan, 134,139 square miles; 1,400,000 population. Language, Iranian and Indian dialects. Religion, Mohammedan. Government, republic (part of Pakistan) and province of Iran.

Balzac, Honoré de

Honoré de Balzac was a great French writer of novels and stories. Some people consider him the greatest novelist that ever lived. He was born in 1799 and was educated as a lawyer, but soon he turned to writing novels and short stories. He lived in Paris, the capital of France, most of his life. Probably no writ-  er ever wrote as much as Balzac. He slept a few hours every evening and then wrote from midnight all through the night to the afternoon of the next day. His first few novels were failures and it was not until he was 30 years old that his novels began to interest the public. He spent the next 20 years of his life writing a tremendous collection of novels and short stories that he called "The Human Comedy." Balzac's aim was to picture the life of all the people of France. He wrote about the old and the young, the rich and the poor, the good and the bad, the working class, the middle class, the aristocrats, artists, writers, lawyers, priests, and everybody he could think of. He had a keen understanding of human nature and a great imagination. Some of the best known of his novels are: *Cousin Bette, The Rise and Fall of César Birotteau,* and *Père Goriot* (which means "old man" or "Father" Goriot). Balzac was very extravagant and was usually in debt. A few months before his death he married Evelina Hanska, a noblewoman from Poland, to whom he had been writing letters for 18 years. He died in 1850.

bamboo

Bamboo is a plant that grows in the warm parts of Asia, Africa, and South America. There are many different kinds. Bamboo looks like a tall tree but is actually a kind of grass. It usually reaches a height of 25 to 50 feet, but may reach 150 feet. The bamboo plant has many

stems or shoots growing together in thick clumps or groups from one underground root. The slender stems are pale yellow in color and hard as wood, with knuckle-like joints all along the length about 8 to 12 inches apart. The stems are hollow between the joints and very strong.

In the eastern part of Asia, especially in China and India, bamboo is used for both food and wood. The shoots, or very young plants, are soft and tasty and the Chinese boil and slice them for use in salads and stews. The seeds of the grown-up trees are small and look like grains of wheat. They are eaten by the people of China whenever there is a shortage of rice. The Hindu people of India like to eat bamboo seeds mixed with honey. Bamboo stems, which are one to six inches thick, are easily split and woven into furniture or tied together to make walls of huts. Bows and arrows, boats, writing pens, cages, chairs, beds, canes, and many other useful things are made from bamboo.

banana

The banana is a large plant that grows in the tropical parts of Central America, South America, Asia, and Africa, where the climate is warm and damp the year round. It grows 10 to 40 feet high and has enormous, broad green leaves that are sometimes 10 feet long. The banana plant has a hollow stem that is 8 to 15 inches thick. Another stem, which grows through the hollow stem, bears the flowers and the fruit. The flower bud is very large and shaped like a heart. As it grows it slowly unfolds and shows from 50 to 150 small blossoms, which are long and narrow and grow together in clusters or groups. Some of these clusters grow into great bunches of fruit. Each bunch is called a "hand" because it looks almost like a hand with the separate bananas like fingers.

The fruit is cut off the plant while it is still green and unripe and is taken by rail to the nearest port. There it is loaded on special refrigerator ships on which it is kept at the right temperature. The flesh of ripe bananas is soft, sweet, and of a pale cream color. Banana plants are cut down after harvesting, because they bear fruit only once. A new plant is grown from a piece of the root. It will bear fruit after two years.

There are more than sixty different kinds of banana. One kind, called a "plantain," is much larger than ordinary bananas and is not sweet. It is often boiled or fried, just like a potato. Many people in Central America and in the West Indies eat plantains.

The first shipment of bananas arrived in the United States about 1865. Since then millions of bunches have been shipped to the United States every year. Nearly all of them used to come from Central America but Ecuador in South America has become a big supplier.

Bancroft, George

George Bancroft was an American writer of history. He was born in the year 1800 in Worcester, Massachusetts, and became a history teacher. He later held several important government posts. He was Secretary of the Navy and minister to Great Britain and to Germany. His principal work was a ten-volume *History of the United States*. He died in 1891.

band

A band is a group of musicians playing different kinds of instruments. There are small bands with just a few players, and large bands with one hundred or more players.

The principal difference between a "band" and an "orchestra" lies in the *instrumentation*—the type and number of instruments played by the musicians. In a band, the wind instruments (those played by mouth, such as cornets and trumpets, trombones and tubas, clarinets and saxophones) are most important. There are no stringed instruments (except in some large symphonic bands, as we shall see later). In an orchestra, the stringed instruments are most important. Dance orchestras are often called bands because the early "jazz bands" had been formed from small street bands, to which were added a banjo and piano. The woodwind instruments (flute, oboe, clarinet, and piccolo) are played in both bands and orchestras. "Brass bands" are composed of brass wind instruments, and drums, and are meant to play as loudly as possible. They play in street parades and in outdoor shows and fairs.

THE MILITARY BAND

The first bands, during the Middle Ages, were groups of wandering minstrels and players, who joined together whenever they met at fairs and state occasions. As time went on, these groups became organized, and were supported by the rulers of European kingdoms, duchies and states. Town-supported, or "municipal," bands began to appear by the year 1200, and as early as 1288, in Vienna, the first musicians' guild, or "union," was formed. This was the Brotherhood of St. Nicholas, a society of professional bandsmen. The idea spread, and soon there were bands in most of the cities of France, England, Germany, and Italy. These were also the first military bands, for their purpose was to inspire soldiers in the field, and to give them a marching beat.

Soon after the invention of the piston-valve (see the article on TRUMPET) for brass instruments, a German bandleader named Wilhelm Wieprecht began to use these instruments in the Prussian army bands. This was about 1830, and marked the birth of the modern military band. During the next few years a Belgian instrument maker named Adolphe Sax (the inventor of the saxophone) introduced his new "Saxhorn" into the French military bands, and this horn became an important band instrument. The earliest military bands in the United States were fife-and-drum corps, but in 1802 the Marine Band added wind instruments. Although all the armed services have their own bands, the Marine band is the official military band of the United States. It makes its headquarters in Washington, D.C., and it furnishes the music for most important government ceremonies.

SYMPHONIC (CONCERT) BANDS

The symphonic, or concert, band differs from the military band mainly in the type of music that it plays, though it sometimes uses additional instruments. Symphonic bands often add a harp, string basses, and cellos, and may add a vocal chorus, and even pianos.

Among American concert bands, the most famous were those conducted by Patrick Sarsfield Gilmore, who founded the first one in 1859, and established a worldwide reputation; and John Philip Sousa (there is a separate article on SOUSA), who wrote *The Stars and Stripes Forever* and many other famous marches, and was known as "The March King." Sousa's band made its first appearance in 1892, and from that day until his last world tour in 1911, no band was ever so popular.

During the same year that Sousa was making his last world tour, Edwin Franko Goldman organized the great Goldman Band of New York City, for the purpose of giving free summer concerts. The Goldman Band of today, and also the Band of America, led by Paul Lavalle, are symphonic bands. All over the United States and Canada there are bandstands for free concerts in the main squares of cities and towns.

BAND MUSIC AND MUSICIANS

There was a time, not many years ago, when the only printed music available for bands was limited to a few marches, overtures, and selections, of the simplest type. Those bands desiring to play more elaborate music were forced to make their own arrangements, or else try to play music written for orchestra. The modern symphonic band, however, has at its disposal an almost complete catalog of the world's finest music, with parts available for all the instruments. Band concerts can be made interesting and held at a high musical level, and it is not necessary to play "old stand-bys" over and over.

SCHOOL BANDS

In high schools, preparatory schools, and colleges, there is always great interest in band music. Contests, held on both a local and national basis, do much to add to this interest, and also to raise the standard of playing. Most high schools have a band as well as an orchestra, and it is not unusual for certain students to play in both organizations. Many social groups and veteran organizations have bands. Sometimes these bands are made up entirely of members of the organizations. At other times, professional musicians are hired to play in the bands.

bandages

A bandage is a piece of cloth used in first aid or medical work. Bandages are of several kinds. One familiar kind is the small piece of gauze fastened to a piece of adhesive tape; the best-known brand is the Band-Aid. This is applied to a very small cut or scratch. *Roller bandages* are usually made of thin cotton gauze wound up into a tight roll. *Triangular bandages* are made of muslin cut into the shape of a triangle. The triangle is usually a yard long on each side. *Elastic bandages* are made of cloth woven with rubber fibers to make it elastic. These are made either in rolls or in special shapes to fit some joint of the body, such as the wrist, ankle, elbow, or knee.

They are used mostly in athletics, to give special support to a weak or injured part.

THE ROLLER BANDAGE

The roller bandage is chiefly used to hold a compress or dressing in place. A compress or dressing is a piece of sterile cloth, usually gauze, which is placed over a wound. (*Sterile* means that there are no germs on it. A piece of cloth may look clean but may have huge numbers of germs on it.) A bandage should never be placed directly on a wound. Only a sterile dressing should be placed on the wound itself.

There are many ways of applying roller bandages. On parts of the body that do not taper, such as the finger, you can simply wind the bandage around in circular fashion. Where the body is uneven in width, such as the arm, the bandage is wound around and then given a half twist on itself every time around. This is called a *spiral reverse bandage*.

Around the wrist and thumb a *figure-eight bandage* is used. You apply this around the thumb and wrist so that it makes the shape of an 8 on the hand.

The roller bandage can be used for tying splints in place, but the triangular bandage is stronger and better.

THE TRIANGULAR BANDAGE

The triangular bandage is the most useful bandage for first-aid work. It is strong and can be used for a variety of purposes

Often the triangular bandage is folded as a *cravat bandage*. It is opened on the table and the point is folded over to touch the base. Now the bandage is again folded back to the base, and then a third time. This will produce a "cravat" about 3 inches wide and a yard long.

The cravat can be used for holding a dressing in place: It is simply tied around the wounded part of the body and a square knot made of its ends. The cravat can be tied around the forehead during athletics, to keep sweat out of the eyes; or soaked in cold water and used as a compress; or used to hold a compress or dressing on an eye.

The cravat can be used to support a sprained ankle. Place the middle of the cravat under the heel of the foot. Then bring the bandage up in back of the heel and around to the front of the ankle. Now criss-cross it in a sort of figure-eight form around the ankle. Tie it firmly in front of the ankle.

The cravat can be used as a pressure bandage. This is called a *tourniquet*. When a person has a cut artery, so that the blood spurts out strongly, it is important to stop the bleeding at once. Tie a cravat around the limb, close to the wound, but not touching it. Tighten the bandage until the bleeding stops. Get the injured person to a doctor as quickly as possible. A tourniquet is a *very dangerous* kind of bandage. It should be used only in cases of extreme emergency. (See the article on FIRST AID.)

The triangular bandage makes a good sling to support the arm. Place the triangle under the arm, with the point of the triangle extending away from the body. One end of the bandage is placed over the opposite shoulder. Then the other end is brought up over the shoulder of the injured man. It is tied in back of the neck to the first end. The point can now be tucked in and pinned at the elbow.

bandicoot

The bandicoot is a small animal of Australia and nearby islands. It is a marsupial, that is, the young are born not fully developed and then are carried in a pouch on the mother's belly. The bandicoot is about a foot long, plus a tail like a rat's. It has a sharp snout and large, rabbitlike ears. It eats insects and plants. Some kinds of bandicoot are eaten as food in Australia. They taste like rabbit.

bandit

A bandit is a robber. In the eyes of the law, or of the government of his country, he is a criminal. And nearly all bandits of history have been true criminals—cruel, violent, murderous men who robbed only for their own benefit and did not care what happened to their victims. But there have been some bandits who were revolutionaries against oppressive governments, or who were fugitives from unfair punishment and robbed to get even with the law. In legends, and sometimes in actual fact, these men have been heros, not villains. Therefore the word bandit is not used for the usual kind of criminal but only for a special kind.

Bandits usually live in groups, or gangs. They live in hiding, in out-of-the-way places; in former times these were mountains or forests. Bandits are also called *outlaws*. From time to time the gang of bandits swoops down from its hiding place to rob—formerly a bank or a train, today a bank or a factory payroll. Any traveler who stumbles on the bandits' lair or encounters them on the road is sure to be robbed and perhaps killed.

The most famous bandit in legend is Robin Hood, who is also the greatest hero. He supposedly stole from the rich to give to the poor. But he may never have existed. In the New World the greatest bandit was the Mexican, Pancho Villa, from about 1914 to 1923, when he died. He had so many followers that they were a real army, and he captured and robbed entire cities. Villa did help to overthrow a bad Mexican government, and to Mexico's poor people he was a hero, but he was also a heartless and dishonest man as nearly all bandits are. The most famous of many outlaws of America's "Wild West," in the 1870s, was Jesse James. With his brothers and a few other followers he made daring robberies. He is often pictured now as a victim of circumstances, but he was a real criminal.

Russian revolutionaries, in the years before 1917, often formed bandit gangs and robbed banks to get money for the Communist Party. Josef Stalin, who became the Communist dictator, was once in such a bandit gang. They considered that they were at war against the Russian government, and in war robbing the enemy is not criminal if the robbers are acting for their own government and do not keep the money themselves.

There have been many permanent bandit gangs, in which whole families are professional bandits and membership in the gang passes from father to son. The Thugs of India were such a gang. For hundreds of years they lived by murdering and robbing travelers—except children, whom they captured and sold as slaves. British troops finally destroyed them, about 1835. Even today there are many bandit tribes in Asia and parts of Africa. There were many in China until the 1920s. The National Government of China got rid of most of them and the Communist government has wiped out the rest.

The best-known of all bandit gangs is the Mafia of Sicily. The Mafia is no longer very powerful in Sicily but the worst criminals in the United States grew out of a Mafia branch founded here.

There have been few real bandit gangs in the United States in the last fifty years and all were soon broken up. The principal one was headed by a woman named "Ma" Barker in Missouri. She trained her four sons and even her sons-in-law and daughters-in-law to be criminals. The F.B.I. caught and killed or convicted them all.

Highwaymen were robbers of travelers on British roads. They were not real bandits, because they usually worked alone or in pairs and they came from the underworld of London. Bandits, especially those who live in tribes, are also called *brigands*. The same kind of robbers at sea are called *pirates*. See the articles on ROBIN HOOD, JESSE JAMES, VILLA, MAFIA, and PIRATES.

Banff

Banff is a famous resort town in the Canadian Rocky Mountains. It is in the southwestern part of the province of Alberta, on the Bow River. About 2,500 people live in Banff all year but many thousands more go there every winter and summer to enjoy the magnificent scenery and the sports. There are skiing in winter, mountain-climbing in all seasons, tennis, golf and horsebackriding in summer. Nearby are beautiful Lake Louise and many hot sulfur-water springs. There is a hot sulfur-water swimming pool in Banff. Banff is in the huge Banff National Park. See other pictures of Banff in the article ALBERTA.

Bangkok

Bangkok is the capital city of Thailand, the country that often is called Siam. It is on the Menam River, north of the Gulf of Siam. About 1,500 years ago, this area was under water. Silt, or soil left by the river, raised the bottom of the gulf and made dry land. In another 1,500 years, Bangkok may be a distant inland town!

Bangkok is a colorful city of canals and islands. The sights include the king's palace, with a 2-foot statue of Buddha carved from a single piece of the gem called jasper, and the "floating town," hundreds of houses moored in the river and canals.

Most of Bangkok's businessmen are Chinese and Europeans, who outnumber the Thailanders. Great quantities of rice are grown in the area around Bangkok. Much of this rice is shipped from Bangkok to people in many other places in the Far East. Other exports are rubber, tin, teak wood, and tungsten.

Bangkok is known for its sparkling

temples, called *wats*, which often have several roofs, one over the other, with long, graceful, curved rafters at the corners. In the chapels are images of BUDDHA, about whom you may read in another article.

Loi Krathong is one of Bangkok's fascinating festivals. It happens on the full-moon night of October. On that night, tiny boats made of banana leaves and filled with flowers and lighted candles are set adrift. They twinkle across the dark river and canals like fireflies. The festival is held to give thanks to the spirits of the waters, for providing the monsoon rains so that the people can grow their rice. It is the same kind of celebration as Thanksgiving Day in the United States.

BANGKOK, THAILAND. Population (in 1975) 3,967,081. Capital of Thailand.

Bangor

Bangor is a city and port in southern Maine, at the point where the Kenduskeag River flows into the Penobscot River. The Penobscot is navigable up to that point. The river flows through Bangor and there are several bridges across it. Bangor is a center for water, railroad and air transportation. Dairy products, lumber and frozen foods are shipped from Bangor. A hundred years ago Bangor was famous for the wood of Maine pine trees, shipped to places the world over. Today Bangor's chief activity is the making of wood pulp and paper.

BANGOR, MAINE. Population (1970 census) 33,168. Third-largest city in Maine. County seat of Penobscot County. Settled in 1791.

banjo

The banjo is a musical instrument that used to be very popular but is no longer played very much. It is somewhat like a guitar, but the "head" of a banjo is like a drum—a skin stretched tight over a round hoop. Attached to this is a long "neck." All along the neck are little metal bars called *frets*. There are strings running across the head and to the end of the neck. With the fingers of one hand, you hold down the strings at various fret points; with the fingers of the other hand you pluck the strings. Plucking the strings makes the sound. To produce different notes, you press the strings down against different frets.

There have been several kinds of banjo. The *tenor banjo* was very important in the early Dixieland jazz bands and is now almost the only banjo used. It has four strings and is tuned like the viola—C, G, D′, A′. Some earlier banjos had five strings.

No one is sure who invented the banjo, or how long ago the first one was made. Probably it was invented by American Negroes in the southern states, and their ancestors in Africa may have had an instrument like it.

Bankhead

Bankhead is the name of a family that is very prominent in the state of Alabama. John H. Bankhead was a United States senator from Alabama. He was born in 1872 and died in 1946. His brother, William B. Bankhead, was Speaker of the House of Representatives.

He was born in 1874 and died in 1940. Tallulah Bankhead, the daughter of William B. Bankhead, was born in 1903 and became one of the best-known American actresses. She died in 1968.

bank holidays

According to the laws of England, all banks must be closed on certain days of the year, besides Sundays. These days are Christmas and the day after, Easter Monday, and Good Friday. They are called *bank holidays*, which means the same thing as *legal holidays* in the United States. Any day on which banks are closed is also a day when no business is done. For the businessman it is important to know when bank holidays will occur because on those days he does not have to pay any money he owes.

banking

A bank is a place where money can be put for safekeeping. This alone is enough to make banks one of the most important parts of modern civilization. Few people can risk having all their money lost or stolen. But banks perform other services that are equally important. In a country such as the United States the entire way of life is built around the banking system.

The most important service of a bank is lending money, but there are various other bank services, which will be described later.

KINDS OF BANK

Most banks are *depository banks*—banks in which people can place (deposit) money, to be taken out when they need it. The amount of money a person has "on deposit" is called his *balance*. The principal kinds of bank are:

SAVINGS BANKS. These pay interest on money deposited with them. (See the article on INTEREST.) Money deposited in a savings bank can be drawn out by going to the bank but not by writing a check. Savings banks lend money chiefly on real estate (mortgage loans), but they make other *secured loans*, as explained below.

COMMERCIAL BANKS pay interest on deposits also. In addition, they offer an important service, the *checking account*, as explained below. Commercial banks make *unsecured loans*, chiefly to business firms.

TRUST COMPANIES are banks that are chartered (licensed) by the state to manage people's money for them. Often a trust fund is named to manage the estate of a person who has died, paying the income to his heirs. Most trust companies accept deposits and make commercial loans, but they cannot lend trust funds as unsecured loans.

SAVINGS AND LOAN ASSOCIATIONS, or building and loan associations, are like savings banks but are chartered under special Federal and state laws. The Home Owners' Loan Act passed by Congress in 1933 provided for the chartering of savings and loan associations and helping them with government money.

PRIVATE BANKERS usually do not accept deposits. They conduct banking services, chiefly lending, with their own money. There once were many private banks, but since the early 1930s, when many of them failed, most of the survivors have changed to one of the other plans.

MUTUAL BANKS are not conducted for the profit of investors but belong to their depositors. Most savings banks are mutual banks.

The names of many commercial banks include the words "national bank." Formerly, national banks were allowed to print and issue their own paper money. The national banking laws have been changed since then (see the article on the FEDERAL RESERVE SYSTEM) but national banks must still conform to certain standards and are subject to regulation and inspection by the Federal government.

TYPES OF BANK LOAN

Many persons do not like to borrow money and "be in debt," but a business firm cannot afford to feel that way. The bigger and richer a business is, the surer it is that the business owes a great deal of money to banks. Usually it can be said

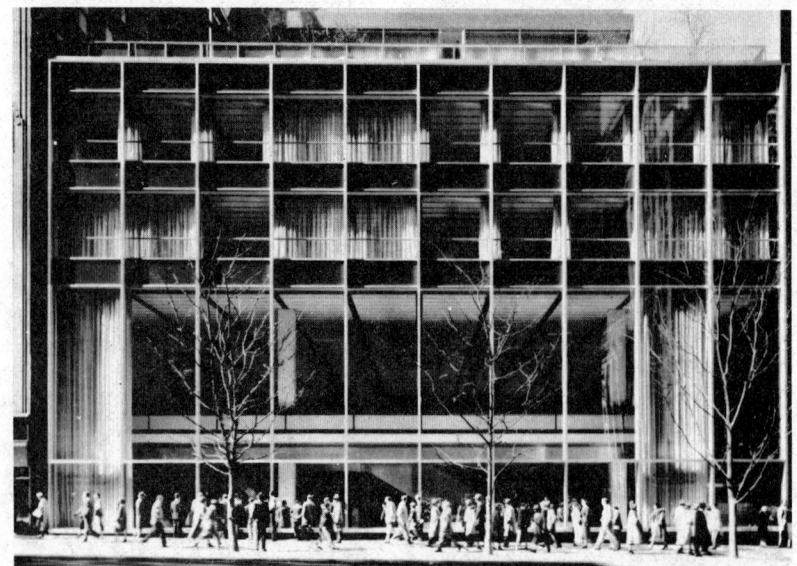

Ezra Stoller

The ultramodern bank building of Manufacturers Trust Company, at 43rd Street and Fifth Avenue in New York, built in 1954. Passers-by can see the huge vault (lower left).

that if a business does not owe money to banks it is not being well managed.

A good example of the commercial loan can be found in the toy business. Most toys are bought between October and December, to be given as Christmas presents. Therefore they must be completely manufactured and in the stores by October. This means the toy manufacturer must make them during the summer months, paying for his materials and his workers, and then wait till December to collect what people pay for them. If the toy manufacturer has only $100,000 of his own, he can make only $100,000 worth of toys, on which he will make perhaps $5,000 profit. But he goes to the bank and borrows an additional $100,000. Now he makes $200,000 worth of toys. In December, when he has collected, he pays back the bank's $100,000 plus about $1,000 interest. Everybody profits—the manufacturer because he made $9,000 instead of $5,000; the bank because it collected $1,000 for the use of the money; and even the public, because without bank loans of this kind there would not have been enough toys to go around. Many bank loans are *seasonal loans* of this kind.

Equally important are the mortgage loans that banks make on real estate. Most people who want to own their own homes do not have the large amount of cash required. Banks supply the rest of the money they need. Of more than twenty million American families that own their own homes, nearly half (46%) owe money on mortgage loans and half of the others originally had loans to help them but have since repaid them.

Farm loans are a third big class of bank loans. Farmers borrow money to pay for seed, fertilizers, and labor while the crops are growing and repay the loans when the crop is harvested and sold.

Other bank loans are made for installment buying of automobiles, refrigerators, and other personal possessions. Banks also make *personal loans,* for example to people who need extra cash because of a serious illness or to pay for their children's education; but these are a small part of a bank's total business.

A loan is said to be *secured* when the borrower agrees that the bank can take some particular part of his property in case he does not pay. The security he offers is called *collateral,* a word that actually means "being at the side of." That is, *besides* his promise to pay, he puts up this property. It may be real estate, stocks or bonds, merchandise in a store, or something else of value. Usually the borrower keeps and uses the property, just as one keeps and uses an automobile he is buying on the installment plan, but legally it belongs to the bank until the loan is repaid.

Nearly all commercial loans are *unsecured* loans. The bank accepts the business firm's note, or promise to repay. It does this when the firm's financial statement (see ACCOUNTING) shows that it is a good, profitable business; and when the bank's officers are satisfied that the firm's managers are men of good character and would not borrow money unless they were sure they could pay it back.

THE BANK AS A BUSINESS

A bank is a business house trying to make a profit as any other business house does. Nearly all the bank's income is from interest on the loans it makes.

The bank gets the money it lends from three sources: *Capital,* the amount of money originally put up by the owners of the bank, to start it. *Surplus,* additional money belonging to the owners of the bank, often being previous profits they have not taken out. But by far the greatest part of the money the bank lends is the money placed with it for safekeeping by its depositors.

The bank keeps plenty of money on hand—a *reserve*—to pay any depositor who wants to take his money out. But since depositors put their money in the bank for safekeeping, it can be taken for granted that most of them will not want to take it out. In fact, people want to add to their savings if possible. Therefore most of the money deposited should not be left idly in the bank but should be put to work helping businesses and others who need to borrow it.

The bank charges borrowers enough interest to pay the expenses of the bank and have something left over for profit. The interest cannot be higher than the "legal rate," which is established by state law and in most states is 6% per year ($6 on every $100 borrowed for a year). In the case of big loans, the interest rate is much less, even as low as 2%. The rate depends on the "money market." When there is plenty of money available to be borrowed, banks charge low rates of interest, so they pay low rates: A savings bank may pay its depositors 2% and lend the money at 3½% or 4%. But when money is "tight" interest rates go up, and a savings bank may try to attract depositors by offering 4% or 4½% or even more and lending the money at 5% or 6%.

SAFETY OF BANK DEPOSITS

For hundreds of years it has worried many people to know that the banks take the money they deposit and lend it to others. Occasionally in the past, especially in times of business depression, people would lose confidence in a bank. All the depositors would try to take their money out at the same time. This is called "a run on the bank." No bank keeps enough cash to pay all its depositors in full, and when a bank cannot pay a depositor it must close its doors and is said to have failed. Hundreds of banks that were actually in sound condition have failed because people lost confidence and started a run on the bank.

To prevent such cases, in 1933 Congress passed a law authorizing the Federal Deposit Insurance Corporation. Now nearly every bank deposit in the United States is insured up to $10,000. Unless a depositor has more than $10,000 in a bank, he cannot lose his money. Before there was deposit insurance, there were many bank failures; between 1920 and 1934 there were 15,000, and more than 9,000 of them were in the years 1930 to 1933. Since 1934 there have not been fifty failures altogether.

OTHER BANK SERVICES

By far the most convenient bank service, and the most costly to the bank, is the checking account. A person with a checking account need not risk carrying much cash. He can safely pay his bills by mail. All he has to do is write a check —an order to the bank to take money out of his account and pay it to someone else. A check is also a receipt for any bill paid, because the person receiving the check must *endorse* it, sign his name on the back to acknowledge that he has received the money. For a customer who keeps a good-sized balance, the bank does not charge anything for handling checks. If his balance is small, it is usually put in a *special checking account* and the bank charges 5 or 10 cents per check. When the service is free, it is the bank's way of paying the depositor for the use of his money, just as the savings bank pays interest for the use of the money.

Safe-deposit boxes are another bank service. The customer can rent a box that is kept safe and fireproof in the bank's big vault, or safe. Valuable papers, jewelry, cash, and any other small items can be kept in the box.

For foreign travelers, banks issue *letters of credit,* which enable the traveler to draw money from banks in other countries. Many banks also handle *foreign exchange,* changing foreign money for American money. Banks often enter into legal agreements with their customers to pay or guarantee payment of money due to others. *Acceptances, escrows* and *trust receipts* are examples of these agreements. For each of these various services the bank charges a fee.

HOW A BANK OPERATES

Except for a few private banks, every bank is a corporation and is managed much like other corporations (see CORPORATION). The owners elect a board of directors and the directors control the management of the bank. The directors elect officers—a president, various vice presidents, a treasurer or cashier, and a secretary—to do the actual management.

The employees of a bank are divided into three main groups: officers, tellers, and bookkeepers.

There are *loan officers,* who decide whether or not to make loans that customers request, and *general officers,* who take care of other services of the bank. The officers are usually seen sitting at desks behind a railing, or in private offices. In the case of very big loans, a special loan committee of the board of directors must make the final decision.

The tellers handle the actual currency, or cash. They are usually seen standing behind grilled windows. They accept deposits and pay out cash withdrawals.

Bookkeepers can seldom be seen in a bank, for usually they work in a room separate from the public banking office. They make the records of every depositor's account—how much he has deposited, how much he has withdrawn, and what balance he has left. Once each month they make up a *bank statement* for each depositor and mail it to him. The bank statement is a record of the transactions—deposits and withdrawals—for the month. With the bank statement are sent all checks drawn by the depositor and paid by the bank during that month.

In a big city there is usually a *clearing house,* operated by all the banks. If there were no clearing house, each bank would have to send a messenger to each other bank to collect cash for checks drawn on that bank. The clearing house takes all the checks deposited in all the banks and finds out the net amount that each bank owes to or is owed by each other bank. A check that has gone through the clearing house and has been paid is said to have *cleared.* Until a deposited check has cleared, a bank calls it *uncollected funds* and will not pay cash for it.

Ezra Stoller

The vault of the Manufacturers Trust Company bank. The door is 22 inches thick and weighs 30 tons. It is protected by four time locks and two combination locks.

Bank examiners are accountants who represent the state. From time to time—usually without advance notice—they drop in at a bank and audit its books. They will almost always detect a dishonest employee who is stealing money from the bank. In rare cases, they will find that by making unwise loans or lending too much money a bank has left itself in dangerous condition, and in these cases they have authority to close the bank at once. But almost always they find nothing wrong, because banks are among the most carefully managed of all businesses.

Most bank bookkeeping is now done by automatic calculating machines. A depositor in a savings bank has a *bank book,* also called a *passbook,* and when he puts in or draws out money his passbook is put in a machine that stamps the transaction in the book and also records it. People who have checking accounts used also to have bank books, but these are not often used now. Instead, the depositor receives a duplicate deposit slip—a copy of the slip of paper he must fill out each time he makes a deposit—which is a receipt for his deposit.

HISTORY OF BANKING

The word bank comes from an Italian word, *banco,* meaning "bench." The earliest bankers were simply money-changers, who weighed and changed gold and silver coins. Then there came to be a demand for *drafts* (checks) that could be carried instead of money, for the highways were full of robbers and it was dangerous to carry money from one city to another in order to do business there. Great merchants began to accept deposits of money and issue drafts or receipts that could be used as cash, for the public had confidence in the wealth and honesty of the merchants.

Banking was slow to arise in Europe, because the Christian Church disapproved of usury—charging interest for money lent. Gradually this religious law was changed and now usury means charging too much interest. In Florence, Italy, a rich man named Giovanni de' Medici, who lived from 1360 to 1428, became the first big banker; his family became so rich and great that they were kings, queens, and popes. By the 1600s there were many money-lenders but still few banks. Banks of the modern kind arose in the early 1700s. The most famous were founded by the Rothschild family of Germany, who had big banks in the principal cities of Germany, Austria, France, England, and Italy. (See ROTHSCHILD.) In the 1800s banks came to be as important as they are today.

The first bank in the United States was the Bank of Pennsylvania, which in 1780 printed money to finance George Washington's army. The first real bank (and the oldest American bank, for it is still in business) was the Bank of North America, founded in Philadelphia by Robert Morris in 1781. This bank lent money to the new United States government and kept the government's deposits. In 1789, when Alexander Hamilton became Secretary of the Treasury, he suggested a national bank owned and operated by the government. The Bank of the United States was authorized by Congress and opened in 1791. It was closed in 1811 because Congress did not think it was working out well, but another Bank of the United States was authorized in 1816. It was opposed by Andrew Jackson and when he became president in 1832 he forced it to close. While they were operating, the Banks of the United States issued money and did much of the work now done by the Treasury Department and the Federal Reserve Banks.

There followed a period of "wildcat banking." Bankers issued money without proper reserves to make it good, and they used deposited money carelessly or even dishonestly, until people lost confidence in paper money and in banks. Some states even outlawed banks. This condition was repaired by the National Banking Act, passed by Congress in 1863, which made banks subject to inspection and put the issuing of paper money under strict control. This was a great improvement but there were still many things wrong with the banking system. After some years of prodding by Senator Carter Glass of Virginia and others, in 1914 Congress passed the present Federal Reserve Act.

During this century banks have been growing bigger and bigger. Most banks in big cities have many branches in different neighborhoods, and each branch operates more or less as though it were a separate bank. There have also been many mergers, the combining of two or more big banks, to form even bigger ones. Since the 1940s the biggest American bank has been the Bank of America, in California, where the state law permits a bank to have branches anywhere in the state. In New York, banks may have branches only in their own city. Two banks in New York City, the Chase-Manhattan Bank and the First National City Bank, are the next-biggest banks after the Bank of America. Such banks have as much as ten billion dollars in deposits.

See BANK OF ENGLAND and FEDERAL RESERVE SYSTEM.

Bank of England

The Bank of England is a big bank in the city of London, England. In some ways it is like a big American bank, because it takes care of deposited money and makes loans to businessmen; but also it is connected with the British government. It prints paper money, controls the sale of government bonds, and carries out laws by which British bankers must work. It also has the same sort of duties as the FEDERAL RESERVE SYSTEM (about which there is a separate article) in the United States. The Bank of England is more than 250 years old, dating from 1694. It has branches in all British nations, but its main office is on Threadneedle Street in London, and for this reason it has been nicknamed "the old lady of Threadneedle Street."

bankruptcy

When a person owes more money than he can ever hope to pay, he can go to court and have himself declared *bankrupt.* He turns over to a person called a *receiver,* who is appointed by the court, all the money and anything else valuable that he owns. The receiver divides this fairly among the bankrupt person's creditors—the people he owes money to. The bankrupt person is then *discharged,* which means that legally he no longer owes any money. He can make a fresh start.

As recently as a hundred years ago, a person could be put in jail for being in debt. Of course, as long as he was in jail he could not earn any money, so his condition was almost hopeless. The great English novelist Charles Dickens wrote about this in his novels *Little Dorrit* and *David Copperfield,* and people began to realize how unfair it was. Today, nobody in any modern country can be put in prison for failing to pay an honest debt.

A person's creditors may force him into bankruptcy, or the person may himself go to court and ask that a receiver be appointed, this being called *voluntary bankruptcy.* All states and the United States Government have special laws governing bankruptcy.

Bannister, Roger

Roger Bannister is the name of the first person to run a mile in less than four minutes. For years, runners had been trying for the "four-minute mile," and some had come close to it. Bannister was a medical student at Oxford University, England, and knew a great deal about how the human body worked. He trained very carefully. May 6, 1954, the day of the race, was cold and windy. It was hardly the kind of weather for fast running. Bannister exerted himself to the utmost, and when he crossed the finish line he fainted from exhaustion, but he had run a mile in 3 minutes and 59.4 seconds. The mile has been run in less than 4 minutes many times since. The first American to do it was a 20-year-old college student, Don Bowden of California, on June 2, 1957. His time was

3:58.7. A human being cannot run a mile in less than 3:30 to 3:40.

United Press Photo
Roger Bannister at the finish line.

Bannockburn

Bannockburn is a village in Scotland where, on June 24, 1314, King Robert the Bruce of Scotland defeated the English army of King Edward II. Bruce had only 40,000 men against England's 100,000, but he won by trapping the English cavalry into pits he had dug in advance. See the article on BRUCE.

Banting, Sir Frederick G., a Canadian physician. He was one of the men who discovered INSULIN. He was awarded the Nobel Prize in 1923 for this. He was born in 1891 and died in 1941.

Bantu

The Bantu languages are spoken by most of the people who live in central and southern Africa. These people are members of one of the three great races of the earth, the Negroid or "black" race, from which American Negroes are descended. The languages in this group are very much alike, but also have some differences. *Bantu* is a word for "men" in this group of languages.

It is not known how old the earliest Bantu language is. It is thought that almost three thousand years ago a powerful tribe of Negroes in the heart of Africa pushed south through the jungle. They spoke the original Bantu and gave their language to the tribes they met.

In the English language, we learn that a word may have one of three *genders*. It may be *masculine*, for a man (for example, *he*); or *feminine*, for a woman (*she*); or *neuter*, for a thing (*it*). The Bantu languages have as many as eight different genders! There are different genders for human beings, plants, and animals, and even for round objects, long objects, and so on.

banyan tree

The banyan tree is a strange kind of fig tree that grows in India, Indonesia, and many islands of the Pacific. The branches of the tree send down young shoots or roots. These shoots take root when they reach low enough to touch the soil, and serve as additional trunks.

A banyan tree may be 70 to 100 feet high with a main trunk 10 to 12 feet thick. It may cover an acre of land and look like a large grove of trees. A very sticky liquid is obtained from the bark of the banyan. It is used to catch small birds, which cannot free themselves once their feet have touched it, and also to make varnish. The word *banyan* means merchant and comes from the Sanskrit, a language of ancient India. Because the banyan tree covers so much ground and gives a great deal of shade, it is often used by native merchants as a sort of outdoor shop. Monkeys live in banyan trees and eat the small, figlike fruit.

Some people in India consider banyan trees sacred.

baobab

The baobab is one of the largest trees in the world. It grows in Ethiopia, Senegal, and other parts of Africa and the islands near it. It grows to be almost 60 feet high, and its trunk is sometimes as much as 30 feet thick. The baobab has large, dark green leaves and beautiful white flowers. The bark of the baobab can be shredded and woven into cloth or twisted into strong ropes. The Negro people who live in Senegal make spices and medicines from its leaves. They call the fruit of the baobab "monkey bread." The natives use the soft, pulpy part of the fruit to flavor other food, and they drink the juice of this fruit. Sometimes a living tree is hollowed out and used as a house. Some baobabs are more than a thousand years old.

baptism

Baptism, in Christian churches, is the putting of water on a person to wash his sins away. John the Baptist baptized Jesus, and Jesus told his disciples to baptize persons to make Christians of them. There are different methods of baptism in different Christian churches. In most churches, the minister or priest pours or sprinkles water on the person who is to be baptized, and says, "I baptize thee in the name of the Father, and of the Son, and of the Holy Ghost." Some churches believes that baptism must be by *total immersion*, that is, that a person to be baptized must be dipped completely under water. Some churches believe in *infant baptism*, while others do not baptize a person until he consciously becomes a Christian.

Very often a child is baptized and given his Christian names at the same time. This is also called *christening*.

In some churches, a child being baptized must have at least one godfather and one godmother, who promise to see that the child will have proper religious training.

Baptist Church

Baptist Churches have more members than any other Protestant Christian church in the United States. The total membership in 1970 was over 26 million. (The next biggest Protestant church, the Methodist, had nearly 13 million members.) There are about twenty branches of the Baptist Church, but they all agree on certain things. According to their belief no one should be baptized until he is old enough to understand and believe in the teachings of Jesus. Baptists do not baptize babies as many other Christian churches do. Baptists also believe that the rite of baptism requires "total immersion." That is, the whole body must be put under water. Personal freedom and freedom of belief are important in the Baptist churches. They have no official creed, for they believe that the Bible itself is the only guide to religion, and that we should be free to read and understand it as we choose. Every Baptist congregation manages it own affairs without control from a higher church authority.

The Baptist movement began with the Anabaptists in Central Europe, in the early 1500s. Anabaptism is "baptizing again," or rebaptism. About 1606 an English clergyman, John Smyth, who had become convinced that adult baptism is necessary, led a group of the first English baptists to exile in Holland to escape persecution at home. In the same way, Roger Williams in 1635 fled from persecution in Massachusetts, founding what became the state of Rhode Island and also the first Baptist church in the United States. Other Baptist churches were opened in the 1600s and 1700s but rapid growth did not begin until about 1800. In 1845 the Southern Baptist Church broke away from northern groups that opposed slavery; it is now the largest single Baptist group, with more than 9,700,000 members. Since 1905 there has been a Baptist World Alliance at whose meetings representatives of many countries exchange advice.

bar and Bar Association

Among other things, a *bar* is a barrier or railing. Because courtrooms for centuries have had some kind of a barrier to separate the judge and lawyers from the prisoners and spectators, the lawyers who sat "beyond the bar" came to be known simply as "the bar," or "members of the bar." Therefore, "the bar" is "the legal profession." A person who has just graduated from law school must pass a *bar examination* before he is licensed to charge money for legal advice. A society of lawyers is a *Bar Association,* and every state recognizes an official Bar Association that prepares the bar examinations and decides what it is proper and honest for a lawyer to do. In British countries, a lawyer who is licensed to argue cases in court is called a *barrister.*

Barabbas

When Jesus was sentenced to be crucified in Jerusalem, one of the other prisoners sentenced to be crucified was a robber named Barabbas. It was the custom that the Jewish people of Jerusalem could ask that one prisoner be pardoned. Pontius Pilate, the Roman governor, asked them to choose between Jesus and Barabbas. The priests, who were against the Christian religion, persuaded the people to ask for Barabbas. So Barabbas was released and Jesus was crucified. The story is told in the 27th chapter of Matthew, in the New Testament.

Barbados

Barbados is an independent country in the West Indies. Settled by the British in 1627, it became a British colony in

1885; was granted internal self-government in 1961; and became fully independent in 1966. Over 248,000 people, mostly blacks live on its 166 square miles of land.

Barbados is a tropical island (the easternmost in the Caribbean Sea), but is cooled by breezes from the Atlantic Ocean. The Portuguese explored the island hundreds of years ago and called it Barbados, which in their language means "bearded," because they found so many bearded fig trees growing there.

Most of the people of Barbados are farmers who grow sugar cane and cotton. Others work in factories which make rum, molasses, cigarettes, and biscuits. Still others are fishermen. Most blacks in the country were slaves until 1834, when the British outlawed slavery in all their possessions.

Barbados is a member of the British Commonwealth. About 11,500 people live in the country's capital city, Bridgetown.

Barbarossa

Barbarossa is an Italian word meaning "red beard." Frederick I, the German or Holy Roman emperor about eight hundred years ago, was called Frederick Barbarossa because of his red beard. Barbarossa was also a nickname for two famous red-bearded brothers who were pirates in the Mediterranean Sea, about four hundred years ago. One was named Koruk Barbarossa and the other was Khair ed Din Barbarossa. They were Greek Christians who became converted to the Mohammedan religion. They attacked European ships in the Mediterranean Sea, robbing them and selling the Christians they captured in the slave markets of Algiers, a city on the north coast of Africa. See BARBARY STATES.

Barbary ape

The Barbary ape is a large monkey, about 2 to 3 feet in length, found in Morocco and Algeria, which are countries on the northern coast of Africa. Barbary apes also live on Gibraltar, a gigantic rock on the southernmost tip of Spain. Gibraltar belongs to Great Britain, which has built a mighty fortress on the huge rock. There is a legend or story that the fortress will never be captured as long as there are Barbary apes on the Rock of Gibraltar. The Barbary ape has no tail. It is a light yellowish-brown on the back and yellowish-white on the belly. It walks on all fours, never climbs trees, and lives in packs among rocks. The Barbary ape is sometimes called a *magot*, because it belongs to a class of monkeys called *macaques*. Like most monkeys, the Barbary ape is a mischief-maker. It often steals fruit from people's gardens.

Barbary States

Between the years 1500 and 1830, merchant ships sailing the Mediterranean Sea were always in danger of being attacked and captured by Barbary pirates. The Barbary countries were Morocco, Algeria, Tunisia, and Tripoli, on the northern coast of Africa. They were called Barbary countries because most of the people living there were Berbers. The Barbary pirates were believers in the Mohammedan religion and hated all Christians. The Christian men, women and children that they captured in these raids were sold as slaves, or—if they were rich—held for ransom. The powerful countries of Europe were usually too busy fighting each other to destroy the pirates. Instead they paid the pirates a certain amount of money each year not to attack their ships.

From 1801 to 1805 the United States was at war with the Barbary pirates of Tripoli. The pirates were defeated by the American fleet and agreed to ask for no more money from the U.S. Government and not to harm American ships. While the United States was busy fighting England during the War of 1812, the Barbary pirates broke their promise. In 1815 the United States Government sent a squadron of nine ships under Commodore Stephen Decatur to punish the pirates. Decatur quickly defeated the pirate fleet and sailed into the harbor of Algiers. The dey, or ruler, of Algiers immediately surrendered and gave in to all of Decatur's demands. All American prisoners were released and the pirate cities of Algiers, Tunis and Tripoli paid large sums of money to the United States for the harm they had done to American ships and citizens. They also agreed not to demand any more money from America. But not until 1830, when France conquered Algiers, was the piracy of the Barbary countries ended forever.

barbecue

A barbecue is an outdoor feast where food—especially meat—is cooked on a frame over an open fire, or on a rod or spit that is turned in front of the fire. The fire is made in barbecue pits, which may be several feet deep. Some pits are permanent and are lined with brick or fire-clay. Straight sticks, peeled and pointed at both ends, or iron rods, are run through the center of the meat, which then is laid across the top of the pit.

Barbecue sauce is poured over the meat while it cooks. It is very spicy and sharp to the taste. It may be a mixture of some or all of the following: garlic, pepper, tabasco, onions, vinegar, tomatoes, paprika, bay leaves and cloves. There may also be a barbecue stew, cooked in huge iron kettles.

The word barbecue means "from beard to tail" and is used because an entire animal is roasted. Many restaurants serve "barbecued" meats, but these are usually pot-roasted beef or pork.

barber

A barber is a person who makes his living by cutting hair and shaving men's faces, but until the last century barbers did much more than that. They also pulled teeth, and opened the veins of sick people to let some of their blood out—a former way of treating the sick.

The barber's shop, about two hundred years ago, was a favorite social gathering place for men who were not busy. Here men got together to discuss the latest news. Musical instruments were kept on hand for those who liked to amuse themselves with music. The sign in front of the barber's shop was a red-and-white striped pole, with a metal pan or basin hanging from the top. The red stripe was painted on the pole to remind one of the ribbon used to bandage up the arm when bleeding was to be stopped. The basin was used to catch the blood. Today the basin is no longer seen on the barber's pole but the red and white stripes are still there. Many men still like to gather in the barber shop to talk and even sing. Usually, when four men join in song they form what is called a barber-shop quartet.

Today, a barber must receive training before he is allowed to work and he must get a license before he can open a shop.

Barber of Seville

The Barber of Seville is a comic opera with music by the Italian composer Gioacchino Rossini, based on a famous play by the French writer Beaumarchais. The opera was first sung in Rome, in 1816. The words are in Italian.

STORY OF THE OPERA

Figaro is a jolly and clever barber in Seville, Spain. His friend Count Almaviva is in love with a beautiful girl named Rosina, but Dr. Bartolo, Rosina's guardian, plans to marry her himself. Figaro suggests that Almaviva disguise himself as a soldier and claim to be billeted (assigned for lodging) at Bartolo's house. As barber to Bartolo, Figaro is often in the house and helps the lovers meet. Don Basilio, Rosina's music teacher, tries to help Bartolo. Almaviva twice gets into the house, once disguised as a soldier named Lindoro and again disguised as a music master. Figaro manages to get the key to Rosina's window and takes Almaviva into her room. Don Basilio arrives with a notary to marry Bartolo and Rosina, and Almaviva forces the notary to marry him to Rosina. The wedding is completed just as Bartolo dashed in, too late to stop it. The most famous song is in Act I—"La-la-la Figaro," in which Figaro introduces himself as the man to whom everyone in Seville turns for help in love affairs.

barberry

The barberry is a shrub or plant grown as a decoration around homes and in gardens. It has bright red berries, which remain on the plant the year round. When boiled with sugar, the berries make an excellent preserve or jam. The green leaves have sharp little points, like thorns, all around the edges. The barberry has pale yellow or pink flowers, which bloom for a short time. The American barberry plant is not grown in those parts of the United States where wheat is raised because *rust*, a disease of wheat, is carried by barberry. Japanese barberry, on which rust will not grow, is often planted instead.

barbiturates

Barbiturates are a group of drugs that doctors give to patients to relieve their pain and to help them fall asleep. There are dozens of drugs in this group. One of the commonest ones is called *phenobarbital*. In most states barbiturates cannot be bought without a doctor's prescription. The drug slows down the action of the nervous system. An overdose is very dangerous.

Barbizon School

A group of painters who were famous in France about a hundred years ago were called the Barbizon School, because several of them worked or met

in a French village named Barbizon. Among the most famous painters of this group were J. F. Millet, Camille Corot, Rosa Bonheur, C. F. Daubigny, and Théodore Rousseau. They painted simple, natural scenes such as landscapes, rather than portraits of kings and nobles.

Barcelona

Barcelona is the second-largest city in Spain. It is on the Mediterranean Sea and is the chief seaport of the country. It is the capital of the province that is also called Barcelona. More than a million people live in the city. Many of them work in factories, making machinery, paper, woolen goods, and other products. Some of the finest Spanish wine is also made in Barcelona. The old section of Barcelona has narrow, winding streets, but the modern part of the city has fine wide streets and beautiful buildings. One of the most beautiful of these is the Spanish National Palace, which has great staircases and sparkling fountains. Although Barcelona is a busy commercial city, it also has an excellent university and several famous churches and a cathedral. One of the most interesting places to visit is the Maritimo Museum, where there is a collection of ship models that go back hundreds of years.

Barcelona was founded more than two thousand years ago, and it has been ruled by the Romans, Goths, and other conquering nations. The city was the capital of the government forces against General Franco, late in the Spanish Civil War. It was finally captured in 1939.

BARCELONA, SPAIN. Province, area 2,975 square miles, population 2,215,901; and city, its capital, population 1,690,000.

bards

The ancient poets of the Celtic peoples were called *bards*. The Irish, the Scots, and the Welsh people who live in Wales, a country on the west coast of Britain, are descendants of Celtic peoples. Hundreds of years ago, bards were very important people in these countries. In Wales they all belonged to a separate society with special rights which were passed from father to son. They did not have to pay taxes or fight in the king's armies. It was their duty to sing hymns praising God and songs about their country's great victories in war. A great yearly festival or holiday meeting called an "Eisteddfod" was held in Wales, at which all the bards sang in competition for prizes and honors. Princes and nobles were the judges at these contests. The custom of holding an Eisteddfod each year died out for a time, but was begun again in 1820.

In Ireland, bards were also a separate group with special rights that common men did not have. The Irish bards were greatly respected and admired. They were often brought over to Wales to teach singing to Welsh bards.

Barents, Willem

Willem Barents was a sea captain from Holland who explored the Arctic Ocean, along the north coast of Europe,

about 350 years ago. In 1594, 1595, and 1596 he made voyages to the Arctic coasts of Norway and Russia. Barents hoped to find a sea route to eastern Asia, which was then important to the merchants of Europe as a place where spices, silks and precious jewels could be bought. On his last voyage he accidentally discovered a large group of islands in the Arctic Ocean, now known as Spitsbergen. Then his ship was trapped in the ice, and he spent the winter in the frozen Arctic. In the spring of 1597 he and his crew left the ship in the ice and set out in two small boats for the mainland. His crew arrived safely but Barents died on the way, in 1597. His birth date is not known. Part of the Arctic Ocean is named the Barents Sea in his honor.

barge

A barge is a flat-bottomed boat with low sides. It is used to carry freight on rivers and canals. Most barges have neither engines nor sails, and are towed or pushed by tugboats. Some barges, called "lighters," are used to unload cargo from ships in harbors where the water is not deep enough to allow an ocean freighter to enter. Barges carry freight much more slowly than railroads and trucks, but they are the cheapest way to send goods from one place to another.

In many countries of the world there are canals that connect great rivers, or rivers and lakes, and tugboats can haul a train of barges for hundreds of miles along these man-made waterways. In the United States barges can travel by canal from Texas along the Gulf of Mexico and Atlantic coasts to New York City and from there to Lake Erie.

Huge steel barges carry thousands of tons of wheat, steel, bricks, iron ore, and all sorts of goods across the Great Lakes. Every day great fleets of barges tied together with steel cables and chains are hauled up or down the Mississippi River by powerful tugboats.

Some barges have small cabins where the bargemen live. In some countries, especially in Asia, there are whole families that live all their lives on barges.

bark

The bark of a tree is the outer covering of its trunk and branches. Bark protects a tree in the same way that skin protects an animal. It keeps the softer, more tender parts from being harmed. Bark is made up of an outer layer called the *cork*, and live inner tissue called *phloem*, through which food is carried to all parts of the tree. This food consists of the dissolved minerals or chemicals that the roots have sucked up from the soil. The fibers in the inner bark are called bast. In some countries a kind of cloth is made from the soft bast of certain trees and is called bark cloth. The fig, breadfruit and paper mulberry trees supply the best bast for bark cloth. The bast of these trees is cut into narrow strips and soaked in water for a long time and then pounded with a wooden mallet that has grooves in it. The bast is soaked and beaten many times until the fibers of the bark

become thin and very soft, and mat together. The bark cloth is used for clothing, draperies, and bedding.

In the bark of acacia, chestnut, oak and some other trees there is tannic acid, used in the tanning or preservation of leather. Cinnamon, a spice used as a flavoring, is obtained from the bast of a small evergreen tree of the laurel family, found in Ceylon, Brazil, and other tropical countries. Quinine, a valuable drug that cures malaria, is obtained from the bark of cinchona trees that grow in South American countries. Many other useful medicines and dyes for coloring cloth are obtained from the bark of trees.

The American Indians of the northeastern United States once made light, strong canoes from the bark of certain birch trees. The bark of the cork tree, which grows mostly in Spain and Portugal, is very light and spongy. It is used for bottle stoppers (corks), life preservers, and many other things.

Barkley, Alben W.

Alben W. Barkley was Vice-President of the United States from 1949 to 1953, when Harry S. Truman was President. When Barkley was vice-president, he invented the name "Veep" for himself. "Veep" comes from the initials of the words vice-president.

Barkley was born in 1877, in Kentucky. He became a judge, then a Congressman, then a Senator, and then vice-president. In 1954 he was again elected to the Senate, where he served until his death in 1956. He was always noted for his skill as a speaker and story-teller.

barley

Barley is an important food crop that is grown in almost all parts of the world. Like wheat, rice, and corn, barley belongs to the family of plants known as "cereal grasses." It has been grown for thousands of years, and was known to the ancient Romans, Egyptians, Chinese, and Greeks. Barley is grown as a food for both men and animals. There are three different kinds. One has two rows of seeds, a second has four rows, and a third has six. Tremendous quantities of barley are used in the manufacture of beer. Barley is a very hardy plant and is not as easily attacked by disease as other cereal grasses, although it sometimes suffers from such plant diseases as smut and rust.

bar mitzvah

Bar mitzvah is a Hebrew phrase meaning "Son of the Commandment." A Jewish boy is called a "bar mitzvah" when he reaches his thirteenth birthday. After that, he is allowed to take part in the religious life of his people. In some Christian churches this is called a *confirmation*. The Jewish celebration for a bar mitzvah is the same kind of occasion. First the boy goes to the synagogue (which is the Jewish house of worship) and joins with the grown men in prayer and in reading from the part of the Old Testament called the Torah, or Law of Moses; or from the books of the Prophets. Then the "bar mitzvah" makes a speech. And later the boy's family gives him a party and he receives presents. The cele-

bration usually takes place on the Saturday after the boy's thirteenth birthday. Saturday is the Jewish Sabbath.

Although bar mitzvah really refers to the thirteen-year-old boy, many people nowadays call the celebration itself the bar mitzvah.

Barnabas

Barnabas was a good friend and helper of the twelve Apostles of Jesus. He too came to be called an apostle and made missionary trips with St. Paul. In the Bible, in the Book of Acts, it says that Barnabas had great power because of his loving and cheerful nature.

barnacle

The barnacle is a small sea animal with a shell. It attaches itself to ships' bottoms and to underwater timbers and rocks along sea shores. Whales and giant sea turtles sometimes have barnacles on parts of their bodies.

There are two kinds of barnacle. One is called the *acorn barnacle*, the other the *goose*, or *ship*, *barnacle*. The acorn barnacle is two to three inches long and has a cone-shaped shell resembling an acorn. The goose barnacle is one to two inches long and has a strong, leathery stalk by which it attaches itself to the bottom of a ship. On one side of its shell it has six pairs of feathery legs, with which it pushes water carrying bits of food into its mouth. The stalk has such a powerful suction grip on whatever it attaches itself to that it can be loosened only by killing the barnacle.

Barnacles are a very serious problem for the owners of ships. After a ship has been in sea water for three or four years, barnacles may become so thick on the bottom that they can slow the ship's speed by as much as four or five miles per hour.

To get rid of the barnacles, a ship is taken into a drydock, which is a huge concrete basin filled with water. The water in the basin is pumped out and the ship settles down into a huge "cradle" with steel arms that hold it in place. Then the barnacles are hacked off with sharp steel tools. All this is very expensive. Certain kinds of paint that contain powdered copper are used on ships' bottoms. This paint is a poison to barnacles.

Am. Museum of Natural Hist.

Barnacles on rocks are usually dead and no longer have these feathery feet.

Barnard College

Barnard College is a very fine college for women in New York City. It is a part of Columbia University. Barnard College was founded in 1889, and became a part of Columbia University in 1900. It has about 1,425 students, and about 500 girls enter the freshman class each year. Most of the students take all their courses at Barnard, but more advanced students frequently take courses at Columbia University. Some Columbia University professors teach also at Barnard College. Barnard College was named for Frederick Barnard, an educator, who was born in 1809 and died in 1889. He favored more education for women.

Barnum, Phineas Taylor

P. T. Barnum was the most famous showman and circus manager of all time. P. T. Barnum was born in Bethel, Connecticut, in 1810. He started working when he was a boy. He went to New York City and worked there and in Brooklyn until he was 18 years old. He returned to Connecticut and went into business with the money he had saved. He got married when he was 19, and he became a newspaper editor. He was accused of libel—a printed statement that insults somebody unjustly—and was found guilty and put in jail for two months.

After getting out of jail he left Connecticut, a poor man. One day, while he was visiting Philadelphia, he saw a Negro slave woman named Joyce Heth, who said that she had been the nurse of George Washington. Her owner said that she was 161 years old. Barnum borrowed $1,000 and bought Joyce Heth. He advertised in many newspapers, saying that he owned George Washington's nurse. People flocked to see her and paid Barnum a lot of money. But when Joyce Heth died the following year, the doctors found that she was only eighty years old. People didn't seem to mind this very much. Barnum saw that people liked to be fooled, as long as he gave them a good show for their money. He is supposed to have said "There's one born every minute"—meaning "one sucker."

For the next several years Barnum traveled through the South with small shows. None of them was very successful. Then he bought a museum and he heard about a very small person, a midget, less than two feet tall, who lived in Connecticut. Barnum made arrangements to show this midget around the country. He called the midget General Tom Thumb and he made a great deal of money exhibiting Tom Thumb in the United States and then on a tour of Europe.

A few years later Barnum arranged to have a very famous Swedish opera singer named Jenny Lind come to America. Miss Lind was known as "the Swedish Nightingale." She toured the country under Barnum's direction, and both of them made a great fortune. Barnum paid Jenny Lind $1,000 for every night she sang—a huge amount in those days.

During the next several years Barnum put most of his savings into several businesses, but they all failed. He took Tom Thumb on a new tour of Europe and made enough money to return to America. He bought two museums, both of which burned down. Then, in 1871, Barnum set up the great traveling circus that he called "P. T. Barnum's Greatest Show on Earth." No one had ever seen anything like it. In this circus Barnum exhibited a great elephant that he called Jumbo. He included clowns and unusual animals that could do tricks. His circus was later called Barnum & Bailey, and still later was combined with the Ringling Brothers circus. Barnum died in 1891, at the age of 81.

barometer

A barometer is an instrument used to measure air pressure. The article on AIR explains how air presses on the surface of the earth. There are nearly 15 pounds of air pressing on each square inch of the earth's surface. This is called *normal atmospheric pressure*.

The barometer was first thought of by an Italian scientist named Torricelli, in 1644. A simple experiment showed him that air had pressure, and that this pressure could be measured. He took a glass tube about 3 feet long, closed at one end; some mercury (a metal sometimes called quicksilver); and a small dish. He filled the tube and the dish with mercury and turned the tube upside down in the dish. This made a *mercury barometer*.

The mercury in such a tube drops until it is about 30 inches above the dish. Fifteen pounds of air pressure, which is normal, will usually hold up about 30 inches of mercury. If the air pressure is lower, the height of the column of mercury will be less than 30 inches. If the air pressure is greater, the column of mercury will be higher than 30 inches.

A mercury barometer can be used to help predict the weather. When the column of mercury begins to fall rapidly, it usually means that bad weather is ahead, because windy, rainy weather usually follows a drop in air pressure. After a storm is over, the mercury will climb back to 30 inches.

Water could be used instead of mercury, but water is so much lighter than mercury that it would take more than a 34-foot tube of water to measure air pressure. Three hundred years ago, a German named von Guericke made a water barometer that was taller than his house. He had to cut a hole in the roof so that it would fit.

THE ANEROID BAROMETER

Even a mercury barometer is too big to carry. There is a smaller barometer that can be carried in the pocket. This is the *aneroid* barometer (*aneroid* meaning "without liquid").

An aneroid barometer looks somewhat like a clock. It contains a small metal box from which most of the air has been removed. The sides of the box move in and out as the air pressure changes. The box is attached by a spring to a pointer on the dial of the barometer. The higher

the air pressure against the box, the further the pointer moves along the dial.

An aneroid barometer can be specially marked so that it will tell how high above sea level you are—for example, when you are up in an airplane. Such a barometer is also called an altimeter. There is a separate article on ALTIMETER.

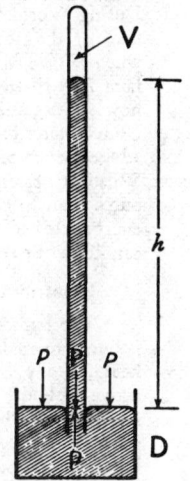

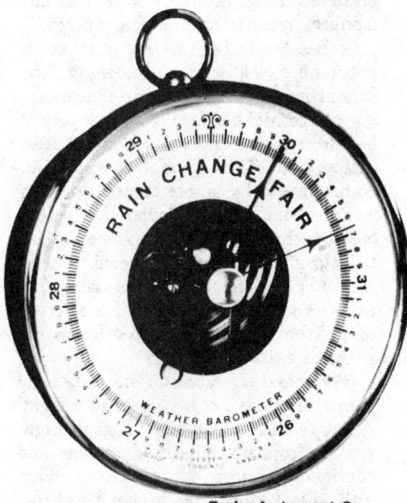

Taylor Instrument Co.

The dark pointer on this aneroid barometer is set in line with the light one. When the light one moves to the left, it means that the air pressure is dropping. A great drop in pressure is a sign of rain.

baroque

Baroque is a style of art that is very fancy, with curlicues and swirls and frills, with Cupids and wreaths of flowers. Baroque art started in Europe about four hundred years ago and was popular for more than two hundred years. Every branch of art was affected. More trills were added to music, more gold was used in furniture, people wore clothes with many more ribbons and ruffles, and buildings had more columns and statues and high domes. The height of the baroque style was found in Italy. In France, this style was called "rococo" by those who thought it was too fancy.

barracuda

The great barracuda is a ferocious fish. It is found mostly in the warm waters around the West Indies and off the Florida coast, but sometimes roams as far north as Massachusetts. A barra-

cuda may be as much as ten feet long and have a big mouth with rows of *canine* (doglike) teeth—long and sharp. When it bites, it shakes and "worries" its victim as a dog does. It also has another trait of the dog: it will chase a moving object. The barracuda will attack any fish or animal in the water, and it is particularly dangerous to bathers who swim out too far from the beach.

The giant barracuda is seldom used as food. Several smaller kinds, especially one found along the Pacific Coast, are good food fish. All barracuda are "game fish," prized by fishermen because they put up a good fight when hooked.

barrel

A barrel is a round container, longer than it is wide and bulging in the middle. It is made of long, curved pieces of wood called *staves*. These staves are placed side by side and are held together by round metal bands called *hoops*. There are usually three hoops, at the top, at the bottom, and in the middle. The barrel is flat at the top and bottom. The making of barrels is called *cooperage*, and a person who makes them is a *cooper*.

Barrels are used to store and ship beer, pickles, wine, butter, pork, flour, etc. Barrels come in many sizes. Standard sizes vary in different countries. In the United States a standard barrel of flour filled to the top weighs about 196 pounds and a beer barrel can hold 31½ gallons of beer, which is about five hundred glasses of beer. Small barrels, half the size of a standard barrel, are called *kegs*. A *hogshead* is a barrel that can hold twice as much as a standard barrel. Wine is stored in barrels called *casks* or *tuns*. A tun can hold about ten times as much as a standard barrel, or about three hundred gallons. Metal containers like barrels, but in the shape of a cylinder, are called *drums*.

Barrels are sealed tightly at both the top and bottom. Wine and beer barrels are filled through a hole called a *bunghole*. The bunghole may be at the top or at the side of the barrel. When the barrel is filled, a wooden plug called a *bung* is stuck in the hole. To get the beer or wine out of the barrel, the bung is knocked into the barrel.

barrel organ

The barrel organ is a mechanical music maker. It is usually operated by turning a crank. The name comes from the barrel-like cylinder inside, which slowly revolves when the organ is played. There are pegs on the surface of the cylinder that open organ pipes as the cylinder is turned. The pegs are arranged so that they open the organ pipes in the proper order and play a tune.

The first barrel organs were made more than two hundred years ago and were used in churches. A small barrel organ is called a *hurdy-gurdy* or *hand organ*. "Organ grinders," playing hurdy-gurdies, with trained monkeys to collect coins from bystanders, may still be seen in some cities, but generally the barrel organ has been replaced by the phonograph record, played through a loudspeaker.

Barrie, James M.

James Matthew Barrie was a famous British writer of plays and novels. He was born in 1860, in Scotland, and became famous as a writer when his book *The Little Minister* was published in 1891. After 1902 he stopped writing novels and began to write plays. One of his best known plays is a fairy tale called *Peter Pan*. In this play Peter Pan, the "boy who never grew up," has adventures in a wild, faraway place called Never Never Land.

Other famous plays by Barrie are *The Admirable Crichton, Dear Brutus*, and *What Every Woman Knows*. His best-known novel is *The Little Minister*.

Barrie was made a knight by the British government, an honor that entitled him to be called Sir James. He died in 1937.

Barry, John

Captain John Barry was a great hero of the United States Navy during the Revolutionary War. He was born in Ireland in 1745, came to America at the age of 15, and settled in Philadelphia. Here he became a very successful trader and sea captain. Soon after the Revolution began, Barry became commander of the American warship *Lexington*. He captured a small British ship named the *Edward* on April 17, 1776. This was the first British ship captured by an American warship during the Revolution. In 1781, while in command of the *Alliance,* Barry captured the British ships *Trepassy* and *Atalanta* after a fierce fight. In 1794, after the United States had become independent, Barry was given the rank of commodore in the new Navy. He died in 1803.

Barrymore

Barrymore is the name of a great family of American actors. The family name began with Hugh Blythe, an English actor who took the stage name of Maurice Barrymore and became a great success in the United States. He married Georgiana Drew, an actress who was the daughter of John and Louisa Drew, famous American actors. The children of Maurice and Georgiana Barrymore were Lionel, Ethel and John Barrymore, who became even more famous than their parents.

Lionel Barrymore, the oldest son, was born in 1878. On the stage he was a great success as Macbeth, in the play by Shakespeare. He was one of the first great stage actors to act in the movies. He also starred in radio. Every year millions of people listened to his reading of *A Christmas Carol*, by Charles Dickens, on Christmas Eve. He died in 1954.

Ethel Barrymore was born in 1879. She was both a beautiful woman and a great actress, and she starred in many plays, in a few movies, and on radio and television. She died in 1959.

John Barrymore, the youngest son, was born in 1882. He made a great reputation as an actor in the plays of

Shakespeare, especially *Hamlet,* and he acted in many movies. John was an extremely handsome man and was sometimes called the "Great Profile" because a side view of his face showed his almost perfect features. He died in 1942.

Bartered Bride, The

The Bartered Bride is a comic opera with music by the Czech composer, Bedrich Smetana. The opera is usually sung in German or English. It was first sung in Prague, Czechoslovakia, in 1866.

STORY OF THE OPERA

A girl named Marzhenka is to marry Vazhek, son of a rich farmer, Micha. She really loves Yenyik, but he is a stranger, and her parents do not approve of him. A marriage broker, Kezal, wants Marzhenka to marry Vazhek; so he pays some money to Yenyik, who promises that he will give up Marzhenka, provided she marries *the son of Micha.* (Yenyik is really Micha's eldest son, but he has been away so long that everybody has forgotten him.) Vazhek, in the meantime, falls in love with Esmeralda, a dancer in a show that is playing in town. Micha recognizes Yenyik as his long lost son and Yenyik marries Marzhenka, which is according to the agreement. It all ends happily for everyone except Kezal, the broker, who has lost the money he paid to Yenyik. When the opera is sung in German the names are changed to Marie (for Marzhenka), Hans (for Yenyik), and Wenzel (for Vazhek).

Bartholdi, Frédéric Auguste

Frédéric Auguste Bartholdi was a French sculptor. He designed the famous Statue of Liberty, which stands in the harbor of New York City. He was born in 1832 in France. There is another fine statue in New York by Bartholdi. It is a figure of Lafayette, the French officer who commanded French troops under George Washington during the Revolutionary War. Statues by Bartholdi of Lafayette and Washington stand in Paris, the capital of France. Bartholdi died in 1904.

Bartholomew, Saint

St. Bartholomew was one of the twelve Apostles, or disciples of Jesus. He is thought to be the same as Nathanael. After the death of Jesus, Bartholomew preached the Christian faith in Armenia. At that time, nearly two thousand years ago, Christians were often killed for their beliefs. Bartholomew was killed with a knife. For this reason the great painter Michaelangelo portrayed him with a knife in his hands. His day is August 24.

The Massacre of St. Bartholomew took place on that day, August 24, nearly five hundred years ago, in 1572. It happened in France, when wars were being fought between the Protestants and Catholics. Catherine de' Medici, a queen of France and mother of two kings of France, was a Catholic. She wanted to murder an important Protestant who was influencing her son, the king. This started a terrible massacre of Protestants in Paris, and it soon spread all over France. Some say that more than 30,000 Protestants were murdered.

Bartok, Bela

Bartok was a Hungarian composer. He was born in 1881 in a place called Nagyszentmiklos, which means "Great St. Michael." Bartok studied Hungarian folk music and his own music was influenced by it, though his music is very modern. He wrote for orchestras, including ballets, and for small instrumental groups. He settled in the United States in 1940 and died in New York in 1945.

Bartolommeo, Fra

Fra Bartolommeo was a painter who lived in Florence, in northern Italy, about four hundred years ago. He was born about 1472. His full name was Bartolommeo de Pagholo del Fattorino. He was called Fra (meaning Brother) because he was a member of the Dominican order, a society of Roman Catholic Monks. His paintings are on religious subjects. His masterpiece, or greatest painting, is his picture of *St. Mark.* Other great paintings of his which are world famous are: *Madonna with Six Saints*, in the San Marco Museum in Florence; *God the Father Adored by Mary Magdalen and Saint Catherine*, in the museum of Lucca, Italy; *The Marriage of St. Catherine*, in the Louvre museum in Paris, France; and *The Last Judgment*, in the Uffizi Palace in Florence. Fra Bartolommeo died in 1517.

Barton, Clara

Clara Barton was the great woman who founded the American Red Cross. When Clara Barton was a little girl she dreamed of being a nurse. She wanted to help the sick and the wounded, homeless and hungry. All her life she did just that.

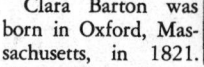

Clara Barton was born in Oxford, Massachusetts, in 1821. When she was 15 years old she became a schoolteacher, and when the Civil War began in 1860 she became a nurse. Soon after that, she started an organization that sent needed things to soldiers in camps and hospitals. President Lincoln asked her to try to trace soldiers who were missing in action. By the time Clara Barton had finished her job she had been able to identify almost all of 13,000 graves at a National Cemetery in Georgia.

After the Civil War, Clara Barton went to Geneva, Switzerland, where she learned about the International Red Cross. During the war between France and Germany in 1871-2, she helped provide refugees with food, clothing, and shelter. In 1873 Clara Barton came back to America. Her hope was to start an American Red Cross. It took her eight years to convince America that it is as important to help people who suffer in peacetime as it is to help them in wartime. She served as president of the American Red Cross until 1904, and died in 1912.

Baruch, Bernard Mannes

Bernard Baruch is the name of an American who became known as the "Adviser to Presidents." He was born in 1870, in Camden, South Carolina, the son of a noted physician, Simon Baruch. Bernard Baruch was educated at the College of the City of New York, and then became a trader in stocks and bonds and an official of many business companies. He made a fortune within a few years. During World War I Baruch was chairman of the War Industries Board and when World War II broke out 23 years later Baruch advised the government on how to organize the industries of the United States for war production. Baruch advised seven presidents, from Woodrow Wilson to Eisenhower, and also worked out a plan to control the use of atomic energy. He came to be called the American "Elder Statesman." He died in 1965.

basal metabolism

The body uses food as fuel, which it burns to make energy. This produces heat, as any burning does. The more active the body, the more energy is needed and the more heat is produced; the less active the body, the less heat. A basal metabolism test measures the heat produced when the body is as inactive as possible. (Basal means "lowest" and metabolism means "change into energy.")

A basal metabolism test is taken at about nine o'clock in the morning. The patient may not eat anything that morning or the night before. First the patient lies on a couch and relaxes for at least half an hour. Then a rubber clamp is put on his nose so he cannot breathe through it. For about fifteen minutes the patient breathes through a tube into a can called a calorimeter (which means "heat-measurer"). The calorimeter automatically tests the breath and makes a record of it, from which the doctor learns the patient's basal metabolism.

The basal metabolism of a healthy person depends on his age and weight. A baby's basal metabolism is at its highest. It drops sharply in the teens and continues to drop as one grows older. Tall, thin people have higher basal metabolisms than short, fat ones. If the basal metabolism is too high or too low, certain glands such as the thyroid gland may not be working properly. Medicine can be given to correct such a condition.

basalt

Basalt is a kind of rock. Most of it was formed millions of years ago from red-hot material called *magma.* The magma flowed up from deep beneath the earth's crust through great cracks or through volcanoes. Basalt is usually black, dark brown, or greenish-black, although sometimes it may be gray. Scientists believe that basalt forms a layer under all the continents and oceans. They also believe that many hundred million years ago all the rock in the world was basalt. Then great heat and pressure and weather changed most of the basalt on the earth's surface to all the other kinds of rock we find today. Basalt is very hard and makes a good building stone.

The great cliffs called the Palisades, along the Hudson River near New York City, are basalt. The Hawaiian Islands are basalt mountains that rise from the floor of the Pacific Ocean. Unlike many basalt mountains, they have sloping sides

and fairly level tops. In Ireland there is a row of six-sided blocks of basalt, sticking up through the ground, called "the Giants' Causeway." The blocks are so perfectly formed that they look as though some race of giants had carved them to use as stepping stones.

bascule bridge, a kind of drawbridge; see BRIDGE.

baseball

Baseball is the national game of the United States. People all over the United States are more interested in baseball than in any other game or sport. Boys learn to play it when they first go to school, men play it as long as they enjoy exercise. Millions of people watch baseball games every summer day, or listen to them on the radio, or see them on television. Many Americans are so interested in the game that they talk about it all winter, when no games are played

Although baseball has always been called the great American game, it has become more and more an international sport. In both World War I and World War II, American soldiers taught baseball to people in other countries where they were stationed. For years baseball has been popular in Japan, Central and South America, and the West Indies.

HISTORY OF BASEBALL

No one knows for sure how baseball came to be the game it is and whether it was invented or just developed from other games. It used to be thought that a man named Abner Doubleday invented baseball in 1839, when he was a cadet at the United States Military Academy, West Point, and that he laid out the first baseball field at Cooperstown, New York. For quite a few years it has been known that this is not so, but still the National Baseball Museum was placed in Cooperstown.

Baseball began with the English games *cricket* and *rounders,* brought over to the American colonies before the United States was an independent nation. In both games, a player had to hit a ball with a bat and then run. In other ways they were much different from baseball.

The first game that really began to look like baseball was called *town ball.* Boys who lived in the country could not always get enough friends to play a large game. Whenever a few boys got together they played what they called *one old cat.* In this game the batter, after hitting the ball, ran to a base and then scored by running back to *home,* the place he had started from. When more boys played, the game was called *two old cat* because there were two bases instead of one. Only in the towns were there enough players to have three bases and nine men on a team, so the three-base game was called town ball. It was played in the early 1800s.

In all these early games the scoring was the same. The batter who got back to the home base, whether from one, two, or three other bases, scored a run, and the team that scored the most runs was the winner.

It seems most likely that a man named Alexander Cartwright laid out the first

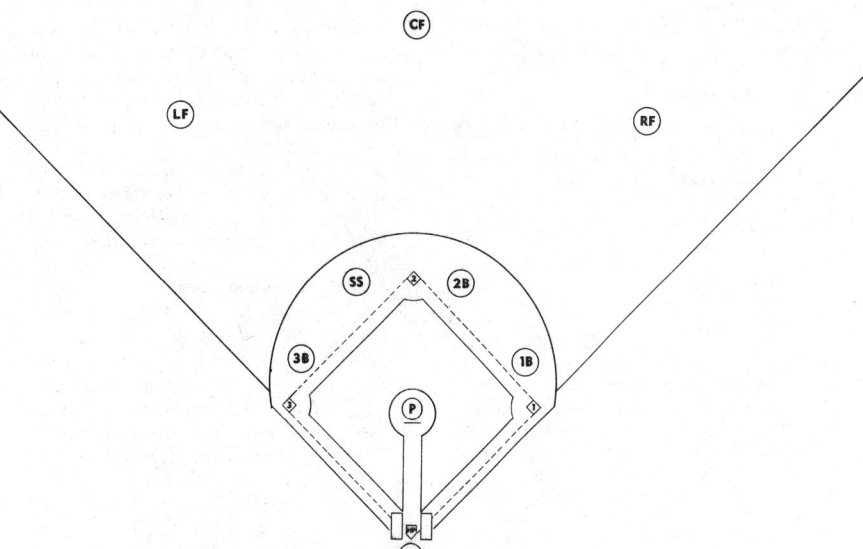

Baseball field. The players of the team "at field", usually station themselves in the positions shown by the circles, but may play deeper (farther from the home plate), closer in, or more to the right or left, depending on where they expect the batter to hit the ball. The foul lines extend from the angle formed by the home plate (HP) to the outfield fence, a distance of 250 to 350 or more feet. The diamond (inside the dotted lines) and the base paths (sandy paths around the diamond) are the infield; all the rest is the outfield. The batter may stand in either of the batter's boxes beside the home plate. The area where the pitcher (P) stands is raised a few inches, forming a mound.

real baseball field in 1846, in Hoboken, New Jersey. The game became more and more popular, and during the Civil War it was played in many army camps. When the Civil War was over, baseball soon became the national game of the United States.

The rules that govern baseball have been changed from time to time, but the game is basically the same that our great-grandfathers played and watched.

HOW THE GAME IS PLAYED

Baseball is played out-of-doors, in warm weather, on any large, level field. A baseball field is divided into an *infield* and an *outfield.* The entire baseball field may be any size, but the infield part of it is always the same size. The infield is actually a square, but it is called a "diamond" because from "home" it looks diamond-shaped. The distance from one base to another is 90 feet. For boys' or girls' games this distance may be made shorter. The infield and outfield together are called *fair* territory. Everything outside the lines is *foul* territory.

The ball must weigh 5 to 5¼ ounces and be 9 to 9¼ inches around. The bat must be all wood, not more than 2¾ inches thick or 42 inches long. (See also the article on SOFTBALL.)

Baseball is a game between two teams. There must be nine men on a team and these nine men must play in certain positions. The positions are pitcher, catcher, first baseman, second baseman, third baseman, shortstop, left fielder, centerfielder, and right fielder. When one team is "in the field," the other team is "at bat." The nine men on the team at bat must go up to the plate in turn and try to hit the ball. When these batters have finished their turn at bat, they go into the field and the fielding team becomes the batting team. Each time both teams have had a turn at bat, one inning of a baseball game has been completed. When the teams have played nine innings they have completed an official game of baseball.

The players of the team that is at bat take turns, strictly in accordance with a "batting order" that is decided before the game begins.

The team in the field takes positions as shown in the picture. They are called *fielders.* A member of the team at bat stands in the batter's box. He is called the *batter.* The pitcher throws the ball toward the catcher. The batter tries to hit the ball.

The batter's object is to advance around the bases—to first base, then to second base, then to third base, then home again—without being *put out.* If he does this, he scores a *run.* The team that scores the most runs wins the game. There are several ways a batter can be put out:

1. The batter is out if the pitcher throws three strikes while he is at bat. A *strike* is a pitched ball that passes over the home plate, no higher than the batter's shoulders and no lower than his knees. It is also a strike when the batter swings at it and does not hit it, or when he hits it into foul territory and it is not caught before it lands. This is called a *foul ball.* But a foul ball never counts as a third strike. Any pitched ball that is not hit or struck at, and that does not pass within the "strike zone," is called a *ball.*

2. The batter is out if any ball that he hits is caught before it lands. This is called a *fly ball.* A ball that hits the ground too soon to be caught is called a *ground ball.*

3. The batter is out if the team in the field can "field" a ground ball that he hits into fair territory, and get it to first base before the batter can get there. A player may "touch" a base with any part of his body, including the tips of his shoes.

The batter can reach first base safely in several ways. The principal ways are:

1. If the pitcher pitches four balls (pitches that are not strikes and are not hit with the bat). In this case the batter is said to *walk,* or to get a *base on balls.* (The same thing happens if any pitched ball hits the batter.)

2. If a fair ball is not caught on the fly, or does not reach first base before the batter gets there. In this case the batter has made a *hit,* or a *base* hit. If his hit takes him to first base

it is a *single;* to second base, a *double;* to third base a *triple;* and all the way home, a *home run.* A fair ball that lands outside the playing field is an automatic home run.

If a batter reaches any base safely, he becomes a *baserunner.* A baserunner may run from base to base—from first to second, second to third, and third to home—whenever he wishes but he can be put out in the following ways:

1. A baserunner is out if he is *tagged* (touched) with the ball when he is not touching a base.
2. A baserunner may also be *forced out.* The rules for a *force-out* are the same as the rule for putting a player out at first base. A baserunner on first base is out if a ground ball is fielded and is held by a fielder touching second base before he gets there. When there are baserunners on both first and second bases, there can be a force play at third base, and when there are baserunners on all three bases there can be a force play at home.
3. When a fly ball is caught, each baserunner must "tag up"—touch the base he was on. Then he may try to run to the next base, but he may be tagged out before he gets there. If a fly ball is returned to his base and held by a fielder touching that base before he tags up, he is out.

The team in the field tries to catch fly balls, and to catch ground balls and throw them to the proper bases to put baserunners out.

When three members of the batting side have been put out, the "side is retired" and the other team comes to bat.

There is always at least one *umpire*—and in professional games there are two, three, or four—to decide whether a pitch is a ball or strike, whether a baserunner is out or safe, and what other rules apply. (There are many rules in baseball, so that few people know them all.) When there is only one umpire, he stands behind the pitcher. When there are two or more, one stands behind the catcher and calls balls and strikes and the other stands near the bases and calls plays in the field.

ORGANIZED BASEBALL

There are many baseball players in the United States who play on teams that represent large cities. These teams are organized into what are called *leagues.* There are two "big leagues," or "major leagues," in the United States. They are the American League and the National League. There are other leagues in the United States that are less important and are called *minor leagues.* The most important minor leagues are rated AAA ("triple A"); then come AA, A, B, C, and D. Each league is made up of some four to eight teams. In each league the teams play each other over and over again until the season is completed. A season in the major leagues consists of 162 games; in minor leagues it varies.

The team that wins the most games in each league during a season wins the *pennant* for that season. The pennant-winning teams in the American and National Leagues play each other in the *World Series,* early in October.

Another important baseball event is the yearly *All-Star Game.* The best players in each of the two major leagues are elected or appointed and the American League all-stars play the National League all-stars about the middle of July.

All men who play in these baseball leagues are called *professional baseball players,* which means that they are paid salaries to play. Other men who play for money but do not play in regular leagues are called *semiprofessional baseball players.* Organized baseball consists of all the professional baseball leagues, and it is the highest form of baseball that is played. Organized baseball is governed by a national baseball commission. Each league is run by a president and several assistants. The league presidents appoint the umpires and see to it that the teams play baseball according to the regular schedule and that they all observe all of the rules. Each professional baseball team has its own ballpark or stadium, which may hold up to 100,000 people.

Amateur baseball is played by schools, army camps, and club teams. When a boy has shown baseball skill he usually moves up from either a club or college team to a minor-league team, and if he continues to show skill he eventually reaches the major leagues, which are the goal of every young American baseball player. Boys and young men who play on fields and lots and pastures all over the country are playing what is called *sandlot baseball.*

Most boys about 12 years old who play baseball play in what is called the *Little League.* In the Little League the baseball fields are smaller than regulation fields —the distance between the bases is 60 feet instead of 90 feet. The game itself is basically the same as regulation baseball. It is played with the same kind of balls and bats and gloves.

The American Legion for many years has also encouraged baseball for boys. Legion posts all over the United States give the boys uniforms and equipment.

THE BASEBALL HALL OF FAME

The Baseball Hall of Fame is part of the National Baseball Museum at Cooperstown, New York. In the museum are pieces of baseball equipment that figured in famous games or were used by great players. Members of the Baseball Hall of Fame are great players and pioneers of the game. They are elected by Ameri-

can sportswriters and for each there is a plaque with his sculptured likeness and a brief record of what made him famous.

Basel or Basle

Basel is a large city in Switzerland. More than 200,000 people live in Basel. The Rhine River, which divides the city, becomes wide and deep enough at Basel for ships to sail all the way up to the North Sea. The city of Basel stands at the point where Switzerland, France, and Germany meet, and at one place in the city there is a small three-sided marker that says France on one side, Germany on another, and Switzerland on the third.

Basel is a historic city. The Council of Basel was an important church conference in 1431 between the Roman Catholic Church and the Hussites, an early Protestant group. Basel has remained a Protestant section. Most of the people speak German. The famous University of Basel was founded in 1460.

BASEL, SWITZERLAND. Population, 378,300. Capital of Baselland Canton. On Rhine River.

basenji

The basenji is a hunting dog that comes from central Africa. It is known as the "barkless dog" because for centuries no basenji had ever been known to bark. Then, at a dog show in London in 1953, a basenji actually barked.

Basenjis were used for hunting in ancient Egypt, and they are still used for hunting in Africa. In the United States, people keep them as pets because they are playful and gentle. The basenji has an unusual habit. It washes itself all over, like a cat.

The basenji is a medium-sized dog, about 16 or 17 inches high at the shoulder. It weighs about 20 pounds. Its tail curls up tightly over its back, making a complete ring. The forehead of the basenji is deeply wrinkled and its ears are round and upstanding.

A basenji's coat is short and silky and may be reddish brown and white, golden brown and white, black and white, or black, tan, and white.

Basic English

The English language is spoken in more different countries than any other language. Many people want the world to have a "universal" language, one that everyone can speak. Some of these people would like to see English become the universal language, but they agree that it is a very difficult language to learn. So in 1920 two Englishmen—a language expert named C. K. Ogden and a literary critic named I. A. Richards—invented a simpler form of English that is called Basic English.

Basic English is made up of 850 English words that can be used to express most of the everyday things that people talk about. The largest English dictionaries contain about 500,000 words. About 20,000 of these are words which most educated English-speaking people use often. That is too many words for someone who is just starting to study a language. So Ogden and Richards selected only the words that a person must know to express simple things clearly. The

This bronze plaque of Babe Ruth hangs with those of other stars in the Hall of Fame.

word *basic* stands for British-American Scientific International Commercial.

Basic English follows the same rules of grammar as regular English. The main difference is that there are only eighteen verbs. These are called *operators*. Some of those included are: *come, go, get, make, put, take, be, do, say, see*. Besides the verbs, other words having to do with action are also called *operators*. These include prepositions, conjunctions, pronouns, articles, some adverbs, and the words *yes, please, north, south, east, west, tomorrow*, and *yesterday*.

Basic English has six hundred nouns (names of things). These include two hundred *picturable* things—of which an artist could draw a picture—such as *ant, apple, army*. There are four hundred *general* things—such words as *act, behavior, account*.

Adjectives and adverbs are called *qualifiers*. Some adverbs are made by adding *-ly* to adjectives, as we are used to doing (*cheap, cheaply*). Comparisons are made with *more* and *most* (*beautiful, more* beautiful, *most* beautiful) or with *-er* and *-est* (*hard, harder, hardest*, or *near, nearer, nearest*). So you can see that the original 850 words grow into quite a few more.

Basic English also uses words for measurements, numbers, days of the week and months. There are extra lists of words for special subjects. One hundred special words for poetry and fifty for religion were used in a Basic English translation of the Bible. Science calls for one hundred extra words, and there are three hundred "international" words, such as *radio, hotel*, and *bank*, which are much the same in most languages.

Even with the special lists, Basic English still gets along with many fewer words than regular English. One way this is done is to use a few simple words combined in different ways to take the place of more complicated words. For example, in Basic English a puppy is a *young dog*, a kitten is a *young cat*, a sapling is a *young tree*. You don't *climb* a tree, you *go up* it.

See also the articles on ESPERANTO and LANGUAGE.

basilisk

Basilisk is the name of several kinds of lizard found from Mexico to Ecuador, South America. In ancient times it was believed to be a fearful, ugly monster that lived in caves and cracks in rocks and could kill a person just by looking at him. But actually the basilisk is only a harmless lizard about 2 to 3 feet long. The male has a spiky fin, or crest, on the back of its head. The basilisk is yellowish-brown on the back and white underneath its body. Some basilisks have black and white stripes on the sides of the neck and back. The basilisk feeds on beetles and other insects. It can run fast if it has to, but it usually moves slowly. It has an unusual trick of "walking on water"—it glides across water with its forelegs folded, using its tail as a balance.

basket

A basket is any container that is made by weaving or coiling strips of flexible ("bendable") material together. Baskets can be made of twigs, straw, wicker, bamboo, grass, palm leaves, cornhusks, twisted paper, rope, thin wire, and many other materials. Some of these are not flexible when they are dry, but they are flexible when they are wet. A thin twig, for instance, will snap if you bend it when it is dry, but it may be curved and twisted when it is thoroughly wet. For this reason, some baskets are made while the material is wet. Then they dry and are baskets.

Two skilled basket weavers in Jamaica.
Jamaica News Bureau

Baskets are among the oldest things made by man. People who lived thousands of years ago were just as skilled in basket-making as we are today. Primitive people, who do not travel very much, make their baskets from the materials they find growing around them. That is why the primitive people of Africa make baskets of palm leaves, while the American Indians use cornhusks.

Sometimes no tools at all are needed in basket making. When tools are needed, they are tools that man invented many, many thousands of years ago, such as the knife, the needle, and the awl (a tool used for punching holes).

KINDS OF BASKET

Baskets can be made in many different shapes and sizes, as well as of many different materials. But no matter what the shape or size of material is, there are certain special ways of making baskets. Woven baskets are made by crossing two or more strips of material over and under each other. The pattern is made by the way the strips cross each other.

Primitive people do beautiful work in the decorating of their baskets. Sometimes strips of the material are dyed different colors, and the design is made by weaving in the different colors. Sometimes the color is not changed, but the weaving or coiling pattern is changed. Sometimes both the color and the pattern are changed. Very often, the designs have special meanings for the maker or for his whole tribe. There may be certain religious or magical ideas attached to the designs.

In some sections of India, the people make boats of basketwork covered with animal skins. Some South American Indians make baskets that are watertight and can hold liquids. Certain South Sea Island tribes make shields for their soldiers out of basketwork. In many North American Indian tribes, mothers carry their babies on their backs in cradle-boards made of basketwork. Men used to make huts by weaving twigs together and covering them with clay.

Some baskets dug out of the sand in Egypt were made four or five thousand years before Jesus was born. That makes them between six and seven thousand years old! The Bible tells us that the infant Moses was hidden in the bullrushes in a basket.

The Potawatomi Indians, who lived in Wisconsin, have a myth about baskets. The Potawatomi believe that there is an old woman up in the moon who spends all her time weaving a basket. When the old woman finishes that basket, the world will come to an end. But fortunately there is a little dog in the moon, too, and every so often he jumps up and spoils the old woman's work, and she has to start her basket all over again. The Potawotami believe that they can tell when the little dog jumps out, because his jumping is what makes an eclipse of the moon. So the Potawotami are happy every time they see an eclipse.

Baskets are made in factories in many parts of the world, but most of the work is still done by hand. This is just a short list of baskets we use every day: laundry baskets, clothes hampers, shopping baskets, sewing baskets, berry baskets, bread baskets.

basketball

Basketball is the most important indoor game in the world. It is played in nearly all countries. Girls as well as boys can play it. It can be played in schools, clubs, and churches. Only five players are needed to make up a team. Tall men have an advantage, and many professionals are nearly seven feet tall, but some of the greatest players of all time have been short men. The equipment is inexpensive, and any school that can afford a gymnasium can afford a basketball team. Basketball is also played outdoors, but it is most important during the winter months, when it is too cold for most athletic games.

HOW BASKETBALL STARTED

Dr. James A. Naismith was a physical director at the International Training School of the Y.M.C.A. in 1891, in the last century. He was worried because the boys were not attending the gym very regularly. He wished he had a game that would be as exciting as football or baseball. He needed a fast game, but one that would not be too rough on a hard wooden floor.

Dr. Naismith went into the gym and stood there a long time thinking. He remembered an old game that boys played, in which the members of one group pass a ball around and try to keep the members of another group from getting it. Then his eye caught the balconies at each end of the gym, and all of a sudden he had an idea. He got two empty peach baskets, knocked out their bottoms, and fastened one on each end of the balcony, so that they were about ten feet above the floor of the gym. Then he got two teams ready for the first game. Before the game started he wrote down thirteen rules and pinned them on the school's bulletin board. The full rules of basketball are now very long, and official committees change them almost every year, but Nai-

George Kalinsky

The New York Knickerbockers play the Boston Celtics at the "new" Madison Square Garden (which opened on February 11, 1968) in New York City.

smith's original thirteen rules were so basic that twelve of them are still used.

HOW BASKETBALL IS PLAYED

Basketball is played between two teams of five players each, with a leather ball blown up with air, and 30 inches around, on a court 94 feet long and 50 feet wide. (It does not absolutely *have* to be this large, and many courts are quite a bit smaller.) Along the sides of the court are the *side lines,* and at each end there is an *end line.* There must be a space of at least three feet running all around the outside of these lines, and when the ball goes off the court into the outside space, it is said to be *out of bounds.*

The *baskets,* two hoops, are attached ten feet above the floor. Behind them are *backboards* which are six feet wide and four feet high. Sometimes the backboards are made of wood, and sometimes they are made of heavy plate glass so that the people sitting behind them can see the game through them. There is one basket at each end of the court.

When the game is about to start, each team lines up with two men at one end of the court, two men at the other, and the fifth player in a circle in the very center of the court. To start the game, the referee tosses the ball straight up in the air between the two players in the circle, and blows his whistle. The players, called *centers,* jump up as high as they can and each tries to tap the ball toward a member of his own team. At the same time the *timekeeper* starts to time the game with a stop watch. A regulation game consists of four 10-minute quarters with a 15-minute intermission between the second and third quarters. In high-school basketball they play 8-minute quarters, and in professional basketball, 12-minute quarters.

The timekeeper is kept busy, for there are numerous "time outs" called, usually to give the players a chance to rest for a minute or to get advice from the coach. When a "time out" is called, the timekeeper stops his stopwatch. He starts it again when play begins again. When ten minutes have gone by on the stopwatch, the quarter is over.

Basketball is really a simple game. Each team tries to keep the other team from dropping the ball in its own basket, and at the same time tries to drop the ball into the other team's basket.

A player is not allowed to run with the ball, but may *dribble,* which means that he must bounce the ball against the floor with one hand as he runs. He may pass the ball to a member of his own team. A player may not hug the ball to his body, but must hold it in his hands.

Only the ball is supposed to be touched. When two players each have both of their hands on the ball so that neither one has to give up, there is *jump ball* at that point on the court, like the one at the start of the game (and at the start of the third quarter.) This is called a *held-ball.*

When the ball goes out of bounds it is given to an opponent of the player who last touched it, and he throws it back on the court. It is thrown back in at the point at which it went out of bounds.

There are two kinds of fouls in basket-

Walt Frazier of the New York Knickerbockers.

Photos by George Kalinski

ball, and they are very important. A *personal foul* occurs when a player charges, trips, holds, or is rough with another player. A *technical foul* occurs when a rule is broken. When a player makes a foul, a player on the other team receives one or two *free throws*, or sometimes a throw-in from out of bounds. In making a free throw, the player stands on the *free-throw line*, which is 15 feet from the basket. He is allowed to throw for the basket, and the other team may not in any way interfere. His team scores 1 point for every free throw that goes into the basket.

The score is 2 points for every basket that is made from the field. When a team has scored, the other team puts the ball back into play by a throw-in from behind the other team's end line. At the end of the game, the team that has the most points is the winner. In case of a tie, a short overtime period is played. It may be a set period such as 5 minutes, with another overtime period if the score remains tied; or it may be "sudden death," with victory going to the team that first scores.

LEAGUES

There are leagues of college teams and professional teams. During the regular season—December, January and February—the college teams play against other teams in their leagues, and also against outside teams. In March, tournaments are held for the league winners. These include the National Collegiate Tournament and the National Association of Intercollegiate Athletics. There are also invitation tournaments—several during the Christmas holidays and the National Invitation Tournament at Madison Square Garden in New York City in March.

In professional basketball there is one "big league"—the National Basketball Association, whose teams are made up chiefly of former college All-Americans—and some smaller leagues. Professional basketball is a faster game because of its "24-second rule": When a team gets the ball it must shoot within 24 seconds or lose possession. In college games a team that is ahead can "freeze" the ball, passing it around among themselves.

One of the first great professional teams was named the Original Celtics. They toured the country in the 1920s, playing against any team, and beating most of them.

By far the most successful team is the Harlem Globetrotters, founded in 1927. They have traveled all over the world and have helped to make basketball popular in countries other than the United States. Basketball is an international sport and is played in the Olympic Games.

In the early years of basketball, the five members of a team had positions assigned to them—center, two forwards, and two guards—and they usually stayed in these positions during most of the game. In modern basketball, all players play the entire floor.

Basques

The Basques are a people who live in the northern part of Spain, in the Pyrenees Mountains, and in southern France, on the other side of the mountains. The three small provinces or states of Alava, Vizcaya, and Guipuzcoa, in northern Spain, are called the Basque Provinces because most of the Basque people live there. The Basques have dark hair and eyes and are usually of stocky build and medium height. Basques are not related to the Spanish or French people. Nobody has ever been able to discover where they originally came from. They learn Spanish in school, but it is not their native tongue. Their own language is different from Spanish and from every other language in the world.

The Basques are Roman Catholics and most are very religious. St. Ignatius of Loyola, who started the Society of Jesus (Jesuits), was a Basque. St. Francis Xavier, a priest who went to India and Japan to convert the natives to Christianity, four hundred years ago, was also a Basque.

The Basques are fine sailors and excellent fishermen. Most Basques live on small hilly farms and work very hard for their living. They grow wheat and vegetables, and raise cattle and sheep. There are some Basque shepherds in the western part of the United States. They take care of large herds of American sheep.

The little cap called a *beret* comes from the Basques, and most of the men still wear it. The fast and exciting game called *jai-alai* is the national game of the Basques. It is played against a wall, as handball is, but the players wear wicker basket scoops on their arms and use them to drive the hard rubber *pelota* (ball) against the wall.

BASQUE GOVERNMENT

The Basques have always enjoyed democratic self-government, even when the rest of Spain was ruled by a king. The kings of Spain agreed to respect the rights of the Basques, and in return for this the Basques gave the king their loyalty and obedience. Under these rights the Basques elected their own representatives to the *junta*, or assembly, of their state. These assemblies used to meet in the open, under trees. The most famous of these trees is the oak of Guernica, in the province of Vizcaya. The rights of the Basques were often written down in a charter or constitution called *fueros*. When a new king of Spain came to the

These men are doing a Basque folk dance, The Dance of the Sticks.

throne he would swear to uphold the fueros in return for the loyalty of the Basques. When General Francisco Franco became the dictator of Spain in 1939, he wiped out the rights of the Basques for the first time in hundreds of years.

There are about 800,000 Basques in Spain and France, most of them in Spain.

bas-relief, a form of sculpture, in which the figures are slightly raised from the background: see SCULPTURE.

bass

Bass (pronounced like *base*) is a word used in music that means the lowest or deepest part of a musical composition or the lowest voice, or instrument, in any musical group. In music for piano or organ the bass is the part sounding the lowest note. The left hand of the pianist plays the bass, while the organist plays the lowest notes with his feet. (There are separate articles on PIANO and ORGAN.) Each family of musical instruments has a bass member, usually named in this manner: *bass* drum, *bass* viol (see VIOLIN), *bass* clarinet, *bass* trombone, etc. A *bassoprofundo* is a man with the lowest and deepest kind of singing voice.

bass

Bass is the name of several kinds of food and game fish. Some of these are salt-water fish. The sea bass is one example of the bass that live in the ocean. A close relative, the *striped bass*, is one of the most highly prized ocean fish. It can be caught by fishing from a boat, or by surf-casting from the beach. This fish gives you a good battle when you hook it and it is delicious to eat. Striped bass may be 2½ feet long and weigh 20 pounds or more. "Stripers," as they are usually called, can be caught all along the Atlantic coast. *Rock bass* of deeper waters may be two or three times as large.

The fresh-water bass are members of the sunfish family. There are two main types, the large-mouthed black bass, and the small-mouthed bass. They are smaller than sea bass, averaging 6 to 10 pounds. Both are excellent game fish. They are found in fresh-water lakes and in some rivers. When they are hungry they will strike at worms, frogs, or grasshoppers used for bait. But the expert fisherman feels that it is a better test of skill to get them to strike at artificial flies or plugs.

The fresh-water bass, like their sunfish relatives, lay their eggs in depressions in the sand of a lake. The female fish clears out a little hollow and then lays the eggs in it. Then the eggs are fertilized by the male and the bass stand guard and chase off any other fish that approach.

Bass, Sam

Sam Bass was a famous bandit and outlaw in Texas about a hundred years ago. He was born in Indiana in 1851.

When he grew up he left Indiana and went to Texas to become a cowboy. He soon tired of the hard life of a cowhand and became a bandit. He robbed stagecoaches, banks, and travelers. Sam Bass was a daring outlaw, quick on the draw and a deadly shot with a six gun. The government of Texas was determined to get Sam Bass. Some of the state's fa-

mous law officers, the Texas Rangers, were sent to hunt him down. They surrounded him while he was robbing a bank in Round Rock, Texas. Sam Bass tried to shoot his way out, but he was killed by the Rangers. This was in 1878. There are many legends or stories about Sam Bass in Texas and the Southwest, and there is even a song about him called "The Ballad of Sam Bass."

basset hound

The basset hound is a short-legged hunting dog that has been used for centuries in France and Belgium. It is used in the United States to hunt rabbits, foxes, pheasant, and raccoons. It is also kept as a pet, because it is very good-natured and gentle, and devoted to its master. It is a one-man dog.

Basset hounds are fine for trailing. They have a keen sense of smell—better than that of any other dog except the bloodhound.

The basset is a large dog with very short, slightly crooked legs and a thick, heavy body. It stands between eleven and fifteen inches high at the shoulder, and is between twenty-eight and thirty inches long. It usually weighs between twenty-eight and forty pounds. The ears of a basset are extremely long, and hang down to its shoulders. Its face is long, wrinkled, and sad-looking, with drooping cheeks. Its tail is long and straight, and is held almost straight up in the air. The basset's coat is smooth—neither silky nor wiry—and it may be almost any color or combination of colors.

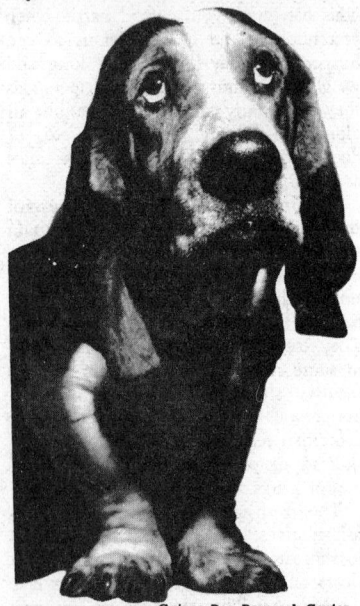

Gaines Dog Research Center

The basset hound is one of the most popular dogs on television because of its sad look.

bassoon

The bassoon is a musical instrument. It is a woodwind instrument (a kind of horn, made of wood) and has the bass, or lowest and deepest, notes of the "double-reed" family. A pipe almost 11 feet long, made up of several sections fitted together, is folded to make an instrument about four feet long. The Italians call it the *fagotto* ("bundle of sticks"). The range is from B♭ in the third octave below middle C, to E♭ in the second octave above. Music for the bas-

soon is most often written in the bass clef, using the treble clef for the highest notes. The *contra bassoon* has a pipe 192 inches long and sounds an octave lower. Some great composers, for example Beethoven in his *Pastoral Symphony* and Dukas in his *Sorcerer's Apprentice,* used the bassoon as a "comical" instrument to make funny-sounding deep notes: but other composers have used it for sad and melancholy music. See ORCHESTRA for illustration.

basswood

The basswood is a large tree found in almost all parts of North America and Europe. It is as well known by another name, *linden,* and is also sometimes called *limetree* and *whitewood.* The tree grows to be 75 to 100 feet tall, and is "deciduous," which means that it loses all its leaves in the fall. The flowers are small and so fragrant that they have been used in making tea and perfumes. Bees use the nectar to make a highly-valued honey. The seeds of the basswood hang in clusters from the center of special leaves, quite different in shape from the other leaves of the tree.

The wood of this tree is used for many purposes. It has strength, but is light and easy to cut and shape. Venetian blinds, chopping bowls and salad bowls, furniture, beehives, and many other light wood products are made from basswood. Because the wood has no odor, it can be used to make many different containers for food. The tough inner bark of the tree is used in making mats and rope.

bast, the fibers, inner part of the bark of a tree: see BARK.

Bastille

The Bastille was the famous old prison in the city of Paris, France. It was a solid fortress, with towers, containing seventy or eighty dark cells, and deep, damp dungeons. The fortress was surrounded by a wide ditch, called a moat, that was filled with water and was crossed by a drawbridge. The word "bastille" means any fortress, but it came to mean this particular fortress. Early kings of France stored their treasure there; and later it became a prison. People were often imprisoned there for years without having committed a crime, without a trial, without much food, and without visitors. Many were there because they were personally disliked by the king of France or his friends. The people of Paris felt that the Bastille represented the injustice and cruelty of the king and his government. On July 14, 1789, crowds stormed the gates and released the prisoners. This was the beginning of the FRENCH REVOLUTION, about which you may read in another article. The Bastille was destroyed soon afterward. Bastille Day, July 14, is still celebrated in France, much as the Fourth of July is celebrated in the United States.

Basutoland

The new independent kingdom (as of 1966) named Lesotho, in Africa, had for many years been known as Basutoland, a British Protectorate since 1867. Its area is 11,716 square miles, about the size of the state of Maryland, and in 1976, about a million people lived there. It is

an enclave (a country wholly surrounded by another country) within the Union of South Africa. The capital is Maseru, a city of about 14,000.

The Territory is mountainous. The people are Basutos, a Bantu Negro tribe. Most of them are farmers or work in South African mines and factories.

bat

Bats are small furry animals with wings. They fly like birds, but they are quite different. Bats are mammals, which means that they have babies and nourish their young with milk, just like cows or dogs or human beings. Bats are the only mammals that have wings.

Bats live together in caves or other dark places during the day. Just before dark, or before the sun rises, they come out, and the sky may be darkened by great clouds of them. A bat has huge wings for its size and is a wonderful flier. As it chases insects in the dark a bat twists and turns in the air better than almost any bird. It snaps up small flying insects in its mouth, but if it finds a big beetle, or other large insect, a bat may catch it between its wings for an instant and bite through its shell to kill it.

Bats can fly great distances. They have been found hundreds of miles out at sea. Bats cannot stand or walk well, because their knees bend backward instead of forward. They rest by hanging upside down from the roof of a cave or a barn or from a small branch of a tree. They hang by their big toes, which are very strong, and wrap their wings around their heads and bodies. Even very young bats can hang in this way.

Baby bats are born once a year, usually in late spring. Most bats have only one baby at a time. They build no nests, and the father bat has no interest in his young; the mother has to look after her baby all by herself. She carries it wherever she goes, clinging to her breast. The baby is quite helpless at first, but as it grows older the mother leaves it hanging up, and brings back insects for it to eat. After three or four weeks the baby bat is grown up and flies away on its own. Sometimes a baby bat falls down to the ground and squeaks for help. Then the older ones swoop down and try to pick it up. If they cannot do so, it will die. In caves which are lighted up for visitors the attendants often pick up hundreds of dead young bats.

HOW BATS FIND THEIR WAY IN THE DARK

People have always been puzzled by how bats see small insects in the dark, and how they avoid bumping into things as they fly around in the dark. Two hundred years ago an Italian, called the Abbé Spallanzani, made an experiment to find how they did it. He caught a lot of bats and covered their eyes with wax so they could not see. Then he let them loose in a room in which many bells were hanging on wires. If a bat touched a wire the bell would ring. But the bats flew to and fro in the room and avoided all the wires. The Abbé was puzzled. He was sure only that bats had some special sense. This special sense was only recently discovered when scientists found out that bats *hear* their way about. Their

eyes are small and weak, but their ears are more powerful than those of any other creature. As bats fly about they squeak. The squeak is so high-pitched that a human being can hardly hear it, but bats can. The sounds echo or bounce back from an object and are picked up by the bat's ears. Bats can hear the tiniest echo. They can hear the echo that comes back from a wire or a flying beetle and can tell exactly where the echo is coming from. Sonar, the device used by ships to detect submarines and obstructions such as icebergs, works in a similar way. See SONAR.

KINDS OF BATS

Most bats live in warm places. Some are very strange: there are brightly colored, even spotted, bats. Some grow very huge. The flying fox of Malaya and Australia is a reddish bat with wings that measure five feet from tip to tip. It feeds on ripe fruit and flowers. The vampire bat lives in South America. It feeds on blood and will bite a human being and drink blood from the wound. Lately a kind of bat has shown up in America that carries rabies, making it dangerous to man.

In North America there are some common bats that you can easily recognize. The little brown bat and the red bat are both small. The first is dull brown, the second is bright orange-red or chestnut. The hoary bat is bigger and is pale gray or yellowish, with brown wings. It flies high in the air, and is unusual because it has four babies at a time.

It is wrong to believe that bats will try to fly into a person's hair. In fact, a bat will fly up and down a room in a desperate effort to get away from anyone there. Bats are very timid and gentle creatures and one need not be afraid of them. They can easily be tamed but are a lot of trouble to keep as pets because they need so many insects for food. All the bats in North America eat quantities of insects such as beetles. They are friends of mankind and should never be harmed.

Bataan

Bataan is a mountainous peninsula on the island of Luzon, in the Philippine Islands. It was here that American and Filipino soldiers bravely made their last stand in the Philippines against the Japanese army, early in World War II. Although they finally had to surrender, other American and Filipino soldiers returned later in the war and recaptured Bataan from the Japanese.

Bataan is 517 square miles in size, which is half as large as Rhode Island. More than 90,000 people live there. Most of the people live along the low, eastern coast, where they grow rice and cotton. Most of Bataan is mountainous and rocky. Mt. Mariveles, in the southern part, rises to 4,700 feet and is the highest point on the peninsula. There are also forests and jungles in the central and western regions.

When World War II began, the Japanese army quickly captured all the Philippines, except Bataan. American forces led by General Douglas MacArthur began making their last stand

there in January, 1942. MacArthur had only about 50,000 men, while the Japanese had five times as many. The American and Filipino soldiers had little ammunition, food or medical suppiles, but they fought heroically for more than three months. MacArthur was flown out to take command of all the forces in the Pacific. A small group under Lt. General Jonathan M. Wainwright held Corregidor Island, off the tip of the Bataan peninsula. Those on Bataan surrendered to the Japanese on April 9, 1942. Corregidor fell to the Japanese the following month.

Lt. General Masaharu Homma was the Japanese general who captured Bataan. He was a cruel man, and he forced all his prisoners to march day and night for more than 60 miles to a concentration camp. Many died along the way, and many were killed by the Japanese soldiers. This terrible journey became known as the Bataan Death March. After the war, Homma was put on trial for his war crimes. He was found guilty and executed.

Batavia, a former name for Jakarta: see JAKARTA.

bath

Taking a bath is the act of washing the body all over. People in civilized countries know now that keeping clean is one of the best ways to be healthy and escape diseases. This was not always known. Still, in ancient Greece and Rome, two thousand years ago and more, the people took many baths and kept themselves clean. Then, paying no attention to the lesson they should have learned, people in Europe and in America for hundreds of years bathed very seldom. Less than fifty years ago in the United States, most of the people thought once a week was often enough to bathe, and the "Saturday night bath" was a standard joke. Very few American houses had bathrooms, which were thought to be an extravagance for the rich.

Most Americans know only two kinds of bath—the tub bath and the shower bath. Actually there are dozens of ways of bathing.

The Finnish bath, used also by people in the Scandinavian countries and in Russia, is a steam bath. It is taken in a separate bathhouse, usually a hut near the dwelling. Stones are heated and brought into the bathhouse, where cold water is poured on them. The water becomes steam, and bathers sit in the steam, and wash themselves with water. In the winter, when the ground is always covered with snow in those northern countries, they often leave the bathhouse and roll in the snow.

The Turkish bath may be found in many big cities of the United States, as well as in Turkey and other countries of the Near East. A Turkish bath is taken in stages. One stage is a steam bath. In another stage, the bather is rubbed and massaged and has hot air blown on him. The last stage of a Turkish bath is to sleep for some hours.

MEDICINAL BATHS

Many kinds of bath are taken for the sake of health. Some mineral waters—salt water, sulfur water, and so on—

have been used for bathing for many years, in the belief that they make the bathers healthier. The city of Bath in England, Baden ("bath") in Germany, and many other places known as *spas,* are places where people have gone to bathe for their health.

A bath in hot water is very relaxing. The *Sitz* bath is a tub of hot water, as hot as a person can stand, in which one sits. Mental patients are sometimes kept in tubs of water to make them relax.

ANCIENT BATHS

In cities of Greece, Rome, and other civilized countries, thousands of years ago, there were usually public baths to which anyone could go. The Romans built the biggest and most magnificent baths. They were great buildings of marble, beautifully decorated and very comfortable. These buildings were called *thermae* and had swimming pools, steam rooms and hot-air rooms for sweating, hot baths, rooms for dressing and undressing, and rooms for massages where the body was rubbed with perfumed oils. Some of the Roman public baths even had gymnasiums, theaters, and libraries.

When a Roman citizen entered a public bath he first entered a room called the *spoliatorium,* where an attendant took his clothes. Then he might go to the *frigidarium,* or cold room, where he could dive into a swimming pool filled with cold water. After this he would go to the *tepidarium,* a warm room where he could sit on a bench and get used to the heat. The walls and floor of the tepidarium were hollow and heated by hot air from a furnace below. While in the tepidarium he might get a massage and have his body rubbed with oils and ointments, or he might go to a special room for this purpose called the *alipterium.* From here he could go to the *calidarium,* or hot room, where there were tanks of hot water in which he could bathe. After the hot bath he could go to a separate chamber called the *laconicum,* heated by hot, dry air, where he could sit and bake himself while discussing politics with his friends. Then came a plunge in the cold pool, after which he would dress and leave. The cost of this was only a few pennies and some public baths were free. The baths of the emperor Caracalla were in a building so huge that each of its four sides was more than 1,000 feet long.

Bath

Bath is a resort town in England, one of the most famous resorts in history. It is also a manufacturing city with a population of over 84,700. There are warm springs at Bath and about 1,900 years ago when the ancient Romans colonized England they made Bath a watering place and built a fine bath there. (See the description of Roman baths in the preceding article.) The Anglo-Saxons later destroyed the Roman bath. In the 1700s Bath became a resort for the British nobility. Richard Nash (called "Beau" Nash) was the social leader and conducted a gambling house. Bath was heavily bombed in World War II.

BATH, ENGLAND. Population 84,700. On the Avon River.

Bath, Maine, is a historic shipbuilding city on the Kennebec River, 12 miles from the Atlantic Ocean. It has an excellent harbor. The population in 1970 was 9,679.

Bathsheba

The story of Bathsheba is told in the Bible, in the Old Testament. Bathsheba was the wife of Uriah, a soldier in King David's army. King David saw Bathsheba and wanted to marry her. He caused her husband to be sent to the most dangerous part of a battle. There Uriah was killed. King David then married Bathsheba, but all his life he was troubled in his heart, knowing that he had caused the death of Uriah. The great king Solomon was the son of David and Bathsheba.

bathysphere

A bathysphere is a hollow steel ball in which scientists go deep into the ocean to learn what life is like there. A bathysphere must be very strong and very heavy. It must be very strong because when it goes very far down the weight of all the water above it, plus the pressure of the air above that, would crush most hollow things. It must be very heavy. The scientists want to go down as far as possible.

The first bathysphere was built in 1930 by a man named Otis Barton, and he made the first descent in it with Dr. William Beebe, who has been the greatest underwater explorer. Barton's bathysphere was a ball made of steel 1½ inches thick. It weighed 5,000 pounds. The inside of it was only 54 inches, or 4½ feet. In this space two men had to huddle, along with all their scientific instruments. There were two windows in the ball, made of fused (melted) quartz, the strongest transparent substance known. Two tanks of oxygen were carried inside the bathysphere, so that the men could breathe. The bathysphere was lowered from a ship, and later lifted to the surface, by a steel cable ⅞ inch thick.

Beebe and Barton made many descents in this bathysphere. The deepest dive they made was 3,028 feet, or more than half a mile. The farther down they went, the less light there was. At 2,000 feet, the human eye could not detect the faintest glimmer of light. They photographed the fishes and other living things with powerful searchlights.

Other bathyspheres were made, much like the first one, but able to go deeper. Auguste Piccard was another great scientist who explored underseas in a bathysphere. His bathysphere went down 4,500 feet. In 1960 his son, Jacques Piccard, and a U.S. Naval officer, Lt. Don Walsh, set the world's record by descending to a depth of 35,800 feet in the North Pacific in a *bathyscaphe*. This is a bathysphere attached to a boat-shaped container of gasoline that makes it heavier. To rise, they let out the gasoline and make the bathyscaphe lighter.

batik

More than a thousand years ago the people of Java, an island of Indonesia, began to put pictures of fruits, flowers, and birds on their clothes. They knew that wax would resist water, so they covered the designs they had made on the cloth with melted wax. When the wax was stiffened the cloth was dipped into a cool dye made from vegetables and fruits. After the wax was removed by melting it again with hot water, the light pictures showed clearly against the dyed, colored background. Today this process, as well as the cloth itself, is called *batik*. Many batiks are very artistic and valuable.

Batista, Fulgencio

Fulgencio Batista y Zaldivar is the name of a Cuban president and dictator ("y Zaldivar" gives the name of his mother's family, in accordance with Spanish custom). He was born in 1901. In 1933 Batista led a revolt against the government of Gerardo Machado, who had been elected president in 1925 but had become a dictator. The revolt, which was called "the Sergeant's Revolt" because at that time Batista was a sergeant in the Cuban Army, was successful. After the army had run the country for a while, new presidents were elected between 1935 and 1940, but Batista controlled them all. In 1940 Batista himself was elected president for a four-year term.

The Cuban constitution does not allow a president to be reëlected. In 1944 Batista's term expired and the candidate he supported was not elected, so Batista was out of power. But in 1952 Batista again led a revolution and overthrew the elected government. In 1957 a strong rebellion against Batista was begun under the leadership of Fidel Castro. The rebels were successful and on January 1, 1959, Batista resigned and fled into exile. He died in Portugal in 1973.

baton

A baton is the wand, or stick, that the conductor of an orchestra holds in his fingers when he conducts. "Baton" is a French word meaning "stick." At first, a heavy stick, or cane, was used by the leaders of musical groups, and they pounded on a desk in order to keep time. That is where we get the expression "to beat time." Before the time of Beethoven, most orchestras were conducted by the first violinist, who would often stop playing to conduct with his bow. This probably led to the use of the light baton, which has been used by almost all conductors for more than a hundred years.

The baton of the "drum major," the leader of a marching band or drum corps, is a heavy cane, usually with a brass "head," like a ball, at one end, and tapering to a point at the other. It is used to keep time for the band or drum corps, to signal marching movements, and for display, or "show." Many drum majors, as well as drum majorettes, are able to perform many tricks of twirling, throwing in the air and catching, changing from one hand to the other, and passing the baton around the body, between the legs, etc., while on the march. There are standard books of instruction on the use of the baton.

Baton Rouge

Baton Rouge is the capital of the state of Louisiana. It is on the east bank of the Mississippi River and is 80 miles north of New Orleans. It was one of the earliest settlements made by French colonists. The settlement was made in 1719 on what was said to have been the site of an old Indian village.

Baton Rouge is a beautiful city, with flowering magnolia trees, picturesque lakes, and dignified mansions. It has 94 chemical plants and is known as "the Chemical Center of the South." It also is near oilfields and has one of the largest oil refineries in the world.

Across the Mississippi River from Baton Rouge are great sugar plantations. This region is known as "the Sugar Bowl of America." In Baton Rouge there are sugar refineries where the cane is made into granulated sugar.

The Louisiana state capitol is a beautiful building. It was built with marble from almost every marble-producing country in the world.

BATON ROUGE, LOUISIANA. Population (1970 census) 165,963. Capital of Louisiana.

battering ram

A battering ram was a military machine used, in the days before cannon were invented, to batter or break down the walls of forts and walled cities that were being attacked by enemy armies. It was a long, heavy, wooden beam with a metal cap on one end shaped like the head of a ram or male sheep. In the beginning, crews of one hundred or more soldiers used to swing the heavy beam and strike walls with the metal end. But arrows and stones from the defenders of the walls would kill many of the crew.

The ram was then improved to give the attackers protection from the arrows and stones of the defenders. A platform was built of wood and provided with wheels. A thick wooden roof supported by posts standing on the platform acted as a shield against arrows. The wooden beam, sometimes as long as 120 feet, was then hung from the underside of the roof by two very thick ropes. A crew of soldiers would take hold of the beam, and pull it back as far as they could, and let it go. The huge beam would then swing forward and strike against the wall with its iron head.

This was continued day and night with one crew relieving another when it got tired. No wall could withstand the terrific pounding of a battering ram for very long. Knowing this, the defenders tried in every way to destroy the ram before the wall broke down. Sometimes they tried to smash the roof in and kill the crew by dropping a heavy rock upon them. Another method was to throw down a heavy rope with a grapnel at the end. The grapnel was a long iron hook with five or six sharp curved claws on it. With this they tried to catch the head of the ram and pull it up over the wall. The name *ram* was used because a ram, or male sheep, attacks by charging forward and striking its enemy with its head.

battery

A battery is a container in which electricity can be made and stored. When the electricity is needed it will flow out of the battery to do useful work such as lighting a flashlight and creating a spark to burn the gasoline in an automobile's

engine. When one battery does not supply enough electric current, two or more batteries can be connected together. In fact, the battery got its name because the first batteries were made by putting together a group of electricity-producing devices, just as a battery of artillery is a group or row of cannons.

The article on ELECTRICITY explains how an electric current flows. There are tiny *negative* particles of electricity, called electrons, and there are tiny *positive* particles of electricity, called protons. The negative particles will flow toward the positive ones if there is a conductor, or substance that conducts electricity through which they can flow. A battery "makes electricity" by causing the negative particles to flow toward the positive ones. For larger quantities of electricity an electric GENERATOR is used, but the battery was the first device for making electricity.

The battery was invented in the year 1799 by an Italian scientist, Alessandro Volta. It is often called the *Voltaic cell* in his honor.

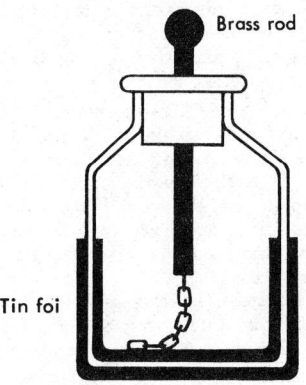

Brass rod

Tin foi

Leyden Jar

CONDENSERS AND THE LEYDEN JAR

For more than fifty years before Volta's invention of the battery, scientists had been experimenting with devices for "capturing" and storing electricity. Benjamin Franklin stored electricity in two pieces of tin foil on opposite sides of a piece of glass. One piece of tin foil held a negative charge, the other piece of tin foil a positive charge; and the glass between acted as a *dielectric*, or insulating material. When the pieces of tin foil were connected by a wire, a spark flew between them as the negative particles flowed toward the positive.

From this came the *condenser*, or device for storing electricity. The first condenser was the *Leyden jar*, made in the city of Leyden, Holland, in 1745. It was a simple glass jar with tinfoil coatings outside and inside. A brass rod through the top was connected to the inside tin foil. When a positively charged wire or rod was touched to the brass rod, the inside tin foil became positively charged— that is, it had more positive than negative particles of electricity in it. When the outside tin foil was connected to the ground it became negatively charged, with more negative particles in it. The Leyden jar would then store these different charges for a long time, but when the two pieces of tin foil were connected a spark would result.

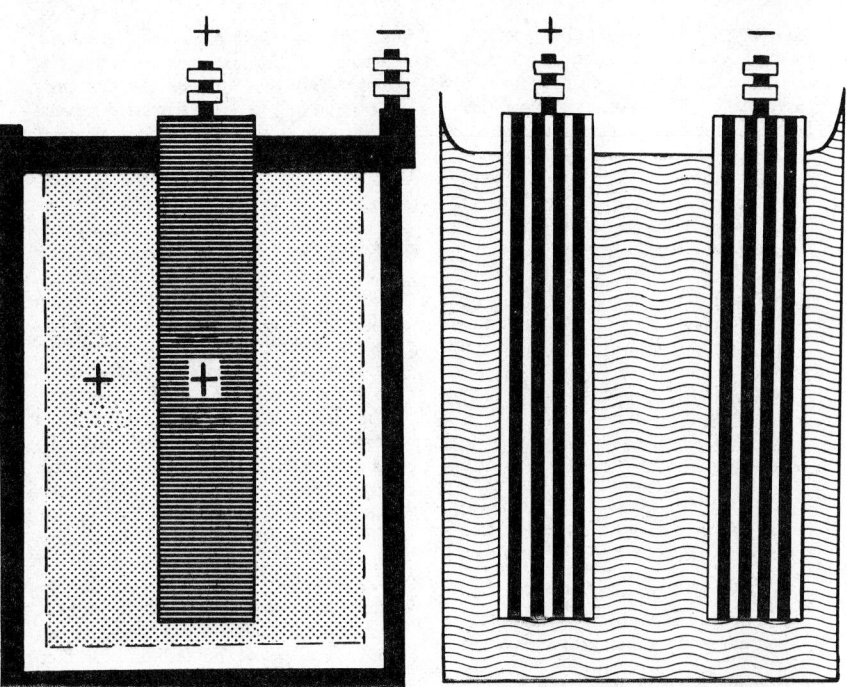

Left: A dry cell. The positive (+) pole of carbon lies in the chemical paste, or *electrolyte*. Between the zinc of the container and the paste there is a partial insulator, of cardboard or cloth, which does however let through some of the chemical to work on the zinc. The black across the top is not zinc; it is an insulating substance such as pitch to separate the positive and negative poles. In this picture the negative pole, like the positive one, ends in a terminal (connected with the zinc) to which a wire can be attached; but on a flashlight battery there is no terminal and the connection is made simply by touching a wire to any place on the zinc case. *Right:* A wet cell. The positive and negative poles are in the same chemical solution.

Condensers are still much used for storing static electricity, but a condenser will not produce a flow of electricity. It will produce a spark only until the two pieces of tin foil have balanced, or neutral, positive and negative charges. Then it will stop.

THE FIRST BATTERY

Volta's invention of the battery was based on two previous experiments. In 1752 a German scientist noticed that electricity will flow between two different metals on which certain chemicals are working. For example, if a clean copper penny and a clean silver dime are placed together and the tongue is touched to a place where their edges join, there will be a bitter taste caused by the flow of electricity. The saliva, which contains salt, produces the necessary chemical action. In 1786 Luigi Galvani, a great Italian scientist, observed that the leg of a dead frog, hung by a copper wire and allowed to touch a piece of iron, would move even though the frog was dead. This too was caused by a flow of electricity.

By correctly interpreting the reasons for both these seemingly strange effects, Volta made his first batteries. He used strips of zinc and copper and a solution of salt. Later he used a solution of sulfuric acid. In 1800 he announced his first real battery, which he called a "crown of cups," or series of electricity-producing cells. It was a row of cups filled with weak sulfuric acid. The cups were connected by strips of zinc and copper, dipped into the acid. The end of a copper strip at one end was the positive pole and the end of the zinc strip at the other end was the negative pole. These poles are called *electrodes*. Wires from the two poles, if brought together, produced a continuous flow of electricity.

The modern batteries that have resulted from Volta's invention can be either *wet cells* or *dry cells*.

THE WET CELL

A wet cell is a box made of a nonconducting substance, such as asphalt, containing sulfuric acid. (There are always several separate cells within the box, connected together.) The positive pole is made of lead oxide and the negative pole is made of spongy lead and both are in the acid. (Other metals can be used.) Electrons form on the negative pole, and when the electrodes are connected the electrons will flow toward the positive pole as long as there are any electrons to flow.

The wet-cell battery most often used is called a *storage battery*. It can be recharged by connecting the poles to a direct-current (DC) generator. In an automobile, the battery is always connected to the generator and if the engine is running the battery is being recharged at the same time that it is discharging electricity for the automobile's ignition, lights, horn, radio, or cigarette lighter.

Each wet cell within the battery box produces about 1½ volts and automobile batteries contain enough cells, connected together, to supply 6 to 12 volts in all.

THE DRY CELL

A dry cell is not as powerful as a wet cell but it can be carried because it is light and it has no liquid to spill out.

The dry cell is a zinc cylinder. Inside is a paste made of ammonium and zinc chloride (or there are other chemicals that can be used). Running into this paste is a pole of carbon. The zinc is the negative pole, the carbon the positive

one. The chemical action causes electrons to form on the zinc but to flow out of the carbon, leaving it with a positive charge. A wire from the zinc to the carbon pole therefore carries a current of electricity (that is, a flow of electrons).

A dry cell cannot be recharged. Gradually the zinc is "used up"; the chemical action causes holes to form in it. Then the flow of electrons stops.

When a dry cell is used, as in a flashlight, the circuit should be broken—that is, the current should be turned off—occasionally. Electrons may flow from the zinc faster than they can be replaced. After a momentary rest, the battery will again deliver full power.

See: ELECTRICITY; GENERATOR; INDUCTION.

battle. For any battle whose name begins with the words "Battle of," see the other name, for example WATERLOO.

Battle Above the Clouds

The Battle Above the Clouds was a battle that was fought between the Northern and Southern armies during the American Civil War. It was part of the important Chattanooga Campaign in 1863. The Northern army captured Lookout Mountain by charging up the sides of the mountain in a heavy mist. There were clouds floating between the mountain top and the valley below. Eight thousand Southern soldiers at the top of the mountain were killed or taken prisoner.

Battle Creek

Battle Creek is a city in Michigan, on the Kalamazoo River. It is best known as a center for the manufacturing of breakfast cereals. Battle Creek was founded in 1831 and soon became known as a health resort. The Battle Creek Sanitorium was founded in 1866. Cereal companies were started there by Charles W. Post in 1895 and by W. K. Kellogg in 1906. The population in 1970 was 38,931.

battledore and shuttlecock, a game very much like badminton: see BADMINTON.

battleship

For hundreds of years the battleship was the biggest, heaviest and most important ship of a fighting navy. It carried the biggest guns and was called also a *big-gun* ship or a *capital* ship. During World War II the aircraft carrier became more important and most navies have not kept their battleships active. Bombers instead of big guns have become a navy's chief artillery.

Early battleships were sailing vessels, made of wood. They were called "ships of the line of battle," which was shortened to "ship of the line" or "battle ship." The greatest of these ships were the ones used by the British admiral Lord Nelson at the Battle of Trafalgar against France in 1805. They had three decks lined with rows of cannons. The guns were fixed in place and the captain had to turn his side toward the enemy to fire a *salvo* (many guns firing at once).

Two great advancements were made during the American Civil War, when the *Monitor* and *Merrimac* were built. These were the first armored or *ironclad* ships, and the *Monitor* had its guns mounted in a rotating turret so it could point them in any direction. Wooden battleships went out of date overnight. At the same time steam-powered ships were replacing sailing ships.

The *Dreadnought,* a British battleship of 1906, was the first modern battleship. It was an "all big gun" ship, with ten 12-inch guns. It was 490 feet long. Later, battleships were built more than 800 feet long and the guns were 16-inch or even 18-inch. They were protected by armor of the hardest steel, 14 to 18 inches thick. The size of a battleship increased from about 16,000 tons to 45,000 tons. The crew numbered more than 2,500 men. No more powerful fighting machine was ever known.

But in World War II battleships proved to be of little use except to bombard an enemy shore—and even that required command of the air by carrier-based planes. The United States and Japan had great battleships but they never met in battle. After the war the United States began to put its battleships "in mothballs"—out of commission, but ready to bring out again in case of war. The most famous was the Missouri, called the "Big Mo," on which the Japanese surrender was received in 1945. It is a battleship of the *Iowa* class, the latest and largest battleships. The *Missouri* was retired in 1955. The last U.S. battleship to remain in service, the *Wisconsin,* was retired in 1957.

Baudelaire, Charles

Charles Baudelaire was one of the great French poets. He was born in 1821, and when he was 21 years old he inherited a large amount of money. But he was so extravagant that his family arranged it so that he got only a little bit of his inheritance at a time. For the rest of his life, Baudelaire had little money.

Gale Research Co.

In 1857 was published the book of poems for which he is most famous, called *Les Fleurs du Mal* ("The Flowers of Evil"). People were shocked by some of the poems and the book was forbidden to be sold until he took out certain poems. Baudelaire died in 1867, poor and unappreciated. Today, his poems are considered very beautiful and not at all shocking.

Baum, L. Frank

Lyman Frank Baum wrote the popular children's book, *The Wonderful Wizard of Oz.* Both children and grownups have enjoyed this story since 1900, when it was written. L. Frank Baum was born in Chittenango, New York, in 1856. He worked as a newspaperman in New York and South Dakota. He wrote many books, including his famous Oz books. *The Wonderful Wizard of Oz* was made into a musical comedy in 1901, and a moving picture many years later. Baum died in 1919.

Bavaria

Bavaria is one of the states of Germany. It is in the southeastern part, and both the Rhine and Danube Rivers run through it. It has many lakes and mountains, and its beautiful scenery has made it a popular place for vacations. Bavaria is the second-largest of the German states. Its area is more than 27,000 square miles, which is about as big as the state of South Carolina. There are more than 10,853,000 people living in Bavaria, or about four times as many as live in South Carolina.

The capital and largest city of Bavaria is Munich.

THE PEOPLE OF BAVARIA

The people in Bavaria are mostly farmers and they own the best farmlands in all of Germany. The farmers raise wheat, barley, hops, and fruit. They also have cows, pigs, chickens, and geese. The people who live in the larger cities work in factories. They make automobiles, airplanes, and many other things. In the city of Nuremburg, in Bavaria, are the best toy makers in the world. Other Bavarians work in mines that produce coal, iron, salt, lead, quicksilver, copper, and other minerals.

Bavaria is a beautiful place. There are high, snowy peaks of the Bavarian Alps in the southern part, near the border of Switzerland. In the forests there is hunting of wild boars and, in the winter, chamois that come down from the Alps to seek food. About a third of Bavaria is dense forest.

The October Festival in Munich is a gay holiday. In the streets and public halls there are orchestras, and gay, laughing people in the peasant costumes of the country. During the festival it is considered proper to misbehave.

BAVARIA IN THE PAST

At one time Bavaria was a part of the Roman Empire. Afterward it was part of the vast territory ruled by the great Emperor Charlemagne for a time. Still later it was made up of many different towns and counties. For more than 700 years, from 1180 until the end of World War I it was a kingdom ruled by members of the Wittelsbach family, but it was also part of the German Empire. In 1918, at the end of World War I, Bavaria became an independent republic for a few months, then it became part of Germany again. After World War II it was occupied by American troops. Many Bavarian cities, with large airplane factories and other industries, were greatly damaged by bombing in World

War II. In 1949, Bavaria became a member of the Federal Republic of West Germany.

BAVARIA, a state of the Federal Republic of West Germany. Area, 27,119 square miles. Population, 9,371,000. Language, German. Capital, Munich (1,065,104).

bay

The name bay is given to a number of different shrubs and trees. Some are evergreen trees of the laurel family. The glossy bay leaves are used as decorations and in ancient times were made into wreaths or garlands with which victors were covered. Other bay leaves have an agreeable fragrance and are used in flavoring foods. See also BAYBERRY.

Bayard, Pierre du Terrail

Pierre Bayard was a noble soldier who lived in France almost five hundred years ago. Bayard was a knight: a skillful, courageous soldier; a religious, kind and gay person. He fought under three French kings. In the great battle of Mézières, a city in France, he defended the city with 1,000 men against 35,000 soldiers. His stubbornness and courage saved central France from invasion by the soldiers of Spain. Bayard became a national hero, whose story has been written in books and songs from his time to ours. He was killed in battle, as had been nearly all his male ancestors for two hundred years before. He was born about 1475 and died in 1524.

bayberry

The bayberry is an American shrub that grows about 18 to 20 feet high. It may be cultivated, but is usually found growing wild. It is found mainly along the eastern seacoast. The plant has many small gray berries on it. These appear on the plant in the fall and frequently stay on through the winter. The berries are used for making bayberry candles. The berries are gathered in the fall. Then they are boiled to get out the wax. The wax is remelted to make it purer and then it is poured into molds to make the candles. The candles have a greenish color and a pleasant fragrance. Sometimes the wax is used in making scented soap. It has also been used to make sealing wax. The bayberry is sometimes called the *wax myrtle* and the *candleberry*. Another kind of bayberry, grown in the West Indies, is used to make bay rum, the after-shave and skin lotion.

Bayeux Tapestry

The Bayeux Tapestry is a picture story on linen of one of the most exciting events in history. It shows, in 72 scenes, the conquest of England by the Normans in the year 1066. The tapestry is a strip of cloth 20 inches wide, and it rolls out to a length of 231 feet. The tapestry was forgotten for centuries. Later, it was found again among the treasures of the Cathedral at Bayeux, in France.

The importance of the tapestry is that it was probably made by people who lived when these events took place. As a result, we are able to see how men of that time dressed, fought their battles, and died. It shows the weapons, the armor, and the kinds of ships that were used eight hundred years ago. The English wear mustaches, and the hair of the Normans is shaved all the way up the back of their heads. There are 1,512 figures of buildings, men, ships, trees, horses, dogs, and other animals. The figures are worked with a needle over the linen, like embroidery. (In a true tapestry, the pictures are part of the cloth.) Eight colors of smooth wool were used. The artist used his color boldly. A man's hair may be made green or blue, yellow or red.

The tapestry shows Duke William and his Normans crossing the English Channel; the battle against King Harold and the English; the horsemen, the archers, the foot-soldiers with battle-axes. Every phase of the battle is shown: Charges, defenses, dying men trampled underfoot. Finally Harold is killed by an arrow. The English have no leader and flee. The battle is over and the tapestry ends.

The tapestry is still kept in Bayeux.

Bayonne

Bayonne is a city in New Jersey, on a thin strip of land in the water that lies between New York City and Newark. The population in the 1970 census was 72,743. Bayonne has great oil refineries and shipyards. A bridge links Bayonne and Staten Island, which is part of New York City.

Bayreuth

Bayreuth is a city in Germany, forty miles northeast of Nuremburg. It is on the Red Main River, in the state of Bavaria. Almost every summer for more than 80 years, people from all over the world have gone to Bayreuth to hear its famous music festival, at which many fine artists perform the operas of Richard Wagner, one of the great German composers, who lived in Bayreuth.

Bayreuth was once a very beautiful city, with wide streets and fine buildings, but most of these were destroyed in World War II. The Wagner Theater, where the music festivals are held is on a hill overlooking the city. The theater was planned by Wagner himself. Wagner's grave is there, as is the grave of another great German composer, Franz Liszt.

Bayreuth is an industrial city. The people manufacture sewing machines, musical instruments, and china. There are more than 60,000 people living there.

bazooka

A bazooka is a special kind of gun. It was first used by United States infantry against enemy tanks, during World War II. The German tanks were covered with a steel armor so thick that no rifle or machine-gun bullet could go through it. Only a direct hit from a heavy cannon could stop them. What was needed was a weapon so light that a soldier could easily carry it, yet able to deliver a blow as powerful as that of a medium-sized cannon. The answer to this problem was the bazooka.

The bazooka is not really a gun. It is a rocket-launcher. It is a steel tube about five feet long and open at both ends. There are two handles attached to the bottom of the tube and a pair of sights on top, through which the soldier can look at his target. The forward handle is for the left hand and the rear handle has a trigger for the right hand.

Bazookas are usually fired by a crew of two men. The man who aims the bazooka holds it by its two handles and places the rear end of the tube on his right shoulder so that it sticks out past his back eight or nine inches. Then the second man puts a small rocket into the rear of the tube and pushes it down into the firing place. When the trigger is pressed, the rocket gives off a stream of smoke and flame from its tail, which rushes out of the rear of the tube, while the rocket itself flies forward with great speed toward the tank. There is an explosive charge in the nose of the rocket.

The word *bazooka* was the soldiers' name for the rocket-launcher. The name comes from a homemade horn made of a long, thick pipe, on which a famous radio comedian, Bob Burns, used to play. He called it a bazooka.

beacon

A beacon is a warning signal light on a high place where it can easily be seen. Hundreds of years ago people were warned of the coming of an enemy army by fires lighted on the tops of hills or mountains. Sometimes a chain of beacon fires lighted on one hilltop after another could signal a warning for hundreds of miles. Mount Beacon on the Hudson River in southeastern New York State got its name from the signal fires that were lighted on its top by American soldiers during the Revolutionary War.

Today a beacon is a light to guide or warn ships at sea or aircraft flying at night. The light is placed in a high tower, often at an airport, or in a lighthouse on a seacoast. The light is so bright that it can be seen for many miles. It may flash on and off, turn around, or just shine steadily. A magnifying mirror behind the lamp concentrates the light so it will be as bright as possible. Formerly, beacons in lighthouses were oil or gas lights with extra air blown on them to make them brighter. Now electric arc lights or powerful searchlights are used. The light may be white, green, red, or a combination of these colors.

bead

A bead is a hard little ball with a

This section of the Bayeux tapestry shows the crossing of the English Channel.

small hole through it. A string is put through the hole and many beads are fastened together on the same string. Beads are made of pretty materials and are usually used as jewelry, or to ornament clothing. But the word *bead* comes from an Old English word, *bede,* which meant "pray." In the Catholic Church and in some other churches, people count little beads on a string as they pray. A string of beads used in praying is called a *rosary.* Beads were useful in ancient times in the abacus, a device for counting. (There is an article on the ABACUS.)

Beads made out of shells, ivory, bones and stones have been found in the tombs and graves of people who lived thousands of years ago, before history was written down. Very ancient "eye-beads" have been found in Asia. Long ago people wore these beads because they thought they were magic charms that would keep the wearer from getting sick, and would also keep evil spirits away. Beads like that are a little bit like the good luck charms that people wear now.

About five hundred years ago, the glassworkers of Venice, Italy, made beautiful glass beads in many colors and shapes. Most glass beads are now made by machine. More expensive beads are made out of pearls, or amber, or semi-precious stones. Tiny glass beads are still sewed on women's clothing. This is called "beading." Larger glass beads are made into necklaces or bracelets.

The most famous beads in the history of America were made out of glass. They were the beads that Peter Minuit used in 1626 to buy all of Manhattan Island from the Indians. These beads were worth only $24, but to the Indians they were worth far more. The Indians used shells and beads as money, or "wampum." The Indians' beads were made out of shells, stone, horn, wood, and dried seeds.

beagle

The beagle is a small hound or hunting dog that is very popular as a pet in the United States. No one is certain as to just how long the breed has been in existence, but everyone agrees that it is one of the oldest in history. In England and the United States, it is used for hunting hares, cottontails, and jackrabbits. The beagle is a good pet, because it is generally good-natured and gentle, and it can easily be trained to obey orders.

The beagle is 12 to 16 inches high at the shoulder and weighs 20 to 30 pounds. It has long, hanging ears and a curved

E. P. Lehnert
This beagle, named Ardale's Rising Cloud, has won many blue ribbons at dog shows.

tail. Its coat is smooth and hard like other hounds', and it may be brown, tan, black, or white, or a combination of those colors.

bean

Beans are the seeds of certain plants called *legumes* (plants that have their seeds in pods). Beans are grown in most parts of the world and are an important food crop for both animals and humans.

When beans are kept in a warm, dry place, they become hard and dry and will last a long time without spoiling.

Before dried beans are used as food, they are usually soaked in water for several hours, then cooked. In some countries dried beans are fed to horses. Beans contain a great deal of protein, an important food element found in meat and cheese, and they are sometimes used as a substitute for meat. Beans and bacon are a favorite food of poor people in England.

In the United States, especially in New England, beans are baked slowly for many hours with pork and molasses. The beans used in this dish are called *pea beans* or *navy beans,* and are small and white. *Kidney beans,* which are red in color and about half an inch long, are used in many dishes. *String beans* or *snap beans* have a long green pod, or cover, with small gray beans inside; the entire pod is cooked and eaten and the pod is more important than the small beans inside. "String" beans got their name from the stringy fiber that runs along the length of the pod. This string used to be very tough and spoil the eating of the beans, so strains have been developed with a small and tender fiber that is hardly noticed. *Wax beans* are one of the "stringless" types.

Lima beans or *butter beans* are grown in warm climates and are an important crop in California. The pods or "shells" are removed and the beans are eaten. They are green and flat.

Soy beans have been grown in eastern Asia for more than five thousand years as a main food crop. They are dried and ground into flour, and provide many different kinds of food, such as vegetable oil, vegetable cheese, and a white juice that looks like milk and is drunk by many people in Asia the way Americans drink milk. In the United States large quantities of soy beans are grown in the midwest. Americans raise soy beans for oil, flour, cattle feed, and fertilizer. The oil is used in the manufacture of paint, soaps, linoleum, printing ink, and other products.

Bean, Roy

Roy Bean lived in the "wild west" of the United States when it was a territory of fierce Indians and self-reliant white men who usually took the law in their own hands. Bean was elected justice of the peace in Langtry, Texas, and because. this town is west of the Pecos River, he called himself "the law west of the Pecos." He owned a saloon, and there he held court. His regular opening speech announced that the court of law for the land west of the Pecos was open. He said that anyone who wanted a drink should have it then, and get it done with, so that the court could go about its business. The

speech went on to describe the crime of the prisoner on trial, and what the judge thought about him. He usually told the jury what decision it should reach, and the jury usually did as it was told. Judge Bean would then pronounce sentence. If a man stole a horse, or shot another man, the sentence was hanging. Although Judge Bean's methods were sometimes unjust, he helped make his district peaceful. He was born in Kentucky in 1825 and died in Texas in 1903.

bear

The bear is a large, fur-bearing animal found mainly in northern countries. It is related to the dog, but a bear can be a dangerous animal. Most bears, however, will not harm a person, unless the bear is wounded, or cornered.

When the bear walks it steps down on the entire sole of his foot, as a man does. This kind of walking is called *plantigrade.* The bear has large, strong claws. It uses these for digging ants out of logs, for catching fish in streams, and for climbing trees. Bears will eat almost anything. They eat the meat of other animals. They like fruits and roots and other vegetable matter. Honey is their special delight. When they find a log where wild bees have built a hive, they rip the log open with their claws to get at the honey. They do not mind the bee's sting, because their thick shaggy fur protects them.

The bear has a very short tail, so short that some people think it has no tail at all. The bear looks clumsy, but when it wants to it can run very fast. A bear has been known to run as fast as thirty miles an hour, which is almost as fast as a racehorse. Most bears can climb trees. Their long, strong claws help them in this. The larger, heavy bears seldom climb trees.

HOW BEARS LIVE

In places where it gets very cold in the winter, bears eat a lot in the summer and fall and store up fat for the winter. When the severe cold weather comes, they go into caves or other protected spots and go to sleep. The sleep may last all winter. It is a kind of hibernation, for the bears stay alive on the fat that they have stored during the summer and fall. Sometimes a bear will come out of its winter sleep if there is a warm spell during the winter. But then when it gets cold again he returns to his warm cave and goes back to sleep until the spring.

Bears usually give birth to twins. The young cubs are usually born during the winter, while the bear is in hibernation. They are not completely developed when they are born. The mother bear takes care of them until they are able to take care of themselves. The young bears are called cubs. They are very playful and full of mischief, just like children. If the cubs are caught and raised in captivity they can frequently be taught to do tricks. They are popular animals in circuses and zoos. They have a remarkable sense of balance and so they can be taught to roller-skate and ride a bicycle. In a zoo the bears quickly learn to beg for peanuts and other things to eat. They particularly like apples.

197

A mother bear and her cubs.

The largest bear of all lives in Alaska. It is a huge brown bear, known as the Kodiak bear. It is the largest living flesh-eating animal. These bears sometimes weigh as much as 1,500 pounds and stand 11 feet high.

The polar bear lives in the far north. It has white fur. This makes it almost invisible against the snow and ice of the Arctic regions, and helps it to sneak up on its prey. The polar bear is a good swimmer and it catches most of its food in the water. It eats fish, seals, and other arctic animals. Polar bears do not hibernate. They remain active during the entire year. The mother bear burrows in the ice or in snow drifts when the cubs are born. It takes several months before the cubs are able to get around and take care of themselves. The polar bear can walk on the ice because the soles of its feet are covered with long hairs. This keeps them warm and prevents them from slipping. Polar bears may be very large, up to 9 feet long and nearly 1,000 pounds.

In Europe the brown bear used to be very common, but now it is almost extinct. A few are still found in some of the heavily-forested parts of the continent. Large numbers of these bears still live in Russia and in northern Asia. They are closely related to our grizzly bears.

The only bear found in South America is the "spectacled bear," which lives in the Andes Mountains. In Africa there is one kind of bear. It lives in the north, in the Atlas Mountains. Very few of these Atlas bears have been found in recent years and it is feared that they will soon become extinct. In the highest parts of the Himalaya Mountains, in Tibet, lives the Tibetan black bear. Few people have ever seen this animal.

Polar bears of the Arctic region.

Beard, Daniel Carter

Daniel Carter Beard was a founder of the first Boy Scout organization in the United States. At first he started an organization of boys called "the Sons of Daniel Boone." It was named for the famous American pioneer and Indian fighter. In 1910 it became part of the BOY SCOUTS OF AMERICA (see the separate article). Daniel Beard was born in 1850. He  was an artist, writer, teacher, and student of nature. He made drawings for many books and magazines. He was also chief of the school of woodcraft known as the Dan Beard Outdoor School. He wrote many articles on nature and outdoor sports for magazines. He also wrote such books as *American Boy's Book of Wild Animals, Field and Forest Handy Book,* and *Wisdom of the Woods.* Mount Beard in southern Alaska was named in honor of Daniel Carter Beard. He died in 1941.

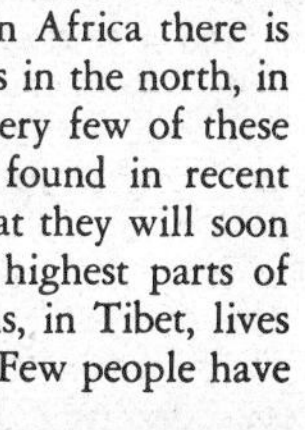

KINDS OF BEAR

In North America there are a number of different kinds of bear. The commonest bear is the black bear. This bear lives in the woods and mountains from Canada to Mexico. He usually weighs between two and three hundred pounds.

The brown bear is simply a black bear of a lighter color. Sometimes the brown bear is called the cinnamon bear.

The large bear of the western United States is the grizzly bear. The fur of the grizzly may be any shade from bright brown to a blackish-gray. Sometimes the tips of the hairs are a silvery gray. Such bears are known by the name *silvertip.* The grizzly may weigh as much as 1,000 pounds and be 9 feet long. Some authorities believe the grizzly can outfight any other animal including the tiger. Grizzly bears have been so ruthlessly hunted that they have almost become extinct. They are found now mostly in the national parks, where they are protected. One of the spectacles that thrills the tourists in Yellowstone National Park is to watch the grizzly bears being fed, early on a summer evening.

beards and mustaches

The hair that grows on a man's face is called his beard. When he lets it grow long on his chin he is said to have a beard. Hair that grows on the upper lip is known as a mustache.

Beards and mustaches are out of style in the United States, where most men shave their faces clean, but a great many American men wore beards and mustaches until about fifty years ago. Abraham Lincoln wore a beard, and two of the most famous generals who commanded the Southern armies during the American Civil War, Robert E. Lee and Stonewall Jackson, both wore beards, as did many other generals. General A. E. Burnside, one of the commanders of the Northern armies during this war, used to wear "side-whiskers," or hair that grew down both sides of the face, while he shaved his chin. After the war many American men used to wear this kind of beard, which they called "burnsides."

A short, pointed beard on the chin, known as the "vandyke," is still popular in France, where beards are much more common than in America. This beard is named after Anthony Vandyke, the great painter of Holland, who often painted men with short, pointed beards.

Napoleon III, who became emperor of France about a hundred years ago, used to wear a pointed tuft of hair on his chin and a stiff, straight mustache with waxed points. This pointed tuft of hair on the chin came to be called an "imperial," and is still popular with some European men. Paintings of Jesus often show him with a short beard.

The man who wears a beard is usually proud of it. To pull a man's beard is often a deadly insult. In the Bible there is a story of how David, king of Jerusalem, sent friendly messages to Hanun, king of the Ammonites, a near-by tribe. Hanun shaved off half the beards of David's messengers and sent them back to their king in disgrace. With their beards half shaven off the men were too ashamed to return to the king, so David allowed them to stay in a place called Jericho until their beards grew back. For this insult to his messengers and to himself, David made war on the Ammonites and destroyed them.

bearing

In many machines there is a shaft or axle that is constantly turning, or rotating. A part that carries the weight of a rotating shaft is called a *bearing*. The purpose of a bearing is to carry the weight of the shaft without slowing it down any more than is necessary.

The shaft, as it rotates, must rub against the bearing. This produces FRICTION (about which there is a separate article) and friction produces heat. The purpose of a bearing is to reduce the friction and the heat.

The smoother a surface is, the less friction there is when something rubs against it. Oil and grease reduce friction. Things that roll, such as rods and balls, reduce friction as shown in the illustration.

The simplest kind of bearing is a *journal bearing*. In machinery, the word *journal* means the part of a shaft that touches another surface while it rotates. A journal bearing is a hole into which

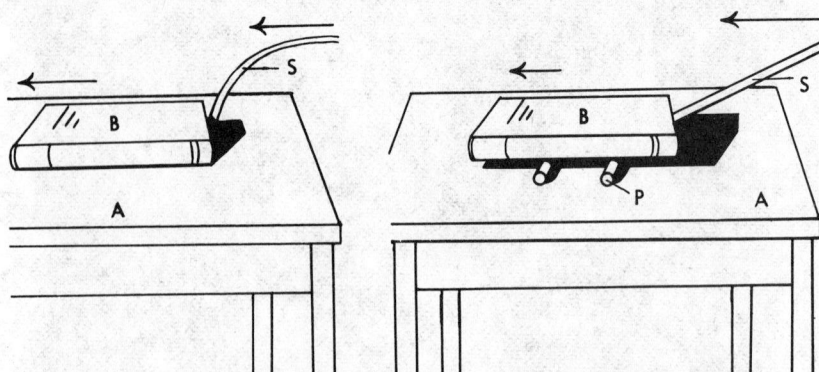

Left: If you push a book (B) across a table (A) with a thin stick, the stick will bend, because the book rubs against the table and does not slide easily. Right: Place some pencils (P) under the book, and it will roll easily, instead of rubbing on the table.

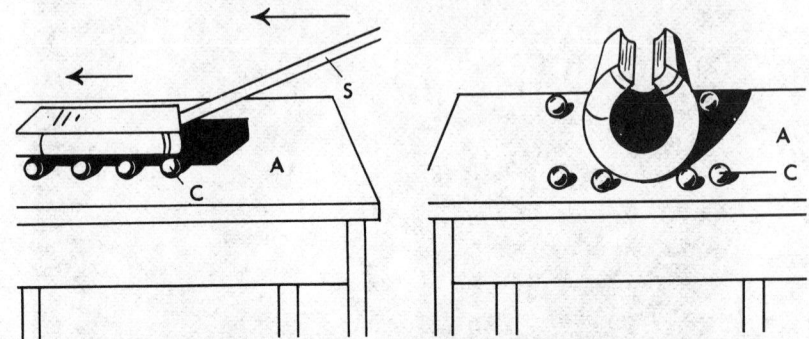

Left: If you place small steel balls (C) under the book, instead of pencils, it will roll even more smoothly, because balls roll better than pencils. Right: If the book could be rolled up into a perfect circle, it would be like the inside ring of a ball bearing.

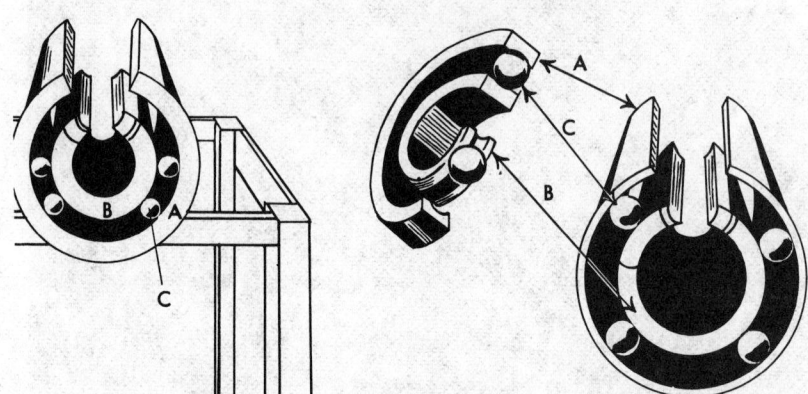

Now if the table top could be rolled into a circle around the balls and the inside ring, the design would be exactly the same as a ball bearing. (Of course, the circles are closed and form complete rings.) A regular ball bearing (right) has a groove, called a *cage*, in which the balls roll, and there are enough balls to fill the space between the rings.

the shaft is fitted. This hole is usually lined with a metal—bronze, or a special metal called *Babbitt*—that has been made very smooth. The bearing is "packed" with grease to reduce the friction still more.

The greater the weight borne by the turning shaft, the greater the friction. The bigger the surface that must slide or roll, the greater the friction.

The *ball bearing* is the most effective kind of bearing. It consists of two rings, between which there are enough steel balls to fill the space, perhaps ten to fifteen balls. The outer ring bears the weight. The shaft goes through the inner ring, which turns with it, helped by the balls. When a ball rolls, only a very small part of its surface touches the surface it rolls on, so the friction is the least possible.

But when a load is very heavy, the weight is enough to flatten a ball just a

little, even when the ball is made of the hardest steel. Therefore, for the heaviest loads *roller bearings* are often used. A roller bearing is like a ball bearing except that steel rods instead of balls go between the rings. The weight is distributed along the longer surface of the steel rod, so the weight at any point is less and the rod will not flatten as easily as a ball would.

A bearing must withstand not only the weight above but a sideways force, called *thrust*. This force tries to make the balls or rollers fly out from between the two rings. To overcome the thrust, tapered roller bearings are often used. In these bearings the rods are bigger around at one end than the other. The thrust is resisted by the bigger end.

In a watch, jewels are used as bearings. A "17-jewel watch" has seventeen bearings made of jewels. These are the same kind of jewels as are used in

rings and other jewelry, except that they do not have to be beautiful jewels. A jewel can be made so smooth that no oil or grease is needed, and it is so hard that friction will not cause it to wear out for many years.

Beatitudes

The Beatitudes are blessings that Jesus gave in his SERMON ON THE MOUNT, about which there is a separate article.

The Beatitudes describe what a man should be like in order to be blessed. He should be meek (which means not proud), he should be merciful, he should want to be righteous (which means honest), he should mourn (which means he should have sympathy for others), he should have a pure heart, he should be a peacemaker, and he should be willing to be made fun of or even punished for teaching and doing what is right. The Beatitudes also say that the poor will be blessed.

Beatrice

Beatrice is the beautiful lady who guides Dante through heaven in Dante's great poem called *The Divine Comedy,* written almost seven hundred years ago. The Beatrice of the poem probably describes Beatrice Portinari, a lady of Florence, Italy, whom Dante first saw when he was just nine years old. *The Divine Comedy* was written as a lasting memorial to her, for she died before it was written. She was born in 1266 and died in 1290, when she was only 24 years old.

Beauharnais

JOSEPHINE de Beauharnais, about whom there is a separate article, was the wife of the great French emperor Napoleon I. Her son Eugène de Beauharnais, who was born in 1781, was adopted as a son by Napoleon and held many high offices as a soldier and government official. He was a very capable man and deserved these high offices.

As a general in the French Army, Beauharnais helped Napoleon to win several important victories. In 1807 he was made Viceroy of Italy and would have become its king if Napoleon's power had continued. Beauharnais commanded part of the French Army when Napoleon unsuccessfully invaded Russia in 1812, and he did more than anyone else to save the army when it had to retreat. Napoleon later said, "Every one of us committed blunders; Eugène alone committed none."

After Napoleon was finally defeated in 1814, Beauharnais lost his power in Italy, though he remained a rich man. He died in 1824, only 43 years old.

Beaumarchais

Beaumarchais was the name with which Pierre Augustin Caron signed the books and plays and articles he wrote, and it is the name by which he is known. Beaumarchais lived in France during the time of the American Revolution and of the French Revolution. He played an important part in both revolutions. He helped the American cause in the Revolutionary War by persuading the king of France to sell guns secretly to the reb-

els. At the Battle of Saratoga, which many believe to have been the turning point of the war, nine out of every ten guns on the American side had been made by the French and shipped to America by Beaumar-  chais. In Europe, Beaumarchais is best remembered for two plays he wrote, *The Barber of Seville* and *The Marriage of Figaro,* both of which have been made into famous operas. Beaumarchais was born in 1732 and died in 1799.

Beaumont

Beaumont is a large city in southeast Texas. It is a port on the Neches River. Beaumont has vast oil refineries and also plants that process foods and make chemicals and synthetic rubber. The city grew after oil was discovered in the nearby Spindletop fields in 1901.

BEAUMONT, TEXAS. Population (1970 census) 115,919. County seat of Jefferson County.

Beaumont and Fletcher

Francis Beaumont and John Fletcher were partners in writing plays in England more than 350 years ago, in the time of Shakespeare. Beaumont and Fletcher together wrote more plays than any other great English author. They wrote so well together that it is hard to tell which man wrote which part. Francis Beaumont died young and it is thought that he worked on seventeen of the plays. He was born about 1584 and died in 1616. John Fletcher used many of Beaumont's ideas in writing other plays. Fletcher was born in 1579 and died in 1625. He wrote one play with Shakespeare, *The Two Noble Kinsmen.* Beaumont and Fletcher's plays were written in poetry. The most famous are *The Maid's Tragedy* and *Philaster.*

Beauregard, Pierre

Pierre Gustave Toutant Beauregard was an outstanding general in the Confederate, or Southern, army during the Civil War. He was born near New Orleans, Louisiana, in 1818, and graduated from the U.S. Military Academy at West Point when he was 20. Then he served in the U.S. Army until 1861, when Louisiana seceded. When the war was about  to start, he joined the Confederate army and started the opening campaign against Fort Sumter. Three months later he won the Battle of Bull Run. At the end of the war, in 1865, he was present at the final surrender of the South to General William T. Sherman. He retired to live in New Orleans, where he died in 1893.

beaver

Beavers are furry animals that live near water and are famous for their ability to build dams across streams, and houses, or "lodges," in which they live. Beavers, like mice, are *rodents,* which means that they gnaw with their teeth.

A beaver may grow as big as a large dog, about 50 pounds in weight; but it

is long and low, with a very flat, scaly tail, which serves as both an oar and a rudder when the beaver is swimming. The beaver's head is short and rounded, with small ears, and its hind feet are webbed and have special claws with which it combs out its thick, soft fur. This fur is double, with a dense mass of short hairs under long, coarse ones.

THE BEAVER'S LODGE

Sometimes beavers live in holes in river banks, but mostly they build large "lodges" in the middle of a stream or pond. A lodge is made of logs and branches, weighted down and tightly plastered together with stones and mud. It usually has several underwater entrances and an emergency escape hole, but the main part is a large circular room, most of it above water level, in which twenty or more beavers live.

If the water is not deep enough to protect the entrances to their home, the beavers deepen it by damming up the stream. With their huge sharp front teeth they fell trees, gnawing their way through their bases so neatly that the wood looks as if it had been cut with chisels. If the tree is too heavy, or to far from the water for the beaver to drag it, he will dig a special canal up to it and float it out. Choosing his site carefully, the beaver fixes his logs so that they cannot be washed away, wedging them securely between roots and weighting them down with stones and mud. Sometimes the finished dam is a giant structure that raises the water level many feet. Whole stretches of the Canadian countryside have been altered by the work of beavers. Not all the trees felled by beavers are used in making dams or houses. Many of them are sunk to the bottom of the water, near the house, where they can be reached in winter by swimming under the ice. These form a reserve of building material and of food, for the beaver's chief food is the soft bark of trees such as willows, poplars, birches, and alders, as well as water plants.

Beavers are very shy animals, hard to see at work; as soon as they sense danger they dive below water, hitting the surface a loud smack with their tails as a warning to other beavers.

Beaver fur is very valuable. At one time their furs were used as money, for they were the most important furs of the great fur trade that opened up large parts of North America. For nearly four hundred years they have been hunted so mercilessly that now they have to be protected, or they would be wiped out, as they have been over most of Europe. Beaver fur is used chiefly in making coats, but one hundred years ago it was more often made into hats.

Bechuanaland

Bechuanaland is a large territory in southern Africa, divided into two parts.

The new independent republic (as of September, 1966) named Botswana comprises the larger part of the territory, with an area of about 275,000 square miles and a population (in 1964) of about 243,-000. The designated capital is Gaberones, a city of about 15,000. This part of Bechuanaland was a British Protectorate from 1885 to 1966 but received self-govern-

ment in 1965.

The other part of Bechuanaland is a district in the Republic of SOUTH AFRICA. Its area is 52,393 square miles and its population about 223,000.

Nearly all of Bechuanaland is on a plateau—a high, level region about 4,000 feet above sea level. Most of it is desert. The people are Negroes who live in villages or small communities. Some of them go to Johannesburg and other cities in South Africa to work in mines or factories for a few months every year. There is some gold mining but most of the people live by farming and raising cattle.

Becket, Thomas à

Thomas à Becket was the Archbishop of Canterbury during the 12th century, when Henry II was king of England. These two men, one the head of the church, the other the head of the state, were the most powerful in all of England. They had been close friends, for earlier Thomas had been Henry's chancellor. But they took opposite sides in a great struggle between church and state. Thomas à Becket was murdered in his own cathedral by friends of the king. So great was his popularity with the people that the place of his murder became a shrine, at which even Henry II, who was indirectly responsible for his murder, had to repent. The famous long poem *Canterbury Tales* by Geoffrey Chaucer describes some of the pilgrims journeying to the shrine. Thomas à Becket was born about 1118 and was murdered in 1170. In 1172 he was named a saint.

bed

A bed is a piece of furniture to sleep on. It usually has a frame of wood or metal holding a soft pad or mattress.

Thousands of years ago, before man began to live in towns and cities, he lived in caves, and his bed was usually a pile of leaves with skins of wild animals on top. As man became more civilized he learned to raise his bed above the ground. The bed had become a fine piece of furniture five thousand years ago. The ancient Egyptians had high beds into which one had to climb with the aid of five or six steps. For a headrest they used a half-round piece of stone, wood, or metal. The ancient Greeks had beds with a wooden frame and a board at the head. The frame had bands of animal hide laced across it and over this lacing animal skins were placed.

The ancient Romans had very high beds with attached steps. Mattresses used by the Romans were stuffed with hay, reed, wool, or small feathers. Small cushions were placed at the head of the bed. The bed covers used by the rich were costly, usually purple in color, with beautiful designs embroidered in gold thread. The Romans even had a special funeral bed on which the dead person lay for seven days, in his best clothes, surrounded by flowers. This bed had short ivory legs and was covered with purple blankets.

About the year 1300, the *tester,* or canopy bed, became popular in Europe. This was a bed with a tall post at each of the four corners of the frame. The tester was a cloth cover that was spread over the tops of the four posts and held up in the center by a rope attached to the ceiling. Sometimes these beds had curtains on all sides. After the year 1400 these beds became very large, often 7 or 8 feet long by 6 or 7 feet wide. Some of them were so large that they were almost a room within a room. Louis XIV, king of France, had 413 beds in his different castles and palaces. Some of his beds were carved by great artists of that time and the crimson velvet curtains that hung from the tester were richly embroidered in gold thread and pearls.

After the year 1700, feather beds, or what are called "comforters" in the United States today, were used in Germany as coverings. Iron beds appeared in Europe and became popular because they were easier to keep free of bedbugs. After 1850 the mattress was usually supported by a bedspring. This was a mesh of interwoven steel wire or flat steel bands in a light steel frame.

MODERN BEDS

The modern bed is a boxspring plus an innerspring mattress. The length of each is 6 feet 3 inches to 6 feet 6 inches, and the width is: single bed, 30 inches; twin bed, 36 inches; double bed, 45 to 48 inches. The bedspring has about 32 upright coil springs, each being about 12 inches high; in a box spring these are completely enclosed in a cloth cover, with thin pads over the springs. Innerspring mattresses have several hundred soft coil springs, 1½ to 2 inches in diameter and about 8 inches high, around which is stuffed cotton, horsehair, or kapok, or any combination of these. Kapok is a light, fluffy material that looks like cotton and comes from the seeds of the silk-cotton tree on the island of Java.

Foam rubber mattresses are favored by many Americans although they are somewhat expensive. These are cream-white in color and made of springy, spongelike rubber. They do not have any springs or stuffing. Like other mattresses they are covered with a strong cotton cloth called ticking.

bedbug

The bedbug is an insect that lives in or near beds and bites people while they sleep. It feeds on blood. The bedbug is equipped with a mouth that is formed like a hollow needle. With this sharp tube the bedbug punches a hole in a person's skin and sucks out blood. But a bedbug may live for years without blood, because it can also eat cellulose from wood.

The common bedbug is a flat insect. It is reddish-brown in color and it would take about five of them to measure an inch. The bug gives off an unpleasant smell. In addition to man, the bedbug may attack other animals and poultry. The bedbug attacks by night. During the day, bedbugs hide in mattresses and beds, or in cracks in walls, floors, or furniture.

The loss of blood is not the only harm the bedbug brings to man. The bites itch fiercely and may become infected and cause trouble. The bug may also carry disease germs.

When bedbugs have gotten into bedding, it may be necesary to clean it with steam. Spraying the room with insect-killing chemicals is the method most used. Sometimes the entire room or house is *fumigated,* that is, all windows, doors and cracks are sealed, then a poisonous gas is set free in the room. This is dangerous and must be done by men who are experts in handling the poison gas.

Bede, the Venerable

Bede was the first great scholar to live and write in England. He was born about 674 and died in 735. Bede was a clergyman and was called the Venerable (saintly) Bede. He lived in a monastery, taught Latin, Greek, and Hebrew, and wrote. His most important work was his *Ecclesiastical History of the English People,* a history of the church in England. He wrote chiefly in Latin but he could also write in Anglo-Saxon, the language of the people, and translated the Gospel of St. John into it.

Bedlington terrier

A Bedlington terrier is a medium-sized dog that looks somewhat like a small sheep, because of the shape of its head and nose, and its woolly coat. It was named for the place in England where it was first bred, the shire (county) of Bedlington. Bedlingtons were first used as rat-catchers, and they used to be very scrappy dogs. Today they are lively but gentle and are popular as pets in both England and the United States.

A Bedlington is a slender, graceful dog. It stands about 15 or 16 inches high at the shoulder, and usually weighs about 23 pounds. It has long, hanging ears with a fringe of hair at the bottom, and a fluffy puff of hair on the top of the head. The Bedlington's tail is medium-long and slightly curved. Its coat is unusual. It is more like sheep's wool than dog hair. It may be a blue-gray, tan, or sandy in color, or a blend of these colors.

Bedouin

The Bedouins are an Arab people who live in the deserts of North Africa and Arabia. They are nomads (wanderers) who raise sheep and goats and move from place to place to find grassy pastures, living in tents. Bedouins consider themselves the "purest" in blood of all Arabs, directly descended from the original Arabs of thousands of years ago without intermarrying with other peoples.

A Bedouin man wears a long cotton shirt that reaches down below the knees and is open at the throat. Around the waist, over the shirt, he wears a broad leather belt or girdle. When it gets cold at night, as it often does in the desert, the Bedouin wears a loose black or black-and-white striped cloak made of woven camel's hair. His hat is a black or yellow-and-red striped cloth folded once and held in place by a rope of twisted camel's hair around the head. A Bedouin woman wears wide loose pants, a long shirt, and over this a wide piece of dark blue cloth that covers the head and entire body and trails on the ground behind her. Children wear no clothes at all until the age of about seven. Few of the Bedouins can read and write.

The Bedouin's tent is about 8 feet high by 20 feet long. The cloth covering of the tent is woven from goat hair dyed black and is stretched over a few light poles. The tent of the *sheik,* or chief of

the tribe may be 40 feet long. Usually there is a part curtained off for the women and children. A rough carpet or mat is spread on the ground inside the tent. Cooking is done outdoors on open camp fires. Bedouins get meat and milk from their herds, and they buy rice, vegetables, and honey from city Arabs on the edge of the desert. They also eat the giant locusts or grasshoppers of the desert and certain kinds of lizards.

Every Bedouin carries a rifle and a dagger and a great many of them carry long lances which they handle with great skill. They are all believers in the Mohammedan religion but do not pay too much attention to it. Women are treated with respect but work very hard, cooking meals, baking bread, weaving cloth on looms, mending tent covers, and doing other household duties, while the husband sits in front of the tent smoking his long pipe.

bee

The bee, like the ant, is a social insect. That is, it lives in groups in which every bee does certain work that helps the other members of the group. The bee is a wonderful insect. It knows how to make wax, and it knows how to gather nectar from the flowers and turn it into honey. It is the only insect in the world that makes something that man can eat.

In the beehive there are three kinds of bees: the *queen bee,* the *drones,* and the *workers.* It is the workers who really run the hive. Without them, there would be no hive at all, no babies, no queen, not even a drone. The worker bee is a female, and is about half an inch long. She has six legs and two pairs of wings. On her flat head are two feelers, and she uses them as we use our fingers when we are feeling our way in the dark. At her back, just where a tail might be, is a stinger. When she stings someone, the stinger is torn from her body, and she dies. But the worker loves her hive and her queen so much that she is willing to die protecting them.

When dawn comes and the flowers open, the worker bee leaves her hive to begin the day. From morning till night, she visits the flowers, sucking the nectar from them and gathering pollen as she goes. The nectar is the sweet juice buried in the flower. Pollen is the golden dust seen in the center of the blossom.

THE HIVE

The bee picks up as much nectar and pollen as she can, and flies back to her hive to store them. Sometimes she lives in the hollow of a tree. Sometimes she lives in a hive that has been made by a farmer. The hive the farmer builds looks like a box of drawers. All through the hive are little six-sided rooms, side by side, as well as on top of each other. These rooms are called cells, or *honeycombs,* and the walls are made of very thin wax. The wax that the bees use to build their cells oozes out of the underside of their bodies. As a flat piece of wax comes out, the worker bee tucks it under her chin like a napkin. There the wax stays soft. When the bee passes an unfinished cell, she places the piece of wax on it, smooths it, and polishes it.

The cells at the bottom of the beehive form the nursery. In some, little bee eggs are hatching. In others, the queen bee may be laying eggs that will grow into more queen bees, workers, or drones. The honey cells are higher in the beehive. Here, the worker bees are packing the honey and pollen that they will use for food during the winter when the flowers are gone.

THE QUEEN BEE

The queen bee is the largest of all the bees in the hive. Her stomach is especially large because the many eggs she lays each day are stored there. Like the workers, she has a stinger. All day long, as the queen lays her eggs, there are worker bees attending her. They clean her and feed her, because she does not leave the hive to find her own food. The worker bees even chew her food for her, because she must have so much food to make eggs that she needs help to digest it.

As the queen lays her eggs in cell after cell, the workers follow her to make sure that the eggs are safe and warm. In each cell they place food so that when the egg hatches, the baby bee will have something to eat. Then they close the cell with wax, and let the egg lie there until it hatches. After a while, out comes something that looks like a worm. This is called the larva. The larva eats all it can and falls asleep in a sort of shell that has grown around its body. While it sleeps, it grows. And while it grows, it changes. At last when it awakens, its warm robe falls off, and there is a beauti-

ful young bee. Some eggs hatch into worker bees; some hatch into drones; and some hatch into queen bees. The eggs that are going to hatch into queens are placed in larger cells. Worker eggs are put inside, and a special kind of food called "royal jelly" is spread around the inside of the cells. It is this royal jelly that makes the worker egg grow into a queen bee.

When the first young queen steps out of her cell, she looks for any queen eggs that haven't been hatched. If she finds any, she kills them, so that she will be the only queen in the hive. But the old queen is still there. Sometimes the young queen kills her. Sometimes they live together in peace for a while. But that cannot last long, for the hive would become crowded with two mothers and all their children. The old queen finally leaves, and her loyal followers go with her.

THE DRONES

The drones do nothing during all this activity. They just fill themselves with the sweets the workers carry in. They get big and fat, and are waiting for only one thing—to be married to the new queen. The worker bees let the drones live in the hive and eat all they want until the wedding. They know that one of the drones must marry the queen so that there can be more young bees. A few days after the queen is born, she leaves on her wedding, or *nuptial,* flight. She meets one of the drones in the air, and when she returns she is ready to lay her eggs. After the wedding, all the drones are driven out of the hive.

The queen bee lives two to three years,

1. Bees sometimes build hives on a branch of a tree, or in hollow tree trunks.
2. This beekeeper is showing the correct way to hold a hive frame with bees on it.
3. Smoke makes bees fill up on honey. They eat so much honey they become sluggish, and they can be handled much more easily in that condition than when they are alert.
4. The various stages in the building of a honeycomb and filling it are shown here.

but the workers live only about six or seven weeks. They work all the time and never rest. Their work is making honey from the nectar they have gathered during the day.

Beekeeping is a large business for many farmers. But the farmers have very little work to do, since the bee does all the work and manufactures the honey herself. The farmer has to have his hives near where the bees can get nectar, and he must also see that the bees have enough to eat in the winter. The farmer must also keep his eyes open for swarms, which are great numbers of bees all leaving the hive at once.

SWARMS

Bees can swarm for many reasons. Perhaps there are two queens in the hive, and one of them is leaving with her followers. The farmer tries to prepare for the swarming time by putting empty hives in places where the bees can see them. Then they will not fly too far away. The farmer knows, too, that if he can pick up the queen bee and place her in a new hive, all the others will rush after her, make her comfortable, and begin building new cells again.

Bees will also swarm if they do not like their hive, or if there is not enough food nearby. Sometimes they just want to return to the wilderness and live in trees again. The farmer will often try to prevent swarming by cutting the queen's wings. He knows that the swarm will not go far away from the queen. If the queen cannot fly away, the farmer will always be sure of capturing the swarm again. But if the farmer takes care of his bees, they will not fly away from him. Bees like comfortable homes and hardly ever move away without a good reason.

ENEMIES OF BEES

Like men, bees have enemies. There are some bees that do not like to work for a living, so they try to get into another hive to steal food. When a robber bee comes near a hive, she goes very slowly at first, and then suddenly darts into the hive. Now, if she had gone into that hive as if she always lived there, the other bees would never have noticed her. But a robber always acts like a robber. When the other bees notice the robber, they all rush at her and off she flies at full speed, to save her life.

Bees have worse enemies than robbers. In the southern part of the United States, there is a kind of ant that attacks the beehives and destroys every bee in it. Farmers take special care to protect their hives from these ants.

KINDS OF BEES

The bees that make the honey are called *honeybees*. There are other kinds. Some, like the honeybee, are social and live together in large numbers. Others live alone. These are called solitary. The *miner bee* is a solitary bee. She makes a hole in the ground, builds a nest there, and lays her eggs. *Carpenter bees* are very much like miner bees, but they bite into solid wood to make their nests. *Bumblebees* are social bees, and they also make honey, but it is not very good to eat. However, bumblebees are very useful to the farmers. They carry clover pollen from one blossom to another.

Wasps and hornets are not bees, though they are related to bees. See WASP.

Beebe, William

William Beebe is the name of an American naturalist, most famous for his studies of underwater life. He was born in Brooklyn in 1877 and first he studied birds. Then he became interested in life in the ocean and made several descents in bathyspheres, including one in 1934 that set a record of 3,028 feet. (Since then, men have gone much farther down; see BATHYSPHERE.) Beebe's expeditions to study birds and other animals have taken him to many parts of the world. His many books have been very popular; they include *Half Mile Down* (1934), and *High Jungle* (1949). He died in 1962.

beech

The beech is a large tree found in Europe, Asia, and the eastern part of North America. It is a deciduous tree, which means that it loses all its leaves in the fall. The beech usually grows 70 to 80 feet high, but many grow as high as 120 feet. The tree is most easily recognized by its bark, which is smooth, and light gray in color.

The wood of the beech tree is hard and strong, and is used in making furniture and utensils, and in the construction of houses. It also makes fine, long-burning firewood. The fruit of the beech tree, called beechnuts, are sweet and tasty. They used to be eaten as nuts, but are now fed to animals, or used as a source of cooking oil.

Beecham, Sir Thomas

Sir Thomas Beecham, a noted English conductor of symphony orchestras, was born in 1879. As a young man he organized and conducted his own orchestra in 1906, and in 1932 he organized the famous London Philharmonic Orchestra. He was perhaps most famous as a conductor of grand operas. He was often a guest conductor for American orchestras. He inherited wealth and his title of baronet from his father, manufacturer of Beecham's pills, which were advertised with one of the earliest singing commercials, based on a Christmas carol: "Hark, the herald angels sing,/Beecham's pills are just the thing./Peace on earth and mercy mild,/Two for man and one for child." He died in 1961.

Beecher, Henry Ward

Henry Ward Beecher was a famous American preacher. He was born in Litchfield, Connecticut, in 1813, and his father, Lyman Beecher, was one of the country's best-known preachers, but as a boy Henry Ward Beecher was not religious. Then he had a revelation and entered the ministry, first as a Presbyterian and then, for many years, as pastor of the Congregational "Plymouth Church" in Brooklyn, New York.

Dr. Beecher was noted chiefly for his eloquent sermons and made several tours to preach and lecture throughout the United States, but he also wrote books and for some years he wrote articles that appeared in many newspapers. He was extremely popular, and not only his congregation but the entire city of Brooklyn remained faithful to him when he was accused of having stolen the affections of a Mrs. Tilton from her husband. He died in 1887. Harriet Beecher Stowe, the author of the famous book *Uncle Tom's Cabin*, was his sister.

Beelzebub

In the Bible, Beelzebub is used as another name for Satan. Beelzebub is the lord of all the devils. His name means "Lord of flies" in the Hebrew language. The ancient Hebrew people thought that devils brought diseases, and that flies were really evil spirits or imps. One Hebrew book says: "The evil spirit lies like a fly at the door of the human heart."

beer

Beer is a drink that is made from grain (usually barley) that is mixed with water, made to ferment by adding a special kind of yeast to it (which turns it into a mixture called *malt*), and flavored with a plant called *hops*. The process of making beer is called *brewing*, and it is one of the most important businesses in the United States. Many people think it is wrong to drink beer, because there is alcohol in it, and alcohol can often be harmful. Many other people say this is not important, because most wines have three or four times as much alcohol as beer, and whiskey has more than ten times as much alcohol. More than half of the adults in the United States drink beer. But everyone agrees that no one should drink beer until he is grown up.

People have been drinking beer for thousands of years. It was known in Egypt more than five thousand years ago. The northern countries, especially Germany and England, became the biggest beer-drinking countries, while in countries farther south, such as France and Italy, wine is a more popular drink.

There are many kinds of beer, but in the United States the most important kinds are *lager beer* and *ale*. Lager beer is a clear-colored beer that is aged, or stored, for several weeks or months after it is made and before it is sold. Ale is the same kind of beer except that a different kind of yeast is used. Beer is often called "dry." This means it has very little sugar in it. In America people like dry beer. In some parts of the world people like a sweeter beer. Also, Americans like beer very cold and people in other countries prefer it cool but not icy. As with any other food or drink, it is all a matter of taste.

There are other kinds of beer: *Bock beer,* usually made in March or in another early spring month, is dark and sweet. *Dark beer,* or *Munich beer,* is a beer very much like bock beer, made all year 'round. *Porter* is a dark ale with roasted malt added for extra flavor and color. *Stout* is even darker and maltier than porter. Both porter and stout are most popular in British countries. Any dark beer often has caramel added to it, making it both sweeter and darker.

Beersheba

Beersheba is a town in southern Israel. The expression "from Dan to Beersheba" is often used in the Bible. It

means the whole of Palestine (modern Israel), because Dan is a town at the extreme northern boundary and Beersheba is at the extreme southern boundary. During World War I, Beersheba was the first city captured by the British in the Palestine campaign.

beet

The beet is a vegetable that has been grown since ancient times. There are many different kinds of beet. More than fifty .kinds are raised. The beet is mainly grown for its large root. Some beets have ball-shaped roots. Other beets have long, tapering roots. Most beets have red roots. The root is cooked and eaten. The leaves of the beet, or beet-tops, also are cooked and served in the same way as spinach and other "greens."

One kind of beet is the sugar beet. It is grown in the southwestern part of the United States. When the roots are ripe they are crushed in large machines to squeeze out the juice. This juice is mixed with lime, so it will not be too acid, and is then heated in large pans. This evaporates the water and raw sugar remains. This sugar is brownish in color. It is then dissolved in water and treated with charcoal, after which it comes out white. Then it cannot be told from the sugar made from sugar cane.

Beethoven, Ludwig van

Ludwig van Beethoven was one of the greatest composers of all time. He wrote wonderful music even when he was deaf and could not hear anything he wrote. He composed music in every style that was known in his time, and he explored new and entirely original forms of composition. He was known as the "great musical liberator" because he made people learn to respect musicians as they did writers and scientists.

Gale Research Co.

Beethoven was born in 1770 in Bonn, the city that is now the capital of West Germany. His grandfather and his father were musicians. Before Ludwig was five years old he showed signs of musical talent and his father immediately started to give him music lessons. When he was 10 years old he wandered into the cathedral and begged to be allowed to play on the big organ. The organist was highly impressed by his talent, and began to give him lessons. By the time he was 12 years old Beethoven was acting as organist, and the next year he became a player in the court orchestra and had his first work published.

When Beethoven was 16 his mother died and he had to become head of the family. Beethoven got a job as viola player in the court orchestra. In 1792, when he was 22 years old, Beethoven moved to Vienna, where he made his home for the rest of his life. At first he lived in a garret, then the Prince and Princess Lichnowsky invited him to come and live at their house. His compositions did not attract attention until 1800, when his First Symphony was played. At this time he was gradually becoming deaf.

Beethoven was a plain-looking man, who rarely smiled. Yet, his music expresses great warmth and emotion. To show his love for one woman, Giulietta Guicciardi, he dedicated his "Moonlight Sonata" to her. Beethoven was in love several times, but never married. Despite a reputation for a hot temper and irritability, he could be a warm and caring person. He had a great number of friends who were devoted to him throughout his stormy life. A strong man, Beethoven overcame deafness, financial disasters, and personal unhappiness, to become one of the most outstanding figures in the history of music.

Beethoven wrote nine great symphonies, the best known being the *Third*, or "Eroica," which he had dedicated to Napoleon Bonaparte, only to take back the dedication when he learned that Napoleon had made himself Emperor of France; the *Fifth*, whose opening measures spell the letter V in Morse code, so that it became the musical symbol of "V for Victory" during World War II; the *Sixth*, or "Pastoral," which showed his great love of nature; and the *Ninth*, with a great vocal chorus that he never heard (for he had become deaf). Beethoven died in 1827, at the age of 57

beetle

Beetles are a kind of insect. Most beetles have a hard, shiny outer skin or shell, and two pairs of wings. The front wings are of the same shell-like substance as the body, and are held out sideways when the beetle is flying. The hind wings are thin and transparent, with few veins, and are the ones the beetle flaps when it flies.

Beetles are the most numerous of all insects, and form the largest order of the entire animal kingdom. More than 250,-000 kinds have been named, ranging in size from some so small that they can barely be seen to some that are more than six inches in length. They are found all over the world.

Although certain beetles are very useful, many of them are enemies of mankind. Young and adults alike, they attack crops, damage stored food, and cost millions of dollars each year.

Among the worst of the pests, or harmful beetles, are the various "weevils." Among these are the apple-blossom, pine, palm, and cotton-boll weevils, which attack living plants. Others, together with the young of another beetle called the mealworm, are the worst destroyers of stored grain and dried foods. The bark beetles kill forest trees. The chafers, such as the cockchafer, the June bugs, the figeaters, the Japanese beetle, and the rose beetle, attack plant roots in their early life, and eat the leaves when adult. The young of the click beetles, called wireworms, do untold damage to cereal roots and root crops such as potatoes. The Colorado beetle attacks potatoes. The deathwatch beetle is found in old houses. The powder-post beetles live in wood. There is even a beetle in California that eats the lead in telephone cables, and is known as the short-circuit beetle! The corn flea, the cucumber beetle, and others, not only attack the plants themselves but also transmit diseases. However, certain beetles, such as the "ladybirds," are very useful to man because they eat other insect pests. An Australian beetle saved the orange and lemon industry of California from the attacks of an insect called the fluted scale; and other beetles are important in keeping down gypsy and browntail moths, houseflies, banana and palm weevils, and mealy bugs.

WAYS OF BEETLES

In their search for food and a safe place in which to lay their eggs, some beetles have acquired strange ways of life. Some live in ants' and termites' nests, and even look like those insects. Some, living in caves or under huge boulders embedded in the earth, have no eyes. Others can no longer fly, and have their outer wings joined together. There are beetles that live on the seashore and are under water whenever the tide comes in. There are beetles that are found only in museums, eating the stuffed specimens; or in hides and furs, or even in the corks of poison bottles. Beetles have many enemies—other insects, including flies, bees and wasps; birds and mammals, fish and reptiles, and human beings.

For protection, apart from their hard shells, some beetles are colored so that they look like moss or dead twigs. Weevils pretend to be dead when touched, and drop to the ground, where they lie still with legs folded, looking like seeds or grains of soil. The bombardier beetle gives off a puff of blistering smoke at its tail end, like a miniature explosion, when it is disturbed. Other beetles emit an unpleasant smell. The wasp beetle deceives its enemies by looking like a wasp. The flea beetle leaps away out of danger, ground beetles run or burrow, and tiger beetles run or fly away. Some beetles can make a noise, squeaking by rubbing different parts of their bodies together, as the longicorn beetles do, or by grinding their teeth, as cockchafer grubs do. They may do this as a warning to other beetles, or to attract their mates. Fireflies ("lightning bugs") attract their mates by flashing their lights on and off; certain tropical kinds even have special lights that they turn on when landing on a leaf!

THEIR STRANGE LIFE STORY

Most beetles lay only a few eggs at a time. Weevils lay single eggs, and may drill a hole for each; ladybirds lay them in batches, on leaves. A scarab collects a ball of dung, digs a hole, buries it, and lays its eggs in it; burying beetles do the same with the bodies of birds and small mammals. Chafers lay their eggs in the soil, bark beetles in wood, and some water beetles in a special case that they fasten to an underwater leaf. When the egg hatches, no little beetle comes out; instead there appears a curious little wormlike grub, or *larva*. Sometimes the grubs are active, running about and eating other creatures (as do ladybirds do), or eating plants, as do the grubs of bark beetles and click beetles ("wireworms"). Or the larvae may be legless and sluggish, as are those of weevils. Perhaps the most interesting is the grub of the oil, or "blister," beetle. It lies in wait on flowers, holds on to the legs of bees, and is carried back to the beehive, where

it eats the bees' eggs and honey.

As it eats and grows, the grub "molts" from time to time, shedding its old skin and growing a new, bigger one. It may stay in the larva stage only a few weeks, or several years, as with cockchafers and stag beetles. Then, at one of its molts, it turns into a *pupa* (that is, it develops a protective skin and lies quiet for a while). Inside this pupa skin, the larva is changing into a beetle. When it comes out it is fully grown, complete with wings, and ready to go out searching for food and a mate. This complicated life-story is called METAMORPHOSIS, about which there is a separate article.

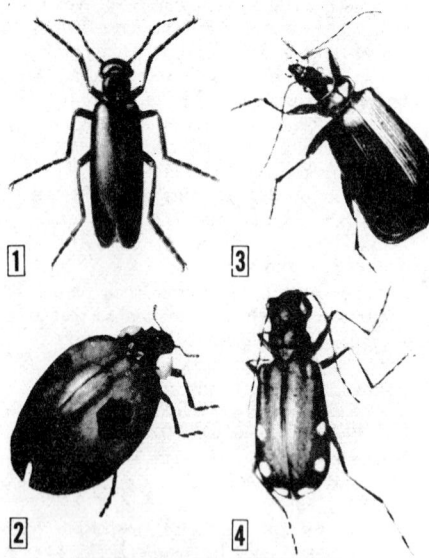

The group of beetles shown are all found in the United States.

1 is the black blister beetle. 2 is the ladybird; it helps farmers by attacking many harmful insects. 3 is the ground beetle. It feeds on snails. 4 is a tiger beetle, which destroys insects.

THE KINDS OF BEETLES

In North America more than 22,000 different beetles are found, of many different kinds. Among the best-known kinds are:

The brightly colored *tiger beetles*, which run about on paths on summer evenings, and whose larva waits at the mouth of its hole to catch passing insects.

The *water beetles*, some of them very large, with a larva that may eat fish; others such as the *whirligigs* and the little black *water beetles*, quite small.

The brightly spotted *ladybirds*, which are nearly all very useful.

The shining, metallic-colored *leaf beetles*, including the *asparagus beetle* and the yellow-and-black *Colorado potato beetle*, which are enemies of man.

The black-and-orange, or black-and-red, *burying beetles*, and the black *carrion beetles*.

The scarlet, or scarlet-and-black, *cardinal beetles*.

The *fireflies*, whose females are often wingless, called *glowworms*.

The *deathwatch, bark,* and *powderpost beetles*, which destroy wood.

The *scarabs* or *chafers*, including the sacred beetles of ancient Egypt, the *goliath, unicorn, rhinoceros,* and *ox beetles*, the *tumblebugs*, the *figeater*, the *June bugs*, the hairy, yellow-brown *rose chafer*, and the green-gold *Japanese beetle*, most

of which are enemies of man because their young eat plant roots.

The fierce-looking *stag beetle*, whose larva lives in decaying wood.

The *click beetle*, which can jump into the air with a "click" if it is lying on its back, and whose larva, called a "wireworm," is a great destroyer of root crops.

The *rove beetles*, or *devil's coach-horses*, which have very short outer wings, and which are mostly useful, living as scavengers in decaying matter; or which sometimes lead strange lives in ants' or termites' nests.

The *oil*, or *blister, beetles*, some of which are used in medicine.

The *weevils*, with their long-beaked heads, which are some of man's worst enemies.

The *black beetle* of cellars (not to be confused with the cockroach), whose larva is the destructive "mealworm."

The *longicorn*, with its tremendously long feelers, whose larva tunnels in wood; and the beautiful, metallic *Buprestis*, whose outer wings are used by native women as jewels.

beggars

People who do not work, but ask other people to give them money and food, are called beggars. Today, beggars are looked on with suspicion, because people feel that many of them could get jobs if they wanted to. But hundreds of years ago, in the Middle Ages, beggars were religious men who were very much respected.

The first beggars are supposed to have been a group of religious people called the *Beghards*, who lived in Europe about six hundred years ago. Many monks felt that they were honoring God by giving up all their possessions and taking a vow of poverty. These monks wandered through the cities, begging in the name of the Church. People believed that giving *alms*, or charity, to these religious men was a way of obtaining future happiness. These monks were called mendicant friars, which means "begging brothers." They used the money to help the sick and the poor. But many other people, who were greedy, and who saw in this custom a way to make some easy money, used begging to get rich without doing any work. More and more people who did not belong to the Church began to beg, until there were beggars all over Europe.

Countries began to pass laws forbidding people to beg, but little could be done to stop it. Some countries whipped beggars, or put them in jail if they were caught. Today begging is forbidden in many countries, but the laws are not strictly enforced. In the United States nearly every state, city and town has laws against begging.

begonia

The begonia is a plant with bright pink, red, or white flowers, and shiny rich green leaves. Some begonias are very small, less than a foot high. Others grow to be more than eight feet high. The smaller begonias make very pretty house plants. They can be grown in baskets or window boxes. They also make fine plants for the garden. Begonias should be planted in rich soil, with some sand

mixed in. They grow best in a shaded spot. Some begonias are known as Christmas Flowering Begonias because they have been trained to flower in December. Begonias can be grown without seeds by taking a single leaf on its stem and putting the stem in deep sand. In a few days the stem will send out roots. When the stem has roots it can be transplanted to a garden.

Beirut or Beyrouth

Beirut, also spelled Beyrouth, is the capital city of the republic of Lebanon. It is an important seaport on the Mediterranean Sea, for the shipment not only of the products of Lebanon but also oil from other countries, which is brought across Lebanon by pipelines. In the 1950s Beirut became one of the fastest-growing cities in the world. The population in 1973 was about 800,000. Beirut has factories that make soap, and thread of silk, gold, and silver.

Some sections of Beirut are very old, but most of it is modern and luxurious, with big apartment houses and fine hotels and restaurants. There are almost as many automobiles on the streets as in an American city. Because Beirut has two main religions, Christian and Mohammedan, there are both churches and mosques. There are three great universities, one founded by Arabs, one by Americans, and one by the French. Beirut's mild, warm climate and good water supply make it a very healthful city.

Beirut is very ancient. It was a seaport of Phoenicia 3,000 years ago and it has been ruled by ancient Greeks and Romans, by Arabs, and by Turks. Its ancient names were Berothai and Byrutus. In the year 551 it was wiped out by an earthquake and tidal wave. It became the capital of Lebanon after World War I, when Lebanon was put under French control, and remained the capital when Lebanon became independent in 1941. In the Lebanese insurrection of 1958 there was little open fighting in Beirut but there were some assassinations and minor bombings by small revolutionary groups. United States Marines stationed in Lebanon in 1958 spent their leaves in Beirut.

BEIRUT, LEBANON. Population 800,000 (1973 estimate). Capital of Lebanon.

Belasco, David

David Belasco was one of the most famous men of the American theater. He was born in San Francisco in 1854. His parents came from England, and went to California because of the great Gold Rush of 1849.

When he was still a child, young David became interested in acting and in writing plays. He appeared on the stage before he was ten years old. When he was only fourteen, he wrote a play called "Jim Mack, or The Regulator's Revenge," and he put it on in a hall in San Francisco. By the time he left San Francisco he had appeared in more than 170 parts, had written more than 100 plays, and had directed more than 300 plays.

In those days, just as now, New York was the center of the theatrical world. When he was 29 years old, Belasco decided to go to New York and try his fortunes there. In New York he became

an even bigger success than he had been in San Francisco. He gave up acting and turned all his attention to writing and producing plays and to managing actors and actresses. Many of today's methods and standards in the theater were originated by Belasco. Belasco worked up to the very end of his life. He died in 1931, when he was 77 years old.

Belfast

Belfast is the capital city of Northern Ireland. Northern Ireland is not part of the Republic of Ireland; it is united with Great Britain. Belfast is one of the important ports of the world, and it has one of the world's largest graving docks. A graving dock is a dock where the sides of ships are cleaned and repaired. Belfast is the most important commercial and manufacturing city in all of Ireland. For more than three hundred years the people of Belfast have been making some of the world's finest linen. There are also large tobacco and rope factories in Belfast, and many shipbuilding yards. The famous ship *Titanic* was built there.

Most of the people of Belfast live in brick houses, and the streets are wide and well-lighted. The sights of the city include beautiful botanical gardens, fine parks, and the famous Albert Memorial Clock Tower, a memorial to Prince Albert of England. More than 400,000 people live in Belfast.

Belfast was founded about 800 years ago, when a castle was built on the River Langan. About 160 years later, a band of Irish chiefs attacked the castle, and burned it and the town around it to the ground. The town was rebuilt and later grew into a city of great importance. During World War II, the Germans bombed Belfast because it had so many big factories. Many ships carrying American soldiers to Europe landed at Belfast.

BELFAST, NORTHERN IRELAND. Population, 450,000. Seaport on the North Channel of the Irish Sea and capital of Northern Ireland.

Belgian Congo (Zaire)

Zaire is an independent country in central equatorial Africa. Prior to its independence in 1960, Zaire was a Belgian colony and was called the Belgian Congo. When the country became independent, its name was changed to the Democratic Republic of the Congo. Unfortunately, the newly formed country was shaken by violence and political upheavals for nearly 6 years. In 1966, political stability was achieved under a new leader, President Mobutu. The country was renamed Zaire, and the Congo River became the Zaire River. The country's capital is Kinshasa, which was formerly called Leopoldville.

Zaire is rich in tropical vegetation, mineral resources, and abundant wildlife. The country is 905,328 square miles in size, which is larger than Alaska and Texas combined, and is subdivided into 9 provinces. The country's population is primarily Negro, and they represent more than 200 different Bantu tribes. Besides the Bantus, there are also tribes of Pygmies, a primitive jungle-dwelling people. The people speak many different languages, but Swahili is widely used. French is the official language.

In recent years, the economic conditions of the country have improved. Zaire depends primarily on agriculture and mining for its livelihood. Efforts are being made to expand industry in the country. Many of the people are farmers, and they raise cotton, rubber, bananas, and coffee for export. Corn and sweet potatoes are grown for eating. Mining is important, and many people work in rich uranium, copper, and diamond mines. Some of the people prefer to work in offices and factories in the cities.

LIFE IN ZAIRE

The Bantu tribes live in villages with houses of either reed or brick. The Pygmy tribes live in shelters made by covering twigs with large leaves. Other people live in the cities in modern homes.

Geographically, Zaire is made up of a low plateau in the country's center, which is surrounded by higher land. The central region is tropical rainforest and contains valuable wood such as mahogany. Also from the forest, the country receives rubber, palm oil, and nuts. The mountains of eastern Zaire contain rich mineral deposits. One of the longest rivers in the world, the Zaire River, begins its flow in the southeast corner of the country.

The Zaire River and its tributaries provide the chief means of transportation. The country also has over 3,600 miles of railroad, 22 airports, and 115,000 miles of road. More transportation is needed. Much of Zaire is tropical with a hot humid climate. However, in the higher mountain regions, the climate is cooler. The animal life of Zaire includes lions, elephants, monkeys, crocodiles, and other species.

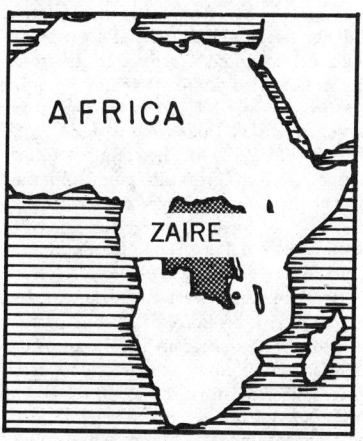

HISTORY OF THE CONGO

Until almost a hundred years ago, Zaire was a wild, unknown part of Africa, where no white men lived. When the famous explorer, Henry Stanley, returned from Zaire and King Leopold II of Belgium learned about the great wealth that was there, the king used his own money to send Stanley back to start trading stations along the Zaire River. In 1885 Leopold organized the territory with himself as king, but it was his personal property, not Belgium's. He called it the Congo Free State and allowed all nations to trade there if they paid fees or taxes to him. This did not work out well for the people of Zaire, who were treated like slaves. In 1908 Leopold gave control to Belgium, which ruled until Zaire became independent.

Uranium, important to atomic energy, was discovered during World War II and miners rushed to Zaire.

During the bloody years between 1960 and 1967, many white settlers and natives were killed. U.N. troops patrolled Zaire for 4 years to try to prevent civil war. In 1966, the then General Mobutu and the army took over Zaire. Despite another revolt attempt, the country remained in Mobutu's control. In 1970, he was elected to a seven-year term as President.

ZAIRE (KINSHASA). Area, 905,381 square miles. Population (1973 estimate) 22,500,000. Capital, KINSHASA. Languages, Kiswahili, Swahili, Tshiluba, Lingala, Kikongo.

Belgium

Belgium is a little country in Europe, between France and Germany. Belgium and the Netherlands together are called the Low Countries because much of the land is flat and lies below sea level. In both World War I and World War II, Belgium was invaded by the Germans, and many stories are told of how the Belgian people courageously fought the enemy. In size Belgium is not much larger than Maryland, but more than nine million people live there, which is about three times as many as there are in Maryland. Belgium has more people in it for its size than any other country in Europe.

THE PEOPLE WHO LIVE THERE

The people of Belgium are divided into two groups, the *Flemish* and the *Walloons*. The Flemish speak a language that is much like the Dutch language; some Walloons speak a language that is more like French. Almost all Belgians can speak French.

The Walloons are descended from the ancient *Belgae*, who were the original settlers in this region thousands of years ago. Many of the Walloons came to America and were among the early settlers along the Hudson River. The Flemish people are a Germanic people, and most of them live in the northern part of the country.

Most of the Belgians are Roman Catholic.

The Belgians are a very energetic and hardworking people. After World War II many parts of their country were in ruins, but the people quickly got to work and within a short time they had rebuilt these sections. The Belgians are extremely clean and neat. Their houses are always well-scrubbed and tidy, and even their streets and sidewalks are kept spotless.

Most of the people of Belgium live in cities and work in large factories. The Belgians are famous for their lace, carpets, and glassware, which are bought by people all over the world. The Belgians also manufacture large quantities of woolen goods, machinery, leather, and chemicals.

Many of the people in the cities own shops, and Belgium has sometimes been called a nation of shopkeepers. The owners usually live in rooms in back of the shops. They open for business very early in the morning and stay open until late at night.

Other Belgians work in the rich coal mines in the central and northern parts of the country. Still others are farmers. Though there is a fertile region in central Belgium (Flanders), the soil is poor in the southern and eastern sections. The farms are small but they produce most of the fruits and vegetables the country eats. There are many cattle, especially dairy cattle.

Everyone has to go to school between the ages of 6 and 14. There are also schools where boys and girls can learn various trades. Two universities are run by the government at Liège and Ghent, and there are other important universities at Brussels and Louvain.

Both grownups and children love sports in Belgium, though few sports are played in the schools. Football (which is what Europeans call *soccer*) is very popular throughout the country. The name of the national team is the "Red Devils." The most popular sport in Belgium is bicycle road-racing, and children follow the success of their racing heroes the way children in the United States follow the batting averages of their favorite players. Almost everybody owns a bicycle.

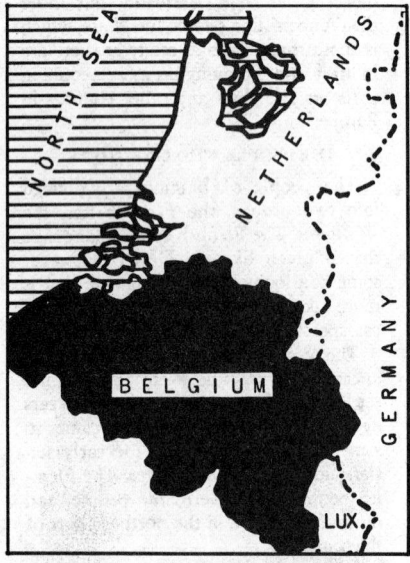

WHAT KIND OF PLACE IT IS

Belgium is mostly a low, level country, with many rivers and canals. The country is so low in the northwest that the people have had to build strong walls of stone and earth, called *dikes,* to keep the North Sea from flooding the land. In the southern part of Belgium the Ardennes Mountains rise to 2,200 feet.

The people living in the low plains along the coast and rivers have a climate that is fairly even. The average temperature is about 50 degrees; but the summers are hot, and in the hills the winters are very cold.

The rivers and canals of Belgium are very important to the people. They ship goods on the Meuse and Scheldt Rivers and through the canals, which connect many of the large cities. The canals are also used to irrigate the land, particularly in the northern region. Equally important for transportation are the many railroads, which reach all parts of Belgium. For its size, Belgium has more miles of railroad than any other country in the world. There are airports in the chief cities.

CHIEF CITIES OF BELGIUM

The leading cities of Belgium are:

Brussels, population 166,920 (including suburbs, (1,069,005), the capital. There is a separate article about BRUSSELS.

Antwerp, population 234,099 (671,872 including suburbs). See ANTWERP.

Liege, population 142,796 (438,825 including subrubs); manufacturing and coal mining center, in the eastern part of Belgium.

Ghent, population 223,145 (472,222 including suburbs); seaport and textile center.

HOW THE PEOPLE ARE GOVERNED

Belgium is a constitutional monarchy, which means that it has a king, a parliament that makes the laws, and a written constitution that protects the rights of the people.

The parliament is composed of two houses, the Senate and the Chamber of Deputies. The Senate has 178 members, who serve a four-year term. Some of them are elected, and some of them are appointed. Princes of the royal family automatically become senators when they are 18 years old. The Chamber of Representatives has 212 members, elected for a four-year term. The country is divided into nine provinces.

Every man over 18 years old must serve in the army for 12 months. There are only 70,000 soldiers in the regular army, but others who have been trained can be called if they are needed. The Belgian constitution forbids the army to attack another country, unless it is attacked first. There is a very small navy and an air force.

BELGIUM IN THE PAST

In ancient times Belgium was part of a big province of Rome, but the Romans did not develop it as they did many of their colonies and German tribes from the east settled there. Belgium became one of the small German nations that were controlled from time to time by a German emperor or by France. From about 1550 to 1700, Belgium and the rest of the Low Countries were ruled by the kings of Spain, but the Spanish rule was often a cruel one. Then for a hundred years it was ruled by Austria.

Belgium was always important to the big countries of Europe because it was so often a battlefield in their wars. The Belgian people always wanted independence, and often revolted against foreign rule, but the big powers always decided what government Belgium would have. While the French emperor Napoleon I was in control in Europe, from about 1800 to 1815, Belgium was ruled by France. Napoleon's final defeat came in 1815 at the Battle of Waterloo, which is a town in Belgium. The big powers then made Belgium part of Holland, but in 1830 the Belgians rebelled again and this time the powers let them have their own nation. Leopold, prince of the small German state of Saxe-Coburg-Gotha, was elected Belgian king. All the big countries agreed that Belgium would be neutral in any war and that none of them would attack it.

Belgium soon became one of the best-governed and most prosperous countries in the world. But when World War I came in 1914, Germany broke the agreement and invaded Belgium. The Belgian

king, Albert, resisted bravely but the country was soon overrun. For more than four years its farms were battlefields, its cities were destroyed or damaged, and its people almost starving. Americans contributed food and money to the Belgian people and also rebuilt the famous library at Louvain, which had been destroyed in the war. The Belgians rebuilt their country and became prosperous again.

In World War II, Germany again invaded Belgium. This time the Belgian king, Leopold III, surrendered after 18 days. The Belgians resisted the Germans through their "underground" until the American and British forces invaded Europe in 1944. Then again Belgium was a battlefield until Germany surrendered in 1945. Once again the Belgians have rebuilt and have recovered their prosperity. But they would not keep King Leopold, who had surrendered. From 1945 to 1951 the government ran the country without a king. In 1951 Leopold abdicated, or gave up the throne, and his son Baudouin became king.

Belgium, an original member of the United Nations and NATO, in 1948 became one of the BENELUX countries.

BELGIUM—SUMMARY

Area. 11,779 square miles. Greatest length 180 miles; greatest width 100 miles.

Population. 9,690,991 (1973 estimate). About half Flemish, half Walloon.

Language. French and Flemish are both official languages (and, in some places, German).

Religion. Principally (98%) Roman Catholic. Full freedom of religion.

Principal Cities. Brussels and suburbs (1,071,194, est. in 1973); Antwerp (226,-570); Ghent (149,265); Liège (147,277); Deurne (80,112).

Government. Constitutional monarchy. King has limited powers. Government conducted by premier and cabinet appointed by parliament, which has two houses: Senate, with one member for every 200,000 inhabitants, 60% elected by councils of provinces, 40% elected by people; and Chamber of Representatives, one member for every 40,000 inhabitants, elected by people. Both serve 4-year terms. Universal suffrage, with a fine for failure to vote. Provinces: Antwerp, East Flanders, West Flanders, Hainaut, Brabant, Limburg, Liège, Namur, Luxemburg.

Currency. Monetary unit, the franc, worth about 2 cents (U.S.).

Military. Universal military training, 12 months service at age of 18; total service in reserves, 25 years. Member of North Atlantic Treaty Organization.

Commerce. Chief industries mining (coal, metals) and manufacturing (iron and steel, glass, cotton goods). Exports, chiefly steel products and cotton goods, about $3,767,880,000; imports, chiefly machinery, meats, and grain, slightly more.

Transportation. 10,659 miles of railroad; 7,300 miles of highways; 983 miles of navigable rivers and canals.

Topography. Low, level country in north, averaging 100 feet above sea level, with marshes in west; rising in south to hills and low mountains of 500 to 2,000 feet (plateau of Ardennes Mts.). Principal rivers, the Scheldt and Meuse.

Natural Resources. About 35% of land can be farmed; 35% is suitable for grazing. Chief crops oats, rye, wheat, barley, potatoes, sugar beets. Minerals: rich deposits of coal, iron, zinc. Woodlands, 21.8%; forest products are important.

Climate. Average temperature 50°. Mild and rainy in low lands, drier and cooler in south.

General information. Flag, three vertical bars, black, yellow, red.

Belgrade

Belgrade is the capital city of Yugoslavia. It is located where the Danube and Sava Rivers meet, and it has been a place of importance since Roman times. Belgrade has been the scene of many battles because whoever held the city could control the Danube river shipping between central Europe and the Black Sea. Its famous fortress, which is many centuries old, still overlooks the two rivers. Inside the fortress are prisons and an old torture chamber.

Over the centuries, Belgrade has been ruled by many nationalities including the Turks, Greeks, Bulgarians, Hungarians, and Germans. Before World War I, it belonged to Serbia (later part of Yugoslavia). It was a modern city, with wide streets and beautiful buildings. But the Austrians bombarded it in World War I and reduced it to ruins. The city was rebuilt, but in World War II it was greatly damaged again by the Germans, who captured it. The Yugoslavs and the Russians retook the city in 1944.

Many of Belgrade's fine old buildings still stand, including the former royal palace, beautiful churches, a cathedral, and a fine theater.

BELGRADE. Population (1973 estimate) 697,000. Location, northeastern Yugoslavia. Capital of Yugoslavia.

bell

A bell is an instrument which, when struck, makes a ringing sound. There are many different kinds of bells. Among these are church bells, door bells, clock bells, fire-alarm bells, dinner bells, cow bells (hung around the cows' necks so that their tinkling sound helps the farmer to find them), musical bells (played in an orchestra), chimes and carillons, Christmas bells, school bells, burglar-alarm bells, and many others.

People have always made and used bells, as long as they have known metals. The first ones were made of sheets of brass or another metal, hammered flat and fastened together with rivets. But it was not long before men learned how to "cast" bells, by pouring liquid metal into a mold, or form, and letting it get cold and hard. This was first done in China, where the bells were believed to have a magical effect upon evil spirits.

BELL FOUNDING

The casting of bells is called "bell founding," and a most important part is the metal that is used, called "bell metal." The metal must be just hard enough to have plenty of *resonance,* or ring, but it must also be flexible enough not to break easily from vibration and from being struck. A mixture of copper and tin, with varying amounts of zinc and lead, is considered the best bell metal. More copper is used in large bells, however, than in small ones. Other metals such as iron, nickel, and steel do not make good bells, and the expression that is often heard, "as sweet as a silver bell," does not mean that bells are ever made of silver, for silver has very little "ring."

When the bell is cast, the molten bell metal is poured into a mold that is shaped like the bell. The inside mold is solid, and is called the "core," for it shapes the inside of the bell. The outside mold is called the "cope," and it shapes the outside of the bell. The shape of a bell is of great importance, for if it is too narrow, or too broad, the tone will be poor and lack carrying power. When the bell has cooled, the molds are taken off, and then tuning and finishing begin. The bell is tuned by shaving off bits of metal, as it is slowly turned around and around. This must be done very carefully, because once the metal is shaved away it cannot be replaced.

CAMPANOLOGY

The art of bell-ringing, as practiced in churches, is called "campanology," after the *Campania,* a district of Italy where the Bishop of Nola is said to have "mounted" the first large bell, about the year 400. Bells are hung in three different ways: (1) the bell is allowed to swing, and the "clapper," hanging down inside, strikes against the sides; (2) the bell itself does not move, but is struck inside by a movable clapper; and (3) the bell does not move, but is struck on the outside by a hammer. Ringing a bell by pulling on a rope is called "clappering," and it is still preferred by some campanologists. The stationary, or fixed, bell has many advantages, however. A better tone is produced, and there is less stress and strain on the bell tower and mounting.

CARILLONS AND CHIMES

Carillons and chimes are sets of bells that sound the different tones of the musical scale, just as the strings of a piano do. Chimes are simple sets of bells, sounding 5 to 10 tones. They are rung by pulling ropes to make the bells swing and ring. Usually teams of men play chimes, each man being assigned to pull the ropes for one or perhaps two bells. The teams practice until they can pull their ropes and ring their bells in perfect order and in perfect time. A tune or arrangement of tones is called a set of "changes" and "ringing the changes" has been a favorite recreation for hundreds of years. A carillon is more elaborate than chimes. The bells are stationary. The carillon-player, usually a fine musican, has a keyboard and a set of pedals with which he makes the clappers strike the bells. A carillon may have as many as 60 bells, giving it almost as wide a range as the piano. There are hundreds of famous carillons in the world. In the United States these include the ones at the Trinity and Riverside Churches in New York, at Scituate, Massachusetts, at Dayton, Ohio, and in many other places.

Chimes and carillons are usually placed high in *bell towers* and their music can be heard for miles around. Today the music of the carillon is realistically reproduced by electronics.

GREAT BELLS OF THE WORLD

The largest bell in the world is the Kremlin Bell, known as "The Great Bell of Moscow." It was cast about two hundred years ago, and although it weighs more than two hundred tons, it was hung on big wooden beams. When Moscow

caught fire, in 1737, the wooden beams burned, and it fell to the ground. A great piece broke out of one side, but it has never been moved from the spot where it fell. One of the most famous bells is "Big Ben," which is hung in the tower of the Houses of Parliament, in London. It was named for Sir Benjamin Hall, the official who installed it. When it was first cast, in 1856, they discovered a crack while it was being tested, and so it was melted again, and recast. (The big clock in the tower is also called Big Ben.) In Independence Hall, Philadelphia, is America's most famous bell, the "Liberty Bell." It was cast in 1751, and cracked as soon as it was struck. It was recast, and cracked again, but not enough to matter, and in 1776 it was rung in celebration of the signing of the Declaration of Independence. It has engraved upon it a text from the Bible, "Proclaim liberty throughout all the land unto all the inhabitants thereof." The crack later became larger, and the bell can no longer ring, but Americans love it because of its history. It is not the largest bell in America, however, for Montreal, in Canada, has a bell which weighs thirteen tons. Other large and famous bells are at Wroclaw (Breslaw), Poland; Rouen, France; and Vienna, Austria.

Dayton Chamber of Commerce

The Deeds Carillon in Dayton, Ohio, plays concerts on summer evenings. It is over two hundred feet high.

Bell, Alexander Graham

Alexander Graham Bell is most famous because he invented the telephone, but he was also a teacher of deaf and dumb people and a distinguished scientist. He was born in Edinburgh, Scotland, in 1847. Bell worked with his father, Alexander Melville Bell, who invented a system of lipreading for the education of deaf mutes (people born deaf who never know what speech sounds like, and so are unable to  learn to speak). In 1871, Alexander Graham Bell came to the United States from London to teach this new way of educating the deaf to students at Boston University. Here he continued his work

on an invention to send sound over wires. Bell's interest in sound and vibration as they helped him in his work with the deaf probably had a great deal to do with his work on the telephone.

Bell worked on his idea for sending messages by electric waves for about ten years, but it was not until 1875 that the way it might be done came to him. On March 10, 1876, while Bell was working in his laboratory, he spilled something on his suit and called to his assistant two floors above, "Mr. Watson, come here; I want you." This was the first telephone message. Bell spoke these same words to Watson again in 1915 when the first cross-country telephone call was made. But this time Watson could answer and said, "It would take me a week now."

Many other men worked on the idea of sending sound over wires, but Bell's telephone was the first to send spoken messages and to allow two people to talk to each other. Earlier telephones had a single opening through which a person spoke and listened. Modern telephones are more private, but the basic idea of the telephone is much the same as Bell first planned it. Bell died in 1922.

belladonna

Belladonna is the name of a plant that grows wild in England and the eastern part of North America. It is also called *deadly nightshade*. The plant is best known as the source of a drug called *atropine*, which is made from its poisonous black berries. Atropine is used to treat people suffering from heart trouble, asthma, hay fever, and other diseases. The plant grows best in damp, woody places.

Bellini

Bellini was the name of a family of great painters who lived in Venice during the Renaissance, or rebirth of art, about 500 years ago. All painted religious subjects.

Jacopo Bellini was the first. He lived from about 1400 to about 1465. His works include several Madonnas and paintings of the Annunciation and Crucifixion. Jacopo had two sons, both born sometime between 1425 and 1430; it is not definitely known which was older. **Gentile Bellini**, who died in 1507, and **Giovanni Bellini**, who died in 1516, often worked together. Giovanni became important in the Venetian government in addition to his importance as a painter. The works of the younger Bellinis included not only Madonnas and other religious subjects but also some portraits and other secular (nonreligious) paintings.

Bellini, Vincenzo

Vincenzo Bellini was an Italian composer of grand operas. He was born in Sicily in 1801. He started to write operas before he was 20 years old and was only 29 when he wrote *La Sonnambula* for La Scala opera in Milan, Italy. The same year his *Norma* was first heard. The rôle of Norma is considered one of the very greatest in all opera. It was first sung by Giuditta Pasta, a famous Italian soprano, and in America by the equally famous Rosa Ponselle. Other well known operas by Bellini included *Il Pirata* and *I Puritani*. He died suddenly while in France, at the age of thirty-four. His gift of sweet melody was outstanding, and it is known that he strongly influenced Chopin, and, for a time, Wagner.

Bellows, George

George Bellows was a famous American artist who was born in 1882. He loved baseball and he painted many pictures of tennis, polo and other sports. One of his best-known paintings shows Jack Dempsey and Luis Firpo in an exciting moment of their famous heavyweight championship boxing match. When he was only about thirty, George Bellows was the most famous member of a group of young artists who lived in the poorer and more crowded sections of New York City. These artists painted what they saw in these sections—backyards, crowded streets, or even the ashcans in the streets. Some artists who painted only very pretty things jokingly called Bellows and his friends "The Ashcan School" and they are still known by that name. George Bellows died in 1925.

Belshazzar

Belshazzar, in the Bible, was the last king of Babylon, a most important ancient city. On the night of Belshazzar's great feast, handwriting mysteriously appeared on the wall. It told of evil times to come. That very night Belshazzar's kingdom was conquered by his enemy, King Cyrus.

Benedict

Benedict is the name of fifteen popes of the Roman Catholic Church. The first Benedict was pope about six hundred years after Christ. The last, Benedict XV, was pope during World War I. He did not favor either side during the war, but worked very hard to make peace.

One of the most interesting of these popes is **Benedict XI**. He was pope for only one year, 1303–1304, but during that short time he did a lot of good. He was a great peacemaker. One thing he did was to have France and Rome get along together in a more friendly way. Benedict XI believed that people should be humble. One time when his mother came to see him, wearing jewels and a beautiful dress, he refused to recognize her until she put on plain clothes.

Benedict XIV was one of the best popes of all. He was a very learned man. He founded schools of physics, chemistry, and mathematics in Rome. He had all the best books written in English and French translated into Italian. He built many fine buildings. He was a very kind and cheerful man. He often said things that made people laugh. He was pope for 18 years from 1740 to 1758.

Benedict XV was born in Italy in 1854. His name was Giacomo della Chiesa. He was pope from 1914 until his death in 1922. He had become a priest when he was 23 years old.

Benedictines

Benedictines are monks of the Roman Catholic Church who live in monasteries according to the rules set down about 1,500 years ago by an Italian monk named St. Benedict of Nursia. The first and most famous monastery founded by St. Benedict was at Monte Cassino, Italy.

It has been destroyed four times, the last time during World War II in 1944. It has since been rebuilt. There are many other Benedictine monasteries all over the Western world, including the United States. One of the best known is at Atchison, Kansas. At Fécamp Abbey, in France, the monks make a famous liqueur (sweet alcholic drink) called Benedictine.

The Benedictines are also called the *Black Monks*, because they wear black robes instead of the brown or white robes worn by most other monks. Nuns as well as monks can be Benedictines. There are more Benedictines than any other kind of monks and nuns. All Benedictines live in monasteries or convents, which they promise never to leave. They spend their time working, studying, and praying.

Benelux

Benelux is a customs union of three small but rich countries in western Europe: Belgium, the Netherlands, and Luxembourg (the smallest, by far). Customs are taxes that a country charges when goods are shipped into it from a foreign country. This tax is also called a tariff, or duty. When two or more nations form a customs union, it means that no taxes will be charged on goods that the citizens of one of them sell to the citizens of another of them. Benelux was formed in 1948. Its name comes from the letters beginning the names of its members (*Be*-Belgium, *ne*-Netherlands, *lux*-Luxembourg).

Benes, Eduard

Eduard Benes was one of the leading statesmen of Czechoslovakia and was its last president while Czechoslovakia was a free country. When Benes was a young man, Czechoslovakia was still a part of the large Austro-Hungarian Empire. A group of Czechs led by Thomas Masaryk were exiles from their country, working to make it independent. Benes joined this group of exiles in 1915, when he was 32 years old. After World War I Czechoslovakia became independent and Benes served as its foreign minister (and for a brief period as premier, or head of the government) until in 1935 he was elected president. In 1938 Adolf Hitler, the German dictator, was trying to control Czechoslovakia and Benes opposed him, but Hitler was too strong and Benes had to go into exile again. After World War II Benes returned to Czechoslovakia as president, but this time the Communists of Russia used their power to rob his country of freedom. The Communists seized control in 1948 and Benes, heartbroken, died a few months later. He was born in 1887 and died in 1948.

Benét, Stephen and William

Stephen Vincent Benét and William Rose Benét were two brothers, both writers. Stephen was born in Bethlehem, Pennsylvania, in 1898, and he became famous as a poet and writer of short stories. His most popular story is *The Devil and Daniel Webster*. In 1929, he won the Pulitzer Prize for his book-length poem *John Brown's Body*. He died in 1943, and his unfinished poem *Western Star* was awarded the Pulitzer Prize in 1944.

William Rose Benét was born in New

York, in 1886, and he became an important editor and poet. His poem *The Dust Which Is God* won the Pulitzer Prize in 1942. He died in 1950, at the age of 64.

Bengal

Bengal is a former state of India on the Bay of Bengal. In 1947, the independent nation of Pakistan was created out of two parts of India. A large section of northwest India became West Pakistan, while the eastern part of Bengal became East Pakistan. (In 1971, East Pakistan became the independent nation of Bangla Desh, severing ties with West Pakistan). The part of Bengal that remained in India was called West Bengal. Its capital is Calcutta. The whole of Bengal used to be 84,000 square miles in area, which is about one-third as large as Texas. West Bengal is 33,928 square miles in size with a population of over 41 million. The people of West Bengal speak Bengali, and nearly all of them are Hindus.

Most of the people are farmers. Although modern methods of farming are now rapidly being introduced, many of the peole still use the crude methods of their ancestors. But the soil is very rich, and the farmers raise large quantities of rice. They also raise corn, tea, and tobacco. Others work in the cities in silk and cotton mills, and jute and tobacco factories. Some of the people are very skilled at carving ivory and stone. Most of the people live in villages in low huts with thatched roofs made of palm leaves and twigs. The climate of Bengal is hot and damp, and there are frequent severe storms called cyclones.

Unations

On a tiger hunt, in Bengal, everybody rides on elephants. The men sitting on the heads of the elephants are called mahouts.

In this Bengal village a woman health inspector is telling the villagers that they must be given blood tests to see if they are diseased and need treatment.

Most of Bengal is low country, not very much above sea level. The land is very fertile because there are heavy rains and because the Ganges and Brahmaputra Rivers, which flow from the high, snow-covered mountains in the north, overflow their banks every summer. Sometimes the floods are very severe and destroy houses and wreck the crops.

In the southern part of Bengal there is a large swampy region called the Sundarbans. It is a great jungle, where tigers and other wild animals roam. The Bengal tiger is very fierce and may enter a village at night and kill people. In the northern part of Bengal there are mountains, where coal, copper, and iron are mined. These mountains are part of the Himalayas, the highest mountain range in the world.

Although their high school has very little equipment, these Bengal children are anxious to learn, and study hard.

Most of Bengal can be reached by roads, railroads, rivers, or canals. Calcutta is the largest and most important commercial city, with over two million people living there.

Like other parts of India, Bengal has been ruled by many native kings and foreign conquerors. British traders began to settle there in 1620 and gradually got control. From 1765 to 1937, Bengal was governed by Great Britain; in 1937 Bengal became self-governing in local affairs; and in 1947, when all of India became independent, Bengal was divided. The Moslem portion went to Pakistan, and the Hindu portion remained with India.

BAY OF BENGAL. Arm of the Indian Ocean between India and Burma. About 600,000 square miles.

EAST BENGAL. Area 54,501 square miles; population 50,840,000. Former state of Pakistan. Capital, Dacca (population 740,000).

WEST BENGAL. Area, 33,928 square miles; population, 41,000,000. State of India. Capital, CALCUTTA.

Benjamin

The story of Benjamin is told in the Bible, in the book of Genesis. He was the youngest son of Jacob or Israel, who founded the Israelites (Jewish people), and he was the best-loved son; the name Benjamin, which means "son of the right hand," describes the youngest or the pet. Benjamin's brother Joseph became the most powerful man in Egypt and moved Jacob and all the brothers there, but first he scared his brothers by making them leave Benjamin with him. The descendants of Benjamin, the Benjamites, were one of the twelve tribes of Israelites that

became slaves in Egypt and were led to freedom by Moses; their territory in Palestine included Jerusalem and they were one of the three tribes from whom most Jews of today are descended. St. Paul boasted of being of the tribe of Benjamin.

Benjamin, Judah Philip

Judah P. Benjamin was a statesman of the Confederacy, or South, during the Civil War in America, and was also a famous lawyer. He was born in 1811 on the island of St. Croix, in the West Indies, of Jewish ancestry. As a child he was taken to Charleston, South Carolina, and as a young man he settled in New Orleans, Louisiana. There he became a prominent lawyer. As a Senator from Louisiana he tried to persuade the United States Senate to let the South secede in peace; but when war broke out anyway he stayed with the South and served as Secretary of War and then Secretary of State in the Confederate cabinet. When the South lost the war he went to England, studied English law, and became one of the most successful lawyers in London. He died in 1884.

Bennett, Arnold

Arnold Bennett was an English novelist. He was born in 1867 and died in 1931. Most of his novels were about the "Five Towns" district of central England, where most of the people work in potteries, making chinaware. Bennett's most famous novel was *The Old Wives' Tale*, published in 1908.

Bennett, Floyd

Floyd Bennett, an early United States flier, was Richard E. Byrd's pilot on the first flight ever made over the North Pole, on May 9, 1926—the first time either pole had been crossed over by aircraft. Byrd and Bennett received many decorations for their achievement, including the Congressional Medal of Honor. They next planned to fly from New York to Paris, but their new plane crashed in its test flight and Bennett was seriously injured. This delayed Byrd's plans, and meantime Charles A. Lindbergh had made the first solo nonstop flight across the Atlantic. In 1928, Byrd and Bennett were planning to fly over the South Pole when news came that three transatlantic fliers coming from Ireland were stranded on Greenly Island in the Gulf of St. Lawrence. Bennett, though ill, attempted to fly to their rescue, but contracted pneumonia on the way and died soon afterward in Quebec. Brooklyn's first airport was named for him in 1931.

Bennett, James Gordon

James Bennett was an American newspaperman who lived more than a hundred years ago. He was the founder of the New York *Herald*, one of the two papers that became the *Herald Tribune*. Bennett was born in Scotland in 1795, and he came to the United States when he was 24 years old. He worked on several newspapers until 1835, when he started the *Herald*. He had only five hundred dol-

lars to begin with, and he published the newspaper from a basement. It cost one cent, and it had only four pages. Bennett made many enemies, but with lively news he built his newspaper into a great success. He was the first to hire foreign reporters, who sent him news from other countries. He was also the first to publish a newspaper every day in the year. When Bennett died in 1872, the *Herald* had become one of the most famous newspapers in the country. His son, also named James Gordon Bennett, carried on the publishing of the *Herald*. He is best remembered for having sent Henry M. Stanley to Africa to find Dr. Livingstone (see STANLEY). He was born in 1841 and died in 1918.

Benton, Thomas Hart

Thomas Hart Benton is the name of a well-known American painter. He was born in Missouri in 1889, and grew up in the Midwest. His most famous paintings are of people and farm life in that part of the United States that he knew so well. When he was 17 years old, he got a job as a cartoonist on a newspaper in Missouri, but later he gave this up for painting. One of his best-known paintings is called *Cotton Pickers*. Benton also painted murals (large paintings on walls). Some of Benton's best murals are in the state legislature buildings of Indiana and Missouri. He died in 1975.

Thomas Hart Benton was the grand-nephew of a famous American statesman, who had exactly the same name, and who lived about 150 years ago. This Thomas Hart Benton was Andrew Jackson's personal assistant in the War of 1812. After the war he moved to Missouri and founded a newspaper called the *Missouri Inquirer*. But his most important work was as a United States Senator. He was a Senator for 30 years, and several of his speeches in the Senate are famous. He was born in 1782 and died in 1858.

benzene

Benzene is a chemical composed of hydrogen and carbon. It is used in making many dyes and explosives.

Benzene is of particular interest to chemists because the atoms in it form a sort of ring, called the *benzene ring,* that is also found in many other chemicals. There is also a different chemical, called *benzine,* that is somewhat like gasoline. It is used as a cleaning fluid and can also be used in automobiles.

Beowulf

Beowulf is the hero of the earliest known poem that was written in the Anglo-Saxon language spoken in England more than a thousand years ago. The poem is a saga, or epic—a long poem that tells a story about a hero. Beowulf, a Norse prince in Sweden, went to Denmark and killed a monster, Grendel. Later he became king in his own country. He died finally killing another monster, a dragon. *Beowulf* is of great importance to students of the Old English language.

Berbers

The Berbers are a large group of people who live in North Africa. They were one of the earliest groups to settle in that part of the world, and over the centuries they have become mixed with Arabs, Europeans, and Negroes. Because of this mixing, they are usually identified by their language rather than on a racial basis. There are about 9 or 10 million Berber-speaking people, or about half the population of North Africa. Some Berbers have light skin and fair hair, but most are dark-skinned, with dark hair and eyes. Most of the Berbers are farmers, and they live in tents, huts, or stone houses. The people belong to different tribes, each with its own chief. They are Moslems, but their religion is partly pagan.

Berchtesgaden

Berchtesgaden is a beautiful resort town high in the mountains of Bavaria, in southern Germany. Here Adolf Hitler, dictator of Germany, built a house in 1936. No one dangerous to Hitler could reach the house, for to get to it one had to go by secret tunnels cut in the rock and take hidden elevators up through the inside of the mountain. On September 15, 1938, Hitler held a famous meeting there with Prime Minister Neville Chamberlain of Great Britain, one of the Conferences that led to Germany's taking part of Czechoslovakia. An old legend says that a great German king, Frederick Barbarossa, who was killed while returning from a Crusade about eight hundred years ago, did not really die but is still sleeping in a cave at Berchtesgaden. When he awakes he is supposed to bring Germany peace and power. See ALPS.

German Tourist Office

Berchtesgaden scene. The children are dressed as the three Magi, for a Christmas festival.

Berezina River

The Berezina is a river in Russia, 350 miles long. It is a branch of the important Dnieper River, and boats going between the Black Sea and the Baltic Sea travel over it. In 1812, Napoleon, the emperor of France, invaded Russia and tried to conquer it. He was forced to retreat, and at the Berezina River he was severely beaten by the Russian armies. In World War II, the Berezina was again the scene of furious fighting during the German invasion of Russia.

Beria, Lavrenti

Lavrenti P. Beria was one of the leaders of the Communist government in Russia for several years. He was head of the M.V.D., the powerful secret police in the Soviet Union. When the Communist dictator, Josef Stalin, died in 1953 Beria wanted to take his place, but the leaders of the Communist Party and the Red Army were too strong for him. They accused him of being an enemy of his country and had him killed. Beria was born in 1899, so he was then about 54 years old.

beriberi

Beriberi is a disease that a person gets when the food he eats does not have enough vitamin B_1, which is called *thiamin.* Beriberi can result in paralysis and damage to the heart and muscles.

Beriberi used to be common in the Orient—China and other countries of eastern Asia—where people ate rice that had been polished, removing all its thiamin. There is plenty of thiamin in unpolished rice and in other whole grains (such as whole wheat and other cereals), lean meats, eggs, and liver.

The cause of beriberi was discovered by scientists experimenting with animals, such as pigeons. One group of pigeons was fed on whole rice. A second group was fed polished rice. Polished rice is rice from which the hull or shell has been removed. The hull contains the vitamin B_1. The birds that ate the polished rice got beriberi. When they were then fed a broth made from the rice polishings, they recovered.

Bering, Vitus Jonassen

Vitus Jonassen Bering was a famous Danish explorer who lived about 250 years ago. Bering Sea, Bering Strait and Bering Island are named after him. These are all near Alaska.

When Bering was a young man he joined the Russian navy, and he showed great bravery in a war Russia was fighting with Sweden. Peter the Great, the ruler of Russia, was so impressed with young Bering that he made him the leader of an expedition to explore the North Pacific Ocean, off the coast of Siberia. Bering made several important trips through these icy waters, which were later called the Bering Sea. On one trip he traveled through a body of water between the tip of Asia and Alaska, and discovered that Asia and North America were not connected as people thought. This body of water was later called Bering Strait. In 1741, Bering's ship was wrecked on Bering Island, where he died.

The **Bering Sea** is the most northern part of the Pacific Ocean, between Siberia and Alaska. It is more than 875,000 square miles in area, the fourth-largest sea in the world. For many months during the winter and early spring, no ships can get through these waters because of the ice and fog.

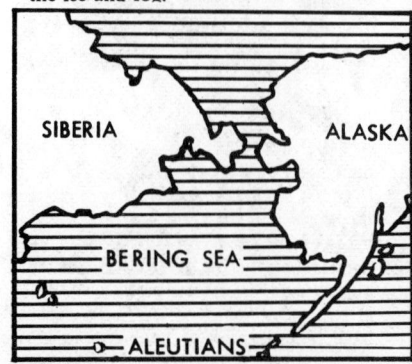

Bering Strait is a shallow body of water, about 50 miles wide. It connects the Bering Sea with the Arctic Ocean to the north; it also separates Asia from North America. The shores are bare and rocky and the weather is very cold. The strait is frozen over except between late June and October. The American Indians probably came from Asia originally by crossing the Bering Strait when it was frozen.

About ninety years ago, a dispute arose between the United States and Great Britain about the right to hunt the many seals in the Bering Sea for their fur. So many seals had already been caught, that it seemed as if soon there would be none left. A group of judges from various countries set a zone of sixty miles around the Pribilof Islands, which belong to the United States, and declared that no one could capture seals in that area.

Berkeley

Berkeley is a city in California. Many people who live in Berkeley go to work in San Francisco, which is only seven miles away. Berkeley was named for George Berkeley, who was a Catholic bishop. He said, "Westward the course of empire takes its way." In 1868 when this new city was being settled in the Far West, the people remembered what Bishop Berkeley had said.

Berkeley is a very large educational center. The University of California is there, one of the largest universities in the world. There are also several other colleges in Berkeley, including the California State College of Agriculture. Some of the things that are manufactured in Berkeley are leather, glass products, and chemicals.

BERKELEY, CALIFORNIA. Population (1970 census) 116,716.

Berkshire Hills

The Berkshire Hills are a range of low, beautiful mountains in Massachusetts. They join with the Green Mountains of Vermont. The highest peak is Mt. Graylock, 3,500 feet high, which is the highest point in Massachusetts. In the Berkshire Hills are many beautiful vacation resorts and many camps for boys and girls. At Stockbridge there is one of the oldest summer theaters. One of the most popular summer attractions each year is a music festival at Tanglewood, called the Berkshire Festival. The Boston Symphony Orchestra, one of the greatest orchestras in the world, plays at this music festival. The American author Nathaniel Hawthorne wrote part of his books about Greek mythology, *A Wonder Book* and *Tanglewood Tales*, while he was visiting at Tanglewood. There is also a summer dance festival at Jacob's Pillow.

Berlin

Berlin is the biggest city in Germany, and until 1945, when World War II ended, it was the fourth-largest city in the world and the capital of all of Germany. More than four million people lived there. Berlin is still one of the biggest cities in the world, but it is split in two parts; many of its fine buildings have become piles of rubble; and half its people are under Communistic rule and have lost their freedom.

In Berlin there are two "zones." West Berlin is controlled by the Federated German Republic, which is usually called "West Germany." East Berlin is the capital of the "East German Democratic Republic," and is under Communist domination. All of Berlin lies within the territory of East Germany, so about two million people who live in West Berlin cannot leave their part of the city with the assurance of being able to return safely.

During World War II, United States heavy bombers by day and British heavy bombers by night dropped "blockbusters" (bombs weighing a ton apiece or more) on Berlin. This did as much as anything to break down German resistance, but unfortunately it also destroyed large parts of a beautiful city.

In 1945, when Germany was beaten and its armies were falling back before Allied and Russian forces, the Russians captured Berlin. Hitler was in the city but killed himself. Defeated Germany was divided into four zones, one each to be governed by the United States, Great Britain, Russia, and France, and Berlin lies in Russia's zone. Berlin also was divided into four zones. In 1954 West Germany became independent again and took over the government of West Berlin.

On April 1, 1948, the Russians refused to allow the Allies to ship food or coal into West Berlin by highway or railroad. They could do this because Berlin was surrounded by the Russian zone. The two million people in West Berlin were in danger of starving—and of freezing the next winter. But the United States and British Air Forces set up a famous "airlift" and flew more than two million tons of food and fuel into Berlin, until on September 30, 1949—nearly a year and a half later—the Russians decided to let the roads and railroads be used again.

In June, 1953, major anti-Communist riots broke out in East Berlin. So many East Germans were using Berlin as an escape route to freedom in the West that the Communists finally built a wall in 1961 that divided the city in two.

BERLIN AS IT WAS

Famous parts of Berlin that were destroyed or badly damaged in World War II include the palace where the former emperors of Germany lived, the University of Berlin, cathedrals and opera houses, and one of the most famous streets in the world, called *Unter den Linden*, which means "under the linden trees." This wide avenue, lined with trees, had many important buildings along it. The Brandenburg Gate, a huge arch, still stands at one end of *Unter den Linden*. It was only partly destroyed.

About 700 years ago, Berlin was made up of two fishing villages on the Spree River, Berlin and Kölln. Later, they were made into one town. About 250 years ago Berlin began to grow into a city of importance. It became the capital of the kingdom of Prussia. The Prussian king, Frederick I, built many beautiful buildings there. Prussia grew into one of the most powerful countries in Europe, and Berlin grew with it. When the German Empire was created in 1871, Berlin became its capital.

Before and during World War II, Berlin had great factories that made furniture, iron and steel, machinery, chemicals, cotton and woolen goods, and many other products. It was the railroad center for northern Germany and a shipping port on the Spree River. Many of its factories have been repaired or rebuilt and are operating again.

BERLIN, GERMANY. Population (1973 estimate), 3,217,019. Capital of East Germany.

Berlin, Irving

Irving Berlin is the name of a writer of hundreds of popular songs. Many of his songs, including "White Christmas," "Easter Parade," and "God Bless America," are known to almost every American, and throughout the world. Irving Berlin was born in Russia in 1888, and was brought to America when he was only four years old. He became a singing waiter in a New York restaurant and wrote his first published song when he was eighteen years old. "Alexander's Ragtime Band," published in 1911, was the first of his many "hit" songs. In all of Berlin's songs both the words and the music are by him. His works include musical comedies and motion pictures. In 1926, in one of America's most famous romances, he wooed and married Ellin Mackay, daughter of a rich and famous family. He wrote the song "Always" to her.

Berlioz, Hector

Hector Berlioz was a French composer, or writer of original music. When he was a little boy he taught himself to play the flute and guitar. One day he came across a book on how to write music. From this book he taught himself enough so that when he was 15 years old one of his pieces was published. Though *Gale Research Co.* Hector's father wanted him to be a doctor, while Hector was going to medical school he decided that he wanted to be a musician instead.

Some people like Berlioz' music very much and others do not like it at all. This is because he tried many new experiments with instruments. He wrote operas that are like music to be played instead of sung, and symphonies that tell a story, like an opera. He called these the *dramatic symphony*, for example his *Romeo and Juliet*, and *opéra de concert*, for example his *Damnation of Faust*. Berlioz was born in 1803 and died in 1869.

Bermuda

Bermuda is the name given to a group of coral islands lying off the east coast of the United States, about 570 miles east of Cape Hatteras, N.C. They are one of the most popular vacation resorts for people from the United States.

The Islands cover less than 20 square miles. They were first discovered by the English, in 1515. The shipwreck of Sir George Somers in 1609 made the islands famous, especially in England. Somers and his companions spent about five

months in the Bermudas, until they could build a boat, and the book about their adventures provided the great English playwright Shakespeare with a setting for his play, *The Tempest*.

The Bermuda islands are the top of an underwater mountain. On the sides of the mountain the water quickly reaches great depths, which makes Bermuda a good place to study all kinds of sea life. Some people use glass-bottomed boats and others wear divers' helmets and walk around on the ocean floor.

Houses in Bermuda are usually built of blocks cut out of the coral that forms the islands. These blocks make strong, cheap, cool and dry buildings, and it would be hard to find a cleaner material. Mark Twain, the American author, said that the Bermuda house "is exactly like the white of the icing of a cake."

Bermuda is a beautiful place, with many colorful flowers. The weather is pleasantly warm and sunny, except for a short rainy season in late winter, and tourists go there all year round.

During the Civil War, Bermuda was a transfer point for shipments between England and the South. Today, yachting is a favorite sport and the Bermuda Cup races are a major sailboat event. The islands are a British colony. The people make their living mostly by making and selling things to tourists. There are almost no automobiles on the islands; bicycles and horses are used.

BERMUDA ISLANDS. Group of more than 350 islands in Atlantic Ocean. Area, 20 square miles. Population 43,500. Capital, Hamilton (population about 3,000).

Bern

Bern (or Berne) is the name of a canton, or state, in Switzerland. It is also the name of the capital city of Switzerland. The canton of Bern is the second-largest in the country in area and has the largest population. The people raise cattle and also manufacture cheese, clothing, shoes, watches, and clocks. More than half the clocks for which Switzerland is famous are made by the people who live in Bern.

The city of Bern is the capital and fourth-largest city in Switzerland. More than 166,800 people live there. Most of them work in factories making woolen and cotton clothing, chocolates, and machinery. In Bern there are many buildings hundreds of years old and there is a magnificent view of the Alps.

BERN, SWITZERLAND. Canton: area, 2,658 square miles; population 889,523. City: population, 166,800. Capital of Bern canton and capital of Switzerland.

Bernadette of Lourdes

Bernadette of Lourdes was a French girl named Bernadette Soubirous. She lived about a hundred years ago, in Lourdes, a small town in the mountains of southwestern France. One day when Bernadette was a young girl, she was playing in the caves, or grottos, in Lourdes. Suddenly she believed she saw the Virgin Mary before her. Bernadette was frightened but she listened and thought she heard Mary say that the waters of Lourdes could heal the sick. Bernadette told the townspeople of her vision, and

though some did not believe her, many did. Since that time sick people have come from all over to be healed by the waters of Lourdes, and many miraculous cures have been reported. Bernadette was born in 1843 and died in 1879. She was named a saint by the Roman Catholic Church and her feast is celebrated on February 11. Franz Werfel, a German writer, wrote a book called *The Song of Bernadette*, which was made into a movie.

Bernadotte

Bernadotte is the name of a family that is important in Swedish history. Jean Baptiste Jules Bernadotte was a Frenchman who became king of Sweden. First he was a general in France under Napoleon. He was such a good military man that he was made a marshal of France. In 1810 Sweden was without an heir to the throne, and the king, Charles XIII, was growing old. The Swedish States in Council looked around for someone to become king. Because he was such a good leader, they picked Bernadotte. King Charles XIII adopted him and gave him the name Charles John. A few years later Charles XIII died and Bernadotte became king. He was then called Charles XIV, King of Sweden and Norway. He ruled for 26 years and was a good king. When he died his son Oscar became king.

Since that time the Bernadottes have been rulers in Sweden. Many of them have married into other royal families in Europe. In 1948 Count Folke Bernadotte, a Swedish prince, was chosen by the United Nations to be a peacemaker between the Israelis and the Arabs in Palestine. He was killed while there and was mourned by both sides.

Bernard, Saint

Saint Bernard was a French monk. He lived in the Middle Ages—he was born in 1091 and died in 1153. Bernard's parents died when he was a young boy, and when he was 22 years old he entered a monastery. Bernard spent years in work and study, and lived the hard, simple life of a monk. He was a fine speaker. People listened to him because he spoke honestly and with deep feeling. Bernard traveled throughout France and Germany, urging people to go to the holy city of Jerusalem and help win it back from the Mohammedans, who then ruled it; this led to the Second Crusade (see CRUSADES). Saint Bernard founded more than a hundred monasteries. The most important one was at Clairvaux, France. He wrote religious songs and a great many sermons. Some monks are called the Bernardines, in memory of Saint Bernard. He was named a saint in 1174 and his feast day is August 20.

St. Bernard of Cluny was a monk of the Benedictine order who lived from about 1122 to 1156. He was English, though he was born in France. St. Bernard of Cluny wrote a famous long poem about "the wicked world." The hymn "Jerusalem the Golden" is taken from it. St. Bernard wrote the poem to urge people, especially priests and other clergymen like himself, to be less sinful. This St. Bernard is often called "St. Bernard of Morlaix" (the place where he was born) and the other, greater St. Bernard is called "St. Bernard of Clairvaux."

Bernhardt, Sarah

Sarah Bernhardt was a French actress—perhaps the greatest of her day. Two of her outstanding roles were Marguerite in *La Dame aux Camélias* (The Lady of the Camellias) by Alexandre Dumas the Younger; and the young Napoleon in Edmond Rostand's *L'Aiglon* (The Eaglet). Sarah was born in Paris in 1845. Her parents were French and Dutch. Her real name was Rosine Bernhardt. She was of Jewish descent, but was baptized and became a Catholic. People who saw her act always remembered her wonderful talent and her "voix d'or" (French for *voice of gold*). She acted in many countries all over the world and appeared in several American plays. In 1912, she became the first great stage actress to appear in the movies, which were then very young. As a result of an accident, one of her legs was amputated in 1915, but this did not keep her from performing for the front-line troops in World War I. In 1922, at the age of 77, she played the part of a young man in a new drama. The "Immortal Sarah," as she was called, died in March, 1923.

Berry, Martha McChesney

Martha McChesney Berry was the founder of the Berry Schools for Mountain Children, in Mount Berry, Georgia. Miss Berry was born in Georgia in 1866, and saw mountain children growing up without knowing how to read and write. The parents of these children did not have enough money to send them to school, and there were no free schools. In 1902 Miss Berry started a school for these children. In the beginning the schoolhouse was a little log cabin, and there were only five pupils. Now there are about a thousand students and the Berry Schools have a waiting list of five thousand students.

Every student at the Berry Schools does some useful work like cleaning, or farming, or helping to cook the meals, to pay for his education. The main subjects taught are farming, nature, and the Bible.

Martha Berry received many medals and honors for the help she had given to the poor mountain children of Georgia, and in 1931 she was named one of the twelve most important women in the United States. She died in 1942.

Bertillon, Alphonse

Alphonse Bertillon was a French scientist who was born in 1853 and died in 1914. He was very interested in a science we now call physical anthropology, which is concerned with the measurement of various parts of the body. He was also very interested in police work and crime detection. When Bertillon was still in his twenties, he became the Chief of the Bureau of Identification of the Paris Police Department. At that time he invented a system of identifying criminals by physical anthropology. This system is called the Bertillon System.

THE BERTILLON SYSTEM

Bertillon knew that there are certain body measurements that do not change after a person has reached his full growth. When a man is sixty, these body measurements are the same as they were when he was twenty. A man may lose or gain a lot of weight but these measurements stay the same. Bertillon figured out that if you could take these measurements on a criminal and keep a record of them, you would always be able to identify the man. The Bertillon System measures such things as these: the length of the head, the width of the head, the length of the middle finger, the length of the left foot. These measurements and certain others are put on a card, together with pictures of the criminal's full face and his profile. The cards are filed in such a way that the measurements of a man who is suspected of a crime can be easily checked against those of known criminals.

The Bertillon System was popular with police departments, but some remarkable coincidences, in which different men had the same measurements, appearances, and even names, occurred to prove that the system does not always work. Meanwhile Bertillon had become interested in fingerprinting, which was a new idea at that time. Today a combination of fingerprinting and Bertillon measurements is used.

beryl

Beryl is a mineral. It is light green, blue, or pink, and sometimes it has no color at all. The precious gem called emerald is a type of green beryl. Beryl was used by women of ancient Rome, in earrings and other jewelry. Some beryl is called aquamarine. Various kinds of beryl have been found in many places. The finest emeralds are mined in South America and Australia. Other kinds of beryl are found in New England, South Dakota and California in the U.S., and in Canada and South Africa. One piece of beryl discovered in New Hampshire weighed 2½ tons but it was not very valuable. The important things are clearness and brightness, not size.

Bessarabia

Bessarabia is the old name of a region in Russia, bordering on Rumania. It is now called the Moldavian Socialist Soviet Republic. About 2,880,000 people live there, and they are of many different nationalities. There are Poles, Bulgarians, Tartars, and Russians. Most of the people are farmers. They grow grain, tobacco, and fruit in the rich, black soil. Some of the people raise cattle. Others work in factories, making wine and soap. Most of Bessarabia is flat and fertile, and in the central part there are valuable forests of oak and beech.

Though Bessarabia is a small region—about 17,000 square miles—it has been invaded many times. About 100 years after Christ, a Roman emperor named Trajan conquered it. Since then, many different peoples have occupied the region. The Russians and Turks fought over it for a hundred years. Between 1711 and 1812, the Russians recaptured Bessarabia five times. After World War I, Bessarabia was given to Rumania, but it was taken back by Russia in 1940. It then became the Moldavian Republic. The capital is Kishinev, a city of 214,000.

bessemer steel, iron that has been rapidly changed into steel by a special process: see IRON and STEEL.

betatron, a machine used in atomic research to drive a stream of beta rays, or electrons, at high speed. See the articles on ATOMIC ENERGY and CYCLOTRON.

betel

The betel nut is the seed of a tree, the betel palm, that grows in southern Asia, especially in Ceylon and Malaysia, and in certain tropical forests of America. The betel palm is also called the *areca nut palm.* Many peoples of the East, especially the Malays, chew betel nuts, much as people of the West smoke cigarettes or use chewing gum. Slices of the nut are squeezed (not really chewed) in the mouth. This makes saliva flow, so that constant spitting is necessary. The nut is prepared for chewing in many different ways, mostly with spices. The saliva of the person "chewing" it is colored red, and some of the flavorings used with betel may blacken the teeth.

People have been chewing betel nuts for more than two thousand years. Today one out of every ten people in the world chews betel nuts. In some tribes betel-chewing is part of the most important ceremonies—weddings, births, deaths, and religious feasts. Some people also believe that betel-chewing clears the stomach and brain, and strengthens the gums and teeth.

Bethlehem

The "little town" of Bethlehem is celebrated as the birthplace of Jesus Christ, nearly 2,000 years ago. Today it is a city of about 22,450 people in Jordan. During the SIX DAY WAR of 1967, Israel captured part of Jordan which included the city of Bethlehem.

Ancient Bethlehem was the scene of the story told in the book of Ruth, in the Bible, and it was the birthplace and early home of King David, but still it was little known when, about 700 B.C., the prophet Micah foretold that the Messiah or Christ would be born there. At the time of Jesus's birth an inn near Bethlehem was a regular stopping place for travelers going from Palestine to Egypt, that being the reason that Joseph and Mary went there, according to the gospels.

With the growth of Christianity, Bethlehem became important again. About the year 330, Constantine the Great, the first Christian emperor of Rome, built the Church of St. Mary in Bethlehem. This made Bethlehem a great pilgrim shrine, second only to the Tomb of Christ in Jerusalem, five miles south. Constantine's church, the oldest monument built by Christians, was later enlarged. A convent now covers the original "Cave of the Nativity," in which visitors are shown relics such as the trough or "manger" in which the Christ Child was placed.

A silver star fitted into the marble paving in the shrine is said to be the central point of the earth—the birthplace of Jesus—and around the star are set fifteen lamps that burn night and day.

Bethlehem means "house of bread" in Hebrew. The sacred bread used on religious occasions was baked in Bethlehem. The town stands in a fertile district among olive and fig orchards and vineyards of grapes. The people carve and sell religious tokens—crucifixes, beads, boxes, and shells—made of mother-of-pearl, olivewood, and Dead Sea stone.

Bethlehem, Pennsylvania, is a manufacturing city located in the Lehigh Valley, 60 miles northwest of Philadelphia. It is one of the largest steel-making cities in the United States. The great Bethlehem Steel Company has its principal plant there. Bethlehem is the national headquarters for the Moravian religious sect. They founded the city in 1741. In the 1970 census the population of Bethlehem was 72,686.

Better Business Bureau

The Better Business Bureau is an organization that tries to keep people from being cheated by dishonest businessmen or fooled by dishonest advertising. It was founded in 1911.

There are offices of the Better Business Bureau in 106 cities in the United States and Canada. They read the advertising, including letters that are sent through the mail asking people to buy something or to contribute to a charity. If they find anything dishonest, they report it to the police or other people that enforce the law. The Better Business Bureau is not a law-enforcement agency.

The expense of running the Better Business Bureau is paid by business firms and by Chambers of Commerce, which are groups of businessmen. More than 75,000 firms contribute.

Anyone who is suspicious of a business firm can get information by calling the nearest BBB office.

Beverly Hills

Beverly Hills is a city in California. It is part of greater Los Angeles and is famous because so many movie stars live there. Only about 33,416 people live in Beverly Hills, but many people come from all parts of the United States to visit. They hope they will be able to see their favorite movie stars shopping on Wilshire Boulevard, one of the city's streets. They also come to look at the homes of the actors and actresses. Not everyone who lives in Beverly Hills is in the movies. There are factories that make gas furnaces, varnish, and insecticides (chemicals for killing insects).

Bhutan

Bhutan is a small kingdom in Asia, in the Himalaya Mountains, with Tibet on its north, and India on its south. Its area is about 18,000 square miles, about half the size of Indiana. About a million people live there. Until 1960, when a road was built from India into Bhutan, one could get into the country only through mountain trails. The northern part is mostly tundra, snow, and ice, and is occupied by monks who live in isolated monasteries. The animal life there includes deer, bears, and yaks. The central part of Bhutan contains fertile valleys where farmers who own their own land raise rice, the most important crop, and wheat, barley, mustard, and potatoes. They also raise sheep, yaks,

cattle, and ponies. Wild elephants and tigers live in the southern regions. Money is not important to the Bhutanese, who raise their own food, weave their own cloth, and build their own homes of stone, mud, and wood. There are only a few villages. The only electric generators belong to radio stations, a few sawmills, and the Royal Palace at Thimbu, the capital. The Bhutanese are of the Mongoloid race; their language is a dialect of Tibetan. Most of the people are Buddhists. Since the 16th century, Bhutan has been under the control first of Tibet, then China, Great Britain, and, most recently, India. It is now an independent country, and in 1971 it became a member of the United Nations.

Biarritz

Biarritz is a little fishing village in the southwest of France, near the Spanish border and the Pyrenees Mountains. It is on the Bay of Biscay which is part of the Atlantic Ocean. Biarritz has warm, sunny weather and swimming almost all year. It is a very fashionable resort town.

Napoleon III, French emperor about one hundred years ago, built a house in Biarritz for his wife, the Empress Eugénie. This house, called a *villa,* is so close to the water that on rough days the waves splash right up onto the porch. The villa is now used as a public bathhouse. About 22,900 people live in Biarritz all year round. There are many fine hotels and restaurants.

Bible

The Bible is the Holy Book of the Christian religion. The first part of it, called the Old Testament, is the Jewish Holy Book, or Scriptures, that Jesus followed. The second part, called the New Testament, was written after Jesus had been recognized as the Christ, or the Savior. Altogether, the Bible took more than a thousand years to write. The last part of it was written more than 1,800 years ago. Our word for it, *Bible,* comes from a word of the Greek language meaning "the Books." St. Jerome, the great translator of the Bible into the Latin language, called it "the divine library," and so it is, for there are many books in the Bible. Three different languages were used in writing these books. Some of them were written in Hebrew, the language of the ancient prophets. Some were written in Aramaic, the language that Jesus spoke. The rest were written in Greek, the language of the most civilized people during the time, long ago, when Jesus was on earth. However, the Greek of the New Testament was not exactly the same as the Greek in which the earlier Greek poets and thinkers had written. It has been described as "Hebrew thought in Greek clothing."

Most of the books of the Christian Bible are called *canonical.* They belong to the *canon,* or the whole mass of writings that Christians believe to be inspired by God. The other books of the Bible are called *apocryphal,* which means "of unknown authority." Many Bibles do not include these books. There is a separate article on the APOCRYPHA.

THE OLD TESTAMENT

The Old Testament is the longest part of the Bible. It is more than three times as long as the New Testament. The Jews divided the Old Testament into three parts: the *Law;* the *Prophets;* and the *Writings.*

THE LAW includes the first five books, the five books of Moses: Genesis, Exodus, Leviticus, Numbers, and Deuteronomy.

THE PROPHETS include some books that tell the history of the ancient Jews, and so are called the *Historical Books* (Joshua, Judges, Samuel, Kings), but which were written by prophets; the *Major Prophets* (Isaiah, Jeremiah, Ezekiel, and Daniel); the *Minor Prophets* (Hosea, Joel, Amos, Obadiah, Jonah, Micah, Nahum, Habakkuk, Zephaniah, Haggai, Zechariah, and Malachi); and the *Books of the Chronicles,* which tell a great deal of history (Chronicles, Ezra, Nehemiah, and Esther).

THE WRITINGS include the poetry and beautiful literature of the Bible: Job, Psalms, Proverbs, Ecclesiastes, Song of Solomon (or Canticles). The Lamentations of Jeremiah is usually included in this group, as are all or parts of the books of Ruth, Ezra, and Daniel.

The first five books ("the Law") are also called the *Pentateuch,* or five-volume book. Moses is credited with the writing of all five books. The first book, Genesis, tells how the world began, and what happened to the early leaders of the Jewish people. The second book, Exodus, tells how the Jews were led out of Egypt, where they had been slaves, to find a new home in Palestine, in the "Promised Land," the land promised to them by God; and it also gives some of the most important laws, including the Ten Commandments. Leviticus is chiefly a list of laws to be followed, and Numbers is partly history of the times. Deuteronomy means "a repeating of the law," and has in t three lessons given by Moses to those who were too young then to remember when the laws had first been given.

THE NEW TESTAMENT

The New Testament is the part of the Bible that tells of the life of Jesus, his teachings, the reasons why Christians should follow him, and the ways in which Christians can live according to his teachings.

Like the Old Testament, the New Testament can be divided into three parts:

THE GOSPELS are the four books (Matthew, Mark, Luke, and John) that tell of Jesus' life and teachings. To these four books are added THE ACTS, which gives the earliest history of the Christian Church.

THE EPISTLES OF ST. PAUL, written by St. Paul to the newly-formed Christian Churches, and also to other apostles and ministers of the Christian faith.

THE GENERAL EPISTLES, written by James, Peter, John, and Jude, and addressed to Christians everywhere.

There is one other book, the last book of the New Testament, that does not fit into any of these three classes. It is the Revelation of St. John, or the Apocalypse, which prophesies what will happen when the world comes to an end. There is a separate article about the APOCALYPSE.

THE GOSPELS

Though the four gospels all have one subject, the life of Jesus, they tell about it in different ways and so are all needed. The first three gospels, Matthew, Mark, and Luke, are called *synoptic* ("seen through the same eyes"). Mark is a brief biography, or life-story, of Jesus. Matthew tells the life-story and also devotes several chapters to the teachings of Jesus, including the Sermon on the Mount, the greatest lesson ever taught. Luke tells many of the good deeds that Jesus did. John tells why Jesus was recognized as the Son of God.

The Bible contains more than three-quarters of a million words, but many people have read it through and some have read it through several times. Many people begin their reading of the New Testament with the Gospels.

KINDS OF BIBLE

The books of the Bible began to be written down about 3,000 years ago, on leather at first and then on papyrus, the earliest paperlike material. Some parts had been memorized and handed down from generation to generation long before they were first written down; some books did not yet exist. The written copies wore out, or were lost, and were replaced many times. Until recently there were no early copies that went back before 350 A.D. Since then earlier copies of some parts, dating back as far as 200 B.C., have been found in Israel near the Dead Sea (for which reason they are called the Dead Sea Scrolls).

The Bible has been translated into hundreds of different languages, and in some of these languages, including English, there are many different translations. Between 250 B.C. and 50 B.C. Jewish scholars translated the Old Testament from Hebrew into Greek; this translation is called the *Septuagint,* meaning it was done by 70 scholars. About 400 A.D. St. Jerome translated both the Old and New Testaments into the vulgate, the conversational Latin of that time; his translation is called the *Vulgate.* The earliest translations into English were made by John Wycliffe about 1380 and by William Tyndale about 1530. Wycliffe followed the Vulgate but Tyndale went back also to Greek and Hebrew texts.

The English translation still most popular with Protestants is the "King James" or Authorized Version of 1611. It was done by 47 scholars. Like Tyndale, they went back to the Greek and Hebrew. The most popular Catholic translation into English, until recently at least, was the Douay Bible, published at Douay, a town in France, in 1609. It and all Catholic Bibles followed the Vulgate until 1952, when the Confraternity Bible was published. It is a Catholic Bible that uses the earliest available sources, Greek and Hebrew as well as Latin.

Revised versions of the Protestant Bible have come out from time to time, the latest having been published in 1951. In 1961, the New Testament in a new translation from Hebrew and Greek was published, and is called "The New English Bible." The translation was done by British Biblical scholars. There have been many other translations of the Bible into English. Edgar J. Goodspeed did a noted one in the American language during the

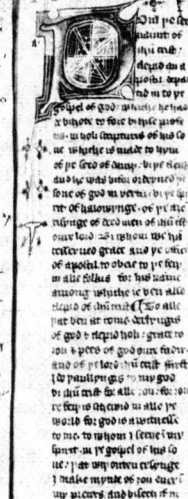

Am. Bible Society

Above is a page of Psalms from one of the oldest Bible manuscripts in existence. It is written in Greek. At right is a page from the Epistles to the Romans, in an old English Bible. It was handwritten—printed by hand, not from type.

Above: Miles Coverdale, Bishop of Exeter, England, who made an early English translation of the Bible in 1535. At the right is part of his translation of the Song of Solomon.

Left: William Tyndale was an English minister who translated the New Testament and parts of the Old Testament into English, from about 1525 to 1535. He was persecuted by church leaders because he used Greek and Hebrew originals instead of following the Latin translation. The title page of Martin Luther's version of the New Testament is shown below. He translated it into German so that most of his followers could read it.

Am. Bible Society

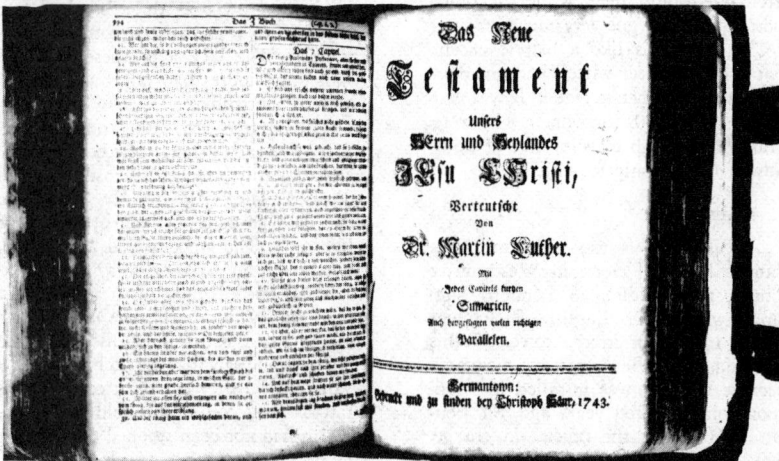

1920s. A translation sponsored by the Roman Catholic Confraternity of Christian Doctrine was being issued during the 1950s and 1960s.

Bibles are usually published as *text Bibles* and *reference Bibles*. A text Bible gives only the words of the Bible itself. A reference Bible adds thousands of notes that show how different passages of the Bible are related to one another. There are tens of thousands of books about the Bible. A *concordance* is an index that shows where every important word or verse in the Bible is to be found. Many Bibles have special indexes, reading guides, maps, and other features that are called "helps."

BIBLE ASSOCIATIONS

The American Bible Society is an organization that works constantly to have the Bible read by as many people as possible throughout the world. It has the Bible translated into new languages, and it prints and gives away millions of Bibles and New Testaments. There are also several organizations whose purpose is to put Testaments into people's hands. The Pocket Testament League is one.

The Gideons are an organization that puts Bibles into hotel rooms so that people may read the Bible while they are traveling.

There are other articles in this encyclopedia on the different books of the Bible and on many of the persons and places in it. See also the article on GUTENBERG, who printed the first Bible from type. A Gutenberg Bible is the most valuable of all books.

During the "Dark Ages," more than a thousand years ago, when printing was unknown to the Christian world and almost no one except priests and monks knew how to read and write, Bibles were handwritten by monks and were *illuminated,* which means that the pages were decorated with pictures and fancy designs in colors and gold. Some of the most beautiful Bibles in existence were made by hand during that period.

In this century, the finest printed books are Bibles. They are often bound in the finest leather and printed on India paper, which is the thinnest paper made. The greatest artists of all time have painted scenes from the Bible.

bicycle

A bicycle is a machine to ride on. It is also called a "bike" or a "wheel." It has two wheels, one behind the other, and that is how it got its name, because *bi* means "two" and *cycle* means "wheel." The wheels are held in line by a metal frame. The rider sits on a little seat that is attached to the frame. He steers by holding onto handlebars that turn the front wheel of the bicycle. He makes the rear wheel turn by pushing pedals up and down with his feet, and that makes the bicycle go forward. There are more than twenty million bicycles in the United States, and in Europe there are more bicycles than automobiles.

Many boys and girls ride their bicycles to and from school and use them for errands. They also go on trips with them. In many countries there are special bi-

cycle paths with small houses along the way, called *hostels,* where bicycle riders can rest and eat. Bicycle riding is a very popular sport. In European countries many more people ride bicycles than in America. Men ride them to work and women to shopping. Whole families take long trips on bicycles.

Schwinn Bicycle

This bicycle, with a short frame, high handlebars, and a long seat, has become popular among youngsters because of its unusual design and its ability to make fast starts and quick maneuvers.

Riders in the National Champion Amateur Bike Race are shown here at the starting line, ready to go. They reach a high speed on their light bicycles.

This modern sports bicycle features racing handlebars and a ten-speed gear shift.

RIDING A BICYCLE

Most people from six to sixty can ride a bike, or can be taught to ride in a few hours. One of the most important things to learn is how to keep your balance, but this is soon learned.

When the pedals of the bicycle are pushed up and down, they make a little wheel go around. This little wheel is attached by a chain to the bigger rear wheel of the bicycle, so the rear wheel turns too and drives the bicycle. Most bicycles have "coaster brakes." Pressing the pedals part of the way backward disconnects the chain and the rear wheels turn freely while the little wheel, operated by the pedals, does not turn at all. This lets one "coast" down a hill without moving his feet on the pedals. Then if he presses still farther backward on the pedals he applies a brake to the rear wheel (see the article on BRAKE) and

this will slow down the bicycle or stop it completely. Some bicycles have other brakes, called caliper brakes, that are operated by gripping a lever on the handlebars.

A bicycle permits the rider to go much faster and yet more easily than he can on foot. He can go faster because of the gear arrangement of the little and big wheels: It is about 75 inches around the big wheel and less than 20 inches around the little wheel, but every time the little wheel turns, so does the big wheel. And there are two main reasons why a bicycle makes it easier for a person to travel under his own power. First, he sits down. Second, he can take advantage of his forward motion and can coast. When walking, a person cannot coast because of the friction between his feet and the road. Modern bicycles have gear-shifts that combine the two advantages: When the bike is already rolling along, the rider can shift to a higher gear and either go faster or pedal less hard, whichever he prefers. (See the article on GEARS.)

Early forms of the bicycle were made more than a hundred years ago. The first bicycle resembling modern ones was made in Franc about 1870 and was a *velocipede*—a name now used for a young child's tricycle. The velocipede had a big front wheel, because the chain drive had not yet been invented and the bigger the driving wheel, the faster one could go. (See the picture on page 675.) The chain-drive bicycle, with front and rear wheels the same size, was first made in England about 1885. Like the modern bike, it had sprocket wheels (wheels with teeth) to connect the small driving wheel to the big rear wheel. The most important developments since that time have been ball bearings in the wheels, the pneumatic (air-filled) tire, and the coaster brake. Bicycling was a popular sport in the 1890s and "tandem bikes" were popular. They had seats and pedals for two, three, or even four or five persons sitting in a row.

Bicycle racing is still one of the most popular sports in Europe. It was very popular in the United States but no longer is. Racing bikes are very light and have a smaller pedal wheel, which increases the gear ratio and makes them go faster. There are road races and indoor races. A popular kind of indoor racing in America was the Six-day Bike Race. A pair of drivers, riding as a team, kept going day and night for six full days; often one would sleep while the other rode but neither got very much rest.

The tricycle is like a bicycle except that it has two rear wheels and one does not have to balance to ride it. It was first made in the 1880s for women who were afraid of the high bicycles of that time. Now it is used only for children.

Big Ben

"Big Ben" is the nickname of a famous bell and clock in Westminster Palace, the building in London, England, where the English Parliament meets. It is high in the tower of this building. "Big Ben" got its nickname because when it was installed in 1856, about one hundred years ago, Sir Benjamin Hall was the official in charge. The bell measures 9 feet across and

weighs 13½ tons. See the article BELL, in this volume.

bighorn

The bighorn is the nickname for the Rocky Mountain sheep. It got this name because of its heavy, curving horns, which are considered a great prize by hunters. The bighorn lives high up in the Rocky Mountains, all the way from California to Alaska. It stands about three and a half feet high, and is grayish-brown in color. Its horns measure about 42 inches from the tip of the horn on one side to the tip of the horn on the other side.

The bighorn is as nimble-footed on the rocky peaks as a mountain goat, and it is very hard to catch. It is very alert. It not only has to look out for hunters, but for wildcats, wolves, and coyotes, which like the delicious flesh of the bighorn. But these animals know better than to chase it. The bighorn has led many of them to their death, high up among the crags and peaks of the mountains. The bighorns wait for the cold and heavy snows of winter. Then they come down from the mountains in herds in search of grass and shrubs. Far from the safety of the peaks, many mountain sheep are killed. Some are killed by hunters, but the bighorn has to be especially on guard against the swift attack of the eagle. This great bird is the only enemy that can follow the bighorn among the high peaks. The eagle cannot hurt the grown sheep but it is able to kill the lambs. A bighorn usually stands on guard, and when it spies an eagle, it gives a warning signal. Then the entire herd flees, dashing nimbly from crag to crag.

The male bighorn is called a *ram.* The female bighorn is called a *ewe.* In the early winter, the herds of rams join the herds of ewes and the rams have fierce fights and batter each other with their heavy horns to see which will win the females.

Although the bighorn is hard to capture, many have been captured and they can be seen in zoos in cities in this and other countries.

big tree

The big tree is the oldest and tallest tree in the world. It is a member of the redwood (or sequoia) family.

The big trees once grew in many parts of the world, but today they are found only in California. Some big trees are three or four thousand years old. The big trees grow over three hundred feet high, which is as high as many city skyscrapers. The largest of these trees are sometimes more than one hundred feet around the trunk.

The big trees are strong and powerful. They live such a long time because they are not easily attacked by insects or tree diseases. They also quickly heal from any damage done to them by storms or lightning. The wood is red and brittle, but it does not burn or decay easily. Nature did not kill most of these trees, but men did. When the settlers moved west to the Pacific Coast they discovered the big trees and saw that the timber was very valuable. So they cut the trees down as fast as they could, and sold the wood. If this had not been stopped there might be no big trees left today.

The government finally set aside many groves of big trees as national parks, and cared for them, and protected them. These trees are still in some danger, however. Visitors who come to California to see these giant trees trample the ground under the spreading branches until it is packed hard. The roots of the big tree end in many tiny rootlets that lie very close to the surface. The ground around these rootlets must be kept soft and moist for them to live and grow. So the government asks visitors to be very careful where they walk when they visit the big trees.

Bikini Atoll

The Bikini Atoll is the Pacific island where two atom bombs were exploded in July, 1946, to test the effects on ships and airplanes. This was called "Operation Crossroads." Bikini is in the northwestern part of the Marshall Islands group, which is about halfway between Hawaii and New Guinea. Bikini is a coral atoll (a ring of small coral islands around a lagoon, or a pool of still water). There are 27 islands in Bikini Atoll. In 1946, the native population of Bikini was removed to another island. About seventy Japanese and old American ships were left in the lagoon. The ships had five thousand animals on them, as well as many scientific instruments. Representatives from the United Nations and from the newspapers of all the major countries went to Bikini. They watched the explosion by television on nearby ships and airplanes. The first bomb was exploded above water, the second one below water. Many of the ships were entirely destroyed. The terrible explosions and the deadly rays released by the bombs killed the plant and animal life on Bikini and on the ships anchored nearby. Airplanes without pilots were sent through the bomb "cloud" to see how much radioactivity was in the air. The Bikini test showed how human beings and their ships and airplanes can be protected against some of the effects of an atom bomb explosion.

Bilbao

Bilbao is one of the chief seaports in Spain. It is on the Nervion River, seven miles from the Bay of Biscay, part of the Atlantic Ocean. Bilbao is one of the most important manufacturing cities in the country and more than 411,000 people live there. Many of them work in factories making steel, glass, and paper. There are also large ship-building yards and nearby there are rich iron mines. The Nervion River runs through Bilbao, and divides the city into two parts. On the right bank of the river is the very old part of the city; on the left bank is the more modern section.

Bilbao was founded more than six hundred years ago. When the Spanish Civil War broke out in 1936, Bilbao remained loyal to the government but was captured by Franco in 1937, after being badly damaged.

BILBAO, SPAIN. Population 411,000 including suburbs. Capital of Vizcaya province.

bile

Bile is a golden-yellow juice that is made within the body and works on fatty foods, to change them into the form that the body needs for building its tissues. Bile is made in the liver. It is stored in a sac called the gall bladder (*gall* is an old word that means *bile*). From the gall bladder the bile goes into the intestines, where food is digested, and mixes with the fats there. Although bile is very important to life, it is a very unpleasant substance—very bitter-tasting.

Sometimes the bile gets sluggish and thickens. It might turn dark and greenish and it might even thicken into a hard substance. The patient may be suffering from "gallstones" and when these little stones try to get out, through the little bile tube, the patient has pain and the doctor must start treatment. If the gallstones are large they usually are removed in an operation.

See also the articles on DIGESTION and LIVER.

billiards

Billiards is the name of various games played with solid balls on a special table. The full-size billiard table is 10 feet long and 5 feet wide, but most tables are 9 feet long and 4½ feet wide, or smaller. The top of the table is a smooth, level piece of slate, covered with heavy green felt. It is enclosed on all four sides by a *rail*. Each rail is faced on the inside with a *cushion*, a thick strip of rubber from which the balls bounce when driven against the rail.

For most games, the balls are a little less than 2½ inches in diameter. They are made of ivory or a plastic.

A player drives the balls with a long tapering stick called a *cue*. A right-handed player holds the heavy *butt* of the cue with his right hand, and directs the other end toward the ball with a kind of crook, called a *bridge*, formed by the fingers of the left hand. This smaller end of the cue has a rounded leather tip, which is rubbed from time to time with blue chalk to reduce slipping when it hits the highly-polished ball.

Carom billiards is a game for two players, with two white balls and one red ball. Each player uses one of the white balls as his own throughout the game. He tries to drive his own ball in such a way that it will touch the other two balls (*object balls*), making a *carom* or *billiard*. His turn continues so long as he makes a carom every shot. When he misses or fouls, the turn passes to his opponent. Each carom counts 1 point. Beginners play a game of 25 points. A popular form of this game is *three-cushion billiards*, in which a carom does not count unless the player's ball has hit a rail at least three times before it hits the second object ball.

Pocket billiards, which is usually called *pool*, is played on a table having six pockets in the bed of the table, one in each corner and one in the middle of each longer side. There are 15 colored and numbered balls, plus one white *cue ball*. To begin a game, the colored balls are racked together in a triangle near one end of the table. Each player in turn tries to drive the colored balls into the pockets by driving the cue ball at them. A player's turn continues so long as he pockets a ball, thereby scoring 1 point. In expert play, the player must name the ball which he intends to put in the pocket: his shot counts only if he succeeds. The turn ends when the player misses or when he fouls. The chief foul stroke is a *scratch*—pocketing the cue ball, or failing to hit any ball. A scratch takes 1 point off the score.

Many other games are played on billiard tables, especially on pool tables. In *rotation pool,* a player must first hit the lowest-numbered ball on the table or he cannot score in that turn. The number of the ball is the score earned for pocketing it. This game is popular when more than two players participate and some are much more expert than others.

PRINCIPLES OF PLAY

The cue ball will always travel in the direction in which the cue is pointed.

To make the object ball travel in a certain direction, have the cue ball strike it at the point where the cue would strike it to send it in that direction.

To make the cue ball keep on rolling after it strikes the object ball, strike the cue ball above its center. This is a *follow shot.*

To make the cue ball return after it strikes the object ball, strike the cue ball below its center. This is a *draw shot.*

When the cue ball is to strike a cushion, strike the cue ball on its right to make it rebound to its right, and on its left to make it rebound to its left. This is called *English.* With no English, the cue ball will rebound at the same angle at which it struck.

Bill of Rights

A "bill of rights" is a list of rights or liberties that the people of a country have and the government cannot take away from them. In the *Magna Carta,* or "Great Charter," that King John of England was forced to sign in the year 1215, the people of the country were guaranteed the right of trial by jury, the right of a speedy trial (see HABEAS CORPUS), and protection against paying any taxes that a legislature had not approved. In the United States, the Bill of Rights is the first ten amendments to the Constitution. These are:

AMENDMENT 1. Congress shall make no law respecting an establishment of religion, or prohibiting the free exercise thereof; or abridging the freedom of speech or of the press; or the right of the people peaceably to assemble and to petition the Government for a redress of grievances.

AMENDMENT 2. A well-regulated militia being necessary to the security of a free State, the right of the people to keep and bear arms shall not be infringed.

AMENDMENT 3. No soldier shall, in time of peace, be quartered in any house without the consent of the owner, nor in time of war but in a manner to be prescribed by law.

AMENDMENT 4. The right of the people to be secure in their persons, houses, papers, and effects, against unreasonable searches and seizures, shall not be violated, and no warrants shall issue but upon probable cause, supported by oath or affirmation, and particularly describing the place to be searched, and the persons or things to be seized.

AMENDMENT 5. No person shall be held to answer for a capital or other infamous crime unless on a presentment or indictment of a Grand Jury, except in cases arising in the land or naval forces, or in the militia,

when in actual service, in time of war or public danger; nor shall any person be subject for the same offense to be twice put in jeopardy of life or limb; nor shall be compelled in any criminal case to be a witness against himself, nor be deprived of life, liberty, or property, without due process of law; nor shall private property be taken for public use without just compensation.

AMENDMENT 6. In all prosecutions, the accused shall enjoy the right to a speedy and public trial, by an impartial jury of the State and district wherein the crime shall have been committed, which districts shall have been previously ascertained by law, and to be informed of the nature and cause of the accusation; to be confronted with the witnesses against him; to have compulsory process for obtaining witnesses in his favor, and to have the assistance of counsel for his defense.

AMENDMENT 7. In suits at common law, where the value in controversy shall exceed twenty dollars, the right of trial by jury shall be preserved, and no fact tried by a jury shall be otherwise re-examined in any court of the United States than according to the rules of the common law.

AMENDMENT 8. Excessive bail shall not be required, nor excessive fines imposed, nor cruel and unusual punishments inflicted.

AMENDMENT 9. The enumeration in the Constitution of certain rights shall not be construed to deny or disparage others retained by the people.

AMENDMENT 10. The powers not delegated to the United States by the Constitution, nor prohibited by it to the States, are reserved to the States respectively, or to the people.

The Fifth Amendment is the one that is most often in the news. The Supreme Court has held that a person need never answer a question "that might tend to degrade or incriminate him"—that is, expose him to disgrace or punishment—and many people have used this right to refuse to say whether they have ever been Communists.

Billy the Kid

Billy the Kid was a famous American outlaw who was born about a hundred years ago, in 1859. His name was William Bonney, but everybody called him Billy the Kid because he was so young.  He was a dangerous person, and it is said that he killed his first man in New Mexico when he was twelve years old, because the man insulted his mother. By the time he was eighteen years old, he had killed twelve men.

When Billy the Kid was living in New Mexico, a group of men tried to get control of all the cattle grazing land. They hired Billy to help them. He stole cattle, and killed some ranchers. When the sheriff tried to arrest him, he escaped to the hills, and gathered a gang of desperadoes around him. These outlaws, led by Billy, fought many battles with the sheriff's men who tried to arrest them. Finally a sheriff and a group of men surrounded Billy in a house, and forced him to surrender. He was put in jail and sentenced to be hanged. But he killed two of the prison guards, and escaped. Officers of the law followed him to Fort Sumner, New Mexico. They saw Billy as he was about to enter a house. The officers shot him dead (in 1881). Billy was 21, and he had boasted that he had killed a man for each year of his life.

Bingham, George Caleb

George Caleb Bingham was an American painter who lived about a hundred years ago. He was noted for painting commonplace scenes and people, which artists seldom did in those times. Bingham was born in Virginia in 1811, but his family moved to Missouri when he was a boy. He studied art in the East and in Europe. He painted portraits, for which there was great demand then (before the days of photography) but his best paintings were of scenes in and near Missouri; the most famous include *The Jolly Flatboatmen* and *Raftsmen Playing Cards*. Bingham was also prominent in Missouri politics and held several high offices. He died in 1879.

Binghamton

Binghamton is a city in southern New York State, at the meeting of the Chenango and Susquehanna rivers. It has many factories where shoes, machinery and other products are made. The city grew after being joined by canal to Utica in 1837.

BINGHAMTON, NEW YORK. Population (1970 census) 64,123; with suburbs, 212,-815. County seat of Broome County.

bingo

Bingo is a very popular game that is played for prizes. Large crowds of people can play at the same time. Each player has a card (or one player may play several cards). Each card has five rows of numbers on it, and no two cards are the same. Someone is in charge of the game. He draws one number at a time from a big container. Everyone having that number on his card puts a marker on it. When anyone gets five numbers in a row, going either across or down, he calls "Bingo!" and wins the prize. Then a new game begins. Bingo is a form of an old game called *Lotto*. It is also played under the name *Keno*. In the 1930s, when business was bad, motion-picture theaters began to have "Bank Nights" when they would stop the picture while the audience played the game (under the name *Screeno* and other names) for prizes given by the theater. Then in many cities bingo games came to be held for the benefit of lodges, volunteer fire departments, Roman Catholic Churches, and others. In the 1950s several states passed laws permitting these bingo games, but in other states bingo remained illegal under anti-gambling laws.

binocular

A binocular instrument is one that you look through with both eyes, to make things look larger. There are binocular telescopes, binocular microscopes, and so on, but the word is usually applied to a "field glass," which is small and light enough to hold to your eyes with your hand, and which allows you to see things that are far away.

The field glass is actually two tubes, or small telescopes, joined together at the top. Each tube has a *lens* at both ends. The lens lets the light through and magnifies the picture carried by the light. The lens at the bottom end is called the *objective lens*.

In a modern, or prism, binocular, the light goes straight in and hits a *prism*. A prism is a piece of glass cut at angles so that it forms a sort of triangle. The prism sends the light to another prism beside it. From here the light goes to the lens in the eyepiece, through which you look.

The prisms are very important, because they change the direction of the light. As light from an object enters the objective lens it is upside down, but

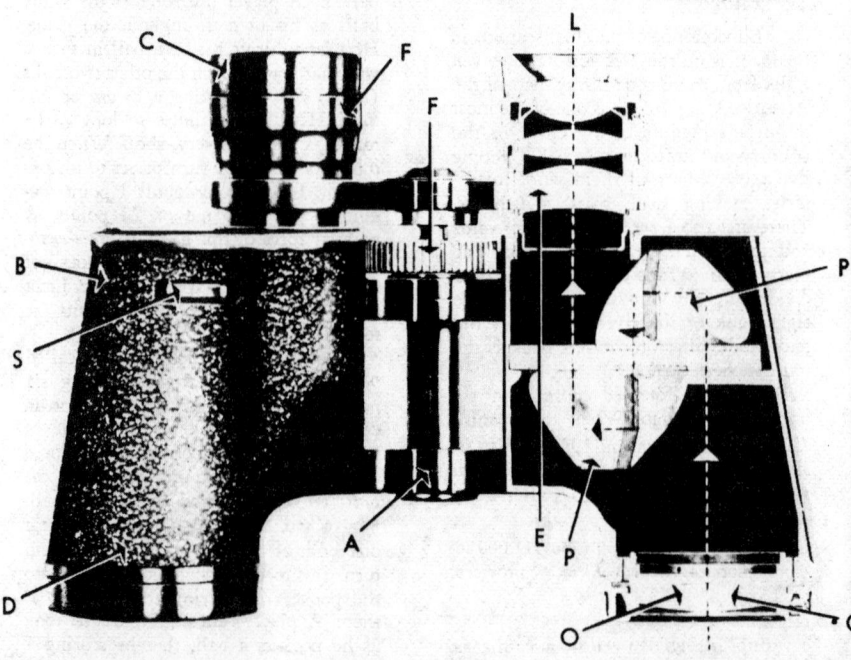

Binoculars are used to make faraway things look near. They are really two small telescopes one for each eye, attached at a hinge (A). The eyepiece caps (C) are placed to the eyes as the body of the binoculars (B) are held in the hands. To make things look clearer you turn the focusing disks (F). Light rays enter the front of the binoculars (D), through the objective lens (O) and strike a prism (P) and then pass up into the eyepiece (E) where you see the enlarged picture (L). For ease in carrying binoculars, there is an eyelet on each side (S) so that a strap may be attached, for carrying over the shoulder.

Bausch & Lomb

This picture of a mother bird feeding her young was taken through binoculars.

Bausch & Lomb

the prisms turn it right side up again. The prisms also make it possible to see a wider view. The objective lenses are farther apart than the eyes, and the prisms bring the light inward to the eyepieces, which are closer together.

A binocular is described by its *power* and its *field*. A "six-power, thirty-five" binocular (written 6x, 35) makes things look six times as big as they seem to the naked eye and has an objective lens that is 35 millimeters in diameter (almost an inch and a half across). The most useful binoculars for everyday use are six- to eight-power, and the best field on these is 50-millimeter. Some binoculars used in the army and the navy can enlarge an object as much as 144 times.

biochemistry

A chemist studies different substances to find out what they are made of and what effect they have on other substances. A biochemist does the same kind of work, but only with the substances that living things are made of, such as flesh and blood and bone. His work is called *biochemistry* because in the Greek language bio- means "life."

The body is composed of a great many different substances. Some of them stay in the body, as the blood and the juices of the stomach and intestines do. Other substances—waste products, such as perspiration and urine—are given off daily. All these substances have been examined in the laboratory by chemists, so it is known what they contain when one is normally healthy: how much salt, how much sugar, how much acid, and so on. When a laboratory test shows that a body substance is not normal, it is usually a sign of disease. For example, too much sugar in the urine is often a sign of the disease called DIABETES (about which there is a separate article).

Today every hospital has a biochemical laboratory. Analysis of blood, urine and other body fluids is a routine part of the medical examination of every patient.

biography

A biography is the written story of a person's life. When a person writes his or her own life story, it is called an autobiography. A biography or autobiography tells where and when the person was born, what he did, and what happened to him all through his life.

In ancient times, most biographies were written either to teach a moral lesson or to explain something about history. These ancient biographies were not always correct, but many of them were very interesting to read. The *Lives of the Greeks and Romans* by Plutarch are probably the most famous.

The most famous biography in the English language is the *Life of Samuel Johnson* by James Boswell, written nearly two hundred years ago. One of the most famous early American autobiographies is that of Benjamin Franklin. The most modern type of biography tells everything that is known about the subject, whether it shows him to have been a good man or a bad one. Older biographies often left out important facts, because they would have seemed unkind.

A brief article about a person, in a magazine or in an encyclopedia such as this one, is a form of biography.

biological warfare

Biological warfare is a recent development. The idea of it is to start sickness in the enemy's country—either to make his citizens sick or to poison his cattle and the crops that are his food. The idea is that sick people or hungry people are soon willing to surrender. Another name for biological warfare is *germ warfare*, because it consists of spreading germs in enemy territory.

Spreading germs is not as easy as it may seem. Most of the diseases that are easiest to spread, such as smallpox, would not work because people in civilized countries are vaccinated and inoculated to make them immune against such diseases. Experts on biological warfare find rare kinds of germs that enemy countries are not prepared for. These germs could then be dropped from airplanes, or can be spread by spies and traitors.

No country has ever used biological warfare. The United States has developed biological warfare, but only as a threat against other nations that might use it. See also CHEMICAL WARFARE.

biology

Biology is the study of living things —not only of all the different kinds of living things, but how they eat and breathe, grow and reproduce, and their habits of life. Biology is no longer a single science—it is a word that covers a great number of different subjects that are now known as the *biological* or *life sciences,* which deal with matter that has life.

All living things, except viruses, are either plants or animals or fungi. A scientist who studies plants is a *botanist;* one who studies animals is a *zoölogist;* and one who studies fungi is a *mycologist.* There are also scientists who deal with particular kinds of plants and animals and fungi. In zoölogy, for instance, an *ornithologist* is a person who studies birds, and an *entomologist* is a person who studies insects. All these scientists are people who want to increase knowledge. They ask questions—and try to find out the answers. Here are some of the questions they ask, together with the names of the sciences that study them:

How are the different kinds of living things related to one another, and how should we name them? *Systematics* or *taxonomy*

What are their ways of life? *Ecology*

What are their parts, and how are these parts related (for example, is the eye of a snail of the same nature as a human eye?)? *Morphology*

Where are the different parts located, and what is their structure? *Anatomy*

What are the tissues of which these parts are made? *Histology*

What are cells made of? *Cytology*

How do the different parts work? *Physiology*

What are the chemicals in living things? *Biochemistry*

What are the diseases of living things? *Pathology*

How do living things reproduce themselves? *Genetics*

How do the unborn things develop? *Embryology*

What is the history of living things? *Paleontology* and *paleobotany*

These are only a few of the many biological sciences.

Aristotle, the Greek philosopher of 2,400 years ago, was one of the first men to study biology. He and his pupil Theophrastus wrote books on animals and plants. Galen, a Greek, was the first notable anatomist and physiologist, and his works were used until four hundred years ago; Leeuwenhoek, by inventing the microscope, made possible many great discoveries; Linnaeus was the founder of modern taxonomy. Schwann showed that all living things are built up of cells; Darwin, with his theory of evolution, showed that all living things could be related to one another; and Mendel showed how living things inherit their characteristics from their parents.

birch

The birch tree is both useful and beautiful. There are about thirty different kinds of birch, and they grow in North America, Europe, and Asia. The trunk of most birch trees is slender, and some reach a height of almost 70 feet when they are full grown, although most of those we see are usually no more than 30 feet high. Every birch tree has a thin, smooth bark that peels off easily. Birch trees are usually white or gray in color. The best known and most beautiful is the *paper birch* that grows in the United

States and Canada. The American Indians used the bark of the paper birch to make baskets and birch-bark canoes. Birch wood is used to make furniture, and it is also used for firewood. Charcoal made from birch is sometimes used for smoking meat and fish. Its smoke has a tangy smell that adds to the flavor. The sap of the birch is used in making a soft drink, "birch beer," that tastes like root beer. The oil of the birch tree is used in tanning certain kinds of leather.

bird

Field Museum of Natural History

Birds are animals with feathers, and this is the thing that makes them different from all other animals. Birds have two feet, and wings instead of arms or front legs. Like men, birds are warm-blooded, which means that the temperature of a bird's body stays the same no matter how hot or cold the weather may be. Also, like man, the bird is a vertebrate animal (has a backbone). The female bird lays eggs that have a hard shell. She then sits upon them to keep them warm until the baby chicks are ready to hatch.

These are ways in which all birds are the same, but there are more than eight thousand kinds of birds, and in many ways they are as different as people. There are fierce eagles and gentle doves, there are dignified owls and saucy bluejays, there are busy orioles and lazy cuckoos. Most birds can fly, but some cannot. Some birds like company and other birds do not. The hummingbird is as tiny as a small mouse, and the huge albatross can spread his wings 12 feet from tip to tip. Sparrows are a dusty brown color and birds of paradise have brilliant bright feathers. Birds live everywhere in the world. They make their homes in the jungles and the deserts. In the coldest north there are some birds, and on the highest mountains, and even in the middle of the ocean.

BODIES OF BIRDS

Every part of the bird's body is made so that the bird can fly as well as possible. The bones are hollow and light. The breast muscles are very powerful, because these are the muscles the bird uses to flap its wings and help take off from the ground, stay in the air, and land easily. Some birds have long, narrow wings and others have broad wings that are short and flat. The hummingbird can beat its wings so fast that it is able to stay in the air in one place for a long time. Some birds are able to soar and glide without flapping their wings. When there are wind currents to support them, birds such as the buzzard can glide back and forth in the sky for several hours without flapping their wings. Many birds have their own special way of flying. A few birds do not fly. The ostrich has funny little wings that it cannot use, and the penguin's wings are somewhat like paddles, making the penguin one of the world's best swimmers.

Scientists believe that millions of years ago birds came from reptiles. There was a flying reptile, the pterodactyl ("wing finger"), and the earliest birdlike animal, the archeopteryx ("ancient bird") was in many ways like a reptile. The legs of birds are still covered with scales that look like the skin of a lizard or snake. Scientists also believe that the soft feathers that cover the bodies of all birds were once scales. Feathers make a very warm coat for a bird, and the wing feathers help it fly. At the bottom of a bird's tail there are little glands that contain oil. As the bird moves his feathers, this oil comes out and helps make the feathers smooth and waterproof.

Birds have hard beaks instead of the soft mouths that many other animals have. They do many things with their beaks. The woodpecker's beak is a very handy hammer for tapping the trunks of trees. Many birds use their beaks to defend themselves against their enemies, and almost all birds use their beaks to clean their feathers, and to gather material for a nest, and to build the nest itself. But the most important thing birds do with their beaks is get food.

Hummingbirds have long thin beaks that can easily search the insides of flowers for nectar and tiny insects. The heron has a long sharp beak that is very good for catching fish. The pelican also eats fish and it has a kind of sack under its beak where it stores the fish it cannot swallow immediately. A very funny sight is a flamingo having its lunch. It eats with its head upside down in the water, swinging its curved beak between its legs and scooping up mouthfuls of water and mud. Then it strains the water and mud through the sides of its beak and finally it eats the small animals that are left.

One of the strangest beaks is the beak of the skimmer, which gets its name because of the way it eats. The lower part of the skimmer's beak is longer than the upper part. The skimmer uses this lower beak to scoop small fish and other water animals from the surface of the water, as it flies along; it does not have to stop to have a meal.

Bird's feet are as different as their beaks, and are just as useful in getting their food. Sparrows and thrushes and most of the birds that are often seen in a garden are called perching birds. Their feet are specially made so that they automatically curl around a branch or twig when these birds perch and rest their weight on their feet. Herons and ibises are wading birds, and they have long legs and thin toes so that they can stand on the soft muddy bottoms of rivers and run very fast in shallow water. The jacana is a South American bird whose toes are so long and thin that it can walk on top of the leaves of floating water plants. Ducks and geese that spend most of their time in the water have webbed feet, and the plover, which dives for his dinner, has winged toes. Eagles and hawks have sharp claws so that they can snatch and tear apart the animals they catch.

THE FOOD OF BIRDS

Birds need all the help their fine beaks and claws can give them in catching food, because they use up so much energy that they need a lot of food. Some birds eat almost their own weight in food every day, and they have to search constantly for all of it. The nuthatch is a little bird that eats the insects it finds in the bark of trees, but it takes so many tiny insects to make a meal for a nuthatch that it has to spend all day at it. It runs up and down the tree, eating as it goes. The owl sits quietly on a branch of a tree and waits. After a while, it may see a field mouse stirring on the ground and it swoops down and catches the little mouse for dinner. A hungry crow may steal the eggs from another bird's nest and eat them if it has a chance. The heron eats frogs and snakes and is a very good fisherman. Birds that live in the tropics eat fruits and nuts and some fierce hawks eat smaller birds. Eagles are hunters and live by catching rabbits and other small animals.

THE NESTS OF BIRDS

Some birds are very careful to build their nests where they are hard to find. Eagles and hawks make their nests at the very top of high trees. Bank swallows and kingfishers dig holes in the side of a river bank. Birds that live in places where there is little danger of anyone's disturbing their nests do not try to hide them. Gannets and loons lay their eggs on the rocky ground of the far North. Many shore birds just scrape out a little hollow in the sand and use that for a nest. A woodpecker may build its nest in a hollow limb.

Some birds are not very careful about the kind of nests they build, some put their nests together any old way, and the cowbird does not build a nest at all. The female cowbird lays eggs in other birds' nests. Birds may use many different things to build their nests, grass and twigs and pieces of bark, bits of string, paper, hair, roots, cloth, and whatever they happen to come across. Robins use mud, and cover the mud with soft grass to make the nest comfortable for the chicks. Sometimes the nest is lined with feathers to make it soft.

The oriole builds a beautiful little nest that hangs like a delicate basket from a tree. When the wind blows, the nest swings back and forth but does not fall. Then there are birds that build their nests together. The weaver bird lives in Africa and many weaver birds build one nest that is like a bird apartment house. The tick birds in South America lay their eggs in one nest and the females take turns sitting on the eggs. Wherever birds build their nests and however comfortable they are, the nest is the place where the female bird lays its eggs. Some birds lay as many as twenty eggs and other birds only one or two. Everyone knows what a chicken's egg looks like, but other kinds of eggs are so carefully hidden away that many peo-

ple never have a chance to see them. Eggs may be speckled or light blue, pale yellow or faint pink, red, black, or brown, and sometimes eggs are pure white. They may be long and thin or almost round, and large or small. An ostrich egg is so big that five very hungry men could make a meal from one egg but a hummingbird's egg is only about the size of a pea.

Whatever the color or size or shape of the egg, the mother bird must sit on it until the baby is ready to hatch, and this may take a few days or several weeks. Some father birds help hatch the eggs, and some do not. Once the baby birds are born the parents are very busy getting food for the hungry family, and then when the little birds are strong enough, the parents have to teach them to fly.

CHARACTERISTICS OF BIRDS

The female in the bird world is usually much duller in color and less attractive-looking than the male. The male rose-breasted grosbeak has a bright rose-colored breast while the female is a pale mouse color. There are similar differences between the two sexes in most birds.

The advantage of this is that the female has to sit on the nest and if she were very brightly colored it would be easier for enemies to find the nest. The bright-colored male can attract the attention of dangerous enemies and keep them away from the nest.

The brightly colored males are proud of their plumage and they are likely to be most popular with the females. Some very conceited turkeys and birds of paradise fluff out their feathers and do a little dance to show the females how beautiful they are.

Birds are most often more brightly colored in the summer than they are in the winter. Birds change their feathers (molt) one or more times every year. The scarlet tanager is one of the brightest summer birds, with its bright red feathers, but in the fall it gets a dull olive-green coat so that it can hide itself against the dull winter scenery.

One of the things that people like best about birds is their singing. Canaries are very popular pets because they sing so well. Some birds have sweet and gentle songs and others are cheerful chirpers. Crows have hoarse voices that sound very funny to us, and some birds sound very mournful and sad. It seems as if birds are talking to each other, and when a hawk comes near, most birds will set up a loud and frightened calling that warns other birds of danger. Scientists think that male birds sing in order to find a mate, and it seems as if the male birds that do not have the most beautiful feathers are likely to be the best singers. Some birds are very good at imitating sounds and they can learn each other's songs, and even learn to talk. Parrots are the best talkers, but Deacon, a famous crow at the Bronx zoo in New York city, learned to say "hello" to visitors. The brown pelican and the frigate bird do not make any sound at all.

MIGRATION OF BIRDS

Each fall in North America we see birds of all kinds flying south and in the spring we see them once again as they fly north. These flights are called *migrations*.

Until recently nothing much was known about why birds migrate and how they go about it. Scientists who have studied birds now think that birds migrate not because they cannot stand cold weather but because when winter comes to a place the birds find it almost impossible to get food.

Many birds migrate. Some merely fly from Canada and northern United States to the southern United States and Central America. Other birds travel long distances each year. The Arctic tern flies from its summer home above the Arctic to its winter home near the Antarctic Circle, 11,000 miles away. When it flies back again in the spring, it has completed a round trip of 22,000 miles.

One of the interesting things about bird migration is the fact that a bird will follow the same path or route each time it migrates. There are several main routes that birds take on their way south and on their return trip to the north. Their main air highway is over the central United

Black Star

Netherlands West Indies Tourist Comm.

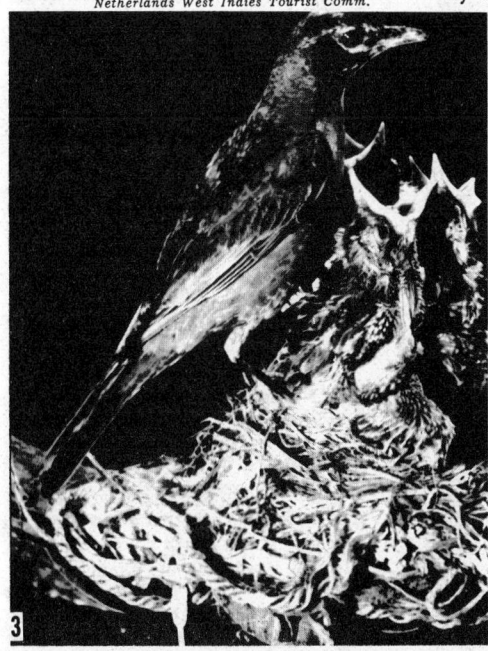

States and the Mississippi River. Some birds fly at night and rest during the day; other birds do just the opposite. The birds band together on these long flights, and some of them, such as wild geese and ducks, even fly in regular formation.

The most remarkable thing about the migration of birds is how they can tell direction and how they will always return to the same places they left the season before. Some birds even return to the same nest or nesting place. How they do this is still unknown to man.

BIRDS' USEFULNESS TO MAN

Birds are useful to man in many ways. Since earliest history men have kept tame birds like chickens and ducks and have raised them for food. Birds have also been kept in cages for their beauty and their lovely songs. Man has used the feathers of the eider duck and a few other birds to stuff pillows and quilts and mattresses. The plumes of many birds have been highly prized for their beauty in women's hats and in fans.

Birds have been most useful to man in their destruction of insects. As the many insect-eating birds go about getting their food, they destroy millions of insects that are harmful to man's crops. If there were no birds, the insects would increase so tremendously that most of the food that man grows for himself would be destroyed. Man has not always realized how important birds are in this respect. In some places birds have been ruthlessly killed, because they were considered to be pests. In these places man soon learned that the birds were not nearly as pesty as the insects that destroyed the crops. The insects increased in numbers with no birds around to eat them.

bird of paradise

The bird of paradise is the name given to a group of the most beautiful birds in the world. Some are bright green and yellow; others are a brilliant red. But the most beautiful thing about a bird of paradise is the fanlike tail made up of long, feathery plumes that grow from its back. These magnificent plumes are usually a deep golden-yellow, though some

Black Star

1. This peewit is sitting on four eggs, though you cannot see them. It takes sixteen days for the eggs to hatch. The peewit is known for the great care it takes in watching over its eggs and its young.

2. This downy baby flamingo is going to look very different when it grows up. It will have fine pink feathers and a very long neck and legs.

3. Two hungry baby robins waiting with open mouths for their mother to feed them.

of the birds have white or black plumes. Well-dressed women used to wear hats that were adorned by these plumes. The bird of paradise lives in New Guinea and on other nearby islands in the South Pacific. It is about two feet long. It feeds on fruits and insects. Only the males are brilliantly colored. During the first year of life, both the male and female are a coffee-brown in color. After this, the male gradually changes, until in its fourth year it has the splendid plumes that make it famous. Despite its great beauty, the bird of paradise is closely related to the crow. Little was known about it until one hundred years ago, when the first bird of paradise was brought to Europe. Until then it had been thought that this bird had no wings or feet and that it floated through the air, supported by its trailing plumes. It was also thought that the bird of paradise never touched the earth until it died, and that it then floated down to the ground. None of this was true, of course. The bird of paradise can be seen in the bird houses of many zoos.

bird-watching

Birds are such interesting and beautiful creatures that all over the world there are thousands of people whose hobby is watching them. Some of them form societies, such as the Audubon Society, and others enjoy watching birds just to see how they live and to discover unusual kinds of birds that are seldom seen.

It is best to go bird-watching alone, to avoid frightening the bird. It is best also to wear dull-colored clothing, and to move very slowly and cautiously. A bird-watcher should have binoculars, so that he can see the birds clearly without being so close that he might frighten them away. Experts say that a 6-power binocular is best for bird-watching.

Even in a big city it is possible to be a bird-watcher. In the heart of New York there are people who have seen some of the country's rarest birds in the parks and private gardens.

Many books are available that describe birds, often with pictures in color, and tell what the habits of different birds are. The birdwatcher's greatest thrill comes from seeing a bird that rarely occurs in his locality, or in the season in which he sees it. He may report this in a letter to a local zoo or newspaper.

Birmingham is the largest city of Alabama and the largest industrial center in the "deep south." It was named after Birmingham, an important industrial city in England.

Birmingham, Alabama, lies in the heart of one of the richest coal and iron districts in the world. Because these raw materials were so near, Birmingham grew into the leading iron and steel manufacturing city in the south. There are great steel mills, and huge blast furnaces that light up the sky at night. That is why Birmingham is called "the Pittsburgh of the South." More than 300,000 people live there. They not only work in the steel mills, but also in large factories that make cast-iron pipe, machinery, stoves, and chemicals.

Birmingham is not just a city of mills and factories. In the spring, parts of Birmingham bloom with beautiful roses, and dogwood trees that have white, fragrant blossoms. There are also 48 parks and playgrounds, and several colleges. Birmingham is the youngest of all the great cities of the United States. It was not founded until 1871, but it rapidly grew into one of the most important cities in the South.

BIRMINGHAM, ALABAMA. Population, 300,910 (1970 census). County seat of Jefferson County. Near the Warrior River. Settled in 1871.

Birmingham, England, is in the central part of the country, 113 miles north of London. It is the second-largest city in England and a great manufacturing center for metal products. Most of the country's coins are made in Birmingham. The people also manufacture guns, tools, automobiles, toys, and many other products.

Although Birmingham, England, was a town more than nine hundred years ago, it did not become a city until 1889. Today, more than one million people live there. In World War II, many of the buildings were severely damaged by German bombings.

BIRMINGHAM, ENGLAND. Population, 1,074,900, urban area, 2,525,000. Location, central England.

birthstones

Long ago, the peoples of many lands such as India, Egypt, Babylonia, China, Arabia, and ancient America, felt that precious stones or gems had the power to protect and help people. This was especially true of a stone associated with the month of one's birth.

Birthstones are used in jewelry by both men and women. The gem may be set in a ring or a pin, or simply carried on the person. Each birthstone is said to bring its wearer a particular virtue or special good fortune. Here is what is said of some of the stones in the list below: garnet—constancy; amethyst—sincerity; aquamarine—wisdom; diamond—innocence; emerald—love; pearl—wealth; ruby—freedom; peridot—friendship; sapphire—truth; opal—hope; topaz—loyalty; turquoise—success.

There are different lists of birthstones, partly because we cannot be sure today just which stones the ancients meant by their names for the various gems. Here is one list:

January	garnet
February	amethyst
March	bloodstone, aquamarine
April	diamond
May	emerald
June	pearl, moonstone
July	ruby
August	sardonyx, peridot
September	sapphire
October	opal, tourmaline
November	topaz
December	turquoise, lapis lazuli

Biscay, Bay of

The Bay of Biscay is a large arm of the Atlantic Ocean that sticks into Europe along the coasts of France and Spain. The bay covers about 100,000 square miles of water and stretches from the little Finistère peninsula of France to Cape Finisterre of Spain, the westernmost points of the two countries; both names mean "land's end." Bordeaux is considered the principal French port on Biscay and Bilboa the principal Spanish port, but actually each of these cities is on a river several miles from the sea. Other Biscay ports include Brest, Lorient and Nantes, France, and Gijon, Spain. The French coast has low sand dunes and the Spanish coast is steep and rocky. There are islands in the northern part. Often there are heavy storms and high waves in the bay. The southern French coast of Biscay is a popular resort area, the principal resort being Biarritz.

Bismarck

Bismarck is the capital city of North Dakota. It is on the Missouri River, in the central part of the state. More than 34,000 people live there. Most of them work in the large flour mills and packing plants. Other manufactures are tile, brick, and gravel. The city is surrounded by a fertile farming region. The farmers send wheat, oats and potatoes to Bismarck, which is an important trading center. It was settled in 1872 and became the capital of North Dakota in 1889.

The North Dakota State Capitol in Bismark is a new, modern building. The old building was destroyed by fire in 1930 and the present capitol was completed in 1935. It is made of gleaming white limestone. Next to it is an 18-story skyscraper, containing the offices of state officials.

BISMARCK, NORTH DAKOTA. Population, 34,703 (1970 census). Capital of North Dakota. County seat of Burleigh County. On the Missouri River. Settled 1872.

Bismarck, Prince Otto von

Otto von Bismarck was a skillful statesman who changed Germany from a group of small, independent kingdoms into a single nation. He was so ruthless in his desire to unite the German states into an empire that he was known as the "Iron Chancellor." A chancellor, like a prime minister, is the highest official in some governments. Bismarck was born in 1815, in Prussia, a north German country that was noted for its warlike and militaristic spirit. At that time, the separate German states were loosely joined in a confederation that included Austria. Austria was powerful, and Bismarck looked upon it as Prussia's rival. William I came to the throne of Prussia in 1861 and made Bismarck his foreign minister and the head of the cabinet. Bismarck began to plan to unify Germany and he declared, "Not by speeches and resolutions of majorities are the mighty problems of the age to be solved . . . but by blood and iron." By this he meant wars would have to be fought.

Bismarck used three wars to gain his ends. He defeated first Denmark, then Austria, and finally France. Now King William of Prussia was emperor of the new Germany, which included all the German countries except Austria. Bismarck was made a prince and served as the first chancellor of the empire. Bis-

marck looked upon the citizens as "children" of the Father State. The State was to arrange and direct their lives, and the good of the State was much more important than the individual citizen. Later, this point of view was greatly admired by Hitler and the Nazis. The Emperor William—Bismarck's great friend and supporter—died in 1888. His son, William II, wanted to rule Germany without Bismarck's advice. Bismarck resigned a few years later, and died in 1898.

Bismarck Archipelago

The Bismarck Archipelago is a group of islands in the Pacific Ocean. They are just north of the eastern end of New Guinea and they are governed by Australia. They are named after the famous German statesman Prince Otto von Bismarck. There are more than two hundred islands in the group. They cover about 20,000 square miles but less than 200,000 people live there.

Most of the people are Papuans, a primitive, black-skinned people found also on New Guinea. They live by farming and fishing. The islands are mountainous and on some there are volcanoes that still erupt. The climate is hot and moist. The largest islands include New Britain, New Ireland, and the Admiralty Islands. (See ADMIRALTY ISLANDS.)

Chicago Natural History Museum
A tribal warrior on the island of New Britain, in the Bismarck Archipelago.

About seventy years ago, the Bismarck Archipelago was placed under German rule. During World War I, the Australians took over the islands. Early in World War II, the islands were seized by the Japanese. They built many airfields and supply bases there. They were driven out by the Allies in 1944.

BISMARCK SEA

Bismarck Sea is a name given, during World War II, to about 70,000 square miles of the Pacific Ocean lying within a circle formed by the Bismarck Archipelago and New Guinea.

One of the big defeats for the Japanese in the war took place at the Battle of the Bismarck Sea, in March 1943. A large convoy of Japanese ships was carrying thousands of soldiers to a big Japanese base in New Guinea. They were suddenly attacked by the United States Air Force. The airplanes bombed the ships for three days until the Japanese convoy was completely destroyed. Fifteen thousand Japanese soldiers were killed, and 22 ships were sunk.

BISMARCK ARCHIPELAGO. Group of about 200 islands in Pacific Ocean. Area, 19,200 square miles. Population (1973 estimate), 163,000.

bismuth

Bismuth is a silvery-white, brittle metal with a touch of red in it. It is a chemical element (see ELEMENT). It is harmless to the human body, unlike the poisonous arsenic and lead with which it is often found. More than thirty medicines are made from bismuth. Most of these medicines are used in treating people who have stomach trouble. Doctors also use bismuth to prepare a patient's stomach and intestines for x-rays. The patient drinks a bismuth mixture that looks like a malted milkshake. The doctor then takes his x-ray pictures. The bismuth mixture makes the stomach and intestines appear more clearly in the x-ray pictures.

By itself bismuth is too breakable for any use, but when it is melted together with other metals, such as tin and zinc, it forms valuable alloys. (See ALLOY.) These alloys are used a great deal for making printing type because they melt easily and are quite hard when cool. Certain bismuth compounds are used as coloring matter to give different shades of orange to porcelain and pottery.

Like most metals, bismuth is found in ores in the earth. It is found all over the world, usually together with ores of silver, lead, and cobalt. It is mined in large quantities in California, Bolivia, and Australia. Heat and chemicals are used to separate the pure bismuth from the rest of the ore.

Bismuth was not known in ancient times. In the Middle Ages the alchemists knew about it, though they often got it mixed up with zinc, tin and lead. About two hundred years ago a Swedish chemist, Torbern Olof Berman, finally gave the world the first clear description of bismuth.

bison

The bison is a large American animal related to the cow and other cattle. It is the largest animal found in the Americas. Usually the bison is called a buffalo, but that is not correct; it is related to the buffalo, but the only real buffaloes live in Asia and Africa, and formerly in Europe.

A full-grown male bison may be 10 to 12 feet long and 6 feet high at the shoulder and weigh 2,000 pounds. The female is smaller, about 1,200 pounds. The bison has a large hump on its shoulders and its head hangs low, almost to the ground, as though it were too heavy to hold up. It has curved, hollow horns about a foot long. Under its chin it has a pointed beard and on its head and for several feet up its back it has a mane of long, shaggy hair. Thick hair also covers the front of its body. The bison's tail is short and is a guide to the bison's feelings: When the bison is contented the tail droops; when the bison is excited or angry its tail stands up, almost as a cat's tail does.

Though it is big and powerful, the bison is gentle and timid. It is not very intelligent and is easily trapped and killed. The bison normally lives 30 to 40 years. Bison do not multiply very fast, for the bison cow, like the domestic cow, usually has one calf at a time, once a year.

When the white men first came to America, millions of bison in huge herds roamed what is now the central part of the United States, from the Rocky Mountains to the Appalachians and from Canada to Mexico. They grazed the northern prairies in warm months, then in the winter moved hundreds of miles south to find more grass. The Indians hunted the bison for its meat, which is like beef; its skin, used for robes, blankets, and leather; and even its hair, which can be spun into thread for weaving. Some tribes of Indians literally lived on the bison, which they killed with bow and arrow. As the white man's civilization moved westward, the bison was pushed westward too. By 1800 there were few bison left east of the Mississippi River, but late into the 1800s travelers to the Far West would see herds of thousands of bison. Then the hunting of bison became a mass slaughter. Many were killed for meat; during and after the Civil War soldiers, railroad-building groups and others were fed bison meat, which became so plentiful that in the 1870s it sold for a cent a pound. "Buffalo Bill" Cody was one of the famous hunters. Hunting the "buffalo" was also a popular sport. Millions were killed.

By 1900 there were only 2,000 bison left. The United States and Canada then set aside reservations, places where bison could live safely, to save the rest. The principal reservations are in western Montana and in the Yellowstone National Park in Wyoming. By the 1960s the number of bison had risen to more than 20,000.

bitumen, any of various tarlike substances that are used for roofing, making ships watertight, and paving streets: see ASPHALT.

bivalve

A bivalve is a kind of shellfish that has a soft body protected by a hard shell, which usually is in two parts, hinged together. Most bivalves live in the ocean, though some live in fresh water, rivers or lakes. The most familiar bivalves are oysters, clams, mussels, and scallops, because they are very valuable as food to people who live near the ocean. There are separate articles about these, and about SHELLFISH. The cockle is another bivalve, but it is not used for food in America and the fancy shell called a cockle-shell is actually the shell of a scallop.

Oysters and mussels attach themselves to rocks; clams burrow in sand or mud;

shipworms bore into wood; cockles attach themselves to the sea bottom or to rocks; and scallops swim about freely and are the only bivalves that have eyes.

Bivalves feed by means of siphons, or tubes. They suck water in through one siphon, filter it to trap the tiny living creatures or decaying particles on which they feed, and then shoot out the waste through their other siphon. In this way they are very useful for purifying water.

Each bivalve is both male and female. As many as two million eggs are released into the water by an individual. They hatch into tiny creatures that swim by tiny lashing hairs. After a while this creature grows a flap on each side of its mouth. Then its shell begins to form, and it becomes too heavy to float and sinks to the bottom. Those that find themselves in a suitable place grow; the others die. From the lines on their shells you can count how many years old they are. Mussels live to be about ten years old. The giant clam of Australia may live for sixty or even a hundred years.

Bizet, Georges

Georges Bizet was a famous French composer of operas and other music. He was born in Paris, France, in 1828, and took his first music lessons from his father, who was a teacher of singing. When Bizet was nine years old he started to study music at the Conservatory in Paris. When he was fourteen years old he

Gale Research Co.

won first prize for his piano-playing, and the next year he won another prize for playing the organ, and for writing a fugue, a musical composition combining different melodies. Bizet's most famous composition is the opera *Carmen.* People did not like it very much at first, but now it is one of the most popular of all operas; in the United States it is the most popular opera. Bizet died near Paris in 1875.

blackberry

Blackberry is the name Americans give to a berry that grows on small, pretty bushes. Each berry is a cluster of tiny black knobs. In England the people call them *brambleberries.* As blackberries grow they change from green to red to black. They are not ripe until they are black all over. Loganberries and boysenberries are forms of blackberries.

The blackberry bush grows about 3 feet high. Its branches are covered with sharp thorns. The bush grows best in deep, rich, moist soil. The bush should be pruned (its branches trimmed) each fall. The berries ripen in August. They are eaten with cream and are canned as jellies and preserves.

blackbird

The red-winged blackbird is a small songbird (slightly smaller than a robin) found in North America. It is black except for red shoulders bordered with yellow, which cannot be seen when its wings are folded. Blackbirds build their nests in the low bushes of swamps or beside ponds. The female lays four to six eggs, blue with patches of black or violet.

black death

The "black death" was what people called a disease that killed millions of people in Europe and Asia about six hundred years ago. It is also called the *plague,* and though people then did not know what caused it, we know now that it was the *bubonic plague,* a disease that was spread by rats on ships. Lice on the rats would bite them and pick up the disease germs, and then would bite people and pass the germs along.

The bubonic plague causes a swelling, called *bubo,* in some glands of the body. The same infection that causes the swelling will usually kill a person within a few days. More than 60,000,000 people died from the "black death" in the 14th century. Nearly everyone ran from every sign of the plague, so very often no one would even bury the dead. The same kind of plague has visited Europe and Asia every few hundred years throughout history. The last time was in the 1890s, when the plague killed millions of people in India.

Until recently, no cure for the bubonic plague was known. Countries protected themselves by watching incoming ships very carefully, so that rats could not bring the infection in. Also people have become much cleaner personally than they used to be, and the plague spreads chiefly in conditions of filth. Some of the new antibiotic drugs will usually cure the plague.

black-eyed Susan

Black-eyed Susans are bright yellow flowers with a dark center. They are a kind of daisy and grow wild in most parts of the United States and Canada. The petals grow like the petals of a daisy, and the leaves are the same as a daisy's. The flower has a dark brown center that looks blackish at a distance. That is why it was called the "black-eyed" Susan. At times it is also called the *yellow daisy,* or the *oxeye daisy.* It is the state flower of Maryland. See COMPOSITE PLANTS.

Blackfoot Indians

The Blackfoot Indians were one of the tribes of ALGONQUINS (about which there is a separate article). The Blackfeet, or sometimes they were called Blackfoots, lived originally near the Rocky Mountains where the Missouri and Yellowstone Rivers have their source, chiefly in the region that is now the state of Montana. They did not call themselves Blackfeet. That name was given to them by French explorers because they wrapped their feet and legs in buffalo leather that was so dark it looked black. The Blackfeet's own name for their tribe was Siksika. There were two branches of their tribe, the Kaina (also called "Blood Indians") and the Piegans.

The Blackfeet were hunters of buffalo (bison) and trappers of beaver and otter, whose fur was so fine that many fur-traders made trips to Blackfoot territory.

In American history the Blackfoot Indians are important because they controlled the northwest passes through the Rocky Mountains and on their friendship or peacefulness depended the safety of settlers traveling to the territories that are now the states of Washington, Oregon,

and Idaho. The Blackfeet were seldom peaceful for any long period and finally the U. S. Army subdued them and resettled them in reservations, where about 4,800 of them still live. At one time there were about 50,000 Blackfoots.

Black Forest

The Black Forest is a mountainous region in southwestern Germany, rising above the Rhine River where it marks the German boundaries with Switzerland and France. The Black Forest is actually a low mountain range about 90 miles long and 25 miles wide, covering in all nearly 2,000 square miles. The mountains are from 2,000 to almost 5,000 feet high. They are covered with pine trees so dark that they look black.

There are many fairy tales and legends set in the Black Forest. To keep their children from wandering in the forest and getting lost, parents used to tell of a witch who lived there and changed lost children into trees; but there also was a kindly giant who helped the children.

The people of the Black Forest have retained many quaint costumes and customs from the Middle Ages. This fact and the beauty of the mountains make the Black Forest a favorite tourist resort. The best-known of many resort towns is Baden-Baden, at the extreme north of the region. There is hunting of wild boars in the forest.

Lumbering and woodcutting are important industries. Cuckoo clocks, toys and musical instruments are made of the wood.

Black Hand

The name "Black Hand" describes a kind of secret society of men, called "terrorists," who threaten to do violent things unless they can have their own way. Some of the secret societies have been patriotic organizations in countries that were under foreign rule and wanted independence. Other have been societies of criminals, or gangsters. *Black Hand* means "evil power."

Famous Black Hands include a society of anarchists in Spain, about seventy-five years ago (see the article on ANARCHISM); another society of the same kind in Serbia, which may have started World War I by assassinating the Austrian archduke (or prince) Ferdinand in 1914; and the Mafia in Sicily, which is an organization of criminals that has branches in the United States. (See MAFIA.) Except for the Mafia and a few bandit gangs (see BANDIT) there has been no active Black Hand society since before World War I.

All Black Hand societies kill or beat people, destroy their property, kidnap them, or commit other violent acts, to make people pay them blackmail or "protection money."

Black Hawk

Black Hawk was a chief of the Sac and Fox Indians and their leader in the Black Hawk War against the United States in 1831 and 1832. He was born in 1767 and became chief when he was 21. At that time the Sac and Fox Indians lived in what is now Illinois. In 1804 the United States made a treaty with most of

them to move westward across the Mississippi River.

Black Hawk refused to accept the treaty. He remained in Illinois and in the War of 1812 he and 500 of his warriors fought for the British against the United States. After the war Black Hawk was forced to sign the treaty but he did not consider himself bound by it and until 1830 he often attacked white settlers in Illinois.

THE BLACK HAWK WAR

Then, in 1830, the United States made several promises to persuade Black Hawk to sign a new treaty and finally he moved west. The promises were not kept and a year later Black Hawk recrossed the river. The Black Hawk War was then begun (Abraham Lincoln was a young militia officer in it) and the U.S. Army fought it very cruelly, with several unnecessary massacres of the Indians. Black Hawk was captured in 1832 and kept in prison for a year. When released he returned to his tribe, which was settled in Iowa, and lived peaceably until his death in 1838. He was a hero to the Indians and was respected by many of the whites.

Black Hills

The Black Hills are a group of mountains in South Dakota and Wyoming. They look black because there are dense, dark, pine forests on them. They are very rough and rocky. They cover about 6,000 square miles in area, and some of them in the central part are more than 5,000 feet high.

The highest peak, Harney, is 7,242 feet high. On Mt. Rushmore are carved 60-foot-high heads of George Washington, Thomas Jefferson, Abraham Lincoln, and Theodore Roosevelt. This is the Mt. Rushmore National Monument. The sculpture on it was supervised by Gutzon BORGLUM, about whom there is a separate article.

The Black Hills territory once belonged to the Sioux Indians. Then gold was discovered there. The Indians were removed, white settlers arrived, and between the years 1875 and 1901 about a hundred million dollars' worth of gold was taken out. The Black Hills have since become popular as a vacation resort.

Black Hole of Calcutta

The Black Hole of Calcutta was a small room in Calcutta, India, in which many men died about 200 years ago. At that time English traders were doing business in Calcutta, protected by a small fort with a garrison of English soldiers. On the night of June 20, 1756, Surajah Dowlah, the Indian ruler of Bengal, attacked the fort. He took 146 prisoners and shut them up all night in a tiny dungeon that had only two small, barred windows. Some say that the room was not big enough for more than ten men. The prisoners suffered cruelly all through the night from heat, thirst, and lack of air. In the morning only 23 men were still alive. This dungeon became known as the Black Hole of Calcutta. The following year the English recaptured the fort. They built a monument fifty feet high in front of the door of the tiny dungeon, in memory of the men who suffered there.

blackjack

Blackjack is a card game that is popular in many parts of the world. It is also called *twenty-one*, and in France it is called *vingt-et-un*, which means twenty-one in the French language. It is a very old game, played for more than 300 years. Blackjack is a popular home game because from two to as many as twelve may play.

RULES OF BLACKJACK

Use a regular pack of 52 cards or two packs mixed together. One player is the first dealer, decided in any way. (It is a great advantage to deal, but the dealer changes often, as explained below.) Chips or other tokens are used.

The object of each player is to have, in two or more cards, a count of 21 or as near to 21 as possible without going over 21. Each face card or ten counts 10; each number card counts its number; but an ace counts either 1 or 11, whichever the player wishes. When a player "busts" (goes over 21) he loses immediately.

The dealer gives each player, including himself, one card face down. Each other player looks at his card and makes a bet against the dealer—for example, one, two or three chips, depending on whether he thinks his first card is poor, fair, or good. The dealer can then double—make every player double his bet. If the dealer doubles, any player may redouble his own bet if he wishes.

The dealer then gives each player, including himself, one face-up card. If any player has a count of 21 in two cards—an ace and a face card or ten, called a *blackjack* or *natural*—he wins immediately and is paid double the amount of his total bet. If the dealer has a natural, everyone pays him double—except that if the dealer and an opponent both have naturals, their bet is called off.

If the dealer has no natural, he begins with the player nearest his left. That player may *stand* if he is satisfied with his count, or he may take another card by saying "Hit me." The dealer continues to give the player cards, face up, as long as the player asks for them. A player may stand after any card. Whenever a card puts a player over 21 he must pay his bet to the dealer and turn all his cards face down. The dealer settles with each player before going to the next. When every other player has either stood or busted, the dealer turns up his face-down card and may deal additional cards to himself. If he goes over, he pays every active player his bet but keeps any bets he has already collected. If the dealer stands with 21 or less, all active players turn up their face-down cards. Dealer pays anyone who is closer to 21 but collects anyone he beats or ties.

Change of dealer. Any player who is dealt a natural becomes the dealer at the end of the current deal, unless the dealer has a natural too. If two or more players have naturals, the one nearest the dealer's left is the next dealer (for he got his natural first). A player may sell the dealership at auction if he wishes to.

New Shuffle. There is a new shuffle when the next-to-last card of the pack has been dealt. (It is customary to turn the top card face up and put it on the bottom of the pack, before the first deal. This is called "burning" a card. When the face-up card is reached, the dealer takes all cards from previous deals, plus the cards of all players who have busted in the present hand. He shuffles these cards, burns a card, and continues dealing. There is also a new shuffle of all the cards when the dealership changes.

Special rules. There are many special rules that are used in some games and not in others, but in nearly all games the following are used:

"One down for doubles." If a player's first two cards add to 10 or 11, he can turn both up, double his total bet, and draw one card face down—but no additional card.

Splitting pairs. If a player's first two cards are a pair, as two sixes or two jacks, he may place the amount of his total bet on each and play them as two separate hands; but a natural in this case pays only singly and does not win the deal.

"Five and under." If a player's count in five cards is 21 or less, he is paid double. For making 21 with three sevens he is paid triple, and for making 21 with 8-7-6 he is paid double.

The dealer cannot use any of these special rules.

Pointers. An ace, 10-point card or nine warrants a high bet, an eight or seven a medium bet, a lower card the lowest bet. Dealer should double on an ace or 10-point card. A player should redouble on an ace. It usually pays to take one down for double and to split a pair unless the dealer has a high card showing. It does not pay to split pairs of face cards, tens, or fives, and in many games a player is not allowed to split aces.

blacklist

Blacklist means "a list of bad people (or companies)." Labor unions used to make a list of companies that were not fair to their employees, and the unions urged everyone to stop buying from those companies. Big companies made lists of men who caused them trouble, and asked other companies not to give jobs to men on the blacklist.

More than one hundred and fifty years ago, in their wars against Napoleon, the British made a blacklist of companies that were doing business with the enemy and so could not do business with British companies; the same kind of blacklist was used by the British and Americans in World Wars I and II. Most people now consider blacklists to be unfair, except in wartime. Blacklists are illegal in labor disputes (see the TAFT-HARTLEY ACT).

blackmail

Blackmail is an unlawful way of forcing someone to pay money he does not owe, by threatening to do him harm if he does not pay. The usual form of blackmail is that one person discovers that another person has committed some crime. He says, "If you do not pay me, I will tell the police about your crime." Very often the criminal is so frightened that he pays.

Lawyers do not usually use the term blackmail. They call it *extortion*. It has many other forms, but all of them are threats. For instance, "If you do not pay, I will throw a bomb into your house," or "If you do not pay, I will kidnap your child." The "mail" in blackmail has nothing to do with letters. Long ago, *black* meant "evil" and *mail* meant "money."

black market

A black market is not any particular place where goods are bought and sold. It is a condition that exists whenever there are laws to control the selling of scarce merchandise, such as food in wartime, and to fix the prices at which this scarce merchandise may be sold. (See the article on RATIONING.) At such times people will

pay high prices to buy things they want but cannot buy legally, and when they buy merchandise that is not supposed to be sold or pay more for it than the law allows they are said to buy it "on the black market."

The United States has never had much of a black market compared to European countries, but during World War II cigarettes were sold in the United States at two or three times the price the law allowed and many butchers kept their best beefsteak "under the counter" and sold it for $2.50 a pound when the law said they could not charge more than 75¢. In all parts of Europe, during and after World War II, nearly everything had two prices, a legal price at which it was never to be had and a black-market price that was much higher. The black market is one of the results of INFLATION, about which there is a separate article.

The term "gray market" was used in the United States for a brief period after World War II. It described a condition in which buyers would pay bribes to get certain merchandise, such as steel, that was scarce but that it was not illegal to sell.

Blackmore, Richard Doddridge

Richard Doddridge Blackmore was an English novelist. His most famous novel was *Lorna Doone*, an adventure story about a family of outlaws and about a man who fell in love with the daughter of one of the outlaws. Richard Blackmore was born in Berkshire, a county in England, in 1825. He became a lawyer, but because he loved nature and gardening he gave up the law and became a fruit-grower. During his life he wrote fifteen novels and several books of poetry. He died in 1900.

Black Mountains

The Black Mountains are a group of mountains in the western part of North Carolina. They are part of the Blue Ridge Mountains in the Appalachian range and include the highest point in the Blue Ridge Mountains, Mt. Mitchell, which is 6,684 feet high. It is the tallest mountain east of the Mississippi River.

blackout

A blackout is the complete darkening of a city at night, to protect it against air raids. The word *blackout* is also used to describe a sudden fainting spell or loss of consciousness.

Blackouts of cities were first tried in the 1930s just before World War II, when it became clear that there would be much bombing of cities if war came. At first everyone in the city was ordered to put out all lights, but this did not work well, because not everyone obeyed. When the war came, most people got "blackout curtains" to cover windows so completely that no light could show through. Air-raid wardens patrolled the streets to make sure no light showed. Even the striking of a match can be seen from aircraft miles up in the air and can help locate a city. Nearly every city and town in Europe was blacked out every night for the full 5½ years of the war.

The fainting spell called a blackout is like falling asleep very suddenly. Aviators sometimes "black out" when they pull out of steep dives at high speeds. The blood rushes out of their brains and for a short time they are unconscious. Some pilots have died because of blackouts but usually the blackout lasts only a few seconds and the pilot recovers consciousness in time to bring his plane under control again.

Black Sea

The Black Sea is a large body of water between Europe and Asia, almost completely surrounded by land. It is 168,000 square miles in size and more than 7,000 feet deep. North of it is a bay called the Sea of Azov. The Black Sea is connected with the Mediterranean Sea in the southwest, by the BOSPORUS, the Sea of MARMARA, and the DARDANELLES, about which there are separate articles.

Many rivers from Europe and Asia flow into the Black Sea. The most important are the Danube, Dniester, Don, and Dnieper. The Black Sea has few islands. The largest one is in the western part opposite the mouths of the Danube. It is called Adassi, which means "isle of serpents." In the summer the Black Sea is usually calm, and ships can travel through it safely, but in the winter fierce storms make it dangerous. There is also danger in the winter from floating ice. The Black Sea has so many rivers flowing into it that it has less salt than the ocean and freezes more quickly. In the winter the Black Sea is often covered with heavy fog.

The Black Sea was important for navigation even to the ancient Greeks and Romans (who called it the Euxine, or friendly sea). Many nations have controlled the Black Sea; Turkey controlled it for more than 400 years, from 1450 to 1850, and even then held the passages through which ocean-bound ships must pass. Since World War I the sea and entrance to it have been open to all nations.

Important Black Sea ports are Odessa, Batum and Sevastopol in the Soviet Union and Batum in Turkey.

blacksnake

The common blacksnake is one of America's fastest animals. It moves along the ground as swiftly as a horse. It is an even, dark color, and is five to six feet long. There are many blacksnakes in states east of the Mississippi River, from Alabama to Connecticut. The blacksnake eats small animals such as mice, frogs, and birds. It can climb trees and glide over bushes easily. It likes to eat eggs and sometimes steals them from poultry farms. The blacksnake will bite when it is annoyed, but its bite is not poisonous. Some are kept as pets.

There are blacksnakes in many countries. Most of them are harmless, but the blacksnakes that live in Australia and Tasmania, an island off Australia, are dangerous because they have poisonous fangs.

The scales of a blacksnake make it look like a woven rawhide leather whip. For this reason it is often called a whip snake.

Blackstone, Sir William

William Blackstone was an English lawyer who wrote a book that has taught law to thousands of lawyers since his time. When he was born in 1723, the English law was very unorganized. To most people the law was very mysterious. Blackstone was the first man to attempt to make the English law of his own day understandable. Because he did this so well in his book, *Commentaries on the Laws of England*, some books on law still have his name on them, though most of the law has changed since his time. He died in 1780.

black walnut

The black walnut is a handsome tree that will grow to be 50 feet tall if it is planted in rich soil. Sixty years ago the black walnut was very common and grew all over most of the eastern United States. The wood from the black walnut is highly valued for making furniture. The wood is very hard and has a rich, dark brown color when it is polished. Today the wood of the black walnut is hard to get and is very expensive because the forests where it grew have almost all been cut down. Most black walnut trees are now found growing along the streets of towns and cities, because they are good shade trees.

Blackwell, Elizabeth

Elizabeth Blackwell was the first woman doctor in the United States. Her struggles and her success opened the way for other women who wanted to do more than nursing. She was born in England more than a hundred years ago—in 1821—and her family moved to America when she was 11 years old. The Blackwell girls received the same education as their brothers. This was most unusual in those days. Their father died young, and they had very little money to live on. Elizabeth and her sisters taught school.

Then a woman dying of cancer urged Elizabeth to study medicine, saying that a woman doctor would have saved her from her worst sufferings. Elizabeth had a strong will. Nearly everyone said a girl should not go to medical school, but she managed to enter Geneva College, in New York State. She graduated in 1849 at the head of her class, receiving the first medical degree ever given to a woman.

Next, Dr. Blackwell went to Paris, France. Her only chance of training was

in a hospital where women came to have their babies. Four months later, while she was working in the French hospital, her left eye became dangerously infected. She lost the eye and had to have a glass eye put in. This accident meant she could not study anatomy and surgery. But she was soon back at work again, this time in London, England, where she made many important friends.

In 1851, Dr. Blackwell was back in New York City. Hospitals did not want a woman doctor, and few men doctors would help her. She gave lectures and very slowly came to have friends and patients. Her young sister, Emily, had meanwhile followed in her footsteps and was now a well-trained surgeon. By this time Elizabeth had enough money and help to open a hospital. She called it the New York Infirmary for Women and Children. The public was prejudiced against women doctors. Several times, when a patient died, ignorant mobs threatened her life. But gradually the hospital earned respect. It is still one of the best and most famous hospitals in the United States.

Elizabeth Blackwell never married, but she adopted a seven-year-old orphan, Kitty Barry. Kitty grew up to be a happy and faithful companion to her.

In 1859, Elizabeth Blackwell was officially recognized as a doctor in Great Britain—the first woman to be so honored. She was the inspiration of Elizabeth Garrett, who began the women's medical movement in England. Florence Nightingale, founder of the practice of nursing by women, was another of her friends. Dr. Blackwell died in 1910, at the age of 89.

bladder

The bladder is a sort of bag in the *pelvis,* or lowest part of the abdomen. Urine is held in this bag until the time comes to get rid of it. When the bladder is full, the muscle that closes it can be relaxed and the urine passes out of the body by way of a canal called the *urethra.* The bladder is balloon-shaped. The skin of the bladder is different from that in other parts of the body. It is able to stretch a great deal. For that reason, animal bladders have been used to hold liquids or gases.

The word *bladder* may mean any balloonlike object, for example the rubber bag that holds the air inside a football.

bladderwort

The bladderwort is a kind of plant. It is most often found in marshy places or floating on water. It is one of the strange plants that eat animals. Bladderworts have tiny hollow bladders among threadlike leaves. These bladders have little trapdoors that allow tiny water animals to pass in, but not out. Once inside, they are digested by the plant. Some tropical bladderworts have showy flowers and are grown in orchid houses, but most kinds have very small flowers, which are on tall thin stems above the rest of the plant. They are yellow, violet, or purple.

Blaine, James Gillespie

James G. Blaine was an American political leader who served in Congress, was twice Secretary of State, and almost became president in 1884, when he was the Republican candidate. He was defeated by Grover Cleveland. J. G. Blaine was born in West Brownsville, Pennsylvania, in 1830, but he moved to Maine and for 20 years represented Maine in the House of Representatives. He died in 1893.

One of the things Blaine did as a congressman was to write an important part of the Fourteenth Amendment to the Constitution of the United States. This amendment gave equal rights as citizens to Negroes, who had been slaves in the Southern states only a few years before the amendment went into effect in 1868. In 1954, the United States Supreme Court used this amendment as a basis for ruling that Negroes and whites cannot be forced to go to separate schools.

Blake, William

William Blake was a great English poet and painter who lived about two hundred years ago. It is very unusual for a man to be a good poet and painter too, but Blake was both. He was born in 1757, and though his family was poor, his father sent him to art school when he was 10 years old. He learned to make drawings on copper plates, called *engravings.* Later, when he wrote poems, he made beautiful drawings to go with them. These were colored in a secret way known only to Blake and his wife. One of his best-known pictures has the funny title, *Ghost of a Flea.* Blake printed many of his own poems, with only his wife to help him. He was usually very poor but he lived a full life. He died in 1827.

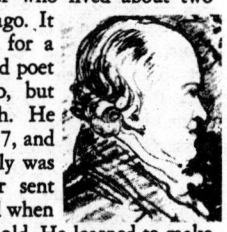

Blake saw beautiful pictures in his mind and he tried to write and draw them so other people would see what he did. He called one of his earliest books of poems *Songs of Innocence.* Many of them are about animals and children. A famous poem is called *The Tyger.*

blanching

Blanching is the name of a process used in gardening to make vegetables look whiter than usual. (The French word *blanc* means white.) Plants make their green coloring matter, called *chlorophyll,* by using sunlight. If light is kept off vegetables when they are growing, they will not develop so much chlorophyll. But they must have some sunlight or they will not grow. Blanched vegetables are grown in a bed with a cover that has holes in it to let in just a little light. This is often done with celery and with salad greens such as endive and chicory. Blanching is also a term used in cooking. It means to remove the skin of a fruit or vegetable by dipping it in boiling water.

blank verse

Blank verse is poetry in which the lines do not rhyme but do have a regular meter, or rhythm. Some of the greatest of all poetry is written in blank verse. William Shakespeare wrote most of his plays in blank verse, and so did other playwrights of his time.

A line of blank verse is supposed to have ten syllables, with every second one stressed, or accented. This is called *iambic pentameter.* An iambic is two syllables with the second one stressed, as in the word *because,* and pentameter is a line of five iambics. Shakespeare's line that says a rose "by any other name would smell as sweet" is in iambic pentameter. If all the lines are exactly like this, the rhythm becomes monotonous, so writers of blank verse put in an occasional line that is slightly different. Often they add one unstressed syllable at the end, as Shakespeare did when he wrote:

"To be or not to be—that is the question."

See the articles on METER and POETRY.

Blarney Stone

Blarney Castle is an ivy-covered castle 500 years old at the town of Blarney in south Ireland. A visitor can climb up a narrow staircase with 118 winding, sloping stone steps; lie down on a platform at the top; squirm out through a hole in the low wall at the edge, with two men holding his legs; take hold of two rusty iron bars, stretch up, and kiss a stone that hundreds of thousands of people have kissed before. Then he has kissed the Blarney Stone, and forever after he is supposed to have the gift of smooth talk—pleasant flattery or agreeable conversation, or even "tall tales," that make people like him.

But the Blarney Stone is more than just a popular tourist sight. Irish legends describe it as a piece of the famous *Lia Fail,* the "Stone of Destiny," over which the ancient kings of Erin were crowned. The biggest part of this historic stone is now called the Coronation Stone, and English kings and queens have been crowned over it for many hundreds of years. According to one belief, the "Stone of Destiny" is famous in the Bible as the "pillow" the prophet Jacob was resting on when he dreamed of angels climbing to Heaven on a ladder.

blasting

Blasting is the use of explosives to break up big masses of rock, or heavy masses that are too big to carry or move. Blasting is done in three stages. First, several holes are drilled into the rock. Second, an explosive is placed in the holes. Sometimes the holes are filled again with loose earth. Third, the explosive is *detonated,* that is, caused to explode. This breaks the rock or other solid material into small pieces that can be carried away.

Various explosives are used, depending on the size and hardness of the mass to be broken up. (See EXPLOSIVES.) A small amount of explosive will break up a solid wall of coal, which is soft; hundreds of tons may be needed to break up a huge rock to open a river channel or in bridge- or roadbuilding.

For small blasting operations, dynamite or a similar explosive is used. It is made to explode by fire (or an electric spark) or by heat. The holes are drilled by electric or pneumatic drills (powered by compressed air). The dynamite, which is made in "sticks" about the size of bananas, fit into the holes. A detonator or fuse is usually added; this is a small container of an explosive that can be set

off even more easily than the dynamite. An electric wire, to make a spark, may be laid to a point far enough away to be safe from the explosion; or a long tube about the size of macaroni may be used to carry fire to the explosive. This tube, which also is called a fuse, burns very slowly and gives the workmen time to run to a safe distance before the fire reaches the explosive.

For big blasting, great quantities of cheaper explosive such as gunpowder may be used. Bags of this explosive are laid in tunnel-like cavities (which may be made by smaller blasting operations). Not only detonators but also quantities of dynamite may be used to start the explosion.

Chemical explosives such as gunpowder have been known only for about 600 years. Long before that, men knew ways to break up great masses of rock. A favorite way, for any rock that is at all porous, was to saturate it (soak it) with water just before freezing weather came. When water freezes, it expands; so the forming of ice inside the rock made it crack, split, and sometimes even break into chunks. See also EXPANSION AND CONTRACTION, which was used in warm seasons or in warm climates where water seldom freezes.

bleaching

Bleaching is a way of removing the color from cloth, paper, and some other things, so as to make them white, or nearly white. People have known for thousands of years how to bleach things. Sunlight bleaches; that is why clothes fade in the sunlight, and a person's hair will become lighter in color if he spends a lot of time in the sun. Sea water can also bleach things, and strong soaps bleach clothes. Chemicals that cause bleaching are called *bleaching agents*.

Chlorine is an important bleaching chemical. The gas *sulfur dioxide* is another. Hydrogen peroxide is a chemical that is used in bleaching. The white rice that people eat was originally brown. The wheat that is used to make loaves of white bread was also brown. Both flour and rice are bleached with sulfur dioxide before they reach the grocery store. Paper is made from a brownish wood-pulp, but the pages of this book are white because the wood-pulp was bleached in large vats before it was made into paper. Cotton, linen and wool are all bleached by being boiled in tanks of water that has one of the bleaching chemicals in it.

The chemical reason why a bleaching agent works can be understood from the section "What Color Is" in the article on COLOR. The bleaching agent has a chemical effect on whatever substance reflects the colored light rays. Sunlight has this chemical effect also; see the article on ACTINIC RAYS.

Blenheim

Blenheim is a village in Bavaria, on the Danube River. Near this village, about 250 years ago (on August 13, 1704) British and Austrian armies won a great victory over the armies of France and Bavaria. This was in the War of the Spanish Succession, in which the British, Austrians and Dutch were fighting as allies to keep France from controlling Europe.

The British commander at Blenheim was the Duke of Marlborough, who was an ancestor of Winston Churchill. The Austrian commander was Prince Eugene (or Eugen). The French and Bavarians had 56,000 troops at the battle and lost 25,000 of them. The British were so grateful to Marlborough that they built him a great house, one of the finest in England, which was called Blenheim Palace in honor of the battle. Visitors to England may see Blenheim Palace at Blenheim Park, Oxfordshire. The War of the Spanish Succession lasted from 1701 to 1713, and the British and their allies won it.

Blennerhassett, Harman

Harman Blennerhassett was a man important in American history more than 150 years ago. He was born in England in 1765, came to America when he was about 32 years old, and built a fine estate on an island in the Ohio River near Parkersburg in what is now West Virginia. At that time Burr was plotting to set up an independent country along the Mississippi River and Blennerhassett became his friend and helped him. Blennerhassett's Island became the headquarters for Burr's army. Nothing came of the plot, and Burr and Blennerhassett were both arrested but both were freed. Blennerhassett returned to Europe and died there in 1831.

Blériot, Louis

Louis Blériot was a French aviator. He made the first flight in an airplane across the English Channel, on July 25, 1909. He flew in a monoplane he had designed and built himself, and the crossing took about half an hour. Blériot's flight has been called the beginning of military aviation. The English Channel had protected England in many wars. Blériot's flight showed that Britain could be attacked across the Channel. During World War I, Blériot was an airplane manufacturer. His plant built about 10,-000 planes for the French army. One of them was the famous "Spad" fighter. Blériot was born in 1872 and died in 1936.

blights and rots

Blights and rots are a family of plant diseases that destroy a great many trees, fruits, and vegetables every year, in nearly all parts of the world. Some of these diseases are caused by bacteria, just as some of the diseases which people get are caused by bacteria. Many other blights and rots, however, are caused by certain types of plants called fungi. (See the article on BACTERIA and the article on FUNGUS. Blights and rots are harder to cure than diseases of people; a blight such as the fire-blight of apples cannot be cured but can only be controlled. A blight or rot is controlled by burning all the plants that have become infected.

blindness

A person who cannot see anything is said to be *blind*. Some persons cannot see because they have no eyes; others do have eyes, but an injury or disease has made the eyes useless. Some persons are born blind, and never learn what the world around them looks like. Others lose the power of sight after having enjoyed it for any number of years. A person may become temporarily blind. That is, he may lose his sight for some period of time, then get it back.

A person is *totally* blind when he cannot see anything at all, even dark and light. Some other blind people are able to tell dark from light, but this does not help much if they cannot see anything else. Blindness is one of the greatest misfortunes possible, but it has been proved that blind people can live useful and happy lives. There used to be very few kinds of work that blind people could do. Among these were basket weaving, brush making, and piano tuning. Now there is hardly any kind of work the blind cannot do, and there are many things they can enjoy: reading, the radio, phonograph records of literature and music, card games, and some sports.

Amer. Foundation for Blind
The most famous blind person of the twentieth century was Helen Keller. See the article on HELEN KELLER.

WHAT MAKES PEOPLE BLIND

One of the most common causes of blindness is injury to the outer covering of the eyeball, called the *cornea*. The cornea is like a window, through which light enters the eye. When it is injured, a scar forms, which prevents light from getting through. The result is somewhat like being shut up in a dark room without any window. The cornea can be injured by an accident, or it can become infected with disease germs.

Infection used to cause some babies to become blind at birth. But now doctors can usually prevent this by putting a medicine called *silver nitrate* into the eyes of all newborn babies, or by using an antibiotic.

A *cataract* is a sort of film that grows over the lens of the eye. It is another cause of blindness, and may be caused before birth, from an injury afterwards, from infections, or from old age. *Glaucoma* is the name for a disease that causes

pressure within the eyeball, usually causing blindness.

HELP FOR THE BLIND

Hundreds of years ago, in Europe, bands of the blind used to roam the countryside, putting on "shows," where crowds gathered to laugh at their clumsy actions and to throw them a few coins. Many years ago, a wealthy young Frenchman named Valentin Haüy saw them, and was overcome with pity. He made up his mind to spend his money on helping the blind. First, he founded the Institute for Blind Youths, in Paris, where he taught blind boys to read and write. In 1784, Haüy published the first book for the blind. The printed letters were raised so that the blind pupils could feel them with their fingers. One of the pupils at Haüy's school was named Louis BRAILLE, about whom there is a separate article. Braille perfected a better system of reading and writing for the blind. The *Braille system* consists of raised dots. The blind "read" the dots by touching them with their fingertips.

In America, the Perkins Institution and Massachusetts School for the Blind was founded in Boston in 1829, under the direction of Dr. Samuel Gridley Howe. In 1837 a little girl from a farm was brought to Dr. Howe. The child's name was Laura Bridgman. She had been blind since she was a baby. She was also a deaf-mute—she could not hear or speak. Dr. Howe began to teach Laura by "spelling" out single words, then whole sentences, into the palm of her hand, and encouraging her to answer him in the same way. Laura stayed at the Perkins Institution most of her life, and was the first blind deaf-mute to receive an education. There have been many others since then. The most famous is Helen KELLER, about whom you can read more in a separate article.

There are now many schools and organizations for the blind in the United States. One of them is the Lighthouse, in New York City, where blind people meet and are taught. The Lighthouse also runs a store where articles made by the blind are sold.

HOW THE BLIND "SEE"

Blind people can usually develop their senses of touch, hearing, and smell until they are far superior to most people's. A blind person may get along by tapping a cane on the street. His ears tell him when he is near a wall or other obstruction, by how long it takes the echo of the tapping to get back to his ears. This is similar to the way a bat finds its way around. (See the article on BATS.) The hands of blind people often become so sensitive that they can feel what a person or a thing looks like.

Another great aid to the blind is the "Seeing-Eye" dog, which is specially trained to guide blind people. There is a separate article on SEEING-EYE DOGS.

EYE-BANKS

It has become possible to restore sight to some blind persons whose trouble is in the cornea. By a very delicate operation, a healthy cornea can be taken from one person's eye and put into the eye of a blind person. The healthy cornea can

Am. Foundation of the Blind

In reading Braille, a blind person feels the letters with the fingers of the right hand, while the left hand guides the right to keep it on the correct line in the book.

The Braille cell has place for six dots. The black circles in this diagram show where the dots are placed to form the letters of the alphabet. The outline circles show the positions in each cell that are left blank.

be taken from the eye of a person who has just died. Some people's wills say that they would like, after their death, to have their eyes used for the blind. These eyes can sometimes be placed in an "eye-bank," and saved until they are needed.

Even a slight accident to the eyes may cause blindness. Firecrackers are very dangerous to the eyes. Guns, bows and arrows and other weapons used as toys should never be used where anyone might possibly be hit.

There are some kinds of "blindness" that limit but do not destroy the sight. A person with *color blindness* cannot always tell the different colors apart, but may have no other trouble with his eyesight. *Night blindness* makes it hard to see things quickly in the dark. This is often helped by eating carrots and other foods that are rich in Vitamin A. *Snow blindness* is usually only a temporary blindness caused by the brightness of sunlight reflected from the snow.

blister

The skin is made up of several layers. When something causes the outer layer to stretch and pull away from the layers under it, a blister is formed. This is a kind of bubble. It fills with a watery fluid, because the body is full of fluids, which flow into any space where there is room for them. Heat will cause the skin to wrinkle and stretch, so a burn is likely to become a blister. Rubbing also stretches the outer skin, so when a shoe does not fit and rubs the foot, a blister may appear. Blisters are not dangerous unless they become infected, but since they leave an opening into the body, the danger of infection is great. If left alone, a blister will heal itself and dry up. A blister should not be broken on purpose. If it does break, a disinfectant should be put on and it should be kept bandaged until it heals.

Also any kind of bubble on the surface of paint, or on a plant, is called a blister because it looks like one. There is a disease called *blister* that attacks some pine trees. It is one of the most serious plant diseases in the United States and threatens to destroy some of the greatest forest reserves. About one out of every ten pine trees has it. The disease has two stages. First, it attacks gooseberry and currant bushes, appearing as orange patches on the undersides of the leaves during the summer. The infection from these patches is spread by the wind onto pine trees, and three or four years later the orange-colored blisters appear on the pine needles and the tree begins to die. To stop the spread of this disease, many states have passed laws forbidding the growing of the bushes that are subject to it, at least near pines. The blister disease is a form of RUST, about which there is a separate article.

blitzkrieg

Blitzkrieg is a German word meaning "lightning war" (*Blitz* means lightning and *Krieg* means war). A blitzkrieg is an attack that is so powerful and so sudden that the enemy cannot resist it. The word came to be much used in English-speaking countries during World War II, when Germany used its powerful air power and armored divisions to defeat

Poland, Norway, the Netherlands, Belgium, and France, each in a matter of days, when major campaigns had previously required years or at least many months. The English used the word *blitz* to describe the bombing attacks on London and other cities in England.

blizzard

A blizzard is a severe snowstorm in which howling winds drive the snow along with such force that anyone who goes out of doors may be unable to reach shelter again and may freeze to death. Sometimes villages and towns are cut off from the rest of the world for days or even weeks. Nowadays they are not in such danger as in former years, for supplies can be dropped to them by air.

blockade

A blockade exists when the navy of one country stops any ships from entering or leaving the ports of another country. Usually the two countries are at war. The purpose of a blockade is to make the enemy weaker by stopping it from getting the food and supplies it needs from abroad.

About 150 years ago the French emperor, Napoleon, declared a blockade against England, which was at war with France; but he did not have a strong enough navy to back it up, so no country would obey it. The United States and other countries called it a "paper blockade."

A blockade helped the North, or Union, government to win the American Civil War from the South, or Confederate, government. The South wanted to buy iron and various war supplies from other countries, and had cotton that other countries wanted to buy. At first, the North had only six good warships to back up its blockade, but it quickly built a strong fleet. Then very few ships could enter or leave any Southern port. Some shipowners made a lot of money sending small, fast ships called "blockade-runners" through the blockade, but these ships could not carry enough to save the South. Many blockade-runners were caught by the Union navy.

In 1908 the countries of the world had a naval conference in London, the capital of England, and tried to agree on rules to govern blockades. The rules they agreed on were: 1, The government that declares a blockade against a country must let all neutral countries know about it. (A neutral is a country that is not taking sides in the war.) 2, The blockade has to be kept up without interruption. 3, The blockade has to be backed up by a navy strong enough to maintain it. 4, The government that declares a blockade must give an early warning to all ships that might enter or leave the blockaded ports.

In World War I the British navy successfully blockaded Germany. The German and Austrian people could not get enough food or supplies by sea, and this helped to defeat them. Germany tried to blockade England with submarines and were almost but not quite successful. After World War I, the use of airplanes changed the nature of blockades. They made a naval blockade more difficult, for scarce supplies can be flown into a coun-

try by an "airlift"; but a country at war can seldom get all the supplies it needs by air. In another way airplanes made blockades easier, for even a country without a strong navy can attack enemy shipping from the air. During World War II German bombing planes attacked many ships carrying supplies to Russia but most of the ships got through.

An *embargo* is like a blockade, but it forbids the people of only one country to carry on business with the people of another country.

block and tackle, a set of pulleys and ropes used for hoisting and hauling heavy loads: see PULLEY.

block printing

Block printing was the first kind of printing. It was used by the Chinese more than a thousand years ago, soon after they invented paper, and it was the only printing known to Europe until Johannes Gutenberg invented movable type about 500 years ago. (See PRINTING.) Today block printing is used by artists who want their original designs to be reproduced exactly as they made them, and by many others as a hobby.

A block print is made from a carved block of wood or some other substance that is neither very hard nor very soft. (Today linoleum is most often used.) The design is carved backwards; it looks as the intended printed result would look in a mirror. From the carved block can be printed cloth scarves, skirts, and so on; pictures for framing; Christmas cards; bookplates; letter paper; and any number of other things.

HOW TO MAKE A BLOCK PRINT

The materials needed are paper, a pencil, a block of linoleum about ¼ inch thick and the size of the desired picture, for example 4 by 6 inches; a knife, preferably a special wood-carving tool; block-printing ink; watercolor paint; a stiff-haired brush about ½ inch wide; a heavy board; and a table to work on.

The picture can be drawn on transparent paper and traced backward (by turning the paper over) on the linoleum; or it can be drawn directly on the linoleum, in which case it must be drawn backward (and the linoleum can be held up to a mirror from time to time to see how the finished print will look). It is good to paint the block with white watercolor before drawing or tracing on it, so that the black lines of the drawing will be easy to see and carve. The drawing should be one that is easy to carve; a pencil will make a long, sweeping curve but a knife will not.

The block is then carved with the knife or tool. Any part of the block that is *not* cut away will show in the print, so for a black-on-white print everything *except* the drawing is cut away and for a white-on-black, or reverse, print the drawing itself is cut away. The block should be held securely while it is being carved. The cutting should be sharp and clear, and deep enough so that ink will not fill the carved parts.

The cloth or paper to be printed is laid smoothly and securely on the board—it is best to tack it down. An inexperienced person should start with a heavy paper that is not too shiny. The ink is brushed on the block (or can be put on with a rubber roller called a *brayer*). If block-printing ink is not available, poster paint can be used. The inked block is pressed very hard against the paper and when it is lifted the print is made. The pres-

sure must be even on all parts of the block and the block must not be allowed to move while it is touching the paper. Some block-printers prefer to hold the block securely, face-up, and lay the paper on it, then press the paper down evenly with a roller. Many prints can be made from one block. The block should be washed after it is used.

block system

The block system is a signaling system to prevent railroad accidents. This system is used on all the important railroads in the United States and Europe. A railway is divided into a number of sections called "blocks." The object is to keep trains a certain distance apart, so they cannot run into one another. A signal is placed at the entrance to each block. This tells the engineer if there is another train in the block ahead. The block signal is usually given with colored lights, like traffic lights. Red means stop; green means go; yellow means proceed with caution. Semaphore signals are also used. See the article on RAILROADS.

Blondel

Blondel was a minstrel, or strolling singer, in French and English legends of almost 800 years ago. He was a favorite of King Richard I ("the Lion-hearted") of England and went with Richard on the Third Crusade (see CRUSADES). After the Crusade Richard was captured by the King of Austria and held secretly in a castle. Blondel found him by going from one castle to another, standing outside, and singing a song that Richard knew no one else could sing. Finally, at the Castle of Dürrenstein, when Blondel sang the song he heard Richard singing it too, from a dungeon in the castle. Blondel took the news to England, where the people raised money and ransomed Richard. Blondel (called Blondel de Nesle for the French place from which he supposedly came) was the name of a real French minstrel and poet of those times, but this story is probably only a story.

blood

Blood is a sticky red liquid that is necessary to the lives of human beings and many other members of the animal kingdom. It flows through the body in tubes call blood vessels. From the lungs it takes oxygen breathed in, and from the digestive organs it takes food substances, and it carries these to all parts of the body. It carries back waste products, chiefly carbon, which is breathed out in the form of the gas called carbon dioxide. It carries disease-fighting cells to all parts of the body. It carries necessary substances to the liver and other glands and vital organs (parts of the body that are necessary to life).

When blood stops flowing through a body, it dies. When blood stops flowing to a part of the body, such as a hand or foot, that part dies; it is said to be affected by gangrene. If the brain's supply of blood is shut off even momentarily, the person loses consciousness.

CIRCULATION OF THE BLOOD

There are five to six quarts of blood in the human body. The blood constantly circulates, or flows around and around

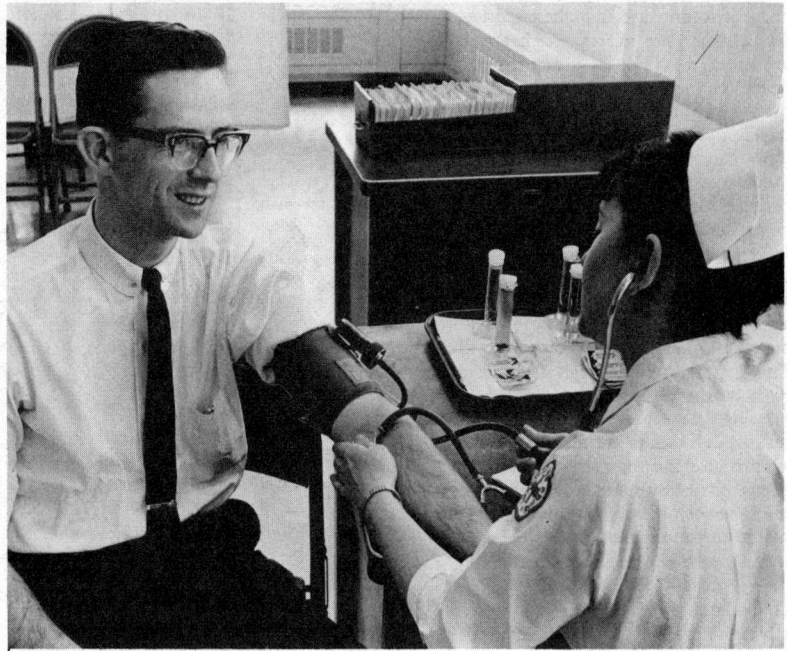

American Red Cross

A man's blood pressure is checked by a registered nurse of the American Red Cross.

through the body. The heart acts as a pump to keep it flowing. All the blood in the body passes through the heart at least twice a minute. It flows away from the heart through large blood vessels called arteries, back to the heart through smaller blood vessels called veins, and to any parts of the body through very tiny blood vessels called capillaries. The circulation of the blood is explained in the articles HEART, ARTERY, VEIN, and HUMAN BODY.

Sir William Harvey, a noted British physician, discovered in 1616 that the blood circulates. This was one of the greatest advancements in the history of the medical profession.

WHAT BLOOD IS

Blood is mostly water, but in the water many substances are dissolved and in this fluid float specks of matter that do not dissolve.

The liquid part of blood greatly resembles sea water. It contains salt, sodium, potassium, calcium, and other minerals.

The specks of matter that float in the blood are of three kinds:

1. Red corpuscles, also called red cells. The red cells carry oxygen and proteins, a necessary food substance, to all parts of the body. In the red cells there is *hemoglobin,* a substance that contains iron (which gives its red color) and that attracts oxygen. As the oxygen is distributed the blood gradually loses its red color, so that when it returns to the heart through the veins it has become a purplish blue. There are 4½ to 5 million red cells in even a small drop of blood.

2. White corpuscles, also called white cells. The white cells can absorb other living cells. This is important to health, because the white cells fight disease by absorbing the disease germs; but at times the white cells can be dangerous by swallowing or destroying cells that are necessary to live, such as the red blood cells. When white blood cells die in the course

of destroying bacteria they form the white matter called pus, which is found in boils and abscesses. There are far fewer white than red cells in the blood. A drop of blood in a healthy body contains fewer than 10,000 white cells. When disease strikes the body, the white cells multiply greatly and there may be 20,000 or more in a drop.

3. Blood platelets. These look, under a microscope, like tiny disks. In combination with a protein in the blood called fibrinogen, the platelets cause the blood to clot when it is exposed to the air. Without the platelets a person might bleed to death from a tiny cut.

All the bits of solid matter are very small. It takes about 3,000 white cells to measure an inch. The red cells are about the same size, very slightly smaller. The platelets are only about one-third as large.

The liquid part of the blood without these solid particles, but including the various chemicals in the blood, is called *plasma.* This is often very important in blood transfusions, as explained later in this article. While the plasma does not include the white cells, it does contain the antibodies that the body manufactures to combat disease.

Blood *serum* is the liquid that remains after blood clots. It is like plasma except that it does not contain the proteins that go into making the blood clot. Serum cannot be used in blood transfusions but it does carry the disease-fighting antibodies. For that reason it is used in inoculations and vaccinations. Serum from the blood of an animal that has had a disease, and so has built up antibodies against the disease, is injected into a person or animal that has never had the disease. The person or animal that is injected now has the same antibodies and will seldom if ever catch the disease.

BLOOD PRESSURE

Blood pressure is the force with which the heart is pumping blood through the

body. The pressure is highest in the arteries, which are nearest the heart; it is lowest in the veins as it returns to the heart, for much of the original force has been spent in sending the blood through the capillaries to the body tissues. A person's blood pressure is often "taken" (measured) in a physical examination because blood pressure that is too high or too low is usually a sign of illness.

To measure the blood pressure, the doctor fastens an airtight bag around the arm and pumps air into it. This creates air pressure in the bag, and the pressure makes the bag tighten around the arm. The doctor listens through a stethoscope to the flowing of the blood. When the air pressure has caused the bag to tighten just enough to stop the flow of blood, the air pressure and the blood pressure must be the same. By measuring the air pressure, the doctor knows the blood pressure.

Air pressure is measured by how high it will push a column of mercury in a tube. Normal blood pressure is equal to about enough air pressure to push the mercury up 120 to 150 millimeters (4½ to 5½ inches). Therefore blood pressure is expressed in millimeters, for example 126 or 133.

Often the blood pressure is expressed by two different figures. The heart beats with a pulsating, or throbbing, action. First it reaches a point of high pressure, called the *systole,* in which it spurts blood with great force into the arteries; then it falls to a point of lower pressure, called the *diastole,* in which it gathers strength for the next high point. When the systolic pressure is 130, the diastolic pressure may be only 80. This would be expressed as "one-thirty over eighty."

DISEASES OF THE BLOOD

High blood pressure, called *hypertension,* is perhaps the most usual ailment connected with the blood, but it is actually a disease of the blood vessels. If the blood vessels have shrunk, or have become coated inside so as to make the passages smaller, they will not let enough blood through. The heart must work harder to force the blood through, and this may damage the heart. If the blood pressure becomes so high that it bursts a blood vessel in the brain, one is said to have a "stroke" and may die or lose some or all of his mental capacity. Arteriosclerosis, or "hardening of the arteries," is another disease that may cause high blood pressure. It is a disease of old age. As people grow older, the walls of the arteries harden, become less elastic, and will not let so much blood through. If the walls of arteries near the heart harden, the patient may die.

Anemia is a disease in which the blood does not have enough hemoglobin, so the body does not get enough nourishment through the blood. There is a separate article on ANEMIA.

Blood poisoning is a diseased condition of the blood when it contains bacteria (disease germs) or poisons. The disease is called *septicemia* when the blood is infected with bacteria and *toxemia* when it is infected with poison. There are several poisons, for example from the bite of a poisonous snake, that infect the blood directly.

Leukemia is a disease in which the

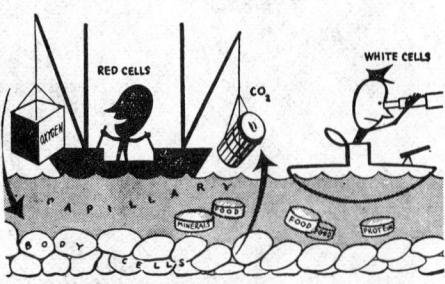

Red corpuscles, white cells, and food, traveling through the capillaries, service the body cells. The red corpuscles bring oxygen and take away carbon dioxide.

The white cells stand guard. They are the body's warriors in the fight against disease. They attack and destroy harmful bacteria in the bloodstream.

Public Affairs Comm., Inc.

blood has too many white cells and they destroy the red cells. Leukemia is a serious form of cancer and usually causes death.

Hemophilia is a disease in which the blood does not have enough platelets and necessary proteins to make the blood clot. If a person with hemophilia cuts himself even slightly he may bleed to death. Hereditary hemophilia is a strange form of the same disease. It afflicted many of the royal families of Europe in times when most European countries had kings. Only a man could have this disease, and he could inherit it only from his mother, not from his father.

Embolism is the forming of a blood clot in one of the blood vessels, so as to stop the flow of blood. Such a clot is called an *embolus.* Embolism frequently causes death. *Thrombosis* is a similar disease, consisting of a blood clot, the only difference being that different substances in the blood form the clot. The most dangerous form of this is *coronary thrombosis,* in which the clot forms in the heart at the entrance to an artery.

BLOODLETTING OR BLEEDING

In former times—up to nearly a hundred years ago—one of the ways of treating certain diseases, especially in fat persons, was to open a vein and let a pint or more of blood out of the patient's body. This treatment was called bleeding, bloodletting, or phlebotomy (which means "vein-cutting"). Doctors thought this treatment removed some of the cause of the disease; actually, without knowing it, they often dangerously weakened their patients. The danger was made greater by the fact that nothing was then known of disease germs and there was no effort to make the operation antiseptic. Often the bloodletting was done by barbers, who had never heard of sterilizing their instruments. The barber's pole is a reminder of the times when he practiced bloodletting (see BARBER).

Today bloodletting is practiced very seldom. A small amount of blood may be drawn out to improve the appearance of a "black eye," but otherwise blood is usually taken out of the body only in the tiny quantities needed to make a laboratory blood test. Instead, every effort is made to prevent the loss of blood, for a person with too little blood cannot so well resist disease and may go into a dangerous state of shock. When a person has too little blood he is given a blood transfusion.

BLOOD TRANSFUSIONS

When a person has lost a great deal of blood because of hemorrhage (bleeding), or when illness has weakened his own blood, so that for example it does not contain enough red cells, the usual treatment is to transfer some blood from a

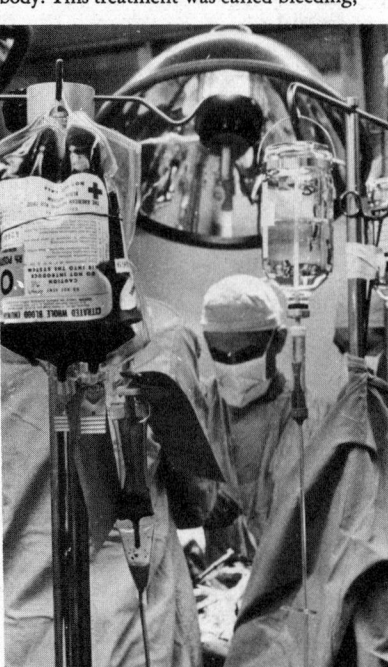

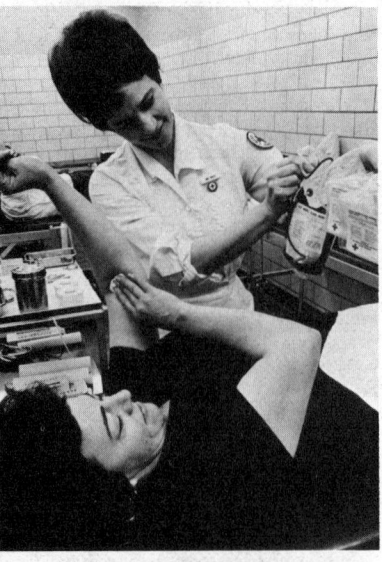

As this donor's smile suggests, giving blood is safe and painless for a healthy person.

During this open-heart operation, a plastic bag of donated blood stands ready for transfusion into the patient.

233

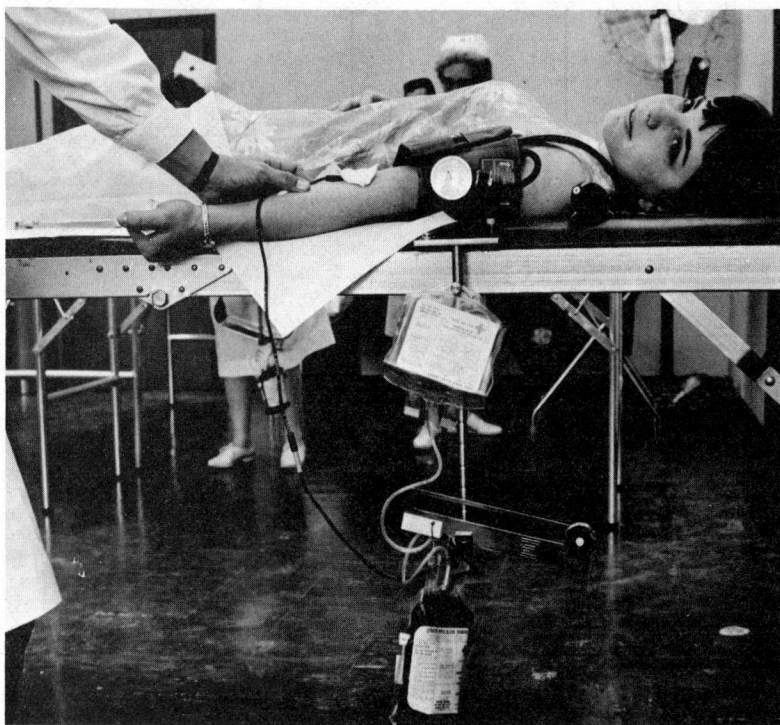

American Red Cross

The blood donated by this young lady is flowing from her arm to the plastic bags beneath her.

healthy person into his veins. This is called a blood transfusion.

The amount usually transferred is one pint, which is allowed to drip into the patient's vein very slowly, a drop at a time. The person from whom the blood is taken is called the *donor*. Some donors are paid for their blood, perhaps $25 a pint, but most donors are volunteers who give their blood freely. It is neither painful nor dangerous to give a pint of blood and a healthy body will bring its own blood supply back up to normal within a week or less. Sometimes, in great emergencies, there is a direct blood transfusion. The blood is drawn from the vein of the donor and allowed to drip, through a tube and hollow needle, directly into the vein of the patient. But this is seldom necessary and usually the blood is taken from the donor and kept in a container until it is used for the patient.

However, most transfusions are emergencies and a donor is not always available when needed. Therefore most hospitals have *blood banks* in which blood is stored for immediate use if necessary. The Red Cross also maintains blood banks, as do military organizations in time of war.

Whole blood, as it comes from the body, will not keep for much more than a week, even in a refrigerator. The blood plasma can be kept in storage almost indefinitely. Therefore blood banks contain quantities of plasma. The plasma can even be dried and shipped in powdered form; when it is needed for a transfusion, it is dissolved in sterilized water. Plasma is not as effective as whole blood in many cases, for it does not include the red cells or any other of the solid particles, but one advantage of plasma is that it can be given to a person of any blood type.

BLOOD TYPES

The idea of blood transfusions is nearly

a hundred years old and blood transfusions have been made for more than fifty years. It was discovered almost at once that only human blood can be used, and not long after it was discovered that not all human blood will do. There are four types of human blood. Some types are *compatible* with each other, that is, they may safely be mixed. Other types are not compatible and if they are mixed the red blood cells will agglutinate (form clumps), which often causes death.

All people are therefore classed as belonging to one of four *blood groups*. In the system used in the United States, these groups are called O, A, B, and AB.

"O" type blood does not clump when mixed with any other blood. It can cause other blood to clump, but this is unlikely when a small amount of "O" blood is mixed with a large amount of the other blood, as in a transfusion. Therefore a person whose blood is "O" type is sometimes called a "universal donor," because his blood can be used for a transfusion to almost anybody with reasonable safety. However, a member of the "O" group cannot safely be given blood from anyone but another O-group member.

"A" type blood can be given to another "A," and "B" type blood to another "B," and either can be given with reasonable safety to members of AB group. Members of the AB group are called "universal recipients" because their blood does not cause any other blood to clump. But it is not wholly safe for any patient to receive a transfusion from anyone but a member of the same blood group.

About half of all human beings belong to the "O" group and nearly all the rest belong to the "A" group. Groups B and AB are quite small.

THE RH FACTOR

Another thing affecting blood transfusions is the Rh Factor. Most people

(85%) are called Rh-positive and the rest are called Rh-negative. An Rh-positive can safely be given the blood of any donor of the same blood group; but with an Rh-negative person this is not enough. If an Rh-negative person receives Rh-positive blood, even though it belongs to the same blood group, the Rh-negative blood builds up antibodies that will cause Rh-positive blood to clump. For the time being this does not harm, but two or more transfusions from an Rh-positive donor may kill the Rh-negative recipient. Therefore doctors try to give an Rh-negative person only Rh-negative blood.

A person's blood group, and the Rh Factor, are inherited from his parents.

In spite of the complications, blood transfusions are safe because blood tests are always made before the transfusion is given and no transfusion is given unless the blood is known to be compatible.

BLOOD TESTS

Blood tests are made as part of every thorough physical examination and also when certain diseases are suspected. Some blood tests are made in criminal investigations.

The blood is drawn out of a vein in the arm or from the thumb. It is examined under a microscope to get a *blood count*, a count of the white cells, for if there are too many white cells it is a sign of infection in the body. At the same time the trained laboratory worker sees if there is anything abnormal, or unusual, about the blood.

The blood is mixed with blood of various types until its own type is found—the one with which it will not cause clumping. Many people make a record of their blood type and carry it with them, to save time in case an emergency transfusion should ever be needed.

The blood is often mixed with bacteria, or disease germs, to see if it will kill them. If it will, the blood contains antibodies to that disease and the person is said to be immune to it. Other tests of the same kind are made, with bacteria and with chemicals, to find out if the blood contains any disease germs or poisons it should not have and if it contains all the properties it should have. Only a small

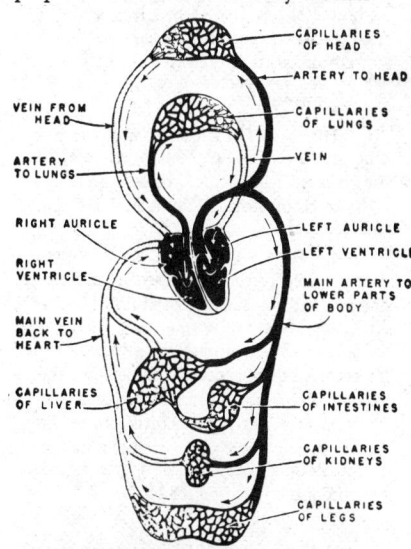

Blood circulation in the human body. From George Schwartz's Outline of Text Biology published by Oxford Book Company, N.Y.

amount of blood is needed for all these tests, for usually no more than a drop of blood is required for each.

In criminal investigation, blood tests are often important. For example, a test by microscope will show whether blood is human blood or the blood of some other animal. The easiest way to tell this is by the size of the red cells. The red cells are different sizes in all animals. For example, an elephant's red cells are bigger than man's but a man's red cells are bigger than a dog's. People suspected of crimes, because of blood found in their automobiles or homes, have sometimes been cleared when blood tests showed that the blood came from chickens or from meat such as beef.

bloodhound

When someone is lost in the woods, or when a convict escapes from prison, the police often use bloodhounds to find him. These dogs have a keen sense of smell and can follow a trail for miles, even when it is so old and faint that no other dog can even find it. Once they get on a trail, they keep following it until it leads to the person they are looking for, or until the trail gets lost completely. When the bloodhound finds the person it is looking for, it loses interest. Other dogs used for tracking will either attack or guard the person whose trail they have been following, but not the bloodhound. To the bloodhound, all the sport is in following the trail itself.

Bloodhounds were used in Europe before the time of Christ. They got their name because as long as eight hundred years ago great care was taken to keep the breed pure. For this reason, they were called "blooded hounds" in England. This meant they were hounds whose blood was not mixed with that of other breeds.

A bloodhound is very gentle and dependable, and makes a very good pet even though it is very large. It is about two feet high at the shoulder and weighs 80 to 110 pounds. It has long, soft ears and a deeply wrinkled face, with skin that hangs in loose folds. Its tail is long and low-hanging.

The bloodhound's coat is smooth and its hair is short. It may be black and tan, reddish-brown and tan, or sandy-colored, sometimes with tiny white spots.

Bloomer, Amelia

Amelia Jenks Bloomer was a leader among American women who worked for greater rights for women. She was born at Homer, New York, in 1818 and she lectured and wrote in favor of woman suffrage (the right to vote, which women did not then have) and also for temperance. She is best remembered for "bloomers," a woman's costume that included loose pantaloons instead of a skirt. Mrs. Bloomer did not invent these but she favored them so much that they came to be known by her name. Until late in the 1920s, girls' teams wore bloomers in several athletic games, including basketball. Mrs. Bloomer died in 1894.

Bloomington

Bloomington, Illinois, is a city in central Illinois. It is a manufacturing city, especially for metal products such as household appliances, and it is the business center for a rich farming area. Bloomington was founded in 1822 and has long been noted as a center of culture. It is the home town of Adlai Stevenson, Democratic candidate for president in 1952 and 1956. Illinois Wesleyan University is at Bloomington, and Illinois State Normal University is in near-by Normal. The population in 1970 was 39,992.

Bloomington, Indiana, is in the south of the state. It is the seat of the University of Indiana, one of the largest universities in the country, and is also a manufacturing city and a business center for a rich farming area. There are large limestone quarries near Bloomington. The population in 1970 was 39,992.

blowgun

A blowgun is a long tube used as a weapon. Blowing into one end forces a dart out at the other end.

Blowguns are used by Indian tribes in South America and by some peoples of the Malay Peninsula (part of southeast Asia) and islands in the Pacific Ocean. These tribes are very primitive, or backward.

A blowgun is about seven feet long and is made out of wood. It is about one inch wide at the blowing end and narrows to three-quarters of an inch at the other end. A dart, about as long as a steel knitting needle, is put in at this end. Sometimes the darts are dipped in poison, and sometimes they are cut with little notches, which stick into an animal as a fishing hook sticks into fish.

The article on AIR GUNS tells why blowguns can shoot a dart very fast. They work very well at short distances, but are not very useful at long distances.

blowpipe

A blowpipe is a small tube. It is used to blow air on a flame and make the flame hotter. All burning requires oxygen, a gas that is in the air. Blowing air on a flame gives it more oxygen, so it burns faster. Blowpipes are used by jewelry-makers and by others who must melt metals in very small quantities but need a very hot flame. A simple blowpipe is about 7 inches long and is usually made of glass or brass. It is about ½ inch wide at the end you blow into, and much narrower where the air comes out. Often there is a bend in the pipe about 2 inches from the small end. A special use of the blowpipe is in making GLASS, about which there is a separate article.

blowtorch

A blowtorch is a device for producing a very hot flame at a point where it is needed. It is a closed can equipped with an air pump and a nozzle. Gasoline is put in the can and high air pressure is built up inside with the pump. When the nozzle is opened a fine spray of gasoline mixed with air is forced out by the air pressure, and when lighted this spray makes a jet of flame whose heat is more than 2,000° Fahrenheit, which will melt most metals. Alcohol and other fuels may be used.

Blücher

Gebhard Leberecht von Blücher was a Prussian general who helped the English defeat Napoleon, the French emperor, in the Battle of Waterloo, in 1815. This battle ended Napoleon's career. Blücher was born in 1742 and served for years in the army of Prussia (in Germany). He was such a driving commander that he was nicknamed "Marshal Forward" by the Russians. He was 73 years old when he took part in the final battle against Napoleon. He fought so well that a new military honor—the Order of the Iron Cross—was created especially for him in 1815. He died in 1819. Read also the article on WATERLOO.

blue baby

Before a baby is born, the blood in its body does not receive oxygen from the air, because the baby is not yet breathing. There is a passage that carries the blood through the heart without taking in air from the lungs. When the baby is born and begins to breathe, this passage closes. Then the blood passes through the heart so as to take in oxygen from the air in the lungs. Sometimes something goes wrong and the passage does not close. Then the baby does not get enough oxygen. It looks blue all over—the color of the veins, which carry blood whose oxygen has been used up. Such a baby is called a "blue baby." It is a very dangerous condition and often the doctor has to operate to close up the passage.

Bluebeard

Bluebeard is a character in a well-known children's story. It tells of a man with a blue beard who murdered his wives and kept their bodies in a locked room. He would test the curiosity of each wife by going away and leaving her with a key to a certain room which he told her not to enter. During his absence, the wife could not resist the temptation to use the key, and so when Bluebeard returned and found she had opened the forbidden door, he killed her. The same thing happened to the next wife, and the next, until the seventh wife was rescued at the last moment, and Bluebeard himself was killed.

In 1697, a Frenchman named Charles Perrault wrote a book of famous fairy tales and *Bluebeard* was one of them. There have been actual men who murdered several wives and these men are called Bluebeards.

bluebell

The bluebell is a wild flower. It grows in meadows and pastures during July and August. It is found in Scotland and is sometimes called the "Bluebell of Scotland." It also grows in Alaska and in the Rocky Mountains of the United States. The small bell-shaped flower droops from a very thin stem. Some people think it looks like a sewing thimble and call it a "witch's thimble."

The bluebell has a very sweet smell. Some people have used a perfume made from crushed bluebells. Bluebells were once considered weeds, but people now grow them in gardens.

blueberry

Blueberries are a favorite fruit in many parts of the United States. They are ball-shaped, about the size of big pearls or beads, and bright blue in color. They grow on a bush, the blueberry bush, which has bright bluish-green leaves. Huckleberries are berries that grow in other parts of the United States and that look like blueberries but are smaller and deep purple in color. Farmers in New England, New Jersey and New York grow blueberries for market, and the bushes are found growing wild in many places.

bluebird

The bluebird is a small bird that is seen in most parts of North America. It is sky-blue on top and has a dull red breast. Just beneath its tail is a touch of white. Its bill and feet are black. A bluebird is seen in earliest spring and may stay in one place all summer if there is a small bird-house for it. It will also live in the hole of a tree, perhaps where a woodpecker lived last year. It lines the hole with grass and feathers.

The bluebird is about 7 inches long. It eats insect and fruits. It has a sweet song that sounds like "Purity, purity."

bluebottle

The blue bottle is a kind of house-fly, but it is much larger than the usual fly—bluebottles are about half an inch long—and also it makes much more noise when it flies. The bluebottle lays its eggs in food and they become wormlike maggots, which spoil the food. See INSECT.

bluefish

The bluefish is a medium-sized fish, shaped like a cigar. It is about three feet long and weighs 5 to 15 pounds. The bluefish is a bright bluish color on top and has a silvery belly. It is a very fast swimmer. The bluefish is found in all the oceans of the world. Nobody knows where the bluefish lays its eggs. Large schools of bluefish swim along the Atlantic coast hunting for food. They have strong sharp teeth and they feed on a smaller fish, the *menhaden*.

Bluefish are among the most valued food fish. Small bluefish are called *snappers*. In some parts of the world the bluefish is called the *skipjack*.

bluegrass

Bluegrass is a grass that has tiny blue flowers that make the fields look very blue when it is flowering in the spring. Bluegrass looks bluer than most grass at all times, because the blades are bluish green.

There are more than 150 kinds of bluegrass. The best known is Kentucky bluegrass, which grows in central Kentucky. It is excellent food for horses and cows and it makes good hay. It can live with very little water. Kentucky is called the Bluegrass State. Texas bluegrass is much like Kentucky bluegrass. Bluegrass makes good lawns except that it turns brown early in the fall. It is also called *June grass* and *spear grass*.

Originally bluegrass grew wild in Europe and Asia but it was not known in America before the white men brought it.

bluejay

The bluejay is the bird of the jay family most often found in North America. It is a bright blue color and the male has a crest. It is 9 or 10 inches long. The bluejay is feared by smaller birds and it will chase them and take their food or even their nests. Its usual cry is an unpleasant sound somewhat like a crow's. See JAY.

Blue Laws

In the early days of New England, the heads of the church were also the leaders of the town governments. These were Puritans, very religious men who had left England and come to America so they could follow their religion as they wished to. They had very strict ideas of right and wrong. Some of the laws they passed made it a crime to read on Sunday, ever to play cards or dance, or even to kiss your wife or husband at certain times. These laws were called Blue Laws. Some of them are still laws, because they have never been repealed (canceled), but very few of them are enforced now. There are various stories to explain why they are called "blue" laws but no one really knows why.

Blue Mountains

The Blue Mountains are a range of mountains in Oregon and Washington. The highest peak is Rock Creek Butte; it is 9,097 feet high. Another range called the Blue Mountains, is in Pennsylvania, New York, and New Jersey (where they are part of the Kittatinny Mountains). In New South Wales, Australia, there are also Blue Mountains, that rise to a height of 4,460 feet. Another mountain range with the same name is in Jamaica, in the West Indies. They run the entire length of the island and are over 7,000 feet at their highest point.

blueprint

A blueprint is a copy of a drawing or plan or printed page, but the copy is seen as white lines on bright blue paper. Making a blueprint is somewhat like making a photograph. The original drawing or printing is put on very thin paper that light will shine through, or on photographic film. The blueprint paper is white to begin with, but is treated with chemicals. After it has been treated, or *sensitized*, any light that falls on it will turn it blue. Therefore, blueprint paper must always be stored in a dark place until it is ready to be used. The drawing that is to be copied is placed in a machine. There are lights on one side of the drawing. The blueprint paper is put on the other side of the drawing. The light shines through the original drawing. It turns the chemically-treated paper a bright blue. But the light cannot shine through the dark lines of the drawing. Therefore the blueprint paper remains white wherever lines have been drawn on the original drawing or plan. The blueprint is then washed to get all the chemicals off. This is called "fixing." After this, the drawing is there to stay. Blueprinting is much used because it is a very inexpensive way of making copies.

Blue Ridge Mountains

The Blue Ridge Mountains are part of the great Appalachian Mountains in the eastern part of the United States. They extend southward from the border of Pennsylvania and Maryland, through Virginia, West Virginia and North Carolina, and end in northern Georgia. The highest point is in North Carolina at Mt. Mitchell, which is capped with snow and is 6,684 feet high. It is the highest peak east of the Mississippi River. The Blue Ridge Mountains are a favorite vacation place because of their beautiful woods and scenery. From a distance they seem to be a pale blue. See BLACK MOUNTAINS.

Blue Sky Laws

Blue Sky Laws are laws to stop the dishonest selling of the stocks and bonds of corporations. The laws got their name because some salesmen of stocks and bonds used to make such false and extravagant claims that "only the blue sky was the limit." Most Blue Sky Laws require any company selling stock to report the facts about the company to state authorities. Stock cannot be offered for sale without permission and there is a limit to the profit that can be made by "promoters" who organize a company and sell its stock. Every state except Nevada and Delaware has Blue Sky Laws. See also SECURITIES AND EXCHANGE COMMISSION.

blushing

Blushing is a reddening of the face and neck, caused by embarrassment or anger. Usually when a person blushes he also feels his heart pound and his face grow warm.

This is caused by two little knobs, or glands, at the top of the kidneys. These are the *adrenal glands*. They pour a powerful chemical into the blood when one is angry or embarrassed. This chemical makes the heart beat faster. As a result, blood pressure goes up, blood is rushed into the head, and more blood reaches the tiny blood vessels, making the skin turn pink or red.

B'nai B'rith

B'nai B'rith is the name of an important Jewish organization. In Hebrew the name means "Sons of the Covenant." This organization was founded in New York City about 120 years ago, in 1843. B'nai B'rith works to see that Jewish people are treated fairly and that people everywhere are told the truth about Jewish history and customs. It does this with printed material and lectures. An important branch of B'nai B'rith is the Anti-Defamation League, which fights against all racial and religious prejudice. There are about 470,000 members of B'nai B'rith in many countries. Most of them are men, but women also belong and there is a children's branch named Hillel, for a famous Jewish rabbi (teacher) who lived shortly before the time of Jesus.

boa

A boa is a kind of large snake. Most boas live in South America. All boas are *constrictors*. This means they wrap themselves around other animals and keep constricting or tightening their coils until they crush the animal to death. Boas

are not poisonous. They are very useful to farmers in certain sections, because they kill mongooses that steal farmers' chickens.

The South American boa is also called the *boa constrictor*. It is an expert tree-climber. It sometimes grows to a length of about twenty feet.

The Cuban boa is like the boa of South America, but it has a wilder and more disagreeable disposition. It is hard to keep the Cuban boa in captivity. However, it is useful to Cuban sugar planters because it kills both rats and mongooses.

Another type of boa is the *sand boa* of India. It seldom grows longer than three feet. It lives mainly underground and gets its food by crawling into rat holes and the burrows of other rodents.

Still smaller is the *rubber boa*. This gets its name from its appearance. It looks like a two-foot length of rubber hose. The rubber boa lives on the Pacific coast of the United States and in mountainous regions. It is a very gentle, timid snake.

Emerald tree boas are about four feet long, and can be found in Brazil and the Guianas of South America. See also the article about SNAKES.

The boa constrictor is very powerful. Its great coils can crush a man to death.

boar

Any male of the pig or swine family may be called a boar but the name usually means a wild boar. The wild boars of America and Europe are not large animals, only about two feet high and four feet long, while the boar of Asia may be six or more feet long and weigh 400 pounds, but all are very fierce. A boar might easily kill a bear or tiger. The boar has razor-sharp tusks in its mouth. Its body is covered by bristles, which are short, very stiff hairs.

There are wild boars in Central Europe, in Russia, and in America. All the boars in England were killed hundreds of years ago.

The wild boars that now live in America were brought to North Carolina about fifty years ago by an English sportsman. He wanted to raise them so he could hunt them on his estate. Some of them escaped. Now they wander over a large area of dense forest in the southern part of the Great Smoky Mountains, in Tennessee and North Carolina.

Hunting the wild boar has been a favorite sport of man for many thousands of years. In India, the boar is hunted with spears and the sport is known as "pig-sticking." Most often the boar is hunted on horseback, with rifles and a pack of specially trained brave dogs. The dogs chase and tire the boar until the hunters arrive. A wild boar is so strong and courageous that even when it is shot through the heart and is dying it will stay on its feet and kill anyone who comes near.

The wild boar is the ancestor of the domestic hog.

boat

A boat is a vessel that floats on water because it is shaped to be full of air. Usually a boat is small enough to be moved by the strength of men, applied to oars or poles. However, many vessels that use sails or engines are also called boats.

The raft, made of logs bound together, which floats merely because the wood is lighter than water, probably came before the boat; but that was so long ago that no one can say. Men were making boats thousands of years before written history began. (See the article ARK.)

One of the first boats used on the streams and rivers of what is now the United States was the *birchbark canoe* of the Algonquin Indians. The Alonquins first made a framework of split saplings, tied together with strong cord. Over this framework they stretched large square pieces of birch bark, sewed together with bone needles and thin strips of hide. Seams and holes were "calked," or smeared with waterproof gum from evergreen trees.

Another kind of boat invented by an Indian people is the *kayak,* a kind of canoe used by the Eskimos of Alaska. It is about 16 feet long and 16 inches wide and has a light framework of thin strips of wood covered with sealskin from which the fur is removed. The kayak is pointed at both ends and is covered on top, so that the sealskin forms a deck. The Eskimo lowers himself into the kayak through a hole in the deck. There is loose skin around the hole and he laces it around his body so that no water can get into the boat. A double-bladed paddle is used to move the kayak.

In many parts of the world primitive peoples make a boat by hollowing out a tree trunk and pointing both ends. Often the tree trunk is hollowed out with red-hot rocks, which burn away the inner part of the wood. This type of boat is called a *dugout* and is used by people in the islands of the South Pacific Ocean. They often add outriggers to it, to prevent it from turning over. The outriggers are a pair of curved wooden arms, each about 5 feet long, attached to the sides of

the dugout and fastened at the outer ends to logs about 3 inches thick and as long as the boat. The log or boom floats on the surface of the water alongside the dugout and steadies it.

As men learned to saw logs into boards, they began to make flat-bottomed boats that looked like long, watertight boxes with square ends. Later the square ends were raised somewhat higher above the water. This kind of boat, called a *punt,* is pushed through shallow waters with a long pole. It is still used in some countries.

CARVEL— AND CLINKER—BUILT BOATS

Boats may be built out of boards or planks in two different styles. If the boards are laid edge to edge, the boat is *carvel-built.* If the boards overlap, the boat is *clinker-built.*

Among the larger kinds of carvel-built boats are *launches, pinnaces* and *cutters.* Many of these are as much as 36 feet long and 8 to 10 feet wide. Launches are open, or undecked, boats. They are used by ships to carry supplies and sailors to and from the shore, and large launches are sometimes used as pleasure boats on lakes and rivers. A pinnace is a light sailboat. It was used in the past as a tender, or supply boat, for larger ships. A cutter is a broad boat with a square stern or rear end. It is driven by oars, motor, or sails. Cutters used to be carried by ships, to move supplies and persons in harbors. Today a cutter is either a large, heavy rowboat carried on big steamships and driven by ten oars, or one of the large, fast, steel boats used by the United States Coast Guard. A Coast Guard cutter is a light warship of some 2,000 tons, powered by diesel engines and equipped with a small cannon.

Among the best known clinker-built small boats are the popular *dinghy, gig,* and *whaleboat.* A dinghy is a small rowboat about 6 to 10 feet long, propelled by oars, and used either as a pleasure craft or as a service boat for larger sailboats and motorboats. Big motorboats may tow their dinghies behind them or have them fastened down on the deck. A dinghy is used to ferry people between the larger boat and the dock.

THE GIG AND WHALEBOAT

A gig is a fast, light boat carried on board a ship. It is driven by oars or sails. In the days when all big ships had sails, the commanding officer or captain always had a gig reserved for his private use, to carry him to and from his ship when it was anchored in the harbor away from a pier or dock.

A whaleboat is a long, narrow rowboat that used to be carried aboard whaling ships. It is sharply pointed at both ends and is extremely strong and easy to handle. It is propelled by four to six oars and can be steered by an oar at the rear. In the days when whaling was carried on by sailships, several whaleboats were lowered and sent after a whale that had been sighted from the ship. Two or three men rowed, one steered with an oar in the rear, and a specially chosen man stood in front with a harpoon to hurl into the whale.

THE VIKING SHIP

The Viking ship was more than a boat. It was 75 feet long and 15 feet wide, or larger. It had a sail on a mast about 40 feet high and it carried 70 to 100 men. Of these, thirty men at a time were oarsmen; the others could rest unless they had to be fighting. In such boats the Norsemen went viking—raiding—swooping down on seaside towns or attacking other ships at sea. Such ships regularly crossed the North Sea to England and in one of them Leif Ericsson crossed the North Atlantic to America. The Viking ship had a small cabin, but most of the men had no shelter, even when sleeping or in storms.

SPECIAL KINDS OF BOAT

One of the oldest known types of boat is the Chinese *sampan*. It is about 20 feet long, with low sides and a small cabin up forward, and is driven by a single oar from the rear. The oar is moved back and forth in the water with a motion like that of a fish's tail. Although it is slow, it is strongly built and is an excellent craft for rivers, harbors, and coastal waters.

Another boat that is propelled by a single oar is the Venetian *gondola*. It has high, flat posts that sweep up from the front end, or prow, and the rear end, or stern. A gondola is flat-bottomed, about 30 feet long, and some 4 feet wide. It has a curtained cabin in the middle that can hold 4 to 8 persons. The man who drives the boat with an oar from the rear is called a gondolier. He stands on a small deck at the back of the boat. The gondola has been used for more than nine hundred years in the canals of the Italian city of VENICE, about which there is a separate article.

All ocean steamships carry lifeboats, which can be loaded with passengers and crew and quickly lowered to the water in case the ship is wrecked and begins to sink. These boats are about 32 feet long and have broad bottoms. A lifeboat will hold about sixty people. It has airtight metal compartments along the sides and at the bow (front) and stern (rear), so that it will not sink even when filled with water. The underside is weighted with cast iron, to make the boat self-righting if it should happen to turn over.

Most laws require all lifeboats to carry life preservers, oars, ropes, hatchets, matches, a compass, a lantern with a fuel supply, red night signals, fresh water, and preserved food. Lifeboats must be placed on the ship's deck in such a way that they can be lowered to the water in the shortest possible time.

Special lifeboats are kept at shore stations of the United States Coast Guard for rescue work when ships are wrecked near American shores. These boats also are self-righting and unsinkable. They are about 36 feet long and hold as many as 100 persons.

See also SHIP, SAILING, and BOATING.

boating

Boating is a popular and rapidly growing sport in the United States. In most cases boats powered by gasoline (or sometimes Diesel) engines are used and the sport is similar to yachting except that it does not require the wealth associated with yachting. Almost 600,000 boats are sold each year. In 1972 there were nearly 7,000,000 power boats in use for pleasure in the United States, plus more than two million sail boats, rowboats, dinghies, and canoes, and at least 46,000,000 Americans enjoyed boating regularly on U.S. waterways.

Of the powered pleasure craft in 1972, a few (perhaps 20,000) were genuine yachts, 40 feet or more long and with sleeping accommodations for eight or more persons. But most of them were MOTORBOATS (about which there is a separate article) used for short trips on inland waters or near the shore at sea. The vast majority (5,420,000 in 1972) were powered by outboard motors.

The great increase in the popularity of boating is due partly to the building of huge dams on many rivers, creating large new lakes that bring water sports to inland states such as Tennessee.

bobcat

The bobcat is a small wildcat. It rarely grows longer than 3½ feet. The fur of the bobcat is usually a rusty brown color. It is striped and spotted with black. The bobcat is a hard animal to find. It hides and sleeps during the day, and hunts for food at night. The bobcat feeds on whatever small animals it can catch, such as birds, mice, and rabbits. Bobcats are found in the Rocky Mountains, and also in the east of the United States and Canada, as far south as Florida and as far north as Nova Scotia.

U.S.D.A.
The bobcat is named for its short, stubby tail.

bobolink

The bobolink is a bird a little bigger than a sparrow. The male is a dull black except for patches of brown and white on its back. The bobolink is famous for its loud and cheerful song, which sounds like "bobolink." Bobolinks live in flocks and usually are found in country meadows. They make their nests out of twigs and grass. The nests are built on the ground and are so well hidden that they are hard to find. In the fall the male bobolink changes color and becomes all brown like the female. This change is called molting. The old feathers drop out and new ones grow in. The American poet William Cullen Bryant wrote a popular poem about the bobolink, in which he called it "Robert of Lincoln."

bobsled

A bobsled is a racing sled that can coast at very high speeds. Bobsledding is one of the most exciting of winter sports, because of the tremendous speed.

Bobsleds were first made in Switzerland, where there are high, icy mountains to coast on. A bobsled has a plank or platform on which one or more persons can sit, with two separate sets of runners, one pair in front, and one in back. The runners have steel edges, to cut into the icy track and keep the sled on its course, and at the same time to allow it to go as fast as possible. The front runners steer the sled, and a brake is attached to the back. The brake consists of

This two-man bobsled team begins its race at St. Moritz, Grisons, Switzerland.

The team is here seen sliding down the famous Cresta run at St. Moritz.

Swedish National Tourist Office
While traveling at such high speeds, the bobsledders must maintain constant concentration on the track ahead.

iron claws that dig into the ice and snow to slow down or stop the sled. The man at the back, called the *brake*, is not supposed to apply the brakes unless he gets an order from the *steersman* in front to do so. Many modern bobsleds have steering wheels, though in Europe many bobsledders prefer to steer with ropes.

There are two-man and four-man bobsleds. The four-man sled is faster, because its heavier weight makes it slide downhill faster. The two men in the middle of a bobsled team are carried only for their weight. The men at the front and back guide and control the sled. The sled may weigh as much as 500 pounds. In a bobsled race, only one sled goes down the run at a time, and its speed is accurately clocked. The next cannot be sent from the starting gate until the starter has received word that the track is clear and that the sled that went out before has completed its run.

Formerly a sled was given a running start at the beginning of a race by having one man push it as he ran beside it, jumping on only when the sled had picked up speed. Now there are starters that operate with handles, giving the sled a push to get it rolling with all men on board.

Bobsled runs are built of stone that is covered with blocks of ice, then flooded with water to form a thick, smooth coat of hard ice. The curves are steeply banked, that is, built up on one side so that a sled turning a curve rushes high up the slope but does not skid sideways.

Bobsledding is a sport for grown men. The weight is necessary, and the tremendous speed at which they travel would be dangerous for the lighter weight of children or most teen-agers. Only the weight of fairly heavy men holds the sled firmly on the track.

Since 1924, bobsledding has been a regular part of the winter Olympic Games. Four-man bobsleds sometimes go nearly 120 miles per hour. They average over 60 miles per hour, and two-man bobsleds over 40 miles per hour. The usual run is 1 to 1½ miles.

bobwhite

The bobwhite is a small, fat bird with a bright brown body, a striped head, and a little black tail. It belongs in the family with partridges, pheasants, and quails. It is about 10 inches long.

The bobwhite lives on the ground of the prairies, where it builds its nest and scratches for food. It eats insects, berries, and seeds. Each year the bobwhite raises a brood of ten or fifteen chicks that hatch from pure-white eggs. Bobwhites live in flocks and they usually have a leader for each flock. They rest and sleep together in little circles with their heads pointing out. If they are alarmed by hunters they quickly fly away in different directions. The bobwhite is hunted because it tastes better than chicken.

Boccaccio, Giovanni

Giovanni Boccaccio was an Italian poet and storyteller who lived about six hundred years ago. He lived most of

his life near Florence, Italy.

When Boccaccio was only 15 years old, he was sent to Naples, Italy, to learn about business. He was more interested in having a good time there than in working. He fell in love with a beautiful princess named Maria d'Aquino, whose father was King Roberto of Naples. Their love affair was very unhappy, and soon Giovanni returned to Florence. He wrote his saddest and most beautiful poems about Maria. Boccaccio's greatest book, however, is not at all sad, nor is it poetry. It is a collection of one hundred humorous stories called the *Decameron*.

Boccaccio was born in the year 1313. He died in 1375.

Bodleian Library

The Bodleian Library is one of the oldest, best and most famous libraries in the world. It is at Oxford University in England. It was named for Sir Thomas Bodley (born in 1545), who gave the library many books, valuable manuscripts, and a great deal of money to be used after he died.

Sir Thomas also worked in the library for the last 17 years of his life before he died in 1613. The original Oxford library had belonged to Humphrey, the Duke of Gloucester, but was mostly destroyed during the REFORMATION, in the 1500s, when there was much religious fighting.

The Bodleian Library today is much larger than it was then. It has a collection of three million books and forty thousand manuscripts (books that were not printed, but written by hand). The library gets about twenty-five thousand more books every year. Many of these are received free because there is a law in England that requires publishers to give a copy of every new book to each of the most important libraries in the country. The books in the Bodleian library are kept in several buildings. The newest and largest building was started in 1937 and was finished and opened in 1946.

body, the physical structure of an animal or person: see HUMAN BODY.

body temperature

The use of food in a living body is much like the burning of a fuel, and like any other burning it produces heat. Like any other heat, body heat is measured by its temperature.

Human beings and many animals have a built-in system for controlling their body temperature. These are called *warm-blooded* animals. Their body heat remains the same whether they are at the North Pole or at the equator. Mammals and birds are warm-blooded.

Other animals, such as reptiles and fish, depend for their body temperature on the warmth of the air or water around them. These are known as *cold-blooded* animals.

Normal temperature for a human being is between 97 and 99 degrees on the Fahrenheit scale. With most people, it is 98.6 (a little over ninety-eight and a half) degrees. This is *oral temperature*, taken by a thermometer held in the mouth. Inside the body the temperature is somewhat higher, so that a person's *rectal temperature* may be as much as a degree higher than his oral temperature. Body temperature also varies at different times of the day. It is lowest, for example, between two and five o'clock in the morning, when nearly everyone is asleep, and highest in midafternoon. Most warm-blooded animals, for example dogs, have higher normal temperatures than human beings.

HOW TEMPERATURE IS CONTROLLED

Body temperature is controlled from a center in the brain called the *hypothalamus*. Messages come to the hypothalamus from nerve endings in the skin, called *hot,* and *cold, receptors.* In hot weather, the hot receptors send the message to the hypothalamus, which then orders the sweat glands to open up. The skin is cooled by perspiration from the sweat glands. At the same time, more blood is sent to the surface of the skin. This keeps the blood from becoming too warm. In cold weather, the cold receptors send messages to the hypothalamus, which then orders the blood vessels in the skin to narrow or close down altogether. As a result, less blood is brought in contact with the cold surface.

When the temperature of the human body rises above 99 degrees, it is called a FEVER, about which there is a separate article. A rapidly rising temperature usually is a sign of infection somewhere in the body.

Boeotia

Boeotia was a territory in central Greece, in ancient times; it was most important about 2,590 years ago. Boeotia was next to Attica, the territory that included Athens, and the Boeotians and Athenians fought several wars against each other. The Boeotians were farmers and warriors but not scholars and artists like the Athenians. Boeotia covered about 1,000 square miles. The territory included the largest lake in Greece, Lake Copais. The principal city was Thebes. Boeotia is now one of the provinces of modern Greece.

Boer

The country that is now the Republic of South Africa was settled about 300 years ago by Dutch people from Holland. They came to be called *Boers,* which means "farmers" in the Dutch language. (They now call themselves *Afrikaaners.*) The Boers were Protestants and some of them left home to escape religious persecution, like the pilgrims who settled Massachusetts, but most of them simply wanted the fine farmlands that were free in the new country.

The Boers worked hard and became prosperous, but part of their wealth was due to the fact that they made slaves of the native Negro peoples. In 1815 Great Britain took over control of South Africa and many British people began to settle there. The Boers did not like to be gov-

erned by *Vitlanders* (their word for "foreigners") and when in 1834 Great Britain outlawed slavery throughout all its territories the Boers decided to move out. Between the years 1835 and 1840, in a famous overland journey called the Great Trek, most of the Boers moved their entire households 500 or more miles to the northeast and founded two new states, Transvaal ("across the Vaal River") and the Orange Free State.

There was peace for about 50 years. Then in 1885 big deposits of gold were found in the Transvaal. This made the territory valuable to the British, and when the Boers tried to keep it for themselves the British went to war.

THE BOER WAR

The war, known in England as the Boer War, broke out on October 11, 1899. The quarrel was between Great Britain and Transvaal (which was then called the South African Republic), but the Orange Free State joined in the war on the Transvaal side. The British territory in South Africa was called the Cape Colony.

Though Great Britain was then the strongest power on earth, South Africa was far away and the Boers knew the country better, so for several months the Boers seemed to be winning. They had specially trained soldiers called Commandos who did not fight with the regular army but made sudden raids on the British. (During World War II, the British used this name, Commandos, for their own raiding units.) For four months the Boers kept an entire British army besieged in the city of Ladysmith. Gradually the British took the chief Boer cities—Johannesburg, Bloemfontein, and Pretoria—and made the Boer armies surrender. The last Boer army surrendered in September 1900, not quite a year after the war began. But large numbers of Boers fought on as guerillas (see GUERRILLA WARFARE) and it was not until March 1902 that the war was finally over.

The chief Boer leaders were their president, Paulus Kruger, who was called "Oom Paul" (meaning "Uncle Paul"), and General Louis Botha. Jan Smuts, who later became a good friend of Great Britain, was a commander of Boer guerrillas. The chief British generals were Lord Frederick Roberts and Lord Horatio Kitchener. See the articles on KRUGER, SMUTS, and KITCHENER.

After the Boer War, Great Britain made the Transvaal and Orange Free State British possessions but gave them local government and tried to be friendly with the Boers. However, most of the Boers were still angry and in World War I they favored Germany; some even favored Germany in World War II. The treatment of Negroes is still a question on which the British and Dutch South Africans disagree; see SOUTH AFRICA, REPUBLIC OF.

bog

A bog is ground that is very wet and soft. It is made up of decaying mosses and other plants, and usually it is covered with grass. In Europe, the bogs are usually made up of peat. Coal is peat from millions of years ago, pressed by nature into the black, rocklike form that we use as fuel. Peat is soft and wet, but when dried it burns as coal does, though not so well. Nevertheless, thousands of people take peat from the bogs, dry it, and use it as fuel.

Bogotá

Bogotá is the capital city of the republic of Colombia, in South America. The city is built on a plateau, a high, level region; it is about 8,000 feet above sea level. The eastern Andes Mountains surround the city and protect it from the cold winds. This makes the climate mild, like May weather in most of the United States. In spring and fall there are heavy rains that last about two months.

Bogotá is a large and busy city. More than 2,500,000 people live there. The land of the plateau is very rich and has many farms that raise wheat, potatoes, and coffee. Some people work in mines. Others work in factories in the city, making such things as cloth, matches, and rope. Bogotá is a very interesting place to see. The San Francisco and the San Augustin Rivers divide the city into four sections, like a pie. There are museums, colleges, and universities. The most important is the University of Bogotá.

The city was founded more than four hundred years ago by Spanish explorers. They called it *Santa Fe de Bogotá*. For a long time Bogotá was one of the most difficult capital cities to get to, because one had to sail up the swampy Magdalena River and climb high mountains. Now, it has modern highways and railroads.

BOGOTÁ, COLOMBIA. Population, about 2,512,000. Capital of Colombia.

Bohème, La

La Bohème is a grand opera by the Italian composer Giacomo Puccini. The story is based on a French novel by Henri Murger. *La vie bohème* means "Bohemian life," the carefree life that many artists lead. *La Bohème* was first sung in Turin, Italy in 1896.

STORY OF THE OPERA

La Bohème is about a group of "Bohemians" in Paris, France, about 130 years ago. Rodolfo, a poet, and his friends Marcel, a painter, Colline, a writer, and Schaunard, a musician, live together. They are very poor and hungry, but they are trying to make a joke of it. One night Schaunard comes in with money, food, and wood for the stove. He has been paid for music lessons he gave to a rich pupil. Then the friends go out to celebrate, but Rodolfo stays behind to finish writing a poem.

While he is alone in the studio, Mimi knocks at the door. She is a pretty girl, and Rodolfo falls in love with her. Another girl, Musetta, has been in love with Marcel, but they have quarreled, and she has a new friend named Alcindoro, who is old and rich; but she is really in love with Marcel.

In the next part of the opera, Marcel and Musetta make up again, and then quarrel again, for that is their way; and Rodolfo quarrels with Mimi all the time, because he is jealous. Then Mimi, who has been ill for a long time, becomes much worse, and it is plain that she is dying. Rodolfo is sad, for he really loves her; and all the friends are sorry and very sad. They sell everything they can, to buy medicine and pay the doctor, and Colline even pawns his overcoat and Musetta her earrings. It is too late for the medicine to help Mimi, and she dies.

The best-known arias, or important solos, in the opera are: "Che gelida manina" (Thy hands are frozen), sung by Rodolfo; "Mi chiamano Mimi" (My name is Mimi) sung by Mimi; and "Musetta's waltz," sung by Musetta.

Bohemia

Bohemia is part of the country of Czechoslovakia. The land in Bohemia is very hilly and has a beautiful landscape of farms and forests. The people who live there are called *Czechs*. They have a long and proud history.

About seven hundred years ago, Bohemia was an independent kingdom. Some of the Bohemian kings were very powerful, and they became emperors of all Germany. This made Bohemia part of the German Empire. After the year 1620, Bohemia was part of the empire known as the Austrian Empire. The Austrian Empire was broken up after World War I, and Czechoslovakia was created. Read the articles about CZECHOSLOVAKIA and the city of PRAGUE.

Bohr, Niels

Niels Bohr is the name of a Danish scientist. He was one of the scientists who helped most to discover how the atom is constructed. He was born in 1885, and in 1913, when he was only 28 years old, he published some discoveries that made it possible, years later, for other scientists to build the atomic bomb. (See the articles on the ATOM and the ATOMIC BOMB.) Bohr became a professor of physics at the University of Copenhagen, in Denmark. He was awarded the Nobel Prize for physics in 1922. In World War II, the Germans invaded Denmark, and Bohr escaped from the country in a rowboat. He came to the United States, and helped to work on the atomic bomb. He returned to Denmark in 1945, after the war in Europe was over, to teach again at the university. Also he was made head of the Danish atomic energy control board. He died in 1963.

boiler

A boiler is a tank in which is stored a liquid that can be boiled to make steam. The long, barrel-like part of a steam locomotive is its boiler. Every house that is heated by hot water or steam has a boiler next to its furnace. Even when a house is heated by hot air, it is likely to have a boiler in which its hot water is made.

When water becomes so hot that it boils and turns to steam, it expands. That is, it needs much more space than it did when it was in liquid form. When the steam is kept in a tightly closed space, such as a tank, it presses against the sides in its effort to get out. This pressure is very useful, because it can be used as power to run machines. But it also requires that a boiler be very strong to hold it. Boilers are made of heavy steel metal sheets or "plates." These are welded together (or in some cases riveted) so there will be no leaks.

TYPES OF BOILER

There are two chief types of boiler. One is called the *water-tube boiler*. It is used in large buildings and for running large engines. The water-tube boiler is made of many steel pipes or tubes, running through a furnace. The flames in

the furnace heat these pipes so that the water inside becomes steam. Water-tube boilers are good because only a little water is needed to make steam. The steam then passes through a pipe called the *steam main*. The steam main carries the steam to the section where it can be used for power. After steam has been used for power, it can be cooled so that it will change back into water. This cooling process is known as *condensation*.

The other type of boiler is called the *fire-tube boiler*. It is a water-filled tank with tubes running through it. Instead of being filled with water, the tubes are filled with heat. They run from the furnace through the water. They heat the water to the boiling point and make steam. Fire-tube boilers are used in locomotives and in small factories, but they do not make as much steam power as a water-tube boiler.

Water is not the only liquid that can make steam. The *mercury-vapor boiler* uses mercury, which is a liquid metal. Mercury-vapor boilers cost more, but the mercury can be re-used.

Just as a balloon bursts when too much air pressure is put in it, a boiler will burst if the steam pressure becomes too great. Therefore every boiler has a safety valve. This is like a little door that is so tightly closed that great force is required to open it—but not quite as much as it would take to burst the boiler. Therefore, before the boiler can burst the valve opens and lets some of the steam escape. This reduces the pressure inside. As soon as the pressure is low enough to be safe, the safety valve automatically closes.

boiling point

When a liquid becomes hot enough, it boils, which means that it changes from the form of a liquid to the form of a gas. This is what happens when water boils and turns to steam. Any other liquid can be made to boil in the same way—if there is enough heat. The temperature at which a liquid boils is called its boiling point.

This temperature depends on the liquid. It takes a high temperature to melt iron—that is, turn it into a liquid—and it takes still more heat to make this liquid iron boil. But "liquid air" will boil when it is still much colder than ice.

The boiling point of water is 212 degrees Fahrenheit (the temperature scale we use in ordinary life) or 100 degrees Centigrade (the temperature scale most often used in science). However, this is the boiling point only at "standard air pressure," which is not quite 15 pounds per square inch (see the article on AIR).

EFFECT OF AIR PRESSURE

When a liquid boils, it escapes into the air. This means the air must somehow make room for it. The greater the air pressure, the more resistance it will offer, and the higher the temperature must be to make the liquid boil. So, every time the air pressure changes, the boiling point changes.

"Standard air pressure" is the pressure at sea level. The higher up you go—to a mountain top, or in an airplane—the lower the air pressure is, and the lower the boiling point becomes. The difference between air pressure at sea

level and in very high places makes it possible for scientists to measure the heights of mountains by boiling water there and testing its temperature. For every 550 feet of altitude the boiling point of water goes down 1° Fahrenheit. At Mexico City, which is 7,000 feet above sea level, water boils at only 200 degrees instead of 212. When an English scientist named Dr. Hooker climbed Donika Mountain in the Himalayas in India, he found that water boiled at the low temperature of 180 degrees and he was thus able to estimate that the mountain was 18,000 feet high. Mountain climbers have to cook their food much longer. Eggs have to be boiled for as long as 10 or 15 minutes, and sometimes the boiling water never gets hot enough to cook the food. But a *pressure cooker*, used in many households, cooks food very fast because the pressure inside becomes so high that the boiling water or steam is much hotter than 212 degrees.

Many liquids, including water, will turn into gas without heating, but much more slowly and by a different process called *evaporation*, or *vaporization*.

Boise

Boise is the capital and largest city of Idaho. It is on the Boise River. About 74,000 people live there. In the past, most of the people worked in the mines or were lumbermen. About forty years ago, the government built the Arrowrock Dam near Boise. This dam is one of the highest in the United States, and it irrigates about 170,000 acres of land. The dam made the land rich and now there are many farmers. They grow fruit, grain, and potatoes. There are also factories in Boise. Candy is an important product.

Not far from Boise there are some hot-water springs. The hot water from these springs is carried in pipes to the city and people use it in their homes. Buildings are heated by the hot water from these springs.

Fort Boise was originally a fur trading post on the Oregon Trail, west of the present site of the city. Almost a hundred years ago, when people were beginning to go west, Boise became one of the stations of the famous Pony Express. Later Boise became an army post, and in 1890 it was made the state capital.

BOISE, IDAHO. Population 74,990 (1970 census). Capital of Idaho. County seat of Ada County. Settled 1863. The Arrowrock Dam is located near Boise.

Bok, Edward William

Edward Bok was a little Dutch boy, 6 years old, when he first came to America. His family was poor, but after he graduated from high school in Brooklyn, New York, he continued his education at night school. He worked very hard, and when he was only 26 years old he was offered the job of editor of the *Ladies' Home Journal*. He stayed in this important job for thirty years. He wrote a famous autobiography, a book telling the story of his own life, called *The Americanization of Edward Bok*. It was awarded the Pulitzer Prize as the best book of its kind in 1920. After World War I, when everyone longed for world peace, Edward Bok offered

$100,000 for the best plan for world peace. Unfortunately, no plan was able to prevent World War II. Bok died in 1930. His life was one of many that prove how a poor immigrant boy can become a great man in the United States.

bolero

Bolero is a word that has three different meanings. It is a kind of Spanish dance, in which the dancers hold castanets—little wooden shells that make a clicking sound when struck together. Then, "the Bolero" is a famous piece of music that Maurice Ravel, the French composer (writer of music) wrote for a ballet. Finally, a bolero is a kind of short jacket, originally worn in Spain and still worn by Spanish dancers. This jacket has long sleeves, but comes only to the waist and has no buttons down the front.

Boleyn, Anne

Anne Boleyn was a queen of England, more than four hundred years ago. She was one of the six wives of King Henry VIII. He met her when she was lady in waiting to his first wife, Catherine of Aragon. Anne was a lively and pretty girl, and Henry wanted to marry her. So he asked the Pope to annul his marriage (declare that he was not legally married to Catherine). The Pope refused, so Henry left the Roman Catholic Church and founded the Church of England. This Church annulled his marriage to Catherine, and Henry then could marry Anne. They had one child, who became Queen Elizabeth I. After three years of marriage to Anne, King Henry grew tired of her. He accused her of being unfaithful to him and had her beheaded in the year 1536, when she was 29 years old.

Bolingbroke

Bolingbroke was a nickname of King Henry IV of England. He was called "Henry of Bolingbroke" because he was born at Bolingbroke Castle in England (in 1437). Shakespeare, in his historical play Richard II, calls the future King Henry "Bolingbroke."

The castle of Bolingbroke is near the town of Spilsbury in Lincolnshire, a county in the east of England.

Bolívar, Simón

Simón y Ponte Bolívar was a great South American soldier and statesman. He is called "the Liberator" because he led the revolutions that gave many of  the South American countries their liberty, nearly 150 years ago. These countries had belonged to Spain. The ones that were freed by Bolívar and his armies were Venezuela, Colombia, Ecuador, Peru, and Bolivia.

Gale Research Co.

Simón Bolívar was born in the city of Caracas, which is in Venezuela, in 1783. His family was very rich, and he was sent to Europe for his education. While he was at law school in Spain he fell in love and got married. He was only 18 years old at that time. He took his wife back to Caracas with him, but

very soon after they arrived she became ill and died. Bolívar was deeply unhappy, and he went back to Europe to try to take his mind off his sorrow. He spent some time in Europe and he also visited the United States, which had won its independence from England only a few years before.

When Bolívar saw that a democratic independent government was working out well for the United States, he decided to spend his life working to bring independence to the Spanish colonies of South America. There already was a secret movement for independence in most of these colonies. Bolívar went back to Venezuela and joined the revolutionaries. He used his own money to help supply the army and to pay for the revolutionary battles.

THE REVOLUTIONS

In 1811, there was a revolt against Spanish rule in Venezuela, and Bolívar played an important part in it. But the revolt was not successful, and Bolívar had to run away to the island of Curaçao, in the West Indies. He went back to South America about a year later and led another great revolt against the Spaniards. This revolt went on for nearly two years, but it was finally beaten and Bolívar again had to run away to the West Indies. But Bolívar would not give up. Once more he went back to South America and led an army against the Spaniards.

While Bolívar and his army had been fighting for the independence of Venezuela, other armies had been fighting for the independence of other Spanish colonies in South America. These different armies got together, and Bolívar was made the head of all the revolutionaries. After many bitter battles, the revolutionaries won independence for Venezuela and Colombia. The two countries were joined together under the name of Colombia and Bolívar was elected president of the new republic. He continued to help the other Spanish colonies until the last independent country was formed, in 1825. That country called itself Bolivia, in honor of Simón Bolívar.

BOLIVAR'S TROUBLES

Soon there were disagreements inside the governments of the new republics. Venezuela decided to separate from Colombia, and they broke up into two different countries. Bolívar had written the Bolivian constitution, but it was very unpopular with the people and was replaced by another constitution. Bolívar himself became less and less popular. The people began to accuse him of being a dictator. The Venezuelans themselves, who had won their independence under Bolívar's leadership, turned against him. In 1830, they asked him to leave the country.

Bolívar was hurt and unhappy. He had given his whole life and all his fortune to the fight for independence. He had no family or home. And the people, instead of being grateful, were angry with him. He had worked and fought so hard for South American independence that he had become ill, and very soon after he was sent into exile he died, in 1830. He was only 47 years old.

But only a few years after Bolívar died, the people began to realize how much he had done for them. They built statues to his memory and honored his name in many ways, as one of the greatest American heroes. In North America Bolívar is honored too. One statue of him stands just outside New York's Central Park.

Bolivia

Bolivia is one of the largest countries of South America. It is about five thousand miles from the United States. It has an area of about 400,000 square miles, which is about two-thirds as big as Alaska. More than five million people live in Bolivia. It is the biggest independent country on earth without a seacoast. It is not a rich country, but it has the biggest tin mines in the world, and this made some of the people very rich until in 1952 the government nationalized (took over ownership of) the mines.

THE PEOPLE WHO LIVE THERE

As in all the Americas, the first people in South America were Indians. More than half of the people in Bolivia now are Indians. Some of these, called the Lowland Indians, are still quite primitive and live today much as their ancestors did thousands of years ago. They speak their own languages and have their own customs.

About one in every seven of the people of Bolivia belongs to the "white" race. The white people are descendants of the Spaniards and Portuguese who went to South America hundreds of years ago. They are the most powerful and richest group in the country. The next most powerful group is called the *mestizos*. A mestizo is part white and part Indian. More than a quarter of the people of Bolivia are mestizos.

The Lowland Indians live in forests and valleys far from the cities, and get along by hunting and fishing. The other Indians, called Highland Indians, work at mining, farming, and sheep herding. Tin-mining is the most important industry. The farms produce cocoa, coffee, and grains, and there are many rubber plantations.

The biggest city in Bolivia is La Paz. More than 679,000 people live there. Most of the government offices of Bolivia are in La Paz, but it is not officially the capital of the country. The official capital is Sucre, which has only about 84,900 people. The only government building in Sucre is the Supreme Court building. Life in La Paz and Sucre is very much like life in North American cities.

WHAT KIND OF PLACE IT IS

A high mountain range, part of the Andes, runs through Bolivia. Most of the people live on the high plains between the mountain peaks. This high part is called the Altiplano. The cities of La Paz and Sucre are on the Altiplano. There is a beautiful large lake on the Altiplano, called Lake Titicaca. It is the largest lake in South America. Many steamships travel back and forth across Lake Titicaca. No other lake at such a high altitude can be used for commerce. The climate on the Altiplano is cool and pleasant. There is a rainy season and

Braniff International

The llama has always been very valuable to the people of Bolivia for the many services it performs for them. The llama's strength makes it able to carry loads even in the thin mountain air of the Andes.

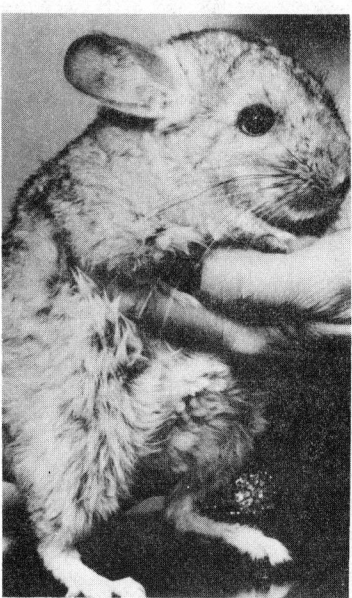

National Archives

The small chinchilla, only ten inches in length, is prized for its fine fur. Once found high in the mountains of Bolivia, it is quite rare in the wild due to overhunting.

a dry season.

Higher up in the Andes mountains it is always cold, and there is snow all year round. Shepherds live on the mountains. They tend flocks of llamas, vicuñas, and chinchillas. These animals have valuable hair and furs. In the valleys and jungles where the Lowland Indians live, it is hot and wet, very much as it is in the jungles and valleys of Africa.

Bolivia is a very beautiful place, with many different kinds of country and many different kinds of wild life. There are colorful birds flying through the tropical jungles. Fierce wild animals roam around the dense forests—jaguars, wildcats, and others.

HOW THE PEOPLE ARE GOVERNED

Bolivia is a republic. It has a president, a congress, and a supreme court, as the United States has. Both men and

women are allowed to vote — married people can vote at age 18, but unmarried ones cannot vote until they are 21. Bolivia has been a republic for more than one hundred years, but it has had many stormy revolutions to decide which party will hold power.

Every man goes into the army at the age of 19 to serve two years, and until he is 49 he must serve for short periods in various army duties. Also, boys and girls between 14 and 18 are given what is called "pre-military training." The Roman Catholic religion is the official religion in Bolivia, but people who believe in other religions are allowed to worship as they please.

Every child in Bolivia must go to grammar school. After that, he can leave school and go to work. Many people in Bolivia do not know how to read and write, but the government is working very hard to teach them. One of the problems the government has is that many of the Indians who live in Bolivia do not speak Spanish, the official language, but speak their own Indian language.

BOLIVIA IN THE PAST

About a thousand years ago, the country that is Bolivia today was part of a very powerful Indian kingdom in South America, called the Inca Empire. The Incas had a wonderfully advanced civilization, but they did not know about gunpowder. When the Spaniards went to South America about four hundred years ago, they were able to defeat the Incas. Like the other countries of South America, Bolivia came under Spanish rule.

In 1825, Bolivia gained independence from Spain and became a republic. The name Bolivia was chosen in honor of the leader of the fight for independence, Simón Bolívar. There have been many stormy fights and arguments among the people of Bolivia, and one war with the neighboring country of Paraguay about which country should control a section called the Chaco. (See the article on GRAN CHACO.)

BOLIVIA. Area, 424,162 square miles. Population (1973 estimate) 5,065,000. Language, Spanish. Religion, Roman Catholic. Government, republic. Monetary unit, the boliviano, worth 8½ cents (U.S.). Flag, three bars going across: red, yellow, green.

boll weevil

The boll weevil is an insect of the beetle family. It is about a quarter of an inch long, and lives on cotton plants. Every year the boll weevil causes losses of more than $100,000,000. The boll weevil has a long snout, which is a kind of beak. With this snout it bites into the blossom buds of the cotton plant and destroys the flower. It also feeds on the young bolls and lays its eggs in some of the holes it makes. The eggs hatch into little, white, wormlike things, called *grubs,* which also feed on the bolls.

The boll weevil originally came from Mexico or Central America. Until about sixty years ago there were no boll weevils in the United States. Then gradually the boll weevils invaded all the states where cotton is grown. Chemicals have been found that will kill the boll weevil but many escape and manage to do a great deal of damage.

Bologna

Bologna is a city in Italy. It lies at the foot of the Apennine Mountains, about 185 miles northwest of Rome. Bologna has been a center of culture for nearly two thousand years—since the time of the Roman Empire. It is known for its churches, which are beautiful and which contain thousands of art treasures. At one time the University of Bologna was a famous law school, and it later became famous as a medical school.

The people of Bologna manufacture many things, including soap, silk, candles, and musical instruments. A kind of sausage from Bologna has become famous as "baloney."

Bologna was the place where Allied troops broke through into the Po Valley of Italy during World War II. The city was badly damaged then, but most of its beautiful buildings may still be seen. Its population in 1973 was about 490,000, which makes it about the same size as Atlanta, Georgia.

Bolshevism is a former name for the policies of the present Communist Party in Russia. See COMMUNISM and UNION OF SOVIET SOCIALIST REPUBLICS.

bomb

A bomb is a container that holds an explosive or some other substance to hurt people. Most bombs hold powerful explosives. Police sometimes use *tear bombs,* which release gases to make people cry so hard that they are blinded and can easily be captured. *Stench bombs* release a gas that smells terrible but is not harmful. Gangsters sometimes use bombs to kill their enemies. But most bombs are used in warfare, and in modern warfare they are dropped from airplanes or carried by rockets.

In World War II, Germany was so badly hurt by bombs dropped from Allied planes that she had to give up. The most powerful of these bombs held about two tons of the explosive called TNT. It was called a "blockbuster" because it would destroy a whole city block. But the atomic and hydrogen bombs that have been developed since then are more than twenty thousand times more powerful.

There are four main parts to most bombs, the outside shell, or case; the explosive or fire-producing material inside; the tail fin, which helps it move through the air or water; and the fuse, which sets the bomb off when it hits a target.

THE MAIN TYPES OF BOMBS

There are five main types of bombs; demolition, fragmentation, incendiary, armor-piercing, and atomic.

The *demolition bomb* has a thin case and a large amount of explosive inside. It was the most destructive bomb used generally in World War II. Demolition bombs often weigh as much as two tons. The fuse that sets off the bomb acts very fast. When the bomb hits the target it immediately explodes with a great blast. The "blockbuster" is a demolition bomb. These bombs are used to blow up factories, bridges, and other big targets.

The *fragmentation bomb* is a small bomb which is dropped on enemy troops by an airplane that often flies close to the ground. The fragmentation bomb has a metal case that scatters in small pieces when the bomb explodes. The pieces serve as bullets when they hit soldiers. The fuse that sets this bomb off works more slowly than the fuse of a demolition bomb. An airplane can drop these bombs while flying close to the ground and still have time to get away before the bomb explodes. This type of bomb usually weighs no more than 50 pounds.

The *incendiary bomb* is not explosive. Its purpose is to start a fire. There are two kinds of incendiary bombs. One kind weighs only a few pounds and has a case made of magnesium. This kind of incendiary bomb is used at night, because magnesium is a metal that burns very brightly and lights up the target. When the target is lit up other airplanes can see it and drop large demolition bombs to destroy it. The other kind of incendiary bomb weighs about twenty-five pounds. It has a thin case, and is filled with a gasoline jelly. When this bomb hits the target the gasoline jelly is set on fire and scattered. This bomb is used to burn down buildings.

The *armor-piercing* bomb is a large bomb with a very strong, heavy case. It weighs about half a ton. The armor-piercing bomb is used against warships. This bomb is made to go through the steel decks of a ship. It does not explode until it gets inside the ship. Ordinary TNT would explode too quickly because TNT is a very sensitive chemical. This bomb is filled with a chemical that is much less sensitive than TNT.

There are two types of atomic bombs, the ATOMIC BOMB and the HYDROGEN BOMB. There is a separate article about each. These are the most terrible weapons of war that have ever been invented. A single atomic bomb is powerful enough to destroy a whole city. The hydrogen bomb is even more powerful.

OTHER TYPES OF BOMBS

A *guided missile* is a demolition bomb that has its own engine and fuel for flying and is guided to its target by radio. No guided missiles of this kind were used during World War II.

The *depth charge* and the *torpedo* are two important types of bombs used in naval warfare. The depth charge is a bomb used against submarines. In World War I the depth charge was called an "ashcan" because it looked just like one. But the depth charge that people use today looks like a huge black teardrop. Depth charges are fired in pairs from the stern (rear end) of a ship that is chasing a submarine. This bomb does not have an ordinary fuse. It explodes when it reaches a certain depth under water. It is the pressure of the water that sets off the depth charge. When it explodes near a submarine the submarine is crushed by the blast.

A torpedo is a large and powerful bomb that submarines, torpedo boats and airplanes fire at a ship. Torpedoes are sometimes more than twenty feet long. Some of them cost twenty thousand dollars to build. Torpedoes travel as boats do, across the water or underwater to their targets. The front of the torpedo

carries the explosive and is called the warhead. In the rear are the engines that drive the torpedo and a gyroscope that steers it.

A *time bomb* is usually a small bomb that is set off by an electric current. It is called a time bomb because it is attached to a clocklike instrument. When the hands of this clock reach a certain time, the electric circuit is closed, causing the bomb to explode. This bomb is much used by spies and saboteurs because it can be placed somewhere and be made to explode hours after the spy or saboteur has escaped.

A *hand grenade* is a small bomb that soldiers carry and throw at the enemy. It is nicknamed "pineapple" because it looks somewhat like one. The fuse that sets it off is a little button that the soldier pulls out before he throws it.

PROXIMITY FUSE

The United States had one great advantage over its enemies in World War II—the proximity fuse. This is a device that will explode a bomb when it gets close to its target. A built-in radar device sets off the bomb.

BOMBSIGHT

A bomber flying at several hundred miles per hour at heights several thousand feet above the target needs very delicate aiming instruments. These instruments are called *bombsights.* They work out automatically and mathematically where the bomb will land.

The United States has had the best bombsights in the world for about twenty years, and this helped to win World War II. The best bombsights have always been military secrets. They are built with little bombs inside them. If a plane crashes, or is in danger of being captured, the bomb explodes and destroys the bombsight so that the enemy cannot take it and copy it. Before World War II, the Sperry bombsight was the best. During World War II an improved design called the Norden bombsight was used. Better bombsights have been developed since World War II.

Bombay

Bombay is a great city on the western coast of India, and a seaport on the Arabian Sea. It is the largest city in Western India and, with Calcutta, is one of the two largest cities in all of India. Each is bigger than any American city except New York and Chicago. Bombay is built on an island, with a harbor that is the finest in India and is also closer to Europe than any other. Bombay was also the name of what was formerly India's largest state, and the city of Bombay was the capital of that state. But in May, 1960, the state of Bombay was divided into two states: Maharashtra, and Gujarat, giving India 15 states. The temporary capital of Gujarat is AHMEDABAD (see separate article), and Bombay is the capital of Maharashtra.

The people of Bombay are of many different origins. Thousands of Englishmen and other Europeans live and work there. A Hindu people called Mahrattas make up the largest single group in the population. Parsees, although there are only about a hundred thousand of them, have an importance out of proportion to

their number; many great businesses and much property is in their hands. Besides these groups Bombay has Arab traders from the Persian Gulf, Afghans from Afghanistan, tall Sikhs, Tibetans from the northern frontier, Senegalese, Jews, Japanese, and many other nationalities.

The two main languages of Bombay are Mahrathi and Gujarati, but almost everybody also speaks and understands a local language called "Bombay Bat," which includes words from several languages.

Most of Bombay's people follow the Hindu religion but there are many Mohammedans and Buddhists and there are some Christians. The Parsees are a separate religious group.

The name "Bombay" comes from *Mumba,* a goddess who was worshipped on Bombay and neighboring islands at about the time of Christ. King Bhima, a Hindu ruler, built the first town on Bombay Island. About five hundred years ago, Mohammedan invaders captured it, and about two hundred years after that it was ruled by Portugal. England acquired Bombay when King Charles II married a Portuguese princess. It remained under British control until India became independent in 1950.

Bombay has a big university, founded in 1857, and many fine buildings and parks.

BOMBAY, INDIA. City. Population (1973 estimate) 5,950,000. Capital of state of Maharashtra.

Bonaparte

Bonaparte was the family name of the French emperor, NAPOLEON, about whom there is a separate article. He made many members of his family kings or noblemen, about 150 years ago.

All of the Bonapartes are descended from Napoleon's father and mother, Carlo and Letizia Buonaparte. The Buonapartes were an old Italian family that had moved to the island of Corsica, nearly three hundred years before Napoleon was born in 1769. Corsica was taken over by France in 1768, so Napoleon and his younger brothers and sisters were all born French citizens. It was Napoleon who changed the spelling of the name to a French way, Bonaparte.

Joseph Bonaparte was the oldest son of Carlo Buonaparte. He was born in 1768, a year older than Napoleon, and the two brothers were very close. Joseph served in the French army under Napoleon in 1796. Napoleon made Joseph King of Naples, and later King of Spain, when those countries came under French control. Joseph was very active in government and politics until 1815, when Napoleon was finally beaten and sent into exile. Joseph retired from government work, came to America, and became an American citizen. He later returned to Europe, where he died in 1844.

Lucien Bonaparte was another brother of Napoleon. He was born in 1775. In 1797 he became a member of one of the groups that ruled France after the Revolution of 1789. This group was called the Council of the Five Hundred. For a while Lucien and Napoleon got along well, but Lucien believed in democracy and was disturbed because Napoleon wanted to be emperor. The two brothers had many quarrels, and Lucien was the

only one of the Bonaparte brothers who was not made a king. Lucien died in 1840.

Louis Bonaparte was Napoleon's next-youngest brother, born in 1778. Napoleon was very fond of Louis, and kept Louis with him during many of his battles and campaigns. But later the relations between the two brothers became very unfriendly. Louis was made king of Holland in 1806. He was married to Napoleon's stepdaughter, Hortense Beauharnais. One of their sons, named Charles Louis Napoleon, became president and then emperor of France in 1852. He was known as NAPOLEON III, and there is a separate article about him.

Jerome Bonaparte was Napoleon's youngest brother, born in 1784. Napoleon made him King of Westphalia. Before that, Jerome was married to an American girl, Elizabeth Patterson, from Baltimore. Napoleon was very angry about this. He made Jerome divorce her, and she went back to the United States, where there have been several prominent descendants of Jerome and Elizabeth.

Napoleon also had three sisters, Maria-Anna Elisa, Pauline, and Caroline. He gave them all many honors. But at that time women were not as active in public life as they are today.

bond

A bond is a written agreement to pay a certain amount of money in the future. Bonds are used to borrow money for long periods, such as 20 or even 50 years. The best-known kind of bond is the *mortgage bond,* which is one of the documents a person signs when he borrows money to buy or build a house (see MORTGAGE). Billions of dollars are borrowed by governments, by public utilities such as gas and electric companies, and by big businesses such as railroads and manufacturers, by issuing bonds. The borrowed money is used to put up big buildings, build highways and bridges, buy heavy machinery, and for other long-term investments.

Usually the whole amount of money borrowed is split up into bonds of $1,000 each. A firm of brokers called *underwriters* may buy the entire issue of bonds, making a profit by reselling the bonds to the public at a higher price. A bondholder, or owner of a bond, may sell it at any time, but the price is not necessarily the face value (such as $1,000). A bond may rise or fall in value like any other property, depending on how sure it seems that the borrower will be able to *redeem* it (pay the promised amount) when it *matures* (becomes due), and will pay the interest in the meantime.

All bonds bear interest, ranging from 2½% to 7% (see INTEREST). On many bonds, *coupons* are printed on every bond and once or twice a year the bondholder clips off a coupon and the issuer of the bond gives him money for it, that being his interest for the period. Some bonds are *discounted*—that is, the interest is taken off the purchase price. An example is Series E Savings Bonds of the United States. The buyer pays $18.75 for the bond and receives $25 seven years later, the difference of $6.25 being his interest for seven years. (It is about 4-1/7% per year.)

A *secured* bond names some particular

property as security or *collateral;* if the borrowed money is not repaid, the bondholder may take the property. Usually, as in the case of a mortgage bond, the security is real estate, but it may also be income such as the tolls from a bridge or highway, or such things as a railroad train or machinery. An unsecured bond, also called a *debenture,* is backed by the borrower's total assets, or net worth, but not by any particular property.

A *negotiable* bond, like paper money, belongs to whoever has it; a *registered* bond is payable only to the person whose name is recorded with the corporation that issued the bond. However, both kinds may be traded—bought and sold—and the buyer of a registered bond simply has his name recorded in place of the previous owner's.

Real estate bonds are like mortgage bonds except that the total amount borrowed is split up into bonds of $1,000 each so that there may be many lenders. *State* and *municipal* (city) bonds, which are issued for such purposes as building schools and other public buildings, are taxfree securities, which means that the bondholder does not have to pay income tax on the interest he receives. They pay low interest rates but are much in demand by rich people whose income taxes are high.

All national governments issue bonds of several different kinds, especially to finance wars. The United States financed World War I with Liberty Bonds and, after the war was won, Victory Bonds. To rearm for World War II it issued Defense Bonds, then War Bonds, and later Savings Bonds. After a series of expensive wars a government may have to turn its bonds into a permanent bonded fund, with no redemption date for the bonds. The British government, after its costly wars against Napoleon in the early 1800s, issued bonds called *consols* (because they consolidated, or combined, previous bonds) and these are still bought and sold. The government redeems some of them whenever it wishes. Many issues of corporate bonds (issued by private companies) are redeemed a few at a time, the company drawing lots to see which it will redeem.

OTHER FORMS OF BONDING

Another kind of bond is an agreement to pay a certain amount of money if some event does or does not occur. This kind of bond is usually issued by a *bonding company,* which is a kind of insurance company.

A *fidelity bond* is a guarantee that a trusted employee will remain honest. Bank tellers, cashiers, collectors, and others who handle money are usually bonded. If they steal, the bonding company makes good. A *bail bond* is a promise to pay an amount established by a court if a person charged with a crime runs away instead of facing trial. A *performance bond* is a promise to pay a certain amount if a person does not do what he agrees to do. For example, a contractor agrees to finish a building by a certain date and posts (supplies) a bond that is payable if the building is not finished by that date.

A *bonded warehouse* posts a bond that it will keep goods in storage until taxes are paid on them.

bone

Bone is one of the tissues of the body. It is the hard substance of which the skeletons of animals such as fish, reptiles, birds and mammals are made. In young animals, before bone is formed, the skeleton is made of a tough elastic material called cartilage. Then the body uses various substances—salts of calcium, phosphorus, and other minerals—to make it hard.

In the human body there are about 212 bones of various shapes and sizes. The long thin bones, such as arm and leg bones, are specially important because they are hollow and filled with marrow, which makes part of the blood.

Bones are not solid. They are full of tiny holes and canals; and on the outside, bones are covered with a tissue full of blood vessels and nerves that feed them and keep them alive.

Bonheur, Marie Rosalie

This French painter is always called "Rosa," a nickname for Rosalie. She is best known for one picture called "The Horse Fair." It is a painting of big farm horses being led home after being bought at an auction. There are all kinds of different colored horses in the picture. Some of them are big, strong white ones, others are brown, black or gray. The picture is filled with movement and you can almost see the horses walking. Rosa Bonheur was born in France in 1822, and spent most of her life there. She came from an artistic family. When she was quite young, she became the head of a school for girls in Paris. Before Rosa Bonheur died in 1899, she had become world-famous as a painter of animals.

Boniface

Boniface was a missionary who set out from England to teach the Christian religion to the people of Germany, France, and Holland. All this was long, long ago, about the year 700, when the people in most of Europe were still barbarians. St. Boniface, whose name was Wynfrith before he became a saint, built so many churches in Germany that he is called the Apostle of Germany. His special day is June 5.

Nine Popes, or heads of the Roman Catholic Church, have taken the name of Boniface. The first was Pope just about four hundred years after the time of Jesus Christ; the last Boniface was Pope almost six hundred years ago.

Bonn

Bonn is a city in Germany. It is on the Rhine River, about 16 miles southeast of Cologne. Since 1949, it has been the capital of the Federal Republic of Germany (West Germany). About 144,300 people live there. Most of them work in factories, making chemicals, machinery, and musical instruments. Bonn is a very old city, and its most famous building is a church that is more than eight hundred years old. If you visit Bonn, you can see the famous Friedrich Wilhelm University, and the house in which the great German composer, Ludwig van Beethoven, was born. You can also see the grave of another famous German composer, Robert Schumann. A beautiful bridge crosses the Rhine

River at Bonn, and along the river you can see fine houses, called villas. In World War II, much of the city was destroyed or damaged.

Bonneville Dam and Lake

Bonneville Dam and Bonneville Lake were both named for Benjamin Bonneville, an American military engineer and explorer who lived in the early 1800s.

Bonneville Lake is not a lake at all. It is a desert in the state of Utah. Many, many, thousands of years ago it was a very large lake. It had an area of 20,000 square miles and was 1,000 feet deep in some places. It almost dried out once, but it refilled naturally. Then it dried out again and it has never been refilled. It turned into a desert. Its shore lines can still be seen, high on the mountainsides.

Bonneville Dam is a real dam. It is on the Columbia River, between the states of Washington and Oregon. Its main purpose is to supply electric power for the people of those two states. Bonneville Dam was built by the United States Army Engineer Corps, and is operated by the United States Army. There are many salmon in the Columbia River, and they all go upstream in the spring to lay their eggs. The Bonneville Dam has a special ladder for the salmon, to help them jump over the dam.

bonus

The word *bonus,* in the Latin language, means "good." We use it to mean extra money that is paid to a person, besides any regular wages he may have earned.

A government often gives special money to men who have served in the army or other armed forces. This is called a "soldier's" (or veteran's) bonus. Many businesses give bonuses to their workers at Christmas time. These bonuses are like Christmas presents. If a worker does a particularly good job, his company may give him a bonus.

If a company has made a very big profit, this extra money may be distributed to the owners of the company. Very often a company gives a "stock bonus." Instead of money, it gives extra shares of stock (ownership) in the company.

book

The purpose of a book is to save mens' best thoughts so that other men may make use of them. Civilization and science depend more on books than on anything else.

A book must record thousands of words and still be small enough to store and handle easily. The earliest writing was on stone slabs or clay tablets and there could be no real books, for these were too bulky. The first real "books" were long rolls of thin animal skins such as parchment or an early kind of paper called papyrus; the reader unrolled the long roll, reading as he went along. The first books of the modern kind, a sheaf of pieces of paper bound together, were made a little more than a thousand years ago. Today, about 10,000 to 15,000 new books are published each year in the United States and about the same number, more or less, in each other civilized country.

A book may be intended to entertain, as a story book or novel does; or it may

be intended to instruct, as a schoolbook does; or it may be intended to make a record of things that might otherwise be forgotten. A blank book, such as a diary or a bookkeeping book, becomes a record book when things are written down in it, just as it would be if those things were printed in it to begin with.

All modern books are printed. A separate article on PRINTING tells how the type is set and how the paper is printed in a press. When a book is printed, a big sheet of paper is used. As many as 128 pages may be printed at one time.

To see how this is done, take a sheet of paper and fold it in exact halves. Then fold it again. And then again.

The place where you last folded it is where the back of the book will be. Take a pencil and number all the separate flat surfaces into which you folded the large sheet. You will find that there are sixteen of these. They will be the pages of the book.

Now unfold the sheet again. You will find that pages 1, 8, 9, 16, 12, 13, 4, and 5 are on one side of the big sheet, and pages 2, 7, 10, 15, 3, 6, 11, and 14 are on the other side. The printer makes up his type so that each page is arranged in the proper position to print in the proper place on the sheet; this arrangement of the type is called the *imposition*. He prints one side of the sheet, then the other. Then he folds the sheet, just as you did, and he has sixteen pages in the proper order to make one section of a book. This section is called a *signature*.

Fold your sheet again, and with scissors trim off the outside and bottom edges. You will find that you have a booklet whose pages open properly and read in order from 1 to 16. There are only eight separate leaves, but each leaf makes two pages.

What you have just done is the same thing a printer does when he prints a book, except that he does it in a more complicated way because his books must have hundreds of pages and he must make thousands of them at a time.

BOOKBINDING

Usually the printer does not do the folding of the book. He ships the big printed sheets to a bookbinder. The bookbinder takes care of all the other steps that go into the making of the book.

First, the bookbinder puts the big sheets on an automatic folding machine. This machine has arms that lift edges of the sheet, and rollers that fold them over much more smoothly than it can be done by hand. Even though 64 or 128 may be printed on one sheet, the folding machine folds them in signatures of only 16 or 32 pages.

These signatures are then *gathered*— that is, put in proper order so that page 17 will follow page 16, and page 33 will follow page 32, and so on through the book, and also arranged so that the edges are even at the ends and sides.

When all the signatures have been assembled in proper order, they are taken to a sewing machine and the backs of them are sewed together. This is very much like the sewing that a housewife does on her sewing machine at home, except that of course the bookbinder's sew-

ing machines are specially built to handle books. If the cover has come off a book of yours, you can see how it is sewed. Or if you take nearly any book and count off the first eight leaves (which make sixteen pages) and open the book wide, you can see the thread.

You now have a *sewed book*. A single folded sheet of heavy paper is now pasted to the back edges of the first page and last page of the sewed book. These are the *end papers*. They will later be used to fasten the book to its cover.

The next operations are: The book is *smashed;* that is, a heavy weight is dropped on it in a special press, to flatten it out all over. Then the book is *rounded and backed;* this means that the backbone of the book is formed into a rounder shape, which is more attractive than a flat back, and then a piece of cloth is glued to the backbone to strengthen it. On a well-made book, *headbands* are added at the same time. That is the piece of decorative woven cloth you can see at the top of this book.

The sewed book is now ready for *casing-in.*

N.Y. Public Library

Monks in the Middle Ages made bindings for books with great care and skill. It sometimes took years to finish the beautiful binding of a book.

MAKING THE CASE

The cover of the book is called a *case*. The bookbinder takes two heavy pieces of cardboard to make the front and back covers. He wraps this in bookbinder's cloth, which is specially made to be attractive, long-lasting, and resistant to soil and water. Bibles and some other books are bound in leather, or in various artificial leathers made of cloth and plastics. A case-making machine automatically wraps the cloth around the pieces of cardboard and glues down the edges, and also leaves a portion in the center that will be the back of the book. From this book you are reading, you can see the re-

sult of these operations.

The case is then *stamped*. Heavy metal dies, which are like printing plates but much stronger, stamp colored inks, or gold, or other metals, on the book, so that its name can be read and also to give it beauty. This book requires three separate stampings to make the lettering and the design on its cover.

When the case has been made and the sewed book is complete, they meet at the casing-in machine. Both the end papers of the book are coated with a very strong glue. Then they are pressed to the inside of the case. The book is now complete. Nearly every step has been done by automatic machinery.

PAPERBOUND BOOKS

There are other methods of bookbinding that are much cheaper. The principal one is called *perfect binding*. A perfect-bound book is not sewed. The folded signatures are trimmed all the way around. Then glue and a piece of light cloth are added to the back, to hold the pages together. This is the same way a writing tablet is made. The telephone books in all big cities are bound in this way. So are the paperbound books that sell for 25 cents or 35 cents at newsstands. It is because so much money is saved in the binding that the publishers of these books can give such great values for so little money.

Many magazines are folded just as books are, but are not sewed. Instead, heavy staples are driven through the sides. Then a paper cover is pasted over the entire magazine. Still other magazines are saddle-stitched, which means that the staple is driven through the center of the fold.

HANDMADE BOOKS

Bookbinding is a hobby with some people, and it is an art with some very fine bookbinders who make beautiful books that can cost hundreds of dollars. The finest leathers are often used, or cloths of rare weaves and patterns. The lettering and designs on the covers are put on by hand, with brass types and instruments that are heated and pressed into the covers. This is called *hand-tooling*. Of course, very few handmade books are made, because they are so expensive. In the early days of books, hundreds of years ago, many more books were made by hand, and some of them are still among the most beautiful of all books.

HOW BOOKS DEVELOPED

Thousands of years ago, when warlike nations such as Greece and Rome would capture the educated men of other countries and make slaves of them, books were written by hand, by slaves who were forced to be copyists. Of course, that was long before printing was invented.

Then came the Dark Ages. They were called dark because men forgot the advantages of education and became ignorant. Only the Christian Church kept learning alive. In the monasteries of Europe, monks worked for years making copies of the Bible and other books that were worth preserving. This went on for nearly a thousand years—from the time

Left: A page from a book made in Italy almost 500 years ago. These early books were very beautiful and they had many fine woodcuts and pictures. *Right:* A woodcut from a 15th-century book. These early books are very rare and are kept in museums.

when the Roman Empire was conquered by barbarians, in 476, to the time when the Renaissance, or "rebirth of learning," began in the 1300s.

During this period, the monks of Europe made some of the most beautiful of all books. These are called *illuminated manuscripts*. The *manuscript* part means they were written by hand, and *illuminated* means decorated with beautiful designs and pictures in brilliant colors. These books were usually written on *vellum*, which is calfskin, or on *parchment*, which is sheepskin or goatskin, prepared in a smooth, white finish that is very beautiful, easy to write on, and very long-lasting.

The Chinese invented printing, but printed books didn't appear in Europe until about five hundred years ago. They were made from wood blocks on which an entire page was carved. Then, about the year 1455, Johannes Gutenberg, at his printing press in Mainz, Germany, made the first book ever printed from movable type. He printed the entire Bible, and it took him six years to do it. Today there are several copies of the Gutenberg Bible in existence, and they are the most valuable of all printed books. Gutenberg Bibles have been sold for prices as high as $200,000.

Movable type made it much easier to make many books, and by the end of Gutenberg's century, there were more than 150 printers in Europe making books from movable type. One of the most famous of these was Aldus Manutius, who lived about the year 1500 in Italy. He printed editions of the great Greek and Latin writers whose works had almost been forgotten. His books are called Aldine editions, and some of those are still in existence and are very valuable. William Caxton was the first printer of English books. He printed books of more different kinds than any other printer. Between about 1475 and about 1490, he printed books on chess, medicine, history, religion; schoolbooks, poems, and romances. In all he printed

about eighty books.

After the year 1600, books were being printed all over Europe. Booksellers' shops began to be seen on the streets, and it became worthwhile for men to make a profession of writing, for the booksellers would pay them.

In America, the first book printed was the Bay Psalm Book. It was a book of psalms, and was printed in Massachusetts in 1640. A copy of this very rare book has sold for $150,000.

Up to about a hundred years ago, only one to three thousand copies of a book were printed at one time. After the Civil War, better printing presses were invented. Books could be made cheaper. More people went to school and learned to read. As a result, books began to be sold in much greater quantities. Today, as many as 750,000 copies of a book are printed at one time. It is not unusual to print 50,000 or 100,000 copies of a book in the first edition (the first time it is printed) and a book may be reprinted many times.

HOW BOOKS ARE PUBLISHED

Until about the year 1800, the printer of a book was also the bookseller and the publisher. Then some companies began to make a business of publishing books (having them set in type, printed, and bound, but not selling them to the public). Other companies were booksellers only. They opened bookstores to sell the books of other publishers.

That is the way the publishing business works today. The author of a book takes it to a publisher. If the publisher likes the book and thinks it will sell, he pays all the expense of manufacturing the book. He pays the author a certain amount of money, called a *royalty*, on each copy that is sold. He sells the book to booksellers all over the world, and they resell the books to the public. When a book sells in a bookstore for $2.50, it means that the bookseller paid about $1.50 for it. The publisher received the $1.50. He paid the author a royalty of

25 cents to 35 cents. Out of the rest of the money, the publisher paid the cost of manufacturing the book.

Mass production and quantity sales can reduce the cost of books, just as they have reduced the cost of automobiles and other things. Sometimes a publisher makes millions of books at one time, and puts them on sale in supermarkets and such stores where nearly everyone goes. The stores accept much less profit than usual, and the authors are paid very tiny royalties or none at all, and as a result people get great bargains in books.

Many other books are offered for sale by mail, or are sold by book clubs, which pick books they think their members will want to read, and sell those books to their members. Still other books are sold by salesmen who represent the publishers and bring the books right to your house.

BEST-SELLERS

When many copies of a book are sold, it is called a *best-seller*. The biggest of all best-sellers is the Bible. So many million copies of it have been sold that no one knows how many.

There are many books of which several million copies have been sold. Some of these are "standard" books, such as dictionaries and encyclopedias and cookbooks. Every few years there may be a novel that sells a million books or more. Several American best-sellers have had sales of more than ten million copies in all editions, but most of these large sales are in paperbound copies at low prices. The best-seller among books for boys has been *Treasure Island*, by Robert Louis Stevenson, and the best-seller among books for girls has been *Little Women*, by Louisa May Alcott.

bookkeeping

Bookkeeping is writing down a record that has to do with money—how much you have received and where you got it; how much you spent and what you spent it for; how much you owe, and how much is owed to you. It is called bookkeeping because these records are written into blank books. A bookkeeper is a person who does this work for a living, and millions of Americans make their livings as bookkeepers; but every other man, woman, or child who jots down notes or reminders about money is doing a kind of bookkeeping.

The first and greatest importance of bookkeeping is to put things down so they will not be forgotten. If you lend a friend a dollar, you do not have to write it down. You will not forget it. But if you were to lend money to fifty different friends, in amounts ranging from thirty cents to a dollar and forty-two cents, you would have to write them all down or you would surely forget some of them. That is why a store or other business house, to which hundreds or thousands of persons may owe money, has to have bookkeeping. If you have five dollars in your pocket and want to buy something that costs four dollars, you know you can afford it—except that you remember something you have to do on Saturday that will cost you two dollars, so you can't afford it after all—unless you remember that on Friday you will be get-

ting another three dollars, so you can afford it after all. Businesses that are constantly receiving money from many different places and that have dozens of bills to pay at different times in the future cannot trust to figuring out such things without written records called bookkeeping.

Bookkeeping can be very simple or very, very complicated, depending on the kind of records that have to be kept, but the job of bookkeeping is always to write the figures down. The job of telling what those figures mean—how much profit a company has made, or how much it has lost—is not bookkeeping but ACCOUNTING, about which there is a separate article.

SINGLE-ENTRY BOOKKEEPING

In the earliest and simplest form of bookkeeping, you take a blank book and use one page of it for each person you do business with. (Each page is said to represent one *account*.) Suppose you own a grocery store, and you have a customer named John Smith. At the top of one page you write "John Smith." Then your record will be something like this:

May 18	He bought groceries worth	$ 3.87
May 22	He bought groceries worth	12.66
	Now he owes	16.53
May 25	He paid	15.00
	He still owes	1.53

Of course, you wouldn't bother to write out so fully the explanation of the figures you put down; you might simply jot down, "groceries," "1 ham," "canned goods," and so on. But that is how your bookkeeping would work, and you could always look at the book and tell how much John Smith owes.

Most people who have checking accounts at banks do their personal bookkeeping in the same way. It is just as though they had a page in the bookkeeping book with "Bank" at the top, except that actually the record is kept in the checkbook. It may read something like this:

May 18	Opened bank account by depositing	$500.00
May 22	Made out check for groceries	15.00
	Money left in bank	485.00
May 25	Made out check for taxes	212.00
	Money left in bank	273.00
May 28	Deposited in bank	200.00
	Money now in bank	473.00

If you stop to consider for a moment, you will realize that the money in the bank is money that the bank owes you and must pay you whenever you ask for it; therefore the bookkeeping record is the same kind as the one that showed how much John Smith owed for groceries.

This is called single-entry bookkeeping because each figure is written down only once. An amount of money recorded in a book is said to be *entered* in the book, and each amount written down is called an *entry*.

The method of single-entry bookkeeping shown above, in which every entry is put in the same column, is very simple but takes up a lot of space. So, hundreds

of years ago, bookkeepers figured out a new way. Each account still had its own page, but the page was divided down the middle, so that there could be a column of figures on each side. The column on the left was called the *debit* column, and the column on the right was called the *credit* column. (In the Latin language, *debit* means "he owes," so a person who owes something is called a *debtor; credit* means "he entrusts," so a person to whom something is owed is called a *creditor*. The abbreviation for debit is *dr.,* and for credit is *cr.*)

In the debit column is written down anything the person owes you, or any money you pay him. In the credit column is written down anything he pays you or you owe him.

Here is the way the account with the bank would look if it were done in the two-column system instead of in the single-column system shown above:

BANK

	DR.		CR.
May 18	500.00	May 22	15.00
May 28	200.00	May 25	212.00

To find out how much money you have in the bank at any time, you add up the two figures in the debit column, which come to $700.00, and the two figures in the credit column, which come to $227.00. You subtract the smaller figure and it gives you $473.00, which is the same figure you arrived at by the other system. This figure is called a *balance*. Since it is in the debit column, it means that the bank owes you that much money. At any convenient time, such as the end of a month or the end of a year, or when the page is full and a new page must be begun, the two columns are added up and the difference between the totals begins a new account. For instance, at the end of May you might total up the columns shown above, then begin a new page and enter in its debit column, "May 31, Balance, $473.00." The $473.00 would be included when you add up the columns on the next page.

DOUBLE-ENTRY BOOKKEEPING

Single-entry bookkeeping is simple enough, but there are several ways in which it is not good enough for a business firm of any size. A simple mistake in adding up a column might not be noticed for months. The system could show a businessman how much money he had, owed, and was owed, but it could not show him how much profit he was making at any given time. To solve these and other problems, double-entry bookkeeping was invented.

Three principles are the key to understanding double-entry bookkeeping:

1. Not only people and companies, but also properties such as furniture and business ideas such as sales, or profit and loss, have their own pages, or accounts, in the bookkeeping books.

2. Every figure entered *must* be entered *twice,* once in the debit column of one account and the second time in the credit column of another account.

3. The total of all the debit entries must be exactly the same as the total of all the credit entries. This cannot fail to be the case if the same figure is entered

twice, once in each. Therefore if the totals are not the same, there is a mistake somewhere and the bookkeeper must keep looking until it is found.

Suppose you open an office to carry on your business. First, you buy $1,000.00 worth of furniture for it. You do not have to pay for it in cash; the furniture store simply sends you a bill, which you must pay next month. You credit the store with $1,000.00, because that is money you owe. At the same time you debit an account called *Furniture* with the same $1,000.00. This means that the furniture owes your business $1,000.00, because that is what it cost.

Then you receive a bill for the first month's rent, which is $100.00. You credit your landlord with $100.00, because you owe it to him, and you debit an account called *Expense,* or perhaps you will choose to set up a special account called *Rent,* with the same $100.00.

All the money you owe makes an account called *Accounts Payable,* and all the money that is owed to you makes an account called *Accounts Receivable.* When the time comes to pay for the furniture, you make out a check and send it to the store. You credit your bank with $1,000.00, because it has paid back that much that it owed you. You debit Accounts Payable $1,000.00, because you owe your Accounts Payable that much less. Again there are two entries that are exactly the same in amount—they *balance* each other.

At certain times a *trial balance* is taken by a bookkeeper. All the columns on all the accounts are added up. All debit balances are added together, and all credit balances are added together. If the totals are the same, the books are in balance. If the totals are not the same, there must be a mistake and enough searching will find it.

On the trial balance, all debit balances are called *assets,* meaning values or amounts you own or that are owed to you; and all credit balances are called *liabilities,* meaning amounts that you owe.

The double-entry bookkeeping system is based on a principle called the *accrual basis.* The idea of the accrual basis is that there is no real difference between money you have in cash and money that is owed to you and will be paid to you sooner or later; and that there is no real difference between bills you received and have paid for, and bills you received and have to pay for later. In other words, if you have $10,000.00 in the bank and owe $5,000.00 you are no better off than if you have $5,000.00 in the bank and do not owe anything.

Many special accounts go on the books to show how much a business is actually worth, but these are jobs for the accountant and not for the bookkeeper. See the article on ACCOUNTING.

THE BOOKS USED

Bookkeeping is done in books that have specially ruled paper—that is, paper with lines drawn at the proper places to make bookkeeping easier. Usually these are looseleaf books, so that pages may be changed as often as necessary.

There are two main types of books. One is called the *journal* and the other is

called the *ledger*. Journal comes from the French word *jour,* meaning "day"; a journal is a day book, in which every separate item of business is entered. A journal is called a *book of original entry.* It is used to make immediate records, and show what they apply to. Many separate journals are kept, depending on the size of the business. There are the *cash receipts book,* to record all money received; the *cash disbursements book,* to record all money paid out; the *sales book,* the *purchases book,* and finally the *general journal,* in which you record anything for which you do not have a special journal.

The other type of bookkeeping book is the ledger. There are usually three ledgers. The *accounts receivable ledger* has a page for every customer who owes money to the company. The *accounts payable book* has a page for everyone from whom the company buys. The *general ledger* combines all the bookkeeping information that is in all the journals, or books of original entry. The bookkeeper first makes the entries in the journal, then transfers them—it is called *posting* them —to the proper page in the general ledger. This book has a page for every account; for example, Cash (how much money is in the bank); Sales (the total of all the goods sold); Purchases (the total of all the goods bought); and so on.

When an amount in one of the columns is to be subtracted from the total, instead of added to it, the amount is written in red ink. When a business has lost money, the amount of the loss is shown in red ink, and that is why a business is said to be "in the red" when it is losing money. Sometimes red ink is not handy and then the bookkeeper puts a circle around the figure. This gives us another phrase you often hear, "in the hole," which means the same thing as "in the red."

MACHINE BOOKKEEPING

In big companies, there is so much business that it would be a waste of time for bookkeepers to make all the entries by hand. For such companies, special machinery has been made to do much of the job of bookkeeping. The "bookkeepers" often type the names of the accounts, and the amounts of the entries, on an electric machine, and then the machine does the rest. Even for quite small companies, there are machines that save them a great deal of time and work. But these machines do not alter the fact that double-entry bookkeeping is being used. The system is exactly the same. The machines have merely been built to do the work mechanically.

boomerang

The boomerang is a weapon that was used by the savage people who lived in Australia before any white men went there. It is a curved piece of wood, rounded on one side and flat on the other. A boomerang is held at one end and thrown at an animal one is hunting, or at an enemy in warfare.

One kind of boomerang is called the *return boomerang.* It is used for hunting. When the return boomerang is thrown, it will fly straight for about thirty yards. Then it will curve and fly back to the man who threw it. It can be used to kill birds when they are flying.

The man who throws it must be careful not to be hit by the boomerang when it returns to him.

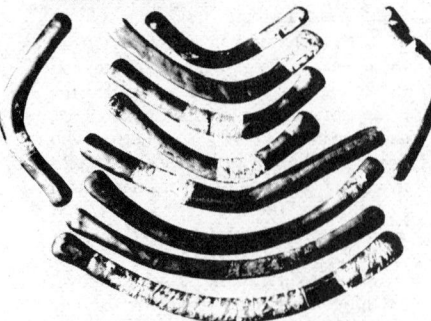

N.Y. Public Library
These boomerangs are very old. Some were used for hunting and others were used in tribal ceremonies. Sometimes the people bound them with bark or painted them.

The *nonreturn boomerang* is bigger and heavier than the return boomerang. Sometimes it is as long as four feet. It is used in war. As it flies through the air, it makes a whistling sound. It travels so fast that it can kill a man if it hits him.

Some of the native people of Australia still use boomerangs. The Hopi Indians, who live in Arizona, once used the boomerang, and so did the ancient Egyptians.

Boone, Daniel

Daniel Boone went into Kentucky more than two hundred years ago, when no one lived there but savage Indians who attacked every white man that came along. The whole territory then was covered with thick forests. Only an expert woodsman could travel through them without being lost or killed. Daniel Boone led new settlers into Kentucky, helped them to fight the Indians, and opened up that part of the western United States.

There was no United States when Daniel Boone was a young man. He was born in Pennsylvania, which was then a British colony, about the year 1735. When he was just a boy he learned to hunt and to trap wild animals. All his life he was a famous hunter. He probably didn't go to school, and knew just a little about reading and writing and arithmetic. But he learned all about the wilds and the streams, about hunting and fishing and exploring. He learned how to find his way through trackless forests, and how to hunt out the wild animals. He could move as silently as an Indian, making no sound and leaving no tracks. The thing he loved best was to live alone in the woods. Nothing frightened him. No hardship seemed too great.

When Daniel Boone was still a boy, his family moved to North Carolina. There Boone worked as a farmer, grew up, married, and tried to settle down. But he liked to live away from settled places. In 1769, when he was 35 years old, he went as leader of a small group on a long trip into the frontier wilderness, the western country that had not been explored. The party crossed the Appalachian Mountains through a passage that is called the Cumberland Gap, into land that is now part of the state of Kentucky. After two years they returned, bringing with them many valuable animal skins, and telling wonderful stories about the beautiful land and their fights with the Indians.

After this, Daniel Boone became famous as a guide and Indian fighter. He was sometimes hired to lead people to the frontier, and to help them settle there. He lived in Kentucky for many years, hunting and exploring. He was a brave leader in battles with the Indians. Once he was captured by the Shawnee Indians, and taken far to the west. The Indians liked him. They treated him well, and they even adopted him as a member of their tribe. But Boone was always loyal to his friends. One day he heard that the Indians were planning to attack Boonesborough, the Kentucky settlement he had founded. He managed to escape from the Indians. Traveling on foot, he covered more than a hundred miles in a few days. He managed to reach Boonesborough in time to warn the people. With his help, the people beat off the Indian attack.

When he was almost 65 years old, Daniel Boone moved farther west, to land that is now part of the state of Missouri. There he continued to hunt and trap animals. There is a story about Daniel Boone's great honesty: When he left Kentucky, he owed money to many people, but could not pay them. He saved carefully for a long time. Then he went back to Kentucky to pay all his old debts. Afterward he had nothing left at all, but he was very happy.

Daniel Boone died in the Missouri country, in 1820. He was very famous in his own time, and is still remembered as a man who helped America become a great country.

Booth

Booth was the name of a famous American family of actors. Junius Brutus Booth was an English actor who came to the United States in 1821 and spent the rest of his life traveling about the country giving plays. Two of his sons were John Wilkes Booth and Edwin Booth. When they were children they appeared with their father in small parts in his plays.

John Wilkes Booth was the man who shot Abraham Lincoln. He was born in 1839. During the Civil War he believed strongly in the Southern cause. When the war ended Booth was very angry because the South had been defeated. In revenge he planned to shoot the president, the vice president and all of the cabinet. His first target was President Lincoln. On the evening of April 14, 1865, Lincoln and his wife were watching a play in Ford's Theater in Washington. Booth slipped past the guards in the theater and entered the box where Lincoln was sitting. He shot Lincoln in the head. When he jumped from the box down to the stage he broke his ankle. He escaped through the stage door, leaped on a horse and rode toward Maryland. He stopped to have a doctor fix his ankle and then rode on into Virginia. But on April 20 he was cornered in a barn at Bowling Green. He was shot trying to escape.

Edwin Booth, John Wilkes Booth's older brother, was born in 1833. He became America's first great Shakespearean actor. For many years he had to live

down the fact that his brother had shot Lincoln. After Edwin had appeared in his father's troupe as a child, he formed his own company. He made a great name for himself in *Hamlet, Othello,* and other plays by Shakespeare. During his life he appeared with all the famous actors of the time, both here and in Europe. He died in New York in 1893.

Booth, William

William Booth was the founder of the Salvation Army. He was born in Nottingham, England, in 1829. From the time he was 15 years old, Booth was very religious. He liked to travel around the country reminding people to love God. After Booth married, he and his wife, Catherine Mumford Booth, did this together. One thing they did was gather together a group of men and women who had been bad but who now believed in God. These men told others what had happened to them. This group was called a "Hallelujah Band."

In 1878, Booth founded the Salvation Army. It was organized somewhat like a military army. Booth was called "General." The Salvation Army preached and sang about God on street corners and in parks. They visited prisons and hospitals, and tried to help sick and unhappy people everywhere. In the beginning it was very difficult, but General Booth believed in what he was doing and the Salvation Army grew bigger and bigger. Organizations were set up in the United States, Australia, Europe, India, Africa, South America, and many other places.

William Booth died in 1912. The Booths had eight children, and all but one of them became important leaders in the Salvation Army. Evangeline Booth, their daughter, born in 1865, became general of the Salvation Army in the United States in 1904 and world commander in 1934. She died in 1950.

bootlegging

Bootlegging is making or selling alcoholic liquor when that is against the law. For many years, bootleggers were simply men who made whiskey and would not pay the government tax on it. Most of these bootleggers lived in mountain and country districts. The whiskey they made was called "moonshine," or "bootleg liquor" (perhaps because they carried bottles of it in the high boots that they wore). The law was enforced by "Revenuers," detectives of the Internal Revenue (tax-collecting) branch of the United States Treasury Department.

From 1920 to 1933, the United States had a Prohibition law that forbade all making and selling of liquor. During this period bootlegging became a national problem. Bootleggers formed big criminal gangs and became rich by selling bootleg liquor. Some of the liquor was smuggled in from foreign countries and some was made in the United States.

Since 1933, when the Prohibition law was repealed (canceled), there has again been much bootlegging of liquor on which no tax is paid. In states and districts where local laws forbid the sale of liquor, there are bootleggers who bring in liquor from other states or districts and sell it illegally.

borax

Borax is a chemical that is used as a water softener, as a cleanser, and in the making of glass, shellac, and glazes. It looks like little grayish-white transparent crystals. Borax is found in nature and also is made by man.

Man has known about borax for many hundreds of years. Most borax used to come from the salt lakes of Tibet, where it is called *tincal.* The natural borax that we use today is mined in California and Nevada in the United States, and in the South American desert of Atacama. Borax can be manufactured by combining boric acid with another chemical, sodium carbonate.

When borax is heated to a very high temperature it melts into a glasslike substance. This is why it is good for making glazes.

Melted borax has another quality that is very useful. It changes color when it touches metallic oxides. When a chemist is not sure what a particular metal is, he can find out by combining the metal with melted borax and seeing what color the borax turns. If, for instance, it turns green or blue, the chemist knows that the metal is copper. If it turns amethyst, the metal is manganese; and if it turns brown, the metal is nickel.

Bordeaux

Bordeaux is an important city in France. It is on the Garonne River, and although it is about 75 miles from the Atlantic Ocean, it is the busiest Atlantic seaport in the southern part of France. This is because the Garonne River is deep enough for ocean-going ships to sail all the way up the river to Bordeaux. The harbor is very large, and a thousand ships can get into it at one time.

Bordeaux is about the size of Richmond, Virginia. About 271,000 people live there. Many of them work in the shipbuilding yards and in factories. Others make Bordeaux wines, which are famous all over the world.

The city is very old and in it there are churches that were built more than seven hundred years ago. Bordeaux University was founded before Columbus discovered America. Three times Bordeaux has been the capital of France, when the regular capital, Paris, was threatened by German armies and the French government had to move. The last time was during World War II. Bordeaux harbor was bombed many times during the war because it was a favorite hiding place for German submarines.

BORDEAUX, FRANCE. Capital of the department of the Gironde. Population, 257,946.

Borden, Gail

Gail Borden was the first man to find a good way of making evaporated milk. This is milk which is heated until most of the water goes off into steam.

Evaporated milk can be kept much longer than fresh milk because it does not spoil if kept in sealed cans. Before Borden's invention, people could have no milk at all unless they lived near a farmer who had cows, or in a place where fresh milk could be bought in stores. Fresh milk does not stay sweet for very long, and Gail Borden realized how useful it would be if there were some way to preserve the food values in milk, so that people on long journeys or soldiers in battle could have milk to drink and to cook with.

Gail Borden was born in Norwich, New York, in 1801, and one of his first jobs was as a land surveyor in Mississippi. He later went to Texas with Stephen A. Austin, and laid out the plans for the city of Galveston. Later he returned to the East and worked for years trying to develop a process for evaporating and canning milk. At last he succeeded, and got a patent for his invention in 1856. This was just in time for the soldiers in the Civil War to benefit from his idea, and the invention was very important in the development of the food-packing industry. Borden died in 1874.

Borden, Sir Robert Laird

Sir Robert Laird Borden was prime minister of Canada at the time of World War I. He was born in 1854 at Grand Pré, Nova Scotia, and held many government jobs before he became prime minister in 1911. After World War I, he worked hard to help Canada become one of the world's important independent nations. He was responsible for the start of Canada's parcel-post system. He also helped a great deal in getting Canada a seat in the League of Nations as an independent country instead of just as part of the British Commonwealth's delegation. At one time he was a member of the Canadian government's embassy in Washington. He died in 1937.

border

The boundary or frontier between two countries or states is called the border. In the history of the United States, borders were important at several different times. The Border War was a bitter fight in Kansas that started in 1854 and lasted for more than six years. Kansas was about to become a state, and the question was whether it should be a slave state or a free state. Slavery was a big problem all over the country at that time. The people who were in favor of slavery and the people who were against it both sent men to live in the Kansas Territory so they could vote for their side. An open war broke out, and terrible violence followed. Many people were killed, and the territory became known as "bleeding Kansas." The Border War ended when Kansas was admitted to the United States as a free state in 1861.

In the Civil War, the "border states" were the states that were between the North and the South and had many sympathizers for each side. The states were Delaware, Kentucky, Missouri, and Maryland. President Abraham Lincoln was very anxious that these important states should not join the Confederacy, or South. He arrested the leaders of Maryland who wanted their state to secede.

In the United States today, "South of the Border" means "in Mexico."

The Border is also the frontier between England and Scotland. Many poems and stories have been written about the battles that took place there

long ago. The most famous writer about the Border was Sir Walter Scott.

Borgia

Borgia was the name of a famous family in Italy about five hundred years ago. The name *Borgia* always makes people think of poison and murder, and the most famous man of this family certainly deserved such evil fame. He was Cesare Borgia, and even in a time when war and cruelty were common, he was outstanding. When he wanted something he would use the most terrible ways to get it, including murder.

Cesare Borgia was born about 1475. His father became Pope Alexander VI. Cesare used his father's power to get what he wanted, and schemed against many of the Italian rulers.

Italy was then made up of many little states, each governed by a ruler who really owned the country. These rulers were almost always fighting with one another, each trying to conquer as much as he could. Cesare Borgia set out to fight the local rulers of Romagna, which was an area in northeastern Italy. He conquered many small states and captured forts and castles, usually killing the rulers. Sometimes he did not bother with wars. He just had people murdered and then seized their property. Poison was his favorite way of murdering. Finally he was lord over a large territory and he became Duke of Romagna.

Cesare was very powerful and very lucky. But plots were always being made against him. In 1503 his father died, and Cesare himself was very ill. The new Pope was an enemy of his and Cesare had to give up all his castles and leave Rome. For a while he was a prisoner of the king of Spain, but he escaped. He commanded an army for the king of Navarre, and in 1507 he was killed in a battle.

Another famous member of this family was Lucrezia Borgia, sister of Cesare. She was very beautiful and intelligent. But she was suspected of helping her father in his crimes.

There are many stories of Lucrezia's wickedness. One story tells of a marvelous ring she wore. It was said to have a secret compartment under the stone where Lucrezia kept a little poison—just in case she should need it suddenly! It is very hard to tell whether these stories are true. Nowadays many people who have studied history say they are not true, but others still believe them.

Lucrezia was born about 1480. She was married several times. Her father arranged several of her marriages, but often he would change his mind and break the marriage off.

There is a story that one of her husbands was murdered on the order of her brother Cesare. In 1501 Lucrezia was married to the son of an Italian ruler, who later became the Duke of Ferrara. From that time on her life was peaceful. She had several children. She became noted for helping people. Many artists and writers lived and worked at her court, and she was always friendly and helpful to them.

Borglum, Gutzon

Gutzon Borglum was an American sculptor. He is most famous for making a mountain into a national monument. He carved huge heads of George Washington, Thomas Jefferson, Abraham Lincoln and Theodore Roosevelt out of the peak of Mount Rushmore in South Dakota. Congress passed a law authorizing him to do this great work, and it is now called the Mount Rushmore National Memorial. Borglum needed to be an artist and also an engineer to do this unusual task, and he was both. He made the largest sculpture ever done by any man.

Borglum was born in Idaho in 1871. He learned his art as a boy from his father who was a Danish wood-carver. Borglum also carved the statue of Lincoln which you can see in the Capitol in Washington, D.C. Many other of his statues are in museums. The work on the Mount Rushmore National Memorial was almost complete when he died in 1941, and his son, Lincoln Borglum, finished the monument.

boric acid

Boric acid (which is sometimes called *boracic acid*) is a very weak acid that can be found in nature or manufactured. It looks somewhat like powdered sugar. It is often used as an antiseptic, which means something that kills germs. Boric acid is either dissolved in water or made into an ointment or salve. The ointment is often used to relieve the sting of a burn or a scratch. The powder can be dissolved in water and used as an eyewash. Boric acid is also used in industry, chiefly for making glazes and enamels. It is chemically related to BORAX, about which you can read in another article.

Boris Godunoff

Boris Godunoff is a Russian grand opera. It was based on a historical play by the Russian poet Pushkin and was first sung in 1874, in St. Petersburg (now Leningrad), which was then the capital. The music was written by Modeste Moussorgsky, and he changed it several times. His friend Nicolai Rimsky-Korsakoff, who was also a Russian composer, helped him change it in some places.

STORY OF THE OPERA

The story is about a czar, or emperor, of Russia named Boris Godunoff, who lived about 350 years ago. He became ruler of Russia by murdering Dmitri, the real czar's brother, who would have become czar when the real czar died. Then Boris went to live in a monastery (where men live a religious life) so that the people would think that he did not really want to be czar. But Boris had many followers and when the czar did die, they knew what to do. They made a lot of people gather together and beg Boris to come back and rule over them.

Meanwhile Gregory, a young man who was just the same age as the murdered Dmitri, pretended that he was Dmitri. Many people believed him, and he was able to raise an army to fight Boris. Even Boris was afraid that Gregory really was Dmitri, and that he had come back to be the rightful ruler of Russia.

Fear and a guilty conscience had made Boris so unhappy that all he could do was pray and hope that God would forgive him for his awful sin. At the end of the opera he sings a farewell to his son Feodor, telling him to be a good and kind czar, and then he kills himself.

Borneo

Borneo is a large island in the East Indies, southwest of the Philippine Islands. It is the third-largest island in the world. Although it is about the size of Texas, not half as many people live there. Most of the people of the forests are natives called *Dyaks*. There are different tribes of Dyaks, and all of them are very backward and uncivilized. They live in the jungle in low huts, and they farm, hunt, and fish. Another group in Borneo are the Malays. They are more civilized than the Dyaks. Most of them live on the coast, and are farmers and fishermen. There are also many Chinese in Borneo.

Borneo is an unusual place because parts of it are very wild and other parts are quite modern. The cities have schools and well-built houses, and there are quite a few automobiles. Many of the people who live in the cities work at mining coal, gold, and diamonds. Others work in the oil fields, and in rubber and tobacco factories. The central part of Borneo is a dense, wild jungle, with valuable forests of ebony and teak trees. Elephants, leopards, orang-utans and other wild animals roam through the jungle.

Borneo has many mountains and rivers. The rivers are important because they are one of the best ways for people to get from one place to another. The weather in Borneo is hot and sticky. Very often there are heavy rains, and sometimes there are small earthquakes.

Borneo was discovered by the Portuguese about 450 years ago. Later the Dutch moved in and drove the Portuguese out. About a hundred years later the British came and also settled. They controlled the northern part of Borneo, and the southern part (about three-quarters of the island) was owned by the Dutch. During World War II the Japanese invaded the island and stayed there for four years. When Japan surrendered to the Allies the Japanese left the island. In 1950, Dutch Borneo became part of the independent state of Indonesia, and in 1963 British Borneo, consisting of Sarawak, Brunei, and North Borneo, became part of Malaysia.

BORNEO, island in the East Indies. Area, 290,012 square miles. Population 4,958,000. These figures are divided into: Malaysian Borneo, area 81,726 square miles; population, 1,258,000. Indonesian Borneo, area, 208,286 square miles; population, 3,700,000.

Borodin, Alexander

Alexander Borodin was a great Russian composer, or writer of original music. He was born in 1833 in St. Petersburg, which is now called Leningrad. He started to study music as a very small boy. When he was only 9 he composed a polka, which is the music for a kind of dance. When he was older

he studied medicine and became a doctor and scientist, but he never stopped writing music. We sometimes wonder how he was able to do so many things and do them all well, for he also wrote many books. His most famous pieces of music are three symphonies (music for a big orchestra), and a grand opera called *Prince Igor*. Borodin died in 1887.

A. Brock

This beautiful borzoi has won many prizes at dog shows and at exhibitions.

borzoi

One of the fastest-running dogs in the world is the borzoi, or Russian wolfhound. Borzois are slender, graceful dogs. They were developed in Russia more than three hundred years ago and were used in wolf-hunting by Russian noblemen. They are still used for hunting, but in the United States they are often kept as pets because they are very beautiful, gentle, and quiet.

The borzoi is a tall, long-legged dog, with an arched back. It stands about 2½ feet high at the shoulders, and it may weigh between 75 and 110 pounds. Its head, for a large dog, is narrow and rather small, with tiny, pointed ears. The borzoi's tail is long, and curves down low under its body. Its coat is long and silky and is sometimes brown, tan, or white, or a mixture of white and any other color.

Bosch, Hieronymus

Hieronymus Bosch was a Dutch painter who lived more than four hundred years ago. His pictures are filled with demons and monsters and all kinds of weird places. Some of the pictures are of religious subjects, like *The Temptation of St. Anthony*. Bosch tried to make everything look as real as possible in his paintings. Sometimes it seems that you can actually feel the cloth in his pictures. Bosch was born in 1470 and died in 1530. He spent part of his life in Spain. The Spanish king, Philip II, bought many of Bosch's paintings to hang in his palaces. They still hang there and every year many people go to see them.

Bosnia-Herzegovina

Bosnia-Herzegovina is the name of a part of Yugoslavia, on the Balkan Peninsula. It is more than 19,000 square miles in size, which is about twice as large as Maryland. More than three million people live there. Most of the people are farmers, and they raise grain and cattle. Others work in the valuable copper, iron and chromium mines in the northern part of the country. In the cities

people work in factories where they produce sugar, prepare chemicals of various kinds, and manufacture iron products. The capital and also the largest city of Bosnia-Herzegovina is Sarajevo. It was in this city that the Archduke Ferdinand of Austria was assassinated in 1914, and it was this event which set off World War I. For more than four-hundred years, Bosnia-Herzegovina belonged to Turkey, but in 1878, it was given to Austria-Hungary. After World War I, in 1918, it was given to Yugoslavia.

BOSNIA - HERZEGOVINA, YUGOSLAVIA. Area, 19,909 square miles. Population, 3,277,948. Capital, Sarajevo.

Bosporus

The Bosporus is a narrow *strait*, or channel, in Turkey, that connects the Black Sea and the Sea of Marmara. It also separates the continents of Europe and Asia. Although the Bosporus is very small, it is of great importance to trading ships. Together with the Dardanelles, it is the only way to sail from the Black Sea to the Mediterranean. (You can read about the DARDANELLES in a separate article.) The Bosporus is about eighteen miles long, and about one mile wide. It has swift currents and fogs that make it dangerous for ships, and lighthouses have been built to help vessels get safely through the strait. The region around the Bosporus is very beautiful. Along the high shores, you can see woods, old castles, and ancient villages. The famous city of Istanbul is at the southern end of the Bosporus.

For the past five hundred years, the Bosporus has belonged to Turkey. No warships of other nations are allowed to pass through the strait without the permission of the Turkish government. During World War II, Turkey allowed German ships to pass through the strait. Later, toward the end of the war, they also allowed Allied vessels to ship war supplies through the Bosporus to the Russians.

Boston

Boston is the capital and the largest city in Massachusetts. Its nickname is "the Hub" because for many years it was the center of American culture. Boston is an important seaport on Massachusetts Bay and a great business and manufacturing city. It has the principal wool market and the largest shoe industry in the country. There are also huge fisheries, printing plants, and business offices and shops.

Boston itself has a population of more than 641,000 crowded into an area that is hemmed in by suburbs and cannot grow. With its suburbs Boston has almost three million people and is seventh among the biggest metropolitan areas in the United States. Among the famous sections of Boston are Beacon Hill and the Back Bay (a former sea marsh that was filled in). There are many fine hotels, and shops.

COLLEGES AND UNIVERSITIES

Boston has long been a center of education. In the city of Cambridge, just across the Charles River from Boston, are some of the country's most famous schools. They include Harvard University, Radcliffe College, and the Massachusetts

Institute of Technology (or M.I.T.). Important colleges in Boston include:

Boston College. Enrollment 10,214 in 1971. One of the largest Roman Catholic colleges in the United States.

Boston University. Enrollment 23,826 in 1971.

Boston Conservatory of Music. Enrollment 450 in 1971.

Northeastern University. Enrollment 42,-149 in 1971.

Simmons College, for women. Enrollment 2,216 in 1971.

Tufts College. Enrollment 4,810 in 1971.

BOSTON IN THE PAST

Boston is one of the oldest cities in the United States. It was settled in 1630 by colonists who came from Salem, in the Massachusetts Bay Colony. Two years later Boston was made the capital of the colony. The people of Boston were among the leaders in the Revolutionary War, and the Battle of Bunker Hill took place in Boston in 1775. After the war the city grew rapidly, and about one hundred years ago it was the center of American learning.

Boston still has many historic buildings and monuments. Some of them are: the Old North Church, from which Paul Revere received a signal telling him that British soldiers were going to attack the American colonists; Paul Revere's house, the oldest house in Boston, built in 1676; and Faneuil Hall, called "the cradle of Liberty," where the colonists planned the Boston Tea Party. The Massachusetts State House, on Beacon Hill, is a famous old building. Boston Common is a famous park in the heart of the city.

In the late 1800s so many people from Ireland settled in Boston that it was once called "the biggest Irish city in the world." More than half a million people in Boston and its suburbs are of Irish ancestry. The largest group in Boston, however, is of New England ancestry.

BOSTON, MASSACHUSETTS. Population (1970 census) 641,071. Capital of Massachusetts.

Boston Massacre

A massacre is the cruel killing of a number of helpless persons. The Boston Massacre was called that because it happened at a time when the people of the American Colonies were very angry with the British and were always ready to think the worst of the British soldiers, but it was more like a street fight than a massacre. It happened on March 5, 1770, before the American Revolution really began. Some of the people of Boston were constantly tormenting the British soldiers who patrolled the streets. One day a British soldier became frightened when a crowd started to make fun of him and throw things. He called for help, and other British soldiers came running. They fired at the crowd of Americans and killed four people. The British soldiers were tried for murder, but John Adams and Josiah Quincy were the lawyers for the defense, and the soldiers were found not guilty.

Boston Tea Party

The Boston Tea Party was one of the first acts of rebellion by the American Colonies against the rule of England. It took place about a year before the American Revolution. The British had put a

heavy tax on all the tea that was sent from England to America. The Americans thought this tax unfair and did not want to pay it. Then some British ships carrying tea came into the harbor at Boston, Massachusetts. The company selling the tea had agreed to pay the tax itself. But the Americans did not want the tax to be paid by anyone. Late on the night of December 16, 1773, a group of Americans dressed up like Indians and boarded the ships. They didn't get excited or noisy, but very quietly dumped all the tea overboard.

Boston terrier

The only breed of dog that originated in the United States is the Boston terrier, named for the city of Boston, Massachusetts, where it was first developed. It came from a cross between the English bulldog and the English white terrier, but the dog that resulted from this combination was like neither of these other two breeds. It became popular very quickly, and now there are many homes in the United States and Canada where the Boston terrier is kept as a gentle, loyal, affectionate pet.

It stands about 11 to 14 inches high at the shoulder, and weighs between 15 and 25 pounds. It has a short tail, and a straight, sturdy body. Its head is round, and its ears are small, and stand up close to the head. The Boston terrier's coat is short and smooth, with a satiny shine. In color it is a dark "brindle," which is a combination of black and brown hairs, with large white markings, usually on the head, chest, legs, and underside.

Boswell, James

James Boswell was a Scotsman who was famous for writing one of the best biographies in the English language, *The Life of Samuel Johnson.* A biography is the story of a person's life. JOHNSON himself was a very famous Englishman, and you can read about him in a separate article. Boswell was born in Edinburgh in 1740. He was the son of a judge with the title of Lord Auchinleck. When his father died, 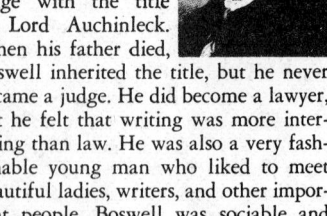 Boswell inherited the title, but he never became a judge. He did become a lawyer, but he felt that writing was more interesting than law. He was also a very fashionable young man who liked to meet beautiful ladies, writers, and other important people. Boswell was sociable and friendly, and many people called him by the nickname "Bozzy."

When "Bozzy" was 23 years old, he went to London where he became friends with Johnson. He also traveled to Holland and to France. One of Boswell's first books was about his visit to the island of Corsica. Then he returned to Edinburgh, and in 1769 he was married. He took many trips to London to see Johnson. One year Johnson came to Scotland, where he and Boswell visited the Hebrides islands, and Boswell wrote a book about this trip, too. Johnson died in 1784 and the next year Boswell published his biography of him. The book made him famous immediately, but for

a long time after he died, in 1795, people thought Boswell was important only because he wrote about Johnson. Today we know more about him because other books that he wrote have just been published for the first time. From these we learn that he was truly a great writer.

botany

Botany is the study of plants and how they grow. It is a branch of BIOLOGY, which is the study of all living things, and which you can read about in another article. Plants are different from all other living things because they make their own food out of chemicals, building up living tissue out of matter that has never lived. By using *chlorophyll,* they use the energy of sunlight to make food out of air and water. This is one of the most wonderful facts in nature, even though it is happening every minute all around us. Man has never been able to do this, and all animals including human beings depend upon plants for food. Without plants, life could not exist on earth. The study of plants, therefore, is very important to us because it helps us to live better. Botany is the foundation of all agriculture, forestry, and gardening. Through botany man has been able to increase the fertility or growing power of the soil, to produce bigger crops, and to control the insects that attack them.

Men have grown some plants, such as wheat, barley, rice, flax, hemp, the date palm, olive, fig, apple, and grape, for more than four thousand years. You might say that the first botanists were these first farmers, the first men who studied the plants they used for food. The Greek scholar Aristotle and his pupil Theophrastus wrote the first scientific descriptions of plants. Then people became interested in the use of plants in medicine. Dioscorides, in the 1st century, gave a list of four hundred plants which could be used as medicine. This list was used for 1,500 years.

Many men were puzzled by the problem of how to name plants. This was settled by Linnaeus, a Swedish botanist who lived about 200 years ago. Linnaeus had the idea of giving each plant two names in the Latin language. *Pisum sativum,* for example, is the garden pea. *Pisum* means pea, and *sativum* tells how it is different from all other kinds of pea. Linnaeus named 5,950 plants. Since then more than 300,000 have been described, and nearly 5,000 new ones are named every year by men called *systematists* or *taxonomists.* These men not only name plants, but they try to find out how plants are related to one another in their various families. Since Linnaeus, other botanists have made schemes for grouping or classifying plants. The system most used today was devised by a German named Adolf Engler.

bo tree

The bo tree is a fig tree found especially in India and Ceylon. It grows to great size and age, and its leaves have long flexible stems so that they rustle in the slightest breeze. The bo tree is sacred to those whose religion is Buddhism. Its name, *bo,* or *bodhi,* means "tree of wisdom." Gotama Buddha, the founder of the Buddhist religion, is said to have

gained his wisdom while sitting under the bo tree. Buddha also died under the bo tree after many years of teaching. The original bo tree was in Gaya, India. A slip from this tree was planted at Anuradhapura, Ceylon. This "daughter" tree is one of the oldest living trees; crowds of people come to visit it. In Ceylon, there is a bo tree planted near every temple.

Botswana: see BECHUANALAND.

Botticelli, Sandro

Sandro Botticelli was one of the greatest painters who ever lived. He was born in 1444 in Florence, Italy. When he was a very young boy he worked for a goldsmith, or jewelry maker. He showed great artistic talent and began to study painting with a famous teacher named Fra Filippo Lippi. He learned all he could about painting. When he was about twenty years old, Botticelli started to paint in the style for which he became famous. His paintings were full of lovely and delicate detail, and rich and beautiful colors. Botticelli often used gold to make them even more magnificent. The paintings were mostly portraits (pictures of people), or about religious subjects. The faces Botticelli painted were beautiful and angelic. A very wealthy and powerful family called Medici liked Botticelli's painting. They bought many of his masterpieces, and also gave him money to continue his painting. When the Medici family was driven out of the country, Botticelli was given help and encouragement by a famous Italian priest named Savonarola. Some of Botticelli's best-known paintings are *Spring, Birth of Venus,* and *Portrait of a Youth,* which is now at the Metropolitan Museum of Art in New York City. Botticelli died in 1510.

N.Y. Public Library

One of Botticelli's most famous paintings, *The Birth of Venus,* shows the goddess Venus rising from the ocean in a sea shell.

bottle, a container for holding liquids and other things: see the articles on BOTTLING and GLASS.

bottled gas

Bottled gas is gas that is put into steel tanks to be delivered to homes far

out in the country where there are no gas pipes. Bottled gas is also used in making chemicals and other things. When all the gas is used up, the empty tank can be refilled. The gas is usually PROPANE or BUTANE, about which you can read in separate articles.

bottling

Bottling is the process of filling bottles with liquid. Bottles are used as containers for many kinds of liquid, such as soft drinks, medicine, and milk. They are also used for many foods, such as pickles and olives. Many foods and drinks are sold in enormous quantities, so bottling is very important and must be very efficient.

The first and most important thing in bottling is to make sure that the bottles are absolutely clean. After careful washing and rinsing, they are made *sterile,* or free from harmful bacteria and other germs. Then the bottles are ready to be filled. They are placed on a conveyor, or moving belt, which carries them to the large vat containing the liquid to be bottled. The belt stops for a moment as each bottle comes under the vat, and the bottle is filled through a tube attached to the vat. Then the belt moves on and another bottle is filled. The filled bottles move on to a section where they are covered with metal caps or cardboard covers.

Many liquids that used to be packaged in bottles are sold in other kinds of containers nowadays. Bottles are good for liquids that have to be shipped a long way between the place where they are made and the place where they are sold. But milk is often put in cardboard containers because it has only a short distance to travel. Soft drinks, which can be made and packaged at one end of the country and sold at the other end, are usually put in bottles, though some manufacturers recently have begun to use cans. Certain liquids, like shampoo, are now packed in plastic bottles. These do not break as easily as glass bottles. They are easier to use because the liquid is not poured out, but is squeezed out like toothpaste from a tube. This is a convenient kind of bottle when only small amounts of liquid are needed at one time.

Nat'l Dairy Council

In a modern plant, milk is bottled and capped very swiftly by large machines.

Boulder Dam, one of the largest dams in the world: see HOOVER DAM.

Bounty, Mutiny on the

The *Bounty* was the name of an English ship on which a famous mutiny took place. When a group of soldiers or sailors decide they are not going to obey their commander, it is called a mutiny, and this is a very serious crime.

The *Bounty* was making a peaceful voyage in April, 1789. It was carrying a cargo of plants from Tahiti to the West Indies. The *Bounty* had been at sea three weeks when without warning the mutiny broke out. A sailor named Fletcher Christian was the leader, and he and most of the crew forced the captain, William Bligh, and eighteen men into a small open boat and set them adrift in the Pacific Ocean, very far from any shore. They had no map, and very little food or water. Christian and the crew never expected to hear of them again, but that is not the way things turned out. With good luck, and because Captain Bligh was a very fine seaman, these men managed to sail four thousand miles to safety. They landed at Timor about six weeks later, and not one man was lost.

Captain Bligh returned to England, and wrote all about what had happened. At first everyone admired his courage and felt very sorry for him. They began to search for the wicked crew. Some of the men had returned to Tahiti, and they were quickly caught and most of them were executed. But the *Bounty* and some of the crew had disappeared, and for ten years no one could find them. It was only by accident that the *Bounty* was discovered, when an American ship landed at Pitcairn Island, a small island in the Pacific Ocean. Only one man of all the crew was still alive. By this time people had found out that Captain Bligh was a cruel man, and they understood why there had been a mutiny on the *Bounty.* There is a famous book, *Mutiny on the Bounty,* by two American writers, Charles B. Nordhoff and James N. Hall.

Bourbon

Bourbon was the name of a French family. They took their name from the part of France they came from. This section was called the Barony of Bourbonnais about a thousand years ago. For two hundred years before the French Revolution in 1789, the kings of France were all members of the Bourbon family. For nearly a hundred years after that, the government of France was very unsettled, but there were several more Bourbon

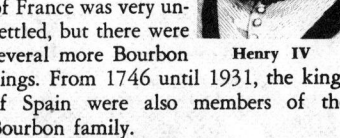

Henry IV

kings. From 1746 until 1931, the kings of Spain were also members of the Bourbon family.

All of the Bourbons were descended from King Henry IV, who became the first Bourbon king of France in 1589. His grandson was King Louis XIV of France, and one of Louis' grandsons was Philip V, who became the first Bourbon king of Spain. Louis XIV was king of France from 1643 to 1715. He was a strong king, and under his rule France became very important and powerful. Louis XVI, who was king at the time of the French Revolution, was the great-great-great-grandson of Louis XIV. He was executed during the Revolution.

Later two of Louis XVI's brothers, Louis XVIII and Charles X, became kings of France. The last Bourbon king of France was Louis Philippe. He ruled until the Revolution of 1848.

The Bourbon rule in Spain was much more peaceful than the Bourbon rule in France. Until 1931 there were only two important interruptions. The first was in the early 1800s, when Napoleon took over Spain. The second was in the late 1800s, when Spain became a republic for a short time. In 1931, there was a revolution in Spain. Alfonso XIII, the king, gave up his throne, but his son or grandson retained a chance to regain it.

bourgeoisie

Bourgeoisie is a French word meaning "the people who live in towns." It comes from the word *bourg,* which means "town" in French. When the word *bourgeoisie* was invented, the people who lived in towns and cities were mostly shopkeepers, craftsmen, doctors, lawyers, and so forth. They were the people we call the middle class. Bourgeoisie has come to mean all middle-class people, no matter where they live.

The bourgeoisie were very important in the French Revolution, which took place in 1789. Before the Revolution, the nobles and the church ran the French government. The bourgeoisie wanted to run their own government. They knew all about the American Revolution, and they wanted to have the same kind of democratic government that the people in America had won.

After the French Revolution, the bourgeoisie became very powerful all over Europe and America. Many people felt that the bourgeoisie had also become much too self-satisfied and narrow-minded. They began to use the word *bourgeois* to describe anyone who had those qualities, no matter what class he came from.

bow and arrow

The bow and arrow is a weapon that men have been using for many thousands of years, in hunting, in warfare, and in the sport called ARCHERY (about which there is a separate article). The weapon shoots the arrow—a sort of slender, sharp-pointed spear—with great force, to strike and pierce its target. There are three parts—bow, bowstring, and arrow.

The *bow* is made of wood. It is a very springy stick that will bend without breaking, and is usually about as long as you are tall. It is thicker in the center than at the ends. At each end there is a notch, called a *nock,* to which the bowstring is fastened.

The *bowstring,* or *string,* is made of strong cord—now usually of linen—and is a little bit shorter than the bow. You can *string your bow* in one of two ways: 1, you tie the string to one end of the bow and tie a loop at the other end of the string. Then you bend the bow while you hold the bottom against your foot, and slip the loop into the nock at the top of the bow; or, 2, you tie a loop at each end of the string; then you put it on the bow just as you would in the first way.

When the bow is strung, there should be about five or six inches between the middle of the string and the middle of

the bow, and the string should be very tight.

The *arrows* are made of wood. They are round like pencils, but thicker, and as long as several pencils—about as long as your arm. There are different kinds of arrows. To go hunting you need arrows with sharp steel points, but to shoot at a target you use arrows with plain points. Arrows are "fletched"—that is, feathers are stuck on them at the opposite end from the point. This makes them fly straight. Each arrow has a notch, or *nock,* at the end where the feathers are.

You may also have a *quiver,* or long, narrow bag, to keep your arrows in. A quiver is made of leather, or canvas, or plastic, and has a strap on it, so that you can hang it over your shoulder It should hold ten to twenty arrows, depending upon how wide it is. As you shoot each arrow, you reach into the quiver and get out a new one.

SHOOTING A BOW AND ARROW

When you shoot a bow and arrow you hold the bow in one hand so that it is straight up and down and in front of you. The hand that you hold the bow with should be just below the middle of the bow. Then you take an arrow in the other hand and fit the nock at the end of the arrow into the string on the bow. Then you rest the front end of the arrow over the finger of the hand that holds the bow, *never over the thumb,* and pull back the arrow.

When you pull back the arrows, put three fingers on the string Hold the the arrow between the top finger and the string just at the tips of the fingers, with next-to-the-top finger. Now you turn sideward toward where you want the arrow to go, the "mark" or target you are shooting at. Straighten the arm that holds the bow (but not too stiff!), and pull back the arrow until the hand holding the string and arrow is just below your chin. Sight along the arrow and let go. The string will snap, and the arrow will fly toward the mark.

MARKSMANSHIP

Marksmanship is the ability to make the arrow go where you want it to. This takes practice as well as knowledge of the right way to shoot.

No two bows are exactly the same. The "pull" of a bow is measured in pounds, and it means that if the bow is put on a solid place, it would take a weight that weighed that many pounds to make the string go down and bend the bow as far as you would to shoot an arrow. The proper pull is about 30 to 40 pounds for men (although bows for big-game hunting go up to 100 pounds and more, which takes a very strong man); 30 to 40 pounds for women; 12 to 30 pounds for boys 10 to 14 years old; and 10 to 25 pounds for girls 10 to 14 years old. You have to learn by experiment where the arrows go with each bow.

If the target is far away, you aim above the place you want to hit, because the arrow *falls* as it flies through the air. The stronger the pull of the bow, the less fall there is, but you find this out by practicing. When you can picture in your head the curve that the arrow makes as it flies through the air, as soon as you are

used to the bow, you can shoot at something and hit it most of the time.

Bowie, James

James Bowie was a man who lived in Texas more than a hundred years ago. He became a colonel in the Texas army and helped Texas to win independence from Mexico, but he was killed in the battle of the ALAMO, about which there is a separate article. He was born in 1796 and died in 1836. A kind of hunting knife, the Bowie knife, is named for him. It has a blade about 10 inches long, sharpened on one edge, and it is kept in a sheath. Millions of people since his time have used Bowie knives. James Bowie is said to have made the first knife of this kind in 1827, grinding it into shape from a steel file.

bowlegs

Bowlegs is a condition in which a person's legs are curved outward. It is usually caused in childhood by a disease called *rickets*. Children get this disease when their bodies lack calcium and phosphorus (the minerals that build bones), or vitamin D (the substance that enables the body to use calcium and phosphorus). The bones of young children are quite soft. A child should never be forced to walk too young, or to put too much strain on his legs. But some poor children do not get foods that contain minerals and vitamins, or enough sunlight to make vitamin D in the skin. They develop rickets. Their bones become so soft that their legs bend under the weight of their bodies. They become bowlegged or knock-kneed (so that their legs are curved inward), and even their back-bones may become curved. Once the bones have hardened out of shape it is a very long and difficult process to get them right again. With modern knowledge of medicine, there is no need for anyone to have rickets, and such things as bowlegs are becoming less common every year.

bowling

Bowling is one of the oldest games in the world. It goes back to ancient times and has been played in some form ever since. The Dutch settlers brought the game with them to what is now the state of New York, more than three hundred years ago. In the story of *Rip van Winkle,* by Washington Irving, we read about the

The front pins struck by the ball fly back and knock down other pins. In the picture, all ten pins will go down—a strike. To get a strike, the bowler must make the ball hit "in the slot"—between the 1 and 3 pins.

A "four-step" bowler.

"thunder" of bowling.

The game of bowling as it is played in the United States is also known as *ten pins*. The object is to roll a ball and knock down "pins," or bottle-shaped wooden pegs. It is America's most popular indoor game, and is played by millions of people.

Until about three hundred years ago, the game was called "ninepins" because only nine pins were used. There were a great many people who thought all games were wrong, and they passed laws against playing "ninepins." So the bowlers simply added another pin and kept on playing, because there was no law against playing "tenpins."

There are two kinds of bowling, called *big-pin,* and *duck-pin* bowling. The rules and scoring are the same, and the same alleys may be used. The difference is in the size of the ball and pins, which are

Position of the bowler from the front.

much smaller in duckpins. Big-pin bowling is too hard for very young people, because the ball weighs between 10 and 16 pounds and is too heavy for them to swing. Duckpins is very popular with young people in schools and YMCA bowling alleys. Grownups often play duckpins too, and it used to be called "summer bowling."

Bowling is done on a long, narrow wooden *alley* with a hardwood floor. It must be highly polished and very level, so that the balls roll straight. The alley is almost 63 feet long and about 41 inches wide. Several alleys are usually built side by side, and along the sides of each alley there is a *gutter,* or trough, so that when a ball rolls off the alley it will not go into the next alley. At one end of the alley where the players stand there is a *foul line* (over which the player must not step), and behind that a runway about 15 feet long. At the other end the pins are set up in rows of 1, 2, 3, and 4, a few inches apart. They form a triangle with the "single," or No. 1, pin in front. Behind the pins there is a *pit,* and when the pins are knocked down they fall into the pit. There may be a *pin boy* in the pit to set up the pins again and roll the bowler's ball back on a chute beside the alley, or all this may be done by automatic machinery.

Here is how you keep score. A game is made up of ten *frames,* or turns at rolling the ball. You "throw" your first ball down the alley at the pins. If you knock down all ten pins with this throw, it ends the frame; you have a *strike* and you score 10 points plus the number of pins you knock down in your next two throws. If your first throw does not knock down all the pins, you get a second throw in the same frame. If your second throw knocks down the rest of the pins you have a *spare.* You score 10 points plus the number of pins you knock down in the first throw of the next frame. When you do not have a strike or spare, your score for the frame is the number of pins you knock down in two throws. A strike in the tenth frame entitles you to two more throws, so a perfect score is 300, made up of strikes in all ten regular frames and in both extra throws. A spare in the tenth frame entitles you to one extra throw. Few bowlers can average much more than 200 per game.

There are many bowling teams in the United States. Some are made up of men, some of women. Usually they are clubs made up of persons who work for the same company or go to the same school. Rules and regulations for tournaments and matches are made by the "A.B.C.," or American Bowling Congress, by the Woman's International Bowling Congress, and by other organizations.

bowls

Bowls is the name of a game that was very popular in England hundreds of years ago. It was played in America before the Revolution, and gave the name Bowling Green to many places. Today bowls is still popular in England as well as in Scotland.

Bowls is played outdoors on a bowling green or indoors on matting. The bowling green is a lawn about 120 feet square, with a ditch running around it. The game is played with big balls called bowls and one small white ball called a jack. The jack stands in one place, and the object of each player is to roll his bowl closest to the jack. The jack is like the pins in bowling, but in bowls the player must not touch the jack. Another difference is that bowling is an indoor game, and bowls is generally played outdoors. Bowls is probably an older game than bowling.

boxer

The boxer is a dog whose name comes from its unusual way of fighting. When a boxer fights another dog, it strikes with its front paws as a man does with his fists. Boxers are sturdy and faithful dogs. They were first bred in England, about a hundred years ago, but were later developed in Germany. They are a mixture of mastiff, terrier, and bulldog. In the United States people keep them as watchdogs and as pets, because they can be trained easily. Boxers are often used as Seeing Eye dogs for the blind.

The boxer is a large dog. It stands about 21 to 24 inches high at the shoulders, and it may weigh between 60 and 65 pounds. The boxer's head is somewhat like that of a bulldog, but its muzzle is a bit longer, and the jowls are less drooping. The ears are clipped, which makes them stand up in small points close to its head. The tail is cut short.

The boxer's coat is smooth and shiny, with short hair. It can be light tan, reddish brown, or "brindle," which is a combination of black and brown hairs.

Boxer Rebellion

In the year 1900, when the Boxer Rebellion took place, China was a very poor, weak country, even though it was so large. Other countries owned large parts of it or had extensive financial interests there. Among them were Great Britain, Germany, France, Russia, the U.S., and Japan. China wanted to be fully independent, but the Chinese people did not agree on how to go about it. One group of Chinese wanted to modernize the country peacefully. Another group wanted to kill all the foreigners. In this group was a secret society, the "Order of Literary Patriotic Harmonious Fists," whom the English nicknamed "the Boxers." They attacked all the foreign people living in Peking (now called *Peiping*), which was the capital of China. The foreign powers sent an international army that stopped the rebellion and forced China to pay a great deal of money for the damages the Boxers had caused. The United States returned to China a large part of this money, to be used to give more Chinese children an education. The Boxers were disgraced, and the other group did a great deal to improve China in the years that followed.

boxing

Boxing means fighting with your fists, according to rules. This makes it a sport, instead of really fighting. There is a story that it got its name, boxing, from St. Bernard, when he was a young priest in Italy, seven hundred years ago. He was worried because the boys were fighting with knives, so he taught them how to use their fists. They would try to "box

up," or corner, their opponents, so they called the sport *boxing*. Boxing is also called *pugilism*, because in the Latin language *pugil* means "a fighter with the fists."

BOXING IN ANCIENT TIMES

In ancient Rome and Greece, two thousand years ago and more, boxing was such a brutal sport that the fighters usually continued until one or the other was dead.

On one of his hands a fighter wore a leather strap studded with brass spikes. This was called a *cestus*.

Today the cestus is no longer used but boxing can still be a dangerous sport. A blow may land in a certain spot so that a nerve center, or the brain, suffers damage. Some consider boxing a brutal sport, but many people like it.

PRIZE FIGHTERS

In England, about two hundred years ago, groups of men would sometimes put some money into a "purse," or prize, and then two fighters would compete for it. These boxers were known as prizefighters. People began to be interested in the sport, and soon there had to be rules. A fighter named Jack Broughton wrote up a set of rules, and later a group of officials had a meeting and adopted the "London Prize Ring Rules." They contained many rules that are in use today, such as "no hitting below the belt," and "no hitting a man who is down," and they had a referee in the ring to make the fighters obey the rules.

The first champion was James Figg, in England. He beat all comers, and eventually had to retire because no one would fight him. He opened the first gymnasium for boxers, known as "Figg's Academy for Boxing." About this time boxing began to be very popular, and spread from England to America.

BARE KNUCKLES TO GLOVES

For more than 150 years after James Figg's time, all the fights were with bare knuckles, and they were fights to the finish. You could not win except by a knockout, and the fight continued until a knockout was scored or one of the fighters gave up. When we read about those old-time fights that ran 50, 60 or 75 rounds, we must remember that a round in those days ended every time there was a knockdown, after which there was a 30-second rest period. So, if a fighter needed some rest, he simply dropped down, and then took his 30 seconds, and could repeat this any number of times. Today's fights, in which every round lasts three minutes, are much harder on the fighters.

Bare-knuckle fighting was illegal, and the police were always raiding the fights, arresting the fighters, and making the spectators go home. Then, in 1865, a rich English nobleman, the Marquis of Queensberry, introduced a famous set of rules, which are still the basis for all rules today. These rules include the use of boxing gloves, a limited number of three-minute rounds, no gouging or wrestling, and the rule that if a fighter is knocked down, and cannot rise within ten seconds, he loses the bout.

CLASSES ACCORDING TO WEIGHT

Boxers are classified according to weight as follows:

Professional:

Flyweight	not over 112 pounds
Bantamweight	" " 118 "
Featherweight	" " 126 "
Lightweight	" " 135 "
Welterweight	" " 147 "
Middleweight	" " 160 "
Light-heavyweight	" " 175 "

Heavyweight, from 175 pounds upward.

Amateur:

The A.A.U. (Amateur Athletic Union) recognizes the following classes: 112, 119, 125, 132, 139, 147, 156, 165, 178, and heavyweight, anything over 178.

TRAINING

When a boxer has set the date for a fight, he goes into training. His success or failure will depend upon what condition he is in. Condition means good health and strength so that he will not get tired or slow down. The best boxer in the world is likely to lose unless he is in good condition.

First of all, training consists in getting plenty of good food and plenty of sleep, because the exercise is using up so much energy. A boxer in training avoids all tobacco and alcohol.

Boxers who can afford the cost, such as champions, set up their own training camps out in the country. Others find the necessary equipment at a local gymnasium, the Y.M.C.A., or a club or school. There are light and heavy punching bags, wall pulleys, weights, and a boxing ring.

The light bag is the one like a pear-shaped basketball, blown up with air. It is used to develop speed and to train the eye. With the light bag you learn to punch to the head.

The heavy bag is made of canvas and filled with sand or shot. It is used to develop power for body blows, and to hit fast in infighting (fighting close together).

Roadwork means running, to strengthen the legs. Many boxers time their roadwork like the rounds of a bout, 3 minutes running, and 1 minute walking, or rest.

Rope-skipping and shadowboxing are exercises to develop footwork.

Boxers are careful to avoid what is known as overtraining, which means that they have trained too hard, and are so tired that it will take them a long time to rest their hearts and muscles. Overtraining is just as bad for a boxer as under-training.

After each training period, the boxer goes a few rounds with one or more *sparring partners*. These are fighters who are paid to give the boxer practice in actual boxing, and they must be very good themselves. Joe Walcott was once a sparring partner for Joe Louis, and then became world's champion himself.

GLOVES AND BANDAGES

Before putting on the gloves, or even before punching the bag, boxers usually tape, or "bandage," their hands. This protects the bones in the hand against breaking. The bandages are plain gauze, and they are wrapped loosely so as not to stop circulation, but not loosely enough to slip. They are never wrapped between the fingers or over the thumb. The thumb is used only to close the hand, and is never used in punching, as it is easily broken. All punches except the uppercut are delivered with the knuckles up and the thumb out of the way.

There are four different weights of gloves. For sparring and exhibition boxing, 14-ounce gloves are used. There are light gloves for punching the light bag, and heavy gloves for the heavy bag. Then there are the 8-ounce gloves for fighting, and 6-ounce for championship bouts.

Most boxers use a rubber mouthpiece during the fight, so that their teeth will not be knocked out or their lips cut. Head protectors are used in sparring, to protect the eyes and ears, but never in an actual fight.

Amateur (A.A.U.) rules require 8-ounce gloves for all classes below 147 pounds. In intercollegiate boxing, no glove lighter than 12 ounces is permitted, and interscholastic rules require 10-ounce gloves up to the lightweight class, and 12-ounce gloves in all heavier classes.

DEFENSE AND ATTACK

Scientific boxing consists of trying to protect yourself from being hit, and at the same time to hit your opponent.

Defensive tricks include *blocking,* by putting your arms and gloves in the way of a punch; *ducking* and *weaving,* so that the punch cannot land; *parrying,* which means to turn the blow with another blow, or ward it off; *sidestepping,* in which you avoid the blow, and at the same time surprise your opponent; and *slipping,* which means that you turn your head slightly, or move over a few inches, so that your opponent's blow misses its mark.

Offensive tactics are those of attack. They include: the *straight right* (or *left*), which is just what it sounds like, a straight punch to either the body or the head. It is usually used immediately after a left jab, and is the favorite knockout punch when it lands on the jaw. The *right cross* is a blow at about elbow height, with the elbow raised and bent. The body weight is thrown behind this punch, and it is a powerful punch when it lands right. The *left cross* is the same, but with the left arm. *Jabs* and *hooks* are most important, and a good boxer can be recognized by his use of these blows. The jab is a short, hard, poke with the arm almost straight out in front of you, and the power comes from the shoulder, as if to throw the shoulder a little to one side. You will notice that most boxers keep one arm slightly out, as a "lead," at all times, and jab with this arm. The hook is considered hard to learn, but is a knockout punch when it connects with the jaw. The *uppercut* is delivered by bringing your arm up close to your body, with the knuckles turned out. It is often used when infighting, and can be a knockout blow.

RULES USED IN BOXING

In the United States, most of the states have their own laws governing professional boxing, and this leads to a few special rules that apply in some states but not in others. Some of the principal rules may be described briefly as follows:

Each *round* is 3 minutes of fighting, with 1 minute between rounds for rest.

The *referee* is in complete charge while the fight is under way. He may award the fight to one of the fighters if he judges that the opponent has committed a foul, or is too badly hurt to keep on fighting without serious risk (called the *technical knockout*), or refuses to fight. There is usually a *timekeeper* who not only times the rounds but also counts off the seconds, up to ten, when a fighter is knocked down. When the fight ends without a knockout, there are usually two *judges* plus the referee, making three judges in all, who vote to decide which fighter has won, or if the fight was a *draw* (not won by either).

A *foul* includes hitting the opponent below the belt, or when he is down; using the knees to hit with; wrestling; and various other acts that break the rules.

A *knockdown* occurs when a fighter is lying on the floor of the ring, or when his weight is resting on any part of the body except his feet—for example, when he is kneeling. Technically, it is a knockdown even when a fighter slips and falls, so long as he is not on his feet. When a knockdown continues for 10 seconds, it is a *knockout*, ending the fight. But if the round ends before the count of ten is reached, it is not a knockout if the fighter is able to begin the next round.

Each fighter has one *corner* of the ring. Their corners are diagonally across from each other. The other two corners are *neutral corners*. When a fighter knocks his opponent down, he must go to the farthest neutral corner before the count begins, and must stay there until his opponent is on his feet again. Between rounds, the fighters go to their own corners, where their *seconds* (helpers) give them water and help them prepare for the next round.

A *clinch* occurs when either opponent is held so that he cannot move his arms freely. The referee taps both fighters on their shoulders and they must *break*—separate without any further blows, and be at arm's length before they start fighting again.

boxwood

Boxwood is a very strong, heavy, hard wood. It comes from a small tree called the box tree. There are several kinds of box tree, growing in Europe and Asia, but most of the wood comes from England. Because it is the smoothest, finest-grained wood known, it is the best wood for wood engraving. This means carving a picture on wood, then putting ink on the carving and printing a picture from it. Many pictures in books are made this way, and when boxwood is used the carving can be very delicate and show many details. Boxwood can be polished beautifully, and it is used in making scientific and musical instruments.

The box tree grows very slowly, and it makes beautiful hedges. It can be clipped into all sorts of wonderful shapes. The art of training and clipping hedges in this way is called *topiary*. If you see a small tree that is the shape of a peacock, for instance, it may be a box tree. The box tree keeps its leaves in winter. They are small and glossy, but they are poisonous, so you should never put them in your mouth. The flowers are small and whitish. They can be seen near the ends of the branches when the tree is in flower.

boycott

When a group of people object to the way a person is acting or want to force him to do something, they sometimes get together and decide not to do business with him. This is called a boycott. If a group wants to boycott a store owner, they refuse to buy anything from him and try to keep other people from trad-

ing with him. In the early days of labor unions, the union members used to boycott certain employers when they thought the employers were being unfair to their workers or were not paying them enough for their work. Sometimes they even boycotted other businesses that dealt with their employers. They hoped to hurt these businesses and so to hurt their employers. This was called a *secondary boycott,* and in 1947 the United States passed a law making secondary boycotts illegal. But the boycott did not work very well, and the unions had to find other ways of trying to get the improvements in working conditions that they thought the workers should have.

Boycotts are sometimes political. A group of people who object to the policies and actions of a country will declare a boycott against the whole country. Some Americans and people of Allied nations boycotted German and Japanese goods during World War II by refusing to buy anything made in Germany or Japan.

The word boycott comes from a man's name. Captain Charles Boycott was the land agent for an English nobleman named Lord Erne, who owned a lot of property in Ireland about 75 years ago. A land agent is the man who collects rents and takes care of property for an owner. At that time Ireland was ruled by England, and English people owned much of Irish property and business. The Irish people did not like this. And the people who rented land from Lord Erne resented England and resented the way they were being treated by Captain Boycott. They thought he was unfair in evicting some of the tenants with hardly any warning. So they refused to work the farms for Lord Erne, and refused to pay their rent to Captain Boycott.

Boyne, Battle of the

The Battle of the Boyne was fought in Ireland on the Boyne River, about 250 years ago. It was a very important battle because it decided that the Protestants instead of the Catholics would rule Great Britain. James II was king of England, Scotland and Ireland in 1688. He was a Catholic. He was a very unpopular king, and some of his enemies asked the Protestant William of Orange and his wife Mary, who was the daughter of James, to be their king and queen. James was put off the throne, but he was allowed to escape to France. But the Catholics wanted him to be king again, and so James went to Ireland and got an army together to fight the Protestant supporters of William III, who were called Orangemen. James was beaten and fled to France, never to return. You can read JAMES II and WILLIAM III in separate articles.

Boys' and Girls' Clubs

A boys' club or girls' club is a group of young people who meet to play or learn or work with one another. Members of a club learn how much better it is to be together than to live and play and work alone. They learn that two or more heads are better than one when there is a problem to be solved, a game to be played, or a camp to be set up. Young people all over the world join clubs. Usually they pay dues, a small

amount of money each year that is used to buy equipment or pay for trips for the club members. They may have uniforms or dress alike. Their clubs may have special flags and mottoes. They may meet in their own clubhouses or in their school or church. Grownups' clubs, like the Lions Club or the Rotary Club, often help children's clubs by buying sports equipment for them or maintaining their summer camps.

Members of some boys' and girls' clubs meet only to play together. Others, like the Boy Scouts, go to camp together and study nature together. Members of 4-H clubs learn all about farming and homemaking. Many clubs are independent, which means they are not connected with other clubs. The Camp Fire Girls are a nationwide organization, with clubs all over the United States. The Boy Scouts and Girl Scouts are part of an organization that has spread all over the world. Boy Scout groups have been formed in about fifty countries. The World Association of Girl Scouts and Girl Guides covers thirty-two nations. There are Girl Scouts in Alaska, Guam, Hawaii, Puerto Rico, and the Canal Zone.

HOW CLUBS STARTED

Families used to be much bigger than they are today, and there would be so many children in each family that they always had someone to play with. But nowadays families are smaller and they are often far apart whether they live on farms or in city apartment houses. Farm children and city children do not meet each other very often. Sometimes they know only a few children of their own ages. Even children who go to school together may live far apart. Clubs bring all these young people together.

There is another good reason for boys' and girls' clubs. In a free country like ours, it is important for the children to learn how to get along with other children of different religions and races. It makes a country strong when its citizens get along well with all kinds of people. This is especially true in a country as large as the United States, where there are so many people of different regions, races, and religions.

In boys' and girls' clubs children learn to be good citizens in many ways. They learn to be "good sports," which means playing your best whether you win or lose. They learn to help others. In New York City recently 50,000 Girl Scouts gave about 170,000 hours of their spare time to hospitals, homes for the aged, and centers for child care. Perhaps the best way club members learn to be good citizens is by learning to talk over different ways of doing things and accepting the decision of the majority, which means doing things the way that most of the members think is best. They find out that this is the way to make their club a good and happy one.

There are many boys' and girls' clubs in the United States. The national ones are Boy Scouts, Girl Scouts, Camp Fire Girls, Boys Clubs of America, 4-H Clubs, the YMCA, YWCA, YMHA, YWHA, and many others. There are separate articles on each of these organizations.

Boy Scouts

The Boy Scouts are an organization of boys which was started in England in 1908 by an English general, Sir Robert Baden-Powell. In 1910, the Boy Scouts of America was founded by a group of men including Daniel Carter BEARD, about whom you can read in a separate article. Since then the Boy Scout movement has spread throughout the world and every four years scouts from many different countries come together for a two-week meeting called a World Jamboree. The aim of all Boy Scout organizations is to help young boys be good citizens and to train their minds and bodies while teaching them how to enjoy outdoor life. All scouts learn camping, woodcraft, nature lore, lifesaving, sports and good citizenship.

BECOMING A SCOUT

To become a scout a boy must be at least 11 years old. Usually he applies for membership in a neighborhood group of scouts called a *troop.* At the head of each troop is a scoutmaster, a man specially trained in scouting. The scoutmaster tells the boy what he must do to become a candidate scout. He must learn the scout oath, the twelve points of the scout law, the scout motto and slogan, and the scout sign, salute, and handclasp. Having learned these things, he becomes a member of a *patrol.* There are five to fifteen boys in a patrol, and two or more patrols make up a troop. Each patrol is named after a bird or animal and has its own flag or pennant and secret animal-call known only to its members. The patrol has a leader and assistant leader, a scribe who keeps a record of the patrol's activities, a treasurer who collects dues, and a quartermaster who has charge of equipment. The patrol is a small group which is part of the troop, or "big team." Each troop has its own flag with its colors and number.

Scouts wear uniforms that include a khaki overseas cap, shirt, and trousers, with brown shoes and a colored neckerchief. In the summer they wear shorts and short-sleeved shirts. They wear emblems and badges on their shirts which show their rank, patrol, troop number, and any honors they have won.

Boys Scouts are divided into three ranks or grades. The lowest is the *tenderfoot.* Next is *second-class scout* and the highest is *first-class scout.* Scouts must pass an examination to go into a higher grade. The candidate scout also must pass a test before he can become a tenderfoot.

WHAT SCOUTS DO

At the weekly scout meeting the boys play games, study to pass tests for the next rank, pay dues, make plans for hikes and camping trips and community events. They learn that the scout is expected to do his best at whatever he tries. He is expected to be faithful to his religion and attend his church or synagogue, and to respect the religion of others. He is taught to do a good turn every day and to be helpful to the people of his neighborhood. He takes part in parades with his troop, helps in safety drives, directs traffic in emergencies, plants trees to beautify his community, joins in all kinds of cam-

paigns to help the poor and the sick, and is expected to be brave, courteous, loyal, obedient, thrifty, and clean.

As he works his way up through the ranks, the scout learns more and more about outdoor living. By the time he is a first-class scout he can take care of himself in the outdoors like an Indian scout of the old frontier days. He knows how to pack a knapsack expertly, what clothing to wear and what to take along when he goes camping or hiking. He can tie all sorts of knots that never untie or loosen and knows which one is best for any special use. He has learned all about the plants in his region of the country and knows which ones are poisonous and which can be eaten in an emergency. The scout learns all about different birds, snakes, animals, and insects.

SCOUTS AND WOODSMEN

The scout is trained in tracking and stalking. He can recognize and follow the tracks of wild animals. He can walk silently through the woods and can approach any animal or person without being seen. One of the tests he must pass is to trail another scout who knows he is being followed and keep up with him through woods and fields without being seen. A trained scout can find his way through unknown territory because he knows how to use a compass, measure distances, read or make a map, keep on a straight course, and find his way at night by placing the North Star in the sky.

Knowing how to light a fire may seem like a simple thing, but scouts must learn to do it with only one match or with no match at all. If he has no matches he must be able to start a fire by striking a piece of steel against a hard stone called a *flint*. The scout learns that there are many different ways of building fires for cooking. Instead of building a huge bonfire, the scout knows how to broil, bake, or boil his food over the right kind of fire using only a small amount of wood. He knows how different foods can be cooked out of doors, what foods to take along, and how to work out a good menu. If he runs out of vegetables a well-trained scout knows which wild plants are safe to eat raw, boiled, steamed, or baked.

Camping outdoors can be fun but if you don't have a good shelter you can be very uncomfortable. The scout's shelter is his tent and he is taught how to set it up without poles inside and how to stake it down so that it will not blow over in a storm. He knows how to prevent water from seeping under it and how to keep dry while sleeping in rain or snow.

FIRST AID AND HOBBIES

Scouts are probably the youngest group

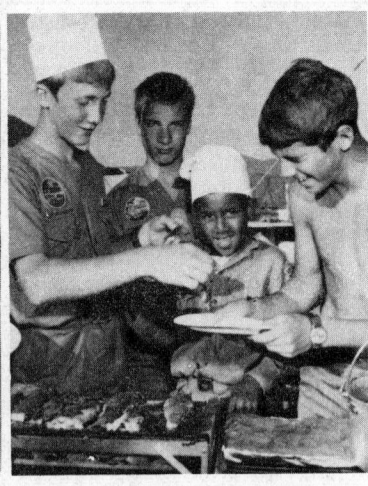

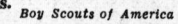

Scouts take part in a wide variety of activities. *Boy Scouts of America*

to be trained in first aid. They are taught first aid because when an accident happens on a hiking or camping trip there may be no doctor nearby, and quick first aid may be the difference between life and death. A first-class scout must know artificial respiration so that he can get a person breathing again, if he has stopped breathing. He also must know what to do about broken bones, serious bleeding, dog bites, snake bites, sunstroke, frostbite, heat exhaustion, fainting, and poisoning.

Not only must a scout learn swimming but he must also be able to get off his outer clothing in twenty seconds and rescue a drowning person. Scouts also learn how to rescue people who have fallen through ice.

Another unusual thing that scouts learn to do is to signal in Morse code by means of blinker lights at night and wigwag flags in the daytime. In Morse code each letter of the alphabet is made up of dots and dashes. At night a dot is a short flash and a dash is a long flash. In wigwag

signaling a two-foot white flag with a red square in the center is waved to the left and right. A wave to the right is a dot, a wave to the left is a dash. In these ways scouts are able to signal emergency messages over long distances.

Scouts are encouraged to learn useful hobbies and to do them well. There are more than a hundred hobbies or skills from which a first-class scout can choose. After passing a test in his hobby, or skill, he is awarded a merit badge which he can wear on his uniform. Merit-badge subjects include such things as stamp collecting, plumbing, sheep farming, poultry raising, metalwork, music, art, dramatics, botany, insect life, chemistry, public speaking, athletics, horsemanship, farming, and aviation.

After a first-class scout has earned a number of merit badges, he may take tests to rise even higher and become a *Star Scout,* then a *Life Scout,* and finally the very highest rank—an *Eagle Scout.*

OTHER SCOUTS

For younger boys, aged 8 through 10, there are Cub Scout groups, called packs. When a Cub Scout reaches the age of 11, he can graduate to a regular Scout Troop. After 14, he can be a Senior Scout, a more advanced grade. Senior Scouts are also called Explorer Scouts, and some are Sea Scouts. They may go on trips in study and exploration groups either on land, on the water, or in the air. All are part of the general Boy Scout activities, from the Cubs to the Explorers.

Boys Town

Boys Town is the most unusual village in the United States. It is a school and home for boys who have no homes of their own. The only people who live in Boys Town, near Omaha, Nebraska, are the boys who go to school there and their teachers.

Boys Town has not always been a village. It started as just a small house in Omaha. This small house was rented by Father Edward J. Flanagan in 1917. Father Flanagan was a Catholic priest. He believed that all children should be given an equal chance, whether they were rich or poor, black or white, Catholic, Protestant, or Jewish. He believed that if homeless boys were given a good home and good schooling, they would grow up to become just as fine citizens as boys with homes and families of their own; but if they had no homes or were badly treated they might turn out to be very poor citizens, or even criminals. So Father Flanagan made up his mind to do everything he could to help homeless boys. He borrowed ninety dollars from some friends to rent the house, and he turned it into a home and school for boys who had no families of their own. At first only a few boys lived with Father Flanagan, but the news of his wonderful work spread very quickly and boys began to come to him from all over the country. Pretty soon the little house in Omaha was too small. Father Flanagan's friends decided to help him again.

They found a farm just outside Omaha, and gave it to Father Flanagan. The farm was very large, and soon enough build-

This great group of buildings is Boys Town, in Nebraska. It was once just a two-story house, but more and more boys came to enjoy the benefits of this community, and more buildings were needed. This large farm was finally bought to take care of all the boys who came there to live. In this view from the air, you can see the cottages where the boys live, the schools, post office, stadium, and student farm.

Boys Town Photos

ings were built on it to take care of nearly five hundred boys. These boys come to Boys Town when they are very young, and live there until they are old enough to make their own way. At Boys Town they go to school, work on their own farm, and learn trades that will help them make their own livings when they are grown up. The farm at Boys Town grows nearly all the fruit and vegetables the boys need for their own meals. There are several school buildings in Boys Town, and a library, a gymnasium, dormitories, and an administration building. Boys Town has its own postoffice. The boys have their own orchestra and chorus. They have baseball and football teams.

Boys Town became a village in 1936. Since that time it has been governed by the boys themselves, just as any other village is governed by the people who live in it. The boys elect their own mayor and a council of six to help him see that everything is run smoothly and properly, and that Boys Town remains a good place to live in.

Father Flanagan was at Boys Town from the time he started it in 1917 until he died, in 1948. After he died, his wonderful work was carried on by Father Nicholas H. Wegner. People all over the United States think so much of Boys Town that they send money to support it, because they know that these boys will one day be among the finest citizens in the United States.

Bozzaris, Marco

Marco Bozzaris was a hero in the War of Greek Independence, when Greece freed itself from Turkish rule, about 125 years ago. Bozzaris was killed in the famous Battle of Carpenisi, when he led 350 Greeks against an army of 4,000 Turks and Albanians, and defeated them. His brother, Kosta, lived to become a senator in independent Greece.

Brabant, Duchy of

Brabant is a territory about the size of Connecticut and Rhode Island put together. It lies partly in Belgium and partly in Holland, and contains several large cities, including Brussels, Antwerp, and Louvain. It no longer has its own government, but hundreds of years ago it was an important and powerful duchy, which is a territory governed by a duke. From 1190 until 1430, when the last duke died, Brabant was one of the most

prosperous states of Europe, famous for its fine wools and other cloths. The merchants of the towns became so rich by this trade that they were able to force the duke to agree not to make war or coin money without their consent. Today the eldest son of the king of the Belgians is called the Duke of Brabant, just as the male heir to the throne of England is known as the Prince of Wales.

bracelet

A bracelet is a band or chain of metal or stones or beads, worn around the wrist or arm as a decoration. Bracelets have been worn by men and women in every country as far back in history as we know. Three thousand years ago the Egyptians wore many gold and jeweled bracelets at the same time, several on each wrist and several more high up on their arms.

Today bracelets are mostly made for women. They are made of many materials, such as gold and silver bands or chains, diamonds and pearls and other jewels, and glass or plastic beads. Some chain bracelets have tiny ornaments made in various shapes, such as musical instruments, animals, coins, dice and other things that are intended as good-luck charms. These are called charm bracelets. During World War II every American soldier wore a chain around his neck with a tag on it giving his name, number, and army group. This was called an identification tag, and it started a fashion for identification bracelets on which the owner's name and sometimes his address were engraved. Identification bracelets are worn mostly by men, though some women and children like to wear them.

The handcuffs that policemen put on the wrists of persons they have arrested are sometimes nicknamed bracelets.

Braddock, Edward

Edward Braddock was a British general who came to America in 1755, when the states were still British colonies, to fight against the French. He led a force against the French fort called Duquesne, now Pittsburgh, Pennsylvania. George Washington was a volunteer aide. Near the fort, Braddock's troops were attacked by the Indi-

ans and French. The Indians hid behind trees, while Braddock's troops marched in columns. George Washington tried to tell him the proper way to fight Indians, but Braddock would not take his advice. More than half of Braddock's soldiers were killed, and Braddock was so badly wounded that he died.

Bradford, William

William Bradford was one of the Pilgrims who came to America on the Mayflower in 1620. He was the second governor of the Plymouth Colony (in what is now Massachusetts), which the Pilgrims started when they landed in America. He was a very good governor. He got along well with the Indians, and he knew how to guide the Pilgrims in all the problems of making their way in a new country.

The people thought so much of Bradford that they elected him governor over and over again. He was governor until just a short time before he died, in 1657. He wrote a book called *The History of Plimouth Plantation*, which tells the whole story of what happened in those exciting times. You can also read about the PLYMOUTH COLONY and the PILGRIMS in separate articles in this encyclopedia.

Bradley, Omar

Omar Bradley is the name of a great American soldier. Like General Eisenhower, he became a "five-star," or highest-ranking general. He was born in Missouri in 1893, and he married his childhood sweetheart. He went to West Point and to many other army schools. In

World War II, he was in charge of all the American soldiers in the invasion of Europe. Field Marshal Montgomery was in charge of the other Allied troops in the invasion, and General Eisenhower was in command of the entire invasion. More than 1,300,000 men served under General Bradley. After the war, he was put in charge of the Veterans Administration, and then was made chairman of the Joint Chiefs of Staff, which is made up of representatives of all the armed forces of the United States. He resigned from that position in 1953 and retired from the Army.

Brady, Mathew B.

Mathew B. Brady was one of the earliest American photographers. He was born about 1823 and began experimenting with photography when he was sixteen. Very little was known about it then, but he was quick to use the discoveries of other inventors and often added his own improvements. Brady set up a studio in New

York City in 1842. He photographed many famous and important people, including President Abraham Lincoln, and won World's Fair prizes in London and New York for his photography. Brady is best known for the wonderful pictures

he took of officers, soldiers, camp and battle scenes during the American Civil War. Although Brady had only crude equipment, his photographs are considered to be some of the finest examples of craftsmanship in photography. Brady died in 1896.

Brahma and Brahmanism

Brahma is the name given to God in the Hindu religion, which is the chief religion of India. This religion has several other gods and goddesses, but the three most important are called Brahma, Vishnu, and Shiva. They make up what is called the Hindu *triad,* or group of three. Many of the Hindus do not believe these gods are real persons, but think that the names stand for ideas of what is true, or right and wrong.

Brahma is the oldest god in the Hindu triad. Hindus believe that he is the creator of the universe. Vishnu is the Preserver and Shiva the Destroyer. Of these gods, Vishnu is the most worshiped.

The Hindu religion is called *Brahmanism.* The priests of the Hindu religion are called Brahmans. They are the only ones who are allowed to preach and explain the scriptures. The Brahmans of India are the best educated, most intelligent and the strictest Hindus. They usually live fairly well, but often they become servants and do other things that bring them close to the common people.

The CASTE SYSTEM (about which there is a separate article) is an important part of Brahmanism. The Brahmans are the highest caste. Others are the *Rajanya* (warriors) and *Vaisya* (farmers and other workers).

HOW BRAHMANISM BEGAN

The ancient Hindu religion had many gods and goddesses. Some of these represented things in nature. There were gods of the sky, sun, light, fire, winds, heaven, and hell. Some of these were good and some were evil. There was even a goddess of luck. In fact, there were so many gods and goddesses that things were quite confusing all over India. Some Hindus worshiped certain gods in one part of the country, while in other parts different gods were worshiped. This ancient Hindu religion was written down in a book called the VEDA, and you can read about it in a separate article. The Veda goes back nearly 3,500 years, when India was invaded by the Aryan peoples from the north in about 1500 B.C.

Brahmanism began about a thousand years later, when the Brahmans wrote a book, called the *Brahmanas.* This book explains the other Hindu holy books and tells people how to worship the gods and also how to behave. Perhaps the most important thing that the Brahmans tried to do was to get rid of some of the old gods and persuade people to worship Brahma as the most important god of all.

The Brahmans were quite successful, though other forms of religion sprang up from time to time and challenged some of the things that the Brahmans believed. One of the most important of these other religions was BUDDHISM, which you can read about in a separate article. The Brahmans, however, wrote another book called the *Laws of Manu* which helped to make them almost as strong as ever. Today Brahmanism is believed by fewer

people, but the Brahmans themselves are still considered the highest class of Hindus.

WHAT BRAHMANS BELIEVE

The Brahmans believe in the existence of one supreme god, whom they call Brahma. They do not believe he ever appeared on earth in human form, but they do believe there have been several men called "atavars," men with the spirit of Brahma, sent to earth to teach men something about God and His rules. Brahmans believe the human soul endures forever but that only those who repent their sins will be able to "join Brahma" (go to Heaven). Brahmans believe prayers to Brahma help them to become better people and they think it wrong to pray for such things as riches or happiness. They hold public religious services, but not on any special day, such as Sunday, nor at any special time of day.

The Brahmans have no Bible, but they do have several books that are holy to them, including the *Bhagavad-Gita,* the *Upanishads,* the *Brahmanas* (which has already been mentioned), and several others.

Brahmaputra River

The Brahmaputra River is one of the largest rivers in India. It is 1,800 miles long, but ships can sail on only 800 miles of it. The river starts high up in Tibet, in central Asia, flows down through India, and empties into the Bay of Bengal, which is an arm of the Indian Ocean. In the summer, the Brahmaputra River is filled with rushing water from the heavy rains. The river becomes so full that it overflows its banks, and floods hundreds of square miles of land. The flooding every year makes the soil very fertile, especially for rice-growing.

Brahms, Johannes

Johannes Brahms was a very great German composer, which is a writer of music. He was born in 1833. His father was a musician in Hamburg, and was his first music teacher, but later Johannes studied with a famous teacher named Eduard Marxen. When the boy was only 13 years old he began to play the piano at concerts and was very well liked by those who came to hear him. He began to write music before he was 20, and though other musicians liked his compositions, most people found them hard to listen to. Young Brahms could not make much money by writing music, but he got a job as teacher and choirmaster at the court of the Prince of Lippe-Detmold, a state in Germany.

When he was about 30 he went to live in Vienna, where he became very well liked and successful. He began to make more money and to write his most important music. Another famous composer named Robert Schumann, and his wife Clara, became his best friends. Brahms never married, and many people thought that he was in love with Clara Schumann, but they were only good friends. You can read about Robert and Clara SCHUMANN in a separate article.

Brahms is one of the "three B's." That is the way the great conductor Hans von Bülow spoke of the three greatest German composers, Bach, Beethoven, and Brahms. Brahms wrote all kinds of music except opera. As a composer of symphonies (music for a big orchestra) he ranks next to Beethoven (the greatest of all), and no one wrote better songs. The songs are in the German language and are called *lieder,* the German word for songs. One of the songs is "Wiegenlied," which means "Cradle Song." You may know it as "Brahms' Lullaby." Some of his best-known compositions are the *German Requiem,* the *Second Piano Concerto,* and a group of Hungarian dances. Brahms played in many taverns and cafes, and learned to use gypsy melodies in his music. He died in Vienna in 1897, at the age of 64.

Braille, Louis

Louis Braille was the inventor of a special system of writing for the blind. This system is called Braille, after him. There was a system of writing for the blind before Braille, but it was not easy to learn, and only a few people used it. With the Braille system, blind people can read and write almost as well as those who can see. In Braille, raised dots like little bumps are used for letters and numbers. There is a different pattern of dots for each letter and number. Blind people read Braille by running their fingers over these patterns of dots. They write by punching tiny holes in paper which is stretched across a frame. (See BLINDNESS.)

Louis Braille was born in France about 150 years ago, in 1809. He became blind when he was only 3 years old. When he invented Braille, he was only twenty years old. He was also a fine musician, and became known all over France for his organ playing. He died in 1852.

brain

The brain is the part of the body that we think with. No one knows *why* it works as it does, but scientists know a great deal about *how* it works. It consists of a mass of nerve fibers, in the form of thin, white strands, at the top of the head. These nerve fibers connect with other nerve fibers that stretch from the brain to all parts of our bodies. They carry messages to and from the brain in less time than it takes to bat an eyelash.

Nearly all animals have some kind of brain. Some, like the ape, have brains which in many ways are like our own. Yet it is man's brain that puts him above all other animals. It enables him to think, to learn, to make decisions. It gives him knowledge of himself and the world in which he lives. In short, it makes him master of the earth. What is this amazing instrument that we call the human brain? How does it differ from the brains of all other creatures?

Let us look at the human brain. It is shaped somewhat like cauliflower, with ripples called *convolutions.* The brain has a coating of grainy gray stuff. This is called the *cerebral cortex,* or simply "gray matter." The gray matter is gathered into many dips and folds called *convolutions,* which give the surface of the brain a furrowed look, something like a walnut shell.

Let us also look at the brain of an animal, for example, the ape. Seen side by side, the two show a number of likenesses as well as differences. They are shaped the same, but the human brain is larger and heavier. Also, the human brain has more dips and folds than the ape's brain. Since each dip and fold is lined with gray matter, the human brain contains more gray matter than the ape's.

You may have heard the expression, "Use your gray matter." When you use your gray matter, you are *thinking.* At this very instant, as you read this article, you are using your gray matter. With the *cerebral cortex* or gray matter of the brain we do the complex things that are called perceiving, thinking, learning and forming judgments which add up to what we call our human intelligence. Special centers inside the cerebral cortex also control our senses, such as sight, hearing, taste, smell, and touch. When one of these senses is damaged by injury or disease, another usually takes over. For example, if a person goes blind, his hearing and touch become sharper to help him overcome his handicap. In this way the brain not only controls our actions, but also helps us to survive. We may say, therefore, that the most important part of the brain, the part that sets us apart from other animals, is the cerebral cortex or gray matter. The brain also contains a layer of *white matter,* consisting mainly of closely packed white nerve fibers. There is also a third or inner layer, which contains quantities of gray matter.

The brain itself consists of the forebrain, the midbrain, and the hindbrain. The forebrain is the largest of the three. It is divided into halves called the *right* and *left hemisphere.* Each of these controls the opposite side of the body, that is, the *right hemisphere* controls the *left* side, and the *left hemisphere* controls the *right* side. If the left hemisphere is injured, paralysis of the right side may take place. The paralysis, or inability to move, may be temporary or permanent, depending on the seriousness of the injury and on the amount of gray matter destroyed. Some parts of the brain control our muscles, and other parts control our various inner organs, such as the heart or lungs.

Nature has provided special protection for the brain by placing it in the skull, or brain case, which shields it from injury. In addition, the brain is covered by three sets of thin but strong sheaths called *membranes,* separated from each other by a liquid which also protects the brain by acting as a cushion against sudden shock. For example, if you bump your head, the liquid around the brain prevents it from being violently thrown against the bones of the skull.

The brain must have a constant supply of oxygen to keep up its many activities. This is ordinarily provided by the many blood vessels that pass through the brain. If the steady flow of oxygen is cut off for as long as three to four minutes, the brain can become severely damaged, and the body begins to come to a standstill. Death follows if all oxygen is cut off from the brain for ten minutes—sometimes less.

Brain Trust

When Franklin D. Roosevelt was elected president of the United States in 1932, he appointed a number of college professors as his closest advisers. This was considered very unusual, since most of the presidents before Roosevelt appointed businessmen and persons with experience in politics to help them run the country. James Kiernan, a writer for *The New York Times,* a newspaper published in New York City, jokingly called these college professors a "Brain Trust." A *trust* is a company or a group of companies that has a "monopoly" or complete control over the sale of some product. Brain Trust therefore meant a group of men with a monopoly of brains in the nation. The name Brain Trust was used to describe the president's advisers by people who felt he had made a mistake in appointing a group of men who were brainy or clever but had no practical experience in government or business.

brake

A brake is any device which is used to slow something down or to stop it from moving. All moving things need brakes to control their motion. Machines need brakes to stop them from turning or to make them turn slower. Automobiles need brakes; so do airplanes. Brakes may be of many different kinds. Most brakes work by rubbing against something. This is called *friction.* When you ride a scooter and let one of your feet drag along the ground, the friction of your foot against the ground slows you down.

Instead of a brake applied directly to the ground, it is much easier to rub something against the wheel of the scooter. This was how the first brake worked. It was used on old-fashioned wagons that were drawn by horses or oxen. A piece of wood was connected to a handle so that when the handle was pushed forward, the wood rubbed against one of the wagon wheels. This prevented the wheel from turning and stopped the wagon.

Such brakes were not good enough when the automobiles were first invented. A man was not strong enough to stop the fast and heavy car wiith a hand brake. Instead of a wood block rubbing against the outside of a wheel, a new kind of brake was developed. This brake applied pressure to the inside of the wheel. This prevented the tires on the outside of the wheel from being worn away. A hollow metal drum was fitted inside the wheel around the axle. Inside the drum were two metal bars lined with hard rubber or asbestos. They were called *brake shoes.* When the brake handle in the car was pulled back, or a pedal was pressed down, the brake shoes would press against the sides of the drum and slow down the wheel. The stronger the pull on the brake handle, the more brake shoes pressed on the drum.

These brakes were called *mechanical* brakes. They depended on the strength of the driver's leg or arm muscles. They are still used as parking brakes on automobiles. They stop only the back wheels.

New brakes have been developed for trains and large trucks which relieve the engineer or driver of using his strength to apply the brakes. These brakes are called AIR BRAKES. You can read about them in a separate article. Most automobile brakes are operated by liquid pressure. These are called HYDRAULIC BRAKES, and there is also a separate article about them.

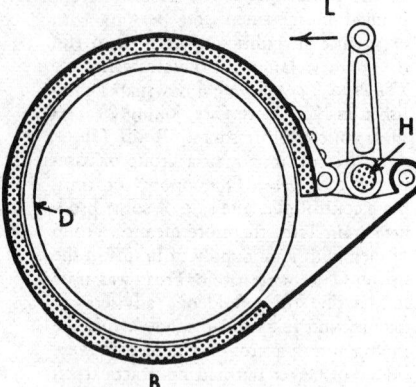

A band brake is used on heavy machinery and large trucks. When the lever (L) is pushed forward, it turns on a hinge (H). This tightens a leather or rubber band (B) around a moving drum (D). When the band is tight, the drum cannot turn.

An airplane has brakes to slow it down when it is coming in for a landing. These are the flaps on the front of the airplane wings. When they are turned forward, air strikes against them and slows the forward motion of the plane. A parachute is also a kind of brake. When a pilot jumps or bails out of a plane, he opens his parachute which balloons in the air like a giant umbrella. As it comes down, air is caught in the silk and slows the parachute. This prevents the pilot from hitting the ground at high speed and being killed. Parachutes are sometimes used as brakes on the airplane itself. They are attached to the plane and thrown out behind it. As they trail behind the plane, they catch air in their silks, thus slowing down the plane.

brake or bracken

Brake is a kind of fern with big, rough leaves that grow as high as a person's waist. It is found nearly all over the world, growing in open fields or in thin woods where there is plenty of light. Nearly everywhere it is regarded as a pest, because it chokes the grass and tree seedlings, and because cattle and sheep get sick if they eat too many of its leaves. In many places it is cut back each year and poisoned. Unless you dig into the ground, all you can see of the brake is its leaves. The main stem is underground, and grows as much as a hundred feet long, though it is always quite thin. The leaves are used as bedding for animals, and for making thatched roofs. In the fall the leaves turn golden, and hillsides are made beautiful by their color.

bran

Bran is the outer coat of cereal grains that is removed when the grain is ground into flour. Many people eat wheat bran as a breakfast cereal. It is rich in minerals and vitamin B, the energy-giving vitamin. Bran is also taken from rye, oats, and rice, but wheat bran is most commonly used. All brans are used as food for farm animals.

Brandeis, Louis D.

Louis Dembitz Brandeis was a great judge in the United States Supreme Court. He was born in 1856 in Louisville, Kentucky, and was graduated from Harvard Law School. He went into law practice in Boston, Massachusetts, and was very successful. Among the important cases he argued were cases for the people against big corporations and against states. President Woodrow Wilson made Brandeis a Supreme Court Justice in 1916. Brandeis knew a great deal about the United States Constitution, and he believed in it very deeply. He was greatly respected, and was known as the "people's attorney." He lived to be 85 years old, and he was in the Supreme Court until two years before he died, in 1941.

Gale Research Co.

Brandeis University, in Waltham, Massachusetts, was named for Justice Brandeis. It was founded in 1948 and one of its principal objects was to provide a higher education for students regardless of their religious beliefs. In 1973, its enrollment was about 2,000 undergraduates and 800 graduates (men and women).

Brandenburg

Brandenburg is a part of Germany, and was once a province of Prussia, the biggest German kingdom. It belonged to the Hohenzollern family, from which came the kings of Prussia and then the German emperors until Germany lost World War I to the Allies in 1918.

Berlin, the biggest city in Germany, is in the Brandenburg territory, but the capital of Brandenburg is Potsdam, a famous old city, now a suburb of Berlin, where Prussia had its military academy for training officers in its army.

Brandenburg is now a part of East Germany and has a population of about 2,500,000. Brandenburg is also the name of a city in this province, with a population of about 87,700.

Brandt, Willy

Willy Brandt achieved world-wide prominence as the anti-Communist mayor of West Berlin. He was born Herbert Frahm in 1913 in Lubeck, Germany, but changed his name when he fled the Nazis in 1933 because of his activities in the Social Democratic youth movement. Taking refuge in Norway, he worked as a journalist for Scandinavian newspapers. He was active in German and Norwegian resistance movements during World War II and returned to Germany after the war. Elected Mayor of West Berlin in 1957, he became Vice-Chancellor and Foreign Minister of West Germany in 1966. Three years later, after the elections of 1969, he replaced Kurt Georg Kiesinger as Chancellor.

brandy

Brandy is a strong alcoholic drink that is made from fruit instead of from grain (as whiskey is). Most brandy is distilled from wine, which is made from grapes.

The world's best brandy is said to come from grapes grown in the Cognac region of France. Other brandies are made from apples, cherries, apricots or peaches, and other fruits.

Brant, Joseph

Joseph Brant was a famous chief of the warlike Mohawk Indians. He fought on the British side in the American Revolution, but later became a good friend of the new United States.

Brant was born on the banks of the Ohio River in 1742, and was given the Indian name of Thayendanegea. Sir William Johnson, the British official in charge of dealing with the Indians, sent him to a school for Indians in Connecticut. When the colonies revolted, Brant became a colonel in the British army. He led Indian braves who came whooping down on New York settlements.

After the war Brant helped the new government make peace treaties with western tribes. He became a Christian missionary to the Indians, and translated the Episcopal Prayer Book and St. Mark's Gospel into the language of the Mohawks. He even went to England and raised funds to build the first Episcopal church in Upper Canada. The British government rewarded him with an estate on Lake Ontario, where he died in 1807.

Brasilia, see BRAZIL.

brass

Brass is one of the oldest metals that people knew about way back at the beginning of the BRONZE Age. (See the article on ARCHAEOLOGY.) They used to make it from copper and *calamine,* a kind of rock that is mostly zinc, and charcoal. About 175 years ago a man named James Emmerson found a way to make brass by melting copper and zinc and mixing them together. Then the brass is poured into a mold made of sand or iron, and when it gets cold it is ready to use. See the articles on BRONZE and COPPER.

Braun, Wernher von

Wernher von Braun is a brilliant physicist whose experiments with rockets were major factors in enabling the United States to become the first nation to land men on the moon. Born in 1912 in Wirsitz, Germany, he attended various schools in that country since his father, Baron von Braun, was required to move from place to place as Secretary of Agriculture under German President von Hindenburg.

In 1930, Wernher von Braun joined the German Society for Space Travel, a group of inventors who made and tested rockets. At the age of twenty, he received a bachelor of science degree in mechanical engineering from the Berlin Institute of Technology. Two years later he was awarded his doctorate in physics at the University of Berlin.

As a result of the experiments conducted by Dr. von Braun at the University, he was hired in 1934 by the German Ordnance Department as a rocket

development engineer. By early 1937, his staff was developing a rocket designed to reach an altitude of 15 miles.

Dr. von Braun surrendered to the Allied Powers at the end of World War II and came to the U.S. to direct firings of captured V-2 rockets. He became an American citizen in 1955. The following year, he became Director of the George C. Marshall Space Flight Center in Huntsville, Alabama. Dr. von Braun's team launched the Western World's first satellite of the earth (Explorer I, in 1958) and of the sun (Pioneer IV, in 1959). They also performed the first successful recovery of animal life from space. In 1970, Dr. von Braun became Chief of Planning of the National Aeronautics and Space Administration.

Brazil

Brazil is a huge country that covers almost half of South America. Its coast, bulging out into the Atlantic Ocean, is thousands of miles long. Its boundaries touch every other country on the continent except Chile and Ecuador. Its population of over 98,000,000 is equal to that of all the rest of South America. Although Brazil is bigger than the United States, it has less than half as many people. The people of Brazil speak the Portuguese language. Almost everywhere else south of the United States, the language is Spanish.

Brazil was discovered more than 450 years ago. It has grown from a small colony of Portugal to a big independent republic. But Brazilians believe that their history as a great nation is only just beginning. Because of the enormous natural riches that lie in the earth and in the forests, waiting to be put to use, Brazilians speak of their country as "the land of the future."

During World War II the United States built several large airfields in Brazil. These were very useful in transporting men and supplies to North Africa and Europe, because Brazil is much closer to the Eastern Hemisphere than the United States is. The distance from Brazil to North Africa, across the narrowest part of the Atlantic Ocean, is less than 2,000 miles. In Italy, Brazilian troops fought side by side with United States soldiers against the Germans. Brazil was one of the first countries to join the United Nations. The United States of America and the United States of Brazil (for that is its full name) have always been good friends.

THE PEOPLE OF BRAZIL

The people of Brazil come from many races and origins. Probably no other country has so mixed a population. Brazilians are proud of this fact. They say that in Brazil they are gradually producing a new civilization, made up of all the races of mankind.

Before the Portuguese explorers came, the only people in Brazil were Indians. There were few of them and they lived in small villages far apart from one another. They wore very little clothing and

painted their bodies. They lived mainly by hunting birds and wild animals in the forests, and fishing in the great rivers like the Amazon. Some were killed by the white conquerors, and some married whites or Negroes. But some others have been protected from change by the dense jungles around them. Even today there are Indians living in parts of the Amazon Valley exactly as their ancestors did hundreds of years ago.

When the settlers came to Brazil, they needed workers to clear the forests and farm the land. They made slaves of the Indians, but so many of them escaped or died in slavery that the settlers began to bring Negroes over from Africa as slaves. By the time the slaves were freed, more than fifty years ago, there were about two million Negroes in Brazil.

Meanwhile the white population was growing. French and later Dutch followed the Portuguese to Brazil to battle for possession of the country. Tales of Brazilian gold and diamonds brought adventurers from all over western Europe. In 1818 a large Swiss group arrived. From then on, the number of people who came to seek their fortunes increased steadily. Italians, Spaniards, and Germans came to settle the vast and empty land. From the Far East, Japanese, Chinese, and Malayans came or were brought in. Today the flow of people into Brazil still continues, particularly from southern Europe.

Because there have been so many marriages between members of one group and members of another, there are not very many "pure-blooded" people left in Brazil. About one Brazilian in every five is Indian or part-Indian; about one in seven is Negro or part-Negro; and the rest are white or nearly so, except for a small number of Orientals.

The great majority of Brazilians are Catholics. There are only about a million and a half Protestants in the country. Like Americans, Brazilians are free to follow the religion of their choice.

HOW THE PEOPLE LIVE

How people live in Brazil depends mainly on what part of the country they live in. In the vast Amazon region in the north, through which the equator passes, the weather is too hot and muggy for most white men, and there is little industry. Most of the people live by hunting and fishing. Some gather sap from the bark of rubber trees in the great forests and sell the crude rubber or exchange it for food. Others farm small patches of land on which they grow sweet corn, sweet potatoes, and other vegetables. Products of the forests include tapioca from the cassava tree, the beautiful wood mahogany, indigo (used in making dyes), and quinine (a drug used to treat malaria).

Farther south, where the land is higher and it is not so hot, a number of crops are grown. Most of the Negroes of Brazil live in this central region, which in places is like the southern states of the United States. At one time sugar cane was the most important crop. Some sugar is still grown there, but most of the fertile land now is used to grow coffee. Brazil grows more coffee than any other country. More than a million Brazilians earn their living from coffee—raising it, harvesting

the coffee beans, or transporting it to the coast to be shipped abroad. It is not surprising that coffee is Brazil's favorite drink.

Many thousands of Brazilians work in the fields growing cotton or rice; thousands of others grow oranges, bananas, pineapples, or corn. On many farms the tools are still very simple and old-fashioned, but many landowners have begun to use tractors and other modern machines.

About two Brazilians out of every three make their living from the land. Yet only a tiny part of the land has been put to use for farming. So you can see that Brazil can be very useful to grow food for people in countries where there are too many people and too little land to raise food for all of them.

Nobody knows how much iron, bauxite, gold, and other minerals will one day be dug from beneath the soil of Brazil. In the southern part of the central region, many Brazilians work as miners. Some work for themselves, panning the streams and rivers for gold and diamonds. This is a risky trade, but a man can become rich overnight if he is lucky.

In the southern part of the country wheat is grown, as well as the crops already mentioned. The vast plains that stretch south to Argentina are like our old West. It is a frontier region where cowboys in colorful costumes watch over huge herds of cattle. But the most interesting part of the south is the cities. Here the weather is cooler. There are many more people here than in the other regions of Brazil, and most of them are white. They work at many businesses, trades, and industries. Outside the big modern city of Sao Paulo, for instance, are cotton mills and cement plants, and factories where tires are made and automobiles are put together. The people here look and dress much like people in American cities and towns.

Brazilians enjoy music and dancing. Some famous dances, such as the samba and others, originated in Brazil. The four days of carnival and the Mardi Gras celebrations in the big cities are famous all over the world. Opera, the kind of play that is sung instead of spoken, is very popular. Brazilians get very excited about their national sport, football, which is soccer, not the game that is called football in North America.

All boys and girls in Brazil must go to grammar school. In some areas there are not yet enough schools and teachers, but in the advanced states there are many elementary and high schools, and some universities. The University of Brazil, in Rio de Janeiro, is the biggest of these.

WHAT KIND OF A PLACE IT IS

Brazil is made up of three kinds of land. In the north is the vast, low Amazon Valley. In the center, spreading over half the country, is tableland crossed by chains of low mountains. This is the great Brazilian plateau. In the south, the land slopes down to form part of the La Plata River valley, along with the neighboring countries, Paraguay, Uruguay, and northern Argentina.

Counting the many rivers, small and large, that flow into it, the Amazon is the biggest river in the world. Most of it is

very deep and wide. Where it empties into the Atlantic, it is 150 miles across. The land through which it flows is covered with dense jungle. Because all of the Amazon Valley lies on or near the equator, and is not very high above sea level, it is hot and damp all year round. It is a very rainy region.

The great Brazilian plateau in the central part of the country has a much more pleasant climate, partly because it is farther away -from the equator, but mostly because it is higher. It is partly forest and partly open prairies. It makes a very fine place to live so that the plateau is often called "the real Brazil," meaning the place where Brazil's future lies. One reason why this region has been so little developed so far is that it is cut off from the coast by a chain of steep, high mountains, called the Serra do Mar.

Between the Serra do Mar and the Atlantic Ocean there is a long narrow strip of land. To the south, this strip widens out. All of Brazil's great cities are on this coastal plain.

The Pampa region of Brazil, at the southern edge of the great plateau, is much higher than the Amazon Valley. Its climate is healthful. Much of it is covered by grassy plains, ideal for cattle ranching.

Although Brazil lies almost entirely within the Torrid Zone, not all the country is hot. The height of the land above sea level makes a great difference. So do wind, rain, and distance from the sea. The climate of the Brazilian coastal plain and of parts of the great plateau is quite like that of the southern Atlantic States of the United States. Since Brazil is south of the equator, summer comes in December, January, and February, and winter—sometimes even with snow—comes in June, July, and August.

HOW THE PEOPLE ARE GOVERNED

Like the United States, Brazil is a federal republic. The country's first constitution, issued in 1889, was written to be like the Constitution of the United States and the present Brazilian constitution is still like the United States one, though it has been changed several times. The President is elected by all the citizens over the age of 18. He serves for a term of five years. Laws are made by a National Congress, which has two houses, a senate and a Chamber of Deputies (like the U.S. House of Representatives). Senators are elected for eight years, Deputies for four years. In 1961 the constitution was revised to give all power to a Prime Minister elected by Congress.

The Brazilian constitution set up a Federal District, much like the District of Columbia, around the original capital, Rio de Janeiro, and a law passed in 1956 created a new Federal District around the new capital, Brasilia. The rest of the country is divided into twenty-two states and four territories. The states elect their own governors and their own law-making bodies, but the territories are ruled by governors appointed by the President. The territories are chiefly backward areas whose people have not yet learned how to govern themselves.

BRASILIA, THE NEW CAPITAL

In 1956 Brazil decided to build an entirely new capital city and move its government there, from Rio de Janeiro, in 1960 and 1961. The name selected for the new capital was Brasilia. The site selected was in the central part of the country, about 600 miles from the sea, on high ground (about 4,000 feet above sea level) overlooking the central jungle territory that has never been developed as other parts of Brazil have been.

Brazil is the third great country to build a new capital in this century, the others being India (New Delhi) and the Philippines (Quezon City); but both these other capitals were built in well-populated regions near the old capitals. Brazil placed its new capital so as to encourage development of a new region. The planners of Brasilia estimated its population at 500,000. They designed the city to be the most modern in the world. The government provided $345,-000,000 to build Brasilia.

The chief cities of Brazil, with population figures from the United Nations, 1970, are:

Brasilia, the new capital, 410,000.

Rio de Janeiro, population 4,344,000, the original capital, the chief seaport and cultural center, and long the biggest city. It is in the southern part of the country, on the Atlantic Ocean. See RIO DE JANEIRO.

São Paulo, population 6,339,000, Brazil's leading industrial center and in recent years its biggest city, probably the fastest-growing big city in the world. See SÃO PAULO.

Recife, population 1,195,000, an important seaport on the Atlantic Coast, in the north near the easternmost point of the bulge.

Salvador, population 975,000, an Atlantic seaport 750 miles north of Rio de Janeiro.

Porto Allegre, population 1,026,000, 750 miles south of Rio de Janeiro, a port on the Lagoa dos Patos, a large lagoon with an outlet to the Atlantic Ocean.

BRAZIL IN THE PAST

Brazil was discovered and claimed for Portugal by the explorer Pedro Cabral in 1500. In 1532 the first permanent settlement was established. The French and the Dutch controlled small areas for a short time, but Brazil remained a Portuguese colony until 1808. At that time Portugal was invaded by a French army under Napoleon. The King of Portugal and his family escaped to Brazil, and for a time Rio de Janeiro became the capital of the Portuguese empire. When Napoleon was defeated, the King returned to Portugal, but his son Pedro stayed behind, and in 1822 proclaimed the independent Empire of Brazil.

Dom Pedro I, as he was called, was not a popular ruler, and in 1831 he was forced to give up the throne. His son, Dom Pedro II, became ruler of the only kingdom in the western hemisphere (all the other Latin-American countries had become republics after revolting from Spain). Dom Pedro II was just and popular, and he reigned for fifty-eight years.

In 1888 Dom Pedro issued a royal decree freeing the slaves. The rich landowners and others who had supported him now turned against him. After a brief and bloodless revolution, Brazil was declared a republic. Since then, Brazil has had a peaceful existence compared to nearly all the other South American countries. The first president, General Fonseca, tried to become a dictator in 1891 but was overthrown in 1893. Brazil declared war on the side of the Allies in both World Wars but has settled all its disputes with its South American neighbors peacefully.

Coffee and rubber brought great wealth to Brazil around the beginning of the 1900s. But coffee sales dropped when other Latin-American countries produced more coffee, and the use of lower-priced rubber from the Far East almost wiped out Brazil's rubber trade. Since then Brazilians have learned not to depend on just one or two crops.

There was another revolution in 1930 when Getulio Vargas seized power (see VARGAS). But though Vargas ruled as a military dictator, he did not suppress all opposition as most dictators do. In 1934 he permitted elections and was himself elected president. He continued to rule as a dictator and the Army forced him to retire in 1945. In 1950 Vargas was elected president again and in 1954 the Army forced him to retire again. This time Vargas killed himself.

Since 1954 Brazil has had several political crises and a serious inflation (see INFLATION). In 1964 the Army, having forced two previous presidents to resign, made General Humberto Castelo Branco president. His moderate, anti-Communist government succeeded in reducing the inflation somewhat.

THE UNITED STATES OF BRAZIL (*Estados Unidos do Brazil*). Area, 3,288,042 square miles. Population, 99,000,000 (1973 estimate). Capital, Rio de Janerio until 1960, thereafter Brasilia. Language, Portuguese. Religion, chiefly Roman Catholic. Government, federal republic. Monetary unit, *cruzeiro*, worth about 1/20 cent (U.S.). Flag, green, with twenty-two white stars forming the constellation of the Southern Cross on a blue circle superimposed on a gold diamond

Pan Am. World Airways

Rio de Janeiro has one of the most famous harbors in the world. Many people come to the fine beaches and hotels there.

in the center; a white band running across the blue circle bears the motto "Order and Progress" in Portuguese.

Brazil nut

The Brazil nut grows on very tall trees in South America. These trees grow as high as 120 feet, and are found not only in Brazil, but in Venezuela and Guiana. The nuts, which are really seeds, grow in huge, round seed pods that are as large as basketballs. The pod is so hard that you have to hit it with a hammer to break it open. Inside the pod, there are fifteen to twenty nuts. The Brazil nut is white and very delicious, and it is sold to countries all over the world. The natives also get oil from these nuts, and they use it as fuel for their lamps.

Brazzaville

Brazzaville is the capital city and the commercial center of the People's Democratic Republic of the Congo. The city lies on the western shore of the Zaire (formerly called Congo) river. The city was named in honor of the French explorer Count Brazza, who founded the city in 1880. During World War II, it was the African headquarters of the Free French, who continued to fight against the Germans after France had been beaten and occupied. Since the war, the city has become very important. Today, Brazzaville has schools, office buildings, and factories. The city's population in 1973 was about 137,000.

bread

When grains, cereals, or seeds are ground or mashed into flour or meal, and then mixed with water and baked, we call it bread. Bread is made of many different things, such as wheat, corn, rye, oats, barley, millet, sesame, rice, potatoes, soy beans, and nuts. It may be that the first bread was made by pounding acorns or nuts and adding water to make a paste, which was dried by the fire. We don't know, because the first bread was made long before man had learned to write, and so there is no record of it. Some historians think it might have started in China, because they had underground "ovens" so long ago. In ancient Egypt bread was baked in ovens, and there were bakeries where people bought bread. Most historians believe that bread-making was invented in many parts of the world at about the same time, when our ancestors first learned to eat grains and cereals, and to plant crops.

Bread has been so important to people everywhere that sometimes the word is used to mean all food, not just bread itself. In the "Lord's Prayer," when we say, "Give us this day our daily bread," we surely do not mean bread alone.

At first every home made its own bread, but when bakeries started to sell bread in Europe, the first "pure-food laws" came into use. Pure-food laws regulate the sale of things we eat. All those who make and sell them must be clean, and must put in the right ingredients. A long time ago, when a baker made bad bread he was sometimes punished by being publicly whipped, or put in a pillory, a kind of wooden board with holes for his hands and feet, where people passing by made fun of him. Nowadays he may lose his license and not be allowed to make and sell bread for some time.

TYPES OF BREAD

There are two main types of bread, called "yeast breads" and "quick breads." The difference is in the speed with which the *leavening* takes place. Now let us see what leavening is and how it works.

In the Bible, "unleavened bread" is often mentioned. Unleavened bread is made of flour and water, and it is heavy and solid, instead of light and full of little air bubbles that make it porous. Most crackers are unleavened, also the *tortilla* Spanish people like, sea biscuit or hard tack, and the matzoth that is eaten by Jewish people on religious occasions. The Biblical meaning is that unleavened bread stands for purity. Leavened bread, on the other hand, is made by adding something to the flour and water, or dough, so that it will "rise" and become light and porous.

When yeast is used as a leavening agent, the bread is slow-rising, or yeast bread, and this group includes our familiar loaves of white or whole-wheat bread, rolls, coffee cake (really a kind of bread), pumpernickel (a slightly sour, dark rye bread), and many others.

Quick breads are made with baking powder, or soda and sour milk, and they rise very quickly. This group includes muffins, biscuits, gingerbreads, waffles, griddle cakes, and cornbread; and there are many, many varieties of all of these.

HOW BREAD IS MADE

1. *Yeast breads* are made in many sizes and shapes and flavors. For instance, there is raisin bread, bread with nuts in it, and other kinds. But there are some steps in the making of yeast breads that are the same for all of them. If you were a baker and were to bake some bread, here is what you would do:

First you would mix the flour, water, and other ingredients to make the dough. The flour might be the kind called "bread flour," or the kind known as "all-purpose flour." You would add the flour to water until the dough became rubbery and sticky. You might use milk instead of water, if you were making a special kind of bread.

Then you would add a little salt, and usually a little sugar and some fat, although not everybody uses sugar and fat. Next comes the yeast, called "bakers' yeast." It is sold in three forms, as a dry cake, or as a moist cake, but today almost all bakers use "crumbled yeast." Then you would start to knead the dough, or push, pull and squeeze it with your hands until it is smooth and all the ingredients are well mixed. In large bakeries a machine does the kneading, but at home it is done by hand on a board. As you kneaded the dough, you would see it changing. Little bubbles appear and the dough becomes less sticky and more rubbery.

After you had kneaded the dough, you would put it in a warm place, so that the yeast could begin to ferment. This is called "letting the dough rise." When it has become about twice the size that it was before, you would knead it again to break up the big gas bubbles, and shape it into loaves. Again it would rise until doubled in size. Then you would put it in the oven and bake it to a golden-brown color.

2. Quick breads can go into the oven as soon as the dough is well mixed. In most of these breads there is no kneading, although biscuits are usually kneaded slightly. The ingredients are almost the same as those used in yeast breads, except that some quick breads contain eggs and more sugar. They may also contain a large amount of fat, or shortening. This is also true of many cakes and pastries, so that sometimes it is hard to decide whether to call them bread or cake.

See also the articles on YEAST, BAKING POWDER, and FLOUR.

breadfruit

Breadfruit is a kind of fruit that grows on a big tree. The fruit is about as big as a small loaf of bread, but it is egg-shaped. When the fruit is baked, it looks and even tastes something like bread, with a slightly nutty flavor. It is a very healthful food, and thousands of people in hot tropical countries raise breadfruit trees. These trees grow well in hot climates like Malaya, the South Sea Islands, and Indonesia.

You can bake breadfruit, or boil it, or dry it and grind it into flour, or cut it into slices and fry it. In the South Sea Islands the natives used to bake it in a hole in the ground filled with hot rocks. Then they would peel the breadfruit and eat it. There is a pit in the center that you throw away. The *jack fruit* tree often seen in Botanical Gardens is another type of breadfruit tree.

breakwater

A breakwater is a kind of barrier made of stones and concrete blocks that sticks out into the sea around a harbor. It protects ships and docks in the harbor by "breaking the water," that is, by checking the rush of waves during a storm. Some harbors, like San Francisco or New York, are almost entirely surrounded by land. In natural harbors like these, breakwaters are seldom needed. But other harbors, Los Angeles for example, have been made out of a straight shoreline by building breakwaters out into the water.

breast

The babies of certain animals live on milk provided by their mothers, and the special part of the body that gives the baby its milk is called the breast. The Latin word for breast is "mamma," and that is why this group of animals is known as "mammals." We human beings belong to this group, and so do horses, cows, dogs, and cats. Not every mammal lives on land; the whale is a mammal, with breasts to feed milk to its baby whale. Even though whales live in the sea and look like fish, they are not fish, because fish are not mammals. Fish come out of tiny eggs, and after they hatch out they must find their own food. Chickens and other birds do not feed their young on milk; their young are also hatched out of eggs. So neither fish nor birds have breasts.

A breast has one wonderful thing about the way it works; it never forms milk until there is a baby to need it. The

female breast stays rather small until the female is ready to have a baby, and then the breasts get slowly larger. When the baby is born, the breasts of the mother are ready with the milk that the baby needs to grow on. The best milk for the baby is naturally the milk of its own mother, but if there is any reason why it cannot have its own mother's milk, some other can be used. That is why human babies are sometimes fed with cow's milk. A cow does not have any milk until it has had its own baby calf. But a cow is such a big animal and has so much milk, that its own calf does not need all of it and the farmer can sell the rest.

breastwork, a protective wall that is quickly put up: see FORTS AND FORTIFICATIONS.

breathing

You breathe when you take air into your lungs. This is necessary to life, because the air contains the gas called oxygen, without which you could not live. But one of the strange things about nature is that you do not have to try to breathe. You do it without thinking about it.

There are really two parts to breathing. Expanding the chest and allowing air to get into the lungs is the outside part, called *external respiration.* (Respiration is another word for breathing.) Lungs are like great sponges. If you squeeze a sponge and then let it expand under water, you can see how it soaks up the water. That is how the lungs soak up air when your muscles swell up your chest.

The second important part of breathing is what takes place after your lungs are filled with air. This is the inside or unseen part of breathing, called *internal respiration.* The lungs are full of tiny tubes into which the air goes. At the ends of these lung tubes are tiny sacs

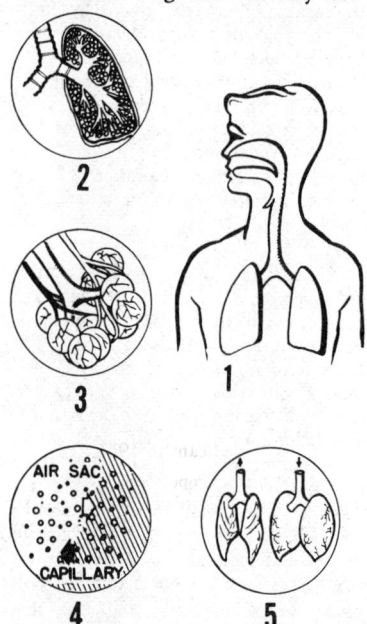

1. This is the path breath takes from the mouth to the lungs. 2. A bronchial tube ends in many air sacs. 3. Air sacs swell when they are filled with air. 4. The air sac and capillaries exchange oxygen and carbon dioxide at the same time. 5. Lungs shrink when air is expelled, and swell like balloons when air is taken in.

called *alveoli.* Each sac is surrounded by a blood vessel that has very thin walls. The walls are so thin that the oxygen of the air can go right through them into the blood. The blood carries it to every part of the body. (See the article on BLOOD.)

The body does not use all the oxygen in the air we breathe in. Some of the oxygen combines with carbon from the body to form the gas called *carbon dioxide.* This gas is part of the air we breathe out. This is an equally important part of breathing, the same two steps only backward. The blood carries the carbon dioxide back to the lungs, to the thin-walled alveoli. It passes through the thin walls of the blood vessels, and back into the tubes. When you squeeze the air out of your lungs, out goes the carbon dioxide, and you are ready for your next breath, ready to take in fresh oxygen and start all over again. You do this, without thinking, about 20 times a minute.

A person who stops breathing for too long will die, but the articles on ARTIFICIAL RESPIRATION and IRON LUNG tell some of the ways that have been found to save the lives of those who have lost the power to breathe for themselves.

Breckinridge, John

Breckinridge is the name of a very prominent family of Kentucky. Several members have served as congressmen and senators. The most famous was John Cabell Breckinridge, who was the Democratic candidate for president in 1860 and lost to Abraham Lincoln. He then turned to the Confederate States, serving as a major general in the Confederate Army and (in 1865) was Secretary of War in the cabinet of President Jefferson Davis. He was born in 1821 and died in 1875.

Breda, Treaty of

Breda is the name of a city in Holland that is famous in history because many important political conferences took place there. One of these conferences was in 1667, at the end of a war between the Dutch and English. The treaty that they signed, together with France and Denmark, was called the Treaty of Breda.

Under the terms of the treaty, the Dutch kept Dutch Guiana in South America; the French got New Brunswick, Canada; and the English got the American colonies of New York (New Amsterdam), New Jersey and Delaware, and several islands in the West Indies. See the separate article on the DUTCH WARS.

breeding

Breeding is a way of making our plants and animals better by carefully choosing their parents. For example, if you are raising corn you want all of it to be good, with large, healthy ears of corn. You would save the seed from the plants with the best ears. Then the next year you would plant only that seed. It would grow into another crop of corn,

and this time the corn would be better than the year before because the seed came from the best plants. This is called "selected seed." Now you would do the same thing again, so that the third season your corn would be even better, because it came from better seed. You could do this any number of seasons, and each time the seed would be taken from the best plants and your corn would keep getting better.

Now let us suppose that you live in a very cold country, and it is hard to grow corn because the frost kills it. But you notice that the frost does not kill all the corn; a few plants grow pretty well in spite of the cold. So you take the seed only from those hardy plants, and next season you plant that seed. Another crop grows, and this time there are many more plants that can survive the cold. You do the same thing again, and after a few seasons you have bred corn that will grow in a cold climate.

All living things, plants and animals and human beings too, inherit certain traits from their parents. In a family, some of the children look like the father, some look like the mother, and some look a little like each. See the article on HEREDITY.

Suppose you are raising horses, and you need two kinds. You want one kind to be very fast for racing, and the other kind to be big and strong to pull heavy trucks and wagons. You would see that the parents of the race horses were fast runners, and not too big and heavy.

You would want your truck horses to be heavy and strong, even if they could not run fast like the race horses, so you would select big, strong parents for them.

Now suppose you wanted a horse that had some of the qualities of the race horse and some of the qualities of the truck horse. You wanted a type of horse to pull a light wagon fairly fast. The race horse would be too nervous and high-strung, and not strong enough; and the truck horse would be too big and heavy and slow, and would not need half its strength. You would therefore breed horses from a combination of the race horse and the truck horse, so that some of the colts would inherit part of the speed and part of the strength of their parents. Then by breeding only those colts with the right combination of speed and strength, you would eventually get the kind of horse you wanted.

WHAT BREEDING IS USED FOR

Breeding has been known since ancient times. Modern scientific breeding is based upon the discoveries of Gregor Johann Mendel, about ninety years ago, called the "Mendelian Law" of heredity. Today we breed sheep so that they will give us more and better wool, cattle for better milk and meat, and hogs, dogs, and almost every kind of domesticated animal. When no further change is wanted, the breeders keep the "strain" by always using the same type of parents. Then we have what is called a "pure-bred" strain of animals, or "pure-line" plants.

When we "crossbreed," or mix parents of pure strains, we have what is known as a *hybrid.* Hybrids can be stronger and better than either parent.

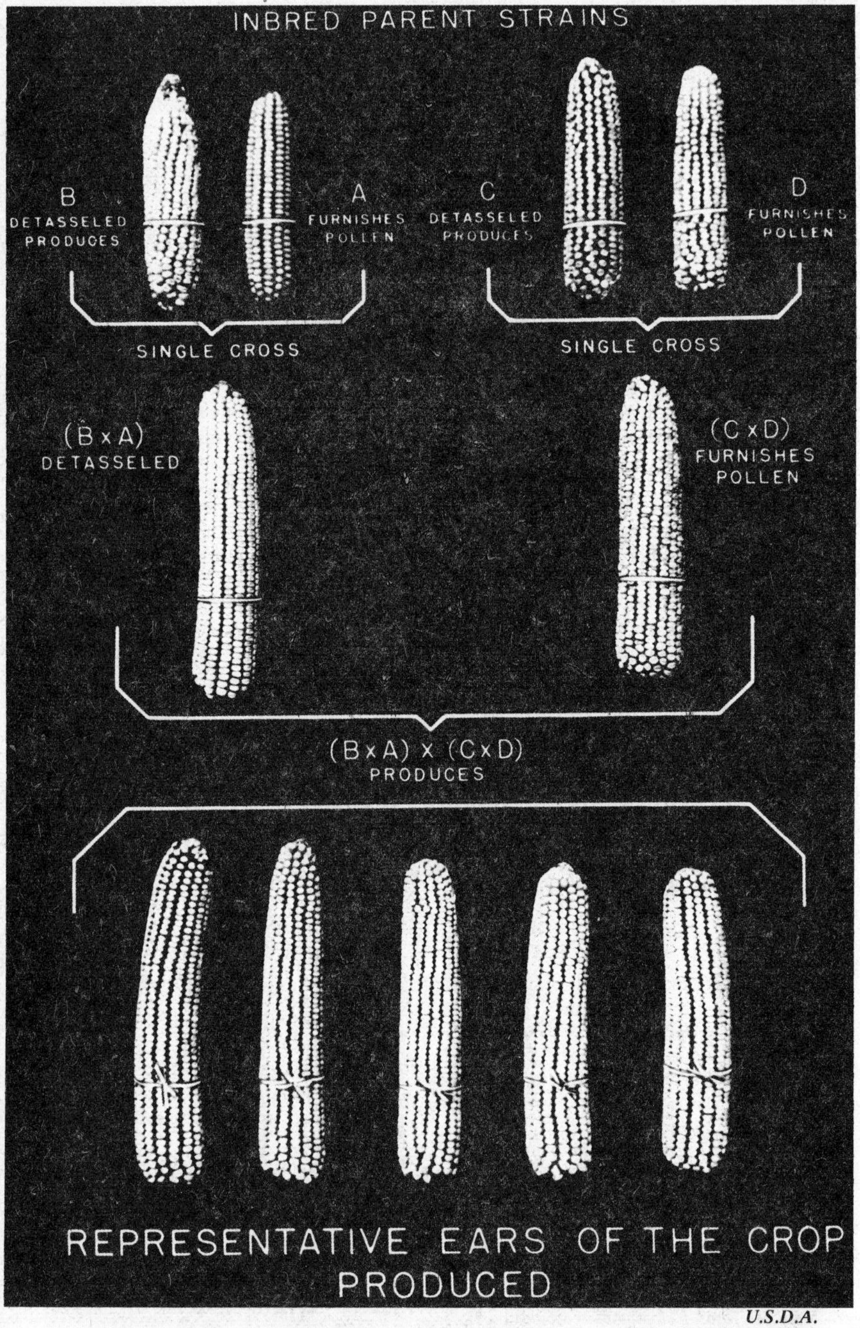

INBRED PARENT STRAINS

B
DETASSELED
PRODUCES

A
FURNISHES
POLLEN

C
DETASSELED
PRODUCES

D
FURNISHES
POLLEN

SINGLE CROSS

SINGLE CROSS

(B x A)
DETASSELED

(C x D)
FURNISHES
POLLEN

(B x A) x (C x D)
PRODUCES

REPRESENTATIVE EARS OF THE CROP PRODUCED

U.S.D.A.

Crossbreeding of good corn has resulted in bigger and better crops. The two kinds of corn in the upper left were crossbred, as were the two in the upper right. Each crossbreeding produced a new corn (center). Then these two new corns were crossbred, and from that came the fine corn crop at the bottom. Hardier and better crops of all kinds have been developed by farmers through crossbreeding. It is a delicate process that farmers have learned through modern farming.

U.S.D.A.

A tomato that is excellent for canning and a tomato that can resist certain diseases were crossbred. It resulted in this big tomato that has both qualities.

Bremen

Bremen is one of the largest, most important cities in West Germany. It has a population of over half a million. Bremen is chiefly a trade center. It is on the Weser River, which is not deep enough for big ships. Ocean freighters dock at the North Sea port of Bremerhaven, 46 miles away.

Bremen is more than 1,100 years old, and some of its streets and houses date back hundreds of years. In the Middle Ages it joined other towns in a strong trade association, the HANSEATIC LEAGUE, about which there is a separate article. Much of Bremen was destroyed during World War II, but it has since been rebuilt.

BREMEN, GERMANY. Population 607,184. Trade center on the Weser River.

Brenner Pass

For hundreds of years the Brenner Pass has been the most important route across the Alps, the highest mountains in Europe. Although it is 4,000 feet high, the Brenner Pass is the lowest gap in these great mountains. It connects Innsbruck, Austria, with Bolzano, in northeastern Italy. In 1772 a road for carriages was built across the pass, and in 1867 a railroad was opened.

In the village of Brennero at the top of the pass, Hitler and Mussolini, the German and Italian dictators, held a meeting on March 18, 1940. They met in a train standing in the railroad station, and agreed on plans for Italy to enter World War II on Germany's side. They held several other conferences in the Pass during the war.

Breslau

Breslau is the German name for the Polish city of Wroclaw in the region called Lower Silesia. It is now a city of about 523,000, on the Oder River. A thousand years ago Breslau was a Polish city; but many Germans settled there and in 1742 Breslau was made part of Prussia. It became almost entirely a German city, a large and important one. Just before World War II in 1939, Breslau had a population of more than 600,000; it was a manufacturing center for woolen and cotton goods, jewelry, machinery, and many other products, and it had beautiful churches and other buildings and a famous university.

In 1945 when Germany was losing World War II, Breslau was almost wholly destroyed by Russians attacking the city and Germans defending it. After the war the city was given to Poland and resumed its ancient name Wroclaw. Nearly all the Germans left the city and the population dropped to about 100,000. The Poles then rebuilt the city and nearly all of the present large population is Polish.

Brest

Brest is an important seaport city in France, on the tip of the peninsula of Brittany. It is on the Bay of Brest, which forms one of the finest harbors in the world. The only way ships can get from the Atlantic Ocean to this bay is through a narrow channel, scarcely a mile wide, called *Le Goulet*. More than 154,000 people live in Brest. Many of them work in factories, making paper, cork, candles, and soap. In World War II, the Germans captured Brest, and made it an important submarine base. The base was greatly damaged by bombings, and was recaptured by the Americans in 1944.

BREST, FRANCE. Population 154,023. In the department of Finistère.

Breugel

Breugel (sometimes spelled *Breughel*) was the name of a family of artists. The most famous were Pieter Breugel and his two sons, Pieter the younger, and Jan. They all were given nicknames which indicated how differently each of them painted. The father was called "Peasant" because instead of painting portraits of important people, he painted farmers working in the fields, children

at play, peasants dancing, and other ordinary subjects. Peter the younger was called "Hell" because his pictures were full of devils and witches. The other son, Jan, was called "Velvet," because of the beautiful flowers and garden scenes he painted.

The Breugels are called Flemish artists because they lived in Flanders, once part of Holland but now in Belgium. Their three lives covered about a century: the father lived from about 1525 to 1569, Pieter the younger lived from 1564 to 1637, and Jan from 1568 to 1625.

Your local museum or library may have copies of Father Breugel's famous picture *Children at Play,* in which you will recognize games that are still being played after four hundred years.

breviary

The breviary is a book of daily prayers used in the Roman Catholic Church. It contains hymns, psalms, and prayers for each day of the year. It is also divided into four parts for spring, summer, autumn, and winter. It was once very long, but about 700 years ago, Pope Gregory IX ordered that it be shortened. The Latin word for short is *brevis,* and that is how the book got its name.

brewing, a process for making ale or beer: see BEER.

Brewster, William

William Brewster was the religious leader of the Pilgrims, who came to America in 1620. He was born in England in 1566. In those days people who

did not believe in the Church of England were not allowed to worship in their own way. When Brewster set up his own church, he was put in jail. Later he and others went to Holland, hoping to find religious freedom. When they did not find it there, these people, the Pilgrims, set sail for the New World. (You can read about the PILGRIMS and their ship, the Mayflower, in a separate article.)

In Plymouth Colony, Massachusetts, Brewster became the head of the church, and for nine years he was the only one to hold religious services. He was one of the most respected men in the community when he died in 1644. Many of his descendants are still living in New England.

Briand, Aristide

Aristide Briand was a French statesman famous for his work toward world peace. He suggested in 1927 that war be called an international crime, and that a nation which declared war should be

treated as an outlaw. This idea became the Briand-Kellogg Pact, which by 1929 had been signed by 45 nations. Unfortunately, some of the nations later broke their word and started wars.

Briand was born in 1862. His first fame came in 1905, when he wrote the law separating church and

state in France. The French government had favored the Catholic religion, but this new law gave a person of any religion, or none, the same rights as any other citizen.

Briand was French premier eleven times, more often than any other man of his time. He served twenty-five times as a cabinet minister. In 1926 he won the Nobel peace prize for his work on the Locarno Treaty, which was another attempt to prevent wars in Europe. Briand also suggested what the American patriot, Thomas Paine, had proposed a century before—a United States of Europe. Briand thought nations should settle their differences by discussion and cooperation, instead of by war. He died in 1932, at the age of 70.

bribery

Getting someone to do a wrong thing by offering him special favors or money is called bribery. The favor or money is called a bribe. Bribery is very wrong, and is a serious crime. Both the man who offers a bribe and the man who takes it are criminals. When people talk about "corrupt" men, they may mean that these men are willing to take bribes. A corrupt judge, for instance, would take a bribe to free a prisoner who is guilty and should be punished. A corrupt athlete would take a bribe to lose a game. The man who bribed him would probably be a gambler who had bet a lot of money on the athlete's opponent to win.

brick

A brick is a block of clay that has been baked to make it hard. Bricks have been one of the best and most popular building materials for thousands of years. First, men used sun-dried bricks, which you can read about in the article ADOBE. Then men learned that bricks would last hundreds of years longer if they were baked under great heat in an oven called a *kiln.*

Modern bricks are made by machinery, but the method is not much different from the one used for handmade bricks in past centuries. First, wet clay is pressed into the desired shape, which is usually 8 inches long, 3¾ inches wide, and 2¼ inches thick. Many of these bricks are put in the kiln and are baked for days or even weeks at a temperature of 2000 degrees (on the Fahrenheit thermometer) or even higher. Different kinds of clay produce different colors of brick—red, yellow, brown, and other colors. Red brick gets its color from iron in the clay. This clay is the most plentiful, so most bricks are red. A brick weighs 4 to 5 pounds.

BRICKLAYING

Putting bricks together to make a wall or other structure is called *bricklaying.* A bricklayer is a skilled craftsman. He takes a brick, strikes it with his trowel to see if it "rings" (because a cracked brick will give a dull sound), and lays it in place. With the same trowel he spreads *mortar,* a kind of cement, which will harden and hold the bricks together. Bricklayers trying for a record have laid as many as two thousand bricks in a day, but usually a bricklayer lays about six hundred bricks a day.

Some of the earliest houses in America were made from bricks brought from Europe as ballast in the holds of ships.

bridge

A bridge is a roadway that goes over a body of water, a valley or ravine, or a highway or street. It is used by people on foot, in automobiles or on railroad trains. A bridge that is used by people only is called a footbridge. A bridge used by cars only is called a highway bridge. A bridge used only by railroads is called a railway bridge. Some bridges can be used by both people and cars, by people and railroads, or by all three.

Bridges are made of wood, stone, concrete, or steel. The first bridge that man ever used was a fallen log. Thousands of years ago a tree fell over a stream, connecting one bank with the other. A man probably saw it and found that he could go across the stream by walking on the log, instead of swimming or wading. He soon learned that he could chop down a tree and place it across a stream that he wanted to cross.

Then he learned that he could place logs across any stream. If the stream was very wide, he would place two or maybe three logs end to end, with large rocks in between them to hold them up. He would place a log from one shore to a rock or a pile of rocks in the stream, and a log from the rocks to the other shore. These rocks were the first bridge *piers.* A pier is a stone, wood, concrete or steel structure placed in the middle or near the middle of a river or stream to support a bridge. The pier is usually sunk deep into the rock or earth beneath the water to hold it steady. The top of the pier sticks out of the water and holds up the bridge. By using piers, it is possible to make a bridge over a stream no matter how wide the stream is.

The first log bridges were sometimes difficult to walk over. A log is round, and can be slippery when wet. Many persons would tumble into the water when trying to walk over a narrow log. In order to make it safer to cross a stream, several logs were placed across the stream, side by side. This made the bridge wider and easier to cross. To keep the logs from slipping apart, pieces of wood were tied or nailed across them. This type of bridge is still used across small streams in the country. It is called a *girder bridge.*

At first, bridges were anchored to the shore by sinking them into the ground or fastening them to rocks. But when there were no rocks nearby and the ground was too hard to sink a log into, something else had to be done. Logs and rocks were placed near the edge of the water, against the bank. This kept the earth from sliding into the water, and made a firm support for the ends of a bridge. Such a support is called an *abutment.* An abutment supports a bridge at its ends. Nowadays it is made of concrete or stone, instead of logs.

All bridges that go across water have some kind of abutment at each end to support them. But only bridges that go across wide rivers and streams have piers. Very few of the bridges we see about us look like the first girder bridge that was made thousands of years ago. Since the

first bridge was made, many different kinds of bridge have been built. Bridges must be strong enough to carry heavy loads, often hundreds of thousands of pounds. They must be able to stand up against high winds, and extreme changes in temperature. In order to do this, bridges are usually made of steel with a concrete or paved roadway. Different types of bridge have different ways of supporting the roadway. These types have different names. In the pictures with this article, you can see many types of bridge. The most important types will be described in the rest of this article.

Bridges are either *fixed* or *movable*. A movable bridge is one which can be opened in order to let high boats and ships pass beneath them. Bridges which do not open are called fixed briges. There are five types of fixed bridge.

INDEPENDENT SPAN BRIDGE

An independent span bridge is a fixed bridge which extends from one abutment to another without any pier to support it. The only supports for the bridge are the abutments at the ends. The span of a bridge is that part which is between two supports. An independent span bridge has a roadway supported by steel beams or trusses. Trusses are constructed in a crisscross fashion like a lot of x's next to one another. The trusses are usually above the roadway.

CONTINUOUS SPAN BRIDGE

The continuous span bridge is a fixed bridge with a long concrete roadway supported by several piers placed in the water between shores. These piers are long steel or concrete pillars or columns. They are sunk deep into the bottom of a river when the bridge is over a river. When the bridge goes across a highway, the piers rest on the highway below.

ARCH BRIDGE

The arch bridge is a fixed bridge, and is one of the oldest types of bridge in the world. It is also one of the most graceful. It was used as far back as the times of the Romans, more than two thousand years ago. It is made of steel, stone, or concrete. In concrete, steel, or stone arch bridges, the arch is underneath the roadway, and supports it from below. In some steel arch bridges, the arch rises into the air somtimes 500 feet above the water. The roadway is beneath the arch.

The George Westinghouse Memorial Bridge on the Lincoln Highway in Pittsburgh, Pennsylvania, is one of the best examples of a bridge with arches below the roadway. The Kill van Kull bridge, connecting Bayonne, New Jersey, with Staten Island, New York, is the longest arch bridge in the world. It has a steel arch above the roadway and is 1,652 feet long.

LONDON BRIDGE

In ancient times, the arch and the roadway were the same and were made of stone. They went over small bodies of water, and were usually less than 100 feet long. The Old London Bridge in England, built more than seven hundred years ago, was an arch bridge. It had towers at either end to prevent enemy soldiers from going across the bridge.

Santa Fe Ry.
Nature made this magnificent bridge in Utah, called Rainbow Bridge.

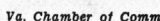
Va. Chamber of Comm.

Left: Coleman Bridge, in Virginia, is made of steel. The two parts of the bridge swing open and shut by machinery.

Port of N.Y. Authority

Below: A bridge with a steel arch and a roadway suspended from it. *Left:* Bayonne Bridge, New Jersey, the longest of this kind.

Below: A steel suspension bridge. *Left:* The George Washington bridge spans the Hudson River between New York and New Jersey.

Canadian Pac. Railway

Below: A cantilever bridge has a system of steel girders supported by steel beams. *Left:* The Quebec Bridge in Canada.

Below: A railroad trestle bridge supported by steel legs. *Left:* Chesapeake Bridge, Maryland, is of similar construction.

Bethlehem Steel Co.

Soldiers were placed in the towers to guard the bridge entrances. Homes and stores were also built on the bridge. In the middle of the thirteenth century, some of the homes caught fire and blocked both entrances to the bridge. To escape the fire about three thousand persons jumped off the bridge and were drowned.

CANTILEVER BRIDGE

The cantilever bridge is a fixed bridge with long steel arms extending outward from opposite shores. These arms or *cantilevers* are made of steel girders which support the roadway from above and below. The cantilevers rest on steel piers. The longest bridge of this type is the Quebec bridge in Canada over the St. Lawrence River. This bridge is 1,800 feet long.

SUSPENSION BRIDGE

The suspension bridge is a fixed bridge, and is the longest type of bridge in the world. It is made of long, strong, steel cables which are connected to the shore, and which rise up to high steel towers. These towers are supported by cables anchored in the banks. From the steel cables hang strong vertical steel cables which hold up the roadway of the bridge. The roadway hangs or is suspended from the cables, and this is why the bridge is called a suspension bridge. The longest suspension bridges are the Verrazano bridge over the Narrows between Brooklyn and Staten Island in New York City, with a span of 4,260 feet, and the Golden Gate bridge over the water separating the Pacific Ocean from San Francisco, California, with a span of 4,200 feet.

The largest bridge in the world is actually the Bay bridge that connects San Francisco with Oakland, California. It is a combination of suspension bridges and cantilever bridges. The entire bridge is 8 miles long. It was finished in 1936.

The George Washington bridge, spanning the Hudson River between New York and New Jersey, is another famous suspension bridge. It is 3,500 feet long.

There are three important types of movable bridge. None of these bridges is very long, the longest being about 500 feet.

SWING SPAN BRIDGE

The swing span bridge is a movable bridge with a large pier in the middle supporting it. When boats or ferries wish to pass beneath it, the bridge swings around in a semi-circle on the pier, like a swivel chair. The boats can then pass on either side of the pier through the section that the bridge previously occupied.

BASCULE BRIDGE

The bascule bridge is a movable bridge with two sections of roadway, separated at the middle and each half connected to opposite abutments. These sections are called *leaves.* The leaves can be raised straight up into the air. There is a famous painting by Vincent Van Gogh, called *The Drawbridge,* which shows an old-fashioned bascule bridge in Holland. A bascule bridge with only one section is called a drawbridge. It was used during medieval times to span moats surrounding castles. These moats were small streams that separated the castle from the surrounding land.

VERTICAL LIFT BRIDGE

The vertical lift bridge is a movable bridge which has a roadway that can be raised and lowered by an elevator at each end of the bridge. One of the most famous bridges of this type is the Buzzard's Bay bridge over the Cape Cod canal. It is 544 feet long.

MILITARY BRIDGES

When soldiers wish to cross a stream where there is no bridge, they put together a kind of floating bridge called a *pontoon* bridge. The pontoons are bags of rubber or skin filled with air so that they can float on the water. They are a kind of floating pier. Mostly, however, wooden or aluminum floats are used for heavy traffic. They are placed a few feet apart from one shore to the other. A wooden roadway is then set on them so that soldiers and equipment can be taken across.

Although such bridges are mostly used for military operations, there are a few which have been constructed for civilian traffic. The most famous is across Lake Washington, at Seattle.

The Bailey bridge, invented by Donald Coleman Bailey of England, is another type of bridge used in military operations. It can be easily put together and stretched across a stream. It is strong enough to carry heavy trucks and tanks.

bridge, a game of cards: see CONTRACT BRIDGE.

bridgehead

An army must often cross a river to attack an enemy. To do this, it must build a bridge. The engineers build the bridge, but other units of the army—the infantry and the artillery—must first control a place on both sides of the river, so that the engineers can build the bridge and the rest of the army can be safe when they cross it. A position on a river that is controlled by the attacking army is called a *bridgehead.*

Bridgeport

Bridgeport is an important manufacturing city in Connecticut, on Long Island Sound, 56 miles northeast of New York City. Bridgeport is the 2nd-largest city in Connecticut, with more than 156,000 people living there. Most of the people work in factories and plants that make more than five thousand different products. Bridgeport manufactures typewriters, sewing machines, electrical supplies, and many other useful things.

Bridgeport also has many beautiful parks and fine schools. One of the most interesting places to see there is the Barnum Institute, which is a museum filled with things that belonged to P. T. Barnum, the man who started the famous Barnum and Bailey circus. You can read about P. T. BARNUM in a separate article.

Bridgeport was settled more than three hundred years ago, and rapidly grew into a thriving town. In World War I and World War II it supplied the armed forces with guns and ammunition.

BRIDGEPORT, CONNECTICUT. Population, 156,542 (1970 census). On Long Island Sound. Settled 1639.

Bridges, Robert

Robert Bridges was an English poet. He was also a doctor, and he practiced medicine until he was 38 years old. Then he decided to spend the rest of his life writing poetry.

He was born in 1844. He went to school at Eton and to college at Oxford. His first poems were not very interesting to most people, but he later became more popular. Some of his best poems are very happy and lyrical, but others are also very difficult to understand. They are called "experimental," because in them he tried to work out new ways of writing poetry. They are also called "philosophical," because he tried to combine the ancient beliefs of religion with the new theories of science. His last poem is perhaps his greatest. It is called *The Testament of Beauty.*

Bridges became so famous before he died (in 1930), that his government made him the official POET LAUREATE, which is a very great honor that you can read about in a separate article.

brig

A brig is a small sailing ship with two masts. A two-masted ship of the same kind, but with a different arrangement of sails, is called a *brigantine.* A brig was considered a very fast ship in the days of sailing vessels, and was often used by pirates, who could use it to chase and catch the bigger ships they wanted to capture. The word *brig* is also used for a prison cell on any ship, where prisoners are kept until the ship reaches shore and they can be turned over to the police.

Bright, John

John Bright was a great English

statesman, and a Member of Parliament. He fought against many injustices that rich and powerful men forced upon poor people during his time, which was about a hundred years ago. He is best remembered in the United States because during the Civil War he was for the North and against slavery. Most people in England favored the South. Bright was born in 1811 and was a Member of Parliament from the time he was 32 years old until he was a very old man. He died in 1889, at the age of 78.

Brisbane

Brisbane is the capital city of the state of Queensland, in Australia. About 578,000 people live there, and it is one of the most important cities in Australia. It is a large manufacturing center, as well as a port. The Brisbane River runs through the city and down to the Moreton Bay, about 15 miles away. Many beautiful bridges cross the river. One of the most beautiful is the Victoria Bridge. There are also many parks and impressive government buildings in Brisbane.

When Brisbane was first settled, in 1824, it was a colony for convicts. But the colony was broken up soon after that, and Brisbane became a city about thirty years later. Brisbane is very modern, and living there is much like living in any medium-sized city of the United States.

Australian News & Inform. Bureau
The City Hall in Brisbane, Australia, has a tower 300 feet high. The palm trees show that the city has a warm climate.

bristle

Bristles are short, stiff hairs from the back of a hog, from the manes and tails of horses, or from plants. They are used in paintbrushes, toothbrushes, and many other brushes. Artificial bristles are made of nylon. The United States uses millions of brushes every year, and imports tons of bristles to make them. One reason the United States does not raise its own bristles is that pigs are slaughtered for food before the bristles are long enough. At first, we imported them from Russia, but after the revolution there, the quality

was not as good. We imported them from China after that.

The supply of bristles from China was cut off by World War II. The United States government declared bristles to be a strategic war material. The Air Force flew whatever bristles could be found in Free China over the mountains to India, then they were flown or shipped to America. But we still did not have enough. Horse hair from Argentina, plant hairs from Mexico, and nylon were used instead. After the war, the United States again imported bristles from China. The Korean war stopped this trade, so brushmakers again turned to substitutes. Shaving brushes and paintbrushes made of the finest bristles are very expensive.

Bristol

Bristol is one of the largest cities in England. It is an important port on the Avon and Frome rivers, 119 miles west of London. More than 436,000 people live there, working on the large docks and in factories. Bristol is a busy manufacturing center. It makes airplanes, chemicals, glass, and many other useful products. It is also a very old city, and you can see a cathedral there that was built eight hundred years ago. During World War II, the Germans bombed the large factories in Bristol many times, and many of its beautiful churches are still in ruins. The University of Bristol has a famous museum of English art.

Britain

The name *Britain* comes from the ancient name of the island that is now called Great Britain. The ancient name was *Britannia*, which is Latin. The Romans invaded the island in 55 and 54 B.C., and called it Britannia. Although the native British princes resisted bravely, the stronger Romans eventually succeeded in conquering the island. British culture was far behind that of Rome, but the Romans soon established their culture in the conquered land. The ruins of Roman roads, baths, altars, and houses can still be seen in many parts of England today. Christianity was also introduced by the Romans. Before that time the people had practiced Druidism. This pagan religion is explained in the article on DRUIDS. You can read more about the history of Britain in the articles on ENGLAND, SCOTLAND, IRELAND, and WALES, in other volumes of this encyclopedia.

British Columbia

British Columbia is the westernmost province of Canada. It is covered with great mountain ranges, and its beautiful scenery has made it a popular place for people to go on their vacations. British Columbia is the third-largest Canadian province, having 366,255 square miles, which is more than twice the size of California. In population it also ranks third in Canada, estimated in 1967 to be nearly two million. The province was given its name by Queen Victoria of England. It became a province in 1871. The capital is Victoria.

THE PEOPLE OF BRITISH COLUMBIA

The early settlers of British Columbia came from Great Britain, the United States, and other parts of Canada, to seek their fortunes. Others came from Europe, especially from Germany, France, and the Scandinavian countries. Today, most of the people are Canadian-born. There are about 25,000 Indians living there. Once the Indians were the only people living in British Columbia.

The people work in many thriving industries. More than half the British Columbians live in the cities, working in large saw mills, fish canneries, and in factories making wood and lumber products. Others cut timber in the great northern forests. Many are farmers and raise poultry, fruits and vegetables, and cattle. Still others work in the rich mines. The miners produce almost all the lead in Canada, and more than half the zinc. British Columbia ranks third among the provinces of Canada in the production of copper, gold, and coal.

The Anglican or Episcopal church is the largest church in British Columbia, but there are also United Church of Canada, Roman Catholic, and Presbyterian churches.

WHAT BRITISH COLUMBIA IS LIKE

British Columbia is very mountainous. The Canadian Rockies and the Coast Range and Cascades run through it. There are many towering peaks, vast forests, beautiful waterfalls, and swift rivers, including the Fraser, Columbia, and Peace rivers. Many tourists go to British Columbia to hunt moose, deer, and bears, which are found there. They also fish for salmon, which are caught in large quantities.

In the northeastern part there is a fertile plain where much farming is done.

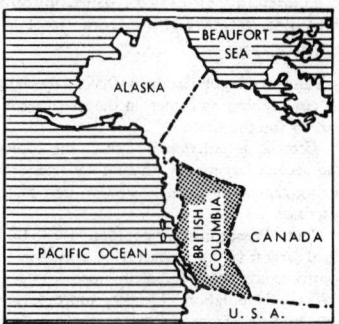

There are also irrigated sections in the central and southern parts where the people raise cattle and crops. Off the southwestern coast of British Columbia is Vancouver Island, which is rich in coal. Victoria, the capital city, is on the island and is an important industrial center. It is one of the busiest ports on the Pacific Coast. The Queen Charlotte Islands are also off the coast of British Columbia.

British Columbia has a warmer climate than any other Canadian province. This is because of the warm winds from the Pacific Ocean. At Victoria, on Vancouver Island, the temperature in summer is about 65 degrees; in winter, about 37 degrees. Flowers bloom there all year round. In the north, however, the climate is much more severe, falling way below zero in winter, and becoming very

hot in the summer. There is a great deal of rain in the western part of the province, but little in the central or eastern regions.

There are railroads throughout most of British Columbia, and the rivers are an important means of transportation. There are also airports in most of the large cities. The Alaska Highway was built across the northeastern section in 1942.

HOW THE PEOPLE ARE GOVERNED

The head of the government of British Columbia is a lieutenant governor, who represents the British Queen. He is appointed by the Canadian federal government. The province is actually run by a premier. He is usually the leader of the political party which elects the most members of the legislature. The premier is assisted by an executive council or cabinet that he selects from among his supporters in the legislature. The premier and his executive council stay in office as long as they can keep the confidence of the majority of the legislature. The legislature is elected for a five-year term. Judges are appointed by the Canadian government in Ottawa, and hold office for life. The provincial government is in the capital, Victoria.

Everyone has to go to school between the ages of 7 and 15. Those children who cannot attend school can get instruction through the mail. Printed lessons are sent to them at home. The children study the lessons and answer the questions. Then they send them back for correction. There is one university, the University of British Columbia, at Vancouver. In 1961 it had 11,621 students. There are four affiliated colleges in various cities with a total enrollment of 1,073.

CHIEF CITIES IN BRITISH COLUMBIA

The leading cities of British Columbia, with population figures from the 1967 estimate, are:

Vancouver, population 410,375, the largest city, a shipping center, in the southwestern part of the province.

Victoria, population 175,000, the capital and second-largest city, trading and manufacturing center, in the southwestern part of the province.

New Westminster, population 38,000, third-largest city, manufacturing center, in the southwestern part of the province.

Trail, population 11,600, fourth-largest city, mining center, in the southern part of the province.

BRITISH COLUMBIA IN THE PAST

When Captain James Cook and his men landed on Vancouver Island more than 175 years ago, they found friendly Indians living there. They exchanged blankets and other articles for furs, and a flourishing British fur trade began at Nootka. However, the Spanish claimed that this part of the coast belonged to them, and they took possession of Nootka in 1789. This almost brought about a war between Great Britain and Spain, but it was finally settled peacefully, and both countries were given equal rights to trade there.

Other trading posts were started by Canadians and men from the United States, and settlers began to come to this region. Arguments sprang up between the British and Americans about who had the right to this territory. Many Americans felt that the United States had the right to the western coast of Canada up to the line on the map marked 54 degrees 40 minutes latitude. The cry in the United States was "54–40 or fight." However, the matter was settled peacefully. In 1846 the boundary between British Columbia and the Oregon Territory was fixed, and British Columbia became a British possession.

Very few settlers came to this territory until gold was discovered in 1858. Then people began rushing to British Columbia to seek their fortunes. The population grew so quickly that it became a British colony in the same year. Vancouver Island was joined to it eight years later, and in 1871 it became a province. However, British Columbia agreed to become a province only on condition that the Canadian government would build a railroad to the Pacific coast. It was very difficult to build the railroad, because of the high mountains, but finally it was completed in 1885.

More people now came to the province, and its mining and lumber industries grew rapidly. British Columbia also became important for its salmon fisheries. Trade flourished and cities grew. In World War II, the province supplied many valuable products to the war effort. Today British Columbia ships products from its mines, factories, and farms to places all over the world.

PLACES TO SEE

Glacier National Park, 521 square miles, in southeastern British Columbia, in the Selkirk Mountains, west of State Highway 95. Snow-capped peaks and glaciers; contains Nakimu Caves and Mt. Bonney, 10,194 feet high.

Kootenay National Park, 543 square miles, in southeastern British Columbia, in the Canadian Rockies, on State Highway 1B. Forests and deep canyons, including Marble Canyon.

Mount Revelstoke National Park, 100 square miles, in southeastern British Columbia, in the Selkirk Mountains, on State Highway 1. Large forest of virgin timber.

Yoho National Park, 507 square miles, in eastern British Columbia, in the Canadian Rockies, on State Highway 1. Waterfalls and lakes, including Emerald Lake; Mt. Gordon, 10,346 feet high.

Mount Fairweather, in the northwest, on the boundary between British Columbia and Alaska. The highest point in the province, 15,318 feet high; slopes covered with glaciers.

Water Route from Vancouver to Alaska, off the west coast of British Columbia. One of the most beautiful boat trips in the world.

[British] Commonwealth

The Commonwealth is the official name for a large group of nations that coöperate in trade and financial matters. It was formerly called the Commonwealth of Nations, and most people call it the British Commonwealth because its members were once part of the British Empire.

Members of the Commonwealth are independent nations, but the Commonwealth also includes *dependencies*. A dependency usually governs itself locally but in some matters is controlled by one of the independent nations.

The Commonwealth is a vast thing, covering one-fourth of all the land and also one-fourth of all the people on earth.

By 1973, thirty-two nations were members of the British Commonwealth:

1. Australia	17. Malaysia
2. Bangla Desh	18. Malta
3. Barbados	19. Mauritius
4. Botswana	20. Nauru
5. Britain	21. New Zealand
6. Canada	22. Nigeria
7. Cyprus	23. Sierra Leone
8. Fiji	24. Singapore
9. Gambia	25. Sri Lanka (Ceylon)
10. Ghana	26. Swaziland
11. Guyana	27. Tanzania
12. India	28. Tonga
13. Jamaica	29. Trinidad and Tobago
14. Kenya	30. Uganda
15. Lesotho	31. Western Samoa
16. Malawi	32. Zambia

The British queen (or king) is the head of the Commonwealth. She is the head of the state in the member nations of which she is queen, but except in the United Kingdom she is represented in each of these nations by a Governor General selected by the country's government. The position of the Queen or Governor General is called "the Crown." The parliament of each country has all the actual power and the Crown must be neutral in politics, but the Crown can often have great influence as an impartial and respected guide when the country's political leaders cannot agree.

DEPENDENCIES

There are several kinds of dependency, and since most of the dependencies within the Commonwealth are those of the United Kingdom, it is easiest to describe the British dependencies first.

A *Crown Colony* is a possession, just like part of the home country. In a *Protectorate* the British government has considerable power. A *Protected State* has made a treaty giving the British government certain rights, especially in foreign affairs and in wartime. A *Trust Territory* is administered (governed) by the British or other Commonwealth nation but under the rules agreed upon with the United Nations.

United Kingdom dependencies are:

1. ANTIGUA—territory with two dependencies: 1) Barbuda
2) Redonda
2. ASHMORE and CARTIER ISLANDS—dependencies of Australia
3. AUSTRALIAN ANTARCTIC TERRITORY—dependency of Australia
4. BAHAMAS—colony
5. BERMUDA—colony
6. BRITISH ANTARCTIC TERRITORY—colony
7. BRITISH HONDURAS—colony
8. BRITISH INDIAN OCEAN TERRITORY—colony (includes the Chagos Archipelago, Aldabra Islands, Farquhar Islands, and Desroches Islands)
9. BRITISH SOLOMON ISLANDS—protectorate
10. BRITISH VIRGIN ISLANDS—colony
11. BRUNEI—protected state
12. CAYMAN ISLANDS—colony
13. CHRISTMAS ISLAND—dependency of Australia
14. COCOS ISLANDS—dependency of Australia
15. COOK ISLANDS—dependency of New Zealand
16. CORAL SEA ISLANDS—dependency of Australia
17. DOMINICA—territory
18. FALKLAND ISLANDS—colony with two dependencies: 1) Santa Georgia Island
2) South Sandwich Islands
19. GIBRALTAR—territory
20. GILBERT and ELLICE ISLANDS—colony
21. GRENADA—territory
22. HEARD ISLANDS and McDONALD ISLANDS—dependency of Australia
23. HONG KONG—colony
24. MONTSERRAT—colony
25. NEW HEBRIDES—Anglo-French condominium
26. NIUE (SAVAGE ISLAND)—depen-

dency of New Zealand
27. NORFOLK ISLAND—dependency of Australia
28. PAPUA and NEW GUINEA—territory of Australia, and U. N. trust territory
29. PITCAIRN ISLAND—colony
30. ROSS DEPENDENCY—dependency of New Zealand
31. SEYCHELLES—colony
32. SIKKIM—protected state of India
33. ST. HELENA—colony with two dependencies: 1) Ascension Island
    2) Tristan da Cunha
34. ST. KITTS-NEVIS-ANGUILLA—territory
35. ST. LUCIA—territory
36. ST. VINCENT—territory
37. TOKELAU (UNION) ISLANDS—dependency of New Zealand
38. TURKS and CAICOS ISLANDS — colony

British Empire was the name given to the part of the world ruled by Britain before the formation of the Commonwealth. See BRITISH COMMONWEALTH.

British Guiana (Guyana)

Guyana, formerly called British Guiana, became an independent member of the British Commonwealth in 1966. In 1970 it became a republic. It is on the Atlantic coast of South America between Surinam and Venezuela. 90% of the people live along this coast, where the capital, Georgetown, is located. The area of Guyana is about 83,000 square miles and the population in 1973 was about 740,000. More than half the people are of East Indian descent; about a third are of African origin. There are about 9,000 Europeans (mostly Portuguese), and the rest are Chinese, native Indian, and mixed races. English is the official language, but Urdu, Tamil, and various dialects are also spoken. Most of the people are farmers who raise sugar, coffee, and rice. Bauxite, gold, and diamonds are mined. The climate is very hot and damp, and in the interior jungles only savages live.

British Honduras (Belize)

British Honduras is a colony in Central America that belongs to Great Britain. In 1973, its name was changed to Belize. It is on the Caribbean Sea, east of Guatemala. It is 8,867 square miles in size, and more than 130,000 people live there. Most of the people are blacks and American Indians, and they grow bananas, sugar, and fruits. Parts of British Honduras are low and fertile, and much of it is covered with forests of valuable mahogany and log-

wood. Off the swampy coast there are dangerous reefs.

The climate is hot and damp; often the temperature goes over 100 degrees. The British have ruled British Honduras since 1783. Belize, the capital, is the largest city and most important seaport. About 33,000 people live in Belize.

British Isles

The British Isles lie northwest of France, a few miles off the mainland of Europe. There are many small islands in the group, but the two chief islands are Ireland and Great Britain. The island of Great Britain includes England, Scotland, and Wales. The island of Ireland contains the Irish Republic, also called Eire, in southern Ireland, and Northern Ireland. Northern Ireland is part of the United Kingdom. You can read more about the countries and divisions of the British Isles in the article about each one in this encyclopedia.

There are several smaller island groups surrounding the British Isles, and they are all associated with the United Kingdom. The Channel Islands are between England and France, in the English Channel. These are the islands of Alderney, Guernsey, and Jersey. The Scilly Islands are southwest of the southwest tip of England. In the Irish Sea, between England and Ireland, is the Isle of Man. Off the northwest coast of Scotland are the Outer Hebrides, Skye, and Mull. To the north and east of Scotland are the Orkneys, and still farther to the northeast are the Shetland Islands.

British Museum

The British Museum in London, England, is one of the biggest, best, and most famous museums in the world. It is the official place where the British government collects treasures of art, literature, and science. These treasures include printed books and manuscripts (which are books that are written by hand), drawings and printed drawings of all kinds, old coins, medals, and statues. However, there are not many paintings.

In 1753 the British Parliament passed a special law establishing the British Museum. For many years the Museum was made up mostly of books and art objects that had been given by King George II and other private collectors. These were kept in Montague House. One part of the present building was begun in 1829. But the central part, which is the reading room of the library, was only completed

in 1857. It is a great circular room many stories high with an enormous glass-domed roof.

The book collection is one of the largest in the world. There are more than six million books. These include a copy of almost every book printed in the English language. The library gets more than fifty thousand new books every year. Many of these books are received free, because the copyright law in England requires publishers to give the library a copy of every new book.

The museum also owns some of the most famous art treasures in the world. There are the ELGIN MARBLES from ancient Greece, and the ROSETTA STONE from Egypt. (You can read about these treasures in separate articles.) Admission is free to the whole museum, but whoever wants to read the books in the library must first get special permission.

Brittany

Brittany is a section in the northwest part of France. Its French name is *Bretagne*. Many English (British) people moved to this part of France about 1,500 years ago, and that is how it got its name. The country is very beautiful, with many rough hills, and rich, fertile valleys. The people of Brittany are not like the rest of the French people. They even speak a different kind of French. It has many words that were once a part of the Old English or Anglo-Saxon that was spoken by the British settlers there. The costumes of the "Bretons," or people who live in Brittany, are quaint and old-fashioned. In some country districts, people look almost the same as their ancestors looked three and four hundred years ago. They kept their old ways and customs longer than the people of any other part of France. Breton fishermen have been famous sailors; one of them was Jacques Cartier, the great explorer.

Brno

Brno, or Brünn, is a city in Czechoslovakia. It is on the Svartka and Svitavy rivers, at the foot of Mt. Spielberg. At the top of the mountain is a castle that is nine hundred years old. More than 306,000 people live in this old city. They work in factories, making woolen goods, leather, machinery, and many other products. Brno is the capital of the province of Moravia, which became part of Czechoslovakia after World War I. In World War II, the Germans captured the city, but it was retaken by the Russian army in 1945.

broadcasting, sending out radio programs from a transmitting station: see RADIO.

Broadway

Broadway is the main street in New York City. More than three hundred years ago, when the city was founded by the Dutch, Broadway was only a cowpath that ran through the "boueries," or farms, at the lower part of the island of Manhattan. But as the city grew, more fine houses were built along Broadway than any other street. Broadway got longer, too—so long, in fact, that it is sometimes called the longest street in the world. It ends officially where it

crosses the city limits at 263rd Street, but it really goes the whole way north to the city of Albany, 150 miles away. There are only two other longer streets in the world. One is the Appian Way in Italy and the other is Watling Street in England. But both of these are very ancient Roman highways, and neither is a modern street like Broadway.

Broadway today is mostly a business or commercial street, and very few of the beautiful old houses remain. Downtown, however, there are several fine old churches, including St. Paul's Chapel, which is the oldest church building in New York. Broadway also crosses Wall Street, which is the financial center of the country. Farther uptown, Broadway runs through the clothing manufacturing district until it comes to 42nd Street and Times Square.

This section is the theater district known as the "Great White Way," because there are so many big electric signs. The theaters themselves are no longer on Broadway, as they used to be. They are on the nearby side streets. Broadway is lined with big movie houses, restaurants, and nightclubs that are visited more by tourists than by native New Yorkers. However, New Yorkers still think affectionately of Broadway, especially when they are away from home. A famous New Yorker named George M. Cohan once wrote a popular song about Broadway in which he "sent his regards" to the street!

Throughout the United States and the world, people often speak of "Broadway" to mean the entire New York theatrical business.

brocade

Brocade is a cloth, usually made of silk, that has rich, colorful designs woven into it or embroidered on it so as to make a raised pattern. The raised design may be of silk, silver, or gold threads. People have been making brocade for more than two thousand years. The damask used today in the finest tablecloths and napkins is a kind of brocade. Until about a hundred years ago, all brocades were made by hand. Then the invention of a special loom, called a Jacquard loom, made it possible to weave complicated designs by machine.

broccoli

Broccoli is a popular vegetable that is closely related to cauliflower. It looks like a small, dark green bush, with a stalk one to two feet high. It has many short branches, each ending in a cluster of little flower-buds surrounded by leaves. When broccoli is ready to be eaten, these tiny buds are green. If the plant is left in the garden, the buds turn yellow and coarse.

Broccoli was brought to the rest of Europe and to America from Italy. Its name in Italian means "little sprouts."

Brock, Sir Isaac

Sir Isaac Brock was a British general who won the title "hero of upper Canada" for his defeat of the United States forces

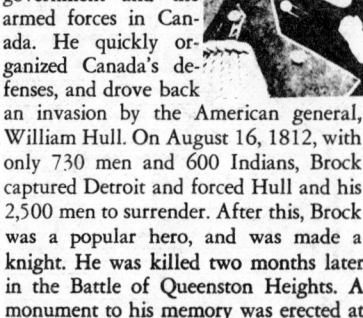

at Detroit, during the War of 1812. When this war between England and the United States broke out, Brock was in charge of the government and the armed forces in Canada. He quickly organized Canada's defenses, and drove back an invasion by the American general, William Hull. On August 16, 1812, with only 730 men and 600 Indians, Brock captured Detroit and forced Hull and his 2,500 men to surrender. After this, Brock was a popular hero, and was made a knight. He was killed two months later in the Battle of Queenston Heights. A monument to his memory was erected at Queenston, and the battlefield is now a public park.

Brodie, Steve

Steve Brodie was a saloon-keeper in New York City. He was not an important man at all, and the only reason he is remembered is that in 1886 he said he had jumped from the Brooklyn Bridge into the East River. The Brooklyn Bridge is 140 feet above the river. Very few people believe that Steve Brodie actually made this jump, but taking a big chance on something is still called "pulling a brodie."

broker, a person who buys and sells stocks and bonds, or grain or cotton, or real estate or insurance, or a number of other things, for his customers and not for himself. He charges his customers a *brokerage fee* for his work. See COMMODITY EXCHANGE and STOCK EXCHANGE.

Bromfield, Louis

Louis Bromfield is the name of an American novelist who was born in Mansfield, Ohio, in 1896. He attended Columbia University, but gave up his studies during World War I in order to serve with an American ambulance corps attached to the French Army. He lived in France for a long time after the war, but in 1939 returned to America to live on a farm near the town where he was born. One of his greatest interests was farming and country life. His first novel and one of his most famous is called *The Green Bay Tree*. He died in 1956.

bromine and bromide

Bromine is a chemical that has many uses. It is a dark brown liquid, but when left standing in a room it turns into a red gas. It smells very bad, and is dangerous because as a liquid it will burn your skin if you touch it, and as a gas it will make your eyes water and give you a sore throat. However it is useful in making certain dyes and drugs. Bromine can be made from salt water by the process called ELECTROLYSIS, about which there is a separate article. Almost all the bromine used now is used in the making of the "ethyl fluid" that is added to gasoline.

The drugs made from bromine are called *bromides.* A bromide is a mixture of bromine with a metal, such as silver, calcium, mercury, sodium, or potassium. A bromide tastes like salt. Most of the drugs that are bromides are used to quiet

people's nerves, to put them to sleep, or in some cases to make them stop vomiting. Bromides should never be taken unless they are prescribed by a doctor. Too many of them can cause skin irritations or extreme weakness.

bronchi

The bronchi are two tubes in your body. They carry air from the back of your throat into your lungs.

The main tube from your lungs to your chest is the *trachea.* The trachea divides into two tubes, one for each lung, and these tubes are the bronchi. The bronchi divide again into many tiny tubes called *bronchioles.* The whole structure looks like a tree with many branches, and so is called the *bronchial tree.*

The inside of the bronchial tree is kept comfortably moist by a thin fluid. That is why breathing is such a pleasant and easy thing to do when we are well. Sometimes germs get into the bronchial tree and this fluid gets thickened and makes us uncomfortable. It might even stop up some of the little tubes, and make breathing difficult. This is called *bronchitis,* and without medicine it can get worse and last a long time. In order to get rid of this thickened fluid, the lungs squeeze violently and suddenly, hoping to throw this thickened material up into the throat. That sudden movement is called a cough.

Bronchitis usually starts with what seems to be a simple cold. Also, smoking can irritate the bronchi, and this can start a chronic (lasting) bronchitis. Workers who have to breathe in a lot of dust also have trouble in the bronchial tree. Nowadays people who work in certain trades wear masks over their mouths and noses to filter out the harmful dust or fumes.

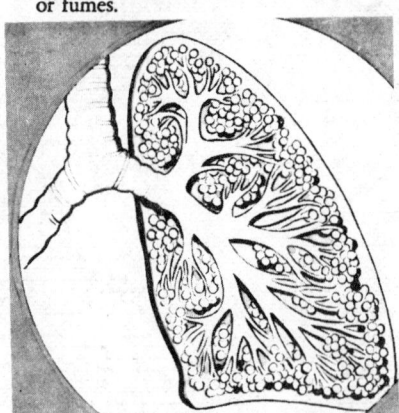

Copyright Curriculum Films, Inc.
The smallest bronchial tubes in your lungs end in tiny bags called air sacs, which fill with air when you breathe in.

Brontë

There were three famous sisters named Brontë. Their names were Charlotte, Emily, and Anne, and they were all writers. They lived in England about a hundred years ago. They were daughters of a clergyman, and had two older sisters and a brother. They went to a very strict school when they were girls, and later they became teachers and governesses. Charlotte's most famous novel was

Charlotte Brontë

Jane Eyre, a story of some of her experiences in school and as a governess. Emily wrote *Wuthering Heights,* a tragic love story that describes the countryside and moors in which the girls were brought up. Anne wrote two good novels, *Agnes Grey* and *The Tenant of Wildfell Hall,* but neither was as great as her sisters.' All the sisters wrote under "pen-names," calling themselves Currer, Ellis and Acton Bell, and for a long time not even their publishers knew who they really were. Charlotte, Emily and Anne all died of tuberculosis at an early age.

Charlotte Brontë was born in 1816 and died in 1855. She was the only sister who married and she lived longest, though she was only 39 when she died. Emily, born in 1818, died in 1848, when she was barely 30, and Anne, born in 1820, died in 1849, aged 29. Their brother Branwell Brontë, whom they loved and admired very much, was born in 1817 and died in 1848.

brontosaurus

The brontosaurus was a huge dinosaur that lived about 130 million years ago. It weighed about 30 tons, and walked on all four feet. Its footprint covered one square yard of ground. It had a thick body, a long neck and tail, and a very small head. Its great weight and its small brain show that it was a slow-moving beast, with not much intelligence. The brontosaurus was a reptile, related to the lizard. It ate plants and spent much of its life in the water. The bones of the brontosaurus have been found in the United States, in Wyoming and other western states.

Bronx

The Bronx is one of the boroughs of New York City. It lies between the East River and Long Island Sound. Nearly one and a half million people live there. Most of the people do not work in the Bronx, but travel by subway and automobile to offices and factories in the borough of MANHATTAN, about which there is a separate article. Most of the people live in large apartment houses, though in the northern part of the Bronx people own large homes.

Attractions in the Bronx include the huge Yankee Stadium, which is the home of the New York Yankees, and one of the world's finest collections of wild animals at the Bronx Zoo. There are many fine parks and universities, and people have called the Bronx "the borough of universities." Among the more famous are Fordham University, one of the largest Catholic universities in the United States, and New York University with its Hall of Fame for great Americans. Another interesting place is Poe Cottage, the house where the noted author Edgar Allan Poe lived and wrote some of his poems.

The first settler of the Bronx was Jonas Bronck, from whom the borough gets its name. For a very long time the Bronx was made up of large farms, and seventy-five years ago a trip to the Bronx was like taking a trip out into the country. Today, more people live there than in most cities of the world. The Bronx became part of New York City in 1898.

BRONX, NEW YORK. Population, 1,472,-216 (1970 census). On the East River and Long Island Sound; settled in 1641.

bronze

Bronze is an "alloy," or mixture, of copper and tin that is used for making statues, church bells, and medals. Bronze is also made by mixing copper and other metals, such as aluminum and nickel, and this is used in machinery, telephone wires, and nuts and bolts. Bronze is a dark, rich, golden brown in color. Men have used it since ancient times to make weapons, household articles, and monuments. In the Middle Ages, about six hundred years ago, it was used to make the great bells and doors of cathedrals. Today, many artists still use bronze for making statues because it is lighter than stone, and it lasts longer than wood. When bronze stands out-of-doors for a long time, it becomes discolored with patches of green, blue, or black. This is called verdigris.

Bronze Age

Bronze Age is the name of a period in history when man first learned to use metals, and to make tools and weapons of them. See the articles on AGE and ARCHAEOLOGY in other volumes of this encyclopedia.

Brook Farm

Brook Farm was a famous community in West Roxbury, Massachusetts, more than a hundred years ago. The small group of people from New England who started Brook Farm hoped that it would become an ideal place, where everybody could live and work together in harmony. Everyone was to share the farm work, and also have time to read and study. Brook Farm was started in 1841 by George Ripley and his wife, and many important people joined them. The most famous was the American novelist Nathaniel Hawthorne. The community lasted for only six years. Some people found the farm work too difficult, and some did not get along so well with the others. Brook Farm was finally given up, but it is remembered as a place where people honestly tried to live cooperatively. Many other cooperative communities like Brook Farm were established in the United States, but few of them succeeded.

Brooklyn

Brooklyn is one of the five boroughs of New York City. It is on New York Bay and the East River at the west end of Long Island. It has the largest population of all the five boroughs of New York with almost three million people living there. Many of them work in factories that make shoes, chemicals, and paints. Others work in the shops and department stores. Still others travel by subway and automobile across the East River to offices and factories in the borough of Manhattan. (There is a separate article about MANHATTAN.) Brooklyn is connected with Manhattan by three large bridges. The most famous is Brooklyn Bridge, which was opened in 1883.

Brooklyn is a borough of homes and churches. People have called it "the city of Churches," and one of the most famous

is Plymouth Church, where Henry Ward Beecher preached for forty years. Also in Brooklyn is Prospect Park, one of the most beautiful parks in the United States. On the southern shore of Brooklyn is Coney Island, the most famous amusement park and beach in the country. On a hot summer day, there are more than one million people on Coney Island's beach and boardwalk. Brooklyn also has several colleges and universities. Brooklyn College has an enrollment of more than 27,500 students.

Brooklyn is a very old region. It was settled more than three hundred years ago by the Dutch, and later by the English. During the American Revolution, General Washington fought the battle of Long Island where Prospect Park now stands. Until 1898, Brooklyn was a separate city. Then it became part of New York City.

BROOKLYN, NEW YORK. Population, (1970 census) 2,601,852. Settled in 1636.

Brooks, Phillips

Phillips Brooks was a very famous minister in the Protestant Episcopal Church. He was born in 1835 in Boston, Massachusetts. He graduated from Harvard College, then studied for the ministry at Alexandria, Virginia. He was for many years the rector at Trinity Church in Boston, a very beautiful church that was built especially for him. He wrote many books on religious subjects, and also wrote the beautiful Christmas hymn, *O Little Town of Bethlehem.* Phillips Brooks was made Bishop of Massachusetts in 1891, two years before his death.

broom

A broom is a brush that is used for sweeping dust or dirt off surfaces. Brooms usually have long handles, which make them easier to use. Most of the brooms we use are made of the stalks of a plant called *broomcorn,* that grows in the Middle West. Cattle eat the flowers of the broomcorn, and the stalks are used for broom-making. The stalks are tied together at the top, so that the broom is shaped like a cone. Then it is put in a vise, and flattened out by being squeezed.

In early days, people used a broom called a *besom.* It was made of the stalks of a plant called *broom* that grows in England and Europe. The broom plant has very short leaves and bright flowers. It grows in sandy soil where other plants cannot grow. It is a wildflower, and is very hardy.

Brown, John

John Brown was a man who lived more than 100 years ago, when Negroes were slaves in the southern states of the United States. He hated slavery and finally gave his life and the lives of his sons in trying to do away with it. Brown was born in New England in 1800, but spent most of his life in the West. In Kansas, he kept a station on the "underground railroad," which was not a real railroad but a secret method of getting Negroes north into Canada where they could be free. John Brown and his sons fought the men who wished to have slavery in Kansas. One night he killed five such men at Pottawatomie. Several months later, he

made a heroic stand against pro-slavery forces at Osawatomie, and from then on he was called "Old Brown of Osawatomie."

Then John Brown had a plan to free the slaves: give them guns and ammunition and let them fight to free themselves. He rented a farm near the town of Harper's Ferry, in the part of Virginia that is now the state of West Virginia. The night of October 16, 1859 (less than two years before the Civil War began) Brown led a party of his sons and friends and captured the arsenal (a kind of fort) at Harper's Ferry. The slaves did not revolt and a company of Marines led by Robert E. LEE (later a Confederate General) killed or captured Brown's whole party.

While the entire nation shook with excitement, John Brown was convicted of treason and hanged at Charles Town (not at Charleston, the capital of West Virginia) near Harper's Ferry on December 2, 1859. In the trial he defended himself calmly and walked bravely to the scaffold to be hanged. His name became a watchword to anti-slavery forces and in the Civil War the Union soldiers marched to the song "John Brown's body lies a-molderin' in the grave . . . "

Browning

Robert Browning and Elizabeth Barrett Browning were English poets who lived about a hundred years ago. They are remembered almost as much for the true love story that led to their marriage as for the great poetry they wrote.

Robert Browning was born in 1812, of a rich family. He became a successful poet and playwright while he was still in his twenties. Elizabeth Barrett was born in 1806, so she was six years older. From girlhood she was an invalid, so she could not go out, and her very strict family did not let her meet men she might marry. She too wrote poetry and had it published while she was in her twenties.

In the years 1841 to 1846 Browning wrote some of his best poems and plays, published under the title *Bells and Pomegranates.* In 1845 Elizabeth Barrett wrote him a letter praising them and he called to see her. They fell in love and, defying the strong opposition of Elizabeth Barrett's father, they were married in 1846. They lived together happily, chiefly

Robert Browning   Elizabeth Barrett

in Italy, until Mrs. Browning died in 1861. Browning lived much longer, dying in 1889.

Mrs. Browning's most famous poems are a series of love poems, *Sonnets from the Portuguese,* which she wrote to her husband. (She was nicknamed "the Portuguese" because she was very dark in coloring.) Browning wrote many famous poems and is now generally considered

the greatest of the Victorian poets, those who wrote during the reign of Queen Victoria of England.

Bruce, Robert

King Robert I of Scotland is also called Robert Bruce, or Robert the Bruce. He lived more than 600 years

ago, but he is still famous because he was one of the Scottish leaders who would not let their country be made part of England. Robert Bruce was born in the year 1274. As a young man he was the Earl of Carrick and supported the English king, Edward I. In 1306 he became king of Scotland, and he carried on constant warfare with England to make them allow Scotland to be independent. He won a great battle over the English in the Battle of Bannockburn, in 1314. At other times the English were winning and he had to hide. On one of these times, according to an old story, he was hiding in Ireland and had almost given up hope of beating the English. He had tried and failed six times. Then he happened to notice a spider trying to spin a web on the ceiling over his head. Six times the spider tried and failed. But the spider tried a seventh time and succeeded. Bruce decided that he too should try a seventh time. He went back to Scotland and led another army against the English. This time he was successful, and in 1328 the English recognized Scottish independence. Less than two years later, in 1329, Robert Bruce died. He is buried at Dunfermline, in Scotland.

Brueghel, another spelling for the name BREUGHEL.

Brummell, Beau

"Beau" Brummell was an Englishman who lived about 150 years ago, and who did much to create the style of men's clothing that is still followed. His real name was George Bryan Brummell and he was born in 1778. He was neither a nobleman nor a rich man, but he went to the best English schools—Eton and Oxford—and made friends with many important people. These included the Prince of Wales, who later became King George IV. At that time men's clothes were changing greatly. The old style had been knee-breeches, very frilly shirts, and bright-colored coats. Young men who were fashion leaders were called *beaus,* or *dandies.* Beau Brummell became the prince's adviser on correct dress. He favored styles that were not too fancy, and he taught many good habits, such as daily baths. Later, Beau Brummell quarreled with the prince and went to France, where he lived in poverty. He died in a charity hospital in 1840, when he was 62 years old.

Brunswick

Brunswick is a district of about 1,400 square miles in West Germany. It is a rich district, with copper, lead and iron mines, fertile farms where cattle, fruits and vegetables are raised, and several manufacturing cities. The German name is Braunschweig. In former

times Brunswick was an independent duchy, ruled by a royal duke, and after World War I it became a state in the German Republic. After being in the British zone of occupation following World War II, it became part of the new German state of Lower Saxony.

Brunswick is also the name of the principal city of the district and the former capital. The city is more than a thousand years old and has been an important trading center for centuries. Now it is a manufacturing city where canned goods, cameras, clothing and machinery are made. Many of the historic buildings and monuments were destroyed by bombs in World War II, but some remain.

BRUNSWICK, GERMANY. District, area, 1,379 square miles; population 782,950. City, population 225,168.

Brussels

Brussels is the capital of Belgium and is one of the richest and most beautiful cities of Europe. It is in the central part of the country, on the Senne River, which carries shipping to the sea through Antwerp, 27 miles to the north. More than 1,000,000 people live in Brussels.

Though Brussels has been a famous city for hundreds of years, in 1958 it became better known than ever to the rest of the world by holding a great world's fair, called the Brussels Universal and International Exposition. Fifty nations built displays of their national life and products at the exposition. The United States pavilion, which cost about $12,-500,000, was one of the most popular with the 35,000,000 tourists who visited Brussels to see the exposition. (See the article WORLD'S FAIR.) The Belgian government spent $300,000,000 on the exposition and an additional $400,000,-000 was spent on improvements and modernizations in Brussels.

Brussels is a great manufacturing city. It is famous for carpets and lace, but there are many other important products, including cotton and woolen goods, automobiles, and bicycles. Most of the people speak French but many speak Dutch.

Most of Brussels is modern, but some parts are very old, with narrow, winding streets and churches and houses that are more than 500 years old. In the modern part there are fine hotels and shops, the royal palace where the Belgian king lives, the government buildings, and the University of Brussels. Brussels has been called "the Little Paris" because it resembles the French capital.

Brussels was founded more than 900 years ago. It was an important commercial city in the Middle Ages and has been the capital of its region for more than 500 years. In 1830, when Belgium became independent, Brussels was made the capital. One of history's most famous battles was fought at Waterloo, a few miles to the south. In both World Wars the Germans captured and occupied Brussels but little damage was done to it.

BRUSSELS, BELGIUM. Population 170,409; with suburbs, 1,071,194. Capital of Belgium.

Brussels sprouts

Brussels sprouts look like tiny cabbages, only an inch or so thick instead of seven or eight inches. They are members of the same family of plants as cabbage, but they are not the same plant. Brussels sprouts are really buds that

grow close together on a thick stem that is usually 2 or 3 feet high. They start to appear as little buttons at the bottom of the stem; then more buds, or sprouts, come out all the way up the stem. Each stem grows about a quart of sprouts. They can be picked all fall, since frost improves their flavor. Brussels sprouts get their name from the city of Brussels, the capital of Belgium, where they were grown and sold more than seven hundred years ago.

Brutus, Marcus Junius

Marcus Junius Brutus was a statesman and general in Rome two thousand years ago, when it was the greatest nation on earth. We remember him best because he was one of the group of Roman senators who killed the Roman leader, Julius Caesar, on March 15, in the year 44 B.C. Before that, Brutus had been considered one of Caesar's best friends, but his group had decided to kill Caesar because they thought he was trying to make himself the emperor of Rome. In one of William Shakespeare's best-known plays, *Julius Caesar,* it is to Brutus that Caesar speaks his last sad words, when Brutus stabs him: "You too, Brutus!"

Brutus was born in 85 B.C. There was a civil war in Rome in 49 B.C., and Brutus fought for Pompey, the general who was Caesar's rival; but Caesar won, and Brutus then joined his side. After Caesar's death, Brutus fought against Mark ANTONY and Octavian, who later became the emperor AUGUSTUS (there are separate articles about both these men). Brutus lost to them in a great battle at Philippi, in Greece, in 42 B.C. When he saw that he had lost the battle, he killed himself by falling on his sword. Brutus was the name of a great family in Rome, and several of Marcus Brutus's ancestors were also famous men.

Bryan, William Jennings

William Jennings Bryan was one of the most famous public figures of the United States in the years from 1896 to 1925. Three times he was the Democratic candidate for president, in 1896, 1900, and 1908, but each time he was beaten by the Republican candidate. He was considered one of the greatest orators, or public speakers, who ever lived.

His most famous

Gale Research Co.

speech won him the nomination for the presidency. Bryan was born in Salem, Illinois, in 1860. After he finished college and became a lawyer he moved to Nebraska, served in Congress, and in 1896 went as a delegate to the Democratic convention where the candidate for president was to be nominated. At that time the United States, like most countries, was on the "gold standard," which means that the government guaranteed that an ounce of gold would always be worth a certain number of dollars. In Nebraska and other western states where silver was mined, people wanted the government to guarantee the value of silver, too. As a Nebraskan, Bryan made a speech in which he said, "You shall not crucify mankind

upon a cross of gold." His "Cross of Gold" speech made such an impression that he was nominated. Bryan was often called "the great commoner."

When Woodrow Wilson was elected president in 1912, Bryan was made Secretary of State. He resigned in 1915 and after that he lectured and wrote until his death in 1925. Bryan was a very religious man and was a leading "fundamentalist," which means he believed that every word of the King James version of the Bible should be accepted as literally true, not merely as a story told to teach a lesson.

Bryant, William Cullen

William Cullen Bryant was a famous American poet who was best known for his lovely nature poems. He

was born in 1794, in Cummington, Massachusetts. Even as a boy, he wrote and published poems that were so good that people found it hard to believe that such a young boy had written them. When he was nineteen, Bryant wrote one of his most famous poems, *Thanatopsis,* a beautiful poem on death. Although he had studied to become a lawyer, Bryant practiced law for only a few years, and then became editor of the New York *Evening Post.*

Most of Bryant's poems are about flowers and wild animals, such as *Death of the Flowers, To the Fringed Gentian,* and *To a Waterfowl.* William Cullen Bryant died in 1878.

Bryce, James

James Bryce was a great British lawyer and statesman who is remembered in the United States because he wrote a book, *The American Commonwealth,* which told how the American government works. This book was written in the year 1888, when a great many people in Great Britain did not know much about the United States, and it helped to make the English-speaking peoples more friendly. Later, from 1907 to 1913, Bryce

was British ambassador to the United States. He was born in Belfast, in Northern Ireland, in 1838, but lived most of his life in England, and served as a cabinet minister and as professor of law at Oxford University. In 1914 he was made a viscount and became Lord Bryce. He died in 1922.

Bryn Mawr

Bryn Mawr is a famous college for women, at the town of Bryn Mawr, Pennsylvania, a suburb of Philadelphia. It was founded in 1885 by the Quakers, but today it is nonsectarian. About 1,000 young women attend it.

Buchan, John

John Buchan was a British statesman and writer. His best-known novel was *The Thirty-Nine Steps,* an exciting

story about spies. Buchan was born in Scotland, in 1875. Although he held many important government jobs, he always found time to write, not only stories but also history. In 1935 he became governor general of Canada. Shortly before he died in 1940, he was given the title Baron Tweedsmuir.

James Buchanan

James Buchanan was the fifteenth President of the United States. He was born in 1791 near Mercersburg, Pennsylvania, and was a lawyer before he entered the field of politics. During his early years as a lawyer, Buchanan was saddened by the death of the girl he was engaged to. He wanted to keep busy in order to overcome his grief, so he decided to become a politician. He never married, and was the only president of the United States to remain a bachelor.

Buchanan became president at a time when the country was faced with the question of slavery and other great problems. His administration did not succeed in straightening out the problems that were facing the country, and Buchanan has often been blamed for many of the events leading up to the Civil War.

When Buchanan was elected president in 1856, the disputes between northern and southern states over slavery had become violent, and feelings were strong. Many people in the North were bitterly opposed to slavery, and wanted to abolish it. Most people in the South wanted slavery to continue.

There were many southerners at the time who resented the Federal government's control over an individual state's government. Some of these people went so far as to say that if the Federal government interfered too much, a state had a right to resign or secede from the Union. These people were known as secessionists. Buchanan appointed several men to his cabinet who were active secessionists, and throughout his administration his feelings were divided between the North and the South. Since he was elected by the Democratic Party, Buchanan tried to be fair to all members of the party, but he seemed to favor the hotheaded southern members.

Any president at that period would have had a very hard time, but a stronger man might have been able to do more than Buchanan. Buchanan could do nothing and the country became more and

more divided. In November, 1860, Abraham Lincoln was elected to succeed Buchanan as president. Buchanan, in a last message to Congress, tried to blame the North for what was happening to the country. He did this even though he knew that the southern states had begun to break up the Union by seceding from it.

Although Buchanan said that no state had any right to secede, he also said that Congress, on the other hand, had no right to try to stop secession. Most people thought that he could not make up his mind as to what was right and what was wrong. As a result, states went on seceding, and the war was finally touched off by the Southerners firing on Fort Sumter. You can read about this in the article on the CIVIL WAR.

After his term as president was over, Buchanan supported the Union side in the war. He felt, however, that it was necessary to explain his presidential policy, and wrote a book called *Mr. Buchanan's Administration*. His life has been the subject of considerable discussion by students of political history ever since he died in 1868.

HIS EARLY YEARS

James Buchanan was born on April 23, 1791, in Mercersburg, Franklin County, Pennsylvania. It was a small country town about ninety miles west of Gettysburg. When he was only eighteen, he was graduated from Dickinson College in Carlisle, Pennsylvania, and he became a lawyer at the age of twenty-one. Buchanan was considered a handsome young man, with thick, wavy hair, and heavy eyebrows.

As a young lawyer, Buchanan was interested in politics but did not become active in this field until after the death of his fiancée. He grieved for her so much that he wanted to keep busy every minute, and working in politics seemed like a good idea. He worked so hard that he became a member of the House of Representatives on the Federalist ticket in 1820, and served for ten years. When Andrew Jackson was a candidate for the presidency in 1828, Buchanan became a Democrat and supported him. After the election, Buchanan became U.S. Minister to Russia, and did very well in that position. He arranged the first commercial treaty between Russia and the United States. It gave the United States important rights concerning American ships entering the Black and Baltic Seas, both of which were entirely controlled by Russia at that time.

When Buchanan returned to this country, he ran for the United States Senate, and became a member of that body in 1834, and served in it until 1845. While he was in the Senate, he argued frequently in favor of allowing each state to choose whether it wanted to have slavery. He said that the national government had no right or power to interfere with the states where people had slaves.

Buchanan was offered the Democratic nomination for president in 1844, but he refused to accept it, and James Polk was chosen instead. Buchanan was Secretary of State during the Polk administration, and he was responsible for many things during that period which have greatly influenced the country's history. They are described in the article about James POLK, in a later volume of this encyclopedia.

When Polk was succeeded by Zachary Taylor as president, Buchanan retired to his farm near Lancaster, Pennsylvania. During this time he adopted his niece and nephew, whose parents had died. In 1853, Franklin Pierce was the new president, and he appointed Buchanan ambassador to England.

In 1856 Buchanan was nominated for the presidency on the Democratic ticket, and he was elected. After his inauguration in the spring of 1857, he announced the names of the men he had chosen for his cabinet. This immediately caused trouble with northern Democratic Party members, because Buchanan had chosen men who were active secessionists, and many Northerners thought secessionists were not loyal to the United States. It was unfortunate that Buchanan had such people in his cabinet, because it caused him to be accused of failing to do his best to preserve the Union. During the four years that Buchanan was president, he accomplished very little, and his weakness as a leader caused much trouble. Instead of uniting the country, Buchanan's policies helped to divide it even more.

By the time Buchanan's term was over, the Civil War seemed certain to be fought, although most people still hoped it could be avoided. James Buchanan left office with his country turned against him.

HIS LATER YEARS

He retired to private life and wrote a book explaining his policy during the time he was president. He attempted to justify his actions in this book, and some people think that he did all that he possibly could under the circumstances. On the other hand, many people think that he could have been more determined to preserve the Union, and could have made decisions that might have helped to prevent the Civil War, although the causes of that war had existed for a long time. James Buchanan died at the age of 77 at Wheatlands, his farm near Lancaster, Pennsylvania, on June 1, 1868.

Bucharest

Bucharest is the capital and largest city in Rumania. It is on the Dambovita River, and is one of the most important manufacturing centers in the Balkan Peninsula. More than one million people live there, and they work in factories, making furniture, leather goods, machinery, paper, soap, and many other products. The Dambovita River runs through the city. The part of the city that is on the right bank of the river is very old, and has narrow, winding streets. The part of the city that is on the left bank is modern, and here you can see beautiful gardens and fine buildings.

Bucharest was founded more than six hundred years ago. A Roman fortress had probably stood on the spot where the city was built. In 1861 Bucharest became the capital of Rumania. In World War II, it was taken by the Germans. The city was taken from the Germans by the Russians in 1944.

BUCHAREST, RUMANIA. Population, 1,-475,050. Capital of Rumania. On the Dambovita River.

Buck, Pearl Sydenstricker

Pearl S. Buck has been famous as an American novelist, and she became best known for her book *The Good Earth*. Thousands of people have read this story of a Chinese family and millions have seen the motion picture that was made from the book. In 1932, *The Good Earth* won the Pulitzer Prize that is given every year to the best novel written by an American. Pearl Buck was the daughter of an American missionary. She was born in Hillsboro, West Virginia, in 1892, and spent her childhood among the Chinese people. Later, she taught at several Chinese universities. Most of her stories are about these people she knew so well. In 1938, Pearl Buck was given the great Nobel Prize which is awarded each year to the most outstanding people in many fields. She was given the prize for her fine writing. She died in 1973.

Buckingham Palace

Buckingham Palace is the London home of the British royal family. It was built about 250 years ago by the man who was the Duke of Buckingham at that time. When George III became king soon after, he liked the palace so much that he bought it, and English kings and queens have lived in it ever since. Buckingham Palace is attended night and day by special troops of the British Army. These troops work in shifts, like all guards. Each time a new shift comes on, there is a very colorful ceremony called the "Changing of the Guard." The bugle call at this time suggested the music for the song that starts, "They're changing Guards at Buckingham Palace, Christopher Robin went down with Alice."

Buckner, Simon Bolivar

Simon Bolivar Buckner was a Confederate general in the Civil War. He was born in Kentucky in 1823. He graduated from the United States Military Academy at West Point. When the Civil War broke out, he joined the Southern army, but in 1862, he was forced to surrender to General Grant. Many years later, he became governor of Kentucky. His son, Simon Bolivar Buckner, was a famous general in World War II. He was born in 1886, and became an army officer like his father. He was the commanding general in Alaska during part of World War II. In 1945, he was made the commanding general in the invasion of the island of Okinawa, in the Pacific. The invasion was successful, but General Buckner was killed only a few day before the Japanese surrendered the island.

buckskin

Originally buckskin meant a soft leather that was made from the skin of a buck, or male deer. American pioneers and frontiersmen wore buckskin breeches and buckskin shirts. Many American soldiers wore buckskin clothing during

the Revolutionary War, and those soldiers were often called "Buckskins." Most buckskin is now made by softening sheepskin in oil instead of tanning it in the usual way.

buckwheat

Buckwheat is a plant that is grown in many parts of the world for grain. It does not grow very high, but it grows very thickly and chokes off anything else where it is planted. Farmers often plant buckwheat to choke off weeds. They use the buckwheat seeds to feed cows, pigs and chickens. They also make buckwheat flour by grinding the seeds. The flour is used mostly for pancakes. The buckwheat plant first grew in Asia, and it was brought to Europe in the Middle Ages. It grows in many parts of North America. Buckwheat usually grows about two feet high, and it has heart-shaped leaves and pale red flowers.

bud

A bud is the part of a plant from which a new flower grows, from which a new plant may develop. A bud, therefore, is a very valuable part of the plant, and in cold climates the trees usually have bud scales which protect their buds from frost in the winter. From the shape of the bud scales, particularly those at the tips of the branches, you can nearly always tell what sort of tree you are looking at, even in midwinter.

With special care, gardeners can grow a whole new plant from a single bud, by "budding," or cutting off pieces which have several buds on them. The "eyes" of potatoes are buds, and you can plant a piece of potato that has two or three eyes, and grow a new potato plant. Some plants, like palms and lilies, have only one bud, and all their growth takes place from it. Palms hold their bud high in the air, and they are easily killed by frost, but lilies, onions, and many other plants with only one bud, keep it safely underground, where it can live through the coldest winter. For more on this subject, see the article on BULB.

The lower kinds of plant, such as seaweeds, and of animals, such as jellyfish, also have buds; from their buds a whole new plant or animal may develop. This is often their chief way of reproducing themselves.

Budapest

Budapest is the capital and most important city in Hungary. It is one of the most beautiful cities in Europe. Almost two million people live in Budapest. They work in the large mills and factories, making flour, metal products, tobacco, textiles, dishes, and many other important articles. Budapest is also the greatest railroad center in Hungary, and the farmers ship most of their crops through this city.

Budapest is really two old cities that grew upon opposite sides of the Danube River, and were finally joined together in 1872. Buda was on the right bank of the Danube, and Pest was on the left bank of the river. When one city was made from these two places, the new name came from joining the two old names. These two parts of the city are joined by many fine bridges. Buda is on high ground, and is built around a great rock called the *Varhegy* (Castle Hill). On this hill is the splendid royal palace, now in ruins, and a cathedral where the emperors of Austria were crowned as kings of Hungary.

Pest is on a sandy plain, so low that walls had to be built to keep the waters of the Danube out. This part of Budapest is very beautiful. Here you can see many fine boulevards, parks, and buildings. People who visited the city before World War II called the *Andrassy Ut* one of the most beautiful streets in the world.

The towns of Buda and Pest are very old. They were both probably founded by Slavic tribes more than 1,500 years ago. The Magyars, who now are the largest group in Hungary, conquered the two towns about a thousand years ago. Buda and Pest were under Turkish rule for almost 150 years during the Middle Ages; when the Turks were driven out in 1686, they left the two towns almost completely destroyed. Then Buda and Pest were rebuilt and were finally joined together. During World War II the Germans controlled Budapest. They defended it against advancing Russian armies in 1945 and many of the beautiful buildings were damaged before Russia captured the city. The Russians set up Communist rule in Hungary and in 1956 the people of Budapest led the nation in fighting to become free again, but they were suppressed by the Russian army. See HUNGARY.

BUDAPEST, HUNGARY. Population, (1973 estimate) 1,950,000. Capital of Hungary. On the Danube River.

Buddha and Buddhism

Buddha is the name of a great teacher who founded the religion called Buddhism. Buddha lived in India 2,500 years ago. His name was originally Siddharttha Gotama (or Gautama). By this name he was known until he was 29 years old. Then he took the title of "Buddha," meaning "the enlightened one." A Buddha is a sort of prophet. Followers of Buddhism believe such Buddhas are born every few generations, to keep the faith of the people alive. Gotama, the Buddha, taught people the meaning of reverence, the love of truth, and the evils of superstition. His followers today number 450 million people, scattered over India, China, Burma, Ceylon, Tibet, Siam, and Japan. He is also honored in the Western World as one of the greatest teachers of all time.

Legend says that Gotama was born the son of a king. When he was 19 he married a beautiful princess, and they had a son. But Prince Siddharttha had seen visions that showed him how vain and useless was the life of a prince. Taking a last look at his young son in the arms of his sleeping mother, he departed from the palace, leaving behind his royal name and all the splendor that had gone with it.

He did not return until seven years later. This time he was dressed in a coarse, yellow robe, and begged for food in the streets. He had come back because his father, wishing to see him once more, had sent for him. But the king was ashamed of his son's begging, and ordered him to stop. Buddha replied, "My noble father, you and your family may claim the privileges of royal descent; my descent is from the prophets of old, and they have always acted so; the customs of the law are good, both for this world and the world that is to come."

He left his home again, and took five pupils with him to study and pray in the wilderness. He fell ill and was believed dead, but he recovered when the kind daughter of a villager brought him food.

His pupils left him, and Buddha himself was tempted by thoughts of his past life, but the religious side of his nature won out in the end. Instead of returning to his old ways, he made up his mind to leave the wilderness and preach to the people. We are told he came to this decision as he sat in the shade of a big tree, eating the food the village girl had brought him. The people of India call this tree the sacred *Bo Tree of Wisdom*.

WHAT BUDDHISM TEACHES

Like all great religions, Buddhism teaches the importance of spiritual or holy values. This religion teaches that if a person has a pure mind everything he does will be pure and decent, and that if he has a pure heart all happiness will come to him. The highest virtue, according to Buddha, is *universal charity*—giving all you can to anybody who needs help.

Buddhists believe in *reincarnation*. This is a religious belief that is common in the East. It means we are born many times, and in each new life we are better than we were before. According to the teachings of Buddha, the good are rewarded by being born into higher forms of goodness, and those who achieve the highest form of goodness finally escape both life and death. These people, having reached their final stage of goodness, are not born again and therefore do not die again, but remain forever and ever in the Buddhist heaven, called Nirvana.

Buddha taught and preached for many years, wandering from city to city. Many noble youths went with him, including his own son and his brother.

He died at the age of eighty, preaching and teaching to the end. He left behind many notable sayings which his followers faithfully wrote down and passed on to others. On one occasion, for instance, Buddha was asked what is the greatest blessing. He listed ten different blessings, some of which follow:

"To serve wise men, and not to serve fools, to give honor to whom honor is due, this is the greatest blessing. To dwell in a pleasant land, to have done good deeds in a former birth, to have the right desires for one's self, this is the greatest blessing. To succor father and mother, to cherish wife and child, to follow a peaceful calling, this is the greatest blessing. To give alms and live righteously, to help one's relatives and do blameless deeds, this is the greatest blessing. They that act like this are invincible on every side, on every side they walk in safety, and theirs is the greatest blessing."

budget

A budget is a way of putting down

on paper the total amount of money that comes in, and then putting down how that money will be spent. One person may make a budget for himself, or a family may make a budget. The governments of cities, states and countries all make budgets. Government officials make a new budget each year to show how much money the government will have to spend, and what the money will be spent for. A personal, or family, budget is usually made for a week, a month, or a year.

A budget helps people to live within their income, which means they plan their expenses so that they do not pay more for food, clothing, entertainment, or other things, than they can afford. People who live on a budget usually do not run out of the money they earn in a week before the week is over. People who do not have a budget sometimes spend all their money before they have bought some things they need. They either have to borrow money (which they have trouble paying back) or they have to go without things until they get their next salary for the work they do.

If you spend all your allowance a few days after you receive it, and then find you need money for something important to you, then you should plan a budget for yourself. Put down the amount you receive as allowance. Then write down all the things you want to spend money on until your next allowance. When the total amount you plan to spend is equal to, or less than your allowance, then you have a good budget. You should always try to save a little money in your budget —it helps take care of things that you may need to do, but had not thought of.

A government budget is a bit different from a personal one. Much larger sums of money are involved. Each year the' person in charge of a government budget plans what shall be done with the government's money during the coming year. The budget for the government of the United States is prepared by a man called the Director of the Bureau of the Budget. He meets with the heads of all government departments and they tell him how much money they will need to run their departments during the coming "fiscal" year. A fiscal year starts on July 1 and ends the following June 30. It is the same length as a regular year, but the government finds it more convenient to have its fiscal or money year start at the beginning of July instead of January.

The Director of the Budget sends his finished budget to Congress. The members of Congress study this budget, and then vote on accepting it. Sometimes Congress makes changes in the budget before it is voted on. Many billions of dollars are spent in a government budget, and Congress must find ways to save money. The income side of a government budget comes mostly from taxes that people pay to the government. Most of the money spent by the government goes for defense (Army, Navy, and Air Force), national parks, aid to veterans, farmers, and friendly nations, and for many other things, including the salaries of all government officials from the president on down to thousands of clerks. In the early days of the United States, the Director of the Budget had to plan for the spending of only a few million dollars. Since then,

the amount has increased every year, and in 1972 the total amount spent by the United States government was $230,-513,992,000.

Buena Vista, Battle of

The Battle of Buena Vista was one of the hardest-fought battles in the war between Mexico and the United States. It took place on February 22 and 23, 1847. It is important because the American force of only 5,000 men won against 20,000 men in the Mexican army.

The battleground was a plateau (a high flat piece of ground) with mountains rising on two sides. The Americans were commanded by General Zachary Taylor. After he won this battle he became so popular in the United States that he was nominated and then elected president. The Mexican army was under General Santa Anna, who was also the president of Mexico. Taylor's army was made up mainly of men who had volunteered and who were not trained soldiers. During the fighting on the first day the Mexicans attacked fiercely and almost drove the American army into a full retreat. But the Americans fought back bravely until the Mexicans retreated in confusion on the following night. The Americans lost only 749 men, while the Mexicans lost more than 2,000.

Buenos Aires

Buenos Aires is the capital of Argentina and one of the biggest cities in the Western Hemisphere, with about six million people living there. It is a historic city, founded by Spanish settlers in 1536.

Buenos Aires is on the wide La Plata River, which is the baylike mouth, or *estuary*, of the Panama and Uraguay Rivers. The city is the commercial and industrial center of Argentina and also of a vast area that includes parts of Paraguay and Uruguay. Many people work in the city's factories, which turn out automobiles, paper, cloth, and chemicals. Others work in meat-packing plants, printing plants, metalworks, and oil refineries.

Buenos Aires (which means "Good Airs" in the Spanish language) is a modern city. It has many fine parks and squares. The best known square is the Plaza del Mayo. Around it stand several impressive buildings, including the official residence of the president of Argentina. The president of the United States lives in the White House, but the president of Argentina lives in the *Casa Rosada,* or Pink House. If you were to visit Buenos Aires, you would see the Avenida del Mayo, a beautiful, broad boulevard lined with trees, that runs about a mile from the Plaza del Mayo to the Plaza del Congréso, where the National Congress meets to make laws. You would also see the Avenue of the 9th of July, which is said to be the widest street in the world.

You can travel to Buenos Aires by railroad, ocean steamer, or airplane. In the city, you could ride on subways, buses, streetcars and taxis. You would find the climate there much like that of most American cities, except that it would be winter in Buenos Aires when it is summer up north, and so on through the year.

BUENOS AIRES, ARGENTINA. Capital city

of Argentina. Population, 5,900,000.

buffalo

The buffalo is an oxlike animal with long horns that is found in Asia and Africa. The Asiatic buffalo, or *water buffalo,* is a large and powerful animal. It is about 7 feet long and 5 feet high at the shoulder, and it has great curving horns. It is an excellent animal for farm work, and it can haul great loads. The tamed water buffalo is gentle and very different from the wild water buffalo, which is savage and fierce and will even attack tigers and elephants. Many of these animals are hunted from the backs of elephants in India. It is called the water buffalo because it loves the water. Its favorite spot is a muddy water hole, where it lies hidden among tall grasses. Another name for the water buffalo that is found in the Philippine Islands is the *carabao*.

The buffalo that is found in southern Africa is called the *Cape,* or *black, buffalo*. It is larger than the water buffalo, and very fierce. It is eight feet long and almost six feet high at the shoulder. Its great horns often measure seven feet from tip to tip. Like the water buffalo, it also enjoys lying in marshy swamps.

The American "buffalo" that once roamed the plains of North America is really a *bison*. You can read about the BISON in a separate article.

Buffalo

Buffalo is an important port at the eastern end of Lake Erie, where the waters of this Great Lake flow into the Niagara River to form, at this point, the boundary between the United States and Canada. Buffalo is the second largest city in the state of New York. It was laid out as a frontier village in 1803 and burned by the British when they tried to conquer the United States in the War of 1812. Buffalo began to grow rapidly when the Erie Canal was opened in 1825, and it became possible to ship furs and forest products eastward by barge to the cities of the Atlantic coast. Settlers thronged through the town on their way west—and a good many of them stayed on.

Today, the people who live in Buffalo include many whose families came from European countries, particularly Poland. They work in huge plants producing steel, pig iron, flour, rubber goods, airplanes, automobiles, plastics, cloth goods, and lenses for cameras and telescopes. On week-ends they often take their children to visit nearby Niagara Falls, the world-famous waterfall.

BUFFALO, NEW YORK. Population 462,-768 (1970 census). County seat of Erie County. On Lake Erie at its Niagara River outlet.

Buffalo Bill, a famous American scout and showman. See CODY, WILLIAM F.

buggy

In the days before automobiles, the buggy was one of the best-known types of carriage that people used to ride in. An American buggy had four wheels, but some English buggies had only two wheels. Some buggies were pulled by two horses, but most of them needed

only one horse. Two or more people rode in a buggy, and they sat under a top, but the sides were open. The best American buggies were made by a man named Carter, who lived in New Jersey more than a hundred years ago. His buggies were much lighter and stronger than other buggies. Carter used light hickory wood instead of the heavier oak that other buggy-makers used. He made his buggies more comfortable by putting very good steel springs between the wheels and the body.

By 1890, hundreds of thousands of buggies were manufactured every year by such companies as Studebaker and Fisher. These companies are now in the automobile business. People called the first automobiles "horseless buggies." When people began to ride in automobiles, the buggy and other horse-drawn carriages began to disappear. Some buggies reappeared during World War II, when gasoline rationing limited the use of automobiles. You may sometimes see farmers driving buggies on dirt roads in the country, or you may see them at a county fair. The word buggy is sometimes used, like jalopy, as a slang word for automobile.

bugle

A bugle is a kind of coiled horn. Its sound is loud and can be heard a long distance away. It is made of brass, and has a separate mouthpiece that fits in the front end of the bugle. There are only a few notes that you can play on a bugle. You play them by changing your lip pressure as you blow into the mouthpiece. A bugle has no keys or valves like a cornet or trumpet. Armies have always used "bugle calls" to signal the troops.

Soldiers learn the tunes of the various calls so that they recognize them and know what they mean. Soldiers get up in the morning when the bugler blows *reveille;* they go to eat when he blows *mess call;* they gather for information when he blows *assembly;* they stand at attention and salute the flag as it comes down, when the bugler blows *retreat;* and they know it is "lights out" and time for bed when they hear the lovely notes of *taps* on the bugle. The Army officially uses trumpets instead of bugles, and the calls are now trumpet calls, but unofficially the soldiers still refer to them as bugle calls.

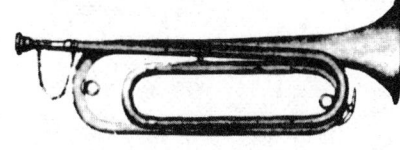

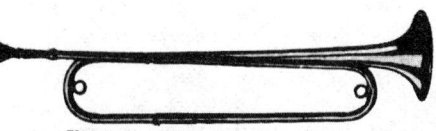

Upper A regulation bugle.
Lower An American Legion bugle.

building

Building is one of the oldest and most important activities of man. It is the way man has used his intelligence, imagi

nation, and strength to put things together to make his life safer and more pleasant. Man has built houses to live in, churches to meet and worship in, theaters and stadiums to be entertained in, and factories, mills, barns, and offices to work in. He has built hospitals, garages, railroad stations, warehouses, and airplane hangars. All of these buildings are shelters. They all have a foundation, floor, ceiling and roof, although what a building looks like depends on what it is used for, and of what materials it is made.

Man also builds many things for purposes other than shelter. He builds ships and railroads, airplanes and bridges, canals and tunnels and docks for transportation purposes. He builds aqueducts to carry water, and pipe lines to carry oil and gas. He builds mighty dams to hold back rushing water, and he builds great monuments, like the pyramids in Egypt, and the Lincoln Memorial in Washington, D.C., to honor famous people. He also builds tremendous atom smashers to make atomic energy and atomic bombs. You can read about most of the things that man has built in separate articles about each of them.

Man is the greatest builder of all the animals, but he was not the first. When early man was still living in caves that he found, or sleeping in treetops, other animals had been building things for millions of years. Birds had been building many kinds of nests. Ants were building anthills with marvelous rooms and tunnels, wasps and bees were building hives, and beavers were building their wonderful dams and lodges. Man probably first began to build by watching some of these other animals, and he soon began to do things better than any of them.

HISTORY OF BUILDING

The first building man did was to make a place to keep himself warm and dry, and he used whatever materials he could find most easily. If he lived where there were many stones, he used them to build a shelter. If he lived in a forest, he used the trees and leaves. He made homes out of dried clay if he lived near a river bank, and if he lived in the far north he made his house of ice and snow. Then when man had a safe, warm place for himself and his family to live in, he wanted company, and soon he began to build larger shelters. He built meeting halls where he and his neighbors could get together to talk things over and have a good time, and he built churches where men could come together to worship God.

Then about 150 years ago man began to build factories and other buildings where many men could work together. Before that most men worked at home. Shoemakers made shoes, and weavers wove cloth, and doctors took care of sick people in the houses where they lived. But when man's busy mind began to discover new and better ways of doing things by machine instead of by hand, he needed buildings large enough to hold the machines and the people to run them. With the INDUSTRIAL REVOLUTION (you can read about this important event in another volume), man started working together with many other men, and so he had to build places to work in—factories, offices, and places to store the things that

he made.

With his new machines, man could build things much better than ever before, and he came to have even more respect for the wonderful builders of ancient times. The people of Egypt had no steam shovels to help them carry the huge stones to build the pyramids. We know that some of these great pyramids were built almost four thousand years ago, and all the work was done by the strong arms of men. The Romans had no bulldozers to help them build their roads, and the Greeks had no complicated machinery to make the temples and other buildings that we can still see standing in magnificent ruins. We know that the Romans found a way to bring water through pipes into their houses, and they built huge aqueducts and public baths. With all this new knowledge and fine equipment, modern man still honors the mighty builders of the past and wonders at their skill. These ancient men knew how to make a building strong and beautiful. You can read about some of the ways they did this in the article on ARCHITECTURE in another volume. You can also read how man's idea of what is beautiful changes all the time, and how he changes the way he builds and develops new styles of architecture.

CHANGES IN BUILDING

Modern man builds higher and faster than the early builders did. He can use the machines he has made to do easily and quickly things that would have taken his great grandfather many hours of hard work to do. Modern man has trains and airplanes to help him and this has made an important change in the way he can build. Long ago, the workmen had to be wherever the building was going on. Now, a man in St. Louis may work on the pipes for a new office building that is being put up in New York City. A man in Seattle may make the nails, and someone in Wisconsin will make the glass. Nails, glass, pipes, and all the other things that are needed for the building can be shipped to New York City by plane or train in just a few hours.

Machines and transportation have made it possible for houses and even huge buildings to be built in factories. Walls and floors and roofs are made in the factory and then sent to the spot where the building is to be put up. Buildings that are made in the factory are called *prefabricated*. Recently in New York City two sides of a tremendous skyscraper were put up in one day in this way, and during World War II whole towns of prefabricated houses were built very quickly and cheaply for men who needed a place to live while they were working in war factories.

One big difference between the way a big city like New York looks now and the way it looked a hundred years ago is that the buildings are very tall. The first modern skyscraper was built in Chicago about seventy years ago. Two important things had happened that made the modern skyscraper possible. Steel and reinforced concrete were two new materials that made a lot of difference in building. (Reinforced concrete is ordinary concrete with steel rods inside of it so that the concrete is much stronger and will

not crack.) Before man learned to make steel he could not make his buildings very tall because the walls had to be thick enough to support the weight of the whole building. But when he learned how to use thin, strong steel he found he was able to build as high as he pleased.

One more thing was necessary before man could make high buildings. If you have ever walked up four or five flights of stairs, maybe you can imagine what it would be like to walk up twenty or ninety flights. Man needed some way to get up and down in these very high buildings, and then about a hundred years ago the first elevator was tried out in New York City. Now man had a way to go up and down, and materials strong enough to hold the weight of many floors. This was a good thing, because with more and more people living together, there was not very much room on the ground any more. One way to go was up, so cities began to climb up into the sky.

Man is finding new kinds of glass, aluminum and many other materials to make his offices and apartment houses, factories, and farms as beautiful and comfortable and safe as possible. Gas, electricity, and now air conditioning, are being used in buildings. Modern homes have been changing too. You may think the newest houses with all glass walls and screens that move in place of any inside walls may look a little funny, but they are designed to make life as healthy and happy as can be for the people who live in them.

THE MEN WHO BUILD

A man can build a little house all by himself, and many men like to do this. But to build the Empire State Building, which is more than 1,200 feet high, many men had to work together. Everyone likes to watch the men who build. The steam shovels pick up large pieces of rock, the bulldozers smooth the ground, men shovel and hack and weld and split and hammer and work machines. It seems that no one pays any attention to what anyone else is doing, and yet you know that out of it all the men who work so busily on some special part of the building are working according to a plan. The architect has made the plan, and everyone else carries it out. The contractor is the man who has to see that the building is done exactly the way the architect planned it. Then there are the bricklayers, the ironworkers, the steamfitters, the plasterers, plumbers, and electricians. All of these men have been trained to do their special work, and all of the work has to be done just right. Every part is important.

First, the foundation of the building must be strong. The Empire State Building is built so solidly that if a wind blew 100 miles an hour against one side, and it blew for two hours, the building would move only 1½ inches. The frame of the building is made of steel columns and crossbeams. The ironworkers have to weld the crossbeams to the columns, and this is dangerous work because it has to be done many stories above the ground. Men are working on all parts of the building at the same time. While the ironworkers are doing their job, bricklayers are laying bricks; on another floor steam-

fitters are busy, and other men are cutting glass, laying floors, and doing all the things that must be done to make the building grow. When the building is ready the painters and plumbers go to work, and even these are not all the men who have to do with the building. Other men, maybe in other cities, are making bathtubs and sinks, light bulbs, paint, chairs and screws. All of these things are part of the building.

Bankers and government officials are interested in the building too. The banker may lend the money to the builder, and the government may promise that if the builder cannot pay back the money, the government will. The builder has had to file plans for his building with the government and the local government must decide whether the plans meet all the safety requirements, and whether it is all right to build in that location.

SOME FAMOUS BUILDINGS

Some of the buildings that man has made are famous all over the world. One is the Pentagon Building in Washington, D.C. Another is the group of buildings called Rockefeller Center, in New York City. The tallest building in the world is the Sears Roebuck Tower, in Chicago. It has 110 floors and is more than 1,450 feet high. The oldest building still standing in the United States is the Palace of the Governors in Sante Fe, New Mexico, which was built about 350 years ago.

bulb

A bulb is a plant bud that develops underground. Like all buds, it is the part of a plant from which a flower, or a new plant itself, will grow. Many kinds of plants grow from bulbs. Some of these bulbs are used by man for food, and some are used to grow beautiful flowers. The onion is the best known food bulb along with other members of its family —garlic, shallot, leek and scallion. Many of our most beautiful garden flowers are grown from bulbs, such as the lily, tulip, daffodil, hyacinth, narcissus, and snowdrop.

Bulbs vary in size, but they are all somewhat round in shape, and they are all hard and tightly packed. Some bulbs, like the onion, are made up of many complete coats, or layers. You can see this by counting the rings of an onion that has been cut in two. Other bulbs, like the lily, are made up of many leaves that are tightly packed together like a firm rosebud. Both the layered and the leaf bulbs contain the life of a new plant. When winter comes, or a dry season sets in, and a plant has withered and died above the ground, the bulb underground still has life. The bulb sleeps in the ground until the warm weather and water comes to awaken it. Then it sends out roots deeper into the ground, and pushes a new plant up through the soil to the surface. In its "sleeping" state a bulb looks dry and lifeless, but it can be taken from the ground, and then when it is replanted it will grow and bloom.

Bulfinch, Charles

Charles Bulfinch was one of the first American architects. He was born

in Boston, Massachusetts, in 1763, and after he was graduated from Harvard College, he traveled in Europe and studied architecture there. He learned to plan and design beautiful buildings. Bulfinch came back to Boston where he built the first theater in all the New England States. He wanted Boston to be a beautiful, clean city so he had the streets made wide and designed a new way of lighting them at night. In 1795, he made the plans for the new State House in Boston, and later designed many other important buildings.

Bulfinch began his most important work in 1818, when he was chosen to be the architect for the national Capitol in Washington, D.C. The work had been started by another architect, but Bulfinch did much of the important work on this great domed building. He died in 1844.

Bulganin, Nikolai

Nikolai Alexandrovich Bulganin is the name of a Russian Communist leader who became premier (head of the government) of the Union of Soviet Socialist Republics.

Bulganin was born in 1896 and joined the Communist Party in 1917. During World War II he was in charge of Russia's armed forces and was made a marshal, the highest rank in an army. After serving several years as Commissar of armed forces (like the United States Secretary of Defense), he was made premier in 1955. However, this was only to win the support of the Soviet Army for the Party Secretary, Nikita Khrushchev, who held the real power. Bulganin and Khrushchev made several "good will" trips together to foreign capitals in the years 1955 to 1957. In 1958 Bulganin was forced to resign as premier and nominate Khrushchev, who was elected premier in his place.

Bulgaria

Bulgaria is a small country on the Balkan Peninsula in southeastern Europe. It is about 43,000 square miles in size, not quite as large as Wisconsin, and more than eight million people live there, about twice as many as live in Wisconsin. For centuries Bulgaria was ruled by Turkey. In 1908 it became independent, but since 1946 it has had a Communist government controlled by Soviet Russia.

THE PEOPLE WHO LIVE THERE

Most of the Bulgarian people are a mixture of two groups of people that settled there many years ago. The first group were Slavs, who came from the north more than 1,700 years ago. The other group were Bulgars, who came from the east about 1,300 years ago, and conquered the Slavs. Both groups of people then lived together peacefully. The Bulgars started doing many things the way the Slavs did them, and they even began to speak the Slav language instead of their own. Many Bulgars married Slavs, and that is why most Bulgarians today are the descendants of this mixture of Bulgars and Slavs. There are also some Turks, Greeks, and Gypsies living in Bulgaria.

The people of Bulgaria are not very tall, but they are very strong and healthy.

They are known for their strength and for the fact that many of them live to a very, very old age. Most Bulgarians belong to the Greek Orthodox Church, to which a great many of the people of Eastern Europe belong. Their language is called Slavonic, and it is something like Russian.

Nowadays, Bulgarians wear clothes very much like ours, but for special occasions they dress in the costumes their ancestors wore. The women wear hand-embroidered blouses and skirts that are colorful and very attractive. The men wear beautifully embroidered shirts and loose pants like knickers.

All Bulgarian children have to go to school from the time they are seven until they are sixteen. Some of them get a chance to continue their education at one of the twenty-six colleges in Bulgaria.

HOW THE PEOPLE LIVE

Most of the people of Bulgaria are farmers. Many of them live and work on farms that are owned by the government. Almost half of them own their own farms. The farmers raise wheat, rye, oats, corn, barley, cotton, flax, and many kinds of fruit. They also raise cattle, pigs, sheep, goats, horses, oxen, and chickens. The soil is very fertile, but not all of it is used for farming. There are long stretches of countryside where nothing is grown, and there are many forests. The Bulgarian horses are smaller than the horses we see in America, but they are very strong and sturdy. The Bulgarian people get most of their milk from their sheep, instead of from cows, and they make a sheep's-milk cheese that some people think is very delicious.

The Bulgarian people have been trying to become more modern. Since the end of World War II, they have tried to build more factories and to produce better crops on their farms. Some of the people who work in factories make modern farm equipment. Other factory workers make machinery, textiles, clothing, and metal products. Most of the houses are old and do not have modern plumbing, heating, or lighting.

The biggest city in Bulgaria is its capital, Sofia. About 840,000 people live there. This is about as many people as there are in Dallas, Texas. The biggest university in Bulgaria, the University of Sofia, is in that city. The next biggest city is called Plovdiv. About 234,500 people live there, which is somewhat fewer than there are in Dayton, Ohio. There are two main seaport cities in Bulgaria. These cities are on the Black Sea, and are called Stalin and Burgas.

WHAT KIND OF PLACE IT IS

There are many mountains, rivers, and forests in Bulgaria. The main mountains are the Balkans and the Rhodope Mountains. The Danube River separates Bulgaria from its neighbor, Rumania, in the north.

The weather in Bulgaria is usually pleasant. The summers are very hot, but very dry, and the winters are short, cold, and dry. It rains a good deal in the autumn and the spring. The rainy spring and hot, dry summers are very good for flower gardening. Roses grow all through Bulgaria. They are very beautiful and

very fragrant. The Bulgarians crush the petals to make a perfume called attar of roses.

There is much coal in Bulgaria, and there is some copper, zinc, and lead. But Bulgaria does not have as many natural resources in proportion to its size as many other countries of the world.

More than one-third of Bulgaria is covered by forests. All kinds of animals live in these forests. There are bears, deer, wild goats, and squirrels. In the marshes near the river banks there are many kinds of wild birds.

HOW THE PEOPLE ARE GOVERNED

Bulgaria has had many different kinds of government. Since 1946, it has been a republic. It has a constitution that was made up in 1947. This constitution is very much like the constitution of the Union of Soviet Socialist Republics (Russia). Bulgaria is actually controlled by the U.S.S.R. in all important matters.

The main governing body of Bulgaria is the National Assembly, which is made up of representatives elected by the people. The National Assembly is elected every four years, and the members of the National Assembly elect the prime minister and the other ministers, who form a body somewhat like the cabinet in other countries.

Since the republic was established in 1946, the government has taken over the operation of most of the industry and farms of the country, but there are still some businesses and farms that are owned by private citizens.

All the men in Bulgaria have to serve in the army. They can be called into the army any time between their eighteenth and sixty-fifth birthdays, and they usually must serve for two years. The Bulgarians have fought in many wars, and although their army is not very big, the men are fierce and good fighters.

BULGARIA IN THE PAST

Bulgaria was part of the Roman Empire nearly 2,000 years ago. It was called Moesia at that time. After the Roman Empire fell, the Slavs came into Bulgaria. Then the Bulgars invaded the country and established a kingdom about 1,300 years ago. The people of Bulgaria

became Christians about 1,000 years ago, when they were converted by missionaries of the Greek Orthodox Church. The Turks invaded Bulgaria about 550 years ago, and for the next five hundred years they ruled the country. The Turks were not Christians, and the Bulgarians were, so there was much bad feeling between the two peoples. The Turks treated the Bulgarians very badly, and their cruelty to the Bulgarians made every one in Europe very angry. Late in the nineteenth century, the Russians went to war against the Turks, and when the peace treaty was signed between the two countries, in 1878, the Turks were made to treat the Bulgarians better. In 1908, a revolution in Turkey gave the Bulgarians the chance to become independent. They established their own kingdom and chose a German prince named Ferdinand as their king.

In World War I, Bulgaria fought on the German side. When the war was over, Bulgaria had to give up some of her territory.

In World War II, Bulgaria once again was on the side of the Germans. Two days before Russian troops entered Bulgaria in 1944, Bulgaria declared war on Germany. Shortly after that the Bulgarians made peace with Russia, Great Britain, and the United States.

After the war was over, the Russians forced the Bulgarians to get rid of their king, and establish a government like the Russian one. This form of government is called a republic, but it is not a democracy like that in the United States. The Bulgarians were allowed to vote, but they could vote only for the candidates selected by the Communist party. Thus Bulgaria, instead of being independent, became very much dependent on the Communist country of Russia.

The United States and Bulgaria did not get along very well after that, and relations between the two countries reached a low point in 1950 when Bulgaria accused the American Minister and members of his staff of spying. The U.S. was so angry that it broke off diplomatic relations with Bulgaria and withdrew its representatives. Diplomatic relations were finally resumed in 1959 when Bulgaria apologized for the unfounded accusations.

BULGARIA. Area, 42,796 sq. mi. Population (1973 estimate) 8,500,000. Capital, Sofia. Language, Slavonic. Chief religion, Greek Orthodox. Government, republic. Monetary unit, lev, worth about 8½ U.S. cents (free rate). Flag, white, green, and red bars across the flag; canton (shield shape) with coat of arms on it.

bull, the male animal of the bovine family: see CATTLE.

bulldog

The bulldog is a ferocious-looking dog but it has a gentle, kind disposition. It has great courage, and is a brave protector and watchdog. Originally the bulldog was bred in England for bull baiting. Bull baiting was a cruel sport in which a bull was tied up on a short rope, and the dogs were supposed to jump up and get a grip on the bull's nose. At that time the bulldog was a strong, stubborn, tough animal, and seemed to feel very little pain, even when badly hurt. When bull baiting became illegal, the bulldog

was bred to be the gentle, easygoing dog that it is today. It is a dog of medium size, but heavier than average for its height.

A bulldog stands about 18 to 20 inches high at the shoulder, and weighs between 40 and 50 pounds. Its head is large, and the teeth on its lower jaw show, because the lower jaw juts out quite a bit in front of the upper jaw. Its face is full of deep wrinkles, and its ears are small, lying close to its head. A bulldog looks slightly bow-legged, but that is only because it has heavy muscles on the outside of its legs, and not because the legs are actually crooked. A bulldog's short tail is some-times straight, and sometimes crooked. Its coat is smooth, short, and soft, and may be solid white, reddish brown, light tan or yellow, or with large splashes of different colors.

bulldozer

A bulldozer is a large and powerful kind of tractor that is used in building or construction work. Most tractors are used to pull loads, but a bulldozer is used to push things. A bulldozer has a great curved blade mounted on its front end. This blade is used to scrape dirt and to push it into large piles. The blade is also used to knock down trees and push aside rocks.

Bulldozers make it possible to do many construction jobs much more quickly than they could be done before. That is why the army uses bulldozers to make air-ports, and why people who build bridges, roads, dams, houses, and athletic fields, all use bulldozers.

bullet

A bullet is a piece of metal that is fired from a pistol, rifle or machine gun. The first bullets were small, round balls of lead that were dropped in the barrel of the gun after the powder charge had been put in the gun. Modern bullets are usually long with a sharp, pointed nose. Bullets for CARBINES (which you can read about in a separate article) have rounded noses. They are made of lead, with an outside jacket of copper and zinc over steel plating. They are held, at the bottom, in a brass case that contains the powder charge. The case, or cartridge, is placed by hand, or fed automatically into the breech of a gun. The breech is the opening at the back end of the gun barrel. You can read more about bullets in the article on AMMUNITION.

bullfighting

Bullfighting is the national *fiesta* (entertainment) of Spain and some Latin-American countries. It is more popular there than baseball or football in the United States. Thousands of people go to watch the bullfights in Spain, Mex-ico, and other places. The fights are held in large circular fields, called arenas, that are completely surrounded by rows of seats. These arenas are very much like the football stadiums in the United States. Before a bullfight begins, there is a won-derful parade of all the men who take part in it, all dressed in beautifully colored costumes.

After the bullfighters have paraded, the arena is cleared, and the bull is let loose. He comes charging out, snorting and pawing the dirt. Then several men called *picadors* come into the arena. They are mounted on horseback and they carry long, sharp lances. Their horses are cov-ered with a thick padded coat to protect them from the bull's horns. The picadors charge the bull and attempt to stick it with their lances. Sometimes the mad-dened bull charges the horses, and wounds them with his horns, even though the horses have the padded coats. When the picadors have stabbed the bull three times and weakened it, they leave the arena, and men on foot called *banderil-leros* come in. The banderilleros wave bright-colored capes at the bull, and try to get close enough to stick sharp darts into the bull's shoulders. The darts have brightly colored ribbons attached to them. When the bull chases the banderil-leros, they jump over a low fence to get away.

When the bull has three pairs of darts, which are called *banderillas,* stuck in his shoulders, the master bullfighter, the *matador,* enters the arena. He carries a sword and a *muleta,* a stick which has a piece of red silk attached to it. The muleta is sometimes called a cape. It is waved at the bull to attract its attention. Bulls, like all animals, are colorblind. They are not maddened by seeing something red, but by movement. Besides, the bull is now furious because of the darts sticking in his shoulders.

The matador tries to make the bull pass as close to him as possible. Some-times he misjudges the distance, and he is gored by the bull's horns. Some mata-dors have been killed in this way. Finally the matador gets set for the last charge. He holds his sword up and when the bull comes close, he plunges the sword into the bull's shoulders.

The art of bullfighting is very com-plicated, just as complicated as baseball or football and many other sports. Bull-fight fans argue with each other about the best ways of doing things and about who is the best matador. Bullfighting is more than just a sport to see who will win or lose. First of all, it is far more dangerous than most sports, because the matador himself is often hurt badly, and sometimes dies. Also, there are rules in bullfighting, just as in other sports, but it is not enough for the bullfighter merely to obey the rules. Bullfighting is also an art, like dancing or acting, and the best bullfighter must also be the most grace-ful.

Bullfighting began in ancient times, in Rome and Greece. It was probably in-troduced into Spain by the Moors of North Africa. Today, it is more popular in Spain than anywhere else. In southern France and Portugal, there is a special type of bullfighting in which the bulls are not killed. But in Mexico and in some other Latin-American countries it is the same as in Spain. The largest bullfighting arena in the world is in Mexico City. It is so big that it holds 47,000 spectators.

bullfinch

A bullfinch is a small bird that lives in Europe and Asia. There are many dif-ferent kinds of bullfinch. One of them, called Cassin's bullfinch, sometimes flies to Alaska from Asia. All bullfinches look very much alike. Mostly they are about the size of a canary, with the same shape of beak—pointed, but stout and strong for eating seeds. The commonest sort lives in woods and is a very pretty bird. It is soft and blue above, with a brick-red breast. Bullfinches make very good pets, and can be taught to whistle tunes. They are often kept in cages, but less often than years ago, because many people think it is cruel to keep a wild bird a prisoner.

bullfrog, a large American frog. See FROGS and TOADS.

bullion

Bullion is gold or silver that has been made into solid bars. The bars are made by melting the gold or silver and pressing it into molds. In some countries you may buy gold or silver bullion if you are going to make some jewelry or use it to fill teeth. In the United States the word bullion is used only for the bars of gold and other precious metals that are se-curity for money. (There is a separate article on MONEY.) These bars are kept in the vaults of the Treasury Department. A *gold certificate* is paper money you can exchange for gold, but it is now against the law to keep gold money or gold cer-tificates. When you need gold for mak-ing things you must apply to the gov-ernment for a special license.

Bull Moose Party

The Bull Moose Party was the nick-name of the Progressive Party, founded in 1912, that nominated Theodore Roo-sevelt for the presidency. At the Repub-lican convention that year, President William Howard Taft was nominated for reëlection, and almost immediately Roosevelt's followers organized the Pro-gressive Party, and nominated Roosevelt to run for the presidency. He and Taft were both defeated by the Democratic candidate, Woodrow Wilson. The name of the party was taken from a remark of Roosevelt's during the campaign. He said, "I feel as fit as a bull moose."

Bull Run, Battle of

Bull Run is a small stream in Vir-ginia, near where two important Civil War battles were fought. The first Bat-tle of Bull Run took place on July 21, 1861. The Union army, under General Irvin McDowell, was defeated by the Confederate army under General P. G. T. Beauregard and General J. E. Johnston. This victory at the beginning of the war gave the South great hope, and showed the people of the North that the war would not be over in a few months as they had thought.

The second Battle of Bull Run was fought on August 29 and 30, 1862. A Union army of 70,000 men attacked a smaller number of Confederates under the famous General "Stonewall" Jack-son. Jackson's troops held off the Union soldiers for one day until fresh troops were brought up by the Southern leader, General Robert E. Lee. Then they coun-terattacked and defeated the Union army. This battle was considered one of the im-portant military victories of Jackson and Lee. In the South, the Battles of Bull Run are called the Battles of Manassas, be-cause they were both fought near the rail-way junction at Manassas.

bull terrier

The bull terrier was the fiercest fighting dog when dog fighting was a popular sport. At that time it was called the "pit bull" because dog fights were held in deep pits. This was years ago, however, and now bull terriers are kept both in Europe and America as pets. They are strong and courageous as watchdogs, but are also usually friendly and playful pets. Very rarely will a bull terrier fight another dog unless the other dog attacks first. Then it will do its best to tear the other dog to pieces.

The bull terrier is a medium-sized dog. It stands about 18 to 22 inches high at the shoulder, and weighs anywhere from 25 to 60 pounds. The bull terrier's eyes are of an unusual triangular shape, and are set very close together. Its tail is short and straight, and slightly pointed. Sometimes the coat is pure white, sometimes it is brown, tan, or black, and sometimes it is one of these colors with white markings. The hair is coarse, and lies flat against the body.

Silverwood Kennels

The white bull terrier is a terror in a fight. It gets a grip and hangs on.

bulrush

The bulrush is a reedlike plant that grows in marshes along the edge of lakes and ponds. It can be found all over Europe, and in parts of the United States. The bulrush grows as high as 9 feet, and is almost leafless. Its stem is the most useful part of the plant. It is used to make mats and the seats for chairs; and, in California, it has been used in packing, to protect wine bottles. The most famous story about this plant can be found in the Bible. The baby Moses was found hidden in the bulrushes in Egypt. The Egyptians used bulrushes to make the paper called papyrus. You can read about MOSES and PAPYRUS in separate articles.

Bulwer-Lytton

Sir Edward George Earle Bulwer-Lytton was a famous English writer. Most of the novels, plays and poems he wrote had historical backgrounds. His most famous book was *The Last Days of Pompeii* which is still very popular today. It tells about the Roman people who lived in the city of Pompeii. The city was at the foot of a volcano called Vesuvius. When the volcano erupted and shot out melted rock and fire, all of Pompeii and the people in it were destroyed. Sir Edward was born in England in 1803 and died there in 1873.

bumblebee, a large, fuzzy, humming bee. See BEE.

Bunche, Ralph Johnson

Ralph Bunche became famous as a peacemaker for the United Nations. He received the Nobel peace prize in 1950,  for the work he did to stop a war between the Israeli and the Arabs. Bunche was the first Negro ever to win a Nobel Prize. He was born in 1904, and when he grew up, he became a teacher. During World War II and for about ten years after it, Bunche held important positions in the United States government, including presidential appointments as a delegate or commissioner to international meetings. He was an Assistant Secretary of State and a delegate to the United Nations. In 1958 Bunche accepted a position in the Secretariat of the United Nations, rather than live in Washington, D.C., where his children might suffer from discrimination. He died in 1971.

Bunker Hill

The Battle of Bunker Hill was the first real battle of the American Revolutionary War. It took place on Breed's Hill, near Bunker Hill, in Charlestown, Massachusetts, June 17, 1775. The battle was between 2,500 British soldiers commanded by General William Howe and 1,500 Americans under Colonel William Prescott. The Americans defended the hill against the British. The British attacked the hill three times, and twice they were thrown back by the Americans. The third time they reached the top of the hill, but more than a thousand of their men had fallen. The British losses were so high because Colonel Prescott told his men, "Don't shoot till you see the whites of their eyes." [That is, let the enemy get very close before you shoot.] Some historians believe the American commander, General Israel Putnam, and not Prescott, gave this order. Whoever said it, Americans have remembered it ever since.

The entire town of Charlestown was burned to the ground after the battle. By capturing Bunker Hill, the British were able to capture and hold Boston. The battle, however, raised the spirits of the Americans, who had shown the British that they could put up more of a fight than the British thought they could.

Bunsen, Robert Wilhelm

Robert Bunsen was a German chemist who became famous for inventing the *Bunsen Burner*. Burners very much like his original invention are still used in every science laboratory. Bunsen was born in 1811, and he had a long and busy life as a scientist, dying in 1899. He made many important discoveries in chemistry and invented scientific appliances that are known by his name. The Bunsen Burner is a metal tube in a holder that burns gas with a very hot, smokeless flame. The high heat is produced by mixing air with the gas. The more air that can be brought

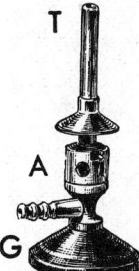

In a Bunsen burner, the gas pipe (G) is connected to a gas jet by a rubber tube. Gas goes into the burner and mixes with air that comes in through the air hole (A). This mixture goes up the tube (T), and burns with a very hot blue flame.

to a flame, the hotter the flame will burn. The Bunsen burner makes it possible to heat things more quickly and to a higher degree of heat. It is used to heat things in glass flasks and test tubes.

bunting

A bunting is a bright-colored bird which looks a little like a finch. Various kinds of bunting are found mostly in England and sometimes in other parts of Europe, Asia, Africa, and America. The *snow bunting* breeds in the north. The *cirl bunting* has a dark-green head. It stays farther toward the south.

The *yellow bunting* is found all over, and the *reed bunting,* which has a black and white head, stays mostly in the marshes.

In America, the *black-throated bunting* lives in the open country of the middle west, and the *bay-winged bunting* lives in the eastern part of Canada and the United States.

The *lark bunting* lives in the far west, and has a brilliant song, unlike some of the other buntings, which have harsh voices.

Bunyan, John

John Bunyan was an English preacher and writer who became famous for writing a great book called *Pilgrim's Progress.* He was born in 1628 in the little town of Elstow,  about 90 miles northwest of London. As a boy he worked at his father's trade of pot-mending or tinkering. After Bunyan was married, he became very religious. He gave up swearing and all kinds of amusements to devote himself to preaching and writing religious books. His first book was published in 1656.

Four years later he was arrested for preaching without a license, which was at that time against the law in England. He was sent to prison for twelve years, and during that time he wrote nine books, and preached to the others in prison with him. He was released in 1672, but five years later he was again arrested, and imprisoned for a short time. During this second time in prison he wrote the great book, *Pilgrim's Progress.* After his prison term was over, Bunyan spent the rest of his life preaching and writing. He died in 1688.

Bunyan, Paul

Paul Bunyan was an imaginary hero who is supposed to have lived about a hundred years ago in the lumber camps of the northwestern part of the United States. The men who worked in these

camps were called loggers or lumberjacks, and they used to sit around their campfires at night and tell "tall tales" about Paul Bunyan and Babe, his great blue ox. Paul was a great giant, the biggest lumberjack of all, and he did many wonderfully impossible things. Babe, the blue ox, was so big that they said it "measured 42 ax handles and a plug of chewing tobacco between the horns."

Nobody knew just exactly when Paul Bunyan lived, but they said that he lived in the imaginary period between the Winter of the Blue Snow and the Spring That the Rain Came Up From China. The character of Paul Bunyan is probably based on a French-Canadian lumberjack with the same name, who became famous fighting against the English and working in the lumber camps. But almost everything in the stories about him is made up. You can read these stories in two exciting and amusing books, each called *Paul Bunyan*, one by James Stevens, the other by Esther Shephard.

buoy

A buoy is a marker that floats in the water to show sailors where there is danger, and where to steer their ships safely. If a ship or boat is going along in a river, bay, or harbor, it might run into rocks, sand bars, cable-crossings, mine fields, and other things, if it were not for buoys. A buoy is held in place by an anchor which is attached to it by a steel cable.

All buoys are not alike, and if you were sailing a ship through a passage marked by buoys, you would have to pay attention to the "markings" and also to the type of buoy. By looking at your chart (a map of the waters through which you are sailing), you would see such marks as "S" meaning a "spar buoy," "N" meaning a "nun buoy," and "C" meaning a "can buoy." Then there are different colors and numbers on the buoys themselves, which mean something to the navigator. Let us see what types of buoy we may find:

(1) *Spar buoys* are made of wood or iron plates and stick up out of the water like poles. The wooden ones are generally cedar, spruce, or redwood logs, bound together by heavy iron bands. Wooden buoys are painted with special paint so that the water and animal life in the water will not damage them. They vary in size from about 20 to 50 feet. The other type of spar buoy is made of iron plates riveted together. They vary in length from 30 to 50 feet. They are cigar-shaped. More of the length of spar buoys is under water than the part that sticks up out of the water.

(2) *Nun buoys* are made of iron plates riveted together. Inside there are two or three airtight compartments, so that the buoy will not sink if it is broken in one place. Nun buoys are of two types, short ones shaped like pears, and tall ones shaped like cigars. They are generally painted red, and have even numbers (2, 4, 6, etc.) painted on them. Short nun buoys sometimes have hollow balls attached to their sides so that they will float upright.

(3) *Can buoys* get their name because the part that sticks up out of the water is shaped like a tin can that food comes

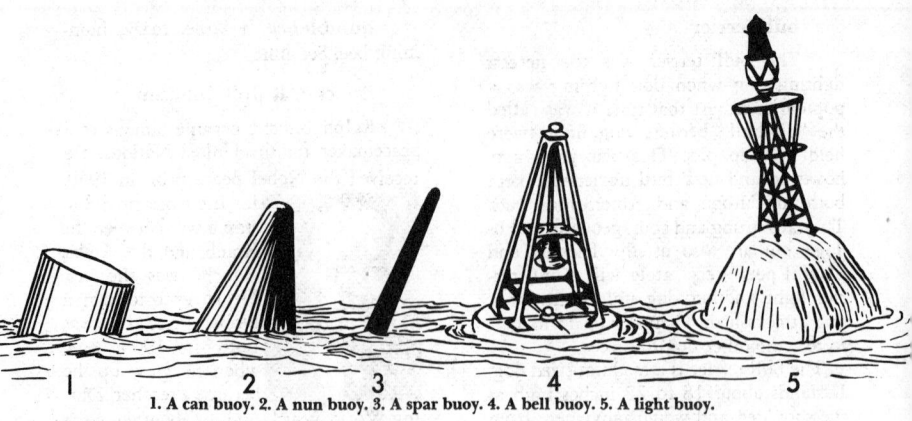

1. A can buoy. 2. A nun buoy. 3. A spar buoy. 4. A bell buoy. 5. A light buoy.

in. The part under water is either rounded, if it is a short can, or cigar-shaped, if it is a tall can. They are generally painted black, and have uneven numbers (1, 3, 5, etc.) on them.

Can buoys and nun buoys are also painted with stripes at times, for different signals, and if they are placed to show a channel or obstruction, there are no numbers.

WHISTLING BUOYS

At some important places it is desirable to have a light or sound to guide vessels at night, or in a thick fog. For these places, there are buoys with lights, bells, or whistles. Here is how they work:

(1) *Light buoys* have lights that burn all the time. Some still have oil lamps, but most of them work on an electric battery. Some have bells or whistles.

(2) *Bell buoys* have a bronze bell. Most of the buoy is a big steel float, under water. The bell part is built over the buoy, and when the waves rock it, the bell rings.

(3) *Whistling* buoys are shaped like short nun buoys, with the upper end more pointed. A tube runs through the buoy from top to bottom. At the upper end of the tube there is a whistle. When the buoy rises and then falls in the waves, the air in the tube (which is open at the bottom) is compressed, as in a pump, by the water pushing up from below. There is no place for the air to go, except up through the whistle, which makes a loud sound.

Burbank

Burbank is a city in southern California. It is a suburb of Los Angeles. More than 88,000 people live there. There are important motion-picture studios and aircraft factories there.

Burbank, Luther

Luther Burbank was a scientist who experimented with plants and became famous for developing new kinds of flowers, fruits, and vegetables. He was born near Lancaster, Massachusetts, in 1849, and grew up on a farm. As a young boy he became interested in working with plants to see if he could make them grow bigger and better. He learned to select the seeds of the best plants to grow new ones, and when he was 24 years old he had devel-

Gale Research Co.

oped the Burbank potato that is still one of the best. Soon after this he moved west for his health. He went to Santa Rosa, northwest of San Francisco, California, which he said was the "chosen spot of all this earth as far as Nature is concerned." There he set up his experimental farm, where he worked for the next 50 years, until his death in 1926. He became famous all over the world, and he inspired many other people to take up plant breeding.

Burbank grew over a million plants a year. Sometimes he had several thousand experiments going on at once—all different. He used both *crossbreeding* and *grafting*. In *crossbreeding* a berry, for example, he took one kind that had a fine flavor but was small in size and mated it with another that was larger. When the result was good, the fruit of the *hybrid*, or new plant, was both large and full-flavored. Burbank made 40,000 hybrids by crossing blackberry and raspberry plants. He also developed a thornless blackberry.

Grafting is a way of giving a weak plant a strong root system. An apple that is good for both eating and baking may grow on a frail tree. Another apple tree may have a strong, healthy growth, but its fruit may be small, bitter, or tasteless. Burbank would take a cutting, or branch, from the frail tree and graft it into a slit in the branch of the sturdier tree. The pieces grew together, and the new branch bore its own fruit. In Burbank's tests, a single tree sometimes carried 600 different grafts. You may have seen flowering trees that have been grafted so that several different kinds of blooms appear on the same tree.

Burbank's work on a single fruit or vegetable might extend over many years. His new varieties included the Gold and Bartlett plums and the Splendor and Sugar prunes. He developed better apples, cherries, peaches, and nectarines, as well as tomatoes, sweet and field corn, squash, and peas. He also grew new kinds of lilies, roses, and the famous Shasta daisy.

burbot

The burbot is the only freshwater fish belonging to the same family as the cod. It is large, shaped like an eel, and has very long fins above and below that extend from its middle to its tail. It has a soft, slimy skin in which there are tiny scales, and a long fleshy feeler under its chin. The burbot is found in deep, cool water in lakes or big rivers in the north-

ern parts of America, Europe and Asia. Some burbots have been caught in Alaska that were five feet long and weighed about sixty pounds. Some people say the burbot is good to eat, but most do not like the way it looks, and refuse to eat this fish.

The burbot is sometimes called *ling* by Americans.

burdock

Burdock is a big, coarse weed. It originally grew in Europe and Asia, but it was brought to America where it now grows wild. It has large, soft leaves, and pink or purplish flowers. These grow in large "heads," like the flowers of a thistle or a dandelion. When they go to seed, this head becomes a big round mass of burs. In Japan the root of burdock is cooked and eaten as a vegetable, which is called *gobo.*

You can see great patches of burdock growing along the sides of roads and in uncultivated fields.

bureaucracy

A government is called a bureaucracy when it is run by many minor officials, or heads of "bureaus" (smaller divisions of the big government departments). When a person says a government is a bureaucracy, he means that he disapproves of the way it is being run. The idea is that minor officials follow the law strictly even when it is unfair, while higher-ranking government officials would use the law more intelligently. Another criticism of a bureaucracy is that all these officials try very hard to keep their jobs, because they could not get better jobs anywhere else. Therefore they look for ways to make more work for their bureaus, instead of less, and this costs the taxpayers money. The very big men in a government are not usually interested in the salaries they get in their jobs, because most of them have made or could make bigger salaries working for privately owned companies.

The word *bureaucracy* means, literally, "government from a desk," or "from an office."

Burger, Warren Earl

Warren E. Burger is the 15th Chief Justice of the Supreme Court of the U.S., appointed by President Richard Nixon in 1969 when Chief Justice Earl Warren retired.

Born on a Minnesota farm in 1907, he spent his early years in St. Paul. After working his way through law school, he graduated *magna cum laude* from the St. Paul College of Law in 1931. He practiced law in Minnesota until 1953 when he joined the Eisenhower administration as an assistant Attorney General. In 1956 he was appointed to the U. S. Court of Appeals for the District of Columbia, the position he held until his appointment as Chief Justice.

burglary

Burglary is the crime of breaking into or entering a person's home with the idea of stealing something. Some states have laws that say burglary can only take place at night. If the same thing takes place in the daytime these states call it *housebreaking.* When the police arrest

a burglar they sometimes say that he is guilty of "breaking and entering," because they can put him in jail for breaking and entering if he opens a closed window or forces a door to get into a house, whether he steals something or not. Some burglars climb up to a porch or window on the second floor of a house because the ground floor is more often locked up. These burglars are called "second-story men."

Burgos

Burgos is a historic city in northern Spain and also the name of a large inland province of which the city is capital. The province is about the size of the state of Georgia and about 400,000 people live there. Most of them are farmers. The city of Burgos is on the Arlanzón River. About 70,000 people live there, working in factories that make woolen and leather goods, and paper.

Spanish Tourist Office
Most of the buildings and sculpture in Burgos are hundreds of years old.

Burgos was already an important city more than a thousand years ago. It was the capital of Castile and León for about 500 years until that kingdom became part of the Spanish kingdom in 1560.

During the Spanish Civil War of 1936 to 1939, Burgos was the headquarters of the forces under General Francisco Franco. At Burgos you can see one of the most famous and beautiful cathedrals in Europe. This cathedral was built in 1221, and one of the most important Spanish heroes, the Cid, is buried there. The Cid lived at Burgos, a fact that still makes the people of Burgos very proud.

BURGOS. Province: Area, 55,350 square miles. Population 390,058. Capital, Burgos, population 69,789.

Burgoyne, John

John Burgoyne was a famous English general during the American Revolution. He was born in 1722 and went  to school in England. After graduation, he entered the army. In 1774 he was sent to America, and in 1777 he was a leader in the fight against the American colonists.

With several thousand English soldiers and a few hundred Indians, he captured Fort Ticonderoga, in New York State. He then lost battles at Bennington, Vermont, and Stillwater, New York, and was badly defeated by the Americans

under General Gates at Saratoga, near Stillwater, in October, 1777. Burgoyne and his whole army were captured. He was later allowed to return to England, and he became commander in chief of the English army in Ireland. His last days were devoted to writing plays and histories. He died in 1792.

Burgundy

Burgundy is a region in eastern France that was formerly a large province. It is now divided into four departments, which are something like states. The departments are Ain, Yonne, Saône et Loire, and Côte d'Or. Burgundy is a rich agricultural country that is especially famous for the wines made from the grapes grown there.

The ancient Burgundians were a German tribe who lived more than 1,500 years ago and formed themselves into a kingdom. Then the kingdom became a duchy, which means that it was ruled by a duke. The dukes of Burgundy were very powerful, more powerful even than the kings of France itself. One of the dukes fought with the English against the French King Charles VII and his army which was led by Joan of Arc. However, the duke was finally beaten and Burgundy became a province of France under King Louis XI. All this happened about 500 years ago.

The largest city in Burgundy is Dijon, which is also the historical capital of the province. There are several beautiful churches and palaces in Dijon as well as in the other towns of Burgundy. In the countryside, there are some very big and famous castles in which people still live.

burial

Burial is the way in which mankind disposes of the bodies of people who have died. Throughout history different peoples in different places have had different ways of disposing of dead bodies. The earliest savage wanderers probably just left bodies lying on the ground. Only when men began to settle down and stay in one place did they probably dig holes and bury the dead. They did this because they found that they could not keep dead bodies lying around to rot away and smell, and attract wild animals. Man also began to bury the dead because he had become religious, and even in his primitive religion, he believed that some respect had to be shown to those who had died.

Many primitive groups believed that people make a long journey after death. So they put certain kinds of tools, or weapons, or food, in the grave when they buried a dead body. When men became more civilized, they still continued to do this. The ancient Egyptians even killed the dead person's horse and pet animals, and buried them with him. Some Eskimo tribes still bury a dead man's dog with him, so that the dog can make this long journey with his master.

There have been tribes throughout history that believed that birth and death are alike in some ways, and that the earth is the mother of all people. These tribes arranged the bodies of their dead in the same position as the unborn child has in the mother, and then buried the bodies in the ground.

People in some parts of the world do not bury the dead in the ground, but build platforms above the ground to hold the bodies. Many Indian tribes have done this, particularly those that lived in the north where the bodies would not rot away so quickly in the cold. Some South American Indians buried their dead high up in the mountains where the ice and snow never melt. In this way, the bodies were kept in a sort of deep freeze and never rotted away.

Many early tribes and many civilized people *cremate* dead bodies. You cremate a body by burning it until nothing is left of it but ashes. The ashes are then either placed in a jar and buried or put in a tomb or place of honor, or they are scattered so that they may mix with the earth from which people believe all life originally came.

Man learned very early in his history how to keep dead bodies from rotting. The Egyptians developed a way of preserving dead bodies, called *embalming,* by injecting certain chemicals into the bodies. They put the bodies in stone tombs. The embalmed bodies of Egyptian kings and queens (called "mummies") were buried in huge tombs called pyramids, that took thousands of workmen years to build. The mummies of some of the kings and queens have been discovered by scientists recently, and these mummies are unusually well preserved. The Greeks and Romans also embalmed their dead before they buried the bodies. In modern countries the law requires that a doctor make out a paper stating what a person died from, before the body can be embalmed and buried.

Most people today bury their dead in the ground or cremate them. Sometimes, if a person dies while he is at sea, his body is sewed in a weighted canvas sack and dropped into the sea.

Burke, Edmund

Edmund Burke was a great British statesman and orator at the time of the American Revolution. He was born in Dublin, Ireland, in 1729. He planned to become a lawyer, but changed his mind and became a writer instead. He lectured on political matters, and wrote many articles about political issues of his day. Burke believed that the American Colonies were being treated unfairly by King George III, and he made a speech before Parliament, the English legislature, in which he said that more justice should be shown to the American colonies. The Americans thought Burke was their best friend in the British government. Burke made many stirring speeches in Parliament, and he was always on the side of the people who were being unjustly treated. He also wrote several books that helped win sympathy for American colonists. He is best remembered for *American Taxation* and *Conciliation with America,* which most students read in high school. Burke died in 1797, at the age of 68.

burlesque

Burlesque is the name given to any exaggerated way of making fun of somebody or something. Whenever you see someone imitate another person's actions in a funny, clownish way you are watching a burlesque. When you read something that makes something seem ridiculously funny, you are reading a burlesque. A burlesque show is one in which the actors make fun of serious things, other shows, or very important people. In John Gay's *Beggar's Opera* produced in London more than 200 years ago, the actors and singers made fun of royalty. For about 75 years, starting about 1850, burlesque shows were musical comedies, or revues, almost like modern musical comedies. In the 1920s they began to use so many naughty jokes and scenes that most people disliked them, and now most places have laws against these burlesque shows.

Burma

Burma is a country in eastern Asia, about halfway around the world from the United States. It is south of China and east of India. It is about 260,000 square miles in area, which is about the size of Texas, and has about 25,000,000 people living in it, which is more than twice as many people as there are in Texas. Life in Burma is very different from life in the United States. The Burmese civilization is very old and is highly developed, but the people of Burma do not have the modern things that we have.

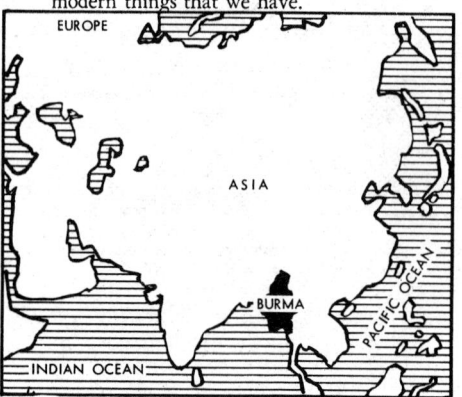

THE PEOPLE WHO LIVE THERE

Most of the people of Burma belong to the Mongolian race, to which the people of China, Japan and Korea also belong. They came to Burma several thousand years ago from China. There are several different peoples in Burma. The largest and most powerful is the Burmese. Most Burmese believe in the Buddhist religion. (You can read about this religion in a separate article on BUDDHISM.) They are not very tall, and most of them are stocky. They are very cheerful, peaceful and even-tempered people. Although they are not very rich or modern in their ways, most Burmese can read and write, and they learn a lot from the Buddhist priests who live in each village. The Burmese are very polite and kind, and the Burmese men treat their women much better than women are treated in most eastern civilizations.

The next most important group of people in Burma is the Karens, who live in the section of Burma which is near the mouth of the great Irrawaddy River. Other Burmese groups are the Chins, the Kachins, the Shans, the Kayaks, and the Nagas of the wild North. Some of these tribes were very primitive until just a short time ago. The Nagas were once head-hunters, and it was dangerous for a stranger to enter their territory. The head-hunting tribes lived by themselves in the hills.

Many Chinese and Indians live in Burma. They went there because their own countries have so many people that it is hard to make a living. Many of the Indians in Burma became rich and powerful because they became bankers and landowners. When Burma separated from India in 1937, most Indian merchants returned to India. The Chinese who live in Burma are mostly craftsmen and merchants.

HOW THE PEOPLE LIVE

Most of the people of Burma are farmers. Their main crop is rice. They live mostly in small villages, and it is not easy to get from one village to another. Not many farmers have automobiles as American farmers do. Very few of them know how to farm in a modern way.

There are only two big cities in Burma. Rangoon is the capital city. About 740,000 people live there, which is about as many as live in New Orleans. There is a very fine university in Rangoon and also one at Mandalay, and many young Burmese study modern ways of doing things and to become scientists, doctors, engineers, and modern farmers. The other big city in Burma is Mandalay. About 186,000 people live there, just about as many as there are in Worcester, Mass. If you were to visit Rangoon or Mandalay you would see many beautiful temples and palaces in both of these cities. Most of the people who live in the cities are tradesmen. Some of the city people work in the different industries the government is trying to develop.

Burma is just beginning to be a modern country. It does not have many big factories or modern plants. But the Burmese government has started on plans to make Burma more modern. Burma can become very rich if the Burmese people learn to take advantage of all the things that can be found there. For instance, there are many rich tin and silver mines in Burma. The most beautiful rubies, sapphires and jade in the world come from that country. A very beautiful tree called teak grows in Burma. Its wood is valuable and is used for making fine and expensive furniture.

WHAT KIND OF A PLACE IT IS

Burma is a very hilly country. It has many high mountains, some of them so high that their tops are covered with snow all year round. Many rivers run through Burma and most of them run from the north to the south. The largest river is the Irrawaddy, and many boats carry goods on it for almost a thousand miles. There are only two seasons in Burma— a wet season and a dry season. In the wet season, there are very heavy rains, and many rivers are flooded. The people who live in villages near the rivers protect their homes from the floods by building them on stilts. It gets quite hot in Burma from February to October. The temperature sometimes goes as high as 100 degrees, but the evenings are usually pleasantly cool. There are many wild animals in the forests of Burma. There are elephants, rhinoceros, and a strange animal called the tapir. There are some very dangerous snakes in Burma, too,

such as the cobra and the python.

HOW THE PEOPLE ARE GOVERNED

Burma is a republic. It used to be part of the British Empire, but it became independent in 1948. Under its constitution, Burma is to be governed by a president, a parliament, and a premier. The premier is the real head of the government. The president just has the honor of leading the government. The parliament is made up of representatives of the different sections of the country. Members of the parliament are elected by the people, and the president is elected by the parliament. But during much of the time since 1958, the Burmese people have actually been governed by military dictators.

BURMA IN THE PAST

For many centuries the Burmese had their own government. This government was ruled by a king, who was very powerful. Burma had very little to do with the Western World until the 18th century, when the British and the Dutch discovered that Burma was rich in precious gems and other things. The British took over the Burmese government in 1885, and Burma became a British colony. The British continued to rule Burma until World War II. In 1942, Japan conquered Burma and held it until the Allies won it back in 1945. After the war was over, Burma became part of the British Empire again, until 1948.

When Burma became independent it had many problems. The Karens wanted to set up their own government, and the Communists were trying to seize power.

A man named U Nu ("U" is a title of respect, just as we might say "Mr. Nu") was premier from 1948 to 1958. In 1958, when the Communist danger became too great, U Nu asked the head of the Burmese Army to run the country. Free elections were held in 1960 and U Nu was again elected premier. But in 1962 the Army took control for a second time, dismissed U Nu, dissolved the parliament, and set up a military government.

Burma is a member of the United Nations. In 1961 a Burmese statesman, U Thant, was selected to act as Secretary-General of the United Nations.

THE BURMA CAMPAIGN

When the Japanese took over Burma in World War II, the Allies lost a very important supply route to China. The Burmese people did not like the Allies but they were not happy under Japanese control, either. The Allies were able to work with Burmese patriots to drive the Japanese out of the country. The British did most of the fighting in Burma. American and Chinese soldiers fought with the British.

The war in Burma was very hard to fight. Most of it took place in the jungle and in hilly places. The soldiers had to fight in heavy rains and in great heat. But the Allies finally drove out the Japanese armies in Burma, and in April, 1945, retook the country.

BURMA. Area, 261,789 square miles. Population (1964 estimate), 24,229,000. Chief language, Burmese. Chief religion, Buddhism. Government, republic. Monetary unit, the kyat, worth 21¢ (U.S.). Flag, red with dark blue shield; white five-pointed star in center of shield, with a smaller star between each two points of the big star.

Burma Road

The Burma Road was built and became known all over the world during the early days of World War II. The Chinese people were fighting a desperate war with the Japanese armies that invaded China, and they could not get supplies from other countries because the Japanese controlled the coasts and ports of China. The only way the Chinese could get supplies was from Burma in the south, and there were no roads leading over the mountains between Burma and China. So the Chinese decided to build a road. While the road was being built, American airmen flew supplies over "The Hump," the name they gave to the high mountains between Burma and China. They flew in many supplies but not nearly enough to help the Chinese in the war.

The Burma Road was begun in 1937, and it took 200,000 workers, both Chinese and Burmese, more than a year to complete it. The men who worked on the road had very little equipment. They did not have any bulldozers or other necessary machinery. Almost all the work was done by hand labor under very primitive conditions, and many of the workers became sick and died.

The Burma Road is 800 miles long. It is very winding, and coils like a giant snake through forests and over mountains. More than 300 bridges were built to carry the road across rivers. The air distance between one end of the Burma Road and the other is less than 400 miles, so you can imagine how the road twists and turns. The Burma Road is not a modern paved highway. It is made of earth and crushed stone, and is difficult and dangerous to travel on.

The Burma Road continued to be an important Allied supply line until the Japanese captured Burma in 1942. Then the road was closed. But early in 1945, the Allies recaptured Burma, and the Burma Road became an important route for supplying ammunition and other war materials to China and other Allied soldiers in China. It is now closed and there is very little traffic on it.

burn

A burn is an injury caused by heat. The heat can be an open flame or a very hot object like the unprotected handle of a pot. When the heat is a very hot liquid, the burn is called a "scald." Like any other injury, a burn can be small, in which case it is no more serious than any other small injury like a bump or bruise. But if the burn covers a large part of the body, it can be serious enough to send the patient to a hospital for many weeks.

Sometimes a burn, even one that covers a large area, is only on the very top of the skin, like a sunburn. That is a burn too, but it does not actually destroy any of the skin, and it is called a *first degree* burn. If the burn is deeper and the outer layer of the skin is really burned off and a great many blisters are formed, it is a *second degree* burn. This, of course, is much more serious and takes longer to heal. The worst kind is a *third degree* burn, when the skin and perhaps the muscles and other layers underneath are hurt. If this third degree burn is wide enough, it can sometimes cause death.

All burns are very painful. Even a bad sunburn is painful. For first degree burns there are a number of cooling and soothing ointments that can be put on at once. Burns should always be kept clean and covered. More serious burns must be treated by a doctor, as quickly as possible, because patients with serious burns go very quickly into a state of "shock" (see the article on BIOCHEMISTRY), and the doctor must do other things to the patient besides treating the burn itself.

There is an old proverb that says, "Never play with fire." While fire is the most useful of all our natural servants, it can get beyond control very easily and then it can cause a great deal of harm. Always be very careful to keep smaller children away from the stove or the fireplace. You show good sense when you are careful with lighters and matches.

Burnett, Frances Hodgson

Frances Hodgson Burnett was a famous writer who was born in England in 1849. She had her first story published in that country when she was only sixteen years old. The Civil War had just ended in America and she and her parents came to live in Tennessee. Frances Burnett went on writing stories and novels for grownups and children for the rest of her life. Her most popular book, *Little Lord Fauntleroy,* was about a little boy who wore velvet suits with white silk blouses, and always behaved himself and had perfect manners. Many other stories were made into plays that were very popular both in England and America.

Burns, Robert

Robert Burns was a great Scottish poet who lived about 200 years ago. He became famous for his songs and poems that were written mostly in the Scottish dialect, the form of English that people

Gale Research Co.

of his country spoke. He wrote *Auld Lang Syne,* the song we all know and often sing when we want to say goodbye, or at the end of the year. The words are Scottish and mean simply "old long since." Burns wrote about ordinary everyday things in a wonderfully simple and beautiful way. The people loved his poems so much that they called him by the affectionate nickname of Bobbie, or Robbie.

Robbie Burns was born in 1759 at Alloway, Scotland, near the town of Ayr. His father was a peasant and so poor that he could not afford to send his Robbie and the six younger children to school. But he was a very fine and intelligent man who taught Robbie almost as much as he would have learned in school. They all worked so hard on the farm that Robbie's health was almost ruined. His early life was so hard that his only amusements were reading books and writing songs and poems. When he was older he began to live in a reckless way that caused people to criticize him.

Robert Burns loved three different girls, Elizabeth Patron, Jean Armour, and Mary Campbell. He was going to marry Mary Campbell, but she died just after his first book of poems was published. He married Jean Armour and they had four children. He tried to make a living as a farmer, but failed. He then became a tax inspector, and kept this job until he died in 1796 when he was only 37 years old.

Not until after he died did everyone realize how great he really was. He made almost no money from his poems and was so poor that just before he died he had to borrow money from his cousin to pay some debts and save himself from spending his last days in jail.

Burnside, Ambrose

Ambrose Burnside was a general in the Union army during the Civil War. He became better known for the kind of whiskers he wore than for anything he did on the battlefield. He was born in Liberty, Indiana, in 1824. He went to the United States Military Academy at West Point.

Gale Research Co.

He resigned from the army, but he rejoined it when the Civil War broke out. He held several important commands in the Union army, and the soldiers easily recognized him because of the special kind of whiskers he wore, which became known as "burnsides," or "sideburns," after him. Sideburns are whiskers that grow on the side of the face. Burnside died in 1881.

Burr, Aaron

Aaron Burr was Vice President of the United States from 1801 to 1805, during Thomas Jefferson's first term as President. Burr was born in 1756, and studied to be a lawyer. He liked politics and soon became leader of a political party that opposed the election of George Washington as President of the United States.

Gale Research Co.

However, Burr is best remembered as the man who shot and killed Alexander Hamilton in a duel, July 11, 1804. Burr and Hamilton were members of two different political parties. They were bitter enemies. After Burr lost the election for governor of New York, he challenged Hamilton to a duel with pistols. He blamed Hamilton for helping to defeat him in the election.

The two men met in Weehawken, New Jersey, across the Hudson river from New York City. When the signal was given to fire their pistols, Hamilton aimed his pistol into the air to avoid hitting Burr. Burr aimed directly at Hamilton, and wounded him so severely that Hamilton died.

Shortly after this, Burr was accused of plotting to take over Mexico and the western part of the United States, and set himself up as a king. Jefferson had him arrested and brought to trial three times for treason, but each time Burr was found

not guilty. Burr then went to Europe. He returned to the United States in 1812 very poor and without friends. He opened a law office and was a lawyer until he died in 1836, at the age of 80.

Burroughs, John

John Burroughs was a famous American writer who wrote many books about nature. He was born in 1837 on a farm near Roxbury, N.Y., and did not receive much education, but he learned much by himself, especially about the wonders and beauties of nature. As a young man, he met the great American poet, Walt Whitman, who became his greatest influence and a very dear friend. Burroughs wrote several books about Whitman and he helped to make the poet popular. Burroughs was also a teacher, a magazine writer, and a treasury official in Washington. But about 1871, he settled on a farm on the Hudson River, in New York, and wrote the first of his twenty nature books. He died in 1921.

Gale Research Co.

Burroughs was a keen observer and a delightful writer. He told of his adventures with birds, fish, flowers, trees, and the seasons of the year and made his readers see things they had never noticed. Many people came to visit him and join his walks through the countryside. Burroughs could show them that "the most precious things in life are near at hand, without money and without price."

Burundi

Burundi is a small kingdom in east central Africa. It became independent on July 1, 1962. Before World War I the territory was part of German East Africa and was called Urundi. Later it became part of the Belgian United Nations Trusteeship territory of Ruanda-Urundi. In area Burundi is about the size of Maryland and has almost the same number of people living there. The chief products are coffee, cattle, and animal hides. The government consists of a king called the Mwami, a premier who acts as head of government, and a legislature. The capital is Bujumbura, a city of 71,000.

The people of Burundi are Negroes belonging to the Bahuto and Watusi tribes. There are also some Pygmies of the Batwa tribe. Most of the people are Bahutos, but for centuries the Watusi have ruled the country. The king is a Watusi. In neighboring Rwanda, the Bahutos drove out the Watusi leaders and gained control of the government; but in Burundi the Watusis kept power. In both countries there has been constant fighting between the two groups and many people have been killed. (See also RWANDA.)

BURUNDI. Area, 10,744 square miles. Population (1973 estimate), 3,600,000.

bus

A bus is a long motor vehicle that carries paying passengers from place to place. It is much longer than a taxicab and carries ten times as many people. Buses that carry passengers within a city or town are called *local buses*. Those that travel from city to city are called *inter-*

city buses. The word *bus* is from the Latin *omnibus,* meaning "for all."

Kings and nobles began to use private horse-carriages more than three hundred years ago. Ordinary people could not afford such luxury, so they demanded public vehicles to carry them about their business. One of the first horse-drawn coaches to carry passengers belonged to the borough of Hackney in London, England. That is where our word "hack" comes from. The French king issued a license for a public coach service in 1662. New York had this kind of bus about thirty years later. It was owned by a Bowery saloonkeeper who gave his patrons special transportation. In 1719, an intercity line started between Philadelphia, New York, and Boston. It took four days to go from New York to Boston. The buses you see today make the same trip in half a day.

THE MOTOR BUS

The first automobile appeared around 1900. Within 25 years, motor buses were replacing streetcars in the cities and had begun to carry passengers who had previously ridden from city to city on railroad trains. The bus lines began to use diesel engines in 1938. These engines give more miles for each dollar's worth of fuel than gasoline engines. (Both engines are described under INTERNAL COMBUSTION ENGINE.)

In 1944, one American bus line alone had 65,000 miles of route, five times more than any railroad. There were more intercity buses on the highways of America than there were passenger coaches on rails. In 1960 there were about 72,850 local and intercity buses in the United States. They carried more than five billion passengers that year. Some cities like San Francisco, Chicago, and Honolulu have trolley buses. Trolley buses, like streetcars, receive their power from overhead electric lines. They are better than streetcars because they do not have to stay on tracks or rails. The coast-to-coast buses go from New York to Los Angeles in three and a half days. They are very comfortable. They are air-conditioned and they have rest rooms. The latest models cost twenty times as much as most new automobiles. There are so many buses going in and out of New York City every day that the world's largest bus terminal was built for them. It is called the Port of New York Authority Bus Terminal. About 180,000 passengers and 6,200 buses use it each weekday.

OTHER USES

Buses are also used for sightseeing. Every day you may see them in great cities like New York, driving slowly past places of interest like the Empire State Building and Grant's Tomb.

In 1960 there were about 178,440 school buses in the U.S. They carried 12,310,000 children to and from school every day. North Carolina has more than 6,000 school buses, the largest fleet in the world. Many parents want their children to ride on these buses because they are sure the children will get to school safely and on time. School buses are usually painted yellow and marked with

large signs that warn other drivers to be careful. In many communities, the law forbids drivers to pass a school bus when it is taking on passengers or letting them off.

Bush, Vannevar

Vannevar Bush became famous as the American scientist who was the head of atomic research during World War II. He was one of the most important people in the development of the atomic bomb. Bush was born in 1890, and became an electrical engineer. In 1932, he was made dean of engineering at the Massachusetts Institute of Technology, and later he became the head of research at the Carnegie Institution of Washington. After World War II broke out, he was made the head of the government Office of Scientific Research and Development. He supervised all the nation's scientists who worked on the atomic bomb and other inventions that helped America and its allies to win the war. He died in 1974.

bushido

Bushido is a set of unwritten Japanese rules on how to behave. It was first used in Japan more than seven hundred years ago. It was like the code of honor that the Knights of the Round Table lived by. Every Japanese noble and warrior in the Middle Ages lived by these rules. They taught him how to live with honor, and also how to die to save his honor. The code covered everything in life, from courage and loyalty to handling a sword and how to dress.

Some of the laws are still lived up to in Japan today. During World War II many pilots of Japanese planes and many soldiers in the Japanese army killed themselves because they thought it was dishonorable to be captured. This was a part of law of bushido. The act of *harakiri* is another part of the same law. This is suicide by cutting open one's own stomach and bleeding to death. Although some of the ideas of bushido still exist today, most of them disappeared after the defeat of Japan in World War II.

Bushman, one of the native peoples of Africa. The natives of Australia are also sometimes called bushmen. See the articles on AFRICA and AUSTRALIA.

bushmaster

The bushmaster is a large poisonous snake that lives in South and Central America. It is known as "the silent rattler," because it vibrates its tail when it

Am. Museum of Nat. History
Would you believe that this bushmaster, curled up in the sun, is nine feet long?

is angry, but the sound produced is no more than a low buzz. The bushmaster is about nine feet long, though some have been found that are twelve feet long. It is pale brown, with large black and brown patches. This snake is dangerous and will attack anything that comes close. It has poison glands in its head and long fangs through which the venom is injected into the creatures it bites.

bushrangers

The bushrangers were a band of thieves and escaped convicts who terrorized Australia about 150 years ago. They got their name because they used to hide in the scrubland, or bush, after their raids. They would raid farms and villages and rob travelers on the roads and highways. When gold was discovered in the southern part of Australia, they used to rob the prospectors and the wagons that carried the gold. They became so bold that in 1815 Australia declared martial law. (That is, the army and the police joined forces to protect the people.) By 1830 laws had been passed against the activities of the bushrangers and to punish them when they were caught. It still took many years to wipe out the last of them, and it was not until about 1870 that the Australian people were sure there were no more of these highwaymen and robbers.

business

Business is any one of many things that people work at to earn money and to do things for other people. It actually comes from the word *busy* and means "being busy with." You would hardly ask a person what he was busy with when you wanted to know what kind of work he did, but you would ask what business he was in.

Business is everything people do that concerns making and selling things. Manufacturing is business, and so are all the other kinds of work concerned with the things that are manufactured—advertising, building, banking, and selling. A *wholesaler* is a businessman who buys large quantities of a product from a manufacturer or producer and sells it to a retailer. A *retailer* is a businessman who sells what he buys to all of us who are customers.

Business really started with the first man who produced more of something than he could use, and then traded it to neighbors who gave him something in return. Perhaps this early businessman had more stone arrowheads than he needed, and his neighbor had an extra piece of fresh meat. When the trade was made the two cavemen had become the world's first businessmen. From that time on business grew. As men produced more and more of a particular thing and built wagons and ships to carry their products, they engaged in bigger and bigger businesses. Modern business has grown from the first simple swap to a point where billions of dollars change hands each year. The more money that is spent in business, the more money there is on hand to pay all the people who work in the many businesses we now have.

Business has grown so big that governments now have laws to control it. Not too long ago, some businessmen used to

be greedy, and they took advantage of everybody they did business with. Government rules now prevent businessmen from taking unfair advantage of the people who work for them, of the people who buy from them, and of the people who are in the same business—their competitors.

Modern business is one of mankind's greatest activities. It provides us with food, clothing, shelter, medicines, transportation, and entertainment. It also provides us with the weapons with which we can defend ourselves when we are threatened or attacked by other countries. Modern business is highly specialized. This makes it possible to produce many things more cheaply and more quickly than they could be made in any other way.

Specialization makes it possible for men to learn to do one thing well, instead of doing many things poorly. It makes us dependent on many people for all the things we need for good living. It also gives jobs to many millions of people. The more people there are working, the more there are with money to buy the things that business provides, and the more jobs there are for other people. Business is good when people are working, earning good wages, and buying many things. Business is bad when fewer people are working, and fewer people have money to spend on the things they need and want.

Busoni, Ferruccio Benvenuto

Ferruccio Busoni was a famous Italian pianist and composer, or writer of music. He was one of the greatest pianists who ever lived, and many people think he was the best of all time. Busoni was born in Italy in 1866. His father and mother were both musicians, and they were his only teachers. When he was seven years old he played in public for the first time, and for the rest of his life he played the piano before audiences all over Europe and America. He composed many things, including a concerto for piano and orchestra, a violin sonata, and a fine opera, *Doctor Faust*. He was also famous for his arrangements of other composers' music so that it could be played on the piano. Busoni's name is often mentioned with that of Johann Sebastian BACH, about whom you can read in a separate article. Busoni took music that Bach had composed for the organ and arranged it to be played on the piano. He died in Berlin in 1924.

butane

Butane is a gas that is found in oil and gas wells. It is a mixture of hydrogen and carbon, and for that reason it is called a *hydrocarbon*. It belongs to the family of hydrocarbons called METHANE, about which there is a separate article.

Butane is very unusual. It boils at the temperature at which water freezes. This temperature is 32 degrees Fahrenheit (32° F.). It is hard to believe that something could boil at such a low temperature. When a liquid boils, it changes into

a gas or vapor. The temperature in oil wells and swamps is usually very much above 32° F., causing butane to boil and become a gas. If the temperature were lower, butane would be a liquid.

Butane can be changed into a liquid by a process called *condensation.* To condense butane, the temperature must be brought below 32° F. A special kind of butane, called *isobutane,* boils at an even lower temperature: 13° F. To change isobutane into a liquid, the temperature must be below 13° F.

Butane is often mixed with *propane,* a similar gas. This mixture is used as fuel for heating homes, and in gas stoves.

There is another gas which is similar to butane. This is *butylene.* Butylene is made by the removal of hydrogen (called "cracking") from butane. Butylene glycol is a compound made from butylene and other chemicals. It can be changed into a gas called *butadiene.* Butadiene is used in making artificial rubber, which you can read about in the article on RUBBER.

Butler, Nicholas Murray

Nicholas Murray Butler was a great educator and worker for world peace. He was born in Elizabeth, New Jersey, in 1862, and was graduated from Columbia University in New York City. He became a teacher and professor at Columbia, and in 1901 he was chosen to be president of that great university. Butler thought that the more educated people there were in the world, the better chance there would be for peace in the world. He worked very hard for peace, and he was given the Nobel peace prize in 1931. He was also a politician. He was a leader of the Republican Party for many years and when William Howard Taft was chosen by that party to run for president, in 1912, Butler was chosen to run for vice president. They were not elected, and Butler continued as president of Columbia University until 1945. He died two years later at the age of 85.

Butler, Samuel

Samuel Butler was the name of two great English writers. One of them lived about a hundred years ago. He was born in 1835. His grandfather was a bishop

and his father a clergyman, so it is not surprising that his family expected him to become a minister too. But at the last moment Butler refused, saying that he was not sure he was fit for the duties of a minister. Instead he went to New Zealand to operate a sheep ranch.

He earned a small fortune from his ranch, and after five years he returned to England. He never married. He was the author of several books. His novel *The Way of All Flesh* tells about a young man who suffers from the cruelty of his minister father. People who knew Butler knew he was writing about himself and his father in this book. Another book he wrote, *Erewhon,* is a long account of a voyage to an imaginary country cut off from the world. As you see, "Erewhon"

is close to being "Nowhere" spelled backward. Butler died in 1902.

The other Samuel Butler lived nearly three hundred years ago. He was born in 1612 and died in 1680. His famous work was a long poem called *Hudibras.* We still quote some of the famous lines from *Hudibras.* One of them is, *"Don't count your chickens before they are hatched."*

butte

A butte is a hill with steep sides, that rises sharply from a plain. Another name for a butte is a *knoll.* In the United States, buttes are usually found in dry regions in the western part of the country. Many buttes are found in the Rocky Mountains, in Montana and North Dakota. In Canada and England, a butte usually means a high mountain peak that is set apart from other peaks.

butter

Butter is a pale- to golden-yellow substance made from the fat in milk or cream. It is one of the most prized of all foods because of its pleasant taste. It is a healthful food, as it contains vitamins and the fat in it is easy to digest. If you shake milk for a long time it will separate into two parts—a layer of butter made by all the tiny drops of fat in the milk joining together, and a thin watery part called BUTTERMILK, which you can read about in a separate article.

Until about a hundred years ago butter was made only on farms or in people's homes, but now most butter is made in factories called creameries. These creameries must be kept very clean and cool, so the butter will be of good quality and safe to eat.

In making butter, the milk is first whirled round and round to extract the cream. The cream is then allowed to stand for a while; it slightly sours and gets the flavor it will have as butter. The flavor is caused by bacteria, which are living organisms so small they can be seen only through a microscope. To make sure the right bacteria are present in the cream, some are usually added to the cream. After the cream has been standing for a while, it is churned to separate the butter. The butter is washed, and usually a little salt is added to it. Then it is stirred to make it smooth.

The natural color of butter depends on what the cows have eaten. When the cows eat lots of fresh grass, their milk makes rich yellow butter. When they have to eat dry hay through the winter months, the butter made from their milk is almost white. If the butter is too pale, artificial coloring is added so that the butter will be yellow.

Butter is then packaged in pound "prints" that are often divided into two or four parts. Some butter is packed in large containers and sold as "tub" butter to large users such as hotels, restaurants, and so on.

There are many different kinds of butter. In some countries it is made from the milk of goats, sheep, and mares. Butter has been made for more than two thousand years, and was known in ancient Egypt and Greece. At first it was used as fuel in lamps, as medicine, and as an ointment for the skin. Today the countries which produce the most butter are the

United States (chiefly in the northern Midwest), Russia, Denmark, Australia, and New Zealand.

buttercup

A buttercup is a kind of wild flower which grows mostly in meadows, though some grow floating in slow-moving streams. They have shiny yellow flowers, the color of butter, with round petals. Their leaves are very pretty—dark green, and deeply cut up into the shape of a tiny hand. Buttercups have sharp, acid juice, so they are not eaten by cows, horses, or other grazing animals. Some people think that if cows eat buttercups, they will give bitter milk. Some buttercups have juice that will blister your skin. Some are so beautiful that they are grown in gardens. One of these is the turban buttercup, which comes in many colors and has "double" flowers.

butterflies and moths

Butterflies and moths are small animals that fly about with big, colorful wings. They are *Insects,* which means that they have six legs and their bodies are divided into three parts—a head, a middle part called the thorax, and a tail part called the abdomen. But they are different from all other winged insects because their wings are covered with scales. If you touch a butterfly's wings, your finger becomes dusty. Under a powerful magnifying glass, this "dust" can be seen to be thousands of flat, wedge-shaped scales. These scales give the butterfly or moth its beautiful colors. Sometimes this is because the scales themselves are colored, but more often it is because they reflect light, in the same way that light is reflected from oil on water. Because of these scales, butterflies and moths are grouped together to form a class of insects called *Lepidoptera,* which means "scaly-winged."

HOW TO TELL THEM APART

There are many ways in which you can tell butterflies from moths. Nearly all butterflies fly only during the day; most moths come out at night. When resting, butterflies usually fold their wings together overhead; moths spread their wings flat, either wide apart, or with the front pair of wings covering the hind pair. The antennas (feelers) of a butterfly end in little knobs; the antennas of a moth are pointed or feathery. Certain butterflies, called *skippers,* are halfway between butterflies and moths.

WHERE THEY ARE FOUND

There are many more kinds of moths than butterflies. About 120,000 kinds of moth are known in the world, about 8,000 kinds in North America alone. Only about 16,000 kinds of butterfly are known in the world, of which only 700 are known in North America.

The most beautiful butterflies and moths of all are found in forests in hot, tropical regions. In Brazil there are giant butterflies with wings of a brilliant flashing blue that measure ten inches across. Other kinds have wings that are as transparent as glass, and there are lovely green-and-white swallow-tailed moths that fly about in the day and behave like

293

Margot L. Wolf

This beautiful Painted Lady butterfly is feeding on the nectar of a flower.

butterflies. In Malaya there are giant bird-wing butterflies, and in India is found the largest of all butterflies and moths, the Atlas moth. The smallest moth, the British golden pygmy, is only one-fifth inch in wingspan.

Here in North America there are many beautiful butterflies and moths—the pale-green Luna moth, the rich-colored, brown-and-red Cecropia moth, the graceful swallowtail butterflies, and many others.

THEIR STRANGE WAYS

If you watch a butterfly or moth as it sits on a flower you will see a strange thing. From under its head a long coiled tube, which looks at first like a watch-spring, unwinds itself and begins to probe about in the flower. This tube is the butterfly's mouth, through which it sucks all its food. Butterflies and moths live entirely on liquids, such as the nectar, or sweet liquid, found in flowers; the juice of fruits; or honeydew (a sweet liquid that oozes from the leaves of some plants). A few butterflies and moths have "spines" on the tips of their mouth tubes, and with these they can dig into ripe fruit.

As the butterflies and moths move from one flower to another, feeding on nectar, they also carry pollen from one to the other. This helps the flowers produce their seeds and fruits.

Most butterflies and moths visit many different kinds of flowers, as each kind opens, but sometimes a moth or butterfly will drink the nectar of only one particular plant. The moth or butterfly depends on that plant for its food, and the plant depends completely upon the moth or butterfly for its pollination. Only the yucca moth, for instance, has a feeding tube long enough to get into the flower of the yucca plant to get at the nectar, and to carry the pollen. After the moth

has sucked up the nectar from one flower, it goes on to another flower carrying pollen from the first, and so on. In each flower the moth lays some of its own eggs. When these hatch, the *caterpillars*, as the young of butterflies and moths are called, feed on some of the seeds of the plant.

Butterflies and moths have many enemies, such as birds, wasps, flies, mantises, and spiders, but they have many different ways of protecting themselves. The Indian Leaf butterfly is colored so that it looks just like a leaf. The owl butterflies have markings on their wings that look like huge staring eyes, probably to frighten away birds. When a swallowtail butterfly is at rest its "tails" look like antennas, to fool an attacker into thinking that the butterfly is facing the wrong way. The little hairstreaks rub their two hind wings together, so that they look like waving antennas. Some butterflies are both evil-tasting and brightly colored; once a bird has eaten one it will never touch another one. The monarch butterfly has this kind of "warning" coloration. The viceroy butterfly protects itself by looking like the monarch, even though it is actually good to eat.

Some butterflies and moths "migrate," that is, they move from one part of the country to another regularly, according to the seasons of the year, just as birds and some fishes do. The painted lady, for instance, spends the winter in southern Europe or North Africa, and in the spring flies north again, often as far as Iceland. The monarch butterflies appear in large numbers in Canada and the northern part of the United States and then, usually in early fall, they all begin to fly south, to Florida, California, or even to the West Indies. More often, however, butterflies and moths will migrate in huge numbers at irregular times and seasons, for no reason that is known.

In many parts of the world large numbers of a certain kind of butterfly or moth will be born year after year in one area, and then suddenly start moving in millions to some other part of the country. This may happen at regular intervals of years, such as every four years, or it may happen once a year.

Some butterflies and moths pass the winter asleep in sheltered places such as hollow logs, or even inside houses. Others die when winter comes, leaving their eggs or caterpillars. The bagworm moth lays its eggs in a silken bag at the tip of a branch. The caterpillars of the viceroy butterfly live through the winter in a rolled-up leaf, those of the cattail moth inside the stalks of the cattail plant, and those of the apple codling moth inside the core of an apple.

The eggs of the butterfly or moth are often so tiny that they can be seen only under a magnifying glass. They may be round little balls, or cores, or rods; they may be egg-shaped, or flat. Whatever their shape, they are nearly always covered with ridges or networks of raised lines in beautiful patterns. Usually the eggs are carefully laid on the leaves or twigs of the kind of plant the caterpillars will feed on. A single butterfly or moth may lay as many as a thousand eggs.

White Peacock butterfly

Minois Semele

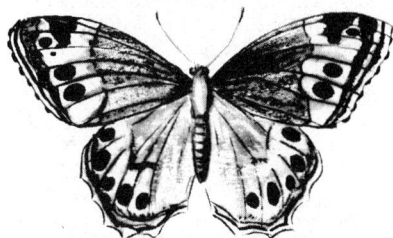

Pearly-eyed butterfly

CATERPILLARS

Quite soon after they are laid, the eggs begin to hatch. Out crowd the baby caterpillars, which begin eating at once. The caterpillars have jaws for biting solid food. They feed mostly on the

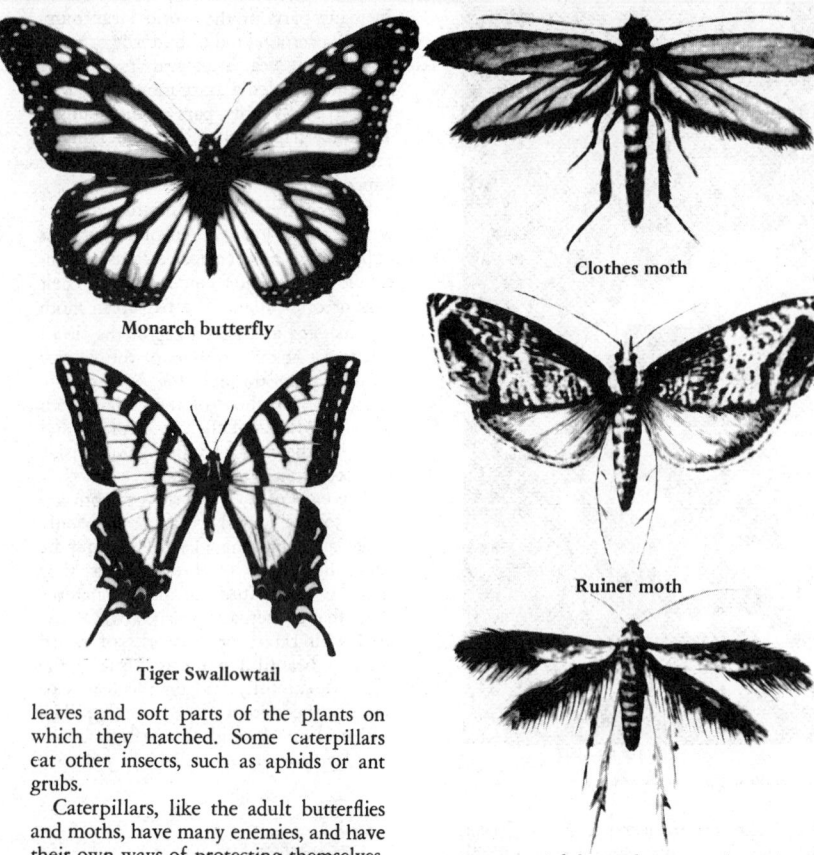

Monarch butterfly

Tiger Swallowtail

Clothes moth

Ruiner moth

Adult case-bearer moth

Sphinx moth

leaves and soft parts of the plants on which they hatched. Some caterpillars eat other insects, such as aphids or ant grubs.

Caterpillars, like the adult butterflies and moths, have many enemies, and have their own ways of protecting themselves. The caterpillar of the hawk moth has a long horn at its rear end, and frightens its enemies just by looking horrible. The "looper" caterpillar disguises itself by looking like a twig. Some caterpillars can throw out jets of acid when attacked, or give off poisonous fumes. The tiger moth caterpillar is so covered with hair that it makes an unpleasant mouthful. Some caterpillars even have hairs that sting. Caterpillars protect themselves best by feeding only at night, and hiding during the day in rolled-up leaves or in special "tents" made out of silk. Caterpillars, like spiders, have special organs in their bodies that produce silk. It comes out as a liquid, hardens at once in the air, and is drawn out into a thread. The "tent" is made of this silk, and caterpillars often use the silken thread as a life-line, dropping off twigs when disturbed and hauling themselves back again later.

A caterpillar's skin cannot stretch, except when new. As a caterpillar eats, it cannot get very much larger unless it gets out of its skin, which is exactly what it does. A new, soft skin forms under the old one. The old one bursts and rolls off like a pullover sweater, while the caterpillar swells rapidly inside the new one before it hardens. In this way a caterpillar grows larger and larger until it has grown as large as it can. Then, if it is a

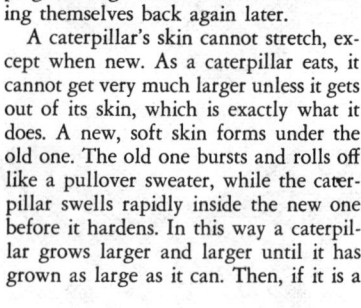

Clearwing moth

butterfly caterpillar, it sticks a small button of silk under a twig, attaches itself to this button, and casts its skin for the last time. What appears now is a strange object, pointed at both ends, with a hard, smooth skin. This is a resting stage in the life of the insect and is called a *pupa*. The pupas of moths are different from those of butterflies. The moth caterpillar usually weaves a fluffy case of silk, called a *cocoon,* around itself. From one such cocoon comes the silk used in clothing; see the article on SILKWORM.

The moth or butterfly may spend weeks or even months as a pupa, but all this time marvelous changes are taking place inside the case. All the organs of the caterpillar become liquid and serve as nourishment for the developing adult cells which will become a complete butterfly or moth. The mature insect looks nothing at all like its larval form. When it is completely developed, the insect splits the pupa and drags itself out. It is still rather soft and damp, and its wings are crumpled. It rests a while, fanning its wings and pumping blood into its veins. Then it flies away. Every butterfly or moth that you see has been through these wonderful changes.

BUTTERFLIES, MOTHS, AND MEN

Adult butterflies and moths are completely harmless. The caterpillars of butterflies, too, are harmless, except for a few that feed on cabbage leaves. The caterpillars of moths, however, do millions of dollars of damage each year. Various caterpillars bore into wood; eat clothing, hair, carpets, and wool; and infest grocery stores, flour mills, and grain stores. Army worms, leaf rollers and loopers are caterpillars that eat the leaves of fruit trees; cankerworms, cutworms and many kinds of borers are caterpillars that attack the roots and stems of food crops; codling moth caterpillars bore into apples; and peach moth caterpillars attack apples, plums, cherries, and peaches.

On the other hand, moths and butterflies may almost repay man by their valuable work in pollinating flowers, eating other insect pests, and giving him silk.

AS PETS

Butterflies and moths are very easy to raise as pets. You may try hatching a pupa, burying it in a jar of earth if you found it underground, or hanging it up in a warm dry place where it can get plenty of air. If you try to raise caterpillars, you must note carefully the plants on which you found them and the part of the plant on which they were feeding, so that you will be able to feed them properly. They must be kept in a warm, dry place from which they cannot escape, but where they will get plenty of air. If you have both males and females of the same kind, and can find out what plant their caterpillars eat, you may be able to watch the whole life story from egg to caterpillar, to pupa, and to adult once again.

buttermilk

Buttermilk is the liquid that is left after butter has been removed from regular milk or cream by churning. Although most of the fat has been taken out, buttermilk is very good for you because it still contains vitamins and other important foods that are in whole milk. Buttermilk has a slightly sour taste that many people like better than fresh milk. Years ago it was thrown away or fed to animals, but nowadays buttermilk is used as a drink, or dried, or condensed, which means boiled down until it is thick. It can then be used in ice cream and custard powders, in chicken feed, and in baking. Sometimes you may be sold a kind of buttermilk that is full of white lumps. This is called *cultured buttermilk* and is made by curdling, or souring, fresh milk with bacteria.

butterwort

The butterwort, or *bog violet*. is a small, pretty, wild plant which grows in damp places. There are many kinds, found in Europe and Asia as well as in North America. They have long, pale green leaves, held flat against the ground in a circle. These leaves are very wonderful things, for with them the plant catches insects and eats them. The leaves are sticky on top, and insects which settle there are caught. Then the edges of the leaves roll in and give off a juice that digests the insect. When the leaf

has absorbed the juice, it unrolls again to wait for another insect. From the center of the circle of leaves the plant sends up a long thin stem, on which there is usually one flower. This is usually purple or white, but one kind of butterwort, which grows in the southeastern United States, has a yellow flower.

button

Buttons are mostly used to fasten or hold different parts of our clothing together. Sometimes they are used just for ornament. Buttons are of many sizes and they can be of different shapes too, but ordinarily buttons are round. Since buttons usually have to be attached to clothing, they are made either with little holes in the middle, or with a piece of metal called a shank on the back, so they can be sewed on with thread. Buttons have been made from metals like steel, brass, iron and even silver and gold. They have also been made from wood, paper, cloth, glass, ivory, bone, horn, paste, celluloid, plastics, pearl and pottery clay.

Buttons are manufactured in many countries, but most of them are made in England and America. Buttons have been made in England for over three hundred years, but they did not become important until about two hundred years ago. At that time, the English button makers covered round metal buttons with cloth. These cloth-covered metal buttons are still made in England and the United States. Brass, steel, gilt, ivory, horn and bone buttons were made in Birmingham England, before the American Revolution. When the Puritans came to America they felt that buttons were too fancy and bright to go with their plain dark clothes, so they decided to wear little hooks and eyes instead. The Amish people who live mostly in Pennsylvania still use hooks and eyes rather than buttons.

Buttons were made by hand at first. Each button was shaped and decorated by a skilled button maker, but gradually people invented ways of making many buttons at one time all looking exactly alike. There are different methods for making buttons of each different kind of material. In Czechoslovakia for instance, glass buttons are made by pressing the heated and softened end of a glass rod into a mold. The glass hardens in the mold and sticks to a shank that has been placed there.

In America the center of the button industry is in Connecticut. Metal, bone, horn, vegetable, ivory, and pearl buttons have been made there a hundred years or more. Pearl buttons are made out of a certain kind of mussel shell which is found in the Mississippi River. These are called fresh-water pearl buttons. Mother-of-pearl buttons are called ocean pearl buttons, and are made from oyster shells. Some of the bone buttons are made from the horns and hooves of cattle and other animals.

Buttons have been found that were made by men who lived many thousands of years ago. Buttons were used as decorations by the Greeks, Romans, and the Chinese who wore them as a sign of high position, but they were first used as fastenings in about the 15th century in Europe. Buttons with special colors and patterns are still worn as decorations or as a sign of membership or high rank in some organization. They are also used in political campaigns so that people can show which candidates they favor in an election.

buzzard

Buzzard is the name given to more than thirty different kinds of hawk. They are all fairly large birds, with long, narrow wings, sharp hooked beaks, and strong, cruel "talons," or claws. European buzzards are mostly brownish-black on top and grayish-white underneath. American buzzards are about the same, except for the buzzard that is also called the *red-tailed hawk*. This bird is also brownish-black with a gray belly, but it has a red tail that is tipped with white. Buzzards build rough nests of sticks in the tops of the highest trees. Three or four white eggs speckled with brown are laid in the nest each spring. Buzzards eat small animals such as field mice, squirrels, chipmunks, smaller birds, and reptiles.

Some people call the vulture a turkey buzzard. Vultures feed on dead animals, and are not at all like the real buzzards. (You can read about the VULTURE in a separate article.)

bylaw

If you join a club or an organization, or work for a company, you have to obey certain rules and regulations that have been passed by these groups. These rules and regulations are called bylaws, because they are not the laws of the country. They do not affect everybody, but only those people who belong to, or work in, the organization that has made the bylaws.

Suppose that you and some of your friends decide to form a club. You may vote on a set of rules and regulations as to how many members your club will have, how often it will meet, what dues will be paid, and so on. These are written down and they become the bylaws of the club. When similar rules and regulations are written into the organization of a town or city, they are sometimes called bylaws.

Byng, Julian

Julian Byng was a British soldier and statesman, who became famous as one of the most important Allied generals in World War I. He was born in England in 1862 and entered the army after his education was completed. He served as an officer in India and Africa, and in World War I he was made commander-in-chief of the British 3rd Army. He led his men to several important victories, and when the war was over he was made a baron by King George V of England. In 1921, the king chose him to be governor-general of Canada, and Byng held this post until 1926. The king made him Viscount Byng when he returned to England. Lord Byng was the head of Scotland Yard, the famous London police headquarters, from 1928 to 1931. He died in 1935.

by-product

A by-product is anything that can be made from the leftovers of an industry. Sometimes a by-product can be used just as it is when the leftover itself is gathered, as in the case of sawdust. As lumber is sawed, the sawdust falls to the ground, and it is collected and used for many things as a by-product of the lumbering industry.

Other leftovers must be manufactured in order to make useful by-products. This is true in the case of soap. Soap is a by-product of the meat-packing industry. The animal fats are used to make soap, and soap has become just as important an industry as meat-packing itself. This is often true of by-products. Many plastics are by-products of lumbering. The resins from lumber are used to manufacture many kinds of plastics, and the plastic business is now a very important industry that started with a by-product of another. Cotton-raising has the by-product cottonseed oil. Flax gives us the by-product, linseed oil.

See the articles on COTTON, FLAX, and PLASTICS.

Byrd, Richard Evelyn

Richard E. Byrd was a famous explorer, the first man who ever reached both the North and South Poles by air. He established the LITTLE AMERICA settlement (about which there is a separate article) on the Antarctic continent. He was a United States naval officer, rising to the grade of rear admiral in the United States Navy. He died in 1957.

Byrd was born in Winchester, Virginia, in 1888, and was graduated from the Naval Academy at Annapolis in 1912. While he was at the academy he injured his left leg, and for this reason was told that he could not pilot a plane, but he persuaded the Navy doctors to let him try, and he became a famous aviator, one of the first men to fly over the North Pole (in 1926) and one of the first men to fly nonstop across the Atlantic Ocean (in 1928). In 1929 he flew over the South Pole, and in 1933 and 1939 he led big expeditions by ship to Antarctica. In his flights across the Atlantic and across the South Pole he had with him another famous explorer, Bernt Balchen.

The Byrd family has been a prominent one in Virginia for many years. Admiral Byrd's brother, Harry Flood Byrd, served as governor of his state and as United States senator.

Byron, Lord

George Gordon Byron was one of the greatest English poets. He lived about 150 years ago. During part of his lifetime he was the most popular English poet. He lived a very interesting life, and died when he was only 36 years old, trying to help the Greek people win their independence from the Turks who had ruled them for hundreds of years.

Byron was born in 1788. When he was 3 years old his father died, and his mother, who brought him up, was not a very sensible person. She would sometimes scold him angrily and then treat him with a great display of love, so that he grew up very confused. When he was 11 years old, the death of his great-uncle gave him the title Lord Byron, which meant that when he grew up he could sit in the House of Lords as a member of the British peerage. He was very proud of

being a lord.

As a boy, Byron was not happy. He was born with a deformed foot, and limped when he walked. He was fat, and most of his life he almost starved himself to keep his weight down. But he tried very hard at whatever he did. At Cambridge University, he became an excellent swimmer and boxer, in spite of his lameness. His first book of poems was published while he was at the university, and most people did not like it, but he did not give up. He kept on writing poems.

After he left school, Byron took a trip through Europe for two years. While he was away he wrote the first part of a long poem called *Childe Harold's Pilgrimage*. This was published in England when he returned, and was a great success. Byron wrote, "I awoke one morning and found myself famous." This was the first of many successful poems by Byron. He made a great deal of money by writing poems. Many consider another long poem, *Don Juan* to be his best.

Byron was a very handsome man, and many women loved him, but when he married, at the age of 27, he and his wife had an unhappy life and separated. This caused a scandal, and everyone blamed Byron. He never went back. He lived most of the time in Italy, where he saw much of Shelley and other famous English poets of that time.

Gale Research Co.

In 1823 he went to Greece to help the people there, but he died of a fever in 1824, before he could join the fighting. He was buried in England, near Newstead Abbey, the house in which he spent his boyhood.

Byzantine Empire

The important city that is now named Istanbul, and is the biggest city in Turkey, was named Byzantium when it was first built, more than 2,500 years ago. It is on the Greek side of the Bosporus, a narrow channel of water that separates Europe from Asia, and for many years it was part of Greece. Then the Roman Empire, which ruled all the civilized world two thousand years ago, took it over. About 1,600 years ago, in the year 330, a great Roman emperor named Constantine changed its name to Constantinople (which means "city of Constantine") and made it the capital of the Roman Empire.

Later in that same century, in the year 395, the Roman Empire was divided into two parts: the West Roman Empire, with its capital at Rome, and the East Roman Empire, with its capital at Byzantium. The East Roman Empire was often called the Byzantine Empire, because its capital had been called Byzantium for so long. The East Roman, or Byzantine, Empire lasted nearly a thousand years longer than the West Roman Empire. Western Rome fell to barbarian armies in the year 476, while the Byzantine Empire finally fell in the year 1453, when Constantinople was captured by the Turks.

The Byzantine Empire had a very

Some of the finest mosaics were made by Byzantine artists. A mosaic looks like a painting, but it is made of many colored stones pasted together.

stormy history during the period of more than a thousand years in which it existed. The emperors and the men who ran their governments were usually evil men, who did not hesitate to murder and steal for their own benefit. The empire was constantly under attack by Mohammedans from the east and savage tribes of Germans and Russians (Slavs) from the north. At first, the empire owned a great part of Asia Minor and some of North Africa, but these territories were taken away from it by losses in wars, and it shrank until it was not much larger than the modern country of Greece.

But even while it was so bad, the East Roman Empire did much to keep culture alive during the Dark Ages (the period of about a thousand years, from the fall of Rome to the beginning of the Renaissance, when learning was nearly forgotten in Europe). The designs and paintings and sculpture of that period are called *Byzantine art,* and although it was quite fancy when compared to the art of today, it created some great masterpieces that can still be admired for their beauty. The buildings of that period are described in the article in this encyclopedia on ARCHITECTURE.

The East Roman Empire also did much to keep Christianity alive in a large region that would otherwise have become Mohammedan. Russia became a Christian country because of the influence of the East Roman Empire, and so did some other parts of eastern Europe. The church of the East Roman Empire became what is now known as the Orthodox, or Greek Orthodox, Church.

This is how a Byzantine building looked 600 years ago.

The remains of this Byzantine arch still stand in Athens, Greece. It was named after the Emperor Hadrian.

Beautiful and brilliantly colored enamel work like this was done on large medals and tablets.

The top of this Byzantine chest was carefully carved out of ivory. It took a skilled artist a long time to do this.

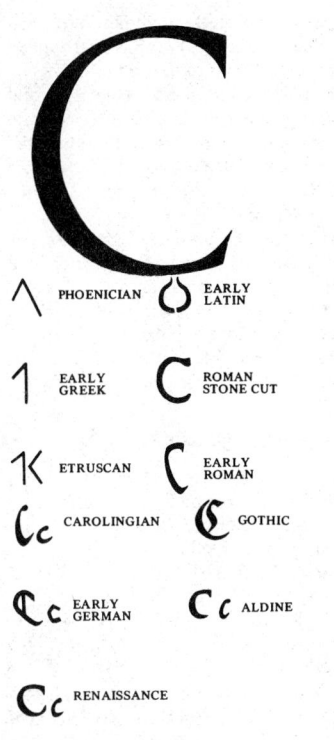

PHOENICIAN   EARLY LATIN

EARLY GREEK   ROMAN STONE CUT

ETRUSCAN   EARLY ROMAN

CAROLINGIAN   GOTHIC

EARLY GERMAN   ALDINE

RENAISSANCE

C or c

The letter C, the third letter of our alphabet, came to us as most of our letters did: First, thousands of years ago, it was one of the symbols used by the ancient Egyptians in their system of "picture-writing," or *hieroglyphics*. In this system a picture of something, instead of a letter, finally came to stand for a single sound. Most scholars believe that the letter C began as a picture of a camel. In the Hebrew language, the word for camel was *gimel*, and the sign for it looked something like the Arabic numeral seven which we use to this day.

Next the ancient Greeks used this letter. But the Hebrews read from right to left, while the Greeks read from left to right, as we do. So the Greeks turned the letter around, and then it looked like the Arabic numeral seven, written backwards.

The Romans were the next to use this letter, and they gave it the rounded form that we use. The Romans had two ways to pronounce C. One way was like the G in *game*. Later on, they put a little tail on the C, and made our present G out of it. The other way the Romans pronounced C was like K. We still do that, in such words as *cave*, and we also pronounce it like S, in such words as *center*. We usually pronounce C as K when the next letter after it is *a, o,* or *u,* and as S when the next letter after it is *e* or *i*.

The Romans used a "small c" which looked very much like the letter "v" which we use today, except that its apex (the pointed end) faced left, rather than pointing downward.

Read also the article ALPHABET.

cabal

A cabal is a group that gets together to plot against others and to work out secret plans for its own benefit. These plans are secret because they are usually against the law, or dishonest. Sometimes the word *cabal* is used to mean the plot or the plans themselves. The name was made up from the initials of five men who were ministers to the English king, Charles II. During King Charles' reign there were many plots, and these men, whose names were Clifford, Ashley, Buckingham, Arlington, and Lauderdale, were often behind the plots.

cabbage

On the coasts of Europe there grows a scraggly-looking wild plant with tough leaves; you would never think so, but it is the ancestor of all the many different kinds of cabbage that we eat. In the common form of cabbage we eat the leaves, which are big and grow packed together in the shape of a ball. Some cabbages have smooth leaves, and some have crinkly leaves. There are red and green varieties of cabbage. They are eaten in many ways. They may be cooked, or pickled, or made into cole slaw. There are also many other vegetables that look and taste quite different from each other but that are of the cabbage family. Among these are: *Brussels sprouts,* in which small edible buds grow along the stem; *cauliflower,* of which the part eaten is the mass of dense white flower buds; *broccoli,* a kind of cauliflower with a looser head of purplish-green buds; *kale,* of which the curly leaves are eaten, and which is also used as a cattle food; and *kohlrabi,* of which the swollen stem is eaten.

Cabell, James Branch

James Branch Cabell was an American writer who wrote a great deal about real and imaginary characters in history. He was born in Richmond, Virginia, in 1879, and was graduated from the college of William and Mary. Many of his stories take place in an imaginary kingdom called *Poictesme,* during the Middle Ages when knights in armor were supposed to have fought dragons, defended beautiful princesses, and searched for such legendary things as the Holy Grail. Cabell described these adventures in an exciting way, but at the same time he made fun of his characters for doing many things that seem silly to us today. For this reason he is called a satirical novelist. His best-known novel is called *Jurgen.* He died in 1958.

Cabinda

Cabinda is, politically, part of the Portuguese province of Angola, on the southwest coast of Africa. Geographically, however, it is separated from the rest of Angola by a small section of the Republic of Zaire (formerly the Democratic Republic of Congo) the capital of which is Kinshasa. See the article on ANGOLA.

cabinet

A cabinet is a committee made up of the heads of the chief departments of a government. In most countries the cabinet is made up from the leaders of the political party that controls the parliament, or lawmaking body. Members of the cabinet are called ministers. Its head is called the prime minister, or premier, and he and the ministers actually run the government.

In the United States government, the cabinet is a group of men who advise the President. The President is the head of one part of the government, called the executive branch, the branch that carries out the laws. To help the President, the Congress set up ten executive departments. Each department takes charge of a certain part of the job of putting the laws into effect. These ten departments are: State; Treasury; Defense; Justice; Post Office; Interior; Agriculture; Commerce; Labor; Health Education and Welfare; Housing and Urban Development; and Transportation. At the head of each is a person who is called the Secretary of that department (except that the head of the Justice Department is called the Attorney General, and the head of the Post Office Department is called the Postmaster General). Together these ten department heads are called the cabinet, when they meet to advise the President.

The cabinet was not set up by the Constitution, as were the Congress and the office of the President. In fact, it has no official place in the government. It is only a matter of custom, but it has a long history as a part of the government. The first President, George Washington, started this custom by asking the department heads to discuss certain problems with him, and every President since then has continued the custom.

cabinetmaking

Cabinetmaking is the trade of building wooden furniture. A cabinetmaker builds many things. The word comes from a French word meaning a "collection of fine things," and a cabinetmaker is one who builds fine things. That is how he differs from a carpenter, who usually does a rougher type of building, such as building houses or repairing them. (See the article on CARPENTRY.) Cabinetmaking includes making furniture, wooden wall paneling, built-in bookcases or shelves, and floors of patterned wood.

A cabinetmaker must know a great deal about the woods he uses and how to match and select them. Mostly he uses hard woods, such as mahogany, walnut, oak, and fruit woods. When a cabinetmaker puts pieces of wood together to make something, he *joins* them instead of nailing them as a carpenter would. This means that he fits the parts together by cutting them with interlocking notches, and then glues the joint. Sometimes you can see the *dovetails* where drawers are put together. Another kind of joint is called a *mortise and tenon*. The mortise is a square hole that is cut into one piece of wood, and the tenon is a tongue cut at the end of another. The tenon fits tightly into the mortise, and they are glued together. There are many other kinds of joints for different purposes.

Nowadays cabinetmakers use electric tools for most of their work, but until about thirty years ago everything was done by hand. Many famous cabinetmakers were also designers. Some of the best known are Thomas Sheraton and Thomas Chippendale, who lived in England about 150 years ago; Jean Henri Riesener, who lived in France about the same time; George Hepplewhite, who lived in England about 200 years ago,

and Duncan Phyfe, who lived in the United States 100 years ago. You can read more about cabinetmaking in the article on FURNITURE.

cable

A cable is a rope or chain. There are many different kinds of cable, and each kind has a different use. The length and thickness of a cable, and the material it is made of, depend on the use for which it is intended.

The first cables were simply ordinary ropes used by seamen to lower anchors into the water or to tie a ship up to a dock. About 150 years ago iron chains began to be used with anchors because they were less likely to break and lasted much longer. Later, wire ropes (cables made up of a number of wires braided or twisted together) came into use for mooring ships. Today all three types of cable are used on ships.

Modern bridges of the type called suspension bridges hang from cables, which in turn hang from bigger cables that are several feet thick. Bridge cables are made up of a great many wires, twisted or straight, and are covered with a casing which protects them from rust. They must support extremely heavy loads, so they have to be very strong. See the article BRIDGE.

Smaller cables are used to carry electrical current. In many cities and towns they are strung overhead to supply power to the streetcars or buses that run beneath them. These are called *trolley cables*. Another example are the cables by which elevators move up and down. The lines that carry electricity from the generator where it is produced to the home or factory where it is used are also cables. Like telegraph cables and telephone cables, power transmission cables are buried underground in most cities and towns, but out in the country they are usually strung on poles.

LONG-DISTANCE CABLES

Most electric cables are made of copper, which bends easily, and aluminum, which is the lightest metal in general use. The light weight of aluminum makes it particularly useful for overhead lines. These cables are often very long. A single telephone cable, for instance, stretches from New York to Chicago for 861 miles. Most of it is strung aboveground on telephone poles. Like almost all overhead cables, it is covered with a sheath of lead to protect it from the weather.

The most famous cable in history was laid between Europe and North America in 1866, after four earlier attempts had failed. Under the leadership of an American, Cyrus Field, the cable-laying group sailed from Ireland on July 13, 1866, aboard the steamer *Great Eastern*. All the way across the ocean the cable unwound from huge drums on the deck, without breaking once. The *Great Eastern* reached Newfoundland on July 28, its job done. On the way back, Field's group found the end of a cable that had been lost in an attempt the year before. They attached it to a new cable and on September 8 they brought the second cable ashore. Since then the number of transatlantic telegraph cables has risen to twenty-one and there are cables across the Pacific and

South Atlantic Oceans and nearly every sea and channel in the world. In 1955 the first telephone cable was laid across the Atlantic.

A special kind of cable that has recently become important is the *coaxial cable*. By means of the coaxial cable a number of telegraph signals, telephone conversations, and television pictures can be sent at the same time in both directions, along each of the several cables of which it is made. This makes it possible to send television pictures across the country, which could not be done before.

cable car

A cable car is a kind of streetcar that is pulled by cables or ropes over ground that is too steep for walking or driving. Most cable cars ride high above the ground, and it is very exciting to ride in them.

The cable car that gave men the idea for all others is used in mining. It is made of buckets attached to a circular chain, or cable, which goes around all the time. The miners put the gold or coal or whatever they are mining into these buckets. The cable pulls them up from the pit, or down from the mountain. The second kind, for carrying people, is a streetcar attached to an underground cable. It was first used in San Francisco in 1873. Before then, horses had pulled the heavy streetcars up the steep hills. The man who invented it, Andrew Hallidie, was in the business of making cables. He put strong clamps or grips under the streetcar and a circular cable underground between the tracks. The conductor attaches clamps on the streetcar to the moving underground cable when he wants the car to move. He releases the clamps when he wants to stop. The third kind of cable car is called an *aerial tramway*. It carries passengers, but it is attached to an overhead wire instead of to the ground. It is like an elevator that goes up at an angle. There is one at Franconia Notch, New Hampshire. Another, called the Cog Railway, runs up Mount Washington. To get to the top of Lookout Mountain, near Chattanooga, Tennessee, you ride in a car that is partly pulled up by the weight of another car that is going down. Most aerial tramways and ski-lifts are pulled up and let down by machines that turn big drums. The turning of the drum winds and unwinds the cable, which is attached to the cable car.

Cabot, John and Sebastian

John Cabot and his son Sebastian Cabot were explorers who lived during the time of Columbus. The Cabots were Italian, but they moved to England when Sebastian was still very young, and they were in England when Columbus made his famous discovery of America in 1492. Columbus had not set out to discover new lands but to find a way of going by sea from Europe to Asia. When John Cabot heard about Columbus' trip, he made up his mind that he would go farther than Columbus and actually find a sea route to the East. In 1496, he and his son sailed all the way from Bristol, England, to the land we now call Nova Scotia, and took possession of the Cape Breton Islands for the British. The Cabots were really the

first to set foot on the mainland of North America, because Columbus had landed only on islands up to that time.

In 1498, the Cabots made a second trip. This time they landed in Greenland and traveled south by ship along the Atlantic coast all the way to Chesapeake Bay. The second trip was very difficult, and the crew mutinied.

After John Cabot died, Sebastian went into the service of the Spanish king. He made a trip to South America, and spent three years there exploring the La Plata River. Sebastian made excellent maps of the routes he and his father had taken to North America, and of his own discoveries.

Cabrini, Saint Frances Xavier

Mother Frances Xavier Cabrini was the first citizen of the United States to be canonized (declared a saint) by the Roman Catholic Church. Mother Cabrini spent her whole life trying to help unfortunate people, especially orphans and the sick. She was born in Italy in 1850, and christened Maria Frances Cabrini. She wanted to be a nun from the time she was a little girl, but she was not very strong, and twice when she tried to become a nun she was refused. Finally she succeeded and was put in charge of a church orphanage in Italy. She came to the United States when she was 38 years old. She died in 1917 and was canonized by Pope Pius XII in 1946. Her title, "Mother," means that she was a nun.

cacao

The cacao is the tree from which we get chocolate and cocoa. It is found in Central America, the West Indies, and the tropical, or hot, parts of South America and Africa. On the trunk of the cacao tree grow large pods, shaped like cucumbers and as much as 12 inches long. These pods are cut off with long knives. Inside there are rows of "beans," from which the chocolate and cocoa are made. When the beans have been cleaned and roasted they are known as *nibs*. Other parts of the tree and its fruit are used as cattle food, and to make *cocoa butter*, which is not really butter but a kind of ointment.

See also the article CHOCOLATE AND COCOA.

cactus

Cactus is the name of a family of about a thousand different plants. Most kinds of cactus have no leaves or very tiny ones. The stem is flat and green, and inside it is often fleshy and full of water. The plant is covered with sharp spines, which are arranged in rows or in small clusters. Sometimes the spines are several inches long, and often they are bright red, purple, yellow, or some other color.

Cactuses grow in very strange shapes. Some look like pincushions, others like footballs, candelabra, or long leathery whips. Some kinds even grow into quite big trees. Their flowers are almost always large and very beautiful. They may be red, yellow, pink, or white. One of the most beautiful is the *night-blooming*

cereus, which is a climbing cactus that flowers once a year and then only at night. The flower of the *giant cactus* is the state flower of Arizona.

Although cactuses can be found growing in places as far north as Canada, and in the dense, steamy forests of the Amazon, most of them grow in deserts or other very dry places where you can find few other plants. Cactuses can live in these places because they store water in their plant tissues. The sharp spikes prevent animals from eating them.

Cactuses are popular as house plants. They also are grown as hedges. The big ones can be used as wood. The fruit and stems of some cactuses, such as the *prickly pear,* are very good to eat. Cactuses grow wild only in America. The plural of the word *cactus* is often spelled *cacti.*

caddis fly

The caddis fly is a small insect that lives near water. It looks like a moth, but it has hairy wings and its young live underwater. There are about 4,500 kinds of caddis fly. They lay their eggs in the water, and the young are called *caddis worms.* Some caddis worms are almost four inches long.

The best-known kinds of caddis worm build themselves cases and crawl around inside them. They build the cases out of bits of twigs, grains of sand, pieces of grass, and so on, bound together with strands of silk which they make themselves. The caddis worms that live in rapid streams make silken cases and attach them to a stone. They also make a silken net with which they catch their food. Some, if they lose their hold on the stone and get carried downstream, can spin out a lifeline and crawl back along it to their homes.

When it is fully grown, the caddis worm closes its case at both ends or spins a cocoon. Inside this it changes to a *caddis fly.* It bites its way out of the case, comes to the surface of the water and flies away. Both caddis worms and flies are eaten by fish.

Cadillac, Antoine de la Mothe

Antoine Cadillac was a French colonial governor who founded the city of Detroit, Michigan more than 270 years ago. He was born in 1658, and came to the New World as a young man. Cadillac was in charge of a frontier post at Mackinac in what is now northern Michigan. He thought a post on the Detroit River would be a better place to defend against the British. So he got permission from King Louis XIV to open a post and trade with the Indians. The settlement started with only fifty people, but Cadillac managed so efficiently and got along so well with the Indians that in two years more than two hundred settlers had come to Detroit. Later Cadillac was made governor of the huge Louisiana territory. In 1716 he returned to France and died there in 1730, at the age of 72.

Cadiz

Cadiz is a city in Spain on the Atlantic coast near the western end of the Mediterranean Sea. It was from Cadiz that Columbus sailed on his second voyage to America. Though most of its buildings are fairly new, the city itself is very old. It was founded eleven hundred years before the birth of Christ by the early Mediterranean traders called Phoenicians. Later Cadiz was ruled in turn by Carthaginians from North Africa, by Romans, Barbarians, Moors, and finally by the kingdom of Castile which became Spain. When Spain was a great world power Cadiz was its chief seaport. Today Cadiz is a clean city of sun-baked white buildings, with straight streets all leading to the sea. It is also a naval base.

CADIZ, SPAIN. Population (in 1973) about 118,000. Capital of Cadiz Province. Major seaport on Atlantic Ocean.

cadmium

Cadmium is a soft metal that is found in ore along with the metal ZINC (about which there is a separate article), and it is somewhat like zinc. It is bluish-white, and can be polished until it gleams like silver. It does not rust or corrode, so it is often used to plate other metals. Cadmium melts at a lower temperature than many metals, so it is mixed with lead and tin to make solder. It is also used in making fuses, batteries, and television tubes. Mixed with other substances, it is used in the manufacture of paint. Cadmium readily absorbs neutrons, therefore it is used in the shielding of atomic piles and in the rods which are inserted into these piles to control the nuclear reaction.

Most of the cadmium in the world is produced and used by the United States. It is also found in Greenock, Scotland, where it is sometimes called *greenockite.*

Cadmus

Cadmus was a character in Greek mythology, the stories the ancient Greeks told about their gods and goddesses. He is famous for having founded the city of Thebes. According to the legend, Cadmus killed a sacred dragon and then pulled out the dragon's teeth and sowed them in the ground like seeds. From these teeth there sprang up soldiers who were ancestors of the later people of Thebes. But Ares, the god of war, became angry because Cadmus had killed the sacred dragon and caused many unfortunate things to happen to him and his family.

Cadmus is also famous because he is supposed to have invented the alphabet. Of course, this is only a story; see the article on ALPHABET.

Caedmon

The first Christian poet who ever wrote in the English language was named Caedmon. He was a servant who took care of the cattle at a monastery in Whitby, England, more than twelve hundred years ago. One night, as Caedmon slept in a shed, a man appeared to him in a vision and commanded him to sing, and he did. When he woke up, he remembered the words of a poem he had sung in praise of God. After that he composed many more poems. Others wrote them down for him, as he could neither read nor write. These poems are written in Old English, or Anglo-Saxon, which is not very much like the language we know today.

Caesar

Caesar was the name of a famous family in ancient Rome. Its name has come to mean an emperor, because of the first Roman emperor, Augustus Caesar. *Czar* in Russian, and *Kaiser* in German, mean "emperor" or "Caesar."

Caesar, Augustus; first Roman emperor, the adopted son of Julius Caesar. See the article on AUGUSTUS.

Caesar, Gaius Julius

Julius Caesar was a very great Roman statesman and soldier. He was born about a hundred years before Christ. Cae-sar's family was rich and powerful, and had always taken a leading part in Roman politics. When Caesar became interested in government, he found that Rome had a very corrupt government that was in need of reform. He was an honest man. He held various important positions in the Roman government while he was still quite young, but he wanted to be even more important so he could do more for his country.

In Rome in those days the best way to do this was to become a military man as well as a politician, so Caesar got himself appointed governor of two Roman provinces, Cisalpine Gaul and Transalpine Gaul. *Cisalpine Gaul* was the Latin way of saying "Gaul on this side of the Alps," and *Transalpine Gaul* meant "Gaul on the other side of the Alps from Rome." These provinces form what is now France. The Germans were trying to take these provinces from the Romans, and the Gauls themselves were trying to win their independence from Rome. But Caesar defeated their armies. He kept Gaul for the Romans after many great battles. He wrote the whole story of his campaigns in Gaul in a book called *The Gallic Wars,* which is still studied by all schoolboys and girls when they learn the Latin language.

When Caesar got home from Gaul, he found that some of his friends were trying to take away his military power in Rome. That would have left all the power in the hands of another Roman general, Pompey, who also had a big army. Caesar had trained and equipped his army so well that it was the greatest fighting force the world had ever known. Caesar found it hard to decide on war against another Roman army, but he finally made the decision. With his army he crossed the Rubicon river in North Italy and marched on Rome. This was in 49 B.C. Pompey also brought his army to Rome, and the two armies fought. Pompey was beaten and fled to Egypt. Caesar followed him there, but before he arrived Pompey had been murdered. Caesar stayed in Egypt for a while, partly because he was in love with the Egyptian queen Cleopatra, and he helped her get firmly established on the throne. While he was in that part of the world he fought battles with many enemies of Rome. One of them was Pharnaces II, king of Pontus, who was threatening to take over some territory

of Rome. When Caesar fought this army he defeated it so easily that he told all about the battle by saying: "I came, I saw, I conquered."

All during this time, Caesar's political power had been growing greater and greater, and when he returned to Rome he was made dictator for ten years. He was given the greatest honors. He was called "Father of his Country," his statue was placed in the temples, coins were made in his likeness, and a month was named for him—Julius, the month that we still call July. But some of the Roman politicians, including his friend Brutus, were afraid that he was becoming too powerful and doing too much for the common people. They plotted to murder him. He was killed on March 15 (which the Romans called the Ides of March) in front of the Senate. Caesar was born in 102 B.C. and died in 44 B.C. One of the greatest things he did was to change the calendar. See the article CALENDAR.

Caesarea

In ancient times there were several very important cities named Caesarea. Two of the most important were in Palestine. One of these, Caesarea Palestinae, was a seaport built by Herod the Great about twenty-five years before Christ was born. During the time of the Crusades, there was a large fort in this city held by the Crusaders. The fort was destroyed by the Moslems in 1265. When Palestine became the new state of Israel, a modern village called Sdot-Yam was founded on the site of ancient Caesarea Palestinae.

The other Caesarea in Palestine was Caesarea Philippi, which was founded by Philip the Tetrarch, ruler of part of the realm of his father, King Herod the Great. This city was in Syria. It is mentioned several times in the Bible. It was also an important city for the Crusaders. A small village called Baniyas now stands where Caesarea Philippi used to be.

cafeteria

A cafeteria is a restaurant where the food is displayed on long counters and the people who come to eat choose what they want and carry it to a table themselves. Cafeterias are so common now that it is hard to believe the first one was opened only a few years before 1900. Before that time, anyone who wanted to eat away from home had to go to a restaurant, and most of the restaurants were very expensive. Many working people could not afford to eat in them, and had to prepare their lunches at home and take them to work.

Then in 1891, a man named H. S. Thompson got the idea for a self-service restaurant. He knew he could serve good food for less money if he did not have to pay waiters or waitresses. He opened a cafeteria in Chicago, Illinois, and it soon became very popular. Many other cafeterias were opened after that. The Young Women's Christian Association (YWCA), for instance, began to operate cafeterias for its members who worked in offices and could not afford to eat in expensive restaurants. Nowadays, many big factories and industrial plants have cafeterias for their workers, and there are cafeterias in many schools and colleges. The Automat is a kind of cafeteria where foods like salads, sandwiches, and desserts, which can be prepared in advance, are kept in little glass cases against the wall. The customer puts coins in a slot and turns a handle, and the glass case opens so that he can take out the food.

caffeine

Caffeine is a chemical substance that is found in coffee, tea, cola, and other drinks. (In tea it is called *theine*.) Caffeine is a stimulant, which means that when you are tired it makes you feel brighter and stronger. Of course, this can be overdone, but in small amounts caffeine does no harm. Tea contains more caffeine than coffee, but more coffee is used per cup, so it evens up. In its pure form caffeine is a crystal, belonging to a group of chemicals called *alkaloids*. It is used as a medicine, and can be made from tea dust and the soot from ovens in which coffee is roasted. Caffeine is also extracted or removed from coffee, which is then sold as "caffeine-free coffee."

Caiaphas

Caiaphas was the high priest of the Jews during the time of the trial and crucifixion of Jesus. In some of the books of the New Testament of the Bible, the story is told of how Jesus was betrayed by Judas Iscariot, and how he was brought before Caiaphas for preaching things that the Jewish priests did not believe. Caiaphas condemned Jesus to death, but the sentence had to be approved by the Romans, who were the rulers of Palestine at that time. Pontius Pilate was the Roman governor, and Caiaphas brought Jesus before him. At this trial the death sentence was confirmed.

Cain, brother of Abel: see ABEL.

cairn

A cairn is a cone-shaped pile of stones, sometimes surrounded by a circle of larger stones set upright in the ground. Cairns are not much used any more except as decorations (in rock gardens, for instance), but at one time they were often put up to mark boundaries. Other uses were to show where an important person was buried, or where a battle had been fought. Many cairns have been found in Ireland and Scotland, and in Norway and Sweden. Mounds of earth found in England and Denmark are the same shape and size as cairns, and served the same purpose. There are many mounds in the United States; see the separate article on MOUNDS.

Cairn terrier

The Cairn terrier is a small dog with a big dog's loyal and protective spirit, and a willingness to work hard at its specialty of catching rats and mice. The breed originated on the Isle of Skye, off the coast of Scotland, and it was originally called the short-haired Skye terrier. It was renamed Cairn terrier because its rough coat and stocky body made people think of a rocky cairn (see the article CAIRN above this one). Cairns are often kept as hunting terriers today, and they can hunt in all kinds of weather because of their coats. The coat is thicker and deeper than that of most terriers. In the United States, the Cairn is usually kept as a house dog and pet.

The Cairn terrier stands about 9½ inches high at the shoulder, and weighs about 14 pounds. Its coat is heavy and coarse, with a soft thick undercoat, and it may be any shade of gray, brown, tan, or black, but it is never white. Its front legs are very straight and stiff, and its tail stands up straight, at right angles to its back.

Cairo

Cairo is the capital of Egypt and the largest city on the continent of Africa. The city lies on the banks of the Nile River, partly on level ground and partly on a rocky range of hills. On top of one

B.O.A.C.
In Cairo, the past and the present meet. Two Egyptians in the desert near Cairo watch a plane flying over the pyramids, built thousands of years ago.

of these hills there is a fortress called the citadel, from which there is a very wide and beautiful view. Below lies the city with its strong walls and high towers. There are gardens, squares, palaces, mosques (the churches of the Moslem religion) with carved domes and minarets, or towers. You can see the broad river Nile with its many islands and the river valley dotted with groups of date trees and palms. Near the city are the great pyramids; to the northwest are fields, villas, and gardens; to the east are barren cliffs and behind them, like a great ocean of sand, lies the Sahara Desert.

Cairo today has a population of about five million. Most of the people are native Egyptians, but there are also many Copts, Negroes, Jews, Turks, Greeks, Armenians, French, and English. Part of Cairo is a modern city with wide streets, but the most famous palaces and mosques are to be found in the older sections. One of the most famous mosques, called El Azhar, is nearly as old as the city itself. In this mosque is the most important Moslem university in the world, with more than 34,000 students. There are many other wonderful things to see in Cairo, such as the Arab and ancient Egyptian museums and the national library. One interesting thing is an instrument more than a hundred years old called the Nilometer. This is a column marked off like a great yardstick. It is used to tell how high the water is in the Nile river. It is on Roda Island, where the baby Moses is believed to have been found in the bulrushes.

Cairo was founded nearly a thousand years ago by a Fatimite general named Jauhar. The Fatimites were descendants of Mohammed the Prophet through his daughter Fatima. You can read about MOHAMMED and the religion he founded in another volume of this encyclopedia. Cairo was attacked many times during the centuries that followed, beginning in the 12th century with the Crusades. The citadel was built to defend the city against the Crusaders, who were Christian soldiers trying to take the Holy Land back from the Moslems. During the 15th century, the city was ruled by the MAMELUKES, whom you can read about in a separate article. Cairo then was one of the busiest and richest cities in the world. Later it became less important and was occupied by the French under Napoleon and after that by the English until 1922, when Egypt became fully independent.

CAIRO, EGYPT. Population (in 1973) about 5,000,000. Capital of Egypt. On Nile River.

caisson

A caisson is a big box, as big as a room, in which men can work under water when they are building a tunnel or the foundations for a bridge. The caisson is a box with sides and a top but no bottom. It is usually made of concrete and steel. The reason it does not have a bottom is that the men in the caisson are going to dig at the bottom, to make room for the tunnel or the bridge foundation.

One section of the caisson is called the *cofferdam*. This section is filled with rocks or other heavy things, called *ballast*. The ballast makes the caisson heavy enough to sink into the water. (There is a separate article about BALLAST.)

This compressed-air caisson is being used to lay a bridge foundation or pier. The caisson has not yet stopped sinking. As the men dig into the floor, the sharp side edges (E) sink into the bottom, forced downward by the concrete load in the cofferdam (D). The men in the working chamber (C) are protected from high pressure by compressed air in the airlocks (A) and in the chamber. The shafts (S) on either side of the main shaft (M) are used to remove soil that has been dug out. The blowout tube (B) removes sand and other materials.

First, the caisson is allowed to sink to the bottom of the water. It is connected with the surface by a shaft, usually with an elevator in it. The men who work in the caisson (and who are called "sandhogs") will enter it through this shaft.

Next, all the water is pumped out of the caisson and compressed air is pumped in. In the article on AIR COMPRESSION you can read how compressed air can be so strong that it will keep the water from flowing back into the caisson. But the men who work in the caisson could not stand such high air pressure without becoming used to it gradually. So they pass through chambers called *air locks* when they go to work and when they leave work. An air lock is airtight, and whatever air pressure is pumped into it, it will stay that way. Sandhogs going to work stay in the air lock while the pressure is gradually increased. When they have become accustomed to the normal pressure of the outside air, they leave the air lock.

The men working in the caisson dig away the mud and rock beneath them. What they dig away is removed from the caisson through the shaft, or through "blow-out pipes" that dump it into the water around the caisson. The sides of the caisson sink deeper as the sandhogs dig. When they have dug enough, concrete is poured onto the bottom. This will be the bottom of the tunnel, or the foundation of the bridge.

There is a disease called "caisson disease," or "the bends," that men sometimes get when they do not wait long enough in the air lock. This disease can be very dangerous. Divers sometimes get it from going too deep in the water. Sandhogs very seldom get it now, because they are careful to use their air locks.

Ammunition wagons for artillery are also called caissons. The official song of the U.S. Field Artillery was named "The Caissons Go Rolling Along."

calabash

A calabash is the dried shell of the fruit of the calabash tree. Calabashes become very hard when they are dried, which makes them useful as dippers, bottles, bowls, or even cooking pots. They often grow as big as footballs. Sometimes they are carved and painted, and used as ornaments. Small ones are filled with seeds and used as rattles or "shak-shaks" by native orchestras.

The calabash tree is a low, spreading tree with very twisted branches, that grows in the West Indies. Its flowers are white, and grow on the branches and trunk. From the flowers grow the huge fruit, full of yellowish juicy pulp which is not very good to eat. The fruit of various kinds of cucumber or pumpkin vine are also sometimes called calabashes, but the real name for them is *gourds*.

Calais

Calais is a seaport on the northern coast of France, just across the English Channel from Dover, England. During the Allied invasion of northern Europe in World War II Calais suffered severe damage from both sides. Since the Germans had strong forces there, the English and Americans bombed the city many times. When the Germans finally retreated they blew up the docks and harbor buildings so that Calais would be useless to the Allies as a port. The old town was completely destroyed. Thousands of people were killed.

Calais was a fishing village until the tenth century. It was fortified by the French about six hundred years ago. Not long afterward the city was besieged and finally captured by the English, who held it for two hundred years until the French retook it. Up to 1940 it was France's greatest center for the making of lace. Although ferry service to Dover and Folkestone across the English Channel started again after the war, Calais found it hard to recover from the effects of being a battleground. The population in 1936 was more than 65,000. The present population is about 70,127.

calamine

Calamine is an ore from which the metal zinc is obtained. (An ore is rock

that has a metal in it, mixed with other substances.) The article on ZINC tells how it is taken from the ore. In the United States, calamine is found in New Jersey, Pennsylvania and Virginia in the East, and in Missouri, Utah and Montana in the West. We also hear the word *calamine* in *calamine lotion,* a white liquid that is spread on skin that is red and itchy from poison ivy or from other causes. Calamine lotion is made with a chemical called zinc oxide, but it is not the same substance as the ore.

calcium

Calcium is a silver-white metal that is found in most rocks and also in the ground. We see calcium every day, but we do not think of it as a metal. Calcium occurs in many compounds. One of them is the hard substance in our bones and in our teeth. It is found in chalk, and got its name because in the Latin language *calx* means "chalk." In one form, calcium carbonate, it makes limestone and marble, and also the pearls found in oysters.

Though calcium is found nearly everywhere, it is never found by itself. It is always combined with other chemicals. Calcium carbonate is one of these compounds —calcium, carbon & oxygen. In its many mixtures, calcium is one of the most useful things we know. It prevents water from freezing in the winter; it fertilizes fields for farmers; it is used to make ACETYLENE, about which there is a separate article; and it is used in dozens of other ways.

Calcium is important to the human body, not only in the bones but also in the blood, where it helps to stop bleeding. Mothers who are expecting babies often take special calcium pills so that the babies will have strong bones. Some salts containing calcium are taken for an upset stomach.

calculating machines

A calculating machine solves problems of arithmetic and saves you the trouble of doing them in your head. It also prints both the problem and the answer, saving you the trouble of writing them down. Some machines can only add. Some can add and subtract. Some can also multiply and divide.

There are hundreds of different kinds of calculating machines, and they are useful in many different businesses and sciences In the articles on BOOKKEEPING and ACCOUNTING you can learn how important it is for business firms to keep track of how much money they have earned and how much they have spent. Bookkeepers used to have to add up long columns of figures. Now machines do it for them—and the machines do not make mistakes. Scientists use calculating machines to multiply figures so huge that you can hardly even imagine them. Banks use calculating machines to show quickly how much money a person has deposited. The Army uses calculating machines to keep track of millions of soldiers. These are only a few of the uses of calculating machines.

Thousands of years ago, men used pebbles to help them do arithmetic. They used the pebbles in a device called the ABACUS, about which there is a separate article. The word for "pebble" in the Latin language, which was used in ancient Róme, is *calculus,* and that is where we get our word *calculate.*

The first modern calculating machine was an adding machine, invented about three hundred years ago (in 1642) by a French scientist named Blaise Pascal. About fifty years after that a German scientist named Gottfried Leibnitz made a machine that could also multiply.

ADDING MACHINES

The calculating machine that is used most often is the adding machine. An adding machine looks like a small typewriter. Some adding machines have even more keys than a typewriter, and the keyboards look more like the fronts of cash registers. In fact, every cash register has an adding machine built into it.

Besides the keys with numbers on them, an adding machine has keys to press when you want to add, or to subtract, or to correct a mistake made by pressing the wrong key, or for other special purposes.

The numbered keys have the figures from 0 to 9 on them. Each key is connected with a little metal bar with the same figure on it. This metal bar will print the number you want on a roll of paper at the back of the machine. After you have pressed the keys you want, you make the number print by pulling a handle on what is called à *manual* machine, or by pressing a button on an electric machine. For instance, if you want to add 963 and 754, first you press the keys for 963 and pull the handle or press the button to print it; then you press the keys for 754 and print that in the same way.

Each time a number is printed on paper, a small wheel is turned inside the adding machine. There is a wheel for each column of numbers. (The meaning of the columns of numbers is explained in the article on ARITHMETIC.) The wheels are lined up next to each other, like small circles side by side. Each wheel has ten little metal points sticking out of it. Each of these points stands for a number from 0 to 9.

After all the numbers you want to add have been printed on the roll of paper, you press a button marked TOTAL Then you pull the handle or press the button the same as to print a number. The answer you want will then be printed on the roll of paper.

Here is how the adding machine adds: when a column of numbers adds up to more than 9, the wheel attached to that column turns the wheel at the left a certain number of points forward. For instance, if the column adds up to 23, only the 3 is printed, and the wheel at the left is turned 2 points forward. If the column adds up to 56, only the 6 is printed, and the wheel at the left is turned 5 points forward. This goes on, with each wheel turning the wheel to the left of it, until all the columns have been added, and the answer printed.

On machines that multiply as well as add, there is a special key marked MULTIPLY. When you press this key, a number will be printed as many times as you wish to multiply it. Then the column will be added. For instance, to multiply 7 by 5 (5 times 7), you first press the key marked 7, then you press the multiplication key until 7 has been printed 5 times. The column of 7's will then be added, and your answer, 35, will be printed underneath it.

ELECTRONIC COMPUTERS

There are other calculating machines that can solve problems in science. Some of these problems are so çomplicated that it would take a man with only a pencil and paper many weeks and even months to solve. Even after he had solved the problem, he would not be sure that his answer was right. A calculating machine would give him the right answer the very first time, and he would not have to check it.

The calculating machines that are used in science are worked by electronic tubes, tubes like the ones used in radio and television sets. These machines are called electronic computers. *Computer* is another name for *calculating machine.* Such machines sometimes have more than 18,000 electronic tubes inside them. They are as big as small houses and weigh more than one hundred tons (200,000 pounds). Some electronic computers can do more than a million problems of multiplication in only one hour.

Most of these big machines are called *data-processing* machines. Data (information or facts) is fed into them and they calculate the correct results. Some of these machines work from *punched cards.* Holes are punched into certain places on a card and the machines will sort thousands of the cards in a minute and perform complicated mathematical processes depending on where the holes are punched. In the *mark-sensing* process, magnetic ink is used to record the data on the card. In the most modern calculating machines, the information is first recorded on tape (as in a tape-recorder that reproduces sound) and the tape then controls the machine. All these machines are being used more and more in business, science, and industry.

calculus

Calculus is one of the ways in which the science of mathematics is used to solve problems. It is such a difficult form of mathematics that no one studies it until he has already studied and mastered all of the other branches of mathematics, such as arithmetic, algebra, geometry, and trigonometry. Calculus has two main branches, called *differential calculus* and *integral calculus.*

Differential calculus is used to solve problems about things that are moving or changing. In simple arithmetic, as when you add 3 and 4 to make 7, there is no change; 3 is always 3, and 4 is always 4, and 7 is always 7. Then suppose a ball is dropped from a building 256 feet high and strikes the ground 4 seconds later. You can divide 256 by 4 and find out that the *average* speed of the ball was 64 feet per second. But how fast was the ball going at the end of the third second? Just before the ball was dropped, it was going zero feet per second, because it was not moving at all. It must have gone faster and faster as it fell; this is

called *acceleration*. Differential calculus is used to solve such problems.

Integral calculus is used to find a total that is made up of things that cannot be measured in the same way. The simplest example is finding the area of a big field with edges that are all kinds of curves and angles and irregular shapes. First the big field is divided into many smaller spaces, all with regular shapes. Geometry teaches how to find the area of each of those regular shapes. When they are added together, the area of the whole field is known. The great Greek mathematician, Archimedes, first used this method more than two thousand years ago, to find the area of a circle. Differential calculus was not used until nearly three hundred years ago.

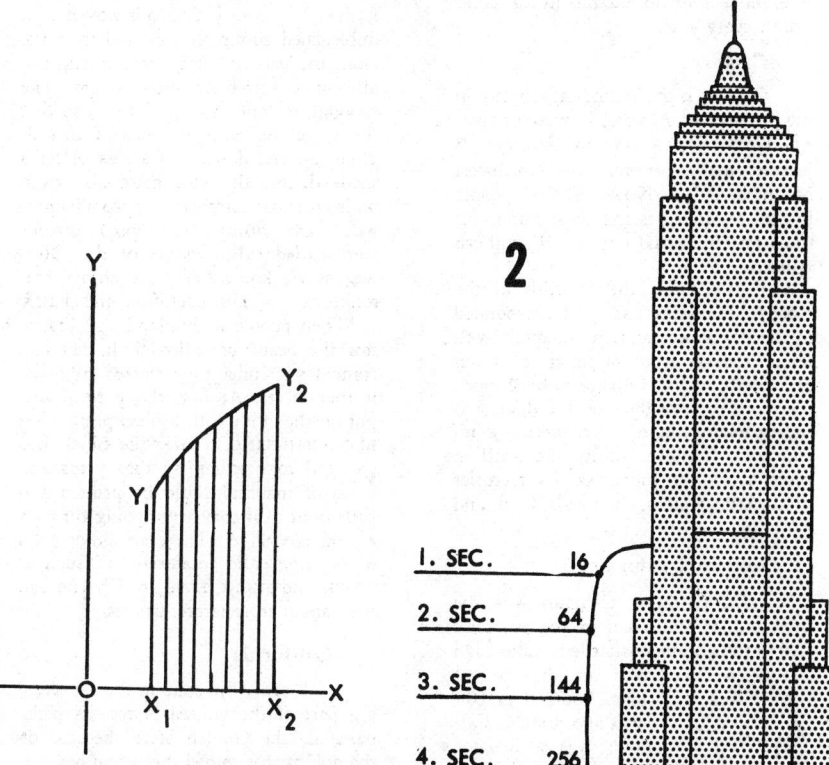

A calculating machine can be compared to a freight train. The problem you want to solve is in one of the cars. It is dumped into a bin, called the *input*. The problem goes into the arithmetic unit, where the problem is solved. The answer comes out at the *output*, on a piece of paper. The man at the controls works the buttons of the calculator as an engineer controls a train. Now he is ready for the next problem.

1. By using integral calculus, mathematicians can find the areas under curves such as Y_1Y_2. First, they draw small strips or rectangles between the lines Y_1X_1 and Y_2X_2. By finding the area of each strip and adding, or integrating, these, they find the entire area. 2. Using differential calculus, mathematicians are able to figure out how fast a ball would fall if it were dropped from the 20th floor of the Empire State building. At the end of the first second, it would be falling with a speed of 32 feet per second; at the end of the next second, 64 feet per second; at the end of the third second, 96 feet per second; and as it hits the ground after the fourth second, its speed would be 128 feet per second. The numbers on the picture show how many feet the ball will have fallen after 1, 2, 3 and 4 seconds.

Calcutta

Calcutta is the largest city in India and the sixth largest city in the world. It is the capital of West Bengal State, and lies on the Hooghly River 65 miles from the Bay of Bengal, which is an arm of the Indian Ocean. Some parts of Calcutta are modern and beautiful, especially along the river. In other areas, however, there is great poverty and overcrowding. There are many fine buildings and places of interest, such as the Maidan (which is a large park), the Victoria Memorial Hall, National Library, Jain Temple, the zoo, and the Botanical Gardens.

Calcutta is a cultural center from which many famous people have come. It is also one of the biggest manufacturing cities in India, with a population of over 3 million. It has factories that turn out metal and other products, and mills that produce cloth and jute (burlap). From Calcutta, rice, oils, jute, and shellac are exported. The city has both a busy port and an international airport.

For many years it was very unhealthy because of bad water, bad sanitation, and large swamps that bred mosquitoes which spread malaria. These problems are still present and very hard to solve because of Calcutta's enormous population, which since 1947 includes thousands of refugees from nearby East Pakistan. From 1772 to 1911, Calcutta was the capital of India, but in 1911 the city of Delhi became the new capital.

Calcutta is often remembered in history because of an incident (doubted by some historians) which is said to have taken place in 1756 when the city was captured from the British by the Nawab of Bengal. (A *nawab* is a Mohammedan prince). The British soldiers who had been taken prisoner were put overnight into such a small, hot, and airless room that most of them died in just that short time. The room became known as the "Black Hole of Calcutta."

CALCUTTA, INDIA. Population (1970 est.) 3,072,196. With suburbs, 4,764,979. On the Hooghly River. Capital of West Bengal state.

calendar

A calendar is a way of dividing time so that all people in a group or country can keep count of it in the same way. There have been many different calendars used at different times in history, but all of them have been based on what we call natural divisions of time. Days, and years are natural divisions of time. The day is the length of time it takes the earth to turn completely around; for example, the time from one sunrise to the next. The year is the length of time it takes the earth to travel all the way around the sun and back to the same place again. The *lunar month* is a natural division of time, from one "new moon" to the next; but the month as actually used in calendars is not a natural division of time, because in most calendars the

month averages about thirty days, while the lunar month is closer to twenty-nine days.

The difficulty in making calendars has always been that the year is not an even number of days or an even number of months. A year is about 12⅓ lunar months. It is about 365¼ days. So calendar-makers throughout the ages have added a few days to months, or an extra month every few years, or an extra day every few years (as we do when we have *leap years*) to make things come out even.

EGYPTIAN CALENDAR

The ancient Egyptians had a calendar that was made up of 12 months of 30 days each. That left 5 extra days each year and 6 extra days every fourth year. The Egyptians counted in the extra 5 days each year, but they paid no attention to the extra day in the fourth year. After a long time of ignoring that extra day, they found that there was something wrong with their seasons. It was dry during months that were supposed to be wet and wet during months that were supposed to be dry. But they did not know how to correct this mistake.

ROMAN CALENDAR

The next important calendar was invented by the Romans many hundreds of years ago. That calendar is the one on which we base our own calendar. The Roman calendar had 12 months, with either 29 or 30 days. The year was 355 days long, instead of 365 as it should have been. In order to correct this, a 13th month of 22 or 23 days was added every other year, and still another extra month was supposed to be added once in twenty-four years. But the officials in charge of making these changes in the calendar were lazy and sometime forgot to do it. Before long the Romans found themselves in the same kind of trouble the Egyptians had been in earlier. Julius Caesar corrected this after consulting with an Egyptian astronomer named Sosigenes. Caesar and Sosigenes worked out a calendar made up of three years of 365 days and one year of 366 days. The year began with the month of January, and went through all the months as we know them today.

We call this calendar the Julian calendar (for Julius Caesar). A few hundred years later, when Christianity had become the official religion of most of Europe, the Church began to date everything from the year when it was estimated that Jesus was born. This estimate was wrong by a few years, but we still follow it.

Unfortunately, the Julian calendar had a mistake in it. There are about 11 minutes each year that were not taken care of by the Julian leap year. After about 1,600 years, the Julian calendar was wrong by about ten days.

Pope Gregory XIII, who was Pope from 1572 to 1585, made another change in the calendar, to correct the mistake in the Julian calendar. His calendar, the Gregorian calendar, is used in nearly every part of the world. In this calendar, every fourth year is a *leap* year (with 366 days) except years ending in even hundreds (like 1900) which cannot be evenly divided by 400. The year 1600

was a leap year, and 2000 will also be one. Dates in the Julian calendar are called "Old Style," or O.S., and dates in the Gregorian calendar are called "New Style" (N.S.).

Many churches have their own calendars by which they date Church holidays. The Julian calendar is still used in the Orthodox Catholic Church, which is the official church in Greece and was in Russia before the Communist rule.

JEWISH CALENDAR

The Jewish year begins in the fall, in their month of *Tishri*. They number their years from the date of the Creation, which they estimate to be October 7, 3760 B.C. The date September 27, 1954, was the beginning of the Jewish year 5715. Another difference is that the Jewish year has twelve months of alternately 29 and 30 days. Seven times in every nineteen years they add a thirteenth month, to make their calendar come out even.

MOHAMMEDAN CALENDAR

The Mohammedan calendar starts from a different time than either the Gregorian or Jewish calendars. The first year of the Mohammedan calendar was the year of a very important event in the Moslem religion. In that year, our year 622, Mohammed was forced to go from the city of Mecca to the city of Medina. In the Mohammedan calendar, there are 12 months. Some have 30 days and some have 29 days. There is a leap year in 11 out of every 30 years. The Mohammedan year does not have the same number of days as the solar year, and so the different seasons do not fall in the same month every year.

Calgary

Calgary is the second-largest city in the province of Alberta, in western Canada. Only eighty years ago, Calgary was just a small fort for the Northwest Mounted Police. Now 181,780 people live there, and it is the most important trade and industrial city in all southern Alberta.

Calgary is near the foothills of the Rocky Mountains and it is surrounded by wide plains and rich mountain valleys. Products from hundreds of miles around are sent to Calgary to be shipped out to all parts of the world. Calgary has meat-packing plants, oil refineries, grain elevators, lumber mills, steel-rolling mills, and iron foundries. Its factories produce machinery, chemicals, food, and clothing.

Calhoun, John C.

John Caldwell Calhoun was the most famous statesman on the Southern side in the argument that led to the Civil War in the United States, more than 100 years ago. John C. Calhoun was a Senator from the state of South Carolina. When he was alive, Negroes were slaves in South Carolina and other states of the South. Most of the people in the North thought that slavery was wrong and wanted the United States Government to set the

slaves free. The Southern states insisted that "States' Rights," according to the Constitution of the United States, left it up to them to decide what would go on in their own territory. There were constant arguments in the Senate about matters connected with this idea. Calhoun always led the Southern senators.

In 1828, when he was 40 years old, Calhoun wrote the most famous argument of its time for States' Rights, and this caused South Carolina to pass a *nullification act* in which the state tried to nullify, or cancel, two tariff (customs tax) laws that Congress had passed. Congress compromised by passing a different law.

Calhoun won many honors in the United States Government. He was born in 1782, while the Revolutionary War was still being fought. He served first in the House of Representatives, from 1811 to 1817. He was Secretary of War under President James Monroe. Then he was vice-president of the United States from 1824 to 1832, and Secretary of State under President John Tyler. Nearly all the other years of his life he was a senator. He wanted most of all to be president, and was very disappointed that he could not be, but the people would not elect a man who was so strongly for slavery and who thought the states should be stronger than the Federal Government. Calhoun died in 1850, nearly eleven years before the Civil War began.

calico

Calico is the name of a flowered cloth first brought from India to Europe in the 17th century. Calico is woven with unbleached cotton threads and then the cloth is bleached, dyed or printed, usually in a small flowered design. The weaving is done in a special way so that there are the same number of threads going up and down and across. After a while all smooth cotton materials woven with an equal number of warp (lengthwise) and filling (crosswise) threads were called calico. Some of the calico weaves we know today are chintz, cretonne, canvas, muslin, chiffon, and challis.

When people in England and France saw the beautiful calico cloth that had come from India they started to make it themselves. At first the pattern was put on the cloth with a blockprint. (See BLOCKPRINTING.) Later the block was changed to a roller, so that yards and yards of material could be printed and rolled out as if they were going through a clothes wringer. There are other ways of printing calico material too, such as BATIK and STENCILING, which you can read about in separate articles.

California

California is a state in the far western part of the United States. Its nickname is "the Golden State" because of the gold that is mined there, and because of the great wealth of golden harvests it produces each year. The name *California* comes from an imaginary island mentioned in a Spanish novel that was written in 1510. It represents an earthly paradise. The state flower is the golden poppy, and the state tree is the redwood.

More people live in California than

in any other state in the United States. There are nearly twenty million people living there. In area California ranks third, covering almost 160,000 square miles. Only Alaska and Texas are bigger.

California became a state in 1850, and was the 31st state admitted to the Union. Its capital is Sacramento.

THE PEOPLE OF CALIFORNIA

The people of California came originally from all parts of the world. Until a little over a hundred years ago, most Californians were Spanish and Mexican, with just a few Americans from the East who worked as fur trappers or traders. After the discovery of gold, thousands flocked to California from everywhere to seek their fortunes. This was followed by the building of cross-country railroads, which drew many thousands more to the state. There were Chinese laborers on the railroads, and most of them remained. When the tracks were finished and trains began to run across the continent, large groups of Europeans settled in California. The Italians began raising grapes for wine, and also went into the fishing trade off the Pacific coast.

Portuguese, Swiss, and Germans joined the Italians, Chinese, Spanish, and Mexicans already there, and California became a land of many nationalities living together. Japanese and Filipino laborers came in considerable numbers, and became farm workers. Now all these different nationality groups have been settled for so long that they have families and homes in all parts of the state, and today almost nine-tenths of the people living in California are native-born Americans.

There are still about 39,000 Indians in the state, though fewer than 9,000 of them live on reservations, where they work chiefly as farmers and cattlemen.

Although almost a third of the state is used for some form of agriculture, more people live in cities than live in rural or country districts. Only about one-fifth of the population lives in the country. The people in the cities work in stores, offices, and factories. Since World War II there have been many large aircraft and machine factories in California, and almost all the cars sold west of the Rocky Mountains are assembled from factory parts in the state of California. The people in rural districts work on farms, in the oil fields, or in the lumber industry.

WHAT CALIFORNIA IS LIKE

California is a state where there is almost every kind of land and climate. It is so big that the different sections might almost be different countries.

Along the northern part of the Pacific coast section there is a double chain of mountains, and the valleys between are rich in all kinds of fruits and vegetables. There are also fine grazing lands in these valleys, where cattle raising and dairy farming are profitable. Toward the border of Oregon, at the far north, are mountains heavily wooded with redwood trees, the state tree of California.

East of the coastal ranges, but still in the northern part of the state, are the beautiful Siena Nevada mountains. These are rugged peaks with snow caps all year around. One section of these mountains is called the Lava Plateau, where the only active volcano in the United States is located. This is the famous Mount Lassen, which erupts occasionally but not very violently.

It is in the Sierra Nevadas also that the largest gold deposits in the state are found.

The Central Valley of California runs between the coastal ranges and the Sierra Nevadas. It is this rich valley that produces the biggest part of California's important agricultural output. This is the northern and central section of the valley. In the southern section are oil fields and plentiful sources of natural gas.

Moving south, you would notice a great deal of difference in the countryside as you went along. There is even a big difference between the eastern and western parts of the state, in the southern section. From fertile coastal plains, the traveler in California can go east over the mountains to the desert country of Death Valley, where nothing is cultivated. Within a few miles of this desolate stretch is the luxuriant Imperial Valley, where huge crops of melons, fruits, and vegetables of many different kinds are harvested each year.

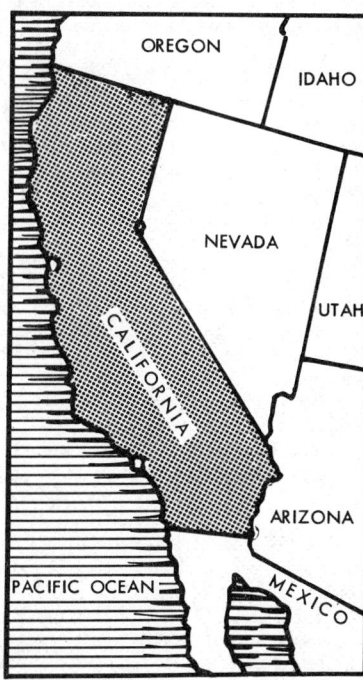

Still farther west, on the other side of the Sierra Nevadas' southern reaches, there is the extremely hot Colorado Desert, where the temperature often reaches 120 during the day. Farther north, in the mountains, the climate is totally different from that of the southern part of the state. The winters are very cold, and long. It is not unusual for freezing temperatures to occur occasionally, even in summer. This kind of weather contrast, and sharp differences in climate, hold true all over the state.

California has a large number of rivers, fed by the mountain streams which start in the many mountain ranges throughout the state. Modern roads have formed a network over the state, and it is no longer a problem to cross either the highest mountain passes or the scorching deserts. Good highways, and ample railroads, go everywhere.

Tourists have found that California is a fine vacationland. There are so many different kinds of climate and so many different kinds of countryside, it is possible for almost everyone to find the recreation he likes, in the type of country that appeals to him.

THE GOVERNMENT OF CALIFORNIA

California, like most other states, is governed by a Governor, a Senate, and an Assembly. The Governor and the Senators are elected to serve four-year terms, and members of the Assembly are elected to serve two-year terms. Judges are elected and serve twelve years. The capital is Sacramento. There are 58 counties in the state. The schools provide textbooks free to pupils. There are about 4,000,000 students attending the public elementary and high schools.

There are many colleges, universities, and technological and professional schools. State, county, and city governments support some of these. Among the largest colleges and universities are:

University of California, with branches at Berkeley, Los Angeles, San Francisco, Santa Barbara, Davis, Riverside, La Jolla (Scripps Institution of Oceanography), and Mt. Hamilton (Lick Observatory). Enrollment 106,035 in 1971. The largest enrollments are at Berkeley (about 27,500 students) and at Los Angeles (about 28,300). The medical school is at San Francisco.

California State Polytechnic College at San Luis Obispo. Enrollment 10,738 in 1971.

Los Angeles State College of Applied Arts and Science, at Los Angeles. Enrollment 22,000 in 1971.

University of San Francisco, at San Francisco. Enrollment 6,457 in 1971.

Stanford University, at Palo Alto. Enrollment 11,193 in 1971.

University of Southern California, at Los Angeles. Enrollment 20,003 in 1971.

California Institute of Technology (men only), at Pasadena. Enrollment 1,451 in 1971.

CHIEF CITIES OF CALIFORNIA

The leading cities of California, with 1970 census figures, are:

Los Angeles, population 2,816, 061. Largest city in the state, and home of the great moving picture industry. There is a separate article about LOS ANGELES.

San Francisco, population 715,674, city of the famous Golden Gate. There is a separate article about SAN FRANCISCO.

Oakland, population 361,561, across the bay from San Francisco, and connected with it by the Bay Bridge.

San Diego, population 696,769, the closest to Mexico of all the important cities in California. There is a separate article about SAN DIEGO.

Long Beach, population 358,633.

Sacramento, population 254,413. There is a separate article about SACRAMENTO.

San José, population 696,769.

CALIFORNIA IN THE PAST

The land that is now California was discovered by a Spanish explorer named Hernando Cortez in 1534. No one settled in the new land until 1683, when

some missionary priests moved to the part now known as Lower California. Upper California, or the part that is now the state, was first settled by the Spanish in 1768. They built a mission at San Diego, and began to convert the Indians to Christianity.

Although a great many Indians made trouble for the Spanish missionaries, the Spaniards did not give up their efforts to convert the Indians. They built many more missions up and down the coast. The first mission on the shores of San Francisco Bay was established in 1776, the same year that the colonies in the East published the Declaration of Independence.

California was a Spanish colony, however, and was not connected at all with the original thirteen colonies that were engaged in the American Revolution.

It remained a Spanish colony until 1822, when Mexico revolted from Spanish rule. California declared its own independence from Spain at that time, and joined with Mexico.

About twenty years later, thousands of easterners moved to California, making the long, dangerous journey by covered wagon. This divided the population of California between eastern Americans and Mexican or Spanish Californians. California was such a rich land that both Mexico and the United States wanted to own it, and in 1846 war broke out between the two countries. The United States won within a year. A few months after the war ended, gold was discovered in California, in February, 1848, and the famous gold rush started.

This drew many thousands of people to California, both from the eastern part of the United States and from Europe. Many of them were lawless and wild. At the time when California was admitted to the Union, in 1850, there was a great deal of trouble in the state because of criminals and outlaws who had been attracted by the promise of great wealth in gold. It was necessary to do something to protect the good citizens, and so a "Vigilance Committee" was organized to restore law and order. Before long, California was again a quiet, peaceful place.

The quiet did not last, however. When the gold rush died down, and people were finding it hard to earn a living because prices were so high, and there were so few jobs, California again went through a hard period. There was plenty of land, but there was a lot of trouble about getting land legally. The Spaniards and Mexicans of California owned great ranches, and they found that squatters were taking this property from them. A squatter was a man who simply settled down on a piece of land and started to live there. Many people settled on land that seemed to belong to no one, and that was all right. But sometimes they settled on land that was part of someone's ranch, and the real owner of the ranch objected to losing good land that way. If they threw the squatters off, that did not help much, because those people had to live somewhere, and a lot of people with no homes can cause trouble any place. Eventually this was all settled, however, by passing many land laws, so that everyone was treated as fairly as

possible, and so that everyone had at least a place to live.

The motion-picture industry made the town of Hollywood famous. Hollywood is a part of greater Los Angeles, and it became the center of the motion-picture industry when small independent producers moved away from New York to avoid legal troubles. A movie trust in the East tried to keep small film companies out of business. There were lawsuits, raids, and riots. To escape from this trouble, one man fled to Los Angeles and made the first commercial motion picture ever produced in California. His name was William Selig, and the picture was *The Count of Monte Cristo,* made in 1908 at Los Angeles. Three years later, the first movie studio in Hollywood was opened. The film company originally went to California just to get away from trouble in New York, but soon the business grew so large that Hollywood suddenly became the movie capital of the world. There is a separate article about the MOTION PICTURES.

During World War II, California became an important war production center, as well as a point of embarkation for the war in the Pacific. Many large aircraft manufacturers established plants in the state, and remained there after the war was over. This increased California's population again, and also added to its importance as a production center.

PLACES TO SEE IN CALIFORNIA

Lassen Volcanic National Park, 163 square miles, in Lassen National Forest, at the northern end of the Sierra Nevada Mountains. It is the area around Lassen Peak, the only active volcano in the United States. It can be reached by State Highways 89 and 44.

Sequoia and General Grant National Parks, the wildest country on the western slopes of the Sierra Nevadas, about 53 miles east of Fresno. It was named for the giant sequoia trees found there. It can be reached by State Highways 32, 180, and 198.

Kings Canyon National Park is directly north of Sequoia National Park, and it can also be reached by State Highway 180.

Muir Woods is a grove of giant sequoias on the west central edge of Sequoia National Forest, on Route 32.

Lava Beds National Monument, in the Modoc National Forest, north central California, an area of about 80 square miles of strange lava formations. There are many caves and frozen underground streams in the area, and lava that hardened into unusual shapes, some of which resemble crude animals. It can be reached by U.S. Route 97.

Yosemite National Park, 752,744 acres, 429 lakes inside the park, and numerous rivers. This national park has accommodations for visitors all year round, and many kinds of sports and entertainment are available at all times. There are hotels, restaurants, cabins, tents, and camping grounds. There is a hospital, and ambulance service. There are even doctors and dentists. Yosemite National Park is so large it is almost like a huge, sprawling, spread-out town.

Death Valley, in the Colorado Desert, has been made a national monument. Al-

though the section that is the actual Death Valley of covered wagon days is comparatively small, the general area covers about 1,500 square miles that have been set aside as a national monument. It extends several miles over the Nevada border. A highway travels the full length of the Death Valley National Monument, and passes through the center of Death Valley proper. In addition, the center of the Death Valley National Monument is crossed by State Highway 190.

FAMOUS PEOPLE FROM CALIFORNIA

Many very famous people have made California their home. Among the famous writers from California are Gertrude Atherton, Jack London, William Saroyan, John Steinbeck, Kate Douglas Wiggin, and L. Frank Baum.

In the music field, there is the composer, Charles Wakefield Cadman, and Lawrence Tibbett, the singer.

The poet Robert Frost also lived in California, and so did the famous publisher, William Randolph Hearst.

Will Rogers, the humorist; Luther Burbank, the plant wizard; Herbert Hoover, the thirty-first President of the United States; and Richard M. Nixon, the thirty-seventh President of the United States, were also residents of California.

CALIFORNIA. Area 158,693 square miles. Population (1970 preliminary census) 19,715,490. Capital, Sacramento. State flower, California golden poppy. State tree, the redwood. Admitted to the Union in 1850. Official abbreviation, Calif.

California, Lower, and Gulf of California

Lower California is a part of Mexico, south of California in the United States. The people who live there call it *Baja California,* which is the Spanish way of saying "Lower California." It is a long, narrow peninsula, which is a piece of land almost entirely surrounded by water. It is about 760 miles long from north to south, with the Pacific Ocean on the west and the Gulf of California on the east. Two ranges of mountains extend the length of the peninsula, one on the east coast and one on the west. The coastline itself is very irregular, with hundreds of bays cut into it. Many small islands dot the shoreline on both the gulf and the ocean sides. The northern section has dense woodlands, the central part has rich, fertile farmlands, and there is a large desert in the south. If you were to visit that desert, you would see enormous cactus plants growing there. Over on the gulf coast you would probably see native pearl divers at work. You might also feel the tremors, or quivering, of a slight earthquake, because Lower California has a great many light quakes.

The people of Lower California are mostly Mexicans who speak the Spanish language and belong to the Roman Catholic religion. In the wild valleys in the middle of the peninsula there are still many very primitive and backward Indians.

Spanish explorers first reached Lower California in 1538, about four hundred years ago. They began to build settlements there and in what is now Califor-

nia in the United States. It was not until about two hundred years ago that the two Californias were separated. The Spanish explorer Hernando Cortez discovered the Gulf of California, and it was first named the Gulf of Cortez in his honor. The gulf is about seven hundred miles long and about a hundred miles wide. In addition to pearl diving, the Gulf of California has a great deal of deep-sea fishing for sharks, whales, barracuda, and other fish.

Lower California is almost equally divided into two sections, Northern and Southern, each with its own capital. The area is not thickly settled. There are only about two people per square mile. Since there would naturally be families of five or six living in one place, you can see that there are large areas with no one at all living in them.

LOWER CALIFORNIA. Region in Mexico. Area, 55,629 square miles. Population (1960 census) 605,000. Divided into two sections. Northern section (a state): area, 27,653 square miles; population, 522,000; capital, Mexicali. Southern Territory: area, 27,967 square miles; population 83,000; capital, La Paz.

Caligula

Caligula was a famous Roman emperor who lived more than 1,900 years ago. He was born A.D. 12. His real name was Caius Caesar Augustus Germanicus, but he was given the nickname of *Caligula,* which means "little boots," because he wore military boots when he was a child.

When Caligula grew up and became emperor, he was so evil that people thought he was insane. He may very well have become insane during an illness. At any rate, he did many mad things. Some of the things that he did were funny. On one occasion he made his horse a consul. But he also had many people tortured and executed. He is supposed to have said that it was too bad everybody did not have the same neck so that it could be chopped off at one blow. All this made the Roman people very angry and he was finally murdered in the year 41, when he was only 29 years old.

caliph

The head of the Mohammedan religion was at the same time a great ruler. He was called the *caliph.* His position was called the *caliphate,* just as the Pope's position is called the papacy.

When Mohammed the Prophet died more than 1,300 years ago, he did not leave any sons, so his followers had to choose a *calif,* or "successor" (which is what the word means). The first caliph they chose was Mohammed's father-in-law, Abu Bakr. He and the caliphs who came after him became also the rulers of the Arab empire and their capital was the city of Damascus. As the empire grew, there were many quarrels over who would become the caliph. At one time there were three caliphs, one in Baghdad, one in Cairo, Egypt, and one in Cordova, Spain. The most recent caliphs were the sultans of Turkey. When the last sultan, named Mohammed VI, was deposed from his throne and went into exile, his cousin became caliph (but not sultan) for a short time. This was in 1922. Two years later the caliphate was abolished, and since then there have been no more caliphs.

calisthenics

Calisthenics is a way of exercising your arms, legs, and body. It is mostly stretching, bending, and other movements of the body. Usually calisthenics is performed in a group, and a leader tells you what to do. For example, the director might say: "Hands on hips . . . PLACE!" and you and everyone else place your hands on your hips, exactly when the director says "place." Suppose the exercise is to be "deep knee-bends." You and the rest of the class would squat down, and rise up, down and up, down and up, beginning when the director said "Exercise!" and stopping when you got the signal to stop. Calisthenics makes the body strong and limber. In the United States Army and Navy and Marine Corps the men do calisthenics every morning. Some people do a few exercises by themselves in the morning, and we say that they are doing their "daily dozen," because there were twelve exercises in a course of calisthenics that was once very popular.

Calixtus

Calixtus was the name that three different Popes took when they were elected to the papacy. No one knows the real name of Calixtus I. He was a Roman who lived about 1,750 years ago. It is believed that he was born a slave about the year 160 and that he died as a martyr in 222.

Calixtus II was a Frenchman whose real name was Guy of Burgundy. He was a relative of the queen of France, the emperor of Germany, and the king of England. In France, he was the Archbishop of Vienne. He was very powerful and became Pope by a battle in which he captured and imprisoned the antipope (or false Pope) Gregory VIII. He died in Rome in 1124.

Calixtus III was a Spanish member of the famous Borgia family. His name was Alonso de Borja. When he became Pope in the year 1455, he was a very old man. He started a crusade against the Turks that was not very successful. The Borgia family in Italy became very powerful partly because of his help.

calla

The calla, which is also called the *lily of the Nile,* is a beautiful plant that is grown indoors, or outdoors in warm countries. It is a native of Africa. It has huge, glossy, dark green leaves, and white or golden heart-shaped "flowers." In the center of each "flower" is a fingerlike golden spike. On this spike are many little knobs, and these are the real flowers. The calla is very much like the jack-in-the-pulpit. They are closely related and belong to the same family of plants called *arums.* Another common arum is the wild calla that grows in ponds in northern America, Europe, and Asia. Its "flower" is very much like that of the cultivated calla, but smaller. The flowers on this spike produce pretty red berries. The leaves of the wild calla are about the size of an open hand, and heart-shaped.

calliope

A calliope is a musical instrument that is played in circus parades and outdoor shows. It is very loud and you can hear it a mile away. It has whistles of different sizes, tuned to notes of the scale like the pipes of an organ, and a keyboard like the one on a piano. When you press down a key, steam blows through a whistle and makes a loud tone. Modern calliopes use compressed air instead of steam. But lots of people think that the old-fashioned calliope, with its steam boiler with smoke and sparks coming out of it, and steam spouting from the whistles, was more exciting. Merry-go-rounds and other amusement park rides often use phonograph records of calliope music.

calorie

How many times have you heard some one say that he is overweight and must stop eating so many calories? Sometimes people also say that they must watch their calories. You are probably wondering what a calorie looks like. You will be surprised to learn that you cannot see a calorie nor can you chew one. A calorie is a unit of heat. It is the amount

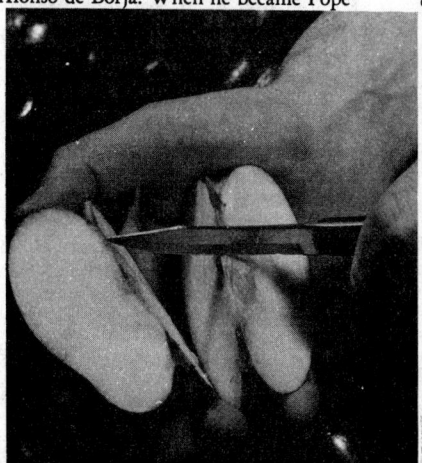

United Fresh Fruit & Vegetable Ass n.

The average apple contains only 80 calories, while one slice of strawberry cream cake has about 300 calories.

of heat that is needed to raise the temperature of one gram of water one degree. Since it takes almost thirty grams of water to make an ounce, you can see that one calorie is a very small amount of heat.

When people talk about how many calories they have eaten, they mean the amount of heat that will be created inside their bodies by the food they have eaten. The food we eat serves as fuel for our body which burns it just as a furnace burns coal. The heat that results serves as energy for our body when it does work. The less work we do the less energy we need and the less calories we should have.

These food calories are each equal to 1,000 small calories. They are called large calories, or *kilo-calories* (abbreviated K-cal). *Kilo* is from a Greek word meaning one thousand. When foods are said to contain calories, this means that when the food is burned inside our body it will give off a certain number of calories of heat to be used as energy. If we do not need the energy right away, the food will not be burned but stored in our body as fat. If we eat foods that contain more calories than we need, we will become overweight. That is why we should eat only enough to keep us healthy and give us energy to do our work.

Each particular food will supply a certain amount of calories. This amount can be found by burning a small bit of the food in a steel container with thick walls, called a *calorimeter*. After the food is burned, the temperature inside the calorimeter is measured and the amount of heat given off is determined. In this way it has been found that one slice of bread supplies 100 K-calories or 100,000 ordinary calories of heat, enough heat to boil a pound of water; an egg contains 80 K-calories; and a potato, 100 K-calories.

Boys and girls usually need about 2,400 calories a day to stay healthy. Of course, the amount of calories you should have depends upon how much exercise you do and also on how much you weigh. You should generally eat about 30 calories of food a day for each pound you weigh. Older people need fewer calories per pound. The amount of calories your body needs when it is completely at rest is called its BASAL METABOLISM. You can read about this in a separate article.

Calvary

Calvary is the name of the place outside the wall of Jerusalem where Jesus was crucified. It is from a Latin word that means *skull*. Calvary is mentioned in the Bible, but today no one knows where the exact place was. Some people believe that it is inside the Church of the Holy Sepulcher, because this church was built on the spot where St. Helena found a piece of wood that was supposed to have come from the cross on which Jesus was crucified. Another spot near the Damascus gate was said to be Calvary by an Englishman, Charles G. Gordon; it is called the *Garden Tomb* or *Gordon's Calvary*. The Hebrew name for Calvary is Golgotha.

Calvin, John

John Calvin was one of the great founders of the Protestant form of the

Presbyterian Historical Society

Christian religion. He was born at Noyon, France, in the former province of Picardy, in the year 1509. At the age of 24 he had what he called a "sudden conversion" from the Roman Catholic Church to Protestantism. Because of this he had to move from one city to another. He finally settled in Geneva, Switzerland, where he changed the church and also the laws of that city. He believed in very strict church discipline. The Puritans who settled New England were Calvinists. Calvin died in 1564.

The teachings of John Calvin influenced many people in western Europe, England, and even in America. There are several Protestant churches that believe in them. These churches are called the "Reformed churches" and the most important one is the Presbyterian Church. Calvinism was a part of the REFORMATION movement, which you can read about in a separate article.

calypso

The people of the islands of Trinidad, Tobago, and the British West Indies, in South America, sing a kind of song called *calypso*. The calypso singers usually make them up as they go along. Later they remember parts of what they sang, and little by little the songs are learned by other people. Usually they use a tune that they know, and make up new words to fit the tune. The words are about all kinds of things, and sometimes they do not fit the music too well. For example, in the song *Sly Woman* it is sung "She's a sly wo-MAN," because that fits the tune better. Calypso also refers to the people who live in the British West Indies, and they say "calypso man," or "calypso woman," as we would say "California man" or "New York man," if that is where they live. Calypso is also the name of a character in the *Odyssey,* the great poem by Homer.

Camacho, Manuel Avila

Manuel Avila Camacho was the president of the Republic of Mexico from 1940 to 1946. He was born in 1897, and when he was still a young man, he became interested in the problems of the Mexican people. At that time, Mexico was a republic, as it is today, but the people were not happy about conditions in the country. From 1911 until 1920, there were revolutions and fighting in Mexico. Camacho joined one of the revolutionary armies. He was an extraordinarily good soldier, and stayed in the army after the revolutions were over. Before he was elected president, he was a division general, the highest title in the Mexican Army. He died in 1955.

Cambodia

Cambodia is an independent nation in southeast Asia. It is one of the countries once called FRENCH INDO-CHINA. After being under Japanese control during World War II, Cambodia won its independence from France in 1955 and became a constitutional monarchy, which means that the king is head of the coun-

try but a parliament and prime minister actually control the government.

In area Cambodia is not much larger than Minnesota; in population, about 6½ million, it is almost twice as large.

Most of Cambodia is level land, but there is a mountain range along the coast with peaks as high as 5,700 feet. There are large areas of jungle that are still wild, and full of tigers, leopards, buffaloes, and elephants. The climate is warm and damp, and there are only two seasons. The rainy season lasts from April to October. The rest of the year is dry.

Most Cambodians are descendants of the Khmer people who established themselves there thousands of years ago. They came from India. Their language, called Khmer, is like Chinese and their favored religion is Buddhism. Cambodians are mostly farmers; they grow cotton, rice (their main food), rubber, and spices, especially pepper. Cambodia has a seacoast on the South China Sea (Gulf of Siam) and fishing is an important industry. Exports include teak and ebony woods.

The children of Cambodia are still taught the arts of their ancestors. Girls of eight and nine learn to perform very complicated dances and boys are taught to carve designs in wood, stone, and bone.

About a thousand years ago the kingdom was called Khmer, and it was very powerful and very modern until it lost many wars. The ruins of the huge city of Angkor, long covered up by the forest, have now been cleared and attract thousands of tourists every year.

In 1947, the Cambodian people were given more freedom than ever before, when a national assembly (parliament) was formed and Prince Norodom Sihanouk was elected Prime Minister. Upon the death of King Norodom Suramarit (Prince Norodom Sihanouk's father) in 1960, Sihanouk became the head of state, although he refused the title of king. In 1970, General Lon Nol overthrew Sihanouk and Cambodia became a republic for the first time in over a thousand years.

Though the government and the name of Cambodia were changed (new name: Khmer Republic) political unrest continued as the Khmer Rouge, supporters of ousted Prince Sihanouk, attempted to regain control of the country. In addition, Communist forces from North Vietnam, using mountain passes, entered Cambodia, and President Nixon ordered troops into that country. More than 30,000 American troops along with 40,000 South Vietnamese fought inside Cambodia until June 30, 1970, when the North Vietnamese offensive was halted and the Communists were forced out. This three-month intervention of Vietnamese soldiers in Cambodia, entangled Cambodia in the Vietnamese War. (See VIETNAM).

Lon Nol was popularly elected President in June of 1972, and when civil war inside Cambodia intensified, the Cambodian government appealed to the United States for extensive military and economic aid. On April 17, 1975, after five years of fighting and the loss of more than 100,000 lives, the Khmer Rouge forces succeeded in their military overthrow of the United States-supported Lon Nol regime.

Though Prince Sihanouk was named Chief-for Life, in reality the Communist leader Khieu Samphan took control. The newly formed government forced many city dwellers to flee to the countryside and jungles. Mass murders of civilians by the Khmer Rouge were reported at this time.

CAMBODIA. Area, [1970] 69,898 square miles. Population, 7,890,000. Government, republic. Capital, Phnom-Penh (population about 600,000). Monetary unit, riel, worth about 2 U.S. cents.

Cambridge

Cambridge is the name of two cities, each the home of a famous university.

Cambridge, England, is an ancient market town on the river Cam. It was originally a Roman fort and later a castle was built there by William the Conqueror. Both the fort and castle have long disappeared, but there are still many old inns, houses and churches in the town. Cambridge University is about 820 years old. It and Oxford University are the most famous universities in England.

CAMBRIDGE, ENGLAND. Population 91,800. On the Cam River.

Cambridge, Massachusetts, is the home of Harvard University, Radcliffe College, and the Massachusetts Institute of Technology. It is on the Charles River, across from the city of Boston. It was first settled by the Pilgrims in 1630, and was called Newtown. Harvard, founded in 1636, is the oldest college in the United States. The first printing press in the United States was set up in Cambridge and on it was printed a translation of the Bible for the Indians.

Cambridge is now a city of many industries; some of the products manufactured there are fine tools, machinery, rubber, chemicals, and candy.

CAMBRIDGE, MASSACHUSETTS. Population (1970 census) 100,361. County seat of Middlesex County.

Camden

Camden is a city in southwest New Jersey, across the Delaware River from Philadelphia. About 117,000 people live there. Camden has many large factories, shipyards, and oil refineries. The American poet Walt Whitman lived in Camden and his house there is now a museum. Camden was settled in 1681.

camel

The camel is a large beast of burden that has served men for the last five thousand years. It is able to carry heavy loads over long stretches of barren desert, and to go for several days without water. The shaggy brown animal is an invaluable friend to traders in Central Asia, North Africa, and Arabia. It is a familiar sight in the deserts and market towns to see the camel, with a heavy burden, plodding along under the hot sun.

Everyone can recognize a camel by the large hump on its back. The camel of North Africa and Arabia has just one hump, and is called a *dromedary*. But the camel in Central Asia has two humps, and is known as the *Bactrian camel*. During the rainy season, the camel enjoys its richest diet, and its hump becomes large

and well developed. But in the dry season the hump is shrunken and small. Usually, the camel eats grass and the branches and leaves of trees. But when this great beast is very hungry, it will eat the skin and bones of other animals, fish, and even a felt blanket.

The desert tribes keep camels in herds. The people drink the camel's nourishing milk, and eat the flesh. They clip the thick woolly hair that grows on the upper part of the camel's body during the winter months, and make it into soft camel's hair cloth. Clothing made of camel's hair is very popular in the United States and Europe. Though this animal is very useful, it is known for its stubbornness and nasty disposition. When it is angry, it kicks and bites, and is dangerous. Unlike other animals used by man, it shows little affection for its master.

camellia

One of the most beautiful shrubs is the camellia. It has dark green, glossy leaves, and large red or pink or white blossoms. Usually these are "double," that is, with more than one row of petals. In the southern United States, you will see camellias growing out-of-doors; but farther north they are grown only in greenhouses. Their native home is in Asia, where some of them grow into trees. They are closely related to the tea plant, and another name for camellias is *tea-flowers*. In fact, from one kind of camellia an oil is produced called tea-seed oil.

Camelot

Camelot was the town in England where King Arthur and his Knights of the Round Table are supposed to have lived more than one thousand years ago. No one knows exactly where this town was located, or if it really existed. But in the stories about King Arthur and his brave knights, Camelot is described as a very beautiful town, with great castles, and flags flying from its high turrets. There were fine roads over which the knights rode away to meet their adventures, and there was also a river that ran past the town. Many poems and stories filled with knights and fair ladies have been written about Camelot. It seems to have been an ideal town of long ago.

cameo

A cameo is a small stone which usually has a tiny face or a figure very delicately carved on it. These stones were first used over one thousand years ago in the Orient. They were attached to the backs of seals which people used to sign their letters. Sometimes the cameos were used, just as medals were, to show the high rank of the people who had them. Some of these cameos can be seen in museums today. The Greeks carved such fine designs on their cameos that people began to wear them on their clothes, and put them on their cups and drinking glasses. Some of the most beautiful cameos made today are carved in Rome, in Italy. They are used as ornaments on brooches, earrings, pins, bracelets and rings. Cameos are carved from semiprecious stones such as sardonyx and agate. These stones have veins in them and the

carver has to know just how to use his tool so that he does not split the stone by carving against this grain.

This beautiful ivory cameo was made by a skilled craftsman in ancient Greece.

N.Y. Public Library

camera, a device for taking pictures: see PHOTOGRAPHY

camera lucida

The camera lucida (pictured on this page, above) was invented more than 150 years ago by an English scientist named Dr. William H. Wollaston. Its name, *camera lucida,* means "light chamber." It is used to draw on paper the outline of objects of almost any size. It is made of a glass *prism* (which changes the direction in which light travels) and a *lens,* or eyepiece, attached to a metal stand. The person using the camera lucida focuses it on the object that is to be drawn and then looks through the lens. Through this he sees not the actual object but an image of it shown on a piece of paper. This image can be adjusted to any size— larger, smaller, or the same size as the object. A perfect drawing can then be made with a pen or pencil.

The camera lucida is very useful to scientists, and to students of art and architecture. It can be used with a microscope to make drawings of very tiny objects, or with a telescope to draw objects that are very far away. Before the camera lucida was invented, another kind of instrument, called the CAMERA OBSCURA, was used to make drawings or tracings. You can read about it in the next article. Since the invention of photography, however, neither one is used as much as formerly.

camera obscura

The camera obscura is an optical instrument that was invented about four hundred years ago by an Italian named Baptista Porta. It was used as a toy, and also to draw outlines of all sorts of objects. Its name, *camera obscura,* means "dark chamber," or box. It has a glass lens at one end. Inside, at the other end of the box, a mirror is placed at an angle. The camera is focused on an object so that its image is shown on a ground-glass plate set into the top of the box. A sheet of paper is then placed on this plate, so that a drawing of the object can be traced with a pen or pencil.

The camera obscura was used a great deal until the invention of the CAMERA LUCIDA, about which you can read in the article just before this one. However, the most important use of the camera obscura was the part it played in the invention of photography. When a piece of photographic paper is used instead of a sheet of drawing paper, a photograph can be taken of the object.

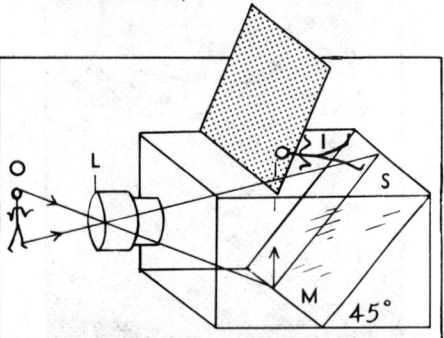

CAMERA OBSCURA. Rays of light from the little figure (O) go through a lens (L) and into a box called a camera obscura. The light then falls on a mirror (M). The mirror is set in back of the box at an angle. This sends the light to a screen (S), where an outline of the figure is seen as an image (I).

Cameroon, Federal Republic of

The Federal Republic of Cameroon (formerly known by its French spelling, Cameroun) is a country on the west coast of Africa. In area it is 184,000 square miles, a little larger than California. Nearly six million people live in Cameroon. The country is composed of two states: the former territory of French Cameroons, which became independent in 1960; and the former territory of British Southern Cameroons, which voted to join the republic in 1961. The government is based on France's government, with a president, premier, and parliament.

The Cameroons area was discovered by the Portuguese toward the end of the 15th century, colonized by the Germans in 1884, and divided between the French and English by a League of Nations mandate after World War I, with four-fifths of the area going to France. Arabs live in the dry northern part of the Cameroons area. In the heavily wooded southern part along the coast, where the weather is always hot, the people are mostly Negroes, belonging to many different tribes. The area produces rubber, ivory (from elephant tusks), and cacao. Other products are peanuts, coffee, bananas, palm oil, and hardwoods. Near the coast is Mt. Cameroon, an ancient volcano over 13,300 feet high.

CAMEROON, Federal Republic of. Area, 183,568 square miles. Population (1973 estimate) 5,800,000. Government, Federal republic. Capital, Yaounde (population 120,000). Largest city and chief port, Douala (population, 210,000). Languages, French, Foulbé Bamiléké, Bantu and many other dialects. Religion, native tribal religions, Christian, Moslem. Monetary unit, franc C.F.A. (African Financial Community), about 277 to the U.S. dollar.

camouflage

Many wild animals, such as the zebra and the tiger, have stripes or coats of other patterns that are very useful as disguises. When the animal wants to hide, in case of danger or in order to attack some other animal, it can stand in bushes or lie down in tall grass so that the pattern of its coat blends in perfectly with the shadows. When this kind of disguise is used by men in warfare, it is called camouflage.

Camouflaged soldiers wear coveralls with irregular colored patterns of brown, tan, green, and olive drab. This helps them to hide from the enemy. Sometimes they also paint their hands and faces with dark colors and put small leafy branches in their helmets so that, when lying down in the tall grass or standing in the forest, they look almost like bushes themselves. When they fight in the winter snow or on the sandy deserts, they wear white or other light colors to conceal themselves. Metal parts of weapons are blackened to prevent them from shining.

Camouflage is also used to disguise buildings, such as forts and factories, and military vehicles, such as automobiles, tanks, and even large guns. Buildings are painted to look like fields or forests. Large guns are covered with nets or wire screen strung with strips of dull-colored cloth that blends into the landscape. It would be almost impossible to hide ships completely. But they are painted in patches of gray or dull green to break up their outlines and to make them less easily seen against the sea and sky. Sometimes they even seem to be going in the opposite direction.

Scientific camouflage was developed during World War I by the French. During World War II camouflage was used by all the big countries, because there was so much bombing by airplanes that it was important to hide factories, airfields, and military bases. Sometimes real targets, like factories, were made to look from the air like fields, and sometimes open fields were made to look like factories. Complete make-believe towns and airfields were built as decoys, with dummy buildings, guns, and airplanes. The use of camouflage in Europe seems to have been very successful, though there is no way of telling exactly how many buildings were saved or how many bombs were wasted on false targets.

campanile

When a set of bells is hung in a separate building instead of in the steeple of a church, the building is called a campanile. The first campaniles were built in Italy hundreds of years ago. The famous "Leaning Tower of Pisa" is a campanile in Italy. The campanile of St. Mark's Church in Venice, and "Giotto's campanile" at Florence, designed by the great artist Giotto di Bondone, also are in Italy. The first campaniles were made round, but later builders made them square. They are generally made of brick and stone, with stairs going up to the belfry where the bells are hung. See the article on BELLS.

campanula

A campanula is a kind of plant with bell-shaped flowers which is often grown in rock gardens. It is also called bellflower. The flowers may be pink or white, but nearly always they are blue. One kind of campanula is called the "bluebell of Scotland," but its real name is the harebell. There are about three hundred kinds of campanula. The best known are the Canterbury bell and the chimney bellflower. The rampion is a kind of campanula whose roots and leaves are eaten in salads. Campanulas grow mostly in the northern parts of the world.

Campbell

Campbell is the name of one of the great clans (families) of Scotland. The heads of the family have been the earls and dukes of Argyll for hundreds of years. The traditional founder of the clan was named Colin. One of the famous Scottish folk songs is "The Campbells Are Coming." See the article on CLANS.

Campbell, Alexander

Alexander Campbell was the founder of one of the important Protestant Christian denominations, the Disciples of Christ (also called simply "the Christian Church" and sometimes "Campbellites"). Campbell was born in Ireland and settled in Washington, Pennsylvania, about 150 years ago. He had been a Presbyterian originally. There is a separate article on the DISCIPLES OF CHRIST. Campbell was born in 1788 and died in 1866.

Campbell, Malcolm

Sir Malcolm Campbell was a former English automobile and speedboat racer. He was born in 1885, and even as a boy he loved racing. He set many records in both automobile and speedboat racing, although these records have since been broken by men driving more modern cars and boats. During World War I, he was a captain in the British Royal Flying Corps. He was knighted by King George V after he had set an automobile speed record of 245 miles an hour in 1931. He set this record in his car, the Bluebird, along the beach at Daytona, Florida. Four years later, at Bonneville Flats, Utah, he was the first person to drive 300 miles an hour. Campbell died in 1949, at the age of 64.

Camp Fire Girls

The Camp Fire Girls are an organization of girls from 7 to 18 years old. The girls learn to play, camp, study, and work together in small groups. They follow their own law, "worship God, seek beauty, give service, pursue knowledge, be trustworthy, hold on to health, glorify work, be happy." Their emblem, or sign, of crossed logs and flame means both the hearth, or home fire, and the camp fire outdoors.

There are three groups in the organization. Girls between 7 and 8 years old may become "Blue Birds." "Camp Fire Girls" are between 9 and 11 years of age. High school seniors join the "Horizon Club," where the girls are between the ages of 15 and 18. Camp Fire Girls may be of any race or religion. Each group has from 6 to 20 members and an adult leader. Groups meet once a week, and also hold outdoor meets. At "cook-outs," the girls learn how to make fires and cook meals outdoors. They also go on nature-study hikes and camping trips.

The Camp Fire Girls follow many

customs of the American Indians. Each girl takes an Indian name that stands for what she would like to become. "Oka," for example, means to paint or sketch. The girl who chooses this name invents a design to go with it, and this design becomes her sign or monogram. She uses it on the special costume she wears at the council fire, which is a special meeting to welcome new members. The costumes are patterned after Indian ones, and so are many of the meetings.

Ceremonial costumes are decorated with colored beads that tell what each Camp Fire girl has learned to do. The girls have many different activities to choose from. These are divided into seven crafts: home, outdoors, creative arts, frontiers (in science), business, sports and games, and citizenship. For every skill or craft the Camp Fire girl learns, she is given a special wooden bead or "honor." A yellow bead means a business honor, green is for creative arts, blue for frontiers, and so on. The Camp Fire girl starts as a Trail Seeker, and as she wins more honors she becomes Wood Gatherer, then Fire Maker. The highest is Torch Bearer, which means a girl who has learned many skills that she is willing to share with others. The watchword of the Camp Fire Girls is *Wohelo*, a word made of the first two letters of the words *work, health,* and *love.*

The Camp Fire Girls organization was started in 1910 by Dr. and Mrs. Luther Gulick. Its program has been copied in 21 foreign countries, including Great Britain, El Salvador in Central America, and the Republic of the Philippines. More than three million girls have joined since the beginning. In 1961, there were about 600,000 members. The President of the United States is honorary president of the Camp Fire Girls.

The girls also join in community projects such as paper drives. During World War II, they helped sell war bonds, and worked in hospitals and nurseries. The headquarters of the organization is in New York City.

camphor

Camphor is a clear white substance that is made from the wood and bark of the camphor tree. It is useful to man in many ways. In the spring when housewives put away the family's winter clothes, they put camphor in with them to protect them against moths and other insects that like to eat cloth. If you have ever watched your mother do this, you probably remember the funny sharp smell that camphor has. Doctors use camphor as a sedative (to make a person relax), and in another form as a stimulant (to make a person feel more lively). Camphor is also used in making celluloid, perfume, and disinfectants. Scientists can make camphor artificially, from pine oil, and most camphor is now made this way. For many years, people in Japan, China, Formosa in the China Sea, and Borneo, have been boiling the bark and wood of the camphor tree and using the vapor to make camphor, which they send to many parts of the world. Camphor trees are now grown in the southern United States.

camping

Camping means living outdoors instead of in a house. A camper sleeps in a tent or on the ground, and cooks and eats his food outdoors. There are some people who camp all the time. They are called *nomads.* They never stay in one place very long because they live by hunting or fishing and they follow the game or fish. Some nomads raise cattle or sheep, and they move their tents wherever their sheep and cattle find pasture and water. The Bedouins of Arabia are nomads who live in desert country, and the Jews in the Bible who lived in the days of Abraham were nomads. So were the American Indians of the Great Plains who lived in *tepees,* or tents made of the hides of animals.

Most of us like to go camping because we can learn interesting things about the woods, rivers, lakes, and seashore. It is a good way to spend a summer vacation. You can go camping with your family, or with a club; with the Boy Scouts or Girl Scouts or Camp Fire Girls; or with the YMCA.

WAYS OF CAMPING

When the early settlers had to go from one place to another, before there were any trains or buses or even any roads, they had to walk. Sometimes a trip might take days or even weeks, and every night they had to stop and sleep wherever they were. They took along only the things they really needed, because anything extra would just be more weight to carry. They took their guns or bows and arrows, a knife, a water bottle, blankets, and a flint-and-steel to make a fire. Sometimes they took some dried corn, called *pinole,* or a meat-paste called *pemmican* that the Indians made. Whenever they saw a squirrel or a rabbit or wild turkey, they shot it and roasted it over the fire. We can learn from them the first important rule of camping:

Take along only what you need.

Today there are many different ways you can go camping. You can go by automobile, by canoe on the lake or river, or by pack train (with your outfit packed on horses). Perhaps you may go on a real exploring trip into wild country. All these things have a lot to do with your "outfit," which means the things you need to take along in order to be dry and warm and comfortable and have plenty to eat.

WHAT YOU NEED IN YOUR OUTFIT

There are as many kinds of outfit as there are places to go. Before you can assemble your outfit you think of where you are going, and how long you are going to stay. Then you decide whether you will go by automobile, train, bus, or on foot. Next you find out if you will be near a store or a telephone. All these things have something to do with your outfit.

Good campers are careful about footwear. In rough and rocky country it is better to have boots or moccasins that come up over the ankles, and an extra pair of soft moccasins to wear at night around camp. Shoes or boots should be large enough so that you can wear wool socks without making them too tight.

Nothing is more important than footwear, because if your feet get blistered or bruised by rocks, your trip will be spoiled. Put a little roll of adhesive tape in your kit, and if there is a place that rubs against your shoe, put a piece of tape over it. This is another important rule for campers: *Always wear shoes or boots that fit well.*

Socks should be made of wool, and have no holes or darned places in them. Cotton holds water, and holes and darned spots will make blisters on your feet. It is very important to take enough extra socks.

In the woods, even in a hot summer, nights are chilly. Be sure you have a sweater, extra underwear, and a warm jacket. All clothes should be strong and lightweight, and they should never be too tight. For winter camping and expeditions you need special clothes that are sold only at sporting goods stores.

Here is a list of things that should be in any outfit:

Knife: You will need a knife, either a belt or pocket knife. One blade, about 3½ inches long, is enough. In some places it is against the law to carry a knife that has a blade longer than 4½ inches.

Handkerchief: You need a big colored handkerchief. It has many uses: as a towel, to tie and carry things in, and to keep the sun and insects off the back of your neck. Never take a white handkerchief during hunting season, or some hunter might mistake you for a deer and shoot you.

Matches: You should carry matches in a waterproof case.

Compass: It is a very good idea to learn how to use a compass, because it can help you if you get lost. See the article on COMPASS.

Whistle: A whistle may help you signal your friends if you get lost.

Snake-bite kit: In any area where there are poisonous snakes you should have a snake-bite kit. You can buy one at sporting goods stores, or where Boy Scout supplies are sold.

Insect repellent: This comes either as a liquid or a paste. When you rub it on your face and legs it keeps insects from biting you for many hours.

First-aid kit: Some bandages, adhesive tape, salve, and iodine should be put in your kit for fixing cuts and scratches.

TENTS AND BEDDING

The kind of tent you need depends on the weather and the ground, and on how you are carrying your outfit. If you are going with your family in an automobile, the tent can be big and heavy. But if you are "back-packing," which means carrying your outfit in a knapsack, and are going by foot, your tent must be very light. The smallest tents, called "pup" tents, are just big enough to crawl into. "Wall tents," or "umbrella tents," are bigger and will hold several people, and there are many other kinds.

Most campers like "sleeping bags," but some like blankets. The best sleeping bags are filled with "down," the soft underfeathers of waterfowl, or a combination of down and feathers. They are really a sort of comforter or quilt folded in half, with a zipper or snap fasteners so that you can fasten yourself in.

Expert woodsmen know how to keep from freezing even without a tent or blankets. One way is to find a slope or big rock that will "break the wind," and then build a fire so that the heat will be

reflected back toward your windbreak. Another kind of shelter is called a "lean-to." It is made by placing some poles against a low branch of a tree, and then piling leaves, brush, bark, or earth on the poles until it makes a windproof wall. Then you build a "reflector fire" against a flat rock or green log, in front of the lean-to. The back of the lean-to should be "into the wind," so that smoke will not blow in.

The ground is cold, even in the hottest summer; and nights are likely to be chilly, even in the jungle. In winter, you can freeze very quickly if you lie on the ground. This brings us to another rule:

Always have more bedding beneath than on top, and never let the body touch the ground—always have a waterproof ground cloth.

The problem of bedding also depends on what kind of camping you do. In an automobile camp, you can use folding cots and mattresses, but they are too heavy for hiking. Air mattresses are lightweight, but they are not warm enough for cold weather. The Indians made beds of willow sticks, laid close together across two logs. "Bough" beds are made of two logs laid about two feet apart and filled in with the tips of balsam or hemlock boughs. Some campers like a "bed-sack," which is a bag that you fill with dry grass and leaves at night. You carry it empty, or use it to carry other things in.

WOODCRAFT AND COOKERY

One of the first things a camper must learn is how to make a good fire, and how to keep it from spreading and causing a forest fire. The campfire should be small, so that it will not be too hot. The best woods are hardwoods, such as maple, birch, white ash, elm, oak, beech, and hickory. Softwoods such as pine, balsam, fir, spruce and cottonwood make good kindling or a quick fire for cooking lunch, but they will not burn down to a lasting bed of coals for cooking dinner and for a night fire.

Learning how to make a fire in the woods is not easy. You need a teacher and a lot of experience. A good camper gathers his wood first, and shaves up a little kindling. Then he clears a space on the ground so that nothing else will catch fire and lays his firebed. He seldom needs more than one match.

Fire regulations are laws that tell us when and where we may build a fire. The laws are not the same everywhere. Usually a permit is required. These laws are important because they are intended to prevent forest fires. Good campers love the woods and do everything possible to avoid setting them on fire. The principal rule about fires is this:

Before leaving a fire, be absolutely sure that it is really out. The best way to be sure the fire is out is to pour plenty of water on it, then rake it over with a stick, then drench it with water again. Unless you get it very wet it can start up again.

Cooking equipment can be any combination of pots and pans. There are special lightweight outfits that are very good, especially if you are back-packing. All the parts fit into each other, and they do not make much weight or bulk. You can do a lot of cooking with a kettle and frying pan and a little "know-how."

Each person in a camping party should have a knife, fork and spoon, and an unbreakable cup and plate.

Before making up a "grub" or food list for camping, learn everything you can about which foods are light and nourishing, and will not spoil without refrigeration. All of these things are important.

WHEN YOU ARE LOST

A good camper never goes into the woods without telling his friends, or perhaps the Forest Rangers, where he is going and how long he expects to be gone. Then if he gets lost someone will miss him and start looking for him. One of the most important rules to observe when you are lost is this:

When you are lost stay where you are.

Every camper should have a compass and know how to use it, and should never be without matches in a waterproof match safe. But if you have neither, and if you have forgotten to tell anyone where you are going, try to find a shelter before it gets dark. Never try to find your way at night, because you might fall and get hurt. If you have a whistle, blow three blasts from time to time. If you have a gun, fire three shots in the air. Three sounds of any kind mean "I am lost!" Above all, do not try to guess where camp is, and try not to be scared. If you know how to build a smoky fire, do that. Searchers will see the smoke and come to you.

WATER

Water is the most important thing in the world when you do not have it. Most of us are used to just turning a faucet when we want water. In the woods there is no running water except a spring or brook, but here is a very important rule:

Never drink water that you find in the woods unless you have boiled or purified it.

The best way to purify water is to boil it, but there are also tablets containing a chemical that purifies the water. You can use them when you have no way to boil the water.

Canaan

In the first book of the Bible, called Genesis, you can read the story of how the Lord promised Abraham a country for his people, who are the Jews. This country was called Canaan, and it lay about where the state of Israel is today. The Bible also tells the story of how Moses led the Jews out of slavery in Egypt, and how after much wandering and many difficulties they finally reached Canaan, the promised land.

Canaan was also the name of a grandson of Noah. He was disrespectful to Noah and was banished.

Canada

Canada is an enormous country that covers all of the North American continent north of the United States except Alaska. The border it shares with the United States is almost four thousand miles long. It has coasts on three oceans: the Atlantic on the east, the Pacific on the west, the Arctic on the north. It is bigger than the United States, and about the same size as China. But while China has a population of about 759,620,000, in all of Canada there are only about 21,406,000 people, or somewhat more than the number living in California. Most of northern Canada is too cold and barren for permanent settlement. In the frozen wastes of the far north, within the Arctic Circle, only the simplest kinds of plants will grow.

Yet in spite of all this, Canada is very rich. Its people live better than those of almost any other country. There is more than enough food to go around. Canada's farmlands are fertile; its forests are full of timber; its rivers, lakes and coastal waters abound with fish. Under the rich soil lie vast quantities of gold, silver, oil, uranium, iron, and many other kinds of natural wealth. Canada's industrial plants and factories are among the most modern in the world. So you can see that Canada could easily support twice as many people as it does now.

Canada is a member of the British Commonwealth. Like the other independent countries in the Commonwealth, such as Australia and New Zealand, it has its own government. Like them, Canada was very important in World War II. The factories turned out war materials of all kinds and the farms produced food for the Allied Forces. The Canadian army, navy and air force fought with the Allies in Europe, North Africa, and the Far East. In the Korean War, Canadian soldiers battled alongside United States and British troops under the flag of the United Nations.

Canada is a member of the North Atlantic Treaty Organization (NATO) and is solidly joined with the other countries of the free world in the fight against communism. The United States and Canada are probably better friends than any other two countries.

THE PEOPLE OF CANADA

The people of Canada are almost all of European stock. The ancestors of almost 40% of them came from the British Isles—England, Scotland, Ireland, and Wales. Next in number are the descendants of French settlers; these number more than four million. The French language is spoken a great deal in Canada, especially in the big eastern province of Quebec. It is one of the two official languages; English is the other. Other Canadian people came originally from Germany, Russia, Scandinavia, Holland, Poland, and Italy.

Before the white men came, there were only scattered tribes of Indians in the vast land. The Indians were of many different types. In the north were the Eskimos. Seagoing tribes lived on the Pacific coast, and hunters and trappers lived in the east. However, there never were very many Indians. Little by little white settlers took their best lands, but they did not treat the Indians badly. Today there are over 238,000 Indians of all kinds in Canada, which is probably more than there were when the country was first seen by Europeans, five years after Columbus discovered the New World.

In religion, the citizens who speak French (called French Canadians) are

almost all Roman Catholics. Most of those who speak English are Protestants. There are more than 8-million Catholics in Canada. The two principal Protestant groups are the United Church of Canada (which has over three million members) and the Church of England, or Protestant Episcopal Church (which has more than two million).

HOW THE PEOPLE LIVE

Canada is such a rich country that its people do not have to depend on only one way of life, such as farming. They make their livings in a number of ways—farming, fishing, lumbering, mining, and manufacturing.

The first settlers who came to the rocky Atlantic coast of Canada almost four hundred years ago found the waters full of haddock, herring, cod, and lobster. Many people still live by catching these and other salt-water fish, particularly in Newfoundland, New Brunswick, Nova Scotia, and Prince Edward Island. These provinces are called the *Atlantic Provinces* because they are on the Atlantic Ocean. Although deep-sea fishing is a big industry in all of them, fresh-water fish like salmon, trout, pike and pickerel are also caught there in great numbers. Thousands of people work in the factories where fish are cleaned and packed in cans, or are frozen while fresh.

Along with the first fishermen, fur trappers came to Canada to hunt the foxes, muskrats, minks, beavers, raccoons, and other animals that brought high prices for their fur. Many Canadians still earn a living in the fur trade. But instead of hunting the animals in the forests, they raise them on big farms so as to have a steady supply of skins to be made into coats, jackets, and collars.

One of Canada's greatest natural treasures is its forests, which cover vast areas. Woodsmen living in lonely forest camps cut down the great trees and roll the logs to a river. The logs float down the river to a lumber mill. There they are sawed into planks for building, or crushed into the pulp from which paper and cardboard are made.

Farming has always been very important to Canada. Farmers use the most modern machines and methods to grow wheat, oats, barley, rye, potatoes, corn, tobacco, and a number of other crops. Dairy farms produce enormous quantities of milk and butter. After Canadians have used all the food they need themselves, there is always plenty left over for sale abroad.

On the western plains that stretch across the provinces of Manitoba, Saskatchewan, and Alberta, the people live much like their neighbors in North Dakota and Montana, just across the border. Big herds of cattle roam over the fine grazing lands. On higher ground shepherds watch over flocks of sheep. The sheep's soft white fleece, or coat, is made into wool. The meat of the cattle is sold for food. The hides become leather, to be used in shoes, belts, and other things.

Underneath the Plains region rich deposits of oil have recently been found. Oil refineries, where the crude oil is made into gasoline and oil for many uses, have been built near the oilfields. Thousands of Canadians work at bringing the oil up to the surface and refining it. In other parts of Canada miners dig for gold, silver, copper, lead, nickel, platinum, cobalt, iron ore, and coal. In northern Saskatchewan miners work the richest deposit of pitchblende in North America. Uranium, which is used in making atomic power, comes from pitchblende.

Across the Rockies from the Plains Provinces, in British Columbia, people work on farms, in factories, and in offices. They depend greatly on the shipping in and out of the Pacific port of Vancouver. In the northern part of British Columbia the Coast Indians still live as their forefathers did, fishing from boats made out of logs, and carving the giant statues of gods or special guardians called totem poles. In the Yukon Territory and the enormous Northwest Territories, which together take in the whole of Arctic Canada, the few white settlers are mostly miners and trappers. Some of the Eskimos have adopted the white man's ways, and live in the tiny settlements and trading posts. But most of them still live as Eskimos have lived for hundreds of years, hunting seals, snow foxes, and polar bears and living in ice huts called igloos.

The biggest Canadian provinces in size and population are Ontario and Quebec. More than half of all Canadians live in these two provinces. Quebec borders on the states of northern New England and New York State. More than three-quarters of its people speak French. Ontario, where most people speak English, borders on Minnesota and on all the Great Lakes except Lake Michigan. The people of both these provinces work at farming, manufacturing, lumbering, and mining. The Great Lakes region of Ontario is the industrial heart of Canada, where many thousands of people work in big, modern factories making machinery, automobiles, trucks, clothing, and leather goods.

WHAT THE LAND IS LIKE

Canada is an extremely varied land. In the east, the rugged, forest-covered Maritime Provinces lie around the Gulf of St. Lawrence, where the St. Lawrence River empties into the Atlantic. The Appalachian Mountains extend from the eastern United States into Quebec and New Brunswick. The many rivers and the beautiful scenery of this region make it a favorite with vacationers, particularly those who like to fish.

Farther west, the St. Lawrence valley opens out to the huge central plains around the Great Lakes. The St. Lawrence River connects the Great Lakes with the Atlantic. It contains thousands of islands, small and large. North of the Quebec farmlands rises the vast tableland called the Laurentian Plateau. This rocky plateau with its forests is sometimes called the "Canadian Shield," because it is really a huge barrier cutting off the northern region around Hudson Bay. It stretches from the Atlantic two-thirds of the way across Canada into Saskatchewan.

From the Great Lakes the central plain rises westward to the Rocky Mountains in Alberta. This region contains many lakes and rivers as well as flat prairie land. Banff and Jasper National Parks, in western Alberta, are world-famous vacation spots.

Along the Pacific Ocean, in British Columbia, are the steep Coast Mountains. Vancouver Island, which is large and covered with mountains, lies off the southwest corner of Canada. Further north a string of smaller islands runs up the coast to the border of Alaska.

Yukon, to the north, is generally mountainous and has an Arctic climate, with very long winters and very short summers. It is not a province, but a territory. It is drained by the Yukon River, which flows into Alaska and on into the Pacific. The important Alaska Highway, built during World War II, winds through the territory. Temperatures as low as 81 degrees below zero have been recorded in Yukon.

The immense Northwest Territories cover most of the northern edge of the North American continent, with vast empty islands out in the Arctic Ocean. There are huge areas of flat or rolling country called *tundras,* where no trees grow and the only plant life is a kind of lichen, or moss. Hudson Bay, a huge arm of the Atlantic Ocean, reaches south about five hundred miles into Canada to the northern edge of the Laurentian Plateau.

HOW THE PEOPLE ARE GOVERNED

Canada is a federation of provinces, as the United States is a federation of states. It is a member of the British Commonwealth of Nations. Elizabeth II is queen in Canada as she is in England. A governor general represents her at Ottawa, the Canadian capital. He is appointed on the advice of the Canadian government.

Laws are made by a parliament consisting of the queen, the Senate, and the House of Commons. Senators are appointed for life, rather than elected for a term. Members of the House of Commons are elected directly by the people. There are now 102 senators and 265 members of the House of Commons.

The prime minister is the leader of the party that has the most members in the House of Commons. He appoints a cabinet of ministers, each of whom usually assumes charge of one of the various government departments. By custom, only members of parliament can be cabinet members.

The provinces govern their own affairs, just as our states do. Each province has a lieutenant governor, appointed by the federal government, and a lawmaking assembly. The territories are governed by officials sent from Ottawa, who are advised by certain elected residents of the area.

Canada has a well-equipped army, navy, and air force. Law and order are enforced by the famous ROYAL CANADIAN MOUNTED POLICE, about whom you can read in the next article.

CANADA IN THE PAST

John Cabot, an Italian sailor in the service of England, reached the Atlantic shore of Canada in 1497. However, it was more than one hundred years later that the first settlement was established, by the French, at Port Royal in Nova Scotia. Later, English settlers came, and the two groups became rivals. The many

wars between France and England in the next hundred years were matched in Canada by wars between the rival colonies. Finally, in 1763, New France was conquered by the British, and all of the settled eastern part of Canada came under British control.

During the Revolutionary War many Americans who still wanted British rule fled into Canada. These people helped to develop the land and to strengthen its ties with England.

Following many exploring trips, the Canadian colonists began to push westward into the wilderness during the nineteenth century. In 1867 four colonies banded together into a kind of union with a federal government. When a railroad was opened all the way to the Pacific coast, many more settlers moved to the west. New provinces were formed and admitted one by one into the Canadian federation. Since then, through two world wars and the Korean war, Canada has kept on growing richer and stronger.

The ten provinces of Canada are: Ontario, Quebec, British Columbia, Alberta, Saskatchewan, Manitoba, Nova Scotia, New Brunswick, Newfoundland, and Prince Edward Island. The territories are: Northwest Territories, and Yukon.

The chief cities of Canada are: Montreal, Quebec; Toronto, Ontario; Vancouver, British Columbia; Winnipeg, Manitoba. The capital of Canada is Ottawa, Ontario. There is a separate article on each of these provinces and cities.

CANADA. Area 3,851,809 square miles. Population (1967 estimate) 20,354,334 Government, self-governing federation within the (British) Commonwealth. Capital, Ottawa. Languages, English and French. Religion, Roman Catholic and Protestant. Monetary unit, the dollar, usually worth within 5% of the U.S. dollar. Flag, red maple leaf on white background, bordered on left and right by vertical red stripe.

Canadian Mounted Police

The Royal Canadian Mounted Police enforce the law throughout the entire Dominion of Canada. The men of the force are popularly known as the "Mounties," and many stories are told of their bravery.

This unusual police force was formed almost a hundred years ago. It was first called the Northwest Mounted Police, because its purpose was to keep order in the great unsettled region in northwest Canada. They protected the settlers from bands of robbers, and saw that there was peace between the Indians and the white men. They wore bright red coats and "campaign hats"—which looked like Boy Scout hats—and they became famous for their daring exploits. It was often said that the Mounties always got their man. Few smugglers or other criminals were able to escape from this police force.

Today, the Royal Canadian Mounted Police maintain federal law in all parts of Canada. They also enforce provincial and even city laws if the provinces or cities wish them to do so. The provinces of Ontario and Quebec have their own police forces, but all of the other provinces now engage the Royal Canadian Mounted Police to enforce their laws. Most large Canadian cities have their own police forces, but many small towns

use the Royal Canadian Mounted Police for local enforcement.

Very few of these policemen ride horses any longer. Instead, they use modern equipment, such as small ships, automobiles, airplanes, and helicopters.

The Royal Canadian Mounted Police are excellent horsemen. They also are trained to track criminals on skis, snowshoes, and dog sleds.

There is no police force in the United States exactly like the Mounties, for they not only fight against many kinds of crime, but they also enforce the laws that protect wild birds, they guard the rights of Indians, they prevent illegal trade in drugs, and they do secret work that in America is done by the Federal Bureau of Investigation.

canals

Canals are waterways made by man. They are among the oldest and most useful things man has ever built. When we speak of canals, we usually mean man-made channels like the Panama Canal or the Houston Ship Canal which ships and barges use. But there are many other kinds of canal. There is the kind that carries water into cities from out-of-town reservoirs. There is the irrigation canal that brings water to thirsty crops. Among the ship canals, there are those that connect one ocean with another to shorten the voyages of ships, those that connect large inland cities directly with the sea, and those that connect lakes and rivers and extend water travel throughout the interior of a country.

BUILDING CANALS

When engineers want to know how much a canal will cost, they examine the ground they have to cut through. Sand, clay, and soft stone are easy to cut through, but then there is the job of dredging. Children have the same problem when they build canals in the sand to bring sea water to where they sit on the beach. The sand falls in from the banks of their canals, and it must be dug out again so the water can flow. This is called dredging. The banks and bottoms of many canals are lined with concrete to avoid the need for dredging.

Much harder to build are the canals which are cut out of solid rock. The PANAMA CANAL took twice as long to build as the SUEZ CANAL although it is only half as long. There are separate articles on these two canals. The United States Army engineers who built the Panama Canal had to blast a path through

mountains. They also had to build locks, so that the ships could go uphill.

LOCKS

Locks are like elevators for ships. They make it possible for a ship to go from a low body of water to a higher one. The ship sails or is pulled into a lock, which is a big tank open at the top. Watertight gates are closed behind the ship. More water is then let into the lock through pipes called *sluices*. As the water gets higher, the ship floats up to the level of the next lock. The gates open, and the ship moves into the next lock. The same things happen again. When the ship is in the last lock it is level with the body of water outside and it leaves the canal. When it comes back, it must go "downstairs" just as it went "upstairs." It enters a lock, the gates close behind it, and the water is let out through the sluice valves until the ship is floating at the level of the next lock. The gates open and the ship sails or is pulled out.

Ships can go through some canals under their own power but in others they are pulled through by engines that run on rails alongside the canal. Men, horses, and oxen used to pull ships and barges long ago, and on some canals in Europe they still do.

CANALS LONG AGO

One of the longest and oldest canals ever built was the Grand Canal in China. It was built almost 2,500 years ago. There was also an important canal between the Tigris and Euphrates Rivers in the land we now call Iraq. The French people built the famous Languedoc Canal several hundred years ago. It was almost 150 miles long, and connected the Mediterranean Sea with the Bay of Biscay. About the same time, the English were starting to build a system of canals which gave the country good waterways for its commerce. For hundreds of years the Belgians and the Dutch have used canals not only for transportation but to drain water off the land which in many places is below sea level. The people who live in the beautiful city of Venice, Italy, have canals instead of streets. They use gondolas and other boats as we use taxis and buses to go from place to place.

After the American Revolution, many people left the eastern cities and moved westward over the mountains. In their new homes, they needed supplies from the East, and they wanted to sell the food they grew and the fur of the animals they trapped. It was too expensive to send these things on slow wagons, so they built canals. The Erie Canal was the first. It stretched across New York State for 363 miles and connected Buffalo on the Great Lakes with Albany on the Hudson River. The Erie made it easier to trade with the new West, and helped to make New York America's largest seaport. The Erie Canal is still in use as a part of the New York State Barge Canal. It is 150 feet wide and 12 feet deep.

During the 1850s, railroads began to take all the passenger and much of the freight business away from the canals. But today canals still carry many tons of freight like coal and oil because it is cheaper to ship it that way than by railroad.

315

A man ties a barge in the Erie Canal to the wall of one of the locks before the water rises until it is equal to the level of water in the next lock.

Some inland cities build canals on which ships and barges can come right up to the city from the sea. Houston, Texas, is fifty miles inland from the Gulf of Mexico, but ocean-going freighters can reach it by using the Houston Ship Canal. The United States and Canada completed a canal system called the St. Lawrence Seaway in 1959 so that ships can sail from the Atlantic Ocean to Chicago, Cleveland and Canadian cities.

Canals make possible one of the most exciting trips you can make in the United States, a voyage through the Intercoastal Waterway. This route follows rivers, lakes, and canals for more than a thousand miles down the Atlantic coast line to Florida and then west to Texas.

Canal Zone, the region around the Panama Canal: see PANAMA CANAL.

canary

Canaries are a kind of small bird, famous for their singing. They are usually yellow, but some are greenish, or a mixture of colors. They were first brought to Europe five hundred years ago from the Canary Islands and the Madeira Islands, in the Atlantic Ocean northwest of Africa. The most famous canaries were bred in Germany, in the Hartz Mountains. Canaries are trained by playing musical instruments or phonograph records to them, or by letting them listen to another canary. Some sing with their beaks almost closed, and give out a long series of trills. They are called *roller* canaries. Others, called *choppers,* sing with their beaks open. Canaries eat seeds, and live happily in cages. They live as long as fifteen years, and may be-

come very fond of their owners.

The cheerful little canary has been a favorite household pet for hundreds of years.

Canary Islands

The Canary Islands are a group of islands off the northwest coast of Africa. They belong to Spain. Like many other island groups, the Canary Islands are old volcanoes of which just the tips stick out of the ocean. One of these mountains on the island of Tenerife is called *Pico de Teide* and is more than 12,000 feet high. It sometimes snows on the top of Pico de Teide, but the weather is usually warm along the coast and on the other islands. All kinds of plants grow on the Canary Islands. Some people work on the banana plantations, some plant potatoes, grain and fruits, and others are fishermen.

In some ancient writings, it is told that sailors visited the Canary Islands even before the birth of Christ. The islands were known to European travelers more

than six hundred years ago. About five hundred years ago the natives, called *Guanches,* were conquered by the Spanish, and the islands have been ruled by Spain ever since. The seven principal islands are Tenerife, Grand Canary, Palma, Lanzarote, Fuerteventura, Gomera and Hierro.

CANARY ISLANDS. Island group in Atlantic Ocean, owned by Spain. Area, 2,912 square miles. Population, 1,047,000. Chief ports, Las Palmas and Santa Cruz de Tenerife.

canasta

Canasta is the name of one of the most popular card games ever played. It was first played about thirty years ago in the South American country of Uruguay. The people of another South American country, Argentina, liked it and began to play it. From them, a few people from the United States learned it and brought it home with them in 1949. Within two years it was the most popular game of the United States, with at least twenty million people playing it.

Canasta is a kind of RUMMY, a card game about which there is another article in this encyclopedia. If you have played rummy, you will find Canasta easier; but the following rules explain everything about Canasta.

WHO MAY PLAY

There are forms of Canasta for any number of players from two to six, but the most popular games are two-handed, where one person plays against another, and four-handed, where one partnership plays against another. We will explain the four-handed game. The partnerships will be called North-South and East-West, and they sit at the table like this:

	NORTH	
WEST		EAST
	SOUTH	

In the explanation, YOU are North, and your partner is South.

The pack of cards used for Canasta is the same as two regular packs of 52 cards each shuffled together, plus four jokers, making 108 cards in all.

We will suppose that West deals first. He gives out cards one at a time to the left (clockwise) until each player has 11 cards. He then puts the rest of the pack face down in the center of the table, forming the *stock*. The top card is turned face up beside it, as the first *upcard*.

You pick up your hand, sort it in the usual manner with highest cards at the left, and this is what you see:

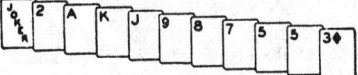

As you sit at the left of the dealer, it is your first turn to play. The turn rotates to the left (clockwise) just like the deal.

You must begin by putting the 3 face up on the table near you, and drawing the top card of the stock to restore your hand to 11 cards.

Red threes are bonus cards and do not count as part of a hand. A red trey must be exposed at once, and if it was found in the original hand or was drawn from the stock, a replacement for it, must be drawn from the stock.

TURN 1. The replacement you draw chances to be a J. You are now ready to begin your turn proper. A turn comprises two or three steps, always in order:

DRAW (always compulsory)
MELD (optional)
DISCARD (may be omitted in going out).

Drawing means taking an extra card into your hand—either the upcard or the concealed card from the top of the stock. If you cannot or do not wish to take the upcard, you must draw from the stock.

The upcard chances to be a K, since you cannot take it, you draw from the stock, getting a Q.

MELDING

Melding means placing cards from your hand face up on the table. When you meld at all, you may meld all the cards you wish, provided that you observe the rules as to valid melds.

A valid meld comprises not less than three cards of the same rank, BUT:

Wild cards may be added to *natural* cards, automatically taking the same rank. A meld must have at least two wild cards.

Black threes may be melded ONLY in going out.

Though you might meld your pair of jacks together with your joker, you do not choose to do so. You end your turn by discarding the 7.

All discards are laid face up in one pile, the top of which is called the *upcard*. The whole discard pile is commonly called *the pack*. This pile must be kept squared up so that only the top card can be read.

TURN 2. The other three players in turn draw and discard without melding, and for your second turn you draw an A. You decide to meld A-A-Joker.

The first meld by a side is its *initial meld*. The initial meld must meet a requirement of *minimum counts* as follows:

PREVIOUS SCORE OF THE SIDE	MINIMUM COUNT REQUIRED
Minus	None
0 to 1,495	50
1,500 to 2,995	90
3,000 or more	120

The *count* of a meld is the total value of the cards melded, according to this table:

POINT VALUES OF CARDS

Each joker	50
Each deuce	20
Each ace	20
Each K, Q, J, 10, 9, or 8	10
Each 7, 6, 5, or 4	5
Each black trey	5

When the upcard is taken for an initial meld, it (but no other card in the pack) may be counted toward the minimum required.

Your meld of A-A-Joker, totaling 90, more than meets the requirement at the beginning of a game. One reason for melding was that you could do so economically, using only three cards. Generally speaking, the more cards you have in your hand the better your chance of running up a big score. But there is little use in concealing meldable aces; aces are not usually discarded early in the play.

You end your turn by discarding the 8, leaving yourself with:

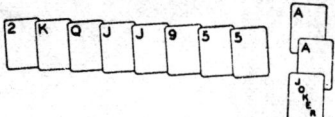

East draws, melds Q-Q-Q-2, then discards a 5. South draws, and before discarding adds an A from his hand to your set.

Any number of natural cards may be *laid off* on a meld (added to a meld on the table). Furthermore, a player may take the pack (when unfrozen) to lay off the upcard on a meld of his side. No card may be laid off on a meld belonging to the opponents.

TURN 3. After West draws, he discards a 9. You decide to take the pack. You expose the 9–2 from your hand, put the upcard with it to complete the set, then take the rest of the pack into your hand, getting K, 7, 6, 5, 4, 8, 5, 4.

The upcard may be taken only to be melded or laid off in the same turn. Having melded the upcard, the player takes the rest of the pack into his hand and may meld all the additional cards he pleases.

The pack is *frozen* for a side before it has made its initial meld. It is frozen for both sides so long as it contains a wild card or a red three. (If such a card is turned for the first upcard, additional cards are turned over on it until a natural appears.)

When the pack is frozen, it may be taken only by matching the upcard with a *natural pair* from the hand. But a player for whom it is not frozen may take it either this way or by matching the upcard with one natural card, using a wild card to complete the set. Also, when unfrozen, the pack may be taken to lay off the upcard.

The pack may not be taken at all when the upcard is a wild card or black three.

This turn brings out the real reason for melding the aces in Turn 2. By making an initial meld you unfroze the pack for your side, though it remained frozen for the opponents until East melded his queens.

Though you now could make some additional melds, you decide not to do so, and end your turn by discarding a 5. (Yes, though you have four 5's, this is your best discard! The important thing is to get the pack as often as possible, and for this purpose a pair is as good as three or four of a kind—better, because discarding the excess leaves more room in your hand to hold other ranks.)

Your hand is now:

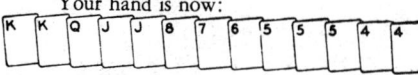

When it comes South's turn, he discards a 2. This freezes the pack again for both sides. His object is to capitalize the fact that your side holds many more cards than the opponents, and so will have a much better chance of pairing the future upcards. (Sacrificing a wild card for this purpose is often worth while.)

TURN 4. You draw an 8 and discard another 5.

TURN 5. The game has proceeded without further melding. West now discards a J. You pounce on it, showing your pair of J's. The pack you get contains: 5, 3, 2, 9, 5, 9, 7. Again you decide to make no additional melds, and discard a 5. leaving yourself with:

In their turns, East lays off a Q and West melds 10-10-10. (The opponents are scared and are beginning to "unload.") West discards a 4.

TURN 6. You take the pack with your pair of 4's, getting also: 5, 8, 6. You decide to do some heavy melding, to prepare for building *canastas*. This is how you stand after you meld, then discard the 3:

MELDED

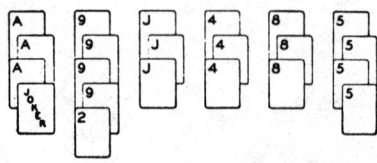

A set of seven or more cards is a *canasta*. Seven or eight natural cards form a *natural canasta*; one containing any wild card is a *mixed canasta*.

A side must have at least one canasta before it can legally go out. Canastas are important also because they earn bonuses additional to the point values of the cards.

South in his turn adds 4-4-4-2 to your set to complete a mixed canasta. He also melds K-K-K and lays off a J.

TURN 7. You draw a 7. You can now go out, and decide to do so. You meld 6-6-2, 7-7-7, lay off the K-K, discard the Q—and you are rid of your entire hand.

You were entitled to consult with South as to whether to go out, but did not do so because he was down to only two cards and you could see a good net score by going out before East-West could complete a canasta.

A player may ask his partner, "Shall I go out?" and is then bound by the reply which must be simply "yes" or "no."

In going out, a player may meld all his remaining cards—*he need not save a card to discard*. When any player gets rid of all cards in his hand, play ceases and the deal is scored.

Now let's score your cards. The first item is the *basic count*, as follows:

For going out	100
For one red three	100
For one mixed canasta	300
Basic count	500

Red threes count 100 each (except that if all four are held by one side they count 200 each for a total of 800). The score is *plus* for a side that has made at least an initial meld, but *minus* for a side that has melded nothing.

The canasta bonuses are: mixed, 300; natural, 500.

To the basic count you now add the total point value of all the cards you have melded, less what remains in your partner's hand.

Your melds total 405; South has left only two 10's, so that the net is 385. Your score for the deal is 500+385= 885.

The subtraction for cards remaining in the hand is done simplest by throwing out cards of equal value from the melds and then counting the residue.

East-West have no basic count at all, only 100 in melds, and cards left totaling 115, for a net score of —15. Your gain is thus 900.

The side that first reaches a total of 5,000 or more points wins a game. There is no bonus for winning a game. Settlement is made on the difference of final scores when a game ends.

TWO-HAND CANASTA

When two persons play Canasta, the differences in the rules are:

Each player is dealt 15 to begin with, instead of 11.

When a player draws from the stock he takes *two* cards, but he discards only one in each turn. (When a player takes the pack, he may not also draw from the stock, but he still discards one card.)

A player needs *two* canastas to go out.

SAMBA

One popular form of Canasta is called Samba. It is played with three regular packs of playing cards, plus six jokers. The big difference between Samba and Canasta is that in Samba you may meld sequences (cards in the same suit that are next to one another in rank, like 10-9-8 of diamonds.) A *sequence canasta,* or *samba* (a sequence of seven cards), counts 1,500 points. You may never take the pack to add the top card to a sequence. A mixed canasta may never have more than *two* wild cards in it. As in two-hand canasta, you draw two cards in each turn and discard only one. You need two canastas (either regular or sequence) to go out.

Canberra

Canberra is the capital of the Commonwealth of Australia. Like Washington, D.C., Canberra is not in any state, but has its own territory which is about the size of Rhode Island. The Capital Territory, as it is called, is within the state of New South Wales, and is between Australia's two largest cities, Sydney and Melbourne.

About seventy years ago the Australian government decided that it wanted a brand new capital city. It sent groups of men to look for a good location and it offered a prize for the best designs for the new city. The location was chosen in 1908 and the plan of an American, Walter Burley Griffin of Chicago, was awarded first prize and was used. The building was delayed by World War I, but by 1927 enough was finished to move the government from its old site in Melbourne to Canberra. It is a very neat and beautiful city, having good roads, many parks, and surrounded by wooded hills. Aside from the many government buildings, Canberra has three colleges, a museum and an observatory.

CANBERRA, AUSTRALIA. Population 174,100. Capital of the Commonwealth of Australia.

cancer

Cancer is one of the most dangerous and most dreaded of all diseases. As you can read in another article, your body is made up of countless tiny CELLS. In cancer, some of those cells begin to grow so fast that they choke off organs of the body that our lives depend on. When those organs can no longer work, a person dies.

Scientists do not know the reason why some cells of the body should suddenly begin to grow in that way. All that doctors can do is to try to kill the deadly cells, or stop them from growing. One of the first ways was by using radioactive substances. Radium was the first one used, and since World War II, when so much was learned about atomic energy, there have been many other radioactive substances that can be used. The radiation kills the growing cells. X-ray is another thing that kills the cells. An even better way is by surgery, to cut out the cells before they can get a good start.

In recent years, two other fronts have been opened up in the fight against cancer. One is chemotherapy or drugs to control or palliate cancer. The other is the field of immunology. This is research to develop vaccines or antisera to prevent or cure cancer. World-wide research into viruses as a cause of cancer is also being sponsored by the Virology Research Resources Branch of the National Cancer Institute of the Public Health Service.

There is one thing on which almost all of the scientists are agreed. When doctors have a chance to examine people regularly, and find out about cancer when it is just beginning, they can save nearly all those who once would have died. In fact, mostly through early detection, one out of 3 persons is cured today compared to one out of 7 twenty-five years ago. A patient is considered "cured" when he lives 5 years after treatment without further evidence of the disease.

Investigations completed in 1956, and continuing in later years, indicated that smoking (and especially the smoking of cigarettes) increases the danger of contracting cancer of the lung. To alert youngsters to the dangers of smoking, the American Cancer Society in 1962 conducted a program in the secondary schools. Many teenagers took part in the program the Society conducted.

Besides the American Cancer Society, many other organizations are active in the fight against cancer. One of these is the Damon Runyon Fund, named for Damon Runyon, a famous writer who died of cancer in 1946. The Memorial Hospital in New York is another organization that has specialized in the treatment of cancer. It established the first department in the world to curing cancer in children.

Cancer

Cancer is the name of a *constellation,* or group of stars, whose pattern in the sky is supposed to look like the shape of a crab. The word *cancer* is a Latin word that means "crab." In geography, the Tropic of Cancer takes its name from this constellation, which marks in the sky the farthest point north of the equator that the sun reaches during the summer. As an imaginary line drawn around the earth, it is the northern boundary of the Tropic Zone, about which you can read more in the article GEOGRAPHY. In astrology, Cancer is one of the twelve "signs of the zodiac," or patterns of stars under which you might be born.

candle

The candle was one of the early ways people used for making a light. It is a long round stick of wax, with a cord through the center and sticking out at one end. This cord is called a *wick,* and it is the part that burns to make light. Nowadays candles are used mostly for decoration and in religious services.

The Romans used candles, and in the Middle Ages candles were burned in churches but they were all made by hand and there were very few of them. Then, about five hundred years ago people discovered easier ways of making candles.

Two kinds of wax are good for candlemaking. They are *spermaceti* (a fatty substance that comes from the sperm whale), and *paraffin,* which is made from perroleum.

If you wanted to make a candle, first

This beautiful building is the Parliament House in Canberra, the capital of Australia. Here the laws are made by the Senate and the House of Representatives.

Australian Gov't Inform. Off.

you would braid some cotton threads to make a wick. If the wick is braided either too loosely or too tightly, the candle will not burn well. Then you melt some wax. You can pour the wax over the wick, or you can dip the wick into the melted wax. Most candles now are made by pouring wax into special molds that hold the wick in place. All of the work is done by machines.

Candlemas

Candlemas is a very old church holiday, always held on the second day of February. It is celebrated by the lighting of candles. Many hundreds of years ago, soon after Jesus was born, His Mother, the Virgin Mary, took him to the temple in Jerusalem. There, a very devout man named Simeon said that Jesus was to become a "light to lighten the Gentiles." The lighting of candles, the Candlemas ceremony, is held in honor of this event and also honors the Virgin Mary. On this day, too, the Roman Catholics bless all the candles that will be used in church services throughout the year.

An old legend says that the ground hog (woodchuck) first comes out of its burrow, in which it has slept through the winter, on Candlemas Day. If the sun is shining and the ground hog sees its shadow, it will go back to sleep, and winter weather will continue for six more weeks.

candy

Candy is a rich, sweet food made mostly of sugar, eggs, butter, cream, and many kinds of fruit, and nuts, and other flavoring. There are now more than two thousand kinds of candy, and people are inventing more kinds all the time.

All candy can be divided into two kinds, hard candy and soft candy. Both fudge and candy canes are made by boiling sugar in water. How hard the candy gets depends on how long you boil it. To find out when it is ready, a bit of it is dropped into cold water. Fudge or any other soft candy will make a soft ball in cold water when it has been cooked enough. Chewy candy, like butterscotch or caramels, will make a firm ball. Hard candies and peanut brittle will make a hard ball.

Fudge is fun to make at home, but it is very hard to make well. It must be stirred for just the right length of time. If it is stirred too long it may get "sugary," which means to taste grainy instead of smooth. Then fudge has to cool in a place that is not too warm and not too cold. Making good candy takes a lot of patience and care.

Most candy nowadays is made by machines, and some of these machines are quite wonderful. Cherries are covered with chocolate by machines. Candy bars are filled with nuts or caramel and covered with chocolate, all by machines. Machines make the designs on fancy chocolates, and other machines make the little chocolate "kisses" and wrap them. All of these machines are very new. Nowadays the United States makes more candy than any other country in the world.

We know that people in ancient times ate candy too. The Egyptians wrote about candy and even drew pictures of what their candy looked like. It was made of honey and was shaped in little mounds. The Romans had some candy too, but it was expensive and only very rich people could afford it. Children in the colonial days of the United States enjoyed eating maple sugar (made from the sap of maple trees), but this was a special treat.

Because candy tastes so good, it is easy to eat too much of it. But a sensible amount of candy helps make a person strong and peppy. When people are going on long journeys and cannot take much food with them, candy is one of the things they take. Admiral Richard E. Byrd, for instance, took a lot of candy for his men, when he made his trip to the North Pole. In World War II the soldiers were given bars of chocolate as part of their rations. This is because the sugar in chocolate gives a person energy.

candytuft

Candytuft is a small plant which is often grown in garden borders and rock-gardens. It has thick, flat-topped clusters of small flowers. The flowers come in many colors, but pink and white are most common. There are many different kinds of candytuft. Some live for a year, others for several years. Some are even small shrubs. The candytuft first came from Europe, near the Mediterranean Sea.

cane

Cane is the name given to tall grassy plants, such as sugar cane, or other big grasses that are fed to cattle and horses. The *canebrakes* of the South are dense thickets of a big bamboo-grass that grows as high as 25 feet. The stalks of this grass are used for fishing poles and bean poles, and the young shoots are sometimes eaten. A Malacca cane is a kind of walking stick made from the stem of a climbing palm called *rattan*. Most palms grow straight, but the rattan has a long flexible stem and can climb up into the top of a tall tree. Its stem may be many hundreds of feet long, though it is quite slender. It is hollow, with joints at intervals, and is very tough. It can be split up into thin strips, which are the cane strips used for making baskets, chair seats, and wickerwork.

cane sugar, the manufactured sugar cane: see SUGAR.

cankerworm

The caterpillars of two kinds of moth are called cankerworms. They are also called *measuring-worms* or *inchworms* because they move about by looping their hind feet up behind their front feet and then stretching out again, just as if they were measuring off the distance. The female moth has no wings; she crawls up the tree trunk and lays her eggs on the bark of the tree. When the young cankerworms hatch they crawl into the foliage and eat the leaves. They are a very serious pest, and can kill a tree. When the caterpillar is fully grown it digs into the ground, and *pupates*. This means that it forms a shell around itself and rests, while inside it is changing into a moth. See the article on BUTTERFLIES AND MOTHS.

Cannae, Battle of

Cannae was a town in ancient Italy where a tremendous battle was fought. More than two hundred years before the birth of Christ the Romans were very badly beaten there. Hannibal, the famous general from Carthage, defeated the Roman army, even though it was twice as big as his army. The Romans are said to have lost more than 45,000 men out of an army of 87,000. Besides that, Hannibal boasted that he took 13,000 prisoners. Very little remains of ancient Cannae. If you were to go there today you would see only the ruins of an open-air theater and a triumphal arch.

cannibalism

When people eat the flesh of other people, it is called cannibalism. The idea of eating human flesh seems very strange and horrible to us, but among primitive tribes this was not an unusual custom. Primitive man had a hard time finding food, and sometimes he had to eat the flesh of human beings to stay alive. It has been said that civilized men who have been shipwrecked and without food for a long time have done this too.

In some primitive tribes eating a person was a way of showing that you respected him. In ancient times among some people in Australia, when a person died the other members of his family would eat some of his flesh. Children in Tibet also did this and used the skulls of their parents for drinking cups. To these people such things did not seem terrible; it was the way they were expected to behave. The natives of Australia thought that if they ate the heart of a person who was brave and good, it would make them brave and good, too. Some Indian tribes in America used to eat their enemies, to make themselves powerful. Cannibalism was part of the religion among some tribes. In Mexico, the people believed that the gods were pleased by human sacrifices, and human beings were eaten by the whole tribe.

canning

Since the earliest days of history men have tried to keep food from spoiling so that they would have it to eat during the long months after the end of the growing seasons. Long ago, men dried apricots and figs, and smoked meat and fish because they had discovered that drying and smoking prevented the food from spoiling. This type of food preservation was all right for small groups of people living in one place, but it did not solve the food problem of great armies. Napoleon Bonaparte, the French emperor whose armies marched all over Europe, said that an army travels on its stomach. He meant that a well-fed army fights well and that hunger can defeat an army as easily as the enemy can. He wanted his armies to carry their food with them so that they would not be dependent in enemy lands. He put scientists to work to find a safe way of preserving food. Nicolas Appert solved the problem by heating food for several hours in loosely corked bottles. The bottles were then sealed, and since no germs could get to the food, it did not spoil.

That was only about 150 years ago. Soon afterward, in the early 1800s, Americans began to can food. Today more

than 228,000 American men and women work in the canning industry, which is one of the largest in the United States. During World War II, they canned 2,000,000,000 pounds of meat for the United States and her allies. Men fighting in the jungles of South Pacific islands and the deserts of Africa ate vegetables, fruit, and meat that had been grown and canned at home.

WHY WE PRESERVE FOOD

The discovery of canning, and then of freezing foods, brought wonderful benefits to people everywhere. Fruits and vegetables can be enjoyed months, and even years, after they have been picked. A family's meals can be varied, healthful and delicious the whole year round. Farmers can raise and sell much more food. People in different parts of the country can buy each other's produce. The growers in California can sell fruit and vegetables in the markets of New York City. Americans now eat more canned food than any other people in the world.

FACTORY CANNING

Many people believe that food cans are made of tin, but this is not true. They are made of very thin sheets of steel coated inside and out with a layer of tin. The work of canning is done in canning factories by many different machines. Machines separate fruits and vegetables according to size. This is called *grading*. Machines shake or wash the dirt out of them. If the factory cans peaches, it has a machine that slices all the peaches the same way and another machine that puts the right number of slices into each can. There are some machines that do all the canning work: they clean and slice the food, and they fill, seal and heat the cans.

Each canning factory has inspectors. They examine the food to be sure it is as good as the Department of Agriculture says it must be. They make certain that the food is the size and quality that is advertised on the label. If the label says that the food is Fancy or Grade A, that is what it must be.

HOME CANNING

Many housewives preserve the food they grow in their gardens or on their farms. There are several good methods of home canning.

cannon

A cannon is a large gun that is used by soldiers in the branch of the army called artillery. (There is a separate article on ARTILLERY). The first cannons were made more than six hundred years ago, after gunpowder had been introduced into Europe from China. They were called *pots-de-feu,* which means "pots of fire," and they really looked like pots. They were narrower at the *muzzle,* where the cannonball comes out, than at the *breech,* or base.

Before long, cannons were mounted on carriages, so that they could be moved easily. About the time of the Civil War in the United States, cannons were made with curved grooves inside the barrel, called *rifling.* These grooves made the shell spin when it left the cannon's muzzle, like a football when it is thrown

properly. The spinning made the shell travel much farther and much more accurately. About the same time, cannons were made that loaded at the breech instead of at the muzzle. That meant the gun crew could load and fire more than twice as fast as before. Better carriages were invented to absorb the *recoil* of the cannon. When a gun fires, it pulls back sharply, and this pull is called recoil. Modern cannons fire shells that are from 3 inches to 16 inches in diameter. During World War I, the Germans fired a cannon called "Big Bertha" that could hit targets 75 miles away.

canoe

A canoe is a light boat, long and narrow, that is sped over the water with paddles. It is very fast because both ends are sharp, and it can navigate very shallow streams, since its frame of canvased wood, or aluminum, sits so lightly in the water. Most canoes are about 16 to 18 feet long and weigh about 70 pounds.

The sides, or gunwales, of some canoes are air compartments to keep them from sinking. Even such a canoe will tip over unless you keep a good balance all the time. When you get into a canoe, you should keep your hands on both sides. Do not try to change places with anyone when you are far from shore.

Canoeing is a favorite sport on the lakes and rivers of the United States. Canoes are very good on hunting and camping trips because they can be carried by car or even by hand from one stream to another. Some people enjoy riding canoes like bucking broncos between the rocks in a rapid river. Other people like to paddle along quietly in a gentle stream. Canoes can be fixed for sailing by adding a sail, a rudder, and special boards (leeboards) on the sides to keep the canoe from slipping sideways when the wind blows against the sail.

The American Indians had canoes long before the white men came to America. They made the frames of branches and covered them with strips of bark from birch trees. They were light enough to be carried in one hand. This was important because the Indians often had to carry their canoes around falls and between rivers. This carrying is called *portage.* The first white explorers and trappers copied the Indians' canoes and used them on their long voyages in America and Canada. Much of America was seen for the first time by men who were paddling canoes.

canon and canon law

The word *canon* is used in Christian churches and particularly in the Roman Catholic Church. It has several separate meanings. For example, when the church decides important matters of faith or conduct, these decisions are called *canons.* The rules and regulations that govern the church courts are also called canons; and when these rules and regulations are gathered together and published, such a collection is called *canon law.* The greatest collection of canon law, called the *Codex Juris Canonici* (Code of Canon Law), was made by the Catholic Church in the year 1917.

The middle part of the Mass is also called the Canon, because it contains

fixed prayers for the consecration of the bread and wine. Some priests are called canons when they are assigned to perform certain duties. A canon is also the name used for official lists, such as the names of the books of the Bible that the church accepts as genuine. Another canon names those persons who are listed as saints by an official church process called CANONIZATION, which you can read about in a separate article.

canonization

Canonization is a process in the Roman Catholic Church in which a dead person is declared a saint in heaven. The person must be proved to have lived a very good life and to have worked at least four miracles to be canonized. The process is a kind of trial. The Promoter of the Faith, called the Devil's Advocate, tries to disprove the evidence presented for the sanctity of the candidate. If the evidence cannot be shaken, the Pope is petitioned to pronounce the person a saint. Only the Pope in Rome has the power to pronounce a person a saint.

cantaloupe, a kind of melon: see MELON.

cantata

A cantata is a kind of music that is sung by a soloist or a choral group, often accompanied by an orchestra. Sometimes a cantata is written for use in church, and sometimes it is like a little opera that tells a story but is not to be acted. Johann Sebastian Bach wrote 295 cantatas, and most other great composers wrote at least one.

Canterbury

Canterbury is a city in England. It is in the county of Kent, 55 miles from London, and it is famous for its beautiful cathedral. It is the headquarters of the Archbishop of Canterbury, who is the head of the Church of England. He is the most important personage in English society, outside the royal family.

The population of Canterbury is about 115,000.

About two thousand years ago England was invaded by soldiers from the

Many famous Englishmen are buried in the great Cathedral at Canterbury.

great Roman Empire. The Roman soldiers founded a town where Canterbury is now. Today you can still see remains of the old Roman walls and roads. There has never been much commerce in Canterbury except for the market where the local farmers sell their goods. Its main attraction has always been the cathedral. In 1130 it was completed but many changes have taken place since then. Fires have swept through it several times. The main steeple, called the "Angel Steeple" has been made higher, and another steeple has been removed. The architecture is Gothic, or the style of the Middle Ages.

Canterbury Tales is the name of a long poem by Geoffrey CHAUCER. You can read about this poem in the separate article about Chaucer.

cantilever

A cantilever is a level beam that is supported at one end so that it can carry a load, and free at the other end. A diving board is one example of a cantilever. A cantilever can be as small as a bookshelf and as large as a bridge. You can read about cantilever bridges in the article on BRIDGE. Cantilevers are very important in building all kinds of things. The design is used in building balconies, airplane wings, and many other things.

Canton

Canton is a city in southern China. It is the capital of the Kwangtung province. About 1,840,000 people live there, somewhat fewer than live in Philadelphia, Pa. Canton is the seventh-largest city in China. It is often very hot, with summer temperatures above 100 degrees.

Canton is a very old city. Many of its streets are narrow and crooked. Canton is on the Pearl River and part of the city is its "Boat Town," where families live in houseboats.

Canton was long the chief trading center of southern China. More than a thousand years ago Arab and Hindu traders sailed there regularly. About four hundred years ago Europeans, first the Portuguese and then others, began to visit Canton to trade for tea, sugar, and silk. Now Canton is a manufacturing city.

In World War II the Japanese captured Canton and held it from 1938 to 1945. Since 1949 the Chinese Communists have controlled Canton.

CANTON, CHINA. Population (1973 estimate) 1,840,000. Capital of Kwangtung province.

Canton, Ohio

Canton, in central Ohio, is a great manufacturing city. There are many large factories that make roller bearings, engines, bricks from clay quarried nearby, and other products. There are also important iron and steel plants. President William McKinley is buried in Canton.

CANTON, OHIO. Population (1970 census) 110,053. County seat of Stark County.

Canute

Canute was a king of England more than nine hundred years ago. He was one of several Danish kings who invaded England and ruled there for a short

time. He was born about the year 994 and died in 1035. Canute is remembered today because of a legend about him. It is said that the nobles of his court believed him to be all-powerful. He wanted to show them that God was a greater power than any king. So he had a throne set on the shore of the ocean, and commanded the rising tide not to wet his feet. But the water kept on rising and his feet got soaked. He leaped up in haste and told his nobles that this proved that no one but God was all-powerful.

canvas

Canvas is a kind of strong, coarse cloth. It once was made from flax or hemp, but today nearly all of it is made from cotton. Canvas is also called duck. Duck got its name from a trademark with a duck on it that was used many years ago by a manufacturer of canvas. Canvas is used for making sails and tents. Artists also paint pictures on canvas. Most of the famous oil paintings that you see in museums are painted on canvas. But it is a special kind covered with a coat of chalk and a chemical called white lead. This coating makes the surface of the canvas smooth. Next, the canvas is stretched tight on a wooden frame, to which it is nailed. It is then ready to be painted on. The canvas used for making the sails of ships is called *sailcloth*. It is carefully and strongly woven so that the wind driving the ship will not tear holes in it. Sailcloth is also used on ships as a covering for lifeboats. A light kind of canvas is much used for embroidering. Another kind of canvas is used for making tapestry, pictures or designs sewed into cloth.

canvasback duck

The canvasback duck is a wild North American duck that got its name because its white back resembles a strip of canvas. The male has a red head and neck, black breast, and white body. The female has a brown head, neck, and breast, and grayish body. Eastern canvasbacks found around Chesapeake Bay, Maryland are considered the tastiest of all ducks, due to their diet of wild celery and other water plants, for which the ducks can dive as deep as 30 feet.

Cape Breton Island

Cape Breton Island is a large island off the coast of Nova Scotia, Canada. It is part of Nova Scotia, but is separated from it by the Strait of Canso. The island's area is 3,970 square miles. More than 169,000 people live there, most of whom are descended from the Scots who settled there in the early 1800's. Many of them still speak the Gaelic language of their ancestors. There are also many people of Irish and French descent, and a few hundred Micmac Indians. Important industries are coal mining, steelmaking, fishing, and lumbering. Because of the many rocks, hills, and forests, there is not much farming. Dividing the island almost in half is a great salt lake called *Bras d'Oro* (Arm of Gold). Beautiful scenery and a fine climate make the island a popular vacation spot, and tourism is a growing industry. The largest city is Sydney, with about 34,000 people.

Cape Canaveral (Kennedy)

After World War II the United States Air Force needed a base for testing guided missiles and selected a small body of land off the east coast of Florida, about 15 square miles in area, called Cape Canaveral. In 1964, soon after President John F. Kennedy was assassinated, the name was changed to Cape Kennedy. All U.S. spacecraft and artificial satellites have been launched from the Cape, and many rocket-powered missiles have been tested there. The space center has been used by the U.S. Army and Navy also. In 1973 the name was changed back to Cape Canaveral, but the space center is still called the John F. Kennedy Space Center. Cape Canaveral City has 4,258 people (1970).

Cape Cod

Cape Cod is part of the state of Massachusetts. It sticks out into the Atlantic Ocean and is shaped like a great big hook. It is 65 miles long. In some places it is only a mile wide, but in other places it is 20 miles across. For three hundred years people had to sail around the ocean side of the Cape, and the currents and tides made this very dangerous. In 1909 work was started on cutting a canal straight across the land. This canal was finished in 1914, and extends from Buzzard's Bay to Cape Cod Bay. Now it is very easy and safe for boats to sail north or south through the canal.

Cape Cod was first visited by white men in 1602. In that year an English sea captain named Bartholomew Gosnold anchored in the bay and named it Cape Cod because he and his men caught lots of codfish there. Ever since then it has been the home base for all kinds of fishermen. Great fleets of fishing boats still leave Cape Cod each day to sail north to the Grand Banks of Newfoundland or out into the Atlantic for large fish.

Cape Cod is known to most Americans as the place where the pilgrims landed in 1620. They were the first permanent colonists to come to North America and they anchored the Mayflower in Provincetown harbor. A monument 250 feet high, called the Pilgrim Memorial, was built in Provincetown in 1910.

All along the southern arm of the Cape is a row of hills, formed when a great ice sheet that once covered New England dropped its load of sand and gravel as it melted. The hills are covered by scrub pine.

The soil on the Cape is sandy. The bogs, or marshes, that dot the entire length of the Cape, and the neighboring land in Massachusetts, produce more cranberries than any other area in North America. People who like sailing, swimming, and fishing think it is a wonderful place for vacations. Artists have painted pictures around Provincetown for many years. Several other towns on Cape Cod have become famous for their industries. The little town of Sandwich is nationally known for its fine glassware.

Cape Hatteras

Cape Hatteras is a piece of land that sticks out into the Atlantic Ocean at the extreme eastern end of North Carolina. It is on Hatteras Island, which is separated from North Carolina by Pamlico Sound.

Sailors find this part of the United States coast very dangerous because of the many sandbanks, gales, and storms. To warn the ships, there is a lighthouse 191 feet high that flashes every ten seconds.

Cape Horn

Cape Horn is the southernmost point of South America, on one of the islands of Tierra del Fuego. It is made up of steep, craggy, cliffs that rise out of the sea. Sailing ships found it dangerous to sail around the "Horn," because of its strong west winds. Steamers today prefer to go through the Strait of Magellan, between Tierra del Fuego and the mainland, which has strong currents. The first person to sail around Cape Horn was the Dutch navigator Willem Schouten, more than three hundred years ago. He named the cape after his native town *Hoorn*, in Holland.

Cape Kennedy, see CAPE CANAVERAL.

Cape of Good Hope

The Cape of Good Hope is a high piece of land at the southern tip of Africa. It is a bare, rocky place that rises almost one thousand feet above the Atlantic and Indian Oceans, which meet at this point. The first person to sail around the Cape of Good Hope was Bartholomeu Dias, a Portuguese navigator, about five hundred years ago. He sailed with two ships down the coast of Africa, hunting for a new way to India. His crew became frightened and would not let him go any farther, and he was obliged to go back. The weather was so stormy that he called the place the Cape of Storms. But when the king of Portugal heard that he had found the end of Africa, he called it the Cape of Good Hope, because he hoped that the way to India was at last found.

caper

The caper is a rambling, spiny shrub with white flowers. It is grown in Greece, Italy and southern France. The flower buds are picked when they are almost ready to burst. They are then pickled in vinegar, and are used for flavoring sauces. Caper sauce is particularly good with fish or lamb.

Capernaum

Capernaum was a town in Palestine where Jesus lived and taught and where he worked some of his wonders, such as curing sick people by a word or a touch. Capernaum was then a busy city on the Sea of Galilee, which is now called the Lake of Tiberias, in northern Palestine. The synagogue (Jewish house of worship) was built for the Jews at Capernaum by a captain of the Roman army. Capernaum is not included on modern maps because nothing but a few ruins remain of this famous Biblical city.

Capet

For many years the kings of France were *Capetians,* or members of the Capet family. They were named after Hugh Capet, who became king nearly one thousand years ago. His father, Hugh the Great, had been king sometime earlier, but the family was not then called Capet. Between the years 887 and 1328 there were 15 Capet kings, each a direct descendant of the king before him. After 1328 the throne of France passed to other families related to the Capets. These families were the VALOIS and the BOURBONS, about which you can read in separate articles.

Cape Town

Cape Town is a city in the Republic of South Africa. It is the legislative capital, which means it is where the laws are made by the legislature. Pretoria is the administrative capital, or seat of the government. Cape Town is near the tip of Africa on the Cape of Good Hope. It has a good harbor, a fine climate and beautiful country around it. A Dutchman, Jan van Riebeeck, in 1652 set up a supply station there so that explorers and trading ships could stop for repairs and supplies. The English have controlled Cape Town since 1806, but many Dutch people still live there. Cape Town has a population estimated to be 1,096,600, including the city's suburbs.

Cape Verde Islands

The Cape Verde Islands are a group of fourteen islands in the Atlantic Ocean, more than three hundred miles off the west coast of Africa. These islands belong to Portugal. Most of the people are farmers, and they raise tobacco, sugar, cotton, and other tropical crops. Some manufacture cotton goods, and others make straw hats and lace. They speak the Portuguese language. The islands are fertile along the coast, but most of them are mountainous. On the island of Fogo there is an active volcano, more than a mile and a half high. The climate is very hot, and sometimes no rain falls for a very long time. In 1832, after a three year drought, 30,000 people died of hunger because no crops could grow. The islands were discovered by the Portuguese about five hundred years ago. In World War II, the United States established air bases there, which at the time were considered vital to the safety of allied shipping against submarine attack.

CAPE VERDE ISLANDS. Area, 1,557 square miles. Population (1973 estimate) 250,000. Capital and chief city, Praia.

capillary action

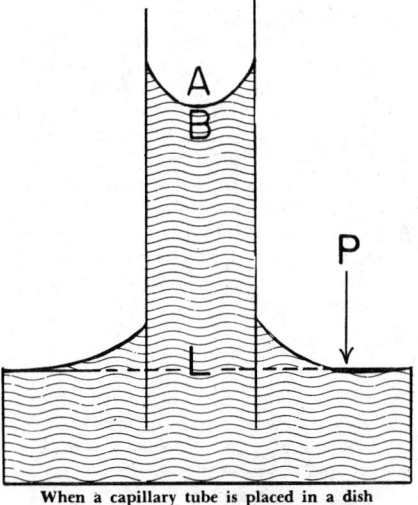

When a capillary tube is placed in a dish of water, the liquid rises to (A). At this point, the weight of the column (B) exerts a force on the surface of the dish (L) equal to 15 pounds per square inch (P).

Capillary action is the force that makes liquids rise in small tubes, makes a towel get wet all over when just one end is placed in a bowl of water, and makes a blotter absorb lots of ink even though only one corner of the blotter touches the ink. All liquids are made up of tiny particles called *molecules*. These molecules cling together, which is called *cohesion*. Some of them try to stick to substances that they touch, which is called *adhesion*. These two forces, working together, make the liquid crawl up the side of a tube.

You can see for yourself how this works. Half fill a straight-sided glass with water. If you look closely, you will see that the water seems to curve up slightly around the edges, where the top surface of the water touches the inside surface of the glass. It seems to climb the walls of the glass for a tiny fraction of an inch. That climbing is the capillary action of the water.

There are other ways in which you can see capillary action. For example, if you dip one corner of a lump of sugar in a cup of tea, in just a moment the entire lump will be wet. This is the capillary action of the liquid on the grains of sugar in the lump. The tea climbs the sides of the grains, and soon coats them all. For another example, pour a large drop of water on a flat plate. Then touch the corner of a blotter to the water, holding the blotter so that it slants up and away from the plate. You will see the drop of water disappear from the plate, while a wet spot will spread over the blotter. This is the capillary action of the water in the tiny spaces between the fibers of the paper of which the blotter is made. Blotting paper is *porous*. That is, it is full of tiny pores or openings, so that water or any kind of moisture can be taken up and held in the fibers of the paper by means of those openings, and the capillary action occurs when a liquid touches them.

The importance of capillary action has been known to scientists for many years, and it has been valuable in the development of many inventions. One of the simplest examples is a cigarette lighter. It is the capillary action that makes the lighter fluid soak into the wick. Without that capillary action, the fluid in the lighter would simply lie on the bottom of the case, and the wick would be dry all of the time. As the fluid in the end of the wick is burned off, more is drawn up, and this continues until the lighter is dry inside. Then it will no longer light, and must be refilled with lighter fluid. Kerosene stoves, oil lamps, alcohol lamps, and anything that uses liquid fuel and a wick, depend upon capillary action.

capital and capitalism

Capital is wealth or possessions that men use for making a profit. A company that manufactures automobiles cannot begin manufacturing them until it has a factory and machinery. The factory and the machinery are the capital with which the company operates its business. Usually, of course, we think of capital as being money, but this is only because money is used to buy the tools with which men make things.

All capital is savings. That is, it is

money that has been earned before and not spent to live on. When a person takes part of his savings and buys stock in a corporation, he is actually putting up part of the capital that corporation needs, and he will receive a profit (called dividends, or interest) for the use of his money. It is the same thing when you put your money in a savings bank and receive interest on it. A bank's "capital" is money, and you have put up part of the money the savings bank uses to make a profit. The savings bank in turn pays you for the use of your money. A capitalist is a person who lives by investing his money—that is, putting it up as capital in various manufacturing and other businesses—and who receives payment for the use of his money.

CAPITAL AND LABOR

You may read from time to time of arguments between "capital" and "labor." In any manufacturing business, two things are necessary. First, someone must supply the capital—that is, build the factory and buy the machines with which things can be made. Then someone has to do the actual work of using those machines and making the manufactured goods to be sold. All the people put together who supply the original money are called "capital," and all the people put together who do the work are called "labor." The capital is paid by profits. The labor receives wages for its work. Of course, the higher the wages are, the less the profit will be. It is perfectly natural for the capital side to want to pay lower wages and make more profit, and for the labor side to want to make as high wages as possible. For hundreds of years, the capitalists—those who have the money—were very powerful, and the laborers were very weak. Wages were low, and laborers had to accept them or starve to death. Labor formed UNIONS (about which there is a separate article) and the unions fought to get higher wages. There was much hard feeling between the capital and labor sides.

In our 20th century, men on both sides have become much more intelligent in dealing with these problems. More and more, they realize that the only way to have a prosperous country is to make sure that capital receives a fair profit for the use of its money, but not too much profit; and that labor receives fair wages for its work, but not wages so high that capital will not want to invest its money. In the biggest companies, the "management" (which means the men in the company who manage it and who represent the capital) and the heads of the labor unions sit down and work out fair agreements that satisfy both sides. There are still arguments and strikes, but they have been becoming fewer and less bitter.

CAPITALISM

Nowadays you will hear the word *capitalism* used to describe a form of government. For example, the United States, Great Britain, Canada, France, and dozens of other countries are spoken of as capitalistic countries. Of course, capital is used in any country, no matter what its form of government is. But in a capitalistic country, the money used for tools and machines and other means of production belong to private citizens. In a country in which *socialism* is the system used, many or all of the means of production belong to all the people put together —that is, to the government itself. People in the capitalistic countries know that capitalism is a better system because men work better and produce more if they have something to gain from it than if they are simply employees of a state and can never increase their profits or make money from their savings, no matter how hard they work. This is proved by the fact that the United States and other English-speaking countries, all of which have capitalism as their policy, have the highest living standards in the world.

There are separate articles on SOCIALISM, and on COMMUNISM, which is a form of socialism.

capital punishment

When a person is put to death as punishment for an illegal act, it is called capital punishment. Hundreds of years ago, capital punishment was quite common. A person might lose his life for stealing, or for insulting a king. Today in the United States and other democratic countries, capital punishment has been abolished. In the United States the Supreme Court decision came in 1972. Formerly, the death penalty was used in cases of murder (intentionally killing someone) or treason (betrayal of one's country). Even so, there are those that feel it is never right to take a person's life, even if he has committed murder.

Many ways have been used to kill a person who has been sentenced to die. The most common way, for hundreds of years, was by hanging—putting a rope around a person's neck and dropping him from a platform called a gallows, so that the neck would break causing the person to die. Previous to the ruling abolishing (putting an end to) capital punishment, the United States used hanging, but more often used either the electric chair or the gas chamber. In the electric chair, a person receives a powerful electric shock so that his body processes stop. In the gas chamber, a person breathes a poisonous gas that fills his lungs so he suffocates (is unable to breathe). In France people are decapitated (heads cut off).

In many countries in which the people have no voice in the government, such as Russia (the Soviet Union) today, or Germany, when it was ruled by the Nazis, a person might be put to death just for criticizing the government.

One argument against capital punishment is that many people have been put to death for crimes they were thought to have committed, and then it was discovered, sometimes years later, that they were innocent.

capitol

A capitol is the chief office building of a government. It is different from a *capital*, which is a city in which a government is located. All states of the United States have capitols. The most important capitol is in Washington, D.C., where the Congress meets. That capitol was built on a hill chosen by George Washington with the help of Pierre L'Enfant, the architect who designed the city of Washington. The capitol building took many years to build. It was started in 1793, but before it was finished it was burned down by the British in the War of 1812. It was later rebuilt. The building was enlarged about one hundred years ago. At that time the present great dome was added, as well as a wing on each side for the House of Representatives and Senate.

In Rome, Italy, the Capitol is not a building, but a hill. It is one of the seven hills of ancient Rome, and on it was built the greatest temple of the city, to the god called Jupiter. For many hundreds of years the Capitol was the political center of Rome.

Capricornus

Capricornus is the name of a *constellation,* or group of stars. The outline of these stars is supposed to look like the front of a goat and the tail of a fish. The word *capricornus* means "goat horn" in the Latin language. In geography, the Tropic of Capricorn passes through the farthest point south of the equator that the sun reaches during the winter. As an imaginary line drawn around the earth, it is the southern boundary of the Tropic Zone, which you can read about in the article GEOGRAPHY. The ancients called Capricornus the "Southern Gate of the Sun" and believed that it brought good luck. In astrology, Capricornus is one of the twelve "signs of the zodiac," or patterns of stars under which you might be born. It has a special sign to indicate the crooked horns of a goat.

capsicum

Capsicum is a small shrub with shiny leaves and little white flowers. It is important for its fruit, which are called *peppers.* There are many kinds of capsicum, some with fruit as big as a grapefruit, others with tiny berries called "bird peppers." Some can be eaten raw, others are so hot that even a taste will bring tears to your eyes. *Cayenne* and *chili* peppers are made from hot kinds, *paprika* and *pimiento* from milder ones. Even before Columbus arrived in America, the natives of the West Indies and Central America grew capsicum in their gardens. There are some kinds with bright-colored, cherry-shaped fruit which are grown in flower pots or in gardens just because they are so pretty.

capuchin monkey

The capuchin monkey lives in South America and is the most intelligent of all the American monkeys. The monkey you see at the circus doing so many wonderful tricks and the cute little monkey who passes the hat for the organ-grinder man are probably capuchins. The capuchin loves to get into mischief, but it is good-natured and makes a fine pet. It is a funny-looking creature, about as big as a cat. It has long arms and legs and a long hairy tail that makes a useful handle for holding on to the branch of a tree or other things.

The capuchin monkey's body is black or dark brown, its face is flesh-colored, and the hair on its head looks like a little hood.

Capuchins

Capuchins are an order of monks of the Roman Catholic Church. Monks are men who devote their lives to religious work. They never marry. The word *capuchin,* in the Italian language, means "the hooded ones." They are called that because of the hoods that they wear with their brown robes. The Capuchins are also famous for wearing beards and going barefoot.

There are Capuchins not only in Europe but also in America, particularly in Canada.

Some Capuchins are hermits, which means that they live alone; they spend much of their time wandering about as preachers and missionaries. The Capuchin order was founded about four hundred years ago by an Italian monk named Matteo de Bascio. It is part of an even larger order of monks called the FRANCISCANS, whom you can read about in a separate article.

capybara

The capybara is the largest living rodent in the world. A rodent is an animal with teeth that are especially good for gnawing and chewing. Mice, rats, squirrels and beavers are also rodents. The capybara is about 4 feet long and weighs about 75 pounds. It lives in South America, and likes to lie on grassy river banks and warm itself in the hot sun. The capybara has reddish-brown fur that is long and coarse, and a short stump of a tail. A curious thing about this rodent is that it has webbed feet, so it is able to swim. When it is frightened, it dives into the water and hides under plants. It is a mild animal that harms no one, and lives on bark and plants. Its hide is used to make gloves, and its bristles are excellent for brushes.

N.Y. Zoological Park
The capybara is the largest of all rodents and is less unpleasant than a rat.

carabao, a water buffalo· see the article on BUFFALO.

Caracas

Caracas is the capital and the largest city of Venezuela. It has a population of about 1,860,000, which is a little less than the population of Philadelphia, Pa. Caracas has a pleasant and healthful climate. The people work at exporting the things produced in Venezuela, such as cacao (from which chocolate and cocoa are made), coffee, tobacco, and oil. Other people work in factories or plants that make cotton goods, shoes, and cigarettes.

Caracas was settled by the Spaniards about four hundred years ago. It was the first South American colony to claim its independence from Spain, in 1811. Simon BOLIVAR, the great South American liberator, was born in Caracas, and the main plaza, or square, is named after him. Around the plaza are most of the government buildings; the *Casa Amarilla* (or Yellow House), which is the home of the president of Venezuela; and the university, the cathedral, and museums.

CARACAS VENEZUELA, Population (1971 U.N. estimate) 1,860,637.

caravan

A caravan is a group of people traveling together, especially across a desert. There are two kinds of caravan, those that are going on religious trips, or pilgrimages, and those that have goods to sell in distant cities. A caravan may have any number of people and animals, but some have as many as one thousand camels. Some have been even larger. One caravan in history is recorded to have had seventy thousand people in it.

When people in Africa and Asia have to travel long distances, they go together in a caravan so that they can protect one another. They need protection because there are often bands of robbers along the way. Before the thieves will let a caravan go, they demand large sums of money or they steal all of the goods the merchants have to sell. Robbers will even attack a caravan of religious people on their way to Mecca. Mecca is the holy Arabian city of the Mohammedan religion. Each year many people make a religious trip there. The robbers know that these pilgrims carry large sums of money to give to the poor at Mecca, so they hold up their caravans hoping to get a big ransom from the travelers.

Some caravans nowadays use jeeps to carry their loads, but camels are usually the beasts of burden. They are very strong and can carry heavy loads. They can walk across the sandy desert for several days without a drink of water, and the heat does not seem to bother them. In a caravan they are tied to one another by a rope and harnesses, and thus they form a long chain. The leading camel does not carry any load. It is gaily decorated with bells and ribbons and ropes. Sometimes the rich people ride horses instead of camels. An ass or donkey usually leads the whole caravan. It is supposed to be the guiding animal, but many people believe it is just there to bring the caravan good luck.

Caravans are usually formed in the spring or early summer, or in late fall. That is because the sun gets so hot in midsummer that even the camels cannot stand the heat. The caravans sometimes travel at night because it is cooler. When they do this, they are lighted by torches carried in square metal boxes. Whether they travel during the day or at night, camels do not move quickly. The average distance covered during a day is between 23 and 28 miles. The entire caravan is governed by a *rais,* or caravan chief who is elected before the journey begins. He sets the route, and decides when to start and stop. When the caravan stops on the desert, the people put up tents. If the caravan stops in a city, it stops at a caravansary, or inn.

In Asia most caravans use horses and donkeys instead of camels. The animals are tied together in the same way. For hundreds of years most of the trade between Russia and China was carried on by caravan. Now that we have quicker ways of transporting goods and people, the caravan has begun to disappear. It is still used in many parts of Africa and the Near East, but it is no longer the only way to travel.

In the United States we have had caravans, too. When the pioneers were crossing the mountains and going to the West they went in covered wagons. They banded together in caravans to protect each other when they were attacked by the Indians. Strings of donkeys, mules or horses were used, too. However, there were never any giant caravans in this country as there were in other parts of the world.

caravel

Caravels were small sailing ships used by the Spanish and Portuguese people about five hundred years ago. Two of the ships Columbus sailed to America in 1492—the *Niña* and *Pinta*—were caravels. If you saw one of these vessels today, you would find it hard to believe that men had actually sailed them across the ocean. They were only twice as long as one of the lifeboats on a modern ocean liner like the *United States.* They weighed about fifty tons. The *United States* weighs 50,000 tons. The caravel had very high decks in the bow and stern. These were called castles. That is why the forward part of a modern ship is called the forecastle, or fo'c'sle.

caraway

Caraway is the name of a plant that grows in Europe, Asia, and the United States. It is about two feet high, and has white or pink flowers. The most valuable part of the caraway plant is its tiny banana-shaped seeds. Caraway seeds are good to eat, especially in rye bread. They are also used in making some kinds of cake and cheese. The oil from the caraway seed is used in making medicine. It is surprising that this oil is useful both as a stimulant (to pep you up), and as an anesthetic (to make you sleepy).

carbine

A carbine is a small rifle that is used by soldiers whose main job is not actually fighting, but who need a weapon to protect themselves. These soldiers might be engineers or medical assistants, for example. The United States Army carbine weighs 5½ pounds, and it fires a .30-caliber bullet. It can be fired accurately at targets up to 300 yards away, and it can be adjusted so that it will fire automatically, like a machine-gun. Carbines were originally meant to be used by cavalry troops, or soldiers on horseback.

carbohydrates

Carbohydrates are present in many of the foods you eat, and they are very important in making you strong and healthy. The foods that have the most carbohydrates contain starches and sugars, so when you eat bread and potatoes,

or sweet things you are eating carbohydrates. They give you energy, so that you can run and jump and work and play and not get too tired. Soldiers who have to fight in battles or march for many miles sometimes eat a chocolate bar to give them energy in a hurry. Athletes do this, too. Your body needs carbohydrates, but if you eat too many starchy or sweet things, your body cannot use all of the energy, and so it stores it as fat. A person who wants to lose weight has to eat fewer starches and sweets, and also he has to exercise more, so that his body can use up some of the stored-up fat.

All carbohydrates contain the chemical elements *carbon, hydrogen* and *oxygen.*

carbolic acid

Carbolic acid is a clear, solid substance that is used in many ways. It is a strong poison, however, and it must be used very carefully. It can be dissolved in alcohol and some other things, but it does not dissolve very well in water. Doctors sometimes use carbolic acid to clean their instruments, because they know it will kill germs. A weak carbolic-acid solution was once used as an antiseptic in cuts and scratches, to kill germs and prevent infection. Now doctors use other things that do this just as well and are not so dangerous. You should never use carbolic acid yourself, because it is poisonous and so strong that it can burn your skin.

Carbolic acid is used to make explosives and dyes. Chemists call it *phenol,* and it is made from coal tar. You can read about coal tar in the article on COAL.

carbon

Carbon is the name of a substance that is found in everything that grows and in everything that is made from things that grow. Pure carbon can look like a piece of coal and it can look like a piece of glass. A diamond is pure carbon and a diamond is clear and smooth like glass. But graphite, from which pencils are made, is also pure carbon; and coal is almost pure carbon. When pure graphite is taken from the ground it is a black, greasy, heavy substance that looks like coal. Millions of years ago when coal was being made, graphite too was being formed. Coal and graphite were made from decaying vegetable matter. But coal still has some of the vegetable matter in it, while graphite is only carbon. It is not easy to understand how pure carbon can look like glass. But scientists have been able to make diamonds by putting graphite under great pressure and very high temperature. This shows that graphite and diamonds are made of the same substance, carbon.

CARBON DIOXIDE

Carbon dioxide is a gas. It has no smell or color but it has a slightly acid taste. Carbon dioxide is made by burning almost any material that contains carbon, such as wood, coal or fuel oil. Carbon dioxide is also made when we breathe. We breathe in air containing the oxygen we need, and we breathe out air containing carbon dioxide that our bodies give off as a waste product. Just the opposite

happens in plants. They need carbon dioxide to live, and they give off oxygen. Although carbon dioxide comes from things that are burned, if enough of it gets into a fire it will put the fire out. This is because carbon dioxide is heavier than air and pushes away the air containing oxygen that the fire needs to make it burn. For this reason carbon dioxide is used in some fire extinguishers. When carbon dioxide is thoroughly mixed with water, it makes soda water, which you can read about in the article SODA WATER. Liquid carbon dioxide is frozen to make DRY ICE, which you can read about in a separate article.

CARBON MONOXIDE

Carbon monoxide is another kind of gas. It is formed when something containing carbon is burned in a place where there is not much air. Carbon monoxide will burn and it is used as a fuel. Like carbon dioxide, it has no smell or color. Carbon monoxide is a deadly poison and much more dangerous than most poison gases because you cannot tell if it is present. Always make sure that there is plenty of air present when you burn something. Never run a car engine when the garage doors are closed, because when the engine burns gasoline, carbon monoxide is formed. Every year hundreds of people die because they run their car engines with the garage doors closed.

CARBON TETRACHLORIDE

Carbon tetrachloride is a heavy, colorless liquid that is used as a cleaning fluid and in fire extinguishers. When a stream of this liquid strikes the base of a fire, it rapidly turns into a heavy gas that smothers the flames. Carbon tetrachloride is also used in the treatment of hookworm. In industry, it is used to dissolve greasy materials, petroleum products, and rubber. If you use carbon tetrachloride as a cleaning fluid, work only in a well-aired place. Fumes from it can be dangerous when breathed in. If you should accidentally drink it a doctor should be called immediately.

CARBIDE

Any metal that has been mixed with carbon is called a carbide. The reason that some metals are mixed with carbon is that carbon makes metal harder and able to stand greater heat without melting. Miners wear lamps in their hats called "carbide lamps" to help them see in the dark mine. These lamps burn a compound of hydrogen and carbon (acetylene).

carbonated beverage, a drink containing soda water: see SODA WATER.

carbon paper

You use carbon paper to make more than one copy of something you are writing or typewriting. When carbon paper is placed between two sheets of paper, anything written on the top sheet is transferred by the carbon paper to the bottom sheet.

Carbon paper is made on an automatic machine. A roll of very thin paper is fed into the machine at one end. The paper goes through two metal rollers that are constantly revolving. Below the bottom

roller there is a pan in which there is a mixture of graphite and a waxy substance. Graphite is a form of carbon. It is the black oily substance that is used in "lead" pencils. For cheaper carbon paper any kind of pigment, or coloring matter, may be used instead of graphite. The bottom roller picks up this black mixture from the pan. As it revolves, a very level blade rubs against it and scrapes off all but a thin, even coating. This coating comes off on the paper as it passes between the rollers. At the other end of the machine is a chopping knife that cuts the paper into sheets. Each of these sheets is coated with the waxy substance, which comes off and makes a mark when you write on it. With thin paper and special typewriters that strike very hard, many business firms make twelve or more "carbon copies" at one time. The bundle of sheets of paper and carbon paper is called a *manifold,* a word that means "many times."

carbuncle

A carbuncle is an infection that forms a painful lump under the skin, usually on the back of the neck or along the backbone. The lump becomes more and more painful, getting red and angry looking. When it is extremely hard, it bursts, and two or more small openings appear in the skin over it, through which infected matter oozes out. At this point, a doctor cuts open the skin and takes out the big hard lump underneath. This leaves a small hole which quickly heals over. However, many carbuncles leave small scars on the skin. A carbuncle can be dangerous, and unless it is treated properly by a doctor it may result in blood poisoning.

carburetor

The carburetor is part of the engine in an automobile. Most people think that this engine burns gasoline, but it really does not. It burns a gas, or vapor, made by mixing gasoline with air. The carburetor is the device that makes this mixture of gasoline and air.

Nothing will burn without oxygen, and the air contains oxygen. The carburetor sprays gasoline into a little chamber where it is mixed with air. An electrical spark makes this mixture burn, and it is the burning of the mixture that gives the engine its power. The best mixture is one part of gasoline to fifteen parts of air. When you hear that the mixture is too rich, it means that there is too much gasoline. When you hear that the mixture is too thin, it means there is too much air and not enough gasoline. In either case, the carburetor needs adjusting so that the mixture will be correct.

A carburetor looks somewhat like a mushroom, and is on top of the engine. The part that looks like a mushroom is actually the air filter, which takes dust out of the air so that only pure air will enter the carburetor. The part of the carburetor that sprays the gasoline is very much like an atomizer with which you spray medicine into your nose or throat.

The accelerator of the automobile, which controls the speed, controls the amount of gasoline that enters the carburetor. The more gasoline, the more air will be mixed with it, if the carburetor is adjusted properly. See also the article on

the INTERNAL COMBUSTION ENGINE.

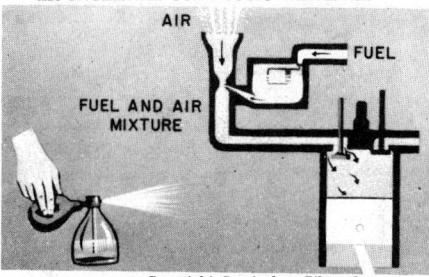

Copyright Curriculum Films, Inc.

The carburetor, like an atomizer, sprays a proper mixture of air and gasoline into the cylinders of an engine.

cardboard, a stiff pasteboard: see PASTEBOARD.

card games

More than four out of five families in the United States play card games at some time or another. There are articles in this encyclopedia about the most popular games that they play. These games are RUMMY, CANASTA, CONTRACT BRIDGE, POKER, PINOCHLE, and HEARTS. There are also articles about games that are very popular with younger card players, for example AUTHORS, EIGHTS, FAN TAN, I DOUBT IT, MEMORY, and MICHIGAN. There is also an article on PLAYING CARDS.

A good card player has a good time and makes friends if he plays the game right and also if he is a good sport. The idea in playing a game is to have fun whether you win or lose. You will not be popular if you grumble when you lose or act too pleased if you win. Sometimes you will lose, sometimes you will win, and the best way to enjoy yourself is to play the best you can whether you are losing or winning.

Cardiff

Cardiff is the largest city in Wales, which is part of Great Britain. About 254,000 people live there, or about as many as in Wichita, Kans., or Tulsa, Olka. Cardiff is in southeast Wales on both banks of the river Taff where it meets the Bristol Channel, and it is a very fine seaport. Rich coal mines north of the city helped make it one of the world's greatest coal shipping ports in the last hundred years as the steamboat replaced sailing vessels. There was a town where Cardiff stands in Roman times, two thousand years ago. Some ancient ruins still can be seen there. Cardiff Castle, where a nobleman named the Marquis of Bute now lives, was built almost nine hundred years ago. But Cardiff really began to be important when the second Marquis of Bute built the docks in 1839. The people work nowadays at ship repairs, in steel and copper works, and in flour mills. Cardiff is a clean city, free from smoke, with fine wide streets and many trees. It has a modern town hall and court buildings. The University of South Wales and Monmouthshire is located there.

cardinal

The cardinals are the highest and most important members of the Roman Catholic Church, after the Pope. They belong to what is called the Sacred College of Cardinals, which acts as a council and gives advice to the Pope. Whenever a Pope dies, the cardinals elect a new one. The cardinals are themselves appointed by the Pope. Their number is limited to seventy, but usually there are far less. Under Pope Alexander IV, about seven hundred years ago, there were only four.

There are three kinds, or classes, of cardinal. First come the cardinal bishops of Rome, of whom there are six. Then come the cardinal priests. There are supposed to be fifty of these. Most of them are the archbishops of big cities throughout the world. At nearly all times several archbishops of the big cities of the United States and Canada are cardinals.

The third class of cardinals are the cardinal deacons. There are never more than fourteen cardinal deacons. They are usually priests in Rome.

Though there are three classes of cardinal, one class does not rank any higher than any other. In electing the Pope, each cardinal has one vote.

The cardinals who live in Rome direct the administration of the church much the way a president's cabinet directs the government of a country. The government of the Catholic Church is called the *Curia Romana,* which is Latin for "the Curacy of Rome." It is divided into departments just like the government of a nation.

People address cardinals as "Your Eminence" when writing or talking to them. A cardinal's insignia resemble what a bishop wears, except for a red, broad-brimmed hat with long tassels. A cardinal is given this hat by the Pope, but never wears it later.

Cardinals are the princes of the church, and rank as such in any gathering of nobility. That is, a cardinal would come after a king but before a duke.

cardinal

If you see a bird which is bright scarlet all over, except for a patch of black on its face and throat, it is a male cardinal or *redbird*. It has a high red crest, and even its bill, which is short and thick, is red. The male cardinal is one of the most beautiful birds in America. The female is not so brightly colored. She is brown, with red patches. Like the canary, the cardinal belongs to the *finch* family of birds, and it has a pretty song. There are several kinds of cardinal in the United States, mostly found in the southern states. They are called cardinals because they are the same color as the cloaks worn by the cardinals of the Roman Catholic Church.

Caribbean Sea

The Caribbean Sea is part of the Atlantic Ocean, to the north of South America. It is about 1,800 miles at its longest point and 900 miles at its widest. It is bordered by a great mountain range, some of which is under water. Some of the mountains rise out of the water, forming the islands we call the Greater and the Lesser Antilles. The mountains of Central America and South America are a continuation of this range.

The water of the Caribbean is unusually clear. It is a beautiful blue in color and is very warm. Submarine mountains get in the way of cold ocean currents that come from Africa. The cold waters rise and get warm when they get to the Caribbean. Then they flow into the Gulf of Mexico. Here again they move over shallows and get even warmer. Finally they become the very warm Gulf Stream.

The Caribbean Sea was discovered by Columbus on his first voyage in 1492.

The sea was named after native tribes called the Caribs who lived on its shores. The Spaniards traveled the Caribbean a great deal, and the mainland around it became known as the "Spanish Main." It was a center for pirates, buccaneers and smugglers who attacked ships on the Caribbean. When the Spanish lost their colonies, the Caribbean Sea became less important, but when gold was discovered in California a hundred years ago it became important again because many people went to California by way of Panama through the Caribbean. When the Panama Canal was built by the United States the Caribbean Sea became one of the world's most traveled seas.

caribou

The caribou, or reindeer, is a strong, small deer, with very large, branching horns. Most caribou are less than 6 feet long and 3½ feet tall. However, the great mountain caribou that live in Alaska and the Canadian Rockies grow to be more than 8 feet long and 4 feet tall. They weigh more than 500 pounds and have enormous antlers. This caribou has fur so dark brown that it looks black. The fur of other caribou is light brown. Caribou are found only in the far north, in Scandinavia, Siberia, and Canada. They have especially sharp hoofs so that they can travel over rocks and ice. Thousands of years ago people in the northern lands tamed the caribou and used them the way other peoples use cows, sheep, and horses. The milk of the caribou is much richer than cow's milk, and a very delicious cheese can be made from it. The Laplanders, who are people of the far north, use the skin of the caribou to make clothes. They also use its horns to make tools.

caricature

Caricatures are pictures and sometimes words which make fun of people and the things that people do.

The word *caricature* is now used for almost any drawing or sketch or story which shows a funny person as even funnier, a sad person as even sadder, an angry person as even angrier than he is. A caricature might show a man who really has a pretty long nose with a nose as long as a city block. Edward Lear was an English writer who drew pictures like this to go with his funny limericks and verses. Thomas Nast and others in America drew caricatures of important people in government. You can read about them

and about the caricatures we see almost every day in CARTOONS and COMIC STRIPS in other articles. The earliest caricatures were not so funny. They were about the devil and skeletons and other dreadful things, but they were very popular anyway. About four hundred years ago the English and Dutch artists began making caricatures of famous people in government and society. Some of the most famous artists in the world were caricaturists. Pictures and stories showed the humorous and even the silly side of people. William Hogarth was a famous English artist who made many drawings about the funny things that can happen to married people. Goya, a Spanish artist, did caricatures of both the sad and the funny things that happen to people.

carillon, a set of bells that can play melodies: see BELL.

Carlson, Evans Fordyce

Evans Carlson was a United States Army officer. He was the leader of a famous group called *Carlson's Raiders,* in World War II. Carlson was born in 1896, and joined the army when he was 16 years old. He fought in World War I and later went to China, where he studied how the Chinese used guerrilla warfare. Guerrilla warfare is warfare in which small bands of men attack the enemy, most often at night, and do not use regular army tactics. This method of fighting was very useful to Carlson when World War II broke out. He became a captain in the Marine Corps, and trained a group of guerrilla fighters. They became Carlson's Raiders, and they performed many daring attacks against the Japanese at Little Makin and Guadalcanal, two islands in the Pacific. Carlson retired from the army after the war. He died in 1947, at the age of 51.

Carlyle, Thomas

Thomas Carlyle was a famous Scottish writer. He is best known today for his history of the French Revolution. He liked to write about great persons and events in history. Carlyle was born in Scotland in 1795. He was a very bright boy and entered the University of Edinburgh at the age of thirteen. He loved to read, and he became very fond of  *Gale Research Co.* German writers. He translated the works of the German poet Goethe into English, and he wrote a biography of another German writer, Schiller. Carlyle and his wife Jane were in bad health and found it very difficult to live together in the same house. When they were apart they used to write very lively letters to each other. These letters are considered some of Carlyle's best writing.

In 1828, Carlyle and his wife moved to a farm near a town called Craigenputtock. Several years later the famous American writer Ralph Waldo Emerson visited there and met the Carlyles. They became great friends and exchanged letters for many years afterward. These letters, too, were published and became very famous.

Jane Carlyle died about fifteen years before her husband did, and he missed her very much. He died in 1881, at the age of 86.

Carmelites

The Carmelites are Roman Catholic men and women who belong to the Order of Our Lady of Mount Carmel. They believe in serving God by living under special rules in monasteries for the monks (men) and convents for the women, the nuns. Monks and nuns do not marry. The Carmelites are supposed to speak very little and to work hard with their hands. They do their own farming and craftwork, and they also copy old and rare religious books.

The Carmelite Order is named for the Virgin Mary and for Mount Carmel in Palestine. In Bible times, the prophet Elijah lived on Mount Carmel. Some think he was the first Carmelite, but this is not certain. The hermits living by themselves in caves on Mount Carmel were first heard of in Europe about seven hundred years ago. Many of them came to Europe in the next century, and Carmelites are now found all over the world. The first Carmelite convent in the United States was started in 1790 in Maryland. Their American headquarters are at Niagara Falls, New York. The most famous Carmelite nun was St. Theresa of Avila who lived in the 16th century. St. Theresa started a stricter group which is called the *Barefoot Carmelites,* because they wear sandals instead of shoes and stockings. In England, the Carmelites are known as "White Friars," because of their white cloaks.

Carmen

Carmen is a French grand opera, a play in which the parts are sung instead of spoken. It is about a gypsy girl in Spain named Carmen. She works in a cigarette factory, and flirts a great deal with many men. A sergeant in the Spanish army is in love with her. His name is Don José, and Carmen has made him desert the army and join a band of smugglers. Another girl, Micaela, is a very sweet, good girl who really loves Don José. She knows that Carmen does not love him, and she tries to get him to go home to see his mother. He does go home, and when he returns he finds that Carmen is now flirting with Escamillo, a bullfighter. When Don José finds Carmen outside of the arena where the bullfight takes place, he asks her to come back to him. She refuses, and he stabs her to death.

Carmen was written by Georges Bizet. The words are by Henri Meilhac and Ludovic Halévy, based on a story by Prosper Mérimée. It was first performed in Paris, France, at the Opéra Comique, about eighty years ago.

carnation

The carnation is a flower grown in greenhouses in the United States and in gardens in both Europe and America. It belongs to the family of *pinks.* The original carnation was the *gillyflower,* which was well-known about four hundred years ago during the reign of Queen Elizabeth I. In those days the gillyflower was put into

wine to flavor it, for some carnations have a wonderful spicy scent, like that of cloves. There are more than two thousand kinds, both double and single. Red, pink, and white are the most common colors. The red carnation is the state flower of Ohio. Carnations are worn mostly on formal occasions, and are a most popular buttonhole flower for men. In the United States boys and men wear carnations on Mother's Day, and there is even a green-dyed carnation for St. Patrick's Day.

Carnegie, Andrew

Andrew Carnegie was a great American. He became famous for building up the huge steel industry, and when he had gotten very rich, he became even more famous for showing how to use money to help everyone.

Carnegie was born in Scotland, in 1835. He had to go to work when he was just a little boy because his family was very poor. But Andrew learned to care for things other than money. His family taught him to enjoy all the interesting and beautiful things in books. All his life Andrew Carnegie loved to read, and to think and talk about books. He even wrote some himself. Another lesson that he never forgot was to care for other people, and to try to help them.

In 1848, the Carnegie family came to the United States. Andrew went to work right away. He was alert, worked hard, and tried to learn everything he could about his job. As a result, he got better and better jobs, and made more and more money. When he was 14 years old, he went to work as a messenger boy for a telegraph company. Gradually he worked his way up until he was in charge of part of a great railroad company. Then Andrew Carnegie formed a company of his own. This grew to be one of the biggest steel companies in the world. Carnegie was a great businessman because he knew how to work hard, and how to make other people like him and want to work hard for him. In 1901, he sold his steel company for hundreds of millions of dollars. From nothing, he had become one of the richest men in the world.

Andrew Carnegie believed that rich men have a duty to spend their money in a way that will help everybody. He spent his own money in many different ways. He set up many public libraries, in cities all over the United States. He set up many organizations, for different purposes. Some of them are: the Carnegie Institution of Washington, which carries on all kinds of scientific studies; the Endowment for International Peace, which tries to work out ways of preventing war; the Hero Fund, which gives awards to people who do brave and dangerous things to help others; and, the largest of all, Carnegie Corporation of New York, which gives money for educational purposes chiefly to colleges and universities. Andrew Carnegie died in 1919.

carnival

Carnival is a time of fun and merry-

making just before Lent. Lent is the period of fasting and prayer before Easter. Carnival usually starts three days before Ash Wednesday, the day on which Lent begins. During those three days everyone is supposed to be very gay, go to costume parties, and generally have a good time. In church calendars the season is called *Shrovetide*.

If you were to go to New Orleans just before Lent you would find everyone celebrating Mardi Gras. Mardi Gras means "fat Tuesday" in the French language, the last day of carnival. Carnival is celebrated all over Europe, too, especially in Italy and France. Rome and Venice in Italy celebrate carnival with many parades, floats, costume parties and street dances. In Cannes, on the French Riviera, there is always a torchlight parade at night to celebrate the climax of carnival.

In the United States the word *carnival* has also another meaning. It is used for a small traveling amusement park. These traveling shows have Ferris wheels, side shows, games to play, and booths where different kinds of food are sold. It is easy to see why they are called carnivals, because the people who go to them expect to have fun and be merry, which is just what carnival has always meant.

Carnivora

Carnivora is the name given to all mammals that eat flesh. Human beings are mammals, and so are all animals whose young are born alive and are fed with milk from the mother's body. The word *carnivora* is from the Latin language, and means "flesh-eaters." All Carnivora have special teeth in both jaws designed for tearing and cutting meat Many carnivores, such as foxes, bears, and skunks, eat a great deal of vegetable matter as well as meat. Carnivores are of all shapes and sizes. Some of them live on the ground, others in trees. Still others spend most of their lives swimming in the sea or in fresh water. They are found wild everywhere on earth, the fewest in Australia.

On land there are seven families of Carnivora: the *dog* family, which includes wolves, foxes, and jackals; the *bears;* the *raccoons,* coatimundis, and pandas; the *weasels,* skunks, minks, badgers, and otters; the *hyenas;* the *civets* and genets; the *cats,* including lions, tigers, leopards, and jaguars.

In the sea there are three families: the *sea lions* and *fur seals,* which have ears and can shuffle about on their hind feet; the *true seals,* which have no ears that you can see and are pretty helpless on land because their hind feet are fused with their tails into one big rear flipper; and the *walruses.* All these water Carnivora have become as good as fish at swimming in the sea, and even their legs have become flippers; but they all still have to come up out of the water to breathe air.

Some carnivores are very useful to man, because they eat such pests as rabbits. Others, like minks and fur seals, provide fur; some, like wolves and tigers, are a menace because they destroy livestock, and may even kill human beings.

carnivorous or **insectivorous plants,** plants which eat insects. See the articles on BUTTERWORT and VENUS'S FLYTRAP.

carol

A carol is a song that we sing at Christmas time. Most carols tell something about the birth of Jesus but others just tell about what Christmas means to people, such as *Good King Wenceslaus,* and *Deck the Halls.* Some carols are very old, and go back to the time before people knew anything about writing music. They used to have carols for all holidays, like May Day, planting, harvest, and Easter. An old custom, still followed in some places, was for groups of singers to go about the streets and sing carols on Christmas. They would go from house to house, and sometimes they would be invited in or given something. Many Christmas hymns are considered carols, though a real carol is more like a folk song. Among the carols of this kind are: *God Rest You Merry, Gentlemen, The First Nowell* (*Noel* is the French word for "Christmas"), *Good Christian Men, Rejoice, Christ was Born on Christmas Day, I Saw Three Ships Come Sailing In,* and *Lo, How a Rose E'er Blooming.* The authors and composers are not known.

Carol I and Carol II

Carol I and Carol II were kings of Rumania. Carol I ruled from 1881 to 1914, after Rumania had become an independent country. Carol II was his grandnephew. Carol II ruled from 1930 to 1940. He was in love with a commoner, that is, a person not of royal blood. Her name was Magda Lupescu, and in 1925 Carol gave up his right to the throne and left his country so that he could be with her. But in 1930 he came back to Rumania and was made king. In 1940, during World War II, Germany occupied Rumania, and King Carol II was driven from the throne. His son Michael became king. Carol II and Mme. Lupescu thereafter married and lived abroad, in Spain, Mexico, Brazil, and at last Portugal. Carol II died in 1953.

Caroline Islands

The Caroline Islands are in the western Pacific Ocean, about 2,500 miles southwest of Hawaii. They are made up of the three big island groups of Palau, Truk, and Yap, the two volcanic islands of Kusaie and Ponape, about 30 atolls, and many islets, or tiny islands. A volcanic island is one that is the peak of a partly submerged volcano. An atoll is a ring-shaped coral reef. The natives of the Caroline Islands are mostly descendants of peoples from Asia. Some of them grow coconuts, sugar cane, and tapioca. Others mine phosphates, bauxite and iron. The Caroline Islands were discovered in 1526 by the Spaniards, who held them for hundreds of years. Germany gained control in 1899, and only a few years later they were taken over by Japan. In World War II Japan had large air and naval bases on the bigger islands of Palau, Truk and Yap which were bombed by United States planes. The Carolines are now protected by the United States.

CAROLINE ISLANDS. Group of islands in the Pacific Ocean. Area, 461 square miles. Population, 50,000 (1973 estimate).

Carolingians

The Carolingians, who are also called *Carlovingians,* were a family of kings. We call a line of kings who come from the same family a *dynasty.* The Carolingians were a dynasty. They ruled over what we now call France more than a thousand years ago, from about 720 to 987. The word *Carolingian* comes either from the name of Charlemagne or from the name of his grandfather, Charles Martel. Charles Martel was the first of the Carolingian Kings. CHARLEMAGNE was the greatest of them. You can read about him in a separate article.

carp

The carp is a type of freshwater fish. It has thick scales, and four soft feelers around its mouth. Originally it came from Asia, but now carp have been introduced into ponds and rivers all over the world. They are very easy to raise, and grow to about 25 pounds in weight. They are usually good to eat. In olden days every monastery and castle had its "stew" pond, full of fat carp. The wild carp was a greenish-brown or yellowish fish, but the carp raised by man can be found in many different shapes and colors, including golden. Carp feed mostly on water plants and insects.

Carpathian Mountains

The Carpathian Mountains are a curved range of mountains in central Europe, about nine hundred miles long. They cover almost as much territory as the Alps, but they are much lower. The highest point is about nine thousand feet. The Carpathian Mountains extend from Poland and Czechoslovakia around through Rumania. They are divided into the Northern Carpathians which include the Beskid and Tatra ranges, the Southern Carpathians and the Transylvania Alps. The mountain slopes are heavily wooded and are rich in minerals such as coal, salt, and petroleum.

carpentry

Carpentry is making things out of wood. Carpenters build houses, fences, and barns. They also repair the inside of houses, make shelves and cabinets, lay the floors, and "hang" doors and windows. There are two kinds of carpentry:

ROUGH CARPENTRY. This means putting up the *frame* of a house. The frame is like the skeleton of an animal, a base on which the covering is fastened. After the foundation is laid, the carpenters frame the house. They use heavy boards and nail them together. They make the doors and window sills, put down the *joists* that the floor is laid on, and erect the *studs,* or supports. They make the rafters for the roof, and brace everything and nail it together.

FINISHED CARPENTRY. When the framework is ready, the carpenters put on the covering, which they call *sheathing* or *siding.* They put in casing for the doors and windows, build stairs, lay the floor, put in the *wainscoting* (wall lining or paneling) and *trim.*

A carpenter must know how to use woodworking tools, such as handsaws, and power saws that work by electricity; planes for smoothing wood, and chisels

for cutting and trimming. He must know how to use a brace and bit to bore holes, and an electric drill. He must be skillful with a hammer so that he can drive nails straight without splitting the wood. He must know how to use a *plumb line,* a weight on the end of a string that tells when something is "plumb," or straight up and down. He must know how to use a *level.* A level is a piece of wood with a little glass tube in it. In the tube there is a bubble. When the bubble is in the center of the tube, then you know that whatever the level is on is level too.

He must know the different kinds of wood, and what kind to use for certain purposes. He must know how to figure the amount of lumber he will need for a job, and how to order it from the lumberyard. Most important of all, he must know how to measure. No job can be good unless the carpenter measures carefully. The tools used for measuring are the *carpenter's rule* and the *steel square,* or *framing square.* The rule is usually six feet long when it is opened all the way, and is marked off in feet, inches, and fractions of an inch. It folds together in a zigzag manner. The carpenter measures the length of board he is going to saw off and marks the place with a pencil. Then he "squares" the board by laying his square snugly along one side so that the other part of the square lies across the board. Then he pencils a line square across the board at the point where he marked the length before. Now if he saws straight across, the board will be cut square. The square also has numbers on it that tell how to estimate the number of *board feet* in lumber. A board foot is a piece of wood one foot long, one foot wide, and one inch thick.

Carpentry is one of the oldest skills and also one of the oldest trades. It began almost as soon as man learned to use tools, and had reached great perfection before the birth of Jesus. Jesus himself was a carpenter. For other kinds of woodworking, read the article on CABINET-MAKING.

carpet

A carpet is a thick piece of material for covering a floor. We do not think of it as cloth because it is so much heavier and thicker, but in many ways it is the same. There is a difference between carpets and rugs in one way, because a carpet is made in strips that can be cut to any size and a rug is a single piece that is not intended to be cut into any other size, but in other ways they are the same.

Nearly all carpets and rugs have been made of wool for hundreds of years, but the latest carpets and rugs are made also of cotton and plastic materials. The finest rugs are made in Oriental countries (countries in Asia) including Turkey, Persia (now Iran), Syria, Armenia, Afghanistan, China, and others. Carpeting is woven on big looms. Carpeting is known by the different types of weaving used on these looms. The most popular weaves are called Axminster and Wilton. A little more than a hundred years ago (in 1841) the invention of the Bigelow power loom, which could do the work of three men working by hand, made carpeting much cheaper, and after that many homes had carpets that could not afford them before.

Broadloom carpeting is woven with a plain pattern that can be pieced together to cover a floor of any size. It usually covers the entire floor of a room, up to the edges, while a rug usually covers only part of the floor and leaves an uncovered border all around. Chenille carpet can be woven up to thirty feet wide. The *pile* of carpeting is the hair that stands up and makes it thick and soft; this pile is sometimes an inch thick. Velvet-weave rugs have very thick piles.

Oriental rugs, and rugs woven by American Indians (especially by the Navajos), and by other peoples who make rugs in their homes, are still woven by hand. The colorful patterns of these rugs are often copied by big factories on their power looms, but the handmade rugs are still considered to be more valuable.

carpetbaggers

Carpetbagger was the name given to some northerners who went South, after the American Civil War. Many people went, to rebuild, to set up new governments, and to help the newly freed Negroes. Some of these northerners were honest and hard-working, really interested in helping the South. But others just wanted to make money. They laid heavy taxes and piled up large debts for the new governments. They gave a bad reputation to all the northerners who went South. A *carpetbag* was a kind of small suitcase used at that time. The name *carpetbaggers* was used to show that these men did not really belong in the South. They were just visitors, with no more belongings than could be carried in a carpetbag.

carpet sweeper

A carpet sweeper is a wooden box that runs on four little wheels. Inside the box there is a brush that turns as you push the carpet sweeper by its long handle. Carpet sweepers are very useful for picking up dust and crumbs and bits of string from the carpet. The carpet sweeper was invented about a hundred years ago. At first it did not work very well. Melvin Bissell is the man who made the carpet sweeper popular, because the one he made worked much better than any other. Now most housewives use vacuum cleaners, but the carpet sweeper is still very handy for making a rug look tidy in a hurry.

Carrel, Alexis

Alexis Carrel was a French doctor and scientist. He is remembered mostly for his work in finding new ways to operate on blood vessels. This helped make it possible to put blood safely into the bodies of people who need it, and Carrel won a Nobel prize for his discoveries about it. Alexis Carrel was born in France in 1873, and studied medicine there. Later he came to the United States and worked as a member of the Rockefeller Institute for Medical Research in New York. During World War I, he developed a new way of treating wounds and preventing infection. With Charles Lindbergh, the famous American flier, Carrel invented an artificial heart, which he used to keep bits of animal tissue alive. Carrel died in France in 1944. In the last years of his life, he was said to have helped the Germans who conquered France. But what we remember him for is his work in medical research. Because of this work our doctors are better able to cure us when we are sick.

carriage

A carriage is a passenger vehicle that is pulled by horses. There is not much chance these days of riding in a carriage unless you know someone who keeps one around a farm, or unless you visit a large city where a few carriages are still used to carry paying passengers through the park and on tours around the city.

The first carriages were the chariots used by the Egyptians and Greeks more than two thousand years ago. A chariot was just a small platform set on two wheels with a waist-high shield in front of the driver. It had no seats or springs. Many years later, the kings and queens of Europe had larger carriages with four wheels. They looked like covered farm wagons and were very uncomfortable. Ordinary people could not afford to own them. At last better and cheaper carriages were made and many more people bought them. Until about 150 years ago, most carriages in the United States came from England. Then Americans began to make their own. They were lighter, stronger, and better-looking than European models. By 1900, when the first automobiles were made, carriage factories were making about two million carriages a year. Almost all of these factories went out of business when people bought cars instead of carriages. Automobiles were called "horseless carriages" for a while.

carrier pigeon, a pigeon used to carry messages: see PIGEON.

Carroll, Lewis, pen name of Charles Lutwidge Dodgson, author of the famous *Alice in Wonderland* and *Through the Looking Glass* books: see the article on Charles L. DODGSON.

carrot

The carrot is an orange-colored root that is eaten as a vegetable. It is one of the most healthful vegetables, because it is full of vitamins and sugar and salts. It helps you to see well at night. The carrots we eat developed from wild carrots that had long stringy roots. They have probably been known for as long as two thousand years. They first became popular in England about four hundred years ago as flavorings in soups and stews. Horses and rabbits love to eat carrots, but mostly they are too expensive for animal food. A substance in carrots is sometimes used as a coloring for butter.

Carson, Christopher

Christopher (Kit) Carson was one of the great heroes of our American frontier—a guide, hunter, soldier, and friend, of the Indians. He was born in 1809 in Kentucky. He was only a boy when he went West on his first hunting expedition, and he remained there the rest of his life. Sometimes he was hired by a new town to be its official hunter. Many times

he guided people to the unknown lands of the West. As a guide on General Fremont's expeditions, in the 1840's, he played a big part in making California a part of the United States.

Kit Carson never went to school. He never learned to read and write until he was more than fifty years old; but he knew more about Indians than any other white man in the United States. He lived with them and learned to speak their language. He knew their ways of fighting and all their customs and habits of life. The American government put him in charge of some Indian tribes in New Mexico. Because he knew so much and because he was so wise and friendly and calm, he did very good work in that job. He helped to make treaties to prevent wars between the Indians and the United States. He helped Indians and Americans to understand each other and to get along together.

Kit Carson died in 1868. We remember proudly this great American who helped to open the West for settlement. He knew how to fight bravely, but he worked hardest to help people live together peacefully and happily.

Carson City

Carson City is the capital of the state of Nevada. Both the city and Carson River Valley, in which it lies, are named after Kit Carson. In the early days, the pioneers who passed through the valley on their way from Salt Lake City to California stopped at a trading post named Eagle Station. It was here that Carson City was laid out in 1858. Gold miners also bought their supplies at the trading post, and when the Comstock silver lode was discovered in 1859 Carson City became famous. (A lode is a place in the earth that is very rich in some mineral.) The city later became the terminal of a railroad used principally to ship out ore. In 1861, when the Territory of Nevada was created, Carson City was made its capital; and in 1867 a United States mint, for making coins, was built there. It was incorporated as a city in 1875.

CARSON CITY, NEVADA. Population (1970 census) 15,468. Capital of Nevada. County seat of Ormsby County.

cartel

When big companies in several different countries make an agreement that only they can manufacture certain things that people need, and that they will not let anybody else manufacture these things, these companies are called a cartel. For many years there were famous cartels in the industries that make drugs and dyes, ammunitions and chemicals. These cartels were made up of big companies in Germany, England, the United States and other countries. They went on operating right up to World War II.

A cartel is very much like what is called a trust when all the companies are in one country. You can read about trusts in the article on MONOPOLIES. When there are cartels the manufacturers can keep the prices very high and make the people pay more than the goods would be worth if many different manufacturers were allowed to make them. That is why it is not good to have cartels.

Jimmy Carter

Authenticated News International

Jimmy Carter became the 39th President of the United States on January 20, 1977 after defeating President Gerald Ford in one of the closest Presidential elections of the twentieth century.

Jimmy Carter was born James Earl Carter, Jr. on October 14, 1924 in the village of Plains, Georgia. His parents, the former Lillian Gordy and James Earl Carter, Sr. later had three more children: Gloria, Ruth, and Billy.

Jimmy Carter graduated from Plains High School in 1941. He studied for a year at Georgia Southwestern College and then for another year at the Georgia Institute of Technology. In 1943, he entered the United States Naval Academy from which he graduated in 1946. Shortly afterward, he married Rosalynn Smith. They had four children: John, James Earl 3rd, Jeffrey, and Amy. During his seven years in the Navy, Jimmy Carter worked on nuclear submarines and took courses in nuclear physics at Union College in Schenectady, New York. When his father died in 1953, he left the Navy to manage the family peanut business.

In 1962, Jimmy Carter decided to run for the Georgia Senate as a Democrat, and won. He was re-elected two years later. In 1966, he ran for Governor of Georgia and lost, but four years later ran again and won. At his inauguration, he pledged an end to racial discrimination. In 1974, he announced he would run for President. He traveled around the country for the next two years, promising to try to give the voters "a government as good as the American people." In 1976, he and his running-mate, Senator Walter Mondale of Minnesota, defeated President Ford and his running-mate, Senator Robert Dole of Kansas. Jimmy Carter thus became the first person from the Deep South to win the Presidency since the Civil War.

Carter, Nick

Nick Carter was a fictitious detective hero of thousands of "dime novels" written in the 1890's by John Coryell and later by Frederick Van Rensselaer Dey, Thomas Harbaugh, and others.

Carteret, Sir George

George Carteret was an English statesman. He was born in 1610, on a little island in the English Channel called Jersey. He was trained to be a sailor and he served in the British Navy. Later he became governor of the Isle of Jersey. Charles I was king of England at that time, and he and his family had many enemies. Carteret was friendly to the king and his followers, and many of them, including the king himself, went to Jersey to get away from people who wanted to harm them. Charles made Car-

teret a knight, and he was then called "Sir." Later, Carteret and Lord Berkeley were given some land in America, between the Hudson and Delaware Rivers. This land was called New Jersey, in honor of Carteret. Carteret died in 1680, at the age of 70.

Carthage

Carthage was an ancient city on the north coast of Africa. It was about ten miles from the modern city of Tunis. If you were to go there today you would find very little but ruins of a once beautiful city.

Carthage was founded more than two thousand years ago and was a hundred years older than the city of Rome. A people called the Phoenicians founded the city. They were great sailors and they built a huge empire by trading with other countries. Their home ports were at the eastern end of the Mediterranean Sea. They built Carthage as a base from which to trade with the people at the western end of the Mediterranean.

After Carthage became important as a trading center, it began to grow and cover more territory. Soon the people of Carthage were living on the island of Sicily, in southern France and Spain (which was called Gaul), and on the island of Sardinia. As they became more powerful in commerce, they also became more powerful in a warlike way. Their armies and their navy grew. Soon they were at war with the Greeks and later they went to war with the Romans. Their most famous general was Hannibal, who tried to conquer Rome, but failed. It was the Romans who finally destroyed Carthage in the three Punic Wars. These wars began 264 years before Jesus was born and lasted 118 years. At the end of the wars the Romans burned the city and plowed the ruins into the ground. The Roman senator Cato the Elder was famous for saying, in every speech, "Carthage must be destroyed!"

Julius Caesar established another city of Carthage in the same place. That was in 29 B.C. It grew into a great port, but it was again completely destroyed, by the Arabs, more than seven hundred years later.

Carthusians

The Carthusians spend more time alone and in silence than any other group of Catholic monks. Monks are men who devote their lives to religious work. They never marry or try to make any money from their work. The rules of the Carthusians have been the same since they were founded by St. Bruno in the 11th century. St. Bruno built the first monastery in the mountains of Chartreuse, near Grenoble in the southwest of France. The Carthusians spread to other countries and to England, where the monasteries were called "charterhouses." In 1901, the monks at Chartreuse were driven out of France into Italy. They still make the well-known liqueur called *chartreuse,* an after-dinner drink which has a yellow-green color.

Cartier, Sir George Étienne

Sir George Étienne Cartier was a Canadian statesman who lived about a hundred years ago. When Cartier was a

young man, both the French- and English-speaking sections of Canada were under the control of Great Britain, but they were not joined together. Cartier worked very hard to bring them together, and it was partly through his efforts that Canada was united. Cartier and Sir John Macdonald served as joint prime ministers of Canada from 1858 to 1862. One of the things that Cartier was very interested in was improving transportation in Canada, and he did a lot to bring about the building of the Canadian Pacific Railway.

Cartier, Jacques

Jacques Cartier was a French sailor and explorer. He is famous because he discovered the St. Lawrence River in Canada. Cartier was born in 1491, just one year before Columbus discovered America. He made three trips to Canada. He set out in 1534 with two ships, to explore the island of Newfoundland, and he claimed Canada for the French government. The next year Cartier sailed down the St. Lawrence River to an Indian village called Hochelaga. He climbed a mountain and the view was so beautiful that he called the mountain Mount Royal. This is the place where the city of Montreal now stands. A few years later, Cartier again went to Canada, to try and settle a French colony there. This plan did not work out, but Cartier's important discoveries were honored by the French people, and he was made an adviser to the French navy.

cartilage is a tough, flexible, whitish substance that connects bones and muscles in the body: see HUMAN BODY.

cartoon

Today when we think of cartoons we think of funny drawings of people or animals doing funny things. But cartoons were not always funny. The word *cartoon* was first used about four hundred years ago to describe the outline drawing which an artist made as a plan before he painted a picture on a wall or a ceiling. Cartoons were also used at that time as patterns for weavers to follow when they made large rugs or tapestries to hang on the walls. Famous artists, Michelangelo and Leonardo da Vinci and others, made cartoons.

DEVELOPMENT OF THE MODERN CARTOON

In England about a hundred years ago there were some artists who liked to do drawings that made fun of some of the strange things people did. These drawings were called CARICATURES and you can read about them in another article. At first these caricatures were printed separately. Later when many of them were printed together in a magazine they were called cartoons. *Punch,* an English magazine which is still published, was the first magazine to print these cartoons. Very often they made fun of important people. Sometimes the cartoons were especially drawn to change people's minds about things that happened in the government. In America these artists were called political cartoonists. Thomas Nast and Art Young were two of the most famous American political cartoonists.

Many American newspapers have po-

litical cartoons on their editorial pages. These cartoons can often make the editors' opinions clearer than words could. Since 1922, Pulitzer Prizes of $500 each have been awarded for the best political cartoon of the year in the United States.

N.Y. American—J. Luzzatto
You do not need any words to explain the joke in this modern cartoon.

In the years before and during World War II, David Low became the most famous cartoonist on international politics. He was born in Australia but drew his cartoons for newspapers in London, England. It was said that he was worth more to England than a battleship.

The most familiar cartoons today are the COMIC STRIPS, about which there is a separate article.

One of the most famous cartoons in America, "Mickey Mouse" by Walt Disney, is also in the movies. When cartoons are in the movies, they are called ANIMATED CARTOONS, which you can read about in a separate article.

Cartwright, Edmund

Edmund Cartwright was an English inventor who lived about 150 years ago. He was born in 1743 and he was trained to be a minister, but when he was in his thirties he became interested in inventing. He invented a loom for weaving wool and cotton thread into cloth called the power loom. This loom was much better and easier to operate than the looms that were being used at that time. The looms used today were developed from the one Cartwright invented. At first Cartwright's loom was very unpopular with the workers because it did the work of many men and they were afraid they might lose their jobs. One factory that had put in a great many of the power looms was burned to the ground one night and the workers were suspected of having set the fire.

Cartwright also helped Robert Fulton with his experiments that led to the invention of the steamboat.

Caruso, Enrico

Enrico Caruso was a very famous opera singer, one of the greatest singers of all time. From 1903 to 1920, he was  the leading tenor at the New York Metropolitan Opera. The son of a machinist, he was born in Naples, Italy in 1873. While growing up, he sang at churches to earn money to take voice lessons from Guiglielmo Verdine. He then worked for a very small opera company, but received no recognition until his performance in Giordana's opera *Fedora*. Caruso's voice was warm, lyrical, and very thrilling. His fame spread, and in 1903 he came to America. Here he became a member of the Metropolitan Opera Company. Caruso was the greatest tenor in the world during the "Golden Age" of grand opera. He created many roles, and sang altogether about fifty. He was the first great tenor to make phonograph records, and they are still considered the finest for purity of tone. He died at the height of his career, in 1921, loved by the world as few others have ever been.

Gale Research Co.

Carver, George Washington

George Washington Carver was a great scientist who made important changes in the farming of the southern United States. He won world-wide fame for his experiments with peanuts and sweet potatoes. For many years the southern states had grown almost nothing but cotton. Dr. Carver persuaded the farmers to grow sweet potatoes and peanuts, after he proved that these would be useful crops that would bring in money to the farmers and improve the soil. From these two vegetables he was able to make more than five hundred different products. These products were first made in his laboratory and many of them were put to practical use. From the peanut he was able to make soap, coffee, ink, dyes, cheese, milk, flour, wood stains, and many other things. Dr. Carver made rubber out of the sweet potato, as well as vinegar, molasses, and flour.

Dr. Carver was a Negro, born a slave during the Civil War near Diamond Grove, Missouri, in 1864. All of his younger life was very hard. He worked his way through high school and college. In 1894 he graduated from Iowa State College. He took his Master's degree there, too. In 1896 he was invited by Booker T. Washington, the great Negro educator, to teach at Tuskegee Institute in Alabama. All the time he was there he worked in his laboratory trying to find ways to improve the crops of southern farmers. Dr. Carver established the Carver Foundation just before he died, using his entire life savings of $33,000. From 1940 until he died in 1943, he worked with the United States Department of Agriculture.

carving

Carving is a way of decorating by

cutting designs into things. People have carved for thousands of years, and it is done all over the world. Carved designs can be very beautiful and delicate. They can be made on any material that can be chipped away or cut into, and that will not crack if a knife or chisel is used on it. Marble, wood, ivory and stone are good materials for carving.

Carving can be used to decorate all kinds of things, from the smallest and simplest to the biggest and most complicated. Primitive peoples all over the world still decorate their weapons and tools with carving. Some natives in Africa carve beautiful designs into the handles of their wooden boat paddles, and some North American Indians put beautiful carving on the bowls and stems of the pipes they smoke. The people of India carve little animals out of ivory. The mummies, or dead bodies, that have been found in Egypt very often lie in beautifully carved cases. Some of the most beautiful carving has been done in connection with religion. The ancient Greeks used to carve the marble pillars that supported their temples. Some of these pillars were carved in the shapes of beautiful young girls. About five hundred years ago, in Europe, many stone cathedrals were built. These cathedrals have beautiful carving on the stone and carved wooden pews and altars inside.

Wood carving is much easier than carving marble or stone or ivory. The carver must be careful to follow the grain of the wood when he is doing delicate work. If he does not, his carving may chip off and break. The first thing to do in wood carving is to draw a design on the wood with a sharp chisel. Then with a knife, and a gouge for scooping out the wood, the carver can make many patterns and designs.

Casablanca

Casablanca is a large city in Morocco, a country in northwest Africa, on the Atlantic Ocean. It is an important seaport and the third-largest city in Africa. More than 1,894,000 people live there. It has a beautiful harbor and a modern airport, called the Cazes Airport. It has a section called the Casbah, which is full of narrow winding streets and mysterious passageways. Although Morocco is not a modern country, Casablanca has some very modern sections.

During World War II, President Franklin D. Roosevelt and Prime Minister Winston Churchill of England had a meeting in Casablanca. This meeting was called the Casablanca Conference. Roosevelt and Churchill discussed the ways the Allies would carry on the war against Germany, Italy, and Japan, and the peace terms they would set to bring the war to an end. They agreed that the Allies would not accept any offer of peace unless the enemy gave up completely. This was called the Unconditional Surrender policy. A short time before the Casablanca Conference, the Allies had invaded North Africa, and United States troops occupied Casablanca. Then the Allies turned Casablanca over to the Free French forces.

Casablanca was founded more than four hundred years ago. In 1755 it was destroyed by an earthquake, but it was rebuilt. The French took it over in 1907. In 1957 Morocco became an independent country and Casablanca came under its control.

Casanova

Casanova was an Italian adventurer who lived about two hundred years ago. His full name was Giovanni Jacopo Casanova de Seingalt. He is famous because he wrote his *Memoirs* (the story of his life), and so many exciting things happened to him that people still enjoy reading about them. Casanova never did anything for very long. He was a preacher and writer, and he was in politics for a while. He was put in prison for being a spy, and he escaped. He traveled all over Europe, and made many friends, and also fought many duels. Casanova was very gay and smart, and he dressed very well. Everywhere he went, women fell in love with him. In fact, this happened so often, that if a man now has many women falling in love with him, he is called a *Casanova*. Giovanni Casanova was born in 1725, and died in 1798.

Cascade Mountains

The Cascade Mountains are a range of mountains in the northwestern part of the United States. This mountain range covers about five hundred miles through the northern part of California and the states of Washington and Oregon. The Cascade Mountains are of volcanic origin, and you can see some magnificent mountain peaks that were once huge volcanoes. The highest of these peaks is called Mt. Rainier, which is still steaming, and is almost 15,000 feet high. Fine forests of pine and cedar and fir trees grow on the slopes of the Cascade Mountains. The United States Government owns many of these forests, and takes very good care to see that no one cuts them down and that there are no forest fires.

cascara sagrada

Cascara sagrada is a laxative and tonic made from the bark of the buckthorn tree. Buckthorns are small thorny trees or shrubs. Most of them keep their leaves in winter. They are found in British Columbia and parts of the United States.

case

The word *case* has several different meanings. When you study the correct way of speaking or writing a particular language, you learn one of these meanings. The *case* of a word is the way it is used in a sentence. For example, if you want to say someone is doing something, you say *he* does it; that is the nominative case. If you want to say he owns something, you say it is *his;* that is the possessive case. If you want to say something is done to someone, you say it is done to *him;* that is the objective case. *He, his,* and *him* are different cases of the same word.

In some languages, there is a different spelling for every case of a word. In Latin, for instance, there are always five or six different cases and four different spellings to learn. In English, there are not many different spellings to learn. Every noun (which is the name of a person, place, thing, or idea) has a possessive case. We speak of *John's hat. John's* is the possessive case of *John*. A pronoun (a word such as *he, she,* or *it,* which stands for a noun) usually has three cases, nominative, possessive, and objective, as given in the example above. For other cases we use prepositions. We say a book is given *to John,* or is given *by John.* Latin would have a different spelling of *John* to take the place of the *to* and *by* that we use. They would use their *dative* case where we use *to,* and the *ablative* case where we use *by.*

The word *case* is also used for an argument that is tried in a court of law; and, of course, it also means a box or container.

casein

Casein is one of the substances that make up milk. Other substances in milk are water, fats, sugar, and salt. Casein is the most important of them all, for it is a *protein.* This is a special kind of food that every man and animal needs every day in order to stay healthy. (There is a separate article on PROTEINS and what they mean to man.) Casein makes up only a small part of milk, but it is what makes milk such an important food.

Casein is also useful to man when it is taken out of milk. Farmers know a simple way of getting the casein out of milk. They let the milk stand till it gets sour. Then part of the milk separates into a thick, white, creamy substance. This is called the *curd.* It contains all the casein of the milk and a few other substances. The farmer can make cheese out of the curd. Chemists have a quicker way of separating the casein from milk. They add to the milk a liquid called rennet, or else certain acids. These make the curd separate from the milk. Some factories make paint or glue out of this casein. Other factories add chemicals known as alkalis and formaldehyde to casein. This makes a hard material called *plastic* that can be formed into many different shapes. Plastics made from casein are used to make fountain pens and buttons. Casein added to paper makes the paper shiny. It is often used in paper made for books. You can read more about casein plastics in the article PLASTICS.

cashew nut

The cashew is not really a nut, but the fruit of a tree that grows in tropical parts of America. This fruit is small and shaped like a half-moon. It grows at the end of a pear-shaped part called the "cashew apple." The fruit that we call the "cashew nut" grows in a double shell that contains a blistering black juice. To destroy this the nut must be roasted before it is eaten. From this juice, however, a varnish is made that is used to protect woodwork from insects. From the nut there is squeezed an oil that is like olive oil. It is used in cooking and to flavor wine. The "cashew apple" is like a big juicy fruit. This is most refreshing to eat raw in hot weather, or it can be stewed, or fermented to make wine. The cashew tree grows to about 30 feet high. It has wide-spreading branches, and large stiff oval leaves.

cashmere

Cashmere is a very soft yarn that is made from the hair of the cashmere goat. The goat is found in Kashmir, a state in India, and in Tibet. Cashmere goats have been brought to other parts of the world, but they do not seem to be able to live anywhere but in their native countries. The cashmere goat is quite small. It has long horns and is usually white. Its hair is very long and straight. The outer coat is coarse and stiff, but the under coat is very fine and soft. After the outer coat has been taken off, this soft under coat is combed off, and the hair is spun into cashmere thread. Cashmere is very fine. Because it is hard to make, and because there are not too many cashmere goats in the world, it is also very expensive. The cashmere shawls made in India are sold all over the world. Although real cashmere comes from the cashmere goat, certain fine woolen materials made of other threads are also called cashmere.

cash register

Cash registers were among the first adding machines. They are used to record the amount and number of sales made each day. Every time a clerk makes a sale, he "rings it up" on the cash register. There are numbered keys on the front of the box, and the clerk presses the right keys to make the amount of the sale figures showing the amount of the sales pop up in a little glass slot at the top of the register. Then he presses a lever. At the same time the drawer at the bottom of the register springs open, so that he can put in the money received and make change. The amount is printed and added up on a roll of paper inside the register. In this way the store owner can tell exactly how much was taken in each day, and how much money should be in the cash drawer. When the store is closed for the day, the register is locked and serves as a strong box until it is opened again with a key.

Nat'l Cash Register

This old-fashioned cash register was once used by most storekeepers.

One modern kind of cash register, which you may have seen in a supermarket or large grocery store, can register the price of every small thing you buy, then add them all up and register the total. Another very modern cash register does an additional service. It tells the cashier exactly how much change is due from the size of bill the customer gave him. In this way no mistakes can be made. Most cash registers provide a sales receipt for the customer, as well. Cash registers are a very important part of modern business.

Years ago, before the cash register was invented by James Ritty in 1878, storekeepers had money boxes to hold the day's receipts. Cashiers had to add up each separate sale by writing down the amounts of all the items purchased and adding up the figures. It took a long time, and they sometimes made mistakes. Cash registers make no mistakes, and keep an accurate record of every transaction. With an old-fashioned money box, the store owner had no way of knowing whether the right amount was in the box or not. With a cash register, he can tell exactly.

The cash drawer opens only when a sale is rung up, or when the clerk pushes a key marked "No Sale." He does this when he wants to make change for someone, or wants to open the drawer to see how much money has already come in. The cash drawer is divided into sections for different sizes of money. There are separate places for pennies, nickels, dimes, quarters, half dollars, and bills.

See also the article CALCULATING MACHINES.

Casino or Cassino

Casino is a card game that is very popular with people of all ages. It is good for young children because it is easy to play. It is played by grownups—in fact, it is popular with some of the most expert card-players in the world—because it is a game requiring great skill when it is played well.

Sometimes the name is spelled *Casino* but more often it is spelled *Cassino*, just because many years ago a printer made a mistake and put in an extra *s*, and people who read his book thought that was the right way to spell it.

The game is best for two players, but may also be played by three or four players. When four play, they form two partnerships, and partners sit across the table from each other.

Here is how the game is played:

Use a regular pack of 52 cards. Deal four cards to each player and four face up on the table. The object of play is to take in cards from the table with cards from the hand. You may win cards by *pairing* or *building*. Pairing means matching a card with another of the same rank. You may capture a 7 with a 7, a jack with a jack, and so on. Suppose there are two or three 7's on the table; you may take them all in one turn with a 7 from your hand.

For purposes of building, each card has a point value: ace 1 and the cards from 2 to 10 the same as their numbers. Face cards have no point values.

You may take two or more cards from the table at once if their total point value is matched by a card from your hand. Thus you may take a 5 and a 3 with an 8, or an 8 and a 2 with a 10. Now suppose there is an 8 on the table and you have a 2 and 10 in your hand; at one turn you may lay the 2 on the 8 and say "building 10"; then at your next turn (because you may play only one card at a time) you take in the build with your 10. But if your opponent has a 10, he may capture the build for himself.

DUPLICATING

You may also duplicate pairs and builds. Suppose you have three 6s in your hand. At one turn you may lay down a 6; at the next turn you may lay a second 6 on it (if it is still there) and say "building sixes"; at your third turn you take in the pair with your remaining 6. Another example: you have 3, 10, in your hand and there is 6, 4, 7 on the table. You may put the 6 and 4 together to build 10, play the 3 from your hand and put it with the 7 on the 4 and 6 to make a double build of 10, then at your next turn capture all four cards with your 10.

You may capture a build that your opponent has left on the table, if you have the necessary card. His words decide what a build is: if he puts a 5 on a 5 and says "building ten" you cannot capture the pair with a 5. At each turn you must play one card and only one from your hand. If you cannot win anything with it, you must *trail* by placing it on the table.

REDEALING AND SCORING

After the first four cards dealt are played out, deal four more cards to each hand, but no more to the table. Continue in the same way until the pack is used up. The cards left on the table at the end go to the player who has last captured any cards.

Each player then goes through his pile of cards won and counts his points, as follows:

FOR WINNING	COUNT
27 or more cards	3
7 or more spades	1
Big Casino (♦ 10)	2
Little Casino (♠ 2)	1
Aces, each	1
Sweeps, each	1

You win a *sweep* when you capture all the cards on the table at that time. Mark a sweep by turning a card face up in your pile of cards won.

Whoever wins 21 points first wins the game.

ROYAL CASINO

In Royal Casino, a jack counts 11, a queen 12, and a king 13. An ace counts either 1 or 14, whichever the holder wishes. You can build numbers above 10, and you may take more than one face card at a time.

STEALING BUNDLES

For very young children, there is a form of Casino called Stealing Bundles. It can be played in many ways, depending on the age of the young child. First, play colors only: a red card takes a red card, a black card a black card. When the child is a little older, play suits: a spade takes a spade, a heart a heart, and so on. The next step is to play matching numbers, with no building: a 7 takes a 7, but you cannot take a 4 and a 3 with a 7, because the child has not yet learned to add. In all these games, cards taken in are put face up on the table and the opponent can steal a bundle of cards by matching its top card with one from his hand. Finally, the child will graduate to real Casino.

333

Caspian Sea

The Caspian Sea is the largest inland body of water in the world. It is a salt lake, but is less salty than the ocean. It is between Russia and Iran, and has an area of 169,300 square miles, almost twice as large as all the Great Lakes together. The Volga, Ural, Kura and Terek Rivers flow into the Caspian Sea, but it has no outlet. Its level depends upon how much water flows in and how much evaporates, and there have been great changes even in recent years. In 1954 it was seven feet lower than it was in 1936. In 1962, it was 86 feet below sea level. Russian scientists have been trying to raise the level of the Caspian Sea by digging canals to make more rivers flow into it. It is too shallow now in places for ships to sail. It is believed that in ancient times the Caspian Sea was connected with the Black Sea and the Sea of Aral. Among the many kinds of fish found in the Caspian Sea are herring, sturgeon, salmon, carp, perch, pike, and lobster. The sturgeon is the fish from which we get black caviar. Most of the other fish are smoked and shipped all over Russia. The most important ports on the Caspian Sea are Astrakhan and Baku, which is a very important oil center.

Cassandra

Cassandra is the name of a princess in Greek mythology, the stories the Greeks told about gods and goddesses. The god Apollo was in love with Cassandra, and he gave her a wonderful present, the power of prophecy. That meant that Cassandra would be able to see into the future, and tell what was going to happen. Cassandra did not love Apollo, and when Apollo found this out, he was very angry. He said from that time on, no one would believe Cassandra's prophecies, even if they were true, and that is what happened. Cassandra saw into the future, and knew that the city of Troy was going to lose its war against the Greeks, but no one would believe her.

cassava

Cassava is a plant from whose roots we get tapioca, or cassava starch. This is a very important food, especially in tropical countries. In South America cassava is an important food of the Indians. They bake it, boil it, roast it, or ferment it to make many different tasting foods and drinks. There are two kinds of cassava; bitter cassava, when eaten raw, contains an acid that is a deadly poison. But it is the kind most used, because cooking destroys the poison. The root is grated and the juice squeezed out. This leaves a kind of meal, which is then heated to make tapioca, in flakes or as flour. The poisonous juice is also cooked, and makes a delicious sauce. The second kind, called sweet cassava, is nonpoisonous. It is eaten as a vegetable, cooked in any of the ways potatoes are cooked. In the southern United States, the sweet cassava plant is a tall shrub, with knobby stems and big leaves shaped like a hand. It is used as an animal fodder.

Cassius, Gaius Longinus

Cassius was a general in Rome two thousand years ago, when it was the greatest nation on earth. We remember him best because he was one of the leaders in the plot to kill the Roman leader, Julius Caesar, in the year 44 B.C. Cassius and six other men did murder Caesar, and after that things went very badly for Cassius. He fought against ANTONY (a friend of Caesar's, whom you can read about in another article), and Cassius was defeated. He then forced one of his men to hold a sword, and Cassius ran against the sword and killed himself. This was 42 years before Christ was born. You can read about Cassius in Shakespeare's great play, Julius Caesar. There are some famous lines in the play that are about Cassius. Caesar says: "Yon Cassius has a lean and hungry look; He thinks too much: such men are dangerous."

cassowary

The cassowary, like the ostrich and the emu, is a large bird that cannot fly. It stands about five feet high, and can run very fast. It lives in the forests of Australia, New Zealand, and some of the small islands in that part of the world. On its head is a horny helmet that protects it from low-hanging branches and vines as it runs through the forest jungles. Its large, green eggs can hardly be seen against the bright green moss in which the cassowary makes its nest. It takes two months for the eggs to hatch, and then several pairs of the large birds gather to help each other protect the chicks.

A cassowary eats almost anything, from live grasshoppers and spiders to whole oranges, berries, and figs. In zoos, they have been known to swallow rubber balls, pebbles, bottle caps, and wooden spools. The cassowary has dark brown feathers. Its head is blue, with no feathers at all. On the neck are six or eight bell-like balls of either bright blue or scarlet. The cassowary's legs are very powerful, and a single kick can knock down a strong man. The meat of the cassowary is good to eat, and its skin is used to make rugs.

castanets

Castanets are little wooden cups, like shells. When you strike them together they make a clicking sound. They are used in music, and to make the rhythm for Spanish dances. Spanish dancers hold a pair in each hand by slipping a loop of string over their fingers. The castanets are fastened together with the string, and when the dancers shake their hands, the castanets click. In an orchestra they are played by a member of the percussion section (the musicians who play the drums, cymbals, and so on). The orchestra castanets are attached to a wooden handle, and are played by shaking the handle.

caste

In some countries people are divided into castes. A caste is a group of people who are supposed to do the same work and live in the same way. They are never supposed to do any other kind of work and neither are their children.

Originally all members of a caste were supposed to have the same ancestors. All butchers might be members of one caste, and all carpenters members of another caste. The noblemen had their own caste. All their lives they would be rich and comfortable, and members of the servants' caste would have to wait on high-caste people all their lives. In India, the highest caste of all was the priests, who were of the Brahman caste, and the warrior caste came next. Under these were the castes of merchants, farmers, skilled workers and unskilled workers. Lowest of all were the untouchables. They were outcasts, which means they had no caste at all.

There were very strict rules that could not be changed. For instance, even a king could not ask a member of the carpenters' caste to do a job of plumbing.

India is the country that is most famous for using the caste system. When India got her independence the government started to get rid of the caste system because it is very unfair. People could not rise above their castes. They had no chance to use their talents or their intelligence, no matter how ambitious they might be.

Castile

Castile is a large region in central and northern Spain. The northern part is called Old Castile and the southern part is called New Castile. The two parts are divided by mountain ranges called the Sierra de Gredos and the Sierra de Guadarrama. New Castile occupies most of the high plateau, or level ground, of central Spain, which has dry soil that is very much worn out by centuries of use. It is used mostly for growing grain and sheep-grazing, but some of the better parts of New Castile produce grapes for wine and olives for oil. In ancient times, Castile was an independent kingdom. Its name comes from the many castles that were built by the Christian noblemen who took the country back from the Moors who had conquered the country. Five hundred years ago Castile became the most important part of Spain, and the kind of Spanish that its people spoke was considered the purest and best Spanish. It was called Castilian, and was the language used in all Spanish books.

casting

Casting is a way of shaping metal by melting it and pouring it into a mold. It has become a large modern industry, and is done in big plants called foundries. You can read more about industrial casting in the article FOUNDRY. Sculptors also make plaster castings of their work, and then make the statue of bronze. This is a delicate and difficult process.

Casting is also a method of fishing with rod and reel. A fisherman casts his fishing line across the water to the place where he hopes a fish will be. See the article on FISHING.

cast iron, a commercial kind of iron. See IRON AND STEEL.

castle

Castles were fortified houses, or dwelling places, of ancient times. They were built during the Middle Ages, when there were no nations with armies and police departments to keep law and order. Every nobleman had to protect himself and his property and those who lived with him and worked for him. The land

was divided among these lords and noble-men, and they were constantly at war with each other. In every country there were many little towns, each with a high stone wall and big gates that could be closed when an enemy approached.

Imagine that we are traveling through the countryside of England six hundred years ago. We cross a river and climb to the top of a hill. In the distance we see a great stone building. There is a stone wall about 30 feet high and 8 to 12 feet thick running all around it, and on top of the wall there are several round towers with narrow windows in them. If we look closely we can see the *battlement.* This is a smaller wall broken by open spaces. Archers can aim bows and arrows at an enemy from the open spaces, and then step behind the battlement to keep from being hit by enemy arrows. As we draw near the castle we see the *moat* that encircles the wall. The moat is a ditch filled with water, about 30 to 40 feet wide and 30 or 40 feet deep. The water is about 10 feet from the top. In order to enter the *castle yard,* or court, we must be permitted to cross the *drawbridge.* The drawbridge is made of wood, and it is fastened to the wall at the bottom. When it is pulled up by heavy chains with weights as counterbalance, it closes the wall. In case of an enemy attack, the *portcullis* would be dropped over it. This is a lattice of heavy iron bars and chains, with long iron spikes sticking out of it.

Sentries, or guards, always walk around the top of the wall. When we draw near the castle, they can see that we are not armed, so we are allowed to enter the court. Inside, we see that it is like a little walled village. Here is a blacksmith shop, a stable, a bakery, a chapel, a carpenter shop, and perhaps a vegetable garden. People are seen going about their work, knights playing games or preparing to ride forth, soldiers caring for their weapons, hunting parties returning with meat. Some castles were not very large, and had only a wall and moat and the inside building, but this is a large castle. Inside the court there is another wall; if the outer one is stormed by an enemy, he has still another one to cross. The inner wall encircles a towerlike building called the *keep.* The keep is the strongest part of the castle, and serves as a home for the master and his family.

The keep was a fortress within a fortress. In those days, the people who lived in a castle were in constant fear of attack. When a castle was strong enough to be safe against the kind of weapons they had in those times, such as *catapults,* (machines that hurled rocks), and the *battering ram,* a high, thick stone wall with a moat around it was almost impossible to storm. Gunpowder had not been invented, so there were no cannons to smash holes in the wall. The only way that a castle could be attacked and won was by *siege.* When an enemy laid siege to a castle, he camped outside the wall, far enough away to be out of range of the archers and near enough to prevent anyone from entering or leaving the castle. His army had to be large enough so that the knights in the castle would not dare to ride out to attack. Then the enemy just stayed there.

Inside the castle the storerooms were full of food and supplies, but they could last only for six or eight months. Meanwhile, those in the castle could not reach their fields or go hunting or fishing. They began to run out of food, and grow weaker and weaker with hunger. At this point the besiegers would attack the castle by placing "scaling" ladders against the wall. They would fill the moat with rocks and logs so they could cross easily, and roll a "tower" up the wall and swarm up to the top. Inside, the defenders fought with their last strength. From the top of the wall they poured boiling water and oil on the attackers, and rolled huge stones down upon them. It was a cruel and awful way to fight.

LIFE IN A CASTLE

In the castle the rooms are cold and drafty. There are few windows, because safety is more important than light and sunshine. The walls and floors are of stone. The bedrooms are at the top, reached by long, winding stairs. In the center is a big room called the *hall.* It has a high ceiling, with a hole in the middle to let smoke out, because right in the middle of the floor there is a big open fireplace. The fire is used for cooking and for warming the hall. Sometimes there were real fireplaces, with chimneys and flues, and some of the bedrooms had fireplaces; but usually there was just an open fire in the middle of the hall.

The walls of the hall were hung with beautiful cloth called *tapestry.* Some tapestries were embroidered with threads of pure gold. Many are preserved today, and are very valuable. These tapestries were not only for decoration, however. They were to prevent drafts and keep the people warm.

All life in the castle centered in the hall. Suppose we are invited to dinner. First benches and tables of wood are brought in and set in place. At one end there is a raised platform called the *dais,* where the master and his family and the important people sit. Dinner is very elaborate. It begins about noon, and may last three hours. Whole deer and pigs are roasted and placed on the table. There may be wild fowl and pheasant, fish and seafood. A pudding made of crushed wheat and milk, called *frumenty,* is eaten with the bread and meat. There is also meat boiled with various spices, cloves, garlic and onions. Then we are served fruit and nuts and berries, and candied and preserved ginger and sweetmeats. We wash it all down with huge goblets of milk, honey, and wine. The dogs are waiting at our feet, and as we finish a piece of meat, we throw the bones to the dogs. The floor of the hall is always cluttered with bones and refuse, which are swept out occasionally with ashes and water. We eat from a dish called a *trencher,* which is somewhat like a plate and somewhat like a bowl. (The expression a "good trencherman" is still used to mean anyone with a good appetite.) There are knives, but no forks, and we eat with our fingers or with a sort of wooden paddle.

On a balcony, or platform, over the master's table, are the minstrels. While we eat, they play and sing ballads that tell stories about famous knights and ladies, and the history of the land.

After dinner, the tables and benches are cleared away and there may be games or dancing. The ladies sew, or play chess, checkers, or cards, while the men talk or practice with their weapons. Bedtime is early for everyone, unless there is a feast for some very important visitor or a wedding or betrothal. Then the party might last all night, or even longer. Ordinarily, unless the weather is warm, we will sleep right in the hall. Curtains are hung at one end for the bed of the lord of the castle and his lady. The rest of us will put our straw mattresses on the floor, and so pass the night. We will be up early, for the business of the castle begins not long after the sun rises.

Castor and Pollux

Castor and Pollux were heroes in the ancient Greek and Roman legends. They were twin brothers. Their mother was Leda, the Queen of Sparta. According to one legend, their father was the god Zeus. Castor and Pollux were enormous men and wonderful fighters. Castor was famous for training and riding horses, while Pollux was famous as a boxer. It was believed that the brothers would appear in battles to help the side they had chosen. They were also said to go to the rescue of sailors at sea.

castor oil

Castor oil is made from the seeds of the castor-oil plant. The plant has big hand-shaped leaves, and often grows to the height of a tree in hot countries. It grows wild in all the warmer parts of the world, but it probably came from Africa. The castor seeds, or beans, are put into a huge press that squeezes out the oil. The first oil pressed out is used in medicine as a laxative. The rest of the oil is used in many different ways: as a lubricant in brake fluid, as a softener or dressing for leather, and in paints and plastics. The meal that is left is used as a fertilizer or as a cattle food, after it has been treated to remove a poison it contains.

Castro, Fidel

Fidel Castro became premier, and virtual dictator, of Cuba when he overthrew the military dictatorship of President Batista on January 1, 1959. He gained power under the guise of bringing democracy to the island republic, but has since ruled by decree, dissolving Congress and barring elections. In 1961 he proclaimed himself and his rule Communist. Castro was born in Oriente province in 1927 of wealthy parents. He was trained as a lawyer, but opposed the regime of Fulgencio Batista. On July 26, 1953, he led a revolt against the government that failed. After his release from jail in 1955, he fled the country, but returned in 1956 to set up guerrilla operations in the Sierra Maestra Mountains. His "26th of July Movement" gradually gathered strength until it resulted in ultimate victory.

cat

The cat family is one of the families of mammals, that is, animals that nurse their young. Many animals belong to the cat family—the ordinary household cat, the lion, tiger, leopard, bobcat, puma, and many others. Cats are among the best of all mammals at hunting.

Cat's paws have very sharp claws designed for slashing other creatures and for helping the cat climb trees. These claws are different from the claws of other animals because they can be pulled back into a sheath when the cat is not using them. In this way they are kept from getting dull. Cats have round heads with powerful jaws and sharp teeth shaped for ripping and tearing flesh. Watch any cat yawn, and you will see what a large mouth it has. Cats have very keen hearing. If you make a slight noise, your cat will hear and twitch its ears and turn its head; it can hear the footsteps of mice twenty feet away. All cats except the very big ones like lions and tigers have very unusual eyes. They are a wonderful yellow color, and the pupils (the central clear parts of the eyes) are not round as in other animals, but slit-shaped. The pupils are like little window shutters. They adjust themselves to let in a proper amount of light to the back part of the eye, which is the part that sees. As it grows dark, they open up to let in more and more light. The eyes of cats are so made that they can see well when there is very little light. This is very important, for nearly all cats are most active at night.

HOW CATS HUNT

Cats kill their prey either by stalking, which means that they creep up silently and then pounce, or by lying in hiding until an animal passes and then jumping onto it and killing it by biting its throat. A favorite place where cats lie in hiding is at waterholes where animals come to drink. The cheetah, which is a large cat that lives in east Africa, can run faster than any other animal, as fast as 55 miles per hour. It hunts antelopes by chasing them until it catches them. The smaller cats, such as the lynx, the ocelot and margay of South America, and the wildcats of Europe, are great killers of birds, which they catch by stalking, or at night when the birds are asleep.

Wild cats are colored so that they blend with the country they live in. The lion, which is sandy colored, lives in the desert. The tiger is striped orange and black and blends with the background of grasses and bushes among which it hunts. The jaguar, leopard and ocelot are spotted black on white, and their coats look like the spots of light in the branches of the trees or on the ground of the forests in which they live. This kind of coloring is a great help to the cats, for it makes it hard for the animals they are hunting to see them.

A cat may not be able to eat the whole of an animal it has killed. Some cats hide what is left. The leopard, for example, drags what it cannot eat into a tree and leaves it hanging from a branch. But the lion and the tiger, the only cats that are poor climbers, leave their prey where they have killed it, and return later for a second meal. Some cats, such as jaguars, leopards, and pumas, have been known to kill men, but the only dangerous man-eaters are lions and tigers. Most lions and tigers avoid men but some very old animals become too weak to catch other animals; then they start eating men, who are easy to catch. Suddenly, in an Indian village where all has been peaceful, a

tiger will pounce on a child or man and eat him. From then on everyone lives in terror until the man-eater has been killed. In Africa, man-eating lions once killed so many workmen that the building of a railway line was delayed for several months. Large and small cats often do a great deal of damage by killing tame animals such as cattle or chickens. However, the smaller wildcats often do a great deal of good by eating rats and mice and other small destructive creatures.

Cats are all very much alike in their breeding habits. The mother cat finds a well-hidden place where she has her babies, which are called kittens or cubs. The young of most cats are helpless when born, and their eyes are closed. At first the mother feeds them with her milk. As they grow larger she brings them food to eat. If there is any danger, she picks each kitten up by the loose skin at the back of its neck, and carries it to a safe place. After a while she teaches them how to hunt. She brings a wounded animal to her kittens, and shows them how to kill it. This may seem very cruel, but all cats get their food by killing.

WHERE CATS ARE FOUND

Cats of various sorts are found wild in all parts of the world except the polar regions and Australia. In North America there are several different kinds of wildcat. The largest is the puma, which is also called the cougar or mountain lion. The puma is now found only in wild places, like the mountainous parts of the West. Several kinds of lynx or bobcat are also found in North America. They are very strange looking cats, with tufts of hair on the tips of their ears, and short tails. In South America the largest cat is the jaguar, but the puma is also found, and there are many small wildcats. Africa and Asia are the continents on which most cats are found. The largest of all cats is the Bengal tiger, which lives in India. It grows to be 10 feet long from the nose to the tip of its tail, and sometimes weighs over 500 pounds. Almost as large is the lion, which is known as the "king of beasts" because it is so handsome and strong. Because lions are so strong, kings have put paintings of lions on their shields. One of the animals which holds up the crown in the British coat of arms is a lion, and Samson and Hercules are supposed to have proved their strength by wrestling with lions. From the legend telling how Hercules killed the lion of Nemea, and from bones that have been dug up, we know that long ago lions used to live in Europe. Tigers also once lived there, but like the lions they have all been killed. The only wildcats left in Europe are lynxes and a small cat that looks like a tame tabby cat. Very few wildcats are still living, except in remote mountains and forests.

TAME CATS

Most wildcats are very difficult to tame. They are so strong and fierce that even when they seem tame one has to be very careful of them. Lion tamers and zoo attendants know this and they are very careful with wildcats, even when they have known them for years. The most treacherous of all cats are tigers, because they will attack suddenly even

when they do not seem to be angry.

The first men to tame cats were probably the ancient Egyptians, more than three thousand years ago. In Egypt there were many large barns in which wheat and barley and other crops were stored. Probably the Egyptians first began to keep cats to kill the mice that ate this stored food. After a while they became the greatest cat lovers the world has ever known. Their cats were treated like human beings, as members of the family. If anyone killed a cat, he was considered a criminal. When a cat died, its owners went into mourning and it was buried with great honor. Its body was preserved by treating it with various liquids and wrapping it in cloth. Thousands of such preserved cat bodies have been found at a place called Bubastis on the Nile River.

Ever since the times of ancient Egypt men have kept cats to kill mice. But it is only in the last two hundred years that they have begun to love them again. This was because at one time people thought that cats, particularly black ones, brought bad luck. They even believed that cats were in the power of the devil. Sometimes the ignorant people of those days would burn a poor old woman as a witch just because she had a black cat, and they would burn the cat too. Nowadays we know that this was all nonsense, but there are still many people who do not like cats. It is true that sometimes cats are fonder of the house they live in than of their owner, and will stay behind when he leaves. But even so cats are much more affectionate than most people think. They become very unhappy if they are not petted by their owners. If you have a pet cat you must make sure it has all it needs to eat and drink. If it scratches the furniture, you can give it a rough log to sharpen its claws on. One of the nicest things about cats is that they are very clean. One of the first things a mother cat teaches her kittens is how to clean themselves by licking their own fur.

There are many kinds of tame cats. The common short-haired cats we have today are probably descended from the cats of the ancient Egyptians, with a mixture of the blood of the European wildcat. The tortoise-shell cat, the Abyssinian cat, the very small Paraguayan cat, the rare Mexican hairless cat, the tail-less Manx cat, and the Siamese cat are all kinds of short-haired cat. The Siamese cat, which has a pale, creamy-brown body and dark-brown face, legs, and tail, is one of the prettiest and most valuable cats. Short-haired cats are usually slimmer and more lively than long-haired cats. Scientists believe that the long-haired cats, such as the Angora and Persian cats, are descended from a kind of wildcat which lived in the mountains of Persia. The most beautiful cat of all is probably the Blue Persian cat. It has long silky fur that is smoky blue-gray in color, pink lips, and pink pads on its feet. The rarest cats of all are the sacred cat of Burma and the Tibetan temple cat, both of which are long-haired.

Both long- and short-haired cats are sometimes white. If you see a white cat with pink eyes it is what is called an "albino," and is always deaf.

There are separate articles on many of

the different kinds of cat in this encyclopedia.

catacombs

Catacombs are underground rooms and passageways where ancient peoples buried their dead. The Egyptians, the Indians of South America, and some of the early people in Asia and Persia built catacombs. The Christians and Jews who lived in Rome about two thousand years ago built the largest catacombs in the world. If you were to visit Rome, you would probably make a trip to the catacombs on the outskirts of the city. A guide would lead you down about seventy feet underground, where the deepest catacombs cover many miles. The tunnels are so narrow that you would have to go single file, and along the walls you would see holes where the bodies of the dead had been placed. The graves are closed with marble or clay slabs. In some rooms whole families are buried together. On the walls and ceilings there are beautiful paintings.

The people who built the first catacombs in Rome were Christians and Jews who lived about a hundred years after Jesus died. When they were persecuted they used to hold religious services in the catacombs. The catacombs were also very good places to hide in. When the invasions of Rome began, people gradually forgot about the catacombs. About 350 years ago, they were discovered again, and we have been able to learn a great deal about these early people from studying the catacombs.

catalepsy

Catalepsy is the name of a strange sickness in which the body becomes stiff. A person with catalepsy may hold one arm up in the air or have his legs bent a certain way, and he will stay in this same position for minutes, or hours, or sometimes for days. In this state the person is not conscious, he breathes very slowly, and his body is cold. We know that catalepsy can be caused by some disease of the nerves, and also can be caused by certain drugs. Catalepsy is most often connected with mental illness.

Catalonia

Catalonia is a region in northeastern Spain. It is bounded on the north by France and the Pyrenees Mountains, and on the east by the Mediterranean Sea. More than 3 million people live there. Catalonia is made up of four provinces: Barcelona, Gerona, Lerida, and Tarragona. Barcelona is the most important of these provinces, and the city of Barce-

lona is the capital of Catalonia. It is a mountainous region that produces wine, olive oil, wheat, and corn. Its rivers also produce hydroelectric power, which has made Barcelona an industrial city and port of great importance. Catalonia is a very ancient region that took its name from its keepers of medieval castles.

catalpa

The catalpa is a medium-sized tree with big, heart-shaped leaves. It grows wild in the South and in the Middle West, but all over the country you can see catalpas in gardens and along the sides of streets where they are planted for shade. Sometimes they are called *cigar trees,* or *Indian beans,* because of their fruit, which are like huge dangling beans. In the spring, when they produce their big clusters of frilly white flowers, catalpas are very beautiful. The wood of the tree is soft, but it is used for making fence posts and railroad ties because it lasts well. There is a worm that eats catalpa leaves in the spring and is popular as fish bait in the South.

catalysis

Catalysis is a process in which a chemical changes other chemicals without being changed itself. Catalysis is also a process that makes other chemicals change faster or slower than they would by themselves. For example, yeast makes sugar change into alcohol and carbonic acid. The yeast itself does not change, but without the yeast the sugar would not change into alcohol. The yeast, in this chemical reaction, is called a *catalyst.* Another example is the unusual metal vanadium. Vanadium is a chemical catalyst that helps sulfur change into sulfuric acid. When sulfur is burned and passed over vanadium it changes quickly into the gas sulfur trioxide. This gas, dissolved in water, forms sulfuric acid. Without the vanadium, only a small amount of the burning sulfur would change into sulfur trioxide. The vanadium is a catalyst because it makes the burning sulfur change more quickly into sulfur trioxide. The vanadium itself, however, does not change at all. Catalysis is a very important ability of certain chemicals. We would not be able to make many important things such as synthetic rubber, or drugs, or alcohol, if it were not for catalysts.

catapult

A catapult is a machine for throwing things. In ancient times, before guns had been invented, catapults were used in warfare to throw rocks against the walls of cities or castles that were being besieged. These catapults had a heavy wooden base, and soldiers would either pull back or twist large ropes that were attached to the wood. When they let go of them, the ropes would spring forward and hurl a rock that had been placed on the catapult. Some of these machines were really enormous bows and arrows, while others had a long wooden or iron arm like a spoon. When the ropes were released, one end of the spoon, on which the rock was placed, would swing upward, throwing the rock. You can do the same thing yourself with a spoon and a small stone. In modern times, catapults

of a different kind are used on warships to launch airplanes. Modern planes need a long runway to get up enough speed to take off. When a catapult throws the airplane forward, the runway does not need to be so long. These catapults, which are placed just under the decks of aircraft carriers, hook on to the underneath of the airplanes, and they can give them a speed of about 150 miles per hour in a matter of seconds. Most modern catapults are operated by compressed steam.

cataract, a clouding of the lens of the eye that may cause partial or complete blindness: see BLINDNESS and EYE.

catbird

Catbirds get their name from the fact that when they are alarmed or angry they make a noise like a cat mewing. They are gray all over, except for their tails and the crowns of their heads, which are black, and a reddish-brown patch under the tail. They are common birds in North America, living and nesting chiefly in tangled shrubby places. They may eat small fruit, but they are on the whole useful to man because they destroy insects. Like their close relatives the mockingbirds, they are great mimics and can sing beautifully. Some kinds of Australian *bowerbirds* are also called catbirds.

catechism

Catechism means questions and answers. Many great teachers have believed that the best way to teach is by asking questions and then giving the answers to them. Questions and answers are used to teach religion. Usually the catechism is printed in a little booklet. It contains such questions as:

Q. Who created the Heaven and the Earth?
A. God created the Heaven and the Earth.
Q. Who made us?
A. God made us. He created man in His own image.

Catechisms are not all exactly the same, because many churches differ in their beliefs. Martin Luther, who founded the Lutheran Church, wrote one of the early catechisms, more than 450 years ago. The *Book of Common Prayer* used in the Episcopal Church contains a short catechism. Sometimes a catechism is called a "confession," because one meaning of the word *confession* is "a statement of faith, or belief."

caterpillars are a young stage of butterflies and moths: see the article BUTTERFLIES AND MOTHS.

catfish

Catfish are curious-looking fish with soft whiskers, called *barbels,* around their mouths. They feed on the bottom of the water, and use these barbels as feelers. Some catfish grow very big. The Mississippi River catfish grows to weigh as much as 150 pounds, and the *wels,* a catfish of the River Danube, may reach 400

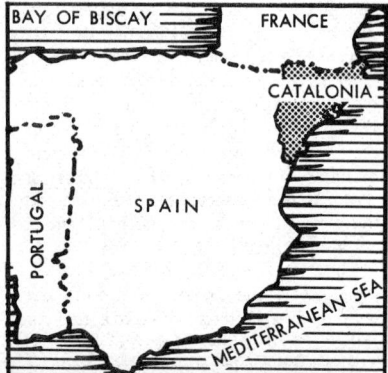

BAY OF BISCAY — FRANCE

CATALONIA

PORTUGAL

SPAIN

MEDITERRANEAN SEA

pounds. Some catfish, like the *tadpole cat* and the *mad tom,* have poisonous spines. Others can make a loud strumming noise underwater, or when they are pulled out, by vibrating an air-bladder. One catfish which comes from Africa can give an electric shock. Most of them are good to eat, but because they are ugly and have soft slimy skin instead of scales, some people do not like to eat them. The South American *armored catfish,* whose bodies are covered with bony plates, are very popular as scavengers in aquariums. A scavenger is an animal that eats waste material. Catfish have interesting ways of caring for their eggs. Some of them lay their eggs in nests. In other types the male carries them in his mouth; in a few very odd types the female rolls on the eggs and embeds them in the special soft flesh of her underside. When the rivers dry up, tropical catfish are not worried. Some burrow into the mud and wait for rain. Others journey overland, wriggling and flipping along, until they find water.

catgut

Catgut is a kind of cord that is made from the intestines of sheep, and sometimes of horses. It is used for the strings of the violin, harp, and other musical instruments. It is also very good for stringing tennis rackets, and sometimes surgeons use it to sew up the incision, or cut, made during an operation. Catgut is made by scraping the sheep's intestines and then soaking them in a special solution. After this the catgut is pulled through different sized holes so that some cords are thicker than others. The finest catgut is made in Italy.

Cathay

In medieval times people had a different name for China. They called it Cathay. It was named after the Khitai, who founded a famous Chinese dynasty, or family of kings. One of the first men to describe Cathay was the explorer Marco Polo. The name has a very romantic sound so that writers about ancient China sometimes still call it Cathay. The name actually does not apply to all of China as we know it today, but only to the northern part above the Yangtse River. (You can read about CHINA in a separate article.)

cathedral

A cathedral is a church that is often very large and beautiful. It is called a cathedral because it is headed by a bishop and is usually the biggest church in the city. It is usually named for the city. Most cathedrals are Roman Catholic or Protestant Episcopal churches. A cathedral usually has one or two high towers, and outside the church there is sometimes a courtyard called a *cloister.* The bishop and priests often live in another building called the *chapter house.*

One of the oldest and most important cathedrals in the world is the Church of St. John Lateran at Rome. It was founded by the Roman emperor Constantine and it is the cathedral of the Pope. Over its main door are written Latin words which mean "Mother and head of all the churches of Rome and the world." No one but the Pope can say Mass at its chief altar, for it covers another ancient altar that is supposed to have been used by the apostle Peter. But the greatest cathedral in Rome is St. Peter's itself. This great church was built on a spot where St. Peter was buried after his crucifixion almost 1,900 years ago. It is the largest cathedral in the world. Next come the *duomos,* or cathedrals, at Florence and Milan, in Italy, the French cathedral at Amiens, and the English cathedral of St. Paul's in London.

There are many other great cathedrals throughout Europe, in England, and in the United States. Most European cathedrals were built hundreds of years ago. The churches built then are among the best examples of a kind of architecture called *Gothic,* although the earlier ones in Italy are frequently *Romanesque.* Later in Italy, Spain, and Germany, they used *baroque* architecture.

(You can read about BAROQUE, GOTHIC, and ROMANESQUE architecture in separate articles.)

In France, the most famous Gothic cathedrals are those of Chartres, Reims, Amiens, Bourges, and Notre Dame of Paris. These cathedrals have enormous stained-glass windows that are very beautiful.

In England, the most perfect example of Gothic architecture is Salisbury Cathedral, which is about seven hundred years old. Most cathedrals are laid out in the shape of a cross, but the plan of Salisbury is a double Latin cross. The largest cathedral in England and the fifth-largest in the world is St. Paul's in London. It was designed and begun in the year 1675 by the famous architect Sir Christopher Wren.

In the United States, there are several modern cathedrals that have been built in Gothic style. One is the Protestant Episcopal Cathedral of St. John the Divine, and another is the Roman Catholic St. Patrick's Cathedral. Both are in New York City.

Catherine

In Europe, there have been three great queens named Catherine. None of them was born in the country she ruled.

One of these queens was Catherine de' Medici, who was queen of France, ruling the country in the name of her son, Charles IX. She was a wicked queen, but was very powerful in France from 1560 to 1570. The Massacre of St. Bartholomew's Day was planned by her.

The other two Catherines who ruled great countries were empresses of Russia, Neither of them was a Russian by birth. They were foreign women who married Russian czars (emperors).

Catherine I of Russia was born about 1680. She was the daughter of a Swedish peasant. She was very intelligent and very beautiful, and Czar (emperor) Peter the Great of Russia married her. When he died in 1725 she became empress. She died in 1727.

Catherine II of Russia, called Catherine the Great, was a German princess. She was born in 1729. Her husband, Czar Peter III, was wicked and stupid. Catherine had him killed and became empress from 1762 until her death in 1796. She too was wicked, but was a very skillful ruler.

There have been several queens of England named Catherine, but none was the ruler of the country.

cathode

An electron is a tiny bit of electricity. It is much too small ever to see with the eye, even under the most powerful microscope. It is one of the smallest of all the tiny pieces of which things are made. Electrons travel in streams. Such a stream is called a *cathode ray.* The point in a battery, in a generator, in a radio or in a television tube from which a stream of electrons flows is called a cathode. You can read more about electrons in the articles on ATOM and ELECTRICITY, and more about the cathode in the article on ELECTRICITY.

It is a cathode ray, passing through solid substances, that gives us x-ray pictures. A cathode ray traveling through a glass tube in which there is a vacuum (no air) hits the sides of the tube with such force that it glows and gives us neon lights. (They are called neon lights because some neon gas is pumped into the tube to replace the air. The presence of neon in the tube makes it glow more brightly.)

Catholic Church: see ROMAN CATHOLIC CHURCH and GREEK ORTHODOX CHURCH.

Catholic Youth Organization

The Catholic Youth Organization, or CYO, is a kind of club for young Catholics, although children of other religious groups are welcome to join in its many activities. There are groups in each *diocese,* or church district, in the United States, and each has its own social, athletic, educational and religious programs. Summer camping, boxing, basketball, swimming, art shows, essay contests and dancing are some of the activities open to CYO members. The CYO is supported by gifts of money from grownups all over the country. The first CYO group was started in 1930, in Chicago, by a Catholic bishop named Bernard J. Sheil.

catnip

Sometimes in a garden you may see cats rubbing themselves against a plant, sniffing it, or eating its leaves. This plant will probably be the herb called catnip, which has a very strong-scented oil in its leaves that cats love. The leaves and stems of catnip are dried and packed in small cloth bags, or in boxes. These are sold in pet shops to people who have pet cats. In the old days, housewives used to make a catnip tea that was supposed to be good for colds.

The catnip plant has velvety, heart-shaped leaves. Its flowers are small, white or purplish, and they grow in clusters among the leaves. The plant grows to be about a foot tall. It is a native of Europe and Asia, but it also grows wild in America.

Cato

In ancient Rome there were two men named Cato, both famous statesmen.

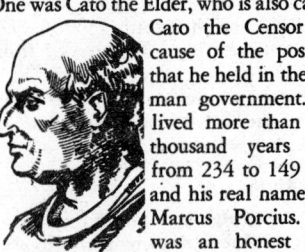

One was Cato the Elder, who is also called Cato the Censor because of the position that he held in the Roman government. He lived more than two thousand years ago, from 234 to 149 B.C., and his real name was Marcus Porcius. He was an honest man at a time when most Roman officials were very corrupt. A famous saying of his is quoted in the article on CARTHAGE.

His great-grandson was Cato the Younger, also called Cato of Utica. He also had a reputation as an honest and wise statesman. He was a general, but not a very good one. He fought with Pompey in the revolution against Julius Caesar, but he was defeated in the year 46 B.C. at Utica. Rather than surrender, he decided to kill himself. He was only 49 years old.

cat's-eye

A cat's-eye is a semiprecious stone used in making jewelry. When it is cut in a rounded shape and polished, a line of light is reflected from inside the stone that looks like the center of a cat's eye, which is how it got its name. Cat's-eyes are usually green, but may be several different shades of greenish blue, greenish gray, or yellowish green. Gems called cat's-eyes are sometimes a type of chrysoberyl, and sometimes quartz. The chrysoberyl is the more valuable of the two. There are separate articles about both CHRYSOBERYL and QUARTZ in other volumes of this encyclopedia.

Catskill Mountains

The Catskill Mountains are a beautiful range of mountains in central New York State, about a hundred miles northwest of New York City. They are low mountains, most of them being about three thousand feet above sea level. Several streams, including the Schoharie and Catskill, begin in the Catskills, and there are many beautiful waterfalls. An aqueduct carries water from the Ashokan Reservoir, in the Catskills, to New York City. This is an important part of the city's water supply, which often has to be more than a billion gallons a day.

The famous story of Rip Van Winkle is laid in the Catskills. Rip was the man who went to sleep for twenty years, in a story in the *Sketch Book* by Washington Irving. There are hotels and resorts of all kinds in the Catskills, and many people from New York visit them both in summer and in winter.

Catt, Carrie Chapman

Carrie Chapman Catt was a famous woman who led the fight to give women the right to vote. She was born in 1859, and even before that Susan B. Anthony and others had been working for this right, called *woman suffrage*. Mrs. Catt joined them in 1890. She spoke at meetings all over the United States and in Europe. Women could not be elected to state legislatures or to Congress where they could help to change the law. They had to persuade the lawmakers to pass new laws. In the National American Woman Suffrage Association, Mrs. Catt taught women how to do this work in politics. The 19th Amendment to the United States Constitution was finally passed in 1919, and women voted for the first time in 1920. Then Mrs. Catt changed the suffrage association to the National League of Women Voters, which today is an important political group. The League studies laws and helps voters understand what they are voting for. Mrs. Catt started the International Woman Suffrage Alliance in 1902, to win the right to vote for women all over the world. She was its president until 1923. In 1925, she gathered many women's groups together to work for world peace, through the National Committee on the Cause and Cure of War. After World War II, she helped place women on the staff of the United Nations, the present international peace organization. She died in 1947, at the age of 88.

cattail

The cattail is a tall reed that grows in marshes. It is also called *reed mace*. It has long narrow leaves, which in one kind may grow to be 9 feet tall. Among the leaves are the flower spikes. At the tips of these are dark brown cylinders, about the size of a corncob, consisting of masses of tiny flowers all closely crammed together. These spikes are used as winter decorations. When the spikes are ripe, they burst into masses of fluff that carry the seeds away on the wind. This fluff was used by the American Indians to stop bleeding, just as we use cotton. The leaves of the cattail are sometimes woven into chair seats. In winter the cattail leaves die, but the underground stem, or *rhizome*, lives on at the bottom of the marsh, and sends up new leaves in spring. These young shoots can be eaten like asparagus, and the Indians ground the rhizome into meal. There are several kinds of cattail, and they are found all over the world.

cattle

Cattle are large animals of a kind that is closely related to the buffalo and the bison. They eat grass, and in most countries they are kept by men for the milk they give, and for meat. Cattle are mammals, that is, they belong to that great group of animals that nurse their young. But they are different from other mammals in many ways. Cattle, for instance, have horny feet called hoofs; most other mammals have paws with toes. Horses also have hoofs, but their hoofs are in one solid piece. The hoofs of cattle are *cloven*, or split, into a right and left half. By this fact you can always tell the footprints of cattle from those of horses.

Another way in which cattle and their relatives differ from other mammals is the curious way in which they eat. Cattle eat grass and other leaves, which are very hard to digest. So instead of swallowing their food once and for all like most animals, they bring it up again as a sort of cake, called a *cud*, and chew it again. If you watch a herd of cattle resting, you will see that nearly all of them are "chewing the cud."

Other animals that have cloven hoofs and chew the cud are sheep, goats, antelopes, deer, buffaloes, bison, and yaks. The last three are the most closely related to cattle. They belong to the cattle "family," which are especially distinguished by the horns its members have. Some cattle have no horns at all, but those that do have curved, pointed, hollow horns. They are never branched, and are permanent, unlike the horns of deer, which are shed and regrown each year. Because they are hollow, cattle horns have been put to many uses in the past. The musical instrument called a horn was originally an animal's horn with the tip knocked off. Gunpowder used to be kept in horns, and horns were used as drinking cups. Wild cattle use their horns for fighting. The females, or *cows*, use them for defending their babies, which are called *calves*. The males, or *bulls*, use them for fighting other bulls. *Domesticated*, or tame, cattle are usually quite gentle, but you must still be careful not to frighten them, or to go too close to a cow with a new-born calf. You should never go into a field where there is a bull, because it may be fierce and may charge you and hurt you. Because bulls are so fierce, only the specially fine ones are kept by farmers, who use them for breeding. Such special bulls are often worth many thousands of dollars. Most of the other bulls, however, are operated on when they are very young so that they cannot breed, and this makes them much gentler. After this operation they are called *steers*, or *bullocks*, or *oxen*, and they are either fattened and killed for meat and leather, or put to work.

DIFFERENT KINDS OF CATTLE

At one time there were wild cattle roaming over large parts of Europe, Asia, and Africa, and men used to hunt them for food. In Europe the chief kinds were the giant aurochs, which stood 6 to 7 feet high at the shoulder, and the smaller Celtic Shorthorn. Both of these are now extinct, which means there are no more of them. Most of the cattle that we know today are descended from them. After a time men began to tame them and use them not only for meat, but for carrying loads, pulling plows and carts, and for riding. Cattle are still used for these purposes in the poorer parts of the world, and even in some parts of America, but in up-to-date places machines do this sort of work. In many of these distant lands cattle are still so important that a man's wealth is measured by the number of cattle he owns, and cattle are used for money. In India, where the cattle come from a different wild stock, and have a hump between the shoulders, they are considered sacred.

The Romans were the first people to try to improve their cattle by breeding, but it was only about three hundred years ago that the types we know nowadays began to appear. At that time, particularly in England, horses began to be used for work, and cattle began to be bred especially for meat and for milk. Most beef cattle were developed in places where there were not many people, and where the soil was too poor for growing crops but good enough for grazing. Yorkshire in England and the Highlands of Scotland were two such places. The

dairy breeds were bred in rich, densely populated places with good soil, like the Channel Islands and Denmark.

Cattle were first brought to the New World by Columbus on his second voyage in 1493. In 1521 the Spaniards introduced longhorn cattle into Mexico. About a hundred years ago cattle ranching began in Texas, with British and Dutch breeds of cattle. Today the United States is one of the world's greatest cattle countries, with nearly eighty million animals. These are of many different kinds and it is very interesting to learn about them and where they come from. Nowadays they are usually kept in fields or corrals, but at one time they roamed wild over the open ranges, as

This great Hereford bull stands patiently while he is brushed by little Johnny, as big sister watches and directs him.

Am. Hereford Assn.

the grazing pastures of the West were called. Owners could tell their own cattle only by the marks branded on them with a red-hot iron. Each year there were fights between owners at the time of the great *round-up,* when each owner counted his cattle, branded his calves, and chose which beasts he was going to drive to market. The life of a cowboy in those days was so hard and dangerous that we still love to read about it in adventure stories. The cattle of the Wild West were all beef cattle. Today, with fencing and improved methods of ranching, there are probably more cattle in the West than ever before. There are many different breeds, the most famous being the Shorthorns, Herefords, and Aberdeen Angus. Brahmans, or Indian humped cattle, are raised in the hotter places. After growing on the ranges, they are moved East into the "corn belt" of the central United States for fattening, and then taken to various centers to be killed. The most important of these centers is Chicago, where much of the meat is packed.

CATV

CATV (pronounced See-A-Tee-Vee) means Community Antenna Television. It is a way of sending clear television pictures to the homes of people who live in places where reception is very poor or where programs cannot be received at all. This system began in the 1950's. Here is how it works:

Let us say that you live in a town near a high mountain. The mountain interferes with television reception and prevents you from being able to watch certain shows. If your town has a CATV company, you can get in touch with a CATV representative. If you agree to pay his company about six dollars a month, he will send a serviceman to connect your television set with the huge antenna which his company has built nearby. This antenna is tall and powerful enough to pick up television signals in the air which are broadcast from stations which are on the other side of the mountain. The signals travel through wires from the CATV antenna to your television set.

Caucasian race, the white peoples of Europe, the Americas, and parts of Asia: see RACE.

Caucasus and Caucasus Mountains

Caucasus is a name given both to a range of mountains in the Union of Soviet Socialist Republics between Europe and Asia, and to the whole area around the mountains. The area is sometimes called *Caucasia.* The Caucasus Mountains are about 750 miles long from the Black Sea to the Apsheron peninsula on the Caspian Sea. They are very rugged mountains. Twenty of them have peaks higher than Mt. Blanc, which is 15,781 feet high, and the highest of the Alps. There are at least 115 glaciers in the Caucasus Mountains. A glacier is a huge river of ice.

These mountains are rather wild and gloomy. Mount Elbrus, which is 18,481 feet, is the highest of all. Some of the favorite vacation spots of the Russian people are in and near the Caucasus Mountains.

There are about thirteen million people in Caucasia. But they are different kinds of people and speak different languages. The people in the mountains raise livestock. The people in the valleys are usually farmers. Some of them hunt in the dense forests for deer, goats, wolves, lynxes and foxes. Around the city of Baku, people work in the oil fields which are among the most important in the world. Some are miners who dig for manganese, copper, silver, and iron.

The Caucasus Mountains were known to the ancient Greeks three thousand years ago. Some of the stories they told took place there, like the story of PROMETHEUS who was chained to a rock. Jason hunted for the GOLDEN FLEECE in the Caucasus. You can read about these stories in separate articles. In modern times not much was known about the Caucasus until two hundred years ago. It is less

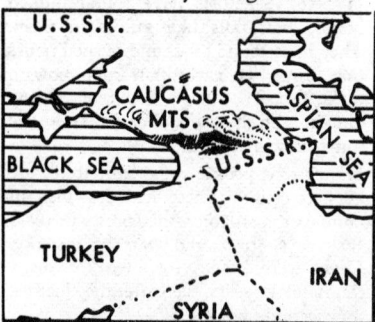

than a hundred years since Russia got complete control there. Caucasia is made up of three states, Georgia, Armenia, and Azerbaijan.

caucus

A caucus is a meeting of members of a political party to decide on a candidate for office, or to talk over party problems and try to work out party politics. Sometimes the word *caucus* is used to describe the action of having a meeting. For instance, a delegate at a political nominating convention may announce that his delegation will caucus at a certain time. This means that these delegates are going to have a meeting to discuss which candidate they would like to see nominated, or what points they would like to have included in the party platform.

cauliflower

Cauliflower is a vegetable that belongs to the cabbage family. It grows best in cool climates where the soil is deep, rich, and moist. As it grows in the garden, it produces leaves more oblong in shape than cabbage. Inside the leaves are clusters of fleshy flower stems that grow very close to each other, finally forming the white heads we eat. When the flower heads are about the size of a teacup, the leaves of the plant are tied up over them with some string, to keep the little heads white until the plant grows large enough to use.

Cauliflower is eaten cooked or pickled, and sometimes raw.

caustic

A caustic is a chemical that can burn or destroy flesh. Sometimes the word *corrosive* is used instead of caustic. An example of a caustic is silver nitrate. Silver nitrate is often used by doctors to remove warts or the extra flesh that grows around an ingrown toenail. Many other chemicals act like caustics, but are too dangerous to use on a person's body. The word *caustic* is also used to describe the way a person writes or speaks. A person who says mean and sarcastic things has a "caustic tongue."

cavalier

Years ago, when soldiers fought on horseback, they were called cavaliers. Groups of such soldiers in an army were called cavalry. *Cavalier* and *knight* meant the same thing. (See the article on KNIGHTHOOD.) But the word also has other meanings. In the English Civil War, supporters of King Charles I were called Cavaliers and their opponents, who supported the Parliament, were called Roundheads.

cavalry

Cavalry is a body of soldiers who fight on horseback. We do not have cavalry in modern armies, because modern rifles and cannon would easily kill unprotected horsemen. The jobs that cavalry used to do are now done by the air force and by tanks and other bullet-proof vehicles. These jobs are reconnaissance (which means finding out where the enemy is and what he is doing), charging

the enemy to frighten him and break through his front line, and pursuing the enemy after he has been put to flight. One division of the United States Army is still called a cavalry division, but it is really an armored (tank) division, and it does not have any horses.

For thousands of years, the cavalry was an important part of the army of almost every country. Alexander the Great of Macedonia, who conquered Persia and India more than 2,300 years ago, used his cavalry to protect the flanks of his army and to charge the enemy and take him by surprise. The army of ancient Rome had very good infantry who could usually protect themselves, and cavalry was less important to the Romans. But after they had been beaten several times by the cavalry of Hannibal, the great leader of Carthage, they too increased their cavalry.

During the Middle Ages, from about the year 500 to 1500, cavalry was much more important than infantry. The knights of Europe put heavy armor on their horses as well as on themselves. It is not hard to imagine how terrifying a cavalry charge must have been, as several thousand men, armed with swords and spears, hurled themselves on the almost defenseless foot soldiers. In the 13th century, a terrible army of Mongols under Ghengis Khan invaded Europe from the East. These soldiers were all cavalrymen, but instead of using swords, they fought with bows and arrows, which they could shoot accurately even when riding at a gallop. In fact, the Mongols fought in very much the same way as the Plains Indians of the West. Their horses were very fast, and they would strike suddenly and then ride out of sight before anyone knew what had happened.

From 1500 to 1900, cavalry and infantry troops usually fought side by side. The usual weapon of cavalrymen was the sword, but many of them also carried pistols or carbines. (The carbine is a small, light rifle.) The horsemen of Russia and Poland, including the Cossack tribesmen from southern Russia, fought with long lances. One special type of cavalry was known as dragoons. They rode swiftly to the battlefield, but once they were there they dismounted, tied up their horses, and fought as foot soldiers.

The cavalry of the United States Army has a proud tradition. In the days of the frontier, a few thousand soldiers had to guard many thousand square miles of wild land against Indian attacks. It was only natural that cavalrymen, who could ride speedily to the scene of any trouble, should be used. Cavalry regiments were divided into squadrons and troops, which were like battalions and companies in infantry regiments. During the Civil War, both the Union side and the Confederacy used cavalry for scouting and for fighting. "Jeb" Stuart and Jubal Early of the South and Phil Sheridan of the North were the most famous American cavalry generals. During the Spanish-American War, Colonel "Teddy" Roosevelt's "Rough Riders" became famous when they charged up San Juan Hill in Cuba. Cavalry was hardly used at all in World War I, and after that it became less and less important in the army. In 1962, the only horsemen left were a small group of mounted military policemen in the occupation of Germany.

cave

A cave is a hollow place in the earth and in rocks. There are caves in most rocky mountainsides and there are caves in rock formations under the earth. Some caves are formed when there is an earthquake that shakes solid rock and makes it crack, and some caves are formed by lava that flows from a volcano and leaves big holes when it cools, but most caves and especially the biggest are formed by *erosion*. This means "wearing away."

These caves are made of limestone, a soft rock that gradually dissolves in water. Underground rivers and other water seeping through the limestone, over a period of hundreds and thousands of years, have cut big chambers or caverns into the stone. Other effects of the water are growths that look like icicles but are formed of limestone. Water dripping from the ceilings of caves dissolves the limestone and makes it hang down in sharp points called *stalactites*. Other water dripping onto the stone floors of the caves carries bits of limestone with it, and this slowly piles up into a kind of spike called a *stalagmite*.

In many parts of the United States you can visit caves in which there are big chambers and strange formations cut by the water. Inside these caves it is usually quite cold, even on the hottest summer day. All caves are dangerous to enter unless you are with a guide who knows his way back to the entrance.

Exploring and studying caves is called *speleology*. It is a science or a hobby with many persons. They are called *speleologists* (or, jokingly, *spelunkers*).

There are caves in all parts of the world. Some of the biggest are in Europe, in southern France and northern Spain. In the United States, the Carlsbad Caverns in New Mexico are the biggest of the caves. Some of the chambers are four or five thousand feet long. There are underground rivers and lakes, and many strange animals, to be found there.

One of the biggest caves in the world is Mammoth Cave, in Kentucky. It is made up of many caves joined together by long winding passages. Some of the separate caves are very large. The largest one is about 40 feet wide, 300 feet long, and 125 feet high. That is as large as a good-sized church. Underground rivers run through Mammoth Cave, and strange fish swim in them. There are many beautiful stalagmites and stalactites in Mammoth Cave.

CAVE DWELLINGS

In his early days on earth, man lived in caves. Scientists have found human bones, and tools like knives in them. They have found ashes and burned bones that prove that early man knew how to make fire. They have also found many drawings on the walls of caves. There are some drawings on the walls of a cave in France that people today still think are very beautiful. These are drawings of animals that roamed the forests in those early days—bison and bears, for instance. Caves were homes for men for many thousands of years, even after they learned how to build houses.

Many animals live in caves. Bears go into caves to sleep during the winter. Hyenas are cave dwellers, too. Many of the wild animals that lived thousands of years ago and can no longer be found on the earth, also lived in caves. We know this because scientists have found their bones in caves all over the world.

There are cave-dwelling animals, insects and fish that never leave their cave homes. These creatures live in the dark all the time. Their sight is usually very poor; some of them are completely blind, but they have a very sharp sense of touch. Also, because they are never in sunlight, their color is usually very dull.

Cavell, Edith

Edith Cavell was a kind and brave heroine of World War I. She was an English nurse, born in 1865. When World War I began, she was the head of a nursing school in Belgium. The Germans conquered Belgium, but they allowed Edith Cavell to stay and turn her school into a Red Cross hospital. In 1915, the Germans arrested her and accused her of treason. She confessed that she had helped a great many English and French soldiers to escape from Belgium and to reach their own armies. The Germans sentenced her to death. She was shot by a firing squad. She remained brave and calm until her death. In the hospital, she had worked hard, taking equally good care of the soldiers from both sides. She was not a spy of any kind, but she tried to do her

Canadian Nat'l Ry.
Mt. Edith Cavell, in Alberta, Canada, is named after the heroic English nurse.

best to help the soldiers of her country and of her country's allies.

caviar

Caviar is a food that is made from the *roe*, or eggs, of a fish called the sturgeon. It is very expensive, and is considered to be a great delicacy. It is eaten as an appetizer, and is usually spread on bread or crackers. Caviar is made by salting the roe after it has been cleaned and strained. The best caviar comes from Russia, but cheaper caviars are made in other countries. Another kind of caviar called red caviar is made from salmon roe.

Cavour

Camillo Benso, Count di Cavour was a great Italian statesman who lived about a hundred years ago. When he was

born in 1810, Italy was not a single country as it is today. It was broken up into a number of small states. These states were weak and badly ruled. Many of them were really controlled by foreign countries. Cavour's great dream was to see Italy free and united. All his life he worked for this goal. He became very important in the government of his own state of Piedmont. He held many offices, and carried out many reforms in his country. He was the leader in the struggle against Austria, which wanted to control Italy. Cavour died in 1861, when he was not quite 51 years old. But he had made his great dream come true. All of Italy, except for two small states, was united into one great country.

cavy

The name *cavy* applies to a whole group of rodents, or gnawing animals. Among them are the *spotted cavy* of Central and South America, and the common *guinea pig*. They are about 8 to 10 inches long, and usually weigh about 2½ pounds. They have no tail. The front feet have four toes, but the hind feet have only three toes each. In the United States, guinea pigs have been used for years in laboratories as experimental animals because litters of baby guinea pigs are born every two months, and there are always plenty of them available. The spotted cavy of Central America, however, is kept in the yard of the home and fed well to fatten it. Then the family has cavy for dinner.

Caxton, William

William Caxton was the first printer in England. He was born in that country more than five hundred years ago. When he grew up he lived for a long time in Bruges, which is a city in Belgium. He became a rich merchant. Printing was invented during this time, and Caxton became so interested in it that he gave up his business and opened a printing shop. Caxton printed the first book in English while he was still in Bruges. Then he moved back to England and set up his shop there. See also the article BOOK.

Cecilia, Saint

St. Cecilia lived at the time of the ancient Roman Empire. She became a Christian, but her parents were pagan, and they arranged for her marriage to a young noble named Valerian. When she refused to worship pagan idols, she was put to death by beheading. She is the patron saint of music, and in Rome today there is a school of music called the Academy of Saint Cecilia. Its orchestra is one of the most famous orchestras in the world.

cedar

The cedar is a graceful, spreading tree. It is often planted for its beauty, and also for its wood, which is very strong, delicately grained, and sweet-scented. One kind, the cedar of Lebanon, is mentioned often in the Bible. Its wood was used to build the Temple and Solomon's house. Another kind, the *deodar*, grows in the Himalaya Mountains. Followers of the Hindu religion call it the Tree of God.

Sweet-scented woods all over the world are often called cedars. The South American cedars are actually close relatives of mahogany trees. In North America all the "cedars" are conifers, as are the true cedars. Conifers are trees that bear cones. The southern white cedar grows in swamps all along the eastern seaboard from Maine to Florida. It has a white, soft wood used in boatbuilding. Inland in the north grow the northern white, and the western red, cedars. Both are lovely trees with flat fanlike sprays of foliage that are often used for hedges. The common eastern cedar is really a kind of juniper. Its wood is used in making pencils, and in chests and closets because its fragrant scent drives away insects. From its wood is made cedarwood oil, which is used in perfumes and medicines, and in microscopes to increase the amount of light passing through the lenses.

Celebes

Celebes is one of the largest islands in Indonesia, which is a country made up of many islands between the Pacific and Indian Oceans. The island is shaped something like a starfish. The capital is Macassar, which is in the southwest part of the island. Celebes is a beautiful island, with many mountains and lakes and waterfalls. It lies on the equator, so the climate is tropical (very hot and damp all year). Some unusual animals such as the *babirusa* (which is like a wild pig) and the *anoa* (a small wild ox) are found in the thick forests. The people are mostly Malayan natives and belong to the Mohammedan religion. They are great sailors, and the seagoing junks (a kind of sailboat) built along the southern coast are known all over southeast Asia. Some of the people are farmers; they grow a great deal of coffee and spices and other crops. Others mine tin, coal, nickel, gold and silver. The Dutch ruled Celebes as part of the Netherlands East Indies until World War II, when the Japanese invaded it. After the war Celebes became part of the independent Republic of Indonesia.

CELEBES, INDONESIA. Area, 72,986 square miles. Population (1973) about 6,288,000. Capital, Macassar.

celery

Celery is a plant with long, grooved leaf stems, topped by curly leaves. The stems are eaten as a vegetable or in salads. Wild celery grows all over northern Europe and Asia, but it is very stringy and tough. The cultivated kinds are very tender. Sometimes they are made even more tender by *blanching*. This means that they are grown in the dark, covered up by boards, paper, or earth, to keep them from becoming green and tough. Another kind of celery is called *celeriac*. Celeriac has large, turnip-shaped roots, which are the parts eaten. It is grown mostly in the north of Europe.

celesta

The celesta is a musical instrument. It has a short keyboard like the one on a piano, and when you press down a key a hammer strikes a little steel plate. There is a plate for every key, and they are tuned to notes of the scale, starting from middle C and going up four octaves. The celesta has a bell-like sound, and is used in the orchestra. In dance orchestras the pianist often "doubles" on celesta, which means that he is able to play either piano or celesta.

Celestine

Celestine was the name taken by five Popes of the Roman Catholic Church. Celestine I was Pope from 422 to 432. In his time the Christian religion was still young. It had not spread much in the British Isles. Celestine I is remembered as the first Pope who was interested in the British Isles and sent missionaries there to teach the people about Catholicism.

The most famous of the five Celestines is Celestine V. He was a monk named Peter, who lived a simple life as a hermit. He was very much admired because of his goodness and the hardships he endured. Many people wanted to imitate him, and he organized them into the Celestine Order of monks. In 1294 Peter was chosen Pope, and took the name Celestine V. But he thought he was not wise enough to be Pope, and after only a few months he gave up his position. He is one of the few Popes who have done that. Some years after his death the Catholic Church made Celestine V a saint. He is known as St. Peter Celestine.

cell

Most living things are made up of parts called cells. Usually, cells cannot be seen without a microscope. Each cell is a tiny bit of living substance, or *protoplasm*. The smallest of all animals and plants consist of just one bit of protoplasm, and that is why we say they are "single-celled." In such a creature this one cell often does many different things that larger creatures do: moves around, captures prey, eats, breathes, gives off waste products, and reproduces itself. The AMEBA is such an animal and you can read about it in a separate article. A common one-celled plant is *Chlamydomonas*. This is the plant that makes still water look green. Sometimes these single-celled creatures live together in groups, and in

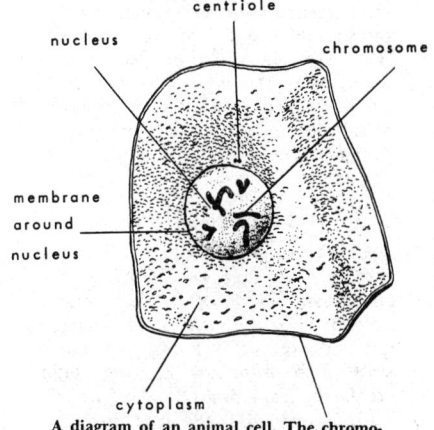

A diagram of an animal cell. The chromosomes are what determine the characteristics of the animal. The centriole is one of the things that make a cell divide.

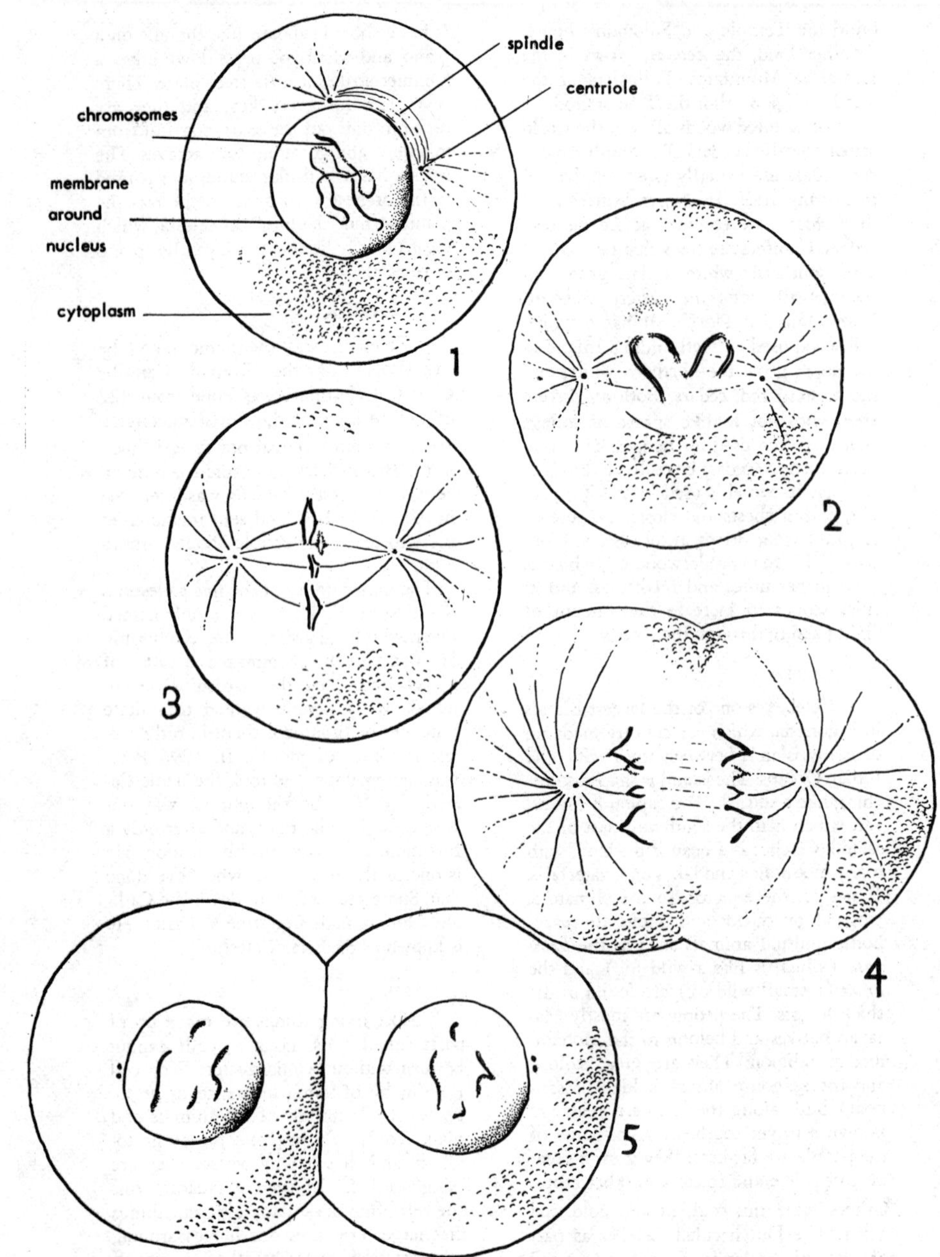

How a cell divides: 1. The chromosomes look like long twisted threads. 2. The centrioles move apart, with the fibers of the spindle between them. 3. The membrane around the nucleus breaks, and the chromosomes split lengthwise. 4. The chromosomes separate into equal groups, one group going to each of the centrioles. 5. Finally, we have two cells formed by division of the original single cell.

some of these groups we find that the cells divide the work, some doing one kind, such as eating, while others do another, such as reproducing. Finally in the larger animals and plants we find cells of many different kinds, grouped together according to the work they do to form *tissues*. Our digestive tissue, for example, consists of millions of cells grouped together in special ways to form our stomach and intestines.

WHAT CELLS HAVE IN THEM

Cells may look very different from one another, but they are built on the same plan. They have a main central portion called the *nucleus*. The nucleus directs the rest of the protoplasm, which is called the *cytoplasm*. This cytoplasm usually builds a protective box, or cell wall, around itself, and it is these cell walls that make living creatures firm instead of jellylike, and that give the cells their shape. Animal cells usually have

rather soft walls, and are filled with cytoplasm, with only a few small spaces in it containing a watery liquid. Plant cells nearly always have hard walls, chiefly of CELLULOSE, about which you can read in a separate article. In plant cells the liquid-filled spaces in the cytoplasm are usually so large that in the center of the cell only a few threads of cytoplasm may cross them. In plant cytoplasm there are always rounded objects called *plastids,* which are usually brightly colored and give the plant their color. The green of leaves and the orange or red of flowers, for example, usually come from colored plastids. The blues and purples may come from colors dissolved in the liquid, or sap, that fills the cell spaces. One function of the green plastids is to manufacture the food of the plant, sugars, from air and water. The cytoplasm of cells does most of the work of feeding, breathing, and excreting, and it is nearly always in motion, streaming round and round in-

side the cells, as you can see if you look at the leaves of any underwater plant under a microscope.

WHAT THE NUCLEUS DOES

Without its nucleus the cell dies, just like an animal without its head, because the nucleus directs all the things the cytoplasm does. It includes nearly everything that makes the plant or animal what it is —its shape, size, color, and kind. The nucleus is needed for sexual reproduction. Single-celled creatures reproduce themselves by doubling the nucleus; then the cytoplasm splits into two, each half keeping one of the nuclei, so that there are two creatures instead of one. Exactly the same thing happens when a plant or animal grows. Its cells multiply to produce more cells. Most higher animals and plants do not reproduce themselves by splitting in two like one-celled creatures. They reproduce by special cells set aside for that purpose, called *sex cells*.

Sex cells each contain only half a nucleus. When two sex cells, one male and one female, meet, they join together to form a whole nucleus again. This is called fertilization. From the whole nucleus a new creature can develop. We do not know how the nucleus builds up this new body. We do not know why a whole new tree can grow from a cutting. We do not know why a crab can grow a new claw to replace a lost one, but we cannot grow a new arm. We do not know how plant cells manufacture their own food using the power in sunlight. All the mysteries of life are in the cell, and we still have many to solve. Among the most famous men who have worked on cells are: Robert Hooke, who gave cells their name; Anton van Leeuwenhoek, who studied microörganisms; Marcello Malpighi, who studied the development of eggs; Matthias Schleiden and Theodor Schwann, who showed that the tissues of plants and animals are built of cells; and Thomas H. Morgan, who studied the way in which the nucleus passes on the characteristics of the animal or plant to its young.

Cellini, Benvenuto

Benvenuto Cellini was an Italian goldsmith, sculptor, engraver and author who lived about four hundred years ago

Gale Research Co.

in Rome. He made cups, plates, vases and even a salt cellar out of gold. He carved beautiful designs on medals and on caskets made for holding a queen's jewels. Cellini carved bronze statues and made portraits out of silver. The kings and the cardinals of his time thought his carvings and his sculpture so wonderful that they paid him a great deal of money and fought for the right to own Cellini's work. Two of the golden cups Cellini made for King Francis I in Paris are now in the Metropolitan Museum of Art in New York City. Cellini was born in the year 1500 and died in 1571.

Benvenuto Cellini wrote a book about his own life. He tells of his adventures, his travels, his quarrels, and his great success which started when he was very young. He was born in the year 1500.

When he was only 15 years old he persuaded his father to let him study with a goldsmith. But Benvenuto had a fiery temper and he was very daring. By the time he was 19 he had fought a duel. He was forced to leave his home in Florence and go to Rome. In Rome Cellini really started to work with the gold, silver, and bronze that he loved. He became very famous and he lived an exciting life full of adventure, even though he worked very hard on his sculpture. He died in 1571.

cello, a musical instrument: see VIOLIN.

cellophane

Cellophane is a thin, shiny material that is used for wrapping. It is transparent, which means you can see through it. All kinds of things that we buy every day come wrapped in cellophane, like packages of food, boxes of candy, toys, drugs, and articles of clothing. Sometimes a box has a little window of cellophane, and if you look through it you can see what is inside.

Cellophane is made of a substance called *cellulose*. Cellulose is the material that makes up a large part of wood, cotton, and other plants. (There is a separate article on CELLULOSE). To make cellophane, chemists add a chemical called *alkali* to cellulose taken from wood. Then they add certain chemicals called acids, and finally a substance called glycerine. Cellophane is made in long, wet sheets that must be dried before they can be used. Dyes can be added to give the cellophane any color.

Cellophane is a useful material for wrapping articles, for several reasons. You can see what is inside a cellophane package. Moisture and gases such as air cannot get through cellophane. When certain chemicals with wax in them are added to both sides of a sheet of cellophane, no water can get through. Thus any article wrapped in cellophane stays clean and dry.

celluloid

Celluloid was the first of the plastic materials that have so many uses today. In 1869 a man named John W. Hyatt, in New York State, was trying to find a substitute for ivory, to use in making billiard balls. He dissolved cotton in nitric acid, and added an oil, camphor, to make the mixture plastic (moldable). He found that this material could be molded into almost any shape, and that it could be made to look like ivory or bone or mother-of-pearl or any color he wanted. He called it *celluloid*. It proved to have hundreds of different uses, including lacquers (paints), photographic film, artificial leather, and explosives. The cotton treated with nitric acid is called *nitrocellulose,* or *cellulose nitrate.* In some forms it is called *guncotton* and is an explosive. When dissolved in a liquid chemical it is called *pyroxylin* or *collodion.* For more than fifty years Hyatt's invention was one of the most useful of all time.

The trouble was that all materials made with nitric acid burn very fast when they catch fire. For this reason a similar material made with acetic acid instead of

nitric acid, and called *cellulose acetate,* has replaced celluloid in many uses. It is used to make photographic film, and to make fine rayon from which clothing is made. Other plastics are made by treating cellulose with other materials, for example *ethyl cellulose.* See the articles on PLASTICS and RAYON.

cellulose

Cellulose is the chief material of which all plants are made. Plants are made of tiny boxlike *cells,* and the walls of these cells are largely made of cellulose. It is manufactured by plants from the sugars that they make from air and water. Like sugar, cellulose is one of the chemicals called *carbohydrates.* It is highly absorbent, which means it can soak up large quantities of liquid. This is something you may have seen for yourself, for the commonest forms of almost pure cellulose are linen, cotton, and blotting paper. Wood, wood pulp and paper are mostly cellulose. It is very important as a raw material from which other things are made. Many of the things around us in everyday life have cellulose in them in some form. Rayon or artificial silk, photographic film, guncotton, lacquers, celluloid and many other plastics are among the things made from it. See the article on CELLULOID.

Celts

The Celts were a great people, made up of many tribes, who lived in central Europe many hundreds of years ago. We do not know exactly where these people came from or what they were like. But we know that the Celts spread out in all directions. Their territory was at its greatest about 2,500 years ago. At that time it extended from the British Isles throughout Europe and as far east as Asia Minor.

The Celts were a bold and warlike people. They were feared everywhere. But they did not know how to join together in one great nation. So when the Roman Empire grew great and strong, the Romans were able to spread out from Italy, and to conquer the Celts and rule over them. The Celts became part of the Roman Empire and died out as a separate people.

Celtic is a name given to the group of languages that were spoken by the Celts. After the Celts were conquered by the Romans, some of their languages began to die out. Some Celtic languages are spoken today. The Welsh, Irish, Scottish (Gaelic) and Breton languages are Celtic. The ancient Celts did not write down their history and religion and poetry. Literature written in the Celtic languages did not begin to grow up until much later. The earliest Celtic literature that we have was written about 1,200 years ago.

The name *Celts* is sometimes spelled *Kelts.* The Romans called the Celtic peoples of western Europe *Gauls.*

cement and concrete

Cement is a powder made from limestone, clay, and some other materials. When it is mixed with water and used to fill in the cracks between stones in buildings, it is called *mortar,* and when it is mixed with water, gravel, and sand, and used in the construction of buildings,

foundations, and roads, it is called *concrete.*

Although the ancient Egyptians knew about mortar, and the Romans could make cement, it was not until 1824 that a cement good enough to build our modern roads and buildings was invented. Joseph Aspdin, an English bricklayer, mixed limestone, clay and some other materials together in his kitchen at home. Then he heated them on his stove until they melted. When the material was cooled it turned to a hard chunk of stonelike material. When this was ground up into a fine powder and mixed with water it made a very good cement. It hardened in the sunlight, and it could harden under water too. He called it Portland cement because it was the same color as the rocks on the Isle of Portland near his home. Because he needed limestone so badly to experiment with his mixtures, he used to steal it from the public roads. Once he was caught and arrested, but he continued working at home until his mixture satisfied him.

About fifty years later, an American named David Saylor changed the mixture slightly to make a much better kind, but he called his "Portland cement" too. Saylor's Portland cement is the kind that is used today.

HOW CEMENT IS MADE

The first step in making cement is to get the limestone. Back in Aspdin's day, limestone had to be dug out of the earth by men using picks and shovels, but today huge machines that weigh twenty tons or more are used to do the digging. The holes that are dug are called *quarries,* and often they are hundreds of feet deep and three or four miles long and wide. Sometimes as much as twenty tons of dynamite are used at one time to blast the limestone loose. When dynamite is used, a tremendous explosion takes place that may shake the ground for miles around. One hundred or more tons of limestone may be loosened at one time. When the smoke and dust from the explosion have cleared away, the huge machines load the fallen limestone rock onto railway cars. As each car is loaded, it is pulled by cable up a steep hill to the mouth of the quarry, and then on to a mill that will crush the stone. As the car approaches a mill, it is again drawn up a steep incline. There it tilts its load into steel-lined baskets that hold thousands of tons of rock. At the bottom of this basket, or hopper, are the crunching jaws of a stone crusher. Rocks the size of a piano, or bigger, come out of the crusher the size of a baseball. From the crusher, the rocks go through two more grinding machines, until they are the size of grains of sand. In these last two machines, other ingredients, such as shale and clay and other kinds of rock, are mixed with the limestone.

At this point, the combined materials are ready to be burned in huge ovens called *kilns.* Although the kilns will do the same thing to the limestone that Aspdin's stove did, you will see that there is quite a difference between the two. A kiln is usually longer than a football field, and wide enough to drive a truck through. It is shaped like a cylinder, and it is surrounded by brick. Inside of the

bricks is a steel wall a foot or so thick, that sits on roller bearings that allow it to spin very rapidly. At either end of the cylinder, gears are attached to huge electric motors that make the kiln spin. The kiln is slightly higher at one end than at the other. At the lower end is a blower that shoots powdered coal into the cylinder; at the higher end, the limestone comes in. As the limestone powder is fed in, the kiln starts to rotate; coal dust is blown in and set on fire, and in an instant, a fifty-foot flame shoots through the kiln, raising the temperature to 3000° F.

At that heat the materials start to melt and flow slowly toward the lower end of the kiln. A cloud of vapor, like a heavy fog, begins to form through the kiln. This vapor is a gas called calcium chloride, containing impurities that have been driven out of the limestone. By the time the materials emerge from the kiln, all the moisture and gas have been driven out. The finely powdered limestone and other matter that went in at the higher end have become a new hard substance, and look like little balls about the size of marbles. This matter is called *clinker*. When clinker is ground up until it is finer than flour, it is called cement.

CONCRETE

Concrete is a stonelike material made from a mixture of cement, sand, rocks, and water. It is the most widely used building material in the United States. Almost anywhere you look in a town or city, you will see something made of concrete. It may be a bridge, a church, a highway, or just a sidewalk.

Concrete is often used as a building material because it is cheap, strong, and fire-resistant. Since it hardly ever needs any kind of repair, it is a very popular and lasting way to build.

There are three different kinds of concrete. The first kind is called *mass* concrete. This is the kind used for highways and for building foundations. It is poured and allowed to stand until it hardens. It needs no other special treatment. The second kind is *reinforced* concrete, and this is used where there are to be heavy weights and other strains put on it. Reinforced concrete is especially strong because it has rods of steel running through it. The third kind of concrete is *preformed* concrete. This means that the concrete is made into slabs or strips all hardened and ready to use, so that the builder can just fit them into place, instead of mixing and pouring his own concrete. Concrete tiles are usually preformed, and so are some of the squares that are used in making sidewalks.

censer

A censer is a small container in which *incense* is burned at church services. Incense is a mixture of gums and spices that is sprinkled on burning charcoal and gives off a sweet smoke. The censer is usually made of metal and looks like a ball, or a cup with a round lid. The lower part holds the charcoal and the incense, and the lid has holes to let the smoke out. The censer is swung by three chains attached to the outside, and the swinging causes the incense to burn more quickly. The motion of the censer also spreads the scent through the air. Censers were used from earliest times among the Jews. They are now used in Roman Catholic and some other Christian churches. The censer is sometimes called a *thurible*.

censorship

Censorship is a way of making people and businesses live up to certain standards in what they do. Censors were government officials in ancient Rome who were in charge of finding out how many Roman citizens there were, and of deciding how the citizens should live and what they should do to help the state. In the United States, there is no government censorship, because we believe that the democratic way is to let people set their own standards, and to trust that they will have good taste and not do anything that will offend decent men and women. Certain businesses in the United States have their own censorship organizations. Moving pictures, radio, and television are censored by their own special boards. In countries that are not democratic, there is a great deal of government censorship. This means that the government examines every book, movie, radio and television program, and newspaper article before it can be presented to the people. In this way, the people get a chance to see only what the government wants them to see.

census

A census is a count of the number of people who live in a certain place. A census is usually taken every certain number of years. Sometimes governments also take censuses of farm produce, of homes, and of other things. All governments need to know these figures so they can provide the proper services and plan what needs to be done. Although *census* is a Latin word, we know that censuses were taken long before the time of ancient Rome. For instance, in the Bible, the Lord told Moses to take a count of the children of Israel before he led them out of Egypt.

The Romans took a census every five years. Each man who was a Roman citizen had to come before two judges, called *censors,* and tell his name, his age, his wife's name and age, and how many children and slaves he had. The government used this information to decide how much money to collect in taxes from each citizen, and also to find out how many men there were who could serve in the army.

The first article of the United States Constitution calls for a census every ten years. The United States census does more than just count people. It counts different occupations, ages, numbers of people in a family, members of farms, schools, hospitals, and so forth. It tells which parts of the country are heavily settled and which are lightly settled. It takes a count of how much people earn, whether they were born in the United States or abroad, whether or not they are American citizens. The 1970 census showed that there were over 204 million people in the country at that time. All the information the government gets from the census is very useful in planning what needs to be done to keep such a big and complicated country running well.

centaur

The centaurs are strange creatures told about in Greek mythology—the stories the ancient Greeks told about their gods. The centaurs were supposed to be part human, part animal. The heads and the tops of their bodies were just like men. But below, they had the bodies of horses, with four legs and a tail. They are usually described as wild creatures who could run like the wind and were great hunters. But they were also friendly to men. The most famous centaur was Chiron, who was very wise. The legends say that he taught Achilles and Aesculapius and other famous heroes about music and medicine and hunting.

center of gravity

The center of gravity is another name for the *balancing point* of an object. If you hold something such as a ruler or a book at its center of gravity, you will balance it. Place a ruler on one of your fingers so that it looks like a small seesaw. Move the ruler along on your finger until it balances without tipping over to either side. The point on the balanced ruler which is directly on your finger is the ruler's center of gravity. It should be about the middle of the ruler.

In the diagram with this article, you will see how to find the center of gravity of a card which does not have straight edges like a ruler or a book.

If you wish to lift a heavy object, it is good to know where the center of gravity is. It is easier to lift something at its center of gravity than at any other point. It is almost as if all the weight was at the center of gravity. Gravity is another name for the pull of the earth on a body—which is what gives it its weight. The

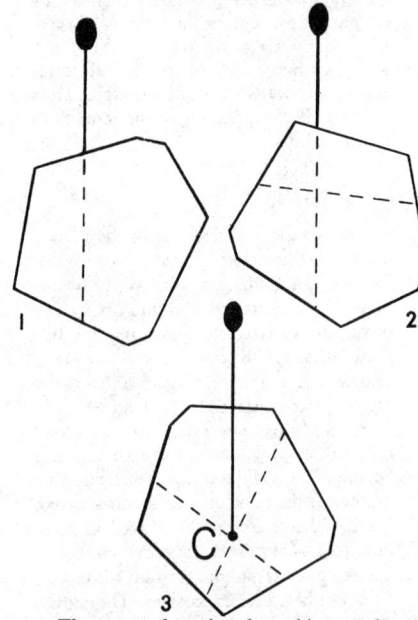

The center of gravity of an object can be found by hanging it from at least two different points on its surface (1 & 2). The vertical lines drawn from these points will cross at the center of gravity (C). The object will hang from this point in perfect balance.

center of gravity is a point on a body where gravity seems to be pulling more than at other points. You can read more about gravity in the article on GRAVITATION.

centigrade thermometer, a scale for measuring temperature: see THERMOMETER and TEMPERATURE.

centipede

Centipedes are flat, wormlike creatures. Their bodies are divided into many segments, with a pair of legs on each segment.

Their name means "hundred-feet," but they never have quite so many. Most centipedes are only a few inches long, but in the tropics there are some that grow to 18 inches. These can give a person a nasty sting. A centipede's front pair of legs has poison claws with which they paralyze the small worms and insects that they eat. Many centipedes live in damp places under stones or leaves, and come out only at night. They are very useful to man because they kill roaches, clothes moths, and other pests. Like insects, they belong to the great group of creatures called *arthropods*.

Central African Republic

The Central African Republic, with a land area slightly smaller than that of Texas, is one of the newest of the African states. It was granted its independence on August 13, 1960, but elected to remain a member of the French Community. Formerly known as Ubangi-Shari, it was one of the four territories of French Equatorial Africa. It was first governed by an Assembly of 50 men, elected for five-year terms, which made David Dacko the first president. In 1966 an Army revolution deposed Dacko, sent the Assembly home, and abolished the Constitution.

The people raise chiefly cotton but also coffee and sesame, plus lumber and diamonds. The principal cities are Bangui, Berberati, and Bambari.

CENTRAL AFRICAN REPUBLIC. Area, 238,-224 square miles. Population, 2,080,000 (1973 estimate). Capital, Bangui (population, 150,000). Languages, French and African languages. Religions, Animist and some Christian. Chief ethnic groups, Bayas, Mandjas, Badas, Saras. Monetary unit, franc C.F.A., worth 4 cents (U.S.).

Central America

Central America is a narrow stretch of land that connects North America and South America. It is really part of North America but people usually speak about it separately. More than eighteen million people live there, or about the same as in the state of New York. There are seven small counties in Central America. Altogether they are not as large as the state of Texas. There are separate articles about each of these countries, HONDURAS, NICARAGUA, GUATEMALA, EL SALVADOR, COSTA RICA, PANAMA, and BELIZE (formerly British Honduras). The United States PANAMA CANAL ZONE is also in Central America, you can read about them in separate articles.

THE PEOPLE OF CENTRAL AMERICA

The people of Central America belong to very different groups now. In earliest times there were many tribes that were different in language, appearance and way of living. The Mayas were the most important, and they had one of the best civilizations in the world about two thousand years ago. They built great cities on the plains of Guatemala, and

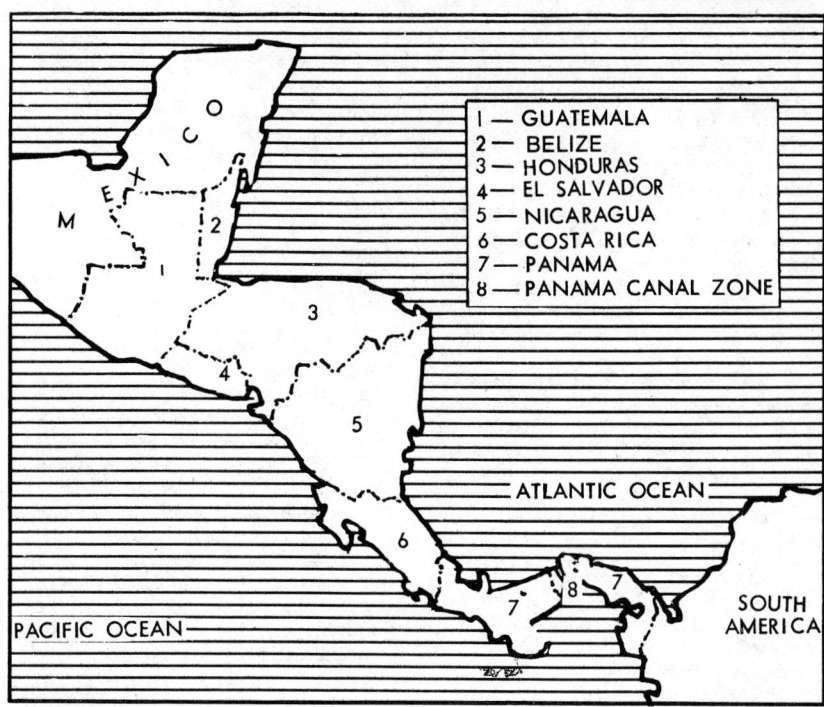

they built temples that look like the pyramids of Egypt. The Mayas began to move away from Guatemala northward into the Yucatan peninsula of Mexico about 1,500 years ago. No one knows for sure why they left. Now their great cities are almost empty. The Aztec Indians from Mexico, who also had a great civilization, overran much of Central America a little later, but they did not stay except for a few small villages. About four hundred years ago the Spaniards began to settle in Central America in large numbers.

Today the people are either white (mostly Spanish), native Indian, or mixed. In Guatemala more than half the people are still pure Indian. In Honduras, Nicaragua and El Salvador the mixed people are in the majority and are called *mestizo* or *Ladino*. There are still some primitive Indians along the coast of the Caribbean Sea who live by hunting and fishing. Nearly all the people of Central America belong to the Roman Catholic religion. They speak Spanish but learn English in school also.

WHAT CENTRAL AMERICA IS LIKE

Central America is mostly made up of a range of high mountains that separate the Atlantic from the Pacific Ocean. Many of the mountains are volcanoes, which are mountains from which steam and melted rock called *lava* sometimes flow. Every country in Central America has volcanoes, and Guatemala alone has more than twenty. The *crater*, or top opening, of Poas Volcano in Costa Rica is one of the world's largest. There are many lakes in Central America. The largest are Lake Nicaragua and Lake Managua. There are also many rivers. On the Pacific side of Central America the rivers are short because the coastal plain is narrow, and they flow almost straight from the mountains into the ocean. On the Atlantic or Caribbean side they are longer because the mountains are farther inland. Along the low, level coast the climate is hot and damp and not very healthful. In the jungle there are many monkeys, parrots and other birds, and

snakes. On the mountain slopes it is cool and pleasant. Most of the people live in the high plateaus, which have a climate that is always like spring.

THE RICHNESS OF CENTRAL AMERICA

Many crops grow well in Central America. This is because the ashes of the volcanoes make good soil. Even before the white man came, the natives grew corn, potatoes, and beans. They found cacao (which gives us chocolate and cocoa), rubber, quinine (a kind of medicine), tobacco, and chicle (from which we make chewing-gum) growing in the jungle. The forests have valuable timber, such as mahogany, cedar, balsa, and pine, but little has been cut yet. Flowers such as poinsettias and orchids grow wild. Gold, silver, copper, tin, lead and iron are found in the mountains, but little has been mined so far.

Most of the people work as farmers. Bananas and coffee are the most important crops. Others are sugar, coconuts, cacao, spices, rubber, and kapok. In Nicaragua, mining, especially of gold, is important.

CENTRAL AMERICA IN THE PAST

The first white man to see Central America was Columbus, in 1502. The Spaniards conquered Central America in 1525 when the army of Cortez came from Mexico and fought the natives. Spain ruled there for almost three hundred years until 1821, when the people revolted.

Central America then became five independent countries—Honduras, Nicaragua, Guatemala, El Salvador and Costa Rica. These countries formed a United States of Central America in 1823 but sixteen years later they split up again. In 1836 the colony of British Honduras was formed. In 1903 Panama separated from the South American country of Colombia and became a country of Central America. The building of the Panama Canal by the United States soon afterward made Central America much more important.

Central Intelligence Agency

The Central Intelligence Agency, also called the CIA, is the branch of the United States defense system that learns what other nations are doing that might affect our safety from attack. It was established in 1947. All of its work must be kept secret from possible enemies. It does its job through espionage and counter-espionage, that is, spying and counter-spying. The CIA sends secret agents all over the world to learn the secrets of foreign governments. They send their information back to Washington, D.C., where it is studied. Such information plays an important part in planning the nation's defense. Then the CIA makes reports to the President and his cabinet through the National Security Council.

centrifugal and centripetal force

Centrifugal and centripetal forces occur whenever a body goes around a curve or turns in a circle. The *centrifugal force* tries to push the body out of the circle, while the *centripetal force* pulls it in toward the center.

If you tie a button to a short string and whirl it in a circle about your head, you will feel the centrifugal force of the button pulling out on the string; the centripetal force of the string on the button keeps the button from flying off in a straight line. If the button is whirled faster and faster, it will finally break the string; this is because the centrifugal force has increased beyond the breaking point of the string.

When a speeding car turns a corner, its tires skid on the pavement. They skid because the car is being pushed away from the curve by the centrifugal force. If the car makes too sharp a turn, the force will become so great that the car will not be able to turn the corner, and instead will skid or crash into the sidewalk. The curves on automobile racetracks and highways are slanted inward or "banked" to prevent the cars from skidding.

Centrifugal force can be put to work in many ways. Machines that create centrifugal force are called *centrifuges*. A clothes dryer in a washing machine is a kind of centrifuge; inside the machine is a round tub that spins around at very high speeds. The centrifugal force presses the clothes against the sides of the tub, and in that way presses the water out of them after they have been washed.

Centrifuges are also used to separate cream from milk and plasma from blood. Plasma is described in the article BLOOD. The blood is put into a centrifuge and a motor spins it around at high speeds. Because it is lighter, the plasma goes to the top and the rest of the blood is sent to the bottom by centrifugal force.

century plant, a Mexican plant: see AGAVE.

ceramics, articles made of baked clay: see POTTERY.

Cerberus

Cerberus is the name of a strange monster in Greek and Roman mythology, ancient stories about gods. Cerberus is usually pictured as a kind of dog, with three heads, the tail of a serpent, and a mane made of the heads of snakes. He was supposed to guard the entrance to the underworld, the place where the spirits of dead people were said to go, so that no living person could enter and no spirits of the dead could leave. It was an old custom of the Greeks and Romans to put cakes in the hands of dead people before they were buried, as a bribe to Cerberus, so that he would not bother them when they entered the underworld.

cereal

Cereal is a food, usually eaten for breakfast. It may be hot, cooked cereal or dry cereal that you eat without cooking it. But when people talk about cereal they sometimes mean the cereal grains, such as wheat, rice, rye, oats, and corn. These grains are the seeds of plants that belong to the same family as the grass on a lawn. The seeds may be bunched in the top or "head" of the plant, or set into a cob or woody stem, as in corn. Grain or cereal plants are found in all parts of the world. Barley and oats can grow even in the Arctic, and rice grows in tropical, or hot, areas. There are separate articles about GRAIN and AGRICULTURE.

The word *cereal* comes from Ceres, the ancient Roman goddess of the earth and agriculture. Man did not always know how to use the grain plants for food. First he learned to pound the grains into flour that could be cooked or baked into bread. Today we use the cereal grains and flour for many kinds of bread, cake, and pastries, as well as for breakfast foods. Dry cereals were produced in the United States by the Kellogg brothers of Battle Creek, Michigan, in the 1880s.

cerebral hemorrhage, the bursting of blood vessels in the brain: see HEMORRHAGE.

Ceres

Ceres was the name of one of the great goddesses in Roman mythology, the stories told about their gods. The Romans learned about her from the Greeks. In Greek religion her name was Demeter. But the Greeks and Romans told the same stories about her. She was the goddess of farming, and of the harvest. They said it was because of her that men could grow the foods they needed. They held festivals and offered gifts to Ceres, so that she would be kind and helpful to them.

A very famous story is told about Ceres and her daughter, Proserpine. Proserpine was carried off by Pluto, the god of the underworld, because he wanted her to be his wife. Ceres wandered all over the world looking for her daughter, and in her sadness she sent too much rain and too much sun. Cattle died, and plants did not grow. But Jupiter, the king of the gods, began to be afraid men would starve. Jupiter decided that Proserpine might return to her mother Ceres. But Proserpine would have to spend part of every year with her husband Pluto. And so that is how it happens: Every year, Proserpine goes to the underworld to her husband, and all the plants fade away and the earth is cold and bare. But after six months she returns to her mother Ceres. And this is the springtime, when Ceres is happy and the earth grows warm, and all the plants and flowers blossom.

Cervantes

Miguel de Cervantes Saavedra was a Spanish poet and writer. He wrote *Don Quixote,* one of the most famous novels in the world. He lived over 400 years ago. We know little about his boyhood or education, but he was the son of a knight and was born in 1547 at Alcalá de Henares, a small town in New Castile, which is part of Spain.

When Cervantes was 25 years old he went to Italy. He worked for a year for the Cardinal Aquaviva, then he enlisted in the army as a private. He was wounded in battle. On his way back to Spain he was captured by the Moors, who were natives of Africa. They held him prisoner at Algiers for five years. His family spent all their money to pay his ransom, so that when Cervantes finally got back to Spain he was very poor—so poor that he was sometimes sent to prison because he could not pay his debts. After he married he wrote many plays, and also some poetry and stories. He published the first part of his great book *Don Quixote de la Mancha* when he was 58 years old. The second part took ten years more. Although Cervantes had many troubles and was poor all his life, he was brave and unselfish, very much like his own hero, Don Quixote. Cervantes died in 1616.

Ceylon (Sri Lanka)

Ceylon is the former name of a large island off the southeast coast of India. Formerly a British colony, it was an independent country in the Commonwealth of Nations from 1948 until 1972, when it became the independent Republic of Sri Lanka. This was its original, ancient name, meaning "great and beautiful island." It is about as big as West Virginia, but has seven times as many people, or more than twelve million.

THE PEOPLE OF SRI LANKA

The settlers of Sri Lanka came from India 2,500 years ago. Their descendants, the Singhalese, form the biggest group of people on the island. They are generally short and slender, and their skin color varies from light brown to dark brown. Other people have Arabian, Portuguese, Dutch or English ancestors, because people of those nations traded with the natives, and then settled there. Still others are descended from a people called the Tamil, who also came there from southern India. The official languages are Singhalese and Tamil.

Most of the people follow the Buddhist religion. There is a mountain on the island called Adam's Peak, and from it Buddha, the man who began the Buddhist religion, is supposed to have gone up to heaven.

Many people of Sri Lanka work on farms where very fine tea is grown. Rubber, rice, and coconuts also are important crops. There are mines from which iron, gold, precious stones and graphite are obtained.

The largest city is COLOMBO, about which there is a separate article. Other cities include Jaffna and Dehiwala-Mount

Lavinia. In the cities there are factories where paper, glassware, pottery, cement, and other products are made.

WHAT SRI LANKA IS LIKE

The island is in the Indian Ocean, about thirty miles from the mainland of India. Along the coast the land is flat, but in the interior there are high mountains. The highest peak is Pidurutalagala, which rises to about 8,300 feet. There are many streams but no large rivers. The forests have banyan, ebony and satinwood trees. There are also many animals, including the elephant, buffalo, leopard, jackal, monkey, deer, bat, and flying squirrel, as well as birds, crocodiles, and snakes.

The island is near the equator, but sea breezes keep the climate moderate. In Colombo the temperature usually ranges from 76 to 86 degrees.

There are 930 miles of railway, owned and operated by the government.

Sri Lanka is a member of the Commonwealth of Nations. (See the article on the BRITISH COMMONWEALTH OF NATIONS.) The laws are made by a unicameral ("one house") parliament. Although there is a president, and the Queen of England is recognized as the head of the Commonwealth, it is the prime minister of Sri Lanka who is the actual head of state in the country.

Education is free, from kindergarten to university.

SRI LANKA IN THE PAST

The island was first settled by peoples from India about 2,500 years ago. The first European settlers were Portuguese. They went there more than 465 years ago, about the year 1505. About 150 years later, in 1658, the island was taken by the Dutch. The Dutch later ceded it to the British, who made it a colony in the early 1800s.

During World War II the island was badly bombed by the Japanese, because of its important position in the supply line to Allied troops and in the defense of India.

In 1948 the colony became an independent nation. In 1956 it became a member of the United Nations. It has taken part in some United Nations projects and has received loans of money and other assistance. It is one of the nations that made the Southeast Asia treaty for defense against Communism.

SRI LANKA. Island in the Indian Ocean. Area 25,251 square miles. Population (1973 estimate) 12,747,000. Capital, Colombo. Official language, Singhalese. Religion, Buddhist. Government, independent republic. Member of the Commonwealth of Nations. Monetary unit, the Sri Lanka rupee, worth about 16½¢ (U.S.). Flag, maroon with yellow border, lion in center; green stripe, saffron stripe on left.

Cézanne, Paul

Paul Cézanne is one of the most famous painters of the last hundred years. He was born in 1839 in France, where he lived and painted all his life. His paintings were not much admired during his lifetime, but his style of painting has since been copied by many artists. He believed that all things in nature, and people, have very simple shapes, such as a cube or cone. Yet he made his subjects look warm and real. Cézanne died in 1906. Today his works are very valuable. They can be seen in museums all over the world.

Chad, The Republic of

Chad, in north central Africa, though it is almost twice the size of Texas, has a population of only 3,800,000. This is because it is almost all desert, except in the southern portion.

Chad became an independent state on August 11, 1960. Before that it was one of the four provinces of French Equatorial Africa. It has been a member of the French Community since 1958. It is governed by an 75-member Legislative Assembly elected for five years, which in turn elects the President and invests the cabinet. The first President and Chief of State was François Tombalbaye.

The chief products of Chad are cotton, peanuts, and livestock. Its principal cities are N'djamena, Fort-Archambault, Moundou, and Abeche.

THE REPUBLIC OF CHAD. Area, 495,794 square miles. Population, 3,800,000 (1973 estimate). Capital, N'djamena (192,962). Languages, French, Arabic, and African. Religions, Moslem, Animist, Christian. Ethnic groups, Arabs, Saras, Peuls.

chaffinch

The chaffinch is a small bird which is often kept as a pet because of its beautiful song. The male is a very pretty bird with a blue-gray crown, pale brown back and reddish underparts, a black tail, and black wings barred with white. The chaffinch belongs to the finch family of birds. Its food is mostly seeds, and it lives in hedges and on the edges of woods.

Chagall, Marc

Marc Chagall became a famous artist because he painted pictures that look like gaily colored photographs of his imagination, or of his dreams. He was born in Russia in 1887, and studied painting there and in Paris before he came to the United States in 1941. Chagall painted things the way he wanted you to see them, and not the way they really look. He may have painted a rooster green and standing on its head, or a cow purple, or a woman with two faces (one sad, and one happy), or a man playing a pink violin. Chagall did this to make you feel a certain way when you look at his paintings —gay, or maybe sad—and he brought new interest and beauty to everyday things. Chagall's pictures may seem a little strange at first, but after you look at them for a while, the stories they tell about Russian peasants, and about the Jewish people, and about animals, become clearer. Paintings by Marc Chagall hang in many of the best art museums in the world.

chain reaction, a reaction that causes further reactions of the same kind: see ATOMIC ENERGY.

chain store

If you own several stores which sell the same kinds of goods, you own a chain. There are more than 5,000 chain-store organizations in the United States. They own or control almost 150,000 stores. Men like Frank W. Woolworth, who founded a chain of 5-and-10-cent stores a hundred years ago, became very rich because their stores were successful all over the country. They were successful because they sold their goods cheaper than anyone else, and they sold more of them. They could sell cheaper because they bought great quantities of the products they wished to sell, and bought them straight from the manufacturer. They could sell quickly because they always rented the busiest location they could find in a city or town. Then they did a lot of advertising to tell people what they had to sell.

Drug stores, tobacco stores, department stores and groceries soon began to form chains. Gasoline filling stations are another example of chain-store selling. Some of the biggest chains had several thousand stores. They bought their merchandise in huge quantities and sold it at low prices.

The single stores, especially in the smaller cities and towns, considered it very unfair for chain stores to come into their territory and sell at lower prices than they were charging, but the public wanted the low prices. Soon the smaller stores found that they could do better by forming chains of their own and buying in large quantities for all the stores that were members of the chain.

Because of chain stores, the prices charged by groceries and other members of chains have dropped, but the stores themselves make as much money because they sell more merchandise.

There are many cases, however, in which stores that are not members of chains sell just as cheaply, because they are big stores and have very efficient management.

chalcedony

Chalcedony is a popular gem stone with many colors and many names. It is a favorite of gem engravers, or carvers, and it is used in rings, pins, bracelets and necklaces. There are white, yellow, green, blue, brown, and red chalcedony. The stone often has a cloudy background. Chalcedony might be called "picture-quartz," because of its circular markings, spots and veins, or streaks of color.

The name *chalcedony* is specially used for the white and gray-striped stones. In *moss-agate* and the *mocha*, or "tree" stone, green or brown particles look like tree rings, leaves, or moss. *Chrysoprase*, also green, is a favorite stone for seal rings. *Carnelian* or *sard* is clear red chalcedony. *Sardonyx* has red, white, and brown bands, and may have ten different layers. It is often carved into cameos, with the design or figure one color and the background another. *Agate* has many colors, and chalcedony itself is sometimes called "white agate." *Heliotrope* or *bloodstone* is a deep green with red spots. The first name is Greek for "turning to the sun," because the Greeks used it for observing the sun. The second name was given many centuries ago, by Christians who thought the red spots were the blood of Jesus. Agate can be stained to improve the color, and green chalcedony may be dyed to imitate emerald and jade. Chalcedony is named after a city in Asia Minor, where the stone was plentiful. Today, it is found in many places, including India, Madagascar, Brazil, and the United States.

Chaldea, a region in Asia more than 3,000 years ago, was one of the earliest places where men became civilized; Abra-

ham, founder of the Jewish people, came from a Chaldean city called Ur. See BABYLONIA and ASTRONOMY.

Chaliapin, Feodor

Feodor Ivanovich Chaliapin was a very famous Russian opera singer. He was a *basso* (the lowest male voice) and a master of *parlando*, which is a kind of singing in which you half talk and half sing the words. Chaliapin was the first to sing the role of Boris in Mussorgsky's opera BORIS GODUNOFF, about which you can read in another article. He was also the first to sing several other important Russian operas. His voice was never considered one of the greatest, but his acting and his personality more than made up for anything his voice lacked. He was born in Kazan, Russia, in 1873, and died in Paris, France, in 1938.

chalk

Chalk is a soft white form of the rock called limestone. Almost every boy and girl has used a piece of chalk to write with on a blackboard in school. That chalk comes from the shells of tiny sea creatures that live on the surface of the water. When they die, their shells drop down to the bottom of the ocean. These shells contain a hard white chemical called *lime*. In time the weight of the water on the shells squeezes them together and they form chalk.

It takes millions and millions of shells and hundreds of years to make a bed of chalk. When the ocean floor rises above the water, great cliffs of chalk are sometimes exposed. On each side of the English Channel, between England and France, there are great, gleaming cliffs of chalk. Some of the biggest are near the English city of Dover and the French city of Dieppe. In the United States, there are big chalk fields in Texas, Kansas, Arkansas, and Iowa. Once the ocean covered these fields. After many centuries, the ocean dried up and the chalk was left.

Farmers mix chalk with their soil when the soil has too much clay in it. The chalk takes some of the stickiness away and also makes the soil more fertile. Chalk is used in making many things such as cement, plaster, putty, paints, rubber goods, and toothpaste.

Another kind of chalk is called *black chalk.* This is not stone like the chalk we have been talking about. It is a kind of black clay. It is found in Scotland, Spain, Italy, and France. Artists make drawings with black chalk and they also use a black paint made out of this kind of chalk.

Chamberlain

Chamberlain is the name of a family that has been important in the British government for many years. Joseph Chamberlain was a British statesman of about 75 years ago. He was a member of the British cabinet. His eldest son, Austen Chamberlain, was born in 1863. Austen Chamberlain was a member of Parliament from 1892 until his death in 1937. He held many important posts in the

government. He is especially remembered for his work for peace in the years after World War I. He tried to make sure there would be no more wars in Europe. He helped to draw up the Locarno Pact between the leading countries of Western Europe. For this work he gained the Nobel Peace Prize in 1925.

Neville Chamberlain, the younger son of Joseph Chamberlain, was born in 1869. As a young man he went into business and was successful and well-known in his home city of Birmingham. He held many important posts in the government of his city, and in the national government. In 1937 he was chosen Prime Minister, which is the top position in the British government. Things were very unsettled in the world at that time. Germany was getting ready to try to take over smaller countries of Europe. Chamberlain hoped to avoid war. He is best remembered for the MUNICH PACT of 1938, which you can read about in a separate article. Neville Chamberlain, with the leaders of France, Germany, and Italy, agreed to let Germany take over a part of Czechoslovakia. He thought that in this way Europe would stay at peace. But he was wrong. In 1939, Hitler invaded Poland. Neville Chamberlain resigned as Prime Minister, and he died soon afterward, in 1940.

British Information Service

chamber music

Chamber music is music to be played by a small group of musicians, in a room that is not too big, and for a small audience. That is how it differs from *orchestral music,* which is written for a large audience. When chamber music first started, more than three hundred years ago, it was just for private performance. A nobleman or king would hire a few musicians to play for his guests or members of the court. They played in his house, and the music was called *da camera,* which is Italian for "in the room."

Chamber music today usually means string trios, quartets, or quintets, that is, music for three, four, or five instruments. Stringed instruments are principally used, and sometimes a clarinet, bassoon, French horn, oboe, or piano.

In chamber music there are no soloists. All the players try to make their music part of the whole. There is no conductor, and there is never more than one instrument to a part. It is a very difficult style of playing. Few musicians have been able to play chamber music well and also excel as soloists.

A period called the "Golden Age" of chamber music began with the composer Joseph Haydn and ended with Johannes Brahms. These two great composers wrote some of the world's most beautiful chamber music.

chamber of commerce

A chamber of commerce is an organization of businessmen who have joined together to improve business in the city where they work. In the United States, there is a chamber of commerce in nearly every important city. The city

chambers are members of the state chambers, and the state chambers are in turn members of the United States Chamber of Commerce. You can see that businessmen have a strong organization that is somewhat like a union for workingmen. The members of the city chambers of commerce work with all kinds of city groups to improve conditions in the cities, to help the poor, to set up clubs for boys and girls, and so on. The United States Chamber of Commerce has no official position so far as the government is concerned. It cannot tell the government what to do, but it can make suggestions and give its own ideas about what would be good for business and for the country. In some of the countries of Europe, the chamber of commerce is part of the government, and its suggestions can become part of the government's program.

chameleon

The chameleon is a small reptile, which means it belongs to a family of lizards. Chameleons are famous for their ability to change the color of their skin. At different times, they can look green, yellow, or gray-black. The skin has very tiny spots of color in it and some black spots that can grow larger and smaller. This makes the light strike the color spots differently, and the chameleon's color changes. This happens when the chameleon moves into light or into shadow, and when it becomes excited. Another unusual thing about chameleons is that they can look in two different directions at once. Each eye can turn in all directions—up, down, around, and back, so that one eye can look backward while the other eye looks up.

Chameleons are 4 to 5 inches long, but their tongue is even longer—it can spring out 6 or 7 inches. You may see a chameleon sitting on the branch of a tree, or moving very slowly toward some insect it wants to eat, such as a grasshopper. Suddenly, the long tongue will flick out, and its sticky tip will catch the grasshopper and carry it back to the animal's mouth. Chameleons have four legs, a long tail, and grasping fingers and toes. This makes them very agile in climbing, swinging, and scampering through the trees in which they live. Some chameleons lay eggs, other have live babies. There are many chameleons throughout Africa and its neighboring Madagascar Island, as well as in the Near East.

In some parts of America, there are little lizards that can change the color of

National Archives
This chameleon from the African country of Kenya, is called "Jackson's chameleon".

their skin. They are also called chameleons, but they really belong to an entirely different family. These little lizards are either brown or green. They are 3 or 4 inches long, and can move about very rapidly.

chamois

The chamois is an animal that looks very much like a large goat. It is light brown, with a black tail, black markings on its face, and a black stripe down its back. It has little pointed horns that are hooked over backwards at the tip. Chamois live in flocks in the mountains of Europe. One of the flock always keeps watch for danger, so it is very difficult to shoot them. In spite of this the chamois has been practically wiped out in the Alps. Although it has hoofs, the chamois is very sure-footed, leaping about agilely among the rocks. It breeds in May and June, spending most of the summer high up near the snow line. Chamois can now be found in New Zealand, where they have been taken and let loose. They belong to the antelope family of animals.

The leather called chamois leather was once made entirely from chamois skins. Now goat and sheep skins also are used, but chamois is still the best. The leather is made from the inner half of the skin. Instead of being tanned with chemicals, it is treated first with lime, then with oil, then the surface is scoured against emery wheels. This makes it extremely soft and good for making gloves and for polishing.

Chamorros

The Chamorros of long ago were a very independent and warlike people who lived on the island of Guam. Guam is in the Pacific Ocean about 1,500 miles east of the Philippine Islands. Almost nothing is known of the Chamorros before the Spanish came with their missionaries about three hundred years ago. The Chamorros had no written history. However, they spoke the language of Indonesia, which shows that in ancient times there had been some connection with the Malay Peninsula on the Asiatic mainland. When the Spanish came, about 50,000 Chamorros were thought to live on Guam. These fierce islanders would not be conquered or converted to a new religion. After many years of fighting almost all of them were killed or forced to leave the island. About the only trace of them left on the island are many thick stone columns twice the height of a tall man. On top of these columns are large stone bowls, which are believed to have been used for burial purposes. The Chamorros who were left mixed with the Spanish and the natives of other islands and have Spanish names. They are a strongly built people with yellow-brown skin. On Guam and on other islands, the Chamorros are now traders.

Champagne

Champagne is a region in northeastern France that was formerly a large province. It is now divided into four departments, which are somewhat like states. The countryside is mostly flat, and is used for grazing sheep. The principal industry is wool, but Champagne is most famous for the sparkling white wine, called *champagne,* that is made there. The grapes from which this wine is made are grown in a small fertile region around the cities of Reims and Épernay. Champagne has been a battlefield in many wars.

Champlain

When Samuel de Champlain was born, about 1570, the North American continent was a wild, unexplored territory. White men from Europe were just beginning to settle it. Champlain was a bold and fearless French explorer. He was the greatest leader of the French settlements in North America called New France. Champlain sailed up and down the eastern coast of North America. The books that he wrote helped to interest people in the New World, and the charts and maps that he drew up were a guide for the people who followed him. The city of Quebec was founded by Champlain, in 1608. He was appointed lieutenant governor of New France, and devoted himself to helping the growth of the colony until his death in 1635. Because he was such a great leader, he is known as the "Father of New France."

On one of his expeditions against the Indians, in 1609, Samuel de Champlain discovered a large and beautiful lake. This lake lies between what are now the states of New York and Vermont. It is more than a hundred miles long. It is called Lake Champlain, in honor of the great Frenchman who discovered it.

chancellor

A chancellor is an official of a government, a college, or a church. The word comes from the name of an official of the Roman Empire. This official, called the *cancellarius,* was a kind of secretary to the emperor, and head of his staff. The *cancellarius* got his name because he sat behind a screen (called a *cancellus*) so that he would not be bothered by the public when they came to ask him to do too many things. In England there is an officer called the Lord High Chancellor. He is the highest judge of Great Britain, and is of higher rank than anyone else in the country who is not a member of the nobility.

Changchun

Changchun is one of the largest cities in Manchuria, which is in northern China above Korea. More than 975,000 people live there, which is more than the population of Baltimore, Maryland. It is an important railroad and trading center. In 1932, when the Japanese invaded Manchuria, they made Changchun the capital of Manchukuo, a puppet regime they created out of part of Manchuria. The Japanese changed the name to *Hsinking,* which means "new capital" in Chinese. The name has been changed back to Changchun.

Channel Islands

The Channel Islands are a group of islands in the English Channel, close to France. The English have owned the islands for more than seven hundred years, but in many ways the islands are more French than English. Most of the people came originally from the nearby coast of France which is called Normandy, and the Channel Islands are sometimes called the Norman Islands for this reason. The people still live like Frenchmen and speak French as well as English. The islands are very small, about 75 square miles in area, which is just a little larger than the District of Columbia. About 104,000 people live there. The soil is very fertile and the climate is mild so the people can grow more food than they need for themselves. They send large amounts of vegetables, fruits and flowers to England. Many people work on dairy farms, too. Some of the finest dairy cattle in the world first were bred in the Channel Islands and bear the names of the larger islands of Jersey, Guernsey and Alderney.

Channing, William Ellery

William Ellery Channing was a great American minister. He was born in 1780 in Newport, Rhode Island, and studied at Harvard University. From 1803 until his death in 1842, he was minister of a Congregational church in Boston. In Channing's time, new ideas were being developed by some people in the Congregational Church. These people believed that God was only one person instead of being a Trinity. Their belief was called Unitarianism. Channing was the great leader of American Unitarianism. He worked hard to form a separate Unitarian Church. Channing was also a writer and knew many of the great writers of his time. He was interested in many reforms. He was opposed to slavery, and he preached and worked to try to have the American slaves freed.

chaparral

Chaparral is a thick growth of shrubs and small trees found in the southwestern United States. It includes such plants as the scrub oak, mountain mahogany, buckthorn, and squawbush. Chaparral country is found where the rainfall is slight (around ten to twenty inches a year), but not slight enough to cause desert. Chaparral is often so dense that it is almost impossible to get through it.

The chaparral cock, or *road-runner,* is a scraggly-looking bird belonging to the cuckoo family. It can fly easily but prefers to run along the ground with its head down, crest up, and long tail held out behind. It got its name from its habit of running ahead of horse-drawn vehicles. It lives in chaparral country, eating insects, mice, small reptiles and birds, and fruit.

chaplain

A chaplain is a clergyman who conducts religious services and performs ministerial duties for men and women who for any reason may be unable to attend regular church services at usual times. All armed services have chaplains. They rank as officers and wear uniforms but never are armed. Prisons, legislatures (such as Congress) and various institu-

tions also have chaplains.

Chaplains were among the most heroic members of the United States armed services in World War II. The most famous example occurred in 1943, when the ship *Dorchester,* a troop transport, was torpedoed in the Atlantic Ocean. The four chaplains aboard gave up their own lifebelts to save other men, and went down with the ship. They were a priest, John Patrick Washington, of New Jersey; two Protestant ministers, Clark Poling of New York and George L. Fox of Pennsylvania; and a rabbi, Alexander Goode of Pennsylvania. The Chapel of the Four Chaplains in Philadelphia and a memorial in Washington, D.C., are dedicated to them.

Chaplin, Charles Spencer

Nearly everyone in the world who has seen a motion picture knows Charlie Chaplin. He is famous as the little man with a black derby, tiny mustache, floppy trousers, worn-out shoes, cane, and a funny way of walking. Most of his early films were silent, with the conversation and descriptions of the action printed on the screen between pictures. The music came from a piano played in the theater. Some of his most famous films are *The Tramp, The Kid, The Gold Rush, City Lights,* and *Modern Times.* The first film in which he spoke was *The Great Dictator.* His other talking films include *Monsieur Verdoux* and *Limelight.*

Charlie Chaplin was born in 1889 in London, England, where he began acting as a music-hall comedian. But he has done most of his work as a motion-picture actor, director, and producer in the United States. He now lives in Europe

Chapultepec

Chapultepec was a strong fortress built on top of a steep, rocky hill just outside Mexico City. Before the Spanish conquerors came to Mexico, it was the home of the Aztec rulers of that land. The Battle of Chapultepec took place in 1847, during the war between the United States and Mexico. (There is a separate article on MEXICAN WAR.) The American forces, led by General Winfield Scott, had marched toward Mexico City, but the fortress of Chapultepec stood in their way and prevented them from entering the city. First the American artillery bombarded Chapultepec for a day, and then the soldiers charged up the steep slope, climbing up to the fortress by ladders that they had brought with them. The Mexicans fought bravely, and there was fierce hand-to-hand fighting before Chapultepec finally fell. The Americans marched into Mexico City four days later.

charade

A charade is a kind of puzzle or riddle. The person who asks the riddle tries to get someone else to guess a word by giving certain clues. He chooses a word, and divides it up into its syllables, or parts. Then he gives a clue to each syllable. He can give clues by making up a little poem or story about them. Or, he can act out the clues, with a little scene that is a hint for each syllable.

This is an example of a charade in the form of a poem:

My *first* is the head of the
family;
My *second* sounds like part of
the head:
My *third* is a song about
"Mammy;"
And my *whole's* what you wear
in bed.

The word that this charade tells about is: pa — ja — ma.

The same word, pajama, could be used in an acted charade. In the first scene, to give the idea of *pa,* a man could walk in, and a little girl could run up to him and say, "Hello, Daddy." In the second scene, someone would open and close his mouth, and point to his jaw, to hint at the syllable *ja.* In the third scene, a woman might move her arms back and forth as if she were holding a baby; this would suggest *ma.* To give the idea of the whole word, *pajama,* someone would yawn and stretch and act sleepy; then he might pretend to be getting undressed and to be putting on pajamas.

Charades are not very easy to play. They take hard and quick thinking. But they are a great deal of fun. People have played this game for many years—perhaps more than two hundred. The acted kind of charade is popular at parties, where people can divide up into two teams, to try to see which team can make up the hardest and cleverest charades.

charcoal

A valuable substance called carbon forms a large part of such materials as wood, bone, and sugar. Charcoal is a pure form of carbon that is left when wood, coal or sugar is burned without allowing much air near the fire. The oxygen in air is what makes things burn. When wood, for instance, is burned to make charcoal, it must not burn to ashes, but only part through. That is why the fire must not have too much air. The fire drives off the water and the gases that are in the material being burned. What is left is the black, spongy substance called charcoal.

An old way to get charcoal was to cover a pile of wood with earth (to keep off the air) and then set the wood on fire. But in this way the gases were lost. When people learned that these gases were valuable, a new way to make charcoal was found. It is still used today. Wood is placed in an iron vessel called a *retort* and heated to a very high temperature. The gases flow out into special chambers. Later, valuable chemicals are taken from the gases. Alcohol, acetic acid, and creosote are some of them.

USES OF CHARCOAL

When gases or odors touch charcoal, the charcoal makes them part of itself (absorbs them). Charcoal also absorbs the color that may be in a liquid. Because it can do this, charcoal is used for taking coloring and other impurities out of water and sugar. It is also used in gas masks. Bone black (charcoal made from bones) is used for making black paints and enamels. Lampblack (powdered charcoal made from oils or fats) is used to make printing ink. Artists use sticks of charcoal made from willow wood to

make drawings. Burning charcoal gives off twice as much heat as the same amount of wood. People who live where coal is hard to get often use charcoal for heating and cooking. The smoke from charcoal gives a fine taste to meat or fish that is broiled over it. Many people today have special outdoor fireplaces called barbecue pits for broiling meat.

chard

Chard is a kind of beet in which the leaves and stalks, instead of the roots, are eaten. The leaves, which grow up to two feet long, are boiled and eaten like spinach. The stalks may be eaten like asparagus. Chard is popular because it comes late in the year, in hot weather, after the spinach is gone. The plant grows very well in cool weather.

Charge of the Light Brigade,

a famous incident in the Crimean War: see BALACLAVA.

chariot

A chariot is a light carriage that was used in warfare or for riding in ancient times. Its introduction more than a thousand years before the birth of Jesus meant a complete change in warfare. We hear of battles in which several thousand were used on each side. Chariots did many of the same things that tanks do in modern war. The chariots would charge into the enemy lines in order to confuse and frighten the soldiers. Chariots were usually pulled by a team of two horses, and manned by two or three men. The driver would stand in the chariot, and he would often fasten the reins around his waist so that his hands would be free to help fight off attacks. Sometimes the men in the chariots would be armed with bows and arrows and sometimes with long spears. Chariots had two wheels, and they looked like small carts. The backs of the chariots were left open, so that the soldiers could jump off quickly and fight the enemy on foot when they had to. Some chariots that were used by the Persians had sharp knives attached to the wheels, so that anyone coming close to the chariot when it was moving would be killed. Chariots were seldom used in war after the days of the ancient Greeks and Persians, but they were used for hunting and in big processions.

charity

Charity is giving to those who need help. Giving money to poor people is charity, but so is kindness in any form. St. Paul, in the New Testament, says that real goodness is faith, hope, and charity or love—and that is what charity is. It is love, love of God and of one's fellow men. The Christian religion is not the only one in which charity is so important. The Mohammedan religion makes charity one of the requirements for getting to heaven.

In modern civilizations, charity is giving money or other valuable possessions, such as clothing, to the poor. Other words for this are *philanthropy* and *altruism,* both of which mean "love of other men." Huge organizations have sprung up to

collect money from charitable persons and use it for the benefit of those who are poor and need it. Often there are so many worthy organizations asking for money that a person cannot possibly give to all of them and does not know which to give to. To make things simpler, some cities have Community Chests, or United Funds. The citizens are asked to make one large contribution each year, instead of many small ones. The large contribution goes to the Chest, or Fund, and it divides the money among the different charities. In 1960, the Community Chest and United Fund campaigns raised more than $458,000,000. The Red Cross always asks for separate contributions, apart from the Community Chests, and some other charities do the same.

Charlemagne

Charlemagne, or *Charles the Great*, was a famous king of 1,200 years ago who united many peoples in Europe under one system of law. Charlemagne was born in 742 at Aachen, in what is now West Germany. His father and grandfather had been kings of the Frankish Empire, which took in most of what we call France and Germany. Charlemagne became king in 768. By years of campaigns and conquests, he added to his territory part of what is now Italy, Bavaria, Austria, northwestern Germany and northern Spain.

In those days, kings were usually harsh and warlike. They governed without any particular rules and did not care whether or not they were just. Charlemagne was one of the first kings to believe that the peasants, or farm laborers, should have their lives and property protected by law. He tried to pick honest and courageous men for his governors, and he wanted them all to follow the

Gale Research Co

Charlemagne encouraged the study of religion, literature, history, and the arts. His efforts brought civilization to a kingdom of barbaric tribes.

same laws. For the first time in northern Europe laws were written down. Charlemagne himself sent long letters of advice to his officials. He kept messengers traveling through his kingdom to report on how his laws and orders were being carried out. Twice a year, officials from

the different sections met in a general assembly to discuss their problems.

Charlemagne believed strongly in the Christian religion. His favorite book was St. Augustine's *City of God,* which urges all Christians to love God. Charlemagne brought the Christian religion to the countries he conquered. He protected the Pope and the city of Rome when they were attacked. In 800, Pope Leo III crowned Charlemagne emperor—the first emperor of western Europe since the time of the Western Roman Empire, more than three hundred years before. (See also the article HOLY ROMAN EMPIRE.)

In Charlemagne's time, there was almost no education outside the Church, and even the priests were often ignorant. Charlemagne changed all that. He brought together famous men of learning from every corner of Europe, England, and Ireland. He had the churches begin their own schools. Children of the poor were taught, as well as children of nobles. The Palace School, for the sons of the king and his aides, traveled with his own camp. All his life, Charlemagne was an eager student of many subjects such as languages, music, and astronomy. He is said to have composed the hymn, *Veni, Creator Spiritus,* and he hired teachers to improve church singing. Today, France, Holland, Belgium, Germany, and Switzerland have schools begun by Charlemagne.

Charlemagne was married four times and had many children. Of his three sons, only one—Louis I—lived after him. Charlemagne died in 814. Twenty-nine years later his empire was broken up, and Europe was never again so united. Many stories were told and sung about him and his twelve knights. The *Song of Roland* is about one of Charlemagne's commanders.

Charles

Charles is the name of many kings. Some of the kings named Charles were good men and wise rulers, and some of them were bad; some were warlike, and some were peaceful. There were two English kings named Charles.

Charles I was born in Scotland, and became king when he was 25 years old, in 1625. He believed that God had chosen him to be king, and that he had divine rights. Parliament (the group of people that makes the laws in England) did not agree with Charles, and this caused much trouble. For a while, Charles I tried to rule without any parliament at all. Charles also had many fights with the Puritans, and finally he was tried and put to death in 1649.

Charles II was the son of Charles I. After his father's death, he became king. He was defeated in a battle with Oliver Cromwell, who was a great leader of the Puritans. (You can read about CROMWELL in a separate article.) Charles II then went into hiding in France for about ten years. After Cromwell died, Charles returned to England and was made king again. During his reign, there was the famous London fire, in which a large part of the city burned down. There was also a very serious plague in which many people died. Charles II liked to have a good time, but he was a clever man and during

his reign England gained many colonies and became a great sea power. He died in 1685.

In France there were ten kings named Charles. The first one, CHARLEMAGNE, was so important that there is a separate article about him. Many of the Charleses of France had names that described the kind of ruler, or the kind of men they were. There was Charles the Bald, Charles the Simple, Charles the Fair, Charles the Wise, and Charles the Beloved or the Mad (he was insane). An important king was Charles VII, who was called Charles the Well Served. He was born in 1403. During the time he was king, England ruled most of France. In 1429, the famous peasant girl JOAN OF ARC (about whom you can read in another volume), led the French armies to victory over the English, and she had Charles crowned king at Reims, France.

A very sad French king was Charles IX. He was born in 1550. He became king when he was only 10 years old, and his mother had to rule for him. Charles IX and his mother hated a group of people called Huguenots, who were against the Catholics. On St. Bartholomew's Day in 1572, Charles IX and his mother had many Huguenots killed by soldiers and a mob of angry people. This was called the St. Bartholomew Massacre. Charles IX died two years later, when he was only 24 years old.

Seven emperors of the Holy Roman Empire were named Charles. (You can read about the part of Europe called the HOLY ROMAN EMPIRE in another volume.) One of the most interesting of these rulers was Charles V. He became Holy Roman Emperor in 1519, and at that time he was already king of Spain. Charles V and the king of France were enemies, and there were many wars between them. Also, Charles V was much opposed to Martin Luther and his followers, who were breaking away from the Catholic Church and beginning the religion called Protestantism. Finally Charles V decided he was tired of ruling and fighting, and so he did a very unusual thing. He gave Austria to his brother, Ferdinand I and he gave all of his other titles to his son Philip II. Charles retired to a monastery, where he spent his time fixing clocks.

The kings of Sweden named Charles were good fighters and, on the whole, they were good men. One of the most interesting was Charles XII. He became king in 1697 when he was 15 years old. Many countries thought they could conquer Sweden because the king was only a boy, but Charles XII was a good fighter. He defeated Russia and Poland and Denmark in mighty battles. Later he made war on Russia again, but this time things did not go so well. His army was defeated and Charles had to flee to Turkey. After a few years he was asked to leave Turkey, but he refused. A whole army was sent to put him out and Charles, with only a few men, bravely fought back. Finally he did return to Sweden. He invaded Norway, and was killed by a bullet while besieging a fortress.

Another important Charles was called Charles the Bold. He was Duke of Burgundy and he was a very warlike leader.

He wanted to make Burgundy a great kingdom. He tried to conquer Lorraine and Switzerland, and was defeated by the Swiss. He was killed in a battle in 1477. Charles the Bold and Louis XI, king of France, were enemies, and they were constantly at war with each other. After Charles the Bold died, Burgundy became part of France.

One of the earliest rulers named Charles was Charles Martel. He was never really king, but he told the king of France what to do, and since he was so powerful, the king did whatever Charles Martel said. He was called Mayor of the Palace. The Moslems were trying to conquer France, and Charles Martel led a very big and important battle at Tours in 732, in which the Moslems were defeated. The name Martel means "hammer," and Charles was called this because he was such a good fighter. He was the grandfather of Charlemagne.

Charleston

In the eastern part of the United States there are a number of towns and cities named for King Charles II of England. The two most important Charlestons are in the states of South Carolina and West Virginia.

Charleston, South Carolina, is a seaport on the Atlantic coast where the Ashley and Cooper Rivers come together to form a harbor. It was settled in 1670 and established ten years later as Charles Town. Charleston has been the scene of many exciting events. During the Revolutionary War its people twice beat off British attacks, but from 1780 to 1782 the town was occupied by British troops. In 1860, after years of growing bitterness between the northern and southern states, a group of men met in Charleston to declare that South Carolina no longer belonged to the United States. The following year the Confederate attack on Fort Sumter, in Charleston harbor, set off the Civil War. The city was badly damaged by the Union, or Northern, forces and finally fell, after a long siege, shortly before the end of the war. In 1886 a violent earthquake knocked down many buildings in Charleston. At other times hurricanes and tornadoes have caused destruction. Yet a number of old houses built in the days when Charleston was the center of southern culture still stand. Each year many people come to see these fine houses, St. Michael's Church, Fort Sumter, and other historical buildings, and to visit the beautiful gardens that are in bloom most of the year. Many of the people of Charleston are farmers and fishermen. Others work in factories that make cigars, fertilizer, asbestos, paper, cloth, and steel. The United States Navy has its 6th District Headquarters here. The Citadel, a famous military school, is in Charleston.

CHARLESTON, SOUTH CAROLINA. Population (1970 census) 66,945. County seat of Charleston County. Settled in 1670.

Charleston, West Virginia, is a very different kind of city, although it has about the same number of people as the South Carolina city. It lies on the Kanawha River in the Allegheny Mountains, and is the capital of the state. Many of its people work in the huge chemical plants around the city, which make use of the natural riches of the region including coal, oil, and natural gas. Others make guns, boilers, glass, furniture, and boats. Charleston grew up around Fort Lee, a frontier outpost. Daniel Boone, the famous woodsman and sharpshooter, lived there.

CHARLESTON, WEST VIRGINIA. Population (1970 census) 71,505. Capital of West Virginia and county seat of Kanawha County. Settled in 1788.

Charlotte

Charlotte is the largest city in the state of North Carolina, with more than 241,000 population. It was settled about 1750 and named after Charlotte of Mecklenburg, the German wife of King George III of England.

Its county was named Mecklenburg, also after her. In spite of this, Charlotte was a center of opposition to British rule. A year before the Declaration of Independence was signed, a group of patriots in Charlotte drew up the Mecklenburg Declaration of Independence. Today, the people of Charlotte make cotton and woolen goods (especially stockings), machinery, and electrical equipment. Queens College for Women, Charlotte College, and Johnson C. Smith University for Negroes are in Charlotte.

CHARLOTTE, NORTH CAROLINA. Population (1970 census) 241,178. County seat of Mecklenburg County. Settled about 1750.

Charon

Charon was a character in Greek mythology, the stories the Greeks told about their gods. They believed that when someone died his spirit had to cross over the dark waters of the rivers of Acheron and Styx to reach the underworld. Charon had a ferry boat to take the spirits there. He charged a fee, and the Greeks usually put a coin in the mouth of a dead relative or friend so that the fee could be paid. Charon has been shown in pictures as an ugly old man.

chart

A chart is a way of arranging facts so that they can be found quickly. A chart may be a map, or a diagram, or a list. But usually when people say "chart" they mean the kind used by navigators to help them guide their ship safely. This kind of chart is called a *mariner's chart*. Another name for it is *hydrographic chart*. When a ship comes near land, a look at the mariner's chart shows the captain many things he must know if he is to steer the ship safely. The chart shows just where the land is and also every lighthouse, beacon, or signal station. It shows every object a ship might strike in the water—reefs, rocks, sandbars, or wrecks of other ships. The chart also tells how deep the water is all along the coast, so that the captain can steer the ship away from places where the water is shallow.

Coastal charts are not the only ones made. Other charts map out everything that is in a harbor, or a river, or a bay. Still others are maps of great stretches of open sea, with no land near them. A branch of the United States Navy called the Hydrographic Office makes many charts for American waters. Its scientists are always looking for changes on land or sea. When they find them, they correct the charts or make new ones. Another kind of chart is the *celestial* chart. This is a map of a part of the sky, showing how the stars are arranged there.

Weather charts are made every day by the United States Weather Bureau. They are printed in many newspapers. They show the temperature all over the country, where it is raining or snowing, what winds are blowing. They tell what kind of weather may be expected in any part of the country. Farmers, cattle raisers and construction workers find weather charts very useful. If you intend to go on a picnic or a hike, you should look at a weather chart to see if the weather will be good.

Business firms use charts. A glance at a *sales chart*, for instance, will tell the owner of a business if things are going well or not. A *graph* is a special kind of chart used a great deal by mathematicians and statisticians (men who work with numbers). It gives information by means of a diagram that has a number of straight lines, curved lines, and dots. They are laid out on paper ruled into tiny squares. See the article on GRAPHS.

charter

A charter is a written statement in which certain rights are given to a local government, or to a group of people, by the head of a nation or its government. Most of the first thirteen colonies of the United States were settled by people who were given charters by the English king. These charters gave the settlers the ownership of certain land and the right to a certain amount of independent local government. The most famous charter in history was the MAGNA CARTA, which you can read about in a separate article.

Charter Oak

The Charter Oak was a tree in Hartford, Connecticut, in which the charter of the Connecticut colony was hidden from the English governor in 1687. A charter is a legal paper that allows a group of people to have their own government. When America was being settled, England gave charters to many colonies in the New World. But in 1687, the English king, James II, sent Sir Edmund Andros to be governor over all New England. Andros had to get the charters back from the colonies before he could govern them. When he came to collect the charter of Connecticut, it had disappeared. The colonists had hidden it in a hollow of a tree, nearly seven feet wide. Connecticut lost its government anyway, but two years later Andros was recalled to England. Then the charter was taken out of hiding, and Connecticut again was allowed to govern itself. The oak tree became a symbol of the people's freedom. The Charter Oak grew to be almost a thousand years old before it was blown down in a storm in 1856. A stone monument now marks the place where it stood.

Chartres

Chartres is a city in France and the capital of the Eure-et-Loire department. A department is a division of a country somewhat like a state. Chartres is 55 miles southwest of Paris on the Eure

River. It is a very ancient city that once belonged to the Romans. Long before that it was probably used by the druids as a place of sun worship. The druids were the priests of the Celtic peoples. You can read about the CELTS in a separate article.

Chartres is famous for the beautiful Cathedral of Notre Dame that was built about eight hundred years ago. This cathedral has two high spires, fine sculpture, and wonderful stained-glass windows.

Today Chartres has a population of more than 31,000. It is in a farming region, and it is a great grain-trading center. Many of its people work at brewing, cider-making, and tanning.

Chase, Salmon Portland

Salmon Portland Chase was a great American statesman and judge. He was born in 1808, in Cornish, New Hampshire, and studied to be a lawyer. In 1830 he began to practice law in Cincinnati, Ohio, and soon became very successful. Chase was always very much opposed to slavery. He made speeches and wrote articles, and worked for the political parties that wanted to abolish slavery. In 1861, he was appointed Secretary of the Treasury in President Abraham Lincoln's cabinet.

In this post Chase did a very outstanding job in reforming and reorganizing the Treasury Department. He planned new taxes to finance the war, and kept the country's credit good. His greatest achievement was the setting up of the national bank system. After he resigned as Secretary of the Treasury, Chase was appointed Chief Justice of the United States Supreme Court, the highest judge in the United States. He remained in this post until his death, in 1873.

Chase was twice elected to the United States Senate, and twice Governor of Ohio.

chat

The chat is the largest bird in the family of the wood warbler. It has a large beak, a yellow throat and breast, white-rimmed eyes, and an olive-green back. It lives and builds its nest in dense, shrubby places in the United States, and flies south of Mexico and Central America for the winter. Its close relative, the long-tailed chat, lives in the West. Both birds have harsh, jerky songs.

Chateau-Thierry

Chateau-Thierry is a town in the northeastern part of France. The Americans won a great victory over the Germans at Chateau-Thierry during World War I. In July, 1918, the Germans started a big attack near this town. They were stopped by 275,000 American troops. If the Germans had broken through, they would certainly have been able to capture Paris, the capital of France, and they might have won the war. On July 18 the Americans attacked, and they captured Chateau-Thierry three days later. This was the last big battle of the war.

Chattanooga

Chattanooga is an important city in Tennessee. It is near the Georgia line on the Tennessee River, at a point called Moccasin Bend, where the river curves like a moccasin. The name is taken from a Creek Indian word, *chat-toto-noo-gee*, which means "rock that rises to a point." This is how Lookout Mountain appears from a distance. The city is almost surrounded by mountains, including Lookout, Missionary Ridge, and Signal Mountain. At one time the Great War Path of the Indians passed over Lookout Mountain, and a stage route, with a ferry at Williams Island operated by John Brown, a Cherokee, was the only pass between the North and South before the railways were built.

Chattanooga has been an important railway center since before the Civil War. It was because of this that the Confederate, or southern forces, concentrated near the city. They were beaten and retreated into Georgia after the Battle Above the Clouds, fought up the steep slopes of Lookout Mountain, and the Battle of Missionary Ridge. Chattanooga was then occupied by Union forces in September, 1863, and was the base for General Sherman's attack on Atlanta. Fort Oglethorpe, at nearby Chickamauga Park, has been a major Army training station since the Spanish-American War.

Chattanooga is a leading Southern manufacturing city. About 119,000 people live there. They make iron and steel products, chemicals, hosiery, furniture, and many other articles. The Tennessee Valley Authority project brought further prosperity to an already busy city. You can read about the TENNESSEE VALLEY AUTHORITY in a separate article.

CHATTANOOGA, TENNESSEE. Population (1970 census) 119,082. On the Tennessee River. Founded 1841.

Chaucer, Geoffrey

Geoffrey Chaucer was an English poet and the author of one of the most famous books in the world, the *Canterbury Tales*. He was the greatest man in English literature before Shakespeare, and one of the greatest poets in any language. He was the first English poet of such high rank. The English that he used is difficult for us to understand today, but it is very beautiful. Chaucer was also a wonderful storyteller. Although his stories were not written for children, they have since been translated or rewritten in a form that everybody, including children, can understand and enjoy.

Gale Research Co.

Most of the little that we know about Chaucer's life comes from government records.

Chaucer was the son of a wine merchant and was born in London about the year 1340. He was in the service of several princes and after fighting with the army of Edward III in France, he became a member of the king's court. About 1366 he married a lady-in-waiting to Queen Philippa. During the reign of Richard II, he was sent on diplomatic missions to Italy and later held several of-

ficial positions at home. He died the same year as King Richard, in 1400.

Chaucer's writing career is usually divided into three periods. During the early part of his life he imitated the French courtly romances, which were love stories about knights and fair ladies. He translated part of the most famous of these, called *Romance of the Rose*. He wrote his own *Book of the Duchesse* when the duchess of Lancaster died. Her name was Blanche and she was the wife of King Edward's son, John of Gaunt, for whom Chaucer was supposed to have worked as a young man. The second period in Chaucer's literary career came after he went to Italy, where he was sent because he knew Italian and could read Italian literature. During these years the two most important works that he wrote were the *House of Fame* and the *Parliament of Fowls*. He also translated a book written in Latin by the Italian writer Boethius. But the greatest period in Chaucer's life was when he wrote under the influence of a great Italian named Giovanni Boccaccio. Chaucer's long poem *Troilus and Cressida* is a love story in five books based on Boccaccio's story *Filostrato*. His masterpiece, the *Canterbury Tales,* is a collection like Boccaccio's *Decameron*.

THE CANTERBURY TALES

The *Canterbury Tales* are stories told in the form of a long poem. They are told by a group of people who are making a pilgrimage, or holy trip, to the shrine of St. Thomas à Becket at Canterbury Cathedral. The *Canterbury Tales* are important because they are the first great writing in the Middle English language (see ENGLISH). Chaucer got the idea for the stories when he himself went on a pilgrimage and noticed how many different kinds of people there were in the party. In the poem each pilgrim is described, and then he or she was to tell four stories. The stories are based on tales that have been told in many other languages. Chaucer translated them into English poetry. Although it is not complete, the poem is 17,000 lines long.

Chautauqua

Chautauqua is an educational and religious center. Thousands of people visit it to hear concerts and lectures in the summer. It is located on Chautauqua Lake in New York State, about sixty miles from Buffalo. Chautauqua has its own theaters, concert halls, and music studios, besides rooms for classes and lectures. It is "a college that trains men and women everywhere to read and think and talk and do." The Chautauqua Institution is also famous for its year-round programs of home reading for people who cannot go to college. Chautauqua was started by Lewis Miller and John H. Vincent in 1874, so that Sunday-school teachers could study the Bible together on their vacations. The first group camped at the lake for two weeks and combined study with entertainment. Each year the camp grew in size and fame. Speakers came from many countries to give lectures and classes in literature, history, and science. More concerts and plays were added. In 1878, Chautauqua offered the first home reading course, and about 8,700 people joined it. Next, in 1882, Chautauqua

invented the correspondence course. Instead of taking tests in a classroom, students wrote letters answering questions about their reading. Sometimes several students in the same town had weekly meetings. In 1889, Chautauqua started a third new plan—university extension work. This means that regular college classes are given in the evening for people who cannot come during the day. Today there are many correspondence schools and university extensions, and Chautauqua has only the home reading and summer courses. Several other cities have also started chautauquas.

check

A check is a written order to a bank to pay a certain amount of money to the person named on the check. Of course, in order to write a check, one must have money in a bank. Checks are a safe and

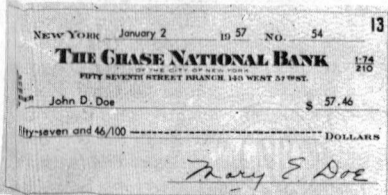

This is how to fill out a check.

easy way to transfer money. Business could hardly be done without them. Checks are usually colored strips of paper, somewhat longer and narrower than a postcard. The paper is specially made so that it will show if anyone tries to erase or change the check. A check must have on it the date; the name of the person to whom the money is to be paid; and the signature of the person who writes the check. Some checks are made payable to "Cash," which means that anyone who has the check may get cash for it. You can read more about the use of checks in the article on BANKING.

checkers

Checkers is a game for two players. It is played on a checkerboard, as shown in the illustrations. Each player starts with twelve pieces, placed as shown in the first illustration.

Black always moves first. The pieces move only on the black squares (but in printed diagrams the black squares are shown white and the white squares are shown black). There are two kinds of moves: simple and jumping. A simple move is made by advancing a piece forward to the next black square, either to the right or to the left. This is illustrated in the upper left corner of the second illustration. The jumping move is illustrated on the right side of the illustration. You may jump only when an enemy piece is on a black square in front of your own, and when the square just beyond it is open. Your piece may jump over the enemy to the open square, and if you can then make a jump from that square you must do so in the same turn. In the illustration, the black piece in the corner can jump three white pieces. All pieces jumped over are removed from the board. You win the game if you capture all the enemy pieces in this way. You also win if you blockade all the enemy pieces so that none can move.

When one of your pieces reaches a

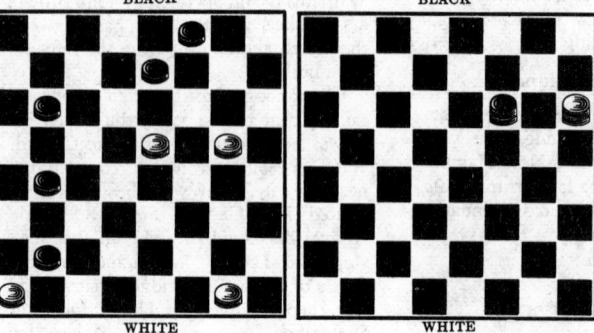

WHITE
Starting position

WHITE
Notation

To start a game, the pieces are set up as shown in the diagram at the left. The pieces are actually placed on the dark squares, but in print they are shown on the light squares. Each square is numbered so that a record can be made of the moves.

WHITE

WHITE

Left: Taking only the pieces at the left, if it is White's move he may jump all three Black men. Taking only the pieces at the right, if it is White's move he moves 16-12 and Black cannot move without giving White a jump. *Right:* A king may move either way. If White moves first, he loses. If Black moves first, it is a draw.

square all the way on the other side of the board from you, it becomes a *king.* Your opponent must immediately *crown* it, by placing an extra piece on top of it. A newly crowned king is shown at lower left in the diagram. A king has all the powers of a single man, plus the right to move backward as well as forward. It may jump several enemy pieces by going both ways in one turn.

If you can make a jumping move, you must do so. If you overlook a jump, and make a simple move instead, your opponent can make you put it back and make the jump instead.

cheese

Cheese is one of the oldest and most valuable foods known to man. It is made from milk. There are many different kinds of cheese, some white and moist, like cottage cheese, and some yellow and thick and heavy, like Cheddar. The milk of many different animals can be used to make cheese. Most of our cheese is made from cow's milk, but we also use goat's milk for certain kinds of cheese, and in some countries in Europe only goat's milk and sheep's milk is used. The early Egyptians used camel's milk, and the Laplanders used reindeer milk. The difference in cheese depends upon three things: the kind of milk used; the kind of "agents" used to change the milk to cheese; and the kind of "curing process," which means the flavoring and ripening of the cheese. Many cheeses are named after the towns or countries where they were first made. Camembert is the name of a town in France, and Cheddar is the name of a town in England, and two famous cheeses are named after them. At one time Swiss cheese came from Switzerland, because that was the only place where they knew how to make it. Today we know how to make all kinds of cheese.

HOW CHEESE IS MADE

"Little Miss Muffet sat on a tuffet, eating her curds and whey," goes the

Mother Goose rhyme. Most of us have eaten curds-and-whey, or *clabber.* It is milk that has soured slowly under certain conditions, not too hot and not too cold. The solid part, the curds, has separated from the watery whey. Now if we further separate the curds by straining and pressing through a cloth (cheese cloth) like a fine net, we can season it as we wish, and we will have cottage cheese. When the milk separates in this way it is called *precipitation,* and the agent is *lactic acid,* which is in the milk itself. There is another agent, called *rennin,* or *rennet,* that is used to make the hard cheeses. It is a substance taken from the stomachs of milk-fed calves or other animals. When it is added to the milk it causes precipitation. Then the curd is drained and separated and pressed into any shape desired—a round ball, or a flat or thick cake that is either round or square. Each kind of cheese is made in a certain shape because people expect it to look that way. Now it is green cheese, which does not mean that it is green in color. but that it is uncured. The green cheese is now ready to be ripened, or cured.

CURING AND RIPENING

Curing and ripening can take from a few months to several years, depending upon the type of cheese. It is put in a place where there is a certain amount of humidity (moisture in the air) and where the temperature is not too hot or too cold, and where these conditions always remain the same. In the old days, before they knew anything about chemistry and air conditioning, they used caves and underground storerooms to cure cheese. Different cheeses are ripened by the action of molds and tiny bacteria, and these forms of life can only exist where the temperature, light, and humidity are to their liking. Caves are still used to ripen cheeses, but modern cheese factories can produce the same varieties of flavor and texture by controlled curing. Processed cheeses consist of blends, or mixtures of

different kinds, pasteurized and packed in airtight containers.

TYPES OF CHEESE

Cheeses are divided into two classes. The hard cheeses are all ripened, and the soft cheeses may be ripened or unripened. Then they are divided as to how they were ripened, whether by molds or bacteria. It is any one or a combination of all of the things we have talked about that gives a particular cheese its appearance and flavor. Some of the best known cheeses are: Cheddar, Edam, Gouda, Emmenthal, Swiss, and Parmesan. (Parmesan is the kind that is often grated to put on spaghetti and salad.) Swiss and Emmenthal are full of holes caused by gas bubbles formed in the curing process. Roquefort (blue cheese), Stilton, and Gorgonzola are hard cheeses ripened by molds, and Münster and brick are ripened by bacteria. Of the soft cheeses, Brie and Camembert are ripened by molds, and Liederkranz and Limburger by bacteria. Cottage cheese, cream cheese, and Neufchâtel are unripened, and are not intended to be kept for long.

Cheeses made from whole milk are rich in protein, calcium, and fats, and can be used as a meat substitute in combination with vegetables and bread. In cooking, cheese is used raw or melted, for sauces, salads, custards, soufflés, and with fish, eggs, and vegetables.

cheetah

The cheetah is an animal that belongs to the cat family. It has yellowish brown fur with black and brown spots, and it looks like a leopard. The cheetah roams through Africa and Asia, and men have used it for years to hunt deer and antelope. That is why it is called the *hunting leopard*. It can be tamed and trained for hunting in about six months, and when it is stalking a deer, it acts just like a hunting dog. It runs faster than any other animal—more than 60 miles an hour. It slinks up to its prey unobserved and then leaps and pins its victim to the ground.

Chekhov, Anton

Anton Pavlovich Chekhov was Russia's greatest writer of plays. He also wrote many short stories. Chekhov was born in 1860. He began to write stories when he was a student, but later turned to writing for the theater. His stories and plays are very simply and beautifully written. They are also sad and sometimes tragic, but Chekhov describes his characters with kindness and a quiet sense of humor. His most famous plays are *The Sea Gull, Uncle Vanya, The Three Sisters,* and his masterpiece, *The Cherry Orchard.* All of these plays and several others have been translated into English and given on the stage many times in the United States. Anton Chekhov died of tuberculosis in 1904, at the age of 44.

chemical warfare

Chemical warfare is the use of chemicals to kill or annoy the enemy. FLAME THROWERS and SMOKE SCREENS (you will find separate articles on these) are examples of chemical warfare, but the best example is poison gas.

The only war in which poison gas was used a great deal was the first World War, which lasted from 1914 to 1918. In April, 1915, the Germans on the Western front in France opened containers of deadly chlorine gas, which was blown by the wind among the French troops. Soon both sides were using chemical warfare, and every soldier in the front lines was given a gas mask to protect himself. Gas masks are made of rubber, and they have a celluloid or plastic screen through which you can look out. The mask fits right over the face, so that no air can get in except through a special opening. Here the poison gases are filtered out, and the man wearing the gas mask breathes only pure air. Some troops also used rubber clothing to protect themselves, and they carried protective ointments that could be rubbed into the skin and eyes to prevent gas from irritating and damaging these parts of the body.

Poison gas can be spread by releasing it when the wind is blowing toward the enemy, by shooting shells and dropping bombs that contain gas, or by spraying it from airplanes. Many people believe that using poison gas is a much worse way of fighting than shooting bullets and shells. No poison gas was used in World War II. Gas was responsible for one third of all the American troops injured in the first World War, but very few of these men died.

Here is a list of the most important poison gases:

Phosgene smells like new-mown hay, and damages the lungs and causes choking.

Adamsite has hardly any smell. It irritates the throat and lungs, but it seldom does permanent harm.

Mustard gas smells like horseradish or garlic. This "gas" is really a brown liquid that causes large blisters on the skin or even in the lungs.

Lewisite smells like geraniums, and it is similar to mustard gas.

Tear gas smells of sour fruit. This gas makes the eyes run with tears and it causes choking, but it is not harmful except in very large amounts. It is used more by police to stop riots than in actual warfare.

Nerve poisons are gases first invented by the Germans during World War II, but they have never been used in warfare. They have no smell, and they are far more powerful than any other poison gases. They attack the nerves and blood stream, and within a few minutes they can paralyze and kill a man.

In the United States Army, chemical warfare is the job of the Chemical Corps. Even though poison gases have not been used for a long time, the Chemical Corps must know all about them, so that the Army and the people will be protected in case an enemy should decide to use them against us.

chemistry

Chemistry is the scientific name for the study of matter and how it changes. Matter is another name for such things as the air we breathe, the water we drink, and the earth we walk on. There are many different kinds of matter and these are all studied in chemistry. Men and women who work in chemistry are called *chemists.* They work in laboratories where they experiment with different kinds of matter called *chemicals.* These laboratories are rooms in which there are all sorts of things that chemists use. Most of the things are made of glass so that the chemist can see what goes on during his experiments. He mixes chemicals together in glass tubes, that are open at one end and closed at the other. These are called *test tubes.* If you were to watch a chemist in his laboratory, you would think he was a magician. He takes two different kinds of powder that do not have any color, puts them in a test tube, mixes them with water and heats them over a flame. Suddenly there is a beautiful red color in the test tube. Magic? No more so than what happens around us and to us every single day of our lives.

THE CHEMISTRY OF NATURE

There are hundreds of things that take place around us every day that are just as amazing and magical as what the chemist does in his laboratory. But we are so used to seeing them happen that we do not think twice about them. These are the chemical changes which nature performs. Nature was the first, and still is the greatest, chemist. She makes things change before our very eyes every day. One of the things she changes is the air around us. Air is very important to us. We need it to stay alive. But the air is always changing. Different things are always being mixed with the air and changing it. Smoke, water from the oceans and lakes, and dust from the ground are always going off into the air and mixing with it. The sun heats the air and the winds cool it. It is almost as if nature were working in a laboratory just like a chemist and air was one of the chemicals she was experimenting with. She makes the air hot or cold, wet or dry, and light or heavy. She puts different things in the air that are sometimes good, sometimes bad for us to breathe.

Nature also does chemical experiments with the water in the oceans and lakes. She mixes salt with water and we have the ocean. She takes salt from the water and we have rivers and lakes. She freezes the water and we have ice; she boils water and we have steam. She mixes so many different kinds of chemicals with the water in the ocean, that if we could take all of them out we would be millionaires. The ocean contains such chemicals as sodium, potassium, calcium, bromine, chlorine, and even some gold, all of which you can read about in separate articles. Some of these chemicals have been taken out of the ocean in small quantities by chemists who have been able to uncover some of nature's secrets. They have learned many lessons in chemistry from her and have used them to make nature give up some of her treasures.

Nature has also put things in water which make people healthy when they drink them or bathe in them. These waters are called mineral springs and contain special salts called carbonates which can also make soda pop fizz. There are many mineral springs throughout the world, and these all were made by nature's chemistry.

However, nature works her most wonderful chemistry experiments with the earth under our feet. The wind blows it,

the sun heats it, and water mixes with it. Underground there are chemistry experiments taking place that are hard to believe. If you could watch them going on you would say that nature was a magician, not a chemist. But it is all done by chemistry. Iron, gold, silver, copper and many other metals are being created under the ground. If it were not for nature's chemistry and the work of chemists in trying to understand her, we would not have any of the things which are made from these metals—stoves, buildings, cars, pots and pans and electric wires, which all contribute to our comfort and pleasure.

Above the ground nature is also at work using chemistry to grow plants and animals. The tiny seed that is planted in the ground and soon grows into a beautiful plant or flower does so by means of nature's chemistry. The seed must have the chemicals nature puts into the ground in order to grow. These chemicals are mixed together by water and heated by the sun. The seed drinks in this mixture and in no time at all changes into an entirely different thing. This is what nature's chemistry can do.

THE CHEMISTRY OF YOUR BODY

Nature is not the only great chemist. Your body is also one. Every minute of the day, it is performing chemistry experiments inside of you which help you grow and become men and women. The food you eat is probably the most important part of the chemistry of your body. When you chew it, it mixes with certain chemicals in your mouth. These make the food soft and easy to go down into your stomach. In your stomach it is mixed with other chemicals which change the food so it can pass into your intestines. In your intestines the vitamins and minerals in your food that make you healthy are sent into the blood stream to be changed into muscle, tissue, and bone. How this comes about few chemists are able to understand. But there are special kinds of chemists called *biochemists* who spend their lives finding out how the chemistry of your body works. You can read more about them in the separate article BIOCHEMISTRY.

The outside of your body is also being used for chemistry experiments. The sun shines down on your skin and changes certain chemicals in it to vitamin D, an important vitamin for giving you strong bones and teeth. Hair growing on your body is another result of your body's chemistry; so are the nails on your fingers and toes, the color of your skin and eyes. Your body is a walking chemistry laboratory.

THE IMPORTANCE OF CHEMISTRY

We have mentioned some of the ways in which chemistry works in nature and in your body. Other examples of chemistry at work are the rusting of iron, the burning of wood and coal, and the decaying of your teeth. But chemists in their laboratories are doing other kinds of experiments every day that help to make us healthy and happy. They study different types of matter and how they change in order to learn something about the things in the world about us. In that way they are able to make new things: the wonder drugs such as penicillin and

streptomycin that have saved many persons' lives by killing germs inside their bodies; anesthetics that are used to keep a person from feeling pain while he is being operated on; disinfectants and antiseptics that kill germs outside our bodies to prevent the spread of dangerous diseases; and vitamin tablets that we take to keep us in good health and able to work and to play.

There are many other important things that chemists have done. They have brought about new and valuable fertilizers that are used in agriculture to help grow bigger and better fruits and vegetables. They have discovered ways to make useful goods out of what once were useless farm products. Plastics from cornstalks, paper cartons from wood pulp, paints and enamels from soy beans, and sugar from sawdust have been some of the chemical changes that chemists have been able to make. This branch of chemistry is called *chemurgy*. Gasoline to run automobiles and airplanes, oil for heating homes, perfumes and cosmetics for women, food, clothing and the roof above our heads—all of these things in one way or another have been brought about by the chemist in his laboratory.

Many chemists are employed by large companies that make food, soap, drugs, candies, and almost anything else that we eat, drink, or use on and inside our bodies. In this way care is taken that none of these products will harm us in any way and that the best possible product will be manufactured.

Other chemists work in laboratories that test our blood. They tell us what blood type we have and if there are any diseases in our blood. Chemists are also employed by the city, state and government to check that our foods are pure and that drugs are being manufactured according to health requirements. Crime laboratories such as those in police departments and the FBI (Federal Bureau of Investigation) employ chemists who examine articles that have been found at the scene of a crime. The examination of parts of clothing, guns, ammunition, and bits of hair and skin that are left behind by a criminal may often help to solve a crime and capture the criminal.

Besides chemists there are other men and women who work in chemistry. They are called chemical engineers. They do not usually work in laboratories but are concerned with designing and building machinery that will be used to manufacture chemicals or products made with chemicals. This machinery must be properly made so that the chemicals will be mixed in the quickest, the easiest and the best way. A chemical engineer must know engineering as well as chemistry. You can read about ENGINEERING in a separate article. Chemical engineers are employed by companies that make plastics, explosives, paper, rubber, food, drugs and iron and steel.

Cheops

Cheops was a great ruler of Egypt thousands of years ago. The Greeks called him Cheops, but the Egyptian name for him was Khufu. Cheops is remembered as the ruler who had the Great Pyramid built as his tomb. The ancient Egyptians believed that men's spirits lived on after

death, and so some of their kings built huge pyramids of stone as tombs for themselves. In those days there was no machinery, so all the work of building the pyramids had to be done by human labor. The Greek historian Herodotus wrote about Cheops and his pyramid. Herodotus said that Cheops spent all his money having his tomb built. He forced everyone to work on his monument. Thousands of men labored for twenty years to build it. Cheops lived about 2650 B.C.

Cherbourg

Cherbourg is a seaport in northwestern France on the English Channel. It is at the end of the Cotentin peninsula, in the Manche department, or state, and once belonged to the province of Normandy. It was settled by the ancient Romans. Cherbourg is important chiefly for its harbor. Some of the largest ships in the French navy and passenger lines have been built there. In time of war, it is one of the best protected harbors in the world. In peacetime it is one of the most important European ports where many Americans land every year on their way abroad. About 38,000 people live there. The principal business besides shipyards is importing coal and lumber, and exporting dairy products and vegetables.

Cherokees

The Cherokees were one of the largest Indian tribes in North America. They originally lived in the highest ranges of the southern Allegheny mountains. Their land included parts of what are now Tennessee, North and South Carolina, Georgia, Alabama, and Virginia. They did not sign a peace treaty with the United States until 1794. At that time, the United States agreed that the Cherokees were to keep their own territory and govern themselves. In 1825, a famous Cherokee named Sequoia invented a written alphabet for the tribe, and soon many were using it. They wrote a constitution and set up a government, published a newspaper, and established public schools.

LATER HISTORY

But the white men wanted their land, and Congress made a law to send the Cherokees away, west of the Mississippi. Gold had been discovered in Cherokee territory. Treaties and agreements were forgotten. The Cherokees were cruelly treated and finally sent to Arkansas. It was winter and many died on the way. A few escaped to the Great Smoky Mountains in North Carolina and Tennessee, where some of the tribe still live. The Cherokees and other Indian tribes were given land in Indian Territory. This later became the state of Oklahoma, and in 1902 the Cherokees became citizens of that state. But some white men continued to use Cherokee property. Finally, in 1934, Congress passed the Indian Reorganization Act, and since then the Indians have been able to live better. There are Cherokees in almost forty states, but the largest number (13,455) live in Oklahoma. Many southern states have towns named Cherokee.

cherry

Cherries are a fruit which grow on shrubs or trees. There are about six hundred different kinds, some sweet and some sour. They can be eaten raw or cooked. Cherry jam and cherry pie are two of the many ways of cooking them. Cider can also be made from them.

All cherry trees have beautiful flowers. The loveliest flowers are those of the Japanese cherry, which is grown only for its flowers and bears no fruit at all. In Japan, cherry-blossom time is a national festival. The Japanese city of Tokyo gave the United States a number of these beautiful trees, and many people go to Washington, D.C., every year to see them in bloom.

There are several wild cherries in America that have pretty flowers, such as the chokecherry, the pin cherry, and the wild black cherry. Their fruit is usually rather sour, but it is sometimes used in jellies. Their leaves are said to be poisonous to animals when wilted. The red wood of some cherry trees is very valuable for fine furniture.

Cherry Valley Massacre

Cherry Valley is a little town in New York State, about fifty miles from Albany. Only about 660 people live there now. During the Revolutionary War, the American settlers of Cherry Valley were the victims of a terrible massacre. On November 11, 1778, the town was attacked by about eight hundred Indians, led by a few Americans who were on the side of the British. They killed about fifty persons, burned all the houses, and carried off about seventy settlers. These seventy were perhaps even more unlucky than those who had been killed right away, for they were tortured by the Indians, and most of them soon died.

cherub

A cherub is a kind of heavenly being, another kind being the seraph. (More than one cherub are called *cherubim*, not cherubs.) The ancient Hebrews thought of cherubim as sphinxlike creatures, with human heads, animal bodies, and wings. The belief was that they served the Creator in various ways. Now we think of cherubim as angels and as beautiful children. Great artists of the Middle Ages portrayed them in that way. See also the article ANGEL.

Chesapeake

The *Chesapeake* was a frigate (a fast, medium-sized sailing ship) that played an important part in American history. In June, 1807, the *Chesapeake* was sailing off the coast of Virginia when she was stopped by the British frigate *Leopard*. The captain of the *Leopard* said he wanted to search the American ship to see if there were any deserters from the British navy on board. Commodore James Barron, the *Chesapeake's* captain, refused, so the *Leopard* opened fire. The *Chesapeake* was not prepared to fight so she was forced to surrender. The British came on board and took off four American sailors. This incident made Americans very angry, and it was one of the causes of the WAR OF 1812 between England and the United States. You can read about this war in another volume of this encyclopedia.

Chesapeake Bay

Chesapeake Bay is a great arm of the Atlantic Ocean that reaches about 200 miles into the east coast of the United States, extending northward into Virginia and Maryland.

The bay is separated from the Atlantic by Delmarva Peninsula, part of which is called the Eastern Shore along the bay. At its entrance to the Atlantic, between Cape Charles and Cape Henry, Chesapeake Bay is thirteen miles wide. A number of rivers empty into it. The most important are the Patapsco (on which is the great port of Baltimore), the Severn (on which is the United States Naval Academy at Annapolis), the Patuxent, the Potomac (on which is Washington, D.C.), the Rappahannock, the York, and the James. Its eastern shore has hundreds of inlets. It is deep enough for ocean-going ships almost everywhere.

Chesapeake Bay is famous as a fishing ground. Oysters and crabs are caught there in great numbers. The bay is the site of the United States Navy's biggest base, at Norfolk, Virginia. Jamestown Island, nearby, is the place where the English established their first New World settlement, in 1607.

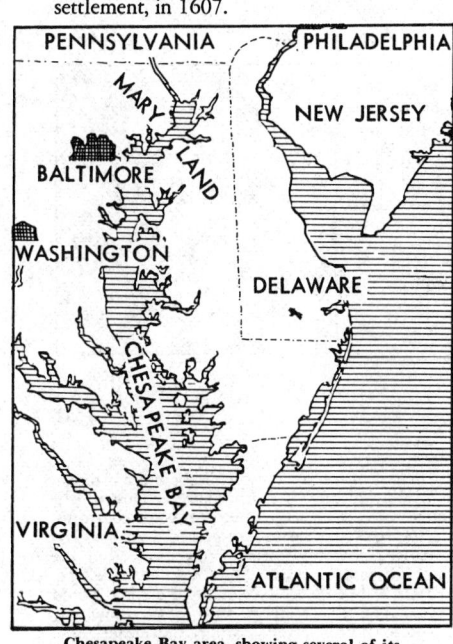

Chesapeake Bay area, showing several of its neighboring states and large cities.

chess

Chess is a game for two players. It is played on a board (chessboard or checkerboard) as shown in the illustration. Each player starts with sixteen pieces. Eight of these are *pawns*, which are all the same and shorter than the others. Two are *rooks* or *castles,* carved like round turrets. Two are *bishops*, sometimes shaped like the pawns but always taller; the bishop has a notched hat that looks like the *miter* (a kind of hat) worn by a real bishop. The two *knights* look like horses. Each player also has one *queen* and one *king*. The king is always the tallest piece, and usually has a smooth crown with a knob or cross in the middle. The queen's crown is shaped with points in a ring around the top.

The illustration numbered 1 shows how to set up the pieces to begin a game. The two players are called White and Black. White always moves first.

The chess pieces are set up this way on the board at the beginning of a game.

THE PLAY

Every kind of piece moves in a different way. The moves are shown in the diagrams. When you move a piece to a square occupied by an enemy piece, you capture that piece. Then you remove his piece from the board and put your piece on the same square. But only the knight may jump over a square on which there is any other piece. All the pieces except the pawn capture in the same way that they move. The pawn moves straight ahead on the file but captures diagonally.

To win the game, you must capture the enemy king. The king is not allowed to move onto a square guarded by an enemy piece. If your king is *checked* (attacked), you must get out of the check in one of three ways: (1) by moving the king to a square that is not attacked; (2) by capturing the enemy piece that checks; (3) if the enemy piece is a queen, rook, or bishop, by *interposing* another of your pieces between it and your king.

IRREGULAR MOVES

There are two irregular moves in chess. One occurs when a pawn moves two squares for its first move, and in doing this passes an opponent's pawn that could have captured it if it had moved only one square. When this happens, the opponent's pawn may capture it anyway, by moving into the square that was passed. This is called capture *en passant*, which in French means "in passing." The other irregular move is *castling*. When a king and a rook have only empty squares between them, and neither the king nor the rook has moved, the king may move two squares to its side and the rook is put in the square the king passed over. You may castle only once in a game, and you may not castle when the king is in check.

HOW TO LEARN CHESS

Chess is the most complex of all games, but there are hundreds of good books written about it. To learn to play chess well you must read the books and also think very hard about making the best moves when you play.

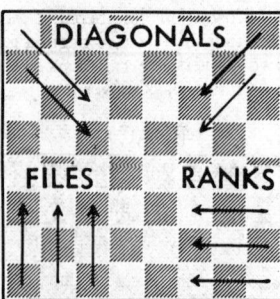

The lines of squares are called ranks, files, and diagonals.

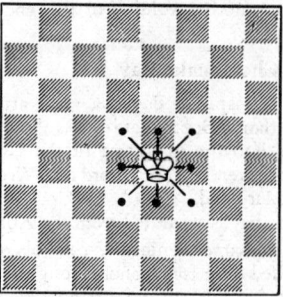

The *king* may move (one square at a time) in any direction.

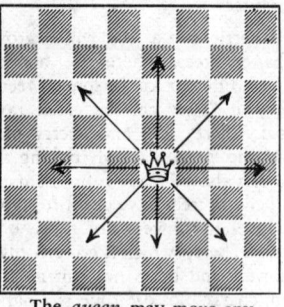

The *queen* may move any distance on the rank, file or diagonal.

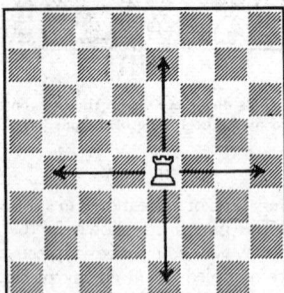

The *rook* may move any distance on the rank or on the file.

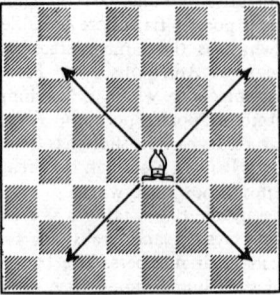

The bishop may move any distance on the diagonal. It stays on the same color.

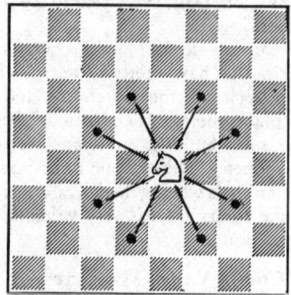

The *knight* may move in a kind of L, jumping over any pieces in its way.

The *pawn* may move forward on the file. (a) At its first turn, the pawn has the choice of moving one or two squares. (b) Thereafter, the pawn may move only one square at a time. (c) A pawn that reaches the farthest rank is replaced by any piece you wish, usually a queen. (d) A pawn captures *diagonally,* not straight ahead. The White pawn is blocked by the Black pawn, but may capture either Black knight. (e) The Black pawn has just made its first move, advancing two squares. The White pawn next to it on the rank may capture it as though it had moved only one square. This is called capture *en passant* or *in passing.*

Castling is a special move made by the king and a rook together, that is allowed only if neither has yet moved. It is made by moving the king two squares toward the rook, then putting the rook on the square passed across by the king. The arrows show how White may castle "on the queen's side." He cannot castle "on the king's side" because the Black bishop guards a square the king would have to cross. The Black kings and rooks show the position of these pieces after castling on either side.

chest

The chest is the part of the body that contains the lungs and heart. It is separated from the abdomen by a large muscle called the *diaphragm.* On the front of the chest is the *sternum,* or breastbone. The ribs form the sides, and are joined to the spine at the back. The medical term for the chest is the *thorax,* and it is nature's protective cage for your lungs, heart, bronchial tubes, and esophagus, the tube that leads to the stomach and through which food is swallowed.

Chesterfield, Lord

Philip Dormer Stanhope was an English nobleman who wrote some fa-

mous *Letters to His Son.* He was born in 1694, the son of Philip Stanhope, the 3rd earl of Chesterfield. When his father died, Lord Chesterfield received the title. He was a member of the House of Lords, which is part of the British Parliament, but he served his country best as lord lieutenant of Ireland. He was famous for his sparkling wit and elegant manner. But he was also very selfish and did many things that most fathers would not think of teaching their sons. Lord Chesterfield died in 1773.

Chesterton, Gilbert Keith

G. K. Chesterton was an English writer who was converted to the Roman Catholic Church and became very famous as a Catholic author. His books were very clever and very popular. He also wrote detective stories in which the detective is a Catholic priest named Father Brown. He illustrated some of his own books, and those of other writers, with very amusing drawings. One of his best-known novels is called *The Man Who Was Thursday.* Chesterton lived from 1874 to 1936.

chestnut

Chestnuts are sweet nuts that grow inside thorny burs on large trees. If you live in a big city, you may have seen chestnuts roasted and sold in the streets. There are several kinds of chestnut trees growing in North America, Europe, and Asia. Some of them grow as tall as one hundred feet, with trunks five feet wide. A disease called the chestnut blight has killed almost all the American chestnut trees. Scientists have developed chestnut trees that can resist this blight.

Chestnut wood looks like oak. It is very long-lasting, and is used for making beams for houses, fence posts, and railway ties. In the southern states there is a small chestnut tree with very good nuts, called the *chinquapin.* The horse chestnut, which has big hand-shaped leaves, is quite different from the real chestnut. The nuts of this tree are poisonous.

chevalier, a knight: see CAVALIER.

chewing gum, chicle that is sweetened and flavored: see GUM.

Cheyenne

Cheyenne is the capital of the state of Wyoming. It is in the southeastern part of the state near the boundaries of Colorado and Nebraska. It was settled in 1867 when the Union Pacific Railroad decided to make a division point there. It became famous in the 1870s as a cattle-raising center and began to grow when the Black Hills gold fields were discovered. Today more than 40,000 people live there. The city is an important shipping center and a market for sheep and cattle, as well as a railroad and highway center. Each year the city holds a Frontier Days Celebration, to remind everyone of its colorful past.

CHEYENNE, WYOMING. Population, 40,-914. Capital of Wyoming and county seat of Laramie County. Settled in 1867.

Cheyenne Indians

The Cheyenne tribe was one of the most famous of the Plains Indians. They fought several wars with the white settlers of the New World about a hundred years ago. Hundreds of them were slain in a massacre by General George Custer and his troops. This started one of the worst Indian wars in the West. In 1876, the Cheyennes and other tribes killed Custer and two hundred of his men at the Little Bighorn River in Montana. You can read more about that battle in the separate article about General CUSTER.

Before 1700, the Cheyenne Indians lived in what is now Minnesota. They raised corn and made pottery. Next, they lived near the Cheyenne River and the Black Hills in South Dakota. When they got horses, they became buffalo hunters. They also raided the plains from northern Montana down into Mexico. They were among the tallest and strongest of the Plains Indians.

THE CHEYENNE WARS

Then came the wars of the United States against the Cheyennes. Their meat, the buffalo, was hunted down by the white man, and the Indians were forced to live on government lands or reservations. They did not have enough food.

Once a year, the Cheyenne and all the Plains Indians joined in a "Sun Dance" that was part of their religion. But the United States Army broke up this celebration, and even killed Indians who took part in it. The Indian tribes started other religious customs. One group, called the Native American Church, had about 25,-000 members in 1947. A Cheyenne Indian of Oklahoma, Alfred Wilson, was head of this church until his death in 1945. There are several thousand Cheyennes today, and they live mostly on reservations in Montana and Oklahoma. Their name is used for the capital of Wyoming and for many mountains and rivers in the United States.

See also the article on PLAINS INDIANS.

Chiang Kai-shek

Chiang Kai-shek became famous as a great soldier and leader of the Chinese people. Chiang was born in China in 1886. He was trained to be a soldier at

Gale Research Co.

Chinese and Japanese military schools. When Chiang was just a young man he met Sun Yat-sen, a great Chinese leader. At that time, China was ruled by an emperor. Sun Yat-sen and his followers wanted to overthrow the emperor, make China a republic, and set up a new government. They thought that China needed many reforms and improvements. Chiang agreed with these aims, and took part in the revolution in 1911. In the following years China was torn by Civil War. Chiang became more and more important as a general and a leader.

After the death of Sun Yat-sen in 1925, he was really the head of the Kuomintang, or Nationalist, party. China was unsettled and divided, and Chiang had the task of trying to unite the country. He had to put down the many different groups that opposed the Kuomintang, and to fight against the Chinese Communists, who wanted to set up their own government. At the same time, both Chiang and the Communists had to fight against the Japanese who were trying to conquer China. After World War II, when Japan was defeated, civil war broke out again in China. This time, Chiang was defeated again and again by the Communists. He was driven back until finally he had to leave the mainland of China, and move his army and his government to FORMOSA, which they call Taiwan. They called their government the Nationalist government, which until 1971 was a member of the United Nations. Chiang died in 1975.

Chiang's wife, Madame Chiang Kai-shek, also became a famous person. Her name before her marriage was Mei-ling Soong, and her family was very powerful in China. Madame Chiang was educated in the United States, and she took back to China many American ideas about health improvement and sanitation and the care of children. She had worked to help spread these ideas in China. She had also helped her husband in his work. Madame Chiang had written articles and books to tell the people of the West about China. During the war against Japan, Madame Chiang was a leader in relief work to help women and children. She always tried to find ways to help orphan children whose parents were killed in the war.

Chicago

Chicago is the second-largest city in the United States and one of the largest cities in the world. It is located on Lake Michigan, in Illinois, and it is one of the greatest shipping and railroad centers, with 22 railroad lines coming into the city. Chicago is a very busy place. It is the largest grain and livestock market in the world, and the greatest meat-packing city. More than 3 million people live there, and like New York City, it has people of many nationalities. There are Poles, Germans, Russians, and those from many other European countries, who came to work in the large industries of Chicago. There are also large groups of Chinese and Negroes. Each of the different groups settled in a com-

munity of its own, so if you travel through Chicago, you will find an Italian section, a Czech section, a Swedish section, and many others. Each group has kept some of its European customs, and many of the people still use their native language, although they also speak English.

HOW THE PEOPLE LIVE

Chicago is located in the great farm and cattle region of the Middle West, and every year, the farmers send millions of head of cattle to the city. Thousands of people work in the great Chicago slaughter houses and meat-packing plants, and these are of great interest to visitors. A famous Illinois poet, Carl Sandburg, wrote a poem about Chicago in which he called the city "hog butcher to the world."

But Chicago also has many other industries. Many people work in the large grain markets. Others work in some of the biggest printing plants in the world, in iron and steel mills, and in factories that make many useful articles. People manufacture all kinds of machinery, furniture, clothing, candy, soap, and many other products that people use in their homes every day.

WHAT CHICAGO IS LIKE

Chicago is a bustling city, with many different sections. The largest section is called the South Side. Here you can see the great stockyards and many factories. But there are also the University of Chicago and many apartment houses. The main business and shopping district is called "The Loop," with beautiful department stores, skyscrapers, office buildings, and hotels. State Street is the most famous shopping street. If you want to see the financial section, you have to go to the La Salle Street district. Here you will see many banks, the Stock Exchange, and the Board of Trade, which is one of the highest buildings in Chicago. There are many big buildings in the downtown area: the Wrigley Building, the Carbon and Carbide Building, and the Tribune Tower. The Merchandise Mart building is not a tall building, but it is one of the largest office buildings in the world. It is almost a city in itself.

The most beautiful part of Chicago is the North Side, with many fine homes and hotels along the lake shore. The Lake Shore Drive is the most beautiful boulevard in the city. Beyond this part of Chicago are suburbs, Evanston (the home of Northwestern University) and others.

Thousands of people come every year to see the many places of interest in Chicago. There are museums, and parks, and historic statues. You can visit a very fine zoo in Lincoln Park, and watch the Chicago Cubs play at Wrigley Field or the White Sox play at Comiskey Park. You can also visit the many beaches along the lake, and the excellent golf courses and tennis courts.

CHICAGO IN THE PAST

The first American settler of Chicago was John Kinzie, who built a log cabin there in 1803. In the same year Fort Dearborn was built. But the Indians in that part of the country did not like the white people taking their land, and there were many fierce Indian raids. In 1812,

the Indians attacked Fort Dearborn and massacred most of the people living inside the fort. For many years Chicago was just a fur-trading station, but gradually more people settled there after a peace treaty was signed with the Indians. The town grew so quickly that by 1837, Chicago became a city. After the Civil War, it grew rich and important, but in 1871, the great Chicago fire destroyed a large part of the city. For two days the fire raged and destroyed thousands of homes and millions of dollars worth of property. Almost three hundred people lost their lives in this disaster. However, the people got to work, and in two years Chicago was rebuilt into a much finer city, with wider streets and buildings of stone and steel. After that, Chicago grew into one of the greatest cities in the country.

The city had other troubles over the years. In 1886, there was a big strike among the workers. A large meeting was held in Haymarket Square, which the police tried to break up. A bomb was mysteriously thrown, and a riot started. Eleven people were killed and one hundred were wounded. This became known as the famous Haymarket Riot. Again, in 1894, there were riots during the Pullman strike, and President Cleveland had to call out the United States troops to restore order. But Chicago has also had more pleasant events in its history. The city held a large World's Fair, in 1893, and in 1933 it celebrated its 100th anniversary with a Century of Progress Exposition, which you can read about in a separate article. It was so successful, it reopened the following summer. Since World War II, Chicago has grown even larger and continued to expand its industries.

CHICAGO, ILLINOIS. Population, 3,366,-957 (1970 census). County seat of Cook County. Settled in 1803.

Chichen-Itza, an ancient ruined town on the Yucatan Peninsula of Mexico. It contains fine examples of Mayan architecture: see the article on MAYAN.

chickadee

The chickadee is a tiny bird that lives in the United States and Canada, and got its name because of the sound it makes. The chickadee has a gray back and a white stomach and a black cap and throat. This little bird likes to make its nest in a hollow tree, and lays seven or eight small spotted eggs. The chickadee does not fly South in the winter and you can see it hopping around in the snow looking for small insects. The chickadee is a very friendly and cheerful bird, and will eat crumbs or peanuts out of your hand.

Chickamauga

Chickamauga is a city in Georgia, ten miles south of Chattanooga, Tennessee. Here was fought a big battle in the Civil War. This battle was part of the Chattanooga Campaign. Fort Oglethorpe, an important United States Army base, is nearby. Chickamauga and Chattanooga National Military Park are in Georgia and Tennessee, the larger part being in Georgia. The Park Commission has rebuilt the roads as they were during

the Civil War, and the Army War College sends its officers here to study how soldiers fought in the Civil War.

Chickasaw: see MUSKHOGEAN.

chicken, a barnyard fowl: see POULTRY.

chicken pox

Chicken pox is a disease that most children are apt to get, and most grownups seldom have. Very few people ever get the disease after the age of ten. Chicken pox is not a dangerous disease, but it is an extremely uncomfortable one. It is infectious, which means you can catch it from someone who has it. If you have been near a child who has chicken pox, you will not know whether you have been infected until two or three weeks have gone by. The disease shows itself after that time when your body breaks out with hundreds of small blisters. About twelve hours later you get another crop of blisters, and a third and last crop twelve hours after the second crop. The blisters then begin to dry up and form scabs. At this time you itch all over, and are very uncomfortable. Do not scratch, because if you do you may infect the scabs and leave scars all over your body.

Chicken pox is caused by a tiny germ, called a *virus,* that is so small it cannot even be seen under a microscope. If you have had chicken pox you will almost surely never get it again.

chicle, the chief ingredient of chewing gum: see GUM.

chicory

Chicory is a tall, coarse, straggly plant with bright blue flowers. It grows wild in North America, particularly along roadsides, but it is a native of Europe. There it is cultivated for the roots, which are roasted and ground and mixed in with coffee, or used as a substitute for coffee. The leaves, "blanched" by growing them in the dark, are delicious in salads. They are known as *French endive,* and the true endive is a close relative. Chicory is sometimes also cooked as a vegetable or herb.

chigger

The chigger is the larva, or young, of the redbug, or harvest mite, that is something like a red spider. When you go out in the woods they sometimes get on your clothes or body as you brush against bushes or when you sit on a log. They dig their way into the skin, and cause itching and red spots. When you scratch the spot that itches, they manage to stay there. As a rule they are more a nuisance than a danger, but they do sometimes cause infection. They usually go away by themselves in about a week. The best thing to do if you are going into the woods where there may be chiggers, is to use one of the insect repellants sold in drugstores or brush some sulfur on your ankles and clothing, especially below the waist.

Chihuahua

The Chihuahua is one of the smallest dogs in the world. It is a toy dog with a lively disposition and an alert, intelligent nature. The Chihuahua also has a trait that is unusual among dogs. It seems to like playing with other Chihuahuas better than with dogs of other breeds, and it actually seems to know the difference.

It is one of the oldest breeds of dog in the world, and many people believe that it has existed for over a thousand years. It is named for the state in Mexico from which it came. Hundreds of years ago, the Chihuahua is supposed to have been used in religious rites. When its master died it was often sacrificed and buried with him. Today, however, people in the United States and Mexico keep Chihuahuas as pets. There are two kinds: one has a short, smooth coat; the other has a long coat. The smooth-coated type is slightly smaller than the long-coated.

A Chihuahua stands about 8 to 10 inches high at the shoulder; the short-haired type weighs between one and six pounds, and the long-coated type weighs between two and eight pounds. The eyes of both are large and round, and the ears also are large. They too are round and stand up straight, widely spaced on the head. The tail is curved and its body is gracefully slender, with slim legs. It is a very swift runner. In color a Chihuahua may range anywhere from white to black, or may be a combination of colors.

Mike Smith, N.J.

The chihuahua makes a friendly house pet.

chilblain, an inflammation of the skin, usually of the hands, feet, or ears, caused by frostbite: see FROSTBITE.

child

If you are a child, it means that your body and mind are growing and changing. When you were born you weighed about 6 or 7 pounds, and were about 20 inches tall. You couldn't hold your head up, or tell anyone what you wanted, and your parents and other people had to do everything for you. It takes a long time to grow from the tiny helpless baby you once were into the strong and useful person you want to be when you are fully grown. You may think by the time you are 14 or 15 years old, and have learned so much, that you are already grown up. In many ways that is so, but your body is not through growing and there are still a lot of things for you to learn. The law says that until you are 21 years old, you are still a child. (In some places the law is different, and you become an adult at 18 years.) As long as you are a child,

there are some things you cannot do. You cannot vote or sign any legal papers, and your parents are responsible for you. That means that if you borrow money and do not pay it back, the law can make your parents pay it back for you. If you do something to break the law, your parents may be blamed for it.

PHYSICAL GROWTH

There are some periods in your life when your body grows very quickly. You do not remember when you were a baby, but if you watch a baby now, you can find out some things about what you were like when you were very young. During the first year of your life, you spent almost all of your time eating and sleeping, and maybe it looked as if you were just taking it easy, but you were really very busy growing. By the time you were a year old, you weighed almost three times as much as when you were born, and you had grown about ten inches taller. This is more growing than you will ever do in one year again. Of course, you did go on growing later, too, but a young child does not grow nearly as fast as a baby does. During the time when a boy or girl is changing into a man or woman, there is another very important growing period. This is called ADOLESCENCE, and you can read about it in a separate article. If you are a girl about 12 or 13 years old, you may feel funny, because many of the boys in your class at school are shorter than you are. This is nothing to worry about, though, because in another year or so, the boys will catch up, and before you know it, they will be taller than you are.

You probably do not remember much about it, but the first five years of your life were a very important growing and learning time. Everything you learned helped you to learn something else. You learned to sit up, and pretty soon you were crawling around on the floor and poking into everything, and by the time you were two years old, you could walk very well. You found out that spoons were good for something besides banging on tables, and, little by little, you began to feed yourself. You learned how to put on your clothes and button them, and to wash your face and brush your teeth. You began to have a good time cutting paper with scissors, and building big forts with blocks. You found out about your own body, and some of the wonderful things it could do. You could skip and jump and turn a somersault. All of these things were part of your physical growth.

MENTAL GROWTH

All the time your body was growing bigger and stronger, your mind was growing, too. You spent a lot of time watching your mother and other people, and you began to copy the things you saw them do. You listened to the sounds they made, and you imitated them. By the time you were two years old, you knew the names of quite a few things, such as "watch" and "cookie," and you knew that you were called "baby." When you were five, you could say about three thousand words and put them together to make sentences. You liked to play with other children, and you liked to sing songs and listen to stories. You knew the difference between stories you made up and what really happened, and you were pretty good at figuring out the best way to do a puzzle. You had already asked your mother and father so many questions that you were smart about a lot of things. Then when you were about five, you began to go to school, and maybe you can remember what a very big time that was for you. One of the most exciting things that happened in school was that you learned how to read. All of this is part of your mental growth.

CHILD TRAINING

You learned a lot of things by yourself, but some of the most important things your parents had to teach you. Your father and mother taught you how to feed yourself, and they carefully explained to you why you should not put everything you found on the floor into your mouth, or play with matches, or lean out of windows. They had to teach you how to go to the bathroom by yourself and help you learn not to wet your bed at night. All of these things that your parents taught you were part of your training.

Some parents try to teach these things to a child while he is too young to learn them. Now we know that this is wrong, and that when a child is ready to learn new things, he will want to learn them, and it will be much easier. Some people have thought a great deal about the best way to help children grow up, and there are a lot of books about it. Maybe your parents have read some of these books, though most parents do what they think is sensible, and things usually turn out all right that way.

CHILD GUIDANCE

Growing up is a lot of fun, but it is also hard work, and sometimes things happen that make you and your parents unhappy. Perhaps you do not like to go to school, or you cannot learn to read no matter how hard you try. Maybe you feel shy and do not like to play with other children very much. These things are called problems and a lot of children do have problems. Your parents may take you to a place where there are people who understand children very well and know how to help them with problems. These people are called psychiatrists, psychologists, and social workers, and the places where they work are called Child Guidance Clinics. Until about fifty years ago there were no places like this where you and your parents could go and get help with things that bother you. Now this is one of the ways that parents are able to help their children have an easier time growing up.

childbirth

Most children have wondered at some time how they happened to be born, and what goes on inside their mothers when a new baby brother or sister is coming.

Everyone who has ever lived on the earth came into the world through childbirth. Man is a mammal, which means an animal that bears living young, nursed by the mother. All mammals have to be "born," which is what makes them different from birds, because a bird is developed inside an egg shell, and is hatched outside its mother's body. Baby mammals are developed inside the mother's body, and are born when the development is complete.

First, there must be a mother and father. In the mother's body there is everything needed for the growth of the unborn baby, and everything that is needed for the birth of that baby when it is ready to come into the world. Without a father, however, the baby could not be conceived, which is the word for the beginning of a new baby's development. There must be a father as well as a mother, or there could never be any babies.

GROWTH IN THE MOTHER'S BODY

In your mother's body there is an organ called a *uterus*, in which you lived for nine months before you came into the world. Near the uterus also there are two other organs called *ovaries*, because they contain *ova*, or eggs. Each month one egg is mature, which means ready to leave the ovary so that it can start to develop into a new baby. The father has to fertilize the egg. If you could see this under a microscope, you would see a tiny, round object lying in the tube between the ovary and the uterus. This is the egg that has just left the ovary. Then you would see a much smaller object that looks like a tiny polliwog or tadpole. It wriggles and moves along until it reaches the egg and joins with it. At that moment, the life of a new baby has begun.

Whether you were to be a boy or a girl was decided right then and there. If there were any way to see, the doctor would have known at that instant whether your mother was going to have a boy or a girl baby, but no one actually knew until you were finally born.

About two months after you were conceived, you had already grown to about an inch in length. At this stage, you were an *embryo*. You weighed only about a thirtieth of an ounce, but you had a big head and a human face, with eyes, nose, and mouth. You had fingers and toes, elbows and knees, and your bones had started to form. Just one month later, you were more than three inches long, and weighed about an ounce. At three months, you were no longer called an embryo, but a fetus. At four months, you had grown to six and a half inches, and weighed nearly four ounces. By the time five months had passed, you were about ten inches long, and your weight had increased to eight ounces.

At the five-month stage, your mother could feel you starting to move inside her uterus, and the doctor could hear your heart beating with his stethoscope, which he placed on the outside of your mother's abdomen. By the time six months had passed, you looked just like a baby, but you were thin and wrinkled. You were about one foot long, and weighed about a pound and a half. By the end of seven months, you had grown a great deal, and were about fifteen and a half inches long, with a weight of perhaps two and a half pounds. You could have been born and lived at this stage, but you would have been very delicate, and would have needed very special care. You probably would have been placed in an incubator, which is a warm, comfortable place in which babies born early are placed. It is

made to be as much like the inside of the mother's uterus as possible. Usually a baby is not born until the end of nine months, when it is about twenty inches long, and usually weighs from seven to seven and a half pounds.

During the months while you were growing and developing inside your mother's uterus, you were enclosed in a small sac called the "bag of waters," and were surrounded and protected by a fluid that acted as a shock absorber against any bumps or jolts your mother might have received. Your mother took care of your nourishment by means of the foods she ate. In the wall of the uterus was a mass of tissue called the *placenta,* to which you were attached by means of your *umbilical cord.* This is a tube that leads from the placenta to the navel of an unborn baby, and through this tube the baby's blood enters its body from the placenta. It reaches the placenta through the blood vessels in the mother's uterus, and the baby's nourishment is carried from the mother's blood to the walls of the uterus, is there transferred to the placenta, and from the placenta goes to the baby. After a baby is born, the umbilical cord is tied. If it weren't, the baby would bleed to death. Soon afterward, the tiny fragment of cord dries up and drops off, as the navel closes.

Before you were born, you did not breathe. Your mother provided oxygen for you, through the placenta, just as she provided nourishment.

THE TIME OF BIRTH

When you had grown big and strong enough to breathe and eat for yourself, you were born. At the end of the uterus there is an opening called the *cervix* which had been tightly closed all during the time your mother was pregnant. When it was time for you to be born, the cervix opened, and the uterus started to contract. It is a large muscle, and it can contract and relax just like any other muscle. The opening of the cervix allows the baby to be pushed out of the uterus by those contractions. When your mother felt the contractions, she knew that you were being gently pushed forward into a special pathway waiting for you, called the *birth canal.* All the time your mother was pregnant, nature was getting the cervix and the birth canal ready for your birth.

When birth is taking place, nature provides the right kind of muscular contractions to carry the baby out into the world. This is called the baby's *delivery,* and the doctor sometimes has to help the mother at this point. Many women have their babies with no difficulty at all, however, and need no help in the delivery. If the mother finds it painful to have a baby, the doctor can give her something to keep her from having pain.

Immediately after the birth is completed, the uterus and birth canal start to return to their original condition. They shrink back to normal size, and the mother is the same as she was before she became pregnant.

While you were growing and developing in your mother's uterus, something else was happening to her body. Her breasts became larger and firmer, and they developed milk, so she could nurse

you. Most women have plenty of milk to feed their babies, but sometimes there is not quite enough, and then the baby is raised on a bottle, with a formula prescribed by the doctor. The formula is usually a combination of cow's milk with a little water and sugar added, and with some of the cream removed, to make it closer to the kind of milk the mother would have provided if she had been able to do so.

FROM TWINS TO QUINTUPLETS

Sometimes two ova are released at the same time by the ovaries, and both are fertilized. This is one way in which twins occur. In this case, they would be called *fraternal twins,* and they might be either two boys, two girls, or a boy and a girl. Another way in which twins occur is when the ovum splits, and each half becomes a separate embryo. These twins would be called *identical twins,* because they both came from the same ovum, and they would be either both boys or both girls, never mixed. The doctor can tell at birth whether the twins are identical or fraternal, because identical twins are both encased in the same sac, while fraternal twins have separate sacs. In the same way, triplets, quadruplets, or even the very rare quintuplets and sextuplets are born. The most famous quintuplets of all time, the Dionne quintuplets, born in Canada in 1934, were identicals (all girls); a single egg split five times.

Siamese twins, or *conjoined twins,* are twins who have grown together in the uterus. Sometimes they are joined by bones that have grown together; sometimes both together have only one important organ, such as the stomach. Twins of this kind are called "Siamese" because of two famous conjoined twin brothers named Chang and Eng, who were born in Siam (Thailand) in 1811. They were joined at the hips and had only one large intestine, which both used. They were never cut apart and lived to be 63. Attempts to cut Siamese twins apart has usually resulted in death for one or both.

CAESAREAN SECTION

There are certain cases in which a woman is unable to give birth to her baby in the natural way, because of some peculiar bone structure she happens to have. In such cases, the doctor will deliver the baby for her by what is called *Caesarean section.* This is the way many people believe the great Roman general, Julius Caesar, was born. The baby is removed from the mother's uterus by means of an operation. Many women have had two or three babies in this way.

child labor

When people talk about child labor, they mean the employment of children to do hard jobs in factories and mines and stores. They do not mean the work that children do in school or the chores they do at home, which are a normal part of the life of boys and girls. But it is not good for children to go to work when they are young. Working prevents children from getting the education and rest and exercise that they need.

At one time it was usual to hire children for all kinds of jobs. Little boys 9 and 10 years old went to work in coal mines, and children of all ages were hired

in factories. But after a while, people began to think this was wrong, and they began to work for laws that would forbid this. The first law against child labor was passed in England, about 150 years ago. Since then many other countries have passed laws like it.

There are different kinds of child labor laws, but they all aim to protect children against work that might harm them. Some laws say that no one under a certain age may work at certain jobs. Other laws limit the number of hours that children may work. In the United States there are many different child labor laws because every state makes its own laws. For certain industries, the laws are made by the national government. Some people want to amend (change) the Constitution so that Congress can make laws for all the children of the United States, but not enough states have agreed to pass this amendment. In most states children of certain ages may work only if they have special permits, called "working papers."

children's courts, law courts where children's cases are heard: see JUVENILE DELINQUENCY.

Chile

Chile is a South American republic that extends north and south along the west coast of the continent. It lies between the Pacific Ocean and the Andes Mountains, which cut it off from its neighbors, Peru, Bolivia, and Argentina. From tip to tip Chile is about 2,600 miles long, but in most places it is only about 100 miles wide. It looks like a big string bean on the map.

Chile owns several islands in the Pacific, including the two Juan Fernandez Islands, four hundred miles to the west, and mysterious Easter Island, more than two thousand miles westward. There is a special article about EASTER ISLAND and its strange stone carvings.

A mountainous country, Chile is very rich in minerals, particularly copper. Its farms produce many kinds of food and other crops. But its factories cannot yet produce all the things its people need, and Chileans must buy automobiles, machinery, and other manufactured goods from other countries.

During the last fifty years, Chile has been on good terms with its neighbors and with the United States. In World War II Chile broke off relations with Germany, Italy, and Japan, and declared war on Japan in 1945.

THE PEOPLE OF CHILE

Almost all Chileans are of European or part-European origin. Like most other Latin American countries, Chile was once a colony of Spain, and Spanish is the national language. Many natives of Chile dwell in the rugged mountain regions, where much of the mineral wealth of the country is to be found. Some native Chileans are of mixed blood, though pure-blooded Indians are not uncommon.

The earliest inhabitants of what is now Chile were the Araucanian or Mapuches Indians. They were a fierce and warlike tribe who resisted the influence of both

the Inca civilization and the Spanish colonists, and were only brought to terms in the late 19th century. There are about 130,000 of them left, mostly in the south. Further south, on the islands of the Tierra del Fuego (Land of Fire) region, live a certain number of Fuegian Indians. The people of Easter Island (there are only about 1,100 of them) are Polynesians belonging to the same racial group as the inhabitants of most South Pacific islands.

The majority of Chileans are Roman Catholics, although some, chiefly descendants of English and German settlers, are Protestants. In the wild parts of the Andes, far from the cities, Indians are being taught modern ways of living, working and worship.

HOW THE PEOPLE LIVE

Most of the people of Chile depend for their living on minerals, which make up three-quarters of all the goods they send abroad for sale, or on the products of the farm. In the dry northern part of the country is the nitrate region. Chilean nitrates are an important product of the country, for domestic and foreign trade. Nitrates are natural salts that have many uses in industry. One of the principal by-products in the manufacture of nitrates is iodine, the dark red liquid used in treating cuts. Chileans produce about seventy per cent of the world supply of iodine.

Thousands of Chileans work in mines, digging copper and iron ore from the rocky earth. The copper deposits of Chile are among the richest in the world, and the country produces more of the metal than any other country except the United States. South of the city of Valparaiso, other Chilean miners dig for coal. Among the other minerals mined in Chile are gold and silver, zinc, manganese, and mercury. Workers with pick axes chip away in quarries for the shiny mica, for marble, and for onyx, a precious stone much used in the making of jewelry.

Farming is particularly important in the central region of Chile, which has a climate like that of Italy or California, and whose soil brings forth the same crops. Whole families, including the children, work in the vineyards picking the grapes from which fine Chilean wines are made. On large and small plantations other Chilean farmers raise oranges and lemons, olives, figs, and melons. From Chilean farms come large amounts of apples, peaches, plums, apricots, and other fruits. As in most countries of Latin America, the farmers of Chile grow wheat, which they make into bread, and corn, which they eat themselves and feed to their cattle.

Chile has many cows. On dairy farms, some of them high up on the slopes of the Andes, cows give milk and cream to be made into butter and cheese. On the plains of southern Chile cattle are raised for meat. Cowboys called *huasos* ride herd over the cattle as they do across the Andes in Argentina. Huasos and their families live out-of-doors most of the year. They are a rugged and hardy group.

Besides beef cattle, sheep are also raised in Chile. Their meat makes very good eating. Wool from the sheep's coat is one of the most important products that Chile sells abroad. Chileans send most of the goods they sell to other countries by ship from Valparaiso, the biggest and most important port on the whole Pacific coast south of San Francisco.

Although they were founded four hundred years ago, Valparaiso and the capital city of Santiago, which has more than 2,500,000 people, both look quite modern. Each has many fine buildings, parks, and squares. The people look just like Americans except that a large number of them have Indian features in their faces. In the southern part of Chile, however, you might see actual Indians dressed in their traditional costumes, with gaily colored blankets wrapped around their shoulders. They would probably be in town to trade at the market.

WHAT KIND OF PLACE IT IS

The chief feature of Chile is the Andes mountain range which forms its land border. In some places the mountains come down almost to the sea. The Chilean Andes include several very high peaks, among them Mounts Tupungato, Tocorpuri, Llullaillaco, all more than 20,000 feet high, and half a dozen others that are taller than any mountain in North America. For the most part these are dead volcanoes whose tops are covered with snow all year round.

A great number of rivers cross Chile from east to west, running down from sources in the high mountains to the ocean. In the famous lake district of the south there are many beautiful lakes, including lakes Villarrica, Ranco, and Llanquihue. A few of the volcanoes in this area are still active. From time to time disastrous earthquakes have shaken Chile, destroying towns and killing many people.

THE CLIMATE

The greater part of Chile's coastline is straight, but south of the port of Puerto Montt it breaks up into a great number of small islands, ending in the big island of Tierra del Fuego at the southern tip of South America. Punta Arenas, on Tierra del Fuego near Cape Horn, lies farther south than any other city in the world.

From north to south, Chile is divided by climate into three main regions. In the deserts and barren mountains of the north, there is little rain; in some places it rains no more than once in ten years. The fertile central valley, where nine out of ten Chileans live, has a good balance of rain and sunshine; the summers are warm and the winters are moderate. In the south, far from the equator, the winters are colder and there is more rain.

HOW THE PEOPLE ARE GOVERNED

Chile has a form of government much like our own. The president is elected every six years. Laws are made by the senators, who serve for eight years, and the deputies, who serve for four. Until recently women could vote only in elections for city officials, but now all citizens over 21 can vote in all elections—city, provincial, and national. The island colonies are governed by officials appointed by the Chilean government.

Chile has a small army and air force. Its navy is quite large for so small a country, because it has such a long coastline to defend.

CHILE IN THE PAST

The territory that is now Chile was first entered in 1536 by an aide of the Spanish explorer Pizarro. Pedro de Valdivia founded Santiago in 1541 and went on to found several more towns, including Chile's second- and third-largest cities, Valparaiso and Concepción.

The Spanish colonists, failing to find the gold and silver they sought, set up a farming and cattle-raising way of life in Chile. Indians were enslaved as workers. The unprotected coast was frequently raided by pirates sailing under the Dutch and English flags.

Like the rest of South America, Chile was swept by the spirit of independence in the early 19th century when Spain was invaded by Napoleon. Liberty was finally won in 1818. Among the three men whom Chileans revere as the founders of their country, two were Irishmen, named O'Higgins and Cochrane, and the third was Juan Martinez de Rosas. During the 19th century Chile fought wars with Bolivia and Peru over boundaries. In 1929 Chile peacefully returned to Peru a piece of territory it had taken in a war fifty years before, and since then its borders have remained the same.

CHILE. Area, 286,396 square miles. Population (1973 estimate) 9,780,000. Capital, Santiago. Language, Spanish. Religion, chiefly Roman Catholic. Government, federal republic. Monetary unit, escudo, worth about 7½ cents (U.S.). Flag, red and white horizontal bars with a white star in a blue canton.

Chillon

Chillon is the name of a famous castle at the eastern end of the Lake of Geneva, at Montreux, Switzerland. It is built on a rock by the edge of the lake and is entirely surrounded by water. The only entrance, except by boat, is across a drawbridge. François de Bonnivard, a church official and patriot, was kept prisoner in the castle for many years, because of his religious beliefs. Byron wrote a famous poem about Bonnivard called *The Prisoner of Chillon*. The castle is very picturesque and is now used as a museum.

chimes, a set of musically tuned bells: see BELLS.

chimney

A chimney is the passage, called a *flue*, that carries away the smoke and gas from a fire burning inside a house or factory to the outside air. Ancient people had no chimneys. They seldom built fires in their houses but warmed their rooms with live coals. These coals were brought in a pan or small stove that was easily carried in and out of the house. During the Middle Ages and until a few hundred years ago only rich people could afford to build chimneys in their houses. A hole was made in the roof of most houses to carry the smoke away. When people began to live in large houses and in cities they needed to have chimneys in order to carry the smoke above the tops of the houses. House chimneys in cities sometimes do not work well because the higher buildings near them turn the wind and make it blow back down the flue. People can often make such a chimney work. They put a revolving bent pipe on the

top of the chimney that will turn its mouth away from where the wind is blowing. Chimneys also have to be kept clean inside in order to work well. There is a very famous essay by the English writer Charles Lamb about chimney sweeps. A chimney sweep was a young boy or man who kept house chimneys clean by going into them and sweeping out all the soot that had fallen into the cracks and holes of the flue.

The reason why smoke goes up a chimney is that the smoke is warmer than air outside and warm air always rises. If a chimney is too wide or too high the heat may be used up before the air and smoke get to the top. Then the smoke will come back into the room where the fire is. Certain factories that burn poisonous chemicals have to build chimneys hundreds of feet high so that the gas and smoke will not poison the air close to the ground.

chimpanzee

The chimpanzee is a member of the ape family, which are the animals that look most like human beings. A chimpanzee is not nearly as big as a gorilla, which is the largest of the apes, though a big chimpanzee can be as big as a medium-sized man. Usually a chimpanzee is between 4 and 5 feet high. Chimpanzees are more intelligent than most animals, and can be taught to do things that human beings do: eat with a knife and fork; dress and undress themselves; ride bicycles, and skate; smoke pipes; and many other things. At home in Africa, the chimpanzee spends much of its time in trees, but will frequently come down to the ground and walk around (usually on all fours). When a chimpanzee walks on its hind legs, its arms hang down below the knee.

The chimpanzees live in families— one male with several females. The male will fight to keep single males from breaking up his group. Chimpanzees feed mostly on fruits and vegetables, and banana growers have to post guards to keep them off the crops when the fruit is ripe. Chimpanzees build leafy shelters in trees to sleep in at night. They have a well developed sense of rhythm, and enjoy drumming on logs and performing a kind of stomping dance. This primitive "music" is accompanied by shrieks and howls. Female chimpanzees have one baby at a time, once a year. Chimpanzees are timid, and will run away from men. After seven or eight years in captivity, the chimpanzee becomes dangerous and bad-tempered.

See also the article APE.

China

China, in the eastern part of Asia, is the third largest country in the world in area. (The Soviet Union is first, Canada second.) In population, however, it is much bigger than any other country, with perhaps as many as 850 million people living there—more than four times as many people as live in the United States.

China's Communist government came into power in 1949. They call their country the People's Republic of China, and refuse to admit the existence of the National government on TAIWAN. They think of Taiwan as part of China that is not yet "liberated."

China is divided into 22 provinces (including Taiwan)and the five autonomous(self-governing)regions of Tibet, Inner Mongolia, Sinkiang-Uigar, Kwangsi Chuang, and Ninghsia-Hui. The provinces and regions are divided into *districts*, which are subdivided into *cantons*.

THE PEOPLE WHO LIVE THERE

The people of China, like many other people of Asia, belong to the Mongoloid race. About 94 per cent of the population belong to the *Han* nation, which they consider to be the "true" Chinese, descended from the original inhabitants of the Middle Kingdom, as they called their country about 3,000 years ago. Under the rule of the Han dynasty, roughly 2,000 years ago, a great
civilization arose, comparable to that of the Roman Empire. The name "China" was used by travelers and scholars from India and Persia, and seems to be derived from the name of the Ch'in Empire, which preceded the Han Empire. There are about fifty minority nationalities living in china, including Mongols, Manchu, Tibetans, and many mixed groups. These minority nationalities are not Chinese, although they all belong to the Mongoloid race and have typically straight, black hair, and other characteristics in varying degrees, such as prominent cheekbones, broad faces, dark eyes, and skin color ranging from pale yellowish or ivory to bronze, like the American Indian.

Since more than two-thirds of the country cannot be cultivated, the vast majority of people live in the southeastern part of China where conditions are very crowded, with over 4,000 people per square mile. In the western and northern regions there may be only about two people per square mile. The government of China has been gradually increasing the amount of farmland and has moved many thousands of families further inland, but this has not helped very much.

HOW THE PEOPLE LIVE

About eight out of ten Chinese are farmers who are engaged in the production of food for China's huge population. This means that about 500,000,000 people are working on the 15% of land that is available at the present time. They have worked out efficient methods of making the best use of the land, and have developed a system of communes. Each peasant has a plot of land for his own use, as well as a small house. There is not enough farm machinery to go around, so much labor is done by hand, or with the help of farm animals such as the water buffalo, just as in centuries past. In the north of China, where it is dry, the farmers raise wheat, barley, and other grains; in the south, where it is wet, they raise rice, sugar, cotton, and silkworms. They produce more than 30 million pounds of raw silk per year.

Most of the Chinese workers, both men and women, wear simple and comfortable garments consisting of trousers, a shirt and jacket, or a short straight blouse. Even the children wear this kind of an outfit. In the cities most people have adopted western style clothing. Farmers in the field wear wide straw hats to protect against the sun.

Chinese meals are usually quite simple, but they are well balanced and include many fresh vegetables. Meat is usually a luxury. The national drink is tea. Very few Chinese are fat. The Chinese have made an art of cooking for thousands of years, much longer than any other people. The Chinese eat their food with *chopsticks,* two thin sticks of wood about a foot long. They hold the chopsticks with their thumbs and fingers and pick up pieces of food with them, as we do with forks. They do not use knives at the table, so their food is always cut into small pieces before being served. Fowl, fish, and pork are eaten more than beef.

China is just beginning to develop modern industry and the natural resources of the country. There is a great deal of coal in China, as well as tin, salt, oil, and iron ore. One of the things that has kept China from developing her industries is poor transportation. Village people often spend their whole lives in the village where they were born. The roads have never been very good, and up to very recently the railroads covered only a small part of the country. Both the railroads and the roads are now being improved, but it will take some time before China's transportation system is completely modern.

The Chinese people have been good merchants for thousands of years. Some of the world's biggest trading companies are in Chinese cities. Many Chinese have become successful merchants in other countries, such as the Hawaiian Islands, Burma and other places in Asia, the eastern and southern parts of Africa, and the United States and Latin American countries.

There are many large cities in China. Shanghai has almost eleven million people. Peking, the capital, has more than seven million. The cities are much more modern than the farming villages. Shanghai has tall buildings very much like those we see in our American cities. There are motion-picture theaters and restaurants. But the poor Chinese in the cities live in very crowded quarters and health and sanitation conditions have in the past been very bad. However, in recent years there has been great improvement. There are automobiles and buses in the cities, but many people travel on bicycles. The old-fashioned *jinrickshas* (little passenger-carts pulled by men on foot) were banned in 1959 and replaced by a similar cart driven by a man pedaling what looks like a very large tricycle with passenger seats.

China is trying hard to become more modern. All Chinese children have to go to school. Many doctors, engineers and other scientists are being trained in the colleges and universities. One of the important things these men and women can do is to help the people understand mod-

365

ern ways of living.

WHAT KIND OF PLACE IT IS

China is a very rolling country, with many mountains and valleys. There are three great rivers in China, which rise from the mountains in the west and flow across the southern part of the country to empty into the Pacific Ocean. These rivers are the Hwang Ho ("Yellow") River, the Yangtze, and the Si-Kiang. The whole western section of the country is very mountainous. There are many high peaks that are covered with snow

all year round. One mountain range cuts across China from the far west to about seven hundred miles from the east coast. This mountain range is called the Tsingling. The northeastern part of the country is very mountainous, too, and for that reason not many people live there. Most of the people of China live south of the Great Wall, which was built nearly two thousand years ago to keep out invaders from the west. The section south of the Great Wall is called China Proper, and it is only one-third of the whole country.

The mountains and rivers of China have a great deal to do with the country's weather. The Tsingling mountains cut the north off from the south, and keep the damp air and rain from the south from coming across into the north. This is one of the reasons that the south is the section for crops like rice, which have to be grown in fields flooded with water, while the north is the section for wheat, which takes less moisture to grow.

In the north the winters are clear and cold; in the south they are chilly and wet. In the summer the weather is hot in both the north and the south, but the north is dry while the south is rainy.

HOW CHINA IS GOVERNED

In 1949 a Communist government came into power on the mainland, where nearly all the Chinese people live. When this happened, the Chinese people lost most of their personal freedom. Like other Communist countries, China became a dictatorship (under Mao Tse-tung, the head of the Communist armies, with Chou En-lai as the second most important leader). The previous government, under CHIANG KAI-SHEK (about whom there is a separate article) held on to the island of Taiwan (in the U.S., often called Formosa). The United States at first refused to recognize the new Communist government, and the Nationalist government of Chiang remained as the Chinese member of the United Nations, but the Communist government was recognized as official by Soviet Russia and other Communist

countries as well as some non-Communist countries.

The Communist government of China at once seized all property of Christian and other churches, and the estates of big land-owners. They took away the people's freedom of speech and right to move from one place to another or to change jobs. Every part of the country is ruled by members of the Communist Party, and the people merely follow whatever orders their rulers give them.

Confucianism, Buddhism, and Taoism have been religions in China for many hundreds of years, but now all religion is very much discouraged, and in 1974 the teaching of Confucianism was actually forbidden, except in Taiwan. (There is a separate article on CONFUCIUS.) There are nearly three million Christians in China, and about 2½% of the people are Moslems.

Every Chinese man must serve in the military forces. In 1976 there were over two and a half million men in the Chinese Communist army.

CHINA IN THE PAST

China has a history that goes back for more than four thousand years. The Western world knew practically nothing about China less than five hundred years ago, but China had a high civilization when the countries of western Europe were still overrun by barbarians. China had strong kings, and was the most powerful country in the east.

A great Chinese thinker, Confucius, lived about five hundred years before Jesus. His teachings are still well-known, and are the basis for many of the ideas of the Chinese people, but they are no longer allowed to read his writings.

The Chinese invented gunpowder more than two thousand years ago, and were the first to invent printing. The Chinese knew how to print from wooden blocks almost 1,200 years ago, which is hundreds of years before the people of Europe knew anything at all about this art.

During all this time, China had nothing to do with the Western world. She was busy building her own civilization. Chinese poets and painters produced beautiful works of art. Chinese emperors tried to strengthen their country and expand its borders. The Chinese dynasties (a *dynasty* is a family of rulers) were very powerful and strong. There were many dynasties in Chinese history, from the earliest period up to 1911, when China finally became a republic. Some of these dynasties ruled for hundreds of years. The Ming dynasty, which ruled from 1368 to 1644, was the dynasty that was in power when the West finally learned about China.

At about the time that Columbus discovered America, there was a great period of exploration and discovery on the part of all the countries of Europe. European ships sailed all over the world, looking for new trade routes. The first western country to reach China by sea was Portugal. A Portuguese ship arrived in China in about 1550. Then the way was opened for many other western nations. From that time until the end of World War II, China was never free of foreign invaders. Some came to make war and some to trade.

About a hundred years ago, the European powers had become so strong in China that they controlled many Chinese cities. The Chinese government, which was in the hands of the Manchu dynasty, was not strong enough to control the European nations and keep them out, but it was strong enough to be very strict with the Chinese people. The people were very dissatisfied during this period. They did not like the idea of having foreigners owning their land and running their cities. England, France, Germany, and Russia all controlled cities in China, and some nations of the West were keeping troops in China.

In 1850, the first great revolt against the government and the foreigners broke out. This revolt was not successful, but it led the way to other revolts, and finally to the Chinese revolution. In 1900, there was another great revolt. This was called the BOXER REBELLION, about which you can read in a separate article. It failed too. But soon after the Boxer Rebellion, Sun Yat-sen, the great Chinese patriot, started a movement to turn China into a republic.

In 1911 the Chinese Revolution took place, and a republic was set up in China. But the country's troubles were far from over. There were many disagreements among members of the government as to exactly what policies should be followed and exactly how China should be governed. These disagreements helped to keep China a weak and poor nation. First she had been troubled by the foreigners, and then her own government was so busy quarreling that very little was done to help the people. China was so busy with wars and internal disagreements that she did not even have a chance to build up her industries and her farming.

China was one of the Allies during World War I, and after the war was over, some of the European countries that had occupied Chinese cities were forced to give them up. Even though this was something the Chinese had wanted for a long time, their trouble continued. A revolution was begun by Sun Yat-sen and accomplished by Chiang Kai-Shek in 1928. After that, China was governed by the National government of the Republic of China, with Chiang as its head. However, troubles developed between the National government and the Communists. Civil war started again.

Then, in 1931, the Japanese invaded Manchuria, which was one of the provinces of China. From that time until the end of World War II, the Japanese were at war with China. The Communists pledged themselves to support the National government in order to fight together against the Japanese invasion, but their promise was not completely carried out. Japan had a stronger and better equipped army than China, and got control of practically every important Chinese city. But the Chinese people did not give up. After World War II began, China continued to fight, with assistance from the United States, and shared in the Allied victory. When World War II was over, Japan was forced to give up all its territory in China.

Then there was civil war in China. Communist forces helped by the Soviet

Union fought the Chinese National Party (Kuo-min-tang) headed by Chiang Kai-shek and defeated it. Fighting went on from 1946 into 1950. Mao Tse-tung was the leader of the Chinese Communists and became dictator of the country after the war was won. Chiang and his army fled to the large island of Taiwan, or Formosa, and also held a few small islands off the shore of China, but the Communists controlled all of the mainland. During the Korean War (see KOREA) the Communist government of China fought against United Nations forces, including the Americans.

After 1960, Communist China became less friendly toward the Soviet Union which was beginning to get friendlier to the United States than it had been in many years.

In 1971, the United Nations voted to exclude Nationalist China as a member and to include, instead, Communist China.

In 1973, President Nixon met Mao Tse-tung in Peking to start normalizing relations between America and Communist China.

CHINA (People's Republic of China). Area, 3,759,181 square miles. Population (1976 estimate) 850,000,000. Capital, Peking. Government, republic (Communist dictatorship). Language, Chinese (Mandarin in the north, Cantonese dialects in the south). Religions (discouraged), Confucianism, Taoism, Buddhism. Monetary unit, the yuan, worth about 45 cents (U.S.)

REPUBLIC OF CHINA (Taiwan). Area 13,905 square miles. Population 1976 census) 16,000,-000. Capital, TAIPEI. Government, republic. Monetary unit, New Taiwan dollar, worth 2½ cents (U.S.).

China Sea

The China Sea is part of the North Pacific Ocean. The larger part, called the South China Sea, has about 1,000,000 square miles. It runs as far south as Borneo, and as far north as the island of Formosa, and it lies between the China mainland and the Philippine Islands. Through the Formosa Strait, it opens into the East China Sea, of about 500,000 square miles, which runs as far north as Korea.

Many large rivers of east Asia flow into the China Sea. There are many large bays in the China Sea, and some important port cities are on these bays. Canton and Hongkong, for instance, are on the China Sea. Manila, in the Philippine Islands, is on Manila Bay, which is part of the China Sea.

chinaware

The name *chinaware* is given to fine dishes and ornaments. Long ago the finest kinds of pottery were made in China. The article POTTERY tells about porcelain, china, and bone china. The word *china* is used also for all kinds of tableware.

Chinaware can be very thin, and look almost transparent, yet be very strong. This is because it is made from a fine clay, KAOLIN, about which there is a separate article. Kaolin was first found in China nearly 2,500 years ago. European potters did not find out about it until about 250 years ago, though it was available in their own countries. The best kaolin deposits of some countries have been almost used up. The finest kaolin today is found in the United States.

Fine chinaware is often known by the name of the place where it is made. *Limoges* and *Sèvres* are French chinaware made in the towns of Limoges and Sèvres. *Cologne, Dresden* and *Meissen* are German chinaware named after towns. *Delftware,* which is particularly known for its lovely blue and white coloring, is made in Holland. There are also many fine English chinas—*Wedgwood, Spode, Royal Doulton, Chelsea,* and others.

American chinaware is among the best, and most expensive, in the world. Some of the finer chinawares made in the United States are Lenox, Syracuse, Castleton, and Franciscan.

Many dishes of good quality are called "china" but are not really porcelain. Experts call them "earthenware," or "dinnerware"

chinch bug

Every year this small insect destroys great quantities of corn, wheat, grasses, and other grain in the central United States, in the valleys of the Mississippi, Ohio, and Missouri Rivers. Another form, the *hairy chinch bug,* is a lawn pest in New England. Both feed on sap, and pass the winters in sheltered places. Two generations are born each year, and when they have destroyed one field, they walk on in thousands to the next. They are trapped by digging deep trenches or painting creosote bands on the ground in their path. The adult chinch bug is quite a pretty insect: it has a black body about one-fifth of an inch long, red legs, and black and white wings. It belongs to the group of insects called *Hemiptera,* or true bugs.

chinchilla

Chinchillas are small animals that look rather like rats. They have long hind legs on which they jump about like miniature kangaroos. They live wild among the rocks high in the Andes Mountains in Peru and Chile. They have lovely soft silvery gray fur, from which some of the world's most expensive fur coats are made. Even before Columbus, the fur was worn by the Inca kings. So many chinchillas were killed by fur trappers that they almost disappeared entirely, but now they are protected by law. Nowadays there is less need to hunt them, for they are specially bred on farms in North and South America.

Chinese language

The Chinese language, or the *Han* language, is spoken by 90 per cent of the Chinese people. More people live in China than in any other country—about 850,000,000—more than four times as many as live in the United States—and all over that vast country the people use about the same words, but they do not all pronounce them the same way, so a person from North China sometimes cannot understand what a person from South China is saying. They can still hold a conversation by writing the words, and sometimes they do this by drawing a picture of the writing in the air, with their fingers.

There are many words in the Chinese language, because the Chinese people have been scholars and scientists long-er than any other people. The official "common speech," called *Puthonghua,* is based on the scholarly and widely used *Mandarin* dialect of North China. The writing system is the same throughout the country, but it has been greatly simplified. In addition, in 1958 a 26-letter Roman alphabet was introduced, making it even easier for many more people to learn to read and write.

CHINESE PRONUNCIATION

The Chinese language is different from the English language, and from other languages spoken in Europe and America, chiefly in the way they accent their words. We use what is called *stress* accent. We pronounce some syllables or words louder than others. In the word *entrance,* meaning a doorway, we stress the first syllable, and in the word *entrance,* meaning to charm, we stress the second syllable, and we have no difficulty telling the words apart. The Chinese use what is called *pitch* accent. They pronounce words in different tones, as though they were singing them. The same word in Chinese means room, stone, eat, lion, and scholar, but each one is said in a different tone. It is hard for an American or European to learn Chinese because he is not trained to listen for different tones, but of course it is not hard for the Chinese.

CHINESE WRITING

The Chinese use "picture writing." We use letters to stand for sounds, and they use letters to stand for whole words. This difference is explained in the article on ALPHABET. Many of the symbols that the Chinese use in writing do not look like pictures to us, but some of them we can recognize. The word for man looks somewhat like a man, and so does the word for tree, or sun. In the Chinese character for the word meaning "peace" you can see, if you look closely, a picture of a woman under a roof, that is, in a home. In the Chinese character for the word meaning "friendship," you can see two hands clasped.

Chinese writing begins at the right-hand side of the page, instead of at the left as in our books, and it runs up and down from top to bottom of the page and from right to left, instead of running across the page as our writing does.

Not nearly so many Chinese as Americans can read and write, because it takes so many years to learn the written Chinese language. We have only twenty-six letters in our alphabet. They have several thousand word-symbols in theirs. Now that the simpler Roman alphabet is being taught in schools, many more people than ever before are acquiring a good education.

Chinook

The Chinook Indians were famous fur traders and fishermen of the Columbia River region in the Pacific Northwest. From their language came the "Chinook jargon," a trade language understood by all Indian tribes along the Pacific Coast. The Chinook settlement began at the mouth of the Columbia River and continued for fifteen miles along its north shore. The Chinooks were very skillful at handling canoes. Usually several families lived together in large wooden

houses, and they kept slaves. The Chinook had the custom of head-flattening. Babies were carried on boards swung over the mother's back, and the child's head grew flat because it was tied so tightly against the board. The chief foods of the Chinook were salmon, roots, and berries. In the early 19th century, the tribe suffered terrible epidemics of measles and scarlet fever. These were brought by the white man, who also taught the Indians to drink liquor. Disease and drink destroyed most of the tribe. The rest were forced off their hunting and fishing grounds and sent to United States government reservations. Today, almost no Chinooks are left.

The name of *chinook* is given to the Columbia River salmon, the commonest and most valuable salmon of the Pacific coast. The *chinook winds* are warm currents that blow over the northwest United States and British Columbia. One chinook wind is wet, one is dry, and one is a mixture. These winds melt snows rapidly, and make the weather like spring. They are felt as far east as Alberta, Canada, and the state of Montana.

chipmunk

Chipmunks are animals like small squirrels, but they live in the ground. There are several kinds found in the northern United States, Canada, and east Asia. The common kind is reddish or grayish brown, with black and white stripes down its back. It has a long flat bushy tail, and is about ten inches long. Chipmunks are very pretty, lively little creatures and are very easily tamed. They eat seeds, nuts, berries, insects and grubs, which they carry about inside their large pouchlike cheeks. When winter comes they store food in the underground burrows in which they live. The entrances to their burrows are usually well hidden. They stay underground from about November, sleeping through the coldest months, and come out again in the spring.

Chippendale, Thomas

Thomas Chippendale was a famous English furniture designer and cabinet-maker who lived about two hundred years ago. Mr. Chippendale lived right next to his factory, and he worked and made pictures of his new designs there all his life. Some of the new ideas he had for making beds, chairs, tables, mirrors, bookcases, washstands, china closets and lots of other things, were so unusual and beautiful that he published a book of furniture designs called *The Gentleman and Cabinet Maker's Director*. You can recognize a Chippendale sofa or chair by the legs, which are shaped in quite fancy curves and are finely carved. A Chippendale china closet very often has diamond-shaped pieces of glass on the doors. Thomas Chippendale designed chair backs which looked like graceful ladders. Furniture designers today still use many of Thomas Chippendale's ideas about how furniture should look.

Chippewa

The Chippewa or *Ojibwa* were the largest and most important tribe of the Algonquin family, which lived in the northern United States. They are famous because many white men became ac-quainted with them and learned about their way of life. The Chippewa had wonderful storytellers and medicine men, or magician-doctors, as well as wise and cunning chiefs. Their customs and beliefs were used in Longfellow's *Hiawatha*, even though the name Hiawatha is Iroquois. In the 18th century, the Chippewa covered almost one thousand miles in the Great Lakes region of the United States and in southern Canada. They were timber people. They hunted caribou, moose, deer and beaver, and they fished. They gathered wild rice from shallow lakes, and also made maple sugar. Their wigwams were made of birch bark or grass mats. The Chippewa wore leather clothes except in the winter, when they wore furs and traveled on snowshoes or on toboggans. The Chippewa rarely fought the white men because few settlers came to their country. They now live on reservations, but have not been removed from their original territory.

chipping sparrow

The chipping sparrow is a bird which is very common in all parts of North America east of the great plains and south of Labrador. It is a small bird, chiefly brown and gray in a streaky pattern, with a reddish-brown cap and a white or blue-gray breast. It spends the winter in the South, coming North early in the spring and building its nest in tangled bushes. The nest is very neat, and almost always lined with horsehair. It contains four or five blue, brown-speckled eggs. The chipping sparrow may have three broods in a single spring. It feeds its young on quantities of caterpillars and harmful insects, and eats the seeds of weeds, so it is very beneficial to man. It gets its name from its pretty trilling song.

chiropody

A chiropodist treats many of the troubles that make people's feet hurt. His work is called chiropody.

Many of the foot troubles treated by chiropody are caused by wearing shoes that do not fit properly. These and other ailments are explained in the article on the FOOT. The chiropodist is trained to cut away the hard spots called corns and calluses, to cut out ingrown toenails, to treat the feet with medicines that relieve rashes of the skin and diseases such as athlete's foot, and to care for the feet in many ways. In most parts of the United States a person must be a high-school graduate and then must go to a school of chiropody for at least four years before he can be licensed to practice chiropody. A chiropodist has the title "doctor" but usually does not have an M.D. degree (doctor of medicine). *Podiatry* is another word for the scientific treatment of ailments of the feet.

chiropractic

Chiropractic is a special kind of treatment for diseases and pains. A person who is trained to practice chiropractic is called a chiropractor.

Chiropractic was introduced more than fifty years ago by a Canadian named D. D. Palmer. His belief was that diseases result when the little bones of the spine, or backbone, get out of place. Many nerves pass between these small bones, and when the bones are out of place they press against the nerves. Chiropractors do not give medicines as physicians do. They use their hands to push the bones of the spine back into place. They also work on bones in other parts of the body. Dr. Palmer set up a school in Davenport, Iowa, which is still the world headquarters of chiropractic. His son, B. J. Palmer, carried on the school after him. To become a chiropractor, a person must have been graduated from high school and then must take a four-year chiropractic course. Many people believe in chiropractic, though most medical doctors are against it.

Chisholm Trail

We often hear the cowboy folk song, "The Old Chisholm Trail." There is a real Chisholm Trail that goes from San Antonio, Texas, to Abilene, Kansas, where the railway ended 125 years ago. Below Abilene there was no railway, and not even any roads. Oklahoma was Indian territory, and the Texas ranchers had a hard time getting their cattle to market. Then Jesse Chisholm drove his trading wagon over the trail, and the wheels left marks in the grass and ruts in the earth to mark the way. Jesse's father was a Scotsman and his mother was a Cherokee Indian. He was born in Tennessee and never was a cattleman or cowboy, but his trail showed that it was possible to drive the great herds of Texas longhorn cattle to market, on the hoof, all the way up from the Rio Grande.

chivalry

Chivalry was a set of rules and customs that knights were supposed to follow hundreds of years ago. Knights were the principal fighting men of Europe. They fought on horseback, and their rules of behavior are called chivalry because the French word *cheval* means "horse." Knights were members of noble or important families.

The code of chivalry required a knight to be fair in fighting and to show mercy to a defeated knight. At all times a knight had to be religious and to dedicate all his warlike actions by prayer. He had to obey the nobleman to whom he owed allegiance, and to serve him with all the spirit and bravery that he possessed. Chivalry required a knight to be polite and gracious to the lady he loved and to fight bravely in her defense. A knight had to be gallant and well-mannered toward all noble-women, and he had to be ready to rescue any lady in distress.

There are famous stories of chivalry. Sir Walter Raleigh, an English knight who lived more than four hundred years ago, once spread his cloak over a mud puddle so that Queen Elizabeth of England would not get her shoes muddy.

There is another story of chivalry told in "The Glove and the Lion," by the English poet Leigh Hunt. Robert Browning, another English poet, told the same story in the poem called "The Glove." Both these poems tell how a knight and his lady were watching lions battle in an arena. The lady, to test the knight's chivalry and his love for her, threw her glove into the pit where the lions were

fighting. Without hesitation the knight jumped into the pit and retrieved the glove. He climbed back to his seat and then instead of handing the glove to his lady he slapped her face with it. The king, sitting nearby approved of the knight's action. The knight had shown his chivalry by braving death to retrieve the glove, but the lady deserved the slap for making him risk his life. Today most of our manners are based on the early code of chivalry.

chive

Chives are small onionlike plants whose thin tubelike leaves are used for seasoning in salads, stews, omelettes, and other dishes. Sometimes they are planted in borders for their pretty, pale purple flowers, which grow in a ball-shaped mass at the tip of a long stalk. Chives grow wild in Europe and Asia, and are grown in nearly all of the United States.

chlorine

Chlorine is one of the most important chemical elements that people use. It is a yellowish green gas that has an unpleasant, suffocating odor. It was discovered by the famous Swedish chemist Karl Wilhelm Scheele about 175 years ago. All people and animals need some chlorine in their bodies. The ordinary table salt you use to flavor meat and vegetables is a chemical compound, or mixture, of chlorine and the soft metal *sodium*. The salt that gives the ocean its peculiar taste is mostly this salt of chlorine, which is also known as *sodium chloride*. By itself, however, chlorine gas is a very powerful and dangerous chemical. During World War I this gas was used in bombs because it could cripple and kill people. But all the countries of the world agreed that chlorine was too terrible to use for that purpose.

The thing that makes chlorine so useful is that it is a very active chemical element. People never find chlorine free by itself. Other gases that are not as active as chlorine, such as oxygen or nitrogen, are found free in the air. But wherever people find chlorine it is mixed with other chemicals. The only way to get pure, free chlorine is to make it in a chemical laboratory.

Chlorine is very important in the bleaching industry. It is also used to make many useful drugs, such as CHLOROFORM (which you can read about in the next article) and chloral. Chloral is a powerful drug that doctors often use to put their patients to sleep. Chlorine and the element hydrogen combine to make a very valuable acid called *hydrochloric acid*. This acid is used to make hundreds of important chemical compounds such as dyes and rayon. Also, thousands of gallons of hydrochloric acid are used every year to clean the surface of iron that is going to be galvanized. Galvanizing is a way of coating iron with tin and zinc so that the iron will not rust.

chloroform

Chloroform is a sweet-smelling liquid that looks like water. It is a chemical compound of chlorine, carbon, and hydrogen. The major use of chloroform is as a solvent for oils and fats.

Chloroform is a powerful drug that can quickly put people to sleep if they breathe it. A person who has been given chloroform sleeps so deeply that he feels no pain while the doctor is operating on him. Chloroform was discovered a little more than one hundred years ago, but it was not used as an anesthetic until many years later. Anesthetics are drugs that put a person to sleep, and you can read more about them in the article ANESTHESIA.

chlorophyll

Chlorophyll is a substance found in plants. It gives them their green color. It also makes it possible for plants to use sunlight in making food. That is why plants can make all the food that they need out of earth, air, and water. No animal can do this. That is why all animals need plants for their food. Even animals that don't feed on plants have to eat other animals that *do* feed on plants. Only the parts of a plant that receive sunlight contain chlorophyll. Plants that do not contain chlorophyll must live on other plants the way animals do. The plants that do contain chlorophyll are able to convert carbon dioxide gas from the air and chemicals from the earth and water into a form of sugar that a plant needs to live and grow on. The plants take the carbon out of the carbon dioxide gas, and give off oxygen to the air. This is important to all animal life. Humans and all the other animals would not have enough oxygen to breathe if it were not for green plants. And these plants would not give off oxygen if it were not for the wonderful substance called chlorophyll. So you can see why scientists sometimes say that chlorophyll is the wonder chemical of life. In recent years scientists have been able to produce chlorophyll in laboratories. It is used to treat infection, and has helped to purify air and to sweeten bad breath.

chocolate and cocoa

Chocolate and cocoa are foods made from the fruit of the cacao tree. Cacao trees first grew in South America, but now about two-thirds of the world's chocolate and cocoa comes from trees grown on the west coast of Africa.

The fruit of the tree is a large pod, or shell, about ten or twelve inches long. Inside the shell are many rows of seeds, or "cocoa beans." Chocolate and cocoa are made from these beans.

HOW THE BEANS ARE PREPARED

When the pods are ripe, men cut them off the trees with sharp knives. The knives have long bamboo handles, because some of the pods grow high up on the tree. The pods are laid in rows on the ground and are cut open. Then they are left to ferment (turn sour). At this point the pod is firm and the beans are green and would taste very bitter if eaten. The fermentation makes the pod become soft and mushy, so that the beans can easily be separated from it. The beans turn brown and lose much of their bitter taste.

When the beans are taken from the pods they are dried in the sun or in special ovens and then are roasted in ovens. Each bean has a shell-like covering and this is peeled off, leaving the softer center, or

"cocoa nib," of the bean. The nibs are ground and mashed to make *chocolate liquor*, a kind of thick paste from which all the other products are made.

COCOA PRODUCTS

Bitter chocolate cakes or blocks are hard chocolate made from the dried liquor.

Sweet chocolate, or chocolate bars, are sweetened and flavored before they are pressed into cakes.

Cocoa is chocolate with most of the oil pressed out by squeezing it between two big steel plates, and then grinding it into a powder. This is what we use to make "cocoa" for drinking. Hot chocolate, as a beverage, is richer and has a creamier flavor.

Cocoa butter is the fat that is pressed out of chocolate when cocoa is made. It is not made to be eaten, and is used for salves and ointments and in the making of cosmetics.

THE DUTCH PROCESS

The Dutch process is a way of preparing chocolate that makes it a darker and richer brown color, and when it is made in this way it is easier to make into candy and syrups. The reason is because "Dutched" chocolate mixes with flavoring extracts and other ingredients better than ordinary chocolate. When the beans are prepared in other ways the chocolate is slightly acid, but "Dutched" chocolate is not. This process started in Holland, and that is how it got its name. Confectioners and candy makers like to use this kind of chocolate.

USES OF CHOCOLATE

Chocolate, as a food, was known to the Aztec Indians before the discovery of America. The Spanish explorers first took it back to Europe. For a long time it was used only as a drink or beverage. About eighty years ago a man named M. D. Peter, who lived in Switzerland, found a way to make "milk chocolate," like our candy bars of today. Now chocolate-making is a big and important industry. We use chocolate to make candies such as fudge, chocolate drops, chocolate bonbons, caramels, and chocolate bars; we use it for icing cakes, making sauces, for sundaes, frosting, cookies, cakes, custards and puddings; to make hot chocolate and cocoa to drink; and to make an alcoholic beverage called "creme de cacao." Chocolate is a very healthy and nutritious food, and is carried as an emergency ration by explorers and by our armed forces in the field. The best beans are considered to be those from the Chouao region of Venezuela.

Choctaw, a tribe of Muskhogean Indians: see CREEKS.

choir

A choir is a group of people who sing together in church. The singing is part of the church service, and the singers occupy a special part of the church called the choir loft, or stall. Sometimes the choir consists only of boys, and is called a *boys' choir*. When there are men and women in the choir it is called a *mixed choir*. The word *choir* is also used to mean any group of instruments of the same type, such as a choir of woodwinds,

meaning flutes, clarinets, oboes, and bassoons.

cholera

Cholera is a disease of the digestive system. It can kill a person in one day. It is also called Asiatic cholera. It is caused by a germ called a *comma bacillus* because it has a tail and looks somewhat like a comma. This germ usually enters through the mouth. It is most often carried in food and drink. The disease first shows itself through violent bowel movements, vomiting, fever, and cramps in the arms and legs. Death comes from extreme loss of water. About one out of two will die if there is no medical treatment. Lives are often saved by injecting gallons of a salt-and-water mixture into the veins.

Cholera is very catching, and it has often spread over entire continents. It is believed to have existed in Asia thousands of years ago. In India it still takes many lives. Most deaths there occur near the River Ganges, which is used by the people for drinking water. Cholera is still dangerous in China and the Philippines. Several times cholera has spread uncontrolled in parts of the United States. The first cholera epidemic in the United States was in 1832, in Kentucky. There has not been one since 1873.

Preventative controls have made cholera no longer a danger in the United States. Injections of dead cholera germs are now used to protect people from the disease. A person can be protected this way for about six to twelve months. Usually, these injections are taken by people who travel in parts of the world where there may be much cholera. They renew this protection with another injection every six months.

Chopin

Frédéric François Chopin was a great composer of music for the piano. A composer is anyone who writes original music. Most people consider him the greatest piano-composer of all time. His father was French and his mother was Polish. He was born in 1810, near Warsaw, Poland, but went to Paris, France, when he was a young man. He lived in Paris all the rest of his life.

Gale Research Co.

Much of Chopin's music was Polish, called *polonaises* and *mazurkas*, which were music written in the rhythm of dances with the same names. He started to study music when he was only 4 years old, and by the time he was 15 he was a famous pianist. He was never able to make much money, and he was too shy and nervous for a concert artist's life. His health was never very good, and he was not strong. Then one night he played for some very rich people, and they were so impressed by his genius that they formed a committee to see that he never needed money. In return, he gave lessons, but always had time to compose. He got tuberculosis, however, and his health got worse and worse. He died in Paris when he was only 39 years old.

Much of Chopin's music is well known to the whole world, wherever there are pianos and musicians to play them. Among his best-known works are *A♭ Polonaise, Nocturne in E♭ major, C♯ Minor Waltz, Fantasy-Impromptu, Revolutionary Étude,* and of the longer works, the *Sonata in B♭ minor* containing the "Funeral March" that is played all over the world.

chorale

A chorale, or *choral,* is music written for a church choir. A chorale is like a hymn. The first chorales were sung in German churches at the time of Martin Luther. *Ein Feste Burg* (A Mighty Fortress) is a chorale written by Luther. Johann Sebastian Bach wrote four hundred chorales, and many other composers wrote chorales and used their melodies for other works. Palestrina, the Italian composer, also was famous for many beautiful choral compositions. See also the articles CHOIR and CHORUS.

chord

A chord is what you hear when three or more musical tones sound at the same time. We usually think of a chord as having a pleasant or agreeable sound. In music, the study of *harmony* explains the use of notes to form different chords. You can read about HARMONY in a separate article. Chords have names, such as *tonic, dominant, seventh, ninth,* etc. A *discord* is a chord that does not have an agreeable sound.

choreography, the art of planning dances: see BALLET.

chorus

A chorus is a group of people singing together. That is what we usually mean when we use the word *chorus,* but we also use it to mean quite different things. In a musical show or motion picture, the chorus is the group that sings together and also dances. In an opera (a play in which the conversation is sung, not spoken), the chorus is the main body of singers, not including the soloists. A chorus may number as many as three hundred voices.

The music for a chorus is arranged in four-part harmony, or five-part, eight-part, or even ten-part. (See also the article on HARMONY.) A *double chorus* means that the music has been arranged for eight-part harmony, not that there are eight singers.

When we speak of the chorus of a song, we usually mean the main part of the song itself. But a long time ago, when folk songs were new, a song was divided so that one singer, as a soloist, sang the verses. The verses told a story, and after each verse there was another part called the *refrain.* Everyone joined in on the refrain, and because a lot of people sang it together they called it the chorus. Popular songs used to have verses and choruses, but now they seldom have verses, and we call the song itself a chorus.

Chosen, the Japanese name for Korea: see KOREA.

chow

Chow, or chowchow, is the name of one of the oldest breeds of dog known to man. Ancient pictures drawn hundreds of years before the birth of Jesus show dogs much like present-day chows. The chow is a calm, dignified dog, usually devoted to the members of its own family, and very patient with children. It is a fine watchdog. It has one unusual feature. All chows have a blue-black tongue, instead of the pink tongue of other breeds.

The chow stands about 17 to 19 inches high at the shoulder, and it usually weighs between 65 and 75 pounds. It is a large, heavy dog, and looks even heavier and larger because of the thick straight hair that sticks out from the skin like a teddy bear's plush, instead of lying down flat as most dogs' hair does. There is a deep collar of extra thick, longer hair around its neck and head that creates a lionlike appearance. Chows are all solid colored, and may be anything between light tan and solid black.

Christ

The word *Christ* in the Greek language and *Messiah* in the Hebrew language mean the same thing: "the anointed one." In early days, a king was anointed with oil (had oil touched to his head) as part of the ceremony that made him king. The Jewish people expected a Messiah sent by God to lead them to victory over their enemies. When Jesus was born, he was recognized by many of the people as the Messiah, or Christ. See the article on JESUS.

Christian

Christian is the name of ten kings who ruled Denmark, Norway, and Sweden. The first King Christian ruled about five hundred years ago. Christian II became king of Denmark and Norway in 1513, and king of Sweden seven years later. He believed that people from noble families were not any better than ordinary people, and this made the noblemen of his time very angry. Christian II was in love with a Dutch girl. When she died, he made her mother Sigbrit his chief counsellor. Sigbrit did a good job, but the noblemen were very angry at having her put above them. When Christian II became ruler of Sweden, there was a big ceremony in Stockholm, Sweden. After it was over Christian II had many of the Swedish noblemen put to death. This was known as the Stockholm Massacre. The Swedish people chose another king three years later. Christian II was put off the throne of Norway and Denmark by the people. Years later he tried to get the throne back but was captured and spent the rest of his life in prison.

Christian IV was also an important ruler of Norway and Denmark. He was king from 1588 to 1648. He did a great deal to build up the navy and industry of his lands. Christian IV was a very brave man. When he was 66 years old, Sweden attacked Denmark. During a fierce sea battle, the king was hit by cannon shot. He was struck in thirteen places, but he immediately jumped to his feet and called to his men that he was all right. In spite of his wounds, he stayed in his place for the rest of the battle. In Denmark there are many stories and songs that tell of the great bravery of Christian IV.

The last Christian was king of Denmark during World Wars I and II. In World War II, the Germans occupied Denmark, but Christian would not work

with them, and he helped his people to resist them. Christian was also king of Iceland, but in 1944 the people of Iceland voted to become independent of even this connection.

Christian Church, a name often used for the Protestant denomination, DISCIPLES OF CHRIST, about which there is an article in anoi

Christian Endeavor

The Christian Endeavor, also known as the *United Society of Christian Endeavor,* is the largest Protestant Christian young people's association in the world. Members of different denominations may belong, and there are branches in many Protestant churches. The association is also international, and there are many branches in foreign countries, including China and Japan. The purpose of the Christian Endeavor is to interest young people in church activities, but meetings are often like parties. Games are played, there is singing, and those who attend usually havè fun.

Christianity

Christianity is the religion of all Christians. It is founded upon the life, sayings, deeds, death and resurrection of Jesus Christ, as told in the New Testament. If you will read the articles on JESUS and CHURCH, you will learn how Christianity started, and how it grew from a little group of men who had followed Jesus while he was living on earth. Less than 300 years later, Christianity was the religion of the great Roman Empire. Despite persecution of the early Christians, the religion was spread to all parts of the world. Today Christianity is followed by about one-third of the world's population.

DENOMINATIONS

There are many different denominations, or branches, of Christianity. Sometimes people wonder how they can seem so different in their beliefs and in their forms of worship, and still all be Christian. It is because there are certain basic Christian beliefs which all Christians share.

Jesus never wrote a book, but the words that he spoke were written down by his followers and are to be found in the four Gospels in the New Testament. The teachings of Jesus in many cases quoted the basic religious writings of the Jewish religion, and these writings, which are now called the Old Testament, are part of the Christian Bible. Jesus taught about God and man's relationship to God in a way that stirred men's hearts.

WHAT ALL CHRISTIANS BELIEVE

Then what is Christianity, and what do all Christians believe? Here are some of the basic beliefs shared by all Christians, no matter how their doctrines may seem to differ:

They believe in one God, the Creator of all things, Who is merciful and just.

They believe in the teachings of Jesus, and almost all Christian groups believe in his divinity (that he was the Son of God).

They believe in the "Beatitudes," or the blessings spoken by Jesus in the Sermon on the Mount, which is in the Gospel according to St. Matthew.

They believe that we should love our fellow men, even those who are our enemies, and forgive them as we want God to forgive us.

Almost all Christians believe in Baptism and in some kind of union with Jesus through what is variously called the Lord's Supper, the Eucharist, the Mass, and Holy Communion.

ST. PAUL

One of the outstanding followers of Jesus in the first century was St. Paul the Apostle. He was also called Saul. He was a Jew, but his father was a Roman citizen and he was born a Roman citizen, which was then a thing highly prized. He tells how he persecuted the Christians until he was converted by a miracle. Thereafter, he became a missionary. He traveled to many countries, converting people to Christianity and setting up churches. He afterwards wrote letters to the people he had visited. These letters, called "epistles," arc in the New Testament. Much Christian theological (religious) writing is based on them.

In his epistles Paul taught that Jesus was the promised Christ, or Messiah, written about in the Old Testament. The Messiah, according to the prophecies and the promises, was to be from the tribe of Judah, and from the family of David, and he would be the savior of the world. Many of the Jews recognized Jesus as the Messiah, though the leaders of the Jews did not. All the first Christians were Jews. Paul also taught that Jesus saved the world by the sacrifice of his life.

A GREAT DECISION

It was about three hundred years after the birth of Jesus that the Roman emperor, Constantine, permitted the Christians to preach and practice their faith openly. Constantine himself died a Christian. There had been small groups that disagreed with the main body of Christians before his reign, but it was while he was emperor that a great division occurred. There were Arians, who said that Jesus was not truly divine in the same sense as God the Father. Others said that in God there were three persons, the Father, the Son, and the Holy Ghost, and all were equally divine. Finally a great council was called at Nicaea, a city in Asia Minor, in the year 325. More than three hundred bishops came to the council from many places. At this council the Arian teaching was condemned and an important *creed,* or statement of belief, was drawn up. It is called the Nicene Creed.

THE APOSTLES' CREED

Another important creed is the Apostles' Creed. It came into wide use about five or six hundred years after the birth of Jesus. In many churches it is used as a statement of faith before baptism. Not all Christian churches accept the entire Apostles' Creed, but it is so nearly a worldwide statement of Christian belief that it is given here in full:

I believe in God the Father almighty, creator of heaven and earth;

And in Jesus Christ His only Son our Lord;

Who was conceived by the Holy Ghost, born of the Virgin Mary,

Suffered under Pontius Pilate, was crucified, died, and was buried; he descended into Hell,

The third day he arose again from the dead:

He ascended into heaven, sitteth at the right hand of God the Father Almighty;

From thence he shall come to judge the living and the dead.

I believe in the Holy Ghost;

The holy Catholic Church; the communion of saints;

The forgiveness of sins;

The resurrection of the body;

And life everlasting. Amen.

The Apostles' Creed is not usually divided into twelve different sections as it is here, but some have liked to divide it in this way for the twelve Apostles, so as to make one section for each of them.

CHRISTIANITY IN THE WORLD

Christianity is the prevailing religion of all of Europe, the Americas, southern and western Africa, and Australia. Islam (the Mohammedan religion) and Buddhism are the principal religions of the other parts of the world.

Missionary work (preaching the Christian religion to non-Christian peoples) and charity are important works of the Church. See the separate articles on MISSIONS and CHARITY.

Christian Science

Christian Scientists are members of the Church of Christ, Scientist, a Protestant Christian religion. This church was founded by a woman named Mary Baker EDDY, about whom there is a separate article.

Many people think of Christian Science as the religion, whose followers "don't believe in going to the doctor when they are sick." It is a fact that Christian Scientists do not go to doctors or take medicine, but there is a great deal more to their religion than that.

In the New Testament we read that wherever Jesus went sick people came to him and he healed them. He spoke lovingly to the blind and their eyes were opened, to the lame and their limbs became normal; and he did all this by the power of his spiritual understanding, without drugs or surgery. His disciples, too, healed all sorts of disease in the same way. For two or three hundred years after Jesus left the earth it was quite common for Christians to heal the sick by prayer.

People call the wonderful healings performed by Jesus and his early followers "miracles." By this they usually mean special signs of God's power and favor bestowed on a few persons. Jesus promised that whoever believed in him should do these same works, but most people have assumed that this was true only in the early days of Christianity.

About a hundred years ago Mary Baker Eddy gave a lot of thought to this question. She was in very poor health and she investigated many different methods of healing. She studied what the Bible teaches about healing. She gave much thought to Jesus' statement, "Ye

shall know the truth, and the truth shall make you free."

MRS. EDDY'S ACCIDENT

In 1866, Mrs. Eddy slipped on the ice and hurt herself so badly that it looked as though she might not live. She turned to the Bible and prayed to God with her whole heart. And suddenly she felt God's goodness and His power so strongly that she was able to get out of bed and walk.

For three years she studied the Bible and thought deeply about it. She lived in a scientific age when people had learned that there is an explanation for all things and that things do not just "happen." So she felt that she must learn the spiritual laws that brought about her own healing and the miracles of the New Testament. Then they would not be regarded as "miracles" any more but as the natural results of divine law.

She called this discovery Christian Science and began to teach it. In 1875 she published her textbook. *Science and Health with Key to the Scriptures,* in which she gave her conclusions on how God's law can free man from every form of evil—from sin, sickness, ignorance, and fear. A few years later she founded the Church of Christ, Scientist, as a local church in Boston, Massachusetts. Some years later she established the present world-wide organization. Before she died in 1910, when she was almost 90 years old, her Church had spread all over the world.

It is composed of the First Church of Christ, Scientist, in Boston, Massachusetts, and more than three thousand branch churches in the United States and other countries. One of Mrs. Eddy's last acts was to found *The Christian Science Monitor*—a famous daily newspaper that is read by many people of all faiths.

Services in a Christian Science Church consist of readings from the Bible and from the book *Science and Health.* Instead of ministers, they have readers. One is called "First Reader" who reads from *Science and Health,* and one is called "Second Reader" who reads from the Bible. At the midweek service members relate their experiences and give what is called "testimony." Thanksgiving Day is an important church holiday.

Christmas

Every year, on December 25, we celebrate Christmas. We get Christmas trees and decorate them with shiny ornaments and electric lights. We give presents to our families and friends, and they give presents to us. Christmas cards are mailed to people we know, and the little boys and girls write letters to "Santa Claus." Garlands and wreaths of holly and mistletoe are hung on the doors and windows. We sing Christmas carols and hymns, and there are special services in churches. And we have a feast with turkey or perhaps a goose; there are nuts and candies to eat, and cider to drink. The young children hang up stockings on Christmas Eve so that "Santa Claus" ("Father Christmas," in England) can fill them full of toys.

We are celebrating the Nativity, or the birthday of Jesus, who was born in a stable because there was no room at the inn. We sing of the Wise Men who came from the East, following the star of Bethlehem, bringing presents to the new-born Babe. At Christmas time we try to put behind us, if only for a few days, all the selfishness and hatred that we are too weak to master most of the time.

Our calendar, by which we reckon the days, months, and years, is dated from the first year after the birth of Jesus. We call this the Christian Era. But as we study and read, we will learn that Jesus was not really born on the 25th of December, but probably in April or May, and perhaps three years earlier. The Christmas holidays come at the time of year known as the *winter solstice,* when the harvest is over and the meat slaughtered and stored in ice or brine. In ancient times, this was the season of revelry and feasting, the season of plenty. The early Christian emperors of Rome decided to hold the Christmas celebration to offset the "saturnalia," the festival of the god Saturn, which had become rather wild. The pagan revel gave way to Christmas as the merrymakers became Christians, but we still say to each other "Merry Christmas." It does not matter that Santa Claus is called St. Nicholas and Father Christmas. He is a real person, however, for he is the spirit of Christmas.

Christophe, Henrì

Henrì Christophe was born a Negro slave and lived to be king of Haiti, an island in the Caribbean Sea. He was born in 1767. Early in his life Christophe bought himself out of slavery and he helped his people win freedom from the French who ruled them. A few years after the people of Haiti won their independence, they elected Christophe president and later crowned him king of Haiti. He lived in splendor in a magnificent palace called Sans Souci, but he was cruel to the people Finally they turned against him, and Henrì Christophe shot himself to death with a silver bullet, to escape their anger.

Christopher, Saint

Saint Christopher is the Christian patron saint, or protector, of travelers. Medals stamped with his picture are often carried by travelers on trips. Christopher lived in Syria, in Asia Minor, about 1,600 years ago. He is supposed to have been a huge and very strong man. He became a Christian, and decided to serve his religion by carrying travelers across a stream where there was no bridge. The story is told that one day he carried a child who seemed to grow so heavy that the saint could hardly reach the other bank. When he finally got across the stream, he said he felt as if he had carried the whole world on his back. The answer was that he had "carried both the world and the one who made it" for the child was Jesus. From this story the saint received the name Christopher, which means "christ-bearer." His festival is celebrated in the Roman Catholic Church on July 25.

chromatic scale

A chromatic scale is twelve musical tones, including all the half-tones, or sharps and flats. For example, a chromatic scale beginning on Middle C would be: C, C-sharp, D, D-sharp, E, F, F-sharp, G, G-sharp, A, and so forth. Coming down, you would use flats, like this: C, B, B-flat, A, A-flat, G, G-flat, F, E, E-flat, D, D-flat, C. On the piano, you get a chromatic scale by playing every note, black and white, in order. In modern music, chromatic means those tones in the music which are not a part of the diatonic scale. You can read more about this in the article SCALE.

chromium

Chromium is a hard, bright-gray metal. It is one of the chemical elements and was discovered about 150 years ago. Until recently pure chromium was very difficult and expensive to prepare, and it was not used very much. But scientists found that chromium formed many valuable alloys, or mixtures, with other metals. A little chromium added to iron and steel makes them much stronger and harder to scratch, and for this reason it is often used as a coating for other metals. Chromium also stops other metals from rusting. The shiny bumpers of automobiles are plated with chromium.

Besides its use as a metal, chromium has other uses. It forms brilliant green, red, and yellow compounds with other chemical elements. For this reason chromium is used in the making of dyes and paints. Lead chromate, for instance, is the famous color chrome yellow that artists use. Small traces of chromium compounds are what give the emerald its bright green glow. A little bit of a chromium compound is what gives the ruby its red color. Another important chemical made from chromium is chromic acid, which is used in the tanning of leather.

chromosome, the part of a cell important in heredity: see CELL.

Chronicles

The Chronicles are two books in the Old Testament that come after the books of the Kings in Christian Bibles. They were the last books in the Hebrew Bible. The writer of Chronicles wanted to provide a different version of the early history of the Jews than was given in the books of the Kings. He wanted one that would be less historical and more religious. So he wrote the Chronicles from a religious point of view, leaving out many things found in the books of Kings and supplying new things not found there. He described the temple of Jerusalem, and wrote of David, Solomon, and others as saintly people. The purpose of Chronicles was to teach the people to be good and obedient in their lives as followers of the Jewish religion.

chronology

Chronology is the science that has to do with dates and time. Its purpose is to arrange all the events in the history of the world into one system of time. To do this, there must be a standard unit of time. The year was decided upon because it is a natural unit of time based on the movement of the earth around the sun. Different countries have used various dates for the year one. They always started counting from some important event. You can read more about this in the article CALENDAR. Most countries now start counting years from the birth of

Jesus. Counting forward from the birth of Christ, we put the letters A.D. before the year. A.D. means *Anno Domini,* or "in the Year of Our Lord." Counting back from the birth of Christ, we put B.C. after the year. For example, 100 B.C. means one hundred years before the birth of Christ.

chronometer

A chronometer is a special clock that is very accurate. It is used on ships and planes, and also by astronomers. A chronometer is different from an ordinary clock because it is made so that jarring and changes of temperature will not change it more than a few seconds in a year. The modern chronometer is a development of the watch. Among the many people who contributed to its perfection were John Harrison of England and Pierre LeRoy of France.

chrysalis

A chrysalis is the strange-looking creature that you find inside a cocoon. It is what the caterpillar changes into in the autumn. During the winter the chrysalis changes little by little, turning into a butterfly. It does not move or eat. It hardly looks alive. But wonderful changes are going on within its body. The chrysalis is growing wings, and legs, and feelers called antennae. All these new parts of its body are kept folded up and attached to the breast of the chrysalis. Then, one day in the spring, the chrysalis splits open and a large moth or butterfly comes out of the cocoon.

chrysanthemum

A chrysanthemum is a plant with large white, pink, or yellowish flowers. Most of the beautiful kinds of chrysanthemum grown in the garden originally came from China and Japan. The different sizes and shades of color have made chrysanthemums very popular plants in gardens or as cut flowers. Chrysanthemums bloom from late summer until early winter. Some are very hardy plants. The flowers are of different kinds, ranging from flat daisylike blooms to big shaggy heads.

Chrysler, Walter Percy

Walter Chrysler was one of the greatest American manufacturers of automobiles. He was born in Kansas in 1875,  and his family was very poor. Walter had to go to work when he was very young. His first job was as an apprentice in a machine shop and he rose from that to become the founder of the Chrysler Corporation, one of the three biggest automobile manufacturing companies in the United States.

Before he started in his own business, Chrysler was an important official of another one of those three big automobile companies, the General Motors Corporation. Chrysler built the Chrysler Building in New York City, second in height only to the Empire State Building. He died in 1940.

chub

Chubs are small fish belonging to the same family as the carp and minnow. They have broad heads and strong jaws, and they feed on smaller fish and insects. The best-known American chub is the creek chub, which lives in streams from the Rocky Mountains eastward. It grows to be nearly a foot long. The male makes a nest for his mate to lay her eggs in, digging a large pit in the bottom of the stream, and piling the sand or mud out of it in a long ridge upstream. The male of another kind, the river chub, builds a nest of pebbles, which he carries in his mouth. There are several other chubs, among them the Columbia River chub. The chub of England and Europe is a different fish, which grows to be more than two feet long and weighs up to twelve pounds.

Chungking

Chungking is a city in China, in Szechwan Province. It is also called Chungching. It is the capital of a vast territory known as Southwest China. The city stands on a rocky hill on the great Yangtze River at the point where the Kialing River flows into it. Chungking is almost nine hundred miles up the river from Shanghai on the Pacific Ocean. Chunking is the market for the products of Szechwan, such as tea, tung oil, hog bristles, silk, and hides. It is a busy port and shipping center. Along its waterfront boatmen live with their families aboard crowded barges.

In 1937 Chungking became the capital of all China. In World War II, China was joined by the United States, England and the other Allies in its war against the Japanese invaders, and Chungking grew in importance. Many industries were established in Chungking, partly with American help. Today, more than two million people live in Chungking. They produce silk and cotton goods, paper, iron, matches, steel, and chemicals, in mills and factories built during the war.

In 1946 the government of China moved from Chungking to Nanking. Four years later Communist forces took over the city.

church

There are several meanings of the word *church,* but all of the meanings have to do with the Christian religion. Sometimes the word is spelled with a capital letter and sometimes it is not. One meaning of the word is a building where Christians go to worship; that is what we mean when we say we are "going to church." In another sense, a Church is a particular group of Christians who are organized into what we call a *denomination,* or *sect,* and whose beliefs are in some way different from the beliefs of other Christians; that is what we mean when we speak of the Presbyterian Church, or the Roman Catholic Church, or the Lutheran Church. And finally, "the Church" is all Christians, all believers in Jesus as the Christ and the Saviour.

Jesus himself used the word "church" twice in his words as recorded in the New Testament. He promised that the Holy Spirit would come to be the soul of the Church, and the day recognized as the coming of the Holy Spirit is called Pentecost, which is fifty days after Easter Sunday, the day that marks Jesus' resurrection (rising from the dead). Jesus ordained twelve Apostles to teach and preach the Christian faith to all nations, and to one of them, Simon, called Peter (which name means "rock"), he said, "Thou art Peter, and upon this rock I will build my church, and the gates of hell shall not prevail against it."

After the death, resurrection and ascension to heaven of Jesus, upon the coming of the Holy Spirit, the Church was born. The Acts of the Apostles in the New Testament tells of the earliest days of the Church in Jerusalem and of the church in Antioch.

THE CHURCH AT ANTIOCH

Antioch is a great city of ancient times, now a part of Turkey. It was known as a center of learning, where many Jews, Greeks and Romans came together, and there was much talk and discussion. It was here that the followers of Jesus were first called Christians. These were mostly Jewish Christians who had left the synagogue, and they and the Greek, or *Hellenistic,* Christians shared many beliefs. Among the members of that early church were the disciples Paul and Barnabas, who were named as missionaries to go forth and preach the gospel. (*Gospel* means "good news.")

The most important missionary of all time was Paul. He traveled to many countries, preaching the gospel and setting up churches. Then after he left he wrote letters to the people whom he had visited, giving them advice and counsel. These letters are called the "epistles," and are found in the New Testament.

In the early churches the service, or worship, consisted of prayer and the chanting of hymns, reading from the Bible, and sometimes a sermon. Sometimes the Lord's Supper was celebrated with bread and wine, and on occasions baptism was administered.

PERSECUTION UNDER THE ROMAN EMPERORS

During the first three hundred years it took great courage to be a Christian. Christians were looked upon by the Romans as enemies of the state. They disapproved of the bloodthirsty games and amusements of the Romans, such as the gladiatorial contests in which one or the other warrior died in the arena to entertain the citizens. Christians believed in the absolute equality of all men. This appealed to the many thousands of slaves held by the Romans, and the Romans feared a revolution. Worst of all, the Christians were taught by the Bible that they could worship only one God, while the Romans had many gods, including most of their emperors. When Christians refused to worship the emperor, the Romans often put them to death. The Christian "churches" in those days were usually secret chambers in the catacombs, which were underground burial places near Rome. Roman police sometimes found the Christians in these underground churches and arrested them. When they could not be made to renounce their faith by torture, they were often thrown to the wild beasts in the

arena as a show for the Romans. And yet, so strong was their faith that they met the most awful death without a sign of fear. They are called the Christian martyrs. But in spite of persecution, Christianity spread and grew stronger. Finally, almost three hundred years after Jesus had died on the cross, the Roman emperor Constantine became a Christian himself. Christians were protected by law, and a new age was born that was to lead to the church-state, and the time in history of the Holy Roman Empire.

There followed a period of more than a thousand years in which the Church grew in importance as well as in the numbers of its members. The great empire of Rome, after five hundred years of civilization, was falling to barbarians. These were crude, cruel and uneducated tribes. They had no respect for learning or for things of beauty. The Christian Church proved to be the only civilizing force that could save Europe. One by one, the barbarian kings and their tribes were converted to Christianity. When they were converted, they recognized the Church as a mightier power than they were, and this prevented them from committing many acts of destruction and cruelty. At the same time, the priests and monks of the Church kept reading and writing and other learning alive, when few other people could read or write.

During much of this period there were only two main Christian Churches. During the eleventh century the Roman Catholic Church, headed by the Pope in Rome, and the Orthodox Church, headed by the Patriarch of Constantinople, separated. The countries of western Europe followed the Roman Catholic Church. Greece, Russia, and some other parts of eastern Europe followed the Orthodox Church.

When the Roman Catholic Church came to have so much power and influence, certain greedy and wicked men saw an opportunity to enrich themselves. By becoming priests, bishops, abbots, and other important men in the clergy, they could use its power for their own selfish purposes. Before long, many crimes were being committed in the name of the Church.

Good people in the clergy and laity cried out for reform. A Dutch priest named Erasmus wrote a work called *In Praise of Folly,* in which he made fun of some of the selfish things that were being done in the name of Christianity. This was published in 1509, and though Erasmus himself remained a faithful member of the Roman Catholic Church, his work encouraged others to question the acts and some of the doctrines (beliefs) of the Church.

In the year 1517 a German priest named Martin Luther nailed a list of ninety-five theses (statements of belief) to the door of the church at Wittenberg. This was a usual way for people to publish their ideas in those days. Luther's act might be called the beginning of the movement that led to the Protestant Churches. Christians who agreed with Luther, and who had other ideas of their own that were different from the doctrines of the Roman Catholic Church, began to form groups, or sects, of their own. Eventually these groups came together to form separate Churches.

THE RISE OF DENOMINATIONS

There followed a period of more than two hundred years in which many different denominations were formed.

A few years after Martin Luther made his first protest, King Henry VIII of England broke away from the Roman Catholic Church and formed the Church of England. This was in 1527. The Church of England was still an "established" church, which means that it was the official church of the nation.

Other Christians did not believe that there should be an official church. They formed other denominations that were not officially connected with any state government. Literally dozens of these denominations came to exist within less than a century. Others continued to arise, and the process is still going on.

THE CHURCHES TODAY

The Roman Catholic Church has the largest membership of Christian Churches in the United States and throughout the world. In the United States the largest body of Christians are Protestants, but they belong to dozens of different denominations. There has been an effort to combine all or nearly all the denominations into one large Protestant Church. Many of them belong to a joint organization called the National Council of Churches of Christ in the United States of America. The largest Protestant Churches in the United States are the Baptists, Methodists, Lutherans, Presbyterians, and Episcopalians (Protestant Episcopal Church).

The Eastern Orthodox (originally Greek Orthodox) Churches in the United States have more than two million members. The Russian Orthodox branch of this Church had more than a hundred million members in Russia alone until the Communist government there made it difficult for Christians to attend any church.

There are independent state Churches in several countries, for example Syria and Ethiopia. Several of these Churches are allied with either the Roman Catholic or Greek Orthodox Church.

Churchill, Sir Winston

Sir Winston Churchill was one of the great Englishmen of all time. By his courage, brilliance and leadership he may have contributed more than anyone else to winning World War II. He was prime minister, the highest position in the British government, from 1940 to 1945 during the war and again from 1951 to 1954. When he died in 1965, more than 90 years old, he was the most honored man in the world. Kings and presidents went to London to attend his funeral.

Winston Leonard Spencer Churchill was born in 1874 to Jennie Jerome Churchill, an American, and to Lord Randolph Churchill, a descendant of the first Duke of Marlborough. As a child, Churchill was fascinated by soldiers. He went to Harrow, a famous school for boys, and also attended the well-known Royal Military College at Sandhurst, which is like the United States Military Academy at West Point. When he was

21, Churchill first saw active fighting with the Spanish in Cuba. He also fought in India and in the African Sudan, under the famous British general, Lord Kitchener. During the South African war he was a newspaper correspondent. He was captured by the Boers, but escaped and became an army combat officer. These years were very adventurous for Churchill. He wrote about them in an exciting book called *A Roving Commission: My Early Life.*

HOW HE BECAME PRIME MINISTER

After the Boer War in South Africa, Churchill came back to England and decided to enter politics. He was 26 years old in 1900 and already well known. He was elected to Parliament as a member of the Conservative party. In 1906, he changed parties and became a Liberal. He was appointed Undersecretary for the colonies. Later he became president of the Board of Trade (which is like our Department of Commerce), Home Secretary (like our Secretary of the Interior) and then First Lord of the Admiralty.

When World War I began, a naval force was sent to save the Belgian city of Antwerp from the Germans. Churchill went with this force, but they failed. The navy failed again when, together with the French, it tried to break through the Dardanelles strait and capture the Turkish city of Constantinople. Because of this failure, Churchill lost his position as First Lord of the Admiralty. He then fought for a while with the army in France. When David Lloyd George became prime minister, Churchill was made minister of Munitions and later Secretary for War and for Air.

After the war, he again became a member of the Conservative party and served as Colonial Secretary in 1921. He also ran for Parliament and was defeated twice before his election to the House of Commons (like the House of Representatives). From 1924–29 he was Chancellor of the Exchequer (Secretary of the Treasury). Then he retired for ten years. He strongly opposed the policies of Prime Minister Neville Chamberlain, who tried to avoid war with Germany by appeasing, or giving in to, the German dictator Adolf Hitler. Chamberlain, together with the French, allowed Hitler to invade Czechoslovakia. But when Hitler broke his promise and began to invade other countries, England and France had to declare war. When World War II began, September 3, 1939, Churchill was again appointed First Lord of the Admiralty. Several months later, Chamberlain was forced to resign and Churchill became prime minister.

THE STRUGGLE FOR VICTORY

In May 1940, England was in great danger. The Germans had already captured Poland, Denmark, and Norway. In the same month they overran Luxembourg and invaded Belgium, the Netherlands, and France. France fell in June when the Allied army was driven into the sea at Dunkirk and had to retreat across the Channel to England. Churchill then showed himself to be a great and inspiring leader. He made many wonderful speeches. He led his countrymen during

the terrible bombings of the Battle of Britain and the campaigns of North Africa and Italy. He met President Franklin D. Roosevelt on the high seas and together they wrote the Atlantic Charter, which stated the peace aims of the Allies. Churchill has visited the United States several times, twice during World War II. He also visited Moscow and attended most of the famous international conferences.

AFTER WORLD WAR II

Germany was finally defeated and surrendered in May, 1945. Churchill was still very popular, although many Englishmen did not like certain policies of the Conservative party. His party was defeated the same year by the Labour party. Churchill resigned and Clement Attlee became prime minister. Churchill then became leader of the opposition in the House of Commons, where he criticized the new government and warned the world against the threat of Soviet Russia. He again became prime minister when his party won the elections of 1951.

In 1953 Churchill was made a Knight of the Garter, which is England's most famous order of knighthood, and so he became Sir Winston Churchill. In 1955, when he was 81 years old, he resigned as prime minister but he remained a member of Parliament. He refused an offer to make him a duke, because a nobleman cannot be a member of the House of Commons. After World War II, Churchill wrote a six-volume history, *The Second World War*. In 1953 he was awarded the Nobel prize in literature, the highest possible honor for a writer.

Church of England

The Church of England is the state Church of that country. It was one of the first Protestant Churches, being more than four hundred years old. It is sometimes called the Anglican Church (Anglican means "English"), but that word is more often used to include all the Churches of the same general beliefs throughout the world. In the United States, the Anglican denomination is called Episcopal, or Protestant Episcopal.

The Church of England was founded in 1527 when the King of England, Henry VIII, maintained that his marriage to his queen, Catherine of Aragon, was not valid, and contested the decision of Pope Clement VII that it was. So Henry VIII created a separate church in England, of which he became the head. Since that time, the English king or queen has been the head of the Church of England. The Archbishop of Canterbury is the next-highest in the Church of England, and the Archbishop of York is third.

The Church of England developed the Authorized Version of the Holy Bible, known as the King James Bible, which is the Bible used by most English-speaking Protestants throughout the world, and also the Book of Common Prayer, which is used by members of Episcopal Churches in all English-speaking countries.

THE ANGLICAN COMMUNION

The Anglican Communion is a union of all the churches in the world that are founded upon the Church of England.

They include the Protestant Episcopal Church in America, the Church of England in Canada, the Scottish Episcopal Church, the Church of Ireland, and Episcopal Churches in Australia, New Zealand, and Africa. Every ten years there is a meeting of bishops from all of these churches at Lambeth, England. These meetings are known as Lambeth Conferences. They are held at Lambeth Palace, the headquarters of the Archbishop of Canterbury.

ANGLICAN BELIEFS

Members of the Church of England believe in the Apostles' Creed, the Nicene Creed, and the Athanasian Creed, and have a statement of faith called the Thirty-Nine Articles. Anglicanism is divided into:

(1) a "High Church element," which believes in Apostolic Succession, or that bishops of the church are successors of the original Apostles of Christ and in the Real Presence, which means that the body and blood of Jesus are actually present during the Lord's Supper;

(2) a "Low Church element," which gets along with the minimum of ritual; and

(3) a "Broad Church element," which steered clear of religious controversy and sought to link itself with a liberal and progressive spirit.

Church of Jesus Christ of Latter-day Saints, the official name of the Mormon Church: see the article on MORMONS.

Church of Rome, see the article on ROMAN CATHOLIC CHURCH.

churn

Butter is made from cream by a machine called a churn. A long time ago, the only way to churn butter was to put cream into a bag of goatskin or sheepskin, and shake it until the butter was separated from the cream. Then the simple churn was invented. This is a sort of barrel, about two feet high and one foot in diameter. Inside there is a piston, or plunger, which means a round plate attached to a handle. The round plate fits exactly inside of the barrel, with just enough room to slide up and down. The lid has a hole in the center for the handle. Cream is put into the barrel, and the lid is fastened on. Then you sit down with the churn between your knees, and work the handle up and down until you feel the butter beginning to form inside. That is what happens to cream when it is churned. It makes butter, and buttermilk is left over. Today most butter is made in large creameries. They use big machines and make a lot of butter at a time. But in the early days every farm made its own butter, and many homes kept a few cows and made their butter at home.

cicada

The cicada is an insect that makes a shrill sound by moving a drumlike membrane, or skin, near its stomach. You can often hear cicadas in the summertime, but it is hard to find them because the sound seems to come from another

place, and what we hear is often the echo. In late summer the female cicada cuts open a twig and lays eggs in it. After a few weeks the *nymphs* (the young of an insect) hatch from the eggs and fall to the ground. Then they burrow into the earth, sometimes as much as ten feet deep, and live there twelve to thirteen years. Then they change into a slightly different form and live underground another one to five years. In the northern cicada, this underground period lasts seventeen years, and the insect is called the seventeen-year cicada. The southern type has a thirteen-year cycle. When the underground period is over, the nymph digs its way to the surface. Its skin comes off, and it is now an adult with long wings. But the adult lives only a few weeks.

Cicadas are sucking insects and live on the juice of plants. They are harmless to animals and other insects but cause damage to trees and other plants.

U.S.D.A.
The cicada has a large head, bulging eyes, and two pairs of sheer membrane wings.

Cicero

Cicero was the greatest orator, or public speaker, of ancient Rome. He was also famous as a politician, thinker, and writer. His letters are very interesting to read, and they describe the ways of Roman life and politics better than anything else that was written at the time. Cicero's fine style of writing Latin has had great influence on English and on many other languages.

Cicero lived more than two thousand years ago, from 106 B.C. to 43 B.C. His full name was Marcus Tullius Cicero. He is also called Tully. He was a member of the party in the Senate that supported Pompey and opposed Caesar. He approved the killing of Caesar but had nothing to do with the plot. At the same time he was a bitter enemy of Marc Antony and replied to Antony's attacks in the Roman Senate with some of his most famous *philippics*, so called because they were like the speeches that the great Greek orator Demosthenes delivered against King Philip. But when Antony became one of the three men who ruled Rome, Cicero was banished, then killed by Antony's men before he could escape. You can read more about POMPEY, CAESAR and ANTONY in separate articles.

Cid

The Cid was a famous Spanish hero whose real name was Rodrigo Díaz de Vivar. He lived about nine hundred years ago and became such a great warrior that his countrymen called him the *Cid* or the *Cid Campeador*, which means the

375

CINERAMA

"Lord," or the "Lord Conqueror." He was first a soldier of the city of Burgos in the province of Castile. Then under the Moorish king of Sargossa he fought against other Moors and against the Christians in Spain. In the year 1094 he conquered the city of Valencia, which he ruled until his death in 1099.

The Cid was also famous as a perfect Spanish gentleman, whose chivalry, courtesy and generosity have become the ideal in Spanish history and literature. He is the hero of *The Song of the Cid*, which was written by an unknown Spanish author during the 12th century. He is also the hero of two famous plays, one by the Spanish author Guillen de Castro, and the other by the great French dramatist Pierre Corneille.

cider

Cider is the juice pressed from apples. It is good to drink. We often have cider with turkey dinners, especially for Thanksgiving and Christmas. Cider is made in a *cider press*. This is a machine with a big screw on top, with long handles. The apples are put into the machine, and when you turn the handles, out comes the juice. It is put into wooden casks and left to ferment to produce vinegar. When pears are used instead of apples, the juice is called *perry*. "Champagne cider" is a sparkling wine made from apples in Spain, France, and England.

cigars and **cigarettes,** two tobacco products used for smoking: see TOBACCO.

Cimabue, Giovanni

Giovanni Cimabue is often called the "father of Italian painting." Though some of his work is well known, he is probably most famous as the teacher of another Italian painter, Giotto. The story is told that Cimabue was walking in the mountains one day and met a shepherd boy. While tending the sheep, Giotto used to draw pictures on flat rocks with pieces of charcoal. Cimabue took the lad back to his studio and trained him. He taught him painting and drawing, and later Giotto became famous as one of the first great Italian painters.

If you go to Italy you can see some of the works of Cimabue in churches there. All of his pictures are of religious subjects. For many years experts could not be sure which paintings were Cimabue's and which were not. The only one that he signed is *St. John the Evangelist* in the cathedral at Pisa. X-rays for examining pictures have established more paintings as Cimabue's. He was also known for making pictures by putting little pieces of colored stone and marble into wet cement. These pictures are called *mosaics*. Cimabue was born in 1240 and died in 1302.

Cimbri

The Cimbri were the first of the many fierce Germanic tribes that invaded Italy. They swept down from the North Sea and wiped out four Roman armies. This happened about a hundred years before the birth of Jesus. Their wives and children followed the army in chariots. The Cimbri warriors wore helmets decorated with the feathers and skins of wild birds and animals. The trained Roman soldiers were frightened at the sight of the wild Cimbri. Between battles, the Cimbri used to slide on their shields down the steep ice of the Alps. The Cimbri were finally annihilated by the Romans.

cinchona

The cinchona, or chinchona, is a tree that grows high in the Andes Mountains of South America. It is also grown in other places for the quinine made from its bark. Quinine is a drug used in the treatment of the disease malaria. The Dutch and English planters raised cinchona trees in Java and India, and almost all the world's supply of quinine came from these places instead of South America, where the tree came from. The American Indians knew about its uses long before the white settlers came. The bark is also known as Peruvian bark, and Jesuit's bark. During World War II the supply of quinine from the Far East was cut off, and South America started to cultivate cinchona trees on a wide scale. Another drug also used for malaria, is made from the bark. It is called totaquine.

Cincinnati

Cincinnati is a city on the Ohio River, opposite Covington, Kentucky. Next to Cleveland, it is the biggest city in the state of Ohio. Cincinnati was called Losantiville when it was first settled in 1789, but a year later it was given its present name in honor of the great republican leader of ancient Rome, Cincinnatus. Cincinnatus was plowing his fields when he was called to lead the army in defense of the Roman republic. The veterans of the American Revolutionary War, nearly all farmers themselves, saw a likeness between their experience and his.

Cincinnati is the trade center of a wide area that takes in parts of Ohio, Indiana, and Kentucky. More than 450,000 people live there, many of them of German and Irish descent. They make whiskey, soap, machine tools, chemicals, plastics, watches, and a variety of meat products. Downtown Cincinnati has often been badly damaged by floods. The city is sometimes called "the Rome of America," partly on account of its name but mainly because, like Rome, it is built on hills.

CINCINNATI, OHIO. Population (1970 census) 452,524. County seat of Hamilton County. On the Ohio River opposite Covington, Kentucky. Settled in 1789.

Cincinnati, Society of the

The Society of the Cincinnati is the oldest military society in America. It was started in 1783, by officers who fought in the American Revolutionary War. When the war was over, they returned to their farms, just as the famous general Cincinnatus had done in Roman times. That is why the society was named after him.

The Cincinnati started a fund to help needy members, which was the first pension system in the United States. George Washington and the Marquis de Lafayette were two famous generals connected with the Cincinnati, which also had a branch in France. When a member of the society dies, his eldest son or male heir takes his place. Cincinnati, Ohio, was given its name because some of the society's original members settled there.

Cincinnatus

Cincinnatus was the hero of one of the legends of ancient Rome. So many stories have been told about him that it is impossible to be sure what is true and what is merely legend. His full name was Lucius Quintus Cincinnatus and he was born nearly 2,500 years ago, about 519 B.C. He was a farmer who became consul of Rome once and dictator twice. According to the story he first became dictator when he was called from his farm to save the army that was trapped by the enemy. In a single day he is supposed to have raised troops and saved the army. He was appointed dictator of Rome the second time when he was 80 years old, in order to defeat an ambitious man named Spurius Maelius, who was suspected of trying to seize control of the government. Within 21 days Cincinnatus had Maelius killed and again retired to his farm.

Cinderella

Cinderella is a fairy tale written by the Frenchman Charles Perrault about three hundred years ago. Grownups as well as children like to hear it. Cinderella ("little Cinder Girl") is an orphan with a wicked stepmother and two cruel stepsisters. They have been invited to the Prince's ball, leaving Cinderella at home to work. However, Cinderella's fairy godmother appears and waves her magic wand over Cinderella. At once she finds herself dressed in a beautiful gown. A pumpkin has changed into a carriage to carry her to the ball. Her fairy godmother warns her that she must leave the ball at midnight, because then her clothes and carriage will again become simply rags and a pumpkin. The Prince is dazzled by the unknown girl and they dance together all evening. Cinderella is so happy that she forgets to leave soon enough. At the stroke of twelve, she rushes away, leaving only her slipper. The Prince vows he will marry the girl who owns the slipper. Cinderella's foot is the only one that fits the shoe. They marry and live happily ever after.

Cinerama

Cinerama is a kind of motion picture that makes a person think he is seeing an actual live scene instead of only a picture of it. Very often Cinerama is called a kind of "3-D" motion picture, but it is not. No picture can really show three dimensions (height, width, and depth) as a person sees them with his eyes. What Cinerama does is to spread the picture out to the width that a person actually sees. In actual use of his eyes, a person sees clearly something straight ahead of him, and at the same time he sees everything on each side within about a semi-circle, or half a circle. He does not see clearly on the sides, but he sees well enough so that if there is any movement he will notice it and can move his eyes to it. Cinerama imitates this by using a curved screen that covers very much the territory that a person sees naturally. It does this by photographing every scene from three directions, once from straight

ahead and once from each side. Then it uses three projectors to throw the three films on the wide curved screen. It also uses "stereophonic sound," which is sound coming from the front and from both sides, which is just as a person hears it in real life.

The first Cinerama show was put on in New York City on September 30, 1952. It included a ride on a roller coaster, a scene from an opera, an airplane ride over the Rocky Mountains, and several other scenes. It was a tremendous success and soon there were other Cinerama theaters in very big cities throughout the United States.

cinnabar

Cinnabar is a mineral taken from mines in the ground. It is the ore from which we extract mercury, the metal that is used to make the backs of mirrors, thermometers, vapor lamps (sun lamps) and many other important things. It is deep red in color, and is used to make paint and ink. We call the color vermilion. Most of the mines are in Spain; there are others in Italy, and in the United States in Colorado and California.

cinnamon

Cinnamon is a sweet, fragrant spice that comes from cinnamon shrubs. These shrubs grow mostly in Ceylon and the Malabar Coast. They have bright green leaves and little yellow flowers. The spice comes from the inner bark, which is peeled, scraped, rolled into sticks and bound into bundles called "pipes." This is sold as "stick cinnamon." It is also ground into a powder and sold in little boxes. Cinnamon is used to flavor cakes and cookies, to make perfumes and incense, and to scent soaps, drugs, and medicines. In large amounts, cinnamon is a poison.

Cassia, or Chinese cinnamon, is a kind of cinnamon used in oriental countries in cooking meat. Cassia is not quite as strong as the cinnamon we know.

Cinnamon and cassia were known to the early Egyptians, 3,500 years ago. This is one way we know there was trade between China and India, because these spices grow only in the Orient. Cinnamon and cassia are mentioned in the Bible.

C.I.O.: see CONGRESS OF INDUSTRIAL ORGANIZATIONS.

cipher and **code writing**, messages written in a secret code: see CRYPTOGRAPHY.

Circe

Circe was a goddess in Greek mythology, the stories the ancient Greeks told about their gods and goddesses. Circe was the daughter of the sun god Helios. She lived in a palace on the island of Aeaea and she had the magical power to change men into beasts. The most famous story about Circe is told by Homer, in the *Odyssey,* a story (in poetic form) about a hero named Odysseus or Ulysses.

The hero, Ulysses, and his soldiers were sailing home after they had won the Trojan War. On their way they stopped off at Circe's island of Aeaea. Circe invited Ulysses' men to dine in her palace. All agreed except one, Eurylochus. After

the soldiers had feasted, Circe turned them all into swine. Eurylochus saw what had happened and hurried back to tell Ulysses. The god Hermes suddenly appeared and told Ulysses to threaten Circe to make her free the soldiers. Ulysses did this and succeeded in freeing his friends. Afterward Circe liked Ulysses and he and his men stayed with her a year.

circle

A circle is a curved line, every point of which is the same distance from a point within, called the center. The simplest way to draw a circle is to use *compasses,* a special kind of instrument made for this purpose. If you have no compasses you can draw a circle with a pencil tied to a piece of string. You hold the free end of the string firmly on the paper with your finger. This point will be the center of the circle. Then you pull the string out to its full length, and move

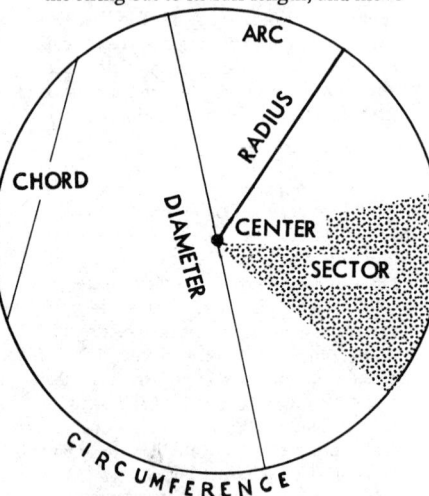

the pencil all the way around your finger until the beginning and end of the line you are drawing meet. This line is the *circumference.* The length of the piece of string, from your finger to the pencil, is called the *radius* of the circle. A straight line that goes from one point on the circumference to another and passes through the center is called a *diameter.* You can see that a diameter is twice as long as a radius. A straight line that goes from one point on the circumference to another is called a *chord,* and the part of the circumference that lies between the ends of that line is called an *arc.*

In any circle, the length of the circumference can be found by multiplying the length of the radius times two, and then multiplying that number by a number we call *pi,* which is 3.1416. The area of a circle can be found by multiplying pi times the length of the radius, and then multiplying that number by the length of the radius again.

circulation of the blood, the way the blood moves through the body: see BLOOD and HUMAN BODY.

circumcision

Many boy babies are circumcised when they are only a few days old. The word *circumcise* means "to cut around." Circumcision is the removal of a small fold of skin on the penis that is called the "foreskin."

The Jews have made it a strict law

that all boy babies must be circumcised. It is a requirement of the Covenant granted by God to Abraham and his descendants, as described in the Book of Genesis in the Bible, Chapter 17. Circumcision takes place when the baby is eight days old. At one time only specially trained holy men performed the rite of circumcision, which is an important religious ceremony, in Jewish homes. Now, however, though it is still a religious ceremony that is always observed by Jewish people, the operation itself is often performed by a doctor.

circus

A circus is a big show in which there are many different acts put on by acrobats, clowns and other performers, dogs, horses, and wild animals of many kinds. The show is given in a huge, high tent called a "Big Top." On the ground there are one or more circle-shaped areas, called rings, in which the main acts are put on. There may be one, two or three rings. The biggest circuses are three-ring circuses, with three different acts usually going on at the same time.

Circuses go back more than two thousand years, to Roman times. Roman circuses were held in open arenas, usually U-shaped. Rows of seats rose on the sides of the arenas, as they do in a modern circus tent. On the ground inside the arena was a wide track for chariot races, which was the favorite attraction of the circus. The chariots were pulled by horses. Sometimes there were four horses hitched to each chariot, but in most races there were three horses to each chariot.

Another great favorite in the Roman circuses was a fight between a man and an animal. Sometimes the man, called a gladiator, fought a bear. Other times he fought a lion, or some other wild animal.

The circuses in Rome were always held on the eight festival days throughout the year. There were four circus arenas in Rome. The most famous one was the Circus Maximus. It was rebuilt many times after fire destroyed the rows of wooden seats. The emperors or rulers often made changes in the decorations of the arena to suit their fancies. Before the decline of Rome the circuses had become very ornate and colorful. They looked almost as gaudy then as the modern circus does today.

THE CIRCUS IN THE MIDDLE AGES

From the Middle Ages to the present day circuses have been traveling shows. They are always spoken of as "nomadic," which means that they roam around the country and are not permanent. During the Middle Ages the circus consisted mainly of acts of fancy horse riding. Occasionally a trained bear was thrown in as an added attraction. The clowns in those days spoke to the audiences. They told jokes and acted out stories. After the performance was over, someone would "pass the hat," that is, they would take up a collection from the crowd that had gathered in the town square. Those medieval circuses always played in the open air. They had no tents or arenas.

At the end of the 18th century there was a permanent circus in London. It was

housed in an enormous building like a large theater. It was run by a man named Philip Astley. He imported all kinds of talent from all over the world. The show he put on was more like a theatrical performance than it was like the circus as you know it today. There were dancing girls and spoken words, as well as trained horses. The animal acts were not as important as the human talent. There were Italian "rope walkers," who walked across a tightly held wire. Their costumes were decorated with so many plumes and lace, it is a wonder they kept their balance.

The first circus in the United States was run by John Bill Ricketts. His circus was primarily horse acts. One of the horses in his circus had been bought from George Washington before he became our first president. After Washington was elected, the horse he sold to Ricketts became one of the main attractions of the show.

The menagerie (an exhibition of wild or strange animals) was made a regular and permanent feature of the circus during the 19th century. At that time many ministers had told the public that circuses were "instruments of the devil." In order to drum up business, and at the same time fight this wrong impression, circus owners began to import animals from all over the world. In their advertising they told about the "wonders to be seen in the menagerie." They called this an "educational feature" of the show. Some managers even went so far as to quote passages in the Bible where animals are mentioned. This made the public think it was perfectly all right to go to the circus because these things were to be found in the Bible.

One person who did more to change the circus than any other man was P. T. BARNUM, about whom there is a separate article. He was a great American showman who was always thinking up new ways to catch the public interest. Once he advertised that he had in the side show a "cherry-colored cat." People flocked to the circus, paid their money, and went into the tent. There they found an ordinary black cat. When some people complained, Barnum said he had been eating black cherries all his life, and that the cat was the same color as those cherries. On another occasion there were so many people in the tent that Barnum thought it was going to collapse and hurt everyone. He quickly made a sign that read: "To the Egress." The crowd got curious and began to move toward the door where the sign was posted. When they got through the door they found they were outside and there was nothing to see. "Egress," you see, means "exit." P. T. Barnum made his circus "the greatest show on earth." He enlarged the wagons in which the show traveled, made them more eye-catching and gaudy. He brought new methods into the actual performance in the ring. In general, he revolutionized the circus.

In 1919, Barnum's circus, Barnum & Bailey, was combined with another large circus, Ringling Brothers, to make by far the largest circus in the United States. It has been called "The Greatest Show on Earth." The Ringling Brothers, Barnum & Bailey Circus travels in a 70-car train, in three sections. The circus carries 1,400 people.

By the end of the 19th century there were over a hundred circuses traveling around the United States. When they moved from place to place, everything was carried in gaily painted wagons. Because these wagons frequently got stuck in the mud, the circuses became known as "mud shows." The wagons were painted many different colors, with lots of gold on them. They had so many curlicues that they looked like elaborate cakes. The two biggest ones were the one for the band to ride in, and the calliope. The calliope is a series of whistles, tuned like the pipes of an organ, through which steam rushes. It plays a wheezy tune. In many cases the wagons had big bright paintings on their sides, showing what was inside. The animal wagons opened on two sides to let the people see the animal in a cage inside the wagon. All of the tents, banners, and other equipment were carried in the same kind of gaudy cart. The performers—the acrobats, the clowns, the animal trainers, and the bareback riders—had their own separate wagons. In each wagon was a place to sleep and a place to keep costumes. There was a table with a lighted mirror over it. Here the performer put on his grease paint and make-up. All of the performer's life, outside the ring, was spent in his wagon. He even ate there. Nowadays all the performers eat together in a huge "cookhouse." It has rows of long tables and benches at which the performers eat. The kitchens are housed in an adjoining tent.

THE MODERN CIRCUS

Today circuses travel in trucks and by railroad. They still have the gaily painted wagons for use in the menagerie and in street parades. They are also used in the ring in the Grand Parade that opens and closes the show. They are not used now, though, to transport everything as they used to be.

All photos: *Ringling Bros. and Barnum & Bailey Circus*
Colorfully-decorated performing horses such as these are an important act in all circuses.

Men and women who perform "ballet" on horseback must not only be well-coordinated, but strong and graceful as well.

Coco and Coconut are father and son.

One of the most exciting things about the show, before it comes to town, is the circus poster. When these brightly colored sheets of paper are pasted all over a city, people begin to get "circus fever." The posters and handbills show lions and tigers and elephants looking very wild. Sometimes they picture acrobats or tightrope walkers high above the crowd. Many years ago they were even more exciting. In those days they would show an animal trainer with his head in a lion's mouth, or a lady acrobat hanging from the trapeze by one toe.

Today when you go to the circus you often sit in a tent with an arched canvas roof and canvas walls. It was only about 150 years ago that the first tent was used. No one wanted to stand around in the rain watching a circus, so a circus owner put up a tent, brought people in out of the rain, and still made money on a rainy day. The next step was to give evening performances. First pine torches were burned to light the inside of the tent. But that was too smoky. Next candles were used and after that they had kerosene lamps. Now the millions of circus lights are powered by huge electrical plants that the circus carries in big trucks. These power plants supply all the electricity needed to run the "Big Top."

A main attraction at the circus is the side show. This is a special tent that is set apart from the rest of the show. In the side show you can see the strong man, the fat lady, the snake charmer, and many freaks of nature. The fire-eater always used to draw a big crowd to the side show, but today the man who swallows neon lights does even better. Siamese twins are another good drawing card, as are the tatooed lady and the India-rubber man.

When you go into the main tent, you find in the arena three big rings. Very often there is something exciting going on in all three places at the same time. The same thing is done high above the audience where the acrobats fly through the air on trapezes. Quite frequently there will be several acrobatic acts going on at the same time. But when there is something very special to be seen, all the other activity stops and all the spotlights play on the center ring.

Acrobatic acts today are much more daring and exciting than they used to be. Clowns are much funnier, too. It is harder to be a clown nowadays. Years ago they used to speak and make funny remarks. But today they have to make you laugh without saying a word, which is very hard to do.

One of the most breath-taking animal acts is that in which all kinds of wild animals that are supposed to be enemies are brought together. Leopards, black panthers, lions, and tigers are often used. Sometimes the animals get into a fight that is hard to break up. The trainer cracks his whip or fires blank cartridges into the air to force the animals onto their perches placed around the cage. Trainers are often clawed or bitten by the animals. One of the most famous early animal trainers was Clyde Beatty, but there are many such fine acts now.

Traveling with the circus is easier now than it used to be. The performers ride in specially designed railroad cars. The men who put up the tents, called "rousta-bouts," have machines to help them. Years ago they used to depend on elephants to lift the heavy tent poles and push large objects around.

By 1957, the bigger circuses had given up appearing in tents and were using arenas, such as New York's Madison Sq. Garden, and it was apparent that The Big Top was on its way to becoming a thing of the past.

Cistercians

Cistercians are monks of the Roman Catholic Church who belong to an even larger order, or group, of monks called the Benedictines. The Cistercians are also called the White Monks, because they wear white robes instead of the black robes worn by other Benedictines, who are called the Black Monks. The laws of the Cistercian order were drafted by St. Stephen Harding more than 850 years ago. The order was founded by St. Robert, abbot of Molesme. Cistercian monks live in monasteries in lonely places. They grow all their own food, and work very hard in the fields. They spend the rest of their time in study and prayer.

citadel

A citadel is a fortress, in or very near a city, that was once used to protect the people in the city from attacks by an enemy. Citadels were usually built on the highest ground in the city, so that they could be most easily defended. The soldiers in the high citadel could see the enemy from all sides, and could fire down on him. Citadels often had two complete walls around them, one inside the other, and usually the space between the walls was filled with water. In olden days, wars were fought almost all the time, and cities that were not defended were in great danger of being robbed or burned down by enemy armies. When the people learned that their city was in danger of being attacked, they all went into the citadel, and carried many of their belongings with them. They even drove their cows, pigs, horses and sheep into the citadel. Most citadels were built just like castles, with strong walls, drawbridges, narrow openings through which the soldiers fired their weapons, and great towers at each corner that were used for observation.

citizenship

Citizenship means membership in a country. Not everyone who lives in a country is a citizen of that country. People may live in a country without being citizens. They may be just visiting. Each country has its own rules for deciding who can be a citizen.

UNITED STATES CITIZENSHIP

In the United States, there are two different ways in which people can become citizens. One is by birth. A person who is born in the United States is a citizen of the United States by birth. Also a person is a citizen by birth if his parents are citizens, even if he is born in another country.

The other way of becoming a citizen of the United States is by *naturalization*.

A person who is not born in the United States must live in the United States for five years before he can become a citizen. He must swear that he will not be loyal to any country except the United States. He must know something about the government and must agree to support it. After he has done this, the government accepts him as a citizen, with all the rights and duties of a native-born citizen.

THE RIGHTS OF A CITIZEN

The rights of a citizen are different in different countries. In the United States, one of the most important rights of a citizen is to vote and choose the people who run the government. The president and the members of the Congress and other officials are elected by the people, and only citizens can vote in elections. A citizen also has the right to be elected to a government office.

Only citizens have the right to work for the government, in the civil service. Citizens have the right to get passports, so they can travel in foreign countries. And when they are traveling they can ask the government to help them, if they have any trouble. These are some of the rights of a citizen.

THE DUTIES OF A CITIZEN

A citizen of a country has certain duties to perform. Each country makes its own laws about what the citizen has to do. Part of the duty of the citizen is to respect and obey the laws of his country. A country needs money to run the government, so it is the duty of the citizens to pay taxes. Another duty of the citizen is to help protect and defend his country. When his country needs him, he must serve in the armed forces.

BEING A GOOD CITIZEN

A country runs well only if its people are good citizens. Boys and girls study civics to learn to be good citizens. They must learn while they are young how the country is run, so that when they are grown up they will know how to help run it.

citric acid

Citric acid is the substance in oranges, lemons, limes and grapefruit that makes them taste sour. These fruits are called citrus fruits, and the citrus acid is sometimes removed from them and used for flavoring other foods, and for other purposes. People buy citric acid at a drugstore when they need it for cooking. You might think that it comes in liquid form like most other acids, but citric acid comes in crystal form, somewhat like rock candy or uneven lumps of sugar. Men who make blueprints use citric acid. You can read about BLUEPRINTS in a separate article.

citron

A citron is a fruit like the lemon, orange, grapefruit and others that we call citrus fruits. Very little citron grows in the United States. Most of the supply comes from Italy, Albania, and North Africa. The citron has a thick yellow skin, and is larger than a lemon. The rind, or skin, has a bitter taste. Some people make candy by soaking the rind in salt water to remove the bitterness. Then

they boil it in sugar water. This makes it crisp and gives it a sweet sharp taste.

citrus fruits

Citrus fruits are the group of juicy, sour-tasting fruits such as lemons, oranges, grapefruits, tangerines, citrons, and limes. Most citrus fruits are good to eat, but some are very bitter, and the trees are used for other purposes. All of the different kinds originally came from China or India, but they are now raised in large quantities in Florida, California, Mexico, Italy, Spain, Sicily, North Africa and most other tropical countries.

The trees upon which citrus fruits are grown, and the fruits also, are unable to stand cold weather, and even a slight frost can damage or destroy a crop. People who grow citrus fruits must be prepared to fight frost immediately. They use many small cans that burn tar or oil. These are called *smudge pots*, and as they burn they make a cloud of thick black smoke which helps to protect the citrus plants. When there is a severe frost nothing can help, and the crop is lost.

Citrus fruits have a lot of vitamin C in them. We need vitamin C in our daily food in order to keep strong and healthy. You can read about the different kinds of citrus fruit in separate articles on CITRON, GRAPEFRUIT, LEMON, LIME, ORANGE, and TANGERINE.

city

A city is a busy place where many people live and work. In ancient times, most people lived on farms. The cities were like fortified castles to which they could run for protection against invading enemies. Now, in countries as modern as the United States, more people live in cities and towns than on farms. These modern cities are huge; they have thousands of different buildings and, sometimes, millions of people.

A city is such a big and wonderful thing that men often try to find a new way to describe it. They say it is like an enormous machine that works smoothly and efficiently year after year and never stops. Musicians describe it as an orchestra that makes a symphony out of whistles, horns, voices, and other sounds it makes all day and night. Teachers often tell their students that a city like New York or San Francisco is a melting pot: people who come from different countries and speak different languages are mixed in the pot and come out Americans. For example, take those two cities, which are three thousand miles apart from each other. Each one has a Chinatown and a Little Italy side by side. On any day of the week, you can walk through New York's lower East Side and hear men speaking Chinese, Spanish, Yiddish, Italian, Russian, and other languages. For this reason New York is also called a "United Nations in miniature." When you read later on how a city is run, it may seem more like a corporation or a small country with its own government and army. Actually, a city is all of these things.

HOW CITIES GROW

There are many reasons why some towns have grown larger and larger and have become great cities, while other towns remain small. People have built cities at places that have natural harbors and seaports. Other people have built cities at the place where important rivers meet, or where main highways cross. Some cities have grown because they were close to great supplies of natural resources like coal or oil. Others have become large because they were near natural sources of power like water falls.

About two hundred years ago, around the time of the American Revolution, New York City was less important than Boston and Philadelphia. Then men built the Erie Canal between Buffalo and Albany to carry freight and passengers between the East and the West. This canal made New York the most important seaport in the country because it was right on the Hudson River which connected the Atlantic Ocean with the Canal. Trade from Europe and the southern states had to pass through New York on its way to the West; and trade from the West came back the same way.

As a city grows in size, the job of running it becomes more difficult. New York City has grown from a tiny settlement on the tip of Manhattan Island to a gigantic city of over seven million people. There is very little land to build on and that land is very expensive. For those reasons, men construct tall buildings. After the elevator was invented about one hundred years ago, New Yorkers made their buildings higher and higher. Not only did they build the city upward into the sky—they built it downward, too. A good part of a city's life goes on beneath the streets you walk on. Gas, electric, and telephone wires are never seen unless the sidewalk or street is torn up for repairs—they were put out of sight in the ground long ago. The motor traffic is so heavy and slow that underground railroads, called subways, are built to carry people quickly around a large city. Many shops and some theaters are built underground, too. You can enter large department stores and other buildings directly from the subway platform. In fact, it is possible for a man to live his entire life in New York and other large cities without ever going out on the street.

HOW MEN RUN A CITY

Like the state and country of which it is a part, a city has its own government. The government of the United States has a president and his cabinet, a congress, and courts. Similarly, most cities have a mayor and his assistants, a council, and their own courts. The mayor and the council are elected by the voters of the city just as the president and the congressmen are elected by the voters of the entire country. Some of the city's judges are appointed by the mayor, and the others are elected by the people. Like the federal government, the city has a budget which tells how much money it can spend to run the city and where the money comes from. Usually the money comes from taxes on land and business within the city. That money is spent on the city's departments, like the Police Department and the Fire Department, whose chiefs are appointed by the mayor. Among the other departments is the one which takes care of the public parks and bathing beaches, the one which runs the schools, the department of hospitals and prisons, the department of sanitation, and several others. Many cities have their own small air forces. The pilots may be policemen who watch traffic coming in and out of the city and make reports to the central police station. These reports enable other policemen on the ground to direct trucks and autos to take different roads to get around traffic jams, accidents, and anything else which may block traffic. Cities have small navies of fireboats and police-patrol boats. The Department of Sanitation is one of the most important in a city. Its job is to keep the city clean and a healthy place in which to live. When the weatherman predicts a heavy snowfall, the head of the department hires hundreds of extra snow-shovellers and sweepers and tells the drivers of the snowplows and trucks to be ready for work. When the storm strikes, thousands of men fight it day and night to keep the city business and activity from being slowed up or stopped by deep snow. The Sanitation Department does much more than keep the streets clean and clear. Its inspectors protect everyone's health by investigating food markets and restaurants to make certain that they, too, are clean, and that the food they sell is of good quality.

The officials of the city work under a charter issued by the state. This charter explains what powers the officials have and how far these powers reach. For example, it tells them what cases their policemen can work on and which cases must be turned over to the state or federal police.

CITIES IN THE PAST

As you read earlier, the first cities were not much more than forts to protect the people of the region from invaders. Then kings or important nobles made their headquarters or capitals in certain towns. The capital towns grew larger as trade and population increased and the rulers built big temples and palaces to show off their power or to please their gods. These great cities appeared first in Babylonia and in the valley of the Nile River in Egypt. When trade and power shifted to the Mediterranean Sea, powerful and prosperous cities appeared around its shores. Some of the great cities of the past were Babylon and nearby Nineveh, Memphis and Thebes in Egypt, Athens in Greece, Rome in Italy, and Carthage in North Africa. Most of these cities were destroyed, but modern cities have been built on the ruins of some of them.

CITY-STATES

Some cities in ancient times were completely independent and not part of countries. They were city-states. The nation we call Greece today was once upon a time divided into many separate and independent cities, such as Athens, Sparta and Corinth. They had their own armies and navies and they were all surrounded by great walls. All of the citizens who lived in them could meet together to make laws for themselves. We owe much to the people of these city-states for the kind of democracy and government we have today.

Venice, Florence, and Genoa in Italy became rich and strong city-states after the Crusades, which were wars between

Christians and Moslems for control of the Holy Land. The Crusades brought many people and much trade to these cities.

CITIES IN MODERN TIMES

When Christopher Columbus discovered America, England, Spain, France, and Holland became the most powerful nations, because they were on the Atlantic coastline of Europe. Trade between these countries and the New World made cities out of small towns. Then the steam engine and other inventions appeared. Men opened new and bigger factories. Thousands of people moved from the country to the cities to find work. At the time of the American Revolution, most Americans were farmers. In 1960, most of the people (seven of every ten Americans) lived in cities or big towns. One reason why American cities grew so fast was that millions of men and women came from Europe to make new homes for themselves and their children. Old industries grew larger and new ones were opened to feed and house all these new citizens. In sixty years the population of Houston, Texas, for instance, jumped from 25,000 to 600,000. Elsewhere the growth was even more spectacular.

Aerial bombardments during World War I and World War II severely damaged many large cities in Europe and Asia. Then the atom bomb appeared. Two of these bombs destroyed most of Hiroshima and Nagasaki in Japan. Now a hydrogen bomb can cause even more terrible damage. Leaders of governments have made plans to decentralize the cities, that is, move important industries away from them. This will reduce the population of cities because many people must follow the factories. It will also make it harder for the enemy to destroy a country with a few bombs. Long ago, people in the country ran to the fortified cities for protection against the enemy. Modern warfare forces city people to flee into the country.

city manager

A city manager is a man who runs a city the way a business is run. He is somewhat like a mayor except that he is not elected and takes no part in politics. The people of a city hire him just as the owner of a factory hires a factory manager. The city manager then hires the best possible men to help him run the affairs of the city.

More than five hundred American cities now have city managers. The argument in favor of the city manager is that he does not depend on votes to keep his job, so he does not do favors for politicians at the expense of the other citizens as the mayors of some other cities often do. Some cities that were run by dishonest politicians have had clean and economical government since they put in the city manager plan. There were many other cities in which the mayor was honest and efficient, but when these cities and mayors saw how well the city manager idea was working out, they adopted it for their cities. Some cities have both mayors and city managers. The mayor usually heads the council that makes the city laws, and the city manager carries them out.

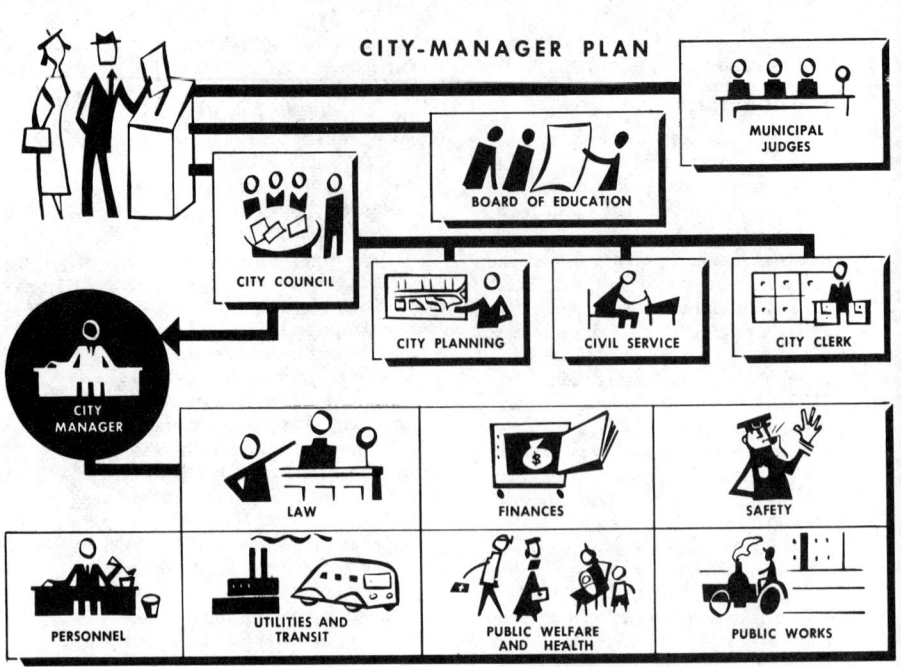

CITY-MANAGER PLAN

MUNICIPAL JUDGES

BOARD OF EDUCATION

CITY COUNCIL

CITY MANAGER

CITY PLANNING   CIVIL SERVICE   CITY CLERK

LAW   FINANCES   SAFETY

PERSONNEL   UTILITIES AND TRANSIT   PUBLIC WELFARE AND HEALTH   PUBLIC WORKS

Graphics Institute for "Your Life as a Citizen" by Smith; Ginn & Co.

A city manager is appointed by a city council, and these are some of the departments he is in charge of. If your city has a mayor, he is elected by the people.

Netherland Inform. Service

City planners build a model of the city with little wooden houses and trees to help them plan new cities, or to make changes in old sections being rebuilt.

city planning

When a man decides to build a farmhouse and barns, he must think of how large a family he has, how many trucks and cars and tractors he will need, how many pigs and cows and chickens he will keep, how much rain and snow fall in his neighborhood every year, and many other things. When he has answered these questions, he can plan the size and shape of his house and barns.

City planning commissions do very much the same thing. They study the census (a count of how many people live in a city or country) to figure out how the population may grow. They make plans for new suburbs to house these additional people. They predict how many cars, trucks and buses will use their city's streets and highways in the future, so that

they may widen old streets and build new ones. Perhaps the city planners decide that the city will need a new airport in five years. There will have to be new roads to the airport. The planners tell people that they cannot build houses or factories where the airport and the roads will be.

The first American city to be planned from the beginning was Philadelphia, Pennsylvania. When William Penn was asked to lay it out in 1682, there were no buildings at all. He was able to plan the city just the way he wanted it. Washington, D.C., was planned that way, too. Both these great cities are very orderly and attractive for that reason. But some cities just grew, and as a result, there are not enough parks or playgrounds; streets are too narrow and there are not enough

parking spaces; factories are too close to homes and schools.

URBAN DEVELOPMENT AND SLUM CLEARANCE

City planning is now concentrated on two goals: First, to tear down the old, unsanitary houses called "slums," where very poor people live in overcrowded and unsanitary conditions, and to build instead new, clean, light and airy houses where people can live in comfort even if they do not make much money. Second, to build superhighways leading into big cities, and inside big cities, so that the millions of automobiles will not cause constant traffic jams and also poison the air that people breathe.

Nearly every big city has made progress. In the biggest city, New York, more than 500,000 people have been moved from slums into modern housing, but in 1965 there were still nearly a million New Yorkers living in substandard dwelling places. Several cities, such as Hartford and New Haven, in Connecticut, almost completely rebuilt their central or business sections. Most of the very big cities — Boston, Detroit, Chicago, and Los Angeles, among others — solved many of their traffic problems with express highways or "freeways," but they still had many problems.

The United States Congress in 1965 voted to establish a new government department, the Department of Housing and Urban Development. In 1966 Robert Clifton Weaver of New York was appointed Secretary of this department. He was the first Negro to become a member of the Cabinet of the U.S.

Ciudad Trujillo

Ciudad Trujillo was the name given to Santo Domingo, capital and largest city of the Dominican Republic, from 1936 to 1961. *Ciudad* means "city" in Spanish, and it was named after the Dominican dictator, Generalissimo Rafael L. Trujillo. However, when Trujillo was assassinated in 1961, the city was renamed Santo Domingo, the name it had had for hundreds of years.

civet

The civet is a catlike animal that roams through Africa and Asia. It has the body of a large cat, with dark gray fur, and its head looks like that of a fox. It is related to both the cat and the mongoose. The civet does most of its prowling at night, and hunts small animals. When there is no prey for it to eat, it can get along on insects and fruits. The civet is chiefly hunted and kept in captivity for a fatty substance it secretes, called civet, that is used in making perfumes.

civics

Civics is the study of the citizen and his rights and duties under his government. When we study civics, we learn about how our city or town runs. We learn about the police departments that are needed to take care of the city. We also try to find out what a good citizen should do to make his city or town a better place to live in.

The study of civics teaches us other things too. We study the governments of the state and the nation. The governments of city and state and nation each have separate jobs to do. Civics teaches us what these jobs are, and how the governments are organized to do them. We learn what a good citizen can do to help these governments run well, and to improve the state and nation.

Today most children study civics in school. In a democratic country like the United States, people must know how the government works to take part in the activities of the community. But grownups can be good citizens only if they begin learning when they are young. For this reason, boys and girls study civics. They read books about how the government runs. They also learn civics by practice, when they elect their own governments to run the school. Civics classes visit the departments that run the city. They see how the city gets its water supply and what is done to keep the city clean. They find out what can be done to prevent fires. In some big cities specially chosen boys and girls take over the city for one day each year, acting as mayor, members of the city council, and so on. This gives them a real idea of how the city is run and what its problems are. All this is part of civics.

Civil Aeronautics Authority: see AVIATION.

civil defense

There was a time when wars were fought only by armies and warships, but modern warfare is just as likely to hurt men, women and children who stay at home and do not fight. A bomb dropped on a city will destroy buildings and start fires that can hurt anyone. Therefore the people who are not part of the armed services must help to protect themselves and their neighbors if an enemy attacks. This work by people who are not part of the armed forces is called *civil defense.*

Most civil defense workers are trained to guard a city against an air raid. In the United States, it would take as many as fifteen million persons to fill all the jobs that would have to be done if an enemy began to attack the country by air. More than twenty thousand first-aid workers would be needed to take care of the people who could be wounded by just one atomic bomb.

An air-raid siren gives warning when a city is likely to be bombed. At that point the civil-defense organization takes charge. The air-raid warden is in charge of his section. He wears a white helmet. Everyone should obey his orders. The plans for civil defense have made some places air-raid shelters. They are the safest places during an air raid. Everyone should go to the nearest shelter unless he has some other official job to do. When a "blackout" is ordered the lights should be turned out in every house. Enemy planes can aim their bombs better if they can see lights. The police and fire departments will need many helpers to do their jobs if there is an air raid.

One important branch of civil defense is "skywatching." The Ground Observer Corps is a group of many thousands of persons who look out for airplanes that might be attacking enemy planes. A skywatcher must be trained, because it would cause a lot of trouble if he could not tell enemy planes from friendly planes. Many members of the Boy Scouts and Girl Scouts are members of the Ground Observer Corps.

The British people were the first to have an organized civil defense, early in World War II when the Germans were making many air raids. The United States organized civil defense when it entered the war. There have never been quite enough workers in civil defense, and volunteers are needed.

civil engineering, the designing and building of bridges, roads, etc.: see ENGINEERS and ENGINEERING.

Civilian Conservation Corps

The Civilian Conservation Corps (CCC) was an agency set up by the United States government to give work to young men who had no jobs. During the business depression that started in 1929, millions of young men could not find work. They felt useless and discouraged. President Franklin D. Roosevelt decided to do something about this. He felt that if business could not give the young men jobs, the government should do so. At his request Congress set up the CCC in 1933. Any male between 17 and 33 could enroll in one of the CCC's 2,600 camps. Here he learned how to plant trees, lay telephone wires, build roads and bridges, and to do other useful work. He got $30 a month and his keep.

The CCC gave work to about three million men. They built thousands of fire observation towers, planted millions of trees, helped to protect wild life and the soil. They added many millions of dollars to the wealth of the country. The CCC ended in 1943 when business improved.

civilization

Civilization is all the ways man has found to make his world more beautiful and to make himself more comfortable and happy. Man has built his civilization by changing the world around him, by learning to control it, and by learning to use the materials that nature supplies. Because man is the only living creature that knows how to change the world, he is the only living creature that has a civilization. Your dog, for instance, cannot build a fire to keep himself warm, or cut his fur in summer to keep himself cool. Birds make nests of twigs and leaves, but if there are no twigs and leaves around, they do not know how to build homes for themselves by making brick and steel. They have to fly away in search of a place where they can find the only kinds of building materials they know how to use.

EARLY MAN

In his very earliest days on earth, man had no civilization either. But gradually man began to find ways to make his life easier. He learned, for instance, how to make himself stronger than the wild animals by making weapons such as bows and arrows, and tools such as axes made by chipping away at pieces of stone. He learned how to build fires and how to keep himself warm by wearing the skins of the animals he killed. He learned how to take shelter, either in caves or in huts built of twigs and stones. He began to develop ideas and speech. These helped him to understand other men.

Man did not learn much more than this for hundreds of thousands of years. It was about seven thousand years ago that man made one of the most important discoveries in his history. He learned how to farm, and how to keep farm animals for his own use. That meant he no longer had to go wandering around in search of food. He no longer had to worry from day to day whether he and his family would have enough to eat. He could grow food in the summer and store some of it to be eaten during the winter months. when nothing could grow. He learned how to spin cloth, and to make clothes to keep himself warm, and he no longer had to depend on the wild beasts for his clothing. He learned how to harness cattle to plow his fields. At some time during this period, he discovered the principle of the wheel. Perhaps he discovered this by watching a fallen tree trunk roll down a hill. When he saw how easily the log rolled, he may have realized that if wheels were attached to a cart, it would be easier to move heavy loads. When man first learned to farm and to stay in one place, communities began to grow stronger. People realized that they had to have laws and government to keep things running smoothly. They began to see that people could do different kinds of work in the community, and that each man could benefit from the work his neighbor did. One man could hunt or fish, another could be a farmer, and a third could be a potter, who made bowls and dishes.

The invention of writing was the next big landmark in the growth of civilization. That took place about five thousand years ago. Before they learned how to write, men had no way of keeping records, or of spreading their ideas further than the sound of their voices. Once they learned to write, men could hand down their knowledge to their children, they could increase learning, and they could send their ideas out to the rest of the world.

Before they learned to farm, men lived in very much the same way all over the world. Men in China and men in Egypt had the same customs and ways of living. But after man learned to farm, to tame and use animals, and to build governments, he had many more choices in his ways of living. Civilizations began to differ in different parts of the world. The civilization of China and the civilization of Egypt were so different that an Egyptian would not have known how to get along if he had suddenly been transported halfway across the world to China. Actually, what happened is that two entirely different kinds of civilization did grow up. Our civilization today comes from a civilization that started somewhere in Asia Minor, near where Iran is now. The civilizations of Asia developed differently. These differences are shown in the ways people live, and also in their ideas, which are an important part of civilization. The idea of freedom for the individual, for instance, is a Western idea. In the East, people think much more in terms of duty than they do in terms of freedom.

The great civilization of Egypt was one of the first civilizations of the Western world. The Jews gave the idea of one god to Western civilization. This Jewish idea developed many thousands of

years ago but it did not become powerful for a very long time, even after the birth of Christ. The Egyptian civilization was followed by the Greeks, who first developed many of our ideas of liberty and justice. Then came the Romans. The Romans controlled most of the Western world for a long time. But the Romans quarreled among themselves, and savage tribes from Western Europe made war on them and destroyed their empire. For about a thousand years, from 500 to about 1500, there was very little advance in civilization in Europe. This period is often called the Dark Ages, because men added little to their knowledge, the poor were badly treated, and ideas of liberty were practically unknown in the west.

The modern period of civilization began about the time Columbus discovered America. This was a time of travel and exploration, and men from different parts of the world learned from one another. Civilization has advanced rapidly since then, because men can trade knowledge better.

Civil liberties and civil rights

Civil liberties and civil rights are almost the same thing, but in the United States they have come to have different meanings, especially since 1954.

Civil liberties cover the right every citizen has to receive fair treatment from his government. The BILL OF RIGHTS, about which there is a separate article, names the things the United States government may not do to its citizens. In 1920 the American Civil Liberties Union, a private association to protect Americans against persecution by government officials, was founded by a large group of distinguished persons including Jane Addams, John Dewey, Helen Keller, Norman Thomas, and many others. The ACLU has done many things to protect citizens against unfair laws or treatment.

Civil rights (some of which used to be called *social rights*) cover the right of a citizen to receive fair treatment from other citizens and from local governments. Many laws have been passed by Congress and by some states saying that a person could not be prevented from voting, or going to a school, or being admitted to a public restaurant or hotel, or belonging to an association, because of his race (as a Negro, or an oriental such as Chinese, Japanese, or Filipino) or because of his religion (as a Jew or Roman Catholic). The first such law was passed in 1866 but the Supreme Court said it was unconstitutional (see CONSTITUTION). In 1868 an amendment (see FOURTEENTH AMENDMENT) gave Congress the power to pass such laws but the Supreme Court did not insist that they be enforced. State laws were usually enforced and many private institutions, such as colleges, did away with racial and religious barriers without being forced by law, but this did not occur in the South. In 1942, under wartime rules, many Americans of Japanese ancestry lost their property and liberty in spite of the Fourteenth Amendment. In 1954 the Supreme Court, reversing its earlier decision, ruled that Negroes could not be prevented from going to school with white children, but as late as 1965 very few Southern schools had obeyed this order. In 1964 Congress passed a Civil

Rights Act admitting Negroes to parks, swimming pools, theaters, hotels, restaurants, and other public places.

Civil Service

A civil servant is a person who works for the government without being elected to his office. He is hired by an elected official, such as a mayor or governor or president. All such persons together are called the Civil Service.

Once people got Civil Service jobs by politics. This was called the "spoils system." When the Republicans had won the last election, all the government employees were Republicans. If the Democrats won the next election, all the Republicans were fired and Democrats replaced them.

About a hundred years ago, people began to see how much their government lost by giving up experienced, capable employees just because they did not belong to the winning political party. So the Civil Service Law was passed. Now a government employee must pass a test to get his job. He cannot lose his job just because his party loses an election. Jobs are given out to people from all states and the states having the most people get the most jobs. It is against the law to make a person in the Civil Service give money or do work for any political party.

HOW CIVIL SERVICE WORKS

The Civil Service system is run by the Civil Service Commission, which is part of the government. The Civil Service Commission makes rules and gives tests. It decides which people should be hired, and what kind of jobs they would be good for. It trains people for their jobs, and promotes them to better jobs when they deserve it. The Civil Service system has improved the running of the government a great deal, and more and more people are hired in this way. Now, about 2,500,000 government jobs in the United States are filled by the Civil Service examination system.

Each state of the United States has its own Civil Service system. Many city governments also hire people through a merit system. Great Britain also uses this system. But not all countries give tests. Sometimes the term *Civil Service* is applied to all the people in government jobs, no matter how they have been chosen.

Besides the Civil Service in the governments of different countries, there is also an international Civil Service. The International Civil Service is made up of the people who are hired to work for the United Nations organization. The International Civil Service also gives tests to find out which people will best be able to do the work. These tests are given in all countries that belong to the United Nations, and people are hired from all of these countries.

Civil War

A civil war is a war within a single country. It is like a bad family quarrel, and it can be more terrible than a war between nations, because in civil wars men sometimes kill even their own brothers. Civil wars are usually very fierce, for they are mostly caused by disagreements over

very important beliefs, such as religion or how the country should be governed.

There have been many civil wars in history. In ancient Rome there was almost continual civil war for eighteen years between 49 B.C. and 31 B.C. In England, a civil war called the "Wars of the Roses" raged from 1455 to 1485. This war was fought between two branches of the English royal family, the House of Lancaster and the House of York. (You can read more about this war in the article WARS OF THE ROSES in another section.) In France there was civil war between the Protestants and Catholics from 1562 to 1598. Another English civil war took place between 1641 and 1647. This war, which ended in a victory for the supporters of the English parliament over the supporters of King Charles I, is called the PURITAN REVOLUTION, and there is a separate article on it. The SPANISH CIVIL WAR, which lasted from 1936 to 1939, was won by the Falangists, who were led by General Franco, over the Loyalists. (There is also an article on this war, which many people call a kind of dress rehearsal of World War II.)

AMERICAN CIVIL WAR

The American Civil War, which lasted from 1861 to 1865, was the biggest civil war of all time. More than 600,000 Americans died in it. There were many causes for the war, but the most important one was that the United States had split into two sections, with completely different ways of living and thinking. In the South, the main activity was growing cotton. This was done on large plantations where the workmen were Negro slaves who had been brought from Africa. In the North, there were small farms of all types, and modern industry was beginning to grow up in the big cities. In the years before the war, the West was rapidly being settled. Every time a new state was admitted to the Union, there was a big argument in Congress over whether it should be *slave* (meaning part of the South) or *free* (part of the North). All over the country, the arguments became more and more fierce, and clubs of Abolitionists, who wanted to end slavery entirely, were formed in northern cities. In 1860, Abraham Lincoln was elected president. He was a member of the new Republican Party, which was against slavery. The people in the South felt that with Lincoln as president, their whole way of life was in danger, and all of the southern states seceded (broke away) from the United States. The main reason why the North fought was to bring the southern states back into the Union.

FIRST YEARS OF THE WAR

The first shots of the Civil War were fired at Fort Sumter, South Carolina, a Federal army fort on an island in the harbor of Charleston. The southerners demanded that the troops in the fort surrender, and when they refused the guns at Charleston opened fire. Fort Sumter surrendered the next day, April 13, 1861, and the Civil War had begun.

Both sides thought that it would be a short war. In the North an army was quickly gotten together and brought to Washington, D.C. In July 1861, this army marched south toward Richmond,

Virginia, which was to be the capital of the Confederate States of America. It met an army of southerners at Bull Run Creek, a few miles south of Washington. Both armies had had too little training to fight well, but the Confederates had better leaders and they defeated the Union forces, which retreated to Washington.

After the Battle of Bull Run, both sides realized that the war could not be won unless real armies were organized and trained. A young general named George B. McClellan was made commander of the Army of the Potomac, as the North's forces were called. He spent months drilling the army until it was in fighting shape. In March 1862, the Army of the Potomac boarded ships and was taken down to the York Peninsula, which is just east of Richmond. But McClellan was a better organizer than a fighter, and he advanced toward Richmond much too slowly and carefully. Perhaps a quick bold stroke would have captured Richmond and ended the war. The Confederate forces were under General Robert E. Lee, who was a brilliant and daring army officer. Lee, his second-in-command General Thomas J. "Stonewall" Jackson, and his cavalry leader J. E. B. Stuart, drove back McClellan's men and forced them to return to Washington by ship as they had come.

After this defeat another general, John Pope, was given a chance to win a victory for the North. In August 1862, he led an army south from Washington, but he was beaten by Lee and Jackson in the second Battle of Bull Run. Lee then decided that it was a good time for the South to attack. The Confederate army invaded Maryland, but in August 1862 the Union forces, led again by McClellan, stopped Lee in the Battle of Antietam. Again McClellan was too cautious. He had a chance to trap the Confederate army, but instead he allowed Lee to slip back into Virginia. In December 1862, the Army of the Potomac, now under the command of General Ambrose Burnside, tried again to take Richmond. This time it was very badly beaten at the town of Fredericksburg, Virginia.

Meanwhile, the war was also being fought in Tennessee and along the Mississippi River. Out there two generals of the Union army, Ulysses S. Grant and William T. Sherman, were becoming known as hard-driving soldiers who won victories. In April 1862, an army under Grant invaded western Tennessee. The Confederates attacked, but they were beaten back in the Battle of Shiloh, one of the bloodiest fights of the war. A few weeks later a fleet of ships under Admiral David Farragut sailed into the mouth of the Mississippi and captured New Orleans. In 1862 there also took place the first battle between ironclad warships, the MONITOR and the MERRIMAC. (There is a separate article on this battle.) It ended in a "draw."

THE WAR IN 1863

In May 1863 the Union army tried to capture Richmond again. A new leader was found, General Joseph Hooker, but he was no more successful than the others. Lee and Jackson trapped Hooker near the little village of Chancellorsville in

Virginia, and once again the Union army was completely defeated. Now Lee got his forces together and marched north into Pennsylvania. If the Confederates were successful this time, the North might have to ask for peace. Still another general was found to command the Army of the Potomac, George Meade, a man who was dependable rather than brilliant. The armies met on July 1, 1863, near the Pennsylvania village of Gettysburg. For three days the Confederates attacked the Union defenses. If they could break through, Washington and other great cities of the East would lie almost undefended. But Meade's men held firm, and finally the beaten southerners were forced to retreat into Virginia. They never invaded the North again.

Not much happened in the East during the rest of the year, but the Union forces in the West made steady gains. On July 4, 1863, Grant captured the Mississippi town of Vicksburg, and the whole river now belonged to the North. The Confederacy was split in two, and the people of the South began to feel a new enemy—hunger. From the beginning of the war, the United States Navy had put warships outside all the southern ports, so that there could be no trade between the South and the outside world. This blockade was beginning to be felt, for the Confederacy could not produce enough food or guns for its own needs, and it could not buy or sell goods abroad. Now with Union gunboats cruising up and down the Mississippi, nothing could be brought from the West either. Besides this, another Union army had advanced into eastern Tennessee and captured Chattanooga. In September 1863, the Confederates under General Braxton Bragg beat the northerners near Chattanooga in the Battle of Chickamauga, but Grant now took charge and brought in more troops. In November he won the Battle of Chattanooga and drove Bragg back into Georgia.

THE FINAL DRIVES

In March 1864 Grant became commander-in-chief of all the Union forces, and Sherman was made head of the Union armies in the west. In May the Army of the Potomac began driving toward Richmond again. There were troops moved forward steadily. All of Lee's skill and the courage of the southerners could not stop them now. Richmond itself was very well defended, so Grant's soldiers circled around the city and besieged Petersburg, 22 miles to the south.

Meanwhile Sherman drove into Georgia and captured Atlanta on September 1, 1864. Then his men marched southeast to the sea, burning farm houses, destroying crops, and tearing up railroads so that the South could not produce or move any of the food that it needed to continue fighting. Sherman reached Savannah, Georgia, on December 20, 1864, and then his army turned to the north and invaded South Carolina. The main Confederate army around Petersburg and Richmond was being hemmed into a smaller and smaller circle. In the Shenandoah Valley in northwestern Virginia, General Philip Sheridan, the Union cav-

NORTH

Abraham Lincoln

Gen. Ulysses S. Grant

Gen. William Sherman

Gen. George McClellan

The Civil War was a great struggle between the Union or Northern army and the Confederacy or Southern army. The Confederacy seemed to be winning the war at first. But as you can see from this map, the South had far fewer men and far less supplies for their army. This is partly why they lost the war. The South manufactured very few things at the time of the Civil War, and soldiers suffered from lack of clothing, shoes, and blankets. The South also lacked enough railroads to ship the supplies to the fighting men. Both the soldiers and the civilians in the South suffered from the lack of food. They had far less grain and livestock than the North, and by the end of the war, people were weakened by starvation.

The Confederacy   The Union

POPULATION
29% | 71%

VALUE OF MANUFACTURED PRODUCTS
8% | 92%

MILES OF RAILROAD TRACK
28% | 72%

PRODUCTION OF GRAINS
30% | 70%

VALUE OF LIVESTOCK
35% | 65%

Library of the Congress Photos   *Graphics Inst. of Am.*

SOUTH

Jefferson Davis

Gen. Robert E. Lee

Gen. Stonewall Jackson

Gen. Joseph Johnston

alry leader, did the same thing Sherman had done in Georgia.

The Confederate soldiers were tired and hungry. They did not have enough shoes, or bullets for their guns, but they put up a strong fight until the very end. On April 2, 1865, Grant's forces broke into Petersburg. Lee realized that he would be trapped if he kept his army around Richmond, so he headed west. He hoped to join what was left of the Confederate army of General Joseph Johnston, which had been fighting Sherman's men, but on April 7 Grant's forces surrounded the weary southerners. Two days later Lee and Grant met in a farmhouse near the village of Appomattox Courthouse, Virginia, and the Confederate commander surrendered the remnants of his army. The war was over.

clam

The clam is a kind of mollusc that lives in sand or mud, burrowing by means of a large organ called a "foot." It is a *bivalve*, which means it has two shells. There are many kinds of clam, most of them living in salt water. The giant clam of the Indian and Pacific Oceans grows to weigh five hundred pounds, but all other clams are quite small. In America the best known kinds of clam are the *hard-shell clam*, from the shells of which the Indians made "wampum," which they used as money; the *littleneck* or *cherrystone clam*, which is a young hard-shell clam; the *razor clam*, which lives chiefly on mud flats; the *surf clam*, which is used for bait; and the *soft-shell clam*, which is found only as far south as Cape Hatteras off North Carolina. It is the clam chiefly used in the famous New England clambakes. A hole is dug in the ground, stones are put into it and a fire lighted to heat them. Then the fire is raked out and quantities of clams are piled in, often with corn, potatoes, and fish. The whole lot is covered with masses of seaweed to keep the heat in while the clams cook.

clan

The word *clan* means a group of people with the same last name, who believe they can trace their families back to the same person, or ancestor. You and your family have the same last name, and if you wish you can call yourselves a clan. This is no longer as necessary as it was hundreds of years ago when living in a clan was the only way to have law and order.

The members of a clan were led by a chief, and they had certain rights and duties among themselves. They also swore to fight for each other. Some members of the clan had higher positions than others, and they showed this by the way they dressed. Slaves, for example, were allowed to wear clothes of only one color, while a chief could wear clothes with as many as six colors. Each Scottish clan had its *tartan*, cloth woven with cross bars of several colors, like the plaid skirts that many girls wear now. You can still see men in Scotland proudly wearing the tartan of their clan. The clans of Scotland were once very powerful, and they ruled themselves. About two hundred years ago, they revolted against the English king, and he punished them by taking away their power.

HOW THE CLANS BEGAN

Long ago, in Ireland and Scotland, there were tribes of people who lived in one place, so they did not need to have a last name to show they were related to each other. A person was simply called something like "Donald, son of Daniel." Then the tribes were broken up by wars, and the growth of towns. People still wanted to show that they were related to each other, so they chose the name of one of their great ancestors and said they were sons of that man. This was how clans started. "Mac" in Irish and Scottish meant "the son of," so people began to use last names like MacDonald or MacDaniel.

Scientists now use the word *clan* to describe groups of people very different from the clans in Scotland. For example, among primitive peoples there are totemic clans, or groups of people who believe they are descended from insects or animals like grasshoppers or cows, and some clans even believe they are descended from vegetables.

clarinet

The clarinet, sometimes spelled *clarionette* in England, is a musical instrument. It is about two feet long, and usually made of wood, but some clarinets are made of metal. It has holes in it that are covered by keys. When all the keys are open, the holes are open. Then if you blow through the mouthpiece you get the highest possible tone. As you press down the keys to cover the holes, the pitch gets lower. When all the keys are

The clarinet was invented in Germany almost 300 years ago, and is now one of the most important instruments in an orchestra.

down, you can play the lowest possible tone.

In the orchestra, the clarinet is a member of the woodwind section. Clarinet usually means the standard B-flat clarinet. The other members of the family are the E-flat clarinet, which is smaller and high-

The people of different clans in Scotland wear special plaids to show which clans they belong to. Here are the plaids of two Scottish clans. They have been worn for centuries.

er and is used mostly in military bands; the E-flat alto clarinet, and the B-flat bass clarinet. The clarinet is a "double" in a dance orchestra. This means that it is played by a musician who also plays another instrument, usually the saxophone.

Clark, George Rogers

George Rogers Clark was an American soldier and frontier fighter whose victories against the British during the American Revolution-ary War helped win the Northwest Territory for the United States. The Northwest Territory was north of the Ohio River and west of Pennsylvania. It included what are now the states of Ohio, Indiana, Illinois, Michigan, Wisconsin, and part of Minnesota. At the time of the Revolutionary War, the territory belonged to England, and English forces attacked the colonies from this western front. Clark fought many battles and won support from Indian tribes, who gave him the name "Big Knife." When the peace treaty with England was made in 1783, the Northwest Territory went to the United States.

Clark was born in Virginia in 1752. He first worked as a surveyor, mapping out land in Kentucky, which bordered on the Northwest Territory. When war broke out, Kentucky was attacked, and Clark organized its defenses. Then he invaded the British territory and captured some of their forts. His success gave the colonies their chief claim on the territory when the peace treaty was made. Clark became famous and was given many honors. He died in 1818.

Clark, Mark

Mark Wayne Clark is the name of an American general who fought in North Africa and Europe during World War II. He was born in 1896, and he graduated from the United States Military Academy at West Point when he was 21. In 1942, the United States and British armies were preparing to land in North Africa, but they did not know if the French who were there would be friendly or not. So Mark Clark landed about a month before the landings, and made an agreement with the French so that they would not fight against the Allies. Later Clark was commander of the American troops who were fighting the Germans in Italy. During the end of the Korean War, in 1953, he was in command of all American troops in Korea, Japan, and the rest of the Far East. In 1954 he retired from the army and became president of The Citadel, a military school in Charleston, South Carolina.

Clark, William, an American explorer: see LEWIS AND CLARK.

classics

Classic is a word used to describe the finest kind of writing or art; that is, the writing or art that all other works of the same kind are compared to when you are trying to find out how good they are. When we speak of the classics we sometimes mean the books written by the Greeks and Romans at the beginning of our civilization, between 1,500 and 3,000 years ago. Aesop's *Fables* are a Greek classic, for example. Hawthorne and Mark Twain have written American classics.

classification

Classification is the arrangement of things into groups, in such a way that we can easily know in what ways things are the same and in what ways they are different. In biology, which is the study of living things (plants and animals), the science of classification is called *taxonomy.*

Everyone uses some form of classification in everyday life, even if he does not know he is doing it. For instance, everyone who lives in a town or city classifies the stores that are there. He knows that some are groceries, some are hardware shops, some are bakeries, and so on. He has classified the stores according to what they sell.

To the scientist the right classification is very important. In fact, there could be no such thing as science without classification. Carl Linnaeus, a great Swedish scientist and botanist, was one of the first men who tried to show how important classification is to science. About two hundred years ago, Linnaeus showed that all the flowering plants in the world could be put in order if they were classified according to the kinds of flower that they had.

Claudius

The name Claudius was borne by many famous Romans. In ancient Rome, a person's whole name included not only the name of his family, but also the name of his *gens,* that is, the tribe to which he belonged. The first Claudius, the founder of that *gens,* settled in Rome about five hundred years before Jesus was born. Many members of the *gens* became famous men. One of them was Appius Claudius Caecus, who lived about 2,200 years ago. He is remembered as the builder of a famous road, the Appian Way, which is named after him.

The most famous Claudius was an emperor. His full name was Tiberius Claudius Drusus Caesar, but in history he is usually known just as Claudius. Claudius was born in 10 B.C. As a child he was weak and sick and grew very slowly. Because of this, people always made fun of him. They said that he was stupid and simple-minded, and even that he was an idiot. But this was not true. Claudius was always interested in studying and writing, and he wrote several books of history. Claudius became emperor when he was about fifty years old. He tried to be a good ruler, and many of the laws that he made were helpful and wise. He did much to build up the city of Rome and make it more beautiful. But other things that Claudius did were not so good. He was always afraid that people were plotting against him. He would have people killed and take their property away, to protect himself. Also he let other people tell him what to do. His wife Messalina and several friends had great influence on him. When Claudius died in the year 54, it was said that he was poisoned by his second wife, Agrippina, who wanted her son Nero to become emperor.

clavichord

The clavichord is a musical instrument that looks like a piano on the outside. It has a keyboard with black and white keys and a square boxlike cabinet. But inside it is quite different. The

strings are struck by brass wedges, instead of felt hammers as in the piano. This gives the clavichord a metallic tone. Johann Sebastian Bach wrote a famous composition called *The Well-tempered Clavichord* consisting of 48 preludes and fugues. The clavichord was popular for about two hundred years, from the 1500s through the 1700s.

clay

Clay is a kind of earth made up of very fine grains of two chemicals, aluminum oxide and silica. It is usually found mixed with other chemicals that give it colors such as white, yellow, red, brown, blue, or gray. When clay is mixed with water it is easily made into a kind of putty or "dough." It can then be shaped into bricks, or pottery, or dishes, and baked to make it permanently hard.

There are many different kinds of clay. Some are very coarse and can be used only for making bricks, rough pottery, and the flat drain tiles that you see on some houses. Potter's clay is a slightly finer clay that is used for making flower pots. Sculptors also use potter's clay for modeling statues. Pipe clay is a purer kind of potter's clay. Fine stoneware is also made from potter's clay. Fire clay is another kind of clay that is used for lining stoves and fireplaces because it is very hard to melt.

The very finest clay in the world is called kaolin. It is used for making beautiful porcelain cups, dishes, and pottery. It got the name kaolin because some of the most famous Chinese porcelain is made of a clay that comes from a hill in China called Kao-ling. Kaolin is white or creamy yellow and it is softer and more crumbly than other kinds of clay. Good kaolin is found in many parts of Europe. In the United States you can find some of the best kaolin in Vermont, Delaware, South Carolina, and Georgia.

Clay, Henry

Henry Clay was a great American statesman. He was one of the most famous members of the Congress of the United  States during the fifty years before the Civil War. These were very important years in the growth of the United States as a country, and Henry Clay had much to do with what happened during those

Gale Research Co. years. He was born in Virginia in 1777. His father died when Henry was a boy, so Henry had to stay on his family's farm instead of going to school, but he was eager to learn and he read as much as he could. He studied law books in a lawyer's office and when he was 20 years old he moved to Kentucky and became a lawyer. In less than two years he was one of the best-known and most successful lawyers in Kentucky.

HENRY CLAY'S CAREER

The people of Kentucky elected Clay to several positions in the state government. Later he was elected to both the House of Representatives and the Senate of the United States. He was always considered one of the outstanding men in both houses of Congress. Henry Clay was a great orator, and whenever he spoke people listened and were impressed. He is best remembered for the work he did to save the country from possible civil war on three different occasions. For years before the Civil War was fought there were hot-headed people in both the North and the South who wanted to have their way about important problems such as slavery, even if it meant breaking up the Union. Clay was able to work out solutions, or compromises, at these different times, and get the people who were arguing bitterly to agree. The most important compromises were called the MISSOURI COMPROMISE and the COMPROMISE OF 1850. You can read about these in separate articles. Both of them were mainly about whether new states that were about to be admitted to the Union would permit slavery. Henry Clay became known as *The Great Compromiser* for his work in settling these great arguments. He never attained his highest goal, however. He wanted to become President of the United States, and he was a candidate in several elections. The people liked him and respected him, but they never elected him President. Clay's most famous saying was, "I would rather be right than be President." He died in 1852.

claymore

A claymore is a double-edged broad sword that was used long ago by Scottish soldiers. Since a claymore is sharp on both sides, it is a very dangerous weapon. The Scottish soldiers used to hold it with both hands and swing it from side to side. There are regiments of Scottish soldiers in the British army today, and their officers carry claymores when these regiments are on parade, although the claymore in no longer used as a weapon.

Clayton-Bulwer Treaty, a treaty signed in 1850 between the United States and Great Britain that finally led to the building of the Panama Canal. See the article on the PANAMA CANAL ZONE.

clematis

The clematis is a flowering vine that grows on garden walls and on fences. In the summer most clematis vines are covered with many flowers which may be pink, white or purple depending on the kind planted. Clematis will grow in most kinds of soil, which should be kept on the dry side. There are more than a hundred different kinds of clematis that grow all over the world. The clematis belongs to a large and important family of flowers that includes the buttercup, the peony, and the columbine.

American Peony Society
This peony belongs to the large classification of flowers that includes the clematis.

Clemenceau, Georges

Georges Clemenceau was a great French statesman and an outstanding writer. Clemenceau was born in 1841. He studied medicine and became a doctor. But he did not practice as a doctor very  long. When Clemenceau was a young man, France was ruled by a king. Clemenceau was always against that kind of government. He wanted the country to become a republic, and he thought the government should be chosen by the people. The king was overthrown by a revolution in 1870. Clemenceau held many posts in the government of the French Republic. For many years, he was the premier, which is the head of the French government. Clemenceau was also famous as a writer and editor of newspapers and magazines. Whatever he felt was wrong he attacked fearlessly, and for this reason the people called him the "Tiger." During World War I, Clemenceau was the great leader of his country. He was an old man at that time, but he never became tired or discouraged. He worked very hard to lead the French people to victory. Success came to him with the help of the Allies, which included England, the United States, Italy, and other countries. Clemenceau represented his country at the Peace Conference of Versailles, in 1919, after the war ended. He was chairman at the conference table. Though he retired in 1920, he worked for peace until his death in 1929.

Clemens, Samuel

Samuel Langhorne Clemens was an American writer. Some people think he was the greatest American writer who ever lived. Most people know him best by the name *Mark Twain*. Clemens was born in the little town of Florida, Missouri, in 1836. When he was 12 years old, his father died, and he began to travel. He went out west and  *Gale Research Co.* lived in mining camps and tough frontier towns. He worked as a printer and a newspaper reporter, and for a while he took a job as a riverboat pilot on the Mississippi. As he traveled up and down the river, he could hear the river boat men calling out "mark twain," as they measured the water. This meant that the water was two fathoms deep. Clemens liked the way these words sounded so much that he began to call himself *Mark Twain*.

Clemens made friends wherever he went, and rich people and poor people, old men and children liked to talk to him. When he wrote his books, he wrote about all of the people he knew and the places where they lived, just the way he remembered them. His two most famous books,

387

The Adventures of Tom Sawyer and The Adventures of Huckleberry Finn, are about two boys who grow up in a small river town, very much like the place in Missouri where Clemens lived when he was a boy. Tom Sawyer and Huckleberry Finn have many exciting adventures, but a lot of things that happen to them are ordinary things that happen to all children. This is one reason why people of all ages have been fascinated by these stories. Clemens wrote about the time he spent on the Mississippi, and when you read his book, Life on the Mississippi you can find out many things about the hard work, fun, and excitement of the days when river boats steamed up and down the great river. Another book Clemens wrote is about a modern mechanic, who dreams he is a knight back in the days of the wonderful court of King Arthur, and all of the funny and wonderful things that happen to him. This book is called A Connecticut Yankee in King Arthur's Court. One of the most beautiful stories that Clemens wrote is called The Prince and the Pauper. It is about a prince and a poor boy, who change places with each other. Most of these great books have been made into motion pictures that millions of people have seen.

Clement

Clement was the name of fourteen Popes, or leaders of the Roman Catholic Church. The most famous one was Clement I. He was one of the earliest Popes. He was Pope about sixty years after the death of Jesus. There are a great many books and articles that Clement I was said to have written. He probably did not write most of them, but they are still called by his name. They are known as the Clementine writings. It was said that Clement I was a martyr—that is, he was killed because he was a Christian. Clement VII, who was Pope from 1523 to 1534, is remembered because he was a member of the great Italian family of Medici. He was often criticized and accused of trying to do what was good for the Medici, rather than what was good for the Catholic Church. Clement XII was Pope from 1730 to 1740. He is remembered because he was interested in art and in learning. He gave many fine things to the museum and the library in Rome. He also had some beautiful buildings erected in Rome.

Cleopatra

Cleopatra, the most famous queen of Egypt, was born just 69 years before the birth of Jesus. Her name Cleopatra was the usual name for a queen in her family, the Ptolemy family, which ruled Egypt at this time. Because she was too young to rule when her parents died, she was put under the care of two Egyptian nobles named Pothinus and Achillas. These men did not allow Cleopatra her share in the government when she became older, as they should have. Fortunately for her, Julius Caesar, the greatest of all Roman generals, invaded Egypt at this time. He met Cleopatra and was captivated by her charm, intelligence, and beauty. He helped her rule as queen of Egypt, and she returned to Rome with him. Then Caesar was murdered, and Cleopatra went back to Egypt.

An ancient stone carving shows Cleopatra, the famous Egyptian queen.

While Caesar was alive, Cleopatra felt that her country would be treated well by the great Roman Empire. She wanted Egypt to be a partner and not a slave of Rome. When Caesar died, the fate of Rome and Egypt became uncertain. Many men, especially a Roman general named Mark Antony and Caesar's nephew Octavian, wanted to take Caesar's place as the ruler of the Roman Empire. Mark Antony visited Egypt and met Cleopatra, and they fell in love. Antony hoped that Egypt's wealth would help him become the ruler of Rome, and Cleopatra hoped that Antony would help her make Egypt a powerful country. But their hopes were never realized. The soldiers of Octavian met those of Antony and Cleopatra in a great sea battle at a place called Actium in 31 B.C. Antony and Cleopatra handled their navy badly and Octavian won the battle. Soon afterwards, Antony lost another battle at Alexandria, and he stabbed himself and died in the arms of Cleopatra. Cleopatra was grieved at Antony's death and afraid that Octavian would treat her cruelly, so she too killed herself, by letting an asp (a small poisonous snake) bite her. The story of Cleopatra has been told in the plays Antony and Cleopatra by William Shakespeare, All for Love by John Dryden, and Caesar and Cleopatra by George Bernard Shaw.

Cleopatra's Needle, the name of two Egyptian obelisks: see OBELISK.

clepsydra, a water clock: see CLOCKS AND WATCHES.

clergy

The clergy are all the priests, ministers of the Christian Churches and rabbis of the Jewish religion. Members of the clergy are called clergymen, and they may have special names in the different churches-not only priest, minister, or rabbi, but also preacher, pastor, and in some churches dean, deacon, bishop, and various other names. A person who is not a clergyman is a layman and is said to be a member of the laity.

Hundreds of years ago, clergymen were also called clerks. In those days, almost no one except a clergyman knew how to read and write, and after a while anyone who could read and write was known as a clerk, even if he was not a member of the clergy. People who worked in offices, doing bookkeeping or writing letters, were called clerks, because they had to be able to read and write; and gradually the word came to be used for many different kinds of employees in offices and stores.

In the Catholic Church and in many non-Catholic churches a man is ordained to holy orders. There are different grades in holy orders. The most important ones are bishop, priest, and deacon. A church that has bishops is called an episcopal church. All Catholic Churches, and also Protestant Episcopal and Methodist Episcopal Churches, have bishops. A bishop is in charge of a certain territory, or diocese. In the Roman Catholic Church, archbishops are bishops who are in charge of very important dioceses, called archdioceses. (Arch means "high.") Cardinals are the highest-ranking members of the Roman Catholic clergy. The cardinals elect the Pope, who is the pontiff, or head of the Church. There is a separate article about CARDINALS.

In most Protestant churches, a minister is called, which means that he both feels a divinely inspired order to become a member of the clergy, and also is summoned to a particular church or duty by the ruling body of his Church. There is a separate article on the MINISTRY.

Cleveland

Cleveland is the largest city in the state of Ohio, and an important port on Lake Erie. It was founded in 1796 by Moses Cleaveland, who gave it his own name. As the years passed people forgot to include the first "a" in writing the name, and the present spelling came to be correct.

In pioneer days, before any real roads reached so far inland as Ohio, people in the surrounding territory brought the products of farm and forest to Cleveland, either by river or by rough country roads, to ship them east on barges. When the railroads came, Cleveland's trade increased. If you were to visit Cleveland's docks, you would see big cargo steamers unloading iron ore from the mines of Minnesota that will be used to make steel in the great mills of Cleveland. Other ships may be loading up with lumber, coal, or grain.

There are many people in Cleveland who came from European countries. They work in steel mills, lumberyards, oil refineries, machine shops, and meat-packing plants. Among the goods they turn out are airplane engines, cement, auto-

mobile parts, electrical wares, and machine tools.

There are several colleges and universities in Cleveland, including Western Reserve University. The people of Cleveland have many beautiful places to enjoy such as the Museum of Art, several lovely gardens, and the zoo. They may hear great music played by the Cleveland Symphony Orchestra and take books from one of the best public libraries in the country.

CLEVELAND, OHIO. Population (1970 census) 750,903. County seat of Cuyahoga County. Founded in 1796.

Grover Cleveland

Only one man in the history of the United States has been president for two different terms that did not come one immediately after the other. Many presidents have been re-elected to the office, but only Grover Cleveland has ever been elected at two different times, after another man had served as president between these two times. The first and third times Cleveland ran for president he won. The second time he lost to Benjamin Harrison. This made Cleveland both the 22nd and the 24th President of the United States.

As a president, he had many difficult and serious problems, and he solved them well. No one ever had any doubt that he was completely honest and a good man, although many people did not always agree with him.

Cleveland was a large man, tall and heavy-set, with a long white mustache and white hair. He was very distinguished in appearance.

He died with the knowledge that all his life he had been a man of the highest honor and integrity and that he had sincerely done his best for his country in the high office that had been given him.

HIS EARLY YEARS

Grover Cleveland was born in Caldwell, Essex County, New Jersey, on March 18, 1837. His full name was Stephen Grover Cleveland, but he did not use his first name.

His father was a Presbyterian minister and moved with his family to New York state in 1841. They lived near Syracuse for a time and then moved to Clinton. When Grover Cleveland was only 16

years old, his father died, and the young Cleveland had to go to work. His first job was with the New York Institute for the Blind. An uncle of his, Lewis F. Allen, arranged to get him another position with a law firm in Buffalo, and Cleveland went there to study law. He became a lawyer in 1859, when he was 22 years old. His political career started four years later when he became Assistant District Attorney of Erie County in 1863. He ran for election as District Attorney in 1865 but was defeated. Five years later he was elected to the office of county sheriff, a position that he held for the next three years. He then went back into private law practice and was very successful. During this period there was trouble in the city of Buffalo with dishonest politicians who were running the city badly. Grover Cleveland was nominated for mayor of the city on a reform ticket in 1881, and he won the election and served well. His reform administration in Buffalo won him a fine reputation. Because of his good record he was nominated governor of New York and was elected to that office in 1882.

HOW HE BECAME PRESIDENT

When the Democratic Party was looking for a good man to nominate for the presidency in the fall of 1884, the fine record of Grover Cleveland as governor of New York made him an excellent choice. He was nominated at the Democratic convention and defeated James G. Blaine, the Republican candidate in the election that year. He was inaugurated in March, 1885.

Cleveland was the first president to be married in the White House. On June 2, 1886, he married Frances Folsom, a year and three months after he was inaugurated as president. They had five children, four girls and one boy.

Throughout his first term as president, he was firm in opposing bills that he thought unworthy, and he fought against many private pension bills. He did not approve of passing acts of Congress merely to make sure that someone with political connections would have a government pension on which to live for the rest of his life. This was the act of an honest man who would not let tax money be used for private gain, but nevertheless it made many congressmen angry.

After one term he was defeated for re-election by Benjamin Harrison, a Republican. There is an article about Benjamin HARRISON in a later volume of this encyclopedia. The election fight was an unusual one. Although Cleveland received a much larger popular vote than Harrison, the electoral college gave the election to Harrison. The way the electoral college operates is explained in a separate article called ELECTORAL COLLEGE. Because so very many people had voted for him that time, the Democratic Party thought that he would have a good chance of being elected four years later, and they nominated him again. This time he was elected with a substantial majority of both popular and electoral votes.

One of the first important things Cleveland did after his second inauguration was to call a special session of Congress in the summer of 1893. He fought for the repeal of the Sherman Silver Purchase Act, which had been passed while Harrison was president. At the time when Cleveland fought to have this act repealed, it was costing the United States government millions of dollars a year. Under the terms of the act, the government had to buy a great deal of the silver that was mined in this country. Cleveland and many other people thought the country did not need all this silver. The Silver Purchase Act was repealed.

The next year a big railroad strike in Chicago threatened to interfere with the United States mails. Trains could not move out of the Chicago station even if they had important mail on board, and Cleveland felt that the government could not allow a strike to stop the flow of mail from one part of the country to another. He called out federal troops to keep the mail moving, which was the first time government troops had ever taken part in a labor dispute.

Although his second administration occurred at a time when the country was having a great deal of difficulty with unemployment, he refused to consider the idea of having the government set up projects to give men work. No president had ever done that up to his time, and he did not think it was the government's place to make jobs for people. Partly because of this, and partly because many people did not like his policy on how the money matters of the country should be handled, he was not nominated again for president, but retired at the end of his second term.

HIS LATER YEARS

Grover Cleveland retired to Princeton, New Jersey, where he lectured at Princeton University. He also wrote a book called *Presidential Problems* which was published in 1904. While he was living in Princeton he was appointed to an important position as one of the trustees of the Equitable Life Assurance Society. He died in 1908 at the age of 71.

MRS. GROVER CLEVELAND

Mrs. Grover Cleveland was the daughter of the man who had been Cleveland's law partner in Buffalo. Her maiden name was Frances Folsom, and she was born in 1864. Her parents were Oscar and Emma Harmon Folsom. She was 22 when she became mistress of the White House in 1886. Five years after Cleveland died, she married a scientist at Princeton, New Jersey. She died in 1947 at the age of 83.

click beetle

A click beetle is an interesting kind of beetle that jumps into the air with a "click" if it falls on its back. There are about five hundred different kinds of click beetles in North America. One of the most common ones has a long, narrow body, of pepper-and-salt color, with a ridged back and two dark "eyespots" near the front end. The young of click beetles are known as *wireworms,* and they are one of the serious insect pests. They live in the ground, feeding on the roots of plants. Each year they destroy millions of dollars worth of corn, wheat, grasses, potatoes, beets, carrots, and other crops.

cliff dwellers, an American Indian people who lived in the Southwest of

what is now the United States. See the article on PUEBLO INDIANS.

climate

Climate is the name for the total effect of all the weather conditions of an area over a period of time. Climate is made up of the amount of sun, rain and snow an area may have, the high and low temperatures, and the direction and strength of the winds over the course of a year. The earth is divided into zones of climate by latitudes, which are imaginary lines drawn around the globe. In the center, around the biggest part of the earth, runs the line called the equator. The areas just north and just south of the equator are called the *torrid zones,* which are always very hot. Just north and just south of the two torrid zones are two *temperate zones,* which are medium in temperature. At the North Pole and at the South Pole are two areas called the *frigid zones,* which are always very cold.

As the earth spins on its own axis and moves around the sun, it is sometimes at a very different angle when receiving the sun's rays. For this reason the amount of sunlight that falls on the earth is changing constantly as the position of the earth and its angle toward the sun change. This gives the earth its four seasons, spring, summer, autumn, and winter. The amount of sunlight that reaches the equator and the North and South Poles does not change very much during a year, and so the weather of those places does not change very much either. The frigid zones are usually very cold, and the torrid zones are usually very hot. But in the temperate zones between the poles and the equator, the weather changes a great deal from season to season.

Three other very important things that affect the climate of a country are how close to the ocean it is, what ocean currents flow near it, and how high it is above sea level. Distance from the ocean is important because the sun heats the land much faster than it does the ocean, and the land loses its heat much faster than the ocean at night and during the winter. This makes places far inland have extremes of climate. Cities like Kansas City, Kansas, and Butte, Montana, have temperatures of more than 120 degrees in summer, and temperatures below zero in winter. But the climate of cities near the ocean, like New York City and San Francisco, California, is much more even. In places high above the level of the sea, the air is colder. Even in the hot tropics, the tops of mountains are often covered with snow. For instance, the climate in the valleys of the Andes Mountains in South America is like a hot, tropical jungle, but at the top of the mountains it is freezing cold. There are ocean currents that bring warm water from the tropic regions to the polar regions, and currents that bring cold water from the polar regions to the tropic regions. Countries that lie near these ocean currents have their climate affected by them, becoming either warmer or colder.

Winds are also important to climate. Some winds move in definite routes, just as if they had their own highways. The winds that come from cold polar regions bring cold air with them, and cool the

areas they pass. Warm winds come from the tropic regions and warm the air in the cold places they pass.

The moisture in the air, and the amount of rain that falls determines whether a country has an arid (dry) or humid (moist) climate. The amount of rainfall determines what kind of plants will grow in any area. In very wet climates there will be thick, dense jungles. In very dry climates there will be deserts.

CLIMATE AND MAN

Climate has a great deal to do with the way people live, eat, dress, and work. Hot climates make it difficult for people to work hard. Cold climates make it hard for a person to think well, although he will have plenty of energy for hard work. A moderate, changing climate seems to be best for people. The temperate climates of the United States, Europe, China and Russia have encouraged the people of these countries to be creative and hard-working. A temperate climate is also important in growing such crops as wheat, rice and barley which are necessary for an active people.

Climate has a great effect on health. Too much dampness or too much dryness, or too much heat or cold are bad for health.

clinics and dispensaries, places that are usually parts of hospitals, where people who are not sick enough to be kept in a hospital can receive medical care. Most of these people pay nothing, or pay the amount of money they can afford: see the article on HOSPITAL.

Clinton, DeWitt and George

DeWitt Clinton was a great governor of the state of New York. He was born in 1769. He became a lawyer and

entered politics when he was a young man. He was elected to many posts in the government of New York City and New York state. DeWitt Clinton is especially remembered for the leading part he had in the building of the Erie Canal. This great canal ran from Lake Erie to the Hudson River. Clinton saw that a canal would help to make New York state great and prosperous. For many years he worked tirelessly to have the canal built. He was successful and his dream was made true. He saw the great canal finished and opened five years before he died in 1828.

George Clinton was the uncle of De-Witt Clinton. George Clinton was born in 1739. When he was a young man, the American colonies still belonged to England. George Clinton believed that the colonies should be free, and he fought for the colonies in the Revolutionary War against England. While the war was going on, New York state formed a new government, to be independent of England. George Clinton was elected the first governor of New York under the new state constitution. He was so popular that he was re-elected to his post many times. In 1804 he was elected vice-president of the United States, and four years later he was re-elected. He died in 1812.

Clinton, Sir Henry

Sir Henry Clinton was an English general in the Revolutionary War that gave the American Colonies their independence from England. Clinton was born about 1738. His father was the English governor of New York. Henry lived in New York, and was a soldier in the New York militia. But he was always a loyal Englishman, and when his father went back to England, Henry Clinton went with him and joined the English army. When the Revolutionary War began, he returned to North America as an officer in the English army. He took part in the English capture of New York. For several years, he was commander-in-chief of the English army in the war. After he returned to England, he was elected to parliament, the English congress. Later, he was made governor of the English colony of Gibraltar, but he died very soon afterward, in 1795.

Clio, the muse of history: see MUSES.

clipper

Not much more than a hundred years ago, it took nearly fourteen days by sailing vessels to go from the United States to Europe. This may seem slow today, but the ships that made this time were the fastest sailing vessels ever built. They were called clippers. They were built for speed, and had long, narrow hulls, or bodies, and sharp, overhanging bows or fronts. A clipper carried many sails on its three tall masts that sloped backwards. A clipper scudding along under full sail was a beautiful sight.

Baltimore was the great American center for the building of clippers. The first one was constructed there in 1832. Clippers were much used in the tea trade with China, and to take people back and forth from Europe as fast as possible. The evil men who captured African Negroes for slaves brought them to America on clipper ships. The clippers began to lose their importance after the Civil War when steamships were improved and could go faster and carry bigger loads than the clippers. The men who sailed the clippers were great sailors and were so hardy and strong that people used to speak about these ships and sailors as "wooden ships and iron men."

Clive, Robert

Robert Clive was one of the great leaders in the English conquest of India.

He was both a general and an outstanding governor. Clive was born in 1725. When he was only eighteen years old, he went to India to work for the East India Company. This company was a trading organization that bought things in India to sell in Europe. It made agreements with the native Indian rulers and it controlled some of the lands in India.

When Clive went there, India was almost always at war. The many different Indian rulers fought among themselves. Both the French and the English were trying to get control. Clive was a bold and

skillful leader in war. Most of the time he had fewer soldiers than his enemies, but he won all his battles. Clive defeated both the French and the native Indian armies and really won control over India for England. After this Clive worked to improve the way the East India Company was running the government. He made the government better and more honest. Because of his work, many people who had been making money in India in illegal ways hated Clive. They accused him of doing many wrong things himself. He was brought to trial in England. After his trial, the British government said that he had sometimes been wrong but that he had done a great service for England. Clive had very often been sick, and this trial made him so worried and depressed and unhappy that he killed himself, in 1774.

clocks and watches

Clocks and watches are the two latest devices for telling what time it is. Clocks are about 600 years old, and watches about 400 years old, but other devices for keeping time go back thousands of years. In the modern world nearly everything depends on accurate timekeeping—in some scientific works the time must be accurate within a small fraction of a second—but as recently as 50 years ago it was almost unheard-of for the farmer and the laboring man to carry a watch and usually they did not have clocks in their houses. The farmer knew about what time it was from the sun; the laborer and his family knew the time by whistles blown by the factory in which he worked. Church bells, summoning people to church, date from the times when people did not have clocks or watches. Only about 150 years ago, when only rich men owned watches, a rich man might carry eight or ten watches—just as women wear jewelry—to show how rich he was.

The first timepieces were the *sundial,* the *clepsydra* or water clock, the *hour glass,* and burning ropes or candles.

Before 2000 B.C., men in ancient Babylonia stuck sticks in the ground and measured time by the length of the shadow cast when the sun shone on the stick. This led to the development of sundials that were very scientifically designed and built; but though sundials are still used, they cannot be very accurate. The sun's position in the sky is slightly different every day and besides the sun does not shine every day and never at night. However, from these early sundials we got the division of time into 12 hours, 60 minutes and 60 seconds. The number 12 was a "magic number"; that is how juries came to have 12 members, the "dozen" became a standard number, and Jesus had 12 disciples.

The first water clock was a big water-filled pot with a little hole at the bottom. It took a measurable amount of time for the water to empty out, drop by drop, and unlike the sundial the water clock could be used at night and on cloudy days. On one ancient Greek water clock, the water dropped into a tube in which there was a little toy man on a piece of cork. As the toy man floated up, he pointed to the hour, marked on the tube.

The hour glass used the same principle as the water clock, measuring the amount

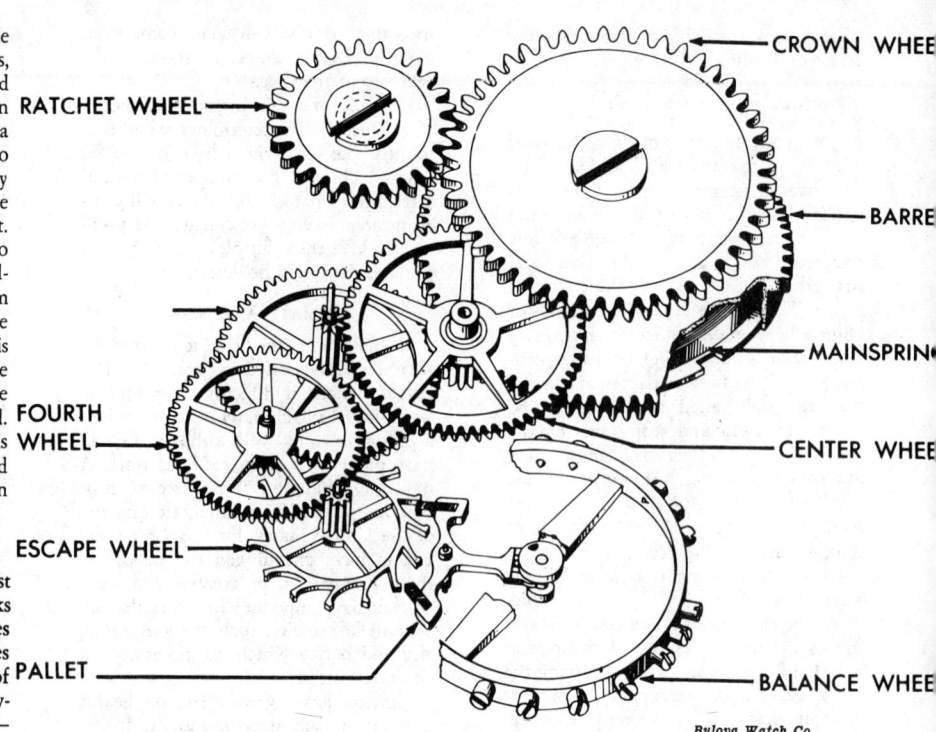

RATCHET WHEEL

CROWN WHEEL

BARREL

MAINSPRING

FOURTH WHEEL

MAINSPRING

CENTER WHEEL

ESCAPE WHEEL

PALLET

BALANCE WHEEL

Bulova Watch Co.

Basic parts of a watch or small clock. The unwinding of the mainspring causes the series of geared wheels, called the *train,* to turn. One gear causes the "hour hand" to turn once in 12 hours; another turns the "minute hand" twelve times as fast as the hour hand; another turns the "second hand" sixty times as fast as the minute hand. The *escape wheel* or *escapement* makes the balance wheel swing back and forth five times every two seconds, creating the sound called "ticking" or "tick-tock." The screws on the balance wheel may be screwed in or out to make the wheel swing back and forth in a desired length of time.

of time it takes sand to run through a tiny hole. Ancient Romans used hour glasses. Slaves were made to watch the hour glass and turn it over as soon as all the sand had run through.

In China, men kept time by burning a long rope with knots tied in it. A known amount of time was required for the rope to burn from one knot to the next. Europeans, in the Middle Ages, kept time by cutting notches in candles and observing how far down the candle had burned.

THE EARLIEST CLOCKS

Clockmaking originated in Southern Germany and Switzerland, and these regions are still noted for their fine clockmakers and watchmakers. About 600 years ago (about 1360) the first clock was made by a German named Henry de Vick. His clock had a dial that showed the hours and also rang a bell every hour. (Our word "clock" comes from a Latin word meaning "bell.") As in a modern clock, there was a dial with a hand that moved around the dial to show the time. The hand was kept moving by gear wheels in the mechanism and the gear wheels were kept running by a weight attached to a cord that was wound around a drum, or cylinder. As long as there was still some cord wound around the drum, the dropping weight continued to turn the drum. The cord would be wound up on the drum to keep the clock going.

Clockwork was the next great advancement. About 1500, a German named Peter Henlein devised a way to provide power for a clock by winding up a coiled spring. As the spring tried to unwind, it provided power that made the gears of the mechanism turn. Clockwork is still used in all watches and in many clocks,

and it was widely used for many other machines—for example, phonographs—before inexpensive electric motors were developed.

The next great advancement came when the great Italian scientist Galileo happened to see a chandelier in a church swinging back and forth in a breeze. He observed that each swing took the same amount of time, whether the breeze was brisk and made the chandelier swing far or died down and let the chandelier swing only a small distance. From this, Galileo derived the principle of the *pendulum,* or moving arm, which is still used to make clocks and watches accurate. Christian Huygens, a Dutch scientist, is credited with first applying this principle to clocks (in 1656). In the first clocks that kept good time, weights were used to keep the pendulum swinging. The "grandfather's clock," which is still popular, works on this principle. In smaller clocks and in watches, the swinging of a pendulum is replaced by the back-and-forth swinging of a balance wheel (see the illustration on page 1256).

TYPES OF CLOCK

Since the earliest clocks were made for rich men or for cities and towns, they were very fancy and expensive. Many of them had automatons, statues of men or animals that pointed to the hour or that seemed to announce the time through ringing a bell or tolling chimes. The chimes—four characteristic notes—ring every 15 minutes; every half-hour the bell strikes and every hour the bell strikes the number of the hour, for example ringing six times when it is 6 o'clock. The automaton clock is still seen in "cuckoo clocks." Every hour a toy bird called a

cuckoo comes out of the clock and "sings." Many huge "tower clocks," with elaborate automatons, were built in the Middle Ages—hundreds of years ago—and some are still in use. Some old clocks had as many as 100,000 parts. Such complexity has not been necessary since electric motors were invented.

The CHRONOMETER, about which there is a separate article, is simply a very accurate clock that is run by a clockwork motor. Chronometers are not really different from the small clocks; they are simply made much more carefully.

The *alarm clock* has been made since 1700. It has a separate mechanism so that when the hour hand reaches a certain time, a bell rings. Hundreds of millions of persons throughout the world use alarm clocks to wake them up in the morning.

Several kinds of clock have been called *electric clocks*. One kind is simply an ordinary clock that is kept wound by a small electric motor. Electric clocks in automobiles are of this type. Another kind is a clock that is connected by telegraph wires to a master clock and that shows the same time as the master clock, which is always kept at the correct time. But since about 1930, the term *electric clock* has been applied chiefly to a clock that is powered by a synchronous motor. This kind of motor is operated by the constant reversals of direction of ALTERNATING CURRENT, about which there is a separate article.

All clocks and small watches operate on much the same principle. The hands are connected to the train by special gears and move with the train. The escapement is made so that the train can move only once for each motion of the pendulum. The rest of the time the train is stationary. The hands move forward a little bit each time the train moves and in this way there is a record of the amount of time that has passed.

One type of clock, then, is just a pendulum with machinery to keep it going and to record how long it has gone. Not all clocks are of this sort. A pendulum has to be fairly long and has to be kept level, so a clock using one must be large and immovable. For smaller clocks and for watches, another device is used in place of the pendulum. A wheel is mounted so that it can turn back and forth easily, and a light spiral-shaped spring is mounted on the same axle. If this wheel is turned in one direction, it will wind up the spring and the wheel will swing back in the other direction, winding the spring the other way. So the wheel will oscillate (swing back and forth), and will take about the same time for each oscillation. This device is more compact than a pendulum, and so is used for smaller clocks and watches. The wheel used is called the balance wheel, and the light spring mounted with it is called the hairspring.

For small clocks and watches a weight also would be impossible, so the power is supplied by a heavy coiled spring. When it is wound up, it pushes on a wheel that acts on the train.

Electric clocks do not depend on the action of a pendulum or a balance wheel to provide the uniform motion on which any timekeeping device depends. Instead they make use of the alternations in electric current, which are very carefully controlled at the power station.

TAKING CARE OF YOUR WATCH

If you own a watch, you should take it to a repairman at least every two years for cleaning and oiling. Try to wind it up at the same time every day. If your watch gets wet, dip it in benzine and take it to a repair shop. Some people learn to clean their own watches and make the study of watches a hobby.

FAMOUS CLOCKS AND WATCHES

There are many wonderful and strange timepieces in the world. On one London clock tower, for instance, there are two life-sized wooden bell ringers called Gog and Magog. Each quarter-hour they bang on bells with great war clubs. Such figures are called *jacks*. There are many kinds of jack. Some come out of a door, move along a runway, bang on a bell, then disappear through the door again till the next hour needs striking. There are several jacks in New York City's Herald Square. Then there is the famous "Big Ben," the 13-½-ton bell in Westminster Clock Tower in London, England. But the biggest clock of all is in the United States. It is the Colgate-Palmolive-Peet clock in Jersey City, New Jersey, which measures 50 feet across. Its minute hand weighs 2,200 pounds and is 27-¼ feet long. There is a watch that tells the time of day in split seconds, plus the day of the week, the month, and the moon's phases, among other things. It even gives the position of the stars over New York, according to season.

NAVAL OBSERVATORY CLOCKS

There are very few clocks or watches so finely made that they keep absolutely accurate time. Among the *most* accurate are the Naval Observatory Clocks in Washington, D.C. These are maintained by the government, and they provide the standard time for all the clocks in the country. These clocks are kept under glass in underground chambers in direct contact with solid ground. They have pendulums that are made of a special nickel steel that will not expand or contract with changes in temperature. They are regulated by slight changes in the pressure of the air surrounding them.

In the late 1940s the National Bureau of Standards developed an atomic clock that is so accurate that in 3,000,000 years it will gain or lose only one second. Actually, it is a large electric clock, but it is regulated by an atomic attachment that tunes it to the ammonia atom.

cloisonné

Cloisonné is a way of decorating jewelry, vases, bowls, and boxes. The name cloisonné is also used for the objects themselves. The method was used hundreds of years ago by the Persians and the Chinese, and it is very much the same today. If a gold bracelet is being made, the design is outlined by attaching paper-thin strips of gold onto the bracelet. These strips are called "cloisons." The spaces between the strips or cloisons are filled with a paste made of colored enamel, and then the whole bracelet is heated so that the enamel and the gold will stick together. This is slow work and it has to be done many times over so that every little space will be filled with enamel. The colors in cloisonné are usually dull white, green, rich violet, and turquoise blue. The last step in making perfect cloisonné is to polish it until it is smooth and glossy.

Cloisonné was used on the covers of some of the earliest books ever made in Europe. In France cloisonné was used about eight hundred years ago to decorate statues. Very beautiful vases were made of cloisonné in China during the Ming dynasty of emperors. They are called Ming china. Cloisonné jewelry, book covers, bowls and sculpture can be seen in museums today.

cloister

A cloister is a covered walk that runs around the inside walls of a group of church or college buildings. The cloister surrounds a central garden or yard, and the open side of the walk is a series of arches. There is a picture of a cloister next to the article on ABBEY. The cloister connects the different parts of the monastery, such as the church, dining hall, study rooms, and sleeping rooms. The cloister is also used for exercise, and classes can be held there. Religious processions or parades move around the cloister on special days. Sometimes a cloister has small alcoves or window seats where a person can read and study.

Cloisters were most popular several hundred years ago. Some of the famous ones are in old buildings in Spain, Italy, France, England, Peru, and Mexico.

The Cloisters at Fort Tryon Park in New York City are part of the Metropolitan Museum of Art. The cloisters there were made with stones and arches from the ruins of French monasteries that were built more than 500 years ago.

closed shop

When a group of workers persuade their employer to hire only members of their labor union, their factory is called a *closed shop*. Some unions think it is better to let the employer hire anyone he wants, but they insist that all new employees join the union in a certain length of time. This is called a *union shop*. When the employer hires anyone he wants and new employees do not have to join the union, it is called an *open shop*.

Sometimes the company and the union agree that as long as a person is working for that company he must remain a member of the union and pay his dues. This is called a *maintenance-of-membership* agreement. The idea of the closed shop is not a new one. There were closed shops almost two hundred years ago. Some people oppose the closed shop because they believe it is unfair to keep an employer from hiring a man who prefers not to join a union. This is called the "right to work" principle. In 1947 the United States Congress passed the Taft-Hartley Act, under which any state may have a right-to-work law, making the closed shop illegal.

cloth, a woven fabric: see the article on TEXTILES.

clothes moth

The clothes moth is one of the worst insect enemies of man. The moth itself is very small and may be brown, black, or gray. It is not the moth but the larva, or worm stage, of this moth that feeds on clothes and does all the damage. It feeds on clothes that contain wool, mohair, feathers, down, fur, or hair. The moth lays its eggs in these materials, and when they hatch into larvae they stay right there eating until they turn into moths. These larvae destroy several hundred million dollars worth of clothing each year.

You can help save your clothes from this insect by keeping them very clean. Closet walls and shelves should be sprayed once or twice a year with a weak solution of DDT to kill the moths or larvae. Woolen clothes that are put away for the summer should be protected with crystals of *naphthalene* or by the chemical called *paradichlorobenzene*. A pound of these crystals scattered throughout a trunkful of clothes will help to keep the moths away.

clothing

Man lives in every climate, from Iceland to the steaming hot jungles. Only man of all the animals makes his permanent home in all kinds of climate. One reason he can do this is that he knows how to protect his body with clothing.

Other animals must be able to live in the climate where they are born, or else they die, except for some birds that fly south to avoid the cold winters of the north. But you can tell from pictures of ancient people just what kind of climate they lived in. Their clothes are the clue.

CLOTHING FOR CLIMATE PROTECTION

The earliest pictures we have are from Egypt. This country is in Africa, which has a hot climate. We could guess that, because the ancient Egyptians wore only two thin garments, a loose skirt and a short cape.

Although Arabia is just as hot, much of that country is a desert, without any trees for protection from the sun. When the hot sands blow against the skin, it is painful. So the desert Arab wrapped himself in a long cape with a hood. This *burnoose* was made of wool, which keeps out cold as well as heat better than other fabrics. It was white, because white throws off heat better than any other color.

History tells us that when Julius Caesar went north to conquer England, he found the people there wearing leggings made of cloth and leather. Later someone had the idea of sewing these leggings up and they became stockings and boots. Such protection was necessary in their cold climate. Eskimos are able to live in the coldest regions because of the fur skins which they use for clothing. For thousands of years men who lived far apart from each other had no contact with each other at all. Yet whenever their climate was the same they all developed the same type of clothing for protection.

Modern man is learning to control the climate he lives in. He is learning to make rain when he wants it. Our indoor life is changing because we can air-condition our buildings for cold and heat. We travel in comfortable temperatures by land and sea and air. Someday our schools and homes and offices may all have complete temperature controls. This will change our future clothing needs. We may be able to use just one kind of indoor clothes in any climate. Only outdoors will we still need special clothing for climate protection.

CLOTHING FOR SPECIAL PROTECTION

Man also uses clothing to protect himself against his enemies. Steel helmets and suits of armor once shielded his body from arrows and stones. But when guns and bullets began to be used in warfare the thin armor could be pierced. If it was thick enough for protection, the armor became too heavy for soldiers to wear in battle. So today, a soldier jumps into a foxhole, or he rides in an armored tank.

Every boy and girl is familiar with the padded uniforms of football players. This is an example of protective clothing for sports.

Men need special kinds of protective clothing for certain jobs. Tunnel builders called "ground hogs" wear helmets to protect their heads from falling stones. Fire-fighters at airports wear fireproof asbestos suits so they can go right into a burning plane to rescue the passengers and the crew. A diver wears an air-filled suit for protection against the pressure of the deep sea.

Man is continually developing new types of clothing to protect himself against all kinds of dangers.

EARLY CLOTHING MATERIALS

In earliest times, man had to use anything that was handy for his clothing. He wore leaves. He stripped the bark off trees. He picked long grasses and braided them together. When he killed animals for food, he used the skins for covering.

In time, instead of depending on nature, he made nature work for him. He learned how to plant seeds and grow cotton and flax (linen). He learned to make tools and used his tools to build spinning-wheels and weaving looms. At last, he could spin the cotton and linen into threads, then weave the threads into fabric.

Instead of tossing an animal skin over his shoulders, he learned to cut off sheep's wool and he wove woolen fabrics too. He mixed wool with gluey liquids from plants. By pounding them together, he made felt. Animal hides used to rot away, but man learned how to preserve them by "tanning," and they became leather.

After European men learned about silk from the Chinese, silk became the favorite clothing fabric of the rich. These materials we have mentioned were the only materials man used for his clothes until recently.

MODERN CLOTHING MATERIALS

Today, scientists have learned how to make fabric yarns by chemistry. They are made of coal, milk, glass, wood, soybeans, and other products. Most of these new fabrics are easy to wash, dry quickly, and need little or no ironing. So the care of clothing can be much easier now. When we buy clothes made of rayon, acetate, Nylon, Orlon, Dacron, and plastics, we are wearing these man-made materials. Because of these fabrics, modern clothes are more interesting; they vary in weight and in quality, and some of them are cheaper than ever before.

CLOTHING COLORS

Man first made colors from the juices of berries and flowers, of plants and tree bark. He dyed his fabrics by hand, with crude tools. Colors were dried outdoors. The sun was sometimes bright and sometimes weak, so the colors often came out uneven.

Today, dyes are made chemically. We can have many more colors and tints and shades. These colors are not streaked, they can be made so that they do not "run" in washing, and they cost less.

In every age and in every country, certain colors have been worn for special occasions. We still have such customs. Our bridal gowns are usually white. In China, a girl wore red for her wedding dress. White was the color the Chinese used for mourning clothes, but this custom is changing. Many people no longer wear a special mourning color. Color customs do change, even though many of them did last for centuries.

In hot climates, where the sunshine is very bright, people prefer to wear bright-colored clothes. In our climate, with its many seasons, we wear all kinds of colors. Most clothes worn today have brighter and lighter colors in the summer, and darker colors in the winter.

When we buy new clothes, we can usually choose any color we like. But in ancient times, clothing colors were often regulated by law. In Rome the slaves could wear clothes of only one color; royal families could wear seven colors. Only a senator (ruler) could wear a robe with a purple border or tie his sandals with black laces. So the colors of a man's clothes were a mark of his rank. Today, it is impossible to tell what kind of work a man does from the color of his clothes.

WAYS OF FASTENING CLOTHES

Man first used cloth by wrapping it around his hips and fastening it with a belt. The Greeks and Romans used a longer piece which they draped loosely around their bodies. A kind of pin held it on the shoulders. They also wore capes that were fastened with big decorative pins.

The Persians were the first people who cut and sewed fabric so their clothes would fit the shape of the body. As many more people came to wear shaped and sewed garments, the clothes were fitted more tightly by lacings of ribbon and string.

In time, fashionable clothes became very complicated. Both men and women wore stiff corsets. Women also wore wire cages over their hips to make their skirts stand out. The costumes of that age had many garments. Then the button came into use. Buttons were used not only as fastenings but also as decorations. Then hooks and eyes were invented and garment fastenings could be hidden.

A few hundred years later, clothing began to be more simple and more comfortable. And the most convenient fastening of all was invented, the zipper. This makes clothing much easier to put on and take off.

It is interesting that every kind of clothes fastening ever used from earliest times is still in use today.

TROUSERS AND SKIRTS

Nowadays we are used to the idea of skirts for women and trousers for men. But once men wore long-skirted robes just like women. This was natural when people just wrapped a piece of cloth around their bodies. But the custom continued for thousands of years, even after man learned to sew and fit clothes.

In Asia, there were warrior tribes who fought their battles on horseback. These men wore trousers for riding comfort. We know that when men settled in northern climates they wore trousers for warmth. We know also that Persian men wore trousers as a national custom. Only in Turkey and China have women worn trousers as a national custom. In Turkey the women's trousers were full and loose; in China they hung straight.

Gradually, most men took to wearing trousers for easy motion. Since women worked in the home and were less active physically, they kept their skirts.

At first, men's trousers fitted tightly, like the long underwear of today. They were called "trunk hose" because they covered the trunk of the body as well as the legs. Then the trunks and the hose became separate garments. The trunks became puffed and worn high on the thigh. As times changed, the trunks again became tight-fitting down below the knees. George Washington wore such "knee breeches."

The long trousers that men wear today came into use right after the French Revolution. The people wanted to change all the old customs. French clothes, which had been very elegant and elaborate, became simple. Men gave up knee breeches and began to wear long, straight trousers. The style was copied in many other countries. Today, men in most civilized countries wear long trousers.

MODERN TYPES OF CLOTHING

During World War II, women began to work in big factories for the first time. Their loose skirts were dangerous around the machinery, so they took to wearing slacks. When the war ended, women continued to wear slacks, for lounging and gardening, and outdoors in winter for warmth. Today, many girls in America wear dungarees and shorts just as their brothers do. Both girls and women wear trouser fashions for special work or as sport clothes.

Sport clothing is a modern idea. Fifty years ago men and women played tennis in their everyday clothes. Our grandmothers went swimming in dresses just like their street dresses, except that they were only knee-length instead of ankle-length.

Today, many people have shorter working hours, with more time for sports. They wear special clothing for every sport. Because sport clothes are designed for the greatest comfort, many people have taken to wearing them when they are just relaxing.

Another change is taking place in men's clothing. Their sport clothes are now made in bright, gay colors. Pink, orange, green and yellow are popular colors for shirts and slacks. This is very different from the dark suits and white shirts that men wore for many years. We know that long ago, men's clothing was just as colorful as women's. Perhaps by starting with bright sport outfits, men will soon be wearing more colorful clothes for everyday too.

There is one outstanding difference between past and present clothing. Today, you cannot tell by looking at a man whether he is rich or poor. You cannot even recognize a president or a king by the clothes he wears. In past ages, you could tell at a glance whether a man belonged to the rich "upper class" or the poor "lower class." The rich dressed beautifully, in the latest fashion. The poor people often owned only plain working clothes.

This is still true in many parts of the world. In backward countries where most of the people are very poor, they are happy to have any clothes at all, and of course they look very different from the few rich people.

In a modern country, most of the people are neither rich nor very poor. Everybody wears the same kind of clothing. The richer people may have more clothes of better quality, but they usually do not look different. Clothing does not divide people into groups or classes.

You may want to know more about many of the points mentioned in this article. Read also the articles on FASHION, GARMENTS, and TEXTILES.

cloture, the stopping of a debate by parliamentary rule: see FILIBUSTER.

cloud

A cloud is made up of millions of tiny droplets of water in a big group. A cloud may be just above the surface of the land or the ocean, or it may be several miles up in the air. Fog is a very low-hanging cloud. When you can see your breath on a cold winter day, it is really a tiny cloud. The moist, warm air of your breath strikes the cold, drier air outdoors, and the moisture in your breath is condensed into droplets so small you cannot see them without a powerful microscope. The clouds you see in the sky were formed when a mass of warm, moist air rose from the earth and reached a section of colder air. The moisture in the air condensed and made a cloud, just as your breath condenses on a cold day.

There are many different kinds of cloud. When clouds seem to cover the entire sky, they are *stratus* clouds. *Stratus* means "layer," and a stratus cloud may be low, as in the case of a fog, or it may be several miles in the air.

The big, fluffy, white clouds that look like heaps of cotton are called *cumulus* clouds. Thin, light, feathery clouds are *cirrus* clouds. Instead of being composed of water droplets, cirrus clouds are made of tiny ice crystals. The warm air rising from the earth reached very cold high air and froze immediately, as fast as it condensed.

When a cloud becomes so heavy with droplets that it can no longer hold them, it spills over, and we have rain. A rain cloud is called a *nimbus* cloud. A cumulus cloud that becomes so heavy that it spills over is called a cumulo-nimbus. The dark-looking thunder clouds you often see in hot weather are also cumulo-nimbus clouds.

You can read more about clouds, rainfall, snow and storms in the article on WEATHER in another volume of this encyclopedia.

clove

Cloves are the dried flower buds of the clove tree. They are an important spice used in cookery and in medicines. The clove tree is beautiful, both in shape and in color. The flowers are pale red, and the leaves bright green. When the buds appear they are white, then green, and finally bright red. The dried buds are dark brown. They are used whole for cooking hams and legs of mutton, or ground into powder for seasoning pickles, relishes, and chutney.

The clove tree originally came from the Spice Islands, or Moluccas, in Indonesia. Today it is also grown in Malaya, Madagascar, and East Africa.

Artificial vanilla is made from cloves. Oil of cloves is used in toothache remedies, and for perfuming soaps and cosmetics. The dried fruit of the tree is milder and less fragrant. It is called "mother-clove."

clover

Clover is a three-leaved plant that grows in the fields. Farmers plant clover to give their fields a rest from growing other crops. The clover will help to nourish the soil and make it good for growing other crops again. It is also good "forage," or animal feed, and makes good hay to feed cattle. When a field is "in clover" it is visited by honey bees. The bees make honey out of the nectar in the clover blossoms, and clover honey has a very good flavor.

The ancient Greeks made garlands and wreaths out of clover, and thought that it was a sacred plant. Some people think that a four-leaved clover will bring them good luck. When people say "I'm in clover" they mean that things are going well with them.

The state flower of Vermont is the red clover. There are several hundred different kinds of clover, and more than fifty kinds are grown in the United States and Canada.

Clovis

Clovis was king of the Salian Franks about 1,500 years ago, when the Roman Empire ruled most of the civilized world. He was born about the year 465 and died in 511. The Franks were the Germanic tribe from which modern France got its name and the name Clovis was an early form of Louis. Clovis became king when he was only 15 years old and led the Salian Franks to many victories in battle.

After his soldiers had won a great victory over another German tribe called the Alemanni, Clovis gave up his pagan religion (belief in strange gods) and decided to follow Christianity, which was the religion of his wife, Clotilda. On Christmas Day in the year 496, Clovis and about 3,000 followers were baptized. After this, Clovis was recognized as king and was supported by Rome. He founded the kingdom that became France and made Paris the capital of the country.

clown

A clown is a man who wears a funny costume and does funny things to make people laugh. Clowns paint their faces white, and then add dark lines and spots of bright paint, and perhaps a funny nose. Most clowns are seen today in circuses. In ancient times kings usually had clowns called *jesters* as members of the court. It was their job to cheer the king or amuse him when he was worried or unhappy. In the plays of William Shakespeare, the jester is often one of the principal characters.

Clowns of America Club
This smiling face exhibits the white make-up, the exaggerated mouth, and the silly costume typical of an Auguste clown.

TYPES OF CLOWN

There are three types of traditional clown. One is the *Charlie* type, who is always in trouble. He makes us laugh, but we feel sorry for him too. Charlie Chaplin was a *Charlie*. The *Auguste* type is the one we generally think of when we use the word clown. He wears white makeup and a funny nose and enormous shoes. He is always falling down or getting bumped. The *Joey* type is usually an acrobat, juggler, or horseman. He makes us laugh by seeming to bother the other performers.

clubfoot

A clubfoot is a foot in which some of the muscles and tendons are too short and twist the foot out of shape. A person with a normal foot can walk easily because the muscles and the tendons, or cords, that hold the muscles to the foot are just the right length to let the foot move properly. If the muscles and tendons are too short, however, the foot gets twisted out of shape, and walking is very difficult. The scientific name for this condition is *talipes*.

A clubfoot is sometimes twisted so that the sole faces backwards and the person can walk only on the tips of his toes. Sometimes the foot is twisted so that the sole faces forward and the person can walk only on his heels; and sometimes the foot is so deformed that he can walk only on the outside or inside edge of the foot. People who have clubfoot are usually born with it. An accident to the bones of the ankle or foot can cause it later in life. An attack of infantile paralysis may also cause a clubfoot. Doctors can cure many cases of clubfoot. The important thing is to start treating the foot while the muscles and tendons are still soft; then the doctor can stretch them until

they are the right length. The doctor who treats clubfoot is called an orthopedic surgeon. Sometimes he massages the foot, or he tapes it, or puts it in a cast. At other times he must perform an operation on the foot. If clubfoot has been left alone too long, the short muscles and tendons will make the bones of the foot or ankle grow into wrong shapes. In this case, the surgeon must operate to make the foot normal.

Clyde

Clyde is the name of the most important river in Scotland. The mouth of the river where it empties into the sea is almost forty miles wide, and is about as long as the rest of the river itself. This mouth is called the Firth of Clyde, and on it lies the city of Glasgow, Scotland's greatest seaport and shipbuilding center. The river has many waterfalls that provide power for factories. So many products were manufactured in this region that it was a target for many bombings in World War II.

coal

Coal is a mineral that looks like black rock, and it is sometimes called "the rock that burns." It is made of trees, ferns, and other foliage that fell to the ground and decayed many millions of years ago. The story of how coal was made from these ancient plants takes us back in time to a period about 280,000,000 years ago. At this time there were many towering trees and other plants. These plants grew very rapidly, became very big, and died, all in a short space of time. This was because the earth was still warm, the air was very wet, and great bodies of fresh water covered much of the land. Wherever there was a dry spot, jungles of tangled plants sprang up. As this process of growth and death continued, great piles of decaying plants accumulated. Sometimes these piles were thousands of feet high and miles long. Often such a stack of decaying plant material would be covered by soil and rock when the surface of the earth exploded because of the tremendous heat still left under its crust. The hundreds of tons of soil and rock lying on top of the decayed plants created great pressure and great heat; so much heat, in fact, that a change took place, and the old plant materials gradually changed to carbon or coal.

DIFFERENT KINDS OF COAL

Not all coal is the same, since it takes many thousands of years, and much heat and pressure, to change plants into coal. During these thousands of years coal goes through many stages. In some places, coal is still in the first stages of formation. This first stage takes place in swampy, wet areas called *bogs*. A bog is very much like the swamps back in the Carboniferous Age when coal was first being made. There are many plants and trees, and the air and soil are moist. Sometimes in a bog a wet, brown substance can be found that looks more like wood than coal, but it is really the first stage in the formation of coal. This substance is called *peat,* and it burns with a very hot fire after it has been dried. Peat is found in many parts of the world, but it is used chiefly in Ger-

many, in Russia, and in Ireland and other parts of the British Isles.

The next stage in the formation of coal is called *lignite*. Like peat it is brown and moist, but unlike peat it need not be dried before it is burned.

Bituminous coal is the next stage, and it is much harder and blacker than either peat or lignite. This is the first material that really looks like what we know as coal.

Bituminous coal is easy to set on fire, and it burns with a much hotter flame than either peat or lignite. It is better in some ways than peat or lignite, but in other ways it is not as good. For instance, peat and lignite are clean and burn with very little smoke, while bituminous coal is very dusty and gives off clouds of black, oily fumes when it is burned.

After bituminous coal comes *cannel coal*. This is the kind of coal people use in their stoves and fireplaces. It is dull black in color, and burns very easily and quickly with a bright, clean flame.

The last stage in the formation of coal is *anthracite,* or "hard coal." This is the hardest and blackest kind of coal. It is not easy to set it afire, but it burns for hours, gives off great heat, and is almost smokeless. People like to use it for heating their homes because it is the cleanest coal.

HOW WE MINE COAL

Coal, like other minerals, is mined, or dug out of the ground. But before it can be mined, it must be found. A prospector (a person who searches for minerals in the ground) knows many ways to find coal. Usually his job is quite simple because most coal is on the surface of the earth, or very close to the surface. If the coal is a few feet underground, he can still find it easily because one or two chunks will be found on the surface, or perhaps clinging to the roots of an overturned tree. The coal is in the ground in long strips that are sometimes fifty feet wide, fifty feet deep, and several miles long. These strips are called *veins* or *seams.*

When coal has been discovered, bulldozers or earth movers, cranes, steam shovels, and other large machines are moved into the area before the mine shaft is sunk. The mine shaft is a large hole that sometimes goes more than a mile straight down into the earth. Branching off from the shaft are tunnels that are often three or four miles long. The tunnels are wide enough for a small railway, and it is in these tunnels that coal is mined. The floor, the ceiling and the walls of the tunnels are all coal. The railway is used to carry the coal from far away in the tunnel back to the shaft, where it is carried by elevator to the earth's surface.

BLASTING

In the past men dug coal with picks and shovels, but today there is a much easier way. The miners use long electric drills to make deep holes in the wall of the tunnel. Then they put gunpowder in the hole and blast the coal loose. Even the shovels that put the coal into the railway cars are now run by machines.

When coal reaches the surface, there are a great many processes that it still must go through before it is usable. At first, coal was used just as it came from

the mine. One load of coal might contain pieces as big as a football and pieces as small as a pebble. Mixed with it could be rocks and dust loosened by the blasting. But today because of *breakers* and *tipples* this no longer happens. A breaker is a building several stories high. Anthracite coal is taken to the top and very large lumps are cracked by rollers. Then the cracked coal is dumped onto screens and only coal smaller than a certain size will go through. A tipple, used for bituminous coal, is very much the same as a breaker except that it only sorts the coal by size and does not break it into small pieces. Different sizes of coal go into separate bins. From the bins the coal is loaded into long trains of coal cars and hauled away to be used. To get rid of dust and rock the coal is cleaned by streams of water or air.

THE USES OF COAL

The most important use of coal is as a fuel. It is used to make the steam that turns the generators that give us our lights and radio and television. It makes the steam that drives the railroads. Even more important are all the things that can be made from it. There are more than 200,000 products that are made from coal. Among these many products are the mercurochrome that we put on cuts and scratches, sulfa drugs that fight infection, cosmetics, and adhesive tape. The most important industrial use for coal is coke, which is used in the manufacture of iron and steel, gas, and tars. You can read more about COKE in a separate article.

COAL GAS AND COAL TAR

Coal gas and coal tar both are made from bituminous coal in a process called "destructive distillation." Bituminous coal is put into airtight ovens and baked for a long time at a very high temperature. When the coal reaches a temperature of about 1000° Centigrade, it starts to disintegrate, that is, to fall apart. As it disintegrates, gases are given off, and these gases are called *coal gas*. Coal gas is sometimes used in stoves. A ton of bituminous coal will yield about 100,000 cubic feet of coal gas. Coal gas also is used in the manufacture of explosives and medicine.

Coal tar is also made by destructive distillation. If coal gas is cooled in a closed bottle, a strange thing happens. Two liquids appear, one at the top and one at the bottom. At the top of the bottle, ammonia is formed. At the bottom of the bottle a black, heavy, sticky, bad-smelling oil appears; this is coal tar. It is not at all the same as the tar that is used to pave roads. That is asphalt and does not come from coal at all, but is found already made in nature. Asphalt is found in huge pools called asphalt lakes. Although coal tar itself has few uses, there are hundreds of products that can be made from it, such as medicines, explosives, and dyes.

THE HISTORY OF COAL

Coal is one of the oldest minerals known to man. The ancient Hebrews knew of it and so did the Greeks, but no one knew how to use it. It is not known exactly when coal was first used as a fuel, but some historians think that the American Indians used it for heat long before

the white men came. The most important reason coal was not used as fuel was because there was plenty of wood. Coal is harder to find than wood, and much harder to set on fire. People were also afraid of the "black rocks that burn" and some thought that they were an invention of the devil.

In the course of time, coal came to be used more and more, and today it has almost entirely replaced wood as a fuel. The first coal mine in the United States was opened in 1750, but because of the poor roads and the abundance of wood for fuel, the new industry did very poorly. It was the farmers who really started the coal industry in this country. Farmers working in their fields might find a small deposit of surface coal and sell it to a local blacksmith to use in his forge.

The Soviet Union produces more coal than any other country; out of a total world production of about two billion metric tons in 1960, the Soviet Union produced 513,600,000 tons. The United States was second with 372,200,000 tons, the United Kingdom was third with 196,800,000 tons. West Germany, China, and Poland also produce much coal.

Coast and Geodetic Survey

The Coast and Geodetic Survey is one of the main divisions of the United States Department of Commerce. It was established almost 150 years ago by President Thomas Jefferson, and was called the U.S. Coast Survey until 1878 when it started to measure the body of the land and not just the coasts. The purpose of the Coast and Geodetic Survey is to help sailors, airplane pilots, and the civil engineers who build automobile highways, bridges, and tunnels. The engineers and scientists of the Coast and Geodetic Survey prepare maps that show all the lakes, hills, and valleys in the United States. In order to do this, scientists explore and measure the land. The information they get is then sent to Washing-

The Coast and Geodetic Survey has men who prepare maps showing the lakes, hills, and other physical features of different parts of the country. This information is of great use to engineers and pilots.

U.S. Coast & Geodetic Survey

ton, where the maps are made by another group, the Geological Survey. Another important job of the Coast and Geodetic Survey is to make charts of the ocean to guide sailors and fishermen. It has about twenty ships that explore the ocean and collect information for these charts. Other charts of airports and radio towers are prepared for the use of pilots.

Coast Guard

The Coast Guard is a body of men who are responsible for the safety and order of United States ships and crews on the high seas, and of all shipping along the coasts of the United States and its overseas territories. Its main purpose is to prevent loss of life and property; its other purpose is to enforce laws. Unlike the other branches of the armed forces, such as the Army, Navy, and Air Force, the Coast Guard has no government department of its own. In peacetime it is part of the Treasury Department, and in wartime it becomes a part of the Navy. During World War II the Coast Guard not only continued to perform its regular duties but also took part in sea battles and invasions all over the world.

Although it is much smaller than any of the three regular armed services or the Marine Corps (which is at all times part of the Navy), the Coast Guard has an enormous number of jobs to do, year in and year out, in all kinds of weather. Thus, while the other services are mostly training and preparing for a possible war, the Coast Guard is actively safeguarding the peace. At the same time it keeps itself in constant readiness for war, for it must be ready to become a part of the Navy at any time.

SAVING LIVES AND PROPERTY

Many of the regular Coast Guard's 31,000 officers and men serve aboard the Coast Guard's cutters and other vessels, which constantly cruise up and down the coasts of the United States, Alaska, and Hawaii, and in other United States waters, looking for ships in trouble. To help this seagoing rescue service, there are about 135 lifeboat stations, at which the Coast Guardsmen keep a watch out at all times for ships in need of help. In storms and hurricanes the Coast Guard can sometimes save hundreds of people from drowning. Sailors of the Coast Guard have to know how to handle a longboat in a rough sea, how to swim with a drowning person (who may be half crazed with fear) on their back, how to bring people who have lost consciousness back to life with artificial respiration. They must know how to use all of the complicated mechanisms involved in rescue at sea, such as the breeches buoy, which is a line shot from a special gun and attached to a high point on the sinking ship, usually the mast, along which passengers may be carried to safety in a seat called a boatswain's chair.

In order to make sure that ships are not wrecked by a simple error on the part of the men commanding them, the Coast Guard maintains and operates a great number of aids to navigation—some 48,000 in all as of 1973. Aids to navigation include lighthouses and lightships (float-

ing lighthouses on ships anchored at a particular spot), buoys of all kinds, lighted and unlighted beacons (markers on the shore), fog signals, and radio beacons. All these aids help a captain to locate the position of his ship with relation to the coast, as well as to such hidden dangers as underwater rocks and shoals or sunken ships. During and since World War II the development of radio and radar resulted in new kinds of aids to navigation, effective over very great distances. These are:

LORAN (*Long Range Aid to Navigation*). Loran stations automatically send out radio impulses which are received aboard ship on the screen of a special device that is much like a television set. By comparing the impulses from two or more Loran stations, the ship's navigator or captain can find out exactly where his ship is, even though he may be many hundreds of miles from any shore.

RACON (*RAdio BeaCONs*). Racon stations send out a continuous beam which enables the navigator of any ship or plane within 120 miles to find out how far away from a station he is, and in what direction from it.

Since the United States has become increasingly conscious of oil pollution in our waters, it has become the job of the Coast Guard to check into this problem. They watch to see if there are any oil spills and if there are they are cleaned up immediately. They have developed airborne pollution controls that can be flown quickly to the scene of any potential oil pollution incidents.

Besides preventing accidents with aids to navigation and rescuing victims when accidents occur, the Coast Guard carries out its principal mission of saving lives and property in a number of other ways. Coast Guard teams remove sunken ships and other menaces to safe navigation from harbors and other much-traveled waters; Coast Guard inspectors carefully go over merchant ships to make sure of their safety; Coast Guard transport doctors go to the aid (often by breeches buoy) of seamen stricken with some sickness or hurt in the performance of duty. Coast Guard planes assigned to the International Ice Patrol scout the North Atlantic keeping track of the movements of floating ice blocks and sending out the information they gather to all ships that pass through the area. Since the Coast Guard took charge of the Ice Patrol in 1912, after the steamer *Titanic* was sunk by an iceberg, not a life has been lost by collision with icebergs or ice fields.

ENFORCING THE LAW

A leading function of the Coast Guard, in peace and war, is to prevent smuggling by sea; that is, to make sure that nothing is brought into the country or its possessions illegally by ship or boat. Smuggled goods include everything from such valuable things as jewels, whose owners want to avoid paying duty on them at United States Customs, to dangerous narcotics. Smugglers have even tried (sometimes successfully) to land immigrants in the United States. During the first year after the United States entered World War II, a German submarine landed a half-dozen Nazi spies on a beach near Amagansett, Long Island. They were quickly caught.

During Prohibition, from 1920 until 1933, when the 18th Amendment to the Constitution (forbidding the sale of alcoholic beverages) was in effect, the Coast Guard had to cope with the enormously complicated problem of stopping the "rumrunners"—the swift motorboats, often heavily armed and armored, in which smugglers tried to bring illegal ("bootleg") liquor into the United States.

OTHER DUTIES

Coast Guard cutters patrol the North Pacific Ocean and the Bering Sea, near Alaska, to make sure that no one takes more than the legal limit of fish and fur-bearing sea animals. They also visit remote Arctic settlements on the coast, bringing medical aid and supplies. In frozen northern waters blunt-nosed Coast Guard icebreakers push a path through the thick surface ice so that other ships may follow. And in lonely outposts in the Pacific and the Atlantic, Coast Guard weather station vessels patiently record information on weather conditions so that a complete picture of world climate can be pieced together in Washington.

Regulations governing where and when a ship may anchor in United States waters are enforced by the Coast Guard. The Coast Guard is also charged with maintaining order at boat races and naval parades.

Since 1942 the Coast Guard has been responsible for order and discipline aboard ships of the merchant fleet. The Coast Guard keeps a record of the conduct of each officer and man in the Merchant Marine, and may take action against an offender if it finds it necessary to do so.

THE COAST GUARD IN WORLD WAR II

Even before the Japanese attack on Pearl Harbor brought the United States into World War II, a United States Coast Guard patrol had made the first American naval capture of the war. On September 12, 1941, it seized the Norwegian ship *Buskoe* and the Nazi radiomen she had landed in east Greenland. Thereafter, during the dark days of 1942 when the waters off the Atlantic coast were so full of enemy submarines, Coast Guard cutters and airplanes kept up a constant search for the marauders, together with elements of the Navy. During this period the Coast Guard saved thousands of lives and much precious cargo; its losses in men and ships were exceptionally heavy.

As United States production became geared to war, more and more ships were launched in the nation's shipyards. Meanwhile the Coast Guard, now part of the Navy, grew rapidly. By the end of the war it numbered some 171,000 officers and men, including 10,000 members of the women's auxiliary known as SPARS (the name was taken from the Coast Guard motto *Semper Paratus*, which is Latin for "Always Ready"). Coast Guardsmen had manned 351 Navy vessels, 288 Army vessels, and 802 larger cutters (of the Coast Guard). They had served aboard destroyers, destroyer escorts, troop transports, and landing craft. They had hunted submarines and done escort and patrol duty in the North Atlantic; and they had taken part in every invasion in the war. At the

same time they had continued, as in peacetime, to patrol some 40,000 miles of American coastline. In all, 1,868 members of the Coast Guard were decorated for bravery in action.

On January 1, 1946, the Coast Guard was returned to the Treasury Department, resuming its peacetime strength.

VIETNAM

In 1965 the Coast Guard assisted the Navy in patrolling the Vietnam coast to suppress the infiltration of men and supplies from the north by sea. They were later aided by an additional nine cutters and experts in the fields of explosives loading, port safety, aid to navigation, and law enforcement. Helicopter pilots worked along with the Air Force, as well, to aid the war effort.

COAST GUARD TRAINING SCHOOLS

For young men entering the Coast Guard as seamen, the first step is the recruit receiving center at Cape May, New Jersey. After a period of intensive training there, recruits who have shown ability in certain fields are sent on to one of several service schools for further training.

Young men seeking careers as officers in the Coast Guard may apply for admission to the United States Coast Guard Academy at New London, Connecticut. When admitted, they become cadets. During his four years at the Academy a cadet will take courses in engineering, military science, cultural and other professional subjects. Upon graduation a cadet is commissioned by the president as an ensign in the Coast Guard, with the same pay, allowances, and privileges as an officer of similar rank in the Army, Navy, or Marines.

HISTORY OF THE COAST GUARD

Although the Coast Guard did not officially come into existence until 1915, when it was created by an Act of Congress out of the United States Revenue Cutter Service and the United States Lifesaving Service, it traces its origin back to 1790. In that year Secretary of the Treasury Alexander Hamilton asked Congress for a fleet of "ten boats" with which to protect the customs, an important source of revenue for the young country, from smugglers. On August 4, 1790, President George Washington signed the bill creating the Revenue-Marine, which became the only American force afloat until the Navy was organized a few years later.

The Coast Guard has served with distinction in every United States war except the war with Tripoli. Of 22 enemy vessels seized during the differences with France, in 1798 and 1799, 18 were captured by the Revenue-Marine. The first capture afloat in the War of 1812 was made by a revenue cutter. During the early 19th century the Revenue-Marine played the leading role in stamping out piracy in the Gulf of Mexico. Vessels of the Revenue-Marine served in the Seminole Indian War, the Mexican War, and the Civil War. Revenue cutters fought alongside Navy ships in the Spanish-American War.

When the United States entered World War I, the Coast Guard for the first

time passed into the naval establishment. Its men and vessels took part in just about every phase of naval activity. The sinking of the Coast Guard cutter *Tampa* by a German submarine on September 26, 1918, with the loss of every one of its 115 officers and men, was the second worst American naval disaster of the war.

Coast Ranges

The Coast Ranges are a series of mountain chains along the Pacific coast of North America. They extend from British Columbia, Canada, down through Washington, Oregon, and California in the United States, and help to form the peninsula of Lower California, in Mexico. Most of the mountains of the Coast Ranges are steep and rocky. Many are covered with valuable timber and rich in minerals. One of the highest points in the United States Coast Ranges is Mt. Pinos, in California, which is 8,831 feet high.

coati

The coati is a small animal that lives in the jungles of Central and South America. It is about three feet long. It is closely related to the raccoon. It has a long snout and tail, and its soft, heavy, brown fur is used to make fur coats. Coatis are fine hunters and skillful tree-climbers. They travel through the jungle forests and swamps in large numbers, like an army. When a group of them is attacked, they keep their ranks solid and make an orderly retreat. These bright little animals feed on insects, lizards, and young birds, and often live in the hollow limbs of giant trees. With some patience, the coati can be made into a pleasant house pet.

coat of arms, the crest of a family or person: see HERALDRY.

cobalt

Cobalt is a metal of a silvery-gray color. It is an element, which means that it is not made by combining other substances. Like iron, cobalt is magnetic—it attracts other metals. Alloys, or mixtures, of steel and cobalt are used to make hard tools that will resist melting under heat. Cobalt is also combined with chemicals to make various pigments and coloring matters, used in dyes, inks, and paints. The most powerful new HYDROGEN BOMBS, about which there is a separate article, are called cobalt bombs.

Cobb, Irvin S.

Irvin S. Cobb was an American writer of amusing stories and plays. Cobb was born in Paducah, Kentucky, in 1876. When he was only 19 he became an editor of the Paducah newspaper, and later he wrote for New York newspapers. His most famous stories are laid in Kentucky. They are called the *Judge Priest* stories and are filled with good common sense and hearty humor. Cobb died in 1944.

Cobb, Tyrus

Tyrus Raymond Cobb, better known as *Ty Cobb,* was one of the greatest baseball players who ever lived. He was born in Georgia in 1886. When he was only 19 years old he joined the Detroit Tigers,

in the American League, as center fielder. He stayed with the Tigers for 22 years, and finally became manager. Then he spent two seasons as a player with the Philadelphia Athletics. He retired from baseball in 1928. "The Georgia Peach," as he was called by millions of fans, had a lifetime batting average of .367. He made 4,191 major-league hits, stole 892 bases, and led the American League in batting for twelve seasons. In 1936 he was the first player to be elected to the Baseball Hall of Fame. He died in 1961.

Cobden, Richard

Richard Cobden was an English political leader who lived about a hundred years ago. He is remembered for his fight against the Corn Laws, which were laws  that put a tax on grain that was brought into England from other countries. This tax made food very expensive, and many people in England were hungry and dissatisfied. Cobden was a manufacturer who believed in *free trade,* that is, he thought there should be no taxes on things brought in from other countries. He wrote many articles and made speeches in Parliament on this subject. He convinced many people, and finally the laws were repealed. Cobden had worked so hard in Parliament that he had not been able to attend to his business, and it was ruined. But people were so grateful for his work that a great deal of money was collected to help him. Cobden spent the rest of his life working for free trade and peace with other countries. Cobden was born in 1804 and died in 1865.

cobra

Cobra is the name of several different snakes, all in the cobra family. They are all poisonous, and all have hoods. This is a part of the neck that can be puffed up to look like a hood when the cobra is angry or frightened. The largest is the king cobra of southern Asia, which grows to a length of twelve feet. Other cobras are between six and ten feet long. The spitting cobra of Africa squirts poison at its enemy's eyes, and its aim is extremely accurate. Unless it is washed away, the poison can blind a man. Unlike the venom of rattlesnakes, the cobra's venom is not contained in its fangs. The cobra gets a good firm bite on its victim. There, from special sacs in its mouth, it releases poison that flows into the wound made by the biting fangs.

coca

Coca is a plant from which the drug cocaine is made. Cocaine is a very strong *narcotic,* which means a drug that relieves pain and puts a person to sleep. Doctors use cocaine for patients who are very ill, or have had painful operations. But it is a habit-forming drug, and is very dangerous to use without a doctor's direction. You can read more about cocaine in the article NARCOTICS.

The coca plant is a shrub that grows in South America. The Indians knew about it long before the white man came. They used to dry the leaves and chew them like tobacco.

Coca sounds like cacao, the tree from which chocolate comes, but they are entirely different.

Coca-Cola

Coca-Cola is a drink that has become unusually popular in America and throughout the world. It is a trade-marked name and is manufactured by only one company. It was first made only about seventy-five years ago, but it is almost as well-known as such drinks as beer, which has been known for thousands of years. Coca-Cola is a syrup made with sugar and various flavorings including cola (or kola), the nut of a tree grown in tropical countries. One part of the syrup is mixed with five parts of carbonated water to make the drink. In the standard glass or bottle of Coca-Cola, there is one ounce of syrup and five ounces of carbonated water, making a six-ounce drink, or less than the usual glass of milk (which is eight ounces, half a pint). A druggist in Atlanta, Georgia, first made Coca-Cola in 1886. Until 1899 it was sold only at soda fountains. Then the bottling of it began. Since then Coca-Cola has been so successful that many other "cola" drinks have been put on the market. The best-known of the others is Pepsi-Cola, a similar drink, which has competed with Coca-Cola by selling a similar drink in a bottle twice as large (twelve ounces) for the same or a slightly higher price. For years people called Coca-Cola "coke" and the company that makes Coca-Cola did not like it, but finally the company gave in to the people and trade-marked the name "Coke" also. In some European countries Coca-Cola has been considered so much a symbol of the United States that when people were angry at the United States they attacked Coca-Cola.

cocaine, a drug made from the leaves of the South American coca shrub, that is used to relieve pain: see the article NARCOTICS.

Cochin China, a former state in Indo-China: see FRENCH INDO-CHINA

cochineal

Cochineal is the name of an insect that lives on a certain kind of cactus. These tiny little insects can be made into bright red dyes for silk and wool. They can also be made into silver-gray or black dyes. The insects are placed on the branches and joints of the cactus, which is a desert plant. They breed and grow, and about two or three times a year they are brushed off into bags or baskets. The best scarlet dyes are made from cochineals, but it takes so many insects to make even a little bit of dye that nowadays most red dyes are made from coal tar because it is so much less expensive.

cockatoo

The cockatoo is a brightly colored bird that belongs to the parrot family. Many of them are pure white, with long, bright red or yellow feathers on their heads. Other cockatoos have a darker plumage. These birds have strong, curved beaks; the great black cockatoo can break the hardest nut with its bill. The cockatoo

is noted for its harsh, screechy voice. It is found chiefly in Australia and on a large island group between the Indian and Pacific Oceans called the Malay Archipelago.

The beautiful white cockatoo can be taught to speak a few words like a parrot.

N.Y. Zoological Society

cocker spaniel, a dog with large, drooping ears: see SPANIEL.

cockfighting

Cockfighting is a sport in which two roosters are made to fight each other. They are a specially bred type of rooster called gamecocks. They are smaller than most of our barnyard roosters, but are much more ferocious. The fight takes place in a round *pit,* or stage. The cocks are held close together so that their beaks almost touch, and then they are released. They fight until one or the other is killed, or is too badly hurt to fight, or gives up and will not fight any more. Sometimes the cocks wear steel spurs on their feet. The spurs are sometimes two inches long, and are as sharp as knives. Cockfighting is against the law in the United States and in many other countries, but in Asia and Latin America it is still popular.

cockroach

Cockroaches are a kind of insect. They are a form of water beetle, and are found where there is dampness and little or no light. They do not like light, and run away when a light is suddenly turned on them. There are cockroaches all over the world, in cities, on farms, and even in the woods. Many millions of years ago, when the earth was covered with big fern-like trees, there were hundreds of different kinds of cockroaches. They will eat anything that we eat, and they will also eat books, papers, clothes, carpets, and furs. After they have crawled through some dirty place, they may next crawl over our food and make it spoil. If we eat that food we may get sick. Cockroaches breed in filth, and the best way to get rid of them is to keep the kitchen and bathroom very clean. Sometimes it is necessary to exterminate them, which means killing the cockroaches and destroying their eggs so that no new cockroaches can hatch. There are many different ways to exterminate them. The most usual way is to put poison where they will walk over it and get their feet in it. Powders and sprays are sold for this purpose, and traps are also used. Cockroaches have an unpleasant odor, which many people can recognize. A big cockroach is sometimes as long as two inches, but most of them are much smaller. They cannot bite, but they can carry disease germs and spoil our food.

cocktail

There are two kinds of cocktail. One is the kind that is served before dinner. It may be tomato juice, or a fruit cup, or oysters or shrimp with a peppery sauce to dip them in. Another kind is made with gin, brandy, rum, or whisky, mixed with fruit juices, vermouth (a kind of spiced wine), grenadine (a sweet red syrup made from the fruit called pomegranate), eggs, or bitters made of various roots, bark, and herbs soaked in alcohol. The two most popular cocktails are the *Martini,* made with gin and French vermouth, with an olive or small onion in the bottom of the glass, and the *Manhattan,* made with rye whisky and Italian vermouth, with a cherry in the bottom of the glass. Good bartenders sometimes know how to mix more than a hundred different cocktails.

cocoa, a powder made from the cacao seed: see CHOCOLATE AND COCOA.

coconut

Coconut trees grow in all of the tropical and semitropical countries of the world. Wherever the weather is always warm and summery, there you will find coconut palms. They are usually near the ocean, and along the coast of Florida and California they are sure to be seen. In the South Sea Islands the coconut palm is a very important tree. Its fruit furnishes the natives with food and a kind of milk that is inside of the fresh, or green, coconut. The tree itself provides shade and shelter and wood for building. From the bark the natives make rope and cordage, and from the leaves they make mats and baskets. The coconut itself is a large nut, about the shape of a football, but a little smaller. On the outside of the nut, there is a thick, stringy husk. The fibers from this husk are dried and made into a tough and hard-wearing material called *coir.* Coir is used to make doormats, bumpers for boats, stuffing for mats, and upholstered furniture. When you take off the outer husk you see a round brown nut with a hard shell. This shell must be broken or sawed in half, and inside there is the white meat of the coconut. When the coconut is green, it is full of milk. The milk is good to drink, and very healthful. The meat is the most important part, for it contains the valuable coconut oil used in making soap and many things to eat.

COPRA

After coconuts are cut open, they are dried in the sun. The dried meat is called copra, and in this form it is shipped to the factories to be made into oil. After the oil has been pressed out, there is a sort of mealy material left. It is called *coco cake* and is used for feeding cattle. Coconut oil makes soap that will lather better and clean better than ordinary soap, and it is in great demand. Many countries such as India, Malaya, Ceylon, and parts of Indonesia, raise coconut palms.

USES OF COCONUTS

There are more uses for the coconut tree than for any other tree in the world. If you were cast away on a desert island you could get the following articles from these trees alone: the meat of the coconut, for food, and also the young shoots and stems, and the buds, called palm cabbage; cups and bowls from the shells; ropes and cordage from the coir; milk to drink from the young nuts; sugar from the boiled flowers; hardwood for building, from the trunk; baskets, mats, and thatched shelters from the leaves; and you could use the husks and what is left to make a fire for cooking and keeping warm.

The search for copra led to much exploration and discovery in the South Pacific. It is a big industry, and millions of fresh coconuts are eaten every year, while shredded coconut is a familiar sight on cakes and pastries and candy.

cod and cod liver oil

Cod are a kind of fish found in the North Atlantic and Pacific Oceans. They are long, soft-skinned, with very small scales, and grow to eighty pounds in weight, though usually they weigh around

National Archives

The gentle nature of the cocker spaniel makes it a loving pet. It is also an excellent bird-hunting dog.

It takes a skillful climber to pick coconuts that grow high above the ground.

ten to thirty pounds. They are one of the world's most important food fishes, and great quantities of them are caught each year, chiefly on the Grand Banks of Newfoundland and off New England, Norway, and Iceland. Rudyard Kipling's wonderful story *Captains Courageous* is about cod fishing on the Grand Banks. In America, Massachusetts has been the center of the cod-fishing industry since the days of the early settlers. The flesh of the cod is white and flaky and rather tasteless when cooked fresh, but salt cod has a very strong flavor. This is one of the main foods in South America, Portugal, and the West Indies, where it is cooked in a large variety of ways. The oil made from the livers of codfish is very important in industry: it is used in tanning leather, in tempering steel, and in making cheap soap; and refined cod liver oil is very important in medicine because it is full of vitamins that are necessary for health. Cod are free-swimming fish which feed chiefly on other small fish. They lay their eggs in the water in mid-ocean, and the eggs develop into young fish while floating about near the surface of the water. The word *cod* is also used for many other fish in the cod family.

code, a system of words or symbols used to represent words: see CRYPTOGRAPHY.

codeine

Codeine is a drug used to relieve pain. It is also a sedative, which means that it has a soothing or quieting effect. Codeine and morphine are both made from the opium poppy, but codeine is milder and less habit-forming than morphine. In large amounts, codeine is a dangerous poison; but in small amounts it is one of the most important and useful drugs that we know.

Code Napoleon

A code is a set of laws by which a country is governed. When Napoleon was emperor of France about 150 years ago, he introduced a set of laws for France that was called the Code Napoleon. The people of France thought a new law code

was needed because there were many different kinds of laws, some old and some new. Some laws had grown up in France itself, and others had been brought by the Romans when they ruled France. Still other laws had been made by the French kings. After the French people had overthrown their king in a war called the French Revolution, they wanted a new set of laws that would be the same for the whole country.

In the century after the Code Napoleon was drawn up, many new governments were being formed all over the world. They all wanted to draw up new and clear law codes, and they studied and imitated the Code Napoleon. It became a model for the law codes of the whole world.

codling moth

The codling moth is the best known, and probably the most important, insect enemy of the apple-grower. The adult moth is a beautiful little creature with bluish-gray wings. The pink or white larva of the codling moth is the worm that people find feeding at the core of rotten apples. The codling moth is also a pest of pears, quinces, and English walnuts. A large part of the damage that these insects do is controlled by farmers who spray their fruit trees with DDT powder after the trees have blossomed.

Cody, William F.

William Cody is the real name of the famous Buffalo Bill. Cody was born in Iowa in 1846, and he lived a long and

Buffalo Bill Historical Center
exciting life. When he was a young boy, Cody went out to Colorado, where he spent a lot of time among the Indians. During the Civil War, he was a brave and clever scout and a good soldier. After the war, Cody arranged to supply the men who were working on the railroads with meat. In less than two years Cody shot almost five thousand buffalo. This is how he got the name Buffalo Bill. Cody, dur-

ing this time, was not only shooting buffalo, but also raising them.

Buffalo Bill was a man who could do many things. One thing he did very well was to put on a good show. When he was a young man, he acted in plays in Chicago. Later, he collected some cowboys and bucking broncos, some Indians and buffalo, and this became Buffalo Bill's Wild West Show. He traveled all over the United States and Europe. Everywhere he went, kings and queens, children and grandparents loved to see Buffalo Bill and his Wild West Show, and Cody became famous.

Cody wrote quite a few western stories, and he also wrote his autobiography (the story of his life). The events of his life are not all told just the way they happened, but people have liked to read his stories anyway. After he was famous, Cody was given a piece of land in Wyoming, where he raised cattle. The town of Cody, Wyoming, is named after him, though most people remember William Cody as Buffalo Bill. He died in 1917.

coeducation

The word *coeducation* means the teaching of boys and girls together in the same school. Americans are used to the idea of coeducation, because in almost all of the public schools in the United States boys and girls go to school together. But this is not true everywhere in the world today, and many years ago, it was not true anywhere. For hundreds of years, girls were hardly educated at all. People thought that women should stay at home and keep house and cook and sew. Girls should learn these things from their mothers. Only men went out into the world to get jobs, and run the government, and fight in wars, so only men needed to be educated. People thought that women were not strong enough or smart enough to do these things, so all the schools were for boys. If the girls had any education at all, they got it at home, or from private teachers.

But finally these ideas began to change. More and more people began to think that girls should be educated as well as boys. At first new schools were set up and boys and girls went to school separately. After a while people began to think about coeducation. They thought that all children should learn the same things, and they thought that it would be good for boys and girls to work and play together. Women wanted to be able to go to the colleges and universities. The idea of coeducation began to spread and become more popular. But even today it is not practiced everywhere. In some countries, especially in the Orient, there is still almost no education for girls. In many places in Europe, boys and girls still go to separate schools. But in the United States, coeducation is found everywhere, and girls and boys are given the same chances to learn.

coffee

Coffee is a drink made from the seed of the coffee tree. This seed, or bean, is roasted and ground. Then it is made to give up its flavor to boiling water. It has become the favorite drink of the people of the United States. The coffee tree can grow to the height of twenty feet. It has

white, sweet-smelling flowers. The fruit of the coffee tree looks like a ripe cherry. Inside the coffee berry, there are two beans. The coffee tree looks more like a beautiful ornament than a food plant. With its glossy, green leaves, and loaded down with rich red berries, it could make an excellent Christmas decoration. It takes about five years for a new tree to grow enough beans so that it is profitable to pick and sell the coffee. There are several kinds of coffee tree. The one that gives the best tasting coffee is the Arabian coffee tree. This tree is the one most grown for the market all over the world.

HISTORY OF COFFEE

Coffee has been used for at least five hundred years in Arabia. It is believed to have originated long before this in Abyssinia, where it still grows wild as a weed. There is a story about the discovery of coffee. We are told that long ago a shepherd found that his sheep were acting strangely at night. They did not sleep much and were surprisingly lively. After several nights of this behavior, the shepherd decided to spy on them during the day. He found the cause of the friskiness of his sheep. He saw them eagerly eat the blossoms and fruit of a tree he had never noticed before. The shepherd tried this food on himself. This threw him into such a feeling of gaiety that his neighbors thought he was drunk. It is said that when he told them of his discovery they all agreed that it was a gift of God, and should be used. From Arabia, the use of coffee spread to Constantinople, in Turkey. In Arabia and in Turkey the people follow the Mohammedan religion. Some of the Mohammedan prayers are very long. Some of the people started to take coffee to keep themselves lively and awake during these prayers. The priests were furious. They had coffee forbidden for a while. The priests said that coffee was like wine and liquors which are forbidden by their religion. In spite of this, the coffee habit spread all over Arabia and neighboring countries. In the 16th and 17th centuries, coffee houses appeared in Europe, where coffee found much opposition. In Germany, anybody who wanted to roast coffee had to have a special license. In England, coffee houses became meeting places for people who talked very much about many things, including politics. This worried the king, and he had all the coffee houses closed for a while.

THE USE AND PRODUCTION OF COFFEE

For a long time, the world's coffee was grown in southern Arabia, in an area called Mocha. This is why light brown coffee, and cake icing of this color, are called mocha. Though Arabia still grows coffee for the world market, it now produces only a tiny amount of the world's coffee. The greatest coffee-grower is now Brazil, with Colombia second. The first coffee tree in Brazil was grown in a garden by a monk. Brazil now grows over 44 million 132-pound bags of coffee a year. This is about half the total world production of coffee.

The people of the United States are the biggest coffee consumers in the world. If the total amount of pounds imported is divided by the entire population, we find that the United States uses over sixteen pounds of coffee per person each year. The total amount of money that the United States pays for its coffee comes to more than it pays for any other thing it buys from abroad. This makes coffee an extremely important part of world trade. Other large coffee-producing countries are Mexico, El Salvador, Guatemala, and Indonesia.

Although the coffee tree can grow wild in some parts of the world, it is important that coffee for the market be grown with great care. The young trees are very delicate. They must be carefully tended. When the coffee grows, the amount of sun, and rain, and the kind of soil all contribute to the final taste of the bean. The flavor and smell of the coffee comes from an oil in the bean. Before coffee is roasted, the beans are green, and taste nothing like the coffee we know. It is the roasting that brings out the coffee flavor. While roasting, the bean swells up somewhat, but it also decreases in weight.

Roasting takes great skill. Too little or too much roasting destroys the quality of the coffee. After the coffee is roasted, it will lose its flavor quickly like anything else that has been cooked. It must be used soon after roasting, or else packed into airtight cans.

Coffees from different kinds of trees, and coffee grown in different countries, have very noticeable variations in taste. Experts decide upon a particular flavor for a popular brand of coffee. Then they take the different kinds of coffees available in the market and mix or blend them in order to keep that chosen flavor. There are people whose job it is to taste coffee. They do this every day. The coffee tasters pour boiling water upon some ground coffee at the bottom of a cup. They suck up some of this coffee as quickly as they can. When they do this, they make a loud noise, like people with bad table manners. But, after they have the coffee in their mouth, they do what even people with bad table manners would never do. They immediately spit out the coffee. The tasters do this because they find that this is the only way they can get the real flavor of the many coffees they must taste. The quality of each coffee sample is written down.

There are different ways to make a cup of coffee. It can be boiled in a pot. But many people now use newer methods called the drip method, the percolator method, and the vacuum coffee-maker. For each of these different ways of making coffee, there is a special way to grind the bean.

Coffee has become more expensive, but even when it was cheap, many people in the world could not afford to buy it. There is an amazing story that, in one of the great coffee-growing countries, the coffeeberry pickers could not afford to buy the beans to make their own coffee. The price of coffee is one of the main reasons why there are many coffee substitutes used instead of coffee. The seeds of various other plants are sometimes roasted and ground. Sometimes they are mixed with real coffee. The most popular substitute for coffee is the roasted root of the chicory plant. Some people in Europe would rather have a chicory mixture than pure coffee. A new development in coffee is the use of "instant coffee"—coffee powders that dissolve in hot water. They are made by brewing coffee from the ground beans, then removing the water that is used to do this. When this is done, a powder or paste is left. Water is added again to this powder when coffee is desired. When the price of coffee rises, more people drink milk or tea. But a person who has the coffee habit finds it hard to give up the pleasure of a cup of coffee.

cofferdam

Cofferdam is a kind of room used when workmen have to build something under water. They put temporary walls of steel or wood in the water. These walls reach from above the surface all the way down to the bottom, and completely enclose the place where the work is to be done. Then the water is pumped out and the workmen can go down to the bottom. Sometimes cofferdams are built against the sides of big ships so that repairs can be made without putting the ship in dry dock. Cofferdams are also used in building piers and wharves. When the work must be done where the water is very deep, CAISSONS are used. You can read about them in another article.

Cohan, George M.

George Michael Cohan was one of the most beloved men in the American theater. As a "song and dance" man, he charmed audiences with his light, gay and happy routines. He was also well-known as a writer and producer of plays. Among the forty plays he wrote are *Seven Keys to Baldpate, Forty-Five Minutes from Broadway,* and *The Song and Dance Man.*

Cohan always said he was born on July 4, America's Independence Day. Actually he was born three minutes before midnight on July 3, 1878. His mother and father were actors, so it was natural that he should go into the theater when he was still very young. By the time he was 15, he was writing songs and skits. His family performed them in their vaudeville act.

During World War I he composed the song "Over There!" which was tremendously popular. He was awarded the Congressional Medal for writing it. Altogether, he wrote more than five hundred songs. He made only one motion picture, *The Phantom President,* which was produced in 1932. His life story was made into a movie with James Cagney playing Cohan. It was called *Yankee Doodle Dandy,* a name Cohan often applied to himself. He died in New York in 1942.

cohesion

When you say that any single thing, like bread dough, or iron, holds together, you are saying that it has cohesion. If you hit iron, it is cohesion that makes it keep its shape. This is very different from adhesion, which happens when you stick one thing to another thing. It is adhesion that makes water stick to, or wet, your hand. Scientists usually explain cohesion by comparing the way liquids act in a glass tube. Mercury is a heavy metal that is usually a liquid. If you pour it into a

glass tube you can see its strong cohesion, because it would rather hold to itself than stick to the glass. This forces the surface of the mercury to bulge up in the middle. If you pour water into a tube, you will see it act in just the opposite way, because its adhesive force is stronger. Its surface curves downward because the water sticks to the glass at the sides, while it sinks at the center. If you use very narrow glass tubing, you can see the water pull itself up the length of the tube, as it wets the glass all the way to the top. On the other hand, it is easy to see that mercury would rather keep to itself. If you drop mercury on the floor, it does not wet the floor like water, or alcohol. It scatters into many tiny balls. You can make these balls into one mass of mercury again just by pushing them against each other and letting cohesion pull them together. They would rather be one piece than stick to anything else.

Everything has both adhesion and cohesion. Even water has cohesion, as you can see when you sprinkle it and it pulls itself into drops. When you dig in your garden and the earth forms into clods or large pieces when it is broken, this means the earth has cohesion. Soil with little cohesion breaks into small, almost sand-like, pieces.

coinage, the term used to describe the manufacture of all but paper money: see the article on MONEY.

coin collecting, a hobby in which the hobbyist tries to find unusual and valuable coins of all kinds: see the article on NUMISMATICS.

coir, a fiber prepared from the outer husk of the coconut: see COCONUT.

coke

Coke is a grayish-black, spongy fuel that burns at a great, steady heat. People use coke because it burns with very little smoke and leaves little ash. Coke is made from coal. To make it, an oven is filled with coal and heated. Air is kept out of the oven, because air would make the coal burn to ashes. The heat drives everything out of the coal except the carbon, which is what the coal is mostly made of. What remains is coke. The heat also drives off many useful materials, which we call by-products because they are not the main thing that is produced. Special coke ovens are used that separate and hold by-products such as tar and cooking gas, when the heat sends them out of the coal.

Coke has been used for hundreds of years. American manufacturers built their first large coke ovens about a hundred years ago in Pennsylvania. They steadily improved the ways of making coke until they were able to get seven pounds of coke from ten pounds of coal. Now, more than 57,000,000 tons of coke are made a year. Steel manufacturers use coke in their blast furnaces.

cola

Cola, or *kola,* is the name of a tree that comes from Africa, but is now grown in many tropical countries, especially Brazil, India, and the West Indies. The fruit of the tree is a pod containing seeds called cola nuts, which are chewed by the natives of these places. The cola nut acts as a stimulant, that is, it freshens one up when one is feeling tired. For this reason cola nuts are an important article of trade. They are exported to America and Europe, where they are used in medicine and in soft drinks such as Coca-Cola and Pepsi-Cola. The stimulating substance in cola nuts is the drug *caffeine,* which is also found in coffee and tea. The flavor comes from an oil. They also contain a substance called *kolanin* which turns to sugar.

cold

Almost everybody catches at least one cold during the year, and many people have two or three. Children have more colds than adults. The cold is not a dangerous disease but it is a very important one. Each year working men and women in the United States lose many millions of dollars because of the time they are out of their jobs with colds.

You all know when you have a cold. Your head aches, your nose begins to run, you sneeze, your eyes water. Your throat may be sore and perhaps your ears ache. You have caught this cold in just one way. You have caught it from some other person. Most doctors believe that a ·cold is caused by a kind of VIRUS, which is the tiniest kind of germ. A person who has a cold carries with him a great many of these viruses. Everytime he sneezes or blows his nose he spreads the viruses. If you are near him you may inhale them and get the cold yourself. You can also catch these cold viruses by kissing a person who has a cold, by drinking out of a glass that he has used, or by using a towel that he has used. A handkerchief used by a person who has a cold is full of germs. Here are some rules to follow if you do not want to get a cold.

1. Stay away from people with colds if you can. Do not stand close to them when they cough or sneeze.

2. Do not use a drinking glass or a towel that may have been used by a person who has a cold.

3. Wash your hands often, especially before eating and after being near a person with a cold.

4. Keep as healthy as possible because then you will not catch a cold so easily. Always change your clothes at once if you get wet. Do not get too tired. Eat good food.

If you catch a cold the best thing to do is to go to bed. You will feel better and you will not spread the viruses you have caught. Keep very warm and be sure to put on your slippers and bathrobe if you get up. Drink plenty of liquids such as soup, water, milk, and fruit juices. Eat foods that you like that are good for you. Do not blow your nose too hard and always use paper handkerchiefs. Drop them into a paper bag when you have used them. Then nobody else will have to touch them. Sleep as much as you can. You will probably be over your cold in less than a week.

MEDICINES

Doctors do not have any medicines that will cure the common cold. They do have medicines that will make you feel better. They can give you nose drops that will make it easier for you to breathe, and they can give you pills that will make your headache go away. If you have a temperature that lasts more than a day or so, you should call the doctor. Perhaps you have something more serious than a cold. Many diseases, such as measles, seem to be colds when you first catch them. If you have an earache, you should call the doctor right away because an infection in your ear can be very dangerous.

cold storage is keeping something cold so that it will not spoil: see the article on REFRIGERATION.

cold war

A "cold war" is not really a war, because there is no shooting. It is a period when two countries are very unfriendly, and each is arming and trying to line up allies for itself in case the unfriendliness should break out into actual warfare. After World War II, the United States and Russia (the U.S.S.R.) became so unfriendly that people said they were having a "cold war."

Coleridge, Samuel Taylor

Samuel Taylor Coleridge was a famous English poet who lived about 150 years ago. Many famous poets were his friends. With one of them, William Wordsworth, he wrote a book of poetry called *Lyrical Ballads.* One of Coleridge's poems in this book, "The Rime of the Ancient Mariner," is one of the best known poems in the English language. Coleridge is also known for other poems such as "Kubla Khan" and "Christabel" and for his most important book, *Biographia Literaria,* his literary autobiography. He was born in 1772 and died in 1834.

Gale Research Co.

Coligny, Gaspard de

Although Gaspard de Coligny had the title of admiral, he was more often a commander of soldiers than of sailors. During the French wars of religion about four hundred years ago, he was a leader of the Huguenots (French Protestants) against the Catholics. De Coligny was a French nobleman who was born in 1519. When he was young he showed great bravery in battle. The Protestants saw that he was not only brave but wise and honest as well, and they made him their leader. For a while it seemed as if de Coligny would be able to make peace with the Catholics and end the wars, but in 1572 he was killed in Paris in the St. Bartholomew's Day Massacre. See the article about ST. BARTHOLOMEW.

colitis

Colitis is the name of a sickness in which the colon becomes inflamed and does not work properly. The colon is the large intestine that helps to digest the food you eat. When you have colitis, you have pains in your stomach, and either you cannot move your bowels, or you need to go to the bathroom too often.

Usually colitis is not very serious, although it is very uncomfortable. You have to be very careful not to eat food that is fried or spicy or rich, because that makes the colitis worse. There is a certain kind of colitis that is much more serious, but it is not common. Doctors are not sure what causes colitis, but they believe that people who are very nervous and worry a lot are likely to get it.

collaborationist

During World War II the Germans conquered and occupied several countries — France, Norway, Belgium, the Netherlands, and others. Most of the people of these countries kept on treating the Germans as their enemies, but there were some of the people who made friends with the Germans and helped them to run the government. This was called "collaborating with the enemy," and the people who did it were called *collaborationists*. Collaborationists were considered traitors to their country. One of them, a Norwegian named Vidkun Quisling, was a major in his country's army and yet helped the Germans to conquer Norway and later became head of a Norwegian government controlled by Germany. Such a government is called a "puppet government." Traitors of this kind are sometimes called "quislings."

When Germany lost the war and the people of the occupied countries were back in control, some of the collaborationists were brought to trial and punished.

collards

Collards are a kind of cabbage, with round leaves that never form a head. They are cooked and eaten like spinach or used raw in salads. Collards are very rich in vitamins and minerals. They are easy to grow. Collards are grown chiefly as a winter vegetable in the South and as a spring crop in the northern states.

collateral security

Collateral security is something valuable we give to a person who lends us money, so that he can keep it if we do not pay the money back. If a boy borrows ten cents from his brother, and gives him his marbles to keep in case he does not pay back the ten cents, the marbles are collateral security. When we borrow money from a bank, we usually have to give the banker more than our promise to pay him back. The banker wants to be sure the bank will not lose any money. He does this by asking for collateral security, which is usually stocks or bonds or something valuable that he can sell to get his money if we do not pay him back.

collective bargaining

Collective means "for a group." A labor union, or association of employees, is said to bargain collectively when a few men representing the union meet with the employers to agree on wages and working conditions for all the members of the union. In fact, it is for the purpose of collective bargaining that the union is formed.

For many years, employers opposed collective bargaining. Since 1935, United States law has required (by the National Labor Relations Act) that employees be permitted to bargain collectively when they want to. Even before that, in 1926, the Railway Labor Act assured collective bargaining to employees of railroads.

The process of collective bargaining is: Representatives of the union meet with members of the management (representatives of the owners of the company). They agree on how many hours a week the employees will work and how much they will receive per hour's work. Often there are different rates of pay for men in different jobs, depending on the skill required. The least the employer can pay for each kind of job is called the *scale*. The union and management representatives also settle matters of vacations, pension funds, seniority (which members of the union have first choice of jobs), and such things. A contract is then signed to put all these agreements in writing. The contract may run for one, two, or more years. When this time ends, the representatives of union and management meet again and agree on a new contract.

colleges and universities

Colleges and universities are schools for people who want to learn more after they have finished high school. A college is a school where advanced subjects are taught. A university is a school that is made up of many colleges and has some courses of study even more advanced than college courses. However, people usually mean the same thing when they use the words *college* and *university*.

Going to college is very different from going to grade school or high school. Nobody has to go to college as children must go to grade school. In fact, some colleges are very hard to get into. People who go to college often come from cities all over the country, and even from foreign countries. Most colleges have buildings for students to live in, as well as libraries, gymnasiums and stadiums, newspapers, museums, and hospitals. A college is sometimes like a small city.

WHY COLLEGES ARE IMPORTANT

Colleges and universities train people for most of the important jobs. They train the school teacher, doctor, dentist, and minister, the architect and engineer, and even the farmer. Most of them would not be able to do their jobs as well as they do if they had not learned to do them at a college or university.

Another reason why colleges are important is that we live under a democratic form of government. This means that we all share in the leadership of the nation. Colleges help students to be good citizens and leaders by teaching them to think for themselves and to understand the world and the other people in it.

HISTORY OF COLLEGES AND UNIVERSITIES

In ancient times there were many schools, such as the Academy of Plato (see the separate article on ACADEMY), that were similar to colleges, but it was not until the University of Salerno was started about a thousand years ago in Italy that the modern university came into being. After Salerno, such famous universities as those at Bologna in Italy, Paris in France, and Cambridge and Oxford in England were built. Students from all over Europe came to study at these universities. Most of these universities were for study of medicine, law, or religion. When the New World was discovered and settled, colleges were started here. The first ones were in Mexico and Peru in 1551. The earliest ones in the United States were Harvard College in 1636, the College of William and Mary in 1693, and Yale College in 1701. One of the first and best known universities in Canada is McGill, begun in 1821.

In many European countries the government owns all the universities. In America the states and some cities have their own colleges. About a hundred years ago, the United States Congress passed the Land Grant Act that helped all the states to form their own state universities. These are now called land-grant schools.

WHO GOES TO COLLEGE

Until about a hundred years ago only men who wanted to be doctors, lawyers, or ministers went to college. Little by little women were allowed to attend. The course of study, which is called the *curriculum*, began to include new subjects such as business and agriculture. Today there is hardly a trade or a profession for which college training is not helpful. Anyone who wishes to have a better knowledge of any special job and anyone who wants to learn more about the world should want to go to college. Colleges and universities have worked out a system of entrance requirements by which they can tell if you are the kind of student who would benefit by going to their school.

COLLEGE ENTRANCE REQUIREMENTS

Colleges want students with good character, good health, and the ability to learn. Colleges usually ask people who know you, such as your minister or teacher or doctor, to tell them whether you are intelligent, reliable, honest, and friendly. Colleges usually want students to be over 17 years of age. Most colleges want you to have a physical examination to see if you are healthy enough to study well. If you plan to go to college, you should study history, English, mathematics, science, and a foreign language in high school. All colleges want to know if you were a good student in high school, and when you apply for admission to a college you must ask your high school to send a copy of your record to them.

Sometimes a college will want students to take an entrance examination or to take a test of the same kind given by the College Entrance Examination Board. This is a test given throughout the United States and Canada each year. It provides a single, uniform way to see if a person will do well in college.

DIFFERENT KINDS OF COLLEGE

Most of the world's colleges teach such subjects as history, science, literature, and mathematics. These are called *liberal arts colleges*. Every university is sure to have a liberal arts college. Such colleges as Dartmouth College and Smith College are liberal arts colleges. Schools that train teachers are also very impor-

tant, and are called *teachers colleges.* Teachers College of Columbia University is the largest and oldest in the United States. Schools that teach such subjects as engineering and architecture are called *technological schools.* Massachusetts Institute of Technology and California Institute of Technology are important technological schools. Schools that train men to become ministers are called *theological schools,* or *seminaries,* and are almost always part of a university. Other colleges teach agriculture, business, medicine, and dentistry.

Another way these schools are different is in the length of time you must study. The usual college course is four years, at the end of which you get a diploma, or a degree. This is a piece of paper that says you have passed all your college work. A degree from a liberal arts college is called a Bachelor of Arts or a Bachelor of Science degree, depending on what you have studied. Some engineering courses take five years instead of four. Here you get a Bachelor of Engineering degree. If a student wishes to study more after he receives his Bachelor degree, he attends a university which has a school only for people who have been graduated from college, called a *graduate school.* If you study a year or two in a graduate school you will usually get a Master's degree in the subject you study. If you study even further you will get the degree of Doctor of Philosophy, which is called Ph.D. for short. If you go to a special school such as law school or medical school, you will get a special degree such as Doctor of Medicine, which is called M.D. for short, or a lawyer's degree, a Doctor of Laws, or LL.D.

Junior colleges are for students who want to learn college subjects but want to study for only two years. Junior colleges do not give degrees.

At most colleges the men and women students go to the same classes. These are called *coeducational schools.* Some colleges have only women students, or only men students. Vassar, Wellesley and Bryn Mawr Colleges, for example, are only for women. Dartmouth and Williams Colleges are only for men. Other colleges have both men and women, but have separate classes for them. At Columbia University there is a school for women called Barnard College, and a school for men called Columbia College. Harvard, Brown and Tulane Universities also have this arrangement.

Some colleges, and especially seminaries, are owned by Churches. The University of Notre Dame, Southern Methodist University and Yeshiva University are among these. Others are owned by the public, such as all the state colleges, many city colleges, and most teachers colleges. But the greatest number of colleges are privately owned. Wealthy men often give these colleges gifts of money for new buildings and to pay the teachers' salaries. These gifts are called endowments. All privately owned colleges must also charge their students a fee because the endowments are never enough. The money you pay to a college is called tuition. Tuition fees are usually between $600 and $1,700 a year. In public colleges, you pay little or no tuition fee. Some students who need help in paying

their tuition fees, and others who are very good students, are often given scholarships. These are sums of money to help them through college. Other students work part of the time, or during the summer vacation.

WHAT COLLEGE IS LIKE

The typical college is made up of classroom buildings, a library, a gymnasium, laboratories, and an athletic field. All this together is called the college campus. At most colleges the students live in buildings called dormitories. The dormitories usually have everything you need to live comfortably, sleeping rooms, dining rooms, living rooms, game rooms, and so on. College is often the first time students live away from home, and they find that dormitories are very pleasant places to live in. However, some prefer to join clubs called fraternities (for men) and sororities (for women), and to live in houses that are owned by these clubs.

The most important part of college life, of course, is studying and learning. College courses are taught by highly trained people who are sometimes world-famous scientists or authors. Young teachers are called instructors. Older ones are called assistant professors, associate professors or full professors. All the men and women who teach in college are called the faculty. The faculty tries to help you learn as much as possible. Sometimes they teach classes of one hundred or more students in large rooms called lecture halls. Usually the class will have about 25 students. In very advanced studies there are sometimes very few students and everyone sits around a table and discusses the subject. This kind of class is called a seminar, and sometimes a professor will have the seminar meet in his own house. Science classes meet in a laboratory where experiments can be done. But in college you do most of your learning and studying alone, either in your room or in the library where there are books to help you find out things for yourself.

It is not all work and no play at college, though. There is time to join many clubs, such as a drama club, where you help put on plays and act in them. Or you can work on the school newspaper or play sports and exercise. When you play on a team against your friends at school, it is called intramural sport. If you are very good at a sport you can join the college team, which plays other colleges. This is called intercollegiate sport. Intercollegiate sports such as football are very popular, and colleges build large stadiums so that there will be room for everyone who wants to see their team play. Some football stadiums seat almost 100,000 people, and are among the largest stadiums in the world. Many of the people who come to watch a college team play are people who used to go to that college. These people are called the alumni of the college if they are men, and the alumnae if they are women. Many people join alumni clubs after college so they will see many old friends they made at school.

In the United States alone there are more than three-and-a-half million college students, about as many people as

live in Chicago, Illinois. Almost half a million people get degrees from American colleges each year. The U.S. government helped many veterans to go to college with the "G.I. Bill of Rights." Most countries have exchange arrangements so students and teachers from one country can study and teach in another. Colleges are becoming more important, and every year more students go to college. If you are interested in learning more about any special college, you can write and ask for the college catalogue, a booklet all colleges print, which tells about the courses that are taught there, what the buildings are like, how much it costs to go there, and other such information.

collie

The collie is a working dog. In Scotland, where the breed originated, it has been used to herd and guard cattle and sheep for over three hundred years. Now collies are used in the United States and Canada as well as in Europe, and they still work at their business of herding flocks of animals. Many are kept also as watchdogs and pets, and they are gentle, even-tempered dogs, patient with children.

There are two kinds of collie. The more familiar is the rough-coated type, but the smooth-coated collie is equally useful to herd owners. Except for its coat, it is just like its rough-coated cousin.

Collie Club of Am.

The collie is one of the best dogs for herding and guarding sheep.

A collie stands about 24 to 25 inches high at the shoulder and weighs between 60 and 75 pounds. The smooth-coated type has hard, short, straight hair; the rough-coated type has thick, straight hair with a big fluffy collar around its neck and a graceful, feathery-looking tail. Collies may be golden and white to dark brown and white in color; or black and white with tan around the head and legs; or blue-gray or black and white, also with tan markings.

Collins, Michael

Michael Collins was an Irish patriot and a great leader in the Irish revolution against England. Collins was born in 1890. In his time, Ireland was ruled by England. Many Irishmen wanted their country to be free and independent. Michael Collins joined these people, and

became an outstanding leader. The English arrested many of the other leaders, but Collins was not caught. All by himself he organized the battle that forced the English to make peace. In 1921 he went to England to sign the peace treaty. Then he came back and helped to set up the Irish Free State, which was to be a dominion; that is, it would still be connected with England, but would have its own government. Collins thought this was the best settlement that could be made. Through his work and his writings, he persuaded most of the Irish people to accept the treaty. But many people were still against it. One of these people shot and killed Michael Collins in 1922, when he was only 32 years old.

collodion

Collodion is a clear, thick liquid with a very sweet smell. It is made by dissolving guncotton in a mixture of ether and alcohol. When the collodion dries a clear, thin, transparent film is left. People once used collodion to make photographic films. Today doctors use collodion to cover and protect cuts from germs. Surgeons also use collodion for this purpose after operating on people. Scientists who work with microscopes use collodion to glue something they want to study onto a microscope slide.

colloid

A colloid is a mass of tiny particles of a substance spread throughout a liquid or a gas. Fog is a colloid. It is made up of very fine drops of water dispersed, or spread about, in air. Another example of a colloid is whipped cream, which is a dispersion of air bubbles in cream. Milk and mayonnaise are other common colloids. A colloid is different from a solution or a suspension. In a solution the particles become really a part of the liquid they are mixed with. In a suspension they keep their own form, and will settle to the bottom if the liquid is allowed to stand. In a colloid the particles remain mixed, but they still keep their own form.

If you shine a light through a true solution, such as table salt dissolved in water, the solution looks perfectly bright and clear. But if you shine light through a colloidal solution, as soap dissolved in water, the solution looks hazy and glows a little. The reason for this difference is that the particles of soap dissolved in water are each much bigger than the particles of salt dissolved in water. The colloidal soap particles are big enough to scatter the light as it hits them, passing through the solution. Although colloidal particles are too small to be seen even under a strong microscope, they are bigger than the particles of salt that dissolve to make a true solution. Muddy water is an example of a suspension of particles of mud in water. If the muddy water stands a while, the particles of mud will settle to the bottom. However, the particles in a colloidal suspension, like fog, never settle out. A true suspension has much larger particles than a colloidal suspension.

Many colloids form gels, such as the jelly that you eat. Many colloids have also been found in the cells of plants and animals. These colloids are so important to living things that some scientists believe we will really understand life only when we learn more about colloids.

Cologne

Cologne is one of the leading cities in West Germany. It is in the west central part of the country, on the Rhine River. It is an important industrial center, and is famous for its beautiful cathedral.

The city forms a vast half circle on the western bank of the Rhine. It has the same general shape now that it had when the Romans founded a town there 1,900 years ago. If you were to go there today you would find very little left of the older parts of the city. They were destroyed by bombs in World War II. The cathedral was not seriously damaged during the war, however. The building of the cathedral was started in 1248 but the work went very slowly and it was not really completed until 1880. The spires are trimmed with lacy ironwork.

Cologne is a great shipping and railroad center. Before World War II it was famous for making a toilet water, or perfume, known as *Eau de Cologne*. There are about 780,000 people living there. Many of them work in factories, making metal products and chinaware.

Colombia

Colombia is a republic in South America. It is the only country in South America that has both an Atlantic and a Pacific seacoast. Colombia has an area of almost 440,000 square miles, which means it is about the size of Texas, Oklahoma, and New Mexico put together. Over twenty-one million people live in Colombia, which is about 6 million more people than live in these three states. Colombia is named in honor of Christopher Columbus, the great Italian explorer, who landed in South America almost five hundred years ago.

THE PEOPLE OF COLOMBIA

Most of the people who live in Colombia are part Spanish and part Indian, and they are called *mestizos*. Many Negro people live in Colombia, and there also are some Europeans and Indians who make their homes there. Some of these Indian tribes are fierce and wild, and they will attack any stranger who comes near their land, but most of the Indians are friendly. You can see them in the market places of the big cities trading with the mestizos, and they look very gay in their brightly colored clothes. The people of Colombia are proud of their cities, with modern streets and fine buildings and homes, but many parts of the country are backward, and the people have to work hard to earn their living. Everyone who lives in Colombia speaks Spanish, and most of the people are Roman Catholics. You can go to school in Colombia without having to pay any money, but the law does not make every child go to school, and so some children grow up without knowing how to read or even write their names.

HOW THE PEOPLE LIVE

Most of the people of Colombia are farmers, and they have made the country famous because they raise more coffee than any other country in the world except Brazil. On the mountain slopes, where the weather is not too hot and not too cool, these men work all year around, and they grow excellent coffee beans that make a rich, mild coffee that tastes very good. People in many countries drink coffee every morning that has come from Medellín and from other parts of Colombia. Farmers who live higher up in the mountains grow wheat and potatoes and corn, and in the valleys, where the weather is very hot, they grow bananas and sugar cane and cotton. All of the farmers in Colombia have to work very hard, because they do not have much modern machinery to help them.

Many people in Colombia make their living working in mines. They mine gold, silver, coal, and platinum, while other men work in the valuable oil fields. Colombia is the only country in the western hemisphere where the finest emeralds are found, and for four hundred years men have been mining this stone. A few people work in factories, where they make cement, rope, candy, and cigarettes. The people of Colombia need many things that they cannot make in their factories, and they must buy machinery, tools, medicine, and many other things from the United States. In return, the United States buys coffee, oil, and other products from Colombia.

There are several important cities in Colombia. Bogotá is the capital of the country, and it is a busy, modern place. (You can read about BOGOTÁ in a separate article.) One of the most exciting cities is Cartagena, which is called the "walled city." If you go there, you can see the tremendous fort and thick wall that is so wide that several automobiles can drive on it, side by side. The Spaniards built this strong fort and great wall more than four hundred years ago to protect the city from pirates, who often came to rob the city of its gold and silver. Cartagena is an important seaport on the Caribbean Sea, and most of the precious gold and silver of the country is shipped from there to many parts of the world.

WHAT THE COUNTRY IS LIKE

A visitor to Colombia will find that it is a country of high mountains, long flat plains, and marshy swamps. You can visit steaming tropical jungles, and places that are so cold that the snow never melts. Most of the people live in the western part of Colombia, where they make their homes on the slopes of three great ranges of the Andes Mountains. On these mountains, there are many little villages, where the farmers work all day in the hot sun, taking care of their crops. The nights are cool, and the climate is very healthful. Great forests of mahogany and other valuable trees grow on these mountains.

In the long valleys, between the mountains, the weather is very hot, and people raise bananas and other crops that grow best in a hot climate. You can see many kinds of palm trees and magnificent orchids growing in the valleys, and there are strange tropical birds, alligators, and other jungle creatures.

If you travel east, from the mountains,

you come to the great plains that are called the *llanos*. Here you can travel for many miles without seeing a single tree. The weather is even hotter than in the valleys, and the grass is thick and good for grazing, so you will see many sheep and cattle.

It is very difficult to travel in Colombia because of the jungles and the high, steep mountains. For hundreds of years the best way to get from one place to another was by water. The Magdalena River is still very important to the people of Colombia, and every day boats travel up and down this water highway, carrying rubber and sugar and potatoes from the farms to the cities. The journey is not easy because there are dangerous waterfalls, and part of the trip has to be made by train, but this is still the only way to get to some parts of the country. The air-

plane has been very useful to the people of Colombia, and you can make some trips now in a few hours that once would have taken you many days of hard travel. But airplanes cannot carry everything that the people have to send from one end of their country to the other. In some places, you can see cable cars on strong wire. The farmers use these cable cars to send their crops from the mountains down into the valleys.

HOW THE PEOPLE ARE GOVERNED

Colombia is a republic, which means that the people elect representatives to rule them, and they have a written constitution. This constitution says that the people of Colombia can have any religion they choose, and there is freedom of the press, as well as other important rights like the ones given by the Constitution of the United States. The people of Colombia are very proud of their constitution, and they feel that the year 1886, when it was signed, is a very important time in their history. The government is very much like the government of the United States. There is a Congress, made up of a Senate and a House of Representatives, and every four years the people elect a president. The women of Colombia received the right to vote and to hold office in 1954. Every man in the country who is between 21 and 30 years old must serve for one year in the army. The country also has an air

force and a navy. The people of Colombia did not like the way their country was being run, and in 1957 they overthrew the cruel regime of General Gustavo Rojas Pinilla. A military junta maintained control until free elections were held in March, 1958.

CHIEF CITIES OF COLOMBIA

The leading cities of Colombia, with populations from 1973 estimates, are:

Bogotá, population 2,293,919, the capital and largest city. There is a separate article about BOGOTÁ.

Medellín, population 967,825, the second-largest city in the country, and the leading manufacturing center.

Cali, population 820,809, the third-largest city.

Barranquilla, population 816,706, the fourth-largest city, and an important seaport.

COLOMBIA IN THE PAST

The first Spanish people landed in Colombia more than 450 years ago. In 1536 a Spanish explorer named de Quesada went to Colombia. He fought some fierce battles with the Chibcha Indians, who lived there then, and won the rich land for Spain. Colombia reminded de Quesada of his own country, and he named it New Granada, after the part of Spain that he came from. For more than three hundred years Colombia, including the countries that are now Venezuela, Ecuador, and Panama, was ruled by Spain. The people did not like this. They wanted to be free to rule themselves. Simón Bolívar is a great hero to the people of Colombia because he helped them to win their freedom, and in 1819 Bolívar founded the Republic of Greater Colombia. When the people of Colombia did not like the way things were going, they sometimes revolted, and there have been several revolutions. Colombia fought on the side of the Allies in World War II, and has been friendly with the United States for years.

Although Colombia is an undeveloped country, the people are very busy building roads and schools, railroads and hospitals.

COLOMBIA. Area, 439,519 square miles. Population (1973 estimate) 21,791,000. Language, Spanish. Religion, mostly Roman Catholic. Government, republic. Monetary unit, peso. Flag, yellow horizontal band above narrow blue and red stripes.

Colombo

Colombo is the capital and largest city of Sri Lanka (formerly called Ceylon). It is an important seaport on the Indian Ocean. About 558,500 people live there—almost as many as live in Phoenix, Arizona. Next to shipping, the most important industry is handcrafts, fine things that people make in their homes and small shops. The city was founded by Portuguese traders in 1517 and named for Christopher Columbus. During World War II the British set up a defense base there.

COLOMBO, SRI LANKA (formerly Ceylon). Population (1973) 558,500. Capital city of Sri Lanka. Settled in 1517.

colonial life in America

The colonial period in America was the time when the settlements still were colonies and belonged to England. The period lasted 169 years, from the found-

ing of the first colony at Jamestown, Virginia, in 1607, until the colonies declared their independence in 1776. Through the years, the colonies were growing steadily and new settlements were constantly being made. The English colonists in North America were building a new world for themselves, and carving a home in the wilderness. They had a difficult job to do and great hardships to endure. But the colonists were brave and strong and determined. Where there had once been a forest wilderness, they built a great new country. But it was a life different in many ways from the lives of Americans today.

A COLONIAL HOME

The homes of the people in colonial times were different in many ways from our homes today. Most of the people lived on their own small farms. There were a few big cities in the north, and in the south there were some very large plantations.

There were some stone houses, and in the cities some people had fine brick homes. But most of the farmhouses were made of wood. The colonists could not buy their wood at a big lumberyard like the ones found in the cities today. They chopped down the trees themselves. In this way they cleared land for the farms and got wood for their houses. There were no great steam shovels and tractors, and no building companies in those days. The colonists had only their strong arms and their helpful neighbors. Often all the people nearby would come to help with the house-raising. Afterward they would have a big party.

Inside the colonial home, things were much different from our homes today. The colonists had no electricity, and no furnaces or stoves. Instead they had only great fireplaces. The boys had to chop great piles of wood to keep the fires burning. Over the fireplace hung the great pots and kettles. The fireplaces gave heat for cooking. They also gave some light. For more light, the colonists had candles that they made themselves by dipping long cords into tallow, which is melted animal fat.

The furniture was plain and strong and made of wood by the farmer himself. Only the rich people could afford to have their furniture brought over from England, and there were no factories to make furniture. So people had to make their own furniture at home. They also made many of the other things they needed. Their wooden dishes, their farming tools, their shoes, were all made at home by the farmer and his sons. The farmer's wife and daughters spun thread and wove cloth, and then sewed clothing for the whole family.

The food that the colonial families ate came mostly from their own farms. There were no grocery stores, or bakeries, and no canned foods could be bought. The family raised vegetables and some animals. They hunted in the woods for game and caught fish in the streams. At home the women cleaned and cooked all the food. The farmer's wife and daughters baked the bread for the family. Water for cooking and washing had to be drawn from the well near the house. The colonists had to get everything they needed by their own labor.

Travel was very difficult in those days. There were few good roads, and there were no railroads or automobiles. On land, the colonists had to travel on foot, on horseback, or in horse-drawn carriages. Travel was easier by water, but still it was not very fast. On lakes and rivers there were canoes and boats that could be rowed. On the ocean, the only ships were great sailing vessels.

There was no telegraph in those days, and no radio or telephone. News and letters had to be carried by people who were traveling to different parts of the country. Travelers on horseback or carriages that were going long distances would carry letters and papers for people in the towns along their way.

MAKING A LIVING

The country that the colonists found was rough and untamed. Great forests spread out everywhere. The soil in most places was good and fertile, but it had never been farmed and had to be cleared and cultivated. In some parts of the New England colonies the soil was so rocky that the people had to work very hard to grow anything at all. But the country also had many good things to offer. After it was cleared, the land was very good for farming. The woods were full of wild animals that the colonists could hunt for food and furs. The seas held great stores of fish. The forests provided a great wealth of lumber for homes and ships.

The early years in the colonies were very difficult. The people had to labor constantly and tirelessly. The land had to be cleared. Crops had to be grown in climate and soil that was sometimes different from that in England. Everything the people needed had to be brought across the ocean from England. The winters were long and cold and difficult. In those early years, many people died of cold and hunger and hardship. Many of the people died of disease, and besides all the hardships of life in a new land, there was the constant danger of the Indians. At any time the Indians might come streaming out of the forests, killing and destroying and setting fires, trying to drive away the white men who had moved into the Indian lands. The colonists' first years were a time of constant struggle and hardship.

But they were brave and persistent, and gradually they began to flourish. All up and down the coast of North America were towns and settlements. Cities grew up at ports like Boston and New York and Philadelphia. A great shipbuilding industry began to grow, and traders sent their ships to England, to the West Indies and to Europe. The New England fishermen sent fish all over the world. Men trapped in the forests and traded with the Indians for valuable animal furs. In the middle colonies, in Pennsylvania and New York and New Jersey, there were prosperous farms. Grain and fruit trees and livestock were grown. In the south, great plantations grew tobacco and rice. Everywhere the colonists on their own farms grew the foods that they needed for their daily life.

LIFE IN THE COLONIES

Since the colonies belonged to England, they were ruled by the English government. Both the English king and Parliament had some say in running the colonies. To take charge in North America, a governor was sent to each of the colonies. This governor was an Englishman, usually chosen by the king. To assist the governor there was a council, and usually the governor chose the men who were on the council. The judges of the courts were usually chosen by the king. But each colony also had an assembly that was elected by the colonists. The assembly helped to make the laws for the colony, and tried to see that things were run the way the people wanted them. An interesting part of the government was the town meeting. This was a meeting where the people of the town got together to discuss their problems and to decide how things should be run in the town. Everyone who was allowed to vote could come to the meeting and give his opinion.

Religion was another important part of colonial life, especially in New England. A great many of the colonists there had left England for freedom to follow their own religion. The churches were very important in the life of the New England colonies. Often the ministers and the most important church members really ruled the towns. These people were not always very willing to give other people religious freedom, and often they did not allow any other churches except their own in the towns. But in the other colonies the people were more free, and slowly the New England towns grew freer. There were people of every religion in the colonies. There were Quakers in Pennsylvania, Catholics in Maryland, Puritans in New England, and many others. All of these people found in America the religious freedom that they did not have in England.

COLONIAL CHILDREN

Most boys and girls in colonial times had a great deal of work to do. On the farm, boys had to chop wood and draw water. They had to work with their fathers in growing food, taking care of the animals, and making things for the house. They had to hunt and fish for food. The girls worked at home. They had to help with the cooking and baking. They learned as children how to spin and to make clothes. In some parts of the country there were very few schools. This was true especially in the South, where there were very few towns and cities. The children of wealthy plantation owners had private tutors to teach them at home. The other children often had no schooling at all.

NEW ENGLAND SCHOOLS

In New England all the children went to school. The schools of those days were not like the big fine school buildings that we have today. They were small wooden houses that must have been very uncomfortable and cold. But boys and girls in those days were not always working or going to school. They had time to play, too, and they played some of the same games we play today. Many things about their life would seem strange to us, but they played tag and hopscotch and marbles, went ice-skating and flew kites, just as children do today.

colony and colonization

A colony is a country that belongs to another country and is controlled by it in some way. There are two main kinds of colonies, and they become colonies for different reasons. One kind is a colony that is formed by a group of people who leave their own country to settle somewhere else. These people are discontented in their own country for some reason. Sometimes they want to leave because their home country has become too crowded and it is difficult to make a living. Some of the people decide to go to a new place and form a colony. This is called colonization and the people who form the colony are called colonists. Sometimes they leave because they want more freedom. They may want to be able to follow their own religion instead of being forced to follow a religion that they do not believe in. Other people may want political freedom. That is, they want to have a say in how the government is run. Some people who are poor at home may want to go to a colony so that they will be able to have their own land and make a better living.

The colonists go to a place where there are not too many people. They find some place where there is room for them to build their own towns and cities, and to have their own land. Ancient Greece sent out many colonies like this. The cities of ancient Greece would become too crowded. Then a group of people would join together to form a new city somewhere else. By this kind of colonization, the people of ancient Greece spread out far from the Greek mainland, all around the Mediterranean Sea and into Asia Minor. England also sent out many colonists about three hundred years ago. Groups of English people sailed westward to the New World, and many settled in North America. These colonies grew and spread. After many years, thirteen of the colonies joined together and revolted against England. They became the independent country of the United States of America. Colonies of this kind usually become independent countries when they have grown big enough.

The other main kind of colony is different. It is not settlement of people from one country in a new place. It is the rule of one country over another. The purposes of such colonies are trade and money-making. One country that is powerful manages to get control of a more backward country and makes it a colony. This means that the more powerful country rules over the colony. The ruling country does not send out groups of people to settle and build new cities. Instead it rules over the people who already live in the colony. Sometimes in the past, colonial people have really been slaves of the ruling country. For example, when Spain first sent conquerors to South and Central America, they made slaves of the Indians. They used the Indians to work in mines and on farms from which the products were shipped to Spain. Thus, countries tried to control colonies from which they could get the things they needed. At the same time they could use their colonies as markets. That is, they could sell in the colonies the things they manufactured at home. For many

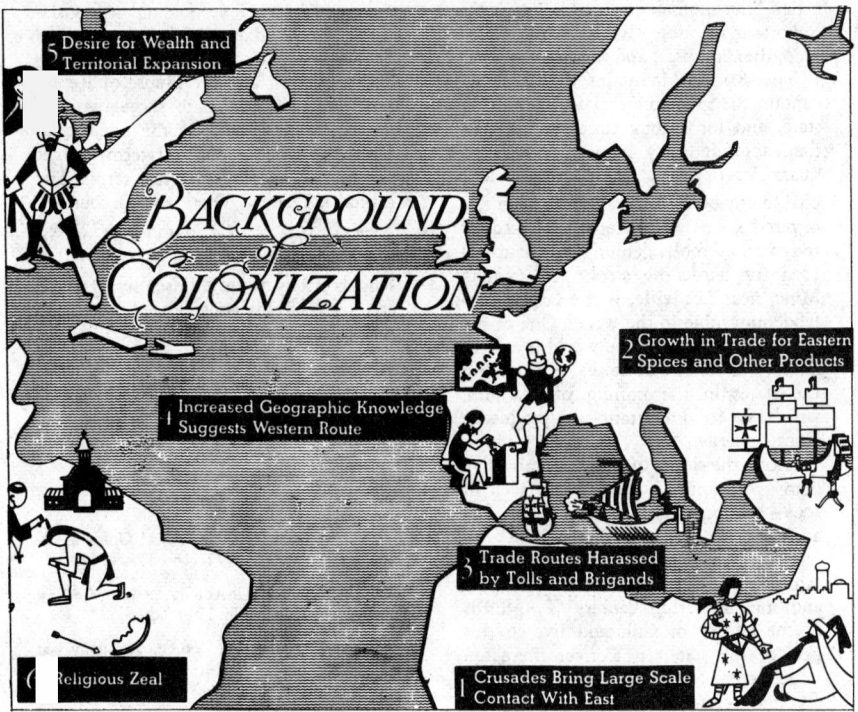

This map shows how colonies came to be established in America.

years, all the countries of western Europe tried to get colonies. The United States did, too. The backward, undeveloped lands of Africa and of the east, and the islands in the Pacific Ocean, all became colonial countries under the control of other countries.

Then, as the native people of the colonial lands became more civilized and better educated, they began to want to control their own governments. Some of these colonies fought wars of rebellion and won their freedom. Some fought but lost, and remained colonies. In some cases the colonies were given independence voluntarily.

Many countries that were once colonies have now become free and independent nations. The countries that still rule colonies are supposed to try to help their colonies to grow and develop, so that someday they can be independent. The United Nations has an organization, called the Trusteeship Council, that tries to see that colonies are helped, and that the people in the colonies are well treated. It hopes that someday all the colonies will have their own governments and take charge of their own affairs.

color

With the help of color, people can appreciate the beauty of the world in a way that they could never do otherwise. Since ancient times people have known that color could help make life cheerful and lovely. Walls have been painted, clothing has been dyed, dishes have been colored, all because people have felt that color was necessary for a full, happy life.

People also use color to show who they are. Armies carry colored flags and banners with them into battle. So long as the bright flags are kept flying the army knows that its leaders are still there fighting. Whole families have taken certain

arrangements of color to stand for them. You can read about this in the article on HERALDRY. The artist, especially, has found that color is a great and wonderful thing.

While people have thought that colors were very beautiful, they have sometimes been afraid of colors. The Puritans who helped to settle America thought that color was too beautiful, and that bright colors were a temptation from the devil for people to do bad things. The Puritans disapproved of anyone who dressed in bright, attractive clothes.

COLOR IN NATURE

Color is one of the most important things about the world we see. Color helps people to tell the difference between things that would otherwise look alike. For instance some birds are the same size and shape, but we tell them apart by their color. Not all animals have eyes that can see color. Dogs, for instance, are color-blind. They see the world in black and white and shades of gray. Certain birds and fish are also color-blind.

To many animals color is very important. The ermine that lives in the snow-covered Arctic region needs its white fur so that it cannot be seen by its enemies. White fur also helps the animals of the north to stay warm because a white surface loses heat very slowly. The bright colors of many animals that live in the jungle and in the mountains make them look like the plants and rocks where they live. This is called protective coloration and it helps animals to hide from their enemies. Color is also very useful to plants. Brilliantly colored flowers attract insects to them. These insects are needed by the plants because they carry the pollen for fertilization from one plant to another so that new plants can grow. In these and other ways, color plays a very important part in nature that people are only beginning to understand.

WHAT COLOR IS

Ordinary white light, such as the light that comes to the earth from the sun, actually has in it all the colors of the rainbow. The famous scientist Isaac Newton proved this about 250 years ago. He let a beam of sunlight fall on a special kind of glass called a prism. The white light that came in on one side of the glass was separated inside the glass and came out on the other side as a kind of rainbow. Scientists call this rainbow a *spectrum.* The reason for this spectrum is that ordinary white light is made up of very small waves of light that are many different sizes. Our eyes cannot see every different wave of light. Nor can our eyes separate the different colors that are together in white light. But those colors that we do see are the waves of light that have been separated by different things before they reach our eyes. For instance, a blue bath towel is blue because the dye in the towel has separated all the white color from the sun or the light bulb, and has allowed only the waves of light that cause a blue color to remain and reach your eyes. Scientists say that the blue towel has absorbed all the red and yellow that is in the white light. If only yellow or red light shines on a blue towel, the towel will look black, because there is no blue light left to reach your eyes. In the same way, if only blue light falls on a yellow towel, the yellow towel would also look black because there would be no yellow light left to reach your eyes. You can prove this by taking a piece of blue cellophane and holding it over a yellow towel. Where the light comes through the piece of blue cellophane and falls on the yellow towel it will look black. When all the different waves of light that make up colors are absorbed, no color is left except black. Black, therefore, is not a color, but is the absence of color.

Colorado

Colorado is a state in the western part of the United States, high in the Rocky Mountains. Some of the tallest peaks of these mountains are in Colorado, making it one of the most beautiful states. It has been nicknamed "the Centennial State," because it was admitted to the Union in 1876, just one hundred years after the United States won its independence from Great Britain. Colorado ranks eighth in size among the states, having more than 100,000 square miles. In population it ranks thirtieth; over two million people live there. The name *Colorado* comes from the Spanish, meaning "colored red." It was first given to the Colorado River because of the reddish tint of its waters.

THE PEOPLE OF COLORADO

Until about one hundred years ago, very few white people lived in Colorado, except for some fur traders and trappers. The territory was mostly occupied by Indian tribes who roamed through the wilderness. Then Spaniards and Mexicans moved into Colorado and settled around San Luis Valley. These people still speak Spanish and observe Spanish customs.

With the discovery of gold, thousands flocked to Colorado from all parts of the

country in search of fortunes. The discovery of silver, coal, and lead brought many more people from Europe to settle in this region. The English worked in the gold mines; the Slavs worked the coal mines; and farming was started by Italians, Russians, Scandinavians, and Mexicans, to provide food for the mining camps. However, all these different people have been settled for so long that they have families and homes in all parts of the state. Today, nine-tenths of the people living in Colorado are native-born Americans. There are still about 4,288 Indians in the state who live on reservations, working as farmers and cattle raisers.

More than half the people of Colorado live in the cities. Many work in plants for smelting and refining metals. Others work in factories making iron and steel products, and in meat-packing plants. The people living in the country work on farms, raising crops and cattle, while others work in the rich mines and oil fields.

WHAT COLORADO IS LIKE

Although Colorado is noted for the beauty of its mountains, it is not all mountainous. The large eastern section of the state is a flat, smooth plain, where the people are farmers. However, the soil is very dry, and so the people have to use irrigation. One can see great wheat fields, like those in the Middle West, and miles of grassy plain, where herds of cattle and sheep graze. The farmers grow fruits and vegetables; and more sugar beets are raised on these plains than anywhere else in the United States. Some of the most delicious cantaloupes also come from the southern section of the state.

The central part of Colorado lies in the Rocky Mountains, and it is this section that has made the state famous. It is a favorite vacation place because of its great beauty and because of the fine fishing, hunting, and skiing. The high mountains are covered with evergreen trees to the 10,000-ft. mark, or *timberline,* and the tops of the mountains are covered with snow all year round. The highest peak is Mt. Elbert, 14,431 feet high, the second-highest mountain in the United States. Many clear rivers and streams run down the mountain valleys, and these rivers have cut deep canyons in the rock. The most famous canyon is the Royal Gorge, which is more than a thousand feet deep. More rivers rise in Colorado than in any other state, and so it is

called "the mother of rivers." The most important of these rivers are the Colorado, the Arkansas, and the South Platte.

The Rocky Mountains in Colorado contain the great mineral wealth of the state, and for a long time mining was the leading industry. In addition to large quantities of gold, silver, copper, and coal, many other minerals have been discovered. Colorado produces two-thirds of the world's molybdenum, a rare metal used for hardening steel. The Climax Mine, near Leadville, is the largest molybdenum mine in the world. One of the largest zinc mines in the world is at Gilman; and Colorado ranks first among the states in the mining of uranium, which is so important in producing atomic energy.

Along the slopes of the mountains live many wild animals that can be seen in zoos—the bear, lynx, western red fox, and deer.

In the eastern part of the Rocky Mountains are two of the most important cities and manufacturing centers. Two-thirds of the people of Colorado live in this part of the state. In Denver there are large factories that make mining machinery and refine beet sugar. In Denver, Colorado Springs, and Pueblo are large meat-packing plants; and Pueblo also has some of the biggest factories for making iron and steel products, so that it has come to be known as "the Pittsburgh of the West."

This Rocky Mountain section is not all mountainous, however. There are also flat, fertile sections where the people grow vegetables and fruits and raise cattle and sheep.

The western part of Colorado is a plateau. A plateau is a region that is high, like a mountain, but level, like a plain. This part of the state is very dry and is used largely for cattle grazing. However, the farmers do grow apples, cherries, and peaches, and vegetables like onions, carrots, and tomatoes.

Both this plateau and the mountain area are covered with great forests that are carefully watched by the United States government, so that the trees will not be cut down too rapidly.

The climate of Colorado varies greatly, depending upon what part of the state you are in. It is much cooler in the mountains than in the plains, but because the air is so clear and dry, people find it quite comfortable in all parts of the state. The average temperature in summer is 67 degrees. The days are warm, but the nights are always pleasantly cool. In winter the average temperature is 24 degrees, but again because of the dry air, it is not uncomfortable. Colorado does not get much rain, and the state is noted for its wonderful sunshine.

Colorado once was covered only with trails which the settlers traveled over in ox-drawn wagons or on horseback. With the great rush of miners, roads and railroads were gradually built, so that today Colorado has about 76,000 miles of state and county roads, and almost 4,000 miles of railroad. There are also airports in all the important cities.

THE GOVERNMENT OF COLORADO

Colorado, like most other states, is

governed by a Governor and a Legislature. The Legislature is composed of a Senate and a House of Representatives The Governor and the House of Representatives are elected to serve two-year terms; the members of the Senate are elected to serve a four-year term. Judges are elected and serve ten-year terms. The capital is Denver. There are 63 counties.

There are about 338,000 students attending public elementary and high schools. Many of the children living in the country go to big consolidated schools, to which they are taken in school buses.

Among the principal colleges and universities are:

University of Colorado, at Boulder. Enrollment, 29,857 in 1971 (co-ed).

Colorado College, at Colorado Springs. Enrollment, 1,694 in 1971 (co-ed).

Colorado School of Mines, at Golden. Enrollment, 1,553 in 1971 (co-ed).

Colorado State University, at Fort Collins. Enrollment, 14,500 in 1971 (co-ed).

United States Air Force Academy, at Colorado Springs. Enrollment, 3,500 in 1971 (men only).

University of Denver, at Denver. Enrollment, 8,087 in 1971 (co-ed).

CHIEF CITIES OF COLORADO

The leading cities of Colorado, with populations from the 1970 census, are:

Denver, population 514,678, the state capital and largest city. There is a separate article about DENVER.

Pueblo, population 118,238, the third-largest city in the state, iron and steel center, in the south central part of the state.

Colorado Springs, population 135,060, the second-largest city, a popular resort, in the central part of the state.

Greeley, population 38,902, the fourth-largest city, trade and shipping center, in the north central part of the state.

COLORADO IN THE PAST

More than four hundred years ago, the Spaniards, under Coronado, were the first white men to explore the region of Colorado. They were searching for precious metals, but they did not find any, and so they moved on and did not settle in the territory. Other explorers followed, but none of them stayed, and Colorado remained uninhabited except for Indian tribes.

In 1803, the United States bought a large section of land from the French, called the Louisiana Purchase. It included part of Colorado. Three years later, an expedition led by Zebulon M. Pike discovered the famous peak which now bears his name. You can read about PIKE'S PEAK in a separate article. In 1848, after the war with Mexico, the United States got the rest of the Colorado territory, partly from Mexico and partly from Texas.

Colorado remained an unknown wilderness, except for some trading posts, until about a hundred years ago, when gold was discovered. Men rushed from the East in great numbers to Pike's Peak, near where the gold had been found, and their slogan was "Pike's Peak or bust!" Later, when silver and lead were discovered,

more and more miners poured into the territory. Mining camps sprang up in many places, and Colorado became a rough and lawless part of the country, where men built fortunes and spent their money quickly. People built expensive houses, wore expensive clothes, and showed off their new wealth. One man, who made a fortune in silver, was known as "Silver Dollar" Tabor. He built a big opera house in Denver and had the entire floor of the lobby made out of silver dollars. About this time, the largest silver nugget ever found was discovered at Aspen, in the Mollie Gibson mine. It weighed 1,840 pounds, and was worth $22,000. Some of the mining towns like Denver, Idaho Springs, Golden, and Boulder, later grew to become important cities in modern Colorado.

In 1861 Colorado was made into a separate territory, and in 1876 it became a state. However, by the end of the century, the rush for gold and silver was over, and people had to find another way of living or return east. They saw that there was fertile land for farming and cattle raising, and so they settled on farms. They also discovered other valuable minerals in the mountains, which they began to develop.

Colorado grew rapidly after that, both as a farming and mining state. The people also began to manufacture many products, which added to their prosperity. Today Colorado is also a favorite place for tourists because of the scenery and fine climate. Every summer there are plays and concerts in cities which once were only mining camps. In World War II, Colorado had many war plants and a large training school for fliers, near Denver. Since the war, Colorado has been expanding its industries.

PLACES TO SEE IN COLORADO

Mesa Verde National Park, 51,017 acres, in the southwest, about thirty miles from Durango, on U.S. Route 160. Most notable and best preserved prehistoric cliff dwelling of early man in the United States.

Rocky Mountain National Park, 254,-575 acres, in north central Colorado, 23 miles north of Boulder, on U.S. Route 34. One of the most magnificent sections of the Rocky Mountains, with 65 peaks more than 10,000 feet high.

Black Canyon of the Gunnison National Monument, 13,176 acres, in west central Colorado, about 10 miles north of Montrose, on U.S. Route 50. Awe-inspiring canyon; the deepest in Colorado; its sheer walls rise 3,000 feet at their highest point.

Colorado National Monument, 18,120 acres, in the west, six miles west of Grand Junction, on U.S. Routes 6 and 24. Sheer-walled canyons and caves filled with huge stones, strangely shaped.

Dinosaur National Monument, 190,-962 acres, in the northwest, partly in Utah, 35 miles north of Rangely, on U.S. Route 40. Fossil remains of giant reptiles and other creatures of past ages; magnificent deep gorges.

Great Sand Dunes National Monument, 35,908 acres, in south central Colorado, about 31 miles east of Monte Vista, north of U.S. Route 160. Among largest and highest dunes in the United States,

deposited over thousands of years by winds; visible for seventy miles; colors of the sand change constantly with the light.

Hovenweep National Monument, 410 acres, in the southwest, partly in Utah, 28 miles west of Cortez, west of U.S. Route 160. Four groups of remarkable prehistoric towers, pueblos, and cliff dwellings.

Yucca House National Monument, 9 acres, in the southwest, 10 miles south of Cortez, on U.S. Route 666. Unexcavated ruins of large prehistoric Indian pueblo.

Cave of the Winds, in central Colorado, 8 miles west of Colorado Springs, on U.S. Route 24. One chamber of the cave is known as "Old Maid's Kitchen"; legend has it that if a girl leaves a hairpin here she will be married within a year; thousands of hairpins are heaped against the walls.

Buffalo Bill's Grave, in north central Colorado, on Lookout Mountain at Golden, on U.S. Route 6. Grave of William F. Cody, Indian fighter.

Million Dollar Highway, in the southwest, part of U.S. Highway 550, south of Ouray. This section of the highway has gold in the gravel that covers the surface.

Mount Evans, in north central Colorado, 36 miles west of Denver, east of U.S. Route 6. Highest automobile road in the United States; leads to the top where Cosmic Ray Laboratory of the University of Denver is located; highest laboratory in the world (14,260 feet).

Air Force Academy, at Colorado Springs. (See the article on AIR FORCE ACADEMY.)

COLORADO. Area, 103,922 square miles. Population (1970 census) 2,207,259. Capital, Denver. Nickname, the Centennial State. Motto, *Nil Sine Numine* (Nothing Without the Deity). Flower, Rocky Mountain columbine. Bird, lark bunting. Song, "Where the Columbines Grow." Admitted to Union, August 1, 1876. Official abbreviation, Colo.

Colorado River

Colorado is the name of a great river in the southwestern part of the United States. On its journey from the Rocky Mountains to the Pacific Ocean, the Colorado travels about 1,400 miles and is joined by several smaller rivers. The names of some of the most important of these rivers are the Gunnison, the Green River, and the Gila. As the Colorado River has worn away the earth for many centuries, it has made deep canyons. People come from all over the world to Arizona so they can see the Grand Canyon, one of the largest canyons in the world. You can read about the GRAND CANYON in a separate article. If you stand at the top of the Grand Canyon, you can look down to where the Colorado River flows five thousand feet below. It looks like a tiny silver thread.

People who live near the Colorado River have been able to use the river in many ways that have helped to make life better. In some parts of California, where it hardly ever rains, the land was so dry no crops would grow. In other places the river would overflow its banks and good soil was washed away. Then the United States government began to build dams. These dams made big lakes

where before there had been only the river. Water flowing over the dams turned great generators that brought electric light and power to cities. The dams also put an end to floods. The largest of these dams was called Hoover Dam, and it was finished in 1936. Farmers in California can now grow winter vegetables. The Colorado River empties into the sea only at flood time. Most of the water is carried by canals into the Imperial Valley, which is one of the best farming places in the country because of the water from the Colorado River. The Colorado River was discovered by Hernando de Alarcón, a Spanish explorer, in 1540.

Colorado Springs

Colorado Springs is a city near the center of the state of Colorado. In 1954, the United States Air Force chose it as the site for the United States Air Force Academy. The Academy was established to train the future officers of the Air Force, just as West Point and Annapolis train the future officers of the Army and the Navy. About 135,800 people live in Colorado Springs, and many people come there for vacations, where they enjoy the magnificent scenery and the fine air, and drink the healthful waters from the mineral springs.

coloratura

Coloratura is a style of singing that is filled with long runs and trills. In the 18th and 19th centuries composers wrote arias, or songs, with many very difficult parts for the singers. This music, which is very high and rapid, is coloratura music. Nowadays coloratura means a very high soprano voice. Originally coloratura music was written for any voice, alto, tenor, soprano, or baritone. But sopranos extended the vocal range, so composers wrote most of their coloratura music for sopranos. Some of the best known coloratura sopranos have been Lily Pons, Amelita Galli-Curci, and Luisa Tetrazzini.

color blindness

When a person cannot see colors as they are, we say he is color-blind. Most people who are color-blind have trouble recognizing red, green, and blue, and there are a few people who cannot see any color at all. For these few, the world has only shades of black and white, without any blue sky, green grass, or brightly colored flowers. About three or four out of every hundred people are color-blind, and about forty men have color blindness

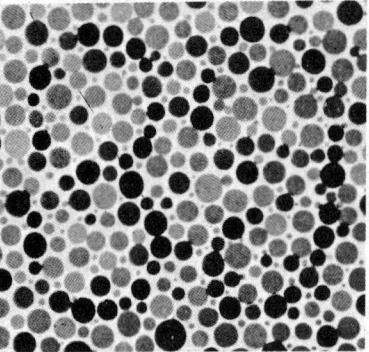

Better Vision Inst., Inc.

A person who is color-blind cannot see the number 89 when this chart is made up of red, green, yellow and blue dots.

Your eye contains about 130 million nerves called "rods" (R), on the surface of your retina. With these you see only black and white.

Your eye also has about 7 million "cones" (c) in the center. With these nerves you see color.

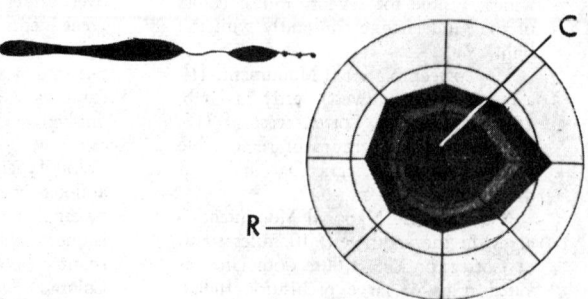

Better Vision Inst., Inc.

for every woman who has it. Color blindness has also been called Daltonism, because a doctor named John Dalton described his own color blindness in 1794.

Some people become color-blind from diseases of the eye, or accidents. Other people are born color-blind. Doctors have said that a person can become color-blind from drinking too much alcohol. Generally, they believe that when a person is color-blind, a part of the eye that is necessary for seeing color is either missing or diseased.

Doctors use several tests to find whether a person is color-blind. In some of the tests a person has to match colors. In another simple test, the person is asked to read numbers which are formed out of colored dots. If the numbers are made of green dots, and the rest of the card is covered with blue dots, a person who is color-blind will not be able to see any numbers at all. It is dangerous for color-blind men to take certain jobs where they must be guided by color, as in the case of a railway engineer, who must see red "stop" lights, and green "go" lights. There are now laws against hiring color-blind men for this kind of work on railways and on ships.

color guard

In the army, the flags of the different regiments are called colors, and the men who march with these flags are the color guard. Regimental colors used to be carried right into battle. It was considered a disgrace to let them be captured by the enemy, so a few men were always assigned to guard the colors. Today the colors are carried only in parades and military ceremonies. Smartly dressed soldiers, carrying rifles, march on either side of the colors, which are carried on the left side of the American flag.

Colosseum

The Colosseum was the largest amphitheater ever built in ancient Rome. An amphitheater is a big, open-air arena like our football stadiums today. The Colosseum was several stories high, and had 50,000 seats. It was beautifully decorated with stonework, gold, and jewels. Curtains somewhat like kites were put up near the top to give shade.

The Colosseum was built in the first century after the birth of Christ, when life in most of Europe was still uncivilized. For about four hundred years, many Roman emperors celebrated victories and holidays by having men and animals "hunted" and killed in the Colosseum. Animals such as lions, tigers, elephants, bears, bulls and ostriches were assembled —some from far-off India and Africa.

Sometimes the animals were trained to do tricks. But usually they were either killed for sport, made to fight, or used to kill people the Romans did not like. Often the victims were Christians—members of the new religion that taught peace and good will, instead of war. Rome considered them enemies. At the Colosseum, dozens of Christians might be thrown to the lions in one day. There were also gladiators, the Roman prizefighters. Mock battles were another way of getting men killed. But the power of Rome crumbled, and earthquakes destroyed parts of the Colosseum. Many of its stones and carvings were used in newer buildings. Yet, after almost 1,900 years, some of its walls still stand. See the article AMPHITHEATER for an illustration.

Colossians, one of the Epistles of St. Paul in the Bible: see EPISTLES.

colossus

A colossus is an enormous statue. Our word *colossal*, meaning very large, comes from colossus. One of the most famous statues of this kind was at Rhodes, an ancient Greek island. It was made of bronze, and was supposed to be the sun-god Apollo. This Colossus of Rhodes was 105 feet tall, or about as high as a ten-story apartment building. The statue was destroyed by an earthquake in 224 B.C. and it is not known exactly how it looked. There is a story that it stood in the harbor of Rhodes holding a torch, and was so big that ships entering the harbor could sail between its legs. The statue was made by the sculptor Chares. He worked on it for twelve years. It was one of the wonders of the ancient world.

The Statue of Liberty is also a colossus made of bronze. It is larger than the Colossus of Rhodes. It was designed by the French sculptor Frédéric Bartholdi. The statue is so large that people can climb inside it all the way to the top, where they have a view of New York and the harbor.

Colt, Samuel

American history would be very different if Samuel Colt, the inventor of the revolver, had never lived. The revolver, which could fire six bullets without having to be reloaded, was one of the most important weapons used in the West against the Indians. Colt's invention, with a few improvements, is still used today. Samuel Colt was born at Hartford, Connecticut, in 1814. When he was 14 years old he ran away to sea, but he soon became interested in firearms. He invented his revolver in 1835, and he soon became famous. In 1852 Colt opened a large factory in Hartford, where thousands of re-

volvers were made every year. He died in 1862. There is a separate article on REVOLVER.

Columbia

Columbia is the capital of South Carolina. It is in the center of the state, on the Congaree River. Columbia is a very pretty place, with parks and trees, and fine old churches and homes. More than 113,000 people live there and work in cotton, fertilizer, and printing plants. South Carolina University is there, and also several other schools. Columbia became the state capital in 1786. During the Civil War, General William T. Sherman marched into Columbia, and a large part of the city was burned to the ground. Woodrow Wilson, one of the presidents of the United States, grew up in Columbia. His home is now a museum.

COLUMBIA, SOUTH CAROLINA. Population (1970 census) 113,542. Capital of South Carolina. County seat of Richland County. Settled in 1700.

Columbia River

Columbia is the name of a big and important river that rises in British Columbia, Canada, and winds for 1,300 miles through the state of Washington and into the Pacific Ocean. It forms most of the border between the states of Washington and Oregon. The Clark Fork, Snake, Willamette and other rivers flow into the Columbia. The countryside along the Columbia is mountainous, and the river has cut deep gorges to make its way through the Cascade and Coast ranges.

The river drops sharply in several places, flowing over steep rapids and dropping over beautiful waterfalls, such as Celilo and Multnomah Falls. At Celilo Falls, American Indians for hundreds of years have speared salmon as the big fish leaped up the cataract to their spawning, or egg-laying, grounds. Along much of its route mountain peaks overhang its shores, adding to the beauty of the scenery. The river is tidal, that is, it rises and falls with the ocean tides, to Vancouver, Washington, about a hundred miles from the mouth.

The Columbia is the greatest source of hydroelectric power in the United States. Four huge dams have been built along its course by the United States government, to supply electric power and provide irrigation and flood control to the entire countryside. One of these, the Grand Coulee Dam in the north central part of Washington, is the largest dam in the world, 550 feet high. It was completed in 1942. Bonneville Dam, in northwestern Oregon, is 187 feet high. It was completed in 1938. Two other large power projects are the McNary Dam, completed in the 1950s, and The Dalles Dam, which was nearing completion in 1961. When The Dalles Dam is completed, the beautiful Celilo Falls will be buried under tons of water. The United States government is paying millions of dollars to the Indian nations that will lose their ancient fishing grounds. At Hanford, Washington, the United States has built an important plant for the manufacture of plutonium, a chemical element used in the atomic bomb. The water of the Columbia River supplies the power to drive the huge tur-

bines and generators of this plant. Many other industries have grown up along the river, including lumber, plywood, and alumina.

The Columbia River was discovered in 1792 by Robert Gray, an American sea captain. He named the river for his ship, the Columbia, and claimed it for the United States. Outside the mouth of the river was a huge sandbar, which hid the opening of the river. The sandbar has long since been cleared away, to make shipping easier. The great explorers Lewis and Clark were the first white men to reach the Columbia overland. They were followed by Canadian fur traders, who established a thriving business. The river became the center of the settlements that formed the state of Oregon.

In 1954 the Columbia River Highway was opened to traffic. This breathtaking road winds among mountain peaks and along the river's edge from Portland to The Dalles, in Oregon, for almost a hundred miles.

Columbia University

Columbia University is one of the largest and oldest universities in the United States. It is on Morningside Heights in New York City, and has a beautiful campus with many handsome buildings. If you want to be a lawyer, a doctor, an engineer, a teacher, or a member of many other leading professions, you can go to Columbia University and get the very best training. More than 30,000 students go to this school. There are about twice as many men as women students. BARNARD COLLEGE, about which there is a separate article, is the women's branch of Columbia University.

This great university was founded two hundred years ago by George II, King of England. At that time it was called *King's College.* During the Revolutionary War all classes were stopped. After the war, the school was called *Columbia College,* and it has been growing steadily ever since. In 1896 the school again got a new name, Columbia University. Many important men have been president of Columbia University. Among the most famous were Nicholas Murray Butler and Dwight D. Eisenhower, who was president of Columbia University before he became President of the United States.

columbine

Columbines are very beautiful flowers that grow wild and in gardens. They have dark green leaves, and their flowers, which have long spurs, grow on tall thin stems. In the East the columbine is also called the *rockbell* because it grows in rocky places. It has red and yellow flowers. The Indians made a tea from its seeds to cure headaches and fever. The blue-and-white columbine of the Rocky Mountains is the state flower of Colorado. These flowers are often visited by humming birds. Most of the columbines grown in gardens came from the European wild columbine.

Columbine is also the name of the girl loved by Harlequin in Italian and French pantomimes and comic operas. See the article COMMEDIA DELL' ARTE.

Columbus

Columbus is the capital of the state of Ohio. The city is on the Scioto River, in the center of the state. More than 539,000 people live in Columbus, and the city is a very busy manufacturing place. They make airplanes, cigars, railroad cars, shoes, and many other things. There are three airports in the city, and quite a few railroads and large highways come to Columbus. There are also several schools. The most important is Ohio State University. Columbus was made the capital of Ohio in 1816, and it is now the third-largest city in the state.

There is also a large city in Georgia named Columbus. It is on the Chattahoochee River. It is a cotton-manufacturing center. About 154,168 people live there.

COLUMBUS, OHIO. Population (1970 census) 539,677. Capital of Ohio. County seat of Franklin County. Settled in 1812.

Columbus, Christopher

Christopher Columbus is famous as the discoverer of America. In 1492, he sailed from Spain and landed in the West Indies. In those days, the people of Europe thought Europe, Africa and Asia were the whole earth. They knew little about the Atlantic Ocean, and nothing about the American continent or the Pacific Ocean. When Columbus found land west of the Atlantic, he believed he had reached Asia. Here was proof that the earth is round: you could "sail west to get east." About 25 years later, Ferdinand Magellan made the first voyage all the way around the world. Then it became known that Columbus had opened up a New World, four times as large as Europe.

The story of Columbus is as full of unknown things as the great ocean he crossed. He never clearly told who his parents were, when and where he was born, or what his early life was like. We think that Columbus was born in Genoa, Italy, between 1446 and 1451, and that he was the son of a wool weaver and tavern-keeper. He had two younger brothers, Bartholomew and Diego. Columbus is described as being tall and having blue-grey eyes. His hair had turned white when he was 30. Columbus had two sons. As a person, he was dignified, honorable, and had a convincing manner.

How much schooling did Columbus have? Some say very little. Others say he made good maps and charts and was a trained navigator. At least, he knew of the wonderful adventures of Marco Polo, a hundred years before, who had seen China's gold roofs and the unbelievable riches of the Orient. Columbus probably had never heard of the Scandinavians like Leif Ericsson, who had explored North America in the 10th century. Columbus is said to have visited Iceland in 1477, and he may have talked there to people who knew about these early voyagers. The papers or orders given him by the Spanish king and queen for his first voyage said he was sailing "for certain islands in the sea" which he knew existed.

It was very important to find a new route to India and Asia. The Mohammedan Arabs had shut off the eastward land route to Asia, and Portugal's explorers had not yet completed the passage around Africa.

THE VOYAGES OF COLUMBUS

Columbus had dreamed of sailing west for twenty years. He tried first to get help from the king of Portugal. About 1485, he turned to King Ferdinand and Queen Isabella of Spain. But the Spanish were fighting to drive out the Moors, who were Moslems. Columbus had to wait. Meantime, in 1486, his brother Bartholomew sailed with Diaz on the first trip around the Cape of Good Hope in Africa. In 1488 Columbus sent his brother to try to interest the English and the French courts. But in January 1492, Spain finally defeated the Moors, and at last Columbus could be given ships for his daring journey.

On the first voyage, Columbus sailed from the Spanish port of Palos with three ships. They went south to the Canary Islands, near Africa, and then headed directly west. The ocean was calm, and the weather was warm and favorable, but still it was an anxious and fearful voyage. The crews were a wild lot—mostly daredevils and former criminals. They had heard dreadful stories about the Atlantic. For example, many people thought the sea boiled at the equator! But Columbus expected to reach land about 2,800 miles from Spain and this they did.

On October 12, after a month on the open seas, they landed on one of the Bahamas islands, northeast of Cuba. Columbus named the island *San Salvador,* meaning "the Saviour." Because he thought he was near India, Columbus called the natives Indians, and the region became the West Indies. Of course, the Spaniards and the natives could not understand each other. But Columbus tried to find out from them where China and India were, so he could load his ships with gold and spices. The natives took him to other islands, and he discovered Cuba and Haiti. But he could not find Asia.

On Haiti, Columbus started a small colony, the first in his "New World." In January he left for Spain, reaching Palos in March. He brought with him pieces of gold, parrots, cotton, other new plants and animals, and a few of the natives—the first "Americans" to be seen in Europe.

Before going on his voyage, Columbus had insisted that he was to be governor of the new lands and share in the profits from them. But the profits were mostly troubles. When he returned to Haiti in the fall of 1493, he found the little settlement burned to the ground, and no white man left alive. Greed for gold and their pride in being Christians and superior to the ignorant savages made cruel men of the European settlers. Treachery, robbery, and murder were the law in the New World.

Diego, his youngest brother, went with Columbus on his second voyage, and in 1494, Bartholomew joined them and was made lieutenant governor. But Columbus met with continual hardships and was often deserted by those he trusted. He made a third voyage, and then an agent of the king sent the three brothers home in chains. In Spain, Ferdinand and Isa-

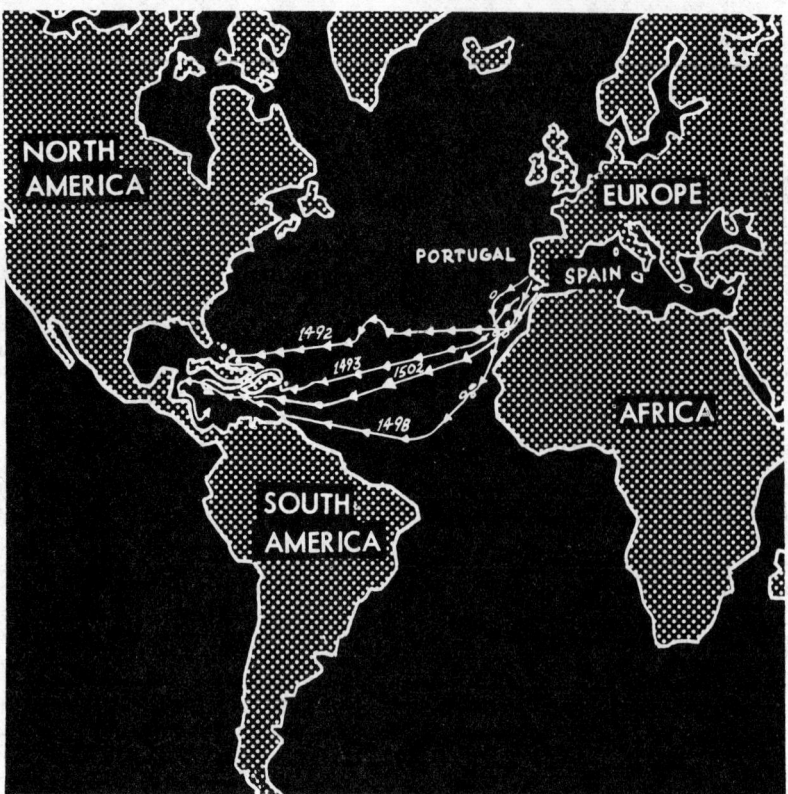

Columbus made four trips to the New World from Spain. This shows the routes he took.

bella said the brothers were innocent. Columbus sailed again. He explored the South American coast, and Central America almost as far as Panama. But when Columbus died in May 1506, few noticed the event. Not until later did Columbus become famous.

A story is told of how some men made light of his discovery, saying that anyone could have done what he did. Columbus passed an egg around the table, and asked for someone to make it stand up. When no one was able to, he tapped the shell on the heavy end, where there is a little air-pocket, and made the egg stand. "Anyone can do it," said Columbus, "after I have shown the way."

Columbus Day

Columbus Day, October 12, is a holiday named in honor of Christopher Columbus for his discovery of America on October 12, 1492. On Columbus Day, schools, banks and business houses are closed in many parts of the world. There may be parades and special ceremonies or meetings. In the United States, Congress made Columbus Day a national holiday in 1892, four hundred years after the famous voyage from Spain to the West Indies. Columbus Day is also celebrated by cities of Spain and Italy, by countries in Central and South America, and by parts of Canada, India, and Kenya, East Africa.

Columbus, Knights of

The Knights of Columbus is a society for Roman Catholic men. It is an American society, named after Christopher Columbus, who planted the flag of the Church on the soil of the New World. The society was founded in 1882 at New Haven, Connecticut. Members promise to be good citizens and good Catholics, and to help each other all they can.

column

A column is a rounded or many-sided upright support for a roof. The first columns were probably trees pulled out of the ground, smoothed on the top and bottom, and used to hold up a roof. The first column, as we know it today, was used in Egypt. About two thousand years before the birth of Christ columns were used in the temples of Egypt. They were decorated with drawings. These pillars had smooth surfaces and were broader at the bottom than at the top. Thousands of years ago columns were used in Persia, too. They were more slender than the Egyptian kind and were spaced farther apart.

The Greeks were the people who used columns most. First their columns were made of wood, but later they were carved from stone. They were carved in sections and then the sections were placed one on top of another. It is said that when the Greeks put the sections together you could never see the dividing line because they were so perfectly carved and matched. You may have seen pictures of the Parthenon, the beautiful temple in Athens, which has columns on all four sides. Other Greek buildings had them just across the front. They were used inside houses for decoration, too.

There are three kinds of Greek column that are still used today. The Doric column is the oldest. It is a plain shaft that is fluted, that is, it has grooves that go from top to bottom all the way around. At the top of the shaft is the capital, which on the Doric column has several rings and grooves around it. Later the Greeks designed the Ionic column. It also is fluted or grooved all around, but it has a square base on which the shaft stands. At the top of the Ionic column the capital is carved with scrolls. The most elaborate of all the pillars used by the Greeks is the

Corinthian. It is similar to the others, but rows of acanthus leaves are carved around the bell-shaped capital.

The Romans copied the Greeks in the use of pillars and columns. They took the same designs but changed them slightly for their own buildings. During the Middle Ages these three kinds of column were not used very much. The builders of Gothic churches and castles used pillars with smooth surfaces. They often had bases, but seldom was a Greek capital used. The top of the column often went right into the framework of the roof. About five hundred years ago builders started using the classic columns again, and they have been very popular ever since. In Washington, D.C., columns are used on many public buildings, among them the White House, the Capitol, and the National Gallery.

Columns are used in the Far East, too. In India the pillars are of carved stone. Sometimes there is not an inch of space that is not covered with some kind of design. In China and Japan they make their columns of wood and then paint them with a heavy, shiny paint called lacquer.

The memorial column is another kind of column. It is a single shaft that rises from a decorated base. This kind of column is used as a monument or decoration in a public square.

coma, a period of unconsciousness: see the article on FAINTING.

Comanche

The Comanches were the finest horsemen and buffalo hunters among the Plains Indians. They were famous for their fierce wars against Texas and Mexico. Many Indian tribes lived on the plains between the Mississippi River and the Rocky Mountains. The Comanches first lived in what is now southern Wyoming, but they were driven south by other tribes. They settled in northwest Texas where they learned from the Mexicans how to use horses. The Plains Indians had been makers of pottery, baskets, and rugs. With horses, their lives changed completely, and they became nomad (or wandering) buffalo hunters. They lived in skin wigwams, or tents, and wore clothes made of deerskin or buffalo hide.

The Comanches were noted for their fine costumes and saddles, decorated with quills, feathers, and silver. They wore a feathered headdress or war bonnet and carried a shield of bison hide. The Comanche weapons were a short, strong bow with a double curve, and the spear. They were expert marksmen. In the 19th century, white settlers in Texas took over their best hunting-grounds, the great Texas Panhandle. Comanches warred against Texas for forty years, and the famous Texas Rangers were organized to fight them. It was not until 1875 that the Comanches finally settled on a government reservation in southwest Oklahoma.

Combat Team, Regimental

Regiments in the army are mostly made up of infantry troops. Every now and then a regiment is sent out to do a job for which other than infantry troops are needed. Perhaps engineers are needed to build a bridge, or artillery to bombard the enemy. In this case the regiment will

often be strengthened by adding to it the extra men that it needs to do its job. This strengthened regiment is called a regimental combat team. It is a well balanced fighting outfit that contains just the troops necessary for the job at hand. An ordinary regiment has three battalions of infantry, a company of tanks, a company of mortars, and a medical company. In addition to all of these, a regimental combat team will often have a battalion of artillery, a company of engineers, a company of signal men (who are specialists in telephone, radio, and other kinds of communications), and perhaps one or two batteries of anti-aircraft artillery. It all depends on exactly what is needed. There are usually about four or five thousand men in a regimental combat team.

combustion

Combustion means "burning," and it is also a way many chemicals combine to form new chemicals. Fire is an example of combustion. When a piece of wood is burning, the chemicals in the wood are combining with the oxygen in the air to form many new chemicals, including water and the gas carbon dioxide. The heat released when the wood burns is so great that the escaping gas glows. It is this hot, glowing gas that we call the flame. Actually, combustion can take place without any flame at all. When iron rusts under water it is slowly burning, that is, it is combining with the oxygen in the water. However, the iron is burning so slowly that the heat it gives off cannot be felt.

Sometimes a house or a barn burns down when people are careless about oily rags, or piles of hay. What happens is that the oil in the rags or the bits of hay burns very slowly and gives off a little heat. No one notices that anything is burning. In time, the heat builds up, and suddenly the rags or hay burst into flames. This is called *spontaneous combustion* and it is very dangerous. The best way to avoid a fire from spontaneous combustion is to make sure there are no piles of oily rags around. Farmers can prevent spontaneous combustion in their haystacks by making sure the hay is thoroughly dry and not green before stacking it.

When gasoline burns in an automobile engine it explodes with great energy and changes into gas. This gas is very hot and it expands with a lot of force, called gas pressure. This gas pressure drives the pistons in the engine. The pistons supply the energy to the wheels and it is this energy that makes the car move. This type of combustion is called rapid combustion. It is very important in many industries where engines are used as a source of power. The steam engines that drive great locomotives get their power from the combustion that takes place in their furnaces where coal or oil is burned.

Until about 150 years ago scientists thought that combustion was caused by something they called *phlogiston*. They thought that when wood or metals burned in air they lost the phlogiston that was in them. They thought that flame was the phlogiston. But the famous French scientist Antoine Lavoisier proved that there was no such thing as phlogiston. Lavoisier showed that when things burned they

combined with the oxygen that was in the air.

See also the articles on INTERNAL COMBUSTION ENGINE and on FUELS and HEATING.

comedy, a light, amusing play that ends happily: see DRAMA.

Comenius

John Amos Comenius was a great teacher who lived about three hundred years ago. He was born in Moravia, which is now a part of Czechoslovakia. When he grew up he became a minister. Comenius is best known for his ideas about teaching children. These ideas are all part of the way children are taught today, but in his own time they were very advanced. Comenius believed, for instance, that schoolbooks should be written in simple language, that pictures should be used to help children understand what they were learning, that children should be taught science and nature study through experiments and through going out on field trips, and that they should be taught languages through conversation instead of just through grammar.

comet

A comet is a bright object in the sky that looks rather like a star. A comet is usually a bright point of light surrounded by a softly glowing cloud. A few comets have long tails of light streaming from them. The strangest thing about comets is that we see them for a short while and then they disappear. Sometimes they are visible for only a few days, and sometimes they stay for a year or two. Because of this, men in the old days were frightened whenever a comet appeared. They thought that the comet was a messenger from God to warn them about something terrible that was going to happen—a war, or a disease, or a famine. A big comet was seen in 1456, and men prayed, "Oh God, save us from the devil, the Turk, and the comet."

WHERE COMETS COME FROM

In the old days, people did not know where comets came from or where they would go. Edmund Halley was the first man to prove that comets moved around the sun. He was an Englishman who lived about 250 years ago. He worked out the paths of 24 comets, and noticed that the paths of big comets that had been seen in the years 1456, 1531, 1607, and 1682 were the same. He said that it was really the same comet and that it came back every 76 years. He predicted that it would come again in 1758. It did come, just as he said that it would, and people named it Halley's comet.

Other comets were found that returned, and people then knew that comets move around the sun just as the planets do. There is one difference. The paths of the planets are nearly circles, with the sun at the center. The paths of the comets are like rings that have been pushed somewhat flat. The sun is near one end of the ring. The path of a comet is longer than the path of the earth. We know one faint comet that goes around its path in a little over three years, and there are other faint comets that go around in four to ten years, but the big, bright comets with tails take much longer. It may take hundreds or even thousands of years for them to go all the way around.

WHAT COMETS ARE MADE OF

The small, bright end of a comet is called the head. The head is made up of little pieces of stone or iron, very far apart. Most of the pieces are probably no larger than marbles, and each piece may be half a mile from the other pieces. Between the little pieces there is very thin gas. The head may be very large, even bigger than any of the planets; but because the pieces are so small and so far apart, a comet does not weigh much.

The tail of a comet is made up of dust and gas, like air, but very thin air. The tail always points away from the sun. A comet acts like a person in the pres-

Yerkes Observatory

A special camera pictured this comet as it shot through the heavens at great speed.

ence of a king. He must never turn his back to the king, so he goes forward when he enters, but backs out. When a comet goes around the sun, the tail is behind as it comes in; when the comet leaves, it backs out, tail first. The dust and gases in the tail are pushed out of the head by light and heat waves from the sun. So the head is always between the sun and the tail.

BIRTH AND DEATH OF A COMET

Sometimes the tails of big comets pass over the earth. In 1910 the earth passed through the tail of Halley's comet. But comet tails are so thin that people never notice anything unusual when the earth passes through them.

Comets are brightest when they are close to the sun. Part of their light is sunlight that is reflected from the solid pieces in the comet's head and from the gas. More of the comet's light is its own light; when the comet comes close to the sun, rays of sunlight are absorbed by the tiny particles in the head and tail.

Halley's comet last passed the sun in May, 1910. Astronomers who watched for it first saw it with telescopes in September, 1909; it looked then like a faint, fuzzy star. By May 4, 1910, it could easily be seen without a telescope, and its tail seemed as long as the whole Big Dipper. On May 18, the tail was longer than from the horizon to overhead, and it was very wide. On May 19, the comet passed the sun and went into the evening sky. Astronomers followed it with telescopes until July, 1911.

There are thousands, perhaps millions, of comets. The paths of about five hundred are known, and more are found every year. No one knows when the next bright comet will be seen, but astronomers hope that there will be several before Halley's comet returns in 1986.

comic opera

A comic opera is a kind of musical show. Many of the lines are spoken, and some are sung. There are songs, duets, trios, and choruses which are all part of the story. One important thing in comic opera is that the words must be understood by the audience, because the words are funny. Comic opera is not as serious as grand opera, but the quality of the music and singing is very good. That is the difference between comic opera and musical comedy. A good example of comic opera is found in the works of Gilbert and Sullivan. The French *opéra comique* simply means opera that is not grand opera (in which all of the words are sung). Classical Italian comic opera is called *opera buffa. The Barber of Seville* is a good example of this.

comics

"The comics" are stories told in pictures and words. Comic means "funny," and the first comics were intended only to be funny.—to tell jokes. The pictures were drawn in what is called cartoon style. When a person said something, his words were printed inside a curved line that is called a "balloon." This same style is used in all comics today, but the comics have come to tell adventure stories, and every other kind of story besides jokes.

There are *comic strips* and *comic books*. A comic strip is just a few scenes, or panels. Comic strips are published in newspapers, and are also called "funny papers." A comic book is a magazine in which a longer story is told by using many more panels.

The comics have become very popular all over the world, and especially in the United States. Nearly everyone, young and old, reads comic strips in newspapers. Comic books are read mostly by children.

It has been shown that comic books can do a lot of harm. Some of them deal with crime and other wicked acts in such a way as to make children think they should act in the same way. Also, some comic books do not have pictures that are well drawn or words that are well written, and so they do not help children to learn good taste in art and literature. For this reason, many persons are against all comic strips and comic books. But the comics remain popular because they are so easy to read and understand. They appeal both to the eye (with their pictures) and to the ear (with the words), and no other kind of literature does this. Many responsible publishers of comic books make sure that there is nothing in their books that can give readers ideas that are dangerous and untrue.

HOW THE COMICS BEGAN

There had been CARICATURES and CARTOONS for thousands of years (you can read separate articles about these), but the first real "comic" appeared about sixty years ago. It was called *The Yellow Kid*, and was drawn by an artist named Richard F. Outcault. It was published on February 16, 1896, in a New York newspaper (the *World*), and it was so successful that within ten years there were comic strips in dozens of big-city newspapers. One of the early comic strips, the *Katzenjammer Kids*, began in 1897 and is still popular. *Mutt and Jeff*, begun in 1909, and *Bringing Up Father*, begun in 1913, are others. These comic strips told a different story, usually a joke, each time.

The first comic book appeared in 1911, and by 1915 there were many of them. Most of them reprinted, in magazines just like modern comic books, a hundred or so of the comic strips that had already been printed in newspapers. By 1920, comic books were so popular that the artists were drawing special comic strips to be used in the magazines and not in newspapers.

In the early 1920s, comic strips began to tell connected stories that went on from day to day. Several of those comic strips are still among the most popular— *Gasoline Alley, Orphan Annie, Moon Mullins, The Gumps, Harold Teen, Smitty, Winnie Winkle,* and many others. "Action comics" such as Terry and the Pirates began in the early 1930s.

Some of the comic strips poked fun at everyday life, and were considered fine art and literature by many critics. The ones most admired were *Krazy Kat*, by George Herriman, which began in 1909; *Li'l Abner*, by Al Capp; *Blondie*, by Chic Young; and *Pogo*, by Walt Kelly.

HOW THE COMICS HAVE GROWN

In 1945, nearly 35,000,000 comic books were being sold every month; by 1961 it was around 45,000,000. The biggest sale began when *Superman* first appeared in 1938. This appealed to the "dream world" of every child. Other publishers rushed to bring out comic books that would have the same appeal. There is nothing real about the stories in such comic books, and for that reason grown-ups are often against them, but children love them.

By 1950, publishers had learned that they had made their comic books so different from reality that they might do a lot of damage. Children were reading in them about things that do not exist, and were being made to believe things that were wrong. The biggest publishers knew that there are many stories and many heroes and heroines who are just as interesting but who are real. Since 1950, these publishers have been making most of their comic books deal with real characters or believable stories. But there are still many publishers who are not so honest. Some schools and libraries have lists of the comic books that are enjoyable to read but will not give a lot of misinformation.

Cominform and **Comintern,** international Communist organizations: see COMMUNISM.

commando

Commando was a word that made many German soldiers shudder during World War II. The commandos were the toughest part of the British army—men who were especially trained to sneak up on the enemy silently and to kill either with knives or with their bare hands. By the time the enemy realized what had happened, the commandos had disappeared. During the early part of the war, when the Germans held almost the whole continent of Europe, small groups of commandos would land at night on the shores of Norway and France. They would blow up bridges, ammunition dumps, and other enemy strong points. Sometimes they would take prisoners, so that they could find out information about the enemy. The most famous raid of the commandos took place in August 1942, when they landed at Dieppe, France. Many Canadian and British commandos were killed in this raid, but the Allies were able to find out how strong the German defenses really were. When the American and British armies landed in France in 1944, the commandos were their shock troops. They went first and did some of the hardest fighting.

The commandos were divided into units of about 450 men. Their training was very hard. Sometimes they marched more than sixty miles in a single day. They swam rivers, climbed cliffs, and learned how to live in the open, finding and cooking their own food. Few troops in the British army were better fighters than the commandos, and it was a great honor to be allowed to wear the maroon beret (a beret is a soft cap) that was part of their uniform. In the American army, the RANGERS are very much like the commandos. You can read about them in a separate article in this encyclopedia.

commedia dell' arte

Commedia dell' arte was a form of Italian comedy that was popular about four hundred years ago. These plays had always the same characters. The actors usually made up the story as they went along. They danced, and sang, and sometimes acted in pantomime, which is acting without words. All of the characters wore masks and fancy clothes. Among them were Harlequin, who was dressed in motley (which means "made of many colors") and who carried a bat; Scaramouche, dressed all in black, who was always getting hit by Harlequin's stick; Pantaloon, a mean old man wearing pantaloons and spectacles; Clown; and the girl Columbine, to whom Harlequin makes love.

commencement

Commencement Day is the day that students finish school and are graduated, but the word commencement means beginning and not ending, as you might think. That is because in olden days most of the people who were well educated became teachers, and they started teaching as soon as they finished studying. So graduation was the beginning of their work, rather than the ending of their school life. At first, the word commencement was used only to describe graduation from a college or a university. Nowadays we use it to describe graduation from any school. On Commencement Day the students receive their diplomas, and there are ceremonies and speeches for the graduates, their families, and their friends.

commerce

Commerce is the part of business that has to do mostly with the buying, selling and transportation of goods between different states or countries. For the full story about commerce, see the article on TRADE.

Commerce, Department of

The Department of Commerce is a branch of the United States government set up to help businessmen. It was established as a separate department in 1913 and today employs more than 30,000 men and women. The head of the Department is called the Secretary of Commerce. He is a member of the President's cabinet.

The Department of Commerce has many bureaus, or offices, to gather different kinds of information that businessmen may need.

The Bureau of Foreign and Domestic Commerce collects facts and figures about trade and industry all over the world. Every day it answers hundreds of questions asked by American and foreign businessmen.

The Civil Aeronautics Administration, or CAA, controls all flying in the United States. Its job is to keep airplanes and airports safe. To do this the CAA makes and enforces rules about training pilots, landing and taking off, and many other aspects of flying.

The Bureau of the Census counts the number of people living in the United States. This is done every ten years. The first census, made more than 150 years ago, took nine months. The 1960 census took one week.

The Coast and Geodetic Survey gathers and gives out information about high and low tides, dangerous rocks and reefs, the depth of the water around ports and coastlines, earthquakes, and so on.

The Inland Waterways Corporation tries to persuade people to use the lakes, rivers and canals of the United States for travel and for commerce. It also manages the barges owned by the government.

The Patent Office grants patents on new inventions. It makes sure that no one else has made the same thing before and then it issues a patent which forbids anyone to use the new invention without the inventor's permission.

The National Bureau of Standards makes certain that you get your money's worth when you buy a can of peaches, an automobile, a suit of clothes, or anything else manufactured in the United States. It also keeps the weights and measures on which all our scales and rulers are based.

The Weather Bureau studies weather conditions all over the country and tells people what to expect. Airlines, shipping companies, people going on vacation, and many others depend on the services of the Weather Bureau.

There are separate articles on most of these bureaus.

Commission, Government

When the government gives a group of men a certain job to do or a problem to study, this group is called a commission. The people who work on the commission are called commissioners. Sometimes the President appoints a commission to study a problem and keep him informed. Sometimes the commissions are appointed by Congress. In the United States there are many commissions. Some work for the Federal government; others work for state governments. Commissions can be either permanent or temporary. The Interstate Commerce Commission, set up in 1887, is a permanent commission. So is the Federal Communications Commission, set up in 1934. Each has a permanent job to do. The War Manpower Commission was a temporary commission. It had a wartime job of finding people to work in war industries.

commission, military

A military commission is a document signed by a king, president, or other official, saying that a man or a woman is an officer in the Army, Navy, or Air Force. These men and women are called commissioned officers. In the Army, the Air Force, and the Marines, they are lieutenants, captains, majors, colonels, and generals. In the Navy, they are ensigns, lieutenants, commanders, captains, and admirals. Lower officers who do not have commissions are called sergeants and corporals (non-commissioned officers) in the Army and Air Force, and petty officers in the Navy.

In the United States, commissions can be obtained by graduating from West Point or Annapolis, by graduating from Officers' Candidate School, or by joining the Reserve Officers' Training Corps in college. In addition, some men and women that the armed forces need very badly for their skills or experience are

given direct commissions. Today anyone with a good enough education, intelligence, character, and physical health and condition can get a commission. This was not always so. In Europe it used to be that only men who were nobles or who were very rich could be officers, and for a long time it was possible to buy a commission for a large sum of money.

commission selling

Commission selling is done by commission merchants who do not own the goods they sell. The farmer or manufacturer ships goods to the commission merchant, whose job is to sell the merchandise at the highest price he can get. He then takes his commission, or charge for selling, from the sales price of the goods. He sends the remainder of the money to the farmer or manufacturer who shipped him the goods. The commission merchant is responsible if the man to whom he sold the goods does not pay.

Commission selling is still very important in the cloth industry, and in the canning industry. It is not used much in other trades nowadays because shippers do not want to take the risk of big price changes between the time they ship the goods and the time they are sold. Also, the buyers do not mind taking the goods directly from the farmer. Better methods of shipping and storage make it more certain that the goods will arrive in good condition.

In large cities, commission markets are still very much used. Vegetables and other foods can be shipped to a large commission market in or near the railroad yard. The fruit-store owners and other buyers come early in the morning and buy what they need.

Committees of Correspondence

The Committees of Correspondence were groups of men formed in America before the Revolutionary War. These Committees were led by such patriots as Samuel Adams, Thomas Jefferson, and Patrick Henry. They were against British rule, and they wanted the American colonies to be independent. Their main purpose was to get as many people as possible to feel the way they did. Whenever the British put a new tax on the colonies, the Committees of Correspondence would write letters and make speeches against the tax. They persuaded many colonists that the taxes were unfair. Samuel Adams, one of the most active members, helped to organize the Boston Tea Party. The British had put a tax on tea. When a British company sent over three ships loaded with tea, Adams got the people of Boston to dump the tea into the harbor. Little by little the Committees gained many supporters. The Revolutionary War would have taken place without the Committees, but they undoubtedly brought it about sooner.

commodity exchange

A commodity exchange is a place where such commodities as wheat, coffee, cotton and lard are bought and sold. When the farmers harvest their crops, they must sell large quantities of whatever they produce. The exchange is a place where the men who sell and the men who buy meet. The thousands of

bags of wheat that are sold every day are not piled on the exchange floor. They are kept in warehouses, and a buyer just gets a piece of paper giving him the ownership of the wheat. The commodity exchange also deals in *futures*. This means the buying and selling of crops that have not yet been grown. A chocolate manufacturer, for example, sells chocolate all through the year, and he must make sure that he will have a steady supply of cocoa from which to make it. To do this, he can go to the exchange and buy cocoa for immediate delivery, or he can buy cocoa futures, which will be delivered to him during some future months.

The Chicago Board of Trade is the largest commodity exchange in the United States. It was started in 1848, and there are now five hundred members who buy and sell there. The members of the Board of Trade who deal in futures do their trading in "pits" on the exchange floor. These pits consist of a series of rings that rise like steps. The buyers stand on these steps where they can be seen in the pit, and make offers and purchases by signs with their hands. Each step stands for a different month of delivery. There are different pits for wheat, corn, rye, cotton, oats, and soy beans. There have been commodity exchanges for a long time. Merchants formed an exchange more than four hundred years ago in Antwerp, Belgium, but it was only a hundred years ago that commodity exchanges of the modern kind became possible. These exchanges were needed to speed the steady flow of commodities to the cities and manufacturers. When the farmers planted larger areas of land, and the growing cities began to need a large and steady supply of food, the commodity exchange became necessary.

common carrier

Common carriers are trucks, railroads, wagons, ships, pipelines, cabs, and buses that are for hire by the public. They are required by law to carry all freight that is offered to them. If they do not have a good excuse for refusing to carry anything, they can be sued in court.

This century has seen many changes in common carriers. Trucks and planes carry much of the freight that the railroads had carried before. In 1960 there were more than twelve million trucks and busses carrying goods and people over the highways of the United States.

The law requires that common carriers must carry the goods safely. If they do not, they can be sued for damages. Carriers of passengers, however, are only required to take great care. Injured passengers cannot collect damages unless they can prove that the railroad or bus company was careless. Private carriers are usually owned by the companies that use them to ship. For example, a gasoline company usually has its own trucks for city delivery. They are not for public hire, and therefore are not common carriers.

common law

Common law is the large mass of unwritten law in England and the United States. The written laws are called statute laws. The common law is based on *precedent*—that is, what another court decided in a case of the same kind. Judges in the United States often follow English judges of many hundreds of years ago. The judges and the lawyers look up what was decided in previous cases of the same kind in order to know how to decide the case before them. Some of the common law has now been written down into statute laws.

Commons, House of, one of the two houses in the British Parliament: see PARLIAMENT.

commonwealth

A commonwealth is a government made up of representatives of the people. A country or state that is a commonwealth usually is part of a group of countries. Four of the states of the United States are officially called commonwealths. These states are Massachusetts, Pennsylvania, Virginia, and Kentucky. Many of the countries that used to be part of the British Empire are now members of the Commonwealth of Nations. Not all these countries were independent in the empire, but under the Commonwealth they are. They have their own governments, but all of them accept the British king or queen. About three hundred years ago, the English forced their king to resign and set up a government without a king. This government, which lasted about ten years, was called the Commonwealth. Its leader was Oliver Cromwell.

commune

Commune is the name given to the smallest division in France that has a local government. A commune is governed by a council elected by the people who live in it. It is like a town in the United States. The French people have often called democratic governments communes. For instance, a commune was set up in 1792, during the French Revolution, when the government was changed from rule by king to rule by elected officials.

The most famous commune was set up in Paris in March of 1871, when France was at war with Germany. France was losing the war, and the French government was quite unsettled. A group of Frenchmen took over the government of Paris and set up a commune. The government officials who had been thrown out laid siege to the city and forced the commune leaders to surrender. Thousands of people were shot. The commune was broken up and most of its leaders were executed.

communication

Communication is the sending and receiving of messages. It is talk, signals, telephone calls, telegrams, radio, or television. Almost anything that we do depends in some way on sending thoughts or orders from one place to another, and from one person to another. Without our wonderful communication systems, our civilization could not exist. We communicate with each other across the sea, from ship to shore, from airplanes to the ground. We pick up a telephone, and in a moment we are talking to someone who is many miles away.

Our ancestors of 25,000 years ago, the people we call cavemen because they lived in caves and wore the skins of animals to keep warm, used to paint pictures on the stone walls of their caves. Many of those early drawings can still be seen. Perhaps the cavemen did not intend it, but their pictures tell us many things about them, how they lived and what they did.

Most of us have seen a rebus, a kind of riddle in which pictures suggest words.

EYE   SAW   YOU

That is the way writing began. When people first learned to live together in tribes, cities, and other communities, they started learning to write. It took a long, long time. At first everything had to be carved in stone. That took a long time, and the stone was heavy. Then they used soft clay, and wrote on it with a metal stylus, or pointed instrument. After the clay had been baked, it was hard enough to last. It was also light enough so that a runner could carry a message to another group of people. After a while, paper and ink were invented; and the horse took the place of runners. Soon messages could be sent ahead of the slow lines of camels and horses, or the marching armies. Roads were improved, and news became important to more and more people. Then, about five hundred years before the birth of Christ, King Cyrus of Persia started a regular postal service. It worked just like the Pony Express of frontier days in the United States.

EARLY COMMUNICATIONS

Among many of the peoples who did not develop the art of writing, there were various ways to communicate. The American Indians used smoke signals. On the top of a high hill they built a fire. As it burned down, they put some wet leaves or moss on it to make a thick smoke. Then they held a wet blanket or a big piece of bark over the fire for a moment, then lifted it away so that a big puff of smoke rose to the sky. By a sort of code, or dot-and-dash system, they could send messages as far as the smoke signal could be seen. At night they used a signal fire. Where there was no hill, they sometimes built a tower of stones and made a fire on top. Our lighthouses of today, signaling to ships at sea to protect them from dangerous rocks and shoals, use the same principle as the primitive fire-tower, or beacon fire.

Drums have been one of man's earliest means of communication, for the sound of a drum can be heard for great distances. In Africa drummers are able to "talk" as easily as if they were close together. There is a drum-language, and the rhythms and patterns of the beats have a real meaning in words. Each drum station picks up a message, and relays it to another, and so on. Usually the stations are about 15 miles apart but the drums can be heard even farther. Sometimes the drum is partly underground, for the earth is a better conductor, or carrier, of sound than the air.

One of the first means of communication ever discovered was the homing pigeon. This is a breed of pigeon that can be trained to fly straight home from wherever they are taken. Written mes-

sages are tied to the bird's leg. These birds have been used almost as far back as we know. During the days of castles and the siege of walled cities, no runner or horseman could escape through the lines of a besieging enemy, and pigeons were often sent for help. The enemy trained hawks to catch them, but the pigeons could fly faster than the hawks and usually got through.

MODERN COMMUNICATIONS

Today almost all communications are organized on a world-wide basis. We write a letter to someone in South America, England, or any part of our own country, attach a stamp that costs only a few cents, and drop it in a mailbox. Within hours, it is on its way by fast train or ship. If we wish the letter to arrive in a hurry, we use an airmail stamp and it goes out on an airplane. On the train, ship, or plane a mail clerk sorts out the mail so that no time is lost, but this is nothing compared to the speed with which news is transmitted by electricity.

About one hundred years ago Samuel Morse invented the telegraph, which changed the world. Before that, no message could be transmitted faster than it could be sent or told. Now it was possible to flash news in an instant to far distant places. When submarine cables were installed on the ocean floor, cablegrams could be sent to and from all the world's capitals. For many years the Morse Code was used, a system of dots and dashes to spell the letters of words. Today an operator simply types the message on a special typewriter, and in another telegraph office many miles away, even around the earth, an automatic typewriter reproduces the message.

In 1897, Guglielmo Marconi of Italy first flashed a wireless message from shore to a ship at sea. Now communication needed no wires, no messengers, no relays. All that was needed was an operator at each station with the necessary knowledge and equipment. The steamships were the first to realize the importance of wireless, and before long hardly a ship was without it. The letters S–O–S were chosen as the signal that a ship was in danger. It was easy to click out the letters in Morse code – 3 dots, 3 dashes, and 3 dots. Later the signal was abbreviated to dot–dash–dot.

For more than twenty years only dots and dashes could be sent by air. Then experiments with what was called the wireless-telephone led to the invention of radio. Now words and music and sounds of all kinds could be sent through the air. We turn a dial and listen to announcers who are speaking in France, England, Italy, China or India. Even transoceanic telephone calls are changed from local telephone lines to powerful radio transmitters, and sent across the ocean in the form of radio waves. Then they are converted again to local telephone lines. This is called radio telephony.

TELEVISION

Today we see baseball games, parades, football games and other special events at almost the same instant they take place. In politics, speeches are made before television cameras, and we are able to size up the speaker and make up our minds whether or not we like him. We can send a photograph across the country by television, at almost the speed of light. Television combines all of the methods of communication we have discussed in this article, sound, sight, light, and immediate reception.

communion

In Christian churches there is a ceremony that acts out the Last Supper of Jesus with his disciples. The story of the Last Supper is in the New Testament, in the Bible. Communion is called a sacrament because it is a ceremony begun by Jesus when he was on earth. Bread and wine are usually used, since Jesus said: "This is my body," when he broke the bread at the Last Supper, and "This is my blood," when he gave them the wine. In Roman Catholic doctrine, during the ceremony, which is part of the Mass, the bread and wine are marvelously changed into the real body and blood of Jesus. This miracle is called *transubstantiation,* which means changing of substance. Those worshipers who are to receive communion go forward from their seats to the communion rail, which is before the altar. They kneel there, and the priest places a small wafer, known as the Host, on the tongue of each. This is the Blessed Sacrament, or Eucharist, of the Roman Catholic Church.

During the Reformation, when the Protestant churches were breaking away from the Roman Catholic Church, they refused to believe in transubstantiation. However, members of the Church of England believe in the Real Presence, which means that Jesus is actually present during communion. This is called *consubstantiation.* Some Anglican Churches accept transubstantiation. Read also the article LORD'S SUPPER.

communism

Communism is a form of government. Once, long ago, a communistic community was one in which all the people owned everything together, and no one had any private property except perhaps his clothes and a few personal possessions. This is not a description of communism as we know it today. Both Russian and Chinese communism are a combination of two systems of government: socialism and fascism.

In communism as in socialism, it is the state (that is the government rather than the individual people) that owns all property that can be used to make a profit. The state owns the farms, factories, mines, railroads, stores, houses, telephone, electric and gas companies, and nearly everything else. In communism as in fascism, the government is controlled by one political party (which in a communist country is the Communist Party). The head of the Communist Party is also the head of the country. He is a dictator having absolute power and authority. The organization of opposing political parties is against the law. The people vote, but this practice is useless because there is only one list of candidates. Parties do not run against one another as Republicans and Democrats do in the United States. People who criticize the government, de-

pending on their influence and the extent of the criticism, risk a possible jail sentence. There is a great deal of censorship (forbidding certain information to be made public) in communist nations. After Stalin died in 1953, Nikita Khrushchev became the leader of the communist movement in Russia. He tended to liberalize such things as education, political criticism, and working conditions; this led the country toward a freer society. Despite this, the Russian people do not have the freedom to travel or work, as do citizens of non-communist countries. There are, as well, instances of people being arrested, imprisoned, or even executed without a fair trial. Communist governments do not let life and liberty stand in their way if their political system seems threatened.

The Union of Soviet Socialist Republics is a communistic country. That is the country we usually speak of as Russia, because Russia is the largest part of it. All communist countries were forced or helped by Russia to become communistic. In the other communist countries of Europe—Poland, Czechoslovakia, Rumania, Hungary, Albania, Bulgaria, and Yugoslavia—Russia used armed aggression or the threat of it to drive out governments elected by the people and put in communist bosses. Aided by Russian arms and men, a few communists in China, North Korea, North Vietnam and Cuba were able to control large armies composed chiefly of men who are not communists, and so bring all these countries under the control of a Communist Party that supports a "party line" favorable to Russia. (China, Yugoslavia and Albania are no longer so friendly with Russia).

WHAT MAKES PEOPLE COMMUNISTS?

There has long been a feeling of distrust between the United States and Russia, due to their different political systems. It is true, however, that communist parties exist in freedom-loving countries like the United States and Canada. The reason for this is that for a long time the communist nations have wanted to gain power over the democratic nations. However, Khrushchev did, in 1956, announce a policy of peaceful co-existence with the west, which was quite an impressive statement for a communist leader. Another reason for the existence of communist parties in democratic countries is that in many such nations, the very poor people are not paid enough to live comfortably and the idea of a classless society usually appeals to them. They want a change of government because they hope they will be better off under a communist government.

People often confuse the ideas of Marx which are very utopian (ideal), with the ideas of the Russian Communists today, which are very different. Originally Marx wanted a classless society where all men are equal, but we can see a great deal of economic inequality in Russia today. The communism that many people think will solve their problems is Marxist communism, not Russian communism. Marx felt that the impoverished working class would turn to organized revolution and form a Socialist economy where all the production would be shared equally.

Young men and women, especially when they are in college, often like the idea of communism. The communists have many arguments that sound good. They say, "In a communistic country, no one is rich or poor, because the people all together own everything. The only way to make money is by working for it. No one has to be afraid of losing his job. No one can make a profit on work that other people do." This all appeals to a person's sense of fairness. The only trouble is, this does not exist in Russia. People who start out admiring communism often grow suspicious of it and eventually turn against it altogether.

HOW COMMUNISM BEGAN

For thousands of years, there have been men who wanted all property to belong to all the people together. "Then," they thought, "no one would have any reason to be ambitious or selfish or dishonest or cruel to his fellow men."

From time to time, groups of people have formed communities to live in just that way. Many religious communities have been communistic. One of them was the SHAKERS, in the United States. More than a hundred years ago, a group that was not a religious sect tried a communistic plan at BROOK FARM in Massachusetts. There are separate articles on both these groups. There have been many other communistic groups. None of them succeeded well enough to last.

The founder of modern communism was a German named Karl Marx. Marx and another German named Friedrich Engels, who helped him, are great heroes in Russia and other communist countries today. In 1848 Marx published a booklet that he called *The Communist Manifesto*. It is from this booklet that modern communism got its name, but even though the communists believe much of what Marx wrote, the communism of today is quite different from Marxism. Later, Marx published a long book called *Das Kapital*, which in German means "Capital," and is about the system of business and government that we call capitalism.

These were Karl Marx's chief ideas, which are still the ideas of communists:

1. Men who own *capital* (factories and farms and tools and machinery) make a profit on the work of men they hire to use this capital.

2. Because of this, there are two classes. One class is the capitalists, or owners of the factories and farms. The other class is the workers in the factories and on the farms. These two classes constantly struggle against each other.

3. At first, the capitalists will be ahead in this "class struggle," and they will take advantage of the workers, who will be poor and suffering while the capitalists live in luxury. But the working class will gradually grow in power. As it does, the capitalistic system will become weaker and weaker and finally will not be able to make profits.

4. At this point the working class (called the *proletariat*) will unite and take over the factories, and the peasants, or workers on the farms, will join them, and they will make a "classless society" in which everyone is a worker and no one profits from another man's work.

5. The greatest enemy of the working class is not the very rich people. It is the middle classes, called the *bourgeoisie*. These people are neither rich nor very poor. They cling to their small amounts of property, and they are powerful because there are so many of them. Besides, when a working man becomes somewhat successful he wants to become a member of the bourgeoisie himself.

Karl Marx's theories were called *dialectical materialism*, which means a logical explanation of what has happened and will happen among men, based on actual conditions. Materialism is opposed to religion, and communist governments are always enemies of all religions and churches.

THE INTERNATIONAL

Marx and Engels had said that the working class must unite, and in 1864 a number of men who believed in their ideas met and formed an international organization of working men. This is now called the "First International." It was the first real Communist Party, though its members then called themselves socialists. Later there was a Second International, organized in 1889. The socialists in several European countries said they did not believe in different nations but only in the two different classes, capitalists and workers, that Karl Marx had written about. However, when World War I broke out most of them supported their own countries and the international organization broke up.

At the time of World War I there were communists in nearly all countries of Europe and America, but they were strongest in Russia. This was natural, because Russia had not advanced as much as other countries, and the factory workers and peasants were very poor and in many cases were not much better off than slaves.

The leaders of the Russian Communists then were V. I. Lenin and Leon Trotsky. In 1917, when Russia was losing World War I and the czar (emperor) had become very unpopular with the people, Lenin and Trotsky helped win a revolution against him, and in November of 1917 they seized complete control of the Russian government. Their party was called the Bolshevik Party (*bolshevik* means "majority") and for a long time communism was also called *bolshevism*.

THE NEW COMMUNISM

So in 1917, for the first time in history, a big country had a communist government. Lenin was the head of the government. At first, it is possible that he really wanted to help the people. But he and the other communists persuaded themselves that they had to murder their enemies ruthlessly "for the good of the working class." Soon Lenin learned that he enjoyed having such power. He became a worse tyrant than the czars.

That has been true of every Communist dictator since. Joseph Stalin, who chased out Trotsky and seized power in Russia when Lenin died, and who remained the dictator until he died in 1953, had millions of people murdered and millions more sent as slave workers to prison camps, mines and factories. He also liked to be treated as a god.

In 1919, with Lenin in power, the Russians formed the "Third International," which they called the *Comintern* (Communist International). The Comintern tried to help other Communist Parties in all countries to start revolutions against their governments. In 1943, Stalin pretended to drop the Comintern, so that other countries would help him in World War II, but after World War II he started another organization, called the *Cominform* (Communist Information Bureau) to do the same work.

For many years, communists all over the world obeyed the orders that came from Moscow, the Soviet capital, and supported all of Russia's acts of aggression and cruelty against its own people and against weak foreign countries. In the 1960s, Red China began to criticize Russia as not being communistic enough —because Russia often compromises with capitalistic nations—so now many communists in Europe and Asia feel free to criticize Russia. But all communists side with communistic countries against capitalistic countries—even against their own countries. This is called "following the party line." Many persons who pretend not to be communists follow the party line. Others, called "fellow travelers," are not members of the Communist Party but usually help the communists to accomplish what they are trying to do.

Communists are often called "Reds," because red is the color of their flag. Therefore some "fellow travelers" are spoken of as "pink"—almost red.

In the United States, the Communist Party never had many members, so it did not have much political power. However, the American communists got control of several important labor unions. After World War II they were voted out of office in nearly all these unions, and some of the communist leaders were convicted of trying to overthrow the United States government and were put in jail. In 1954 the United States Congress passed a law that denied the Communist Party recognition as a political party and that required members of the Communist Party to register as agents of a foreign country (the U.S.S.R.).

THE AIMS OF COMMUNISM

The United States has found through frequent dealings with Communist nations that they are not honorable in their dealings with other countries. Previously, before the various arms limitation pacts, the Soviets made it quite clear that they wanted to lead the rest of the world under communist rule, by starting wars if necessary. This, however, is no longer true. The change has occurred mainly because today's weapons have such a destructive capacity that they could annihilate (wipe out) the entire population of the world.

To protect themselves against the danger of an attack from Russia, several European and American nations formed NATO (the NORTH ATLANTIC TREATY ORGANIZATION, about which there is a separate article) and in 1954 Yugoslavia, Greece, and Turkey made a treaty to fight together if any of them were attacked, and nine free countries of eastern Asia made a similar treaty, the SOUTHEAST ASIA TREATY. (See also the articles

on UNION OF SOVIET SOCIALIST RE-
PUBLICS, CAPITALISM, and SOCIALISM.)

community

A community is made up of a group of people who live together or near each other and carry on the same type of life. If you go to a camp and live with other people who are camping, you are living in a camping community. Everyone there is doing the same type of thing you are doing. If you are living with your family in an apartment in a big city, you are living in another type of community. This community has many more people, but they are all usually living the same type of life. They live in apartments, and they go to work in offices that are usually in big buildings. Their jobs may be very different, but the way in which they live is similar. They work at about the same time. They eat the same type of food. And if they want to entertain themselves, they all do it about the same way. A community does not have to be any special size. As long as a group of people in a certain area live in a certain way, the group is called a community.

There are many types of community. An agricultural community is one where the main interest of the people is farming. The people in an agricultural community usually have to get up in the morning much earlier than someone who does not live in an agricultural community. Their way of living depends on the weather, and their work is done outside. An agricultural community is completely different from a large city community. The center of the agricultural community may be only a small store or a church or a small town. Even the storekeeper in a small town depends on the type of life in his community. In an agricultural area, he may keep his store open late at night so that the farmer, who must work during the day, can buy from him.

Some people live and work in mining towns such as Scranton, Pennsylvania. These are communities built around one industry. Almost everyone there works in the mines or in offices connected with the mining industry. Some people live in suburban communities. Their offices and places of work are often in a nearby city, and they all have to take a train into the city every day. Some communities are made up of people with one special interest. Sun Valley, Idaho, for example, is made up of people who like sports.

Often the people of a community like to get together to talk and to share their interests. In a small town or village people may go to a store where they can find other members of the community to talk with, and hear what other people are doing. This is an informal type of meeting place and it is used because it is convenient. Many communities, however, have started community centers. These centers are a room or a building where people can meet. They use the room or the building for entertainment and recreation. They use it to hold meetings about community plans. It is a center of community activity. Every person in any community should be interested in the community, and should take some responsibility for making it a better place to live. Community centers where people

Italian State Tourist Off.

Lake Como in Italy is surrounded by hills and mountains that are reflected in the blue water. On the slopes of the hills are beautiful groves of figs and oranges.

may meet and talk together make this possible.

community chest

The community chest is made up of a group of people and various charity organizations in the community. These charity organizations may be local, such as one organized to get funds for a new hospital. Or they may be national ones such as the YMCA or the Boy Scouts. They join together for the purpose of raising money to carry on their good work. Each of these organizations will get a certain portion of the money that is raised during the community chest campaigns. Everyone who contributes to these campaigns knows that it will be spent wisely. The community chest also tries to get everyone interested in the groups connected with it. It helps the groups plan their work so that one group is not doing the same work that another group is doing. The first community chest was organized in Cleveland, Ohio, in 1913. Five years later a national organization of community chests was set up. It serves as an information center for all community chests in the United States.

Como, Lake

Lake Como is one of the most beautiful lakes in the world. It is in northern Italy, at the foot of the Alps, and its very clear water reflects the high mountains around it. The lake is about thirty miles long and almost three miles wide in some places. The ancient city of Como is located at the southern end. The beautiful scenery and wonderful climate of this region have made the shores of Lake Como a famous resort for tourists.

compass

A compass is a device or instrument for finding direction. It is used by explorers, mountain climbers, the captains of ships, airplane pilots, and anybody else who has to be sure in which direction he is moving or facing.

Hundreds of years ago nobody had any way of finding direction. If a person was lost in a woods or on a desert, for instance, he had no way of knowing if he was walking toward home or going farther away with every step. Then somebody made an interesting discovery. He found that a small piece of the iron ore called magnetite, or lodestone, when floated on a cork in water would point in only one direction: north. Later on somebody tried this trick with a needle. He stroked the needle with a piece of lodestone, then floated the needle in water on a splinter of wood. The needle, too, pointed steadily north. A needle treated in this way by a lodestone was said to be *magnetized*. (See the article MAGNETISM.) Other ways of magnetizing needles have been found.

These floating lodestones or needles that always pointed north were the first compasses. Some scholars think the Chinese invented them. Others think the compass was brought to Europe by the Arabs. Still others claim it was invented in Italy towards the end of the Middle Ages. We do not know for sure. We do know for certain, however, that the compass was being used by European mariners after the 12th century.

HOW THE COMPASS CHANGED HISTORY

Before they had compasses, mariners were afraid to sail far from shore. Once they were away out on the ocean, how could they tell in which direction they were sailing? With land out of sight they might sail off so far they would never get back to their home port. Of course, good seamen could find direction by the position of the sun or certain stars. But what

An ancient compass supposed to
have been used by Columbus.

Ships use a compass card that
floats in a liquid so that it will lie
flat at all times.

Some small compasses can be carried in a person's pocket.

could they do when storms or fog arose
and they could not see these heavenly
bodies? The compass solved this problem. By means of this instrument they
always knew where north was and could
steer their ships accordingly. They ventured farther and farther from land and

made discoveries that would have been
impossible otherwise. Such voyages as
that of Columbus to the New World and
the one Vasco da Gama made around
Africa to India would never have taken
place without the compass.

THE POCKET COMPASS

Every Boy Scout and Girl Scout can
use a pocket compass. It consists of a
round card on which north, south, east,
and west are marked. These are called
the principal, or *cardinal*, points of the
compass. In the center of the card a magnetized needle is mounted on a pivot.
The needle, free to move in any direction,
points north. If you are lost, a map and
a compass together can help you to find
your way. On most maps, north is at the
top of the map; if not, there is usually a
symbol that indicates the direction of
north. When you make the needle of the
compass line up with the north direction
on the map, you can then locate the points
or places indicated on the map.

Use the compass needle or degree
reading on the compass to locate a landmark—a high tree, a rock or a building
in the direction in which you want to
travel. Turn around and pick another
landmark in the exact opposite direction.
This will give you a straight line. If you
are moving toward an established point,
always keep two landmarks in sight.

THE MARINER'S COMPASS

The mariner's compass is a kind of
compass used on many ships. It is much
more complicated than the pocket compass.

The ship's compass is fixed in a large
brass bowl called the compass bowl or
binnacle. The binnacle is located near
the ship's steering wheel. On top is a glass
window.

When you look through the window,
you see a large circular card made of
mica. It is marked with a large star that
has 32 points. The four cardinal points
are marked, and also the directions between them. Some of the latter are northeast, northwest; north-northeast, north-
northwest; and northeast by north, northwest by north. In addition, the edge of
the card is marked by the 360 degrees of
the circle, beginning with zero at north
and going clockwise. Calling off all the
points in order, going either forward or
backward, is known as "boxing the compass." Good seamen can do this.

No needle is visible on the card. How
then does this compass work? It actually
has two to eight needles. They lie parallel to each other, and are attached to the
underside of the card by means of silk
threads.

The needles always point north and
keep the point of the star that is marked
north steadily pointing in that direction.
Many needles are used so that the card
will hold steady, and in case one of the
needles gets out of order. The card is often floated on a quantity of water mixed
with alcohol. The liquid absorbs shocks
that might make both card and needles
shake and make the card hard to read. In
addition, the compass is supported by a
number of metal rings known as *gimbals*.
They hold the card so that it remains
horizontal no matter how the ship may
plunge or tilt.

THE FAULTS OF THE MARINER'S
COMPASS

Useful as it is, the mariner's compass
has two bad faults. We have been saying
that a magnetized needle always points
north. This is not strictly true. Such a
needle does not really point to true north,
that is, to the North Pole. It actually
points to a spot about 1200 miles south
of the North Pole. This spot is called the
magnetic North Pole. The difference, expressed in degrees of the circle, between
true north and magnetic north is called
the "variation" or "declination" of the
compass. The captain of a ship has charts
that tell him how much variation from
true north his compass shows at any particular part of the earth's surface. He
finds out how many degrees of variation
exist at the particular spot his ship has
reached and corrects the compass reading to determine true north. Then he
steers his ship accordingly.

A second difficulty arises because of
iron or steel objects in the ship. These
may become magnetized and pull the
compass needles off direction. To prevent
such a pull, which is known as "deviation" of the compass, small magnets are
sometimes placed on the outside of the
binnacle. They take up the magnetic pull
of the iron or steel in the ship and keep
it from affecting the needles. The more
iron and steel used in a ship the harder
it is to correct the deviation. In modern
ships with their steel construction and
huge engines made of steel, such correction is a very troublesome matter indeed.
For a long time scientists tried to make
a compass that would not be subject to
either variation or deviation.

THE GYROCOMPASS

Such a compass was invented in 1911.
It is called the gyrocompass. It does not
depend on magnetized needles. It makes
use of a scientific instrument called the
"gyroscope." (Read the article GYRO-
SCOPE). The principal part of a gyroscope is a wheel that rotates swiftly on
an axis. If a gyroscope is mounted on another body that is also rotating on its
axis, the gyroscope will set and keep its
own axis parallel to that of the other
body. The earth is a revolving body. It
turns completely on its axis once every
24 hours. The axis of the earth is a line
running north to south. A gyroscope once
set into motion will set its own axis parallel to that of the earth—that is to say,
directly true north and south.

The gyrocompass takes advantage of
this. It consists of a large heavy wheel
that is kept rotating steadily (8,500 revolutions per minute) by a motor. As we
have said, its axis points true north and
south. By a number of devices it keeps
the north point of a compass card pointing steadily in the same direction—true
north. There is no variation or deviation
to worry about. The gyrocompass is used
on all warships and on large passenger
and freight vessels and on airplanes. For
small ships the mariner's magnetic compass still works well enough.

OTHER KINDS OF COMPASS

Surveyors use a compass that has a magnetic needle. The compass card has many markings. The instrument is so mounted that while in use it is always in a horizontal position.

Like the gyrocompass, the compass known as the earth-induction compass is free of the errors of the magnetic compass. The earth-induction compass consists of a coil of wire in which the magnetism of the earth generates an electric current. This current keeps the needle pointing true north. This type of compass is used a great deal in airplanes.

The radio compass is a receiving set with a loop aerial. It is used on ships to receive signals sent by radio. If another ship is sending out distress signals by radio, they will be strongest on the receiving set when its aerial is in line with the direction from which the signals are coming. The radio operator turns the aerial until the signals are coming in very strong. Then he knows the direction where the endangered ship lies and his own ship need lose no time in going to its rescue, by following the "beam."

compass plant

The compass plant or rosinweed is a large coarse plant of the prairies with jagged-edged leaves that turn edge up and often point north and south. It has a thick sap and large flowers like sunflowers, and is sometimes grown in gardens. Apart from rosinweed, other plants called compass plants are found in different parts of the world, and are used by cattlemen and travelers to find their direction if they are lost.

Compiègne

Compiègne is a town in northeastern France, about 50 miles from Paris. Several very famous events have happened there. It was at Compiègne that St. Joan of Arc, the girl who led the troops of France into battle, was captured by the English in 1430, to be tried for witchcraft and burned at the stake.

Many years later, on November 11, 1918, the armistice that ended World War I was signed in a railroad car near Compiègne. And in June, 1940, after the Germans had beaten the French at the beginning of World War II, the French generals were forced to surrender in the same place in the very same railroad car. This was the Germans' way of getting revenge for their defeat in 1918. Four years later, in August, 1944, the Allies captured Compiègne from the Germans.

About 22,000 people live in Compiègne. The town is over a thousand years old. There are factories there that make cloth and ladies' stockings.

complex

People who study the mind, called psychologists, say that we have complexes that make us act the way we do. A thing is complex when it is made up of many connected parts, usually complicated and difficult to understand. The psychologist means that our minds hold many memories of things that have happened to us, but some of these memories are of unhappy things and our minds keep them buried so that we are not even aware of them. If these buried memories are not too unhappy, they do not bother us. But sometimes a person can become very upset and even mentally sick if these memories are too painful. When we say a person has an inferiority complex, we mean that he has buried memories of things that happened to him that make him think he is not as good, or as intelligent, as other people.

composite plants

Composite plants are plants, such as daisies and chrysanthemums, whose "flowers" are heads made up of many individual flowers massed together.

Most composite flower-heads are made up of two kinds of flower. Around the edge are *ray* flowers, each a single long petal. In the center of the flower-head are a large number of flowers called *disk* flowers, each made up of five tiny petals forming a long tube.

There are more plants belonging to the family of composites than to any other. This may be because of the many seeds they produce. The seeds of some have tiny parachutes of hairs that carry them in the wind. Others are bristly or barbed and stick to fur or cloth.

Composites are commonest in cool climates, where they are chiefly herbs with rosettes of leaves at the base. In the tropics they are sometimes trees or climbers.

Many composites are very beautiful and are grown in gardens. Some are used for food, and some for medicine. Among the best known are: both sorts of artichoke, chicory, sunflower, dandelion, goldenrod, camomile, marigold, thistle, daisy, aster, dahlia, chrysanthemum, and lettuce.

compound

When two or more chemicals come together and form a new chemical in which we cannot see the parts, we call this a compound. If you look at table salt, you do not see the two different parts that have combined, or come together, to make the salt, but it is really a compound of two chemicals called *sodium* and *chlorine*. If you tasted either one of these two chemicals, you would die, because they both are deadly poisons. But salt is harmless because the chemicals changed and made a compound, which is something different from the two parts of the salt.

When you pour sugar and sand into a bowl, you have a mixture, not a compound, because the sand still remains sand, and the sugar remains sugar. You can pick out grains of sand and grains of sugar. Sugar itself is a compound. If you divide a lump of sugar down to the smallest grain you can see, it is still sugar. Smaller than you can see, there is the *molecule* of sugar, which is the finest you can divide sugar and still have it remain sugar. If the molecule is broken, you no longer have sugar, but only the parts that came together to make it. There are a tremendous number of molecules in a small lump of sugar. Each tiny molecule is a compound. It contains carbon, hydrogen, and oxygen.

compound interest

Interest is payment for the use of money that belongs to somebody else. When a person borrows money from a bank he has to pay interest. When he puts money into a savings account in a bank the bank has to pay him interest, because the bank is using his money.

Compound interest is interest paid not only on money that is put in the bank but also on the interest that the bank pays. Suppose you put $100 in a savings bank and the bank pays you 2% (two percent) interest. That means the bank will pay you $2 every year for the use of your $100. But the bank agrees that it will pay you compound interest and will pay it every six months, which is half a year. At the end of six months the bank adds $1 to your $100, because that is the interest your money has earned in half a year. Now you have $101 in the bank. At the end of the next six months, the bank pays you another $1 on the $100 and also pays you 1 cent on the $1. In other words, they pay you 2% interest on your $101 instead of on the $100 you put in when you opened the account. During the next six months the bank will pay the interest on $102.01. This makes your money earn more when you leave it in a bank for a long time. Some banks compound the interest quarterly, which means every three months.

United States Savings Bonds and some other government bonds pay compound interest. In 1961 interest rates on Series E and H savings bonds were raised to 3¾% a year, compounded semi-annually.

Compromise of 1850

The Compromise of 1850 was an effort to settle the question of slavery in the western territories before the Civil War. From 1850 until the Civil War started, the major question was slavery. The South wanted slavery in the West; the North did not want slavery. The compromise was a settlement between the North and South. It stated that California would be a free, or nonslave, state. But the Mexican territory (land the United States got from Mexico at the end of the Mexican War, in 1848) would be either free or slave. It would be entirely up to the settlers whether or not they wanted slavery. On the other hand, the Compromise said that if any Northerner found an escaped slave, he must return the slave to his owner.

There was much discussion and conflict leading up to this compromise. Southern leaders such as John C. Calhoun of South Carolina were in favor of slavery anywhere in the country. Northerners such as William Seward of New York did not want it in any part of the country. Henry Clay of Kentucky and Daniel Webster were both in favor of this in-between, or compromise, settlement. It was mainly through their work that the compromise was brought about.

This compromise delayed the Civil War for several years. Both the North and South got something, although not everything they wanted. In the end, however, it was better for the North.

Compton, Arthur Holly and Karl Taylor

Arthur Holly Compton and Karl Taylor Compton, two brothers, both became celebrated as scientists and teachers.

A. H. Compton

They were born in Wooster, Ohio, Arthur in 1892 and Karl in 1887. Both stayed in Wooster until they were graduated from college. Then they both went on to do advanced study at Princeton University. Both of the Compton brothers did a lot of teaching in colleges and universities. Karl Compton became president of the Massachusetts Institute of Technology. Arthur Compton won the Nobel prize in physics in 1927 for his work in X-rays. Karl died in 1954, Arthur in 1962.

comptroller or controller

The comptroller is an officer of a corporation. He is in charge of its accounting records. The corporation's accountants work under him. He has authority over the general accountant, the tax accountants, and the cost accountants. Financial reports receive his attention, and he must approve of a report before it is passed on to the treasurer of the corporation. The comptroller actually handles much of the detail work that would be the job of the treasurer. The treasurer is then able to devote himself to working out the larger financial problems of the corporation. City governments can also have an elected official called a comptroller. His work is similar to the work of the comptroller of a corporation.

Conan Doyle, Sir Arthur

Sir Arthur Conan Doyle was a famous English writer who is best known for his stories about Sherlock Holmes, one of the greatest detective characters ever created. Holmes and his friend Dr. Watson, who tells the stories, both seem almost like real people. In fact, many readers, when they visit London, try to find the house in Baker Street where Sherlock Holmes is supposed to have lived. When you read these stories, it is very easy to picture Sherlock Holmes telling Dr. Watson how he solved some very difficult and mysterious crime. When Dr. Watson expresses admiration, Holmes says, "Elementary, my dear Watson!" You can read about this famous detective and his friend Dr. Watson in several books, including A Study in Scarlet, which was the first story about him, published in 1887.

Sir Arthur Conan Doyle was born in Edinburgh, Scotland, in 1859. He became a doctor, but later decided that he would rather write instead. Besides the Sherlock Holmes stories, he wrote many other novels, short stories, plays, poems, and histories of the Boer War in South Africa and World War I. Sir Arthur's oldest son was killed during World War I and Sir Arthur afterwards believed that he could communicate with his son's invisible spirit. Beliefs like this are called spiritualism, and Sir Arthur became a well-known spiritualist before he died in 1930.

Conant, James B.

James Bryant Conant, an important American educator and diplomat, was born in 1895, and when he grew up he became a professor of organic chemistry at Harvard University. He made many experiments in this field, and wrote several important books. From 1933 to 1953 he was president of Harvard University. In 1953, Conant left Harvard and was made United States High Commissioner to Germany. When West Germany became independent in 1955, Conant was made the first United States ambassador. He retired from this position in 1957.

concentration camp

A concentration camp is a kind of prison, but it is out in the country instead of in a city as most prisons are. Many countries have used concentration camps in which to keep large numbers of prisoners of war, but people remember concentration camps especially because of the evil ones kept by the Germans before and during World War II. In these camps the Germans put persons who criticized the government, and members of races they did not like, especially Jews. Prisoners in these German camps received very cruel treatment. They were fed so badly that they slowly starved and were made to work so hard that many died. In addition, many prisoners were tortured. Among the most notorious of these camps were Buchenwald, Belsen, and Auschwitz. After World War II, an international court tried to punish the Germans for the cruel things they had done, but most Germans said they had never heard of the concentration camps and the ones who were brought to trial said they were following orders from higher-ranking officials. The Russians and other Communist countries have labor camps at which prisoners receive the same kind of cruel treatment.

concert

A concert is playing or singing by musicians, such as an orchestra, band, or chorus, before a lot of people. Most concerts are held in public places, halls, auditoriums, and theaters. Originally the word meant "playing together" or "in concert." A modern concert has a program of several pieces of music. Great care is given to the selection of music so that everyone will like the program. When only one musician or singer performs it is really a recital, but many soloists are also said to be giving concerts.

concertina

A concertina is a little music maker. You hold it in your hands and squeeze it together. When you squeeze it, air blows through a number of metal "reeds," or flat, flexible pieces of metal. The reeds vibrate and make the sound. There are rows of keys on the six-sided boxes at the ends. When you press down the keys, or different buttons, you can play a tune. There are several different sizes of concertina, but the soprano, a small one, is the kind most often seen. The tone is beautiful, and there have been many artists who learned to play so well that they became famous. You can play violin, flute, or oboe music (parts) on the concertina, and there are also many pieces written especially for the instrument. See ACCORDION.

concerto

A concerto is music written for a solo instrument, such as a piano, violin, violoncello, or clarinet, and the orchestra. The object is to give one instrument the full opportunity to express itself. In a concerto we are shown what the instrument (and the player) can do. The first concertos were written as church music, about 400 years ago. In the early concerto grosso there were several instruments, or a group of soloists, accompanied by the full orchestra. The cadenza, or solo passage, where the player is all by himself, began about the time of Handel. Most of the cadenzas were made up by the players; but later the composers (who wrote the music) wrote them into the music.

Johann Sebastian Bach wrote his famous "Brandenburg Concertos" in a style more like symphonies (see SYMPHONY) or the concerto grosso. The modern concerto started with Mozart, who wrote nearly fifty, for piano, violin, horn, flute, oboe, bassoon, clarinet, and other instruments. Beethoven's piano concertos and his violin concerto are considered masterpieces. Practically all composers have written concertos. Two famous piano concertos are by Grieg and Tchaikovsky; famous violin concertos include those by Bruch and Mendelssohn.

conch

Conchs are a very large kind of snail that crawls about on the bottom of shallow tropical seas. Their huge spiral shells, which may be a foot long and weigh many pounds, are usually white outside and a deep rosy pink inside, and are sometimes used as door-stoppers. In some islands the tip is cut off, and they are blown like horns, giving a wonderful resonant sound. Sometimes the shells are used for making pearl buttons, or for cameos, or they may be ground up and used as lime for porcelain-making. Conch meat is tough, but makes a delicious soup. The eggs of the conch, which are laid in leathery chains, are sometimes called "sea necklaces."

Concord

Concord is a town near Boston in Massachusetts. Its population is 16,148. Beside a bridge in Concord there is a monument, and on the monument are these words from a poem by Ralph Waldo Emerson: "Here once the embattled farmers stood, and fired the shot heard round the world." Concord and its neighbor, Lexington, are towns where the first battle of the American Revolution was fought on April 19, 1775. British troops were trying to capture military stores that the colonists were keeping in Concord, but the colonists fought off the attacking Britishers, and drove them back to Boston. The story of how the colonists were warned that the British were on their way is told by Longfellow in his famous poem, "Paul Revere's Ride."

A little over a hundred years ago, some of the most famous American writers and thinkers lived in Concord. Among them were Thoreau, Hawthorne, Emerson, and Bronson Alcott and his daughter, Louisa May Alcott. The house the Alcotts lived in is still standing, and if you go to Con-

cord you can visit it and see the place where Louisa May Alcott's books *Little Men* and *Little Women* were written.

Concord, New Hampshire

Concord is the capital city of the state of New Hampshire. It is on the beautiful Merrimack River. About 30,000 people live in Concord.

They work in factories, making silverware and cloth and electric motors. Some people work in printing shops, and many men work in the granite quarries (where men take the rock from the earth), near the city. Concord is an interesting place to visit. You can see the place where Franklin Pierce had his law office before he became President of the United States, and you can visit the state capitol building. You can also enjoy the beautiful campus of St. Paul's School for Boys, and you can have a good time looking at all the things in the State Historical Society building.

Concord is an old city that began as a trading post more than two hundred years ago. Some settlers from Massachusetts built a little village that they called Pennycook, but in 1765 the people who lived there changed the name to Concord. Concord was made the state capital in 1808.

CONCORD, NEW HAMPSHIRE. Population (1970 census) 30,022. Capital of New Hampshire and county seat of Merrimack County. On Merrimack River.

concrete, a stonelike building material, made with cement: see the article on CEMENT.

condensation

Condensation means the changing of a substance to a more concentrated form. We mostly speak of gases condensing to liquids. Dew and fog are condensed water vapor from the air. When you see drops of water on the outside of a cold pitcher, you know that some of the moisture in the warm air has condensed on the pitcher. In the grocery store you can buy cans of condensed milk. This kind of milk is made by removing some of the water from ordinary milk, so that it becomes thicker. A writer can also condense a story or an article by making it shorter.

condor

The condor is one of the largest known birds. It lives in high mountains and is a strong and beautiful flier, but it is best known for the way it feeds. The condor is a member of the vulture family, and it feeds on the dead bodies of animals. Flying high in the sky, the condor can tell a carcass or a dead body from a great distance away. It swoops down and starts tearing the flesh from the bones with its sharp, curved beak. You may have seen pictures of the prairies showing the bare bones of cattle that have been picked clean by vultures. But the condor also kills and eats lambs and calves.

The condor is three to four feet long, and may have a nine-foot wingspread. It is not a pleasant sight. Its head and long throat are bare and red, and its feathers are black. Condors do not make a nest. The female lays two large white eggs on bare rock in a high, out-of-the-way place, and then the male and female birds take turns sitting on the eggs. Condors cannot take off into the air to fly unless they have space to run first. People who want to trap them set bait in a small, fenced-in place. The bird can land in the enclosure, but cannot leave it because it has no room for the run that helps it get into the air. Condors have no voice, and can only make a rasping hiss or snort.

The California condor lives in the mountains of southern California. Once there were many of these condors, but today very few are left alive. Most condors live in the high peaks of the Andes Mountains of South America. They look like the California condor, except that they have a white ruff at the base of their necks.

conducting

Conducting is a musical term that means leading an orchestra, band, choir, or any group of singers or musicians. The conductor stands in a place where all the musicians can see him, usually on a raised platform called the podium. He keeps time for the music by motions of his arms. Most conductors use a stick, which is called a baton, but many just use their hands and arms. Conducting is the hardest thing to learn in music. The conductor must know the score, which is the music with all the parts in it, and he must be able to hear what every musician is doing, all at the same time. With signals and gestures, he lets each player know when he is playing too loud or too soft, or just right. At the same time he controls the tempo of the music so that it is not too fast or too slow, but just right. Conducting is very important in music, for no matter how good an orchestra may be, it cannot play well without a good conductor.

conductor

A conductor is something through which electricity can flow easily. We usually mean a metal when we talk about conductors, but many other things, even your body, will conduct electricity. The best metal conductor is silver, but it costs so much that we usually use copper, which lets electricity flow through it almost as easily as silver. The opposite of a conductor is an insulator, which is a material that will not let electricity flow through it.

A good example of both conductors and insulators is the cord that runs from the wall socket to a lamp in your home. In the center of this cord there is a copper wire (usually two of them) which lets the electricity flow from the socket to the lamp. Covering this wire is a layer of rubber or a plastic that acts as an insulator so you can touch the cord without getting a shock. You can find out more about how conductors and insulators are used by reading the separate article in this encyclopedia on ELECTRICITY.

cone

An ice-cream cone is so called because it is just the shape of what mathematicians mean by a cone. Think of the ice-cream cone filled up and solid; the cir-

cular mouth then becomes the *base*. A line joining the center of this base with the *apex* (point) of the cone is the *axis*. Since this axis is at right angles to the base, and the base is a circle, the cone is called *right circular*. If the axis is not at right angles to the base, the cone is *oblique*. The base may be an oval, or any other curved shape (but not outlined by straight lines, for then the solid is called a pyramid).

The right circular cone has interested mathematicians since the time of the ancient Greeks, because cutting it produces certain important curves called *conic sections*. If you cut it in half parallel to the base, the section is of course another circle, smaller than the base. But tilt the cut a little and you have an *ellipse*, a kind of oval. Tilt even more so that you cut into the base and the section is an open curve called a *hyperbola*, or, in the special case where you made the cut parallel to the side of the cone, a *parabola*.

A cone (3) is a shape you can see in an ice-cream cone or in a carrot. It has slanted sides (S) and the distance from top to bottom is called its altitude or height (H). If you cut the cone with a knife (P) to the base, you will make various conic sections: an ellipse (E4); a hyperbola (H1), and a parabola (L2).

cone, the fruit of trees called conifers, such as pine and spruce: see the article on CONIFERS.

Conestoga wagon, a broad-wheeled covered wagon named for Conestoga, Pennsylvania, in the United States: see the article on COVERED WAGON.

Confederate States of America (the Confederacy)

The Confederate States of America, or the Confederacy, is the name taken by eleven states that seceded (withdrew) from the United States, formed their own government, and fought a war against the United States in the years 1861 to 1865. That war is now called the Civil War, but at one time the people who lived in the states that were members of the Confederacy preferred to call it the War for Southern Independence, or the War Between the States. The original United States, also spoken of as the Union, or the North, won the war and so the Confederate States of America came to an end.

REASON FOR THE CONFEDERACY

All the states of the Confederacy were

southern states. In these states Negroes were slaves and worked in fields raising cotton, on which the prosperity of the South depended. For fifty years there had been arguments in the United States between people of the North, who thought slavery was wrong and wanted to outlaw it, and people in the South, who wanted to keep their slaves. In 1860 Abraham Lincoln was elected President of the United States and the southerners believed he would try to outlaw slavery, which he opposed. The southern states said that they had joined the United States of their own free will, and so they had a right to leave it if they wanted to. In December, 1860, a month after Lincoln was elected, South Carolina seceded. By February, 1861, six other states had seceded—Florida, Georgia, Alabama, Mississippi, Louisiana, and Texas. Representatives of these states met in Montgomery, Alabama, and formed the Confederate States of America, with Montgomery as the first capital. Jefferson Davis of Mississippi was elected President and Alexander Stephens of Georgia became Vice-President.

President Lincoln and the Congress of the United States did not agree that these states had a right to secede. Lincoln raised an army to force the southern states back into the Union, and the Civil War had begun. Four other southern states then seceded and joined the Confederacy—Arkansas, North Carolina, Virginia, and Tennessee. The capital of the Confederacy was moved to Richmond, Virginia.

The Confederate States adopted a Constitution much like that of the United States, except that it gave the states more rights and made sure that no law could be passed against slavery. The Confederate government issued its own money and raised armies much as the North did.

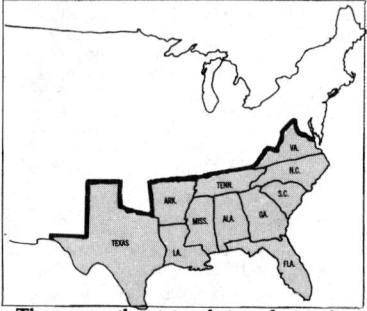

These were the states that made up the Confederate States during the Civil War.

Map by Keville Foley

PROBLEMS OF THE CONFEDERACY

The big problem of the Confederacy was to persuade foreign countries to recognize it as an independent country and to lend it money. The best chance was England, because many English manufacturers of cloth needed the cotton grown by the Confederate states. But many other people in England were against slavery, and besides the Union forces had such a strong navy that they could blockade southern seaports and prevent the South from shipping cotton to England. The Confederacy did sell $15,000,000 worth of bonds in England.

Unable to enlist foreign help, the Confederates had to fight the war all alone. The North was much stronger in the resources that count in warfare—factories, iron ore, and coal—and the Confederate armies never really had a chance.

Many of the wisest statesmen and best generals were southerners, and they chose to be loyal to their states rather than to the Federal government; but they quarreled among themselves and many mistakes were made in running the Confederate government and fighting the war. Confederate cotton rotted in the barns and Confederate money and bonds became worthless. By 1865, the North had won the Civil War. Most of the Confederate statesmen and generals were threatened with imprisonment, but nothing was actually done to them. The Confederacy just ceased to exist, slavery was ended, and the southern states rejoined the United States.

There are separate articles about the important men of the Confederate States, especially DAVIS, STEPHENS, Robert E. LEE, Judah P. BENJAMIN, and others. See also the article on the CIVIL WAR.

Confederation, Articles of, the first constitution that was agreed on by the thirteen original states of the United States in 1781: see the article CONTINENTAL CONGRESS.

Confucius

Confucius, a great Chinese religious teacher, is famous for his rules of good government and of daily conduct. He 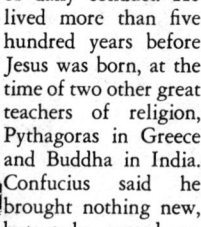 lived more than five hundred years before Jesus was born, at the time of two other great teachers of religion, Pythagoras in Greece and Buddha in India. Confucius said he brought nothing new, but only passed on what the ancients knew. He believed that the wisdom taught in the past could help men in the present and bring about a happy or Golden Age. He traveled over China, teaching, studying, and gathering followers. He taught this good rule: "What I do not wish men to do to me, I also wish not to do to men." Confucius thought that people should learn to find the true rule of life within themselves, helped by the directions of wise men.

Congo, People's Republic of the

Situated in west central Africa, the People's Republic of the Congo became independent in 1960. Formerly it was one of the four territories of French Equatorial Africa and had the name of Middle Congo. The People's Republic of the Congo has an area of 132,046 square miles, which is about twice the size of Missouri. Brazzaville is the capital city.

The economy of the country is based mainly on its agricultural exports such as palm oil, cocoa, bananas, coffee, and peanuts. Rain forests cover a large amount of land, and their wood products are also important exports. Efforts are being made to industrialize the country. The vast majority of the population is made up of different tribal groups, and they speak different variations of Bantu language.

At the present time, the People's Republic of the Congo favors SOCIALISM, a form of government in which the people share the work, the property, and the profits. The country's first two presidents were overthrown, and now the president's power is limited.

PEOPLE'S REPUBLIC OF THE CONGO. Area, 132,046 square miles. Population (UN estimate 1973) 960,000. Capital, Brazzaville (population 136,200).

Congo (Zaire) River

The Congo River was the name used for the Zaire River before October 27, 1971. Nearly 3,000 miles long, it is the second-longest river in Africa. David Livingstone was the first white man to explore its tributaries and Sir Henry Stanley was the first to sail all the way to its mouth.

Congregational Church

Congregationalists are members of a Protestant Christian denomination. The Congregational Churches were first established in England about 350 years ago. Their members were first known as Puritans because they believed that the state church of that day needed to be purified. They were persecuted, and many of them fled to Holland. In 1620 some of them sailed for the New World on the Mayflower. They are known in history as the Pilgrim Fathers. The Congregational Churches had the largest membership in New England, and from there spread to all parts of the world. About two hundred years ago, during the period known as the Great Awakening, religious revivals swept over the United States. Such Congregationalists as Jonathan Edwards, the religious writer, were very important in promoting religion. Congregationalists founded many important colleges, among which are Harvard, Yale, Dartmouth, Amherst, Oberlin, and Hampton Institute. In the Hawaiian Islands, Congregational missionaries taught the people to read and write.

UNITED CHURCH OF CHRIST

In 1931 the Congregational Churches merged with the General Convention of the Christian Church and in 1957 they merged with the Evangelical Reformed Church, forming a combined Church called the United Church of Christ, which had 2,022,090 members in 1960. One of their official publications, *Missionary Herald,* is the oldest religious magazine in the United States. In this Church each congregation decides its own doctrines, based on fundamental Christian belief.

Congressional Record

The Congressional Record is a sort of newspaper published by the United States government every day the Congress meets to do its work of making the laws of the country. The Record tells what laws Congress has talked about or passed each day and who has voted for or against each. It also prints every speech that any member of Congress makes. A member may also have printed in it a speech he has written but did not actually make. These daily reports are then gathered together and bound into big books that form a permanent history of each session of Congress. Often a Congressman will want the people of his district to know what he has been doing. He sends them copies of the Congressional Record with a speech of his in it. The Congressional Record got its name in 1875. Before that time the records of Congress had other names, such as Annals of Con-

gress, Register of Debates, and Congressional Globe.

Congress of Industrial Organizations

The Congress of Industrial Organizations, also called the C.I.O., was one of the two big organizations of labor unions in the United States. The other was the American Federation of Labor (A.F. of L.). In 1955 they united.

A labor union is a group formed by men who do the same kind of work. It tries to get better wages, shorter hours, and other good working conditions for its members. There are two kinds of labor union, the craft union and the industrial union. Members of craft unions usually have a skilled trade. Printers, carpenters and musicians belong to craft unions. Members of an industrial union usually work in factories or mills. Steel workers and clothing workers are examples of people who belong to industrial unions.

The A.F. of L., which was formed many years before the C.I.O., was made up mainly of craft unions. In 1935 millions of factory and mill workers did not belong to any labor union. Several leaders of the A.F. of L. wanted to bring these workers into A.F. of L. unions. Other A.F. of L. leaders did not want these people in their unions because they were not craft workers. Then eight unions left the A.F. of L. and started the Committee for Industrial Organization. They quickly took thousands of workers into what they called the C.I.O. Later, when the C.I.O. was big and well organized, they wanted to change its name to something that sounded more permanent, but they wanted to keep the initials C.I.O. because everybody knew them. So they decided on Congress of Industrial Organizations.

The C.I.O. has done much to help factory and mill workers make a good living. In 1953 about five million people belonged to the unions that made up the C.I.O. The three largest unions were the United Automobile Workers (about 1,350,000 members), the United Steel Workers (more than 1,000,000), and the Amalgamated Clothing Workers (about 385,000). In 1938 the C.I.O. elected its first president, John L. Lewis. When Lewis resigned in 1940, Philip Murray became president. When he died in 1952, the C.I.O. elected as president Walter P. Reuther, who became vice-president of the combined A.F.L. & C.I.O. in 1955.

Congress of the United States

The Congress of the United States is the law-making, or legislative, part of the government. It represents everybody in the country, and every citizen of voting age can vote for the people he wants to represent him. Congress is divided into two houses. One of them is called the House of Representatives and the other one is called the Senate. Every member of Congress is really a Congressman. Those who are in the House of Representatives are called Representatives. Those who are in the Senate are called Senators. Each Congressman receives a salary of $30,000 a year. The Representatives are elected for two years. The number of Representatives from each

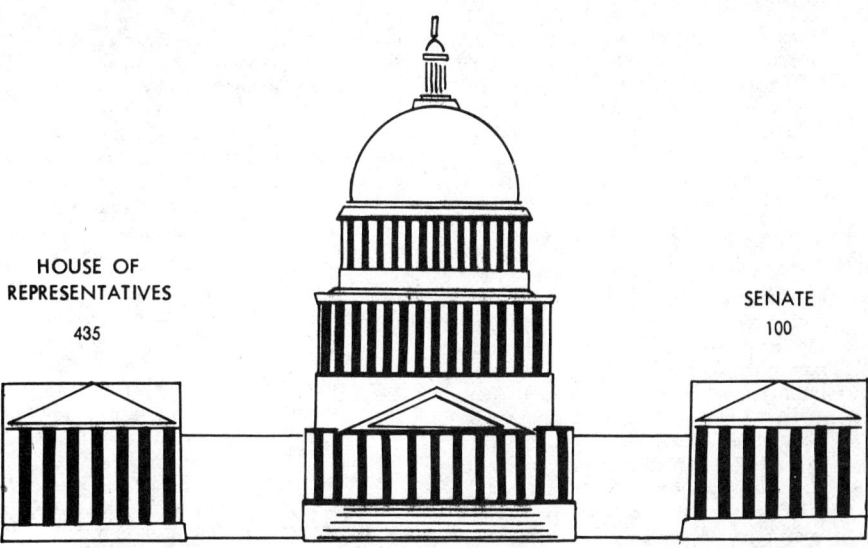

HOUSE OF REPRESENTATIVES
435

SENATE
100

A chart showing the two houses of Congress and the number of members in each house. Both houses meet in the Capitol, the most famous building in Washington, D.C.

state is based on the number of people living in the state. Senators are elected for six years. There are always two from each state. Therefore a small state has as much power in the Senate as a large state. But a state with many people in it has a better chance to express its opinions than a state with fewer people, because the state with more people has more Representatives in the House. Congress is required to meet at least once a year. The President may call special sessions after the regular one is over.

POWERS OF CONGRESS

Congress has the right to make laws. When Congress was first organized under the Constitution, some people wanted the state governments to have the greater power, and other people wanted the Federal government to have the greater power. Finally they decided that the central government should be stronger than the state, and they gave Congress the power to do certain things. Congress can make tax laws. It can borrow money and coin, or make, money. It can regulate foreign trade and trade between the states. It can declare war and set up an army and a navy. One of the most important powers of Congress is merely suggested by the Constitution, which says that Congress can make any law that is necessary to carry out the other powers the Constitution has given it.

The House of Representatives has certain powers that the Senate does not have. When the country wants to raise money, the House of Representatives must take the first move. Since there are more members in the House of Representatives, it is actually the people of the country who control the purse strings. The House is the only part of the government that has the right to accuse the President or other Federal officials of a crime. In some cases, the House may also elect the President. This happens when no candidate receives a majority vote in the Electoral College. It has happened only once (in 1824).

The Senate has certain powers and duties that the House does not have. The Senate has the right to approve or disapprove of anyone the President may appoint to a high office Two-thirds of

the Senate must approve of any treaty made with a foreign power. This gives the Senate much power in the field of foreign relations. The Senate may elect the Vice President when the Electoral College has not done so. When a President or Federal official is accused of a crime or impeached, the Senate acts as the jury to decide whether or not the accusation is true.

The House of Representatives and the Senate are both equally important, however. Sometimes the House is said to lean on the Senate for stability. The Representatives come up for election every two years, so they have to pay more attention to the voters in their states than Senators who are elected every six years. Sometimes a Representative will ask for a law that only a few people in his state want. The Senators may block this law if they feel that not enough people want it. But no law can be passed unless both the Senate and the House of Representatives want it.

ORGANIZATION OF CONGRESS

Congress has a large amount of work to do every year. Without some sort of organization, this work could never be completed. To help organize the work of Congress, there is a leader for the House and for the Senate. The leader of the House is called the Speaker. The Speaker is usually chosen by the party that has more members in the House at that time. The Vice President of the United States is president of the Senate. The Senate also chooses a president who takes the Vice President's place when he is not there.

The House has different rules from the Senate. The Speaker of the House has more authority than the Vice President has in the Senate. He can refuse to call on someone who wants to talk. A member of the House of Representatives may talk for only one hour. A member of the Senate may talk for as long as he wants to. If a Senator does not want the Senate to vote on some bill, he can hold up the voting by talking. He does not have to say anything important just as long as he talks. This is called a filibuster. The only way to stop a filibuster is to use the cloture rule. This rule says that if two-thirds of the Senate agree, the speaker can be limited to one hour, as in the

House. You can read more about this in the article FILIBUSTER.

Congress does much of its work in committees. There are fifteen committees in the Senate and nineteen in the House. These committees study all the bills and make a report on them. It saves the time of many people.

HOW A BILL IS PASSED

Committees play a very important part in lawmaking. For example, a bill for raising money starts in the House. The House will vote on it. If it is passed, it is sent to the Senate. The Senate gives the bill to the Senate Finance Committee to study and report on it. If the committee likes the bill, it sends a favorable report to the Senate. The Senate then votes on it. If a majority of the Senators like the bill, it goes to the President to be signed. Sometimes, however, the Senate Finance Committee may not like the bill. Usually then the Senate will not pass it. The committee may make changes or amendments to the bill and send it back to the House. Sometimes a special conference committee is set up, with members from both the House and the Senate. They will try to reach an agreement. If the committee makes changes the bill must be voted on again, both in the House and Senate.

Sometimes it is hard to understand how Congress can get so much work done. It represents every person in the United States and many different ideas and interests. But Congress is well organized, and Congressmen realize that they cannot always get what they want for their own states or sections. They know how to compromise, and most of them try to do what is best for the people as a whole. They are elected by the people and they are governing for the people. It is only through the Congress that this can be done.

conifer

Conifers are a large group of trees and shrubs that bear their seeds in cones or small fleshy fruits. The pine and fir trees are conifers. The fruit of these trees are typical cones. The yew and the juniper, also conifers, have berries instead of cones. Some conifers have both male and female cones, and the female cone is fertilized by pollen blown from the male cone. Often this pollen fills the air and covers the countryside with a yellow dust. When the seeds of the conifer develop, they also are scattered by the wind. Conifer berries are scattered by birds.

Most conifers grow straight and tall, in the shape of a Christmas tree. They have long needle-shaped leaves that are evergreen, that is, they are not shed in the fall. However, there are exceptions to these rules. The yew, for example, has ordinary looking leaves, and the larch sheds its leaves. Conifers grow chiefly in cool climates, where they form vast forests. Their wood contains resin, but it is light, strong, and of even grain. It is the most important wood in the world for building, furniture, and other wood products, and is the chief source of pulp for making paper, cardboard, processed wood, and many other things. Conifers are often very beautiful, and are planted in parks and gardens, in hedges, and to shelter other plants from the wind.

There are about a hundred kinds of conifer in North America, including the arbor vitae, cedar, cypress, fir, hemlock, larch, redwood, spruce, and the southern pines. The southern pines furnish about half the wood used for making paper, and nearly all the turpentine and rosin.

conjunction

Conjunction means the joining together of two things. In grammar, which is the study of the forms of words, a conjunction is a word used to connect other words or groups of words. *And, but,* and *or* are conjunctions that can connect independent clauses (groups of words that can stand alone), as in the sentence: "Mary is good, but John is bad." *Because, though* and *if* are conjunctions that can connect an independent clause with a clause that cannot stand alone, as in the sentence, "I will go if he comes."

The word *conjunction* is also used in astronomy, which is the study of the stars. When we say stars and planets are in conjunction, we do not mean they actually come together. Though they look close to each other, they are really millions of miles apart. We mean that they pass each other, so that we see them directly below or above each other. Astronomers have found that once a month the sun and the moon are in conjunction. An eclipse, when we see the moon pass across the face of the sun, is another kind of conjunction.

conjunctivitis

Conjunctivitis is an inflammation or soreness of the lining of the eyelids. This inflammation does not affect your ability to see, but it causes a painful swelling and itching of the eyelids. The eyes water, and a sticky matter collects in the corners. This may cause your eyelids to stick together, especially when you wake up in the morning.

The important thing is not to rub your eyes, or touch them with your fingers. A doctor will give you an eyewash or salve that will clear up the inflammation, usually in a short time.

Connecticut

Connecticut is one of the New England States in the eastern part of the United States. It was one of the thirteen original colonies, and its laws were so well planned that they were used as a model for parts of the Constitution of the United States when it was written. That is why Connecticut is nicknamed the "Constitution State." There is an amusing story about how it also came to be called the "Nutmeg State." Many years ago, so it is told, the Connecticut peddlers would travel to little towns and settlements, selling all kinds of useful articles to the people. One of the things they sold was nutmeg, which was used by the women in cooking. These salesmen were clever people, but not always as honest as they might have been. Some of them made the little brown nutmegs out of wood and sold them for real ones to the housewives. That is why Connecticut is called the "Nutmeg State."

Connecticut is very small and ranks 48th in size among the states, having 4,899 square miles. In population it ranks 24th; nearly three million people live there. The name Connecticut was first given to the Connecticut River by the Indians, who called it *Quonectakut,* which means "long river." Later it became the name of the state.

THE PEOPLE OF CONNECTICUT

Until about three hundred years ago, Connecticut was a wilderness, where Indian tribes roamed. The first white people to explore the territory were Dutch traders, but the first people to settle there were Puritans who had first come to Massachusetts from England. They mostly became farmers, though some of the people became the earliest manufacturers in the United States. The people of Connecticut have always been known as peace-loving, steady and hard-working. Since the Civil War, Connecticut has become a great business and manufacturing center, and people from many European countries have flocked to this state to work in the factories. They have come largely from Italy, Poland, Germany, Canada, and England, and today about one out of every five persons living in Connecticut is foreign-born.

The people living in New England were called "Yankees," and the Connecticut Yankee was known for his shrewdness and for his great ability to invent things Many of the things people use every day were invented by someone from Connecticut. Eli Terry and Seth Thomas improved the modern clock; the locks people have on their front doors were invented by Linus Yale; and a machine to make pins and needles was built by John Ireland Howe. Samuel Colt of Connecticut invented the revolver. Other men from Connecticut built the first steamboat and improved the submarine.

So many things were first made in Connecticut that it is difficult to imagine what people would have done without this little state. It was the first to make silk thread, tacks, bicycles, hats, carpets, shaving soap, inexpensive watches, and nuts and bolts, among many other things. Today three out of four people live in the cities, working in offices, and in the factories that produce some of the most important articles used all over the country.

Many people are also farmers in the fertile valleys around the rivers. They produce dairy products and raise tobacco, fruits, and vegetables. Other people who live in the southern part, along the coast, depend on fishing in the Atlantic Ocean and Long Island Sound, where oysters and lobsters are found.

The largest Church in the state is the Roman Catholic. The largest Protestant Churches are the Congregational and Episcopal.

WHAT CONNECTICUT IS LIKE

Connecticut is a beautiful state, with a wide, fertile region in the central part, and with hilly, wooded regions in the eastern and western parts. The central region is in the valley of the Connecticut River, where the farmers raise tobacco, eggs, chickens, fruits and vegetables. The tobacco they grow is a special kind called

New Haven, Connecticut.

Connecticut broadleaf. It has to be covered with white cheesecloth to protect it, so, from a distance, these tobacco fields look like fields of snow. In this section you can also see the great tobacco sheds where the tobacco leaves hang from the ceiling to dry, and give off a very pleasant, sweet odor.

The eastern part of the state has low hills covered with trees. There are also some fertile valleys. The western section is somewhat the same, with rocky soil that makes farming difficult. Bear Mountain is in the western part of Connecticut and is the highest point in the state. The southwestern corner of Connecticut is so near New York City that people can live in Connecticut and work in New York by traveling back and forth on fast trains. This has given Connecticut the name of the "Suburb State."

Connecticut is not important for its mining, but some granite, sandstone, and limestone are found in the hills. An unusual sport is enjoyed in the Black Rocks Hills, outside Waterbury, where people practice mountain climbing because the rocks are so much like those in the high Rocky Mountains and in the Alps.

People found that the Connecticut River and the Housatonic River had rapids and waterfalls, which could supply water power, and so they built the first factories along these rivers. Today in many parts of the state, there are large cities which are the chief source of Connecticut's wealth. In Waterbury, persons can see the largest brass-producing factories in the United States. At Thompsonville is the largest carpet manufacturing plant in the country; and Connecticut ranks first in the making of needles and pins, typewriters, and clocks. One of the largest submarine bases in the world is at Groton; there are more insurance companies in Hartford than in any other city in the world. It can be seen, then, how important Connecticut is. Among its many other products are hats, cotton and woolen goods, and airplanes.

The climate of Connecticut is healthful and varied. The winters are cold and severe, with heavy snows in the mountains. The temperature can drop as low as 15 degrees below zero. In the summer, the temperature can rise to 100 degrees, though it is usually about 69 degrees.

The New York, New Haven, and Hartford railroad goes through Connecticut, carrying people to most parts of the state. There are also airports; and the rivers can be used by barges and oil tankers.

THE GOVERNMENT OF CONNECTICUT

Connecticut is governed by a Governor and a legislature called a General Assembly. The governor is elected for a four-year term. The Assembly is composed of a senate and a house of representatives, the members of which are elected for a two-year term. Judges are appointed by the Assembly, and they serve eight-year terms. The capital is Hartford. There are eight counties in the state.

From the very earliest days, the people of Connecticut were concerned about giving their children an education, and they quickly built free schools for them. They were the first to build a children's library and a school for girls. Elementary education is free for all children between the ages of 4 and 16 years, and compulsory between the ages of 7 and 16 years. There are about 646,000 pupils enrolled in the public elementary and high schools. Among the most important colleges and universities are:

University of Connecticut, at Storrs. Enrollment, 17,510 in 1971 (co-ed).

Trinity College, at Hartford. Enrollment, 1,840 in 1971 (co-ed).

Wesleyan University, at Middletown. Enrollment, 1,435 in 1971 (co-ed).

Connecticut College for Women, at New London. Enrollment, 1,695 in 1971.

Yale University, at New Haven. Enrollment, 8,665 in 1971 (men only).

CHIEF CITIES OF CONNECTICUT

The leading cities of Connecticut, with populations from the 1970 census, are:

Hartford, population 158,017, the state capital and largest city. There is a separate article about HARTFORD in this encyclopedia.

Bridgeport, population 156,542, second-largest city, manufacturing center, in the southwestern part of the state.

New Haven, population 137,707, third-largest city. There is a separate article about NEW HAVEN in this encyclopedia.

Waterbury, population 108,033, fourth-largest city, manufacturing center, in the west central part of the state.

CONNECTICUT IN THE PAST

The story of how Connecticut grew is part of the dramatic history of how the United States itself grew. Although it is not as old as Massachusetts, where the first English settlers came, it is not many years younger.

Connecticut was a territory of Indians until the Dutch came and set up trading posts. However, the first permanent settlement was made in 1633, by Puritans from the Massachusetts Bay Colony. They were dissatisfied with the strict laws in the Bay Colony, and they had heard about the fertile soil in Connecticut. A small group made the difficult journey in winter, but when they arrived, they discovered that the river was frozen, preventing their supply ship from reaching them. That winter the settlers suffered. Sometimes they had nothing to eat but acorns, and many of them died.

In the next four years, other people from Massachusetts came and started settlements in Connecticut, but they wisely made the journey in summer. Some of the settlements joined together to protect themselves from Indian attacks; and finally they all joined into the colony of Connecticut, under a charter given to them by Charles II of England. This charter allowed the people to govern themselves, without interference from the king.

However, when the next king of England, James II, came to the throne, he tried to take back the charters of the American colonies, and he put these people under the rule of a royal governor, Sir Edmund Andros. When this governor came and tried to seize the charter, the people put out all the lights, and quickly carried the charter into the woods, where they hid it in the hollow of a large oak tree. Ever since, this tree has been known as the Charter Oak. You can read about the CHARTER OAK in a separate article in this encyclopedia.

The people of Connecticut took an active part in the American Revolution, sending 30,000 men to fight under General Washington against the British. Connecticut contributed more men and money for its size than any other colony. One of the outstanding patriots of the Revolution was Ethan Allen, who organized the "Green Mountain Boys." You can read about ALLEN in a separate article. One of the most dramatic stories of the war was that of Benedict Arnold, an army officer born in Connecticut who tried to betray the American army to the British. You can read about ARNOLD in a separate article.

After the Revolution, Connecticut was the fifth state to adopt the United States Constitution.

The people of Connecticut were strongly against the War of 1812, but they contributed men and money to it.

In the Civil War, the soldiers from Connecticut distinguished themselves on all the battlefields; and the governor of the state, William A. Buckingham, was one of President Lincoln's most trusted advisers.

After the Civil War, Connecticut grew rapidly from a farming state into a prosperous manufacturing and business center. Today it not only leads in manufacturing many articles, but it has also become a favorite vacation spot because of its beautiful scenery, its fine beaches, and its fishing and boating.

FAMOUS PEOPLE FROM CONNECTICUT

More famous inventors have come from Connecticut than from almost any other state. In addition to the men mentioned in other sections of this article are John Fitch, who made the first steamboat, Samuel Colt, who perfected the revolver, Charles Goodyear, who discovered a practical way of hardening rubber, called vulcanizing, and David Bushnell and Simon Lake, who made improvements on the submarine. Eli Whitney, who invented the cotton gin, made his home in Connecticut.

The famous circus man, Phineas T. Barnum, was born there, as was Noah Webster, who wrote the first American dictionary.

Many important people also made Connecticut their home, including the writers Harriet Beecher Stowe and Mark Twain.

PLACES TO SEE IN CONNECTICUT

Devil's Hopyard State Park, 860 acres, 7 miles east of East Haddam, on State Highway 85. Rugged ravine, five waterfalls, unusual rock formations; hiking trails and picnic grounds.

Fort Shantok State Park, 177 acres, 4 miles south of Norwich, on State Highway 12. Once the site of an old Mohegan Indian village. Contains the remains of the old Shantok Indian fort, and the Shantok burial ground, now surrounded by a log stockade.

Colonial Museum, in Israel Putnam Memorial Campground, 5 miles southeast of Danbury, on State Highway 58. Contains many interesting relics from the Revolutionary War.

Barnum Institute of Science and History, in Bridgeport, on U.S. Route 1. Contains personal belongings of P. T. Barnum, born in this city, and of Tom Thumb, the 26-inch midget who was the star attraction of Barnum's circus.

Travelers Tower, in Hartford, on U.S. Route 6. The highest building in New England, 527 feet high.

Children's Museum, in Hartford, on U.S. Route 6. Contains fossils, shells, insects, birds, animals, and things of interest about the Indians of North America.

CONNECTICUT. Area, 4,899 square miles. Population (1970 census) 3,031,709. Capital, Hartford. Nickname, the Constitution State. Motto, *Qui Transtulit Sustinet* (He Who Transplanted Sustains). Flower, mountain laurel. Bird, robin. Entered the Union, January 9, 1788. Official abbreviation, Conn.

Connecticut River

The Connecticut River is the largest river in the New England region of the United States. The river flows south from the Canadian border, in northern New Hampshire, and forms the border between New Hampshire and Vermont. It continues south through Massachusetts and Connecticut and empties into Long Island Sound halfway between New Haven and New London, Connecticut. People have built factories along the Connecticut River because the dams at many places furnish water power to make electricity. Farmers who live in the river valley in Massachusetts and Connecticut have some of the best, most level land in New England. They grow many crops including tobacco, vegetables and grains. Early settlers and fur traders used the river as their chief passage between the northland and the sea. Steamers can go up the Connecticut River as far as Hartford, Connecticut, and small boats as far as Holyoke, Massachusetts.

Conrad, Joseph

Joseph Conrad was born in Poland in 1857 and went to school there. His name was really Teodor Jozef Konrad Korzeniowski, but when he went to England as a young man  he decided his middle names would be enough. He went to sea when he was only 17, and he became a master mariner in the British merchant fleet ten years later. Two years later he became a British subject. After twenty years at sea, his head was full of his adventures, and his heart was full of a desire to share them with others. He retired from the sea and became a writer of adventure books. Among his greatest books are *Almayer's Folly, An Outcast of the Islands, The Nigger of the Narcissus* (which was first called *The Children of the Sea*), and *Lord Jim.* Although English was not his native language, he wrote very well, making use of his experiences at sea, as well as his own vivid imagination. His books are favorites to this day with everyone, young or old, who loves adventure. He died in 1924.

conscientious objector

A conscientious objector is a person who does not believe in war and refuses to become a soldier. Some people are conscientious objectors because of their religion. Others do not believe that war solves any problems. A true conscientious objector is convinced that he is right in refusing to become a possible killer of other men.

Conscientious objectors first became a problem in the United States during World War I, because the draft law said that male citizens had to serve in the armed forces. There is a separate article about DRAFT in this encyclopedia. Before the draft, soldiers were volunteers who wanted to fight. But in World War I the government needed so many men that it had to draft them. There were no plans for men who refused to join the army, so most of the conscientious objectors were sent to jail. People called them "slackers" who were afraid of battle.

WORLD WAR II RECORD

In World War II, another draft law was passed, and this time the government made allowances for the conscientious objectors. About 100,000 of the men drafted in the United States were objectors—four times as many as in World War I. Some of these men were willing to be members of medical units, where they did not have to carry guns. These conscientious objectors drove ambulances and tended the wounded at the front lines. Some volunteered for dangerous medical experiments, firefighting, and work in mental hospitals. This showed they were sincere in their beliefs. Other conscientious objectors were sent to government camps.

conscription is the drafting of men into military service: see the article on DRAFT.

conservation

Every country has what are called natural resources. These natural resources are the wealth of the country itself. Coal, iron, copper and other minerals are natural resources of the United States. So are the mighty forests that cover parts of the land; the rich soil on which crops can be grown; and the rivers that wind through the countryside. If all the minerals had been dug up or wasted, the forests cut down, the rich soil blown or washed away, and the rivers dried up, the United States would be a very poor country and could not support its millions of people. All this can easily happen if the citizens of the United States do not take care of their natural resources.

Conservation means "saving." With minerals, it means not mining more than we need and not wasting any that we mine. With forests, it means planting enough trees so that every year there will be as many new trees, ready to cut, as are needed. With farm lands, it means taking care of the soil so that it remains fertile and so that it will not be blown away by the winds or washed away by the rivers.

HOW NATURAL RESOURCES ARE WASTED

Much of America's natural wealth has already been wasted. When the first European settlers arrived, most of the land was covered with forests of huge trees. Most of the trees were cut down and until about fifty years ago no new ones were planted to replace them. Even today, not enough new trees are planted and there is danger that the forests will soon be used up. As an example of how much wood is used, every day that a big newspaper is published several thousand trees have to be cut to make the paper.

Trees are also important because in various ways they protect the soil. Their roots hold the soil together and prevent it from being washed away. Then their branches break the force of the rain and hold a lot of the water, so that it only drips slowly to the ground. This is very important, because where trees have been cleared the water runs off the ground so fast that it carries a great deal of the soil with it. This is called erosion. Every year erosion strips America of as much soil as there is on 73,000 farms of 40 acres each. When the water runs off the ground very

Hopefully, this scene of natural beauty will be preserved, so that future generations can also enjoy its scenic splendor. Fortunately, more and more people recognize the need to preserve the remaining spots of unspoiled beauty.

fast it also causes floods. Floods occur when the river channels cannot carry away all the water that comes down at once. Every year America loses millions of dollars from floods. Most of these floods would not occur if the forests that used to hold back the rain water had not been cut down.

Another result of cutting down forests is that the climate becomes drier. In southeast Australia much less rain falls each year than fifty years ago. This is because the forests have been cleared. Scientists believe that even the great Sahara desert once had trees growing on it. In the sands of the Sahara there are buried cities that show that the desert was once a rich and fertile land. Probably many of the great deserts of the world have been caused by men who did not understand the need for conservation.

In America there are vast regions where there is too little rain for forests to grow. Instead the country is covered with grass. These grasslands are called the prairies. They are even more easily turned into desert than forest country. When too many cattle are grazed on the prairie, the grass is all eaten away and the soil is left bare. Too much plowing also can leave the soil bare. When the soil is bare it becomes dry and turns into dust. Then the dust is blown away by the wind. This has happened in huge parts of the central United States that are now called the Dust Bowl. Because the soil has blown away, the farmers in the Dust Bowl cannot grow their crops.

There is no reason except thoughtless greed for any of this waste. If we are wise we must try to stop it by showing the farmers how they can use their land without destroying it. This is all part of conservation.

CONSERVING MINERALS

We can grow plants again, but what are we to do about our mineral resources? Once we have dug up minerals we can never put them back in the ground again.

There is only one way to conserve our minerals, and that is to use them carefully and wisely. Our greatest mineral resources are oil, iron, coal, natural gas, copper, lead, zinc, gold, and silver. Already America has to import many of these to meet her needs. We can no longer produce enough ourselves. By mining these minerals in better ways, and by saving what is now wasted, we will be able to do a lot to conserve our mineral wealth.

WHAT WE HAVE DONE

Conservation can be practiced only if we understand the laws of nature. Usually conservation requires many years of hard work. It cannot be begun and then stopped, then started again. For all these reasons it is best if conservation is done by the government of the United States or of the various states of the Union. Because the United States is so rich, we wasted many of our resources before we even began to think of conservation. Poorer countries had conserved their resources for hundreds of years. But people in America began to think of conservation only about fifty years ago. While Theodore Roosevelt was president, the National Conservation Commission was set up, and huge sections of land were set aside as forest reserves and National Parks. Since then many other things have been done to save our wealth, but even now there are huge losses every year from forest fires, waste, and bad methods of farming. Because the future of our country depends on conservation, every citizen should do what he can to help it.

Conservative Party

The Conservative Party is one of the two main political parties in Britain. The party was started about a hundred years ago by Benjamin Disraeli, a British statesman. It carried on the ideas of the Tory Party which had started two hundred years earlier. Conservatives liked old and traditional things. They liked the king.

They thought that the aristocracy, or upper classes, should rule because they always had ruled. They wanted the Church of England to be the most powerful church in England because it had been for the last several centuries.

But the Conservatives realized that they had to do things for everyone, not just the wealthy classes. So they took ideas from the opposing political party, the Liberal Party, and they used these ideas for their own. It was the Conservative Party that gave the working man the right to vote. Today the Conservatives have became more and more like the Liberals. They are democratic and try to help the lower classes as well as the aristocracy. Sir Winston Churchill became the leading Conservative. The opposite of the British Conservative Party today is the Labour Party. The Labourite wants government ownership and management of industry. The Conservative wants private ownership and management.

A person who is cautious about new ideas and seems to like the old ones better is sometimes called a conservative. This does not mean that he is a member of a special political party. It simply describes his way of thinking.

consonant

A consonant is a sound that you make by moving your tongue, teeth or lips in certain ways to stop or interfere with the flow of air out of your mouth. All the letters of the English alphabet are consonants except a, e, i, o, and u, and sometimes y and w, which are called VOWELS and are the subject of a separate article. Different consonants have special names, such as *dentals* (made by using the teeth, as *d* or *t*); *sibilants,* or hissing sounds, such as *s* and *z; gutturals,* or sounds produced partly in the throat, such as *k;* and many others.

Constantine the Great

There have been several rulers named Constantine, but the one who is best known was the first, called Constantine the Great, who was a Roman emperor more than 1,500 years ago. He is remembered especially because he helped the Christian religion to grow and spread in the Roman Empire. At that time Christianity was still a new religion. Most emperors  before Constantine were against it. The Christians were often tortured and killed because of their beliefs. In the year 313, Constantine issued his famous Edict of Toleration, which said that everyone could follow his own religion. Christians would not be killed any more, and the property that had been taken away from them would be given back

In Constantine's time, Rome often had two emperors, and sometimes there were several other men who claimed to be emperor. Constantine's soldiers elected him emperor in 306, but he had to fight many other men who wanted to be emperor. By about 325, Constantine had defeated all his enemies, and was the only Roman emperor. He decided to move his capital away from Rome. He

went to the east, to where the city of Byzantium had been. This city he rebuilt and made more beautiful, and he renamed it after himself, Constantinople. The city's name has been changed again; now it is Istanbul. Constantine the Great died in 337. He had helped Christianity all his life, and just before he died he was baptized a Christian.

Constantinople

The biggest city in Turkey is now called Istanbul, but it has had two different names in the past. First it was called Byzantium. Then about 1,650 years ago the Roman emperor Constantine changed the name to Constantinople (which means "city of Constantine"). Constantine was the first Roman emperor to become a Christian. Several of the early meetings of bishops and other leaders of the Christian Church met in Constantinople to define correct Christian beliefs. These meetings were called Councils of Constantinople. The first of them was held in the year 381, about fifty years after the emperor Constantine died. Constantinople's name was changed to Istanbul in 1930. See the articles on ISTANBUL and BYZANTINE EMPIRE.

constellation

A constellation is a grouping of stars that makes it easy to identify them. The stars in the sky are now divided into 88 constellations. As far back as ancient times, shepherds, sailors, and people with imagination gave names to groups of stars they could see. These constellations seemed to have the outlines of different animals, persons, and things, and were named after them. The most famous is the Great Bear, or Big Dipper, which you can see on any clear night. Other constellations were named after mythological characters, such as Hercules. By the time Jesus was born, 48 constellations had been named. Astronomers have named the new groupings of stars that they have discovered with more powerful telescopes. Today, every star in the northern and southern skies has been put into some constellation. Star maps show how the sky is divided into these groups.

Constellation, the name of a United States frigate, sister ship to the *Constitution.* See the article on CONSTITUTION. You can also read about the

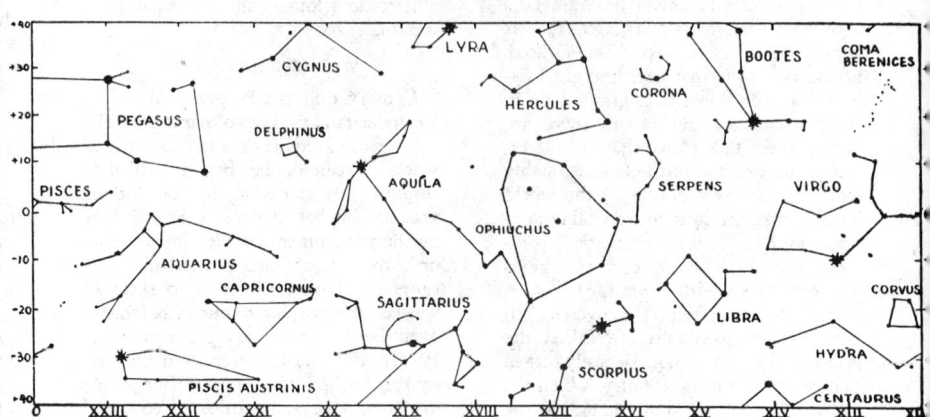

These charts show the stars that can be seen south of the equator. Most of the stars are in groups called constellations. The constellations seem to change their positions in the sky with each hour that passes. This is because the earth spins on its axis. The constellations also seem to change their positions with each season of the year. In winter, new constellations seem to appear in the east and the old constellations move off into the west. This is due to the rotation of the earth about the sun.

Constellation in the article on JOHN ADAMS.

Constitution

Constitution is the name of a famous American ship. This frigate (warship) was built in 1794, along with the *Constellation* (see above). The *Constitution* fought and won some important battles for the United States, and after 33 years, she was declared unseaworthy. Oliver Wendell Holmes, an important poet, wrote a poem called "Old Ironsides" that was about the *Constitution.* People were very much stirred up by the poem, and felt that the *Constitution* should be saved. It is still on display at the Charlestown Navy Yard at Boston, Massachusetts.

Constitution, United States

The constitution of a country is its supreme law. In the United States, the Constitution is the basis of the national government. No act of the government, no law passed by Congress, and no law in any state, city or town can conflict with the Constitution.

Experts consider the Constitution of the United States one of the most remarkable documents in all history. It was written well over 150 years ago, but it works just as well today as it did then.

The Constitution was written at a Constitutional Convention that met in Philadelphia in May, 1787. The American states had just won their independence from England. They had been working under a loose agreement called the Articles of Confederation, in which every state was treated as a separate, independent country. The convention met to change the Articles of Confederation, but soon they decided to start all over and create a Federal (united) government.

BACKGROUND OF THE CONSTITUTION

The Constitution was a compromise between two different ideas. One of the ideas was the Virginia Plan. The men in favor of the Virginia Plan were from the larger states. They wanted the larger states to have more power in Congress. The opposing idea was the New Jersey Plan. The men in favor of this plan wanted each state, whether it was large or small, to have the same amount of power. For many weeks the Constitutional Convention tried to decide how to satisfy everyone. At last, a compromise settlement was proposed by William Samuel Johnson of Connecticut. This settlement, called the "Connecticut Compromise," was used. The Connecticut Compromise set up Congress as it is today. There would be two houses in Congress, the House of Representatives and the Senate. The number of members in the House of Representatives would depend on the number of people in each state. The Senate would have only two members from each state. A bill (a plan for a law) must be approved by both the House and the Senate. If a small state like Rhode Island did not like a bill, it could still fight against it in the Senate. The small state would have just as much power in the Senate as the large state.

Before the Constitution could be used, nine of the original states had to ratify (agree to) it. Many small farmers and people in the poorer classes did not like it. Virginia and New York did not like it. Finally they agreed to it when the Bill of Rights was added. The Bill of Rights is actually the first ten amendments to the Constitution. They guarantee certain rights for the individual, such as the right of freedom of speech.

BASIC IDEAS OF THE CONSTITUTION

It is one of the basic ideas of the Constitution that the people are the most important part of the government. The government is to be run for and by the people. They are to have the final power. The writers of the Constitution divided the government into three branches. One was Congress, which represents the people and makes the laws. One was the executive branch, the President, who carries out the laws and sees that they are enforced. One was the judiciary, or the Supreme Court. The Supreme Court was to be the final judge of any difference between state and national governments. This three-part division is called the separation of powers. But each division is supposed to check up on the other. The President, for example, can veto any bill passed in Congress. If the President vetoes, or objects to, a bill passed in Congress, Congress may pass the bill again. But this time two-thirds of both the House of Representatives and Senate must vote for the bill. Only a majority (one more than half) must vote for a bill the President does want. The Supreme Court has the right to check up on Congress. If Congress passes a law, the Supreme Court has the power to declare it unconstitutional, or illegal. Congress has the right to check up on Federal officers, even the President. If Congress thinks that the President or some other Federal official is guilty of a crime against the United States, Congress can remove him from office.

CHANGES IN THE CONSTITUTION

It is amazing that the Constitution of the United States has lasted so well. However, it has been changed to meet the needs of the modern world. There are several ways in which these changes are made. One of them is by means of the Elastic Clause. Congress has the power to do certain stated things. It also has the power to pass any laws that are necessary for carrying out some of the stated powers. For example, Congress has the power to set up post offices and courts. This is a stated power. But Congress also has the power to take land for public purposes. This is an "implied" power. The Constitution does not say in so many words that Congress may take land. But it makes sure that Congress is able to take land (and pay for it, of course) to put up a public building like a post office.

The Constitution has also changed through amendments. This is hard to do, but it has been done several times. Three-fourths of the states and two-thirds of both the Senate and the House of Representatives must agree to an amendment. It took about fifty years to bring about a constitutional amendment allowing women to vote.

Sometimes the Constitution changes without any written amendment or implied powers. This is shown by the way in which the President is selected. The President is chosen by the Electoral College, which is made up of men from each state. Originally, these men did not have to vote for any particular candidate. They could choose the candidate they wanted, no matter whom the people in their state might have voted for. Voters in a presidential election still vote for the men who will be members of the Electoral College, but they know that these men will vote for the candidate the people chose. There is no constitutional amendment for this change. It has simply happened in the course of history.

consul

A consul is a person who has the

HOW THE CONSTITUTION ESTABLISHED FEDERAL POWER

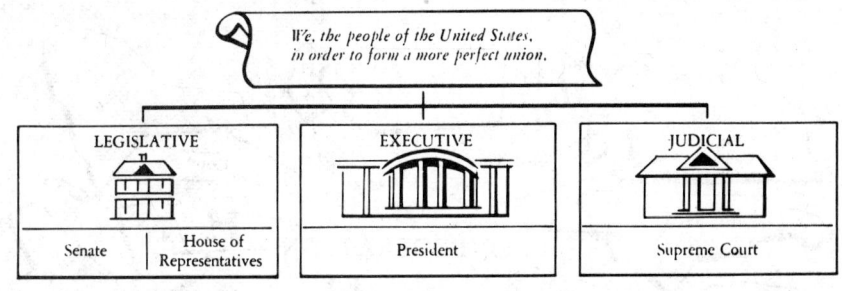

We, the people of the United States, in order to form a more perfect union.

LEGISLATIVE	EXECUTIVE	JUDICIAL
Senate | House of Representatives	President	Supreme Court

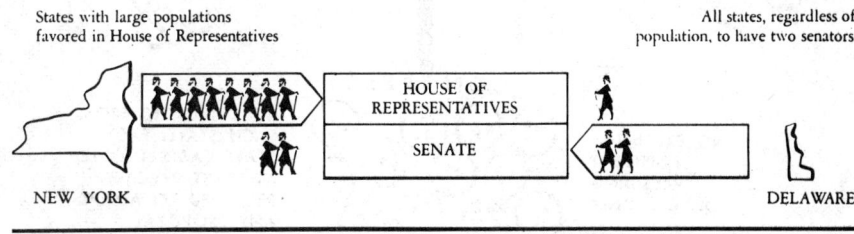

States with large populations favored in House of Representatives

All states, regardless of population, to have two senators

HOUSE OF REPRESENTATIVES

SENATE

NEW YORK   DELAWARE

Congress to regulate foreign and interstate commerce

No duties on exports

Graphics Inst. of America

The Constitution established the three main branches of the United States government. It also stated how representatives and senators should be selected from the states. The Constitution also made clear the duties of the Federal government.

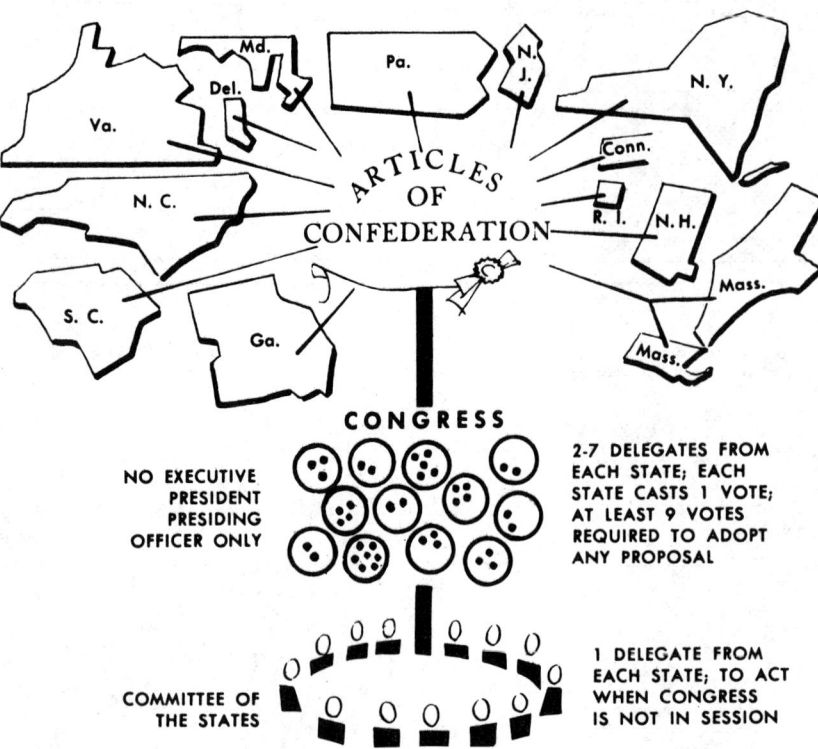

ARTICLES
OF
CONFEDERATION

Va.   Md.   Pa.   N. J.   N. Y.

Del.

N. C.   Conn.

S. C.   R. I.   N. H.

Ga.   Mass.

Mass.

CONGRESS

NO EXECUTIVE
PRESIDENT
PRESIDING
OFFICER ONLY

2-7 DELEGATES FROM
EACH STATE; EACH
STATE CASTS 1 VOTE;
AT LEAST 9 VOTES
REQUIRED TO ADOPT
ANY PROPOSAL

COMMITTEE OF
THE STATES

1 DELEGATE FROM
EACH STATE; TO ACT
WHEN CONGRESS
IS NOT IN SESSION

Graphics Inst. of America

The Articles of Confederation, the constitution of the colonies after they broke away from England, made the Continental Congress the first American governing body.

job of helping people when they are traveling in a foreign country. The consul is sent by his government to live in another country, and he knows about the laws and the way business is carried on there. The United States consul in France, for example, writes a report about French business and trade, and businessmen in the United States find this report a big help in carrying on business with France. The consul also does many other things to help travelers. He can help you with a passport and other important papers, and he can sometimes act as a judge. The consul's job is important, and all consuls for the United States have to pass examinations. You can read more about what a consul does in the article on the DIPLOMATIC SERVICE.

contact lenses are glasses made to fit directly over the eyeballs: see the article on GLASSES.

contempt of court

Contempt of court is disobeying the rules or procedures of a legal court. You can read more about COURTS in another article, later in this volume. Since a court represents the government, disobeying the rules of a court is the same thing as disobeying the rules of the government, and a man who acts in contempt of court has committed a crime. The punishment for contempt of court can be either a fine or a jail sentence. Contempt of court includes such things as refusing to answer questions, trying to bribe the judges or the jury, or hitting anyone in the courtroom.

continent

If you look at a map of the world, you will see that there are six bodies of land that are larger than any others. These bodies of land are called continents. One of them, Eurasia, is usually considered as two continents, Europe and Asia. The other continents are: North America, South America, Australia, Africa, and Antarctica. Of all the continents, only Antarctica, which is down at the South Pole, has no people living on it. Even though the continents are very large, they do not take up as much of the earth's surface as the oceans. There is a separate article on each of the continents.

Continental Congress

There were two Continental Congresses. The First Continental Congress was formed by the American colonists just before the Revolutionary War. Its purpose was to protest against British rule over the colonies. It was held in Philadelphia, Pennsylvania, in September, 1774. At that time, the members of the Continental Congress did not actually want to break away from the British. When the Congress ended a month later, it had made a list of what the colonists did not like about the British rule. This document was called a *Declaration of Rights and Grievances*.

The Second Continental Congress met in May, 1775. By then fighting had started, and the members of the Congress wanted to break away from the British. The most important thing the Second Congress did was to write the Articles of Confederation. This was actually the first constitution of the United States. Always before, the states had had complete power. Now the Articles of Confederation gave the Continental Congress certain powers over the states. The Congress

was allowed to borrow money, issue money, and make treaties with other countries. It could also form an army and a navy. This was the first time that the states had ever had a central government. From 1775 to 1781, the Second Continental Congress served as a central government. In 1789 the Constitution of the United States was adopted.

Continental Divide

The Continental Divide is an imaginary line on a ridge in the Rocky Mountains that separates the rivers flowing west into the Pacific Ocean from those that flow east into the Atlantic Ocean or Mississippi River. The Continental Divide for years represented a line of division to the pioneers in the old West. If they could cross the divide, they felt that they had achieved a great triumph. The actual crossing of these mountains was difficult to the wagon trains, and when they finally accomplished it and settled the west-coast region, it marked an important step in making the United States a great country. The Continental Divide also goes through Canada.

contraband of war is war goods supplied by countries which are not at war to the countries that are fighting. See the separate articles on BLOCKADES and NEUTRALITY.

contract

A contract is an agreement between two or more persons or groups. The persons or groups who make the agreement are called parties to the contract. One party to a contract promises to do something, and the other party agrees to accept what is done. For instance, if a man writes a book and signs a contract with a publisher, the writer promises to deliver a book within a certain period of time, and the publisher agrees to accept it, to publish the book, and to pay the author a certain amount of money. If one party does not live up to the contract, the other party can bring him to court and sue him for what is called *breach of contract*.

contract bridge

Contract bridge (usually called simply "bridge") is a card game that is played by nearly forty million people in all parts of the world. Since 1932 it has been the most popular of all card games. Now and then people will prefer a new game, such as canasta, for a few years, but they always go back to bridge. Even before 1932, other forms of bridge were the most popular games. Some of these earlier games were auction bridge, bridge-whist, and whist.

Contract bridge is not an easy game to learn, and it is even a harder game to play very well, but many younger players become quite good at it, and it is very popular in high schools and colleges.

THE FIRST STEP

Bridge is played by four players. Two are partners against the other two. You may decide in any way who will be partners, but in a serious game a pack of cards is spread face down and each of the four players draws one card. The two players drawing the highest-ranking

cards will be partners against the other two. The suits rank: spades (highest), hearts, diamonds, clubs. The cards in each suit rank: ace (highest), king, queen, jack, 10, 9, 8, 7, 6, 5, 4, 3, 2.

The partners sit across the table from each other. The player who drew the highest card is dealer. After him, the next dealer is always the player who sits at the left of the player who dealt last.

The dealer gives one card at a time to each player until all the cards are dealt. Each player then has thirteen cards.

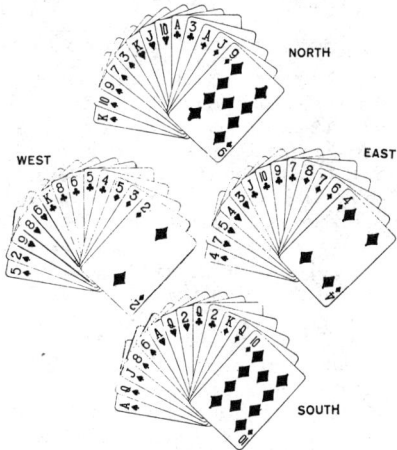

The next two stages of the game are *bidding* and *play*.

In the play, one player (the *leader*) puts a card face up in the center of the table. This card is the *lead*. Each player in turn after him must play one card. When all four have played, the four cards are a *trick*. The object in bridge is to win tricks. Each player must *follow suit* (play a card of the suit led) if he can. If he does not have a card of this suit in his hand, he may play any card from his hand. One suit is the trump suit. A trick is won by the highest trump in it, if it contains a trump. If a trick does not contain a trump, it is won by the highest card of the suit led. The player who wins a trick leads to the next trick. So the play proceeds until all thirteen cards in each hand have been played.

THE BIDDING

Before the play begins, there is bidding. The dealer has the first turn to bid. Then the turn to bid passes to his left. Each player in turn must make some *call*. A call may be a *pass*, a *bid*, a *double*, or a *redouble*.

Whenever you bid, you contract (promise) to take a certain number of tricks. Unless you have some high cards in your hand, you probably will not win many tricks, so you are not strong enough to bid. In that case, you pass. If you have a strong hand, you bid.

To bid, you name the suit you want to be trump, and the number of tricks you expect to win. However, in bridge you must win at least six tricks before your tricks begin to count toward your contract. So when you bid "one spade" you mean that you want spades to be trumps, and that you think you can win at least seven tricks (6 + 1) if spades are trumps. The highest bid you can make is seven, because there are only thirteen tricks altogether (6 + 7). A bid of six is a *small slam* (a bid to win all but one of

the tricks). A bid of seven is a *grand slam* (a bid to win all the tricks).

If you are strong enough to bid but do not want to have any trump suit, you may bid *no-trump*. No-trump ranks higher than any suit. A bid of one no-trump will overcall (is higher than) a bid of one in any suit, but a bid of two clubs will overcall one no-trump. Each bid must be higher than any bid that was made before it, either in its rank or in the number of tricks it names.

If an opponent has made the last bid and you do not think he can win as many tricks as he bid for, you may *double*. Then if he does not make his bid (win that many tricks) you will score more than you would have if you had not doubled. If an opponent has doubled a bid made by you or your partner, and you think you can make your bid, you may *redouble*. This will increase your score if you make the bid, and increase your loss if you do not.

The bidding (called the *auction*) ends when any call (bid, pass, double, or redouble) is followed by three passes in a row.

When the auction ends, one player becomes the *declarer*. He is decided by the trump suit (or no-trump) named in the last bid. He is the player who first named that suit (or no-trump) for his side, even if his partner made the last bid. His partner becomes the *dummy*, and the opponent on his left becomes the leader. As soon as the leader has led a card, the dummy puts his hand on the table, face up. The declarer then plays the cards from both his own hand and the dummy hand, but he plays from each hand in proper turn.

WHEN TO BID

There are many books that tell when to bid in bridge, because it is a very complicated game. However, most authorities give the following advice:

Count every ace in your hand as 4 points, every king as 3, every queen as 2, and every jack as 1. If you have 13 or more points, you should usually bid. The bid should be one in your longest and strongest suit. (The suit should not be less than four cards long.) If you have 16 to 18 points and high cards in all four suits, you may bid one no-trump.

When the two hands of a partnership have 26 or more points, they should reach a contract as high as three no-trump, four spades or hearts, or five diamonds or clubs, whichever they think will be the best trump suit or contract for the hand.

When your partner has made the first bid, if you have 6 to 10 points, you should "keep the bidding open" by bidding one in your best suit or one no-trump. If you have 11 or more points, and your best suit is lower-ranking than your partner's suit, you should bid two in that suit.

PLAY AND SCORING

The play of the cards was described above. As each trick is finished, a player of the side winning it takes in the four cards, turns them over, and keeps them in front of him. One player on each side takes in all the tricks for his side.

When all thirteen tricks have been

played, they are counted. If the declarer has won at least as many tricks as he bid for, he has made his contract. The tricks he bid for are scored toward *game*. A game ends when either side has scored 100 or more points in tricks that it both bid for and made. Then a new game is begun. A *rubber* ends when either side has won two games.

When the declarer's side does not win as many tricks as it bid for, its opponents score undertrick *penalties*. These penalties are higher when the declarer's side is *vulnerable* (has won a game in that rubber) than when it is not vulnerable. The penalties are also higher when a contract was doubled, and still higher when it was redoubled.

There are several *bonus* or *premium* scores that do not count toward game. These include the values of tricks that were won in addition to the tricks bid for; bonuses for making slams, winning the rubber, or holding *honors* (any four or all five of the A, K, Q, J, 10 when there is a trump suit, or all four aces at no-trump); and penalties for defeating an opponent's contract. Tricks scored toward game are said to be scored "below the line," and bonuses or premiums are scored "above the line." This is because the contract bridge score sheet has a line drawn across it to keep these scores separate.

HOW TO LEARN BRIDGE

There are many other rules in bridge. The best way to learn is to play as much as possible with experienced players. If you can, take lessons from a bridge teacher, and read books. It is a great pleasure to be able to play bridge well, so it is worth anyone's time.

To see how the scoring is done, follow through the description of the following rubber, and see how the scores are put down on the specimen score sheet shown in the illustration.

(a) We bid two hearts and win nine tricks, scoring 60 points below the line (trick-score) for two tricks at hearts bid and made (30 each), and 30 points above the line (honor-score) for one overtrick at hearts. We now have a *part-score* of 60.

(b) We bid two clubs and make four (that is, we win ten tricks). We score 40 points trick-score for two tricks bid and made (20 each). This completes a game (100 points), so a line is drawn across both columns to show the end of the first game of the rubber. We also score 40 points for two overtricks at clubs (20 each), and 100 points for four honors in one hand (one of us held A-K-J-10 in clubs). *We are now vulnerable.*

(c) We bid four hearts and are doubled. We win only nine tricks, so we are "down" one trick. They score 200 for defeating our contract, because we are vulnerable.

(d) They bid four spades but take only nine tricks, being down one. We score only 50 points as a penalty, for they are not vulnerable and we did not double. One of them held spade A-Q-J-10 (four trump honors in one hand), so they score 100 points for honors even though they did not make their contract.

(e) We bid and make one no-trump. This scores 40 points for us below the line. Now we need only 60 points more to make a game.

(f) They bid and make three no-trump, scoring 40 for the first, 30 for the second, and 30 for the third trick over six (100 points below the line), a game. Another horizontal

line is drawn across both columns, marking end of second game. Our part-score no longer can count toward a game for us; we start afresh. *Now both sides are vulnerable.*
(g) We bid two spades. We are doubled and are down three tricks and the opponents held 100 honors as well. They score 800 for defeating us and 100 for the honors.
(h) We bid and make six diamonds, a small slam, scoring 120 points trick-score, giving us the third game of the rubber and entitling us to the rubber premium of 500 points. We also score the vulnerable small-slam premium of 750 points.
Adding the score for both sides, we have 1,730 points, they have 1,300; we therefore win the rubber by 430.

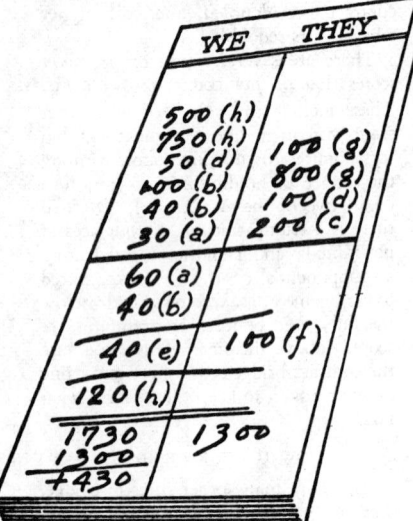

Reprinted from CONTRACT BRIDGE FOR BEGINNERS, by Josephine Culbertson, by permission of the John C. Winston Co., Publishers.

Cook, Frederick Albert

Dr. Frederick Albert Cook was an American explorer who said he discovered the North Pole a year before Peary reached it in April, 1909. You can read about Robert E. PEARY in a separate article in this encyclopedia. Cook, who was born in 1865, had been a surgeon on several expeditions and then led other trips himself. He also claimed he had climbed Mount McKinley. He wrote books and gave lectures about his supposed discoveries. But both "discoveries" were proved false. Cook was afterward sent to jail for some dealings in an oil business. He died in 1940.

Cook, Captain James

Captain James Cook was a famous English explorer who lived about two hundred years ago. His adventurous life began when he joined the British navy at the age of 27. He surveyed the St. Lawrence Channel and the coasts of Newfoundland and Labrador before he was given his own ship, the *Endeavor*, to command. He sailed this ship all the way around the world, exploring the coasts of eastern Australia and New Zealand on the way.

After returning to England he set out again for the South Pacific with two ships, the *Resolution* and the *Adventure*, and explored the icy Antarctic Ocean. He explored the New Hebrides Islands and discovered the island of New Caledonia in the Pacific Ocean off Australia. He was very strict about giving his men good food. In this way he kept them from get-

ting a disease which had always made sailors sick on long sea voyages. He searched the coast of North America for a passage from the Pacific to the Atlantic, but of course he could not find one and had to turn back. On his way home Captain Cook was killed by natives of the Hawaiian Islands. He was born in 1728 and died in 1779.

cooking

Cooking is exposing food to heat, to make the food more tender, easier to chew, and easier to digest, and to make it taste better. Men probably found out how to cook soon after they learned to use fire. By experiments they learned what foods were helped by cooking and what foods were hurt by cooking. They also discovered that adding certain things to the food that is being cooked, such as oils, fats, salt, and spices and other flavorings, makes the food taste better. In the course of thousands of years cooking has become one of the greatest arts in the world. Whole encyclopedias have been written about cooking.

METHODS OF COOKING

There are many ways in which food may be cooked. The most common are baking, roasting, broiling, boiling, and frying.

Baking is cooking by dry heat. Food is baked in an oven. In the oven the air is very hot but the food does not come near the fire.

Roasting is cooking in front of an open fire. Meat is put on a spit and turned slowly so that the fire can heat all sides of it. (See the article on BARBECUE.) Today meat is also said to be roasted when it is baked in an oven. Some vegetables, such as corn or potatoes, are roasted if they are cooked with the meat or if they are cooked in the open fire on hot coals.

Broiling is cooking over or under an open flame. This may be from burning wood, or from a gas or electric burner in the broiler of a stove.

Boiling is cooking food in boiling water. *Frying* is cooking food in hot fat or oil. Since oil and fat boil at a much higher temperature than water, they are often hot enough to cook food before they boil. There are two kinds of frying. When the food is covered with fat, the cooking is called *deep frying*. When the fat does not cover the food, the cooking is called *pan frying*.

NATIONAL FASHIONS IN COOKING

Different countries have different styles and ways of cooking, and in each country there are certain foods that are not often eaten in other countries. Often the food that is the fashion in a country depends on the kind of food that is grown there. In eastern countries, such as India, China, and Japan, rice is the principal food, whereas in Europe and the United States wheat is the principal food. Latin America uses corn as its main food, as the United States did in earlier times.

Three of the principal kinds of cooking are Oriental, French, and Germanic. The oriental peoples were the first to develop cooking as an art, and the Chinese carried the art farther than any other people. For hundreds of years oriental cooks have used seasonings and flavorings that the people in Europe and America are just beginning to discover. Asiatic countries such as Japan and India were influenced by the Chinese style of cooking. Rice is served at every meal, and the meat dishes are almost always in the form that Americans would call stews.

The most famous style of European cooking is called French cooking. Many people consider it the best cooking in the world. This style started in Italy about

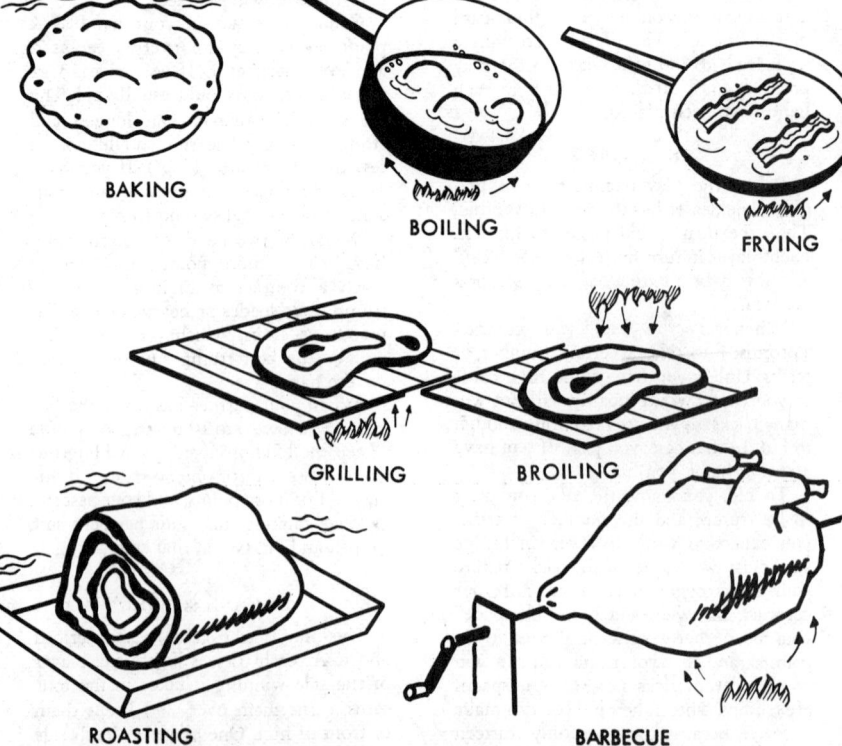

BAKING

BOILING

FRYING

GRILLING

BROILING

ROASTING

BARBECUE

When you learn to cook, you have to find out all the different ways food can be prepared. Certain things need baking, others need roasting, frying, or boiling. Cooking food properly can be fun, and can mean delicious meals that everyone will enjoy.

five hundred years ago. From Italy it was brought to France. Most "French" restaurants are run by Italians. French cooking uses many sauces, and often these sauces are made with wine.

The German style is the cooking that Americans and the English often call "plain cooking." It is done with fewer sauces and seasonings, and the meat and vegetables are usually cooked separately by baking or boiling.

There are as many variations of these kinds of cooking as there are good cooks. Each country has its own cooking habits. Spanish and Mexican food is highly spiced, while food in Greece, the Balkans, and the Near East is cooked with a great deal of oil. The Scandinavian cooks are famous for their appetizers, called *smörgasbord,* and the Hungarians are famous for their pastries. In a big city such as New York or London there are restaurants where you can sample almost any kind of cooking.

Calvin Coolidge

Calvin Coolidge was the thirtieth president of the United States. Coolidge became president in 1923 when President Warren G. Harding died in office. This was between World War I and World War II, when the country was very prosperous, and the world in general was at peace. Coolidge was known for his habit of saying very little, which earned him the nickname of "Silent Cal."

Throughout his administration Coolidge made it clear that he did not believe in wasting government money any more than he believed in wasting his own. The prosperity of the country was high, but he did not feel that this was any reason to spend a lot. In fact, he did at least one thing that no other president has done either before or since. He reduced the national debt two billion dollars in three years. This made many people believe that Coolidge was one of the most practical and sensible business men ever to hold the office of president of the United States.

Coolidge's term was filled with arguments about foreign relations. There were disputes concerning tariffs, immigration, war debts, the League of Nations, the World Court, and many smaller matters. He opposed plans that would cause the United States to get mixed up in expensive foreign affairs, and favored plans that kept the United States rich and in-

dependent. As long as he was president, this was the case, but a few months after he left office, the wave of prosperity stopped suddenly with the Wall Street crash of October, 1929. Many people said this was due to lack of foresight on his part, and that he might have helped prevent it if he had been wiser.

After Coolidge's retirement from politics, he was a familiar sight in the streets of Northampton, where he often walked home carrying small packages. He built a beautiful home called "The Beeches," where his widow lived after he died.

In spite of having held the country's highest office, Coolidge never lost his simplicity and naturalness. He was always modest and unassuming and never foolishly extravagant.

HIS EARLY YEARS

Calvin Coolidge was born on July 4, 1872, at Plymouth, Vermont — a town so small that it is not even shown on many maps. His full name was John Calvin Coolidge, but he did not use the first name. His father was a storekeeper and later became a Justice of the Peace. Coolidge attended Amherst College and was graduated in 1895. He studied law and was admitted to the Massachusetts bar in Northampton in 1897. He had practiced law there for only two years when he was elected to the city council. A year after that, in 1900, he was made city solicitor and later held several other offices.

Coolidge married Grace Anne Goodhue of Burlington, Vermont, in 1905. They had two sons: John, born in 1906, and Calvin, born in 1908. Tragedy struck the Coolidge home when young Calvin died at the age of 16 as the result of an infection in his foot. A small injury developed into a serious infection, which spread to general blood poisoning.

Calvin Coolidge was a man of medium height and slender build. His hair was straight and thin, medium brown in color. His general appearance was that of a New England businessman, shrewd and frugal.

He was mayor of Northampton, then state senator, Lieutenant Governor, and at length Governor of Massachusetts. It was while he was governor that the famous Boston police strike occurred. In 1919 the police refused to work unless their wages and hours were improved. Coolidge became famous all over the country for his prompt and decisive action. He called out the militia to break up the strike and wrote a telegram to Samuel P. Gompers, president of the American Federation of Labor, in which he said: "There is no right to strike against the public safety by anybody, anywhere, anytime."

HOW HE BECAME PRESIDENT

When the Republican Party held its convention in 1920, Coolidge's popularity had grown so much that he received 34 votes for the presidential nomination on the first ballot. There was considerable division in the Republican Party at that time between Governor Frank Lowden of Illinois and General Leonard Wood. For several ballots the convention was deadlocked between these two men, but finally it decided on a compromise candi-

date whom both factions would accept. They chose Warren G. Harding, and Calvin Coolidge was nominated as vice president to run with him. They were elected the following November.

Coolidge was at the home of his father in Plymouth, Vermont, in 1923 when the news of Harding's death reached him. His own father administered the oath of office to him at three o'clock in the morning. No other father in American history has had the honor of doing that for his son.

Later, in Washington, Coolidge was given the oath of office again, by a Supreme Court justice, and formally took over his duties as the President of the United States.

Before his first term expired Congress passed a bill to give cash bonuses to veterans of World War I. This was called the Soldiers' Bonus Bill, and Coolidge vetoed it. This made many veterans angry, and they never liked Coolidge afterward. However, Congress passed it over his veto, and it became a law.

He was opposed to the League of Nations because he felt that it would give the United States too much responsibility in the affairs of Europe.

In the election of 1924 Coolidge was re-elected by a large majority. The Democratic candidate, John W. Davis, received about half as many votes as Coolidge, and Robert M. La Follette, a member of the Progressive Party, received about half as many as Davis.

Coolidge was a practical, businesslike president. At the time he was in office there was a great deal of discussion about European war debts. Almost every country in Europe owed the United States money that had been borrowed during World War I. Many people thought it would be better to collect part of the money than none at all, and suggested that the U.S. should tell each country that it owed only a part of the debt and that the rest was canceled. Coolidge did not think this was at all a sensible idea. His only comment was, "They hired the money, didn't they?" Although this was true, of course, it did not help to collect debts from people or countries that simply did not have the money to pay. Only Finland kept up all payments regularly. Although Coolidge was as busy as all presidents are while they are in office, he still found time to go to celebrations given by several Indian tribes. He was made an honorary member of these tribes, and the newspapers often printed pictures of him receiving and wearing the elaborate feather headdress that some Indian tribes wear.

During the latter part of Coolidge's administration, the prosperity of the country had been increasing steadily. The year of 1926 has often been considered the ideal time, when prices and income were in good balance, and most people earned enough to provide themselves and their families with a good living. His businesslike administration was credited by many with being one of the reasons for the prosperity of these years. Others declared that he should have made some attempt to control prices and stock market activities. The people who felt that way seemed to think that if he had done so he might have helped to prevent the stock market crash that occurred in October of 1929,

seven months after Herbert Hoover became president.

"Coolidge prosperity" has been used as a phrase to describe the great boom of the 1920s. Although Coolidge could probably have been re-elected in 1928, because the country was so prosperous, he turned down the offer of nomination. This was another occasion when he made one of his famous short statements. He said merely, "I do not choose to run for president in 1928." He was known to be a determined man, and no attempt was made to persuade him to change his mind. Herbert Hoover ran instead, and was elected. There is an article about Herbert HOOVER in a later volume of this encyclopedia.

HIS LATER YEARS

After his presidential term expired, Coolidge retired to Northampton, Massachusetts, and wrote articles which were published in many places. He also became a director of a life insurance company, and lived quietly until his death in January, 1933. He was 60 years old when he died. He was buried in Plymouth, Vermont, the town where he was born and where he was first sworn in as president of the United States.

MRS. CALVIN COOLIDGE

Mrs. Calvin Coolidge was born in Burlington, Vermont, on January 3, 1879. Her maiden name was Grace Anne Goodhue, and she was the daughter of Andrew and Lemira Goodhue. In 1902 she was graduated from the University of Vermont and she later taught in the Clarke School for the Deaf. On October 1, 1905, she married Calvin Coolidge. They had two sons. John Coolidge was born in 1906 and later married Florence Trumbull, daughter of a governor of Connecticut. Calvin Coolidge, the younger son, was born in 1908 and died in 1924 as the result of blood poisoning. Mrs. Coolidge died in 1957.

Cooper, James Fenimore

James Fenimore Cooper was one of the first great American writers. He was born in 1789, when the United States was a new, young country, and American writers usually copied the writers of the older countries of Europe. Cooper was one of the first Americans to write about American subjects—about the people and the country of the United States. His books told exciting stories about the American scouts and trappers who explored the frontier. He wrote about the wild, unsettled forests of America, and about the Indians who lived there. He told what life was like for the first white pioneers and settlers in the new land.

New York State Historical Association

Cooper is most famous for his *Leatherstocking Tales,* which is a series of five books. These books tell about the adventures of a brave and bold scout named Natty Bumppo. The hero is sometimes also called Pathfinder, and Leatherstocking. The names of these five books are *The Deerslayer, The Pioneers, The Last of the Mohicans, The Pathfinder,* and *The Prairie.* Cooper also wrote a great many other books. When he was young, he was a sailor for many years, and he wrote exciting books about the sea. One of these is called *The Pilot.* James Fenimore Cooper lived most of his life in Cooperstown, New York, a town that his father founded. He died in 1851, at the age of 62.

Cooper, Peter

Peter Cooper was an American businessman who lived from 1791 until 1883. His family was very poor, and he had practically no education. When he became rich, he made up his mind to help other poor boys get schooling. In 1859 he established a school in New York City, called The Cooper Union, that is still in existence today. The Cooper Union gives free courses in engineering and art. The students who graduate from the school of engineering get degrees just like those given in any other college. The students that complete the art courses are given certificates. The school also has a very fine museum and library, and it gives free lectures for the public. One of the first men to lecture at The Cooper Union was Abraham Lincoln, who spoke there in 1860. His lecture was so good that many people thought he would make a good President of the United States.

Cooper was very interested in transportation, too. In 1830, he built the first locomotive that was used in the United States. It was called the "Tom Thumb." He ran for President of the United States in 1876 on the Greenback Party ticket, but he was not elected.

cooperative

A cooperative is a group of people who work together to get something they need. (The word is spelled coöperative or co-operative in other senses, but in this sense it is more often spelled cooperative and sometimes is called and pronounced a "coop" or a co-op.) Most cooperatives are groups of people who buy food and clothing cheaper than they can get it in the stores. They can do this if they open their own store, and sell to themselves without having to make a profit.

Groups of people in Great Britain started the modern type of cooperative about two hundred years ago. One of the men who did most to build the cooperatives was Robert Owen. He was a mill owner who tried to help his workers have a better life. He was not able to build successful cooperative groups, but the people who later did succeed used some of his ideas. This group called themselves the Rochdale Society of Equitable Pioneers. Cooperatives today still follow rules and ideals that are almost the same as those set down by the Rochdale Pioneers in 1844.

COOPERATIVE IDEALS

The cooperative movement is not only a way you can get more for your money; it is also a way of living a better life. The main rule of cooperatives is that people must be fair. The 27 English workingmen and one woman who called themselves the Rochdale Pioneers started

something that has spread all over the world. Their original aims, or ideals, have been used by every true cooperative. They decided that any man or woman could become a member, no matter what his race, color, or religion. The members had to run the cooperative in a strictly democratic way. Each member had only one vote, no matter how much money he had put into the cooperative, and no one could cast the vote of another person. The managers of the cooperative had to give regular reports to the members, and the books and records could be seen at any time by any member. People were free to join or leave the cooperative whenever they wished, and to buy from the cooperative only if they wanted to. Hundreds of thousands of cooperatives using these ideals have spread all over the world.

HOW COOPERATIVES WORK

Cooperatives work very simply. The people in a cooperative own the store from which they buy what they need. The money that a cooperative store or factory has left at the end of the year is not considered as profit. The members believe it comes from charging too much, and they divide this money among the members according to how much each bought. The more one buys, the more one gets back. A man who bought $1,000 worth of goods would receive more than a man who bought $100 worth of goods.

There are many different kinds of cooperatives in the United States. You can join cooperatives that will sell you goods, or a house to live in, or medical care. A person can also borrow money at very little cost, or get telephone or electric service, or insurance from a cooperative. Also, there are farmers, fishermen, and manufacturers who form their own cooperatives. When they work as a group they are able to bring their goods to the market more cheaply and to get a better price for them.

coot

The coot is a running bird, which means it runs over the ground more than it flies. The coot is about half the size of a small chicken, but it has longer legs and large, fleshy toes. Therefore, a coot can wade, swim and dive as easily as a duck can. Coots feed mostly on seeds and plants. They build a large nest near the water's edge, and the female lays creamy-colored eggs that have dark spots on them. The coot is slate-gray in color and against this background you can see its white bill very clearly. Coots can be eaten, but they are not used for food as much as ducks are. Coots are found all over the world. The American coot lives as far north as Alaska in North America and as far south as Ecuador in South America. It is sometimes called a mud hen.

Copenhagen

Copenhagen is the capital of Denmark and is a busy Baltic seaport. Part of the city is built on the island of Sjaelland and part on the island of Amager. There is a very fine harbor in between. Nearly a million and a half people live in Copenhagen and its suburbs. Many people work at building ships, and some make fine porcelain vases and cups and saucers

that are famous all over the world. Some people make dairy products and work in factories brewing beer. The University of Copenhagen has an excellent library and is one of the oldest and best universities in Europe. The Christiansborg Palace, where the Danish parliament meets, is built on a little island. Nearby is the Thorvaldsen Museum, in which are some of the great statues made by the Danish sculptor, Bertel Thorvaldsen. There are many other museums where you see great works of art as well as swords and armor that were used by the ancient Danish warriors.

Copenhagen is a very old city that was founded about seven hundred years ago, and it was made the capital of Denmark in 1443. Copenhagen has been attacked several times in its history, and in 1940 the city was occupied by the Germans. The Danish people were very angry at this and were always thinking up ways to show the Germans how they felt. Finally in 1945, after World War II, Copenhagen was liberated from the Germans.

COPENHAGEN, DENMARK. Population (in 1973) 623,300; with suburbs, 1,381,312. Capital of Denmark.

Copernicus, Nicolaus

Nicolaus Copernicus was a Polish astronomer who lived about four hundred years ago. He became famous for stating  that the earth moves around the sun. This was a daring thing for him to say, because people wanted to believe that the sun and all the stars move around the earth. Copernicus was born in 1473, in Poland, Later he moved to Frauenburg, Germany, where you can still see the tower from which he studied the stars. Copernicus wrote a book on money, and he also was a painter and a doctor. His medical services were always given to the poor. His greatest book, on the movement of the stars and planets, was not published for many years. The first printed copy was placed in his hands as he lay dying in 1543.

Cophetua

Cophetua was the name of an African king in a poem written hundreds of years ago. King Cophetua fell in love with Penelophon, a poor beggar girl, and finally he won her love'and married her. The idea of a powerful king marrying a simple girl is something that people have always liked to hear about. The story of Cophetua has been used by other great writers. William Shakespeare wrote about Penelophon, and the English poet Lord Tennyson wrote a poem about the lovers, Cophetua and Penelophon. His poem is called "The Beggar Maid."

copper

Copper is a reddish-yellow metal that has been known since very ancient times. It is rustproof and can be bent or stretched to almost any shape. It can be mixed with other metals to form valuable alloys (mixtures of two or more metals). When it is mixed with tin it becomes bronze. Bronze is such an important metal

that there is a long period in history called the Bronze Age. For hundreds of years weapons, chariots, armor, and almost all metal things were made of bronze. Brass is an alloy of copper and zinc. Musical instruments such as the trumpet and the trombone are made of brass, and so are most clocks. Even some coins are made of a copper alloy, for example the penny.

The most important uses of copper are in the electrical industry. Half of all the copper made goes to manufacturers of electrical equipment. Telephone and telegraph wires, and the wires that supply our homes with electricity are made of a copper alloy. Copper is used so much in the electrical industry because it is one of the best conductors of electricity. This means that electricity flows easily through it.

WHERE COPPER COMES FROM

Like other metals, copper is found in the ground. It is usually found in rocks called copper ore, although sometimes it has been found in a pure form. Copper is found in many places in the world. It is found in mountain ranges, in jungles, in water, and even in straw. There is also copper in some of the food we eat, and there is a little of it in our own bodies. It may seem that it should be easy to get as much copper as we need, but that is not true. There are only a few places where copper is found almost pure. When it is found in this state, it is called native copper. One of the largest native copper fields in the world is in Michigan, near Lake Superior. The Indians knew of this copper bed. In some places the copper lay right on the surface of the earth, and they used to break off big pieces with stone hammers.

Copper would be easy to get if there were many copper beds like the one in Michigan. But usually the metal is found in rock deep in the earth. Rock with metal in it is called ore, and the ore field is called a lode.

COPPER MINING

Copper mining is done in one of two ways, depending on whether the ore lies close to the surface or deep in the ground. When it is mined close to the surface it is called a surface or open-pit mine. From a distance a surface mine looks like a number of steps cut into the ground. Each step is shaped like a horseshoe, and the horseshoe becomes larger and larger for each higher step When you are close to an open-pit mine, however, you can see that the steps are from thirty to fifty feet high, and they are wider than an ordinary road so that huge machines can travel on them. Railroad tracks are laid on them for the trains that carry ore to copper mills. The miners call these steps *benches*. The benches are not dug with picks and shovels; they are blasted. The miners use explosives for the actual mining, too. They use it to loosen the ore from the walls of the benches. First they bore holes about twenty feet deep into the walls. They do this with air drills that work like the drills used by repairmen on streets and roads. They then put explosives in these holes. When everything is ready, the miners run to safety. The explosive is set off from a distance

by electricity. There is a roar loud enough to hurt your ears. The ground is ripped open and a great mass of ore shoots high into the air like a huge fountain of black water and then it crashes back down to earth again in a shower of broken rock and dust. Then power shovels put the loosened ore into railway cars to be taken to the copper mill.

SHAFT MINING

The other kind of copper mining is called shaft mining and it is more expensive and dangerous than open-pit mining. Shaft mines are dug when the ore lies hundreds of feet underground. To reach the ore, a tunnel must be dug straight down into the ground a thousand feet or even deeper. The tunnel is called a shaft and inside it is an elevator.

A copper shaft mine looks very much like a coal mine, but it is not so dangerous because there are no poison gases to harm the miners. Every hundred feet or so in the shaft a big flat place is cut, called a *station*. From the stations, tunnels are dug like roads to the ore. These tunnels are lighted by electricity and in them are railroad tracks to carry ore cars, just as the benches of an open-pit mine do. Dynamite is often used in the shaft mine to loosen the ore, though in much smaller amounts than in open-pit mining. Some of the work still has to be done with pick and shovel.

When the ore has been loosened, the miners place it in little cars, and these carry it along the tracks to the shaft station. Here it is dumped into big bins, some of which hold as much as 150 tons. When a bin has been filled with ore, it is carried up the shaft on a mine elevator, or a cage, as the miners call it. In big mines the shaft has two or more cages. Then one cage is used to carry ore, while the other is used to carry men and supplies.

CRUSHING THE ORE

Mining is only the first of many steps that the ore has to go through before it is copper. When the ore goes up the shaft it does not look like the copper in a bright new penny. It must be cleaned and made pure.

From the railway cars at the mill, the copper is dumped onto a moving conveyor belt that carries it to giant crushing machines. These will break it into small pieces so that the dirt can be removed more easily. There are several kinds of crushing machines. The jaw-crusher has huge mechanical jaws that close upon the rock and grind it as our teeth grind food. Another kind of crusher is the stamp mill, which is a tremendous hammer weighing many tons that drops with terrific force upon the rock and smashes it into thousands of small pieces.

After this the pieces of ore that contain too much dirt must be separated from the good ore. The crushed ore is placed in a big tank in which there are water and oil. The whole mixture is stirred rapidly by machinery. The oil floats on the water because it is lighter. During the stirring the oil coats the pieces of metal, but does not coat the dirt. The dirt and water become a muddy mess. When the stirring stops, the metal pieces covered with oil are on the top.

Then they are skimmed off, just as cream is skimmed off milk.

SMELTING

Now the ore is ready for a further cleaning. This is done by melting. People have found that it is very much easier to get rid of all other materials in this way. This is called smelting.

It takes great heat to melt copper ore, so special furnaces have to be built for smelting. They burn coal, but they become much hotter than a home furnace. Before the ore is melted, it is first roasted until it becomes red hot. The ore passes in at one end of the roasting ovens, and comes out at the other. Then it is fed into the top of a smelting furnace.

The smelting separates the copper ore into two parts. One part is the copper itself, called *matte.* The other part is made up of dirt and ashes and many other things that were in the ore. This is called *slag.* Before the matte becomes cold and hard, air is blown through it to make it even purer. When the copper cools it is full of tiny air holes and for this reason it is called *blister copper.*

Blister copper may still have very small amounts of gold, silver, iron and perhaps other metals in it. So it is smelted again, this time in smaller furnaces. Then the liquid copper is run out into molds. This is one of the last steps in making copper. Each mold may weigh more than five hundred pounds. Manufacturers who need copper buy it in these molds or in fabricated shapes.

copperhead

The copperhead is a poisonous snake that lives in the eastern part of the United States. This snake got its name because of the reddish brown color of its head. The rest of the snake's body is brown, with darker brown patches on it, and it is about three feet long. The copperhead is a quiet snake that would much rather crawl under a log than fight, but if you step on it or disturb it in some other way, it will bite, and this can be very dangerous. The copperhead lives in forests and places where there are rocky ledges that are good for hiding. It eats mice and frogs and birds and other snakes. Young copperheads also eat insects.

copra is the dried meat of the coconut: see the article on COCONUT.

copyright

A copyright is an exclusive right to print and sell copies of the work of a writer or artist. A publisher gets a copyright on any book he prints so that no one else can print the book and sell it. The publisher gets a copyright by sending two copies of the book, with $4.00, to the Office of Copyright, which is a branch of the Library of Congress in Washington, D.C. When this is done no one else can print any part of the book without the publisher's permission. In the United States, the publisher's copyright lasts for 28 years. At the end of that time, the writer of the book can have another 28 years of copyright for himself. The notice is printed on the back of the title page of a book or on the title page itself. On the back of the title page of this volume you will see a "copyright notice."

Before the invention of the printing press, about five hundred years ago, people had no need for copyrights. In those days, it took weeks to make a single written copy of a book. After the printing press was invented, people were able to make many copies of any book very quickly. For a long time, printers were able to print any author's book without paying him for it. Writers complained that the printer made the money, while they themselves got nothing for their work. To protect the rights of authors, most nations passed copyright laws. The Berne Convention, an international treaty first signed at Bern, Switzerland, in 1886, protects authors of most countries and their heirs for fifty years after the author's death.

Not only printed work but also pictures, music, plays, motion pictures and designs for materials may be copyrighted.

coral

Coral is a kind of tiny sea creature. We know coral mostly because of its skeleton. Corals live all their lives in the same place. Sometimes they live together in such vast numbers that their skeletons form reefs hundreds of miles long, and even islands, which are called atolls when they form a ring with a lagoon in the center. A lagoon is an area of shallow water like a pond.

There are many kinds of coral. There is the solitary coral that lives in northern waters. Many different forms of coral live on the reefs of warm seas. Among these are the brain corals, which form round humps covered with wavy ridges; the organ-pipe corals, which form tall pillars; and the branching-tree corals.

Perhaps the most famous coral of all is one that lives in the Mediterranean Sea. Since the days of ancient Greece its red and pink skeletons have been very valuable for making beads, necklaces, earrings, cameos, and other ornaments. Today the coral fishermen work chiefly from Naples and Genoa in Italy, going as far

Marine Research Laboratory, State of Florida

This greatly magnified photograph depicts the skeletons of large star coral. Star coral is found in many Florida coral reefs.

south as the coast of North Africa. They haul up the coral in *drags,* which are drawn over the bottom of the sea.

The skeleton of corals is chiefly made of calcium carbonate, or limestone, mixed with other substances which may color it black, yellow, or red, though white is commonest. Corals feed on tiny marine life brought to them by the ocean currents. For this reason they grow more strongly on the outside of the reef or atoll, where the current is strongest. Many scientists have tried to explain the nature of the coral reefs and atolls of tropical seas. It is generally believed that the atolls, or rings of coral, used to have an island in the center. The island sank below the waves in the course of time, while the coral animals continued to build upward and outward. The world's longest coral reef is the GREAT BARRIER REEF of Australia, more than 1,200 miles long; there is a separate article about it.

Coral Sea

The Coral Sea is a part of the Pacific Ocean just east of Australia. A great victory of the United States and Australian navies over Japan in World War II took place here. In May 1942, the Japanese sent a big fleet with three aircraft carriers into the Coral Sea. They were attacked by two American aircraft carriers, an American cruiser, and two Australian cruisers. Actually the two fleets never came close enough to see each other. The battle was fought by airplanes from the aircraft carriers. They flew over to bomb the other fleet. The Allies sank a Japanese cruiser, damaged most of their other ships, and shot down 80 planes, and finally the Japanese retreated. The Americans lost one aircraft carrier, the *Lexington,* and 66 planes. If the Japanese had won the battle, they would have been able to attack Australia and New Guinea.

coral snake

The coral snake is a bright-colored poisonous snake with cross-bands of bright red, yellow (or white), and black. It somewhat resembles colored corals. It is sometimes mistaken for one of the non-poisonous king, or "milk," snakes. This snake has similar colors but the bands are arranged differently. The red bands of the coral snake are always bordered by yellow or white; the red bands of the king snake are always bordered by black. Coral snakes have two hollow teeth called fangs that are attached to the upper jaw and through which they shoot out venom.

Coral snakes are narrow and may be from 2 to 4 feet long. Their scales are iridescent, which means they reflect many colors. The female lays from two to four oval eggs. You do not often see a coral snake because it is usually underground, or under the bark of trees, hunting its food—lizards, small snakes, and insects. Coral snakes live in the southern parts of the United States and especially in Mexico. They are relatives of the cobras, the deadly snake of Asia and Africa. Africa, Asia, and Australia also have coral snakes.

Corbett, James John

James J. Corbett, known as "Gentleman Jim," was a heavyweight boxing champion. He was the first official cham-

pion under the "Marquis of Queensberry" rules. He gained the title in a fight with the famous John L. Sullivan at New Orleans in 1892. Sullivan was the bare-knuckle champion, and this was the first championship fight with gloves. It was really an elimination contest, which means a fight between two boxers who are considered the best around. Sullivan's bare-fisted title was not at stake.

Jim Corbett was born in San Francisco in 1866. He learned to box by practicing with his brothers. He was also an actor, and when his fighting days were over he appeared on the stage and in motion pictures. He also wrote a book and a number of articles. He lost the title to Robert Fitzsimmons of Australia in 1897. Corbett died in 1933.

Cordilleras

Cordillera means "little rope" in Spanish. It is a name given to a long chain of mountain ranges that begins at northern Alaska and passes down through Canada, the United States and Mexico, and ends at Panama. The Cordilleras in the United States include the Rocky Mountains, the ranges of the Great Basin, the Sierra Nevada, and the Coast Ranges. The word Cordillera was first used by the South Americans for their own chain of mountain systems which begins at Panama and runs along the western coast of South America as far as Cape Horn at the very bottom of the continent. They are usually called the *Cordillera de los Andes*, or just the Andes. Sometimes the word *cordillera* is used for any long chain of mountain ranges.

Cordoba or Cordova

Cordoba is an ancient town on the Guadalquivir River in Spain. It was founded shortly after the time of Jesus, probably by Phoenicians from the African side of the Mediterranean Sea. Later the Romans and Moors invaded it. During the Middle Ages Cordoba was famous as a city where many scholars and artists lived. At that time, it had nearly one million inhabitants and many large beautiful buildings. Today there are only about 181,000 people living there, and many of its ancient buildings are in ruins. It is rambling and picturesque with its crooked streets and beautiful gardens, brilliant with color. When the Moors went to Cordoba, they built beautiful mosques. These are buildings where Moslems worship. The largest and most beautiful of the mosques in Cordoba has now been made into a fine cathedral. Its bell tower is over three hundred feet high. The leather and silver products of Cordoba are among the finest in the world. Cordovan leather has been famous for hundreds of years. It is especially good for making men's shoes.

Corinth

Corinth was the name of a famous city in ancient Greece which was founded about 2,600 years ago. This city was on the Isthmus of Corinth. The Isthmus is a narrow strip of land nearly twenty miles long and from four to eight miles wide. It connects the lower peninsula of Greece, which is called the Peloponnesus, with the Greek mainland to the north. On the west of the Isthmus of Corinth is the Gulf of Corinth, which is an inlet of the Ionian Sea, seventy-five miles long. On the east of the Isthmus is the Saronic Gulf. The city of Corinth grew to be very rich because it controlled the trade and travel routes between the Peloponnesus and the main part of Greece in the north, and between the two gulfs on either side of the Isthmus.

Corinthians are the New Testament letters or epistles written by St. Paul to Christians at Corinth: see the article on EPISTLES.

cork

Cork is a tough, springy substance made from the bark of certain trees. It is made from birch in Russia and from a tree called *abemaki* in Japan. The greatest amount of the world's cork comes from the cork oak. This is a tree that grows as high as forty feet. It is raised chiefly in Spain, Portugal, Morocco, Algeria, and Tunisia, though some were planted during World War II in the southwest United States.

The trees are harvested from June to August. Two circular cuts are made round the trunk, then cuts are made down it so that the bark is divided into long slabs. These are then pried off the tree with the wedge-shaped handles of the cutting axes. Care is always taken to see that none of these cuts goes through to the inner bark, which would hurt or kill the tree. The cutters have to be very skilled men. The slabs are then softened by boiling, which removes the bitter-tasting tannins from the bark and allows the rougher parts to be scraped off. In years when the price is good the larger branches may also be stripped. The first harvest is usually taken when the trees are between fifteen and twenty years old, and from then on at intervals of eight to ten years, until the tree gets too old, which is usually when it is around 150 years old. The quality of the cork improves during the first five or six harvests, and then keeps steady. The wood of the tree is too tough and brittle to be of much use except as firewood.

WHAT CORK IS USED FOR

Cork is a wonderful substance, and nothing else has its strange properties. It weighs about a quarter as much as water, and so floats buoyantly.

For this reason, it is used a great deal in floats and life jackets. Unlike wood, which soon soaks up water and sinks, cork is impervious to both air and water. It can be used again and again for long periods. It is used in making floats for gasoline and other tanks to show the height of the liquid, and as a seal for liquids.

Its most famous use is for bottle-stoppers. This use depends upon another property as well, its springiness when squeezed. It can be pressed into a bottle top and will hold its place for hundreds of years without letting a drop of liquid out. This springiness makes it a wonderful shock and sound absorber, and it is used in making fenders for the sides of even the largest ships, in mounting heavy machinery, in making flooring materials like linoleum and cork tiles, in artificial limbs, in shoe heels and soles, and in making rooms and buildings soundproof.

Cork acts as an *insulator,* or barrier to hot and cold, and it is used in all cold-storage plants and refrigerators, in insulating bricks, and in the wall and floor linings of air-conditioned buildings.

It is the properties of the cork itself which are important, and they come from its peculiar structure. Cork is about half air by volume: it consists of millions of minute air-filled "cells" (there are about two hundred million of them in a piece of cork an inch square and an inch thick). The cell has cellulose walls that have been reinforced with a waxy material, and this gives it its unusual combination of strength with springiness, and its powers of insulating and softening vibrations.

Cork

Cork is the name of the largest county in Ireland. It is on the southern coast of the island, and its area is 2,881 square miles, which is just a little larger than the state of Delaware. Cork has had a great many invasions in its history, and has been the center of fighting and trouble for more than a thousand years. Many thousands of Irish people from County Cork moved to the United States during periods of great poverty that occurred in Cork in the late 1800s. During those years the potato crops in Cork and other parts of Ireland were very poor, and since the people depended on potatoes for much of their food, there was great starvation. About 350,000 people now live in Cork, mostly farmers and fishermen. About 80,000 of them live in the largest city, also named Cork.

cormorant

The cormorant is a fishing bird that can swim and dive after its prey. In the East and in England, cormorants are trained to help fishermen catch fish. The birds are tied to fishing boats, and their throats are partly closed with a loose collar so that they cannot swallow the fish. They can follow the fish for some distance underwater and are known to go about forty feet down. This bird eats almost half its weight in fish each day, but it usually does not eat the fish preferred by man. The cormorant is three feet long, about the size of a goose, and is black in color. Its neck and wings are long, and its bill has a sharp hook at the end. Some have tufts on the top of their heads, and others have red faces. The female lays two to four oval eggs of a whitish-blue color. Cormorants live in most of North America. In South America, the Peruvian cormorant or guanay deposits guano—bird dung that is a valuable fertilizer for farmers. There is a separate article about GUANO in this encyclopedia. The Harris's cormorant, which lives on the Galápagos Islands, cannot fly. Its wings are small and its feathers are like hair.

corn

Corn is one of the big grasses whose seeds, called *grain,* feed the world. What is called corn in the United States and Canada is called maize, or Indian corn, in other parts of the world. When British people speak of corn they usually mean wheat, or perhaps all kinds of grain including wheat, barley, rye, and corn. American corn, or maize, was unknown to

Am. Museum of Natural Hist.

U.S.D.A.

Above left: American Indians grew corn or maize in the western world long before the white man came. This bag, filled with popcorn, was found some years ago attached to the belt of a mummy in Chile.
Left: Corn was an important food of the Incas of South America more than 600 years ago. This Inca pottery has a design representing ears of corn.
Above: Different kinds of maize were grown by North American Indians and later by settlers from Europe.

the rest of the world before Columbus discovered America, but it was already the chief food of American Indians.

Not only is American corn the most important agricultural crop raised in the United States, but the United States grows more corn than all the other countries of the world together. In 1959 world production of corn was about 242,000,000 short tons and of these the United States produced 122,112,000 tons. In some years the corn grown in the United States is worth more than all the other vegetables produced and more than all the iron, steel, gold, and silver produced.

Corn looks very much like sugar cane or other big grasses. There are more than a thousand different kinds of corn. The smallest kind grows only 18 inches tall, the largest grows 25 feet. Most of the corn grown in America is about 7 to 10 feet high. It is a very beautiful plant, with long, dark green, pointed leaves growing all the way up the stalk. Corn has two kinds of flower. The male flowers grow at the top of the stalk. They form a tuft that looks live several heads of wheat. The female flowers grow alongside the cob and hang out of the end of the ear in long threads called corn silk. From them develop the fruit, which are called ears. Each ear is made up of a thick stem, which is called the cob. On this there are hundreds of seeds arranged in long, straight rows. These seeds are the part which human beings eat. There are green leaves closely wrapped around the whole ear. These are called the husks.

Since the time of Columbus corn has been taken to all the different parts of the world. It can be grown in almost every climate except the coldest. The Indians themselves had many different breeds of corn. Some of these were grown by the Indians in the hottest parts of Mexico, others high up in the mountains of Peru, and in the hot, wet climate of the Amazon valley. Many new kinds of corn have been bred by scientists and farmers since the days of Columbus.

The most important kinds of corn grown in America are: flint corn, which is grown chiefly in the northern parts of the country; sweet corn, which is grown to be eaten by human beings; popcorn, which is a special kind of corn that is heated until the seeds burst, then eaten like candy; and dent corn, which is the commonest of all kinds of corn grown, and is fed to cattle and other farm animals. Most of the corn planted in America nowadays is hybrid corn, which means corn that has been specially bred to grow in a certain place. Hybrid corn is not one kind of corn, but is a cross between two or more kinds, which make the cross stronger than either kind. Since farmers started using hybrid corn they have been able to grow twice as much corn in the same fields.

WHERE CORN IS GROWN

Corn is very important in nearly every warm country in the world. Argentina, Brazil, China, Russia, India, Italy, South Africa, Hungary, Yugoslavia, Rumania, Bulgaria and Turkey are among the many countries that grow a great deal of corn. The United States grows more corn than any other country. It grows more than half of the world's corn. Most of this is grown in the valley of the Mississippi River, particularly in Iowa and Illinois. Other states that grow a lot of corn are Indiana, Minnesota, Ohio, Nebraska, Missouri, and South Dakota. Because so much corn is grown in this part of the country, it is called the corn belt.

In America practically all the work of growing corn is done by machines. There are special machines that dig the soil, plant the seeds, cut the corn when it is ripe, and even take off the husks. The corn is cut at different times depending on what it is to be used for.

More than three-quarters of all the corn grown in America is used for feeding animals, chiefly cattle and pigs. Nearly all the animals we eat are fattened in the corn belt before they are taken to market. For this reason, if it is a year in which the corn has grown well, there is plenty of meat. If the corn crop has not been big, meat is poor in quality and costs a lot. Much of the corn fed to animals is cut when it is still young and soft. The animals eat not only the ears, but the stems and leaves as well. Sometimes they eat the corn plant when it is still fresh, but often it is stored in a special building called a silo and then fed to the animals during the winter. In the silo the corn turns brown, but it is still good for animals to eat. A lot of the corn, however, is left until the ears are ripe and dry. When this is done only the ears are picked and kept; the stalks and leaves are thrown away. The grains of corn on the ears are used for making many things. The outside shells of the grains are taken off by machines. This is called corn bran and is fed to cattle. The inside of the grains contain a great deal of oil. This oil is squeezed out by machines. It is used in salads and cooking; it is made into soap and paint and glycerine, oilcloth, varnish, and many other things. Sometimes it is even used in making a kind of rubber. After the oil is squeezed out, what is left is called oilcake, and this is the best of all foods for cattle. Sometimes the oilcake is ground up. Then it is called oil meal. The part of the grain called the kernel is usually removed before the oil is squeezed out. The kernel is full of starch and a substance called *gluten*. Gluten is used to make glue, such as the glue on postage stamps. Gluten is also mixed with corn bran and fed to cattle. The starch from corn is used in many ways: as food, in making explosives, fireworks, shoe polish, and many other things. Syrup is the most important product made from cornstarch. To make syrup, cornstarch is mixed with acids. These acids turn the starch into sugar. Corn syrup is used in making jams and candy, vinegar, artificial silk, caramel, and beer, to name only a few things. Even the corncobs are not thrown away. They are made into gum, and corncob pipes, which some people say are the best of all pipes to smoke.

Even with all these thousands of uses, a great deal of the corn plant is often thrown away. Many men believe that these parts could be made into useful things—paper, cardboard, and alcohol. When these leaves and stems are used, another great industry will spring up in America.

Many different kinds of insects attack corn plants. The worst of these are the CHINCH BUG and the CORN BORER, which you can read about in separate articles. A fungus that damages corn is called RUST FUNGUS, about which there is also a separate article.

corn borer

Corn borers are the "caterpillars," or young stage, of several kinds of moth. They bore into the stems of growing corn and do great damage. In 1927, Congress decided to spend ten million dollars to try to control one kind of corn borer, the European corn borer. This borer first came to America in 1917, when it was found near Boston. It has now spread as far west as the Mississippi River. In Europe, certain other insects were its enemies. In an effort to control the corn borer, some of these insects were brought to America. They kill many corn borers, but not enough, and the European corn borer is still a great pest.

cornea is the thin, transparent layer on the outer surface of the eyeball: see the article on EYE.

Cornelia

Cornelia was the devoted mother of two important Roman tribunes or political officers. The story is told that when a lady asked to see Cornelia's jewels, the mother brought out her two sons, and said, "These are my jewels." Cornelia lived in the 2nd century B.C. She had twelve children, and when her husband, Tiberius Gracchus, died, she was left to bring up the family alone. However, only a daughter and two sons, "the Gracchi," lived to grow up. Cornelia was highly educated and was admired as a great lady. She gave her sons exceptional training. They became famous, but did not live long. After her second son was murdered, Cornelia devoted herself to literature and the company of writers and scholars. When she died, the Roman people put up a statue to her memory, calling her "the mother of the Gracchi."

Cornell, Katharine

Katharine Cornell was a famous American actress. She was born in Germany in 1898, but she acted on the American stage from the time she was 19 years old. She was married to Guthrie McClintic, a fine director who directed her in most of her roles until his death in 1962. Katharine Cornell had a beautiful low voice, and people have been thrilled by watching her on the stage. One of her most famous parts was Juliet in Shakespeare's play, *Romeo and Juliet*. Miss Cornell has been called "the first lady of the American stage." She died in 1974.

Cornell University

Cornell University is one of the largest universities in the eastern part of the United States. All of the colleges that make up the university are in Ithaca, New York, except for the Medical College, which is in New York City. The University also operates a large aeronautical research laboratory at Buffalo, and

Ezra Cornell

an agricultural experiment station at Geneva. The campus at Ithaca is on a hill above Lake Cayuga. It is famous for its beautiful grounds, its deep gorges, and the bridges over them. It was founded in 1865 by Ezra Cornell and was for a long time only for men, but now it is coeducational, having both men and women students.

cornet

The cornet is a musical instrument that you blow like a horn. It is made of brass, and is called a *brass instrument*. It has a cup-shaped mouthpiece at one end, and the other end has a flared bell, where the music comes out. There are three valves, or pistons, in the center. These are like plungers, and when you press down the valves in different combinations it changes the pitch and you can play any tune. Sometimes the valves are rotary valves like the ones on a French horn. These valves have keys, instead of pistons. The difference between the trumpet and cornet is in the amount of conical tubing. Conical tubing is like a cone; it gets larger and wider as it gets longer. The cornet is composed mostly of conical tubing, while the trumpet is more cylindrical, or shaped like pipe. Cornets are used mostly in military bands, in which they are very important, and also in many small jazz bands.

cornflower

Cornflower, which is also called the *bachelor's button,* is a European plant of the daisy family. It is grown in many American gardens. The flowers are white, pink and blue, with many beautiful shades ranging from pale mauve to the deepest royal blue. They grow at the ends of slender stems up to three feet tall. The leaves are long and jagged-edged. The cornflower is the national flower of Germany.

Cornwall

Cornwall is a county at the extreme southwestern corner of England. It is a peninsula that sticks out into the Atlantic Ocean and English Channel. At its very tip there is a long, rocky part known as Lands End. Cornwall is famous for its tin mines, pasture lands, and fishing. The county seat is Bodmin. Its main rivers are the Tamar, the Fowey, the Fal, and the Camel, whose valleys are very beautiful and fertile. The coast has a fine climate and is very popular with tourists, who come to see the picturesque old towns about which there are many legends of knights and pirates. On the coast of Cornwall is the district called Penzance, about which the Gilbert and Sullivan operetta *The Pirates of Penzance* was written. One of the titles of the Prince of Wales, the heir to the British throne, is Duke of Cornwall.

Cornwallis, Lord Charles

Lord Charles Cornwallis was an English general who is remembered by Americans because of the part he played in the American Revolution. Cornwallis was born in 1738. His father was an earl, and after his father's death Charles Cornwallis inherited the title. He served in the army, and rose to the rank of general. In Parliament, he was against the English policies that made the colonies fight to be

independent. But when the Revolution started, he came to America with the English army.

Toward the end of the war, he commanded the English forces in the South. For a while his army was successful. But in 1781 the French and American armies cornered him at Yorktown. After a siege, he surrendered. That was really the end of the Revolutionary War In his later years, Cornwallis was English governor-general and commander-in-chief in India. He was also at one time viceroy of Ireland. He was attempting to settle some disputes in India when he died there, in 1805.

corona is the name of the ring or halo of light seen around the sun at the time of a total eclipse of the sun: see the article on SUN.

Coronado, Francisco Vásquez de

Francisco Vásquez de Coronado was one of the leaders of the Spanish explorations in North America. He was born in Spain sometime around the year 1510. In the years following Coronado's birth, Spain was making her first discoveries and conquests in the New World. The lands she took were called New Spain. Coronado went to New Spain, and was made governor of a part of Mexico.

As a ruler, Coronado was able but was often harsh and cruel to the Indians. His great work was as an explorer. The Spaniards in Mexico had heard many exciting stories about cities to the north, called the Seven Cities of Cibola. These cities were supposed to be very beautiful and fabulously rich. Coronado was sent to lead an expedition to find these cities, and to seize their riches for Spain. With his men, Coronado traveled far to the north, and explored the lands that now form the southwestern states of the United States —New Mexico, Arizona, Texas, Oklahoma. But the "rich cities" of the stories turned out to be only poor Indian villages of the Pueblo Indians. Coronado had to return to Mexico, where he died in 1554, disappointed in his search for gold. The Spanish government was disappointed too. It was not until many years afterward that people realized what a great journey Coronado had made, and what a great territory he had conquered for Spain.

coronation

The coronation is the splendid and stately church service at which a king or a queen is crowned. Once there were many kings, queens, and coronations, but now England is the only kingdom that uses its coronation service. The most recent coronation was that of Queen Elizabeth II, on June 2, 1953. It is not the crowning that makes a king or queen. Elizabeth became queen in February 1952, upon the death of her father, George VI. When a king dies, the saying is, "The King is dead, Long Live the King!" The kingdom is never without a ruler, even though the coronation may not take place until many months after the ruler comes to the throne.

The coronation is a very sacred occasion, and every part of it is a reminder of some power or duty of a king. Some parts go back to the first kings we know of—

in ancient lands like Egypt and in the Bible. The English coronation service is almost a thousand years old, and has been repeated for many kings and queens. The rich colors and beautiful costumes are like those of the Middle Ages, when knights and their ladies lived by the code of honor called chivalry. In the coronation service, the king or queen is first made a minister of the church, with special powers. In olden times, this was supposed to be the reason why the "king's touch" could cure certain diseases. The crowning itself is the second part of the service.

Since 1066, England's coronations have taken place in London's Westminster Abbey. For the coronation of Queen Elizabeth II, thousands of people assembled there—the royalty and nobility of the British nations and other countries, as well as representatives of the Church of England. The first act of the ceremony is the recognition. The Archbishop of Canterbury, the highest churchman in England, asked if all recognized Elizabeth as their "undoubted Queen." This is a reminder that the ruler must have the consent of his subjects. The people answered, "God save the Queen!"

Then the Archbishop began the Communion service, which means a sharing of the body and spirit of Jesus. Next, the Queen took the coronation oath, promising to govern according to law and to "defend the Faith" of the Church. This oath is taken so seriously that George III (who was king at the time of the American Revolution) said, "I can give up my crown and retire from power; I can quit my palaces and live in a cottage; I can lay my head on a block and lose my life; but I cannot break my coronation oath."

After the oath came the anointing, one of the most ancient parts of the service. The Archbishop touched the Queen's head, breast and the palms of both her hands with a special oil. An anointed person is supposed to have holy powers. Next, various tokens or signs of a ruler were given to the Queen. She received golden spurs, and the jeweled swords that stand for justice and mercy. Also, the "Orb," a small gold ball with a cross set on top, showing that the world should be ruled by Christ. A ruby ring was placed on her finger. This is the "wedding ring of England," for the Queen is united with her people. Then she held scepters. The ancients called these "rods of power," and they stand for the power and justice of the ruler.

The final mark or symbol of a monarch is the crown, which the Archbishop placed on the Queen's head. This is the actual moment of coronation. Trumpets blew a fanfare. Outside and in all the cities of the land, as well as in other Commonwealth cities, guns fired a salute. Inside the Abbey, the old and thrilling ceremony of homage began. Homage is the special respect and faithfulness given to a king or leader. High officials from the different orders of the Church and the kingdom came forward, one after the other. Each one knelt before the Queen, and took an oath of loyalty. Then he rose, touched the crown, and kissed the Queen's hand. The archbishop next completed the Communion service, and the Queen brought gifts of a cloth and a bar of gold to the altar of the church.

Another special relic from the past is part of the coronation. This is the Stone of Scone, set under the coronation chair where the Queen sat for her anointing and crowning. There is a separate article about the Stone of SCONE.

Corot, Jean

Jean Baptiste Camille Corot was a great French landscape painter. He was born in Paris in 1796. His mother and father had a hat shop in Paris, and later his mother was appointed official hat designer to the court of Napoleon. Corot never lacked money as so many artists have. He started to paint at the age of 26. He made many trips to Italy, where he painted landscapes. He liked best to paint at twilight. He died in 1875.

corporal punishment

Corporal punishment is any type of punishment that is done to the body. Whipping, being sent to prison, and death by execution are forms of corporal punishment. However, a punishment that is intended to cause death, such as hanging, is also called a capital punishment. A punishment that is intended to injure, but not kill, a person is what we usually consider a corporal punishment. Whippings or floggings used to be common means of punishment, but now they are illegal. Sailors, for example, used to be punished by a certain number of lashes. Spankings, given to punish a child, are a form of corporal punishment.

corporation

A corporation is a group of people who get permission from the government to do business under one name. Most corporations are formed to do business and make a profit. A corporation has several advantages for the persons who form it. For example, if a corporation fails and has not enough money to pay its bills, people can sue the corporation for their money, but they cannot sue the owners of the corporation themselves. Therefore a person can lose only the money he put into a corporation, and not his personal money. Also, a corporation can keep on doing business under the same name even though it may be sold to other people. Another advantage of a corporation is that thousands of people can own part of it. The ownership of a corporation is divided into shares. By selling these shares, or stock, a corporation can gather great sums of money.

A corporation is said to be *incorporated. Limited liabilities company* means the same thing as corporation. Companies show that they are corporations by using Corp., Inc., or Ltd. after their names.

Corpus Christi

Corpus Christi is a city in southern Texas, on Corpus Christi Bay of the Gulf of Mexico. It is an important seaport. Corpus Christi has large oil refineries, canneries, and textile plants that make cotton cloth. Corpus Christi is a year-round fishing and bathing resort. Corpus Christi developed greatly after its new, deep port was opened in 1927. It is a modern, beautiful city.

CORPUS CHRISTI, TEXAS. Population (1970 census) 204,525. County seat of Nueces County. Founded in 1840.

corpuscles, the small particles or cells in the blood: see BLOOD.

Corregidor

Corregidor is an island fortress in the Philippines. It lies at the entrance of Manila Bay, just off the Bataan Peninsula of the great island of Luzon. Before World War II most people had never heard of Corregidor, but the events that took place there in the spring of 1942 made its name famous all over the world.

On January 10, 1942, the Japanese invaded Bataan with 200,000 men. The much smaller American and Filipino forces were steadily pushed back. By early April these forces were forced to surrender Bataan, sending 3,500 men to Corregidor. There, on the tiny island of only two square miles, Wainwright's little army held out for almost a month against a continuous Japanese bombardment from land, sea, and air. Finally, with their food and supplies exhausted and with no hope of relief, the island's heroic defenders had no choice but to give themselves up. On May 6 they came out of Corregidor's tunnels and turned over to the Japanese the last remaining bit of free Philippine territory.

Corregidor was reoccupied by American forces in 1945, and became part of the new Philippine Republic in 1947.

Corsica

Corsica is the name of a large mountainous island lying between the southeast coast of France and the northwest coast of Italy in the Mediterranean Sea.

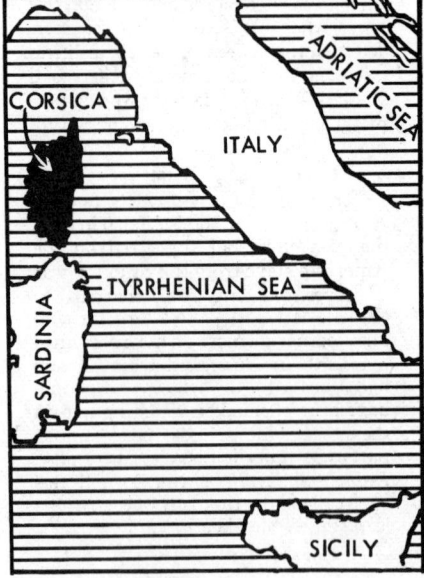

It is the fourth-largest island in the Mediterranean Sea, about three times the size of the state of Rhode Island, but has only 269,831 inhabitants. Although the people of Corsica speak mostly Italian, the island has belonged to France for about 150 years. The capital of Corsica is Ajaccio, which is famous as the birthplace of Napoleon Bonaparte. There is very little commercial activity in Corsica, but there is some export of chestnuts, wine, olive oil and timber.

Cortez, Hernando

Hernando Cortez was a great Spanish soldier who is remembered as the conqueror of Mexico. Cortez was born in 1485. He started to study law, but decided it was not exciting enough. He wanted adventure, and set out to the New World to find it. Mexico had just been discovered, and Cortez was sent to explore and conquer it. The native people of Mexico were Aztec Indians. They had developed a great civilization, and their capital city was noted for its beauty and splendor, and for its great wealth. But these native Indians of Mexico had never seen great ships and horses and guns like those the Spaniards landed with, in 1519. They thought the Spaniards must be gods, and received them with gifts. Cortez set up a new town, Vera Cruz, and left some of his soldiers there. Then he burned his ships, so that the soldiers could not run away. He marched toward the capital city. At first, the Mexican emperor, Montezuma, received Cortez with honor. But later he ordered an attack on Vera Cruz and when some of the Spanish soldiers were killed, the Mexicans were no longer afraid. They knew that the Spaniards were not immortal gods, but only men like themselves who could be killed. When Cortez heard of the attack on Vera Cruz, he acted quickly and boldly. He seized Montezuma and imprisoned him. Montezuma was forced to recognize the Spanish king Charles V as ruler of Mexico, and give to the Spaniards a great gift from his huge wealth of gold and jewels.

Gale Research Co.

There was much fighting in Mexico in the following years. Cortez wanted the Mexicans to become Christians and to stop worshiping their own gods and sacrificing human beings to the gods. This human sacrifice seemed very cruel to the Europeans. However, many of the things that Cortez did were just as cruel. He was a brave and able man, but he was fierce and completely ruthless in crushing all resistance and in keeping the conquered Mexicans down. By 1521 Cortez had a firm hold on Mexico. He had won a great country for Spain, but he was very little rewarded. Many men were jealous of his fame and wealth and power. The king was persuaded to take some of his rewards away from Cortez. Hernando Cortez died in Spain in 1547, a bitter and neglected man. But he lives in history as one of the greatest explorers. His name is also spelled Cortes.

corundum

Corundum is the name of a mineral that is found in the United States, in Canada, and in Asia. Corundum crystals are very valuable, and the deep red rubies and the clear blue sapphires in a king's crown or a precious bracelet are kinds of corundum. Now scientists have found a way to make these jewels in a factory. Another kind of corundum is emery, which is gray or black. Paper and cloth coated with emery are used for smoothing and polishing, as sandpaper is.

Read also the articles on ABRASIVES and ALUMINUM. Corundum is the hardest mineral we have, except for the diamond.

cosmetics

Cosmetic means "producing beauty," and many preparations that women use in an effort to make themselves more beautiful are called cosmetics. The things most often thought of as cosmetics are face powder, lipstick, cold cream, nail polish, rouge, and other things that women put on their faces and hands. Many other things, including soap and toothpaste, are really cosmetics. Some are used to help the hair grow, some to smooth out or cover up wrinkles, some to keep the hands soft and white, some to change the color of the hair. Today nearly every grown woman in the United States uses some form of cosmetics. Perhaps she uses only face powder, or dusting powder after a bath, or only toothpaste. All these are cosmetics, and so are the preparations that check perspiration in certain areas so that clothes will not get stained.

The use of cosmetics started in ancient times. Makeup boxes have been found in the tombs of Egyptian princesses. They contained large collections of cosmetics of many types. The ancient Egyptians used eye shadow, pencils to outline the eyebrows and circle the eyes, rouge for the cheeks, tints for the lips, colored nail polishes, and even hair dyes. The sculpture and painting left by the people of ancient Egypt show women with their faces elaborately made up with cosmetics.

When the Greeks invaded Egypt, they took the custom of using cosmetics back to Greece. From there it spread to Rome and so on through Europe. In France the art of makeup became very important during the 1700s, and French women of that time spent hours in putting on their makeup. They had very little soap then, and bathing was not particularly fashionable. A woman often went for several days without brushing her hair or

Some women use "eye shadow" to add a little color above their eyes.

This woman is using a new kind of powder for absorbing excess oil and perspiration.

In the bottle is liquid make-up that can be put over other make-up or right on the face.

This model is holding a tube of cream make-up with moisturizers to keep the skin soft.

"Eye-liner" is a dark, liquid make-up for the eye lid.

Mascara is applied to the eye lashes to make them look darker, thicker, and longer.

Women are able to buy lipstick and nailpolish in matching colors.

Nailpolish is made in colors which will look best with the clothing that is in style.

Max Factor
This model shows how soft her hair is after using a new shampoo.

washing her face. After all, she had spent the better part of a day in arranging her hair and putting on her makeup, and she wanted the result to remain as long as possible. Soap was a cosmetic that had not become very popular. Today soap is one of the first necessities, and a clean, well-washed face needs very little makeup to make it attractive. Soap is one of the most important of present-day cosmetics.

From France, the interest in cosmetics spread to England. When the colonists first came to America, however, they did not bring with them the custom of using artificial color on women's lips or cheeks. The Puritans would have been horrified at any such vanity. It was not until many years later that some kinds of cosmetics and makeup started to be used in this country. Young ladies found that beet juice tinted their lips and cheeks becomingly. If eyebrows were too thin or light, a bit of charcoal or a burnt cork darkened them enough to make a great difference. There were other things that women found useful, too. Mutton tallow, the grease that comes from sheep, could be made into a cosmetic cream that removed dirt from the face and at the same time made the skin feel soft and smooth. Today the same grease is used in many different cosmetics, but now it is called *lanolin*.

THE COSMETICS BUSINESS

From the simple vegetable coloring and homemade creams and lotions that young women used at the time of the Civil War and even later, the cosmetics business has grown into a gigantic industry worth billions of dollars. Today women could still make their own cold creams, lotions, and nail polishes for a few cents, if they wanted to take the trouble to find out the ingredients and how to blend them, because the actual cost of ingredients in cosmetics is usually extremely low. In most cases the production, manufacture, packing, distribution, advertising and sales expense makes the price many times higher than the value of the finished product.

THE ART OF MAKEUP

Makeup experts try to create the most natural-looking makeup possible, unless of course they are making up a young person to play the stage role of a great-grandparent, or something of that sort. Ordinarily, experts say that the best makeup is the most natural makeup. Women and girls who follow the advice of experts in using cosmetics will make it a point to use the most natural-looking makeup possible. The purpose of cosmetics is not to hide the features and create a "false-face" effect, but to make your features look as attractive as possible while still looking like you.

Girls usually do not start using makeup of any kind until they are in their teens.

cosmic rays

Cosmic rays are very powerful bits of energy that come from somewhere in outer space. Some scientists say that they come from a distant star (like our sun, but much brighter) where a gigantic explosion took place, like a million hydrogen bombs going off at the same time. Not very many of these bits of energy ever reach the earth because when they hit the earth's atmosphere (the place where the earth's air begins), they lose their energy by striking small particles of air and dust. Artificial satellites sent into the skies in 1958 revealed that cosmic radiation is very heavy about 600 miles above the earth's surface. These bands of radiation are called Van Allen Belts, after their discoverer. They are thickest over the equator. The heaviest cosmic ray shower ever recorded was in 1961 near Albuquerque, N.M., when an estimated 20 billion particles struck the earth.

"WEATHER MAP" OF SOLAR SPACE

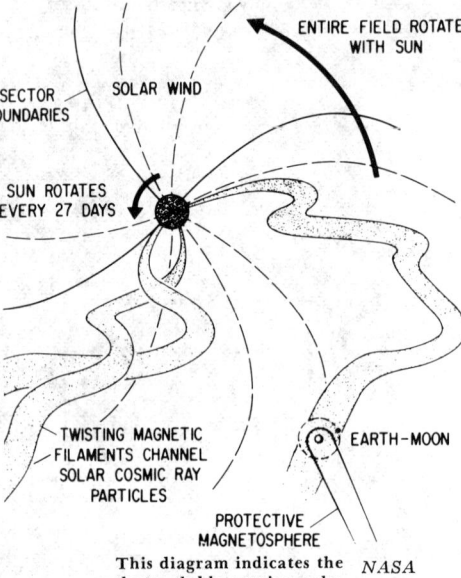

(VIEW LOOKING DOWN ON SUN'S "NORTH" POLE)

THE AVERAGE ANGLE OF MAGNETIC FIELD LINES TO THE EARTH-SUN LINE IS ABOUT 45° CAUSED BY SOLAR ROTATION. ONCE A MAGNETIC FILAMENT ROTATES PAST THE EARTH, THE HIGH-ENERGY PARTICLES IT CHANNELS WILL MISS THE EARTH.

ENTIRE FIELD ROTATES WITH SUN

SOLAR WIND

SECTOR BOUNDARIES

SUN ROTATES EVERY 27 DAYS

TWISTING MAGNETIC FILAMENTS CHANNEL SOLAR COSMIC RAY PARTICLES

EARTH-MOON

PROTECTIVE MAGNETOSPHERE

NASA

This diagram indicates the paths traveled by cosmic rays between the earth and the sun.

cosmos

Cosmos is a pretty, flowering plant rather like a daisy and closely related to the dahlia. One kind of cosmos that flowers in the fall sometimes grows into a bush ten feet high. The leaves of cosmos are delicate, feathery, and few in number, and the flower heads are at the ends of long, thin stems. Each has a single row of about five frilly-edged petals. The petals are usually pale pink, though sometimes they are crimson or white or yellow with a small yellow center. Cosmos are all natives of Mexico. There are many kinds, and they are grown in gardens all over the world.

Cossacks

The Cossacks were a group of tribes in Russia who were known for their horsemanship and fierce military spirit. They wore large fur hats, wide trousers, and boots with spurs. In the old Russian Empire, each Cossack had to spend twenty years in the army. In World War I, the Cossack regiments had more than 300,000 men, each with his own horse. In return for their military service, the emperor gave them land, and they paid no taxes. The Cossacks now live under the new Russian government, but they still have their own part of the army. The Cossacks were often very cruel in battle. Because the Cossacks were handsome and had beautiful uniforms and wild ways, many exciting stories have been written about them.

Costa Rica

Costa Rica is a small country in the southern part of Central America. It is bordered on the north by Nicaragua and on the south by Panama. Costa Rica is about the same size as Vermont and New Hampshire put together, but more people live there. When Columbus visited America for the fourth and last time, one of the places at which he landed was in Costa Rica. This place now is called Puerto Limón, or Lemon Port. He and his sailors would never have believed that one day Costa Rica would be served by great steamships and have two airports for airplanes from all over the world.

Costa Rica has a short, nearly straight coastline on the Atlantic Ocean side, but on the longer Pacific Ocean side the land forms two duck's heads, one smaller than the other. Under the larger duck's chin is the Gulf of Nicoya, while the baby duck peers over the Golfo Dulce, or Sweet Gulf.

Costa Ricans are very proud of their Poas Volcano, because it has in its top one of the biggest craters in the world.

THE COSTA RICAN PEOPLE

The people of Costa Rica are descendants of the Spanish who conquered their country in 1563. Although some of the conquerers married the Indians whom they found in Costa Rica, most of the Indians went up into the mountains so as to escape from them. For that reason, the Spaniards could not make farm workers of the Indians as they often did in other conquered countries in South and Central America. Instead, they had to content themselves with small pieces of land which they could farm themselves. Since about 1800 when the first coffee was planted in Costa Rica, it has become the country's most important product. It is an especially good coffee, and has helped Costa Rica to live up to its name, which is Spanish for "rich coast." Next to coffee, the people grow more bananas and cocoa than anything else, but they also have corn, sugar cane, rice, tobacco and potatoes. There are a lot of things which they have to buy from other countries, such as flour for bread, textiles to make clothing, machinery to help in their work, gasoline, leather and hardware.

WHAT THE LAND IS LIKE

On the coast of the Caribbean Sea the land is low and has a tropical climate. It is hot and humid. The interior, the part away from the coastline, is about 4,000 feet high and flat, and is called a plateau. In that part the climate is neither too hot nor too cold; it is temperate. The main mountain range of Central America crosses Costa Rica and is divided into several chains called *cordilleras* in Spanish. There are the Guanacaste Mountains in the north and the Talamanca in the south. In the middle is the Cordillera

Central, which has volcanoes towering above it. These volcanoes are not very active. They have Indian names such as Irazú, Turrialba and Barba. Terrible earthquakes have often shaken Costa Rica. San José, the capital, is on the central plateau 3,838 feet above the level of the sea and has lovely weather all year round. About half of the country is wooded and in the lowlands near the coasts the jungle is crowded with balsa, cativo, rosewood, guayacan, cedar, dyewood, sandalwood, mahogany, oak, and rubber trees.

HOW THE PEOPLE ARE GOVERNED

Costa Rica has been independent from Spain since 1821 Although the government has been upset by revolutions for short periods of time and there have sometimes been dictators, Costa Rica is mostly democratic in its ways.

The constitution, adopted in 1949, has done away with a permanent army. The people vote for a president every four years as well as a Chamber of Deputies, which is like our Congress. All the people must vote, and the same man cannot be president twice in succession.

COSTA RICA. Area 19,647 square miles. Population (1973 estimate) 1,860,000. Government, constitutional republic. Capital, San José (population 203,148).

costume is a name sometimes given to clothing: see the article on CLOTHING.

cotton

Cotton is a white, fluffy substance that is obtained from a small bush called the cotton plant. It is very important because cloth and many other things are made from it. More cloth is made from cotton than from wool, or linen, or any other material. In many parts of the world, particularly hot ones like India, China, and most of Africa and South America, the people seldom wear any cloth other than cotton cloth.

The cotton plant is a small bush that usually grows about three feet high, though some kinds grow to be twelve feet high. It has dark green leaves and large flowers. At first the flowers are white, but they slowly turn yellow or pink. From the color you can tell what kind of cotton is being grown. After a while the flowers die and fall to the ground. Then, where each flower was, a fruit (called a boll) begins to grow. Then they burst open, and inside each boll there is a round white puff of cotton. This puff is full of seeds. In nature the fluffy cotton helps the seeds to be scattered by the wind. But where cotton plants are grown by men the fluff is picked before it begins to blow about. There are many kinds of wild cotton. They are found in India and Africa and America, but always in the hot sections.

DIFFERENT KINDS OF COTTON

Several kinds of cotton are grown. The most important difference between them is in the kind of fluff they have. Sea Island cotton is the best kind of all. It comes from a very tall plant that was first grown on the Sea Islands off South Carolina. Not much of it is grown in America any more, because the plants are nearly always damaged by an insect called the BOLL WEEVIL, which you can read about in a separate article. The fluff of Sea Island cotton is made up of very long, soft fibers. Cloth made from Sea Island cotton feels almost as smooth as silk, and is very expensive. The next best kind is Egyptian cotton. A little Egyptian cotton is grown in America, but most of it still comes from Egypt. It is made into good quality cotton thread, stockings, underclothes, and dresses for women. Peruvian cotton is another important kind, but in America nearly all the cotton grown is called upland cotton. Sometimes this has very long fibers, but mostly they are short. The United States grows about one-third of the world's cotton — in 1964, more than 15,000,000 bales out of a world production of 50,000,000 bales.

HOW COTTON IS GROWN

Most of the cotton in America is grown in Texas and the southern states. It is grown in huge fields, and is a beautiful sight when it is in flower or when the little balls of fluff cover the plants. As soon as the cotton is ripe, thousands of workers set up camps near the fields and begin picking it. The bolls do not all ripen at once, so the same fields have to be picked over and over again. Nowadays a lot of the picking is done by machines.

HOW COTTON CLOTH IS MADE

After the cotton is picked it is taken to a factory where it is thrown into a machine called a cotton gin. This machine separates the fluff from the seeds by pulling the fibers through slots on the teeth of round, flat saws. The slots are so close that the seeds cannot go through them, but the small fibers can. Then the light, fluffy cotton is pressed into huge blocks called bales, and bound up with iron bands. At one time the seeds used to be thrown away. Now they are kept, for they are very important too. Many different things are made from cotton seeds, which will be described later. The cotton bales are sent to factories in the South or in New England, or even in England, France, or Japan. There the bales are opened. Each bale weighs about five hundred pounds and is only four or five feet long. Yet when the bale is opened, the fluff from one bale fills a large room, First the fluff is combed out so that all the fibers lie in one direction, in the form of a thick, soft sheet. Then the sheet is divided into strips, and each strip is rolled over by a machine. As each strip is rolled, it turns into a thick rope. As this rope is twisted more and more tightly, it becomes a cord, then a thread. Then several of these threads are twisted together. This makes the thread that is finally sold. This whole process of making thread is called SPINNING, and there is a separate article about it.

According to the kind of cotton it is made from, and the kind of thread it is, this thread is made into many different things. Most of it is made into cloth. The way this is done is described in the article on WEAVING. Cotton is made into many different kinds of cloth. Some of the commonest kinds are voile, organdy, cheesecloth, muslin, calico, cretonne, drill, and canvas. The most delicate kinds of these are so thin that you can see through them. The strongest, canvas, can be used for the sails of large boats and will not tear in a high wind. Each kind of cotton cloth has its special uses. Some kinds are made into sheets and pillowslips, others into shirts and dresses, hospital bandages, belts for machines, or the cording under the rubber in motor-car tires. Besides all these kinds of cloth, there are many other ways in which cotton is used.

SPECIAL USES OF COTTON

Cotton is almost pure cellulose, which is a chemical substance. Many things can be made out of cellulose, such as rayon, paper, photographic film, and celluloid. Sometimes cotton is treated with chemicals and made into these things. You can read more about this in the article on CELLULOSE.

Sometimes cotton fibers are soaked in acids and then dried. This makes what is called guncotton, which is a very powerful explosive. It is used in war, and also by engineers. There is always some waste material left over when cotton is made into cloth. This cotton waste is kept and sold for cleaning oily machinery.

HOW WE USE COTTONSEED

At one time the seeds of cotton were thrown away or burned. Nowadays there are hundreds of factories that make things from them. First of all the shells are removed by machines. These shells are sometimes mixed in with food for cattle and horses, but mostly they are burned to ashes. The ashes are full of chemicals that make plants grow well. They are spread on the ground as fertilizer, to make the soil more nourishing to plants.

After the shells have been taken off, the seeds are squeezed in huge machines called presses, to remove the oil. After the oil has been forced out, a hard mass is left behind. This is ground up into cottonseed meal. Like the shells, it is used for feeding animals or as a fertilizer. It is even better for animals and for the soil than the shells are.

The most important part of cottonseed is the oil. When this is pure it has a very nice taste. It is used as salad oil, in cooking, and for making lard, lipstick, margarine (imitation butter), and many other things. Not all cottonseed oil is good enough to eat. Most of it is used for making paint, soap, putty, artificial leather, oil cloth, tar, and all sorts of other things.

Even after the cotton and the seeds have been picked, the plants are not always wasted. In some places the stems are made into pulp, and this is made into cardboard. Because of all the ways cotton is used, it is hard to imagine how we could live without it.

THE HISTORY OF COTTON

Most of the kinds of cotton we use now came originally from India. For this reason scientists believe that the first cotton cloth was probably made in India. The oldest cotton cloth we know of was found in tombs in Egypt. It is three thousand years old, yet it is as beautiful as any that is made today. From India and Egypt traders carried cotton cloth to all parts of their world. The people of ancient Greece and Rome wore cotton from Egypt. It was only about a thousand

years ago that the first cotton was grown in the south of Europe. It was grown by the Arabs, who at one time ruled Spain.

When Columbus discovered the New World, he found cotton growing wild in the West Indian islands. And when the Spaniards conquered Mexico and Peru, they found that the people in those countries made beautiful cloth from cotton. In fact, some people think that the loveliest of all cloth was made by the people who lived in Peru a thousand years ago.

Cotton was first grown in the United States soon after the first settlers began to live in the South. But at first very little was grown, because it was very expensive to separate the seeds from the fluff. In one day a man could separate only one pound of fluff. Then in 1793 an American named Eli Whitney invented a machine that did this as fast as a hundred men.

This machine was called the cotton engine. Now it has come to be known as the cotton gin. As a result of this invention, cotton soon became one of the most important industries in America. Nowadays America grows more cotton than all the rest of the world put together.

Because new ways to make use of cotton are always being found, more cotton is grown every year. Other countries that grow a lot of cotton are India, Burma, Egypt, Brazil, China, and Russia, but even these countries sometimes buy cotton from the United States.

cottonwood

Cottonwood is a tall graceful tree of the aspen or poplar family. It has grayish-brown bark, heart-shaped glossy leaves, and long yellow catkins of flowers in the spring. It gets its name from the round green fruit that bursts when ripe and lets loose masses of white fluff that carry the seeds away on the wind. The wood is white and soft, but is used in making boxes, matches, barrels, and paper. Cottonwoods grow wild throughout the central and northeastern parts of the United States and Canada. They grow chiefly near streams, and are often broken and partly fallen. Sometimes they are planted for shade in cities.

cougar

The cougar is the largest of the "big cats" in the Americas except for the jaguar. Cougars are 6 to 8 feet long and weigh about 160 pounds. They are very strong and can drag about five times their own weight. The cougar has a small head, a long, heavy tail, and is gray or sand-colored like the rocks and caves where it lives. The cougar hunts deer and farmers' livestock, such as cattle horses, sheep and pigs. Cougars sleep during the day and prowl at night, springing silently on their prey. They can leap twenty feet in one bound, and sometimes jump from sixty feet above the ground. They can also swim across rivers. If the cougar does not eat all of its kill in one night, it covers the rest with brush and returns to it for later meals. Cougars have a terrifying shriek. They do not attack man, but man often hunts the cougar for sport and to protect other animals. Cougar kittens, usually three in a litter, are born at almost any time of the year.

How to Detect Counterfeit Coins

DROP COINS ON A HARD SURFACE

Genuine coins have a bell-like ring. Most counterfeit coins sound dull.

FEEL ALL COINS

Most counterfeit coins feel greasy. COMPARE questionable coins with known genuine coins of the same denomination.

F.B.I.

CORRUGATED OUTER EDGE

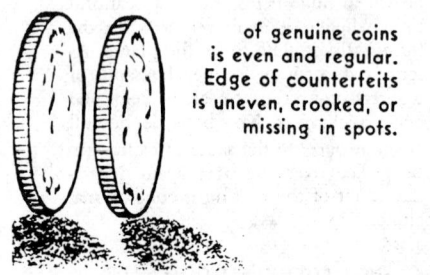

of genuine coins is even and regular. Edge of counterfeits is uneven, crooked, or missing in spots.

They are about a foot long, weigh a pound, and are blind at birth just like the kittens you know. You can read more about the habits of these animals in the article on CAT in this encyclopedia.

The cougar is sometimes called a catamount in the eastern United States. In the West and Southwest, you hear them named pumas, panthers, or mountain lions. Many cougars used to live in the Americas, roaming the forests all the way from southern Canada to the bottom of South America. Today these big cats are found only in the wild parts of Florida and Louisiana and in the West from British Columbia to Mexico. Central and South America still have many cougars.

counterfeiting

Counterfeiting means making an imitation of something in order to cheat people. The word is usually used to describe the crime of making false money and cheating people by spending it as if it were real money. Counterfeiting has been done ever since money was first used thousands of years ago. In ancient times anyone caught counterfeiting was put to death. In the United States, a counterfeiter can be sent to prison for 15 years. You can tell if a coin is counterfeit by listening to the sound it makes when you drop it. Good coins sound clear and sharp. Bad coins sound flat and dull. If you compare counterfeit paper money with real money, you will find that the pictures and numbers on counterfeit bills do not look as neat and as beautiful as those printed by the government.

counterpoint

Counterpoint is two or more melodies written so that they can be played or sung together. All of the parts can be heard separately. Sometimes there is a main melody, and the other melodies form a sort of accompaniment. There are five kinds of counterpoint; one note against one note, two notes against one, four notes against one, syncopation (which means that the accents are on different beats), and florid counterpoint, which is a mixture of the four other forms. Johann Sebastian Bach is considered the greatest master of counterpoint in modern times.

Count of Monte Cristo

The Count of Monte Cristo is a famous storybook nobleman whose adventures were told by Alexandre Dumas the elder, a French writer. Edmond Dantès, the Count of Monte Cristo, has an exciting time escaping from his prison in the Chateau d'If on an island off the French coast, searching for hidden treasure, punishing his enemies, and rewarding his friends. Dumas made the small Italian island of Monte Cristo famous by giving its name to the hero of his book.

county

A county is an area of land which has its own local government. The number of the counties ranges from two, as in Delaware, to 254, as in Texas. In Louisiana a county is called a parish. The purpose of the county is to carry out the state laws and help the state govern the area within its borders. The county also looks after its own schools, highways, and health and welfare activities. England and Northern Ireland do not have states. Their counties are similar to our states. And they have much the same powers that our states have.

court

A court is a place where questions of law are settled. Since laws are rules of government, a court is a branch of the government. (See the article LAW.)

We use the word *court* because in olden days, judges used to sit in enclosed yards, called courts, when they were trying a case. In the days when government and religion were closely connected, courts often took care of both religious and legal questions. Often the judge was an official of the church as well as an official of the state. Very often, too, the man who ran the government, the man who made the laws, and the man who enforced the laws, were all the same person. A very powerful king, for instance, had complete control of the gov-

ernment. He was the president, the congress, and the judges all rolled into one.

As governments became more complicated, it became harder for one man to handle all the problems that running a nation involved. It also became clear that one-man rule in every field was not always fair. One way to see that all men had an equal chance for justice was to give one group of men the job of making the laws, and another group the job of enforcing and explaining them. Another safeguard was to set up a system of *trial by jury,* that is, a system in which a man's guilt or innocence would be decided not just by one professional judge, but by twelve ordinary people.

Both of these safeguards were used by the men who founded the United States and wrote its Constitution. They were careful to separate the three great powers of government from one another, and to keep them completely independent. The executive branch (the president is its head and it runs the government), the legislative branch (the houses of Congress which make the government's laws), and the judiciary branch (the judges and the courts which enforce and explain the laws), are three equal partners in the American system. The Constitution provides, also, that any man who is accused of a crime has the right to a trial by jury, so that he can be sure that his fate is in the hands of ordinary people who have no hidden motives of power or politics behind them.

In the United States, there are both federal courts, which handle questions of national law, and state courts, which handle questions of state law. The federal courts are provided for in the United States Constitution, and the state courts are provided for in the various state constitutions. These two kinds of court are almost completely independent of each other. One way in which they are not independent is that the United States Constitution comes before any state law that might conflict with it. Therefore the Supreme Court often decides cases that began in state courts.

The federal court that has the final word on all matters of the federal Constitution is the Supreme Court. It is the highest court in the country. Under the Supreme Court are the district courts and the circuit courts of appeals. If a man is brought to trial in a district court and is not happy about the verdict, he can ask the circuit court to hear the case and give its decision. The decision of the Supreme Court is final. The judges of the federal courts are appointed by the President of the United States and must be approved by the Congress. They remain in office as long as they want to and are considered fit.

In the state courts, the same general idea is followed as holds in the federal courts. That is, there are lower courts and higher courts, and a man can appeal his case from the lowest state court to the highest. One difference between the federal and state courts is that in the federal courts most kinds of cases, criminal, constitutional, tax evasion, are tried in the same courts. In the state courts, on the other hand, there are different courts that handle different legal problems. Another difference between the federal courts and the state courts is that the judges in state courts are elected by the people of the state and serve for only a certain specified period of time.

The main idea of the United States system of courts is to see to it that every man who is accused of breaking the law shall have the right to a fair trial and shall have the right to appeal the decision of the court to the highest possible authority. Since we believe that every man is innocent until he is proved guilty, our court system is carefully organized to give all citizens an equal chance to defend their innocence before the courts.

court-martial

A court-martial is a special military court convened under the rules of military justice to decide whether the persons brought before it are innocent or guilty of the crimes with which they are charged. In the time of ancient Rome courts-martial often dealt out heavy punishment to soldiers found guilty; but during the Middle Ages there were no regular systems of courts-martial in the armies and fleets of various countries. Present military law is based on a series of laws drawn up in England during the 17th century to govern soldiers and sailors.

Courts-martial deal not only with military offenses, but also with all crimes committed on an army post or by a soldier overseas. By far the most frequent court-martial offense is being AWOL, or *a*bsent *with*out *leave.*

The Uniform Code of Military Justice, a set of rules enacted by Congress in 1948, provides for three kinds of courts-martial; the *Deck* or *Summary,* consisting of one officer and empowered to sentence an offender for a period up to one month; the *Special,* consisting of three officers who can sentence a man up to six months; and the *General,* of five officers or more, that can impose very severe penalties, including death. Under UCMJ an enlisted man accused of a crime has the right to demand that one third of the court-martial that is trying him be made up of enlisted men.

covenant

A covenant is an agreement between people to do certain things and not to do other things. But there is a difference between a covenant made between equals and one granted by a superior to an inferior. In the latter case the superior dictates the terms. In the Bible we hear of covenants granted to men by God. One of the most important was that given Israel at the time of Moses. God agreed to watch over the people of Israel but required that the people obey His laws. Earlier God had made covenants with Abraham, Noah, and other important Jewish leaders.

In Scotland about three hundred years ago a group of people were called Covenanters. They had signed a covenant saying they would keep the Presbyterian religion in the Church of Scotland. For fifty years the English, who were united with Scotland, wanted the Scottish people to accept the Church of England, but they would not break their covenant, even though they were pressed to do so by the English. Finally, in 1743, the Presbyterian Church was established in Scotland.

Covenant is also a word in law that means a written promise made between people saying they will do something or will not do something. It can be used as a verb, "I do covenant to do so and so."

Coventry

Coventry is a very famous old town on the Sherbourne River in the center of England. During World War II many of Coventry's old houses and churches, built more than five hundred years ago, were destroyed by bombing. Because Coventry was the first English city to be bombed heavily in World War II, for some time after that bombing a city and destroying it was called "Coventrizing" it.

Coventry has long been famous for its textile manufacture. After World War I other kinds of industry grew, such as the manufacture of airplanes, automobiles, bicycles, plastics, explosives, electrical equipment and tools. It was because of these industries that Coventry was so heavily bombed by the Germans.

In ancient times Coventry was famous as a religious and political center. About the year 1043 a Benedictine abbey was founded by Lady Godiva and her husband, Leofric. You can read about Lady GODIVA in a separate article. The famous Coventry miracle plays were given here during the 15th century. The town is also mentioned in Shakespeare's play *Richard II.* There is a famous expression about Coventry. Whenever anyone is "sent to Coventry," it means that person is no longer accepted by society.

covered wagon

In the days before the railroads were built, and even before there were many roads, heavy loads were moved in wagons. These were freight wagons pulled by teams of four, six, eight, and sometimes up to twenty horses or mules. Over one hundred and more years ago, when people started to move westward in big waves, they took household goods, stoves, beds, building materials, and livestock.

Most of the wagons used were of the type known as covered wagons. They were long and narrow, and made something like a boat, with a curved bottom rising at both ends. The reason for making the wagon box in this shape was to keep the freight from shifting as the wagon went up and down hill. It was balanced on high wheels and bow springs to add further to this design. Over the top was a canvas hood stretched over curved wooden staves. The hood followed the general lines of the box, and was higher at each end than in the center. There was a seat for the driver at one end, and a round opening at the other, like the mouth of a bag. The appearance was something like a bonnet. There was a good reason for the cover, as well as for the shape of the wagon box. Being of canvas, it added little extra weight for the team to pull, but served to keep out sun, dust, and rain. It could be removed for easier loading and unloading. The original covered wagons were called *Conestogas* or *Conestoga wagons,* because they were first made in a town in Pennsylvania named Conestoga.

THE PRAIRIE SCHOONER

When settlers started to journey across

the Great Plains, they used a small model of the Conestoga wagon. Instead of teams of six or eight horses they used two or four, and often they used oxen instead of horses. Oxen were really preferred in many cases, because they were stronger, required less care, and could eat grass while hitched to the wagon. The settlers had to travel very long distances—sometimes more than three thousand miles.

They went through unknown country where there were hostile Indians and other dangers. It took many months of traveling to reach the end of the journey, and they had to take everything they owned with them. It was because of this that the wagon train was developed.

Here is how a wagon train was organized: Suppose you are in St. Louis, Missouri, about 150 years ago. You and your family want to go to California to settle there. You would "sign up" with a party of other people going the same way, and all travel together. That would be called a wagon train, and it might be from twenty to one hundred families, with all of their belongings. The wagon train would be like an army on the march. Officers would be elected, and the services of a professional guide secured. Certain powers would be given to the officers and committee in charge, and they would see that the rules were obeyed. You would sign an agreement to obey the rules or be punished. This was necessary for the safety of everyone. Every day hunting parties would ride out on fast horses to find meat such as antelope, deer, and buffalo. Scouts would ride ahead to find water to locate the best route for the slow-moving wagons. There was plenty of work to do and everyone had a job, even the children. At night the wagons were parked in a circle, with all the animals and people within, and guards were placed on duty to warn of danger. Wagon trains were always made as large as possible, because the larger the number traveling together, the greater was the safety.

cow is the female of several different kinds of animal, but the word usually refers to the milk-giving animal of the cattle family. See the articles on CATTLE and DAIRY FARMING.

cowbird

The cowbird is an American bird of the same family as the starling. It is also called *lazybird* and *corn bunting*. It lives in flocks in which there are more males than females, and is peculiar because it makes no nest. The females lay their eggs in the nests of other birds, one egg to a nest, and leave their young ones to be hatched out and raised by the foster parent. Usually these parents do not seem to notice anything strange about the young cowbird, which may be twice the size of their own chicks. The foster parents selected are usually warblers and other small birds. However, they sometimes do take alarm and leave the nest and their own young, and build a new one somewhere else.

cowboy

American cowboys are famous the world over—so famous, in fact, that they are called by their English name in many foreign languages. In the early days of the Wild West, they led very dangerous and difficult lives. They spent most of their time on horseback taking care of the cattle. They drove the herds to pasture, branded them with red-hot irons at roundup time, and protected them from rustlers and wild animals. They still do these things, but their work today is much easier since the great western ranches are now fenced in, and there are not as many thieves and cattle rustlers as there were formerly. However, most cowboys are still fearless and skillful horsemen. You can see them at work either on the ranches or at rodeos. There are separate articles about RANCHES and RODEOS. And they still wear the same picturesque costumes, with broad-brimmed hats, bandannas, chaps, high boots with spurs, and lassos. These costumes are not just for decoration. They are also very useful, as anyone who has seen a cowboy at work can tell. Although the cowboys of the United States are famous all over the world, there are other cowboys in South America who are just as famous. These cowboys are called GAUCHOS, and you can read about them in a separate article.

Cowpens, Battle of

Cowpens is a small town in South Carolina far in from the seacoast of that state. In January 1781, an important battle of the Revolutionary War took place near Cowpens. At this time the British, who were fighting the Americans, were trying to take all the southern states away from the Americans. They took the cities on the seacoast, then marched inland. At Cowpens about 1,000 American soldiers stopped about 1,000 British soldiers. The Americans defeated the British and killed many of them. Those who were left marched back to the coast as quickly as they could. From then on the British did not try to capture the inland parts of the southern states but kept to the coast. The story of many other battles of the Revolution is told in the article REVOLUTIONARY WAR.

Cowper, William

William Cowper was a famous English poet. He was born in 1731 and died at the age of 69 in 1800. As a young man he studied law, but never practiced because he suffered from a mental disease called melancholia that made him feel miserable, unhappy, and afraid. He was very fortunate, however, to have a  devoted friend named Mrs. Unwin to take care of him. Cowper lived for some time in the small village of Olney, in southern England. He was a very religious man, and his curate, or pastor, Henry Newton, encouraged him to write many fine poems and hymns. The hymns are called the Olney Hymns. Cowper was also famous as a writer of brilliant personal letters, and you may have read one of his best-known humorous poems about "John Gilpin's Ride."

cowpox

Cowpox is a disease of cattle. Human beings can also get it; when they do, it is a very mild illness. In 1796, a scientist named Edward Jenner discovered that people who had ever had cowpox would not get smallpox, a very serious disease. He developed a method of using fluid (vaccine) from cowpox blisters to protect humans from getting smallpox. This method is called VACCINATION. There is a separate article about it, and also an article about SMALLPOX.

cowslip

There are many different kinds of plant called cowslip. The English cowslip is a kind of primrose in which the flowers grow in a bunch at the top of a stalk about six inches high. They are like little brownish-yellow bells, and the leaves, which grow in a circle close to the ground, are long and crinkly, like pale-green rabbit's ears. The plants grow mostly in damp meadows.

The American cowslip is a very pretty kind of primrose that is called the *shooting star* in the West. The *marsh marigold,* a kind of buttercup that grows in damp places, is also commonly called cowslip. It has large golden-yellow flowers, and its leaves are sometimes used as a vegetable. Another cowslip is the *bluebell,* or *Virginia cowslip,* which belongs to the lungwort or borage family of plants.

Cox, James M.

James M. Cox ran for President of the United States on the Democratic ticket in 1920, against Warren G. Harding. Neither Cox nor the man who ran with him for Vice-President, whose name was Franklin D. Roosevelt, was elected. Before he ran for President, Cox was a member of Congress. He was governor of Ohio for six years, and was governor of that state at the time he ran for the presidency. Cox was born in 1870 in Ohio. He became a newspaper reporter and later, when he was 28 years old, bought a newspaper and became its publisher. He was very successful, and bought several more newspapers, both in Ohio and in Florida. He died in 1957.

Coxey, Jacob

Jacob Sechler Coxey was an American politician who lived from 1854 to 1951. When he was still young, Coxey became interested in the problems of the working people who, at that time, had bad working conditions and were often unable to get jobs. During a serious depression in 1894, Coxey led a march of unemployed men to Washington to ask the government to lend money to the local communities so the unemployed could be put to work on public improvements. This group was called Coxey's Army. It did not succeed in getting what it wanted, and Coxey and some of the other leaders were arrested for walking on the lawn in front of the Capitol.

coyote

The coyote or the prairie wolf is known in the western United States for its continued yelping, barking, and howling during the night. The Aztec Indians named it "barking wolf," and its cry carries long distances. Coyotes are about half the size of their relatives, the gray wolves. The coyote is 21 inches high,

weighs twenty to thirty pounds, and is almost four feet long, of which about one-third is tail. The coyote's color is gray or yellow-brown, with black markings and white on the under parts. Coyotes hunt rabbits, mice, gophers, birds, insects, reptiles, and carrion or dead animals, but they also eat fruits and vegetables and even catch fish. The coyote has been called a pest to man because it kills sheep, chickens and calves, but it also helps man by killing rodents and rabbits that would otherwise eat much of the grass needed for grazing.

The coyote can run as fast as 45 miles an hour and therefore can catch even the jackrabbits and also escape its enemy, the gray wolf. But wolves, eagles and owls often catch the young coyotes. Coyote pups are born in the spring, with from 6 to 15 in a family. They are born in a cave, a hollow tree, or a burrow in the ground, and stay there with their mother for six weeks or so. The father brings their food but does not come into the den. After two months, the young are trained to hunt, and in the fall they must look for their own hunting range. Coyotes are found in the western and central parts of North America, north to Alaska and south to Central America. Coyote fur is used for lap robes, gloves, and coats.

crab

Crabs are hard-shelled animals with roundish, flattened bodies and five pairs of legs, the front pair of which end in large claws. With the lobsters, crayfish and shrimps, they belong to the group of jointed-legged animals called *crustaceans*. They have eyes on the ends of stalks, and are famous for their way of running sidewise. Most crabs live in the sea, some of them swimming with paddle-shaped legs. A few are found in fresh water, and some spend most of their lives on dry land. These do so by carrying water around with them to keep their gills moist. The land crabs of the West Indies are found even on top of high mountains, but they return to the sea once a year to breed. As crabs get bigger, they have to shed their hard shells every so often, for the shell stops them from growing. Their new shell is soft at first, and in it the crab grows rapidly. It is helpless to defend itself, however, so it hides during the few days it takes the shell to harden.

Crabs eat all sorts of food, chiefly decaying material. The robber crab of the Pacific Ocean climbs coconut palms and eats their fruit. The racer crab of the West Indies sucks the juice of sugar cane. Hermit crabs live in the empty shells of sea snails, moving to another shell as they grow bigger.

The horseshoe, or king, crab is not a true crab at all, but is related to the spiders. Its shell is in two parts, hinged together and ending in a long, pointed tail. It spends its life burrowing in sand and mud in search of the small worms and shellfish that it eats. Most of the time it lives in deep water, but it comes into the shallows to spawn, or lay its eggs.

crab apple

Crab apples are apples that grow on various wild apple trees. The apples are small, often irregular in shape, and acid in taste. They are often used for making jams and jelly. There are many kinds of crab apple tree in America, the best-known being two from the central and eastern parts of the country: one with narrow leaves, which grows as far south as Florida, and a more northern kind with a sweet-scented, yellow-green fruit. Another very good kind grows in Bitter Root Valley in Montana.

crab grass

Crab grass is a common grass all over the United States. In the North it is considered a pest because it is difficult to kill, but in the South it is cultivated for hay. It is a native of Europe, where it is also grown for hay and for its seeds, from which a kind of porridge is made. It has both upright and creeping stems, and in summer grows two or three feet high, with tall spikes of delicate flowers or fruit.

Cracow

Cracow is a very old city on the Vistula River, in the south of Poland. It was the ancient capital of Poland, and many Polish kings are buried there. The people of Cracow are proud of their splendid cathedrals and great works of art. Cracow University, which was founded almost six hundred years ago, is the largest university in Poland.

The city of Cracow is the capital of Cracow province, a rich farm region. The main crops are wheat, rye, and oats. There are large deposits of rock salt in mines just south of the city.

The city was held by the Germans during World War II, and in 1945 the Russians occupied it. About 479,000 people live there. The name is spelled Kraków in Polish.

crafts are art trades or special skills, such as leathercraft or wood carving: see the article on HANDCRAFTS.

Craig, Sir James Henry

Sir James Henry Craig was a well-known British military officer who fought in the American Revolutionary War. He was born in 1749 at Gibraltar, a famous British fort at the entrance to the Mediterranean Sea. At the age of 14 he entered the British army with the rank of ensign, and later he fought as a captain in the American Revolutionary War. He was wounded in the Battle of Lexington and the Battle of Bunker Hill. He afterward rose to the rank of general and served with the British army in many other parts of the world. In 1807 he was appointed governor-in-chief of Canada, but he had so many difficulties with the French Canadians and was such a poor governor in other ways that he was replaced after four years in office. He then returned to England, where he died in 1812.

cramp

A cramp is a sudden, painful tightening of a muscle. A cramp can occur when a muscle is tired, or when its circulation is cut off, or when it is suddenly chilled. Any of these things can make the muscle tighten up painfully in one spot. It seems as if there were a knot in the muscle. When you bend your arm to make the muscle stand out in the upper part of your arm, you are tightening that muscle on purpose, and it does not hurt. You can make it relax just as easily. When you have a muscle cramp, the cramped part of the muscle tightens all by itself; you cannot make it relax. It will gradually relax and smooth out all by itself, just as it tightened up all by itself, but you can speed this up by gently massaging the cramped place. Massage in the direction of the heart, and you will help the circulation to return, so that you will feel the knotted or cramped muscle straighten out and relax.

cranberry

A cranberry is the fruit of a plant that belongs to the same family as the blueberry. But the blueberry plant is a bush, while the cranberry plant creeps along the ground. The cranberry plant grows wild on wet moorlands and boggy places. For this reason cranberries are sometimes also known as *moorberries,* or *mossberries.* The berries are round, about the size of large peas, and most kinds are bright red. They are rather sour, but they have a delicious flavor. They are made into cranberry sauce and cranberry jelly, which people eat with meat and poultry such as geese and turkeys. In the United States people eat cranberry sauce with turkey on Thanksgiving Day.

A number of kinds of cranberry are found in North America, Asia, and Europe. The American kinds have the biggest berries. Because people eat so many cranberries—over a million bushels a year—they are now grown by gardeners, mostly in Wisconsin, New Jersey, Cape Cod in Massachusetts, Washington and Oregon.

crane

The crane is the tallest of the wading birds. It stands four or five feet high and looks like a stork. Wading birds have long, thin legs and beaks and spend part or most of their time in shallow water. Cranes eat insects, frogs, and also the young shoots of grain and grass, and they usually swallow small animals whole. If you could watch cranes during their mating season, you would see them do a dance, hopping, skipping, and jumping about, making a croaking sound. The female bird lays from two to four eggs, and the baby birds in the shell have an "egg tooth" for cracking their way out. After only a few weeks, the young ones can run so fast that you would have a hard time catching them.

The tallest American crane is the whooping crane, a graceful white bird, which has been almost entirely killed off. Its name comes from the croaking call it makes while flying. A flock of cranes flies in a long straight line. Smaller, brown American cranes are the sand-hill and the little brown cranes. They are found in the American Northwest and Canada, as well as in the southern United States and in Cuba. Cranes may live to be forty years old, which is a very long life for a bird. These birds have been known to man for many centuries, and myths and folk tales are told about them.

crane

When it is necessary to lift something heavy and put it in a high or awkward place, a crane is usually used. A crane is a device or machine that has a long arm attached to the ground; at the other end there is a pulley. The object to be lifted is tied to a rope. The other end of the rope is put through the pulley. When the rope is pulled, the object will be lifted to the end of the long arm. The long arm can then be swung into whatever position is desired, and the heavy object can be let down. Cranes are useful for building houses where building materials must be carried to the second floor or higher.

Cranes are similar to derricks, except that derricks have a system of pulleys on one end. This makes them able to lift objects too heavy for cranes. There is a separate article in this encyclopedia about DERRICKS. Derricks are useful for loading ships and constructing steel buildings where the load is very heavy.

Crane, Stephen

Stephen Crane was an American short story writer, journalist, and poet. He was the author of one of the most famous novels of the Civil War, *The Red Badge of Courage,* which he wrote at the age of 22 without having had any war experience himself. He also wrote two series of exciting stories for boys, called the *Whilomville Stories* and *The Black Riders.* He was born in 1871 at Newark, New Jersey, and attended Lafayette College and Syracuse University. He died of tuberculosis at the age of 29 in Germany.

crayfish

Crayfish or crawfish are animals very much like lobsters. But lobsters live in the sea, while crayfish live in fresh water. They have hard shells and five pairs of legs. The front two legs have large claws on them like a crab's claws. Crayfish lurk under stones or in holes during the day. At night they come out and walk about on the bottom of the stream or lake in search of food. They eat fish, water snails, worms, insects which fall into the water, and rotting animal matter.

A crayfish can swim, and if it needs to escape from an enemy it can jerk itself backward through the water by flipping its tail. Its tail is broad, and the mother crayfish carries her young under it for a while. Because crayfish need calcium for their shells, they are usually found in districts where there is plenty of limestone rock or chalk, both of which are full of calcium that dissolves into the water of the rivers. Crayfish sometimes damage dams across rivers and canal banks, because they burrow so much. They are very good to eat, and in some parts of England people prefer them to any other dish. There are many kinds of crayfish found in different parts of the world. In America there are about thirty kinds, the largest of which may be about eight inches long. Like crabs and lobsters, crayfish belong to the group of hard-shelled animals called CRUSTACEANS, about which there is a separate article.

crayon

A crayon is a kind of pencil made out of wax or chalk or charcoal. You can draw on a blackboard with chalk, and you can make a very fine picture with black charcoal on white paper. But if you like bright colors, you can have the best time using wax crayons, because you can buy wax crayons of so many beautiful colors. Some people like to draw with colored chalk. These drawings are called pastels, and they are very pretty. If you like pale yellow and pink and light blue, you will enjoy making pastel drawings.

Crazy Horse

Crazy Horse was a famous Indian chief of the Oglala Sioux. The Oglala tribe belonged to the western branch of the Sioux who called themselves the Dakota. When the white men tried to make the Oglala tribe go to a reservation, Crazy Horse and his tribesmen would not go. They were brave fighters, and Crazy Horse was a good general At the battle of Rosebud River in Montana, Crazy Horse defeated the United States army of General George Crook. This was early in 1876. Later in the same year the Sioux tribes joined together under the leadership of Sitting Bull and wiped out the forces of General George A. Custer. You can read about this battle, called "Custer's Last Stand," in the article on General CUSTER. Crazy Horse was second in command to Sitting Bull. In 1877, his village was destroyed in a battle with the United States army under General Nelson Miles. A few months later his tribesmen, hungry and sick, surrendered to the government. Crazy Horse was shot by the guard when they came to arrest him for planning a revolt.

cream

Cream is the rich, fatty part of milk. Usually the cream in the milk rises and floats on top, but in homogenized milk the cream is mixed so completely with the milk that it will not separate out. Cream is a very nourishing part of milk, and a good grade of milk has a lot of cream in it. People who want to gain weight often drink milk with extra cream added to it. Most of the cream that is removed from milk is used to make butter. You can read about the making of BUTTER in a separate article.

The amount of cream in milk depends on the kind of cow the milk comes from and the food the cow eats. Good herds of cows, like the famous Holstein, give a very rich, creamy milk when fed properly. Goat's milk is very rich in cream, and for this reason some of the finest cheeses in the world are made from it.

Crécy

Crécy is a small town in northern France near the English Channel. A great English victory over France took place there about six hundred years ago, during the Hundred Years' War between those two countries. An English army, led by King Edward III, had landed in France, and in August 1346 it was attacked by the French, who were led by King Philip VI. Most of the French were on horseback, and they wore heavy armor. The English, who fought on foot and wore very little armor, had a new weapon called the longbow. Their arrows went right through the armor of the French. The English also used cannon, which was a very new weapon in those days. About 1,500 French knights were killed, while only 50 of the English lost their lives. This battle made England an important military nation for the first time.

credit

Credit is an arrangement under which a person can buy something and pay for it later. The plan is based on the seller's belief in the honesty of the buyer. If we think a person will pay his bills, we say his credit is good. The charge account that a woman may have with the grocer or with a large department store is a credit arrangement. She buys what she needs for a week or a month, and takes the goods home with her. Then at the end of the credit period the store sends her a bill for all her purchases, and she can pay it all at one time. The storekeeper and the manufacturers buy on credit, too. In this way they can buy large quantities of goods to sell, or raw materials to make into products to sell. They may not have enough cash to pay for these things when they are needed. Credit makes it possible for them to get the goods and pay for them when they have taken in enough money to do so. For instance, if a grocer bought $500 worth of milk on credit during a month, and sold this milk for $700, he would have the $500 to pay for the milk at the end of the month and have his $200 profit besides. Banks also are giving credit when they lend money to persons or businesses who sign a *note,* or a promise to pay back the loan.

Cree Indians, a branch of the Algonquin family of American Indians: see the article on ALGONQUIN.

creed

The word *creed* comes from the Latin word *credo,* which means "I believe." Therefore a creed is a statement of a person's beliefs. It is usually used in connection with religion. In many Christian Churches there are creeds, or statements, of the basic beliefs and ideas of these Churches. One of these statements, the Apostles' Creed, is given in full in the article CHRISTIANITY.

Creeks

The Creeks or *Muskogeans* were the great family of Indians in the southeastern United States. In the 19th century, the Creek confederacy, or union, ruled many different tribes and almost controlled the Cherokees and Choctaw. Then came the famous Creek war against the United States, in 1813. The American general, Andrew Jackson, finally defeated the Creeks after violent battles. Like other southeastern tribes, the Creeks were sent off their land and onto the "Trail of Tears," which was a dreadful forced journey to Indian Territory, now the state of Oklahoma. They were many times cheated of their land and their goods by the white men. Later, the white men called the Creeks one of the "Five Civilized Tribes" in the territory.

In the early 18th century, Creek towns were scattered all over the present states of Alabama and Georgia, where there are many streams or creeks. They had "white towns" for peace ceremonies or meetings and "red towns" for war. Their

houses had curved roofs made by bending young trees to form the rafters and covering them with thatch or bark. On their farms they grew maize, sunflowers, pumpkins, melons, and tobacco, as well as fruit. They wore almost no clothing, but they made beautiful deerskin costumes and turkey-feather hoods or capes. The Creeks were probably sun-worshipers who believed the sun was the greatest symbol of God.

creeper

A creeper is a small bird that runs up and down the trunks of trees searching for insects. Usually a creeper will start at the bottom of a tree and work up to the top.

The creeper spends its time hunting up and down the trunks of trees for insects.

It looks very much like a mouse as it runs rapidly about hunting in all the crannies of the bark. The tail feathers of creepers are stiff and pointed. They stick into the bark and prop up the bird as it clings with its claws. There are many kinds of creepers. One that is often seen in North America is the brown creeper, which is about the size and color of a sparrow, but has a longer beak. It builds its nest in cracks and holes in trees.

Crémazie, Octave

Octave Crémazie was a French Canadian poet who lived about one hundred years ago and became famous as a patriotic writer. Many of his poems were published in newspapers. His poem, "The Old Canadian Soldier," won him the title of official poet of Canada. He had a great influence on other French Canadian poets both through his own work and personally. He and his brothers owned a bookshop in the city of Quebec where other writers and poets would gather to talk. He was born in 1827 and lived most of his life in Quebec. But in 1862 he got into business troubles and went to France, where he lived under a different name and died very poor in 1879.

Creole

A Creole is a person who is born in America or the islands of the West Indies, but who is a descendant of early French or Spanish settlers. The French first used the word Creole to describe a person of French ancestry and French culture who was not born in France.

In America most of the French settlers came to Louisiana, in or near the city of New Orleans. Later the Spanish settled in the same places and married the Creoles already living there. The word Creole then came to mean anyone born in the New World of mixed French and Spanish ancestry. In New Orleans, those people who can trace their ancestry back to these early settlers call themselves Creoles. The Creoles are high in society in New Orleans, and Louisiana is called the Creole State. Some people in Louisiana speak a kind of French dialect, or patois, that is also called Creole.

In Mexico, people who have only Spanish or Portuguese blood are called Creoles. In South and Central America, Creoles also hold a high position in society.

creosote

Creosote is a sharp-smelling oil that makes your eyes water. People get creosote from the sap of the beechwood tree and also from coal. This oil is very useful. A small amount of creosote stops meat from spoiling. It is also used to stop wood from decaying. When wood is soaked in creosote it turns black and smells like tar. Most of the wooden piles that are used to build docks and bridges are protected first with creosote. Doctors sometimes use creosote to treat certain diseases of the stomach and intestine.

Crerar, Henry Duncan Graham

Henry D. G. Crerar is a Canadian general who commanded his country's overseas forces during World War II in Europe. He was born in 1888 in Hamilton, Ontario, and attended Upper Canada College at Toronto, and the Royal Military College at Kingston. He served during the first World War and afterward held several important military positions. During World War II, he served first as a brigadier (general) and senior officer at Canadian military headquarters in London, from which position he rose to the rank of full general and to the position of commander of the Canadian army overseas. He retired in 1946.

crescent

The crescent is an emblem or symbol that looks like the outline of a new moon. The word *crescent* means "increasing." The crescent was used as a symbol many years ago by the Byzantines in Constantinople, and became the emblem of the Ottoman Turks when they captured the city five hundred years ago. Today the crescent is not only a Turkish emblem. It is a symbol for most of the Mohammedan people, just as the cross is a symbol for the Christian people, because the Sultan of Turkey was at the same time considered the caliph, or head of, the Mohammedans everywhere.

The crescent is used in the flag of Turkey.

Crete

Crete is the largest of the Greek islands. It is in the Mediterranean Sea 60 miles southeast of the mainland. It is 160 miles long. It is a rugged, mountainous island whose highest peak, Mt. Ida, is over 8,000 feet. Like Greece, Crete produces olive oil, wine, raisins, citrus fruits, vegetables, and dairy products.

The history of Crete is older than that of Greece and goes back to one of the earliest civilizations in the world. It is called the Minoan civilization and was named after the legendary King Minos, who is supposed to have founded early Crete. In the ruins of the ancient palace at Cnossus there have been found many clues to this civilization, which reached its period of greatest power and wealth about the year 1600 B.C., more than 3,500 years ago. It had a peculiar writing, which has recently been deciphered, and the language has been recognized as an early form of Greek. Then suddenly the Minoan civilization collapsed, no one knows why. Other Greek tribes later settled on the island, and through the centuries it was fought over and controlled at one time or another by the Romans, Byzantines, Genovese, Arabs, Venetians, and Turks. After the Greco-Turkish War in 1896–97, Crete was returned to Greek control, although it was occupied by other European troops until 1909. In 1913, after the Balkan Wars, Crete officially became a part of Greece.

During World War II, Crete was used as a British base until a German airborne invasion captured it in May, 1941. It was recaptured by the British in 1944, and after the war it was returned to Greece.

CRETE. Area 3,234 square miles. Population (1973 estimate) 456,208. Government, nome (province) of Greece. Capital, Canea.

Cribbage

Cribbage is a card game for two players. It is an English game and according to some stories it was invented by Sir John Suckling, an English poet who lived about three hundred years ago, but probably he did no more than to make some changes in a game that was already being played.

In Cribbage the regular pack of 52 cards is used. Six cards are dealt to each player. Of these six cards, each player puts aside two (face down), making four cards that form the *crib,* or extra hand, which belongs to the dealer. A player does not show the cards he puts in the crib.

The undealt cards are cut into two packets, and the top card of the second is turned face up. This is the *starter.* It is later counted as though it were part of both hands and of the crib.

THE PLAY

The player who did not deal now plays a card face up on the table, and announces its number. Face cards and ten count 10 each; aces count 1 each; other cards count the same as the numbers printed on them. Each player in turn plays a card and adds it to the total of the cards previously played, announcing the new total. For example, the first player puts down a three and says "Three"; his opponent puts down a seven and says "Ten"; then the first player puts down a queen and says "Twenty"; and so on. A player cannot take the total to more than 31. If he cannot play without going over 31, he says "Go," and his opponent scores a point. Then the player puts down a card to start a new series of numbers. This goes on until both players have played all their cards.

SCORING

In Cribbage you keep score on a "cribbage board," as shown in the picture. Each player has two pegs. Each time he makes a score he moves the backward peg that many holes ahead of the forward peg. The game is usually won by the player who first reaches 61, but some players prefer to play "twice around," in which case game is 121. Scoring is called *pegging.*

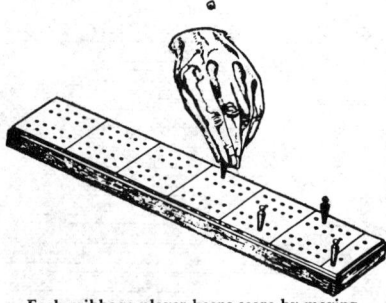

Each cribbage player keeps score by moving his two pegs on the cribbage board.

You score for cards that make the following combinations:

Pair. Two cards of a kind, as two queens: peg 2.
Pair royal. Three cards of a kind: peg 6.
Double pair royal. Four cards of a kind: peg 12.

Run. Three or more cards in sequence, as 4-5-6: peg the number of cards in the sequence. Suits do not make any difference.
Fifteen. Any two cards totaling 15, as 8 and 7, or face card and 5: peg 2.

In the play, whenever the last two or more cards make one of these combinations, the player who played the last of the cards makes a score. For example: The first play is a six, the second a seven, the third a five; the player who put down the five pegs 3, for the run 5—6—7. The next player now puts down a five and pegs 2 for the pair of fives.

When the play is completed, each player counts all the combinations in his hand plus the starter, five cards in all. He counts every combination that requires a new card; that is, for 7-6-5-5 he would peg 8, counting 3 for each different run of 7—6—5 and 2 for the pair of fives. The dealer counts up the crib plus the starter in the same way and gets that score.

Some special scores are:

Flush. If all four cards of a hand are in the same suit, the holder scores 4; if the starter is also the same suit it adds 1, making the score 5. If the crib and starter are all of the same suit the dealer scores 5, but he does not score if only the four cards of the crib are the same suit.
His heels. If the starter is a jack it is called "his heels" and scores 2 for the dealer.
His nobs. If the jack of the same suit as the starter is held in either hand or in the crib, the owner scores 1 point for "his nobs."
Muggins. Some play that if a player pegs fewer points than he is entitled to, his opponent may say "Muggins" and score the difference.

Cribbage is sometimes played by three or four players. There are complete rules of Cribbage in many books on games.

cricket

A cricket is a small dark brown insect, about an inch long. It has long, thin hind legs with which it can jump like its cousin the grasshopper. Unlike grasshoppers, crickets hide under stones or in dark places during the day. They feed chiefly on vegetable matter such as plant stems. They lay their eggs in loose earth in the fall and the young crickets hatch in the spring. There are many different kinds of cricket; the common sort lives in houses and gardens. People associate crickets with coziness at home because of the cheerful chirping sound the males make by rubbing their wings together, and the fact that they often live near fireplaces. The great author Charles Dickens wrote a book called *The Cricket on the Hearth.*

A different sort of creature is the mole cricket, which has spadelike front feet with which it burrows in the earth. Mole crickets are often destructive insects, because they eat the roots of plants such as grasses.

cricket

Cricket is one of the games from which the American game of baseball was developed. In England and some other British countries, cricket is almost as popular as baseball is in the United States. Some cricket games are played in the United States and Canada.

There are eleven men on a cricket team. The field must be at least 500 feet

square. The ball is very much like a baseball.

Two batsmen go to bat at one time. They stand at wickets 66 feet apart. A wicket is a stump in the ground. On top of each wicket is a piece of wood called a *bail.* The *bowler* (the same position as the pitcher in baseball) bowls (throws) the ball in an effort to knock the bail off the wicket. If the batsman hits it, he and the other batsman must exchange places before the fielders can return the ball to the wicket and knock off the bail. There are no foul balls as in baseball, so the fielders are placed all around the wickets. Whenever the two batsmen can exchange place safely, they score a run. When a batsman is put out (by having the bail knocked off a wicket before he can reach it), the next batsman takes his place. An inning does not end until all eleven members of a team have batted, and often a batsman will score a *century* (100 runs or more in his turn), so an inning may last for hours and a game may last for several days.

The biggest cricket match, equivalent to the World Series in baseball, is the Test Match between English and Australian teams.

crime

A crime is an act that breaks a law. If the law has been made by people who have the best interests of the people at heart, the act will not be a crime unless it hurts somebody else. For thousands of years men have been arguing about what is a crime and what is not. In wartime, soldiers do many things to hurt the enemy that would be the worst possible crimes in peacetime; they kill, burn buildings, and take what does not belong to them, and these are crimes of murder, arson and stealing (larceny) according to the laws of all countries. When a king or dictator has control over a country he may have the power to pass laws and say it is a crime to tell the truth or to disagree with him, and these are not crimes in countries where men are free. But people who are lucky enough to live in the United States or Canada or other free countries can be sure that the laws are passed for the good of the people, and that it is a real crime to break the law.

The worst crimes are called *felonies.* These are usually crimes that hurt or may hurt other people physically or that take important property away from them. Homicide (killing a person), arson (intentionally burning down a building), or grand larceny (stealing a large amount of money or something of great value) are felonies under nearly all laws, and other things are felonies in different states or countries. A felon (person convicted of a felony) is usually sent to prison and in most states he can no longer vote.

An unimportant crime is a *misdemeanor.* It is an act that breaks a law but does not hurt anyone very much, though it may make things inconvenient for other people. An example is parking a car too long in one place. The usual punishment for a misdemeanor is a fine (an amount of money that must be paid to the government of the city, state, or other place where the misdemeanor occurred).

A person who commits a crime is a *criminal,* but this word means several different things. Some persons try to make their livings by committing crimes, and they are called *habitual criminals* or *professional criminals.* Usually they are suffering from some form of mental illness. An *occasional criminal* does not think that crime is the best way to make a living; he breaks the law for some other reason. (He is not a person who breaks the law "every now and then," but a person who breaks the law on some particular occasion; it may be only once in his lifetime.) Perhaps an occasional criminal is tempted just once to take a large amount of money that does not belong to him, and is not strong enough or smart enough to resist the temptation; or perhaps he is just careless and does something that hurts other people when he really did not intend to do it. Psychologists and scientists in several other fields have spent many years studying criminal behavior. They hope that someday they will learn enough so that there will be very few crimes.

CRIME DETECTION

As long as people may commit crimes, there have to be police forces and detectives to prevent crimes and to catch and punish criminals. Many stories have been written about how crimes are solved, and how clever and skillful detectives are. Although these stories are not true, the police departments of the world are just as skillful as the stories say they are, and in some cases even more so.

Usually, crime detection is just careful study and hard work. There are several ways in which the police go about solving nearly all crimes. These are the most important ones:

1. *Witnesses.* Usually someone has seen the crime committed and can tell what happened. When no one is known to have seen the crime, the police visit one person after another who *may* have seen it, until they find someone who did.

2. *Type of crime.* The police keep records on all known criminals. Certain professional criminals almost always commit crimes of the same kind and in the same way. The records show what known criminals may have been guilty of a particular crime. These are the persons the police look for.

3. *Informers.* Criminals are almost never honorable men (though some stories falsely say they are), and usually a criminal who knows about a crime will sell the information to the police, or trade it for favors—if he is not guilty himself.

4. *Scientific study.* Police work uses many sciences. A criminal can sometimes be identified by his fingerprints. The gun from which a bullet is fired can sometimes be identified by ballistics. (There are separate articles about FINGERPRINTS and BALLISTICS.) Chemistry helps to make sure that certain traces left by the criminal belong to him alone. Radar has been used to catch automobile speeders. Nearly every modern science is used by up-to-date police departments.

Experience has shown that no threat of punishment will stop everyone from committing crimes, but it does frighten some criminals and make the number of crimes fewer. The combination of better crime detection and psychological knowledge can reduce the number of crimes.

Crimea

The Crimea is a part of southern Russia. It is a peninsula, which means that it is a piece of land surrounded on three sides by water. The Black Sea is on the west and south; and the Sea of Azov is on the east. It is attached to the southern part of Russia on the north by a small piece of land about five miles wide. This connecting land is called an isthmus, the Isthmus of Perekop. The Crimea is about 10,000 square miles in size, just a little larger than the state of Vermont. Since 1783 the Crimea has belonged to Russia. Until 1945 it was an independent province of Russia, but in 1945 Russia took over its government.

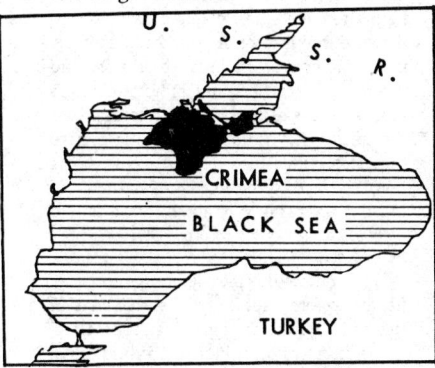

The cities in the south are ideal vacation and health centers. Yalta is one of these cities. It was the setting for an important political conference in 1945. The Crimea has many forests of cedar and magnolias, pastures for sheep and horses, and a good climate for grain, cotton and tobacco. Iron, coal, marble, silver and limestone are other industries of the Crimea.

CRIMEAN WARS

The Crimea has been an important battle area in two wars. The first was the Crimean War of 1854–56. Turkey, France and England fought Russia because they were afraid Russia was getting too powerful. "The Charge of the Light Brigade," a poem by Alfred Tennyson, tells about one of the Crimean War battles. It took place at BALAKLAVA, a city in the Crimea, about which there is a separate article. During World War II, Sevastopol, another Crimean city, was attacked by the Germans. The Germans occupied it for two years before Russia could get it back. It was almost destroyed in the fighting.

Crittenden Compromise

For many years before the Civil War started in the United States, there were men who believed that the question of slavery could be settled peacefully. They tried to make compromises, or agreements, between the Northern states that wanted to abolish slavery, and the Southern states that wanted to preserve it. Henry Clay of Kentucky was a senator who succeeded several times in preventing the start of the war. After he resigned, his good friend John Jordan Crittenden was appointed to take his place as senator. Crittenden tried very hard to get the Senate to make constitutional amendments (changes in the laws) to settle the problem of slavery. This plan was called the Crittenden Compromise. The plan failed, and the war started. Crittenden was born in Kentucky in 1786 and died in 1863.

Croatia

Croatia is one of six republics that are joined together to form the country of Yugoslavia. The other five are SERBIA, SLOVENIA, BOSNIA-HERZEGOVINA, MACEDONIA, and MONTENEGRO. There are separate articles on all of these republics, and on the country of YUGOSLAVIA, in other parts of this encyclopedia.

Croatia is in the northwest part of Yugoslavia, and now it includes most of the Yugoslav coastline, which is called Dalmatia. Behind the coastline, the Croatian countryside is quite mountainous and rugged. Croatia is about 22,000 square miles in size, and it is the home of over 4,442,000 people. That makes it about as large as the state of West Virginia, with over twice as many people living in it. These people, called Croats, are Slavs, like most of the people of eastern Europe.

The Croats have lived in that section of the world for nearly 1,500 years. During most of that time, there was a kingdom called Croatia, but its borders were not the same as they are today. The Croatian kingdom had the same king as Hungary, but it had its own parliament and laws. For centuries, part of Croatia was ruled by the Turks. After World War I, Croatia became part of the larger country of Yugoslavia, which was ruled by a king. During World War II, the Germans occupied Croatia, but many of the Croatian people joined with the "partisans" to drive the Germans out of their land.

CROATIA. Area, 21,611 square miles. Population (1973 estimate) 4,442,564. Language, Serbo-Croatian. Religion, predominantly Roman Catholic. Government, constituent republic of Yugoslavia. Capital, Zagreb, population (in 1973) 566,084.

crochet

Crochet is handiwork done with a hook, called a crochet hook, and a single strand of yarn or thread. It is easy to crochet once you have mastered a few simple stitches. These few stitches can be combined in hundreds of different ways, and beautiful things can be made in crochet. You can make tablecloths, potholders, sweaters, hats, handbags, rugs, ties, and even complete dresses.

Many materials are used for crocheting, from fine silk thread to heavy rug yarns. When you buy crochet cottons or yarns, you will see complete instruction books with commercial patterns for whatever you want to make at very small cost. By following the instructions exactly, you will be able to make anything you wish. Instruction books also show you how the simple stitches are made, as well as the variations to make more complicated stitches.

A person who has never crocheted before can make a potholder in *single crochet* by following the simple instructions here. Buy a ball of cotton rug yarn, and

a large crochet hook—size G. It will be so marked. Loop the yarn around the first finger of your left hand and then pull the string through the loop and make a slip knot. Next, hold that loop in your left hand and take the crochet hook in your right hand. Use the hook to catch hold of the string, and draw it through the loop, making a second loop. You now have two links in a row of *chain stitch*. Pull each loop as you make it, to keep them all about the same size. Keep on making links, or chain stitches until you have fifteen of them. You are now ready to start doing single crochet. Make two extra loops, or chains, and then turn your row of chain stitch around, ready to go back. Draw the thread, with the hook, through the third loop back from the end. You will now have two loops on your crochet hook. Pick up the thread with your hook again, and draw it through both of the loops on the hook. You have now completed a stitch of single crochet. Continue all the way back to the very beginning, putting a single crochet in each loop of the original row of chain stitches. When you reach the last—which will be the first loop you made—make your single crochet in that final loop. Then do two chain stitches. Turn around, and crochet back across the entire length again. Keep going back and forth until you have made a complete square. It will not take long. When you think it is wide enough to be used as a potholder, or when it looks square, pull through the last loop and cut the thread in the middle of the loop. Pull the end tight, and it will not unravel. You now have a hand-crocheted potholder, made in single crochet. After you have had a little practice, you will be able to do many other interesting things.

It should now be easy for you to read and understand the directions in commercial crochet pattern books. They will tell you how to do *double* and *triple crochet* and how to do fancy stitches.

Crockett, Davy

Davy Crockett was a famous frontiersman in the early days of the West. He was born in Tennessee in 1786 and

fought with General Andrew Jackson in the Creek War of 1813–1814. Then he traveled around the frontier, as the Mississippi Valley region was called in those days. He was a fur trader for a while, and got to know the Indians and their customs. Then he went back to Tennessee, and was elected to the United States Congress. He served three terms, and while he was in Washington the people found that he was a very intelligent man even though he talked like a frontiersman and dressed in leather clothes and a squirrel-skin hat.

There are many stories told about Davy Crockett, for he was something of a legend even while he was alive. He wrote, or was supposed to have written, several books. They are stories of his adventures, but many people think that he did not write them himself. He did write many letters that tell us interesting things

about American customs and history of that time. In 1834 he went to Texas, where he joined the Texas Revolution and fought for its independence against Mexico. He was killed in 1836, at the famous battle of the ALAMO, about which you can read in a separate article.

crocodile

The crocodile is a large reptile or crawling animal that lives in the water. It is found on all the continents except Europe and Antarctica. Snakes and lizards are also reptiles, and the crocodile looks like a huge lizard. Crocodiles and alligators are in the same family, but crocodiles have a few overlapping teeth in their lower jaw that fit outside the upper jaw. There is a separate article about the ALLIGATOR in this encyclopedia.

Crocodiles are from ten to twenty feet long and have a heavy, horny skin. When they are looking for an animal to capture, they can float with only their eyes and nostrils out of the water. The crocodile's tail, which is almost as long as its body, can strike down an animal or lash it to bits. Crocodiles feed on fish, birds, other animals, and sometimes on human beings. If a crocodile is not hungry, it will often hide away an animal it has killed by covering it with mud.

The crocodile lays its eggs on dry places, where they hatch by the heat of the sun. It lives in warm or tropical regions, like southern Florida in the United States. The Nile crocodile is one of the most famous, and is found in different parts of Africa. The Egyptians and other ancient peoples used the crocodile as a symbol for some of their gods.

You may remember the crocodile who cries in the story of Peter Pan, by Sir James Barrie. When the crocodile's mouth is full, the food presses against the glands that cause tears. So the crocodile is not unhappy when he cries, and we say a person cries crocodile tears when he is only pretending to be sad.

crocus

A crocus is a pretty plant related to the iris. As soon as the snow melts in the early spring, crocus flowers begin to appear just above the ground. They have six petals, and are very beautifully colored, usually yellow or white or purple. After a while the leaves begin to push up above the ground too. They are long and thin, like grass leaves. The crocus only flowers for a few weeks, but the leaves last until the fall. Then they die away, and the bulb of the crocus, which is deep underground, lives on through the winter. Unless the winter is so cold that the frost kills the bulb, the crocus will produce more flowers and leaves the next spring, and may live for many years.

Crocuses are mostly natives of Europe and western Asia. There are many different kinds, three of which are wild in England. Because they are so pretty and appear before almost any other flower in the spring, people with gardens love to plant them. They are now found in all the cooler countries of the world.

Croesus

Croesus, king of Lydia, was famous for his wealth. Lydia was an ancient country in Asia Minor, and although Croesus lived 2,500 years ago, we still say "as rich as Croesus" when we want to speak of a very rich man. Before Croesus became its king, Lydia was a small part of what is now Turkey. Croesus extended his kingdom on all sides, especially toward the East, where he added Phrygia. According to legend, Phrygia had once had a king named Midas, whose touch was supposed to turn everything to gold. Midas did not enjoy his gift—even his food became gold before he could eat it. So he washed away his golden touch in a river called Pactolus. The great wealth of Croesus was said to come from the gold sands of this river, which is now called Baguli.

Lydia was threatened by Cyrus, king of Persia, a much larger country. Croesus went to Delphi, Greece, and consulted the famous Oracle. The Oracle was supposed to answer questions about what would happen, but the replies were sometimes like riddles. Croesus was told he would destroy a great empire. He thought this meant that he would conquer Persia, and so he attacked Cyrus without enough troops. Croesus was defeated and then Cyrus captured Lydia's capital. Croesus had destroyed a great empire, his own. He was the last King of Lydia.

Crompton, Samuel

Samuel Crompton was one of the greatest English inventors. He was born in Lancashire, England, in 1753. As a young boy he helped his mother weave cotton in their home and he became very interested in the machines that spun the cotton. At the age of 21, he invented a machine that could draw, twist, and wind many strands of cotton into a very strong, fine yarn. He received only a little money for his invention; many other people who used it made great fortunes. He died a poor man in 1827.

Cromwell, Oliver

Oliver Cromwell was Lord Protector of the British Commonwealth between 1653 and 1658. This position actually made him a military dictator for a period

Gale Research Co.

when England had no king. Cromwell was born in 1599, but not much is known about his early life. By the time he was thirty, he had become a Puritan. This was a religious group which did not like the Church of England. The Puritans thought that the Church of England was too much like the Catholic Church. It was not until he was about forty that Cromwell became very active in politics. At about this time, too, he became very active in the army.

The period in which Cromwell lived was a time of conflict between the king, Charles I, and Parliament. The king thought he should have absolute power over his people. But Parliament thought it should have more authority in the government. Parliament was gradually becoming more influential. Many of its members were wealthy people, and many of them were Puritans. The king favored the Church of England. Cromwell was a member of Parliament, and as a Puritan,

he did not like the king's power. In 1642 the Puritan Revolution started and the king's army was defeated. In 1649 Charles I was beheaded; that same year the Commonwealth was set up. There was to be no king. Cromwell led the armies of the Commonwealth. He defeated all opposition to the Commonwealth.

In 1653 the first written constitution was set up. It was called the Instrument of Government. Cromwell was made Lord Protector for life. He was a very strong leader. In the five years he ruled, the army supported him, and brought great prosperity to England. He died in 1658 leaving his son, Richard, to rule. Richard was not very capable. But by 1660 the English people were tired of Puritan rule, and they restored a king (Charles II, the son of Charles I) to the throne.

Cronos

Cronos was the god of time in the Greek myths, stories that were told thousands of years ago. The myths described how the earth began and how human beings first came upon it. The gods and goddesses were special, powerful beings who were said to cause the happenings in nature. Cronos was chief of the Titans —giants born from Heaven and Earth. He dethroned his father, and then was told that one of his sons would take the throne away from him. So Cronos swallowed his children to prevent them from growing up. But one son, Zeus, escaped, and after a great war among the gods, Zeus became king. Cronos is sometimes pictured as Father Time, with a scythe and an hourglass, an old instrument for telling time by the trickling of sand. Just as the scythe mows grass or grain, Cronos or Time, was said to be the Great Reaper, who brought man the results of his acts, as the harvest from his crops. The story that Cronos swallowed his own children is explained as meaning that time brings an end to all things that have a beginning. Cronos was also the father of Demeter, who was called Ceres by the Romans.

croquet

Croquet is an outdoor game, usually played on any fairly level lawn. The object of the game is to strike balls with mallets so that they will roll through a series of hoops, or wickets, and back to the starting point. There may be any number of players from two to eight. When there are four, six or eight players, they usually play in partnerships, two players being partners. The player or partnership that first gets back to the starting point is the winner.

Almost anyone can enjoy playing croquet, but there are experts who play very well and very seriously. In many parts of the country they have their croquet courts lighted so that they can play at night.

The official court is 30 feet by 72 feet. The balls should be 3⅝ inches in diameter and may be made of wood or of a hard rubber or plastic. They weigh from half a pound to a pound. The mallets are made of wood, with long handles and a solid wooden head that is cylindrical (shaped like a thin tin can). The wickets are hoops of wire or pipe, as narrow as

four inches wide in expert games but usually seven or eight inches wide.

A player starts at the home stake. He tries to drive his ball through the two wickets in front of it, then through the first wicket at the right of the court, the center wicket, the second wicket at the right, and the two wickets at the other end of the court. At this point he must hit the stake at the other end. He then returns toward the home stake by the same series of wickets on the other side of the court. When he has gone through the two starting wickets again he may hit the home stake and end his round, but as long as he does not hit the home stake again he may continue to play as a rover.

Each time a player goes through a wicket, he has another shot coming to him. When he shoots and does not go through a wicket, his turn ends and the next player in turn plays. Hitting the ball of another player (or going through two wickets with one shot) gives two more shots. When a player has hit another player's ball, he may put his ball against it, hold his ball with his foot, and drive the opponent's ball away by hitting his ball with his mallet. He will still have one shot left, but he may not use this shot to hit the opposing ball again. He is said to be "dead" on that ball until he has gone through another wicket.

A good croquet court has some area outside the 30 by 72 feet of the official court, so that opposing balls can be driven far away. In the game of *roque,* there is a concrete curb around the court that keeps the balls inside. When you want to hit another player's ball, but find a wicket in the way, you may be able to reach it by bouncing your ball off the curb.

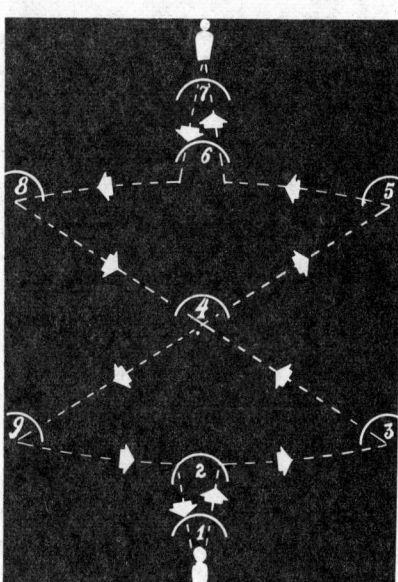

Croquet grounds are arranged in this way. You have to knock your ball through each of the numbered arches in turn. You begin at the starting stake behind Arch 1.

Crosby, Bing

Bing Crosby is the name of one of the most popular and famous entertainers who have ever lived. As both a singer and

an actor he has made millions of people like him. He was born in 1904 in Tacoma, Washington, and he was named Harry Lillis Crosby. He started singing when he was about 21, with dance orchestras in his home town. He became a member of a trio (three) of singers called the "Rhythm Boys," and they joined Paul Whiteman's orchestra. Not long afterward he made his first "hit" record, and in 1931 he started his own radio program. Within a year he had made a successful motion picture, and had become a "household name," which means that almost everyone had heard of him. His singing was always relaxed and pleasant to listen to. His phonograph records have probably been played on the radio more than those of any other single performer.

Crosby, Fanny Jane

Fanny Jane Crosby was a writer of hymns and gospel songs. She probably wrote more songs than anyone else who ever lived, for it is believed that her total number was about eight thousand. She was born in 1820 in Putnam County, New York. When she was only six weeks old, she became blind because the wrong medicine was accidentally put in her eyes. She studied at the New York City School for the Blind, and stayed there as a teacher for eleven years During this time she met Grover Cleveland, who later was president of the United States, and they became friends for life. She married a blind musician named Alexander Van Alstyne, and many of her hymns are signed F. J. Van Alstyne. Her best-known hymns include: *Jesus, Keep Me Near the Cross; Pass Me Not, O Gentle Saviour; To the Work; Blessed Assurance; Close To Thee.* She died in 1915 at the age of 95.

cross

We usually think of the cross as a symbol of Christ and Christianity, but actually, crosses were used long before Christ was killed on the cross. They have been found as far back as the Stone Age and long before the birth of Jesus they were used all throughout Europe, sometimes on medals and coins. The first time that the cross was used as a Christian symbol was during the reign of Constantine, an early Roman emperor. During the Middle Ages Crusaders used the cross as their symbol. Crusaders were Christians who were trying to get the Holy Land, Palestine, away from the Moslems. At about the same time, many crosses began to appear on churches. Some churches are designed in the form of a cross. The long, center aisle represents the upright part of the cross. The aisle just before the altar represents the crossbar of the cross. Crosses have also been used in churchyards and on gravestones. They have appeared even on village greens and market places. Crosses have been used in religious ceremonies for a long time. Often they are carried before the archbishop in a procession. It has been only in the last two centuries that people have begun to wear crosses about their necks. A cross is

Ten of the many varieties of cross: 1. The original cross, used by the ancient Greeks. 2. The later Greek cross. 3. St. Andrew's cross. 4. The swastika. A different form of swastika was the emblem of Germany before and during World War II. 5. The Greek Orthodox cross. 6. The Cross of Lorraine, used by the Free French in World War II. 7. The Jerusalem cross. 8. The Maltese cross. 9. The Latin cross. 10. The patriarchal cross.

sometimes called a crucifix because it represents Christ's crucifixion. Many societies or fraternities in Christian countries have flags or banners with crosses on them.

There are several forms of the cross. One is called the Latin cross. It is formed by one piece that goes straight up and another piece set across the top of the first. Christ was crucified on a Latin cross. A second cross is called St. Anthony's cross. It is shaped like a T. Another is called St. Andrew's cross. It is shaped like the letter X. Whenever we see the word *Cross* capitalized, we know that it is referring to the cross on which Christ was crucified.

crossbill

The crossbill is a bird of the canary family. Its beak looks twisted out of shape, because the two parts of it cross one another instead of meeting. This strange beak is very useful to the crossbill, for with it they can pry open the scales of pine cones to pull out the seeds with their tongue. These seeds are the crossbill's chief food. Their beaks are so powerful that they can tear their way out of a wooden cage. The story is told that they got their beaks crossed when trying to pull the nails out of the cross on which Jesus was crucified.

The European crossbill, which is found all over Europe, northern Asia, and parts of North Africa, is a beautiful bird. The male is crimson-colored, with patches of bright scarlet. The female is yellow-green. In captivity the male soon fades to an orange-yellow. The American red crossbill differs from the European in having a smaller beak. The white-winged crossbill is smaller, rose-pink in color,

with bands of white on the wings. Crossbills are seldom seen outside of pine forests. Their nests are very roughly built of pine twigs and plant fibers.

cross-breeding

When scientists develop a seed from plants of different kinds, or cause animals of different kinds to have offspring, it is called cross-breeding.

It often happens naturally that the pollen, which is the male part of a flower, is carried by a bee or butterfly to the stigma, or female part, of a different kind of plant. This is called cross-fertilization. Seeds produced by cross-fertilization will grow into plants that look a bit like one parent and a bit like the other. Scientists often find two plants, each of which has something they like. For instance, one plant of a certain kind may have blue flowers and small leaves, and the other blue flowers and very big leaves. In order to get a new plant with big leaves and also blue flowers, the scientists will cross-fertilize them. When cross-fertilization is done on purpose it is called cross-breeding. See the article on POLLINATION.

Scientists and others also mate different breeds of the same kind of animal, in order to produce an animal that combines good features of both its parents. A familiar example is the mule, which is produced by mating a jackass, or male donkey, with a mare, or female horse. A donkey can work better than a horse but is not as big and so is not as strong. The mule gets its endurance from its father and its size from its mother. See also the article on EVOLUTION.

A cross-bred plant or animal is called

a hybrid. Many of the beautiful flowers in our gardens, and many of the finest kinds of tame animals have been produced by cross-breeding.

cross-eyes, a defect of vision that makes one eye or both eyes turn toward the nose: see the article on STRABISMUS, in another volume of this encyclopedia.

crossword puzzle

A crossword puzzle is a game of finding words that fit a list of definitions (meanings). One person "works" a crossword puzzle by himself, except that it is all right to ask someone else for help when a word is hard to think of. The puzzle is a lot of squares. Some are white squares, and in each white square you write a letter of the word that fits the definition. Some are black squares, and these show where words end. Half the words go "Across" (or *horizontal*) and the other words go "Down" (or *vertical*). Each definition has a number. The same number in the crossword puzzle diagram shows the square in which the word begins. Then you can count how many white squares follow that number and know how many letters there are in the word.

In American puzzles, every letter is part of two different words. Such a letter is said to be "keyed." This means that when you find one word, every letter in it is a key that helps unlock the mystery of another word. Suppose the definition for a three-letter word is "household pet." That might be either a dog or a cat. But the first letter of the word begins another three-letter word for which the definition is "time between sunrise and sunset." You decide this word is *day,* and write it in the blank squares. Now you know the first letter of the household pet is D, so it cannot be a cat and must be a dog. You write in the word *dog.* Every word you get helps you to get other words.

The ancient Romans had puzzles somewhat like crossword puzzles, nearly two thousand years ago, but the crossword puzzle as it is known today was begun about 1920 in a New York newspaper, the *World.* A few years later a new book-publishing company, Simon and Schuster, brought out a book of these puzzles and they became very popular all over the United States and in many foreign countries. Since then, nearly every newspaper and many magazines have printed crossword puzzles.

Experts at solving crossword puzzles sometimes do "diagramless puzzles." The definitions are given, but the solver (person who is doing the puzzle) has to figure out not only the words but where the white and black squares go in the diagram. Another kind of puzzle that is like a crossword puzzle is called a "Double-Crostic." Definitions are given for the words, and when you find out what the words are they spell out a quotation from a book, and also the name of the book and the name of the person who wrote it.

crow

The crow is a sly, curious, and clever bird found all over the world. It lives in places where other birds of its family cannot live, such as the Hawaiian Islands and Australia. Ravens, jays, and

¹P	²A	³S	⁴S	
⁵A				⁶
⁷I		⁸		
⁹L		¹⁰		
	¹¹			

In an "American-style" crossword puzzle, every letter is part of two different words. A number shows where each word begins. A definition tells what this word means. To solve the puzzle, you must think of the word that fits the definition, and write the letters of this word into the proper blank spaces. For the puzzle drawn here, the definitions would read like this:

ACROSS
1 Go by
5 Table in a church
7 A thing
8 Behold!
9 According to law
11 Traveled on horseback

DOWN
1 Bucket
2 Change
3 Street (abbreviation)
4 Dish of raw green vegetables
6 Part in a play
10 Move away from where you are

magpies are all members of the crow family. Crows are about 1½ feet long, are shiny black in color, and have a long, cone-shaped beak. Their wings spread to 3 feet, and they are exceptional fliers. In the air they move in a straight line, and from this we get the saying, "as the crow flies." Crows nest in trees and build very comfortable homes. The female crow lays three or more eggs. Crows live on insects, mice, rats, young rabbits, corn, nuts, and the eggs and young of other birds. Crows also like to feed on carrion, the dead bodies of animals. The crow's greatest enemy is the great horned owl.

You would have a hard time trying to catch crows, for they are clever at avoiding traps. Farmers put up scarecrows, or straw figures, especially in corn fields, to keep crows away. But often the crows learn that the scarecrow is not really harmful, and they go back to stealing the corn anyway. Crows usually manage to stay out of range of gunshot. A crow likes bright objects such as pieces of metal or glass and will hide them away. Crows sometimes play amusing tricks, and tame crows have been trained to say a few words. The crow's sound is a harsh "caw."

Crow Indians, a branch of the Sioux tribe of American Indians: see the article on SIOUX.

crown and crown jewels

A crown is a fancy headpiece worn by a king or other ruler. A crown is usually set with precious stones or gems called the crown jewels. In Great Britain there are seven crowns, and every year about three hundred thousand people go to see them in the Tower of London. The most important crown is St. Edward's, the crown of England, used for the coronation. This crown was made about three hundred years ago, and is a solid gold circle, decorated with rubies, emeralds, sapphires, diamonds, and pearls. It weighs almost seven pounds, and on state occasions the king or queen wears a lighter silver crown, the crown of state. Among the jewels on this crown is the third-largest diamond in the world. The other crowns were made for the king when he visited India, for several queens, and for the Prince of Wales.

The most famous of the crown jewels are the *Black Prince's Ruby* and the *Koh-i-noor* and *Cullinan* diamonds. The ruby is at least six hundred years old. The Koh-i-noor, or *Mountain of Light*, is said to be five thousand years old, and was found in India. It passed among many Oriental kings and conquerors before Queen Vic-

toria received it in the 19th century. The Cullinan, the largest diamond ever found, was discovered in South Africa, in 1905. The stone was cut into 9 large and 96 smaller gems, and the largest are called *Stars of Africa.* Besides the crowns, other tokens or signs of royalty are decorated with gems. There are scepters or rods, bracelets, spurs, and the Orb, a golden ball. Altogether the crown jewels are valued at about thirty million dollars.

crucifixion

Crucifixion was a method of putting people to death in ancient times. The old Romans used this form of capital punishment (punishment by death) for their slaves and lowest criminals. The person was often whipped first. Then he was either tied or nailed to a cross and left to die.

The best-known crucifixion was that of Jesus Christ. Whenever we see the word Crucifixion written with a capital C, we know that it refers only to the execution of Christ. Saint Peter was also crucified.

Cruikshank, George

George Cruikshank was a famous English illustrator and cartoonist. He is most famous for his drawings in the novels of Charles Dickens and his funny cartoons in *Punch* magazine. His illustrations for *Oliver Twist* by Dickens won him worldwide fame. He did many caricatures of famous people. Caricatures are drawings that exaggerate people's bad points and poke fun at them. Cruikshank used to draw fat people that looked like balloons, and very thin people that looked like broom handles. He probably illustrated more books during his lifetime than any other artist. He was born in 1792. Both his father and grandfather were artists, so it was only natural that he should become one too. After a busy life he died in 1878.

cruiser

A cruiser is a medium-sized warship whose guns are almost as powerful as a battleship's and that is nearly as fast as a destroyer. There are separate articles on BATTLESHIPS and DESTROYERS in this encyclopedia. There are *heavy cruisers,* which may displace 9,000 to 17,000 tons and have 8-inch guns; and *light cruisers,* which may displace 4,000 to 14,000 tons and have 6-inch guns. About two thousand sailors live on the biggest cruisers, while there are about five hundred on the smallest ones. In the

United States Navy, cruisers are named after cities. Heavy cruisers are usually named for the big cities, and light cruisers are named for smaller cities. There used to be *battle cruisers,* as big as battleships, but they are no longer built.

Crusades

The Crusades were wars fought hundreds of years ago, from the year 1096 to the year 1291. At that time, America had not been discovered. The people who lived in Europe were Christians. The Holy Land where Jesus had lived and had been crucified, including the city of Bethlehem where he was born and Jerusalem where he died, belonged to people who followed the Mohammedan religion. The Christian people of Europe sent armies to try to win the Holy Land back from the Mohammedans. These were the Crusades.

There were four big Crusades, and some smaller ones. For a time, the Christian armies were successful. They captured Jerusalem and set up a Christian kingdom there. But in the end the Mohammedans won. They still had the Holy Land when the last Crusade ended.

Many of those who went from Europe to fight in the Crusades were religious men who wanted to win the Holy Land back to Christianity. But some of them were young, bold, adventurous men who just wanted a good fight; and some were clever businessmen who could see profit from winning new territory.

THE FIRST CRUSADE

In the year 1095 the Pope, head of the Christian Church in all of western Europe, told the kings of the European countries that they should go and conquer the Holy Land. Many brave men started out at once. But they did not plan well, and they did not have good enough training or equipment to fight the great armies of the Mohammedans. They were soon defeated and many of them were killed. But after them came a big army led by the best soldiers in Europe. This was called the First Crusade. It was the only one that was really successful. In nearly three years of fighting it drove back the Mohammedan armies and captured Jerusalem in 1099.

The victorious Crusaders formed four states from the territory they had captured. These were called Jerusalem, Antioch, Edessa, and Tripoli. The new states became very rich, and traded with the cities of Europe.

THE LATER CRUSADES

The Crusaders were far from home, where their supplies and weapons came from. The Mohammedans kept on attacking them. Bit by bit, the Crusaders gave ground. By 1147, a Second Crusade was needed to save the Christian territories of the Holy Land. The Second Crusade was led by the kings of France and Germany. There was hard fighting for two years, but the Crusade was a failure. The kings went back home. The Mohammedans kept on fighting, and in 1187 they captured Jerusalem again.

The loss of Jerusalem caused the kings of Europe to try a Third Crusade. The great King of England, Richard the Lionhearted, was one of its leaders. This Cru-

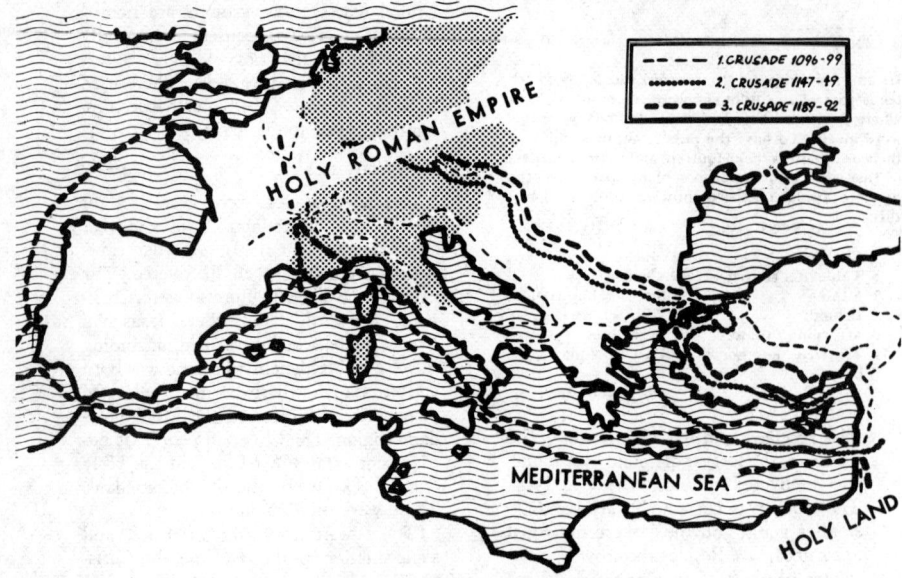

Seven Crusades were made many hundreds of years ago to the Holy Land in Palestine. This map shows the routes taken by the Crusaders in the first three Crusades.

sade lasted from 1189 to 1192. There were fierce battles between the Crusaders led by Richard and others, and the Mohammedans led by their famous king Saladin. But the Third Crusade did not recapture Jerusalem and neither did the Fourth Crusade, which lasted from 1202 to 1204. The Crusaders of the Fourth Crusade did little besides capture the city of Constantinople, which was disgraceful because it was a Christian city and their only purpose was a greedy one —to plunder it, because it was a very rich city.

The saddest story of the Crusades is the "Children's Crusade." In 1212, hundreds of European children started out on a Crusade. Most of them were from France and Germany. They did not have a chance to conquer the Mohammedan armies, and they did not even get close to the Holy Land. Most of them died of disease, starvation, or the hardships of the long march, and others were captured and sold as slaves.

By 1291 the Mohammedans had conquered all the lands that had been won from them in the First Crusade, and the Crusades were over. Many lives were lost in the Crusades, but they did some good for Europe. The Crusaders brought back with them a better knowledge of the world, and of the science that was being developed in the East, and this helped Europeans to become better educated.

crustacean

A crustacean is an animal with a hard shell and several pairs of jointed legs. The legs of a crustacean except the first pair are divided into a long outer part and a short inner part. The first pair of legs usually end in claws. Lobsters, crabs and shrimps are typical crustaceans, but there are many other kinds that look quite different. Some crustaceans are so small that you can see them only under a magnifying glass. Altogether there are about ten thousand kinds. Most of them live in the sea, but some live in fresh water and a few live on land. Because of their hard shells, crustaceans cannot grow in the same way as other animals. Instead, they have to burst out of their old

shells and grow rapidly before their new shell hardens. This takes a few days. During this time they hide, because without their hard shells they can easily be eaten by other animals.

Crustaceans lay eggs. Some kinds, such as lobsters, carry their eggs under their tails until the eggs hatch. Often the eggs just float away in the water. When the young ones hatch, they sink to the bottom if they are crustaceans that walk about like crabs; or else they go on swimming if they are of a kind that spends its life swimming. Even though they have hard shells, crustaceans are eaten by other animals. Some of the small swimming kinds are the most important food of certain fishes. All over the world the big crustaceans are a favorite food of human beings.

crying

Crying is what you do when you have a strong feeling about something. If you are very sad or mixed up or angry, there is a good chance that you will cry, and many people also cry when they are very happy. Crying can make you feel better, though some people think it does not help very much to cry, and they may tell you, "There is no use crying over spilt milk." When you cry, a salty fluid called tears comes out of your eyes. These tears come from a gland under each of your eyebrows that is called the *lachrymal,* or tear, gland. This gland keeps your eyes a little moist all the time, and this helps them to stay clean and free of tiny bits of dust. When you cry the gland works much harder, and makes many more tears. You can read more about crying in separate articles on EYES and GLANDS.

cryptography

Cryptography is the art of secret writing. It is the writing of messages that are not intended to be understood by anyone who does not know the secret or *key.* A cryptogram, or cipher, usually looks like a jumble of letters:

FRPHK HUHTX LFNOB

This is written in a simple *substitution cipher,* in which some letter of the alphabet always stands for some other letter.

The key is to count back three letters in the alphabet from each letter of the cipher, so that D means A, F means C, and so on. The message says, "Come here quickly." (A cryptogram is usually written in groups of five letters, no matter how many letters there are in each word of the real message, which is called the "clear.") This kind of substitution cipher is called "Caesar cipher" because Julius Caesar is supposed to have used it in writing home to Rome when he was far away with his army.

Of course, a system of *encipherment* must be much more complicated than this to defeat a *cryptanalyst*—one who tries to find the hidden message in a cipher, without knowing the key.

Another kind of encipherment is illustrated by:

EOHMC QRUEE LCYKI

which also says, "Come here quickly." This is a *transposition* system, the letters of the plain message being jumbled on a regular plan to make the cryptogram. The ancient Spartans used a system of this type. When a Spartan general wished to send a message back to the city, he wrapped a narrow strip of paper or a cord spirally around a rod called a *scytale.* Then he wrote his message across the turns, down the length of the rod. When the paper was unwound, the message was reduced to disconnected fragments. Presumably it could be read only by someone having a scytale of the same diameter and knowing that he must wrap the strip upon it.

The need for cryptography has always been greatest in warfare, when written messages may be captured, and messages sent by telegraph or radio may be intercepted. But secret writing is extensively used also by statesmen, diplomats, and businessmen, in peacetime as well as in war. Here we find the systems mostly *codes.* In a typical code, COME HERE QUICKLY might be rendered:

PXVM JOLG TSIU

Each four-letter group stands for a word, but there is no "key" except a special "dictionary," consisting of from 5,000 to 20,000 "meanings"—letters, words, phrases, or whole sentences—with the group of four or five letters that represents it. Businessmen often use public commercial codes in sending telegrams or cables. The chief purpose is to save on the cost of the message by using short words to stand for longer words or sentences.

Since the earliest days of military communication, there has been continual battle between cryptographers and the enemy cryptanalysts. The "Black Chamber," as the military cryptanalysts are often called, has often won out, for the cryptographers are usually hastily trained men who cannot be trusted with very safe but complicated systems. During World War I, the Russians sent many messages to their troops "in the clear," because they found that the cipher clerks took longer to decipher under the cumbersome system than it took the German cryptanalysts to break the intercepted ciphers. In 1920 and again in 1940, United States cryptanalysts broke Japanese codes and so gained important knowledge of Japan's plans.

But in World War II the cryptographers forged ahead. They devised new and extremely secure systems, some of which seem to be unbreakable.

crystals

If you find a rock that looks like glass, or has straight sides and is all of one color, you probably have found a crystal. These crystals were formed millions of years ago, but it is possible for you to see a crystal forming right before your eyes. Dissolve a little table salt in a tiny bit of water, and watch it dry. You can see the salt form itself into tiny crystal shapes. The shape of a crystal depends on what it is made of. Some look like building blocks with flattened corners, and others come to a point at each end. Long ago, people kept crystals because they believed these rocks had magic powers. Now some people collect crystals because of their beautiful shapes and colors.

EXAMPLES OF CRYSTALS

The word *crystal* comes from a Greek word meaning "ice." For a very long time, people thought that only rocks that looked like ice, or glass, were crystals. Later, scientists found that dark rocks could also be crystals. We often see the clear crystal that we call quartz, or rock crystal. Skilled craftsmen have used this clear crystal to make beautiful drinking glasses.

Another crystal that we often see in jewelry is the diamond, and the spoonful of sugar that you put on your cereal is a heap of tiny crystals.

HOW CRYSTALS GET THEIR SHAPES

Scientists now know how crystals get their shapes. The crystal shapes we see are built of many tiny crystals of the very same shape. The sides of the smaller crystals run in the same direction as the sides of the larger chunk of crystal we can see. This is the reason why light and electricity will travel easily through a crystal in one direction, and have great difficulty getting through a crystal in another direction.

It is almost like the difference you would find between pouring water through a pipe lengthwise, and trying to

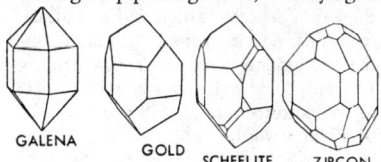

GALENA   GOLD   SCHEELITE   ZIRCON

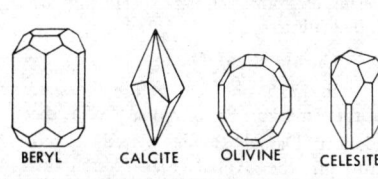

BERYL   CALCITE   OLIVINE   CELESITE

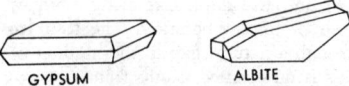

GYPSUM   ALBITE

Crystals of different substances have different shapes. When some of these crystals are stretched or squeezed slightly, they produce an electrical current. Because of this, crystals are used in electrical equipment and in radio sets.

get water through the walls of the pipe. Inventors have used the way electricity flows in a crystal to make better radios and telephones.

Cuba

Cuba is the largest island in the West Indies and is almost as large in area as the state of Pennsylvania. In 1973, the island's population was estimated to be over 8 million people. Because of its natural beauty and pleasant climate, the island is known as the "Pearl of the Antilles." Christopher Columbus discovered Cuba in 1492; he believed it to be part of China. Cuba remained a Spanish possession until, after the Spanish-American War in 1898, it became a republic. Cuba has many fine harbors including its capital city, Havana.

Cuba lies at the entrance to the Gulf of Mexico, between Florida and Central America. Florida is only 90 miles north. Cuba's location inspired the Spanish to call it "the key to the New World."

Cuba and the United States were good neighbors until 1959. Cuba became a Communist dictatorship under Fidel Castro. Diplomatic relationships were broken off. The United States stopped buying Cuban sugar and Havana cigars. Some actual fighting occurred briefly.

THE PEOPLE OF CUBA

The original inhabitants of Cuba were Arawak Indians who were made slaves by the Spanish and treated very cruelly. Most of the Indians died and the Spaniards then brought Negro slaves over from Africa. About 12 per cent of the present population is Negro. Most of the others are descendants of Spanish immigrants, although about 200,000 were born in Spain. There are some Europeans and Chinese. Spanish is the official language, but more and more people are learning English. By law, education is compulsory between the ages of 6 and 14. In 1964, the Cuban government declared that illiteracy was officially eliminated.

At the present time, Cuba has both public and private schools. Due to a strong national effort to improve the country's educational system, the number of public schools has grown rapidly. Private schools are largely Roman Catholic, although the influence of the Catholic Church has been limited under Castro.

WHAT THE LAND IS LIKE

Most of Cuba is low, rolling country with few hilly parts. The eastern end is mountainous. Most of the south shore is very flat and suffers from hurricanes that drive in the waves. The highest mountain peak is Pico Turquino, in the southeast. Its altitude is 6,560 feet. From the east the land drops suddenly under the sea. Most of the coastline is low and rocky, fringed with coral reefs. There are lagoons and salt marshes in many places, some so large that they resemble fine harbors. There are very few inland lakes, and the only navigable river is the Rio Cauto. Cuba has a tropical climate with enough rain for most agricultural purposes. It is generally healthy, mostly due to the conquest of malaria by Carlos J. Finlay and Walter Reed early in this century.

Cuba has many natural resources, such as copper, iron, manganese, nickel, and salt. There is some manufacturing of rayon, cement, naphtha and gasoline, chemicals, and beverages. Agriculture is the leading industry. Cane sugar is the most important farm product and Cuba the world's chief producer. Tobacco is the second leading crop, and the famous Vuelta-Abajo district in the Pinar del Río province produces some of the most valuable tobacco in the world. Other products of Cuba are coffee, bananas, pineapples, and citrus fruit. There is also much cattle and poultry raising and vegetable growing. The sugar plantations are crisscrossed with about 7,500 miles of private railway lines, plus 3,700 miles of public railways.

Under its Communist government, Cuba has had less money and its people have had less to eat and to wear. The big Communist countries have not bought as much Cuban produce as the United States did and there are no more American tourists, who used to spend heavily in Havana, a favorite winter resort.

THE GOVERNMENT OF CUBA

Cuba's constitution calls for a president and vice-president elected for four-year terms, and a congress composed of a senate of 54 members plus a house of representatives with one member for every 35,000 persons. But seldom has Cuba had a truly democratic government. Several times revolutions have upset the elected government, and some elected presidents have become dictators. Castro, whose title is Premier, is a dictator, ruling by decree. Soon after he came to power he dissolved Congress, and no elections have been held since that time.

CUBA IN THE PAST

Cuba was discovered by Columbus in 1492. It was settled in 1511 by his son, Diego Columbus, who founded the city of Santiago three years later. Spain ruled the island with such cruelty that many insurrections broke out. Cuba became free when the United States helped Cubans win the Spanish-American War in 1898.

In 1935 a young sergeant in the Cuban Army, Fulgencio Batista, led a revolt against the government of Gerardo Ma-

chado, who had been elected president in 1925 and had become a dictator. Soon Batista too was a dictator. Batista's government was corrupt; the rich people and politicians prospered while the working people went hungry; and in 1959 a young lawyer named Fidel Castro won a new revolution, with most Cubans secretly on his side. So was the United States, which knew Batista's government was bad and did not know Castro was a Communist.

Castro soon announced that he was a Communist, and became more of a dictator than Batista had been. His political enemies were shot or forced to flee. Cuba declared itself an enemy of the United States and allied itself with Soviet Russia, Red China, and other Communist nations. The United States, supported by the Organization of American States (OAS), broke off relations and trade with Cuba.

Cuban exiles formed an army and tried to invade Cuba (at the Bay of Pigs) in 1961. The invasion was a total failure and more than 1,000 of the Cuban exiles were captured. President John F. Kennedy admitted that the Central Intelligence Agency (CIA) of the U.S. had planned and helped the attack, and with government encouragement American firms gave Castro more than $50,000,000 worth of drugs and food to ransom the prisoners.

In 1962, U.S. reconnaissance planes discovered that Russian nuclear missiles were being installed in Cuba by Russian experts. President Kennedy placed a naval embargo on all shipping to Cuba and threatened invasion unless the nuclear missiles were withdrawn. The Soviet Premier Khrushchev took the nuclear missiles back to Russia.

By 1973, Russia, China, and Cuba were becoming friendlier with America. Cuba agreed to return American airplane hijackers.

CUBA. Area, 44,218 square miles. Population (1973 estimate) 8,660,000. Language, Spanish. Religion, Roman Catholic. Government, republic. Capital, Havana. Monetary unit, the peso, worth one dollar (U.S.). Flag, three blue stripes separated by two white stripes; at the mast, a large white star inscribed in a red triangle.

cube

Many familiar objects are cubes, for example toy blocks, and ice. In geometry a cube is defined as a solid having six faces, squares of the same size, with each pair of opposite faces parallel. You can find the volume of any cube by multiplying the length of any side by itself three times. A cube 5 inches on the side will contain $5 \times 5 \times 5 = 125$ cubic inches. A short way to express this is to write $5^3 = 125$, the little number above and after the 5 showing the number of times to multiply. The little number is called an *exponent,* and in every case where it is 3 the expression is read "the cube of 5 (or whatever number) is 125 (or whatever)." In contrary way, 5 is called the cube root of 125 — the number that has to be *cubed* in order to make 125. This fact can be written: $\sqrt[3]{125} = 5$. The little number 3 is called the root.

cubism

Cubism is a kind of painting in which the outline of objects is simplified. The objects become more like blocks, or ice cream cones, or round balls. For instance, a painter sees a perfectly natural object such as a bottle. On the canvas he may paint it as a triangular shape. The purpose of cubism is to let the objects take whatever shape the painter thinks best, not the shape that is real. This gives the impression of what the object is, without the whole object being there. Shapes and forms in cubism are generally flat and made up of angles. They seldom have a real, or three-dimensional, quality.

Georges Braque and Pablo Picasso were cubist painters. Cubism was a favorite style of painting in France from about 1910 to 1920. It is still popular among certain artists.

cuckoo

The cuckoo bird gets its name from the sound of its cry. In Europe, the cuckoo's song is so melodious that its call is a favorite sign of spring. Cuckoo clocks are made to imitate the sound. Each hour and half-hour a little mechanical bird pops out of a door in the clock, and the cuckoo note marks the time. Most cuckoos are brownish in color and have long tails and strong, curved bills. Their feet are shaped for grasping tree branches, and they feed on caterpillars and other insects in the trees. The cuckoo usually lays its eggs in the nests of another bird and takes no further care of them. The cuckoo eggs hatch earlier than the eggs of the bird the nest belongs to. Then, in its first few days of life, the young cuckoo pushes the other eggs or young birds from the nest. But the American cuckoos usually build their own nests and care for their own young.

There are about a hundred kinds of cuckoos, some the size of a sparrow and others as large as a chicken. The cuckoo is found all around the world but especially in Africa and the tropics of India and Malaya. The road-runner of the American Southwest is a ground cuckoo, which means that it does not do much flying. It can run as fast as a deer and is known for its ability to kill rattlesnakes. Cuckoos usually move south for the winter, returning north in the spring. The bronzed cuckoo of New Zealand lays its eggs in the nest of the flycatcher bird and then travels west to Australia and north to the Solomon and Bismarck Islands— a total distance of 1,300 miles. When the young cuckoos are able to fly, they make this same trip alone.

cucumber

The cucumber is the fruit of a vine that grows along the ground. It is not a sweet fruit, but is eaten in salads and as pickles. The cucumber has a skin of green, or yellow, or green striped with yellow. The yellow varieties are not grown as generally as the all-green ones. On the surface of cucumbers will be found small white or colored spines that are not sharp and that rub off easily when handled. The seed must be planted every year in warm, moist, fertile soil. A frost can easily kill the vines. Some kinds of cucumber have fruits that grow 6 to 8 inches long and are sliced for eating in salads. Some kinds produce fruits that do not grow over 2 or 3 inches long and are used 'for making sweet, sour, and dill pickles. Cucumbers

grow wild in the East Indies, but have been grown in gardens all over the world for thousands of years. The cucumber belongs to the family of pumpkins and melons.

Culbertson, Ely

Ely Culbertson is a man who made the card game of Contract Bridge famous throughout the world, and who also made a system for world peace. He was born in Russia, in 1891, but he was an American citizen and happened to be born in Russia because his father, a mining engineer from Pennsylvania, went there to work for the Russian government. Culbertson became a very fine Bridge player and wrote many books to teach other people how to play the game. After he had become famous as a Bridge player, he wrote other books on how to make war impossible. He died in 1955.

Culloden Moor

Culloden Moor is a famous battlefield in the county of Inverness-shire, Scotland. In 1746, the English were at war with France. The Scottish prince, Prince Charles Edward Stuart, who was known as "Bonnie Prince Charlie," thought that while the English army was busy fighting the French, he had a good chance to seize the thrones of Scotland and England, which the English had taken away from his family. He assembled an army of Highlanders, who were men who came from the Scottish mountains, or Highlands. Bonnie Prince Charlie and his Highlanders won several important battles, but they were finally defeated at the battle of Culloden Moor by an English force led by the Duke of Cumberland. On Culloden Moor today, you can see a monument called the Cumberland Stone after the Duke of Cumberland. It marks the place of the battle.

culture

The word *culture* means the entire way of life of any group of human beings. Such cultures are studied in the science called ANTHROPOLOGY, about which there is a separate article. Often culture means the development of education and the arts among people. A person who is very polite and well-educated is often said to be "cultured," but "cultivated" would be a better word.

The word *culture* has other meanings. For example, specially grown groups of germs, used for scientific experiments, are called cultures.

Cumberland Gap

In 1775, one year before the start of the American Revolutionary War, the pioneer Daniel Boone blazed a trail through the Appalachian Mountains. Boone followed the signs of an old Indian path, and also the marks made by many herds of bison (buffalo). The trail led through a natural gap in the mountains. This is now called Cumberland Gap, at the downward slope of the Cumberland Plateau. It is part of the Appalachian Mountain chain, where the states of Kentucky, Virginia, and Tennessee meet. For many years Boone's trail was called the

Wilderness Road, and it was the only passable wagon route through the mountains during colonial days. The gap was discovered by Thomas Walker, an agent for a land company, in 1750. The old Wilderness Road is now a part of the Dixie Highway, U.S. Route 25. A new park was opened to the public in 1956. It consists of 10,000 acres in Kentucky, 7,400 in Virginia, and 2,000 in Tennessee.

Cumberland Road

The Cumberland Road was the first highway in the United States that led to the West. More than 150 years ago, there was talk in Washington about building such a road. They started to build it in 1811, but the following year the War of 1812 brought the work to a halt. When the war was over work was resumed, and in 1818 the first section was opened for travel. It ran from Cumberland, Maryland, to Wheeling, Virginia (now in the state of West Virginia). The Cumberland Road followed a natural path, or trail, through the mountains over which buffalo had migrated, and the Indian warpath that connected the South with the North. This is known as "Nemacolin's Path" because it was blazed and cleared by the Delaware Indian chief, Nemacolin, about 1750. It was over this route that General Braddock drove his famous wagon train in the French and Indian Wars, building the roadway as he went. George Washington used this route when he traveled west, using the road built by Ebenezer Zane, an early settler who with his brothers founded Wheeling.

Today's U.S. Route 40 passes over much of the old Cumberland Road. At various places along the way you can see statues of the *Madonna of the Trail,* in remembrance of the women who traveled the route to the West when the great migration started.

cumin

Cumin, or *cummin*, is a pretty, low-growing plant with delicate threadlike leaves. It is grown for its fruit, which is very tiny and looks like caraway seed. The fruit is used to flavor bread, curry powder, and soup. It is also crushed to squeeze out its oil. This oil is used to flavor special wines called liqueurs, and medicines.

Black cumin is another plant whose seeds are used in cooking. It is quite a different plant from true cumin. It is related to the garden flower called love-in-a-mist.

Cunard, Sir Samuel

Samuel Cunard was a Canadian shipbuilder and owner who founded the famous Cunard Line. He was born in 1787 at Halifax, Nova Scotia. He began with sailing vessels, but became interested in the development of steam navigation and owned shares in the *Royal William,* which in 1833 was the first Canadian steamboat to cross the Atlantic to England. In 1840, Cunard formed a partnership that started the first regular steamship service between America and Europe. Out of this company grew the Cunard Line, which later became the present Cunard White Star Line. Cunard was made a baronet in 1859 and lived the last

part of his life in England, where he died in 1865.

cuneiform

Cuneiform is a wedge-shaped kind of writing that was invented by the ancient Sumerians and was used by various other ancient peoples. Cuneiform writing was first used nearly four thousand years ago. It was invented to be written on clay with a pencil called a stylus. It was a complicated form of writing, and was not widely used after the East was conquered by the Greeks under Alexander the Great and the people learned the simpler alphabet of the kind that is used today.

Immense quantities of cuneiform tablets have been discovered in cities of Assyria and Babylonia. During the last 150 years scholars have studied them and have worked out a way of reading and translating them.

The most famous cuneiform writing in the world is at Behistun, a mountain in Iran, carved in the rock high on the mountain. Together with pictures also carved in the rock, it tells about the ancient Persian king, Darius I, who lived nearly 2,500 years ago. The writing is in three languages, Babylonian, Elamite, and Persian. In most museums there are clay tablets, cylinders, and other objects upon which you can see this ancient form of writing.

Cupid and Psyche

The story of Cupid and Psyche tells how the god of love himself lost his heart to a beautiful princess, who had to go through many trials to prove she was fit to be his wife. The story is one of the Greek myths told thousands of years ago, when people believed that the happenings in nature were caused by special, powerful beings called gods and goddesses. Cupid was the the son of Venus, the goddess of beauty, and his magic arrows made both gods and men fall in love. Psyche, the daughter of a king, was so beautiful that people adored her instead of Venus. This made Venus angry, and she ordered Cupid to make Psyche fall in love with some horrible creature. But when Cupid saw Psyche, he loved her himself and married her.

Cupid came to Psyche only at night, and said she must never try to see his face. But one night after he was asleep, Psyche lighted a lamp and saw the beautiful god. Cupid awoke and immediately left her, saying that love could not live where there was no trust. Psyche was heartbroken and searched all over the world for him. Finally, she went to Venus, who gave her several impossible tasks to do. But Psyche was always secretly helped, by ants, by a reed in the river, by an eagle, a tower, and finally by Cupid himself. Then Zeus made Psyche immortal, so that she would live forever like the other gods and goddesses.

Curaçao

Curaçao is the largest island of the Dutch West Indies. It is about twenty miles long and lies near the northern coast of South America, off Venezuela. It is a hilly island, largely covered with cactus bushes and thorny shrubs because of its dry climate. There is very little land

on which to grow crops, so most of the food eaten on Curaçao has to be brought from other countries.

Curaçao is only about 182 square miles in size, but it has about 145,700 people living on it. Most of the people work in the oil refineries, for which Curaçao is famous. In these refineries crude oil (oil just as it comes out of the earth) is purified and the different things of which it is made up are separated. The oil refined in Curaçao comes from Venezuela and Colombia. The refineries make Curaçao very rich. Phosphates, which are used to make the soil grow more crops, and salt are two things that we get from Curaçao. At one time a famous drink called Orange Curaçao was made there, but most of it is now made in Holland.

Curaçao, and two islands close to it called Aruba and Bonaire, have been ruled by the Dutch since 1634. The last Dutch governor of New York, Peter Stuyvesant, was governor of Curaçao before he came to New York. The capital of the islands is Willemstad. It is one of the prettiest towns in the West Indies.

CURACAO. Area, 182 square miles. Population (1970 census) 145,707. Capital, Willemstad, population 94,133 with suburbs.

curare

Curare is the name of a poison made by certain Indian tribes in the part of South America called Guiana. The Indians put it on the tips of the darts and arrows they use for shooting animals. The poison kills the animal quickly, and does not cause it any pain; nor does it spoil the animal for eating. This is because the poison does no harm if you eat it, only if you get it in your blood. But in your blood it is deadly, and there is no known cure. If a person is poisoned by curare the only thing that can be done to save his life is to try to keep him breathing even after he has lost consciousness. Sometimes this can be done by artificial respiration. If artificial respiration is given for several hours the poison may wear off and the person get well again. The Indians always make curare in secret, so for a long time nobody knew what was in it. Now scientists have found out many of the ingredients. They have found that some of them are very useful in medicine. Nowadays doctors use drugs made from curare in treating some kinds of heart disease, and to get better muscular relaxation in patients that are being operated on.

curfew

Curfew is a law or rule that after a certain time at night no one may be in the streets. Sometimes during war or revolution a curfew is imposed so that the police or soldiers will not have to watch so many people. In many cities there is a curfew for young people and after a fixed hour they must not be on the street unless they are with a grownup. Originally, *curfew meant* "cover the fire." It started many hundreds of years ago when people first started to live in cities and were afraid of fires because there were no fire departments. Every night at a set hour a bell would be rung as a signal, and everyone would put out the fire so that while they slept no fire could spread and set the city

on fire. Sometimes we speak of any evening bell as the curfew.

Curie, Pierre and Marie

Pierre and Marie Curie were two great scientists. Pierre, a Frenchman, was born in 1859. His wife-to-be, Marie Sklodowska was born in Poland in 1867. She saved all her money and moved to Paris to study at the Sorbonne, the famous French university. While a student, she experimented with uranium and learned new facts about the rays it gives off. She named this property of giving off rays, RADIOACTIVITY. When Pierre and Marie were married, they began to work together on the mystery of radioactivity. They discovered two new elements, *radium* and *polonium*. In recognition of this discovery, they were awarded the Nobel Prize in 1903.

French Embassy Press
Pierre Curie

Tragedy struck in 1906. Pierre was hit and killed by a heavy wagon. After his death, Marie took over his position as Director of the Physical Laboratory at the Sorbonne. Marie continued her work with radium and was once again awarded the Nobel Prize in 1911. She became the first person to be given two Nobel Prizes. A tireless worker, she headed the Curie Institute of Radium and also founded a laboratory to study radium in Poland. She died on July 4, 1934.

French Embassy Press
Marie Curie

The Curies had two daughters, Irene and Eve. Like her mother, Irene became a scientist and married a scientist. Irene and her husband, Frederic Joliot-Curie, became important scientists. The second daughter, Eve, chose writing for her career and wrote a book about her mother.

curlew

The curlew is a small bird that is usually found around ocean shores and beaches. It is one of that group known as wading birds, because it spends part or most of its time in the water. Curlews have long, thin legs and beaks that they use to catch fish, worms, and insects. The curlew also eats the snails, clams, and oysters it finds on the beach. The curlew's head and breast are gray or ash-colored, but it has red and white spots on its back and underparts. The female lays its eggs, usually four, on the ground in a lightly-built nest or in a tuft of rushes or long grass. The curlew's cry is like a whistle.

Curlews live in many different climates from the Arctic to the tropics. One kind of curlew nests in Alaska and flies some two thousand miles to the Hawaiian Islands for the winter months. The common curlew of Scotland, or the *whaup,* is found all over Europe, and some of the birds take yearly journeys as far as New Zealand in the south Pacific Ocean.

Am. Museum of Nat. History
The curlew uses its very long bill to dig worms and insects out of the ground.

curling

Curling is a game that is played on ice (but not on skates), usually indoors on a curling rink. It is played by teams of four. The players are called *lead, second man, third man*, and *skip* (or captain), who calls the plays. A regulation rink is 42 yards long. At each end there are circles marked off. These are 38 yards apart at the centers, and are called the *house.* The object of the game is to slide a heavy stone so that it comes to rest on the *button*, the small center circle in the house. The stone is 4½ inches thick, 36 inches around, and weighs 38 pounds. There is a hole in the center, and a handle is attached to a bolt that goes through the hole. One side of the stone is smooth and the other side is grooved. If the player wants to change sides of the stone, he can switch the handle to the other side by unscrewing the bolt that holds it.

When the game starts, the skip takes his broom (a regular broom) and points to the place where he wants the stone to stop. Then a teammate shoots for that point. He can give the stone a twist to the right or left as he releases it so that it spins as it slides along, and the spin will make it *curl,* or curve in that direction. One point is scored for each stone that stops within the circles called the house; but if a member of the other team slides a stone that stops near to the button, it cancels the point. The broom can also be used to sweep in front of the stone as it slides toward the house, but the player may not touch the stone itself. Sweeping the path of the stone smooths the ice and may make the stone slide farther.

Curling is an important sport in Scotland and in parts of Canada where there are people of Scottish descent. There are several American curling clubs, and there are annual tournaments attended by teams from Canada, Scotland, and the United States, at which international champions are chosen. The largest tournament is the Manitoba Bonspiel held at Winnipeg, in Canada.

currant

A currant is a small round, red, white or black fruit that grows in a loose bunch like grapes. Red currants have a rather sharp flavor, and are chiefly used in making red currant jelly, but some are made into wine, also. Red currants grow on small shrubs that grow wild in southern Europe, Turkey, and the United States, but they are also grown in home and commercial gardens. White currants grow like the red currant but are not as popular because they do not make as pretty a jelly or wine as the red ones. Black currants have a strong musky smell. They are made into jelly and are used in pies. They first grew in Europe, but are cultivated in America. They are not as important as the red currant. The word currant is sometimes also used for a small raisin that has no seeds; and also for the pretty pink-flowered shrub called the flowering currant.

Currie, Sir Arthur William

Sir Arthur W. Currie was a Canadian military officer who commanded his country's forces during World War I. He lived from 1875 to 1933. He enlisted as a private in 1895 and rose steadily in rank until he was a lieutenant colonel when World War I began. Currie was one of the first Canadians to volunteer for active service in Europe. Shortly after he was sent over as a brigadier general, he succeeded Sir Julian Byng as commander of the Canadian Army in France. Under his command the Canadians won many important engagements and after the war General Currie was knighted for his services. From 1920 until his death he was principal and vice-chancellor of McGill University in Montreal, Canada.

Currier and Ives

Currier and Ives were American print makers. Their prints were called *lithographs.* Lithographs are pictures that have been printed from a carved or etched stone. They are colored by hand. The lithographs or prints made by Currier and Ives are very much sought after today. When they were first printed they sold for one or two dollars each. Today they bring as high as five hundred dollars each. They depict frontier scenes and Indian wars, steamboat races, disasters at sea, and many other current events of the 19th century. Other prints show the everyday life of the people at that time, such as skating on the pond or arriving at a farmhouse in a sleigh.

Nathaniel Currier was born in Massachusetts in 1813 and died in 1888. At 22 he started his own lithographing business. James Ives was his partner. Ives had first been hired by Currier as a bookkeeper, but as he was an artist he soon began to hand-color the prints that Currier made. James Ives was born in 1824 and died in 1895.

curry

Curry, or *curry powder,* is a seasoning for food. It is made of several spices, onions, garlic, ginger, chili, cumin seed, coriander seed, turmeric, fenugreek, cardamon, cloves, and pepper. The ingredients are mashed up together, and then dried. At first the color is reddish, but later it becomes a beautiful golden yellow. When you cook food with curry it has a rich golden color.

The first people to use curry were the Chinese, but today we think of curry as

an Indian seasoning. In Indonesia it is so important that the word *curry* almost means "dinner." Fish, meat, chicken and vegetables are cooked with curry and served with rice. In Java the *rijst-tavel*, or "twenty-four boys," curry means that there are 24 separate dishes, each one brought to the table by a separate waiter (not necessarily 24 waiters). In cooking, just the correct amount should be used, or the food may be too "hot" because of the pepper and ginger in the curry.

Curry, John Steuart

John Steuart Curry was an American painter. He liked to paint scenes of American life. He was born in Kansas in 1897 and always liked to paint pictures of things in his home state. One of his most famous pictures shows dark and threatening storm-clouds over a farm. You can almost feel the wind rushing through the trees and see the distant flashes of lightning. After he went to the Kansas and Chicago Institutes of Art he became an illustrator for magazines that specialized in Western stories. In 1936 he was appointed "Artist in Residence" at the University of Wisconsin. He died there in 1946. Curry painted murals in several of the government buildings in Washington, D.C. He considered the mural he painted in the state capitol in Topeka, Kansas, his finest work.

Curtiss, Glenn Hammond

Glenn H. Curtiss was a famous American inventor and aviator. He was second only to the Wright brothers for his contributions to the science of aviation. He lived from 1878 to 1930 and made many daring flights and brilliant demonstrations. His most famous and spectacular flight was from Albany to New York City to win a prize of $10,000 offered by a newspaper, the New York *World*. His best-known invention was the *flying boat*, or seaplane. Like many American inventors, Curtiss became interested in mechanical contraptions while he was still a boy. He first started a bicycle shop that grew into a factory for the manufacture of motorcycles. He was experimenting with airplanes at the same time as the Wright brothers. He gave some of the first public demonstrations and in 1909 started the first flying school.

Cushing, Cardinal

Richard James Cushing of Boston, Massachusetts, became a cardinal, or Prince of the Roman Catholic Church, in 1959. Cardinal Cushing was born in Boston in 1895, of a poor family (his father was a blacksmith), and was ordained a priest in 1921. His outstanding ability was recognized almost at once, and he was raised to the rank of bishop when he was only 43 years old and became Archbishop of Boston when he was 49. But though Boston is one of the largest archdioceses in the world, Archbishop Cushing was not made a cardinal throughout the reign of Pope Pius XII, a fact that caused much murmuring of dissatisfaction among Boston's Catholics and non-Catholics alike, to all of whom Archbishop Cushing was a revered hero. Even as an archbishop, Cushing persisted in performing the pastoral duties of a simple priest, visiting jails, hospitals, poor people's

houses, and gatherings of the people. Pope Pius did not consider such acts consistent with the princely dignity of a cardinal. When John XXIII became Pope in 1958, one of his first acts was to name Archbishop Cushing a cardinal. In 1970, Cardinal Cushing died of cancer only one month after his retirement. He had been Archbishop of Boston for twenty-six years.

Custer, George Armstrong

George Armstrong Custer was a famous general of the United States Army. He was graduated from the United States Military Academy at West Point in 1861, the year the Civil War began. He saw action almost immediately, and soon became the youngest general in the Union, or Northern, army. He led a cavalry charge in the Battle of Gettysburg, one of the most important battles of the war, and he was a member of General Grant's staff at Appomattox, when the Confederate, or Southern, army surrendered. After the Civil War he was assigned to the 7th United States Cavalry, where he remained until his death.

United States Military Academy Archives

Custer was popular with the public, and very much talked about. He had a habit of making decisions without asking his superior officers, and this kept him in constant trouble. One such mistake resulted in a court-martial or military trial in which he was found guilty of leaving his post without permission. His friend, General P. H. Sheridan, under whom he had served in the Shenandoah Valley campaign of the Civil War, got him reinstated. Then he promptly did something wrong again. He went on a raid against the Cheyenne Indians and other tribes and killed them after they were defeated. During this battle he was accused of leaving a party of his soldiers who were all killed by the Indians.

When the United States was at war with the Sioux, about 75 years ago, Custer received information that a large party of Indians were camped on the Little Bighorn River, in Montana. Without waiting to ask his commanding officer, he led about two hundred men into a trap. They were all killed, including Custer himself. This battle is known as "Custer's Last Stand." He was born in Ohio, in 1839. He was killed in 1876, and is buried at West Point.

customs duties

Customs duties are special taxes on goods or merchandise that pass from one country to another. Such taxes, which are also called *tariffs*, probably date back in history to the time of ancient Greece. Originally they were payments for the use of ports and even market places inside the country. During the 18th and 19th centuries, however, these two kinds of taxes were separated, and one kind was called *excise taxes* and the other kind was called *customs duties*. Customs are now collected only at the boundary of a country. The reason they were called customs is very simple. In England for many years, the Crown (government) argued with the Parliament (congress) over which had the right to collect taxes. The Crown

argued that it had been collecting such taxes for so long that it had the right by custom; and so, when the Crown finally won, the name customs duties was kept. The first customs house in England was built at London in 1304. The first one in the United States was built at New York in 1799.

Anyone who imports goods into a country is liable to pay two sorts of customs duties. One kind, called *ad valorem*, is worked out according to the value of the merchandise. For example, if you import an automobile from England, the United States government will charge you a certain percentage of what the automobile cost in the first place. The other kind of customs, called *specific*, is worked out according to the weight and number of things imported. For example, a big heavy automobile will cost more to import than a small light one; and several low-priced automobiles will cost more than one or two expensive ones.

cutlery

Cutlery is the word we use to describe small tools used for cutting, such as knives, razors, and scissors. Sometimes the word *cutlery* is used to describe the other tools that are used for eating. These include forks and spoons as well as knives.

Early men knew how to make knives out of flint and stone. Scientists have found many flint and stone knives that were made by our primitive ancestors hundreds of thousands of years ago. Later on, when metals were discovered, man began to use metals to make his cutting instruments. Men used knives for cutting and eating their food much earlier than they used forks. But until about five hundred years ago, even knives were not supplied by a host to his guests at dinner. Each guest was expected to bring his own knife with him when he went out to eat. At about the same time that hosts began supplying knives to their guests, forks were brought into use. Before forks were used, people either ate with their fingers or speared the food with their knives and carried it to their mouths on the knives. Even the most polite people, such as kings and queens, had table manners that we would think quite bad.

The best and sharpest scissors, knives and razors are made from steel. There are four steps in making cutlery from steel. First the steel must be forged. That is, it must be hammered into the shape that is wanted from the short square bar the steel originally comes in. Then the forged steel must be put into an extremely hot oven (this is called *tempering*) and removed and cooled by dipping it into cold water (this is called *quenching*). When this is done, the steel becomes very hard. As a matter of fact, it becomes so hard that it cannot be used. It will snap and break too easily. So it is again tempered and quenched, but this time the oven is not as hot as it was the first time. When this part of the process is finished, the steel is just the right consistency, neither too hard nor too soft. The consistency that is wanted depends on what instrument is being made. A razor must be fairly soft, because it is very thin, and can therefore be bent very easily. If it were too hard, it

would snap instead of bending. Knives are next to razors in softness, and scissors are the hardest. This is because they are usually the thickest, and therefore very hard to bend. For that reason they can be made quite hard without fear of their snapping and breaking easily.

cutter

Cutters are small ships that are used by the Coast Guard. These sleek gray vessels do many different jobs. Some cutters go out to sea with instruments that are used to tell what the weather is going to be like, others look for icebergs in the Atlantic Ocean and warn ships about them, others rescue shipwrecked sailors, and still others keep a lookout for smugglers. The biggest cutters, which are named after past Secretaries of the Treasury, are 327 feet long, while the smallest ones are 83 feet long. You have to be a good sailor to be a Coast Guardsman and live on a cutter, because these ships go out to sea in the roughest weather. In the days of sailing ships, a cutter was a vessel that could carry a great amount of sail, and could go much faster than most ships.

cuttlefish·

A cuttlefish is a sea creature with a pear-shaped body, a thick neck, and a round head. Attached in a circle round the mouth are ten arms, two of which are much longer than the others. These arms are covered with round suckers, except for the longer two, which have suckers only at the tip. Cuttlefish eat fish and other marine animals. They hold them in their arms and tear them to pieces with their jaws, which are very strong and shaped like a beak. Cuttlefish have big eyes, and they have the largest brains of all the lower animals, that is, animals that have no backbones. Actually cuttlefish do have a sort of bone inside their bodies, but it is not a true backbone. This is the cuttlebone that is put in birdcages.

Cuttlefish have a fin on each side of their bodies, and they are very good swimmers. As they move through the water they change color so that they are difficult to see. If they are swimming over sand, they become sandy-colored; if over black rocks, they become black; if far out at sea, they become silver to blend with the water. When they want to move fast, they swim backwards, propelling themselves by squirting water out of their funnel, which is what they breathe through. If a big fish chases them, they can throw out a cloud of black ink through this funnel. This hides the cuttlefish and gives it a chance to escape.

Cuttlefish lay eggs. The eggs look like bunches of small purple grapes. When the young cuttlefish hatch they can swim around and look after themselves.

The people who live around the Mediterranean Sea and in Japan are very fond of eating cuttlefish. Most cuttlefish grow about a foot or two long. They are closely related to the much larger SQUIDS and OCTOPUSES, about which there are separate articles. All these animals are molluscs, and there is a separate article on MOLLUSCS also.

cutworm

A cutworm is the caterpillar, or young stage, of a small moth that flies at night. Cutworms are often serious pests in gardens and fields. By day they hide in the soil, but at night they come out and feed on plants such as wheat, corn, or garden vegetables. They chew through the stems close to the ground, causing plants to fall over. Another kind of cutworm climbs up into the branches of trees and cuts off the buds and leaves. When you see dying leaves on the ground, or plants that have been cut off at the base, and you are sure this is caused by cutworms, you should either dig up the ground and kill the cutworms or spray the ground with poison. If you do not kill the cutworms, they will kill most of the plants in your garden.

cyanide

Cyanide is a powerful poison that comes in powder or liquid form. Although we are most likely to come across cyanide in murder mysteries, where villains use it to kill people, this chemical is actually useful in a number of other interesting ways. It is used in the case-hardening (or toughening) of metals such as steel; in the killing of rats and insect pests; and in getting gold out of crushed rock or gravel. There are several kinds of cyanide, made usually from such metallic elements as sodium and potassium.

cyclamen

The cyclamen is a small plant that grows wild in countries bordering on the Mediterranean Sea and it is raised in greenhouses farther north because of its beautiful heart-shaped leaves and colorful flowers. The flowers of cyclamen may be white, pink, lilac, or crimson. They bloom in the winter and early spring. Cyclamens have many natural enemies such as rots and eelworms, and they must be watched carefully. The most serious pest of the cyclamen is a very small insect known as a mite that feeds on the tips of the plant and on its flower buds. People sometimes spray sulfur dust on cyclamens in order to kill these insects.

cyclone, a violent windstorm: see the article on HURRICANE.

Cyclops

A Cyclops was a character in Greek mythology, the stories the ancient Greeks told about their gods and goddesses. It was a huge fierce giant, who sometimes ate men. A Cyclops looked somewhat like a human being, but instead of having two eyes, as human beings do, it had only one eye—a large round one, placed in the center of the forehead. According to the stories, its special work was to make the thunderbolts and lightning that Zeus, the king of the gods, hurls across the sky in a storm.

cyclotron

An atom is so small that it cannot be seen, yet it is made up of still smaller parts called protons, electrons, and neutrons. For years scientists tried to find a way to split atoms into these smaller parts. The problem was finally solved in 1931 when an American scientist named E. O. Lawrence invented a machine called the cyclotron.

The cyclotron is a machine in which protons—particles of the atom with positive electrical charges—are shot round and round in spirals, so that they look like a whirling eggbeater. Each time they go around they move faster because of the electrical energy that is pushing them. After they have reached a tremendous speed, they are shot out through a hole in the outside of the largest ring of their spiral. On the other side of the hole is a piece of metal that is the target, and the extra high-speed protons hit that target and dive into it. This shakes up the atoms in the metal of the target. The target is then radioactive because its atoms are all shaken up. It will remain radioactive until its atoms settle down. In almost the same way a common horseshoe magnet gradually becomes weaker and weaker until it is finally no good at all because all of its magnetism (magnetic power) has worn off. In the case of the cyclotron's target, it is back to normal and no longer radioactive when all its atoms are completely settled down again. Before this happens, however, it can be used in the treatment of disease, and medical science has found many cases in which radioactive materials are very helpful.

A *betatron* produces the same general effect on its target as the cyclotron does, but in the case of the betatron it is electrons—particles of the atom with negative electrical charges—that gain speed and shake up the atoms in the target.

cylinder

If you take a piece of paper and roll it into the shape of a straight pipe, you have made a cylinder. Some cylinders are hollow like the roll of paper, others are solid like a piece of chalk, and some hollow cylinders have closed ends. One kind of closed-end cylinder that you can see every day is the usual can of vegetables. The top and the bottom of this kind of cylinder are equal circles, and one circle is exactly above the other. We have many uses for cylinders, and we see this shape in cigarettes, stove pipes, soda straws, and containers. There are many reasons why we use cylinders. One reason is that you can roll something into the shape of a cylinder without tearing or crinkling it. A cylinder is also easy to handle and easy to clean. There are holes that are called cylinders in automobile engines, where gasoline explodes and gives power to the car.

cymbals

Cymbals are a musical instrument. They are made of brass and shaped like a very shallow bowl. When you strike them together with the hollow sides against each other, they make a loud crashing sound. If you strike them together and hold them there, they make a loud shushing sound that stops suddenly. Cymbals are used in the orchestra to emphasize certain beats. When a band plays a march the cymbals are sounded on each beat.

There are many different sizes of cymbals. They were invented in the Orient, probably in China, many thousands of years ago. Chinese and Hindu music makes much use of cymbals. A long time ago the word *cymbals* meant a kind of

DULCIMER, about which there is a separate article. The cembalo is a stringed instrument like a dulcimer played with hammers. It is used in Hungarian orchestras.

Cynic

The Cynics were a group of ancient Greek philosophers. They believed that virtue was the only good thing in life. They thought that a person could be virtuous only by being independent. Later the Cynics became very intolerant. They criticized everyone who was not a Cynic. They thought that anyone who did not follow their beliefs and actions was not good. Today we sometimes hear a person called a *cynic*. A cynic is a person who distrusts the actions of other people. He does not believe that someone will do something because he wants to help others. A cynic distrusts human nature. A person who does not believe in the sincerity of others is said to be cynical.

cypress

A cypress is a tree related to the pine and fir trees. Pines and firs have needle-shaped leaves, but the leaves of a cypress are very tiny, flat, and overlapping. They completely cover the ends of the branches, and make them look very neat and delicate. Like pines and firs, cypresses belong to the group of plants called CONIFERS, about which there is a separate article. The flowers of cypresses are in round cones, but these are very small.

There are many different kinds of cypress; some are found in Europe and China, but most of them are natives of the west coast of North America. One of the prettiest of these is the Monterey cypress, which is often grown as a hedge. The most famous cypress is the common cypress of Europe. It grows tall and very thin, in the shape of a cigar. Because of its dark color, beautiful shape, and the fact that it points up into the sky and is an evergreen, this cypress is often planted in graveyards. For hundreds of years it has been thought of in connection with sorrow and its branches were at one time carried at funerals as a sign of mourning.

Cypress wood is dark reddish-brown in color. It is sweet-smelling and even-grained. It is used in making small boxes and chests. The doors of St. Peter's church in Rome were built of cypress wood. They lasted 1,100 years before they had to be replaced. In the United States, the most important kind of cypress is the bald cypress, which grows in the southeast. It is not a true cypress, but is related to the sequoia or redwood tree. Unlike the true cypresses, which are all evergreen, it sheds its leaves in winter. The bald cypress has strange roots called knee roots. These stick up out of the ground like hoops. When the tree is old the roots become very thick, and these roots may help the underground parts of the tree to breathe. There are still huge forests of bald cypress, but the larger trees have mostly been cut for their timber. The wood is valuable because it lasts well even when wet, although it is soft, and because the tree can be cut into large-sized planks.

Cyprus

Cyprus is one of the largest islands in the Mediterranean Sea. It is in the eastern part of the Mediterranean Sea, and lies south of Asia Minor and north of Egypt. Cyprus has an area of 3,572 square miles and about 633,000 people live there.

War between Greece and Turkey over Cyprus seemed near late in 1967 but efforts by Cyrus R. Vance, sent by American President Lyndon B. Johnson, secured a temporary peace.

Archbishop Makarios remained President until July 15, 1974 when the Cypriot National Guard, commanded by officers of the Army of Greece, seized the government. Nikos Sampson became President while Makarios fled to safety. Five days later Turkey invaded Cyprus and occupied almost half the island. The matter was brought before the United Nations, yet the world organization was unable to effect a reconciliation.

Greek Cypriots and Turks engaged in battle. By August 16, Turkish troops occupied the northeast third of the island. In a riot in the capital city of Nicosia, the United States Ambassador to Cyprus was slain by a bullet. By December, Makarios was reinstated as President.

Turkish Cypriots voted on June 8, 1975 to establish a separate Turkish Cypriot state.

ANCIENT CYPRUS

Cyprus was settled more than four thousand years ago. It has been controlled by many nations at one time or another. The Phoenicians, the Greeks, the Persians, the Egyptians, the Macedonians and the Romans all ruled Cyprus at different times. It was taken over by Turkey in 1571, and remained under Turkish control until the British came to power in 1878.

The main industry on Cyprus is farming, and the most important crops are barley, cotton, fruit and olives. There are some good railroad lines between the capital city, Nicosia, and other sections of the island. On the whole, Cyprus is not very modern. Nearly one-third of the population, mostly older people, do not know how to read or write.

CYPRUS. Area, 3,572 square miles. Population (1976 estimate) 666,000. Government, republic. Capital, Nicosia (population 115,000). Languages, Greek, Turkish, English.

Cyrano de Bergerac

Cyrano de Bergerac is most famous as the hero of a play by the French writer Edmond Rostand. Actually Cyrano de Bergerac was a heroic and romantic Frenchman who lived about three hundred years ago. As a soldier, he did many remarkable deeds. There is a story that he fought single-handed against one hundred enemies. He was often involved in duels, and it seems that he never lost, but he must have been wounded many times. Cyrano was said to have had a very large nose. Through a lifetime of fighting, his nose was much disfigured by saber cuts. Besides fighting, the real Cyrano wrote some plays, and two books which were a kind of early science fiction. He died in 1655.

Cyrenaica

Cyrenaica is a part of LIBYA, a country in North Africa, about which there is an article in another part of this encyclopedia. Nearly 3,000 years ago, Cyrenaica was a colony of Greece. Its capital city, Cyrene, was one of the most important cities of the ancient world, and in Cyrenaica today you can see the ruins of many beautiful buildings and temples that were erected when Cyrene was at its height. Another city of Cyrenaica has been important in modern times. That is the city of Tobruk, which was the scene of bitter fighting between the Allies and the German Afrika corps under Field Marshal Rommel in World War II. The present capital of Cyrenaica is Bengazi.

Cyrus

Cyrus is the name of two famous men of ancient Persia. Cyrus the Elder was a famous king about 2,500 years ago. He was the founder of the Persian Empire. He conquered several countries in the Near East, including Babylonia, which had been a rich and powerful country. The city of Babylon fell to Cyrus in 537 B.C. At that time the Jewish people were captives of the Babylonians, who had conquered them. According to the Bible, Cyrus freed the Jews from the Babylonian captivity and sent a group of them back to rebuild the temple at Jerusalem and begin life amid the ruins of their city. Cyrus died about 530 B.C. His mausoleum, the tomb in which he was buried, still stands near the city of his birth and is regarded as a holy place by the tribesmen of Iran, the modern name of the country that used to be Persia.

Cyrus the Younger was a Persian prince who lived about 2,350 years ago. He was the son of Darius II, who was king of Persia, and when his father died, he tried to kill his older brother, Artaxerxes II, so that he could become king. But he was unsuccessful and it was only because his mother begged for his life that he was forgiven. Later, he formed an army and with the assistance of many thousand Greek mercenaries went to war against his brother, but he was killed during the battle of Cunaxa, a small town near the Euphrates River. The leader of the Greek force was Xenophon, who wrote a book about "going up" with Cyrus. The book is called the ANABASIS, and there is a separate article about it. Cyrus the Younger died in 401 B.C.

Czechoslovakia

Czechoslovakia is a country in central Europe. It is about 50,000 square miles in area, which is a little larger than New York State, and about 14,000,000 people live there, which is a little less than the population of New York State. Czechoslovakia is similar to New York State in other ways too. It is a land of beautiful mountains and winding rivers. It has rich farm country and a great many manufacturing cities.

Czechoslovakia is a landlocked country; that is, it does not lie on any ocean or sea. Czechoslovakia is surrounded by Germany, Poland, Austria, Hungary, and the Soviet Union. For many hundreds of years, the lands and peoples that now form Czechoslovakia were ruled by one or another of these countries. Czechoslovakia now has a Communist government, and no one is able to find out much about what goes on there.

THE PEOPLE WHO LIVE THERE

The people of Czechoslovakia are Slavic people, formed mainly of two groups, the Czechs and the Slovaks. You can easily see how the names of these two groups were joined to form the name of the country. These Slavic peoples have lived in that part of Europe for hundreds of years. The Czech and Slovak languages belong to the group of Slavic languages, which are part of the Indo-European family of languages. Besides the Czechs and Slovaks, there are small numbers of people from many of these countries around Czechoslovakia. Before World War II, there were a great many Germans living in Czechoslovakia. Most of these people returned to Germany after the war ended.

About three-quarters of the people of Czechoslovakia belong to the Roman Catholic Church. Some people belong to the Greek Orthodox Church; others are Protestants, and there are followers of various other beliefs. When the independent country of Czechoslovakia was first formed in 1918, the government said that everyone should be free to follow his own religion. But now, as in all Communist countries, it is difficult in Czechoslovakia to follow any religion freely.

The western part of Czechoslovakia is chiefly the country of the Czechs, who have always been industrious and enterprising. The region has the best land and the most minerals, so it is highly developed. Most of the large cities of Czechoslovakia are in the western section. There are great manufacturing cities, like the cities of western Europe and the United States. The eastern part of the country is poorer, and not so well developed. There are fewer people there, and most of them are farmers.

Czechoslovakia has a heritage of very good folk songs. Two of its greatest composers or writers of music, Bedrich Smetana and Antonin Dvorák, used these songs as inspiration for their music.

The schools belong to the state and they are free. Czechoslovakia also has many fine scientific schools and universities. One of these, the University of Prague, is more than six hundred years old.

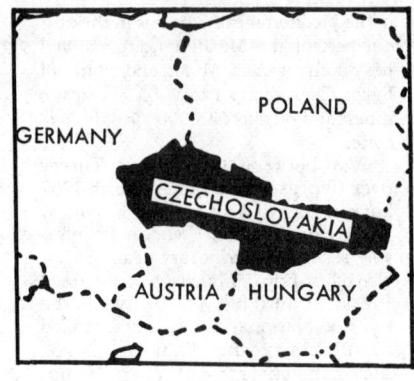

HOW THE PEOPLE LIVE

Czechoslovakia is a rich and varied country. It has many different kinds of resources, so there are a great many kinds of work for the people to do. About half of the people are farmers. Czechoslovakia has fine farm areas, and is able to produce almost all the food used by her people. The chief farm product is grain—wheat, rye, barley, and oats. The farmers also raise sugar beets and potatoes, and the hops used in making beer. The beer from Czechoslovakia has been famous in Europe for hundreds of years.

Some parts of the countryside are covered with forests, and great industries have grown up to use the wood. There are paper and lumber mills and factories that make furniture and fine woodwork.

Czechoslovakia is also rich in mineral resources. It has great coal fields, iron, copper, and other metals. Some semiprecious stones, natural gas, and oil are also found in Czechoslovakia. Many people work in the mines. Great factories turn out war materials and machinery. Other factories turn out chemicals, cloth, fine china and porcelain. The glassworks make bright beads and bracelets, and sparkling Christmas tree decorations. About one-half of the Czechoslovakian people work in their country's industries.

WHAT KIND OF PLACE IT IS

There are two main mountain chains in Czechoslovakia. Toward the east are the Carpathian Mountains. In the west, on the German border, are the Sudeten Mountains. The west is plains country, with mountains surrounding it. It is around these western mountains, where the valuable minerals are to be found, that most industry has developed. Here are the larger cities, and more people. The Carpathian areas have fewer people. They are best for farming and raising animals.

Many rivers wind through the country. The chief rivers are the Oder, the Elbe, the Moldau (or Vltava), and the Danube.

The climate varies in different parts of the country, but on the whole it is a good climate, not too cold in winter nor too hot in summer. The winters are usually fairly dry. Most of the rain comes in the spring and the fall.

Manufacturing needs a great deal of power, and Czechoslovakia has this power. The rich coal deposits provide one kind of power. Electric power comes from the steam-electric and hydroelectric works. Czechoslovakia has many railways and good roads.

CHIEF CITIES OF CZECHOSLOVAKIA

The leading cities of Czechoslovakia, with populations from 1973 Czechoslovakian estimates, are:

Prague, population 1,102,060, capital of Czechoslovakia and its largest city. Prague, or Praha, is in the western section, on the Moldau River. It is a great manufacturing city. It has beautiful churches, and fine museums and theaters.

Brno, population 335,935, second-largest city. Brno is the leading textile manufacturing city.

Bratislava, population 283,234. It lies in southern Czechoslovakia on the Danube River, very close to the Austrian border. Bratislava is a rail and shipping center.

Ostrava, population 273,280, a leading rail center. Ostrava is in the north central section, not far from the Polish border. Many metal industries are located there.

HOW THE PEOPLE ARE GOVERNED

After World War II, the Communists were the strongest of the many political parties in Czechoslovakia. In 1948, they got control of the government. They formed a new constitution which set up a dictatorship that they called a "People's Democratic Republic."

There is a parliament, and members of it are elected by the people. But in fact only one political party is allowed to exist. The real control of the government is in the hands of top-ranking members of the Communist Party. The Communists have complete control of the country and the people. The people have no real voice in their own government, and there is no personal liberty as it is known in the United States.

CZECHOSLOVAKIA IN THE PAST

The independent country of Czechoslovakia was first formed in 1918, but the peoples who were joined together to form the new nation had a long history before that. First among these peoples were the Czechs. They lived in the part of central Europe called Bohemia. The kingdom of Bohemia was established about a thousand years ago. It was one of many small states in Europe that made up the HOLY ROMAN EMPIRE, about which there is a separate article.

For a long time, Bohemia was fairly independent. But about 350 years ago, there began to be trouble. There were many religious wars going on at the time, and the Czechs of Bohemia were opposed to the religious ideas of the Hapsburgs, the rulers of Austria. In 1620, at the great Battle of the White Mountain, Bohemia was defeated by the Hapsburgs. From that time on, the Hapsburg rulers of Austria controlled and governed the Czechs of Bohemia.

About a hundred years ago, many of the people of Europe began to want freedom. Among them were the Czechs of Bohemia and the Slovaks. The Slovaks had been conquered by the Magyar peoples of Hungary in the year 907. For hundreds of years they had been ruled by the Hungarians. There were also Slavs in the regions of Moravia and Ruthenia who wanted to be free of their Austrian or Hungarian rulers.

When World War I began (1914) these peoples tried to win freedom by siding with the Allies (England, France,

Russia, and later the United States). Some escaped and fought for the Allies. The two great Czech leaders, Thomas Masaryk and Eduard Benes, in exile in the United States, planned a government for a new, free and independent republic.

The dream came true. Four groups of Slavs — from Bohemia, Slovakia, Ruthenia, and Moravia — set up a democratic nation, which soon became one of the happiest and most prosperous in Europe. But this nation remained free for only twenty years.

In the Sudeten mountain region of Czechoslovakia there were many people of German origin. Under the rule of the Nazi party, Germany demanded during the 1930s that these people, the Sudeten Germans, and the region in which they lived, be taken from Czechoslovakia and given to Germany. In the famous MUNICH PACT of 1938, Germany's demands were granted; but a few months later, Germany broke its word and sent in armies to take over all the rest of Czechoslovakia. Again Czechoslovakia was under foreign rule.

The Czechoslovakian people suffered much under German rule. When their Underground was successful in acts of sabotage, the Germans killed prominent Czechoslovakian citizens in reprisal. After the German official Reinhard Heydrich (a man so cruel he was called "The Hangman") was murdered by the Underground, the Germans retaliated by slaughtering all of the men and most of the women of the village of Lidice, and sending the remainder to slave camps.

Russian armies drove the Germans out in 1945 and the Republic of Czechoslovakia was organized again. But Russia kept its military forces in Czechoslovakia and in 1948, by threat of armed aggression, forced the elected government headed by Benes to resign. Jan Masaryk, son of Thomas Masaryk, committed suicide or was murdered. A Communist dictatorship under Klement Gottwald took over. The country was then actually controlled from Moscow.

In August of 1968, when the government of Czechoslovakia under Communist Party Chief Alexander Dubcek was allowing the people more liberties than ever before, the country was invaded by troops of five allied nations: the Soviet Union, Poland, Hungary, East Germany, and Bulgaria. The Soviet Union, which had organized the invasion, had been afraid that, if more and more freedoms were given to the people of Czechoslovakia, the citizens of the Soviet Union and of the other Communist countries of Eastern Europe might eventually also demand these freedoms, leading to the end of Communism in Europe. Very little fighting occurred during the invasion, but as a result of it, the Czechoslovak government was forced to put an end to certain freedoms it had been permitting.

CZECHOSLOVAKIA. Area, 49,366 square miles. Population 14,500,000 (1973 estimate). Language, Czech, Slovak, and others. Religion, about 75% Roman Catholic, 25% others. Government, republic. Monetary unit, koruna, worth about 14 cents (U.S.). Flag, two stripes, white above, red below, with blue triangle from mast to middle of flag.

Czolgosz, Leon F., was the man who killed President McKinley: see the article on William McKINLEY.

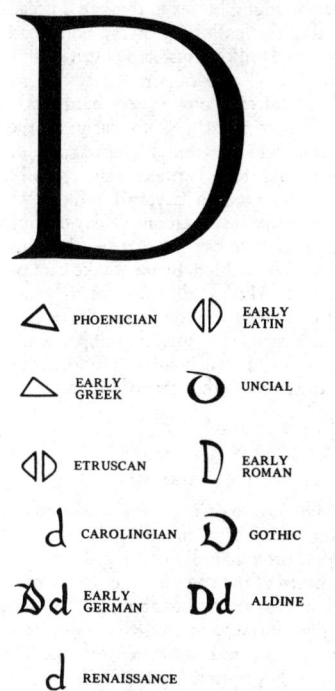

△	PHOENICIAN		EARLY LATIN
△	EARLY GREEK	O	UNCIAL
	ETRUSCAN	D	EARLY ROMAN
d	CAROLINGIAN	D	GOTHIC
	EARLY GERMAN	Dd	ALDINE
d	RENAISSANCE		

D or d

The letter D is the fourth letter of the alphabet. It can be traced all the way back to the earliest writing known to man, in Egypt thousands of years ago. In the Canaanite dialects (one of which is the Hebrew that the Old Testament was written in) the letter is called *daleth,* a word that means "door." The ancient Greeks took over this same letter and its name, calling it *delta.* The name was taken from the Canaanites of the Palestine seacoast and Syria.

The Hebrew letter *daleth* looks like an equilateral triangle (one with all sides of equal length) with its base running horizontally. The earliest Greek *delta* was really the Hebrew *daleth* tilted a little to the right. In the Canaanite language, as in most Semitic languages, writing runs from right to left. But the Greeks followed the custom of the Assyrians and other peoples, and they wrote from left to right, as we do today. In the history of writing, letters often get turned sideways or upside down. The later Greeks tilted the *delta* even further to the right, so that it became a *daleth* lying on its right side. The result was a letter closely resembling the capital letter D which we use today.

Read also the article ALPHABET.

dab

Dabs are flatfish of the same family as the flounder. They can easily be recognized because the midway line along their sides is arched just behind the head. They are a brown or gray color, speckled and mottled like the sandy bottom of the shallow seas where they live. Like all flatfish, they are born looking like ordinary fish; then one eye starts to change its position until, in the dab, the left eye has moved over to the right side of the body. This side becomes the top of the fish, which now lies flat on the bottom on its left side. Both eyes are raised a little above the rest of the body, to give the fish a good view, and they can move independently of one another. The rusty or sand dab is the common kind found off the coasts of North America.

Dachau was one of the worst concentration camps in Germany during World War II: see the article on CONCENTRATION CAMP.

dachshund

The dachshund is a hunting dog bred in Germany to hunt badgers. The name *dachshund* is a German word that means "badger dog." Its extremely short legs made it possible for the dog to go right down into the badger's burrow. Dachshunds are still used for hunting in Germany, but they are kept mainly as pets and house dogs in the United States and Canada. They are lively and affectionate, with good dispositions. They are useful watchdogs because they bark vigorously whenever a stranger comes to the house. There are three kinds of dachshund —the smooth-haired, which is the most common, the wire-haired, and the long-haired.

A dachshund stands between 6 and 12 inches high at the shoulder. The difference is big because there are miniature as well as standard size dachshunds. For the same reason, their weight varies a great deal also. They may weigh as little as 5 pounds, or as much as 25. The color of all three types (smooth, wire-haired, and long-haired) varies widely too. Some are black and tan, some reddish-brown, some striped reddish-brown with darker streaks, and some grayish, brownish, or white with big splashes of dark gray, brown, rust or black.

Dadaism

Dadaism is a style of art. It was popular in France during the 1920s. It is a kind of art that uses the fantastic or the foolish with a serious purpose. If you lined a bathtub with fur and put a lady dressed in fish net in the bathtub, and then exhibited the whole thing in a museum, that would be an example of Dadaism. In many cases it was intended to be amusing or to shock people. However, some of the more serious artists in France combined Dadaism with another form of art called surrealism. Surrealism is a form of painting that uses weird and fantastic objects that are seen in a painter's dreams.

daddy-longlegs

Daddy-longlegs is a name given to two different kinds of small animal. One, related to the spider, is called a harvestman. It has a small round body and eight very long and thin legs. It feeds by sucking the juices from fruit and vegetable matter, and also from insects, which it is said to catch and kill. Daddy-longlegs are often seen in fields or barns where hay is stored. The other kind of daddy-longlegs is the crane fly, which is an insect like a very large mosquito, and may be an inch long. It is common in summer in damp pastures.

Daedalus

In the stories of the ancient Greeks, Daedalus was a great artist and inventor.

There are many stories about Daedalus. It is said that he made wonderful statues and built beautiful temples. He invented many of the carpenter's tools and found new ways of building ships. The most famous story is about how Daedalus flew. He and his son Icarus were prisoners. To escape, Daedalus built two pairs of wings. He made them of birds' feathers, and fastened them together with wax. On the flight, Icarus flew too close to the sun. The wax of his wings melted, and he fell into the sea and was drowned. The place where he was said to have drowned was called the Icarian Sea. Daedalus was more careful, and with the wings that he had made he soared through the air to safety.

daffodil, a white or yellow flower of the narcissus family: see the article on NARCISSUS.

daguerreotype, an early kind of photograph: see the article on PHOTOGRAPHY.

dahlia

A dahlia is a plant of the daisy family. It grows about four or five feet high, and has long stalks at the ends of which are the flower heads. These are very beautiful, and of many different colors, particularly shades of red and yellow. Sometimes they are as small as buttons and sometimes as big as soup plates. There are many kinds of dahlia. All of them are natives of Mexico; but since they began to be cultivated 150 years ago, gardeners have bred many new kinds which are only found in gardens. Dahlias are grown chiefly because they are beautiful, but sometimes a kind of sugar is made from their roots.

Dahomey, The Republic of

The Republic of Dahomey, on the west coast of Africa between Togo and Nigeria, became independent in 1960. It had been an Overseas Territory of French West Africa since 1904. The people of Dahomey are Negroes of several tribes and are farmers, producing palm oil, coffee, karite (vegetable oil), cotton, kapok, phosphates, peanuts, and tobacco. Dahomey was planned to be governed by a legislative assembly of 70 members and a President elected by the Assembly, but in 1965 the Army of Dahomey took over the government.

THE REPUBLIC OF DAHOMEY. Area, 44,-696 square miles. Population (1973 estimate). 2,760,000. Capital, Porto Novo (74,600). Ethnic groups, Fons and Adjas, Boribas, Yorubas, and Mahis. Languages, French and African. Religions, Animist, Christian, and Moslem. Monetary unit, French franc.

dairy farming

Dairy farming means raising animals for the milk they give. In this country we usually think of cows in connection with a dairy, but goats and sheep have also been kept for their milk. In France the dairy farmers make a very popular type of cheese (called Roquefort) from sheep's milk.

Some of the earliest historical writings that we have found mention butter and cheese, so we know that dairy farming is very old. Butter is said to have been discovered when an Arabian nomad put a bag of milk on his horse and rode for many miles across the desert. When he stopped and opened the bag to take a drink, he found butter in the bag, instead of milk. The galloping of the horse had shaken the milk up just as a churn would, turning it all into butter.

Dairy farming now is very hard work. The farmer must get up early in the morning and see that his cows are all milked and fed. Farmers usually milk their cows twice a day; all milk cows must be milked at least once a day or they become sick. After the farmer has his herd milked and fed, he must take care of his crops. Almost all dairy farms grow their own feed for the cows. There is a separate article in this encyclopedia on AGRICULTURE which will tell more about how the farmer takes care of his crops.

THE DAIRY HERD

Man has kept cows for thousands of years, and used their milk. During most of that time man did nothing to improve the breed of the cows in order to get more and better milk, but about 1770 some English farmers noticed that some cows gave much more milk than others. The farmers began to breed best milk-producing cows and to use the others for beef. They kept this up for many years and developed pure-bred cows. Now there are several different breeds of pure-bred cows which have been named after places in England. Some of the breeds which have been brought to the United States are the Jersey, Guernsey, and Ayrshire. Another good milk cow, the Holstein Friesian, came from North Holland, or Friesland province, and the Brown Swiss came from Switzerland.

Jersey cows are small in comparison to the others, but the milk that they give is very rich. They are usually cream-colored or light brown cows, and they will live in almost any climate. The Guernsey cows are larger than Jerseys, and they are reddish-brown with white markings. The milk they give is very yellow in color. Holstein cows are black-and-white spotted, and while they give a lot of milk, it is not very rich. Ayrshire cows can be almost any color, but you can tell them because their horns are curved up and back. They like to live on rocky land and seem to do quite well even on poor pasture land. The Brown Swiss cows are brown in color, as you might expect from their name; they like to live in the same type of surroundings as the Ayrshire cows. Their milk is about average in quantity and richness.

There are about 30,000,000 cows in the United States today. The average cow gives about 5,500 pounds of milk a year, which is about 640 gallons. Milk is measured in pounds because the farmer is paid by the pound when he brings it to the dairy. One of the champion milk cows, a purebred Holstein, gave 39,000 pounds of milk in one year. That is almost twenty tons of milk. It is enough to give almost 90,000 children four glasses of milk each. But production from even the average cow has been increasing each year because of better breeding. A dairy cow normally gives milk for five or six years.

GOVERNMENT SUPERVISION

Government inspectors go around to all the farms to see that the milk is kept pure and clean. They see that all of the cows are fed properly and that their stalls are clean and sanitary. Then they check all of the dairy equipment to see that it is cleaned and sterilized after each use. They test the cows to see that they are healthy and free from disease. The milk is then checked as it comes from each cow.

After a farmer milks his cows, he strains it into large milk cans and stores the cans in a cool place until he can take them to a dairy. At the dairy the milk is pasteurized. This means that the milk is heated until it is almost boiling, so that any germs that might be in it are killed. Most of the milk is then delivered to homes and stores while it is still fresh. However, some of it is made into butter, cheese, ice cream, or other dairy products.

THE DAIRY FARMER'S TOOLS

Not too many years ago all cows were milked by hand, and this was hard work and took a long time. Milking machines now do the work of many people and do it in less time. The milking machine is one of the most important machines the dairy farmer can use. It has a suction pump connected to a pipe which runs to each stall in the barn. This pipe ends in a soft rubber fitting which goes over the cow's teats. The milk flows from the cow, through the pipe and into a big vat. The milking machine is a great help to the dairy farmer because it is much faster and more sanitary than milking by hand. Many farmers who use milking machines strip, or finish milking, the cows by hand.

Another important device is the cream separating machine. It is shaped like a big bowl; when the milk is poured into the bowl, it starts spinning very rapidly. Since the milk is heavier than the cream, it is forced to the outside of the bowl and allowed to flow into a sterilized can. This is called skim milk. The cream is then taken out of the bowl and bottled.

Early dairy farmers found that if the milk got warm, it would sour very quickly. The milk cooler was invented to keep the milk fresh and cool until it can be delivered. The milk is poured over a long strip of stainless steel which has cool water flowing under it. This not only cools the milk but airs it, allowing any odors which may have gotten in the milk to escape.

THE FARMER'S DAY

If you were living on a dairy farm, the farmer would get you up at about five o'clock in the morning so you could help milk the cows. If the farmer had a very large herd of cows, you might not get to eat breakfast until eight o'clock, because every cow must be milked and fed before you can eat. A good farmer always takes care of his animals before he takes care of himself.

After a good, big breakfast there is plenty of other work to do on a dairy farm. Barns and stalls have to be cleaned, the cows have to be cleaned and fed at different times, and the milk has to be prepared for market. Heavy milk cans have to be made ready to be taken to the

milk plant nearby or to the railroad to be shipped farther away.

CARE OF COWS

Cows do not get very many diseases, but those that they do get are usually very serious. Sick cows are usually killed and buried immediately, so the rest of the cows do not catch the disease.

Most modern dairy farms wash their cows frequently during the summer months with a mild disinfectant so the flies won't bother them too much. Some farms have long, deep troughs which they fill with water and disinfectant; then the farmer makes the cows all walk through the trough. Some farmers prefer a kind of shower system, usually in the barns, where the cows just have to walk under a stream of water. If your farmer has neither of these systems, your arms are going to be stiff from washing cows with a bucket and sponge.

Around three or four o'clock in the afternoon the cows will be ready for another milking. This will take a few hours or longer, if you have to load a truck and drive the milk into town. Supper would be waiting for you when you got back, and after that, around seven or eight o'clock, you would be very happy to go to bed.

daisy

The daisy is a small white flower with a yellow center. It came originally from Europe, but it grows wild in most parts of the United States. In different parts of America other flowers such as the marguerite, the black-eyed Susan, and the wild aster are also called daisies. The true daisy belongs to the COMPOSITE family of plants, about which there is a separate article. What makes these plants different from others is the fact that their flowers actually are made up of many tiny flowers growing together as a head. If you look closely at a daisy you will see this is so. The wild daisy is only about four inches high, but gardeners have bred many larger kinds. Daisies have always been loved by people because they are so pretty and they make the fields beautiful. We say "simple as a daisy," or "humble as a daisy," but in the old days the daisy was a sign of true and faithful love.

Boutrelle

If you walk through a field in the country, you will see many daisies growing wild.

Dalai Lama

The Dalai Lama is the highest priest of Lamaism, the religion of Tibet, which is a country in the Himalaya Mountains between China and India. Lamaism is a form of the Buddhist religion, and the lamas are the monks, or priests. Followers of Lamaism believe in reincarnation, that is, they believe that when a living thing dies its soul is immediately born in another living thing. They believe that when one Dalai Lama dies, his soul has passed into a baby that was born just as he was dying. The lamas go out looking for that baby, and when they find him he is the next Dalai Lama. For centuries, the Dalai Lama was not only the high priest but also the ruler of Tibet. He lived in a palace-monastery at Lhasa, the capital city of Tibet. When the Communist government gained control of China, it sent an army into Tibet. This was in 1950. The Chinese soon controlled Tibet and captured the Dalai Lama, who was then about 16 years old. When a revolt against the Chinese in 1959 failed, the Dalai Lama fled to India.

Dali, Salvador

Salvador Dali became famous as an artist who specializes in a kind of painting called surrealism, which shows things as they might look in a dream. A painting by Dali might show watches that look like pancakes and that are hanging on the branch of a tree or dripping off a table. Even though he painted unusual objects, he painted them very carefully. Some of his pictures are almost like photographs.

Dali was born in Spain, in 1904, and spent his early life there. He visited the United States for the first time in 1936 and has lived here most of the time since then. He designed some window decorations for a store on Fifth Avenue in New York. In these windows he put fur-lined bathtubs and kitchen utensils made of fur. Besides his surrealistic paintings he paints serious religious pictures. He has also designed jewelry.

Dallas

Dallas is second only to Houston among the largest cities in the state of Texas. Dallas is on the Trinity River, which is formed in the city by the junction of the Elm Fork and the West Fork. It is also one of the greatest rail centers in the state and is served by ten different railroads. It is an industrial city, famous particularly for its cotton and oil products; but its citizens are also proud of their city's broad, clean streets, handsome buildings, and fine parks.

Dallas was first settled in 1841 when a man named John Neely Bryan built a hut on the Trinity River. It was named Dallas in 1845 in honor of George M. Dallas, Vice President of the United States. Many of the early inhabitants were French colonists. The city grew most rapidly after the coming of the railroads in the 1870s.

Dallas is the center of many business, educational, and cultural activities. The Texas State Fair is held there every year. The cotton and clothing industry have made Dallas a style center that is well-known not only in Texas but in many other parts of the country. Dallas is also the home of Southern Methodist University and of a United States Air Force flying school.

In 1963 President John F. Kennedy was assassinated in Dallas.

DALLAS, TEXAS. Population (1970 census) 844,401. County seat of Dallas County. Settled in 1841.

Dalmatia

Dalmatia is a section of Croatia, one of the six republics that make up the country of Yugoslavia. Dalmatia is on the western side of Yugoslavia, on the Adriatic Sea. Almost all of Yugoslavia's coastline, from Fiume in the north to Kotor in the south, is in Dalmatia. Dalmatia extends back from the coast about fifty miles to the Dinaric Alps, which are among the tallest mountains in Yugoslavia.

The Dalmatian coastline is one of the most beautiful regions of Europe. There are hundreds of little islands dotting the sea. The shoreline is winding and forms many coves, bays and harbors. Yugoslavia's main ports are on the large har-

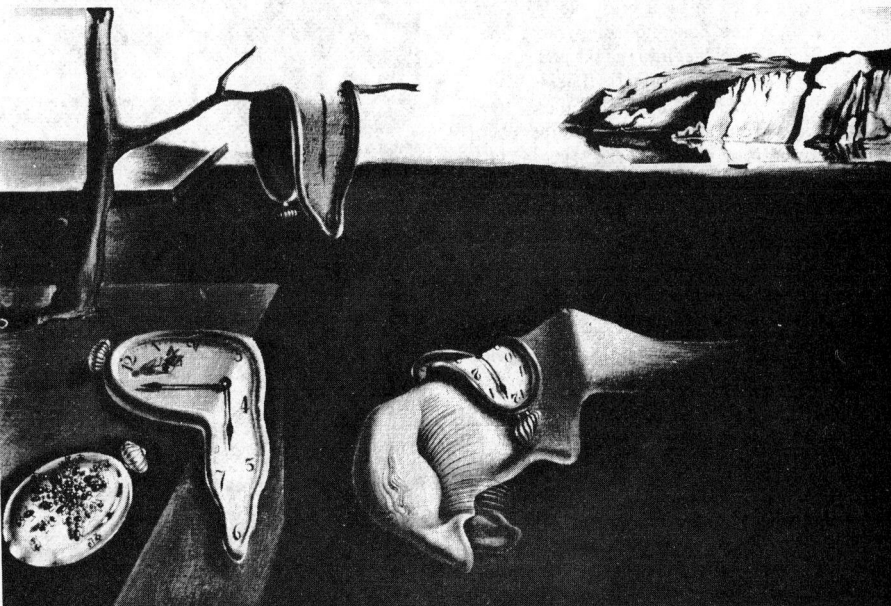

Museum of Modern Art

Salvador Dali's famous painting *The Persistence of Memory* shows the strange way this artist paints his pictures by making things like watches look unreal.

bors of Dalmatia. Many vacation resorts are in Dalmatia, too.

Most of the people of Dalmatia are a Slavic people called the Croats, who have lived in that section of the world for nearly 1,500 years. For most of that time, until 1919 when Dalmatia became part of Yugoslavia, they were under foreign control. The Serbs, the Venetians, and finally the Austrians were the rulers of Dalmatia.

Dalmatian

The Dalmatian dog was a familiar sight in the days of horse-drawn fire engines, as it ran alongside the horses or beneath the carriage. This breed of dog has had many different kinds of jobs, and almost as many different names. It is called a Dalmatian because records seem to indicate that the dogs lived originally in Dalmatia, a province of Yugoslavia. At various times it has also been called *coach dog, English coach dog, carriage dog, plum pudding dog* (probably because someone thought its spots looked like large raisins) and *firehouse dog.*

Dalmatians have done many different jobs. They have done sentinel duty during wartime; they have been sheepherders; they have been hunting dogs and rat catchers; they have been stage and circus performers. Today many Dalmatians still do all of these things, but in the United States and Canada they are popular mainly as house dogs and pets, and are gentle and patient with children.

A Dalmatian stands about 19 to 23 inches high at the shoulder, and weighs between 35 and 50 pounds. Its hair is short and smooth and it looks a little like a hound, with long drooping ears, and a long tail. It is a white dog, with brown or black spots all over its body.

dam

A dam is a thick, strong wall that is built across a river to hold back the flow of water. A dam can be just a couple of six-foot logs that you use to dam up a tiny brook trickling through your backyard, or it can be a great block of dazzling white concrete rising more than five hundred feet into the sky and stretching as far as fifteen football fields.

America has more of these huge concrete super-dams than any other country in the world. Each year, in fact, thousands of American and foreign tourists come to visit these dams and admire their size and beauty. But dams are much more fun for you to visit if, in addition to admiring their beauty, you also know something about how they are built and how we use them to stop floods, to water our farm lands, and to make our electricity.

WHAT DAMS ARE USED FOR

For many thousands of years men have been putting up dams to hold back the flood waters of rivers and lakes.

Most dams are built to control floods, but they also save and store up water for farms. Suppose you had a large farm with a good-sized stream running through it. During very hot summers you would not sit by and watch the sun scorch your corn and tomato crops, while thousands of gallons of good fresh water flowed along

U. S. Bureau of Reclamation

The Shasta Dam and Reservoir in California.

your stream and emptied out into nearby rivers. Instead, you would look for a place on your property where this stream flowed through a little valley between two hills. There you would build a log or concrete wall across the stream and up the sides of the hills. The stream's water, hitting this wall, would begin to form a great pool which would be held in by the wall and by the two hillsides. Even if no rain fell, you would still have a big supply or reservoir of water for your crops. You would dig a ditch, or run a concrete water pipe, from the reservoir to your corn and tomatoes. This way of watering your crops, even when rain does not fall, is called *irrigation.*

For thousands of years, men have built dams to make sure they had reservoirs of drinking or irrigation water. In ancient Ceylon, near India, the people once built a dam that was eleven miles long, thirty feet thick on top, two hundred feet wide on the river bottom, and seventy feet high. The Romans, Babylonians and Egyptians were not far behind the Ceylonese as dam builders. Today we have found an entirely new use for dams that the builders of ancient times never dreamed of. We use the water stored up by dams to make electricity. In the article on ELECTRICITY you will learn how electricity can be made if you rub together a pair of special wire "brushes."

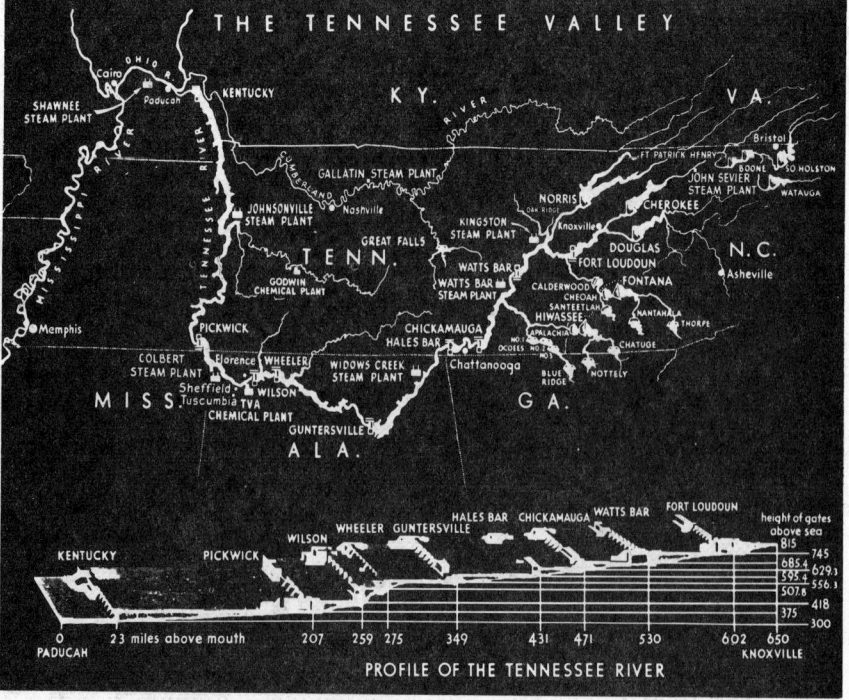

One of the great projects in the United States was the building of dams in the Tennessee Valley region to provide a system for flood control, electricity, and navigation. Dams were built along the Tennessee River and its five main branches. This map shows where they are located. At the bottom of the map are the dams in the Tennessee River.

Four huge generators in the powerhouse at the Pickwick Dam on the Tennessee
The water power turns turbines in the dam, the turbines run the generators, and the generators make electricity that power lines carry to houses, factories, and farms.

The Aswan Dam in Egypt is an unusual combination of small dams within larger ones. To protect the great temples with their gigantic statues of gods and kings, carved out of rock cliffs, the waters of the small artificial lake around them will be kept at a lower level than the big artificial lake between the main Aswan dams.

Civil Engineering Magazine

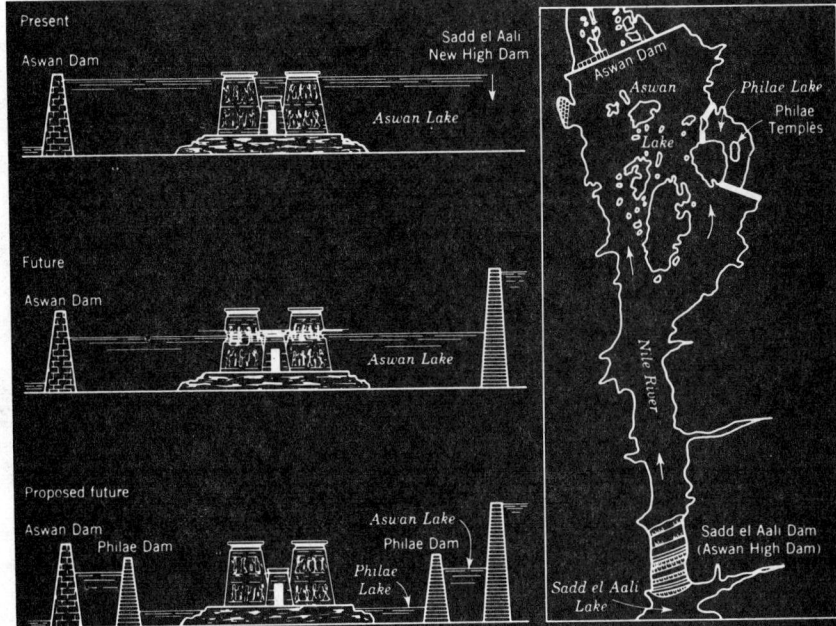

If you allow some of the water in a dam to go shooting through a wide pipe and spin a great wheel hooked up with several of these wire brushes, you can make enough electric current to keep the lights going in a small town. Such an electricity-making machine is known as a turbine, and the current created by a turbine from water power is called hydroelectric power. Probably the most modern hydroelectric center in North America is the giant St. Lawrence Seaway project, which was recently completed by the United States and Canada. You can imagine how much this giant hydroelectric plant would amaze the old-time dam builders.

HOW DAMS ARE BUILT

These same old-time dam builders would also find that we have made many changes in the way our dams are built. In olden times, dams were often four times as thick as they were high. This was because the dam builders were not sure exactly how strong a dam had to be to hold back the tremendously strong thrusting power of a great river. They made them extra thick and strong just to make sure. About a hundred years ago a French expert named de Sazilly worked out a way of telling just how thick a dam had to be, and how it should be shaped. Today our dam builders (or engineers) need use no more material in dams than is actually necessary to hold back the water. The dams you see today are usually one of the following types:

Earth dams. These are built up out of layers of soil which are packed down tight by heavy rollers. Seen from the side, such a dam looks like a great mound of earth, very wide at the bottom, and slanting up to the top like a Boy Scout tent. Since the swirling river waters quickly eat away even closely packed soil, the side or "slope" of the dam facing the water has to be protected with a smooth covering of hard concrete or stone. The best thing about earth dams is that they cost very little. Earth is cheap, and it is usually found near the location of the dam.

Rock-fill dams. Like earth dams, rock-fill dams are built where a concrete dam would cost too much. The inside of such a dam is filled up with heavy rocks, then covered with a layer or "skin" of smooth concrete, to keep the flowing river water from pushing in between the rocks and washing them away. This concrete skin is about one foot thick at the top of the dam, and three feet thick at the bottom.

Gravity dams. These are made of concrete, or of large heavy stones fitted together. Many of our greatest dams are of this gravity type. If you look at a gravity dam which is only half full, you will see that the side facing the stream (the "upstream side") is flat, and almost straight up and down. But the side away from the water presses extra hard on the bottom of the dam. This is one of the secrets discovered by de Sazilly.

Horizontal arch dams. These dams are built in fairly narrow river valleys called gorges. Instead of being flat, the side of the dam which touches the water bulges out. This bulge, or arch, makes the dam stronger because the heavy push of the water is held back not only by the dam's thick bottom, but also by the rocky sides of the gorge against which the sides of the horizontal arch are braced. With this double protection, you can build very tall, very strong dams.

Multiple-buttress dams. The upstream side of these dams is covered with a number of arches, or bulges. Only the two ends or "feet" of the arch feel the force of the water, and it is behind these feet that we place heavy supports called "buttresses."

Floodgates. Many big dams have huge doors, called floodgates, which can be opened to let more water flow out of the dam. If a county far downstream needs water to irrigate its farms, the floodgate is opened enough to send just as many millions of gallons as the county needs.

Without our big dams we could not have so many fruits and vegetables, or the pure drinking water that nearly all Americans have. We would not be able to use so much electricity, and we would have many more floods.

SOME FAMOUS DAMS

America has a great number of amazingly large and complicated dams. For instance, our Hoover Dam, on the Colorado River, is 726 feet high, which makes it the world's tallest dam. If you visit Hoover Dam, you will recognize it as the curved gravity type, built of solid concrete. It took five years to build and is used for irrigation, flood control, and hydroelectric power. Then there is our Grand Coulee Dam, on the Columbia River in the state of Washington, which is the largest concrete dam in the world. This is the dam, mentioned in the first part of this article, that is 550 feet high,

and as long as fifteen football fields. It has 18 giant turbines for making electricity, and it irrigates more than a million acres of land. Another giant dam is Fort Peck Dam, in Montana, on the Missouri River. Fort Peck is 9,000 feet across, or the length of thirty football fields.

The Aswan Dam is on the Nile River in Egypt, near a town called Aswan. The United States and Soviet Russia both gave Egypt money to help build the dam, which will be one of the world's largest. Some ancient monuments had to be cut from the solid rock in which they were carved and lifted hundreds of feet so that the flood waters would not cover them. No matter where you live in America, you should be able to find at least one big, exciting dam that is in your section of the country. It is possible that the lamp by which you are reading this article is lighted by electricity made at a hydroelectric plant not too far from the town in which you live.

See also the article DIKES AND LEVEES.

Damascus

Damascus is the capital and the largest city of Syria. It is mentioned in Genesis and in other books of the Bible and is supposed to be the oldest city in the world that has been continuously inhabited. Today, however, little remains of the ancient city except its two most famous sights, the Great Mosque and the medieval Citadel (fortress).

Damascus is a beautiful city on the Barada river, whose waters are used to irrigate the fine gardens and orchards of apricots, dates, almonds, and pomegranates. It is a famous tourist center and also important for trade, its chief products being silk, wool, and damask fabrics, furniture inlaid with mother-of-pearl, and elegant glass and jewelry. In the past the city was famous for its steel, from which wonderful swords were made with blades so flexible and edges so hard that they have never been equaled. The city is also noted as the place were St. Paul was converted to Christianity.

Damascus is one of the three great holy cities of Islam. It has an old Oriental appearance with its mosques (Moslem places of worship), souks (covered streets for bazaars), and khans (public inns). There is the famous "Street Called Straight," and there are many low houses that may be dirty on the outside but are clean, and often rich and elegant, inside.

During the centuries of its history, Damascus has been ruled by the Jews, Persians, Greeks, Romans, Arabs, and Turks. During World War I it was freed from the Turks by the British, although the independent republic of Syria with Damascus as its capital was not firmly established until World War II.

DAMASCUS, SYRIA. Population (1973 estimate) 835,000. Capital of Syria.

damask

Damask is a rich fabric with designs of flowers, animals, or landscapes woven into the material. Both the design and the background are usually the same color—white—but two colors can also be used. When you look at a white damask cloth, you can see the design because it is slightly raised and has a shinier finish than the rest of the cloth. The design in damask shows on both sides of the cloth. Damask may be linen, silk, cotton, rayon, or a combination of two of these. Fine white linen tablecloths and napkins are made of damask, and so are some window curtains and fine hand towels. Damask is named after the city of Damascus, capital of Syria in the Near East, where this kind of cloth first came from. People made damask on hand looms until the 18th century, when a power loom was invented. This new loom was perfected about 150 years ago by a French inventor named J. M. Jacquard.

Damien, Father

Father Damien was a Catholic missionary who was born in Belgium more than a hundred years ago. He went to the Hawaiian Islands in 1873, and he asked to be sent to the island of Molokai, which was a settlement for people who had the disease called leprosy. In those days, people were very frightened of leprosy. They had many superstitions about the disease and about the people who suffered from it, and the lepers who lived on Molokai were treated very badly. Father Damien believed these people should have as good a life as possible. He did a great deal to improve the terrible conditions on Molokai. He got leprosy himself, and died in 1889, when he was only 49 years old.

Damocles

Damocles was a character in the legends of ancient Greece. He may have been a real person, for his homeland of Sicily was a real country, and his ruler Dionysius the Elder was a real person. But we do not know whether what is told of Damocles is history or just a story. The legend says that Damocles was always telling Dionysius how fortunate he was to be so rich and powerful. One day, Dionysius invited Damocles to a great feast, to show him what it was like to be as happy as a king. Damocles was enjoying everything very much, until suddenly he saw something that made him fearful through the rest of the feast. Over his head was a sword, hanging by just one thread. Then he understood the constant worry and fear of being a ruler. When someone nowadays says that something is like the sword of Damocles he means that it is something dreadful that he is afraid may happen, something that seems to hang over his head like a sword about to fall.

Damon and Pythias

The story of Damon and Pythias is a famous example of a perfect friendship. Damon and Pythias were followers of Pythagoras, a Greek teacher whose pupils learned the highest rules of action and conduct. Pythias had been condemned to death by Dionysius I, the cruel ruler of Syracuse on the island that is now Sicily. Dionysius accused Pythias of plotting against him and condemned him to death. Pythias asked to be allowed to go to his family before he died, to arrange for their care. Damon offered to stay in prison himself as a guarantee that his friend would return at the promised time. But Pythias was unexpectedly delayed, and Damon was led to the place of execution. It is said that people along the way felt sorry that Damon should trust his friend so far, for they believed Pythias had probably escaped and was not coming back. Damon was ready to die in place of Pythias, but Pythias returned just in time. Then each asked to die so the other could go free. Dionysius was so struck by their feeling for each other and by their sense of honor that he pardoned both of them, and asked to be taken into their brotherhood. That is, he wanted to become a follower of Pythagoras. The story of Damon and Pythias has been made into many plays and poems.

Damrosch

The name Damrosch was borne by three men who were important in American music. They were a father and his two sons.

Leopold Damrosch, the father, was born in Posen, Prussia, in 1832. He studied medicine in Germany and became a doctor, but he decided to make music his profession. He had already become an important orchestral conductor in Germany before he went to New York in

N.B.C.
Walter Damrosch

1871. In New York he founded the Oratorio Society and the Symphony Society, and was the conductor of both. He also conducted the Philharmonic Society. He died in 1885.

Frank Heino Damrosch, elder son of Leopold, was born in Breslau, Germany, in 1859. He came to America with his father when he was twelve years old and became an American citizen. He was a choral conductor of exceptional ability, and after several successful years in Denver, Colorado, he became chorus master at the Metropolitan Opera. In 1897 he was made director of music in the New York public schools. He founded the Institute of Musical Art in New York in 1905, and was its director until his death in 1937.

Walter Johannes Damrosch, younger son of Leopold, was born in Breslau, Germany, in 1862. He came to America with his father and became a citizen. He studied music with his father and with the famous conductor Hans von Bülow. When Leopold died in 1885, his son Walter succeeded him as conductor of the Oratorio Society and the Symphony Society, and finished the season as conductor at the Metropolitan Opera. Walter Damrosch was a pioneer in radio. In 1925, he conducted the first symphonic concert ever to be broadcast with the New York Symphony Society. In 1927, he organized the NBC Music Appreciation Hour for school children. He also composed many operas, choral works, and songs. He died in 1950.

Dan

You can read about Dan in the Old Testament of the Bible. It is the name of a man, a city, and a tribe. The man, Dan, was one of the twelve sons of Jacob, and he was the ancestor of the tribe of Dan, which was one of the twelve tribes of Israel. One of the most famous members of the Tribe of Dan was Samson, the

strong man whose strength left him when the Philistines cut off his hair. The Danites were so hard-pressed by Philistines that they migrated from their homes and founded a new city named Dan near the source of the Jordan River, at the northernmost tip of Palestine. The southernmost city in ancient Palestine was Beersheba. That is why we use the expression, "from Dan to Beersheba," to mean from one end of the land to the other.

Dana, Richard Henry

Richard Henry Dana was an American lawyer. He was the author of one of the most famous of all sea adventure stories, *Two Years Before the Mast.* He  lived from 1815 to 1882. His father was a well-known poet and essayist, and his grandfather was an English historical and landscape painter. Dana was educated at Harvard, but left college after two years to work as a common sailor on a voyage around Cape Horn to California. Afterwards he went back to Harvard and was graduated in 1837. Three years later he published the story of his adventure, in which he told about the hard life at sea in the days of sailing ships. During the rest of his life, Dana was a lawyer and wrote mostly about legal matters, some of which had to do with the sea.

Danae

Danae was a character in Greek mythology, the stories the ancient Greeks told about their gods and goddesses. Danae was a very beautiful girl. She was the daughter of King Acrisius. An oracle had told Acrisius that his grandson would kill him. To prevent this, Acrisius wanted to make sure that his daughter Danae would have no children. So he kept her shut away from everyone. But Zeus, the king of the gods, loved her, and turned himself into a shower of gold so that he might visit her. When Danae had a son, Acrisius put them out to sea in a great box. But they did not drown, as he had hoped. They floated safely to an island. Danae's son, Perseus, grew up to be a great and brave hero. And, as the oracle had foretold, he did kill his grandfather Acrisius. It happened while Perseus threw a discus in an athletic contest. The discus struck Acrisius in the foot and caused his death.

Danaus and the Danaides

Danaus was a character in the legends of ancient Greece. According to the story, Danaus was king of Libya. He had fifty daughters, who were called the Danaides. Danaus's brother Aegyptus had fifty sons, who tried to take Danaus's kingdom away from him. Danaus and his daughters fled far across the sea. Later the sons of Aegyptus came to Danaus. They wanted to forget the past, and to marry Danaus's daughters. Danaus agreed but he could not forget his fear and hatred of the fifty brothers. He gave his daughters swords, and told them all to kill their husbands. On their wedding night, all but one of the Danaides took swords and cut off their husbands' heads and threw them in the river. After the daughters died they went to the underworld, which was the Greek version of hell. As punishment for the murders, the Danaides had to try forever to draw water from a well in sieves.

dancing

Dancing is a way of moving the body in rhythm—that is, so as to keep time to music or to the beating of a drum. Today dancing is done for fun or to entertain spectators, but dancing among primitive peoples was very serious indeed, for it was part of their religion and magic. They had dances that were actually prayers for rain, fair weather, victory in battle, and success of their harvest. When there was a wedding, they danced in celebration; and when a member of the tribe died, they danced to show grief.

We know how they used their dancing as a religious ritual by studying certain peoples who preserved primitive customs until recent times. The American Indians taught us many important things about the history of dancing.

Dancing is man's oldest art. It is older than language or music, and even little children dance when they hear music, and jump up and down when they are joyful, or angry, or want something. Even animals and insects dance.

DRUMS AND RHYTHM

Dancing is rhythmic movements of the body. In the primitive tribes everyone took a part. These people had to have some means of keeping everybody in step. That is why the drum was invented. At first the drums were just hollow logs, beaten with sticks. Then people found that the dried skin of an animal, stretched over a frame, made a better sound. That is how music and dancing were born, and they are still bound together.

Some of the earliest dancing we know about was practiced by the Egyptians almost five thousand years ago. It was derived from African tribal dancing. The tribal dances were symbolical dances, in which movements and gestures were used to represent real thoughts. A good example is seen when we shake our heads from side to side to signify *no*, and nod them up and down to mean *yes*. As time passed by, the gestures and movements became more complicated. Various peoples developed different styles of dancing, just as they developed different spoken languages. From these sources came the national dances which today are called folk dances.

Folk dances expressed the lives of the people. They were symbolic of great historical events, legends, and exploits of their heroes. Then little by little language and music began to take over the sacred and symbolical meanings of the ceremonial dances. But the people never forgot the significance of certain typical movements, and they became part of their tradition. These steps and movements took on national individuality, like language and dress. They became unmistakably Italian, German, Chinese, English, Russian, Polish, American, Japanese, and so on.

Students of ancient history have no trouble in tracing the origin of Greek drama to choral dances in honor of the mythological god, Dionysus; and in Japan the Noh drama, a kind of dance drama, originated in ancient religious dances. In Europe, during the Middle Ages, the Dance of Death, or Danse Macabre, was often performed. It was a semi-religious dance on the subject of morality.

CLASSICAL AND NATIONAL DANCES

Most dancing today is of the social type. It is meant for a good time, for people to get together, get acquainted, and enjoy dancing to the music of an orchestra. Such dancing began with the waltz, derived from the earlier French minuet, in 3/4 time, and the volta. Social dancing was quite formal for a time. The art of music was developing, and orchestras were able to offer a varied program of rhythms. Many of the rhythms used by the great composers were originally meant to keep time for dancers.

The mazurka, named after the Mazur Lakes of Poland, is in 3/4 time with the accent on the second beat. It is the national dance of Poland. You stamp your feet and click your heels together as you dance. The polka is more spirited, in 2/4 time. *Polka* means "Polish girl," but the dance is Czechoslovakian. It has ten figures, or steps, but in crowded ballrooms they are not all required. The polonaise, made famous by Chopin, means "Polish dance." It is in a slower 3/4 time, and was originally used for processions and fancy balls.

From France came the gigue (jig), played in a fast 6/8, as is the spirited Italian tarantella, which represents the movements of a large poisonous spider. The Spanish fandango is colorful and bright in a fast 3/4 time, danced to the accompaniment of clicking castanets and singing dancers. The gavotte was a French peasant dance, used by Lully in his court ballets for Louis XIV. It is in a measured 4/4 time.

Beginning in the 1500s, and until many years after the Civil War, the cotillion was used at the close of a ball. It was a combination of the waltz, polka, and mazurka.

In the article on FOLK DANCING you may read about the Morris dance, in which such characters as Robin Hood and Maid Marian were depicted; the czardas from Hungary; the bolero from Spain; the Highland fling from Scotland; and the reel and jig from Ireland.

From America came the Virginia reel, usually danced to "Turkey in the Straw"; the Paul Jones; and the square dance.

MODERN BALLROOM DANCING

The dances that are commonly used today in Europe and the United States began about 65 years ago with the one-step, a fast 2/4, and the two-step, a slower 2/4. These dances set the basic style for all of the variants that came after, including the turkey trot, bunny hug, and the fox trot. The fox trot appeared in 1912 and is still the most popular ballroom step. These dances started in the United States, with the spread of ragtime and jazz music. The music is cut time, written in 4/4. It can be fast or slow, and the dancers adjust to the music.

The Charleston, black bottom, shag, Lindy hop, and all kinds of jitterbug steps

were based on the 4/4 beat. They were more acrobatic and violent forms.

Beginning about 1936, Latin American dances became very popular in the United States and in Europe. The Argentine tango is a graceful and beautiful dance, but its glides and pauses make it unsuitable for crowded dance floors and it has found a place as an exhibition dance. In the rhumba, or rumba, a highly syncopated dance with African flavor, in 8/8 time, the body moves more than the feet. The samba and mambo are strenuous and exciting variations of it.

In the 1960s, new dances became popular — first the *twist,* then variations on it such as the *watusi, frug,* and others — in which the dancers stand apart and move their bodies rhythmically. These dances were seen most often at *discotheques,* which originated in France: cabarets for dancing, drinks, and refreshments, with music supplied by phonograph records instead of a live orchestra, and entertainment by professional dancers demonstrating the latest methods of dancing. See also the article BALLET.

dandelion

The dandelion is a very common weed that grows in lawns and in fields. Its leaves grow in a circle close to the ground. They are long and very deeply notched along the edge. Because these notches are shaped like teeth, the French call the plant *dent de lion,* which means "lion's tooth." From this we get the word dandelion. From the middle of its circle of leaves the dandelion sends up several stalks eight or nine inches tall. Each of these stalks carries a large bright yellow flower head. This flower head looks like a single flower, but actually it is made up of many small flowers growing close together. Sometimes in summer the meadows are made bright yellow with thousands of these flower heads. When they mature, these flower heads turn into large balls of fluff. Each of these balls consists of dozens of little umbrella-shaped pieces of fluff. When the wind blows, these float away in the air. Each one has a seed attached.

Young dandelion leaves are good to eat in salads or cooked as greens. There are many different kinds of dandelion that grow wild in North America, Europe, and Asia. Some kinds are used in making medicines.

Daniel

Daniel is the name of a book in the Bible. It is also the name of the man whose story and prophecies are told in this book. He is supposed to have been taken to Babylon when its king, Nebuchadnezzar, conquered the Jews. Babylon was the chief city of Babylonia, a country northeast of Palestine and now part of Iraq. Daniel remained faithful to the religion of the Jews, even while he studied in Babylon, which was known for its great astrologers. His three friends, Shadrach, Meshach and Abednego, were thrown into a fiery furnace for not praying to the gods of Babylon, but they walked out unhurt.

Daniel read the meaning of a dream Nebuchadnezzar had, and told the king about the great empires that were going to follow him. The next king, Belshazzar, saw a hand writing words on the wall, and these Daniel explained by saying that the king's days and those of his kingdom were almost over. That night the king was killed and his kingdom captured by a neighboring king, Darius. Because of this story, the phrase "the handwriting on the wall" is often used to mean that the end, or defeat, is near.

Daniel was thrown into a lion's den for praying to the God of the Jews. But he was still alive the next day, and he said his God had sent an angel to shut the lions' mouths. Daniel also had visions of the future. He said there were four kingdoms, the golden, silver, bronze and iron, and that after them would come the Kingdom of Heaven. The visions of Daniel gave the Jews great hope for the future, and his story shows how a man can live his religion even when he is away from his own people.

Dante Alighieri

Dante Alighieri was an Italian poet, author of *The Divine Comedy,* and one of the greatest poets who ever lived. He was born in Florence in 1265 and lived there until 1302, when he was banished after the side he was on lost in a civil war. He died in Ravenna in 1321.

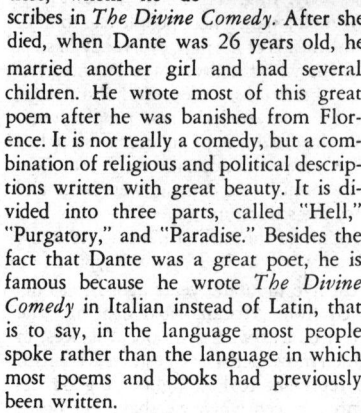

When he was only nine years old he fell in love with a beautiful girl named Beatrice, whom he describes in *The Divine Comedy.* After she died, when Dante was 26 years old, he married another girl and had several children. He wrote most of this great poem after he was banished from Florence. It is not really a comedy, but a combination of religious and political descriptions written with great beauty. It is divided into three parts, called "Hell," "Purgatory," and "Paradise." Besides the fact that Dante was a great poet, he is famous because he wrote *The Divine Comedy* in Italian instead of Latin, that is to say, in the language most people spoke rather than the language in which most poems and books had previously been written.

Danton, George Jacques

George Jacques Danton was an outstanding figure in the French Revolution. He was born in 1759, and was educated to be a lawyer. He always favored overthrowing the French king and setting up a new government. In the revolution he became a great leader. He was very brave and clever, and he seemed

Gale Research Co.

to be able to encourage and inspire others. Danton was the leader and planner in defending France against the Prussian army that tried to put down the revolution. Wherever he went, he seemed to make the people more patriotic, and to encourage the army to fight better. He was a leading figure in the government for a while. But he disagreed with some of the other leaders in the revolution. His enemies had him arrested, and he was beheaded on the guillotine in 1794.

Danube River

The Danube River is the second largest river in all of Europe. The only one that is larger is the Volga. The Danube is about 1,770 miles long. It starts in the Black Forest, which is in southern Germany, and flows through Germany, Czechoslovakia, Austria, Hungary, Yugoslavia, and Rumania, until it empties into the Black Sea. It is a very beautiful river, and a boat trip down the Danube is a very wonderful experience. There are rolling fields, deep forests, and beautiful cities on the banks of the Danube. The cities include three great capitals of nations: Vienna (Austria), Budapest (Hungary) and Belgrade (Yugoslavia). The most famous of all waltzes, by Johann Strauss, is called "The Beautiful Blue Danube." Like many other great rivers, the Danube is blue and beautiful near its source, but by the time it reaches the big cities it is muddy and brown.

The Danube carries much important freight, on ships and barges. Canals connect the Danube with other great rivers in Europe, including the Rhine and Elbe in Germany and the Vistula in Poland. For more than a hundred years all nations through which the Danube flows agreed not to close the river to the freight of other nations, but since World War II the river from Vienna to the sea has been controlled by Communist nations.

Wherever the Danube goes, its waters irrigate the land and make it fertile. For this reason land on the Danube has always been considered very desirable. For many hundreds of years invaders from many parts of Europe and Asia came to the plains around the Danube to settle, bringing with them many different ideas and ways of living. Because so many different peoples have traveled down the Danube and settled on its banks, the river is sometimes called *The Highway of Races.*

Danzig

Danzig is a city in Poland. It is on the Baltic Sea and at the mouth of the Vistula River. Over 369,900 people live in this important Baltic seaport, and many of them are shipbuilders. Some trade in lumber, grain, and coal. Danzig is more than a thousand years old, and until about five hundred years ago it was a free (independent) city. The people of Danzig made their own laws and fought their own battles. About 180 years ago (in 1793) the Free City of Danzig became part of Prussia.

In 1920, after World War I, the Treaty of Versailles made Danzig a free city again, but this only made more trouble for Danzig. The Germans and the Poles both wanted to control this valuable seaport, and in 1939 Hitler demanded that Poland give Danzig to the Germans. When Poland refused, Hitler invaded Poland, and Danzig became German. The Russians invaded Danzig in March, 1945, and for several weeks there was fierce fighting. Finally Danzig fell to the Russians, but most of the city, with its fine old cathedrals and beautiful buildings, was destroyed. The Potsdam Declaration of 1945 says that Great Britain, Russia, and the United States agree that Danzig should be part of Poland.

Daphne

Daphne was a beautiful nymph, or nature spirit, who was turned into a tree to save her from the god Apollo. The story is one of the Greek myths told thousands of years ago, when people believed that all parts of nature were connected with special, powerful beings called gods and goddesses. Daphne was the daughter of a river god, and she liked hunting in the woods so much that she did not want to give up her freedom and marry.

One day the god Apollo saw Daphne, and he fell in love for the first time. Daphne ran away from him, and the god chased her, begging her not to be frightened and telling her that it was a god who loved her. Apollo almost caught her, but Daphne was near her father's river, and called frantically for help. Immediately she was changed into a tree to save her. Her hair became leaves, her arms branches, her body was enclosed in bark, and her feet were roots. Apollo was very sad, but he said that the tree, a laurel, would be known as his, and he would wear the leaves as his crown. This is said to be the reason why the Greeks gave wreaths of laurel to the winners of games held in honor of Apollo. In Rome, great conquerors were crowned with laurel wreaths.

Daphnis

Daphnis was a shepherd whose beauty won the hearts of the Greek goddesses and nature spirits. Different stories are told about Daphnis in the Greek myths, which were stories about special beings called gods and goddesses who could do things ordinary people could not do. The Greeks connected trees, rivers, mountains, and so on with nature spirits or nymphs. One of these was the sweetheart of Daphnis. In some stories, Daphnis is the most faithful of lovers, and even Aphrodite, the goddess of love, cannot win him away from the nymph. But in another story, Daphnis is unfaithful, and the nymph blinds him or turns him into a stone. Daphnis was beaten in a contest with a cruel farmer, Lityerses, who always killed those who could not reap as much as he could. But the gods saved Daphnis and killed Lityerses instead.

Daphnis is said to have made the first songs and poems about shepherds and herdsmen of cattle. He was called Daphnis because he was found in a grove of laurel trees, which are connected with the nymph DAPHNE, about whom there is a separate article.

Dardanelles

The Dardanelles is the name of a narrow strip of water, about forty-five miles long and three to four miles wide, that joins the Sea of Marmara with the Aegean Sea and separates Turkey in Asia from the Peninsula of Gallipoli on the European side. The Dardanelles were called the *Hellespont* by the ancient Greeks, and the word *Dardanelles* comes from the name of an old Greek city called Dardanus which was located on one side of the strait. The Dardanelles are the continuation of the waterway that connects the Black Sea with the Mediterranean Sea by way of the Bosporus, the Sea of Marmara, then through the Dardanelles into the Aegean Sea which is really a part of the Mediterranean Sea. Since the Dardanelles control the entrance to the Sea of Marmara and also the Black Sea, they have always been very important as a military objective, and many battles have been fought to capture them. Today the Dardanelles are controlled by Turkey, and both sides of the narrow strait are heavily fortified in case of war.

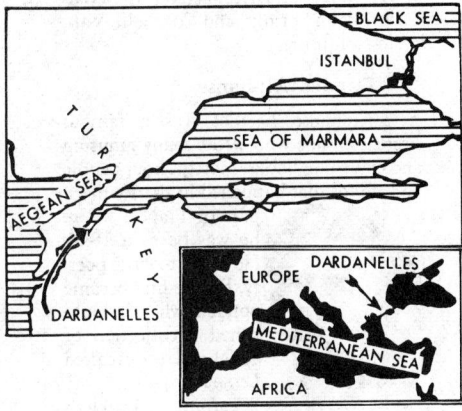

Dare, Virginia

Virginia Dare was the first child born in America of English parents. She was born on August 18, 1587, at Roanoke Island in the colony of Virginia (it is now in the state of North Carolina). Virginia Dare was granddaughter of John White, the governor of the colony, who had been sent out to begin a farming center in the New World. White's daughter Eleanor was married to Ananias Dare, the governor's assistant. The baby was born only a month after they landed in America, and was called Virginia in honor of the new colony. On the 27th of August, White sailed back to England for more supplies. A war between England and Spain prevented anyone from getting back to the colony until 1591. By then, there was no trace left of the settlers. So we know of only nine days in the life of Virginia Dare. You can read more about the colony of Virginia in the article LOST COLONY in another volume of this encyclopedia.

Darius

Darius was the name of several ancient Persian kings. The most important was Darius I, who was born about 2,500 years ago. He is often called Darius the Great. The Persian empire under Darius I was so large, that he divided it into *satrapies* or provinces, and then placed a satrap (governor) over each province to represent him. Darius built many good roads between his cities and at certain regular distances on these roads there were stations where fresh horses and food could be obtained. These stations were used by the king's messengers, who would gallop day and night to all parts of the empire delivering the messages of the king, stopping only to change horses and then go on again. This messenger system

Darius III

was like the Pony Express in the United States, in the days of the early West.

Another Darius was Darius III. He was king for only a short time, and was defeated in battle by Alexander the Great nearly 2,300 years ago. Shortly after his military defeat, he was treacherously killed by one of his own officials.

Dark Ages, see the article on MIDDLE AGES.

darning needle, see the article on DRAGONFLY.

Darnley

Henry Stuart, Lord Darnley, was the second husband of MARY, QUEEN OF SCOTS, about whom there is a separate article. He was the father of James I, who was the first king of the united kingdom of England and Scotland. Darnley was a distant cousin of both his wife, Mary, and Queen Elizabeth I of England. He was born in England in 1545 and was married to Mary in 1565. Darnley was a very disagreeable and jealous young man. He aided in the plot to kill Queen Mary's secretary and advisor, a man named Rizzio.

Darnley was blown up by powder kegs in a house called Kirk o' Field near Edinburgh in 1567. When his body was discovered afterward, it was found that he had first been strangled. It has never been proved, but people said the queen knew of the plot to kill her husband. The Earl of Bothwell, who was in on the plot, later became Mary of Scotland's third husband.

Dartmoor

Dartmoor is a region in Devonshire in southwest England. It is mostly wasteland used for grazing, but it is also very picturesque and interesting. The central portions are occupied by the ancient Royal Forest. Above the plain and the trees of the forest there rise bare granite peaks called *tors*. There are also granite quarries, tin, copper, and iron mines. At Princetown there is the famous Dartmoor Prison built in 1806. When the United States and Great Britain were at war, in the War of 1812, many American prisoners were held captive at Dartmoor Prison.

Dartmouth College

Dartmouth College is a school for men in Hanover, New Hampshire. About three thousand young men go to Dartmouth College, and along with the regular courses they can study to be doctors or engineers. Dartmouth College began as a school for Indian boys. In 1769 it became a regular college and was named after the Earl of Dartmouth, because he gave so much money to the school. At Dartmouth College you can get a fine education and also enjoy winter sports. Every year they have a winter carnival, with skiing and skating, and the Dartmouth Winter Carnival has become famous.

Darwin, Charles

Charles Robert Darwin was a great English scientist who lived from 1809 until 1882. He is the most famous one of a family of many well-known people.

From the time he was very young, Darwin was interested in the study of plants and animals. After he finished his education, he went on a scientific trip on a ship called the  *Beagle,* to study the plant and animal life of lonely islands in the Pacific Ocean, where few men lived. Darwin was interested to see if there were certain kinds of animals on those islands that differed slightly from their relatives on near-by parts of continents. He concluded that plants and animals are not all alike in all places where they occur. He thought that young animals born into the world differed from each other, and since there was not room enough for all of them, those that survived were better able to fit into the world around them than the ones that did not survive. He thought the survivors in the competition lived on because they chose mates that insured stronger and healthier offspring. This enabled the young to make their way in the world. Darwin called this process "natural selection," by which plants and animals gradually change through the ages. He explained this process in a famous book, *Origin of Species.* Natural selection insures survival of the fittest, according to Darwin's theory. The changes occurring in this process he called EVOLUTION, about which there is a separate article.

date line

The international date line is the name of an imaginary line passing roughly north and south through the Pacific Ocean. We change the date one day forward if we cross the date line traveling westward, and one day backward if we travel eastward. For example, if the date on a ship on the United States side of the date line was August 21, the date on a ship a few miles away on the other side of the line would be August 22. This change of date has to be made because a whole day is either lost or gained by traveling completely around the globe. The United States asked to have the date line bent to include Alaska on the United States side of the line. Otherwise some parts of Alaska would have had the same time as Asia.

date palm

The date palm is a tall and beautiful tree. It grows wild in the deserts of North Africa, Arabia, and Persia. Its trunk is tall and straight, and may be as much as sixty feet high. All the leaves grow at the top of the trunk. They are feather-shaped, and grow to about fifteen feet in length. Date palms are very famous because of their fruit, which are called dates. There are male and female date palms, and the fruit grows only on the female palms. It grows in huge bunches hanging just below the leaves. Each date is about two inches long and contains a long, hard seed. Dates are very important, because they are the chief food of the men and women who live in the desert. Sometimes the pulp of the date is eaten fresh, but mostly dates are dried and squeezed into cakes. As cakes, dates keep for months, yet they are very nourishing. Sometimes

the Arabs, who are the people who live in the desert, make a kind of date wine that they drink at their dances.

Date palms have been grown by the Arabs for more than 2,000 years. Often they are the only plants that grow beside the springs of water in the desert. These springs are called oases. From the oases in Africa and Asia, date palms have been brought to the United States. Date palms can be seen in Phoenix and Salt River Valley in Arizona, and Imperial Valley, Palm Springs, and Coachella Valley in California.

Daudet, Alphonse

Alphonse Daudet was a famous French author who wrote many amusing and charming books, mostly about people and things that happened in the southern  part of France, where he was born in 1840. He began to write poetry, but he first became popular when he published a collection of delightful stories called *Letters from My Windmill.* Daudet's most amusing stories, however, are about a very funny character named Tartarin who is supposed to have lived in the French town of Tarascon. Tartarin likes to boast and brag all the time about the big fish he has caught and other things he has done, but his stories sometimes get him into trouble. Other people make fun of him and play jokes on him because he believes almost everything he hears. But he is really a very harmless and lovable character. You can read about him in three of Daudet's books, *Tartarin of Tarascon, Tartarin in the Alps,* and *Port Tarascon.* Although Daudet was born in southern France, he lived and wrote during most of his life in Paris, where he died in 1897.

Daughters of the American Revolution

One of the most important patriotic organizations in the United States is known as the D.A.R., which are initials that stand for the Daughters of the American Revolution. Membership in the D.A.R. is open to women who are citizens of the United States and who have one or more ancestors who fought for or helped the American cause during the Revolutionary War. This society was organized in 1890 at Washington, D.C., where it also has headquarters in a fine large memorial building known as Constitution Hall.

dauphin

The eldest son of the former kings of France was called the dauphin. This title was sold with the province of Dauphiné to King Philip VI in 1349 by the Dauphin Humbert II of Vienne. The dauphin was therefore a kind of count or prince. The word itself means dolphin, or porpoise, which is a kind of ocean fish. A drawing of a fish was probably first used as a heraldic device on the family coat of arms.

If the French dauphin died before the king, the dauphin's son inherited the title. The last dauphin was Louis Antoine,

the Duke of Angoulême. The eldest son of Louis XIV was called the Great Dauphin, because he was a good military leader. When Louis XVII disappeared, he was supposed to have come to America; he is known as the Lost Dauphin.

David

David was the "Shepherd-King" who united Israel. His family or dynasty ruled it for four hundred years. He is remembered for killing the giant Goli-  ath, for his friendship with Jonathan, and for losing his son Absalom. David probably lived a thousand years before the birth of Jesus. Saul was king of Israel, and David was a shepherd boy. But one day the prophet Samuel heard a voice saying that David would be king after Saul. When the Hebrews were fighting the Philistines, the enemy giant Goliath challenged anyone to come out and fight him. David went out alone and killed Goliath with a stone he cast from a sling. David was then taken to King Saul. The king was pleased by David's beautiful playing on the harp.

David became great friends with Jonathan, the king's son. Saul made David the head of the army, but later Saul became jealous and tried to kill David. Then both Jonathan and Saul were killed in battle. One of the many songs or psalms said to be written by David tells his grief: "How are the mighty fallen!" David and his followers fought against the followers of Saul. After several years, they won, and David was crowned king of all Israel. He made Jerusalem the capital, and the religion of the Jews became more powerful. David's son Absalom tried to take the throne away from him, but when Absalom was killed, David mourned, "O my son Absalom, my son, my son Absalom! Would God I had died for thee, O Absalom, my son, my son!" Another son of David ruled after him. This was Solomon, who built the famous temple.

David, Saint

Saint David was a popular preacher who became the patron saint of Wales, a country west of England. His festival is celebrated on March 1st. A patron saint is a protector, and people pray to him especially when their country is in trouble. David, or *Dewi,* had a great deal to do with bringing the Christian religion to southern Wales in the 6th century. More than fifty monasteries and churches are called by his name. Monasteries are religious houses for those who devote their lives to the Church. Very little is certain about the life of St. David, but after he died many people came to visit the shrine where he was buried. About 1120 he was made a saint. On St. David's Day, the Welsh usually wear a leek, their national plant. This is in memory of a famous battle the Welsh won from the English. On the day of the battle, the Welsh soldiers picked leeks from the fields and wore them so they would be different from the Saxons, or English.

Davidson, Jo

Jo Davidson was a famous American sculptor. He was born on the lower east side of New York City in 1883. He was interested in drawing and painting from the time he was a child, but he did not plan to be a professional artist. He intended to become a doctor, and he went to the Yale Medical School for his training. While he was there, he realized that sculpture was his real interest, and he left medical school and began to study it. In 1907, he went to Paris to continue his studies and he lived there until World War II, when he came back to the United States. He is most famous for the bronze busts (statues of a person's head and shoulders) he made of famous people. Among the people who sat for him were two Presidents of the United States, Woodrow Wilson and Franklin Delano Roosevelt, and his other models included Will Rogers, George Bernard Shaw, John D. Rockefeller, and Helen Keller. Jo Davidson died in 1952.

Davis, Jefferson

When the Confederate States of America was formed as the government of the southern states during the Civil War, Jefferson Davis was chosen as its President. He was born in a cabin in Kentucky, the tenth child of a pioneer tobacco planter, in 1808. His birthplace was less than one hundred miles from that of Abraham Lincoln. When he was still a child, his family moved to Mississippi; then as a young man he returned to Lexington, Kentucky, where he received his education at Transylvania University. He was appointed to the United States Military Academy at West Point, and graduated as an officer of the army in 1828. In the Black Hawk War against the Sac and Fox Indians he served as a junior officer.

Davis's first marriage, to the daughter of the great general Zachary Taylor, was very tragic. His bride died after three months and Jefferson retired to his Mississippi plantation, where he spent the next ten years. His plantation, called Brierfield, was a beautiful expanse of rich land overlooking the Mississippi River. As a slaveholder he was considered just and kindly. He introduced a system of

self-government among his slaves, who tried their own members by slave juries. There were schools and churches, and the plantation was an example of slavery at its best. Davis was nevertheless a strong believer in the expansion of slave territory and a champion of what was then called Southern rights.

In 1844, Davis married Varina Anne Howell, the daughter of a wealthy Mississippi planter. The same year he was elected to the House of Representatives, and his political career began.

One year after entering politics Davis joined General Zachary Taylor in the Mexican War, as commander of a Mississippi Regiment. There he distinguished himself in the siege of Monterrey, and at the battle of Buena Vista. He returned a war hero, and was soon appointed to the Senate.

When the Civil War started, Davis was made president of the provisional government at a convention of Southern leaders held at Montgomery, Alabama, in 1861. He was inaugurated as regular president at Richmond, Virginia, in 1862. Throughout the Civil War he was in constant disagreement with the high command of the Confederate Army. Because of his early personal military exploits he had fancied himself a great strategist, When Robert E. Lee surrendered and the war ended, it was against the wish of Davis, but Lee had no choice. His army was trapped and without supplies.

Div. of Pub., Frankfort, Ky.
Jefferson Davis Monument in Kentucky.

HIS FINAL YEARS

Davis was taken into custody in Georgia in 1865. He was held for two years at Fort Monroe, while the government prepared an elaborate set of charges against him as a war criminal. He was charged with treason, the penalty for which is death. The case dragged on for years, but was finally dropped in 1869, after President Johnson issued his proclamation of unconditional amnesty, restoring constitutional rights to all who had supported the Confederacy. Davis lived for twenty years after his trial ended. He died in 1889 and was buried in New Orleans, but his body was later moved to Richmond, Virginia.

Davis, John W.

John William Davis, one of the most notable of American lawyers, was the Democratic Party's candidate for President of the United States in 1924 but was defeated by Calvin Coolidge. Davis was born in Clarksburg, West Virginia, in 1873, and attended Washington and Lee University. He served as ambassador to Great Britain from 1918 to 1921. After 1924 he retired from political life and headed a large firm of lawyers in New York City. He tried many important cases before the United States Supreme Court. He died in 1955.

Davis, Richard Harding

Richard Harding Davis was an American short-story writer, novelist, playwright, journalist, and famous war correspondent. He was born at Philadelphia in 1864. His mother was a popular novelist and journalist, and his father was the editor of the Philadelphia *Inquirer*. He went to Lehigh and Johns Hopkins universities. He first became famous with a story called "Gallegher." As a journalist he covered many wars, especially the Spanish-American and Boer wars. He also wrote several popular plays and many novels and short stories, some for children. He died in 1916.

Davy, Sir Humphry

Sir Humphry Davy was an English chemist who was born more than 150 years ago, in 1776. He became interested in chemistry when he was very young, and by the time he was 20 he had started making his many chemical discoveries such as finding out what plain earth is made of. He saved the lives of many coal miners by inventing the miner's safety lamp, which warned the miners of the presence of firedamp, a deadly, explosive gas that killed men in coal mines. He was also a fine speaker, and many people enjoyed his interesting talks on chemistry. The King of England honored him by making him a knight. He died in 1829.

Dawes, Charles G.

Charles Gates Dawes was an American lawyer, banker, statesman, and vice-president of the United States under President Calvin Coolidge. He is best known for the Dawes Plan, which he presented in 1924 as a method of collecting money, known as reparations, that Germany owed the Allies for damage done during World War I. For this plan Dawes was awarded the Nobel Peace Prize in 1925. He was born in Marietta, Ohio, in 1865 and died in 1951. He had a busy private career as a lawyer, banker, and businessman. During the war he served in France on General Pershing's staff and afterward held many government positions, including that of ambassador to England.

Dawson, Sir John

Sir John William Dawson was a Canadian geologist and educator. He was born in Pictou, Nova Scotia, Canada, in 1820. His parents were Scottish, and he was sent back to Scotland for his education at the University of Edinburgh. At an early age he became interested in geology, and in 1842 he accompanied the famous geologist Sir Charles Lyell on an expedition to examine the fossil forests of Nova Scotia. In 1855 he was made principal of McGill University in Montreal, where he was also a professor. He was the first president of the Royal Society of Canada and also served as president of the American Association for the Advancement of Science. He died in 1899.

day

Day is a word that can mean either the time of light and sunshine, which lasts about 12 hours, or it can mean the kind of day we count on the calendar, which is one period of light and one night together, or 24 hours. The earth takes 24 hours to spin completely around once. This means your home faces the sun, and is in daylight, for about 12 hours, and then is turned away into the darkness we call night for another 12 hours. The length of the night and day we have depends on where we live, and someone

living at the North or South Pole would have only one period of night and one of day in a year. Each usually lasts six months, because the Poles at the top and bottom of the earth tilt six months toward the sun, and six months away from the sun, as the earth spins its way around the sun.

Day, Clarence

Clarence Shepard Day was an American writer who became most famous after his death in 1935 because of the play *Life with Father*. The play was written by Howard Lindsay and Russel Crouse, but it was based on stories that had been written by Clarence Day. He was born at New York City in 1874. He graduated from Yale University and then went into business. However, he became ill and had to spend much of the rest of his life in bed, where he wrote many stories.

daylight-saving time

Daylight-saving time is a way we save millions of dollars in electricity by using more of the daylight hours when the days grow longer in spring and in summer. We do this by pushing the clocks one hour ahead at two o'clock in the morning on the last Sunday in April, and then pushing them back to regular time at two o'clock in the morning on the last Sunday in September. In some sections of the country, daylight-saving time has been extended to the last Sunday in October. Daylight-saving time was thought of in 1907 by an Englishman named William Willett.

day lily

The day lily is a beautiful lily with trumpet-shaped yellow flowers that have a sweet odor. They grow on the end of a tall, branched stem that rises out of the ground from among a mass of long and narrow leaves. Two kinds of day lilies are grown in gardens, both of them from Eastern Europe and Turkey. They are called day lilies because the flowers only last while the sun is up.

Dayton

Dayton, a city in Ohio, is one of the most important manufacturing cities in the United States. Its skilled workers make airplane parts, cash registers, electric motors, bicycles, boilers, golf clubs, automobile parts and tires, and many other articles. The city is on the Great Miami River, in the southeastern part of Ohio, sixty miles from Cincinnati. In 1902, the Wright brothers, Orville and Wilbur, invented the airplane at Dayton. Today the city has one of the biggest airfields in the world. It is called the Wilbur Wright Field and is owned by the United States government. There United States Air Force engineers try out the latest inventions for airplanes.

Dayton is also noted for the five dams it built in the Great Miami River. These dams stop the water from overflowing the banks to flood the country. In 1913 the people of Dayton stopped electing a mayor to run their city. Instead, they elected a group of men called a council, who then hired the best man they could find to run the city. Such a man is called a city manager. Many people think a city manager is better than an elected mayor. A mayor may be a popular man but that

does not always mean he knows a great deal about running a city. A city manager must know all there is to the business of governing a city. Otherwise he would not be hired to do this job. Dayton was the first large city in the United States to be run by a city manager.

DAYTON, OHIO. Population (1970 census) 243,601. County seat of Montgomery County. Settled in 1796.

DDT, a poison used to kill harmful insects: see the article INSECTICIDES.

Dead Letter Office, see POST OFFICE DEPARTMENT.

Dead Sea

The Dead Sea is a very large lake that lies between Israel and Jordan. It is about 46 miles long and 8½ miles wide. It is in a deep valley and is nearly 1,300 feet below sea level. The most interesting thing about the Dead Sea is that it is very, very salty, so salty that no fish can live in it. It is probably called dead because it contains no life at all. The saltiness makes the Dead Sea very easy to swim in. It is almost impossible to sink in such salty water. The bad thing about swimming in the Dead Sea, though, is that your body gets all covered with salt and you feel very sticky and uncomfortable when you come out of the water.

The Dead Sea is mentioned in the Bible, but there it is called the Salt Sea. The Bible says that the wicked cities of Sodom and Gomorrah were near the Salt Sea. Some people think that when those cities were destroyed by God they were buried underneath the Salt Sea.

The Dead Sea Scrolls are copies of books of the Bible, written on thin sheets of copper and parchment (goat or sheepskin specially prepared for writing). Over a period of years starting in 1947, these 2,000-year-old fragments were found in eleven different caves in the Dead Sea area. They are very valuable to Bible students. (See BIBLE.)

Deadwood

Deadwood is a city in the Black Hills of South Dakota. It is the county seat of Lawrence County in the western part of the state. It was settled in 1876 after the discovery of gold nearby the year before. It had a famous history in the days of the Wild West and you can see there the graves of such famous characters as Wild Bill Hickok, Calamity Jane, and Deadwood Dick. The city is now famous as a tourist center and shopping point for the miners and ranchers.

deafness

Deafness is a handicap that people have to bear when they cannot hear at all, or cannot hear as well as the rest of us. In order for you to understand deafness you also have to know a little about sound, which is made of little unseen vibrations that travel through the air like waves across the water. The ear has three parts, and when the sound vibrations come to the first part, the *outer ear*, they are collected by its funnel-like shape and carried through the ear passage to the eardrum which actually is just like a tiny drum. The drum then vibrates against

the delicate little bones called the *middle ear*. These bones, in turn, carry the message to the *inner ear* which is the most delicate of all, but is also the best protected part because it is so far inside the head. The inner ear is made up of many little nerves inside a tiny shell, and these nerves sort out different sounds for you. Connected to the inside of the inner ear is a large nerve which carries the final message to the brain so that you can hear. If anything goes wrong with any of these three parts of the ear, you will have deafness.

OUTER EAR DEAFNESS

Troubles that happen to the outer ear are the least serious, and this kind of deafness usually lasts only until a doctor can clean out the ear passage. The ear passage may get clogged up by small beans or buttons, or by insects or cotton, but it is easy for a doctor to take these things out so that you can hear again. Perhaps a pimple or a boil has grown there, or maybe too much protective wax clogs the ear passage. These cause trouble for only a day or so, until your doctor can clean them out, so nobody ever stays deaf long from trouble in the outer ear.

MIDDLE EAR DEAFNESS

You should be careful with troubles of the outer ear mainly because they might affect the middle ear. Most deafness happens when the sound vibrations cannot be carried through the three little bones of the middle ear. This may happen because a hole has been made in the eardrum that germs can go through when careless people have tried clumsily to get something out of the ear passage. Sometimes it happens because the germs of a cold or some more serious disease have worked their way up the tubes that connect the middle ear with the back of the inside of your nose. When germs get into the middle ear they cause an infection. If the middle ear becomes sore and inflamed, those three bones cannot vibrate against each other the way they are supposed to, and the vibrations do not get to the inner ear at all. Until the trouble is all cleared up, you are deaf. If the disease is a serious one, such as scarlet fever or diphtheria, sometimes the middle ear can never work right afterward. Another cause might be a serious accident such as a blow on the side of the head, which could break the eardrum so badly that it could never again carry its message across the bones of the middle ear to the inner ear.

INNER EAR DEAFNESS

It is not very often that young people become deaf from troubles of the inner ear. If they do, it is because loud noises or explosions have injured the nerves, or because a serious disease has harmed them. In every person, the nerves of the inner ear become slowly weaker as he grows older, so real old people always become at least a little bit deaf.

The usual cause of deafness is something that is wrong with one of the three parts of the ear. A few children, however, are actually born deaf, just as some children are born blind. This means that one of the parts of the ear did not grow right before the baby was born. Children who are born deaf are almost always children of deaf parents.

In the United States there are probably 23,000,000 people who are partly deaf. Since we have about 185,000,000 people, it means that every time you counted eight people, one of them would be partly deaf. The number of completely deaf people is about 69,000.

Deafness is an unpleasant thing to live with, and children who are deaf have a most difficult time getting along with other children. A child needs to hear well in order to learn well. If a child cannot hear well, he may get into a habit of being confused lots of times when the other children around him are not. Soon he may come to think he is not quite as good as other children and if he cannot change this way of thinking, it may become a habit. Most of the habits of grown-ups come from good or bad habits they had as children. It is very important that parents or teachers should discover bad hearing in children as early as possible.

Parents can tell if a child is deaf because he or she does not learn to speak at the age when other children normally do; teachers can tell if children are partly deaf by giving tests with a machine called an audiometer. When doctors find out that something is wrong with a child's hearing they try to repair the part of the ear that is causing the trouble. Sometimes operations are necessary (they can perform a wonderful new operation on the middle ear called the "window operation"). Even if the doctor cannot help, there are still many things that can be done. Assistance is given by societies to help deaf children, such as the Society for the Hard of Hearing in Washington, D.C. Children who cannot hear at all can learn to speak and to understand by carefully watching and studying other people's mouths while they are speaking. Children who can hear a little bit, but not well enough to understand, can wear hearing aids which make ordinary sounds much louder so that words can be understood.

The important thing to remember is that something can always be done for deaf people; and they, most especially, have to want to help themselves.

DEAF-MUTES

People who are born deaf have been called deaf-mutes or "deaf and dumb." They can neither hear nor talk. A child learns to talk by hearing other people. Deaf-mutes cannot hear other people, and therefore never learn how to talk. Most deaf-mutes have to "talk" with a sign language. They use their fingers to make signs that mean letters and words.

In the last hundred years ways have been found to teach deaf-mutes to talk. The most famous example of a deaf-mute who learned to talk is Helen Keller, who was also blind. Before her the great example was a girl named Laura BRIDGMAN, about whom there is a separate article. The articles about Samuel Gridley HOWE, Thomas Hopkins GALLAUDET and Helen KELLER tell more about this subject.

There are separate articles about the EAR, SOUND, HEARING, and HEARING AIDS.

Dean, Jerome Herman

Jerome Herman ("Dizzy") Dean was one of the most famous baseball pitchers of all time. He is in baseball's Hall of Fame. He is also known as Jay Hanna Dean, which may be his real name. A right-hander, with a fast ball and a wide variety of curves, in 1934 he won thirty games for the St. Louis Cardinals of the National League, losing seven. In 1937 his arm was injured, and he left the major leagues in 1940. He was born in Lucas, Arkansas, in 1911. In addition to his value as a pitcher, he was one of the most colorful and picturesque personalities ever known. After retiring from active playing of baseball he became a sports broadcaster, and his back-country speech gained him an enthusiastic following. Dizzy Dean died in 1974.

JAY HANNA (DIZZY) DEAN
ST. LOUIS (N.L.) 1932-1937
CHICAGO (N.L.) 1938-1941
ONE OF FOUR N.L. PITCHERS TO WIN 30 OR MORE GAMES UNDER MODERN REGULATIONS. PITCHED IN 1934 (ST.L.) 1938 (CHICAGO) WORLD SERIES. LED LEAGUE IN STRIKEOUTS 1932-33-34-35. SINGLE GAME RECORD WITH 17, JULY 30, 1933. FIRST PITCHER TO MAKE TWO HITS IN ONE INNING IN WORLD SERIES. MOST VALUABLE N.L. PLAYER IN 1934.

Baseball Hall of Fame

In the Baseball Hall of Fame you can see this plaque of Dizzy Dean, one of the greatest baseball pitchers of all time.

Dearborn, Fort

Fort Dearborn is a United States army post that was built more than 150 years ago on a site now surrounded by the city of Chicago. It was named after General Henry Dearborn, who was then Secretary of War. It was built on the Chicago River, by the southwest shore of Lake Michigan. During the War of 1812, Fort Dearborn was threatened by Indians. The troops were ordered to leave together with some civilians including women and children. As they were leaving, however, they were attacked by the Indians, who killed many of them and captured most of the others as prisoners. The fort, which was also destroyed, was rebuilt a few years later and formed the center around which gathered cabins and trading posts that increased to become the city of Chicago. You can read about CHICAGO in a separate article.

Fort Dearborn, which is in the state of Illinois, should not be confused with the city of Dearborn, Michigan. Dearborn city, which also is named after General Henry Dearborn, was formerly a village settled in 1795 on the Rouge River, west of the present city of Detroit. It is famous as the birthplace of Henry Ford, who built his automobile plants there. Ford also built there a typical American town called Greenfield Village, at which one can see such interesting things as the original workshops of Thomas Edison and other inventors.

Death Valley

Death Valley is a deep and dry desert region in southern Nevada and southeastern California. It lies between two mountain ranges, the Panamint Range on the west and the Funeral Range on the east. It is about 150 miles long and varies between 10 and 30 miles in width. One place, called Badwater, is 276 feet below sea level and the lowest point in North America. The temperatures in the summer are among the highest in the world. Less than an inch and a half of rain falls a year and the two streams, Furnace Creek and the Amargosa River, are swallowed up by the dry desert sand.

The region was called Death Valley by a group of prospectors, most of whom died here during the rush to the gold fields in 1849. Miners have since found some gold, but the most valuable mineral there is borax. The only group of people who have been able to live in Death Valley are the Panamint Indians, for whom the government has set up a special village. In 1933, the valley was made a national monument in order to preserve the many small animals and peculiar desert plants that manage to survive there. You can see some of these in a wonderful film by Walt Disney called *The Living Desert*. Another sight is the castle of Death Valley Scotty, a former prospector named Walter Scott, whose publicity stunts and supposedly secret wealth did much to make Death Valley famous.

debate

A debate is a formal discussion, or argument, that is carried on between two persons or two teams of opponents. Before a debate begins, a subject is chosen for discussion. The subject to be discussed is usually stated in the form of a resolution, such as, "Resolved, that democracy is a better form of government than fascism." Sometimes the subject of debate is presented as a question instead of a resolution, such as "Should the voting age be lowered from 21 to 18 years of age?" In other one side is called the *affirmative* and the other side is called the *negative*. Each side tries to gain agreement with its point of view by presenting arguments stronger than its opponents'.

When two debating teams meet, the first speaker for the affirmative always begins the debate. The first speaker for the negative follows next. Then the second speaker for the affirmative presents more arguments for his side, and so on, until everyone has spoken once in turn. These speeches may be prepared in advance or may develop from the opponents' arguments. In some debates there are rebuttals, in which each speaker has a second chance to reply to the arguments of the other side. These rebuttals usually consist of attempts to support one's own arguments that have been attacked, or they may be attacks on the opponents' arguments, or they may be a combination of both. Finally the leader for the negative side

summarizes the arguments for his side, and the debate ends with a similar summary by the leader for the affirmative. The winner of most debates is decided by three judges, who decide in favor of the side that has presented the most and best points and has best answered in rebuttal the arguments by the other side.

To have a good debate, it is necessary not only to choose good speakers, but also a good subject that gives each side a fair and equal chance to win. The resolution or question must also be clearly stated, so that it can be easily understood. If it is too vague or too general, the arguments become confused and the debate breaks down.

The purpose of a debate is to permit free and public discussion of important topics of general interest. Debating is an old American custom and very useful in the practice of democracy. In the 19th century, public officials debated much more than they do today. Some of the most famous of these debates were held in 1858 between Stephen A. Douglas and Abraham Lincoln before Lincoln became president. In a series of seven debates they discussed the problem of slavery with the result that Lincoln became nationally famous and Douglas lost much of his popularity.

Debating is also excellent training for young people. It trains them to think logically, to judge honestly, and to express themselves as public speakers. It also teaches them to look up the necessary facts with which to debate and increases their store of knowledge. Most schools have debating teams that meet once or twice a year, to give students the opportunity to learn how to debate.

Debs, Eugene V.

Eugene V. Debs was an outstanding American labor leader. He was born in 1855. His first job was on a railroad, and he was always a leader in the railroad unions. He was one of the founders of the Socialist Party of America, and five times he was the Socialist candidate for President. You can read about the SO-CIALIST PARTY in a separate article. He did a great deal of writing for magazines and newspapers put out by unions, and by the Socialist party. During World War I, Debs thought and said that the United States should stay out of war. Because of these ideas, he was put in prison for some years. After he got out, he wrote many articles telling about bad conditions in the prisons. Debs was a fine speaker, and often traveled around the country making speeches. When he spoke, he made people interested and excited. Eugene Debs died in 1926. Many people had liked and respected him, even when they did not agree with him, because he was an honest and sincere man who wanted to help people.

Debussy

Achille Claude Debussy was a great French composer. A composer is a writer of original music. He is known as Claude

French Embassy Press

Debussy because he took the Achille off his name when he grew up. For a time he also signed his name De Bussy. He was one of the founders, and his work is an outstanding example, of the type of music called impressionism. This is music in which tradition and the obvious are ignored and chords and sounds are used to represent a mood or to represent ideas that have no direct meaning in words. Debussy was born in Saint-Germain-en-Laye, near Paris, France, in 1862. He died in Paris in 1918. Among his most popular compositions are *Clair de Lune*, from the *Suite Bergamasque; La Mer; L'Après-midi d'un Faune;* and the opera *Pelleas et Melisande*. He also wrote numerous songs and literary works.

decathlon

The decathlon is an event in the Olympic Games, the international athletic contests held every four years. A single competitor engages in a group of ten events. Scoring is by the number of points gained in the entire group, according to the number of first places won, second places won, and so on. The separate contests are: 100-meter dash, 400-meter run, 1,500-meter run, 110-meter hurdles, high jump, broad jump, pole vault, discus throw, shot put, and javelin throw. This event is sometimes included in other large athletic contests.

Decatur, Stephen

Stephen Decatur was a naval hero and American patriot in the early years of the United States. He was born at Sine-puxent, Maryland, in 1779, and entered the United States Navy as a midshipman when he was 19 years old. At that time there were many pirates attacking American ships in the Mediterranean Sea. They came from Mohammedan countries on the "Barbary Coast" of North Africa, and were called the Barbary pirates. Decatur fought bravely against the pirates of Tripoli, one of the Barbary countries, and for this he was promoted to captain in 1804. In the War of 1812 against England, Decatur commanded a frigate (warship), the *United States*. He captured the English frigate *Macedonian*, and for this Congress awarded him a gold medal. Finally Decatur commanded a squadron of nine ships against other Barbary pirates, and made their owner, the bey (ruler) of Algiers, sign a treaty agreeing not to attack American ships again.

U.S. Naval Academy Museum

In 1815 Stephen Decatur was made a naval commissioner, a very high office. But he had an enemy, Commodore James Barron, who had been suspended from the Navy by a court-martial of which Decatur was a member. In 1820, Decatur and Barron had a quarrel and fought a duel, which was the custom of those times. Decatur was shot through the hip, and died the next day from the wound.

Stephen Decatur is best remembered for saying, at a dinner at Norfolk, Vir-ginia, in 1816: "Our country! In her intercourse with foreign nations may she always be in the right; but our country, right or wrong!"

December

December is the twelfth and last month of our modern calendar. The Romans began their year with March, and so December was their tenth month. The name "December" comes from the Roman word *decem,* which means "ten." In the Northern Hemisphere, this month contains the shortest day and the longest night of the year, December 21st, when the sun passes through the winter solstice. This means that the sun's path is farthest south of the equator. There is a separate article about SOLSTICE in this encyclopedia. December 21st is the beginning of winter in our Northern Hemisphere, but in the Southern Hemisphere, this day is the beginning of summer—the longest day and the shortest night of the year. Long ago, December 21st was celebrated as the "birth of the sun," and of the sun gods. There were festivals of lights to show that the dark winter was passing away.

decimal system is a system of numbers based on ten or tenths. See the separate articles on ARITHMETIC and NUMBERS.

deck tennis

Deck tennis is a game that was first played on the decks of large ocean liners, where there was space enough only for games that could be played in comparatively small areas. It can be played anywhere there is room for a small court that is laid out in the fashion of a tennis court, and where there is room to hang a net like a volley-ball or badminton net. Deck tennis is played with rings that look like quoits. The rings are about six inches in diameter and usually made of rubber.

Two or four people may play, the same as at tennis or badminton. The ring is tossed from one side of the court to the other. It must be caught by the player on the opposing side before it hits the ground and tossed back immediately. The play goes back and forth until one player fails to catch the ring, or a player holds it without throwing it back immediately, or until the ring lands on the ground out of bounds—behind the end line of the court, or outside of the side lines of the court. Every such "miss" counts as a point for the other side, and the first team or side to get 21 points wins the game.

Declaration of Independence

The Declaration of Independence is one of the most important documents in history. It explains the ideas of government that were held by the American colonists during the time of America's revolution against British rule, it lists the complaints the Americans had about the ways the British were treating them, and it announces the fact that the colonies consider themselves free and independent, and not part of the British Empire.

The Declaration of Independence was written mostly by Thomas Jefferson, who later became the third President of the United States. Jefferson, John Adams, Benjamin Franklin, Roger Sherman and

Pa. Chamber of Comm.

The famous Independence Hall in Philadelphia is where the Declaration of Independence was signed. The Liberty Bell rang out the joyful news on July 4, 1776.

on such principles and organizing its powers in such form, as to them shall seem most likely to effect their safety and happiness."

In other words, according to the Declaration of Independence, all men are born equal, and all equally have the right to live their lives in liberty and as happily as possible. The job of government, says the Declaration, is to give all men liberty, safety, and a chance at happiness. Government is at all times responsible to the people, who have a right to change it if they are not satisfied with it. We today hold these very same beliefs, and the democratic governments of the world are based on these beliefs.

But the governments of Europe at the time of the American Revolution were based on very different ideas. They were based on the idea that the kings and the nobles were superior to the common people, and that the government had no obligation to satisfy the needs and wants of ordinary people, or to represent them in any way. The notion that the wishes of a shoemaker were just as important as the wishes of an earl, seemed dangerous and ridiculous to the rulers of Europe at that time.

Of course, Jefferson and the other members of the Continental Congress were not the first men to express these ideas. Important thinkers and philosophers all over Europe had stated these same ideas of life and government many years before the Declaration of Independence was signed. But the Declaration of Independence was not just a statement of beliefs, it was actually a way of bringing about a kind of government that would put these beliefs into action. It was a chance to find out if these ideas would work in practice. Because the American Revolution and the new government were successful, the words and ideas of the Declaration and of the new American nation were a real inspiration in all parts of the world, from France to South America and Asia, in the establishment of democratic governments.

After the explanation of the kind of government the colonists believed in, the Declaration of Independence goes on to list all the complaints the colonists had against the British king, George III. These complaints include the fact that the king has permitted unfair laws to be passed, has permitted the colonists to be taxed unfairly, and has kept a standing army in the colonies. The Declaration then goes on to say that the colonists have asked the king, over and over again, to change these unfair practices, but that he has refused to. Therefore, the Declaration says, the colonists have no choice but to declare themselves a free country, independent of Great Britain.

The Declaration that was passed by the Continental Congress was different in certain ways from the Declaration that was proposed by the committee. When the committee brought the Declaration to Congress on June 28, it included a long paragraph attacking slavery, and accusing the English king of encouraging the slave trade. The members of the committee wanted this paragraph to be in the Declaration, but the Continental Congress took it out. In the final official version of the Declaration of Independ-

Robert R. Livingston were appointed by the Continental Congress (which was made up of delegates representing the thirteen American colonies) on June 10, 1776, to draw up a statement announcing America's independence from Britain. The committee gave Jefferson the job of doing the writing, and worked with him on the Declaration until it was finished, on June 28. Then it was brought before the Continental Congress. The Congress made a few changes in it, and passed the changed version on July 4, 1776.

At that time the American Revolution was already under way. It had really started in April, 1775, with the Battles of Lexington and Concord. Two days before the Declaration of Independence was signed, on July 2, 1776, the Congress had passed a resolution stating that the colonies "are, and of right ought to be, free and independent states."

Actually, therefore, the Declaration of Independence was, in part at least, only a formal public statement of facts that everyone knew: that the American people were no longer willing to be under

British control, and were ready to fight to get and keep their freedom from England. But the Declaration was really much more than just a public statement of facts that everyone knew. It was also the first public statement of a brand-new idea of government, which became a model for countries and people all over the world, and which was very different from the idea that lay behind the governments of Europe at the time the Declaration of Independence was written.

This new idea is explained at the beginning of the Declaration:

"We hold these truths to be self-evident, that all men are created equal, that they are endowed by their Creator with certain unalienable rights, that among these are life, liberty, and the pursuit of happiness. That to secure these rights, governments are instituted among men, deriving their just powers from the consent of the governed. That whenever any form of government becomes destructive of these ends, it is the right of the people to alter or to abolish it, and to institute new government, laying its foundation

A Declaration by the Representatives of the UNITED STATES OF AMERICA, in General Congress assembled

When in the course of human events it becomes necessary for one people t dissolve the political bands which have connected them with another, and to sume among the powers of the earth the separate and equal station to which the laws of nature & of nature's god entitle them, a decent respect to the opinions of mankind requires that they should declare the causes which impel them to the separation;

We hold these truths to be self-evident; that all men are created equal & independent; that from that equal creation they derive rights inherent & inalienable, among which are the preservation of life & liberty, & the pursuit of happiness; that to secure these ends, governments are instituted among men, deriving their just powers from the consent of the governed; that whenever any form of government shall becomes destructive of these ends, it is the right of the people to alter or to abolish it, & to institute new government, laying it's foundation on such principles & organising it's powers in such form, as to them shall seem most likely to effect their safety & happiness. prudence indeed will dictate that governments long established should not be changed for light & transient causes: and accordingly all experience hath shewn that mankind are more disposed to suffer while evils are sufferable than to right themselves by abolishing the forms to which they are accustomed. but when a long train of abuses & usurpations [begun at a distinguished period & pursuing invariably the same object, evinces a design to reduce them] under absolute Despotism, it is their right, it is their duty, to throw off such government & to provide new guards for their future security. such has been the patient sufferance of these colonies; & such is now the necessity which constrains them to expunge their former systems of government. the history of the present king of Great Britain is a history of unremitting injuries and usurpations, [among which appears no solitary fact to contradict the uniform tenor of the rest all of which have in direct object the establishment of an absolute tyranny over these states. to prove this let facts be submitted to a candid world [for the truth of which we pledge a faith yet unsullied by falsehood]

Thomas Jefferson wrote this rough draft of the Declaration of Independence. Benjamin Franklin and others then helped put it in its final form.

ence, there is no mention of slavery at all.

THE SIGNING

When the Declaration was passed on July 4, 1776, it was signed by two men: John Hancock, president of the Continental Congress, and Charles Thomson, its secretary. A month later, a beautiful copy of the Declaration was made on parchment, and all the members of the Congress signed this copy. Independence Hall, where the Continental Congress met and passed the Declaration of Independence, is still standing in Philadelphia. It is now a museum and is open to the public.

Decoration Day, see the article on MEMORIAL DAY.

deed

A deed is an important paper that is used to make a record of the sale of land or buildings. When a person wants to sell a piece of land or a building that he owns, he must give the buyer a deed. The deed is worded very carefully and tells where the property is, how large it is, and most important of all it contains the statement that the man who is selling the property owns it and has a right to sell it. The person who is selling the property must sign the deed, and the person who

is buying the property must also sign. Another person must attest it, which means that he signs a statement on the deed that he has seen the deed and heard the agreement between the seller and the buyer. In most places a deed must also be signed by a public official and a copy must be placed with the clerk of the county in which the property is located.

deer

The deer is a graceful, swift animal with long, slender legs. Deer are hunted for sport and for their flesh or meat, which is called venison. The deer family is known for its antlers, the bony branches that grow on top of a male deer's head. Antlers are different from horns because they are solid instead of hollow, are usually branched, and are new every year. Each winter or spring, the deer's antlers fall off, and a new set grows by autumn. Antlers are mostly used in the autumn, the mating season, when the male deer, the stags or bucks, battle for possession of the females, the does. You have probably seen pictures of a stag fight.

The deer is a mammal, that is, it gives birth to live babies and nurses its young, which are called fawns. Deer live in forests and eat grass or the young, tender bark, twigs, and shoots of trees. Like

a cow, a deer has a separate stomach "paunch" or sac for partly digested food. In its leisure, the deer brings up this food or cud, and finishes chewing it.

Each year the male deer sheds its large antlers and then grows new ones again.

There are almost 100 kinds of deer, and the family includes the elk or wapiti, the moose, and the caribou or reindeer. In the Americas, the most common deer is the white-tailed deer, found all the way from southern Canada down to Peru and Bolivia in South America. This deer holds its tail straight up when it runs, showing the white underside. The white-tailed deer may be about 5 feet long and 4 feet high. The mule deer is about the same size, but it has long ears. Mule deer live in western North America. The largest deer is the moose, which grows to a height of six feet and weighs over half a ton. The deer you may know best from pictures and stories is the red deer of Europe, Asia, and Africa. Deer have been known to man for so long that some of the oldest drawings we have, which were made by cavemen thousands of years ago, show wonderful pictures of them. You can read more about deer in the separate articles on CARIBOU, ELK, MOOSE, and REINDEER.

Defense, Department of

The Department of Defense is one of the main branches of the United States Government. The purpose of the Department is to defend the country in case of war. This means the Department must always be ready to fight any enemy who comes to the United States. It must also fight our enemies in their own countries or wherever else they may be. The Department of Defense was established in 1947. Its head is the Secretary of Defense. He is one of the most important officials in the government. He is a member of the President's cabinet. Only one man in the government has more to say in matters of defense than the Secretary of Defense. This man is the President himself, who is commander in chief of all forces in the United States that fight in case of war.

The Department of Defense is divided into three main sections or departments and each has its own chief, also called a secretary. The three sections are the Department of the Army, the Department of the Navy, and the Department of the Air Force. The secretaries are called Secretary of the Army, Secretary of the Navy, and Secretary of the Air Force. The Secretary of Defense must work together with the other three secretaries. He must make sure that the three departments are always ready for war and that they will work together well when they have to fight the enemy. The Joint Chiefs of Staff, composed of the generals and admirals who head the various services, also report to the Secretary of Defense. Each year Congress votes money to be spent for the defense of our country. The Secretary of Defense is in charge of this money. He must see to it that it is spent wisely. In 1961 this money amounted to about 47 billion dollars. The President appoints the Secretary of Defense. In 1947 President Harry Truman appointed James V. Forrestal as the first Secretary of Defense. Since that time a number of men have held this post.

Defoe, Daniel

Daniel Defoe was an English writer and the author of one of the most famous adventure stories in the world, *Robinson Crusoe*. He was born in London in 1660. His early life was difficult because he was a dissenter, which means that he refused to accept the authority of the Church of England. He wrote many political articles and several other novels besides *Robinson Crusoe*, but none of them became as popular. *Robinson Crusoe* tells the adventures of an Englishman shipwrecked on a desert island. It is based on the real story of a man named Alexander Selkirk. Defoe died in 1731.

De Forest, Lee

Lee De Forest was a famous American inventor, called the father of radio. He was born at Council Bluffs, Iowa, in 1873, and studied at Yale. He made more than two hundred inventions but the most important was the radio tube, which he called the Audion. Without this invention talking pictures ("movies"), radio, and television would have been delayed many years. Dr. De Forest, who had many college degrees, also improved the telephone, wireless, and telegraph. His tube made it possible to amplify sound (make it louder) so that weak sounds sent electrically through the air can be heard. He died in 1961.

Degas, Edgar

Edgar Degas was a great French painter and sculptor. Especially famous are his paintings and statues of ballet dancers. Degas would sit in the theater, in the wings just off the stage, to watch the dancers at work and at rest. He would make sketches, and then go back to his studio to paint or make sculptures of the scenes. All of his pictures and statues of dancers have a light, floating feeling.

Degas was born in Paris in 1834. His first success came with his pictures of race track horses. In these paintings the horses seem to run right out of the frames. He also liked to paint scenes of his native Paris, where he lived most of his life. Before he died in 1917 he came to America. His mother had come from New Orleans. While he was visiting there he painted a well-known picture of Negroes loading cotton on river boats.

Degas loved to paint and draw ballet dancers. This picture was done with crayons.

de Gaulle, Charles, see the article on GAULLE, CHARLES DE.

De Grasse, Count François

De Grasse was a hero of the American Revolutionary War, though he was a Frenchman, not an American. He was an admiral in the French navy and was sent with a fleet of ships to help the Americans fight the British. De Grasse prevented aid from reaching Cornwallis at Yorktown by fighting British naval vessels, and he stopped Cornwallis from escaping. He received a vote of thanks from Congress for this. He was finally defeated and captured by the British in the West Indies. Later he was allowed to return to France. He died in 1788.

degrees

Students who complete their courses in a college or university are given a degree when they are graduated. The degree is a way of saying that the student has learned what is required. There are three main divisions of degrees. The first is the *bachelor's degree,* which is given when a student is graduated from college, usually after four years of college attendance. Then comes the *master's degree.* It is given to a student who does a certain amount of specialized work in a university after graduation from college. The highest degree is the *doctor's degree.* In order to get it, a student must do a great deal of very advanced studying. He must pass difficult tests and must write a paper that shows he has done a lot of thinking and studying in his special subject. As a student moves on from the bachelor's degree to the more advanced degrees, his work becomes more and more specialized. By the time he has a doctor's degree, he is a real expert in his subject. In olden days, most people who went to college became teachers, and degrees were something like licenses to teach.

dehydration

Dehydration is a word that means the drying of something so that all or most of its water is removed. During World War II, scientists found that they could dehydrate large quantities of food such as milk, eggs, and potatoes. The armed forces used these foods because they did not spoil quickly. Also, with the water out of them, they had less weight and bulk and could be shipped easily. The dehydrated-food industry is now very large, and even our frozen fruit juices are dehydrated to a quarter of their original weight.

Deirdre

Deirdre is the heroine in a famous Irish story. When she was born it was predicted that her life would be unhappy. She was brought up secretly to become the wife of King Conchobar of Ulster, but one day she accidentally saw a boy named Naoise and fell in love with him. Together with Naoise and his brothers she fled to England, where they all lived happily for a long time. King Conchobar, however, finally tricked them into returning to Ireland. The brothers were killed and Deirdre was so unhappy that she killed herself. Many Irish writers have told the story of Deirdre, but the best version for children is by James Stephens.

de Kalb, Johann, Baron, see the article on KALB, JOHANN, BARON DE.

de la Mare, Walter

Walter de la Mare was an English novelist and poet who was born in 1873. For many years he earned his living as a bookkeeper and had very little time to write. His first book of poems, called *Songs of Childhood,* was published in 1902. De la Mare later received a government pension, which made it possible for him to retire and spend all of his time writing. Much of his poetry is written for children or about children. Most of his poems and stories are about imaginary things and are written in a charming and delightful fashion. One interesting novel he wrote is called *Memoirs of a Midget.* He died in 1956.

de la Roche, Mazo

Mazo de la Roche is a Canadian novelist. She was born in Toronto, Canada, in 1885. She first became famous for her novel *Jalna,* which was published in 1927 and won an *Atlantic Monthly* book prize. *Jalna* was a novel about a family named Whiteoak, which is further described in a series of novels. Miss de la Roche also wrote a play called *Whiteoaks* that was very popular, and in 1935 a film called *Jalna* was made. Both the play and the film were based on the earlier novels. She died in 1961.

Delaware

Delaware is a little state in the eastern part of the United States, on the Atlantic Ocean. It was one of the thirteen original colonies and the first to become a state. Thomas Jefferson called Delaware "a jewel among the States"; and a Delaware poet wrote that it was like a diamond, small but of great value. Perhaps

for these reasons, Delaware is called the Diamond State. It is also called the Blue Hen State, because the blue hen was known for its fighting spirit, and during the American revolution a famous company of Delaware soldiers carried these hens along with them as pets. Later, all Delawareans came proudly to be called Blue Hen's Chickens.

Delaware ranks 49th in size among the states, with 1,978 square miles. Only Rhode Island is smaller. In population it ranks 46th, with 548,104 people living there. The state was named after Lord de la Warr (or Delaware), the governor of Virginia, who sailed up Delaware Bay almost 350 years ago.

THE PEOPLE OF DELAWARE

Most of the people of Delaware used to be farmers like their English ancestors, who settled in the territory about 300 years ago. As Delaware began to grow into an industrial state, people from many European countries came to the cities, particularly to Wilmington, where they worked in the factories and stores. Many people in Delaware come from these Italian, Russian, German, and Polish immigrants. Today, six out of ten people live and work in the cities. Negroes make up about one-seventh of the population, and most of them live in Wilmington.

The Delawareans have always been very proud of their little state. In the southern region, the farmers have not had much to do with other people until the last fifty years, when radios and automobiles made such communication easier. These people have kept many of the customs and habits of their English ancestors, and they even pronounce words somewhat differently from those who live in other parts of the state. The children still like to play old English games such as "London Bridge Is Falling Down," and "Oh, Dear, What Can the Matter Be?" The people still believe that certain things will bring them good or bad luck, and in some parts of Delaware the first articles carried into a new house are the Bible and a saltshaker for good luck. Most of the people in the small towns and villages love to tell "yarns," or stories, that are humorous or, sometimes, fearful, such as the story of Fiddler's Bridge. You can read about Fiddler's Bridge in the section "Places to See in Delaware."

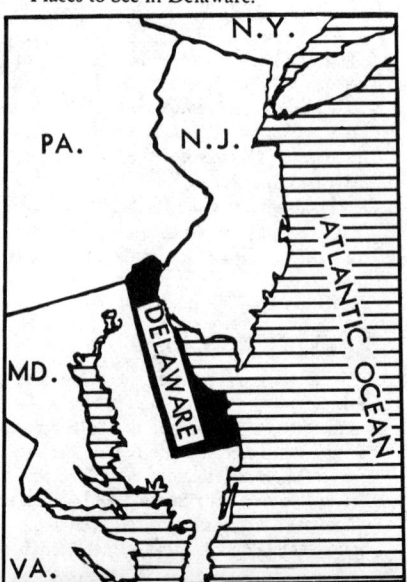

The churches are very important in the social life of the people. Especially in the small towns, people have their clubs and parties through their churches. The largest church in Delaware is the Methodist, and others include the Presbyterian, Roman Catholic, and Episcopal churches.

WHAT DELAWARE IS LIKE

If you visit Delaware, you will find that the northern and southern parts of the state look very different. In the north are low hills, but the southern part is flat and has many swamps. Along the eastern coast it is marshy.

The hills have many fertile valleys with farms where the people raise dairy products, chickens, wheat, and corn. In central Delaware, farmers grow fruits, and the state is famous for its peach and apple orchards. In the southern sandy areas vegetables and broiling chickens are grown. The broilers and vegetables of Delaware are shipped to many of the large cities in the eastern states. Along the southern border, you can see the Great Pocomoke Swamp.

Delaware has only a few important cities, which are mostly in the north, but they are prosperous, and manufacture many important and useful products which everybody uses. Wilmington is one of the biggest chemical manufacturing cities in the world. Its factories produce nylon for clothing, paint, dyes, and cellophane, which is used to wrap so many things. Clothing is made in large factories, and special leather for gloves and shoes is manufactured. The du Pont family has been responsible for the tremendous growth of Wilmington as an industrial city.

The climate of Delaware is mild, and there is a good deal of rain for the crops. Railroads and highways reach all parts of the state, and there are airports in the principal cities.

THE GOVERNMENT OF DELAWARE

Delaware, like most other states, is governed by a Governor and a Legislature, called the General Assembly. The Governor is elected for a four-year term. The Assembly is composed of a Senate, the members of which are elected for a four-year term, and a House of Representatives, whose members are elected for a two-year term. Judges are appointed by the Governor with the approval of the Senate for a twelve-year term. The capital is Dover. There are three counties.

SCHOOLS IN DELAWARE

Delaware's public schools were founded in 1829 by Willard Hall. There are about 130,000 students attending the public elementary and high schools.

The colleges and universities are:

University of Delaware, at Newark. Enrollment, 13,327 in 1971 (for men and women).

Delaware State College (for Negroes), at Dover. Enrollment, 1,276 in 1971 (for men and women).

Wesley Junior College, at Dover. Enrollment, 771 in 1971 (for men and women).

CHIEF CITIES IN DELAWARE

The leading cities of Delaware, with populations from the 1970 census, are:

Dover, population 17,488, the state capital and third-largest city in the state. There is a separate article about DOVER.

Wilmington, population 80,386, the largest city in the state. There is a separate article about WILMINGTON.

Newark, population 20,757, the second-largest city, in an agricultural region, in the eastern part of the state.

Elsmere, population 8,415, the fourth-largest city, a suburb of Wilmington, in the northern part of the state.

DELAWARE IN THE PAST

Delaware was a territory inhabited only by Indians when Henry Hudson discovered Delaware Bay about 350 years ago. Hudson did not land in Delaware, but continued northward in his ship to discover the Hudson River, which is named after him. The first people who actually settled here were the Dutch, who started a colony many years later, but then were killed by Indians. Later, a group of people from Sweden and Finland came to Delaware and built a fort, which they called Fort Christina, after their queen. They called this part of the country New Sweden. But the Dutch, living at New Amsterdam, saw this as an invasion of their territory. They finally seized the whole Swedish settlement.

When New Amsterdam was taken from the Dutch by the English, Delaware was claimed as part of English territory. William Penn, who had settled Pennsylvania, bought the English rights to Delaware, and made it part of Pennsylvania. After some years, it became a separate colony. Although the other colonies suffered from Indian wars and attacks, Delaware had almost no trouble because it was in a corner by the sea, out of the path of the trouble.

During the American Revolution, the Delaware soldiers were among the best and bravest of General Washington's troops, and they were called "the Blue Hen's Chickens." After the war, the people of Delaware were the first to adopt the Constitution, and so became the first state in the Union.

At the time of the Civil War, many people in the state owned slaves who worked in the fields. Although other slaveholding states seceded from the Union because they did not want the Negroes to be freed, Delaware did not secede. However, many people were sympathetic to the South, and joined the Confederate army, while others fought in the Union army. Delaware was not too pleased when the slaves were freed by President Abraham Lincoln, and for many years afterward there was an unfriendly feeling toward the Negroes.

The people enjoyed prosperity after the Civil War, and industries and commerce grew rapidly. In the last fifty years, many modern schools and roads have been built, and manufacturing has become the chief source of Delaware's wealth. People have also found the state a fine vacation place because of its excellent fishing, boating, and beaches.

PLACES TO SEE IN DELAWARE

Amstel House, at New Castle, on U.S. Route 13. A typical colonial house, with many exhibits, including complete kitchen furnishings of colonial times.

Brandywine Park, in Wilmington, on

U.S. Route 13. A beautiful natural park with gardens, a children's zoo, and playgrounds.

Elephant Rock, at Talleyville, off U.S. Route 13, 4 miles north of Wilmington. A large natural formation, resembling an elephant asleep.

Fiddler's Bridge, at St. George, 6 miles south of New Castle, on U.S. Route 13. A dark and gloomy place, where, according to legend, a mad Negro fiddler used to sit on the bridge rail, and play sad tunes. One night he fell into the water and was drowned. It is said that if a person drops a silver coin into the water, exactly at midnight, the fiddler will play his violin again.

Old Dutch House, in New Castle, on U.S. Route 13. Believed to be the oldest house in the state; built before 1700.

Rehoboth Beach, on the east coast, 5 miles from Lewes, on State Highway 14. Best known resort in Delaware; fine, sandy beach, swimming, canoeing, horseback riding.

Octagonal Schoolhouse, in Leipsic about 5 miles north of Dover, on State Highway 9. Odd little stone building, used as a public school until about fifty years ago. Two circles of desks; the outer circle for boys facing the wall; inner circle for girls facing the center.

Redden State Forest (1,133 acres), between Milford and Georgetown, on U.S. Route 113. Only large state forest in Delaware; beautiful scenery, trails, picnic areas.

Society of Natural History of Delaware, in Wilmington, on U.S. Route 13. Museum with collections of birds, plants and minerals.

Fenwick Island Lighthouse, 10 miles east of Selbyville, on U.S. Route 113. 80 foot tower; its light can be seen for 15 miles at sea.

DELAWARE. Area, 1,978 square miles. Population (1970 census) 548,104. Capital, Dover. Nickname, the First, or Diamond State. Motto, Liberty and Independence. Flower, peach blossom. Bird, blue hen chicken. Admitted to Union, 1776, ratified Constitution, December 7, 1787. First state in the Union. Official abbreviation, Del.

Delaware Indians, a branch of the Algonquin family of American Indian tribes: see the article on ALGONQUIN.

Delaware River

Delaware is the name of one of the most important rivers in the eastern part of the United States. If you want to travel the whole length of the Delaware River, you have to start in the Catskill Mountains of New York state. Then you go south about three hundred miles to the New Jersey coast, where the river flows into Delaware Bay. Some important cities you would pass on the way are Trenton, New Jersey, and Philadelphia, Pennsylvania. There are many shipyards along the banks of the river, and rich green farmlands. Ocean-going ships can sail up the river to Philadelphia, and all the way to Trenton. The Delaware River has cut a deep valley through the Kittatinny Mountains of New Jersey and Pennsylvania. This is called the Delaware Water Gap, and it is famous for its beautiful scenery.

People come here for their vacations from many parts of the United States.

The Delaware River was named for Baron De la Warr, who was the governor of Virginia almost 350 years ago. This river is very important in the history of the United States, because on Christmas Eve in 1776 George Washington and his men crossed the Delaware, and won one of the important battles of the American Revolution. A picture of this, painted by an artist named Leutze, has helped to make the Delaware famous.

Some of the water supply for New York City is carried in aqueducts from the Delaware River.

Delhi

Delhi is an ancient city in India, on the Jumna River. It was the capital of the Mohammedan Empire in India. About 3,629,800 people live in Delhi. It is a city of many temples and mosques. One of the largest of these is the Jama Masjid, or Great Mosque, built by the Mohammedan Emperor Jehan 300 years ago. When the English took control of India, they moved the capital to the port city of Calcutta. Later, in 1912, Delhi was again made capital of India, and about the same time a new city was started near Delhi. It is called New Delhi. New Delhi is now the capital of the Republic of India. There is a separate article on NEW DELHI.

Delilah was the woman in the Bible story who betrayed Samson: see the article on SAMSON.

della Robbia, a famous family of Italian artists: see the article on ROBBIA.

Delphi, Oracle of

The Oracle of Delphi in Greece was believed to be the voice of a god who gave people help and advice. Kings and commanders went to Delphi from many countries to find out their fortune in war and peace. The Oracle was consulted about famines and epidemics of disease, as well as about marriages, births, children, and the finding of lost property. The Temple of Delphi was in high and beautiful country near Mt. Parnassus, and in the Greek myths it was always a holy place. Myths are stories about great beings called gods and goddesses who can do things ordinary persons cannot do. People thought the gods sometimes talked to men and women, especially to priestesses like those at Delphi. The priestess made herself ready to hear the voice of the god by clearing her mind. She probably used incense, the smoke from burning spices and herbs. But it is also said that she changed the magnetism of her body and put herself into a sleep.

Over the door of the Delphic Temple were the words, "Man, know thyself and be divine." To the ancients, this meant that each one could learn to listen to the god within. Perhaps this is why the words of the Oracle could not be understood right away by the questioner. Sometimes he jumped to the wrong conclusion about what the Oracle meant, or refused to believe that the words would come true. In the story of CROESUS in this encyclopedia, you can read about one of these messages. The Delphic Oracle was said to go back

to 1400 B.C. By the 4th century A.D. it was silent. The Temple at Delphi also contained a sacred stone, the Omphalos, which was supposed to mark the exact center of the earth.

delta

A delta is a triangular or fan-shaped piece of land formed at the mouth of a river by the mud, sand, and stone the river has collected as it moves along. The river then leaves this collection of earth and stone at its mouth, as it empties into the sea. If you visit the Mississippi delta, you can see places that were once on the coast line and are now many miles inland. The river has built this delta into the Gulf of Mexico at the rate of over a mile every twenty years. Other famous deltas are at the mouth of the Nile in Egypt, the Po in Italy, and the Ganges in India. We call these new pieces of land deltas because the river forms them into a triangular shape like the Greek letter *delta*.

deluge

A deluge is a very heavy rain that sweeps away earth and trees and rocks. Most of the peoples of the world have stories about great deluges that have nearly destroyed the entire earth and everything on it. The Babylonians and Greeks and the people of India had legends about deluges, and most of the ancient stories are based on the Babylonian legend.

In the Bible, in the Book of Genesis, it tells about the great deluge of rain that God brought down on the earth for forty days and forty nights. Everything on earth except those people and animals that were with Noah in his ark were destroyed. You can read more about NOAH and the ARK in separate articles in this encyclopedia.

demarcation, line of

The year after Columbus discovered the New World in 1492, the two countries of Spain and Portugal began to argue over the rights to land in South America. They finally asked Pope Alexander VI to settle the argument. He then took a map of the Americas and drew a line, called the Line of Demarcation, running north and south, at a distance six hundred miles west of the Azores and Cape Verde Islands, which lie off the coast of Africa. Spain was supposed to keep all lands west of the line and Portugal all lands east of the line. But maps were so inaccurate in those days that the line drawn by the Pope actually went down the middle of the Atlantic Ocean, thereby giving Spain all of America, and Portugal just the tip of Brazil. So a year later the two countries moved the line nearly six hundred miles farther west. By this arrangement Portugal got most of what is today Brazil and Spain got the rest of South America, which explains why Brazilians speak Portuguese and other South Americans speak Spanish.

Demeter was the Greek goddess of farming and the harvest. She was called Ceres by the Romans: see the article on CERES.

De Mille, Cecil B.

Cecil Blount De Mille was a famous

American motion-picture director and producer. He was born at Ashfield, Massachusetts, in 1881. He went on the stage in 1900 and was active for a number of years as an actor, playwright, and producer. His biggest success as a producer came in staging the plays of David Belasco. When movies became popular, he formed a partnership with Jesse L. Lasky and made his first film in 1913. He died in 1959.

De Mille made nearly a hundred films, for both silent and talking pictures. Many of these were spectacular epic or historical films that gave De Mille a reputation as the most lavish director and producer in Hollywood. He used hundreds of people in his casts and spared no expense in creating great banquet scenes, battles, operas, circuses, and other spectacles. His first great film of this kind, which was made in 1915, was based on the opera *Carmen*. Other famous films include *The Ten Commandments*, *The King of Kings*, *Madam Satan*, *The Sign of the Cross*, *This Day and Age*, *Cleopatra*, *The Buccaneer*, *Union Pacific*, *The Greatest Show on Earth*, and many others in technicolor as well as black and white.

democracy

Democracy is a form of government in which all the people together have the power to decide what the laws will be and how the government should be run. The United States is a democracy, and so are Canada and Great Britain and France and Sweden and many other countries.

Of course, the millions of people who live in a country cannot get together and talk things over and then decide what to do, as the members of a club might. So the people go to the polls and vote for a person to represent them—that is, to act for them—in running the government and making the laws. That is what is called *representative government*. The people elect their representatives—the President of the United States, and members of Congress, and Governors of states, and even the dogcatcher, in some towns. Then it is up to the representative to do what he thinks best. But it is still the people who rule the government, because if the people don't like what their representative does, at the next election they can elect someone else to take his place.

That is what makes a democracy different from any other form of government. Under other forms of government, if the people are dissatisfied they can do nothing but grumble—and they had better not grumble too loud or they will be put in jail for criticizing the government. In the United States and other democracies, they can change governments until they get one they like.

We are so used to our democratic form of government that we seldom stop to think how fortunate we are to have it. In some countries of the world, the people do not control the government; a few of the people, who are rich or noble or powerful in a big political party, can decide what all the other people must do. Throughout the history of the world, nearly every country has been governed in that way.

Even today, many countries that call themselves "democracies" are not really democracies at all, because most of the people who live in them have no power.

REPUBLICS AND DEMOCRACIES

There is a difference between a republic and a democracy. A republic is any country that does not have a king. The United States is both a republic and a democracy. But British countries, which are kingdoms, are also democracies; while communist countries such as Russia and China, which are republics, are not democracies because the people cannot change governments when they want to.

Since the people rule in a democracy, they can have the government run any way they please. If they wanted to, they could decide to take away all their freedoms. They could decide that everybody would have to go to the same church and read the same books and newspapers. They could decide that no one could criticize the government or travel from town to town without a passport or quit his job. They *could*—if they wanted to. But men value liberty more than anything else, and as long as the people have the power they are not going to vote to turn themselves into slaves.

For that reason, a democracy is a country of free men and women. In any democracy, the people have a certain number of rights that keep them free.

FREEDOM IN A DEMOCRACY

The first important thing about a democracy is that the people have *freedom of opposition*. They can belong to political parties that are against the government. They can go to the polls and vote for the candidates of their political party. If enough other citizens agree with them, they will elect their candidates and have a government they agree with. In countries with governments that we call communist or fascist, no opposition political parties are allowed.

Hand in hand with freedom of opposition goes *freedom of speech*. In a democracy, when a person thinks he is right and the government is wrong, he has a right to say and write what he thinks. In this way he may persuade other people that he is right, and in the next election they will vote the same way he does. A person is not allowed to tell lies that would hurt someone else, but he is allowed to tell the truth and to say what his opinion is. Without freedom of speech, there can be no democracy. In communist countries today, and in the fascist countries that the United States and its allies defeated in World War II, men lost their freedom of speech and when they did, they lost their own freedom.

There are other freedoms that men can be expected to have in a democracy, where they have the power to protect their freedom. People in the United States, Canada, and other real democracies have all these rights: Everyone can follow whatever religion he chooses. No one can be put in prison without a trial under the laws that the people themselves have made. Anyone can leave a city, or a job, whenever he pleases, and can freely travel in or out of the country. In fact, anyone can do about anything he pleases, as long as he does not hurt someone else. Again, these are things we take for

granted and often forget to appreciate, yet in communist and fascist countries today, and in most of the countries of history, people did not have any of these rights.

HOW DEMOCRACY DEVELOPED

The word *democracy* comes from ancient Greece, 2,500 years ago. It means "government by the people." At that time nearly every country was under an absolute ruler—a king, or tyrant, or dictator—who had power of life and death over the people. Most of the people on earth were slaves or little better off than slaves.

But in Athens, a city and state of ancient Greece, men were trying the first real democratic government. There was no king and no dictator. All the citizens of Athens—about 30,000 of them—could listen to both sides of an argument and then vote to decide what should be done. Democracy in Athens was far from perfect. There were 450,000 people in the city and only 30,000 could vote; in fact, at least half of the people were slaves who had no rights at all. But Athens came closer to democracy than any other big state could come for more than two thousand years afterward.

After the time of Athens, most countries were run by either kings or noblemen. A country in which the government was ruled by the noblemen was called an *aristocracy*.

The first modern democracy was Switzerland. For nearly three hundred years, the people of Switzerland have elected representatives to make their laws and run their government. But until about a hundred years ago Switzerland was not exactly the kind of democracy the United States is. It was broken up into small "cantons," or countries, and in each of those the people controlled the government just as people do in a small American town. No one had yet proved that a democratic government would work for a big country.

Most men who were wise in politics said that democracy could not work in a big country. "The masses of people do not know enough to govern themselves," they said.

In the American colonies of Great Britain there were other wise men who thought democracy *would* work. These men included Thomas Jefferson, who wrote the Declaration of Independence; and Benjamin Franklin, one of the greatest thinkers of his century; and many other patriots who helped America to win independence in the Revolutionary War and then to adopt the Constitution of the United States, which created the first great democracy. Everyone has since had a chance to see that democracy works, for the United States became the richest and happiest country on earth.

Other experiments showed that a country does have to be "ready" for democracy. If most of the people of a country cannot read and write, and are ignorant in other ways, it is easiest for dishonest politicians to fool them and take their liberties away. France tried a democracy when it had a revolution and threw out its king and its noblemen in 1789, but it was nearly a hundred years before France had a democracy that really worked. Great Britain has been a real democracy for more than fifty years. It kept its kings and queens,

but all the power of the government belongs to members of Parliament who are elected by the people. Germany failed in its first effort to have a democracy, from 1919 to 1933, and let a dictator, Adolf Hitler, take the power away from the people and make himself the dictator. In Sweden, Denmark, and Norway, democracy has worked well for a hundred years, but in Russia, which was the most backward country in Europe, a democratic government lasted less than a year (in 1917), and then a tyrannical communist government grabbed the country and has run it ever since.

HOW TO MAKE DEMOCRACY WORK

There is a famous saying, "The price of liberty is eternal vigilance"; it is based on something that an American, John Curran, said during the first year of American independence. The right to live in a real democracy has been given to very few people in the history of the world, and many who have had this right have lost it because there were always greedy and dishonest men waiting for a chance to take it away and make them slaves again.

History has also shown that when a strong man—a Napoleon, a Hitler, a Lenin—asks for complete power "for a short time," until he can straighten out the affairs of the country, he never seems to want to give up that power later.

But when the people are educated, when they keep up with what is going on in their government, and when they use their privilege of voting in every election, they are unlikely to lose their freedom and their democracy.

Democratic Party

The Democratic Party is sometimes called the party of Thomas Jefferson, just as the Republican Party is called the party of Abraham Lincoln. This description is not complete nor entirely accurate, but it does indicate something about the nature and separate origins of the two major political parties in the United States. First of all, it indicates that the Democratic Party is older than the Republican Party. It goes back to the beginnings of the United States under the Presidency of George Washington when political parties first arose. There were then two political groups, one headed by Jefferson and the other headed by Alexander Hamilton. Hamilton's group was called the Federalist Party and it was opposed by Jefferson's group, which was called the Republican Party because it stood for the republican ideals of the French Revolution. The Republican Party that we know today, however, has no connection with this early party of the same name. When Jefferson's party won the national elections of 1800, it was called the Democratic-Republican Party, or sometimes the Democratic Party. By 1828, it was officially known simply as the Democratic Party. In the early days, therefore, the Republican Party as we know it today did not exist. Instead, the two major parties were the Democratic Party and the Federalist Party, which soon disappeared.

For many years the Democratic Party was split up into different factions, or groups within the party that disagreed with each other. Several of these factions joined together and called themselves the National Republicans and elected John Quincy Adams President. The famous Whig Party, which elected Presidents William Henry Harrison and John Tyler, was similarly created out of quarreling Democratic factions. But with these exceptions, the Democrats remained in power from the time Andrew Jackson was elected President in 1828 until the election in 1860 of Abraham Lincoln, the first Republican President.

During and before the Civil War, the Democratic Party divided sharply between northerners and southerners over the issues of slavery and secession. This split between northern and southern Democrats continued after the war, but Republican Reconstruction policies were hated so much in the South that nearly everyone turned Democrat. The "solid South" has since then almost always voted entirely Democratic. The Republicans nevertheless remained in power for many years, except for Democratic Presidents Grover Cleveland and Woodrow Wilson. Only when Franklin D. Roosevelt was elected President in 1933 did the Democrats finally become a strong party again. Roosevelt was in office for four successive terms, and when he died he was succeeded by Harry S. Truman, who was re-elected once. The Democrats lost the elections of 1952 and 1956, but won once again when John F. Kennedy was elected President in 1960.

The Democratic Party originally stood for Jefferson's principles, which favored the farmers. The Democrats also opposed high tariffs, which were advantageous to business and industry. But for many years, the Democrats were really more in agreement with the Republicans than against them. The present Republican Party is probably more conservative than the Democratic Party, but the two are not so sharply opposed to each other in principle as are the Labour and Conservative Parties in England or the many different political parties in France, Italy, and other countries.

De Molay, Order of, see FREE-MASONS.

Demosthenes

Demosthenes was a great political thinker of Greece who was famous for his oratory or public speaking. He lived about 2,400 years ago.

In Demosthenes' day, the different Greek states had become weak and divided. King Philip of Macedonia, a country north of Greece, was gradually gaining control of the separate Greek states. Demosthenes wanted Athens to become the center of a free Greek union. He warned that Philip intended to conquer all of Greece. The people of Athens did not listen to Demosthenes until it was too late and Philip had taken away the liberty of the Greeks. Demosthenes was the chief defender of Athens. Therefore the Macedonians wanted to capture him so he could not go on arousing the Greeks to fight. But when the Macedonians thought he was finally in their hands, Demosthenes took poison and escaped them by death.

Before the days of newspapers and news broadcasts, a man who wanted to bring his ideas to the public had to speak or write them himself. At first Demosthenes had a weak voice and some speech defects. But by long and strenuous efforts he trained himself to talk easily and clearly, and to find powerful, simple words for what he had to say. He taught himself so well that he is often used as an example of the perfect orator.

Dempsey, Jack

Jack Dempsey held the heavyweight boxing championship of the world from 1919 to 1926. His full name is William Harrison Dempsey and he was born in Manassa, Colorado, in 1895. He was often called the "Manassa Mauler." In 1926 he lost his title to Gene Tunney. In 1927 he fought Tunney again and seemed to have won by a knockout, but a technical rule of boxing gave Tunney a "long count" of fourteen seconds instead of the usual ten and Tunney recovered and won the fight. Dempsey in his fighting days was 6 feet 1½ inches tall and weighed about 195 pounds. At first the people did not like him, but later he became one of the most popular athletes of all time. After his retirement from boxing he ran a restaurant in New York City.

Denis, Saint

St. Denis was the first bishop of France and is its patron saint. A patron saint is a protector, and people pray to him to help their country.

St. Denis lived in Rome about three hundred years after the birth of Jesus. He was sent to France (then called Gaul) to spread the Christian religion. He made many converts or believers, but the Roman emperor murdered and beheaded him for preaching Christianity. Four hundred years later a famous monastery was built over his tomb, and for a long time the French kings were buried there. St. Denis is usually pictured as carrying his head in his hands. His feast is celebrated on October 9th.

Denmark

Denmark is a small country in the northwestern part of Europe. Together with Norway and Sweden it makes up the region called Scandinavia. Some include Finland in Scandinavia.

Denmark is a peninsula plus about five hundred islands that cluster around the peninsula. A peninsula is a piece of land surrounded on three sides by water. The total area of Denmark is about 16,500 square miles, which is about twice the size of the state of Massachusetts. Although the country is twice as big as Massachusetts, it has fewer people living in it. Only about four and one-half million people live in Denmark.

In its early days, the seafaring kingdom of Denmark was a very powerful and warlike country, and it was feared throughout Europe. Today Denmark is no longer as

powerful as it used to be, but it is very modern, peaceful, and prosperous. The Danish people have a high standard of living, and they are liked and respected throughout the world.

THE PEOPLE WHO LIVE THERE

The Danish people are the descendants of a people who used to be called Vikings. These men and women wandered all the way from the southeastern part of Europe to its northwestern tip about 2,500 years ago. They settled in Scandinavia and slowly built up their civilization. The Danes, like all the Scandinavian people, have light complexions. Many of them have blonde hair and blue eyes. They are both good looking and healthy looking. The Danes are known all over the world for their friendliness and good spirits. Of all the Scandinavians, the Danes are the most light-hearted. They are gay and cheerful, and at the same time they are very hard-working and industrious and clever. If they were not, they would never have been able to make their country, which is not rich in natural resources, so prosperous and happy.

The Danes have given the world many famous artists and scientists. One of the world's greatest atomic scientists, Niels Bohr, is a Dane, and every child knows of the famous Danish storyteller, Hans Christian Andersen.

Most of the people of Denmark are members of the Lutheran church. Lutheranism is the official religion in Denmark, but members of other religious groups have complete freedom to worship as they please.

All Danish children must go to school from the time they are seven until they are fourteen. After that, they can go on with their education at schools called gymnasiums, which are like our junior colleges, and when they are graduated from the gymnasium, they can go to a university.

Many boys and girls in Denmark spend a few months at a school called a folk high school after they have finished their primary education. The folk high schools are not like our high schools at all. First of all, all of them are boarding schools. Secondly, there are no examinations or report cards at the folk high schools. Thirdly, students at the folk high schools do not learn regular subjects as they do in our high schools. Instead of teaching mathematics and geography, the teachers at the folk high schools try to give their students an understanding of the dignity of work, and the relationship of people to one another and their responsibility to their community.

The Danish language, like Norwegian and Swedish, comes from an old form of German. So does English, so our language is a kind of cousin to the Danish language. Although many of the words are similar, it is not easy for an English-speaking child to learn Danish.

HOW THE PEOPLE LIVE

The most important business in Denmark is farming. About one-third of the Danish people make their livings through farming, and nearly three-quarters of the land in Denmark is given over to farms. Most Danish farms are quite small, but they are very efficient. Danish farms pro-

duce all kinds of meats, vegetables and dairy products. Most of the meat and vegetables are sold inside Denmark, but many of the dairy products are sold abroad.

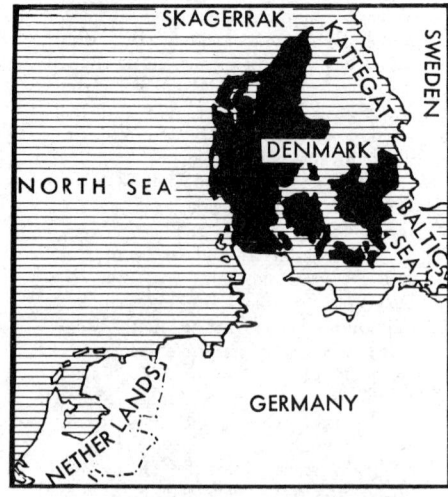

Most Danish farmers are members of cooperatives. Cooperatives are organizations that are owned and supported by their members. The idea of cooperatives started in Denmark about a hundred years ago. It spread around the world, and now there are cooperatives in many countries. You can read more about COOPERATIVES in a separate article.

In Denmark, the farm cooperatives own most of the machinery for grading, packing, and shipping farm products such as milk, butter, cheese, and bacon. There are about 1,300 cooperative dairies in Denmark.

There are also cooperatives that handle the buying and selling of many other kinds of goods, such as clothing, food, furniture, and so on. These cooperatives are called consumer cooperatives. Nearly half the population of Denmark belongs to consumer cooperatives.

About two-thirds of Denmark's working population makes its living by working in factories, offices, or stores, or as lumbermen, sailors and fishermen. The Danes have always been good seamen, and many Danes are fishermen or merchant sailors who work on the ships that transport Danish products around the world. The factory workers make machinery, electrical goods, paint, shoes, paper, and many other important products. The Danes are known for their beautiful craftwork in porcelain and silver, and for their skill in furniture and textile design.

WHAT DENMARK IS LIKE

As we said earlier, Denmark is made up of a peninsula called Jutland and about five hundred islands. There are people living on about one hundred of these islands. The other islands are wooded and wild, and are used as a source of lumber. Some of the inhabited islands are near the peninsula of Jutland and are joined to it by bridges. The largest island, called Sjaelland, is quite far from the mainland and is reached by boat. The capital of Denmark, Copenhagen, is on Sjaelland. Copenhagen is a lovely city (see COPENHAGEN). The town of Helsingor, or Elsinore, the scene of Shakespeare's Hamlet. is on Sjaelland.

Wherever you go in Denmark, you will find people riding around on bicycles. Although there are many automobiles in Denmark, most of the people travel by bicycle.

Both Jutland and the islands are quite flat. There are no high mountains in Denmark, but there are many low hills and rolling plains. There are many lakes in Denmark, and streams and rivers that flow out to the ocean. The largest of these rivers cut deep into the earth, and are called fjords.

The Danish winter may be cold and snowy, though it can also be mild for long periods, and the autumn and early spring

Denmark's Queen is Margrethe II. She took over the throne on January 15, 1972, after the death of her father, King Frederik IX.
Royal Danish Ministry

are rainy and damp. During the winter, the days are extremely short. The sun rises very late and sets very early in the afternoon. But during the summer, when the weather is clear and gentle breezes blow, the sun never really goes down at all. Even at midnight in summer, Denmark is bathed in a kind of twilight glow.

The Danes are always excited to see the storks, which come flying to Denmark every spring from Egypt where they have spent the winter. The storks make their summer homes in Denmark. When the first stork arrives, the Danish people come from miles around to see it, for it is a sign of good weather to come.

HOW THE PEOPLE ARE GOVERNED

Denmark is a constitutional monarchy. It has a queen, a parliament that makes the laws, and a written constitution that protects the rights of the people. Margrethe II became Queen in January, 1972.

All Danish citizens can vote when they are 23 years old. The voters elect the officers of their local government as well as the members of the Danish Parliament, which is called the Folketing.

The Danish government is very liberal in aiding its citizens. Health insurance is private but is supported by the state. Unemployment insurance is paid for by both the employers and employees and receives additional help from public grants.

Denmark's young men take part in universal military training. There are about 24,000 men in the Army, 7,000 in the Navy, and 10,000 in the Air Force.

DENMARK IN THE PAST

Denmark has been settled for about 2,500 years, but we know very little about the earliest period in Danish history. We do know that for a good part of that time, until about a thousand years ago, the Danes were not Christians, but, like the other Scandinavian peoples, they believed in a religion in which there were many gods. Odin was the chief of these gods, and Freya was his wife. There are many stories of the Scandinavian gods and goddesses.

About a thousand years ago, several important things happened in Denmark. The first Danish king, King Gorm, brought together under his rule all the different tribes that were living in Denmark. King Gorm also became a Christian. His son later converted all of Denmark and Norway to Christianity. Even before the rule of King Gorm, the Danes had been very powerful and warlike. Their ships sailed to England, France, Iceland, and Greenland. The Danes raided France and England, and they established colonies in all of the countries to which they traveled.

Under King Gorm and his son, Harold Bluetooth, the Danes continued to raid the shores of England. Harold Bluetooth's grandson, Canute, finally defeated the English in a fierce battle, in 1014, and made himself a king in England as well as in Denmark. After Canute died, the Danes lost England and many of their other colonies, but Denmark continued to be one of the most powerful countries of Europe. It ruled over most of Scandinavia more than four hundred years ago.

Gradually the other countries of Europe became stronger and Denmark became weaker. As it became weaker its kings became more strict and the Danish people were treated very poorly. About 150 years ago Denmark fought and lost several wars with Germany and with England. In 1849, the Danish people forced King Frederik VII to give them a constitution, and Denmark became one of the first democracies of the modern world.

After their bad experiences in war, the Danes were afraid to get into any more fighting. They were neutral in World War I, and they intended to remain neutral in World War II, also. But the Germans, who occupied Denmark, treated the Danish people so badly that a strong Danish underground grew up. It was so strong that the Allies considered Denmark no longer a neutral, but an ally in the fight against the Axis powers.

Denmark joined the United Nations in 1945. It is also a member of the North Atlantic Treaty Organization. It lives in peace with its neighbors, and its citizens are happy and prosperous.

DENMARK. Area, 16,619 square miles. Population (1973 estimate) 4,970,000. Language, Danish. Religion, Lutheran. Government, constitutional monarchy. Monetary unit, the krone, worth 14.5 cents (U.S.). Flag, white cross on a red field.

density

The denseness of a material is a matter of how heavy it is for its size. A piece of iron weighs much more than a piece of wood of the same size, which means that iron is more dense than wood. A cubic foot of water, which is enough water to fill a box one foot long, one foot wide and one foot high, weighs 62½ pounds. That is how density is usually measured, by the cubic foot. Therefore the density of water is said to be 62½ pounds. Things that have less density than water will float in it. The density of cork is only 16¼ pounds, so cork floats easily; the density of lead is 708 pounds, so lead sinks. A cubic foot of air weighs less than one ounce, and so is 600 times less dense than water, but there are other gases, such as hydrogen and helium, that are less dense than air. That is why balloons filled with these gases will float in the air.

dentistry

Dentistry is the science and study of the mouth and teeth. It is closely related to medicine, and this means that the dentist is a doctor who takes care of the mouth and teeth. The dentist cleans teeth and fills cavities, and when teeth are growing crooked, he straightens them. Sometimes the dentist has to pull teeth, or a person loses some teeth in an accident, and then the dentist makes new, or false, teeth. Dentists also perform operations on the teeth and jaw, and treat the mouth and gums, when they are infected. The dentist needs a great deal of scientific knowledge and mechanical skill to do this work, and he must have a long and careful training.

THE TRAINING OF DENTISTS

A person who wants to become a dentist must first attend a regular college for two or three years, and take certain science courses. He then goes to dental school for four years, where he takes many courses like those given in medical school. He studies the heart and lungs and other organs of the human body, and learns about the bones and how the muscles and joints work. He must know the diseases of the human body, because bad teeth can cause diseases. Very often the dentist and medical doctor consult with each other to find a cause of illness.

The dental student spends a great deal of his time learning all about the mouth and teeth. He also studies chemistry, and the way that different drugs can affect the body. He learns about metals, which later he will use when he fixes teeth. When he graduates from dental school, he receives the degree of Doctor of Dental Surgery. Then he must take a special examination that is given by the state in which he lives. When he passes this examination, he receives a license and is permitted to practice dentistry. Before he opens up his own office, he may spend some time working in a hospital as an interne, the way a doctor does, and some young dentists get some experience by working in the office of an older dentist for a while.

THE TOOLS OF DENTISTRY

When you go to the dentist, you sit in a special chair that the dentist can move up and down, and tilt back, so that you are in just the right position for him to see into your mouth easily. Next to the chair, there is a tall stand with many instruments on it, and this is called a unit. There is a basin with running water, and a tray that holds instruments, and has a small gas flame. The most important instrument on the unit is the dentist's drill, which runs by electricity. The dentist uses this drill to clean out the decayed parts of your teeth. Dentists have been experimenting with a tiny sandblaster and a rapidly vibrating tool that they hope will replace the drill. A dentist has many burrs and sandpaper disks that fit onto the drill, and he uses these to smooth the rough edges of your teeth. There are tiny brushes that fit on the drill that can clean and polish your teeth. On the unit, there are several tubes with nozzles attached to them. One of these blows air into your mouth, and the dentist uses this to dry a tooth or blow away little particles, while he is cleaning out a tooth. Another tube squirts warm or cold water to clean your mouth. Before the dentist uses any instruments in your mouth, he makes certain that they have been sterilized.

X-RAY IN DENTISTRY

Usually, before the dentist begins to work on your teeth, he takes some pictures, which are called x-rays. (You can read about the X-RAY in a separate article.) The dentist puts a small, square film in your mouth, and the invisible ray makes a picture of your teeth and jaw on this film. Then the dentist can see if there are any deep cavities in your teeth, and he can see how the roots of your teeth are set in your jaw. The x-ray has made the dentist's work much easier, because the pictures show him how much work he has to do. When he has to pull a tooth, and he sees that the roots are growing crooked, he knows that he will

have to cut the gum. If the roots of the tooth are straight, he knows he can pull the tooth out another way.

THE WORK OF DENTISTS

When a person had a toothache one hundred years ago, it was a very serious thing. The dentist did not know so much about the teeth and jaw, and he had only crude tools to work with. He also did not realize how important it is to use instruments that are sterilized, and many people who went to the dentist got infections. Dentistry, like medicine, has made tremendous strides in the last one hundred years, and today the dentist has many fine instruments to help him in his work. Now, if a person gets an infection, the dentist uses penicillin and other miracle drugs that can clear up most infections very quickly.

One hundred years ago going to the dentist was a very painful experience, and many people did not go until their jaws swelled up, and they had terrible toothaches. Now people know how important it is to see the dentist regularly, and it is not painful, because the dentist uses anesthetics that kill pain. There are two kinds of anesthetic that the dentist most often uses. He may give his patient an injection of novocain, which is a drug that makes the whole area that he is going to work on numb. When he is going to pull a tooth, he may give the patient a little gas, so he will go to sleep while the dentist is doing his work.

Some dentists do many kinds of work on the teeth, and some specialize in one particular kind of dentistry. There are specialists who pull teeth, or make false teeth, or straighten teeth. The dentist who straightens teeth is called an orthodontist.

When you go to an orthodontist, he will take some x-rays of all of your teeth. Then he fills a small, round tray with soft plaster. You bite into this plaster. When it hardens, and the dentist removes the tray, the plaster shows the exact shapes of the holes that your teeth made when you bit into it. This is called an *impression*. Then the dentist fills these holes with another kind of plaster, and when it hardens, he will break away the impression, and he will have a model of all your teeth. This model makes things much easier for you and for the dentist. He can do a lot of the necessary work on the model of your teeth, while you are at home. The dentist will fit wires and bands of platinum and silver, and perhaps little hooks and rubber bands, onto the model of your teeth. Then, when you come back for your next appointment, everything will be ready, and he will fit the appliances into your mouth. Slowly they will move your teeth into the proper places. This takes a long time, and you will probably have to go to the orthodontist for several years, before your teeth are straightened.

Naturally, it is nice to have straight teeth that look well, but straight teeth are also very important for good health. If you have spaces between your teeth, or they are too crowded, you cannot bite correctly, and as you grow older, this can do your teeth a lot of damage.

If one of your teeth hurts when you eat something hot or cold, it means that you probably have a cavity, which is a hole in your tooth made by decay. (You can read about how this happens in a separate article on TEETH.) As you grow older, you will probably have fewer cavities, but almost every person has some cavities that have to be filled. First, the dentist carefully removes all of the decay from your tooth, and when he has cleaned and dried the cavity, he is ready to fill it. Very often, he will fill the tooth with a mixture of mercury and silver that is called amalgam. (You can read about AMALGAM in a separate article.) If you have a very large cavity, the dentist may make a particular kind of filling out of gold which is called an *inlay*.

The dentist first fills the cavity of your tooth with warm, soft wax, and when it hardens, he removes the wax, which will be exactly the shape of the hole in your tooth. He covers this wax (called an impression) with plaster, and heats it. The wax melts and runs out of a small channel in the plaster covering (called a *mold*). When all of the wax is gone, the dentist pours melted gold into the hollow plaster mold. The gold hardens, and when he removes the plaster, he has a piece of gold that will exactly fit the hole in your tooth. He polishes this gold inlay and cements it into your cavity, and you have a filling that is strong, and will last for many years.

If you have a cavity in one of your front teeth, the dentist will fill it with a kind of plastic or porcelain. Some people have very white teeth, and others have teeth that are a bit yellowish. Your dentist has a card with more than thirty different tooth colors on it, and he will pick the color that best matches your own teeth, so that the filling will not show.

When a person loses any of his teeth, he can go to a dentist who makes false teeth. This dentist has to be both an artist and a fine mechanic, because he must make teeth that look well and fit properly. When a person needs some new teeth, the dentist will first make an impression out of plaster, and then he will make new teeth to fit in the space. This is called a *bridge*. Some bridges can be taken out and cleaned every night, and these are called *removable* bridges. Other bridges are cemented to the remaining teeth, and are called *fixed* bridges.

If a person loses all of his upper or lower teeth, the dentist will make a *full denture*. (Most people call a complete set of upper or lower teeth a plate.) If a person loses all of his teeth, the dentist must make two full dentures. He takes impressions of the gums, so that the dentures will fit the gums exactly, and the new teeth will work as well as possible. Once, dentists made teeth out of elephants' tusks and wood, but now they use porcelain and many kinds of plastic that fit well, last a long time, and feel quite comfortable in the mouth.

Even if you think there is nothing wrong with your teeth, it is very important to visit your dentist at least twice a year. When you do, your dentist will clean your teeth. He has special instruments that can reach places under your gums and between your teeth, where your toothbrush does not reach. Sometimes the dentist has a woman assistant, who has been especially trained to clean teeth.

She is called a dental hygienist. She can teach you the best way to brush your teeth, and explain to you how brushing your teeth carefully and regularly is one way you can prevent decay and infections in your mouth.

Besides the work your dentist does when you go to his office, he must spend many hours in his laboratory, where he works on models and impressions and inlays that he will later fit into your mouth. Some dentists send out part of this work to people called dental mechanics. They have spent one or two years learning how to make bridges and dentures and inlays, and they are very useful to the dentist, although they do not work on a person's teeth directly.

HISTORY OF DENTISTRY

More people have had toothaches than any other pains, and dentists have always been important to man's health and happiness. When we read the books of early Greek and Roman writers, we learn that ancient man had toothaches, and there were dentists then who knew how to pull teeth and make new teeth. We have found some of the crude instruments that these early dentists used, and we know that the work dentists do has changed very much since ancient times.

Pierre Fauchard was a French doctor, who is famous because he wrote the first complete book about dentistry, more than two hundred years ago. He is called the father of dentistry, because when people read his book, they began to realize what an important science dentistry is. In 1840, the first school of dentistry in the world began. It was called the Baltimore College of Dental Surgery, in Baltimore, Maryland. This was an important event, because it meant that a dentist could go to school and receive special training for the work he had to do.

Dentists now are studying new and better ways of caring for the mouth and teeth. More than 113,000 men and women in the United States belong to the American Dental Association, a society that has regular meetings and publishes a monthly magazine, in which dentists write articles about new scientific discoveries, and methods of caring for the mouth and teeth. Dentists have been very important during wartime, and in World War II thousands of dentists traveled everywhere with the soldiers. They fixed teeth and performed operations, and learned many things that have helped them in their work.

Denver

Denver is the capital city of the state of Colorado, and is situated on the South Platte River. Denver is sometimes called "the mile high city," because it is one mile above sea level. It is famous for its fine weather and fresh air. People who are sick come from all over the United States to enjoy the healthful climate and get well at Denver, and there are many hospitals there. About 514,000 people live in Denver. It is the largest city in the state. Nearby there are gold and silver and coal mines, and there are factories that make tools for the miners to use. Other plants manufacture rubber products and scientific instruments. Many young people

go to the University of Denver and several other colleges there, and many young men are stationed at the large Air Force base and technical school in Denver. Denver is a very nice place to visit. You can see beautiful mountain parks and fine museums and libraries.

Miners who wanted to make their fortune went to Denver to look for gold many years ago. These men were rough and wild, and there was much shooting and fighting. James William Denver, governor of the Kansas territory, did a lot to bring law and order to the territory, so when Denver was settled about one hundred years ago the people decided to name the city for him.

DENVER, COLORADO. Capital of the state of Colorado. Population (1970 census) 514,-678. Situated on South Platte River. Settled in 1858.

deodorant

A deodorant is made of chemicals that remove or disguise unpleasant odors. Some of these chemical combinations are *aluminum chlorhydroxide* and *aluminum oxide.* Our bodies give off unpleasant odors when they are not clean. Some deodorants combine with the substances our bodies give off and make them odorless. Other deodorants clog our pores and prevent body odors. Perfumes and colognes cover up unpleasant odors with pleasant ones. They are not successful deodorants because when their odors wear off our body odors reappear. Deodorants are used to remove odors other than bad odors. Bottles that have a wick and a liquid containing the wonder chemical chlorophyll, which absorbs smells, are used to rid our homes of unpleasant odors caused by cooking and garbage. The wick soaks up the liquid in the bottle and spreads the deodorant through the air. Gum, candy, and toothpaste with chlorophyll in them are used to remove unpleasant odors of the breath.

department stores

Department stores are places where a person can buy almost anything he wants. They are like many different kinds of store put together under one roof. As you walk through a department store you see toys, furniture, sporting goods, books, clothing, candy, perfumes, dishes, drugs, and many other kinds of things for sale. You will not find them all in one room, as they might be in a small store. Instead they are separated into large departments, or sections, and you may have to walk to a different room or floor for each kind of thing sold. A great deal of space is needed for this, and some department stores are larger than several apartment buildings put together. As many as eight thousand people can work in one department store, and they may have their own clubs, cafeterias, ball teams, doctors, and newspapers. Some people have called a department store "a city within a city," but from the eyes of the customer, it is a great big show. Each department is a separate, enjoyable act, and some people, who have the time, come down to the department stores just to spend the day. They like the colors and beautifully decorated windows, especially around Christmas time. Long moving stairways carry people from one floor to another, and the way the goods are arranged can keep them interested for hours. The men and women who run department stores must be able to handle the billions of dollars worth of sales they make every year, so, besides being expert showmen, the managers of a store must also be very good businessmen.

HOW DEPARTMENT STORES BEGAN

If you pass through a country town, you may still be able to see the small general stores that are called the fathers of the modern department store. They were small, but they sold everything from bacon to pajamas. They had their cracker barrel, their apple barrel, and rolls of dress goods were on the counters. People did not need a department store in those days. First there had to be large cities, and then people had to have better ways of traveling, before a department store could exist in any city. The United States did not have larger cities and railroads till about one hundred years ago, around the time of the Civil War. Some of the biggest department stores in New York, Chicago, Philadelphia, and other cities all started about that time. Once people had better roads and railways, they were able to come to the stores. Also goods could then be shipped cheaply and quickly.

If it were not for this, customers would have continued to do all their shopping in stores near their homes, even if they could not buy everything they wanted. New inventions—the telephone, elevators, moving stairs, electric lights, and bookkeeping machines—helped to make the modern kind of department store possible. But cities have now become too crowded, and there is little place for a department store to increase its size. Even more important, the tremendous number of cars on the roads makes it impossible for anyone to park his car near the department stores in the great cities. In order to overcome this difficulty, the big stores had to build branch stores outside of the cities. Here they have huge parking lots, and a customer can drive to the store, then drive away with what he bought. The men who planned these branch stores used the newest ideas for building beautiful stores, and you can see them outside the cities with their great glass and brick fronts facing the main roads.

HOW A DEPARTMENT STORE WORKS

A customer might think that most of the work in department stores is done by the sales people. Actually, there are many more people working for a department store than those we see selling behind the sales counters. Even an umbrella must pass through many steps before it can be sold. First, the head of the department must feel that the customers would like to buy that kind of an umbrella, and he must know how many he will have to order from the manufacturer. Men must inspect, ship, and put the umbrellas in storage until the right time. Then the people who know how to make beautiful arrangements of the goods on sale use lights, signs, and colored paper to put the umbrellas into a design or display that will catch the customer's attention. People must take care of these umbrellas from the time they are delivered to the store until they are sold and delivered to the customer. There are other people in the store who have the job of putting advertisements for the sale of umbrellas in the newspapers, or on the radio, or even on television. You can see how many people must work on even one umbrella before it can be sold.

It is usual to divide the work of a department store into four parts. There are the merchandising people who buy and sell; the publicity staff who advertise the goods to be sold; the control worker who takes care of the money records of the store; and the service employees who are in charge of all the other work which has to be done, like delivery, cleaning, hiring, and putting goods into and out of storage. The general merchandise manager is sometimes the owner of the store. He has the most important position, and he is in charge of buying and selling for the whole store. He has to decide questions about what kind of store he will run. What kind of goods will be sold? Will they be high-priced, or bargain-priced goods? What departments should grow, and which should get smaller? What new departments should be started, and which should be discontinued? With the help of the men in charge of the four main parts of the store, he must answer these questions and many more. The general merchandise manager may have assistants who tell him what is going on in departments. Each department has its own chief who is called a buyer. He must buy what is most saleable, and he must make sure that he sells it. He is really the manager of the department. The buyer has assistants who are called junior buyers and assistant buyers. They help the buyer take care of his department. Below the assistant buyers there is a man who is called the "head of stock." He takes care of keeping the goods in storage, and he tells the buyer which things are almost sold out and must be reordered. Below all the merchandising staff are the salespeople who must meet the customers and sell.

Department stores have grown to be one of the biggest businesses in the country. Their sales run to billions of dollars, and they employ many thousands of people. Many young people in the colleges are taking merchandising, management, and other business courses that are training them for jobs in department stores. They will try to become assistant buyers, and they have hopes of getting better jobs in the merchandising section. Other people must be trained to hire many kinds of workers. A department store also needs its own advertising staff which works together with the independent advertising agencies. For untrained people, there are thousands of jobs in sales and other work. A department store has a great variety of goods to sell, and jobs to offer.

Departments of the United States are the branches of the federal government in Washington, D.C. See the separate articles on the individual Departments: AGRICULTURE; COMMERCE; DEFENSE; HEALTH, EDUCATION, AND WELFARE; INTERIOR; JUSTICE; LABOR; POST OFFICE; STATE; and TREASURY.

depression

A depression is a time when business is bad all over the country, and people are afraid of not having enough money to buy food, or have good clothes, even though these things would become very cheap. Many of your neighbors would be poor and out of work. People who had their own homes and businesses would lose them, because they could not pay their bills. Economists, men who study such things, have found many causes for depressions. They say that one main cause happens when manufacturers and farmers produce more goods than people can buy. If a boy's father worked for a manufacturer when this happened, he and many others might lose their jobs, because the manufacturer would close down part of his factory until he sold the goods he had piled up in his warehouse.

When many people are losing their jobs all over the country, they have even less money to buy goods. The manufacturer must make still less goods, and so he fires more people. This can continue until businessmen cannot pay their bills and must close the doors of their factories. When this starts to happen, many more people lose their jobs and they have to be given food and shelter by charities and the government. We usually do not have good business again until people are brave enough to start hiring men and producing goods. Then, there is a slow turn back to better conditions for everyone.

During the depression that lasted from the end of 1929 to 1934, about 14,000,-000 people could not find jobs. Their families suffered so much that the government, and professors of universities, have been working very hard to find out how to prevent these terrible depressions. For this reason, the government has been trying to put some controls on business, such as limiting the amount of money banks can lend, and controlling prices, wages, building, and farming. The government also tries to do a lot of public work such as building highways, bridges, dams and other things when a depression starts. In this way the government hopes to keep most people working and earning enough money until business can again provide enough work for everybody.

depth bomb, a bomb that explodes under water: see the articles on BOMB and SUBMARINE.

derrick

A derrick is a special type of crane used for lifting or moving heavy objects. When a ship is loaded, small steam engines operate this special type of crane, which can pick up heavy pieces of cargo and swing them aboard a ship. The small engine supplies power with which the derrick, using a tackle and a system of pulleys, picks up the cargo. The tackle enables the derrick to pick up much heavier loads than it could without tackle. Derricks are also in use around oil wells and in the construction of buildings. See also the separate article on CRANE.

Descartes

René Descartes was a great French mathematician and philosopher. A philosopher is a man who tries to understand the meaning of life and knowledge, and  the relationship between ideas and things. Descartes was born in 1596 and died in 1650. He is sometimes called the Father of Modern Philosophy, because he used methods and ways of thinking that have been the basis of philosophy ever since.

Descartes was not satisfied just to believe what he was taught. He believed in asking questions and testing ideas until they were proved to be true or false. He tested all the ideas he had been taught, and he decided that the only thing he knew to be true without any doubt at all was the fact that he was alive, and the only way he knew he was alive was through his thinking. His philosophy was based on that idea, which he expressed as: "I *think,* therefore I *am.*" He believed that ideas and things are in two entirely separate groups that have little relationship to one another. His ideas are explained in a book he wrote, called *Discourse on Method.* Followers of Descartes are called Cartesians.

Descartes was also interested in mathematics, and invented a special branch of that subject which is called *analytic geometry.* Analytic geometry is a combination of algebra and geometry, and is a very important part of mathematics.

desert

A desert is a barren, sandy waste where there is no rain and no water under the soil—where almost nothing grows, and where the only wild life consists of the few desert animals that can survive the intense heat of the day and the dryness of the land. There are other kinds of wasteland that scientists also call deserts. They are the icy plains of the polar regions where the snow never melts and plants cannot grow, and the rocky stretches in various parts of the world where the ground is solidly covered with layers and heaps of rock through which very little vegetation can grow.

WHAT MADE DESERTS DRY

Long, long ago, the deserts of the world were not dry wastes, but fertile, well-watered land. Many things caused the land to dry up. The settling of the earth's surface caused great mountain ranges to be pushed up in many places, and the land on the side of the mountains that was farthest from the sea gradually dried and became desert, because the moist air blowing in over the ocean was stopped by the mountains and dropped its rain on the side of the hills nearer to the sea. The rain never reached the inland side and so the inland side dried up, as in the case of the desert of western Nevada, just east of the Sierra Nevada mountains. Other mountains formed rings around a flat, level stretch of land and prevented the rainy winds from reaching the land inside the ring. For a long time, the moisture in the soil there rose in the form of vapor, made rain clouds in the colder air high above the earth and rained back on this land. Over a period of time, however, this ground grew drier and drier as some of that moisture sank far into the ground instead of rising into the air to form rain clouds. Thus there was less and less rain, and the land became more and more dry, until finally there was no moisture at all left in the ground and no more rain. The land then turned into a desert and its plants died off.

Man has also been the cause of turning fertile land into desert. People have cut down forests for timber and to clear the land for farms and towns and cities. The roots of trees helped to hold moisture in the ground; when the trees were gone, the land started to dry up and became desert. In parts of Asia, flocks of goats did enormous damage, and ruined as much fertile land as man ruined with his axes and saws. The goat herds devoured trees, shrubs, grasses, vines, and flowers, stripping the land and killing the vegetation that the land needed to hold its moisture. Deserts now existing in Asia were caused in this way.

When soil becomes dry and powdery, windstorms blow it away, leaving only the rocky subsoil that is less fertile, less tillable, and very dry. This is what happened in the dust bowl of the United States, in Kansas, Nebraska, and Oklahoma, as it has happened in other areas throughout the world.

A great deal has been done toward restoring the usefulness of this land, which was once valuable farm country. Irrigation, crops to hold the soil in place, planting to retain moisture, and contour ploughing to prevent valuable water from flowing downhill and disappearing, with other conservation measures, have made much of the land fertile again. The desert land of Israel is being steadily reclaimed in the same way. Irrigation makes it possible for plants to grow, and the roots of these plants, after the crops have been harvested, decay and combine with the sand. Eventually the sand becomes enriched and turns into fertile soil. Deserts can be reclaimed in many parts of the world, if people are willing to use scientific methods and work hard to make them fertile again.

WHAT DESERTS ARE LIKE

The great sandy deserts of the world are alike in several ways. They are all sandy, rainless, and barren, and they are all hot during the day and cold at night. The great Sahara Desert in Africa, the Gobi Desert in Asia, the central desert of Australia, and the Great American Desert in the southwestern United States are the largest of the world's many deserts. On the Sahara there is a vast, treeless expanse of sand extending for miles in every direction. Here and there a traveler arrives at a small patch of land with trees and water, like a tiny island in a great ocean of sand. These patches are called "oases," and caravans crossing the Sahara stop at each oasis to refresh themselves and their animals. Camels are used on the Sahara because they can go for a long time without water. This is due to the fact that a camel has two water storage compartments in its stomach that hold enough water to last for several days. Camels' feet are also well suited for travel over sand. They are wide, flat, and well padded, and they can walk over soft sand without sinking in deeply. The bottom of camels' feet have somewhat the same effect on the surface of sand that

snowshoes have on the deep, soft snow of northern countries.

Travelers on the Sahara often see "mirages," and think that they see a distant oasis. A mirage is a reflection of a far distant scene—one that may be hundreds of miles away—visible in a layer of hot air rising from the desert that acts like a mirror. Many people have seen mirages. It is not their imaginations, as some people used to believe, but an actual reflection due to the overheated air rising up from the hot sands of the desert. The caravans crossing the desert are always looking for a real oasis, and when they reach one, it seems like the most beautiful sight in the world. The green of the date palms and the other tropical plants seems like the most beautiful color imaginable, after the endless brown of the sand over which the caravan has been traveling.

The Great American Desert has been famous in American history since pioneers first tried to cross it more than a hundred years ago. They lost their way frequently, and many died of exhaustion and thirst. The fortunate travelers were those who came upon water holes. When they did, it was usually more a matter of luck than anything else, because there were no roads, no guideposts, no paths, and no maps to help them reach their destination. The first pioneers to attempt this difficult journey were not even sure what they would find on the other side of the desert.

They learned that they could not travel in the heat of the day, because toward noon the desert becomes unbearably hot, and people perspire so much that they need large quantities of drinking water to make up for what their bodies have lost in perspiration. When it is difficult to carry enough water for the barest necessities, anything that causes extra need for drinking water is to be avoided.

The only time the pioneers could travel with any degree of comfort was in the early morning hours or for a short time after sunset, while it was still light. After dark, the desert becomes cold very quickly. It may be over a hundred degrees in temperature during the day, and drop almost to freezing at night. The sun on the sand during the day makes the daylight hours very hot, but as soon as the sun goes down the sand cools quickly because it is so dry. Water takes longer to heat than sand, but it holds the heat for many hours longer once it has been warmed. The water in the leaves of trees and in grass makes a grassy place stay warm after the sun goes down, but the desert gets cold because there is no foliage. The sudden cold, after the intense heat, caused early pioneers a great deal of discomfort.

Today there are roads across the desert, and travelers know about the heat of the day and the cold nights. Still, it is a difficult journey, and it can be dangerous. If you are driving your car across the desert, everything in the car should be thoroughly checked, and you should be sure it is in perfect condition. A breakdown on the desert could mean that you would be unable to reach water, and there are no garages for hundreds of miles at a stretch. The driver of a car that broke down might very possibly die of heat prostration and thirst before anyone else came along to rescue him.

LIFE ON THE DESERT

Travelers on the American desert today will see many of the same desert animals that early prospectors and pioneers observed. The only animals that can live there are those able to get along on little or no water. Many animals on the desert drink no actual water at all, but get the necessary liquid from the foods they eat. There is a small amount of moisture in the desert plants, which seem able to extract it from the air although the air itself is almost totally dry. Insects eat the moist leaves of plants, and snakes and lizards eat the insects. The moisture in the body of the insects provides them with their water. Larger snakes eat smaller snakes and small lizards. Larger lizards eat small ones. There are several kinds of desert lizard. The horned toad is a lizard, not really a toad at all. Another desert lizard is the basilisk. Both horned toads and basilisks are completely harmless to humans, but the gila monster, another type of desert lizard, is dangerous. Its bite is poisonous enough to kill a small animal and to cause great discomfort to human beings, although people do not usually die from the bite of a gila monster.

Lizards and snakes have dry, scaly skins, and can stand the heat and dryness of the desert with a minimum of discomfort. They usually prefer to remain in their burrows or under rocks during the hot day. At night, they come out to hunt for food. Lizards can run very fast when danger approaches, in spite of the fact that their legs are quite short in comparison to the length of their bodies. There are desert mice and kangaroo rats, bobcats, jackrabbits, and various birds of prey, in addition to the snakes and lizards of the desert. There are insects and large members of the spider family, such as tarantulas and scorpions. Snakes and lizards eat other snakes and lizards and insects. Bobcats eat the rats and mice, and the rats and mice eat the snake and lizard eggs. The birds of prey—hawks and owls—eat any small animals they can catch, and the vultures that soar over the desert eat any dead animals they find. The chaparral cock, or road runner, is a desert bird that runs after lizards and small snakes. There are some wolves and coyotes that prey on the jackrabbits and smaller animals.

For years scientists have dug deep into the sands of the deserts to find out what lies below their surfaces. Often they find proof of past life, and even of past civilizations. In the Gobi Desert of Asia, they uncovered ruins of cities that existed thousands of years ago, proving that once this was fertile land, and that man lived there centuries before the desert took over.

Scientists in 1954 discovered the ancient tomb of Cheops, near the Pyramids of Egypt in the Sahara, and will continue to learn about the past history of man and of the world by studying the deserts of the earth and the secrets they conceal beneath their shifting sands.

design

When a person plans the best way to make a thing, and how to arrange the shapes and colors and lines and spaces, so that the thing will look as beautiful as possible, he is making a design. If you look at a great painting, you will be seeing the work of a great designer, but a painter is only one kind of designer. All of the beautiful things you see around you every day were designed by someone, who planned how to make them so they would work well, and give you pleasure to look at them.

The famous Empire State Building in New York City, the public library in your town, and the house you live in, were designed by men called architects. A woman wears a dress that is pretty because the color of the dress, the material, and the way the dress is cut, go well together. A person called a fashion designer planned all of these things. (You can read about FASHION DESIGNING in a separate article.) Someone designed the spoons you use, and the glasses you drink out of, and the chair you sit on. If you go to a play, and you like the scenery and the costumes, it is because the stage designer and the costume designer did their jobs well. Some people are called industrial designers. They plan the machines that factory workers operate, and they design utensils and tools, and even the packages that cornflakes and other foods are packed in.

THE WORK OF DESIGNERS

A designer must know how to draw, because this is the way he makes his ideas clear to other people. This is very important, because often the designer does not actually work on the thing he has designed. An architect who designs a swimming pool does not dig the hole and fill it with concrete himself. He puts his plans down on paper, so that other men will know what he intended, and they can build the swimming pool just as he designed it.

A designer must also understand a great deal about materials, so he will know the best material to use for his design. A rug should look nice, but it also has to be made of a material that is strong and will not tear easily. If a costume designer thought of some beautiful costumes for a play, but the actors could not walk comfortably in them, then the designs would not be good. If a person designed an automobile that was very powerful, but cost so much to make that very few people could afford to buy it, that would not be a good commercial design.

HISTORY OF DESIGN

Men have been designing things for thousands of years. The first man who took some clay and hollowed it out to make a bowl was a designer. Then other men made bowls that were shaped better for holding things, and looked more graceful, and they began to decorate the bowls. All of these people were designers. Early designers made weapons and tools to work with, and ancient man designed cloth and jewelry and better shelters to live in. A designer planned the Egyptian pyramids, and someone designed the beautiful buildings of Greece and Rome.

Very often, many people would work on the design that one person had made.

In China, some families became famous because they made beautifully designed dishes, and for many generations the members of the family made these dishes in the same way. Long ago, paintings were worked on by many artists. The designer, who was called the master, would draw the outlines for the painting, and then his students, who were called apprentices, would work on it. People learned to recognize the designs of the master, and paintings that were done in his style were said to belong to a particular school of painting. Some schools of painting, like the Flemish and the early Italian schools, have become very famous.

The first regular school where a student could take courses about the principles of design, and learn what makes a design good, began in Paris, France, about three hundred years ago. It was called the Royal Academy of Fine Arts. Now there are schools in many large cities all over the world, where students can study design. Some of these schools teach painting and sculpture and stage designing, and they are called Fine Art Schools. A person who wants to learn how to design tools and machines and household equipment goes to a School of Industrial Art. People who want to design clothes can go to a school that teaches fashion design. Many universities have a special course for a person who wants to be an architect and design buildings. All of these students learn how to design things that will be useful and beautiful.

Des Moines

Des Moines is the capital of the state of Iowa. The Des Moines River runs right through it and you can walk from one side of the city over to the other on any one of twelve bridges. Trains carry people over six more bridges. The city was first a little town that grew up around Fort Des Moines, which the United States built here in 1843. By 1857 the town had grown so large it was made the state capital.

Des Moines is a very busy place. More than 200,000 people live there. Not far away are big farms that raise corn, and also some coal mines. Farmers and coal operators sell their products in Des Moines or ship them from Des Moines to other places. To help do this seven important railroads run through the city. The farmers and miners do their shopping here and keep their money in the banks of Des Moines. Many insurance companies have their main offices in this city. If you walk along the river front you will see many beautiful buildings. The largest building in the city is the state capitol. It is on a hill in the middle of a large beautiful park. Drake University, where both young men and women study, is in Des Moines.

The Des Moines River rises in the state of Minnesota and then goes into Iowa and runs right through the state until it reaches the Mississippi River. The Des Moines River is about five hundred miles long. Boats can use its upper part, but in the lower part the current is so rapid that the river cannot be used by boats. These swift waters are used for making electricity to run the machinery in factories.

DES MOINES, IOWA. Capital of the state of Iowa, and county seat of Polk County. Population (1970 census) 200,587. Situated on the Des Moines River. Settled in 1843.

de Soto, Hernando

Hernando de Soto was a great Spanish explorer. He was born about the year 1500. At that time, Spain was sending great expeditions to explore and conquer the New World. When de Soto was just a young man, he took part in these expeditions. At one time, he sailed to Darien, which is now in Colombia. At another time he went with the expeditions that explored Central America. In 1532, de Soto marched with the explorer Pizarro into South America, to Peru. The people of Peru were Inca Indians. They had a great and rich civilization. The Spaniards conquered the Incas, and took a great deal of treasure from them. De Soto returned to Spain with a large fortune.

A few years later, people in Spain heard stories of a wonderful country called Florida, and of the great riches that could be found there. Florida was the name given then to the whole southern part of the United States. De Soto decided to go to Florida, in search of gold. He spent much of his treasure in fitting up an expedition. The king of Spain made him governor of Cuba and Florida, and de Soto sailed for the New World again. He landed in Florida in 1539. For about four years he explored the country. He marched north, through what are now the southern states of the United States. He turned west, and discovered the Mississippi River. Farther west and farther north he pushed, but nowhere did he find gold. He was returning from his explorations, going south down the Mississippi, when he died in 1542.

despot, a ruler who has unlimited power: see the articles on DICTATOR and TYRANT.

Dessalines, Jean Jacques, born a slave, he became emperor of Haiti: see the article on HAITI.

destroyer

Destroyers are small warships, fast and light. Because the steel plating of their sides is very thin, to give the ships greater speed, destroyers are known as "tin cans" among the men who serve aboard them. The destroyer was first built to combat torpedo boats; it was called a torpedo boat destroyer. In World War I, destroyers were first fitted for and used in anti-submarine work. But these ships soon proved that they could do many other jobs as well. In today's Navy destroyers are called upon to perform a greater variety of tasks than are the ships of any other class.

In World War I the familiar type of United States destroyer was the four-piper, so called because it had four stacks. Most four-pipers have been scrapped, but a few survive, having been converted to other purposes, such as mine-sweeping. In World War II a new type of destroyer, called the *destroyer escort*, was developed from British plans. This ship, usually referred to by its official abbreviation as the DE, was smaller and lighter than most modern destroyers. Its purpose was to guard convoys of troop-ships and cargo ships from submarine and aircraft attacks.

Today's destroyers are bigger, but still very small by comparison with aircraft carriers. The two types most often seen have displacements of about 2,100 and 2,400 tons. But new, much heavier types — the *destroyer leader* and an atomic-powered destroyer — have been adopted by some navies.

Destroyers are armed with batteries of 3- or 5-inch anti-aircraft (AA) guns. Smaller AA guns cover all available deck space. On the main deck near the stern are the K-guns, holding the big, barrel-shaped depth charges. Some destroyers still have torpedo tubes, but on others the torpedoes have been removed to make room for radar and fire-control stations.

Destroyers sometimes operate in groups (as in the famous hunter-killer packs of World War II which sank many German and Japanese submarines), sometimes in task groups with other types of ships (as in numerous battles in the Pacific), and sometimes alone. Among the jobs a single destroyer might be assigned over a period of time are patrolling a given sea area (picket duty), bombarding an enemy coast, assisting in landing operations, standing by an aircraft carrier to pick up pilots whose planes crash, transporting men and supplies, rescuing the crew of a stricken freighter, gathering scientific information (taking soundings of the sea bottom to determine its depth, charting uncharted coasts, etc.), visiting a foreign port on a good-will tour, and testing out new equipment.

LIFE ABOARD A "TIN CAN"

The center of life on a destroyer is the bridge, from which the Officer of the Deck directs the ship's movements. Information is relayed to him from radar scopes in CIC (Combat Information Center), from underwater sound gear in the sonar "shack," from the radio "shack," from the signal bridge, from the engine rooms, from the fire-control stations, and from gun emplacements.

A modern destroyer usually has a crew of about three hundred men and fifteen to twenty officers. The captain, usually a commander by rank, has his own cabin and sea cabin (a small room on the bridge where he can retire and still be within instant call if needed). The officers sleep and eat in "Officers' Country," meaning the ward room and adjoining staterooms. The enlisted men, including petty officers of all ratings, seamen ("deck apes"), and firemen ("the black gang"), live in compartments below decks. Enlisted men sleep in bunks three or four deep that can be folded back against the wall (called *bulkhead*) when not in use. A compartment forward doubles as the mess hall on most tin cans. Each man has his own locker in which he keeps his uniforms and other necessary gear.

In spite of the discomfort and danger of life aboard a tin can, many men prefer it to duty aboard larger ships. A destroyer is big enough to be important, yet small enough so that everyone can know everyone else. The crew works as a team.

Consequently morale and efficiency can be very high even though discipline may be relaxed.

detective, a person who tries to find out who has committed a crime: see the article on POLICE.

detective story, an exciting story about a crime that has been committed, and who did it: see the article on MYSTERY STORY.

detergent, a substance used for removing dirt: see the article on SOAP.

Detroit

Detroit is a city in the state of Michigan. It is the largest city in the state and the fifth-largest city in the entire United States. About 1,500,000 people live there. It lies on the Detroit River, a stream thirty-one miles long that runs between Lake St. Clair east of Detroit and Lake Erie to the south. More automobiles are made in Detroit than in any other city in the world. That is why Detroit has the nickname "Motor City." Packards, Lincolns, Cadillacs, Chryslers, and Plymouths are some of the automobiles manufactured there. On the nearby River Rouge you can see some of the factories of the Ford Motor Company. The city also has factories that make many other things, such as tires and tubes, vacuum cleaners, aircraft parts, and television sets. Ships carry the articles Detroit makes to other cities on the Great Lakes both east and west of Detroit. Ten railroad lines have stations in the city.

A visitor to Detroit will find many interesting things to see. One is the Ambassador Bridge between Detroit and the city of Windsor, Canada, on the other side of the Detroit River. Another interesting place is Cadillac Square in downtown Detroit, with its modern skyscrapers towering above the beautiful, old-fashioned City Hall. Other places to see are Belle Island Park on Belle Island in the Detroit River, and Briggs Stadium, where the Tigers, Detroit's baseball team in the American League, play their games. Among the many fine schools and colleges in the city are the University of Detroit (for men and women) and Marygrove College (for women only). The Detroit Institute of Arts, which is run by the city, is one of the finest museums in the United States. It has more than 1,000 paintings.

Detroit was not always an American city. Long ago the French owned all the land in what is now the middlewestern part of our country. They founded the town of Detroit in 1701. The British took the city from France during the French and Indian War, and then the Americans took it from the British during the Revolutionary War. The city was quite large and prosperous during the nineteenth century. However, it really started to grow fast when the automobile was invented, and automobile factories were built in Detroit. Since about 1900, hundreds of thousands of people have come to live and work in this city.

DETROIT, MICHIGAN. Population (1970 census) 1,511,482. County seat of Wayne County. Largest city in the state, and fifth-largest in the United States. Situated on the Detroit River, between Lake St. Clair and Lake Erie. Settled in 1701.

Deucalion and Pyrrha

Deucalion and Pyrrha were characters in Greek mythology, the stories the ancient Greeks told about their gods and goddesses. Deucalion was a king of the country of Phthia, and Pyrrha was his wife. At one time, Zeus, the king of the gods, sent a great flood to the earth. The rains fell, and the seas rose higher and higher. All the people on earth were drowned except for Deucalion and Pyrrha. They floated in a ship for nine days and nine nights. Finally they landed on the top of a high mountain, Mt. Parnassus. The flood started to recede. Deucalion prayed to Zeus, asking that there be people on the earth again. Deucalion was told that he must walk along throwing his mother's bones behind him. Deucalion decided that this meant the stones of "Mother Earth." Deucalion and Pyrrha walked along, dropping stones behind them. The stones dropped by Deucalion turned into men, and the stones dropped by Pyrrha turned into women.

Deuteronomy

The Fifth Book of the Old Testament, in the Bible, is called Deuteronomy. Together with the first four books, Genesis, Exodus, Leviticus, and Numbers, it makes up the books of Moses, which are called the *Torah*, or book of Jewish law. The book of Deuteronomy is the story of how the great leader, Moses, preached to the Jews just before they came to the Promised Land of Canaan. Most of the book of Deuteronomy is made up of Moses' words, which tell about the laws that the Lord made for the Jews, and about the troubles and hardships the Jews suffered during their long journey from Egypt to the land of Canaan.

The book also tells how Moses, knowing he was to die, turned over the leadership of the Jews to another great man, Joshua. The last chapter of Deuteronomy is the story of the death of Moses. The Lord planned things so that Moses would lead his people right up to the Promised Land, and they would cross over the river Jordan into Canaan, but Moses himself would die before they made that crossing. He died, and was buried in Moab, across the river from Canaan.

Deutzia

Deutzia is a shrub that came originally from Asia. It was named for a Dutch botanist, Jan Deutz, and for many years it was grown only in greenhouses. Since the early 1900s, however, it has been used widely in the United States, and in other places with moderate climate, as an outdoor shrub. It blossoms in the spring, with large numbers of attractive blooms that may be white, pink, purple, or blue. You may have seen it many times without knowing its name. It is a thick bush about three feet high, with many clusters of blossoms. It has no noticeable scent. One kind of Deutzia has very rough leaves covered with spiny hairs. Woodworkers in Japan use them to polish wood, as American carpenters might use sandpaper.

de Valera

Eamon de Valera is the name of an Irish patriot and statesman. He was born

in New York in 1882 of an Irish mother and a Spanish father. He went to college in Dublin and then taught mathematics in Ireland. At this time many Irishmen were trying to win the independence of their country from Great Britain, which had ruled Ireland for many centuries. De Valera became one of these Irish patriots.

During Easter Week, 1916, the Irish fought a bloody battle against British soldiers in Dublin. De Valera was one of the Irish leaders in this battle. The Irish lost and de Valera and others were given prison sentences. He was soon freed, and then again arrested. This time he escaped from jail. He went to the United States and raised a large sum of money to help free Ireland. Through the never-ending efforts of de Valera and other patriots, Ireland (except Northern Ireland) finally managed to win independence. In 1948 it became a new nation, known as Eire or the Republic of Ireland. De Valera was premier of Ireland several times while it was still a British dominion and after it became independent. In 1959, when he was 78 years old, he retired from active politics as premier and was elected President of Ireland. He died in 1975.

Devil's Island

Devil's Island is a small island near the coast of French Guiana, in South America. It is one of three islands called the Safety Islands. These islands belong to France and for about a hundred years were used for prison camps to which France sent some of its most dangerous criminals. Escape from the islands was almost impossible. In 1946 France decided to stop using the islands for prisoners. The 2,800 prisoners on the island were returned to France.

The area of Devil's Island is about three square miles.

dew

In the air there is always some water you cannot see. When air cools it can hold less water than it did when it was warmer, so some water comes out of the air in tiny drops that we call dew.

You can often see the grass wet with dew in the early morning, because at night the grass loses the heat it gets from the sun during the day, and moisture settles on it out of the air. On a warm day you can also see dew on the outside of a cold glass of milk or water.

dewberry

The dewberry plant is a sort of bramble. It is a thorny, trailing plant that looks like a blackberry, but its canes grow along the ground instead of upright. One kind is called the "running blackberry." Dewberry fruit is usually black, and some varieties have fruit larger than blackberries.

There are several kinds of dewberry, most of them native to North America, and some kinds are found in Europe. Dewberry fruit is very good to eat. It can be made into jam, or it can be preserved by canning or freezing. The loganberry

may be a kind of dewberry, as are the boysenberry and youngberry.

Dewey, George

George Dewey was a famous American naval commander. He was born in Montpelier, Vermont, in 1837. He graduated from the United States Naval Academy, then served in the Union Navy in the Civil War. After the war he rose from captain to the rank of commodore.

In 1898 the United States declared war on Spain to help Cuba, a Spanish possession, to win independence. Dewey was in command of the United States Asiatic Squadron of six ships at the time. The squadron was at Hong Kong, China, the day war was declared. Dewey acted swiftly. He rushed his ships to Manila Bay, in the Philippines, where he knew a Spanish fleet lay. He stole into the bay after midnight. At dawn of May 1st he turned to the captain of his flagship. "You may fire when you are ready, Gridley!" he said. By noon the American ships had sunk the entire Spanish squadron of eight ships. Not an American vessel was lost. No Americans were killed, eight were wounded.

For this victory Dewey was known as the hero of Manila. When he returned to America a great parade took place in his honor in New York. The nation gave him a large estate. Congress made him an admiral, a rank given to only a very few naval officers up to that time (see the article on ADMIRAL), Dewey was still active in naval affairs when he died, in 1917.

Dewey, John

John Dewey was an important American philosopher and teacher. He was born in Burlington, Vermont, in 1859. He taught at Columbia University in New York City from 1904 to 1930, when he retired. He died in 1952. Dewey's ideas have been important in education, and he wrote many books about them. He did not believe that children should be taught by memorizing things. Instead Dewey believed  that children could learn best by doing things for themselves when they really wanted to do them. His ideas have been put into practice in many schools that are called progressive schools.

Dewey, Thomas E.

Thomas Edmund Dewey is an important American statesman who twice was the candidate of the Republican Party for the Presidency of the United States. He served as Governor of New York and as District Attorney of New York City.

He made his big reputation as a special prosecutor of the rackets that were making New York City politics very dishonest. He was so successful in breaking up these rackets that his name became known all over the United States. People admired him particularly because he was so young. He was only 33 years old at the time.

Thomas E. Dewey was born in Michigan (in 1902) but became a lawyer in New York City. He was appointed as special prosecutor in 1935 and served in this job until 1937. In 1938 he became District Attorney. He was elected Governor of New York in 1942 and again in 1946 and 1950. He ran for President of the United States in 1944 against Franklin D. Roosevelt, and again in 1948 against Harry S. Truman, but he was defeated both times. After his defeat in 1948 he said he would not run for President again, and in 1954 he said he would not run for governor. He died in 1971.

diabetes

Diabetes is the name of a disease in which the body is not able to use sugar as it should. Sugar comes from the food we eat (especially starches, such as potatoes and bread, and cake and candy), and it is very important because, as our bodies burn sugar, we get heat and energy. If the body cannot use sugar it will get rid of it through the urine, so one important way the doctors find out if a person has diabetes is to test the urine to see how much sugar there is in it. Doctors also test the blood to see if there is more sugar than ought to be there.

There is in the body a special substance called insulin that helps the body burn sugar. When a person has diabetes, it means that he does not have enough insulin. A person with diabetes learns how to give himself injections of insulin, and this has helped people with diabetes a great deal. Two other things that are important for a person with diabetes are to keep to a special diet that the doctor works out carefully, and to have just the right amount of exercise. If a person with diabetes is careful and listens to what his doctor tells him, he can live a happy and busy life. Diabetes is most common in people who are over forty years old.

diamond

A diamond is the hardest substance known to man. It is a stone that is almost pure carbon, but it is much different from some other substances that are almost pure carbon. These include the coal that is burned in furnaces, the soft, oily graphite that is used in the "lead" in pencils, and charcoal or ashes from a fire. Nature has subjected the diamond to such tremendous heat and pressure that it is clear and bright and sparkling. The polished diamond is the most desired of all precious stones. The diamond ring is a symbol of love, and a man usually gives a diamond ring to the woman who has promised to marry him as a symbol of their engagement.

USES OF DIAMONDS

There are two principal uses of diamonds. One of these is for jewelry. The diamond, which is almost five times harder than any other natural substance and four times harder than any substance made by man, is equally important in industry. Many industries use diamonds in cutting, drilling and polishing tools. In time of war diamonds increase in value because every country needs them in order to make heavy machinery and armaments. During World War II the Allies were fortunate because Great Britain had control of the diamonds in South Africa and the United States had access to the diamonds in Brazil.

Another use of diamonds is for phonograph needles. The diamond phonograph needle will not wear down as easily as phonograph needles made of other materials.

GRADING OF DIAMONDS

The grading of diamonds, which determines their value, depends upon their size, their color, and their clarity (clearness). Usually the bigger a diamond is, the more valuable it is. A very white diamond, which is called a blue-white diamond, is worth more than a yellowish or cloudy diamond, though occasionally a yellow diamond is found that is clear and flawless and then it is very valuable. Most diamonds have little spots or holes called *flaws* that make them less valuable. Diamonds are measured in units of weight called *carats*. A diamond that weighs one carat is about the size of a very tiny pea.

Cartier/Wagner International

This diamond, weighing over 69 carats, was purchased by actor Richard Burton for his wife, actress Elizabeth Taylor.

CUTTING AND POLISHING

Diamonds are cut in various ways. A diamond has a grain, and an expert cutter can split a diamond along its grain. Most of the beauty of the diamond is the way in which it reflects light. A well-cut, clear diamond will reflect all the colors of the rainbow. The diamond is usually cut so that it has many different flat surfaces called *facets*. The most popular cuts are brilliant, emerald, and marquise.

Diamonds are polished with a wheel somewhat like the wheel used by a dentist for polishing teeth. The wheel has a surface that looks like sandpaper, but this surface is actually covered with diamond dust. Only diamonds are hard enough to polish other diamonds.

SOURCES OF DIAMONDS

Diamonds are formed by the heat and pressure of the earth on fallen trees. Over a period of millions of years, carbon is formed. The diamond is pure carbon in the form of crystals. Often diamonds are found around ancient dead volcanoes where at one time the heat and the pressure of the earth was very great. Diamonds have been found in many parts of the world, and princes in India and China were wearing diamond jewelry thousands of years ago. Today the biggest diamond mines are found in South Africa and in the country of Brazil in South America. Most of the gem stones come from South Africa.

Diamond mines were discovered in South Africa in 1867. Two Englishmen named Barney Barnato and Cecil Rhodes set up the first big diamond mine, which was called the DeBeers Consolidated Mines. Today this famous mine has been closed, but the same company has mines in South Africa. The chief mines are Dutoitspan, Premier, Jagersfontein, Bultfontein, and Wesselton.

DIAMOND MARKETING

The diamonds from the mines in South Africa are shipped to Antwerp, Belgium, to Amsterdam in the Netherlands, to London, England, and to a few other cities. These cities are the diamond centers of the world. Here the raw diamonds are separated and prepared for sale. The best ones are cut and polished and sold for gems. The others are sold for industrial purposes at a much cheaper price.

Most jewelers who sell diamonds do not own the diamonds themselves. The diamonds are sold by a method called *consignment*. The big diamond merchants let the jewelers have the diamonds to sell at a certain price. If the jeweler does not sell them he merely returns them to the merchants.

Certain large diamonds have become very famous. The Koh-i-noor diamond is one of the crown jewels of England. The Cullinan diamond was one of the largest ever found; when it was finally broken into many smaller stones, the largest of these weighed 516½ carats and 309½ carats. The Hope diamond was supposed to bring bad luck to anyone who owned it, and the Jonkers diamond, bought by Harry Winston of New York, was studied for several years before it was finally cut so that the split would be exactly right.

Diamonds brought into the United States are subject to a tax called *customs*. This tax is very high. Often in the past big groups of criminals tried to smuggle diamonds into the country without paying this tax. Today the Treasury Department has many ways to catch smugglers, including the use of x-ray machines, and smuggling of diamonds has been greatly reduced.

Diana

Diana was a great goddess in Roman mythology, the stories the ancient Romans told about their gods and goddesses. She was the same as the goddess whom the Greeks called Artemis. Diana was young and strong and beautiful. She was the daughter of Leto and Zeus, king of the gods. She was the twin sister of Apollo. Apollo was god of the sun, and Diana was goddess of the moon. She was also the goddess of hunting. She loved to live in the woods, and to chase the wild animals. She carried a bow and arrows, and rode in a chariot drawn by great stags with gold antlers. Diana was the protector of the young animals in the forests, and of the flocks. She would be most angry with anyone who killed baby animals. In Rome, Diana was also the protector of slaves. Diana never married. Some stories say she never loved anyone. The priests and priestesses in her temples were devoted to her. They were not allowed to marry.

diaphragm

The diaphragm is a large, dome-shaped sheet of muscle in the body. It is the "floor" of the chest cavity, or thorax, and the "roof" of the abdominal cavity. (In the chest cavity are your heart and lungs, and in the abdominal cavity are your stomach, intestines, liver, and other vital organs.) The diaphragm is the muscle that helps you to breathe. As you breathe in, the top of the diaphragm's dome goes down, and the space inside your chest cavity gets bigger. This lets air be drawn into the lungs, and they fill up. As you breathe out, the dome of the diaphragm is pushed up, and it presses the lungs so that air is pushed out.

If you place your hand at the point where your ribs separate in the front, and cough, you will feel a muscle harden there. That is your diaphragm. If you were suddenly hit in that spot, the blow would make you gasp, and your breath would burst out in a "whoosh." That is because the blow would strike your diaphragm, and push it in so that it literally "squashed" the air out of your lungs.

You can read about the lungs, chest, abdomen, and other organs in the article on the HUMAN BODY.

diarrhea

When you have to go to the bathroom to move your bowels quite a few times a day, you have diarrhea. If you are very excited or upset about something, this is likely to happen, and as soon as things are quieter, the diarrhea will disappear. However, diarrhea may be a warning that something else is wrong with you. If it continues, see a doctor. Sometimes infants get diarrhea when they are still in the hospital. For some reason that scientists do not yet understand, babies who have just been born seem to catch diarrhea from each other in the hospital, and when a very new

N.W. Ayer & Son, Inc., Photos
A diamond cutter marks the stone with India ink to show where it should be cut.

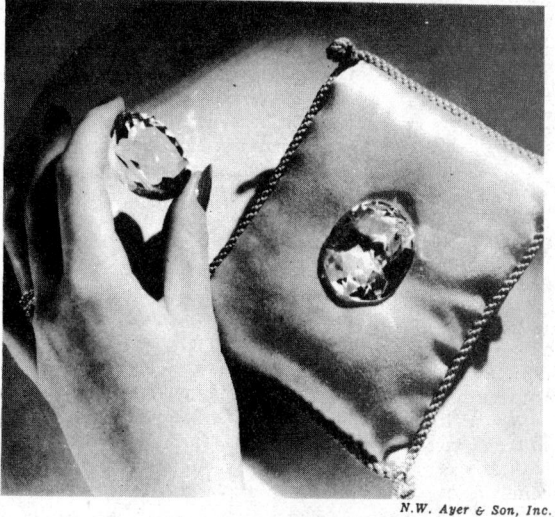

N.W. Ayer & Son, Inc.

On the left is the famous Koh-i-noor diamond as it looked when it was presented to Queen Victoria of England about 100 years ago by the East India Company. It then weighed 186 carats. The Queen had it recut, as it appears on the cushion, and it then weighed 109 carats. It is worn only by English queens and is now in the Queen Mother's crown.

baby has any sickness, including diarrhea, it is serious.

Dias, Bartholomeu

Bartholomeu Dias was a great Portuguese explorer about five hundred years ago. Before his time, people traveled to India and the other countries of the Far East over land, in camel caravans across the deserts. In Dias's time, they were looking for a new route, a way by which they could sail all the way to the east. Africa was an unexplored country, and no one had ever sailed around it. Portugal sent out many expeditions, to sail southward down the west coast of Africa. In 1486, Bartholomeu Dias sailed from Lisbon as commander of an expedition. He sailed far to the south, until he reached the cape at the very southernmost tip of Africa. From there, the ships could begin to go north and east. Dias had discovered the new water route to the East. The cape that Dias discovered was called the Cape of Good Hope. He was on another expedition in 1500, when he was drowned near the cape that he had discovered.

diatom

A diatom is one of the many very small plants that live in water. These plants all belong to the class called the ALGAE, about which you can read in a separate article. Diatoms are so small that they can be seen only under a microscope, which is the most powerful kind of magnifying glass. Under a microscope you will see that diatoms are very beautiful. Each diatom consists of a single cell, instead of the thousands of cells that are in bigger plants. This single cell has a hard shell called the cell wall, which is made of a substance like glass. The cell wall usually has a very fancy shape; it may be like a star, or a half-moon, or a cartwheel. Each one of the thousands of different kinds of diatom has a differently shaped cell wall, by which it can be told from the others. The color of diatoms is another way to tell them from other kinds of tiny water plants. Most tiny water plants are green, but the living diatom inside its cell wall is bright golden-brown.

Sometimes you will see that the mud on the shores of the sea or a lake, or even the water itself, is yellow. Almost always this is caused by millions of diatoms, floating or living on the mud. Diatoms are eaten by small animals, which in turn are eaten by larger and larger animals. Finally these may be eaten by the fishes we ourselves eat for food. By finding out where the most diatoms are, scientists in Britain are able to tell the fishing fleets where to go to catch the most herring.

Diatom cell walls are so strong that they last for millions of years after the plant has died. The bottoms of some of the oceans are covered with a thick layer of diatom skeletons. In some places such ocean bottoms have become dry land. Their earth is called *diatomaceous earth*, and it feels rough. This kind of earth is used for many purposes. For instance, it is used for polishing, and dynamite is made from it by soaking it in the liquid explosive called nitroglycerin. Both dead and alive, the invisible diatoms are of great importance to men.

Diaz, Porfirio

Porfirio Diaz was a Mexican leader who was president and dictator of Mexico for 35 years, from 1876 to 1911. He was born in the state of Oaxaca in 1830; like many of the Mexican people, he was a mestizo, which means that he was part Spanish and part Indian. Diaz's parents were very poor. They wanted him to become a priest, but he was more interested in law and government, so he became a lawyer. He later served in the Mexican Army. He fought against the United States in the Mexican War of 1847, and then joined with Benito Juarez in helping to establish a liberal government in Mexico. But he did not remain a liberal, and when he was elected president in 1877, he was a conservative. As president and dictator, Diaz did a great deal to help Mexico become a modern country by developing its industries and transportation. But the common people were not well treated under Diaz's rule. They were very poor and most of them were completely uneducated. In 1911, they rebelled against Diaz and threw him out of office. He ran away to France, where he died in 1915.

dice

Dice are by far the oldest of all things men have made to play games with. They have been found in buried cities that are six and seven thousand years old. Ancient peoples in all parts of the world have made and used dice. The American Indians made dice that looked like sticks; the Chinese made dice that looked like dominoes; but most dice, even thousands of years ago, looked just the way they do today: Each die, which is what each of the dice is called, is a cube, or block. On one side of the die there is one dot, or another side two dots, and so on, up to six dots. At one very early period, long before written history began, men made dice from the knuckle bones of sheep and other animals, and marked the dots on those.

The priests of ancient religions used dice when they asked advice of their gods: They would throw out the dice, believing that the gods would answer the question by controlling the way the dice would land. Of course, gamblers have used dice through the ages. And dice are very useful in many games, such as Parcheesi (which itself is a very old game), to decide how far you can move in your turn.

Dice have been made out of many materials, including ivory. Modern dice are usually made of plastics, such as celluloid.

dickcissel

The dickcissel is a bird very much like a sparrow. It has a dark back, a reddish-brown patch on its wing, a yellow belly, a white throat, and a black band across its breast. It builds its nest on the ground, under a tuft of grass, or low down in a tree. Most of the year it lives on the prairies of central United States, but in the fall it flies down south to Texas, where it spends the winter. Then in spring it flies north again. It feeds chiefly on seeds and small insects. It gets its name from its call, which sounds like "dick-cissel! dick-cissel!"

Dickens, Charles

Charles Dickens was one of the greatest and most famous of all English novelists. He wrote more than twenty novels and other books that for years were more widely read and loved than those of any other English or American writer. He is still very popular for his exciting stories, wonderful characters, and descriptions of life in London where he lived more than a hundred years ago. You can learn a good deal about Dickens' early life by reading several of his books that are partly based upon his own experiences. His parents were very poor and his childhood was miserable and unhappy. But later, when he wrote about many queer characters that he met and unpleasant things that happened to him, he made them seem exciting and often very amusing.

Charles Dickens' father was a poor navy clerk in Portsmouth, England. Charles was born in 1812 in nearby Landport. In 1814, the family moved to London; Charles' father, who was sure that something better would "turn up" there, never found a good job. Once when Charles was twelve years old, his father was put into prison because of unpaid debts, and Charles had to go to work in a shoe-polish factory. The experience, which he describes in his novel, *Little Dorrit,* was so unpleasant that he never forgot it. His father became the model for a wonderful character named "Mr. Micawber" in the novel *David Copperfield*, just as his mother appears as "Mrs. Nickleby" in *Nicholas Nickleby.*

Charles was able to attend school only for a few years, but at other times he went to the library and read as much as he could. He later worked in a lawyer's office, and at the age of nineteen became a newspaper reporter. His first stories and essays were called *Sketches by Boz,* and these were so popular that he wrote some others very much like them called *The Pickwick Papers.*

If you want to meet some of Dickens's most wonderful characters, read *The Pickwick Papers.* These characters are described so sharply and clearly that they stand out almost like living cartoons. Their names describe the kind of people they are. There are Mr. Perker, old Buzfuz, Jingle, Job Trotter, Sam Weller, and others. Some are silly and stupid, some pathetic and lovable. All seem more exaggerated than people we meet in real life, but that is partly because people like this really used to exist in England, and partly because Dickens describes them with such magnificent word-pictures. Some of the other characters and things Dickens describes in his other novels, however, are more unpleasant and frightening. Whenever he saw people being badly treated, he became angry and wrote about what he saw. His descriptions of bad conditions in schools and prison, for example, were so powerful that the gov-

ernment was forced to reform them. Dickens's writing has many faults, but most readers do not mind because he can make them laugh and cry over stories about characters who seem more human than people they meet in everyday life.

Dickens made lots of money from his novels and from trips that he made in both England and America, to read from his works. In 1836 he married Catherine Hogarth. The next year the first of their ten children was born. He was the editor of two different magazines, managed his own amateur theatrical society, and wrote several other books including *A Child's History of England*. But he worked so hard that his health broke down, and he died in 1870 without finishing his last novel, *The Mystery of Edwin Drood*.

Dickinson, Emily

Emily Dickinson was a great American poet. She was born in Amherst, Massachusetts, in 1830, and she lived there all her life. In fact, as she grew older, Emily Dickinson hard-ly went out of the house where she was born, except to walk in the garden. She saw almost no one besides her family, and she would not even allow her poems to be published. Only three or four of Emily Dickin-

Amherst College

son's beautiful poems were printed while she lived. People have wondered why Emily Dickinson shut herself away from the world. Some people have said she was very shy. Others think she may have had an unhappy love affair, or some other great sadness. People have been sorry that they do not know more about the life of this great poet. She died in 1886, when she was 56 years old.

The poems of Emily Dickinson are about birds and butterflies and blades of grass. They are about love, and there are many poems about life and death, and what they mean. Some of these poems are very clear, and children have enjoyed reading them. Emily Dickinson wrote the way she wanted to. She did not care whether her poems were written in the way most poetry is. People have always been puzzled by her poetry, but they all agree that she was one of the greatest poets America has had.

dictating machine

A dictating machine is a device that records the voice (or any sound) on tape, on a record, or on a belt. Businessmen "talk" their letters and memorandums into the machine, and later the recordings can be played back and the messages typed. This saves a great deal of time for both the businessman and his secretary, as she is free to attend to other duties while he is dictating into the machine.

Thomas A. Edison invented the first dictating machine in 1878. His machine recorded the words, or "dictation," on a record made of wax. Two different companies sold the dictating machine he invented, under the names Ediphone and Dictaphone. Since World War II, these and other companies have put out machines that use the latest methods of re-

cording on tape and on disks that are the same as phonograph records.

The person who is dictating the letter talks into a *microphone,* a mouthpiece that electrically transfers his voice to the tape or disk. When the tape or record is "played back," the typist hears what he has said.

See also the article on RECORDING.

dictatorship

A dictatorship is a form of government in which one man, called a *dictator,* has the power to do just as he wishes with the country and all the people who live in it.

A person who lives in a dictatorship can never feel free or safe, because the dictator can have him arrested and imprisoned and tortured and executed if he wants to, even if there is no legal reason to do so. The same thing has often been true of governments called *absolute monarchies,* in which a king or emperor had power of life and death over the people in his country, but a dictator is not a king. That is, he does not get his power by birth but by political importance. The most powerful dictators of modern times, Benito Mussolini in Italy, Adolf Hitler in Germany, and Josef Stalin in Russia, were born into poor and unimportant families, and became dictators because they were the heads of powerful political parties. People who live in free countries such as the United States and Canada have always been opposed to dictatorship of any kind, and many of them (or their ancestors) came to America to get away from dictatorial governments in which the people had no freedom.

dictionary

A dictionary is a book that tells how words should be spelled and pronounced, and what they mean. Nearly all well-educated persons have what is known as the "dictionary habit." That means they have learned how to use a dictionary, and whenever they have the slightest doubt as to what a word means, or how it should be spelled or pronounced, they go at once to a dictionary and look up the word. If you get the dictionary habit, you too will have made an important step toward becoming a well-educated person.

There are hundreds of different dictionaries, large and small, old and new. Some are made especially for use by children. These are just as "correct" as dictionaries made for adults, but they try to give the meanings of words so that children can understand them more easily. Dictionaries for children are very useful, but they do not have as many words in them as do most dictionaries for adults. If you are reading and come across a word you do not understand, and if that word is not in your own dictionary, you should not give up but should find a bigger dictionary in the school or library, if you do not have one at home. The most important thing about the dictionary habit is never to pass over a word you do not understand, but look it up at once.

The first step in acquiring the dictionary habit is to know how to use the dictionary. There are slight differences between dictionaries, but all of them follow about the same arrangement.

ALPHABETIZATION

The word you are looking for in the dictionary will be printed in a bigger, blacker type than the other words. This is called *boldface* type. Each word in boldface type is called an *entry* word, or "finding word."

These words are listed in alphabetical order. They follow the order of the alphabet, beginning with A and ending with Z. In alphabetizing, the editors of the dictionary first separate all the words according to their first letters. That gives them, as a starting group, all the words that begin with A or a. Then they take only the second letters of the words, and put the "A" words in alphabetical order by their second letters, so that they have all words beginning with aa, then all words beginning with ab, and so on. They then take all the words that begin with the first two letters and put these in the order of their third letters. They keep on doing this as long as necessary, through the fifth or tenth or even the fifteenth letter. Finally all the words are all in alphabetical order.

SPELLING

The first thing you learn from the entry word is how to spell it. This includes more than the letters used in spelling the word. The dictionary will also show you when a word should begin with the capital letter and when it should not. It will show when a word should be spelled with a hyphen, as *self-confidence* is, or without a hyphen, as *antifreeze* is, or with an apostrophe, as *don't* is.

Sometimes there are two different ways to spell a word, and both of them are correct. A dictionary will give both ways, but the spelling it gives first is the one its editors like better. That is called their *preferred* spelling.

SYLLABIFICATION

In most dictionaries, each entry word is divided into syllables. These short hyphens should not be confused with the hyphens used in spelling a word. The dots or short hyphens are there only to show you how to divide the word into syllables.

It is important to know how to divide a word into syllables. When you come to the end of a line and do not have room to get an entire word on the line, you can divide it with a hyphen and put the rest of the word on the next line. But the only proper place to divide a word is at the end of a syllable, as shown in the dictionary. Some words, such as *ground* and *dipped*, have only one syllable and cannot be divided at all. The entire word

must go on one line. A word such as *be-lieve* must be divided *be-lieve*. It would be wrong to make it bel-ieve.

The syllabification of a word follows sensible rules. Usually it is divided just as it is pronounced. But it is always safer to make sure by looking up the word in the dictionary. Especially for girls who want to become stenographers or secretaries, it is important to learn the proper dividing of words into syllables.

PRONUNCIATION

The next thing the dictionary tells is how the word should be pronounced. Here again there may be more than one correct way to pronounce a word, and the dictionary will give every correct way but will put the preferred one first.

In showing the pronunciation, the dictionary will probably use *stress marks*, also called *accents*, to show which syllables should be emphasized. In the case of *believe*, it will use the mark ´ after the *-lieve* to show that you emphasize that syllable. Many words have two or more syllables that should be emphasized, but one is emphasized more than the others. The one that is emphasized most is marked with the , which is called *primary stress*. Another syllable that is emphasized but not so much is marked ", which is called *secondary stress*.

The rest of the pronunciation is usually shown by *diacritical marks,* or *accent marks*. These are marks added to a letter to show how it is pronounced. There are many different methods of marking the pronunciation of letters. Most American dictionaries use about the same method. For example, if the letter *a* is marked ä it should be pronounced like the *a* in *father*, and if it is marked ā it should be pronounced like the *a* in *gate*.

Sometimes it takes a person a while to catch on to easy reading of the diacritical marks, but if you are willing to try just three or four times you will find that it will always be easy for you after that.

DEFINITION

The dictionary will give you one or more definitions for each word. A definition tells what the word means.

Many words have more than one sense, or meaning. In most dictionaries, each different sense will be numbered. You may look up a strange word and find that it has several different senses. You should read them all and see which one makes the best sense in the sentence in which you read it. That will tell you what the sentence means, and at the same time you will have learned some extra information about that word.

The test of a good definition is this: If you put it into the sentence in place of the strange word, the meaning should become clear and the sentence should still follow the rules of good grammar. Suppose you come across this sentence:

He wrote a didactic book.

You don't know what *didactic* means, so you look it up in your dictionary. The dictionary says it means "intended to teach or instruct; instructive." That would make the sentence mean:

He wrote a book intended to teach.
or
He wrote an instructive book.

1. Dr. Samuel Johnson's dictionary, published in 1755.
2. The Oxford Dictionary gives the date when each word was first used.
3. One of the early English dictionaries defined words in Latin because scholars knew it better than English
4. An early English dictionary with English definitions.

[1] ABI'DER. *n. f.* [from *abide*.] The person that abides or dwells in a place; perhaps that lives or endures. A word little in use.
ABI'DING. *n. f.* [from *abide*.] Continuance.
We are strangers before thee and sojourners, as were all our fathers: our days on the earth are as a shadow, and there is none *abiding*. *1 Chron*. xxix. 15.
The air in that region is so violently removed, and carried about with such swiftness, as nothing in that place can consist or have *abiding*. *Rawleigh's History of the World.*
A'BJECT. *adj.* [*abjectus*, Lat. thrown away as of no value.]

[2] Discriminator. [a. L. *discriminator* (Tertull.), agent-n. from *discriminãre* to DISCRIMINATE.] One who discriminates.
1848 COLEBROOKE in *Trans. R. Asiat. Soc.* (1830) II. 183 He [the judge] discriminates, and is, consequently, the discriminator (*vindex*).
Discriminatory, *a. rare.* [f. L. type *discriminãtõri-us*, f. *discriminãtor*: see prec. and -ORY.] = DISCRIMINATIVE.
1848 W. FIELD *Mem. Dr. Parr* II. 414 Proofs of a pure taste and a discriminatory judgment. 1892 *Columbus* (Ohio) *Dispatch* 1 Mar., The Government still hoped for discriminatory rights with Great Britain.
Discriminoid. *Math.* [f. after DISCRIMINANT: see -OID.] A function of which the vanishing expresses the equality of all the integrating factors of a differential equation. Hence Discriminoidal *a.*
1879 SIR J. COCKLE in *Proc. Lond. Math. Soc.* X. 111 It will be found convenient to give a name to the functions □ and □. Let us call them discriminoids. *Ibid.,* This first species of discriminoidal solution

[3] ¶ the Heele. Calx, cis, Dub.g. Calcáneus, nei, m.g. & Calcáneum, nei, n.g.Virg. Talus, li, m.gen. Le talon.
* That commeth downe to the heele, or ancle. Taláris, & re, om.g. vt, Tunica talaris. Cic.
¶ Heifer. Vide Haifer.
¶ an Heigh, or shrill sound. Extentus sonus. Plin.
* Length: tallnesse: heigth. Procéritas, f.g.Cic.
¶ Height, or highnesse: the top. Summitas, & Sublimitas, tatis, f. gen. Hardieur, fomite, Sommer. Vide High.
¶ an Heinous matter, a wicked & detestable thing: a wicked act. Nefas, indeclin.n.g.Ouid.

At the same time your dictionary will tell you how to pronounce *didactic,* and how to divide it into syllables.

ETYMOLOGIES

An etymology is the history of a word. It tells how that word happened to become part of the English language. There is a separate article on ETYMOLOGY in this encyclopedia. Many smaller dictionaries, and many dictionaries made especially for children, do not give the etymologies of words. Usually the use of etymologies is not taught before high school or college. Etymologies can help a person to speak and write better English and to spell and pronounce words better. To many people they are very interesting besides.

THE MAKING OF DICTIONARIES

Dictionaries of the English language have been written for more than four hundred years, but the early ones were very small and not very good.

The first great English dictionary was written by Dr. Samuel Johnson, who was the greatest scholar of his time. The dictionary was published about two hundred years ago, in 1755. All English dictionaries since that time have followed the lead of Dr. Johnson.

The first great American dictionary was written by Noah Webster more than a hundred years ago, in 1828. Dozens of

[4] M
Maccerate, to steepe in water, or make cleane
madefie. dip. make wet
maffle, stammer, or stut
magicke, inchaunting, coniuring
magistrate, gouernour
magitian, (g) one using witchcraft
magnanimitie, valientnes, courage
magnificence, sumptuousnes
magnifie, to extoll, or praise highly
magnitude, greatnes
§ mayre, leane

dictionaries still bear the name Webster, although the English language has changed a great deal since his time and he did not actually write any dictionary

that is published today. One company bought the legal right to publish Webster's dictionaries, and still uses his name.

A dictionary is also called a *lexicon,* and the making of dictionaries is called LEXICOGRAPHY, about which there is a separate article.

Dido was the Queen of Carthage, according to Roman legend. The Trojan prince Aeneas was shipwrecked near her city, and she fell in love with him. He left her, and she killed herself in despair.

Didrikson

Babe Didrikson was one of America's most famous women athletes. Her real name was Mildred, but she was called "Babe" ever since she was a little girl. She was born in Texas in 1913. When she was only sixteen, she became a member of a famous girls' athletic club called the Golden Cyclone Athletic Club, and she traveled all over the United States playing basketball and running in track meets. In 1932 she was in the Olympic Games, where she broke the world's record for women in throwing the javelin and in the eighty-meter hurdle. She was a champion in every sport she tried except table tennis. Later she decided to concentrate on golf, and she became America's best woman golfer. In 1953, she had a very serious operation, but that did not prevent her from continuing her career in sports, and she went right on winning golf tournaments. She married a man named George Zaharias, who used to be a professional wrestler. She died in 1956.

Dieppe

Dieppe is a town on the coast of France, across the English Channel from England. About 30,000 people live there. During World War II, when France was occupied by the German army, Dieppe was raided by Canadian soldiers. Five thousand Canadians, who had been especially trained as commandos, landed at Dieppe on August 19, 1942. (There is a separate article about COMMANDOS.) The Germans had put guns on the cliffs and in the houses around the town, and they killed many of the Canadian soldiers who were getting out of the small boats that

had brought them and were wading ashore. Some of the Canadians managed to approach the town, but they soon had to leave because the Germans there were very strong. Of the 5,000 Canadian soldiers in the raid, 3,369 were either killed, wounded, or taken prisoner in the raid. This heroic fight of the Canadians was very useful to the Allies, because now they had learned how difficult it would be to land in France.

diesel engine, an internal-combustion engine that burns oil. It was named for a German engineer, Rudolf Diesel, who invented it. See the article on IN-TERNAL COMBUSTION.

diet

A diet is another name for a congress or a legislature. The Japanese people, for instance, call their lawmaking body the diet. It is made up of two houses, the House of Councilors and the House of Representatives. There have been two other very famous diets in history. One was the diet of the Holy Roman Empire. This diet was the lawmaking body for the powerful empire that ruled over most of the central part of Europe for nearly a thousand years, between 962 and 1806. Once, this diet met for a special purpose at Worms, in Germany. This special meeting took place in 1521, and it is called the Diet of Worms. The Diet of Worms met to try to straighten out differences of opinion about religion between an important man called Martin LUTHER (you can read about him in a separate article) and the Catholic Church. The Diet of Worms did not succeed. Shortly afterward, Luther and his followers broke away from the Catholic Church and the Protestant movement in the Christian religion began to grow.

diet is what a person eats and drinks: see FOOD and NUTRITION.

dietary laws

The dietary laws are religious laws observed by many members of the Jewish religion (Judaism). These laws concern food. For example, certain meats such as pork, and shellfish such as lobster, may not be eaten at any time. Meat may not be eaten at the same meal with dairy foods such as milk and butter. The Bible states these laws in a very general way, but they are explained in *Shulchan Aruch*, a book of Jewish law written about four hundred years ago. See also the article KOSHER.

differential gear

Before people had automobiles they rode in carts drawn by horses. You have seen pictures of the way people went along the winding trails to the Wild West in covered wagons. Since the wagons were pulled by horses, they could not go very fast around the curves. Later, when the first autos were invented, people started to go much faster than they could in horse-drawn wagons. When they went around turns they discovered something not very pleasant. They skidded around every turn.

The cause of that skidding is very simple. It is just that whenever a car goes around a curve to the right, the left rear

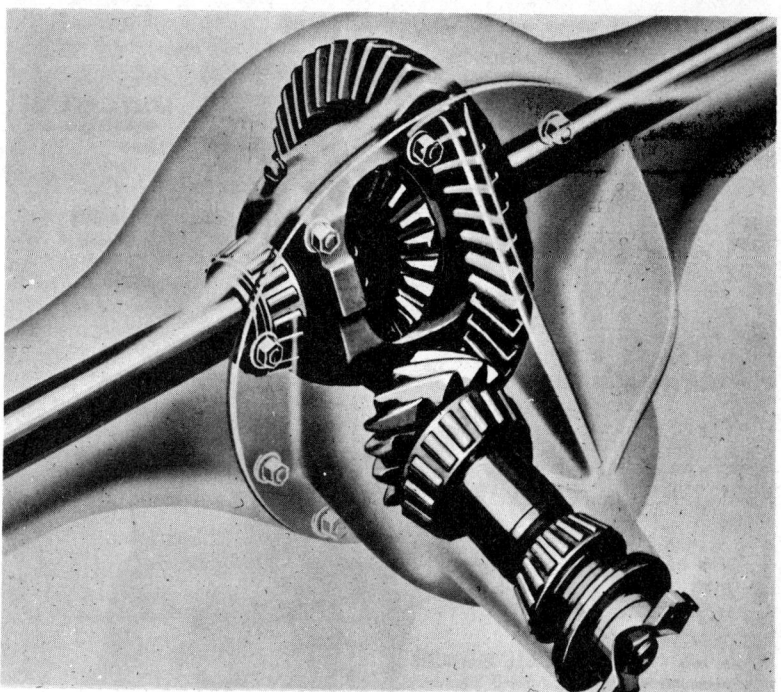

General Motors Corp.

These gears are called a differential. They are connected to a shaft that turns the rear wheels of an automobile and makes it move. The differential is important in turning corners because it makes the outside wheel turn faster than the inside wheel. This prevents the car from skidding and saves the tires.

wheel must turn faster than the right wheel. Think of what happens when you go walking with two of your friends and you all walk in line. Now suppose you have to turn a corner to the right. If you were on the outside and your friends were closest to the corner you would have to run in order to keep up with them. It was not so simple to get rid of the skidding—another part for the car had to be invented. The name for that part is *differential,* or *differential gear.* It is found between the two rear wheels of the car and looks somewhat like a pear. Just as you might guess from its name, it lets the rear wheels travel at different speeds. It does its work whenever a car goes around curves.

diffusion

Diffusion is spreading out, as a fluid does.

When a bottle of perfume is opened you can smell the sweet odor after a little while, because the perfume mixed with the air by diffusion finally reaches your nose. When you pour vinegar into a bowl of water the vinegar quickly spreads, by diffusion, until the entire bowl of water tastes sour. Diffusion happens whenever the tiniest parts of something, known as molecules, mix with the molecules of something else. Sometimes different molecules will not mix, and if you pour olive oil into a glass of water you will see that the oil stays together and floats on top of the water. Luckily, however, a great many things will diffuse in water. For instance, the food that we eat is changed in our stomach so that the nourishing things in the food will diffuse through the water in our bodies and keep all our muscles and other tissues healthy. Young growing plants need rain because the water makes it possible for the plant food in the soil to diffuse through the roots of the plant and nourish it.

digestion

Digestion changes the foods you eat into liquids, so that they can be absorbed by the body. Your teeth start the change from solid to liquid by grinding up food into small particles. If you had no teeth you would have to live on liquids or food that had been ground into mush, doing the job that your teeth ordinarily do while you are chewing food. However, that food is being mixed with the saliva in your mouth, and saliva contains chemicals that also help to turn the food to liquid. When you swallow, the muscles in your mouth and throat push the chewed food into your esophagus, on the way to your stomach. You can swallow even if you are standing on your head, because food does not merely drop or slide down into your stomach. It is forced there by the muscles in your throat.

When food gets to your stomach, the next step in digestion takes place. On the inside of your stomach's lining are many tiny glands called "gastric glands." These release gastric juices, in much the same way that tear glands in your eyes release tears when you cry. As the food reaches your stomach, the glands start working, and at the same time your stomach's walls toss the food around in your stomach, like the whirling bowl of a food mixer without the beater inside. This way the food is thoroughly mixed with the gastric juices. At the bottom of your stomach is a small muscle that opens or closes the tube leading to your small intestine, where the food goes next. When your partly digested food reaches this opening, the muscle there pushes it through into the small intestine. On the inside of the small intestine is a wavy surface covered with millions of hairlike projections that work constantly, and whip the food through the intestinal tube, breaking it down as it goes. At the same time, more juices are released, to join with the partly

Cross section of your whole digestive plant

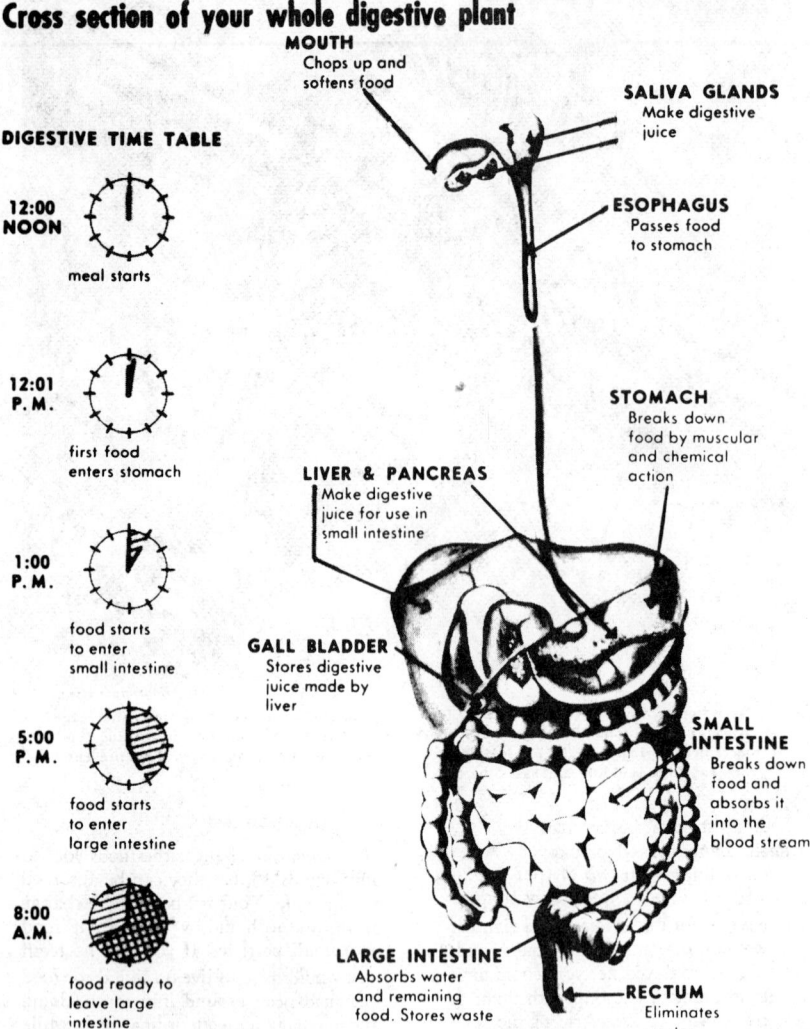

MOUTH
Chops up and
softens food

SALIVA GLANDS
Make digestive
juice

ESOPHAGUS
Passes food
to stomach

STOMACH
Breaks down
food by muscular
and chemical
action

LIVER & PANCREAS
Make digestive
juice for use in
small intestine

GALL BLADDER
Stores digestive
juice made by
liver

**SMALL
INTESTINE**
Breaks down
food and
absorbs it
into the
blood stream

LARGE INTESTINE
Absorbs water
and remaining
food. Stores waste

RECTUM
Eliminates
wastes

DIGESTIVE TIME TABLE

12:00 NOON
meal starts

12:01 P.M.
first food
enters stomach

1:00 P.M.
food starts
to enter
small intestine

5:00 P.M.
food starts
to enter
large intestine

8:00 A.M.
food ready to
leave large
intestine

Graphics Institute for *Pageant Magazine*

digested food, and digest it still further, making it more liquid, and breaking down the chemicals in the food at the same time. In the small intestine are many capillaries, which are small blood vessels with porous walls. Through them, the digested food passes into the bloodstream, and from there travels to different parts of your body, feeding the cells and tissues with the nourishment that makes them strong and healthy.

After passing through the small intestine, the digested food is liquid, and in this liquid state goes into the large intestine, or colon. Here most of the water is removed from it, and it becomes the waste material that finally passes out of your body.

You can read more about digestion, and how body cells are built and replaced, in the article on the HUMAN BODY.

dik-dik

A dik-dik is a tiny antelope found in Africa. It is only about fourteen inches high, and weighs six or seven pounds. It is so small that it can run swiftly through the underbrush where larger animals cannot follow. Its speed does not protect it from human hunters, however. Each year thousands are captured in nets, and the skins are used for making fine gloves for women. Gloves made of "antelope leather" are often made of dik-dik skin.

dikes and levees

Dikes and levees are fences or barriers built to keep river and ocean waters from overflowing. If you lived in a country like the Netherlands, which is mostly below sea level, you would see dikes almost everywhere. They are huge mounds of earth, sometimes covered by stone or concrete, that hold the ocean back from the land. If a dike broke, the land would be flooded and people and property would be destroyed. There is a very famous story about a boy who saved the lives and homes of many people in Holland by stopping up a hole in a dike. The dike, so the story goes, would have broken if it were not for the courage of this boy who stayed up all night long, plugging the hole with his hand. He did this because a small hole in a dike will soon grow so big that the whole dike will be worn away.

People build levees to keep rivers from overflowing their banks. Every spring the river waters rise several feet because of the spring rains and melting snows. Sometimes the river will overflow its banks and the homes of people living near by are destroyed. To prevent a river flood, people make the banks higher by piling dirt, sand, concrete, or asphalt on them. Then when the river rises, it cannot overflow the banks and the levee, too. Sometimes the levees are not high enough and people build temporary levees by piling sandbags on the river banks. In 1947, the

Mississippi River overflowed its banks and people and property were washed away. During this flood men, women and children worked night and day piling sandbags on the levees to hold the water back. The worst river disaster happened about seventy years ago when the Hwang Ho, or Yellow River, in China overflowed its banks and washed away its levees. A part of China bigger than New York State was flooded and a million people were drowned. See also the article on DAMS.

dill

Dill is a plant of the carrot family. It grows to a height of three or four feet. Housewives use it as a flavoring in foods, especially in sauces, and in making dill pickles. From the seeds, two things are made—an oil used as a flavoring, and a laxative called dill water. Dill is a native plant of Europe and Asia. It has been used for thousands of years, and is mentioned in the Bible, where it is called anise. In years gone by, superstitious people used it in making charms which they thought would protect them from witches and evil spirits.

DiMaggio, Joseph Paul

Joe DiMaggio was one of the greatest baseball players of all time. He was born in Martinez, California, in 1914 and grew up there and in San Francisco. When Joe was still a boy he had already attracted attention as a baseball player on the sand-lots in San Francisco. Soon many major-league baseball clubs were after him to play on their teams. He became a member of the New York Yankees, and from 1936 to 1951 he was their outstanding player. He hit over 300 home runs, led the American League in batting several times, was chosen as the most valuable player in the league in three different years, and played in the All-Star game thirteen times. His greatest achievement was getting at least one hit in 56 consecutive games. This is so unusual a record that it may be a long time, if ever, before another player does better. DiMaggio was also a great centerfielder. He could run fast and make wonderful catches, and he could throw a ball far and accurately. He did everything on the field with graceful ease.

dime novel

Dime novel was the name given to a kind of story of love or adventure that used to be sold for a dime and read by many people in the United States. The first two dime novels appeared in 1860. One was entitled *Malaeska, or The Indian Wife of the Frontier*. The other was *Seth Jones, or The Captive of the Frontier*.

Later well-known characters in dime novels include Deadwood Dick, Buffalo Bill, Nick Carter, and the boy heroes of Horatio Alger Jr. Many parents did not want their children to read dime novels. They said the stories were too exciting and frightening. Today parents make the same kind of objection to some comic books.

Dinah

One of the stories in the Old Testament, in the Bible, is about Dinah, who was the only daughter of Jacob. Jacob had twelve other children, all of them boys, who became the founders of the Twelve Tribes of Israel. Dinah's brothers were very fond of her. Once she was badly treated by a prince named Shechem. Dinah's brothers swore to avenge her. When Shechem later fell in love with Dinah and wanted to marry her, the brothers pretended to agree to the marriage, provided Shechem did certain things. Shechem lived up to his part of the bargain, but Dinah's brothers killed him, destroyed his city, and made off with all his possessions.

dingo

A dingo is a wild dog of Australia. It looks like a wolf, with ears that stand up straight, and a big, bushy tail. It is found running wild in Australia, as it was when the English settlers first went to that continent, but many dingoes have been tamed and are kept as house dogs now. The wild dingo howls like a wolf, instead of barking, but the dingoes that have been tamed soon learn to bark when they hear other domestic dogs do it. Australians use the dingo for hunting, and as watchdogs. A dingo is about the size of a small German shepherd, and approximately the same colors, from light tan to almost black.

dinosaur

Dinosaur means "terrible lizard." Once dinosaurs ruled the world. There are no dinosaurs now, but we know from bones we have found, and footprints we have discovered in stone, that 150 million years ago these creatures roamed the earth. Some dinosaurs were as small as roosters, but many of them were as big as houses. The Brachiosaurus that lived in the swamps of Africa and North America was the largest land animal that ever lived. Some were more than 80 feet long, and it is believed they weighed up to 95 tons. It has been learned that there were two kinds of dinosaurs. Some were built like birds and others were more like lizards. Some dinosaurs walked on two legs, had a large tail to help them sit, a comparatively tiny head, a great long neck, and an enormous body that was often covered with scales like those of a snake. Some dinosaurs ate plants and others ate meat.

About 65 million years ago, the dinosaur disappeared. The climate was getting colder, and scientists think one reason why the dinosaur died out is because it could not stand cold weather. You can see what the BRONTOSAURUS (an American dinosaur) looked like, and read about it, in a separate article. There are skeletons of some huge dinosaurs in museums in New York City and Washington, D.C.

Diocletian

Diocletian was a powerful Roman emperor about 1,700 years ago. He was born in the year 245, and was chosen emperor by his soldiers in 284. During his rule, Diocletian worked to reorganize the empire. He divided it into four parts, and chose three other men to help him rule it. The capital of the empire was the city of Nicomedia, in Asia Minor. He worked out a system for running the government more efficiently throughout the empire. Diocletian is also remembered for trying to wipe out the Christian religion. He thought the government would be stronger if people returned to the old Roman religion. Many Christians were tortured and killed. Diocletian retired in 305, and lived quietly until his death in 313.

Diogenes

Diogenes was a famous Greek philosopher who lived about four hundred years before Christ, and he was a Cynic. The Cynics believed that things that make man too comfortable are dangerous, and a good man should stay away from them. Diogenes wore very simple clothing, and ate only enough food to stay alive. He even gave up drinking from a cup, when he saw a peasant boy drinking water from his hands.

Diogenes used to walk in the market place in Athens at noon, carrying a lantern. When the Greeks asked him what he was doing, he told them he was looking for an honest man. Diogenes wanted to be very careful that he was not making himself too comfortable, and finally he began living in a tub. There is a famous story that tells how one day Diogenes was sitting in his tub, when Alexander the Great came by. Alexander asked Diogenes what he would like Alexander to do for him. Diogenes answered that he would like the mighty ruler to move, because he was standing between Diogenes and the sun.

Diogenes was captured by pirates and sold as a slave in Crete to Xeniades. He became the tutor of Xeniades' two sons, and he lived in the household as an equal for the rest of his life. Diogenes died in the year 323 B.C., when he was 89 years old.

Dionne

Dionne is the name of five sisters who are famous because they were quintuplets, that is, all five were born at the same time. The parents of these sisters lived in Callender, Ontario, in Canada. When the five babies were born in May, 1934, they weighed only about two pounds each, and no one expected them to live. Dr. Allan Roy Dafoe took care of them, and he saved all of the little girls and their mother. The whole world was excited about this very unusual happening, and people have been interested in the lives of the five sisters ever since. The sisters were named Annette, Cecile, Emilie, Yvonne, and Marie. Marie was the smallest of the five.

The quintuplets received a great deal of money from people all over the world and they became wards of the province of Ontario. They received the very best care while they were growing up. Many people visited the little town of Callender, where they were allowed to see the children through a glass window, although the little girls could not see them. When the quintuplets were twenty years old, Emilie died. She had been sickly since she was a little girl of three. Marie died in 1970.

Dionysius

Dionysius was the name borne by two famous tyrants who ruled in the city of Syracuse in Sicily about twenty-three hundred years ago. The Greeks called tyrant any ruler who seized all power for himself, without being chosen according to the laws.

Dionysius the Elder was the first of these tyrants of Syracuse. In his time, the great country of Carthage was trying to conquer all of Sicily. Dionysius managed to become chief general of his city of Syracuse. With the power that this gave him, he took control of the government. That was about 405 B.C. Dionysius the Elder ruled for almost forty years. He conquered many of the cities of Sicily. He led his country against the Carthaginians and several times he won great victories. He conquered many cities in southern Italy. But Dionysius was not only a fighter. He was also interested in poetry and learning. Many famous poets and philosophers visited his court. He even wrote some poetry himself. Dionysius the Elder made his city great and powerful. But he also made it miserable. He was a cruel man. He had absolute power, and gave his people no freedom.

When Dionysius the Elder died, in 367 B.C., he was followed by his son, Dionysius the Younger. The second Dionysius was not a strong leader like his father. He was easily influenced, first by one person and then by another. The philosopher Plato visited Syracuse, and

Diogenes, the Greek philosopher, once lived in a tub to prove how simply man could exist. Here he speaks with Alexander the Great, the mighty ruler of ancient Greece.

tried to teach Dionysius the Younger to be a good ruler. But Dionysius soon got tired of the hard work of study. He was interested only in living a life of pleasure and ease. Civil war soon broke out, and Dionysius the Younger was forced to leave Syracuse. He returned some years later, but was again forced to leave, in 343 B.C., and lived the rest of his life in exile.

Dionysus, the Greek god of wine: see the article on BACCHUS.

Dioscuri, the name for the twins Castor and Pollux, in Greek legend: see the article on CASTOR AND POLLUX.

diphtheria

Diphtheria is the name of a disease that is caused by a bacterium (a one-celled plant so tiny that you can only see it through a microscope) that grows in the body. It is very easy for one person to catch diphtheria from another person, and so for a long time when anyone got diphtheria it was a very serious thing. Now doctors are able to give people certain injections so that they will not get diphtheria, or if they do catch it, they will only have a very mild case. Most children begin to have these injections when they are only a few months old, and they may have them several times before they are 14 or 15 years old. No one likes injections very much, but these injections were a wonderful discovery, and helped man to be healthy. Some of the signs of diphtheria are a sore throat, fever, and a headache.

diplomacy

Officials appointed by a nation to deal with other nations are called *diplomats,* their work is *diplomacy,* and together they form the *diplomatic service.*

In the Middle Ages when a ruler in Europe had something to talk over with another ruler, he sent someone to do the task for him. This man was called his agent. When the agent was finished he went back to his own country. After a time the rulers of the great Italian cities, such as Venice, had so many questions to take up with each other that each kept an agent living in the city of the other all the time. This agent was known as a *resident.* The custom spread and soon all European governments had residents of this sort.

AMBASSADORS

If some unusually important problem arose, however, a nation sent a more important official than the resident to take care of it. This man was called an *ambassador* or *envoy.* In time the envoy took the place of the resident agent altogether, remaining in the foreign country permanently. The different countries gave different titles to their diplomats. A title that was considered important in one land might not be so regarded in another. To make sure all nations would use the same titles and that these would receive the same respect everywhere, the European nations got together and made a list of titles in order of importance. They all agreed to use these for their diplomats and no others. This was done in 1815 and 1818. Later the United States also agreed to this list.

First in rank in the diplomatic service of any country is the *ambassador.* He takes care of the most important political matters that come up between his country and the one to which he is sent. (Read also the article, AMBASSADOR.) Second in rank is the *minister plenipotentiary* and *envoy extraordinary.* His duties are much the same as those of the ambassador but not quite as important. The diplomat third in rank is called *minister* or *resident minister.* He deals with matters still less important than those given to the first two diplomats. Fourth in rank is the *chargé d'affaires.* He deals with minor matters.

Members of a diplomatic service are entitled to many privileges. They are not subject to the laws of the land in which they serve. They may not be arrested or imprisoned for any reason. If they commit a crime, however, they may be expelled from the country. They do not pay taxes to the foreign country in which they live. In case war breaks out between this country and their own, they must be permitted to go back to their own country unharmed. They may worship as they please no matter what rule about religion the country they are in has made for its own citizens.

FOREIGN OFFICE

The diplomatic service of a country is run by a branch of the government called the Foreign Office or the Office of Foreign Affairs. In the United States, the diplomatic service is one branch of the Foreign Service. The other branch of the Foreign Service is the consular service. The consular service takes care of business matters for Americans in foreign countries. (Read also the article CONSUL.) The diplomatic service deals with political matters. If you want to know if you can sell a particular kind of goods in a certain foreign country, you ask the consul for that country. If you should happen to be in trouble with the police of a foreign country because they say your passport is not stamped correctly, you could appeal to the nearest American legation. The members of the diplomatic corps located there will help you.

Both the diplomatic and consular services—the entire Foreign Service—are run by the Department of State. Its head is the Secretary of State. His superior is the president. The president nominates or appoints all diplomatic agents, who must then be approved or confirmed by the Senate. In a recent year the United States had 42 ambassadors and 15 ministers representing it in foreign lands, as well as numerous lesser diplomats. Most of these officials were men who had worked their way up in the American diplomatic service. Such officials are known as career diplomats, which means that they have chosen diplomatic service as their life work. The others were appointed because they had shown great ability in other fields such as business or politics.

Dipper

The Big Dipper and the Little Dipper are constellations, that is, groups of stars that can be seen in the sky at night. Each of these constellations has a shape that reminds people of a dipper or ladle, though the same shape has reminded people of other things, such as a plow, a wagon, or a bear. They are best known by the names Big Bear and Little Bear (or, in Latin, *Ursa Major* and *Ursa Minor*). The two end stars in the Big Dipper are called the *pointers* because a line connecting them points to the North Star (Polaris). See the article CONSTELLATION.

direct current

Electricity flows through a wire in the same way that water flows through a pipe or in a river. Just as the movement of the water is called a current, the movement of electricity through a wire is called an electric current. When you turn on a light, electricity must flow through the wire that leads from one of the two outlets of the plug, through the electric lamp and back again through the other wire to the plug.

This electric current comes from a generator in a powerhouse. The generator is a big machine that produces the current. Some generators produce current that always flows only one way. That is, it flows into the lamp from one of the wires and out of the lamp through the other wire. Electric current that does not change its direction of flow is called direct current. Direct current is not used too frequently in houses, but it is still very useful in factories. Automobiles, flashlights, and portable radios all use direct current.

See also the separate article about ELECTRICITY.

Directory

During the French Revolution, the French people got rid of their king and tried to set up a republic. In 1795, they gave the main governing power to five men who were called Directors. This group, called the Directory, was supposed to have the same power and do

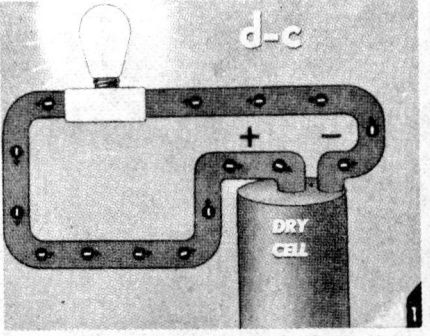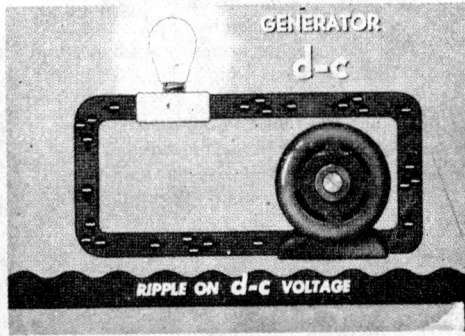

General Electric

**Direct current from a battery (1) or from a generator (2) always goes in one direction.
It flows continuously from the negative pole (−) to the positive pole (+).**

the same work as does the President of the United States. The Directory was in power until 1799, when it was overthrown by Napoleon. Two of the members of the Directory, Sieyès and Barras, worked against the Directory and the government to help Napoleon sieze power. There are separate articles about the FRENCH REVOLUTION and NAPOLEON.

dirigible

The word *dirigible* means "directable," or "capable of being steered." A certain type of balloon—cigar-shaped, driven by engines and propellers, and steered by rudders—is called a dirigible. The same kind of balloon is called an airship, or a Zeppelin. Dirigibles are described in the article on BALLOONS AND AIRSHIPS.

disarmament

Disarmament is one of the methods by which men have tried to prevent wars. Every war begins when one nation attacks another. A nation would not attack if it did not think its armed forces—army, navy, and air force—were strong enough to win the war. If all nations could be persuaded to disarm, then wars might never begin.

Every country, and especially every big country, wants its armed forces to be strong enough to defend it against attack. Therefore no big country will disarm unless all other big countries do. The problem has been to get all the big countries to agree to disarm at the same time.

After World War I, the League of Nations tried to get the big countries of Europe, America and Asia to disarm. France refused to reduce its army because Germany had many more people, and if both countries had started rearming at the same time Germany could have become much stronger than France. There was some success during the 1920s in naval disarmament. Great Britain, the United States and Japan agreed on a "5-5-3 ratio" in which Great Britain and the United States were allowed to have five warships of any particular size and kind for every three that Japan had. However, Japan secretly built more and bigger ships than it had agreed to build.

After World War II, the great nations of the world again tried to work out some plan of disarmament, this time under the leadership of the United Nations. The United States and Great Britain were willing to reduce their armed forces if Russia would, but Russia immediately began to build bigger armed forces than ever and so the United States also kept big armed forces for fear Russia would attack. Bernard Baruch and later President Eisenhower suggested that atomic weapons be limited, but Russia refused to permit United Nations inspectors to watch to see if Russia kept its word and limited its supply of atomic weapons, and the other countries did not trust Russia to keep its word, so every country continued to build atomic weapons. See also WAR and WORLD GOVERNMENT.

Disciple, a follower of Jesus: see the article on APOSTLE.

Disciples of Christ

The Disciples of Christ are members of Protestant Christian Churches that together form one of the largest Protestant groups in the United States, with about two million members. They have called themselves simply "Christians" (because they do not believe in having different denominations or sects in Christianity), and they have also been called Campbellites because their early leaders were Thomas and Alexander CAMPBELL about whom there is a separate article.

The Disciples of Christ share basic Christian beliefs with other sects, but accept no creeds as conditions for membership in the Church. The Bible is considered the only guide for faith and practice, and each member has the right to interpret it for himself. They believe in the baptism of believers by total immersion. (See BAPTISM.) A group that was related to the original Disciples of Christ, organized as the Christian Church, merged with the Congregational Church in 1931.

discount

A discount is the amount of money that is sometimes taken off the price of things you buy. If you go to a store and buy a book that is supposed to cost one dollar and the storekeeper says you can have it for 90 cents, he is giving you a discount of 10 cents. In this case you would be getting a 10 percent discount. If the storekeeper charged you 85 cents for the book, you would then be getting a 15 percent discount. Every time you buy from a store that is having a "sale" you are getting a discount.

Retail stores and wholesale dealers make their profits from the discounts allowed to them by the manufacturers of the merchandise they sell. Usually a retailer gets a discount ranging from 40 percent on manufactured goods down to 20 percent on food. That is, if he sells a pair of gloves for five dollars he pays only three dollars for them. Out of the extra two dollars he pays his rent, the sales clerks' salaries, and other expenses, and anything that is left is his profit. A wholesaler, who buys larger quantities from the manufacturer and resells them to retailers, will receive an extra 10 or 20 percent.

Many businessmen allow discounts "for cash." The bill will usually have a discount printed on it. It may say 2/10 EOM, which means the customer may take 2 percent off what he pays the manufacturer, if he pays within ten days after the end of the month in which the bill is sent to him. If the customer does not pay his bill within the time given, he may not discount the bill (take off anything from what he pays). The reason discounts are given in business is to get people to pay their bills quickly.

Banks also use a form of discount. When you borrow money from a bank, you must pay interest on the money. Interest is what the bank charges you for the use of the money. If you borrow $100 from a bank, and the interest on the loan is 5 percent, the bank usually discounts the loan by taking off the 5 percent before it gives you the money. In this case you would receive only $95, and when you repaid the loan to the bank you would have to give back $100.

discovery and exploration

Exploring is going to a new place and looking it over thoroughly, so that you find out all there is to know about it. Every human being is an explorer. He starts exploring even in his childhood days. A city boy or girl who lives on a certain street wonders what the next street or neighborhood is like. One fine day he or she makes his way to that next street or neighborhood and finds out. A boy or girl living in a valley in the country wonders what things are like on the other side of the mountain that shuts him in. Sooner or later he goes exploring to find out.

Just wondering what things are like somewhere else is not the only thing that makes people go off exploring. In very ancient days, before there were cities, men lived in tents on great grassy plains. They raised cattle; the milk and meat of the cattle were their food. When their herds ate up all the grass in one place, no matter how well the people liked it there, they had to look for another place that had good grass for their cattle. They became explorers because otherwise the cattle would have died and they would have had no food.

THE WORLD GROWS LARGER

After men settled in cities and formed nations, the known world was a small place. The ancient peoples we know most about lived in such places as the valleys of the Tigris and Euphrates Rivers, the valley of the Nile, and in Palestine and Greece. What land lay beyond these places nobody knew. There were rumors that a great nation called Cathay (China) lay far beyond the deserts and mountains to the east. Strange tales were told of monsters that lived in the waters to the west and north. But nobody in particular did any exploring until the Phoenicians started doing it about 2000 B.C.

Phoenicia was a small country at the eastern end of the Mediterranean Sea. It did not have enough food for all its people or enough work for them all to do. To find new places for its people to live was one reason the Phoenicians went exploring. Another reason was to find people to whom they might sell the goods they made, such as glassware and dyed cloth. They built ships and sailed them westward on the Mediterranean, as well as to other places, looking for good locations for colonies and for people to trade with. They even sailed out of the Mediterranean, north as far as Britain, and south down the African coast. They started many colonies. The most important was Carthage, which was settled about 800 B.C. on the African coast of the Mediterranean, near present-day Tunis. Carthage itself became a great nation and sent explorers to the Atlantic coasts of Spain and Africa.

The Greeks, too, needed new places for their people to live and went exploring to find them. They settled colonies on the shore of the Black Sea, in North Africa, and on the island of Sicily.

Desire for new lands to rule was another reason that made people become explorers. Alexander the Great conquered lands little known to Europeans, such as Afghanistan and India, and in doing so found out many new things

about them. In becoming a great conqueror he had to become a great explorer too.

The Romans, the best fighters of ancient times, did a lot of exploring as they fought. They learned about the lands and peoples bordering the Rhine and Danube Rivers. Under Julius Caesar, they conquered Britain and explored and settled the country up to the borders of Scotland. By the time the Roman Empire was at its height, much more was known about the world than had been known when the first Phoenicians set sail to see what the world was like. And yet there remained a great deal to be explored.

Little of this was found out during the early Middle Ages. People were too busy trying to defend themselves from attacks by the barbarians to worry much about the outside world. Nevertheless at this time the Norsemen or Vikings of Scandinavia discovered Iceland and Greenland, and in the year 1000 actually found and explored parts of North America. A little later people all over Europe became explorers for a new reason. During the Crusades thousands of them armed themselves and went off to Palestine to take the Holy Land away from the Arabs. In traveling and fighting they learned a great deal about the lands of eastern Europe and western Asia. It was a religious reason chiefly that made explorers out of them.

Two Franciscan monks of the Middle Ages also became great explorers for religious reasons. In 1245 the Pope sent the Italian monk Giovanni de Piabo Carpini on an expedition to the Great Khan, ruler of far-off Mongolia, a part of China. Carpini was the first European to write a book about China. In 1253 the French monk Guillaume Rubruquis was sent by his king to central Asia. He explored many new places, converted many Asiatic people to Christianity, and wrote a great book about the new lands and peoples he had visited. The greatest explorer of the Middle Ages was Marco Polo, a Venetian. He went farther into Asia and lived there longer than any other European of his time. The book he wrote, called *The Book of Marco Polo*, made many other people want to become explorers. One of the people who read Polo's book and became excited by it was Christopher Columbus. You will find more about early exploration in the articles: PHOENICIA, CARTHAGE, GREECE, ALEXANDER THE GREAT, ROME, NORSEMEN, CRUSADES, and MARCO POLO.

THE AGE OF DISCOVERY

At the close of the Middle Ages, the people of Europe wanted to learn new things, enjoy new pictures and books, and eat new foods. Also they wanted to find new places, see new sights, trade with new peoples, or find new ways to reach the peoples of Asia with whom they had been trading for many years. From the end of the 15th century to the end of the 18th century more exploration and discovery took place than ever before in the world's history. This period is called "The Age of Discovery."

When that age began, ignorant people thought the earth was flat. If you sailed away from land and kept on sailing long enough, they thought you would get to the edge of the earth and fall off into empty space. It can be easily understood then, why sailors did not want their ships to get far away from land. Another reason was that once they were out on the open seas, far from land, they had no way of knowing in which direction they were sailing. Perhaps they were sailing toward land, perhaps they were heading for the edge of the earth. Toward the end of the Middle Ages, several instruments were invented or came into use by navigators that made sailing to distant places much safer. They were the *compass*, in which a needle always points north, and two instruments called the *quadrant* and the *astrolabe*, which enable a navigator to tell how far north or south of the equator he is. You can read more about these instruments in the articles COMPASS and NAVIGATION. When a captain and his crew set sail, they were sure that with the help of these instruments they would be able to return home.

THE ROUTE TO ASIA

There were other reasons why exploration was so important during this Age of Discovery. For about a hundred years the Europeans had been trading with eastern countries such as India and China. This trade was carried on partly by sea, and partly by land. The goods were loaded on ships that traveled across the Mediterranean Sea and through the Dardanelles, a narrow strait (passage of water) that connects the Mediterranean to the Black Sea. After the ships had crossed the Black Sea, the goods were loaded on caravans and carried thousands of miles across land to India and China. The traders exchanged their goods for spices, silks, ivory, and other rare articles from India and China, which too had been carried by caravans to the edge of the Black Sea.

In 1453 the Turks, a Mohammedan people, captured Constantinople, the most important city on the Dardanelles. The European traders feared that the Turks would refuse to let their ships through the Dardanelles. They were also bothered by many pirates in the Mediterranean and by bandits who attacked the caravans on land. If they could ship their goods all the way to the East by water, the shipping would be much less expensive and much safer. For these reasons the traders were very anxious to find a way to go to India and other Eastern countries by water. They began to send out explorers to find out if there was such a way.

One of the first to try was a Portuguese prince called Henry the Navigator. He did not do much exploring himself, but he sent out many ships to find a new way to the East. It was his idea that if a ship sailed down the west coast of Africa and around the southern end of that continent and then sailed north, it would get to India. Starting about 1420, he sent many expeditions down the west African coast. His sea captains discovered many new islands off the coast and many new places on the coast. Year by year they went further south. Even after Henry died in 1460, Portuguese expeditions tried to find that route around Africa to India. In 1498, Vasco da Gama finally sailed around Africa and then north to India. There was great excitement in Portugal and the rest of Europe when this news became known.

DISCOVERY OF AMERICA

A few years before this, there had been a discovery that was even more important. The Spanish, too, wanted to find that new route to India. In 1492 the King and Queen of Spain gave the Italian navigator, Christopher Columbus, three ships. They were called the *Pinta*, the *Niña*, and the *Santa Maria*. With these he set out to find a short waterway to the Indies. He did not try to reach the Indies by sailing around Africa, as the Portuguese were trying to do at this time. Columbus knew that the world was round. Since this was so, he thought, it must be possible to reach the Indies by sailing west from Europe. He was right, of course. You are able to get to Asia from Europe by sailing west long enough. But long before you reach Asia you reach another continent, North or South America. After sailing west for 69 days, Columbus finally saw land on October 12, 1492. He was sure he had reached the East Indies. He even called the natives Indians. But Columbus was wrong. This land was not part of Asia. These people were not Asiatics. He had found a new world—the Americas. For the story of how this new world got its name, read the article AMERIGO VESPUCCI.

After Columbus had opened up this new world, many new discoveries and explorations followed. In search of a passage to eastern Asia through the New World, Fernando Magellan sailed through the Straits of Magellan at the southern end of South America. Keeping on through the Pacific and then around Africa, his ships finally reached their home port in Spain. Magellan died on the way home, but his sailors were the first ever to sail completely around the world. This was in 1522. Sir Francis Drake, the great British sea captain, also sailed around the world (1577–80). Among the many places he explored on the way was the coast of California.

In the 17th and 18th centuries, exploration and discovery went on at a great pace. Driven by desire to find gold and to establish Christianity, Spanish explorers and soldiers conquered and explored most of Mexico, Central America, South America, and the southern part of what is today the United States. The English, Spanish, and French, the Dutch and Swedes, explored and settled different parts of both the sea coasts and the interior of North America. In the 18th century Captain James Cook, the most famous of Pacific explorers, explored part of Australia, New Zealand, Hawaii, the Bering Sea, and even the Antarctic Ocean. By the beginning of the 19th century the known world was indeed an immense place compared to what it had been in the days of Columbus. But even then there were many places in the world still unknown. For more information on the Age of Discovery read the articles on COLUMBUS, MAGELLAN, CORTES, BALBOA, PIZARRO, DE SOTO, PONCE DE LEON, CABOT, DRAKE, CHAMPLAIN, CARTIER, HUDSON, DUTCH WEST INDIA COMPANY, EAST INDIA COMPANY, and James COOK.

AFRICA AND THE POLES

One of the regions still unknown at the beginning of the 19th century was the interior of Africa. On the northern coast of this continent were lands that had been settled for centuries, such as Egypt, Cyrenaica, and Tunis. On the western and eastern coasts were settlements made by the Portuguese, Dutch, Spanish, and English for trading in ivory, gold, and slaves. But the interior of the continent was a mystery. Few Europeans except slave traders ever traveled inside Africa. The huge Sahara Desert kept those on the north coast from traveling south. Those on the western coast who tried to go inland found the hot, steamy, jungle and swift waterfalls blocking their way. Nevertheless, little by little brave men worked their way into the interior.

Mungo Park, a Scottish surgeon, was one of the first. He discovered one of the largest rivers in Africa, the Niger, and lost his life by drowning while trying to sail down the Niger to find out where the river ended. Another great explorer, David Livingstone, discovered the Zambesi River, the Victoria Falls, a number of lakes, and explored much other territory. Wherever he went he tried to put an end to the slave trade. The natives loved him and helped him all they could. Henry Stanley, a newspaper reporter, became interested in African exploration when he was sent to find Livingstone, who had disappeared into the heart of Africa in 1871. Stanley found him and then explored many parts of Africa himself. These three men are only a few of the hundreds of explorers who made Africa known to us in the 19th century. By 1900 most of Africa had been mapped out, and the great nations of Europe had colonies in every part of it.

While brave men were pushing through steamy jungles and over blazing deserts in Africa, other explorers were fighting bitter cold at the two ends of the earth, the North and South Poles. Two purposes led them to explore the regions around the North Pole. The first was the hope of finding a short way from Europe to Asia, either by sailing around Europe to the northeast, or by going northwest through some passage leading through North America. Many brave explorers lost their lives trying to find either the Northeast or the Northwest Passage. A Swedish explorer, Baron Nils Nordenskjold, was the first (1878–80) to make his way from Europe to Asia by going around the northern edge of Europe.

In 1853, a British explorer named Robert J. McClure discovered an all-water passage from the Atlantic Ocean to the Pacific Ocean, but it was unnavigable because of ice. The first to actually make the passage by water was Roald Amundsen, a Norwegian explorer, in 1903. In 1954, two United States "icebreakers" succeeded in going through McClure Strait, which had been named for its discoverer. Now Northeast and Northwest passages had been discovered.

Explorers tried for many years to reach the North Pole, and many failed. Finally in 1909 an American, Robert E. Peary, did it after a dangerous dogsled ride for five days over crackling ice. The South Pole was reached in 1911 by Amundsen, who got back safely and did much more

exploring. A month later an Englishman, Robert Falcon Scott, reached the South Pole but he and his party lost their lives in a blizzard on the way back. Advancements in science opened new ways for explorers. Admiral Richard E. Byrd used the airplane to reach both the North and South Poles (see ANTARCTICA). The American atomic submarines *Nautilus* and *Skate* both went under the North Pole in the Arctic Sea in 1958.

Scientists seeking more knowledge have been among the greatest explorers, even when their chief purpose was not to go where other men had never gone. Charles Darwin and Baron von Humboldt found places not known before because they wished to study plant and animal life. Vilhjalmur Stefansson discovered new places when he went to learn how people live. Auguste Piccard explored the air ten and more miles above the earth and ocean waters hundreds of feet deep, and William Beebe explored even deeper in the ocean. Roy Chapman Andrews went into deserts and jungles where no man had gone before to learn more about strange animals of the present day and the ages millions of years ago. Thor Heyerdahl sailed in a raft across much of the Pacific to find out if people living on Pacific islands came from South America. His book *Kon-Tiki* tells about it.

Many women have been famous explorers: Gertrude Bell, who explored the deserts of Arabia; Rosita Forbes, who did the same in the Sahara; and Osa Johnson, who with her husband Martin Johnson went far into Africa to photograph animals.

EXPLORATION OF SPACE

For hundreds of years, since first astronomy showed what the universe is really like, advanced thinkers among men have planned ways to reach the moon, nearby planets such as Mars and Venus, and someday perhaps the stars beyond. Since the end of World War II the two countries with the most money for research and the greatest number of scientists, the United States and the U.S.S.R., have each tried to outdo the other in exploring space. The Russians have usually been first with new developments, followed within a few months by Americans. Some original American developments have had more useful value.

The age of space exploration began when on October 4, 1957, the U.S.S.R. put the first artificial satellite into orbit. The United States succeeded in orbiting an artificial satellite on January 31, 1958, but it was a smaller one. After being first to test, with a dog named Laika, on November 3, 1957, whether space travel was safe for living animals, Russia was first to put a man into orbit. He was an Air Force officer, Yuri Gagarin, and he became a national hero in the U.S.S.R. The United States matched both feats not long after, sending monkeys named Able and Baker into orbit, after which an orbital flight was made by John H. Glenn on February 2, 1962. Men sent into outer space came to be called "astronauts." Russia put the first woman into orbital space flight. Her name is Valentina Tereshkova and the date was June 16, 1963. (See the article ARTIFICIAL SATELLITE.)

Russia was first also in sending spacecraft to the moon to photograph it, with the United States not long behind (see the article MOON), and Russia was first to have a man step out of a spacecraft into empty space and return safely to the spacecraft. The man was Aleksei Leonov and the feat was accomplished on March 18, 1965.

The United States led in making practical use of spacecraft by means of the "Telstar," which accepts and rebroadcasts radio or television signals, making possible television transmission throughout the world.

In 1969, the United States sent its Apollo 11 mission to the moon. Three astronauts, Neil A. Armstrong (civilian commander); Colonel Edwin E. Aldrin, Jr. his co-pilot (from the Air Force); and Lieutenant Colonel Michael Collins, command module pilot (also from the Air Force) were first launched into earth orbit from Cape Kennedy, Florida on the morning of July 16, 1969. They then blasted their combined command and lunar modules out of earth orbit and toward the moon. They entered lunar orbit on the afternoon of July 19th. On July 20th, Collins remained in the command ship 69 miles above the moon while Armstrong and Aldrin climbed into the lunar module, separated it from the command ship, and guided it to a moon landing.

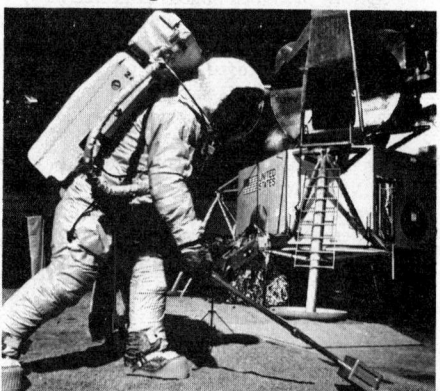

NASA

Apollo 11 Lunar Module Pilot Edwin E. Aldrin demonstrates the collection of samples of lunar surface material. Aldrin was the second man ever to step onto the surface of the moon, July 20, 1969. The first man was Neil Armstrong, who preceded Aldrin by 20 minutes.

discus

A discus is a piece of wood with a metal rim. It looks somewhat like a round, flat plate. The ancient Greeks began the sport of discus throwing more than two thousand years ago, and discus throwing is still one of the important events at the OLYMPIC GAMES. (You can read about this great sports competition between many countries in a separate article.) A discus weighs almost five pounds, and a person must have great power and skill to throw it well. The thrower must stand in a circle that is about eight feet wide, and throw the discus as far as he can. If you have the opportunity to watch a person throw the discus, you will see that he holds the discus in one hand, and swings it backward and forward to gather speed. Then he whirls in a complete circle, and throws the discus with all of his strength. The

faster he whirls, the farther he can throw the discus. There is a very famous statue of an athlete with his arm in position to throw the discus. This statue was made by Myron, a great Greek sculptor, and it is called the *Discobolus,* which means "discus thrower" in the Greek language.

disease

Any kind of sickness or illness is called a disease. A disease may be caused by tiny germs, called bacteria or viruses, that are attacking the body; this is called an *infectious disease.* Or it may be due to the fact that some part of the body is not built exactly as it should be; this is called an *organic disease.* Or it may be due to the fact that some part of the body is not working properly; this is called a *functional disease.*

There are other kinds of disease. All the different kinds will be explained later in this article. All of them are caused by something wrong inside the body. An injury received in an accident, or a wound received in battle or in a fight, is not called a disease, though of course it can cause just as much damage.

There are thousands of different diseases. Some of them are very serious, which means that they can cause death or some damage that can last the rest of your life. Some diseases are not usually serious at all, for example the common cold.

Disease has killed billions of people in the history of the world, but people living today have less to fear from disease than people who lived in any other age. Many diseases that once caused many deaths are almost unknown today; an example of this is smallpox, which is prevented by vaccination. Many diseases that once caused many deaths can now be controlled by drugs; examples of this are pneumonia and meningitis. There are still some diseases that scientists have not learned to control, but the number of them is reduced every year.

COMMUNICABLE DISEASES

A disease that can be passed from one person to another is called a communicable disease. All communicable diseases are caused by bacteria or viruses. When these attack the body or a part of the body, the body is said to be *infected.*

Sometimes the infection is likely to stay with the person who has the disease and not pass to others who are near him. In other cases a person who comes near him, or who touches something he has touched, may catch the disease. A disease that passes from one person to another is said to be *contagious.*

Influenza is an example of a contagious disease. It is caused by a virus, a tiny bit of living matter even smaller than the bacteria that can be seen only under a microscope. A person who has influenza may spread germs by coughing or sneezing, and another person may breathe them in and get the disease.

Yellow fever is a disease that is communicated in another way. A mosquito bites a person who has the disease, then bites another person and transfers the germ to him.

There are many diseases of this kind. Most of them are under control. Influenza stopped being so dangerous when drugs were discovered to cure it. Yellow fever was stopped by killing all the mosquitoes that carried it.

CONGENITAL AND HEREDITARY DISEASES

Congenital means "connected with birth." There are some diseases that a person gets before he is born, or due to some accident while he is being born. A "blue baby" has a congenital trouble with his heart and it keeps him from getting enough oxygen when he breathes. A "spastic" person may have had his nerves injured while he was being born.

A *hereditary* disease is passed along from parent to child. Not many diseases have been proved to be hereditary. The fact that a father has a disease of the liver or kidneys does not mean that his son is likely to get the same disease. Nevertheless, there are some diseases that are inherited. Just as a child might inherit a big nose from his father, he might inherit big teeth; and just as he might inherit small feet from his mother, he might inherit a small mouth; and if he has big teeth in a small mouth, it might cause a disease of the gums or bones. There are also some cases in which a child might have a hereditary weakness in his glands or heart or some other part of the body that will finally cause disease.

DEFICIENCY DISEASES

Some diseases are caused by failure to eat proper food. Among these diseases are scurvy, rickets, and beriberi. Through the study of these diseases, scientists found out about vitamins, because it is by not eating food that contains the right kinds of vitamins that people get these diseases. By eating the proper foods, people have almost eliminated these diseases. There are other cases in which proper diet (the right kind of food) cures diseases. Goiter, a disease of the thyroid gland, disappears when a person gets a bit of iodine in his food; anemia, a lack of red corpuscles in the blood, is controlled by a diet that includes liver.

DISEASES OF OLD AGE

The branch of medicine that studies diseases of old age is called *geriatrics.* For thousands of years it has been taken for granted that as a person grows older he will have certain diseases because parts of his body will become worn out and unable to work as well as they once did. Among these diseases are hardening of the arteries (arteriosclerosis), some heart diseases, and arthritis. Medical science has found no proof that diseases of old age can be prevented, but doctors do not agree that all of them are necessary.

DISEASES OF CHILDREN

There are some diseases that children usually get and grownups usually do not. Among these are measles, German measles, chicken pox, whooping cough, and mumps. None of these is often a dangerous disease. Diphtheria, which used to be a dangerous disease of children, is now prevented or cured by inoculation with an ANTITOXIN, about which there is a separate article.

One of the most dangerous children's diseases, infantile paralysis (poliomyelitis), was on its way to being conquered in 1955, with the development of a vaccine by Dr. Jonas A. Salk. By 1957, this vaccine had been proved to be so effective that polio no longer was considered the major threat to children.

MENTAL DISEASE

Mental diseases are a special class of disease. When a person is mentally ill his mind does not work properly. He may not understand things the way most people do, and he may imagine that certain things exist when they do not. A person can probably become mentally ill when there is nothing wrong with any part of his body; worry or some other feeling may cause his illness. The science that studies diseases of the mind is *psychiatry.* There is a separate article on MENTAL DISEASE.

FIGHTING DISEASE

The science of medicine is engaged in preventing disease before it can make a person sick, and in curing disease after it has made a person sick. In this work more has been done in the last fifty years or so than in all the other thousands of years of man's history.

Many diseases that killed people for hundreds of years seldom happen today because of preventive measures or are readily cured by new drugs or methods of operating.

Methods that prevent disease include vaccination and inoculation. Some drugs prevent disease, as for example quinine prevents malaria. Other drugs cure diseases, as for example penicillin or other antibiotics cure pneumonia. It is always necessary to see a doctor for the proper drug or treatment, but in most cases there will be one.

The best methods for combating disease are cleanliness and good habits (explained in the article HYGIENE) and regular examinations by doctor and dentist, about once every six months. There is a separate article about PHYSICAL EXAMINATIONS.

There are separate articles in this encyclopedia about nearly all the principal diseases, and see also the articles on MEDICINE, INFECTION, MENTAL DISEASE, and HUMAN BODY.

dish, a vessel that is used for serving food: see the articles on CHINAWARE and POTTERY.

disinfectant

A disinfectant is a chemical that removes something that might cause disease. Usually it removes bacteria (germs) or viruses, for these are living things that often cause disease. Another word for a disinfectant is *germicide,* which means "germ killer." ANTISEPTICS (about which there is a separate article) also kill germs, but an antiseptic is a drug that is put on a place that is already infected (attacked by germs), while a disinfectant is used to kill the germs before they can attack people. Cleanliness is the best defense against germs, so soap and water and sunlight are usually good disinfectants. A room in which a sick person has been used to be fumigated (which means "treated with smoke"), by burning in it a chemical such as formaldehyde that can kill many kinds of bacteria, but the modern method is simply to keep such a room clean and filled with fresh

air. Water used in swimming pools is often disinfected either by adding a small amount of a chemical called chlorine or by passing the water under rays of ultraviolet light from a special lamp, since these rays kill bacteria. Anything on which there can be no living thing that could cause disease is said to be *sterile,* and since boiling water can kill all disease-causing germs, surgeons' instruments are sterilized in boiling water before they are used.

dislocation is what happens when a bone in the body is put out of its correct relation with another bone in the body: see the article on FIRST AID.

Dismal Swamp

Dismal Swamp is partly in Virginia and partly in North Carolina. A swamp is an area of mud and water, with thick forests and dense underbrush. Dismal Swamp is about 25 miles long and 10 miles wide. Near the center, on the Virginia side, is Lake Drummond, which is about five miles long. The Dismal Swamp is only a few miles from the Atlantic Ocean, and the surface water is just about at sea level. More than two hundred years ago it was visited by William Byrd, upon whose land the city of Richmond, Virginia, was founded. About thirty years later, in 1763, George Washington helped to organize a company to drain the swamp. In 1828, a canal was opened, joining Chesapeake Bay with Albemarle Sound. The swamp is still being drained, and year by year it shrinks in size; some day it may be gone entirely. Dismal Swamp is the scene of a novel called *Dred,* by Harriet Beecher Stowe, who wrote *Uncle Tom's Cabin.*

Disney, Walt

Walter E. Disney is famous as the creator of Mickey Mouse, Donald Duck, and other characters in ANIMATED CARTOONS (about which there is a separate article), and also as a producer of movies that have won many prizes and always are interesting to both children and grown-ups. He also founded Disneyland at Anaheim, California, the world's most famous amusement park.

Disney was born in Chicago in 1901. He studied art in Chicago, then became an artist for magazines and newspapers. When he was 22, he went to Hollywood, California, and started to make his animated cartoons. The first one was *Oswald the Rabbit.* Next came *Mickey Mouse.* That little character became famous all over the world and audiences everywhere loved him. As Disney's cartoons became popular, he had to hire more and more people to help him. Now he has an enormous studio and hires hundreds of people.

Disney has made cartoons of many of the stories you have known all your life. Among them are *The Three Little Pigs, Cinderella,* and *Pinocchio.* His first cartoons were in black and white, but now they are always in color. His cartoon of *Snow White and the Seven Dwarfs* was the first full-length movie cartoon

ever made. Disney made another experiment with a movie called *Fantasia.* This was a combination of animated cartoons and great music by such composers as Beethoven, Stravinsky, and others. In the 1950s he began a series of motion pictures about animals and how they live. Some of these have been about seals, beavers, and the creatures of swamps, deserts and prairies. He died in 1966.

Disraeli, Benjamin

Benjamin Disraeli was a great British statesman. He was born in London in 1804, a member of a distinguished Jewish family. At first he studied law; then he became a writer. He wrote novels in which he gave his ideas on how the country should be governed. These ideas helped him win election to Parliament. When he made his first speech there, everybody laughed at him. He was dressed in very

Gale Research Co.

fancy clothes and kept using long, hard words. He had to stop his speech and sit down. But he was not discouraged. "You may laugh at me now, but some day you will listen to me!" he said.

He was right. He became the leader of his party, the Conservative Party. Finally he was made Prime Minister, the highest office in the country. He did everything he could to make Great Britain strong. He helped to raise the money with which Great Britain got control of the Suez Canal in Egypt. Most ships going from Europe to Asia must go through this canal, and pay a toll for doing so. He gave Queen Victoria the title of Empress of India. This showed the world that Great Britain was now a great empire. As a reward for all Disraeli did for his queen and country, Queen Victoria made him a nobleman with the title of Earl of Beaconsfield. He died in 1881.

distemper

A puppy should usually be lively and cheerful. If one day you see his eyes are dull, he does not want to play or eat, he coughs and sneezes and shivers and has a high temperature, take the puppy to a veterinarian (animal doctor) as quickly as possible. Probably the puppy has distemper, a disease like influenza in human beings, but much more dangerous.

Distemper is one of the worst diseases a dog can catch. Its cause is not known. Dogs from two to twelve months old are most likely to get it, although older dogs can get it too. Many dogs die of distemper, or of the pneumonia or convulsions that sometimes come with distemper.

To cure a dog with this disease the veterinarian will give the animal an injection. Then the dog should be kept in a dry, warm, quiet place. You may feed him simple food, such as beef broth, eggs, and milk. The disease lasts about four weeks. Even after the animal gets better, it is usually very thin and weak and should not run or jump too much.

A good way to keep a dog from catching this disease is to have it vaccinated when it is about four months old.

distillation

If a liquid like water is heated until

it boils, it will change into a gas. When this gas is cooled it will become a liquid again. Distillation is the name of this process.

When people talk of distillation, they usually mean the distillation of alcohol. Alcohol is usually made from a mixture that includes both alcohol and water. Alcohol boils at about 175 degrees, while water boils at 212 degrees. So the mixture is heated until the alcohol has all boiled away while all the water is left because the temperature has not yet reached 212 degrees. The alcohol gas is trapped and cooled until it is nearly pure liquid alcohol.

Distillation is also very important in the petroleum industry. Petroleum, which is the name of oil as it comes from an oil well, is a mixture of gasoline, kerosene, and a great many other chemicals such as tar and asphalt. In order to separate all the different things that are in petroleum, a special kind of distillation is done in a very large tower.

distribution

Distribution is a word that means the dividing of something among a number of persons, or even among places or things. For example, you can distribute books to several people, or a general can distribute soldiers along different parts of a battlefield, or you can distribute clothing among closets, dressers, and chests. In business, we use the word *distribution* to describe the movement of goods from the many farmers and manufacturers, through the stores, to the consumer or final user of the goods.

district attorney

In the United States, a district attorney is an officer of the government whose job it is to present and bring to trial the cases against people accused of breaking the law. United States district attorneys are appointed by the President and work under the Attorney General of the United States, the chief law-enforcement officer of the national government.

State district attorneys are usually elected by the people. They work under a state attorney general, the chief law-enforcement officer of the state government.

District of Columbia

The District of Columbia is the federal territory of the United States in which the capital city of Washington is

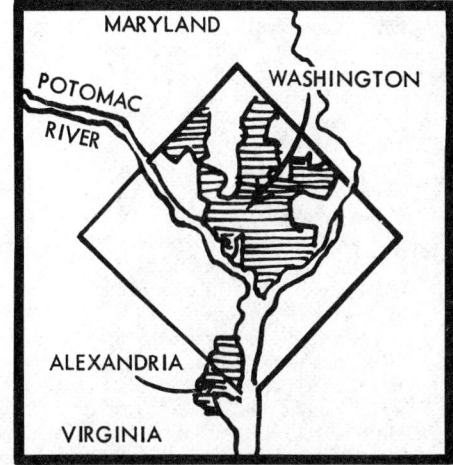

located. The Founding Fathers thought that the nation's capital should not be a part of any one of the states, and so Virginia and Maryland gave up some of their lands to make a separate territory. The District of Columbia was formed in 1790. About one hundred years later, the city of Georgetown in the District was made part of the city of Washington. Today when we speak of the District of Columbia and the city of Washington, we mean the same thing. You can read more about the territory in the article on WASHINGTON, D.C.

dividend

Dividend is a term used in arithmetic. It means the result when one number is divided by another. If you divide 10 by 2, the dividend is 5. You will often hear that someone receives a dividend from a company in which he owns a share. This means that the profits of the company have been divided among the owners of the company. Suppose the company makes a profit of $1,000 and there are five persons who own equal shares in it. The $1,000 profit is divided by 5 and each owner receives a dividend of $200.

divine right of kings

The divine right of kings was the name given to an idea that people used to have about government. They thought that in each country a certain family had been chosen by God to rule. The head of the family had the right to rule because God gave it to him. He should have complete power over all the people. No one had the right to criticize what he did, or to say that he was wrong. When he died, his son or some other member of his family should inherit his right to rule and his power. This idea was especially popular in England three hundred years ago, and in France two hundred years ago. Nowadays, not many people think that way. Most people today think that every ruler gets his power and his right to rule from the people of his country. Then the people have a right to criticize him, and to take his power away from him if he uses it wrongly.

diving

Diving is jumping into deep water. There are two kinds of diving. One kind is a sport. People practice ways of diving that are fancy or difficult or unusual. This kind of diving is described in the article SWIMMING AND DIVING. The other kind of diving is used for money-making or for science.

A diver goes under water to study the ocean bottom, to find gold and other sunken valuables, or to do work. Divers make underwater repairs, help build foundations for bridges, and repair damaged ships and cables. They are even helping us to learn more about ancient civilizations. In the waters off Greece, divers have found broken bits of pottery, money and other things in ships that sank thousands of years ago. These discoveries tell us about ancient peoples.

The first divers went under water with no special equipment at all. They just went under water and held their breath for as long as they could. A good diver can hold his breath for about four minutes. This is not long enough to do much

work under water, especially if the diver has to go down very deep. Four minutes, though, is plenty of time for a pearl diver or sponge diver to get down twelve or fifteen feet and do the work he has to do. A sponge diver goes down in shallow water with a knife between his teeth. When he gets to the bottom, he cuts the living sponge from the rocks and coral it clings to and comes right back up. A pearl diver, too, does not have to spend much time on the bottom. He dives in shallow water and cuts oysters loose from the rocky bottom. Then he brings the oysters to the surface and opens them there.

Divers using special equipment can go under water and stay as long as they want to. One man stayed in 40 feet of water for over 24 hours. Of course this takes some kind of equipment that lets the diver breathe under water, such as a diving suit and helmet. The suit is made of heavy waterproof canvas or rubber that covers the diver's whole body except his hands. A heavy leather belt is wrapped around the waist of the suit and lead weights are hung from it to keep the diver from floating to the surface. The neck of the suit has a metal ring around it and the diving helmet is screwed on the ring. The helmet looks like a brass fish bowl. It is round and has a glass front so the diver can see out.

An air-hose leads to the back of the helmet and air is pumped to the diver through the hose. When the diver breathes out, the air goes out through a valve in the helmet's top. This valve will let air out, but lets no water in. Sometimes a second hose leads to the helmet. It carries a telephone wire so the diver can talk to the people on the surface. Another kind of diving helmet does not need to have air pumped to it from the surface. The diver carries compressed-air bottles on his back and breathes the air from them.

SKIN DIVERS

For shallow dives of thirty to forty feet the diver does not need a suit. Diving without a suit is called skin diving. Skin divers just carry bottled compressed air on their backs, and breathe it from a hose they hold in their mouths. This is the kind of diving the Navy "frogmen" do. Many people skin dive for pleasure, too. They go to the ocean bottom in warm water to look at the beautiful fish and plants. They sometimes carry spears, which they use to kill fish for sport. The Navy uses divers for underwater salvage work, too. Some of the ships that the Japanese bombed at Pearl Harbor were repaired under water and made to float again. You can read more about this in the article called SALVAGE.

THE BENDS (CAISSON DISEASE)

Years ago, men working in diving bells and suits would get violently ill when they came up from great depths. (You can read about diving bells in the article CAISSON.) They would be in great pain and sometimes they would lose consciousness. This illness is called the "bends." People found that the great pressure of water more than 40 feet down caused a lot of gas that the body does not use to be put into the blood. When the

diver came up quickly, this gas formed bubbles which caused the pain. These bubbles caused by changing pressure are just like the bubbles formed in soda water when the pressure is changed by taking the cap off the bottle. People learned that divers have to come to the surface slowly in order to prevent the bends. Another way to prevent them is to have the diver breathe a mixture of helium and air.

divining rod

A divining rod is a forked or Y-shaped stick that is used to find water in the ground. Some people believe that the divining rod really works, but scientists think that if water is found with its help it is just luck. When a person wants to find water under ground so that he can dig a well, he sometimes hires a *dowser*. A dowser is a person who uses a divining rod. The dowser holds the divining rod in both hands so that the long part points straight out in front of him. When he walks over the spot under which there is water, the stick is supposed to turn all by itself and point to the ground.

division, a form of arithmetic: see ARITHMETIC and FRACTIONS.

divorce

When a husband and wife can no longer get along together and want to end their marriage, they often get a divorce. They must go to a court and prove to a judge that their marriage should not continue. If he agrees, he will grant them a divorce, which cancels the marriage and leaves both of them legally free to marry again. He may also award the wife money which is called alimony. There is a separate article about ALIMONY in another volume of this encyclopedia. A divorce is different from an *annulment,* which is a declaration by a judge that the marriage never legally existed at all. Divorce is a very serious thing and a husband and wife must have good reasons for wanting a divorce before a court will grant them one.

Dixie

The song named "Dixie" was the favorite song of the Confederacy, or Southern states, during the Civil War. It was written by Daniel Decatur Emmett in 1859, and there are several stories about the origin of the word Dixie. One story is that a man named Johaan Dixie, who owned land on Manhattan Island, New York, sold some slaves to a southern plantation. The slaves while working in the hot sun and remembering the easy life they had in the North, would sing: "I wish I was in Dixie's land." Another story is that ten-dollar bills printed in New Orleans had on them the French word *dix*, which means "ten." These bills were called dixies. The name Dixie came to be used to mean all southern states.

Dixiecrats, a name used for members of the STATES' RIGHTS Party.

Dnieper

The Dnieper is a river in Russia and it is the third-largest river in Europe. The Dnieper flows 1,400 miles south from the Valdai Hills that lie between Moscow and the Baltic States, and empties

into the Black Sea. On the banks of the Dnieper are many large towns and cities. Kiev, one of the oldest cities of Russia, with a population of nearly a million people, and Dnepropetrovsk, the capital of the Ukrainian Republic, are both on the Dnieper River. One of the world's largest dams, the Dneprostroy, is on the Dnieper. During the winter, the Dnieper freezes for about a hundred days and many people travel over it on sleds.

Dniester

The Dniester is a river in southeastern Europe, nearly nine hundred miles long. It flows from the Carpathian Mountains in Czechoslovakia to the Black Sea, which is between Europe and Asia Minor. A great many fish are caught in the Dniester, including carp, pike, and salmon. The fish caught in the river form an important part of the diet of the people who live in that part of Europe. The Dniester once formed the boundary line between Russia and Rumania. For many years after the Russian Revolution of 1917, armies on both banks of the Dniester patrolled its banks and prevented any trade between the two countries. In 1940 Russia took over that part of Rumania, and today the Dniester is entirely inside Russia.

Doberman pinscher

The Doberman pinscher is a fairly large dog that was bred in Germany about eighty years ago as a watchdog and guardian. It was such a good watchdog, and learned so quickly and easily, it was soon used in police work and later as a war dog in both World War I and World War II. Dobermans are kept in all parts of the world today both as pets and as watchdogs. They are fond of the children in their own family, and will protect their own people bravely at all times. Many Dobermans are used as Seeing Eye dogs for the blind.

The Doberman pinscher stands about 25 inches high at the shoulder, and weighs between 55 and 65 pounds. Its tail is cut off short, and its ears are clipped to make them stand up straight. You will recognize a Doberman by its reddish-brown eyebrows, throat, chest, and legs. The rest of the dog may be brown, black, or bluish black, but it always has the red markings.

docks and wharves

A dock is a water area in which ships can moor, or be made secure, in order to load or unload supplies or to be repaired. A wharf is a kind of platform, made of wood, bricks, stone, or some other material, where ships dock and moor. Some wharves are built along the shore; others stick out into the water. The water along a wharf, to which the ships come, is always a dock.

The opposite, however, is not true; that is, not all docks have wharves next to them. For there are several kinds of docks. The simplest kind, described above, is a *tidal dock*. It is found wherever the difference between the level of the water at high tide and at low tide is not very great, as in most ports along the Atlantic and Gulf of Mexico coasts of the United States. In ports which have a greater difference of tides, such as London, Cape-

The busy docks in New York City are used by large ships carrying people and products to and from all parts of the world.

town, or Hong Kong, *wet docks* are used. These are huge basins with high walls and a gate by which water can be let in or pumped out, so that ships can enter the dock or leave it whether the tide is high or low.

DRYDOCKS

A *drydock* is a special kind of dock used for repairing ships. It is a deep, wide trench dug in the earth next to a harbor, and lined with thick slabs of cement so that water cannot seep in when it is in use. It is connected to the harbor by a gate. When a ship is to "go into drydock" for repairs, the gate is opened and water from the harbor flows in, flooding the drydock. Then the ship is floated in through the gate. Finally, the gate is shut again, and all the water in the drydock is pumped out into the harbor, leaving the ship high and dry on blocks, ready to be worked on.

During World War II, our Navy developed huge "floating drydocks," strange-looking ships with hollow hulls that were capable of receiving vessels as large as a battleship for repairs.

doctor, a person who has a license that permits him to treat sick people: see the article on MEDICINE.

dodder

The dodder is a plant with thin yellow stems that twine around other plants. Because the dodder has no leaves, it looks like a tangle of yellow threads. You will often see dodders growing on hedges. The dodder is a *parasite,* which means that it feeds on the juices of other plants. The plant that gives a parasite its juices is called the "host" plant. The dodder gets its food by sending small roots into the stems of the host plant. Sometimes the dodder takes so much juice from the host that it seriously weakens or even

kills the plant. For this reason, in order to get rid of the dodder seeds, farmers sift the seeds of certain crops such as clover, alfalfa, and flax before planting them. The young dodder starts from the ground. It climbs up into its host plant and pushes its roots into it. Then it dies away behind. As it grows older, it produces masses of small white flowers. Dodders belong to the same family of plants as the morning glory. There are many different kinds, and they are found in countries all over the world.

Dodecanese

The Dodecanese are a group of small islands in the Aegean Sea, southwest of Turkey in Asia. Only about twelve of the islands are inhabited. Rhodes, one of the largest islands, is the capital. Most of the people who live in the Dodecanese are Greek, but the islands have belonged to many nations in the past. They were occupied for many years by Turkey, and after World War I they became a possession of Italy. However, in 1948, as a result of an international conference, the Dodecanese were given to Greece.

Dodge, Mary Mapes

Mary Mapes Dodge was a writer who knew the kind of stories that children like to read. Her most famous book is *Hans Brinker, or The Silver Skates.* This is a story about a little Dutch boy and his friends and how they live. There are sad things in the book, and funny things. The book has been translated into many languages, and children have enjoyed reading it very much. Mary Mapes Dodge was born in New York City in 1831. She wrote many stories and poems for children, and some stories for grownups, too. She was editor of a popular magazine, called *St. Nicholas,* for 32 years, until she died in 1905.

Dodgson, Charles Lutwidge

Charles Lutwidge Dodgson was the real name of the author of *Alice in Wonderland* and *Through the Looking-Glass*. Lewis Carroll was the name he signed to his children's books. Dodgson formed this pen name from his first two names, Charles Lutwidge, which are names that mean "Carroll Lewis" in other languages. Charles Dodgson's chief work was as a mathematician, or a person who deals with numbers. He lectured at Oxford University for 26 years and wrote books about all kinds of mathematical problems.

Lewis Carroll is known all over the world because of "Alice." The stories about the little girl who dropped down a rabbit hole were invented for a real little girl named Alice Liddell. When she and Lewis Carroll went rowing on the river he also told her stories of how Alice stepped through a mirror into a make-believe land where flowers talked. Many grownups enjoy the adventures of Alice even more than young people. That is because most of Lewis Carroll's nonsense books are *satires*. Satires are pieces of writing that poke fun at well-known people or famous authors or popular works of art.

There are several poems in *Alice in Wonderland*, all parodies of well-known poems of Carroll's day, and *Through the Looking-Glass* is a story of a giant chess game in which all the characters are part of the game.

Dodgson was born in Cheshire, England, in 1832, and died in 1898.

dodo

The dodo was a large bird that you might think was not a bird at all, for the dodo could not fly. The bird was discovered by Portuguese sailors in 1507, on Mauritius Island. This island is in the Indian Ocean, about 500 miles east of Madagascar, which is near Africa. When the sailors told about the strange bird that could not fly, you can imagine that people hardly believed their story. A few dodoes were brought to England in the 17th century, but no dodoes have been

seen alive for two hundred years. The settlers on Mauritius Island found the flesh of the birds so good to eat that they killed all the dodoes. Pigs brought to the island also preyed on the dodoes. This is the reason for the saying, "as dead as a dodo."

The dodo seems to have been of the pigeon family, and was almost as large as a turkey. It had thick, stubby legs, a tremendously big head, and a hard, deeply-hooked bill.

You may remember reading about a dodo in Lewis Carroll's *Alice in Wonderland*.

dog

Wherever you go you see dogs of every size, shape, and color. It has been estimated that there are about twenty-two million dogs in the United States alone. This means that just about every other family owns a dog.

BREEDS

There are more than two hundred breeds. There are more different kinds of dog than there are different kinds of cat, horse, or any animal that lives close to man.

Why are there so many dogs in the world? Because in return for its friendship, man has always taken care of the dog and let the number of dogs get bigger all the time.

The United States alone has about 115 pure breeds of dog. (This encyclopedia has an article on each important breed.) We say a dog is purebred if both of its parents were of the same breed, and their parents, and their parents' parents also. Of the twenty-two million dogs in the United States, more than four million are purebred. The rest are of mixed breeds, that is, one parent is of a different breed from the other.

Whether pure or mixed, all dogs have certain things in common.

All dogs have compact bodies and slender legs. No matter how much they differ in size, all dogs have the same number of bones in their body. Each front foot of a dog has five claws and there are four claws on each hind foot. Dogs are carnivorous, that is, they live chiefly on meat. They have many teeth, most of them growing very sharp in order to tear meat easily, the others used for chewing.

Nearly all dogs have large ears. They are able to hear many sounds that a man cannot hear. Their sense of smell is even better than their sense of hearing. However, their eyesight is not usually very good. A dog cannot make out one color from another. The world looks black or white or gray to them. There are no pores in a dog's skin by which it can perspire as a human being can. When it is hot, a dog pants. When it pants its tongue perspires and it cools off. The mother of a dog carries its young for sixty-two days. She gives birth to several at a time, called a litter. A dog is full-grown by the time it is two years old, and lives to the age of ten or twelve, sometimes even older.

FROM THE BEGINNING OF TIME

Scientists believe that dogs have been on earth for millions of years. Some scholars think that the dog originated from

two other animals that are like it in many respects, the wolf and the jackal. They think the first dog that ever lived had a jackal for a mother and a wolf for a father. Other scholars believe the dog came from some animal like the wolf, but not from the wolf itself. It is not likely we shall ever know the real origin of the dog. One thing we do know, however, is that hundreds of thousands of years ago, man tamed the wild dog and took it to live in his home with him. In those days that home was a cave. The dog guarded the cave, went out hunting with its master, and fought its master's enemies. How do we know this? Our chief proof is that in caves men used in the Stone Age, we have often found bones of men and dogs lying together.

All this was in prehistoric times, the period before written history began. When man began to write about his doings, he frequently mentioned the dog. The Egyptians used a large dog like our greyhound for hunting antelopes. Pictures of this dog, and others, have been found on Egyptian tombs five thousand years old. American Indians painted pictures of their dogs on their pottery centuries ago. The ancient Ethiopians respected dogs so much that once they chose a dog to be their king; they did whatever they thought it meant when it barked. The Greeks and Romans used dogs for hunting and as pets. In the Middle Ages knights kept packs of hounds to hunt the deer and fox. In modern times countless stories have been written about the dog, its usefulness, intelligence, faithfulness, and heroism. Anyone who owns a dog undoubtedly has a lot of similar stories of his own to tell.

THE KINDS OF DOG

The dogs of the world may be divided into two classes, the wild and the domesticated. Australia is the home of a wild dog known as the dingo. It preys on sheep, usually in packs. The wild dog of India, the dhole, forms a pack with others of its kind, and they hunt tigers. The African hyena dog hunts antelopes. Other wild dogs live in China, Japan, Burma, and Siberia. All these dogs look more like wolves than dogs. Unlike domesticated dogs, they do not bark; they howl instead.

It has been said that domesticated dogs learned to bark because they tried to imitate human speech. Of course we do not know this for certain. But we can be sure that most dogs love and admire their masters above anything else in the world. They are not happy unless they have a human master to whom they can be a companion and helper. Domesticated dogs are of so many kinds, and do so many different things for man, that it is easier to tell about them if they are divided into six groups.

1. *Sporting dogs.* These dogs are trained or bred to help in hunting small game, such as quail or geese. They do not actually attack the game. They only find where it is hiding and show their master where it is. Some do it by "pointing," that is, they stop short and become stiff with their nose pointing to the spot where the game is (pointers). Other sporting dogs also point their noses towards the game, but crouch or "set" as they do so (setters).

Am. Museum of Nat. History

The funny-looking dodo no longer exists, but once there were many of them on islands in the Indian Ocean.

Another type is used only to find game that has been shot and to bring it to its master (retrievers). Sporting dogs are also known as field or bird dogs.

2. *Hounds.* This is another kind of hunting dog. Instead of hunting birds, these dogs hunt wild animals, such as foxes. Sometimes they hunt alone, sometimes in packs. Some hounds trail their quarry by their sense of smell. They are known as "scent hounds." Others follow game by their keen eyesight, and are called "sight hounds."

3. *Working dogs.* This class of dog does all sorts of work for man. You may read more about this farther down in this article.

4. *Terriers.* These are small or medium-sized dogs once used to hunt small game. They were particularly able to dig rats and other such animals out of holes in the ground. The word "terrier" comes from the Latin word *terra,* meaning "earth." Today terriers are kept mainly as pets. Their small size makes it easy to keep them in small apartments.

5. *Toy Dogs.* The smallest dogs belong to this group. They are used only as pets. Some are merely small varieties of larger dogs. Others are definite breeds and no larger dog like them exists.

6. *Miscellaneous* or *Non-Sporting Dogs.* Most of the dogs in this group were once used for some kind of sport or work. Today they are used only as pets, with rare exceptions.

WHAT DOGS DO FOR MAN

No animal in the world does more for man than the dog. There is one group of dogs that performs all sorts of tasks for man. The collie, for instance, helps the sheep herder and cattle raiser with his animals. By day the dog keeps the livestock together as it grazes, and protects it from wild animals. At nightfall the collie drives the animals home.

In far northern countries such as Alaska and northern Canada, the Eskimo dog is invaluable to man. It leads its master to places where seals and bears are hidden, so that the master may kill them for food. When a man wants to travel in winter, he hitches a pack of Eskimo dogs to a long sled and the dogs pull him swiftly wherever he wants to go. Without the help of this dog it would be impossible to travel any distance in winter in those countries.

Policemen everywhere use dogs to help them. The principal breeds trained for this work are the German shepherd and Doberman pinscher. The police dog goes along with its master as he makes his rounds and protects him if someone attacks him. The dog also is trained to chase after people the policeman wants to catch for breaking a law. The dog will grab the suspected criminal and hold him till its master comes up. The bloodhound also is used by policemen. This dog has a sense of smell better even than that of most dogs. It can follow a trail by smell for as much as a hundred miles. It is used to find criminals who have escaped from jail, and also to find people lost in woods or swamps.

Dogs are used to help soldiers. They are trained to act as sentries, carry messages, bring medicines to the wounded, go on patrol with soldiers, find land mines, and even to attack enemy soldiers. In World Wars I and II thousands of dogs were used on both sides. The United States had a special name for its army dogs in World War II. They were called the K-9 corps, because another name for dog is "canine."

Dogs are used to save lives. The St. Bernard dog is trained to find travelers lost in the snow in the Swiss Alps. One St. Bernard dog named Barry saved more than forty people during his lifetime. The Newfoundland dog, a fine swimmer, has saved many people from drowning. Another wonderful thing the dog does for man is to act as guide for a blind person. This dog wears a special kind of harness which its master grips at the top. The dog is trained to conduct its master through crowded streets and traffic, and to take him to such places as elevators, subways, and classrooms. Such dogs are called "Seeing Eye" dogs. German shepherd dogs are the ones usually chosen for this work.

Other working dogs are the Belgian sheep dog, which takes care of sheep and is often used to pull carts; and the Dalmatian, which goes to fires with fire engines and often helps firemen save people from burning buildings. But even if a dog does no work and is only kept as a pet, it is very useful to man. A pet dog is a fine friend and playfellow for a child. An old or lonely person will have someone to give him companionship and love if he adopts a dog. In the United States few dogs do any work. It is because they make life so much more pleasant for everybody that they are kept as pets.

WHAT MAN CAN DO FOR A DOG

If you own a dog it is your duty to give it the best of care. The more you do for your dog to keep it healthy and well-behaved, the happier both you and the dog will be.

There are five principal things you must take care of for your dog: its food, shelter, training, grooming, and health.

1. *Food.* A pup feeds on its mother's milk for six weeks after it is born. When you start taking care of it, at this time or a little later, the pup needs a great deal of food. Until it is six months old it should be fed four or five times a day. Among the foods it may be given are milk and dry cereal, raw egg in milk, chopped beef or horse meat, and a small amount of cooked vegetables. A dog fifteen months or older should eat only one meal a day, towards evening. About one-third of a dog's daily food should be meat. Do not give your pet fish bones or chicken bones. They may splinter and get stuck in its throat or stomach. Also do not give it starchy foods (bread, rice, or potatoes); the dog cannot digest them. A pan of drinking water should be kept where the dog can get at it easily. The water should be changed frequently.

2. *Shelter.* Puppies should have a low basket or wooden box to sleep in. A blanket should be spread on the bottom. A larger dog should sleep on a blanket in a convenient place in the apartment or house, or in a kennel. It should never be permitted to sleep on a bare stone or wooden floor.

3. *Grooming.* A dog's owner should bathe his animal with water and a dog soap once every two weeks in winter and once a week in summer. Bathing takes away any smells the skin may have, and helps keep the animal free of fleas or mites. The dog should be brushed daily with a comb and brush. You should clean out your pet's ears every week or so with a bit of cotton soaked in camphorated oil, and now and then clean its teeth with a cloth soaked in salt water.

4. *Training.* The first training a pup should get is to relieve itself in the places you want it to use, not any place it chooses. This training is called housebreaking. Right after feeding the pup, place it on a floor that has been covered with newspaper, or take it outside the house. After the dog has finished, be sure to praise it highly. A young pup must be placed on paper or taken outside several times a day: right after it wakes up in the morning, after each meal, and just before going to bed at night. If your dog makes a mistake, do not hit it. Make it smell what it has done while you say sternly, but not angrily, "No, no, bad dog!" As a dog is always anxious to win praise, not blame, from its master, your pup will soon realize what is wanted of it.

A dog should also be trained to behave. It must learn to obey orders such as "Come!", "Stop!", and "Sit!" It must be trained to walk on a leash. When walking off leash, at its master's command "Heel!", the dog should come and walk at its master's left side and stop whenever he does. It takes common sense and a lot of patience to train a dog but the result is an obedient animal that will escape many dangers and troubles. In addition to training a dog themselves, some people take their dogs to a dog school once a week. There experts teach dogs how to obey, and their masters how to get obedience from them.

5. *Diseases of Dogs.* Dogs are subject to a number of sicknesses. The most serious are distemper and rabies. (Read the separate articles on DISTEMPER and RABIES.)

Pups often have worms. Sometimes you can see the worms in the dog's bowel movement. Sometimes you will know it has worms because the dog vomits a lot, and drags its bottom across the floor or bites at its tail in an effort to scratch or get rid of the worms. Do not try to treat a case of worms yourself. Take your pup to a veterinarian.

A common trouble of dogs is constipation. If your dog does not move its bowels for a day or two, feed him some milk of magnesia (a teaspoonful) before breakfast. Also exercise the dog more and mix a spoonful of mineral oil in his meal. If the constipation continues, take the dog to a veterinarian.

Fleas and lice sometimes get into a dog's coat and make it scratch a lot. The best way to get rid of these insects is to give the dog a good bath with dog soap. Ticks sometimes fasten on a dog's skin and will suck its blood. They must be found and pulled off one by one. Do not pull them off by hand. You may catch a disease from them. Use a pair of tweezers to pull them off, and then burn them.

Among other sicknesses of a dog are such skin troubles as eczema, mange, or ringworm. Or a dog may be poisoned by

eating rat or roach poison or by licking fresh paint. The best thing to do in all these cases is to take it to a veterinarian without loss of time.

TRIBUTE TO THE DOG

A dog is the most wonderful animal companion a man or boy can have. Many years ago Senator Vest of Missouri made a speech that tells what every dog owner feels about a dog. Here is part of that speech:

"The one absolutely unselfish friend that man can have in this selfish world, the one that never deserts him, the one that never proves ungrateful or treacherous, is his dog. A man's dog stands by him in prosperity and poverty, in health and sickness. He will sleep on the cold ground where the wintry winds blow if only he may be near his master's side. When all other friends desert he remains. When riches take wings and reputation falls to pieces, he is as constant in his love as the sun in its journey through the heavens. And when death takes the master in its embrace, and his body is laid away in the cold ground, there by the graveside will the noble dog be found, his head between his paws, his eyes sad, but open in alert watchfulness, faithful and true even in death."

dogfish

A dogfish is a kind of small shark. It has a pointed nose and rows of small teeth. Like a dog, it finds its prey by scent. There are many kinds of dogfish, the largest growing up to five feet in length. Most kinds are a sandy color or a dark grayish- or blackish-brown. Fishermen do not like dogfish because they eat large quantities of valuable fish. The flesh of dogfish is dry and rather stringy, but it is quite nice when fried. Sometimes shops cut it into little cubes and sell it as a substitute for scallops. On the Pacific Coast there are small factories that make oil out of dogfish livers. This oil is very nourishing. The skin of dogfish is very rough when you stroke it one way, but smooth the other way. This makes it valuable for polishing wood.

Dogger Bank

Dogger Bank is a big sand bar lying in the middle of the North Sea between England and Denmark. The bar is about 160 miles long and 40 miles wide. The bar does not stick up out of the water to making sailing there dangerous for ships, since 100 to 150 feet of water lie over it. Codfish are found in great numbers in these waters, and fishermen from England and Europe come here in boats to catch them. Several naval battles have been fought near the Dogger Bank. In World War I a British fleet won a big battle there over a German fleet.

dogtooth violet

The dogtooth violet is not a violet, but a kind of lily. It has a scaly bulb, out of which grow two glossy green leaves that are often splotched with brown. In spring a short stalk grows out between the leaves. At the end of this stem a single flower opens. The flower may be purple, white, or yellow, depending upon which kind of dogtooth violet it is. The dogtooth violets grow wild in moist woods

in the northern United States and Canada.

dogwood

Dogwood, or cornel, is the name of a large group of flowering trees or shrubs. They grow wild in North America, Europe, and Asia. One of the best-known kinds is the flowering dogwood. If you drive into the country in spring, you will see masses of its beautiful white or pink flowers by the roadsides or in the woods. Yet actually what you are looking at is not a flower at all, but a special kind of leaf that is colored white or pink. Four of these leaves grow in the shape of a cross. The real flowers are in the center, and they are small and not very pretty. Most dogwoods do not have these special leaves, so you scarcely notice when they are in flower. The cornelian cherry, which is grown in North America for its pretty scarlet berries, is another kind of dogwood. Its home is in Europe, and there the berries are made into jams and used for flavoring drinks. The fruit of the dwarf cornel, or bunchberry, is also very good to eat.

Sometimes dogwood bark is used for tanning leather or made into medicines. When quinine is hard to get, a substitute for it is made from the bark of the Florida dogwood. This is good for treating malaria and other kinds of fever. The wood of the Florida dogwood is smooth and close-grained, and is made into tool handles, golf club heads, and shuttles for weaving cloth.

The blossoms of the flowering dogwood tree.

doldrums

The doldrums are places in the ocean near the equator. There, at certain times of the year, no winds blow and the waters are entirely calm. In the days when ships used sails they depended on good breezes to reach the port. Sailors were very much afraid of the doldrums. Sailing ships that were driven into these perfectly calm parts of the ocean would sometimes drift helplessly in them for several weeks until a strong current of water, or an unexpected change of the wind, would bring them out of the doldrums.

doll

Dolls have existed as long as there have been people. Almost any material you might mention has been used at one

time or another to make dolls. There have been dolls of clay, rags, plaster, corn husks, wood, china, wax, papier maché (wet, shredded paper that is packed around a mold and allowed to dry in the shape of the mold), rubber, plastic, and many different combinations of various materials.

DOLLS IN HISTORY

Although most people have thought of dolls only as playthings, they are used for many other purposes, and have been since ancient times. The people of ancient Egypt made dolls to represent important people who had died. They also made dolls to look like the servants, friends, and family of the dead man. They buried these dolls with him, thinking that this would provide company for his spirit.

Down through the ages, dolls have been made to represent people, and often dolls have been used to raise money for various causes. A doll representing the wife of the famous Polish pianist, Ignace Paderewski, was made in 1917 and thousands were sold, with all the profit going toward the relief of Polish refugees.

There has long been a doll festival each March in Japan, where dolls are made to look like the emperor, the empress, and all their court. The clothes are beautifully made and carefully exact in every detail, because it would be disrespectful to the emperor if everything were not absolutely correct.

DOLLS AS AMBASSADORS

You can learn how people all over the world are dressed by means of dolls from each country, completely clothed in the costumes of that country. In fact, nearly every country makes many dolls in native costume, just so the rest of the world can become better acquainted with their people through the exchange of dolls. In toy stores you may see hand-carved wooden dolls from the wilds of Africa dressed in strange straw or leather clothes. These costumes would be actually what natives of that section would normally wear. Or you might see daintily dressed dolls from Holland in the elaborate, full-skirted costumes of that country, possibly wearing six or seven petticoats and a big ruffled hat or bonnet with embroidery and other ornamentation. At the same time, people in other parts of the world can learn what the American Indian looks like by means of dolls made in full Indian costume with feather headdress. People in other countries learn about Americans from their dolls.

VOODOO DOLLS

Although dolls are usually made for the pleasure of someone, there are places in the world where dolls are made for a very different reason. Certain savage tribes make dolls to look like their enemies. Usually they will imitate one particular feature of the enemy—a certain man's large nose, or another man's extra powerful arm, or something to make the likeness to a particular person very clear. When the doll is made, the witch doctor does something to it that would hurt a real person if the same thing were done to him. For example, he might break the doll's leg or arm, or stick a pin in its chest. According to the beliefs of some

tribes, this will make the person the doll represents hurt in the same place. Although this seems very foolish to people in the United States, many tribes believe that it actually happens. There are different names for this custom in different parts of the world where it is practiced, but the most familiar name is "voodoo."

DOLLS AS FASHION MODELS

Before the days of photographs and fashion models, dolls were used in France to show the new styles in clothing, hats, and jewelry. Doll makers of that time made beautiful dolls and dressed them in the latest fashion from head to toe. The model dolls were taken from town to town so the people in each place could know the latest styles. These dolls' wardrobes were very expensive, and everything was exactly the same as it would later be made for a real person to wear. Earrings, bracelets, pins, and ornaments were made in miniature, with real jewels. Even the underwear was exactly like the full-sized garment. In 1396, in the reign of Charles VI of France, a single doll's wardrobe cost 459 francs, which would be about the same as $1,000 in America today. Nowadays, women who want to find out what the newest fashions will be can go to fashion shows, where live models show the new creations. Back in the time of the French fashion model doll, there were no fashion shows, and the doll took the place of today's live models.

MODERN DOLLS AND THEIR CLOTHES

Until 1844, most dolls were made to represent grown people. There were men dolls, and women dolls, in full grown-up costume of the time when they were made. In fact, when the designers of costumes for motion pictures and plays want to be sure about how people dressed at certain periods of history, they often examine the clothes of dolls from those periods.

About 1844 the first known "baby" doll appeared, and it became popular very quickly. Eighteen years later, the first "unbreakable" doll was made in the United States. Before then, dolls' heads had been made of china or wax. The wax dolls grew soft if they were overheated by accident, and china dolls broke very easily. A doll of composition might chip, but it could be repaired. Now dolls are made that not only are unbreakable but are made of a material that feels almost like real human skin. In fact, dolls become more lifelike all the time. Today a little girl can have a baby doll that opens and closes its eyes, talks, cries, drinks water, and wears real diapers. If she likes a doll that looks more like a little girl than a tiny baby, she can have a doll with hair that can be washed, curled, and set in different styles. It can even be given a permanent wave and there are dolls' hair dyes, so that a little girl can change her blonde doll to a redhead or a brunette.

Of course, a doll's wardrobe can be as complete as her owner wishes. She may have playsuits, school dresses, party clothes, and bathing suits. There are complete bridal outfits for many dolls. A doll may have a beautiful white wedding gown with a veil and train, and a bouquet

A doll dressed as Elizabeth, wife of Edward IV of England.

Priscilla, one of the Pilgrims who arrived on the *Mayflower*.

Molly Pitcher, a heroine of the American Revolution.

Betsy Ross, who is supposed to have made the first American flag.

Martha Washington.

Mary Todd Lincoln.

of tiny flowers to carry for her make-believe wedding. Dolls also have nightgowns or pajamas, with bathrobe and slippers to go with them. Many little girls make clothes for their dolls, and learn to sew well in that way.

Not only can you make clothes for your doll, but you can make dolls for yourself as well. Rag dolls have been popular for hundreds of years, and they are easy to make. You may need help to make your first rag doll, but after that you can make more for yourself and as gifts for your friends. Even little boys may like dolls, before they grow too big for that sort of thing. In fact, many little boys have stuffed animals they take to bed every night. Soft dolls or stuffed ani-

mals made of rubber, plastic, or a waterproof material, are best for small babies, because very little children often chew on a doll. Of course it must be made of something that will not hurt the baby. Also, babies have a way of throwing things from their cribs or highchairs, and their dolls should be soft and unbreakable.

DOLLS SEEM LIKE REAL FRIENDS

Children usually name their dolls. Whether it is a stuffed animal, a rag doll, or a fancy walking, talking, crying doll, it will usually be given a name. Once a doll has a name it seems to become part of the family. The longer a little girl has a doll, the more she loves it. Even when

she gets a new doll, she still loves her old one. Sometimes grownups don't understand this, and they think she ought to be willing to give the old doll to some less fortunate child, especially when she has just received a beautiful new doll for Christmas or for her birthday. It is not that the little girl is selfish or greedy; to ask her to give away her dear old doll is almost like asking her to give up a friend. Soon, however, the new doll will probably seem just as dear, and then perhaps she will not mind letting some other child have the older doll.

If your doll is hurt, or accidentally breaks an arm or a leg, you can take her to a doll hospital. The experts in doll hospitals understand how important it is for a little girl to have her doll fixed, and they work carefully to make that doll look just the same as she used to look. There are doll hospitals all over the country.

DOLL-MAKING

Making dolls is a big business in the United States. Dolls may be only about an inch high, or they may be three or four feet tall. There are dolls to represent motion-picture stars and cartoon characters. There are dolls that look like famous people in the government or the army. There are dozens of different special dolls like these, and many thousands that are just dolls with no particular name and made to look like no one in particular. But little girls love them and give them names of their own. Not only are there dolls that walk and talk, but there are mechanical dolls that ride bicycles, do acrobatic tricks, and perhaps even operate tiny sewing machines. This is made possible by means of machinery inside the dolls that moves their arms and legs in the right direction at the right time. It is quite complicated machinery, but it is very easy to operate. All you have to do is turn a key somewhere on the doll, and it will keep on doing its tricks until the spring runs down—just the way the spring of a mechanical car runs down and makes the car stop until you wind it up again. Still other dolls sing songs, recite prayers, and say whole sentences. These have tiny phonographs or record-players built inside their bodies, which is where the sound comes from.

DOLL COLLECTIONS

For many years, Germany was the most important doll-making country in the world, and German dolls were beautifully made. They were elaborately dressed, and their hair was arranged in fancy, complicated styles with braids, curls, ribbons, and all kinds of expensive ornaments. If you happened to have an antique German doll now, it might be worth a great deal of money. There are many people who collect dolls as a hobby, the way other people collect stamps or coins, or antique furniture. Some doll collections are worth thousands of dollars. In most museums you can see antique dolls, and there are often special shows at which people exhibit their doll collections. The next time you see in the newspaper that there is going to be a doll show, perhaps you would like to see it, and look at the many different kinds of dolls that will be on display.

HOW DOLLS CAN BE USEFUL

Dolls are often very useful, in addition to being toys and collectors' items. Large baby dolls are used to teach young husbands how to hold and carry a baby, how to pick it up, and how to change its diapers. Then, when the mother gets home from the hospital with a new baby, he can help in taking care of it, and the doll will have helped him to learn.

Little girls can also learn a great deal through playing with dolls. They learn how to set a table and give tea parties, by playing house with a family of dolls around a small table, with a set of dolls' dishes. They even learn something about arranging furniture attractively when they play with the furniture in their dolls' houses. You can read more about dolls' houses and other playthings in the article on TOYS, in another volume of this encyclopedia.

Another kind of doll that has been very popular for years is the paper doll. Children cut paper dolls out of books or magazines, and have a great deal of fun dressing them in different costumes. They often make new and original dresses out of paper, as well as using the costumes that came with the doll in the first place. Making new clothes for paper dolls is very easy, and it is fine for playing indoors on a rainy day.

In fact, dolls give a great deal of pleasure to people of all ages. As long as there are children, there will always be dolls. And that is the same thing as saying that there will always be dolls.

dolomite

Dolomite is a rock often used for building because it has an attractive texture and can be polished to a pearly luster. Dolomite may be white, red, green, black, brown, yellow, or colorless. It is found in all parts of the world. Many famous buildings are built of this colorful stone. The Houses of Parliament in London are of gray dolomite which has darkened with the years. The stone was quarried in England. St. Patrick's Cathedral in New York City is of gray dolomite that was quarried in Westchester County, New York.

The Dolomite Alps, in northern Italy, are so named because they contain great quantities of dolomite. Some sections are red, some green, some brown, some yellow, because of the different colors of the dolomite of which they are composed.

dolphin

A dolphin is a kind of animal that swims in the sea and looks like a fish. But dolphins are not fish. They have babies and nurse them with milk, so they are mammals, just like dogs or cats. They have to come up to the surface of the water often because they breathe air. Dolphins are related to whales, but their closest relatives are the PORPOISES and the NARWHAL, about which there are separate articles.

There are many different kinds of dolphin. The common dolphin lives in herds in seas all over the world, though it is commonest in the Mediterranean. It grows up to ten feet in length, and has a mouth shaped like a short beak. It is usually black above, paling to white below. If you go for a sea voyage you will almost

certainly see herds of the common dolphin. It is a wonderful sight to see them plunging and playing in the water. They swim so fast that they can easily keep up with the ship. Often, just for fun, they will race the ship, swimming just beside the bow. Off the coasts of America you may easily see other kinds of dolphins, such as the bottle-nosed dolphin, the black dolphin, or the spotted dolphin. If you ever travel up any of the huge rivers in Africa, or India, or South America, you may even see dolphins that live in fresh water.

Dolphins can hear very well. Sailors say that they are so fond of music that they will come to swim beside a boat in which music is being played. Perhaps it is because they knew this that the ancient Greeks considered dolphins sacred to Apollo, the god of music. Sailors do not fear dolphins, for they never hurt men. In fact sailors consider them friends, and for thousands of years there have been tales of how dolphins rescued men from shipwrecks and carried them ashore on their backs. But these stories are probably not true, though there are wonderful and perfectly true tales of how dolphins have been friendly with individual men, or have guided ships through dangerous rocks.

Dolphins eat fish and other marine animals such as molluscs. They probably do some damage by eating herring and other fish we eat for food. The flesh of dolphins does not taste very good. The only people who eat it are the Laplanders who live in the north of Norway and Finland. Sometimes an oil is made from the fat of dolphins. It is used for lubricating delicate machinery such as watches.

The name dolphin is often used wrongly for a large fish called the coryphene. This is related to the mackerel, and lives in warm seas all over the world. Like the true dolphin, it is common in the Mediterranean Sea. When this fish dies it slowly changes its color, going through many marvelous hues. The ancient Romans loved to watch this sight at their feasts.

dome

A dome is a rounded cap on top of a building. It looks somewhat like a ball cut in half. Some domes are almost perfectly round, and others curve to a point.

Men have put domes on the tops of buildings for thousands of years.

St. Peter's cathedral, in Rome, Italy, has one of the most beautiful and famous domes in the world. It was designed by the great artist Michelangelo. The Pantheon, in Rome, was built about 1,800 years ago; it has one of the largest and

Italian State Tourist Office
The famous dome of St. Peter's at Rome.

finest domes in the world. The Capitol Building, in Washington, D.C. has a dome that rises high above the rest of the building. This dome is 90 feet across. Many of the state capitols in the United States have domes.

A dome is built by putting a number of arches together to form a VAULT, about which there is a separate article ·

Domesday Book

The Domesday Book is a set of two large volumes that contain a list of all the property owners of England in the time of William the Conqueror, almost nine hundred years ago. King William ordered his men to make this list because he wanted to collect all the tax money he felt the people should pay. He sent a group of men into all the districts of England, and they were so strict when they questioned people about what they owned that the people called it *Domesday*, which means "Day of Judgment," the day when God is supposed to question people about their sins. The king's men finished their list in 1086, and you can still see the Domesday Book in London.

domestic animals

Domestic animals are those that man has tamed and trained to provide for his needs. No one knows when a primitive man first captured a wild animal and tamed it for his own use, because even in prehistoric times people had domestic animals. Probably the first animal that people tamed, or domesticated, was some kind of cow, for the sake of the milk. It is also quite likely that people did not use domestic animals for food in those first days of taming animals. There was no need to do so, because men were hunters then, and there was plenty of game for their families to eat. As civilization advanced, however, people began to realize that animals were useful in many other ways, in addition to giving milk. Today people everywhere in the world keep domestic animals for different purposes. Some are kept to give milk; some to provide meat; some for the wool made from their hair; some for their hides; some for eggs, as in the case of poultry; some as beasts of burden, used to draw wagons and plows; and some as pets. Some are even kept to help man care for other animals, as in the case of sheep dogs, and still others are kept to help man in hunting.

Besides the domestic animals, there are some animals that people keep, feed, and protect, but never really domesticate. Animals that will stay at home even if they are set free are truly domesticated. This group includes dogs, cats, cows, pigs, sheep, goats, chickens, and horses. Animals that will run away if they are set free are only partly domesticated. This group includes rabbits, caged birds, hamsters, guinea pigs, pet mice, lizards, turtles, and pet monkeys.

DOMESTIC ANIMAL WORKERS

Since long before the time of Jesus, people have kept domestic animals to work for them. Pictures of oxen pulling plows in the days of ancient Greece, Rome, and Egypt show that man kept work animals in those days. All over the world animals are still used for that purpose. People of the United States and Canada use horses, donkeys, mules, and oxen. If you visited South America, in many sections you would see a strange kind of pack animal, a llama, used for carrying loads in the mountainous districts. In Europe, in northern countries such as Finland, Ireland, Northern Norway, and Russia, you would see reindeer working, pulling sleighs. The people of Asia and Africa use horses and donkeys as do the people in other parts of the world, but they also keep elephants, camels, and oxen for their heavy work. In Egypt, India, other parts of Asia, and on the Philippine Islands many people use the water buffalo to pull plows and wagons. Although a wild water buffalo is a dangerous and vicious animal, the tame ones are extremely gentle, and even a small child can lead them around without danger. Another strange animal used to carry heavy loads is the yak of Tibet. The people of this rocky and mountainous country depend upon the sure-footed yak to climb the steep hills where there are no real roads, and no rail lines.

ANIMALS FOR TRANSPORTATION

Long before there was such a thing on earth as a car, a train, or an airplane, people either had to walk from one place to another, ride on horses, camels, or other strong animals, or ride in carts or wagons drawn by such animals. Domestic animals were actually the first means of transportation that people had for land travel. Of course, they could use boats where there were waterways, but on land animals were the best means of transportation. Even in the days of the Old West in the United States, people crossed the continent in wagons drawn by horses, oxen or mules. In many countries of the world donkey carts, pony carts, and horse-drawn wagons are still used a great deal. In Arctic regions, dogs are an important means of transportation. During most of the year, the dog sled is the only practical way of getting around. In the African and Asiatic desert country, camels are as important to the people as dog sleds are important to people in the far north. The people of Belgium and the Netherlands use dogs to pull small carts.

DOMESTIC ANIMALS FOR FOOD

Various domestic animals are raised throughout the world for food. In some cases, the flesh of the animal itself is eaten. This is true of cows, pigs, sheep, poultry, goats, rabbits, camels, and reindeer.

These animals today are not very much like the animals of the same families in the distant past. When people started to tame and domesticate animals, they gradually improved and altered the breeds. If a man had a few cows that gave a great deal of milk, and were better-looking than the rest of his herd, he would keep the calves of those cows, and use the other cows' calves for meat. This way his herd kept getting better all the time, and then his son's and grandson's herds became better yet, and so on through the ages. A cow or a sheep, or any kind of domestic animal of today, looks very little like that same kind of animal as it might have appeared two thousand years ago.

Another great change in the world's manner of living came when large herds supplied many families with meat and milk, and one farm took care of many people who lived nearby. Raising domestic animals as a business became more important as time went by, and today is one of the most important industries in the world. The domestication of animals was an extremely important step in the advancement of civilization. Animals that could help in farm work made it possible for one farmer to do more and to grow more. As he was able to produce larger quantities of everything, other people were free to do different things, and different kinds of work—to make and build things, and to study and invent.

The meat-producing animals are useful to man in other ways. Of course, milk and eggs come from animals that are also used for their meat. Cows, goats, sheep, and reindeer give milk, while chickens and poultry lay eggs. The usefulness of these doubly valuable animals does not even stop there. The hides of most can be used to make leather. Goats, sheep, and rabbits have hair that makes wool, which is an additional way these animals are useful to man. Animals, and the products that are made from animal hair and hides, are responsible for the great leather, felt, woolen, and shoe industries. These are just a few of the world's developments that are directly due to the domestication of animals.

DOMESTIC ANIMALS AS PETS

As long ago as two thousand years before the beginning of Christianity, cats and dogs were kept by the people living at that time. They were sometimes pets, sometimes sacred animals in ancient religions, and sometimes they were used in hunting, as in the case of dogs. Man has done a great deal toward developing new types and breeds of both cats and dogs. Very few breeds today look as they did even a thousand years ago. Many kinds of dog have been bred for definite purposes, such as police work, trailing, hunting, sheep and cattle tending, guarding the home, and lately as dogs to lead the blind. Cats are kept in homes all over the world today, mainly as pets, although they do a useful work in killing rats and mice. There are many members of the cat family that have never been domesticated at all. Although they are often friendly and playful while they are kittens, such cats as tigers, lions, bobcats, and cougars become wild and dangerous when they grow up.

Birds as pets have been domesticated for centuries. However, they have to be caged or they will fly away and disappear. A bird that has been kept in a cage usually dies if it escapes, because it is not able to look after itself and find food, or to protect itself from its natural enemies. When an animal has been kept in captivity all its life, it seems to lose some of its natural ability to get along on its own.

Domestic animals in general are dependent upon human care and require it in order to survive. In return for the care man gives them, domestic animals supply people with food, clothing, countless industries, transportation, and beasts of burden to help man in his heavy labors.

domestic science, the science and art of making a home: see the article on HOME ECONOMICS.

Dominic, Saint

Saint Dominic was a priest of the Roman Catholic Church who lived about eight hundred years ago and who founded a great religious order, the Dominicans. St. Dominic was born in the year 1170 and founded his order in 1216, at the city of Rome. The purpose of the order was to protect the Church against heresies—beliefs that the Church did not approve. Dominicans wore black cloaks, and have often been called the "Black Friars." St. Dominic died in 1221. His feast is celebrated on August 4.

Dominicans have held many high Church offices, and four have been Popes. The order had several famous teachers, especially in the 13th century. The Italian painter, Fra Angelico, and Savonarola, the reformer of Florence, Italy, were Dominicans. So was the first American saint, St. Rosa of Lima, who died in 1617. There are also many Dominican Sisters, who spend their lives teaching, going on missions to spread the Catholic religion, and doing social work. The Dominican Order has members in many parts of the world.

Dominican Republic

The Dominican Republic is a small country that occupies almost two thirds of the island of Hispaniola. The remaining third of the island, which is to the west of the Dominican Republic, is called the Republic of Haiti. The entire island is often called Haiti instead of Hispaniola.

The island of Hispaniola is located between Puerto Rico and Cuba. It is the second largest island of the Greater Antilles, which is a group of islands in the Caribbean Sea. The Dominican Republic has an area of 18,700 square miles, and more than four million people live there.

THE PEOPLE WHO LIVE THERE

The first people to live on the island of Hispaniola were the Indians. Then, nearly five hundred years ago, Spanish colonists began to settle in the eastern part. This part of the island is now called the Dominican Republic. After the Spaniards arrived, they brought Negro slaves to the island to work in the mines and on the large plantations. Soon the three different races became mixed; now about 70% of the people of the Dominican Republic are called "mestizos," which means they are a mixture of the Spanish, Negro, and Indian races.

The language of the Dominican people is Spanish, but English is taught in all schools and is spoken by many people in the large cities. Almost the entire population is Roman Catholic, although there is complete freedom of worship in the Dominican Republic as there is in the United States and Canada.

The people of the Dominican Republic are mostly farmers or workers on the large plantations. Many are still poor and uneducated in comparison to the American farmer, but during the past few years they have made great progress. There are adequate hospitals, pure drinking water everywhere, and many new indus-

tries. Today, children are required to go to school and there is free education for both children and adults. However, it may still be some time before the Dominican Republic can be called a truly modern country like the United States or Canada.

WHAT THE LAND IS LIKE

Much of the Dominican Republic is mountainous, with deep valleys between the mountains and lowlands near the sea. In the valleys and lowlands the climate is quite warm, and the earth is very fertile. This is why the Dominican Republic is primarily an agricultural country. Sugar cane is the most important crop grown, but tobacco, cocoa and coffee are also cultivated. There are many minerals that can be found in the valleys and mountains of the Republic, especially salt, gypsum, bauxite (aluminum ore), gold, silver, copper, iron and nickel ores. However, mining is still very undeveloped, and it has only been during the past few years that steps have been taken to develop this industry.

HOW THE PEOPLE ARE GOVERNED

The people of the Dominican Republic are supposed to have a democratic form of government, with a president who is elected every four years, and a National Congress made up of a Senate and a Chamber of Deputies. Every person over 18 years old has the right to vote. The capital is Santo Domingo.

The main program of the government is supposed to be the education of the people and the development of the country. Some steps have been taken to create new industries and to modernize and develop mining so that a drop in sugar prices will hurt the country less than previously, but the fact is that the country has never had a truly democratic government that has done what it should do.

DOMINICAN HISTORY

Christopher Columbus landed on the island of Hispaniola in one of the earliest discoveries he made in America. His son Bartholomew Columbus founded the city of Santo Domingo before the year 1500. Within a few years many Spaniards arrived, hoping to become rich with large plantations and mines. They were very cruel, killing or enslaving many of the native Indians. Later Frenchmen settled the western end (now Haiti).

The people who have lived in the Dominican Republic have not had a very happy life at many times in the past 450 years. The early Spanish and French settlers did become very rich, and politicians who have ruled the people in the past hundred years also became very rich.

Pan Am. World Airways
This towering white monument in Santo Domingo is 200 feet high and was built to honor the renaming of the city in 1936.

After the year 1550, French and English pirates often raided the island and in one attack the English admiral Sir Francis Drake almost destroyed the city of Santo Domingo. Wars in which England, France and Spain were constantly fighting caused control of the country to change hands several times in the next 250 years. In 1801 TOUSSAINT L'OUVERTURE (see the article about him), after winning control of Haiti in a revolution, gained control also of the Dominican Republic. Sometimes the island was ruled by France, which called the island Saint Dominique, and sometimes by Spain, until they agreed to divide it into a French part, Haiti, and a Spanish part, Santo Domingo. In 1844 the Dominican Republic became independent but there were still times when Spain or the United States controlled it. At other times the people were under the control of dictators. There were frequent revolutions, but the people did not gain from them. A revolution meant only that power was transferred to another dictator. The most famous of these was Rafael Trujillo (see the article about him). After Trujillo was killed, the Organization of American States insisted on free elections. These were held in 1962 but the Dominican politicians, all eager for power, did not give a democratic government a chance. The first elected government was deposed by a revolution in 1963. In 1965 there was another revolution, this time with rioting and much bloodshed. The United States sent soldiers and marines to keep order, then the Organization of American States sent ambassadors to try to give the country a freely elected government and to prevent revolutions.

DOMINICAN REPUBLIC. Area, 19,333 square miles. Population (1973 estimate) 4,190,000. Capital, Santo Domingo. Language, Spanish. Religion, Roman Catholic. Government, republic. Monetary unit, the peso. Flag, two red and two blue squares formed by arms of white cross.

dominion

A dominion is an independent country that chooses to be closely and permanently allied with another country or

group of countries. The word, which is not used much any more, referred to all the countries which recognized the king or queen of Great Britain as their head of state. These countries are Canada (which, until 1949, was officially called the Dominion of Canada), Australia, New Zealand, Barbados, Fiji, Jamaica, Malta, Mauritius, Sierra Leone, and Trinidad and Tobago. They are said to have "dominion status" in the British Commonwealth of Nations.

Dominion Day

Dominion Day, July 1st, is the "birthday of Canada." It is a holiday celebrating the day in 1867 when the provinces of Canada were joined to make a dominion of the British Empire. The holiday is a quiet one, not like July 4, which is Independence Day in the United States. Students in the schools in Canada usually celebrate Dominion Day with Empire Day, May 24, because school is out before July 1. After World War II, the name of the holiday was officially changed to "Canada Day," but many people still speak of it as Dominion Day.

dominoes

Dominoes are little blocks of wood used in playing games. They are very old, hundreds of years and maybe thousands, and were invented by the Koreans or by the Chinese. Each domino is called a *bone,* and has two ends. Each end is either blank or is marked with one, two, three, four, five or six dots.

The most popular game to play with dominoes is called simply "Dominoes." You take all the dominoes (there are twenty-eight of them in a standard set) and turn them face down. Then you shuffle them—mix them around. Then

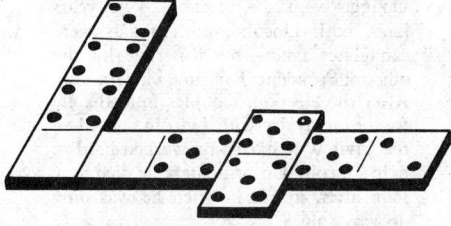

each player pulls out a number of bones (seven bones each, if there are two players) and puts them on their sides in front of him so that he can see their faces but his opponent cannot.

One player plays first. It is well to take turns playing first. He puts any bone face up in the center of the table. His opponent must now fit the end of a bone from his hand to an end of the bone on the table. The ends must match. If the first play was a 6–1, and he has a 6–4, he may play his 6 against the 6–end on the table. A doublet (both ends the same, as 6–6) is usually placed crosswise, and most persons play that you can play off its open side or off either end. When a person cannot play from his hand, he draws from the "boneyard"— the bones that were left over at the start —until he can play. The first player to have played all his bones is the winner. If no one has "gone out" in this way, and neither player can make any play, the game ends. Each player counts up all the spots on his unplayed bones. The one with the lower count wins.

Three or four may play. The turn to

play passes from player to player around the table. When three play, they start with six bones each; when four play, they start with five bones each.

Don

The Don is one of the great rivers of Russia. It is more than 1,200 miles long, or about the length of the Colorado River in the United States. If it ran in a straight line, it would reach from New York City to New Orleans, Louisiana. The Don flows from tiny Lake Ivan, near the city of Tula, to the Sea of Azov, which is really a gulf of the Black Sea. Many rivers empty into the Don. The largest is the Donets, or "Little Don," which runs through the rich coal basin called the Donbas. Russia gets most of its coal from this area. Boats can go up the Don about 800 miles from the sea.

Even though the river is often very shallow and is frozen over three or four months every year, it has more shipping on it than any other river in south Russia.

Many of the people on the banks of the Don live in fishing villages and fish for sturgeon, herring and salmon, which they ship to many other places. One of the world's greatest delicacies is caviar, made from the sturgeon's eggs.

When the Don river is frozen the fishermen catch fish through holes they cut in the ice. The fish freeze alongside the holes.

The fertile black soil of the Don district stretches out into long plains, called steppes, on which the Don Cossacks live and raise their fine horses and sheep. The Don Cossacks are among the best horsemen in the world. The land is also good for farming, and the people of the district raise large crops of grain, sunflowers, and tobacco. The seeds of the tall sunflowers are used for food, and the oil is pressed out of some of the seeds to be used for cooking. The largest city on the river is Rostov-on-Don.

Donatello

Donatello was the first great sculptor of Italy during the period called the Renaissance. His figures and statues have influenced every sculptor from Michelangelo down to the present day. You may have seen pictures of his most famous statue, David. Donatello was born in Florence in 1368. His full name was Donato di Niccolo di Betto Bardi. Before he started to carve figures, all statues had been very stylized, or unrealistic. He broke all traditions and rules and made his works lifelike. After 1425 he was influenced by statues that remained from great Roman sculptors. He did a statue of a warrior on a horse (called an equestrian statue) which is in Padua. It is considered to be the first bronze statue in the modern style. Donatello died in 1466.

Don Juan, or Don Giovanni

Don Juan is a legendary lover. His story is Spanish in origin. He is supposed to have been very bold and reckless. He made love to a great many ladies and then left them. As the most widely accepted story goes, Don Juan killed the father of one of the ladies in a duel. Months later, not feeling a bit sorry for it, he invited a statue of the father to come to dinner with him. The statue arrived

and dragged Don Juan down to hell in punishment for all of his past sins. Many authors and composers have liked the story of Don Juan and have written about him. Mozart wrote an opera called *Don Giovanni,* Richard Strauss wrote a tone poem called *Don Juan,* Molière wrote a play about him, and so have many others. Lord Byron's poem called *Don Juan* is also about a lover but not the legendary one.

donkey is a name for the domesticated ass. Its name comes from the word *dun,* which is the color of dull brown. See the article on ASS.

Don Quixote

Don Quixote is the title of one of the most famous novels in the world. It was written about 350 years ago by the great Spanish author, Cervantes. The hero of the novel is a somewhat odd country gentleman named Alonso Quijano who lived in the Spanish province La Mancha. He loved to read about the deeds of knights in the tales of chivalry, and one day he decided to imitate them. So he put on his great-grandfather's armor, mounted his bony old nag of a horse, and set off in search of adventure. He called himself Don Quixote de la Mancha. Accompanied by a simple-minded peasant named Sancho Panza, who acted as his squire, Don Quixote made himself ridiculous by pretending that the most common everyday things were exciting and romantic. When he saw a windmill, he pretended that it was a giant; but when he attacked it, his lance got stuck in an arm of the windmill and threw him off his horse.

Cervantes wrote about Don Quixote partly to make fun of people like him in real life who are too romantic. But the true greatness of his novel comes from the wonderful characters of Don Quixote and Sancho Panza, who represent much that is both silly and important in human nature. In many ways the character of Don Quixote resembles that of his creator, CERVANTES, whom you can read about in another article. The word *quixotic* is applied to anyone who, like Don Quixote, is too romantic and unpractical.

Doré, Gustave

Gustave Doré was a famous French artist who was born in Strasbourg more than a hundred years ago. When he was about fifteen years old, he worked as an illustrator for a French magazine of humor. He wanted to become famous as a painter of religious pictures, but although his painting was generally well thought of, his greatest fame came as a book illustrator. He was much better at drawing than he was at painting. He made illustrations for many beautiful editions of famous books, such as Dante's *Divine Comedy,* Cervantes' *Don Quixote,* Milton's *Paradise Lost,* and La Fontaine's *Fables.* He made one piece of sculpture that became very well known, a statue of the famous author, Alexandre Dumas. Doré was born in 1833 and died in Paris when he was 50 years old.

dormouse

The dormouse is a small rodent or gnawing animal found in Europe, Asia, and Africa. It is about the size of a squirrel, and although it is a closer relative of the mouse, it looks more like a squirrel. Its hair is silky, and its tail is long and bushy. It has a round head, with bright-looking black eyes. The dormouse sits up on its hind feet to eat, as a squirrel does, and it has the squirrel's custom of storing up food for the winter. How this food is used is hard to tell, because the dormouse hibernates for almost six months a year, simply sleeping through the cold winter like a bear.

Dormice almost never leave their homes during the day, and so comparatively few people have ever seen them. They became familiar to millions of readers, however, who were charmed by the sleepy dormouse in *Alice In Wonderland*, by Lewis Carroll. Dormice breed twice a year, and have two to four young in each litter.

Dorr's Rebellion

Dorr's Rebellion took place in the state of Rhode Lsland in 1842. It is called after its leader, Thomas Wilson Dorr. At the time of Dorr's Rebellion, Rhode Island had a constitution that had been drawn up nearly two hundred years earlier. This constitution was not democratic at all. Under it, a poor man could not vote, and small towns in the state had more representatives in the state legislature than did larger ones. Dorr led a revolt of thousands of citizens of Rhode Island who set up a new government with new laws. This government was put out by the United States Army, but the rebellion was really successful, because a new and democratic constitution was put into effect in Rhode Island in 1843, just after Dorr's Rebellion was ended.

Dos Passos, John

John Dos Passos is an American writer. He has written plays, novels and travel books. In his writing he is very realistic. He makes you think that you are part of the story and that what is happening in the story is happening to you. He draws a wide, sweeping picture of current events and puts his characters into those events. In that way he makes the events influence the characters. Two of his best-known books are *Manhattan Transfer*, and *U.S.A.*, which is three separate stories that make one big book. He was born in Chicago in 1896. He graduated from Harvard University in 1916 and has traveled all over the world.

Dostoevski, Fedor Mikhailovich

Dostoevski was a great Russian writer who lived about a hundred years ago. He understood people very well. He saw how a person can often do bad things, even though he wants very much to be good. He saw that the world can seem cruel, and that it can also be very beautiful. Dostoevski wrote novels that have become very famous. His best-known

Gale Research Co.

novels are *The Brothers Karamazov* and *Crime and Punishment*. Dostoevski had a hard life, and he described many of his adventures in books he wrote. As a very young man he was sentenced to be shot for plotting against the government, but at the very last moment he was pardoned. He was then sent to prison in Siberia, where he stayed for five years. Dostoevski was born in 1821 and died in 1881, when he was sixty years old.

Dougherty, Dennis

Dennis J. Dougherty was one of the few Americans who became cardinals of the Roman Catholic Church in the United States. Next to the Pope, the cardinals hold the highest offices in the Church. Dennis Dougherty was born in 1865, and studied in Montreal, Canada; in Pennsylvania; and at Rome. In 1903 he became the first American bishop to serve in the Philippine Islands. He was made Archbishop of Philadelphia, Pennsylvania, in 1918. An archbishop is the highest-ranking bishop. In 1921, Archbishop Dougherty was appointed a cardinal. The College of Cardinals then had 70 members chosen by the Pope, who is head of the Catholic Church on earth. (See the article on CARDINALS.) At Cardinal Dougherty's death in 1951, there were only three other cardinals in the United States.

Douglas fir

The Douglas fir is a large evergreen tree that grows in the northwestern part of the United States and in western Canada. It was named for David Douglas, a Scottish scientist, who first studied it. The trees are cut for timber and are used instead of pine in some sections of the lumber industry. Douglas firs grow to a height of 180 to 250 feet and may be 4 to 6 feet thick. The cones are 3 to 4 inches long, with forklike tongues that stick out between their overlapping scales. The needles are about an inch long, and are flattened and slightly twisted at the base. More than half of the timber in the western United States is Douglas fir. The cones of the tree are often used as Christmas decorations.

Douglas, Sir James

Sir James Douglas was the chief founder of British Columbia, a province in southwestern Canada. He was born in 1803, and in 1824 he organized the northwestern property of the Hudson's Bay fur-trading company. This company bought furs from the American Indians and from other trappers in the Northwest. Douglas started many forts to protect the fur-trading business of his company, and Fort Vancouver, his headquarters, is now the city of Victoria, British Columbia. In 1851, Douglas became the governor of Vancouver Island, which later was made a British colony. In 1858, he was appointed governor also of British Columbia. Douglas won the confidence of the Indians, and was fair with the white settlers who came into the region. He built many roads that helped the growth of

British Columbia. Douglas was knighted in 1863. He died in 1877.

Douglas, Stephen Arnold

Stephen Arnold Douglas was a great American political leader about one hundred years ago. He is remembered as one of the people who tried hardest to find a compromise between the North and the South that would prevent a Civil War.

Stephen Douglas was born in 1813, in Vermont. As a young man, he studied to be a lawyer. In 1833 he

Gale Research Co.

moved west, and settled in Jacksonville, Illinois. Douglas had always been interested in politics. In Illinois he became prominent very quickly as a lawyer and political leader in the Democratic Party. He held one important post after another, and in 1843 he was elected to Congress.

The greatest problem of that time was slavery. The South wanted slavery to be allowed to spread into the new territories that were added to the United States. The North thought that slavery was bad, and should be kept out. Douglas worked hard to try to find a compromise. He thought the most democratic way to decide would be to have "popular sovereignty." This meant that the people in the territories should be the ones to decide whether they wanted slavery. In the election of 1858, the two Illinois candidates for U.S. Senator were Stephen Douglas and Abraham Lincoln. In the campaign, these two men appeared together at public meetings to talk about the problem of slavery. These Lincoln-Douglas debates are very famous. Douglas won the election. Two years later, both Lincoln and Douglas were candidates again—but this time for the office of President. This time Lincoln won. After the election, Douglas immediately forgot his rivalry with Lincoln and when the Civil War started he worked hard to help Lincoln. Unfortunately he died very soon after, in 1861, when he was only 48 years old.

Stephen Douglas was a very short and frail man, but he had a large head, and a great brain inside it. For this reason, people called him "The Little Giant." Douglas was a very energetic and a very clever man. He worked all his life to help make his country united and great.

Douglass, Frederick

Frederick Douglass was a great American who was born a black slave and grew up to be a famous writer and statesman. He was born in Easton, Maryland, in 1817. When he was 21 years old, Douglass escaped from slavery and went to Massachusetts. He began to make speeches against slavery, and people who heard him respected him very much. Douglass wrote the *Narrative of the Life of Frederick Douglass*. This was his own story of what it was like to be a slave, and many people were affected by his book. Douglass was afraid he would be captured and sent back to the South, so he went to England, where he stayed for several years. When he came back to the United States, he had enough money to buy his freedom. He founded a news-

paper called the *North Star*. This paper printed many articles against slavery, and Douglass was its editor for seventeen years. During the Civil War, Douglass organized two regiments of black soldiers to fight for the North. After the war, he held many important jobs. In 1889, he was appointed minister to Haiti, which means he was the representative of the United States to the people of that country. Douglass died in 1895, when he was 78 years old.

dove

The dove is a small bird of the pigeon family. It is famous for its affection toward its mate. When one dies, the other mourns for a long time. The kind you probably know best is the mourning or turtle dove, which is brownish gray or white with lavender spots. Doves do much billing and cooing in the spring, when they are mating. This is what is meant when the Bible says, "The voice of the turtle is heard in our land." The dove is used as a symbol of peace, or for a person who is innocent, tender, and loving. Doves are found all over the world, but especially in the tropics, where they originally came from. You can read more about the dove in the article on PIGEON in this encyclopedia.

Dover

Dover is the capital of the state of Delaware. It is on the St. Jones River, which runs into Delaware Bay. The city is in a rich farm country, where peaches, strawberries, apples, and grapes grow plentifully. Farmers bring their produce to Dover. Some of it is canned or dried there, and the rest is sent fresh by railroad to all parts of the United States. Some of the people of Dover work in factories that make automobile bodies, baskets, and plumbing supplies. Many work at repairing airplanes. The state of Delaware is governed from the State House. This building, put up in 1722 and rebuilt later, is one of the oldest state houses in the United States. Dover was settled in 1717 and became the state capital in 1777. It is a beautiful little city with many churches and other fine buildings of the 18th Century.

DOVER, DELAWARE. Population (1970 census) 17,488. Capital of Delaware. County seat, Kent County. Settled, 1717.

Dover and Strait of Dover

Dover is a port city in England. It is also a very popular seaside resort. About 35,000 people live there all year round, but many more live there during the summer holiday months. The city is on a bay that lies beneath high white chalk cliffs that are among the most beautiful sights in England. Dover is the English city that is nearest France. It is separated from France by the Strait of Dover, which is only 21 miles wide, and which lies between the English Channel and the North Sea. Because Dover is so close to France, smugglers used to bring their loot into England across the Strait of Dover and hide it in the large caves under the chalk cliffs. During World War II the people of Dover used these caves as shelters against German long-range guns that were fired at Dover from German bases in France.

Doyle, Sir Arthur Conan. See the article on CONAN DOYLE, SIR ARTHUR.

Draco

Draco is famous as the first Greek writer of laws. He lived in Athens about 2,600 years ago. Before his time, the laws were not written down. The upper class ran the government. The rulers could do anything they wanted to. When Draco wrote down the laws, it was a good thing for the people. Then everyone knew what the laws were and even the rulers had to follow them. Most people think that Draco's laws were very harsh and cruel, because the punishment for most crimes was death, but that was common everywhere in those days. Draco did not make up those laws. He just wrote down the usual customs and rules.

draft

When a nation goes to war, it is often necessary to raise a large army in a short time. To get a great many men into the armed forces in a hurry, governments usually "draft" male citizens. This means that the government tells the person it drafts (the "draftee") that he will have to become a member of one of the military services, the Army, Navy, or Air Force, or the Marines or Merchant Marine. The draft is also called *conscription*.

It is illegal not to enter one of the military services when the government orders you to. A man who does not go into the service when he should is called a "draft dodger." Some people are excused from wartime service if they believe it is wrong to fight or go to war. They are called CONSCIENTIOUS OBJECTORS and you can read about them in a separate article.

THE DRAFT IN THE UNITED STATES
The first time a draft was used in the United States was during the Civil War. Both the North and the South drafted troops. Men were drafted again in World War I. President Wilson himself picked the first man to go into the Army. All the men of draft age had been given numbers. President Wilson reached into a fish bowl containing thousands of numbers and pulled one out. The men who had their numbers picked were the first draftees of the war. The next time America drafted men was in 1940, just before World War II started. This was the first time the United States had drafted men in peacetime. When the war was over, the draft was stopped, but it began again in a few years. When the Viet Nam War started, men were still being drafted. Because the government felt that a large Army was still necessary, today the United States has an all volunteer army.

See also the article on SELECTIVE SERVICE.

dragon

Dragons are mythical creatures that never really existed except in the imaginations of men. They were supposed to have been enormous in size, up to forty feet long. They had wings like a bird's, scales like a reptile's, claws like an eagle's, and long tails like an alligator's. They breathed fire. It was once thought that certain immense dinosaurs may have remained on earth until a few thousand

years ago, and were remembered by men, but geologists assure us that this is impossible.

According to an old legend St. George, the patron saint of England, slew a dragon. The dragon also figures in the early English poem *Beowulf* and the German legend *Nibelungenlied*. It is the national emblem of ancient China, and the emblem of Wales.

dragonfly

Dragonflies are insects that hunt insects. They prey upon mosquitoes and other small insects, which they catch and eat. A dragonfly can fly swiftly and overtake the tiny insects it wants to eat. It folds its legs into a basketlike shape, scoops up the smaller insects in flight, and devours them immediately.

Dragonflies lay their eggs on water plants in ponds, lakes, and swampy places. The young of the dragonfly is called a *nymph* or *naiad*, and lives under water. It is one to two inches long, and looks like a wingless grasshopper. The nymph destroys the larvae of various insects in the water, and sometimes devours very young trout or salmon, which are only a fraction of an inch long when they are first hatched. Some kinds of dragonfly are fully grown in a year, some not for four or even five years. When the nymph has grown to full size, it climbs out of the water and dries off in the air. Its shell splits open, and it emerges as a full-grown dragonfly, spreading its two pairs of stiff wings for the first time. It is brightly colored, and has eyes that can see in all directions at once. Its body is about two and a half inches long, and is thin, like a large needle. That is why it is also sometimes called the "darning-needle." It does not sting people.

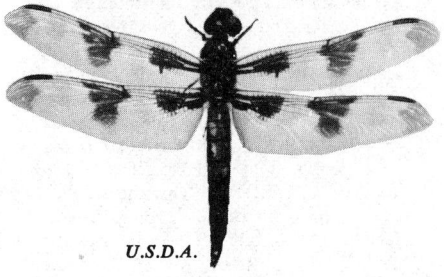

U.S.D.A.

Dragonflies have been timed at sixty miles per hour over a short distance.

dragon of Komodo

The dragon lizard of Komodo is the largest living lizard. It grows to a length of about ten feet, and is found on the island of Komodo, in Indonesia, and on several small islands in that area. Although this lizard has been known to the natives of its islands for many hundreds of years, and has been on the earth for countless thousands of years, it was not until 1912 that modern-day scientists first learned of its existence. A scientific expedition at that time made a blind behind which to hide, and left a herd of dead pigs and deer out in the open to attract the animals. The lizards appeared and devoured huge quantities of meat, swallowing bones and all. Ordinarily, they prey on the small deer and other small

animals of the islands. They live in sandy, rocky country, and sleep during the night in burrows under rocks or in the midst of tree roots. They are afraid of people, and are seldom seen unless elaborate traps are set to capture them.

Dragon lizards are not dragonlike in appearance, but look like any extremely large lizard with rough, scaly skin. The adults are a brownish gray in color, and the young have yellowish stripes on the tail and spots on other parts of the body which disappear as they grow older. Like the Nile monitor lizard, dragon lizards lay their eggs in the ground. It takes these eggs ten months to hatch, and the young break out some time in November.

drainage

When good farm land is covered over by water that keeps the crops from growing, the work of getting rid of the water is called drainage.

In most countries drainage is a very important activity, since there is seldom enough good farm land to go around. Luckily, most nations have millions of acres of seemingly worthless swampland that can be drained of their water and turned into rich farm country. In England, for instance, water keeps oozing up out of the ground from deeply buried wells and rivers, or collecting in great puddles after heavy rains. So farmers often build low fences of earth around their fields and then get rid of the water in ways we will describe further on. In Holland, the farmers have for hundreds of years built great walls (called "dikes") right in the ocean, just offshore, and then have pumped all the sea water out and used this "reclaimed" soil as rich farm land. The sea pushes and batters against these dikes, high over the farmers' heads, but Hollanders go on tilling the soil.

Another kind of drainage is used when you give your land a gentle slope, or slant, downward. Most major-league baseball fields, for instance, are built somewhat like a turtle's back, slightly raised in the center near the pitcher's mound, and gently sloping downhill past the foul lines. This slant helps the rainfall to "roll off the back" of the playing field. Too much rainfall is especially bad for farm land because it "drowns" the plant roots.

The soil that is just below the surface of the ground (it is called the *soil-root zone*) needs a certain amount of water, but too much of it is harmful. If you cut a ditch through gently sloping farm land, any extra water will drain off through this ditch into nearby wasteland. Such ditches are known as open-channel, or gravity, drains. Another way to remove water is to pump it out with gasoline or electric pumps, or even hand-pumps. Sometimes water collects on a farm because its drainage ditches get clogged up with soil ("silt"), and the water cannot flow through. In this case the silt is often blasted out with dynamite. Perhaps the best way to remove water from farm land is to put tile or concrete drainage pipes under the ground. Water collects in the pipes and runs off harmlessly.

Such a drainage system costs quite a lot; but it deepens the important soil-root zone, keeps water from washing good soil away from the land, helps the soil to breathe by allowing it less water and more air, and prevents the growth of mosquitoes in puddles of surface water. For these reasons, at least 99,000,000 acres of American farm land have installed drainage systems, and there are about 40,000,000 acres that badly need them. In addition, America has fully 25,000,000 acres of swamp land which will some day be "reclaimed" by drainage as rich farm land.

Drake, Sir Francis

Sir Francis Drake was a famous English seaman. He had an exciting life both as a privateer and as an admiral in the Navy, and he is one of Britain's greatest naval heroes. He was born in Devonshire, England, in about 1539, and was apprenticed to a shipowner. They sailed many times to France and Holland, and Drake inherited the ship after the owner died. He continued to sail, and Queen Elizabeth I gave him a commission to sail to the West Indies. It was the first of his privateering voyages. For years he raided towns, and raided other ships, and always brought home a rich cargo. Much of his loot went to the royal treasury, but he grew very rich also. One of his voyages took him completely around the world. He sailed to the West Indies, down around Cape Horn at the southern tip of South America, up the west coast of that continent, where he raided towns in Chile and Peru, and on up as far as San Francisco. He took formal possession of the land in the name of the Queen, and then set sail across the Pacific to Java. He went through the Indian Ocean, around Africa, and back home to Plymouth. This time his cargoes of booty were fabulous. Soon the Queen ordered him to destroy part of the Spanish Armada, which was then getting ready to invade England. He reached the port of Cadiz, in Spain, one morning, and by nightfall had destroyed a hundred ships. His booty was fabulous again, but he was not content, and sailed toward the Azores in the hope of encountering another ship to plunder. He was successful, and returned to Plymouth with a rich cargo. The grateful Queen Elizabeth rewarded him with the title of vice admiral under Lord Howard, in the fleet that scattered the Spanish Armada and broke Spain's naval power. You can read more about the Spanish ARMADA in a separate article. Drake had an important share in making the British navy master of the seas. He died in 1595 at Portobelo, Panama, and was buried at sea.

drama

A play that you see being acted on a stage (or that you may have acted in, as in a school play) is called a drama.

A drama may be a *comedy* or a *tragedy*.

A comedy is any drama with a happy ending, but a comedy is usually a funny play, written to make you laugh.

In a tragedy the hero dies, or at least there is an unhappy ending. Shakespeare's *Hamlet* is a famous tragedy.

When men began to live together in groups thousands of years ago, drama began. In those far away days they used to have tribal dances. Some of these dances were Death Dances. There was weeping and moaning and sadness. That was a form of tragedy. There were other dances of happiness and joy and thanksgiving. That was a kind of comedy. Hundreds of years later men began to put their feelings into words. These words were spoken by a few people for an audience. That was the beginning of drama as we know it today.

Many hundreds of years passed and these spoken words began to be written down and the written words were called a play. These plays were passed on from generation to generation.

DRAMA IN ANCIENT GREECE

The ancient Greeks loved to watch dramas. They built huge theaters out-of-doors and sat on stone benches while actors performed on a stage. The Greeks had both comedy and tragedy. They used to offer prizes for the best play written during the year, just as we do now in the United States. Some of these plays are still acted today and are considered very fine examples of comedy and tragedy. Aristophanes was a great Greek comedy writer. Euripides was a great Greek author of tragedies. Both of these men are called dramatists, or writers of drama.

The Romans expanded the Greek idea of drama. They added more actors to the plays and even had a few pieces of scenery, or backgrounds for the players. The Romans also loved the drama and went in for more elaborate productions.

MYSTERY AND MORALITY PLAYS

During the Middle Ages there was very little drama written or acted. The Church disapproved of plays unless they were based on religious subjects. There were bands of actors who went from place to place putting on plays that were called Morality or Mystery plays. Dramas showing scenes from the Bible were called Mystery plays. They were not like detective mysteries you see in the movies or on television. They were plays that depicted the miracles that happened in the Bible. Morality plays were always about Good and Evil and had a moral ending. That is, the ending showed why it was right to be Good and bad to be Evil.

THE RENAISSANCE PERIOD

The period after the Middle Ages was known as the Renaissance. During that period, which lasted several hundred years, the drama became much greater. Everyday problems were the plots of the plays. Everyday language was used to tell the story. This made the drama much more understandable to the audience. Sometimes weird and fantastic stories were used for pure entertainment. The man who combined all of these talents was William Shakespeare. He is the most famous figure connected with the drama.

MODERN DRAMA

During the 1700s most of the drama was comic. The tragedies of earlier days were repeated and revived, and many new

comedies were written. In the 1800s a new type of play called a melodrama was introduced. This kind of drama had a happy ending but there were many sensational events before the final curtain. Early motion pictures made in Hollywood were often melodramas with scenes which were thought to be very suspenseful. They often included train wrecks, burning buildings, runaway horses, stagecoach robberies, chase scenes, and duels. Sprinkled throughout the pre-Hollywood melodramas were songs, dances, and performances by musicians. In fact, the word melodrama means "musical drama".

In the twentieth century, drama is very realistic. The characters in the plays might be your next door neighbors. The Norwegian dramatist Henrik Ibsen was the first great realistic dramatist. Two modern realistic dramatists who wrote plays in English were Eugene O'Neill and George Bernard Shaw. See the article on THEATER.

drawing

Drawing is the art of making a picture. When you take a pencil in your hand and make the outline of a box or a cow or a tree on a piece of paper, you are drawing. Drawing is the foundation of all art. You have to be able to draw before you are able to paint. A sculptor has to be able to draw before he can carve a statue. An architect has to be able to draw before he can start to build a house.

Drawing seems to be almost an instinct. An instinct is something you do without being taught to do it. Every young child picks up a pencil or a colored crayon and starts to draw something without being taught to do it. Perhaps we can not immediately recognize what the picture is, but if the child tries again and again to draw the same thing, the picture will become better. Not all of us have an equal talent for drawing, but all have had the urge and the satisfaction of putting down on paper something we have seen. This is called an artistic urge.

EARLY DRAWINGS

Thousands and thousands of years ago, when the race of man was very young, people lived in caves in the hills and mountains. The urge and desire to draw was so strong in those cave men that they made pictures on the walls of their caves. They used charcoal to draw the pictures. Charcoal is a soft willow wood that has been burned. It is the oldest form of drawing material. The cave men drew pictures of animals. Recent discoveries of caves in Spain and southern France show that cave men especially loved to draw pictures of bulls and deer. These were animals that they knew and saw every day. Some of the drawings in these French caves show the animals running. They are very lifelike and real. It is amazing to consider that some of these pictures were drawn more than ten thousand years ago.

WRITING WITH DRAWINGS

As man began to grow up he began to use pictures for communication. Drawing was actually the first form of writing. If a man wanted to send a message to someone, he would draw a picture of what he wanted. Then men began to draw pictures to decorate public buildings. The ancient Egyptians used drawings for

decoration and for writing at the same time. These drawings are called *hieroglyphics*. If you were to go to Egypt you would see them all over the ruins of ancient buildings.

After writing was invented man continued to draw pictures for his pleasure. Many time these drawings were used for religious purposes. The Chinese and the Persians drew pictures of their gods and worshiped in front of them. The Greeks and Romans used drawings in their houses as well as in their temples. In the ruins of many ancient Roman cities you can still see beautiful drawings that were made two thousand years ago. You can still see the colors that were used and the heavy dark outlines of the figures.

From Roman times until today drawing has been part of our everyday lives. Not only do you have pictures hanging on the walls of your home, but you see drawings in magazines and newspapers, you see pictures in your class room at school, and you find drawings in most of the books you read.

LINES AND SPACES

The actual art of drawing is made up of lines and spaces. There are beautiful lines and there are ugly lines. A beautiful line is one that is smooth and graceful and reminds you of something lovely. Gentle curves and round lines are beautiful lines. Ugly lines are those that make you feel uncomfortable. They make you think of something unpleasant. Crooked or squiggly lines are not beautiful. Jagged lines are not pretty lines by themselves. They remind you of knives and broken windows.

Many times a line is beautiful or ugly depending on how it is placed in the space around it. A beautiful line can be made ugly by not giving it enough space to show off. Take a piece of paper and draw a circle. See how nice the circle looks all by itself on the paper. Now draw a square or a triangle as close as you can around the circle. You can see now that the circle has lost a great deal of its beauty and shape because it does not have enough room to show off in. So it is in all kinds of drawing. The line has to be given enough space to be beautiful.

ANATOMY

In all drawing the shape of an object has to be studied completely before it can be put on paper. This study is called anatomy. Anatomy is the knowledge of each of the little separate bits and pieces of an object, and their relation to one another. All of the little bits and pieces make up the structure of the object. In order to draw well you have to know the structure, or make-up, of an object, and in order to know the structure you have to know the anatomy, or the little bits and pieces. This sounds complicated, but it is not. You know when you look at a tree that it has roots and branches and leaves. When you look at the tree you study where and how the roots go into the ground. Then you study the direction that the branches take. You look to see where the leaves are placed on the branches. When you draw the tree you know that the whole tree is the structure. And you know that the anatomy is the

roots, branches and leaves, and how they flow into one another.

PROPORTION

When you are drawing a picture you have to study two other things before you start to put pencil to paper. One is called proportion. Proportion means the size of one object in relation to another. Let us pretend you are going to draw a skyscraper and a tree in the same picture. You do not draw the tree larger than the skyscraper, do you? The skyscraper is five times larger than the tree, so you draw the tree five times smaller than your drawing of the skyscraper. That is proportion.

PERSPECTIVE

The other thing you have to know about is perspective. Perspective is what gives the drawing a three-dimensional quality and makes it look real. It is the way you see angles meet that gives you a feeling of depth and distance. When you stand in the middle of a perfectly straight highway you will see how perspective works. The road is very wide where you are standing. As it goes off into the distance the sides of the road seem to come closer and closer together. Finally in the far distance the sides of the road seem to meet in a point. This gives you a feeling of distance and of depth.

Drawing is also a matter of light and shade. When the light falls directly on an area of an object, that area is called a highlight. The darker areas around it are called shadows. In drawing, the highlights are made lighter in color. This sets them off from the shadows, which are darker in color. Many people who draw make their most effective pictures by using highlights and shadows.

A sketch is a kind of drawing, too. It is a picture that is done quickly. All of the details are not filled in as they are in a regular drawing. Many painters make lots of sketches before they settle down to draw their pictures. In this way they can decide which one of several sketches is the best and will make the best finished drawing.

MATERIALS

Nowadays there are many different kinds of paper and cardboard that professional artists use for their drawings.

The first material that men drew pictures with was charcoal. Now there are many other drawing materials. An ordinary pencil is often used. There is a red chalk called Sanguin that makes very effective drawing (especially on gray paper). Another type of pencil is called silver point. It is a graphite pencil that makes a very silvery-looking picture. Pen and ink make a very definite line that is harder to handle. Many children love to use crayons made of a waxlike material, or they use colored chalks.

Drawing has become very popular in America in recent years. Many people have started to study drawing and have then gone on to painting and sculpture. It is a favorite hobby of many famous people. (See drawings on next page.)

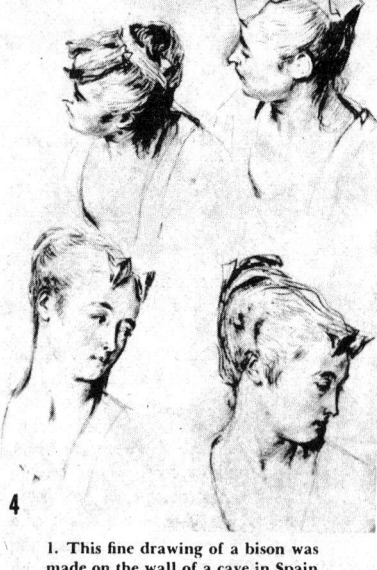

1. This fine drawing of a bison was made on the wall of a cave in Spain thousands of years ago.
2. A beautiful drawing by the famous German artist Albrecht Dürer.
3. A sketch by the great Rembrandt.
4. A head drawn in four positions by the French artist Watteau.
5. This drawing of a dancer gives one the feeling of motion and grace.

Rafaello Busoni

dream

Dreams are pictures and stories that go through our minds when we are asleep. All of us have dreams at one time or another. Sometimes we can remember exactly what we dreamed, and other times we know that we dreamed, but we cannot remember what we dreamed. No one is exactly sure how long dreams last. Most scientists think that dreams go on for a long time, others think that even when dreams seem to be very long, they are really short and take place just before we wake up. Dreams usually seem very real when they are happening, and for that reason people have been interested in them for many thousands of years. Until recently, people believed that dreams foretold the future, and that certain kinds of dream meant that certain things would happen. We know today that this is just superstition. Most scientists agree that dreams reflect the things that we think and want when we are awake, and instead of foretelling the future, dreams tell us something about our pasts. They therefore believe that they can learn a great deal about a person from his dreams. For example, if you are unhappy about something, you may have a bad and frightening dream, which is called a nightmare. The things that happen in your nightmare can give scientists a clue about what is disturbing you during the day and making you unhappy.

dredge

A dredge is a machine that digs up the ground under water to clear away sand and mud and rock and other materials. Most dredges are operated by electricity, and there are several different kinds. The dipper dredge looks very much like a steam shovel. It has a long boom, with a big dipper at the end, which can be lowered into the water from a barge. This dipper scoops up the material that is to be cleared away. Another kind of dredge is made of a series of buckets that are lowered, one after another, into the water, and each bucket scoops up some of the material. A suction dredge is especially useful in clearing away soft mud and sand. A pipe that is connected to a powerful pump is lowered into the water, and the mud and sand are pumped up through the pipe into a barge.

Dredges are used to clear and widen harbors and channels, so that boats can navigate easily. Dredges greatly helped the men who built the Panama Canal and many important harbors all over the world. The simplest dredge is the kind that oyster fishermen use. They make a large bag or net that is held open at the top by a metal ring. This bag is attached to a long pole that the fisherman holds while he drags the bag along the bottom of the sea, searching for oysters. The first steam dredge was invented by Oliver Evans, who also invented the steam engine, and it was used in the United States more than one hundred and fifty years ago.

Dred Scott Decision

Dred Scott was the name of a Negro slave who lived about a hundred years ago, before the Civil War in the United States freed the slaves. Dred Scott was the servant of a doctor in the United States Army named John Emerson; by the law of that time, he "belonged" to Emerson. In his travels, Emerson went from the "slave state" of Missouri, where he lived, to the "free state" of Illinois and to the "free territory" of Wisconsin, where slavery was not allowed. He always took Scott with him. Later, when Scott had been taken back to Missouri, he sued in court for his freedom. His reason was that taking him to Illinois, a free state, had made him free. Dred Scott began his lawsuit in 1846. It lasted for years and interested millions of people. The Supreme Court finally ruled, in 1857, that Dred Scott had no right to sue in the courts because he was not a citizen. He lost the case and remained a slave. Eight years later the Fourteenth Amendment to the Constitution wiped out slavery in the United States.

Dreiser, Theodore

Theodore Dreiser was a great American writer. His novels are very long and not very cheerful. His most popular book is called *An American Tragedy*.

Dreiser was born in Indiana in 1871. His family was very poor and very strict. He had a succession of jobs in many different cities, including editing magazines and working on newspapers. His first novel, *Sister Carrie*, was withdrawn shortly after it was published because some people did not approve of it. After that he had to work at many different jobs again before he had another book published. In his books and novels he expressed the idea that people are not always able to do what they want because things they cannot control work against them. *An American Tragedy* and *Sister Carrie* have

both been made into popular motion pictures. Dreiser died in 1945.

Dresden and Dresden China

Dresden is the capital city of the district of Saxony, in East Germany. Nearly half a million people live in Dresden, which is about as many as live in the city of Atlanta, Georgia. Many of the people of Dresden are skilled craftsmen, who make such things as optical instruments and machine tools. About two hundred years ago, Dresden was one of the most important art centers of Europe. In Dresden there were many beautiful cathedrals, castles, and museums, in which there hung some of the most famous paintings in the world. During World War II, most of these buildings were destroyed by Allied bombings.

Dresden is also the name of a very beautiful kind of porcelain called "china." It was not manufactured in Dresden itself, but in Meissen, which is a city near Dresden. For that reason, it is sometimes called Meissenware. It is made in lovely soft colors, and many of the pieces have delicate raised designs of flowers or of people. The best Dresden china was made during the period of Dresden's artistic importance.

dress, a kind of garment: see the article on CLOTHING.

dressmaking

Dressmaking at home is a pleasant hobby, and a way to have beautiful clothes without paying tremendously high prices for them. When a girl makes her own clothes, she can have just what she wants, in the color, style and material she chooses, made to fit her exactly. What is more, she gets a tremendous amount of satisfaction and pleasure from the fact that she "made it herself."

Although today it is possible to buy just about anything ready-made, this was not always true. Until about seventy years ago, women had to make their own clothes, unless they could afford to hire seamstresses or tailors to do it for them. There were no clothing stores where a woman could step in and try on as many dresses as she wanted to before deciding which one to buy. When most women needed dresses, they had to make them. Home dressmaking then was very necessary. It was also quite slow and difficult until about a hundred years ago, because there were no sewing machines, and everything had to be sewn by hand. That took a great deal of time.

If a mother had to keep all the members of a large family clothed, she could not make many dresses or suits for each one. In those days, styles did not change very fast. A dress was still fashionable after three or four years, and this was fortunate, since most dresses had to be worn for three or four years at least. Men and boys were expected to wear their suits and overcoats for several years, too, and when the older boys in a family outgrew things, the younger ones wore them. Younger sisters wore things outgrown by the older girls in the same way, and everyone tried to make clothes last as long as possible, because it was hard work to make new things.

HOW SEWING MACHINES HELPED DRESSMAKING

Today women make clothes for themselves because they can have more changes in their wardrobes, and spend less money than if they bought everything ready-made. Also, they can make things of better quality material than they could buy in ready-mades for the same amount of money. Now, however, they do not have to spend hours and hours for hand sewing. They simply use their sewing machines, and in a few hours the new dress can be finished and ready to put on.

When Elias Howe invented the sewing machine in 1846, he started a new way of life for women who had been slaves to the sewing box, needle, and thimble. Sewing machines made a tremendous difference in home dressmaking, even though those first machines broke down frequently and were hard to operate. On those machines, one hand was kept busy turning the wheel that moved the needle, which left only one hand free to hold the material and guide it for stitching. When Isaac Singer brought out the foot treadle machine, another big step forward was made in home dressmaking. The foot treadle type of operation left both hands free to hold and guide the material as it was being stitched. The latest electric machines are as much better than those early foot treadle machines as the foot treadles were better than the hand-turned wheel type. On a sewing machine today you can stitch as slowly or as fast as you wish—or you can stitch frontward, backward, sideward, or in zig-zags. With the help of the box of attachments that comes with every sewing machine, you can make buttonholes, ruffles, gathers, tucks, or pleats. You can hem, and put on binding tape, or you can embroider. It is well worthwhile to study what can be done with attachments. They can save you hours of time in hand-sewing.

PATTERNS AND MATERIALS

A person can make a dress even if she has never done it before by following the instructions on a pattern. The most important first step is to choose both pattern and material carefully. Some materials are unsuitable for certain patterns, and some materials are hard to work with. Some ravel badly, some are so soft they are hard to handle, and some are too stiff to fall into graceful folds when they are made into clothing. For example, you would not think of making a blouse of stiff upholstery material, or an evening dress of flimsy mosquito netting. That is an exaggeration, of course, but you can see how different textures and types of materials are suitable for somethings, but not for others.

When you start thinking about your pattern, you should keep in mind that the simpler the pattern, the more easily an unexperienced dressmaker can put it together. Many pattern companies have groups of patterns called "Easy to Make," or a similar name, which are designed for the beginner. Usually the pattern maker suggests materials suitable for the pattern you select. You will see a list of these suggested materials on the pattern envelope. It is wise to pay attention to those suggestions. The salesperson in the store where you buy your pattern will

tell you how to judge your correct size, and you should also pay attention to what she says. Do not assume that because you

Above: The diagram on the pattern shows how to alter hem and waist length.
Below: The same pattern size, with adjustments, will fit several different figures.

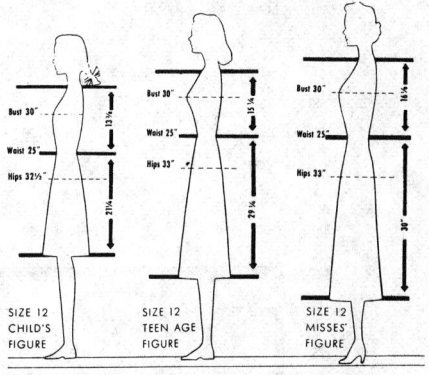

SIZE 12 CHILD'S FIGURE   SIZE 12 TEEN AGE FIGURE   SIZE 12 MISSES' FIGURE

wear a size fourteen dress that you should buy a size fourteen pattern. Commercial ready-made dress sizes are often different from pattern sizes. Let the woman in the store measure you, and give you the size you should have in that particular pattern. On the pattern envelope, it will tell how many yards of material you will need to make a dress in your size. After you have bought your pattern and your material, you are ready to start dressmaking.

CUTTING OUT YOUR DRESS

First, the material must be cut out. For this you need a large, flat surface, on which you can lay out the entire pattern at once. The pattern instruction sheet will include a diagram of where to place each individual pattern section on our material. Follow it carefully. Pin the pattern pieces in place, with ordinary straight pins, at intervals of no more than two inches around the edges. When you have it all carefully pinned in place, you are ready to cut. You will use either pinking shears or ordinary dressmaking shears. Pinking shears are useful if the material is inclined to ravel, and they also make an attractive seam finish even on non-raveling material. Either type of shears will do on most materials, however. Cut carefully, according to the pattern's

35" FABRIC ALL SIZES

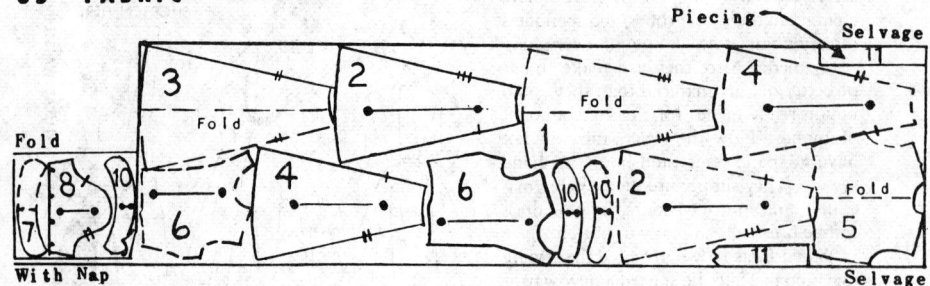

Piecing

Selvage

11

3

Fold

2

Fold

4

Fold

1

Fold

5

Fold

8

10

7

6

4

6

10 10

2

11

With Nap

Selvage

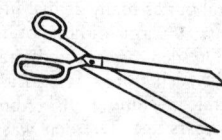

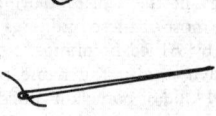

PLACE LINE ON FOLD

SEAM LINE

CUTTING LINE

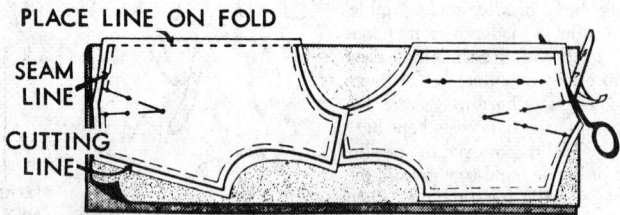

Above: Be sure to notice where the edge of a pattern piece should be placed in line with a fold of material.

Below: Marking darts, and stitching them carefully is important to the shaping and fit of your dress or blouse.

BACK DART

BACK DART

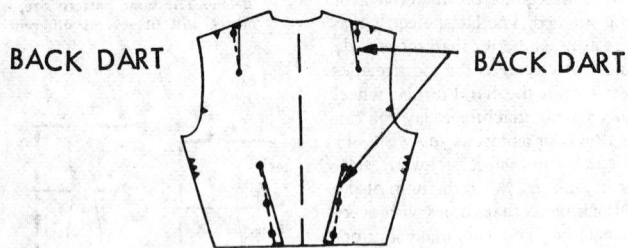

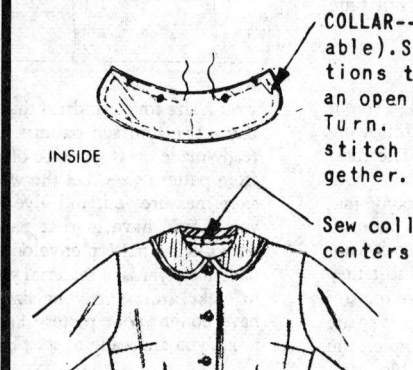

INSIDE

COLLAR--View A (Detachable).Stitch two sections together; leave an opening. Trim seam. Turn. Press. Slip-stitch open edges together.

Sew collar to neck edge, centers matched.

OUTSIDE

INSIDE

CUFF--View A (Detachable)--Stitch two sections together at upper edge and ends, continue stitching 1/4 in. from lower edge. Trim seam. Turn. Press.

Slip-stitch open edges together.

Sew cuff to sleeve facing.

instructions. Some patterns have a black line on which you are told to cut, and some patterns are cut exactly along the outside edge of each piece. Just be sure to follow the manufacturer's instructions, because otherwise you will cut the pattern either too small or too large for a good fit.

After you have cut out the entire pattern, you will have to make marks on the material wherever there are marks or little holes in the pattern. All of those marks are there for a reason. Some dressmakers use French chalk because it can be brushed off the cloth and leaves no permanent mark. Others run straight pins through the material to mark the places where the pattern has special markings. The notches in the edges show where one edge should be matched with

the other edge. A single notch on one edge will match the single notch on another piece's edge, and a double notch on one will match with a double notch on another. The dots on a pattern sometimes indicate the line on which your seams should be made, or they sometimes show you where to make a dart or a tuck, to shape the garment in spots where it should be curved to fit the shape of your body. Again, you simply have to follow the pattern directions carefully, and join the different pieces exactly as the instructions tell you.

FITTING AND FINISHING YOUR DRESS

Fitting comes after you have basted the first main pieces together, before you stitch them on the sewing machine. Slip the dress on, and see if the fit is right. You may prefer it to be a little more snug, or a little looser than it is. In that case, you put in a few pins to show where you want to have each seam, and then you take it off and put in new bastings where you have decided you want the seams. Then you stitch it up on the sewing machine, and put the rest of the pattern together. You will soon be ready for the finishing and hemming. Most finishing will be done automatically in the course of putting the parts of the pattern together in the correct order, but you may have to make buttonholes, or put in a zipper, or something of that sort. Also, you may have to face the neckline. That means you put in a small lining around the inside at the edge. The pattern will have a part marked "neck facing" if this is necessary, and it will tell you how to put it in.

Hemming a new dress is just like hemming anything else. Usually a pattern that has been put together accurately and carefully will have markings where you should turn up the hem, and this will usually make a perfectly straight hem on the skirt. However, if you are a little taller or shorter than the average, or if the pattern was put together a trifle unevenly, the hem may have to be measured and marked off by someone else. This is called hanging the skirt, and although it takes a little time, it is very easy to do.

Now your new dress is ready to be pressed, and ready for any special decoration or trim you want to put on it. A colored scarf, a few decorative buttons, a fancy belt, or an initial embroidered somewhere near the shoulder—any or all of these things are simple decorations, and you will probably think of many more.

You can learn to make beautiful clothes, and you can have the pleasure and satisfaction of knowing that you are well dressed at all times. No one else will have clothes exactly like yours either, because you will have made your own. Dressmaking is a wonderful skill for a girl to have, and one that she will enjoy throughout her life.

Drew, John

John Drew was a famous American actor. His family has been called America's Royal Family of the Theater. His father was a well-known actor, his mother was an actress and a successful manager of a theater, and his nieces and nephews were the famous Barrymores, John, Ethel, and Lionel. He was born in 1853 and ap-

peared when he was very young in his family's theater. He played opposite many of the famous figures in theatrical history, both in the United States and in England. Drew was very handsome and much admired by the ladies who attended matinees (afternoon performances) and was called a matinee idol. He is famous for his polished performances in modern comedies. He died in California in 1927. He was playing in a revival of *Trelawney of the Wells* at the time.

Dreyfus, Alfred

Alfred Dreyfus was a French soldier. He became famous, not because of what he did, but because of what was done to him. In 1894 Dreyfus was accused of having betrayed his country by telling certain secrets to the Germans. Dreyfus was tried and found guilty, and he was sent to Devil's Island. Dreyfus's family kept on saying that Dreyfus was innocent. After two years, some new evidence was discovered that showed that Dreyfus was really innocent, but none of the officials would do anything about it. A lot of honest people became interested in the Dreyfus case. They said that the reason Dreyfus was treated so unfairly was that he was Jewish. Emile Zola, a successful French writer, wrote an angry article against the French government, called "I Accuse." He accused the French government of anti-semitism (being against a person because he is Jewish). This article is still famous, and because of it Zola was put in prison.

Finally, after four years, Dreyfus was again tried, and he was again found guilty. Ten days later, he was pardoned by the French President. It was not until five years later that a thorough investigation showed that Dreyfus was so plainly innocent that no one could doubt it any more. Dreyfus was born in 1859 and died in 1935.

dromedary is the one-humped camel: see the article on CAMEL.

drowning

A person drowns when he cannot breathe because his head is covered with water or some other liquid. People have drowned in bathtubs, or some other unusual way, but most drownings happen when a person is swimming in an ocean or a lake or a pool. Swimming is a lot of fun, and very healthy, but it can be dangerous. Every summer people drown at beaches, because they are careless, and do not pay enough attention to the rules for safe swimming. One of the biggest reasons why people drown is that they get frightened, and begin to thrash around in the water, until they are too tired to stay afloat any longer. An important thing to remember when you are swimming is that if you relax in the water and stretch out, your body will float for quite a long time. When a person is drowning, there are some things that will help save his life. You can read about some of these things in separate articles on ARTIFICIAL RESPIRATION and FIRST AID.

drugs

Drugs are chemicals that are taken into the body for some useful purpose. There are thousands of different kinds and mixtures of drugs, and there are

many different reasons for taking them, but most drugs are used as medicines, that is, as remedies for illness. Drugs may be dry, as pills are, or liquids, or salves. They may be swallowed (taken internally) or put on the outside of the body (applied externally) or injected under the skin with a hypodermic needle. Most drugs, no matter how useful they are, can be poisonous if they are taken in the wrong way or if too much is taken, and there are very, very few cases in which it is safe to use drugs at all without the advice of a physician.

Drugs may be made from minerals, such as iron or mercury; or from plants; or from animals. There are separate articles in this encyclopedia about many different drugs and how they are made. There are also articles about MEDICINE and PHARMACOLOGY that tell more about how drugs are made and mixed and used.

HOW DRUGS WORK

There are three chief ways in which drugs can be useful in the body.

One way is by killing germs that cause disease. Iodine has this effect when it is put on a cut. It kills germs and keeps the cut from becoming infected. Drugs that kill germs in this way may be called antiseptics, or disinfectants, or germicides. They are never intended to be swallowed. Among the drugs that are taken internally to kill disease germs are the new "wonder drugs," or "miracle drugs," about which you can read in the article on ANTIBIOTICS and in other articles about particular antibiotics such as PENICILLIN.

Another way in which drugs work is by making some organ of the body work better, or work differently. An example of this use is an anesthetic, which deadens the nerves so that a person will not feel pain. Some drugs are stimulants, and make some part or parts of the body work more quickly. Other drugs are depressants, and cause some part or parts of the body to become less active, so that a person will be less nervous, or can go to sleep. The famous drug called *insulin* supplies to the body a substance that the body has become unable to make for itself.

In a few cases, drugs supply food to the body. Vitamin tablets are an example of this. The body needs vitamins, and sometimes a person does not get all the vitamins he needs from the food he eats. In that case he can take extra vitamins in the form of drugs.

There was a time when many people used the word *drugs* to mean only narcotics, which are habit-forming and very dangerous when they are not prescribed by a physician. A person who formed the habit of taking narcotics was called a "drug addict."

There is a separate article about NARCOTICS.

Druids

The Druids were priests in the religion of the ancient Celts. You can learn more about these people in the article on CELTS. The Druids had a very important place among the people. They were not

DRUM

528

only priests. They were also the teachers who educated the children. They were the scientists who studied nature, and scholars who knew all about the history of their people. They were sorcerers and practiced magic. Among some of the Celtic peoples they made the laws and acted as judges. All questions were brought to them for decision. Some of the Druids were called *Bards*. These Bards knew all the stories and history and poems of the Celts and would recite or sing them. The Druids worshiped the sun as their chief god. They also had other gods. They believed that when people died their souls continued to live in other bodies. The Druids did not have churches or temples. They worshiped outdoors, usually near oak trees. The Druids never wrote down their history and poetry and religious beliefs. These things were taught by the older Druids to the young ones, never put into books. It is too bad that they did this, because it would be interesting to know more about what they were like.

drum

The drum is the oldest musical instrument. Every primitive tribe had some form of drum, and almost every one of us discovered the drum as soon as we found that we could strike some object with another and produce a sound. The first drums were hollow logs or blocks of wood. The true drum is a frame over which is stretched a skin, or membrane, called the drumhead. Drumheads are made from the skins of calves and other animals. The first important use of the modern drum was as a military instrument, with drum and fife corps and other bands. Soldiers marching to a drumbeat do not tire easily.

In the modern orchestra there are the tympani, or kettledrums. These have definite pitch and can be tuned to notes of the scale. They look like huge kettles, over which are stretched calfskin drumheads. Some have screws to tighten the drumhead, and others have foot pedals, with which rapid shifts of pitch can be made. The bass drum, the snare drum or side drum, the tambourine, and the Chinese drum are also used in bands and orchestras. They belong to the percussion section. Each type of drum has a different type of drumstick and a different method of playing. Playing the drum looks easy, but no greater mistake can be made than to think it is. Good drummers must have an exceptional sense of rhythm, a good sense of tone color, and a high degree of control. A bass drummer, for instance, may have only one note to play in an entire concert; but it must be played at precisely the right instant, with perfect poise, or the whole concert may be spoiled.

Druses

The Druses are a religious sect of the Near East. Most of them live around the mountains of southern Syria. The Druses are named for their founder, the Syrian apostle Darazi. This sect first developed about nine hundred years ago. Its beliefs are a mixture of different things adopted mostly from the Jewish, Christian and Mohammedan religions. The Druses believe in one God, that things are always getting better and better, and

that the soul is born into another body after death. They number a little over 150,000. The land where most of them live is called the Jebel Druze, or Druze Mountains, located in southern Syria at the Jordan border.

Dryads

The Dryads were characters in Greek mythology, the stories the ancient Greeks told about their gods and goddesses. The Dryads were nymphs, that is, minor, or not very important, goddesses. The Dryads were lovely maidens who lived in trees. Each one was born when her tree was born, and died when her tree died. The Dryads loved to dance and sing in the forests. They were friendly to human beings, and were especially helpful to people who protected their trees. But people who destroyed trees for no reason at all were hated and punished by the Dryads.

dry cleaning

Dry cleaning is the process by which clothing and other materials are cleaned without the use of water. Because it was invented in France in the nineteenth century, it is sometimes called French cleaning. The reason that some materials are dry cleaned and not washed in soap and water is that water will shrink or change the shape of some kinds of cloth and soap sometimes will wash the color out.

When you send your clothes to the dry cleaner's he puts them in a machine that looks like a big washing machine. Instead of putting soap and water in the machine, he puts in a chemical "cleaning fluid," usually naphtha, benzine, or carbon tetrachloride. These all are clear liquids that look like water but that will dissolve greases and oils. If there are any grease spots on your clothes the cleaning fluid will take them out without hurting the cloth or fading the color. In the washing machine the clothes and the cleaning fluid are jumbled together until all the dirt is out. Hot air is forced through the clothes until they are dry. Then they are pressed and ready to wear again.

Dryden, John

John Dryden was a famous English poet who lived about three hundred years ago. He was very well known during his lifetime, and was made the poet laureate (chief poet) of England, and was chosen to be the special writer of the history of the king and his family. Still, Dryden's life was not entirely happy. His wife had a very bad temper, and the mar-riage was unhappy, although they had three sons. Also, during Dryden's lifetime, the English people were deciding what kind of government and what kind of religion they wanted. Many people accused Dryden of changing sides when it seemed the best way to take care of himself. After his death, people saw that this was not true, but during his life he had many enemies. This made him sad.

Dryden wrote many poems in a clever and sharp way that showed people some of the bad things that were going on in the country. These poems are called *sat-*

ires. He also wrote many plays that people still enjoy reading, although they are not acted on the stage so often now. One of the best of Dryden's plays is a comedy about marriage, called *Marriage-a-la-Mode.* Dryden was born in 1631 and died in 1700, when he was 69 years old.

drydocks are docks where ships are repaired: see the article on DOCKS AND WHARVES.

dry ice

Dry ice looks like a piece of ordinary ice that has been covered over with a coat of silvery-white snow frost. It gives off a thin white smoke. No doubt you have seen chunks of dry ice packed around boxes of ice cream sold in the summer by peddlers with bicycle carts. Dry ice is a gas called carbon dioxide that has been frozen solid. Because it is light in weight, much colder than ordinary ice, and melts away into a harmless, invisible gas, dry ice is widely used to keep different kinds of food from spoiling. However, no matter how cool and delicious dry ice may look to you in hot weather, it is not at all good for eating, and should never be touched with bare hands. Above all, do not put dry ice into a bottle and close it up, for the great amount of gas it gives off may burst the bottle and explode splinters of glass into your face and eyes.

Dublin

Dublin is the capital of the Republic of Ireland. It is on the central eastern coast of Ireland. It is the leading city of the country and is an important railroad center. All of the farmers for miles around bring their goods to Dublin's markets, which are very fine. Dublin is the headquarters of the Roman Catholic Church in Ireland. The city is connected with the River Shannon (spoken of by poets and song writers) by the Royal and Great Canals. It has fine large docks for commercial boats and passenger ships. Today more than 568,000 people live in Dublin.

In 150 A.D. the Romans and the Greeks knew that a small town existed where Dublin is now. St. Patrick is said to have gone there in the year 448. More than nine hundred years ago the Danes invaded Dublin, but in 1171 the English threw them out. Ever since then the story of Dublin has been a bloody one.

Throughout its history it has been involved in fights, battles and strikes to gain Irish freedom from England. In 1922 Ireland gained its independence and the treaty with England was signed in Dublin.

Dublin is the home of the National University and Trinity College, which was founded by Queen Elizabeth I. It has a beautiful cathedral. The famous Abbey Theatre was in Dublin. It was started by Lady Gregory, an Irish writer. The purpose of the Abbey Theatre was to encourage Irish writers. After it burned the Gate Theatre took over the work of the Abbey. Dublin is the center of culture and commerce in Ireland.

DUBLIN, IRELAND. Population (1973 estimate) 568,800; with suburbs, 650,200. Capital of the Republic of Ireland. Capital of County Dublin. Irish Sea port on the Liffey River.

duchy

A duchy, or a dukedom as it is sometimes called, is land that is ruled by a duke. The wife of a duke is called a duchess, and sometimes a duchess can rule a duchy in her own right. In Roman times, a military leader was called *dux,* the Latin word for "leader." Such leaders governed parts of the country and still later got to own much of it themselves. The importance of dukes at the present varies greatly. In Luxembourg it is the Grand Duke or Grand Duchess who rules. In England a duke is after a prince in importance. In Italy the title of duke is almost worthless, and a person can sometimes become a duke simply by buying certain pieces of land.

duck

Ducks are water birds, found in all parts of the world. They live on lakes, ponds, and rivers. Ducks have webbed feet, and are expert swimmers. They are also powerful fliers, and some breeds have been known to fly as fast as sixty miles an hour. In their wild state they are migratory birds, which means that they move in flocks from north to south in the fall, and back again in the spring. They fly in perfect formation, as if they were directed by a squadron leader. Some wild ducks in flight look like a giant letter V, and when the point of the V—which is the front of the flock—changes direction, the rest of the flock goes along without ever breaking formation.

Ducks are a domestic fowl as well, and are raised both for their eggs and for their meat. You can read about domestic ducks in the article on POULTRY, in another volume of this encyclopedia.

Wild ducks live on snails, water plants, and small insects. They sometimes dive under the surface of the water for food, and often go all the way down to the bottom of the river or pond to find favorite morsels. Ducks' feathers are covered with a natural oil that keeps the water from soaking them. You have probably heard the expression: "It rolls off like water off a duck's back." This is an accurate way of describing anything that refuses to stick, because water will literally roll off the duck's oily back feathers without soaking through to the downy undercoat that keeps the birds warm.

Among the most familiar kinds of wild duck in North America are the mallard, the canvasback, the green-winged teal, the redhead, the black duck, and the wood duck. Some nest in hollow trees, some on the ground near water in a place that is well protected by reeds or other plants. Baby ducks leave their nests when they are just a day or two old, and follow their mothers to the nearest body of water. They can swim immediately.

In the past hunters killed so many wild ducks that the government had to pass laws to protect them. The government also built shelters where the ducks could live safely, and make their nests. Many of the ponds and swamps that had been their homes were drained for building and land developments, and waterfowl were suffering because they had too few places for breeding and raising their families. Now they have plenty of ponds and lakes in which they are perfectly safe, and where the water is left undisturbed.

Baby ducks can swim when they are just a day or two old.

duckbill, another name for the platypus: see the article PLATYPUS.

duel

A duel is a fight between two persons, usually men, over a point of honor. The custom is now illegal in all civilized countries, but less than one hundred years ago it was widespread in Europe and America. A general custom was for friends of the injured, or insulted party, to act as seconds and challenge the person who had caused the insult or injury. That person had to accept the challenge or suffer dishonor and be thought a coward. He was permitted a choice of weapons, either swords or pistols, and then selected friends to act as his seconds. The seconds of both parties made all arrangements, and at an appointed time the challenger and the challenged party met for the duel. The intention was usually to draw blood, after which the offended challenger considered his honor avenged, and the fight stopped. Occasionally, however, one or both of the duelists were killed.

dugong

The dugong is a large mammal like a seal that lives in the water. A mammal is an animal that gives birth to live babies, and that nurses its young. The dugong has one pair of short flippers for front limbs, and a flat, broad paddle tail. The full-grown male reaches about nine feet in length. Dugongs have a thick hide and blubber of fat underneath it that altogether is about an inch deep. Their tusks keep growing all during their life, and they are hunted for their hide, tusks, oil and meat. There are not any dugongs in America, for they live in warm coastal waters of the East, from the Red Sea near Arabia to the Indian Ocean, and around northern Australia. The Australian natives catch the dugong with a harpoon, which is like a spear attached to a rope, and then they put wooden plugs in its nostrils to stop its breathing. The dugong does not seem to be able to breathe through its mouth, so it suffocates. The Israelites in Bible times are said to have covered the Ark of the Covenant with dugong skins. The Ark of the Covenant carried the laws God gave to Moses.

Dukhobors

The Dukhobors were a Russian religious sect that came into being nearly two hundred years ago. Their beliefs were somewhat like those of the Quakers. They recognized no authority except that of God, so they would not obey the laws of Russia, and they refused to join the army, saying war is a sin. Dukhobors was not their real name; it means "wrestlers of the spirit," and their enemies called them that sarcastically. Today they are called the Christians of the Universal Brotherhood. Because they refused to do military service they were banished from Russia. Between 1890 and 1900 most members of the sect settled in the province of Saskatchewan, in Canada. Their leader was Peter Veregin, and after him they were led by his son, also named Peter Veregin. They had trouble with the Canadian government because they would not pay taxes, join the army, or send their children to public schools. Peter Veregin the elder was killed by a bomb in 1924. When Peter Veregin the younger died, in 1939, he left a letter to his people, telling them they would have to obey the laws, but never to give up their religion.

dulcimer

The dulcimer is a musical instrument made up of wire strings stretched across a boxlike soundboard. It is played by striking the strings with drumsticks or hammers. This instrument and the psaltery, of which the modern form is the zither, belong to the harp family of stringed instruments. A type of dulcimer known as the cembalom, or zimbalom, is very popular in the Balkan countries, and is much used in Hungarian and gypsy orchestras. It is tuned to the chromatic scale (see the article SCALE), and is mounted on a stand, or console. On some, the strings are damped, that is, the sound is deadened, by hand, and on others there is a pedal like the ones on a piano.

Duluth

Duluth is a city in the state of Minnesota. It lies on the western end of Lake Superior. It has a large harbor that is always full of ships coming and going. Duluth's chief business is sending goods out to other cities on the Great Lakes. Most of the shipments are iron ore that comes from the famous iron mines of Minnesota. Railroads bring the ore to Duluth and from there ships take it to cities that use it for making steel. Read the article on Lake ERIE. Duluth also ships out wheat and coal.

The city got its name in the seventeenth century from a French explorer, Daniel du Luth. The settlement that grew into the present city was made by Americans in 1852. Today Duluth is the third-largest city in Minnesota. Its population is about 100,600.

Dumas

There are two famous French writers named Alexandre Dumas. One is the father, called *Père,* and the other is his son, called *Fils. Père* (pronounced "pear") and *Fils* (pronounced "feece") are the French words for father and son.

Dumas père is the author of many wonderful adventure stories. Most people have read some of them. The two most popular ones today are *The Three Musketeers* and

Dumas Père

The Count of Monte Cristo. Dumas wrote about three hundred books altogether. Thirty of these were books about all of his marvelous trips to different places, but he is primarily remembered today for

his exciting historical novels. Dumas loved to invent stories about events that had happened in history. He thought up all kinds of wonderful heroes and desperate situations. It is said that he had the most vivid imagination of any French writer. He was born in 1802. His father was a general in the French Revolution. His writing earned him much money, but he died penniless in 1870.

Dumas fils was a writer, just like his father. This Alexandre Dumas is world-famous as the author of the play *Camille*. The play is about a lovely lady who slowly dies of tuberculosis. It has been seen all over the world and translated into many languages. Actresses have always loved playing the part of Camille. It has been made into several movies. The most famous one was made by Greta Garbo. In his other plays Dumas tried to set right many wrongs that existed at the time. He tried to get equal rights for the women of his time. He was born in 1824 and died in 1895.

du Maurier, George

George du Maurier was an English writer and illustrator. He is remembered today for two books, *Peter Ibbetson* and *Trilby*. He was born in France in 1839. His father was French and his mother was English. He divided his time between the two countries, being very happy in either one. He became an artist at an early age and used to send drawings to the English magazine *Punch*. He feared he was going to go blind and not be able to draw very much longer. So he started to write novels and to draw a few pictures to go along with them. In his pictures and books he idealized everything. In other words, he pictured everything as being pure and perfect. Both *Trilby* and *Peter Ibbetson* have been made into plays and movies. *Peter Ibbetson* was also the subject of an opera by Deems Taylor. Du Maurier died in 1896.

Daphne du Maurier is the granddaughter of George du Maurier. She is a popular English novelist. She was born in 1907. She has written many novels, but the most famous one is *Rebecca*. It stayed on best-seller lists for more than a year and was later made into a movie and a play. Many of her novels have historical settings.

Dunant, Jean Henri

Jean Henri Dunant founded the Red Cross as an international society for the aid of men wounded in battle. This was the beginning of the Red Cross you know, which helps people in many other disasters and emergencies, such as fires, floods, and earthquakes. Dunant was born in 1828 in Geneva, Switzerland. During the War of 1859 between Italy, Austria, and France, he visited the battlefields and was shocked to see men dying because there was no way to take care of their wounds. Dunant spoke to many people and also wrote about the need for medical aid to wounded soldiers. Finally, in 1864, representatives or officials from various European countries met in Ge-

American Red Cross

neva, and the Red Cross was formed. Twenty-six governments agreed to respect the wounded, no matter what army or country the soldiers belonged to. The nations also agreed not to destroy military hospitals, and to protect Red Cross workers. In 1901, the first Nobel Peace Prize was given to Dunant for starting the Red Cross. Dunant received the prize together with Frederic Passy, a French pacifist, or worker for world peace. Dunant gave a great fortune to charity. He died in 1910.

Dunbar, Paul Laurence

Paul Laurence Dunbar was an important poet. He was born in 1872 in Dayton, Ohio. He was a Negro, and his father and mother had both been slaves, before the Civil War. Dunbar became well known when a book of poems called *Lyrics of Lowly Life* was published. His most popular poems were written in the way that the Negro people in the south really talk. This is called *dialect*, but he wrote many other kinds of poems, too. Dunbar also wrote some short stories and novels. He died in 1906, when he was 34 years old.

Duncan, Isadora

Isadora Duncan was an important dancer. She was born in San Francisco in 1878. She developed a new kind of dancing that was very simple and was based on the Greek style of dancing. Scarves were used to help express the meaning of the dances. At first people did not like this new kind of dancing and they poked fun at it. But Isadora believed in what she was doing, and this did not stop her. Finally, people did see the beauty in this kind of dancing, and schools were set up in Paris and Berlin and Moscow to teach this new dancing to many people. Isadora Duncan and her pupils danced in many places in Europe and the United States, and people were pleased. Isadora Duncan was a beautiful woman, and though she was finally successful, she did have a sad life in many ways. You can read about her life in a book she wrote called *My Life*. She died in 1927 in a strange automobile accident when a scarf she was wearing got caught in the wheel of a car.

Dunkards or Dunkers

The Dunkards, or Dunkers, are a Protestant Christian religious sect who baptize by "total immersion." That is, they believe that the person being baptized must be completely covered by water, not only sprinkled. The believer kneels in the water and is dipped, or immersed, three times by the minister, in the name of the Father, Son, and Holy Ghost. This is called *trine baptism*. The sect was founded in Germany in 1708; they were then called the Brethren (brothers). They were persecuted in Germany and fled to America, settling at Germantown, Pennsylvania, in 1719. There they founded the Conservative Dunkers, or Church of the Brethren. This group and other groups of Dunkards have spread through the United States. They are opposed to war and to the use of alcohol and tobacco.

Dunkerque

Dunkerque is a city in northern France, on the Strait of Dover. In English the name is spelled *Dunkirk*. Many fishermen sail their boats from its harbor to fish for herring and cod in the Atlantic Ocean. The people of Dunkerque also make fine leather goods, soap, and rope, and build ships. Dunkerque was founded more than a thousand years ago. It has had many rulers, Spanish, English, and finally French. Dunkerque is most famous for what happened there in the early part of World War II. In 1940 the Germans drove a big Allied army out of Belgium and France to the seacoast around Dunkerque. The Germans would have killed or captured all of this army if help had not come.

Hundreds of British boats rushed over from England and took the Allied soldiers away. They did this even though the Germans were shooting at them all the time from the shore and from aircraft overhead. More than 335,000 men were saved in this way and were able to fight again later.

duplicating machines

A duplicating machine makes copies of something that has been written by hand or on a typewriter, or that has been drawn. A few copies can be made with a typewriter and carbon paper, but in many businesses and associations it is necessary to have several dozen or several hundred copies of a letter or report. Yet not enough copies are needed to go to the expense of printing with regular type on a printing press. A duplicating machine makes a smaller number of copies inexpensively. Nearly every big office uses some kind of duplicating machine.

There are several different kinds of duplicating machine. Some are sold under well-known trade-marked names, and those names will be used here, but there are other machines that work in the same way but whose names are not as well known.

The *hectograph* is one of the oldest methods. A "master" is written or typewritten with a special kind of ink. This master is pressed against a sheet of gelatin and the ink comes off on the gelatin. After that, blank sheets of paper are pressed against the wet gelatin. Enough of the ink comes off on each of them to make a copy of the master. It is just like a blotter soaking up ink.

A duplicating machine that uses a similar principle is called the Ditto, but this kind of machine makes more copies and makes them faster, and they are not wet as sheets from a hectograph are. In this kind of machine, the blank pages press against the master itself and pick up enough ink to come out as copies of it.

In the stencil duplicator, the master has had the writing or type cut through a special paper. Then ink is pressed through the stencil against the blank paper, making a copy of what is on the master. The best-known machine of this kind is the Mimeograph.

A machine called the Multigraph used to be much used. It is a kind of printing press, but it can print its type through a ribbon as a typewriter does, and so it makes copies that look like typewritten letters. The same company that made the Multigraph makes a machine called the Multilith, which is an offset printing

Xerox

Xerox machines make copies by transfering powdered ink from an electrically-charged drum to sheets of paper, after a special camera has photographed the original document.

press (as described in the article on PRINTING) but is small enough and easy enough to work so that it is used in many offices.

Many duplicating machines use the principle of photography. One example is the BLUE PRINT, about which there is a separate article. Other modern duplicating machines shine a light through the typewritten "master" onto a sheet of paper that has been chemically treated for photography, and the sheet of paper comes out as a copy of the original. The PHOTOSTAT, about which there is a separate article, works on the same principle; it makes better copies, but it takes longer to make them. See also the entry on XEROGRAPHY.

There are several types of machine that print only addresses. These are called addressing machines, and they are used by magazines to address copies to their subscribers, by business firms to send notices or catalogs to their customers, and by clubs to send letters to their members.

du Pont

The du Ponts are an important American family that originally came from France. They started one of America's biggest chemical plants, E. I. du Pont de Nemours and Co. The first member of the du Pont family to come to the United States was Pierre du Pont, who arrived in 1800 with his family. In France he had been a diplomat, and soon after the American Revolution he helped to arrange the terms by which Great Britain recognized the inde-

Pierre du Pont

pendence of the newly formed United States. One of Pierre du Pont's sons, Eleuthère Irénée du Pont, started the family business in 1802, three years after he arrived in the United States with his father. He opened a gunpowder manufacturing plant in Wilmington, Delaware.

One of Pierre's grandsons, Samuel du Pont, was an officer of the United States

Navy during the Civil War. Many other du Ponts have been important in public life and in business.

The Du Pont Company has done a great deal to help the United States. It has manufactured and invented various chemicals and chemical products, both for war and peacetime use. Although it remained a manufacturer of gunpowder, its other products have been more important to people all over the world. Cellophane is a du Pont product that became so widely used that many other companies now make it also. Nylon was first made by du Pont.

The du Pont family has retained control of the du Pont Company and is noted also for having invested in General Motors Corporation in the early years of that corporation, so that members of the du Pont family controlled General Motors until, in 1957, the U. S. Supreme Court ruled that under the anti-trust laws they could no longer do so.

Duquesne, Fort, a French fort built where the city of Pittsburgh, Pennsylvania, now is: see PITTSBURGH.

Duralumin

Duralumin is the name of a very strong metal that is also light and hard. Duralumin is an alloy that is made from aluminum, copper and some other metals. (See ALLOY.)

In the building of aircraft, there has always been a need for metals that are strong enough to bear heavy weights and still are light enough to be easily lifted off the ground. Duralumin is important in the history of aviation because it was the first alloy that was suitable for this purpose.

Durban

Durban is a city in the Republic of South Africa. More than 570,000 people live there, making it about the size of San Diego, Calif. Durban is on a bay in the Indian Ocean and is the country's chief seaport. Ships carry many products from its harbor, including coal, corn, and sugar. Durban is a beautiful city, and because it does not get cold in winter many people from colder parts of Africa spend

winter vacations there. Durban has fine beaches, parks, and theaters. Along the bay runs a beautiful, palm-lined walk called the Victoria Embankment. On high ground above the bay are pretty houses with gardens that have tropical trees and gorgeous flowers.

DURBAN, REPUBLIC OF SOUTH AFRICA. Population, 571,100; with suburbs, 655,370. Seaport on Indian Ocean.

Dürer, Albrecht

One of the greatest figures in the history of art is Albrecht Dürer. He was

Left: A self portrait by Albrecht Dürer.
Right: A portrait he made of his mother.

a German painter, engraver and woodcut designer. The way he drew the human figure in his pictures has been a model for all painters who came after him. He brought the Italian style of painting into Germany and other northern countries.

Before Dürer started to paint, all works of art in the northern countries had been very stiff and wooden. He introduced the softer and more delicate Italian style into paintings. In his pictures he made human figures appear more like real human beings and less like statues. Dürer was born in Nuremburg in 1471. His father was a goldsmith from Hungary. When he was fifteen he was made an assistant to an artist who painted altar pictures. In 1490 he made a tour of the cities of Germany learning many different things about art. In 1495 Dürer went to Italy. His style changed very quickly after he had been there for a while. The Italians admired his work very much and liked his engravings and pictures. Between 1516 and 1520 his style changed again. He spent those four years in his home town and had little contact with the outside world. His work was not influenced by new ideas and it became difficult to understand. In 1520 he went to Holland for the crowning of Charles V and his interest in painting was renewed. He received many royal favors before he died in 1528.

Durham, Lord

John George Lambton, Lord Durham, was a famous British statesman. He was born in London in 1792. When he was 20 years old he ran away from home, and only six years later he was famous in English politics. He is most famous for his "Report on the Affairs of British North America," which he read to Parliament in 1839. In 1839, Canada was divided into two parts, Upper and Lower Canada. Upper Canada now is the province of Ontario and Lower Canada is the province of Quebec. In 1837 he was made Lord High Commissioner and Governor General of Canada. His job was to unify the colony; that is, he was to do away with the two governments that Canada then had and organize a single government for the whole area. He died in

1840, and in 1849 Canada was unified largely because of his efforts.

Duryea, Charles E. and J. Frank

The Duryea brothers, Charles and Frank, were among the first Americans to manufacture an automobile driven by a gasoline engine. This kind of car was invented in Germany in 1885, and the Duryea brothers started to manufacture it in America in the 1890s. Their factory used to turn out one car a week. It cost about a thousand dollars. One of their cars won the first American automobile race in 1895. It was driven by Frank. The brothers manufactured the Duryea car for about twenty years, and both brothers stayed in the automobile business after that. Charles died in 1938.

Duse, Eleanora

Eleanora Duse was one of the greatest actresses in the past hundred years. She was an Italian and was born in 1859. All of her family had been in the theatre. Her grandfather, her mother and her father were all actors. Duse, as she was always called, made her first appearance on a stage as Juliet in *Romeo and Juliet*. She was 14 years old at the time. For many years she had to struggle very hard to make a name for herself in the Italian theater, but by 1896 she had won great fame in her native country. Then she took the big step. She went to Paris in 1897 and appeared in Alexandre Dumas' play *Camille*. This was a very difficult thing to do because there was a French actress named Sarah Bernhardt who had almost made that same play her own private property. However, so great was Duse's talent that she took Paris by storm. After that she had great success everywhere. For many years she acted in the plays of an Italian writer and soldier named D'Annunzio, who became her close friend. When Duse was 42 years old and at the height of her fame she retired from the stage. Twenty years later she needed money so she came back to the theater and toured the United States, England, France, and Italy. She died in 1924 while playing in Pittsburgh, Pennsylvania.

dust and dust bowl

Dust is the name of the tiny bits of smoke, earth and cotton that you find floating in the air or settled on things. If you live in a large city where the air is very dusty, you can see dust on your furniture every day. Germs are carried around on bits of dust, and it is bad for our health to breathe the air that has a lot of dust in it. A lot of dust can also stop the delicate parts of a machine from working. Each year many people have a jeweler remove the dust that has gotten into their watches.

One of the most terrible things that ever happened to farmers in the United States was the dust storms of the 1930s in Oklahoma and parts of Texas and other states. The farmers had used poor farming methods and most of the topsoil in this region dried out, forming a crumbling powder. The dry winds came and blew all this powdery earth into the air making terrible dust storms. People called this part of the United States the Dust Bowl. You can find out more about the Dust Bowl in another article on AGRICULTURE. A famous book, *The Grapes of Wrath*, by the American writer, John Steinbeck, is all about what happened to the farmers who left the dust bowl and went, with their families, to California.

Dutch Guiana: see the article on SURINAM.

Dutchman's breeches

Dutchman's breeches is the name of a wild flower that grows in most parts of the United States and southern Canada. It is named "Dutchman's breeches" because the blossom grows in two plump-looking sections that look somewhat like a pair of breeches of the kind worn by Dutchmen who live in Holland, or the Netherlands. These breeches have full, baggy legs and tight ankle cuffs. The flower is white, with a yellow tip at the "cuff" end. It is a perennial plant, which means that it grows from the same roots year after year.

Dutch West India Company

The Dutch West India Company was a group of Dutch businessmen formed (1621) to trade with places in North and South America and Africa which were owned by the Dutch government. The government gave permission to this company to send settlers and soldiers to these places. In return, the company had to pay the government large sums of money. The most important thing this company ever did was to make trading posts along the Hudson River. This river had been discovered for the Dutch by Henry Hudson in 1609. The company's settlers came with tools, seeds, clothing, and food. They traded with the Indians for furs. These settlements later became New York state.

The Dutch West India Company also built Fort Amsterdam on Manhattan Island. A town called New Amsterdam grew up here; later it became New York City. The Company also made an important settlement called Curaçao in the West Indies, and one in South America called Surinam. The Company went out of business in 1674 and the Dutch government took its place.

Dvořák, Antonin

Antonin Dvořák was a great Bohemian composer. A composer is a writer of original music. He was born in Nelahozeves, Bohemia, now Mühlhausen, Germany, more than a hundred years ago. When he was only a child he played the violin to entertain people who stopped at the inn. He studied music, and by the time he was 18 years old he had already written many works. He destroyed many of his early compositions. One that he forgot to burn, his *C Minor Symphony*, was discovered in 1923.

Dvořák was very successful by the time he was fifty years old, in Europe and in his own country. In 1892 he came to New York to take a position as director of the National Conservatory. Here he became enthusiastic over American folksongs, Negro musicians, and Indian music. His famous *Symphony From the New World* is based upon American themes, one of which, the English horn solo, is the melody used in the song "Goin' Home." His "Songs My Mother Taught Me" is well-known all over the world. He was born in 1841 and died in 1904.

dwarf

A dwarf is any plant or animal or human being that stops growing before it reaches a normal size. The Chinese and Japanese people are famous for the tiny gardens of dwarf trees and flowers that they grow in pots. Some people raise varieties of plants, like the marigold, that do not grow as large as ordinary marigolds, and they are called dwarf marigolds. A human being who is a dwarf may have a head that is too large for his body, or his legs may be too short, but many dwarfs are perfectly shaped. People often call these tiny persons *midgets*. General Tom Thumb was a famous dwarf. He was only about two and a half feet high when he was full grown. He traveled all over the world with the circus, and thousands of people got to know him. Dwarfs were popular in many courts of Europe, where they used to entertain the king and his followers. People of many countries have stories about dwarfs. One of the most famous stories is called "Snow White and the Seven Dwarfs," and it was made into a cartoon motion picture that many people enjoyed.

dyes and dyeing

Dyes are materials that are used to color all kinds of fabrics. Until they are dyed, all fabrics—silk, wool, cotton, or any other—are a whitish color. Men have known about dyes and dyeing for thousands of years. There is a color called Tyrian purple which was used to dye the clothes worn by the priests and nobles in ancient Phoenicia, three thousand years ago. This color became so famous that purple has ever since then been considered the royal color. There are many stories in the Bible that show that dyes were known in Biblical times. One of the most famous is the story of Joseph's coat of many colors, which was given to him by his father, Jacob, and which made Joseph's brothers so jealous that they tried to kill him.

Until about a hundred years ago, dyes were made from things that are found in nature. Tyrian purple, for instance, was made from certain shellfish. A famous blue dye, called indigo, was made from a plant called indigo tinctoria. But not all natural dyes were permanent, and many of them were very expensive. When scientists discovered how to make dyes out of coal tar and other chemicals, the dyeing industry became very important. This industry was most highly developed in Germany and was a great help to that country during World War I, because many of the processes and chemicals used in making dyes can also be used in making explosives and other war materials. After World War I was over, the United States and Great Britain took steps to develop the dye industry in their own countries, and nowadays both have many dye producing factories.

The general process of dyeing is to put the material to be dyed in a bath of liquid combined with dye. This bath is then

heated to a particular temperature, depending on the dye and the material being dyed. In the case of some materials, the dye is absorbed right into the fibers of the fabric; in others the dye produces a chemical reaction in the fabric which makes it change color.

Some materials, such as cotton, cannot be dyed directly. In dyeing these materials, a substance called a mordant must be used. The mordant acts somewhat like a glue that holds the material and the dye together. Sometimes the mordant is applied before the dye, sometimes they are applied at the same time, and sometimes the mordant is applied after the dye. The order of the dyeing operation depends on the mordant used, the composition of the dye, and the kind of material being dyed.

dynamics is the science of force and motion, and is part of physics and mechanics. See the article MECHANICS.

dynamite

Dynamite is a white powder. It is usually wrapped in paper sticks and used by engineers and miners for blasting tunnels and breaking up large rocks that have ores of valuable metals in them. You can read about BLASTING and MINING in separate articles. There is a very sensitive chemical in dynamite called nitroglycerine. When this chemical is shaken it breaks up suddenly and with a great force known as an explosion. Many difficult jobs such as building the Panama Canal would have taken many years longer if people had not had dynamite to help them blast through the rock that was in their way. Dynamite was invented about ninety years ago by the great Swedish scientist Alfred Nobel.

dynamo is a machine for making

electricity: see the article on GENERATOR.

dysentery

Dysentery is a disease of the bowels. If you have dysentery you have to go to the bathroom often, and it is painful to do so. You may have a mild case of dysentery and not even know it, but you may have a high fever, be very thirsty, and have pains in your stomach. Wherever many people have to live together in places that are hard to keep clean, and where there are many flies and no good sewage system, there is a danger of dysentery. It is very easy for people to catch this disease from one another, and during World War I and World War II, the army had a hard time controlling it. Doctors now know of some drugs that are helpful in curing anyone who has this disease.

Atlantic Chemical Corp.

A typical plant process used in the manufacture of dyestuffs.

Hanes Hosiery, Inc.

Stockings are placed in bags and dyed in drum-like machines.

E

∃ PHOENICIAN	ΛΕ EARLY LATIN
Ε EARLY GREEK	Ε UNCIAL
Ε ETRUSCAN	Ε EARLY ROMAN
℮ CAROLINGIAN	Ε GOTHIC
Ε EARLY GERMAN	Ee ALDINE
℮ RENAISSANCE	ℰ PAPAL

E or e

The letter E is the fifth letter of the alphabet. It can be traced all the way back to the earliest writing known to man, in Egypt thousands of years ago. In the Hebrew language, in which much of the Bible was written, the letter was called *he,* which was the closest thing to an *e* sound in that language. The ancient Greeks took this same letter and called it *epsilon.*

At the top of this page, at the far left, you can see what the Greek letter *epsilon* looked like in its very early stages of development. In those early times, writing was not read from left to right as it is today in our culture, but from right to left. However, the later Greeks changed this system and began to read from left to right. When this change was made, the Greeks also turned the individual letters around. That is, whereas previously the letters (from our present point of view) faced right, they were made to face left. Epsilon thereafter looked much like our E.

Read also the article ALPHABET.

Eads, James Buchanan

James Buchanan Eads was an American engineer who made an ocean port of the city of New Orleans, Louisiana. This city is 107 miles up the Mississippi River from the Gulf of Mexico. Eads invented a system of jetties or breakwaters to keep the river deep enough so that ocean liners could travel to New Orleans. Eads was born in 1820. When he was 21, he invented a diving bell to help in finding boats sunk in the river. During the Civil War he constructed a fleet of gunboats that helped the northern states win. If you ever visit St. Louis, Missouri, you will see the Eads Bridge he built. Eads died in 1887.

eagle

The eagle is a large bird that lives in the United States and Canada. There are two kinds. One has a white head and tail feathers, and is very handsome. From a distance this eagle's head looks as if it were bald. This bird is called the *bald eagle.* The other kind, when mature, has a golden head and is called the *gold-*

The American bald eagle is the national emblem of the United States, and stands for courage, power, and great dignity.

Am. Museum of Nat. History

en eagle. It is sharp-eyed and strong of claw and has the great wingbeat of a powerful flier. Eagles build huge nests in tall trees or on cliffs near the water. The eagle's nest is so big and strong that it can hold a man. The female eagle lays one or two eggs, and when the baby eagles are hatched, the parents take good care of them for about two months. Eagles eat fish that they catch by diving into the water from great heights. They will also steal the food of other birds. An eagle will circle around just below a sea hawk, until the sea hawk drops his dinner, and the eagle catches it in midair.

In 1782, when Congress made the bald eagle the United States national emblem, Benjamin Franklin said no bird with such habits should represent the country, but most people thought that because the eagle is strong and proud and free, it was a very good emblem for the United States. Its picture is on the United States 25¢ piece.

Eakins, Thomas

Thomas Eakins was an American

Metropolitan Museum of Art

One of Thomas Eakin's famous paintings, *The Surgical Clinic of Professor Gross.*

painter. During his lifetime he was not appreciated as much as he is today. He was considered very radical for his time, because his pictures are very realistic. When you look at his paintings, you feel that you are right in them and are a part of them. Among his best-known pictures are *The Surgical Clinic of Dr. Gross, The Cello Player,* and *The Chess Player.* He was born in Philadelphia in 1844. After living for some time in Paris, and a trip to Spain, he returned to the United States in 1870. Eakins taught art in Philadelphia, where his methods of teaching were considered too advanced. He died in 1916.

ear

The ear is the part of the body with which animals hear. Man is not able to hear as well as many other animals that can turn their ears in the direction of a sound, but hearing is a very important way that human beings learn. You probably think of your ear as the funny, twisted thing that sticks out from the side of your head. This is only part of your ear, the outer ear. You can bend your outer ear and twist it, because it is made of movable tissues called cartilage.

Besides the part of your ear that you can see, your outer ear also has a tube or canal that leads to your eardrum. Your eardrum is a thin delicate tissue that separates your outer ear from your middle ear. In the middle ear there are three tiny bones that are shaped like a hammer, an anvil, and a stirrup, and so they are called by these names. They are the smallest bones in your body. You also have an inner ear in which there is a fluid and some tiny fibers that help you to keep your balance, as well as to hear. The outer ear, the middle ear and the inner ear are all important in hearing. You can find out more about the wonderful way your ear works in separate articles on HEARING, DEAFNESS, and SOUND.

You should take very good care of your ears, and that means you should never put anything smaller than your finger and a washcloth into your ears. Small things like pencils or toothpicks can pierce your tender eardrum and cause a lot of trouble. You should try not to get water into your ears. If you have wax in your ears that won't come out with soap and water, your doctor can get it out for you, and that is much better than trying to do it yourself. If you have an earache, you should go to the doctor right away.

Earhart, Amelia

Amelia Earhart was a very brave woman flier. Her first flight was with two men, when they flew from Newfoundland to Wales. In 1932 she flew from Newfoundland to Ireland all alone. This was the first time a woman had flown across the Atlantic Ocean alone. It was an important event in the history of aviation. Then three years later Amelia Earhart flew from Hawaii to California alone, and this was the very first time anyone had ever done this. The next thing she planned was a flight around the world. She started out from Miami, Florida, in June, 1937. About a month later, Amelia Earhart and the navigator who was with her were flying toward Howland Island, a tiny spot in the central Pacific Ocean, when the plane disap-

Eight-year-old Tyler Nelson of Boise, Idaho wears a heavy leather gauntlet when his tame golden eagle, Clyde, perches on his arm. This protection is necessary since the eagle has talons (claws) that enable it to defeat a mountain lion in battle.

Idaho Dept. of Commerce and Development

Amelia Earhart in Atchison, Kansas in 1935, two years before her fateful flight.

Kansas State Historical Society, Topeka

peared. No one knows just what happened to this courageous woman flier, and no trace of the plane was ever found.

Amelia Earhart was born in Kansas in 1898, and she was a teacher until she gave this up to become one of the greatest woman pilots. She wrote some books about flying and her experiences, and she was married to George Putnam, a publisher.

earth

The earth is the planet we live on. A planet is a body that travels around the sun. The earth is shaped like a ball. It is about 8,000 miles in diameter and 25,-000 miles around. (More exactly, 7926½ miles and 24,903 miles.) Although this seems very large to us, the earth is really a small planet. There are nine planets, and four of them are bigger than ours. For a long time men thought that the earth was the center of the universe and that all the stars circled around it. (The universe is space with all the planets and stars there are.) But scientists now know that the sun is the center of our solar system. The solar system is the sun and the nine planets that travel around it.

For thousands of years men thought that the earth was flat. The people in India thought that it was shaped like a pancake, and that it was held in the sky by four elephants riding on the back of a turtle who swam in an endless sea. At least two thousand years ago the Greeks learned that the earth was round. They noticed that when a ship got farther and farther from shore, it seemed to sink lower and lower. The last part of the ship they could see would be the top of the mast. Because this could happen only on the surface of a ball or sphere, they knew that the earth must be round.

HOW THE EARTH BEGAN

Scientists and other people have always been interested in the question of how the earth began. As astronomers (men who study the stars and planets) learned more and more about the universe, they came to the conclusion that the earth had come from the sun. This explanation was first given about 1800. Since then they have suggested various explanations of how this might have happened, and when. The present explanation of how the earth was formed is this:

Scientists think that the stars and planets were formed at the same time. About five billion years ago there was a huge cloud of dust that was contracting. As

Alaska Development Board
More than a million years ago, large portions of the earth were covered by great glaciers. This one in Alaska still remains.

NASA
This view of the earth greeted the first astronauts to orbit the moon. The photograph was taken at a distance of 240,000 miles from our planet.

the dust particles fell toward the center they started the cloud spinning. Then the cloud grew hot. You know how a nailhead gets hot when you hit it with a hammer. The dust particles get hot in the same way when they hit against each other. After about a billion years the cloud was hot enough to shine, and it became the sun. Some smaller parts, left outside, became planets. Still smaller ones were trapped around the planets as moons. All stars are thought to have been formed this way. Planets are thought to have been formed in some cases with stars (like the planets in our solar system) and in other cases, without stars nearby. However, none of these "sunless" planets has ever been detected. Stars are always being formed, growing old, and "dying."

OUR CHANGING EARTH

In the five billion years that have passed since the earth was first formed, many changes have taken place. At first the earth was very hot, so hot that nothing could live on it. There was no water, but only hot gases surrounding the entire globe. When millions of years had gone by, some of the hot gases cooled and made water that then covered all of the earth.

There have been other important changes in the earth since its beginning. When the earth was completely covered by water, great heat and pressure in its center occasionally caused great portions of the floor of the ancient seas to be pushed up into the air. This gave us the dry land. Sometimes the land would sink back into the sea again and reappear millions of years later. Scientists believe that

Alaska was once joined to Asia by a strip of land that has now sunk back into the ocean. They also think that the people now known to us as American Indians came from Asia to this continent over that connecting strip of land. In some places out in the midwestern part of America, far from any ocean, scientists have found fossils (remains of ancient life imbedded in rock) of shellfish and other sea life, showing that at one time those areas were covered by a sea.

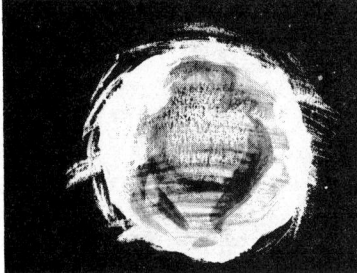

For millions of years the earth was a whirling mass that was bombarded by smaller bodies also thrown off by the sun.

According to one theory, the earth was formed when part of the sun was pulled off by the magnetism of a passing star.

About three million years ago, the climate turned very cold and great sheets of ice, called glaciers, formed at the poles. The glaciers slowly grew and spread until about one-third of the earth was covered with ice from one to two miles thick. The last great glaciers melted from the North American continent about 8,000 years ago. (This entire period is called the ICE AGE, about which there is a separate article.) As the ice spread over the earth it gouged out valleys, rivers, and lakes. It covered nearly all of North America to the Ohio and Missouri Rivers, and covered most of Europe. Antarctica is still ice clad. No one knows what started the ice to form, nor why it finally melted.

About 400 million years ago, the earth was mostly covered by shallow seas. The low-lying land was bare and rocky with no life on it except tiny rootless plants that clung to the stony shores. During the next several hundred millions of years, the face of the earth was vastly altered by volcanic eruptions, earthquakes, and internal pressures that upraised the mountains. These powerful forces caused the breaking and crumbling of the rocks, which were then worn down still more by rain, wind, floods, and glaciers. Generations of animals and plants evolved, died, and decayed. Their remains thus enriched the rock grains and fragments, creating and building up soil in an endless cycle. Some decayed matter, under pressure, became coal.

If we could cut the earth right through the center and look at one of the halves, we would see that in it there are three layers of different kinds of material.

Each time the earth revolves around the sun, it rotates 365 ¼ times on its axis like a spinning top, with the axis tilted.

The earth moves at the tremendous speed of 60,000 miles per hour around the sun. The path that the earth takes is an ellipse.

The outermost layer is called the *crust*. It is a thin shell of rock varying in thickness from about five miles under parts of the ocean to about fifty miles under some parts of the land. The next layer is called the *mantle*. It is believed to be composed of several kinds of dense rock about 1,800 miles thick. The point where the crust and the mantle meet is called the Mohorovicic Discontinuity (or "Moho"), named for its discoverer. Finally, there is the *core* of the earth, about 4,000 miles thick, composed of molten iron. Estimates of its temperature range from about 2000°F. to about 9000°F. Some scientists think there may be another inner core that is solid.

About three-quarters of the earth is covered by water.

The ATMOSPHERE, about which there is a separate article, is a layer of various gases surrounding the earth to a height of at least 700 miles.

THE MOVEMENTS OF THE EARTH

As you already know, the earth moves around the sun. The path it follows is called an orbit, and it is shaped like a slightly flattened circle called an ellipse. The earth travels along this path at a rate of about 60,000 miles an hour, and it takes a full year to complete its journey all around the sun. In addition to this motion of the earth around the sun, there is another motion the earth makes. It is spinning around like a top on its axis. The earth's axis is an imaginary line drawn from the North Pole to the South Pole. The speed of the spin is over a thousand miles an hour. This spin has bulged the earth out a little bit at the

equator and slightly flattened it at the poles. The bulge is very small, for the distance through the earth at the equator is only twenty-seven miles longer than the distance from pole to pole. The spin also causes night and day. The earth makes one complete turn in twenty-four hours, and in that time each part of it is turned toward the sun and lighted about half the time, and away from the sun and in darkness the other half.

The turning of the earth on its axis makes day and night. While half the earth facing the sun has day, the other half has night.

SOLIDS (SOIL ROCKS)

LIQUIDS (WATER)

GASES (AIR)

The surface of the earth is made of solids and liquids. It is completely covered by a blanket of gases that form the atmosphere.

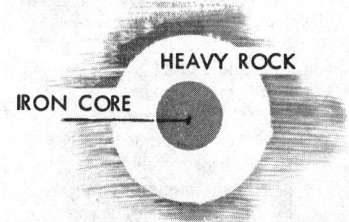

HEAVY ROCK

IRON CORE

Scientists believe that the interior of the earth is made of an iron core surrounded by dense heavy rocks that are 1,800 miles thick.

The seasons of the year result from the inclination, or tilt, of the earth's axis. Nearness to the sun does not cause summer. Summer is caused by the angle at which the sun's rays strike the earth, and in the Northern Hemisphere it happens when a portion of the earth is farthest from the sun.

As time goes by, geologists, astronomers, and other scientists who are interested in the earth are learning more and more about it. Someday we may know the answers to how the earth was formed, why the glaciers started to move, and the other questions that scientists are curious about.

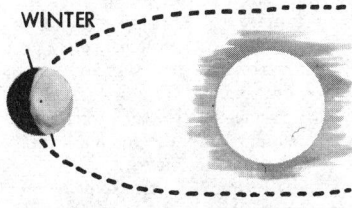

WINTER

In winter, the North Pole is tilted away from the sun, and the northern hemisphere receives fewer direct rays, making it colder.

SUMMER

In summer, the North Pole is tilted toward the sun, and the Northern Hemisphere receives more of the hot sun's direct rays.

earthquake

An earthquake is a sudden trembling and shaking on the surface of the earth. Sometimes huge cracks hundreds of feet long and many feet wide appear in the ground during an earthquake. Some earthquakes are so severe that whole cities can be destroyed as buildings fall, streets split open and other property is shaken to pieces. The most famous earthquake of all was in Lisbon, Portugal in 1775. The whole city was destroyed and forty thousand people lost their lives. At the same time a tidal wave covered Lisbon. Tidal waves are caused by earthquakes on the ocean floor. The San Francisco fire of 1906 was caused by an earthquake, too. It destroyed almost all the downtown business section of the city and the fires burned for three days without stopping. Five hundred people were killed.

The city of Tokyo, Japan, has had many earthquakes. The people in Tokyo live in houses made of paper and wood. These materials bend easily and do not crack and fall when an earthquake comes. The Imperial Hotel in Tokyo has a specially built foundation that will not crack during an earthquake. When most of the stone buildings fell in the 1923 earthquake, the Imperial remained standing. It was designed by the American architect, Frank Lloyd Wright.

Although the earth may be billions of years old, it is still going through a great many changes. Mountain ranges are gradually sinking and other ranges are slowly rising up, and the rock underneath the surface of the earth is always changing its position.

Earthquakes are caused by the moving rock under the ground. Underneath the soil and going down for about forty miles are layer upon layer of different kinds of rock. Sometimes one of the layers will crack because of the weight of the other rocks on top of it. When a layer cracks, other rocks will fall into the crack and tons of stone will all be falling at once, miles under the ground. Sometimes the underground crack will appear on the earth's surface, but even if it does not, the earth shakes or quakes for miles around due to the weight of the falling rock.

Sometimes earthquakes are caused by explosions underground. There is hot melted rock deep in the earth that sometimes shoots up to the surface with such force that mountains can be split apart by it. Such great force can make the ground shake, too. You can read more about this in the article on VOLCANO.

earthworm

An earthworm is the kind of worm that you find when you dig in a field or garden, and use for bait when you go fishing. Many people call the earthworm an angleworm, because it is bait for angling (fishing). The earthworm has a soft body, and it has no eyes or ears or arms or legs. The earthworm's body is made up of many rings or segments, so that it can stretch itself to great lengths, and this helps it to move. It also has tiny bristles on its underside, so that it can crawl very well, even on smooth sidewalks. It is a pink or brown color, and lives in almost every part of the world.

Earthworms stay underground during the day, but they come out of the ground at night to eat decaying leaves and plants. They are very useful to man, because they are constantly digging and turning over the earth, and for this reason they have been given the name, "nature's ploughmen."

earwig

The earwig is a small black or brown insect. It got its name because many people used to believe that it would crawl into the ear of a sleeping person.

The earwig looks like a beetle, and the male is always larger than the female. It has pincers like tiny arms at the end of its abdomen. These are very useful in catching other insects. Many earwigs, however, eat only flowers and ripe fruit. The earwig lives in the southern part of the United States and on the west coast, and in many parts of Europe. There are some earwigs in tropical climates, and they are brightly colored. The earwig makes its home in the decayed bark of trees and under stones, and comes out only at night.

East Anglia

East Anglia was a kingdom formed in the eastern part of central England in the 6th century by a people called the Angles. They came from northeast Germany and conquered the Britons, who then lived in this part of England. At this time there were six other kingdoms also in what later became England. All seven kingdoms fought with each other. First one and then the other won. Then fierce fighters came from Denmark and defeated all these seven kingdoms. In 878 the Danes made one of their number, Guthrum by name, king of East Anglia. Little by little the seven kingdoms won their freedom back from the Danes and later joined together to make up one kingdom, England.

The land that formed East Anglia today makes up Norfolk and Suffolk counties.

Easter

Easter is a day of rejoicing for all Christians. It marks the anniversary of the resurrection, or the day on which Christ rose from the grave. Easter falls on a Sunday between March 22 and April 25. The date was determined by the early Christians, from the Jewish calendar. They knew that Jesus entered Jerusalem, a week before he was crucified, during the Jewish Passover, or Spring Festival, which fell on the fourteenth day of the Jewish month of Nisan. Their Easter, therefore, fell on the Sunday nearest to that date. About three hundred years after the birth of Jesus, a council of the Christian Church decided that Easter would fall on the first Sunday following the first full moon after the spring equinox. The spring equinox is the day in the spring in which there are twelve hours of daylight and twelve hours of darkness, and it comes about March 21. Today some churches celebrate Easter on different days from the one marked on the calendar used in America.

Before the time of Christ, some people used to worship gods and goddesses. One goddess was the Goddess of Spring, who was named Eastre. Because Easter comes in the spring, we have named it for this goddess. We have brightly colored eggs at Easter, because eggs stand for the beginning, or birth, just as spring itself is a birth each year. Early Christians celebrated Easter as the New Year, and they often gave gifts at this time. Ever since ancient times, men have had a feast day at the coming of spring. The Easter custom of dressing up in new clothes and having a happy time is very old.

Easter Island

Easter Island is a small, triangular, volcanic island in the South Pacific about 2,300 miles from the coast of Valparaiso, Chile. Named for the day it was discov-

Am. Museum of Nat. History

Nobody knows who made the ancient stone statues that are found on Easter Island.

ered in 1722 by a Dutch explorer, Jacob Roggeveen, the island is famous only for the hundreds of strange statues that were carved from volcanic rock by an unknown people who lived there about 800 years ago. They also left stone tablets with carved picture-writing that has not yet been deciphered. It is the only form of writing ever discovered in all the Pacific islands. In 1888 Chile took over Easter Island. It is governed by the Chilean Navy, which also operates the island's only organized industry, a sheep farm that provides meat for the people and wool for export. Once a year a naval transport brings supplies to the island and picks up the annual wool crop. The Navy also keeps a station there to record data on earthquakes, weather, and tides. The 64-square-mile island has about 1,100 inhabitants, believed to be of Polynesian origin. There is only one village, called Hanga Roa. Many islanders earn money by selling small copies of the ancient statues.

Eastern Star, see ORDER OF THE EASTERN STAR.

East India Company

East India Company was the name of several groups of European businessmen of the 17th century, formed to trade with the East Indies and other lands of eastern Asia. Their governments gave them permission to send out ships with traders, settlers, and soldiers. They bought such articles as pepper and silk very cheaply and sold them in Europe for good prices.

One such company was formed in England in 1600. It was called the English

or British East India Company. It set up trading posts in the East Indies, but the Dutch who were already there drove the British out. The British Company then made many settlements in India. The native Indians did not want them as rulers but the company's strong army defeated them. After a time the company ruled nearly all of India. Its members became very rich. Many people felt that a private company should not rule a large country like India. The British government itself became the ruler of India in 1858, and the company broke up a few years later. British rule in India lasted until 1947, when India became a free nation. (Read the article on INDIA.)

Another famous company was the Dutch East India Company, formed in 1602. It made strong trading posts in the islands of the East Indies, especially at the city of Batavia. From that city it traded also with Japan, China, Persia, and other places. As in India, the natives of the East Indies did not like to have Europeans as rulers. Over and over they revolted against the company. French and English traders tried to take away the Company's business too. In 1798 the company let the Dutch government take its place. The government was able to fight the natives and other enemies much better than the company could. The natives gained their freedom from Dutch rule in 1949. (Read the article on INDONESIA.)

The French East India Company was founded in 1664. It made trading settlements chiefly in India. The strong army of the English East India Company under the British general, Robert Clive, defeated the French in several battles. The French had to be satisfied to rule only a few very small parts of India. The company came to an end in 1769.

East Indies

The East Indies is a general name given to the many islands that are now grouped together and called the Republic of Indonesia. The name East Indies was first used more than 350 years ago by many Dutch, English and French shipping companies that traded with these islands. They used the name East Indies to make a difference between these islands south of the Chinese mainland and the West Indies in the Western Hemisphere. The West Indies were mistakenly named the Indies by Columbus, who thought he had reached the Orient. (See the article on INDONESIA.)

Eastman, George

George Eastman was a famous American inventor and industrialist. He was born in 1854, and at the age of 26 he perfected the photographic dry plate with which many professional photographers take pictures. Four years later he patented flexible film, which is used in most cameras today. He also invented the Kodak, the first simple and successful box camera ever placed on the market. Anyone could take pictures with the Kodak, without special training and without expensive equipment. He established the Eastman School of Music, in Rochester, New York. Eastman never married, but he was interested in helping children to get musical educations, and he

contributed musical instruments to public schools. He also helped the Rochester Orphan Asylum, and such schools as the University of Rochester, Massachusetts Institute of Technology, and Tuskegee and Hampton Institutes. He was also one of the first employers to take a strong interest in the welfare of his workers. He died in 1932, at the age of 78.

East Prussia

East Prussia is a territory in northeastern Europe on the Baltic Sea. Most of its people are farmers. They raise potatoes, oats, and flax, and also cattle and horses. East Prussia was ruled by the Teutonic knights, a religious order, in the 13th century. For a long time it was part of Germany. When Germany lost World War I; East Prussia was separated from Germany by a narrow strip of land that was called the Polish Corridor. It ran from Poland to the Baltic Sea. This strip was called the Polish Corridor. It was made to give the Polish people, who have no seacoast, a route to the port of Danzig. In the early part of World War II the Germans took the Polish Corridor and Danzig. Later, however, the Russians took both of them away from the Germans. After World War II, the northeastern part of East Prussia was given to Russia and the rest to Poland. Danzig is today a Polish city. The capital of East Prussia was Königsberg, with a population of nearly 400,000. This city now belongs to Soviet Russia, which gave it the Russian name, Kaliningrad. East Prussia (when it belonged to Germany) had about 14,000 square miles and its population was about 2,500,000.

Eban, Abba

Abba Eban is an eloquent Jewish statesman. He was born in South Africa  in 1915 but grew up in England. He served with the British in the Middle East during World War II. In 1945, he moved to Jerusalem, becoming Israel's delegate to the United Nations in 1948. In 1958, he was elected to Israel's Knesset (Parliament). He was also made Minister of Education and Culture and has been a Deputy Premier. In 1966, he became Minister for Foreign Affairs and he is now a member of the Knesset.

Ebro River

The Ebro, the only large river in Spain that empties into the Mediterranean Sea, is about 480 miles long. This river was the scene of much bloody fighting in the Spanish Civil War, 1936–39. The Ebro flows southeast across the northeast of Spain, at the foot of the Pyrenees mountains between Spain and France. Beginning in Santander Province on the Bay of Biscay, the river enters the Mediterranean at Tortosa, south of Barcelona. The river has been a source of irrigation, or water for farming, since a thousand years ago when the Moors ruled Spain. The Ebro also furnishes power to make electricity.

Ecclesiastes

Ecclesiastes is the name of a book in

the Old Testament, in the Bible. Its name comes from the word *ecclesiast*, which means "preacher." The great king Solomon is often said to be the author, but the book was not actually written down until hundreds of years after Solomon died. The book contains some beautiful poetry and much wise advice. We use the word *ecclesiastical* for things having to do with the Christian religion or the Church.

echidna

The echidna, or *spiny anteater*, is an animal that looks very much like a big hedgehog. An echidna has longer spines than a hedgehog, and it has a very long, pointed snout. At the tip of this snout is its mouth, which is only a tiny hole. Through this hole the echidna pushes out its tongue, which is long and thin and very sticky. With this tongue it licks up ants and other small insects. Echidnas sleep most of the day; during the night they come out and search for their food. They have short, strong legs and sharp claws with which they dig deep burrows underground.

Echidnas are very strange animals. They are mammals, which means that they nurse their young. Most mammals bear their young alive; but the echidna lays eggs that are hatched in a pouch on the mother's body. After the young have hatched, they remain in the pouch for a few weeks, feeding on the mother's milk.

The only other mammal that lays eggs is the PLATYPUS, about which there is a separate article.

echinoderm

An echinoderm is a sea animal that belongs to a large group of animals called the *Echinodermata*. Although there are more than three thousand different kinds of echinoderm, they differ from all other animals in that they are circular in shape, like a wheel. In the middle of the circle is the animal's mouth. Very often echinoderms have long arms all around the edge.

The word *echinoderm* means "spiny-skinned." Many kinds of echinoderm have needle-shaped spines that protect them from other animals.

Some echinoderms that you might see at the seashore are starfish, sea urchins, and sea cucumbers. Starfish have short spines with which they crawl about on the bottom of the sea. Some echinoderms such as the sea lilies and brittle stars are never seen on the shore; they live only in deep water.

Echinoderms feed on seaweed and on other sea animals. They lay their eggs in the water; the eggs float about for a while before hatching and developing into young echinoderms.

echo

When you look in a mirror you see yourself because the surface of the mirror reflects the light waves that hit it. The same principle of reflection operates with sound.

When a sound wave hits a reflecting surface, the sound reflects back just as the light does from a mirror. That reflection of sound is what we call an echo. If you walk through a long, wide tunnel or through a cave, for instance, any sound

you make will hit the walls and bounce back at you in the form of an echo. Sometimes the sound bounces from one wall to another several times and then you will hear your words repeated several times. This is called reverberation.

You will hear an echo only if you are a long distance away from the reflecting surface. Sound travels at the rate of 1,100 feet every second. If you are 550 feet away from a reflecting surface, it will take one second for the sound to reach that surface and then travel back to you, so, you will hear your echo one second after you have finished speaking. If you are so close to the reflecting surface that it takes less than a quarter of a second for the sound to come back to you, an echo will be formed, but you will not be able to tell it from the original sound. This is because the human ear cannot distinguish between sounds that follow each other so quickly.

The word echo comes from the name of a nymph about whom there is an ancient Greek legend. It tells how she once helped the chief of the Greek gods, Zeus, by chattering away at Zeus's wife, Hera, so that Hera would not be able to pay any attention to a wrong thing that Zeus was doing behind her back. As a punishment, Echo lost the power of speaking for herself, and the only words she could say were the last words spoken by someone else.

eclipse

An eclipse is what happens when the moon passes between the earth and the sun, called a *solar eclipse,* or when the earth passes between the moon and the sun, called a *lunar eclipse.* There are other eclipses, such as when the brightest moons of Jupiter pass into the shadow of that planet.

If you place your hand in front of a light bulb, you are making a kind of eclipse. You are blocking out the light from the bulb and keeping it from reaching your eyes.

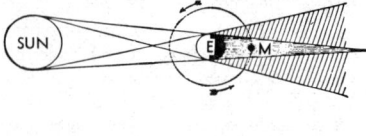

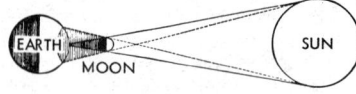

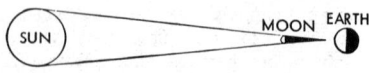

Smithsonian Inst.

1. An eclipse of the moon occurs when the earth comes between the moon and the sun.
2. An eclipse of the sun occurs when the moon comes between the earth and the sun.
3. An eclipse of the sun that occurs when the moon is farthest from the earth causes a ring of light to be seen around the dark body of the moon.

When the moon completely blocks out the light from the sun, it is called a total solar eclipse; when only part of the light is blocked out, it is a partial solar eclipse. Eclipses cannot be seen in all parts of the world at the same time. Sometimes an

eclipse can be seen best in the United States, other times in England, and still other times in Africa. There are often two solar eclipses in a year, sometimes as many as five. There can be as many as five lunar eclipses, but sometimes more. Scientists have a list telling them when and where an eclipse will occur.

Eclipses happen because the sun, earth, and moon are always moving in the heavens. Thousands of years ago people believed that eclipses were caused by evil spirits.

ecology

Ecology is the study of the relationships between living things and their environments. It is a branch of biology, and the word means "study of the house"—the "house" being, in this case, the world we live in. The actual livable space covering the earth is only a thin layer of air, soil, and water called the *biosphere,* which supports all life. On land this layer extends from the tops of the highest trees to the depths of the deepest roots; although birds and insects can soar above the tallest trees, they do not actually live up there, and must always return to the earth. Life in the ocean can exist at a depth of five or six miles, but nearly all sea life is concentrated in the top 500 feet of water. In the limited area of the biosphere live more than 1,300,000 kinds of animals and plants. There are many different environments: grasslands, forests, arid deserts, steamy jungles, frozen tundras, freshwater ponds, salty oceans, and areas of perpetual snow, to name a few. Each supports a characteristic assortment of animal and plant life, and this community is called a *biome.* Each biome has its own pattern of rainfall, as well as typical changes in temperature, humidity, seasons, and lengths of days. All these factors together determine the kinds of plants growing there, which in turn influence the animal life in the biome. Biomes on land are named for the dominant vegetation that develops and thrives there, but as other types of plants also exist there, biomes are divided into smaller units called *habitats,* each with its own group of life forms. Each life form in a habitat has its own special needs in the way of shelter, food, and relationships to other forms in the habitat. Each living thing, plant or animal, has its own place, called a *niche,* in the total balance of life in the biome. Due to many factors, both natural and man-made, this balance is constantly but slowly changing. A pond, for example, may once have been a lake; as its edges become overgrown, dying vegetations fills it in, the shrinking pond becomes a swamp, and finally dry land, with a totally different plant and animal community.

economics

Economics is the science that tells us how men get the things they want and need. An economist, a person who studies economics, studies the economic problems of families, towns, cities, and governments. Economics is a very important science because all of us want and need many things.

There are two kinds of objects or commodities that people want. One kind is called *free goods,* and the other is called *economic goods.* Free goods are commodi-

ties that do not cost anything. Such things as fresh air and sunshine are free goods. Economic goods are commodities that we have to pay for, such as clothes and food. Sometimes things that are free goods in one place are economic goods in another place. If you lived on an island in the tropics where there was plenty of food, and it grew on trees and all you had to do was pick it, food would be one of the free goods. Unfortunately, most of us do not live on such an island. We must pay, somehow, for the food we eat because somebody worked hard and spent money to grow it for us. The way we get the money to pay for the things we want is called *economic activity.*

Suppose you want a candy bar and it costs ten cents. Why does it cost ten cents and not more or less? What gives it a value of ten cents exactly?

Let's suppose that your candy bar is made of chocolate, sugar, and nuts. The manufacturer of the bar had to get his chocolate from an importer who probably got the chocolate from South America. The sugar came from a hot country in the south, probably Cuba. The nuts came from India or Brazil or the southern part of the United States. The candy bar also has a wrapper made of colored, printed paper with wax on it to keep the candy fresh. The manufacturer had to pay for the printing, coloring and waxing of the paper, too. But his biggest cost is labor. Labor is the word economists use when they mean all the people who work in business and manufacturing. Naturally, everyone who works at a job has to be paid. The wages paid to labor are the biggest part of the cost of manufacturing something.

In addition to the cost of the labor, there is the cost of the machines that are used to mix the candy and nuts and sugar together to make a candy bar, and to wrap it. The manufacturer has to pay for the machines and keep them in good running condition. He must also have a building to put them in. He must either buy the building or pay rent for it. After the manufacturer has put the chocolate, sugar and nuts together, and paid for all the operations performed on them to make a candy bar, and wrapped the candy bar, he has to sell it at a profit. If he did not sell it at a profit, he would not have the money he needs to feed and clothe himself and his family.

How does he know how much profit he has to make to keep in business and to make a living at the same time? The amount of profit he makes is controlled by two things. It is controlled by the cost of production, and the prices charged by the other makers of candy bars. The cost of production is the amount of money it costs him to make candy bars plus overhead. Overhead is the rent he pays and the cost of repairing machines and such other things as taxes and insurance. The other candy-bar makers are his competitors. If he charges more for his candy than they do, most people will not buy his product but will buy the ones that cost less, unless his candy bar is much better and therefore worth more.

Suppose that when the candy bar is finally made it has cost five cents and that the manufacturer has to make a two-

cent profit to pay for the cost of his own living and have enough left over to buy more chocolate, sugar, and nuts. He must charge seven cents for the bar. The dealer, or retailer, who buys from the manufacturer pays seven cents and charges you a dime. He has made three cents profit, which will help pay the rent and the cost of running his store. If he charges more than ten cents he will make more profit, but if all the other candy stores charge only a dime, no one will buy from him. If he charges less he may not be able to make enough money to pay all his expenses.

ECONOMIC LAWS

Economic laws describe what happens at different times in the field of business or economics.

One of the best-known economic laws is called the *law of supply and demand*. The word *supply* means how much of a commodity there is available to be sold. If all the candy-bar manufacturers in the country made a million candy bars in one year, the supply of candy bars that year would be one million bars. The word *demand* means how much of a commodity people want or are able to buy. If the people only wanted half a million of the million candy bars made, the demand for candy bars would be half a million. Since people wanted fewer candy bars than the manufacturers made, economists would say that the supply was greater than the demand. When this happens, all of a commodity that is in the stores cannot be sold, and the manufacturers must stop making the commodity. This is very bad for business. The manufacturer must do something to keep on making and selling his product. He usually lowers the price of his commodity. The oversupply of candy bars would be sold for less money. When the price of something is lowered, the demand for it is increased, because more people can afford to buy things that are cheaper than they were before. The demand for the candy equals the supply when all the bars that are manufactured are bought by the people.

When more people want a commodity than there are pieces or packages of that commodity, the economists then say that the demand exceeds the supply. When this happens, the price of the commodity is raised. Then fewer people can afford to buy the commodity, and the demand for it drops. It is not always easy to know whether demand is greater than supply or supply greater than demand. Sometimes it takes some time before a businessman can tell. At other times something happens very suddenly to change the normal good balance between supply and demand. Supply usually is greater than demand during times when business is bad and fewer people are working and earning money. This means that fewer people are able to spend money, so the demand for things drops. Demand usually exceeds supply during wartime when manufacturers are busy making war materials and there are fewer things on the market that people want and need. People are working and earning much money at these times and they demand or want things, but there is only a small supply of these things available. That is why prices are so high during wartimes.

Another important economic law is called the *law of diminishing returns*. If a farmer puts a pound of seed and a bushel of fertilizer on a one-acre field, he will grow a hundred pounds of vegetables. If he puts three pounds of seed and three bushels of fertilizer on the field, he will grow three hundred pounds of vegetables. But if he puts ten pounds of seed and ten bushels of fertilizer on the field, he will not grow a thousand pounds of vegetables because the field is not big enough to grow that much. If he doubles these amounts, he will grow even less, for by now the vegetables will be choking each other for space. This is an illustration of the law of diminishing returns. Beyond a certain point, the more that is put into some process, the less the return becomes.

The study of economics includes TAXES, BANKING, TRADE, ACCOUNTING, and MONEY. You can read about these subjects in separate articles.

Ecuador

Ecuador is a small country on the Pacific coast of South America. It is larger than Arizona, having an area of more than 106,000 square miles, and more than six million people live there, or over three times as many as there are in Arizona. The Galápagos Islands belong to Ecuador and are about 500 miles off the cost in the Pacific. (You can read about the GALÁPAGOS in a separate article.)

Ecuador is a land of many contrasts and colors. It lies on the equator, the imaginary line that runs around the center of the earth, from which it gets its name. It has snow-capped mountains, and its landscapes range from grey misty moors and many-colored fertile valleys, to dry yellow desert, green moist jungles, and sandy beaches.

THE PEOPLE WHO LIVE THERE

The land, and the people who live on it, are divided naturally into three parts by the Andes, a very high mountain range that cuts through the center of the country. On the east side there is an interior jungle section called the Oriente. In the center are the mountains, or highlands. The people belong to many different tribes and have different origins, but almost everyone follows the Roman Catholic religion.

Most of the Negroes and many of the mestizos (half Indian, half Spanish) live in the coastal region. These people probably once made up the Esmeralda and Manta tribes, but they were conquered by the Spaniards. There are no records to tell us if they were all killed, or if they became mixed with their conquerors through marriage.

About three-quarters of the people of Ecuador live in the mountainous highland region. Here is where the Quitus Indians once lived, the tribe that gives Quito, the capital of Ecuador, its name. Almost a thousand years ago the Quitus were conquered by a tribe called the Caras, who still later were conquered by the Incas. Almost all the people in the highlands are descendants of these tribes and more than a million speak the Quechua language.

In the Oriente, the eastern jungle section, there are very few people, but they are very interesting. These tribes have had little contact with our civilization, and still live much the same as they did before America was discovered. There are the Jivaros, who used to shrink the heads of their battle victims for trophies. Here too, live the Cayapa and the Colorado Indians, so called because they paint their bodies in bright colors, especially red and black.

HOW THE PEOPLE LIVE

About half the people in Ecuador are farmers, but there are two types of farming. On the northern coastal plain the people grow most of the crops which are sent to other countries, such as the important cacao crop, from which chocolate and cocoa are made, the increasingly important banana crop, rice, kapok, rubber, coffee, and the tagua nuts which are used as a substitute for ivory. More balsa wood comes from Ecuador than from any other place, and during World War II, the Allies used large amounts of it to make life rafts and a very lightweight bomber called the "Mosquito."

Most of the vegetables and fruits eaten by the Ecuadorian people are grown in the highland region. Some people here work in small factories making textiles, shoes, cement, soap, and furniture. Many others work at home where they make most of the Panama hats in the world, which do not come from Panama at all. Ecuador is almost self-sufficient; the only things its people must get from other countries are items like paper, chemicals, machinery, and trucks.

The people are very cheerful and like to wear brilliant colors. In the large cities bullfighting is a favorite amusement, and all through the highlands men play a game called *pelota*. This game is played with a ball and a large *guante*, or glove, which is tied to the right wrist. It is sometimes called a tennis game for giants.

According to the law, children between the ages of 6 and 14 must go to school, but some mountain villages are so isolated that it is hard to enforce the law. There are high schools where boys and girls can go to if they like, and there is a university in each of the large cities.

WHAT KIND OF PLACE IT IS

Ecuador is a country that has mountains, jungles, plains, and every kind of climate. There are many peaks almost as high as Mount Chimborazo, which is more than twenty thousand feet high; the Andes are among the highest mountains of the world. Many minerals such as copper, iron, gold, lead, silver and coal are in the Andes, but because they

are so hard to get at, they have not been mined much. Some of the higher mountains are snow-capped, even though they are near the equator. Others are volcanoes, some of which are active. Except for the Pan-American Highway through Ecuador, and a railroad connecting the capital city of Quito with the port of Guayaquil, few good railroads or highways have been built because of the mountains. Mule trains and the strange-looking animals called llamas are still used to carry things in the mountains. On the hillsides the climate is like spring all year, and in Quito, a city almost two miles above sea level, the climate is so wonderful that people who are sick with tuberculosis go there to be cured.

There are probably more earthquakes in Ecuador than anywhere else. The cities of Quito and Guayaquil have been severely damaged in the past, and in 1949 an earthquake destroyed the town of Ambato, killing six thousand people.

To the west of the mountains is the Pacific coast. The important Guayas and Esmeraldas rivers come down from the mountains and flow through this hot, unhealthy forest region. Trees used for making furniture, balsa, and chinchona (for the medicine quinine) are sent down these rivers which become swollen during the rainy season from December to May.

To the east of the Andes lies the wild Oriente section. Here is dense jungle filled with beautiful and dangerous plants and animals. There are large, wonderfully colored butterflies; giant ants that eat anything in their way; anacondas and boas, snakes that are sometimes 38 feet long; crocodiles, pumas, jaguars, deer, monkeys, and other animals. Many of the natives live by hunting them, but the Oriente is not a safe place for anyone to be.

HOW THE PEOPLE ARE GOVERNED

The government of Ecuador is similar to that of the United States. The president is elected directly by the people and he serves for four years. The Congress is made up of 52 Senators who serve for four years, and a Chamber of Deputies or Representatives (one for each 80,000 people, or about 72) who serve for two years. However, Ecuador has nothing like the state governors elected in the United States; the local government is controlled by the central or national government in Quito.

People over 18 *must* vote, provided they can read and write. This law bars many people from voting. Social security helps those who are sick, old, or have had accidents. Labor laws guarantee workers a minimum wage and a 44-hour working week. All men must serve in the armed forces.

Ecuador is becoming more and more friendly with the United States and other American nations. It was on the Allied side in World War II and allowed the United States to build a big air base on Seymour Island in the Galapagos Islands, to help protect the Panama Canal. Ecuador was one of the first to join the United Nations.

ECUADOR IN THE PAST

The history of Ecuador has been filled with constant struggle. The Indians fought among themselves before the Spaniards came, making it easier for the army of Francisco Pizarro to conquer them (about 1530). But then the Spanish soldiers began to fight among themselves for the treasures they had found, and law and order was not established for more than twenty years.

When the people of South America rose up in revolt against Spanish rule, about 150 years ago, Ecuador joined the fight, and in 1830 became an independent republic. In the early years of the new nation the country was divided into two camps. The Conservatives supported the Roman Catholic Church and the army, and the Liberals wanted to give the people more liberty and limit the power of the Church, especially in the schools. For many years there were bitter fights between these two parties. Then in 1861 Gabriel García Moreno, a Conservative, became president. For fourteen years he gave Ecuador an orderly government, and he did good things for the country, building roads and public buildings. Moreno would not allow anyone to disagree with him, however, and he made many enemies. Juan Montalvo, a Liberal, wrote many articles against Moreno, and when Moreno was murdered in 1875, Montalvo said, "My pen has killed him." After this, the Liberals held power for many years. Their most famous president was Eloy Alfaro, who has been compared with Abraham Lincoln. He began schools to train teachers, allowed women to work for the government, and made sure the Indians got equal treatment.

With modern farming methods, Ecuador has doubled its food production since 1948. At the Rio de Janeiro Conference in 1942, Ecuador and Peru finally settled a long-standing border dispute. With Colombia, Venezuela and Panama, Ecuador signed the Quito Charter in 1948, promising to work out their problems.

THE CHIEF CITIES IN ECUADOR

Quito is the capital and the second-largest city in Ecuador, having more than 528,000 people. It is the center of Ecuador's political and educational life.

Guayaquil is the largest city in Ecuador, having more than 794,000 people. It is on the Guayas River near the ocean and is a very important port.

ECUADOR. Area, 106,178 square miles. Population (1973 estimate) 6,300,000. Language, Spanish. Religion, Roman Catholic. Government, republic. Monetary unit, the sucré, worth about 4 cents (U.S.). Flag, wide yellow bar over smaller blue and red bars; coat of arms in the center.

ecumenical council

An ecumenical council is a meeting at which representatives of different Christian Churches, or of different branches of the same Church, try to settle their disagreements. Famous meetings of branches of the Catholic Church, such as the Council of Nicaea (a city in Asia Minor) in 325 A.D.; the Diet (assembly) of Worms (a city in Germany) in 1521, and the Council of Trent (a city in Italy), from 1545 to 1563, solved some problems but never all. Most other ecumenical councils have been among representatives of Protestant Churches and have not succeeded in combining more than a few of the hundreds of different Protestant denominations. In 1959 John XXIII, then the Pope, called for a new ecumenical council in the Roman Catholic Church. This council met in 1962 and again (under Pope Paul VI) in 1963. It succeeded in solving some questions in Church government and adopting a more liberal attitude toward persons who are not Catholics.

eczema

Eczema is a disease of the skin. It causes the skin to become red and perhaps pimply, and to itch. Doctors use the name eczema for such a skin condition when they do not know what causes it. Eczema may be caused by an allergy, or by rough clothing that irritates the skin, or by some other disease, or even by a mental condition such as worry. The first step in treating eczema is a series of tests to find out what is causing it. Eczema is not contagious; that is, you cannot catch it from someone else.

Eddas

The Eddas are collections of songs or poems that tell about the ancient Norwegian gods and goddesses, and about the beginning of the earth. There are two kinds of Eddas, and they were written down in the 13th century, in Iceland. The songs of the older Edda had been sung for hundreds of years before that. The young Edda is about poetry, which in those days really meant religion. That is, a poem was a "soulful song," or a song about man's soul, and it contained the ideas you learn in church, or from holy books. Poetry was supposed to come from a god who could answer all questions. One of the most famous poems in the Eddas is about a seeress who could see into the Past and the Future. See MYTHS AND MYTHOLOGY.

Eddy, Mary Baker

When Mary Baker Eddy was a little girl in New Hampshire, her stern, religious father believed that God punishes most human beings forever and chooses only a few to be saved after death. But her mother taught her to lean on God's love and go to Him in prayer.

As she grew up, Mary searched constantly for the truth about God and man and bodily health. She had become convinced that if she could discover the spiritual law behind Jesus' healings, the same healings could be done in her times. After an accident in which she was dangerously hurt, she was suddenly sure she had found the truth; and her injuries were healed.

Christian Science Center

After this she spent years studying the Bible, writing, and testing her discovery. In 1875 she published her famous book, first called *Science and Health* but afterward entitled *Science and Health with Key to the Scriptures*. People began to come to her to study. She called her discovery Christian Science, and in 1879 she founded the Church of Christ Scientist, in Boston, Massachusetts. In 1892 she established the present worldwide organization, The First Church of Christ, Scientist, in Boston, Massachusetts, and its branches.

Mrs. Eddy lived a very busy life, conducting the affairs of her Church, writing books and articles, and receiving visitors from all parts of the world. When she was 87 she founded the daily newspaper *The Christian Science Monitor*. She died in 1910, when she was 89.

See also the article CHRISTIAN SCIENCE.

edelweiss

Edelweiss is the name of a flowering plant that grows high up in the Swiss mountains. It is about six inches tall, and has a small yellow flower that is surrounded by leaves that are covered with white fuzz. These leaves make the edelweiss look like a soft, white star from a distance. The edelweiss is a rare flower, and there are many stories about brave men who have tried to climb the rocky Alps to pick the edelweiss, and have lost their lives. The Swiss people have made this flower their national emblem, and it is now against the law to pick it in Switzerland. Many people in Europe and the United States grow the edelweiss in their gardens. In the German language, the word *edelweiss* means "noble white."

Eden, Anthony

Sir Anthony Eden is the name of an important English statesman who became prime minister in 1955, succeeding Winston Churchill. Eden was born in 1897. His full name is Robert Anthony Eden. He was a captain in the British Army during World War I, and after the war, when he was about 25 years old, he began his career as a statesman. Eden held many different government positions including prime minister. He was the chief British representative to the League of Nations in 1935. Three times, beginning in 1934, he was British foreign minister, which is about the same as Secretary of State in the United States government. He was foreign minister during the important years of World War II. In 1955, Eden became prime minister. He resigned this high position and retired from politics in 1957, partly because of ill health but also because his government had failed in its effort to take control of the Suez Canal from Egypt. In 1961 Eden was made Earl of Avon.

Ederle, Gertrude, the first American woman to swim across the English Channel, on August 6, 1926.

Edinburgh, Duke of, see Prince PHILIP.

Edinburgh

Edinburgh is the capital of Scotland. It is in the south of Scotland, two miles south of the Firth of Forth. Edinburgh was first settled in the 7th century. It did not actually become a city until it was given a charter by the Scottish King Robert I (Robert Bruce). This happened in 1329. It became the capital of the country in 1436. Many kings and queens of Scotland made their home in Edinburgh. They lived in a castle built on a rock more than 400 feet high in the western part of the city. Edinburgh Castle may still be seen, high up on its rock.

Some of the Scottish rulers lived in another place, Holyrood Palace, a mile to the east of the castle. The city grew up between the castle and the palace. The eastern part is called the New Town. The western part is the Old Town. Between the two ran a stream called the Nor' Loch. It was filled in with earth, and trees and bushes were planted there. Today one of the most beautiful streets in the world runs alongside where the stream used to run. It is called Princes Street and is the business and shopping center of the city.

Edinburgh is a center for printing and publishing. Its factories make paper, rubber goods, rope, soap, and other things. The city has a famous university, Edinburgh University, and two medical schools, the Royal College of Surgeons and the Royal College of Physicians.

EDINBURGH, SCOTLAND. Population 464,-764 (1973 estimate). Capital of Scotland. County seat, Midlothian County. Settled, 7th century; chartered as a city, 1329.

Edison, Thomas Alva

Thomas Alva Edison was one of the greatest inventors of American history. Among his most important inventions are the electric light bulb, the phonograph, and the talking motion picture. During his long life Edison had 1,099 patents granted to him by the Patent Office in Washington, D.C., and he worked on at least a thousand other inventions.

HIS EARLY YEARS

Thomas Edison was born at Milan, Ohio, on February 11, 1847. When he was seven his family moved to Port Huron, Michigan. Edison only went to school for three months. Because his teacher did not understand him, Edison's mother, who had been a schoolteacher before her marriage, taught him at home.

Edison was an unusual little boy, always observing and investigating. He never believed anything until he proved it by experiment. When he was six years old, his father found him sitting on a nest of goose eggs, trying to hatch them. At the age of nine he started making scientific experiments in a laboratory that he set up in his cellar. All his money was spent on chemicals, which he kept in bottles on the shelves. The bottles were marked "Poison," so that nobody would disturb them.

When Edison was 12 years old he became a newsboy on a train that left Port Huron in the morning and returned there in the evening. Edison set up a laboratory in the baggage car of the train because he did not want to waste any time. Later he bought a printing press and set it up in his laboratory on wheels. He published a weekly paper, which he sold for three cents a copy. At the same time Edison spent many of his free hours reading in the public library. He started to read the library through, book by book, shelf by shelf.

The laboratory on wheels came to a sudden end one day when a stick of phos-phorus fell on the floor of the train and exploded. The conductor became very angry and put Edison off the train at the next stop.

Edison was partially deaf most of his life. He once wrote, "I haven't heard a bird sing since I was 12 years old." Speculation has been made that his deafness was caused by a blow to the ears or from his childhood bout with scarlet fever. He said his deafness resulted when a trainman grabbed him by the ears and pulled him onto a moving train.

After this Edison became a telegraph operator, at first around his home town and later in Boston, Massachusetts. Shortly after Edison arrived in Boston he decided to give up telegraph operating and devote all his time to inventing. With only enough money for his boat ticket, he set out for New York.

EARLY INVENTIONS

In New York York Edison became a manager of one company and later a partner in another company called Pope, Edison & Co. When this company was bought by Western Union, Edison was asked to sell several of his inventions to the new owners. Edison was 22 years old at the time, and he had never sold any invention before. He decided to charge $3,000 and when Western Union offered him $40,000 he nearly fainted.

With this money Edison opened a shop in Newark, New Jersey, where he continued with his inventions. Edison, unlike many inventors, always had men to help him. He planned the experiments and the other men worked on them.

Between the years 1870 and 1876 Edison patented 122 inventions. Many of these inventions had to do with telegraphy, but other inventions were the mimeograph, a machine to copy letters, and district call boxes, used today for police calls and fire alarms. He also had a part in developing the typewriter.

While in Newark, Edison married Miss Mary G. Stilwell. In 1876 the Edisons moved to Menlo Park, New Jersey, where Edison founded a laboratory that became world-famous.

THE WIZARD OF MENLO PARK

One of the first inventions at Menlo Park was the carbon transmitter. This transmitter made the telephone, invented by Alexander Graham Bell, practical for wide use. It also made possible the later invention of the microphone used in radio.

Edison's favorite invention was the phonograph, the first patent for which was issued in 1878. This invention made Edison famous throughout the world.

In 1878 Edison started to work on the problem of electric lighting. At that time the huge arc light was the only electric light. Edison wanted to make electric lights in small units or "divided" lamps. To do this he had to produce a filament, or tiny wire, that would stay hot for a long period without melting. He tried many materials, including carbon, platinum, and other alloys, but in each case the wires melted after they had been lighted for a short time.

For months about fifty men worked

day and night at this invention. Edison himself always worked 18 or 19 hours a day, sleeping only a few hours now and then. Finally Edison tried carbonized thread as a filament. The carbonized thread was put in the bulb, which was emptied of air and sealed. The current was turned on, and there was light! The incandescent lamp, the modern electric light, was invented. The date was October 21, 1879.

At this time Edison was only 32 years old, and he had become known as the "Wizard of Menlo Park" because of all his inventions.

THE MOTION PICTURE

Edison's first wife died in 1884, and in 1886 he married Miss Mina Miller. In 1887 he moved his laboratory to West Orange, New Jersey.

In 1889, with the aid of the new transparent celluloid roll films introduced by George Eastman, Edison produced the first practical motion picture camera, and the first projector to throw pictures on the screen. In 1912, by using the phonograph and the motion-picture camera, Edison produced the talking motion picture.

EDISON'S LATER YEARS

Once Edison was asked the secret of his success and he replied, "Hard work, based on hard thinking." Edison continued to work hard and to think hard in his later years. His inventions included the alkaline storage battery, the telescribe, which makes automatic records of telephone conversations, and the transophone, which is a kind of dictating machine. During World War I he worked on the Naval Consulting Board. At the age of 80, Mr. Edison was experimenting on the rubber content of various kinds of plants, hoping to find a way to produce rubber.

On October 21, 1929, the fiftieth anniversary of the electric light, President Herbert Hoover and other important men in the United States met at Dearborn, Michigan, to honor Thomas Edison. Here Henry Ford had reproduced the old wooden laboratory at Menlo Park where Edison made so many famous inventions.

Thomas Edison died on October 18, 1931, when he was 85 years old. He was buried on the fifty-second anniversary of the invention of the electric light. At ten o'clock that evening, at the suggestion of the President, millions of lights all across the United States were put out for one minute, in honor of the man who had invented them.

Edmonton

Edmonton is the capital city of the province of Alberta, in southwest Canada. Alberta borders on the state of Montana in the United States. Edmonton is on the North Saskatchewan River. Over 438,000 people live there. More railroads and airlines meet in Edmonton than in any other city of the Canadian Northwest. There are rich farm lands and coal mines in the region around Edmonton, and the farm produce and coal are shipped from that city. Edmonton has also been a fur-trading station since it was first settled in 1795 as a fort and post of the Hudson's Bay Company. This company bought furs from the Indians in all parts of the Northwest. If you visit Edmonton, you can still see the ruins of the fort on a bluff or cliff overlooking the town. At Edmonton, besides the government buildings, are the University of Alberta and a Jesuit college for training priests of the Roman Catholic Church. Gold, silver and platinum are mined in the region.

EDMONTON, ALBERTA. Population, 438,-152 (1971 census). On the North Saskatchewan River. Settled 1795.

education

Education is the process by which each generation of human beings learns the things that were known by human beings before them. Education includes both the teaching and the learning of this knowledge.

It is largely education that makes the difference between men and animals. In every generation men learn new things, and none of the new knowledge is ever lost because it is taught to the next generation. Education is more important than anything else in the world. Men have been able to survive and become civilized and build powerful nations mainly because of education.

SCHOOLS

Most people become educated by going to school. For hundreds of years only the very rich people or the nobility and members of the clergy went to school. The common people did not even learn to read and write. It is only within the last few centuries that the world has realized that education is important to all people.

From the time when the United States first became a country, the leaders in the government have believed that education for everyone was important. At first only the boys were given a free education, but later both boys and girls were included. Today all state governments promise free education to all children from 6 to 16, and many of the states provide for education beyond that age.

KINDS OF SCHOOL

For many years educators have studied the best ways to organize schools and the best ways to teach. Many different ideas have been followed and many different ideas have been tried. In most places the schools have been organized along the following lines:

Kindergarten, a pre-school or play school. In kindergarten the child learns to work well with other children and to become accustomed to going to school. A four- or a five-year-old child goes to kindergarten. There are play schools for children as young as two.

Elementary school, sometimes called grammar or grade school. Elementary school generally has eight grades. The child begins the first grade when he is 6 years old, the age at which he is ready to read. At the end of eight years the child has learned to read, to write, and to do simple arithmetic. He has learned a little about many other subjects, such as history, geography, and science. Up until about fifty years ago an elementary-school education was considered sufficient for most people. In more recent times, people have become convinced that more education is desirable. In the United States today most people go on from elementary to higher education.

High school, a four-year course beyond elementary school. Some high schools are divided into junior and senior high, and in such cases grades seven and eight of the elementary school become part of the junior high school. There is a separate article on HIGH SCHOOL. The high school prepares the student either for higher education or for a job.

College, education for those who wish to go beyond high school. People usually go to college for training in business or in one of the professions, but recently more and more people are going to college because they feel the additional education is worth while. The college course is also a four-years course, at the end of which a student graduates and receives a bachelor's degree. The student may do advanced study in some special field to earn a master's or a doctor's degree. There is a separate article on COLLEGES AND UNIVERSITIES.

WHAT IS TAUGHT IN SCHOOLS

Once the subjects taught in schools were classical. The literatures and languages of the Greeks and the Romans were considered the most important thing for the schoolchild to learn. For many years schoolchildren spent long hours memorizing Latin verbs and reciting Latin poetry.

Gradually this curriculum, or course of study, was replaced by a more practical curriculum, although classical subjects were considered of first importance until about fifty years ago. Up until that time any person who went to high school learned at least one language, usually Latin, and studied some kind of higher mathematics, usually algebra. He also read some of the great works of literature of the past.

Today there are many subjects taught in the schools. By the time a student reaches high school he has some idea of what he is interested in learning. He studies the subjects about which he wishes to learn and by which he will be helped in the future.

METHODS OF TEACHING

For centuries people have been trying to decide how best to teach children. They have realized that children should like to learn and that they should remember what they have learned. There have been many different methods used. For example, Cardinal Mazarin, a great French statesman, taught the boy King Louis XIV by playing card games with him. The cards were marked with things that Mazarin thought the young king should know.

For many years teachers taught students by the catechism method. The teachers asked certain questions and the students were taught to give certain answers. In this way all students learned certain facts that their teachers thought necessary.

MNEMONICS

The mnemonics system has been the most widely-used method of teaching. In this method the teacher presents facts to

the student to memorize. The student then repeats these facts from memory whenever he is tested on them. This method of teaching has been criticized by many educators. They say the student sometimes does not understand what he is memorizing and does not know why it is important. Today many teachers continue to use this method, particularly in the elementary schools.

The lecture system has also been used, particularly in high schools and colleges. The teacher lectures to the students, who take notes about the important things the teacher says. Then the student reads more about the subject in outside books.

PROGRESSIVE EDUCATION

One new method of education is called *progressive education*. Progressive educators believe children should be taught a subject only if they are interested in studying it. Instead of learning reading, writing, and arithmetic by a series of sounds, rules, and tables, the classroom has a rich supply of materials. An example is the learning of arithmetic through an imaginary grocery store.

The child who studies in a progressive elementary school may not learn the alphabet or the multiplication tables. He may learn to write by keeping a diary of his own actions from day to day, and he learns to spell words only when it is necessary for him to use them in his writing.

The child with a teacher's guidance decides upon his own curriculum. If he becomes interested in Indians, for example, his teacher will help him find out about everything connected with Indians, how they lived, dressed, and worked, and how they built their houses, and what they ate. Probably the class will do other projects which relate to Indians.

There is still much argument about whether progressive education is a good way to teach schoolchildren.

SEGREGATION IN THE SCHOOLS

For many years the southern states and those states near the south did not allow black children to go to the same school with white children. The black children were segregated, or kept apart, from the white children. The black people and others said that this was against the constitution. In 1898 the Supreme Court of the United States ruled that separate schools were not against the constitution as long as the schools for the black children were as good as the schools for the white children.

For more than fifty years the southern states relied upon this "separate but equal" decision. Separate schools were maintained, but most of the black schools were not as good as the white schools. The black people and others said black children would never receive an equal education as long as their education was a separate one. In the late 1940s and the early 1950s, when it seemed likely the Supreme Court would change its decision, the southern states raised a great deal of money to build new black schools that would be equal. However, in 1954 the Supreme Court ruled that segregation is against the

constitution, even if the separate schools are equal. Today, children of all races and creeds are integrated in schools. This was accomplished through the efforts of the Civil Rights Movement in the 1960's. There still are many problems concerning the issue of busing children to achieve integration.

Edward, King of England

The name Edward has been borne by eleven kings of England, but only eight of them have been numbered, since the other three were Anglo-Saxon kings who ruled before William the Conqueror and the Norman conquest in 1066.

The first Anglo-Saxon king named Edward was called Edward the Elder (the oldest Edward). He ruled from 899 to 925. He was the son of King Alfred the Great, and is famous because he fought the Danes (people of Denmark) and won back a large part of England that they had taken from his father.

Edward the Martyr ruled for only three years, from 975 to 978. His stepmother, Queen Elfrida, is supposed to have had him murdered so that her own son, Ethelred, could become king. He was called Edward the Martyr (a martyr is a person who is killed because he will not give up his beliefs) and also considered a saint because when his body was moved after his death, three miracles are said to have occurred.

Edward the Confessor ruled from 1042 to 1066.

Edward I, the ninth king of England after William the Conqueror, was born in 1239. He belonged to what is called the House (family) of Plantagenet and was the son of Henry III, whom he succeeded as king in 1272. Edward I was one of the greatest kings that England ever had. He limited the Church's civil power and established more law and order. The English Constitution was developed under his reign, and he also set up a system of courts of law. Probably his most important act was to put all power of raising taxes in the hands of a "Model Parliament" (Congress), which was the first parliament of its kind in England that represented the people. During Edward's reign Wales was united with England, and the title "Prince of Wales" was created for his oldest son, who became Edward II. (This is the same title that has since been given to the king's oldest son or any other male heir to the throne.) Edward I was a fine soldier and a handsome, charming man, so tall that he was called Edward Longshanks. He died in 1302.

Edward II was born in 1284 and became king in 1307 when his father, Edward I, died on the way to Scotland to fight the army of the Scottish leader, Robert Bruce. Edward promised his father to carry on the fight against Scotland, but he was a coward and a poor leader. Robert Bruce completely defeated him. Edward was the first English king who was forced to give up the throne. Everybody hated him because he was such a weak king. The great nobles finally forced Edward to give up the throne to his son, Edward III, in 1327. In the same year he was murdered by Roger de Mortimer, a friend of Queen Isabella, his wife.

Edward III was born in 1312. He succeeded his father, Edward II, when he was only 15 years old. In 1330, he seized control of the government, which until then had been held by his mother, Queen Isabella, and her friend Mortimer. Edward had Mortimer executed and forced Isabella to leave the court. Edward then led an expedition against Scotland, but the French soon interfered, so he invaded their country too. This invasion of France marked the beginning of the Hundred Years' War, which began in 1337 and kept Edward busy during most of his reign. He and his famous son, Edward the Black Prince, won many brilliant victories, but the war was very hard on England. (You can read about EDWARD THE BLACK PRINCE and the HUNDRED YEARS WAR in separate articles.) Before Edward died in 1377 he had much trouble with his son and with Parliament (Congress), which he was dependent upon for money and supplies. During Edward's reign there was a terrible plague, or disease, called the "Black Death" that killed nearly half the people in England.

Edward IV was the first member of the York family to become a king of England. He was born in 1442, the son of Richard, Duke of York, a descendant of Edward III. He became king in 1461 during the WAR OF THE ROSES, which you can read about in a separate article. During this war, the York party, which Edward led after his father was killed, defeated the Lancaster party, which was led by King Henry VI. Henry was a very weak king, so Edward put him in the Tower of London and made himself king. In 1470 Henry was rescued from the Tower by the Earl of Warwick. Edward fled to France, but returned the next year with an army and defeated Warwick. He then put Henry back in the Tower, where he soon died. Edward was a strong king and very popular. He died in 1483 and was succeeded by his son, Edward V.

Edward V was only 13 years old when his father died. As soon as he became king his cruel uncle, Richard, Duke of Gloucester, had himself appointed protector of the kingdom. Gloucester then put him with his young brother, Richard, the Duke of York, in the Tower of London. Most people believe that they were murdered there by order of their uncle, who made himself King Richard III. Much later, the bones of two children were found buried in the Tower, probably those of Edward and his brother.

Edward VI was only 10 years old when he became king, but he was very intelligent and advanced for his age. He was born in 1537, the son of Henry VIII. He tried to carry out the religious changes begun by his father and he was helped first by his uncle, the protector, Edward Seymour (later Duke of Somerset), then by John Dudley (later Duke of Northumberland). But Edward was king for only six years and died in 1553, at the age of 16.

Edward VII was born in 1841 and was 60 years old when he became king. He

was the son of Queen Victoria and Prince Albert. In 1863, he married Princess Alexander, daughter of King Christian IX of Denmark. They had six children, the second of whom became King George V. Edward be-

Gale Research Co.

came king when his mother, Queen Victoria, died in 1901, and he himself died only nine years later. He was very popular and helped his country a great deal in its relations with foreign countries.

Edward VIII was born in 1894. He succeeded his father, George V, on January 20, 1936, and after he had been king for only ten months, he abdicated (gave up his throne) on December 10. He studied at the Royal Naval College. He was made Prince of Wales in 1911. During World War I, he served in France, and later in Italy and Egypt. After the war, he traveled a great deal all over the world until his father died in 1936. Ten months after his accession, he announced his intention of marrying an American-born woman, Wallis Warfield Simpson. A great crisis arose when the British government opposed the king's wish. Edward thereupon abdicated and his younger brother became King George VI. Edward himself was granted the title of Duke of Windsor. He went to France, where he married Wallis Warfield Simpson. When World War II began, the duke served briefly in France as a major general, then as governor of the Bahama Islands from 1940 to 1945. He later moved to France but traveled much and made frequent trips to the United States.

Edward the Black Prince

Edward the Black Prince never became king of England, but he served his country during the Hundred Years' War between England and France. The title of "Black Prince," which probably referred to his black armor, was not given him until long after he died. Edward, the son of Edward III of England, was born in 1330. The prince joined his father's army as a young man, and soon showed himself to be a successful leader. In 1356, Prince Edward won a great victory at the battle of Poitiers, a town in central France. He took King John II of France a prisoner.

The prince married Joan, "the fair maid of Kent," in 1361, and a year later he became governor of some provinces in southern France that then belonged to the English. In 1367, he led an army into Spain to help the king of Castile regain his throne, but this war brought Edward great losses. War with France broke out again. Edward became ill, and had to return to England. He opposed the dishonest government of his brother, John of Gaunt. The Black Prince died in 1376. His only son later became King Richard II.

Edward the Confessor

Edward the Confessor was the last of the Anglo-Saxon kings of England. He was called "the Confessor" because he was a very religious man. He was the first English king to use the touch of his hand to cure a skin disease called "the King's

evil." Edward was born about 1002, and was brought up in France, because at that time the king of Denmark also ruled England. Edward became king of England in 1042. He gathered together the rules of justice that people had followed in England, and made them into laws. During the last years of his life, he built Westminster Abbey, the great cathedral of London, England. You probably remember that Queen Elizabeth II was crowned in the Abbey, as many of England's rulers have been. Edward died in 1066, and his successor was William the Conqueror. There are separate articles about WESTMINSTER ABBEY, ELIZABETH II, and WILLIAM THE CONQUEROR.

Edwards, Jonathan

Jonathan Edwards was a well-known American preacher about two hundred years ago. He was born in 1703, and both his father and grandfather were Protestant ministers. Jonathan was a bright student. When he became a preacher, his sermons were so exciting that hundreds of new members came into his church, but Jonathan's ideas were too harsh for most of his congregation. He believed for example that even little children were wicked until they joined the Church. Jonathan Edwards was born and preached in Connecticut, but in 1757 he became president of the college that is now Princeton. He died in 1758.

eel

The eel is a very long, thin fish that looks like a snake. The eel has very tiny scales, and some eels have no scales at all. The eel's body is so smooth that people sometimes say that something or someone is as slippery as an eel. The eel is a very interesting and unusual fish. Eels spend their early lives in the warm oceans of the world, except the western Pacific. As they grow older, eels move into the fresh-water lakes and rivers of North and Central America and Europe. When mature, they return to the sea to lay their eggs. There are more than twenty different kinds of eels, and some of them are brightly colored fish that grow to be about ten feet long, while other eels look like little worms.

For many years no one understood how the eel laid its eggs. Now we know that all eels lay their eggs in salt water. This means that the female eel that lives in the fresh-water rivers of Central America must travel to the sea to lay its eggs. The female begins this journey in the fall, and part of the time it must travel overland. It can do this, because it is able to breathe through its skin. The journey takes about six months. Males live nearer the coast, and do not have to make this great trip. When the female reaches the Atlantic Ocean, it lays its eggs, and then it dies.

The newborn eel does not look anything like its parent. It is a small, flat creature that is transparent, which means that you can see through it. This little fish begins its journey back across the Atlantic, and this trip takes about a year and a half. At the end of this time, it is shaped like a grown eel, although it is still transparent, and it is now called an elver. Most eels live to be more than fifteen years old, and some people have cap-

tured and raised eels that have lived to be more than fifty years old. Some American and European eels are good to eat, and people enjoy them smoked, pickled, and fried.

egg

An egg is a cell from which animals of all species, including man, grow. The egg exists in the female of every species. There are some animals in which the egg is developed inside the parent. The egg is fed inside the mother's body through a tube, and when it is well enough developed it is born. Animals like this are called mammals. Dogs, cats, cows, and almost all four-legged animals with hair are mammals.

There are other creatures that lay their eggs before they are hatched. These eggs are usually in a shell or, in the case of fishes, they are often protected by some form of jelly. Bird eggs are the most familiar, and chicken eggs are probably a very common sight to you. The egg is surrounded by a shell. This shell forms a short time before the egg is laid. Inside the shell is the white of the egg, or albumen. Inside the white is the round yellow yolk. At the top part of the yolk is the cell which produces the baby chicken. You see only a tiny white speck because the eggs you eat are fresh; but if left to hatch, the white speck would grow and nourish itself on the yolk and the white of the egg. When the baby chick has eaten all the nourishment that the egg contains, it is ready to hatch and it pecks its way out of the shell.

Many birds lay eggs that are very large in comparison to the size of the parent. Bird eggs vary greatly in appearance. Kingfisher eggs are glossy. Ducks lay waxen eggs. An ostrich's egg has deep pits in it, and is also the largest of all eggs. Eggs laid in dark places are white or extremely light in color. The eggs of wild birds often have elaborate markings on them, so the parents can identify their own nests. Waterfowl like ducks lay from ten to sixteen eggs. Many seagoing water birds lay only one egg a year. The number of eggs laid by different creatures seems to be based on the animal's chance of survival. Nature seems to have worked it out very well for the survival of all species, but she did not count on the destructive powers of man. Several species of animals have been destroyed by man.

EGGS OF FISHES AND REPTILES

Most birds hatch their eggs. After the eggs are laid, the parents keep the eggs warm for a period of time until the embryo inside is developed. Amphibians and fishes generally lay their eggs in a protective jelly and leave them to develop by themselves. Reptile eggs are much like bird eggs but are usually buried in the ground. An exception is the python, which lays from fifteen to a hundred eggs and broods them until the young hatch. A catfish lays a few eggs and carries them around in its mouth until they hatch. But in most cases the eggs are left to the heat of the sun. The codfish lays nine million eggs. Salmon also lay an enormous number of eggs. They travel far up inland streams, fighting rapids and waterfalls, to leave their eggs in the sheltered headwaters.

A few species of fish lay their eggs on rocks or in clumps of weeds between high and low tide, so their eggs will be exposed to light and air twice a day when the tide is out. Several kinds of fish eggs are very good to eat. Perhaps the most famous is caviar, which comes from a sturgeon. Caviar is a great delicacy and very costly. Shad roe is another popular fish egg.

EGGS OF INSECTS

Insects lay from one or two eggs up to thousands. Bees and wasps lay their eggs in the compartments of mud or wax combs. They raise their young in these compartments. The eggs of butterflies and moths have an outer coating of delicate membrane that holds the egg and a food supply for the developing egg.

EGG INDUSTRY

Eggs for food are a world-wide industry. About seven hundred million dozen eggs are sold every year. Most eggs used for food are chicken eggs, but more and more people are using duck and goose eggs. Eggs have very nourishing things in them and are very good for you. An egg is usually better if it is not cooked too much.

PRESERVATION OF EGGS

Eggs can be preserved for a long time. The modern way of preserving eggs is by cold storage. They do not have to be frozen, but if kept in refrigerators they will last for several years. Eggs will also last for a year or more if they are coated with the chemical sodium silicate, which is usually called "waterglass." The Chinese bury eggs for about a year, and in this period the eggs become hard as though they had been hard-boiled but do not spoil. The Chinese call them "hundred-year eggs," which is quite an exaggeration, but they are considered very good to eat.

Candling eggs is a way of testing them to see if they are still good to eat. The egg is held in front of a strong light, and if the yolk and white of the egg can be seen to be the same as they are in a fresh egg, the egg is good.

Eggleston, Edward

Edward Eggleston was a well-known American novelist. He was born in 1837 at Vevay, Indiana. In some of his novels he tells the story of what it was like to go to school a hundred years ago in Indiana. In other novels he tells how he became a young Methodist minister and he rode about on horseback and preaching in one town after another in Indiana and Minnesota.

Before Eggleston died in 1902, he completed part of a history of the United States that was used for a long time in many schools all over America.

eggnog

An eggnog is a kind of thick drink that is made with a raw egg. People are very often given an eggnog when they are sick. It is very good for you and helps you gain weight. Lots of people drink eggnog because it tastes so good. You make an eggnog with sugar, raw egg, and milk or cream. You put all of these things in a bowl and beat them for a long time. The mixture becomes very frothy and is a very pale yellow color. After it has become frothy you put it in the refrigerator to cool. After it is very cold you pour it into a glass and sprinkle a little spice called nutmeg on top of the froth. Lots of people like to drink eggnog around Christmas time. It is served at many parties during the holiday season. Some people like to have liquor added to eggnog. Whisky or brandy is usually the liquor used.

eggplant

The eggplant is a plant that grows wild in India and other countries where the climate is warm. It grows about two feet high and has a thick, woody stem. People in many parts of Europe and the northern United States raise eggplants, because the fruit is very good to eat. The fruit is shaped like an egg, and may be about the size of a hen's egg, although many eggplants bear fruit that is seven or eight inches around. The fruit may have a shiny dark purple skin, or it may be white. Eggplant as a vegetable is usually boiled or fried. Many people like to eat it with cheese and tomato sauce.

egret

The egret is a graceful, white heron. During the breeding season, the bird grows beautiful plumes on its back. Plumes are large, long feathers, and women use them for decorating their hats and dresses. Thirty years ago, the white silky plumes or "aigrettes" were so popular that the egret was almost hunted out of existence. Then the United States government said that egrets could no longer be killed for their feathers, and since then there have been more and more egrets. The two American egrets are called the common egret and the snowy egret. There is also one called the reddish egret that lives on the coast of the Gulf of Mexico and in Latin America.

Egrets, like herons, are tall, with very thin legs and long necks. They are wading birds that spend much of their time in the water. They feed on frogs and small fish, which they spear with a quick thrust of their pointed bills. In late summer and early fall, the egrets often fly as far north as southern Canada.

Egypt

Egypt, known officially as the Arab Republic of Egypt, is a country in the northeast of Africa, with a long coastline on the Mediterranean Sea. The area of Egypt is about 386,000 square miles, about half again as big as the state of Texas. About thirty million people live in Egypt, nearly three times as many as live in Texas. Almost all Egyptian people live in a narrow strip along the Nile River, which flows through the country and irrigates it. The rest of the country is mostly hot, dry desert.

The earliest of all civilizations probably began in Egypt. Five thousand years ago the Egyptians were putting up big buildings, observing the stars and making a calendar, and learning to write. They put up great tombs (the pyramids) and statues, such as the Sphinx, that remained the biggest structures built by man for more than four thousand years. They learned to use metals and their craftsmen made jewelry that is still beautiful. The study of ancient Egypt is so important to scholars that it is a science all by itself, called Egyptology.

In modern times Egypt has been important for several reasons. The Suez Canal, which connects the Mediterranean Sea with the seas south of Asia and makes possible the shortest sea route from Europe to the Asiatic countries, runs through Egyptian territory. Egypt is an Arab country and a Mohammedan country, and it has taken the lead among the Arab and Mohammedan countries in trying to become completely independent of the European countries that once controlled them.

Egypt is important in Christian history, because the Jewish people were slaves of the Egyptians for many years until the Jewish leader, Moses, led them out of Egypt to freedom, as told in the book of Exodus, in the Bible.

THE NILE AND EGYPT

The Nile, one of the greatest rivers in the world, is responsible for Egypt's long history and early greatness. The Nile comes from African mountains far to the south of Egypt and runs northward through the country to empty into the Mediterranean. Most of Egypt is desert

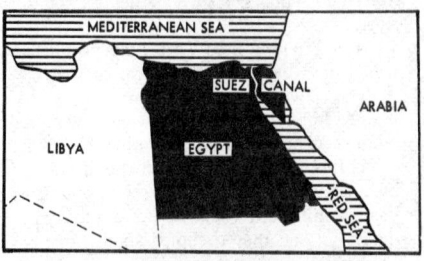

where it almost never rains and where useful plants cannot be grown, but where the Nile flows the land is rich and fertile. As it nears the Mediterranean, the Nile branches into several rivers, in a form called a *delta*.

The Nile carries rich soil along with it. Every year in September the Nile floods and covers its banks, and when the flood waters go down they leave rich soil in which the farmers raise their crops.

Most of the land near the Nile River is level. Mountains in the east rise to more than 7,000 feet above sea level. The Libyan Desert on the west has high, rocky hills and great sand dunes.

The weather of Egypt is dry and warm. Usually there are cool winds from the north, but occasionally a south wind, called the khamsin, brings unpleasant dust and even sandstorms. There is never any snow and the rainy season each year is the Egyptian "winter."

ANCIENT EGYPT

About five thousand years before the birth of Christ, people began to settle on either side of the river. They were a farming people, and they discovered that the fertile banks of the Nile were easy to cultivate and gave a good harvest. They called the land *kemi*, which meant black earth as against the red desert lands on both sides of the valley.

1. One of the most famous sights in Egypt is the great stone pyramid at Giza, built thousands of years ago as a royal tomb.

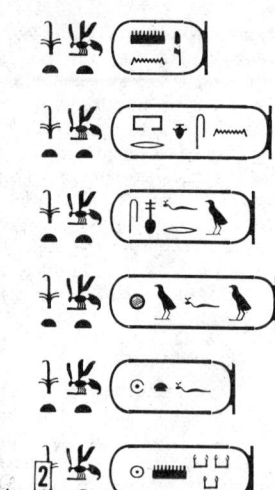

TWA Photos

2. The Egyptians did not have an alphabet and used picture writing, called *hieroglyphics*, that has been found on the walls of ancient tombs and buildings.

At first these settlers of the Nile valley lived in small groups or tribes. Often one tribe would go to war against another tribe, and the winner would take over the villages and lands of the loser. This warfare continued for many years. Then, nearly 5,300 years ago, Egypt was united under the rule of a powerful king whose name was Menes. He built his capital in the Nile delta, and called it Memphis. Memphis was the capital of Egypt for many years, and then the capital was moved to Thebes, a city farther up the river.

After Menes united Egypt, the people were ruled by many different dynasties. A dynasty was a family of kings that remained in power from generation to generation. When a king died without leaving children, or was forced off the throne by another powerful family, a new dynasty would start. There were about thirty dynasties, and they occupied about three thousand years in history.

Beautiful Egyptian sculpture was used to decorate tombs and important buildings.

The king of Egypt was called *Pharaoh,* which means "great house." The king was given this title because he owned all the land of Egypt, and was master of all the people that lived there. The Pharaoh

was even thought to be a god, and the people worshiped him as a divine being. The king was unable to rule the country alone, so he allowed a small number of people to help him. They were called *nomarchs* and collected the taxes, acted as judges, and kept peace among the people.

The Pharaoh and his nomarchs lived in great palaces made of stone or bricks. The many rooms of the palaces were decorated with brightly colored cloths or glazed tiles. Often a high wall separated the palaces and their grounds from the outside, and the common people were not allowed to enter those walls unless they were slaves or servants of the Pharaoh or nomarch who lived inside.

THE GODS, PRIESTS, AND BELIEFS OF ANCIENT EGYPT

The ancient Egyptians believed in many gods, and built many temples to honor them. Usually each village and town had its own private god or gods. The most important god was called Ra, and later Amon-Ra. He was the sun god. The next god of importance was Osiris, god of the dead. The god of the Nile was also worshiped, and there were such other gods as the lion god, the hippopotamus god, the turtle god, and the hawk god.

Since Pharaoh was a god, his helpers. were considered priests. They made a calendar, chiefly so that they could tell the farmers when the Nile was due to flood and make the fields ready for planting. They invented a style of writing with pictures so that they could keep records. This writing is called *hieroglyphic* (which means "carving by priests") and you can read more about it in the article ALPHABET. It was hard to learn, and this led to a new group of professional men, called *scribes* (writers). At first the scribes carved their writing into stone or clay tablets. Then they learned to use the skins of animals, usually sheepskins (called *parchment*). More than five thousand years ago they learned to make a kind of paper from a reed called the *papyrus* that grows near the Nile, and much of their writing was done on papyrus.

The priests and scribes used a device called the *nilometer* to measure the floods. The nilometer was a slab of stone with

marks cut in it. Nilometers were placed beside the Nile, and the marks showed how high and how fast the river was rising. These are still used.

The scribes also learned a kind of surveying, because the floods would wash away boundary marks between different farms and the scribes would have to mark the boundaries again. The scribes collected a part of each farmer's crop as a tax, which was sent to Pharaoh. There was no money in ancient Egypt.

The early Egyptians believed in a life after death, and like other ancient people, they built great tombs for their Pharaohs and nobles. Before a powerful Pharaoh was buried, he would be embalmed, which meant that his body would be treated with certain chemicals and wrapped in many feet of linen cloth to preserve it. We call a body that has been treated in this way a mummy. The Pharaoh, before his death, would have many slaves and workers build a great tomb where his body would be placed after his death, along with many weapons and food. Even his servants were buried with him to help him in the other life. The most famous tombs that we can still see today are called the pyramids. The Pharaoh Cheops, or Khufu, built the largest one almost five thousand years ago. It is nearly five hundred feet high, and its base covers almost thirteen acres of land.

THE LIFE OF THE COMMON PEOPLE

In early Egypt, the life of the common people was very different from that of the Pharaoh and his nobles. Many of the people were slaves, and even those that were free lived a hard life under cruel masters. Children were forced to go to work when they were still very young.

The largest number of people in ancient Egypt were farmers. They worked the land with hoes or used wooden plows drawn by oxen.

Besides the farmers who worked in the fields, there were the herdsmen who tended the cattle and sheep. They were usually slaves. The Egyptians had many kinds of livestock. Oxen were raised for work animals, and cows for meat and milk. The Egyptians were very fond of milk and their cows were carefully raised and watched over. Beekeeping was another important job, because the Egyptians used honey not only as a sweet, but in many of their medicines.

There were still many other workers. The potter made bowls and pots, and even discovered the art of making small glass jars and bottles. Many men worked as metalsmiths, making swords, knives, plates, and even jewelry, from copper, gold, silver, and iron. The weaver made beautiful cloths from wool, cotton, and linen. The stonemasons and builders carved the great statues, sometimes 90 feet high, from huge blocks of granite often weighing thousands of tons. Even today we are amazed at the ability of the early Egyptians to transport these great blocks of stone from the quarry where they were obtained, to the distant cities where they were used.

Egyptian civilization did not change for hundreds of years. Then, nearly 3,500 years ago, Egypt became a warlike nation and began to conquer other distant lands.

The capital of Egypt was moved to Thebes, and the great temples of Karnak and Luxor were built. One of the advantages of these conquests was that Egyptian civilization was spread to other lands.

During this period Egypt was ruled by Pharaohs whose names are still known, often because their tombs have been opened and their mummies and jewels and other possessions have been studied. Names of famous Pharaohs include Amenhotep, Ikhnaton, and Tut-ankh-amen. One of the most famous was a woman, Hatshepsut, who is remembered for sending ships through the Red Sea to open commerce with the land of Punt (present Ethiopia and Somaliland).

Egypt finally weakened. Alexander the Great conquered it about 2,300 years ago, in 332 B.C. It was ruled by the Greek Empire and then for hundreds of years by the Roman Empire. Egypt still had its Pharaohs—several of them named Ptolemy, and one famous one, the queen CLEOPATRA, about whom there is a separate article—but they were weak rulers.

About the year 640, Arab armies conquered Egypt and introduced the new religion of Mohammed. Egypt has been a Mohammedan country ever since. It was part of the Turkish empire for about four hundred years, and was ruled by governors called *khedives* who represented the Turkish sultan (emperor). The history of Egypt since that time is considered part of the modern history of the country and a later section in this article tells about it.

The articles on ALEXANDRIA, ALEXANDER THE GREAT, and ROMAN EMPIRE tell more about ancient Egypt. Read also the article on the MAMELUKES.

THE PEOPLE OF MODERN EGYPT

Egypt has been invaded by the armies of many different nations, and many soldiers of these armies settled there and raised their families. These families, in turn, have mixed with the rest of the population, and as a result, there is no pure Egyptian race. The invaders who changed Egypt the most were the Arabs, who conquered Egypt about 1,300 years ago and settled down in great numbers. The language of the Egyptian people is a form of Arabic.

The only important group of people in Egypt who are not Mohammedans are the Copts. The Copts are Christians, and are the last descendants of the ancient people who lived in Egypt before the Arab invasion. More than one and a half million Copts live in Egypt. There are also a small number of Jews and Europeans, but they live mostly in the large cities.

The Egyptian man or woman who lives in the large cities looks very much like an average American man or woman, though perhaps with a darker complexion and blacker hair. The man might wear business suits just like an American's, and the woman wear dresses that might have come from New York or Paris. Some of the men wear the fez, or cone-shaped cap, instead of a hat, and sometimes you might see a woman wearing a veil, but this is not common now.

In a small village up the Nile River, the people look and dress much differently. The man might wear a long robe and have a flowing beard. The women wear long robes and always wear veils over their faces.

HOW THE PEOPLE LIVE

Most of the people of Egypt are farmers, as they have been for thousands of years. The Egyptian farmer is called a *fellah*. He is very poor, and usually lives in a small mud house in a village near the Nile banks. Often he does not own the land he cultivates, but works for a large landowner who pays him very little. The fellahs of Egypt are now being helped by the Egyptian government. Schools have been built for their use, and many have been given land of their own. The rich landowners must pay fair wages to their workers, or be fined by the government.

The most important crop in Egypt is cotton. Egyptian cotton is often said to be the finest in the world because of its softness and strength. Other crops are wheat, sugar cane, vegetables, and fruit. The people of ancient Egypt had to depend on the yearly overflow of the Nile River to water and irrigate the land, but in recent years large dams have been built to regulate the supply of water. One of these, the Gabel Awlia, is one of the largest dams in the world. Construction of another dam, the Aswan High Dam, was started in 1960.

There are still some people in Egypt who are nomads, people who wander from place to place. They live near the Upper Nile valley or in the oases, the small, fertile watering places in the great deserts. They are mostly sheep herders or camel raisers, and belong to different Arab tribes. They are often called Bedouins.

There are several large cities in Egypt. Cairo, the capital, is very modern and is the largest city in Africa. The second-largest city in Egypt is Alexandria, a busy port on the Mediterranean Sea. Other important cities in Egypt are Port Said, Suez, and Assouan or Aswan.

If you lived in one of these large cities, you would find it not very different from living in the United States. There are many large hotels and restaurants, theaters, and even movie houses where you could see an American movie. The Egyptian people like to go to the movies, and Egypt has become the largest producer of films in the Arabic language in the world.

Most of the people who live in the large cities, Cairo or Alexandria, are not native Egyptians. They are Greeks, Turks, Italians, Frenchmen, and Englishmen, who have settled there recently, or have come to open or represent different businesses. Most Egyptians, almost eight out of ten, live outside the cities.

There is still little industry in Egypt, but the people are skilled rug makers and work at many other types of handwork. They make beautiful jewelry and metal vases and dishes. The women are well known for making beautiful shawls and other handmade woolen and cotton products. There are some minerals found in Egypt and also some petroleum, but both mining and oil drilling are undeveloped.

HISTORY OF MODERN EGYPT

Like many other Mohammedan countries, Egypt for many centuries was supposedly subject to emperors far away—first to the caliph who ruled in Baghdad, and then to Turkish sultans—but actually Egypt was governed by its own kings and merely paid taxes or tribute to these emperors. Under the caliphs, the Egyptian rulers were called viziers. They ruled from about 900 to 1250. The most famous Egyptian vizier was Saladin, who was a great warrior against the Christians in the Crusades. Then for more than 250 years Egypt was ruled by men called Mamelukes. The Mamelukes had been slaves of Turks who captured them in wars. They were so able that they were entrusted with the management of the government and they were so clever that they soon took over the country.

In 1517, the Ottoman Turks conquered Egypt and Egypt remained part of the Ottoman Empire (usually called Turkey) until World War I in 1914. Even during this period, Egypt actually had its own rulers, called khedives, who paid the Turkish sultans a small tax each year. France tried to win control of Egypt when Napoleon invaded the delta region in 1798, but after three years the French withdrew. Throughout the 19th century Egypt was ruled by a khedive named Mohammed Ali and his descendants, but British and French influence was great because of their ownership of shares in the Suez Canal. In 1882 the British seized control of Egypt, and when World War I broke out in 1914 and Turkey became an enemy of Great Britain and France, the British officially made Egypt a British protectorate. The British did permit Egypt to have its own king and government. Fuad became king of Egypt in 1922 and his son Farouk succeeded him as king in 1936. But the British were in control until 1949. Then Egypt became an independent country, except that British troops remained to guard the Suez Canal.

The Egyptian people were still dissatisfied, partly because Farouk's government was corrupt and partly because of the British troops that remained. In 1952 there was a revolution in which the Egyptian Army made Farouk leave the country. In 1953 Egypt became a republic with Gen. Mohammed Naguib as president, and in November 1954 Col. Gamal Abdel Nasser became premier. Soon Nasser was in effect a dictator in Egypt and the most powerful man in the Arab League.

In 1954, Great Britain yielded to the wish of the new government and withdrew its troops from Suez, but Great Britain and France still owned large shares of stock in the canal. In 1956 Egypt seized full ownership of the canal, violating a treaty. The United States disapproved of this illegal action and withdrew an offer to lend Egypt a large sum of money to build a new dam at Aswan. Nasser became very angry at the United States and began to trade with the Soviet Union and other Communist countries.

Like other Arab countries, Egypt fought in 1948 and 1949 to prevent Israel from becoming an independent country. Israel won that war and the other Arab countries stopped fighting but Egypt considered itself still at war with Israel and Egyptian guns continued to fire on shipping that tried to reach Israeli ports through the Red Sea. In 1956, Israel

invaded Egyptian territory to put a stop to this, and France and Great Britain joined on the side of Israel. Egypt was not able to offer any great resistance, but the United States government disapproved and, through the United Nations, persuaded Israel, France and Great Britain to restore peace and withdraw their forces.

In 1958, Egypt, Syria, and later the kingdom of Yemen joined to form the United Arab Republic. This union was dissolved in 1961, but Egypt kept the name United Arab Republic. In 1973 on Yom Kippur the Syrians and Egyptians attacked Israel. Egypt then changed its name to its present name, the Arab Republic of Egypt. See ISRAEL.

EGYPT (Arab Republic of Egypt). Area, 386,100 square miles. Population (1973 estimate) 34,130,000. Capital, Cairo (4,961,000). Language, Arabic. Religion, Mohammedan.

eider

The eider duck lives in the cold coastal sections of the Arctic in North America and Europe. There are large numbers in both Norway and Labrador. Under the eider duck's outside plumage there is a thick coat of soft feathers, called *down*, that is so light and warm it has become a favorite material in many lands for making quilts, and for lining clothing. The female eider duck plucks this down from its own breast when it is building its nest and lines the inside of the nest to protect the eggs from the bitter cold. The down also helps to conceal the eggs from enemies. People of Europe take the down from the inside of the eider ducks' nests and use it for eider-down quilts. They take only a small amount of down from each nest, leaving enough to protect the eggs.

The male eider is a handsome black and white bird, with green feathers on its neck or head. It is about 26 inches long, with a wing spread of about 11 inches. The female is a plain brown color, so that it is not too noticeable as it sits on the nest. Eiders are expert divers, and sometimes go down to the bottom of water 50 or 55 feet deep in order to get food. They do not fly South for the winter, but stay in the cold North all year round.

Eiffel Tower

The Eiffel Tower is the greatest landmark of Paris, France, visible from almost any part of the city and the first thing visitors see when they approach Paris by air. The tower is built of steel framework and is 948 feet high, not including the television transmitting tower on top of the structure, which raises its over-all height to 1,056 feet. From the time it was built (in 1889 for the great Paris Exposition of that year) until the Empire State Building was completed in 1931, it was the tallest man-made structure of history. The tower has four legs 620 feet high, which come together in a more slender shaft. There is a spiral stairway to the top, but there are also elevators to platforms at three different levels. The Eiffel Tower was built by Alexandre Gustave Eiffel, who was born in 1832 and died in 1923. Though Eiffel built his tower as a curiosity for visitors to the Exposition, his great engineering achievement contrib-

uted greatly to the modern skyscraper. See the article on PARIS for a picture.

Eights

Eights is a popular card game. Some people call it Swedish Rummy, but it is neither Swedish nor related to any game of Rummy. Sometimes it is called Crazy Eights, the word *crazy* meaning the same thing that "wild" means in other card games. The same game, with other cards wild, is called "Crazy Jacks," or "Crazy Sevens," or any number of other names.

The game is best for two, three, or four players. The regular pack of fifty-two playing cards is used. The dealer gives one card at a time to each player, face down, until each player has seven cards if two are playing; five cards if three or more are playing. The rest of the pack, the undealt cards, is placed face down in the center of the table. The top card of this pack is turned face up and placed beside the pack.

After this, each plays in turn, beginning with the player at the left of the dealer. Each player must put down a card that is either the same suit or the same rank as the card played previously. The first player must match the starter in one of these respects. For example, if the three of hearts is the last card played, the next player must put down a three or a heart. Suppose he puts down the three of clubs; then the player at his left must put down either a three or a club.

All eights are wild and may be played in any turn. When one plays an eight, he may say to the player at his left, "Play a heart" (or any other suit). He may not name a rank of card, such as a king or a nine.

When a player cannot play because he does not have the proper card in his hand, he must draw from the stock, one card after another, until he can play.

SCORING

The object of the game is to play all the cards in your hand. When any player has played out all his cards, the game ends. The winner collects for all cards that remain in the hands of his opponents: 50 points for each eight, 10 for each face card (king, queen, or jack), one for each ace, and the number of the card for each other card that an opponent holds. The first player to reach a score of 100 points or more wins the game.

Einstein, Albert

Albert Einstein was considered the greatest scientist of the 20th century and one of the greatest of all time. He is best remembered for his theory of relativity, an idea difficult to understand but one that has had as much influence on modern science as any other idea in the last three hundred years, especially in astronomy and atomic science.

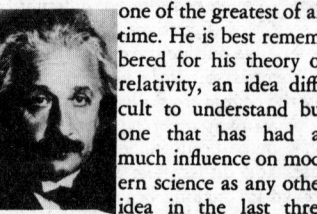
Gale Research Co.

Einstein was a physicist, which means that he studied matter (anything that has weight and takes up space) and the physical changes it undergoes, such as motion, changes in weight and size, changes from a solid to a liquid, and so on. He

often was called a theoretical physicist, which means that he thought up ideas that later were tested by experiments carried out by other scientists called experimental scientists.

Einstein was born in 1879 in Ulm, a city in Germany. By the time he was 12 years old, he was reading books about science and mathematics. He studied and taught in Switzerland, where in 1905 he published his first paper on relativity and also explained how light falling on certain metals can cause electricity to flow. (For this work he received the Nobel Prize in physics in 1921.)

In 1914, he once again became a German citizen and was made director of theoretical physics at the Kaiser Wilhelm Institute in Berlin. He traveled and lectured all over the world, and in 1933 went to the United States to lecture at the California Institute of Technology.

Because Einstein was a Jew, his property and German citizenship were taken away by the Nazi government in 1934 and he settled in the United States, becoming a professor of physics at the Institute for Advanced Study at Princeton, New Jersey. He became a U.S. citizen in 1940.

Einstein's favorite pastime was playing the violin. With his long, flowing white hair and his sad-looking face, he became a favorite subject of painters and photographers. He died in 1955.

THE THEORY OF RELATIVITY

In 1905, Einstein set forth his first or special theory of relativity, in which he showed that the speed of an object must be measured against some other object, either moving or standing still. It is meaningless to say that an object is moving at 60 miles an hour unless you say with what you are comparing its speed. A car may be moving at 60 miles an hour compared with the highway, which is standing still, but the car will be moving only 20 miles an hour compared with another car moving in the same direction at 40 miles an hour. In this sense, all motion is relative, which means it must be measured in comparison or relation to some standard that is thought of as standing still.

From some point of view, we can say that all matter is in motion. Since energy is another name for matter in motion, matter is just another way of saying that something has energy. Matter and energy are really two ways of looking at the same thing. When we talk about matter as if it were at rest, we say that it has potential energy. When we talk about matter as if it were moving, we say that it has kinetic energy.

There are many different kinds of energy. A moving truck has mechanical energy. Little bits of matter called molecules striking hard against each other have heat energy. Air molecules moving back and forth have sound energy. Smaller particles of matter called atoms moving through the air like ocean waves in bundles called photons have radiant energy; examples of this are light, radio waves, x-rays, and so on. Tiny particles called electrons, found in all atoms, move rapidly through wires and have electrical energy. Protons and neutrons, found at

the center of atoms, move violently apart and have atomic or nuclear energy.

Einstein tried to explain how these different kinds of energy are related to matter and to each other. He explained why, when photons of light strike certain metals, electrons are released from these metals in the form of electrical energy. This is called the photoelectric effect and is the basis of the photoelectric cell, commonly called the electric eye, about which you can read in the article ELECTRONICS. To explain this effect, Einstein used an idea first thought of in 1900 by the German physicist Max Planck. This is called the *quantum theory*. You can read about it in the article on Max PLANCK.

The faster something moves the greater its energy. Einstein showed that the highest speed anything can reach is the speed of light. This speed was found to be about 186,300 miles a second. Therefore the largest amount of energy anything can have would be if it were moving with the speed of light. This energy can be found by multiplying the mass (in pounds) of the object by the square of the speed of light (186,300 times 186,300).

If a piece of matter moves at almost the speed of light, its energy will increase. Since matter and energy are the same, its mass will also increase. If its velocity should equal the velocity of light, both its mass and energy will become infinitely large (impossible to measure). Because this is impossible we say that no object can travel with the speed of light, except light.

Einstein also developed a more complete theory of relativity to explain all motion in space. You can read more about this in the article GRAVITATION.

Eire is a Gaelic or Irish name for Ireland: see the article on IRELAND, REPUBLIC OF.

Dwight D. Eisenhower

Dwight David Eisenhower was elected President of the United States in November, 1952, and took the oath of office in January, 1953. He was the 34th President of the United States; he was the third man to become President after commanding the United States Army in a great war (the other two being George

Washington, after the Revolutionary War, and Ulysses S. Grant, after the Civil War); and he was the second West Point graduate to become President, General Grant having been the first.

Before becoming President, Dwight D. Eisenhower had a long and brilliant military career. He was Supreme Commander not only of the United States but of all Allied forces in Europe in World War II, and attained the rank of General of the Army, the highest rank possible in the United States Army. He was respected and honored throughout the world. In 1948, many members of both the Democratic and the Republican Parties asked him to become the candidate for their parties, but he refused. In 1952 he accepted the nomination of the Republican Party, and he was elected by a large majority, defeating Adlai Stevenson, the former governor of Illinois, who was the candidate of the Democratic Party. In 1956 he was again nominated as the Republican candidate and again he defeated Stevenson by a very large majority.

When he became President, Eisenhower selected for his principal assistants many men who were leaders in the biggest business and manufacturing firms.

At the same time he was very active in international affairs, the dealings of the United States with other countries of the world. One of his most important acts, in a speech delivered to a United Nations meeting in 1954, was to propose a plan for using atomic energy chiefly for peaceful purposes instead of for warfare.

President Eisenhower's great personal charm helped him to get such big votes in the 1952 and 1956 elections. Even strangers felt drawn to him when they heard him speak. Millions of people came to think and speak of him as "Ike," the nickname by which his friends had always called him. Many men felt they had something in common with him, because of his liking for bridge and golf and for trout-fishing and aviation. He earned a private pilot's license while he was stationed in the Philippines with General Douglas MacArthur in 1936.

President Eisenhower's interest in food and cooking is well known, but many people do not know that he taught his bride how to prepare meals when they were first married. Mrs. Eisenhower was only nineteen at the time, and she had never learned to cook. His interest in cooking continued throughout his military life, and when he became Chief of Staff during Harry Truman's administration, he always inspected the kitchens of the army posts he visited. He said once that he would like "to be remembered as the Chief of Staff who did something about the army's cooking."

Dwight Eisenhower's service was freely recognized by many different countries. He was decorated with high honors by 22 countries in addition to the United States, and Canada renamed a mountain peak Mount Eisenhower in his honor. In his speech of appreciation he showed the sense of humor that was one of his well known traits. He remarked, "One thing I feel thoroughly certain of—it must be a bald peak." He was referring, of course, to the fact that he did not have very much hair himself. His hair started to thin out when he was only about 30.

Dwight Eisenhower was a very handsome young man, with blue eyes and medium brown hair. He was tall and well-built, and while at West Point was assigned to the company that had the tallest men in his class. He was always powerful physically and was a better-than-average athlete. He played on the West Point ("Army") football team.

HIS EARLY YEARS

The Eisenhower family was originally German, but had been settled in Switzerland for many years before coming to America in 1741. David Eisenhower, the President's father, was born in Elizabethville, Pennsylvania. His family moved to Kansas when he was 15.

President Eisenhower's mother was born in Mount Sidney, Virginia, a town near Staunton. Her name was Ida Elizabeth Stover. She remained in Mount Sidney until she was 20 years old. Her parents had died when she was quite young, and she had lived with her cousin, Mary Ann Link. When her cousin was married and moved to Kansas, Ida Stover went along. In Kansas she met David Eisenhower, whom she married in 1885. They lived in Hope, Kansas, for four years and then moved to Denison, Texas, where Dwight David Eisenhower was born on October 14, 1890.

He was the third of seven sons, but one of his younger brothers died while he was a baby. Growing up in a family of six boys, however, he learned to get along with other people and to take care of himself in a rough-and-tumble while he was quite young.

Denison is a town about seventy miles north of Dallas, on the border of Oklahoma in the northeast part of Texas.

In the early days of the West this section was a center for traders, buffalo hunters, and cattlemen. A stagecoach line went through Denison before the railroad was built. After the rail lines reached Denison, it became a shipping center for the farm products of the Red River Valley. Dwight Eisenhower's father, David Eisenhower, was a railroad worker on the line between Denison and Tyler, Texas.

Most people think of Dwight Eisenhower as a native of Abilene, Kansas. Actually, however, the family did not move to Abilene until he was two years old. His name was originally David Dwight, but his mother always called him Dwight, and so he finally turned his names around and called himself Dwight David, which he kept as his official name. The nickname "Ike" started in early childhood. In fact, he and all of his brothers were called Ike, from the first syllable of the name Eisenhower.

He and his brothers attended grammar school and high school in Abilene, and he was graduated from Abilene High School in 1909. His older brother, Edgar, was a member of the same class, and they both wanted to attend college. That was expensive, however, and they had to think of some way to earn money in order to do it.

The plan they finally hit upon was an unusual one. Each brother agreed to work a year, and attend school a year. The year one worked, he would pay the other's expenses at college, and then the next year they would change places. Ed-

gar started first, entering the University of Michigan, while Dwight worked in a dairy plant. He became night manager. The plan to alternate years at college, however, was changed when a friend persuaded Dwight to take an examination and try to enter either Annapolis or West Point. This he did, and came through the examination with a very high rating. He was willing to attend either academy, but he discovered that he was too old for Annapolis because his twentieth birthday had passed just a few months earlier. West Point, however, did not have that age limit, and when a senator in Kansas gave him the appointment to West Point, he entered the academy in June of 1911.

Throughout his four years at West Point, he was a good student, and was in the top third of his class when he was graduated as a second lieutenant in June, 1915. Three months later, he was stationed at Fort Sam Houston in Texas, and it was there that he met his future wife.

Mamie Doud was visiting Texas with her family for a winter vacation in San Antonio at the time. Her full name was originally Mary Geneva Doud, and she was one of a family of four girls. When she first met Second Lieutenant Dwight Eisenhower, she was just nineteen. Her birthday had been in November. They fell in love almost immediately, and on St. Valentine's day their engagement was announced. Mamie's engagement ring was an exact duplicate of Dwight's West Point ring, especially made to fit her hand.

A little less than five months later they were married, on July 1st, in Denver, Colorado. A little over a year later their first son was born. His name was Doud Dwight, but he died of scarlet fever when he was only three years old. Another son, John Sheldon Doud Eisenhower, was born August 3, 1922. The Eisenhower grandchildren that were shown during the presidential campaign in many newsreels and newspapers were the children of this son and his wife, the former Barbara Jean Thompson.

HIS MILITARY CAREER

After his marriage, Dwight Eisenhower lived the typical life of an officer in the regular army. His first big responsibility came when he was placed in charge of 6,000 men at Camp Colt, Gettysburg, Pennsylvania. He did his job so well that he was awarded the Distinguished Service Medal. By then he had been promoted twice, and was a captain. After his service in the tank instruction school at Camp Colt, he was promoted again, and became a major at the age of 29. For the next few years, the home life of the Eisenhowers consisted in moving from army post to army post all over the United States. Then, in 1927, Major Eisenhower was sent to France as a member of the American Battle Monuments Commission. The Commission's job was to prepare a guidebook and map of all the places where battlefields were located, so that Americans traveling in Europe might visit them.

After living in Paris and the Panama Canal Zone, the Eisenhowers returned to the United States, but the major was soon ordered to join General Douglas MacArthur's staff in the Philippines. Their purpose, on the American Military Mission, was to draw up a Philippine National Defense Act. While he was there, in 1936, he became a lieutenant colonel.

When World War II started on September 3, 1939, many changes occurred in the United States Army. Lieutenant Colonel Eisenhower was ordered back to the United States to help in establishing defenses along the Pacific Coast. Toward the end of this service he was appointed a full colonel, in March, 1941. A few months later, he became Chief of Staff of the Third Army at San Antonio, Texas. In the fall of 1941, he conducted war maneuvers in Louisiana, which gave him an opportunity to demonstrate how he would have defeated enemy forces under similar circumstances.

His strategy and planning were so well organized and so skillfully carried out that he was promoted to the temporary rank of brigadier general in September of 1941. Shortly thereafter, on December 7, the Japanese attacked Pearl Harbor, and Eisenhower's life was changed again. He was made Chief of the War Plans Division on the General Staff of the War Department, and he was now personally engaged in making important decisions with regard to carrying on the war. In June, 1942 he was given great responsibility as Commanding General of the European Theater of Operations.

General Eisenhower directed the African invasion in November of 1942, and then was made Supreme Commander of the Allied forces preparing to invade Europe, with rank of full general. The way he did this tremendous task is described in the article about WORLD WAR II. Complete German surrender took place on May 6, 1945, and General Dwight Eisenhower was the hero of the hour.

When he returned to London after this wonderful event, he was given a gigantic welcome, and hundreds of thousands of people thronged the streets to get a glimpse of him. At a dinner in his honor, he made one of the most famous speeches of his career up to that point. He said, "To preserve his freedom of worship, his equality before the law, his liberty to speak and act as he sees fit, subject only to provisions that he trespass not upon similar rights of others, a citizen of London will fight. So will a citizen of Abilene."

In November, 1944, he was given the highest military rank the United States has to offer, General of the Army. This rank is known as "Five Star General."

HOW HE BECAME PRESIDENT

In November, 1945, after the war in the Pacific was over, President Truman appointed him as Army Chief of Staff, to succeed General George Marshall. The appointment was confirmed unanimously by the Senate.

It was almost two years later that he was offered the presidency of Columbia University, and in July, 1947, he decided to accept. He did not take office immediately, however, because he wanted to write his memoirs of the war. The book was published under the title *Crusade in Europe* and a million copies were sold.

In February, 1948, General Dwight Eisenhower resigned as Chief of Staff. The following October he was formally installed as president of Columbia University.

When the 1948 election for the United States Presidency approached, many members of both the Republican and Democratic Parties wanted Eisenhower to accept the nomination. He refused to give them any encouragement, and in January 1948 he wrote a letter in which he said positively that he would not be a candidate. Even this did not stop some people from forming a "draft Eisenhower" committee as late as the Democratic National Convention in July 1948. He still refused, and President Truman, who was re-elected in 1948, made him the first Supreme Commander of the Allied Forces in Europe under the NORTH ATLANTIC TREATY, about which there is a separate article. Eisenhower held this position from 1950 to 1952.

In 1952 Eisenhower accepted the Republican Party's nomination and was elected President. He soon came to be recognized throughout the free world as the leader in the effort to bring longlasting peace to the world. Re-elected in 1956 despite the fact that he suffered a heart attack in 1955 and underwent an ileitis operation in 1956, he served two full terms. He died in March, 1969 and was given a State Funeral in Washington, D.C. He was buried in Abilene, Kansas.

MRS. DWIGHT D. EISENHOWER

Mrs. Dwight Eisenhower was born in Boone, Iowa, on November 14, 1896. Her maiden name was Mary Geneva Doud, and she was the daughter of Jon Sheldon Doud and Elvira Matilda Carlson Doud. Mrs. Eisenhower is called Mamie by her family and close friends. In the winter of 1915, she met Dwight Eisenhower. They became engaged in February and were married on July 1, 1916.

In September, 1917, their first son was born and named Doud Dwight. He died during an epidemic of scarlet fever at Camp Meade, Maryland, in January, 1921.

Their second son was born on August 3, 1922. His name was John Sheldon Doud Eisenhower, and he married Barbara Jean Thompson.

eisteddfod

Every year the people who live in Wales have a music and poetry contest that is called the eisteddfod. Wales is part of the British Isles. The eisteddfod is also held among Welsh people who have moved to other countries like the United States. The contest usually takes a week. Many people come to hear different poets, writers, and musicians read or play their works. The best ones receive special honors. Another purpose of the eisteddfod is to keep alive the beliefs, stories, and customs of Wales. The meeting goes back to ancient times, probably long before the year 1. In the Middle Ages, the eisteddfod chose the official bards, or traveling poet-singers. These minstrels moved around the country as a kind of "living library" before books were known. On their journeys, the bards had the right to lodging in the homes of the nobles.

eland

An eland is a very large antelope that lives in Africa. A full-grown eland is

Chicago Park Dist.

A baby eland stays close to its mother.

about 6 feet high at the shoulder, and weighs about 1,200 pounds. It is about the size of a horse. The eland is a bright brown color, and has straight horns that twist into a graceful spiral at the top. It also has a large loose fold of skin that hangs from its throat almost to its knees. (This is called a dewlap.) Once the eland was very common, and traveled in large herds over the plains of Africa. But the eland was not a very fast runner, and it could not defend itself or get away from its enemies, so large numbers of elands were killed and now there are very few of them left in Africa.

elasticity

Elasticity is the ability of a thing to return to its original shape after being stretched. A rubber band is very elastic; we can stretch it almost as much as we want to (without breaking it, of course) and when we let go it will snap back to its original size and shape. On the other hand we would not call a lump of moist clay elastic. Although it will stretch almost as much as a rubber band, when you let go it will not return to its original shape.

There is some elasticity in nearly everything. Steel is very elastic; the

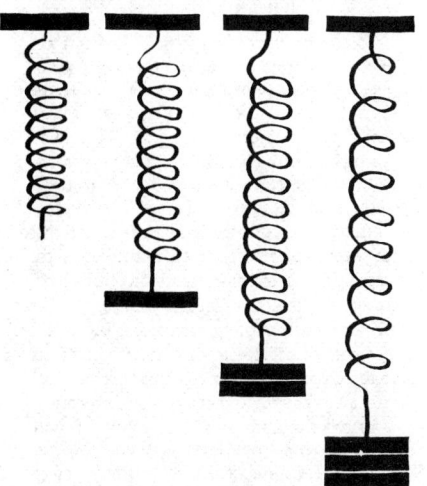

You can see how the elasticity of a spring makes it stretch as more and more weight is attached to it. *1* has no weight. *2* has one pound pulling it down. *3* has two pounds, and *4* has three pounds stretching it.

springs on an automobile are an example of this. The air we breathe is also very elastic, or we would not have air compressors and paint sprayers. (There is a separate article on AIR COMPRESSION.) Another good example of an elastic material is your skin; if you pull on it and let go, it snaps right back into place.

Elba

Elba is a small mountainous island in the Tyrrhenian Sea, nearly six miles off the western coast of Italy. Elba is famous in history because it was the place of exile of Emperor Napoleon I of France. Napoleon was sent to the island in exile after he lost the important Battle of the Nations in 1814. However, shortly afterwards, Napoleon escaped, and returned to France to try to win back his empire.

Elbe River

The Elbe, one of the most important rivers of Europe, begins in Czechoslovakia as the Labe, and flows north through central Germany to the North Sea. Its longest part is in Germany. In April 1945, at the end of World War II, the Russian armies from the east and the Allied troops from the west met at the Elbe, completing the conquest of Germany. Part of the Elbe now forms the border between the Federal Republic of Germany in the West and the Communist controlled German Democratic Republic in the East. The Elbe, about 720 miles long, is a major waterway for shipping. You can travel over 500 miles on it by boat. Canals connect the river with the Baltic Sea and the Oder River of Germany and Poland. The German cities of Dresden, Magdeburg and Hamburg are on the Elbe. The Elbe has tidal waters at Hamburg, and has been deepened to 40 feet for a fifty-mile stretch here.

elder

The elder is a shrub or small tree that grows along the roadside in many parts of Europe and the United States. The fruit of the elder is a purplish black berry that makes a very good wine. Elderberries also make delicious jam and jelly and many housewives use them to make pies. The elder has a creamy white flower that blooms in June or July, and both the flower and berry are used to make certain medicines. The elder flowers are also used in making perfume, and in some parts of Europe people pickle the flower buds and eat them. It is easy to hollow out a young elder branch, because it has a soft pith (the spongy tissue inside the stem of many plants). Many boys know that an elder branch makes a very good popgun or whistle. There are several different kinds of elder, and some of them have red berries that look very pretty, but are not good to eat. People in many countries have stories about the elder. In some places it is supposed to bring evil spirits, while in other places the people believe the elder stands for good luck.

El Dorado

El Dorado, meaning "the golden," was a fabulous treasure city of gold that many Spanish explorers in the New World were looking for about four hundred years ago. Pizarro, the Spanish con-

queror of Peru, discovered a great golden temple of the sun at Cuzco, Peru, and this may have been the "El Dorado" that native tribes in America told of. But other explorers kept on looking for a treasure-city long after Cuzco was found. Hunting for El Dorado, they explored south from Central America, and traced the course of the Orinoco and Amazon rivers in South America.

El Dorado also means the "gilded" or gold-covered man. There really was such a man, for a certain South American king-priest covered himself with gold dust once a year. He probably did this at a lake near Bogota, the present capital of Colombia, but the treasure in the lake was gone before the Spanish reached it. You will often hear "El Dorado" used to mean a place where a person can get rich quickly, and several cities in the United States have this name.

election

Whenever a group of people get together and form an organization, whether it is a government, a social club, a church, or a business association, they must have leaders. These leaders can be chosen in many ways. If they are chosen by vote, we call that an election. Election is not the only way of choosing leaders. Leaders can be appointed, or can inherit their jobs, or can be chosen by lot, but election is considered a much better and fairer method in most cases.

The elections we hear most about are elections of government officials, but there are many other kinds of election. For example, the Pope, the leader of the Roman Catholic Church, is elected by the College of Cardinals. In many schools, students elect class and student council officers. Organizations like trade unions, business associations, and social clubs have officers who are chosen by election.

Election is a very old way of choosing government leaders. It was used in ancient Greece and in the Roman republic more than two thousand years ago. But after that, for many hundreds of years, elections were not common. People were governed by kings and lords who were thought to have the right to govern by birth. In many countries there were elected groups, too, which were supposed to represent the interests of the common people, and to work together with the king and nobles. But these groups had very little power.

In the early days of the United States, not every citizen could take part in elections. Many of the state constitutions (which set up regulations about which citizens of their state are to be allowed to vote) originally contained provisions that made it impossible for poor men to participate in elections. These provisions, which made it necessary for a man to own a certain amount of property before he was allowed to vote, have since been changed. It took a great war, the Civil War, to make it possible for Negro citizens of the United States to vote. The Constitution of the United States was amended in 1868 to give Negroes the vote. Another constitutional amendment, in 1920, gave the vote to women in the United States for the first time. The United States was ahead of many other countries in giving the vote to women.

In Japan, for instance, women were not allowed to vote until 1945. Now women vote in most of the civilized countries of the world. The voting age varies from country to country, and in the United States it varies from state to state. In most of the states, people are allowed to vote when they reach the age of 21, but in some states they can vote at 18.

Before citizens can vote for any candidates, these candidates have to be chosen. In the United States, candidates may be chosen in primary elections, which are elections in which all the voter-members of a political party get a chance to vote for the candidates they would like to see running on election day. Primary elections take place some time before the regular elections, which are held on the first Tuesday after the first Monday in November.

REGISTRATION

A few weeks before any election, each person must *register*. He goes to a place selected by the government, gives his name and address, and takes a simple test to prove he can read and write. If he does not register, he is not allowed to vote when Election Day comes. Every state requires a voter to be able to read and write and to live in his voting district for some number of months before the election. *Permanent registration* means the voter has to register only once, unless he changes his place of residence.

TERMS OF OFFICE

Officials can be elected for different lengths of time. These lengths of time are called terms of office. In the United States, the term of office of the President and the Vice President is four years. Both of them are allowed to run for re-election once after that, but the President is not allowed to serve for more than eight years. The term of office of a senator is six years, and of a member of the House of Representatives, two years.

KINDS OF ELECTION

Elections can be either direct or indirect. A direct election is one in which the voters vote for the candidates who are running for office. Senators and members of the House of Representatives in the United States are elected by direct elections. An indirect election is one in which the voters vote for representatives who will then vote for the candidates who are running for office. The President and Vice President are elected by indirect elections, through the ELECTORAL COLLEGE (see the separate article). In many countries, the head of the government is elected indirectly by the members of the senate or parliament. For example, in France, the premier is elected by the members of the National Assembly, which is like the United States House of Representatives.

When citizens vote, their vote is secret. A secret vote is called a ballot. The ballot is used all over the civilized world. (You can read about the BALLOT in another article in this encyclopedia.) The secret vote is important to ordinary people because it protects them from the threats of a strong or vicious leader and gives them a chance to vote exactly as they please. But the open vote is just as important in the case of elected officials,

because these people are not acting as individuals, but as representatives of a political party or a geographical section, and are themselves responsible to the party or section they represent. The open vote is also used in the Congress of the United States when a piece of legislation is being decided on.

electoral college

The electoral college is the group of men and women who actually elect the President and Vice President of the United States. When a person votes on Election Day, he does not vote directly for President and Vice President. Instead, he casts his vote for a group of electors from his state, who have promised to vote for the candidate of the voter's choice. The size of the group of electors a person votes for is different in different states, because each state is allowed as many electors as it has Senators and members of the House of Representatives. The law would permit the electors to vote for anyone they wish, but they always do vote for the candidates in whose names they were chosen as electors.

Electra

Electra was a character in the stories of ancient Greece. She was the daughter of Agamemnon, the king of Mycenae, and his wife Clytemnestra. Electra had a brother named Orestes. While Agamemnon was away leading the Greek armies in the Trojan Wars, Clytemnestra fell in love with a Greek prince named Aegisthus. When Agamemnon came back, Clytemnestra and Aegisthus murdered him. They would have murdered Orestes too, but Electra had sent him far away. Electra was horrified by the murder of her father. She was always thinking of revenge. She often sent messages to her brother Orestes to remind him that it was his duty to avenge the murder. When Orestes was grown up, he returned to his home with his friend Pylades. Electra helped them to plan a way to get into the palace. Once inside the palace, Orestes killed Clytemnestra and Aegisthus. The murder of Agamemnon was avenged. Later, Orestes' friend was married to Electra. The three greatest Greek dramatists, Aeschylus, Sophocles, and Euripides, all wrote plays about Electra and her brother.

electric eye: see the article on ELECTRONICS.

electric fish

Electric fish are strange fish that have special muscle tissues that produce electricity. There are several different kinds of electric fish. Some of them have their electric power located near the tail, and others have muscular tissues in their heads that produce the electricity, while there are some fish that are electric all over their bodies. If you were to touch an electric fish, you would get an electric shock. All electric fish live in waters that are warm and tropical. The electric eel of South America is about six feet long, and it can produce about two hundred volts of electricity, which is enough to stun a large horse. The electric catfish lives in the water of the famous Nile River of Egypt, and in southern Europe

there are electric fish called torpedo fish. These fish use their electric power to defend themselves against enemies, and to kill other fish for food.

electricity

Just as tiny bits of matter that together form water will flow in a current, so do the tiny particles of matter that we call electrons flow in a stream or current that we call electricity. And just as the flow of water supplies force that can be put to useful purposes, so does the flow that we call electricity supply useful force. The difference is that the electrons are so small that they can never be seen, so that electricity is invisible. For this reason, men discovered electricity thousands of years after they had discovered other ways to produce force, or power.

Today, electricity is the best servant of man. It allows us to push a button or throw a switch and instantaneously to bring light, heat, and entertainment into our homes. It makes us comfortable, makes our jobs easier to do, and gives us more time to play and enjoy ourselves.

Electricity is used in almost every part of the world. Nine out of ten people in the United States use electricity every day of their lives.

Although electricity was known more than two thousand years ago, it was not until the beginning of the 1800s that anyone could discover a way of making an electric current. At that time an Italian scientist named Alessandro Volta made the first electric battery, in which electricity could be stored for use when needed. (See BATTERY.)

Thirty years after the invention of the electric battery, an English scientist named Michael Faraday discovered that large amounts of electric current could be made by moving a magnet through a coil of wire. This discovery led to the invention of the electric generator, which is used to supply electric current to houses, factories, farms, and other places requiring large amounts of electricity. The current used in most homes is so large that it would require about 75 batteries connected together to produce it.

ELECTRIC CIRCUITS

Electric current can flow only from an electric battery or generator, called an electric source, through a wire that leads from the source to some electrical device and back to the source again. The path along which electric current flows is called an electric circuit. Current can flow only through a complete path called a closed circuit. An electric bulb will light up only when there is an unbroken path from an electric source to the bulb and back to the source again. If one of the wires should be disconnected, no electricity will flow. (Such a circuit is called an open circuit.) When you turn off an electric switch, you are breaking a connection and opening an electric circuit. When you turn on an electric switch, you are making a connection and closing an electric circuit.

A *short circuit* occurs when electric current flows through a closed circuit without going through any electric device. This happens, for instance, when an electric

National Film Board of Canada
The Sir Adam Beck power generating station on the Niagara river at Niagara Falls, Ontario.

General Electric Co.

In an electric battery, electricity flows through a wire or conductor from the negative pole (−) to the positive pole (+). This is called current electricity.

light cord is frayed and the two wires of the circuit touch each other.

Electricity can flow only through substances called *conductors*. To conduct electricity from a battery or generator, silver, aluminum or copper wires are most often used because they are the best conductors. *Insulators* are substances through which electricity cannot easily flow. The wires in an electric light cord are kept from touching by being covered with cotton and rubber, substances that are good insulators.

An electric current may have various other wires connected to the two main wires of the circuit. If a wire is connected to one or both of the main wires, so that part of the current flows through the wire, the circuit is called a parallel circuit. The wire can be taken out of the circuit without affecting the flow of electric current through the circuit. When you plug an electrical appliance into a wall socket in your home, you are making a parallel circuit. Pull out the plug or turn the switch off on the appliance, and electricity will still flow to other appliances.

When a wire is connected into a circuit so that all the current flows through the wire, the circuit is called a series circuit. Disconnect the wire from the circuit, and no electricity will be able to flow through the rest of the circuit.

POSITIVE AND NEGATIVE POLES

The electrons, which move in a stream to form an electric current, are said to be *negative*. There are other particles of electricity called *protons,* and they are said to be *positive.* When any substance has more electrons than protons in it, it is *negatively charged;* when it has more protons than electrons, it is *positively charged.* When it has exactly the same number of electrons and protons it is said to be *neutral.*

Only the electrons, the negative particles, can move. They will always move toward anything that is positively charged. Any battery or generator has a negative pole and a positive pole. The electrons move toward the positive pole, and this creates the current or flow of electricity.

There is no particular reason why the word *positive* should describe the electricity that does not move. These words got their names long ago, when people did not know as much about electricity as they know now. In other uses, *negative* means "no" and *positive* means "yes," but

this has nothing to do with their meanings in electricity.

HOW ELECTRICITY FLOWS

When an electric circuit is closed, electricity flows through the circuit at the amazing speed of 186,000 miles a second. Because there are so many electrons in a circuit there is very little room for them to move about, so they strike each other with great force and each pushes the other forward through the circuit. At any point in an electric circuit, there are more than three million million million electrons flowing past every second. Because of the cramped quarters, the electrons themselves cannot move more than an inch every five or six minutes.

The electrons can move forward or backward. When the electrons move only forward through a circuit, the current is called DC or direct current. When the electrons move first forward and then backward, the current is called AC or alternating current.

Most houses in the United States are supplied with alternating current because

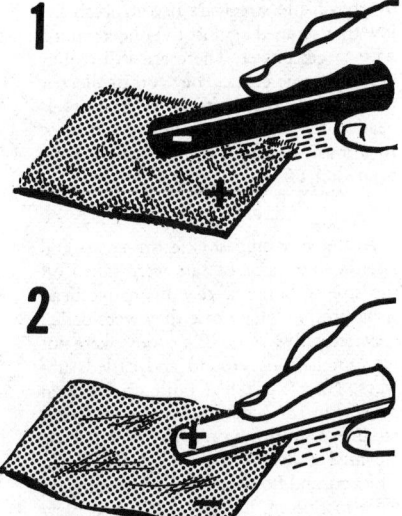

When a hard-rubber rod is rubbed with a piece of fur (1) it takes little bits of negative electricity called electrons from the fur. Negative electricity is on the rod (−) and positive electricity on the fur (+). When a glass rod is rubbed with silk (2) it gives electrons to the silk. The glass is then positive (+) and the silk negative (−). This is called static electricity.

it can be sent more easily over long-distance power lines. After it is sent through these lines, the current is increased by a special device called a transformer and then sent to your home. This cannot be done with DC current.

Most household appliances are made to work on either AC or DC current, but some will only work on one type of current and not on the other. An electric clock will not run on DC current, nor will an electric phonograph or steam iron. Most appliances that work on DC current will also work on AC current. In cases where the appliances are made for AC current and the only current available is DC, a special device called an inverter must be used to change the current from DC to AC. In cases where the appliances are made for DC and the only current available is AC, a special device called a rectifier must be used to change the current from AC to DC.

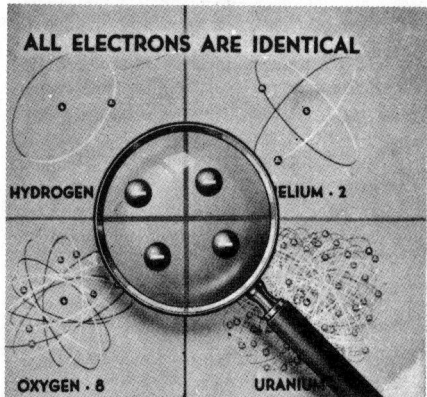

All things have electrons in them, and all electrons are alike. But some things have more electrons than others. The flow of electrons through a wire makes electricity.

HOW CURRENT IS MEASURED

Electric current is measured in units called *amperes.* These amperes are measured by a special device called an ammeter, which tells how fast a certain number of electrons, called a coulomb, is flowing through a circuit. A coulomb is equal to more than six million million million electrons. An ampere is the same thing as a coulomb of electricity flowing through a wire every second.

The force pushing these electrons through a circuit is called the electromotive force (EMF) and is measured in electrical units of force called *volts*. A volt is the amount of force needed to move one coulomb through a circuit. Most of the electricity supplied to homes has an EMF of 110 or 120 volts. When electricity is sent through long-distance power lines, more than 100,000 volts are used.

When one ampere is multiplied by one volt, the result is one *watt*. Most electrical appliances have numbers on them that tell how much voltage they can use and how many watts of power they use, which is another way of telling how fast they can use electricity. A light bulb marked 50 watts will use up electric power twice as fast as a light bulb marked 25 watts. An electric iron may be marked 575 watts, a waffle iron 800 watts. A watt is the amount of power needed to lift a pound almost three-quarters of a foot in one second. The watt was named in honor of James Watt, an English scientist, who invented the first practical steam engine.

The amount of electricity that you use in your home is measured in units called watt-hours or kilowatt-hours (thousands of watt-hours). A watt-hour is the amount of electricity needed to keep a one-watt bulb burning for one hour. Because thousands of watt-hours of electricity are used every month in homes, electric companies use the kilowatt-hour as a more convenient unit of measurement.

Kilowatt-hours are measured by an electric meter connected to the electric wires that enter your building. An electric meter has a small motor that turns whenever electricity is used in your home. The more electricity you use the more the motor turns. When the motor turns it moves four pointers on four dials on the face of the meter. Each dial stands for one number. Once each month a man from the electric company comes to read the meter. He looks at the dials and puts a number down in the book he carries. He subtracts this number from the reading he took the previous month. A bill is sent from the electric company to you telling how much electricity you have used for the month and how much you must pay for it.

Most electricity in the United States costs about three cents for every kilowatt-hour that is used. That means that it costs about three cents to operate an electric toaster for an hour. It costs less than one cent to burn a 60-watt light bulb for five hours.

Read also the articles on ATOM, BATTERY, GENERATOR, and INDUCTION.

electric railway

Any car or train that runs on tracks and whose engine is powered by electricity is called an electric railway. For a long time the electric railway was the most important type of transportation in cities in the United States. It is still important, but most of the electric cars have been replaced during the last twenty years or so.

TROLLEY CARS

The first kind of electric railway was the streetcar, which was also called the trolley car, and in England was called the tram. Electric current from a generator was kept constantly running through a wire over the street, and the car had a sort of pole going up to the electric line. At the top of the pole was a little wheel that picked up power from the electric wire. This wheel was called a trolley, and the car was named for this trolley.

The first trolley car was used in Kansas City, Missouri, in 1884, and within twenty years or so every big city in the world had many miles of tracks on which streetcars ran, carrying passengers to and from work, shopping, and school. In those days the interurban electric car was very important, carrying passengers between nearby cities. *Interurban* means "between cities." For long distances people used railroads, but for travel between cities ten, twenty, or even fifty miles apart they took the interurban. Finally you could go from one end of the country to the other by taking different interurban lines, just as you can today with buses.

The usual streetcar was about 30 or 40 feet long, and could carry 50 to 60 passengers. It was driven by a motorman and there was a conductor who collected fares, but in later years one man did both jobs. The motorman stood in front and operated the car by a switch that controlled the speed. There were usually two speeds forward, and the car could be backed up by reversing the motors. In the early years streetcars had handbrakes, but later they always had airbrakes. The cars had driving equipment at both ends so that either end could be the front and the car did not have to be turned around at the end of its run.

In many of the biggest cities, such as New York, there came to be so many overhead wires on the streets, with the telephones and trolley cars and electric lights, that all the wires were put underground. Then instead of having trolleys overhead, the streetcars had a brush below that scraped against the underground wire to get power. There are still trolley buses in some cities. They run by electric motors and take their power from overhead wires, but they do not need tracks. In almost all cities, the old tracks have been dug up.

RAPID TRANSIT

In the very biggest cities streetcars and later whole trains of cars were taken off the streets. Some were put on overhead structures, in which case they were called elevated railways, or "Els"; some were put in tunnels underground and called subways. New York had built an elevated railway in 1867, but it used regular steam engines to pull the cars. The first electric elevated railways were in New York, Chicago, and Boston, and the first subways were in Boston, London, Paris, and New York. There is a separate article about the SUBWAY. In many cities there were rapid-transit lines that ran on the surface, but the tracks were fenced in so that the cars never crossed traffic or had to stop at corners as automobiles do.

ELECTRIFIED RAILROADS

The first suggested use of electricity in railroads came when an electric locomotive was displayed at the Chicago World's Fair in 1883, the year before the first streetcar line was built. This electric locomotive had the same purpose as the steam engine—to pull a train of cars, not to carry passengers itself. It took power from a third rail, just as the subways and elevated trains do today. This third rail runs alongside the two rails on which the train runs, and a little wheel attached to the car rolls over it and picks up current. Trolley lines seldom carried more than 1,000 volts; third rails carry up to 3,000 volts and sometimes even more.

The railroads first put electric locomotives into use when New York City passed a law that steam locomotives could not enter the city because they made too much smoke. The Pennsylvania Railroad finally put in complete electric railroad service all the way from New York to Washington, D.C. Most other cities use electric locomotives for commuter trains in which people who live in suburbs travel to and from work every day. As you can read in the article on LOCOMOTIVES, although the electric locomotive is more efficient than the steam locomotive, it is less efficient than the Diesel engine, and so for a number of years there has been no new electrification of railroad lines.

electrocardiograph

An electrocardiograph is an electric machine that tells you how strongly your heart is beating. The *cardio* in the word means heart, and *graph* means to draw, so that actually an electrocardiograph is a machine that draws a kind of picture of how your heart works.

Your body is really a walking generator or maker of electricity. When your muscles and nerves move, they send out small bits of electricity.

The electrocardiograph can measure the amount of electricity that your heart muscles are making when your heart is beating. It is a special kind of electric machine, called a GALVANOMETER, about which there is a separate article. The galvanometer or electrocardiograph is connected to the patient's body by wires called electrodes, at his left and right arm and on his left leg. A wire in the galvanometer moves whenever electricity goes through it from the patient's heart muscles. The movements are caught on a mirror, aimed toward a motion picture camera. The camera takes pictures of these movements on special motion picture film.

The pictures are thick, black lines that go up and down, and look like small mountains separated by flat ground. These mountains or "peaks" are made every time the heart beats. By looking at the picture, a doctor can tell if your heart is working properly. Some electrocardiographs have a pen connected to the galvanometer, and the pen moves along a special piece of paper tracing out the action of your heart.

electrocution

Electrocution is being killed by an electric current that passes through the body. Every year many persons are electrocuted accidentally by touching lines that carry a lot of electric power, or by be-

ing struck by lightning, or even by working a light switch while they are in the bathtub. In some states, murderers used to be put to death by electrocution as a form of punishment.

When electricity flows through an electric heater, it makes the wires of the heater red hot. This is because the wires carrying the current to the heater are good conductors of electricity and the wires in the heater are not such good conductors. In the heater wires, the electricity meets with resistance in its effort to pass through it becomes hot, just as you become hot when you make a great effort in an athletic game.

Just as electricity makes the heater hot, it makes you hot when it tries to pass through your body, because your body is not as good a conductor of electricity as the wires are. If there is enough electricity, it can burn a person badly—perhaps enough to kill him.

Electricity can kill you in another way. If you have ever stuck your finger in a "live" socket, you received a shock that made you tingle all over. A much more powerful electric current can shake a person's nerves loose from his spinal cord. This stops the workings of his body and he dies at once.

The force with which electric current flows is measured in volts; the amount of current flowing through a wire is measured in amperes. Either a lot of volts or a lot of amperes, or a combination of the two, can kill a person. Therefore it does not always take "high voltage" to electrocute someone. When a person's body is wet, he is in more danger when he touches an electric current. Water is a good conductor of electricity and will carry the current to much more of the surface of the body.

Sometimes an electric shock stops the breathing but does not kill the person at once. In such cases a person may be saved by ARTIFICIAL RESPIRATION. If the person is still touching the electric wire, it is dangerous to touch him directly, because the electricity will flow from him into anyone who touches him. He can be wrapped in a blanket and pulled away from the wire, or pushed away with a dry stick.

ELECTRIC CHAIR

Until 1972, many states of the United States used electrocution as a means of CAPITAL PUNISHMENT, about which there is a separate article.

New York was the first state to use electrocution, under a law passed in 1888 (changed in 1965 to eliminate the death penalty in all but a few special cases). The first person ever electrocuted died in the prison at Auburn, New York, on August 6, 1890. At one time electrocution was thought to be the least painful way to put murderers to death, and twenty-four states adopted it, but some of these states later decided that suffocation in a gas chamber is quicker and more humane.

When a murderer is electrocuted, he is strapped into a large chair. A metal band is put around his head, at a spot that has had the hair shaved off, and another metal band is put around his ankle. These bands are moistened with a salt solution, because it conducts electricity well.

Through these bands about 2,000 volts of electricity are sent. The criminal loses consciousness almost at once and usually dies in less than a minute, but the whole process lasts about five minutes before he is taken from the chair and examined by a physician, who pronounces him dead.

electroencephalograph

An electroencephalograph (called EEG for short) is an instrument to study electric waves that come from the brain. The electric waves are called brain waves. They are tiny electric currents produced by the activity of the cells in the brain. Wires attached to the scalp take up these brain waves, enlarge them, and record them on paper. This record is called an *encephalogram*. Different people have different kinds of waves, and the same person shows varied kinds of waves at different times, as, for example, when he is awake as compared to when he is asleep. The encephalogram has been able to show if people have epilepsy, tumors, or brain injuries, by the type of brain waves they have. A great deal of testing, using this instrument, is now being done by doctors. The electroencephalograph was invented by Hans Berger, in 1926.

electrolysis

Electrolysis is a way of separating the molecules of a chemical compound by passing electricity through it.

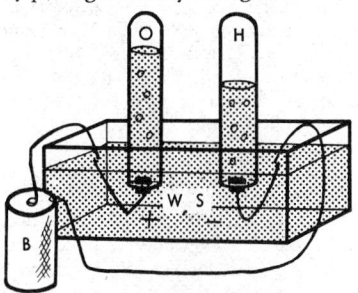

Above: In electrolysis of water, current from a battery (B) flows through a mixture of water (W) and sulfuric acid (S). This breaks up the water into oxygen (O) and hydrogen (H). There is twice as much hydrogen formed as there is oxygen.

The molecules in a solution can be either positive or negative ions (charged particles). If you put both positively and negatively charged particles in a solution, the positive ions migrate to the negative charge and the negative ions go to the positive charge. The new combination of ions become new molecules completing the process of electrolysis. Some substances can only be produced through electrolysis. To find out if a solution is an electrolyte (separating into ions and conducting electricity) we can perform this experiment. If we take a dry cell battery and connect it to a light bulb with two pieces of wire, we can then immerse the two ends of wire into a solution (salt, sugar, etc.) and see if they conduct electricity. If they do the bulb will light up and the solution can be classified as an electrolyte. When a certain material dissolves in water it dissociates into either positive or negative ions. This solution will then conduct an electric current. This is very useful to the scientist and chemist. If a chemist wants an element alone he

can usually get it by using this process of electrolysis. Electrolysis has other uses besides separating of chemical compounds.

Electrolysis is used in making tin plate. After the tin has been extracted from the ore, it is purified in a great blast furnace and then is refined by an electrolytic process shown here.
Republic Steel Corp.

Another important use for electrolysis is in *electroplating*. The shiny chrome on automobiles, the brass doorknob and certain kinds of silverware are electroplated. To silverplate a spoon, for example, all we have to do is to replace the negative carbon rod with a steel spoon, and replace the salt with a liquid that has silver in it. Then the longer the electricity flows the thicker the silverplating will be, until the liquid gives up all of its silver.

Electrolysis is also used for making printing plates, or electrotypes. First a mold is made of an entire page of printing type. Next, the mold is covered with a very fine graphite powder that will conduct electricity. The mold is then put into a liquid that has copper in it and the negative wire from the battery is connected to the graphite coating. The copper from the liquid is deposited on the mold. When this becomes thick, it is called a shell. A melted metal is poured into this shell to make it strong. The result is a printing plate that will print the same thing that the type would print and will last longer because it is made of harder metal.

The same system is used in making phonograph records. First a "master" is cut by a needle on a disk made of a plastic material. The master is electroplated to make a metal shell. This metal shell is "backed up" with a hard metal, just as a printing plate is. This forms a "stamper." When pressed against a soft plastic material, it makes a duplicate of the master record. The plastic then hardens and forms the record you buy in a store.

electromagnet is a magnet that works by electricity: see the article on MAGNET.

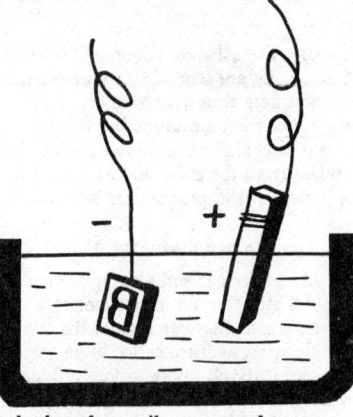
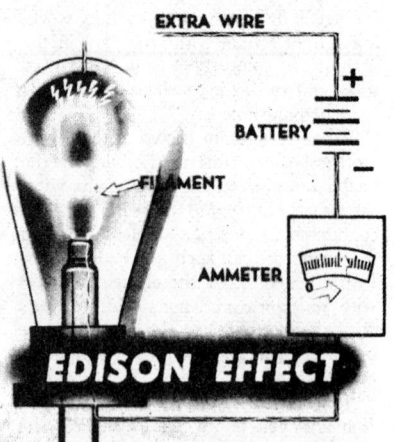

Left: Silverplating a fork by electrolysis. A fork and a bar of pure silver connected to a battery are placed in a solution containing sodium, silver, and cyanide. The electric current causes the silver in the solution to attach itself to the fork. More silver is added to the solution from the silver bar. *Right:* Making letters for printing by electrotyping is done in the same way. A copper bar and a mold for a letter are connected to a battery and placed in a solution. The current breaks up the copper, which fills the mold of the letter.

electronics

Electrons are particles of matter, so tiny that they can never be seen but so powerful that their movement along wires produces the electricity that lights our homes and runs our factories. Not many years ago, scientists discovered that electrons can also move through air, gases, and even a vacuum (no air or gases). The study of the movements and uses of electrons is called electronics.

The science and industry of electronics has made possible radio and television, tape recording, and the "sound track" (tiny marks on a strip of photographic film) that produces the voices in talking motion pictures. It has made possible the guiding of an airplane in which there is no pilot. It has made possible the photoelectric cell ("electric eye") that opens and closes doors automatically, detects more than two million different color shades (when the human eye can detect only ten thousand), and inspects metals and other materials for flaws the eye cannot see. It has given us x-ray and thousands of other modern devices.

All these are due to the vacuum or gas-filled electronic tube. These tubes now range in size from tiny globes of fingertip size to long cylinders twenty-five feet high.

HOW ELECTRONICS BEGAN

The beginning of electronics came about through an accidental discovery made by Thomas A. Edison about seventy-five years ago. One day in 1883 Edison was experimenting with the electric light bulb, which he had invented not long before. He observed that sometimes there was a glow inside the bulb, between the two sides of the filament, the loop of wire that made the light.

Investigating further, Edison sealed a metal plate inside the bulb between the two sides of the filament. He connected this plate to the positive side of an electric battery and he connected the filament to the negative side of the battery. Edison found that when the filament became hot ("warmed up") it released electrons and an electric current flowed across the space between the filament and plate. This became known as the "Edison effect" —the basis of modern electronics.

However, Edison did nothing with his discovery. Twelve years later an English scientist, J. J. Thomson, proved that the

current between the filament and the plate was a stream of electrons. The filament had gotten so hot that it had thrown off electrons toward the plate. When they hit the plate, they produced an electric current.

THE DIODE

It was not until nine years later that anything was done with the Edison effect. In 1904 an English engineer, J. A. Fleming, made the first electronic tube (or *valve*, as it is called in England). It was a vacuum tube with a filament made from a metal that easily gave out electrons, and a thin metal plate sealed inside the tube to catch these electrons. The electrons produced current in the plate, and the current flowed out of a prong in the bottom of the tube.

Both the filament and the metal plate in an electronic tube are called *electrodes*. The filament is the negative electrode, called the *cathode*, while the plate is the positive electrode, or *anode*. Because Fleming's tube or valve had only two electrodes, it was called a *diode*, meaning "two electrodes."

Diodes are used to change AC current (electricity that changes its direction) into DC current (electricity that goes in one direction). Diodes are often called rectifiers. The first use of the diode was in wireless telegraphy. The wireless signals are sent through the air in the form of AC current. To be received and heard by a receiving set, the signals must be changed to DC current. This is done by a diode.

Here is why the rectifier changes AC current to DC current: The electrons can flow only from the filament to the plate, never from the plate to the filament. Since the electrons flow only one way, the current coming from the plate must also flow one way and is therefore direct current.

THE TRIODE

Soon after Fleming's invention, an American inventor named Lee De Forest placed a small fine wire screen, called a *grid*, between the filament and plate. De Forest found that when the grid was given an electric charge, by electricity supplied by an outside battery, it could control the quantity of electrons flowing from the filament to the plate. Because it had three electrodes, De Forest's tube was

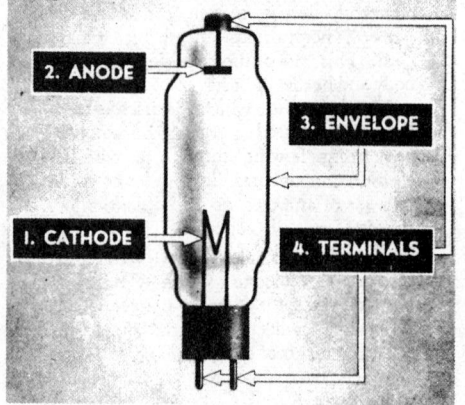

In 1883, Thomas Edison discovered that he could make electricity pass from a hot wire or filament to a metal plate. This is known as the Edison effect, and is the basis of all electronic tubes, especially the radio tube. The filament and the plate are in a glass tube and connected to a battery. The movement of the dial on the ammeter (a device for measuring current) shows that electricity is flowing inside the glass tube.

General Electric Co.

An electronic tube has a cathode or negative electrode from which electrons flow to an anode or positive electrode. The electrodes are contained inside a glass tube or envelope. Most of the air has been removed from the tube so that the electrons can flow more easily. The tube in this picture is called a diode because it has only two terminals or electrodes. When it is connected to a source of current, electricity flows through one terminal to the cathode, across to the anode, and out the other terminal. Electricity can flow in only one direction in such a tube. For this reason it is often used to change alternating current (AC) to direct current (DC). Such tubes are called rectifiers or current changers. Some tubes have a wire screen, called a grid, between the anode and cathode to control the flow of current in the tube. They are called triodes. They are used in radios to increase or amplify the radio signals sent out by radio stations.

known as the *triode,* meaning "three electrodes." He called it the Audion tube.

The triode was used by another American scientist, E. H. Armstrong, to increase the strength of radio signals coming from a radio station to a radio receiver. This made possible the loudspeaker that is used today. Before about 1920, earphones had been used on all radio sets, because the sound was too weak to be heard throughout a room.

ELECTRIC EYE

So far we have discussed how heating a filament with electricity can cause it to give off electrons. Light falling on certain metals can do the same thing. This is the

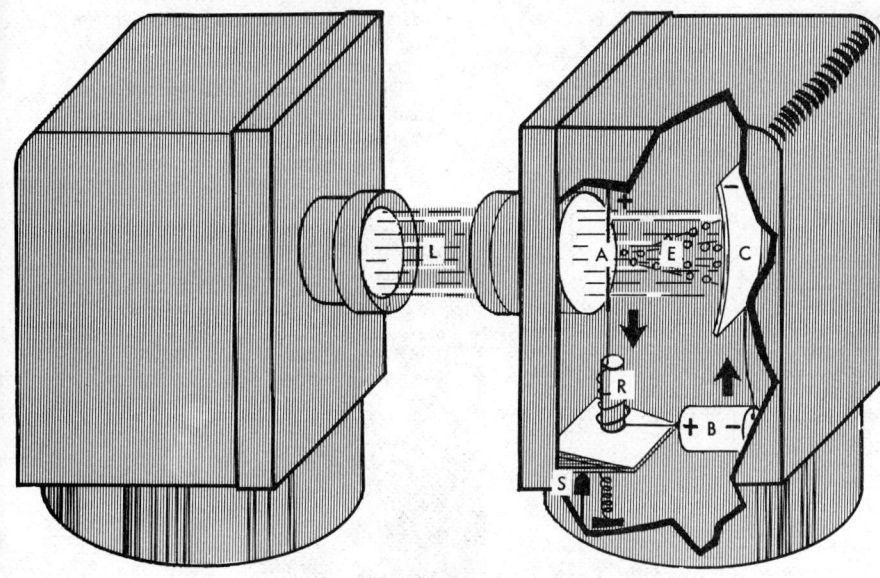

Above: The electric eye sees all and says nothing. It uses a special kind of light called infrared that you cannot see. The light (L) passes from one box to another. When it falls on a special piece of metal of the cathode (C), it knocks electrons (E) off. They pass to the wire anode (A) and flow to a relay (R), a kind of electromagnet, that can turn a switch (S) on and off. A battery (B) sends current back to the cathode. A person blocking out the light will stop electrons from flowing and turn the switch on, opening a door or ringing a bell.

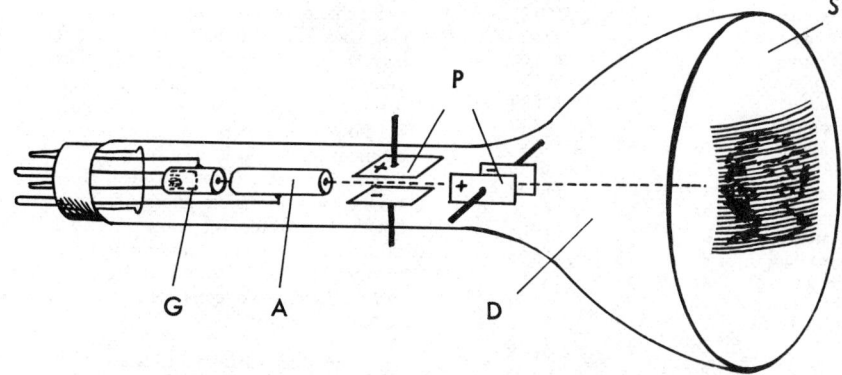

An electronic tube called a kinescope is the heart of your television set. A picture is sent from the television station in a form of electricity and goes into the kinescope, where an electron gun (G) shoots it into an anode (A) or positive plate. The electrons pass between two sets of plates (P) and are changed into a beam at another anode (D). The beam falls on a special screen that lights up when electrons hit it. The picture you see is the result.

basis of the photoelectric cell, or "electric eye."

The light acts in the same way as the electricity in a diode or triode. There are many different metals, called alkali metals, that will give off electrons when struck by light. The metal called caesium is very sensitive to ordinary light. The metal called potassium is very sensitive to blue light. The metal called zinc is very sensitive to ultraviolet light (light that cannot be seen with the naked eye).

The inside of the glass tube in a photoelectric cell is coated with a metal that is sensitive to light. The metallic coating is connected to the negative side of a battery. A loop of wire or a thin metal rod is set in the center of the tube and is connected to the positive side of the battery. Light entering the tube strikes the metal coating, which gives off electrons. These electrons are caught by the wire loop, resulting in a flow of electric current. When the light is turned off, electrons

no longer are given off by the metal coating and the current stops flowing. Often photoelectric cells are filled with helium or argon gas to increase the flow of current.

In the electric eye used to open and close doors, a beam of light is directed toward a photoelectric cell in front of a doorway. As long as the light strikes the cell, the electric current that it produces will keep the door closed. When someone walking toward the doorway steps in front of the light beam, electric current will stop flowing and the door will open.

electron microscope, a special kind of microscope designed so that scientists can see the greatly magnified shadows or silhouettes of substances through which a stream of electrons cannot pass. See the article on MICROSCOPE.

elegy

A poem that tells the way the writer feels about some sad thing that has hap-

pened is called an elegy. Most elegies are about someone who has died, or about how it feels to love a person who does not love you. Sometimes elegies are about the unhappiness in the world. Thomas Gray wrote the most famous elegy in the English language, and it is called "An Elegy Written in a Country Churchyard." Walt Whitman, the great American poet, wrote a beautiful elegy about Abraham Lincoln's death, which is called "When Lilacs Last in the Dooryard Bloomed."

The first elegies were funeral songs that were written in a special rhythm, and for a while all poems that were written in this rhythm were called elegies. The Greeks wrote very fine elegies about love and war, and there are also fine elegies written in Latin by the Roman poets. Ovid was a Roman poet who wrote elegies that people still read with pleasure.

Some great elegies in English poetry are Spenser's *Astrophel* (about Sir Philip Sidney), Milton's *Lycidas* (about a college classmate named King), Shelley's *Adonais* (about the poet John Keats), and Tennyson's *In Memoriam.*

element

Everything in the world is made up of tiny particles, much too small to see, called atoms. Most substances contain atoms of different kinds, and these are called *compounds.* When a substance is made all of the same kind of atom, it is called an *element.*

At least a hundred different elements are known to exist. An element can be a gas, such as the oxygen in the air that we breathe; or a liquid, such as mercury; or a solid, such as iron or aluminum.

The difference between elements is the difference between the atoms of which they are made. Every atom is made from the same bits of electricity. These are electrons, protons, and neutrons. An atom always has exactly as many electrons as protons, but it may have any number of neutrons. An atom with one electron and one proton will always be different from an atom with four electrons and four protons (or any other number), so the elements formed by the atoms will also be different. Neutrons in the atom will add only to the weight of the element.

A list of the known elements is shown after this article. It also gives the following information:

Symbol. This is only an abbreviation of the name of the element. It is shorter and therefore easier to write *Bo* than *boron.*

Atomic number. This is the number of electrons in each of the atoms that form the element. (It is also the number of the protons, for they are always the same.)

Atomic weight. This is the number of protons and neutrons in the atom of the element. The weight also takes into consideration the electrons in the element, but the electrons are so light that they are hardly worth counting. One proton or neutron weighs about as much as 1,800 electrons.

The exact atomic weight is found by considering that the atom of oxygen weighs 16, and comparing the weights of other atoms to it. For example, an atom of atomic weight 32 would weigh exactly twice as much as one oxygen atom.

CHEMICAL ELEMENTS

Element	Symbol	At. No.	At. Wt.	Element	Symbol	At. No.	At. Wt.
Actinium	Ac	89	227	Mendelevium	Mv	101	256
Aluminum	Al	13	26.97	Mercury	Hg	80	200.61
Americium	Am	95	243	Molybdenum	Mo	42	96.0
Antimony	Sb	51	121.76	Neodymium	Nd	60	144.27
Argon	A	18	39.944	Neon	Ne	10	20.183
Arsenic	As	33	74.91	Neptunium	Np	93	237
Astatine	At	85	210	Nickel	Ni	28	58.69
Barium	Ba	56	137.36	Niobium	Nb	41	92.91
Berkelium	Bk	97	247	Nitrogen	N	7	14.008
Beryllium	Be	4	9.02	Nobelium	No	102	254
Bismuth	Bi	83	209	Osmium	Os	76	191.5
Boron	B	5	10.82	Oxygen	O	8	16.000
Bromine	Br	35	79.916	Palladium	Pd	46	106.7
Cadmium	Cd	48	112.41	Phosphorus	P	15	31.02
Cesium	Cs	55	132.91	Platinum	Pt	78	195.23
Calcium	Ca	20	40.08	Plutonium	Pu	94	242
Californium	Cf	98	249	Polonium	Po	84	210
Carbon	C	6	12.01	Potassium	K	19	39.096
Cerium	Ce	58	140.13	Praseodymium	Pr	59	140.92
Chlorine	Cl	17	35.457	Promethium	Pm	61	146.0?
Chromium	Cr	24	52.01	Protactinium	Pa	91	231
Cobalt	Co	27	58.94	Radium	Ra	88	226.05
Copper	Cu	29	63.57	Radon	Rn	86	222
Curium	Cm	96	247	Rhenium	Re	75	186.31
Dysprosium	Dy	66	162.46	Rhodium	Rh	45	102.91
Einsteinium	E	99	254	Rubidium	Rb	37	85.48
Erbium	Er	68	167.64	Ruthenium	Ru	44	101.7
Europium	Eu	63	152.0	Samarium	Sm	62	150.43
Fluorine	F	9	19.000	Scandium	Sc	21	45.10
Fermium	Fm	100	253	Selenium	Se	34	78.96
Francium	Fr	87	223	Silicon	Si	14	28.06
Gadolinium	Gd	64	156.9	Silver	Ag	47	107.88
Gallium	Ga	31	69.72	Sodium	Na	11	22.997
Germanium	Ge	32	72.60	Strontium	Sr	38	87.63
Gold	Au	79	197.2	Sulfur	S	16	32.06
Hafnium	Hf	72	178.6	Tantalum	Ta	73	180.88
Helium	He	2	4.002	Technetium	Tc	43	97.8
Holmium	Ho	67	163.5	Tellurium	Te	52	127.61
Hydrogen	H	1	1.0078	Terbium	Tb	65	159.2
Indium	In	49	114.76	Thallium	Tl	81	204.39
Iodine	I	53	126.92	Thorium	Th	90	232.12
Iridium	Ir	77	193.1	Thulium	Tm	69	169.4
Iron	Fe	26	55.84	Tin	Sn	50	118.70
Krypton	Kr	36	83.7	Titanium	Ti	22	47.90
Lanthanum	La	57	138.92	Tungsten	W	74	184.0
Lawrencium	Lw	103	257	Uranium	U	92	238.07
Lead	Pb	82	207.21	Vanadium	V	23	50.95
Lithium	Li	3	6.940	Xenon	Xe	54	131.3
Lutetium	Lu	71	175.0	Ytterbium	Yb	70	173.04
Magnesium	Mg	12	24.32	Yttrium	Y	39	88.92
Manganese	Mn	25	54.93	Zinc	Zn	30	65.38
				Zirconium	Zr	40	91.22

The atomic weights give you a good idea of how heavy the elements are. For example, you can see that gold, whose atomic weight is more than 197, is much heavier than iron, whose atomic weight is hardly 56, and iron is much heavier than aluminum, whose atomic weight is less than 27.

ISOTOPES

Elements with the same atomic number can have different atomic weights. This means that their atoms have the same number of protons and electrons but that there is a difference in the number of neutrons. Two forms of the same element that differ in atomic weight are called isotopes. They are the same element in everything except their atomic weight. You can read more about isotopes in the article ATOM.

Read also the article CHEMISTRY, which explains how men found out about elements.

elephant

The elephant is the largest and strongest animal that lives on land. Afri-

can elephants grow to be about twelve feet tall and they weigh about six tons. Indian elephants are somewhat smaller. Another kind of elephant, called a pigmy, grows to be only about four feet high. Elephants have long trunks (which are part of the nose), huge, flapping ears, tiny eyes, and sharp ivory tusks that sometimes weigh two hundred pounds each. Most elephants are gray. A few are grayish-white; some people believe that these white elephants bring good luck, and in some countries they are sacred.

The elephant's long trunk is so powerful that it can pick up huge logs, and yet it is delicate enough to pick up a peanut. The trunk is useful in many ways. The elephant depends for its safety on its sense of smell and it can sniff danger with its trunk very quickly. A trunk is very useful to eat with, and an elephant must eat about five hundred pounds of green plants and drink about fifty gallons of water every day. An elephant's trunk is also a good spray and elephants have a good time spraying themselves and each other with water or dust. When a baby elephant is born, its mother has to teach it how to use its trunk. It takes about 25

years for an elephant to be fully grown, and some Indian elephants live to be 150 years old.

These enormous animals are useful to man. In ancient times, elephants were used in battle very much the way we use tanks now. African natives use elephants to haul logs and other heavy loads.

Margot L. Wolf

Elephants captured for the circus have been taught to do many tricks and stunts.

Elephants are very popular at the circus, where they play ball and balance on barrels and do many wonderful tricks. Female elephants are gentle and good-natured, and they are very good at learning how to do things. The most famous elephant in the world was Jumbo. P. T. BARNUM, a great circus showman about whom you can read in another volume, bought Jumbo from the London Zoological Society for $10,000 and brought her to America about seventy years ago. You can see Jumbo's skeleton in the Museum of Natural History in New York City.

elevated railway, railway tracks built on a high framework so that street traffic can pass under them. See the article on ELECTRIC RAILWAY.

elevator

An elevator is a cage or platform that can be lifted or lowered to different floors or levels. It moves up and down in a shaft. It must have a device for lifting and lowering, such as a cable connected to machinery. Power of some kind drives that device.

Elevators were used in ancient times and in the Middle Ages. They were pulled up by means of ropes. Sometimes strong men pulled the ropes to make the elevator go up, sometimes animals were used, and sometimes the ropes were tied to a wheel that was turned by a swift current of water. In the United States elevators did not come into use until about 1850. The first ones were worked by power from steam engines. On top of the elevator shaft was a revolving drum. The rope or cable to which the elevator was attached was wound over this drum. A belt ran from the steam engine to the drum, and when power was applied the belt made the drum turn and this made the rope go up or down.

Another early kind of elevator was the hydraulic elevator. The cage was mounted on a steel plunger. This fitted into a cylinder that went down into the ground. When water was forced into the cylinder, the pressure of the water pushed the plunger up and that pushed the cage up. When water was let out of the cylinder, the car went down. It was not practicable to make the plunger and cylinder very long, and so this kind of elevator only went up a few stories. It took time for the water to be forced in and out of the cylinder, and for this reason the hydraulic elevator moved rather slowly.

Elevators of today have intricate machinery that is driven by electricity. They are able to go up any number of stories and to move very fast. Without this kind of elevator no one would have bothered putting up the very tall buildings known as "skyscrapers." The first electric elevator was made in 1880 by a German inventor. This first one had to be improved a great deal before electric elevators could be used in really tall buildings, but such improvements were made, and electric ele-

Below: The more common traction-sheave elevator balances the car (C) against a weight (W). A sheave (T), which is turned by a motor, moves the cable and the car by means of friction or traction.

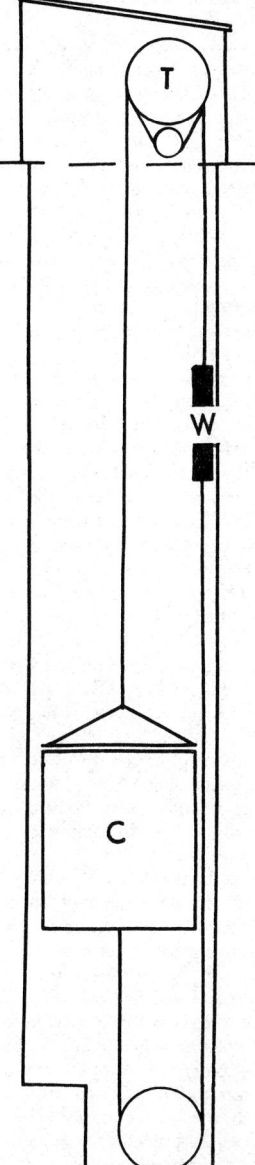

vators now go to any height desired and at a very high rate of speed. In addition, the elevator of today has safety devices that make it almost impossible for it to get out of order. You can travel as safely in an elevator as in any other vehicle.

Elgin Marbles

The Elgin Marbles are a collection of marble statues and carvings from ancient Greek temples. There are statues and pieces of statues of Greek gods and goddesses, and also of horses. The carvings are a long series of picture-stories that the Greeks used to decorate the fronts of the temples. The collection is kept in the British Museum in London, England. The Marbles were named for Thomas Bruce, Lord Elgin, who bought them in Greece about 150 years ago. The British Government bought the Elgin Marbles in 1816. Many casts or copies have been made of them, and one set of copies is owned by New York City.

Eli, Eli

Eli, Eli means "My God, my God." It is the title of a traditional, or very old, Jewish song. The first words of the song are taken from the twenty-second Psalm, in which the crucifixion of Christ is foretold. The first words of this Psalm are, "My God, my God, why hast thou forsaken me?" On the cross Jesus said these words in Aramaic, the language of the Old Testament: "Eli, Eli, lama sabachtani?"

The words of the song express the sorrows of the Jews. The song is not a religious song, although people often consider it one. It is often used as a concert song.

Elijah and Elisha

Elijah and Elisha were two important men in the Bible. The books of Kings, in the Old Testament, tell about them. Elijah came first. He lived about eight hundred years before Jesus was born. At that time the king of Israel, Ahab, was married to a Phoenician princess named Jezebel, who worshiped the Phoenician god, Baal. A lot of people thought it was fashionable to do the same. Elijah went before the king and told him he should make his people pray to the true God. Elijah said that unless the king did this, God would not let it rain in the kingdom. The king did not listen to him, and there was no rain. To escape the king's anger, Elijah went to live alone in the wilderness.

Later Elijah went back to the king. A great contest was held on Mount Carmel between Elijah and the priests of Baal. The people sided with Elijah and his God, and then the rain fell again. But Jezebel wanted to destroy Elijah, so he had to flee into the wilderness of Mt. Horeb, or Sinai.

God told Elijah that he should call Elisha for a successor. This he did and then was "translated," or taken away, by horses and chariots of fire.

Elisha went on doing great things just as Elijah had done. Elisha healed the chief general of the army of Damascus from a sickness called leprosy, by telling him to go and bathe in the River Jordan. The Bible says he brought a dead child to life, but he once sent the bears after some bad boys who made fun of him for being

bald. People think of Elijah and Elisha together because they lived during the same time and did about the same kind of work.

Eliot, Charles W.

Charles W. Eliot was an American educator. He was president of Harvard University in Cambridge, Massachusetts, from 1869 to 1909. He was born in 1834 and was graduated from Harvard in 1853. Eliot taught mathematics and chemistry at Harvard for ten years before he was appointed president in 1869. Until that time all the presidents of Harvard had been Protestant ministers.

Harvard is the oldest college in the United States, founded in 1636, but Eliot did much to make it into the great school it is today. He brought great scholars and teachers to Harvard and improved the medical and law schools. He was also the first American university president who allowed students to choose some of their subjects, instead of having to study only what they were told.

Eliot was much interested in high school education. Until 1892 students in high schools in different parts of the country did not always study the same subjects. Because of Eliot's influence, high schools in the United States standardized their courses so that students everywhere in the nation studied the same subjects. He also believed that fifteen minutes of daily reading of the great literature of the world would educate a man. He selected a series of books that are sold under the name of the "Harvard Classics." These volumes took up just five feet on a bookshelf and were called Dr. Eliot's Five-foot Shelf. Eliot died in 1926.

Eliot, George

George Eliot is the pen name of a woman who was one of the greatest of all English novelists. Her real name was Mary Ann Evans. When she wrote her first novel, she was so afraid it would not succeed that she did not want people to know who had written it, so she published it under a man's name. After she had written several novels that were very popular, she told people her real name but continued to publish her novels under the name of George Eliot.

One of her most famous novels is called *Silas Marner.* Other novels by George Eliot include *Adam Bede, The Mill on the Floss,* and *Middlemarch.*

George Eliot (Mary Ann Evans) was born in 1819. Her mother died when Mary Ann was only 16 years old, so that she had to take care of her father and the big country house in which they lived. When her father died, she went to London and got a job as assistant editor of a magazine called the *Westminster Review.* She also fell in love with the editor-in-chief, George Henry Lewes, with whom she spent a happy married life. It was Lewes who encouraged her to write her first novels. Lewes died in 1878, and two years later Mary Ann Evans mar-

ried an old friend, John Walter Cross. But she herself died only six months after this marriage, in 1880.

Eliot, John

John Eliot was the first missionary to convert some of the New England Indians to Christianity. He was born in England in 1604 and attended Cambridge University. Eliot went to Boston in 1634 and became a teacher in the church at the nearby town of Roxbury, where he lived until his death in 1690. He learned the language of the Indians near him and his great achievement was translating the Bible into their language. The whole Bible was published in this Indian language in 1663, the first Bible to be printed in North America.

Eliot, T. S.

Thomas Stearns Eliot is the name of an English poet, one of the most important poets of this century. He was born in the United States (in St. Louis, Missouri) in 1888, and studied at Harvard, but then he continued his studies in England and became a British citizen. The book of poetry that first made him famous was *The Waste Land*, published in 1922. Eliot was also the author of several books of criticism, or comment on the writings of others. In 1949 he wrote a play, *The Cocktail Party*, that was very successful. In 1948 he was awarded the Nobel prize in literature. He died in 1965.

Elisabeth, Saint

Saint Elisabeth, or Elizabeth, was the mother of John the Baptist and the cousin of the Virgin Mary. The first chapter of the Gospel of Luke, in the New Testament, tells how Elisabeth and her husband, the priest Zacharias, in their old age, had their son John; how Mary visited Elisabeth before Jesus was born; and how Elisabeth said to Mary the words now most familiar in the prayer *Ave Maria* (Hail Mary!): "Blessed art thou among women, and blessed is the fruit of thy womb."

Elisha, see ELIJAH AND ELISHA.

Elizabeth

Elizabeth is a city in northeastern New Jersey, on Newark Bay. Many of the people work in nearby Newark and New York City. Elizabeth has factories that make machinery, sewing machines, and airplane and automobile parts. The area was bought from the Indians in 1664. Elizabeth was the scene of fighting in the Revolutionary War, and the *Minute Man*, a statue, honors Elizabeth's heroes.

ELIZABETH, NEW JERSEY. Population (1970 census) 112,654. County seat of Union County.

Elizabeth, Queen of England

In 1953, a young woman named Elizabeth II became queen of England, and millions throughout the world saw her coronation in movies and on television. She is called Elizabeth "Second" because about four hundred years ago there was another Queen Elizabeth of England, who is now called Elizabeth I.

The first Queen Elizabeth was one of the greatest rulers England ever had. The time when she reigned is called the Elizabethan Age, and it was a long period, forty-five years, when England became

very rich and powerful. When Elizabeth II came to the throne the British people rejoiced and hoped there would be another Elizabethan Age like the first one.

ELIZABETH I

The first Elizabeth was born in the year 1533. Her father was Henry VIII, who married six different times. Elizabeth's mother was his second wife. Her name was Anne Boleyn. When Elizabeth was only two years old, Anne Boleyn was accused of unfaithfulness and other serious crimes. The accusations were probably not true, but Henry believed them and had Anne Boleyn executed. Elizabeth grew up without a mother. Much of her girlhood was very unhappy.

King Henry died when Elizabeth was 14 years old. First her half-brother, who was only 10 years old, became king. He died while he was still a boy, at the age of 16. Then Elizabeth's half-sister Mary, who was seventeen years older than she was, became queen.

At that time the people of England were trying to decide whether the country should be Catholic or Protestant. Mary was a Catholic. While she was queen, the Catholics had power in the government. In 1558 Mary died and Elizabeth became queen, at the age of 25. Elizabeth was a Protestant, and England has been a Protestant country ever since.

Elizabeth was called "the Virgin Queen" because she never married, though she had many suitors.

When Elizabeth was queen, the greatest of all English writers, William Shakespeare, wrote his plays and poems. Many other great English poets and writers lived in the Elizabethan Age. Elizabeth's reign was a peaceful one for those times, but she had some troubles. First, the Scottish queen, called Mary, Queen of Scots, was accused of plotting to kill Elizabeth and become Queen of England herself. Mary was Elizabeth's cousin, and she had asked Elizabeth for help when her own people turned against her, but Elizabeth's courts said she was guilty and Elizabeth let her be put to death. The following year, in 1588, the king of Spain, Philip II, sent a great fleet of warships called the Armada to try to conquer England. But the English navy, led by Lord Howard and two other great admirals, Sir John Hawkins and Sir Francis Drake, chased the Armada away, and England remained safe.

Elizabeth I died in 1603, when she was 70 years old and had reigned 45 years.

ELIZABETH II

Elizabeth II was born in 1926, the daughter of the Duke of York, later King George VI. As princesses, she and her younger sister, Princess Margaret, were very popular. They were both Girl Guides, which is like being Girl Scouts in the United States. During World War II, Elizabeth served in a special military branch called the ATS (Auxiliary Territorial Service). In 1947, she married Philip Mountbatten, who became Duke of Edinburgh, and the next year their son, Prince Charles, was born. Their second child, Princess Anne, was born in 1950. Two other sons, Prince Andrew (1960) and Prince Edward (1964) were

born to them. Elizabeth and Philip were visiting the Union of South Africa when King George VI died in 1952. They returned to England, where Elizabeth succeeded to the throne. Her coronation, on June 2, 1953, was a magnificent spectacle broadcast by television throughout the world, plus a technicolor film.

After she became queen, Elizabeth II became very busy doing all the many things that a modern queen must do, such as seeing important people, signing government papers, and appearing at public ceremonies. She was helped in many of these duties by the Duke of Edinburgh. She and her husband also traveled to Australia, New Zealand, and several other British dominions and colonies. An innovation by the Queen and Duke was in sending their children to public schools. Prince Charles attended school in Australia in 1966.

Elizabethan Age was the time of Queen Elizabeth I: see the separate articles on ELIZABETH, LITERATURE, and ENGLAND.

elk

The elk is the largest member of the deer family, except for the moose. An elk stands 5 feet 4 inches at the shoulder, and sometimes weighs 1,000 pounds, or half a ton. The elk, also called by the Indian name of "wapiti," once ranged over most of the United States and southern Canada, but it was hunted so much for its meat, hide, and teeth, that it is now found only in the Rocky Mountain region and the far western states. The elk's coloring is yellowish brown, with gray, white, red, and black markings. It feeds on grass, but does not digest it right away. The half-chewed food is swallowed and stored in its first stomach, or "paunch." The elk brings this food or "cud" up again later to chew it completely.

Elks live in herds, and in the autumn, during the mating season, the bulls or males fight each other for the possession of the female elks. This is when the bulls use their antlers—the bony branches on their heads. Antlers are different from horns because they are solid instead of hollow, are usually branched, and are new every year. The elk's antlers may be five feet wide.

Elks

The Benevolent and Protective Order of Elks, the B.P.O.E., is a club or society in the United States. It has about 1,508,000 members. The purpose of the society is to help its members, to assist the government of the United States, especially in wartime, and to help poor people, who need not be members of the society.

The Elks have about 2,146 branches. Each is called a lodge and has its own meeting place, often a building of its own. Every year members from all over the country get together and elect a leader. His title is Grand Exalted Ruler. During World War II, the Elks raised a great deal of money to help the United States fight. The society also opened many of its buildings to soldiers and sailors for games and entertainment. Since the war it has helped thousands of wounded veterans. The society spends millions of dollars a year to help poor people in the

various cities in the United States in which it has lodges.

Ellis Island

Ellis Island is a small island in New York Bay. It lies about a mile southwest of Battery Park, which is at the south end of Manhattan Island. Ellis Island once belonged to a New York merchant named Samuel Ellis. Since 1808 it has belonged to the United States government. For many years the army used it as an arsenal, that is, a place where guns and ammunition are kept. In 1892 the government found another use for it. At this time thousands of people were coming from Europe to make their homes in the United States. Those that came in through New York had their admission papers examined in a building called Castle Garden, at the Battery. When this building proved too small for the great numbers of immigrants, buildings on Ellis Island were used instead. In 1954 the government stopped using Ellis Island as an immigration center.

Ellsworth, Lincoln

Lincoln Ellsworth became famous as an American explorer who flew over both the Arctic and Antarctic regions. He was born in Chicago in 1880, and studied engineering at Yale and Columbia. He was a surveyor and an engineer in railroad building for a time, and later went to Canada as a mining engineer. He joined with Roald Amundsen, the Norwegian polar explorer, and flew with him in 1926 on the dirigible *Norge* over the North Pole. (See the article on AMUNDSEN in another volume.) In 1935, Lincoln Ellsworth flew over the Antarctic continent in an airplane. (The map of his route is shown in the article on ANTARCTICA in another volume of this encyclopedia.) He also wrote several books describing his explorations. He died in 1951.

elm

The elm is a fine shade tree that grows in many parts of Europe, the United States, and Canada. The stately trees that you can see lining the streets and in the parks of many cities in the eastern part of the United States are probably white elms. Many of these trees were planted by the early settlers more than two hundred years ago, and now some of these great elms are more than one hundred feet tall. In the early spring the elm has small clusters of flowers that disappear before the first leaves begin to grow. The leaves are jagged at the edges and are a dark green color. People use the strong, hard wood of the elm in building ships and making furniture. Some elms that grow in western Canada and near the Mississippi River in the United States are called slippery elms. The bark and leaves of these trees produce a sticky substance that is used in making medicine, and some people like to chew the bark.

El Paso

El Paso is a city in western Texas, on the Rio Grande. A bridge joins it with Juárez in Mexico. El Paso is the largest city on the border, and many of the people are Mexican. It is a center for shipping goods and has large oil and copper refineries. People visit El Paso because of the fine climate and to see the many Spanish-style buildings. Fort Bliss, a guided-missile testing station, is nearby. El Paso was settled by Spaniards in the 1860s. There are pictures of El Paso in the article TEXAS.

EL PASO, TEXAS. Population (1970 census) 322, 261. County seat of El Paso County.

El Salvador

El Salvador is the smallest republic in Central America. It is on the Pacific side of Central America, and is the only Central American republic that has no Atlantic seacoast. El Salvador is about one third as large as the state of Indiana, and more than three and a half million people live there.

THE PEOPLE OF EL SALVADOR

Most of the people who live in El Salvador are part Indian and part Spanish, and they are called *mestizos*, which in Spanish means "persons with mixed blood." There are also people of Spanish ancestry and some full-blooded Indians.

The city of San Salvador is the capital of El Salvador and is the largest city in the republic, with a population (in 1973) of 349,333. You can fly there in a few hours from New York City, or you could travel there by train. In San Salvador, one sees native women walking down the street, gracefully balancing baskets on their heads, and other women who look very much like women in any city in the United States. Some people ride in oxcarts, and some in automobiles, and almost everyone speaks Spanish.

Every young person has to go to school, and children who live in far-off villages are visited by traveling teachers.

Most of the people of El Salvador are farmers. They raise coffee and sugar cane, and almost every farmer grows some corn, because corn is one of the most important foods that people in El Salvador eat.

In the jungles, some people make their living getting balsam from the trees. (Balsam is a valuable sap that is used in making many kinds of medicine.) A few men work in factories, making cigarettes and rope and refining sugar, but the factories are small and very simple.

WHAT EL SALVADOR IS LIKE

Most of the country is a plateau (high like a mountain, but flat like a plain), about two thousand feet above the sea. Because of the high altitude, the weather is quite pleasant most of the time, with temperatures in the 70s, much like a June day in a United States city. The plateau is crowded with farms and villages and cities. Many rivers help to keep the land rich and moist, though most of these rivers are shallow and rocky and boats cannot travel on them. The largest and most important river is the Lempa, which is deep enough to be used by boats.

The El Salvador plateau lies between two mountain ranges, and some of these mountains are volcanic. Very often there are severe earthquakes, and the people who live near the mountains have learned to build strong houses out of steel and concrete so that they will not crumble when the earth shakes.

EL SALVADOR IN THE PAST

El Salvador was discovered by Pedro de Alvarado in 1524. For a while it was part of the republic of Guatemala, and later it became a state in the Central American Federation (an organization of all of the Central American states). Finally, in 1839, El Salvador became an independent republic. During its history El Salvador has had many different kinds of government, and there have been revolutions when the people wanted to change the government. The people now elect a president every five years. During World War II, El Salvador fought with the Allies against Germany.

EL SALVADOR. Area, 7,722 square miles. Population (1973 estimate) 3,534,000. Language, Spanish. Religion, Roman Catholic. Government, republic. Monetary unit, the colon, worth 40 cents (U.S.). Flag, three alternating bars, two blue and one white, coat of arms on white.

Elysian Fields

The Elysian Fields was a place told about in the legends of the Greeks and the Romans. It was a beautiful place, and a happy place. Lovely flowers bloomed there always and the sun shone brightly. When great and good men died, they did not go to Hades, which was the Greek and Roman version of hell. Instead, they were taken to the Elysian Fields.

Emancipation Proclamation

Emancipation means "setting free." In 1862 the northern states of the United States and the southern states, which had organized a separate government as the Confederate States, were fighting each other in the Civil War. In the southern states, Negroes were slaves; in most of the northern states they were not. On September 22, 1862, President Abraham Lincoln made an announcement called the Proclamation of Emancipation, in which he announced that slaves living in the southern states would all be freed.

This Proclamation did not end slavery. In Maryland, West Virginia, and other slave-owning places that had remained loyal to the United States, Negroes remained slaves. In most of the southern states the Negroes remained slaves because President Lincoln had no control over them. But the Proclamation of Emancipation did tell the world that several million slaves would become free if the Union (northern) forces won the war. The Union forces did win the war, in 1865, and all slaves were then set free.

embalming is the preparation of a dead body for burial: see the articles BURIAL and MUMMY.

embargo

An embargo is an order by a government stopping ships from entering or leaving its ports. During a war or when there is a threat of war, a country tries in every way it can to make its enemy suffer. By placing an embargo on supplies to its enemy, the country can make its enemy do without important and needed things, such as food for its people, guns for its soldiers, and gasoline and oil for its machines.

The United Nations placed an embargo on its enemies, North Korea and China, during the Korean War. The embargo prevented them from getting many supplies. In a case such as this where a country forbids supplies to its enemy, it is called a *hostile embargo*. A country can also put an embargo on goods moved on other kinds of transport such as trains and airplanes. Another kind of embargo is a *civil embargo*. If cows in a certain state become sick, a civil embargo may be placed on that state to keep milk from those cows from being sent to other states and spreading the disease or making people ill.

embroidery

Embroidery is a kind of sewing in which the stitches are used for decoration. It is sometimes called "painting with a needle." Embroidery can be a simple act of putting an initial or an outline picture on an apron, a towel, or pot-holder, but elaborate pictures and designs also can be made with needlework, using many different colors and several kinds of stitch. Choosing and combining the colors are as important in embroidery as in painting. A fine piece of embroidery is a work of art.

Embroidery stitches must be made carefully and exactly. The difference between embroidery and plain sewing is that in embroidery the stitches must show, and in plain sewing the stitches are used to hold the material together at the seams, and the stitches themselves may show or they may not. The name embroidery comes from a word meaning "border." Embroidery stitches are often used to decorate the edges and borders of clothes, linens, curtains, and spreads. Some of the stitches can also be made on a sewing machine, with special attachments.

An embroidery stitch is the part of the thread that shows on top of the material after you pull the needle and the rest of the thread through. The simplest embroidery stitch is the running stitch, and you make it by pushing your needle in and out of the cloth in a straight line. The stitches are the same size and the same distance apart. You will often see this stitch on quilts, where two pieces of material are sewed together with a filling like lamb's wool inside.

Another easy stitch is the outline stitch, a closed straight line, used for tracing the outline of a design. You can easily try this stitch yourself. Ask your mother for some cloth or material to use as a practice-piece. Then get a needle and some heavy colored thread or yarn. Decide what design you are going to use.

Perhaps you want to do an animal design, a cat or an elephant, for example. Draw or copy a simple picture of the animal, and trace this lightly on the material with chalk or pencil. Then sew carefully along the outline, placing the stitches so that they overlap a little and form a continuous line on top of the cloth. When you have gone all around your design, you will have finished a piece of embroidery. If you want to try other stitches, there are booklets and books that show you how.

You can also buy aprons, napkins, tablecloths, and other articles already marked with a pattern for you to embroider. You may wish to start with a wool thread or yarn, and work up gradually to the finer embroidery threads. As a rule, the finer your thread is, the smaller your stitches have to be.

DIFFERENT KINDS OF EMBROIDERY

There are several hundred embroidery stitches, but they are variations of a few main kinds: flat, linked, blanket or buttonhole, and knot stitches. The flat stitches are like those we have already mentioned. They lie on top of the cloth, without being knotted, looped, or linked. You probably know the cross-stitch, which looks like this: XXXXX. The linked or chain stitches leave loops of thread lying on top of the material. The blanket or buttonhole stitch keeps the edges of cloth from fraying or coming apart. You make knot stitches by winding the thread around the needle before sticking it down through the cloth. The little knobs form a rough, raised surface.

A single piece of embroidery usually combines several stitches. Sometimes one thread will be sewn into the material and another one laced or woven through that one, on top. Or a thread too heavy to be drawn through the fabric will be fastened down with a smaller thread. Gold and silver threads are put on this way. Braids or narrow strips of cloth are embroidered on uniforms or colorful peasant costumes. Cut-out pieces or designs, as well as pearls, beads, and jewels, may be sewn on. Smocking is a way of gathering cloth in regular folds, so as to make it narrower. You may have smocking on some of your clothes, at the neck, shoulders, or waist.

Embroidery is one of the oldest crafts or arts. The work takes only threads, needles, scissors, and a frame for holding the material even. Therefore, you can easily do it at home. Many fabrics, from silk to leather, can be embroidered, and there are silk, cotton, metal, and leather threads. Special needles of various sizes are used with the different threads.

During the Middle Ages, especially from the 9th to the 16th centuries, embroidery was a way of "writing down" history. One famous piece, called the Bayeux Tapestry, shows the Norman Conquest of England in the 11th century. Elizabeth I, queen of England in the 16th century, had thousands of embroidered dresses, and many queens were famous for their needlework. Church decorations and the costumes of the people were covered with beautiful embroidery. Some of the finest pieces still come from China and India, where the art is at least

five thousand years old. Long before the time of pattern books, samplers that showed the different stitches were passed down from mother to daughter.

embryo, a living animal before it is born: see the article on CHILDBIRTH.

emerald

Emerald is the name of a precious stone that comes from the mineral beryl. (You can read about BERYL in a separate article.) The emerald is a beautiful deep green color, and is so precious that a bracelet with one emerald stone in it might cost many thousands of dollars. Emeralds in ancient times were found in Egypt mostly, and you can still see the ruins of these old emerald mines. Now emeralds are found in South America, Australia, and Russia, and in the United States some emeralds have been found in North Carolina. People who are born in the month of May have the beautiful emerald as their birthstone.

Emerson, Ralph Waldo

Ralph Waldo Emerson was an American writer who lived about a hundred years ago. He was born in Boston, Massachusetts, in 1803. Emerson came from a long line of Protestant ministers and was brought up by a brilliant maiden aunt, Mary Moody Emerson, who had a great influence on his education and thinking. He was in school after the age of two and entered Harvard University when he was only fourteen. He was not a very good student and concentrated only on the subjects he liked. Emerson studied to be a minister and became minister in the Old North Church (Unitarian) in 1829. Some of his ideas about religion seemed too radical and strange to his congregation and in 1832 he decided to leave the church. He made two trips to England and visited the poets William Wordsworth and Samuel Taylor Coleridge. He became a very close friend of the great English historian Thomas Carlyle. He married Miss Lydia Jackson in 1835 and went to live with her at Concord, Massachusetts.

Gale Research Co.

Emerson spent most of his life as a public lecturer. He was very popular and always had a big audience for his talks on art, literature, poetry, politics, religion, and other subjects. These talks were usually given in Boston. Emerson is best known today for his essays, short articles in which he discusses and explains his ideas. Emerson also wrote two books of poetry. Many have considered him the greatest American writer. He died on April 27, 1882.

emery, a coarse form of corundum: see CORUNDUM and ABRASIVES.

emigration is leaving one's native country: see the article on IMMIGRATION.

Emmaus

Emmaus was the name of two or three places in ancient Palestine. Today, it is hard to tell exactly where they were. At one Emmaus, Judas Maccabaeus won

his great victory for the Jews over the Syrians in the 2nd century B.C. Syria is a country near Palestine. Another Emmaus is mentioned by St. Luke as the place where Jesus appeared to two travelers after His rising from the tomb. You can read this story in the Gospel of Luke in the Bible. The third Emmaus was the name given by the Greeks to the hot springs near Tiberias, on the Sea of Galilee. These springs were famous for their healing power.

Emmet, Robert

Robert Emmet was an Irish patriot who led an unsuccessful rebellion in Ireland against England in 1803. He was born in the Irish city of Dublin in 1778, and was educated at Trinity College. In Emmet's time, Ireland, which today is an independent country, was still ruled by England. Emmet and other Irish rebels made plans to attack Dublin Castle and other English strongholds. Unfortunately the English knew all about the plans from the very beginning. On July 23, 1803 Emmet and eighty poorly armed men attempted to seize Dublin Castle. This foolhardy and impractical attempt was easily beaten off by the English and Emmet fled to County Wicklow, another part of Ireland. He unwisely returned to Dublin to be near a young woman he loved, and was captured by the English, who tried and hanged him. Emmet became a hero to all Irish patriots.

Emmy Award

The Emmy Award is a small statue which can be seen in the photograph below. It is presented by the National Academy of Television Arts and Sciences to people who have made outstanding contributions to various areas of television production. The Emmy is to television what the Oscar is to motion pictures. (See the article on Academy Awards.)

The award, first presented in 1948, was designed by Louis McManus and named by Harry R. Lubcke, the Academy's third

president. The name "Emmy" comes from the word "immy," an engineering term relating to the Image Orthicon camera tube.

The Emmy is also known as the Television Academy Award. The main categories for which the Emmy is presented include: outstanding achievement in various news and documentary productions; outstanding entertainment program achievements; achievements by performers, writers, directors, composers, art directors, scenic designers, set decorators, cinematographers, electronic cameramen, and film editors; achievements in children's and daytime programming, sports, music, visual and graphic arts, and electronic production. Certain other special awards are also presented each year.

emotion

Emotions are feelings that make you sad, happy, ashamed, disgusted, excited, angry, or frightened.

You cannot see, hear, smell or taste an emotion or feel one with your hands. Emotions are feelings that you have only in your mind. Scientists tell us that emotions make certain glands in our bodies act differently.

If you feel the emotion of grief or sadness, your body supplies tears by means of your tear glands, so that you can express that emotion through crying. If you have the emotion of fear or anger, your body's glands supply you with a substance called adrenalin that makes it possible for you to hit harder or run faster than you can when you are not afraid or angry.

In every emotion you feel, some gland has a definite reaction. If you refuse to cry when you are very sad, you are keeping your body from doing what it naturally tries to do under the strain of that emotion. This may not be good for you.

It is best to keep a balance between expressing emotions reasonably and going into wild displays of temper, tears, anger, or fright over nothing.

It is good to laugh when you are happy and amused, good to cry a few tears when you are very unhappy or badly hurt, and good to have some hard exercise when you are angry. These things all help you to get rid of the disturbing emotion. Even if you do not discharge the emotion in one way or another, the emotion gradually fades away with time.

empire

An empire is a group of kingdoms or other separate countries, each with its own king or other ruler but all under a more powerful ruler called an emperor. There have been many empires in history. In most cases they have been formed because one powerful nation conquered many smaller ones and made them subject to the rule of the emperor. But in some cases smaller countries have voluntarily joined together to form an empire.

The greatest empires of the ancient world were the one formed by Alexander the Great about 2,200 years ago, and the one formed by Rome about 2,000 years ago. Alexander the Great was the king of a small country named Macedon in Greece, but before he died he controlled

territory from Greece all the way to India. The Roman Empire began as a country centered on the city of Rome in Italy, but it controlled all the countries around the Mediterranean Sea, all of western Europe, and England.

About 1,300 years ago, beginning about the year 650, the Arabs went out to spread the Mohammedan religion, and they built up an empire under a ruler called the caliph. This empire included the Near East and North Africa, and much of Spain. Later on, the Turkish Empire included most of these countries except Spain, and parts of the Balkans in Europe.

VOLUNTARY EMPIRES

Examples of voluntary empires are the ones in the Germanic nations. The first was called the HOLY ROMAN EMPIRE, and there is a separate article about it. It was formed of a group of German kingdoms whose kings were called electors because they elected their emperor. In 1871 the kings of the German countries, with the exception of Austria, formed a new empire and made the king of Prussia their emperor. The German Empire lasted until 1918, when Germany was defeated in World War I.

The most powerful empire of modern times was called the British Empire. In 1876 India was made part of the territory of the British queen, Victoria, and because India had many different countries with their own rulers, Victoria was called Empress of India. After World War I, most of the British countries changed the arrangement to make a Commonwealth of independent nations.

The word *imperial* means "of an empire." When a country is very greedy to take in other independent countries, it is said to be imperialistic. There is a separate article about IMPERIALISM.

employment

Employment is having a job. When a person has no job, he is unemployed, and when many people in the country are out of work, there is unemployment. The prosperity of a country depends on employment. When a man has a job he gets money to buy things for himself and his family, and this keeps other men and women employed making the things he buys. When many people are unemployed, the people who are out of work cannot buy things they need. They themselves suffer and at the same time they cause other people to lose their jobs. Sometimes the companies they work for have to go out of business. When this happens on a large scale we say there is a depression in the country.

When nearly everyone who wants a job can get one, there is full employment in a country. There have not been many times in the recent history of the world when there has been full employment. Wartime is usually an exception. During World War II there was not only full employment, but actually a shortage of labor. Many people were afraid that when the war ended there would be unemployment. Others believed the opposite—that there would be a great period of prosperity. Henry Wallace, who was then Secretary of Commerce, predicted that there would be sixty million jobs in

peacetime America. Some people thought this was an impossible figure to reach, but the postwar years proved that Wallace had actually been cautious in his prediction, for full employment in the United States came to mean that about sixty-three million people have jobs.

LAWS ABOUT EMPLOYMENT

Many laws have been passed in the United States to protect working people. One law sets up a minimum wage, that is, the least amount employers can pay for every hour of work. The same law says that people cannot work more than forty hours at this rate of pay; if they work more than forty hours, they must be paid one and a half times the regular rate. There are special laws about the employment of children and women. When children under a certain age (usually 16) want to work, they have to get working papers, which give them legal permission to work. Also, children are not permitted to be employed at certain kinds of work, such as mining. Women too may not work in certain industries, and there are laws in some states that say that women must receive the same rate of pay as men when they do the same kind of work. Other laws say that when a worker is hurt on the job, he is entitled to special pay called *workmen's compensation*.

When a working man or woman loses his job in the United States he gets a certain amount of money for each week he is out of work, up to a definite number of weeks. This is called *unemployment insurance*. The money for unemployment insurance is contributed in equal amounts by people when they are employed and by their employers. This money is paid into a fund that is managed by the United States government. During and after World War II, when there was very little unemployment, this fund grew very large, since so few people had to ask for unemployment insurance.

In the United States, people have often not been able to get jobs because of their religion or race. To put an end to this, some states have passed fair employment practices laws and have set up fair employment practices commissions to see that these laws are carried out. Many attempts have been made to have the Federal government pass a similar law (called the F.E.P.C. law) for the whole United States.

emu

The emu is an Australian bird that cannot fly. Next to the ostrich, the emu is the largest bird in the world. Emus are about five feet tall, and although they cannot fly, they are fast runners and powerful swimmers. The emu has a small head, a long neck, and a big body, but its legs are shorter than the ostrich's. The female lays six or seven dark green eggs. The male emu, smaller than the female, sits on the eggs until they hatch, and then tends to the young. If you lived in Australia, you might eat part of an emu egg. One egg is large enough to make a meal for a whole family. The Australian natives also eat the flesh of the emu. The emu has a pouch or bag attached to its windpipe, the passage between the throat and the lungs. This pouch makes the emu's call unusually loud and booming.

Emus feed on grass, like cattle. This bird is becoming scarcer every year.

enamel

Enamel is a coating material which contains the mineral silica. It is applied to pottery or to metal. Silica is found in clean white sand and is used in making glass. Enamel may be transparent, which means you can see through it, or opaque, which means you cannot see through it. It may be colored or without color. It has been used for many centuries to put a glaze or thin glassy surface on clay pottery.

Ground silica and other mineral colors are mixed in powder form with water, and the resulting paste is brushed or blown from a metal tube on the surface of the pottery. The clay vessel, vase, jug, or dish is then placed in a special kind of furnace by a skilled worker. The heat melts the enamel mixture, which forms a hard, glassy surface when it cools.

Powdered enamel, called *frit*, is mixed with water and applied to steel which is put in a furnace at very high heat. The steel gets red hot and the frit melts and forms a smooth, very hard, glasslike surface on the metal. So strongly does the enamel stick to the metal that only very hard blows will make parts of it chip off. This kind of enamel is known as porcelain enamel, and is used on many kitchen pots and pans and on bathroom fixtures.

The word enamel is also used for paints that dry with a smooth, glossy surface. Enamel paint is usually used in kitchens and for interior woodwork trim because it can easily be cleaned with a damp rag.

encyclopedia

An encyclopedia is a set of books that gives the important facts about any person, place, thing, or idea that a person is likely to be interested in. There are books giving more information about nearly everything man knows, but no one could afford to buy so many books, or find space for them in his house, and it is not possible to drop everything, go to the library, and read an entire book, every time you want the answer to a simple question. An encyclopedia solves all these problems.

There are hundreds of encyclopedias published. Some are in several volumes, some are in only one volume. Some are for grown-ups, some are for children. Some answer questions about a particular subject, such as music, or sports, or religion; some cover all subjects.

Long ago, when men had not learned nearly as much as they know today, it was possible for one man to write an encyclopedia. The great Greek scholar Aristotle, who lived nearly four hundred years before Christ was born, wrote seventy books all by himself and set down nearly everything that men knew about nature and science. Nearly two thousand years ago a Roman scholar, Pliny, wrote a set of thirty-seven books that told nearly everything that was known about geography, mathematics, botany, metals, and many other things. A hundred years after Pliny's time another Roman scholar named Marcus Varro wrote a set of nine books about music, medicine, mathematics, and other scientific subjects. These were the first encyclopedias.

The first real English encyclopedia was written by a man named Ephraim Chambers in 1728. (He called it a *cyclopedia*, but that means exactly the same as *encyclopedia*.) The Chambers encyclopedia had two volumes. It was the first encyclopedia to use cross-references, which are notes telling the reader what other articles he should look up to get more information on the same subject. There are still English encyclopedias called "Chambers' Encyclopedia," though of course none of them was written by the original Chambers, who died about two hundred years ago.

The success of Chambers' cyclopedia caused two great French scholars, Denis Diderot and Jean d'Alembert, to put out a famous *Encyclopédie* in French. It was published between 1751 and 1772, in twenty-eight volumes. This encyclopedia had a great deal of information in it that made the people see that the government of France, under the kings and noblemen, was very bad. Seventeen years after its publication was completed the French Revolution broke out, and the government was overthrown.

The Encyclopaedia Britannica was first published in 1768. It is still one of the most famous encyclopedias. The policy of the Encyclopaedia Britannica was to find a noted scholar who was an expert on each subject, and ask him to write the article. This system had its good points, but when there was a disagreement on some subject the reader would get only one point of view and might never hear about the others.

Until about fifty years ago there were no encyclopedias for children. Now there are several good ones. The one you are reading is one of the newest. It has been written to make each article understandable by those who knew nothing about the subject before.

Endecott, John

John Endecott was the assistant governor of the Massachusetts Bay Colony, the first English settlement in New England. He held this office from 1628 to 1644 when he died. He did his best work during the colony's first two years and had everything running smoothly by the time the governor, John Winthrop, arrived from England in 1630. For a time he was military leader of the colony, but he handled himself poorly as a commander and brought about a war between the colonists and the nearby Pequot Indians. He was a stern and intolerant Puritan who hated both the Church of England, to which all loyal Englishmen in the mother country were supposed to belong, and the Roman Catholic Church. Although Endecott had left England in order to have freedom of worship, he did not believe in the same religious freedom for anyone who was not a Puritan.

endive

Endive is a small plant that was first found growing in India, China, and Japan. It grows a little less than one foot high and has clusters of leaves that look like leaf lettuce. It is a hardy plant that grows very well in any good garden soil in both Europe and the United States. People enjoy the crisp, slightly bitter taste of the leaves, and use them in making salads. They are also chopped fine and used in soup. Some plants have broad, flat leaves, and others have curly leaves.

The curly-leaved varieties are the ones commonly grown in gardens. The center leaves of the endive are white or a very pale green, and the outer leaves are a darker green in color.

Endymion

Endymion was a character in Greek mythology, the stories the ancient Greeks told about their gods and goddesses. Endymion was a very handsome young shepherd. One night as he was sleeping, Selene, the goddess of the moon (whom the Romans called Diana), looked down and saw him. He was so beautiful that the goddess fell in love with him. She kissed him, and watched over him. Endymion lay there forever after, always asleep and always beautiful. Selene took care of his sheep. Every night the moon goddess could look at the beautiful Endymion and kiss him with her silver rays. Keats wrote a beautiful poem about Endymion.

energy

Energy means the ability to do work. We use energy to press a spring together. When we release the spring, energy forces it to snap back to its original shape. Anything that does work uses energy. Some examples of energy are: a magnet drawing an iron filing toward itself; gunpowder exploding to force a bullet from a rifle; a battery supplying power to a motor.

Energy exists in either of two forms, *potential* and *kinetic*. An example that shows both of these forms of energy is a pile driver. This is a big machine having a heavy weight which is drawn up to a height of ten or twenty feet, and then let go. The weight comes down on a post and drives it into the ground. Energy is used to pull the weight up to the top of the pile driver. When the weight gets to the top and stops moving, it has potential energy. As soon as the weight is released, the potential energy changes to kinetic energy, because the weight is moving.

Potential energy is energy that can do work; kinetic energy is energy that is doing work. All energy is in one of these forms or the other. When we eat food, our bodies turn it into potential energy; when we walk upstairs, our bodies turn the potential energy to kinetic energy.

Engels, Friedrich, a German Socialist who helped write the Communist Manifesto: see the article about Karl MARX.

engine

An engine is a machine to do work. It takes energy from the burning of a fuel such as oil or gas, or from the movement of water or steam, and it changes this energy into mechanical energy, so that the engine can move other things. There are many different kinds of engine. You can read about some of them in the articles on INTERNAL COMBUSTION, STEAM ENGINE, and JET and ROCKET ENGINES. An engine whose energy comes from electricity is usually called a *motor*.

engineer and engineering

An engineer uses expert knowledge of physics, mathematics, mechanics, chemistry, and other sciences to make men's work more useful and safer. Engineering knowledge goes into nearly everything that is built or made by man and into nearly every new invention.

The word *engineer* is also used for persons who do other work, such as the driver of a railroad locomotive or members of certain branches of armies, but this article is about the kind of engineer who has studied for his profession in a college or university, just as a physician or lawyer must.

An engineer is said to design and build things, but professionally he is more interested in the usefulness than the appearance of the things he designs. For example, an architect may design a building to show how he wants it to look but an engineer must decide how strong the steel girders must be to carry the load, and how deep the foundations must be dug, and so on. Then a contractor carries out the actual building, from the plans made by the engineer. Engineers decide scientifically how many persons a bridge or an elevator will safely hold, how heavy a wire must be to carry a certain amount of electricity, how long a time is needed to make a certain kind of metal, and literally millions of questions of this kind.

These engineers are sometimes classed in more than thirty different fields, but there are five main branches: civil, mechanical, electrical, chemical, and mining.

CIVIL ENGINEERING

A civil engineer is one who designs, builds, and repairs buildings, highways, railroads, bridges, dams, airfields, canals, water and sewage systems, harbors, and tunnels. The Suez and Panama Canals, the Golden Gate Bridge, the Empire State Building, and the New Jersey Turnpike are examples of the kinds of structure designed and built by civil engineers.

A civil engineer may have many different titles. He may be called a highway engineer, bridge engineer, sanitation engineer, airport engineer, and so on. A municipal engineer is a civil engineer who plans cities by laying out streets, parks, and business and residence areas to promote better living conditions.

Civil engineers are employed by construction companies, or by the government. There are about 100,000 civil engineers now working in the United States, more engineers than there are in any other branch of engineering.

MECHANICAL ENGINEERING

A mechanical engineer is one who designs, builds and repairs machines, engines, boilers, automobiles, trains, airplanes, and ships. Jet engines, atomic-powered submarines, and all kinds of machine tools are among the things designed and built by mechanical engineers.

A mechanical engineer may have many different titles. He may be called an automotive engineer, jet propulsion engineer, production engineer, tool engineer, plant supervisor, industrial engineer, and so on. An industrial engineer studies how industries and businesses are organized and thinks of ways in which machinery, workers and money can be used to improve production and business.

Mechanical engineers are employed by industries making automobiles, airplanes, ships, and machinery, or by government.

ELECTRICAL ENGINEERING

An electrical engineer is one who helps produce and send out electricity. Also, electrical engineers design and build motors, generators, and other instruments that produce or use electricity. Telephones, radios, television sets, radar, electronic tubes, guided missiles, and all kinds of lighting equipment are among the things designed and built by electrical engineers.

An electrical engineer may have many different titles. He may be called a television engineer, a power-plant supervisor, an electronics engineer, a lighting engineer, a telephone superintendent, and so on. An important part of the work of an electronics engineer is building automatic calculating machines, often called "giant brains," for solving problems in mathematics that would not even be attempted by a human being with pencil and paper.

Electrical engineers are employed by the radio and television industry, the electronics industry, and the government.

With the development of electronics and atomic energy, electrical engineering is the most rapidly expanding branch of engineering today.

CHEMICAL ENGINEERING

A chemical engineer is one who designs and builds plants and machines in which chemicals are manufactured or used. He also studies and plans the uses of the chemicals themselves. Vitamins, wonder drugs such as penicillin and cortisone, synthetic rubber, and many plastics are some of the things that chemical engineers have helped produce.

A chemical engineer may have many different titles. He may be called an atomic energy scientist, a petroleum engineer, a plastics plant manager, an industrial chemist, a sales engineer, and so on. A sales engineer helps sell the products made by the chemical industry, and therefore must have some knowledge of what they contain. There are sales engineers in all the main branches of engineering.

Chemical engineers are employed by food industries, the rubber industry, the petroleum, coal, leather, and plastics industries, and others. They also are employed by the government.

MINING ENGINEERING

A mining engineer is one who helps locate and take out coal, iron, oil, uranium, and other valuable substances found in the ground. A mining engineer also helps find ways of purifying these substances so that they can be used to manufacture other products. Such a mining engineer is often called a metallurgical engineer. Steel, copper, lead and other metals are some of the things that are produced by the mining engineer. Asbestos, asphalt and mica are some of the non-metals that are produced by the mining engineer.

A mining engineer may have many different titles. He may be called a materials engineer, a rolling mill superintendent, a welding engineer, a manager of a smelter, a foundry engineer, a mine superintendent, and so on.

Mining engineers are employed by the Atomic Energy Commission to help mine uranium ore for atomic energy. Mining engineers also are employed by mining

companies, and by companies that manufacture materials made from substances that are mined.

THE BEGINNINGS OF ENGINEERING

Engineering probably began thousands of years ago when the first cities were being built. Most engineering was for the protection of these cities against outside enemies. Huge walls were built around the cities. Weapons and all sorts of devices for warfare were made. This sort of engineering was called military engineering.

There were also the huge pyramids in Egypt, irrigation systems, roads, bridges, and tunnels, which had very little to do with military warfare. This kind of engineering was called civilian or civil engineering to distingush it from military engineering, but it was not called civil engineering until about 1770, when an English engineer signed himself John Smeaton, Civil Engineer. In 1818, the British Institution of Civil Engineers was founded. In 1852, the American Society of Civil Engineers was founded. In the next twenty-five years, mining, mechanical, electrical, and chemical engineers formed separate organizations to distinguish themselves from civil engineers and from one another. As new machines were invented other engineers, such as aeronautical (airplane) and automotive engineers, formed separate societies. There are now sixty separate engineering societies in the United States, and about 700,000 engineers.

England

England is one of the three countries that make up the island of Great Britain. This island and Northern Ireland together form a country called the United Kingdom. The United Kingdom, in turn, is only one of the parts of the far-reaching group of English-speaking nations that together form the (British) Commonwealth. Yet England is so important in history and in the government of all these nations that often the entire United Kingdom, and even the entire Commonwealth, is spoken of as "England."

The capital of England, the city of London, is the home of Queen Elizabeth II, who is queen of all the British countries. It is also the seat of the Parliament, the English lawmaking body, whose laws for hundreds of years have established and safeguarded principles of liberty that people enjoy in all English-speaking countries.

England is about 50,331 square miles in area, which is a little larger than the state of North Carolina. In that comparatively small area, however, there are about 45,870,062 people. That is almost as many people as there are in all the east coast states from South Carolina to Maine. London is the capital of England, and has a population of about 7,612,280, ranking next under the total populations of New York City and Tokyo.

London is the center of the government of the British Commonwealth. The palace of Queen Elizabeth, Buckingham Palace, is located in London, and so are the Houses of Parliament where the British government representatives meet to make the laws.

WHAT ENGLAND IS LIKE

Most of the land is gently rolling country, with no big hills or mountains. The land is more rugged and slightly rocky in the northern section, toward the border between England and Scotland. There are a great many rivers, and most of them are deep and wide enough to be used for shipping products to a seaport. A large system of canals connects the rivers.

The climate of England is mild in most parts, but very damp. The land is low, and because the island is small, the moist air from the sea on all sides drifts over the land, creating considerable rainfall, and frequent fogs.

Many villages in England look almost the same today as they did three hundred years ago. The narrow, winding streets, the old houses with big, heavy beams, the stone cottages with ivy-covered walls, all these seem like a picture-book story of old England.

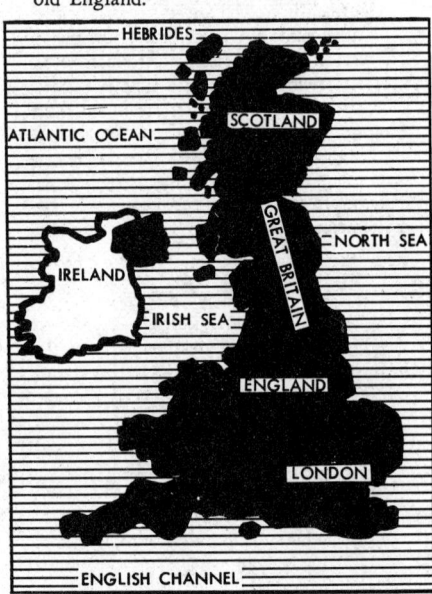

THE PEOPLE OF ENGLAND

About two thousand years ago the people living in England were a branch of the Celtic people who were early settlers of Europe. These early English people were called Britons. The neighbors of England in Wales, Scotland, and parts of northern France are closely related to the old Britons, but the English people no longer are. About 1,900 years ago armies from the Roman Empire conquered England and settled there. Then, about 1,500 years ago, Germanic peoples called Angles and Saxons settled in England (and the name of the country comes from the Angles). Other Germanic peoples, Jutes and Danes from Scandinavia, came a few hundred years later. In the year 1066 England was conquered by a Norman (French) king, called William the Conqueror, and he brought many Frenchmen with him. The English people of today are descended from all these different peoples and the English language includes words from the original languages of all these people.

English people have spread to all parts of the world. There are many reasons for this. People who live on comparatively small islands are usually seafaring people, and good sailors. England is an island, and English people have always sailed the seas. They have sailed as traders, they have sailed as explorers, they have sailed as pirates, and they have sailed as fishermen. When the people at home heard stories of the fabulous lands beyond the seas, often they became so interested that they organized groups to establish colonies in those far lands. The people of these possessions and colonies throughout the world seldom stop thinking of England as home. They are an intensely patriotic and loyal nation, and have often fought bravely to protect their little island and their precious rights as British citizens.

HOW THE PEOPLE LIVE

Many English people work in shops, stores, offices, and factories. In England there are three distinct classes of people. The biggest and by far the most important group is the great middle class. The nobles, or titled people of England, are a comparatively small group, and the very poor are also a comparatively small group. There are many millions of people who are neither rich, titled, nor poor.

There are huge steel plants, automobile factories, and manufacturing plants of all kinds in every section of the country. England is one of the world's largest producers of manufactured articles.

Mining is a large industry in England, also. The coal and iron mines provide work for hundreds of thousands of people, and at the same time supply necessary materials for the manufacturing industries. Among the important manufactured products England makes are machinery, electrical goods, automobiles, textiles, aircraft, chemicals, pottery, and cutlery. All these things are exported in foreign trade, and some of the largest shipyards in the world are located in England.

Farming and cattle raising are also important. English cattle are noted for rich, creamy milk, and English horses are among the finest in the world. The farms of England are not operated in the same way as American farms. Most farmers do not own their own land, but rent it from large landholders. The soil itself has been used for so long that large amounts of fertilizer are necessary. This makes it more costly to raise garden crops there than in countries where the soil is reasonably fertile already. A large part of the farming country is grazing land for the cows and sheep that are important to the farmers. Most farms raise both cattle and crops.

In addition to manufacturing and farming, England has a large merchant marine and fishing fleet. Englishmen are noted sailors and their ships carry more passengers and freight than any other country's.

In the cities of England, people live about as they do in the cities of the United States and Canada.

There are fewer automatic refrigerators and washing machines than there are in the United States and Canada, but more than there are in most of the countries on the continent of Europe. People in England drive smaller cars, as a general rule, than the American brands. They drive on the left-hand side of the road, which is confusing for American drivers who visit England. Their cars have the steering wheel on the right.

In England all children must go to

The famous guards march in front of Buckingham Palace, the home of the royal family in London.
British Tourist Authority

school from the time they are five years old until they are sixteen. A great many children go to church schools, but free education through high school is provided by the government.

There is complete religious freedom in England, but the Established (official) Church is the Church of England, which is Protestant Episcopal. The king or queen of England is the head of the church.

HOW THE PEOPLE ARE GOVERNED

England is a monarchy, which means it has a king or a queen, but the English people govern themselves by electing members to their Parliament. Parliament makes the laws of the country. You can read more about the operations and functions of PARLIAMENT in a separate article. There are two houses of Parliament, but only the members of one house are elected by the people. The two houses are the House of Lords and the House of Commons. The House of Lords is composed of people who have titles in England. They are not elected but become members of the House of Lords because of their inheritance of their titles. They may be royal dukes, dukes, marquesses, earls, viscounts, or barons. All archbishops of the Church of England and all bishops are members. There are more than 900 members.

The House of Commons is entirely elected. The building in which its members meet is the one building in all of England that the king or queen is never permitted to enter. No one with a royal title may go inside the doors of the House of Commons.

The people elect representatives from their local districts to sit in the House of Commons. The party with the largest membership is called the majority party. The leader of this party is invited by the queen to accept the title of Prime Minister, and the Prime Minister chooses a cabinet to direct the affairs of the country. The Prime Minister is always a member of the House of Commons, and he is as much the head of the government as the President of the United States is the head of its government.

Women have voted in England since 1918, and they can be elected to Parliament.

ENGLAND IN THE PAST

England has had a long and exciting history. It is especially interesting to English-speaking people, because so many events of English history are mentioned in English books. There are separate articles in this encyclopedia about most of the famous kings, queens, and great men of England, and about many of the historical events. The following paragraphs give a brief outline of its history.

There were prehistoric men living on the British Isles ten thousand years ago and more, but the first people about whom anything is known were the Celts. These were a people who crossed over from the continent of Europe about four thousand years ago. They were a simple farming and fishing people two thousand years later, in the year 55 B.C., when the great Roman Empire ruled most of the civilized world and the Roman general Julius Caesar invaded England to see if it would make a good Roman colony. About a hundred years later, in the year 43, the Romans did turn England into a colony. (The land was called Britain then.)

The Romans built cities and paved roads and fine buildings. In 1954, excavations in the city of London brought to light the ruins of a Roman temple that had been buried for more than a thousand years. The Romans kept a big army in England to drive off Germanic tribes that wanted to capture England from the sea and also to fight the original Celtic tribes that were unwilling to be ruled by Rome. A British queen named Boadicea led one Celtic army against the Romans in the year 61, but the Romans beat her. Some of the fierce Celtic tribes, the Scots and the Picts, were never conquered, but the Romans drove them north into the land that is now Scotland and built a wall, called Hadrian's Wall after the man who was then emperor of Rome, to keep them out. Still other Celtic peoples remained quietly in the region that is now called Wales. The present Scottish and Welsh peoples are descended from the Celts.

In the year 410, Rome itself was so heavily attacked by barbarian armies that the Roman soldiers were recalled from Britain. Germanic tribes called the Angles, the Saxons, and the Jutes then conquered Britain, which came to be called England (Angle-land). England was divided into seven separate kingdoms, called Northumbria, Mercia, Essex, Wessex, Sussex, Kent, and East Anglia. In 597 a priest of the Roman Catholic Church, Augustine the Monk, brought Christianity to England.

Other invaders from Europe, this time the Danes (men from Denmark), sought to conquer England. Toward the year 900 a great king of the West Saxons (Wessex) named Alfred divided the country with the Danes, giving them a northern territory called the Danelaw. The sons of Alfred later conquered the Danes and united the country, and England first became one single kingdom under Alfred's grandson, Edgar, in the year 959.

A little more than a hundred years later, after an English king called Edward the Confessor died, two men claimed the right to be the next king of England. One was a Saxon, Harold; the other was William, duke of the French territory of Normandy. In September, 1066, William invaded England with a Norman army and defeated Harold at the Battle of Hastings. William, known as William the Conqueror, became king of England and his victory is called the Norman Conquest.

The Norman Conquest is considered the beginning of modern England. The Anglo-Saxon England that William conquered was far different from the England of today. Powerful noblemen called earls owned most of the land in big estates. Most of the farmers were called churls, and they were little better than slaves. They wore iron collars to show that they belonged to an earl. Some of the working men were free, but not many. Life was rough, and most of the earls lived in "mansions" built of wood. William took the lands away from the earls and gave them to the French noblemen who had helped him. The French language and French customs influenced the English language and customs. The Normans built great stone castles, some of which may still be seen.

The next four hundred years of English history were filled with wars against Scotland and France, with struggles among the descendants of William the Conqueror for the English throne, and with struggles between the English kings and the English noblemen and people.

Like the Romans, England failed in many attempts to conquer Scotland. About the year 1300, the English kings claimed the throne of Scotland but were finally defeated by Robert the Bruce. The English kings also claimed parts of France and fought a series of wars, called the Hundred Years War, which lasted from 1337 to 1453, before they gave up their claims.

In their strivings for the throne of England, members of the royal family often killed or made war on one another. During one period, from 1455 to 1484, two branches of the royal family (called the House of Lancaster and the House of York) fought a series of battles called the Wars of the Roses to decide which branch should be the kings. In 1485 these struggles ended when Henry VII, a member of the Tudor family, became the king.

In the struggles between the kings and the noblemen, the noblemen finally won. In 1215 they forced King John to sign the *Magna Carta*, or Great Charter, which gave them and even the common people certain rights that were unusual in those days, such as a right to trial by jury. In 1295, under King Edward I, the Parliament was established and eventually it came to rule England completely. There were later periods in English history when the king had more power than

the Parliament, but this never lasted very long.

Under the Tudors—Henry VII, Henry VIII, Edward VI, Mary I, and Elizabeth I—England became very strong and prosperous. This was a time when religion was causing great argument. Henry VIII, who was king from 1509 to 1547, made England a Protestant country in 1534. His daughter Mary, who became queen in 1553, was a Catholic and made England a Catholic country again. When she died in 1558 her sister Elizabeth changed it back to a Protestant country and it has been a Protestant country ever since. Religious differences had much to do with causing war between England and Spain, in 1588. In this war Spain sent a great fleet of ships, called the Armada, to conquer England, but it failed.

Under Elizabeth I, England produced some of its greatest literature with such writers as Shakespeare, Spenser, Marlowe, and Francis Bacon. English explorers settled parts of America that eventually became the United States. They also began trade with India, from which came much of England's wealth in later years.

The death of Elizabeth I, in 1603, united England and Scotland for the first time. The nearest heir to the throne of England was James VI of Scotland, a member of the Stuart family. He became James I of England. England and Scotland have had the same king ever since, but it was not until 1707 that they were officially joined as one country, under the name Great Britain.

The Stuart kings caused a great deal of trouble in England. James I believed the king should have supreme power, while Englishmen expected Parliament to have at least some of the power, and a new religious group, the Puritans, wanted the king's power reduced even more. Under Charles I, the son of James I, the people rebelled. Charles I was beheaded in 1649 and the Puritans set up a republican government called the Commonwealth. The Puritan leader, Oliver Cromwell, became a dictator under the title Lord Protector. He fought wars against the Scottish, who supported the Stuarts, and against the Irish, who did not want to change religions. Cromwell was even a harder ruler than the kings had been, and when he died in 1558 the English people soon called back Charles II, son of Charles I, to be king. Charles II became king in 1660. This was called the Restoration.

There was more trouble when Charles II died and his brother, James II, became king. By this time England was a confirmed Protestant country, while James II preferred the Catholic Church. Mary, the daughter of James, was married to William of Orange, a Dutch prince. Some English noblemen invited William to come fight for the throne and William accepted. He invaded England in 1689, James II fled to France, and William and Mary became king and queen. Mary was a reigning queen, not merely a queen consort. James II and the Jacobites (see JAMES II) tried to regain the throne, supported by English Catholics and most of the Scottish and Irish people. Several times they raised Scottish and Irish armies to fight for the throne, but they never succeeded.

In 1714 the last Stuart to reign in England, Queen Anne, died. The next in line was a king of the German country of Hanover, and he became George I, king of Great Britain. During his reign Sir Robert Walpole became the first Prime Minister of England, establishing the form of government that England and other British countries still use.

Under George III, grandson of George I, the American colonies won their independence in the Revolutionary War, and became the United States. Napoleon became ruler of France, and Great Britain fought against him for about fifteen years. With the defeat of Napoleon in 1814, and in the reign of Queen Victoria from 1837 to 1901, Great Britain became the richest and most powerful country on earth. It had the biggest navy, the most merchant ships, and the busiest factories. It ruled the most territory.

Queen Victoria's reign was the most prosperous in English history. There were two great statesmen who served her as Prime Minister. Benjamin Disraeli, a member of the Tory Party (which became the Conservative Party) added to British wealth and possessions abroad. William Ewart Gladstone, a member of the Liberal Party, made the British people better off and freer at home. But as Victoria's reign neared its end, Germany arose as the strongest European nation since Napoleon's France and began to threaten British trade and possessions. This put Great Britain on the side of Germany's European rivals, France and Russia, and when World War I broke out in 1914 the British were Germany's strongest enemy. Though Great Britain was on the winning side in this war, it was very costly.

David Lloyd George, a Welshman, was British Prime Minister during World War I. He was the last prime minister of the Liberal Party. The Labour Party became stronger and elected its first Prime Minister, Ramsey MacDonald, in 1924.

Just as Great Britain was recovering from World War I, it was forced to fight World War II. By that time (1939), Germany had become the most powerful European country. Under the gallant leadership of Winston Churchill, the British people held out against Germany for nearly two years, almost without help, until the United States entered the war and supplied the power needed to defeat the Germans.

Again Great Britain had been on the winning side, but World War II was even more costly than World War I and the country was weakened even more. After World War II it lost some of its most valuable possessions, notably India. But England, and especially its capital, London, remained the financial and political center of the great British Commonwealth of Nations.

Since 1927, when Ireland became an independent country, the official name of England has been the United Kingdom of Great Britain and Northern Ireland.

During World War I, George V was king, and during World War II his son George VI was king. In 1952 George VI died and Elizabeth II, his daughter, became queen.

ENGLAND. Area, 50,331 square miles. Population (1973 estimate) 55,344,658. Language, English. Religion, principally Protestant (Episcopal). Government, constitutional monarchy. Monetary unit, the pound, worth about $2.40 (U.S.). Flag, Union Jack (blue ground with crosses of St. George, St. Andrew, and St. Patrick superimposed).

English Channel

The English Channel is the body of water that separates England and France. It runs between the Atlantic Ocean and the North Sea, and is about 350 miles long and from 22 to about 100 miles wide. On the English side of the Channel are such cities as Plymouth, Portsmouth, and Southampton. French channel cities include the big seaports of Le Havre and Cherbourg. For many decades various plans have been discussed to make transportation of passengers and goods between the continent and England easier by building a bridge across the Channel or by digging a tunnel under it. So far nothing has been done about it.

There have been many athletes who tried to swim across the Channel and a few have succeeded. The first man to swim it was Captain Matthew Webb, an Englishman, in 1875. The first woman who swam across was an American girl, Gertrude Ederle, in 1926.

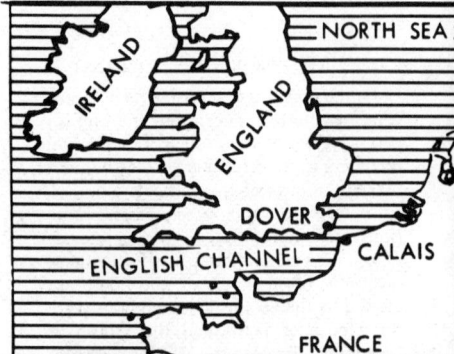

English horn

The English horn is not English and it is not a horn. It is a musical instrument of the oboe family, in the alto range, or five tones lower than the oboe. The double-reed mouthpiece, which looks a little like a pipestem, is bent backwards slightly, and there is a bulb-shaped bell at the end. There is usually one in every symphony orchestra. The tone is sad and sweet, and many composers have used it for important solo passages.

For instance, the English horn is heard in the Largo in Dvořák's symphony *From the New World*. It is heard also in Tristan's theme from Wagner's *Tristan and Isolde*.

English language

The English language is spoken by more than 333 million people throughout the world. The only language that is spoken by more people is Chinese.

People who speak English live chiefly in the British Isles (Great Britain and Ireland), the United States and Canada, and other parts of the world that are or used to be parts of the British Empire—Australia, New Zealand, South Africa, and India. There are millions of others who have learned English as a "second language." That is because it is the most valuable language in business. At least five million Europeans know some Eng-

lish, and another five million in China, Japan, and other oriental countries.

These people speak English with many noticeable differences. They have different "accents" and pronounce many words differently from one another. They use different words for certain things, as when an American speaks of an "elevator" and an Englishman calls it a "lift." But they can all understand one another, and they can all read the same books and newspapers.

This is a very important fact in world history. In the past the English-speaking peoples have often fought against one another, as when the United States fought England in the Revolutionary War and the War of 1812, and when the North and South of the United States fought in the Civil War; but these wars have been much like quarrels in the same family. More and more, English-speaking peoples have come to feel a kinship that makes them stand together against outside enemies. They have learned from the same books and other writings, so they feel the same way about basic things. In the past century the great German statesman, Prince Otto von Bismarck, said that the most important thing in world affairs was the fact that the English and American people speak the same language. It turned out to be true when the United States entered both World Wars on the British side.

WHAT THE LANGUAGE IS LIKE

Since you are reading this encyclopedia, which is written in the English language, it is probable that English is your native tongue—the language that you learned to speak and understand as a child. If so, you probably think that English is "easy" and that other languages are "hard." To those who did not learn English as children, it does not seem that way at all. English is one of the hardest languages to learn.

One reason is that English has more words than any other language. Of course, this makes English the best language for writing fine literature or scientific books, because the writer can express his meaning more exactly. Still, it makes the language hard to learn.

Another reason is that in English there are so many words that sound alike, or are spelled alike, but mean different things. *Bear* means carry and also an animal, and sounds the same as *bare*, which means unclothed. *Him* and *hymn*, or *to*, *two*, and *too*, are among hundreds of cases in which a native speaker has no trouble but anyone else would.

The biggest complaint of foreign-born speakers of English is about the spelling. In many languages the same letters, or groups of letters, are always pronounced the same way. In English they can be pronounced in many different ways. The *-ough* in *though*, *through*, *rough*, *cough*, has so many different pronunciations that almost anyone might be confused, and there are a few other, special, ways in which these same letters can be pronounced, for example *hiccough* (where it sounds like "up") and *hough*, which is pronounced "hock."

Many people think that English should be made an official international language, to be spoken by people every-where, but most of them agree that the spelling must first be made more simple.

HOW ENGLISH GREW

The English language of today has developed gradually through a period of just about two thousand years. In the year 54 B.C., when Julius Caesar first entered England with his Roman armies, the people there spoke a Celtic language that was related to the languages one can still hear in Ireland and Wales (see the articles on CELT and GAELIC). About a hundred years later the Roman Empire occupied England, and until the year 410 the people spoke a combination of their old Celtic language and the Latin language brought in by the Romans. But very little of this old language has remained in the English language that is spoken today.

Modern English is a Germanic language, and a member of the Indo-European family of languages. Nearly all the languages of Europe, and therefore the languages of America, are members of this Indo-European family. English is most closely related to the Scandinavian languages (Swedish, Norwegian, Danish, and Icelandic), to the Dutch languages, and to German.

This came about because the people who settled in England after the Romans left (in 410) were Angles and Saxons, Danes and Jutes, who were Germanic and brought their German languages with them. (We call the language English, and the country England, because of the Angles.)

THE THREE PERIODS

Scholars divide the history of the English language after this into three periods. Until about the year 1100 the language spoken in England is called *Old English*, or *Anglo-Saxon*. From about 1100 to 1500 it is called *Middle English*. After 1500 it is called *Modern English*, though during the 1500s and 1600s it was still enough different from the present language to be called *Early Modern English*. This is the language in which Shakespeare wrote.

OLD ENGLISH

You could not understand Old English if you read it or heard it spoken today. Many of our most common words come from it, but few of them were pronounced as they are today. Old English was an *inflected language*, which means that the same word had several different forms depending on how it was used in a sentence. This continues to be the case with some of our words, such as *I, me, my, mine*. In Old English it was true of most words. Besides, so many of the words were altogether different from our present words that in every sentence there are likely to be words you cannot understand. You can read more about this in the article on ANGLES AND ANGLO-SAXON.

Students of languages today know a great deal about Old English. Enough books and other writings have remained to give them about thirty thousand words. This is not many, of course, compared to the half-million or more words of the modern English language.

MIDDLE ENGLISH

In the year 1066 England was conquered by William of Normandy, called William the Conqueror. He was French and brought with him his French noblemen and soldiers. These people spoke French, while the common people, who had been conquered, spoke the Old English (Anglo-Saxon) that they had spoken before. French was the language of the king's court and the nobleman's castle for more than two hundred years. But gradually the two languages grew together and become a single language in which some of the words were from the Anglo-Saxon and some were from the Norman French. This was Middle English. The greatest writer in Middle English was the poet Geoffrey CHAUCER, who lived and wrote his poems between 1350 and 1400, and about whom there is a separate article.

You could understand Middle English a bit better than you could Old English, but not much. The words and the way they were pronounced changed a great deal before they became Modern English.

MODERN ENGLISH

One big difference between Modern English and the earlier forms of English is this: Modern English was not formed by an invasion of England in which a conquering people brought their own language with them. Modern English grew gradually out of the languages that were already there.

By the year 1500, the English in which books were written had changed enough so that you would understand much of it today. By 1600, the time of Shakespeare's plays and the "King James" Bible, it had changed enough so that you could understand most of it. Still, there were many words you would not understand. Some of these words are now said to be *obsolete*. That means they are no longer used. For example, Shakespeare used a word *disme*, meaning "a tenth." If you came across that word you would not know what it meant, and that would make it hard for you to understand the sentence. Some other words used in Early Modern English are now called *archaic*. That means they are still understood but are so old-fashioned that they are very seldom used. Writers sometimes use the word *varlet*, meaning a rascal or scoundrel, but they do this only to give the sentence an old-fashioned sound, as though it had been written or spoken hundreds of years ago.

The principal developments that have made Modern English are these: 1, the grammar has been made much more simple; instead of saying "I have," "thou hast" and "he hath," as speakers of English used to, Modern English has only two forms of *have* ("have" and "has"). 2, as science and learning grew, writers needed more words to express their thoughts. Many of these words they invented; others they took from the classical languages, Greek and Latin, or from the languages of other countries. 3, as English-speaking people traveled to other places and settled in other parts of the world, they adopted words spoken by the natives of those places. Many new

words came into the language from the Indians of India and the American Indians of America.

The style of writing in Modern English dates from about the time of John Dryden, one of the great poets of his century, who did his important writing after the year 1660. The spelling of English words became standardized when Samuel Johnson published his dictionary in 1755. There have been many changes since those times, just as new words have been added and are being added every year. The English language, like all languages, changes constantly.

engraving

Engraving is the art of cutting lines, words, designs, or pictures on metal or wood with a steel tool. It may be done for decorative purposes on jewelry, silverware, watches, armor, or any metal surface, in which case it is called *chasing*. Artists also engrave pictures on wood blocks or flat metal plates that are later inked and used as printing plates to transfer the picture to paper. Wood engravings are usually called *woodcuts*. The artist draws a picture with a soft, black pencil on a smooth, flat block of wood about an inch thick. Using a very sharp, pointed knife and other wood-carving tools called *gouges*, the artist cuts away the background of the picture, leaving the lines of the picture standing up like ridges. Printer's ink is then spread over the surface of the woodcut with a rubber roller. Since the background has been cut down below the surface of the wood block, only the raised ridges or lines of the picture take the ink. When the inked surface of the woodcut is pressed against a sheet of paper, the picture is transferred to the paper. This is called *cameo* printing.

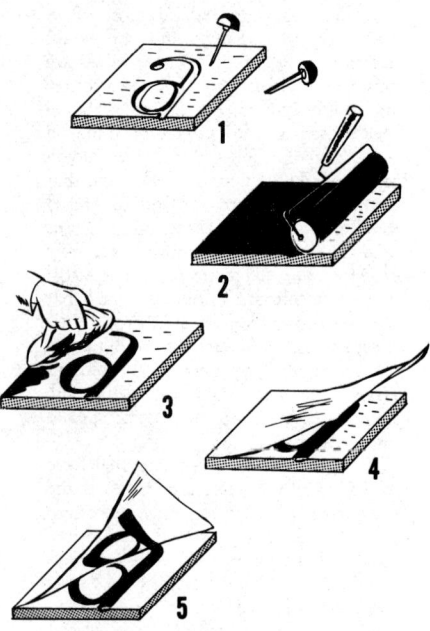

1. You start an engraving by cutting the figure you want into the metal. 2. Then you ink the surface with a roller. 3. You wipe excess ink off the surface but enough remains in the lines you have cut. 4. Now you press a sheet of paper over the engraving plate. 5. When you lift the paper carefull , the inked engraving is printed on it.

Engraving on metal is done on flat plates of copper, zinc, or steel. The artist traces his drawing on the plate and then cuts lines into the metal with a *burin*, a sharp steel tool used by engravers. The background is left untouched and the lines, instead of being ridges as in wood engraving, are grooves in the metal. The artist inks the surface of the plate with a rubber roller and then wipes away the ink. This removes the ink from the surface but leaves it in the hollow lines or grooves. A damp sheet of paper is placed over the metal plate and held against it with great pressure by a press. The ink in the grooves of the plate is absorbed or sucked up by the damp fibers of the paper. After a few minutes the paper is removed and has a perfect copy on it of the picture on the metal. This is called *intaglio* printing.

Engraving on metal is also done by a method in which the lines of a picture are eaten into the metal by an acid. For a description of this method see the article under ETCHING.

Eniwetok

Eniwetok is the name of a small atoll in the group of islands known as the Marshall Islands. The atoll of Eniwetok is made up of a number of coral reefs that form a large circle, and within the circle is a fairly deep lagoon. Eniwetok and Bikini, which is another atoll in the Marshall Islands, have been used by the United States as the place for atom bomb experiments. The few people who lived on Eniwetok were mostly natives who lived by fishing and growing coconuts. When the United States wanted to use the island for A-bomb tests, these people were given another island to live on and were taken there on Navy ships. Today, because of the atomic and hydrogen bomb explosions, the waters around Eniwetok are very dangerous because of their high radioactivity.

Enoch

Enoch was one of the so-called Patriarchs before the Flood, in the story in the Bible. He is said to have lived 365 years. He was the father of Methuselah, who lived to be 969 years old. The Bible says, "Enoch walked with God and was not, for God took him." This means that he did not die, but was "translated," that is, transported to Heaven.

After there were no more prophets among the Jews, there arose some authors who wrote books under the names of famous men of olden times. One of these wrote a Book of Enoch. Such books are called *Pseudepigrapha*, or "false" writings. Jewish legend makes Enoch the inventor of writing, mathematics, and astrology.

entente

An entente is an agreement between two or more countries to work together and help each other. In French, *entente* means understanding, and the Triple Entente was the name of a very important understanding between France, Great Britain, and Russia. These three countries agreed in 1907 to look out for each other's welfare and protect each other. When the first World War broke out, all three countries promised not to make

peace unless all agreed. During World War I, these countries were called the Allies. (You can read about the ALLIES in another article.) In 1917, Russia had a revolution, and this broke up the Triple Entente. You can think of the Triple Entente as a team. There was another team, called the Triple Alliance, with Germany, Austria-Hungary, and Italy as the members. This alliance was formed in 1882 and lasted until World War I. Italy refused to fight in the war on the side of the Alliance and so it broke up.

After World War I, there was another entente between the countries of Czechoslovakia, Rumania, and Yugoslavia, and this was called the Little Entente. The Little Entente made some agreements with France, who was big and strong enough to help these smaller countries. The Little Entente wanted to make sure that they would not be taken over by more powerful countries, but in 1938 Germany entered a part of Czechoslovakia, the Sudetenland, and the Little Entente was not able to do anything to stop the Germans, and so it broke up.

entomology, the study of insects: see the article on INSECTS.

environment

Environment is everything that surrounds a plant or animal or human being, and affects the way it grows. The air you breathe, the sun, the laws of gravity, the plants that grow near you, are all part of your environment. The kind of home you live in, the things you see around you, and the people you know, are the parts of your environment that affect you most. The kind of person you are depends upon certain things that you inherit from your parents (you can read about HEREDITY in a separate article), and on your environment. A good environment is one that helps you to grow up healthy and happy.

Every living thing is surrounded by land and water and air, and these are called the physical environment. An animal or plant survives when it is so made that it can be safe and healthy in this environment. The polar bear gets along well near the North Pole; it is healthy there because it can stand very cold weather and it is safe there because its white fur cannot easily be seen against the white of the snow and ice, which protects the bear against hunters. Brown bears could not stay alive so far north. Many animals can live well in different environments, or in the course of thousands of millions of years they change so that they can stand a particular environment better. This is called adapting to the environment. Many thousands of years ago there was an animal called the mammoth. It was an ancestor of the elephant. The mammoth had long hair. It lived in cold climates and the hair kept it warm. The climate gradually grew warmer and the mammoths died, but their descendants, the elephants, could live comfortably in such hot countries as Africa and India because they have thick skins and almost no hair.

Sometimes plants or animals cannot adapt to their environment. Millions of years ago there were many huge animals

called dinosaurs on the earth. Then the climate grew colder. The dinosaurs were not able to get used to the colder weather, and so gradually they died out.

Man can live in more different environments than any other animal except the rat. Man can live at the North Pole, and then he can move to the tropics. Of course, it would take his body time to get used to such a big change, but man's body can stand very hot weather and very cold weather, and many other kinds of physical change.

Man can also change his environment, and he has learned how to irrigate deserts and drain swamps so that new plants can grow and he can have the best possible physical environment. Sometimes man changes his environment by building dams that make large lakes or by cutting down forests, or changing prairies into great cities.

The study of how living things get along in their environment is called ECOLOGY, on which there is a separate article.

enzyme

An enzyme is a chemical compound that is made by living cells to speed up chemical reactions. An example of how an enzyme works is the way sugar turns to alcohol in the presence of yeast. If left by itself with no yeast added, the sugar would eventually turn to alcohol anyway, but this might take years. By adding yeast, the sugar turns to alcohol in a very short time due to the action of an enzyme, *zymase*, produced by the yeast.

Some enzymes are given off by the cells; others act right inside the cells. An enzyme called *ptyalin*, found in saliva, changes starch to sugar so that it can be digested easily. In 1969, an enzyme was, for the first time, synthesized (made by chemists) in a laboratory. That enzyme is called *ribonuclease*.

Eos

Eos was the "rosy-fingered" goddess of the dawn in the Greek myths. The myths are the stories the ancient Greeks told about their gods and goddesses. Eos was the mother of the winds and the stars. She drove her chariot across the sky to tell of the coming of the sun. Eos loved Tithonus, prince of Troy, an ancient city near Greece. Eos asked Zeus to make Tithonus live forever like the gods did, but she forgot to ask that Tithonus would always be young. So Tithonus got older and older, and shrank until only his voice was left. Then he became a grasshopper. The Romans called Eos by the name Aurora.

Ephesians, the New Testament letters or epistles written by St. Paul to the Christians at Ephesus: see the article on EPISTLES.

Ephesus

Ephesus was a great city on the west coast of Asia Minor. A Greek legend says that the town was founded by Ephesus, the son of a river god, and was named for its founder. The first people who lived there were Greeks. Ephesus grew very rapidly, and became one of the most important ports of Asia Minor. When the Romans ruled that part of the world,

Ephesus was the capital of a province that was called Asia, though it took in only part of what we now call Asia Minor.

Ephesus was most famous for its great and beautiful temple of the goddess Artemis (whom the Romans called Diana). The temple was built and rebuilt many times. The most magnificent building was made of marble, and was built about 2,500 years ago. It took more than a hundred years to build. Many great Greek artists made statues and pictures to decorate the temple.

The city of Ephesus was overrun in many battles. Now nothing remains except a heap of ruins.

One of the books of the Bible is called Epistle to the Ephesians. It is a letter written by St. Paul to the Christians of Ephesus.

Ephraim

Ephraim is the name of a district in ancient Palestine and of the powerful tribe that inhabited it. The tribe of Ephraim was believed to be descended from a man of that name. You can read about him in the Old Testament, in the Bible. Ephraim was the younger son of Joseph, whose story everyone knows. His elder brother was Manasseh. When Jacob, their grandfather, was dying, he gave his blessing to Ephraim.

The district of Ephraim was in north central Palestine, in the region afterward called Samaria. The tribe of Ephraim was probably the most warlike in Israel. Joshua, the conqueror of the Holy Land, was an Ephraimite, and so was the prophet Samuel. For a long time the tribe of Ephraim kept the Ark of the Covenant, containing the tablets of stone with the Ten Commandments, and the Tabernacle or Holy Tent of God, at Shiloh, one of their towns.

epic, a long poem that tells about the adventures of a great hero: see the article on POETRY.

Epicurus and Epicureanism

Epicurus was a famous Greek wise man and teacher who lived 2,200 years ago in the city of Athens. Epicurus bought a fine garden and used it as a school to teach his own ideas about the way people should live. According to Epicurus, the most important thing in life is pleasure. There are, of course, different kinds of pleasures. Epicurus believed that the intellectual pleasures, such as come from reading a good book, were better than the physical pleasures, such as come from eating or drinking. The idea became very famous and was called Epicureanism after the man who taught it. But in modern times, the meaning of the word epicurean has changed and is applied to any one who seeks the physical pleasures.

epidemic

When many people get a disease at the same time, it is called an epidemic. If one child in a school has the measles, and then many children catch it and children who live in the next town get the measles too, the doctors may say that there is a measles epidemic. The most terrible epidemic in history was called the Black Death. This epidemic spread

over all of Europe and Asia, more than six hundred years ago, and millions of people died. You can read more about epidemics in the articles on the BLACK DEATH and DISEASE.

epidermis, see the article on SKIN.

epigram

An epigram is a short, witty poem or saying. The first epigrams were written by the Greeks, who were imitated by the Romans and then by many famous writers in Germany, France, and England during the 18th century. Alexander Pope was a great English master of the epigram. Here is a prose epigram by Oscar Wilde, who was very famous for his wit: "A cynic is a man who knows the price of everything and the value of nothing."

epilepsy

Epilepsy is the name of a disease. A person with epilepsy feels fine until he gets an attack. Some people with epilepsy only get an attack about once a year, but others have them much more often. When a person has an epileptic attack, he becomes unconscious and his body grows stiff, his muscles twitch, and he may froth at the mouth. An attack of epilepsy lasts only a few minutes, but afterwards the person feels very tired, and usually sleeps for an hour or more. Some people who have epilepsy can tell when they are going to have an attack, because they get a funny light feeling, which is called an *aura*. Other people do not get any warning ahead of time.

Doctors are still studying the causes of epilepsy. They know that sometimes it comes from an injury to the brain, but in other cases there does not seem to be any physical cause. Doctors can give people who have epilepsy some drugs that help prevent attacks. A person with epilepsy can live a useful, happy life, although he should be sure to get plenty of good food and rest. Julius Caesar, the great Roman leader, and Dostoevski, the Russian novelist, and some other famous people, had epilepsy, which used to be called "the falling sickness," because the person usually falls to the ground during an attack of epilepsy.

Epiphany

Epiphany is a day of celebration in most Christian churches. It comes on January 6, the twelfth day after Christmas, and is sometimes called Twelfth Day, or Little Christmas. The night before it is called Twelfth Night and is also a time of celebration. Epiphany marks the end of the Christmas season. In the Eastern churches the day was originally celebrated as the day of the Nativity, or birth of Jesus. Some people give gifts at Epiphany, as most of us give gifts on Christmas.

Epiphany is observed by Christians in memory of three things. The first is the baptism of Jesus, as told in the first chapter of the gospel of Mark in the New Testament. The second event is the visit of the Magi, or Wise Men, who recognized Jesus as King of all people. The third event is the miracle that Jesus performed at the marriage feast at Cana. You can read about this in the second

chapter of the Gospel of John, in the New Testament.

Epirus

Epirus is a great region in the northwest of Greece. The Ionian Sea is on its west and Albania borders it on the north. Epirus has many high mountains and swiftly flowing rivers. Its people are mainly farmers and they raise wheat, olives and tobacco. Its chief city is Ioannina, in the northern part of the region. In ancient days Epirus was part of the Roman Empire. In modern times it belonged to Turkey for a long time. Greece won part of it from the Turks in 1881, and part in 1913 and 1919. During World War II Italian soldiers coming in from Albania tried to take Epirus, but Greek soldiers drove them out.

Episcopal Church: see the article on CHURCH OF ENGLAND.

epistle

An epistle is a special kind of letter that used to be written on special occasions. Most epistles were formal letters, which means that they were written in an elegant or official style. Most epistles were also intended for publication so that they could be read by many people. The most famous epistles are those in the New Testament of the Bible. Altogether there are twenty-one books in the New Testament that are called Epistles. Most of them were written by Saint Paul and are called the Pauline Epistles.

Most Biblical epistles were real letters written by teachers to distant churches, and were intended as instruction in faith and godly living. The epistolary form has sometimes been used as a device by authors. In an epistolary novel, the story is told by a series of letters that are usually exchanged among two or more persons. One of the first and most famous epistolary novels in English was *Pamela,* written by Samuel Richardson more than three hundred years ago.

epsom salts

Epsom salts are a medicine that is mixed with water and drunk as a laxative or put on a swelling (such as a sprained ankle or wrist). The swelling usually goes down and the injury feels better. Epsom salts got their name from a famous spring in England. For centuries people went to this spring at Epsom and bathed in its waters because they always felt much better afterward.

Epworth League, formerly a young people's society in the Methodist Church. Its name came from Epworth, a town in England, where John and Charles Wesley, the founders of the Methodist Church, were born. The Epworth League is now part of the Methodist Youth Fellowship, about which you may read in the article on METHODIST CHURCH.

equation

The word equation is used in mathematics, the study of numbers, and in chemistry, the study of the nature of matter. A mathematical equation is a statement that two quantities are equal. For instance, the mathematical statement $2+4=6$ is an equation. An equation like this one, which contains only numbers, is called a numerical equation. If we said $2+F=6$, this would be an equation, too, in which F stood for 4. An equation that contains letters as well as numbers is called a literal equation. Almost all mathematical problems can be put in the form of equations. Read the article on ALGEBRA to learn more about this.

In chemistry, the word equation is used to show what happens when two or more chemical substances are brought together. For instance, $NaOH+HCl \rightarrow NaCl+H_2O$ is a chemical equation. The letters are ways of naming the chemical substances. NaOH stands for sodium hydroxide, which is often called lye, and is a strong cleaning soda. HCl stands for hydrochloric acid, which is a strong acid often used for cleaning metals. The equation says that if you bring together these two very powerful substances you get a very harmless substance called salt water. NaCl means salt, and H_2O is water. An arrow is used in a chemical equation to show that the equation describes a process. Read the article on CHEMISTRY to learn more about this.

equator

The equator is an imaginary line drawn around the earth halfway between the North and South Poles. The half of the world north of the equator is called the Northern Hemisphere; the southern half is the Southern Hemisphere. In order to measure distances from north to south or south to north, we draw ninety lines parallel to the equator from the equator to the North Pole, and ninety similar lines from the equator to the South Pole. These lines, which run from east to west, are called parallels. See the articles on GREAT CIRCLE and MAPS.

Equatorial Guinea

Equatorial Guinea is an African republic. It covers 9,828 square miles—about the size of Vermont. Over 300,000 people live there.

The country is made up of the province of Rio Muni (on the mainland) and Fernando Po (consisting of the islands of Fernando Po and Annobon in the Gulf of Guinea). The capital and largest city is Santa Isabel.

The region was discovered by the Portuguese in the 15th century. In 1778, Spain acquired it. Rio Muni and Fernando Po became, in 1904, the West African Territories, later known as Spanish Guinea. From 1959 to 1968, Rio Muni and Fernando Po were Spanish Provinces. In 1969, the country gained independence.

equinox

The equinox is the time of year when there are just as many hours of daylight as there are of darkness. The word equinox means a day that has an equal night. The equinox occurs twice during the year: the vernal, or spring, equinox comes about March 21, and the autumnal equinox about September 23. At these times the sun is shining directly on the earth's equator. It rises directly in the east and sets directly in the west, and all over the earth there is equal day and night. At the vernal equinox, the sun is ready to move north of the equator. This gives to the northern half of the earth spring and summer. At the autumnal equinox, the sun begins to move south of the equator, and fall and winter begin.

Erasmus

Desiderius Erasmus was a great Dutch scholar. He was born in Rotterdam about the year 1466. He went to school in a monastery, became a Catholic priest, and later studied at a college in Paris. At that time a German priest, Martin Luther, said there were many things wrong with the Catholic Church and started what became the Protestant Churches. Erasmus agreed that there were things wrong with the Catholic Church, but he thought Luther went too far in starting a new religion. Erasmus remained a Catholic although he wrote a book pointing out what he thought was wrong with the Church. The book is called *In Praise of Folly.* He wrote many other books. Most of them were translations or new editions of old Greek and Roman books. Erasmus was always more interested in helping people understand the learning of ancient Greece and Rome than in religion. He died in 1536.

Gale Research Co.

Erebus, a place of utter darkness on the way to Hades: see HADES.

Ericsson, John

John Ericsson was a Swedish-American engineer and inventor who designed and built the *Monitor,* the first iron-armored ship used by the United States Navy. During the American Civil War the *Monitor* forced the *Merrimac,* a Confederate ironclad ship, to withdraw after it had destroyed two wooden northern battleships. For an account of the famous battle between these two ships see the article on MONITOR AND MERRIMAC. Ericsson was born in Sweden in 1803. He came to the United States in 1839 to build ships for the United States Navy. The U.S.S. *Princeton,* which he completed in 1844, was the first warship in the world to have a screw propeller. During the Civil War he built several other ships like the *Monitor* for the United States Navy. Later he built warships for other nations. He made many improvements in naval guns, marine engines, and engines driven by heated air. Ericsson died in 1889.

Ericsson, Leif

Leif Ericsson landed and lived on North America about 950 years ago, so he is called the first discoverer of America. Leif was an Icelander, and his people came from Norway. Iceland is a small island northwest of the British Isles. Leif was a son of Eric the Red, who discovered and settled Greenland, the large island halfway between Iceland and North America. (There

is a separate article about ERIC THE RED.) Leif was also named "The Lucky" because he rescued a group of shipwrecked people on one of his journeys.

The old sagas or hero tales of Iceland tell how Leif sailed west from Greenland and landed at several new places. He probably put ashore on Labrador near what we call Newfoundland. Some people think that he reached Nova Scotia on the coast of Canada and may even have landed in New England, perhaps where the state of Massachusetts now is. The next year, Leif's brother Thorvald sailed farther south, possibly as far as Nova Scotia.

The Norsemen did not stay on North America, but the story of their discovery was remembered and told in Europe before Columbus sailed for the New World.

Eric the Red

Eric the Red discovered and named Greenland about a thousand years ago. He was a Norseman who had been banished from Norway for killing a man. Eric was sent to Iceland, but he was banished again, for the same reason as before. About the year 982 he decided to sail west from Iceland. In the North Atlantic Ocean he found a large island almost covered with ice, and he named it "Greenland." Eric hoped the name would attract settlers. He started two settlements there, and they lasted several hundred years. Eric had three sons, Thorvald, Thorstein, and Leif. There is a separate article about Leif ERICSSON.

Erie

Erie is a large city in northwest Pennsylvania, on Lake Erie. It is an important port for fishing and for shipping such goods as coal, oil, and lumber. There are factories that make machinery, household appliances, and railroad equipment. Mercyhurst College is in Erie.

ERIE, PENNSYLVANIA. Population (1970 census) 129,231. County seat of Erie County. Founded, 1795.

Erie Canal

The Erie Canal was a waterway made to carry freight from Lake Erie at Buffalo, New York, to the Hudson River at Albany, New York. Before it was built, freight wagons carried goods over dirt roads, which often were muddy and could not be used. The wagons were expensive, and it cost ten dollars to send a barrel of flour from Buffalo through Albany to New York City. In 1817, Governor De Witt Clinton of New York had the building of the canal started. In 1825 the "big ditch" (the name given it by opponents of the canal) opened.

The Erie was 363 miles long and 40 feet wide. Canal boats pulled by horses or mules moved goods through the canal, and passengers sat on their decks enjoying the beautiful scenery.

The canal was successful, because it cost only thirty cents instead of ten dollars to ship a barrel of flour from Buffalo to New York City. But after the 1850s railroads took its place. Part of the canal is still used. Since 1919 it has been part of the canal system called the New York State Barge Canal.

Erie, Lake

Lake Erie is a large lake in the north of the United States. It is one of the five Great Lakes. There are many large cities on the United States shore of Lake Erie. Among them are Buffalo, New York; Erie, Pennsylvania; and Cleveland and Toledo, Ohio. Ships from these cities sail through Lake Erie and then through the lakes west of it carrying passengers and goods to and from such cities as Detroit, Michigan; Chicago, Illinois; and Duluth, Minnesota. The most important thing the ships bring back to the cities on Lake Erie is iron ore from Minnesota. Out of this ore steel is made for buildings, automobiles, and thousands of other uses. Many of the ships carry wheat and coal across Lake Erie. The lake is 240 miles long and up to 57 miles wide. From the end of December to the end of March it is partly frozen over and not all ships can use it.

In the War of 1812 between England and the United States a great naval battle took place on Lake Erie. After a hard fight the American ships, commanded by Commodore Oliver Perry, defeated the British. You can read more about this in the article on Oliver Hazard PERRY.

Eris

Eris was a character in Greek mythology, the stories the ancient Greeks told about their gods and goddesses. Eris was the goddess of discord, which is disagreement and hatred between people. She was the sister of Ares, the god of war.

Once all of the gods and goddesses were invited to a great feast, all except Eris. She was very angry. She went to the feast uninvited. In the midst of all the guests she threw a beautiful golden apple. On the apple was written "To the Fairest." Three of the goddesses claimed the apple, for each one thought she was most beautiful. This caused great discord. A Trojan prince named Paris was asked to decide who deserved the apple. He chose the goddess Aphrodite, and this later led to war, as you can read in the article on PARIS.

Eritrea

Eritrea is a large territory, part of Ethiopia, in northeast Africa. It runs for 670 miles along the Red Sea. More than a million people live there. The part near the sea is very hot and does not get much rain. Tropical trees and other plants grow high and thick. Lions, panthers, antelopes, and elephants live in the forests. Back from the sea the land rises, and in this region the weather is much cooler and more comfortable. Many different kinds of people live in Eritrea. Some have Egyptian blood, some are part Negro, some are Arabs, and there are a number of Italians. The people are mostly farmers. They grow cotton, coffee, linseed, and wheat, which they export along with furs and leather.

In ancient times Eritrea was part of the kingdom of Ethiopia lying to the southwest. In the 16th century the Turks took Eritrea, then the Egyptians, and then the Ethiopians again. In 1890 soldiers from Italy made Eritrea an Italian colony and many Italians settled there as farmers or businessmen.

During World War II the British drove the Italians out of Eritrea. The country was under British rule from 1941 to 1952. Then the United Nations decided that Eritrea should join in a federation with Ethiopia. The Federation lasted from 1952 until 1962 when Eritrea voted for complete union with Ethiopia.

The capital of Eritrea is Asmara. Before World War II it had a population of about 85,000, of whom 50,000 were Italians. Since the war most of the Italians have left. The city now has about 190,500 people.

ERITREA, province of Ethiopia. Area, 48,350 square miles. Population (1973 estimate) 1,235,000. On the Red Sea.

ermine, a kind of weasel that turns white in winter, or its fur: see the article on WEASEL.

Eros, the Greek god of love: see the articles on CUPID and PSYCHE.

erosion

Erosion is the wearing away of rock and the wearing away of soil by wind and water. Geologists (scientists who study the earth) say that there are three causes of erosion. The most important cause of erosion is running water. You have probably seen what the running water after a rain can do to the soil. There are small ditches, a few inches deep and several feet long, all over the ground. These ditches are caused by the rain water streaming over it. As the water flows over the ground it wears away, or erodes, the soil. River beds are worn into solid rock in the same way. Of course it takes a long time to wear rock away with running water. It may take hundreds of years just to wear an inch away. If you have seen pictures of the Grand Canyon, you will understand what a powerful force running water is. The Grand Canyon is an old river bed. It was cut out of the rock by running water. It took mil-

S.C.S. Photo

These deep gullies in Wisconsin, caused by erosion, ruined acres of valuable farming land.

lions of years for the water to cut the canyons out of the rock. Ice, a form of water that is found over millions of square miles of the earth's surface, is also very important in wearing away rocks.

The wind is another cause of erosion. As the wind blows, it picks up small particles of earth and stone and carries them along with it. These little pieces of wind-carried stones and earth blow over rocks and help to wear them away even more than water. The wind acts almost like a sandpaper because of the little chunks of matter it carries with it. The strange shapes of the rocks in the Badlands of South Dakota were made by wind and rain going over them for thousands of centuries.

The third important cause of erosion is rapid changes in temperature. During the daytime, rocks are heated by the sun. When the rocks get hot they expand and sometimes crack. Then, when it rains, water gets into the cracks made by the heat of the sun. When winter comes, the water in the cracks freezes and expands and breaks the cracks all the way open. As the seasons go by, one rock can be broken up so many times this way that all its pieces become as small as grains of sand.

Each year erosion costs the government and farmers millions of dollars. See also the article SOIL.

Esau

Esau, whose story is told in the Bible (book of Genesis) was the twin brother of Jacob, or Israel, the founder of the Israelite or Jewish peoples. Esau was a few minutes older and so was entitled to take the place of their father, Isaac. Once when Esau had been out hunting without success, and was so hungry he thought he would die, he staggered into the lodge of Jacob, who was a shepherd. Jacob had a nourishing soup (pottage) on the stove but refused to give Esau any unless Esau gave him the first right to inherit Isaac's great kingdom and power. So Esau "sold his birthright for a mess of pottage." Esau seems to have had no intention to keep his promise, so later Jacob cheated him again, disguising himself as Esau so as to get Isaac's blessing. Jacob did become head of the Jewish people, but Esau also became a great king and ruler of the Edomite nation. (Esau was also called Edom, which means "red," because Esau had red hair. Esau means "hairy.")

escalator

An escalator is a moving stairway. The steps of such a stairway are connected by a chain in the center underneath, or by two chains, one on each side. These chains are made to move up or down by means of an electric motor. Escalators are used chiefly in department stores, subway stations, and big railroad stations. Usually you find two escalators together, one going up and the other going down. Each has a handrail for passengers to hold on to. The handrail travels at the same speed as the steps. The steps of an escalator move at the rate of between 90 and 100 feet per minute. Elevators move upward faster, but one pair of escalators will carry as many people as several elevators during the same time. As many as three people can stand on each step of an escalator. In addition the escalator keeps moving all the time. It does not lose any time stopping at floors as an elevator does.

Esdras, Books of

There are four books of Esdras. The first two belong to the Bible. In Catholic Bibles they are called First and Second Esdras; in Protestant Bibles, Ezra and Nehemiah. The first book tells of the homecoming of the Jews from captivity. The second book tells of the arrival of Nehemiah in Jerusalem and what was done by him and Esdras for the good of the people. The third and fourth books of Esdras, which are not part of the Bible, contain some fanciful stories, including a contest between three boys to answer the question, "What is the strongest force in the world?" One answered "Wine," the next said "The King," but the third said, "Women are the strongest, but above all things truth beareth away the victory." This answer has given us a proverb, "Great is truth and it will prevail."

Eskimo

The Eskimos are people who live in the northern region above the Arctic Circle. They number about 50,000. They live in small villages and groups of a few families scattered from northeast Siberia through northern Alaska, the Aleutian Islands, the Arctic wastelands of North America, and Greenland. Eskimo is an Indian word that means "eaters of raw meat." In their own language they call themselves *Innuit*, which means "the people."

National Archives

The Eskimo hunter uses a kayak, a one-man canoe made of stretched walrus skin, to hunt for seals and walrus. The kayak is so light in weight that this man can lift it with one arm.

Nobody knows where the Eskimos came from, but it is believed that thousands of years ago they crossed the Bering Strait from Siberia to Alaska. The people are short and sturdy, with somewhat dark skin and coarse, black hair. Their features are somewhat like those of the Chinese.

The part of the world where the Eskimos live is cold and barren. There are few plants, and the Eskimos had to learn ways of getting food and staying warm. They lived by hunting and fishing. They hunted the seal and walrus, the polar bear and caribou. They fished for whales and porpoises. All of their clothing, tools, food, weapons, fuel, boats, sleds, and oil for their lamps came from animals and fish. Their fur clothing was the warmest and lightest in weight that man has ever made. They made fur *parkas,* or long hooded outer shirts, that were almost weatherproof. Their sealskin boots, or *mukluks,* were nearly as waterproof as rubber boots are today.

From walrus skins they made boats called *umiaks* and canoes called *kayaks.* The umiak was a large whaleboat. The kayak was a small boat, pointed at both ends; the skin covering had a round hole in the center, with a drawstring. An Eskimo in his kayak, with the drawstrings pulled tightly around his waist and dressed in his waterproof suit, could roll over and over in the water and never get wet. There is a separate article about the KAYAK.

Almost all transportation was by kayak or dog sled. The sleds were made of driftwood and were drawn by ESKIMO

DOGS, about which you can read in the next article.

During the long winter the Eskimo lived in houses made of driftwood and chunks of sod. When they could not get enough of these building materials they made houses out of blocks of snow. These are the snow houses we often hear called igloos, but *igloo* really means any kind of house. In the summer, which is very short in the Arctic but often quite hot, they lived in tents made of skins. All of their cooking, lighting, and heating was done by oil lamps made of soapstone, which is a kind of soft stone that can be worked with simple tools. Seal and whale blubber were burned in the lamps.

When the Eskimo were first discovered by explorers, they were living as men did in the Stone Age more than ten thousand years ago. Today the Arctic is being settled and modernized, and the Eskimo are changing their way of life. The walrus and whales are almost gone, and so are the caribou. About fifty years ago reindeer were brought to Alaska, and now the Eskimo have learned to herd these animals. Reindeer can live in the Arctic where cattle could not survive. They now provide the Eskimo with food and hides.

Read also the articles ALASKA, ALEUTIANS, GREENLAND, and ARCTIC REGION.

Eskimo dog

The Eskimo dog is a large, strong dog that is used for pulling sleds in the far north, or Arctic, regions. It looks somewhat like a chow, but it is larger and heavier. The Alaskan malamute and the Siberian husky are also sometimes called Eskimo dogs. Actually, each is a pure breed, although the three breeds are closely related.

In the cold regions, dog sleds, called *komatiks,* are used to carry men and supplies where no other kind of transportation is possible because of snow or ice. The sleds are pulled by six to eight dogs hitched to the sled, each on a separate line or, more usually, all on a single line. There is a "lead dog" at the front of the line. It takes commands from the driver and controls the other dogs.

The Eskimo dog's coat is made up of long guard hairs that cover a thick, woolly fur underneath. This warm double coat allows the dog to sleep out-of-doors even in the coldest weather. The dog digs into the snow until it is completely covered except for a small air hole just above its nose.

Eskimo dogs vary greatly in size, but they usually weigh about 85 to 100 pounds when full-grown. In color, they are most often gray, white, or white with black markings. Most Eskimo dogs do not bark; they yelp or howl as a wolf does. When properly trained an Eskimo dog seems to enjoy its work.

Esperanto

Esperanto is an artificial language that was invented about seventy years ago by a man who called himself Doctor Esperanto, which is a name that comes from a Spanish word that means "hope." Doctor Esperanto's real name was Dr. L. L. Zamenhof. He was a Polish doctor and scholar who hoped that his new language would be taught in schools all over the world, so that for the first time in history everyone could speak a common language. This idea of a universal, or international, language was not new. There had been other artificial languages. One was Volapük, which was invented in 1879 by a German priest named Johann Martin Schleyer. But Esperanto, which was invented in 1887, has been the most successful attempt so far to create an international language.

Sometimes real languages have functioned as universal languages. During the Middle Ages, Latin was a kind of universal language spoken by priests, scholars, and travelers all over Europe.

Esperanto was created according to a system of selecting words that are used in two or more European languages, such as French, Italian, Spanish, English, German, and so on.

Esperanto is simpler than any real language, so that students can learn it easily in a few months. The vocabulary consists of basic words to which syllables called prefixes and suffixes can easily be added at the beginning and end, in order to change the meaning of the original word. For example, in Esperanto, the word *bona* means "good." By adding the prefix *mal* to the beginning of the word, it becomes *malbona,* which means "bad." *Fermi* means "close," *malfermi* means "open." The word for "boy" in Esperanto is *knabo.* By adding the suffix *-ino* to the root of the word, we get *knabino,* which means "girl."

Here is part of a poem that was written about Esperanto by its inventor, Dr. Zamenhof. With it is the translation into English.

Sur neutrala lingva funamento,
Komprenante una la alian,
La popoloj faros en konsento
Un grandan rondon familian.

On a neutral lingual foundation,
Understanding one another,
The people shall form an agreement
One great family circle.

There have been many magazines and books written in Esperanto, and several hundred people in all parts of the world read, write, and speak Esperanto to some extent. Dr. Zamenhof believed that if everyone in the world could speak the same language, we would all understand each other better and not fight so many wars.

espionage

Espionage is the work done by spies or secret agents. Spies are people who try to obtain the secret military or government plans of one country, and deliver these plans to the government of an enemy country. Espionage is very dangerous work. If a spy is caught, he is usually condemned to die, or sent to prison for many years.

Espionage is very old, and spies were used even in the days of the early Persian Empire, 2,500 years ago. These spies were called the "eyes and ears" of the king, because it was their duty to report to the king on all the happenings that were taking place in the distant provinces of the empire. About five hundred years ago, in Europe, many kings and princes used spies to obtain secret information about their enemies. Often these spies would even be ordered to kill an enemy king or prince. The spy would disguise himself and wear a dark cloak that would cover his face from watchful eyes. Then he would sneak into his victim's home, and in a quick movement stab his victim with a sharp dagger and escape into the night. This is why we often use the nickname "cloak and dagger work" when we mean espionage.

If you wanted to be a spy, you would have to go to special schools for several years. First, the spy must be taught the language of the country in which he will work, and he must learn that language perfectly. When he enters the enemy country, he must pretend to be a native of that country so that he can go from place to place without being caught. A spy is also taught to use tiny cameras, no larger than a cigarette lighter, to take pictures of secret weapons and plans. He must learn to use radio equipment so that he can report to his chief and receive new orders. Other special inventions have been made for spies. There are special tools that can open locks and safes, and there is even a tiny pistol no larger than your hand that the spy can use in case of danger.

When a spy has finished his training, he is given an assignment. This means that he is told what country to enter, and what special information about that country is needed. Sometimes a spy does not enter a country to obtain information, but to destroy a bridge or factory. This kind of work is called *sabotage.* It is usually very difficult for a spy to enter an enemy country. Sometimes he must be dropped by parachute at night, or he may be landed at a deserted beach by submarine.

Once a spy has entered enemy country, he must work alone or perhaps make contact with another spy. He has been taught to recognize another spy from his own country by the use of a code word, or a secret way of shaking hands, or even a secret way of lighting a cigarette. A spy must always be careful of his friends in an enemy country, and he must do his work quickly and quietly. If he makes a mistake, he can easily be caught and either killed or sent to prison, and he will have failed in his work.

Another kind of espionage is called *counter-espionage.* American counter-espionage agents are the men and women who have been trained to discover and arrest the enemy spies who are working in the United States.

essay

An essay is a written composition that expresses the author's personal opinion about almost any subject.

The word *essay* was first used more than 360 years ago by the great French author Montaigne, whose essays on love, friendship, death, and other subjects are probably the finest ever written. The first famous essays in English were written by Sir Francis Bacon, who lived at about the same time as Montaigne. The essays of Joseph Addison and Richard Steele published in the *Tatler* and *Spectator* magazines are also famous. Many other English authors are famous as essay writers and some, such as Charles Lamb with his

amusing *Essays of Elia,* have written for children as well as adults. The most famous American essays were written by Ralph Waldo Emerson.

Essenes

The Essenes were members of a Jewish religious sect that was most active during the two hundred years before the birth of Jesus. The Essenes dressed all in white, never married, and allowed no women in the places where they lived, studied, and worked. The Essenes were farmers, and also made furniture and tools. They were one of the first religious groups to use baptism as a means of cleansing the soul and of assuring its eternal, or everlasting life. The Essenes disappeared about two hundred years after Jesus was born.

Essex

Essex is a county in the southeast of England. Long ago, Essex was a kingdom, with a king of its own. This was back in the 7th century. The people who lived there at that time were called Saxons. They came to England from northwest Germany and set up seven kingdoms, one of which was Essex.

Earl of Essex has been the title of various noblemen in England. The most famous was Robert Devereux. He lived in the time of Queen Elizabeth, in the 16th century.

Devereux was a close and trusted friend of the queen. She gave him much important work to do for England, such as fighting the Spanish and governing Ireland. After a time, however, he quarreled with the queen. He led a revolt against her and was captured and beheaded.

estate

When many people hear the word *estate,* they often think of a large piece of land or property in the country with a fine house surrounded by gardens, fields, and woods. In this sense, the term *real estate* refers simply to any land or property, and a man who makes his living selling or renting property is called a real estate agent. When anyone dies, the property and money that he leaves, if any, is also called his estate. The word *estate* originally came from feudal times in Europe when all the land in a country was supposed to belong to the king. Anyone who owned land privately had only a limited right or interest in the land, and this limited ownership was called his estate. The word was also used then to indicate social and political classes that were called the "estates of the realm." In France there were three such estates: the clergy, the nobles, and the commons. In modern times, particularly in England and in the United States, newspapers are often called the "fourth estate."

Estates-General, the law-making body of France before 1789: see the article on FRENCH REVOLUTION.

ester

An ester is a chemical compound of an alcohol and an acid. Natural fats such as butter, lard and olive oil have esters in them. Almost all of the soap we use is made from esters; they are also used to make fruit flavorings and perfumes. Nature makes perfume with esters, too; they cause the sweet smell of flowers.

Esther or Hadassah

Esther is the heroine of the Book of Esther in the Bible; her name is also spelled Edissa or Hadassah. Esther saved the Jews, who were living in Babylonia, from being killed. Esther belonged to the Persian king Ahasuerus's harem, or company of women. At a certain feast the queen, whose name was Vashti, refused to show her beauty to the king's guests. The king decided to have another queen, and Esther was chosen because she was the most beautiful woman.

At this time, the Jews had been conquered by the Persians, and Esther did not tell the king she was Jewish. After she became queen, the prime minister got the king's permission to kill all the Jews and take their property. Esther and her cousin Mordecai succeeded in saving their tribe. The king allowed the Jews to defend themselves against any who tried to kill them. The result was that for two days the Jews killed thousands of their enemies. Every year, many Jews keep the memory of those days at the feast of Purim, which occurs in February or March.

The Book of Esther was probably written about 2,500 years ago, when the Jews were cruelly treated by the Babylonian king. Babylonia was a country east of Palestine, in the region now called Syria and Iraq.

Estonia

Estonia is a country in the north of Europe. In 1940 it was invaded and taken over by Russia, and it is now called the Estonian Soviet Socialist Republic. However, the United States has never recognized Estonia as part of the Soviet Union.

About 1,221,000 people live in Estonia. Of these, about seventy-five per cent are Estonians, twenty per cent are Russians; the rest are of various nationalities.

Estonia is a small country, about as large as New Hampshire and Vermont together. It lies on the Baltic Sea. It is a low country, but there is a line of low hills running across the land from south to north. Estonia has many lakes and rivers.

Most of the people of Estonia have blue eyes and blond hair. They speak a language of their own, the Estonian language. It is more like Finnish than like most of the other languages of Europe, such as French or German. Most Estonians are farmers, raising wheat, potatoes, flax, and barley. They keep large herds of cows and sheep, and also raise

chickens, pigs, and horses. The capital of Estonia is Tallinn, a city of about 280,000 people (1960 estimate).

Estonia has had many rulers. For five hundred years the Danes, Germans, Swedes and Russians ruled in turn. From 1721 to 1918 it was part of Russia and the czar, or emperor, of Russia was Estonia's ruler. In 1918 it became a republic with its own president. In 1940 Soviet Russia took it. The next year the Germans drove the Russians out, but in 1944 the Russians again took it and have held the country ever since.

etching

Etching is the art of making pictures on metal with acid. Before making the picture the artist takes a sheet or flat plate of zinc or copper about ⅛ inch thick and coats it with varnish or *ground,* a thick mixture of wax, gum mastic, and asphaltum. When the varnish or ground has hardened, the artist quickly smokes one side of the plate over a flame until it is covered with soot. Using a sharp, pointed steel tool, he scratches the lines of the picture on the blackened side, cutting through the varnish right down to the metal. The exposed metal shows up brightly against the soot-blackened background and enables the artist to see his picture more clearly.

The metal plate is then placed in a tray containing a liquid which is half water and half acid. The acid etches, or eats, into the metal wherever the varnish has been removed. The varnish or ground itself is not affected by the acid. From time to time, the plate is removed from the acid with tongs and washed under running water. This stops the acid from further etching of the metal. The longer the plate remains in the acid the deeper the lines of the picture become. To prevent the acid from making the fine lines of the picture too deep, the artist covers them with varnish after the plate has been in the bath for a short time.

When the acid has done its work, the plate is washed in water and the varnish removed with a chemical solvent. Black or colored ink (usually brown) is spread over the plate with a rubber roller. The ink is then wiped off the surface with a rag but remains in the grooves or lines etched by the acid. A damp sheet of paper is placed over the inked plate and pressed hard against it by a machine called an etcher's press. The picture on the metal plate is thus transferred to the paper, which becomes a print.

ether

Ether is a very useful chemical compound made of carbon, hydrogen, and oxygen. It is a liquid that looks just like water, but if you pour a little on your hand you can tell immediately that it is not water. It feels very cold, because it evaporates into the air very quickly.

Chemists often use ether to dissolve chemicals that will not dissolve in water or alcohol, but its best-known use is as a general anesthetic (one that puts the patient to sleep). The patient breathes in the gas that ether forms when it evaporates. This causes him to go into a sound sleep. Then the doctor can operate.

Another meaning of the word *ether* is the substance that exists between the

planets and stars. There is no air in these places, but astronomers (scientists who study the stars and planets) believe that something has to be there for light from the stars to travel through. This unknown substance is called ether.

Ethical Culture Society

The Ethical Culture Society is a religious organization the members of which believe the best way to worship God is by doing good or right acts. The Society has Sunday services with a sermon and the people sing hymns as in most churches. One way that Ethical Culture is different from most religions is that you can join Ethical Culture and still be a member of another religion. The Society has schools, from kindergarten up to college, that are open to everybody. The first Ethical Culture Society was started in New York by Felix Adler in 1876, and now there are Societies in Chicago, Philadelphia, St. Louis, Brooklyn, and Boston, as well as a few in England.

ethics

Ethics is the study of what is right and what is wrong. Philosophers, or thinkers, have been studying this for years, and it is a more difficult question than it may seem to you. In many cases we know without even thinking about it that something seems wrong, or right, but there are other cases in which the question is not so easy to answer. When a person is honest and fair, we say he is an ethical person, and when he is dishonest or unfair we say he is unethical. Sometimes two persons accuse each other of being unethical, and both of them have good arguments, and anyone who tries to decide between them is likely to be puzzled.

Ethics is very closely related to religion. Christian ethics is expressed best in the Golden Rule, which is usually put into the words, "Do unto others as you would have others do unto you." This rule is based on words that Jesus spoke. They may be read in the seventh chapter of Matthew, in the New Testament. The Ten Commandments (in the twentieth chapter of Exodus, in the Old Testament) are a statement of ethics. The word *morals* means very much the same things as ethics, but often there is a difference between the meaning of the two words. It is immoral to behave dishonestly or so as to hurt others. It is unethical to be a bad sport and play unfairly in a game.

Ethiopia

Ethiopia is a mountainous kingdom in northeast Africa. It was once called *Abyssinia*. It is the oldest independent country in Africa, and its independence goes back even to Biblical times. Ethiopia is slightly larger than the states of New Mexico, Arizona and Colorado combined, having an area of about 400,000 square miles. About 22,000,000 people live in Ethiopia, by a 1970 estimate; this figure includes more than a million who live in Eritrea, a small country on the Red Sea north of Ethiopia, to which Ethiopia was joined in 1952. Eritrea was formerly a colony of Italy, but it became independent during World War II. (See ERITREA.)

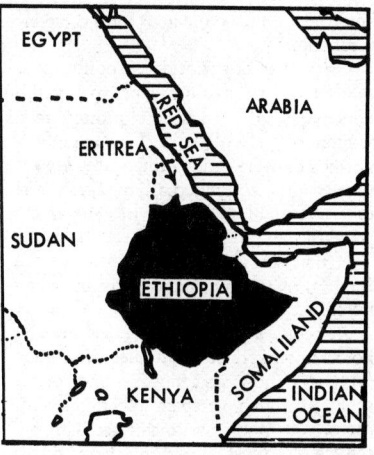

THE PEOPLE OF ETHIOPIA

The Ethiopian people are a mixture of several early African and Semitic tribes. They speak a language that is called Amharic, although other native languages are used. Amharic is a very ancient language and is a branch of the Semitic family of languages. Today, English is the main foreign language taught in the schools, and it is spoken by many educated people.

The Ethiopian people belong to three large religious groups. The largest group are the Christians, who are members of the Coptic Church. The Coptic Church is one of the oldest branches of Christianity and was introduced into Ethiopia more than 1,500 years ago. The next important group are the people who follow the Mohammedan religion, and the last important group are the more than four million Ethiopians that are pagans. The pagans believe in many gods and spirits.

Ethiopia is still an undeveloped nation and many people are unable to read or write. Most of the Ethiopians are farmers, or raise cattle and sheep. Since the end of World War II, the government has been building many new schools and teaching the people new trades and professions.

Ethiopia is a large, high plateau with several high mountains and a small area of lowland in the northeast. The only important river of the country is the Blue Nile, which runs between Ethiopia and the Anglo-Egyptian Sudan. The only important lake is called Lake Tana and is located in the northwestern part of the country. Ethiopia did not have a seacoast until its union with Eritrea.

The temperature of Ethiopia is warm, as it is very close to the equator; but it can be very cold on the high plateau and in the mountains. In the warm valleys and lowlands, coffee, cotton, and date palms are grown. Many minerals can be found in the valleys and mountains, but they are still undeveloped. Ethiopia is also known for its wild and domestic animal skins, which are sent to many parts of the world.

THE GOVERNMENT OF ETHIOPIA

Ethiopia is a democratic monarchy, which means that it has a king, but that the people can vote for various representatives in the government. HAILE SELASSIE became king in 1928. There is a separate article about him. He is called an emperor, because in the country there are many less important kings, whose title is *ras*, or prince.

The capital and principal city of Ethiopia is Addis Ababa. Founded in 1887 by Emperor Menelik II, it did not become the capital until two years later. The population numbers about half a million.

ETHIOPIA IN THE PAST

Ethiopia is a very ancient kingdom. According to tradition, the first king of Ethiopia was the son of the Queen of Sheba and Solomon. His name was Menelik. About 1,400 years ago, Ethiopia was a much stronger nation than it is now. Ethiopian armies were sent into Arabia and at one time even occupied the country now called Yemen, which is in the southern part of the Arabian peninsula.

It was only about a hundred years ago that the European nations made their first important contacts with Ethiopia. These contacts were not always friendly, and there were several battles between the Ethiopians and the English and Italians who wished to gain control of the country. Finally, about fifty years ago, Ethiopia was recognized as an independent nation by England, France and Italy, and a few years later it joined the League of Nations. In 1935, Ethiopia was treacherously attacked by Italy. Although the government of Ethiopia asked for assistance from the League of Nations, Italy conquered and occupied the country. At the start of World War II, Ethiopia was liberated by British armies and regained its freedom. Today, Ethiopia is a member of the United Nations and a friendly ally of the United States.

ETHIOPIA. Area, 398,350 square miles, including Eritrea. Population (1970 estimate) 22,000,000, including 1,040,404 in Eritrea. Language, Amharic (official). Religion, mostly Coptic Christianity. Government, monarchy. Monetary unit, the Ethiopian dollar. Flag, three wide green, yellow, and red horizontal stripes with figure of lion in center bar.

ethnology, the science that studies the races of mankind: see the article on ANTHROPOLOGY.

etiquette

Etiquette is a system of rules that tell you what is the polite way to behave toward other people. The rules of etiquette cover such things as good table manners, and how to introduce one person to another, and what to say or do when someone invites you for a meal or a visit, and many other things.

Some of the rules of etiquette seem silly, because they began hundreds of years ago when things were not the same as they are today. Most of the rules of etiquette are not silly at all. They are based on the fact that you should never hurt other people's feelings or make things unpleasant or uncomfortable for other people. Kindness is always good manners, and unkindness never is.

SOME RULES OF ETIQUETTE

There are "formal" manners in which everything must be done or said in a certain way. For example, if you received a formal invitation and wanted to answer it formally, you would have to write the answer like this:

Miss Jones regrets that she is unable to accept the kind invitation of Miss Smith to dinner on Thursday, March 15.

But it has become more and more unusual to use the formal style, except with people who are in official positions with governments, and today the person invited would probably write a note like this: "Dear Miss Smith, I'm sorry I can't come to your dinner next Thursday, but I have to be out of town that day. Sincerely, Mary Jones."

Here are some of the rules of etiquette that every polite person follows:

Invitations. When you invite someone, always name an exact day and if possible an exact time. It is not polite to say, "You must have dinner with us sometime soon." If you cannot fix a time for the invitation, it is all right to say, "We want you to have dinner with us soon. I will call you next Monday or Tuesday and we will try to fix a day." It is all right to say you will call in two weeks, or even a longer time; but whenever you say you are going to call, you must be sure to do it.

When you are invited, you must either accept or refuse the invitation promptly. If the invitation is in writing, you should write your answer, and you should not wait more than one or two days before writing. If an invitation says R.S.V.P., it means *Répondez, s'il vous plaît,* the French words for "Reply, please," and you must answer in writing. If the invitation is given in person or by telephone, you can either say Yes or No at once or you should call back with your answer within a day or two at most.

You should arrive at the time given in the invitation or a few minutes later. You should not be early, because your host or hostess will probably be busy doing other things.

Table manners. Different countries have different "polite" ways to use the knife, fork, and spoon, and any one of the ways is all right. Only the fork or spoon may be used to carry food to the mouth, and when the table is set with several knives and forks, the one on the outside is always the one to use next. A napkin should be laid in the lap and never tucked into any part of the clothing. It is considered impolite to lean on the table with your elbows. You should not begin to eat until your host or hostess has begun. It is bad manners, because it is ugly, to take too large mouthfuls or to talk while there is any food in your mouth. A bite-size piece of bread or a roll should be broken off and buttered separately. One bite of meat should be cut and eaten before another is cut. These are the principal rules of table manners, but there are many more.

Introductions. Always introduce a younger person to an older one; say, "Mrs. Smith, may I introduce my friend Grace Jones." Among grownups, a man is always introduced to a woman: "Miss Smith, may I introduce Mr. Jones."

When you are with one friend and meet another, you must immediately introduce them if they do not already know each other. When you have been out with a friend and he accompanies you home, you must ask him to come in and meet any members of your family who are there, unless he already knows them. It is

very rude to fail to make or offer these introductions.

Gifts. It is not considered polite for a man or boy to give too expensive or too personal a gift (such as clothing) to a woman or girl unless she is his wife or fiancée. Flowers and candy are always proper gifts, and when a boy takes a girl to any formal party or dance he is expected to send her flowers (usually a corsage that she can wear) before he calls for her, or to take them with him when he calls.

Acknowledgments. Before leaving any house in which you are a guest, you must find your host and hostess and thank them. If you have spent the night with them, you should write a letter within a few days at most, and thank them; this is called a "bread-and-butter" letter. A thank-you letter must also be sent promptly for any gift, and it is polite to do so when you have been at a party or at dinner at somebody else's house.

Courtesy to ladies. It is not polite for a man to remain seated while a woman is standing, unless the woman asks him to. When a woman enters a room, every man in the room should immediately stand up and remain standing until she sits down or asks them to sit down. A man should let a woman go before him through a doorway, or going upstairs, or going downstairs, and he should not get into an automobile until she is in it and the door on her side is closed. In taking places at a table, the men do not sit down until the women are seated.

ORIGINS OF ETIQUETTE

A man tips or lifts his hat as a polite greeting (usually to a woman) because hundreds of years ago knights in armor raised the visors of their helmets so that their faces could be seen.

People shake hands because long ago men held out their empty hands to show that they were not holding daggers or other weapons.

A man walks on the outside of the sidewalk because at one time streets were not paved and were muddy, and by walking on the inside the woman would stand less chance of being splashed by carriages.

A man helps a woman across a street or out of a car because years ago women's skirts reached to the soles of their shoes and they had to hold them up with their hands and also look down to keep from tripping.

There are many books that give the rules of formal etiquette. Most of these rules are seldom needed. Many of them would be ridiculous if used in ordinary circumstances. The ones that are matters of good taste, kindness, and simple good manners are never ridiculous.

Etna, Mount

Mt. Etna is an active volcano on the east coast of Sicily, a large island in the Mediterranean Sea that lies close to the southern shores of Italy. It is 10,758 feet high. On its eastern side, there is a tremendous crater or hole called Val del Bove, three miles wide. The lower part of the mountain up to about 3,000 feet from the bottom has a rich soil and there are many villages and towns in this section. In the next 3,000 feet the mountainside is covered with planted trees. From

6,000 feet to the top there is nothing but ashes and hard lava, which is melted volcanic stone that once poured out of the mountain and hardened. Mt. Etna has erupted violently many times. In 1669, it exploded with terrible violence; molten lava flowed down the mountain and destroyed the nearby town of Catania and its 15,000 people. There were eruptions in 1923 and 1950. To the poor Italians who live on its slopes, Mt. Etna is both a blessing and a misfortune. Its rich soil provides them with food but they can never tell when it will erupt again and send them fleeing from their homes.

Eton

Eton is the name of a small town on the Thames River in England. It is the home of Eton College, one of the oldest and most famous of the private schools of England where boys of wealthy and aristocratic families study in preparation for a university. It was founded by King Henry VI of England in 1440. Although it is really a private school, the English call Eton and other schools like it public schools. The reason for this is that the sons of the aristocracy and the wealthy used to get their primary, or grade school, education at home where they were taught by private tutors. In contrast to this instruction at home, studying at a school with other boys is considered education at a public place.

Etruscans

The Etruscans were an ancient people who had the highest civilization in Italy before the rise of Rome. We know very little about the Etruscan people. Their civilization reached its highest point around 2,500 years ago. From the writings of ancient historians and by studying the ruins of their cities, their beautiful pottery, metal work, and monuments, modern scholars have pieced together the story of the Etruscans. We know that they probably came from Asia Minor (now called Turkey) in ships and settled the west coast of central Italy

Metropolitan Museum of Art

This statue of an Etruscan soldier was modeled in clay more than 2,400 years ago.

about 800 B.C. From here they spread northward to the valley of the River Po, building twelve great cities. They introduced olive trees, grapevines, and two-wheeled chariots into Italy at a time when these were unknown to the less civilized Latin peoples of those days. They knew how to work iron as well as bronze, and their gold jewelry and ornaments show the finest workmanship found anywhere in the ancient world. They were expert farmers and knew how to control rivers to irrigate their fields. The Etruscans reached the height of their power about 500 B.C. After this time, the Etruscan cities lost their power and were conquered one after the other by the surrounding Latin tribes. The most powerful of these tribes, the Romans, conquered and captured the land of the Etruscans, who disappeared forever as a separate people.

etymology

Etymology is the study of the history of words. It is not pure accident that *bread* means something we eat and *break* means destroy or ruin. There is a story behind every word we use. Sometimes this is a fascinating story.

Most of the larger dictionaries have etymologies in them. These are short explanations of where each word came from. Some words we borrowed from other languages. Some we made up by combining other words that we already knew. Some have changed from words our ancestors used. From the etymologies we learn that the word *apron* was once *napron*, but people got mixed up between "a napron" and "an apron," and gradually they changed the word. We learn that the fish *halibut* got its name because *butte* is an old word that once meant "flounder," and *hali* is an old way to spell "holy," and the fish was called a "holy flounder" because people ate it on fast days, when they were forbidden by the Church to eat meat.

It pays to read the etymologies of words you look up in the dictionary. By learning the origins of words you become a better speller, you learn to pronounce words better, and you even learn to know the meanings of words you have never seen before, because you recognize the older words from which they are made.

Eucalyptus

Eucalyptus is the name of a large group of evergreen trees that grow wild in Australia. They have long, narrow leaves and small, fluffy yellow flowers. Some Eucalyptuses are the world's tallest trees. They have been known to reach a height of nearly five hundred feet. This is more than one hundred feet taller than the next biggest tree, the redwood of California. Because gum sometimes oozes out of their bark, Eucalyptus trees are often called gum trees. One kind of Eucalyptus is the tree called the blue gum. It grows very fast and can live in very dry places. Many blue gum trees have been planted in California, Florida, and Texas. Eucalyptus wood is very strong. It is used for boat-building, for furniture, for house-frames, and as firewood. A sweet-smelling oil is made from Eucalyptus leaves. It is also used as a medicine and in perfumes.

Eucharist, the holy wafer that is given in the Communion service: see the article on COMMUNION.

Euchre

Euchre is a card game. Once it was one of the most popular games in the United States, but it is seldom played now. Some of the rules that were used in Euchre are now part of the game of Five Hundred, which is still popular. The rules of Euchre may be found in many books on games.

Euclid

Euclid was a great mathematician who lived in ancient Greece about 300 B.C. Most of the theorems and problems in plane geometry, which every boy and girl studies in high school today, are discussed and explained in Euclid's book, *Elements,* which he wrote more than 2,200 years ago. Not much is known about his life, even though he is one of the great mathematicians of all times. Once Ptolemy, a king of Egypt, asked Euclid whether there was not some way of making the study of geometry easier. Euclid is said to have replied, "There is no royal road to geometry." By this he meant that there was no way to make geometry easy, even for a king.

Eugène, Prince of Savoy

Eugène, Prince of Savoy, was a French-born general who spent most of his life fighting in foreign armies against France. He was born in France in 1663 and was the son of a French nobleman, the Count of Soissons. He applied to Louis XIV, the powerful king of France, for a commission as an officer in the French army, but he was refused, because the king was angry at Eugène's mother.

Disgusted with the king, Eugène went to Austria, a country of central Europe, where his relative, the Emperor Leopold I, accepted him as an officer in the Austrian army. He fought against the Turks and took part in the Austrian capture of Belgrade (now the capital of Yugoslavia), where he was gravely wounded. He had great ability as a military commander and soon became a general in the Austrian army. He commanded Austrian and Allied troops against the French army in the War of the Grand Alliance from 1688 to 1697. In the long and terrible War of the Spanish Succession fought from 1701 to 1714 between France on one side and England, Austria and the Netherlands on the other, Eugène won many battles for the Allies. He served with the Duke of Marlborough, the great English commander-in-chief of the Allies, at the battles of Blenheim in southern Germany, and Malplaquet and Oudenarde in the Netherlands. Eugène died in 1736 at the age of 73.

eugenics

Eugenics is the science that studies how to improve the quality of the human race. Human beings inherit qualities from their parents. For this reason, if only the healthiest, strongest, and most intelligent people were allowed to marry and have children, the human race might become very much finer in a few genera-

tions. However, this would mean that the people who were not allowed to have children would be very unhappy. The most that any government can do is to prevent certain people, such as madmen, dangerous criminals, and people with certain diseases, from having children.

Many states in the United States have laws that require people to be examined by a doctor before they may marry.

Eugénie

Eugénie was the wife of Napoleon III, emperor of the French. Her maiden name was Marie Eugénie de Montijo. She was born in 1826 in Spain and was the daughter of a Spanish nobleman, the Count of Montijo. After 1834 she lived with her mother and sister in Paris, the capital of France. Here she met Louis Napoleon who was then president of the Republic of France and who was later to become emperor of that country as Napoleon III. She was very beautiful, a daring sportswoman who loved to go hunting and could ride a horse better than most men. Napoleon fell in love with her and shortly after he became emperor he married her.

Eugénie was very popular with the French and was a leader of world fashion. In 1856 she gave birth to a son. She took part in the politics of the day and usually advised her husband to be more bold in political matters. When her husband was away at war she sat on the throne and acted for him and was consulted by the French government on important matters. When revolution drove Napoleon III from his throne, she fled with him and her son to England, where she died in 1920.

Eulenspiegel, Till

Till Eulenspiegel was a legendary German who lived about six hundred years ago. Little is known about him, but many stories are told in many different languages about his wild and clownish pranks. His name became well known through the circulation of chapbooks, which were cheap books similar to our modern comic books. Till Eulenspiegel was always pictured as playing tricks on rich people to make them look ridiculous. One of the recent books telling of his pranks was written by Charles de Coster. Richard Strauss wrote a musical tone-poem, *Till Eulenspiegel's Merry Pranks,* and a ballet has been set to the music.

Euphrates

The Euphrates is a river, one of the most important rivers in world history. It begins in Turkey and flows 1,700 miles through Syria and Iraq to the Persian Gulf, a branch of the ocean. It flows through the territory called "the cradle of civilization" because five thousand and more years ago men built some very great cities there. The great cities along the Euphrates were BABYLON and UR, about which there are separate articles.

At that time, the land along the Euphrates was better watered and more fertile than it is now, and there were many

farms. Today there are farms near the river but most of the land of Iraq is desert. The Euphrates used to stop at where the city of Ur was, about a hundred miles above where the ocean waters now begin. Soil carried down by the Euphrates and Tigris rivers filled up the land between there and the place where the Euphrates now flows into the Persian Gulf. The Euphrates is now 1,700 miles long. The most important city at its mouth is ABADAN, where Iran has big oil refineries.

Eurasia

Eurasia is the name given to Europe and Asia together. Since they are one great land mass stretching from the Atlantic Ocean to the Pacific Ocean, some scientists consider them not two continents, but one.

A Eurasian is a person who is part European and part Asiatic. For instance, a boy or girl whose father was French, or Dutch, or English, and whose mother was Chinese, would be called a Eurasian. A Eurasian boy or girl would look partly like a European child and partly like a Chinese. Certain peoples who live in Europe or Asia look part European and part Asiatic. The Finns are a good example. Like most Asiatics they have yellowish skins; broad, flat faces; high cheekbones; and narrow eyes. Yet in many ways they look like Europeans too. That is why they are classed as Eurasians.

Euripides

Euripides was one of the three great ancient Greek writers of the kind of play called a tragedy. The other two were Aeschylus and Sophocles.

In the plays of Euripides, tragic things happened because men and women did bad things or broke the laws of their country or city, not the laws of the gods. Euripides was born in Attica about 480 B.C. He wrote between 75 and 92 plays. Eighteen of them are still known. The best-known is titled *Medea*. Euripides died about 406 B.C.

Europa

Europa was a princess in one of the myths the ancient Greeks told about their gods and goddesses. The god Zeus took the form of a white bull and swam with Europa on his back over to the island of Crete, which is south of Greece. Europa had three children by Zeus. He gave her several wonderful presents—a bronze man (Talos), a dog that never lost its prey, and a spear that always hit its mark. Europa became the wife of the king of Crete. After her death, she was worshiped as the goddess of the earth.

Europe

Europe is one of the seven continents of the world. It is a part of the huge land mass of Asia and Europe, which is sometimes called "Eurasia," but people usually think of them separately.

In area Europe is about the same as the United States with its territories and possessions, but the population of Europe (462,120,000 by a 1973 estimate) is more than twice that of the United States.

The "Straw Bridge" in Venice, Italy.

In comparison with most parts of the United States, Europe is very crowded.

For centuries, Europe was the center of the western world's education, art, and culture. There were even older civilizations and cultures in Egypt and other parts of Africa, and in Asia, but these are considered Oriental civilizations.

When immigrants and colonists went from Europe to America many years ago, they felt that they were going to a new world, and so America became known as the "New World," and Europe, the land these people had left behind, was called the "Old World."

THE COUNTRIES OF EUROPE

Like all continents except Australia, Europe is made up of different countries. There are nineteen wholly independent countries in Europe. They are Austria, Belgium, Denmark, Finland, France, West Germany, Greece, Iceland, the Republic of Ireland, Italy, Luxembourg, the Netherlands, Norway, Portugal, Spain, Sweden, Switzerland, the United Kingdom of Great Britain and Northern Ireland, and Yugoslavia.

There are also ten countries in Europe that are known as the "Iron Curtain" countries, because they are completely ruled or controlled by Soviet Russia. The Iron Curtain countries are Albania, Bulgaria, Czechoslovakia, East Germany, Estonia, Hungary, Latvia, Lithuania, Poland, and Rumania. Part of Russia itself is in Europe, although the greater part is in Asia. A small part of Turkey is also in Europe, and the rest is in Asia.

There are also five tiny independent states in Europe. They are Andorra, Liechtenstein, Monaco, San Marino, and the State of Vatican City—the home of the Pope and headquarters of the Roman Catholic Church.

There is a separate article about each of the countries of Europe.

WHAT EUROPE IS LIKE

Europe has many different kinds of land and countryside, and many different climates. The warm, balmy regions of southern Italy and France are as different from the mountainous, cold land of Norway and Sweden as the Rocky Mountains of Wyoming are different from the mild, warm lowlands of southern Florida.

On the shore of the Mediterranean the winters are mild, and there is plenty of rainfall. In Spain, southern France, and Italy, the climate is similar to the climate of Miami, Florida. The climate in the southern part of the Balkan section is like the climate of California.

Along the southern part of Europe run great mountain ranges—the Pyrenees north of Spain, the Alps north of Italy, and the Balkans and Carpathians to the east. From these mountains the land levels out northward. Almost all of Europe is low, fertile land. As it reaches the North Sea it becomes so low that it is below sea level (in parts of the Netherlands and Belgium). Nearly all of northern Europe and the British Isles (which are considered part of Europe, and were once connected to it by land) can be cultivated, and most of it ranks with the richest farmlands of the world.

The three northernmost countries of Europe's mainland—Norway, Sweden, and Finland—are more rugged and mountainous. Here the people live for the most part by fishing, dairying, lumbering, and some manufacturing. Winters in these lands are very severe, and in many districts the best way to get around when the snow has covered the ground is by skis or snowshoes. The climate of these countries is more like that of Alaska than of other parts of America.

A NEW EUROPE IS TAKING SHAPE

A new Europe quite different from that of the past has risen out of the ruins and the devastation left by World War II. The United States has contributed greatly to bring about this change and to awaken new life in the "Old World" by giving and lending money to the countries of Europe so that their people could rebuild their shattered homes and factories. Without such help the reconstruction of what had been ruined by the war would have taken many more decades. Today, most of the scars of war have been erased.

But it is not only money that the United States has contributed. It has, besides, served as a model. Europeans have begun to imitate what America's founding fathers did almost 200 years ago. After the war, statesmen of those European countries that had not fallen under Communist domination agreed that Europeans had to stop waging wars against one another and that they must unify instead and work together to protect their freedom and to achieve new prosperity for the people impoverished by the war.

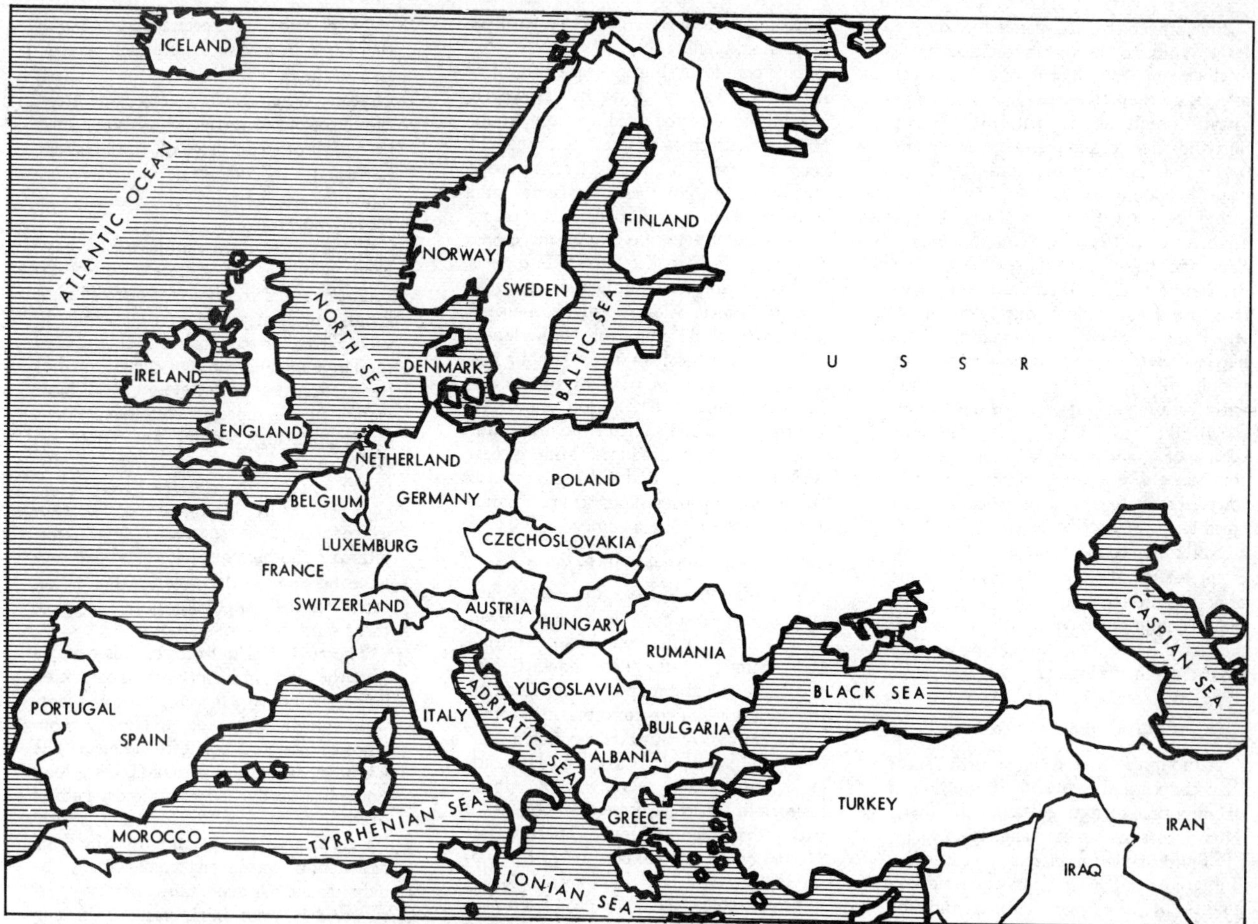

The continent of Europe is not much larger in size than the United States, but its many countries are more crowded.

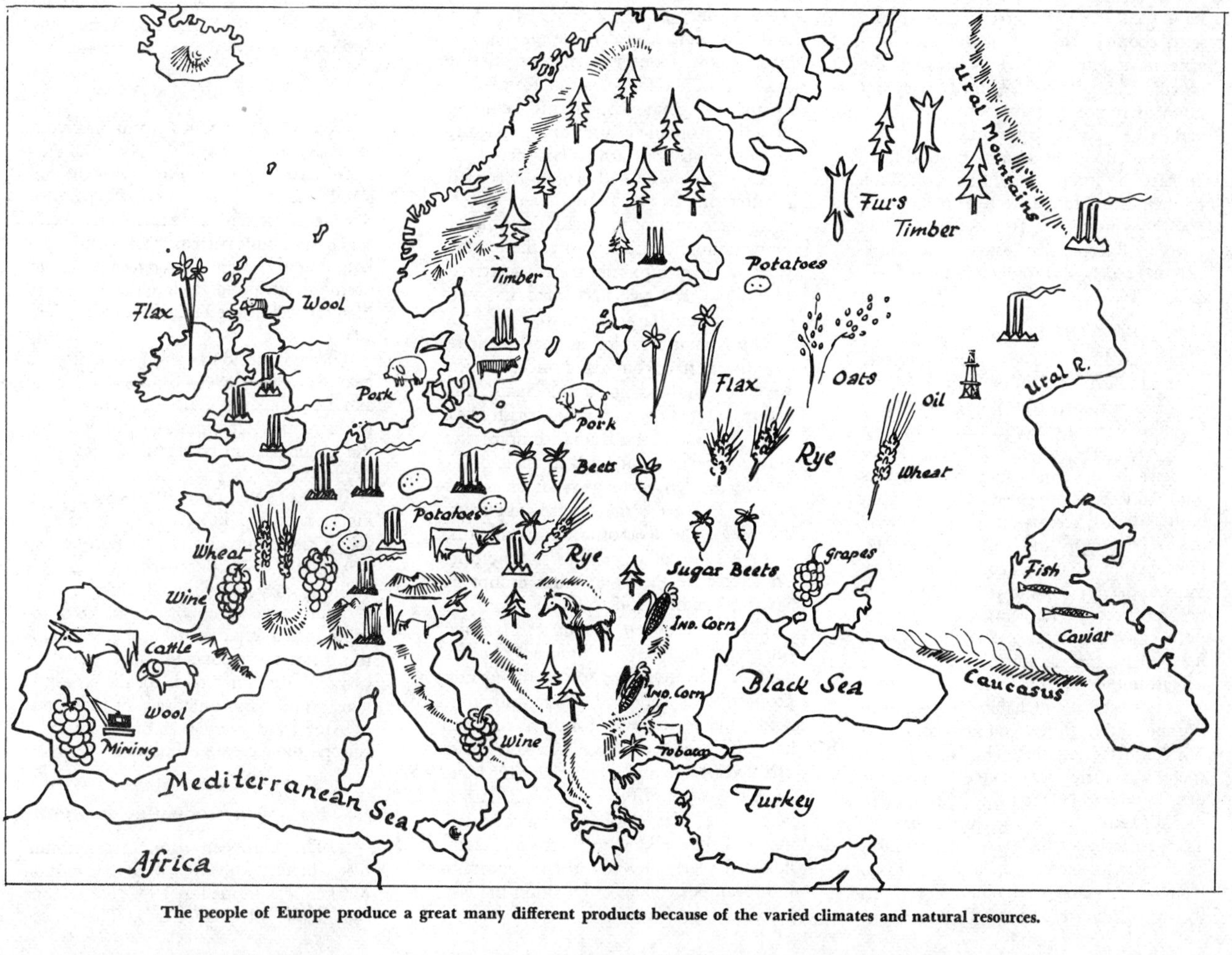

The people of Europe produce a great many different products because of the varied climates and natural resources.

Encouraged by the United States, a large number of European countries have, in the years after World War II, joined in pooling their resources and in forming several organizations with the aim of unifying their economies. The most important of these organizations, the European Economic Community (often referred to as the Common Market), was established in 1957 by Belgium, France, West Germany, Italy, Luxembourg, and the Netherlands. Other European countries are free to join this community, which aims to remove gradually all the barriers to trade and free movement of people among these countries and eventually create a great political federation much like the United States. Customs duties for goods traded between these six countries have already been drastically lowered and are scheduled to be abolished entirely over a period of years. Partly as a result of the cooperation of the European countries, people in some areas of Europe now live better than ever before. Economic conditions have steadily improved, and there has been a shortage of workers instead of unemployment.

THE DIFFERENT LANGUAGES

Although Europe is only a little larger than the United States, there are dozens of different languages spoken there. There are three major language groups, the Balto-Slavic tongues such as Russian, Bulgarian, and Polish, the Teutonic languages of Northern Europe, and the Romance languages of Southern and Western Europe. Often the people of one part of a country find it difficult to understand people from another part of the same country. Not only is there a difference in accent, as there is between the North and South in the United States, but often there are vast differences in words, and in the meanings of words.

Most school children in Europe learn at least one foreign language, in addition to their own. In the Iron Curtain countries, they usually learn Russian. In other parts of Europe, they usually learn English or French, and sometimes both.

HOW THE PEOPLE LIVE

Life in Europe is in many respects quite similar to that in the United States. This is particularly true of large cities like London, Paris, or Rome. Tall buildings have been erected after the war, many modern homes and apartment houses with modern conveniences have been built, but still comparatively few people own refrigerators and washing machines. However, many more people than before the war have cars, and traffic jams have become a severe problem for many European cities. Most Europeans drive small, inexpensive cars because of the high price of gasoline.

The customs and habits of people in Europe often differ considerably from one country to another. This is so because there was little interchange among the people of Europe for many centuries. In recent years this has changed greatly. Travel has been made easy and in most cases visas are no longer necessary to go from one country to another. Europeans by the millions now spend their vacations

in various parts of the continent regardless of national boundaries.

The people of Europe earn their livings in a variety of ways. However, farming is still the leading occupation. Most of the farms are small, but the yield per acre is very high. The leading crops are wheat, rye, potatoes, oats, barley, and corn. In Southern Europe, citrus fruits, grapes, and olives are important crops. Much livestock is also raised. Europe is also noted for its manufacturing. Great Britain, France, West Germany, Switzerland, Sweden, Belgium, the Netherlands, Italy, and Czechoslovakia are among the leading industrial nations of the world. Textiles, wine, watches, iron and steel, and machinery are some of the important products Europe produces. Mining (especially of coal) and fishing are also important industries. Tourists are another important source of income.

EUROPE IN THE PAST

The map of Europe did not always look as it does today. Only since World War II have all the countries of Europe been named as they are now. Before World War I, the map of Europe looked still different. Then there was no Yugoslavia, no Czechoslovakia, no Poland, no Finland. Instead of Austria and Hungary as separate states, there was the single country of Austria-Hungary. There were two independent countries, Serbia and Montenegro, that are now part of Yugoslavia.

Scientists say that there have been people living in different parts of Europe for many thousands of years, and that for most of that time they lived a primitive and uncivilized existence. The first important European civilization that scientists know about was that of ancient Greece, about 2,500 years ago. Rome then became a great conquering empire, spreading Roman culture throughout the lands where Roman armies conquered.

The people who had originally settled in different parts of Europe were developing their own cultures. By the time of the beginning of Christianity, there were tribes and groups of tribes scattered throughout Europe. Each had its own section of land, large or small.

The Roman Empire, at the height of its power, had conquered most of the western mainland, including Spain, and had penetrated deep into the British Isles. After the fall of the Roman Empire, the different tribes went back to their original independent state, as separate groups again. There were the Franks, the Celts, the Slavs, the Teutons, the Lombards, and other Germanic peoples. On the British Isles were Picts and other groups of Saxons, Teutons, and Celts.

These European countries became Christian countries. For hundreds of years they fought invading forces of Asiatic peoples who followed other religions. Arabs and Moors, who followed the Mohammedan religion, invaded Spain about 1,200 years ago and stayed there for hundreds of years, until the year 1492. Turks, who were also Mohammedans, ruled much of the Balkans for more than four hundred years, and lost their important European possessions only within the last hundred years.

Fierce tribes of Tartars and Mongols that came from Asia kept attacking Russia and the Balkan countries for hundreds of years. When the danger became great, the European countries would sometimes help each other to drive off the invaders, but usually the European countries were too unfriendly among themselves to unite for any purpose.

In the course of the centuries there have been hundreds of different European countries ruled by thousands of different kings, but nearly always the people in each particular section have remembered the language and some of the customs of their ancestors of long ago, and have wanted to be separate and independent of neighboring peoples and countries. Kings and other conquerors, greedy for power and wealth, have tried to rule foreign peoples by force of arms. The subject peoples have resisted. One war has followed another. Suspicions and enmities have become so deep-seated that it has often seemed impossible ever to wipe them out.

The two World Wars of this century were the worst in history. European cities, houses, and big manufacturing plants were ruined by bombs, and many thousands of people were left homeless. The job of repairing war damage takes a long time. Just as Europe was almost getting over the damage of World War I, World War II came along, and this time the destruction was even worse. With the help of the United States, however, recovery has been fairly rapid. Through the European Recovery Program (Marshall Plan) alone, aid to Western Europe totalled more than $12,500,000,000. Although some scars remain, today most of Europe is prosperous and strong.

HISTORIC PLACES

From north to south, from the western shore of Ireland to the border of Asiatic Russia, Europe is filled with the relics of history. There are ancient ruins of Roman roads and aqueducts, and medieval castles built perhaps a thousand years later, but also there are modern buildings of more advanced design than you are likely to see in the United States or Canada.

Throughout Europe the country is beautiful: The lovely beaches of France and Belgium, the majestic, snow-capped peaks of the Alps, the lakes of Finland, the rolling countryside of France and England.

In Europe you can still see people living as they did hundreds of years ago, yet in the cities (of which Europe has twenty-two with populations over one million) they enjoy modern life.

Tourists are an important source of income in many parts of Europe, so everything has been done to make traveling easy and life comfortable for the visitor. It is no wonder that hundreds of thousands of Americans every year make a trip to Europe their greatest ambition.

European Economic Community

The European Economic Community, better known as the Common Market, was formed in 1957. Six nations signed the original treaty. They were

France, West Germany, Italy, Belgium, the Netherlands, and Luxembourg. The purpose of the association was to further trade among the nations by reducing tariffs and other trade barriers. They also agreed to have common trade policies toward nations outside the organization. Greece became associated with the group in 1961. Great Britain and Denmark applied for membership that same year but President de Gaulle of France opposed British membership and no new member was taken in. However, on January 1, 1973, Great Britain, Denmark, and the Republic of Ireland were granted membership. Eventually the EEC will unite about 300,000,000 people and form one of the largest markets in the world.

Eurydice, a woman in Greek legend, who was loved by the god Orpheus: see the article on ORPHEUS.

eurythmics

Eurythmics is a system of teaching music and dancing. It teaches the students to move their bodies in time with music. Various exercises and motions are practiced, and after a time the student is able to express what the music means to him through movements that he thinks of himself. The system was originated in 1903 by Emile Jacques-Dalcroze, and it is often called the Dalcroze Method. Singers use it to learn to use their arms gracefully while singing. A Dalcroze Institute was founded in the United States in 1915.

Eustachian tubes

The Eustachian tubes are small pipes that lead from the back of your throat to your ears. They let air into your ears, behind your eardrums, to keep the air pressure the same on both sides of your eardrums. Without the Eustachian tubes your eardrums would probably burst. When the pressure on the outside is a little stronger than the pressure on the inside, it makes the eardrum bulge a little—and that gives you the feeling that your ears are stopped up. You can stop this feeling by opening your mouth, swallowing, or yawning. This opens the Eustachian tubes, and lets enough air into your ears to make the pressure equal again on both sides of your eardrums. The changing air pressure as an elevator moves affects your ears, and you feel the bulging of your eardrums. When you open your mouth and yawn, this should stop immediately.

Your doctor may have warned you not to blow your nose very hard when you have a cold. That is because the germs of the cold may be forced up through the Eustachian tubes to your middle ear, and cause a serious infection there. You can see why this is so if you will hold your nose and then try to breathe out through it. You will feel pressure building up in your ears. The same thing happens when you blow your nose, but instead of just air being forced back into your ears, some of the cold germs may be carried back along with the air.

Evangelical Churches

Protestant Christian denominations that believe in a strict interpretation of the gospels in the New Testament, and in the doctrine of salvation through faith (as stated in John 3:16) are often called evangelical churches; and there have been several churches that made *Evangelical* an official part of their names.

One of these was the Evangelical and Reformed Church, a large organization with 810,000 members and nearly 3,000 churches, which in 1957 merged with the Congregational Church to form the United Church of Christ. The Evangelical and Reformed Church had been formed of other churches founded by German and Swiss settlers in the United States.

The Evangelical United Brethren Church is a Church that was formed in 1946 when the Church of the United Brethren in Christ and the Evangelical Church joined to form one Church. It is one of the youngest Protestant Christian Churches in the United States. Both of the original Churches were founded more than a hundred years ago in Pennsylvania and were much like the Lutheran and Methodist Churches. For many years they used the German language in their services, but they later came to use English. This Church has two organizations, the Women's Society for World Service, and the Brotherhood, that devote themselves to missionary work. The Church maintains many home missions, seven colleges, three seminaries, and several publishing houses. It has about 732,000 members and about 3,970 churches.

evangelist

An evangelist is a person who preaches or writes about religion. The writers of the Gospels of the New Testament, Matthew, Mark, Luke, and John, were evangelists. John Wesley and George Whitefield, founders of the Methodist Church, were also evangelists, as was George Fox, who founded the Quakers.

In Christian churches an evangelist is particularly a preacher who tries to make more people active Christians, often through baptism. He is sometimes called a *revivalist* because he tries to revive sinners, or make them live anew, through a deeper belief in Christ. Dwight L. Moody, Billy Sunday and Gipsy Smith were all evangelists of this type.

A modern evangelist is Billy Graham. Millions have seen or heard him conduct evangelistic meetings on television or radio.

Evansville

Evansville is a city in southwestern Indiana, on the Ohio River. It is a center for a coal-mining and farming region. There are many factories, including several that make refrigerators. Evansville College and a zoo are there.

EVANSVILLE, INDIANA. Population (1970 census) 138,764. County seat of Vanderburgh County. Founded, 1817.

evaporation

Evaporation is the changing of a liquid into a gas at any temperature below the boiling point of the liquid. If you put some water in a shallow dish and leave it uncovered for several hours on a dry day, it will disappear very quickly. What happens is that the water has turned to water vapor, a gas, and risen into the air above it. If water is put into a kettle over a fire, it will boil after a time and turn into a gas that we call steam; and if we let the fire continue to burn, all the water will turn to steam and disappear into the air. Evaporation is much the same process except that the liquid changes into a gas without boiling and does it much more slowly. Heat is needed to bring about evaporation, so the liquid must draw heat out of the materials around it as it changes to a gas. For example, if you put alcohol on your hand and let it dry, your hand will feel very cool because the evaporation of this liquid draws some of the natural heat of your skin. Some liquids, such as alcohol, benzine, gasoline, and ether, evaporate rapidly; others, such as heavy petroleum oils, evaporate very slowly.

Eve, the first woman: see the article on ADAM AND EVE.

evening star, a bright planet that you see after sunset in the western sky: see the article on VENUS.

Everest, Mount

Mt. Everest is the highest mountain in the world. It is in the Himalaya range in south-central Asia, rising on the border between Tibet and Nepal. The top of Mt. Everest is 29,149 feet above sea level. That means it goes up for five and one-half miles.

Many mountain climbers have tried to get to the top of Everest. The steep rocks, seas of ice (glaciers), deep snow, thin air, and terribly icy winds beat them back and many lost their lives. Finally two men did succeed in getting there. On May 29, 1953, Edmond Hilary, an Englishman, and Tensing Norkay, a Nepalese, planted the flags of Great Britain, Nepal, and the United Nations on the summit of Mt. Everest. For more about this record-breaking climb, read the article on MOUNTAIN CLIMBING.

Everett, Edward

Edward Everett was an American statesman. He was born in Dorchester, Massachusetts, in 1794. He studied at Harvard and later became its president. He also was a congressman, governor of Massachusetts, and minister to Great Britain.

Everett was famous for his speeches. One of his best was made at Gettysburg, Pennsylvania, at the opening of a cemetery for soldiers who had been killed in the Battle of Gettysburg. Everett's speech lasted two hours. Then President Abraham Lincoln made a speech that took only a few minutes. Everett said, "President Lincoln has said more in a few minutes than I said in two hours. It will never be forgotten." He was right. Lincoln's speech is the famous "Gettysburg Address." Everett died in 1865.

Everglades

The Everglades is the name of a large tropical swamp, about one hundred miles long and more than fifty miles wide, in the southern part of the state of Flor-

ida. The Everglades is the part of the United States that is most like the jungle. The weather is hot and very rainy. If you visit Florida, you may take a trip to the Everglades. You can travel in a small boat along dark brown, narrow, winding streams. Your guide will often have to push the boat with a long pole, because the water is very shallow and the boat can easily get stuck in the muddy river bottom. You will see many tiny islands that are covered with a special kind of tall grass that is called saw grass. This grass grows as high as a man's head in many parts of the Everglades. You can see alligators and sleepy lizards, and many colorful tropical birds. Clumsy pelicans, blue herons, and graceful pink flamingos make their home in this swamp. In the jungles there are black bears, panthers, wildcats, and many other animals. Many huge orchids and other brilliant flowers grow in the Everglades, and there are thick forests of mangrove and cypress trees and low-hanging deep green Spanish moss.

If you go to the Everglades, you may see some Seminole Indians, dressed in their brightly colored red and yellow clothes. Once there were about four thousand Seminole Indians who made their home in Florida, but after some fierce battles they were driven out of the state. A few hundred Seminoles escaped to the Everglades, where they live in odd-looking huts, with thatched roofs, that they build on tall stilts above the swampy ground. These Indians fish and search in the Everglades jungles for their food.

About fifty years ago, the United States government and the state of Florida spent millions of dollars in the Everglades. They built canals and ditches to drain off the water and make the land useful for farming. After they worked this project for some time, there were some very serious fires in the Everglades, and scientists began to realize that the land had been drained so much that it was becoming dangerously dry, and it could not be made into good farm country. Very few people live in the Everglades. Some of them, who live near Lake Okeechobee, raise sugar cane and vegetables and cattle now that the land has been irrigated, but the Everglades is not a very healthy place to live, though it is a very interesting place to visit. In 1947 the United States government made the Everglades into a national park.

evergreen

An evergreen is any plant that keeps its leaves all the year round. In cool countries most trees shed their leaves in the winter. In hot countries, many trees shed their leaves during the dry part of the year. Both these kinds of tree are called deciduous. Evergreen trees may have leaves that live for several years. As these leaves die, young leaves may already be appearing on the tree. Very often the old leaves of evergreen trees drop one by one, so the tree is never bare. In North America most of the evergreen trees are CONIFERS, about which there is a separate article. Many conifers are huge trees, but their leaves are tough and can stand frost and snow. For this reason conifers grow farther north than any other trees. Evergreens such as holly, ivy,

Everglades National Park is the third largest national park in the United States. It consists of nearly 1½ million acres of land and water. The above photograph shows a section of the park called Flamingo, located on Florida Bay.

myrtle, and boxwood look very much like our deciduous trees.

everlasting flower

Everlasting flower, or *immortelle*, is the name of several different kinds of flower. If everlasting flowers are picked and put into water, they will wither and die. But if they are not put into water, they will dry and keep their shape, and often their colors. Sometimes they will last for several years. This is why they are called everlasting flowers. They are very pretty to have in the house in winter, when there are no other flowers. The common everlasting flower is a plant very much like a daisy. Sea pink, globe amaranth, cockscomb, and strawflower are other kinds of everlasting flower. To preserve the colors best, they should be dried hanging upside down in the shade.

Everyman

Everyman is the hero of an English morality play. A morality play is not exactly like a play you see on the stage, because the people in a morality play stand for ideas like Friendship, Riches, Beauty, and Knowledge, and the hero usually has to choose between Good and Evil. In the Everyman play, Death comes without warning to take Everyman. He tells Everyman to look back and decide what his life has been worth. Everyman wants company on his last journey, but Friendship, Family, and his Possessions all refuse to go with him. Then Knowledge says, "Everyman, I will go with thee, and be thy guide." Good Deeds joins them. So do Discretion (or right choice), Strength, Five Wits (or senses), and Beauty. But at the grave, only Good Deeds stays with Everyman.

We do not know the author or the age of the Everyman play. It was printed about 400 years ago, but the story is much older. It may have been written by a churchman, because many parts are like some of the ceremonies of the Catholic Church, for example, baptism, when a person joins the church, and the Last Sacrament, the final confession of sins

and forgiveness before death. The Everyman play is sometimes given today in cathedrals and churches, as well as on the stage.

evidence, the statements that are made and accepted in a court of law: see the section *trials* in the article LAW.

evolution

Millions of years ago, there was a small four-legged animal that roamed the plains of North America. It was about the size of a fox and had four toes on each front foot and three toes on each hind foot. This creature, which scientists today call *eohippus*, was the ancestor of the modern horse. As time went by the eohippus slowly changed. It grew larger, its legs became longer and stronger, and the toes on each foot grew together to form a single hoof. Gradually it became the big, strong horse we know today.

This change in form in a species or race of living creatures over a long period of time is called *evolution*.

SELECTIVE BREEDING

Men have known for thousands of years that all young animals inherit certain qualities from their parents. Men have used this knowledge to improve the usefulness of domestic animals, such as horses, cattle, sheep, dogs, and hogs. A sheep is more valuable if it has long hair, which makes wool. If two sheep that have long hair are allowed to breed (have babies), the lambs that are born to them will probably have long hair too. In any flock of sheep there are some that have longer hair than others. Shepherds would let the long-haired sheep breed, but not the shorter-haired sheep. Gradually, the sheep were improved until all of them today have much longer hair than their ancestors did thousands of years ago. In the same way, men have bred cattle that give better beef and more milk; horses that are stronger for pulling heavy loads or faster for running; and so on.

An English scientist named Charles DARWIN (about whom there is a sepa-

Chicago Natural Hist. Museum

This chart shows the evolution of the horse. The earliest ancestor of the horse was a tiny, foot-high animal called the *Eohippus*. During millions of years the Eohippus grew larger and developed into the horse as we know it today.

rate article) pointed out about a hundred years ago that the evolution of animals can be explained in the same way. He did this in a famous book called *Origin of Species*, which was published in 1859. Some of Darwin's ideas were not new, having been suggested by other scientists before him; some of his ideas caused long and angry arguments, and later scientists have found that he was mistaken about some things; but altogether he made a great contribution to knowledge.

NATURAL SELECTION

In nature, Darwin said, there is a desperate struggle to live. Big trees crowd out little ones. Meat-eating animals prey on grass-eating animals. In the oceans the big fish devour the smaller ones. Despite this the oceans are full of small fish and the jungles, forests, and plains of the world (where man does not interfere) are full of grass-eating animals. Every race of wild creatures finds a way to protect itself from its enemies and find its food so that it can continue to live. If it does not, it disappears from the face of the earth forever.

The eohippus of the past developed longer legs and became a faster runner; then it could outrun its meat-eating enemies. In the far north of Canada there is a rabbit whose fur is brown in the summer and white in the winter when the snow falls. If this Arctic rabbit remained brown in the winter it could easily be seen against the snow and might easily

be wiped out as a race by its natural enemies. Its thick coat protects it against the intense cold, and its enemies have difficulty seeing it against the snow. How did eohippus and the Arctic rabbit learn to change themselves? Man changes animals by selective breeding. Darwin says wild creatures change themselves by variation and natural selection.

By *variation* Darwin meant that each living creature is slightly different from its parents. It may be slower or faster than its parents, bigger or smaller, lighter or darker. Whatever the variation or change from its parents, it is something over which the animal has no control; it is simply born that way. The change may be so slight that it does not matter. On the other hand the change may be enough to make a great difference in the animal's life. Suppose it can run a little faster than its parents. That extra speed may mean the difference between life and death when it is being chased by an enemy that wants to eat it. Darwin called this process, in which the better-fitted animals survive while the others die, *natural selection*.

The animal that can run faster than its parents may mate with a female of its kind that will bear several young of which perhaps only one or two can run as fast as their father. The slower young animals may never live to grow up because they cannot outrun their natural enemies. In time all the slow animals are eliminated or destroyed and only the

faster ones remain to breed and carry on their race.

Of course, speed is not the only quality that fits a creature to live in its environment. It may develop a color of skin or fur that prevents its enemies from seeing it easily, or a hard armored shell like a turtle's, or an unpleasant smell like the skunk's, or big, powerful jaws and sharp teeth with which it can catch its prey more easily. The creatures that never develop variations of shapes or other changes that may be necessary for continued living just die out. We do not know why the ancient dinosaurs and other great reptiles disappeared from the earth. Some scientists think that there may have been a sudden change in the climate that destroyed their food supply, or perhaps it became too cold for them. In any case, they could not change themselves to fit themselves to the new conditions of life about them. The ants seem to have reached the end of their evolution millions of years ago. Having found a form or shape that enabled them to keep on living despite the many changes in the world about them during the past 50 million years, ants have not changed any more.

exchange, a place where businessmen buy or sell or trade something: see the articles on COMMODITY EXCHANGE and STOCK EXCHANGE.

exchequer

Exchequer is the word used in England for the national purse or government bank account. It is the department of the British government that receives and keeps the tax money paid by its citizens. The treasury is the department of the government that controls the spending of the money in the exchequer on orders from the head of the government. The official in charge of the exchequer in England is called the Chancellor of the Exchequer.

excise tax

Excise tax is a tax on goods produced and bought within the same country. In the United States such taxes may be levied by the federal government in Washington, D.C., or by state governments. The federal government levies excise taxes on tobacco, and every package of cigarettes, cigars, or pipe tobacco must have a stamp attached to it to show that the tax has been paid. There are federal and state excise taxes on liquor and gasoline. Many city governments have excise taxes on sales, usually called a *sales tax,* which may be one cent to three cents on every dollar spent to buy anything in the city except food.

excommunication

One of the meanings of the word *communion* is all the people who belong to Christian churches, or to a particular church in the Christian religion. Any member of a church who does not follow the beliefs of the group excommunicates himself, because the word *ex* means "out of" in the Latin language, and he goes outside of the communion or church when he breaks its laws. In the Roman Catholic Church there may be a public announcement of the excommunication

of a person or even a whole country. This announcement is made by the Pope.

exercise

Exercise is the use of our muscles in order to improve our health and agility. It includes games and sports, calisthenics, swimming, gymnastics, and weight-lifting. Some types of amusement are considered exercise, such as dancing, horseback riding, camping, and boating. When we exercise, it causes better circulation of blood, which nourishes the muscles. Our muscles are intended for use, and when they are seldom used they lose their efficiency.

Most people of all ages are benefited by exercise, but each person should know his own needs and be careful not to .exceed his limit. Very active work, such as mountain-climbing or weight-lifting, would be very dangerous to anyone having a weak heart. When you are out of breath after exercising, it is important to rest, since overexertion can strain the heart by giving it too much work to do.

Schwinn Bicycle Co.

Although this bicycle does not take its rider anywhere, it provides year-round exercise.

Exodus

Exodus is the name of the second book of the Old Testament. The word *exodus* means "going out." This book of the Bible tells the story of how the Jewish people, who were slaves in Egypt, went out of Egypt and became free. Their leader was Moses and he was helped by his brother, Aaron. The book tells the story of the birth of Moses and how God chose him to take his people out of slavery. It tells how God punished the Egyptians with ·sickness and death for being cruel to the Jews, but the Egyptians continued to be cruel. Finally the Jews left the country. They marched day and night, with an Egyptian army after them. The Jews came to the Red Sea. They had no boats, but God made the waters of the sea separate so the Jews could walk over to the other side. Then God sent the waters back and the Egyptian army was drowned.

Moses then led his people through wilderness and desert to the sacred mountain, Mt. Sinai. Here God gave Moses the Ten Commandments and other religious laws. Then Moses led them to the

borders of the land God had promised them for their home. This land is called Canaan, or Palestine. Here Moses died.

Every spring Jewish people everywhere in the world celebrate their exodus from Egypt in a great holiday. The name of the holiday is PASSOVER, and you can read about it in a separate article.

expansion and contraction

Expansion means growing larger, contraction means growing smaller. Most solids, liquids and gases expand when heated, and contract when cooled. In laying railroad tracks, spaces are left between rail sections to allow for expansion in hot weather. If these spaces were not left, the rails would expand and twist out of shape.

For the same reason inch-wide gaps are left between segments of concrete highways, and expansion links placed in the roadways of bridges. The roadway of the George Washington Bridge, a 3,500-foot suspension bridge connecting New York City with New Jersey, may expand or contract as much as thirty feet in extreme temperature changes. This is taken care of by the links in the roadway and expansion joints on the towers from which the cables hang. During very cold weather, the joints will contract, causing the roadway to curve above the water. During very warm weather, the joints will expand, causing the roadway to flatten out. This prevents bumps and cracks from forming in the roadway.

Warm weather also causes the metal parts in a clock to expand, causing the clock to lose time. In cold weather, these parts contract, causing the clock to gain time.

The rocks on the earth are gradually worn down by expansion and contraction. The heat of the day causes them to expand, the cold of the night to contract. This makes them flaky, and causes thin sheets to peel off the rocks.

All matter is made up of small particles called molecules with spaces between them. These molecules are constantly moving about, and pushing against each other. Heat causes them to move more rapidly, cold to move more slowly. When a substance is heated, its molecules push harder against each other. This increases their distance from each other and causes the substance to expand.

Because the molecules of a gas are not held together with as much force as the molecules of a liquid or solid, a gas expands much more than a liquid or solid. The expansion of gases is used in the steam engine, where the pressure of the expanding steam moves a piston in a cylinder. Gas thermometers are more sensitive than liquid thermometers because of the ease with which gases expand with the slightest rise in temperature.

The same rise in temperature will cause different amounts of expansion in different materials. Brass, for example, will expand more than iron. This fact is used in making a thermostat, a device used to regulate temperature in the home. A strip of brass and a strip of iron are welded together to form a compound bar. When heated, the brass expands more than the iron causing the bar to bend in the direction of the iron. This causes the

bar to shut off a gas or oil burner. If the bar is cooled, it will bend the other way, turning on the burner. (There is a separate article on THERMOSTAT.)

EXPANSION OF ICE

At certain temperatures some substances will expand rather than contract when they are cooled. When water is cooled to or near to the freezing point, it will expand. This is why frozen milk will push out through the top of a milk bottle and sometimes even crack it. The expansion of water in the motors and radiators of automobile engines can cause them to crack. A solution of antifreeze is used in cars in winter, to lower the point at which the water in the engine would normally freeze.

The fact that water expands when it freezes means the difference between life and death to fish and other creatures that live in the bottoms of lakes that are about to freeze. When a pond of water cools toward the freezing point, the surface next to the cold air cools first. As it nears the freezing point and expands, it floats. The ice that is formed floats on the surface, forming a protective cover for the water underneath and preventing it from freezing.

Scientists explain the expansion of ice by the fact that water molecules occur in groups rather than singly. When water begins to freeze, these molecules regroup themselves in such a way as to cause ice to expand.

expatriate

An expatriate is a man or woman who gives up citizenship in his own country and becomes a citizen of another nation. For instance, an American who became a citizen of England would be an expatriate, and so would a Frenchman who became an American citizen.

Sometimes a person changes his citizenship because he wants to. Millions of people from Europe have come to the United States and become Americans in this way. Sometimes a man's citizenship is taken away from him because he has broken a law. For instance, an American soldier who runs away and is tried and found guilty of desertion loses his citizenship. If an American leaves the United States during wartime because he does not want to serve in the army, he also loses his citizenship. A boy or girl does not lose citizenship because his or her parents give up or lose theirs. Any child born in the United States remains an American even if his parents become expatriates.

experiment

An experiment is a way of testing an idea. The word *experiment* comes from a Latin word meaning "test," or "trial." When you perform an experiment, you are trying out an idea to see if it works. If it does, the idea is correct; if it does not, it is incorrect.

Modern science is based mostly on experiments. For that reason it is often called experimental science. Chemistry, physics and biology are all experimental sciences. Scientists who perform experiments are called research or experimental scientists. The ideas they experiment with

are thought up by a special group of scientists called theoretical scientists. *Theory* is another word for an idea that has not as yet been experimented with. Some scientists are both experimental and theoretical scientists.

The principle of experimental science is that nothing should be believed simply because "it seems reasonable" or "obviously it must be true." Until it has been proved by experiment, it is only a theory. Scientists will accept it as fact only after experiments have proved it true.

In experimental science, the first requirement is to know the difference between proof and coincidence. Suppose research workers are testing a medicine. They give the medicine to fifty people who have a certain disease. All fifty people get well. That is *not* proof that the medicine cures the disease. Maybe the fifty people would all have gotten well anyway. Now suppose the same fifty people are taken, and twenty-five of them are given the medicine but the other twenty-five are not given the medicine. The twenty-five who were given the medicine get well and the other twenty-five do not get well. This can be accepted as experimental proof that the medicine cures the disease. Such a method is said to give the experimenters a control on the experiment.

When a true scientist experiments, he does not care whether the experiment proves or disproves the theory. He is interested only in finding out what is true. This makes his work "pure science." If he is anxious to prove that a certain thing is true, his wishes may cause him to judge the result of the experiment the way he wants it to be instead of the way it actually is.

explosion and explosives

An explosion is a sudden and violent release of heat, gases, or both, accompanied by a loud noise. Explosions can occur in several ways. They may occur when a gas is under extreme pressure, or when a gas is heated and suddenly expands. Explosions can also occur when certain substances are mixed together and set afire by a flame or a spark. The mild explosion of a mixture of air and drops of gasoline is used to power internal combustion (gasoline) engines. The power is supplied by the rapidly expanding gases that are produced.

Flour dust mixed with air often will explode when a flame is brought near. Ether and air, naphtha and air, benzol and air are some other mixtures that are highly explosive when near a flame. These mixtures burn rapidly and produce large quantities of hot gases.

Other substances such as acetylene gas explode easily without being mixed with air when they are sufficiently compressed and heated.

EXPLOSIVES

There are certain chemicals that when mixed together can be easily exploded. These are called explosives, and may be in the form of solids, liquids, or gases. They may be exploded by heat, by a flame, by rubbing, or by shock. In all cases the pressure of hot gases that are rapidly produced is the cause of the explosion.

The first explosive ever made was gunpowder, a mixture of potassium nitrate (called *niter* or *saltpeter*), sulfur, and charcoal. It is also called black powder or blasting powder. It is used in fuses and for breaking up rocks and ores in mines. It is a *low explosive,* which means that it explodes at a slow speed. It explodes upon burning and gives off a great deal of smoke. The temperature of the explosion is about 4760 degrees on the Fahrenheit scale. Gunpowder was once widely used in small arms ammunition but has since been replaced by smokeless powder, a mixture of nitrocellulose, nitroglycerine, and TNT.

Other kinds of explosives can be exploded very rapidly and without burning. These are called *primary explosives* or *primers* because their explosion is often used to set off other explosives. These include mixtures of nitrogen and chlorine; sulfur and chlorine; and mercury, nitric acid, and alcohol. They can be easily exploded by heat, by rubbing or striking, or by electric current. They explode very rapidly. Rapid explosion often is called *detonation.*

High explosives are exploded by shock waves from primary explosives. They include dynamite, TNT, blasting powder, gelatin (nitrocellulose mixed with acetone), amatol (ammonia and nitrogen), ammonal (a mixture of amatol, aluminum and charcoal), and liquid oxygen in wood pulp. The safest of these is TNT.

High explosives are used for blasting purposes and in bombs, shells, and mines, where great shattering effect, called *brisance,* is needed.

The explosion of atomic and hydrogen bombs is accomplished by the sudden release of millions of degrees of heat. Atomic bomb explosion is caused by atomic fission, hydrogen bomb explosion by atomic fusion. You can read more about this in separate articles on ATOMIC BOMB and HYDROGEN BOMB.

export, sending products from the place where they are made to a buyer in a foreign or distant place: see the article on FOREIGN TRADE.

exposition, a show that is open to the public: see the articles on FAIR and WORLD FAIR.

extreme unction

Extreme unction means "last anointing." Anointing is the rubbing on of oil. In the Roman Catholic Church extreme unction is given by the priest to someone who is dying. The priest uses holy oil, or oil that has been blessed by a bishop on Maundy Thursday, the Thursday before Easter. The priest anoints the eyes, ears, nostrils, lips, hands, and feet of the dying person. This act sometimes serves to ask God to forgive the dying person for sins that he cannot confess. See the article on CONFESSION.

eye

The eye is very much like a camera, for the camera was copied from the eye. Although the camera will never be as delicate and wonderful as the eye, you can learn a lot about how your eyes work by studying what a camera (and especially a motion-picture camera) is and how it works.

SIGHT

Both the eye and the camera work because they collect and make a record of light. Light is made of tiny rays or waves; when all these tiny rays are added together they make what you call light. They can bounce off, or reflect, from many of the things or objects with which we live. When they do this the eye feels them; it collects and records them as the moving colors and shades we call "sight."

HOW THE EYE IS MADE

Your eyes are set in deep bony sockets in your head that protect them from being hit by all but small objects. On the outside of your eye is your eyelid. It protects the eye from too much light and from small things that might fly into the eye. The underside of the eyelid is always moist, to keep the eyeball from drying up, and to wash away tiny specks with the fluid we call tears. Next there is the sclerotic coat, a strong and tough layer that covers the back as well as the front of the eyeball. On the front of the eyeball it is called the cornea and it is transparent, meaning that you can see through it. The white part of the eye that you see in the mirror is also part of the sclerotic coat. Between the cornea and the brown or blue part of the eye is a lens made of fluid and called the aqueous humor; it helps you to focus when you see. It also helps the eye to keep its shape; without it the eye would collapse like a balloon without any air in it.

The black part in the center of the eye is a hole through which the light can enter in order for you to see, and the brown or blue part is a tiny muscle called the iris. The iris gets larger or smaller to allow the right amount of light through for you to see correctly. In a bright light, the black part becomes very small, because too much light will hurt your eye. Inside is the crystalline, or solid, lens of the eye; it can get larger or smaller when pulled by tiny ligaments and muscles which surround it, and this helps you to see clearly when you look at near or far objects. Behind the lens and filling up most of the whole eyeball, but not seen from the outside, is more of the transparent "humor" fluid, called the vitreous humor. This fluid also helps the eye to keep its round shape and is used by you as a lens.

On the back wall of the inside of the eye is the retina, which is a layer of millions of tiny nerves whose endings, called rods and cones, collect all of the light waves together from all the things you are able to see after the outer parts of the eye have prepared the waves. The cones receive colors and shapes, and the rods help you to see movements. Color-blind people have cones that do not work properly. In the center of the retina is a "spot-for-best-vision," which, without thinking about it, you use for looking at one particular thing, such as a word when you are reading; this is called focusing. Below the focusing spot is another called the blind spot; you do not see any light waves that are focused (gathered together) on this spot, for here is where the large optic nerve leaves the back of

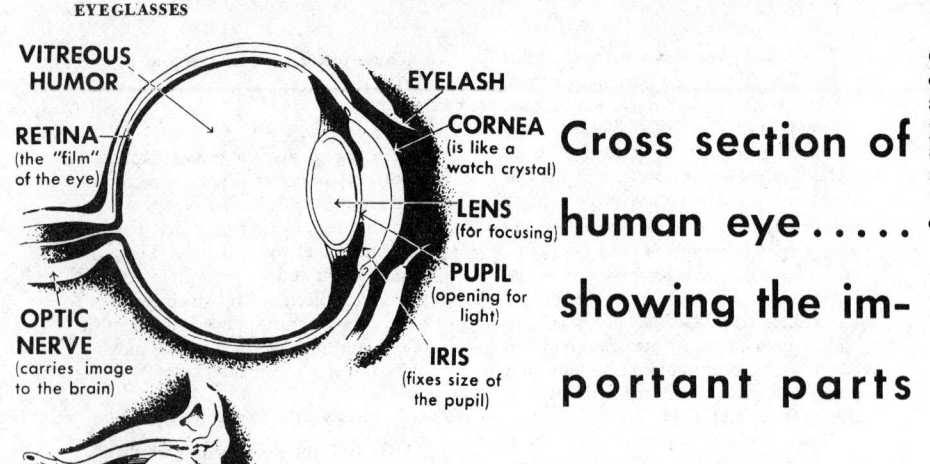

VITREOUS HUMOR

RETINA
(the "film" of the eye)

EYELASH

CORNEA
(is like a watch crystal)

LENS
(for focusing)

PUPIL
(opening for light)

OPTIC NERVE
(carries image to the brain)

IRIS
(fixes size of the pupil)

Cross section of human eye..... showing the important parts

eyewash or water in an eyecup; if that does not get it out, or if something more serious gets into the eye or punctures it, put a cold, wet, clean cloth over the eye and see the doctor. If a chemical, such as an acid or lye, burns the eye, wash it with lots of water while waiting for the doctor.

eyeglasses, see GLASSES.

Muscles move the eye up or down, right or left

Better Vision Inst., Inc.

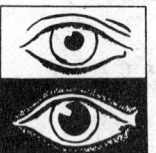

The pupil lets in the right amount of light . . . .

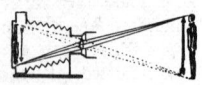

The eye—like the camera "takes pictures" upside down

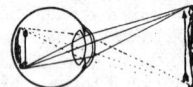

the eye to carry the eye's messages to the brain.

HOW YOU SEE

If you understand the parts of the eye you already know pretty well how you see. The humorous, or fluid, lenses, the crystalline lens, and the iris muscle all work together to let in just the right amount of light waves and bring them together, or focus, at the right place on the retina; the retina sends a series of pictures to the brain very rapidly so that you see things as they move. To make your eyes turn from side to side, up and down, and to help them work together while you are seeing, you have three pairs of small muscles connected to the sides, top, and bottom of the eyes; you can feel them work by looking quickly from side to side. Your eyes also see depth, the third dimension, because there are two of them giving you two pictures all the time; you learn to see and recognize depth because of the slight difference in the two pictures. Close one eye and reach out to touch something in front of you; you will notice that you can't easily tell how far away it is. And did you know that you actually see things upside down all the time? When you were a baby your brain learned the habit of putting things right side up and making the correction for you, so that it is now so automatic that you cannot even think about it.

PROTECTING THE EYE

Never forget how precious your eyes are, for they bring to you most of the wonderful things of your life. If you can

help it, never read by weak light or close to a glaring light. Good light is strong, comfortable, steady light that comes from behind your shoulders; daylight is the best, so do not do eye work at night that you can do in the day. Do not make a bad habit of staring or looking down while reading, for if you do this for several years the muscles and lenses may get set one way and lose their ability to focus themselves on things farther away. The strength of your eyes goes with the strength of the rest of your body, so if you are ill, wait until your body is strong again before using your eyes a lot.

EYE DISEASES AND EYE OPERATIONS

When either the lens or the muscles of the eye are not perfect, a person's sight is not as good as it should be. About one out of every four young people has some sort of eye trouble, and about three out of four people who are more than 50 years old.

If the lenses do not have the right shape, the light will not be properly focused when it reaches the retina. This can lead to nearsightedness, farsightedness, or other conditions that cause objects to appear blurred. Most troubles of this kind can be corrected by proper GLASSES, about which there is a separate article.

If the outer muscles of the eye do not work properly, a person may be cross-eyed. Doctors can usually help or cure cross-eyed children, especially if the treatment is begun when they are young. Read the article on STRABISMUS.

When a crystalline lens is clouded so that a person cannot see clearly through it, he is said to have a cataract. Cataracts can cause blindness, but modern operations can often cure them or replace a bad crystalline lens with a good one. Usually, only older people have cataracts.

A bad cornea, also, may be replaced. See the section on eye-banks in the article on BLINDNESS.

Glaucoma is a disease in which the eyeball hardens. Like cataracts, it seldom occurs in young people. Treatment or an operation to remove excess fluids will often cure or control glaucoma.

FIRST AID FOR THE EYE

Tiny particles or specks that get in the eye can usually be taken out by using

Ezekiel

Ezekiel was a priest and prophet who lived more than 2,500 years ago. A prophet is a person inspired by God to teach and to predict what will happen in the future. In Ezekiel's time, King Nebuchadnezzar of Babylon attacked the Jews and carried many of them into exile in Babylon. Ezekiel was one of them. He began to see visions, and he felt that God was telling him to speak to the people. The book of Ezekiel in the Bible tells the things that Ezekiel taught and prophesied to the exiled Jews. Ezekiel said that the Jews in their homeland were sinful and bad. They had not been loyal to God. Their religion was not pure, and did not follow the old laws. For this reason God was angry with the Jews, and He would punish them. The city of Jerusalem and the great temple would be destroyed by the enemies of the Jews. About ten years later the city was captured by the people of Babylon, and the temple was destroyed. Then Ezekiel tried to lead the Jews in Babylon to keep the true religion. He prophesied that some day all the enemies of the Jews would be destroyed and the Jews would return to their home. A new and good city of Jerusalem would arise, and the temple of God would be rebuilt.

Ezra

Ezra was a great leader of the Jews who lived about 2,400 years ago. In Roman Catholic Bibles he is called Esdras. He is known as the Scribe. A scribe is a writer, and Ezra is thought to be the writer of the Books of Chronicles and the Book of Ezra in the Bible. More than a hundred years before Ezra's time, the land of the Jews had been conquered by the people of Babylon. The great temple of the Jews had been destroyed, and the people had been taken into exile. They lived near Babylon, and there Ezra was born and brought up. In Ezra's time, the king of Babylon decided to let the Jews go back to their home and rebuild their temple at Jerusalem. Ezra was the leader of a large group of these exiles who went back to Jerusalem. In Jerusalem, Ezra worked to reform and purify the religion of the Jews. He was a learned man, and he led the people to return to the old laws of their religion. The Book of Ezra tells the history of the Jews during an eighty-year period, five hundred years before the birth of Jesus. The book of Nehemiah tells what happened next.

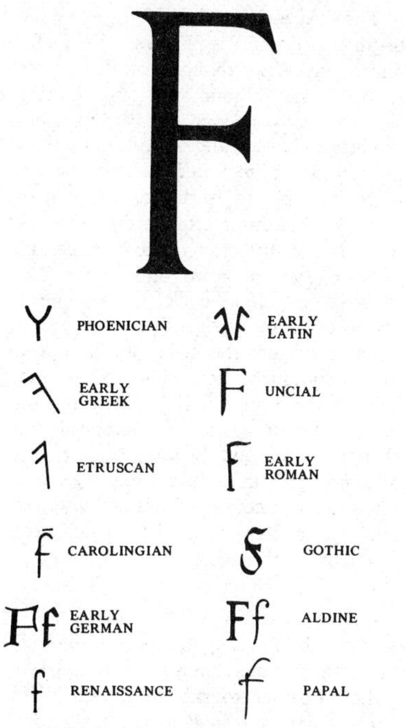
PHOENICIAN
EARLY LATIN
EARLY GREEK
UNCIAL
ETRUSCAN
EARLY ROMAN
CAROLINGIAN
GOTHIC
EARLY GERMAN
ALDINE
RENAISSANCE
PAPAL

The letter F is the sixth letter of the alphabet. It can be traced all the way back to the earliest writing known to man, in Egypt thousands of years ago. In the Hebrew language, in which much of the Bible was written, the letter was *he.* The ancient Greeks took this same letter, removed the lowest of its three bars, and called it *digamma.* In the Greek language the digamma is believed to have had the sound of our *v* or *w.* The letter was dropped out of use by the Greeks and was later adopted by the Romans for their alphabet. It gradually came to have the sound that we know today.

At the top of this page, at the far left, you can see what the early Greek letter *digamma* looked like in its beginning stage of development. In those early times, writing was not read from left to right as it is today in our culture, but from right to left. (In some old languages, such as Hebrew, writing is still read from right to left.) However, the later Greeks changed this system and began to read from left to right. When this change was made, the Greeks also turned the individual letters around. That is, whereas previously the letters (from our present point of view) faced right, they were made to face left. *Digamma* thereafter looked much like our own letter F.

Read also the article ALPHABET.

fable

A fable is a very short story that is intended to teach a lesson. The lesson is called the moral of the story. Most fables have animals as characters, acting as though they were human beings. This is not necessary, and there are many fables in which the characters are not animals.

Almost three thousand years ago the ancient Greeks wrote fables, and the most famous of these Greeks, Aesop, used animals as characters, so that became the style of fable that we always think of first. Many writers since have written the same kind of fable. You can read more about the fable, and read examples of fables, in the articles on AESOP and LA FONTAINE.

Not much more than fifty years ago, an American writer named George Ade wrote a series of stories that he called *Fables in Slang.* They were intended to be humorous and to use many of the new words called slang that the American people were using but that had not yet appeared in dictionaries.

There is a great difference between the fable and the parable, although each is a story intended to teach a lesson. The moral of the fable is usually something that is either humorous or good advice, but it is not intended to teach the lofty kind of lesson that Jesus had in mind when he taught his Disciples by parables.

Fabre, Jean Henri

Jean Henri Fabre was a French scientist. He was born at St. Leon, France,

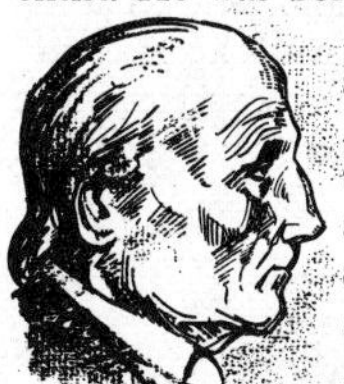

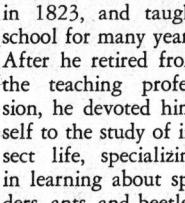

in 1823, and taught school for many years. After he retired from the teaching profession, he devoted himself to the study of insect life, specializing in learning about spiders, ants, and beetles. In 1907 he published a ten-volume set of books describing what he had learned. Parts of it have been printed in English, and his observations were so accurate that they have been used in entomology, which is insect study, for many years. He died in 1915.

face

The face of an animal or a person is the part of the head on which are the eyes, nose, mouth, and ears. These are the organs of four of the five senses: sight, smell, taste, and hearing. Almost everything we know enters the brain through one of these four senses. The fifth sense is the sense of touch.

Often we can tell what part of the world a person comes from by looking at his face. The facial features of different kinds of people are one of the ways used by scientists to classify the peoples of the world.

The face often expresses the thoughts of a person better than the words he speaks. Usually a person cannot help smiling when he is amused or frowning when he is puzzled or displeased. This is not something we learn to do; it is natural to us. On the contrary, we learn to prevent our faces from always showing how we feel, because often it is polite to do so. We also use our facial expressions intentionally to show our feelings. If a person smiles and says, "I am going to hit you," the smile tells you he is only joking.

factor

A factor is a kind of businessman who buys and sells things for other people. One type of factor might represent farmers. The farmer raises food and the factor does the selling of it. The factor takes a part of the money he sells it for. He uses this to pay his expenses and to pay himself for his work. This is called a commission. For example, he might sell a thousand dollars' worth of vegetables for a farmer, keep $250 for his commission, and send $750 to the farmer. Many businessmen who used to be called factors are now more often called agents or brokers, but it is the same kind of business.

One method of lending money is called factoring. This kind of factor is somewhat different from a banker. He often lends money in cases in which bankers are prevented by law or by banking custom from lending money. For example, a businessman might have sold some goods to customers and have sent them bills for it, but the customers are not required to pay him for a month or two. He can take the bills and sell them to a factor. The factor gives him the money at once and gets it back when the customers pay. The factor charges a fee that is like the interest the bank charges on a loan, but it is usually at least two or three times as much as the bank would charge.

Factor is also a term in multiplication, which is a branch of arithmetic. See the article on ARITHMETIC.

factory

A factory is a building in which workmen use machines to make things. Different kinds of factory are called by different names, such as mill, works, foundry, assembly plant, and others, depending on the exact kind of manufacturing they do. There are hundreds of thousands of factories in the United States. Some are very small and some are so huge that they have as many as forty thousand or more people working in them.

Big factories have been known for only about two hundred years. Before then, things were made by skilled workers in little shops. The big factory came in with the INDUSTRIAL REVOLUTION, about which there is a separate article.

The first factories were the cheapest kind of building that men could put up. No attention was paid to the comfort or health of the workmen. Now there is a great difference. Factories are built so that they are the most comfortable and healthful places possible. Modern factories have many conveniences for the workers. They have rest rooms and recreation rooms. Sometimes music is played while the employees are working. There are cafeterias where the workers can buy food, and dining rooms where they can eat lunches they have brought from home. There is a dispensary or infirmary with a doctor or nurse in attendance in case any worker becomes ill or is injured on the job. Many factories nowadays are made with soundproofed walls and ceilings, because research has shown that people work better in quiet surroundings.

PLANNING A FACTORY

There are several things that are considered very important in planning a modern factory. The first is location. The factory must have good transportation so that raw materials can be brought in and the finished products can be shipped to the places where they are to be sold. Usually this means that the factory has to be very close to a railroad. Factories

usually have private tracks, called spurs or sidings, that run into or next to the factory building so that goods can be unloaded and loaded conveniently. The trains may be made up so that a freight car containing certain things stops right beside the department where those things are needed. Some big factories are built on rivers or lakes so that goods can be shipped by water.

Another important thing about location is that the factory must be placed so that the people who work there can get to it easily by streetcar or bus, or in their own automobiles. Factories are often built some distance out in the country so that there will be plenty of parking space and so that the land will not be too expensive.

The second important step in planning a factory is to use the floor space in the best way possible. The floors themselves are a special problem, because the machinery is often very heavy. Engineers have to study how much weight the floor has to carry and then design a floor that will carry that much weight. The factory must be planned in advance so that the machines will be as close as possible to each other in order to use the space economically, but not so close together that the workmen will lack room to move around. This is also a problem for engineers.

Light is very important in most kinds of manufacturing, and for that reason many factories have nearly solid glass sides and skylights to let in as much natural light as possible. The most modern factories are likely to have no windows at all, because artificial lighting is so much better than it used to be. Having no windows also helps insulate the building to keep it warm in winter and cool in summer. In manufacturing of many kinds, air conditioning is used, and it is easier to air-condition a building when there are no windows.

For many years factories often had two or three or even more stories. For the last forty to fifty years, however, almost all new factories have been built with only one floor. This is especially important when the workers have to handle heavy things, so that elevators or conveyors are not needed to move the things up and down between floors.

Nearly every factory is very carefully fenced in, and each employee has a badge and a number. No one can get in without showing his badge. There are three principal reasons for this. One reason is to protect the things in the factory from theft when it is closed down. Another is that if someone who is not an employee wanders in and gets hurt, the factory may have to pay damages. The third reason is secrecy. In many factories, the products are made by secret processes, and the owners do not want anybody to learn about them. In wartime, secrecy is even more important.

Faeröe Islands

The Faeröe Islands are a group of twenty-one islands far north in the Atlantic Ocean. They are about 2,000 miles from the United States and about 250 miles from Scotland. About 33,000 people live there. The islands have their own government, but they are a part of the kingdom of Denmark. The land is too rocky for farming, and most of the people live by raising sheep. The name of the islands means "sheep islands." Many of the people are fishermen. Thorshavn is the capital of the islands. The people speak a Scandinavian language called Faerish.

Fahrenheit, Gabriel

Gabriel Fahrenheit was a German scientist who invented the mercury thermometer. This thermometer is known as the Fahrenheit thermometer, and it measures accurately all temperatures between the freezing and the boiling points of water. On the Fahrenheit thermometer, water freezes at 32 degrees and boils at 212 degrees. The normal body temperature of a human being is 98.6 degrees. Fahrenheit was born in 1686. When he was a young man he became interested in making a more accurate thermometer than the alcohol thermometer used at the time, and succeeded with his mercury thermometer. There is a separate article on THERMOMETERS. Gabriel Fahrenheit died in 1736.

faïence

Faïence is a kind of glazed pottery. It was extremely popular about five hundred years ago. It was used for things around the house, such as bowls and plates. In recent years it has become popular again. Faïence is sometimes called *majolica*. It is sometimes decorated with green leaves, or red apples, or other colored shapes. It was first made, and still is, in a town in Italy called Faenza. In Faenza there is a large museum filled with pottery from all over the world. You can read how faïence is made in the article on POTTERY.

fainting

When a person becomes unconscious for a short time, we say he has fainted, or swooned. Fainting happens because the brain does not receive enough blood to keep it working in the normal way. The medical name for it is *syncope*. Almost always doctors consider that there is nothing serious, and nothing to worry about, in fainting.

Something sudden (doctors call it a shock) occurs before a person faints. It may be something that happens to a person's body, such as a sudden injury, or it may be something that suddenly frightens him. In either case some other part of the body borrows more blood than the brain can spare for a short time. The brain is not hurt by this. Soon the normal amount of blood will be returned to the brain and the person will again be conscious as he was before.

People who are weak from illness, or from lack of food or fresh air, are more likely to faint than those who are strong and healthy.

Also likely to faint are people who have the illness called anemia. Anemic people either have a little less than the normal amount of blood, or else not quite enough good blood. Some people faint whenever something exciting or frightening occurs, and even doctors cannot explain it, for they seem, otherwise, to be perfectly normal and healthy.

The clearest sign that fainting is near, or about to occur, is paleness of the face and hands. Also, though you do not see it, the heartbeat and rate of breathing slow down. If someone actually does faint the first and best thing to do is to put him or her into a reclining position where there is plenty of fresh air, then loosen any tight clothing around the waist or neck. It is even better if the head can be lowered and the arms and legs raised. This brings blood back into the head. Spirits of ammonia is also helpful to get more blood into the head. Spirits of ammonia should be held close to the nose so that the fumes will be breathed in; cold water or ice on the forehead and chest are also good. If doing these things does not help in a short time, then it is likely that something more serious than fainting has happened. That would be a problem for the doctor.

fair

A fair is a large temporary market, where many merchants and tradesmen gather together to show and sell their wares. Fairs were held in the early days of the Greek and Roman empires, two thousand years ago, and they became very important in Europe during the Middle Ages, more than five hundred years ago.

There was little trade between the many cities and kingdoms of Europe at that time. The people depended on the traveling merchants who went from town to town selling the goods they had obtained from many distant lands. Traveling in Europe during the Middle Ages was a very difficult problem. There were only a few roads, and on those roads there were bandits and other difficulties to be overcome. Many merchants began to travel together in groups in order to protect themselves from these dangers. Each time a group of these merchants would enter a new town, they would ask permission from the city authorities to hold a fair. This meant that they would be allowed to set up temporary stalls and small shops to show and sell the goods they had brought with them. As time went by, these fairs became larger and were soon held only in special towns and at certain times of the year.

Not all the visitors who came to the fair came to buy the many different goods. Many came to see their friends, and others came to amuse themselves after a year of hard work. The fair was a place for amusement and laughter as well as a place to buy and sell things. You could listen to musicians and watch actors put on special shows. There were jugglers and acrobats and plays to amuse the crowds. Gay parties were held in the inns of the town where the fair was being held.

The streets would be decorated with colored paper and flowers, and at night they would be lighted with flaming torches. After a few weeks the fair would close, and the merchants would pack up their goods and depart for another town where a new fair was to be held.

MODERN FAIRS

The fairs held in the United States today are usually agricultural fairs. They are held in cities and towns that are near many farms. The farmers bring samples

of their best vegetables and fruits to the fairs, as well as their best animals. The goods and animals are then judged, and the farmers who have the best crops and the best animals win prizes. Sometimes the farmers sell their goods at the fairs. The women bring cooked foods to the fairs, pies and cakes and preserves, as well as samples of their knitted, crocheted and embroidered work. These also are judged for prizes. Then they may be sold to the people who come to the fair. The farm children may bring their pets to the fair to try for prizes, or they may enter special contests with plants and animals that they have raised.

Manufacturers of farm equipment and of feed for animals set up booths at these fairs to exhibit their products and to explain anything new on the market. Representatives of the local or state agricultural groups may give demonstrations to the women, showing them the newest and best ways to preserve food, to make rugs, or to raise chickens.

Often a carnival is also set up at the fairgrounds. There may be a merry-go-round and a Ferris wheel and other rides, and many booths for the amusement of the visitors. There may also be horse racing.

Organizations from the local clubs and churches often serve food to the people at the fair.

Usually the fair ends late at night with a large square dance. Most agricultural fairs are held in the early fall, after the crops have been harvested.

Another kind of fair is the World's Fair, or International Exposition. There is a separate article on WORLD'S FAIR.

Fairbanks

Fairbanks is a city in the center of Alaska. It is on a branch of the Tanana River. About 14,770 (1970) people live in Fairbanks. They make their living by mining, fishing, and lumbering. Fairbanks is a city of comfortable houses and fine buildings. The houses must be built small and light, because otherwise they might sink into the frozen ground. Some of the houses are cracked and tilted because they were built wrong. The University of Alaska is only four miles from Fairbanks. The Alaska Railroad runs to Fairbanks, and the great Alaska Highway ends there. There are several other good highways and an airport. Fairbanks was settled by men who went to Alaska to hunt for gold more than fifty years ago.

Fairbanks, Douglas

Douglas Fairbanks was one of the most famous motion-picture actors from the earliest days of the films until the 1930s. He was a fine athlete, and for that reason he could play parts in which

he had to climb cliffs and make great leaps and fight off many men with a sword. Some of his most famous roles were in *The Three Musketeers, The Thief of Bagdad,* and *Robin Hood,* but he also played in more serious films, including Shakespeare's *The Taming of the Shrew.*

Fairbanks was born in Denver, Colorado, in 1883. He got his first job as an actor when he was 17, but before that he had worked at several other jobs. When he was about 22 he went to Hollywood to enter the new industry called motion pictures. Fairbanks was married three times. The most famous of his wives was Mary Pickford, who was as great a star as he was. He was a founder of United Artists, one of the big producing companies, and therefore he became one of the richest men in the motion-picture industry. Douglas Fairbanks died in 1939.

Douglas Fairbanks, Jr., his son, was born in 1909. He also became a noted motion-picture and television actor, although never as famous as his father was.

Fair Deal

The Fair Deal was the name given to the policies of President Harry S. Truman and his administration when he was President of the United States from 1945 to 1953. Much of this program was the same as the program of President Franklin D. Roosevelt, which was called the New Deal.

The outstanding things that President Truman and his Fair Deal administration tried to have passed into law by Congress were national health insurance, by which everyone would receive medical and hospital treatment, and the Fair Employment Practices Commission, also called FEPC, by which employers could not refuse jobs to working people on account of their race or religion. The Fair Deal administration did not succeed in having these laws passed. Some of the laws that they did have passed were continuation of rent control so that landlords could not raise rents in some places, and an increase in benefits from Social Security and unemployment insurance.

Although President Truman was a member of the Democratic Party and his was a Democratic administration, Democratic as well as Republican Congressmen opposed some parts of his program.

fairy and fairy tale

People have always been trying to understand why things happen as they do. Before so many things were explained by science, people thought that the world was filled with strange creatures, not at all like men, who made the seasons change, rivers flow, men fight or sleep, and so on.

The more powerful and important of these creatures were called gods and goddesses; the smaller creatures with less important jobs were called fairies, elves, brownies, goblins, kobolds, imps, sprites, gnomes, leprechauns, djinns and many other names.

These ideas are very old; they are almost as old as man himself. When little things went wrong man would try to fix them up by calling on the "little people" to help him. Sometimes it was to his "guardian spirit" that he prayed; sometimes it was to his "lares and penates," or spirits of his house, or to his ancestors; sometimes it was to the creatures of the woods or fields that he called for help out of small troubles. He called on the gods for help out of *big* troubles.

At the same time, he began to think that some of the "little people" were causing his troubles, so an idea of careless or "bad" spirits began to be common. You can read about the activities of these bad "little people" in a poem called "Tam O'Shanter" by Robert Burns. In this poem a human being is annoyed or tormented by a group of merry, but evil, spirits.

WHAT THE "LITTLE PEOPLE" ARE LIKE

The *elf* is a mischievous creature, always ready to tangle and break up things. Sometimes bad dreams were blamed on the elves, and when horses were found with the hair of their manes tangled into tight, painful little knots (or "elf locks") the elves were blamed. Sometimes they were accused of putting an elf child, or "changeling," into a cradle after stealing a human child; the changeling would grow up to be a strange, evil child with wild habits. If the elves were treated right, they would sometimes clean your house for you, or help you in your business, but you could never trust them for a moment; they might get playful and wreck your house.

The *kobold* was a kind of tame elf that was supposed to take care of the house and sleep in front of the fireplace and bring good luck.

The *fairies* were a lot like elves. Nowadays people think of fairies as gentle, happy little creatures, but not so long ago people were terribly afraid of them and called fairies "the good people" for fear of what the fairies would do to them if they called them what they really thought of them.

The fairies were supposed to be able to kidnap people who put themselves in their power, and if those people ate or drank anything while they were in the fairy fort, or "rath," they had to stay there forever. The only thing that frightened or hurt a fairy was anything that had iron in it, so many people wore little iron charms for fear of the fairies.

In the story of Aladdin and his wonderful lamp, we read about the spirit of the lamp, the *djinn,* or *genie,* who could grant any wish of his master by magic. A djinn is also a kind of fairy who is bound by a powerful magician and made to use his magic powers for his master.

You could make the Irish *leprechaun* give you his pot of gold by catching him while he was busy at his work (which was always shoemaking), and not letting him go until he would do as you wished. Most of the time, however, the leprechaun would trick his captor into letting him go and would dash away, screaming with laughter.

People tell many stories about the fairies. Many of the most famous were collected by two brothers named Grimm two hundred years ago. Hans Christian Andersen also wrote many famous fairy tales.

Most of the famous fairy tales, such as the Cinderella and Sleeping Beauty stories, are found in many different countries at many different times and, as far as we can tell, seem to be very, very old. Usually the fairy stories begin with "Once upon a time . . ." and end with the good people always winning over the bad people, or the bad fairies losing.

fakir

A fakir is a member of any of several different sects in the religion called Hinduism, which is followed in India. Like some very religious Christians, fakirs believe that they can best show devotion by hurting themselves. Some fakirs sleep on beds made of boards into which nails have been driven with the points upward.

The word *fakir* is taken from the Arabic language, and means "a poor man." There are many men who call themselves fakirs who are not really religious, but who do these tricks to entertain the public, but that is not the real meaning of the word.

Falaise

Falaise is a town in northwestern France, in the region called Normandy. About six thousand people live there. Falaise was important in World War II, when the Allied forces invaded Normandy in 1944. After fierce fighting, the Allied armies trapped the Germans in this region. On August 17, 1944, the Canadian First Army occupied Falaise, completing the encirclement of the Germans. Falaise was badly damaged, but has since been rebuilt. Before World War II, Falaise was known chiefly as the birthplace of King William I of England ("William the Conqueror").

Falange

The Falange is the political party that controls Spain. The government system in Spain is a type of fascism, which means that only the ruling political party is permitted. The head of the party is Francisco Franco, who is called *El Caudillo,* meaning "the leader." Franco was the general who led the Spanish revolution from 1936 to 1939, in which the previous republican government was beaten and the present government took control of the country. See the article on SPANISH CIVIL WAR.

falcon and falconry

The falcon is the name given to several different kinds of bird that belong to the hawk family. The falcon is a bird of prey, which means that it attacks and eats smaller birds and even small animals such as mice and rabbits. It is often considered as one of the strongest and bravest of the birds of prey. The falcon is found in almost every part of the world. The best-known falcon is the peregrine. This is the falcon that is most often used in the sport of falconry.

Falconry is a hunting sport in which falcons are trained to hunt game birds and small animals. It is also called hawking. It is a difficult sport and requires practice and patience. The falcon, usually the female, which is larger and stronger than the male, must be taken from the nest at a very early age. The bird is then taught not to be afraid of its master. This is called *manning* the bird. After the young bird has become accustomed to its master, it starts a period of hard training that sometimes lasts for many months. The falcon must be taught to perch on a special leather wristband that its master wears. It must learn to obey its master's commands, which are given with a small whistle, and to return to its master when called. Then the bird must become accustomed to a small hood that is placed over its head when it is taken into the fields. This hood is removed when the bird is supposed to fly in pursuit of its prey. The falcon must be taught to return immediately to its master after capturing and killing its prey.

Falconry is an ancient sport and was practiced by the early kings of Asia many hundreds of years ago. After its introduction into Europe, it became the favorite sport of the nobles.

Falkland Islands

The Falkland Islands are a British colony in the South Atlantic Ocean, at the very tip of South America. The Falkland Islands are made up of two large islands, East Falkland and West Falkland, and about one hundred little islands. Besides these islands, there are the territories known as the Falkland Dependencies. These include South Georgia, the South Shetland Islands, the South Sandwich Islands, the South Orkney Islands, and some land in Antarctica, the frozen wasteland at the bottom of the world.

Fewer than three thousand people live in the Falkland Islands, and almost half of them live in Port Stanley, the capital. The main reason so few people live there is the wet, cold climate. Heavy winds prevent trees from growing, but sheep can graze there, and their wool is the chief product of the islands.

In 1592, John Davis discovered the Falkland Islands for the British, but they founded no permanent colonies. In 1820 Argentina began a colony. The British retook the islands, but Argentina still claims them. In World War I, British ships defeated a squadron of the German navy in a battle near the Falkland Islands. The Germans lost three cruisers in the battle.

Falla, Manuel de

Manuel de Falla was a great Spanish composer, or writer of music. He was born in Cadiz, Spain, in 1876, and his full name was Manuel Maria de Falla y Matheu. His mother was his first music teacher, and when he was eleven years old he started to play in public. It was then that he shortened his name to de Falla. He was the first Spanish composer of international importance in almost two hundred years. He wrote music for big orchestras, called symphonic works; music for small orchestras, called chamber music; ballets, or stories to be danced, and songs and piano music. De Falla based most of his music upon the folk music of his country, but without using the exact melodies. In the United States, his best-known work is the "Ritual Fire Dance" from his ballet *El Amor Brujo.* Manuel de Falla died in 1946.

falling bodies,

any objects when they are falling from a height to the earth: see the article on GRAVITATION.

fall line

East of the Appalachian Mountains and all along the eastern coast of the United States, the land is close to sea level and there are no mountains or rocky places. This is called the coastal plain, and the line that separates it from the Appalachians is called the fall line. If you take a map of the eastern coast and draw a line through the cities of Trenton, New Jersey; Philadelphia, Pennsylvania; Richmond, Virgina; and Augusta, Georgia, you will have an idea where the fall line is. The reason it is called the fall line is because the rivers which come down from the rocky region to the sandy and gravelly coastal plain form falls and rapids along this line.

Fall of Man

The Fall of Man happened when Adam and Eve ate the fruit of the Tree of Knowledge in the Garden of Eden. The story is told in Genesis, the first book of the Bible.

After God created Adam and Eve and put them in the Garden of Eden, he told them that they could eat everything in the garden except the fruit of the Tree of Knowledge. The Devil, disguised as a serpent, or snake, came into the garden. He told Eve that she should taste the fruit of the Tree. She was very tempted and tasted it. She gave some to Adam, too. Because they did something God had told them not to do, they had sinned, and God made them leave Eden.

fallow

When a farmer plows his land in the spring but plants nothing on it, we say the land is fallow. Farmers sometimes leave land fallow because the land becomes tired and needs rest. If the farmer raises a crop on the land for five or six years without letting it rest, the crops become small and weak. When the farmer lets the land lie fallow, it has a chance to store up moisture and food for the next year's crop.

Sometimes the farmer plants a crop of clover or beans and then plows this crop into the ground. The dead clover or bean plants decay in the ground and make the land much richer for the next year's crop. If the farmer does not want to wait until a crop of clover grows, he may spread fertilizer over the ground and plow it under. The fertilizer then acts like the decaying plants and makes the soil rich and moist.

fallow deer

The fallow deer is a handsome animal that lives in many parts of Europe. The male is especially fine looking, with broad flat antlers that grow from its head in a graceful curve. Every spring the fallow deer sheds its antlers, and by autumn they have grown back again. The fallow deer is tan in summer, with white spots, and it turns to gray in the wintertime. The male deer is about three feet tall and weighs about two hundred pounds. It is a swift runner and can jump over high fences and bushes with ease. In the parks of many cities of Europe you can see herds of fallow deer making a meal of grass and leaves and roots, or strolling slowly among the trees.

Fall River

Fall River is a city in southeastern Massachusetts. It is on Mount Hope Bay,

which empties into the Atlantic Ocean. The city was first settled about three hundred years ago, in 1656, and its first name was Ocasset. Later the name was changed to Fall River, which is a translation of the Indian word, *Quequechan*. The Indians had given that name to the river that runs through the city. During the Revolutionary War there was a great battle between the British and the American colonists in Fall River.

About 100,000 people live in Fall River. Most of the people who live there make their living by working in the cotton mills and other manufacturing plants of the city.

false pretenses

When someone gets you to buy something from him by lying about it or by pretending it is worth more than it is, he is guilty of selling it to you under false pretenses. He may tell you that he is selling you a solid gold ring and after you buy it you find out that it is really only brass. If he is caught, it will not do him any good to say that you should have known it was not gold or that you should not have believed him. He has to return your money to you and he will be punished for the crime of selling under false pretenses. See the article on FRAUD, in another volume of this encyclopedia.

false teeth, teeth that the dentist makes to take the place of a person's real teeth: see the article on DENTISTRY.

family

Our way of living—our "culture," as the scientists call it—is based on the family. Sometimes we speak of a family as meaning all the persons who are related to one another by blood or by marriage; this would include not only parents and children but also grandparents, uncles and aunts, and cousins. However, the family on which modern human culture is based consists of a husband and wife (father and mother) and their children, all living together.

Only human beings have this kind of family, but all mammals have some form of family life. (Mammals are animals whose young are born alive and nursed by the mother.) Mammals have to have some form of family life because the children are helpless when they are born. They would die if the mother did not make a home for them during the early part of their lives. Among most mammals the father is not part of the family. Among birds, which are not mammals, both the father and the mother are usually part of the family life as long as the baby birds are helpless and cannot feed themselves. The difference between the human family and all the other families is this: Among other mammals and among birds, as soon as the young are old enough to take care of themselves the relationship is forgotten and the family is ended. Among human beings the family relationship continues.

THE HUMAN FAMILY

In nearly all civilized countries, the human family today is based on *monogamy,* a word meaning "one marriage," that is, one husband and one wife. We are so used to this system that we take it for granted, but it has not always been the rule, even among civilized peoples.

Among many ancient peoples, one husband would have several wives. This is called *polygyny* (which means "more than one wife"). Many of the ancient Jews, whose stories are told in the Bible, practiced this system. The Mohammedan peoples still are permitted by their religion to use it, though many of them have given it up. The Christian religion does not permit a man to be married to more than one woman at the same time.

Among people whose culture is not so far advanced, the practice of *polyandry* ("more than one husband") is quite usual. The family would consist of a mother and her children living together. The mother might have several husbands. This custom seems very strange because it is unlike anything known in civilized countries today, but to prehistoric and primitive men there is nothing strange about it. A mother must care for her children, so she must stay in one place. Men do not have to bear children, so they can roam as they please. Therefore the house belongs to the mother and she is head of the family.

THE HEAD OF THE FAMILY

A system in which the mother is the head of the family is called *matriarchal.* A system in which the father is head of the family is called *patriarchal.*

Nearly every civilized country for thousands of years has used the patriarchal system. Until the century we live in, the twentieth century, this system was followed much more than it is today. The father was the head of the family, and his wife and children had to obey him. Women could not vote, and any property they owned before their marriage became the property of their husbands. A son or a daughter could not marry without the father's consent.

This system, in most European countries, included the system of *primogeniture,* which means "first born." The oldest son would always become head of the family when his father died. He would own all the family property. His brothers and sisters and their children, as well as his own wife and children, would often continue to live with him, because part of his duty would be to support them. Kings and queens, in countries that still have them, still use the system of primogeniture.

The modern family is much different from any of these systems. The father and mother have equal rights. The children must obey their parents, and the parents are supposed to support their children, until the children grow up; after that the children may go where they please and marry whom they please. The control of parents over their children has become far less strict than it was. Children seldom receive the severe punishment they once did. Psychologists say that this makes more loving families and helps the children to become happier men and women.

FAMILIES OF THE PAST

In ancient Rome, more than two thousand years ago, laws were made to control the rights of the members of families. A family included all persons who were descended from the same ancestor. This large Roman family was called a *gens.* A person could be adopted into a gens, and would then become a member of it just as though he had been born into it. The same is true of adopted children today.

Much like the Roman family system was the clan system of Ireland and Scotland. All the members of an Irish or Scottish clan (which might include everyone who lived in a town or even in a county) would have the same name and claim descent from the same ancestor, though usually this ancestor had lived so long ago that nobody could be sure who his descendants were.

In many countries, ancient and recent, every member of a family has been expected to protect every other member against enemies. Often this has led to *feuds,* which are "wars" between families. If a person is killed or harmed, members of his family are supposed to fight all members of the family of the person who killed or harmed him. Even within the last fifty years, there have been bloody feuds in parts of the United States.

famine

A famine is a time when there is not enough food to feed all the people of a country or a large region, and many people starve to death or suffer from great hunger.

Throughout most of his history, man has had to work very hard just to raise enough food for himself and his family. Only in recent years has scientific agriculture, with farm machines and fertilizers and widespread irrigation, made it possible for land to feed many more people than are required to farm it. Even while this tremendous advance has been made, the population of the world has grown so much that in many parts of the world it is still difficult to raise enough food to feed the people.

In ancient times, and right up to modern times in such thickly populated countries as China and India, any year when one thing or another ruined the crops there would be a famine. There can be any of several reasons for a famine. One is a year in which there is no rain, so that the crops cannot grow. In countries like China and Egypt, where a great deal depends on the big rivers, if the river is low there is not enough water for irrigation, and if the river floods at the wrong time the crops may be washed away.

Exhaustion of the land is another reason for famine. In the early 1930s the wearing out of the land in midwestern states such as Oklahoma and Kansas caused "dust bowls," dry fields in which nothing could grow. In the early days of the world, when transportation was difficult, there would have been a famine and people would have starved to death. Because of modern transportation, food could be shipped in to the dust-bowl states and the people could travel to places where the land was still fertile.

In some areas famines are caused by swarms of locusts that eat the crops, and by other insect pests and diseases that ruin the crops.

There have been many famous famines in history. One of the worst was the seven-year famine in Egypt that occurred more than five thousand years ago. The Nile River, on which the farmers de-

pended for water, had fallen to a very low level. There was almost no food in the entire kingdom.

Ireland also had a terrible famine, about a hundred years ago. The people depended almost entirely on potatoes for their staple food. When the potato crop failed, more than a million people died of starvation, and many thousands had to leave their homes.

The United Nations Relief and Rehabilitation Administration, which is called UNRRA, has done a great deal of work to prevent famines and to feed people where there are famines. Scientists are working constantly on the problem of growing more food so that the population of the world will have enough to eat.

fan

A fan is something that is used to move air. Usually fans are used to make people cooler. When moisture evaporates, heat is reduced. Air absorbs moisture, and if more air passes over a certain place at a certain time, more moisture is absorbed and the place becomes cooler.

The simplest kind of fan is a flat, broad surface that is waved in front of the face. A magazine or a piece of cardboard can serve this purpose, but in the course of history fans have been so fancy that they became practically a piece of jewelry that women carried (and, in some countries, men). Women have carried fans also to give them a graceful appearance.

About seventy-five years ago the electric fan was invented. The electric fan has a motor that makes a set of blades turn rapidly. They pull air from behind them and send it out in front of them in a strong current of air. This current of air makes an entire room cooler.

Fans are also used to cool machinery, as for instance the fan at the front of an automobile engine that sends a current of air over the engine.

Air conditioning to a certain extent has replaced the big fans in public places, but most air conditioners have fans in them, since a current of air is almost as important as the coolness the conditioner creates.

fanatic

A fanatic is a person who feels so strongly about some subject or cause that he becomes very unreasonable in dealing with those who disagree with him. His feeling is called *fanaticism*.

The way we often use the word *fanatic* is an exaggeration.

For instance, we speak of a person who likes baseball a great deal as a "fan" (which is short for fanatic), or we say a person who likes to collect stamps or other things is a fanatic. Actually, a fanatic can be quite dangerous if he has enough power to try to make others feel and act the way he does.

Religious fanaticism has been the most usual kind. In most periods of the world's history there have been people who believed so deeply in their religion that they wanted to kill or torture people who followed other religions and would not give them up. This has led to the killing of thousands of people, as for example the Christians in ancient Rome who were thrown to lions because they would not give up their religion and follow the official Roman religion. In most countries today there are laws that prevent anything of this sort, but there have been examples of political fanatics such as the Communists in Russia, or Adolf Hitler and his followers in Germany, who killed people and started wars to advance their own beliefs.

fandango

The fandango is a dance that originated in the West Indies and has been popular in Spain and many Latin American countries for hundreds of years. The fandango still is one of the most popular dances in certain parts of Spain today. It is danced to the strumming of guitars and the clicking of castanets. Castanets are two hollowed-out wooden bowls that are small enough to hold in your hand. They are held together by a piece of string and when you hold them in one hand and click them together very rapidly, they make a very exciting sound. Many composers of serious music have introduced a fandango into their compositions. Mozart, de Falla, Granados, Rimsky-Korsakov, and Albenez have all written fandangos for large orchestras. The dance is supposed to express love between the man and woman who are dancing it. It was introduced into Spain from the West Indies. When Spanish explorers came to the New World three hundred years ago they were looking for gold. They found the gold, and the fandango, too, and took both back to Spain in the 17th century.

Faneuil Hall

Faneuil Hall in Boston, Massachusetts, is known as the cradle of liberty because it was used as a meeting place by American patriots before the Revolutionary War. When Peter Faneuil, a wealthy merchant, lived in Boston, there was no public market building and meeting hall, and Faneuil thought there should be one. By 1742 he had it built and he gave it to the city of Boston. At first it was a two-story brick building, then a third floor was added and the meeting hall was made larger to seat three thousand people. Later many famous speeches by Daniel Webster, Edward Everett, Charles Sumner and others were made in Faneuil Hall. It is standing and may still be seen.

Fan Tan

There are two games called Fan Tan. One of them is an old Chinese game, and is not often played by anyone outside of China. In this game, a bowl of beans is used. A person takes a handful of beans from it. He puts this handful of beans down on the table, and everyone tries to guess how evenly the number of beans can be divided by four. A person can guess zero, one, two, or three. Then the beans are counted off, four at a time. When there are no more beans left, if the last group is exactly four beans, the people who guessed zero win; if there is one bean left, the people who guessed one win; and so on.

The card game called Fan Tan is not like this at all. This game is often called "Sevens." Here is the way it is played:

A regular pack of fifty-two cards is used. Any number of players from three to eight may play. The cards are dealt out, one at a time and face down, as far as they will go; it does not matter if one player receives more cards than another. The turn to play goes to the left, from one player to another.

The game is best played with chips. Before the cards are dealt, each player puts one chip into a pool. (At the end of the game, all the chips in the pool will go to the winner.) Each time a person is unable to play, he must put one chip into the pool.

A player can always start by playing a seven; there is no other card that the first player can play. Once any seven has been played, then the next player in turn may play a card that is of the same suit and the next card in rank to the seven or to any card that has been played on it.

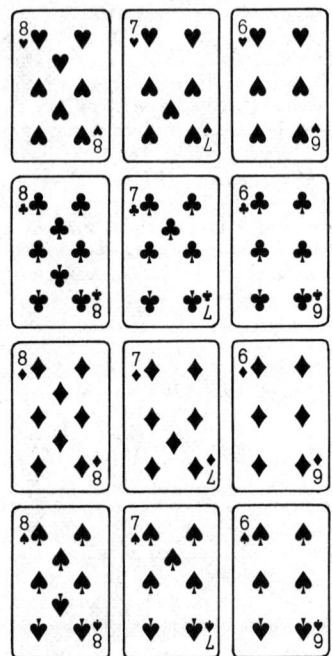

Once a seven is put down, the six and eight of the same suit become playable; if the six has been played the five becomes playable, if the five is played the four becomes playable, if the eight is played the nine becomes playable, and so on. From the sevens, the side including the eights is built up to the king and the side including the sixes is built down to the ace.

When any player gets rid of his last card, the game ends. Each player puts a chip into the pool for every card remaining in his hand. The winner takes the entire pool.

A player must play a card if he is able to do so. If he is able to play and does not, when his error is noticed he must pay a three-chip penalty to the pool. If his failure to play occurred when he had a seven in his hand, he pays the same three chips to the pool, but in addition must pay five chips each to the players who held the six and the eight of that suit. This same game is sometimes called Sevens, or Parliament, or Play or Pay.

fantasy

A fantasy is a story in which something takes place that we know could not really happen. In a fantasy there may be creatures that we know cannot exist, but fantasies are not fairy tales.

Stories about people on other planets are fantasies, because we do not really believe there are such people. Tarzan stories are fantasies because in them Tarzan, a man, is supposed to be able to talk the language of apes.

Alice in Wonderland, by Lewis Carroll, is a fantasy, for we know that it is impossible for any little girl, even one as adventurous as Alice, to meet and talk to a Cheshire cat, Humpty Dumpty, and a March hare.

Faraday, Michael

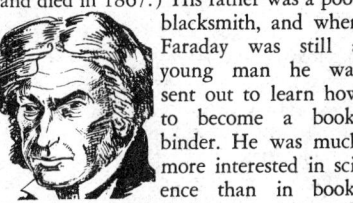

Michael Faraday was a great English scientist who lived about one hundred dred years ago. (He was born in 1791 and died in 1867.) His father was a poor blacksmith, and when Faraday was still a young man he was sent out to learn how to become a bookbinder. He was much more interested in science than in bookbinding, and spent his spare time reading scientific books and studying. When he was about 22 a famous English scientist named Sir Humphry Davy took an interest in him and helped him to get a job as a laboratory assistant at the British Royal Institution. From then on, Faraday gave his entire time to scientific work, and he became very famous.

He discovered many important principles of science in chemistry, magnetism, and electricity. An electrical unit called the *farad* is named after him. Faraday built the first dynamo, which led to the power plants that provide electricity. The telephone and telegraph are also based on principles that Faraday discovered.

Farbenindustrie, I. G.

The I. G. Farbenindustrie was a large industrial organization that existed in Germany until the end of World War II. For many years before the war, the Farbenindustrie controlled the production and distribution of many different products such as chemicals and some metals, not only in Germany but in many other countries. I. G. Farbenindustrie was a member of several world-wide cartels. A cartel is an association of several large companies from different parts of the world that produce the same products. They form agreements as to how much of a certain product should be made and at what price it should be sold to the public.

After World War II, the Allies accused I. G. Farbenindustrie of having plotted with Adolf Hitler's Nazi government to start World War II, and of having cooperated with the Nazis in enslaving and murdering people. The Allies forced I. G. Farbenindustrie to break up into smaller companies and withdraw from all cartels.

farce

A farce is a kind of play or motion picture that is intended to be funny and to make you laugh. Most people think of a comedy as a play that makes you laugh, but a comedy is any play that has a happy ending. Parts of a comedy may not be funny at all. A "situation comedy," which has been one of the most popular types of television show with such stars as Lucille Ball and Jack Benny, is a kind of farce. In motion pictures the type of comedy where people are always falling down and getting custard pies thrown at them is called a farce. This kind of action is known as "slapstick comedy."

People's taste in entertainment changes from time to time, so the farces of one period are not always the same as the farces of another period. Many motion pictures used to have slapstick comedy in them, but very few do now.

The most famous farce of modern times is the play *Charley's Aunt*. This play is always being put on somewhere in the world, and it has been made into several motion pictures. It has also been made into a successful musical comedy called *Where's Charley?*

Fargo

W. G. Fargo

Fargo is the largest city in the state of North Dakota. It is in the eastern part of the state, on the Red River, which forms the boundary between Minnesota and North Dakota. About 53,300 people live in Fargo. Fargo is an important distributing center for all the farm products that come from the northwestern part of the United States. It is also an important railroad center, and a great number of the men and women who live in Fargo work for the railroads. The North Dakota State University of Agriculture and Applied Science is located in this city.

Like most of the cities of the western part of the United States, Fargo is comparatively young. It was first settled in 1871, when the Northern Pacific Railroad was extended from Minnesota across the Red River.

The city of Fargo was named after William George Fargo, who, together with Henry Wells, founded Wells, Fargo and Company in 1852. In the days of the Western pioneers, Wells, Fargo and Company carried both goods and gold in stagecoaches across the United States.

farm bloc

Certain of the states in the United States, such as Kansas, Iowa, North Dakota, South Dakota, and Nebraska, are chiefly farming states. The Senators and Representatives in Congress who represent these states do their best to see that the needs and wants of the farmers in their states are taken care of. These Senators and Congressmen are called the farm bloc, because they usually vote as a unit, or bloc, on all questions that have to do with farm problems, even if they belong to different political parties.

farm bureau

Farm bureaus started in the United States before World War I to help the farmer. At first the bureaus were small groups of farmers who got together to discuss better ways to raise their crops and get them to market. Then the farm bureaus hired experts on agriculture and transportation to advise them. The idea of forming bureaus spread until nearly every state had one.

Then, in 1919, representatives from all of the state farm bureaus met at Chicago, Illinois, and decided to become a nation-wide organization. This way, they would have more influence and be able to get better help from the Department of Agriculture. This American Farm Bureau Federation has grown since 1919 until it has over 1,943,100 members.

Farm Credit Administration

The Farm Credit Administration is a branch of the United States Department of Agriculture. It lends money to farmers so they can improve their farms. Before this administration was begun, it was hard for a farmer to borrow money. Banks did not like to lend money to farmers because if anything happened to the crops the money that had been lent could not be repaid. The Farm Credit Administration was formed in 1916. In 1965 loans outstanding to farmers amounted to about seven billion dollars.

Farmer, Fannie

Fannie Merritt Farmer was a famous cooking expert who was born in Boston, Massachusetts, in 1857. She wrote one of the most popular cookbooks ever published, the *Boston Cooking School Cook Book*. It was first published in 1896. Fannie Farmer became interested in cooking when she was still a girl, and she went to the Boston Cooking School to learn to be a cooking teacher. At that time cookbooks did not have any standard way of describing exact measurements. They would say, "Put in a 'scant' teacup," or "Two 'rounding' spoonfuls." Fannie Farmer first used the idea of measuring ingredients by the level spoonful and cupful. Most cookbooks published today still use this system of measurement.

Fannie Farmer was the director of the Boston Cooking School for a long time, and then she opened her own cooking school in Boston. She died in 1915.

Farmer-Labor Party

The Farmer-Labor Party was a political party in the United States. It was founded in 1920, and in 1944 it joined with the Democratic Party, so that it no longer exists. It was strongest in the middle west, and it elected a governor of Minnesota, Floyd B. Olson, who served from 1930 until he died in 1936. The Farmer-Labor Party was particularly interested in the problems of farmers and working people.

Some parts of the Farmer-Labor Party program were never put into effect at all, but other sections were. One of the parts that were not carried out was the demand that some of the country's large businesses, such as the railroads, be taken over and operated by the government. A part that was carried out was the demand for a social security program. The Social Security law was passed in 1935.

Farmers Home Administration

The Farmers Home Administration is an organization that was set up by the United States government to lend money to farmers who are not able to borrow it anywhere else. About twenty years ago, the United States Department of Agriculture was told by Congress to help these farmers by lending them money.

The Farm Security Administration was established to do this; in 1946, it was replaced by the Farmers Home Administration.

The Farmers Home Administration lends money to farmers for many purposes: to build up and improve their farms; to buy farms; to build or repair their homes and farm buildings; and to buy or repair farm machinery. The Administration has local offices in many parts of the country. The farmer applies to his local office for the loan and explains what the money is to be used for. If the Administration considers the loan a sound idea, the money is lent to the farmer, and he may even be helped to plan the use of the money in the best way. The farmer repays the loan over a period of years, plus an additional amount of money (called interest) that is paid for the use of the loan money.

farming, the work of raising crops or animals: see articles on AGRICULTURE, DAIRY FARMING, CATTLE, POULTRY, HOGS, FARM MACHINERY.

farm machinery

Farm machinery includes machines that do almost every job that is done on the modern farm. There are machines for preparing the soil and for planting the seeds, weeding, and fertilizing. There are machines that cut the crops, separate the usable parts from the unusable ones, sort, and bale.

Thousands of years ago farmers tilled the soil with wooden pegs and crooked sticks, and since all the work had to be done by hand, farms had to be very small. Then the first tools were devised: the ax to clear the land, the spade to turn the soil, the hoe and rake to prepare the seedbeds, and the sickle for harvesting the crops.

Farming remained at this stage for many hundreds of years. Because so little land could be tilled by the primitive methods in use, frequently the people of whole areas or countries would starve to death for lack of farm products. Nowadays such starvation is a rare thing, and even with the vast increase in populations, the farms with their efficient equipment are able to provide enough food for all.

HISTORY OF FARM MACHINERY

Farming was done entirely by hand until about two hundred years ago. Up to that time, the horse had been used chiefly in warfare and as a means of transportation. Then the farmer realized how much lighter his labor could be if he used animals to pull the simple farming machines he had invented. As horses became standard equipment on farms, the farm machinery became more complicated and more efficient, and farms grew larger and larger.

With the invention of the locomotive, inventors began trying ways of using a powered machine to make farming still easier, and in 1892 the first internal combustion tractor was built in the United States. New and better farm machines then followed rapidly. In England an oil engine was made, and in the United States two of the most important farm machines were invented. Cyrus Hall Mc-Cormick invented the reaper in 1831,

and for more than a hundred years it was the leading machine of its kind. It cut the grain and left it on the ground to be bound up by men following the machine on foot. In 1878 a self-binder was invented by John F. Appleby, which made it possible for one man to do the work of eight. This binder reaped the grain and bound it with twine automatically. Better plows and harvesters were devised, and then came the combine, which did the work of both harvester and thresher.

In 1793 Eli Whitney had invented the cotton gin to separate the cotton from the seeds. This machine quickly revolutionized the cotton industry of the southern United States.

New inventions and improvements on existing machines continued to appear, and in 1947 the airplane was pressed into farm use for dusting and spraying crops against insect pests.

As farm machinery became more efficient and less expensive, it made great changes in the lives and labor of farmers everywhere. The acres of soil one man could till, and the number of heads of livestock one man could raise, increased enormously. In the 1950s it was possible for one farmer to feed a family of five and as many as ten other persons by his own work.

TYPES OF FARM MACHINERY

Farm machinery is classified according to the kind of work it does. Some of the most important types are the following:

Soil preparation machinery includes many kinds, shapes and sizes of machinery used for breaking up the soil. The ground must be broken and crushed into small particles. The soil preparation helps to make water and air available for plant growth. The chief machine for soil preparation is the *plow,* and there are three principal kinds of plow. The first is the *moldboard plow,* which has a sort of three-sided wedge for turning the soil. The second is the *disk plow,* which is used for soil that is sticky when wet and crusty when dry, and for soil that is full of stones or roots. The third kind of plow is the *rotary plow,* which has knives that cut down into the soil.

Seedbed preparation machinery is used for much the same purpose as soil preparation machinery. The rotary plow is one of the best machines for seedbed preparation, but it does not always complete the job, and other special machines must be used. Among these special machines are the *stalk cutter,* which cuts stalks left from the previous crop; the *disk and spike-tooth harrows,* which plow under any weeds or plants already in the soil and smooth the soil to receive the new seeds; the *spring-tooth harrow,* which does the same job as the spike-tooth harrow but cuts deeper and can spring up over obstructions in the soil.

There are many other very specialized machines for preparing the soil for the planting of different crops.

Seeding machinery is of many kinds, but all are designed to make planting easier. The machines can plant a certain number of seeds at a certain depth in the ground in rows that are evenly spaced at a certain distance apart. The number of seeds and the distance apart depend on the kind of crop being grown and the kind of soil it is being grown in. Some seeding

machines can even put not only seeds but also fertilizer into the ground.

There are two main kinds of grain seeder, the *broadcast seeder* and the *drill seeder.* The broadcast seeder simply scatters the seeds evenly over the surface of the soil. The drill seeder puts the seeds in shallow trenches and covers them with soil. The most modern seeders are combination machines that can put a dozen or more different kinds of grain and vegetable seeds at the distance and depth desired.

Cultivating machinery includes all the machines that are used to kill weeds, stir and aerate (let the air circulate through) the soil, and mulch the surface. Mulch is straw, leaves and loose earth that are spread on the soil to protect the plants. Seedbed preparation machines such as the harrow are often used as cultivators while the crop is very young. The kind of crop, the condition of the soil, the size of the farm, and the amount of rainfall are important in deciding what cultivating machinery should be used. These machines are made for use by hand, or to be drawn by horses or tractors. They have names that describe the job they are meant to do, such as *scratcher, sweep, scraper-hiller,* and *furrower.*

Fertilizing machinery is necessary for easy and even distribution of fertilizers, whether the kind used is a chemical product or simple barnyard manure. The machines can control the amount of fertilizer distributed, and pulverize, or crush, the fertilizer to make it easier for the plants to make use of its food values. The *manure spreader* is found on almost every farm. It carries manure to the field, shreds it and spreads it evenly over the soil. The *commercial fertilizer distributors* are of special kinds, depending on how the fertilizer must be applied. They may spread the fertilizer on the soil, or put it under the soil near the roots of the plant.

Harvesting machinery is used to reap and collect the crop when it is ripe. There are many kinds of harvesting machines for reaping different crops. Some are horse-drawn, others are pulled by tractors or have their own motors. There are special hay-harvesting machines, such as the mower, chopper, stacker, and bailer. Other harvesting machines are the small-grain machines, the corn and cotton harvesters, and special harvesters for crops that are planted in rows.

Seed preparation machinery is needed to separate the seed from the plants in preparation for marketing. Plants that need such machines are the small grains and peanuts. Corn must be removed from the cob, and cottonseeds must be removed from the lint. Among the machines that prepare seed are the grain threshers, the corn husker-shredders, the cotton gin, and the peanut thresher.

Transportation machinery is needed to take the farm produce to market or to the transportation center. The old-fashioned farm wagon has been replaced by the truck and the auto-trailer. After World War II, the jeep and the pick-up truck became members of the farm machinery family on many American farms.

General service machinery includes all the highly specialized equipment that has been developed to help modern farmers work many acres of land. There are the *fanning mill* for cleaning grains, the

seed recleaner for cleaning oats, the *corn grader* for separating and sorting corn, and various machines for improving the soil and conserving water supply.

The number of farm machines in use in the United States has grown tremendously in the early part of the 20th century. For example, in 1940 American farmers used 1,500,000 tractors, 190,000 combines, and 110,000 mechanical corn pickers. In 1960 they used 4,770,000 tractors, 1,065,000 combines, and 780,000 corn pickers. The total number of acres of land being cultivated has not increased very much since 1920, but the use of power equipment has made it possible to get more crops from every acre with less labor and fewer workers. See also the article on DAIRY FARMING.

Faro

Faro is a card game that has been played for hundreds of years. Once it was called "America's national card game," but now it is not played very often. It got its name because it used to be played with a pack of cards that had a picture of Pharaoh (king) of Egypt on one of the face cards.

In playing Faro, a player would pick any rank (for example, a seven, or a ten, or a queen, regardless of its suit). Then a dealer would turn up the cards of a full pack, one by one. He would lay them in two piles. All the cards in one of the piles would "lose." All the cards in the other pile would "win." If a player's card first showed up in the "lose" pile, he would lose; if it first showed up in the "win" pile, he would win. As the years passed, this simple form of the game was changed so that a player had the right to guess whether his card would win or lose, and could pick any number of different cards in the same game. The complete rules of Faro can be found in many books on games.

Farouk I

Farouk I is the name of the last king of Egypt. He was born in 1920, the son of King Fuad I, and became king in 1936, after the death of his father. At first, the

people of Egypt believed he was going to be a good ruler. However, after World War II, King Farouk began to pay very little attention to the problems of his country and people. He preferred to gamble and give great parties. He allowed his family and friends to run the government, and they used their positions for their own gains. The people grew tired of this bad rule, and in 1953 several army leaders who had the support of the army and the Egyptian people made King Farouk abdicate, which means to leave the throne. Egypt was then made a republic. Farouk was forced to leave the country, and the government took over his great estates. He died in 1965.

Farragut, David

David Glasgow Farragut was an American admiral who fought on the Northern side in the Civil War. He was born in 1801, and he joined the Navy as

a midshipman when he was only nine years old. Although Farragut was quite an old man by the time the Civil War broke out in 1861, he was one of the most daring officers in the Navy. In 1862 he led a fleet that captured New Orleans from the Southerners. The ranks of vice admiral and then admiral were created especially for him. He died in 1870.

Admiral Farragut is known best for leading the Union Navy in the Battle of Mobile Bay. In August 1864 a fleet commanded by Farragut steamed into the harbor of Mobile, Alabama. The old white-haired admiral had climbed up into the rigging of his ship, the *Hartford,* so that he could see better. Suddenly there was a great explosion ahead, and the *Tecumseh,* which was leading the fleet, blew up. The next ship, the *Brooklyn,* turned around to go back. Farragut yelled to the *Brooklyn* to find out what was wrong. The answer came back, torpedoes! In those days, mines, which were put in the water by the enemy to explode when a ship touched them, were called torpedoes. Farragut shouted back, "Damn the torpedoes! Full speed ahead!" The *Brooklyn* turned, and the fleet entered the harbor and captured Mobile.

Farrell, James T.

James Thomas Farrell is an American writer. He is best known for novels that try to give a very true-to-life picture of the way average people live. Farrell was born in Chicago in 1904. As a boy he loved sports, and sports play an important part in many of his novels. While studying at the University of Chicago he began writing. Between 1932 and 1935 his first important work, *Studs Lonigan,* was published. This work was a trilogy (three closely related novels) about people of Irish ancestry living in Chicago. It soon made Farrell famous. He has written several other novels, most of them about life in big cities. He has also written books about his philosophy, or way of thinking, on various subjects.

fascism

Fascism is a form of government in which one political party runs the government and no other political party is allowed to exist. The word *fascism* is fairly new, but it is based on the bundle of twigs, called *fasces,* that was used as a symbol of power in ancient Roman times. The idea is that while one twig can easily be broken, a bundle of twigs cannot be. In other words, in union there is power.

The Italian leader Mussolini used this same word in the name of his political party formed in Italy just after World War I. He called the party *Fascio di Combattimento,* meaning "Union of Combat." Later, members of this political party were called *Fascisti,* or Fascists. At the end of World War I Italy, like most European countries, was suffering from great poverty. The King of Italy and many other people were afraid that the Communists would get power in the government.

Mussolini was against the Communists, and the king made him premier of the country, even though Mussolini's party had only about thirty-five representatives in the parliament, or less than one-tenth of the members. Mussolini at once used his power to destroy other political parties. He imprisoned people who were against his party, and sometimes he tortured and even killed them. Under Mussolini Italy became a dictatorship, with Mussolini as its dictator.

Mussolini made Italy stronger and more prosperous, and for that reason some other countries adopted a Fascist form of government. The principal one was Germany, which became a dictatorship under Adolf Hitler.

Although fascism proved that it could cure some of the ills of a country, it also proved very bad for the people because it took away their liberty, which people in the United States and Canada and other democratic countries value more than anything else. Also, every Fascist government proved to be dishonest and warlike. The Fascist government of Italy built up a large army and navy and went to war against Ethiopia for no reason except that it was greedy for land. Later Italy did the same thing in Albania, and tried to do the same thing in Greece. Finally the Fascists led Italy into World War II against the United States and other democratic countries. The party was wrecked when Italy lost the war.

The world's experience with fascistic countries of this century has made it clear that fascism is one of the worst things that can happen to the people of a country. See the articles on Benito MUSSOLINI and ITALY.

fashion

The particular way that most people prefer to behave or dress at any particular time is called the fashion. We usually think of clothes in connection with fashion—the kind and appearance of the clothes people prefer to wear. Fashions in clothes were once as important to men as they were to women, but in more than a hundred years men have changed their way of dressing very little, so fashion has come to mean the latest style in women's clothes.

WHY FASHIONS ARE ALWAYS CHANGING

When women go shopping they do not want to buy a duplicate of something they already own. They want something different and new. So the fashion industry must keep making new styles. Once a new style is seen, others want it too. Then everyone starts to follow the leader. This is how a new fashion is created.

Most fashion trends change slowly. Each year the spotlight is focused on one part of the garment. One year sleeves may grow wider or longer. Another year the hemline goes up or down. All these changes give women the variety they want in their new clothes.

Once in a while a great fashion change happens overnight. This was true in 1947, after World War II. During the war, the American government had a law called "L-85." It limited the amount of fabric that could be used for all clothing.

fabric that could be used for all clothing. Men's trousers were not allowed to have cuffs. Their suits could not have vests, and could have only a certain number of pockets. Women's fashions were skimpy, with very narrow skirts way up to the knees. By saving fabric on civilian clothes, we had more fabrics for soldiers' uniforms. When the war ended, the L-85 law was dropped. Skirts then promptly dropped from the knees to the ankles.

One popular style may continue for many years, yet look fresh and new because of its new colors and fabrics. This is true of the "shirtwaist dress," which buttons in front to the waistline, and also the "coat dress," which buttons all the way down the front so it can be put on like a coat. Because these same styles have remained popular for many years, they are called "classics."

HOW DESIGN IDEAS START

Designers get their style ideas in different ways. For example, one designer got her idea for a tailored blouse in red-and-white checks from an ordinary checked tablecloth. A famous milliner created a popular hat from an ancient Roman helmet that she saw in a museum. The delicate coloring of a Chinese spoon inspired a fabric designer to use that combination of colors for an evening-dress fabric. Some designers adapt or vary somebody else's design. This is different from deliberately copying a high-priced style to sell for less.

Ideas for new styles often come from fashions of the past. We may call them new because they really are new to us. Because they are combined differently, they do not look at all like ancient costumes, but quite fresh and modern. Everyone who works in the fashion world must know historical fashions.

WHY PARIS IS SO IMPORTANT

For many years Paris, France, has been responsible for most of the changes in fashions. French women are famous for their good taste and their love of fashions. This fact alone would be an inspiration to French designers, but they also have another advantage. They make one style for only one woman. American designers must make a single style for thousands of women.

When you make one style to please many different tastes, and to fit many different figures, obviously you must be more conservative, or less daring. The Parisian designer has no such worries about mass production. Only one woman must approve of each style. Often, this woman is a fashion leader who wants her clothes to be an original design.

Like all other designers, the Parisians guard their new ideas until the seasonal openings. Then we discover that Mr. X is introducing a tight fitting waistline; Mr. Y favors a loose, bloused waist; Mr. Z shows long middy waistlines. It is clear that these world-famous creators did not get together to plan one new trend. In fact, they are all going in different directions. Who is right? Who will start a new trend? We can answer this only after the fashions have been launched by the fashion leaders and accepted or rejected by the average American girl and woman.

FASHION CAREER OPPORTUNITIES

The fashion magazines are continually publishing helpful articles about jobs in the fashion world. There are many schools with special courses for each type of fashion work.

DESIGNING. Making your own clothes is a good start. You learn the best way to use patterns and how to cut, fit, and sew. You discover how to handle fabrics, and what styles should be made of a stiff fabric such as taffeta or a soft fabric such as jersey. You learn to select the best styles for your figure and personality type.

But there is a great difference between designing for yourself and designing for a fashion manufacturer. The professional designer must plan styles that she herself might not like to wear. She must plan styles that her firm can sell. Most fashion firms specialize in one type of clothes. One firm will make teen-age dresses; another will make coats and suits; another will make only formal dresses for evening wear; another will make only tailored dresses. By watching carefully what all kinds of people wear, you train yourself to know about fashions for others. This is called an impersonal, or objective, viewpoint.

With a hundred new styles to create each season, no designer has the time to plan and cut and sew each garment herself. Some designers sketch their ideas and "sample hands" make the first sample from the sketch. Other designers prefer to drape fabrics on a figure and work out the style details by pinning and basting. For girls who have designing talent this is wonderful work. It is creative and pays very fine salaries.

STYLING. The word "stylist" is one title that stands for several different kinds of fashion jobs. There are fabric stylists who work for textile manufacturers. They choose the new colors and the new weaves and prints their firms will make. A store stylist is responsible for giving her store a reputation for fashion leadership. She does this by organizing all the new fashions so that her store can show complete outfits in harmonious color schemes. Because she coördinates, or acts as a go-between among related departments in a store, this stylist is also called a *fashion coördinator*.

Both these jobs involve great responsibility so they must be held by people with experience. To get this experience it is best to start as a secretary to a stylist.

There are photographic stylists, who find accessories for fashion photographs. This stylist often chooses the models and helps arrange the outfits in front of the camera. She may work for a photographer, for a magazine, or for an advertising agency.

MODELING. A fashion model may specialize in posing for photographs. If she does not photograph well but she wears clothes beautifully, she can model for fashion shows and manufacturers. A few fortunate girls combine these talents. Manufacturers' models have steady jobs. Free-lance models register with model agencies and are on call for jobs. To prepare for this career, study models in fashion shows carefully. See how they walk and turn, how they hold their hands, and how they smile. To model clothes

properly you must know just which detail is important in each style you have to wear.

DISPLAY. Store windows are changed at least once every week. The display director usually has assistants who go to all accessory departments to select the proper hats, gloves, handbags and shoes for every fashion on display. A knowledge of current fashion trends is obviously needed for this work. But this job is always supervised, so beginners with good taste are sometimes given the job of a display stylist.

BUYING. Selecting fashions from manufacturers for a store is only one part of a buyer's work. She is also responsible for getting the fashions sold to the public. She trains her sales staff. She keeps her merchandise in good order. To be sure that her budget is not overspent, she keeps careful records. A buyer cannot choose styles she personally likes. She must choose what her customers will want to buy. That means satisfying a variety of tastes and preferences. Buyers must be experts about workmanship and value.

Buying is an ideal job for people who enjoy activity. Buyers are either visiting manufacturers' showrooms in distant cities, or they are supervising the selling in their own departments. Many stores have special training programs to prepare girls and boys for fashion-buying jobs.

ADVERTISING. Fashion advertisements have pictures and "copy" or written parts. Writing fashion copy is one of the jobs in which girls can go as far as boys, or even farther. Knowing how to typewrite is essential for this job. Knowing about fashion trends is necessary because you must know what you are writing about. Fashion copywriters are employed by stores, by magazines, and by advertising agencies.

SKETCHING. Girls and boys both can become fashion artists. By watching the newspaper advertisements, you can learn a lot about the different kinds of fashion sketches. A fashion artist must understand every tiny detail of design to draw clothes correctly and to emphasize the important new style features. Fashion artists can work for stores or advertising agencies. Many use an art studio that acts as an agency to get free-lance jobs.

EDITING and PUBLICITY. All magazines and newspapers report news. Fashion news is also reported free when it is truly newsworthy, such as a "first-time" appearance. This differs from advertising where the space is paid for and the fashions presented may be "classics."

The publicist is the person who brings the fashion news to the editors. The editors in turn reject or select what will interest their particular readers.

Fashion editors and publicists must know fashion trends and how to write about them. Giving fashion shows is often a part of their jobs, so they must enjoy entertaining and talking to large groups of people.

These jobs sound glamorous, and they are; yet every publicist and editor must know how to typewrite. So starting as a secretary is a good way to break into this branch of fashion.

FAMOUS FASHION SILHOUETTES

The outstanding shapes or silhouettes

of past fashions are easy to recognize in historical movies. We connect famous people in history with the typical style worn in every era or age.

Cleopatra and the Sphinx are two of the best known figures of ancient Egypt. The Sphinx's "hat" or kerchief covers the forehead and hangs around the neck. This served as a sun shield and was worn four thousand years ago by men and women. Queen Cleopatra's dress is long, straight, and narrow, and held on the shoulder by a strap. Like all Egyptians, she had her head shaved and she wore a wig of tight curls. The snake on her headband was a sign of power. Egyptian men wrapped short skirts or sarongs around their hips. The hot climate of Egypt did not require more clothing. The turned-up toes of Egyptian sandals have been copied for modern house slippers and play shoes. We also wear wide necklaces and bracelets, taken from Egyptian designs.

Helen of Troy and Julius Caesar are among famous names of ancient Greece and Rome. The same fashion silhouette was worn in both countries. Most boys and girls know the Roman *toga*, the big loose cape pinned on one shoulder. All the garments of these nations were loosely draped, and gathered or pleated. Working men wore their shirts or tunics only to the knees, so they could move about easily. Important men and all women wore long belted dresses or robes. The fabrics were solid colors, usually white, with a simple line-design border. The pleated skirts that girls wear today are like the short skirts of a Roman soldier's uniform.

Ivanhoe, Rebecca, and Rowena are characters we know from the famous story by Sir Walter Scott. They lived during the Crusades, in the time we call the Middle Ages. Fashions were no longer draped around the body, but were shaped to fit the figure. Although their waistlines were fitted, women wore belts low on their hips or high under the bosom. Women's hair was hidden in wire cages over each ear. Later they wore high pointed hats, like dunce caps, with floating veils. For a time coats were sleeveless, like our modern jumpers.

Men wore long trousers that fitted snugly like the tights of a modern ballet dancer. Often each leg was a different color. Jackets tied in back and ended at the hips like short skirts. Shoes had long pointed toes. Many sleeves were so wide at the wrist that they touched the ground. Royalty wore clothes designed like their coats-of-arms, with different emblems and colors on each side of the body. They also wore fur-trimmed garments, and these are still popular.

Shakespeare and King Henry VIII are great personalities of the Renaissance era. The word *renaissance* means "rebirth," or "revival." At that time, people revived their interest in all the arts, including the art of dress. Clothes were designed with cuts and slashes that were filled in with puffs of contrasting fabrics.

Men's tights of the past became stockings worn with short slashed-and-puffed pants. The shape of women's fashions changed to a wide skirt, held out by many petticoats. Waistlines became pointed, and necklines were wide and square.

Toward the end of this age, big stiff collars became fashionable. Around their necks, people wore starched white ruffs like the ones some clowns wear today. Women wore lace collars that stood up like fans behind the head. We can see this in pictures of Queen Elizabeth I when she is stepping on Sir Walter Raleigh's cape, or when she is knighting Sir Francis Drake.

Priscilla and John Alden belong to the 1600s. Most of us know the simple clothes those women wore, with plain white aprons and wide white collars. Puritan men also believed in style simplicity. The slashed-puffed trunks of the past became knee breeches. Their shoes had wide, comfortable toes. Hats were black felt, with high, tapered crowns and broad brims. People who were not Puritans, especially royalty, changed this silhouette by adding lace ruffles, loops of ribbons, bows and fancy buttons. Such elaborate trimmings do not look strange on women, but the men of that period look strange to us. They wore wigs of long, wavy hair, and big feather plumes on their hats.

George and Martha Washington show us the elegant styles of the next century, the 1700s. Everyone knows the white wigs that men wore in those days. The Puritan knee breeches and square-toe shoes continued in fashion, but men's hats became *tricorne,* or three-cornered. Their coats were shaped at the waist and stiffened to flare away in back. Women's silhouettes changed because they puffed out the sides of their dresses with cages. The French called these *panniers,* which means "bread-baskets." Over the wide skirt was an overskirt that could be kept loose or draped up into scallops by pulling a cord. This is called a "polonaise" skirt. To match these complicated styles, women's hats became big and wide with many bows and plumes. Toward the end of this era, in 1789, the French Revolution created another revolution in fashion.

Napoleon and Josephine, who ruled France after the revolution, started a fashion trend of simplicity. It became bad taste to dress like royalty after the king and queen were beheaded. Men stopped wearing wigs. A man would wear long trousers with a cutaway jacket and a high hat. This style is obviously the origin of the formal clothes that men wear today.

The women gave up brocaded satins and silks and began to wear plain cotton fabrics. The silhouettes became slim and narrow, with a very high waistline right under the bosom. Because it came from Napoleon's Empire, we call this the Empire silhouette. It lasted for about thirty years.

The Victorian era is named for Queen Victoria, who ruled England for most of the last century. Two main silhouettes were fashionable: first, hoopskirts and tiny waistlines; later, the back-bustle skirt. Smartly dressed women in all countries followed these fashions. Men's jackets took the shape they have today, except that they were more fitted and they buttoned up high near the neck. Both men and women wore high-button shoes with pointed toes.

Now we come to our own century, the 1900s. At the beginning, a woman's figure was shaped like an hourglass. It was called the "Gibson Girl" silhouette, after the fashion sketches drawn by Charles Dana Gibson. This style had high boned collars, long wide skirts and puffed leg-o'-mutton sleeves (shaped like a leg of lamb). Gradually skirts grew shorter and narrower. Belts began to drop to the hipline. The bosom was flattened with bandeau bras.

The flapper silhouette was the result of these gradual changes. By 1925, skirts were the shortest they had ever been. For the first time, women cut their hair short. A popular hair-do was the windblown bob, and bobby pins came into use. High-button shoes disappeared in favor of pumps. Women began to use makeup freely.

There was an overnight change in 1928. This was a year of great national prosperity, just before the depression of 1929. Most people could afford to buy the new long skirts that replaced the flapper skirt. Although many objected to the sudden change in fashion, they gradually accepted it.

During World War II, from 1940 to 1946, skirts grew short and narrow again and shoulders became wide and squared with big shoulder pads. We explained why, earlier in this article. Then in 1947 Christian Dior of Paris introduced the "new look." Shoulders returned to normal. Skirt length dropped to mid-calf. Hips were rounded, sometimes with pads.

Today our fashions differ from the past because we no longer have only one silhouette. Most women own both slim skirts and full skirts and wear a variety of necklines and collars and sleeves. Modern women get around more than women of the past and wear special clothes for special occasions. In spite of this modern variety, each season of the year some new style detail appears.

fasting

Fasting actually means going without anything to eat or drink, but we often use the word to mean going without certain kinds of foods or drinks. People must eat to stay alive, and fasting completely for too long is dangerous. But eating is more than just a necessity, it is also a pleasure. Because eating is a pleasure, fasting is considered by many religions to be a way of atoning for the bad things that all people do. Jesus fasted forty days and forty nights as an act of devotion to God. In the Jewish religion there is a very important holiday, which comes once a year, called Yom Kippur, or the Day of Atonement. On Yom Kippur Jews do not eat a bit of food or drink a sip of water for twenty-four hours, from sundown on one day until sundown the next day.

In the Roman Catholic Church there are many fast days during the year, but the Catholic fasts are not complete fasts as Yom Kippur is. Usually it is a matter of not eating meat. During the period called Lent, which lasts forty days and ends the day before Easter, members of several Christian Churches go without certain kinds of food. Each person decides what he or she will give up for Lent. The period of Lent starts on Ash Wednesday, which is forty days before Easter, and ends the day before Easter.

The Moslems have fasts, too. There is one season in the Mohammedan calendar during which good Moslems do not eat, drink or smoke from sunrise to sunset.

Fasting is sometimes used by political leaders in order to win their demands. The great Indian leader, Gandhi, who spent his life trying to win freedom for his native country from Britain, frequently fasted in order to force the British authorities in India to do certain things. The Indian people loved Gandhi so much that the British were afraid of what would happen if he died as a result of a fast, so they usually did give in. This kind of fast is sometimes called a hunger strike.

fat

Fat is a tissue that is made by the body, much as muscle tissue and bones are. Food is stored in the fat of your body to be used as your body needs it. If it were not for the fat in your body, you would have to be eating all the time. Fat also acts as an insulation against cold weather. Heat does not go through it easily, so the layer of fat under your skin keeps in the heat of your body when the air is cold.

It is not at all healthy to have too much fat on the body. This is explained in the article on OBESITY.

Fat is also made by plants. It is usually made in the seeds and fruit, and sometimes in the roots. The fat that plants make is somewhat like the fat that animals make, and it is usually easier to extract. Oleomargarine, a plant fat, is used as a substitute for butter, an animal fat. Many different kinds of fats are taken from plants and animals for uses in industry. Plants give fat that is used for making foods, soap, candles, chocolate, drugs, polishes, and perfumes. Animal fats are used for the same things, but the main use of animal fat is for butter.

fatalism

Fatalism is the belief that everything follows a plan that has already been made, so human beings cannot change it. Fatalists, or people who believe in fatalism, think that our actions cannot change things because we are following the plan and we are fated to do exactly what we do. A fatalist thinks that if it is in the plan of things that he have an accident, it will not do him any good to be especially careful while driving because a loose brick from a building may fall on him instead.

People believe in fatalism more in Asia than in Europe or America, and it is part of many religions. In the Mohammedan religion fatalism has a very important place and is called *kismet*. Some Christians are fatalists, too. They say that God knows everything and is powerful enough to do everything, so He must have made the plan for the whole world for all time.

Fata Morgana

If you stand on the sea shore in southern Italy and look across the water to the island of Sicily, it looks as if the houses and trees there are upside down or floating in the air. The name of this strange sight is Fata Morgana, which is a kind of mirage. You see other mirages yourself when you drive on a highway on a hot day and it looks as if the road ahead is wet when it is really dry. People in the desert see mirages when they see trees and water ahead of them when there is nothing but sand. Fata Morgana is named after a fairy called Morgana who is supposed to have made this kind of mirage.

Fates

In ancient mythology, the stories the Greeks and Romans told about their gods, there were three very old women who were called the Fates. These women were very powerful and often cruel, but they were not wicked. They were goddesses, not witches. If they decided who on earth was to have bad luck, they also decided whose luck would be good; if they set the time, place and circumstance of each person's death, they were also the ones who decided what persons would be born, and where and when. Whatever they decided would happen, happened. Nothing could happen to anyone, no matter how important, even a king, which the Fates had not agreed upon. Not all their decisions were fair, but they never changed their minds.

One of these old women was named Clotho. She was in charge of all births. She held a spindle on which the thread of each person's life was spun. The second was named Lachesis. She held straws with which she measured the amount of good or bad luck each person would have. The third was Atropos, who had the power of life or death; she held scissors with which she cut the thread of each person's life when his death was decided on.

The old Norsemen also had stories they told about the Fates, whom they called Norns. In these stories the Fates were called Urd, Verdundi, and Skuld.

fatigue

Fatigue is a condition of the human body when it is unable to function properly until it has rest. When we have worked too hard or too long without sufficient rest, we become tired and lack enough energy for any normal activity.

Doctors tell us that fatigue is produced from poisons in our bodies. This type of fatigue of the body is called *physiological fatigue*. However, too much mental strain can also result in fatigue. Mental fatigue can occur in a person when he has had too much mental activity without enough rest. This type of mental fatigue is called *psychological fatigue*.

In the modern world fatigue is just as dangerous for the worker as bad machines. When the worker is under great strain for a long time he can become a victim of fatigue. When this happens, the worker cannot do his job properly and he becomes a risk to himself and his fellow workers. Industry is trying to do away with fatigue in many ways. The first way is not to have employees work too hard. Secondly, in order to stop mental fatigue caused by boredom from doing the same type of work over and over, many diversions, such as recreation halls and music, are being tried out in factories. In order for the worker to keep interested in his job, pay-raises and bonuses are offered.

Sleep is the state of complete rest and is the best cure for fatigue. Usually, a good night's rest will cause a partially fatigued person to awaken refreshed and rested. A person who is completely fatigued will need days and possibly weeks of thorough rest and sleep. Certain foods are suggested to cut down fatigue. Water, lemonade and oranges are very helpful. These foods passing through the body help to drive away and eliminate the poisons of fatigue.

FATIGUE IN METALS

Metals often weaken when they have been used a great deal, and this weakening is called fatigue. Metal that is constantly bent or hammered is likely to weaken. An example is a steel girder or a bridge. It is so big and thick that it does not seem to bend, but actually every load it carries bends it just a little. In time this may cause the metal to be full of tiny cracks inside, though there may be nothing on the outside to show that it has weakened in any way. Engineers examine and test metal structures regularly to make sure they can still carry loads safely. X-ray can be used to look at the inside of solid metal and see if it is suffering from fatigue.

Fatima

Fatima was a quiet, unknown village in Portugal, like a hundred others, with a little church, a few houses, and farms and pastures in the country around it. Then one spring day in 1917 three shepherd children reported that they had seen the Virgin Mary appear before them while they were caring for their sheep in the field. When they told about seeing her not everyone believed them, but they said the image of the Virgin appeared before them again and again during the summer, six times all together. Finally the priests of the Roman Catholic Church to which they belonged believed that the children really had seen a miraculous vision. Since then many visitors have come to Fatima to see the place where the children saw the Virgin Mary, and a fine new church was built there for visitors to worship in.

Fatima and Fatimites

The Fatimites were an important family of caliphs, or Mohammedan kings, who ruled Egypt about nine hundred years ago. The first caliph of this family claimed to be descended from the daughter of the Prophet Mohammed. Her name was Fatima, and for this reason these caliphs are called the Fatimites. They started their rule in Tunis in northwest Africa and conquered Egypt about a thousand years ago. Soon afterward, they founded the city of Cairo as their capital. The rule of the Fatimites ended in 1171.

Faulkner, William

William Faulkner became famous as one of America's greatest writers of novels and stories. In most of his books,

Faulkner has tried to show what the southern part of the United States was like after the Civil War ended and in the present time. Faulkner does this by writing about the same three or four families, showing how they live and the problems that they have. These stories take place in Yoknapatawpha County, an imaginary place that is a great deal like the country around New Albany, Mississippi, the town where Faulkner was born in 1897. His novels *The Sound and the Fury, As I Lay Dying, Sanctuary,* and others, are read all over the world, and in 1949 Faulkner won the Nobel Prize in literature. In 1954 his novel, *A Fable,* won the Pulitzer prize. He died in 1962.

fault

A fault is a sudden break in the earth's crust. The great pressure caused by the rise of new mountains or the sinking of old ones may make the rocks of the earth's crust break wherever they are thin or weak. You can read about the reasons for the rise and fall of the earth in a separate article on GEOLOGY. When the crust breaks in this way it is called *faulting.* The break may be a sidewise one. There is a great fault called the San Andreas fault that runs the length of western California. One day in 1906, a 275-mile-long section of rock beneath the land along this fault moved sharply sidewise, causing the great earthquake that nearly wiped out the city of San Francisco. The earth's crust may also break so that it moves up and down. The steep eastern slopes of the Sierra Nevada Mountains are the result of faulting that took place millions of years ago. This faulting caused the western parts of Utah and Arizona to sink sharply downward, leaving the mountain sides as great cliffs. When cliffs are formed by faulting, they are called *fault scarps.*

Many parts of the earth are in the process of faulting. Alaska, the sea floor near Japan, Chile, and the floor of the eastern Mediterranean Sea, all are faulting. Faults may be found in any part of the world.

faun

A faun was an imaginary creature that the Romans believed in more than two thousand years ago. The faun was half man and half goat. According to the Romans, a faun liked to play tricks on people, but it was not cruel. It lived in the woods and was friendly and lively. Claude Débussy, the French composer, wrote a musical composition called "The Afternoon of a Faun." Using this music, the famous ballet dancer Nijinsky made a ballet showing how a faun spends its time leaping and whirling through the woods.

Faust

Faust is the name of a grand opera. This is a play in which all the conversation is sung, not spoken, and the music is classical, intended to be played by a symphony orchestra and sung by the greatest singers. The music for *Faust* was written by Charles Gounod, a great French composer. The story of the opera, called the libretto, was written by Paul Barbier and Michel Carré, two French writers who often worked together as librettists. The story of *Faust* is an old German legend. It tells of a Doctor Faust who sold his soul to the devil in exchange for a return of his youth and for magical powers. The famous German poet Goethe wrote a tragedy based on this legend, and the opera retells part of this tragedy. Faust was first presented at the Paris *Théâtre Lyrique* on March 19, 1859. It is still performed in the United States each year and is one of the most popular operas ever written.

STORY OF THE OPERA

Faust is an old man who is famous as a philosopher, or thinker. He is alone in his study when a devil named Mephistopheles appears and offers him love, wealth and power if he will sign away his soul. This means that Faust's soul will belong to the devil when he dies. Faust is not sure he wants to do this until Mephistopheles shows him a vision of a beautiful girl named Marguerite. Faust falls in love with her and agrees to sell his soul. He becomes a handsome young man and wins Marguerite's love. One night Mephistopheles sings an insulting song to Marguerite, and her brother Valentine fights with Faust because of this. Faust kills Valentine, leaving Marguerite very sad because her brother has died blaming her for his death. Faust becomes more and more evil as he becomes more and more friendly with the devil. At the end of the opera Marguerite goes insane. Although Faust wants her with him, she is saved by angels who bear her soul to Heaven. Then Mephistopheles seizes Faust and drags him away.

fauvism

Fauvism is a style of painting that created a sensation more than fifty years ago, in 1905. *Fauve* in French means wild beasts, and the Fauvists were painters who used very bright, unrealistic colors and made their pictures in very simple forms and shapes. They were influenced by the style of Paul Gauguin. Henri Matisse, George Braque and Raoul Dufy were among the famous Fauvists, and Georges Rouault painted some fauvistic paintings. Many of their ideas came from art done by native Africans. As you look at the fauvistic paintings of Dufy and Matisse you get a feeling of lightness and sunshine and gaiety. The fauvistic paintings of Rouault are like the stained glass windows you see in a church. Fauvism was first shown in an exhibition in Paris, France, in 1905. Most of the Fauvists changed to other styles a few years later but good fauvistic paintings are still very valuable, partly because so many fauvistic painters became famous later.

Fawkes, Guy

Guy Fawkes was an Englishman who tried to blow up the Houses of Parliament, the English lawmaking body. Fawkes and his men planted several kegs of gunpowder in a cellar beneath the House of Lords, one of the two houses which make up Parliament. Fawkes' plot was discovered before the powder exploded, and he and his fellow-conspirators were caught and arrested. They were put to death on November 5, 1605. This event of English history is known as the Gunpowder Plot, and each year, on November 5th, the people of England celebrate Guy Fawkes' Day in honor of the day their Parliament was saved.

fealty, the loyalty that a vassal promised to his noble lord: see article on FEUDALISM.

fear

Fear is a feeling of uncertainty or dread that something painful or dangerous is about to happen. When you feel fear your body goes through a physical change. Your eyes open wider. Your heart beats faster. Your blood seems to pound through your body. The muscles in your body react, too. Your jaw tightens and your teeth clamp tightly together, or you may lose control of your facial muscles and your jaw may drop and your mouth hang open.

A different kind of fear, a mental fear, is the cause of most mental illnesses. Almost every case of mental disorder, or nervous upset, is caused by a fear or dread of some unknown or unreal thing. When these causes are discovered and treated by a doctor, the fear is removed and the patient is on the road to getting well.

feast

A feast is a day set aside to celebrate a great or special person or event. All religions have feasts, and many religions celebrate the same ones, such as Christmas and Easter. Christmas is the feast that celebrates the birth of Jesus, and Easter is the feast that celebrates his resurrection from the dead. Many religions observe feast days for each of the saints.

HOLIDAYS and FESTIVALS are sometimes called feasts; you can read about them in separate articles.

feathers, the outer covering of a bird's body: see article on BIRDS.

February

February is the name of the second month in the year. It has 28 days, except every fourth year, when there are 29 days in the month. This is called leap year, and you can read about it in a separate article on CALENDAR. February was not part of the first Roman calendar, and was added, along with the month of January, later. February comes from a Latin word that means "to clean," and it has to do with certain religious ceremonies that in ancient times took place during February. Abraham Lincoln and George Washington were both born in this month. If your birthday is in February, your birthstone is the amethyst, and your flower is the primrose.

Federal Bureau of Investigation

As far back as 1908 the United States government had a special group of men to look into the breaking of its laws. In that year the Bureau of Investigation

was formed. In 1935 the name was changed to the Federal Bureau of Investigation. It is one of the world's best-known investigative agencies. It is often called the F.B.I. and its workers are often called "G-men," which means "government men." There is an office of the F.B.I. in almost every large city in the United States and in United States territories and possessions. The headquarters is in Washington, D.C. The Federal Bureau of Investigation is part of the Department of Justice.

In the beginning the F.B.I. fought against crime that city and state laws could not handle. If someone stole a car in one state and took it to another, F.B.I. men went to work because state police are not allowed to go beyond their state borders. The F.B.I. still does this kind of work, but since World War II it has gone more and more into checking up on people who might do harm to the United States government itself. These include not only spies from other countries, but Americans.

Of course, not everyone the F.B.I. checks up on is thought to be a spy or a person who would harm the government. An F.B.I. man might come to your door at any time and ask questions about someone who lives near you. He would be doing this because that person might have taken work with the government.

If you were to see an F.B.I. man in the street, you would not know he was a law-enforcement officer. He would wear clothes like those worn by everyone else. But if you were to know all the hard work and study he has had to go through to get his job, you would see that he is not an ordinary person, nor an ordinary officer. This is because the F.B.I. men, or Special Agents, as they usually are called, are picked especially to do dangerous work. They also have to be good students, because they go to a special school to learn all the scientific ways of catching criminals.

The F.B.I. will hire only lawyers or accountants between the ages of 25 and 40. They have to be checked up on very carefully to see that they are hard-working and honest. They cannot have any bad habits; and they must not be afraid of doing the dull work of their job any more than the dangerous part. The pay these men get is not very high, yet every year the F.B.I. gets thousands of letters from men who want to become agents. J. Edgar Hoover became the chief of the F.B.I. in 1924. The chief reports to the Attorney General, the nation's highest law-enforcement officer.

The work of the F.B.I. is varied. There is the fingerprint work. There are about 132,000,000 fingerprint cards in the F.B.I. files. These are used not only against crime in the United States, but also in other countries. F.B.I. agents also work in a laboratory where even a hair or a tiny piece of wood can be studied and used to catch a criminal. The F.B.I. runs a police academy, too, for teaching city and state policemen the latest ways of fighting crime.

Federal Communications Commission

When radio came into wide use about thirty years ago, the United States government decided that it would have to be controlled, but the government did not want to own the radio stations, as the governments of some countries do. In 1927 the government started a commission to do the work of controlling radio, but radio grew too fast for it. That is why the Federal Communications Commission was started in 1934. It was given the job of seeing that radio service in the United States was of the kind that would be good for all the people. Now the Commission has power over not only radio but also over telephone, telegraph, and television.

Seven men chosen by the President make up the Commission, which sometimes is called the F.C.C. They hold their jobs for seven years. They decide what methods will give the people the best service. It is possible to send only a certain number of messages by broadcast in one place, so the commission chooses the persons who may use the air.

Anyone who wants to start a broadcasting station for radio, television or wireless must get permission from the Commission. When you hear a broadcasting station sign off at night, you will hear the announcer say that it has been given the right to broadcast by the Commission. If a broadcaster puts programs on the air that break the Commission's rules, or if he tries to broadcast more hours than the Commission allows, he may lose his right to use the air. The Commission also has power over broadcasting to other countries from the United States.

Federal Courts, those courts that are part of the United States government: see the article on COURTS.

Federal Deposit Insurance Corporation

The Federal Deposit Insurance Corporation is the part of the United States government that makes sure that money deposited in banks is safe. Sometimes banks have failed, or have unwisely used the money people have given them to hold. Now, if a bank should close, the Federal Deposit Insurance Corporation would probably pay those who had money in the bank. It also prevents unsafe banking practices, and it may lend money to banks to prevent their closing. In 1960, total assets of the Federal Deposit Insurance Corporation were more than two billion dollars, but they insured deposits totalling more than 260 billion dollars in 23,554 of the 24,954 banks in the U.S.

Federal Housing Administration

The Federal Housing Administration is a part of the United States government. It helps people to live in better houses. A person who builds a house for himself, or who builds an apartment house for several families to live in, usually has to borrow some of the money he needs. People also have to borrow, very often, to repair the houses they own or to buy new houses. The Federal Housing Administration makes it easier for them to borrow the money by guaranteeing to the banks that the money will be repaid. The banker collects interest on the money he lends and pays a small part of this interest to the Federal Housing Administration. The Federal Housing Administration, or FHA, was organized in 1934 and is part of the Housing and Home Finance Agency.

Federalists

Federalists were those Americans who, soon after the Revolutionary War, thought it would be better if the new national government were much stronger than any of the thirteen original states. This was in the years 1787 to 1789, when people were trying to decide whether to adopt the new Constitution of the United States. This Constitution created a strong national government.

In those days many people were more loyal to their states than to the United States, and they feared big national governments. The people who were against the new Constitution were called Anti-Federalists. To convince them that they should approve of the new Constitution, Alexander Hamilton, James Madison and John Jay wrote a series of excellent newspaper articles clearly explaining the importance of the Constitution. They were published as a book called *The Federalist Papers,* and are still widely read. The Federalists were successful and the Constitution became law.

The argument went on for some years after the Constitution was adopted, and the Federalist Party was one of the important political parties. President John Adams was a Federalist. After various problems of government were worked out, the argument became pointless and by 1824 the Federalist Party was dead.

Federal Power Commission

The Federal Power Commission is a part of the United States government. It watches out for the people's supply of electricity and natural gas, and sees to it that the cost of electricity is not too high. If a utilities company wants to build a dam on a river to make electric power, the company must ask the Federal Power Commission for permission. The commission investigates whether the dam will interfere with boats on the river, and whether there is enough water for electric power as well as for drinking purposes and for irrigating farmer's fields. All electric and natural gas companies must make reports to the Commission each year on what they have been doing, how much money they have made, and if they will continue to serve their customers properly in the next year.

Federal Reserve System

The Federal Reserve System is an organization of banks set up by the United States government. The Federal Reserve banks are different from the ordinary banks where individual people keep their money. You can read about these ordinary banks in the article on BANKING. The Federal Reserve banks do most of the things that ordinary banks do, but they are really banks for other banks. They hold money for other banks; they make loans to banks, and collect checks for banks.

The Federal Reserve System was set up fifty years ago. People in the govern-

ment thought that banks, and the money that banks hold, were concentrated too much in one part of the country. Sometimes banks would lend out too much of their money, and not hold enough in reserve in case people asked for it. Also there was the problem of what to do with the money that belonged to the government. Different ways of keeping that money had been tried, but none of them seemed good enough. So in 1913 the Federal Reserve Act was passed, and the next year the Federal Reserve System was set up. Under this system, the United States is divided into twelve districts, with a Federal Reserve bank in each district. This means that banks are spread around the country. Other ordinary banks can join the Federal Reserve System. These banks have to deposit a certain amount of money in the Federal Reserve banks. This means that they cannot lend too much money. The Federal Reserve banks supervise the member banks and see that they are run correctly. The Federal Reserve banks also hold the money that belongs to the United States government. Each Federal Reserve bank has a group of directors who are chosen to run that bank. In Washington a group of directors called the Federal Reserve Board supervise the whole Federal Reserve System.

Federal Trade Commission

The Federal Trade Commission is a part of the United States government set up to control businesses that trade in two or more of the states. The Commission was established by a law passed by Congress in 1914. It is made up of five persons who hold their jobs for seven years. They are chosen by the President of the United States. Not more than three of the five members may belong to the same political party.

The FTC is supposed to keep business from misleading the public or using unfair methods in selling merchandise, and this is a necessary and valuable service, but the FTC has not been very successful. This is partly because the Commission is not well run, but also because the FTC seldom makes a company change its methods until the damage has already been done.

feeble-mindedness

A feeble-minded person is a person whose brain is underdeveloped or damaged so that he cannot do simple everyday things without help. Such a person's state is called feeble-mindedness. It can be inherited from parents, or caused by disease or damage to the brain through an accident before, during, or after birth.

About one out of every 200,000 people in the world is feeble-minded. A feeble-minded person is one of a larger group known as mentally retarded people, who cannot function normally. However, some mentally retarded persons can be taught to earn their livings in very simple ways. Feeble-minded persons can never be taught more than to take care of their own personal needs.

At one time, the feeble-minded were considered to be strange people who had no place in the world. Today teachers and doctors have come to realize that a feeble-minded person can live more or less comfortably and happily. Special classes for feeble-minded children teach them how to keep themselves clean, how to eat properly, and how to perform all the simple tasks of everyday living.

feldspar

Feldspar is a mineral found in many kinds of rock. It is used in the making of porcelain, a kind of pottery that looks smooth and shiny. It is used in concrete to make better roads. It also can produce potash, a substance that is very valuable in the making of soap. Sometimes it is used as a roofing material. Feldspar can be found in nearly all parts of the world. It is found in many different forms and the finest feldspars do not have any color. Many feldspars, however, are white, gray, pink or green in color.

fellah

Fellahs are the peasants or farmers of Egypt and other eastern countries. The fellah of Egypt is very poor and uneducated. He usually lives in a small mud house, and rarely owns land of his own. Instead, he works long hours for the wealthy landowners who pay him very little.

Today the government of Egypt is trying to improve the condition of the fellahs. Schools have been built for them, and the properties of the large landowners have been broken up and divided among them.

The Egyptian fellah wears a garment called a *gallabieh*. It looks very much like a nightgown. It is loose and so is comfortable in the great heat of Egypt.

fellowship

Fellowship is taking part in an activity with others. Persons joined in a fellowship are called fellows. If the activity you take part in is work, you are a fellow-worker to those you work with. If it is school, you are a fellow-student.

Fellowship is often used to mean a special kind of activity; for example a college graduate is given some money, usually by a college or a university, so that he can join in an activity such as research or teaching. The amount of money is about a thousand dollars or more a year, and the fellowship is for a definite purpose. If the person who gets the fellowship is supposed to teach, he is called a teaching fellow; if he is supposed to travel while doing research, he is a traveling fellow. A great many fellowships are also given by organizations begun by wealthy people to encourage research. The Guggenheim, Rockefeller and Ford Foundations are famous organizations of this kind.

The word *fellowship* is also used to mean a group of religious people who worship together.

felony

A felony is a very serious crime. If you kill someone, or rob a person, or burn down a building, you have committed a crime that is called a felony. If you break the law by disobeying such laws as traffic rules or the health regulations, your crime is called a *misdemeanor*. The law in every country says that some crimes are felonies and other crimes are misdemeanors. A felony is always a more serious crime and the law punishes it more severely. In the United States, some states say that all crimes that are punishable by death, or by putting the guilty person in prison for more than one year, are felonies.

felt

Felt is the name of a thick, smooth cloth that is made when many fibers of wool, hair, or fur are pressed together. If you look at a strand of wool, or rabbit's fur, or even a hair from your own head, under the microscope, you will notice that each hair is covered with tiny notches, or scales. When many hairs are pressed together, these notches cause the hairs to cling to each other. The curly wool of sheep makes a very good felt, as does goat's hair. The fur of rabbits and beavers is also used. Men in factories operate powerful machines that roll and steam and beat the fibers until they stick together, and make a thick, soft felt.

Women wear skirts and jackets and belts and carry pocketbooks made of felt. Many slippers are lined with felt. The fur of a rabbit or a beaver makes a very fine felt hat. Felt is used for many things besides clothes. If you look inside a piano, you will see small, hammer-shaped parts that are covered with felt. Many chairs are lined with felt, and strips of heavy felt placed along the frame of a window or door help keep out the cold. An artificial felt is made from paper and wood shavings and other material, and is used in roofing and other construction work.

The first machines for making felt were invented in the United States about one hundred years ago, but people thousands of years ago knew how to make felt by hand. Many people now believe that man knew how to make felt even before he learned how to spin and weave cloth. Ancient writers tell about the art of felt making, and we know that long ago in Asia the people made tents and head coverings and decorations of it.

feminism

Feminism is the belief that women are equal to men and should have the right to vote, to hold office, to go to college, and to work at the same jobs as men. This belief may not seem strange to us now, but for a long time everyone thought that a woman's place was in the home, and she was supposed only to be a good wife and mother. About two hundred years ago, women began to work because there were not enough men for the jobs in new factories. Soon afterwards the American and the French Revolutions were fought for the democratic rights of all men, and some people began to think that women ought to have democratic rights too. Mary Wollstonecraft, an English feminist, wrote a book that convinced many people that women were the equals of men. A little later, around 1850, a group of feminists in the United States issued a "declaration of independence for women." With the help of the famous Susan B. Anthony, the feminists began to be heard. Both in Europe and in America women began to fight for their rights. Sometimes they did extreme things such as wearing mannish

clothing, cutting their hair short, and even taking men's names as did the French woman novelist, George Sand. Gradually the feminist idea grew. When World War I took many men away from their jobs, women took their place and showed that they could do all kinds of work well. The year the war ended England gave women the right to vote, and the United States did the same two years later, in 1920. Now women are taking their places next to men as students, doctors, lawyers, scientists, and executives.

fencing

Fencing is a contest between two persons who use swordlike rods to touch each other and to keep from being touched. In olden times fencing was not so much a sport as a way of fighting. Real swords were used, and a man who did not fence well might be killed by a better fencer. Almost everyone studied fencing, and those who became very good at it became famous. The best part about fencing in those times was the way it kept big people from hurting smaller and weaker ones. In fencing, quickness is usually more important than strength.

The rods that people use now for fencing are called *foils*. A foil is made of steel and it looks very much like a thin sword, but its point is like the head of a nail and is not at all sharp. Other kinds of foil have edges that will not cut. A foil has a handle and a guard to keep the fencer's hand from being hurt.

Fencers wear masks and padded jackets to keep from getting hurt. In most kinds of fencing, they try to touch each other with the points of their foils anywhere between shoulders and hips. Touches on the arms or legs or head do not count.

There are two other weapons that are used in fencing, the *epee* and the *sabre*. The epee is like a foil except that it is longer and stiffer and has a much larger guard. With the epee you can try to touch your opponent anywhere on the body, even the tip of the toe. The sabre has a guard that comes around to protect the fencer's fingers, and it has a dull edge along one side. You are allowed to try to touch your opponent with either the pointer or the edge, and a touch anywhere above the waist counts as a "good touch."

A fencer stands facing the other player with his right foot out and his left foot about ten inches behind it. He holds the handle of his foil at chest height and he aims the point at the other person's eyes. He usually tries to keep the point aimed that way, and he uses the part of the foil nearest the handle to keep the other fencer's point from touching him.

One kind of attack is called a lunge. When a fencer lunges, he stretches out his right arm and moves out his right foot very quickly. If the other fencer can push or beat aside his point, he is said to have been "parried."

Each movement in fencing has a name, and the body of the fencer is marked off into four quarters. Each is named by a number in French. When a player parries at a certain point or lunges in a certain way, there is a double name for the movement. One is for the movement itself, and the other is for the part of the body it is nearest to. This system was in-

vented by the Italians, who fence very fast and hard, and mostly use the forearm to back up the foil. The French took up fencing from the Italians and worked out a less active attack, mostly using the wrist and fingers for greater deception. France and Italy lead the world in fencing. There is also much fencing in American universities. Hungary leads the world in sabre fencing.

Fenian Brotherhood

The Fenian Brotherhood was an Irish-American secret society devoted to making Ireland a free country. For hundreds of years Ireland had been ruled by England, and the Irish were always trying to win their freedom. The Fenian Brotherhood was founded in Boston, Massachusetts, in 1858. Almost all of the members were Irish-Americans, but there were members all over the world. The brotherhood tried to start an uprising in Ireland by causing street fights and breaking windows, as well as by setting fire to public buildings. They even tried to invade Canada. They crept across the border at Buffalo, New York, to capture a fort. Some of the men lost their courage and the group was captured. Many of the Fenians were given long terms in jail. By 1885 the Fenian Brotherhood had almost disappeared.

fennel

Fennel is a plant that people use in cooking because its leaves are highly flavored. The flavor of fennel is somewhat like licorice, a sweet-tasting spice. Fennel is a member of the parsley family of plants. It grows most abundantly in the south of Europe, especially in Italy where it is extremely popular as a food. The lower part of the fennel plant leaf thickens, being smooth and straight. This is blanched and is the part eaten. The plant usually grows to a height of five feet, but in California fennel sometimes grows as tall as fifteen feet.

Fens

A fen is a marsh, or swamp. The Fens is a region of about two hundred square miles in the eastern part of England. Once it was all a marsh, but most of it has now been drained for farming.

Ferber, Edna

Edna Ferber became famous as an American writer. Her stories are known to a great many people because they were popular as books and plays, and also because of many movies that were made from them. Miss Ferber began writing  for a newspaper in Kalamazoo, in Michigan, where she was born in 1887. Later she began to write novels. In 1925 her book, *So Big*, won the Pulitzer Prize as the best American novel of the year. One of her best-loved stories is *Show Boat*, a tale of show people who travel along the Mississippi. This colorful story was made into a fine musical play. Edna Ferber died in 1968.

fer-de-lance

The fer-de-lance is one of the most

poisonous snakes on earth. It is found in South America and in parts of Mexico. The fer-de-lance grows to be eight to ten feet long, and has a black and yellow design on its skin. Its head is shaped like a spearpoint; this is how it gets its name, which means "head of a spear" in French. The fer-de-lance does not have to be coiled up to attack, as some snakes do. Some people say that it can spring ten feet through the air from a stretched-out position on the ground. The female fer-de-lance lays sixty eggs at one time.

Ferdinand and Isabella

Ferdinand and Isabella were the names of several kings and queens of Spain. The most important were Ferdinand V and Isabella I, who lived nearly five hundred years ago. At first, Ferdinand was ruler of the kingdom of Aragon, and Isabella was queen of the kingdom of Castile and Leon. After their marriage, the two kingdoms were united under one crown. This was the first important step in making Spain a single kingdom. Ferdinand and Isabella fought the Moors, the Mohammedan invaders who had ruled much of Spain for hundreds of years. After more than twenty years of fighting, in 1492 Ferdinand and Isabella conquered the city of Granada, the last Moorish stronghold in Spain. In the same year, 1492, they expelled all Jews from Spain, forcing several hundred thousand Jews to migrate to other countries.

Ferdinand and Isabella are best remembered in America for giving ships and men to Christopher Columbus, which enabled him to discover America—also in 1492.

Ferdinand was born in 1452 and died in 1516; Isabella was born in 1451 and died in 1504. They were married when Ferdinand was 17 and Isabella was 18.

fermentation

Fermentation is the action that yeast has on sugar or starch in foods. The best place to see fermentation is in baking bread, which has yeast in it that causes it to rise, or get larger. Bread usually rises the most in the first few minutes after it has been put in the oven. During these first few minutes you can actually see the top of the bread rising in the pan.

This rising is caused by the yeast changing the starch or sugar in the food to alcohol. While this change is occurring, a gas (carbon dioxide) is made inside the bread or cake, and because it cannot escape it causes the food to swell, much like a balloon being filled with air.

The yeast that causes fermentation is a very small living plant. We do not know very much about what actually happens during fermentation. We do know that a little bit of yeast can change a large amount of starch to sugar, and it will change the sugar into alcohol if it is left there long enough. The yeast causes these changes by giving off chemicals called enzymes.

A very famous chemist and biologist discovered that small bits, or spores, of yeast are floating around in the air all the time. This man, whose name was Louis Pasteur, found that these yeast

spores were causing all kinds of food to spoil. He said that if food was heated, these yeast spores would die and the food would not spoil so easily. This process by which food is heated to prevent spoilage is called pasteurization in honor of Louis Pasteur. It is used a great deal, especially in the milk industry.

Fermi, Enrico

Enrico Fermi became famous as one of the scientists who helped the United States develop the atomic bomb during World War II. The United States government awarded him the Medal of Merit in 1946 for his work on this project. Fermi was born in Italy in 1901, and he lived there until 1939. Then he came to the United States because he was not happy living under Mussolini's dictatorship. Fermi taught physics at Columbia University and the University of Chicago Institute for Nuclear Studies. He received the Nobel Prize in physics in 1938. He died in 1954.

ferns

Ferns are a group of plants that are among the oldest in the world, nearly 350,000,000 years old. There are about 8,000 different kinds of fern, varying from a single leaf fern to a towering tree fern of 80 feet, which is about the height of an ordinary eight-story building.

Ferns are found wherever the soil is not covered by snow or ice. The filmy ferns live in rocks beneath a waterfall, getting their water from the spray; other kinds of fern live in the cracks of cliff walls or deep ravines, which are narrow valleys between mountains. They can also be found in a cool, shaded woodland or on the hot, baked ground of a desert.

In the tropics, ferns may live high up on the trees, where their weight, after a heavy rain, sometimes brings the branches down. They are so widespread that they can be found anywhere from north of Greenland (a country near the North Pole) to the hot jungles near the equator. However, ferns are scarce in some regions and abundant in others; for example, there are only 250 kinds of fern in the land north of Mexico while the small island of Jamaica in the Caribbean Sea has more than 500 kinds all by itself. In any event, most ferns are found in the tropical jungles.

Ferns are very leafy. The fern leaves are called *fronds*. Fern fronds never have flowers.

Ferns differ from other plants in their method of reproduction, the way in which all new plant life is grown or reproduced. Most plant reproduction is carried on by germination, which is seed sprouting. Ferns, however, do not have seeds. Ferns have tiny microscopic organs called spores that are contained in holders on the underside of the fern's frond. These spore-holders are called sporangia. Each of these sporangia acts as a kind of gun, or propelling instrument. It shoots out the spores, scattering them some distance from the fern plant. The spore is planted in this way and then begins to sprout like an ordinary seed. The spore plant is heart-shaped and very small. Tiny roots grow from this new plant. Some of these roots are male and some are female. The male and female roots merge

(grow together), causing the spore plant to grow into a fern. The fern method of reproduction is called the cycle of alternating generations.

Some ferns are used by florists in flower arrangements. One kind of fern, known as the Boston fern, is very popular in the United States for its grace and beauty. In the tropics, tree ferns are used for building purposes because they do not decay easily. The fiber of a tree fern growing in the Hawaiian Islands is used for filling mattresses. It is called *pula*.

Ferrara

Ferrara is a very old city in northwestern Italy. The main part of the city is inside a great wall that was built five hundred years ago to protect the people from the armies of neighboring towns. Ferrara was a leading art center in Italy. Poets and painters came from all over Italy to live there.

If you were to go to Ferrara today you would see many of the beautiful paintings and statues that these artists did while they lived there. There are several beautiful palaces, and a cathedral where there are many statues of people who are buried there. Ferrara is three miles from the River Po, one of the most important rivers in Italy. The population today is about 143,000.

ferret

The ferret is a fierce, red-eyed, yellowish-white animal that has been used for centuries to destroy rats and hunt rabbits. It is about fourteen inches long, very strong, with a powerful neck and a long body that can go right into the burrow, or hole, of the rat or rabbit. Because it is so good at digging out its prey, the ferret's name has come to be used as a word meaning "to hunt busily." The ferret is rare today.

Ferris wheel

The Ferris wheel is a ride found in many fairs and amusement parks. It is actually two wheels joined together and is usually about fifty feet high. Between the two wheels there are twenty to thirty cars, each of which can carry two to four passengers. The Ferris wheel is always gaily decorated with colored lights. As it turns, and your car reaches the top of the wheel, you can see the park and the surrounding area.

The first Ferris wheel was built by George W. Ferris, who was an American engineer. He built the wheel for the World's Columbian Exposition held in Chicago in 1893. This first wheel was nearly 280 feet high and had 36 cars. Each car could hold about forty passengers.

ferry

A ferry is a boat to take people or freight back and forth across a narrow stretch of water, such as a river, a lake, or a bay. Today bridges are replacing ferries almost everywhere, except in places where the stretch of water is too wide for a bridge, but there are still thousands of ferries used for shorter trips.

For thousands of years ferries were moved by oars, sails, poles, or tow ropes. Poles were used when the water was shal-

low enough so that the men who ran the ferry could reach bottom with a long pole and push the ferry across. When ropes were used they were tied to trees on the sides of the water, and the crew of the ferry moved the boat from one side of the water to the other by pulling on the ropes.

Robert Fulton, who built the first steamboat, also built the first successful power-driven ferryboat. This boat was built in 1810 and crossed the East River, in New York City, between Manhattan and Brooklyn. It was a "paddle wheeler." A steam engine turned a big wheel that had paddles attached to it. You can read more about this boat in the article STEAMBOAT in another volume of this encyclopedia.

By the end of the 1800s there were dozens of ferries carrying tens of thousands of passengers every day across the rivers to New York City. Even today thousands of people who live in New Jersey take ferries across the Hudson River to their work in New York, in spite of the fact that there are three railroad tunnels, four automobile tunnels and one bridge across the river.

MODERN FERRYBOATS

Many of today's ferryboats are huge vessels 300 feet long. Some of them can carry 1,000 passengers and 80 cars or trucks.

Thousands of visitors to New York City have taken "the world's greatest five-cent ride" on the ferry across New York Harbor to Staten Island. The Puget Sound ferryboat, which travels across Puget Sound at Seattle in the state of Washington, has a 3,000-horsepower engine and can travel at 18 knots (more than 20 miles an hour). It carries 2,000 people and 110 automobiles.

fertilization

Fertilization is a part of the process of reproduction in both plants and animals. There are two types of reproduction: 1, asexual, in which a new organism develops from a part of the parent organism, and 2, sexual reproduction, in which special cells, the *ovum*, or female cell egg, and the *sperm*, the male cell, must be brought together in order to produce a new organism. The bringing together of the ovum and sperm is called fertilization.

In the higher plants the reproductive organs are in the flower. This is where the ovum and sperm grow. While the flower is ripening, a dry, powdery substance called pollen is being produced. Each grain of pollen contains the sperm, and it collects on the ripe flower until finally it begins to drift away. Rain and wind, and the insects that visit the flower, help to spread it; and soon the grains of pollen reach another part of the flower, where the egg cell is waiting. Here the sperm fuses with the egg, and the egg becomes fertilized. Now the fertilized egg contains the two parts that will grow into a seed from which new plants can grow.

Fertilization is the same among most of the animals. Here the ovum and the sperm unite to form a *zygote*. The zygote is the fertilized egg, and it grows into

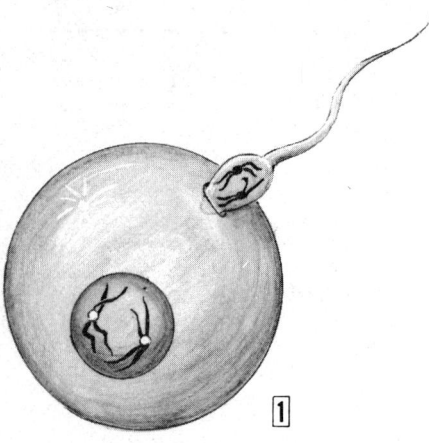

1.

Fertilization in an animal begins when a sperm cell enters an egg cell and moves towards the nucleus of the egg.

2.

Here the nucleus of the sperm cell with its long tail approaches the nucleus of the egg cell in order to merge with it.

3.

The nuclei have merged. The curved black strips are chromosomes that control many things in the baby to be formed.

drawings by D. Millspaugh

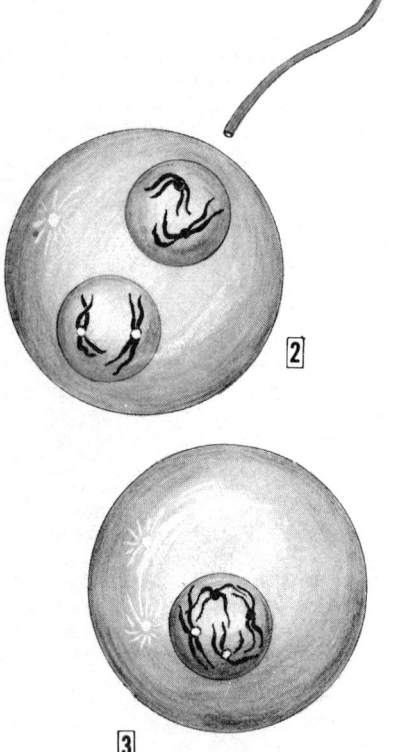

what is called an *embryo*. The embryo is the young of any animal while it is inside the egg, or inside the mother. It grows and becomes the young of the species.

After the egg cell has been fertilized, *cleavage,* or division, takes place. Each cell divides to form two, then these cells divide to form four, and these cells divide and form eight, and so the process continues until the young chick is ready to emerge from the eggshell, or the new baby is ready to be born.

Nearly all animals grow from eggs and develop through cleavage. Ripe sperm, among animals, are contained in a liquid base that is produced by the male animal. Sperm are so tiny that they cannot be seen by the naked eye. They have long tails with which they swim to the ovum or female cells, which they enter to complete the process of fertilization.

fertilizer

Fertilizer is any substance used to enrich the soil for the purpose of giving food to plants. Plants need many different minerals and chemicals in order to grow and bear well. When the soil does not contain enough of one or more of the important minerals or elements, fertilizer is used.

One of the oldest fertilizers is manure, or the droppings of domesticated animals. This is collected and spread over the area that is to be planted. Other types include bone meal, fish meal, and waste matter from the meat-packing houses and food-processing plants.

When a farmer is in doubt about the quality of the soil of his farm, he takes a sample and has it tested. Then he will know what is needed. The plant foods most often missing are nitrogen, phosphorus, and potash. When you buy a bag of fertilizer you will see numbers on it that indicate the amount of these elements, in the order given above. If the numbers are 4–8–12, it means that the bag contains 4 pounds of nitrogen, 8 pounds of phosphoric acid, and 12 pounds of potash. The elements can also be bought separately.

Should the soil contain too much acid, limestone is used as a chemical agent to lessen the acidity. There are many elements that are needed in very small quantities, such as copper, boron, iron, manganese, zinc, sulphur, and cobalt. Sometimes these elements are diluted in water and sprayed on the soil, or they may be mixed with the base fertilizer. The new drugs called antibiotics are also used in modern agriculture to combat plant diseases. These are usually sprayed directly on the crops.

In Peru, the droppings of large sea birds are used for fertilizer. It is called guano, and is sold widely in South America and in many other parts of the world. It is rich in nitrogen.

festival

A festival is a special time set aside for people to mark some particular season or enjoy themselves in a particular way. It may be a single day, or several days, or longer. Festivals have been an important part of people's lives ever since there was any kind of civilization, and the ancient festivals were always a part of the people's religion. There were festivals in the spring, when the earth became green again and the people could grow crops; there were festivals in the fall, when the crops were harvested. When the Christian church came to form the festivals gradually came to mark great events in religious history.

In ancient Greece, one of the greatest festivals was the Olympic Games. These were athletic contests among the strongest young men of the country, and today the Olympic Games are held in very much the same way as they were then.

Another festival we have from ancient times is the May Pole Dance. This festival was started by the Druids, who were the priests and religious leaders in what we now call England, two thousand years ago. It celebrated the coming of spring. A May Pole Dance can be a beautiful thing to see and a great deal of fun to take part in. Streamers of flowers, colored ribbons, or long strips of colored paper are attached to the top of a tall pole. Each dancer takes a ribbon, and they weave in and out around the pole in special ways until all of the streamers are braided around the pole. The May Pole Dance is still danced in England every May 1.

In France, festivals have always been called "fêtes." In Spanish countries they are called "fiestas." At these festivals you will find lots of singing and dancing. Sometimes you might think they were county fairs, because there are many trained animals and gaily decorated booths where you can buy pretty things and special kinds of food.

Most of the festivals we know today are film festivals, music festivals and dance festivals. Movie, or film, festivals are held in many different cities in Europe. At these festivals are shown the best films made by different countries. There are film festivals in Venice, Italy, in Berlin, Germany, and in Cannes, France.

The most popular kind of festival nowadays is a music festival, and several important ones are held each year. One is the Bayreuth Festival. It is in the city of Bayreuth in Germany. You sit in a theater designed by Richard Wagner, the great German composer. He built this theater because he thought there was no perfect theater in the world where his music could be heard at its best. Each summer world-famous singers come to the theater to sing in Wagner's operas. An opera is a play in which the words are sung instead of spoken. Another famous music festival is held in Austria, in the city of Salzburg. Here you can see plays and operas and hear symphony orchestras and many great musicians. You sit in the beautiful Mozart Square for the opening of the festival. Men stand up in the hills surrounding the city. At the right moment they all blow on silver trumpets. This means that the festival can begin, and no matter where you are in the city of Salzburg you can hear the silver trumpets.

In America, the most important music festival is held in the Berkshire hills in Massachusetts, in the town of Tanglewood. The music is performed by the Boston Symphony Orchestra. You can sit under a tree and hear the music being played in a huge building called the "Shed," which is open on three sides. Another kind of festival, the dance festival, has become popular in the United States since World War II. At a dance festival you see ballet, or modern dances, or old folk dances. Sometimes you can see Oriental dances from India and Siam, in which the dancers wear lots of little bells on their wrists and ankles. The most famous dance festival is held at Jacob's Pillow in Lee, Massachusetts.

There is an old mining town in Colorado called Central City. Every summer

hundreds of people go to a festival there. There are plays and operas in a wonderful old-fashioned opera house. Everyone celebrates the memory of this once-famous mining town.

fetishism

Fetishism is the belief that any object can have a magical power or can be treated like a person. The object, which is called a fetish, can be practically anything. Trees, statues, knives, pictures, and clothing can all become fetishes. Fetishism is most common among the primitive tribes of Africa. A native who is ready to go hunting may talk to his spear, telling it how well he has treated it and how much he is relying on it in the hunt. Or he may talk to a river and ask it to upset his enemies' canoes.

Fetishism is found in our everyday life too. The belief that rubbing a rabbit's foot brings good luck is fetishism. Kissing the picture of someone you love or talking to a doll is also fetishism. People everywhere have had fetishes.

feudalism

Feudalism was a system of living that was followed in Europe for nearly 1,500 years. Some of the traces of this system lasted into our twentieth century, and it took the two World Wars to put an end to them. Other countries, especially Japan, have also followed the feudal system in modern times (as recently as a hundred years ago).

In the feudal system, every man and woman had a definite place, and it was almost impossible to change jobs. For example, if your father was a farmer, you would be a farmer too. If you wanted to leave the farm or even to get married to someone who lived on another farm, you would have to get permission from the lord who owned the farm. The lord, who ruled all the farmers on his land, was himself ruled by a more powerful lord or by the king of the country. These lords, who lived in great stone castles, spent a great deal of their time fighting each other. When a war started, the farmers had to leave their land and fight under the lord. Feudalism was a very harsh system. Today, when we want to call a way of ruling a country very bad and old-fashioned, we often say that it is feudal.

HOW FEUDALISM CAME ABOUT

At one time, until 1,500 years ago, all of western Europe was ruled by the Roman Empire. There was an army to keep law and order and most people lived peacefully. Then Rome was conquered by a number of wild tribes from the East and North. No one in Europe was strong enough to keep order. The farmers, many of whom owned their own land, never knew when some group of soldiers was going to tramp over their land, steal their crops and animals, and perhaps even kill them and their families. So the farmers wanted the most powerful landlord in their neighborhood to protect them. The landlord took the farmer's land and made the farmer a kind of slave, called a serf. The landlord and his army protected the farmers from enemy soldiers, but in return the farmer had to give up a large share of his crops.

LORDS AND VASSALS

Every important lord in those days had his own bodyguard. The lord rewarded these men for helping him by giving them a part of his land, with all the serfs on it. The men in the bodyguard became knights. (There is a separate article on KNIGHTHOOD). In return for the land, the knights kneeled down in front of the lord and solemnly swore to serve under him and never to turn against him. This was known as "paying homage." The knights were then called "vassals" of the lord.

Many of the lords had got their land in the same way from the king, and they were his vassals. The knights owned land, but they did not become farmers. The serfs still did all the work, and the knights took a good share of what they produced as taxes. The knights spent most of their time living in the lord's castle and fighting in his wars.

Besides the knights, the lord had other vassals who were not so important. Some of these were called "sergeants," and the modern army rank of sergeant comes originally from feudalism. The sergeants got small amounts of land, and in return they did various jobs for the lord. The king of England had one sergeant who held the king's head if he got sick crossing the English Channel. The job of another sergeant was to cook for the king.

THE CLERGY

In western Europe there was only one Church, which was Roman Catholic. People were very religious, and many important lords gave part of their lands to the clergy (or priests). Some clergymen became feudal lords themselves, and even fought as soldiers. Many men who were very religious wanted to get away from the hurly-burly life of feudalism, so they became monks and entered monasteries where they could pray and work in peace. There were no printing presses in those days, and the monks spent a lot of time copying old books and manuscripts. These have been handed down to us, and they tell us what life was like in those times.

The clergy tried to do what they could to make life less terrible for the people. They ordered soldiers not to kill women and children, and not to fight on week-ends or holy days (the word "holiday" originally meant a "holy day"). These rules were not always obeyed, but they helped make life more pleasant.

FEUDAL TRIALS

If you were a knight and you had an argument with another knight, you would go to your lord to have it settled. The lord would get together a number of knights, and they would decide who was in the right. Sometimes the knights, who were like a modern jury, would hear what both of you had to say, and sometimes they would use other ways of settling an argument. One way was to throw a man who had been accused of a crime into a pool of water. If he floated he was judged guilty, and if he sank he was innocent. This may seem like a silly way to settle an argument, but these men thought that water would not accept a guilty man. Sometimes an argument was settled by having the two men fight, and the winner was judged to have been right in the argument.

CASTLE LIFE

The lord, his vassals, and their families and servants all lived together in a castle. In the cellar of the castle there were dungeons where the lord kept his enemies, often chained to the walls. On the first floor there was just one big room. At one end there was a fireplace that was used for roasting whole animals on a spit and for keeping the castle warm. The floor was covered with reeds or straw, and all the knights and their ladies ate together at long tables. Table manners were not much like today's. Forks had not been invented, and the knights would tear off pieces of a big joint of meat and eat them with their hands. They drank wine or beer out of big glasses called goblets. Some of these goblets held more than a quart. The servants sat around the sides of the room, and when the knights had finished eating they would throw them scraps of food that they did not want.

In summer, the knights would go hunting and riding in the forests near the castle, but in the winter life was very dull. Tapestries were hung a few feet in front of the walls of the room to keep out the cold, and all the garbage would be thrown behind them.

Upstairs all the knights slept in one big room. There was usually only one big bed, with curtains around it, where the lord and his wife slept. The others would sleep on straw that had been placed on the floor. Every now and then, peddlers (who were like traveling salesmen) would visit the castle, and that would be a time of great fun for the lords and ladies. They would buy rich cloths, perfumes and spices that came from the East, and they would listen to gossip from other castles. There were hardly any big cities in Europe where things could be bought in stores, so the arrival of a peddler was a big event. There would also be minstrels who sang songs and told stories. But usually life in a castle was not very pleasant.

FARM LIFE

The life of the serfs was much worse than that of the lords and knights who lived in castles. If you were a serf, you would have to live all your life in one village. It was built near a castle, so that in case of danger you could run into the castle and be protected. The village was made up of a few little hovels that had dirt floors and no windows. Glass had not been invented and it was too cold in the winter to have open windows. You would work in the fields all day. The lord would get a good share of the food you grew as taxes, and another share (known as a "tithe," or tenth) would go to the Church. You would have no money to buy anything, and the clothes you wore would probably be made by your mother or wife. Very often the serfs would live together with the pigs and cattle in their homes. The women would have to go and work for the lord's wife in the castle a few times every year, but they would not be paid for it. Because everyone was

so poor, there was not much meat to eat, except for pork occasionally. Mostly the serfs lived on bread, oatmeal, and similar food. On Sundays there were games and dancing in the village, but all week the work was very hard.

THE END OF FEUDALISM

About six hundred years ago feudalism began to disappear from western Europe. It stayed on in eastern Europe for long after that, and even a hundred years ago many people lived under a system like feudalism. People began to get richer in western Europe, and there was more trade between different countries. Many serfs were able to save up money and then pay their lords to set them free. Others ran away to the towns that were growing up, where they became shopkeepers and craftsmen. The kings of England, France, and other countries conquered the feudal lords and set up central governments with real armies and police forces like the ones we have today. It took a long time, but gradually the life of feudalism disappeared.

feud

A feud is warfare, not between nations or states, but between private groups, tribes, gangs, or families. Nowadays there are laws for our protection, and police to see that the laws are obeyed, but very long ago there were no laws or police. A person had to depend for his safety on his friends or relatives to help him if he were wronged, or to avenge him if he were killed. This meant that every member of a family or group was responsible for what his relatives or his friends did, and this is the way law enforcement began. Of course, one would not allow a relative to kill a member of some other family, if it were sure to lead to a feud in which one might be killed oneself. So people began to urge their closest relatives to respect the lives of others, and law replaced feuds.

fever

When the temperature of the human body becomes higher, meaning warmer, than it usually is, we call it a fever. The usual temperature in most people's bodies is about 98.6 degrees on a Fahrenheit thermometer, although for some people it may be a little higher and for some a little lower. Your temperature will stay about the same unless a disease gets started within your body.

CAUSES OF FEVER

The germs of a disease soon make toxins, or poisons, which they give off, and these toxins excite the nerves and blood vessels throughout the body. Soon the heart beats faster and everything within the body goes faster, so much so that the temperature rises from as little as one degree, as in a simple cold, to seven degrees with more serious diseases. A fever is a symptom, meaning a sign, of some disease that your body is fighting; so if the fever is high, meaning two or more degrees above your normal or usual temperature, or if the fever lasts for any length of time, it means a serious disease and your doctor should treat it at once. The fever by itself is a sign the body has a disease, and also means it is fighting the disease.

TREATING A FEVER

During a fever a large amount of sweating, or perspiring, occurs so that a person must drink more water to replace what is lost. More food is burned up inside the body, so it is usually wrong to follow the old saying, "Starve a fever."

BELOW NORMAL TEMPERATURES

Sometimes a person's temperature may go far below normal. This too may be a sign that something is wrong. It happens when people collapse from working too hard in hot rooms or on hot days.

Fez

Fez is the name of a large city in the kingdom of Morocco, in North Africa. It was founded more than a thousand years ago by a Mohammedan ruler named Idris II. Fez became the home of many important rulers and scholars, and about six hundred years ago became the capital of an independent kingdom. However, three hundred years later it was conquered and became a part of Morocco. Today it is one of the four capitals of that country.

About 220,000 people live in Fez. Most of the people are Moslems, but there are a few Europeans and Jews. The city is divided into two parts, Fez Djedid and Fez-el-Bali. Fez-el-Bali is the oldest part of town. In both parts of the city there are many beautiful monuments and mosques, which are the religious meeting places for the Mohammedan people. The famous Qarawiyin mosque and university attract students from all over North Africa. Fez is known for its beautiful scenery, and the low foothills and plains around the city are covered with gardens and orchards.

fez

The fez is a kind of hat worn by many men in the Mohammedan countries. It is sometimes called the tarboosh. The fez is round, without a brim, and it has a flat top. It is usually made of red felt, and attached to the top there is a black tassel that hangs down to the bottom edge of the hat. The fez was the national headdress of Turkey for many years. However, nearly thirty years ago it became illegal to wear a fez in Turkey, and the men had to change to European-style hats. Many people still wear the fez in other Mohammedan countries in North Africa and in the Middle East.

fiber

Fibers are tiny hairlike bits, usually much shorter and finer (thinner) than hairs. Almost all living things, whether they are plants or animals, have fibers in them, and some fibers are found in minerals. Fibers are very important to our lives. All cloth and other fabrics, and all paper, depend on fibers. So do hundreds of other things, from hairbrushes to certain paints.

The tiny hairlike fibers cling together, forming a sort of chain. This can be drawn out to form thread used in weaving or pressed together to form paper or felt. The longer the fibers are, the stronger the thread, or paper, or other product will be.

A "long" fiber may still be so short that you would hardly notice it. The white, fluffy cotton boll is a mass of fibers. Cotton is graded by the length of its fibers (called the staple). Long-fiber cotton costs more than short-fiber cotton, because it makes stronger cloth. The flax plant has a longer fiber than cotton, and the cloth made from it (called linen) is stronger than cotton cloth. The pulp of a tree has longer fibers than the wood. The cheapest, shortest-lived paper, the kind used in newspapers, is made from the short-fibered "groundwood," while better paper is made from the longer wood fibers and the best paper of all is made from cotton or linen fibers.

WHERE FIBERS COME FROM

The strongest fibers that come from plants are taken from the bast, or inner bark. These fibers taken from hemp and jute make very strong, but coarse, ropes and heavy burlap bags. Often the fibers are naturally combined in the plant, as they are in the reeds used in basket making. In other cases they are spun into yarn, as for cords and ropes.

Natural fibers from cotton are used not only for cloth but also to make plastics (the cellulose plastics) that can resemble ivory, bone, or shell.

Animal fibers include wool and silk. These are made into yarn or thread for weaving. They are stronger than vegetable fibers. Other natural fibers include the bristles, or stiff hairs, used in brushes.

Mineral fibers include asbestos, which can be made into fabrics. Glass can be spun into fibers that make fabrics of great strength.

Synthetic (man-made) fibers include nylon and many others. They can be made from coal or petroleum and from many chemical combinations.

Since these different fibers have many different qualities—in length, smoothness, color, strength, resistance to water or sunlight or wear—when we choose a material for a particular purpose we are actually choosing a particular fiber that best suits the purpose.

fiction, stories that are not true but are fun to read: see the articles on NOVELS and LITERATURE.

fiddle, a name sometimes given to the violin: see the article on VIOLIN.

fiddler crab

The fiddler crab is usually found along the sandy shores of the hot and warm regions of the world. It got its name because the male crab sometimes waves its huge claw as though it were playing a violin (or fiddle). When the ocean's high tide rolls in to shore, the fiddler crab burrows deep into the soft mud. As soon as the tide begins to ebb, the crab scurries from its hole in search of food left by the receding waters; at this time, vast numbers of them can sometimes be seen. The fiddler crab is a very small crab. The biggest one measures only one and one-half inches across its body. It is extremely common along the Atlantic coast of the United States.

fiduciary

Fiduciary is the legal name for a person who holds something in trust—has the duty of taking care of it. A person can be said to act in a fiduciary

capacity, which means that he is holding something in trust, or taking charge of something.

For instance, a child whose parents die has a guardian to take charge of him. This guardian is a fiduciary, and he acts in a fiduciary capacity. A lawyer acts in a fiduciary capacity toward a client, that is, he has an obligation to deal fairly with him. The same is true of two businessmen in partnership; they are entitled to place trust in each other.

Field, Cyrus W.

Cyrus W. Field was an American merchant who became famous for the part he played in laying the first telegraphic cable across the Atlantic Ocean.

Stockbridge Library Association

Field was born in 1819 in Stockbridge, Massachusetts, and he made a small fortune early in life in the paper business. After Field retired in 1853 he became interested in a Canadian idea to put a telegraphic line across Newfoundland. Field knew that Newfoundland was closer to Europe than any other place in North America, so he thought it would be a good idea to extend the line by laying a cable across the Atlantic Ocean. This would allow messages to be telegraphed between Europe and America, instead of depending on slow ships to carry them. After many attempts, a cable was laid in August 1858, and the first message was sent. After only three weeks something went wrong with the cable and Field had to try to get it done all over again. At last, in 1866 the huge ship *The Great Eastern* successfully laid a cable.

Field won many honors, and a vote of thanks from the United States Congress for his great work. Later, he helped to get other cables laid across the Pacific Ocean to Asia and Australia. He died in 1892.

Field, Eugene

Eugene Field was an American writer who is best known as the author of "Little Boy Blue," "Wynken, Blynken and Nod," and many other poems for children. He was born in 1850 in St. Louis, Missouri. After he finished college, he traveled to Europe and worked on several newspapers. Then he began writing a column for the Chicago *Daily News*. He had married in the meantime, and his young children inspired him to write his most famous poems, which appeared in his newspaper column. Grownups as well as children like his poetry. He died in 1895.

Field, Marshall

Marshall Field has been the name of four famous Americans. They have been prominent in business and have given a great deal to charity and good works. Today the name is prominent in the publishing of books and newspapers.

The first Marshall Field was born in Conway, Massachusetts, in 1835. When he was twenty-one years old he moved to Chicago, where he took a job as a clerk in a department store. Within ten years he was one of the owners of the store. At his

death in 1906 he had been its head for many years and it was named Marshall Field and Company. It is one of the largest department stores in the world. Marshall Field gave many gifts to institutions and organizations. He gave money to build the Chicago Natural History Museum (the "Field Museum") and part of the land for the campus of the University of Chicago.

Marshall Field II, his son, was in poor health most of his life, and did not take an active part in his family's business. He was born in 1868 and died in 1905.

Marshall Field III, the son of Marshall Field II, was born in Chicago in 1893. He came to be called simply Marshall Field. He spent much of his youth in Europe, and went to Eton, one of England's finest boys' schools, and to Trinity College at Cambridge University, in England. He served as an officer in the United States Army during World War I and was decorated for bravery. Later he became a banker in Chicago. He always had great interest in human rights, as he explains in his book *Freedom Is More Than a Word*.

In 1940, Marshall Field helped to finance the New York newspaper *PM*. In 1941 he started the *Chicago Sun*, a liberal daily newspaper. Later he bought the *Chicago Times* and combined the two newspapers. He organized a corporation called Field Enterprises to control his many interests in the publication and communication fields. In addition to his newspapers, these interests included several book-publishing firms, radio stations, and the magazine *Parade*.

Marshall Field made many contributions to charitable and civic organizations. To the Chicago Museum founded by his grandfather he gave a 38-story office building in Chicago. The Field Foundation, Inc., which he founded in 1940, helps finance charitable projects. Each year it gives about $600,000 to educational and charitable organizations, particularly those interested in child welfare and in solving social and racial problems. Marshall Field died in 1956.

Marshall Field IV, usually called Marshall Field, Jr., was born in 1916. He went to Harvard University and to the University of Virginia Law School. He was a naval officer in World War II, and became the publisher and editor of *The Chicago Sun-Times*. In 1957 and 1958, Marshall Field, Jr., sold several of the book-publishing firms and also sold *Parade* (to John Hay Whitney); then in 1959 he bought the old and highly respected newspaper *The Chicago Daily News* and merged it with the *Sun-Times*. He and his father owned no share of the department store.

field artillery, heavy guns that are mounted on wheels so that they can move easily to aid infantry in battle: see the article on ARTILLERY.

Fielding, Henry

Henry Fielding is an English writer who is often called the "father of the modern novel." A novel is a very long story in book form. There had been many

novels written before Fielding came along, but he made the books he wrote more lifelike and true. He used everyday people who might be your next-door neighbors as characters, and he used everyday events that could happen to you, as the stories in his books. Fielding was born in 1707. He started writing plays when he was quite young. In his plays he wrote many unkind things about Sir Robert Walpole, who was Prime Minister of England then. Walpole did not like it and had a law passed which made it impossible for Fielding to get a license for a London theater. He had to have a license to produce his plays. So, since he could not get one, he had to find another way to earn a living and support his wife and children.

In 1737, Fielding started to study law. He was appointed Justice of the Peace, which is a kind of judge, in 1748. While he was working as a lawyer and a judge he continued to do a lot of writing. Fielding wrote his novel *The History of Tom Jones* during this time. It has a very complicated plot and many amusing characters. *Tom Jones* and *Joseph Andrews* are the two novels for which he is best remembered. He got tired from all of his work, and took a trip to Portugal to rest. He died in Lisbon, Portugal, in 1754.

field marshal

Field marshal is the highest rank in the British army. It is about the same rank as General of the Army (five-star general) in the United States Army. A field marshal's insignia is a crown with a wreath underneath, with two crossed batons inside the wreath. The baton, which is like the stick that an orchestra leader uses, is the special sign of a field marshal. The first field marshals were appointed by King George II of England in 1736. Ten field marshals were appointed in the British Army during and after World War II. See also MARSHAL.

Field of the Cloth of Gold

After many years of war, England and France were at peace in the year 1520 and King Henry VIII of England met King Francis I of France for a friendly conference. They met on a field near the town of Calais, which is on the French side of the English Channel but which at that time belonged to England.

The meeting was famous for its beauty and was called the Field of the Cloth of Gold. Everyone wore beautiful clothes and gold and jewels. It was so dazzling it looked as though everything had been made of gold. So many people came with each of the kings that a great many tents had to be put up. These tents were very tall and of many gay colors. During each day of the conference there were feasts, games, and dancing. But not very much was accomplished and after about two weeks everyone went home.

fife

The fife is a musical instrument that belongs to the flute family. It is played by blowing across a mouthhole, or *em-*

bouchure. Years ago the fife was a metal or wood tube about twelve inches long. It had six fingerholes and a mouthhole. The modern fife has keys as well as fingerholes. The pitch, or tone range, of the fife is between the pitch of the flute and that of the piccolo. It has a shrill tone and is most often used by fife and drum corps in military parades. Fifes are sometimes used to play reels, marches, and hornpipes.

Fifth Amendment

The Fifth Amendment, in the BILL OF RIGHTS, says that no person may be forced to be a witness against himself. This means that the defendant in a criminal case does not have to go on the witness stand and testify if he does not wish to do so; but also the Supreme Court of the United States has said that a witness in a court trial or formal investigation, even if he is not the defendant and is not accused of any crime, need not answer a question if the answer might "tend to incriminate or degrade him"—that is, to make him seem guilty of a crime or to hurt his reputation.

Many persons in trials or in Congressional hearings are said to "take the Fifth," or refuse to answer a question, because of this constitutional privilege. Some persons have "taken the Fifth" dozens of times in a single Congressional hearing. Very often such persons have "taken the Fifth" by refusing to say whether or not they are, or have ever been, Communists. Actually a person's reputation usually suffers about as much when he "takes the Fifth" as when he answers the question, and some employers dismiss employees who "take the Fifth." Therefore the spirit of the Fifth Amendment could be preserved only if examiners were forbidden to ask any question to which the answer might be incriminating. Occasionally a judge or committee chairman has ruled that the Fifth Amendment does not apply to a certain question, and when the person asked refuses to answer he is cited for contempt of court or contempt of Congress, but in very few cases has a person been punished for this.

fifth column

A fifth column is a group of people who work secretly against their own government in wartime. The expression was first used during the Spanish Civil War, which lasted from 1936 to 1939. In that war, General Francisco Franco led a rebellion against the government. He finally won the war and established the government that rules Spain today. The story is told that early in the Spanish war, one of Franco's generals was asked how he expected to capture the capital, Madrid. He answered: "I have four columns moving against Madrid and a fifth will rise up inside the city itself." He meant that in addition to his troops, who were the four columns, there were many spies, saboteurs, and sympathizers among the civilians inside Madrid, and that these people would help his army.

Fifty-four forty or fight

"Fifty-four forty or fight" was a slogan used by the Democratic Party in the United States in the elections of 1844. At that time, many American pioneers, mostly fur-trappers, cattle-raisers, and farmers, lived among British settlers in a region known as the Oregon Territory. The Oregon Territory started in the American Northwest and stretched into Canada, which was then a colony of Great Britain. Both the United States and Great Britain had claims to this land.

A dispute arose over the boundary separating America from Canada. The American settlers said they owned the land through latitude 54 degrees, 40 minutes, north. Latitude is an imaginary line that measures distances north and south from the equator. It measures distance in degrees; a *minute* is one-sixtieth part of a degree. England disagreed with this boundary. For a time it seemed that war was about to break out between England and the United States. At the last moment, however, President James K. Polk and the British Foreign Minister, Lord Aberdeen, agreed to a compromise on the 49th latitude that was used for most of the existing boundary between the United States and Canada. The American pioneers then joined the United States and later formed the states of Oregon and Washington.

fig

The fig is a pear-shaped, fairly sweet fruit that grows on a tree, the fig tree. The fig is one of the oldest foods in the world. There are about eight hundred varieties of it. Some are purple or black; some, including the Kadota figs of California, are yellow or nearly white. What is called the fruit is really a fleshy, pear-shaped container for the tiny flowers that grow inside the fig itself, and for the seeds that are the real fruit of the fig.

Most fig trees grow in hot countries, such as Spain, Italy, Turkey, and Greece. Probably they first grew in the steaming tropical forests of India and spread many centuries ago all around the Aegean Sea and the countries of the Near East. The ancient Greeks fed their slaves mainly on figs, and there are pictures of figs in the tombs of the old Egyptian kings. Today, Turkey raises the most figs to sell (more than 35,000 tons a year come from the district of Smyrna). California is next in production. Both Smyrna and California export dried figs. These figs are allowed to dry partially on the trees and fall to the ground. The figs are then gathered and the drying is finished on trays in the sun. Sometimes they are shipped in special "sweat boxes" and finish drying as they travel to the dealers. The fig is the only tree in the world that bears two crops of fruit every year.

figure of speech

You are using a figure of speech when you do not say exactly what you mean but you expect everyone to understand you anyway. When you say someone's heart is as hard as a rock, you do not mean that it is really hard. You mean the person is not very kind or sympathetic. But your meaning is quite clear.

There are several different kinds of figure of speech. There are special names for all of them. Most of these names come from the Greek language and almost no one ever uses them. All of them together are called *tropes.* The two figures of speech that are best known by their names are *metaphor* and *irony.*

A metaphor uses one idea to mean another idea. When a person is in a great hurry to get someplace, and he drives very fast, and then he says, "I burned up the road getting here," he is using a metaphor. One kind of metaphor is a comparison, which is called a *simile.* An example was given in the paragraph above. When you compare someone's heart to a rock, you are using a simile. You may say, "It's hot as an oven in here." That is a simile.

Irony is saying exactly the opposite of what you really mean. When it is raining very hard, and you say, "What a nice day it is!", you are saying the opposite of what you really mean. Anyone who hears you say it knows you mean it is a very bad day. Ironical statements are often the same thing as *sarcasm,* but a sarcastic statement is intended to poke fun at someone, or criticize him, and irony does not have to be sarcastic.

Fiji Islands

The Fiji Islands are a group of about 320 volcanic islands in the South Pacific Ocean, about 1,200 miles north of New Zealand. Their total land area is 7,055 square miles, which is a little smaller than New Jersey. Most of the islands are very small, and no one lives on them; about 519,000 people live on only 106 of the islands. 42% of the population are native Melanesians, tall and dark-skinned, with thick, frizzy hair which they comb straight up from their heads. A little more than 50% of the population are descendants of slaves brought to Fiji from India in the 1880's. The rest of the population are Chinese, white, or people from other islands. Although the Melanesians own 83% of the land, it is the Indians who control the business and professional life of the islands.

When Fiji became a British colony in 1874, the natives were warlike, uncivilized cannibals. They have since given up their savage ways, and today nearly all of them are Christians or Hindus. Suva, the capital of Fiji, is a modern city and center of commerce, with hotels, theaters, banks, and the new South Pacific University, which was opened in 1968. After Honolulu, Suva is the most important city in the Pacific Islands. Fiji's climate is tropical, but it seldom gets hotter than ninety degrees. November to April is the rainy season, often with severe hurricanes. Rainfall averages about 10 feet per year. Fiji's most important commercial crops are coconut and sugar, but rice, bananas, pineapples, cocoa, corn, and tobacco are also raised. Gold mining is a very important industry.

The Fiji Islands were discovered in 1643 by Captain Tasman, and later described in detail by Captain Bligh after the mutiny of the *Bounty* in 1789. (See the article on the BOUNTY.) In 1970, after 96 years as a British colony, Fiji became an independent member of the British Commonwealth.

FIJI ISLANDS. Area, 7,055 square miles. Population (1969 estimate) 519,000. Capital, Suva.

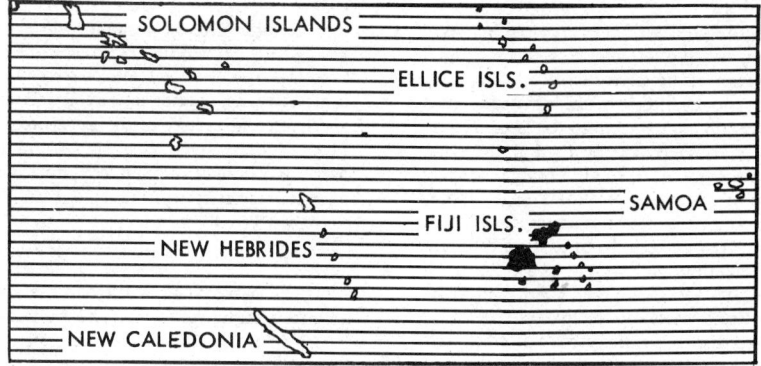

filbert, a nut that grows on the hazel tree in the United States and Europe and is very good to eat: see the article on HAZEL NUT.

filibuster

A filibuster is a very long speech, usually by a United States Senator, for the purpose of delaying a vote on a new law.

Sometimes a senator is very much against a proposed law, and in order to get it changed more to his liking he will make a speech in the senate and not stop until he gets his way. Most often filibusters are used near the end of the Senate's yearly meeting. Then senators talk until the end of the session so that there can be no vote on the law they oppose, and it will have to wait for many months until the next meeting. Sometimes a few senators filibuster and their speeches continue day and night without interruption for a week or more.

The Senate has often tried to stop filibusters by using the so-called cloture rule, which puts a limit on discussion of a new law; but most senators think they should not be stopped from talking all they want to, and the rule is not used often.

The word filibuster used to mean something very different. About three hundred years ago the Spaniards used it to mean a freebooter, or pirate. These pirates, or filibusters, were especially active a little over a hundred years ago. At that time many countries in Central and South America had weak governments, and often citizens of these countries wanted to overthrow their rulers. These men got together a band of piratelike soldiers to invade their own country and try to begin a new government. Some United States citizens led filibustering expeditions. The United States government was not at war with any of the countries who were victims of these filibusters, so the word came to mean a war between a private individual and a country. Some people thought that when a senator or small group of senators delayed the vote of a new law, it was like a war between filibusters and a country. For this reason the long speeches are called filibusters.

filigree

Filigree is a very delicate kind of decoration made of twisted wire. If you look at a piece of filigree you will see strands of gold or silver that are twisted and turned and formed into curlicues. In Asia, particularly India, filigree is very popular. The ancient Greeks used filigree ornaments three thousand years

ago. Almost every ancient race has used filigree work for pins and bracelets and earrings. Men digging in ancient ruins in South America have recently discovered that filigree work was worn there many hundreds of years ago.

The methods of making filigree are not much different today than they were thousands of years ago in Greece. The wires are twisted and curled to form a pattern.

Millard Fillmore

Millard Fillmore was the thirteenth President of the United States. He was serving as Vice President during the term of Zachary Taylor, and he became President when Taylor died in office, in 1850.

Fillmore's administration was short, because he did not become President until about a third of Taylor's term was over, and he was never re-elected.

While Fillmore was President he signed the Fugitive Slave Law, and this turned many northerners against him. Then he opposed the entrance of Texas into the Union as a slave state, and he was in favor of the annexation of Utah and New Mexico as territories without any laws against slavery, which turned many southerners against him. In fact, his policies pleased few people, and he was not nominated for re-election in 1852.

In 1856, the Know-Nothing and Whig parties nominated Fillmore. He was defeated in the election by James Buchanan, a Democrat. John C. Frémont ran on the Republican ticket in that election.

After his defeat, Millard Fillmore retired to private life and became Chancellor of the University of Buffalo. He died in Buffalo, New York, at the age of 74, on March 8, 1874.

HIS EARLY YEARS

Millard Fillmore was born in Cayuga

County, New York, in a section of the state that was still a wilderness. On January 7, 1800, when he was born, the nearest house was four miles away from the log cabin that was his family's home. The cabin was about thirty miles southwest of what is now Syracuse.

His family was very poor, and the only education he received was what the village school could provide. When he was fourteen, his father apprenticed him to a wool-carder, so that he could learn a trade. (An apprentice in those days agreed to work for a man for a certain length of time in order to learn a trade.) He worked to pay for being taught the trade, and after his training was completed he continued to work for a certain length of time in order to pay for the board and lodging he had received while he was learning. When Fillmore was nineteen, he still owed the wool-carder thirty dollars.

During his five years as an apprentice, he studied and read every evening to improve his education. When Fillmore was nineteen, he attracted the attention of a man named Wood, a judge, who took an interest in the young man who was trying so hard to learn in spite of all handicaps. Wood lent Fillmore the money to pay what he owed to the wool-carder. Wood then gave the lad a position in his law office. Fillmore began to study law with the Judge. Fillmore also became a part-time teacher, to earn some extra money.

To save money, he walked all the way to Buffalo at the age of twenty-one. He worked hard there to finish his law training and taught at the same time. Fillmore succeeded in becoming a lawyer, and a member of the New York State Bar in 1823. He practiced in the town of Aurora for several years, and then moved back to Buffalo.

In 1826 Fillmore married Abigail Powers, and in 1828 he began his political career. He was elected to the New York State Legislature, as representative from Erie County.

HOW HE BECAME PRESIDENT

As a member of the New York State Legislature, Fillmore earned a reputation for honesty and competence. He was largely responsible for legislation that made it illegal to throw a man in jail if he could not pay his debts. Before that, the debtor's prison had been a dreadful place to many honest people who simply did not have the money to pay what they owed.

Fillmore's next step up the political ladder was his election to Congress in 1832. He was re-elected several times. For three years, starting in 1844, he worked as a lawyer in private life. In 1847 he was elected comptroller of New York State. In the following year he was nominated for Vice President on the Whig Party ticket, and Zachary Taylor was nominated for President. Their party won in the election of November, 1848.

ABIGAIL POWERS FILLMORE

The first Mrs. Millard Fillmore was the daughter of a Baptist minister in Stillwater, New York. Her maiden name was Abigail Powers, and she was born in 1798. Before her marriage she taught school in Cayuga County, New York. She was an invalid, and because of her

poor health her daughter, Mary Abigail Fillmore, served as the White House hostess. Mrs. Fillmore died in 1853, and her daughter died a year later, at the age of 22.

CAROLINE CARMICHAEL MCINTOSH
FILLMORE

The second Mrs. Millard Fillmore was the widow of an Albany businessman when Fillmore married her in 1858. They had no children, and the second Mrs. Fillmore died in 1889.

film

A film is a thin layer or sheet of some material, and usually—but not always—you can see through it. For example when it rains a little bit and then grows cold, everything outdoors has a thin covering of ice upon it. We say it is covered with a film of ice. If you put a drop of oil in a glass of water, a thin layer of oil covers the surface of the water. We call this layer of oil a film because it is so thin.

When the word film is used by itself, it usually means the kind of film you put into your camera or the kind used to make movies. This kind of film is made of plastic in long narrow strips that are rolled on spools. To learn more about this kind of film, see the separate articles on PHOTOGRAPHY and MOTION PICTURES.

filters and filtration

Filters are devices that are used to separate things. A filter may be a piece of colored glass that will let only one color through, or it may be part of a radio that lets one kind of electricity pass through it. Chemists use filters to separate solids from liquids; in this case the filter may be a piece of paper. Most automobiles have oil filters in them to prevent dirt from getting into the engine. The oil filters may be made of paper, cloth, or even metal with fine holes in it.

Air filters are used for many reasons. In an air conditioner there are air filters that remove dust and dirt from the air. These filters are usually made of metal shreds closely packed together. Some big air conditioners use a spray of water to filter the air. The water collects all the dust and dirt and lets it settle in a large pan in the bottom of the air conditioner.

Air filters are also used in automobiles to clean the air that goes into the engine. Most of these filters use oil to collect the dirt. The stream of air passes over a small pool of oil and into a cloth filter that has oil in it. The oil helps the cloth catch dust because it is sticky.

Light filters are mostly used by photographers, but every time you wear sunglasses you are using a light filter. Light filters are used both in color photography and black-and-white photography. Filters for color photography make it possible to use outdoor film indoors and indoor film outdoors. A color filter also cuts through the haze in the air. In black-and-white photography, filters bring out certain colors that do not register well. Blue skies, for example, do not come out dark enough without a yellow, orange, green, or red filter. See also the article on PHOTOGRAPHY.

Usually paper filters are used in chemistry, but if the chemicals to be filtered are very strong acids that would eat away the paper, filters made of glass, clay, porcelain or stone must be used. These materials may also be used if the solid to be filtered is small enough to pass through paper. Some filters made of unbaked clay are fine enough to prevent the tiniest bacteria from passing through.

Sometimes the liquid passes through the filter too slowly and suction must be applied to speed up the filtration.

See also the articles on TOBACCO and CANCER.

finance

Finance is the management of large sums of money. It is private finance if the money is used in business, and public finance if the money is used by a government.

Banks and stock exchanges do most of the work of private finance. The purpose of private finance is to supply business enterprises with the money they need. This money is called CAPITAL, and there is a separate article about it. A company that has as much money as it needs is said to be properly financed. It gets this money in two ways. First, people invest money in the business. That is, they buy shares of ownership in the business. Investment is therefore an important part of finance. The second way for the business to get money is to borrow it. Nearly every business needs more money than the capital its investors have put into it. It borrows some or all of this money from banks. The rest it may borrow from individual persons who have extra money and want to earn interest. When these persons lend money to a business they receive printed papers called bonds, which are a sort of contract in which the business house promises to pay interest on the money and later to pay back all the money.

Finance is a very big and complicated business itself. Hundreds of thousands of men and women are in some branch of finance.

Public finance is a special form of finance. Like a business house, a government needs money to do the many things it must do for its citizens—provide police forces and fire departments, make laws, maintain armed forces, and many other things. The government's money comes partly from taxes and partly from borrowings. The department of a government that takes care of its financial problems is usually called the Treasury. In the Treasury Department are experts on public finance. They decide how much of the government's money it can get from taxes and how much it can borrow. They decide how much the government can afford to spend on certain things. Then they advise the legislative, or lawmaking, branch of the government (such as the Congress of the United States). The lawmakers then pass laws that control how the money is to be obtained and how it is to be spent.

Government financing is very much like business financing. The government borrows some money from banks. This is usually "short-term financing," which means that the government must pay back the money very soon, perhaps in a few months. The government also borrows from private investors and issues bonds. If you have a United States War Bond, Defense Bond, or Savings Bond, you have lent money to the government. Most of these bonds are "long-term financing," because the money does not have to be paid back for several years. See the article BOND.

finch

The name finch is used to identify a certain family of birds. The birds belonging to the finch family are usually small. Their bills are strong and hard because they are used in breaking seeds, one of the main foods finches eat. There are various kinds of bird in the finch family. Some of them make very nice household pets because they can be kept in cages without too much trouble. Perhaps the best-known finch is the canary. Other kinds of finch are sparrows, bullfinches, chaffinches, and goldfinches. There are more than five hundred kinds of finch, found all over the world.

fine arts, the name given to the highest forms of art: see the articles on ART, ARCHITECTURE, BALLET, DRAMA, MUSIC, PAINTING, POETRY, and SCULPTURE.

Fingal

There are many legends, or stories, in Ireland about a man named Fingal, or Finn MacCumhal (pronounced *ma-cool*), as he is sometimes called. He is the hero of many old folk stories and tales, but he was a real person. He was very tall and powerful, and was also very wise. About 1,700 years ago many armies were trying to invade and capture Ireland. In the year 250 the king, Cormac mac Airt, made Finn the head of an army called the Fianna. They roamed the countryside, protecting people and hunting in the forests. According to one old tale Finn's girl Grania was stolen from him by a member of his band. He hunted for the man all over Ireland and Scotland and finally found and killed him. He is also supposed to have had the help and protection of "the little people," or fairies. There is an enormous cave in the Hebrides Islands off the coast of Scotland that is called Fingal's Cave.

Finger Lakes

The Finger Lakes are a group of long, narrow lakes in the western part of the state of New York in the United States. They are called the Finger Lakes because the five biggest of the lakes are shaped like the fingers of a hand; however, there are more than five lakes. The region surrounding the Finger Lakes is very beautiful and many people go there for vacations. Besides its beauty, this region is also noted for the growing of grapes. A few hundred years ago, the Iroquois Indians, at one time one of the largest of the American Indian tribes, used to live in the beautiful woods around the Finger Lakes. All the lakes have Indian names. The names of the main lakes are Keuka, Seneca, Cayuga, Canandaigua, and Owasco.

PLAIN ARCH

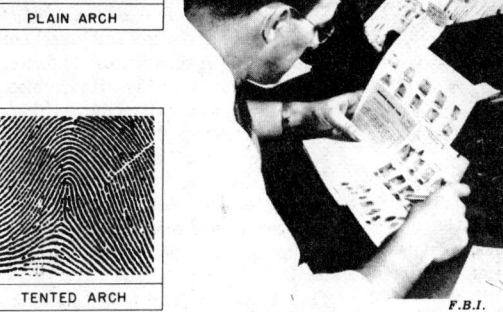

F.B.I.

TENTED ARCH

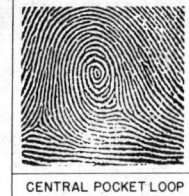

PLAIN WHORL

CENTRAL POCKET LOOP

LOOP

PRESENCE OR EXISTENCE OF WHORLS IN FINGER IMPRESSIONS IS USED AS THE BASIS FOR THE DETERMINATION OF THE CHIEF OR PRIMARY CLASSIFICATION EACH WHORL APPEARING IN ANY OR ALL OF THE TEN FINGERS HAS A CERTAIN ARBITRARY OR FIXED VALUE THE ADDITION OF THE VALUES REPRESENTED BY SUCH WHORLS AND THE INDICATION OF THE TOTAL VALUE IS KNOWN AS THE PRIMARY CLASSIFICATION. ILLUSTRATIONS OF THE WHORL TYPES WHICH ARE THE SAME AS PATTERNS HAVING THE FIGURED VALUE ARE SHOWN ON THE RIGHT OF THIS CHART, ILLUSTRATIONS OF THE OTHER TYPES ARE SHOWN ON THE LEFT.

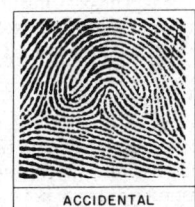

DOUBLE LOOP

LOOP

ACCIDENTAL

fingerprinting

When your hands are dirty and you press your finger tips against a piece of white paper, the marks you leave are called fingerprints. No two persons have the same fingerprints.

If you look closely at your own finger tips, you will see that they are covered with little hills and valleys, and look somewhat like the furrows in a plowed field. Dirt and sweat collect on your finger tips, but when you touch a smooth surface, like a mirror, only the little ridges or hills on your fingers leave behind the marks we call *latent fingerprints*. When these latent fingerprints are dusted with fingerprint powder, the powder sticks to the oily, sweaty traces left by your fingertips. By examining these powdered prints, the police can sometimes make sure who committed a crime.

Though fingerprints had been known for many hundreds of years, it was only about fifty years ago that a Frenchman named Alphonse Bertillon, and two Englishmen, Francis Galton and E. R. Henry, made fingerprinting a science that police could use in their work. Today the Federal Bureau of Investigation has the largest collection of fingerprints in the world. Not all the people who are fingerprinted are criminals. All men and women of the armed forces are fingerprinted. Many banks now ask customers to "sign" their checks with fingerprints. Hospitals take the footprints of a million newborn babies each year, so that mothers can be sure they are taking home the right infant.

One New York fingerprint expert, John Dondero, has taken prints from the noses of dogs and found that no two dogs have the same noseprint.

Fink, Mike

If you had been in Fort Pitt, now Pittsburgh, around 1800, you would have heard of Mike Fink, an American frontiersman. In a time when all pioneers were good shots, Mike Fink was the very best of them. He was born in Fort Pitt about 1770. In 1822 he joined a party that followed the course of the Missouri river to its furthest reaches. The Northwest Indians there had never seen a white man until Mike Fink arrived.

During the course of this expedition, in 1823, Fink was mixed up in a fight during which he killed another member of the exploring party and was himself killed. Mike Fink's bravery and tremendous strength, as well as his shooting ability, are told in many stories.

Finland

Finland is a country in the north of Europe. It is next to the countries of Norway and Sweden, which are called Scandinavian countries, and Finland itself is sometimes called a Scandinavian coun-

try. The area of Finland, about 130,000 square miles, is somewhat less than that of the state of Montana. In shape and size Finland is much like the entire island of Great Britain, but the population is only about four and a half million.

For hundreds of years the Finnish people have had to fight to keep their powerful neighbors, first Sweden and more recently Russia (whether ruled by the czars or by the Communists), from grabbing Finnish territories by force. Between 1940 and the present, Soviet Russia has taken 17,000 square miles of Finnish territory by war or threat of war.

The United States has a very friendly feeling toward Finland, partly because Finland was the only country after World War I that insisted on paying back money it had borrowed from the United States. Americans kept their friendly feeling toward Finland even when the countries were on opposite sides in World War II. In most parts of the United States there are few people of Finnish descent, but millions of Americans know the name of the great Finnish composer Jan Sibelius and also of the Finnish runner Paavo Nurmi, one of the greatest athletes of all time.

THE PEOPLE OF FINLAND

The most numerous of the people living in Finland are the native Finlanders, or Finns. They speak the Finnish language, a language that is related to Hungarian but not to other European languages. Some Finnish people came there, long ago, from Sweden. In fact, Sweden at one time conquered Finland and ruled it for several hundred years. There are some Russian people living in Finland, but they are very few in number. The first settlers were the Lapps, a tribe of people who came to Finland almost 1,900 years ago from Mongolia, which is in Asia. There are about five thousand Lapps still living in the northern part of Finland.

Almost all of the Finns are farmers. The farmers' homes look like the log

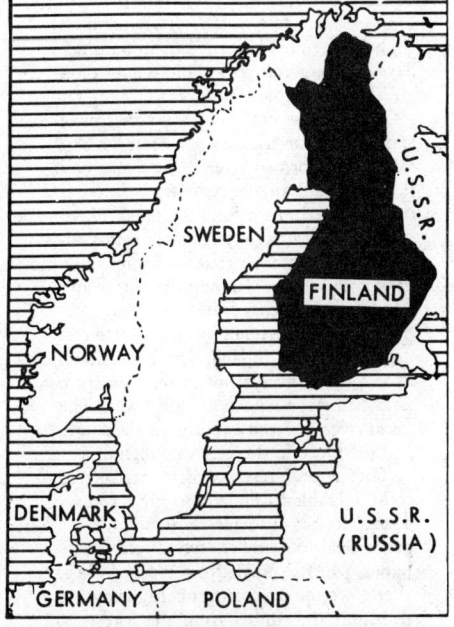

Helsinki, Finland.

Consulate General of Finland

cabins American pioneers lived in a hundred and more years ago.

The people who live in Finland's two biggest cities, Helsinki and Turku, live mostly in modern apartment houses. Helsinki is the capital city of Finland and Turku is a seaport on the Baltic Sea.

Nearly nine out of ten Finns follow the Lutheran religion. When Sweden conquered Finland, it brought Christianity with it. The people who are not Lutherans belong to the Greek Orthodox or the Roman Catholic Church.

Some of the people on the farms wear the same costumes their ancestors wore many years ago. However, the European customs of dress are readily accepted and worn, both by the people living on the farms and by those living in the cities.

All children between the ages of 7 and 14 must go to school. The rate of literacy, the number of people who can read and write, is exceptionally high in Finland.

WHAT THE LAND IS LIKE

Finland is known as the land of a thousand lakes. Actually, the country has about forty thousand lakes and they cover more than one-tenth of the land. There are many swamps and marshes that soak the soil and make it too wet for farming. This is a problem in Finnish agriculture. Although it is a flat country, Finland is spotted with rolling hills. Its highest point is a mountain called Haltia, and that is only 4,344 feet high. The climate is roughly the same throughout the whole country, but there is some difference between the northern section and the southern section. The south of Finland is slightly warmer than the north. Summer days are long and cool while winter days are short and cold.

Throughout Finland, waters that have spilled over or trickled out of the many lakes have formed rivers. The Finns call these rivers drainage systems, as water is continually drained from the lakes. However, these drainage systems are very shallow and boats have great difficulty navigating on them. To improve on water transportation, the Finns have built canals. There are many of these artificial canals all over Finland. The best-known of the drainage systems is the one from Lake Saimaa, a lake in the southwest. The main rivers are the Paijarne in the south, and the Oulu in the west of Finland.

The natural resource that has proved most valuable to Finland so far is forests. These forests provide Finland with a great deal of timber, wood pulp, and paper, which is made from wood. Where there are no railroads or highways to transport the timber from the forests to the industrial centers, the cut trees are floated to their destination in one of the many drainage systems or artificial canals.

Finland grows some wheat in the southeast and some rye in the central area. Potatoes, a very strong vegetable and not readily killed by the cold, can be found in the northern section. Among the chief industries are ship building, mining, textiles, leather and chemicals.

THE GOVERNMENT OF FINLAND

Finland is a republic, which means that it has no king. The people choose and elect their own representatives to make the laws, and have a constitution to protect the rights of the people.

Finland has a president. It also has a cabinet, a group of men who advise the president. The parliament is known as the Eduskunta. There are two hundred members in the Eduskunta, elected by the people.

All people who are 21 years old or more may vote. Freedom of press, religion, and speech, and the right to meet, called assemblage, is guaranteed by the constitution. There is a Supreme Court.

Finland is divided into provinces. There are ten provinces and each one has a governor appointed by the president.

FINLAND IN THE PAST

For almost 700 years, Finland was ruled by either Sweden or Russia; and since it lies between these two countries, which were constantly fighting, Finland was often a battleground and its people suffered greatly. Until 1700, all of Finland belonged to Sweden. Then the Russian czar (emperor) Peter the Great invaded Finland and after twenty-one years of war Russia won southeastern Finland from Sweden. In 1807 Russia defeated Sweden in another war and this time all of Finland was made part of Russia. Finland was made a Grand Duchy, or small kingdom, ruled by the Russian czar.

In 1917 the Russian Revolution overthrew the czar and soon Russia was controlled by the present Communist government. Finland declared itself independent and under the leadership of the Finnish general Baron Carl von Mannerheim the Finns fought off Communist forces that tried to keep Finland a part of Russia. After 1918 Finland became a democratic republic, as it is today. Its first prime minister was Juho Kusti Paasikivi.

Soviet Russia, like czarist Russia before it, continued to try to annex every country that touched its borders. In 1939 Russia made a deal with Germany, which was then ruled by the Nazis under Hitler, whereby Germany was free to start World War II and Russia was free to attack several small countries including Finland. In the winter of 1939 Russia attacked Finland. The Finns fought bravely but Finland was much too small to hold out for long and in 1940 the Finns had to yield several sections of their country to Russia, including the valuable territory of Karelia. Sentiment in the United States strongly favored Finland. In 1941, Germany broke its word and treacherously went to war against Russia. Finland took this opportunity to fight Russia also and try to recapture the territories that had been taken from it. This made Finland an enemy of the United States in World War II, but the American people never blamed Finland and when the war was over the United States protected Finland against Russian control. However, Russia retained the territories it had seized from Finland in 1940 and forced Finland also to give up its northern territory of Petsamo, its only outlet to the open ocean.

Since World War II, Finland has had to be very careful not to offend its powerful Russian neighbor, but Finland has managed to remain a free and prosperous country. In 1955 it was allowed to join the United Nations.

FINLAND. Area, 130,165 square miles. Population (1973 estimate), 4,682,000. Capital, Helsinki. Language, Finnish. Religion, 96 per cent Lutheran. Government, republic. Monetary unit, markka, worth 24 cents (U.S.).

Finnmark

Finnmark is the largest section in the country of Norway. It is also Norway's most northern section, and its climate is cold and icy. Finnmark is a big plateau, a high stretch of land that is flat on top. It is surrounded by huge mountains. Almost all the people living in this vast, cold region are Norwegians. Most of the other people are Lapps, who are descendants of the Mongolians and whom the Norwegians call Finns. The people earn their living by fishing, and by raising reindeer. The chief city of Finnmark is called Hammerfest.

fins

Fins are wide, thin extensions from the body of a fish. The fish uses them for balancing it in the water. They also help the fish to swim. Fins are made of folds in the skin of the fish and are supported by bony rods that are called fish rays.

The two main kinds of fins are called paired and unpaired. The paired fins come out from each side of the body of the fish just as your arms come out from each side of your body. The unpaired fins are attached along the center of the back of the fish. The main means of movement of most fish is the tail fin. Some kinds of fish have a great many fins, while others have only a few. The fins of the flying fish grow much larger and wider than the fins of most fish. They grow so large that they are almost like wings. The flying fish uses his big fins to glide through the air.

fiord

A fiord is a very narrow bay that lies between high cliffs. If you visit the seacoasts of Norway, Greenland, Alaska, Scotland, Chile, southern New Zealand, or certain other lands near the North or South Poles, you will find that their coasts

have many narrow inlets with high, straight rock walls.

These inlets are called fiords. They were formed many thousands of years ago when ice covered the land, and glaciers (ice rivers, or tongues of ice) went down to the ocean. The steep rock walls of a fiord are really the sides of what was once a glacier. When you sail on the waters of a fiord, you are really sailing above the floor of a drowned valley. You may see the word fiord spelled *fjord.* That is because it is a Norwegian word, and sometimes it is not changed when it is used in English.

fir

The fir belongs to the pine-tree family. It bears cones instead of fruit and needles instead of leaves. It stays green all winter, which is a reason why many Christmas trees are firs. The white fir grows as high as 300 feet. It takes 150 to 250 years to finish growing. The cones are made of many overlapping scales, and in each scale are two big seeds. The needles of the fir grow directly from its branches instead of having stems, and this is how the fir differs from other pines. The bark of balsam fir gives a sticky resin, called balsam, that is used in varnishes. The wood is often used in musical instruments and for the masts of ships. Most of the western fir is made into lumber for boxes and houses, but balsam fir is used to make paper. The six most important firs that grow in America are the balsam, the red, silver, and white firs, the noble fir, and the grand fir of the Pacific Northwest. The Douglas fir is not a true fir because it has a different kind of cone.

fire

Fire is the heat and light that you feel and see when something burns. When you see something burn it means that oxygen, a gas that is in the air around us, is combining with some other chemical element. (This is explained in the article on COMBUSTION.) It takes heat to start a fire, but once the fire is started it produces heat and that keeps the chemical process going.

Very little heat is needed to make some chemical elements combine with oxygen. Phosphorus requires very little heat, and for that reason it is used in the tips of matches. Friction (rubbing) produces heat. Just the friction of scraping the head of a match against a rough surface will make enough heat to start the phosphorus burning. This tiny fire makes enough heat to cause the wood in the match to combine with oxygen. The heat from this can be used to set twigs or kindling wood afire, and this will make enough heat to start coal or heavy logs combining with oxygen.

FUELS AND OXYGEN

Once anything starts burning, it usually produces enough heat to keep the oxygen and the other element combining —that is, to keep the fire going. For this, there must be a constant supply of oxygen and of the other element. The oxygen comes from the air, so if a fire is not constantly getting fresh air it will go out just as surely as it will if you stop adding the other necessary element (the fuel) to it. Adding oxygen will make the fire burn better, just as adding fuel will. That is why bellows are used to "fan a flame" in a blacksmith's forge and sometimes in a fireplace. Blowing more air on a fire gives it more oxygen, because the air contains oxygen.

WHY YOU CAN BLOW OUT A FIRE

But you can also "blow a fire out." If a match is burning and you blow on it, you will not make it burn more; instead, you will put it out. There are two reasons for this: First, a moving current of air produces coolness (that is why you fan yourself on a hot day); and second, you blow away the hot gases that are producing heat to keep the fire burning. If the fire is not already very hot, the air you blow on it will reduce its heat below the point necessary to keep it burning. This will make it go out. If the fire is already so hot or so big that the current of air cannot bring it below the burning point, it will keep on burning and the extra oxygen will make it burn even more.

FLAME

The flame that you see in a fire is hot gas. Oxygen is a gas, and there are various kinds of gas in the fuels used in fires, such as coal and wood. When some gases become hot enough they glow, just as iron glows when it becomes "red hot." Different gases glow with different colors, from blue to red to a brilliant white. When fire is used to give light (as in a candle or lamp or gaslight) there must be a fuel containing gases that glow with a white light.

Oxygen will not combine with all the chemical elements. An element with which oxygen will not combine is *noncombustible,* or "fireproof." There are other elements with which oxygen will combine, but such great heat would be required that actually these elements are "fireproof" too. Most fires are made by a combining of oxygen with the element carbon, which you see in almost pure form in coal but which is a part of all living things such as trees, other plants, and our own bodies.

HOW A FIRE STARTS

A fire will start when carbon, oxygen and heat are all present. There are many ways of producing the heat. Since friction (rubbing) produces heat, you can start a fire by rubbing two pieces of wood together until they are hot enough. Every Boy Scout learns to start fires in this way. A spark can be made by scraping the hard rock flint against the hard metal steel, and this momentary heat will start a fire if the fuel is one that burns easily, such as gunpowder or gasoline or even dry leaves. An electric spark has the same effect. The heat from the sun, if a lot of it can be concentrated at one point (as when it shines through a magnifying glass), will start a fire. For thousands of years men simply kept their fires going all the time and started each new fire with a burning coal or log from a fire that was already going.

Men have known and used fire for hundreds of thousands of years. They probably learned about it accidentally, perhaps when lightning struck trees and started them burning. Ancient men had many stories to explain fire. One of these is the Greek story of PROMETHEUS, about which there is a separate article.

Fire has been one of man's best friends. It has not only kept him warm and cooked his food, but it has given him the use of metals such as iron. At the same time fire has been one of man's greatest dangers. You can read more about this in the article FIRE DEPARTMENT and in the section on *Forest Fires* in the article on FORESTS.

firearms is a word that means all types of guns and weapons like guns: see the articles on GUN, PISTOL, and RIFLE.

fireclay

Fireclay is a special kind of clay which is used to make firebricks and to line furnaces. It is called fireclay because it must be able to stand very high temperatures without melting or crumbling. Most fireclay is used for making blast furnaces for steel and glass. Lime kilns and cement furnaces also use fireclay, and most electricity generating stations use fireclay to line the steam generator furnaces that furnish power to the big generators.

Fireclay is dug from the ground near riverbanks in most warm countries of the world.

firedamp

Firedamp is a very poisonous, explosive gas that is usually found in underground mines. It cannot be seen or smelled, so it is very difficult for the miners to detect. In the eighteenth century in England, it was discovered that a very small amount of firedamp in the air would kill canaries before it would hurt the miners. The miners then hung cages of canaries all over the mines; when they noticed a dead canary in one of the cages, they would clear the mine of all workers until it could be ventilated, or have fresh air forced through it. The practice of hanging cages of canaries in the mines was finally stopped because it was cruel to the birds; Sir Humphry Davy invented a safety lamp to take the place of the canaries. This was a gas lamp that burned with a bright white flame unless there was firedamp in the air; then the flame turned blue and warned the miners to leave immediately. Today other devices are used to detect firedamp.

fire department

A fire department is a branch of the government of a city. It is made up of men who are trained to put out, control or prevent fires, and of the equipment that they use. Communities that are too small to have city fire departments have "fire companies" in which most of the firemen are unpaid. Firefighting has become a science and thousands of men are always studying ways to keep fires from doing costly damage.

Until recent years, not one American city had a fire department big enough and good enough to protect it properly from a great fire. Then in 1904 almost the whole city of Baltimore burned to the ground. There were not nearly enough engines and men, and though firemen came from far off as New York City, 2,500 buildings were destroyed at a cost of fifty million dollars. Surprisingly, this terrible

N.Y.F.D.

fire did not teach a lesson to other poorly protected cities across America. In spite of the warnings from fire experts, these cities were not willing to pay out the large sums of money necessary for a well-trained and well-equipped fire department. They paid no attention when the experts protested that one big fire would cost any city many times as much as a good fire department. Then, in 1906, a great earthquake shook the city of San Francisco and started several fires. Just as the experts had warned, San Francisco was helpless. The great city's fire department had only 62 engines, 15 ladder-carrying trucks, and 600 firemen. To make things worse, both the fire-alarm system and the underground waterpipes were crippled by the earthquake. So the great fire roared through the city for three days, as high winds carried sparks from building to building. The damage amounted to 350 million dollars in money, not to mention the dead and the homeless. At last, cities throughout the United States began listening to the experts who had said it would happen. Most of these experts worked for a group called the National Board of Fire Underwriters. They got together with firefighters from all over the country, and helped work out plans for modern, up-to-date fire departments. As a result, such awful disasters as the Baltimore and San Francisco fires are not likely ever again to destroy an American city.

YOUR FIRE DEPARTMENT

Today's fire department is set up somewhat like an army and is able to move with split-second efficiency.

The general plan of your fire department is this: if you stand on any corner in the business section of a city, there is a firehouse within 1,400 yards of you. In a non-business neighborhood, where there are private homes, a station house is always within 1½ miles of you. In country areas, where the homes are more scattered, there is a firehouse within three miles.

In every firehouse there is the following equipment:

One or more engine and hose, which is a big fire truck with lots of bright brass wheels, nozzles, and other gadgets. Since water from an ordinary hydrant, or fireplug, may not shoot through the firemen's hoses high enough to reach the upper stories of a blazing building, the water is first fed into this engine truck. There powerful motors squirt this water out through hoses, often shooting it a hundred feet into the air. In olden times

these engine pumps were run by steam power that came from a large bright brass boiler drawn by horses.

A ladder-truck, which carries the one-hundred-foot ladders that firefighters prop against buildings to rescue people trapped by the flames. In addition, most fire departments have special trucks and equipment for chemical fires, waterfront fires, and other blazes that are especially hard to put out. This special equipment is described further on in this article. However, almost all the fire engines you see in action at the average fire are either engine-and-hose units or ladder-trucks.

The firemen stationed in each firehouse get orders from a lieutenant, who in turn gets orders from a company captain. This chain of command goes right up to the top, through battalion chiefs, deputy chiefs, the fire chief, and the top man, the fire commissioner.

WHAT FIREMEN LEARN AT SCHOOL

A fireman's life is not easy. Besides getting himself into top shape for such feats as carrying fire victims down one-hundred-foot ladders, the fireman must go to school and study fire-fighting as a doctor studies medicine. He must learn all about alarm systems, water supplies, knot-tying, first aid, rescue work, gas masks, and the characteristics, or habits, of fire. If he wants to become a chief, a fireman must have an understanding of civil, chemical, and mechanical engineering, building construction, the law of fire violations, and any number of other subjects. In addition he must know how to give orders to his men, and create confidence in himself.

FIRE-ALARM SYSTEMS

Most cities have fire-alarm boxes on street corners and in big buildings. When a person sees a fire, he opens the door to the box and pulls a handle. This makes a loud bell (called a *fire alarm*) ring in firehouses throughout the city. Each fire-alarm box rings a signal that tells the district in which there is a fire. The firehouse closest to the fire will send out its trucks and men. If the fire is too big for them to put it out alone, other firehouses send trucks and men. A fire is called a "two-alarmer," "three-alarmer," and so on, depending on how many companies must be called out.

The "false alarm" is the most troublesome and dangerous problem of fire departments. Some people have a form of mental illness that causes them to give fire alarms just for the fun of seeing the fire engines go through the streets. (You

can read more about this under *The Firebug,* later in this article.) If a fire company goes out to answer a false alarm, it may not be where it is needed in case of a real fire.

Some cities are putting in new fire-alarm systems with telephones instead of bells. The fire-alarm boxes contain telephones leading direct to headquarters and a person who sees a fire can telephone the information in. This system gives the fire department more information and makes it difficult for anyone to give a false alarm.

FIGHTING A FIRE

When an alarm comes into the firehouse, the men may be asleep or they may simply be waiting until they are needed. It makes little difference, for they will be up and dressed and on their way to the fire in less than one minute.

WE GO TO A FIRE

Suppose there is a fire in a tall warehouse on the waterfront. Flames are shooting straight up through the building, since hot air is lighter than cool, and tends to rise. But as the flames hit ceilings inside the warehouse, they flatten out and begin shooting through the building in all directions. Meanwhile great blasts of hot air are pouring through broken windows out into the night. Hot air alone can set nearby buildings afire. Also, great sparks are floating through the night, threatening to start more fires along the waterfront. Now some firemen reach the warehouse roof and start chopping holes in it so the flames will shoot up and out while they pour water into the holes. But the roof is so high and the fire is becoming so dangerous that the fire captain sends in a second alarm, requesting special equipment. First to arrive is a water tower truck. The truck carries a very tall hose-pipe that quickly begins throwing water high up onto the warehouse roof and into the holes cut by the firemen. Next to arrive is the chemical truck. It seems the firemen have found that a highly inflammable paint, lacquer, is blazing in one part of the warehouse. Water will not put out such a fire, so the chemical truck sprays a coat of foam over the blazing lacquer. This coat of foam cuts off the fire's oxygen so the lacquer blaze soon dies out. The reason for this is explained in a separate article on FIRE.

Next your firemen friends call on the fireboat that patrols the waterfront. This fireboat carries as much equipment as many twelve-engine companies. Sucking water up out of the river, its mighty engines hose the burning warehouse with twenty thousand gallons of water each minute. Meanwhile, a powerful smoke ejector has rolled up and gone into action. Its huge, thick suction hose looks like a giant caterpillar as it reaches into the warehouse to suck out the smoke, which is blinding the firemen. Finally, after much hard, bitter fighting, the warehouse fire is put out. Wearily, the firemen drive back to the station house. Another alarm may call them out any minute.

LIFE AMONG THE FIRE BUFFS

Fire buffs are men, women, and children who love to chase fire engines and

watch firemen put out blazes. Just about every town in America has its fire buffs. Many of them belong to fire-buff clubs, read books on fire-fighting, and often know the workings of the fire department as well as the firemen themselves. When a town has no full-time paid group of firefighters, the buffs run the fire department and are called volunteers. Volunteers are people who leave their jobs when the fire siren sounds, and race to the fire station or drive straight to the fire in their cars. Of course many volunteers are not true buffs; they have joined the volunteers because they feel it is their duty to protect their town whether they like firefighting or not. Without such brave volunteers, most small American towns would be defenseless against fires.

THE FIRE BUG

Next to a four-alarm blaze, there is nothing a fire department fears so much as the man who sets fires either for fun or for pay. Such men are called arsonists, and the crime they commit is arson. There are two main types of arsonists. When a man's store or factory is not making money he may hire an arsonist to burn it down so he can collect the insurance money. Or the arsonist may be a man who, for reasons going back to his childhood, has a very strange and unusual love of fires. This kind of fire bug gets no money for setting fires. His reward is the thrill he gets out of watching fires he has set in other people's homes or office buildings.

The medical word for such a twisted person is *pyromaniac,* which means "a man who likes fires too much." Although pyromaniacs are usually caught, they manage to do great damage every year.

firefly

Fireflies are winged beetles that glow in the dark. There are more than two thousand different kinds of fireflies, and they can be found all over the world. The light is caused by the very slow burning of a special kind of chemical that the firefly makes in its body. Fireflies flash their tiny lights on warm summer nights. The flashing is believed to help the firefly to find a mate. The light is usually a green-white in color and is located on the sides of the stomach. In some of the tropical parts of South America people use fireflies for lanterns. There is another kind of firefly in South America that flashes a red light at each end of the body and green lights along the sides.

fireproofing

Something is fireproof if it will not burn or if it is difficult to make it burn. We fireproof whenever possible to keep fires from starting and from spreading. We make fireproof homes, schools and offices by building them out of stone or brick and by putting in floors, walls and ceilings made of concrete or another material that will not burn easily. We can guard against fire by using fireproof articles within our homes, or by fireproofing any articles that burn easily. For example, curtains, drapes, and clothing, which catch fire easily, can be fireproofed at a very low cost. One simple way to make a fireproofing solution is to mix nine ounces of borax and four ounces of

boric acid with one gallon of water. Any fabrics that are dipped into this mixture and then dried will not catch fire easily, even if a lighted match is held to them.

Firestone, Harvey Samuel

Harvey Samuel Firestone was an important businessman who did a great deal to build up the rubber industry in the United States. He was born in Ohio, in 1868, and his father was a wealthy farmer. Firestone did not want to work at farming, so he went to the city of

Harvey S. Firestone.   H. S. Firestone, Jr.

Columbus, Ohio, and began to work. Soon he started making rubber tires, and in 1900 he organized the Firestone Tire and Rubber Company, which became one of the largest rubber companies in the world. Harvey Firestone died in 1938. His three sons became executives in the company, with his oldest son, Harvey S. Firestone, Jr., its chairman.

fireworks

Fireworks are used in the United States to celebrate Independence Day (the Fourth of July) and in nearly all other countries to celebrate days of rejoicing. Fireworks are explosives that are used to make a noise or to create patterns of bright light and color that are fun to watch.

The foundation of all fireworks is a chemical, niter (also called saltpeter), which is the basis of most explosives. You can read more about it in the article NITROGEN. The first fireworks were made about a thousand years ago in China. At that time the Chinese had just invented gunpowder. They did not have the pinwheels and rockets that are used today. The Chinese used their early fireworks in their festivals and religious ceremonies. If you were to go to Chinatown in San Francisco or New York on the Chinese New Year's Day, you would find them still using firecrackers and other kinds of fireworks to celebrate the New Year. If you take a trip to some of the South American countries you will find that the people there use fireworks to celebrate Christmas. They shoot off fireworks in front of their churches and use them to light religious processions.

THE FIRST FIREWORKS

In Europe, fireworks were never seen until about 700 years ago. Gunpowder was discovered in Europe then. Nothing was added to give the fireworks more color. They were very expensive and only kings and emperors could afford to buy them. When King Louis XV lived in the palace of Versailles he had displays of fireworks very regularly. The poor people would come from miles around and stand outside the palace gates to watch them being shot off.

About 125 years ago, color was added to fireworks. This was done by adding powdered chemicals to the gunpowder. These chemicals make the different colors you see in the sky when fireworks go off. Powdered metals such as aluminum and magnesium were added later to give more brilliance to the colors.

FIRECRACKERS

The simplest kind of fireworks is the firecracker. It is made like this: Different powders are packed into a tube that is made of layers of paper that have been glued together. A short piece of string called a fuse is put into the tube. Then some of the mixed powders are put into the tube and the end of the tube is glued, leaving a bit of the fuse outside. When the end of the fuse is lighted, the fuse burns down through the paper. When the burning fuse comes to the chemical powders, the firecracker will explode.

The most complicated fireworks to make, and the most beautiful ones to see, are rockets. These are the fireworks that rise high in the air, burst with a loud bang, and make a bright shower of color in the sky. They look like colored feathers floating in the air. The pinwheel is another popular kind of fireworks. It is a wheel that you nail to a tree or post. Around the sides of the wheel are little rockets. When the fuse is lighted, the wheels turn around and the little rockets shoot different colored balls of fire into the air. The biggest kind of fireworks display is called a set piece. It is a picture made of fireworks. Perhaps it is a picture of George Washington, or the American Flag, or a bunch of flowers. It is made on a wooden frame to which rockets, pinwheels, and other fireworks have been wired. When the fuse is lighted, the fireworks burst into color and you see the complete picture.

Many cities in the United States have passed laws so that fireworks cannot be sold to boys and girls. The laws were passed because so many accidents happened with fireworks. Both children and grownups were burned or blinded. The only way to stop the accidents was to stop the sale of fireworks. Nowadays there are special companies that do nothing but put on displays of fireworks. They are set off by men who have been trained to do it without getting hurt.

fire worship

Many thousands of years ago our ancestors, who lived in caves, began to worship fire. They thought a god lived in the fire because the fire was able to do marvelous things. It gave warmth, it cooked food, and yet it could burn down a whole forest and destroy a great deal.

Some of the American Indians worshipped fire. Among the greatest fire-worshippers of all were the ancient Persians. If you go to India today you will find some tribes there whose ancestors were ancient Persians, and they still worship fire.

first aid

First aid is the immediate care given to a person who has been injured or become suddenly ill, before the doctor comes. First aid often can save a life, and always can relieve pain, so it is very im-

portant for everyone to know the principal methods of first aid in common types of illness and injury.

There are some things that must be done no matter what the trouble is: 1, keep the victim lying down and try to keep him from being frightened; 2, examine the victim to see if you can find a wound, burn, bleeding, or other sign of injury; 3, do not move the victim unless it is absolutely necessary, because moving can make some injuries much worse; 4, decide calmly what must be done to prevent further injury, to save the victim's life, or to make him more comfortable, but do no more than necessary; 5, send for a doctor.

First-aid treatment for different conditions varies greatly. Below are given the first steps required in various kinds of illness or accident:

SHOCK

Shock is caused by failure of blood circulation because of loss of blood, damage to body tissues, or even emotional upsets. Shock can take the form of a faint, or be so severe that it can cause death. The victim's face is pale and his skin cold and clammy. Breathing is rapid and shallow, and the pulse is fast. The victim may be partly or completely unconscious. *What to do:* Keep the victim quiet and lying down. Wrap him in blankets and apply hot-water bottles or electric heating pads, being careful not to burn him. Make a mixture of 1 quart of water, 1 teaspoonful salt, ½ teaspoonful of soda. Give the victim drinks of this if he is conscious, unless he has an injury to the abdomen. Relieve pain as much as possible.

WOUNDS

A wound is any break in the skin or the mucous membranes within the body. The chief dangers are serious bleeding and infection. *What to do:* In an external wound, that is, a break in the skin, the most important thing is to stop bleeding if it is severe. If the blood flows in quick spurts, it means that an artery has been cut; a steady flow of blood means that a vein has been cut. Bleeding from a vein can usually be stopped by applying pressure directly over the wound. Place a thick pad of gauze or clean cloth over the wound and tie it firmly in place. If you have no bandages, a cloth pad held in place with the hand will help. To stop bleeding from an artery, the pressure point must be found. The pressure points are the spots where an artery crosses a bone. Pressure must be made on the pressure point nearest the wound between the wound and the heart. When the bleeding stops, have someone apply a pressure dressing over the wound, then release the pressure at the pressure point. If the bleeding starts again, pressure at the pressure point must be applied and then released, over and over again, until the pressure dressing alone keeps the bleeding stopped. (See also BANDAGE.)

If bleeding cannot be stopped in a wound in an arm or leg, a tourniquet may be used. Any fairly wide, flat band long enough to go twice around the limb will serve as a tourniquet. Do not use cord, rope, or wire. Wrap the tourniquet around a firm pad placed on the inside of the arm or leg. Tie the tourniquet with a half knot, and then tie a small stick with a square knot over the first one. Tighten the tourniquet by twisting the stick just enough to stop the bleeding. Once a tourniquet has been applied it should not be removed except by a doctor. In internal bleeding, a doctor must be gotten as quickly as possible. In the meantime, treatment should be given for shock. In wounds of the abdomen give nothing by mouth.

SNAKE BITES

The bite of a poisonous snake is followed rapidly by severe pain and swelling. Get a doctor as soon as possible. *What to do:* Keep the victim lying down and quiet, with the injured limb slightly lower than the rest of the body. Above the wound apply a band just tight enough to make the veins stand out, to keep the poison from spreading. With the tip of a knife or razor blade that has been passed through the flame of a match, make a crosscut in the shape of an X about ¼ inch deep over each fang mark. Then apply suction to suck out the poison. If no other suction device is at hand, apply suction by mouth, spitting out the fluid sucked from the wound.

ANIMAL BITES

The chief danger of animal bite is that rabies, or hydrophobia, may develop. Rabies is spread by rabid, or mad, dogs, but any warm-blooded animal may have the disease. A doctor must be seen at once. *What to do:* Wash the wound under running water, using soap to remove the animal's saliva. Then go at once to a doctor for further treatment, and so that he may decide whether the Pasteur treatment for prevention of rabies is necessary.

CHOKING AND STRANGULATION

Choking may be caused by anything that binds the neck, such as a rope in hanging, or by objects stuck in the throat or windpipe, such as bones, coins, or pieces of food. *What to do:* Cut away any constriction around the neck. Slap the victim strongly on the back if something is stuck in his throat. The victim can help by bending forward or lying with his head and shoulders hanging down. If the victim is a small child, hold him upside down by the heels and slap his back. If the object is not dislodged, send for a doctor at once, or rush the victim to a hospital. If breathing is difficult, give ARTIFICIAL RESPIRATION, which you can read about in a separate article.

SUBMERSION

Most drownings happen close to shore. If possible throw a rope or life buoy to the victim, or use a boat. Do not try to swim to the rescue unless you have been trained in lifesaving. Your local Red Cross chapter has courses in lifesaving that you can take. *What to do:* If the victim is not breathing, start artificial respiration at once, and send someone for help. There is a separate article on ARTIFICIAL RESPIRATION, with diagrams showing how it is given.

ELECTRIC SHOCK

Electric shock occurs when an electric current passes through a person's body. This can be caused by faulty electrical equipment, by a live wire or rail, or by lightning. The victim becomes unconscious, and cannot breathe. He may be severely burned. *What to do:* The current must be broken immediately. Do not touch the victim or his clothing with your bare hands, as this may be as dangerous for you as the electrical conductor itself. Turn off the current if possible. If not, stand on a folded dry coat or on newspapers, and with one hand protected by cloth or newspaper or strong rubber gloves, drag the victim away

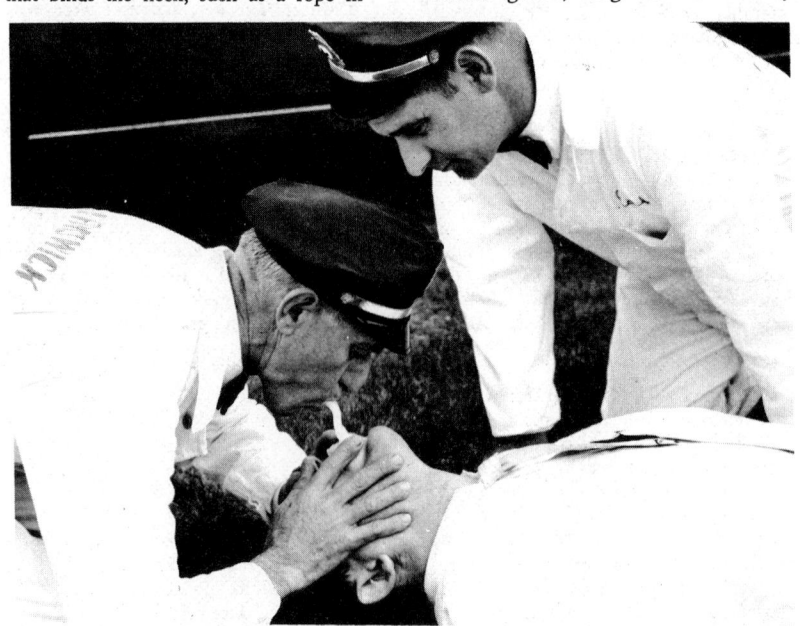

Johnson and Johnson Photos

In the photograph above, two members of an ambulance team demonstrate mouth-to-tube resuscitation, a way of reviving people who have stopped breathing.

from the conductor. If the victim is not breathing, start artificial respiration immediately. You can find out how this is done in the article on ARTIFICIAL RESPIRATION. Have a doctor called at once. Treat burns after the victim has become conscious.

CARBON MONOXIDE

This gas is odorless and a deadly poison. Carbon monoxide gas may escape from loose gas fixtures used for lighting, cooking, or heating. It can also be given off when the gas is burning. The motor of an automobile gives off carbon monoxide gas, and should never be started in a closed garage. *What to do:* In rescuing a victim of carbon monoxide gas, be sure to protect yourself. Use a mask, or tie a rope around your waist and have someone outside hold the end of it and rescue you in case you fall. Get the victim to fresh air at once and call a doctor. If breathing has stopped, start artificial respiration at once. If possible, send for an oxygen inhalator from the police or fire department. Keep the victim quiet and warm. Even slight exercise is dangerous.

POISONS

First aid is most important in cases of poisoning. Every moment's delay means that more of the poison is being absorbed by the victim's system. Call a doctor at once and then take steps to get rid of the poison. Nausea, vomiting, pain in the stomach, cramps, diarrhea, collapse and convulsions are some of the signs of poisoning. Do not waste time trying to find out what poison was taken. Wash out the stomach by causing the victim to vomit, unless the lips, mouth, and tongue are stained or burned, which would mean that a strong acid or caustic alkali has been swallowed. The emetics, or liquids that will cause vomiting, that are easiest to prepare are: 1, a tablespoonful of table salt in a glass of warm water; 2, soapy water made by shaking a piece of mild soap in warm water until good suds are formed. There are special antidotes for all the different kinds of POISON, about which there is a separate article.

BONE, JOINT, AND MUSCLE INJURIES

A fracture is a broken bone. You can read more about FRACTURES and what to do for them in a separate article. A dislocation is a bone out of place at the joint. First aid should not be given. A doctor should be called at once. A sprain is a tearing of the ligaments that connect bones. There is pain, swelling, and usually discoloration. A doctor should be called for all except very slight sprains. *What to do:* Raise the injured joint so that it will get less blood. Apply cold cloths or ice packs.

BURNS AND SCALDS

First-aid treatment of burns is intended to relieve pain, to prevent infection, and to prevent loss of tissue fluid in burns over a wide area of skin. *What to do:* For minor burns where the skin is unbroken, apply burn ointment, olive oil, or mineral oil, and cover the burned area with a sterile gauze dressing. For severe burns call a doctor at once. The danger of infection is great in deep or extensive burns, so it is wise to cover the

mouth and nose with a mask of clean cloth before treating such burns. Cover the burned area with a thick layer of sterile gauze and bandage firmly in place. Keep the victim quiet and warm.

Chemical burns: These are caused by chemicals such as strong acids. Immediately strip off all clothing that has come in contact with the chemical, and flood the skin with large quantities of clean water. Then give first aid according to the seriousness of the burn. If any chemical enters the eye, immediately wash the eye with great quantities of water. If there has been any delay do not use water; call a doctor at once.

Sunburn: This may be treated like any other mild burn. If the victim feels sick, call a doctor.

Sunstroke: The victim feels dizzy and sick, and has pain in the head. He may become unconscious, have trouble breathing and have a high fever. Call a doctor. Put the victim in a cool, shady place on his back, and apply cold cloths or an ice bag to his head. Sponge the body with cold water.

FROSTBITE

Frostbite occurs when a part of the body is frozen. Signs of frostbite are whiteness, coldness, and numbness of the flesh. *What to do:* The victim should be taken indoors and given a warm drink. Warm the frozen part as rapidly as possible by placing it in lukewarm—not hot—water, or by wrapping it in blankets. Do not rub the area, because this may damage the tissues. Call a doctor.

FAINTING

Fainting usually is caused by a shock, such as fear or bad news, but it may occur after slight injuries, hunger, fatigue, or the sight of blood. A person about to faint becomes dizzy, turns pale, and loses consciousness. You can read about FAINTING and what to do for it in a separate article.

EPILEPSY

Epilepsy is an illness in which the victim has "fits." He falls and becomes unconscious. He may stop breathing for a moment and turn blue. *What to do:* Call a doctor. Do not try to hold the victim down more than is necessary to keep him from hurting himself. Lay him on his back and loosen his clothing. Place a cloth pad or a small stick between his teeth to keep him from biting his tongue. Keep him warm with blankets.

fish

Fish are animals that have gills, scales, and fins. They breathe water, and live in water throughout their lives. Water covers nearly three-quarters of the earth's surface, and almost every ocean, lake or stream has at least one kind of fish living in it. Scientists say there are more than thirty thousand kinds of fish.

People have always eaten fish as food. In fact, fish ranks next to agricultural products as the most important source of food for man. Fish meat is extremely healthful since it contains such nourishing substances as proteins, fats, minerals, and vitamins. Cod liver oil and halibut liver oil are valuable as sources of Vitamins A and D. Fish oil is also very use-

ful in the manufacture of candles, soap, paint, and medicine.

People from all over the world catch fish for a living. Countries such as Norway, Japan, the United States and Soviet Russia are noted for their fishing industries. Fishermen are found in almost every country of the world. Fishing is also a sport and many people like to catch fish just for fun.

HOW FISH BREATHE AND SWIM

Like every other living thing, fish need air to breathe. Man breathes by use of his lungs. The breathing mechanism of the fish is called the gill. Fish take in, through their mouths, water that contains bubbles of air. They let it out through their gills. The oxygen in the air is absorbed by blood that flows through tiny vessels in the gills. The blood gives off carbon dioxide, which leaves the fish's gills with the water.

Some fish also store air in another part of the body called an air bladder. By controlling the amount of air stored in the bladder, a fish can balance itself in any particular depth of water.

There are other animals that live at least part of their lives in the water, such as reptiles, amphibians, and mammals. These animals, however, are not fish since they do not have fins and cannot breathe in water. The whale, for instance, is not a fish though it spends all its life in water; the whale is a mammal.

Fins are fishes' limbs. Fins enable fish to swim, to steer, and to balance themselves. With the use of fins, fish get food or dart from place to place to escape an enemy.

Both the fish's tail fins and streamlined body help it to swim. By wriggling its body and at the same time lashing its tail in the water, the fish is able to swim.

HOW FISH ARE IDENTIFIED

Fish are animals with vertebrae, or backbones. Fish are usually identified by shape, form, fins, tail, mouth, teeth, and other characteristics.

Where fish eat and live is another important factor in identifying them. Some fish live in the fresh water of the rivers, lakes, and streams of the world. Some of the more popular fresh-water fish are the whitefish, trout, pike, and bass—all of which are favorite catches for fishermen. Those fish that do not live in fresh water live in salt water, or the sea. The sea is divided into three areas, or zones. These three areas are the tidal or shore zone, the open sea, and the deep sea. Most fish can live in only one of these three zones. Most fish are either tidal or open-sea fish.

The deep-sea fish swim in the black depths of the deep ocean and some of them are blind. Other deep-sea fish have parts of their bodies that light up the dark waters around them.

Another method of identifying fish is by their eating habits. Some fish are surface eaters, which means they get food that floats on the surface of the water. A few of these are the herring, perch, and bass.

Other fish, such as the flounder, catfish, and eel, eat food that is on the bottom. These fish are called bottom eaters. However, the largest number of fish get their food from anything that is between

the water's surface and the ocean floor or river bed.

WHAT FISH EAT

A great part of a fish's diet is plant growth. Seaweed, or algae, is a common food for some fish. However, the greatest portion of plant life eaten by fish is made up of tiny, microscopic plants called plankton. It is a very rich food for fish. Though plankton is found almost everywhere in the open water, it floats in even greater abundance near the shore, and it is there that the fish seek it. Many fisheries are near shore, for the men of this industry know that such fish as the cod, halibut and herring swim there for plankton.

There are many fish that eat other fish, and it is usually the larger fish that feed on the smaller fish. This battle of life usually takes place in the open sea, between the water's surface and bottom. Fish that eat other fish have large mouths and a plentiful supply of teeth. The barracuda, for example, has more than two hundred razor-sharp teeth. Two of the most vicious killers of the open sea are the shark and the manta ray. The smaller fish of the open sea must be very swift to protect themselves against the slower but more ferocious bigger fish.

Sometimes fish eat the eggs of other fish, but nature has a way of protecting their eggs. The minnow lays more than ten thousand eggs at a time so that a few may escape being eaten.

HOW FISH ARE BORN

Fish differ greatly in breeding habits. There are fish that lay their eggs, or roe, on rocks; other fish store their eggs in sand; still others lay their eggs upon the backs of other fish. Cod, for instance, lay their eggs almost anywhere in the water, leaving them to be eaten by other fish. The roe of grunion, a small fish, is deposited in sand underneath shallow waters and is washed out by high tide. When fish lay eggs, they are said to be *spawning*.

When the adult salmon spawns, it returns upstream to the place of its birth, jumping over the swift-flowing rapids and dangerous rocks of rivers. It dies as soon as it has deposited its eggs. The salmon is unusual in another way. It is born in fresh water, swims out to salt water to live, and returns to fresh water to spawn. The shad is another fish that lives in this way.

Eels do just the opposite—they are hatched in the ocean and go up streams of North America and Europe to develop.

fisher

The fisher is a vicious little animal that will attack almost anything. It is a member of the weasel family. It is very important because it produces a valuable fur. It grows to be two or three feet long and has a long, bushy tail. The fisher eats meat, but it does not like fish. Its name comes from *fitchew*, which is an old name for an animal like the fisher. It used to live all over most of North America before there were so many cities and towns. Now it only lives in the wilder northern parts. Its favorite places to live are where hemlock and spruce trees grow.

Fisher, Dorothy Canfield

Dorothy Canfield Fisher became famous as a writer of short stories and novels about people who live in New England. She was born in Kansas in 1879, and she went to Columbia University when it was unusual for a woman to go to college. She married John Redwood Fisher, and they lived in Vermont, where she got to know many of the people she wrote about in her books. Dorothy Canfield Fisher was also very much interested in the best kind of education for children, and she wrote many articles and books about education, and traveled around the country on lecture tours, so that other people would know her ideas. Her book *Something Old, Something New* is for children. She died in 1958.

fisheries

Since earliest times fish has been one of man's most important foods. Primitive peoples caught fish with their hands, or with crude spears. In the northern part of Canada there are Indians who still use these methods, spearing salmon from the shore or by wading out into the water. Thousands of years ago men learned to trap fish. They built dams of stones and sticks or clay across the entrance of a shallow pool or basin. Fish would swim over this dam at high tide, or when the streams were swollen by rains. Then when the water receded they could not swim back over the barrier. This was the first and simplest attempt to catch fish in quantity.

Commercial fishing, or the business of catching fish for a living, is also very ancient. We use the term *fishery* to describe any fishing business, including the catching of the fish and the canning or preserving of it. There were fisheries in Greece, Sicily, and Spain before the birth of Jesus, almost two thousand years ago. In American colonial days, the main business in New England was cod fishing.

FISHING GROUNDS

There are fish in all parts of the ocean, but they are scattered and few in number except in certain locations. These locations are called fishing grounds, and they exist where the water is fairly shallow for some distance offshore. There are places where the land slopes gently and gradually for many miles before it drops off into the ocean depths. In these parts of the continental shelf fish can spawn (lay eggs) and find food.

Some of the best fishing grounds are off the coast of Newfoundland. They are called the *Grand Banks*, the *Green Banks* and the *Banks Pierre*. Enormous quantities of cod, haddock, halibut, herring, and practically every fish known in northern waters are taken there every year. Fishing vessels come from Canada, the United States, and from Russia, England, and France. There are also important fisheries off the coast of Norway, and Japan operates vast fisheries in the northern Pacific. The great shrimp fisheries are found along the Gulf Coast, and sardine fisheries flourish in Portugal and Spain. Salmon fisheries are centered along the northern Pacific coast of North America, and the famous California tuna fleets bring in hundreds of thousands of pounds every year.

METHODS OF FISHING

Modern fishermen, in order to do well in their business, must operate in the right location and must have the most modern of equipment. The fishery must be located close enough to a fishing ground. The boats must be able to go quickly from home port to the fishing grounds and return with a large cargo of fish. The boats must be equipped to haul large nets, and they must have some means of keeping the catch fresh for at least a week. Small boats often use salt water, but more modern fishing craft have refrigeration. Some of the northern Pacific salmon boats are actually seagoing canneries. When the fish are caught they are canned immediately aboard the ship. Modern whalers are also factory ships, and the old way of harpooning whales by hand is no longer used. Today whales and swordfish are shot from the deck by harpoon guns.

NETS

There are hundreds of types of net used for fishing. They vary according to the type of fish sought and its habits, and also according to custom in various parts of the world. However, there are only two basic types of net: 1, those that remain fixed, or stationary, and trap the fish, and 2, those that are towed through the water, gathering in the fish. These two types are divided into special nets for catching fish that live near the surface, and for catching those that live near the bottom.

One of the earliest nets was the *pound net*. It is a sort of trap consisting of square pockets of netting placed upright in the shallow water of bays or inlets. Stretching from the gates, or sides, are long sections of straight net called leaders. When a school of fish approaches the net, it turns to avoid the barrier and follows this leader into the pound where it is trapped. The *gill net* is another form of trap. It is used in open water, across a tidal current, or across running water. In a gill net the meshes, or squares of the netting, can be of any size, depending on the type of fish to be caught. When the fish come to the net they can force their heads through the meshes, but their gills keep them from backing out. Several nets fifty or sixty feet long are connected, and hang down from cork or wooden floats at the top, the bottom being weighted. The nets are suspended across a tidal current for about six hours, and then hauled into the boats.

Stationary nets are seldom used by the large fisheries, for with such nets the fishermen must wait for the fish instead of going after them. Storms and high tides also damage such nets, whereas moving nets can be kept on the boats when the weather is bad.

TRAWLING AND PURSE SEINING

The two most important methods of fishing in modern use are *purse seining* and *trawling*. Purse seining is used to catch surface fish that swim in schools, such as mackerel, tuna, herring, and menhaden. The net is laid in a semicircle

by two skiffs, small boats launched from a bigger vessel called a purse seiner. This is done after a school of fish has been sighted, to try to surround the school and trap it. Then the net is drawn together into a sort of purse, or pocket, by hauling in a rope that runs through rings at the bottom. The top of the net is kept erect by cork floats.

Trawling means dragging a cone-shaped net through the water. There are several types, the most common being the otter trawler. These nets are enormous, sometimes being forty to a hundred feet across the open end. They are drawn across the bottom of the water on iron runners, and are kept open by the force of water against the *otters*, which are big wooden doors that are set at either side of the mouth of the net. Other types of trawls are drawn nearer the surface; these are called *balloon*, or *fly*, *trawls*. The vessels used, called *trawlers*, are powerful and seaworthy ships, ranging up to two hundred feet in length. Smaller trawlers, called *draggers*, are used for inshore fishing.

LINE FISHING

Some commercial fishing is still done by hook and line, although trawling and seining have largely replaced this method. Salmon, halibut, red snapper, tuna and tile fish are the fish usually caught in this manner, by the use of a long line. This is a main line to which shorter lines that carry hooks are attached. As many as five thousand hooks are sometimes baited and set, and the main line may run for miles. Each line is fastened to a buoy, or float, that marks the place. The lines are put out by dories, or rowboats of a special type used by fishermen.

SEA FOOD AND SEA PRODUCTS

Oysters and clams are found in shallow water where there is little current. These areas are called beds, and today there is a vast industry in the farming of oysters and clams. The fisheries transplant them to beds that are fenced in to give the oysters and clams protection, and at the proper time they are harvested like any other crop. Clams are harvested by using a special rake, and oysters are harvested with oyster tongs, made of iron with long wooden handles.

Lobsters and crabs are caught in wooden or wire traps. Most of the best lobsters come from Canada and Maine, as does the largest supply of clams. Oysters are found in the United States in Rhode Island, Connecticut, Long Island and Chesapeake Bay, and scallops are brought up all along the coast of New England.

Other products and by-products of fisheries include sponges, found in the Mediterranean Sea and near the West Indies and Florida; and turtles and tortoises caught for their flesh and for tortoise shell. The shells of abalone furnish material for jewelry and toilet articles, and the flesh is a delicacy. The Mississippi River fresh-water mussels support a huge button-making industry. In Japan certain seaweeds are used as food. Other kinds of seaweed, called kelp and agar-agar, are used medicinally.

fishing

Fishing is one of the most popular sports in the world. It is much different from the business of fishing, about which you can read in the article on FISHERIES. In the sport of fishing, the object is to catch one fish at a time. This is usually done by putting a sharp piece of bent metal, called a *fishhook*, at the end of a light cord called a *fishing line*, and trying to get the fish to take the hook into its mouth. When the fish does this, its mouth catches on the hook, it cannot free itself, and it can be pulled out of the water with the line. This kind of fishing is also called *angling*, because long ago fishhooks were called angles.

The simplest form of fishing is to attach the line to a long pole and dangle it in the water. A small piece of lead, called a *sinker*, is tied to the line to make it sink in the water. Some sort of food that fishes eat, usually a worm, is put on the hook. When a fish tries to swallow the worm it is hooked and is pulled out of the water. This kind of fishing is usually good only for small fish that do not fight to escape after they are hooked. For a fish that will fight, called a *gamefish*, different equipment and usually different bait are needed. Instead of any long branch cut from a tree, a *fishing rod* is used, scientifically designed for lightness and flexibility and strength. Attached to the rod is a *reel*, which holds hundreds of feet of fishing line that the fisherman can let out or pull in (reel in) as he wishes. The bait too is often scientifically designed to appeal to a particular kind of fish. The fisherman learns to *cast* his line—cause it to fly out from the reel—so that the baited hook will land in a particular place. Experts become excellent "marksmen" and have contests in casting (called "skish casting").

PROCESS OF FISHING

The fisherman baits his hook, and casts it into the water at a spot where he thinks there might be a fish. He may use natural bait, such as a worm (night crawler), a bug, or a little fish such as a minnow; or he may use an artificial bait, or lure, made to resemble the natural food of the fish. When a fish down in the water sees the bait, it may *strike* (bite down on it). The fisherman, constantly alert, gives a sudden yank as he feels the strike, and the fish is hooked.

Now the exciting part begins. If it is a gamefish, such as trout, bass, salmon or pike in fresh water or striped bass, bluefish, tarpon, or marlin in salt water, as the fish feels the hook it dashes frantically away. Sometimes it leaps clear of the water in an effort to throw the hook. But the rod in the angler's hands is made so that it will bend without breaking, and it acts as a shock absorber for the first violent rush of the fish. The fish runs, and the line is rapidly stripped from the reel. The fish could easily snap the line if the angler tried to hold back, but there is plenty of reserve line on the reel, and the fish is allowed all it wants.

Now perhaps there are forty or fifty yards of line out (or even much more) and suddenly the fish turns. The angler must at once reel in the slack. Then the fish runs in another direction and again the line pays out. Little by little, as the fish tires, its charges become less strenuous. Always, the angler reels in his line and keeps the slack out of it but never

tries to *horse* the fish in, or pull him in by main strength. The angler takes his time, and finally the fish is exhausted and can be brought in.

Sometimes a net is needed to lift the fish from the water, and if it is one of the large gamefishes a *gaff* is used. A gaff is a big hook attached to a wooden handle. Some fishermen can play a fish so expertly that they can land a fish that weighs more than a hundred pounds on a line with a *pound-test* of less than ten pounds.

METHODS OF FISHING

All methods of fishing are very ancient, for mankind has caught fish for food since the beginning of time. In some parts of the world primitive methods are still used to some extent. The Eskimos and the South Sea Islanders spear their fish, while in Tonga and other places the natives poison the fish. They put a plant extract, such as derris root, into the water. It kills the fish, but is harmless to humans. Probably one of the oldest methods is *guddling*, or catching fish by hand. You put your hands under a rock or log in the water where a fish might be lurking. When you feel a fish, you cautiously slide your hand forward, and suddenly seize the fish just behind the gills. (There is a certain amount of danger in guddling where poisonous water snakes abound.)

Modern angling dates from about the year 1400, with the invention of the steel hook, but as much as six thousand years ago the *gorge* was used at the end of a line. A gorge is a short stick sharpened at both ends and buried in the bait. It is effective only when a fish swallows the bait whole. The first hooks, or angles, were manufactured in England, about five hundred years ago. They were much like the hooks we use today, with an eye, a bend, and a barbed point. England is still the largest hook-producing country, with Norway second. Norwegian hooks are softer and will bend before they break.

There are several times as many books on fishing as there are on any other sport. *The Compleat Angler*, written by Izaak Walton in 1653, is considered the classic of fishing books. As a guide to fishing it is largely outmoded, but it is still widely read, and has passed its 300th edition. Books cannot take the place of practical experience, but it is worth any fisherman's time to read about this sport. He is sure to gain valuable knowledge.

Among the most productive fishing methods in use today are: 1, bait-casting; 2, fly-casting; 3, trolling; 4, surf-fishing; 5, still-fishing; 6, spinning, which is not precisely a method of fishing but rather a type of tackle. Special knowledge, skill and tackle are required for the various methods, including familiarity with the type of fish to be caught. The fisherman must know the feeding habits of the fish he seeks, where and when to fish, and the legal restrictions of the area. There are laws that regulate the season during which you can go fishing, the number of fish you can catch, and the size limitation. Such laws are a necessary part of the conservation program, and vary from place to place. You can get all the information you need by writing to the Fish and Wildlife Service, Washington, D.C. Fishing licenses are required for most fresh-water

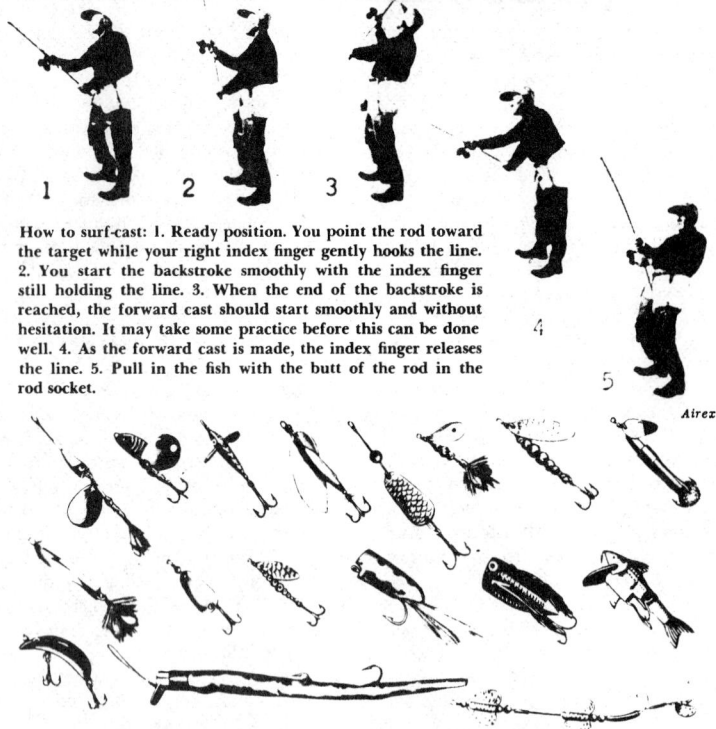

How to surf-cast: 1. Ready position. You point the rod toward the target while your right index finger gently hooks the line. 2. You start the backstroke smoothly with the index finger still holding the line. 3. When the end of the backstroke is reached, the forward cast should start smoothly and without hesitation. It may take some practice before this can be done well. 4. As the forward cast is made, the index finger releases the line. 5. Pull in the fish with the butt of the rod in the rod socket.

Some of the many fresh-water lures fishermen put on their lines to attract fish.

Salt-water lures are usually larger and heavier than the fresh-water lures.

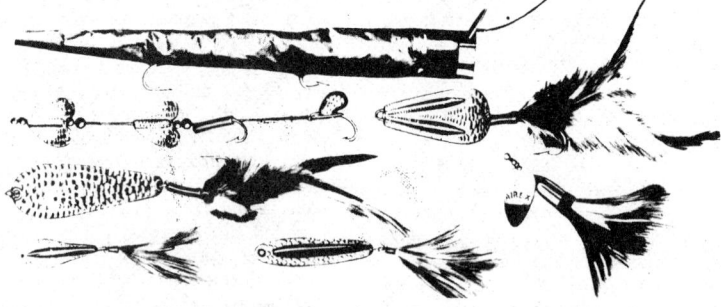

fishing, but not for salt-water fishing. The laws are different in all states, and it is best to ask a few questions before you do any fishing.

A glance at the window of your sporting-goods store, or a look through a fishing tackle catalog, will show you that there is an almost endless variety of rods, reels, leaders, lures, and so on. It is beyond the scope of this article to do more than describe the basic tackle needed for the various types of fishing.

In bait-casting it is the weight of the bait, or lure, that carries the line forward. Therefore the reel is of the utmost importance, and should be of the multiplying type so that you can retrieve your line faster. The reel also should have a level-wind mechanism that distributes the line evenly on the spool. Rods for bait-casting average 5 to 5½ feet in length, and are made of glass, steel, or sometimes bamboo.

Fly-casting is a method in which the line is sent forward in the cast, and the terminal tackle has no weight, consisting of a leader and an artificial insect. Therefore the line itself, and the rod, are of the utmost importance. In fly-fishing the object is to make the fish believe that a choice insect has just fallen into the water. It is a difficult method of angling to learn, and requires many hours of practice, but the rewards are well worth it.

Fisk, James

James Fisk was one of a group of American businessmen who made great fortunes about a hundred years ago. They did not do this by building big businesses of their own. Instead they manipulated (bought and sold) the stocks of businesses, especially railroads, that others had built. Fisk and his group have been called the "robber barons" of their time. They bribed lawmakers (members of state legislatures) to pass laws that would help them make money. Fisk is best remembered for one time, in the year 1869, when he and others tried to control all the gold in the United States. If they could have done this, they would have made a lot of money, but at the last minute the United States government, which was then headed by President Ulysses S. Grant, stopped them. Their attempt still caused so much trouble that thousands of innocent businessmen lost money. This happened on a Friday, which has since been called "Black Friday." Fisk was only 35 years old at this time, having been born in 1834 in Bennington, Vermont. He started life as a peddler, and

later moved to New York City. In 1872, when he was 38 years old, he was shot and killed by another New York man, Edward Stokes. He and Stokes had quarreled because they were both in love with the same woman, and also Stokes was one of those who had lost money on Black Friday.

Fisk University

In 1866, just after the end of the Civil War, Fisk University was started in Nashville, Tennesssee, to help the Negroes of the South get higher schooling. At that time the university had little money. Many of its students were good singers, and these singers traveled around the United States and Europe and sang for money to build a big new building for their school. Now Fisk University has about seven hundred men and women students who can study almost any subject there. Good singers among these students still go out to sing every year.

fission, the name scientists use to describe how atoms are split to produce atomic energy: see ATOMIC ENERGY.

Fitch, John

John Fitch was an American inventor who first had the idea of using the power of steam to make ships go. He was born in 1743 in Windsor, Connecticut. He built and ran many ships, one of which operated between Philadelphia and Trenton. It was the first of its kind to carry freight and passengers. Fitch was unsuccessful in convincing other people of the value of his invention. He died a poor man in 1798, at Bardstown, Kentucky; and a later inventor, Robert Fulton, got the credit for inventing the steamship.

Fitzgerald, Edward

Edward Fitzgerald was an English writer and translator. A translator is a person who takes something that is written in one language and puts the words into another language. Fitzgerald became famous for taking a series of beautiful poems that had been written in Persian and putting them into English. These poems are called *The Rubaiyat of Omar Khayyam.* Fitzgerald did not try to change each Persian word into an English word. He put the feeling, or idea, of the Persian words into English. Fitzgerald was born in 1809 and went to Trinity College, Cambridge. He died in 1883.

Fitzgerald, F. Scott

F. Scott Fitzgerald was a very popular American writer of novels. Most of Fitzgerald's novels are written about the 1920s and give you a very clear picture of how rich people lived during that time.

Fitzgerald was born in St. Paul, Minnesota, in 1896 and went to Princeton University. His first novel, *This Side Of Paradise,* was an immediate and great success. After that he wrote other books but *The Great Gatsby,* his third novel, is considered his best. He died in Hollywood, California, in 1940. He was writing a book at the time called *The Last Tycoon:*

Fitzsimmons, Bob

Robert Fitzsimmons was a prize-fighter who became heavyweight champion of the world. He was born in Cornwall, England, in 1862 or 1863, and lived as a young man in Australia and New Zealand, where he became a very successful fighter. In 1890 he came to the United States, and seven years later he defeated James J. Corbett to gain the heavyweight crown. In his fighting prime he stood six feet tall and weighed between 163 and 170 pounds. He lost the championship to James J. Jeffries in 1899. In 1914, at the age of 52, he fought an exhibition bout. He died in Chicago in 1918.

Fiume or Rijeka

This is a city and seaport on the Adriatic Sea, with a population (1961 census) of 100,989. The city is now part of Yugoslavia and its official name is Rijeka, but for many years Italy held the city and Americans know it best as Fiume, its Italian name.

Fiume is a fine seaport, having two good harbors. Through the centuries many countries have wanted it for a port, and it has been seized again and again. It has been held by France, Austria, Hungary, and Italy. During World War II, it was captured by Yugoslavia, and after the war it was officially made a part of Yugoslavia. Fiume, or Rijeka, is a busy and important city. It is a port and a railroad center. It has shipbuilding, oil-refining and other industries. Fiume combines old and new parts. The old town has narrow crooked streets, winding along a hill. Along the shore the new town is a fine modern city with wide streets and public squares and gardens.

Five Hundred

Five Hundred is the name of a card game. Once it was one of the most popular games played in the United States, and millions of people still enjoy it. It was invented about 70 years ago (in 1904) by the United States Playing Card Company, in Cincinnati, Ohio. This company will send the rules of the game to anyone who sends 25 cents and asks for them. The game is best for three players, but can also be played by four. The rules can be found in many books on games.

Five Nations, a group of Iroquois Indian tribes: see article on IROQUOIS.

Five-Year Plan

The Communist government in Russia first used the Five-Year Plan. When the Communists came into power, in 1917, Russia was a poor country with very little industry and with its methods of farming old-fashioned and undeveloped. The government planned certain improvements it hoped to make within five years, and the way in which it hoped to make these improvements. This was the first Five-Year Plan. It started in 1928. It was not as successful as the government had hoped, but it was successful enough for Russia to continue using such plans. The sixth Five-Year Plan started in 1956, but this was replaced by a new Seven-Year Plan that was adopted in 1959.

flag

Many years ago, kings began hanging a piece of cloth from a tree branch or from a rope in front of their houses. This showed where they were. When a king traveled, he put the same piece of cloth on a long stick. This was the first flag.

The use of flags became so widespread that by about six hundred years ago all kings and nations of Europe and Asia had them. The earliest flags had pictures of animals or of things that told about the king or the country. The most-used animal was the eagle, because it was brave and proud. Later, people stopped using pictures on their flags and, instead, made colored flags in different shapes. These colors and shapes stood for something special in the life of the king or in the country's history.

Because a country's flag is its sign and special mark it is always treated with love and respect by the people of that country. In all countries people salute their flag and use it to show their love for their country. Flags also are used by army groups, and each naval vessel carries a special flag to show the rank of the commander.

FLAGS AS SIGNALS

Flags are used as signals, too. A white flag in war means that the people using it give up or want to have peace for a short time. A yellow flag flying over a fort, ship or hospital shows that its people are sick from a dangerous disease. When a flag is flown halfway up its staff, it means some important person has just died.

Pirates carried black flags with a skull and crossbones, which showed that they were of no nation and would fight to the death. A flag flown upside down means that the people who put it there are in need of help.

THE UNITED STATES FLAG

In the Battle of Concord, American soldiers carried a flag with the words "Conquer or die" written on it in Latin. The flag used at the Battle of Bunker Hill really belonged to Massachusetts. It

showed only a picture of a pine tree. It was not until January 2, 1776, that the American colonies had a flag that looked anything like the United States flag. It was raised by General George Washington, and it had thirteen red and white stripes, one for each colony, and a blue field. On the blue part were the crosses of Saint Andrew and Saint George that stood for the union of Scotland and England, the mother country of the colonies. The English king's colors were used for the crosses to show that the colonies still thought of themselves as belonging to England.

Then, when the Declaration of Independence was signed in July of 1776, the colonists' thinking about their country changed. They decided they should have a flag that showed their new country was free. Congress ordered that the new flag should have thirteen red and white stripes and thirteen white stars on a field of blue. There is a story that Mrs. Betsy Ross of Philadelphia made the first flag, but no one knows if this is true. There was a Betsy Ross who made flags, but no proof has been found to show it was she who sewed the first Stars and Stripes.

The war against England was going on then, and in August, 1777, the new flag first flew in battle. This happened at Fort Schuyler, which stood where Rome, New York, is now. One story says that the flag was made with a white shirt belonging to one of the soldiers, a red petticoat belonging to the wife of another soldier, and a captain's blue cloak. A month later the new flag saw its first battle at sea, and not long after that France became the first foreign nation to salute the flag of the United States.

When two more states, Vermont and Kentucky, were added to the Union in 1791 and 1792, Congress voted to add two more stripes and two stars to the flag. For twenty-three years this remained the flag of the United States; and when Francis Scott Key wrote "The Star-Spangled Banner," our national anthem, he was looking at the fifteen-stripe flag. Because more and more states were being added all the time, it became necessary to

1. When the American flag is displayed with other flags, it should always be on a level with the other flags. 2. The flag should not be raised before sunrise. 3. On Memorial Day, the flag is flown at half-staff until noon and then raised to the peak. 4. In a parade with one other flag, the American flag should always be to the right. 5. When there are many flags, the American flag should be ahead of the others. 6. When the flag is draped over a coffin, the stars should be over the left shoulder of the dead person.

1. At a public meeting where the American flag is displayed with another flag on a platform, the American flag should always be to the right of the speaker. 2. If it is not displayed on a platform, it should be to the left of the speaker. 3. When the flag is hung horizontally on a wall, the stars should appear in the upper left-hand corner. 4. When it is hung vertically, the stars should also be in the upper left-hand corner. 5. When the flag is crossed with another flag, the American flag crosses from right to left. 6. When it is displayed with two other flags, the American flag should be in the middle.

change the make-up of the flag. Otherwise it would be much too big. In 1818 Congress passed a law saying that the flag should have only thirteen stripes and that a star would be added for each new state.

Between then and 1912, 28 states were added, so that the flag had 48 stars. In 1959 and 1960 two more stars were added, making it 50. Until 1916 people made the flag in different shapes. That year the President ordered that it should always be 1$\frac{9}{10}$ times as long as its height and that the blue part on which the stars appear should be seven stripes high. The stars should be five-pointed, the President ordered, with one point directly upward. As the nation grew, other new laws were passed governing the way the flag may be used.

By law, the flag should be flown during school days on every schoolhouse. It should not be spread over cars, trains, or boats; and when it is carried in a parade with other flags, it should be ahead of the others or on their right. When the flag is flown with those of cities or states, it should be put up first and should fly above the others. One of the most important rules is that the flag may not be allowed to touch the ground. When it is old and worn out, it should not be used any more, but should be put away or burned in a private place. Respect for the flag shows respect for the United States itself.

Flag Day

The first "Stars and Stripes" was born on June 14, 1777, when the Congress of the United States passed a resolution that said:

"Resolved, that the flag of the thirteen United States be thirteen stripes, alternate red and white; that the union be thirteen stars, white on a blue field."

Each year, on June 14, Americans honor the anniversary of that day. The flag is displayed in public places and at homes, and many schools have special programs in honor of the flag. Flag Day is not a national holiday, but many states have made it a legal holiday for people living there. See the article FLAG.

flagellants

Flagellants is the name given to people who whip themselves because they want to make up for having done wrong. Thousands of years ago this kind of whipping was done often by people in such places as Egypt and Greece. Usually it was part of their worship of the gods. It has been used in the Christian Church. There were many flagellants in Italy and parts of Southern Germany seven hundred years ago. There are no longer many flagellants.

flageolet

The flageolet is a musical instrument that belongs to the flute family. It is played by blowing into a whistle type of mouthpiece, that is, it is blown from the end and not across a mouthhole. Up until about 250 years ago, the flageolet was used a great deal in orchestras, but now the transverse flute is used in its place. The flageolet has a pleasant and appealing tone and is very much like the recorder.

Flageolet tones are flutelike sounds that can be produced on stringed instruments.

Flagg, James Montgomery

James Montgomery Flagg was a well-known American illustrator. He became famous as an artist who drew pictures for magazines and newspapers. He was born in 1877 and studied at the Art Students League in New York. He wrote the story of his life and called it *Roses and Buckshot.* Flagg died in 1951.

Flagstad, Kirsten

Kirsten Flagstad became famous as a singer in grand opera, a kind of play in which the parts are sung instead of spoken. She was born near Oslo, Norway, in 1895. She made her operatic debut at the age of 18. Soon she began to specialize in operas by Richard Wagner, and in 1935 she began to sing in Wagnerian operas at the Metropolitan Opera House in New York. Though Flagstad was greatly admired as an artist, she lost much of her

popularity because she was accused of being a "collaborationist" when Germany occupied her country, Norway, from 1940 to 1945. In 1953 Flagstad retired from the operatic stage.

flame thrower

The flame thrower, one of the most terrible weapons of war, has a long history. A thousand years ago, the warships of Constantinople shot spouts of flame at the Turkish ships. The American army used flame throwers in World War II to kill Japanese soldiers who had hidden themselves in caves on the Pacific islands of Iwo Jima and Okinawa. A soldier with a flame thrower carries a container of fuel, which is like gasoline, and a container of compressed air on his back. In his hand he holds a hose that connects with the containers. When he presses a trigger attached to the hose, the fuel is forced out by the compressed air. It catches fire from a spark that is made at the end of the hose, and a jet of flame shoots out about forty feet from the nozzle of the hose. Anything in the way of the flame is killed or burned in an instant. Flame throwers are also put in tanks.

flamingo

The flamingo is a beautiful pink bird that lives in many parts of the world where the climate is very warm. In the United States, some flamingos can be found in Florida. They are about five feet tall, and have long thin legs, very long necks, and large curved bills. Flamingos live in flocks, and to watch them eating is a very funny sight, because they have a most unusual way of getting their food. The flamingo stands stiffly in the shallow salt water of the bay or swamp where it makes its home. When it is ready to eat, it bends its long neck, until its head is upside down, and it is looking backward between its legs. Then the flamingo scoops the water with its bill, searching for insects and water plants. Inside the flamingo's bill there is a kind of sieve that is very useful for catching the small creatures the flamingo eats, and with its bill the flamingo can separate the mud from the food. Flamingos are good swimmers and graceful, strong fliers. Like geese, the flamingos fly in a long line or in a triangular formation, and hundreds of these birds make a beautiful pink cloud as they travel swiftly through the air. The flamingo builds a long column-shaped nest out of mud in the shallow water or along the mudbanks of a pond. Some of these nests are about a foot high and it is remarkable that the flamingo can fit into one of them. It curls its long legs underneath its body, and sometimes you can see thousands of flamingos sitting on their nests with their long necks sticking out over the top. The female bird lays one or two white eggs. The parents take turns sitting on the eggs for about a month, and both take care of the young flamingo.

Flanagan, Father

Edward Joseph Flanagan was the first man to say, "there is no such thing as a bad boy." He was born in Ireland in 1866, and he came to America in 1904.

He was a priest and he wanted to help other people. He became interested in homeless boys, and he started his first home for boys in Omaha. He called it Boys Town, and it was so successful that other people soon gave Father Flanagan enough money so that he could continue his work.

Father Flanagan's Boys Town became, over the years, the most famous home for boys in America. Father Flanagan himself knew more than anyone else about homeless boys and how to turn them into happy, useful, decent men. In 1948, while visiting Berlin, Germany, Father Flanagan died. Since that time, motion pictures have been made and books written about Father Flanagan.

Read also the article about BOYS TOWN.

Flanders

Flanders is a region in northwestern Belgium. It is on the North Sea. It is divided into West Flanders, the capital of which is Bruges, and East Flanders, the capital of which is Ghent. The people of Flanders are called Flemings. Flanders is one of the Low Countries, which means that like the Netherlands it is so nearly at sea level that in time of high tides or storm the sea water used to flood the land. For that reason, the country is protected by DIKES, about which you can read in a separate article.

Many of the people of Flanders earn their livings by making lace and cloth. Fishing and farming are also important occupations. Wheat, flax, sugar beets and fruits are grown there.

Flanders has been a battlefield in many wars because it is the easiest way for French armies to get to Germany or for German armies to get to France. Very often the armies have met and fought in Flanders. During World War I there was heavy fighting there, during which the Canadian armies were distinguished by their bravery. Many Allied soldiers are buried in Flanders. The Canadian poet John McCrae wrote a famous poem, usually called "In Flanders Fields," about the thousands of crosses marking the graves of these soldiers in the midst of fields of poppies, for which Flanders is famous.

The language of Flanders is called Flemish. It is a Germanic language, but it is more like Dutch than like German.

flannel, a soft warm cloth that is made of wool, cotton, or other fibers: see the article on TEXTILES.

flare

A flare is a white or colored light that is used in warfare for giving a signal or for lighting up a place at night. During World War II, bombers dropped flares that drifted down by parachute and lighted up the area that they wanted to bomb. Sometimes when infantry troops are going to capture a place, the commander orders that the attack will begin when a flare of a certain color is shot into the air. The defenders then might shoot up their own flares so that they can see the enemy. These flares are fired from

rifles, and they burn for about one minute. In the Navy, flares are used by ships as a way of recognizing each other.

flash point

The flash point of a fuel is the temperature at which it bursts into flame. It is usually found by putting a little bit of fuel, such as gasoline, kerosene, or diesel oil, into a small steel cup. The temperature of the cup is then slowly raised until the fuel bursts into flame. The temperature at which this happens is then recorded as the flash point of this fuel. This test is called the Abel Test; it was named after Sir Frederick Abel, who invented it. Finding the flash point is a safety measure; fuels should never be used in surroundings with a temperature higher than the flash point of the fuel. If this rule is not followed, serious explosions may result.

flatboat

A flatboat is a wide boat with a flat bottom and square ends, used to carry freight. This boat was used by pioneers in the United States about 150 years ago. It was useful to them because its flat bottom helped it float on rapid rivers without touching bottom.

A flatboat could carry heavy loads of farm products, cattle, coal, and furniture. Flatboats were steered by one long oar attached to the rear. The men who worked on these boats were called rivermen. Sometimes the rivermen would use their flatboats as department stores, carrying groceries and hardware to pioneers who were not able to get to stores. Mostly the flatboats were used on the Tennessee, Ohio, and Mississippi Rivers, because these rivers flowed into the fertile valleys of the West where many pioneers were settling. These boats had no sails, so they could only travel downstream, with the current of the river. Once the flatboats reached their destinations, they were broken up and sold for lumber or firewood.

flat feet is an ailment of the feet. See the article on FOOT.

flatfish

Flatfish are thin, flat fish that have both eyes on one side of the head. They swim on their flat sides and sometimes lie on the bottom of the ocean with their eyes facing up. When a flatfish is very small it looks like almost any other fish. As it grows, however, one eye begins to move over closer to the other. The side that now has no eyes begins to lose its color and becomes almost white. The upper side is colored to match its surroundings so that the fish cannot easily be seen. There are many kinds of flatfish, and many of them are food fish such as flounder, sole, and halibut.

Flathead Indians, another name for the Salish Indians, who live in Montana.

Flaubert, Gustave

Gustave Flaubert was a French writer who became famous for his true-to-life stories. Flaubert was born in 1821. As a

French Embassy Press

young man he studied law, but he became ill and could not practice, so he began to write. He was very particular about his writing, and sometimes would spend hours finding exactly the right word to say what he meant. His books included both short stories and novels. His most famous novel was *Madame Bovary*. It was very shocking in those days because it told much more about people's private lives than other novels did, but since then nearly all novels have done the same. He was arrested for writing it, but nothing happened to him and he wrote several other novels that were equally frank. He died in 1880.

flax

Flax is a plant with long slender stems, small green leaves, and bright blue flowers. The thin stem of flax contains the long, strong fibers of which linen cloth is made. People have grown flax ever since the ancient Egyptians learned how to weave this fiber into fine linen more than 5,000 years ago.

Fiber flax, the flax grown by farmers especially for its fibers, grows tall and has not many branches. To harvest fiber flax, farmers pull the plants up by the roots because a machine or cutting instrument may injure the fibers. The way flax grows and is harvested is important to farmers because the fiber used for spinning and weaving is only in the stems. For this reason, special care is given the plant during its cultivation.

Many different kinds of people have raised flax for its fibers. Besides the early Egyptians, the people of Ireland used flax. The weavers of France became very expert during the Middle Ages, especially in the province of Flanders. Flax was the most important fiber plant until two hundred years ago, when cotton began to take its place. But linen is still considered the finest cloth for certain purposes. Today Belgium, France, Soviet Russia and Ireland are the leading producers of flax.

Flax is also grown for its seeds. The flax seed is pressed to obtain linseed oil, a valuable product used in the manufacturing of paints, varnishes, printers' inks, and linoleum. Because linseed oil has become important in people's daily living, many countries grow flax just for its seeds. For instance, the United States is one of the largest producers of flaxseed and linseed oil. See also the article on LINEN.

flea

The flea is a small insect that lives on people or animals and bites them to feed on their blood. The bites can itch and therefore are very unpleasant. Fleas are black or dark brown. Unlike most insects, they have no wings, but they can jump from place to place. The flea is very strong considering its size. If a man were as strong he could jump three hundred feet. No man has ever jumped thirty feet.

The flea is one of the most troublesome of insects and one of the most dangerous. Certain kinds of flea, called "rat fleas" because they live on rats, carry the germs of a disease called plague. This disease killed millions of people in Eu-

rope during an epidemic about six hundred years ago. Fleas especially infest rats, dogs, cats, rabbits, pigeons, and chickens.

There are special soaps and powders that kill fleas on dogs and cats.

Fleming, Sir Alexander

Sir Alexander Fleming is famous as the scientist who discovered the drug penicillin. This drug was discovered in 1928, and has proved very helpful in curing many kinds of infection. Alexander Fleming was born in Scotland, in 1881. From the time he started school he was always an outstanding student. He went to England to study medicine, and there he won many prizes and honors. After he graduated, he became a teacher at the medical school of the University of London, and devoted most of his time to research. He was always interested in learning about the germs that produce diseases, and in trying to find new cures. He made many discoveries.

During World War I, Fleming was a captain in the medical corps of the British army, and he continued his research, trying to find the best ways to cure wounds. In 1928, Fleming was working in his laboratory when he accidentally discovered something that seemed to kill certain germs. It took many years of work by many people before this new drug, penicillin, could be perfected enough to use on human beings. During World War II doctors learned how useful it was, and since then it has helped to save many lives. People everywhere were grateful to Alexander Fleming. He received many honors and awards from Great Britain and many other countries. In 1944, the king of England honored him for his work, by making him a knight. That is why he is called Sir Alexander Fleming. In 1945, Sir Alexander Fleming and two other men who took part in the development of penicillin were awarded the Nobel Prize, which is given each year to persons who do outstanding work in various fields. Fleming died in 1955.

Flemish, the language spoken in Flanders: see FLANDERS.

flicker

The flicker is one of the largest members of the woodpecker family. It is a brown bird with a bright streak of red on its neck. Underneath the tail and wing feathers it is a golden yellow or orange-red. The flicker gets its food by using its beak to get ants and insects from under the bark of trees. It also eats berries and worms. It builds its nest in holes in trees. The yellow-shafted flicker lives mostly in the southern part of Canada and in the eastern United States. The red-shafted flicker lives in the western United States.

flight

The theory of flight is the explanation of why airplanes fly.

This theory explains the forces that are holding the airplane up and moving it along in the air. It explains how something as heavy as an airplane can get off the ground and fly in the air, which is so much lighter than it is.

The scientific name for the study of flight and other movements in the air and gases is *aerodynamics*.

THE FOUR FORCES

An airplane moving through the air has four forces pushing against it. One is its *weight* trying to push the airplane back down to the ground. Opposite to this is a second force, the *lift* of the wings, a force pushing up against the airplane's weight and holding it in the air. This lift comes from the wing's motion through the air. The wing is tilted up at an *angle of attack* to its direction of motion, forc-

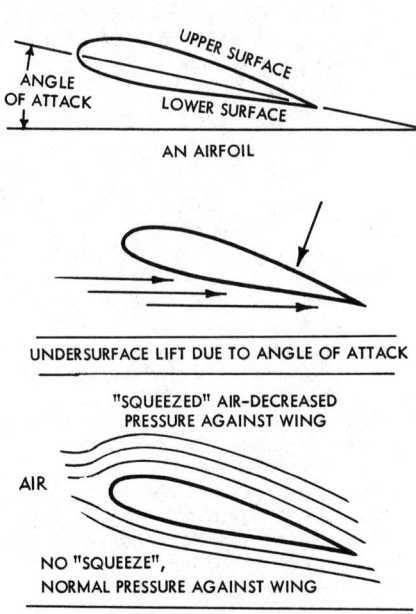

ANGLE OF ATTACK — UPPER SURFACE — LOWER SURFACE

AN AIRFOIL

UNDERSURFACE LIFT DUE TO ANGLE OF ATTACK

"SQUEEZED" AIR-DECREASED PRESSURE AGAINST WING

AIR

NO "SQUEEZE", NORMAL PRESSURE AGAINST WING

LIFT DUE TO THE AIRFOIL

LIFT

The force needed to lift an airplane into the air is created by air flowing over and under the wings. The wings are often called airfoils. They are tilted slightly on the plane so that more air can strike the underside of the wings. The amount of tilt is called the angle of attack. The air against the underside of the wing helps lift the plane in the air. But most of the lift comes from having less pressure on top of the wing than on the bottom. This difference in pressure comes from the greater curvature on top of the wing than on the bottom. This makes the air go faster over the wing than under it. This reduces the pressure on top and gives the plane most of its lift.

ing the air down as the wing passes through it. The air in resisting being moved causes the upward lifting force on the wing.

To get this lifting force the airplane must be pushed through the air by the *thrust* given by its propeller or jet. This thrust is the third force. The fourth force is the resistance of the air against the wings, body, and all other exposed parts of the airplane moving through it. This force is called *drag*. This is the force you can feel if you hold your hand out of the window of an automobile that is traveling fast.

LIFT

One of the most important problems of aerodynamics is the design of wings to get the most lift from them. This is done by very careful design and testing. The airplane wing is not flat like a piece of paper. The top of the wing is arched up in a curve. It is thick near the front edge, rising in a curve and then thinning down to a sharp edge at the rear, called the *trailing edge*. The bottom of the wing is nearly flat. Such a wing shape is called an *airfoil*. Due to the curve of the top surface, the air through which the wing moves is sucked down over the top face and pressed down by the bottom surface. Actually the larger part of the lift comes from the sucking effect of the top of the wing rather than the pressure on the bottom. The amount a wing can lift depends on several things: the shape of the airfoil, the area and spread of the wing, and its speed through the air. So we find that the high-speed racing or fighter planes have small, thin wings, while the large cargo and passenger planes have bigger wings.

THRUST

A propeller or a jet pushes an airplane ahead by pushing air back. In so doing thrust is produced. This is exactly the same as the way a canoe is pushed forward by the paddle pushing the water backward. The more water or air is pushed back and the faster it is pushed, the greater the thrust it gives.

flint

Flint is a very hard, brittle, dark brown or black stone that is found in the chalk cliffs of England and in limestone in many parts of the United States. Now-

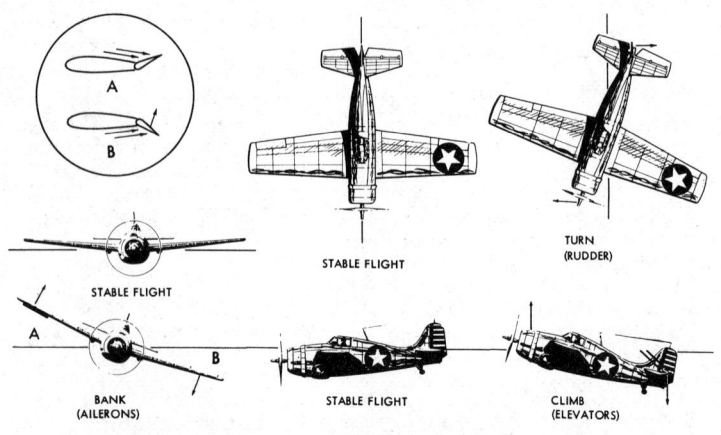

A

B

STABLE FLIGHT

STABLE FLIGHT

BANK (AILERONS)

TURN (RUDDER)

STABLE FLIGHT

CLIMB (ELEVATORS)

CONTROL

An airplane is controlled by the ailerons (A and B), the elevators, and rudder. Raising and lowering the ailerons makes the plane tip to one side, or bank. Raising the elevators makes the plane climb. Moving the rudder makes the plane turn. A pilot uses all these controls to help keep the plane level in different air conditions.

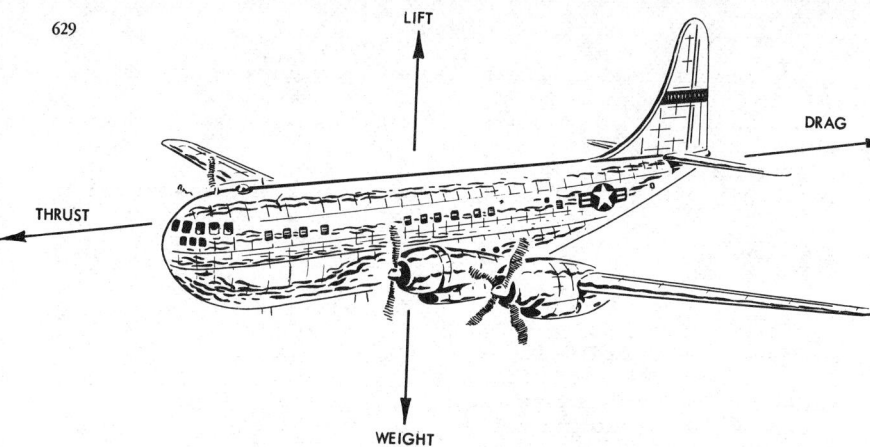

Above: There are four important forces pressing against an airplane when it is in flight. First there is its own weight pushing the plane toward the ground. To keep the plane up in the air, there is a force called lift which must be greater than the plane's weight. The lift is caused by air flowing at a greater speed above the wings than under them. Air flowing against the plane creates a force called drag that pushes against the front of the plane. To keep the plane moving forward, there is a force called thrust. This is made by the propellers that turn like a screw and cut through the air in front of the plane, pulling the plane forward.

Below: The propellers are turned by the giant engines that are the power plants in front of the wings. The wings are attached to the main body or fuselage of the plane. The ailerons are parts of the .wings that can be raised or lowered to turn the plane on its side. The fin on the tail keeps the plane from tipping to one side when it is flying straight ahead. The stabilizer keeps the plane from tipping up and down. By moving the rudder, the pilot can turn the plane right or left. The elevators are raised or lowered to make the plane go higher or lower in the air. When the plane comes down on the ground, its landing gear, or wheels, can absorb most of the shock as the plane lands and rolls to a stop.

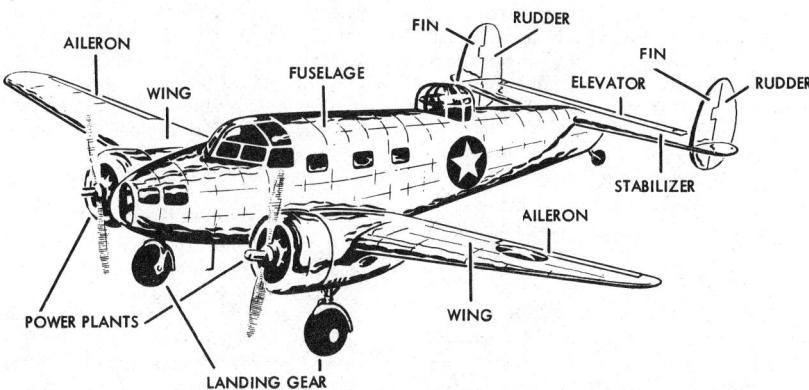

adays we have very few uses for flint, but thousands of years ago it was the only material that man knew how to make into tools. Because flint is so hard and brittle, it was easy for primitive man to chip it into the shapes of spearheads, arrowheads, axes, and awls to punch holes in animal skins.

Ancient man also learned to make fire by striking a piece of flint against iron. This caused a spark that could be caught on some dry leaves and kindled into fire. The friction, or rubbing, of the flint against iron caused enough heat to produce combustion, about which you can read in the article on FIRE.

For a long time guns were fired by sparks made from flint. The flintlock musket was a kind of gun in which a strong spring caused flint and steel to rub together and make a spark, which lighted the gunpowder and fired the bullet. You can read more about the flintlock in the article on RIFLE.

The substance that causes fire in a cigarette lighter is called flint, but it really is made of the metals cerium and iron. When it is struck by steel it produces a spark.

Flint

Flint is a city in the state of Michi-

gan. It is one of the most important automobile manufacturing centers in the United States. Almost 200,000 people live in Flint, and they make more automobiles and motor parts than any other city in Michigan except Detroit. In early days, Flint was an Indian village. It has a museum with many relics from this time. Flint became a trading post, and about fifty years ago, when the first automobile plant was opened, the city began to grow into the busy place it is now.

FLINT, MICHIGAN. Population (1970 census), 193,317. County seat, Genesee County. On the Flint River. Settled 1819.

flintlock, an old-fashioned kind of gun that used flint striking against steel to make a spark and fire the gunpowder: see the article on MUSKET.

floating island

A floating island is a large tangled mass of driftwood, mud and plants that floats on rivers, lakes, and oceans. A floating island is formed close to the shore when driftwood and other floating objects are washed together and held by vines and other plants that grow on them. The tangled mass is torn away from the shore during storms or by flood waters, and it floats away. A floating island may fall

apart when the plants and vines that hold it together die. Sometimes grass grows on the floating island and holds it together for years. Some floating islands have been big and strong enough to hold horses, cows, and men.

Floating island is also the name of a dessert made by floating a foam of beaten egg whites and sugar on a thin pudding.

flood

When a river, a lake or an ocean overflows its banks or shores and covers all the land nearby, we call this overflow a flood. Each year floods destroy hundreds of homes and human lives in America alone. In the year 1421, Saint Elizabeth's Flood drowned 100,000 people in Holland. Again in 1953 the people of Holland were victims of the worst flood of our times. This flood struck at midnight. Driven by howling windstorms, huge waves from the North Sea crashed through the sea-walls, called dikes, that stand between Dutch farms and the ocean. Waves, some of which were over twelve feet high, rolled deep into Holland's rich farm country. When the storm ended and the waves flowed back to sea, they left behind 500,000 acres of once-rich farm land, now spoiled by salt from the water. In this disaster about 1,550 people were drowned, and about a million more had to be moved to homes outside the flood area.

WHAT CAUSES FLOODS

We can best understand how a flood gets started if we look at America's own giant Mississippi River, which has floods each spring. The Mississippi is of course very long and very wide, mainly because hundreds of smaller streams, called tributaries, flow down from high land and feed into the big river. But each spring heavy rains fall on hills to the north of the Mississippi. These rainstorms melt the winter snow still lying on the ground, so an unusual amount of water is shed off the hillsides into the Mississippi's tributary streams below. Soon these streams, choked with water, are pouring millions of extra gallons into the Mississippi itself. Swiftly the big river rises, spills over its man-made sides, called levees, and floods out over the countryside.

Spring rains are the main cause of floods, but there are many others. Windstorms often drive lake or ocean waves up onto the shore, causing great damage each year. In fact, the great Holland flood of 1953, described above, was caused by just such a windstorm. Then, too, sea walls, levees, dikes, dams and other man-made shields against such rising water will sometimes break open, allowing water to come flooding through. Or a giant earthquake will occasionally cause huge tidal waves.

HOW TO STOP A FLOOD

There is no single, certain way to stop a flood. But if we combine several different ways at once, floods can be stopped. We can, for instance, build dams. A dam is a tall wall of wood, earth, or concrete built clear across a stream and up its banks on either side. A hole in the middle of the dam allows normal amounts of water to flow through. But extra-large amounts of flood water cannot get

through. Instead, this water piles up against the dam, forming a large pool or lake, which we call a reservoir. Many such dams are now being built across Midwest rivers to hold back flood water, and prevent them from flowing all at once into the Mississippi. Often, as in the big Tennessee Valley dams of the TVA, this trapped water is used to turn machinery to generate electricity. Another flood-stopping plan is the watershed, which is a stretch of slanting land along which water flows down to a stream. If this watershed land could only soak up the flood water instead of shedding it, floods would not take place. So farmers are asked to run a plow along such land, making little furrows, or ridges, able to soak up the rain water much better than can the smooth, hard ground. The watershed plan also includes planting grass and other crops to help hold back the water. Although dams and watersheds are our main flood-fighting methods, there are several others. Levees, for instance, are man-made walls along the sides of streams instead of across them. Paths called channels can be cut through from the stream to the beds of rivers or lakes now dried up. In flood time, flood water pours harmlessly through these channels into the old river bed instead of into a larger river. If all these flood-fighting methods can be teamed together, we may in our lifetime see an end to the very great damage now done by floods.

Flora

Flora was the goddess of flowers and of the springtime in Roman mythology, the stories the ancient Romans told about their gods and goddesses. Flora was worshiped in Italy for hundreds of years. Even before Rome became a great and powerful city, the country people of Italy worshiped Flora. Every year in the springtime, the Romans celebrated a festival called the *Floralia,* in honor of the goddess. They celebrated the end of winter and the return of flowers to the earth in the springtime.

Florence

Florence is a city in Italy. It is a very beautiful city, but it is even more noted for the great art works that can be seen in its museums and palaces. Many of the most famous artists of all time lived and worked in Florence. Among them were Michelangelo, Leonardo da Vinci, Raphael, and Giotto.

Florence is in north central Italy. Its Italian name is *Firenze.* The city is built on both sides of the Arno River, and the two banks of the river are connected by several bridges. The most famous of these is the *Ponte Vecchio,* which is lined with shops in which you can buy a handkerchief or a piece of lovely old jewelry. The most famous of all metal-carvers, Benvenuto Cellini, once worked on the *Ponte Vecchio.*

The most famous family of Florence was the Medici family, who ruled the city for about three hundred years. There is a separate article about the MEDICIS.

Florence is a very big city with a population of more than 400,000, but it does not have as many factories as most cities of that size. Many people make their livings by taking care of the many visitors.

Some of the buildings and art treasures of Florence were destroyed by the Germans in World War II, and some works of art were carried away, but the people of the city hid most of them in the hills until after the war.

Florida

Florida is a state that forms the southeastern corner of the United States. It is a peninsula, that is, a body of land that sticks out into the water. It extends farther south than any other state, and it has a warm and sunny climate all year round. That is why Florida is called both the "Peninsula State," and the "Sunshine State." The state is one of the most famous vacation spots in the United States, and thousands of people go there to lie on the beautiful white beaches and swim in the blue Atlantic Ocean.

When the Spanish explorer Ponce de Leon discovered this territory on Easter Day, about 450 years ago, he called it Pasqua Florida, which means Easter, or the Feast of Flowers; and Florida is a beautiful sight with its brilliantly colored wild flowers and plants, which bloom all through the year. At the southern tip of the state are the famous Everglades, the most junglelike part of the United States. It is a great swamp with huge trees and thick grass that often grows higher than a man's head.

Florida ranks 22nd in size among the states, with 58,560 square miles. In population it ranks 9th, with about six million people living there. It became a state in 1845, the 27th state admitted to the United States.

THE PEOPLE OF FLORIDA

In the past, the people of Florida were mostly farmers, growing tobacco, cotton, and the famous Florida fruits. Though farming is still very important in the state, two out of three people now live in the cities, taking care of the great tourist trade. Many people from the north saw what a popular vacation place Florida was becoming, and in the past fifty years they have built beautiful hotels, houses, shops, and theaters there. Today, Florida earns more money from the tourist business than from any other industry. However, people in the cities also work in factories. Florida is the leading cigar-manufacturing state.

Visitors to Florida will find many interesting groups of people. In the northern part of the state are farmers whose English-speaking ancestors settled there before the Civil War. These natives are called *crackers,* because in the pioneer days they cracked heavy whips over the oxen to get them to pull the carts filled with heavy loads.

About one-sixth of the people are black. In the Everglades, the Seminole Indians live in villages. Once there were many thousands of these Indians, but today only about seven hundred live in the state. They still make beautiful dolls, miniature boats, and other native products. These are sold by the Indian men because the women are not permitted to speak to white people. These Seminole Indians pride themselves on their independence, and on the fact that they have never signed a treaty with the United States.

In the past 75 years, people from Cuba, Spain, and Greece have also settled in Florida. They live in their own communities, and have many colorful celebrations and holidays. If you visit Tarpon Springs you will find the Greek fishermen, who gather large quantities of sponges from the ocean's bottom along the coast. Florida produces more sponges than any other state. At Key West, an island off the southern coast, are the Spaniards and Cubans, who live as fishermen, catching crawfish and sea turtles.

The leading churches in Florida are the Baptist, Roman Catholic, and Methodist.

WHAT FLORIDA IS LIKE

Anyone who has traveled through Florida knows how low and flat the state is. Along the eastern coast, on the Atlantic Ocean, are a series of sand bars and islands on which have been built some of the most famous resorts in the world, such as Daytona Beach, Palm Beach, and Miami Beach. Although the business districts are often on the mainland, the resort sections are on these islands.

At the southern tip of Florida are the Everglades, which was an unexplored and mysterious region until a hundred years ago. It includes the Big Cypress Swamp, with its junglelike underbrush, great orchids, and wild plant life. In recent years a large section of the Everglades has been drained and is now used for farming.

Off the southern tip of Florida is a curving chain of islands, known as the Florida Keys. These low coral islands are covered with coconut palms, banana trees, and pineapple plants. The most famous of these islands are Key West and Key Largo, and they attract people from all over the country because of the wonderful deep-sea fishing. Connecting these islands to the mainland is the Overseas Highway, the largest over-sea bridge in the world. It is remarkable because it is built on pontoons, so that it is actually a floating bridge.

The west coast of Florida is on the Gulf of Mexico, and has many bays. Off the coast are the Ten Thousand Islands, which are so low that some of them are occasionally covered by water.

Florida has some thirty thousand lakes. Most of these lakes are in central Florida. In this part of the state are large forests

and the springs for which Florida is famous.

The people have developed the rich Florida soil, particularly in the northern part of the state and grow not only fruit, but tobacco, cotton, and sugar cane. Florida ranks first in the production of grapefruits and tangerines, as well as in Irish potatoes, cucumbers, and winter-grown tomatoes. Many oranges and lemons are grown. Important also are the forests, and Florida produces more cypress lumber than any other state. Minerals are also important, and most of the country's phosphate rock comes from Florida.

In the wilder sections and swamps of the state, one can still see deer, bears, some wildcats, and pumas. Florida's most famous animal is the alligator, which is found in all parts of the state. These huge creatures, with their heavy bodies and short legs, can grow to be almost twenty feet long, and may weigh as much as a thousand pounds.

Railroads reach all parts of the state, and there are airlines and ships for the large tourist trade. Florida is one of the main traffic lanes for trade, and ships from all over the world come to Florida ports.

The climate of Florida is generally mild. In winter the average temperature is about 59 degrees, though in the northern parts it can go as low as 32 degrees. In summer, the temperature is about 81 degrees.

THE GOVERNMENT OF FLORIDA

Florida, like most other states, is governed by a Governor and a Legislature. The Governor is elected for a four-year term. The Legislature is composed of a Senate, the members of which are elected for a four-year term, and a General Assembly, whose members are elected for a two-year term. Judges are elected for a six-year term. The capital is Tallahassee. There are 67 counties.

More than a million pupils are enrolled in the public elementary and high schools. Among the colleges and universities are:

University of Florida, at Gainesville. Enrollment, 19,699 in 1971 (co-ed).
Florida State University, at Tallahassee. Enrollment, 16,000 in 1971 (co-ed).
Florida Agricultural and Mechanical College, at Tallahassee. Enrollment, 4,248 in 1971 (co-ed).
Florida Southern College, at Lakeland. Enrollment, 1,620 in 1971 (co-ed).
University of Miami, at Coral Gables. Enrollment, 16,674 in 1971 (co-ed).
Rollins College, at Winter Park. Enrollment, 3,420 in 1971 (co-ed).
John B. Stetson University, at De Land. Enrollment, 2,674 in 1971 (co-ed).
University of Tampa, at Tampa. Enrollment, 2,184 in 1971 (co-ed).
Jacksonville University, at Jacksonville. Enrollment, 2,816 in 1971 (co-ed).
University of South Florida, at Tampa. Enrollment, 13,823 in 1971 (co-ed).

CHIEF CITIES OF FLORIDA

The leading cities of Florida, with populations from the 1970 census, are:

Tallahassee, population 71,897, the state capital. There is a separate article about TALLAHASSEE.

Miami, population 334,859 (with suburbs, 1,267,792), the largest city in the state. There is a separate article about MIAMI.

The 234-foot Singing Tower at Lake Wales contains 71 bells. It stands in a 58-acre sanctuary.

The resort city of Palm Beach is known for its cleanliness, fine stores, and wealthy citizens.

A section of the Palm Beach shoreline.

Tampa, population 277,767 the third largest city, tourist and fishing resort in the western part of the state.

Jacksonville, population 528,865, the second-largest city. There is a separate article about JACKSONVILLE.

St. Petersburg, population 216,232, the fourth-largest city, winter resort in the western part of the state.

Orlando, population 99,006, fifth-largest city, in central part of state.

FLORIDA IN THE PAST

On Easter Sunday, 1513, the Spanish explorer Ponce de Leon sighted the coast of Florida and became its discoverer. He was searching for gold and for a famous fountain he had heard stories about. This fountain was supposed to keep a person young forever if he drank from it. However, Ponce de Leon found neither gold nor the Fountain of Youth, and he was finally killed in a fight with the Indians living in Florida.

Later Spanish explorers came to this territory, and the first permanent settlement was made at St. Augustine in 1565, making it the oldest community in the United States. The Spanish treated the Indians very cruelly, and they were hated ever after by them. Both the French and English also settled in various parts of Florida, but it was the Spanish who gained control of most of the territory. However, they were often at war with the English.

Finally, the Spaniards signed a truce with the English and gave them Florida in exchange for Cuba.

Many English settlers came to this region and saw how fertile the land was. They began to farm and grow prosperous. But it was too difficult for England to hold on to Florida, and shortly after the war with the American colonies, England gave Florida back to Spain. In 1821, the United States bought Florida from Spain, but for many years there were bitter wars with the Seminole Indians, who did not want to be removed from their land. They finally surrendered, however, and most of them moved to what is now Oklahoma.

When Florida became a state in 1845, many people owned slaves who worked in the cotton and sugar-cane fields. Like the people in other slave-holding states, they did not want the Negroes to be freed. After Abraham Lincoln became president, in 1860, and it looked as if the slaves would be set free, Florida seceded from the Union in protest, and joined the Confederacy during the Civil War. Several years after the war, Florida was admitted back into the Union.

Since then, Florida has grown enormously, and its farming and lumbering industries have made the state prosperous. In the past fifty years the wonderful warm climate has attracted thousands of people from the north, and the tourist industry has boomed ever since. In World War II, Florida served as a large training base for soldiers and for navy fliers. During the war it was a familiar sight in cities such as Miami Beach to see soldiers marching and drilling in the streets, and living in the large hotels taken over by the government. Since the war, Florida has been expanding its industries and has been very prosperous.

Today Florida is very well-known because the United States Air Force Missile Test Center at Cape Canaveral is located there. It is the place where most of America's space rockets have been launched. America's first artificial satellite was launched from here in January 1948, and the first manned space flight in May 1961. Col. John H. Glenn, Jr., orbited the earth from here in February 1962.

PLACES TO SEE IN FLORIDA

Everglades National Park, 1,258,361 acres, in Southern Florida, on U.S. Route 41. Largest remaining subtropical wilderness in the United States; open Everglades prairies, mangrove forests; abundant wildlife including rare and colorful birds.

Fort Matanzas National Monument, 227 acres, 10 miles south of St. Augustine, on U.S. Route 1. Spanish fort built in 1737 to protect back door to St. Augustine. Near this site, Menendez massacred two parties of French Huguenots in 1565, thus determining that Florida should remain Spanish rather than French territory.

Fort Jefferson National Monument, 47,125 acres, at Dry Tortugas, 60 miles west of Key West, on U.S. Route 1. Largest all-masonry fortification in western world; built in 1846 for control of Florida Straits. Federal military prison during and after the Civil War. Outstanding bird refuge; extraordinary marine life.

Mountain Lake Sanctuary, 58 acres, in central Florida, 12 miles east of Winter Haven, on U.S. Route 60. Established by Edward Bok as a sanctuary for birds; overlooks some thirty lakes; on Iron Mountain, the highest point in Florida. More than a hundred varieties of birds; beautiful plants, shrubs, and trees. Contains the Singing Tower, where Edward Bok is buried. High up in the tower is a magnificent set of 71 bells.

Highlands Hammock State Park, 3,800 acres, in south central Florida, 6 miles west of Sebring, on U.S. Route 27. One of the most remarkable scenic spots in the state, it adjoins the huge Florida Botanical Garden and Arboretum. A wilderness of dense jungle and swamps, it abounds with wild animals and birds.

Silver Springs, in central Florida, 6 miles east of Ocala, on U.S. Route 27. One of the largest springs in the world. Strange underwater plants, turtles, and fish may be seen from special boats.

Marine studios at Marineland near St. Augustine have thousands of salt water fish of all sizes, including large sharks, on exhibit. Visitors can see them below the water surface through 300 windows.

FLORIDA. Area 58,560 square miles. Population (1970 census) 6,789,443. Capital, Tallahassee. Nickname, the Peninsula State. Motto, In God We Trust. Flower, orange blossom. Bird, mockingbird. Song, "The Swanee River." Admitted to Union, March 3, 1845. Official abbreviation, Fla.

florist

A florist is a person who sells flowers. A florist usually buys flowers from a farm (called a nursery) that raises flowers, and from a greenhouse in the winter. He must know the names of the flowers, and how to keep them fresh for as long as possible. This is usually done by putting them in a refrigerator, but there are some chemicals that can be put in water to make certain flowers last longer, and different flowers require more or less water. A florist must learn what lengths to cut flower stems, and how to pack them so that they will look well and not be crushed in the box. He must learn how to combine different flowers into beautiful combinations and how to arrange them in vases or bowls, how to make ribbon bows to set off a bouquet, and how to arrange ferns and leaves as a background for flowers. He must know how to trim and arrange flowers into bouquets called corsages that are worn by women. There are many special ways in which flowers are used, and the florist must know all these uses and which flowers are most appropriate for each.

flotsam and jetsam

Flotsam and jetsam are valuable goods floating on the waters of the ocean. Flotsam may be remains from a ship that has been shipwrecked, or it may be something accidentally lost from a ship. Jetsam is something that was intentionally thrown from a ship, usually to lighten the load of the ship during a storm. There are many complicated laws dealing with flotsam and jetsam. Usually, if someone finds them and knows who the owner is, he must give them back to the owner but can charge a fee, or claim a reward, for *salvage* (that is, for saving it). If the

owner is not known, the finder of the flotsam or jetsam can keep it.

There is a third class of lost goods, called *lagan*. This is property that has sunk to the bottom. The owner of it is given a certain period of time in which to salvage it. After that, anyone else may bring it up from the bottom, and the law covers cases when the previous owner may reclaim it and pay a salvage fee, and when the person who salvages it may keep it.

flounder

The flounder is a food fish that is eaten by people all over the world. It belongs to a great family of fish known as FLATFISH, about which you can read in another article. There are two kinds of flounder, the winter flounder and the summer flounder, which is sometimes called a fluke. The winter flounder is found in both the Atlantic and Pacific Oceans. However, fishermen catch more winter flounder in the North Atlantic Ocean, especially around Labrador. It eats mostly tiny shellfish which it finds on the bottom of the water. When it is full-grown, it weighs about two pounds. The summer flounder, or fluke, weighs about four pounds. It is most commonly found along the eastern coast of the United States. The fluke feeds on small fish, crabs, and shellfish.

flour

Flour is the finely ground kernels of wheat or other plants, such as rye, potatoes, beans, corn, or rice. All flour, no matter what it is made of, contains many of the nourishing things needed for good health. It contains carbohydrates, proteins, fats, minerals, and vitamins. Flour is the main ingredient of one of man's most important foods, bread. Bread is so important to man that it is often called the "staff of life." Flour is part of many other foods, too: cake, pie, pancakes, macaroni and spaghetti are only a few of the foods that are made from flour.

DIFFERENT KINDS OF FLOUR

The plants people use to make flour are those they find growing most abundantly around them. In India and China, for instance, some of the flour is made from a plant called millet. The North American Indians made their flour of corn, and the South American Indians made theirs from the root of a plant called the cassava or manioc. You know this flour by the name of tapioca. For many hundreds of years the people of central and eastern Europe made their flour from rye. But of all the different grains from which flour can be made, wheat has been most commonly used. There are two important reasons for this. One is that wheat grows in most parts of the world and is a hardy plant. The other is that bread made from wheat flour is finer and lighter than bread made from other flours.

WHEAT FLOUR

Flour that is made from the whole wheat grain is called whole-wheat flour; flour that is made from the inner part of the kernel only is called white flour. Whole-wheat flour is coarser than white flour, but it contains many vitamins and

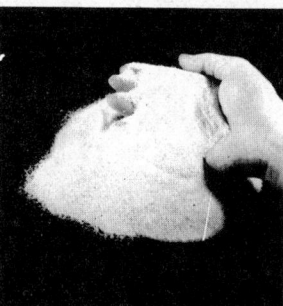

Wheat Flour Inst., Chicago

The grinding of wheat into flour requires several steps. At each step the coarse grain is made finer and finer until at the end we have the smooth white flour.

minerals that are not present in white flour. Nowadays these food elements are often added to white flour. Flour that has had these elements added is called enriched flour; it tastes the same as regular white flour, but it has more food value. About 98% of all the wheat flour that is made in the United States today is white flour, and much of it is enriched.

There are several different kinds of wheat, and each kind produces a different kind of flour. The flour that is used for baking bread usually comes from hard-kernel wheat. The flour that is used for making macaroni and spaghetti comes from durum wheat. The flour that is used for making cake, pie crusts and biscuits comes from soft wheat.

HOW FLOUR IS MADE

Man first learned how to grind grain into flour more than five thousand years ago, at about the time he learned how to cultivate the land and raise crops. At first his method of grinding grain into flour was very simple. He used tools somewhat like the mortar and pestle your druggist uses today in grinding the dry ingredients in a prescription. The grain was put into a shallow bowl and ground as fine as possible with a kind of mallet. Even today some primitive people use this method of grinding grain.

Later, men learned how to grind grain more efficiently between two large stones that had rough surfaces but were nearly flat. The grain was placed on the lower stone. The upper stone, which was called the *quern,* was turned on top of it until the grain was ground fine enough to be used as flour. At first, the quern was turned by men who were harnessed to ropes attached to the rim of the quern. The men turned the quern by walking around and around it. Still later, men discovered that they could use farm animals for this hard, heavy work. During the days of ancient Egypt, about three thousand years ago, oxen and other farm animals were used to turn the quern.

As civilization advanced, men found other, more efficient, ways of turning the grindstone. They learned to use the power of the wind, for example. Many of the windmills for which Holland is famous turn flour mills. The wind turns the wings of the windmill, and this turning power is transferred through gears to the upper grindstone. Water and steam, too, were used to provide the power to turn the grindstone.

About a hundred years ago, a new method of grinding flour, called roller milling, was developed in Hungary. This method spread throughout the world and is the one used today in all modern flour mills.

When flour is made by the roller-milling process, the first step is the cleaning of the grain. Then the grain is dampened and passed through long grooved rollers. In these rollers the *husk,* which is also called the *bran* or the *middlings,* is separated from the inner kernel, which passes through many more rollers. At each stage the coarser grains are separated from the finer ones, and the grains are cleaned. Some grains of wheat cannot be ground as fine as others; in the roller-milling process four separate grades of flour are produced, ranging from the finest to the coarsest. At each stage of the process, the grains that cannot be ground fine enough to become flour at all are separated from those that can. More than a quarter of the wheat is discarded when flour is made; about 72 pounds of white flour can be made from 100 pounds of wheat. The part that is discarded in making flour is used for cattle feed.

The factories that produce flour are called flour mills. The largest flour-producing countries of the world are the United States, Canada, England, Hungary, Argentina, and Australia.

flower

A flower is usually the bright-colored part of a plant. Therefore it is the easiest part of the plant to see. Usually it is also the easiest part of a plant to smell, and often the smell is very pleasant. Most plants, from the daisy to the oak tree, are flowering plants.

The purpose of the flower is to produce the seeds from which new plants grow. Nature has created flowers in many shapes and colors and has provided each with a distinct odor. A bee or butterfly smells the odor or sees the colors and flies to the flower. Pollen from the flower gets on the insect's legs and wings. The insect carries the pollen to other flowers. This is what causes seeds to form and new flowers to grow.

TYPES OF FLOWERS

There are thousands of different kinds of flower. Some flowers, for example water lilies, grow on plants on the surface of water. Some, like mistletoe, are parasites that live on trees. Among the families of flowering plants are the grass family, the rose family, the lily family, and the iris family. One species of iris grows from a *rhizome,* which is a kind of root shaped like a long, thin potato. The rhizome is planted in the ground instead of a seed. Some flowering plants are climbers. They send out shoots that climb walls or along fences. Some are bushes or shrubs.

PARTS OF A FLOWER

A flower has four main parts. The *calyx* is the outside part. It is a kind of cup, usually green, that holds the flower together and is attached to the stem of the plant. Inside the calyx are the *petals.* The petals are the colored part of the flower. The petals taken all together are called the *corolla,* which surrounds the heart of the flower. The heart of the flower is usually a different color from the petals. It is a group of tiny stems with heads on them sprinkled with a delicate powder. The tiny hairs are called *stamens* and the powder is *pollen.* There are usually the same number of stamens in a flower as there are petals, or a number that is equally divisible. The stamens are in a circle and inside the circle is the *carpel,* a small spike. The *ovules,* or eggs that are the seed of the flower, are at the base of the carpel. The pollen on the stamens must get into the carpel and down to the ovules. Bees and other insects help it to do this.

HISTORY OF FLOWERS

Flowers began to appear on the earth early in the Mesozoic Age, about one hundred million to two hundred million years ago. When plants began to grow on the earth, they grew in large numbers. There were great jungles of trees with huge leaves on them. Forests of deciduous trees, that is, trees that drop their old leaves every year and later grow new ones, covered the mountainous parts of the earth. The open places in the forests got enough sunlight and heat so that true flowers began to grow. Insects began to develop at about the same time. Insects quite possibly stayed alive because there were plants for them to feed on, and in turn the flowers stayed alive because the insects carried their pollen. Flowers became more brightly colored and more highly scented, because then they attracted insects better. Their shapes changed as well. This change came about mostly in their petals, which became thicker. They could then better support the weight of the insect as it rested on the flower to suck the sweet juices from it.

FLOWERS AS SYMBOLS

Because of their beauty, flowers have meant a great deal to man. Poets have praised them, nations have chosen them as national emblems, and military conquerors have selected them as badges for their armies or as symbols of victory. The rose, which is called "the flower of flowers," is the national flower of England. The thistle became the national flower of Scotland because an invading army fell on thistles while attacking at night and their cries wakened the defenders of the castle, who drove them off. When St. Patrick brought Christianity to Ireland he used the shamrock to explain the idea of the Trinity. The Irish have kept it as their emblem ever since.

The United States has not yet agreed on a national flower, but the goldenrod has many supporters because it grows in many parts of the country. Some of the

The delicate apple blossoms bloom each May.

Stark Bros. Nurseries

The azalea has clusters of lovely flowers.

Horace McFarland Co.

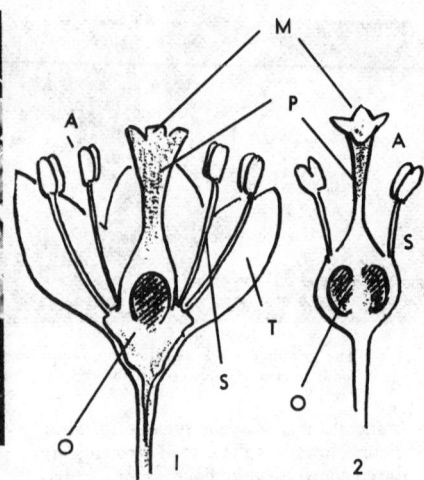
Cutaway views of a flower (1) and its pistil (2). The pistil (P) contains the ovary (O) and the stigma (M), where pollen grains are caught. The ovary contains one or more ovules (O). The stamens (S) have parts called anthers (A) that carry the pollen. The petals (T) fit around the pistil and stamens and may have a bright color or sweet odor.

Margot L. Wolf
A perfect rose blooming on its stem.

Margot L. Wolf
The orchid grows in the tropics.

states have adopted flowers as their emblems. Iowa has the wild rose; Maine, the pine cone and tassel; Michigan, the apple blossom; Nebraska, the goldenrod; Oregon, the Oregon grape; Vermont, the red clover; Colorado, the columbine; Oklahoma, the mistletoe. School children have voted for flowers in some states. In California they voted for the poppy; in Idaho, the syringa; in Kansas, the sunflower; in Minnesota, the moccasin flower; in Nevada, the sagebrush; in Washington, the rhododendron; in Georgia, the Cherokee rose; in New York, the wild rose.

FLOWERS FOR OCCASIONS

Flowers are used for many occasions, both important and simple ones. At weddings flowers decorate the church and the home or reception hall. The bride carries a bouquet of flowers she will remember all her life. A bride's flowers are generally white. Her attendants have flowers that look well with their dresses. At funerals, flowers are sent as expressions of sympathy or grief. Poppies are a traditional decoration for the graves of American soldiers. Distinguished guests, usually women, are greeted with a bouquet of flowers.

Margot L. Wolf
The anemone is a lovely spring flower.

Margot L. Wolf
A tulip loses one of its petals.

FLOWER SHOWS

A flower show is an occasion when flowers are displayed for prizes. It is run by some organization such as a horticultural society, which sets the standards and makes the rules. There are classes in the show for different kinds of flower, for flower arrangements, for small gardens, and other kinds of entries. In the big flower shows, growers from all over the country bring their best blossoms and plants. These are judged by experts who have made a special study of the different kinds of flower, and the best ones win prizes.

LANGUAGE OF FLOWERS

Men have always sent flowers to women they admired or loved, and they still do. They was a time when particular flowers were supposed to have particular meanings. For example, one red rose

Bodger Seeds Ltd.
Giant asters grow well in gardens.

Bodger Seeds Ltd.
The amaryllis has rose-red petals.

A flower sent as a message has the following meaning:

Apple blossom	Preference
Buttercup	Riches
Candytuft	Indifference
Cornflower	Heaven
Cowslip	Youthful beauty
Daisy	Simplicity
Dandelion	Flirtation
Everlastings	Undying affection
Four-leafed clover	Good Luck
Foxglove	Insincerity
Geranium	Deceit
Goldenrod	Encouragement
Heather	Loneliness
Hepatica	Anger
Honeysuckle	Faithfulness
Lilac	Neatness
Marigold	Contempt
Orange blossom	Marriage
Rosemary	Remembrance
Snowdrop	A friend in need
Sweet William	Gallantry
Tulip	Boldness
Violet	Modesty

These are the flowers to send on a person's birthday:

January	Carnation or snowdrop
February	Violet or primrose
March	Jonquil or daffodil
April	Sweet pea or daisy
May	Lily of the valley
June	Rose or honeysuckle
July	Larkspur or water lily
August	Poppy or gladiolus
September	Aster or morning glory
October	Calendula or cosmos
November	Chrysanthemum
December	Narcissus or holly

means "I love you," and the small white roses that brides carry in their bouquets stand for happy love. The lilies that are used in churches and religious ceremonies, and sometimes at weddings, stand for purity. On the next page you will find a list of flowers and what they mean.

fluid

A fluid is anything that takes on the shape of its container. Water is a fluid because when you pour it in a glass, it takes the shape of the glass. Ice is not a fluid, because if you put ice cubes into a glass they are still cubes. The word *fluid* means "flowing," so we can also say that a fluid is anything that will flow. Fluids include gases as well as liquids, because they will flow, too. The air is a good example of a fluid. It always takes the shape of its container, and you can certainly tell that it flows on a windy day.

Some things are fluids part of the time and solids the rest of the time. A candle is a good example of this. Candles are usually solid, but if they become too warm they become fluid. Ice is another good example; if you let an ice cube stand in a warm place, it will become fluid.

fluorescence

Fluorescence is an ability to make visible light from rays that the eye cannot see. Most parts of light are visible, but not all. Sunlight, for example, includes certain rays called ultraviolet rays that we cannot see. When these ultraviolet rays fall on materials called *phosphors,* they cause a glow that we can see. X-rays are other rays that we cannot see unless they fall on one of these fluorescent phosphors.

Some of the important phosphors are made from uranium, zinc, calcium, or beryllium. They are used in the FLUOROSCOPE (about which there is a separate article), in most electric signs, and in fluorescent lighting.

FLUORESCENT LIGHTING

Fluorescent light is made in a glass tube coated on the inside with a phosphor. Inside the tube are argon and nitrogen gas and drops of mercury. At the ends of the tube are coils of wire made of tungsten, a hard metal. The tungsten wire is coated with a material that gives off electrons (particles of electricity) when it is heated.

An electric current is connected to the ends of this tube. It causes electrons to leap through the tube. They cause the mercury to form an arclight, which is a series of electrons leaping through the gas in the tube, from one end to the other. The arclight gives off a large amount of ultraviolet light. Ordinarily this light would be wasted, but when it strikes the phosphor on the tube it glows brightly.

Because the ultraviolet light is saved, the fluorescent tube produces more light with less electricity than the regular incandescent light bulb. It produces much less heat than the incandescent bulb and is easier on the eyes. Fluorescent lighting is the closest scientists have come to creating artificial daylight.

Coating the inside of the tube with the different phosphors, and using different gases inside the tube, will produce different colors. The use of neon gas produces a red color, and for this reason it was the first gas used in electric street signs. Most of these signs are still called "neon signs."

See also the article ARCLIGHT.

fluorine

Fluorine is a greenish-yellow gas that will burn your nose and lungs if you breathe it. It has a sharp, choking smell. When you put most things in fluorine they burn up even easier than they do in oxygen. Even metals burn in fluorine. When a metal burns in fluorine, chemicals called fluorides are formed. Small amounts of fluorides in the water you drink will help to build up your teeth and make them strong and healthy. Fluorides are found in tiny amounts in your blood, teeth and bones. They are also found in rocks called fluorite and cryolite.

fluoroscope

The fluoroscope·is a machine that shows an X-ray picture without having to develop it on a film as most X-rays are developed. With a fluoroscope a doctor can look at a screen placed in front of your body and see a picture of what is going on inside your body.

The fluoroscope screen has been chemically treated so that the X-rays, when they have passed through the body invisibly, will cause visible light rays to appear on the screen. The visible rays, which make up the picture, are a reaction of the chemical substance to the invisible rays.

If a doctor looked for a long time at a fluoroscope without any protection, the X-rays would burn his eyes, so a hood is built around it to protect him.

Doctors have learned to study certain parts of the body by injecting or having the patient drink certain chemicals. The chemicals make a shadow on the fluoroscope telling the doctor where they went, and what is happening that may harm the body.

flute

The flute is a musical instrument. It is also the name of a family of instruments which includes the fife, the flageolet, the recorder, the piccolo, and many others.

All flutes are played by blowing across a mouthhole, or *embouchure.* There are two types. Those of the recorder type are blown from the end and have a

whistlelike mouthpiece. They are called *fipple-flutes.* The other type is blown from the side and has no mouthpiece. It is called a *transverse flute.* The recorder is often called the English flute because it was used in English orchestras long after the orchestras of Europe had begun to use the German, or transverse, flute in its place. Many improvements were made in the flute by Theobold Boehm, a German flutist who lived from 1794 to 1881. He invented a system of mechanical keys that made it possible for the flutist to stop more holes on his instrument. There are separate articles on each of the instruments in the flute family.

The flute is one of the highest pitched of the woodwind instruments. It has a liquid and dreamy tone, and is often used to express the sound of the wind in trees, the sound of flowing water, or other sounds in nature. The modern symphony orchestra generally uses two or more flutists, one of whom may also play the piccolo. In a military band, there are usually two flutes and one piccolo.

fly

There are 75,000 different kinds of fly, but they all have one thing in common: they have only two wings for flight. Their back wings are so small they are used only for balancing the insect in flight.

Flies must breed extremely fast because of their short life span, and they lay eggs. Some flies develop the eggs inside their bodies; the others lay the eggs and leave them to hatch. The eggs turn into maggots, or tiny worms, that have enormous appetites. Some fly maggots feed on rotting animal or vegetable matter, some maggots feed on living animals, and others develop in water. There are also flies that lay their eggs on plants, and their maggots eat away the fruit or the vegetable of the plant, and so ruin the crop.

Gadflies and mosquitoes have sharp mouth parts with which they pierce the skin of an animal and suck blood from it. Some gadflies attack cattle and carry diseases like ANTHRAX, which you can read about in a separate article. The gadfly sucks blood from a sick animal, then goes to another and when biting into its bloodstream spreads the disease. In the same way mosquitoes give human beings malaria and yellow fever.

The common housefly is the fly you are probably most familiar with. It alights here and there all through the house. Because its body is covered with hair it carries a great many germs. It may go from garbage to the food you are eating.

The fight against the housefly never ends. There are sprays, swatters, flypaper, fans, and other methods of fighting it, but in summer there are always some flies to be found where animals or human beings live.

flycatcher

Flycatchers are small, fast birds that catch and eat insects in flight. They are important to man because they eat many crop-destroying insects.

There are more than three hundred different species of flycatcher, and they are found all over the world. Most of them are about the size of sparrows. The biggest one is the *scissor-tailed flycatcher.* Its tail is more than ten inches long, divided into two parts like a pair of scissors. The beak or bill of all the flycatchers is wide and flat. They use their bills like scoops to catch insects in the air.

The *crested flycatcher* has an unusual habit when it builds its nest. It finds a skin that a snake has shed and puts it in the nest. Scientists who study birds say that the snakeskin scares the flycatcher's enemies away. Another interesting kind of flycatcher is the *Australian fantail* that is also called a Willie Wagtail because it is always moving its tail feathers. In Australia and other countries where the Australian fantail lives, the people often find them flying through houses and offices looking for insects.

flying, traveling through the air in an airplane: see the article AVIATION.

flying bomb

The flying bomb was a fearful weapon that the Germans used against the English during the last year of World War II. They fired these bombs, which were like small airplanes that flew themselves, from specially built launching platforms in France. Many of them landed in the middle of London, more than 100 miles away. The English had been bombed before, but these self-flying, or robot, bombs were much more terrifying because they hit without warning. Many people think that if the Germans had had flying bombs earlier, they might have won the war.

There were two kinds of flying bomb, the V1 and the V2. The V1, which was first used in June 1944, had wings that were about sixteen feet across. It flew 300 miles an hour. Many of them were shot down by British planes before they could reach London. But it was not so easy to shoot down the V2, which was first used in October 1944. This bomb was a wingless rocket. You may read about ROCKETS in a separate article. It was 45 feet long, and it flew faster than the speed of sound, 760 miles an hour. There was no defense against this deadly weapon. If you were around when it hit, you would hear nothing at all before it exploded. The V2 could be guided to its target by remote radio control. The flying bombs killed thousands of people in England and damaged almost a million buildings. The attacks of the flying bombs stopped during the winter of 1944–45 when the Allied armies captured the launching platforms from the Germans. See also the articles on GUIDED MISSILES and BOMBS.

Flying Dutchman

The *Flying Dutchman* was a ghost ship, manned by a dead captain and a dead crew, which was supposed to haunt the seas around the Cape of Good Hope. The Cape of Good Hope is at the extreme southern tip of Africa. The sea there is very rough, and storms are frequent. In the past, when ships were not as strongly built as now, and moved by sail instead of steam, the passage around the cape was greatly feared. Sailors became very superstitious about making this passage, for without luck they could not hope to make it safely. A glimpse of the *Flying Dutchman* was supposed to be a sign of bad luck.

According to the legend of seamen, Captain Vanderdecken of the *Flying Dutchman* had been condemned to sail around the cape forever and never enter a port, as punishment for having cursed God.

The German composer Richard Wagner wrote an opera called *The Flying Dutchman,* telling in wonderful music the story of this ghost ship and its unlucky captain.

flying fish

Flying fish are fish that move about as though they are flying. They have no real wings but they use their fins as wings and this gives the impression of flight. The flying fish gathers great speed under water and then jumps into the air. As it does so, the air catches under its spread-out fins, and it soars like a glider plane. Some of the larger flying fish fly, or jump,

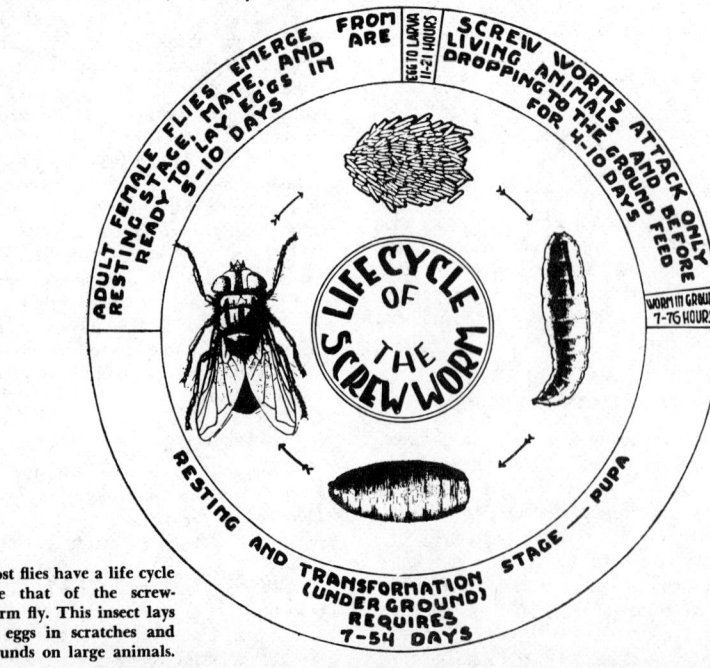

Most flies have a life cycle like that of the screwworm fly. This insect lays its eggs in scratches and wounds on large animals.

distances up to two hundred yards at a time, almost one-eighth of a mile. All flying fish use their power of flight to escape from their numerous enemies, the deadliest of which are sharks and tuna fish. Small varieties of flying fish are found along the Atlantic coast of the United States. The California flying fish, found along the Pacific coast, grows to about a foot and a half in length.

flying fox

The flying fox is not a fox at all. It is a bat, and it is the largest bat in the world. Its body may be as much as a foot long, and its wings spread out to as much as five feet when it is flying. Its face is sharp and pointed like the face of a fox, which gives it its name. Flying foxes live and travel in great crowds, and a colony will roost in one spot for years. Sometimes several hundred of these bats occupy a single tree at a time. They quarrel among themselves as they come in to roost toward dawn, and they fight for the best places until long after daylight. Flying foxes feed on fruit and some small fish. They mate in February and March, and the young flying foxes are born in August or September. Only one baby flying fox is born at a time.

Like all bats, flying foxes are mammals, that is, they nurse their young. The flying fox lives in Australia, on islands in the South Pacific, and in tropical Asia. Those that live in southern districts of these places make regular migrations when the weather gets cool, and go toward the equator for the winter. They also make occasional trips or migrations in search of ripening fruit crops.

flying saucer

Flying saucers is the popular name for many different kinds of mysterious objects that have been seen in the sky. Some look like saucers, balls, cigars, or other solid objects; others look like balls of fire or spots of light. The name comes from a newspaper report of January, 1947. A businessman alone in his private plane was flying across the Cascade Mountains of Oregon, when he suddenly saw in the sky "a chain of saucerlike things at least five miles long, swerving in and out of the high mountain peaks. They were flat like a pie pan and so shiny they reflected the sun like a mirror." Nobody knew what these flying saucers were, and some people doubted whether the man had actually seen them. But reports began to come in of similar things in the sky, from all over the country and then from many other countries. People began to talk of space ships visiting us from Mars, and of secret weapons developed by enemy countries here on earth.

Excitement in the United States became so intense that in December, 1947, the President appointed a commission of Air Force officers to investigate the flying saucers. Their report two years later said that a large number of the 375 stories they investigated turned out to be hoaxes. People had just made up the stories to get their names into the newspapers. In many other cases, people thought things mysterious that turned out to be natural things, such as the bright planet Venus or reflections of light from clouds, or mirages, or weather balloons. But the commission said that some cases remained for which they could find no explanation. The United States government said that it was not conducting any secret experiments that could explain the flying saucers, and it is doubtful whether any other country could keep secret any radically different kind of airplane it had built.

flying squirrel

The most remarkable of all the squirrels is the flying squirrel, which seems to fly although it does not have wings. This animal has a fold, or layer, of skin attached from its front legs to its back legs. When it leaps, it spreads out the fold of skin like a parachute. This helps it glide through the air. The flying squirrel can be found in forests across the continent of North America. There are two kinds of flying squirrel. One is a bluish-gray in color, and the other is brown.

flywheel

A flywheel is a heavy iron or steel wheel that helps an engine give steady power. In internal combustion engines, or engines where the power is created by fuel exploding in a closed space, the flywheel is given a sudden twist by the exploding fuel. It keeps turning after the explosion and provides a turning motion until the next explosion. The engine can not have explosions occurring all the time; the flywheel keeps the engine running between explosions. Flywheels are a part of all steam, gasoline, and diesel engines, and also of air compressors, pumps, and water turbines. Read also the separate article in this encyclopedia on INTERNAL-COMBUSTION ENGINE.

Foch, Ferdinand

Ferdinand Foch was an important French general during World War I. He was born in 1851, and he entered the army when he was 22. He became a brigadier general in 1907. In the war, which began in 1914, he became known as a brave officer who always attacked the enemy, even if the situation seemed very bad. Once, when the Germans seemed to be winning a battle, Foch sent back a report that became famous because it showed that he refused to be defeated. He said, "My right has been rolled up. My left has been driven back. My center has been smashed. I have ordered an attack." In March 1918, Foch was appointed commander of all the Allied armies who were fighting Germany, and he led the Americans, British, and French to victory that November. In 1918 he was promoted to marshal, the top rank in the French army. Foch died in 1929.

French Embassy Press

fog

A fog is a cloud lying on the ground, or hanging so close to the ground that you can walk right through it. Sometimes a cloud is so large that it can cover an entire city. Sometimes the cloud is so small that you can drive through a tiny fog in an automobile and scarcely notice it. Some fogs are so thick you can hardly see your hand in front of you. Other fogs are thin and wispy.

There are different ways in which a fog may be formed. When the day has been sunny, and the air warm, the air absorbs a great deal of moisture from the earth. Then, after the sun goes down, that air may cool quickly, and the moisture it has absorbed from the earth forms tiny droplets around the particles of dust that were drifting around in the air close to the ground. The cooling causes the moisture to condense, because cool air cannot hold as much uncondensed moisture as warm air can hold. You can see how this is if you hold a cool plate in front of the steam coming from the spout of a teakettle. The steam condenses on the cool plate and turns into drops of water. In the case of a fog, the condensation forms such tiny droplets that a fog looks like thin smoke floating in the air, but it is really millions of drops of water too tiny to see.

Another kind of fog is the type that occurs so often in London and off the coast of Labrador. This is fog caused by moist warm air that blows into colder air. When the warm, moist breeze reaches the colder section, the cold condenses the moisture into tiny droplets that form thick fogs. As long as the wind and the temperatures remain about the same, the fog continues to stay over the area. The warm air over the water of the North Atlantic Drift, which many people call the Gulf Stream, causes the fog in London, and in Labrador. Heavy, long-lasting fogs are dangerous, because people cannot see where they are going and often have accidents.

Foggia

Foggia is a city in the south-central part of Italy, near the Adriatic Sea. It is more than eight hundred years old, and most of the buildings and houses are old. Many Americans remember Foggia because it was the great base in Italy for the United States 15th Air Force during World War II.

The city is in the middle of a large plain, and there were more than twenty great airfields in the fields for miles around. Morning after morning, as the airplanes took off to bomb the enemy, there would be more than five hundred great bombers in the air above Foggia, and when they returned in the afternoon or evening they would fill the sky again. British and Canadian fliers were also stationed at some of the airfields. More than five hundred thousand Allied airmen were stationed at Foggia at some time during the war.

The city suffered heavy damage before the Allies took it over. Most of it has been rebuilt and there are now modern factories and apartment houses. About 125,000 people live in the city; they work in the flour mills, chemical factories, and railroad yards. The farmers around the city grow wheat in the fields and raise large herds of sheep.

folk dancing

Folk dancing is the national and characteristic dancing of the people of a country. Some folk dances are very ancient, and have their origin in the history of the nation. They contain special steps and gestures that have a deep meaning to members of one national group, but to the people of another country these

steps may have practically no meaning at all. If you go to a Chinese or Balinese dance recital, you may notice that at certain times the audience cheers and applauds, but unless you have lived in those countries you may not notice anything that makes you feel the same excitement. It is the same with American tap-dancing. When the American audience is applauding loudly, a foreign guest may be completely bewildered. Folk dancing is like a language. It must be learned slowly, from those who understand it.

True folk dancing is accompanied by singing and music. It is believed that the dancing came first, and began in the rites and ceremonies of primitive tribes. From these pagan festivals there arose various forms of expression, combined with shouts and cries that gradually became words and songs. Most national dances are believed to have grown from ancient primitive dances. They have gradually gained form and design and a set pattern of steps. Good examples are the *Viennese waltz*, the *Hungarian czardas*, the *Spanish fandango*, the *Highland fling* (Scotland), the *Bohemian polka* (Czechoslovakia), the *Virginia reel*, and the *Paul Jones* (United States). Jean Baptiste Lully, one of the founders of ballet dancing, often based his works on a French peasant dance, the *gavotte*.

Children preserve many of the oldest folk dances, which they use as games. Among these are "The Farmer in the Dell," "London Bridge is Falling Down," "Here We Go Round the Mulberry Bush," "Ring Around the Rosy," and various versions of the Maypole dance.

Some dances have a long history, such as the *Morris dance*. In England this dance was a part of country fairs and festivals. It usually depicts characters such as Robin Hood and Maid Marian. The steps are complicated and must be learned carefully. This dance originated in Spain more than four hundred years ago, where it was introduced by the Moors. It was called the *Moresque* (Moorish dance).

Many popular dances begin with the people and so become folk dances, although folk dancing really means group dancing rather than dancing by couples. Nevertheless, many modern dances are essentially folk dances, such as the *jig*, *reel*, *tap dance*, and the Latin-American dances such as the *rumba*, *samba*, and *mambo*.

There are several organizations founded to preserve folk dancing. In England there is the English Folk Dancing Society. In the United States, the American Folk Dancing Society holds an annual festival at Madison Square Garden in New York City, where folk dances of every country in the world are performed.

folklore

Folklore is the stories and beliefs that have been handed down from one generation to another without ever being written down and usually without anyone knowing where the stories or ideas began.

Nearly all the fairy tales that children read are a kind of folklore, very often called folk tales. Legends about the great heroes of a country are part of its folklore. For example, the Greek heroes such as Achilles that Homer wrote about in the *Iliad* are part of the folklore of Greece. In England such heroes include Robin Hood. In the United States there are Paul Bunyan, Billy the Kid, Buffalo Bill, and others. The characters in folk tales can be real persons, as Buffalo Bill was (he was a man named William F. Cody) but there were so many stories about them that they become part of the folklore of their countries. Many folk tales tell about spirits such as elves, fairies, and other imaginary creatures.

Scientists find folklore one of the most interesting parts of the study of a people. Sir James Frazer in Great Britain studied the folklore of many different countries and found that the same stories had developed independently among ancient peoples who had never met or heard of each other and could not have gotten the stories from each other. They just happened to make up the same stories. Frazer wrote a famous book about folklore, called *The Golden Bough*. Almost all of the primitive peoples had some story of where their race came from. The Japanese story, for instance, was that the first person came down from the sun.

The arts and crafts of people in the past also are part of folklore. The making of such things as cloth and pottery in some countries is a folk art because the country people make things in the same way and use the same tools as their fathers and grandfathers did.

folk music

Folk music is the music of a people. Much folk music is so old that we do not know when it was made up or who made it up. We do know that men made up songs long before they learned to write them down, and the music itself always tells us a great deal about the people. It is usually simple and direct music, and often tells stories of the things that interested the people, such as tales of unhappy love, important battles, and fears or sufferings. Some folk music is sad, as are the spirituals of the American Negro, while some is very gay and happy, as is the folk music of many of the countries of southern Europe. Folk music does not necessarily have words to go with it, although it often does. Most of our American folk music does have words. The cowboy songs of the West and the songs of the hill people of Kentucky and Tennessee are the best examples of folk music in the United States.

Before music was written it was handed down from one generation to another. A singer might not like the words or the music of some particular song and would change them. He might not remember just how the words went and would have to make up his own words. So our oldest folk songs have come down to us in different versions. The same story may be told, with the words or the music, or both, being changed. Many of the best musicians for hundreds of years have been interested in folk songs. John and Alan Lomax recorded many American Folk songs.

Most folk songs were written so long ago that no one knows who wrote them. All Negro spirituals, such as "Swing Low, Sweet Chariot," are folk songs. In many cases a song can be called a folk song when we do know who wrote it, or part of it. "Annie Laurie" came to be known so well by millions that it is a folk song though we know that a Scotsman, William Douglass, wrote the words. Several songs of Stephen C. Foster are folk songs because millions know and love them.

In many cases the words and music of folk songs are known differently in different places because they were not written down but were learned by children from their parents, who may have forgotten some words or parts of the music and made up their own.

About 1960 folk songs became very popular and many singers and groups became famous for their folk-music concerts and performances.

folkways

Folkways is a word used to describe ways of acting or living that have become customary for people living in the same region or country. For instance, we in America watch the World Series by television or listen to it on the radio, and on Thanksgiving we eat turkey with cranberry sauce. These are American folkways. In England, it is common to interrupt one's work at four o'clock in order to have a cup of tea; so tea at four o'clock is an English folkway.

Folkways are not only the kinds of things done by the people of a whole country. They are also the kinds of things done by local or smaller groups of people who have lived for a long time in one place or region. For instance, the hillbillies of the South have a music different from that of other Americans and a way of telling a story by which one can recognize immediately the part of the country from which they come. People who do the same kind of work also have a way of doing things common only to them. Cowboys, jazz musicians, actors, ballplayers, all have customs common to them alone.

Folkway are not strict. No one is forced to follow them. Americans do not have to have turkey on the table at Thanksgiving. No one forces the English to take tea at four o'clock. Folkways are customs people follow because they like to follow them.

Fontainebleau

Fontainebleau is the name of a town about 35 miles from Paris, France. When we speak of Fontainebleau we usually mean the famous palace there. Many important people and events in French history have some connection with this palace. It stands in a clearing in the Forest of Fontainebleau, just outside of the town. The palace was built for Francis I, who was King of France more than four hundred years ago, and it was a favorite summer home of many kings after him. Francis I was interested in beautiful art and architecture, and he invited many famous artists and architects to visit him at this palace. One of them, Benvenuto Cellini, decorated the inside of the palace. Two kings of France, Philip IV and Louis XII, were born at Fontainebleau. When Napoleon, the great emperor of France, gave up his throne, or abdicated, he signed the document at this palace. In 1927 John D. Rockefeller, Jr., a rich American businessman, gave France a large sum of

The Chateau of Fontainebleau was once the home of French kings but is now a public monument that tourists visit.

money to help restore the palace to its original beauty.

Foochow

Foochow is a city in China, the capital of the province of Fukien. It is in the southern part of the country, near the coast. About 400,000 people live in Foochow, which is about as many people as live in Louisville, Kentucky. Foochow is on the Min River, which empties into the China Sea, and it used to be one of China's most important ports. About a hundred years ago, most of the tea that was shipped out all over the world from China was shipped out from Foochow. The city has become less important as a port, and most of the people who live in Foochow make their living by working in stores and factories.

food

Food is any substance that a living body can change into the cells of which it is composed. A living body can be either a plant or an animal, but plants and animals require different kinds of food. Foods eaten by human beings and other animals must be largely organic matter, which means that they must contain the element called carbon. There is carbon in the air, and plants can use the energy of sunlight to take carbon out of the air and make tissues of it. This is called PHOTOSYNTHESIS, and there is a separate article about it. Animals cannot use sunlight in this way, so they must get their carbon from plants. Some animals eat only meat, but they are still getting their carbon from plants because they eat animals that have eaten plants and changed them into flesh (meat) that contains carbon.

In addition to the carbon, food must supply various other things that the body needs or that the plant needs. In the case of food for human beings and other animals, this includes certain minerals such as iron to make blood, and calcium to make bones; certain chemicals such as iodine; and a large group of organic substances called vitamins. If the food that a person eats does not contain all these things, he will become sick with what is called a *deficiency disease*. Deficiency means lack of something. The lack of iron can cause anemia, the lack of iodine can cause goiter, and the lack of various

vitamins can cause such diseases as scurvy or beriberi.

The entire life of nearly every animal, and the life of man from the day he was created until very recently, has been a struggle to get enough food. Most animals spend their entire waking hours doing nothing but look for food. In parts of the world still, food is so scarce that men have to work from morning to night to get enough food to stay alive. Anthropologists, the scientists who study man from the earliest times that he lived on earth, call the most primitive cultures the "food-gathering stage" of man's development.

TYPES OF FOOD

Men have eaten almost anything that might be nourishing. Some things can be eaten safely and some cannot, and men have experimented to find out which were which. They have also found what kinds of food taste good and what kinds do not, and they tend to eat only the kinds that taste good. There is no way to define taste. Among some South American and African peoples, termites are considered a great delicacy. Termites are a kind of ant, and we might find them disgusting. Some peoples have eaten seaweed and other things that we would never think of as food.

Men have also found, through millions of years of trying foods, which ones are good for them and which ones are not. Certain grasses, for example, are nourishing but they are so tough that the human body cannot digest them and they would make us sick.

The foods that most human beings eat are divided into two kinds: meat and vegetables. These two main kinds are divided into many different groups. We get vegetables from plants not only in the form of roots such as potatoes, seeds such as peas, and leaves such as spinach, but also in the form of chemical substances taken from plants, such as sugar and vegetable oils.

Meat is usually divided into three groups: meat, poultry, and fish. In this grouping, meat is the flesh of animals, such as beef, pork, and lamb, and poultry is the flesh of birds, such as chicken and turkey. Often meat and poultry are grouped together as meat, and fish is made a separate group.

WHAT HAPPENS TO FOOD IN THE BODY

The body takes in food and digests it. This means that through certain chemicals that the body manufactures it breaks the food down into particles or fluids that the blood can carry to all parts of the body. There the food is transformed into the cells that make up the different tissues of the body. Not all the food can be used by the body. Some of it is waste matter and we eliminate it. See also the article on NUTRITION.

FOOD AND RELIGION

Some religions forbid people to eat certain foods. In many cases this arose in ancient times when only the priests knew very much. To keep the people from eating foods that would poison them or make them sick, the priests sometimes made it a matter of religion that people must not eat those foods. The Jews and

the Mohammedans are not permitted to eat pork and the Jews cannot eat shellfish, because without refrigeration these foods spoiled very easily in the hot countries where these peoples lived.

There are other reasons for not eating certain foods. A person who belongs to almost any religion may refrain from eating certain kinds of food as an act of devotion to God. Most religions have fast days, on which certain foods may not be eaten, or no food at all may be eaten.

Food and Drug Administration

The Food and Drug Administration is a part of the government of the United States. The job of the Food and Drug Administration is to see that the laws about pure foods and drugs are obeyed. The purpose of these laws is to protect the American people. About fifty years ago people got very upset about conditions in the food and drug industries. They found that often the companies that packaged and sold foods and drugs were not telling the truth about their products. Tests were made that showed that many foods were not pure and could be very harmful to people. Many drugs had in them ingredients that were harmful and even poisonous. So from 1906 on, several different laws were passed. Finally, in 1938, the Food, Drug, and Cosmetic Act was passed. The Food and Drug Administration sees that this law is obeyed. The law applies to all foods and drugs and cosmetics that are shipped out of the United States, or are sent from one state to another. It says that all foods must be pure and clean and healthy. Foods and drugs must be carefully measured, and the labels must tell how much is in each package. The labels must also tell all the ingredients. If you look at the labels on the packages of foods and drugs at your house, you will see that they list everything that is in the package. You will see that any drug that could be poisonous is very clearly marked, so that you will know how much it is safe to take, and will be careful in using that drug. The law also has regulations about advertising. Food and drug companies must tell the truth about their products, and they may not say that their products can do things that they cannot do. The Food and Drug Administration has many ways of seeing that these laws are obeyed. Because of the work of the Food and Drug Administration, the people of the United States can be sure that the foods and drugs that they buy are pure and healthful.

foot

Feet support the weight of a body and help it to move. All the more highly developed forms of animal life have feet, and they are found in many different shapes. Some animals, such as man and the bear, walk with the whole foot on the ground and have fairly large and flat feet. Other animals, such as dogs and members of the cat family, walk with just their toes on the ground, and have almost no heels at all. Still other forms of animal life, such as horses and deer, walk on just the tip of one or two toes, which form is what we call a hoof.

The human foot is quite complicated. It is made up of a mass of nerves, muscles,

tendons, and bones. There are 26 small bones in the human foot. Seven of these bones, called *tarsals,* are thick, short bones which make up the top of the instep and the heel. Five other bones are known as *metatarsals,* and are curved to form the foot's arch and instep. The rest of the bones in the foot are the *phalanges.* The big toe has two phalanges, and each of the other toes has three. The foot also has a number of strong *ligaments,* which fasten the bones together. The strongest of these is the *plantar ligament,* which runs along the bottom of the foot connecting the heel with the base of the metatarsals in the ball of the foot. The layer of tough skin beneath it is called the *sole.* Just under the sole is a pad of fatty tissue that acts as a kind of cushion to protect the foot against shocks.

The bones of the foot form two arches, the *longitudinal arch* that stretches from the heel to the ball of the foot, and the *transverse arch* that runs across the ball. You can see where the arches are by making a wet footprint on a flat surface. The arches give your foot more strength and spring, help support the body's weight, and ease the force of sudden jars. Sometimes the bones that form one or both of these arches no longer fit together properly, and the arch begins to flatten out. When this happens it is called a *fallen arch,* and we say that a person who suffers from this condition has *flat feet.* Some people are born with flat feet, but flat feet also may be caused by wearing high-heeled shoes too often, or by walking or standing on hard floors or pavements for many hours each day. Children who do not eat the right kinds of food also may get flat feet. A much more serious foot trouble is clubfoot, in which the ankle is badly deformed and the foot is twisted up, down, or to one side.

It is very important to take good care of

Bone structure of right foot seen from below.

your feet. When walking, you should point your feet straight, and shift your weight so that your toes grip the ground at the end of each step. Although a certain amount of walking is good for the feet, you should see that they get enough rest, too. Wear stockings that are smooth and fit well, and, most important, see that your shoes always fit properly. Corns,

bunions, calluses, and many other foot troubles all can be caused by wearing shoes that do not fit. Bathe your feet every day, and take good care of toenails. The best way to cut toenails is straight across. Be careful about walking barefoot in public showers and swimming pools, where it is possible to pick up athlete's foot, a very contagious infection caused by a kind of growth called fungus.

Men and women who are trained to give scientific treatment of ailments of the feet are called *chiropodists* or *podiatrists.* There is a separate article about CHIROPODY. Read also the articles on CLUBFOOT, ATHLETE'S FOOT, and SHOE.

foot and mouth disease, see HOOF AND MOUTH DISEASE.

football

There are several forms of the game of football. The original game of football is the most popular game in nearly all European countries. This is the game that in the United States is usually called SOCCER, and there is a separate article about it. Another form of football is called Rugby. That is a game first played in the year 1823, and it is the game from which American football was developed. American football, too, is played somewhat differently in the United States and Canada. In Canada there are twelve men on a team, and in the United States there are eleven. In Canada the scoring is not exactly the same as it is in the United States.

The game described in this article will be football as it is played in the United States.

FOOTBALL, UNITED STATES STYLE

Football in America began as a game played only in high schools and colleges. During the football season, from September through November, it is the most popular of all games. The star players are heroes and may become nationally famous. Sometimes crowds of 100,000 people go to see college games.

Since the 1920s, football has also become a popular professional game, as

baseball is. The big cities have professional teams that draw crowds almost as big as those that see the college games. Nearly all the professional players were formerly stars on college teams.

The football field is 120 yards (360 feet) long, and 160 feet wide. The side boundaries of the field are called sidelines. Each of the two opposing teams has a goal line. The goal lines are 100 yards apart, and there is an end zone, 10 yards long, beyond each goal line. In high school and college football, goal posts stand at the ends of the end zones; in professional football the goal posts stand on the goal lines. (See the illustration on page 2083.) The posts are $16\frac{1}{2}$ feet apart and the crossbar is 10 feet high. The actual playing field is the 100 yards between the goal lines. It is marked with white lines every five yards. In writing or talking about football, we speak of the "twenty-three yard line," and so on, but the lines are not actually marked more often than every five yards. The 23-yard line is an imaginary line 23 yards from the goal line. The center of the field is the 50-yard line, as shown in the diagram. A team's 35-yard line is the line 35 yards from its own goal line.

HOW THE GAME IS PLAYED

Football is played with a ball made of leather and blown up with air. The shape is not at all like that of any ball used in any other game. The ball is 11 to $11\frac{1}{4}$ inches long and $21\frac{1}{4}$ to $21\frac{1}{2}$ inches around at the center, and it tapers down almost to a point at each end.

The object of the game is to carry the ball across the opposing team's goal line. In trying to do this, a team may run with the ball, throw the ball (called passing it), or kick the ball. There are many complicated rules that tell exactly when and how these may legally be done, but the general idea of the game is not complicated.

There are three kinds of play. At the beginning of each play, the opposing teams face each other across one of the real or imaginary lines. This is called the

NBC

Spalding, Inc.

Left: The type of football used in the United States is shaped for easy kicking. **Right:** Football shoes have cleats on their soles to keep players from slipping.

line of scrimmage. One team "has the ball"; that is, it has the right to try to advance the ball toward the opposing goal. Here are the three kinds of play available to the team that has the ball:

The running play. A player takes the ball in his arms and runs toward the opposing goal. The players on the opposing team try to tackle him so that he cannot continue running. His teammates try to block the opponents out of his path so that he can keep on running. When he is tackled and falls, it is a *down.* Where he fell is the new line of scrimmage.

The pass. A player who has the ball throws it to a teammate so that the teammate can run with it. If the teammate is in front of him (nearer the opposing goal) it is a *forward pass.* If the teammate is beside him or behind him, it is a *lateral pass.* If a forward-pass ball touches the ground before any player catches it, it counts as a down but the ball goes back to the same line of scrimmage for the next play. If a teammate catches it, the play becomes a running play. If an opponent catches it (called intercepting it) the opponent can run with it toward the thrower's goal and possession of the ball goes to the team that intercepted.

The kick. A player may always kick the ball. The usual purpose is to transfer possession of the ball to the other team; this is often good tactics. Such a kick is called a *punt.* The kicker drops the ball from his hands and kicks it while it is in the air. A member of the opposing team may catch it and run back with it, but the act of punting transfers possession to the other team. Much less often, a team will try a different kind of kick as a scoring play. This must be a *placement kick* or a *dropkick,* in which the ball touches the ground before it is kicked. To score, it must go over the crossbar and between the goal posts.

A player who has possession of the ball and drops it is said to *fumble.* Thereafter the ball will belong to whichever team recovers, that is, gets secure possession of the ball.

All running plays and kicks must remain within the sidelines. If a player carries the ball out of bounds, he is down at the point at which he went out. If a punt goes out of bounds, the ball goes to the other team at the point at which it went out.

SCORING PLAYS

Points are scored as follows:
Touchdown, 6 points. For carrying the ball or completing a forward pass across the opposing goal line.

Field goal, 3 points. For a placement or dropkick that goes across the crossbar and between the goal posts. If a try for a field goal is unsuccessful, the opposing team takes the ball on its 20-yard line.

Conversion, 1 or 2 points. After a team scores a touchdown, it is given the ball for one play on its opponents' 2-yard line. In high-school and college games, it can then score 1 point more by making a successful placement or dropkick, or 2 points more by carrying or passing the ball across the goal line. In professional games any of these plays scores 1 point.

Safety, 2 points. If a player carrying the ball is downed behind his own goal line, the opposing team scores 2 points.

CONDITIONS OF THE GAME

A football game consists of 60 minutes of actual playing time. This is divided into two halves of 30 minutes each. Each half is divided into two quarters of 15 minutes each. In high-school play the quarters are 12 minutes each and the half is 24 minutes.

There is "time out," which does not count in the 60 minutes, when a forward pass is grounded, when a scoring play is made, when a substitute player is sent in, when a team wants to rest, or when an official calls time out for any reason. Time does not count until the ball is put into play again.

There are usually at least four officials. The referee is in charge of the game, and the umpire assists him. The head timekeeper keeps track of time and time out. Often there is also a field judge to watch for any case of breaking the rules of the game. Any official can call attention to such cases. The rules are intended to keep either team from having an unfair advantage and to prevent rough play that could cause a player to be hurt. The penalty is almost always that the ball is moved nearer the offending team's goal line.

PROGRESS OF THE GAME

The game begins with a kick-off. One team places the ball on its own 40-yard line and a player kicks it toward the opposing goal. The opposing team catches it and runs back with it. Wherever he is down is the line of scrimmage, and his team has the ball.

To keep the ball, a team must advance it at least 10 yards in no more than four

plays (downs). The first of the plays is "first down and ten to go." Suppose the team tries a running play and carries the ball four yards forward. The next play will be "second down and six to go." If a team carries the ball ten or more yards in four or fewer plays, it has a new first down. In this way it can advance the ball all the way to and over the opposing goal line, scoring a touchdown. But if, after the fourth down, the team has not advanced the ball at least 10 yards, the opposing team gets the ball back at the point where the last down occurred. A team almost never risks having this happen. On the fourth down it will punt, so that the opponents will get the ball much nearer their own goal line. Often a team punts on third down, if it has gained only two or three yards in its first two plays.

The offensive team (the one with the ball) lines up with seven men on the line of scrimmage (the *linemen*) and four men behind the line of scrimmage (the *backfield,* or *backs*). One of the linemen, called the *center,* leans forward over the ball and tosses it back, between his legs, to one of the backs. This back may run with it, pass it, or kick it.

The defensive team usually places a man in front of each offensive man, and stations its own backfield men behind the line of scrimmage to back up (support) the line, defend against forward passes, catch a kicked ball, and so on.

No player can cross the line of scrimmage until the center has passed the ball behind him. If a player does this, his team is offside and the penalty is five yards.

At the end of each quarter the teams change goal lines, but the ball remains in play. If one team had the ball, second down and seven to go on its own 40-yard line, which is 40 yards from its own goal line, at the beginning of the next quarter the ball will be placed 40 yards from its new goal line and play will continue.

At the end of the first half there is a rest period of 15 minutes. Then there is a new kick-off to begin the second half. There is also a kick-off after each score.

If a kicked ball lands behind a team's goal line, it is a *touchback,* which is much different from a touchdown. After a touchback, the ball is given to the receiving team on its own 20-yard line.

SUBSTITUTIONS

The football rules have been changed often to increase or decrease the number of times a team can substitute new players during a game. For several years, the rules allowed unlimited substitutions. A player could be taken out of the game and put in again as often as the coach of the team wished. This led to the "two-platoon" system. Big colleges would have entirely different teams for offensive and defensive play.

The two-platoon system was found to be best for professional football. For college and high-school teams, which may not have such big squads, the rules sometimes limit substitutions so that a player must know how to play on both the offensive and defensive squads.

THE POSITIONS

Each player has an assigned position in the line-up, and an assigned duty.

The line. Beside the center are two *guards,* one on each side; then two *tackles,*

A football helmet can save a player from head injuries in a rough game.

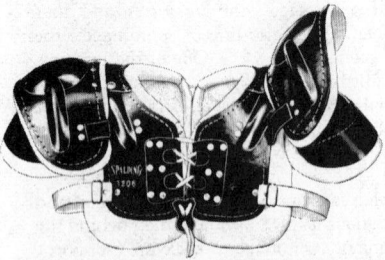

Football shoulder pads are made so that players' arms can move freely.

Spalding, Inc. Photos

The football hip-and-kidney pad protects the torso of the player.

one beside each guard; then two *ends*, one on the outside of each tackle. The guards and tackles, called *forwards*, are expected to block the players who face them. The ends do blocking but also catch forward passes.

The backfield. There are a *quarterback*, whose chief duty in modern football is to throw forward passes, but who also hands the ball to another back who is to run with it, or may himself run or kick. Two *halfbacks* and one *fullback*, who run or kick, complete the backfield.

The two-platoon system has brought into the game positions with other names, for example *linebacker* and *tailback*.

In early football a team lined up like this:

E T G C G T E
Q
H   H
F

Football officials use many signals. These mean: 1. Illegal crossing of the scrimmage line before the ball is passed. 2. Touchdown or field goal. 3. Offensive back illegally moving forward before the ball is passed. 4. Illegal blocking from behind. 5. Illegal interference with the receiver of a pass.

Many other formations, such as the "T," the "split T," the "single wing," and the "double wing," have been used.

TRAINING AND STRATEGY

Football is a rough game and players must be in perfect condition. Teams usually begin practice in August (but sometimes in the spring) for the season that begins in September and lasts through November or into December.

Players must learn and practice complicated plays worked out by skillful

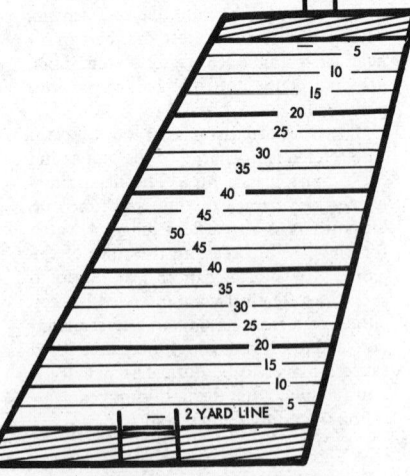

The H-shaped goal posts on a football field are set 10 yards behind the goal lines for college games and on the lines for games between professional teams.

coaches. These plays are kept secret so as to take the opposing team by surprise. For many years the quarterback announced the play out loud, using signals in numbers, for example "45-22-33-12." About forty years ago the "huddle" system was

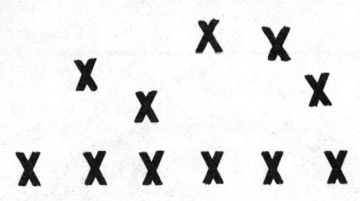

In T-formation, one back is near the center and the others in a row behind.

In the single-wing-back formation the backs are grouped on one side of the lineup.

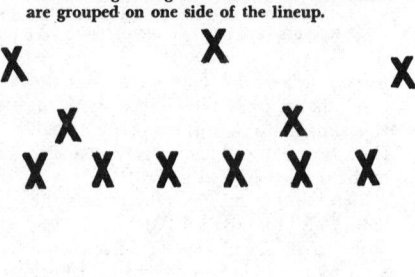

The shoulder block (*above*) is used by linemen near the line of scrimmage. The side-body block (*below*) is used to stop tacklers in downfield runs. Football rules allow players to tackle only the ball carrier.

adopted: all members of the offensive team get together in a circle and agree on the next play.

PROFESSIONAL FOOTBALL

In the 1960s football got ahead of baseball as America's most popular professional sport. The National Football League was the first "big league" and established teams in the biggest cities of the United States, but after 1962 the American Football League was almost as important. In 1964 television networks guaranteed to pay more than $40,000,000 to broadcast pro games during the following five years. A pro team usually

Football rules allow the ball carrier to shove a tackler away with his hand. This type of shove is a "stiff-arm." If his stiff-arm fails, the ball carrier can break a tackler's grip by twisting. Sometimes a tackler puts the ball out of play by pushing the carrier outside (over one of the field's sidelines). Pushing the ball carrier outside is as good as a tackle.

draws a crowd of 40,000 to 70,000. The pro season is much shorter than the baseball season but longer than the college football season.

Quarterback Fran Tarkenton of the N. Y. Giants during a moment of practice.

In each league there is a "draft" of college football stars in the pro leagues, so that only one team of that league can try to sign up a player, but the two big leagues compete with each other. In 1964 the New York "Jets" of the A.F.L. paid $400,000 to a quarterback from Alabama, Joe Namath. Higher bonuses are said to have been paid since then.

BOWL GAMES

Every year, after the regular football season is over, outstanding college teams are invited to play in special post-season games called "Bowl Games." These games are usually played on New Year's Day and are called Bowl Games because most of them are played in big circular stadiums that look like bowls.

The first Bowl Games were played in the Rose Bowl in Pasadena, California. For years, this game was supposed to decide the national championship among college teams. Now the champions of

two conferences (leagues) of college teams, the Pacific Coast and the Midwest ("Big Ten") conferences, play each year. Other important Bowl Games are:

Cotton Bowl, Dallas, Texas
Sugar Bowl, New Orleans, Louisiana
Orange Bowl, Miami, Florida
Sun Bowl, El Paso, Texas
Gator Bowl, Jacksonville, Florida

CANADIAN FOOTBALL

Canadian football is very much like the United States game except that there are twelve men on a side and the field is 110 yards long and 65 yards wide. Touchdowns once were 5 but now are 6 points each.

HISTORY OF FOOTBALL

American football comes from the game that was created in 1823 at Rugby, England, when one of the players, "disregarding the rules of football as played in his time, took the ball in his arms and ran with it across the goal line." The score was not allowed but a stone tablet has been set up at Rugby to commemorate this player.

The first real Rugby match between two American colleges took place in 1869, when a game was played by Rutgers and Princeton Universities. In 1874 McGill University in Canada challenged Harvard to a game of Rugby. Afterwards, Harvard refused to play a return match, holding out for a different version of the game. Then Princeton called a meeting of the big eastern colleges. It was held in 1876 and attended by Harvard, Columbia, Princeton, and Yale.

In almost every year since then, some changes have been made in the game. In the beginning games were long and there were no rest periods. Play was very rough. In the play known as the "flying wedge," nine players would run at full speed toward their opponents' line, trying to carry the ball through them by sheer power. There were many injuries. In 1905, President Theodore Roosevelt saw a newspaper photograph of a battered college football player and said that such brutality could not continue. Changes in the game followed. In 1906 the use of the forward pass was made legal. Until then, one could only advance the ball by kicking it or running with it. Now it was possible to toss it over the heads of the opposing players to a teammate. In 1913, the usefulness of the pass was proved by Gus Dorais and Knute Rockne, who later became a famous coach but was then a player at Notre Dame, when they completely upset an Army team by forward passes.

The idea from then on was to outwit rather than to outdrive the other team.

force

Force is anything that can cause motion, or more strictly, a change of motion. You exert force when you throw a ball, and also when you catch a ball. In both cases the rate at which the ball moves (or does not move) is changed. There are many kinds of force. The wind is a force; it moves the leaves on the trees. If a book slips out of your hand, it falls to the ground; a force called gravity pulls everything around us toward the center of the earth.

A force is a kind of push or pull. It may not actually cause a motion. You may

push against a heavy trunk without being able to move it. You have exerted force, but have been opposed by an equal force, the weight of the trunk and the friction of the floor that keeps it from sliding. An object moves or changes motion only if the forces acting on it in directly opposite directions are not exactly equal.

If you get a friend to help you, and he pushes the trunk from the end while you push from the side, you may be able to move it. But it will not go in the direction which either he or you are pushing, but on a diagonal between these lines. What happens when several forces act on the same object is studied in the branch of science called *mechanics*.

As you can see from the example, the direction in which the trunk will move, and how fast it will go, depend not only on how much force you and your friend exert, and on the friction, but also on the directions in which you push. You cannot add and subtract forces by ordinary arithmetic. Calculations have to be made by a branch of mathematics called *vector analysis*, which takes account of direction as well as amount of force.

When forces are unbalanced they do work in the form of motion. There are separate articles in this encyclopedia about ENERGY and WORK.

Gerald Rudolph Ford

Gerald Rudolph Ford became the 38th President of the United States, upon the resignation of Richard M. Nixon in August, 1974. He is the only man to have held this office without being elected by the people.

HIS EARLY YEARS

Gerald Rudolph Ford was born to Leslie and Dorothy Gardner King in

Omaha, Nebraska, on July 14, 1913, and was named Leslie, Jr. Two years later, his parents were divorced and his mother moved with him to Grand Rapids, Michigan where she met and married Gerald R. Ford. Her second husband later adopted her son and gave him his own name

In his high school years, Gerald Ford played football and was named to all-city and all-state teams. Later, at the University of Michigan, he was named the Most Valuable Player of the 1934 season. Choosing to attend Yale Law School over playing professional football with the Green Bay Packers, Ford graduated in 1941 in the top third of his law school class.

Ford then entered the practice of law, and shortly thereafter he joined the Navy. He served in the Pacific for a period of 47 months and during that service rose to the rank of lieutenant commander.

HIS POLITICAL CAREER

Returning from World War II, Ford resumed his law practice. In the 1948 election, Ford, a conservative Republican, entered public office by upsetting the incumbent Congressman in Michigan's 5th District. (An incumbent is a person already in office.) He went on to serve for twenty-five years in the House of Representatives.

In 1973, Gerald Ford held the position of House Minority Leader, and when Spiro T. Agnew resigned from the Vice Presidency, President Nixon nominated Ford to fill the vacancy. For the first time, the provisions of the 25th Amendment to the Constitution were utilized. On December 3, 1973, Gerald Ford was sworn in as the nation's 40th Vice President.

Soon after his ascending to the Vice-Presidency, Ford's political future took another dramatic turn. Due to increasing pressure over his involvement in the Watergate scandal, President Nixon resigned on August 8, 1974 (See the articles on NIXON and WATERGATE) and Ford was sworn in the following day as the nation's 38th President, the first to hold this office without being elected.

Ford nominated former New York State Governor Nelson A. Rockefeller to be Vice-President, and on December 19, 1974, Rockefeller was sworn in as the nation's 41st Vice-President.

As President, Ford attemped to increase domestic oil production by requesting an end to oil price controls. In addition, he vetoed a farm-support bill and two bills to regulate strip-mining in his first year in office. He also offered conditional amnesty to those draft evaders of the Vietnam War who were willing to work two years in alternative public service.

On September 6, 1974, President Ford declared an unconditional pardon for ex-President Richard Nixon for crimes he "committed or may have committed" while serving as Chief Executive. This issue caused much controversy among the American people.

In 1976, Ford and his running mate Senator Robert Dole of Kansas opposed Governor Jimmy Carter of Georgia and his running mate, Senator Walter Mondale of Minnesota in the presidential election. Carter and Mondale won the close race.

Gerald Ford married Elizabeth Bloomer Warren on October 18, 1948. They have three sons and one daughter.

Ford, Henry

Henry Ford is one of the greatest names in the history of the automobile. He was born more than a hundred years ago, when there were no automobiles. As a young man he liked to tinker with machinery, and he was very much interested in automobiles. By his bold ideas and his hard work, he made the United States "a nation on wheels"—that is, a country in which nearly all the families have automobiles. He founded a company that for years was the biggest automobile manufacturer in the world, and he made himself one of the richest men in the world. Few men in history have done more to change and improve the way people live than Ford did.

Here are some of the things that Ford did:

He decided that if he made a lot of automobiles instead of just a few, he could make them cheaper; and if he made them cheaper, more people could afford to buy them; and if more people bought them, his company would make much more money than if it sold just a few automobiles at high prices.

He worked out methods of making automobiles in large quantities; these methods are now called "mass production," and Ford himself is often called "the father of mass production."

He saw that if he paid his workers higher wages, they could afford to buy his automobiles, and he would turn them into customers. He also saw that if he gave the workers more leisure time, they would want automobiles to use for pleasure trips and for visiting friends. So Ford raised wages and reduced working time.

Other manufacturers thought—and some of them said—that Henry Ford must be crazy to do these things. It turned out that he was so crazy he made millions of dollars, and one by one industries changed their old-fashioned methods and adopted Henry Ford's new methods.

HOW HE DID IT

Henry Ford was born in Dearborn, Michigan, in 1863. His father was a farmer, but Henry was not interested in farming. He liked to fix clocks and watches, and to find out how machines worked. When he was 16 years old he went to Detroit and got a job working in a machine shop. He helped build gasoline engines until he was so good at it that he quit his job and became a traveling repair man. When his father gave him some land with lots of trees on it, Henry opened up a sawmill to cut the trees and sell them as lumber. Then he gave up the sawmill and became chief engineer for the Edison Illuminating Company in Detroit.

It was during this time that Ford became very much interested in the automobile, or the "horseless carriage" as it used to be called. When he was 32 years old he began building automobiles in his spare time. For a while he built racing cars, and sometimes drove them in races himself. Then he went to work for a maker of horseless carriages. The company built very few cars and sold them at high prices. In 1903, he started his own

company. In 1906 he built his first low-priced car and in 1908 he introduced the famous Model T Ford. Eventually he made millions of them. No matter where you went you would see Model T cars.

ASSEMBLY-LINE PRODUCTION

To make these millions of cars Ford used a moving assembly line. This is a slowly moving chain that passes along the factory floor, bringing the work to the men who stand at different points along its path. Each man has a special job to do in building or assembling every automobile. He does only one job and uses only one tool. Then the car moves on to another man along the line so that he can do his special job on it. When all the men have done their jobs, a finished automobile rolls off the end of the assembly line. Before Ford used the assembly line, automobiles were built by a few men doing many different jobs together. They would move from one automobile to another, getting in each other's way and wasting much time. It would often take them several days to finish an automobile. With the assembly line, Ford was finally able to manufacture more than 9,000 automobiles in one day.

Ford saw that if working people had more money to spend they would be able to buy his cars. Before 1914, most working people were earning less than $2.40 a day. For this they would have to work from 10 to 12 hours a day, 6 days a week. In 1914 Ford raised wages in his factory from $2.34 to $5.00 a day, shortened the working day to 8 hours, and later cut the week to 5 days. In time, his idea was followed by other companies and wages were soon raised all over the country.

By the early 1920s, Henry Ford was considered a "billionaire." In one of the first years in which income-tax figures were published, it was shown that Ford's income was $100,000,000 for one year. (He paid $20,000,000 income tax that year; in the 1960s his income tax would have been more than $90,000,000.)

HIS LATER YEARS

Henry Ford was in many ways a simple man, little different from the boy who came off the farm in 1879. But he had strong ideas about many things, and he had enough money to do whatever he pleased. He liked to plan whole cities for his employees. He built the world's biggest factory, on River Rouge near Detroit, Michigan (where Ford founded his company). He was interested in American history, and you can read a separate article about GREENFIELD VILLAGE, which he built.

During World War I, Henry Ford tried to stop the war by sending a "Peace Ship" to Europe, carrying men and women to argue for peace, but this effort was a failure. Then, when the United States entered the war, Ford's company made many kinds of war materials. Henry Ford also built the first real transport airplane, in 1926.

Ford was president of his company until 1919. Then his son Edsel took over. In 1943, when Edsel died, Henry Ford once again became president of the Ford Motor Company. In 1945 he retired and the presidency went to Edsel's son, Henry

Ford II. In 1947, Henry Ford died at the age of 83.

The Ford Foundation is an organization founded in 1936 by Edsel Ford. Edsel and Henry Ford gave it several hundred million dollars worth of stock in the Ford Motor Company. In 1960, the Ford Foundation was worth more than two billion dollars, which is more than any other organization of its kind has. It helps science, education, world peace, and other worthy causes with the money.

Foreign Legion

The Foreign Legion is a branch of the French Army. It is called *foreign* because, except for officers, its soldiers are citizens of nations other than France. Many members of the Legion join because they want to escape unpleasant circumstances (such as political disorders) in their native lands. Others simply like being professional soldiers.

To join the Legion, a man must be between 18 and 40, and must sign up for five years. At the end of that time, he may become a French citizen and an officer.

The Foreign Legion, founded in 1831 by King Louis Philippe who wanted to conquer Algeria without killing French soldiers, is today made up of about 13,000 men. These men used to be stationed in various French territories in Africa and Indochina. Now, though, they are found only in Aubagne, France; in the French Territory of the Afars and the Issas; and in parts of the Sahara. This is because most French overseas territories have become independent.

foreign trade

The food, manufactured articles, raw materials, and other products that a country buys from and sells to other countries make up its foreign trade. When a businessman in Germany buys wool from Australia, he is taking part in foreign trade. When a Canadian paper manufacturer sells paper to a United States newspaper he too is taking part in foreign trade.

Goods that are brought into a country are *imports*. Goods that are sent out of a country are *exports*. Foreign trade is a very important part of the business of most countries of the world. Every year about 120 billion dollars worth of goods are bought and sold in foreign trade.

Foreign trade is important for other reasons, too. Many countries do not produce enough food and other goods to keep their people supplied, and must make up the difference by importing these necessary things from other countries. Great Britain, for example, raises only enough cows to keep a small number of its people supplied with meat, so it must import the rest of its meat from Argentina and other countries. At the same time Great Britain produces more of some products, such as woolen goods, than it can use at home and has to sell them abroad.

TARIFFS

Very often several countries produce the same kind of article. The one that can make it at the lowest price usually has an advantage over the others. For example, both the United States and Switzerland manufacture watches, but Switzerland can make them much more cheaply than the United States, because the watchmakers there are not paid as high wages as watchmakers in the United States. If all the people in the United States bought Swiss watches because they cost less, watchmakers in the United States would lose their jobs. When something like this might happen, a government usually puts a special tax, called a *tariff*, on the foreign goods. When the tariff is added to the price of the foreign article, the cost becomes more nearly like that of the product made at home.

FOREIGN EXCHANGE

When a person in one country buys goods abroad, he must pay for them with the kind of money, or currency, used in the other country. An American dealer who buys toys from Japan pays the Japanese manufacturer in *yen*, which is the Japanese currency. A Japanese businessman who buys American radios is expected to pay for them in American dollars. In order to buy the foreign currency with which to pay for the goods they have bought, the American businessman and the Japanese businessman would buy the foreign currencies from their own banks, or from dealers who specialize in selling foreign currency. This trade in the money of other countries is called *foreign exchange*.

BALANCE OF TRADE

The difference in value between what a country imports and what it exports is known as its *balance of trade*. When a country imports more than it exports, it is said to have an unfavorable balance of trade; when its exports are more than its imports, it has a favorable balance of trade.

In the past it was believed that a country had to have a favorable balance of trade; otherwise it might find itself in a bad business position because too much of its money would belong to people in foreign countries. This opinion is not so widely held any more, and there have been countries which have had unfavorable balances of trade for quite a while without being harmed.

forest

A forest is a large piece of land on which many trees grow. A country can have no greater wealth than its forests. From the wood of the trees buildings and furniture are made. Nearly all the paper used in the world is made of wood. In many sections wood is the chief fuel. In addition there are hundreds of other manufactured products and chemicals that are made from wood. But this is not the only value of a forest. The forest can be even more valuable when the trees are not used for wood. Their roots hold the soil together and keep it from washing away. The roots also make soft earth that soaks up water and prevents floods. The water runs through the trees and evaporates into the air, from which it will later fall as rain. The leaves of the trees give off oxygen that men and other living things need.

The study and care of forests is called *forestry*. Experts in this science divide forests into three main types.

In *deciduous* forests, most of the trees are of the kind that shed their leaves each year. (A deciduous tree is one that sheds its leaves.) Most of the deciduous trees are hardwood trees. They are oak, maple, ash, hickory, birch, beech, walnut, and many others.

In *coniferous* forests, most of the trees are evergreens, such as pine, spruce, hemlock, fir, and cedar. They bear cones and have needles that stay on the tree all year. Their wood is usually soft compared to that of the hardwood trees.

Tropical forests grow in regions near the equator. The trees grow so thickly that they make a jungle. Some of the most valuable of all trees, such as ebony, mahogany, and rubber trees, grow in the tropical forests.

CONSERVATION OF FORESTS

When the first Europeans explored North America, they found the biggest and finest forests men had ever imagined. Nearly all of what is now the United States and Canada was covered with big, healthy trees.

For more than three hundred years after that, North America had the world's finest forests. But as the population grew, men cleared the trees to make level farmlands and cut the trees for fuel and to make paper and lumber. By the time the 20th century came, Americans were beginning to pay the price for their shortsightedness and greed. In vast areas of the west, the fertile topsoil that had been held in place by the roots of trees began to blow away, and in place of good farms there was a "dust bowl" where crops could not be raised. In other parts of the country the topsoil was washed away by rain and streams, and rich farms turned into poor ones. Trees in the forests were cut down and no others were planted, and it became clear that soon the United States would not have as much wood as it needed. It takes twenty or more years to grow a new timber tree.

About fifty years ago, the United States government stepped in to save the forests. Experts on forestry knew that when the trees are gone, and then a drought comes (a long dry spell), good land may become a desert. So the United States Forest Service was formed to protect the forests.

Originally, forty per cent of United States territory was fine forests. In 1905, when the Forest Service was created (as part of the Department of Agriculture), more than half of these forests were in bad or hopeless condition. In 1950, one-third of United States territory was again in fine forests. The Forest Service cares for 155 national forests, with more than 185 million acres, but this is a small part of the total forest land, which is more than two billion acres. Much of this forest land is privately owned, and the state forest-service agencies help the owners to take care of it, prevent diseases that would kill their trees, plant new trees to replace the ones that are cut down, and prevent forest fires.

There are also branches of the Department of the Interior that care for forests and even plant new forests where there were none before. This is especially important on slopes of hills, to hold water

in the soil and to prevent the washing away of soil. During the 1930s, the CIVILIAN CONSERVATION CORPS (about which there is a special article) did much to put the forests of the United States in good condition.

Canada was not settled as fast as the United States was, and the Canadian government was able to observe the way the forests of the United States had been wasted. Therefore Canada passed laws to protect its forests before they were badly hurt. The Canadian forests are now the world's best. They provide wood pulp for the United States and other countries.

FOREST FIRES

The great danger to forests is from forest fires. There are many ways in which a forest fire may start. Lightning may set a tree on fire, and a whole forest will soon be burning. Rotting leaves and other vegetation give out inflammable gases that burn easily, and this can start a forest fire. But most forest fires are caused by the carelessness of human beings. They build fires when camping and do not make sure they are completely put out. They light cigarettes or pipes and toss the matches aside without making sure they are completely put out. Farmers or woodsmen may set fires to clear brush or burn leaves, and the fires may get out of control. Each year America has about 170,000 of these forest fires, and they destroy about 24,-000,000 wooded acres.

Once a forest fire starts burning, it may become so big a blaze that ordinary fire-fighting equipment is powerless to stop it. Millions of dollars' worth of trees can be destroyed in one forest fire. The only way to prevent this damage is to stop the fire before it becomes too big—or not to let it start at all.

The United States Forest Service maintains fire-control agencies wherever there are large forest areas. Lookout stations are placed at high points on mountains and hills, and forest rangers keep a constant watch for smoke that may mean a forest fire is starting. Airplanes and helicopters patrol forest areas. When a forest fire seems to be starting, parachute fire fighters are sometimes flown to the area and dropped from planes. They can be in action in a few hours when formerly it took several days to reach the place of the fire. These "smoke-jumpers" have modern fire-fighting equipment and also use radio to keep in touch with their headquarters. Sometimes fire-fighters spray water or throw soil on the fire, trying to put it out by the direct method. More often they cut down a line or belt of trees and shrubs well in front of the fire. Then when the fire has burned to that point all the trees in its path are gone and the fire dies out. Fire-fighters also build back fires, that is, they get out in front of a fire and start a smaller blaze of their own. This second fire burns its way back to the main fire, and when the two meet, both fires have to go out since there are no trees left to keep them going.

Hundreds of thousands of American boys and girls are Junior Rangers. Together with the Boy Scouts, Girl Scouts, Camp Fire Girls, and many other youth organizations, they are pledged to do everything they can to prevent forest fires. For the younger children, the Forest Service has a "mascot," a kind of teddy bear called Smokey Bear, which is sold in stores as a toy and also stands for the effort everyone should make to fight forest fires.

forgery

Forgery is the use of writing to mislead someone so that he will give you money that you are not honestly entitled to. It is a type of FRAUD, on which there is a separate article. Usually we think of forgery as the copying of another person's signature on a check or contract or will, but as far as the law is concerned, writing a letter that misleads somebody dishonestly is forgery if it causes the person who receives it to give you money.

Faking a painting or a postage stamp, or anything else that is drawn and printed, for the purpose of trying to convince people that it is the genuine thing, is often called forgery.

forget-me-not

The forget-me-not is a pretty flower that is grown in rock gardens and along flower-bed borders. It is a flower you read about in a great many poems and stories. Its name comes from an old German legend of a knight who was drowned while swimming to get some of the flowers for his sweetheart. His last words were, "Forget me not." You will find forget-me-nots growing close to the ground with clusters or bunches of tiny pink, blue or white flowers. The plant has small, oblong, light-green leaves. The stems of the flower have soft little hairs all over them. The forget-me-not carries the idea of faithfulness, and is often used at weddings.

forging

When a metal is heated it becomes soft and will change shape if it is struck hard enough. Hammering hot metal into a desired shape is called forging. A forge is a place where there is the proper fire to heat the metal and the proper equipment with which to hammer it into shape.

Very few things are forged now except tools that have to be very hard. Forging a piece of metal and immediately cooling it makes it very hard, and tools such as the heads of axes and hammers are usually forged.

There are two kinds of forging, hand forging and drop forging. In hand forging, the heated metal is hit with hammers of different shapes against a large block of iron called an anvil. In drop forging, the heated metal is placed on a metal mold and a very heavy weight is dropped on it, forcing it into the mold. Drop forging is used when a large number of pieces of the same shape are needed.

Every town, no matter how small, used to have its forge or smithy, and the man who did the forging was called the blacksmith. He made shoes for horses, and blades for knives, and tools, and even parts for machines. He was a very important part of the community. When the automobile replaced the horse, and mass production in factories replaced the making of things at home, the trade of the blacksmith died out.

formaldehyde

Formaldehyde is a very important commercial chemical. It is a colorless gas with a very sharp smell. One of its largest uses is in manufacturing paper; it is used to make paper towels and tissues stronger when wet. It is also used to tan white leather and to make all sorts of glue.

Some of formaldehyde's other uses are making drugs, rubber and plastics, photographs, insecticides, explosives, and silver mirrors. It is valuable as a deodorant, disinfectant and preservative, and it is also used in the preparation of dead people for burial.

formic acid

Formic acid is a colorless, sharp-smelling liquid. It is found in all animals and most insects, especially ants. Formic acid can also be prepared by chemists, and it is used in cloth mills as a base for dyes, or in leather factories for preparing animal skins to be made into shoes, coats, and luggage.

Formosa or Taiwan

Taiwan is a large island in the Pacific Ocean about a hundred miles off the coast of China. It is the headquarters of the National Government of the Republic of China. This government contests the right of the Communist government to rule the mainland of China. We had called the island Formosa because for years it belong to Japan and that was the Japanese name for it. The Chinese name for the island is Taiwan and the official name is Republic of China, but Communist China does not recognize it as a separate country.

Taiwan has an area of about 14,000 square miles, which is about the size of Delaware and Maryland put together. Over sixteen million people live on Taiwan and the neighboring Pescadores Islands.

A long mountain range stretches all the way down the middle of Formosa from north to south. The highest peak of this mountain range is Mt. Nitaka, which is 14,500 feet high. The land on the east side of the mountains is very steep and wild, but the western part of Formosa is quite flat and the soil is very good for farming. About half the people of Formosa make their living by farming. Their main products are rice, sugarcane, and tea. The climate is warm, and there is heavy rainfall. Some light manufacturing is done, and there are flour mills and sugar refineries.

Life in Taiwan has all the hardships of a nation at war. A large army is maintained, though it has not been used since 1949. There is some sea and air fighting with the Communists. Formosa is governed under the constitution of the Republic of China, which went into effect when Chiang Kai-shek was elected president in 1948. President Chiang was reelected for a third six-year term in 1960, again in 1966 and 1972. All adults in Taiwan can vote. Young men must serve a period in the armed forces.

Taiwan is believed to have been discovered by the Chinese about 1,300 years ago. Portuguese explorers visited it in 1590, and Spanish settlers arrived in the 1600s. The Spaniards were driven out by the Dutch, and they in turn were driven out by the Chinese. At the end of the Chinese-Japanese war in 1895, the peace treaty gave Formosa to Japan, and the island remained under Japanese rule until

The photograph on the right shows an aborigine (native) girl from Formosa whose ancestors have been living on that island for centuries. The photograph on the left shows a girl from Formosa whose ancestors came from the mainland of China.

the end of World War II, when it was returned to China.

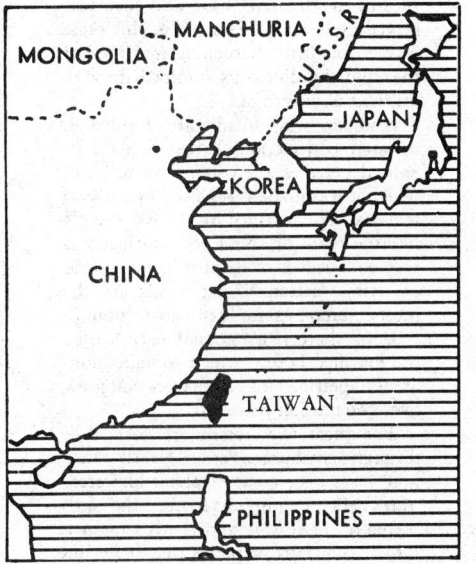

The United States helped Chiang Kai-shek control the economy of Formosa by contributing about $10,000,000 a year until 1965, when this type of aid ended. United States military aid, which has supplied most of the equipment for Chiang's armed forces, has continued. China's seat in the United Nations was held by the Nationalist government until 1971.

FORMOSA (Taiwan). Area (with Pescadores Islands), 13,905 square miles. Population (1973 estimate) 15,000,000. Government, republic. Seat of Chinese Nationalist government. Capital, Taipei (or Taipeh).

Forrest, Nathan Bedford

Nathan Bedford Forrest was a great cavalry general in the Confederate, or Southern, Army during the American Civil War. He was born in 1821 on a small farm in Tennessee and he never had much formal education; he is often quoted as having said that the art of war is to "get there fustest with the mostest men," but in fact the errors in grammar are exaggerated and Forrest was a man of great charm and fine manners.

Forrest joined the Confederate Army at the outbreak of war in 1861. He was promoted to brigadier general in 1862 and to lieutenant general in 1865. After the war he was the first supreme head of the Ku Klux Klan. (This was not the same as the Ku Klux Klan that was formed in this century.) He died in 1877.

forsythia

Forsythia is one of the first shrubs, or bushes, to bloom in the spring. It has masses of yellow, bell-shaped blossoms that come out before its leaves do. Almost as soon as the snow melts, you can cut the branches and force them into bloom indoors by putting the stems in water.

There are two kinds of forsythia, the upright kind of shrub, and the hanging kind that grows on walls and fences. The branches of the hanging forsythia take root by themselves when they touch the ground.

Forsythia grows well in most any soil. After its early blooming in the spring, it has a rich, simple foliage that lasts into late fall. The forsythia plant is unusually free of insect pests and plant diseases. It cannot stand temperatures much below freezing, however, and if it is exposed to extreme cold the blossom may be killed while still in the bud.

Forth River

The Forth is an important river in the southeastern part of Scotland. It is about 170 miles long. Many smaller rivers empty into the Forth, among them the Tiel, Kiel, and Dreel.

The Firth of Forth is the mouth of the Forth River in the North Sea. The Firth is a salt-water estuary, which is a river mouth in which the tide meets the river current. There are a number of islands and deep, sheltered harbors for ships in the Firth.

Because the fishing is so fine—there are many salmon and whitefish in the Forth—many people spend their vacations in the pretty little towns along the Forth and the Firth of Forth.

forts and fortifications

Even longer than history has been written, men have protected themselves against enemies by getting behind something such as a mound of earth or a wall, or a building with very strong walls. These means that man has used to protect himself against attack are called fortifications. When a man builds a house or an army builds a camp protected by any one of these means, it is called a fort.

Nearly all ancient cities were surrounded by walls. For a thousand years, until only a few hundred years ago, kings and noblemen built castles, which were forts with heavy walls and usually surrounded by moats. In the early days of America, forts were built. These were settlements surrounded by walls to protect the people from attack by Indians. As late as World War I cities were surrounded by small concrete mounds or buildings in which there were cannons and machine guns and a group of soldiers (called a garrison) to protect the city against attacking armies. The great city of Paris in France was once a fortified city.

The development of heavy artillery made forts ineffective, and yet as late as World War II the French had a fortification called the Maginot Line that was intended to keep the German armies from attacking France.

The Maginot Line was a series of concrete-and-steel gun positions, with deep underground chambers for storing food and ammunition and for providing shelter for the soldiers. It was thought by many people that the Maginot Line could not be broken, but when the Germans attacked France in 1940 they drove through with tanks and they used dive bombers to wreck the guns. Since the guns of the Maginot Line were pointed only one way, part of the German army merely went around the end of it by attacking through Belgium.

In modern warfare there is no such thing as a fortification in the old sense.

ANCIENT FORTIFICATIONS

The traditional fortification had certain parts that had special names. The walls of the fort or town had round towers called roundels placed at intervals around them. These roundels were large enough to hold several cannon. Later the roundels were made into independent towers not connected with the walls. When it was found that the round shape of the roundel made it hard to fire at the enemy if he came too close, the roundels were made with five sides, one side facing the interior of the fort and the other four sides facing the enemy. These five-sided towers were called bastions. The rampart was the platform around the bastion on which the guns stood, and the parapet was a low wall about the rampart behind which the gunners could be sheltered from enemy fire. In the parapet were slots called embrasures, through which the guns were fired.

Another fortification was the castle, which was really a private fortress for a king or nobleman. Many castles of the Middle Ages are still standing in France and other parts of Europe. They were usually circular in shape because curved walls are stronger than straight ones. They were surrounded by a wide ditch, called a moat, which was kept filled with water. A wooden bridge crossed the moat, and it could be pulled up at night, cutting the castle off completely from the outside world. Big castles had two walls, one inside the other, so that if the enemy succeeded in breaking through the first they still would be stopped by the second.

The tops of the walls were built jaggedly instead of straight, so that there were narrow slots, called crenellations, through which the soldiers could shoot arrows at the enemy without being seen themselves. Sometimes wooden platforms

were built over the edge of the walls. These platforms had holes in the floor, and the defenders could shoot straight down at anyone attacking the castle.

For a long time it was very difficult to capture forts or castles, and the best way was to wait until the defenders' food ran out. Then they would be forced to surrender. This was called a SIEGE, about which there is a separate article.

In modern warfare, the only kind of fortification that is much used is the *pillbox*, which is a concrete shelter to protect machinegunners against enemy fire. There are also field fortifications. The simplest field fortifications are the *trenches* and the *foxholes* that were used in both world wars. It is very difficult to drive a determined enemy out of its trenches, but in World War II the armies moved so fast that there was seldom time to dig trenches. Wherever American soldiers went, they dug the deep holes called foxholes to protect themselves.

fortunetelling

Fortunetelling is trying to guess or predict what will happen in the future. Many people in all ages have believed in fortunetelling, though among the Hebrews it was forbidden. Fortunetelling can be fun if it is played as a game, or used as entertainment on the stage. There are laws in many states against telling fortunes for money.

There are four popular ways to tell fortunes. Some fortunetellers look at the lines on the palms of your hands to tell you what your future will be. This is called PALMISTRY and there is a separate article about it. Fortunetelling by cards is also popular. The person whose fortune is being told may select cards from a deck of playing cards that is lying face down on the table. The cards have meanings for the fortuneteller. The fortuneteller lays down the cards in a pattern on a table and tells the fortune by the order in which the cards appear. The crystal ball is also used to foretell the future. The crystal ball is a glass globe, or ball, in which the fortuneteller is supposed to see a picture of some future event. Some fortunetellers, particularly the gypsies, use tea leaves to tell fortunes. They "read" the future in the patterns that tea leaves make in the bottom of a cup.

Read also the articles on ASTROLOGY and ORACLES.

Fort Wayne

Fort Wayne is the third-largest city in Indiana. More than 177,000 people live there. Many men and women work in large factories in Forth Wayne that make electrical equipment, such as radios and household appliances. Other factories in Fort Wayne make trucks and gasoline station equipment. Fort Wayne was named for General "Mad Anthony" Wayne. President George Washington sent the general to conquer the Miami Indians who had their chief village there. General Wayne defeated the Indians and set up a fort. As the city grew around the fort, it came to be called Fort Wayne. The city, which is only 148 miles from Chicago, has many fine schools, colleges and museums. If you ever visit Fort Wayne you should see the early American stockade and also the remains of the earlier forts with which the French for a time held the city against the Miami Indians.

FORT WAYNE, INDIANA. Population (1970 census) 177,671. County seat, Allen County.

Fort Worth

Fort Worth is the fourth-largest city in Texas. It is also a fast-growing city, for in the years between 1950 and 1970, about 117,000 people came to live in Fort Worth and increased its population to over 393,000. There is a great deal in Fort Worth that makes people want to live there. There are thousands of oil wells nearby; hundreds of the ranches in Texas send their cattle to this city to be sold or slaughtered and packed; grain, to feed cattle and humans, is shipped to and from the city. In addition to oil-refining, its stockyards, and the manufacture of grain products, Fort Worth has many other industries. It is one of the largest egg-drying centers in the world; cowboy clothing is also manufactured here, as well as steel, cement, and wood products. Fort Worth is a beautiful city. Many of its buildings are very modern and made mainly of steel and glass. Its main streets are lined with palm trees. Texas Christian University is located in Fort Worth. The city was named for General William Jenkins Worth, a hero of the Mexican War.

FORT WORTH, TEXAS. Population 393,476 (1970 census). County seat, Tarrant County.

Forty-niners were men (and a few women) who went to California in 1849 and the few following years, just after gold had been discovered at Sutter's Mill. See the article on GOLD RUSH.

forum

Forum in the modern English language means some kind of public discussion. A forum is usually held to discuss some subject that people may have different opinions about. It is often a subject that will interest all the people who live in a certain area, such as what to do about some public problem. Many people meet together and, after someone has spoken on the subject, everyone joins in the discussion. Sometimes the word, forum, is used to mean the place where some public discussion is held. This is like the old Roman meaning of the word. In Latin, the forum was the place where all the business of a city was carried on. The most famous place of that kind was the Roman Forum. It was a large open place in the city of Rome. There were many fine buildings there, and many kinds of decorations, to make the Forum beautiful. There the Roman officials met, there the courts were held, and there the merchants came to buy and sell their wares. You can see the ruins of some of these ancient buildings if you visit Rome.

fossil

Hundreds of millions of years ago, dead plants or animals became buried under earth, and often this earth was formed by millions of tons of pressure into rock. Very often the part of the plant or animal kept its original form in this rock, and if you look at the rock today you can see where a leaf or a bone, or the shell of a shellfish, or even a whole animal, was buried and pressed into rock. Any such remains of times long past are called *fossils*. They are a record of life that existed on the earth millions of years ago.

HOW FOSSILS ARE FORMED

Fossils are formed in three main ways. One way is by the impression long dead creatures made in mud or sand. Suppose a shellfish, for instance, died in the soft mud of a river bed many millions of years ago, and the river itself gradually dried up. The mud around the shell would harden into rock, and on the rock would be an impression of the outside of the shell. The shell itself might decay and disappear, but its impression would remain. Or it could happen that the fish's body inside the shell gradually decayed, and as it decayed, mud from the river bed seeped in and hardened into rock inside the shell. This rock would have on it the impression of the inside of the shell. The footprints of animals which no longer exist, like the dinosaur, have also been preserved as fossil impressions in this same way, through the hardening into rock of the mud the dinosaurs tramped through millions of years ago.

Another way fossils are formed is through petrifaction. When a plant or animal petrifies, the original material of which it was made is replaced by mineral material. The petrified fossil looks exactly like the plant or animal of which it was formed, but it is made of mineral instead of living matter. Wood fossils are the most common example of petrifaction. In Arizona there is a national park, called the Petrified Forest, which contains hundreds of petrified logs from trees that grew over two million years ago.

The third way fossils are formed is through actual preservation. Nearly a million years ago, great elephant-like creatures called mammoths roamed the earth. Some of them were apparently caught in great waterfalls or floods that froze into glaciers and were preserved in huge chunks of ice. Several of these mammoth fossils have been found in the northern wastes of Siberia and Alaska.

WHAT KIND OF PLANTS AND ANIMALS BECOME FOSSILS

There are more fossils of water plants and animals than there are of land plants and animals. Animals or plants that died on land usually decayed or were eaten up by other animals. But those forms of life that lived and died in the water were frequently embedded in the soft mud of the water bed, and became fossilized through the impression process we described earlier. Most of the fossils of land animals or plants were probably formed from animals that fell into bogs or lakes, or from plants that were blown to these places.

WHAT WE LEARN FROM FOSSILS

The study of fossils is important in many ways. From it we can learn a great deal about how life has developed on earth; scientists have found great support for the theory of evolution in the study of fossils. We can learn also about the formation and age of the rocks from the study of fossils embedded in them. Different forms of life were found on earth at different periods in the earth's history, and scientists know, for example, that

Fossil sea lilies resemble those living today.

a rock that contains a fossil dinosaur is much older than a rock that contains a fossil deer, because the dinosaur is an older form of life than the deer. We can also see how the surface of the earth has changed through the study of fossils. If we find fossil snails in the middle of a desert, we can be sure that at some time in the earth's history the desert was a lake or a sea, because snails are water-dwellers.

Foster, Stephen Collins

Stephen Collins Foster was the writer of some of the greatest and best-loved songs in the history of the United States. "Old Black Joe" and "My Old Kentucky Home" are two of Foster's songs that have come almost to stand for America to people throughout the world. In all, Foster wrote some two hundred songs in his short life of 38 years.

Foster was born on July 4, 1826. He was interested in music almost from the time he was a baby. When he was only 2 he used to try to play his sister's guitar. At 7 he taught himself to play the flute, and when he went away to boarding school he had a hard time keeping his studies ahead of his music. His first printed song was called "Open Thy Lattice, Love," and it was published when Foster was 18. It was dedicated to a 13-year-old girl friend.

"Oh! Susanna" was Foster's first big national hit. It spread so quickly that it was heard in England and other countries soon after it had been published in the United States. Foster wrote many songs for the minstrel, or song-and-dance, shows that were popular in those days, among them "Massa's in the Cold, Cold Ground," "Old Dog Tray," and "Old Folks at Home."

Foster made quite a lot of money with his songs, but he always spent more than he earned. He married a girl named Jane McDowell, who was the inspiration for his song "Jeannie With the Light Brown Hair." They had one son, but Foster was difficult to live with and he and Jane were often separated. In the last years of his life he became very poor. He had no home, and he managed to get along by selling songs for very little money. Some of these songs he had written many years before he became known and popular. When he died in 1864 he had only 38 cents in his pocket.

Foster has been greatly honored by his country for his great gift of song. In 1954 a bust, or statue of head and shoulders, of Foster was set up in the Library of Congress in Washington, D.C. The state of Florida has planned a park and museum in his honor on the Suwanee River, which Foster made famous in his song "Old Folks at Home." This song has been adopted as the official state song of Florida. Other Foster memorials have been built in states across the country.

Among other famous songs written by Foster are "Beautiful Dreamer," "Camptown Races," and "Come Where My Love Lies Dreaming."

Fouché, Joseph

Joseph Fouché, the Duke of Otranto, was a French politician who became chief of Napoleon's police and spies. He was born in 1763. When he was 26 the French Revolution broke out, and Fouché became a cruel leader of the revolution and killed many people. He was also the kind of man who would join any side, just so long as it was winning, so when Napoleon became emperor of France, Fouché said he was for Napoleon and not for the revolution. All of France feared Fouché, because his spies were everywhere, and it was almost impossible to say anything against the government that Fouché would not find out. Some people said that even Napoleon himself was afraid of Fouché. When Napoleon was defeated, Fouché was forced to leave France and to live in Italy, where he died in 1820.

foundry

Founding is the pouring of melted metal into a mold so that when it hardens it will have the shape of the mold. A factory where this is done is called a *foundry.* Usually the mold is made of sand because it is very easy to give sand the desired shape, and because it takes such high temperatures to melt sand that the metal poured into it will harden into the shape of the mold instead of melting the sand.

The first step in founding is the carving of a pattern out of wood in the exact shape you want the metal to be. Sand mixed with clay is put into two iron boxes, and one half of the pattern is pressed into each box of sand. When the two boxes of sand are placed together they make a sand mold of the whole piece that is to be made. In the sand there is a tube, called a *sprue,* leading into the mold. The metal is melted and poured through the sprue until the mold is full. The metal hardens as it cools. The sand mold is then taken away and the piece of metal has the same shape as the pattern.

As the melted metal is poured into the mold, gases sometimes form and create holes in the metal. These holes are called *bubbles.* They make the casting weak and such castings are often thrown away.

The same mold can be used to cast many pieces of the same shape, but if this is to be done the pattern must have what is called *draft.* This means that the pattern must be shaped with no projecting parts so that the metal piece can be removed without taking any of the sand with it. Anything on the metal piece that would pull sand out of the mold is called an *undercut.*

Metals with a very low melting point are often cast in molds made of metals that have a higher melting point. For example, a mold can be made of steel, which melts at about 2000 degrees, and in it you can mold lead, which melts at 337 degrees. The melted lead will not be hot enough to melt the steel. Such a metal mold is called a *die,* and the process of casting metal in a die is called *die-casting.*

The printing type from which books and magazines and newspapers are printed is usually cast by machines. The type is made of a very soft metal mixture that is mostly lead, and the dies are made of brass, which has a higher melting point. See the article on TYPESETTING.

fountain

A fountain is a stream of water that is forced out of a spout. Some fountains are made because they look pretty, and others are made because they are useful. An example of the useful fountain is the drinking fountain that sends up a stream of water so that people can drink it. The stream of water itself is called a fountain, and the fixture from which it streams into the air is also called a fountain.

Men have used fountains for many thousands of years, and from the earliest days have decorated the basins from which the fountains flow in very beautiful ways. In the days of early Greece and Rome, fountains were used as sources of water by all the people. The rich had fountains in their own homes, but the poor could not afford to have water piped directly into their own homes and used large public fountains. Even today, in some of the poorer villages of Europe, there are public fountains, wells, or pumps in the village square.

Fountains often had a religious meaning to the ancient Greeks and Romans, too. Springs and fountains were often dedicated to nymphs, who were minor goddesses in the Greek and Roman religions, and small rooms called shrines, where people could pray and leave gifts to the nymphs, were often built nearby.

The most beautiful fountains are those that are built for purely decorative purposes. The idea of putting elaborate decorations on fountains, and of using fountains to enhance the beauty of parks and homes, started about five hundred years ago in Italy. Some of the most beautiful fountains in the world were built in that country at about that time. Among the most famous of the Italian fountains are the Trevi Fountain in Rome and the fountains in the Vatican, where the Pope lives.

In the gardens at Versailles, France, where King Louis XIV built a beautiful palace and laid out beautiful parks about three hundred years ago, there are many lovely fountains throughout the grounds. One of the best known fountains in the United States is decorated with the statue of PROMETHEUS, about whom you can read in a separate article. It is in Rockefeller center in New York City.

Fountain of Youth, a fountain that was supposed to make a person who drank from its waters young again: see the article on PONCE DE LEON.

fountain pen, ball-point pen

A fountain pen is a pen that holds a large quantity of ink, so that a person can write several pages before he has to refill it. Fountain pens were not used until about 75 years ago; until that time people used steel or quill pens, which had to be dipped into an inkwell every few minutes because they held only a small amount of ink on the point.

In the original fountain pen, a rubber tube held ink inside the pen and the ink flowed into the point of the pen so you could write until the tube was empty. Later a sealed barrel made of a plastic material replaced the rubber tube. When the tube or barrel is empty, you dip the point in ink and create a vacuum by pressing a lever or plunger; the vacuum causes the pen to draw in a new supply of ink.

In the ball-point pen, a small steel ball revolves in a socket connected with a cartridge full of ink. As you write, the ball turns, picking up ink from the cartridge and transferring it to the paper. When the cartridge is empty, you put in a new cartridge.

Most people today use ball-point pens, for several reasons. Ball-point pens are much cheaper. Fountain pens often leak, staining fingers or clothes with ink, and ball-point pens seldom do this. Ball-point pens last several months, while fountain pens do not take in much ink. But fountain pens produce better-looking writing on anything but a very glossy paper, and almost all fountain pens work well, while one must usually buy several ball-point pens before he finds a good one. (If the little steel ball is not perfectly round, the ball-point pen will not write well.) Some fountain pens are now made to be filled with ink cartridges, so they will hold more ink.

Four Freedoms

The Four Freedoms was a phrase first used by President Franklin D. Roosevelt in a speech made on January 9, 1941. At that time, France and Norway had been seized by the Germans, and Great Britain was at war with Germany. The United States was preparing for war and was helping to supply war materials to Great Britain, but had not yet entered World War II. The neutral nations and those opposed to Germany were not united, and there was a great need for a statement of the ideals for which the people living in free democracies should be willing to fight. President Roosevelt stated these ideals in words that have been printed and repeated many times since. His way of stating them seemed the best that had ever been found.

President Roosevelt said:

"In the future days, which we seek to make secure, we look forward to a world founded upon four essential human freedoms.

"The first is freedom of speech and expression—everywhere in the world.

"The second is freedom of every person to worship God in his own way—everywhere in the world.

"The third is freedom from want—which, translated into world terms, means economic understandings which will secure to every nation a healthy peacetime life for its inhabitants—everywhere in the world.

"The fourth is freedom from fear—which, translated into world terms, means a worldwide reduction of armament to such a point and in such a thorough fashion that no nation will be in a position to commit an act of physical aggression against any neighbor—anywhere in the world."

Four-H Clubs

The Four-H Clubs are organized groups of young people who are engaged in farming, homemaking, or community activities under the guidance of grownup extension workers and local grownup leaders trained by them.

Any boy or girl between the ages of 10 and 21 who agrees to "learn to do by doing" may join the Four-H Club. The group elects its own officers, plans and conducts programs based on the needs and interests of the members of the club, holds regular meetings, and takes part in community activities. There are Four-H Clubs in practically all counties of every state, and in Alaska, Hawaii, and Puerto Rico.

Four-H Club work is part of the national system of extension work in agriculture and homemaking, in which the United States Department of Agriculture, the state land-grant colleges, and the counties take part.

Four-H has helped to develop nineteen million young citizens since its beginning. The program is helping to increase farm incomes, improve standards of living, increase the satisfactions from community life, and prepare young people for the world ahead.

AIMS OF FOUR-H CLUBS

Four-H stands for Head, Heart, Hands, and Health. By Head, it means trying to give rural young people an intelligent understanding and appreciation of nature and the environment in which they live, to teach them the value of research and develop in them a scientific attitude toward the problems of the farm and the home.

By Heart, it means trying to train rural young people to work together to solve rural problems; and to give them high ideals and standards for farming, homemaking, community life, and citizenship, and a sense of responsibility for reaching these ideals.

By Hands, it means to give technical instruction in farming and homemaking, and to help them "learn by doing" through conducting farm or home enterprises and showing others what they have learned.

By Health, it means to develop in rural young people habits of healthful living, to teach them the intelligent use of leisure, and to arouse in them worthy ambitions and a desire to continue to learn, that they may live fuller and richer lives.

The Four-H has 10 "guideposts" for young people to live by: 1, developing talents for greater usefulness; 2, joining with friends for work, fun, and fellowship; 3, learning to live in a changing world; 4, choosing a way to earn a living; 5, producing food and fiber for home and market; 6, creating better homes for better living; 7, conserving nature's resources for security and happiness; 8, building health for a strong America; 9, sharing responsibilities for community improvement; and 10, serving as citizens in maintaining world peace.

The national Four-H emblem is a fourleaf clover, with a letter H on each leaf. The Four-H pledge is: "I pledge my head to clearer thinking, my heart to greater loyalty, my hands to larger service, my health to better living, for my club, my community, and my country."

Four Horsemen of the Apocalypse: see the article on APOCALYPSE.

Fourteen Points

In January, 1918, toward the end of World War I, President Woodrow Wilson made a speech before Congress in which he announced the fourteen conditions, called Fourteen Points, on which he hoped that all, friend and enemy alike, could agree and thus lay the foundation for world peace. His idea was to give all the nations in the war, especially Germany, reasons why they should stop fighting. The Fourteen Points showed that the United States did not want to make things too hard for the Germans, who by then knew they probably could not win the war and might lose it. After Germany gave up, in November 1918, the chief Allies against them (Britain, France, and Italy) did not accept all fourteen points.

President Wilson said that there should be no secrets when nations made treaties; that everyone should have equal rights to sail the seas; that trade should move freely between nations; that armies should be smaller; that the people living in a territory should decide what nation they wanted to live in and what kind of government they should have; and that all nations should join in an international organization to prevent wars (see LEAGUE OF NATIONS).

Fourteenth Amendment

Between 1865 and 1870, the years just after the Civil War, the 13th, 14th and 15th Amendments to the United States Constitution were adopted. They are called the Reconstruction Amendments because the U. S. was being reconstructed—made into one nation again, after being divided.

Since 1954 the Supreme Court has made the 14th Amendment very important in its rulings, especially in the integration of schools (see the article on EDUCATION).

The 14th Amendment says that no state may favor one citizen over another or deprive a citizen of any rights "without due process of law," which means the citizen must be legally tried and convicted. The 13th Amendment abolished slavery and the 15th says that no state may make it difficult or impossible for a person to vote because of his race or color.

Civil rights laws passed by Congress have been upheld by the Supreme Court because of the 14th Amendment, and in 1965 Congress passed a law, requested by President Lyndon B. Johnson, to force some Southern communities to let Negroes vote who had not been permitted to vote there. See the articles AMENDMENT and CIVIL RIGHTS.

Fourth of July, a holiday that celebrates the day on which the United States

signed the Declaration of Independence, in 1776: see the article on INDEPENDENCE DAY.

fox

The fox is a small animal related to the dog. In many fables it has been pictured as the cleverest of all animals. This may not be so, but the fox is very hard to catch. It may run in a circle several miles wide and then leave the circle without leaving a scent, by running through a stream. In the winter a fox will run over ice that is just thick enough to hold it but too thin to hold its pursuers. One kind of fox, the gray fox, can climb a tree as fast as a cat. Some foxes run as fast as 45 miles an hour.

Foxes in the Arctic travel in packs, like wolves. They are white in winter, when there is snow, but turn brown in the summer, so they are always hard to see.

Foxes live underground when their cubs are being born and raised. The litter of cubs is born in a small burrow that the father digs. Foxes are poor diggers and often use a hole that some other animal has dug and abandoned. As soon as the cubs are old enough to hunt for their food, the whole fox family leaves the den and never returns. While the cubs are in the den, the father brings them food.

Sometimes the fox makes farmers angry by stealing chickens, but also the fox helps farmers by killing rabbits, rats, mice, and insects, which eat the crops.

Years ago, men used to trap foxes and sell their pelts for a living. People now raise foxes on fox farms. Silver and platinum foxes are raised on farms, and the pelt of one of these animals may be worth almost a thousand dollars.

Fox, Charles

Charles Fox was an English statesman at the time the United States won its independence in the Revolutionary War, and he was a good friend of America. He was a great liberal, which means that he believed in personal liberty. He was born in 1749 and became a member of Parliament, the English lawmaking body, when he was only 19 years old. He was for American and Irish Independence, the French Revolution, and religious freedom, and was against slavery. Most of these ideas were very unpopular at the time, but he was so brilliant that he held many important positions in the British government. He died in 1806.

Fox, George, was the founder of the Society of Friends, or Quakers. See the article on the Society of FRIENDS.

foxglove

Foxglove is a tall, spiked plant that grows wild in hilly pastures and along roadsides in Europe. It is best known for a medicine that is made from it. The medicine is called *digitalis* and is given as a stimulant to people who have heart trouble. Foxglove is cultivated in America, where it does not grow wild as in England and European countries. You will often see it in old-fashioned gardens where it is very decorative. The stem of the foxglove is straight and tall. It grows to heights varying from eighteen inches to five feet. The oblong, dark-green leaves are spaced along the stem, and the flowers, which are like classic bells, hang in rows down a large part of the spike stem. These blossoms are white, crimson or purplish. Foxglove blooms in July and its many small seeds ripen in August or September. It is an herb and belongs to the digitalis family from which the medicine takes its name. The medicine comes from the leaf of the two-year-old plant and is taken in the second year of the plant's growth when the blossoms are three-quarters out.

foxhound

Foxhounds are hunting dogs that have been used for over three hundred years in England, the United States, and France for hunting foxes. Sometimes a foxhound goes out with a hunter who plans to shoot the fox; sometimes the dog merely follows trails in competition with other hounds. People on horseback who hunt foxes use packs of foxhounds to trail the foxes across the fields and woods. You can read more about this sport in the article on FOXHUNTING.

There are two main types of foxhounds, the American and the English foxhound. They are very much alike, but the English type is slightly larger and heavier. Foxhounds are not often kept as pets.

An average foxhound stands about 21 to 26 inches at the shoulder and is between 25 and 30 inches long. It weighs between 40 and 65 pounds. A foxhound may be any color, or any combination of different colors. Usually its ears are long and hanging, and its tail is long and curved.

Bryn Mawr Hound Show
"Rowdy" is a prize-winning foxhound.

foxhunting

Foxhunting is the sport of hunting a fox, either on foot or on horseback, using dogs. Some people think it is a good sport because foxes are smart, because they can run fast, and because they are hard to catch. Red foxes are best for hunting because they do not hide in holes or climb trees as often as gray foxes do. People who go foxhunting on horseback almost always wear bright red coats and black boots. One of the rules of the sport is that the fox must never be shot. If the dogs cannot catch the fox, it is let go free. The hunter who first reaches the fox after it has been killed is allowed to keep its tail.

Fox Indian, a member of the Algonquin Indian tribes that lived in the midwestern part of the United States: see the article on ALGONQUIN.

fox terrier

Fox terriers are one of the most popular breeds of pet dog in the world. They are lively, playful, intelligent, and affectionate. Children love them, because a fox terrier will romp and play as long as its master wants it to. They are small dogs, but they are afraid of nothing, and can easily be taught tricks. In fact, most of the trick dog acts you see on television and in stage shows use fox terriers, or dogs that are part fox terrier. The breed started in England about 250 years ago. At that time, the fox terrier's job was to go right down into a foxhole after the fox when a pack of hounds had driven it to cover. They are still used in foxhunting today, but they are mostly kept as pets and as watch dogs, because they will bark loudly whenever a stranger comes to the house. Fox terriers are also expert mouse and rat catchers, which makes them valuable in farms and country homes.

There are two kinds of fox terriers, the smooth-coated and the wire-haired types. They look different because the wire-hair's stiff, shaggy coat gives it the appearance of being heavier and stockier. You have probably noticed the fuzzy front legs of wire-haired terriers. They look as if the dog wore woolly leggings. The smooth-haired terrier has a smooth coat that lies flat and straight on the body. People usually clip the tails of very young fox terrier puppies. Fox terriers are mostly white, with black, brown, or tan markings.

fraction

A fraction is a part of something. In arithmetic, it is a way of using numbers to show how big the part is, or how many parts there are. Anything whole can be shown by a whole number, such as 1 or 2 or 10 or 360. A fraction, or part of a whole thing, must be shown by two numbers, like this: $\frac{1}{3}$. The number above the line is called the *numerator*. It tells how many whole things there were to be split up into parts. In this case the numerator is 1, meaning there was only one whole thing. The number below the line is called the *denominator*. It tells how many parts were made of the whole thing (or things). Each of these parts must be exactly the same size. In this case one whole thing (for example, a chocolate bar) was divided into three parts, each of the same size. The fraction $\frac{1}{3}$ stands for one of these three parts of the chocolate bar. (Often a fraction is written with a slanting line.)

A fraction can stand for several parts of one whole thing or for one part of several whole things. Suppose there is a plot of land with three acres in it and it has to be divided equally among eight persons. If you own one of the shares, your share will be shown by the fraction $\frac{3}{8}$, which means three acres divided into eight parts. Then suppose there is a plot of land consisting of one acre, and it too is to be divided into eight parts, but you own three of those eight parts, your share will still be shown by the fraction $\frac{3}{8}$.

A fraction means simply that the top figure is divided by the bottom figure. The fraction $\frac{3}{8}$ is the same thing as

$3 \div 8$. When the numerator (number on top) is smaller than the denominator (number on the bottom), as in $\frac{1}{2}$, the fraction is called a *proper* fraction. When the numerator is not smaller than the denominator, as in $\frac{5}{4}$, the fraction is an *improper* fraction. If there are five chocolate bars to be divided equally among four persons, each person's share is $\frac{5}{4}$, which is the same thing as $1\frac{1}{4}$—one whole chocolate bar plus a quarter of another.

Fractions that have the same denominator are called *like fractions*. To add like fractions together, you add the numerators: $\frac{1}{4} + \frac{1}{4} = \frac{2}{4}$. To subtract one like fraction from another, subtract the numerators: $\frac{3}{4} - \frac{1}{4} = \frac{2}{4}$. The denominators do not change.

Unlike fractions have different denominators. Before you can add or subtract them, you have to find a *common denominator*. That is, you have to change them into fractions that have the same denominator.

A common denominator is a number that can be evenly divided by the denominators of both the fractions you want to add. One of these denominators may be a common denominator. If you want to add $\frac{1}{2}$ and $\frac{5}{12}$, you can use 12 as the common denominator, because it can be divided by both 12 and 2. In this case you divide the larger denominator by the smaller: $12 \div 2 = 6$. Multiply both the numerator and the denominator of the first fraction ($\frac{1}{2}$) by the result, which in this case is 6: 1×6 and 2×6. The new fraction is $\frac{6}{12}$. Now add the fractions $\frac{6}{12}$ and $\frac{5}{12}$ and the answer is $\frac{11}{12}$.

When neither denominator may be used as a common denominator, as when you want to add $\frac{1}{2}$ and $\frac{1}{3}$, multiply the denominators: $2 \times 3 = 6$. Their product (in this case, 6) will be a common denominator. Now divide the common denominator (6) by the denominator of the first fraction (2): $6 \div 2 = 3$. Then multiply both numerator and denominator of the first fraction by 3, giving the fraction $\frac{3}{6}$. Do the same thing with the second fraction: $6 \div 3 = 2$. Multiply both numerator and denominator of the fraction $\frac{1}{3}$ by 2, which gives you $\frac{2}{6}$. Now add the fractions $\frac{3}{6}$ and $\frac{2}{6}$ and your answer is $\frac{5}{6}$.

To multiply fractions, you multiply their numerators and you multiply their denominators. To multiply $\frac{2}{3} \times \frac{3}{4}$, you multiply 2×3, giving you 6 as your new numerator, and you multiply 3×4, giving you 12 as your new denominator. Your new fraction is $\frac{6}{12}$.

You can always reduce a fraction (to make it simpler) by dividing the numerator and the denominator by the same number. Take the fraction $\frac{6}{12}$. Divide the numerator by 6; 6 divided by 6 is 1, so your new numerator is 1. Divide the denominator by 6; 12 divided by 6 is 2, so your new denominator is 2. You have reduced the fraction to $\frac{1}{2}$. That is, $\frac{6}{12}$ and $\frac{1}{2}$ are the same thing.

The rule for dividing fractions is, *invert the divisor and multiply*. If you want to find out how many times $\frac{1}{4}$ will go into $\frac{1}{2}$ ($\frac{1}{2} \div \frac{1}{4}$), the divisor is $\frac{1}{4}$, to "invert" it you change the places of its numerator and denominator, making it $\frac{4}{1}$, and then you multiply $\frac{1}{2} \times \frac{4}{1}$. The answer is $\frac{4}{2}$, and when you divide 4

by 2 you get a result of 2, which means that $\frac{1}{4}$ will go into $\frac{1}{2}$ twice. ,

DECIMAL FRACTIONS

A *decimal fraction* always uses as its denominator the number 10 or one of its powers, such as 100, or 1,000, or 10,-000, and so on. A dot or period is used instead of a line to show that it is a fraction. For example, .4 is the same as $\frac{4}{10}$, and .40 is the same as $\frac{40}{100}$. See also the article on ARITHMETIC.

fracture

A fracture is a broken bone. There are two kinds of fractures. One is called a *simple* fracture, the other a *compound* fracture. In a simple fracture the bone breaks but the skin is not broken or cut. In a compound fracture the skin is broken or cut, and the bone may push through the cut. The compound fracture is usually more serious because germs may get into the opening to cause blood poisoning or bone disease, and the muscles around the bone may be torn. There always has to be a push, or force, against a bone to break it. In people with weak or diseased bones the force does not have to be very strong, but with healthy children and grownups it takes a bad accident to break any bones. Young children and very old people sometimes get "greenstick" fractures in which the bone twists around and splits along its length.

TREATMENT OF FRACTURES

When a doctor thinks you may have a broken bone he takes an X-ray picture. This answers the question in a few minutes. When he finds that a bone is broken he must set it, which means to put it in the same position it was before it was broken. Then he must put the broken part of the body, the arm or leg for example, in a cast so that it does not move while the fracture is healing, which takes from eight to twelve weeks. A cast is made of wet plaster on long bandages that are wound around and around the injured part. When the wet plaster dries it becomes very hard and holds the leg or arm quite rigid. Nowadays doctors have found another way to hold some fractures until the bone heals, or knits. By an operation, they fasten the bone ends together with a metal plate and screws. These are left in place until the fracture mends, or even after it mends. Often the bone will be stronger than before it was broken.

Skull fractures must be treated differently from other fractures because of the shape of the head. While they can be most serious and cause death, they are usually not as dangerous as most people think, unless the brain is injured. With a simple fracture of the skull and no brain injury a person will usually get well quickly. With a compound fracture the brain might be exposed to germs that could cause infection. Also, such a blow would probably cause bleeding inside the brain. The new "miracle drugs" usually prevent infection in open skull fractures, but if bleeding happens inside the brain it can mean death if a doctor cannot stop it quickly.

FIRST AID

If you must move someone with a frac-

ture to get him to a doctor, keep the broken part from moving so that the fracture will not be made worse. If an arm or leg is broken, make a splint. A splint is anything you can tie to the broken part, such as a large stick or a little board tied to each side of the fracture, to keep it straight. If a person's skull might be fractured do not do anything except to make the person comfortable until you can get a doctor. Whenever you think someone has a fracture remember that you will make it worse by moving the injured part, and only a doctor can make it better.

Fragonard, Jean-Honoré

Jean-Honoré Fragonard was a famous French painter who lived about two hundred years ago. As a boy, he showed such talent that his family permitted him to study art. Years later, the French king became interested in Fragonard's work, and the painter's fortune was made. Fragonard painted romantic scenes, with beautiful ladies and handsome men. The colors are soft and lovely. Fragonard also painted scenes of his family, including some of his son Fanfan learning to walk. After the French Revolution Fragonard was almost forgotten. He died in 1806. Today his paintings are very popular.

France

France, the largest nation in western Europe, lies between the Atlantic Ocean on its west, the English Channel to the north and the Mediterranean Sea on the south. It also touches Spain, Italy, Switzerland, Germany and Belgium. France has been a nation for more than a thousand years. Once France held land throughout the world. Today the French Republic includes mainland France, Corsica, and the overseas departments of French Guiana, Martinique, Guadeloupe, and Réunion. Also France has several territories such as the Afars and the Issas in Africa and French Polynesia in the Pacific.

WHO LIVES IN FRANCE

Long before France became a nation, it was overrun by many different European peoples. There were the Celts, who lived in Ireland, England and in the north of Germany; the Teutons, who come from northern Europe; and the Latin peoples of the Mediterranean. Each of these races left its mark, and the French are about evenly divided between broad, brown-haired people like the Celts; tall blonds like the Teutons; and short, dark people of the Latin type. The language is French in all parts, although there are small groups that also speak Flemish, Basque and Breton.

The Frenchman usually is thought to be quick-spoken, lively and gay; but this is not always true. The people of Paris are like this, more or less; but the country people are more likely to be quiet, serious, and rather slow. For the most part the French people live quiet lives; and they usually are hard-working. Most of them are members of the Roman Catholic Church. About a million are Protestants; and there are about seventy thousand Jews, mostly in the large cities. The gov-

The Chateau of Chenonceaux in the Loire Valley of France.

ernment allows people to belong to any church they please.

In their long and troubled history, the French have somehow found time to become among the most artistic of peoples. They love beautiful things and make many of them. They are proud of the fact that they "know how to live." Women everywhere look to Paris for the latest thing in beautiful new clothes. French cooking, French wines and French perfume are the finest to be found. During the last hundred years, France has led the world in the painting of pictures, and artists from every country go there to study their art.

HOW THE PEOPLE LIVE

About half the people of France earn their living by farming. In fact, about a third of them live in the country. Compared with farms in the United States, those in France are small, because they average only about 25 acres. Most of the farmers own their own land, which is good for the country because they take better care of the fields. These people live in rather small houses, sometimes with the livestock under the same roof. They do not often visit the large cities.

The most important crop is wheat, but the growing of grapes for wine also brings them a large part of their money. French farming is quite modern. The farmers use machinery and other ways of growing better crops. More of the farms of France have electricity than in the United States, but it is not often that a French farmer can have a car or send his children to college. Just the same, if you were to visit a French farmhouse or a small country village, you would find them pleasant places.

In the large cities, Paris especially, the people live a much different kind of life. The cities are much like those in the United States, except that everywhere you can see buildings that were put up in very olden times. The city people dress well and like sports, movies, and the theater. One of the most interesting sights to see in French cities is the sidewalk restaurants. People go there to sit in the open air, sip drinks, eat ice cream and watch the crowds passing by. Usually French cities are quieter than American cities.

The city people earn their living mostly by working in offices and factories. In the northeast part are the iron ore mines, among the world's richest. Also in this part are the coal beds. These together are only about one-twentieth the size of those in Illinois, but from them the French take three-fourths of the coal they need. The most important kind of factory work for the French is making cloth. They make wool, cotton, linen, and silk. The second-biggest kind of factory work is making things out of metal and glass.

Education is good everywhere in France; and students from all over the world go there to study. The Sorbonne, a part of the University of Paris, is especially well known. Many of the girls who go beyond grade school attend schools run by the Roman Catholic Church; but the boys usually are sent to the free government schools. Up to the universities, the boys and girls go to different schools. They usually have to study harder than students in the United States because they take hard subjects at an early age. Almost all Frenchmen can read and write.

WHAT KIND OF COUNTRY IT IS

Most of France is farther north than any part of the United States; but the weather is not especially cold. Water surrounds France on three sides to keep the land from cooling off fast; and the mountains shut out most of the cold winds. Along the Mediterranean in the south is the Riviera, sometimes called the *Cote d'Azur,* or "Blue Coast," where the weather is always warm and people from all over the world come to live and swim in the clear, clean water. In other parts the weather is colder, but not cold enough to make life difficult.

If you were to travel from Le Havre in the north to Marseilles in the south of France, you might think the country is fairly flat. That is because the mountains are mostly along the east and west borders. The Alps separate France from Switzerland; the Jura and the Vosges are in the east; and the Pyrenees divide the country from Spain. The highest mountain in Europe, Mont Blanc, is in the French Alps.

Frenchmen are fortunate to have many fine rivers in their country. These rivers make carrying goods cheap and easy. They also are used for power to make electricity. The best known of these rivers is the Seine, which flows from near Dijon north to the English Channel. The city of Paris is on the Seine. The longest French river is the Loire that flows more than 600 miles through the country. These mountains and rivers divide France into three main basins, or low places. Because the weather is somewhat different in these places, different crops grow in each. For this reason, France is able to grow a large part of almost every kind of food the people need. What comes into France is brought mostly to the ports of Le Havre, in the north; St. Nazaire, in the northeast; Bordeaux, in the southwest; and Marseilles, on the Mediterranean. Many tourists also come through these ports to visit France.

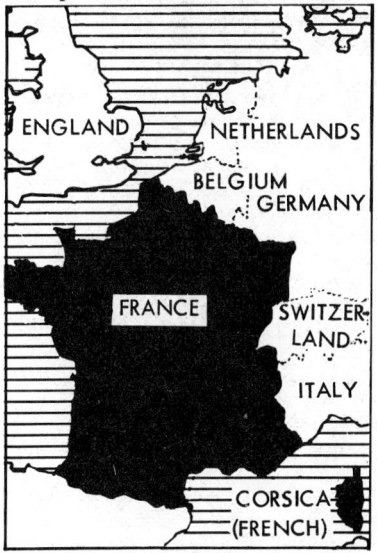

HOW FRANCE IS GOVERNED

France is a republic governed by a president, a cabinet, and a parliament. The constitution for the present or Fifth Republic (see page 2130) was adopted in 1958 and changed slightly in 1960. The president has the greatest power. He appoints the premier, who is executive head of the government. The premier selects the cabinet ministers, or heads of the government departments.

The French parliament, like the United States Congress, has two "houses": The National Assembly of about 580 members and the Senate of about 255 members. The parliament has less power than it once had. It cannot overrule the president's choice of a premier, and except in financial and some other important matters the cabinet (or, in emergencies, the president) can govern by decree — that is, by making their own laws. The premier and cabinet cannot vote in the parliament, making the French parliament different from others (see PARLIAMENT).

The president is elected for a seven-year term. Under the 1958 constitution the parliament and representatives of big cities and government departments elected the president. Charles de Gaulle was elected easily. In 1960 the constitution was changed so that all the people now voted to elect the president. In 1965, de Gaulle was elected for another seven years but not so easily. In French elections, a candidate wins if he receives a

majority of all the votes cast; if no candidate gets this majority, there is a second election in which the winner needs only to get more votes than any other candidate. De Gaulle did not receive a majority in the first election of 1965, although he had the largest vote. He won in the second election.

The president may send the parliament home and call for new elections, but not until the members of parliament have served for at least one year.

France is divided into 90 departments (which are somewhat like states of the United States, except that in France much more of the direct government is controlled by the government in the capital at Paris). These departments, and some other departments in French overseas territories, send representatives to the National Assembly. See FRENCH TERRITORIES.

FRANCE'S DEPARTMENTS

The leading cities in France, with 1975 estimates of the population are:

Paris, population 2,317,227, the capital, largest city in the country.

Marseilles, population 889,000, the second-largest city, commercial center and leading seaport, in the southeast, on the Mediterranean Sea.

Lyons, population 462,841, the third-largest city, manufacturing and commercial center, in the east central part.

Toulouse, population 439,764, the fourth-largest city, manufacturing center, in the south.

Nice, population 392,635, the fifth-largest city, seaport and health resort, in the southeast, on the Mediterranean Sea.

Bordeaux, population 270,996, the sixth-largest city, manufacturing center and seaport, in the southwest, on the Atlantic Ocean.

There are separate articles on all these cities.

FRANCE IN THE PAST

Men have lived in France from the earliest times known to scientists. From the village of Abbeville in the north of France to the Pyrenees mountains in the south, remains have been found of men who lived ten thousand and even as much as fifty thousand years ago. They made rough stone tools and hunted mammoths (a kind of elephant) and other animals that no longer exist.

About 2,500 years ago, the first civilized men reached France. They were sailors from the ancient country of Phoenicia, and they founded a colony (Massilia) where the great city of Marseilles now stands. Later the Greeks and then the Romans ruled this colony. Meanwhile a Celtic people, whom the Romans called Gauls, had settled in most of France.

When Rome ruled almost the entire civilized world, about two thousand years ago, the great Roman general Julius Caesar conquered the Gauls and the land of Gaul became one of the finest Roman possessions, with paved roads and fine cities. This lasted until Rome fell, about 1,500 years ago. Then a Germanic people called the Franks became rulers of the country and it is from them that modern France gets its name. At about this time (in the year 481) a king named Clovis, who today would be called Louis,

became the king of the Franks, and he united the different parts of France to form about the same country it is today.

Clovis and his descendants were called the Merovingian dynasty, or family of kings. Within two hundred years—that is, about the year 700—the Merovingian kings had become very weak. A family of men who governed the country for them, under the title major domo (which in Latin means "mayor of the palace"), became more powerful than the kings. The founder of this line was named Pepin. One of the famous members was Charles Martel ("Charles the Hammer"), who won the Battle of Tours in 732. This battle prevented Mohammedan invaders from conquering France, and so it saved much of Europe for Christianity.

This new family became the next kings of France. They were called Carolingians. By far their most famous member was Charlemagne, or Charles the Great, who in the year 800 was crowned emperor of what later was called the Holy Roman Empire. But France did not remain a member of the Holy Roman Empire. Gradually it grew into a single independent country, and in most periods of the next thousand years it was the richest and most powerful country in Europe.

This did not happen at once. After Charlemagne's death, France broke up into separate kingdoms and territories ruled by powerful noblemen. The descendants of Charlemagne also became weak kings. Finally, in the year 987, a nobleman named Hugh Capet became king and started a new line. His descendants were kings of France until the French Revolution of 1789, when France became a republic. Some of these kings were named Capet, and some had other family names—Valois and Bourbon—but all became kings because they were the closest living descendants of Hugh Capet.

FRANCE IN THE MIDDLE AGES

In the year 1066 one of the most powerful French noblemen, William, Duke of Normandy, became king of England. For hundreds of years after this, France and England were at war from time to time because the English kings claimed the right to rule parts of France. During this period France was not always a powerful nation. By the year 1429 the English had invaded important parts of France. In that year France's greatest heroine, Joan of Arc, led French armies to victory over the English and began a series of successes that made France a united, independent and strong nation. Burgundy, a part of France that had been almost a separate country, was brought under the control of the French king Louis XI in 1480, and in 1558 England's last claim to French territory ended.

Two great cardinals of the Roman Catholic Church, Richelieu and Mazarin, and two strong French kings, Louis XIII and Louis XIV, made France the greatest power in Europe during the 1600s. Louis XIV was so powerful that one of England's kings, James II, was almost controlled by him. (That was one of the reasons the English took the throne away from James.)

France was also the foremost European country in learning. The French Academy, a group of great French scholars, promoted science and literature. Great writers arose in France, the playwright Molière in the 1600s and Voltaire in the 1700s. This continued under the next kings, Louis XV and Louis XVI. But in many ways France had not advanced enough. The king and the noblemen still ruled the country, yet the prosperity of the country depended on the rich tradesmen and manufacturers of the thriving cities. The peasants, or poor farmers, were little more than slaves of the noblemen who owned the lands. France fought one war after another, and these cost many lives and more money than the country could afford. If the people had been stupid and uneducated they could have endured all this, but the French people included the best-educated and most enlightened men in all of Europe. They helped the American colonies win independence and become the United States, and with this example before them they could not let their own country continue as it had been. In 1789 the common people in the French parliament, or lawmaking body, took the power into their own hands. In 1793 they put the king, Louis XVI, to death and France became a republic, a country not ruled by a king.

The events of these times are told in the article on the FRENCH REVOLUTION. The revolutionists had succeeded, but they could not agree among themselves, and all of them were ambitious. While they fought for power, no one was safe. In the midst of the confusion a strong man arose, a general named Napoleon Bonaparte. In 1802 he was given complete control of France and in 1804 he became emperor of France.

FRANCE IN THE 1800s

Napoleon made France the greatest nation in Europe. He gave it new laws that are still followed in many European courts, and he gave the French people rights they had never had before. At the same time, he fought so many wars that France remained poor in the midst of its prosperity, and he tried so hard to unite Europe that Great Britain was afraid for its own safety and most of the kings of European countries were afraid they would lose their thrones. The British fought Napoleon constantly, and finally they united enough European allies to defeat him. In 1814 they exiled Napoleon and gave the throne of France back to a Bourbon king, Louis XVIII, a brother of Louis XVI. Napoleon escaped from exile in 1815 and for a brief period called the "Hundred Days" he threatened to regain his power, but he lost to the British and Germans at the Battle of Waterloo and was exiled again.

France had another revolution in 1830, in which it changed kings, and still another in 1848 in which it became a republic again. A nephew of Napoleon, Louis Bonaparte, became president of the new republic and in 1852 he made himself emperor as Napoleon III.

Once again France was prosperous and powerful; but it was not as powerful as the French people thought. The German kingdom of Prussia, which later was to become the principal part of the country

called Germany, was becoming the greatest power on the continent of Europe. In 1870 the French went to war against Prussia, expecting to win, and in this war, called the Franco-Prussian War, the Prussians won in a few months. France threw out Napoleon III and began a new republic, which it called the Third Republic, and which was very much like the French government of today. One effect of these years was that France and Great Britain, which had been enemies most of the time for hundreds of years, became friendly and have been allies ever since.

MODERN FRANCE

France recovered quickly from the loss of the war with Prussia. Its army officers wanted revenge against Prussia and built a powerful army. France became allied with Russia and Great Britain, other European nations that feared the growing strength of Germany. In World War I, from 1914 to 1918, France was badly hurt by Germany but was saved when the United States entered the war. In World War II France was conquered by Germany, but was again restored to freedom when the United States entered the war and helped to defeat Germany.

During World War II, from 1940 when France surrendered to Germany until 1944 when the Germans were driven out of most of France, there was a new French government. It was called the "Vichy government" because its capital was at the city of Vichy in central France. The Germans occupied northern France, including the capital city of Paris (that is, the Germans stationed an army there and governed that territory). The Vichy government was headed by Marshal Henri Philippe Petain, who had been a hero in World War I but sympathized with France's enemies in World War II; and by Pierre Laval, who had been a French premier before World War II and who also sympathized with France's enemies.

At the same time Frenchmen who remained loyal to their country were organized by an army general named Charles de Gaulle, who had escaped from France when the Germans invaded it. His forces were called the "Fighting French." They helped the allies to invade France in 1944 and drive the Germans out. De Gaulle headed the first French government after the war. In 1946 the French wrote a new constitution and formed the Fourth Republic. When the people elected a new government, General de Gaulle and his followers lost most of their power.

After World War II, France had great problems at home and abroad. Much of the country's wealth had been destroyed in the war. The great colonies of France in Africa and Asia were pressing for independence. France fought a long, expensive war to keep French Indo-China from being taken over by Communists, and by 1954 all the countries of Indo-China had become independent. Among France's North African possessions, Morocco and Tunisia demanded and received independence, while from 1956 to 1962 rebel guerrillas in Algeria fought almost a full-scale war for Algerian independence. This warfare also was very costly to France.

Under the French governmental system in those years, the government was conducted by a premier and cabinet that could retain their positions only if a majority of the parliament voted for them. In the French parliament there are about a dozen different political parties and none ever has a clear majority. Therefore each "government" (premier and cabinet) depended on a coalition, or temporary agreement, of several political parties. Whenever one or two parties became dissatisfied and withdrew from the coalition, the premier and cabinet would have to resign and there would be a period of confusion while efforts were made to form a new coalition. Between 1946 and 1958 France seldom had the same men at the head of the government for more than two or three months. Therefore no government ever had time to solve the important problems that face every nation's government.

Finally all the parties agreed to call back General de Gaulle, the war hero, as a "strong man" to solve the problems. In 1958 de Gaulle was appointed premier. He proposed a new constitution to give the government stability (lasting power). In September 1958, the new constitution was overwhelmingly accepted in France and its overseas territories. In 1959 de Gaulle was elected president and in the years that followed many of France's problems were solved. Many former colonies achieved independence; the war in Algeria was ended and Algeria became independent; and France became an atomic power in 1960. De Gaulle was re-elected president in 1965 and 1968, but resigned in 1969 when voters failed to approve new laws he wanted passed. Georges Pompidou then became France's new president. (De Gaulle died in 1970.)

See also the articles on FRENCH TERRITORIES and FRENCH COMMUNITY.

THE FRENCH GOVERNMENTS

In the history of France, the different periods are usually described by the following names:

Monarchy: 987 (Hugh Capet) to 1792 (execution of Louis XVI).

First Republic: 1792-1804. See FRENCH REVOLUTION.

First Empire: 1804-1814. See NAPOLEON.
Restoration: 1814-1848.
Second Republic: 1848-1852.
Second Empire: 1852-1871. See NAPOLEON III.

Third Republic: 1871-1940.
Vichy Government: 1940-1944.
Fourth Republic: 1945-1958 (constitution of 1946).
Fifth Republic: From October 1958.

FRANCE. Area, 212,736 square miles. Population (1973 estimate), 51,500,000. Language, French. Religion, Roman Catholic. Government, republic. Monetary unit, the franc, worth about 18 cents (U.S.). Flag, three wide vertical stripes, blue, white, and red.

France, Anatole

French Embassy Press

Anatole France was the name that one of the best French writers signed to his books. His real name was Jacques-Anatole Thibault, and his father was a bookseller. France was born in Paris in 1844. He wrote many short stories and books in which he made fun of some of the stupid things people do. He became very famous because he was wise and because he used words beautifully in his books. Among his best books are *The Crime of Sylvester Bonnard* and *Penguin Island.* Three years before France died, in 1921, he won the Nobel Prize in literature, one of the greatest honors given to writers. Even after France died, in 1924, other writers tried to copy his way of writing.

Francesca da Rimini

Francesca da Rimini is the heroine of one of the saddest of all love stories. She was an Italian girl who lived about seven hundred years ago. Her father forced her to marry a man she had never seen. Once married, she discovered that she loved her husband's brother, Paolo. When her husband discovered that she really loved his brother instead of him, he became very angry and killed both of them.

The story of Francesca and Paolo has became known throughout the world because it was told so beautifully in the *Divine Comedy* by Dante, the greatest poet of Italy. Many other writers have used the story, and Tschaikowsky composed a famous piece of music about it.

franchise

The franchise is the right to vote. Everyone who has the right to vote is said to hold the franchise. In the United States, there are two kinds of rules that determine who has the right to vote. One kind is the federal rule that applies to the whole country and is part of the Constitution of the United States. The Constitution says that no one can be deprived of the franchise, that is, kept from voting, because of color or race or sex. The other kind of rule about voting is the state law. Each state has certain laws that determine who is allowed to vote. These laws state such things as the age at which people may be allowed to vote, and the length of time people must live in the state before they can vote.

The word franchise also means a special privilege that the government gives to some person or company to do some special kind of work. For instance, to start a new railroad, or run a ferry across a river, or build a gas company, you would first have to get a franchise from the government. The franchise would give you the privilege of running your railroad, or ferry, or gas company.

Francis, Saint (of Assisi)

Francis of Assisi was a very good man who lived in Italy about eight hundred years ago. He was made a saint by the Roman Catholic Church because of his love for God and the help he gave to

poor people. Francis also had a great love for all living things. One time he even preached a sermon to a flock of birds. He got his name from Assisi, the name of the town where he was born in 1181 or 1182. Francis started a group called the Franciscans. They all lived in poverty and helped others, as Francis did; and there are still many groups of Franciscans. Francis also wrote some poems and stories that were made into a book called *The Little Flowers of Saint Francis*.

Francis was the son of a rich man, and as a boy he did nothing but have a good time. Then he became a soldier, but he got sick and had to come home. He was very unhappy after that; and he changed his way of life. Instead of always playing, he went to the mountains and prayed. When Francis came back, he began to give away his money to poor people. His father was afraid Francis would give all the family money away, so he took his son to court, hoping that would stop him. Francis took off all his clothes and gave them away, and then borrowed a coat to wear. He wanted to show his father he liked to be poor.

Again Francis went to the mountains. There he was joined by twelve men who wanted to live like him. This was the first group of Franciscans. After that Francis traveled in Spain and Africa. But he liked better to stay home preaching to the birds and writing little poems. Two years before his death, Francis went back to the mountains alone. He ate very little for forty days; and it is said that he saw an angel. There is a story that marks, called *stigmata*, appeared on his hands and feet like those on Jesus Christ when he died on the cross. Francis was carried back to Assisi, where he died in 1226.

Francis, Saint (Xavier)

Francis Xavier was a great Spanish religious leader and teacher who lived about four hundred years ago. Xavier came from a noble family, and when he grew up, he went to Paris and became a Catholic priest. He became a Jesuit (a member of the Society of Jesus) and a missionary. Xavier then traveled thousands of miles through India and the East, and he preached about Jesus to the people he met. He was so sincere and had so much common sense that the people believed him. Xavier converted more than a million people to Christianity, and he set up many missionaries in backward places so that other people would have a chance to become Christians. Xavier has been called the "Apostle of the Indies," because he did so much to bring religion to people.

Francis Xavier died in 1552, when he was on his way to China. He was 46 years old. During his lifetime many people believed that Xavier could perform miracles, and after he died he was made a Saint by the Pope, the religious leader of the Catholic people. Now there are many churches named after Saint Francis Xavier, and people all over the world love and honor him.

Francis, King of France

Francis was the name of two kings of France. Francis I became king in 1515, and he has been called the Father of Letters because he did a great deal to encourage the French people to be more inter-

French Embassy Press

ested in books. During the time he was king, France had many wars. Francis was planning to make war against Spain, and he wanted to get Henry VIII, King of England, to help him. When these two kings met, both the English and the French were dressed so splendidly that the place of their meeting has been called the FIELD OF THE CLOTH OF GOLD. You can read about this in a separate article. Henry VIII refused to help Francis, and so the French had to fight the Spanish alone. For twenty years Spain and France fought each other many times.

Francis II was born in 1543. He was the grandson of Francis I. Francis II became king when he was only sixteen years old. He was married to Mary Stuart, who later became MARY, Queen of Scots. You can read about her in a separate article. Because Francis was so young, Mary Stuart's uncles wanted to help him rule. Some French people did not like this, and they made a plot to kill the king's advisers. The plot was discovered, and many of the plotters were executed. Francis II ruled for one year and died in 1560, when he was 17 years old.

Francis Joseph, Emperor of Austria and King of Hungary: see FRANZ JOSEF.

Franciscans

The Franciscans are Roman Catholic men and women, who have devoted themselves to a very strict religious life. The men are called monks, and they live in monasteries. The women are called Poor Clares, and they are nuns and live in convents. The Franciscans were founded by St. Francis of Assisi more than seven hundred years ago. (You can read about ST. FRANCIS OF ASSISI in a separate article.) Many people joined, and within ten years they numbered about two hundred thousand.

The Franciscans lived very simple, humble lives. They did not want to have any things for themselves. They ate only the simplest food and wore a plain brown garment and went barefoot. They did not use money or have any comforts, but devoted all of their time to people who were sick and unfortunate. The Franciscans were very much interested in books and art and beauty. Their teachings about love and gentleness had an effect on many great painters. After St. Francis died, the Franciscans disagreed about whether it was right for them to own any property, even the monasteries in which they lived. Although the Franciscans split up into different groups, the movement continued to grow, and now there are members of this great religious group in many parts of the world.

Franck, César

César Franck was a Belgian-French composer, or writer of music, who lived about a hundred years ago. He was born

Belgian Consulate General

in 1822 in Belgium. He studied music at schools in Belgium and France, and took many prizes for his piano and organ playing, and for composition. In 1872 Franck became professor of organ at the Paris Conservatory, or school of music, and he held this post for the rest of his life.

Franck wrote many different kinds of music, but in almost all his works the organ is an important instrument. He is best remembered for his *Symphony in D Minor*, the oratorio *Redemption*, and the piece for piano and orchestra called *Symphonic Variations*. A symphony is music for a large orchestra; an oratorio is a sacred story sung by a chorus and soloists and played by an orchestra. Franck died in 1890, when he was 68 years old.

Franco, Francisco

Generalissimo Francisco Franco became head of the government of Spain after the Spanish Civil War, which began in 1936 and ended in 1939. Generalissimo means "*chief general.*" Franco is also called *el Caudillo,* which in Spanish means "the leader."

Franco was born in 1892. He became an officer in the Spanish army. Until 1931 Spain had been ruled by kings, but in 1931 the Spanish people forced their king to abdicate (give up the throne) and established a republican government. Franco, like most of the army officers, continued in the army under the new government. By 1935 Franco had become chief of staff of the Spanish army.

In 1936, a group of army officers decided to overthrow the government and started a civil war, leading most of the troops they commanded. They were called the Insurgents. At first General José Sanjuro commanded the Insurgents, but he was killed in an airplane crash in 1936. Franco, as the next-highest-ranking officer, took his place. Franco's forces won the war, but they accepted help from the fascist governments of Italy and Germany, which were enemies of democratic countries, and after winning the war Franco set up a fascist government in Spain. Only one political party was permitted, the Falange, with Franco as its leader.

During World War II Franco remained friendly to Italy and Germany, and helped them in many ways, but did not take Spain into the war. The governments of the Allied countries, which won World War II, remained unfriendly to Franco's government for several years after the war, but in the 1950s they became more friendly.

Francisco Franco has been generally recognized as a man of personal charm and great ability, and after World War II he made many efforts to win back the friendship of the democratic countries.

Franconia

More than a thousand years ago,

Franconia was a duchy in the central part of Germany. A duchy is a place ruled by a nobleman called a duke. Many of the famous old cities of Germany, including Frankfurt, Mainz, and Worms, were in this duchy. Franconia was the most important part of Germany. It was divided into two sections, West Franconia and East Franconia.

Beginning about seven hundred years ago, Franconia was gradually divided among other German states. It is now part of West Germany.

Franco-Prussian War

The Franco-Prussian War was one of the most important wars of the 19th century. Prussia was the biggest state in Germany, and by winning the war it became powerful enough to unite all of Germany, forming the German Empire with the King of Prussia as emperor.

In 1870 Count Otto von Bismarck, the chancellor (which is like a prime minister) of Prussia, wanted to start a war with France, so he cleverly made it seem as if the French ambassador had been insulted by the king of Prussia. When the French people heard about this they were furious. On July 19, 1870, France declared war. But the Prussian army was prepared, while the French army was not. The Prussian forces quickly invaded France and won several battles. They surrounded one French army in the city of Metz in eastern France. Another French army tried to come to its rescue, but it was trapped in the town of Sedan, near the border of Belgium. At this battle the French emperor, Napoleon III, was captured by the Prussians.

SIEGE OF PARIS

Even though their armies had been beaten, the French people kept fighting with whatever weapons they could find. The Prussians surrounded the French capital of Paris, and tried to starve out the people so that they would surrender.

Finally the people of Paris had to give in, and the Prussians entered Paris at the end of January. A peace treaty was signed at Frankfurt, Germany, in May 1871. The Prussians took the provinces of Alsace and Lorraine away from France, and they made the French pay them five billion francs. Napoleon abdicated (resigned as emperor) and France became a republic.

The harsh terms of peace made the French hate the Germans. This hatred continued up to World War I, which broke out forty years later. About 28,000 Prussians and 156,000 Frenchmen were killed in the Franco-Prussian War.

Frankenstein

Frankenstein is the name of a book written by Mary Shelley in 1818. In it Frankenstein, a nobleman, discovers how to make parts of dead people come to life. He puts together a monster that looks like a man; and it comes to life. The monster is very strong and is able to escape from the place where Frankenstein keeps it. Finally, it grows lonely and begins to kill everyone Frankenstein loves. Frankenstein dies near the end of the book and the monster is lost in the Far North where it is very cold. Many

people who have not read the story make the mistake of calling the monster Frankenstein, instead of its maker.

Frankfort

Frankfort is a city, the capital of the state of Kentucky. It is in the northern part of the state, on the Kentucky River. Frankfort was first settled in 1779 by pioneers who traveled westward from the Atlantic states into the wild country beyond the frontier. There are many historical sights in Frankfort. One of them is the grave of Daniel Boone, the great pioneer who helped open the western United States to settlers. Another is a building called Liberty Hall, which was built in 1796 and was probably designed by Thomas Jefferson, who wrote the Declaration of Independence and was the third President of the United States.

Frankfort is a trading center for farm products, and for limestone (which is used in making cement and other building materials). About 21,300 people live there. Many of the people work in shoe factories and in factories where twine is made. Others work in plants where whiskey is made.

The first Capitol building in Frankfort was built in 1827. It is still standing, but it is no longer used. The new Capitol was built in 1909.

FRANKFORT, KENTUCKY. Population (1970 census) 21,356. Capital of Kentucky. County seat of Franklin County. On the Kentucky River. Settled in 1779.

Frankfurt

Frankfurt is the name of two cities in Germany. They are called Frankfurt-on-Main and Frankfurt-on-Oder, because one is on the Main River and the other is on the Oder River.

Frankfurt-on-Main is in West Germany. About 661,800 people live there, about the same number as live in Dallas, Texas. It is a river port and rail-

This tower in Frankfurt-on-Main, Germany, is a famous landmark. It was one of the old gates of the city hundreds of years ago.

road center. Many of the people work in factories that make chemicals, drugs, machinery and clothing. The city was founded almost two thousand years ago. In one of its libraries are the first two Gutenberg Bibles, the first books printed

with movable type. They are more than 500 years old. Frankfurt-on-Main is an important trading, banking, and insurance center. Until 1866 it was a "free city," that is, its government was not under the government of any state in Germany. Then, in the year 1866, Frankfurt-on-Main sided with Austria in a war against the German state of Prussia. Austria was defeated and Frankfurt-on-Main was forced to become part of Prussia. Many of the beautiful old buildings in Frankfurt-on-Main were destroyed by bombs in World War II. After the war, the city became an important headquarters for American soldiers who were sent to occupy Germany.

Frankfurt-on-Oder is a much smaller city. About 57,669 people live there. It is in East Germany, near the city of Berlin. It is also a port and a center for trade. Many of the people work in factories that make machinery, cloth, and foods, especially the kind of sausage called the frankfurter. Three times a year the city holds fairs at which corn, cattle and wine are bought and sold.

frankfurter, a small sausage that is made from either beef, pork, or both beef and pork, and is usually eaten on a roll: see the article on SAUSAGE.

frankincense

Frankincense is a substance that gives off a very sweet odor when it is burned. Because of its sweet odor, it was used as incense in the religious ceremonies of many ancient peoples. Frankincense is a gum resin, that is, a gummy substance that comes from the juices of plants. Frankincense comes from certain trees that are found mainly in East Africa. In ancient times, it was used in many medicines, but today it is not considered useful for that purpose. The name frankincense is most familiar to us today because it was one of the gifts brought by the Wise Men of the East, when they went to worship the infant Jesus.

franking privilege

The franking privilege is the right of sending mail without paying the postage. At one time, many people in the United States had this right, which was given them by laws made by Congress. Many times Congress passed special acts to give the franking privilege to the widows of ex-presidents. Today the laws give Congressmen and other government officials the franking privileges. They may send official letters and papers, things published by the government, seeds given away by the government, and other things, through the mails free.

Franklin, a name first given to the state of Tennessee. See TENNESSEE.

Franklin, Benjamin

Benjamin Franklin was a great American of two hundred years ago. He was one of the men who did the most to make the United States a free and independent country. He was the oldest of the patriots who were called the Founding Fathers. Because he was considered to be the wisest American of his time, and

Historical Society of Pennsylvania
This picture shows the mature Franklin, a famous and respected man in America and Europe.

ing. Finally he opened his own printing shop and started a newspaper.

The name of Franklin's newspaper was the *Pennsylvania Gazette.* People liked it because of Franklin's humorous articles. Franklin also printed an almanac which he called *Poor Richard's Almanack.* It was filled with the wise sayings of Poor Richard, an imaginary person. People bought many copies of the almanac. This, besides hard work and saving, made Franklin rich. When he was only 42, he left business and spent the rest of his life working for his country. He was an agent for the Colony of Pennsylvania in England for fifteen years, and later he was elected to the Continental Congress.

HOW HE HELPED HIS COUNTRY

In 1776, the year the Declaration of Independence was signed and the Colonies began calling themselves the United States of America, Franklin went to France on a government mission. There he helped to make an agreement with France which caused the French to send their fleet to help the Americans fight England for their freedom. He also got the French to lend money to the United States. Franklin was able to obtain all this from the French partly because they liked him and thought he was very wise and humorous. The ladies of the French king's court liked him and often invited him to their homes for dinner. He became so popular that his picture was put on pieces of jewelry and snuffboxes.

After the American Colonies won their freedom from England, Franklin came back home to Philadelphia. There he took part in the most important work of his life when he helped to write the Constitution of the United States. It was hard work, because the men from the different states could not agree on how the government should be set up. Franklin's good humor and clear thoughts were very helpful in getting everyone to agree; and after four months the work was done. Our Constitution contains many of Franklin's ideas.

HIS INVENTIONS AND WRITINGS

Some of the things we use today were invented by Franklin. He got the idea for the lightning rod, and no one ever has found a better way of protecting houses from lightning. Franklin also invented a kind of stove for heating a room. The Franklin stove still can be found in places where people use stoves.

Bifocal eyeglasses also are one of Franklin's inventions. These look much like ordinary glasses, except that the upper and lower part of each lens is ground differently for seeing things close or far away. He founded the first library that would lend books for people to take home; and he organized the first city fire department and the first city street-cleaning department. The idea of paving the streets of Philadelphia and having them lighted and policed also was Franklin's. He thought education was important and helped to establish the first academy in Philadelphia.

The signature of Benjamin Franklin appears on all four of the most important papers that helped the American

one of the wisest men in the world, the other patriots looked to him for advice in everything they did. The new country that was to become the United States relied on him to conduct matters with European countries because he was so respected.

Franklin was the best American writer before Ralph Waldo Emerson. Most of the information about him comes from his *Autobiography,* the book in which he told the story of his own life. He also had great skill and knowledge in science, and he invented some things that we still use.

Franklin was born in Boston in 1706. His father made candles and did not earn very much. There were 16 other children in the family, and this made things harder. When Franklin was 8 years old, his father sent him to school, planning to have him learn to be a minister. But when Franklin's father thought about how much it would cost to send Benjamin to college, he decided the boy should go to a school where he would learn writing and arithmetic only. When Franklin was 10, he left school to help his father. He did not like cutting candle-wicks and running errands. He much preferred to read, and so his father decided he would make a good printer.

At that time Franklin's half-brother, James, had a printing shop, and there young Benjamin went to work. He had a chance to borrow some books while he was learning to be a printer, so he read even more. To get money for buying books he asked his brother to give him half the amount he spent for Benjamin's food. In return for the money, Benjamin promised to eat no meat. With the books he bought Franklin taught himself grammar and arithmetic. He also studied hard to learn how to write well. After a while he began to write articles for his brother's newspaper, the *New England Courant.*

Franklin did not sign his real name to the things he wrote. Instead, he signed the name, "Mrs. Silence Dogood," and slipped them under the door of his brother's shop at night. When the articles were printed in the newspaper, people liked them very much. In spite of this, Franklin kept his secret for several months. Then town officials told Franklin's brother he could not publish the newspaper any more, so the name of Benjamin Franklin appeared as the editor. To do this Franklin's brother had to say that Benjamin no longer worked for him. He wanted to make a secret agreement, though, that would force Benjamin to go on working in the shop. Benjamin refused and left.

HIS LIFE IN PHILADELPHIA

Franklin tried to find work in other printing shops in Boston, but no one would hire him. They had been told by his brother not to give him work. Franklin decided to go to Philadelphia. So, at the age of 17, he arrived in the strange city with very little money. There is a story that Franklin was hungry when he reached Philadelphia and went into a bakery to buy three pennies' worth of bread. He was given three big loaves. With one under each arm and eating the third, he walked down the street. A girl named Deborah Reed thought he looked funny and laughted at him. Franklin remembered her, and seven years later they were married.

The young man soon found work in a printing shop in Philadelphia. The governor of the province (an area a little bigger than a county) advised Franklin to start his own business and promised to lend him the money. To buy printing presses and other machines, Franklin sailed for England. But the money the governor had promised never arrived, so again Franklin was penniless in a strange place. He did find work, though, as a printer; and after a year and a half he returned to Philadelphia. There he took a job as a clerk. When his employer died, Franklin went back to print-

Colonies become the United States. These are the Declaration of Independence, the Treaty of Alliance with France, the Constitution of the United States, and the Treaty of Peace with England. He helped to write or correct all of them. His best-known writings, however, are the Poor Richard sayings, his papers about his scientific experiments, and his *Autobiography,* the story of his life. This is a wise and witty book that is still much read. Franklin died in 1790, at the age of 84 years, about a year after the Constitution was signed.

Franklin, Sir John

Sir John Franklin was an English explorer and a rear admiral in the British Navy. He tried to find the Northwest Passage. This is the route for ships to go from the Atlantic Ocean to the Pacific Ocean, along the northwest coast of North America. Franklin was born in 1786. After he had shown great courage in battles at sea and on exploring trips, the British government gave him command of two ships and asked him to find a northwest passage. He set sail more than a hundred years ago, in 1845, but he and the ships never returned. Later it was found that he had discovered the right route but his ships had been stopped by blocks of ice. He and his crew died, in 1847, of cold and starvation.

Franks

The Franks were the German-speaking tribes that the Romans found living in what is now eastern France and western Germany. The Franks were completely defeated by the Roman emperor, Julian, and were forced to pay tribute to Rome, and even to supply its armies with soldiers. Frankish soldiers fought alongside the Romans in the defeat of Attila, the Hun.

Although all the tribes of Franks spoke the same language, each tribe had its own customs and ruled itself. The Franks were famous as warriors, being very tall, strong, and fierce-looking. Their appearance must have been very frightening. Their hair was generally blond or red, and they wore it long, combing it so that it fell across their foreheads instead of hanging down their backs. They shaved their faces, except for their bristling mustaches. They wore short, tight trousers, and around their waists were leather belts with heavy iron buckles, from which hung one of their famous weapons, the single-edged ax which could be thrown like a tomahawk. They also used iron lances, bows and arrows, and protected themselves in battle with large, wooden shields. The reason we know so much about their weapons is that they buried their dead warriors in their arms and armor.

France takes its name from the tribes of Franks. Clovis, king of one of the tribes, became a Christian in the fifth century. He was helped by the Church to form a united state by conquering the other tribes of Franks and making them Christians. The state founded by Clovis was the beginning of what is now France.

Franz Ferdinand

Franz Ferdinand, or Francis Ferdinand, was an Austrian archduke (prince) who was assassinated in 1914. At that time he was heir to the throne of Austria-Hungary. He was born in 1863. His death caused the outbreak of World War I.

In 1914, Austria-Hungary controlled a large territory in which lived Slavic people related to the Serbs. These people wanted to be independent. On June 28, 1914, Franz Ferdinand and his wife visited Sarajevo, a city now in Yugoslavia but then ruled by Austria. A young Slav named Gavrilo Princip shot and killed both of them as a protest against Austrian rule. Austria-Hungary blamed Serbia, Russia defended Serbia, other nations joined in, and the war began.

Franz Josef Land

Franz Josef Land is a group of about 85 islands between the North Pole and the north of Russia, east of the islands of Spitsbergen. There is no land between Franz Joseph Land and the North Pole. It was first explored by the Austrians, who named it for their emperor, Franz Josef. Later, an English expedition went to Franz Josef Land, hoping to use it as a base from which to travel to the North Pole. Finally Fridtjof Nansen, a great Scandinavian explorer, proved that there is no land connection between Franz Josef Land and the North Pole.

Franz Josef

Franz Josef was the emperor of Austria and king of Hungary for 68 years, from 1848 until 1916. He was the last real emperor who belonged to the Hapsburg family, which once ruled a large part of Europe. He was a kindly man, much loved by those who knew him, and under him the people enjoyed great prosperity. Vienna, the capital city of the empire, was a center of culture and beauty. Franz Josef had much sadness in his family life; his son committed suicide, and other members of his family died tragic deaths while they were still young. Although Franz Josef was emperor of Austria-Hungary during World War I, in which Austria-Hungary fought against the United States and other Allies, most people do not blame him for the war but blame ambitious politicians in his government. Franz Josef was born in 1830. When he died in 1916, Charles I became emperor but he was forced to abdicate, or give up his throne, two years later when the Allies won the war. See AUSTRIA-HUNGARY.

Gale Research Co.

Fraser River

The Fraser River is the main river of British Columbia, which is the most westerly province of Canada. The Fraser River is more than seven hundred miles long. It rises on the west side of the Rocky Mountains, in eastern British Columbia, flows northwest for about 350 miles to the center of the province, and then flows southwest to the Strait of Georgia, which empties into the Pacific Ocean. Ships can travel up the Fraser River for about eighty miles from its mouth. From that point on the river is too wild for navigation, with its many waterfalls and dangerous currents.

fraternities and sororities

Fraternities and sororities are clubs of college students. A fraternity, which means a brotherhood, is a club for men. A sorority, which means a sisterhood, is a club for women. They are called Greek-letter societies because their names are made up of the beginning letters of several words in the Greek language. These words are a secret motto or phrase whose meaning is known only to the members. One such fraternity is called Sigma Alpha Epsilon. These are Greek letters that are the same as S, A, and E in English. This name shows that the words of its secret motto begin with the letters S, A, and E. Sometimes fraternities and sororities are called *Hellenic,* which means Greek.

The original purpose of fraternities and sororities was to provide food and lodging for their members. Each one had its own house, where the members lived together and shared the expenses. Many colleges have a "fraternity row," that is, a street where most of the fraternity houses are. The fraternity house is a center for social activities, such as dances and parties for the members and their friends. The members are "brothers" or "sisters" for life. Members who are no longer at college often stay at their fraternity or sorority house when they go back to visit the college.

RUSHING AND PLEDGING

At the beginning of each school year, the fraternities and sororities choose new members from the new students. There are parties and meetings at the house and new students are invited so the members can meet them. This is called "rushing." Then the old members decide which students they want as new members. If those students want to join, they are "pledged," or become "pledges." For a time the pledges have to learn a number of things, such as the rules of the fraternity. Then they are "initiated," which means they learn the secret mottoes of the club. Fraternities used to make "hazing" a part of initiation. This means that the people to be initiated had to do everything the old members told them to do, and often were beaten or had cruel tricks played on them. Very few clubs still do this. After initiation the new member may wear the club's pin. Each fraternity and sorority has a special pin on which is written its Greek letters and other secret signs. When a fraternity member gives his pin to a girl, it is called "pinning." This means that the couple is "engaged to be engaged," or are "going together."

Some fraternities are local. This means they are not connected with other fraternities of the same name at other schools. Other fraternities are chapters. This means that each is a branch of a national fraternity that has other branches at many different schools. The members pay a certain fee, or membership dues, to their chapter, and the chapters must give a certain part of these dues to the national organization. The national fraternity usually puts out a magazine, and keeps records of all the members of its branches.

There are also honorary and professional fraternities. The most famous honorary fraternity is PHI BETA KAPPA, about which you can read in a separate article. The members of an honorary fraternity are chosen because they do very well in their studies and also take part in school activities, such as working on the school newspaper or playing on an athletic team. Professional fraternities are clubs for people in special professions, such as doctors and lawyers and engineers. They help their members to learn about what is happening in their field in different parts of the country and of the world.

fraud

Fraud is the crime of getting a person to give up money or property by making him think something is true when in fact it is not. There are many ways of defrauding people. Some criminals who practice fraud are called *confidence men*. Sometimes they pretend to be important businessmen. Sometimes they even admit that they are criminals. They tell a person that they have an important business deal, or perhaps that they are going to defraud someone else and will share the money they make with him. They may use gambling games or stock-market trading, and persuade people to risk their money in the hope of making large profits. A criminal called a *swindler* sells things such as a stock, or merchandise, by saying it has great value when actually it has no value at all. Almost anything that is done to obtain money dishonestly, except stealing, is said to be fraudulent.

Fraunces Tavern

Fraunces Tavern is a very famous building in New York City. It was built in 1719 as a home. Then in 1762 a tavern keeper named Samuel Fraunces bought it and opened a restaurant called the "Queen's Head Tavern." This tavern was the headquarters for General Washington's troops during part of the American Revolution. It was in Fraunces Tavern that General Washington made his famous farewell speech to his officers on December 4, 1783. At that time the American Revolution was over, the new country had won its freedom, and Washington, the great general who had led his countrymen in battle, retired from public life to become a private citizen again. Fraunces Tavern fell into disrepair after that, but it was rebuilt and restored, and today the building stands just as it did in Washington's time. There is a restaurant on the first floor of the building.

Frazer, Sir James George

Sir James George Frazer was a Scottish author and scholar. He studied the habits and customs of primitive people. The study of primitive people is part of the science called anthropology. (There is a separate article on ANTHROPOLOGY.) Frazer was born in Glasgow in 1854. His most famous book is *The Golden Bough,* which is a study of religious and magical beliefs among different peoples of the world. He was knighted by King George V of England in 1914 for his important work. Frazer died in 1941.

freckles

The color in our skin comes from a material called pigment. Sometimes large amounts of pigment form right under the skin and appear on the skin in the form of little brown dots. These dots are called freckles. Freckles are usually found on the face and the hands, which are the parts of the skin that are most constantly exposed to the air and the sun. The pigment deposits that show up as freckles are often caused by exposure to the sun. Many people who have no freckles at all during the winter months become very freckled during the summer, when the sunlight is strong. People with fair complexions have freckles more often than darker people. That is because any excess of pigment shows up more on fair skin than it does on dark skin, and fair skin is more sensitive to the sun than dark skin is. Freckles can also be inherited, and parents with freckles very often have children with freckles.

Frederick, Maryland

Frederick is a city in the state of Maryland. About 21,000 people live there. It is best known because of Barbara FRIETCHIE, about whom there is a separate article. Francis Scott Key, the author of "The Star Spangled Banner," was born in Frederick.

Frederick Barbarossa

There were three emperors of the Holy Roman Empire named Frederick. The most famous was Frederick I, who lived about eight hundred years ago. He was called Frederick Barbarossa, which means "Frederick with the red beard." He was born in the year 1123 and became emperor in 1152. He fought against the Pope, the leader of the Roman Catholic Church, but finally gave in and recognized the spiritual leadership of Pope Alexander III. After that, Frederick was made leader of the Third Crusade, a military campaign to drive the Mohammedans from the Holy Land, but he died during the Crusade, in 1190. See HOLY ROMAN EMPIRE and CRUSADE.

Frederick, King of Prussia

Prussia, a German country that was once a powerful independent kingdom, had three kings named Frederick. The most famous of them, Frederick II, was called "Frederick the Great." The last, Frederick III, was also German emperor, but his reign lasted only three months. All the Fredericks were members of the HOHENZOLLERN family, about which there is a separate article.

Frederick I was born about three hundred years ago, in 1657. Under him, Prussia was first recognized as a kingdom, so he was the first king of Prussia and the first Hohenzollern to be a king. He died in 1713.

Frederick II, "the Great," was born in 1712 and was king from 1740 to his death in 1786. He was very skillful in dealings with other countries, and he trained the Prussian army so well that it was considered the best small army in Europe. He was a wise ruler who took away some of the power of the noblemen and gave the common people greater rights and more freedom than they had

in other European countries. He had foreseen the danger of a revolution such as the French Revolution, which began in 1789, three years after his death. The changes made by Frederick the Great prevented any such revolution in Germany. Like his grandfather, Frederick I, Frederick the Great encouraged the arts. He helped the great French writer, Voltaire, who was his guest for years.

Frederick III was born in 1831 and died in 1888. During his lifetime Germany became an empire and Frederick's father, William I, was the first German emperor. When William I died, in 1888, Frederick became king and emperor but he was already dying of cancer and ninety-nine days later he died. His son, William II, was "the Kaiser" against whom the United States fought in World War I.

Fredericksburg, Virginia

Fredericksburg is a city in the state of Virginia. About 13,000 people live there. It is remembered because a terrible battle was fought there during the Civil War, almost a hundred years ago, in the year 1862. A Southern army under General Robert E. Lee defeated a Northern army under General Ambrose Burnside. Almost 18,000 soldiers from both sides were killed.

Frederick William

Frederick William was the name of four different kings of Prussia, which is part of what is now Germany. Frederick William I was born more than 250 years ago, in 1688. He built a strong army for Prussia. He died in 1740.

Frederick William II was born in 1744 and died in 1797. He became king in 1786. He conquered parts of Poland and added them to Prussia.

Frederick William III was born in 1770 and died in 1840. He lost a great battle against the French emperor Napoleon—the battle of Jena in 1806. He was a weak king and he let Napoleon control Prussia, instead of controlling it himself.

Frederick William IV, born in 1795, became king in 1840. During his reign (in 1848) the people had a revolution and forced Frederick William to give them more rights. He died in 1861.

Freedmen's Bureau

At the end of the Civil War, in 1865, in the southern states of the United States there were several million Negroes who had been slaves, and who had suddenly become free men. Most of them did not know how to read and write, and knew only how to work in the fields. To help them, the United States government set up the Freedmen's Bureau as part of the War Department. This Bureau provided teachers to educate the Negroes, doctors to cure their illnesses, lawyers to advise them, and so on. The Freedmen's Bureau continued until 1872.

freedom

Freedom is the right of a person to do what he pleases, as long as he does not hurt anyone else. Therefore, freedom is the opposite of slavery. For thousands of years men were divided into two classes, free men and slaves. Gradually over the past thousand years, slavery was eliminated over almost the entire world,

and the word freedom took on new meanings. In 1941, before the United States had entered World War II, President Franklin D. Roosevelt made a speech to Congress explaining why help should be given to the countries of Europe that were already fighting the Germans. He named Four Freedoms which he said free men everywhere should be able to enjoy: freedom of speech, freedom of worship, freedom from want, and freedom from fear. You can read more about these in the article FOUR FREEDOMS. Most people agree that these freedoms are important, but freedom means even more than that. It means the right to leave something you do not like, freedom to quit a job, or freedom to leave a country if you do not like the way it is being run. This is one of the big differences between the beliefs of a democracy and the beliefs of a Communist country. The Communists say that their people are free because they have job security, that is, they cannot lose their jobs. We think of them as in a kind of slavery because they cannot quit their jobs. In Communist countries a person can be imprisoned for not showing up on his job; he can be shot if he tries to leave the country without permission. One can get that kind of freedom and job security by being sentenced to a life term in prison. He would be guaranteed a job, and he could not leave.

See also the article BILL OF RIGHTS.

freedom of the air

Freedom of the air is the name given to a rule made for radio and television programs in the United States. It means that when one political party or other group states its views over radio or television, its opponents must be given or sold the same amount of time to state its own views. Usually broadcasting companies do this voluntarily—that is, without being forced to. If there are any disputes about this, they are settled by the FEDERAL COMMUNICATIONS COMMISSION, about which there is a separate article.

freedom of the seas

Freedom of the seas is the right of a ship of any country to sail anywhere on the oceans, except inside another country's territorial waters, sometimes called the three-mile limit. The three-mile limit means the waters within three miles (and sometimes up to twelve miles) of any country's coast. To sail inside this limit, the captain must have the country's permission. Other parts of the ocean are the "high seas" and any ship is free to sail on them.

The United States and Great Britain are two countries that have always been willing to fight so that their ships might have freedom of the seas. Once, during the War of 1812, the United States fought against Great Britain because British ships were interfering with American ships on the high seas. Almost fifty years ago, in 1917, the United States went to war against Germany because German submarines were attacking American ships. Nearly every country believes in the right of freedom of the seas, but nearly every country violates it in time

of war. Read also the article on BLOCKADE.

free enterprise

The free enterprise system is the system in which the management of every business can run its business as it pleases, without interference from the government. This is the system under which business is operated in the United States and other English-speaking countries, and in most democracies.

About two hundred years ago, a Scottish thinker named Adam Smith wrote a famous book called *The Wealth of Nations*. Governments in those days had a great deal to say about how businesses should be run. The governments helped certain industries and hindered others. These governments wanted gold more than anything else, so they tried to get businessmen to sell most of their products abroad where they would be paid in gold. Adam Smith said it would be better to let businessmen sell their goods wherever they could get the best prices.

Adam Smith's ideas were adopted in most of the European and American countries, and they worked very well. Then, as populations grew and businesses became bigger and more complicated, some form of government control was needed. The first important laws to control business were the Anti-trust Acts in the United States, about which you can read in the article on MONOPOLY. During the great depressions that followed World War I, the British and then the United States put many other controls on business. The most important of these were the LABOR and SOCIAL SECURITY laws, about which there are separate articles. But business remained free in nearly every respect. A businessman in the democracies remains free to make whatever products he pleases and to shut down his factory if he wants to.

In some countries, however, the government took over complete control of businesses. These are called Fascist and Communist countries. They tell business men how many workers they must hire, what they must produce, and what prices they must sell their products for. A factory that is losing money may not be permitted to shut down if the government does not want it to.

The trouble is, as experience has shown, when business is not free the workers are not free either. Most experts now agree that there have to be some government controls on business, but they agree that there should be as few as possible.

See the article on ECONOMICS.

Freemasons

The Freemasons are a brotherhood, or society, of men. About four million men are members in the United States, where Freemasons are usually called simply "Masons." Each group of members is called a *lodge*.

Freemasonry began more than six hundred years ago, when skilled workers were organized into GUILDS, about which there is a separate article. The stonemasons, who built houses and churches of stone, had a guild whose members were called Free Masons. About three hundred years ago the guild began to accept mem-

bers who were not stonemasons, and these members were called Accepted Masons. In the year 1717 it was decided to call both groups by the same name. In their meetings today, Masons wear aprons that look like the working clothes of the old stonemasons, and repeat secret words that have been handed down from Mason to Mason for hundreds of years. The Masons also have open meetings at which they entertain their families and friends.

A man who joins the Masons progresses through various *degrees*. Most lodges use the *Scottish rite*, in which a 33rd-Degree Mason is the highest. The KNIGHTS TEMPLAR, about whom there is a separate article, are a branch of the Masons but use a different system. The Shrine is not a Masonic order, but only Knights Templar or at least 32nd-Degree Masons can belong to it. Women may not be Masons but may belong to the Order of the Eastern Star, a society that has about 3,000,000 members and is connected with the Freemasons. Boys 14 to 21 years old may belong to the Order of De Molay, and girls to the Rainbow Girls, societies that were founded by the Masons.

Masonic lodges in America support all good works, the equality of all people, freedom, and democracy. They have summer camps to which they invite boys and girls of all faiths. They raise money for research into rheumatic fever, one of the worst diseases of children.

There are more than a million Masons outside of America. Not all of them agree with the views of the American lodges, who insist that the open Bible (or, in Mohammedan countries, the Koran) be on the lodge room's altar during meetings.

free ports

Free ports are ports where ships can land, and unload their cargo, without having to follow any customs regulations. Customs regulations are the rules that a country sets up to regulate bringing foreign products into that country. According to those rules, all goods brought into ordinary ports must be inspected, and sometimes the importer (the person bringing the foreign goods in) must pay a tax, or duty, on certain products. In free ports there are no customs regulations. There is no duty on the goods brought into a free port. But the duty must be paid if the goods are taken from the port into the country.

Free ports began to develop about four hundred years ago, when most countries made so many customs rules that it was sometimes very difficult and troublesome even to land a ship at any port. Nowadays there are not so many rules, and not so many free ports. But free ports are still useful. Ships can land their cargoes at a free port and leave without paying customs duties. Then the goods can be stored or sorted or sent on to some other country, without inspection and duties. In the United States there are just two free ports, one at Staten Island, New York, and the other at New Orleans, Louisiana.

freesia

Freesia is a sweet-smelling flower that grows in the fields and is grown in green-houses. It grows from a bulb and

belongs to the iris family. The bulb sends up tufts of thin, pointed leaves and a branched stem with three or four slender funnel-like blossoms which can be white, yellow, pink, or lavender. You can grow them indoors during the winter by potting the bulb in pebbles or sandy soil in a sunny window. Freesia is very popular for its bright flowers. It belongs to the group of plants called herbs. Originally it came from South Africa.

Free Silver

Gold is the metal that has been used by most nations throughout history for their most valuable money. When a nation is "on the gold standard," it offers *free coinage*. That means it will buy all the pure gold it is offered and pay for it in the same weight of gold coins without charging anything.

When a nation offers free coinage of silver as well as gold, it is using bi-metallism, which means "use of two metals." The United States once used bi-metallism, but gave it up at about the time of the Civil War. People who live in western states, which produce a lot of silver, tried for years to bring back bi-metallism, with free coinage of silver. This was called the Free Silver Movement.

William Jennings Bryan of Nebraska, who ran for President of the United States three times (and was defeated all three times), was the leader of the Free Silver Movement after 1896. He wanted the government to fix values so that gold would always be worth exactly sixteen times as much as silver. But the government never did, and in the 1930s the United States and all other countries gave up the gold standard too.

Read also the article on MONEY.

Free-Soil Party

The Free-Soil Party was a political party in the United States about a hundred years ago. At that time the main national problem in the United States was the problem of slavery in the new territories. The South wanted slavery to expand into the new western territories of the United States, but the North thought that slavery should not be allowed to spread. After the Mexican War, much new territory was added to the United States in the southwest. In 1848, a group of people joined together in the north and formed a new political party. It was called the Free-Soil Party, because the main purpose of the party was to keep the new territories free by keeping slavery out. The Free-Soil party was not strong enough to win the election for President, but it did win some seats in Congress and had much influence. Two of the leaders of the Free Soil Party were Martin Van Buren and Salmon P. Chase. The Free-Soil Party never grew very large. In 1854, it joined with other anti-slavery groups and became part of the new Republican Party.

Freetown

Freetown is the capital city of Sierra Leone, a country in West Africa. Freetown was founded by the British in 1787 as a home for former Negro slaves who had escaped or had been freed. The descendents of these slaves, called Creoles, today make up most of the population of Freetown, which is about 128,000.

Freetown has an excellent harbor on the Atlantic Ocean. Fourah Bay College, the University of Sierra Leone, is located in Freetown.

freezing

When something freezes, it changes from a liquid to a solid. The most familiar example of freezing is the change from water to ice. Almost all liquids are able to turn into solids, if the temperature is low enough. Some liquids also freeze at very high temperatures. Iron is a good example of a liquid that changes to a solid at high temperatures; it freezes at 1500 degrees!

Most liquids become smaller in volume (or contract) when they are cooled or frozen. Water does just the opposite; its volume becomes larger. This expansion causes burst water pipes, when the water in the pipes freezes.

When a liquid freezes, it gives off quite a lot of heat. There are many uses for this heat. When farmers have vegetables stored in their cellars, sometimes a freeze will ruin them. The farmers place large pans of water about the cellar; the heat they give off while the water in the pans is freezing is frequently enough to prevent damage to the vegetables.

Pure liquids freeze more easily than liquids with impurities in them. For this reason ocean waters and river water may still be flowing when the temperature is much below the freezing point of water. This principle can be very useful. If the water in an automobile radiator freezes, it will expand and crack the motor. All we have to do is to add some impurities in the form of alcohol or a commercial anti-freeze, and we lower the freezing point of the water.

freight

Freight is goods or other valuable things that railroads or trucks transport (carry) from one place to another. The same thing carried on ships is usually called *cargo*. Airlines carry a small amount of freight. Freight may be manufactured goods, raw materials, livestock, food, and so on.

Carrying freight is the chief business of the railroads. Most railroads lose money carrying passengers, because the fares paid by passengers are less than it costs to operate the passenger trains. The railroads make their money by carrying freight.

A railroad or truck company is called a *common carrier* when its business is carrying freight for anyone who will pay its charges. If it operates in two or more states, its charges (called tariffs) are set up by the INTERSTATE COMMERCE COMMISSION, about which you can read in a separate article. The tariff depends on the kind of commodity (goods) being sent and the distance it must be carried. For example, it may cost $3.00 to ship a hundred pounds of shoes and only $1.00 to ship a hundred pounds of coal the same distance. One reason for this is that shoes are usually packed in boxes, which take up more space in a railroad car.

FREIGHT LINES

The United States is covered with rail-road tracks. There are very few places that cannot be reached by railroad, but the tracks belong to different companies. Therefore a shipment from one city to another may go over the tracks of two or more different companies.

One company usually acts as the *carloader*. It takes the freight from the *consignor* (the person shipping it) and loads it into a railroad car. It gives the consignor a receipt called a *bill of lading*. The consignor pays this carloader the entire charge for carrying the shipment. The carloader often must pay part of that money to every other company that carries that carload of freight over its tracks.

Usually the shipment stays in the same freight car all the way. A shipment may leave the state of Tennessee in a freight car on a train that carries it to a city in Kentucky. There it is switched to a train on another company's tracks and carried to a city in West Virginia. There it may be switched to still a third line that takes it to a city in Pennsylvania. The carloading railroad company usually tries to keep the freight car on its own tracks as much as possible so it will not have to pay too many other railroads. Some carloading companies are not railroads at all. They are companies that own freight cars, accept freight for transportation, and pay railroads to move these cars.

Trucking companies carry freight under I.C.C. rules very much like the ones that control the railroads. Sometimes a trucking company has to switch some of its freight to another trucking line, but not often. The highways are free; no one owns them as companies own railroad tracks. A single truck can go anywhere in the United States without switching its load to another truck. The reason it switches its load at all is that a company would not send a truck to an out-of-the-way place just to deliver a small package.

FREIGHT CARS

Railroads have many different kinds of freight car. The most familiar one is the boxcar. A boxcar is loaded with goods in packages. It may also carry automobiles or other things that should be kept safe and covered. A refrigerator car looks like a boxcar but is insulated as a refrigerator is. It carries food and other goods that have to be kept cold. Open cars are used for cattle and other live freight that need fresh air to breathe.

The gondola car is a special kind of open car. It has sides but no roof. It is used for carrying coal and other things that do not need to be protected from rain. Many of these are dump cars. Coal is poured into the car through a chute. When the time comes to unload, the gondola car is tilted and the load pours out.

Flatcars are platforms on wheels. They carry logs and other bulky things.

Tankcars carry oil and chemicals and other liquids. Some of them are glass-lined, refrigerated cars for carrying milk.

There are many other kinds of freight car for special loads. There is a separate article about TRUCKS that tells about the different kinds of truck used for carrying freight.

There are *slow freight* and *fast freight*. The trains may travel at the same speed in miles per hour, but fast freight has the

right of way over slow freight. This means that if a train carrying slow freight and another carrying fast freight want to use the same track, the fast freight may use it first.

Even faster than fast freight is *express*. Express shipments are made through a separate company that owns its own cars and pays the railroad company to attach these cars to passenger trains. A passenger train has the right of way over all freight trains.

Every railroad has a special "freight service" for the baggage of passengers. If you are making a trip by rail and have a heavy trunk to take with you, you can *check* the trunk. This means that the railroad puts the trunk in the baggage car and gives you a receipt called a check. You pay the railroad no more than the price of your own fare for this service.

Freischütz, Der

Der Freischütz is the name of a grand opera, which is a play in which all the conversation is sung, not spoken, and the music is intended to be played by a symphony orchestra and sung by the greatest singers. The music for *Der Freischütz* was written by Carl Maria von Weber, a German composer. The words to the opera were written by Friedrich Kind, who based his story on an old German legend. The legend is that a huntsman may sell his soul to Samiel, or the devil, in exchange for seven magic bullets. Six of the bullets will always hit the mark. However, the seventh bullet belongs to the devil, and the huntsman must shoot it whenever the devil directs. *Der Freischütz* was first produced in Berlin, Germany, on June 18, 1821. In 1825 it was presented in English at the Park Theater in New York City.

STORY OF THE OPERA

Der Freischütz means "The Freeshooter." In the opera, Max, a young hunter on the estate of a Prince of Bohemia, is in love with Agatha. Agatha promises to marry him if he wins a certain shooting match. He is very unlucky at the beginning of the match, and a huntsman named Caspar, who has already sold his soul to Samiel, tells him how he may get the magic bullets. Max does not want to sell his soul, but decides it is worth it to have Agatha as his bride. At midnight in the Wolf's Glen, he calls for Samiel and is given the magic bullets. When the time comes for the last and most difficult shot, the Prince points out a white dove as the target. Just as Max takes aim Agatha cries out, "Max, I am the white dove." Max fires, and Agatha falls to the ground. Samiel, however, has no power over Agatha, and has directed the seventh bullet toward Caspar, who is killed. Max is very sorry for his evil bargain, and, helped by the prayers of Agatha, he is forgiven. The prince announces that after one year Max and Agatha may be married.

Frémont, John C.

John Charles Frémont was an American army officer and explorer who

was nicknamed "The Pathfinder." He led many expeditions into the West about a hundred years ago. He was born in Savannah, Georgia, in 1813. As an officer in the Army Engineers, he went on journeys up the Missouri River, across the Rocky Mountains, and into Oregon and other parts of the West that few Americans had ever seen before.

In 1845, he led a small band of men into California. While he was there, the Mexican War broke out. Frémont quickly took command of the Americans in California, and captured that state for the United States. A few years later the people of California elected him to be one of their senators in Washington. In 1856, Frémont became the candidate of the new Republican party for president, but he was beaten by James Buchanan, the candidate of the Democrats.

When the Civil War broke out in 1861, Frémont was promoted to major general and given command of the Union (Northern) Forces in the West. Although he was very skillful as a leader of small groups of soldiers in the mountains and desert, he failed as commander of a large army. He soon got into a bad quarrel with another officer, and in 1864 he resigned from the Army. He was governor of the territory of Arizona from 1878 to 1883. He died in New York City in 1890.

French Academy

The French Academy is an organization that was founded in 1635 by Cardinal Richelieu to purify the French language and set standards of good usage. It is composed of forty members, all of whom are distinguished scholars and writers. When one member dies, another great writer is elected to take his place. It was once considered the highest honor to be elected to the Academy, and its members were known as the "Immortals." However, many great French writers were never elected to the Academy because their thinking was considered too original or revolutionary for their times. Even today many outstanding writers have been passed over because their thinking is considered too liberal. For this reason, and because many Academy members collaborated with the Germans during World War II, belonging to the Academy has lost much of the prestige it once had.

French Community

The French Community is a confederation of the French Republic, including its Overseas Departments and Overseas Territories, and six of the twelve republics in Africa which were at one time colonies ruled by France.

After World War II France gave the people of its many colonies in Africa and other parts of the world more rights and greater freedom. As a first step, the French Union was established in 1946. The former colonies became members and were gradually given almost complete independence.

In 1958, under its new constitution, France took another step in this direction by creating the French Community. This

succeeded the French Union and gave the former colonies further rights. All subjects of the French Community are citizens with the same status as that of French Nationals of Metropolitan France—that is, French people who live in France itself—without regard to their origin, race, or religion.

Those French territories which did not want to retain their ties with France were allowed to become independent countries. Those which did not want to cut their ties with France were allowed by an amendment to the French Constitution adopted in 1960 to become independent sovereign republics without losing their membership in the French Community.

The six African republics which joined with the French Republic in the French Community are the Republic of Senegal, the Malagasy Republic (formerly Madagascar), the Republic of Chad, the Central African Republic (formerly Ubangi-Shari), the Republic of the Congo (Brazzaville), formerly Middle Congo, and the Gabon Republic. See the articles on each of these republics.

The president of France is also the president of the French Community. He is represented in each member state by a High Commissioner. An Executive Council composed of the president and the heads of the governments of the member states coordinates the common affairs of the Community in the fields of foreign affairs, defense, finances, economics, education, and transportation. See also article on FRENCH TERRITORIES.

French, Daniel C.

Daniel Chester French was a popular American sculptor. When he was only 23 years old, he created one of his most famous works, *The Minuteman of Concord*. This statue, of which you have probably seen many pictures, is in memory of the farmers and people in and around Concord, Massachusetts, who upon a moment's notice took up their rifles to fight for independence in the Revolutionary War in 1775. Daniel C. French made many other great statues, and there is one other which almost every American knows: the statue of Abraham Lincoln in the Lincoln Memorial in Washington, D.C. French was born in 1850 and died in 1931.

French Guiana

French Guiana on the northern coast of South America is one of France's Overseas Departments. It has an area of about 35,000 square miles, about the same as Indiana, but only about 46,000 people live there. Much of the country is wild jungle. Most of the people are farmers and live along the coast, where it is hot and rainy. The capital of French Guiana is Cayenne. This city has given its name to a sharp spice called cayenne pepper. Devil's Island, former French prison colony, is near the coast of French Guiana.

French and Indian War

The French and Indian War was really a war between the British and the French. It was fought in the wilderness of North America about two hundred

years ago, when France owned Canada and the part of the United States that is now the Midwest. The American settlers in the thirteen colonies fought on the side of England. The war ended in a great victory for the British and Americans, and the French were forced to leave North America.

In the year 1754, the French and their Indian allies built a fort where the city of Pittsburgh is today. They wanted to take all of western America for themselves and keep the colonists from spreading westward across the country. A young lieutenant colonel of colonial troops named George Washington was sent with a force of 150 men to capture the fort, called Fort Duquesne, from the French. It is said that Washington fired the first shot of the war. But the French were too strong, and the Americans had to retreat.

The next year a British army under General Edward Braddock tried to take Fort Duquesne. Near the fort the British were suddenly attacked by a large number of Indians, who hid behind trees and fired at the bright red British uniforms. The British were used to open battles, but they had never fought in this way before, and they were badly defeated. Braddock was killed. Now it looked as if France would win the war. French troops captured Fort William Henry in upstate New York from the British, and more and more Indians joined their side.

It was mostly a war of small battles and raids. No American settlers in the west felt safe from an attack by Indians. Many farms were burned down, and many men, women, and children were killed. But in 1758 the tide turned in favor of the British. William Pitt, one of the greatest men in British history, became prime minister, and he decided to send a strong force to conquer the French. He chose young and vigorous men to command the British and colonial troops, and soon there were many victories. An army under Lord Jeffrey Amherst sailed to the French fortress of Louisbourg in eastern Canada and captured it. The British and Americans also captured Fort Duquesne and renamed it Pittsburgh, after William Pitt.

The most important French fort in all of America was Quebec, which stood on top of a steep cliff overlooking the St. Lawrence River in Canada. If Quebec could be taken, all of French America would soon fall to the British, because the only way that the French could bring troops and supplies from France was up the St. Lawrence River and past Quebec. In 1759, a British army under a daring commander called General James Wolfe attacked this strong fortress. The French under General Louis Montcalm felt safe from attack, but one night the British climbed the cliffs silently, and in the morning the two armies met. (See the article on Plains of ABRAHAM.) The British won the battle, in which both Wolfe and Montcalm were killed. Quebec now fell to the British, and less than a year later the Canadian city of Montreal was captured. In 1763, the French signed a peace treaty and agreed to leave Canada. America as far west as the Mississippi River then became British.

French horn

The French horn, which is often called just the horn, is a musical instrument that belongs to the family of brass instruments, or lip instruments. The French horn is a brass tube about sixteen feet long that is coiled into a circular shape. It has a funnel-shaped mouthpiece at one end, and a wide, flaring bell at the other. It is played by blowing into the mouthpiece and fingering three valves with the left hand. All other brass instruments are played with the right hand. The French horn player can control pitch, and the loudness and quality of tone, by putting his right hand into the bell and varying the degree of muting. This is called *stopping*.

The French horn was developed from the horn used by early hunters, which had no valves. The valves came into use only a little more than a hundred years ago. Before that, players had to add "crooks," or pieces of tubing of various lengths, to the horn in order to change keys. Four horns are used in the modern symphony orchestra. The French horn is a difficult instrument to play. The horn players must work together closely, and they must be as careful of their physical condition as if they were athletes.

French Indo-China

French Indo-China is a name still used in speaking of a large territory on the southeast corner of Asia that for many years was controlled by France, though the territory now consists of four independent countries. It is also called Indo-China. The whole territory is about as large as the state of Texas, having an area of 286,000 square miles, but it is much more thickly populated than Texas, having a population of about 41,000,000.

Three of the countries that make up Indo-China—Laos, Cambodia, and South Viet Nam—still have some alliance with France, at least in trade relations. The fourth country, North Viet Nam, has a Communist government.

About a hundred years ago, France conquered Cochin China, a kingdom that was then independent but later became part of Viet Nam. France's purpose was to establish a colony that would add to its wealth. Since France had a strong army and navy and the Indo-Chinese countries were weak, France was able in the following forty years to gain control of all Indo-China. During World War II Japan took control of Indo-China, and after the war the Indo-Chinese countries demanded more independence. In Tongkin, another of the old Indo-Chinese countries that had become part of Viet Nam, an army led by Communists started a war against France. France granted Laos, Cambodia and Viet Nam independence, and they decided to remain allied with France, but the Communist army continued to fight and in 1954 they forced France to surrender to them the northern part of Viet Nam.

Most of the people of Indo-China are called Annamese and are related to the Chinese. The rest of the people of Indo-China are more closely related to the brown-skinned peoples of Siam and Indonesia. The language spoken in most parts of Indo-China is related to Chinese but is not exactly the same.

There are separate articles on LAOS, CAMBODIA, VIET NAM, and ANNAM.

French language and literature

The French language is the language spoken in France and in many French territories in other parts of the world. It is also the official language of Haiti and one of the official languages of Belgium (along with Flemish), Canada (along with English), and Switzerland (along with German and Italian). For hundreds of years it was the chief "diplomatic" language of the world; that is, it was used by the ambassadors of nearly all countries. It is one of the five official languages of the United Nations.

Altogether there are about seventy million people in the world who speak French. Only Chinese, English, Spanish, Russian, Hindustani, Japanese and German are spoken by more people. There are four million French-speaking people in Canada. French is taught in nearly all high schools in the United States.

It is not difficult for English-speaking people to learn to read and write French. The arrangement of words in sentences is much the same in French and English. Many French words are familiar because French was one of the languages from which English grew; you can read more about this in the article on the ENGLISH LANGUAGE.

It is much more difficult to learn to speak and to understand spoken French. As in English, many French words are not pronounced in the way you would expect from the spelling. Only about half the sounds that are spelled are actually pronounced at all. For example, a final *s*, or *t*, or even *-ent*, usually is not pronounced. In conversational French there are many slang words and expressions that are not learned in school. French *idiom*, or manner of speaking, is often much different from English; for example, when we would say "It is warm," the French would say "It makes warm."

In French spelling there are certain *accents*, or marks to show how letters should be pronounced. These are the *acute* accent, as in the letter *é;* the *grave* accent, as in the letter *è;* and the *circumflex* accent, as in the letter *ê*. There is also the *cedilla*, a mark under the c that means it should be pronounced like *s*.

ORIGIN OF FRENCH LANGUAGE

French is one of the Romance languages. This means it grew out of the Latin language spoken by the ancient Romans. Two thousand years ago, France was inhabited chiefly by Celtic peoples who were called Gauls. The country became a colony of Rome, and the "popular Latin" spoken by the Roman soldiers combined with the speech of the Gauls to form French. Later, a Germanic people called Franks settled in France, giving both the country and the language their names. (The French word for the language is *français*.)

French has two main branches, *langue d'oil*, spoken in most of France and especially in the north, and *langue d'oc*, spoken in the south. Both of these mean "language of yes." Long ago the word for "yes" was *oïl* in the north and *oc* in the south. It is now *oui* in both sections. The southern language is most often called *Provençal*, because formerly Provence was the name of the southern part of the country. French literature is almost

all written in the northern language. Two other languages spoken in France are Breton, a Celtic language related to Welsh, which is spoken in a northwest region, and BASQUE (about which there is a separate article), which is spoken in a region along the Spanish border.

FRENCH LITERATURE

French literature for hundreds of years has been one of the world's greatest, in poetry and plays and novels and also in science. Until the 1400s the language was Old French, which is no longer very easy to read. Famous poems and ballads were written in Old French. One of the long poems, the *Romance of the Rose,* inspired the English poet Geoffrey Chaucer. This poem was written more than seven hundred years ago. Two hundred years before that, the *Song of Roland,* a long poem telling of heroes who fought with the great king Charlemagne, gave us legends that have been told through Europe ever since.

About the year 1450, the poet François Villon wrote short poems that are still popular. His poems have been translated into English many times. The essays of Michel de Montaigne, who lived from 1533 to 1592, were the great French literature of the next century.

Modern French began in the 1600s when the French Academy was founded and rules were adopted for spelling and grammar. The greatest writer of the 1600s was Molière, whose plays are ranked with the English plays of Shakespeare. The fables of La Fontaine were written in the same century and are still read. Corneille was another great playwright of the century.

The great writer of the 1700s was Voltaire. He wrote great histories, humorous novels, volumes of poetry, and essays that affected the thinking of men all over the world. Jean Jacques Rousseau was another writer of that century who affected men's thinking. He had a great effect on the American and French Revolutions. At the same time Beaumarchais was writing comedies, such as *The Barber of Seville,* that are still acted or performed in operas.

During the 1800s the most famous French writers were novelists. Honoré de Balzac has been rated by some critics as the greatest novelist of all time. Stendhal and Flaubert did not write so many novels as Balzac, but their best novels are among the best ever written. Victor Hugo, whose many works include *Les misérables* and *Notre-Dame de Paris* (The Hunchback of Notre Dame), was almost as widely read in America as in France. So was Alexander Dumas, whose works included *The Three Musketeers,* though he was not considered nearly as great a writer. Guy de Maupassant is considered one of the greatest of all writers of short stories. Emile Zola and Anatole France were among the famous novelists who came some years later. Other great writers of the nineteenth century were Alphonse de Lamartine. Théophile Gautier, Charles Sainte-Beuve (a very influential critic), Alfred de Musset, George Sand, and Alphonse Daudet. Among the poets who greatly influenced modern poetry were Baudelaire, who wrote *The Flowers of Evil,* Paul Verlaine

and Arthur Rimbaud, leaders in the Symbolist movement, and Stéphane Mallarmé, who wrote *The Afternoon of a Fawn.*

In the present century, Marcel Proust has been ranked among the great novelists of all time. His masterpiece is *Remembrance of Things Past,* a brilliant study of French aristocracy as seen through the eyes of a sensitive young boy growing up. André Gide is one of the modern writers whose works have been widely read in English, among them *The Immoralist, Strait Is the Gate,* and *The Counterfeiters.* Several French writers of this century have won the Nobel prize for their work. Romain Rolland, who wrote the long novel, *Jean Christophe,* won it in 1915. The philosopher, Henri Bergson, wrote works that greatly influenced the literature of his day, among them *Creative Evolution* and *Time and Free Will.* He won the Nobel prize in 1927. François Mauriac won the prize in 1952 for his many analytical novels. Other great French writers of this century who have built outstanding reputations are Jules Romain, who wrote a long series of novels called *Men of Good Will;* Jean Paul Sartre, a leading Existentialist who embodies much of that philosophy in his plays and novels; Albert Camus, another Existentialist, who wrote *The Stranger* and *The Plague;* Colette, a woman writer of many romantic short stories and novels, among them *Gigi* and *Cheri;* André Maurois, noted for his biographies, including *Ariel* and the *Life of Disraeli;* and Jean Cocteau, poet, novelist, and dramatist.

French Revolution

The French Revolution was one of the most important events in the history of modern Europe. It began in 1789 and lasted ten years. By the time it had ended its effects had been felt in every country in the Western World.

Before the French Revolution, the governments of all European countries had been controlled by kings and noblemen. There were two other main classes. One was the middle class, called the bourgeoisie, who were the merchants and the professional men such as lawyers and writers. The other was the lower class, the peasants (poor farmers) and workingmen, who were uneducated, very poor, badly fed and badly clothed.

In the French Revolution, the middle class took for themselves the power that the kings and noblemen had always had. The lower classes joined enthusiastically in the Revolution, but they did not start it and it was many years before they gained anything from it. The middle classes had already come to control England without a real revolution. They had won control of the United States through the Revolutionary War. In the fifty years following the French Revolution they came to control all the other important countries of western Europe, especially Germany and Austria.

The first European revolution was in France because the people there were the best-educated and most advanced. The French peasants were poor and oppressed, but they were better off than the peasants in most European countries. The French government was in debt because of many costly wars and extravagant kings, but France was still the rich-

est country on the continent of Europe.

Nevertheless, discontent was widespread in France in the middle of the 18th century. The people had waited until the old king, Louis XV, died, thinking things would be better under a new ruler. But time proved that the succession of Louis XVI did them no good. In 1788 there was a serious crop failure. This brought the people to a mood in which they were ready for rebellion. Jean Jacques Rousseau, Voltaire and other French writers had protested against conditions, and their writings further angered the people. The king had tried several ways to improve matters, and finally he ordered the Estates General to meet in May 1789. The Estates (or States) General was the nearest thing France had to a free Parliament, but it had not met for 150 years. It was made up of three houses, or Estates: the nobility, and clergy, and the middle classes. The houses of the Estates met separately, and each house had one vote.

REVOLUTION BREAKS OUT

When the Estates General met, the middle classes, or Third Estate, demanded that the whole body meet together. This would have given them the biggest voice, because they had more members than the clergy and the nobility. When the other two groups refused, the Third Estate left and declared itself a National Assembly with ruling power. Lacking a place to meet, the National Assembly gathered in an indoor tennis court and vowed not to leave until France had a new constitution. This vow is known as the "oath of the tennis court." Soon, more people defied the monarchy. On July 14, a mob in Paris attacked the Bastille, a prison and a hated reminder of the king's power.

The Bastille was taken, and the mob murdered several soldiers who resisted. Army troops were called out, but they refused to fire on the crowd. The citizens of Paris organized a National Guard, or army of their own, and adopted a red-white-and-blue striped flag, called the tri-color, as their emblem.

Meanwhile, peasants all over the country were rising up; they stormed houses of nobles and burned them to the ground. The king had remained in his palace at Versailles, outside Paris, trying to make peace with the revolutionists. In October a group of men and women marched to Versailles and forced the king to return to Paris with them. The National Assembly proclaimed a constitutional monarchy, which means a government in which the power of the king is limited by a constitution.

JACOBINS AND GIRONDISTS

Many of the revolutionaries had organized political clubs, where they made and discussed plans for taking power. One of these, the Jacobin Club, whose leader was Maximilien Robespierre, wanted to set up a republic and force the king to step down. Another group was the Girondists, who had been members of the Jacobin Club but could not agree with all of their ideas. The Girondists were the strongest group in the Legislative Assembly, which was formed when the National Assembly disbanded. By

The Third Estate (middle class) raised their arms in the "Tennis Court Oath" in 1789, pledging not to give up until France had a new constitution.

French Embassy Press

this time many French nobles had fled to other countries of Europe, and these nobles, called *emigrés,* were urging these countries to invade France and stop the revolution. In April, 1792, the Assembly declared war against Austria.

Paris was still in a very upset condition, and this was now made worse by the danger of invasion from abroad. No one knew from day to day who was in power and what might happen next. In August a mob stormed the Tuileries, a palace where the royal family was living. King Louis and Queen Marie Antoinette were put in prison, and another government under Georges Danton took over. The people of Paris became very frightened and panicky, and wanted to kill anyone who believed in the monarchy. In five days in September, 1,100 persons were seized and put to death.

On September 20, another new government was formed, called the National Convention. It abolished the monarchy and set up a republic. In December the king was tried for treason, and in January, 1793 he was put to death.

REIGN OF TERROR

The National Convention under Danton now tried to do away with all its enemies at home. Robespierre, leader of the Jacobin group, soon gained power again. A Committee of Public Safety, consisting of 12 members, was given police powers, and it acted very cruelly. The guillotine, a machine for beheading persons, became the symbol of the Reign of Terror. In about a year more than 40,000 persons were put to death.

The National Convention made laws to control prices and wages, and gave all men the right to vote, but its leaders quarreled among themselves. In 1794 Robespierre managed to get rid of Danton by sending him to the guillotine. Then it was the turn of Robespierre him-

self, and he was arrested and executed. Gradually the Reign of Terror came to an end.

THE DIRECTORY

In August 1795 a new constitution was passed that once more gave France a change of government. There were two houses in the legislature, like our Senate and House of Representatives, but the real power was held by a council of five men known as the Directory.

Meanwhile the war against Austria was going on under the direction of Napoleon Bonaparte, and the French were winning many victories. However, the French people were tired of war and unrest, and in March, 1797 the royalists won an election. The royalists wanted to make peace with Austria and put the brother of Louis XVI on the throne as Louis XVIII. Before the end of the year, however, the supporters of the republic managed to oust the royalists from the government, and the Directory held power for two more years. By that time Napoleon had become a hero to the French people because of his military successes. In 1799 he overthrew the Directory, and the Revolution was at an end. You can read more about DANTON and ROBESPIERRE, the JACOBINS, and NAPOLEON, in separate articles. Read also the article on FRANCE.

French Somaliland

French Somaliland is the former name of the French Territory of the Afars and the Issas (pronounced uh-FARZ and EE-sozz). It is a member of the FRENCH COMMUNITY (about which there is a separate article in the previous volume). The name was changed in 1967. It lies on the northeastern coast of Ethiopia in Africa. Its area is about 9,000 square miles (about the size of New Hampshire) with a population of 81,000

(about one-eighth of New Hampshire's). Most of the people are Somalis or Danakils, and one in ten is an Arab. The country is hot and dry, though it is a little cooler in the interior where the mountains rise to 4,000 feet above sea level. A little farming is done and livestock is raised, but the chief industry is salt mining. Salt, hides, and coffee are among the principal exports. The country is important chiefly for the railroad that connects its capital city of Djibouti (population in 1972, about 42,000) with the city of Addis Ababa, the capital of Ethiopia. This railroad is Ethiopia's main trade artery with other nations. In 1958 and again in 1967, French Somaliland voted to remain an Overseas territory within the French Community. The territory is governed by a 32-member Assembly and a Governor responsible to the French Government.

FRENCH TERRITORY OF THE AFARS AND THE ISSAS. Area, 8,500 square miles. Population (1974 estimate), 150,000. Capital, Djibouti, Status, Overseas Territory within the French Community.

French Territories

France controls or is allied with a number of regions and countries in different parts of the world.

Some of these are called *Overseas Departments.* People who live in the Overseas Departments have the same rights of citizenship as people who live in France, and send representatives to the French parliament. FRENCH GUIANA in South America, the islands of MARTINIQUE and GUADALOUPE in the West Indies, and the island of RÉUNION in the Indian Ocean are Overseas Departments. (See the separate articles.)

In French Overseas Territories, people have as much personal freedom as people in France but the French government in Paris has more control over the local governments. These territories include the FRENCH TERRITORY OF THE AFARS AND THE ISSAS, and Mayotte Island in Africa; French Polynesia, New Caledonia and the Wallis and Futuna Islands in the Pacific Ocean; St. Pierre and Miquelon near Newfoundland; and French Antarctica. Control of the New Hebrides Islands in the South Pacific is shared with Great Britain. Other French territories have become independent countries. See FRENCH COMMUNITY and FRENCH SOMALILAND.

French Union

The French Union was composed of France and many other territories that belong to France or used to belong to France. At one time, France had many colonies that were ruled by the French government in Paris. After World War II, in 1946, France changed its constitution so as to give all the people of these colonies more rights and greater freedom. In 1958 the constitution was changed again and the FRENCH COMMUNITY was formed to replace the French Union.

French West Africa

French West Africa is a former French federation in Africa, consisting of Dahomey, French Guinea (now Guinea), French Sudan (now Mali), Ivory Coast, Mauritania, Niger, Senegal, Upper Volta, and what is now the northern half of Chad.

freon

Freon is a fluid which boils at low temperatures. This makes it a good cooling substance to use in refrigerators and air conditioners. Freon is not poisonous, has no smell, and will not burn or explode. See the entry on REFRIGERATION.

fresco

The word *fresco* is used to describe a painting made directly on a wall. *Fresco* means "fresh" in Italian, and the painters of Italy four hundred years ago used the word for paintings made on plaster that was newly laid and still wet. However, they also painted on walls on which the plaster was dry, and so they called this *fresco secco*, or "dry fresco." Then they needed another name for the wet-plaster paintings, and they called them *buon fresco*, or "proper fresco."

Fresco painting is one of the oldest ways of painting known to man. The murals (wall paintings) in a palace in Crete, an island off the coast of Greece are fresco. This palace was built more than three thousand years ago, when the Greeks were still uncivilized tribes.

In dry fresco, a paint called *tempera* is most often used. Tempera is a paint in which the color, or pigment, is mixed with a substance called a binder to make it stick. This binder is usually egg yolk, although modern chemists have found other protein substances that work as well. There is a huge mural at the United States Military Academy at West Point for which the artist used thousands of dozens of fresh eggs in mixing his paints. In wet fresco such a binder is not needed, because the lime in the wet plaster mixes with the pigment and serves the same purpose.

The most famous frescos in the world are those in the Sistine Chapel at the Vatican in Rome. These were painted by the great Italian artist, Michelangelo.

Fresno

Fresno is a city in the central part of California, in the beautiful, rich and green San Joaquin valley. Many fruits are grown there and shipped to other parts of the country, especially as dried fruits. The population of Fresno in the 1970 census was 165,972.

Fresno produces more raisins than any other place in the world. Cotton is also raised in the valley, and oil and iron ore can be found nearby. Many of the workers in Fresno are migratory workers who come there for only a month or so a year to pick the fruit.

Freud, Sigmund

Sigmund Freud was a famous Austrian doctor and psychologist, that is, a person who studies the mind and the way in which it works. Freud was born in 1856. He became a doctor, but he was always most interested in research. He began to study the mind and mental illness, and he developed many new theories about both the sick and normal human mind. He thought that many illnesses seeming to show something wrong with a person's body are really caused by worries and conflicts deep in his mind. His way of treating mental illness was to have the patient talk about himself and try to understand his conflicts. This is called psychoanalysis. From his work with sick people, Freud developed a

theory of how the human mind works, in both sick and healthy people. He wrote many books to explain his theory, and how to use the theory in discussing such things as dreams, and art, and religion. Freud was a pioneer in this field, and for many years he worked alone. People everywhere criticized Freud and his work and disapproved of much that he said. But he continued with his work, and gradually many doctors became convinced that he was right. Freud died in 1939, but he is still remembered as a great pioneer in the field of medical psychology.

Frey and Freya

Frey and Freya were a god and goddess in the stories of the ancient Norsemen, the people who lived in the lands that are now Norway, Sweden, Denmark, and Iceland. Frey and Freya were brother and sister, and they were gods of love and marriage, of peace, and of all things that had to do with the growing of plants, such as rain and sunshine and the soil.

Frey owned a wonderful magic ship. It was big enough to hold all the gods, with their arms and equipment for war, but it could be folded up and carried in a pocket. Freya was the most beautiful of the goddesses. The stories tell of several of the evil race of giants who tried to get her as a wife. Half of all the soldiers slain in battle belonged to Freya.

The gods of the ancient Germans were about the same as those of the Norsemen. Frey was told about in both German and Norse mythology. In German mythology Freya seems to be the same as the goddess FRIGGA, about whom there is a separate article.

friar

A friar is similar in many ways to a monk. However, whereas monks live together in monasteries apart from others, friars go about in the world. They serve the religious needs of people and help those in distress. Friars were very poor at one time and lived entirely from gifts. Today, friars are neither so numerous nor so poor as they were hundreds of years ago. The four chief societies of friars are the Dominicans, the Franciscans, the Carmelites, and the Austins.

Frick, Henry Clay

Henry Clay Frick was an American industrialist who did a great deal to help develop the coal and steel industries in the United States. He was born in 1849 in West Overton, Pennsylvania, and went to work in his grandfather's flour

mill when he was only nineteen years old. Two years later he started his own coal and coke business, and later he joined with Andrew Carnegie, another famous businessman, and became chairman of the board of managers, or the highest official, of the Carnegie Steel Company. He had a very beautiful mansion in New York and a wonderful art collection. When he died, in 1919, Frick left his house and his art collection as a museum for the use of all persons.

friction

Friction is the rubbing of any two things against each other. Any matter, whether it is a solid, a liquid, or a gas, resists having something else move over it or through it. Force is required to overcome this resistance. Even when you wave your hand, there is friction between your hand and the air and force is required to overcome it.

Friction creates heat. All things are composed of tiny particles called molecules. The force of two groups of molecules scraping against each other knocks some molecules loose. They fly off in waves. Heat is composed of waves (as you can read in the article on HEAT). When your hands are cold, you can make them warmer by rubbing them together because the friction releases heat.

The rougher a surface is, the more friction there is. Any surface, no matter how smooth it may appear to the naked eye, will be found to be rough when it is seen through a microscope. When one thing moves over another, these rough spots catch on each other. Putting oil between the two surfaces reduces the friction, partly because it spreads out and fills the spaces between the uneven spots and partly because it is a liquid. Any liquid reduces friction because it flows from one place to another and helps to carry the rough surface along with it.

The greater a surface is, the more friction there is. If you lay a book on a table top and tilt the table top a little, the book will not move. Gravity is pulling the book downward, but it is not enough force to overcome the resistance of the friction. If you put a ball beside the book, the ball will at once roll off the table. The ball's surface resting on the table is little more than a single point. The surface of a round pencil resting on the table would be little more than a single thin line. Therefore either would roll when the book would not. You can read about this in the article BEARINGS.

The greater the speed with which two surfaces rub against each other, the greater the friction will be. The air does not seem to offer much resistance, yet when meteors from outer space strike the atmosphere of the earth, traveling as fast as several thousand miles per second, their friction with the air causes so much heat that they quickly burn up and become what we call "shooting stars."

Friction is often much greater than it would seem to be. A ball resting on a flat surface is flattened out just a little at the bottom, because of its weight. When it rolls, it crumples the surface ahead of it just a little. You can see a similar flattening of an automobile's tire where it rests on the road, and a similar crumpling effect when you try to slide a book across a tablecloth. When a hard steel ball rolls over a hard steel surface the flattening and crumpling are so slight that the eye cannot see them.

Because of friction, more power must be put into a machine than comes out of

it. When you feed energy in the form of electricity into an electric motor, the motor will be doing well if it produces 90 percent as much energy. The rest of the energy was needed to overcome the friction of the parts of the motor rubbing against one another. "Perpetual motion," or a machine that runs itself without receiving power from an outside source, is impossible because of friction.

Friction is not wholly a bad thing. Without it we could not walk, because we would be constantly sliding and slipping (as we do on ice). Friction between the tires and the road makes it possible for automobiles to move. Without friction, nails would not hold things together.

There is a kind of friction called internal friction. Gases and liquids have internal friction. The molecules in them are constantly moving, so they knock against one another and create friction. There is some movement of molecules in solids, but so little that it is not important.

Friday

Friday is the sixth day of the week. Its name comes from Frigga, a Germanic goddess of ancient times. For the Moslems, Friday is the sabbath, or day of rest. Roman Catholics do not eat meat on Friday. The Jewish sabbath begins at sundown on Friday and lasts until sundown on Saturday.

Friends

The Society of Friends is a Protestant Christian religious group. Its members are often called "Quakers" instead of "Friends." This is because people once made fun of them for shaking, or quaking, because their religious feeling was so great. They did not object. They even called themselves Quakers, and also the "Friends of Truth."

The founder of the Society of Friends was an Englishman who lived about three hundred years ago. His name was George Fox. He was born in 1624 and died in 1691. George Fox was a shoemaker, but in those days the established (official) Church of England could imprison people who did not agree with its teachings. George Fox spent much of his time in jail.

Gale Research Co. At other times he traveled through England, Scotland, and the English colonies in America, preaching his beliefs. He found thousands of people who agreed with his religious ideas. William Penn, who founded the state of Pennsylvania, was a Quaker, and in Philadelphia and near-by parts of Pennsylvania there are many Friends today. Two United States Presidents, Herbert Hoover and Richard Nixon, were Quakers. In 1972, there were about 127,000 Friends in the United States.

BELIEFS OF THE FRIENDS

The Friends believe in the fundamentals of CHRISTIANITY, about which there is a separate article; but they believe also that each person may interpret the Bible for himself. Because of this, there are many small differences of belief among members of the society.

The Friends believe that God has given to every man an "inner light," and that by thought, pure living, and prayer every man can find salvation. They do not believe that baptism with water is necessary, or that a person can actually be present at the Lord's Supper by taking communion. They do not believe that clergymen should be paid or that there should be a regular form that is always followed at church services. Friends will not swear (take an oath), as for example a witness in a court trial usually does when he swears to tell the truth; the law, which in the United States respects all religions, allows them to "state," or "affirm," that they will tell the truth, instead of swearing.

One strong belief of the Friends is that war is so wrong that they must not bear arms. In spite of this, the Friends have been among the bravest and hardest workers in the front lines of World Wars I and II, and wherever there has been disaster in the world, supplying ambulances and giving medical treatment to the injured. They do this through the American Friends Service Committee, an organization that was created by members of their Church. One hundred years ago and more, the Friends did a great deal to end slavery in the United States.

For a long time, very strict members of the Society of Friends used the old words "thee" and "thou," instead of "you," in addressing another person. There are not many Friends who still do this.

DISCIPLINE OF THE FRIENDS

By discipline, the Friends mean the duties that members of their Church should undertake. Their church gatherings are called *meetings*. At these meetings everyone remains silent unless he feels moved to speak; then he can speak. Their prayers are most often silent. Births and deaths are reported, and couples can be married at these meetings. Members are openly discussed and may be praised or criticized. An accused member may speak for himself and appeal from a criticism.

The Friends have several schools that are considered outstanding. The principal ones are in Philadelphia and its suburbs and in New York City.

Frietchie, Barbara

Barbara Frietchie was an old woman who lived in the town of Frederick, Maryland, at the time of the American Civil War. There is a famous story about her that John Greenleaf Whittier tells in his poem "Barbara Frietchie."

In September, 1862, a great Confederate army under General "Stonewall" Jackson attacked Maryland from the South and marched into Frederick. According to the poem Barbara Frietchie loved the flag of the United States so much that she flew it from her window, even though an enemy army was passing by. When Jackson saw the flag, he ordered his soldiers to shoot it down, but Barbara Frietchie herself went to the window and waved the flag.

"'Shoot, if you must, this old gray head,
But spare your country's flag,' she said."

When he saw the bravery of the old woman, Stonewall Jackson said:
"'Who touches a hair of yon gray head
Dies like a dog! March on!' he said."

So the whole Confederate army marched by under the Stars and Stripes of the Union. It is not known for sure whether or not this event ever really happened.

frieze

A frieze is any long, horizontal panel of carvings or sculptures used to decorate a wall or a building. Friezes are usually carved on churches, state buildings, and museums. There is a frieze running across the front of the Metropolitan Museum of Art in New York City. The most famous frieze ever made is the one carved on the top of the outer wall of the Parthenon, the Greek temple that still stands on a hill outside of Athens, Greece. The sculpture on this frieze is considered to be a perfect example of the Greek sculpture of that time. The frieze itself is considered one of the best pieces of architectural sculpture of all time.

frigate bird

The frigate bird is one of the greatest fliers of all the birds. Like sea gulls, frigate birds are nearly always found at sea or near the sea. Sometimes they fly as far as a hundred miles from any land, but they cannot float on the water like a sea gull so they must stay in the air all the time they are over water. They are bluish or greenish black in color, and sometimes they have a white breast. The male frigate bird has a bright red or scarlet throat that he can puff out to attract a female or to frighten his enemies. Their bodies are about a foot and a half long not counting their twelve-inch tail. Their wings are sometimes more than six feet long from tip to tip, and with them they glide for miles. The male is the one who takes most care of the nest, hatches the single egg, and feeds the young bird. The female helps the male, and one bird is always on the egg to protect it from its enemies. Frigate birds make their nests on rocks and bushes out of twigs and vines. When not in their nest, they roost in trees.

The frigate bird is sometimes called the Man O' War bird because of the way it gets its food. It flies and shrieks at other birds while they are flying and frightens them so much that they drop whatever food they are carrying. With its long, slender hooked beak it then catches in mid-air what the other birds have dropped. It flies fast enough to catch a flying fish jumping out of the water.

Frigga

Frigga was a goddess of the ancient Norsemen. She was the greatest of the goddesses and wife of Odin, the greatest of the gods. She was a kind goddess and helpful to human beings. She was especially the goddess of marriage, and people who wanted to have children would pray to Frigga. The gods of the ancient Germans were mostly the same as the gods of the Norsemen, but in German mythology, the stories the ancient Germans told about their gods and

goddesses, Frigga is possibly the same person as the goddess Freya. See the article FREY AND FREYA.

Friml, Rudolf

Rudolf Friml was an American writer of music who became famous for his operettas. An operetta is a gay and happy story told on the stage in conversation and song. Friml was born in Bohemia in 1881. He studied music with the great composer Anton Dvorák. Friml came to the United States in 1901 and made his home in New York City. He gave concerts as a pianist, and he wrote a great deal of music for the piano, violin, and cello, but he is best remembered for such popular operettas as *The Firefly*, *High Jinks*, *Rose Marie*, and the *Vagabond King*. He died in 1972.

fringed lizard

The fringed lizard is a reptile about thirty inches long, and more than half of its length is tail. It lives in trees and on the ground. Its feet have five fingers each, very much like human hands. Like most lizards, it lives on flies and other insects. The most unusual thing about the fringed lizard is the way it frightens away its enemies. When it thinks it is going to be attacked, it raises a ten-inch fan around its neck. The fan, or fringe, is part of its body and is made of skin. When its fringe is raised and its big red mouth is open, it is certainly frightening to look at. In Australia and New Guinea, where it lives, dogs that will kill other lizards its size are afraid of it because of the fringe.

Frisian Islands

The Frisian Islands are a chain of sand bars in the North Sea. They stretch from Holland along the coast of Germany and up to Denmark. They are divided into three groups: the West Frisian Islands, which belong to Holland; the East Frisian Islands, which belong to Germany; and the North Frisian Islands. Some of the North Frisian Islands belong to Germany and some belong to Denmark. None of the Frisian Islands is very large, but they are all very popular as summer vacation resorts for the people of northwest Europe. Most of the people of the Frisian Islands work either at fishing or at raising cattle. One of the interesting things about the Frisian Island people is their language. It is a form of German, but it is very different from the language spoken in Germany. The English language originally was a Germanic language, too, and of all the Germanic languages, Frisian is most like English.

Frobisher, Sir Martin

Sir Martin Frobisher was a famous English sailor and explorer who lived more than four hundred years ago, during the reign of Queen Elizabeth I. He was one of the many explorers who tried to find a sea passage from the Atlantic Ocean through America to the Pacific Ocean, and on to the Orient. He did not succeed in discovering the Northwest Passage, as this route was called, but he did discover an important bay, called Frobisher Bay, off Baffin Island. He fought against the Spanish Armada with the famous English explorer Sir Francis Drake in 1588, and was knighted for his part in England's victory.

frogs and toads

Frogs and toads are amphibians, that is, they live like fishes and breathe through gills in early life; then they change into air-breathing animals. There are hundreds of different kinds of frogs and toads. They are found all over the world, in forests, fields, swamps, and ponds.

TADPOLES

Like all amphibians, frogs and toads are hatched from eggs. We will take a frog egg as an example. The mother frog lays thousands of tiny eggs in the water; she leaves the eggs and never sees them again.

Soon each egg begins to grow larger, and one end grows larger than the other. This end is the beginning of a head, the other end the beginning of a tail.

In about a week, the eggs hatch. What comes out of each egg is not a baby frog, but a tiny little thing called a tadpole or polliwog. A tadpole is less than half an inch long at this time. It has no mouth or eyes.

In a few hours the tadpole grows tiny fringes at the side of its head. These fringes are gills, with which the tadpole is able to breathe in the water. The tiny tadpole begins to grow. In a few days it has eyes and a mouth. With its mouth it can now eat tiny plants it finds in the water. The tadpole swims by wiggling its tail. Many tadpoles do not live very long because they are soon eaten by faster-swimming fishes.

When a tadpole is about a year old, it is five or six inches long. At this time remarkable things begin to happen to the tadpole. Hind legs start growing near its tail. Its legs become longer and stronger. Front legs begin to grow near its gills. Its eyes bulge, its mouth grows larger and larger, and a big, sticky tongue begins to grow inside it. Lungs begin to form in its chest. Its tail becomes smaller and smaller, and soon disappears. The tadpole is now a young frog. With its tail gone, it is about two inches in length. Within a year or two it will have become a full-grown frog.

THE FOOD OF FROGS

Frogs, like other amphibians, eat insects. A frog catches a flying insect with its long sticky tongue, which is attached to the front of its mouth. Its tongue is very important to the frog and helps him get his food, for it can flip its tongue out very rapidly to catch flying insects. The frog does not chew its food; it swallows it whole.

If a frog catches an insect that is almost too big to swallow, it uses its front legs to cram the insect down its throat. As a frog swallows a large insect, its eyes close and sink in. The frog looks as if it were happy and smiling at this time. Toads eat in the same way.

HOW THEY LIVE

There are many different kinds of frogs and toads, and they are found all over the world. Most frogs live near the water or on swampy ground. Most toads live on land, but they usually stay in damp, cool places where they do not become too dry or hot. Some of them burrow into the ground or mud for shelter or protection.

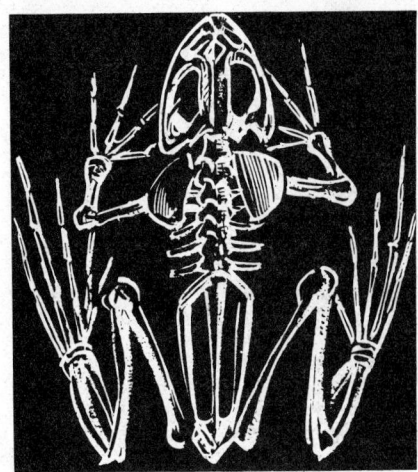
A frog's skeleton is shaped for swimming in water and hopping on land.

Most toads spend most of the day hiding, and come out at night to feed. Some frogs and toads live in trees. They have sticky pads on their feet which help them cling to the bark of a tree. All frogs and toads move around on land by hopping around on their strong hind legs. Frogs and toads are good swimmers. Their webbed hind feet make it easy for them to move through the water.

Frogs and toads look very much alike, but if you know how they differ you can tell them apart. Frogs are thinner than toads. A frog's skin is smooth and moist; a toad's skin is dry and lumpy. A toad's eyes bulge out even more than a frog's. A toad is usually much clumsier than a frog and cannot jump as fast or as far.

HIBERNATION

Frogs and toads hibernate, that is, they sleep through the winter if they live in places where the winters are cold. The frogs that live in or near the water bury themselves in the mud at the bottom of the water. The frogs and toads that live on land find some hiding-place for the winter, and some of them even dig themselves into the ground. The winter-sleeping frogs and toads breathe through their skins. Their hearts beat very slowly. The sleepers awake early each spring. If you live in the country, you will know when the frogs and toads have awakened. Almost the first sign of spring is the sound of the croaking made by the awakening frogs and toads.

Frontenac, Count

Count Louis de Buade Frontenac was a French general who was also governor of the lands France owned in North America before the American Revolutionary War. Frontenac was born in 1620, and he went into the army when he was only 15 years old. He was promoted very quickly, and soon became a brigadier general. He led the French armies in the early days of the French and Indian Wars. He won many important battles. Fort Frontenac in Canada was named after him. He died in 1698.

frontier

A frontier is a boundary. There are two types of frontier. One is a boundary between two civilized countries. The other is where the developed part of some country ends and the undeveloped part begins.

A frontier between two countries that are not friendly usually has armed soldiers of both countries stationed there. It often has watch towers, barbed wire, and other fortifications. Frontiers of this kind have existed between countries for thousands of years.

The most famous of all frontiers, and the longest, stretches three thousand miles across North America. It is the frontier between the United States and Canada. It is famous because it is the only frontier in the world that is not fortified. The United States and Canada have been so friendly that fortifications have not been needed.

In countries where not all sections have been developed, people are always pushing on to develop new areas and build homes there. Almost always, throughout history, beyond these frontiers there have been savage peoples who made war on the pioneers.

About two thousand years ago, when the Roman Empire ruled all the civilized parts of Europe, the Romans had to fight savage German tribes in order to develop more lands. In the United States, as the pioneers pushed westward they had to fight the Indians.

Because of this, frontier life is always thought of as rough and dangerous. The American pioneers lived in log cabins. Often these were built inside of stockades, a kind of fortification made with heavy wooden walls. Sometimes they went out by day to work in the fields, but they returned to the stockade at night. Often the United States Army had cavalry posts at the frontier to protect the pioneers. The last frontier in the United States ended about fifty years ago, when all of the country was developed.

frost

There is always a small amount of water in the air around you. If the air close to the earth becomes suddenly chilled, this water freezes on anything it touches. This frozen water that forms on objects is called frost. The most noticeable frost is the kind that forms on windows. This frost forms into thousands of beautiful shapes that look like ferns, pine trees, and jungles. The different shapes are caused by the amount of water in the air, the thickness of the glass, bits of dust on the window, the currents of air around the window, and many other things. No two shapes, or patterns, are exactly alike. They are made of ice CRYSTALS, about which you can read in a separate article.

Frost is a danger sign to farmers, because if the water in the air can freeze, the juices in the plants may also freeze. When this happens, the plants usually die. Frost usually occurs in the spring or fall, so if the farmer has planted his crops early in the spring, or does not harvest them until late in the fall, there is danger of frost. If it is in the spring and the plants are young and small, the farmer may put little paper tents over each plant to keep the frost from them. If the plants are large, the farmer may set smudge-pots, or cans of burning oil, among the plants. The heat from these pots is usually enough to keep the frost away.

Frost, Robert

Robert Frost is recognized as one of the most important American poets. He  was born in San Francisco in 1875, but as a boy he lived in Massachusetts. Frost attended Dartmouth College and Harvard University, but sometimes interrupted his studies in order to teach or to work on farms. He lived in England for three years, and his first poems were published there. His poems are usually easy to understand, and often portray New England scenes such as a country cottage, the wind and the rain, or the stars at night. One of his most popular poems is "Stopping by Woods on a Snowy Evening." He died in 1963.

Gale Research Co.

frostbite

Frostbite occurs when an extremity of the body, such as toes, fingers, nose or ears, becomes frozen. This usually happens when a person stays out in very cold weather too long. When part of your body is frostbitten, you cannot feel anything in that part. It usually happens to parts of the body farthest from the heart, because warm blood has difficulty getting there. If a frostbitten finger or toe is not given proper treatment immediately, it may turn black. This means that gangrene has set in; gangrene means a small portion of skin has died.

The proper way to treat frostbite is to thaw out the finger or toe very slowly by rubbing it with cold water or snow. Some doctors say that you should not use snow because it has bits of ice in it and they may cut the skin. The water that is used should be slowly warmed, and the frostbitten part should be gently rubbed until the person can feel the rubbing again. If the skin has turned black, a doctor should be called immediately.

frozen foods

Frozen foods are foods that have been quickly frozen while at the peak of freshness and quality, to preserve their food value over long periods of storage. For hundreds of years, foods have been dried, canned, and salted, and this preserved them well enough to be edible, but a great deal of their food value was lost in the process. Frozen foods usually keep their freshness, good taste and food value for many months.

As recently as twenty to twenty-five years ago, most people who lived in cities had never heard of frozen foods, but farmers and people in smaller towns were already using them. In the late 1920s, community locker houses began to appear in farming areas. These were freezing plants where farmers could take all the meat from the animals they had killed and have it quick-frozen and stored in lockers that they rented. Then the meat was available during the seasons when fresh meat was hard to get. They could also take what vegetables they did not need for home use or for sale and store them in the community freezer for use in the winter months. Gradually people in nearby towns began to use the community lockers. They could rent a locker, and then buy big cuts of meat or large quantities of vegetables when they were cheap on the market, and store them to be used throughout the year. Each week or so, they could make a trip to the locker house and bring home enough of their own food to last them until the next trip.

USE IN CITIES

In 1921, an American scientist named Clarence Birdseye thought of a way of putting out frozen foods in small packages that could be sold in stores. This was the beginning of the great frozen-food industry. Freezer cabinets began to appear in grocery stores, and nowadays you can buy everything from a package of frozen peas to whole turkeys ready to roast, in your neighborhood grocery store. Cooked foods are also frozen, and entire meals laid out on plates of aluminum foil can be bought and popped into the oven.

Manufacturers now build home refrigerators with freezer compartments so that housewives can take advantage of good buys on frozen foods and stock up on them. Home freezers are very important. These are big enough so that city housewives can buy and store large cuts of meat and big quantities of vegetables and freeze them themselves just as their farm neighbors do. They can also prepare and freeze baked foods such as bread and pies.

FROZEN FRUIT JUICES

The condensing and freezing of fruit juices, especially orange juice, was a difficult problem for a long time. It was easy to condense, or remove the water from, orange juice and to freeze it; but it was found that the juice was not as good when the water was put back. After many tests and experiments, it was discovered that not all the water could be removed. A little fresh, uncondensed orange juice had to be added to the condensed juice so that the product after freezing and thawing would be as good to drink as the original juice. Now almost every kind of fruit juice you can think of is condensed and frozen in little cans. When the juice is thawed and water is added, it is a delicious drink that is as full of vitamins and other food values as the fresh juice was. As a result, people today drink much more fruit juice than ever before, and this is very important to health.

HOW FREEZING WORKS

Freezing preserves food because it stops the process of spoiling. Most foods, especially garden products, contain a lot of water. Much of their food value is in the minerals and vitamins that are dissolved in this water. As long as the produce is growing, moisture is being drawn from the soil; as some of the moisture with its minerals and vitamins passes off into the air by evaporation, the roots renew the supply from the earth. When fruits and vegetables are harvested, the loss of food value by evaporation goes on, but the moisture is no longer renewed. The food dries out and begins to lose its mineral and vitamin value. At the same time the slow chemical process that we call rotting begins. Much the

same thing happens in meats and dairy products.

If the food is frozen as soon as it is ready to eat, the moisture cannot evaporate and the rotting process is stopped. Everything stays just as it was. The colder the food is kept, the longer it will stay fresh. When the United States Army was building military installations and roads in Alaska, they had to blast out some huge glaciers, or sheets of ice, that were in the way. Under the glaciers they found the carcasses of animals that had died and been frozen there thousands of years ago. Some of these animals were members of extinct species that had not been seen on earth for thousands of years, but their meat was still so fresh that dogs ate it with enjoyment and showed no bad effects from it.

KEEPING FROZEN FOODS

The two most important factors in freezing and storing foods are freezing them quickly, and keeping them frozen at very low temperatures. If food is to be stored for only a few weeks, it will be safe in the freezer compartment of an ordinary home refrigerator. But if it is to be kept for a year or so, it should be stored in temperatures near zero.

The length of time frozen foods can be safely stored depends on the quality of the foods used, and the conditions of packaging and storing. Most frozen meats, fruits and vegetables can be kept for one year. Prepared frozen foods such as pies, casserole dishes, and frozen leftover foods should be used within three to six months.

All frozen foods should be used promptly after they have been thawed, and they should not be refrozen after thawing. Frozen fruits should be thawed slowly in the regular food-storage part of the refrigerator, to prevent them from losing their color. Vegetables are best dropped immediately into boiling water in the frozen state. Meats may be thawed or cooked frozen.

The use of frozen foods of all kinds has added greatly to the health value and the enjoyment of our meals. Fresh corn in December and oysters in July are only two of the hundreds of surprising dishes that can be served to brighten our menus.

fruit

The fruit is the part of a plant that contains its seed. It appears in the same part of the plant where the flower was before it. When you eat an apple you will find pits at the core of it. The pits are the seeds of the apple. There are many kinds of fruit, but they can mostly be divided into two groups. The first kind ripens in a pod or jacket that splits open and drops the seeds out. Many plants that we call vegetables, such as peas or beans, bear this kind of fruit. The second kind is the fleshy fruit that has the seeds at the core, such as peaches, apples, plums, apricots, and avocado pears. Berries also have the seed in the fleshy part, but in berries the seeds are scattered through the fruit.

Although any seed-bearing plant produces a fruit, we usually think of fruit as being the juicy, sweet, delicious fruit we eat. This kind of fruit is a very important part of man's diet, and in certain warm climates the native people live almost entirely on it. In more northern climates fruits are a pleasing and healthful addition to people's diet. Besides tasting good, fruit supplies salts and acids that are very good for you, gives you a good appetite, and is good for the digestion.

Different fruits grow best in their native climates. Dates, coconuts, bananas, and pineapples grow in abundance near the equator. Further away from the equator, where it is not so hot, you will find oranges, lemons and figs. In temperate zones, where there are four seasons in the year, apples, peaches, grapes, and many other familiar fruits grow. Most fruit is also cultivated, that is, planted and grown by man. The North American continent has the greatest variety of fruits concentrated in one section of the globe. When the settlers came here they grew fruits that they had grown in their native countries as well as the fruits they found already growing here. The United States, because of the variety of its climate, can grow almost any kind of fruit. Fast transportation makes it possible for most of us to have fruits from far-off places at any time of the year. Oranges that are picked in California can be sold in New York a few days later, and special grapes can be flown from Belgium to the United States in a few hours.

Fruits can be dried, canned, preserved, or frozen. Dried fruit is kept by evaporating the water from it. Preserved fruit is cooked with or without sugar and preserved in jars or cans. Frozen fruit may go into a deep freeze just as it comes from the vine, or it, too, can be cooked before freezing. Science has done much to improve the preserving of fruit and also the growing of it. Experts have found new ways of fertilizing and feeding plants and of breeding them to get the best results.

Fruit contains starches and sugar, which give fuel to the body. They also contain a carbohydrate called *pectin*. This makes it possible for them to be made into jelly.

fruit fly

Fruit flies are very small flies and there are many species or kinds of them. You have probably seen them in the country around fruit trees. Usually they have brightly colored stripes or spots. They are harmful because they lay their eggs on fruit and the maggots that develop from the eggs feed on the fruit and spoil it for people to eat. Other fruit flies make galls on fruit trees. The gall is a swelling caused by developing larva, or maggots, which grow from eggs that the fly has deposited in a part of the tree, the leaf, or the flower.

fuchsia

Fuchsia is a plant that grows in the woods and forests of South and Central America, as well as in a few places in New Zealand. Most of the fuchsia that you see today is grown in pots in greenhouses, which are buildings with glass roofs, in which all kinds of plants are grown. The fuchsia that is grown in a greenhouse is much more beautiful than the kind that grows in forests. There are over 550 different kinds of fuchsia. Sometimes you will hear people call fuchsia "evening primrose" or "ladies' eardrops." The bunches of blossoms nod in the breeze and look like a lady's dangling earring. The blossoms have four or five petals of lovely colors: deep pink, purple, white, or different reds and scarlets. The stem has a very simple leaf. In South and Central America you will find that some fuchsia grows like a tree and is sometimes forty feet tall. The kind that is grown in pots in greenhouses is usually one to two feet high. In England and the United States fuchsia blooms throughout the spring and summer.

fuel

Fuel is anything that we burn for a useful purpose. The main uses of fuels are, first, to make fire for heat, and second, to provide power for transportation. The principal fuels burned for heat are coal, oil, wood, and gas. The principal fuels burned for transportation are gasoline in automobiles, other oils in Diesel engines, and coal or oil in steam locomotives.

Electricity is also used both for heat and for transportation, but it is not called a fuel.

There are separate articles on all the principal fuels. The food we eat is often called fuel, because our bodies burn it to get energy.

Fugitive Slave Laws

Fugitive Slave Laws were laws that said what should be done about fugitive slaves, that is, slaves who ran away from their masters. In the United States from colonial times up until the Civil War, people could own slaves; so there were always fugitive slave laws. The colonies had laws about Negro and Indian slaves, and indentured servants, or people who were bound to work for someone for a certain number of years. All these laws said that runaway slaves and servants must be returned to their masters. When the colonies declared their independence and formed the United States of America, the Constitution and the Fugitive Slave Act of 1793 provided for the return of slaves to their masters. These laws also said that owners had a right to get their slaves back, and that people who hid slaves from their owners should be fined.

These laws did not work well for long. Gradually, in the northern states all the slaves were freed, and people there began to feel that it was wrong to keep human beings enslaved. So people in the North did not return the slaves to their masters, but instead hid them and helped them to escape. Groups of people in the North began to join together and formed the Underground Railway, which had secret hiding places and helped slaves to get away. The people of the South, who still owned slaves, became very alarmed about this. They were losing many slaves, who were an important part of their property. They wanted better and stronger laws to help them get back their runaway slaves. Finally, in 1850, Congress passed a new Fugitive Slave Law, which said that agents of the United States government would recapture fugitive slaves and that everyone must help them. People who tried to help the fugitives would have to pay heavy fines and even go to prison. The United States did not manage to solve the problems concerning slavery

peacefully, and finally the North and South went to war, in 1861. The Fugitive Slave Law of 1850 was repealed in 1864.

After the Civil War all the slaves were freed, and an amendment was added to the Constitution that said that no one could own slaves.

fugue

A fugue is a kind of musical composition that was first written about four hundred years ago. The fugue is made up of different voices, or parts, which follow one after the other. First the theme, or melody, called the "subject," is played or sung by itself, followed by one or more voices, or parts, that answer in the same melody but at different levels of pitch. The fugue develops in this way until the various voices are brought together in a climax, in which the different parts sometimes overlap like the rounds you sing in school. (The name *fugue* comes from the Latin word for "flight"; the different parts of the music follow one another like a flight or chase.) Johann Sebastian Bach was one of the greatest composers of fugues.

Fujiyama

Fujiyama is the most famous mountain in Japan. Its name means "Fire Mountain." It is also called simply Fuji (fire) or Fujisan, which means "the Honorable Mr. Fire." Fujiyama is about fifty miles west of the city of Tokyo, the capital of Japan. It is a volcano, but it last erupted more than three hundred years ago. It is more than two miles around its crater. When eruptions took place, hot lava poured down the mountainside. Fujiyama is snow-covered in winter and usually has snow on its top even in the summer. Some people say that the volcano suddenly appeared on what was a flat plain one morning more than two thousand years ago. It is sacred to the people of Japan. On its sides are religious shrines and temples. Fujiyama is 12,460 feet high, and many pilgrims climb part way up each year.

Fukien

China is divided into sections called provinces, and Fukien is one of these provinces. It is on the southeastern coast of China, and has an area of about 46,-000 square miles. About 13,000,000 people live in Fukien. This means that the province is about the same size as the state of Pennsylvania, but it has a greater number of people living there. The capital city of Fukien province is Foochow, which is a port on the China Sea. Amoy is another important port in Fukien. The Min River, one of China's largest rivers, flows through Fukien. Many of the people of Fukien are farmers, and they raise rice, sugar cane, tobacco and tea. Others are lumbermen or fishermen. There are rich deposits of coal and manganese in Fukien, but mining is not an important industry because not many of the mines have been developed yet. About a hundred years ago Fukien was known for the fine flower-scented tea that was grown and packaged there; this tea was sent all over the world, and it was among the best known of all Chinese teas. Today, although the farmers in Fukien still grow fine tea, it is used mostly at home, and less of it is exported to foreign countries.

fuller's earth

Fuller's earth is a very interesting type of clay that comes from many places in the United States and Europe. Usually it is in the form of a powder. When anything oily or greasy is mixed with fuller's earth, the oil or grease becomes colorless. This makes the clay very useful in clothing factories, tailor shops, and laundries, because if a piece of cloth gets a grease stain on it, a little fuller's earth rubbed into the stain will remove it completely. It is also very useful in factories for filtering oil that flows through machines. The clay removes any foreign particles from the oil and makes it clean so that it can be used again.

Fulton, Robert

Robert Fulton was the famous American inventor who built the first passenger steamboat ever used in the United States. This boat was called the *Clermont,* and because at first people had very little confidence in it, it was called "Fulton's Folly."

Fulton was born in Lancaster County, Pennsylvania, in 1765. While he was still a child, he showed a great deal of talent and skill in arts and crafts, and his family decided to have him learn the jewelry trade. They sent him to Philadelphia as an apprentice to a jeweler, but he was more interested in painting than in jewelry making. Benjamin Franklin, the great American statesman and inventor, took an interest in young Fulton and encouraged him to go to England to study painting. Fulton did go abroad when he was 21 years old, and he became a very successful portrait painter. But soon he lost interest in painting as a profession, and he turned his talents to inventing. He invented several new kinds of canal boat and devised a method for emptying and filling canals that was more efficient than the old system of locks. Later he went to France, where he worked on the invention he considered most important of all, a submarine. His submarine really worked, but he could not get the American, the French, or the British government to take any interest in it. He returned to the United States and built his ship, the *Clermont.* It made its first successful trip up the Hudson River in 1807. After that, Fulton built several more steamboats that were used for river travel. He died in New York in 1815.

fumigation

Fumigation is the use of smoke or gas to drive away or kill insects, mice, and other pests. When a person decides to have his house fumigated to kill household pests, the house is sealed off completely, and gas is piped into it. The house or room is not entered until all of the gas fumes have blown away. Several gases can be used in fumigation; the most common are cyanide, formaldehyde, and chlorine gas. The fumes of these gases are dangerous to people as well as to insects and rodents, and for that reason it is wise to call in a fumigator or an extermi-nator if you want to have your house fumigated.

fundamentalists

A fundamentalist is a person who believes that every word in the Bible should be treated as literally true, and not just as an example or story which, like the parables of Jesus, was given to illustrate a religious idea. The word comes from a set of books published in 1910, called *The Fundamentals,* which gave as the basic Protestant beliefs: 1, the absolute truth of the Bible; 2, the Virgin birth of Jesus; 3, the Resurrection, or rising from the dead, of Jesus; 4, the Redemption, or saving, of man; and 5, the second coming of Christ.

William Jennings Bryan was the fundamentalist whose name was best known because he was very prominent in public life.

Fundy, Bay of

The Bay of Fundy is a long arm of the Atlantic Ocean that separates Nova Scotia, Canada, from New Brunswick, Canada. It is about a hundred miles long, and it is sixty miles wide at its widest point. It is not easy for ships to travel in the Bay of Fundy because in some places its waves are very wild and rise to great heights. The Bay of Fundy is famous for its fifty-foot high tides, which are the highest in the world. The oldest town in Canada, Annapolis Royal, which was founded by the French in 1605, is on the Nova Scotia side of the Bay of Fundy. The chief port of the Bay of Fundy is on the New Brunswick side. It is called Saint John. Scientists have studied the great tides in the Bay of Fundy to see if the force of the tides can be used as water power to make electricity.

fungus (plural fungi)

A fungus is a plant body without root, stem or leaves. It is not capable of manufacturing its own food and is therefore a *parasite,* or an organism that lives on other living matter, or a *saprophyte,* which lives on dead matter.

A fungus can be a mushroom, the downy, green growth on a stale loaf of bread, or the grey mold you find when you uncover a pile of wet, rotted leaves. A fungus finds a place it likes, settles there and begins to feed on its host. It reproduces itself by sprouting. Some fungi build themselves out into the air into a kind of fuzz; others, like mushrooms, take a more definite shape. Certain fungi are very useful to man. Mushrooms and truffles are a nourishing part of people's diet. Penicillin, which is used to fight germs and infections in the human system, comes from a fungus which is cultivated on wood shavings in a laboratory. Yeast, the ingredient that makes bread rise when it is baked, is a fungus. Some fungi are good simply because they are scavengers and destroy refuse such as rotted wood and leaves or garbage. Some fungi choose harmful insects as their hosts and destroy them. Sometimes a good fungus may feed on a harmful one. The harmful fungi settle on fruit and grain and ruin crops. There is a certain fungus that settles in the intestines of animals and saps their strength. Horses are subject to a fungus that gets in their lungs.

Young fishes in hatcheries can easily be killed off by a fungus disease. Athlete's foot is perhaps the most familiar fungus disease that attacks people, but in World War II a number of soldiers who went to the South Pacific were subject to a lot of unknown fungus diseases. Although scientists have done a great deal of research, many of these fungus diseases remain a mystery.

Fungi belong to the same group of plants as algae. The great difference between algae and fungi is that algae contain chlorophyll, the agent that most plants use to make their own food out of carbon dioxide gas and water, with the sun as a source of energy.

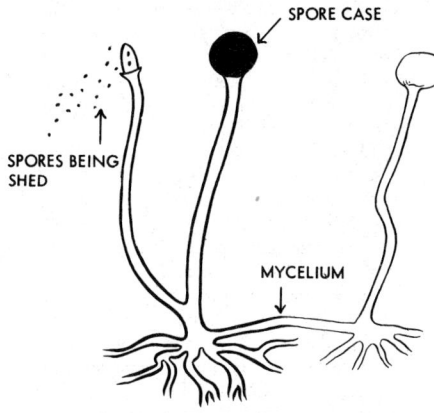

SPORE CASE

SPORES BEING SHED

MYCELIUM

A BREAD MOLD

The mycelium, a threadlike part that absorbs food, grows upward and produces a case that contains spores.

fur

Fur is the hairy skin of certain animals. The animals are trapped, so as not to injure the skin, usually during the winter months when the fur is at its best. After being taken from the traps and killed, the animals are skinned. The salted and dried skins, called *pelts,* are taken to trading posts in the spring. There they are baled for shipment to the factories where they will be made into coats, neck-pieces, and other things to wear.

Furs have been used since prehistoric times. It is probable that man's first clothing was the skins of animals. The natives of many cold regions could not get along without furs. The Eskimos make fur garments that are the warmest and lightest ever devised by man, using the furry hide of caribou, sealskin, polar bear, and Arctic hare. These people, and many northern Indians, could never have survived without furs for clothing, sleeping robes, and floor covering. The fur trade was known to the early Romans, who bought furs from the barbarians of the north and from Africa; and the Greeks bought furs from Russia and Asia.

Soon after the discovery of America, fur trade with the Indians began. Much of the history of North America is tied to the fur trade, for it was the hardy trappers and traders who penetrated the wilderness. Paddling their canoes over inland waterways, they were the first to reach the mountains of the West and the Pacific coast. In 1670, Charles II of England granted a charter to a group of men who wanted to trade with the Indians of the Hudson Bay region. This became the Hudson's Bay Company. This group

divided the wilderness into districts, each having a trading post, or store, and several trappers. Beaver skins were used for money. All furs and other goods were rated as being worth so many "made beaver," or beaver ready for shipment. A gun, a barrel of flour, a blanket, or a steel trap could be purchased with beaver skins or other furs, just as we use money. By 1810 the fur trade in North America had reached a peak. Rivalry between John Jacob Astor's American Fur Company and the Northwest Company reached a condition of actual warfare. There was shooting and bloodshed. Then in 1821 the Hudson's Bay Company merged with the Northwest Company, keeping the name of the Hudson's Bay Company. By that time Canadian trappers had reached Alaska; American traders such as Kit Carson, Jim Bridger, and Thomas Fitzpatrick had crossed the Rocky Mountains and gone on to the Pacific Ocean.

But the peak of the great fur trade passed and it began to decline. By the time of the Civil War there was little left of it. There were many reasons. The country was being settled rapidly. As the forests were cleared to be converted into farm lands, the wild animals were driven out or destroyed. Meantime, the greed of the traders had cut down the supply of fur animals. Some species such as the sea otter became extinct. The same thing might have happened to the fur seal if laws had not been enacted to protect them. Now there are refuges for them, such as the Isle of St. George in the Pribilof Islands, and the hunting of fur seals is carefully controlled.

As prices rose, furs became less popular. The beaver hat went out of style and men all but stopped wearing fur coats. Furs soon became a luxury item for women's coats and neckpieces. Nevertheless, the fur trade is still very much alive. Thousands of people work in the many fur centers such as London, New York, Leipzig, Paris, and Moscow. Fur workers are among the most highly skilled of all craftsmen and there is a large and flourishing retail business.

HOW FURS ARE PREPARED

Most of the world's supply of furs comes from northern Canada, Alaska, Siberia, and China. Natives of these regions, such as Eskimos, Indians, and many others, make their living by trapping fur-bearing animals. The raw furs are shipped in bales to the manufacturing centers, there to be dressed and dyed, matched and cut, and made into clothing. At the factories, the hides are selected according to size and quality. Then they are soaked and washed, and scraped on the inside. Some furs, such as seal, have long coarse hairs called guard hairs. These are pulled out or cut, leaving only the soft underfur. Next the skins are stretched on boards to dry, and then they are ready for leathering. The skins are greased with animal fat and laid in tubs. Barefooted men get into the tub and walk around on the skins, treading on them and kneading them until they are soft and smooth. In many factories this is done by machinery. Now the skins are cleaned and combed until the fur is soft and fluffy. The furs are then ready for cutting. Cutting the skins is a very skillful operation, and it is always done by hand.

Before the furs can be sewed together into garments, they must be matched for color. One coat may be made of hundreds of small pieces, all perfectly matched in color and sewed together so that you cannot tell where they are joined.

PRINCIPAL KINDS OF FUR

There are many different kinds of fur used for clothing. Some furs are preferred because they give greater warmth; some are desired because of their light weight; others are chosen because they wear particularly well. A particular fur may be popular just because it is easily made into styles fashionable at the time. Prices change from season to season depending upon the scarcity of different animals and the demands of fashion.

One of the higher-priced furs is *sable,* which is dark brown in color with dark streaks. The best sable comes from Siberia and is called *Russian sable.* The fur of the *marten* is sometimes called *American sable.* The *stone marten,* found only in Europe and Asia, has fur that wears better and is more expensive than other marten.

Mink is another costly fur, usually dark brown in color. Minks are now usually bred on farms called mink ranches. The natural furs, however, are more desirable, and of these the darker furs are more valuable. In recent years, ranch minks have been crossbred to produce light-colored, or platinum, furs; these have become very fashionable and are the most expensive because they are scarce. *Ermine,* from a relative of the mink, is the traditional fur of royalty. It is trapped in midwinter, when it is snow-white with a black tip at the end of its short tail. *Chinchilla* comes from the Andes Mountains of South America; the soft fur of this tiny animal is dark bluish-gray in color, and it is very beautiful and expensive. *Nutria,* the fur of the coypu, a beaver-like animal, also comes from South America.

Beaver and *seal* are among the most durable of all furs. They are priced below the top luxury furs, making them very popular. Seal is usually dyed black. *Otter* is an extremely durable fur that is almost waterproof. At one time it was very much in demand for the collars of men's overcoats. *Silver fox* is also raised on fur farms, but the wild variety is much more expensive, as is the famous *blue fox,* or Pribilof fox.

Modern fur processing can produce such close imitations that laws now require the true name of the fur to be given. Not long ago, for instance, *muskrat* dyed to resemble seal was sold as *Hudson seal,* but now it must be called *Hudson seal-dyed muskrat.* Natural muskrat is quite popular, as are *skunk, squirrel, marmot, raccoon, rabbit,* and *opossum. Mouton* is lambskin with the hair left on. By an electrical process it is made to look like beaver. *Persian lamb, astrakhan,* and *karakul* are skins of the newly born karakul lamb. The hair is tight and curly, and furriers rate the quality of the fur by the tightness of the curl. The younger the lamb the tighter the curl. Persian lamb is usually dyed black.

There are separate articles in this encyclopedia about the animals whose furs are most used for clothing.

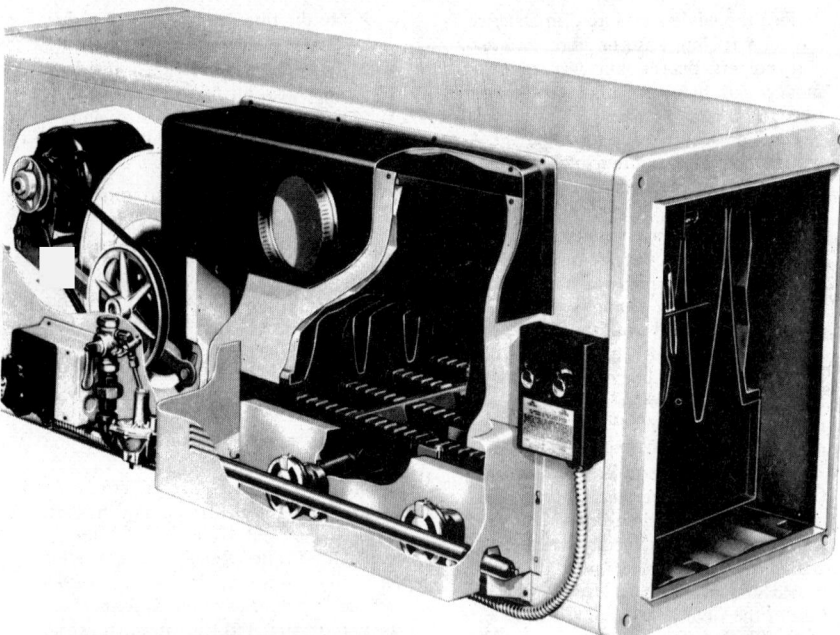

Lennox Furnace Co.

In a gas-burning furnace, the gas comes through a number of jets. The air is blown in by the motor at the left. The gas furnace is one of the easiest to adjust.
Left: In an oil-burning furnace, oil is pumped in by the motor at the bottom, and air is blown in by the top motor.

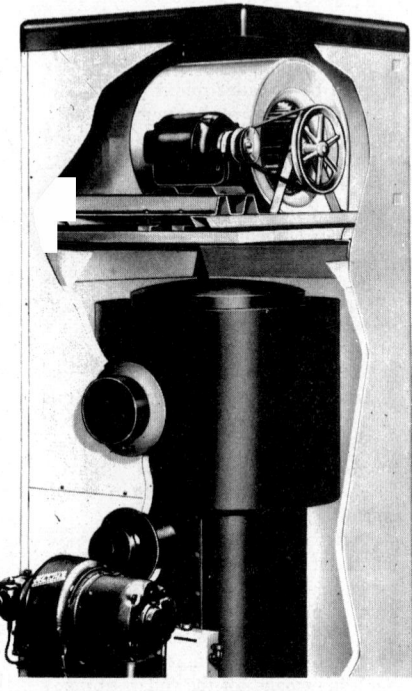

Furies

The Furies were beings in Roman mythology, the stories the ancient Romans told about their gods and goddesses. The Greek name of the Furies was the Erinyes. The Furies, or Erinyes, were avenging goddesses, whose work was to punish criminals. They were described as fearful-looking women with snakes in their hair and blood dripping from their eyes, who lived deep in the nether world. When some crime was committed, they rose to the earth and pursued the criminal. They brought him suffering during his life and punishment after death. Their purpose was to see that justice was done, and nothing could move them from their purpose, or protect the person whom they pursued. They especially punished people who were disobedient to their parents, people who did not show proper respect for old age, and certain other wrongdoers. The Eumenides were also Furies but dispensed justice. The great Greek playwright Aeschylus wrote a play called *The Eumenides,* in which the Furies torment Orestes because he murdered his mother, Clytemnestra, who murdered his father.

furnace

A furnace is a container in which a fire is made to produce heat. The heat may be to warm a building or to melt something, or, as in a steam engine, it may be changed into energy to do work. The most familiar type of furnace is the kind we have in our homes. It burns coal, oil, or gas, and has an opening for the air that is needed to keep the fire burning. You can read more about this kind of furnace in the article on HEATING.

Furnaces that are used for melting purposes require different kinds of fuel. A very high temperature is needed in these furnaces in order to melt metals or even stones. The high heat is usually produced by forcing extra air into the furnace. A blast furnace, which you can read about in the article on IRON AND STEEL, gets its name because air is blasted into the furnace.

The electric furnace produces the greatest heat—up to 7000 degrees Fahrenheit. This type of furnace is used by jewelers and people who work with metals that melt at a very high temperature. All furnaces must be constructed to hold the heat they produce and not waste it. They must also be safe so that the fire and heat is kept burning inside the furnace and there is no chance of fire on the outside. Insulation keeps the heat in a furnace and makes it safe. Asbestos or rock that does not melt is used to insulate, cover and protect a furnace.

furniture

Furniture is chairs, tables, beds, lamps, and all the things used in a house to make it more comfortable. Rugs, pictures, and other ornaments are furniture too, but they are usually called *furnishings,* which are extra things that make a house look attractive. Another class of things that add to the comfort of a house are called *fixtures,* such as built-in bookshelves, chandeliers, and bathroom equipment.

Ancient man did not have furniture. He slept on animal skins and sat on rocks or on the ground. Tables and chairs are mentioned in the Bible, but they were not much like the furniture we have in our homes today. The chairs were a kind of folding campstool, and the tables were very small and light so that they could be packed on an animal's back, because the people in Old Testament days did a great deal of moving around.

One of the first beautiful pieces of furniture that we know about is in the Metropolitan Museum in New York City. It is a bed that was made in Egypt more than five thousand years ago. It is made of wood and is carved and painted with pictures. It has no mattress, only strings stretched from side to side.

Egyptian furniture was very simple. The ancient Greeks and Romans learned almost everything they knew about furniture from the Egyptians. The Greeks used wood for their furniture at first, but later they made much of it out of marble, which was long-lasting and could be carved in beautiful shapes.

The Romans made chairs and tables of wood and ivory, but they did not like to sit in chairs for their meals. At a Roman dinner the guests lay on couches while they ate. The couches were made of marble and had cushions and pillows to make them comfortable. The Romans had floor lamps just as we have today. They were made of bronze and had large bowls that held burning oil. Roman beds were elaborately carved, and they had mattresses and pillows.

During the Middle Ages, which lasted from about the year 500 to 1400, there was very little furniture. What few pieces the people did have were very big and clumsy. They were made of carved wood. The chairs looked like boxes with high backs and arms. The castles and houses in which the people lived were very cold, so chairs did not have legs. They had solid bottoms so that the wind could not whistle around people's feet and ankles. The beds were like enormous tents, with curtains hung around all four sides.

THE RENAISSANCE PERIOD

In the period called the Renaissance, which began about the year 1400 and lasted about 200 years, the people had more furniture and it was much more beautiful. The chairs were upholstered; that is, the backs and seats were padded and covered with some material such as velvet or silk. During this period furniture began to be admired for its beauty as well as its usefulness, and the making of furniture became a kind of art. Carving became very elaborate, and a great deal of inlay work was used. Inlay is small bits of beautiful wood, ivory, gold,

Many different kinds of furniture have been used in different countries through the ages to help people get a good night's sleep. 1. An ancient Egyptian bed. 2. Headrests, used in some parts of Africa, where the people sleep on the floor. 3. A headrest used in Japan. 4. An ancient Roman bed. 5. A canopied bed used in Europe 200 years ago. 6. A canopied bed used during colonial times. 7. A warming pan, used in the colder parts of Europe to heat bedclothes at night before modern methods of heating were invented and made houses comfortable all the time.

or pieces of china that are set into the wood in designs.

The Renaissance started a great interest in furniture that has continued up to the present day. About 250 years ago there was more beautiful furniture made than at any other time in history. Designers such as Thomas Chippendale, Duncan Phyfe, George Hepplewhite and Thomas Sheraton became famous for the designs of their chairs, tables, chests, and other pieces.

When the Pilgrims landed in America in 1620 they brought with them very plain furniture. They did not believe that anything should be fancy or elaborate. This simple furniture is called Colonial style, and it is still popular in the United States.

As time went on, people in the United States and Europe began to want to return to the elaborate styles of the Middle Ages and the Renaissance. The more elaborate a piece of furniture could be made, with curlicues and fringe and brass knobs and ornaments, the better they liked it. By the 1920s this style again passed and furniture became simple and attractive, designed principally for comfort.

MODERN FURNITURE

Modern chairs may be made of plastic, or of plywood, which is many thin layers of wood glued together. Often foam rubber is used to upholster chairs and sofas. Metal and glass have become very important in modern furniture.

The making of furniture has become a big industry. The day of the individual furniture maker has passed, except for special pieces made for very rich people.

Furniture factories turn out handsome and well-made pieces of furniture. The city of Grand Rapids, Michigan, makes so much furniture that its name has come to be almost synonymous with furniture.

fuse

The word *fuse* comes from a Latin word meaning "to pour." A metal is said to fuse when it melts, and the temperature at which a metal such as iron will melt is called its *fusing point*.

Our most familiar use of the word *fuse* is for a safety device used in electrical circuits. As electricity flows through a wire it creates heat. If a lot of electricity tries to get through a small wire that is not heavy enough for it, the heat becomes so great it will cause a fire. But every electrical circuit is run through a fuse, and in the fuse there is a piece of metal that will melt at a much lower temperature than the wire will. Before the elec-

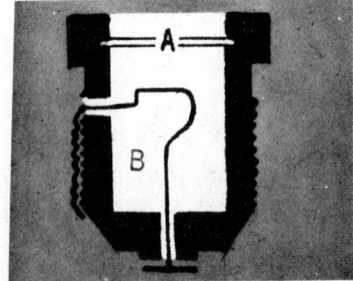

A cross section of a fuse. A window (A) in the fuse makes it possible to see when the aluminum or lead fuse wire (B) has melted or "blown" because too much current has been sent through the circuit.

tricity could possibly cause enough heat in the wire to start a fire, it melts the piece of metal in the fuse. This breaks the circuit; that is, it stops the electricity from flowing. Then the wire cannot heat up and there is no danger of fire. It is very dangerous to use a heavy fuse that will stand more electricity than the wire can.

The word *fuse* has other meanings. Fusing metals, or making them join together, is an important part of FORGING and WELDING, about which there are separate articles.

Another meaning of the word *fuse* is a rod or tube that carries flame to an explosive to set it off. The piece of string on a firecracker is a fuse. A long fuse is used to lead a fire up to a charge of dynamite, so that a person can light the fuse and be far away before the dynamite explodes. This word *fuse* comes from a Latin word that means a "spindle," or thin rod. It is often spelled *fuze*.

fusel oil

Fusel oil is an oily liquid that is produced when alcohol is made. It is a kind of alcohol itself, but fortunately there is very little of it in alcoholic drinks because it is a quick-acting poison. There is not much more than a few drops of fusel oil in a pint of alcohol, and even this is removed before any drink is bottled and sold. Fusel oil is a solvent, a substance that dissolves some kinds of solid matter. It is used in making paint and lacquer.

fusing point

The fusing point of a metal or other solid material is the temperature at which it melts, or changes from a solid to a liquid. The most familiar fusing point on the Fahrenheit temperature scale is 32 degrees, the temperature at which ice turns into water. Some things have fusing points that are much lower than that of ice. Mercury, the metal, has a very low fusing point, so it is usually seen as a silvery liquid. The reason for this is that under normal conditions mercury is at a temperature above its fusing point, which is 39 degrees below zero.

fusion, the name scientists use to describe how hydrogen atoms combine and form helium atoms at temperatures of millions of degrees. See SUN and HYDROGEN BOMB.

Future Farmers of America

Future Farmers of America is the name of an organization of high-school boys who are planning to become farmers when they finish their education. The purpose of the organization is to help the boys to become better farmers and more useful citizens. More than 375,000 boys belong to the organization, and there are 8,644 chapters in the United States and Puerto Rico. They have regular meetings at which they talk about methods of farming and ways of working together. Future Farmers of America was founded in 1928 and has its headquarters in Washington, D.C.

Members of the Future Farmers of America traditionally take part in livestock shows at which they display their own cattle and learn to judge such contests, as well.

Future Farmers of America

677

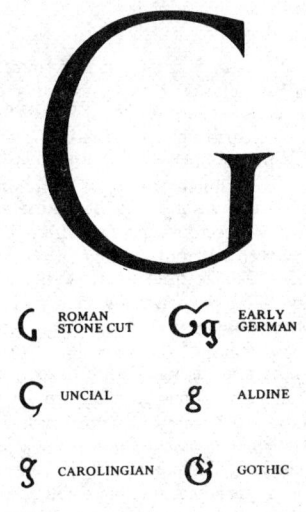

G

G	ROMAN STONE CUT	Gg	EARLY GERMAN
C	UNCIAL	g	ALDINE
g	CAROLINGIAN	G	GOTHIC

G or g

The letter G is the seventh letter of the alphabet. It is different from most of our other letters because it does not come from one of the earliest alphabets. The Romans first used the G as a special form of the letter C when they wanted to make the sound that our G has in the word *game*. The letter C came from the Greek *gamma* and the Hebrew *gimal;* you may read about it in the separate article on the letter C. Today the G is often used to make the J sound.

At the top of this page, at the far left, you can see the Roman Stone Cut equivalent of the letter G. The Roman Stone Cut symbol was gotten from the late Greek letter *gamma* which looked like our letter V with its apex (pointed end) facing left. That letter came from an early Greek form which looked like our number 7 drawn with a right angle. In early times, writing was read from right to left, and in some old languages, such as Hebrew, it still is. But the Greeks changed and began to read from left to right. When they made this change, they turned the letters around so that the letter which looked similar to our 7 became the late Greek *gamma*. It is not hard to see how this evolved into our modern letter G.

Read also the article ALPHABET.

gabardine

Gabardine is a cloth that was originally made of wool, but now is made of cotton and rayon also. The material is tightly woven and has small diagonal ridges in it. Gabardine is a strong cloth that is often used to make raincoats because it keeps out water. Men's and women's suits are often made of gabardine.

In the Middle Ages, more than five hundred years ago, Jews and pilgrims wore loose cloaks that were called *gaberdines*. They were not made of the material that is called gabardine today.

gable

A gable is the top part of the end of a building. It is shaped like a triangle. As you stand at the end of a building and look at the roof, you see that the two sides of the roof come down like the sides of a triangle and meet the upright front and back walls of the building. That roof, which comes to a peak at the top, is called a gable. Often you will see a little win-

dow on the main roof of a house that has a separate little peaked roof of its own. That is a gable window. In Holland and Belgium there are many roofs with gables. These houses are very high and narrow, and the roof gables, which are very steep, make them look like witches' hats. Gables were used in ancient Greece more than 2,500 years ago. The famous Parthenon in Athens had a beautiful gabled roof.

Gable, Clark

Clark Gable was a famous actor in motion pictures. He was born in 1901 in Cadiz, Ohio, attended Akron University, and then worked at many different jobs before he became an actor. He appeared on the stage in several plays and then went into the movies. His first leading  role was opposite Joan Crawford in *Dance Fool, Dance*. His greatest role was that of Rhett Butler in the famous motion picture *Gone With the Wind*. Gable also acted in many comedies, winning an Academy Award in *It Happened One Night*. During World War II Gable flew many bombing missions over enemy territory for the Air Force. He died in 1960.

Gabon, Republic of

The Republic of Gabon gained its independence on August 17, 1960. Previously it had been one of the four territories of French Equatorial Africa. It is located on the west coast of Africa between Rio Muni and The Republic of the Congo (Brazzaville). The people are Negroes belonging to many different tribal groups. The chief products are cocoa; akoume and acajou woods from Gabon's dense forests; and manganese, gold, and uranium. The government consists of a President and a National Assembly.

REPUBLIC OF GABON. Area, 102,300 square miles. Population, 500,000 (1973 estimate). Capital, Libreville (65,000).

Gabriel

Gabriel is one of the archangels or messengers of God. He is known especially as the angel who announces God's will to men. He told of the prospective birth of John the Baptist, and he announced to Mary the forthcoming birth of Jesus. In the Mohammedan religion, it is Gabriel who explained the Koran, the holy writings of Islam, to Mohammed, the prophet. To Moslems, therefore, Gabriel is also an angel of truth. Gabriel is usually pictured with a trumpet in his hand, for it is believed he will blow his trumpet to announce the Day of Judgment. Gabriel's feast day is March 24.

gadfly

Gadflies are greenish or black flies that are larger than the common housefly. One kind of gadfly is also called a *horsefly,* because it bites horses and cattle. Another kind of gadfly is the *botfly,* whose young live as parasites, or unwanted guests, in the stomachs of horses. When you see horses or cows swishing their tails, they may be brushing off gadflies.

Gadsden Treaty

The Gadsden Treaty was an agreement by which the United States bought territory from Mexico. The purchase was 45,000 square miles, or about as much land as the whole state of Pennsylvania. This land is now a part of southern New Mexico and Arizona. Other parts of the treaty gave the United States the right to cross the Isthmus of Tehuantepec, the narrowest part of southern Mexico. This was in the days before the Panama Canal had been built. It was easier and cheaper for Americans to take a ship to the Isthmus, cross the narrow strip of land and take the rest of the journey by ship, than it was to cross the whole width of America by land or to take a ship around South America. The Gadsden Treaty, signed in 1853, was named for General James Gadsden, who was sent by President Franklin Pierce to Mexico to make these proposals to the Mexican government. The United States paid Mexico ten million dollars for these rights and for the land, which is now known as the "Gadsden Purchase."

Gaelic language

Gaelic is a very old language. It is a Celtic language and belongs to the Indo-European family of languages, as do English and most of the other languages of Europe. Gaelic is still spoken in Ireland; by some people on the Isle of Man, where it is called Manx; and in northern Scotland, where it is called Scottish Gaelic.

gag rule

From time to time in any government a small number of people are very enthusiastic about a proposal in which the majority of lawmakers are not interested. To prevent a small group from forcing discussion of their own special interest, which they would like to make law, the House of Representatives in Washington, D.C. has a rule. This rule is called a "gag" rule. If the majority vote in favor of the gag rule, then the proposed law, called a bill, which the minority want to discuss, is put away. The gag rule therefore protects the majority of legislators, or lawmakers, from an argumentative minority.

Gagarin, Yuri

Yuri Alekseyevich Gagarin, a Russian astronaut, was the first man to orbit the earth in a spaceship. His feat was a milestone in man's attempts to conquer space. It took place on April 12, 1961. The name of his spaceship was *Vostok*, which in Russian means "East." Traveling at 17,000 miles per hour, Gagarin circled the earth in 89.1 minutes. He reached a maximum height of 188 miles and a minimum height of 109½ miles in his elliptical orbit. The spaceship landed safely one hour and forty-eight minutes after blast-off by using a combination of parachute and glider. Upon landing, Gagarin reported that he felt fine and that everything went well. His trip proved that man could endure the physical stresses and the hazards of space travel. For his courageous exploit, he was feted in Moscow and in many of the capitals of the world. Gagarin was born in 1934 on a collective farm near Gzhatsk, about 100

miles from Moscow. In 1961 he was a major in the Soviet Air Force.

Gage, Thomas

Thomas Gage was the British general whose soldiers fired the first shots in the American Revolution. He was born in England in 1721. When he was a young man he entered the army. The British  government sent him to America in 1763 and made him commander-in-chief of all the soldiers in the colonies, and in 1774 he was appointed governor of Massachusetts. He became afraid that the colonists were going to revolt against England and he sent his troops to Concord and Lexington to take away the stored guns and ammunition and to capture the leaders of the revolt. The colonists resisted his soldiers, and the American Revolution began on April 19, 1775. The English blamed Gage for starting the war and he resigned from government service. He died in 1787.

Gainsborough, Thomas

Thomas Gainsborough was one of the most famous English painters of portraits, about two hundred years ago. Portraits are pictures of individuals or of a family group. Gainsborough painted portraits of the richest and most fashionable people. He made the women he painted look very beautiful, sometimes more beautiful than they really were. He also painted 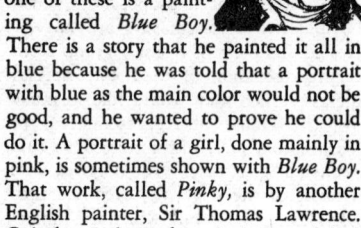 many pictures of children. The most famous one of these is a painting called *Blue Boy.* There is a story that he painted it all in blue because he was told that a portrait with blue as the main color would not be good, and he wanted to prove he could do it. A portrait of a girl, done mainly in pink, is sometimes shown with *Blue Boy.* That work, called *Pinky,* is by another English painter, Sir Thomas Lawrence. Gainsborough was born in 1727 and died in 1788.

Gaitskell, Hugh

Hugh Todd Naylor Gaitskell became leader of the British Labour Party—

and therefore a candidate for Prime Minister—in 1955. He was born in 1906, of upper-class English and Scottish families, but as a young man he decided to try to help the working class. He joined the Labour Party and in 1945 was elected to Parliament. To win control of the party he and his "moderate" branch of the Labour Party defeated the extreme Socialist and anti-American branch led by Aneurin Bevan. He died in 1963, otherwise the Labour Party's victory in the 1964 British elections would have made him Prime Minister.

Galahad

Sir Galahad was the noblest and purest of the knights of King Arthur. He was the son of Lancelot and Elaine. When he was old enough to join the other knights at King Arthur's Round Table, he went directly to the one seat that had always been vacant. This seat had been reserved for the knight pure enough to find the Holy Grail, the cup from which Jesus is supposed to have drunk at the Last Supper. All others who had tried to sit in this chair had been swallowed up by the earth. Sir Galahad joined the quest for the Holy Grail, and found it. See ARTHUR and HOLY GRAIL.

Galápagos

The Galápagos are a group of islands in the Pacific Ocean, almost 650 miles west of Ecuador in South America. They were discovered more than 400 years ago by a Spanish explorer, Tomás de Berlanga, who named them for the giant tortoises that live on the island. The Spanish word for "tortoise" is *galápago.*

The Galápagos now belong to Ecuador, and their official name is the Archipelago of Colón.

The islands are formed of old volcanoes, and the soil came from lava rock. The climate is mild. The people make their living at fishing and farming.

The Galápagos are best known for the rare animals and birds that live there: dragonlike lizards called iguanas that are often four feet long; strange birds that are not found anywhere else on earth, such as the cormorant that cannot fly; and penguins, although we usually think of them as living only in the Antarctic regions. The giant tortoises for which the islands are named sometimes weigh as much as five hundred pounds. So many of these rare animals were killed that the islands are now a protected wild-life reserve.

The largest islands, with their Spanish and English names, are: Isabela (Albemarle); Salvador (James I); Fernandina (Narborough); Santa Cruz (Indefatigable); and San Cristóbal (Chatham). The seat of the government is on San Cristóbal.

GALÁPAGOS. Group of five large and numerous small islands in the Pacific Ocean, belonging to Ecuador. Area, 2,966 square miles. Population (1973 estimate), 3,300.

galaxy

A galaxy is a cluster, or group, of stars. Each cluster is made up of a great many stars, sometimes as many as a billion. The earth on which we live is part of a galaxy which is called the Milky Way. We cannot see all of the Milky Way because we are inside of it ourselves, but we can see a lot of it. The Milky Way can be seen best on evenings in the late summer. People used to think that the Milky Way was the only galaxy there is. But astronomers, scientists who make a special study of the stars, have found out that there are many other galaxies all over the sky. Some galaxies are larger than the Milky Way and some are smaller. The smaller galaxies have only a few million stars. Galaxies are shaped in different ways. Some are round. Some are like very large pinwheels, with a thick cluster of stars forming the center and smaller clusters spreading out from the center like big arms. See the article MILKY WAY.

Galen

Galen was the name of a famous Greek physician who lived in the Greek city of Pergamum about 1,800 years ago. He started to study medicine when he was still very young, and later spent much time doing research and writing on medical subjects. He wrote many books on how to cure different diseases and illnesses with drugs and herbs. Many of his ideas were still used up to a few hundred years ago.

One of the most important studies made by Galen was his study of the human body and its structure. Read also the separate article on ANATOMY.

galena

Galena is a mineral from which we get most of our lead. Lead is never found by itself, but always in minerals that contain lead and something else. Galena is the most important of these minerals. It is a heavy, lead-gray mineral that shines like metal and breaks very easily. It is one of the most common of all minerals. Galena is gotten by mining, just as coal is. It is found mainly in Mexico, Spain, Canada and in the western and mid-western United States. Galena often contains silver, copper, and zinc.

Galicia

Galicia is a region that is partly in Poland and partly in Russia. It is somewhat smaller than the state of Maine, having an area of about 31,000 square miles, but more than six million people

Men with heavy loads cross a typical hanging bridge suspended by long ropes over a river in the Galápagos Islands. The bridge is made of poles fastened tightly together.

live there. Galicia is close to the Carpathian Mountains and extends down to the Dniester River.

Hundreds of years ago Galicia was an independent kingdom. Then for some time it was part of Poland. Almost two hundred years ago Russia and Austria divided it between them. After World War I the Austrian part of Galicia was given to Poland.

The people of Galicia are mostly Slavic. Some of them are Poles and the others are a Slavic people called Ruthenians.

Galilee, Sea of

The Sea of Galilee is in the northeast part of what was once called Palestine, in the new state of Israel. Around the Sea of Galilee are many of the places mentioned in the Bible. It was on the Sea of Galilee that Jesus walked. You can read about this in the Gospel of St. Matthew in the New Testament. Jesus also chose his first four disciples from among the fishermen who lived at the northern end of the Sea of Galilee. They were Peter, Andrew, James, and John.

Near the Sea of Galilee are ruins of many ancient Jewish villages and Roman towns. One of these is the old Roman city of Tiberias. This was one of the biggest cities in that section of the country two thousand years ago.

The Sea of Galilee is not as big as most seas, but is more like a large lake. It is shaped like a pear and is fifteen miles long and seven miles wide at its widest point. The land around the lake is quite bare, except on the west side, where some gardening is done. Windstorms in this area come up without warning and the waves on the Sea of Galilee get very high. It is 686 feet below sea level. The River Jordan flows into it.

Galileo

Galileo was one of the greatest scientists who ever lived. He was born about four hundred years ago in Pisa, Italy. As a young man he had planned to become a doctor, but he found himself so interested in mathematics and the nature of the world that he abandoned medicine and devoted his life to the sciences of astronomy and physics. When he was only 18 years old he made his first important discovery. In the cathedral of Pisa he watched a hanging lamp swinging back and forth. It occurred to him that it seemed to take the same length of time to make a big swing as to make a smaller one. He timed the swings by the beat of his own pulse, and later found his idea was true by other experiments. This was the principle of the pendulum, and its discovery led to the invention of the pendulum clock, about which you can read in the article on CLOCKS AND WATCHES.

Galileo is credited with the discovery that objects of different weights but of the same material and shape fall at the same rate of speed. Supposedly, Galileo dropped a one hundred pound iron ball and a one pound iron ball from the top of the Leaning Tower of Pisa. Both balls hit the ground at the very same time. Thus, Galileo proved his theory.

Galileo was the first to use a telescope to observe the movements of the heavenly bodies. He made improvements on the crude telescope of his time until he had one that was powerful enough to show the craters on the moon. The earlier great astronomer Copernicus had already said that the earth and other planets revolve around the sun, and not the sun around the earth as many people had believed for thousands of years. Galileo with his telescope was the first man to prove that this was true.

The discoveries of Galileo were so different from what men then believed that they were considered dangerous, and he was forced to stop publishing them for many years. But he kept on believing in them, and he kept on with his experiments.

Galileo lived to be an old man, and in his last years, even though he became blind, Galileo used to say that no man had ever seen more than he. He died in 1641, when he was 78 years old.

Gallatin, Albert

Abraham Albert Alphonse Gallatin was a great American statesman. He was born in 1761 in Geneva, Switzerland. When he was 19 years old he came to America to help the colonies fight for freedom and independence. After the Revolutionary War, when he was 23 years old, he settled in Pennsylvania, where he helped to found the town of New Geneva. He became very important in Pennsylvania and was elected to Congress. Later he was Secretary of the Treasury under President Thomas Jefferson. He was very cautious and hated to have the new country spend more money than it could afford.

After the War of 1812 between the United States and Great Britain, Gallatin was the main American representative at Ghent (a city in Belgium) where the peace treaty was signed.

In later life Gallatin became minister to France and to England, and the president of a bank. He was much interested in the American Indians, and he wrote a book about them. Gallatin died in 1849.

Gallaudet

Gallaudet is the name of a family of Americans who did much to help persons who are handicapped by deafness. Thomas Hopkins Gallaudet, born in Philadelphia in 1787 and educated to be a preacher, founded the first American school for the deaf, in Hartford, Connecticut, in 1817. He died in 1851 but his son Thomas Gallaudet, also a preacher, carried on the work by teaching deaf-mutes and caring for those who could not earn a living; he was born in 1822 and died in 1902. A younger son, Edward Miner Gallaudet, born in 1837, established the first college for the deaf, Gallaudet College in Washington, D.C. Edward died in 1917 but the college carried on and in 1964 had about 650 students.

gall bladder

The gall bladder is a small, pear-shaped sac right next to the liver in the abdomen of your body. The liver is a gland that makes bile, or gall, and the gall bladder is used to store some of this until it is needed. Bile is very important because it helps you to digest fatty foods. The liver secretes, or makes, much more

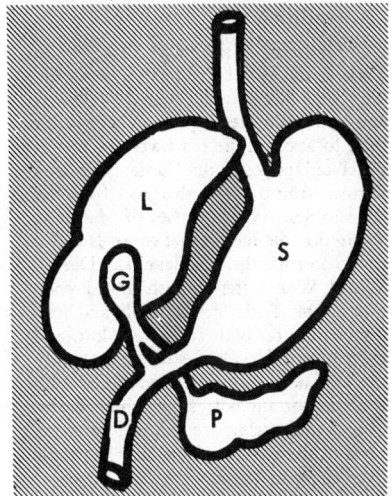

In digesting food, the gall bladder (G) stores bile made by the liver (L) until the food enters the duodenum (D). The bile and pancreatic juices from the pancreas (P) help us digest our food as it passes from the stomach (S) to the intestines.

bile than is needed. Most of it is excreted, or thrown out of the body, but since it is used for digestion, there must always be some bile in the body, and the gall bladder is used as the storeroom. Bile passes from the liver through the *hepatic duct,* which is a small tube from the liver to the gall bladder.

When you have eaten foods with fats in them, for example egg yolks or cream, a muscle in the gall bladder squeezes and forces the bile from the gall bladder through the cystic duct into the intestines, where it can work on the foods you have eaten. Sometimes the bile becomes more concentrated than it should, and the chemicals in it get solid. This means they crystallize, or form small crystals called gallstones. Gallstones are bad because they block up the tubes that the bile has to flow through. Then a doctor can operate on the abdomen to get into the gall bladder or tubes and remove the stones.

galley

The galley was an ancient warship or trading ship used by many ancient peoples. It was a low, flat-decked ship, and was rowed by slaves. These slaves were chained to long benches on either side of the ship, and were guarded by the galley master. When the captain wanted a ship to go faster, the galley master would whip the slaves without mercy, making them row faster and faster. Because the galley slaves were chained to the benches, they would go down with the ship if it sank during a battle with another ship, or in a storm.

Some of these galleys were so large that they could carry many tons of different products. Sometimes they not only used galley slaves, but had large colored sails to move them with the wind.

gallinule

A gallinule is a bird that looks like a small crane. It is only about a foot long. It lives in marshes or swampy places,

around the Great Lakes and in the Mississippi River Valley. You can hear the clucking sound it makes at some distance. The gallinule is often called a mud hen. It is olive brown on its back and a dull black on its underside. It has a red bill. It makes its nest in marshes and has long toes so that it can run easily on soft swampy ground.

Gallipoli

Gallipoli is the name of a city in Turkey, and also the name of a peninsula on which the city is located. The city and peninsula are important because of their location at the northwestern end of the Dardanelles. The Dardanelles is a narrow strait of water that goes from the Aegean Sea to the little Sea of Marmara. Therefore, the nation that controls Gallipoli controls the Dardanelles. During World War I the English and French fought the Turks at Gallipoli and lost. Many lives on both sides were lost, and the city was largely destroyed by bombing and heavy gunfire. Today Gallipoli is an important port from which beans, wheat and barley are shipped to many parts of the world. About 20,000 people lived there in 1960.

gallplant

Gallplant is a common roadside weed. You may call it "butter-and-eggs" or "toad-flax." It is about eighteen inches high and has a straight stem and a long tip covered with yellow and orange blossoms. The blossom looks like a snapdragon. The orange spot at the throat of the flower is the color of the yolk of an egg and the rest is the color of butter. Gallplant came from Europe and somehow it was replanted in America. Once it takes root it is very hard to get rid of, so it can be a troublesome weed.

Galsworthy, John

John Galsworthy was a famous English writer of novels, plays, and short stories. He was born in 1867. He went to Oxford University and studied to become a lawyer, but he never practiced law. Many of Galsworthy's novels are about various members and generations of the Forsyte family, from the middle of the 19th century right up to modern times. One of his greatest works is a trilogy, which means that it is made up of three separate, not related, books. It is called *The Forsyte Saga*. Part of Galsworthy's story of the Forsyte family has been made into a motion picture. John Galsworthy received the Nobel Prize for literature in 1932. He died in 1933.

Galt, Sir Alexander

Sir Alexander Tilloch Galt was a famous Canadian statesman. He was born in England in 1817, and he is remembered today for two important services he performed for the government of Canada. He was among the Canadians in the 1840s who worked for the unification of Canada. This means that he wanted the provinces to be governed by a central government. He is even more famous for defying the British government and gaining economic freedom for Canada. The Canadian government was taxing British imports. Britain told the Canadian government that such a tax was not permitted since Canada was a part of the British Empire. Galt persuaded the Canadian government to defy the British demands that the tax be removed. He died in 1893.

galvanizing

Things made of iron or steel are sometimes coated with zinc to prevent them from rusting. These things are said to be *galvanized,* and the process of putting the zinc on the iron or steel is called galvanizing. One is called "hot dip galvanizing" and the other is called "electrogalvanizing."

In hot-dip galvanizing, the steel or iron articles are first cleaned with acid. Then they are galvanized by dipping them in a bath of melted zinc. Today this kind of galvanizing is used to put a protective coating of zinc on sheet steel, pipes, pails, wire, and other products. When zinc cools on the iron or steel, it leaves small drops of zinc on the article that has been plated. This is why galvanized iron or steel looks spotted and somewhat uneven.

Electrogalvanizing is done by placing iron or steel articles in water that has zinc dissolved in it. By using electricity, we can transfer, or plate, the zinc onto the iron or steel. Galvanizing was named after the Italian scientist, Luigi Galvani, who was one of the first scientists to study the question of how chemistry and electricity are connected with each other.

galvanometer

A galvanometer is an instrument that shows if electricity is flowing through a wire. Sometimes it is also used to measure the amount of electricity. The front of a galvanometer looks like a clock, except that it has only one hand. When the ends of a wire are connected to two metal knobs at the bottom, the pointer will show if there is any electricity in the wire and how much. If the pointer moves to the side, it shows that there is electricity in the wire. If it does not move, then there is no electricity flowing. The numbers on the dial will tell just how much electricity there is.

The galvanometer was invented more than a hundred years ago, in Germany. The galvanometer that is mostly used today was first made by a French scientist, Arsene d'Arsonval, about seventy years ago. It is called the d'Arsonval or moving-coil galvanometer. Inside is a coil of wire between the sides of a horseshoe magnet. Attached to the coil is a pointer that moves along a dial. When the galvanometer is connected to a wire in which electricity is flowing, the coil will turn, moving the pointer along the dial.

When a galvanometer is made so that it can tell how much electricity is actually flowing in a wire, it is called an *ammeter.* An ammeter measures the current in units of electricity called amperes. A *voltmeter* is a galvanometer that measures the force pushing the current through the wire. It measures units of electrical force called *volts.*

There are many other kinds of gal-

vanometer. One special kind was invented by a Dutch scientist, William Einthoven. It is called the Einthoven galvanometer and is used in the ELECTROCARDIOGRAPH, about which you can read in a separate article.

Galveston

Galveston is a city in Texas. It is built on a small island less than two miles from the coast of Texas, and raised roadways and bridges connect it with the mainland. Galveston is an important seaport on the Gulf of Mexico. It is only about thirty miles from Houston, the biggest city in Texas, and many shipments to and from Houston are landed at Galveston. Oil and petroleum products, cotton and chemicals are among the things shipped through Galveston.

Galveston was founded by Spanish explorers nearly four hundred years ago. It was named after a Spanish governor of Louisiana named Galvez. Galveston is popular with vacationists because the swimming and fishing are good there.

GALVESTON, TEXAS. Population (1970 census) 61,809. County seat of Galveston County.

Gama, Vasco da

Vasco da Gama was a great Portuguese explorer who was the first to sail from Europe to India. He was born about 1460, not long before Columbus discovered the New World. He made his first trip in 1497, when he started out from Lisbon, Portugal, with four ships given to him by King Manuel I. He had letters from the king to all the leaders he might meet. Until he reached Calicut, India, da Gama was well received,

Portuguese Tourist & Information Center

but in that port he had to fight his way out of the harbor. When he returned to Lisbon, da Gama had sailed about 24,000 nautical miles, and had made one of the most daring and brilliant trips up to that time. In 1502, da Gama made another trip to Calicut. This time he forced the rajah, or ruler, to submit, and he returned to Lisbon with thirteen ships loaded with jewels, spices and cloths of India. From this time on, trade between Portugal and India flourished and the Portuguese Empire grew. In 1524, Da Gama made his last trip to India. He died the next year.

Gamaliel

Gamaliel is the name of several great ancient Jewish rabbis. (A rabbi is a teacher and religious leader of the Jewish people.) You can read about the first Gamaliel in the Book of Acts in the Bible. He is called Gamaliel the Elder, and he was the teacher of St. Paul. After Jesus died, Gamaliel tried to see that his followers, especially the Apostles, who were the closest friends of Jesus, would not be punished. Gamaliel was the head of the Sanhedrin, the city council of Jerusalem, and he was very much respected. The Jewish people gave him the title of *Rabban,* which is the highest honor a Jewish person can receive. He died about seventy years after Jesus. Gamaliel II, his grandson, was also a very wise and learned man, and a great teacher.

Gambetta, Léon

Léon Gambetta was a French statesman. He was against the government of Napoleon III, for he believed in a more democratic government. When France was attacked by Germany in 1870, and Paris was under enemy gunfire, Léon Gambetta escaped from the city in a balloon. He tried to organize the people of France to fight the Germans with more energy. He opposed the Treaty of Frankfort, which marked the end of the war, and always preached revenge against the Germans. After the war he was head of the new republic, for a short time. Gambetta, born in 1838, died in 1882.

Gambia

The Gambia, a new nation on the west coast of Africa, became independent on February 18, 1965. Except at the coast, The Gambia is completely surrounded by Senegal. It is the smallest nation in Africa in area (4,003 square miles, or a little smaller than the state of Connecticut), and the second smallest in population (about 380,000). It consists of two narrow strips of land, one on each side of the Gambia River, each strip about 10 miles wide and 200 miles long, plus St. Mary's Island in the mouth of the river. Bathurst, the capital city, is on the island.

The people are Negroes belonging to several different tribal groups. Most of them follow the Mohammedan religion. Farming is the main occupation and the chief crop is peanuts. The Gambia was formerly a British Trust Territory. Upon becoming independent it was governed by a legislature, with the Speaker of the legislature acting as the head of the government.

THE GAMBIA. Area, 4,003 square miles. Population (1973 estimate), 380,000. Capital, Bathurst (population 31,800).

Gambia River

The Gambia river is an important river that flows through West Africa into the Atlantic Ocean. It is almost 1,000 miles long. Big ships can sail up it for about 200 miles. It rises in the Senegal mountains.

Gambrinus

Gambrinus was a mythical king of Flanders, which was a kingdom in northern Europe many years ago. Today, the lands of the kingdom of Flanders have been divided between Belgium and Holland. In Germany, Gambrinus was thought of as the patron saint of drinkers. You can often see pictures of Gambrinus that show a fat, jolly man sitting on a great barrel of beer or wine and holding a foaming glass of beer or wine.

game and game laws

Game is a word that means almost any kind of wild animal, bird, or fish that people go hunting or fishing for. Throughout most of the history of mankind, hunting and fishing have been done to get food or to use the fur and skins of animals. Today, hunting and fishing are more often a sport. Unfortunately, men who like this sport are sometimes so greedy that they kill too many game animals. They forget that if they kill all the animals, they can no longer enjoy their sport.

Most states and nations have laws that prohibit the killing of certain animals. Other laws allow the hunter or fisherman to hunt or fish only during certain times of the year, and to shoot or catch no more than a certain number of animals or fish. These laws are called *game laws*.

The first game laws were passed in England. They were not intended to protect wild life so much as to stop common men from hunting and fishing on the lands of the powerful nobles. This was called "poaching." Once it was almost as serious a crime to kill one of the "royal deer" (in the king's forest) as to kill a human being. Of course, that was several hundred years ago. The English game laws today are like those of most other countries.

The United States government has game laws to protect wild animals. The Federal government maintains the Fish and Wildlife Service, which is part of the U.S. Department of the Interior, to protect certain game, such as migratory birds and fish. The different states protect wild life with laws that prohibit hunting and fishing during certain seasons, especially the mating season.

The United States government also protects wild life in National Parks and in National Wildlife Refuges. These are large areas of land that are owned by the government. No hunting is allowed in them, but fishing is permitted in some areas. In one of the most famous parks, Yellowstone National Park, many kinds of animals can be seen. There are bear, moose, bison, deer and elk among the larger animals, and many kinds of fish, birds, and small mammals. National Parks may be visited by campers and other travelers.

Gamelin, Maurice Gustave

Maurice Gustave Gamelin was the commander of the French Army at the beginning of World War II, in 1939. He was born in 1872 and served in World War I, in which his rank was brigadier general. When World War II came he believed that a series of powerful French fortifications, known as the Maginot Line, would keep the Germans from invading France. The Maginot Line failed to keep the Germans out and Gamelin lost his command to General Maxime Weygand. The Germans defeated France, and Gamelin was kept in Germany as a prisoner until 1945. He died in 1958.

games

A game is a kind of play, because it is done for fun, but the player of a game tries to play better than someone else, called his opponent, and he must play according to rules that are agreed on in advance. Human beings have been playing games for almost as long as they have existed on earth, and thousands of different ways of playing games have been invented.

Many of these games are described in this encyclopedia. There are athletic games such as BASEBALL and FOOTBALL, in which physical strength and skill are important; and card games such as CONTRACT BRIDGE and CANASTA, or board games such as BACKGAMMON, CHECKERS, and CHESS, in which good play is important.

In many games a player does not have a particular opponent he is trying to beat. He simply tries to do as well as he can. These are called party games, or parlor games. Here are some of the most famous:

WORD GAMES

Ghosts. There should be several players. One player names any letter, for example, B. The next player in turn must add a letter to it, for example, BE. The next player in turn must add a third letter, for example, BES. When a player finishes a word of four or more letters, he becomes "a third of a ghost" and the next player starts the game again with a new letter. Every time a player adds a letter, he must have a real word in mind. If someone "challenges" him and he cannot name a word, he becomes a third of a ghost. When a player's turn comes and he cannot think of a letter to add, he must challenge the player who last put on a letter. When a player challenges and the previous player did have a good word in mind, the challenger becomes a third of a ghost. When a player has been a third of a ghost three times, he becomes a full ghost and is out of the game. The others continue to play until only one is left.

GUESSING GAMES

Twenty questions. Many radio and television quiz shows are based on this. One player asks the questions. He leaves the room while all the others agree on something that he must guess; it may be a real person, somebody from history, a character in a book, an animal, a piece of furniture, or anything else. When the thing is secretly agreed on, the player comes back into the room. He may ask twenty questions. The answer to each one must be yes or no; other answers are not permitted. The object is to guess what the others have selected. This is a very difficult game when played by expert players. The game is often called *Animal, Vegetable, Mineral*, because experts often start out by finding out which kind of substance the thing is made of.

ACTIVE GAMES

Musical chairs. Place in a row a number of chairs—exactly one chair less than there are people playing. If there are eight players, you need seven chairs. Each chair must face the opposite way from the ones beside it. Someone who is not in the game plays a phonograph record while the others march around the row of chairs. Suddenly the music stops and everyone tries to sit down. One person will be left standing. He is out of the game. One chair is taken away and the music is turned on again while the remaining players parade. This goes on until there are two players and one chair. The one who gets the chair when the music stops is the winner.

Blind Man's Buff. One person is blindfolded. The other players stand in a circle around him. The blindfolded person turns around several times and then stops and points. The person he points to must come to him, and he feels that person's face and tries to guess who it is. If he is right, the person he guessed is the next blind man. If he is wrong, he must try again.

Post Office. This is not really a game, though it is usually called one. It is played by a group of boys and girls. A boy goes out of the room. He knocks on the door and says he has a letter for a girl, whom he names. He tells how much the postage is (a number under ten). The girl goes out and pays for the "letter" with that many kisses. Then the boy goes back into the room and the girl knocks on the door and says she has a letter for a certain boy. This can go on as long as the players wish.

TRACK GAMES

There are hundreds of games for which special equipment is sold. Most of these are "track games," in which the object is to move counters and pieces around a track and get them "home." The ancient game of pachisi is the simplest of these games; it is sold under the name Parcheesi. Many track games, such as Monopoly, have numerous special features added to the basic rules.

gamma globulin

Gamma globulin is a drug that was used to vaccinate children, to protect them against infantile paralysis, or *polio,* before the Salk vaccine was discovered. It was called "GG." It was not very effective and the Salk vaccine replaced it.

Gandhi, Mohandas

Mohandas Gandhi was a great leader of the people of India. They called him *Mahatma,* which means almost the same thing as saint or prophet. Most people think that he deserves more credit than anyone else for the fact that India is now an independent country. He had many disciples who followed him as faithfully as the disciples of Jesus followed him. Hawaharlal Nehru, who became the first head of the Indian government when it became independent; was a follower of Gandhi.

One of Gandhi's beliefs was that force is wrong for any reason, and he did not resist or let his followers resist when they were being mistreated. Gandhi was born in western Asia in 1869. He studied in India and in England, and when he had become a lawyer he practiced in India and South Africa. Many Indians live in South Africa, and Gandhi fought to stop the injustices they were suffering.

When Gandhi returned to his own country he began to preach three main ideas: home rule for India, the development of small home industries, and the abolition of the caste system. India had been ruled for generations by Great Britain. Gandhi believed that India should rule herself. To achieve this, he advocated not war, but "passive resistance," that is constant peaceful disobedience to the laws made by the British. India is a very poor country and has far too many people living in it. Gandhi believed that small home industries would help his people to eat and live better. Gandhi followed the Hindu religion, which forbids eating meat and believes in a simple life. But he did not believe in the Hindu caste system. The caste system means that a way of living is inherited. A person is born into a caste and can work and live only in certain ways decreed for members of that caste. Gandhi was especially interested in the caste of "untouchables," a great number of people in India whom

those of other castes would not touch, and who had to do only the most unpleasant work.

Gandhi was much loved by his own people, and he was respected by the British and everybody else. When he wanted to force the British government to do something that he considered necessary for his people he would decide to "fast unto death," which means kill himself by starvation. The British were afraid that his death might cause the people of India to rebel, so they usually consented to Gandhi's demands. By such means, after many years, Gandhi and his followers won independence for their country in 1947. In 1948, while Gandhi was holding a prayer meeting in New Delhi, he was shot to death by a Hindu who blamed Gandhi for the fact that India had been divided into two countries.

gang

A gang is a group of persons who join together and work toward the same goal. The word has been used for such groups as work gangs on railroads or roads, but in recent times it has come to mean persons grouped together for criminal purposes.

During the early days of the West in the United States, the forces of law and order were still very weak. Cattle thieves and other criminals who had been outlawed by the people of the towns and ranches would join together in outlaw gangs. These outlaw gangs often became so strong that they could rob and steal at will and fight off officers of the law.

Many years later, in the 1920s, the Prohibition Era developed a new kind of gang. This was the period in which it was a crime to make, sell, or transport alcoholic liquors in the United States. Many people wanted to buy liquor anyway, and the demand for it made a wonderful opportunity for criminals. The breaking of the law started with men called "bootleggers," who made and sold liquor in a small way. Then bigger criminals went into the liquor business. They formed gangs, and the members of the gangs were called gangsters. They smuggled liquor from countries where it could be bought legally and sold it in the United states.

Bootlegging was such a profitable criminal business that there was great competition among the different gangs, and gang wars began. A great wave of murder swept over the country, with gangsters being found dead nearly every day. The gangsters used not only pistols but also machine guns and bombs. The expression "take someone for a ride" meant to drive a person out to a lonely spot and kill him, and this often happened. In 1933 the Prohibition law was repealed, but there was no way of repealing the gangs.

When the liquor business was ended the gangsters spread to many other businesses. They started "protection rackets," which forced small businessmen to pay them a certain amount of money by threatening to ruin their businesses or even kill the owners. They smuggled many things into the country, especially narcotic drugs. Many gang activities were turned into organized businesses. Often the leaders of the gangs seemed to have

close ties with the political organizations of the city or state in which they operated, so that it was very difficult to do anything to stop their crimes. At last the United States government stepped in, and government agents such as the "G-men" (agents of the Federal Bureau of Investigation of the Department of Justice), and agents of the Treasury Department, have been very successful in breaking up the gangs and sending their leaders to prison.

JUVENILE GANGS

Another kind of gang is the one formed by children and young people. Many juvenile gangs are intended only for fun and social activities. The gang is a way of finding adventure, and it can develop loyalty and other good traits in its members. This kind of gang is really a sort of club.

But some juvenile gangs turn into the same sort of bad group that the grown-up gangsters belong to. These young gangsters have their gang wars, and these wars often lead to serious injury and death. The gang members fight with stolen guns and homemade weapons and knives. They steal automobiles and use them for wild rides about the city or countryside, often causing accidents that injure or kill other persons. Sometimes they organize bigger thefts from stores and find themselves in serious trouble.

Most of these juvenile gangsters come from poor or unhappy homes, and their chief trouble is lack of love and understanding and proper training. The best way to prevent the crime that grows out of juvenile gangs is to provide good neighborhood centers for them, where they can have fun in useful and healthful ways. The principal thing such young gangsters need is some way to make use of their normal desire for a feeling of achievement and a feeling of being wanted and needed.

Ganges River

The Ganges is a large river in northern India. It rises in the South Himalaya Mountains and flows eastward for 1,500 miles before it empties into the Bay of Bengal. Many of the early civilizations of India began in the fertile Ganges valley, and today millions of people live on both sides of the river. The fields and banks near the river are good farming lands, and large crops of rice and wheat are grown there. Today great irrigation projects are being built near the river to use the water of the Ganges to water more fields, because the people of India need more food than is now being raised.

The people of India also consider the Ganges their sacred river. Every year, many people from all over India go to special bathing places along the river, such as those of the cities of Allahabad and Benares, to bathe in the waters. This is considered a holy act. Sometimes the bodies of dead people are burned on wooden pyres that are built near the river, and then the ashes are pushed into the flowing waters of the Ganges.

gangrene

If deep wounds become infected with germs, or bacteria, or if the blood does not circulate well enough through

a part of the body, gangrene may occur. Gangrene means the death of the tissue in a part of the body, such as an arm or leg.

Soldiers sometimes get gangrene when they are not treated soon enough for deep wounds. Climbers of high mountains may get it if their arms or legs are frozen badly. In severe gangrene the arm or leg may have to be amputated, or cut off, to keep the disease from getting into the rest of the body and causing death.

Old people sometimes get gangrene when the blood supply to their legs and arms is not great enough. There are new drugs that make the blood supply better, and others that fight gangrene itself. The symptoms of gangrene are fever, headache, and pain. There is a darkening of the gangrene spot, and a bad odor.

gannet

Gannets are large sea birds. They are related to the pelicans and cormorants. Gannets have large, strong bills. They feed on fish and their bills are large enough to sweep up a whole fish and hold it until it dies. Gannets are found on seacoasts in different parts of the world.

The common gannet breeds on certain rocky islands on the coast of Great Britain and at Cape St. Mary's in Newfoundland. Gannets generally breed only in these places, but recently a new nesting place on Funk Island in Newfoundland has been reported. When the young gannets learn how to fly, they scatter in all directions. Some of them travel as far as the Gulf of Mexico. The common gannet is pure white, except for a buff marking on the head and black outer wing feathers. The young are a mottled grayish brown. Another kind of gannet is found in Australia and in South Africa. These are the same color except for blue and red marking on the bare skin around their eyes and throat. On certain tropical islands there is a smaller type of gannet called a *booby*.

Ganymede

Ganymede was the most beautiful young man on earth, according to ancient Greek legends. He was the son of the King of Troy. Zeus, who was the father of the gods in Greek stories, looked down from Mount Olympus (which was like heaven, where all of the gods lived) and saw Ganymede. He thought Ganymede was so handsome that he should be in heaven with all the gods. Zeus disguised himself as an eagle and flew down to earth. He picked up Ganymede and carried him back to Mount Olympus, where he was made the cup-bearer of the gods. As cup-bearer he served the gods their water and wine. When he went to Olympus he became a kind of god himself. He was spoken of as the source of all water on earth and was supposed to protect the Nile River in Egypt.

Astronomers, the men who study the stars, named a constellation after Ganymede. It is called *Aquarius,* which means "*water bearer.*"

Garand rifle

The Garand rifle, which is also called the M1, was used by American troops throughout World War II and the Korean War. It was invented by John C. Garand, a civilian who worked for the army, and it was first introduced in 1936. The Garand has been called the best combat rifle ever produced. It is 43 inches long and weighs 9½ pounds. It fires a .30 caliber bullet, which means that the bullet is three tenths of an inch in diameter. The Garand can fire accurately at distances up to five hundred yards. It is loaded with a metal clip of ammunition that contains eight cartridges. All a soldier has to do is to press the trigger eight times. After the last bullet is fired, the empty clip is thrown out of the rifle automatically, and a new one can be loaded. This is called semi-automatic firing. There is an explanation of how it works in the article on RIFLE in another volume of this encyclopedia.

The Garand rifle has been praised because it is simple to fire and easy to clean, and because it seldom breaks down even when it has to be fired in very bad weather.

garbage

Garbage is waste food and other things that are thrown away into wastebaskets and trash cans. In most cities getting rid of garbage is the job of the Department of Sanitation. Sanitation means cleanliness for the purpose of health. In history there have been cases of great cities that ceased to exist because they had no proper way of getting rid of garbage. Disease germs that bred in the garbage caused epidemics.

The Department of Sanitation is one of the largest and most important departments in most cities. In New York City, the Department employs more than 14,000 persons, uses 1,800 trucks, and costs $110,000,000 a year. Engineers, chemists and other scientists are constantly looking for new ways to get rid of garbage more cheaply, and to make it serve useful purposes. One use of garbage is to fill in wastelands such as swamps; this dries them out so they are suitable land for farming and building.

Some garbage is burned in huge furnaces called incinerators. The ashes may be used to fill in land, or are dumped in the ocean if the city is near a coast. Some garbage is chemically dissolved. One way of doing this is to dump it into a big airtight vat and spray it with superhot steam (called live steam). The steam melts the garbage down into a slimy mass, with oil and grease floating on the top. The solid matter underneath may be used as fertilizer, to enrich the soil.

New York City uses ashes and rubbish (bottles, cans, rags, wood, shoes, and metals) to fill in swampland and marshland, changing them into parks and recreation areas. The ashes and rubbish are deposited, sprayed with disinfectant, covered with earth to prevent odors and keep away insects and rats, and brought to a proper grade by the Department of Sanitation. The Park Department then plants grass, trees, and shrubbery, and builds baseball diamonds, benches and play areas to complete the job.

When garbage and rubbish contain too much moisture to burn properly (because they are rain-soaked or because of large amounts of watermelon rinds, corncobs, or similar fruits and vegetables), fuel oil is added. The residue (all unburned material) is then taken to the landfill.

Incinerators are not cheaper to run. Incineration costs $4.75 a ton while the landfill process costs $2.42 a ton.

New York City's Department of Sanitation collection trucks haul three tons of garbage, or the contents of approximately 250 full garbage cans. The trucks average three loads a day, or 750 cans.

Garbo, Greta

Greta Garbo is considered by many to have been the greatest of all motion-picture actresses. She was born in Sweden, in 1905, and her real name was Greta Gustaffson. She became a stage actress in Sweden and made several motion pictures there. In 1925 she went to Hollywood, in the United States, and made a series of successful pictures in the period of silent films. After talking pictures were introduced she made some of her most successful pictures, including *Queen Christina* and *Anna Karenina.* Most of her pictures were very serious, but she made one comedy, *Ninotchka,* and it was very successful. She became an American citizen in 1951. Greta Garbo is famous for being shy, not wanting to be interviewed by newspaper reporters or have her picture taken, and not going to parties. She often wore unfashionable clothes, used false names, and did other things to avoid attracting attention. "I want to be alone" and "I think I'll go home now" are statements she is supposed to have made and they have been widely quoted. She did not marry, though there were rumors that she would.

García

Calixto García y Iniguez was a Cuban patriot. He was born in Cuba in 1836. Cuba was then owned by Spain. García fought for Cuba's independence just as Washington, Adams, Jefferson, and others had fought for the independence of the United States. In 1880 García was arrested and sent to Spain, where he was in prison for fifteen years, but then he returned to Cuba and continued to work for independence.

In 1898 the United States went to war against Spain. The United States wanted to help Cuba win its independence and wanted García's help in defeating the Spanish. The United States Army sent a message to García by a young lieutenant named Andrew S. Rowan. Rowan had a great deal of difficulty in delivering the message and met with much danger and hardship, but he finally got to García.

As a result of the Spanish-American War, Cuba did gain its independence, but García had died in 1898 while he was in Washington to discuss Cuban affairs with President McKinley.

A United States writer named Elbert Hubbard wrote a famous essay about the

heroism of Lieutenant Rowan. The essay is called *A Message to García.* Because of that essay, anyone who overcomes many obstacles to do what he is supposed to do is sometimes said to "deliver a message to García."

gardenia

The gardenia is a flower with a very sweet fragrance and with white or yellow, velvetlike petals and shiny green leaves. Many women like to pin gardenias to their dresses, wearing them as a corsage. The gardenias used in corsages are very large. A single flower may be almost as large as a person's hand. This kind of gardenia is grown in hothouses by florists. The gardenia also grows wild, on bushes in the tropics. The wild garde-

The gardenia has a strong fragrance.

nia is about the size of a half-dollar. The gardenia bush grows as tall as a man and produces as many as one hundred gardenias, one blossom on the end of each branch. There are about sixty different kinds of gardenia.

The plant has many uses, such as gum manufacture, fabric-dyeing, and perfume-making. The cape jasmine that grows in China is a kind of gardenia.

gardening

Gardening is taking care of a garden, a place where flowers or vegetables grow. A person who does this work is a gardener. Some very rich people with big estates pay gardeners to take care of their gardens, but to most people gardening is a hobby. The gardener has a "patch" of land on which he grows vegetables to eat in his own home or flowers to cut and show for their beauty. Thousands of American cities and towns have Garden Clubs whose members try to raise the most beautiful flowers in their communities and win prizes for them in flower shows. During World War II, when the governments of many countries including the United States asked people to raise as many vegetables as they could, millions of people became interested in gardening and now they are proud when they serve corn or beans or peas or other vegetables that they have raised themselves.

VEGETABLE GARDENS

The vegetable garden is generally a flat piece of land where the seeds are planted in even rows far enough apart to walk between them. It is necessary to walk between the rows to weed the plants and loosen the soil around the roots. The quality of a vegetable, that is, the size and flavor, depends on the quality of the soil

in which the plant grows. Most vegetables need rich soil and grow best where the top soil from higher land drains onto them. There must be a good deal of moisture for vegetables, and good drainage, which means that the water should not remain around the roots. If the soil is not good enough it can be strengthened with fertilizer or manure. The vegetables that are easily and often grown in amateur gardens are peas, beans, corn, beets, lettuce, potatoes, tomatoes, squash and many others. An herb garden is an interesting sideline to a vegetable garden. Herbs are used to flavor food dishes, and an herb that is fresh from the garden will give an even better flavor to the dish. Mint is one of the most useful herbs and can be grown in a patch by the kitchen door. Dill and marjoram also can be grown in the garden or even in window boxes in the city.

FLOWER GARDENS

A flower garden is most often used to beautify the land around a house. There are different kinds of flower garden. *Rock gardens* are very popular on slopes and in woody places. A rock garden usually looks wilder and more woodsy than the more formal gardens. The plants grow between rocks that may have been placed to hold up the soil behind them. A rock garden can be planted on land that is already sloped and rocky. Ferns, ivy, climbing roses, low-growing green plants called sedums and small flowering plants are usually planted in rock gardens. *Flower beds* are very often used in laying out a garden. A flower bed is generally long and narrow. It may be curved or lie in a straight line with lawn on either side of it, or it may be against a garden wall. All kinds of flowers grow in flower beds; they may be any color and any size. If a flower bed is against a wall, the taller flowers are best seen if they are in back and the shorter ones planted nearer the edge according to their height. Many flower beds are bordered with a solid row of low-growing herbs or small plants. People sometimes plant according to the season in which the flowers will bloom. Some flowers bloom in the spring, some in the early and late summer, and some in the fall. If the flowers are evenly set out, the flower bed will always have something blooming in it.

Green gardens are quite rare but very effective. A green garden has no blooming flowers in it—only green plants. Usually it is a well-tended lawn enclosed by clipped hedges or rows of trees. Sometimes marble or stone sculpture is placed here and there in a green garden, or a bench or a bird bath. A green garden can be laid out in a long lane framing a view of the sea or mountains in the distance. There are many of these in Italy. They are called *vistas.*

FORMAL GARDENS

Formal gardens are created and kept up by experts. They are laid out by gardeners who are architects. A formal garden takes up a lot of space and surrounds a palace or a public building or is in a park. It consists of flower beds with lawn or stone walks between them. The walks and flower beds seen from a distance make a complicated symmetrical design. Fountains and statuary are often

found in formal gardens. Sometimes there are also *mazes.* A maze is a path or walk through high hedges, so high you cannot see over them. The path is laid out in such a way that once you get into the maze there is only one way out. You have to continue walking until you find that one way out.

FAMOUS GARDENS

Throughout history there have been famous gardens. One of the earliest was the hanging gardens of Babylon. The gardens of Babylon were built in tiers on a hillside and were such an engineering feat for the time that they have become known as one of the seven wonders of the world.

The gardens of Versailles, a palace built by Louis XV, king of France, are as beautiful as any in the world. The gardens of Versailles are so well planned that everywhere you look you see a complete picture of formal beauty. The fountains of Versailles are a main feature of the garden. When the fountains are turned on it is called the "play of the waters." Water shoots in all directions around the elaborate statuary. Kew Gardens in London is famous for the number and variety of its trees and plants. The Pinto gardens in Rome are noted for their shady peacefulness.

In Williamsburg, Virginia, many of the restored houses are surrounded by beautiful gardens that reflect the Colonial period in America.

Garden of the Gods

The Garden of the Gods is one of the greatest natural wonders of the western United States. It is situated near Colorado Springs, Colorado, and thousands of people visit this exciting place every year. If you go there, you will enter the Garden of the Gods through a giant gateway that is formed by two rocks that stand over three hundred feet high. These rocks are a brilliant red. The Garden of the Gods consists of about five hundred acres of dazzling red and white rock that has been formed into many strange and marvelous shapes. Some of these rocks look so much like things we know that they have been given names. You can see "The Seal," "The Bear," and "Punch and Judy." Some of the rocks in the Garden of the Gods have weird and fantastic shapes, and many are very beautiful.

James A. Garfield

James Abram Garfield was the twentieth President of the United States. He was the last President of the United States who was born in a log cabin, and he served in office for only four months before he was killed by an assassin. The only person to serve a shorter term in the presidency was William Henry Harrison, who died a month after his inauguration.

HIS EARLY YEARS

Garfield was the son of a farmer from New York who had settled in Orange, Cuyahoga County, Ohio. Orange was a small town near Cleveland. James was

the youngest of four sons, and his father died when he was only two years old. His mother, Eliza Ballou Garfield, brought up her four sons alone, and early taught them the importance of self-reliance, thrift, and hard work.

As a boy, Garfield worked hard to earn his way through school. He drove the horses pulling barges on Ohio canals, and he also worked as a farm hand. During his school vacation in 1850, he found work as a carpenter.

In 1851, he entered the Western Reserve Eclectic Institute at Hiram, Ohio, and transferred to Williams College, Massachusetts, in 1854. Two years later he was graduated with honor grades. After his graduation, he returned to his old school, the Eclectic Institute, but this time as a teacher. One year later he became the head of the school.

Garfield first became active in politics at the time when the Republican Party was founded, in 1856. He worked on the campaign in Ohio that year, and three years later, in 1859, he was elected to the Ohio state senate. This was at the time when there were sharp differences of opinion about slavery, and Garfield was firmly opposed to it. He felt so strongly about it, in fact, that he spent a great deal of time in trying to impress upon the people of his state how important it was to make ready for trouble.

Trouble came when the Civil War broke out. Garfield volunteered for service, and was appointed lieutenant colonel of the 42nd Ohio Volunteer Infantry Regiment. He was a good officer and commanded his troops through many important battles. He was promoted to the rank of brigadier general in 1862, and became chief of staff the next year.

While the Civil War was still going on, Garfield was elected to the House of Representatives, and he resigned his commission in the army in order to take office.

HOW HE BECAME PRESIDENT

He was very active for the next seventeen years, from 1863 to 1880, as a member of Congress. He was responsible for the law that enforced the drafting of men into the army at a time when the Union forces desperately needed more soldiers.

Garfield supported John Sherman as the man to represent the Republican Party as nominee for President at the time of the Republican convention in 1880. A large group of delegates to the convention backed Sherman, but large groups also were in favor of Grant and

James Blaine. It was a very long, very exciting convention, with ballot after ballot—but not enough agreement for anyone to win the majority of votes necessary for nomination. None of the groups would give up and throw its vote to one of the others. The rivalry was too strong for any of the three to withdraw, and after 33 ballots it was very clear that someone else would have to be nominated—someone who would be acceptable as a substitute, and who could win a majority of convention votes. James Garfield was the final choice, and he was given the Republican presidential nomination at the end of the longest convention fight in the history of the Republican Party. In November, 1880, James Garfield was elected President of the United States, and Chester A. Arthur became Vice President.

THE ASSASSINATION OF GARFIELD

President Garfield was inaugurated on March 4, 1881. Four months later he was assassinated—before he had time to do anything in office except appoint his cabinet and generally get himself and his family settled in the White House.

On July 2, Garfield was about to get on board a train to attend the commencement exercises at Williams College, in Massachusetts, when suddenly a half-crazed man shot him. The man was caught immediately, but the wound proved fatal to President Garfield. He was taken from the railroad station to the White House, and the best surgeons in Washington did everything they could to save his life. For a time it seemed that he might recover, but he grew weaker toward the end of August. The doctors thought that the climate of Elberon, New Jersey, near Long Branch, might be better for the President's chance of recovery, and he was moved by train to New Jersey. It did no good, however, and on September 19 James Garfield died. Chester A. Arthur, who had been his vice-president, succeeded him in office.

His assassin was Charles J. Guiteau, a man who had tried to get a government job when Garfield took office. He was angry because he had been turned down, and he was also mentally unbalanced—perhaps actually insane. He was convicted of the crime, and was hanged in Washington jail on June 30, 1882, just two days less than a year after the fatal shooting.

James Garfield was buried in Cleveland, Ohio.

MRS. JAMES GARFIELD

Lucretia Rudolph Garfield was born in 1832, the daughter of an Ohio farmer. Her mother was a descendant of General Nathanael Greene, a hero of the American Revolution. Lucretia Rudolph was a schoolteacher and she married James Garfield in November, 1858, while he was serving as principal of the Eclectic Institute in Hiram, Ohio. After Garfield's death, the people of the country took up a collection and established a trust fund for the President's widow and children. Three hundred and sixty thousand dollars were raised.

President and Mrs. Garfield had five children—four sons and one daughter.

Mrs. Lucretia Rudolph Garfield died on March 13, 1918.

gargoyle

A gargoyle is a stone waterspout that is carved to look like an ugly monster, or strange animal. If you went to Paris, and looked at Notre Dame Cathedral, you would see gargoyles all around the roof of the church. They are put on buildings to prevent rain water from pouring down the walls in a steady stream, which would eventually wear the walls away. The gargoyles stick out from the roof about three feet, so that when water runs from the roof into the gargoyle, it will pour out of the gargoyle's mouth and miss the side of the building. Gargoyles were used in Greece three thousand years ago. They became very popular during the Gothic period (roughly the years 1000 to 1500). Gargoyles are carved in many strange shapes. They have hideous heads on bodies that look like the bodies of strange birds, and they often have lion's tails and claws.

Garibaldi, Giuseppe

Giuseppe Garibaldi was a great Italian patriot and hero. He was a leader in the movement to unite Italy, which had been divided into a number of small states. Garibaldi was born in 1807 in Nice, France. His father was a shipowner. Garibaldi went to sea when he was quite young. He joined a group of patriots who called themselves "Young Italy" and who were determined to end foreign rule in Italy. Garibaldi took part in an unsuccessful rebellion and was sentenced to death. He fled to France and then went to South America, where he helped other people in their fight for freedom.

When, in 1848, the Italians began to fight against Austrian rule, Garibaldi hurried home. He organized his famous "Red Shirts," an army of volunteers who helped defend Rome against the invading French armies. But Garibaldi's brave soldiers were pushed back, and Garibaldi again had to flee for his life. He came to the United States and worked for some years as a candle-maker in Staten Island, in New York. Garibaldi believed strongly in a republican form of government, but he became convinced that Italy could only be united under a constitutional monarchy, that is, a kingdom with a constitution guaranteeing rights to the people. He then devoted himself to helping King Victor Emmanuel. With his Red Shirt army, Garibaldi won many battles, and gave the lands he liberated from foreign rule to the king. After most of Italy had been united, Garibaldi continued to fight for his country. He died in 1882.

Garland, Hamlin

Hamlin Garland was an American writer who wrote about life on the prairie farms as he really saw it. He was born in 1860, and when he was a boy he loved the country and the free feeling of life on the open plains. He also knew how hard it was to be a pioneer and how often the pioneers were lonely and poor. In his book *A Son of the Middle Border* he tells

us what it was like to be a boy in those days, and in another book, *A Daughter of the Middle Border,* he tells us about his own family when they moved to Chicago. When he died in 1940 he was famous for his honest, interesting writing.

garlic

Garlic is well known for its odor and the strong flavor it gives to food when it is used as a seasoning. Garlic is a form of leek, an onionlike plant. Since earliest times it has been cultivated in Mediterranean countries and later in the Western Hemisphere. The stem of the garlic plant is about two feet high. The leaves are straight and grasslike. At the top of the stem are a few white flowers and a bulb. The bulb is made up of twelve or fifteen oblong sections. This bulb is the part of the garlic plant that is eaten or used as a flavoring.

garment

Garments are articles of clothing usually made of cloth. Shoes and belts and hats are not called garments, but suits and dresses and underwear and overcoats are. Hundreds of years ago people made their own clothes at home, but when automatic machines to spin thread and to weave cloth and to sew fabrics were invented, everybody found it was cheaper and easier to buy clothing ready-made. The garment industry includes all the factories that make clothing and all the people who work in them. It is one of the biggest industries in the world because everybody wears clothing. The business of the garment industry consists of designing, manufacturing, and selling.

HOW CLOTHES ARE DESIGNED

Every manufacturer of garments has at least one designer. It is his job to plan all the articles of wearing apparel so that they will look well and fit and be fashionable. Fashion is what people at a particular time like to wear. This usually is based on passing fancy rather than usefulness. In women's clothes it has been considered for many years that the best fashions come from Paris, and in men's clothing that the best fashions come from London. Although other countries do not agree with this, nevertheless most people still like to wear Paris and London fashions.

The designer works out an idea for a garment and has a model made of it exactly the way he wants it. This model is then made up by hand, and the designer can make any changes that he thinks will improve its appearance. Then a pattern is made from the model. The pattern shows what pieces of cloth of different sizes and shapes must be used to make that particular garment. The original pattern is scaled to make different sizes of the same garment, and then other patterns are made for each size in which the garment is to be manufactured. The patterns are laid out on a large piece of cloth to see just what is the best way to get the most garments out of the least amount of cloth.

When the manufacturer has the pattern, he can buy the material for the garment. The buying must be done very carefully so that he can cut the pieces to fit the pattern and waste as little as possible.

The big bolts of cloth that the manufacturer has bought go to the cutter. The cutter lays the material out in piles of layers that may be as much as a foot high. The pile is put on a machine in which a big knife cuts the material to the shape of the various pieces of the pattern.

When enough pieces have been cut to make dozens or hundreds of garments of that particular pattern, the pieces are turned over to the workers at the sewing machines to be put together into garments. Most of the workers at this job are women. After the garment is put together it goes to the finishers for buttons and snaps and hand sewing, and then to the pressers to be put into final condition to be sold and worn.

GARMENT WORKERS

For hundreds of years the workers of the garment industry were underpaid and had to work very long hours in dark and unsanitary places to make a living at all. The poet Thomas Hood wrote a famous poem called "Song of the Shirt" about these bad conditions. Gradually in the United States people became horrified at the "sweatshops" in which these workers had to do their jobs. The workers joined together into unions, and now these unions are among the strongest in the world. Workers in the garment industry have better working conditions than almost any other group of people in the world. Laws and public health regulations were passed to make sure that no more sweatshops were operated in the United States.

SALE OF GARMENTS

There are considered to be three seasons in the garment industry: fall and winter, spring, and summer. These are the big buying seasons during the year. The manufacturers hold showings in their showrooms, with models to display their new styles for the coming season. Buyers from all over the country, from little specialty shops and huge department stores with many branch stores, come to the showings and look at the models and place their orders. The buying is usually done well in advance of the season, so that the manufacturer can tell from the number of orders he has received how many of each type of garment he should manufacture.

In the United States, New York is the center of the garment industry, although there are other American cities that also have important garment industries. In New York the industry is centered in an area of a few square blocks that represents about one-tenth of one percent of the total area of the city, but it is one of the busiest areas you can imagine. The manufacturing goes on in lofts and tall buildings, and the streets are always thronged with little handcarts in which dresses are hung on rods and trundled from one place to another.

Read also the articles on FUR, SHOE and HAT.

garnet

Garnet is a stone that is used in jewelry. It is a semiprecious stone, which means that it is valuable, but not nearly as valuable as a precious stone such as a diamond or ruby. Garnets are red, black, yellow, brown, green, and almost every color you can think of, except blue. Garnet is a mineral that is found in great quantities all over the world. The deep red garnets that are found in Africa and India, and in Arizona in the United States, are used to make jewelry. Garnet is very tough, and it makes a very good abrasive to polish and smooth leather and wood and metal. (You can read about ABRASIVES in a separate article.) Some people use garnet to remove paint and varnish, especially from automobile bodies. Men who work in glass factories sometimes use garnet to polish glass. The ancient Greeks made garnet bracelets and necklaces and decorated glasses and bowls with garnets, which they called *carbuncles.* The garnet is the birthstone for January.

Garonne River

The Garonne River is an important river in the southwest part of France. It rises in the Pyrenees Mountains and flows in a generally northeast direction until it reaches the large city of Toulouse, where it changes its course and flows northwest. It continues this course until it passes the city of Bordeaux where it joins the Dordogne River, and these two rivers together form the large Gironde River. Most of the smaller rivers of southwestern France flow into the Garonne, but it is not a very large river, and only its lower part can be used by ships.

gar pike

The gar pike is a long, slender fish that is found in the rivers and lakes of North America. Though it is a fish, the gar pike cannot live completely in water; it must come to the surface of the water to gulp air. It gets its food by eating smaller fish. Its long jaw makes it easy for it to catch its prey. Fishermen do not like the gar pike and consider it a nuisance. There are many kinds of gar pikes, and some of them reach a length of more than five feet.

The gar pike swallows smaller fish whole.

Garrick, David

David Garrick was a famous English actor who lived about two hundred years ago. Like many famous actors, he was most famous for the parts he played in the plays of William Shakespeare. Garrick was born in 1717. His father was an Army captain and sent young David to a school run by Samuel Johnson, who later became one of the most famous English writers. Before Garrick became an actor, he studied to become a lawyer; then for a time he was a wine salesman. He soon gave up selling and started acting. In 1741 he appeared as the star of Shakespeare's *Richard III.* He was a great success and was a public favorite until he died in 1779.

Gale Research Co.

Garrick acted at the Drury Lane Theater, a theater in London that he later bought. He himself wrote some farces (comic plays) and acted in them, but

they were never very successful.

Garrick was buried in Westminster Abbey, the great cathedral in London. His body lies next to the statue of William Shakespeare. You can read more about David Garrick in the article on ACTORS AND ACTRESSES.

Garrison, William Lloyd

William Lloyd Garrison was one of the leaders among the abolitionists, people who wanted to end slavery in the United States. This was over a hundred years ago, when Negroes were slaves in the southern states.

Garrison was born in the year 1805, in Newburyport, Massachusetts. When he was only 9 years old he went to work for a shoemaker. When he was 21 years old, he became the editor of the Newburyport *Free Press,* but he was more interested in freeing the slaves. In 1831 Garrison founded his own newspaper, *The Liberator,* which had as its principal pur-

pose the ending of slavery. Many people were afraid that the work of Garrison and the other abolitionists would lead to war, which they wanted to avoid, so Garrison had many enemies. The state of Georgia had a reward for anyone who would prosecute and convict him. Even in the North, people destroyed his newspapers and tried to break up his printing presses.

Garrison was not frightened by this. In the first issue of *The Liberator* he had said, "I am in earnest. I will not equivocate; I will not excuse; I will not retreat a single inch; and I will be heard!" He won his fight 34 years later, when the northern states won the Civil War and Congress passed the Thirteenth Amendment to the Constitution, which abolished slavery. Garrison also campaigned for women's right to vote, for better treatment of Indians, and against liquor. He died in 1879.

Garter, Order of the

The Order of the Garter is the highest order of knighthood in England. It is

Some of the decorations that go with the Order of the Garter are the Star (*top*), Collar (*middle*), and George (*bottom*).

an honor given to the most prominent and highest-ranking persons. A man who receives the Order of the Garter becomes a Knight of the Garter.

The name of this order comes from an

incident that is supposed to have happened about six hundred years ago, when Edward III was king. At a ball, King Edward picked up a garter that a lady dropped while she was dancing. When the people there started to laugh, the King became angry and said "*Honi soit qui mal y pense.*" In the French language this means "Shame on him who thinks evil of it." This phrase became the motto of an order of knighthood, the Order of Saint George, founded by Edward III. This order became the Order of the Garter. On formal occasions a Knight of the Garter wears around his neck a dark blue ribbon edged with gold, with the motto printed on it. It looks like the garter worn by a woman of six hundred years ago.

Only about sixty people are Knights of the Garter. They are the king or queen of England, the English princes, the highest-ranking British noblemen, and other British subjects who have done the most for their country. Sometimes the king of a country that is on good terms with England is given the Order of the Garter. Sir Winston Churchill, the British Prime Minister, was made a Knight of the Garter in 1953.

garter snake

Garter snakes are small, harmless snakes. They are very numerous in North America. They vary in color from light green to olive to black. They usually have three stripes, one along the back and one along each side. The garter snake moves about at night as well as during the day. It eats frogs or toads, insects, and the eggs of birds that nest close to the ground. In the West it helps farmers by eating gophers and young ground squirrels, which eat their crops. A garter snake is very fast, both to catch what it is after and to get away from the larger black snakes or king snakes that eat it.

Garter snakes are full of fight. They may bite or pretend to bite if you handle them, but their teeth are so small the bite only pricks your skin; they are not poisonous. Twenty-five to forty garter snakes are born at a time, and once it was reported that eighty were born at one time from the same mother.

A garter snake sheds its skin in the spring. It scrapes it off by crawling through rock crevices, and the skin peels off from the head backward, inside out.

Gary

Gary is a city in the state of Indiana. More steel is manufactured in Gary than in any other place in the United States except Pittsburgh. About 175,000 people live in Gary, and they also make cement and chemicals. Gary is now a busy, modern city with fine schools and parks and libraries, but fifty years ago it was nothing but sand dunes and swampland. Then the United States Steel Corporation picked this site on which to build their great steel factories. Gary is the second-largest city in Indiana. The city was named for Elbert Gary, chairman of the board of directors of the United States Steel Corporation. If you drive through the city of Gary at night, you can see the fires from the great furnaces of the steel foundries, and it is a very exciting sight.

GARY, INDIANA. Population, 175,415 (1970 census). County seat of Lake County. Settled in 1905.

Gary, Elbert Henry

Elbert Henry Gary was an American lawyer and businessman who organized the great United States Steel Corporation. Gary was born in the town of Wheaton, Illinois, where he served as county judge, and received the nickname of "Judge" Gary. Gary was chairman of the board of directors of United States Steel for many years, and he did a great deal to make it one of the richest and most powerful corporations in the world. Gary was against labor unions, but he did help the workers to get higher wages and better working conditions. He helped to found the big Indiana city named Gary in his honor. He was born in 1846 and died in 1927.

gas

A gas is one of three kinds of matter. You can read about MATTER in a separate article. The other kinds of matter are liquid and solid. A gas is very different from a liquid or solid. A gas has no definite size. Both liquids and solids do have a definite size. If you fill a glass with a liquid such as water, and pour it into a larger, empty glass, there will not be enough water to fill the second glass. But if you fill a glass with gas and then pour it into a larger one, the gas will also fill up the second glass. In fact, if you took a thimble full of gas and emptied it into a tank as large as an office building, the gas would spread out until it filled the entire tank. Of course, the gas would become very thin, but there would be some gas in every part of the tank. The reason is that a gas is able to grow larger or expand no matter where it is. A gas fills whatever space it is put into. The size of the space is called the volume of the gas.

The most important gas in your life is the air that you breathe in and out every day. At one time, gas and air meant the same thing. Then scientists found out that air is actually made up of many different gases, such as oxygen, nitrogen, carbon dioxide, and argon. (There are separate articles on AIR and other gases.) You cannot see these gases because they do not have any color. Other gases, such as chlorine and fluorine, have a color. You can see these gases expand when they are put into a container. Some gases have an odor, and you can smell them even though you cannot see them. One such gas is that used in kitchen gas stoves. If one of the burners on the stove has gas escaping from it while it is unlighted, you will soon smell the gas in the kitchen, and in all parts of the house. If enough gas escapes, you will find it hard to breathe. This is because the gas expands and drives out most of the oxygen. The burner should be immediately turned off, and the windows opened wide to let the gas out into the open air and more air into the house. It is very important that the burners be turned off at all times when the stove is not lighted.

There are some gases that you can

neither see nor smell. Carbon monoxide is such a gas and is very dangerous to have around. Some gases are lighter than others. A lighter gas has less density than a heavier one. (You can read about DENSITY elsewhere in this encyclopedia). A lighter gas will rise above a heavier one. Hydrogen and helium are two gases lighter than air. They are used in balloons that are sent up into the air to explore the atmosphere. Other gases are used for heating and lighting, to put you to sleep when you are in the dentist's chair, to make soda water or "pop," and for many other purposes.

CHANGES IN A GAS

Cooling a gas slightly will reduce its size. If a gas is cooled to a very low temperature, it will change into a liquid or a solid. Heating a gas causes it to expand and increase in size. That is why cakes baked in an oven will rise and get larger. The gas inside the cake, formed by the baking powder, expands during baking, and the cake "rises." When the cake is cut, you see the holes made by the expanding gas.

Gases, liquids and solids are made up of millions of tiny particles called *molecules*. In a gas, these molecules are constantly moving about and hitting each other. In a liquid and solid, the molecules are packed very close together. Many liquids and solids become gases when heated to very high temperatures. The heat separates the molecules and causes them to move about and strike each other like in a gas. Some liquids such as water when boiled change into a vapor or steam. A vapor is like a gas except that it is moist. The heat causes the molecules of water to strike each other so hard that they are knocked into the air and hang there separated from each other. If the vapor is cooled slightly or put into a smaller container, the molecules will be brought together again. The vapor will then be changed into a liquid.

Expansion of a gas when it is put into a larger container makes it cooler. The reason is that there is more room for the molecules and they do not strike each other so often. When the gas is put into a smaller container, the molecules strike each other more often. This heats up the gas. Refrigeration and air conditioning are based on this principle.

Gascony

Gascony is a section in the southwestern part of France. On the south are the Pyrenees mountains and to the west is the Bay of Biscay. It is a place that has had a very exciting history. The territory of Gascony used to be a duchy, which means that it was ruled by a duke. First England owned it, then France captured it, then the English took it again. The English were finally driven out of Gascony five hundred years ago, and it became a permanent part of France in 1451. The area was split into smaller counties in 1790.

The Gascons are said to be very proud, outspoken, and given to rash but brave actions. Two famous characters in fiction are Gascons. One is D'Artagnan, in *The Three Musketeers* by Alexandre Dumas. The other is Cyrano, in *Cyrano de Bergerac* by Edmond Rostand.

gas mask

A gas mask is used to protect the person who is wearing it from breathing harmful gases into his lungs. The mask fits tightly over the face and is held in place with straps. The material it is made of is treated with chemicals to keep out gases. The air that is breathed in must pass through a little can before it gets to the person's nose and mouth. In the little can are chemicals which take out the harmful gases. Only pure air that is not harmful can get through. Gas masks are sometimes used by firemen when they have to enter buildings that are full of smoke, and by people who are doing rescue work in mines. They were used in World War I, but did not have to be used in World War II because poison gas was not used.

gas meter

A gas meter is a metal box that is used to measure how much gas people use in their homes for cooking, heating, and lighting. It measures the amount of gas in cubic feet. (You can read about cubic feet in the article on CUBE.) There are two pipes connected to the meter. One leads from the city gas supply to the meter, the other leads from the meter to the stove or some other gas outlet. Inside the meter are two boxes separated by a partition. The boxes can be pushed out or in by the gas just like an accordion. When gas is being used, one box is emptied while the other is filled. These boxes also work the pointers on the dials in front of the meter by a series of gears which tell the gas company how much gas you have used, so they know how much money to charge you. In some places you must put a coin in the meter in order for it to supply gas to your stove. The coin opens the pipe leading from the city gas supply to the meter. It will give you gas until one of the boxes in the meter has been emptied. Then another coin must be put in; this lets the gas out of the other box.

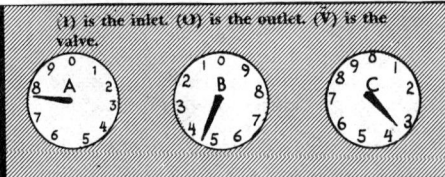

(I) is the inlet. (O) is the outlet. (V) is the valve.

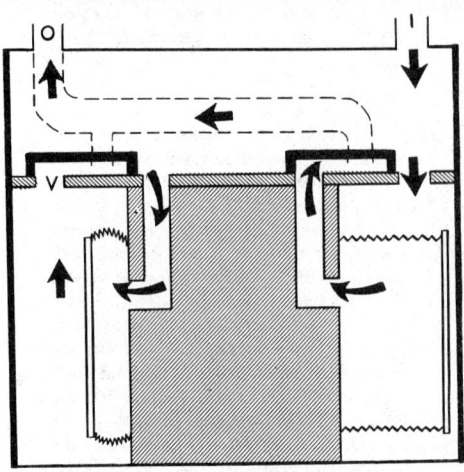

There are usually three dials in the front of the meter. The pointer on the first dial tells how many hundreds of cubic feet of gas have been used; the next dial to the left of it tells how many thousands of cubic feet; and the one to the left of that tells how many ten thousands of cubic feet. A man from the gas company usually comes to read the meter every month. He can tell how much gas you have used in a month by subtracting the reading taken last month from the new reading. If the pointer on a dial is between two numbers, he always reads the lower number. The dials on the meter in the diagram read 743. This means 74,-300 cubic feet of gas have been used.

gasoline

Gasoline is a clear liquid that is used as a fuel in the engines of many automobiles and airplanes and in many other engines. It burns quickly and at great heat. Gasoline is made up of hydrogen and carbon, two chemical elements, both of which burn very well.

The three main kinds of gasoline are called straight run, cracked, and *natural*. Straight run gasoline is made from petroleum, the crude oil that comes from oil wells drilled in the earth. Gasoline boils at a lower temperature than the rest of the crude oil, which makes it easy to separate. The crude oil is heated until the gasoline turns to vapor, just as water turns to vapor (steam) when it is boiled. When this gasoline vapor is collected and cooled, it turns to a liquid again.

The parts of the crude oil that are left engines and also in other engines.

OCTANE RATING

Some kinds of gasoline burn more completely than other kinds and so are better in automobile and aircraft engines. A number called an *octane number* tells how good gasoline is. High octane gasolines will hardly ever cause a "knock" (a noise made when the gasoline is not completely burned in the engine). Automobiles use gasoline with an octane number of about 84. Aviation gasolines have octane numbers well over 100.

gasoline engine, a machine that gets the power to move, and to move other things, from gasoline: see the article on INTERNAL COMBUSTION ENGINE.

Gaspé Peninsula

The Gaspé Peninsula is a tongue of land in the southeastern part of the province of Quebec, in Canada. It is about 150 miles long, and about 90 miles wide at its widest point. The Gaspé Peninsula is famous for its beautiful scenery and its quaint fishing villages. About 25 years ago a highway was built that goes all around the coast of the peninsula, and since that time Gaspé has become a very popular tourist section. Hunters and fishermen especially enjoy going on camping trips through the interior of the peninsula, where there are many lovely forests and clear mountain streams. A range of mountains called the Notre Dame Mountains runs through the Gaspé Peninsula from one end to the other.

Most of the people of the Gaspé Peninsula are fishermen. They catch cod, mackerel, and salmon. Others are farmers or lumbermen, and some work in pulp mills where lumber is turned into paper pulp.

gastric juice, a fluid given off by the glands in the stomach. See the articles on DIGESTION and STOMACH.

gastritis

Gastritis is a condition in which the stomach becomes inflamed. There are two kinds of gastritis. *Acute gastritis* is caused by swallowing something that damages the soft lining of the stomach, which is called the mucous membrane. This is most often food which has begun to spoil. The victim begins to vomit and has a headache, pains in the stomach, and a tongue that feels furry. Attacks of this kind tend to go away after a few days, even though drugs are not of much help. About the only thing which can be done is to suck on small pieces of ice. *Chronic gastritis* may be caused by diseases in the body's other organs or by excessive use of alcohol.

gastropods

Gastropods are a family of animals belonging to the mollusc, or shellfish, class of animals. A gastropod is usually small, but may be about the size of a hen's egg. Its body and its one foot are usually enclosed in a shell, which may have a spiral (coiled) form. Its head has tentacles, or feelers, and one pair of eyes. It may breathe through gills, or, in certain kinds of gastropod, it may have a lung. The snail is probably the best-known gastropod. Other gastropods include slugs, whelks, and limpets. Gastropods are found in all parts of the world.

Gates, Horatio

Horatio Gates was a famous American general in the Revolutionary War. He was born in England in 1727 and he went to school and became an army officer in that country. He was sent to the American colonies where he fought in the British Army in the

French and Indian Wars. Gates was badly wounded and his friend, George Washington, persuaded him to buy a plantation in the South where he could live and get well again. When the colonies declared their independence from England, Gates decided to fight on the side of the Americans. In 1777, the British decided to cut the New England states off from the rest of the colonies. If their plan had succeeded, the Americans might have lost the war. But the plan failed because Gates defeated a great part of the British army at Saratoga, New York. This was such an important victory that the Continental Congress voted a bill of thanks to General Gates. He then was sent to command an American army in the South. He was defeated so badly by the British in South Carolina that Congress thought he had purposely lost the battle. The Congressmen investigated what had happened in the battle, and decided that it was not the fault of General Gates, but they did not give him another command. After the war, Gates sold his plantation and his slaves and moved to New York. He died in 1806.

Gatling, Richard

Richard Gatling was the inventor of the first machine gun to be used by the United States Army.

Gatling was born in 1818 in North Carolina. When he was 25, some of his inventions were patented. He invented some important farm machinery when he was still quite young. When he was 31, he went to medical school. He never practiced medicine after he graduated, but continued as an inventor. In 1886, he invented his famous Gatling gun, a machine gun with six barrels arranged in a circle. The army bought the gun from him and improved it by adding four more barrels. To fire it, a soldier turned a crank that made the barrels rotate in a circle. As each barrel passed a certain spot, a bullet was automatically put into it and fired. The Gatling gun could be fired very rapidly. *Gat,* the slang word for *gun,* comes from the name Gatling. Dr. Gatling died in 1903.

gauchos

The cowboys who ride herd on the huge cattle ranches of Argentina, in South America, are called gauchos. The gauchos are descended from South American Indians who married Spanish and Portuguese settlers. They are expert, daring horsemen. Some people say that they are better riders than America's cowboys or Russia's famed Cossacks. The gauchos ride recklessly across the wide Argentine plains (called the *pampas*), rounding up the cattle that make their country so rich. Years ago the gauchos were equally famous for other feats, such as their fierce fights against savage Indian tribes that lived deep inside Argentina.

In the past fifty years much Argentine cattle land has been bought by farmers who have moved there from Europe, so there are not as many gauchos as there used to be.

The gauchos often put on demonstrations of their skill, as the cowboys of the United States do in rodeos. They are especially skillful in throwing the *bolas.* This is a kind of lasso with three balls on one end. They throw it so that this end twists around a steer's foot.

gauge or gage

A gauge, which is also spelled *gage,* is something used for measuring. Often it is an instrument that shows the measure of something. On the instrument panel of every automobile there is a dial called the *gasoline gauge.* It shows about how many gallons of gasoline there are in the gasoline tank. Thermometers and barometers are kinds of gauge.

The pressure gauge is one of the most familiar forms of gauge. It shows how much steam pressure there is in a boiler or how much air pressure there is in a tank. It works in a way that you can test with a rubber balloon. The more you blow into the balloon the greater the pressure will be inside the balloon and the farther the balloon will stretch away from you. In a pressure gauge, the pressure of steam or air forces a curved metal tube to expand. This moves a needle on a dial. The movement of the needle shows how far the tube has stretched, and this shows what the pressure is.

A water gauge is based on the fact that water seeks its own level. It is an upright glass tube connected with a tank that has a liquid in it. The higher the liquid is in the tank, the higher it will be in the tube. Therefore by looking at the tube you can see how much there is in the tank.

Gauges are also pieces of metal that have been carefully measured to make sure they are some exact length. When machinists are making machine parts that must be that exact length, they compare them with the gauge.

Gauge is also a term used for railroad tracks. Standard gauge tracks are 56½ inches apart (4 feet 8½ inches). Wider tracks (usually 5 feet wide) are called *broad gauge,* and narrower tracks are called *narrow gauge.*

Gauguin, Paul

Paul Gauguin was a great French painter who painted beautiful pictures of the natives of Tahiti. Tahiti is an island in the South Pacific Ocean. His pictures are very simple, with large patches of very bright red and orange. The objects and the people in the pictures have beautiful, simple outlines. Gauguin thought that paintings should not be elaborate and should have a very direct appeal to you when you look at them.

Gauguin was born in Paris in 1848. He became a painter quite late in life. Before that he had been a successful banker. He quit and went off to the South Seas because he did not like the stiff and formal life in France. He lived

French Embassy Press & Information Center

among the natives on the island of Tahiti and married a native woman. In some of his pictures he has painted his wife and child. He never made very much money from his paintings during his lifetime, but since his death they have become very valuable. Gauguin died in the South Seas in 1903. W. Somerset Maugham, the novelist, wrote a story around the events in Gauguin's life. It was called *The Moon and Sixpence,* and was later made into a motion picture.

Gaul

Gaul was the ancient Roman name for the country we now call France. Gaul was conquered by the Roman military leader Julius Caesar and became a province of the Roman Empire. The story of the conquest, which begins with the words "All Gaul is divided into three parts," was written by Caesar in the Latin language, which was the language of the Romans. Many high-school students who study Latin have to read this book as a part of their studies. The people of Gaul were barbarians when the Romans conquered the country, but they soon learned new ways of growing their crops and many men from Gaul joined the Roman armies. The Gauls were a Celtic people related to the ancestors of the people of Scotland, Ireland, and Wales. Their language was mixed with the Latin language of the Romans and became the French language.

Gaulle, Charles de

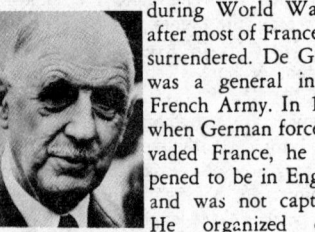

Charles de Gaulle, former President of France, was the principal French leader during World War II, after most of France had surrendered. De Gaulle was a general in the French Army. In 1940, when German forces invaded France, he happened to be in England and was not captured. He organized other French soldiers who had not been captured, calling them the Free French Army. (Afterward they were called the Fighting French.) This force fought alongside the British and Americans and helped to liberate France.

De Gaulle was born in 1890. He became an officer in the French Army and was a captain in World War I, in which he was captured by the Germans. In 1934, as a colonel, he wrote a book called *The Army of the Future* in which he predicted that tanks would be the most important thing in warfare on land. He was made a general in 1939, at the beginning of World War II.

In 1943, de Gaulle and another French general, Henri Giraud, were elected co-presidents of a French Committee of National Liberation. Giraud later resigned. In 1944, when the Germans were driven out of France, this committee became the government of France and de Gaulle was made the president. After two months he resigned, and the next year he became head of a new political party in France, the R.P.F. ("Reunion of the French People"). The party did not win many elections and de Gaulle gradually withdrew from politics. Then, in 1958, de Gaulle returned to politics and was appointed Premier. He was elected President in 1959 and re-elected in 1965 and in 1968. He resigned in 1969 when voters failed to approve various laws which he had wanted them to vote for. He died in 1970. See FRANCE.

gauntlet

A gauntlet is a large, heavy glove. Knights of the Middle Ages wore metal gauntlets as part of their armor. If they wanted to challenge someone to a fight, they threw their gauntlet on the ground. If another knight picked it up, he meant that he agreed to fight. Even today, we use the expression "to throw down the gauntlet" as a way of saying "to challenge someone to a fight." "Running the gauntlet" used to be a punishment for soldiers and sailors. The man who had committed a crime had to run between two lines of men, who hit him with their fists or with sticks as he passed by. The American Indians also used this punishment. The word *gauntlet* here had nothing to do with a glove, but came from a word in Swedish that meant "a running down a lane."

gaur

The gaur is a wild animal that looks somewhat like an ox or bison. Gaurs are sometimes six feet high at the shoulders and can weigh more than two thousand pounds. Except for the buffalo, they are the largest animals in the ox class. Gaurs are found in the forests of India, Burma, and Malaya. The people of these countries have rarely succeeded in taming them because they are so fierce. For many years the gaur has been a favorite target for hunters, and so many have been killed that the species may become extinct.

gavial

The gavial is a fierce-looking crocodile that is found mostly in the northern part of India. It reaches a length of 20 to 25 feet and has huge jaws with many teeth. It will not attack human beings, however, and the people of India consider it harmless and timid. The gavial is a fast swimmer, and its big jaws make it easy for it to catch fish, its main food. A smaller kind of gavial lives in the countries of Borneo and Sumatra. The gavial is also known as the *gharial*, or *garial*.

Gawain

Sir Gawain was the nephew of King Arthur and one of the most famous knights of the Round Table. In that great age of chivalry Sir Gawain was especially known for his courtesy and his wisdom, and he was in all ways an ideal knight. One of the best-known stories of Gawain tells how he agreed to marry a horribly ugly lady to help King Arthur who had been forced to prom e one of his knights for her husband. Because of Gawain's gallantry in marrying her, and then later in allowing her to have her own way, Gawain broke a wicked spell that had been cast on her; her ugliness disappeared, and she became the lovely lady she had once been. You can read more about King Arthur and his knights in the article on King ARTHUR.

Gay, John

John Gay was a poet who lived 250 years ago in England. He became famous for a saucy play called *The Beggar's Opera* that is still acted sometimes because it is funny and full of adventure. John Gay was a poor man who tried to make a living first by working at the court of Queen Anne and then by writing plays. At last his *Beggar's Opera* was a success, and he became rich and admired, although his play made fun of the people he knew at court. But Gay died only four years later, and his epitaph reads:

"Life is a jest and all things show it,
I thought so once and now I know it."

Gaza

Gaza is a town in southern Palestine. In Bible times, it was the principal city of the Philistines, and it was here that Samson was killed when he pulled down the temple on himself and the Philistines who had captured him. This is told in the Book of Judges. The ancient Egyptians made Gaza a great trading center, where caravans of travelers from many countries met and exchanged their goods. Many countries have ruled Gaza, and it was destroyed twice, once about 1,300 years ago, and again in the 1950s when the Jews and Arabs were fighting for possession of Palestine. Today, more than 40,000 people, mostly Arabs, live in Gaza. The town, famous for its pottery, was captured from Egypt by Israel in 1967.

gazelle

A gazelle is a small antelope that lives in the Sahara and Syrian deserts. It looks like a deer, with long, slender legs and horns. The horns of a gazelle are shaped like a lyre (a musical instrument like a harp). The horns are about 13 inches long and the gazelle is about 24 inches high at the shoulder. Gazelles are animals of very delicate appearance. They are light tan in color, with a wide dark brown band on their sides, and their stomachs and hindquarters are white. They have two stripes on their faces.

Gazelles are extremely swift and leap high in the air as they run. When they are going as fast as they can, they seem to skim the ground and resemble birds in flight. The eyes of a gazelle are large and soft with a sad, trusting expression. Poets compare the eyes of the gazelle to the eyes of lovely women. Because of its graceful movements and its appealing look the gazelle is often mentioned in literature.

Gazelles feed at dawn and in the evening, and drink water once in twenty-four hours. This animal is hunted by natives, by other animals like lions, and by people who shoot them as trophies, to stuff them and keep them in a collection. Because of this gazelles are becoming quite rare, but a number of them still survive in the Sahara desert and the rocky plains of Syria. Gazelles are also found in India near the Indus River, in central and south Africa, and on the high Tibetan plateau.

gear

A gear is a wheel with teeth sticking out from its rim (outside edge). Two or more gears are used together. The teeth of one gear fit between the teeth of another gear. The gears are then said to be meshed. If one of the gears is turning, the other gear must turn with it. Sometimes gears are used to make one of the gears turn faster or slower. Sometimes they are used so that the power from a horizontal shaft (a shaft lying on its side) can be made to turn a vertical shaft (a shaft standing upright); this is the arrangement of gears on a hand-operated eggbeater. A gear is also called a *cogwheel*, and the teeth are called *cogs*.

HOW A GEAR WORKS

The teeth on each pair of gears must all be the same size in order for them to mesh. However, the gears themselves do not have to be the same size. One gear may be smaller than the other. In fact, a smaller gear is usually meshed with a larger one. Since the teeth must all be the same size, the smaller gear must have fewer teeth than the larger one. If the small gear is half the size of the big one, it must have half as many teeth. If the big gear has twenty-four teeth, the small one must have twelve. The small gear will make one complete turn when its twelve teeth have meshed with twelve teeth of the larger gear. That means that when the small gear has gone all the way around once, the large one has turned only halfway around. The small gear must go all the way around again before the large one can make a complete turn. Thus the small gear will make two complete turns for every complete turn of the large one. To do this, the small gear must

turn twice as fast as the large one. A shaft turning slowly can make another shaft turn fast by the use of gears.

Although the larger gear turns more slowly than the smaller one, it turns with more force. If it is twice the size of the smaller one, it will turn with twice the force. In many cases, gears are arranged to give a shaft a great twisting force, which is called a *torque*. This helps the shaft to turn large wheels, or lift heavier weights, or drive deep holes in metal or wood. It is much easier to raise a bucket from a well if the bucket is attached to a rope on a large gear, while you turn a crank that is attached to a small gear, than it is to raise it by sheer muscle-power. You may have to turn the crank two or three times to make the large gear turn once, but you will not have to use as much effort to turn the crank as you would to lift the bucket all by yourself.

DIFFERENT KINDS OF GEAR

There are many different kinds of gears and they are used for many purposes. The

Spur gears have perfectly straight teeth.

most familiar gear is the one called the spur gear. It has teeth sticking straight out from its edge. It is the simplest type of gear and the one first used in machines.

Another type of gear is the helical gear. It looks almost like the spur gear except that the teeth are cut sideways. Helical gears work more quietly than spur gears, and for this reason they are used in automobiles to change the speed of a car. Two

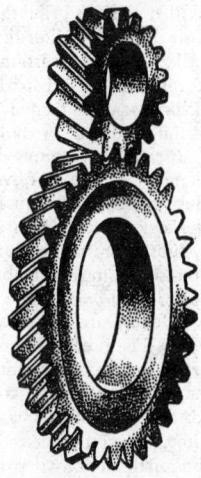

Helical gears have teeth cut at an angle so that they will mesh quietly.

helical gears fastened together side by side are called herringbone gears.

The most powerful gear is the bevel gear. The teeth on a bevel gear are not on the edge but are cut slantwise on the face of the gear. A spur bevel gear has straight

A herringbone gear is like two helical gears put together side by side.

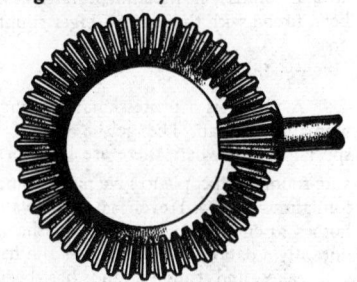

Spur bevel gears have straight teeth set wider apart on one side than on the other.

teeth. A helical bevel gear has teeth that are slanted and curved. Bevel gears are used in the differential gear of an automobile. There is a separate article on DIFFERENTIAL GEAR.

A worm gear is a kind of helical gear but looks more like a long screw. It is usually meshed with a spur gear. The worm gear may be part of a shaft operated by a crank or a motor. A horizontal worm gear can be made to turn a vertical shaft and vice versa. Worm gears are used in pulleys.

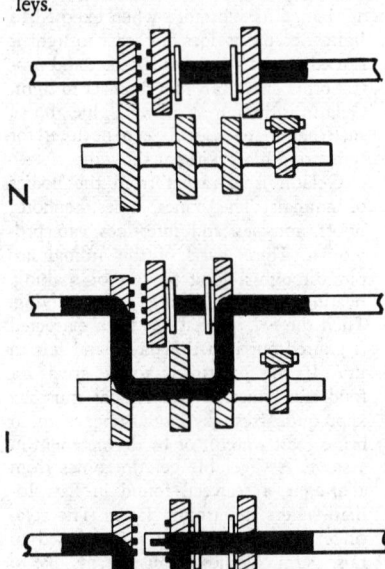

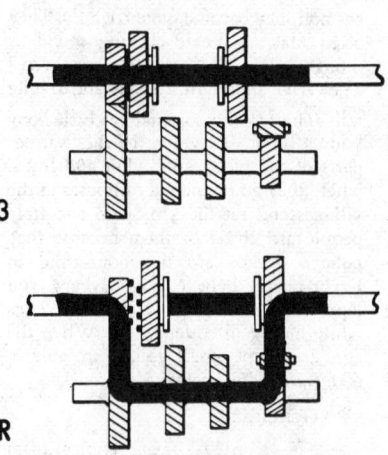

In these views of an automobile transmission the turning parts are shaded. The shaft at the upper right is turned by the engine. When one of its gears is meshed with one of the gears on the lower shaft, the lower shaft is turned and turns the shaft at the upper left. The shaft at the upper left turns the wheels of the automobile. The views show, from top to bottom, how the shaft at the upper right moves to the left or right to mesh the gears in neutral, first, second, third, or reverse positions.

USES OF GEARS

One of the most important uses of gears is in the automobile transmission. The transmission is a box full of gears. It is located behind the engine and its purpose is to change the speed of the automobile. In the diagram, you can see how the gears are meshed with each other when the car is going at different speeds. There is also a reverse gear, which makes the car go backward, and a neutral gear position, used when the car is not moving. After World War II many automobiles were built with automatic transmissions. You can read more about automatic transmissions in the article on TORQUE CONVERTER.

The bicycle was one of the first machines to use a gear. One gear is located between the wheels and is called a sprocket. The sprocket is meshed with a chain that goes around another gear on the back wheel. When you push down on the pedals, the sprocket turns. This moves the chain forward and turns the rear wheel.

Clocks and watches are run by means of small gears. A gear is attached to the hour hand, a smaller gear to the minute hand, and a very small gear to the second hand. These gears are meshed with each other, so that when one turns all the gears turn. The second-hand gear turns 60 times faster than the minute-hand gear. The minute-hand gear turns 12 times faster than the hour-hand gear. This means that the second-hand gear turns 720 times faster than the hour-hand gear.

gecko

Geckos are small lizards, most of them less than a foot long. They can climb up and down window-panes or any smooth surface because they have small suction discs on their feet, and they can move quite fast. Geckos have no eyelids, but some people say that they have a transparent scale like a watch crystal that comes down over their eyes when they blink. They are harmless reptiles—they could not harm you even if they wanted to. You can tame them if you

try, and they become quite friendly. They often make a feeble clicking sound as though they were saying "toco-toco." They have short, thick heads and fragile tails. Their skin is soft and has little bony bumps on it. They live in the warmer parts of the globe, in Ceylon and India, where they go in and out of houses in the villages and eat flies. In Spain and Italy people are afraid of them because they believe geckos are poisonous, and in Egypt people believe that they give you leprosy. Geckos lay two or three eggs while hiding in rotten wood. When the eggs hatch the small geckos are able to take care of themselves.

Gehenna

The word *Gehenna* comes from two Hebrew words that mean "Valley of Hinnom." In the Bible, the Valley of Hinnom was a valley to the south of Jerusalem. It was a place where a huge fire burned all of the time. People would dump their garbage and other things that they wanted to burn up into the valley. Thousands of years ago children were thrown into the fire as sacrifices, or offerings, to the gods. This happened in the time of the prophet Jeremiah, who also refers to a place called Tophet, which lay in the valley of Hinnom, as the location of some of the worst iniquities of the valley. It became known as a dreadful and horrible place, and people began to imagine that Hell was just like that. When the word *Gehenna* is used now it means a place of everlasting doom and woe and torture.

Gehrig, Lou

Henry Louis Gehrig was one of the greatest players in the history of baseball. He was born in New York City in 1903 and began to play baseball in school. Then he went to Columbia University where he also was known as a good football player. He joined the New York Yankees in 1925 and became the first baseman of the team. Gehrig was called "The Iron Horse" because he was big and powerful and for about 14 years never missed a game. He played in 2,130 games in succession. No one before Gehrig came

close to this record, and probably no one ever will. Gehrig was a great hitter and led the American League in 1934 with a batting average of .363. His lifetime batting average was .341, and he hit many home runs. Lou Gehrig was infected with a crippling disease 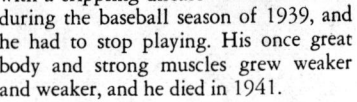 during the baseball season of 1939, and he had to stop playing. His once great body and strong muscles grew weaker and weaker, and he died in 1941.

Geiger counter

A Geiger counter is an instrument that can measure particles of energy as small as an atom. These particles of energy are radiated, or sent out, from substances such as radium, which we say are *radioactive*. The instrument is made of two thin sheets of metal that are rolled into cylinders. One piece is placed inside the other, a few inches apart. Both pieces are placed inside a glass envelope; gases

are pumped into the envelope and it is sealed. A very high negative charge of electricity is placed on the inside cylinder, and a very high positive charge is placed on the outside one. When a particle of radiation enters the instrument, it therefore conducts large amounts of electricity from the outside cylinder to the inside one. This is connected with a noisemaker which clicks every time a particle enters the instrument. The operator hears the click through a pair of earphones. The closer the operator moves toward the source of energy, the faster the clicks become.

People must be very careful when handling radioactive materials because they give a very dangerous kind of burn. Geiger counters are therefore very useful in places where these materials are handled. The instrument is also widely used for locating the radioactive materials in the ground. Many of the uranium deposits (uranium is used for making atomic bombs) in the United States have been found with the aid of Geiger counters.

geisha

A geisha is a professional dancing-woman of Japan. The geisha works in special houses where there are large private rooms for people to give parties, and sometimes she will even go to private homes to entertain guests. The geisha is not only a dancer, but also serves the tea and cakes and candies, and has been trained in the art of conversation. The geisha starts her training when she is still a young girl, and studies for years before she can begin to work. She must be able to play several musical instruments, and to sing many songs. She must also be able to talk with the guests about many different things, and entertain them with stories if they want her to.

gelatin

Gelatin is probably most familiar to you as the flavored, jellylike desert you are given at meals. It has many other uses as well. Gelatin is used in photographic plates because it does not react or change its substance when exposed to light. Because it does not react to light it is used in many ways to conduct and protect other chemicals that do react to light. Gelatin is the purest form of glue and as such has many uses. It can be used for cementing glass without showing.

Gelatin is extracted from the bodies of animals. The bones, hides, tendons, hoofs, muscles and intestines can provide it. These parts of the animal are put through a long process of soaking, heating, washing, drying, and purifying. Then the gelatin that has been extracted is poured out in a thin layer and left to dry. If the gelatin is to be used for food the bones of the animal must be kept quite fresh by preserving them in brine (salt water), or by drying them in a stove. A vegetable gelatin comes from agar-agar, a seaweed found in East Indian waters and around Japan. The gelatin extracted from agar-agar is used to raise germ colonies because germs like to feed and grow on the gelatin.

Gemini

Gemini is the name for one of the constellations, which are groups of stars

in the sky. It was given the name Dioscuri by the people of ancient Greece, to whom this name meant "twins." (In the Latin language, *gemini* means "twins.") People thought that this group of stars looked like twin brothers named Castor and Pollux, characters in the stories the ancient Greeks told thousands of years ago. Castor and Pollux lived in the city of Sparta, in Greece. Castor was the best horse-trainer and Pollux the strongest boxer of the city. The ancient Romans said that when a war was going badly for their side, Castor and Pollux would appear on horseback in the battle and then the luck would change. The sign of the zodiac that stands for the constellation Gemini is ♊; the vertical (up and down) lines look like the twins, who are joined by the horizontal (crosswise) lines to show they are always together. Read also the articles on CONSTELLATION and ZODIAC.

GEMINI is also the name given by the United States to its spaceships that carry two men. See the article SPACE TRAVEL.

gems

Gems are rare and very valuable stones commonly known as jewels. They are used to ornament watches, rings, bracelets, brooches, necklaces, royal crowns, and many other things. Gems were formed millions of years ago when the rocky crust of our earth was soft and terribly hot. The enormous heat and pressure made certain chemicals melt together and harden into stone when the earth's crust cooled. Some of the substances or chemicals that were united in this way became our rare gems.

Gems are dug out of the earth in the same way that coal, gold or iron is mined. The mines may be deep underground, or they may be open pits in the surface of the earth. The gems are usually found embedded in layers of rock or clay. When they are first brought out of the mines they look like small pieces of dull-colored rock or dirty pebbles. To make them into the bright sparkling stones we often see in the windows of jewelry stores, the rough gems are sent to places such as the city of Amsterdam in Holland and the city of Antwerp in Belgium, countries of western Europe. There skilled workers grind them smooth and polish them. Grinding little flat surfaces, called *facets,* all around the gem makes it reflect light and sparkle no matter which way it is turned. Gems are ground and polished by holding them against a rapidly turning disk coated with diamond dust and olive oil. Diamond dust is used because it is the hardest material known to man and thus is the only substance that can cut diamonds.

The rarest and most valuable gems are called *precious stones* while those that are less valuable are known as *semiprecious stones.* The precious stones are: diamond, ruby, emerald, sapphire, Oriental amethyst, Oriental topaz, and Oriental emerald. Some semiprecious stones are: tourmaline, garnet, topaz, moonstone, turquoise, opal, zircon, chrysoberyl, jade, spinel, and peridot. In addition to these stones, there are *organic gems* that are the products of living creatures or ancient plants that have turned to stone. The organic gems are: pearl, amber, coral, and jet.

PRECIOUS STONES

Diamonds are probably the best known of the precious stones to most of us. Like ordinary coal, diamonds are a form of carbon. However, coal contains many other chemicals besides carbon while diamonds are pure carbon formed into the hardest material known to man by terrific heat and pressure. Diamonds are clear or transparent like glass but may be bluish or yellowish or even black. For the complete story of this gem see the article under DIAMOND.

Emeralds are transparent, that is, you can look through them, and they are green in color. Good emeralds are the rarest and most valuable of precious stones. Most of the world's best emeralds come from mines in Colombia, a country of South America. Oriental emeralds that are found in Asia are not as good as the Colombian gems, although they look much the same except that they do not sparkle as brilliantly.

Rubies are blood-red and transparent. They are among the most valuable gems in the world. Rubies are found in Burma, Siam, and Ceylon, countries of southeastern Asia.

Sapphires are transparent blue gems. They are mined in Siam, northern India, Ceylon, Australia, and in the state of Montana in America.

Oriental amethysts are transparent and violet in color. They are found in different parts of eastern Asia and are sometimes called purple sapphires. Many people think amethysts are good luck charms that protect you from thieves, help you in love, and give you peaceful sleep.

The *Oriental topaz* is a yellow sapphire whose color ranges from pale yellow to deep gold. Oriental topaz is found in parts of eastern Asia.

SEMIPRECIOUS STONES

Semiprecious stones, although less valuable because they are not so rare as precious stones, are nevertheless very beautiful and are used for less expensive jewelry. These stones are found in all parts of the world and can be obtained in almost any desired color whether transparent or opaque, that is, a material through which one cannot see. Some are so much like precious stones that only an expert can tell them apart. Very few people can identify all the semiprecious stones.

Try to remember the following descriptions of the different semiprecious stones and then see if you can recognize any of them in a jeweler's window.

Tourmaline is opaque (you cannot see through it). It is flesh-red or dark pink and has a glassy luster. Other colors are violet, red, yellow, black, and blue. Sometimes there are two or more colors in bands with sharp boundaries between the colors.

Topaz is transparent and may be light or dark yellow. It does not sparkle as brightly as the precious stone called Oriental topaz. *Garnet* is transparent and very dark red. *Turquoise* is opaque and greenish blue in color. It is the favorite gem of Mexican Indian silversmiths who like to ornament their silverwork with it. *Moonstone* is a milky white stone with a bluish tint. It is partly transparent and reflects light from its inner layers. *Opal* is a beautiful milky white stone that may be opaque or transparent. It is known for its brilliant changing colors that can be seen inside the gem through its outer partly transparent milky layers. *Chrysoberyl* is transparent and may be colorless, pale yellow, red, or a smoky brownish color. *Jade* is an opaque stone and when polished looks as if it had been waxed. Its color varies from grayish white to emerald green, the emerald green variety being the most highly valued. Jade is considered the most precious of all gems by the Chinese and Japanese. *Spinel* is a very hard transparent gem that may be red, green, blue, brown, or black. The red variety is called *spinel ruby*. *Peridot* is the name given by French jewelers to a transparent olive-green or yellowish green gem. It is also called *olivine* and *chrysolite*.

ORGANIC GEMS

Pearls are the best known of organic gems. They are spheres or balls with a soft, glowing white color and are strung together as necklaces or used separately in rings, earrings, and other jewelry. Pearls are made by oysters lying on the sea bottom. Sometimes a grain of sand gets inside the shell of the oyster. To protect his soft body from the sharp bit of sand the oyster coats it with a fluid (mother-of-pearl) that slowly hardens. After many coats of this fluid a round pearl is formed. Because oysters do this only once in a while, good pearls are rare and very valuable.

Amber is a transparent soft stone with a dark orange color. It is resin (a sticky fluid that oozes out of certain evergreen trees) that hardened into stone after millions of years in the ground. It is used for cigarette holders, pipe mouthpieces, combs, brushes, and other articles.

Coral is an opaque, dark pink stone formed by the skeletons of very tiny creatures of the sea that live together in colonies. After many years the skeletons of the millions of dead coral form mounds of stone from which all kinds of inexpensive jewelry can be made.

Jet is an opaque black stone that takes a brilliant polish. It is a black form of lignite, a brown soft stone that can be burned like coal but is not quite as good a fuel as coal.

gemsbok

A gemsbok is a large antelope, an animal like a deer, that lives in South Africa. It has sharp-pointed, straight horns, and a long, sweeping, black tail, and a short mane that stands up on its neck. It is said that gemsboks never drink water since they get enough moisture from the juicy, bulbous plants they feed on. Like all antelopes they can run very fast. Since airplanes have brought civilization deeper and deeper into the part of the world where gemsboks are to be found, the animal is dying out, except where they live in game preserves.

gender

Gender is a term in grammar that indicates classification of nouns and pronouns as *masculine, feminine,* or *neuter.* In all languages living things are classified according to their sex: male creatures are masculine, female creatures are feminine. Objects (that is, non-living things) are called neuter. There is one other classification for words that may mean either a male or female creature, such as *animal.* This classification is called *common gender.*

The English language follows these four gender groups exactly. For example, *man* is masculine in gender, and it requires the masculine pronouns such as *he, him,* and *his; girl* is feminine in gender, and it requires the feminine pronouns such as *she, her,* and *hers; house* is neuter in gender, and it requires the neuter pronouns *it* and *its.* Common gender covers such animals as *dog, bird,* or *fish,* and such group words as *company, club, Scout troop.* One would say, *The man lost his hat and he is hunting for it.* In this sentence, *man, his,* and *he* are masculine in gender, and *hat* and *it* are neuter. In the sentence. *The girl lost her dog and she is hunting for it,* the words *girl, her* and *she* are feminine; *dog* is common gender because it may be either a male or female dog, and the neuter pronoun *it* is used with the common gender noun. Words meaning a kind of animal that may be either masculine or feminine take pronouns of the neuter gender; for example, *The dog hid its bone.* Words meaning a group of people also take the neuter gender; for example, *The club held its meeting last night.*

When we refer to all the members of a group that includes both sexes, pronouns of the masculine gender may be used, for example, *Every member of the class should wear his class pin.*

In English, many nouns have different forms for masculine and feminine, such as *boy* and *girl, husband* and *wife, king* and *queen.*

Other languages often have different, and sometimes more difficult, systems of gender. In French, words for non-living objects may also be classified as masculine or feminine. For instance, *chemin* means *road,* but it is a masculine noun; *plume* means *pen,* but it is a feminine noun. The German language also uses this way of making inanimate things masculine or feminine, but in German some living things are given the neuter gender. For instance, *mädchen* means *girl* in German, but it is in the neuter gender.

gene

A gene is a part of a cell, the tiny particle of which living things are composed. Genes are too small ever to be seen, even under a microscope. It is the genes in the cell that cause a person's hair to be a certain color or his feet to be a certain size, or that cause a plant to bear white flowers instead of red ones. The combination of different genes in cells is responsible for the kind of plant or animal that is produced from a seed or egg. Genes are inherited. That is, a plant or person or any other living thing gets its genes from its parents, and that is why children tend to look like their parents. A gene can be entirely different from anything a person's parents or any of his other ancestors ever had. Such a difference is caused by a process called *mutation,* which means "change". In 1970, an artificial gene was made for the first time, by scientists at the University of Wiscon-

sin under the direction of Dr. H. Gobind Khorana. The study of genes and how they are inherited is called *genetics*.

genealogy

A genealogist traces the history of a person's family. He finds out who the person's ancestors were, often for hundreds of years back. His work is called *genealogy*, and the line of a person's ancestors is called his *lineage*.

The genealogist traces a lineage by making a family tree. This is a kind of chart that shows what persons were married, who their children were, and the years of their births and deaths.

Many people pay genealogists to trace their families because they hope to learn they are descended from famous people, of whom they can be proud. In the United States there are a number of patriotic societies, such as the Sons of the American Revolution, the Daughters of the American Revolution, and the Mayflower Society, that will not elect a member unless he can prove that he is descended from certain persons. People who want to join these societies often hire genealogists for this purpose. The genealogists do this by looking through old records of births in courthouses and in books. Thousands of books of genealogy have been published. Most of them give the history of one family, but some of them include all the families in a certain county or state. In European countries that have royal and noble families, there are organizations that have kept genealogical records for hundreds of years.

general

Very high-ranking officers in an army bear the title *general*. In the United States, generals are the highest-ranking officers in the Army and also in the Marine Corps and Air Force. The generals wear stars on their shoulders. One star marks a brigadier general, the lowest of the generals; two stars, a major general; three stars, a lieutenant general; four stars, a full general, or simply a general; five stars, a General of the Army (or General of the Air Force), the highest-ranking general. In other armies, a brigadier is a separate rank and is not classed as a general, while the highest rank is not General of the Army, but MAR-SHAL (about which there is a separate article). The Russian Army uses, and the German Army used to use, the title colonel general, which is about the same as lieutenant general in the United States.

Until 1944, the United States had no rank higher than general, except that John J. Pershing, commander of the United States armies that fought in Europe in World War I, was given a special title of General of the Armies of the United States, which no other person has ever held. George Washington was voted the same title by Congress but never used it. During the Revolutionary War he was only a lieutenant general. After the Civil War, the Union generals Ulysses S. Grant, William T. Sherman and Philip H. Sheridan received the rank General of the Army. In 1944, George C. Marshall, Douglas MacArthur, Dwight D. Eisenhower and Henry H. Arnold were made Generals of the Army. Arnold later was appointed General of the Air Force after that service was separated from the Army. See also the article ADMIRAL.

General Education Board

The General Education Board was set up in 1902 to help schools and to encourage education for all, without distinction as to race, sex or religion. A large amount of money was given to the General Education Board, mostly by a very rich man, John D. Rockefeller. Most of it has been spent in improving colleges for both Negro and white students in the southern United States, and in helping high schools and junior colleges all over the country. By 1954 the Board had stopped work because it had reached most of its goals and had spent most of its money.

general staff

General staff is the name given to the group of military officers who assist and advise the commanding officer of a military headquarters and actually run the Army. In the United States the Secretary of the Army, who is in charge of the Department of the Army, receives advice and assistance from the general staff of the Department of the Army. This general staff is made up of a chief and a deputy chief of staff. They in turn are helped by several assistant chiefs of staff who are in charge of the various sections of the Army: Personnel (G-1), Intelligence (G-2), Operations (G-3), and Logistics (G-4).

generator

Electric generators supply all of the electricity we use, except for small amounts obtained from batteries. Generators are even used on automobiles, so that the battery does not have to work all of the time.

A generator's job is to change mechanical energy (such as the energy taken from the driveshaft of a gasoline engine) into electrical energy, which may be used in your home. There are only two important parts in a generator, the *field* and the armature. The field is a series of bar magnets which are placed in a circle with opposite poles next to each other. (There is a separate article in this encyclopedia about MAGNETS which will tell you more about how they work.) There must always be an even number of these field magnets, or there will be two with the same poles side by side, somewhere in the circle. These magnets may be just bar magnets, or they can be electromagnets, which are much stronger. If electromagnets are used, there is a coil of wire wrapped around each one. The electricity which flows through these coils comes from the generator itself.

The armature is made of thin sheets of steel. These sheets are placed on top of each other and formed into a cylinder, or drum. This cylinder is then wrapped with wires which carry the electricity that is generated.

The armature is then placed in the center of the circle formed by the field magnets. Some means of turning the armature is set up. This may be anything from a gasoline engine to a water wheel. When the armature turns, the wires on its surface go past the field magnets. When this happens, the electricity in the magnets sets a current of electricity moving in the wires on the armature. One of the big problems with generators is how to get the electricity from the rapidly spinning armature. It is impossible to take the electricity by means of wires, because they would twist around one another and break when the armature started spinning. There are two solutions to this problem: brushes and sliprings. To use either of these devices, the armature is shaped so that one end has a ring of copper wire-endings from the wires on the surface of the armature. This ring is called the *commutator*.

Brushes are box-shaped pieces of carbon which rest against the commutator. These brushes allow the armature to turn, because they just slide against the commutator. The brushes have wires attached to them which allow the electricity to be carried to the place where it will be used.

If a slip-ring is used, the armature wires end in an actual brush, or it is arranged so that just the bare wires stick out. The wires are adjusted so that they are always touching a circular piece of copper which does not move. These circular pieces of copper are called the sliprings.

ELECTRIC MOTOR

Since the turning of the armature creates a current of electricity, it follows that feeding a current of electricity into the same machine will make the armature turn. This is the principle of the *electric motor*, which is simply a generator to which electricity is supplied.

HISTORY OF GENERATORS

A man named Michael Faraday made the first generator in the year 1831. This first generator was a very simple one. It was just a copper disc which was turned rapidly between the poles of a horseshoe magnet. The generator was developed in many countries by many different men, each adding a new idea. In 1878, Thomas A. Edison put all of these ideas together in what he called the *bipolar generator*. Edison invented the electric light a year later, and as his light came to be used more and more, so did his generator. The design of generators improved, because they had to be made larger and larger as there was more demand for electricity. Engineers are always trying to make generators give more electricity for the amount of energy used to turn them. Atomic generators, for example, are similar to the older ones, but they are turned by atomic engines, which are much cheaper than gasoline or Diesel engines.

Most large dams today have generators inside them. The water which flows through the dam turns a wheel which has many paddles on it to catch the water. This wheel turns the generator. Another inexpensive way to generate electricity is by using steam. The steam is forced from a fine nozzle onto a wheel which has many tiny paddles on it. This wheel then turns the generator, just like the wheel inside the dam.

A question which frequently comes up about generators is this: Why can't you connect an electric motor to a generator, then connect the wires from the generator to the motor? It would seem that the motor would spin the generator and make electricity flow into the mo-

tor. This would keep happening, and the motor and generator would run forever, supposedly. This is not possible because the full amount of energy put into the generator in the form of mechanical energy is never returned in electrical energy.

Some of the finest generators are ninety percent efficient. This means that ninety percent of the energy put into the generator is taken out in the form of electricity. The figure would have to be one hundred percent before the motor would turn the generator forever, and this is impossible. The ten percent that is lost is taken up by friction in the generator.

There are separate articles in this encyclopedia about DYNAMICS, ALTERNATING CURRENT, and DIRECT CURRENT.

Genesis

Genesis is the first book in the Old Testament, in the Bible. Together with the next four books, Exodus, Leviticus, Numbers, and Deuteronomy, it forms the Pentateuch ("five books"), which are called the books of Moses. Genesis tells the story of the creation of the world, the lives of the patriarchs or fathers of the Israelites, and the origin of Judaism, the Jewish religion. Genesis probably was not written down in its present form until four or five hundred years before the birth of Jesus. It is very important in history as well as in religion. The events told in Genesis are covered in the articles on ADAM AND EVE, ABEL, CAIN, NOAH, ABRAHAM, ISAAC, JACOB, and JOSEPH, and in the article on the BIBLE.

genet

The genet is a catlike animal, but it has a big, bushy tail that makes it longer than a cat. Its fur is a muddy grey color with dark spots, and it has a dark stripe down its back and rings of black and white around its tail. The genet can be found in Africa, in southern Europe, and in Palestine. It makes its home near rocks and water. This animal survives by eating smaller animals and birds, which it hunts when it comes out at night. A very unpleasant odor comes from the genet.

Genet, Citizen

Edmond Charles Genet was a Frenchman who was ambassador from France to the United States more than 150 years ago. He was appointed in 1792, when France was in the midst of the French Revolution, in which the French people threw out their king and became a republic. He was called Citizen Genet because Frenchmen at that time used the title Citizen instead of the other titles that the noblemen had used.

The United States was grateful to France, because France had helped the Americans win the Revolutionary War, but Citizen Genet tried too hard to persuade the United States to join France in its war against England and Spain. President George Washington finally asked France to call Genet back and send a new ambassador. Genet did not want to go back, so he stayed and became an American citizen.

Genet was born in 1763. When he was only 12 years old he received a medal from the King of Sweden for translating a French history into the Swedish language. He was only 29 years old when he became ambassador to the United States. He married the daughter of Governor George Clinton of New York and settled on a farm in New York, where he died in 1834.

genetics

Genetics is the study of how animals and plants inherit their appearance and characteristics from their parents, and why they are different from their parents. The "parents" are almost always one male and one female member of the same kind of animal or plant. The offspring grow from seeds or eggs produced by these parents. In these seeds or eggs there are *genes* that give the offspring certain characteristics. These are likely to resemble the characteristics of the parents and other ancestors, but no two individuals are likely to be exactly the same. Certain *variations* occur that cause differences, and often there are *mutations,* or changes, that cause an individual to be entirely different in some way from any of his ancestors. The science of genetics has not yet solved all the problems of how such things occur. See the articles on GENE and HEREDITY.

Geneva

Geneva is a large city in southwestern Switzerland, near the border between Switzerland and France. It is more than two thousand years old. About 170,000 people live in Geneva, which makes it about the size of Nashville, Tennessee. It is one of the most important cities in Europe because so many international conferences have been held there.

Most of the people who live in Geneva speak French, which is the language of the people who live in that part of Switzerland. Some speak German or Italian.

The people of Geneva work in many small factories that make the products for which Switzerland is most famous, such as clocks and watches, scientific instruments, and jewelry. In the older parts of Geneva you can still see buildings that were built hundreds of years ago. The University of Geneva is one of the most famous in the world. It was founded more than five hundred years ago.

After World War I, Geneva was made the seat, or official headquarters, of the League of Nations. Many of the fine buildings that were built for the League of Nations were taken over by sections of the United Nations.

There have been many historic meetings in Geneva. You can read in separate articles how the RED CROSS was founded there and the GENEVA CONVENTIONS were made. In July 1954 a meeting at Geneva ended fighting between French and Communist forces in Viet Nam. In July 1955 President Dwight D. Eisenhower of the United States, Prime Minister Anthony Eden of Great Britain, Premier Nikolai Bulganin of the Soviet Union and Premier Edgar Faure of France met in Geneva to try to find a way to avoid another world war.

LAKE GENEVA

Lake Geneva, which is also called *Lac Leman,* is the largest of the lakes near the Alps. Lake Geneva lies between France and Switzerland. It is more than forty miles long and is about nine miles wide at its center. The Rhone River enters Lake Geneva from the east and leaves it at the city of Geneva on the west. The lake is more than a thousand feet above sea level. The lake is a dark blue color, and it is very beautiful with its background of high, snow-covered mountain peaks.

Geneva Convention

About a hundred years ago (in 1864) representatives of the biggest countries in Europe met in Geneva, a city in Switzerland, and agreed on certain rules to protect wounded men and prisoners of war. These rules are called the Geneva Convention. At this meeting the Red Cross was recognized as an international society to protect such men, and its flag, a red cross on a white background, was adopted as a mark to show that relief work was going on and should not be attacked by either side. Prisoners of war may be made to work if they are enlisted men, but must be paid for their work; officers may not be made to work and must be granted certain freedoms if they give their parole (word of honor) not to try to escape. Red Cross workers may not be captured or hurt. Florence Nightingale, the great Englishwoman who founded the profession of nursing, had much to do with the adoption of the Geneva Convention. Nearly all warring countries since then have pretended to obey it, though some of them (for example, the Japanese, Germans and Russians during World War II) have not obeyed it. In 1949 some new rules were added to the Geneva Convention. The important one was that armies may not take citizens of enemy countries as hostages. A hostage is a person who is held as a prisoner and can be punished or killed if other people disobey instructions.

Genevieve, Saint

St. Genevieve is the patron saint of the city of Paris. She was a girl there 1,500 years ago. When she was seven years old her friend St. Germain asked her to study to become a nun, and she became famous for her kindness and purity. Then Attila, the king of the Huns, came out of Asia and invaded Europe with an army of fierce, wild soldiers. The nun Genevieve told the people of Paris that he would attack their city. She begged them to be brave and said that if they trusted God, Attila could not hurt them. Because these things happened just as she had promised, the people of Paris were grateful to her for showing them how to save themselves, and they still think of her with love.

Genghis Khan

Genghis Khan was a great soldier who almost conquered the world. If you take a map and look at Asia you will be able to see how big his empire was. It stretched from northern China down to northern India, and from China over to Syria and the Persian Gulf. It included a great slice of what we call Russia, almost to the Arctic Circle. It was the biggest empire that anyone had ever ruled, and no one has equaled it since.

In many history books Genghis Khan is called a barbaric Tartar. The Tartars were a very wild and warlike people who

lived in northern Asia and were famous for their cruelty. They were fierce fighters and showed very little mercy to anyone. Genghis Khan was born eight hundred years ago, in 1162. He was the son of a Tartar chieftain. He was called Tennujin then, and was not called Genghis Khan until after he had captured a great deal of land. *Genghis Khan* means "Great Ruler." His father died when he was thirteen years old and he took over the command of his father's tribe. Many of his father's subjects thought that a young boy of thirteen could not rule a country, so they planned to get rid of him. He fled from his country and was taken in by a neighboring ruler. There he became the head of the army, married the ruler's daughter, and became very powerful. There was a plot to kill him there too, but he escaped and returned to his own country. Then he started out to capture all of Asia. In 1215 he swept through northern China and captured it, along with the important city of Peking, now Peiping. By 1223 he and his armies had captured northern India. In some history books they will tell you that if Genghis Khan had taken one more step to the west he could have conquered all of Europe. He died in 1227 while he was fighting another war in northern China.

Genghis Khan was not really a barbarian. A barbarian cannot read or write, is cruel, and lives like a savage. Genghis Khan could read and write, and he had several wise and well-educated men with him at all times to give him advice. He set up a police system throughout his empire, so that you could travel from China to the Mediterranean Sea in safety. He had his empire and its people well protected. He also set up a system of communication that was very rapid for that time. It was not like the telegraph system of today, but news got back and forth very quickly.

When Genghis Khan died his lands were divided among his many children. His three oldest sons got the largest shares.

genie

A genie was a magical spirit that the Persians and Arabians told about in their folk stories. There were good genies and wicked genies, but all of them were supposed to have been created out of fire. There are many genies in the stories of the Arabian Nights. In the story of Aladdin, when the boy rubbed his lamp it was a good genie who appeared to do his bidding. The wicked genies did all kinds of harmful and cruel tricks because they hated human beings. Most genies were thought of as looking like men, but they had a wonderful power of changing their shapes and they could even appear and disappear as clouds of smoke. The Arabians and Persians used a word that we spell *jinn* for the same kind of spirit.

genius

Originally a genius was considered a spirit with greater powers than human beings have. Two thousand years ago, the Romans thought that every person had a genius, a guardian spirit, who watched over him and protected him, and that countries and even buildings each had a genius. Each person worshiped his own genius. The word was much the same as *genie,* the spirit you read about in the Arabian Nights.

Today, the word *genius* is used for some sort of outstanding talent or ability. A person with an I.Q. of more than 135 is called a "near genius," and a person whose intelligence is very much greater than other people's is often called a genius.

We may also say that a person has a genius for painting, music, or some other art or ability. A word more often used today is *aptitude*. See the article on IN-TELLIGENCE.

Genoa

Genoa is a city in northwest Italy. It was the birthplace of Christopher Columbus, who discovered America. In Genoa there are many beautiful churches and palaces. Very narrow streets go up to the hills surrounding the city. Genoa became very famous as a shipping center hundreds of years ago. Next to Venice, it was the most important seaport on the Mediterranean Sea. At that time it was an independent state, governed as a republic. It is still an important shipping center and seaport, and ships from all over the world stop there. More than 750,000 people live there.

The beautiful cathedral in Genoa is made of strips of black and white marble. It was built in 1100. Many of the city's beautiful buildings were damaged during World War II. In the museums and the city hall there are many reminders of Christopher Columbus, including several famous statues. Many of his letters, written more than 450 years ago, are considered great treasures.

genocide

Genocide is the killing of an entire race or national group of people. The purpose is to exterminate them—kill them all. In very ancient times, thousands of years ago, it was not unusual for one tribe to kill all the members of another tribe, but most people thought this could never happen again until the Nazi party, under Adolf Hitler, came to power in Germany in 1933. Part of the Nazi policy was to kill all the Jews in the world. They could not do this because they never controlled the whole world, but in Germany and other parts of Europe that they came to control they killed more than six million Jews. After the Allies won World War II against Germany, a few of the Germans who were responsible for this killing were punished but most of them were not. Most of the nations of the world have since signed agreements that make genocide an international crime.

genre painting

Paintings that show you scenes of everyday life are called genre painting. They are paintings of things that everybody knows about. If you look at a picture painted by Pieter Breughel, you will see a scene of Dutch life painted four hundred years ago. One called *The Country Wedding* shows a whole room full of people at a wedding feast. It is a very colorful scene with lots of reds, yellows, and greens, and you feel that you are right in the picture and know what is happening. If you look at some of the pictures by Grant Wood, an American painter, you will see scenes of farm life in Iowa. These pictures show farmers plowing fields, eating dinner, and washing their hands. They are scenes that you would find on any farm, and Grant Wood painted them so that you would feel as though you were there. Thousands of years ago the ancient Greeks made vases that were decorated with scenes from the lives of people living then. They are a kind of genre art, too.

Genseric

Genseric, who lived about fifteen hundred years ago, was king of the Vandals and a great military leader. Under Genseric, the Vandals, a Germanic tribe, swept down from northeastern Europe as far west as France and Spain, terrorizing everyone. Genseric conquered all of North Africa and made Carthage his capital. His pirate fleets terrorized the Mediterranean. He attacked and practically destroyed Rome, carrying off the Empress and her two daughters, and many art treasures. The Vandals were so destructive and cruel that to this day we call a destructive act an act of *vandalism*.

gentian

The gentian is one of the most beautiful of wild flowers. It grows 10 to 12 inches high. It has a branched stem upon which the flowers appear. The petals of the gentian are delicately fringed at the edge, and the blue of the blossom, which is shaped like an upended bell, has been compared by poets to the blue of the sky. They have called it a touch of the sky on earth. The gentian is difficult to cultivate in America, but it does grow wild and when found, it should not be destroyed or the plant might become extinct. This plant is, however, easily and commonly cultivated in gardens in England and France. King Gentius of Illyria is said to have discovered the medicinal value of the plant. The extract from the root of the gentian is known as *bitters* and is sometimes given to increase the appetite. Also a liqueur or cordial called *gentiane* comes from it. Gentians come from Alpine regions.

Gentile

Centuries ago, in the years before Christianity was first established, the Jews called other peoples Gentiles. The meaning of the word has not changed, and it still means any person not of the Jewish faith. People in one country describe the people of another country as foreigners, because they are not of the same nationality. Jews can describe people of another faith as Gentiles in exactly the same way. The word foreigner is not contemptuous, and the word Gentile is not contemptuous; both are merely descriptive.

Geoffrey of Monmouth

Geoffrey of Monmouth was a monk, or religious scholar, who lived in Great Britain about nine hundred years ago. He wrote a work called *History of the Kings of Britain*. This was supposed to tell the true stories of the kings, but Geoffrey also included many legends, which were not

always true. He was one of the first writers to tell about King Arthur and his Knights of the Round Table. Geoffrey's book became very popular, and many of the greatest English authors, including Shakespeare, Milton, and Tennyson, have gotten ideas for poems and plays from it.

geography

Geography is the study of the earth and the life on it. It tells us about features of the earth, such as land masses and oceans and mountains; it tells about the natural resources of the earth that can be grown or made into things that man needs. It tells about the way man has divided the earth into nations and territories.

The different parts of geography have special names: *physical geography, economic geography,* and *political geography.* All three are important because they give us information about the nature of our earth, the uses we have made of it, and the uses we can make of it.

PHYSICAL GEOGRAPHY

Physical geography studies the surface of the earth, its plains and mountains, rivers and oceans. Before men knew anything about geography they wandered aimlessly over the earth without knowing which places might be good to settle down in, and which might present dangers and difficulties that would make life harder. By knowing physical geography people are able to plan intelligently where to live, where to build factories, and where different crops can be grown to the best advantage.

Physical geography is divided into several branches. One branch is called *geomorphology,* and it deals with the formation of the land, how mountains were raised by volcanic action and how they are leveled by erosion, or wearing away; how rivers were formed and how they have changed the face of the earth by cutting new channels to flow through and picking up earth and depositing it in other places. Another branch of physical geography has to do with mathematical measurements of the earth. It divides the earth into imaginary lines called *meridians* and *parallels.* Meridians are great circles going through the North Pole and the South Pole; parallels are small circles parallel to the equator. Along these lines we measure *longitude* and *latitude,* about which you can read in the article on MAPS. By means of these measurements any spot on the globe can be accurately found.

Other branches of physical geography are *oceanography,* or the study of the seas and their tides and currents; *meteorology,* the study of weather; *hydrography,* the study of bodies of water; and *climatology,* the study of climate.

ECONOMIC GEOGRAPHY

Economic geography enables man to plan his life, his industry, and his agriculture to the best possible advantage. It explores and charts the locations of the greatest mineral resources, where profitable mining for coal, copper, iron, gems, and other vital minerals can be done. It finds out which areas are best for growing certain crops and which are best for other crops. It studies the distribution of raw materials and the availability of power for all kinds of industry. Economic geography also is important in the planning of cities and towns. For example, cities built along the banks of rivers are assured of plenty of water and cheap transportation. In the past, before power could be used from far away, a nearby river was important for power.

The economic geographer also studies the needs of trade and the possibilities for transportation. Through these studies man has learned to build roads through mountains, to build bridges over water, and even to farm in hilly lands. Man fights floods by building dams and dikes, and he brings water to dry areas by irrigation.

POLITICAL GEOGRAPHY

Political geography deals with the man-made divisions of the earth, the countries and their boundaries and their governments. In some cases these political divisions are about the same as the divisions made by nature in the earth. For instance, it is easy to see why Great Britain developed as a separate country, since it is divided from the rest of the continent of Europe by good-sized bodies of water. But divisions like that of the United States and Canada, or the countries of Europe and South America, came about through the relationships of men with each other instead of through natural boundaries such as seas, lakes, or rivers. In the early part of the 1900s a new kind of political geography was devised. It was called GEOPOLITICS, a way of using the principles of geography to predict the course of world politics, and there is a separate article about it.

geology

Geology is the scientific name for the study of the earth. Scientists who study the earth are called geologists. They spend much of their time outdoors gathering samples of rocks and soils. They make maps that show the exact shape and size of mountains, hills, valleys, lakes, rivers, swamps, bays, seas, and other parts of the land and water. These maps almost never show the names of towns or roads or bridges. Most of them do not show the boundaries of states or countries very clearly. These maps, which are called *topographic maps,* are different from the maps you use in studying geography. Geologists also make maps that show where you can find different kinds of rocks.

Some geologists work in laboratories where they examine the rocks and soil that have been gathered outdoors. They grind pieces of rock until they are as thin as paper, and then, to see just what the rock is made of, they look at the pieces through a microscope (an instrument that makes things look hundreds of times bigger than they really are). They study any fossils that the rocks have in them. Fossils are remains of animals or plants that died millions of years ago and then were buried.

Geologists do all these things for the purpose of learning about the materials the earth is made of and how these materials are put together. They also want to learn about the history of the earth. By knowing these things, geologists can find oil, coal, gold, iron, and other valuable materials buried in the earth.

While some geologists are all-around geologists and teach geology in colleges and universities, most geologists work in only one particular branch of the science.

Economic geologists are geologists who explore for oil, gas, metal ores, coal, building stone, and underground water. They do this for companies that want to sell these things. If you were to become an economic geologist, you would examine, identify, and map rocks showing on the surface of the earth as well as those in mines. You would drill deep holes to obtain samples of ores, the kinds of earth that contain metals. You would study maps and reports of geologists who worked before you. You would often use very delicate instruments that help you tell what is deep beneath the surface of the earth without having to dig for it. With all the information you collect you would tell mining engineers what is buried in the earth, and about how much of it is there, and about how much it is worth in money. More than half the economic geologists are *petroleum geologists.* Petroleum is the name for the oil that comes from oil wells. Petroleum geologists search for oil and natural gas deep underground. In this job they spend most of their time out-of-doors. Four out of every five geologists are economic geologists.

You might be a *mineralogist,* a geologist who examines minerals. Minerals are special kinds of rock, and you can read more about them in the separate article entitled MINERAL. The mineralogist puts minerals in different groups depending on what they are made of, and he describes what they look like and how they behave under certain tests. As a mineralogist, the tests you would make include finding out how hard a mineral is, just how it looks when you break it, how much it weighs, what its colors are (the same mineral can have many different colors), and what certain chemicals do to it. You would also use X-rays to learn what kind of crystals the mineral is made of. If you were a mineralogist who studies gems and precious stones, you might be called a *gemologist.*

You could be a *petrologist,* a geologist who studies rocks as they are found in nature. You would learn where the rocks came from, how they have been changed by weather and other natural forces, and how strong they are. You could advise an engineer whether or not certain kinds of rock would be strong enough to build heavy foundations of a building or bridge.

You might be a *stratigraphic geologist* and study the different layers of rock in the earth's crust. You probably have traveled along a road that engineers have cut through a hill. On either side of the road you have seen how the rock they cut through is in layers. It is a very difficult task to tell how the layers of rock came to be where they are, and how many millions of years ago each layer was formed. Learning these things is the job of the stratigraphic geologist.

You may choose to be a *structural geologist* who studies the shapes of masses and beds of rock, especially those which have been folded and pushed out of shape by forces of nature. You will

learn what these forces of nature are, as you read further in this article. You would work closely with the stratigraphic geologist in tracing the arrangement of layers of rock. The results of your work would be of very great scientific interest because they would tell much about the earth before people lived on it. Also, your work would be most useful in searching for petroleum and valuable minerals.

Another kind of geologist you could be is a *physiographic geologist* who studies the action of such erosive natural forces as wind, ice, and water that shape the earth's surface by cutting valleys and wearing down mountains.

Still another kind of geologist that you might be is a *geophysicist*, who uses his knowledge of geology in combination with a knowledge of engineering, physics, and chemistry. Nine out of ten geophysicists are really economic geologists who are prospectors working for mining companies. The rest of the geophysicists are divided up in the following kinds of work:

Some are called *seismologists*. They study the time and place and strength of earthquakes. What they learn about earthquakes is very useful to engineers in choosing safe places to build dams and in designing buildings that will not be shaken down by earthquakes. Other geophysicists are *hydrologists* who study the movement of water both on top of the ground and underground. They map and chart the flow and the amount of the water, and also how much soil it carries along with it. They study glaciers and how they move. What they learn is used to control and forecast floods and droughts. They plan soil and water conservation, so that there will be enough running water in rivers to make electrical current, and enough for irrigating crops, and to keep the water high enough in canals and lakes so that boats can sail on them. Still other geophysicists are called *geodesists*. They use very accurate instruments to make the topographic maps we learned about in the first part of this article. Some geophysicists are *oceanographers* who chart and study icebergs, ocean bottoms, tides, and currents. They make chemical tests to find out what is in sea water and in ocean-bottom mud. They study the shifting sand on the beaches. Their findings are of great use to ship navigators.

Yet another kind of geologist that you might be is a *paleontologist*. This is a geologist who studies fossils, the remains of plants and animals that are buried in the rocks. He does this to tell biologists (people who study plants and animals) what were the ancestors of today's plants and animals. Paleontologists have proved that birds are descended from an ancient species of small reptile called a thecodont, which was also the ancestor of the dinosaurs. Paleontologists also collect fossils for museums and help oil companies find oil by discovering the ages of different layers of rock that might contain oil.

Geologists tell us the earth is more than four billion years old. They have found a "clock in the rocks." This "clock" is the element uranium. Uranium is always changing slowly, beginning with the moment it is created. It gradually be-

comes lead and a gas called helium. To learn more about this kind of change, see the article on RADIOACTIVITY. Geologists know just about how much lead and helium there should be in a piece of uranium after it has been changing for a certain number of years. For instance, when half the uranium has changed to lead and helium, four and a half billion years will have gone by. Geologists have found rocks in which about half of the uranium has changed.

A movie showing the entire history of the earth, but speeded up so that millions of years become one minute, would be something like this:

In the first scene of our movie we see the earth when it was very young. It is a smooth ball of hot rock. High above it are clouds of steam that cover the sky so that the sun never shines down upon the earth. There are no mountains or rivers or seas or soil, and the earth is too hot for anything to live upon it. It rains all the time, but as soon as the raindrops fall on the hot rock, they turn to steam and rise again to the clouds.

Now and then we see great cracks (or fissures, as geologists call them) open in the rock surface of the earth. Out of the cracks pours red-hot molten (melted) rock, called lava. We see the molten rock spread out and become cool. It forms flat high places, or plateaus, on the earth's surface.

Sometimes, instead of fissures, we see small round holes open up in the earth's rocky surface. Out of them shoots hot cinders and gas and smoke, and then lava begins to pour out. The cinders and lava pile up around the hole (which has become much bigger), and make big cone-shaped mounds. And we realize that we have been watching volcanoes form. These volcanoes are like the volcanoes of today.

Now we see a big bulge appear in the earth's surface and a mountain chain grows before our eyes. Let us find out what is causing the mountains to grow. To do this we will have to put an X-ray lens on our camera and look beneath the surface of the earth. When we have gone into the earth for ten or twenty miles, we come to a layer of very hot rock. Although this rock is hotter than lava, it is not molten. It is under so much pressure from the weight of the rocks above it that it is stiff like candle wax. This kind of rock is called *magma*. We see a large amount of magma pushing its way to the surface. Slowly (taking thousands of years) it pushes up to fifteen miles from the surface, then up to ten miles, then eight miles. The rocky surface of the earth bends and strains. The magma pushes up to seven miles, six miles, five miles, but the earth's crust holds, and the magma must stop. In its great push it has made the big bulge that was the new mountain chain we saw.

And now we know the three ways that high places on the earth's surface are made: plateaus are made by lava pouring out of fissures; mountains are made by lava and cinders pouring out of volcanoes, and by magma pushing up big bulges from underneath. To these three things geologists give one name: uplift.

While we were exploring under-

ground, many things were happening on the surface. We see that much of the thick blanket of clouds has rained down and formed puddles. This means that the earth is much cooler, for the rain no longer turns to steam. Two of the puddles are very big. Although they are not shaped exactly the same, they are just where the Atlantic and Pacific Oceans are now. In fact, these puddles are oceans. We can also see at the North and South Poles two white ice caps growing.

We look closely at the mountains, and to our surprise, those that were formed first are much lower than they were; indeed they are gradually disappearing. What could be causing them to disappear? Our camera takes us close to the earth's surface. And we see that because of much bending and breaking; heating by the sun and sudden cooling by rain; hot summers and cold winters; freezing of water in cracks in the rock and the ice splitting the rock; the pounding of the waves of the ocean; and water dissolving parts of the rock and leaving behind the parts it could not dissolve—all these things have broken the rocky surface of the earth into pieces of rock of all sizes. There are boulders, small rocks, pebbles, and grains of sand. These pieces of rock are moved by tides and pounded against rocky shores by waves. They are pushed and rolled along the bottoms of rivers and streams, and the sand grains are blown by the wind. We see that the moving boulders and the bigger stones are acting like hammers smashing to pieces the rock of the mountains and plateaus. The sand is scouring and scraping the rock just like scouring powder and sandpaper do. Deep furrows are worn into the mountains wherever a stream or river runs down their sides. The sides cave into the deep cuts that the rivers make. And, little by little, the mountain wears away, until it is down to the level of the seas. With all the high land worn down, we see the oceans covering most of the surface of the earth.

As we watch, we see a time of great spouting of volcanoes. There are huge lava flows from great fissures. There is much folding of the earth's crust, as mountains are pushed up from below. Then, as millions of years go by, we see all these high lands worn down to the level of the oceans again. This happens time after time as our movie runs on through the ages. This wearing down of plateaus and mountains is called by geologists *erosion*. Uplift and erosion—these two things follow each other over and over again. They make all the changes in the earth's surface.

Our movie has shown us the two most important things that geologists have learned about our ever-changing earth. There are many other things that geologists have learned, such as how there came to be so many different kinds of ROCKS, which you can read about in a separate article.

If you want to be a geologist, you must go to a college or university for four years, and then work with a geologist for a year. Usually, however, geologists go to college for five to seven years. After your education, you will be ready to get a job with a mining company or with the government, doing any one of

the jobs mentioned in the beginning of this article.

1. Glacier National Park.

2. Makoshika State Park. Once a tropical jungle site, Makoshika is an American Indian word meaning "Hell cooled over".

Geometry

Geometry is one of the branches of mathematics. Geometry is used to measure shapes, sizes, and distances. The word comes from Greek words meaning "earth" and "measure." Geometry was used by the Egyptians and other ancient peoples, at least six thousand years ago, to measure land and to build big buildings.

Plane geometry is used to measure a flat surface, such as land or the top of a table. *Solid geometry* is used to measure things that are, or could be, solid, such as a block of stone or a tin can. Geometry is not usually taught before high school, because to learn geometry you should know something about arithmetic and algebra, which are other branches of mathematics. Geometry is used by engineers and architects in planning buildings and other structures such as bridges and tunnels. It is important to astronomers, scientists who study the stars. Surveyors, artists, and many other professional men and scientists use geometry in their work.

Geometry deals with things that have dimensions—length, breadth (width), and thickness. A *point* is simply a place or location; it has no dimensions. A *line*
is a row of points; it has length but no other dimension. A *plane* has length and breadth but no thickness. A *solid* has all three dimensions.

When two lines intersect (come together) they form an angle. A *flat* surface with three sides is a *triangle,* which means that it has three angles. Angles are measured in *degrees.* All the angles that can be formed around a point will have a total of 360 degrees. When you know the length of two sides and the number of degrees in one angle of a triangle, or when you know the length of one side and the number of degrees in two angles, by geometry you can figure out all the sides and all the angles. There is a special branch of mathematics called *trigonometry,* that deals with triangles.

Hundreds of other figures are dealt with in geometry. There are curves and circles; plane surfaces with four, five, or any greater number of sides; solids with four or more sides, or with curved sides, such as the sphere, the cone, and the cylinder. Among the most important are the square, a four-sided plane figure in which all the sides and all the angles are equal; and the cube, a solid with six flat surfaces, all equal.

EARLY GEOMETRY

The earliest great student of geometry was a man named Thales, who lived in Greece more than 2,500 years ago. Another, who came soon after him, was Pythagoras. The greatest of the early writers on geometry was Euclid, who lived in Greece about 300 B.C. Euclid wrote thirteen books on geometry. They are called the *Elements.* Except for the Bible and some other religious books, Euclid's *Elements* have probably been read by more people than any other book in history. Most of the geometry taught in high school is taken from six of the thirteen books. In some countries, including England, geometry is called simply *Euclid.* The geometry taught by Euclid is called Euclidean geometry.

EUCLIDEAN GEOMETRY

Euclidean geometry is based on *postulates* and *axioms.* The postulates are statements in geometry that are taken for granted without further explanation or *proof.* They tell us that one, and only one, straight line can be drawn through two points, and that two straight lines cannot intersect at more than one point. The axioms are other statements that are accepted as self-evident, so obviously true that no proof is needed. For example, "Things equal to the same thing are equal to each other." If $3 + 2 = 5$ and $4 + 1 = 5$, then $3 + 2$ must equal $4 + 1$.

Using these postulates and axioms, Euclid worked out the rules of geometry in a series of *theorems,* or *propositions.* A theorem is something one believes but must prove; a proposition is a statement of what must be proved. Euclid proved his theorems by a kind of reasoning called *logic.* Logical reasoning uses statements that are known to be true and draws conclusions from them.

Many people have studied Euclidean geometry to help them think more clearly. There is a story that Abraham Lincoln, before he became President of the United States, once borrowed a geometry book,
so that he could learn how the theorems were proved in the book. This helped him think more clearly when he was arguing law cases in court.

Special types of geometry, called *projective* and *descriptive* geometry, are important in drawing plans and blueprints for buildings and other structures. Architects and draftsmen study them in college.

NON-EUCLIDEAN GEOMETRY

There are other kinds of geometry besides Euclidean geometry. These are called non-Euclidean geometry. They start out with one or more postulates that are different from Euclid's. One kind is called *hyperbolic* geometry. It was invented by two European mathematicians more than a hundred years ago. It disagrees with Euclid's postulate that one and only one line can be drawn through a point parallel to a given line.

In another kind of non-Euclidean geometry, called *elliptic* or *Riemann* geometry, there is a postulate that says no parallel lines can be drawn. This geometry was used by Albert Einstein when he developed his famous theory of relativity.

geopolitics

Geopolitics is the study of how geography affects politics. It is also called *political geography.* It teaches that the policy of a nation must be to gain or to hold the territory where its people can grow the food and find the minerals that they need, and where they will be safest from attack. Also valuable are places of strategic importance—that is, important only when fighting a war—such as the Rock of Gibraltar, a British possession that is of value only as a naval base.

Germany, especially during the time when it was governed by the Nazi Party of Adolf Hitler, is the country that is most often thought of in connection with geopolitics.

The word geopolitics was first used in 1917 by a Swede named Rudolf Kjellen. Though Kjellen was not a German he thought that all the Germanic peoples, which include the Swedish and other Scandinavian peoples, should get together.

An Englishman named Halford Mackinder, in 1904, had written that a territory in the center of Europe and Asia, which territory he called the "heartland," was necessary to any nation that wanted to control the world. A German general named Karl Haushofer taught these ideas in Germany and they had a great influence on Hitler's government, which came into power in Germany in 1933. Hitler tried to conquer the "heartland" in World War II, but of course he was beaten. The ideas called geopolitics are totally lacking in justice and morality.

George, Lake

Lake George, in the eastern part of the state of New York, is one of the most beautiful lakes in the United States. It is a narrow body of water, 33 miles long and only two or three miles wide. Most of the lake is deep, and the water is unusually clear. The lake is dotted with tiny islands, and along the shore the foothills of the mighty Adirondack Mountains rise to about two thousand feet. Lake

George drains into Lake Champlain. There are fishing and swimming at Lake George in the summer, and skiing and other winter sports in the winter. At Lake George Battleground Park there are ruins of great forts that were used during the French and Indian War and also in the American Revolution. The French discovered Lake George about three hundred years ago. It was named for George III, king of England.

George, Saint

St. George is the patron saint of England. A patron saint is a special guardian and protector. Many of the stories you read about St. George are legends, that is, they are not really true but are marvelous tales. The most famous story about St. George is that he killed a dragon in a terrible fight in order to save a king's daughter. St. George was a real person who died in the year 303. Very little is known about him except that he was known to have been a very holy man and a popular hero.

The Cross of St. George, which is an emblem, or sign, was put on the English flag five hundred years ago and you will find it there today.

George, King of England

There were six kings of England named George. The first four of them belonged to the house (family) of Hanover, the royal family that originally ruled the small kingdom of Hanover, in Germany. The last two English kings named George were members of the House of Windsor, which is the name of the royal family in England today.

George I lived about two hundred and fifty years ago. He was born in 1660, and became elector (king) of Hanover in 1698. In 1714 he became king of England because he was a grandson of King James I of England. George I spoke no English, and was not very much interested in English affairs. Under his rule, the cabinet, which acts for the Parliament, became stronger in England than it had ever been before. George I died in 1727.

George II, the son of George I, became king when his father died. He was a wiser king than his father, but he too was more interested in German affairs than in English affairs. During the reign of George II, England fought several wars and became very powerful. George II died in 1760.

George III was the grandson of George II. He was born in 1738 and became king in 1760, and it was against George III that the American colonies fought and won the Revolutionary War. George III was much more interested in English politics than either George I or George II, but he was not a good king, and was unpopular with his people. During the last years of his reign, George III became insane. His son, the Prince of Wales, took his place and became George IV in 1820, when George III died. George IV was born in 1762, so he was 58 years old before he became king. He was also an unpopular king. He reigned for about ten years, and died in 1830.

George V, the grandson of the great Queen Victoria, was born in 1865 and became king in 1910. Although he was a good and popular ruler, England had

George I   George II   George III

George IV   George V   George VI

to face many serious problems during his reign. Chief among these problems were the rising labor problems of the country, the difficulties of English rule in Ireland and India, and then World War I. During the rule of George V, the royal family of England changed its name to the house of Windsor.

George VI was the younger son of George V. He became king when his brother, Edward VIII, abdicated (gave up the throne) in 1936. George VI was a very popular king and the English people loved him and his family very much. The years of his rule were very difficult years because George VI became king just before World War II, and he died shortly after the war. All through the years of the war, George VI remained with his people, helping them and giving them courage to fight the war to victory. When George VI died, in 1952, his eldest daughter was crowned as Queen Elizabeth II.

George, Henry

Henry George was an American author who became famous by writing one book. It was called *Progress and Poverty*, and in it George told why he thought people were poor and how they could be helped. He felt that a country's land belongs to its people and that all have an equal right to the use of the earth. However, it is not possible or practical for all men to use the land, so George thought that the government should have a single tax, on the land alone, which would be enough to run the country. Henry George was born in Philadelphia in 1839 and later moved to California. After working at many jobs and often suffering from poverty, he moved to New York. Here George became well known as a lecturer and writer. He published *Progress and*

Poverty in 1879. In 1886 he ran for mayor of New York and almost won the election even though the major political parties opposed him. When he died in 1897 huge crowds attended his funeral.

George Junior Republic

The George Junior Republic is a village where all the work is done, and the government is run, by teen-age boys and girls. It is called a republic because, as in a country that is called a republic, the government is run by its citizens, the people who live there. The citizens of the George Junior Republic are boys and girls 16 to 21 years old. They all must work on the farms or in the industries of their village. Everyone has a voice in the government. The George Junior Republic is in New York State, in the United States, so it has to obey the laws of the state and the nation, but when special decisions have to be made about affairs in the village, all the citizens meet to discuss their problems and make their laws.

The George Junior Republic was started in 1895 by a man named W. R. George. Mr. George was looking for a way to help boys and girls who were delinquent, that is, who had disobeyed the law. They were unhappy and uncared for, and they might have grown up to be criminals. George thought that if these boys and girls had a chance to work and to take charge of their own government, they might learn to be good and responsible citizens. So he started the George Junior Republic as a place to try out his ideas. The George Junior Republic has proved to be very successful. People have come from all over to study it. Some other villages like the George Junior Republic have been set up in other places, and it has been imitated by schools and institutions and

prisons. They are helping boys and girls by giving them a chance to support themselves and to run their own government.

Georgetown

For more than a hundred years, from 1714 to 1830, the kings of England were named George, and during this period many towns and settlements in British colonies were named Georgetown in their honor.

George Town is the capital of Penang, a state of the Federation of Malaysia, which is one of the member nations of the British Commonwealth. It is on an island near the Malay Peninsula. The population of George Town is about 235,-000. It is a very modern city and an important seaport. See the articles on MALAYSIA and MALAY PENINSULA.

Georgetown is also the name of a city that is the capital of British Guiana, in South America. It has a population of about 120,000. It is at the mouth of the Demerara River and is an important seaport. In 1940 the British leased some property in Georgetown to the United States for use as a naval and air base.

Georgetown is also a part of Washington, D.C., the capital of the United States. Until 1878 it was a separate town. It is a residential section, with many old houses, some of them dating back more than two hundred years. Georgetown University, the oldest college in the United States conducted by the Roman Catholic Church, is in Georgetown. It was founded in 1789 and is for men and women. In 1971 there were 7,942 students enrolled.

There are several cities in the United States named Georgetown.

George Washington Bridge

The George Washington Bridge is a bridge across the Hudson River, connecting Manhattan, in New York City, and Fort Lee, New Jersey. It is a suspension bridge, which is a bridge held up by cables hung from great towers. The towers of the George Washington Bridge are 600 feet above water, and the cables are each three feet thick. The main span of the bridge is 3,500 feet long.

The George Washington Bridge is one of the longest suspension bridges in the world. It was completed in 1931. Millions of automobiles, trucks, and buses stream across the bridge every year. Because of the growing traffic, a second level was added to the bridge in 1961 and 1962 underneath the original road-way.

Georgia

Georgia is a state in the south of the United States, and was one of the original thirteen colonies. Since the Civil War, Georgia has grown so important as an industrial state that it is now called the Empire State of the South. Georgia was named after King George II of England by the first English settlers.

In area, Georgia ranks 21st in size among the states, with 58,876 square miles. In population it ranks 15th, with more than 4½ million people living there. In 1788, it was the fourth colony to become a state. The capital is Atlanta.

THE PEOPLE OF GEORGIA

About a fifth of the people of Georgia are farmers. They grow large quantities of cotton and corn, and produce more watermelons and peanuts than any other state. The peaches they grow are also famous throughout the country. The people who live in the cities work in factories, making many products such as cotton goods, clothing, peanut butter, and paper.

If you visit Georgia, you will notice that there are almost as many colored people as white people. There are more Negroes in Georgia than in any other state—more than a million. Most of them work on farms or are laborers in factories.

The earliest settlers in Georgia were the English, who came there about 220

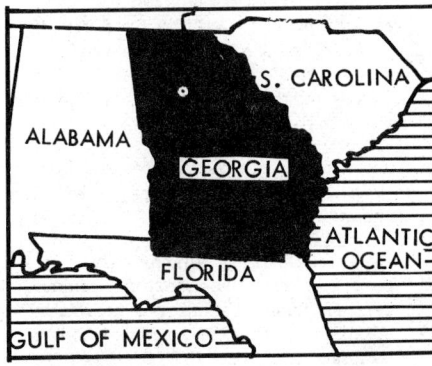

years ago. They were followed by people from Switzerland, Germany, and France, who wanted to escape from these countries because they could not worship God as they pleased. Today, almost all Georgians are American-born. Many are proud that they are southerners and that Georgia was one of the states that formed the Confederate States of America in 1861, and fought against the Union in the Civil War. In Georgia, you will see old Confederate flags in many places, and monuments to soldiers who died in the Confederate armies.

The churches are very important in the social life of the Georgians. Nearly everyone goes to Sunday School and to church, and, especially in the smaller towns, people have their clubs and parties and picnics through their churches.

WHAT GEORGIA IS LIKE

If you travel through Georgia, you will find that the north, central, and southern regions are quite different. In the northern section are part of the Appalachian Mountains, known as the Blue Ridge Mountains. This is a very beautiful part of the state, with deep valleys and steep cliffs covered with valuable timber. It is also rich in minerals, and much gold used to be mined here. The fine marble found in the mountains has been used to build the public buildings in many states and foreign countries.

The central part of Georgia is a plateau. A plateau is a region that is high, like a mountain, but level, like a plain. More people live here than in any other part of Georgia, and some of the most important cities are located in this region. Several rivers flow through the plateau, supplying water power to the manufacturing cities. The farmers grow large quantities of cotton in the fertile areas.

The entire southern part of Georgia is a low plain, where peanuts, watermelons,

and other crops are grown. There are also large pine forests from which the people get turpentine and rosin. Along the coast are marshes, the largest being the Okefenokee Swamp, where many animals and birds live.

As in other southern states, one can see many small fur-bearing animals—the raccoon, the squirrel, and others that people like to hunt. There are some wild animals such as the wildcat, bear, and alligator.

Although Georgia is in the south, it is not as uncomfortably hot as one might think. The climate is varied and healthful. In the mountains, it is quite cold, with ice and snow in the winter. In the plateau it is warm in summer, but not hot. Only in the southern plain are the summers very hot. Most of the state has a mild climate, with an average temperature of 48 degrees in January and 80 degrees in July.

The rivers of Georgia are very useful for transportation. The most important are the Chattahoochee, the Altamaha, and the Savannah. Located on the Savannah River is the famous Savannah River Plant, where one of the most important chemicals for the hydrogen bomb is made. Railroads and highways reach nearly all parts of the state.

GOVERNMENT OF GEORGIA

Georgia, like other states, has a governor (elected for a four-year term) and a legislature, called the General Assembly and composed of a Senate and a House of Representatives with members elected for two-year terms. Judges are elected for six years. The capital is Atlanta. There are 159 counties.

Like other states of the deep South, Georgia tried to evade the laws that require black and white students to attend the same schools, using all legal devices and sometimes illegal violence. By 1966 there was some integration in many of Georgia's elementary schools and high schools, and in most of the colleges and universities, of which the principal ones (some of them famous) are:

University of Georgia, at Athens. Enrollment, 20,500 in 1971 (co-ed).

Georgia Institute of Technology, at Atlanta. Enrollment, 7,262 in 1971 (co-ed).

Woman's College of Georgia, at Milledgeville. Enrollment, 1,400 in 1971 (women only).

Mercer University, at Macon. Enrollment, 1,850 in 1971 (co-ed).

Emory University, at Atlanta. Enrollment, 5,241 in 1971 (co-ed).

CHIEF CITIES OF GEORGIA

The leading cities of Georgia, with populations from the 1970 census, are:

Atlanta, population 496,973, the state capital and largest city in the state. There is a separate article about ATLANTA.

Savannah, population 118,349, the second-largest city in the state. There is a separate article about SAVANNAH.

Columbus, population 154,168, the third largest city, manufacturing center, in the western part of the state.

Augusta, population 59,864, fourth-largest city, cotton trading center, in the eastern part of the state. There is a separate article about AUGUSTA.

Macon, population 122,423, fifth-largest

city, commercial and industrial center, in the central part of the state.

GEORGIA IN THE PAST

More than four hundred years ago the Spanish, under Hernando De Soto, were the first white people to visit Georgia. They were searching for gold, but did not find any, and moved on to the Mississippi River. Some years later, other Spanish explorers came to Georgia, as did the French and English. But the first permanent settlement was not made until 1733, when King George II of England gave James Oglethorpe the right to start a colony there. Oglethorpe wished to start a settlement for people who were poor and in debt, and who wished to begin a new life. He also saw it as a place where Protestants from Europe could live and worship God as they pleased. People from many countries came to the colony, which was located where Savannah now stands. In 1736, the first Sunday School in America was started there and, a few years later, the first orphanage in the country was built.

Georgia was the last of the thirteen colonies to be settled, and for a time it did not flourish. However, land could be bought on very easy terms, and many wealthy South Carolinians moved in, bringing their slaves. Farming and cattle-raising helped Georgia to prosper.

The Georgians fought in the Revolutionary War, though they were so far south that sometimes they did not know how the war was going in New England. In 1788 Georgia became a state.

It was in Georgia that Eli Whitney invented the cotton gin, which made the growing of cotton more profitable than ever. You can read about the COTTON GIN in a separate article. The people in Georgia planted great fields of cotton, and wanted the Negroes to cultivate them. Slavery became very important as Georgia grew into one of the biggest cotton-producing states. There were large plantations whose rich owners lived in fine mansions and owned hundreds of slaves. When Abraham Lincoln was elected president in 1860, and it appeared that the slaves would be set free, Georgia was one of the southern states that seceded from the Union.

In the Civil War, Georgia suffered more destruction than almost any other Confederate state. The Battle of Chickamauga, in September, 1863, lasted two days, and they were called the two bloodiest days of the war. The following year, the Union troops under General Sherman captured Atlanta and set fire to it. With an army of 60,000 soldiers, Sherman then began his famous march to the sea, destroying villages, towns, and countryside as he went. At the end of the war, three-quarters of Georgia's wealth had been destroyed. The state was in ruins and the people were very poor. Carpetbaggers controlled the state government and robbed it of millions. However, the people gradually rebuilt Georgia, though it was not readmitted to the Union until 1871. The state prospered as the Georgians developed their industries.

Several events of importance occurred in Georgia. In 1819, the first transatlantic steamer sailed from Savannah and crossed the Atlantic Ocean to England in 25 days.

The following year the first railroad in America, with horse-drawn cars, was built near Savannah. In this same city, the first American Girl Scout troop was organized in 1912.

Georgia has long since recovered from the hardships that followed the Civil War. Today it is a flourishing farming and industrial state.

Franklin D. Roosevelt is closely associated with Georgia, although he was not born there. He founded the famous Warm Springs Foundation, at Warm Springs, in 1927, to help people who had infantile paralysis.

Several events of importance occurred in Georgia. In 1819, the first transatlantic steamer sailed from Savannah and crossed the Atlantic Ocean to England in 25 days. The following year the first railroad in America, with horse-drawn cars, was built near Savannah. In this same city, the first American Girl Scout troop was organized in 1912.

Georgia has long since recovered from the hardships that followed the Civil War. Today it is a flourishing farming and industrial state.

Franklin D. Roosevelt is closely associated with Georgia, although he was not born there. He founded the famous Warm Springs Foundation, at Warm Springs, in 1927, to help people who had infantile paralysis.

PLACES TO SEE IN GEORGIA

Chattahoochee National Forest, 1,165,-000 acres, in the northern part of Georgia, on U.S. Route 76. Superb mountain scenery; wild turkeys; streams well-stocked with fish; picnic areas.

Fort Frederica National Monument, 210 acres, off southeast coast, on St. Simon Island, five miles from Brunswick, on U.S. Route 17. Built by Gen. James Oglethrope (1736–1748), during the struggle between Spain and England for control of what is now the southeastern part of the United States.

Fort Pulaski National Monument, 5,364 acres, in the southeast, on Savannah Beach, 12 miles west of Savannah, on U.S. Route 80. Early nineteenth century fort, with moat and drawbridge; fired on by Union soldiers in the Civil War; first proved the total ineffectiveness of old-style masonry fortifications.

Ocmulgee National Monument, 683 acres, in central Georgia, in Macon, on U.S. Route 41. Unique remains of mounds and prehistoric towns of an ancient tribe of Indians; museum with Indian relics.

Bethesda Orphanage, in the southeast, in Savannah, on U.S. Route 17. The oldest orphanage in the United States; opened in 1740. During the Civil War it was used as a military hospital.

Kennesaw Mountain National Battlefield Park, 2,883 acres, in the northwest, west of Marietta, on U.S. Route 41. Historic field on which occurred one of the two heavy attacks made by General Sherman on Confederate troops in his campaign against Atlanta.

Slave Market, in Louisville, on U.S. Route 1. Built in 1758, in the center of town; slaves were sold here.

Tallulah Gorge, in the north, on U.S. Route 17. A steep-sided crevice, 1,000 feet deep; may be reached by trail. Along the descent is a stone profile resembling the head of a witch, 35 feet high.

The Little White House, in western Georgia, at Warm Springs, on U.S. Route 27. Used by President Franklin D. Roosevelt during his lifetime. It was here that he died in 1945.

Bonaventure Cemetery, 4 miles east of Savannah, on U.S. Route 17. One of the most beautiful cemeteries in the country; magnificent oak trees, Spanish moss, and flowers.

GEORGIA. Area, 58,876 square miles. Population (1970 census) 4,589,575. Capital, Atlanta. Nickname, Empire State of the South. Motto, Wisdom, Justice, Moderation. Flower, Cherokee rose. Bird, brown thrasher. Song, "Georgia." Joined the Union January 2, 1788; one of 13 original states. Official abbreviation, Ga.

Georgian Bay, an extension of Lake Huron, in the southern part of Ontario, Canada. The bay has many islands to which people go for summer vacations: see the article on Lake HURON.

Georgian S.S.R.

The Georgian Soviet Socialist Republic is a region that is usually called Georgia, which is the same as the name of the state in the United States. It is one of the fifteen republics in the UNION OF SOVIET SOCIALIST REPUBLICS, about which you can read in a separate article. It is less than half the size of the state of Georgia, having about 27,000 square miles, but about the same number of people, about four million, live there.

The people of Georgia speak a language of their own, called Georgian, but other languages such as Russian, Armenian and Turkish are also spoken. For many hundreds of years the women of Georgia have been considered very beautiful. Some famous men have come from Georgia, among them Joseph Stalin, the former premier of Russia.

For many years the Georgians were almost all farmers and raisers of livestock. In the southern part of Georgia, they raised mulberry trees for silk and also grew grapes. During the past forty years other industries have begun to grow. Factories have been built in Tbilisi (or Tiflis) the capital city, and also in Batum, a large port on the Black Sea. The oil industry is especially important at Batum. Georgia has large coal fields, and its manganese mines are among the largest in the world. There are big forests, which are cut for lumber.

In the south of Georgia the climate is warm and moist, and in the east are high mountains and dry plains called *steppes*. The two largest rivers are the Kura and the Rion.

GEORGIA IN THE PAST

Georgia began as an independent kingdom about 2,300 years ago. During most of the last 1,500 years Georgia has been ruled by other nations, and about 150 years ago most of it was taken by Russia. For a short time after 1917, Georgia was an independent republic. In 1921 it became part of the U.S.S.R.

geranium

The geranium is a colorful flower that is grown in the warmer parts of the United States. The flower has small, four-petaled blossoms at the top of a stem.

The leaves are light green with lines of darker green running through them in a pattern.

Geraniums are usually very red, but they can also be white, yellow, rose, or even purple. Potted geraniums (grown in flowerpots or in window boxes) grow from ten inches to a foot and a half high, but in California they may grow to a height of four feet when planted out-of-doors. An oil with a rich, pungent odor is taken from some kinds of geranium. It is used to make perfume and to give a pleasant odor to soap.

geriatrics

Geriatrics is a new branch of medicine that studies diseases of older people. In the past one hundred years medical science has become successful in conquering many diseases that used to kill large numbers of people. As a result many more people are living today in the older age groups. These new large groups of older people have their own medical problems, and the study and treatment of these is called geriatrics. The doctor who specializes in them is a geriatrician.

Of course older people have many of the same diseases as younger people, but they are more likely to get some diseases and less likely to get others; so the geriatrician specializes in the diseases that older people are most likely to have trouble with. These are diseases that have something to do with parts, or organs, of the body which may gradually wear out. Mainly it is the veins and arteries, or blood vessels, that wear out in such places as the heart (causing heart trouble), or the brain (causing cerebral hemorrhage, or bleeding within the brain). Cancer is another disease studied by geriatrics because it is often caused by long wear and irritation in different parts of the body. Also, there is mental disease that can be caused by the wearing out of blood vessels of the brain in older people. It is like mental disease in younger people except that they usually cannot remember things, or think clearly. In all diseases of geriatrics older people need much care and attention.

germ

A germ is the first stage in the life of any living thing. The part of a plant that develops into its seed is called the germ of the plant. The tiny egg that develops into a human being or animal is called a germ cell.

Usually when we say germs we mean disease germs or BACTERIA, about which you can read in a separate article.

German language and literature

The German language is spoken in Germany and Austria, and also Switzerland, where it is one of the three official languages (along with French and Italian). In many other countries to which German-speaking people have emigrated, there are people who speak both German and the language of their new country. This is true of the United States, to which more than five million German-speaking people have moved in a little more than a hundred years. Besides all this, German is taught in most colleges and in many other schools throughout the world. It is a very valuable language to scientists and scholars, because many great scientific

books have been written in German.

Altogether, there are about ninety million people in the world who speak German. Only Chinese, English, Spanish and Russian are spoken by more people.

The modern German language grew out of the languages spoken by the Germanic tribes that settled in northern and central Europe more than two thousand years ago. Several other modern languages are closely related to German. English is a Germanic language, because the Angles and Saxons who moved into England about 1,500 years ago were Germanic peoples. Even more closely related to German are the Dutch language and the Scandinavian languages (Norwegian, Swedish, Danish, and Icelandic).

All these languages, like nearly all European languages, belong to the Indo-European family of languages, called Indo-Germanic by German scholars.

HIGH AND LOW GERMAN

The German word for their language is *Deutsch*. It is spoken in many forms, or dialects, but it has two main branches, *platt Deutsch* (meaning "Low German," the oldest form of the language, which is still spoken in the low, flat regions of northern Germany) and *hoch Deutsch* (meaning "High German," the language spoken in the high, mountainous regions of the south). High German is the language taught in the schools and the language in which German literature is written. Low German is more like English.

The German way of arranging words in a sentence is so different from the English way that sometimes it seems funny to English-speaking people. The great humorist Mark Twain was one of those who poked fun at it. Of course, one way is as good as another; it is all a matter of what you are used to. Where we would say, "At three o'clock we saw the man get into his car," the Germans would say, "At three o'clock have we the man into his car get in seen."

In the German language, separate words can be combined to form one long word. It is as though in English we spoke of a person who is slightly insane as a "partlyoutofhismindperson." These long words, too, can seem funny to a person who is not used to them, but they are really quite easy to understand.

German is more of an inflected language than English is. That means that the words have different endings, depending on how they are used in the sentence. In English, an example of inflection can be found in such words as *he, him, his,* where the same word has different spellings depending on how it is used. In many cases a mark called the *umlaut* is used in the spelling of German words to show a change in the pronunciation of an *a, o,* or *u.* For example, *Mann* is the German word for *man,* and *Männer* is the word for *men.* This is one case in which the same sort of change occurs in English.

In German spelling, a noun (name of anything) always begins with a capital letter.

English used to be the same kind of inflected language German is, until less than a thousand years ago. Gradually, the English people stopped using many of the special forms of their words. The German people kept on using them.

GERMAN LITERATURE

Until the present (twentieth) century, German literature was noted chiefly for its great poetry and its scientific literature. One of the great works of German literature is Martin Luther's translation of the Bible. The poet GOETHE (about whom there is a separate article), who was born about two hundred years ago, ranks among the greatest poets of all time, along with Greece's Homer, Rome's Virgil, Italy's Dante, and England's Shakespeare. Friedrich von Schiller, who lived in the same period as Goethe, wrote great poetry and plays, some of which can be read at their best in English because they were translated by one of England's greatest poets, Samuel Taylor Coleridge. Gotthold Lessing was Germany's great playwright of this same period. Strangely enough, Shakespeare is considered by the Germans to be one of their greatest playwrights because his plays were so admirably translated (by August Wilhelm von Schlegel) that they seem as good in German as in English.

Americans have a particular fondness for the poetry of Heinrich Heine and for the novels of Thomas Mann, because they have been so widely read in their translations, but there is equally great German literature that is not so familiar to English readers. Many great philosophers, such as Immanuel Kant, were German and wrote in the German language. The novel was a neglected form of literature in Germany for many years, though Goethe wrote some novels and E. T. H. Hoffman, about 150 years ago, wrote several fine novels. Hoffman is well-known in English-speaking countries because the composer Offenbach wrote a light opera, *Tales of Hoffman,* based on his stories.

German measles

German measles is a disease caused by a virus, which is a tiny form of life—even smaller than a germ—and can cause disease when it enters the human body. German measles is a different disease from measles, although the signs of it are somewhat the same. Usually a person does not have German measles more than once.

German measles starts in much the same way as a cold, with a headache, a runny nose, and perhaps a slight fever. Later the skin breaks out in a light rash that itches a great deal. A person is likely to have German measles in the winter or spring, and children are more likely to catch it than grownups. German measles does not last more than a few days, and the patient is not very sick.. It is not a serious disease, except that it can be very dangerous to a woman who is pregnant, that is, a woman who is going to have a baby. German measles can harm the unborn child in several ways, particularly by damaging its heart.

German shepherd

The German shepherd is one of the largest, strongest, and at times fiercest of all dogs. It was used for many years in Germany to guard flocks of sheep and cattle, and for police work. The present German shepherd has been bred carefully since about 1900, so all dogs of the breed look pretty much alike. Today German shepherds are trained to guide

the blind. They are also kept as pets, because they are very loyal to their own people, and when they are properly trained are wonderful protectors for children. Many people persist in calling the German shepherd a German police dog, but this is not correct.

The K-9 corps of dogs in both World War I and World War II had great numbers of German shepherds, trained for war work, and many of these fine dogs were awarded medals for special acts of heroism and bravery. Many German shepherds are used as watchdogs in stores, factories, and government buildings, and they do a fine job at that also.

The German shepherd stands about 23 inches high at the shoulder, and it is about 29 inches from the front of the chest to the base of the tail. It weighs anywhere between 65 and 85 pounds. It has ears that stand up straight, and a curved, bushy tail. Males are both larger and heavier than females. Although you can see German shepherds in colors that vary from dark brown or blackish to a light shade of tan, the most common color is wolf-gray and tan, with black markings.

German silver

German silver is a whitish metal made by combining copper, nickel and zinc. A lot of the silverware which we use on the table is made of German silver that has been coated with real silver. German silver is harder than real silver and it can be polished to shine brightly, but it loses its shine very easily. If vinegar or other strong mixtures are mixed with German silver, they form a solution that is poisonous. German silver should not be used with such liquids or with fruits, if the real silver coating has worn off. German silver was given this name because it was first made in Germany.

Germany

Germany is the name used by English-speaking people for a large section of Central Europe where the people speak the German language and are descended from early inhabitants of Europe who were called Germans, or Teutons.

When World War II began in 1939, Germany was a single country, the richest and most powerful in Europe. The German people called it *Deutschland*. About eighty million people lived there, more than half as many as then lived in the United States, though the area of Germany was only about 145,000 square miles, or not quite the size of the state of California.

Germany regained its independence some years after World War II but was divided into two countries. One took the name Federal Republic of Germany, and is usually called West Germany; in this country there is free enterprise. The other part of Germany, the eastern part, came under the control of Russia and has a Communist government; it calls itself the Democratic Republic of Germany, but it is not a democracy as that word is understood in America. This part of Germany is usually called East Germany.

In the past, Germany was made up of many small countries, which often fought

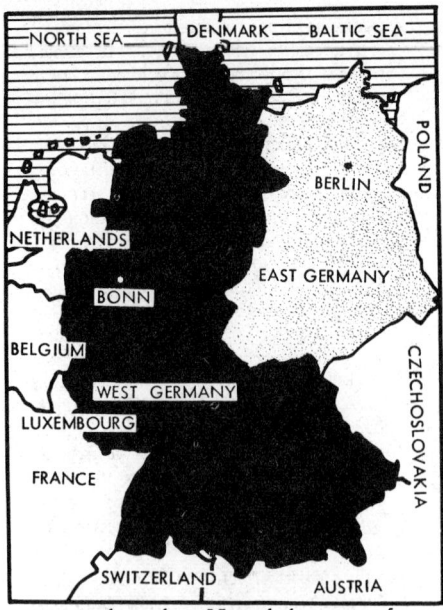

among themselves. Nevertheless most of the people felt that they were one nation, because they share the same language and literature and history. They have never stopped feeling that way, and in the period after World War II, the chief ambition of most Germans has been to unite West and East Germany to make a single nation again.

THE GERMAN PEOPLE

Most of the people who live in Germany are descended from several different Germanic tribes that settled in northern and central Europe more than two thousand years ago. Some of these tribes went to other countries such as France, Spain, England, and the Scandinavian countries (Norway, Sweden, and Denmark). The others became the German people as we know it today.

The people of Germany speak the language called German, about which you can read in the article on GERMAN LANGUAGE AND LITERATURE. There are many dialects, or slightly different forms of this language.

The Germans who live in the north are mostly Protestants, but among those who live in the south there are many Roman Catholics. The largest group of Protestants are Lutherans. Martin Luther, who began this church more than four hundred years ago, was a German.

No people in the world have been better educated or more advanced in science than the Germans. This has been the chief reason that Germany has been so powerful in manufacturing and also in war. Germany's population has often been so big that there was not enough land for all the people, and Germany has tried to take territory from neighboring countries. This has led to wars in which the Germans have fought against several other powerful countries at the same time, and so have lost.

HOW THE PEOPLE LIVE

The people of Germany live very much as do the people of the United States and Canada. Many of them live in large cities and work in offices or factories near by. The industries of Germany are very well developed and produce many different things. Germany has been one

of the leaders in the manufacture of machinery, iron and steel products, chemical goods, and scientific equipment. Germany's factories and cities were greatly damaged and in many cases destroyed during World War II, but the people in West Germany worked very hard to rebuild their country, and by about 1960 they had not only rebuilt but had improved and modernized their industries. Today West Germany is one of the leading industrial nations of the world, and the people live better than ever. East Germany did not match this recovery.

About thirty per cent of the land of West Germany is good for farming. The German farmers are very modern and raise many different crops. In the north they raise potatoes and rye, in the central areas they grow wheat and other grains, and in the south there is chiefly dairy farming and the raising of livestock.

Not only are the German people hard workers, but they have always been great scholars. German scientists have always been among the best in the world. Many of the great books of the world have been written by Germans, and much of the world's most beautiful music was composed by German composers such as Wagner, Bach, and Beethoven.

There are also nineteen important universities in Germany, and many American students go to these universities to study.

WHAT THE COUNTRY IS LIKE

The eastern part of Germany, the Communist part, is mostly level plains lying between the Elbe and Oder Rivers. West Germany, which is more than twice as large as East Germany, with a total area of about 95,000 square miles, is divided into several important regions. The southern part is mountainous. It includes the Bavarian plateau, which averages nearly 1,600 feet above sea level. A plateau is high, like a mountain, but level like a plain. The Zugspitze Mountain, in this region, is the highest point in Germany, almost 9,800 feet high. This part of Germany is noted for its dairy industries. Much of the land is covered with large forests, which supply a great deal of West Germany's wood and timber needs.

The central part of Germany is low, hilly country, with many level plains. This is the largest part of West Germany. The northern part of Germany is a low plain that reaches to the North Sea.

There are several important rivers in Germany. In the south, the Danube rises in the Black Forest and flows eastward through Germany, across the Bavarian plateau, and into Austria. The other important rivers of Germany flow northward. The Rhine, perhaps the most important river in Germany, begins in Switzerland, flows all the way through Germany, and then enters Holland. The Elbe and the Oder, both important rivers in East Germany, also flow north. The Elbe empties into the North Sea and the Oder into the Baltic Sea.

On these important rivers many boats go up and down stream, carrying all kinds of freight. Many canals connect the rivers, and the rivers and canals provide Germany with a network of cheap transportation for all sorts of freight. Important industrial centers and cities are linked by modern *Autobahnen* (thruways).

Germany's extensive network of railroads, greatly damaged during World War II, has been rebuilt and changed almost entirely to electric and Diesel traction. Its fleet of merchant ships, also destroyed during the war, is now larger than it was in 1939. Germany is taking part in civil aviation again and has its own airline.

The climate of Germany is much like the climate of the northern New England states, but it is not as damp. This is the general climate of Western Europe. The average summer temperature is about 65 degrees, and there are usually snows and freezing temperatures during the winter. The people who live in the mountain valleys in the south have a somewhat warmer climate, but there are heavy snows in the mountains. Many people go there to enjoy winter sports.

HOW THE PEOPLE ARE GOVERNED

After the defeat of Nazi Germany, the country was divided into four zones. In 1949, the three zones that had been controlled by the Western Allies (the United States, Great Britain, and France), became the Federal Republic of Germany. The Russians, who dominate East Germany, have refused to permit free elections that might result in a union of West and East Germany as one nation again.

The government of West Germany made its capital in the city of Bonn. The government is headed by a president, who is elected every five years. The lawmaking body is the parliament, which has two houses: the Bundestag, whose members are elected every four years by popular vote, and the Bundesrat, whose members are appointed by the legislatures of the German states. The president of Germany selects a chancellor or prime minister representing the strongest political party in the parliament.

The Democratic Republic of Germany, which is made up of the zone of East Germany and a part of the city of Berlin, has a constitution very much like the constitution of Soviet Russia. The leaders of this government are under the orders of Soviet officials stationed there.

THE CITIES OF GERMANY

The largest city of Germany, Berlin, is divided into two sections: West Berlin, and East Berlin. Berlin was the capital of Germany before the war. There is a separate article about BERLIN.

In West Germany there are several important cities. The largest is Hamburg, which has a population of about 1,818,-600. Munich, the capital of the state of Bavaria, is a city of about 1,302,600. It is an important industrial as well as cultural center. It has an old, famous university and many good theatres. A large number of artists and writers live there. Cologne, famous for its old cathedral, is the third-largest city in West Germany with a population of about 860,800. Other big cities are Essen, which is a steel and machine building center, Frankfurt-am (on the)-Main, and Düsseldorf, both centers of banking, business, and insurance. Bonn, the capital of West Germany, is quite small in comparison with these other cities.

In East Germany, the important cities are Leipzig, which is an important center for publishing and printing as well as commercial trade; Dresden, which is an important railroad center and port on the Elbe River; and Chemnitz, which is an important textile manufacturing city. Chemnitz is now called Karl Marxstadt, in honor of the founder of Communism.

GERMANY IN THE PAST

During the early days of the Roman Empire, about two thousand years ago, the lands that now make up most of Germany were inhabited by many Germanic tribes, some of which came from central Asia. About 1,100 years ago, the Germanic tribes were united into one powerful country under the great king Charlemagne.

After the death of Charlemagne, the eastern part of his kingdom became the kingdom of Germany. This kingdom broke up into small countries, which became part of the HOLY ROMAN EMPIRE, about which there is a separate article. One of these small kingdoms, which was called Prussia, soon became much stronger than the others. In 1871, William I, King of Prussia, was made German Emperor (in German, the Kaiser), uniting all the German countries north of Austria. This was the beginning of the modern German state. Germany's trade and industries were built up, and the country became very strong.

The Prussian leaders of Germany were not satisfied with the development of foreign trade and home industries. They wanted to make a great world empire out of Germany. Their ambition had much to do with starting World War I.

Germany and its allies lost this war, and had to give up most of their land and all their outside colonies. A new constitution was adopted, and Germany became a republic. This new German government was known as the Weimar Republic, because its constitution was adopted at the German city of Weimar.

THE THIRD REICH

In German, the word *Reich* means "realm," or "nation." The First Reich was the old empire, called the Holy Roman Empire, which lasted until the year 1806. The Second Reich was the German empire under the kings of Prussia. The Weimar Republic replaced the Second Reich. It was not a bad government, but in the 1920s and 1930s people in all countries became very poor. Even in the United States, the richest of all countries, there was a great depression. Germany, made poor by its loss of World War I, was in the worst possible condition to stand a depression. The German people were suffering from very bad living and working conditions. The different political parties of Germany were all blaming one another for these problems.

One of these political parties was the National Socialist Party, which is usually called the Nazi Party. In 1933 this party managed to seize control of the government. Adolf Hitler, the Nazi leader, was first made chancellor (prime minister), and then when he had become powerful enough, he made himself dictator. He called the country the Third Reich and called himself *der Führer,* which means "the leader." Under Adolf Hitler and his Nazi Party, the German people lost all their freedoms, freedom of worship, freedom of speech, the freedom of the press, and the other rights of people who live in a free and democratic country. Hitler persecuted and eventually murdered millions of Jews, and he also fought against the Roman Catholic and other Christian Churches.

Adolf Hitler had no honesty in dealing with foreign countries and, by threatening war, he seized Austria and part of Czechoslovakia. He wanted still more territory, so he made a treaty with the Communist government of Russia, which was just as dishonest as he was, to conquer and divide several small countries. In 1939, Hitler started World War II by invading Poland. Most of the German people idolized Hitler, approved of the things he did, and willingly let him lead them into war.

Germany was successful at first. Soon nearly all of Europe was under German domination. Hitler betrayed his Russian friends and invaded Russia too. His fatal mistake was in declaring war on the United States in 1941. Germany was the strongest European power, but American power proved to be far greater. In 1945 the Allies forced Germany to surrender and the four chief victor nations, the United States, Great Britain, France and Russia, took control of Germany. In 1955 West Germany regained independence and in 1959 East Germany officially became independent, though still under Soviet domination.

GERMANY. Area, 137,558 square miles. Population (1973 estimate) 78,330,000. Language, German. Religion, mainly Lutheran and Roman Catholic. Government divided as follows (excluding Berlin):

DEMOCRATIC REPUBLIC OF GERMANY (East Germany). Area, 41,479 square miles. Population (1973 estimate) 17,040,000. Government, republic. Monetary unit, the Deutsche mark, also called Ostmark, worth about 45 cents (U.S.).

FEDERAL REPUBLIC OF GERMANY (West Germany). Area, 95,738 square miles. Population (1973 estimate) 61,290,000. Government, republic. Monetary unit, the Deutsche mark, worth about 25 cents (U.S.). Flag, three wide horizontal bars of black, red and gold.

germicide

Germicides are chemicals that kill germs. Chlorine, which is a chemical put in drinking water in a big city, is a germicide. Chlorine is also used to kill germs in the water of many swimming pools. Iodine is a germicide. We usually speak of germicides as "antiseptics" or "disinfectants." Antiseptic and disinfectant have much the same meaning, but chemicals used for living things are usually called antiseptics and chemicals used on nonliving things, such as dishes, are called disinfectants.

germination

Germination is the process by which seeds grow into plants. We usually speak of it as *sprouting.* Every living thing begins with a germ or embryo. In the case of plants the embryo is in the seed; the outer parts of the seed are food that enables the embryo to grow until it is large enough to burst the outer coat of the seed. The same thing happens in the case of an egg, which contains the embryo of a

chicken and food to feed it. When the chicken is large enough, it bursts the eggshell.

The seed of every plant in the world has the same living parts, or organs, that are necessary for germination. In every seed there is a part that will eventually grow into a root. There is a part called the *hypocotyl* that will grow into the plant's stem. There is a third part that will grow into the leaf or leaves.

Seeds need the right amounts of water and air, and the right temperature, in order to sprout. Too little or too much water or air, or the wrong temperature, may stop the process of germination. For example, many seeds die when too much water stops air from getting to them. This happens when soil in gardens and fields is too wet and does not have good drainage (places to soak up the excess water). The time needed for germination differs in various types of seed. The seed of a grass or vegetable usually takes less time to sprout than the seed of an oak tree. Some seeds have been known to germinate overnight, and the seeds of some mountain plants may take ten years to germinate.

A proper knowledge of germination is necessary for farmers and plant growers.

Geronimo

Geronimo was a famous chief of the warlike Apache Indians. He became famous in the 1870s for his attacks on the villages and settlements of the white men in Arizona. He was captured and put on an Indian reservation, and with the rest of

the tribe he was forced to become a farmer. Farming was something entirely new to the Apaches, since they had always lived by hunting and by raiding other tribes. In 1881, Geronimo and a small band of Apaches broke away from the reservation and began again to live by raiding the white settlers. The government sent General Crook, a famous Indian fighter, to capture Geronimo and his followers, and in 1886 Crook finally caught them. As Crook and his men were taking the Indians back to their reservation, they escaped but were captured soon again. Even though the Indians were far outnumbered by the Army, Geronimo refused to surrender unless the government would allow him and his men to return to their families. After serving two years in prison, Geronimo lived peacefully until he died in 1909 at the age of about eighty-four.

Gerry, Elbridge

Elbridge Gerry was an American patriot who took part in the organization of the first government of the United States. Gerry was born in 1744, in Massachusetts. At that time the American colonies in North America still belonged to England, but Gerry agreed with the people who thought that the colonies should be independent from England. Gerry was elected to the Continental Congress, and when the Congress wrote the Declaration of Independence, which said that the colonies would set up their own

government, Gerry was one of the signers. From that time on, Gerry held many posts in the government of the new country.

During the Revolutionary War, he worked hard at getting supplies needed for the army of the colonies. After the war, he was one of the members of the convention that wrote the Constitution of the United States. He was elected to the first Congress. Later he was sent to France as a representative of the United States government. For a while, he was governor of Massachusetts. While he was governor, some changes were made in the organization of the voting districts of Massachusetts. These changes did not seem very fair, and the people made up a new word, "gerrymander," to describe the unfair changes that were made by Gerry's government. This word is still used today, and people who talk about *gerrymandering* mean changing voting districts unfairly. The last post that Gerry held was the office of vice-president of the United States. He was elected vice-president in 1812, and was still in office when he died in 1814.

Gerry had a grandson, Elbridge Thomas Gerry, who lived from 1837 to 1927. Elbridge Thomas Gerry is remembered as a reformer. He was especially interested in children, and he was a leader in organizing the Society for the Prevention of Cruelty to Children, which tries to see that children are taken care of, and not mistreated.

gerrymander

Gerrymander is a word made up in the United States more than a hundred years ago to describe a special kind of political trickery. Each state in the United States is divided into districts from which members of the House of Representatives are elected. Sometimes politicians change the districts so that their party will get its votes in the districts where the votes will do them the most good. Elbridge Gerry was Governor of Massachusetts in 1812 when the districts in Massachusetts were changed to give his party more power. One of the new districts in Massachusetts was of such a strange shape that a newspaper editor, who was politically opposed to Gerry, called it a "gerrymander" because it was authorized by Gerry and looked like a huge salamander, a lizardlike animal with a long tail. Since that time any changing of the districts of a state for unfair political purposes has been called *gerrymandering*.

Gershwin, George

George Gershwin was a famous American composer. He started as a writer of popular songs but he also wrote some more serious music that is performed by symphony orchestras. He is best remembered now for *An American in Paris* and *Rhapsody in Blue*. He also wrote many musical shows, including *Of Thee I Sing,* for which he received a Pulitzer Prize, and *Porgy and Bess,* one of his most ambitious works. His popular songs include "Swanee" and "The Man I Love." George Gershwin

Gale Research Co.

was born in Brooklyn, New York, in 1898 and died in 1937, when he was only 39 years old.

His brother, Ira Gershwin, became a very successful writer of lyrics for popular songs, including the lyrics for *Of Thee I Sing*. He was born in New York City in 1896.

Gestapo

The Gestapo was the secret state police in Germany when it was ruled by the Nazi party. The word comes from the first syllables of the German words *Geheime-Staats-Polizei,* which means "secret state police."

The Gestapo was formed in 1933, when Adolf Hitler and the Nazis took control of Germany. Members of the Gestapo were not controlled by a "Bill of Rights" as American police are. They arrested anyone who criticized the government or who was against the Nazis, and their spies were everywhere. The Gestapo came to be feared by everyone, even by important officials of the government.

Hermann Goering was the first chief of the Gestapo, but in 1935 Heinrich Himmler got control of it. This gave Himmler more actual power than anyone in Germany except Hitler.

The Gestapo was responsible for the upkeep and guarding of large concentration camps and secret prisons in Germany. Not only did it torture and starve hundreds of people, but it also killed great numbers of prisoners, especially those who were Jewish, in poison-gas chambers.

A branch of the Gestapo was set up in every nation defeated or occupied by the Nazi armies during World War II.

gestation

Gestation is the growth of the young inside its mother. The length of time that this growth takes is called the *gestation period.*

The period of gestation in human beings, the time between the fertilization of the egg inside the mother and the birth of the fully formed baby, is about forty weeks, or about nine months. There is a separate article on CHILDBIRTH.

The animals that have one baby at a time require longer periods of gestation than those that have litters of several young at a time. The animals that are born singly are completely developed and formed when they are born. Animals born in litters may be incomplete in some respect. Baby rats, for example, are born without hair and with their eyes closed. Kittens and puppies are also born with their eyes closed and cannot walk around right away. Baby colts, however, can walk and stand immediately, and so can calves.

An elephant has twenty to twenty-one months of gestation, a horse eleven months, and a cow nine months. Dogs have a gestation period of only 62 or 63 days, cats 55 to 60 days, and squirrels and rats three weeks.

The animals that carry their newborn young in pouches, such as the kangaroo and opossum, have comparatively short gestation periods. This is because the marsupials, as these animals are called, give birth to young when the babies are still not entirely ready to live in the world by

themselves. They must remain in the mother's pouch until they grow a little more, and gain strength. The kangaroo's gestation period is thirty-nine days, the opossum's thirteen days.

Gethsemane

Gethsemane was a garden near the city of Jerusalem. The Gospels of Mark and Matthew in the New Testament tell how Jesus prayed there after he had eaten the Last Supper with his disciples. At that time Roman soldiers were looking for him to arrest him. Because one of his disciples, Judas, betrayed him, the Roman soldiers found Jesus and arrested him, and he was crucified.

Gettysburg

Gettysburg is a small city in southern Pennsylvania. It has become one of the most famous places in American history. Here, from July 1 to July 3, 1863, the Northern army stopped the Confederates, and forced them to give up their plans of invading the North. The Battle of Gettysburg has been called the turning point of the Civil War. For three days the Southerners, who were under the command of General Robert E. Lee, tried to drive back General George G. Meade's Union army, which had taken up a position on a long stretch of high ground just south of the town, called Cemetery Ridge. On the final day, the Confederate division of General George Pickett launched a desperate attack on the center of the line. A few men reached the ridge, but they were soon killed. The rest of the Southern soldiers in this heroic charge were either driven back or were killed or wounded. The Northerners lost 23,000 men out of 97,000 who were in the battle. The Southern losses were 28,000 out of 75,000. The battlefield of Gettysburg is now a National Military Park, and every year it is visited by thousands of people. Nearby is a National Cemetery, where many of the soldiers who died in the battle are buried. Abraham Lincoln made his famous Gettysburg Address here when the cemetery was dedicated four months after the battle. Though the speech consists of only 267 words and lasted only four minutes, it is one of the two most famous examples of great writing in American history (the other being the Declaration of Independence).

GETTYSBURG, PENNSYLVANIA. Population (1970 census) 7,275. County seat of Adams County.

geyser

A geyser is a spring of hot water that spouts out of the ground from time to time. A person watching a geyser first hears a rumbling in the earth below his feet, and then a great roar as the spout of water shoots up into the air. Geysers shoot up at regular intervals. Some geysers erupt every few minutes or hours, but there is one geyser that erupts only once every eight years.

Geysers are found only in parts of the earth where there has been recent volcanic activity, that is, where hot lava from deep inside the earth has burst out close to the surface. Mostly geysers are found only in Yellowstone National Park in the United States, in New Zealand, and in Iceland. Geysers are formed by a deep crack in the earth, into which runs rain water and water from inside the earth. The hot lava heats this water until it turns to steam. When the steam reaches a certain pressure it bursts out of the passage, sending tons of water up with it. The time between the eruptions of a geyser depends on how long it takes for the water to drain into the crack and then become hot.

One of the most famous geysers is Old Faithful in Yellowstone Park. It erupts regularly every 65 minutes in a beautiful fountain as high as 125 feet. The Giant is another favorite of sightseers there. It throws up a column of water five feet across and two hundred feet high, and erupts for an hour and a half. Yellowstone Park has seventy geysers.

Geysers build strange and beautiful deposits around the mouth of the crack. These deposits consist of white silica, a mineral the spouting water brings up with it from the earth below.

Ghana

Ghana is a republic in West Africa. It is one of the youngest independent countries in the world, having been a British colony, called the Gold Coast, until March 6, 1957. Then it became independent, as a member of the British Commonwealth of Nations, and joined the United Nations.

About 8,860,000 people live in Ghana and almost all of them belong to the Negro race. The name Ghana was taken from a great Negro empire that existed in central Africa about a thousand years ago. The area of Ghana is 91,843 square miles—about the size of the state of Oregon. This is made up of 79,000 square miles of the original Gold Coast colony (including the Northern territories and Ashanti), plus British Togoland and some smaller regions that were added to Ghana when it became independent. The capital and largest city of Ghana is ACCRA, about which there is a separate article.

Ghana has a seacoast on the Atlantic Ocean. Its principal river is the Volta. Since Ghana is only a few degrees north of the Equator, the climate is tropical—very hot all year, with a long "rainy season."

Most of the people are farmers. Their principal crop, especially in Ashanti, is cacao, from which cocoa and chocolate come. Ghana has rich deposits of gold and manganese, which are mined, and aluminum, which is not yet mined but can be if the Volta is dammed for hydroelectric power. Most of the people live in villages that are ruled by local kings or chiefs. There are several languages or dialects spoken, but the principal one is Odji, a Sudanese African language. Many of the people follow native religions, but there have been many Christian missionaries in Ghana and especially in the larger cities the children go to Christian schools.

In Ghana, unlike many parts of Africa, all the land belongs to the native people; there are few white residents (about 10,000 in the whole country) and they own none of the great farms and forests.

In 1960 Ghana became a republic. Its first president was Kwame Nkrumah, who had led Ghana's struggle for independence. Nkrumah's rule became more and more that of a dictator; he stamped out all opposition and put many in prison. In 1962 he was made president for life. Nkrumah was also very ambitious; he wanted to be a leader of all the new nations of Africa. But he did not do very much for the people of his own country. By 1966, Ghana, once one of the most prosperous countries in Africa, was heavily in debt. In February 1966, when Nkrumah was out of the country, the Army seized power and exiled Nkrumah.

GHANA. Area, 91,843 square miles. Population (1973 estimate), 8,860,000. Language, Sudanese (Odji). Religions, Roman Catholic, other Christian, and native. Capital, Accra. Government, republic within the (British) Commonwealth of Nations. Monetary unit, the pound, worth $2.80 (U.S.). Flag, red, gold, green, with black star in center.

Ghent

Ghent is an important city in Belgium. It is the capital of the province of East Flanders. About 228,000 people live there. A canal connects it with the North Sea, making it a seaport. Ghent has been an important trade and manufacturing center for hundreds of years. It is still important in manufacturing, especially cloth and lace, and as a seaport. The people of Ghent are Flemish but speak the Dutch language.

The War of 1812 between the United States and Great Britain was ended by a treaty signed at Ghent in 1814. Henry Clay, John Quincy Adams and Albert Gallatin were among the Americans who helped make the treaty. It was agreed that each country would return to the other whatever lands it had captured during the war. The greatest battle of the War of 1812, the Battle of New Orleans, was fought after the Treaty of Ghent had been signed, because in those days it took so long to get the news of the peace to North America that no one knew the war already had come to an end.

A famous English poet, Robert Browning, wrote a poem called "How They Brought the Good News from Ghent to Aix." It tells about bringing the news of a great victory from Ghent to the city of Aix, in France. The story is imaginary, and was wholly made up by Browning.

ghetto

Hundreds of years ago, before civilized countries generally adopted the principle of religious freedom, many European cities required that all Jews live in a certain section of the city. This section was called the ghetto. It was usually a poor and overcrowded section.

Some of the ghettos were surrounded by walls, and had gates that were locked at night, so that the Jews living in the ghettos had to be home by sundown and could not leave until the next morning. In some European cities there were ghettos that were not required by law. Nearly all the Jews of the city lived in them so that they could more easily follow their ancient customs together. But in most cities the Jews had no choice.

One of the most famous ghettos was the one in Rome, established about 1550. It was located on a few dark streets near

the Tiber River, which flooded it yearly. Some Roman rulers were more liberal than others in granting privileges to the Jews, but these ghetto conditions existed in Rome until 1885, when King Victor Emmanuel abolished the ghetto of Rome. Ghettos in other places were gradually abolished after the early 1800s. While the Nazi party ruled Germany and occupied other countries in Europe, the Jews were forced into small sections of the city in Warsaw, the capital of Poland, and Prague, the capital of Czechoslovakia, and these were called ghettos. Also, any section of a big city where nearly all the people are Jews may sometimes be called a ghetto. A famous one was the "Lower East Side" of New York City, from the 1890s to the 1920s.

Ghiberti, Lorenzo

Lorenzo Ghiberti was an Italian sculptor and architect who lived more than five hundred years ago. He is most famous for designing "The Gates of Heaven," two sets of bronze doors for a building called the Baptistry, at Florence, in Italy. He was born in 1378 and died in 1455.

Ghirlandaio, Domenico

Domenico Ghirlandaio was an Italian painter who lived about five hundred years ago. He is famous as the teacher of the great artist Michelangelo. Ghirlandaio painted many scenes from the Bible that were unusual because the people in them are shown wearing the style of clothes worn in Italy five hundred years ago. He did some of the work on the Sistine Chapel in Rome, together with another great painter, Botticelli, and he painted some beautiful frescoes (wall paintings on wet plaster) in the Cathedral of Florence. Ghirlandaio was born in 1449 and died in 1494. His two brothers and his son were also painters.

ghost

A ghost is supposed to be the spirit of a person who has died. Unlike most imaginary spirits, ghosts are not supposed to have any great powers. They can only come back and appear to people in houses, which is called *haunting*. A ghost is supposed to look like steam, so that you can partly see through it. Ghosts are usually pictured in long white robes, and on Hallowe'en people dress up as ghosts in white sheets. Ghosts are supposed to scream, groan, rattle chains, and make other strange noises. This is said to be because they are unhappy to come back to earth, where they are punished for sins they committed when they were alive.

Often the ghosts of murdered people are believed to haunt the place where they were killed. Whole families may be visited by the ghost of a person that an early ancestor killed or injured, or even by the ghost of an ancestor. The Norwegian writer Henrik Ibsen wrote a play called *Ghosts,* which tells about an imaginary family ghost. In Shakespeare's play *Hamlet,* the father of Hamlet appears as a ghost.

There is an organization called the Society for Psychical Research that investigates reports that ghosts have been seen. The Society does this for scientific purposes.

giant

A giant is a creature of human shape but enormously big and strong. There are many stories of giants in the Bible. The giant Goliath was slain by David, and there were whole tribes of giants like the sons of Anak, who were so tall that ordinary people looked like midgets beside them. The ancient Greeks believed in a race of giants called Titans, who fought the gods. The Titans hurled forests and mountains against Olympus, the home of the gods, and laughed at the lightning that Zeus flung back at them. The northern countries have many tales of giants. The Norwegians tell of the giant who had no heart in his body. In India, Cambodia and Ceylon, there were giants who hid their hearts in bird nests to keep them safe. Jack the Giant-killer of the fairy tale was supposed to have lived in Wales. A Cyclops, told about by the great Greek poet Homer, was a one-eyed giant who sometimes helped the gods.

There have been many real giants, too, but they are different from the legendary ones. They are seldom very strong, and they usually do not live long. Many people have grown to be seven feet tall, and some have even reached nine feet. Most circuses have a "tall man," who looks even taller when he stands beside the midget. In the days of ancient Rome an Arabian giant named Gabbaras was captured and exhibited to the people. He was 9 feet, 4 inches tall.

Real giantism usually begins in childhood when a gland called the *pituitary* works too hard and produces too much of the substance that enables the body to grow.

Giant's Causeway

The Giant's Causeway is a strange formation of tall rock columns on the northeastern coast of Ireland. There are about 40,000 of these columns, most of them having five or six sides. All of them stand close together. They were actually formed by a great outpouring of lava, or liquid rock, from the earth many millions of years ago, but there is a legend in Ireland that says the Giant's Causeway was made by a man. According to this legend, there was a great Irish hero named Fingal or Finn MacCool who built the Giant's Causeway nearly two thousand years ago as a road for giants to use in crossing from Ireland to Scotland.

gibbon

A gibbon is a tailless ape that lives in the East Indies. When a gibbon stands erect its arms are so long that they nearly touch the ground. As gibbons live in forests and travel about in the trees a great deal, their long arms are very useful for swinging from branch to branch. In the air these animals move with great ease and grace, but on the ground they move awkwardly. Gibbons are the least intelligent of the apes, and are also smaller and thinner than other apes. They have naked, calloused patches on their backs. They are closely related to orangutans and chimpanzees, other members of the ape family. They are also related to the Old World monkeys.

Gibbon, Edward

Edward Gibbon was an English writer of history who lived about two hundred years ago. He is most famous for a work called *Decline and Fall of the Roman Empire.* In this work he tells the story of Rome, from the time of its greatest glory to its downfall almost 1,300 years later. Gibbon was born in 1737 and died in 1794. You can read more about him in the article HISTORY.

Gibbons, James Cardinal

James Gibbons was a famous American Roman Catholic priest who became a cardinal, or prince of the church. He was born in Baltimore, Maryland, in 1834, and he studied for the priesthood at St. Charles College and St. Mary's Seminary in Maryland. He became Archbishop of Baltimore and was made a cardinal in 1886. He is best known for the help he gave the Knights of Labor. The Knights of Labor was a labor union that was banned in Canada because the Canadian government thought that it was a secret society. Cardinal Gibbons persuaded the Pope to praise the Knights because they were helping laborers. The Knights of Labor were accepted in Canada mostly because of Cardinal Gibbons' efforts. He died in 1921.

G.I. Bill of Rights

The G.I. Bill of Rights is a name by which Public Law 346 is known. The law was passed by the Congress of the United States to aid veterans who served in the armed forces in World War II and Korea.

British Inform. Service

Groups of the stone columns of the Giant's Causeway in Ireland have interesting names such as the Giant's Chimney, the Giant's Wishing-Chair, and Lady Giant's Fan.

Under this law, the government paid a veteran's necessary school costs and helped him support himself while he was in school or training for a better job. Even veterans who work on farms received special training under the G.I. Bill. Almost eight million veterans received benefits from this law.

Another law, which is not part of the G.I. Bill, provides for even greater help to disabled veterans. These veterans, who were hurt during the war, obtain special training to help them overcome their injuries, such as the loss of an arm or leg. This law is called Public Law 16.

Gibbs, Josiah Willard

Josiah Willard Gibbs was an American scientist who made important discoveries about matter. (Matter is anything that has weight and takes up space.) Gibbs lived about 75 years ago, but people did not recognize the importance of his work until after his death. He died in 1903, and was elected to the Hall of Fame in 1950.

Gibbs was born in New Haven, Connecticut in 1839. He studied at Yale University and also in Paris, France and in Heidelberg, Germany. In 1871 he became professor of mathematical physics at Yale. Six years later, in 1877, he developed a rule called the "Gibbs Phase Rule," which described certain chemical changes in matter that had never been explained before. Most of Gibbs' studies were in the field of thermodynamics, the branch of physics that studies heat. He also wrote several books on mathematical physics.

Gibraltar

Gibraltar is a British colony located at the southern tip of Spain. The colony is actually a huge rock formation just over two miles long and about a mile and a half wide, and it is about 1,400 feet high. It is often called the Rock of Gibraltar. It is very important because it guards the Strait of Gibraltar, which is the name of the narrow strip of water connecting the Atlantic Ocean with the Mediterranean Sea. The Strait of Gibraltar separates the southern end of Spain from the northern coast of Africa, and is about seven miles wide at its narrowest point and twenty-five miles wide at its widest point. There is a large naval base at Gibraltar, as well as an important coaling station for ships. Many tunnels have been driven through the rocky ground to connect one part of the colony with another, and large fortifications and gun emplacements have been built there in case of war. Including the soldiers stationed there, more than 25,000 people live at Gibraltar.

Gibraltar has had a very long history. It was captured by the Arabs who crossed into Spain over 1,200 years ago. Later it became a Spanish possession and was

Gibraltar seen from the air.

finally turned over to the English in 1713. Most of the people who live on the peninsula today, aside from English military personnel, are of Spanish or Italian descent. Most of the people work at the naval base or have jobs in the other military installations.

Many of the animals called BARBARY APES are found at Gibraltar. There is a separate article about them.

Gibson, Charles Dana

Charles Dana Gibson was a famous American artist and illustrator. He is best known as the creator of the "Gibson Girl." She was the central figure in a series of drawings. The Gibson girl was very beautiful and was supposed to be the ideal American girl. (Actually these were drawings of Gibson's wife, who was a great beauty.) These pictures showed the Gibson girl at parties, playing tennis, and playing cards. She wore her hair piled high on her head, and wore a blouse with huge sleeves and a long skirt. The drawings really poked fun at the people of the time by showing how silly some of their fashions were.

Gibson was born in Roxbury, Massachusetts, in 1867. He made drawings to illustrate many stories in leading magazines. He later gave up drawing and became the editor of a magazine. Before he died in 1944 he wrote many books about his travels around the world.

Gideon

Gideon was a hero in the Bible. He lived in Israel more than a thousand years before the birth of Jesus. The Jews were troubled then by another desert people, the Midianites, who came into their lands and often killed or stole from them. Once while Gideon was threshing wheat in secret, to hide it from the Midianites, he was visited by an angel who said he could save Israel. Gideon called three hundred friends and relatives to help him fight the Midianites and this little army chased the raiders out beyond Jordan and killed their leaders. The grateful Jews invited Gideon to be king of Israel but he refused.

THE GIDEONS

There is a society called Gideons International that distributes Bibles free of charge to hotel rooms and other places. The society took Gideon's name because of Gideon's obedience to God, as told in the Book of Judges. Gideons International was founded in 1899 in the United States, and has since spread to about thirty countries. It has given away more than two million Bibles to hotels, schools, prisons, ships, and military camps. During World War II the Gideons distributed Bibles among the men in the armed services.

Gila monster

A Gila monster is a poisonous lizard that is found in the sandy deserts of the southwestern United States and Mexico. It is a reptile with a long, narrow, heavy body and thick tail and head. It is called the Gila monster because it was first noticed in the valley of the Gila River in Arizona. A large Gila monster may be nearly two feet long, which is very large for a lizard. It has a rough, warty skin,

usually black and yellow. The Gila monster has large teeth. Some of the teeth have a groove down the side that allows the poisonous saliva to flow into wounds made by the teeth. Human beings have died from its bite. Gila monsters eat worms, centipedes, and bird and lizard eggs.

A Gila monster crawling in the desert.

Gila River

The Gila River, more than five hundred miles long, rises in the mountains of New Mexico and flows westward across Arizona. It flows into the Colorado River. On its way it forms canyons in the mountains and fertile valleys in the flat plains. Southern Arizona would be much drier than it is if the Gila River and its tributaries did not irrigate its dry land.

Gilbert Islands

The Gilbert Islands are in the western part of the Pacific Ocean. There are 16 coral islands in the Gilberts. These islands are called atolls, and about 33,000 people live on them. The islands belong to England, but they were captured by Japan in World War II. Almost two years later, on November 21, 1943, a strong American fleet sailed to the two largest islands, Tarawa and Makin, and landed troops who defeated the Japanese there. You can read about TARAWA in a separate article. The Gilberts were then used as bases for American bombers.

Gilbert, Sir Humphrey

Sir Humphrey Gilbert was the first Englishman to establish a British colony in the New World. He was born in England in 1539, and he went to school at Oxford, one of England's best universities. Later he became an army officer and fought for England in many foreign countries. From his half-brother, Sir Walter Raleigh, he learned to love the sea. He became interested in finding a Northwest Passage across the seas from Europe to China, and he persuaded Queen Elizabeth I of England to outfit him for a voyage.

Gilbert's first trip in search of the Northwest Passage was a complete failure. His second trip was a success, but not the kind he expected. He did not find a Northwest Passage. Instead he landed in Newfoundland, where he founded a small fishing village and claimed the land for England. In 1583, while he was returning to England in his small ship, he was lost in a storm.

Left: W. S. Gilbert. *Right:* A. S. Sullivan.

Gilbert and Sullivan

Sir William Gilbert and Sir Arthur Sullivan were two Englishmen who wrote comic operas together. These are plays with some of the words set to music and much of the story told in songs. In them certain customs and habits, some of them English and others worldwide, were satirized (made fun of). Gilbert wrote the words and Sullivan wrote the music. Their comic operas were by far the most popular written during their time, which was about sixty years ago. Many of them are still so popular that they are constantly being performed.

Among the most popular comic operas that Gilbert and Sullivan wrote together are *The Mikado, The Pirates of Penzance, Trial by Jury, H.M.S. Pinafore, Iolanthe,* and *The Yeomen of the Guard.*

A special theater, the Savoy Theater, was built in London in 1881 by the producer Richard D'Oyly Carte to put on the Gilbert and Sullivan operas. The companies that put them on were often called Savoyards. There is still an English company called the D'Oyly Carte Company that performs these operas.

Sir William Schwenck Gilbert was born in 1836. He was first a military officer and later worked in a government office. He also studied and practiced law. In 1861 he began to publish humorous poetry, which was very well liked. One collection of his poems is called *Bab Ballads.* Then he and Sullivan began writing comic operas together. Even though Gilbert and Sullivan worked together they often quarreled, and sometimes did not speak to each other for weeks at a time. They would send their work back and forth by messengers. In 1890 they had a very serious quarrel and did not speak or work together for six years.

Prominent Englishmen are often rewarded by being knighted and allowed to use "Sir" before their names. Sullivan was knighted in 1883. Gilbert had hurt Queen Victoria's feelings by insulting the British Navy in *H.M.S. Pinafore,* and he was not knighted until 1907, six years after the Queen's death. He died in 1911.

Read also the article about Sir Arthur SULLIVAN.

Gilead

Gilead was the name of a land told about in the Bible. It was also the name of a mountain and a city in that land. Gilead was a region east of the Jordan River. It was an upland region of pastures and woods. It was especially known for the spices and the balm, a sweet-smelling oil or ointment, that came from there. Gilead is mentioned often in the Bible. It was given as a home to the tribes of Reuben and Gad, and to part of the tribe of Manasseh. The great Hebrew prophet and preacher Elijah came from the land of Gilead.

Gilgamesh

Gilgamesh is the greatest hero of Babylonian and Assyrian mythology, the stories the Babylonians and Assyrians told about their gods and goddesses. Gilgamesh was daring in battle, the most handsome man of his time, and the wisest. Other men called him "the Powerful, the Perfect, and the Wise."

All the women fell in love with him and the men became jealous. They asked the goddess Ishtar to create a rival to Gilgamesh, and Ishtar told Aruru, another goddess, to make Engidu his rival. Engidu was as handsome and as wise as Gilgamesh. He was big and unbelievably strong, and knew everything about the past and future. But he did not like people and spent his time in the forest, living with the animals. Engidu was supposed to have had the body of a bull and the chest and head of a man.

When Gilgamesh and Engidu met and fought, the earth shook for miles around. At last Gilgamesh won. Engidu and Gilgamesh became friends after this and fought many battles and had many adventures side by side. When Engidu got sick and died, Gilgamesh learned to fear death. He left the country in search of a magic tree called the Tree of Life, which could make him live forever. He asked a wise man for directions to the Tree and as the wise man gave him directions, he also told him the story of a great flood that covered the earth. Gilgamesh wandered in the wilderness for a long time and had many battles and adventures while searching for the Tree.

gills

Gills are the organs by which fish breathe, just as human beings breathe with their lungs. Gills are tiny blood vessels behind the head of the fish. They take oxygen out of the water that the fish takes in through its mouth. If you look at the throats of most fish, you will see four or five small slits. These openings are called gill slits. The fish opens his mouth at regular intervals and takes in water. When he closes his mouth, the water is forced through the slits over the tiny gills. The blood in the gills takes the oxygen from the water. The oxygen is then carried to other parts of the body by the blood stream. The water is let out of the body through the gill slits, and this is the way fish breathe. The gills of the fish must be wet in order for them to breathe, because dry gills do not work. This is why fish die if they are kept out of water.

ginger

Ginger is a spice used in cooking. It gives food a special flavor and a sharp taste. You can taste this spice in ginger tea, ginger beer, ginger candy, ginger ale, and gingersnap cookies. There are other forms of ginger, the dried ginger root, which lasts for a long time, and the green or young root, which looks like an onion.

All these forms of ginger come from the root of the ginger plant, which grows in the tropics, in England, in India, in Australia, and other parts of the world. The part of the plant that grows above the ground consists of reeds, with leaves and flowers growing on separate stalks.

When the leaves and flowers wither, the native workers take the roots out of the ground. They wash and dry and scrape the roots and then prepare ginger for its many uses. Ginger is ground for use as ginger powder. Ginger root can be dried and bleached in the sun, making white ginger. The green roots can also be preserved in heavy syrup and eaten as a sweet relish.

Ginger has been used as a food and medicine for thousands of years. The Bible mentions ginger, and the ancient Chinese ate it to make them feel warm inside in cold weather.

gingham

Gingham is a cotton cloth woven in Lancashire, England, in Glasgow, Scotland, and in the United States. The manufacturer weaves the colors into gingham. He does not merely print them on the cloth, as he does with calico. Women use gingham for aprons, dresses, curtains, and upholstery. Men use gingham for sport shirts, and children wear gingham clothes. The different types of gingham are: *chambray,* a plain gingham; *nurse gingham,* which has blue and white stripes; *Scotch gingham,* made in Scotland; *tissue gingham,* which has the feel of cord; *zephyr* or *French gingham,* which is thin and soft; and *madras gingham,* which is woven in many brilliant colors.

ginkgo

The ginkgo is a very ancient tree that grows in China and Japan. It is the only tree left of a large family of trees that grew thousands of years ago. It is sometimes called the maidenhair tree. The ginkgo looks just the same today as it did thousands of years ago when it grew in the forests of ancient times.

The ginkgo can live in cities where harmful gases kill many other kinds of tree, so it is being planted more and more in parks and along streets in the eastern United States. The female trees, which bear foul-smelling fleshy fruits, are not desirable as street trees, however. The ginkgo grows to a height of 60 to 80 feet. Its leaves are fan-shaped. They are on flexible stems and wave in the slightest breeze.

ginseng

Ginseng is a plant from which a valuable drug is made. The ginseng is a low plant. It has three leaves divided into five leaflets each and small, greenish-white flowers. Ginseng has a forked root, and a

drug made from the root of the ginseng that is grown in China was used for many years as a medicine. It was so expensive that scientists wanted a cheaper substitute for it. They found one in a member of the same family that grows wild in the United States and Canada. It was then grown commercially for the drug, which is used as a soothing, or quieting, medicine. The ginseng has to be grown in a protected spot because the direct rays of the sun will kill it.

Giorgione

Giorgione was a great Italian painter. He worked with a group of painters in Venice, and so we say he belonged to the Venetian school. Very little is known about Giorgione, and there is only one painting that can safely be called his. There are four or five more that were probably painted by him, but experts are not positive.

The one picture known to have been painted by Giorgione is called "The Tempest." It is a landscape, or outdoor scene, with dark clouds in the background. In the picture are a young shepherd boy and a mother with her child. This was one of the first pictures in which the landscape was important. Giorgione, which means "Big George" in Italian, was born about 1477. He died when he was only 33 years old.

Giotto

Giotto was an Italian artist and one of the greatest painters who ever lived. He lived during the Middle Ages, about seven hundred years ago.

At the time Giotto began to paint all pictures were flat-looking. There was little feeling of depth or distance in painting. The ancient Romans had known how to make painted people look real, but during the Middle Ages painters had forgotten how to do it. Painters made their figures tall and wide, and squeezed as many into a picture as possible. Giotto studied very hard and learned how the Romans had made scenes and people look so natural. His paintings look like scenes taken from a play and tell you a story as you look at them.

Giotto's full name was Giotto di Bondone. He was born in Florence, Italy. He drew the first sketches for the lovely bell tower called the Campanile, in the main square in Florence. Most of Giotto's paintings are frescoes, or pictures painted on a plaster wall while the plaster is still wet. All of Giotto's frescoes are scenes from the Bible. They are in churches and cathedrals in Florence and Padua. By the time Giotto died in 1327 his name was known all over Italy, and his fame had spread through most of Europe.

giraffe

The giraffe is an animal with a very long neck and long legs. It lives in Africa south of the Sahara desert, and it can be seen in many zoos. The giraffe is the tallest of the mammals. (Mammals are animals that nurse their young.) A giraffe may reach a height of eighteen feet, and most of its height comes from its extremely long neck. The giraffe's neck, however, has only seven vertebrae, or

Italian Cultural Institute

Right: The Kiss of Judas, a famous fresco by Giotto. Above: A portrait of Giotto.

form of a cud, which the animal then chews. The giraffe feeds on grass and leaves. It eats a great deal of mimosa, a flowering shrub that grows on the plains where the giraffe lives.

Giraffes are peaceful animals that would rather run away from danger than face it, but they are good fighters if they have to be. They can beat off a lion by kicking their hind legs so fast that it is almost like an explosion in the lion's face. A giraffe can keep up with the fastest horse and outdistance it on uneven ground. It runs by moving both of its legs on the same side at the same time. All four of its legs are the same length, although the front ones look longer. Giraffes were known to the Romans, who exhibited them in spectacles or shows. Thousands of years ago the Egyptians pictured giraffes in their art.

Girard, Stephen

Stephen Girard was an American banker who lived about two hundred years ago. He was born in France in 1750, but when he was 26 he settled in Philadelphia. He made a great deal of money, which he gave generously to the poor.

In his will, Girard left his fortune to build schools. One of these schools is Girard College in Philadelphia, which was intended for orphan boys who wanted to learn a trade. Stephen Girard also lent money several times to the United States government, and in 1814 he paid almost all its war loans himself. He gave his service as well as money. During the yellow fever epidemic in Philadelphia he volunteered to manage a hospital for the sick people, as well as paying for their care. Girard died in 1831.

Giraud, Henri

Henri Giraud was a French general. He was born in 1879. In both World Wars he was captured by the Germans, and both times he escaped. When he escaped in 1941 France had been beaten and occupied by the Germans. Giraud got to North Africa, a French possession that was liberated by British and American forces early in 1942. At that time General Charles de Gaulle commanded the French forces that were not under the

The giraffe's long legs and neck make it easy for it to eat leaves high above the ground. But getting a drink of water is very difficult.

S. Africa Govt. Inform. Office

control of Germany. Giraud and de Gaulle did not agree on many things, but they were persuaded to work together for the benefit of France. Giraud died in 1949, a few years after the war ended.

Girl Scouts

The Girl Scouts is an organization of girls who meet in small groups to work and play together. These girls learn to be good and helpful citizens. At the same time they have a good time with their friends. The Girl Scout organization was started in England, in 1909, by an English general named Sir Robert Baden-Powell, the same person who started the Boy Scouts organization. This English organization of girls was called the Girl Guides. An American woman named Juliette Gordon Low, who was living in Scotland at that time, became interested in the Girl Guides. When she returned home to America she founded the first Girl Scout group in the United States, in 1912. The Girl Guide and Girl Scout movement has spread all over the world, and today groups from more than thirty countries belong to the World Association of Girl Guides and Girl Scouts.

WHAT GIRL SCOUTS DO

Any girl ten years old or more can become a Girl Scout. Girls from 7 to 9 years old can join the Brownies, an organization that is connected with the Girl Scouts. Brownie Scouts could be called Junior Scouts. Girls from 10 to 13 are called Intermediate Scouts. When a girl is 14, she may become a Senior Scout if she has been an Intermediate Scout long enough to pass certain requirements.

The Brownies learn songs, dances and handcrafts, and get an idea of what the Girl Scouts do. They are then ready to become good Girl Scouts when they are old enough.

To become a scout, a girl applies for membership in a neighborhood group of scouts called a troop. At the head of each troop is a captain, or leader, a woman especially trained in scouting. A girl who wants to become a scout must first learn something about scouting. She goes to scout meetings. She learns the scout oath, the ten points of the scout law, the scout motto and slogan, and the scout sign, salute, and handclasp.

Within a troop, a Girl Scout becomes a member of a patrol. A patrol is a small group of scouts who work together. There are about eight girls in a patrol, and two or more patrols in a troop. Each patrol has its own name, usually the name of an animal or plant, and its own flag. The scout troop is run in a democratic way, and girl scouts learn about democratic government by practicing it in their troop. Each patrol elects its own leader. The leader has an assistant. All the patrol leaders, together with the troop captain, the troop scribe who keeps records of meetings, and the troop treasurer who collects dues, form the Court of Honor. This court meets to make its own plans and decisions, and everyone helps by making suggestions and giving her own ideas.

Girl Scouts wear uniforms that include a dark green dress, belt, and beret, and a brightly colored neckerchief. They wear the special Girl Scout pin. They wear emblems and badges which show their rank, their troop, and any office they hold and honors they have won. Girl Scouts are divided into three ranks or grades. The lowest is the tenderfoot. Next is second-class scout, and the highest is first-class scout. A girl must pass a test to show that she knows and can do certain things before she can become a tenderfoot. Then she must pass more tests to go into a higher grade.

Girl Scouts learn to be good citizens and helpful friends. A Girl Scout is expected to be loyal, courteous, obedient, thrifty, and clean. She learns to do a good deed every day, and to be useful and helpful to others.

Scouts hold meetings every week, to learn about scouting, to play games, and to work at their many activities. They make plans for hikes and camping trips. They study to pass tests and earn badges.

Senior Scouts help out with younger scouts and experiment in various fields of work that they may choose as careers. In this group many girls go in for Wing Scouting, in which they learn about flying and aviation, or Mariner Scouting, in which they learn about sailing and navigation.

CAMPING AND OUTDOOR LIFE

Girl Scouts have many outdoor activities, through which they learn a great deal about nature, and about how to take care of themselves outdoors. Often scouts take hikes and trips. They cook their meals out-of-doors, and sometimes they camp out.

Scouts must learn many things that are useful to them in their trips. They must know how to follow trails, and how to make road maps. They learn how to plan their trips, and how to get ready the things they need. A camping trip is a success only if the campers know how to take care of themselves, and how to provide the things they need. So a Girl Scout must know how to light a fire. This may seem like a simple thing, but a scout must learn to do it when she has only two matches and no paper to make the fire burn easily. The scout learns that there are many different ways of building a fire for cooking. The scout knows how to broil, bake, or boil her food over the right kind of fire using only a small amount of wood. She knows how different foods can be cooked out-of-doors and what foods to take along on an outdoor trip.

Overnight camping is not much fun without a good shelter, so scouts learn how to put up a tent that will stay up, even if the wind blows. They know how to prevent water from seeping under it. And they learn how to build a shelter from branches that they gather in the woods in case they do not have a tent.

When accidents happen, a Girl Scout must be prepared. Scouts are taught first aid so they can take care of any accidents that happen when there is no doctor nearby.

First aid may mean the difference between life and death. A first-class scout must know how to give artificial respiration so that she can revive a person who has stopped breathing. She also must know what to do about broken bones, serious bleeding, dogbite, snakebite, sunstroke, frostbite, heat exhaustion, fainting, and poisoning.

Many scouts also learn to signal in Morse code, using blinker lights at night and wigwag flags in the daytime. In Morse code each letter of the alphabet is made up of dots and dashes. A dot is a short flash, and a dash a long flash of the blinker light. In wigwag signaling, a two-foot white flag with a red square in the center is waved to the left and right. A wave to the right is a dot, a wave to the left is a dash. In these ways scouts are able to signal emergency messages over long distances.

A scout who knows all these things can have a good time on a camping trip. She knows how to take care of herself. She learns how to do things safely, and how to care for her camping site so that it will be a pleasant place for other campers who follow her. She learns to work together with the other girls. She comes to know the woods and the fields, and to enjoy being close to nature. She also has a great deal of fun.

LEARNING THROUGH SCOUTING

Girl Scouts also learn many useful and interesting things that they use in their everyday lives. Homemaking is one of the many things that Girl Scouts learn about. A family can enjoy its home only if it is taken care of so that everything runs smoothly. So scouts know how to take care of a house and how to plan the work. They learn how to plan and cook good meals that everyone will enjoy. They know how to sew, and how to make useful things.

Girl Scouts learn how to take care of their health. They know what things are needed for a healthy body, and they develop good health habits. When someone in the family is sick, a scout knows how to be helpful. She studies home nursing, and learns many ways to help a sick person feel comfortable, and get well quickly. Someone who is sick in bed needs special foods and special care, and a scout knows what foods are right. She can help a sick person take a bath in bed. It is not much fun to be sick in bed, but a Girl Scout knows ways to keep a patient comfortable and to entertain a sick person.

A Girl Scout is a good citizen, and she tries to practice good citizenship all the time. She tries to be considerate of other people and to respect their rights. She learns to practice democratic government in her own scout troop. She works on projects that will help her community, and make it a better place to live in. A Scout learns about health and sanitation and safety laws, and she does everything she can to see that the laws are carried out.

Scouts are encouraged to learn useful hobbies, and to do them well. There are more than a hundred hobbies, or skills, that a scout can choose to study. After passing a test in one hobby or skill, she is awarded a merit badge which she wears on her uniform. Merit badges are given in such fields as handicrafts, music, art, dramatics, child care, and nature study.

Girty, Simon

Simon Girty was an American backwoodsman who lived during the time of the Revolutionary War. He was born in Pennsylvania in 1741. When he was a young man he was captured by the Indians and he lived several years with them. He learned their language and ways of living. Then he turned against his own race and became known as "the white renegade." During the Revolution he was in the pay of the English, and led many Indian raids against the American settlers. He was hated and feared by the American frontiersmen for his cruelty, cunning, and savageness. After the war he moved to Canada, where he died in 1818.

Gish, Lillian and Dorothy

Lillian and Dorothy Gish became famous for their acting in some of the first silent movies. In 1915 Lillian Gish acted in the first long movie made by D. W. Griffith, who was one of the earliest movie makers. It was called *Birth of a Nation* and was about the Civil War. Lillian Gish was in other films made by Griffith, including *Way Down East* and *Orphans of the Storm*. She was very pretty and made a great hit with the public and was popular for many years. She was born in 1896

a great hit with the public and was popular for many years. She was born in 1896 and was only 19 years old when she appeared in *Birth of a Nation*. She later became a popular star in television.

Lillian and Dorothy Gish, shown here in the silent movie, *Orphans of the Storm*, were popular stars during the 1920s.

Dorothy Gish, Lillian's sister, was born in 1898. She also acted in many movies and was the star of *Nell Gwyn* and *Madame Pompadour*. She appeared with her sister in the silent movies *Hearts of the World* and *Romola*. She, too, appeared on television. She died in 1968.

gizzard

The gizzard is the second stomach of birds. It has very thick, muscular sides or walls, and a tough, horny lining. Birds use their gizzards to grind their food. First, the food is softened in the first stomach by juices that help digestion. Then it is ground up by the second stomach. The gizzard is located in the back of the bird's stomach. Birds that eat hard food have stronger and usually larger gizzards than birds that eat soft foods. Birds that eat grain usually have the strongest gizzards, while birds that eat insects have less strong gizzards. Birds of prey, such as eagles, that eat very little grain, have weak gizzards. Sometimes small stones are found in the gizzards of birds. The birds swallow them to help them grind up their food.

glacier

A glacier is a stream of ice that slides down from the high fields of snow on the tops of mountains. It is a mass of ice blocks broken by huge holes, and as it moves downward it tears bits of the land and mountain with it, changing the shape of the mountain walls and scooping out great valleys. The snowfields where glaciers begin are piles of snow heaped up on mountains so high and cold that the snow keeps falling faster than it can ever melt. The weight of this snow and the slope of the mountains make the snow pull and slide downward and this moving field of snow becomes the glacier. Glaciers are formed when the snow lies about a hundred feet deep from year to year without melting. The speed of the snowfall and the steepness of the slope control the speed of the glacier. Some glaciers move only part of an inch each day. Some push forward several feet. In the Alps, glaciers move ten or twenty inches daily in summer but only half that fast in winter.

There are four recognized kinds of glacier. The *valley*, or *mountain*, *glacier* is a glacier that falls from the snowfield like a long river into the valley. When it reaches a level warm enough, it melts. It may reach the sea before it melts. The bits that break off the edge of a mountain glacier and float in the sea are called icebergs. A hanging glacier is a special kind of valley glacier. It does not become a river of ice. As soon as it falls away from the snowfield it breaks up into ice-falls, which look like waterfalls. These ice-falls are called avalanches, and they in turn may start new glaciers.

A glacier that is formed at the foot of a mountain is called a *piedmont glacier*. The Malaspina Glacier is a piedmont glacier. The small *ice caps,* which cover mountains and valleys, and the *continental ice sheets,* such as are found in Antarctica and Greenland, are the two other kinds of glacier.

The holes in the glacier are caused by the pull and pressure in the ice sheet that help to break up the ice. Also, the curves or rough outlines of the valley in which it travels will shatter the ice. As the glacier goes down its path, part of the ice is melted by the heat of the earth and the sunshine. This melted snow water tunnels its way under the glacier until it comes out at the foot where it may become a real river. The glacier grinds stones to such a fine floury powder that the melted ice water looks milky. Rivers from the foot of glaciers run white with this powdery water.

HOW THE GLACIER CARVES

A glacier can change the whole look of the country it touches. Its action, which tears and scrapes away at mountains and valleys, is called erosion. The ice clings to the rocks and earth around it and tears them away with it, digging huge basins. These basins may fill with rain or melting snow and become lakes. If a mountain is surrounded by glaciers tugging at its sides it may be cut into such jagged peaks as the Matterhorn in Switzerland or the Teton Range in Wyoming. The glacier can also change the land by rubbing and polishing it. Ice files away at the walls surrounding it, smoothing out V-shaped valleys into rounded, smooth-walled, U-shaped ones. Great rocks sometimes tumble into glaciers and become part of them. The rocks file the landscape over which they slide, and the glacier may drop them far away when the ice that carries them dissolves.

All the rocks and earth that the glacier has plowed up and carried on its way downward are left at the foot of its path. These mounds of rock and earth are called *moraines*. Sometimes a moraine will build into a dam that holds back the water and makes a lake after the glacier has melted. Some glaciers are nearly pure ice, but some are so mixed with dirt and rocks they have gathered that they will become almost entirely frozen earth stuck together with a little ice. New Zealand has several glaciers like that. One kind of moraine left by a melted glacier is called a *drumlin*. This is a small hill rounded like the back of a spoon. Many hills in Wisconsin and Michigan are drumlins; so is Bunker Hill, near Boston, left from the melting of a glacier.

The moving, grinding mountains of ice left scars on all the continents of the world.

Ancient rocks shows marks of glaciers that occurred more than 600 million years ago, when the only forms of life were bacteria and algae. The second glacial period began about 250 million years ago when the reptiles were dominant, but big dinosaurs had not yet appeared. These glaciers covered most of the southern hemisphere. The third and last glaciation was the ICE AGE, about which there is a separate article. It began about 3 million years ago and ended about 8,000 years ago. Some scientists say it has not ended yet. As the huge glaciers moved, they dug out lakes and valleys and altered the landscape. Mountains of New England were buried under such a heavy sheet of ice that their tops were crushed and rounded down. Out in the west the big continental glacier carved the Yosemite Valley out of the mountains. When the ice did begin to melt, the holes it had cut filled with water and made thousands of lakes and rivers. By now this sheet of ice is melted except around the North Pole and the South Pole.

gladiator

Back in the days of the Roman Empire, nearly two thousand years ago, the people went to arenas as people today go to circuses and theaters, and their favorite entertainment was bloody fights that we would consider too cruel to look at. The men who fought in the arena were called gladiators. They were sometimes captives taken in warfare and sometimes citizens who had been convicted of a crime. Unless they fought in the arena they would be put to death, but as gladiators they had a chance to stay alive for a while. Many gladiators were slaves, and if they became very successful fighters they might be freed. Sometimes the gladiators fought wild animals such as tigers or lions, but often one gladiator would fight another. They fought with swords or knives or other weapons until one fell to the ground. Then the victor would look to the crowd to ask whether to kill the wounded man or let him live. There is a tradition that if the people put out their hands with the thumbs turned down, the victorious gladiator would kill his wounded enemy. But if the people turned thumbs up, the wounded man would be allowed to live.

gladiolus

The gladiolus is one of the flowers you see most often in gardens, in flower shops, in bouquets, and in flower arrangements in the house. It is named from the Latin word for "little sword," because the leaf is long and slender and comes to a sharp point. The flowers blossom in a row at the top of a long stem two or three feet high. The buds at the top of the row come out as the blossoms at the bottom die. The gladiolus grows in more colors than almost any other flower. It can be seen in almost every color, from white to almost black. Gladiolus grows from a bulblike base, and most of the gladioli that are cultivated here come from a kind that grows wild in South Africa.

Gladstone, William Ewart

William Ewart Gladstone was a great English statesman who lived from 1809 to 1898. He was only 33 years old when he was first elected to the House of Commons, which is part of the Parliament, or lawmaking body, of the English government. For the rest of his life, Gladstone devoted himself to politics and government.

Gladstone was an outstanding speaker and always impressed the people who listened to his speeches. He quickly became a leader in the Liberal Party. Gladstone held many important posts in the government of England, and four times he was prime minister. The prime minister is the head of the English government. Many reforms were introduced into England when Gladstone was head of the government. The right to vote was given to many more people, so that the government of England became more democratic. Under Gladstone, the first complete educational system was set up, so that all English children had to go to school and there were free schools for everyone. Gladstone always worked especially hard to try to help the Irish people. At that time England ruled over all of Ireland. The Irish people were very poor, and they thought that the English government was very unfair to them. Gladstone led the English government to make important changes and reforms in these laws governing Ireland. Gladstone also had other interests. He was an outstanding scholar, and he found time to write many books on religious and historical subjects.

gland

A gland is a part of your body that either makes a fluid, or liquid, to be used by the body, or a fluid to be given off from the body; both kinds are very important to help your body grow and live in a healthy way.

ENDOCRINE GLANDS

There are eight different kinds of endocrine glands, or glands that make useful fluids. These glands make different hormones, or chemical fluids, that, when given off into the blood, help the different parts of your body to work all during your life; some of them work at certain ages, and some of them work only when you need their services. But they all work together in a wonderful and delicate machine-like system, so it should be easy for you also to understand that if one of these glands does not work properly, the other glands may all be upset by it. Then unusual things may happen throughout the body. Whether they work right or not is one of the most important things that makes you the kind of person you are, such as tall or short, fat or thin, nervous or easygoing. Each gland is very interesting by itself, and study of it helps you to understand yourself.

1. The *thyroid* is a small gland found on the larynx, or Adam's apple, in your neck. It produces a hormone called *thyroxin* that makes you grow properly. If your gland did not give you enough thyroxin as a child you would become a dwarf, and the lack of growth of your brain would leave you stupid; you would

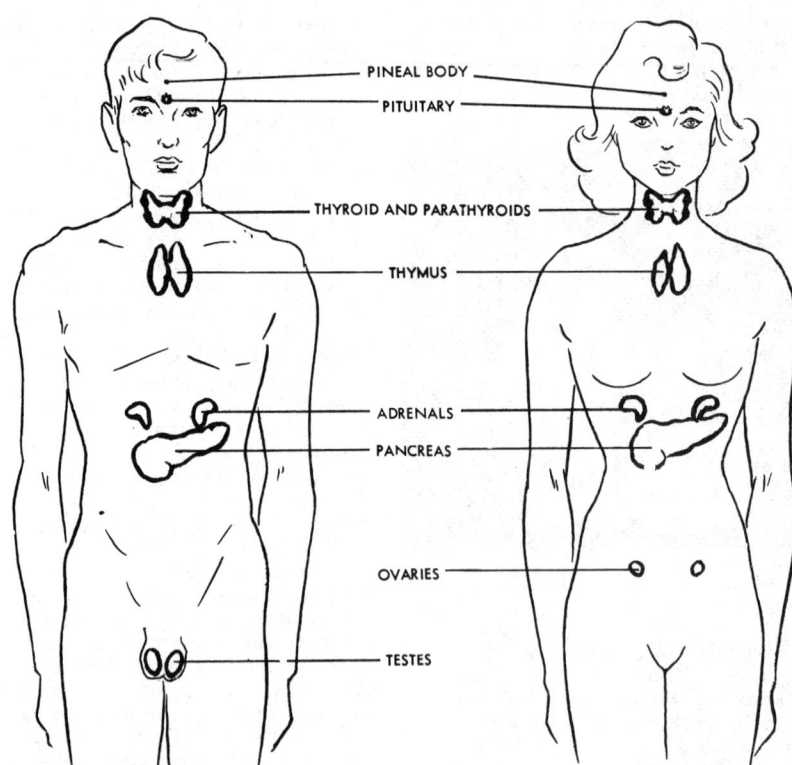

The diagram shows the location of the most important glands in the human body.

be called a *cretin.* If this happened only when you had grown up, you might develop a goiter, which is a growth on the neck. If your thyroid produced too much hormone you would be overactive, very nervous, and thin; some people even develop bulging eyes. Doctors can cure most thyroid troubles, especially if they find out soon enough, by adding iodine, which is needed to make thyroxin, or thyroxin from other animals, to your diet; in more serious cases operations are usually successful.

2. The *parathyroids* are four little glands located within the thyroid glands. These glands work all during your life, and their hormone regulates the amount of calcium in your body. Calcium is important to your bones, teeth, blood and muscles. You would die quickly without parathyroid hormone, but the same hormone from sheep can be used for people whose glands do not make enough.

3. The two *adrenal* glands (adrenal means over-the-kidneys) produce hormones for emergencies: when you need to think and act faster, or when you are suddenly afraid or angry at something or somebody. Your excitement excites the adrenals to give off their hormone, *adrenalin,* which spreads through your body in the blood. All your actions become quicker. Another adrenal hormone, *cortin,* is required by your body to make proper use of the foods you need for your energy.

4. The *gonads,* or sexual glands, are the ovaries in woman and the testes in man. They give off hormones from around thirteen years of age until old age. These hormones cause the differences in your body build and actions that make each person different from any other person. Scientists can make these hormones chemically, and they are very helpful in many cases.

5. The *thymus* is a gland under your sternum, or breast bone, which is believed to guide your growth during childhood.

6. Another endocrine gland, the function of which is not completely understood as yet, is the tiny *pineal* gland near the middle part of the brain. It has been suggested that it helps to slow down growth after a certain time of your life.

7. The *pancreas,* under your stomach, makes *insulin* that controls the use and storing of sugar within your body. Since scientists learned the use of insulin they have been able to control the serious disease diabetes, which is caused by lack of insulin, by obtaining the hormone from animals.

8. The *pituitary* gland, near the middle of the brain, is called the "master gland" because it gives off hormones that cause all the other endocrine glands to work the way they should in order to keep the body healthy. The thyroid gland, the pancreas and the rest must receive hormones from the pituitary before they can do their work. Too much or too little pituitary hormones can make a giant or a dwarf, a thin or a fat person; it can make you weak or strong, intelligent or stupid, nervous or relaxed. Chemists have also learned to make some of the pituitary hormones, which have become important as medicines.

OTHER KINDS OF GLAND

The second kind of gland is one that gives something off from the body. Examples are the kidneys, bean-shaped organs within your lower back, which all during your life clean out the extra water and waste called urine from your body. The urine is passed from the kidneys through tubes to your bladder and then out through your urinary body opening. The kidneys, when healthy, also act to keep the right amount of salt and water in your body. Other glands that give off waste are the tiny sweat glands in your skin.

715

There are other glands that give off fluids important to life. With the *mammary,* or breast, glands a mother feeds her child milk. There is the *prostate* gland, next to the bladder of man, which gives off a fluid that carries the man's seeds into the body of the woman where they join with her egg to grow into a new human being. In the eyes there are *tear*

Ewing Galloway

An overactive pituitary gland helped this giant reach a height of 8 feet 7 inches. The midget with an underactive pituitary stopped growing at only 23 inches.

glands for washing and cleansing the eyeball.

In many parts of the body there are *lymph* glands to keep clean the watery, clear lymph fluid that, in turn, carries off waste and poisons from the millions of tiny cells that make up your body. The digestive glands in your mouth, stomach, liver, and intestines are something like the endocrines because they give off fluids that are used in the body, though not within the blood. These digestive glands give off *enzymes,* or digestive chemicals, that prepare food so your body may use it. There are many other important glands always working to help the wonderful machine that your body is.

glanders

Glanders is a very dangerous disease that attacks horses. When a horse catches glanders it acts much as a human being does when he has a cold. The horse has a runny nose and a fever. It cannot breathe and it may die of suffocation, or smothering. This disease is known all over the world, and both farmers and owners of horses always fear it. Horses

can be tested to see if they carry the disease germs, and some countries, such as the United States, import only horses that do not have any glanders germs. This method has worked, and glanders is rarely found in the United States. Sometimes human beings get glanders, too, but not often. Glanders is also known as *farcy.*

Glasgow

Glasgow is the largest city in Scotland and the third-largest city in Great Britain. For hundreds of years it has been one of the most important shipbuilding centers in the world. The city lies on the banks of the river Clyde, on the west coast of Scotland, and there are several miles of good docks on the river for shipbuilding and trading activities of the city. More than 907,000 people live in Glasgow, and besides working on the construction of ships they work in many large factories that produce iron goods, textiles, and other products. Glasgow, with its good harbor, is in the richest coal and iron district of Great Britain, and has become an important city for manufactured goods as well as a trading center. Prestwick International Airport is a major transatlantic stop for several airlines.

Today much of Glasgow is quite modern, and visitors to Glasgow can see the parks, the large public buildings, and the art museums as well as many of the interesting old buildings that were built many years ago. The famous Cathedral of Glasgow, which is an important landmark of the city, was built more than seven hundred years ago. The University of Glasgow was started in 1451. It was aided by the famous Queen Mary of Scots, and later by her son. Today, many plans are being made by the people and civic leaders of the town to build more new buildings, and also to do something about the smoke that comes from the factories and the iron and steel mills, which is always a problem in an industrial city. GLASGOW. Population (1973 estimate) 907,672. Seaport on the Clyde River.

Glasgow, Ellen

Ellen Glasgow was an American writer. She was born in Richmond, Virginia, in 1874, and she lived all her life in the South. She was too delicate to go to school and educated herself by reading the many books in her father's library. Her novels give us a picture of life in the South from the Civil War to modern times.

She was a realist, which means that she wrote about life as it really was, even when this meant writing about unpleasant things. Because of this, her books were never as popular as they should have been, although in 1942 she won the Pulitzer prize, for her novel *In This Our Life.* The Pulitzer Prize is an award given for good writing. Ellen Glasgow died in 1945.

glass

Glass is a hard material whose greatest value is the fact that it is transparent, that is, it can be seen through. Glass has hundreds of other uses that do not depend upon its being transparent. It is used especially for dishes you drink out of, so much so that you say you drink a "glass

Men found that they could make much better glass from sand that was almost pure silica than from sand that contained dirt and other impurities. It was difficult to find sand without some impurities, so men had to find ways to get rid of them. They learned that if they mixed soda with the sand, and boiled the mixture until it became very hot, the soda made some of the impurities boil away. The mixture of soda and sand is called the *batch.* Then someone added crushed limestone to the batch, and he found that this made it boil more quickly, so all glassmakers began to use limestone. Glass made in this way is called *lime glass.*

Men discovered that when they used lead instead of limestone they could make a glass that was clearer and brighter than any glass ever made before. Lead glass is very clear and it sparkles when it is polished. Men began to make glass ornaments out of lead glass. They found that when they added certain materials to the batch, they could make glass of many colors. Most inexpensive jewelry with glass ornaments that you see in stores now is made from lead glass.

One of the wonderful things about glass is that when it is very hot, it is runny, like syrup. Then when it hardens it will keep whatever shape it had when it was a liquid. Men made molds of clay or metal, and they poured the liquid glass into these molds to cool. As the hot glass cooled, it gradually turned from a liquid into a soft mass that could be rolled. Then it could be shaped into plates and cups and bowls and many other objects.

BLOWING GLASS BUBBLES

Next men discovered that much finer (thinner) glass could be made by blowing glass bubbles. Glass bubbles are blown very much as we blow soap bubbles. Instead of blowing just ordinary round bubbles, a good glass blower learned to blow bubbles into almost any shape he wished. We do not know just when glass blowing began, but ancient Egyptians carved pictures on rocks almost four thousand years ago that show some of the early glass blowers. In these pictures, each glass blower holds a slender pipe to his lips. For thousands of years people blew glass in pretty much this same way. The blower used a pipe about six feet long, and this pipe was shaped like a bell at one end. When the glass blower dipped the bell end of his pipe into the hot batch, a small ball of soft, glowing glass stuck to the pipe.

Then the blower placed the opposite end of the pipe to his lips and began to blow gently. Slowly, the bubble of glass formed, and grew larger. The blower raised the far end of the pipe over his head and began to twirl it. Gradually, the bubble took the shape of a vase or goblet, or whatever he wished to make. For a long time, a glass blower needed great skill to do his own work well, because the shape of the bubble depended on how well he could blow glass. Then, blowers learned how to make their work much simpler. They found that they could blow the glass bubble into a mold, so that the bubble would take the shape of the mold, and all of the objects made from one mold would be shaped exactly alike.

A few people now blow beautiful vases and delicate figures and other objects of glass, and men in factories operate great machines that can blow glass. Blown glass now can be made quite easily and it does not cost very much.

GLASSMAKING TODAY

Glassmaking is one of the biggest industries in the United States, employing about 150,000 persons. The glassmakers first remove all of the loose dirt and other impurities from the sand. This is done by special machines. Then, the materials are measured and mixed to make the batch. The large chamber where the materials are mixed is called the *dog house*. It takes about three weeks to heat the giant furnace that must heat the batch.

Most of the furnaces now are heated by electricity, although some of the older furnaces burn coal or gas.

There are two kinds of furnaces that men who work in glass factories use in their work. One kind of furnace holds the batch in huge pots that are placed on ledges above the fire. Another kind of furnace has one great tank that holds the batch, and the heating system is built around the tank. The floor of the tank slants a little, so that as the glass melts it flows towards an opening at the lower end of the tank. A large tank is about one hundred and forty feet long, and it can hold almost two thousand tons of glass. It takes about two days for the glass to melt in the furnace, and then it is ready to be shaped into windows and many other things.

Once men who made window glass had to pour the melted glass onto a table where they used a tool that looked very much like a rolling pin to roll the glass out into thin sheets. Now machines roll the glass. Some window glass is made by machines that blow huge glass bubbles, and these bubbles are cut open and spread out flat.

Plate glass, which is used for mirrors, automobile windshields, and store windows, is clearer and brighter than window glass. Plate glass is rolled in giant rollers, and then ground and polished until it is very clear.

Machines called *pressing* machines press liquid glass into the desired shapes of dishes, drinking glasses, ashtrays, or bottles. Some machines can press as many as three hundred glass bottles at once. Other machines blow glass electric-light bulbs; more than a billion glass bulbs are blown each year in the United States. Special machines make fine glass for use in telescopes, lenses, and microscopes.

STRONG GLASS

One trouble with glass is that it breaks very easily. Often it cracks when its temperature is changed very suddenly. Modern science has invented many kinds of glass that are hard to break. One of these is a kind of plate glass called *safety glass.* Safety glass is made like a sandwich. It has a thin layer of tough, transparent plastic material between two layers of glass. Sometimes safety glass has as many as five layers of this plastic material. Safety glass will crack but it will not shatter, and it is required in automobile windshields and windows.

Left: A bird painted by Audubon is perfectly reproduced by engraving on the underside of a thin glass dish. *Below:* Light and shadow play on and below the surface of a crystal horse designed by Sidney Waugh. Because glass is light and clear, figurines made of it are a favorite decoration in many homes.

All the natural grace of a fish as it makes its way through the water is caught in the design on the left. The special qualities of glass lend themselves to an illusion of grace and lightness that can be achieved with few other materials. Yet the crystal is very heavy.

There is another special kind of glass that can be boiled and then put on ice, and it will not crack. This kind of glass is called *borosilicate glass,* and it is used to make baking dishes, coffee pots, and other articles that are used in the kitchen for cooking food. Electricity cannot flow through this kind of glass, and so it is used to protect wires and tubes in radios, telephones, and electric power plants.

SPUN GLASS

Men have discovered a wonderful way to spin glass into fibers or threads that can be woven into cloth or fluffed like cotton or wool. This glass feels very fine and silky and it is difficult to believe that it is glass at all. When men make spun glass, they first melt the batch, just as they do to make any other kind of glass. Then the glass is molded into tiny marbles that you can see through. All of these marbles are rolled down a slide into a furnace and melted again. The liquid is sent into a heated chamber that has many tiny holes in the floor, and the glass runs through these holes, and it hardens into soft fine

threads. These threads can be spun together to make fine or heavy yarn, or even thick cord. Glass yarn will not burn or stain. It is light and waterproof, and so strong that it will not wear out for a very long time. Scientists now are finding out many ways to use this marvelous new kind of glass.

glasses

Glasses are worn by people who have poor eyesight. Glasses help them to see things clearly and without straining their eyes. Eye doctors, called *oculists* or *ophthalmologists,* or *optometrists,* who are trained to measure a person's ability to use his eyes, find out what kind of glasses a person needs. There are many kinds of eye trouble, and all but a few of them can be helped by the use of glasses.

Years ago people bought glasses from peddlers or through the mail. What they got were magnifying glasses that simply made things look larger. These glasses did not help people to see more clearly without straining their eyes. In some cases, the glasses only increased the eye trouble.

Modern glasses are especially made for the individual wearer by an *optician* (maker of glasses), who carefully grinds the glass or lens for each eye according to the thickness prescribed by the doctor or optometrist. A frame is fitted to the wearer's face so that it rests comfortably on his nose and ears. The lenses are then mounted in the frame.

Some glasses, called *pince-nez,* are clipped to the bridge of the nose and are not supported by the ears. A *monocle* is a single lens that is held in place in the hollow in front of the eye. A *lorgnette* is a frame with lenses for both eyes. It can be held by hand in front of the eyes for short periods of time.

In *bifocals* most of the lens is ground so that the wearer can see things at a distance. The lower part of the middle of the lens is ground so that the wearer can look at things close to his eyes. A person is usually looking up when he looks at things far away, and looking down when he reads, so he automatically looks through the proper lens. The great American statesman, Benjamin Franklin, invented bifocals about two hundred years ago. Today there are even *trifocals*—three kinds of lens for each eye. They are used by people who must have a lens for very close work in addition to the lenses in bifocals. Jewelers, dentists and others who work with small objects use trifocals.

CONTACT LENS

Contact lenses are worn directly on the eyeball, and because of this they must be specially made for the wearer. If they do not fit exactly they can cause discomfort. They are made of a clear plastic material that is ground into lenses just as glass is.

Contact lenses are better for some kinds of eye trouble than regular glasses. Some actors wear contact lenses for the sake of their appearance, and athletes sometimes wear them because the lenses cannot be broken and therefore are safer. At first, contact lenses were inserted with a special clear fluid in them. The fluid helped magnify and also prevented irri-

If you have normal sight, you can see objects that are near and objects that are far away clearly, as in this picture. The drawing shows how light strikes the eye.

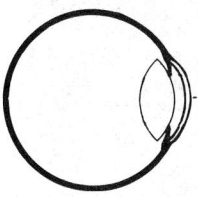

If you are near-sighted, objects that are close up are clear but things far away are blurred, and you need glasses to correct this.

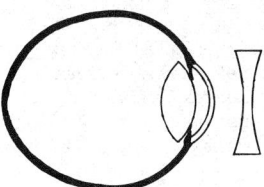

When you are far-sighted, things in the distance are clear, but objects close up are blurred as is shown in this picture of the girl.

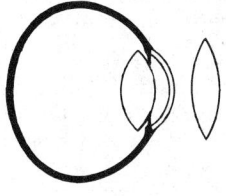

Double vision causes you to see two images of things. In the diagrams, note how the point of light behind the eye falls differently in each instance of faulty eyesight.

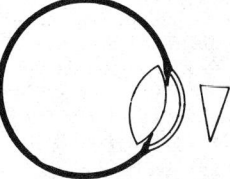

kinds of eye trouble than regular glasses. Some actors wear contact lenses for the sake of their appearance, and athletes sometimes wear them because the lenses cannot be broken and therefore are safer. At first, contact lenses were inserted with a special clear fluid in them. The fluid helped magnify and also prevented irritation to the eyeball. The latest contact lenses do not need fluid. They are made to fit only over the iris, the colored part of the eye, and are much more comfortable and can be worn longer than the old kind.

HOW GLASSES HELP

There is a lens in your eye called a *crystalline lens.* It bends the rays of light that enter your eye and brings them to a point or focus on the back of the eye-

ball called the *retina.* When the focus is right, clear pictures or images of objects are formed by the eye. It is an amazing fact that all images on the retina are upside down. A special part of the brain, called the *occipital lobe,* causes the image to appear right-side up.

Sometimes when the eyeball is too short or the muscles of the eye too weak to control the crystalline lens properly, the light entering the eye is focused too far away from the lens. People who have this trouble are said to be *far-sighted.* They can see distant objects clearly, but not objects that are near by. To correct this defect, slightly convex lenses are used, lenses that are thicker in the middle than at the edges. They help to focus the light at just the right distance from the crystalline lens so that a distinct im-

age of near objects is formed on the retina. The crystalline lens of the eye is a convex lens.

The opposite of far-sightedness is *near-sightedness*, or *myopia*. The light entering the eye is focused too near the lens, in front of the retina, so that a distant object appears blurred. Slightly concave lenses are used to correct this defect. Such lenses bend the rays of light away from each other so that they are focused on the retina. Concave lenses are thicker at the edges than at the middle.

Some people have what is called *astigmatism*. This happens when the eyeball is curved somewhat like an egg instead of like a round ball. In such cases, lines running up and down may be seen quite distinctly, while lines running from left to right may appear blurred. Specially ground lenses must be used to correct this defect.

WHO FIRST MADE GLASSES

The Chinese are believed to have invented glasses about 2,400 years ago. Marco Polo, the great Italian explorer, journeyed to China about 700 years ago and found many Chinese wearing glasses. At about the same time an Italian named Salvino d'Armati was making glasses. He is given credit for being the first to make glasses in the Western world. Most people at that time believed that glasses were instruments of the devil and should not be used on the eyes, which they thought were a gift from God. That is why when d'Armati died, the inscription on his tombstone read: "Here lies Salvino d'Armati of Florence, the inventor of spectacles. God forgive him his sins. Died in the Year of Our Lord 1317."

The invention of printing, about 450 years ago, did much to improve the quality of glasses. More and more people began to read, and more and more of them found their eyesight was not good enough. Scientists began to study the eye and how to make better glasses for it. As they learned more about eyesight and lenses, they were able to provide people with better glasses.

glass snake

The glass snake is a lizard, but it has no feet as other lizards have. It looks somewhat like a snake, but it has movable eyelids and a stiff armor of scales that prevents it from having the graceful movements of a snake. The glass snake is yellow or greenish-brown, and it is sometimes striped. It get its name because its tail, which is twice the length of its body, can be broken as easily as a piece of glass. If caught by the tail, the glass snake can shed part of its tail. This part will go on wiggling and hold the enemy's attention until the lizard can escape. The tail grows back, but it is slow in becoming as long as it was originally. The glass snake has a lizard's head. It grows to be about two feet long. It is found in southeastern Europe. A smaller kind lives in the Mississippi valley and the southern United States.

glasswort

Glasswort is an herb that grows wild along the seacoasts in many parts of the world. The ash of the glasswort that grows around the Mediterranean Sea contains soda, which was at one time used in glassmaking and soapmaking. Glasswort grows to be about a foot high. It has tiny leaves and flowers that turn red in the fall. The stems of glasswort are very thick and become brittle in cold weather. If you walk across a field of glasswort in winter the flowers crackle and break into bits as if they were glass. Glasswort is not often grown in gardens.

Glauber's salt

Glauber's salt is a chemical compound used as a laxative. It is named for a famous German chemist, Johann Glauber, who lived about three hundred years ago. When he was 21 years old, Glauber was attacked by a fever and he was advised to drink the water from a certain well. After he recovered from his illness, he took from the water of this well some large crystals that looked like rock candy. He called these crystals "the wonderful salt." This salt has been used as a medicine ever since. Glauber's salt is found in many parts of the world.

glaucoma

Glaucoma is a very serious disease of the eye. It often leads to blindness. In glaucoma the eyeball gradually hardens. A person with glaucoma first sees flashes of light and colored rings around objects. He gradually sees less and less. Glaucoma is most common in people over forty. There are medicines that help cure the disease, and sometimes an operation is necessary.

Glendale

Glendale is a city in southern California, near Los Angeles. Its population in 1970 was 132,752. Most of the people work in nearby Los Angeles, but Glendale also has factories making airplane parts and petroleum products. Forest Lawn Cemetery, one of the world's most elaborate burial places, and Glendale College are there. Glendale was founded in 1887.

Glenn, John H., Jr.

John Herschel Glenn, Jr. was the first American astronaut to orbit the earth. This historic feat took place on Feb. 20, 1962, with millions following the flight by television and radio. Glenn, a Lt.-Colonel in the Marine Corps, circled the earth three times in his Mercury capsule, *Friendship 7*. He traveled 81,000 miles at a top speed of 17,545 miles per hour, reaching a maximum height of 162 miles. Total time of the flight was 4 hours and 56 minutes. Glenn, a former combat and test pilot, was born in Cambridge, Ohio, in 1921.

glider

The glider is an airplane without an engine. It is sent into the air under power from a tow line, or carried by a powered airplane. Once it is in the air the glider is carried along by natural air currents.

The first glider was built in 1810 by an Englishman named Sir George Cayley. His models were too small to carry anyone, but they proved that gliding was possible. Between 1891 and 1896, Otto Lilienthal made man-carrying gliders, and around 1900 the Wright brothers got their first flight training in gliders. Many of these first models were called "hang gliders" because the pilot actually hung in place by his armpits and shifted his body to control the glider.

Except that it has no motor, the glider is exactly like any other airplane. It has the same type of controls, and is flown the same way. When a glider is ready to be sent aloft, a towing line is attached to the nose, and the other end of the line is hooked to a car or truck, or an airplane. When the glider is towed, it acts just as any airplane would with a propeller, and it rises into the air. When it is as high as necessary, the pilot drops the line. After the glider is in the air, the pilot must look for up-currents to keep him up there, or he would soon glide back to the ground. He knows that the sun shining on flat lands will heat the air over these lands. He also knows that heated air will rise, so he looks for places where these heated air currents are most likely to be found. These hot air currents are called *thermals*. One sign of thermals is flat-bottomed clouds. By staying under these, the pilot keeps his glider in the air.

GLIDERS IN WARTIME

After World War I, Germany was not allowed to have a military air force. When Germany wanted to teach its men how to fly, glider clubs were formed. These clubs were permitted because it was thought that gliders could not be used for war, but this was a mistake. By spending much time in these clubs, German pilots learned how to fly gliders, and when Germany started to build military planes, it had almost 200,000 trained pilots. In this way, Germany had a large air force when it was thought to have none at all.

Other military uses were found for gliders. Since they could be towed by other planes, someone thought of using one powerful airplane as a "locomotive" to pull a "train" of gliders. By using many gliders, large numbers of troops could be flown into combat by only one plane. This was good because gliders are easier and faster to build than airplanes with motors, and cost less. When Germany invaded Crete in 1941, it used glider trains for troops. The United States and England soon caught on to this means of troop transport and used gliders during the invasions of Sicily, France, and Holland. Gliders were also found useful for carrying supplies.

Gliding as a sport has become very popular in the United States, and glider clubs are found all over the country. This is an excellent way to learn to fly, and gliding licenses are issued to people as young as fourteen years of age. For those interested in model-plane aviation, model gliders are among the easiest types to build and fly. People interested in building and flying more complicated types of planes can learn much from gliders.

Many records have been set in gliders. In 1961, Paul F. Bikle of the United States flew a single-place glider up to 46,267 feet. This is higher than some powered planes can go. In 1952, Charles Atger of France stayed up in the air for 56 hours and 15 minutes, which was more than two days of motorless fly-

Schweizer Aircraft Corp. Photos
Gliders are often towed by airplanes. After the cable is released, the glider soars on its own. Note the glider's wide wingspread, which helps it utilize any air currents.

J. Crawford and I. Smith
The Globe Theatre was open to the sky; only those in the balconies left and right of the stage were sheltered if it rained. Shakespeare used no scenery. The balcony above the stage might serve as a tower in *Hamlet* or as a real balcony in *Romeo and Juliet.*

globe

A globe is a model of the earth or the heavens. The globe got its name from the earth, which is a sphere and is sometimes referred to as a globe.

A globe of the earth shows all the lands and waters of the earth, drawn to scale. It is called a *terrestrial globe.* Terrestrial means "of the earth." Being the shape of the earth itself, a globe is therefore much more accurate than a flat map. The distance from one place to another is recorded almost exactly while a flat map could very easily be wrong in that distance. Directions, too, are more accurate than on a flat map.

One of the first terrestrial globes was made by a man named Martin Behaim in 1492, the same year Columbus discovered America. Globes are used in the study of geography. The globe is used in schools to show children and students what the world looks like. There are many globes and they are built in many sizes.

A globe of the heavens shows all the stars and planets. It is called a celestial globe. *Celestial* means "of the sky." It is widely used in astronomy, the science that studies the positions, sizes, and motions of all celestial bodies.

globefish

The globefish is an ocean fish that lives in tropical or warm coastal waters. It is sometimes called rabbitfish because it has sharp teeth like a rabbit's. It eats

Am. Mus. of Nat. Hist.
The globefish looks like a prickly pear with tiny fins, bulging eyes, stiff mouth and tail. It takes in air, and floats, belly up, on the surface of the water.

barnacles and small shellfish. Globefish can grow to be a foot long, but those found along the coast of the United States are much smaller. When the globefish is in danger it sucks air into a bladder in its stomach and blows itself up into a big ball. Then it floats on the surface of the water until the danger is past. Globefish are not good to eat and some of them may even be poisonous. They are often kept in a fish bowl or aquarium.

Globe Theatre

The Globe Theatre was built near London, England, more than 350 years ago, in 1598. William Shakespeare, England's greatest playwright, owned part of the theater and his acting company performed there. The first play to be given at the Globe was Shakespeare's *Henry V,* and most of his great plays were first acted there. Later many other famous plays were acted at the Globe.

The Globe was in Southwark, just across the Thames River from the old city of London. You may read about the construction of the Globe and other early English theaters in a separate article on THEATERS.

In 1613, during a performance of *Henry VIII,* a cannon that was shot off in the play set the roof on fire and the Globe burned down. A year later it was rebuilt, but it was destroyed thirty years after that by the Puritans, who felt that it was wrong for people to go to the theater. Today a small bronze marker on a brick wall shows where the famous Globe Theatre once stood.

glove

A glove is a covering for the hand. The history of the glove reaches back into the earliest days of man's existence. Even the prehistoric caveman used a hand covering that was a kind of glove. The ancient Greeks, Romans and Persians also wore gloves.

The earliest gloves were crude and were more like the mittens that children wear today. They did not have fingers in

before the birth of Jesus—introduced the glove to England.

At first only men wore gloves. For many years they were worn only by members of the nobility or by high church officials. Today both men and women wear gloves, for warmth and for protection. There are many jobs that require gloves to protect the workers' hands from injury. Many women wear gloves to keep their hands clean, and because without them they are considered poorly dressed for most social occasions.

THE GLOVE AS A SYMBOL

In former days the glove played an important part in the laws and customs of nearly all peoples. It was a symbol of faith, friendship, and authority. Historians think that the glove may have become a symbol because of the habit that men started of shaking hands to express their friendship and good will. It came about that kings and other important people, who could not themselves attend an important meeting, began to send the glove of their right hand as a greeting and as a sign of faith or good intention. A king would send his glove to another king as a guarantee for the safe passage of an ambassador or messenger.

As this custom became more common, gloves were passed between people who were making an agreement of some kind. The glove was a sign that each man intended to live up to his agreement. The glove came to have almost as much legal power as a signature. A young man and a young woman who became engaged to be married exchanged gloves. A soldier riding into battle carried his sweetheart's glove for good luck.

The glove was a sign of truth and honor in the middle ages. A man pledged his allegiance to his king or to his lady by swearing on his glove. A man who felt he had been insulted threw down his glove as a sign that he wished to fight the person who had insulted him. From this custom we get the expression "throwing

down the gauntlet" (*gauntlet* means "glove") to show that one person is daring another to fight. If a nobleman committed a serious crime, his gloves were often taken away from him.

Women in England first used gloves about four hundred years ago, during the reign of Queen Elizabeth I. Only those who belonged to the court circles were allowed to wear them. The gloves worn by both men and women·at this time were perfumed and decorated, often with very costly jewels. Queen Elizabeth herself had three thousand pairs of decorated gloves.

KINDS OF GLOVES

Leather has always been the most popular material for gloves. The leather used for gloves must be flexible as well as soft and long-wearing. We get the expression "fitting like a glove" because gloves have to fit the hand so perfectly. Nearly all the leather used in the United States for gloves is imported from other countries. Generally it is found that animals born in high altitudes and cold climates, and those that have coarse, hairy fur, produce a leather of fine texture best suited to gloves.

The most common leather used for gloves is sheepskin. Different types of sheepskin gloves are called capeskins, mochas, degrains, suedes,· and chamois. Other leathers often used are deerskin, wild pigskin, and dogskin. These leathers are made in a grained finish or in a velvet finish. The grained finish has a surface that shows a rough pattern. Many pigskin, goatskin and dogskin gloves have grained finishes. Velvet-finish leathers are smooth but often have a *nap*, a surface of very short hairs. Several kinds of sheepskins and deerskin have a velvet finish. (See the article on LEATHER.)

Gloves are also made from silk, rayon, wool, cotton, and synthetic fabrics such as nylon. Fabric gloves are of two kinds, those that are knit and those that are woven. Fabric gloves are usually less expensive than leather gloves.

GLOVEMAKING IN THE UNITED STATES

The people in the American colonies wore homemade gloves until about 1750. Then a New York landowner, Sir William Johnson, invited a group of Scottish glovemakers to leave their homes and settle in the New World to make gloves. These people settled in upper New York State and called their town Gloversville. People in nearby towns also began making gloves. Today this area is still the glovemaking center of the United States, though gloves are made also in many other places.

glowworm, the larva, or young, of the firefly; see the article BEETLE.

Gluck, Christoph Willibald von

Christoph Willibald von Gluck was a German composer. (A composer is a writer of original music.) Gluck was one of the first great composers of music for opera, a play in which the words are sung and not spoken. He was born in Germany on July 2, 1714, and started to study music when he was a schoolboy. Before his time, operas were not often natural. There was very little relationship between what was happening in the story and the way the music sounded. Gluck wanted to make the music express the same emotion that the story expressed. For example, he did not think that sad music should be put in at a point in the story where a couple were dancing gayly in celebration of their engagement. This seems perfectly natural to us now, because composers make their music fit the mood of a story as a matter of course. In Gluck's day, however, they did not, and he was the first important operatic composer who used this method. Most of his operas were written about mythological characters, or ancient gods. Some famous ones were *Orpheus and Eurydice, Artaxerxes,* and *Iphigenia Among the Taurians.* Gluck died in 1787.

glucose

Glucose is a kind of sugar made from cornstarch. It is also called corn syrup. Since it costs much less to make glucose than it does to make cane sugar, glucose is used a great deal for sweetening candies, jellies and jams.

Glucose is also called *dextrose.* Pure glucose, or dextrose, is found in many plants, especially in grapes and other sweet fruits.

Our bodies also make glucose. The body cannot use most sugars as they are, and so it turns them into glucose, which can be used by the body just as it is. Starches, such as bread and potatoes, and sugars are made into glucose by the body in the course of digestion.

glue

Glue is a strong, sticky substance that holds things together. It is an adhesive; you can read about others in the article on ADHESIVES. Glue is usually made from animal bones, which contain gelatin. There are other kinds of glue, but this is the oldest kind. Marine glue is waterproof and strong, and contains India rubber or shellac instead of the gelatin from animal materials. There are liquid glues that do not become hard at room temperature, as bone glue does. Bone glue has to be dissolved and heated before it can be used, but liquid glue can be used as it comes from a tube or bottle. Isinglass is also a true gelatin glue. It is made from the bladders of fish and it is used to mend glass. Isinglass is one of the oldest forms of glue.

To make glue, the bones or skin or fish substance is boiled and then steamed under pressure. This makes the glue liquor.

The liquor is drained into iron pans, where it sets into a firm jelly. The jelly is sliced into small sheets, so that the air can dry it quckly. The best glue should be a clear amber in color, and should break like glass when it is dry.

Most of the glue in America is made near Chicago, close to the big slaughterhouses from which the bones and skin may be saved for glue. Many large meat-packing companies have their own glue factories.

gluten

Gluten is the part of wheat flour that will not dissolve when the wheat is washed in water. It is one of the most healthful parts of the wheat, and it is used to make a kind of bread called gluten bread, that is used in special diets for persons with certain kinds of sickness. Gluten is tough and rubbery, and has almost no taste.

glycerin

Glycerin is a sweet-tasting, white Glycerin is made from fats. The parts of fat are broken apart by the action of soda and brine in a process called fat-splitting. The glycerin in the fat is washed off with the watery part. If this fat-splitting is repeated several times it produces an extremely pure form of glycerin.

Some substitutes for glycerin have been discovered in the United States and Germany. The German synthetic glycerin is made from fermented beet sugar. But millions of pounds of crude glycerin are produced every year in the United States. Some of this is used in the anti-freeze preparations that keep automobile radiators from freezing in the winter. It is also eaten, for glycerin is used in canning meat.

G-Man, short for government man, a member of the Federal Bureau of Investigation. See the article on FEDERAL BUREAU OF INVESTIGATION.

gnat

A gnat is a small, two-winged fly. It looks like a very small mosquito, and some kinds have a sharp bite. The buffalo gnat that attacks cattle feeds on blood as does the mosquito or the gadfly. While mosquitoes normally come out at night, the gnat flies in the daytime. The eggs of most kinds of gnat are laid in the water, and the maggots, or worms (also called *larvae*), that come from the eggs feed there without destroying fruit or other crops. However, there are gall gnats and fungus gnats that do harm plants by laying their eggs on them. In Florida human beings suffer from a disease called "sore-eye" that is carried by gnats. In England mosquitoes are sometimes also called gnats.

gneiss

Gneiss is a rock that is many millions of years old. It is usually made up of layers of quartz, feldspar, and mica, although it may contain other minerals such as hornblende or garnet. Its color depends upon the minerals found in it. The layers are not always straight and can vary in width. Gneiss is called a metamorphic, or transformed, rock because it was made from granite or from other rocks that melted and joined together again in a different form. It is a very hard rock, and for this reason it is often used for buildings and paving blocks.

gnome

A gnome is an imaginary spirit that is told about in certain fairy tales. Gnomes are supposed to live underground and watch over hidden treasures. They are usually pictured as ugly little men with pointed beards. They are gray all over. They wear long, pointed caps. You can read more about them in the article FAIRY AND FAIRY TALES.

Gnostics

The Gnostics were people who belonged to certain sects, or small religious groups, that developed about 1,800 years ago. The religious ideas of the Gnostics were called Gnosticism. These ideas came from many different places. The Gnostics adopted many Christian ideas, as well as ideas from the religions of Greece, Persia, and Babylonia.

Gnosticism taught that there are two different worlds. One is the world of goodness and light, and this is the world of God. The other is the world of evil and darkness, and this is the world that we see around us. This evil world was not made by God, but by an evil power. The Gnostics said that special knowledge was needed to overcome this power.

The Gnostics thought that only they had the knowledge that was needed to go to heaven. The Gnostics said that they had a special secret knowledge that had been given to them by Jesus and his disciples. Only Gnostics were allowed to learn this. There were many ceremonies and rites for Gnostics. They had to learn certain secret words and formulas, which they said would help them get into heaven. The Christian Church condemned Gnosticism as a heresy, or false belief, and Gnosticism died out.

gnu

A gnu is a kind of antelope. It is native to South Africa. It is as large as a medium-sized horse and has a stiff mane that stands up at the back of its neck. It has a tuft of hair on its forehead and a beard under its chin. The gnu's legs are slender. Its horns are thick at the base and curve down around the eyes before bending up. The gnu may weigh as much as five hundred pounds. Its meat is good to eat. Gnus are still found in great numbers north of the Zambesi River in Africa, but in other parts of the continent they are becoming very scarce.

goat

The goat is a graceful, sure-footed animal that lives in the mountains and rocky places in many parts of Europe, Asia, and North Africa. The goat looks very much like a sheep, and from a distance it is difficult to tell these two animals apart. The goat has a thick coat of hair that may be black, brown, or yellow, and some goats are pure white. The goat has a short tail and a beard under its chin. It has handsome, hollow horns that are flat, and twist backwards at the tips. The goat's hoofs are cloven (divided into two parts), and it can run swiftly up and down steep crags, without slipping. There are many different kinds of goats, and some of them have strange names, such as ibex, and markhor, the largest of the wild goats, that lives high up in the Himalaya Mountains of India. People have believed that goats eat everything, even tin cans, but this is not true. Goats eat grass and leaves and the bark of trees.

DOMESTIC GOATS

People have raised goats since early times. The farmers who lived in Persia about three thousand years before Jesus knew how useful goats were, and some of these people were goat farmers. Now farmers in the United States, Canada, and many parts of the world raise goats. Certain kinds of goats are raised for their milk. Goat's milk is very nourishing, and it is especially healthful for children and people who are sick, because it is easy to digest. Very good cheese is made from goat's milk, and some people eat goat meat. The skin of the goat is made into leather that is called morocco. People in factories make fine gloves and handbags and shoes of morocco leather. One of the most valuable things about the goat is its wool, which is used to make cloth. The Angora goat and the Cashmere goat have especially fine, silky hair. Farmers comb this hair from the animal's coat, and people in factories spin it into soft cashmere sweaters and scarves and other articles of clothing that are prized by people everywhere. The hair of the Angora goat is called mohair.

People in many parts of the world have had stories and legends about goats. Many people who lived on farms kept goats because they believed that a goat could find certain plants that would cure a person who was sick. People also believed that the "billy goat" (the male goat) would bring good luck, and that the female, or "nanny goat," had a magic power that could drive witches and other evil spirits away. Goats are very intelligent and playful animals, and some people keep them for pets.

goatsucker

The goatsuckers are a family of more than seventy different kinds of birds that live in many parts of Europe and the United States. These birds got their strange name because the ancient Greeks believed that they sucked the milk of goats. This is not true, but the goatsuckers have an unusual way of catching their food that explains why these early people got this wrong idea. The goatsucker has a very large mouth, and bristles stick out from the sides of this opening. The goatsucker flies with its mouth open and catches moths and other insects in the bristles.

The goatsucker sometimes searches for insects close to the ground, where goats and cattle graze. The goatsucker has brown and white and black feathers that blend with the leaves and trees, so its enemies cannot see it. The goatsucker is about ten inches long. It has a strange habit of resting lengthwise on the branch of a tree, so that it looks as if it were lying down. It does not build a regular nest. The female bird lays two eggs in a hollowed-out place under a bush. The goatsucker is sometimes called the *nightjar,* because it has a jarring call, and also because it rests during the day and flies at night.

Gobelin

The Gobelin Manufactory in Paris, France, is a factory for the making of tapestries. A tapestry is a cloth that is woven of yarns of different colors into pictures or designs. The Gobelin tapestries are famous for the beauty of the weaving. Many great paintings have been reproduced in tapestries. One of these paintings is *The Assumption,* by the Italian artist Titian.

Hundreds of years ago, a family named Gobelin started a dye business in what is now the Manufactory. In the 16th century the family began making tapestries as well as dyes. Some members of the family bought titles from the

Metrop. Mus. of Art.

Many Gobelin tapestries have historical scenes. Here, the king of France, Henry IV, greets his friend, the Duke of Sully.

king, or served in the government of France. In 1662 the business was purchased by King Louis XIV, and the firm is still controlled by the French government.

Gobi

The Gobi is a vast desert on a plateau in the heart of central Asia. The Gobi covers about 300,000 square miles, which is twice the size of the state of Montana. The waterless part of the desert covers only one-quarter of the whole area, but little grows but grass and patches of scrub anywhere in the Gobi. Most of the people who live in the Gobi are nomads, or wanderers, who move their herds of livestock about the few grassy areas. During rainy seasons when some agriculture is possible, Chinese farmers move into the eastern, more humid parts. The only important towns are located on the edge of the desert.

During World War II, supply routes between the Soviet Union and China crossed through the Gobi desert. Marco Polo, the Italian explorer, crossed in the 13th century.

Some of the earliest men lived in the Gobi desert, perhaps before there were any men in Europe or the western parts of Asia. Archaeologists, scientists who study how the earliest men lived, have made some of their most important discoveries in the Gobi desert.

goblin, an imaginary spirit that plays tricks on men: see the article FAIRY AND FAIRY TALES.

God

God is the name used for the Supreme Being who made the world. He is worshiped not only in the Christian religion but also in the Jewish and Mohammedan (Moslem) religions.

There is a difference between God, spelled with a capital letter, and the many gods and goddesses that appear in the

mythology or religion of ancient or primitive peoples. Some of these peoples worshiped idols (statues) and even animals, thinking that they held the spirits of superhuman beings (beings that had powers greater than those of men). Where science and civilization have developed, the worship of idols and other gods and goddesses has always ended, but the belief in one supreme God has gone on.

Belief in one God is called *monotheism;* belief in many gods is called *polytheism.* Most of the early religions were polytheistic. Men were trying to understand the world around them. They saw many things more powerful than themselves. The sun brought heat and life. Terrible storms, accompanied by thunder, lightning, and great winds, destroyed many things. The mysterious forces of nature made crops grow from the soil. They looked at these things and were filled with wonder. They saw that some of these forces helped men to live and were therefore kind, but that others could destroy.

To help themselves understand these things, men imagined the forces of nature as gods. The ancient Greeks called their god of the sun Helios. Helios had great and shining palaces in the east and west (where the sun rises and sets). He had horses and chariots in which he was carried on his daily journey across the sky. Since there were many forces of nature, people had to imagine many gods. Then they had to imagine a chief, or king, of the gods. The Greeks called their chief god Zeus; the Romans called him Jupiter.

Some of the ancient people worshiped only one god. This one god was the source of all power, and he filled the universe.

The one God that most people in the Western World worship today is different from any god of ancient monotheism. The first people to accept this God were the Hebrew writers of the Old Testament. He is the only true God. He is all-good, and all-just, and all-powerful. He is the God of all men, not the god of one country. Most of all, He is invisible.

THE NAME OF GOD

In the Old Testament God is sometimes referred to by a Hebrew word of that meaning, but more often is given a personal name. It was written with four consonants: YHWH (or JHVH). The Jews came to consider the name too holy to be spoken aloud and so its pronunciation was virtually forgotten. Wherever the name occurred the Jews substituted the word *Adonai,* meaning "Lord," and so the English Bible has LORD. In the book of Exodus, in the Authorized Version of the Bible, the name is given in the pronunciation *Jehovah,* but this is not the way the Hebrews pronounce it. There is some doubt about the original pronunciation, and it seems to have varied in different places and times. A tradition that it was pronounced *Yahweh* (Jahveh) has become widely accepted. But it appears as *Yahu* or *Yaho* in some names, and can be further shortened to *Yah,* as in *Hallelujah* (Praise ye the Lord). In the English Bible *Iah* has often been substituted for *Yahu,* as in the prophet Jeremiah's name, which appears in Hebrew as *Yirmeyahu.*

IDEAS OF GOD

By some, God has been thought of as being totally present in the world. This idea of God is called *immanence,* or an immanent conception of God. Others have thought of God as being outside the world. This is called *transcendence,* or a transcendent conception of God. The immanent view leads to what is called *pantheism,* identifying God with the world, and the transcendent view leads to what is called *deism,* making Him dwell apart from the world, taking little interest in it since creating it. The compromise is that God is both immanent and transcendent. This is called *theism* and is the general view of the Christian church.

Since men can speak about God only in human words, they have most often described Him as having human qualities, yet the whole idea of God makes it clear that His real nature may be beyond human understanding. Biblical language sometimes describes God as baring "His mighty arm" when it wants to show His power or strength, or it speaks of His eyes, hand, or mouth, to show His other qualities in human terms. This way of speaking about God is called *anthropomorphic,* meaning "in the likeness of man." An instance such as the one quoted is an *anthropomorphism.*

PROOFS OF GOD

Many great thinkers have tried to prove that God exists. Usually, Christians, Moslems, or Jews simply accept God as revealed in the holy writings of their religions. This is *belief by revelation.* Others have sought to show that even if there were no revelation, or if a man did not believe in revelation, it would be just as correct to believe in God as it is to believe that one and one make two.

Here are some of the proofs they give for God's existence: They say that there must be a reason for anything that is. In the world around us we see this sufficient reason in the cause of a thing. For example, the cause of a child is his parents and that is why the child exists. But they say, there must be a First Cause. The First Cause would not be caused by something else. It would be eternal—something that always existed and always will. This is called the argument from the First Cause.

Other arguments say that such things as the wonderful order of the stars show us that there must be an infinite Creator whose mind made this design. Or that because men think that there is a God, He must exist. Or that because nothing in the world is necessary (that is, anything in the world could not exist), there must be a necessary being or God outside the world.

But since the time of the German philosopher Kant (late 18th century) these "proofs" have been abandoned. God cannot be "proved," for all our thinking is based on comparison and He is unlike anything. If we could "prove" Him, furthermore, we would have circumscribed Him, and He cannot be circumscribed. The reality of God is experienced by people and after they have experienced it they know it exists.

Read also the articles on BUDDHISM, CHRISTIANITY, JUDAISM, and ISLAM.

Godey, Louis Antoine

Louis Antoine Godey founded the first woman's magazine in the United States. That was about a hundred years ago. The magazine was called *Godey's Lady's Book.* It contained stories and articles on subjects of interest to women, such as fashion, homemaking, and the care of children. It had many illustrations, including pictures of the latest styles in women's clothing. Louis Godey was born in New York in 1804. He became interested in newspaper work and publishing when he was still a young man. He moved to Philadelphia and began working in a newspaper office. In 1830, he started to publish *Godey's Lady's Book.* He also published several other magazines, among them one for children. He died in Philadelphia in 1878.

Godiva

Lady Godiva was the wife of an English lord in the city of Coventry, about nine hundred years ago. Her husband's name was Leofric, and he forced his people to pay such high taxes that Lady Godiva felt sorry for them. She begged her husband to reduce the taxes, and he sarcastically said he would if she would ride naked through the streets. He thought he was safe in making this promise, but Lady Godiva took him up on it. She rode through the streets of the town on a white horse, and her long flowing hair was her only clothing. All the people of the town closed their shutters as she went by, out of respect for a great lady. All, that is, except a tailor named Tom who peeped through his window and was struck blind. To this day we call someone who spies on others a "Peeping Tom."

Godwin-Austen

Mount Godwin-Austen is the name of the second-highest peak in the world. It is also called K-2. It is in the Karakorum range of the Himalayan Mountains in the northern part of Kashmir, India.

After many years in which mountain climbers had tried to reach the top of this snow-covered mountain that rises 28,250 feet above sea level, in 1954 an Italian expedition under the leadership of Professor Ardito Desio at last succeeded. Clouds usually hide the peak, and vast glaciers make climbing very dangerous.

Goebbels, Joseph

Joseph Paul Goebbels was one of the most important men in the German government during the years from 1933 to 1945, when Germany was ruled by the Nazi Party. He was the Minister of Propaganda and Public Enlightenment, and he was considered one of the greatest experts who ever lived in making people believe what he wanted them to believe. Unfortunately, what he wanted them to believe usually was not true.

Goebbels was a short, weak man who walked with a limp. He was one of the earliest followers of Adolf Hitler, the Nazi leader. As Minister of Propaganda he controlled everything that was said in newspapers, on the radio, in

program of propaganda started against the Jewish people, whom he wanted to kill or drive out of Germany. When the Germans were defeated by the Allies in 1945, Goebbels killed himself and his family.

goeduck

The goeduck is one of the largest clams in the world, and some people say that it is also the ugliest. Goeducks are found along the western coast of the United States. The shell of the goeduck is more than eight inches across, and there is a long fleshy part that sticks out between the shells. This part of the goeduck looks like a long neck, but it is called the *foot*. The foot helps the goeduck clam to breathe when it lies buried in the sand, under the water of the ocean. The goeduck eats tiny living things that it finds in the sea.

Goeduck is an Indian name that means "dip deep." The goeduck can dig two or three feet into the sand. Many people like to cook goeducks and eat them.

Goering, Hermann

Hermann Goering was the second most powerful man in the German government during the years from 1933 to 1945, when Germany was ruled by the Nazi Party. He was the only one of the high-ranking Nazis to have been an officer in World War I, which gave him a very high social position. During World War I he was one of Germany's most famous flying aces. When Hitler started the Nazi Party in 1920, Goering became one of his followers. When the Nazis came to power in 1933, Goering was put in charge of the air force, which he built into the most powerful in the world. He was also in charge of heavy manufacturing, and one of the biggest new steel factories that Germany built was called the Hermann Goering Iron Works.

Goering was a very vain man who liked to wear gaudy uniforms. He was also a very cruel man who liked to kill animals and to see blood. He sent tens of thousands of people to death because he thought they stood in the way of his ambition, which was very great. Goering made himself very rich by using his official position, but when Germany lost the war all his wealth was taken away from him. Goering was arrested, and tried and sentenced to death as a war criminal by an International Military Court. Several hours before he was to be hanged, he killed himself with poison. It is still a mystery where he got the poison.

Goethals, George W.

George W. Goethals was the American engineer who was in charge of the construction of the Panama Canal. The Panama Canal permits ships to cross a narrow part of Central America and get from the Atlantic Ocean to the Pacific. When the

United States began to build the canal in 1907, President Theodore Roosevelt put Goethals in charge. It was considered one of the most difficult engineering feats of history, but Goethals completed it in 1914, which was even earlier than had been hoped. After that Goethals was made governor of the Canal Zone, the land around the canal, from 1914 to 1916. Goethals was born in Brooklyn, New York, in 1858, and died in 1928.

Goethe, Johann Wolfgang von

Johann Wolfgang von Goethe may have been the greatest German writer. He lived about two hundred years ago. Goethe wrote stories, plays and poems, but he is best remembered as a poet. His best-known work of poetry is *Faust*, a story about a man who sold his soul to the devil. His best-known novel is *Wilhelm Meister*, in which he gives many of his ideas about life.

Goethe was born in 1749. When he was only 25 he wrote his first novel, *The Sorrows of Young Werther*, which made him famous overnight. The next year he was invited to visit the court of the Duke of Weimar, and he spent the rest of his life there. He became an official in the Duke's court, and he was also the court poet.

During his lifetime Goethe was considered one of the world's greatest writers, and even today his works have universal appeal. He died in 1832.

Gog and Magog

Gog was prince of the land of Magog, told about in the Bible. The Book of Ezekiel says that someday a fierce people will sweep down from the land of Magog in the north. A great army, led by Gog, will attack the land of Israel. But God will protect Israel, and destroy the invaders. The Book of Revelation in the Bible uses the names Gog and Magog to mean all the evil people of the earth, who will gather together to destroy the good people, but will themselves be destroyed at the Day of Judgment.

Gog and Magog are also characters in an old British legend. The story tells about a race of great giants. All of them were killed except for two, Gog and Magog. These two were captured, and were forced to be guards at the royal palace. When they died, statues of them were made to stand in their place. The huge wooden statues of Gog and Magog, fourteen feet high, stood for a long time in the Guildhall in London, England.

Gogh, Vincent van

Vincent van Gogh was a great Dutch painter who lived a very short life and yet is one of the most famous painters who ever lived. He was only 37 when he died. Van Gogh used a lot of oil paint on his canvases, and his pictures look as though the paint had been put on with a knife instead of with a brush. He liked to paint pictures of everyday things. Three of his most famous pictures are *Sunflowers in a Vase*, which is

full of lovely shades of yellow and brown; *The Artist's Room*, a painting of his bedroom that looks like patchwork, it has so many squares of color in it; and *Wheat Fields*, which makes you feel as though you were out in a wheat field in the strong sunshine.

Sunflowers is a famous painting by Vincent van Gogh, noted for its beautiful color and masterful flower arrangement.

Van Gogh was born in the Netherlands in 1853. He was a very religious man and became a preacher to coal miners in Belgium. He did not start to paint seriously until he was about 30 years old. He taught himself almost everything he knew about painting. His brother Theo worked in an art gallery in Paris and sent Vincent to southern France to paint. Almost all of his most famous paintings were painted during the last three years of his life.

Van Gogh became mentally ill when he was only 35. In 1890 he was sure he would never be well again, and he killed himself. During his lifetime he could sell only a few of his pictures, but today one of them would cost you many thousands of dollars.

Gogol, Nikolai

Nikolai Gogol was a great Russian writer of short stories, novels, and plays. He was born in 1809. Gogol was one of the first Russians to write stories of real people in real situations. His ancestors were Cossacks, the colorful peasant-soldiers of Russia, and his first successful stories were romantic tales of these people. Gogol is chiefly remembered for his play, *The Inspector General*, which poked fun at stuffy government officials. Gogol was worried about having this play produced for fear it would make Russian officials angry with him, but the emperor himself ordered it performed, and it has been popular ever since. It has been translated into English and several other languages. One of Gogol's greatest novels is *Dead Souls*, which tells about the unhappy lives of the serfs of Russia in olden times. Gogol

died in 1852.

goiter

Goiter is a disease that occurs when the thyroid gland is not working properly. The thyroid gland is in the front of the neck. It produces a chemical called *thyroxin*, which the body needs.

KINDS OF GOITER

Simple goiter is a swelling of the thyroid gland. This happens when the body does not get enough iodine. The thyroid gland needs iodine to make thyroxin. As a medicine iodine is a poison, but a little of it in your drinking water or food is important. In places near the sea, there is usually enough iodine in the water. In other places people usually get their iodine by using iodized salt.

Exophtalmic goiter (goiter with bulging eyes) occurs if the thyroid gland makes too much thyroxin. The patient becomes very nervous and thin, and does everything so fast that he wears himself out. This disease can be corrected by removing part of the thyroid gland so that less thyroxin is produced. There are also new drugs that help this disease. See also the articles on THYROID and GLAND.

Gold

Gold is one of the earth's most precious metals. It is an element, one of 103 basic substances of which everything in the world is composed. Gold is a soft metal, yellow in color. It is valuable partly for its beauty; partly because it will not rust, and most acids and other substances do not hurt it, so that it lasts a long time; and partly because it has many practical uses for which no other metal is quite as good. Gold is so valuable that for thousands of years it has been the one metal that is used everywhere and accepted everywhere as money.

Gold is usually found in gold ore, either in soil or rocks. In a few places it can simply be picked up off the ground or taken out of the ground in solid chunks called *nuggets*. When gold has been discovered, it is *assayed* to find out how much gold there is in the ore. There is a separate article on ASSAYING.

HOW GOLD IS MINED

There are two principal ways of mining gold. One is by *placer mining*, or washing it from the sand and gravel of streams. Wind and water and air have worn the gold from the rock where it once lay and carried it into the streams. There it sinks to the bottom because it is twenty times as heavy as the water. This gold may be in tiny grains smaller than grains of sand. This is called *gold dust*. Sometimes the gold is in pieces as large as good-sized pebbles. These are called nuggets. The largest gold nugget ever found weighed 183 pounds.

Placer mining used to be done by hand with a simple iron pan. The prospector, the man searching for gold, would scoop up a pan of pebbles from the bottom of the stream and fill the pan with water. Then he would shake the pan and toss out the water, with some of the pebbles. He would repeat this with more and more water until he had tossed out

all the pebbles and only the gold remained. The gold had sunk to the bottom because it was heavier than the water and the pebbles.

Today powerful machinery does the work of placer mining. A hose washes great beds of gravel into a trough, and then into large baskets, which are shaken by motors to toss out the pebbles and the water.

The second method of gold mining is done just the way iron and coal are mined. That is, gold is dug out of the earth. This is called *lode mining,* because the gold is taken from great beds and veins of ore, called *lodes,* beneath the ground. Gold ore must be processed to separate the metal from the rock. This is called refining, and it is done in large plants with complicated vats and machines.

People who work in gold refineries and in places where gold is used in manufacturing usually wear special uniforms that are kept and washed in the plant. This is because a large quantity of gold dust will collect during the day's work in the material of the workers' clothing. The gold dust is recovered by washing.

HOW GOLD IS RATED

Gold is weighed in *carats*. Pure gold, with no other metal in it, is said to be 24-carat gold. If it has 22 parts of gold and 2 parts of some other metal, such as silver, it is called 22-carat gold. The number of parts of gold out of each 24 parts determines the carat count of the metal. The symbol for carat is *k*, so if you see 10*k* on a piece of jewelry it is made of 10 parts of gold and 14 parts of another metal. Because gold is so soft, it is seldom used in its pure form.

WHERE GOLD IS FOUND

The principal sources of gold today are Canada, the southern part of Africa, and Soviet Russia's Ural Mountains and Siberia. Some very rich gold mines were found in the United States, in the far western states such as California and Nevada, and in Alaska and the Yukon Territory of Canada. When gold was found in these places it caused tremendous gold rushes. Thousands of people flocked to the gold fields and soon took most of the gold out of the ground. (There is a separate article on GOLD RUSH.) Nowadays gold mining is very scientific. It is done by elaborate machinery that belongs to big corporations and millions of dollars are invested in mining operations. There are still many prospectors, however, who search for gold in the United States and Canada where some gold ore is known to exist.

USES OF GOLD

Gold is one of the most important metals in the making of jewelry. It is also used in dental work because it makes the best possible fillings for teeth, but it is so expensive that usually other materials are used for filling cavities.

Gold can be made into sheets so thin that a pile of them an inch high would contain more than two hundred thousand separate sheets. These sheets are called *gold leaf* and are used for gilding domes and ceilings of churches and palaces, and for the gold lettering on office and store

windows. Another method of gilding is by electroplating, which is putting a layer of gold over another metal. Long ago, gold plating was done by dipping an object into melted gold. In the modern method, a piece of pure gold is placed in an acid solution, along with the object to be plated. Then an electric current is passed through the solution, and this causes a very thin layer of gold to detach itself from the piece of pure gold and settle all over the surface of the other object in the solution.

GOLD AS MONEY

For thousands of years gold was made into coins. Today most countries do not have gold coins because they do not have enough gold.

In the early days of the West in the United States, gold dust was used as money. It was weighed at the time it was spent, to find out how much it was worth.

In foreign trade, settlement still is finally made in gold. When one country owes another country a large amount of money at the end of a certain period, it settles the debt by sending gold. The United States has almost nine-tenths of the world's reserve of gold used for money. This amounts to about twenty billion dollars. It is stored in an underground vault at Fort Knox, Kentucky. It is in the form of gold bars, called *bullion*. See also the article on MONEY.

After being mined deep under the ground, gold is refined and shipped at great cost. Most of it is then returned to the bowels of the earth in deep vaults like those at **Fort Knox.** Any lucky prospector allowed to stake out a **claim** here could "mine" many billions of dollars in gold.

Ewing Galloway

Gold Coast

The Gold Coast is the southern section of the country of Ghana, in West Africa. Until Ghana became an independent country, in 1957, the name Gold Coast was applied to the entire British territory (including Ashanti and the Northern Territories) that now makes up most of Ghana. The Gold Coast section is on the Gulf of Guinea, a large section of the Atlantic Ocean, and includes the city of Accra, capital of Ghana. Gold and also diamonds, and the metal manganese, are principal products of the Gold Coast.

Golden Age

The Golden Age of a country is a period that is considered the best period in its history, especially in literature and other arts. The ancient Greeks, 2,500 years ago, spoke of an imaginary Golden Age that had happened before, but today the period about four hundred years before the birth of Jesus is considered the Golden Age of Greece. The Golden Age of Rome was about 2,000 to 1,900 years ago. During part of this period Jesus was on earth. The Elizabethan Age in England, the period about four hundred years ago when Elizabeth I was queen, is sometimes called England's Golden Age because Shakespeare and other great writers were living and writing then.

golden calf

The golden calf was an imaginary god that some of the Jewish people set up to worship, as told in the Book of Exodus in the Bible. This book tells how Moses had just led the Jews out of Egypt, where they had been slaves, and then had gone up to Mount Sinai, where God gave him the Ten Commandments and other laws. While he was gone the people became impatient. They melted all their gold jewelry and made a small statue of a calf, which they worshiped. This broke one of the Commandments God had given to Moses, and God punished the high priest Aaron, who was Moses' brother, for permitting the people to worship the idol. When Moses found out what the people had done, he was so angry that he broke the tables, or pieces of stone on which the Commandments were engraved. He ground the golden calf to dust and mixed it with water, which he made the people drink as punishment.

Golden Fleece

In the stories the ancient Greeks told more than two thousand years ago, there was an imaginary ram, or male sheep, whose fleece or hair was made of gold. This golden ram was first heard of when it carried away two Greek children who were the grandchildren of the god Aeolus. For this Aeolus punished the ram by killing it, but its golden fleece was saved and guarded by a dragon. Later Jason and his followers, called the Argonauts, stole the Golden Fleece. You can read about this in the article on JASON.

Golden Gate

The Golden Gate is a narrow body of water that leads from the Pacific Ocean into San Francisco Bay in California. It is five miles long and one to two miles wide. One of the longest suspension bridges in the world crosses the Golden Gate. It was completed in 1937. It has two towers eight hundred feet high, from which hang cables more than three feet thick. The span of the Golden Gate bridge, between the towers, is 4,200 feet long. The bridge is crossed by a six-lane roadway. At night the bridge is brilliantly lighted.

goldenrod

The goldenrod is a yellow flower that grows in many parts of North

The Golden Gate Bridge, one of the world's longest bridges, joins the redwood country to San Francisco. Ships heading toward the Pacific pass beneath it twenty-four hours a day.

America. It is a very strong and hardy plant and can grow in dry soil, so that it brightens roadsides and many barren places where other flowers cannot grow. During the autumn months fields covered with goldenrod look like yellow carpets.

The individual flower of the goldenrod forms a crown of yellow on a green stem that grows two to eight feet high. Green leaves with sharp edges protect the bottom of the stem.

Some persons believe that the pollen of goldenrod causes hay fever, but this is not true. Goldenrod pollen is heavy and sticky, and it is not carried about by air currents. What really happens is that ragweed, the pollen of which does cause hay fever, blooms at the same time as goldenrod, and thus ragweed pollen is dusted over goldenrod, asters, and other fall-blooming plants.

Golden Rule

The Golden Rule was given by Jesus in his famous Sermon on the Mount. You can find the Golden Rule in the seventh chapter of the Book of Matthew in the New Testament. Jesus told the people, "therefore all things whatsoever ye would that men should do to you, do ye even so to them." This is usually simplified in the words "Do unto others as you would have others do unto you." Men in many other religions have been credited with giving this same rule long before Jesus did, but this is not so. The Chinese teacher Confucius, the rabbi Hillel and many others said, "Do not do unto others what you do not want them to do unto you." Jesus was the only one who made the Golden Rule teach people to do kind and pleasant things, and not merely to avoid doing unkind and unpleasant things.

goldfinch

The goldfinch is a bird that looks somewhat like a canary and is about the same size. It is yellow and has touches of black on its wing tips, the crown of its head, and the tip of its tail. The gold-

finch has a beautiful song. When it flies it streaks through the air very fast in a kind of undulating, or waving, flight, and it changes its course frequently.

There are different varieties of goldfinch in the Rocky Mountains and along the Pacific coast and in Mexico. Some goldfinches visit the northeastern United States in summer. The European goldfinch has a bright red throat and is often kept in cages so that people can enjoy its singing.

goldfish

Goldfish are the most popular fish that people keep as pets. Most of them are a golden color or have some gold mixed with such other colors as red. They can be kept in almost any receptacle that holds water and they live a long time if they are properly cared for. You can read more about the care of goldfish in the article on AQUARIUM.

Until a few hundred years ago, nearly all goldfish were a dull green color, with just a trace of gold. The Chinese and Japanese began to breed the brightest-colored of them and gradually they developed the beautiful colors that goldfish have today.

There are many kinds of goldfish in many different groups and colors. For instance, a very popular kind is a goldfish with a huge, sweeping tail, called the *fringetail* or *fantail*. A rare kind of goldfish is the white one. Others have been developed with veil tails, with double or triple fins, and with huge bulging eyes.

gold rush

A gold rush occurs when gold is discovered in an unsettled territory where nobody yet owns the land. Thousands of people get there as fast as they can to find gold and make themselves rich. All kinds of people are likely to join a gold rush. Often they include criminals and dishonest or unprincipled men, so that a gold rush is likely to be a time when there is no law and order. Since the ter-

ritory is unsettled, people live very rough lives, with few of the benefits of civilization. There is always a shortage of food and clothing and other materials, so these sell for very high prices. A single good meal is likely to cost a hundred dollars or so.

There have been many gold rushes in the United States. The most famous one was in California, when gold was discovered at Sutter's Mill in 1848. Most of the people got there in 1849, so they were called Forty-niners. There have been smaller gold rushes in other western states of the United States, including Colorado, Nevada, Idaho, Montana, and South Dakota.

The last big gold rush in North America was when gold was discovered in the Klondike area in the Yukon Territory of Canada. People on their way there found gold in Alaska too. This gold rush took place from 1898 to 1900. There was a gold rush in Australia in the 1850s, and in South Africa in the 1880s.

Goldsmith, Oliver

Oliver Goldsmith was a great writer who was born in Ireland about the year 1730. When he was only 19, he graduated from Trinity College in Dublin. Goldsmith studied medicine for three years but he gave up his studies to travel about Europe, where he sometimes earned money by playing the flute. He finally settled in London, England. Goldsmith's poems, novels and plays are usually about ordinary people and are written in simple, clear language. His most famous work is a long poem called "The Deserted Village," in which Goldsmith describes a lovely little town. His novel *The Vicar of Wakefield* has always been widely read. Goldsmith also wrote plays. *She Stoops to Conquer* is a comedy that is still performed in America. In this play, the heroine, who knows that the young man her parents wish her to marry is shy with well-bred ladies, pretends for a while she is a barmaid in order to see how he behaves normally. Goldsmith died in 1774 from a fever for which he had not taken the correct medicine. Goldsmith was very generous, so he always owed money and he died poor.

Gold Star Mothers

The Gold Star Mothers are an organization of American women who had one or more sons killed in the two World Wars or in Korea. The organization has about eighteen thousand members. It was founded in 1928 and has its headquarters in Washington, D.C. The name Gold Star Mothers comes from the custom of placing gold stars on service flags in honor of men who were killed in war.

Goldwater, Barry

Barry Morris Goldwater was the candidate of the Republican Party for the presidency of the United States in 1964 but lost the election to Lyndon B. Johnson. Goldwater stood for the conservative group in the U.S., being opposed to the participation of the Federal Government in many cases that affect individual citizens.

A. G. Spalding & Bros., Inc.

Irons, by number and name, from left to right: No. 1, driving iron; 2, midiron; 3, midmashie; 4, mashie iron; 5, mashie; 6, mashie niblick; 7, pitcher; 8, pitching niblick; and putter.

Goldwater was born in Phoenix, Arizona, in 1909, the grandson of a famous Arizona pioneer who founded the first store in that state. From the time he was a young man Barry Goldwater made himself known nationally as an outstanding businessman, writer, speaker, and public official; in 1952 he was elected to the U.S. Senate from Arizona and served there until he resigned to run for President.

golf

Golf is a game played by hitting a small, hard, rubber ball with a special kind of club called a golf club. The game is played on a *golf course*, or *links*, in which there are places where a cup, or hole, has been put in the ground. This cup is 4½ inches across and 6 inches deep. Each time a player hits the ball it is called a *stroke*. He tries to sink the ball in the hole with as few strokes as possible.

A golf club is a long, thin, stick made of steel or wood, with a knob or *head* at the bottom. The ball is hit with the flat side of the head, called the *face*. The face may be straight up-and-down or tilted at an angle with the ground. Clubs with straight faces are used to hit the ball long distances. Clubs with tilted faces are used to give the ball a *loft* (that is, to hit it high into the air). A special club with a metal head, called the *putter*, is used to make the ball roll along the ground.

A full set consists of fourteen different golf clubs. Clubs with wooden heads are called *woods*, and clubs with steel heads are called *irons*. Each club has a different shaft length and a different shaped head.

Each club has a number, such as "Number One Iron." Many years ago the clubs were called by different names, such as "brassie," "spoon," "niblick," and "mashie": now they are known by numbers.

THE GOLF COURSE

A golf course is a large plot of ground, specially planned and built usually with eighteen holes. Each hole is marked by a number on the flag of a long wooden stick called a *flagstick*. The hole is in a well-kept part of the course called the *putting green*. The grass on the green is cut very short. About 100 to 600 yards from the green is a mound called the *tee-*

ing ground. Between the teeing ground and the putting green is a section of mowed grass called a *fairway*. On both sides of the fairway are usually trees, rocks, and tall grass. This is called the *rough*. It is more difficult to hit a ball when it is in the rough. Between the fairway and the green, there are usually other places where it is difficult to hit the ball. These places are called hazards, and include bodies of water and pits of sand called *bunkers* or *traps*.

HITTING THE BALL

The way in which the ball is hit with the club is called a *stroke*, or *shot*. There are many different kinds. Some shots are for distance and are called drives. To drive a ball properly, one must hit it squarely with the face of the club. If the ball is not hit squarely, it will curve off to the right in a *slice* or off to the left in a *hook*. Sometimes the club will strike the ball near the top and send it only a short distance. This is called *topping the ball*.

There are other shots that are used to bring the ball nearer or sink it into the hole. A *chip shot* is used when the ball is just off the green. It is a short, low shot. A *pitch shot* is used to bring the ball on the green and near the hole. It is a high shot with some backspin on the ball to keep the ball from rolling too far from the hole. When the ball is on the green, a *putt* is used to roll the ball toward the hole.

PLAYING A GAME OF GOLF

In playing a game of golf, a player must start on the first tee and play each hole in order, from the first to the eighteenth. This is called a *round* of golf. After sinking the ball in the first hole, he moves on to the second tee. From there he tries to sink the ball in the second hole in as few strokes as possible.

At each tee, the player places a little wooden peg into the ground. This peg has a flat top and is also called a tee. The player then places the golf ball on the wooden tee and picks out the club he wants to use. Usually he will pick out the "Number One Wood," also called the *driver*, because that club is good for distance shots. He then gets ready to hit the

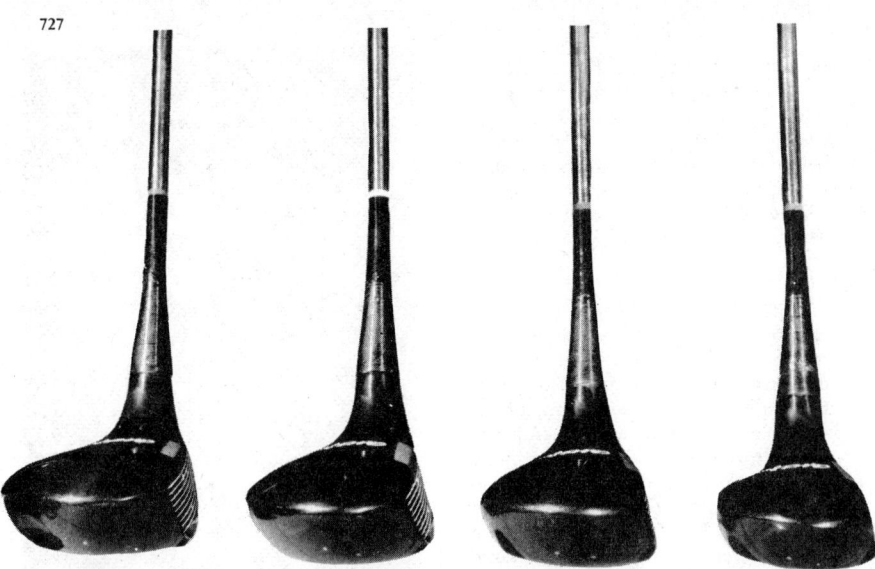

Golfing woods, left to right: driver, brassie, spoon, and cleek. Each wood has a different pitch to help the golfer control the distance and elevation of his shots.

ball, by facing it with the side of his body toward the direction in which he wants the ball to go. He keeps his eye on the ball at all times, and places the face of his club directly in back of the ball. He slowly draws the club back until it is behind his head. He then swings the club down toward the ball and hits it with full force.

If the ball lands on the fairway, the player will next choose one of the woods or irons that will help him hit the ball on to the green. If he lands in the rough or in one of the hazards, he must choose the iron that will help him get his ball back on the fairway or on the green. If his ball is in a sand bunker he might use a special iron called a sand wedge or blaster.

When the ball lands on the green, the putter is the next club the player uses. It has a short shaft and an almost straight face that is best for rolling the ball along the green and into the hole.

THE CADDIE

In most cases, the player will go around the course with a caddie. The caddie is a boy or man who carries the clubs for the player. The caddie often helps the player to choose the right club. The caddie works for the golf course and is assigned to the player by the caddie master. The caddie gets paid for each round he caddies. Many schoolboys earn money during the summer and on week-ends by caddying.

Each golf course has what is called *par* for the course. This is the score one of the best players is supposed to make when he is playing as well as he should. Each hole has a par. A hole that is up to 250 yards from the tee is par 3 (three strokes to get in the hole). A hole between 251 and 445 yards is a par 4. A hole between 446 and 600 yards is a par 5. Over 600 yards, the par is 6.

A *birdie* is a score of one less than par on a hole. An *eagle* is two less than par. A *hole-in-one* is a score of one stroke for a hole. To score a hole-in-one, a player must hit the ball from the tee into the hole. A *bogey* is the score a good average player should make on each hole. Usually it is one stroke above par.

GAMES AND TOURNAMENTS

Golf is usually played by two, three or four players, who go around the course together. There are two ways of scoring, called *medal* or *stroke* play and *match* play. In medal play, the player competes against everyone else on the course and the one with the lowest score for the course wins. In match play the player competes against only another playing against him. Each hole is scored separately. The player who makes the lowest score for the hole wins the hole. The player who wins the most holes wins the round.

In the United States, the United States Golf Association (USGA) governs the playing of golf. It distinguishes between amateur golfers, who cannot accept money as prizes or for teaching others to play golf, and professional golfers, who play for money prizes, teach golf, and sell golf equipment. There are separate tournaments for amateurs and for professionals, and there are open tournaments in which both may play.

Every year there are many big tournaments for professionals and for amateurs. The Professional Golfers Association (PGA) has a yearly tournament in which only professionals may play. The Walker Cup match is played between teams of amateurs representing the United States and Great Britain. The Ryder Cup match is held between the best professional golfers of the United States and Great Britain.

Golf courses are found in most country clubs where members who have paid their dues can play. At most country clubs, there is a professional golfer, or "pro," who teaches golf. There are also public courses in most large cities where you can play for a small fee.

HOW GOLF STARTED

Golf was played at least five hundred years ago in Scotland. Scottish shepherds played it by hitting a leather ball, stuffed with feathers, with the sticks they carried to herd sheep. So many people played the game in Scotland that the government stopped it. The government wanted them to practice shooting their bows and arrows instead of playing golf. With the bow and arrow they could defend their country.

This did not stop the game from being played, and by the year 1600 even the kings were playing it. This gave golf the name of a "royal and ancient game." The most famous golf club is the Royal and Ancient Golf Club of St. Andrews in Scotland. It was begun in 1754. It is the governing body of golf in the British Commonwealth.

In 1895, the first national championships were held in the United States. A few years earlier, in 1888, a group of men began the St. Andrews Golf Club in Yonkers, in the state of New York. Players were brought from England and Scotland to teach golf.

There are about four million people in the United States who play at least ten rounds of golf a year. About six hundred thousand of these people belong to golf clubs. There are more than five thousand golf courses in the United States. Men and women of all ages play golf.

Golgotha

When Jesus was to be crucified, as told in the New Testament, he was taken to a place outside the walls of the city of Jerusalem. The Hebrew name of this place was Golgotha. The Latin name was Calvary.

The word Golgotha means "place of the skull." We do not know why the place had this name, but there are many different ideas about it. There may have been a little hill there that was shaped something like a skull; or it may have been the place where criminals were executed or where there was a cemetery, and so there would be many skulls there.

Goliath

Goliath was a great and powerful giant told about in the Bible. Goliath was one of the Philistines, a people who were at war with the people of Israel. Goliath was the champion of the Philistines. and he challenged the people of Israel to send out a champion to fight alone with him. Whoever won the battle would win victory for his side. Goliath was a fearful warrior, nine feet tall, and King Saul of Israel and all his men were very much afraid. Just then the boy David happened to come to the battlefield bringing food to his brothers who were in the army. When he heard Goliath's challenge, he offered to go out and fight him, to show everyone that God would help the people of Israel. David refused to wear armor, or to carry a sword. He took only his slingshot and some smooth stones. The first stone he aimed hit Goliath in the forehead. The great giant fell down dead, and David cut off Goliath's head with Goliath's own sword.

Gomorrah, a city told about in the Bible: see the article on SODOM AND GOMORRAH.

Gompers, Samuel

Samuel Gompers was a great leader in American labor organizations. He was  born in 1850, in England. When he was still a boy his family settled in the United States. Gompers went to work in a cigar factory and he soon became a leader in the Cigarmakers' Union. From then on he de-

voted his life to trying to improve working conditions.

In 1886, some labor unions joined together to form a new organization of unions called the American Federation of Labor. There are separate articles about the AMERICAN FEDERATION OF LABOR and LABOR AND LABOR UNIONS. Samuel Gompers was one of the leaders in the formation of the American Federation of Labor. He was elected its first president and re-elected every year except one until he died. When World War I began Gompers helped to unite the American working people, and urged them to support the war. After the war, he helped to settle labor problems all over the world. Samuel Gompers died in 1924. Under his leadership the American Federation of Labor had grown and prospered, and American working men had been able to win better working conditions.

Goncourt, Prix de

The Prix de Goncourt is a prize that is awarded each year by the Goncourt Academy for a great work of French fiction. The academy was founded in 1900 under the will of Edmond de Goncourt. Edmond de Goncourt and his brother Jules were famous French novelists who lived and wrote together during the 19th century.

gondola

A gondola is a kind of boat. The best-known type of gondola is used in the city of Venice, in Italy. Venice has canals instead of streets, and the gondolas carry passengers from one place to another just as taxicabs do in other cities. Each gondola is pushed through the water by a man called a gondolier, with a long pole. Many of the gondoliers sing as they work.

A certain type of flat-bottomed river boat is called a gondola, and so is a flat-bottomed railroad car. The car that hangs from a dirigible airship is also called a gondola.

gong

A gong is a round metal instrument that is made of bronze, or a mixture of copper and tin. A gong looks like a shallow dish. When you strike it with a drumstick or a small, padded hammer, it makes a loud, ringing sound. The Chinese and other people of Asia have used gongs for thousands of years. They use them the way we use bells, and many temples of the East use gongs to call the people together. Oriental people like the sound of the gong in their music, and some English and French composers have written music that includes a gong. The gong makes such a clear sound that it can be heard a long way off, and people sometimes use gongs to call others to dinner or to a meeting.

Gonzaga

Gonzaga is the name of an Italian family that became famous about seven hundred years ago. It was a very powerful and rich family. For about four hundred years the family ruled Mantua, a large section of north Italy. Giovanni Francesco Gonzaga was the first person in the family to become rich. He added much land to

that already belonging to the family. His grandson, Francesco Gonzaga, was a great soldier who married Isabella d'Este, a very beautiful and good woman. Together they helped many writers and artists. The family lost its power in 1708 after Ferdinand Charles Gonzaga had lost many wars. The land was taken over by Austria.

Good Neighbor Policy

The Good Neighbor Policy is the name given to the way in which the countries of South America and the countries of North America work together to solve their problems. Years ago, many of the countries of Central and South America did not trust the United States. They were afraid that because the United States was so large and powerful it would attempt to rule them. In 1933 President Franklin D. Roosevelt announced to the world that the United States wanted to be a good neighbor to these smaller countries. The United States would be willing to help them if they needed help but would not try to rule them or tell them what to do. Since that time all the countries of North and South America have been friendly, and in World War II all the Latin American countries except Argentina took the side of the United States. Recently the countries have held conferences, or meetings, at which they discuss what is best for all the countries. You can read about these conferences in a separate article on PAN-AMERICANISM.

Goodrich, B. F.

Benjamin Franklin Goodrich was an American businessman who founded one of the greatest rubber businesses in the world, nearly 100 years ago. He was born in 1841 and became interested in the rubber business when he was still a young man. He failed several times to make a success of the business, but continued to work hard, and finally, in 1880, he founded the B. F. Goodrich Company in Akron, Ohio. He died in 1888.

Goodyear, Charles

Charles Goodyear was an American inventor. His most famous invention was a way of making rubber that is hard, strong, and able to stretch in all kinds of weather. He was born in New Haven, Connecticut, in 1800. After finishing public school, he went to work in his father's hardware business. His father was an inventor of farm machinery, and Charles helped him with many of his inventions. However, when his father lost all his money because of bad business management, Charles had to find other ways of making money. He tried to find a way to make rubber that would not crack or become sticky when the weather changed. The rubber then being used would melt in the summer and freeze in the winter. Goodyear worked for ten years trying to make rubber that would not spoil. Then, in 1839, he found what he was looking for. One day he accidentally dropped a mixture of rubber and sulfur on a hot stove. When he scraped off the mixture, he found that the rubber could be stretched more easily and was much stronger. What was more important, it did not spoil in winter and summer. Heating a mixture of rubber and sulfur is called *vulcanization*. It is named after

Charles Goodyear holds the first piece of vulcanized rubber. The pot in which he accidentally made his discovery is still steaming on his kitchen stove.

Vulcan, god of fire in the religion of the ancient Romans. Vulcanization is used to make most of the rubber in the world today. Goodyear began to manufacture rubber products by vulcanization, but many people used his invention without paying him for it, and when he died in 1860 he had very little money. The Goodyear Tire and Rubber Company, which was formed in 1898, was named after Charles Goodyear but he did not start it.

goose

A goose is a waterfowl similar to the duck in many ways, but larger and with a longer neck. Geese live in all parts of the world, on lakes, ponds, and rivers. They have webbed feet and are good swimmers. They also are powerful fliers, and some can fly as fast as sixty miles per hour. You can read about domestic geese, which are raised for their meat and for eating weeds in gardens, in the article on POULTRY.

Wild geese are migratory, which means they move in flocks from north to south in the fall, and back again in the spring. They fly higher than any other migratory bird. They are very noisy and honk constantly when they fly. A type of Canadian goose is called the *honker*, because it is even noisier than most geese. Like wild ducks, geese are game for hunters.

Laws have been passed to protect them and sanctuaries have been established where they can safely stop to feed during their migrations.

Wild geese live on roots of plants they find in marshy fields, rather than from water plants as ducks do. They usually do not breed until they are 3 years old. They build their nests on an island or a mound in shallow marshy water. They mate for life, and can live from twenty to thirty years. Ganders, the male geese, protect their families and will fiercely attack enemies, such as the fox.

gooseberry

The gooseberry is a berry used in

preserves and in desserts such as pies. It grows on a thorny bush that is found in England, northern Europe, the northern part of the United States, and other places. The shrubs grow wild in most places, but in England they have been carefully cultivated for more than four hundred years, and they yield a large, sweet, plumlike fruit that can be eaten right off the bush. As the fruit ripens its color changes from green to purple. It has many seeds. The gooseberry grown in other parts of the world is usually bitter on the bushes.

gopher

A gopher is a small animal that spends most of its life underground. It lives in the western part of North America. It is seven to fourteen inches long, and is gray, tan, or brown in color. A gopher does not see very well, because it seldom comes out during the daytime and does not need good sight in the underground darkness. Gophers are rodents, or gnawing animals, and are related to rats, beavers, and squirrels.

Gophers live alone, and make tunnels or burrows in which they live. Each gopher's house contains several storage compartments for food to be eaten during the winter, when it would be hard to find the plant roots and bulbs that gophers live on. The gopher has a strange way of carrying its food home. It has two fur-lined pouches or pockets on the outside of its cheeks, and it fills these pockets with the food it wants to store or with materials for its nest. That is why it is often called a pocket gopher.

Male and female gophers live in separate burrows, and never associate with each other except at mating time. If one gopher meets another in a burrow they sometimes fight until one is killed. Baby gophers are born in the late spring. There are from one to nine in a litter, and they are only about an inch long when they are born. When the young gophers are two months old, they leave their mother's home to build their own tunnels and houses.

Farmers of the western part of the United States and Canada find gophers a pest, because they eat the tender roots of many crops. Minnesota is called the Gopher State, because so many gophers used to live there.

Gordian knot

The story of the Gordian knot is told in Greek mythology, the stories the ancient Greeks told about their gods. According to the story, an oracle (one who could see the future) had foretold that the people of a country called Phrygia would get a strong king to solve their troubles. This king would arrive in a wagon. One day a poor peasant named Gordius brought his wagon to the market place, and the people made him their king. He was so grateful for this good fortune that he dedicated his wagon to the greatest of the gods, called Zeus. The pole of the wagon was fastened to the yoke for the animals by a very complicated knot. The oracle also foretold that the man who could loosen this knot would be ruler of all Asia. Alexander the Great came to the city and very simply cut the knot with one blow of his sword. He then declared that he had fulfilled the prophecy. Modern students of history doubt very much that Alexander cut the true Gordian knot; they think that he cut through a copy of it. It is true that he did go on to conquer Asia.

Gordon, Charles William

Charles William Gordon was a Canadian minister who was best known by his pen name, Ralph Connor. Under this name he wrote many novels about his life as a missionary in the lumbering country of the Northwest Territory of Canada. Among the best known of his books were *The Prospector, Corporal Cameron,* and *The Sky Pilot.* Gordon was born in Ontario, Canada, in 1860. After he became a minister, he was sent as a missionary to the Northwest Territory for three years. He lived with the lumbermen, and his books were based on his experiences during this time. Later he became minister of St. Stephen's Church in Winnipeg. He died in 1937.

Gordon, Chinese

Charles George Gordon was a famous British soldier. He is often called *Chinese Gordon* because of his many years of service in China, and sometimes he is called *Gordon Pasha* because of his military service in Egypt. He was born in Woolwich, England, in 1833, and was graduated from the Royal Military Academy when he was about 20 years old. He went to China and took part in the capture of Peking. Later, he helped the Chinese forces to defeat the Taiping rebels.

In 1873, the khedive, or ruler, of Egypt asked Gordon to become governor of the Sudan, which is south of Egypt. Several years later he returned to England, only to be called back to the Sudan again to help the khedive. He was besieged at Khartoum for ten months by rebel forces. Gordon was killed by the rebels only a few days before new troops arrived to help him. It is said that his head was cut off and taken to the chief of the rebel forces as a trophy.

Gorgas, William Crawford

William C. Gorgas was a very famous doctor who became surgeon general of the United States Army. The surgeon general is the chief medical officer of the Army. Gorgas was born in 1854, and when he was a young boy he had two ambitions, to be a soldier and to be a doctor. So  he studied medicine and then entered the Army Medical Corps. While stationed in Texas, he became ill with yellow fever. He recovered and was immune to the disease from then on. After the Spanish-American War, about fifty years ago, Gorgas was made sanitation officer in Havana, Cuba, which was then occupied by American soldiers. Within a short time he permanently rid the city of yellow fever. He was promoted to colonel for this work.

In 1904, Gorgas went to Panama, where the United States government was building the Panama Canal. The land was very unhealthful and many workers were dying of yellow fever and other diseases. Gorgas knew that yellow fever was carried by a certain kind of mosquito, so he immediately set about draining the marshes and swamps, and putting screens on the doors and windows of the houses. His work rid the Canal Zone of yellow fever and made it possible to finish the canal. From 1914 to 1919 he served as surgeon general. Gorgas died in 1920. He is now in the Hall of Fame.

Gorgon

The Gorgons were three fearful-looking women in Greek mythology, the stories the ancient Greeks told about their gods and goddesses. The Gorgons had coiled snakes on their heads instead of hair; they had sharp claws and huge teeth. They were named Stheno, Medusa, and Euryale. They were so horrible-looking that anyone who looked at any of them was instantly turned to stone. Medusa was killed by a Greek hero named Perseus, who killed her while looking at his polished shield as he chopped off her head. Because he did not have to look directly at her, he was not turned to stone as many other heroes had been. He took the head of Medusa to the temple of the goddess Athena as an offering, or gift, because Athena had given him the polished shield that saved his life.

gorilla

Gorillas are the largest of all the apes. A male gorilla may be as much as six feet tall and weigh four hundred pounds. A gorilla is an enormously powerful animal, and other beasts of the jungle usually leave gorillas strictly alone. The gorilla, however, never seems to attack other animals deliberately, and is peaceful unless threatened. Gorillas live mostly on fruits and vegetables.

Gorillas live in family groups, with one adult male, one or two females, their babies, and a few half-grown gorillas. They travel from place to place, and

A large male gorilla pounds his chest. The jungle of the Congo is a rather hot place for him to wear such a heavy fur coat.

make camps for the night as they go. They never live with other families, as baboons do.

There are two kinds of gorilla. The black mountain gorilla lives in the mountain forests of central Africa. The lowland or coast gorilla is iron-gray in color, and it lives in the damp rain forests in the western coastal section of equatorial Africa. Both are covered with hair everywhere

on their bodies except the face, the palms of the hands, and the soles of the feet. They have a strangely human look, but their arms are so long they reach to the middle of the legs when the animal stands upright. Gorillas lumber about on all fours most of the time. See also the article APE.

Gorki

Gorki is the name of one of the most important industrial cities of Russia. It is also one of the oldest cities in Russia, and has often been called the birthplace of the Russian empire. Gorki used to be called Nizhni Novgorod, but the name was changed to honor the great Russian writer, Maxim Gorki. The city is about 260 miles east of Moscow, the capital of Russia, at the point where the Oka and Volga Rivers meet. About 1,170,000 people live in Gorki. They are mostly workers in the iron and steel factories of the city, or in the automobile factory that is one of the largest in Russia.

The city is divided into two parts. The upper part of the town is where the historic cathedrals, the fortress called the Kremlin, and a government palace are located. The lower part of the city, near the river, is the industrial area. Gorki is also an important commercial town. In the Middle Ages, more than six hundred years ago, great fairs were held here.

Gorki, Maxim

Maxim Gorki, whose real name was Alexei Maximovich Peshkov, was born in Nizhni Novgorod, Russia, in 1868. He became so famous as a writer that in 1932 the city was renamed Gorki in his honor. Gorki supported himself from the age of 9, and he traveled all over Russia and Europe, working at all kinds of jobs and meeting many kinds of people. He published his first story in a Russian newspaper. He used the name of Gorki, which means "the bitter one," because he was bitter that so many people had to live in poverty and despair.

Gorki became a journalist and started writing short stories, plays and novels that became popular all over the world. Some of these are *The Lower Depths, Twenty-six Men and a Girl,* and *Mother.* The people he wrote about best were those he had met on  his travels: the poor, the tramps, the unfortunates. He wrote with great force and sadness about their unhappy lives. He gave a broad picture of life in Russia and discussed the many problems people had to face. Gorki supported the Bolshevik revolution and became head of the propaganda bureau, but ill health forced him to go abroad in 1922. He returned to Russia and died there in 1936.

goshawk

The goshawk is a large, handsome bird that lives in many parts of the United States, Canada, and Europe. It is about two feet long, and is blue-gray in color, with a white stomach and gray stripes across its underpart. The goshawk has flashing red eyes and a white streak above each eye. Like all members of the hawk family, the goshawk eats other birds. It also catches rabbits and squirrels, and will swoop down on barnyards and kill chickens.

The goshawk builds a strong nest made of sticks and mud, high up in the trees of pine forests. Every year the goshawk builds a new nest, and the female lays white or pale blue eggs. People in Europe taught captive goshawks to bring the rabbits, or other animals it caught, back to them, and this became a popular sport called *falconry.*

Goshen

Goshen was the name of a territory given by Pharaoh to the Israelites, the Jewish people who had come to Egypt from Israel. There is some question as to the exact location of Goshen, but from the description of it in the Bible it is believed to have been outside of Egypt. The land was very good in Goshen, and all things grew well there. Today people think of the land of Goshen as a place of good things.

Gospel

Gospel means "good news." Christians have used the word for hundreds of years to mean the good news that Jesus Christ, the savior of mankind, had come to earth as promised in the Bible. A preacher is said to "preach the Gospel." Usually we use the word to mean any of the first four books of the New Testament, the books of Matthew, Mark, Luke, and John.

All of these Gospels were written during the first century A.D., which means they were written within less than a hundred years of the time when Jesus was actually on earth. Scholars have considered that each of the four Gospels has a slightly different message. St. Matthew tells of Jesus the preacher who preached the Sermon on the Mount. St. Mark tells a simple story of Jesus' life on earth. St. Luke shows Jesus as founder of the Christian Church. St. John shows Jesus as the Son of God, the spiritual inspiration of men.

The first three Gospels, Matthew, Mark, and Luke, are called the *synoptic* Gospels. *Synoptic* comes from Greek words meaning "the same eyes." The synoptics, as though seen through the same eyes, tell much the same story. The Gospel of Saint John is not so much a biography, or story of Jesus' life, as it is an interpretation of his life.

A "Harmony of the Gospels" is an arrangement of them so that each is shown to tell the same story as the other. The word *harmony* means "agreement." *Harmonics* is the study of the Gospels in such a way as to show that they agree with one another.

Gothic

Gothic is a style of architecture, the design and construction of buildings. The Gothic style came into use in Europe in the Middle Ages, about eight hundred years ago, and developed out of a growing love of beauty and a widening interest among the people in religion. Gothic architecture was originally used for churches, but gradually its style was copied for other types of building.

The pointed arch is a main feature of Gothic architecture. As you can read in the article on ARCH, the Roman arches of earlier times had been rounded with very thick walls and small windows if any. The architects wanted their churches to have more windows to let in sunlight. To have more windows they had to make the walls higher and straighter. The pointed arch

The interior of the Exeter Cathedral in England is a beautiful example of medieval Gothic architecture.

British Railways

gave them the straighter walls that they wanted but they were not as strong as the rounded arch. So they invented the *flying buttress.* The flying buttress is a stone pillar that is propped against the wall to support it.

One of the most famous Gothic churches is in Paris. It is the cathedral of Notre Dame, and it was built almost eight hundred years ago. It has beautiful stained-glass windows showing scenes from the Bible, and a lovely round window called a "rose window" that looks like a blossoming rose. There are many churches in the United States that are built in the Gothic style. St. Patrick's Cathedral and the Cathedral of St. John the Divine in New York City are two of the finest Gothic churches in America.

Goths

The Goths were a Germanic or northern people who lived hundreds of years ago in what is now southern Sweden. From there they slowly moved down across Europe, conquering any tribes who tried to stop them. About three hundred years after Jesus was born they reached the borders of the Roman Empire. Rome at that time controlled most of the civilized world. The Romans fought the Goths for many years. As the Roman Empire became less powerful, more and more of the Goths tried to cross its boundaries. In the year 36 the Goths divided

into two groups. One group, called the West Goths, or Visigoths, crossed the Danube River and were allowed to settle in the Roman Empire. The other group, called the East Goths, or Ostrogoths, remained behind.

The Romans did not treat the Goths well at first, and the wars continued. The

most famous leaders of the Visigoths were two kings named ALARIC; you can read a separate article about these kings. After about thirty more years of war, during which the Visigoths invaded the city of Rome, they moved west to what is now Spain and southern France. Here the Goths founded a kingdom that lasted more than three hundred years. It was finally conquered by the Moors.

The Ostrogoths later came down into Italy and conquered a large part of the Roman Empire, where they ruled for about 35 years. This kingdom was finally taken back by the Romans.

The Goths were fierce and bold fighters. They were not as civilized as the people they conquered, but they were good rulers. They let the conquered people keep their own laws and religions and customs. Often the Goths settled down in the conquered regions, adopted the customs of the empire, and lived in peace with the people they had conquered. They later accepted the Christian religion. Many of the people living throughout southern Europe are the descendants of these northern people.

Gould, Jay

Jay Gould was an American financier and railroad owner who became very rich and powerful. He was extremely clever, but his business methods were not always according to the highest standards. He was born in Roxbury, New York, in 1836. He was a rich man before he was 20. In 1869, Gould and a man named James Fisk tried to buy up all of the gold in the United States. The government stepped in to prevent this so they did not succeed, but their activities caused a great stock market panic that was called the Black Friday Panic. Gould started to buy railroads soon after he moved to New York City, and by 1880 he owned nearly one tenth of all the railroads in the United States and controlled the Western Union Telegraph Company. He died in 1892.

Gounod, Charles

& Information Center

Charles Francis Gounod was a famous French composer, a writer of music. He was born in Paris in 1818. He is best known for his operas, which are plays in which the characters sing the parts instead of speaking. His most famous opera is *Faust,* the story of a man who sells his soul to the devil, and how he is punished for it. He also composed an opera about the story of *Romeo and Juliet.* Gounod wrote a great deal of church music. One of his best-known religious works is *The Redemption,* an oratorio, or music for chorus and soloists. During the Franco-Prussian War, Gounod lived in England. While he was there he founded the Gounod Choir, which was a chorus of men's and women's voices. Gounod died in St. Cloud, France, in 1893.

gourd

Gourd is the popular name for a group of plants that bear hard-shelled fruits of many different shapes. The shells are used as decorations, drinking cups, bowls, and dippers. Some plants of the gourd family may be eaten. Pumpkins and the different kinds of squash that Americans like to eat are members of the gourd family.

Gourds were used as dippers, drinking cups, and bowls by the American Indians long before the white man arrived in the New World. In many American homes small gourds are used as table decorations. They are usually bought at a fruit market and varnished or shellacked to preserve them. This type of gourd cannot be eaten. They make attractive decorations because of their odd shapes and pretty colors. They may be orange, green tan, or cream colored, and a few are green on top and orange below. Some are about the size and shape of a large pickle; others are round and the size of a large apple. Many have thick round bumps on them like warts. The larger gourds are about the size of a small pumpkin. One kind of gourd from which dippers are made is about fifteen inches long and is shaped like a dipper, with a long stem for a handle and a round end that forms the bowl when the top is cut off. The gourd is picked and allowed to dry until the seeds rattle inside it. They cannot be used for hot liquids but serve very well for cold liquids and will last for many years.

gout

Gout is a painful disease of the joints. It is a form of ARTHRITIS, about which there is a separate article. Gout attacks a small joint (usually the big toe), which becomes hot, swollen, and red. The area becomes so tender that even the weight of bedclothes is painful. Attacks of gout usually begin in the night and last from three days to a week. Often there is fever as high as 103 degrees.

Gout is brought on by something in the body that causes too much uric acid to form in the blood. This results in chalky deposits in joints such as the toes. Women usually do not have to worry about getting gout; nineteen out of twenty cases are men, most of whom are over 35. Gout was very common in Europe in the 18th and 19th centuries. It was once known as the "rich man's disease," probably because acute attacks are sometimes brought on by overindulgence in rich food and drink. The best thing to do for gout is to keep the infected joint warm and at a level higher than the rest of the body. Doctors may also prescribe large doses of baking soda and water, or a drug called *colchicine.*

government

Government is the organization set up to keep people from doing harm to each other or to the society in which they live, and to help them lead safe and comfortable lives. There have been many different forms of government throughout the ages, and most of them have benefited the rulers more than the people who were governed. But every American's idea of a good government is what Thomas Jefferson expressed in the Declaration of Independence:

"We hold these truths to be self-evident, that all men are created equal, that they are endowed by their Creator with certain unalienable rights, that among these are life, liberty and the pursuit of happiness.—That to secure these rights, governments are instituted among men, deriving their just powers from the consent of the governed.—That whenever any form of government becomes destructive of these ends, it is the right of the people to alter or to abolish it, and to institute new government, laying its foundation on such principles and organizing its powers in such form, as to them shall seem most likely to effect their safety and happiness."

FORMS OF GOVERNMENT

Beginning with the early Greek thinkers, men have considered and studied different forms of government and tried to decide which is the best one. The great philosopher Aristotle divided governments into three classes: autocracy, aristocracy, and democracy. AUTOCRACY is government by one man; ARISTOCRACY is government by a special group of people who are considered the best people; DEMOCRACY is government by all the people. There are separate articles on these. There are innumerable ways in which these forms of government can be set up, and men have given them dozens of different names. A few of these are: Oligarchy is government by a small group; it is like aristocracy, except that in an aristocracy the governing group holds its position by some special privilege such as inheriting it. Plutocracy is government by the very rich. Theocracy is government by priests; this was quite usual in ancient civilizations.

In the world today there are two main forms of government: democracy and dictatorship. Dictatorship as we have known it is government by a single man or a single political party. You can read about it in the articles on COMMUNISM and FASCISM.

FORMS OF DEMOCRATIC GOVERNMENT

Most of the countries that we call democracies today use either of two systems: the system used in the United States, and the parliamentary system. The United States system is called a system of "checks and balances," because there are three branches of government and none of them has supreme power. They constantly check and balance one another. These branches are the *executive,* the *legislative,* and the *judicial.*

The legislative branch is the Congress, with its Senate and House of Representatives. It decides what should be done, by passing laws. The executive branch consists of the President, his Cabinet, and all the government departments and their employees. It carries out the laws made by the legislative branch. The judicial branch consists of the various Federal courts. It judges whether the laws are proper laws, and whether any of them are being violated.

These three branches depend on each other because each one limits the authority of the others so that no one of them can become too powerful.

The parliamentary system is different in one particular way. Parliament is the lawmaking body, as Congress is, but it has both legislative and executive powers. The President of the United States and

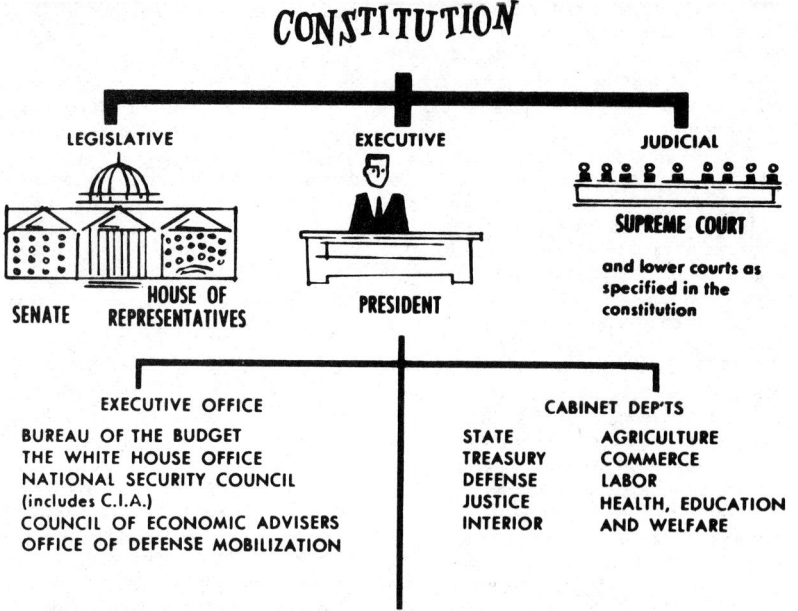

The government of the United States is organized under three branches—the legislative, executive, and judicial. Governments of other nations may be organized differently, but all have branches or departments like those of the United States government.

Left: In a democracy, the people tell the government what to do. *Right:* But in a dictatorship, the government has all the power and tells the people what they must do.

the Prime Minister, or Premier, of a parliamentary country are different because the President is not a member of Congress, while the Prime Minister is a member of Parliament and is the chairman of its executive committee. Nearly every democratic country in the world except the United States follows the parliamentary system. The states of the United States follow the same system as the federal government.

CONSTITUTIONS

A constitution is the basic principles that underlie all the laws and all the acts of any of the branches of government. The United States and many other countries have written constitutions, and no member or division of the government may do anything that violates this basic set of laws. There is a separate article on CONSTITUTION. In Great Britain there is no written constitution, so that any act of Parliament becomes a part of the constitution. However, there are certain basic principles and policies that it would be as impossible for the British Parliament to violate as it would be for Congress to violate the United States Constitution.

LOCAL GOVERNMENT

Every group of people, no matter how small, needs some form of government. In the home, the parents are the govern-

ment, although happy family life requires that there be a certain amount of democracy, with each member having some say in decisions affecting him. In the town, the city, the county, and the state or province, there must be local government to handle matters that do not affect people outside that particular community. Towns and cities have mayors or city managers, as the executive branch, and councils or assemblies to pass laws (often called *ordinances*). Counties have officials such as sheriffs and judges and clerks. States and provinces have more elaborate systems that are very much like a national government.

government ownership

When a country finds that certain things are too large and important for one person or group of persons to own and operate, these things are often put under government ownership. In the United States certain great forests and parks, post offices and the postal system, the Panama Canal, all atomic-energy resources, the Tennessee Valley Authority system of dams and water power for electricity, the Grand Coulee Dam, the Hoover Dam and other great public works belong to the government. They are all supposed to be operated by the government for the benefit of all the people.

State, county, or city governments in the United States operate such things as the public schools, some highway systems, subways, sewers, and electric-light and gas systems.

Some people in the United States believe that the national government should own and operate many more works or industries; others believe the government already owns too many things.

In many countries of Europe, governments own and operate the railroads, the telephone and telegraph systems, radio, coal mines, and banks. In England, under the Labour Party, the government took over the railroads, the mines, and the public-health system. This was done by what is called *nationalization,* the taking over by the nation of what had been owned or operated by private citizens or firms.

At one time United States companies owned many oil wells in Mexico, but the Mexican government *expropriated* them, or took them over to operate itself with the promise of paying the owners for the value of the wells and property.

Under communism as in Soviet Russia, the government owns almost all land and natural resources, and either owns or controls all business, industry, and agriculture. Under socialism, the government also owns many things. (There are separate articles about COMMUNISM and SOCIALISM.)

Government Printing Office

The Government Printing Office is a branch of the United States Congress. It prints the documents and records of the United States government. It was started by Congress almost a hundred years ago. One of the most important things that is printed by the Government Printing Office is the Congressional Record, which tells what Senators and Representatives are doing. The office also publishes many other books and pamphlets that are ordered by Congress or other departments of the government. Many of these publications can be bought from the Government Printing Office. There are about fifty thousand publications available. They deal with everything from how to take care of a baby to how to grow corn. You can obtain information and catalogs by writing to the Superintendent of Documents, Government Printing Office, Washington 25, D.C.

governor

A governor is an attachment used to keep an automobile or truck or elevator or train from moving too fast. It is attached to the engine and slows it down when it reaches a certain speed. The usual type of governor is called a *flyball governor.*

This governor has a shaft with two steel balls that move outward when the shaft turns. These balls are on hinged arms that are held down by a spring. This spring is measured so that an exact amount of pressure is needed to open the spring. When the arms push the spring open and move up the shaft, a lever attached to them shuts off the fuel to the motor, or makes brakes go on. As the car

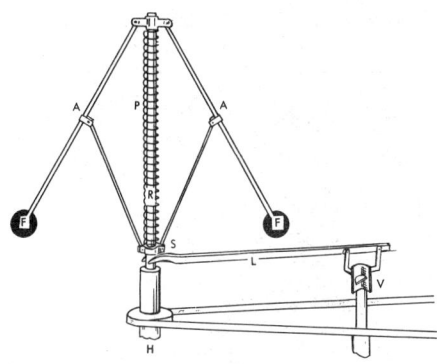

The parts of a governor: Shaft (H), governor shaft (P), balls (F), arms (A), spring (R), slide valve (S), lever (L), and valve (V).

moves, the shaft of the governor turns. The faster the car goes, the faster the shaft turns. As the shaft turns faster, centrifugal force moves the balls outward, and pulls the arms up. If the car is going too fast, the arms move up strongly enough to push the spring open. This makes the car slow down until the shaft also slows and the arms come down again. There is a separate article about CENTRIFUGAL FORCE.

governor

Governor is a title used by the heads of various governments and organizations.

In the United States, the head or chief executive of the government of each state is called the Governor. His position is almost exactly like that of the President of the United States, because the state governments are modeled after the United States government. He can sign or veto laws passed by the state legislature, and he can pardon persons convicted of crimes. He is commander-in-chief of the state's militia, or own army, and he can appoint the heads of the various departments that run the state government. Each state decides what other powers the Governor has, and what his term of office shall be. The term of office is two years in some states and four years in other states. In some states the same man cannot be re-elected as Governor.

Many countries appoint men called Governors to run their colonies and possessions. The President of the United States appoints a Governor for the Virgin Islands and other U.S. territories.

Governor-General

Governor-General is a title used in Canada, Australia, and other dominions that are members of the British Commonwealth of Nations. A dominion governs itself but recognizes the British king or queen as its king or queen. The Governor-General lives in the dominion as personal representative of the king or queen. In the government of the dominion he has the same power that Queen Elizabeth II has in Great Britain. This is not very much power, because the Prime Minister and cabinet, who represent the Parliament, actually run the country, but the Governor-General has a great deal of influence.

Most often the Governor-General of a dominion has been a member of the British royal family or a high-ranking nobleman sent from Great Britain, but

in 1952 for the first time a native Canadian, Vincent Massey, was appointed Governor-General of Canada.

In India, when it was a part of the British Empire, Viceroy was the title of the man in the same position as the Governor-General in dominions.

Governors Island

Governors Island is a small island in New York harbor, less than a mile from the tip of Manhattan. It was bought from the Indians more than three hundred years ago by the Dutch settlers. Later, when the English occupied New York, it was used by the English governors, and this is why it is called Governors Island. Several forts were built on the island, and until 1965 the island was headquarters of the U.S. Army's First Corps Area. In 1966 it became a base for the U.S. Coast Guard.

Goya, Francisco

Francisco José de Goya y Lucientes was a famous Spanish artist and designer. He is best known for his drawings and etchings of bullfights and of warfare, which he made seem very real. He was born in Aragon, in Spain, in 1746. His family was very poor, and he too would probably have been poor if it had not been for a priest who saw him drawing on walls. The priest was impressed by his talents and found a patron, or wealthy man, to help Goya. Goya painted many portraits of Spanish royalty and society, and later produced many religious paintings. Most of his work was designed to show the stupidity, greed, cruelty, and other defects of men. When he was an elderly man he left Spain because he disapproved of the government. He died in Bordeaux, France, in 1828.

Gracchi

Tiberius Gracchus and Gaius Gracchus, together called "the Gracchi," were brothers who lived in Rome more than two thousand years ago. They were statesmen and reformers, and fought for the farmers and other poor people. The

Gracchi were brought up by their mother, Cornelia, an intelligent and proud woman. There is a story that when Cornelia heard all of her rich friends boasting about their gorgeous collections of jewelry, she pointed to her two boys and said "These are my jewels." After fighting in Africa, Tiberius, the elder brother, returned to Rome and became a tribune —one of the rulers who were supposed to protect the common people from the nobles. He was very popular with the people, especially because he persuaded the assembly to pass a law limiting the amount of land any one person might hold and providing that the land left over should be rented to the poor at a very low rental.

Graces

The Graces were three goddesses in Greek mythology, the stories the ancient Greeks told about their gods and goddesses. The Graces controlled the gifts of beauty, elegance, and charm. They were named *Aglaia,* which means brightness; *Euphrosyne,* which means joyfulness; and *Thalia,* which means bloom. They lived on Mt. Olympus with their father, Zeus, king of the gods, and their mother, Eurynome. The Graces are usually associated with the Muses, nine sisters who were goddesses of the arts. Many artists have made statues of the three Graces standing together and holding hands.

grackle

The grackle is the largest of the American blackbirds. It makes its home in the eastern part of the United States and in some parts of Canada. The grackle is sometimes called the *crow-blackbird.* It is usually about one foot long, although some of these great birds are about eighteen inches long. The males are black, and in the sun their feathers shine with green and blue color. The female is a pale grayish-brown color. Grackles build their nests of grass and reeds in swampy marshes, on or close to the ground. The female lays pale blue or greenish eggs with brown spots on them. The grackle

Spanish Tourist Office
Many famous people asked Goya to paint their pictures. The portrait of Queen Maria Luisa on the right is very true to life. These paintings are in the Prado Museum, Madrid.

The grackle has a graceful shape, but its harsh cry very often makes it unwelcome, especially in the early morning.

has a hoarse cry that is unpleasant to hear. Grackles are very useful because they eat many insects, but they can also be a pest to farmers because they are fond of corn.

graduation, the receiving of a certificate or diploma from a school or college. See the article COMMENCEMENT.

Grady, Henry W.

Henry W. Grady was an American newspaperman and speaker. He was born in Athens, Georgia, in 1850, and he studied at the University of Georgia. In 1879, after the end of the Civil War, Grady bought part of the Atlanta *Constitution,* a newspaper he helped make famous. In editorials in the newspaper and in many speeches, he worked hard to help the North and South make up their differences after the war, and to help the South rebuild its life and industry. His greatest speech was "The New South," made in 1886 in New York. Grady died in 1889.

grafting

Grafting is joining a part of one plant to another so that the two plants will unite and grow. Grafting usually gives the farmer new or better plants. Usually a bud or a small branch, called the *scion,* is grafted onto a growing plant or tree which is called the *stock.* The scion and the stock do not have to be the same kind, but they do have to be very closely related and in the same plant family. Grafting a pear variety on another pear variety, an apple on another apple, and so on, gives the best results. You cannot graft an apple and a peach. If an apple scion is grafted on a pear stock, the scion will keep on growing as an apple even though it is nourished by the pear stock.

If you peel off the bark of a twig in early spring you will find a thin layer of plant tissue inside the bark. This is the cambium, and the graft is successful only if the cambium layers of both scion and stock are touching each other. Usually a graft is tied in place to keep the cambiums joined and then covered with a spe-

cial grafting wax to prevent the graft from drying out. Sometimes the trunks or branches of two closely related plants growing close to each other will get pressed tightly together, and a *natural* graft will be made when some of the bark gets worn away and the two cambium layers unite. Natural grafts have been made by farmers for more than two thousand years, and the first man who tried it probably had seen one in the field and got the idea of making one like it himself.

The chief use of grafting is to grow new trees of a kind that do not easily reproduce their kind by seed or that would not root easily when a piece of branch is planted. When a new tree is wanted, a very young tree that grows easily from seed is taken for the stock. Then most of the top is cut off, and a scion, or twig, from the desired tree is grafted on. This kind of grafting is also used if the farmer wants to grow a tree where the soil or climate is not suitable for it. Here he uses a tree that grows well in the soil and climate as the stock, and then grafts the kind of tree he wants onto it.

Sometimes a farmer will have a fairly old tree that produces a kind of apple he does not like. He will cut back most of the branches and graft onto them scions of a kind of apple he does like. When you graft this way, or "top-work a tree," as it is called, you will get fruit quicker than if you wait for a young tree to begin bearing fruit. Sometimes grafting is used for novelties, such as one apple tree that has five different kinds of apples grafted on to it.

There is a separate article about the great scientist, Luther BURBANK, that tells how he experimented with, and produced, many new plants by grafting.

Doctors sometimes are able to graft skin onto people who have been badly burned. See the article PLASTIC SURGERY.

Graham, Billy

Billy Graham is the most successful evangelist of modern times. He was born in Charlotte, North Carolina, in 1918, and his full name is William Franklin Graham. He became a Baptist preacher after acquiring college training in theology, and he delivered sermons on radio, later on television, and in revivals attended by tens of thousands wherever he traveled throughout the world, urging his listeners to make "a decision for Christ." Also he has written much for newspapers, magazines, and books, and has produced many evangelical films. See EVANGELIST.

grain

Grain is the seeds of certain plants, such as wheat, oats, corn, barley, and rice. These seeds are made into flour at mills, or they are used as cereals; sometimes they are fed to animals. Bread, which is made from grain, has been called the "staff of life" because it contains so many important elements which the body needs for growth and health. There is gluten, which is a tissue builder; and starch and fat, which provide heat and energy. Grain also contains certain vitamins and minerals.

grain elevator

A grain elevator is a large bin in which grain is stored until it is needed. Many farmers harvest their grain at the

same time, and some of it must be stored for later use. The elevator is a series of bins set close together, with machinery for lifting the grain, for weighing, cleaning, and drying it, and for unloading it again. Long ago grain elevators were made of wood covered with a layer of bricks, but today they are made of fireproof materials such as steel or concrete.

The farmer sends his grain to the elevator in cargo ships, or by freight train, or in large trucks, and the first job is to get it unloaded. There are two ways of getting the grain up to the top of an elevator. The first way is with a machine consisting of a long circular belt with buckets attached. The grain is scooped into the buckets and the belt carries them to the top where they are emptied. At some elevators the unloading is done in another way. There is a long tube that works like a vacuum cleaner, sucking up the grain with a long nozzle.

At the top of the elevator the grain is cleaned, weighed, and dried, and there it stays until some big mill needs grain. Then it is unloaded and shipped to where it is needed. Some of the biggest elevators can hold up to ten million bushels of grain, as in Duluth, Chicago, and Minneapolis.

grammar

Grammar is the science of the forms of words used in a language. Many things affect the form of the word to be used. These include NUMBER, PERSON, GENDER, TENSE, and CASE, about which there are separate articles.

Sometimes the whole study of language is called grammar. The grammar you study in school may include things that are not really grammar, such as *syntax,* which is the study of how words should be arranged in a sentence, and *rhetoric,* which is the study of the choice of words. There are separate articles on SYNTAX and RHETORIC.

Very often your intelligence, as well as your education and family background, will be judged by the grammar you use, so it is important to learn and use correct grammar.

ENGLISH GRAMMAR

English grammar is easier to learn than the grammar of most other Indo-European languages (the family of languages to which English and other European languages belong). The changes in the form of a word are called *inflections,* and a word has a certain inflection according to its use. The English language has few inflections, and the only words that change their form according to the way they are used are nouns, pronouns, and verbs. These are called PARTS OF SPEECH, and you may read more about them in a separate article.

The pronouns have the greatest number of grammatical forms. The sentence "He sees me and I see him" shows one way in which pronouns change their forms. *He* and *him* stand for the same person, and *I* and *me* stand for the same person, but they have different forms when they are used differently.

The noun in English has only three forms: a form to show that it is one thing, or singular; a form to show that it is more than one thing, or plural; and a form to show that it owns something, or posses-

sive. Both the singular and the plural forms can be made possessive. Thus we say: dog, to mean one animal; dogs, to mean more than one animal; dog's, to mean that one animal owns something; and dogs', to mean that more than one animal owns something. There are some irregular nouns in English that do not form their plurals by adding "s" to the singular. Such a noun is *man*, the plural of which is *men*, or *deer*, the plural of which is also *deer*.

The verb in English has six tenses. Each of these has a special form. Most verbs do not change their form within any tense except the present and then only after he, she, it, or a noun. We say *I see* and *you see*, but we say *she, he*, or *it sees*.

Some irregular verbs follow no such pattern. The verb *be*, for example, changes form in all three persons of the present tense, and is conjugated *I am, you are, he, she*, or *it is*.

GRAMMAR IN OTHER LANGUAGES

In most Indo-European languages there are more inflected forms than there are in English. The Latin language, for example, has six different forms for each verb in the present tense, and ten different endings for each noun. In French, most words are either masculine or feminine and often the form of the word depends on which it is. Ancient Greek had more than a hundred forms for verbs.

In many languages the adjectives also change their form according to their use, and nouns have special endings to be used after certain prepositions or to be used instead of prepositions. The English language was once a highly inflected language, too, but gradually it dropped most of the inflections.

grampus

The grampus is a large animal that lives in the sea. It is the largest member of the dolphin family and is related to the whale. Though it lives in the water, it is not a fish but a mammal. This means that the females bear their children alive and nurse them. The grampus is sometimes more than twenty feet long. It has powerful jaws armed with sharp teeth, and it hunts and roams the sea in packs of more than forty, seeking its food. It will eat anything, even man, and is sometimes known as "the killer of the sea." The killer grampus can swallow dolphins, great tuna fish, or seals whole. Its characteristic round head and glistening black back are signs for other fish to get out of the way. The grampus can be found in all waters of the world, but it is more common in the colder regions.

Granada

Granada is a region in southern Spain. It was once an independent kingdom but is now a province in modern Spain. Granada is also the name of its capital, a city of about 157,000. Most of the people are farmers or raisers of livestock. There is very little industry in the region, which borders on the Mediterranean Sea.

Granada has had a long history. About a thousand years ago most of Spain was ruled by Mohammedan peoples from Arabia and Africa, and Granada was a separate country in Spain. It was called an emirate, and the prince who ruled it

was called an emir. In the city of Granada is the most famous of all the palaces built by Mohammedan rulers, the Alhambra. In 1492 the Spanish king and queen, Ferdinand and Isabella, drove the Moors out of Granada. There is a story that the last emir of Granada, after he had been forced to leave the city, looked back on it from a hill near by. There were tears in his eyes because he had lost the city to the Spaniards, and his mother said to him, "Do not weep like a woman for that which you were unable to defend as a man."

Gran Chaco

The Gran Chaco is a large area of land in South America. The Gran Chaco has no large cities or industries, but a terrible war was fought to control it. Two South American nations, Bolivia and Paraguay, fought bloody battles for more than eight years to gain possession of the Gran Chaco. They both claimed the land on account of old Spanish land grants. Moreover, Bolivia wanted the Gran Chaco, which is on the Paraguay River, in order to have a route to the sea. A treaty was signed in 1935 ending the war, and giving most of the Gran Chaco to Paraguay, but giving Bolivia a strip of land leading to the Paraguay River, so that Bolivia could ship goods to the sea.

Grand Alliance

The Grand Alliance is the name given to the group of nations including England, Holland, Brandenburg and the Duchy of Savoy, which joined together to fight Louis XIV of France. Louis XIV had wanted to make his empire larger by taking over other lands, and the nations of the Grand Alliance went to war against him to prevent this. The war, which began in 1688, lasted for nine years. It ended in the Treaty of Ryswick, in which Louis lost many of his earlier conquests.

Grand Army of the Republic

The Grand Army of the Republic, or G.A.R., was an organization of veterans who served in the Northern army during the Civil War. It was started in Decatur, Illinois, more than 85 years ago. The purpose of the founders was to bring together the men who had fought to save the republic; to take care of the dependents of the soldiers who had died; and to protect the laws and Constitution of the United States. The G.A.R. was the first organization to celebrate Memorial Day in the northern part of the United States.

Every year the G.A.R. would meet, in "encampments," and discuss matters of national interest. The G.A.R. had its largest membership about seventy years ago, when t' ere were more than 400,000 members. It held its final official meeting in 1949.

Grand Banks

The Grand Banks is a large area of shallow water near the coast of Newfoundland. The Banks begin on the southeastern tip of Newfoundland and curve around the coast for about two hundred miles, sometimes extending more than 250 miles into the Atlantic Ocean. The water of the Grand Banks ranges from 50 to 1,000 feet in depth.

The Grand Banks is one of the best fishing areas in the world. The most important catch is cod, which swim in large schools, or groups. The fishermen of many different nations travel to the Grand Banks to catch these fish with nets and hooks. However, the fishermen must face many dangers from icebergs, storms, and fogs. Thick fogs are frequent; they are caused by the warm air from the Gulf Stream meeting the much colder air of the Labrador current, which passes by the Grand Banks.

Grand Canal

There are several canals in the world that have the name of Grand Canal. Two of the most famous of these are the Grand Canal in Venice and the Grand Canal in China. You can read more about Venice's Grand Canal in the article on VENICE.

The Grand Canal in China is the oldest and longest canal in the world. It was started about 2,400 years ago and took almost two thousand years to build. It is a thousand miles long and runs from north to south through the two Chinese cities of Chinkiang and Tientsin. It connects two of China's main rivers, the Yangtze and the Yellow Rivers. The canal was originally built to make transportation easier between the Yangtze River and the North China Plain.

Grand Canyon

The Grand Canyon, in the state of Arizona, is the most famous canyon in the world. The word *canyon* comes from a Spanish word that means "hollow," and the Grand Canyon is a tremendous hollow in the earth. It is more than two hundred miles long, and in some places it is about eighteen miles wide at the top, while other parts are only about four miles wide.

The sides of the Grand Canyon are straight walls of rock. If you stand at the top, you can look down and see a tiny silver thread of water about a mile below. This is the mighty Colorado River. For millions of years the flowing water of the river has worn away the rock and earth and made this gigantic hollow in the earth's surface. You can read about the way this happened in separate articles on EROSION and COLORADO RIVER.

The sunlight and shadows fall on the towering peaks and crags and deep hollows of the canyon, and show the brilliant red, green, blue and white colors of the rock. As the light changes, the rocks glow and change colors. People come from every part of the world to visit the Grand Canyon. About fifty years ago, the United States government turned about a hundred miles of the Grand Canyon into a national park. In 1932, almost two hundred thousand acres adjoining Grand Canyon National Park were set aside by the national government and named Grand Canyon National Monument. You can read more about these in the separate article on NATIONAL PARKS.

Scientists have studied the rocks of the Grand Canyon, and they have learned many important things about how the earth was formed. The Grand Canyon was first visited by Spanish explorers more than four hundred years ago.

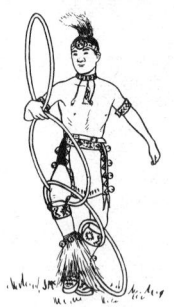

Grand Canyon is the home of many Hopi Indians, and there is a Hopi House on the south rim of the canyon. Here a brave rests before taking part in one of the age-old Hopi dances. On his lap rest the traditional feather headdress and mask. In his hands is a dried gourd. When he shakes it, the seeds inside will keep time with the drums.

Grand Coulee Dam

Grand Coulee Dam is one of the largest dams in the world. It is on the Columbia River in the state of Washington. It is a tremendous dam, 4,173 feet long and 550 feet high. It was completed in 1942, and provides power for industry and water for irrigation.

Grand Coulee has electric generators inside it. As the water goes through the dam it turns big paddle wheels, which turn the generators. The Grand Coulee Dam generates more electricity than any other dam in the world.

This dam is also a very important source of water for farmers. Most farmers in Washington do not have to worry about dry spells, because the water that is stored behind the Grand Coulee Dam is enough to cover ten thousand acres of land with a foot of water.

grand jury, people chosen to decide whether a person who has been accused of committing a crime should be tried in court. See the article on JURY.

Grand Rapids

Grand Rapids is an important city in the state of Michigan. It is on the Grand River and gets its name from the river rapids near the city. Grand Rapids is often called the furniture capital of America because the designing, manufacturing and selling of furniture is one of its main industries. Grand Rapids has a population of more than 197,000 people. Many of them work in various branches of the furniture business. Others work in plants that make metal and paper products, and in the shipping and packing businesses. The city was settled in 1877.

Grand Remonstrance

About three hundred years ago in England, during the reign of Charles I, there was a great struggle for power between the king and the Parliament. Charles thought that he should have sole power to rule the country, but Parliament was always getting in his way by passing legislation that he did not like, or refusing to give him money that he wanted. From 1629 to 1640 Charles ruled without any Parliament. Then he formed a new one, which came to be called the Long Parliament because it lasted nearly twenty years. For a short time it did what Charles wanted, but then, in 1641, it passed a measure called the Grand Remonstrance, which set forth a list of things that the people considered very unfair. The king pretended to accept this measure, but he did not like it and tried to arrest five leaders of Parliament who had voted for the Grand Remonstrance. This made Parliament and the people so angry that it led to civil war in England, and Charles I was put to death.

Grange

The Grange is an organization of farmers that was founded in 1867 by a United States government clerk named Oliver H. Kelley. *Grange* is a word that had been used in England for many years; it means "farm." Kelley called his organization the National Grange of the Patrons of Husbandry, but soon everyone just called it the Grange. Kelley founded the Grange to try to help farmers learn more modern methods so that they could make better livings for themselves and their families. The movement spread very quickly, and by 1875 there were more than 800,000 Grangers in the Midwest. It became so strong that it was able to get laws passed for the farmers' benefit. These were called Granger laws, and they set rates that the railroads could charge for hauling produce.

The Grange continues to be very helpful to its members. Any adult member of a farm family may join, and there are special groups for children under 14. When there are problems to be solved, the members discuss them at meetings and sometimes send representatives to Congress to present their opinions and requests. There are lectures at the meetings, but there is fun too, with parties, dances, and picnics. Sometimes Grangers get together to buy things they all need, such as feed or machinery, because it is cheaper to buy in large quantities. The Grange has members all over the United States, but it is strongest in New York, Pennsylvania, Ohio, New Jersey, and New England.

Grange, Red

Harold E. Grange was one of the greatest American football players. He was three times named an All-American, and is a member of most of the All-Time All-American teams that have been chosen. Many experts rank him second only to the late Jim Thorpe as a backfield star. Grange played under the famous coach Bob Zuppke at the University of Illinois in 1923, 1924, and 1925, and then left college to become a professional football player. He played until 1935 for the Chicago Bears and the New York Yankees, and has been elected to many all-time professional teams. Grange was nicknamed the "Galloping Ghost," and his number, 77, was famous throughout the country while he was playing. His greatest single game was played against Michigan in 1924. He scored four touchdowns in the first twelve minutes, on runs of 90, 60, 45 and 55 yards. Later in the same game he ran for one more touchdown, and passed for still another.

granite

Granite is a kind of very hard rock. It is usually gray, but there is also a great deal of red granite. Scientists believe that it was formed millions of years ago when the liquid rock of the earth's crust cooled and hardened. It is usually found deep under layers of other kinds of rock, but in many places it has been brought to the surface of the earth by the kind of terrific upheaval that created the mountains of the world long before man or animal life existed. Many mountains are almost solid granite. Thousands of years ago in Rome and Egypt granite was used for buildings and monuments. Granite takes a very high polish and is still used as a building stone by modern man.

Ulysses S. Grant

737

GRANT, ULYSSES S.

Ulysses Simpson Grant was the eighteenth President of the United States. He was the head of the Union, or northern, forces during the Civil War. There have been several American generals who became President, but Grant and Dwight D. Eisenhower are the only ones who were graduates of West Point. When Grant became supreme commander of the Union Army in March of 1864, the war had not been going well for the North. It was not until Grant assumed command that the tide turned definitely in favor of the Union. The war was won thirteen months later.

Even in his triumph, Grant was generous and considerate of the defeated Confederate forces. General Robert E. Lee, head of the Confederate Army, was treated with the utmost courtesy. The Confederate soldiers were allowed to keep their horses, instead of being forced to surrender them, because they "would be needed for spring plowing."

In the first presidential election after the Civil War was over, Grant was elected President by a large majority, in November, 1868. He was re-elected in 1872, again by a large majority. During his administration, there was a great deal of difficulty within the government. Some of the officials he appointed were not honest and used their government jobs to make money for themselves. This was done without Grant's knowledge, but it created a bad impression of the administration.

Ulysses Grant was a short, heavy-set man with a black beard. He was a stern military commander, but in private life he was gentle, kind, and extremely fair.

HIS EARLY YEARS

Ulysses Grant was born in Point Pleasant, Ohio, on April 27, 1822. His father was a farmer, and his mother's maiden name was Hannah Simpson. Although Grant was originally named Hiram Ulysses Grant, the registration office at West Point made a mistake, and entered his name on the academy's list of students as Ulysses Simpson Grant instead. He found it easier to change his name than to change West Point records. When he was twenty-one, he was graduated from West Point as a second lieutenant, with a commission in the regular army. Three years later, the war with Mexico broke out, and Grant was assigned to duty there. He received two promotions in recognition of his war service, and when peace came he was a captain. In 1848, when he was 26 years old, he married Miss Julia Dent of St. Louis, Missouri. He remained in the army as a captain until 1854, and at that time it seemed that there was not much prospect of a good future for him in the army. He resigned his commission and retired to civilian life in Galena, Illinois. He believed that he was through with the army for good. He tried farming, did a little real-estate operation, and worked selling leather goods, without much success in anything.

GRANT AS A SOLDIER

When the Civil War started in 1861, Grant immediately offered his services to the government. He was ready to do anything that might be needed, and at which he could be useful. At that time no one knew of his great gifts of leadership, but his offer to serve was welcome. He was appointed colonel of the 21st Illinois Volunteer Regiment. He took whatever duty was given to him, and never tried to get any special favors or easy jobs. Grant never tried to build up his reputation by looking for publicity, but went about his work quietly and efficiently, doing his job well. In fact, Grant did it so well that President Lincoln very soon noticed what a capable officer and soldier he was and promoted him to brigadier general.

He commanded his troops in a long series of battles. At the battle of Belmont, Maryland, the horse on which Grant was riding was shot. Grant was unhurt, however. Shortly afterward he was sent to the Kentucky-Tennessee area to fight under General H. W. Halleck. Grant's forces took Fort Henry on the Tennessee River in the early part of February, 1862, and a few days later attacked Fort Donelson on the Cumberland River near Nashville, Tennessee. It was here that he made the famous speech that gave him the nickname of "Unconditional Surrender" Grant. The general defending Fort Donelson asked what terms Grant would give them, and Grant replied: "No terms other than an unconditional and immediate surrender can be accepted . . ." The capture of this fort was an important victory for the Union Army, and it was the beginning of General Grant's fame as a commander.

About two months after the capture of Fort Donelson, Grant was camped at Pittsburg Landing in the southern part of Tennessee, near the Mississippi border, on the west bank of the Tennessee River. The Confederates attacked him there, and he was slightly wounded in battle. It was not a severe wound, however, and it did not keep him out of the fight. He went on to the Battle of Shiloh, a few miles away, after his men had driven the Confederate army back. Victory at Shiloh gave the Union forces control as far south as Vicksburg, Mississippi. Vicksburg surrendered on July 4, 1863.

Grant's next important step was to attack the Confederate army in the Battle of Chattanooga, in eastern Tennessee. His victory there, in November, 1863, drove the Confederates out of the state.

By this time, Grant was a great public hero. Congress presented him with a special medal in recognition of his skill as a commander, and President Lincoln gave him full command of all the Union forces. On March 9, 1864, he took over his new responsibility, and the people of the country felt that the North could not lose the war with General Grant in command of the army.

General Grant conducted a long and bitter fight against the Confederate Army led by General Robert E. Lee, and it was not until April 9, 1865, that he was able to force the surrender of Lee at Appomattox Courthouse, Virginia.

HOW HE BECAME PRESIDENT

Grant was the hero of the day, and he was generally given credit for having won the war. For the next Presidental election, in 1868, the Republican party nominated him for President and the people elected him with a large majority of votes in his favor. The Democratic candidate that year was Horatio Seymour.

During his first years as President, Grant succeeded in convincing Congress that the South was being harshly treated in some respects. He was as popular as President as he had been as a general of the army. He succeeded in correcting some of the injustices that Johnson's Congress had voted into law. An important achievement was the Amnesty Bill, which gave back the civil rights of all people in the South except a few Confederate leaders. The Fifteenth Amendment to the Constitution was ratified during his first two years in office. This was the amendment that gave all citizens the right to vote, regardless of whether they were white or Negro, or whether they had once been slaves.

President Grant also succeeded in reducing the national debt during his term of office. The cost of the Civil War had been high, and the country was deeply in debt when he became President. The public showed its appreciation of Grant's original administration by electing him for a second time in 1872, when he defeated Horace Greeley, the famous publisher and journalist.

HIS LATER YEARS

After his second term was over, Grant and his family made a trip around the world, visiting many foreign countries. People in foreign countries were not well acquainted with Americans at that time, and his trip did a great deal toward showing them what Americans were like. He was welcomed by the highest officials and rulers of every country he visited, and given the highest honors a visitor could receive.

When Grant returned to the United States at the end of the tour, an influential group of Republicans tried to nominate him for the Presidency for a third time, but there was then a very strong feeling against a third term for any President and he was not nominated.

Grant retired to private life and attempted to conduct a banking business in New York City, but he was unsuccessful. He did not have the kind of experience that is needed in banking, and also he was badly cheated by several people whom he had trusted. They took advantage of his fine name and great reputation in order to make fortunes for themselves. Soon he had lost all his money, and it was necessary to do something in order to provide for his family.

When it became known that the great general and ex-President was poor, the entire country sympathized, and the sentiment was so strong that Congress introduced a bill to award him a pension of $5,000 a year. He asked to have the bill withdrawn, however, and Congress felt that it must do as he wished in this matter.

It was then that Grant started to write his personal life history, in which he included complete stories of all the battles in which he had taken part. He called it his "Personal Memoirs," and worked very hard to finish it. It was extremely difficult, because at this time he was in almost constant pain from cancer of the throat. He finished his book, however, and it is considered by many people to be one of the best military biographies ever written. It brought about half a million dollars to his family, although the general himself did not live to enjoy his painfully earned

money. He died at Saratoga, New York, on July 23, 1885.

Grant's Tomb, on Riverside Drive at 123rd Street in New York City, is a famous monument. It is 150 feet high and 90 feet square. It was built by money contributed by the public, and cost $600,000. Grant's body was removed from the temporary tomb in which it had been placed and transferred to the monumental tomb where it remains. The transfer took place on April 17, 1897, twelve years after his death. The body of Mrs. Ulysses Grant was placed there also when she died.

Mrs. Ulysses S. Grant

Julia Dent Grant was born in 1826, the daughter of Judge Frederick Dent, of St. Louis. She was married to Grant in August, 1848, and they had three sons and one daughter. Mrs. Grant outlived her husband by seventeen years. She died in 1902 and was buried in the same tomb as Grant, in New York City.

granulation

Granulation is making into grains. Ordinary table sugar is an example of a substance that has been granulated. When the sugar is taken from the sugar cane (or sugar beets), it is in the form of a very thick syrup. This heavy syrup is slowly heated and mixed, until all of the water is driven out of it. Then all that is left is the tiny white grains of sugar, which is the form in which we get it from the grocery store. We say that the sugar has been granulated.

Doctors often find a different kind of "grain," called a *granule*, on a wound or sore that has become infected and has begun to heal. The forming of these granules is also called granulation. The granules are made of capillaries (tiny blood vessels) and other parts of the flesh. Eventually they will form a scab.

grape

The grape is a fruit or, more exactly, berry, that grows in bunches on a vine. It is one of the oldest plants known to man and grows in almost every country in the world. It is one of the principal crops of France, Italy, Spain, Germany, and the United States, especially in California.

There are many different varieties of grape, but only a few dozen are widely grown. The most important species (kind) of grapes is the *vinifera* or Old World grape, and most of the grapes grown in the world are of this type. The second most important species of grape is called *labrusca* or New World grape. It can be recognized easily because unlike the Old World grape, its skin slips off easily but the seeds stick to the fleshy part. It is grown in many parts of America.

Grapes may be eaten fresh but some Old World varieties are dried first. Dried grapes are called *raisins* or *currants*. Grapes may also be used to make grape juice and wine. The most common grapes used for eating fresh are the yellow Thompson Seedless, the most important grape grown, the red Tokay, the Malaga, the Ribier, and the Muscat. The Thompson Seedless and the Muscat are also used for raisins, as are the tiny Black Corinth grapes. Wine is made from the Pinot,

Riesling, Mission, Madeira and Muscat grapes, and grape juice from the Concord grape.

Grapes grow well where the winter is not too cold and where there is a long, warm summer that enables the plants to ripen their fruit slowly. This kind of climate is often found near lakes and oceans, and grapes may be planted on nearby hillsides. The soil must be fertile and care must be taken to keep insects and disease away. Grapevines must be carefully pruned each year and the vines are often grown on trellises or tied to stakes.

A good grapevine may live more than fifty years and will produce large quantities of grapes, the amount depending on the variety and where and how it is grown.

grapefruit

The grapefruit is a juicy, round, yellow fruit that belongs to the same family as lemons and oranges and limes. The grapefruit is one of the largest citrus fruits. It is named after the grape, because it often hangs in clusters, which look somewhat like bunches of grapes. Most grapefruits weigh slightly under one pound. The grapefruit first grew in Asia, and the Spanish people began to grow grapefruit in the West Indies and Florida hundreds of years ago. Now people in California, Italy, and many tropical countries raise grapefruit.

People have discovered new ways to improve the grapefruit in the last fifty years. Now you can buy grapefruits that are much larger and have more juice, and do not have any seeds. Fifty years ago people had to use sugar on grapefruit, but now many grapefruits are sweet enough to eat without adding sugar. Some of them have a pink flesh that is especially sweet and juicy. The juice of the grape-

Grapefruit tastes sharp and refreshing, and contains lots of healthful Vitamin C.

fruit is canned and frozen and is a very popular breakfast drink. See also the article CITRUS FRUITS.

graph

A graph is a special kind of picture that can give you a quick idea about different sets of numbers. There are several kinds of graphs, but the main purpose of all of them is to tell a story about numbers easily and clearly.

There are some things that all graphs have. A graph must have a title that tells what the graph explains. A graph must also have a scale, which is somewhat like a ruler.

The scale shows you in regular units of measurement the difference between the things that are being explained on the graph. Every good graph depends on accurate number facts. Sometimes number facts are called statistics. Only when the statistics are accurate, and have been written down in regular order in what is called a *table of numbers*, can you make a good graph. Sometimes a table of numbers has numbers that are too large or too uneven to be compared with each other easily. In these cases, the numbers must be rounded off. This means that they must be brought to the nearest even set of numbers that can be entered on the graph. For example, the number 104 might be made 100, or the number 489 might be rounded off to 500. In this way the figures can be shown in terms of hundreds, which make them easier to understand quickly. Because of this, however, a graph should never be taken as completely accurate. It is meant to give only an approximate idea about number facts.

LINE GRAPH

A line graph is a very good way to show what happens over a period of time. A line graph is drawn on paper that is marked with small squares. Suppose you wanted to show how the population of your town has grown in the last fifty years. Across the bottom of the graph, you would mark off the years. Each square might represent one year. Along the left side of the paper, up and down, you mark off the number of people. Each

The main purpose of any line graph is to show what happens over a period of time.

square might stand for one thousand people. Then, you would make dots on the graph to show how many people there were in your town in each year. When you connect the dots, you have a line that shows how the population has changed from year to year. When a person is sick, the nurse may make a line graph of his temperature. Then the doctor can see at a glance if the patient's fever went up or down.

CIRCLE GRAPH

A circle graph is another good way to tell a number story. Circle graphs are used to show the relation of the parts of a thing to the whole thing. For example, suppose you wanted to make a graph that shows how a family spends its money;

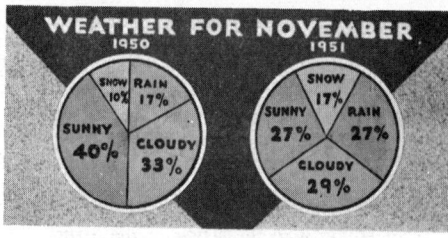

The circle graph shows the changing relationship between parts of a whole.

how much of the family income is spent for food, how much for clothes, how much for entertainment, and so on. You divide the circle into sections. Suppose the income is $5,000 and you divide the circle into 50 parts. Each section stands for $100. If the family spent $500 for food, you would mark off five parts to form a section representing food. Finally the circle would show, by the size of the sections, about how much your family spent for each thing.

PICTOGRAPH

A pictograph is very useful when you want to show things in round numbers. If you wanted to show how many children were enrolled in schools in the United States in 1960, you could make a picto-

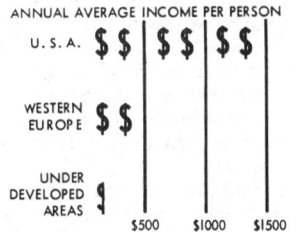

ANNUAL AVERAGE INCOME PER PERSON

The pictograph uses symbols to dramatize statistics. The dollar signs contrast incomes of people in different places.

graph. On the graph you would place tiny pictures of children. Each picture would stand for one million children. If you placed three figures next to ages five to thirteen, you would know that three million children of those ages were enrolled in school in 1960. In a pictograph you have to count the symbols (the little figures) and multiply by the scale (each figure stands for one million children) to find out the number information.

BAR GRAPH

A bar graph, like a line graph, is made on paper with small squares on it. If you

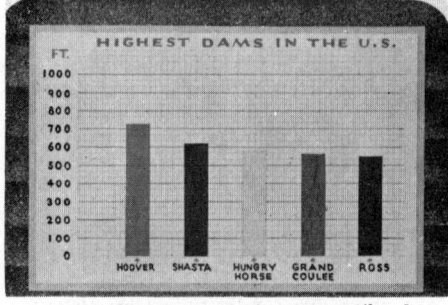

Copyright Curriculum Film, Inc.
A bar graph makes it quite simple to measure by scale and to compare amounts.

wanted to show the number of workers in the factories in your town, you could make a bar graph. Across the bottom of the graph you make a scale of numbers that are rounded off. Then on the vertical lefthand side of the graph, you label the kinds of factory in your town, such as chemical and plastics and automobile factories. Then you can use your scale to mark the approximate number of men who work in each of these factories. A person who looks at the bar graph can tell, without having to measure, which kind of factory employs the most men. When you want to compare several number facts, a bar graph is a clear way to do it.

graphic arts

The graphic arts are the use of any kind of drawing, writing or printing to create something beautiful. The designing of beautiful books has come to be considered as much one of the graphic arts as ENGRAVING and LITHOGRAPHY, which were once considered the principal graphic arts. There are separate articles about these.

graphite

Graphite is a pure form of carbon. It is black or grayish black, soft and greasy, and it has a shine like a metal. Graphite is a good conductor of electricity and does not burn easily or melt even at high temperatures. Because of its resistance to great heat it is often used for *crucibles,* the vessels or pots in which metals are melted. It is very important as a lubricant and is often used where large flat surfaces must rub against each other. Locksmiths sometimes blow powdered graphite inside locks to lubricate them, instead of using light oil which dries out and becomes sticky. The black grease used to lubricate the gears of automobiles is often a mixture of heavy petroleum oil and powdered graphite. The pencils that most students use in school do not really contain lead but a mixture of clay and graphite. Soft pencils that write very black contain a larger amount of graphite than hard pencils. The more clay that is mixed with the graphite, the harder the pencil, and the lighter it writes. Graphite is dug out of the earth as are coal, iron, and other metals or minerals. It is mined in the states of Nevada, Michigan, Rhode Island, Alabama, and North Carolina in the United States, as well as in Great Britain, Europe, parts of South America, and Ceylon in southeast Asia.

graphology, the study of handwriting in the belief that it reveals something about the writer's character and personality: see the article on HANDWRITING.

grass

Grass is the most important family of plants in the world. There is hardly a place in the world where some form of grass does not grow. This family of plants has many members, ranging in size from the inch-high grass on your lawn to the tall stalks of bamboo that grow to be over a hundred feet high. Because it is such a varied family, it has many uses.

THE CEREALS

All cereals are grasses. Cereals include

wheat, corn, rice, rye, oats, and barley. Most of the farmed land in the world is used for raising one or another of these cereals. They are used primarily for food, either for man or animals.

Wheat is the most important single crop. It has been known to man for more than five thousand years, and he has grown it wherever he has gone. It is a fairly easy crop to grow, but without proper care it dies out in a few years. The main use of wheat is in making "the staff of life," or bread.

Rice has been almost as important a crop as wheat, and today it may feed even more people, for it is the chief cereal of India, all of East Asia, Japan, and the South Pacific islands including Indonesia; also it is a big crop in the United States.

Corn (that is, *maize* or *Indian corn*) is important in the Americas as a vegetable and grain for bread, but also as food for animals bred for meat. In England, "corn" means "wheat." It is believed that today's corn, or maize, has been refined over the centuries from a plant first found in North America and used by American Indians long ago. In some parts of North America it is used more than wheat.

Oats are not nearly as important as a cereal as they used to be. The main use of oats was to feed horses, but with the invention of gasoline and diesel engines, the number of work horses has greatly decreased. Oats are a very sturdy grain which will grow on fairly rocky soil where there is not too much sunshine. These qualities make oats very popular with people living in cool, rather barren places, such as Scotland. Oatmeal is considered the "national food" of Scotland. The usual yield of oats is 15 bushels per acre.

OTHER GRASSES

The kinds of grass that grow lower to the ground are valuable for feeding animals. These grasses do not include clover, which belongs to another family. Sometimes these grasses are used for fertilizer, when they are plowed under the ground.

Grass is also very important when used as hay. This is a dried grass that is used for food during the winter months when the animals cannot get green grass. The most important hay crop is a grass called alfalfa. Other grasses used in hay-making are timothy, wild hay, blue grass, and the stalks of the cereals after the grain has been removed.

There are many other uses for grass. Most of these other uses depend upon the particular qualities of the grasses and the region in which they are used. Bamboo is used in the southern Asiatic countries for making everything from houses to writing paper. Other grasses are used for weaving baskets and mats. There is almost no limit to the things that can be made of grass.

GRASS AS A DECORATION

The members of the grass family that we are most familiar with are the grasses that make our lawns and gardens beautiful.

There are many different kinds of lawn grass. Some are used for their color, while some are selected because of the soil to be used. The best way to find out what kind of grass to plant is to have the

soil inspected by an agricultural expert. He will find out what kinds of grass may grow in your soil, and then you may select the particular color you want. Some grasses are much more dense than others; some grow very tall, while some stay very close to the ground and never have to be cut at all. These things should be considered when choosing your grass.

There are two ways to plant a lawn. One way is to "seed" it. The grass seed is bought at a hardware or garden store. The ground is dug up and very carefully raked. Then the seeds are planted. Strips of burlap, or some other cloth, are placed over the seeded area to keep the birds from eating the seeds and to keep the rain from washing them away. If the lawn is carefully watered and not disturbed, in a few weeks the first blades of grass grow up through the burlap.

Another way to start a lawn is to buy strips of sod, or earth which has grass growing in it already. These strips of sod are placed on the ground, watered, and allowed to grow into the soil. This is a much surer way of growing a lawn, because the grass has already started growing and does not need as much care as the seeded lawn.

There are many things that can happen to a lawn to make it die, but usually if a lawn is well watered and taken care of, it will remain healthy. Sometimes a lawn will turn brown in spots. Usually this means that it has not been getting enough water. If careful watering does not make the brown spots turn green again, it is necessary to dig up the spots, rake them out, and either plant more seed or lay a piece of sod down.

When something happens to the lawn that you cannot seem to prevent, the best solution is to have an expert look at it. You may be doing something wrong, and the expert will be able to tell you how to correct it. Most garden stores have men who know all about lawns and can help you out.

grasshopper

The grasshopper is an insect that lives in almost every part of the world. It is a great jumper and with its strong back legs can hop very quickly from one place to another. When they are full-grown, grasshoppers have wings, and some kinds fly hundreds of miles in search of food. They travel in swarms, and in earlier times people reported flights of grasshoppers so huge that they blotted out the sun. Grasshoppers feed on all kinds of plant, and are a great pest to farmers because they destroy the crops. About eighty years ago, grasshoppers east of the Rocky Mountains, especially in the states of Kansas and Nebraska, destroyed hundreds of millions of dollars worth of grain. Farmers now have good ways of killing grasshoppers, mainly by spraying their crops with poisons.

There are many different kinds of grasshopper, but all of them belong to either of two main groups: those that have short feelers on top of their heads, and those that have long feelers. Grasshoppers make various kinds of sound. They do this by striking their wings together, or by rubbing their hind legs against their wings. The most common

The wingless grasshopper found in many southern states looks harmless enough, but does lots of damage when it sets out to eat its way through a crop.

of all grasshoppers is the short-horned insect that makes a noise that sounds like a steady hum.

gravel

Gravel is made up of small pieces of rock. Some gravel is made by the action of rivers and oceans. This kind usually has pebbles that are round in shape because the waters of the rivers and oceans have tumbled them around and over each other for hundreds of centuries. The very tiny chips of stone that are knocked off by this action form the sand that is found on beaches and riverbanks.

A special kind of gravel that is not round is found in deposits in the earth, where it was formed in ancient times when ice covered large areas of the earth. This gravel is dug out in many of the northern states of the United States.

Gravel is very important because it is used in building roads and in making concrete. The United States produces about three hundred million tons of gravel every year.

gravitation or gravity

Everything in the world attracts every other thing in the world—that is, it pulls every other thing to it. This attraction is called gravitation, or "the force of gravity."

Larger things have a greater pull than smaller things. That is why we do not see such things as tables, chairs, stones, or other things coming together just because they are standing near each other. They are not large enough for us to notice their pull. The earth, sun, moon, and planets are constantly pulling on each other. The planets turn around the sun because the sun is larger than any of them and pulls them toward it.

The gravitational pull you are most familiar with is the pull of the earth on you. If you jump into the air, you will always come down again to the ground. The reason is that the earth is pulling you down. Gravity means "heaviness." Be-

cause the earth is so much larger than you are, its pull on you is much greater than your pull on it. When you stand on a scale, the earth pulls your body to the scale. The amount by which your body is pulled down is called your weight.

The earth acts somewhat as a magnet does with a piece of iron. It makes rivers and streams run downhill. The closer something is to the center of the earth, the more it will be pulled down, so the more it will weigh. If something weighs a thousand pounds on top of a mountain about 14,000 feet high, it will weigh one pound more if it is brought down to sea level.

The farther you are from the earth the less you will weigh. If you weigh 100 pounds on earth, you will weigh only 25 pounds 4,000 miles away. If you were on the moon, you would weigh only 17 pounds. The reason is that the moon is so much smaller than the earth, and pulls you down less than the earth does. If you were on the sun you would weigh almost 3,000 pounds, because gravity on the sun is much stronger than the earth's.

SPEED OF FALLING OBJECTS

Because gravity's pull is greater as a weight comes closer to the center of the earth, a falling body increases its speed as it falls. This increase in speed is called acceleration of gravity and it is constant, which means it is always the same. The rate of acceleration is 32 feet per second per second; that is, at the end of every second the falling object is going 32 feet per second faster than it was at the end of the previous second.

Suppose a ball is dropped from a high place. At the moment that it is dropped, it is not falling at any speed. Since it is accelerating at the rate of 32 feet per second per second, at the end of the first second it acquires a speed of 32 feet per second. Its average speed during the first second is 16 feet per second and the distance traveled is 16 feet. At the end of the second second, it acquires an additional speed of 32 feet per second, making its speed 64 feet per second. At the end of the third second, it acquires another 32 feet per second, making its speed 96 feet per second. Since the average speed during these three seconds is 48 feet per second, the distance traveled is 144 feet.

If a one-pound and a two-pound weight are dropped from the same height, the force of gravity is greater on the two-pound weight, but the two-pound weight is also pulling on the earth with twice the force of the one-pound weight. But, since the mass of the two-pound weight is twice that of the one-pound weight the force per unit mass, or the acceleration of the two, is the same. The fact that things of different weight fall with the same acceleration was first proved by the Italian scientist Galileo, more than 350 years ago.

The English scientist Sir Isaac Newton first explained the way gravitation works more than 250 years ago. His explanation is called the Law of Universal Gravitation. He discovered that the pull of the sun on the planets, and the pull of the earth on things on its surface, are alike and can be explained in the same way.

The law of gravitation says that the pull between two things depends on how

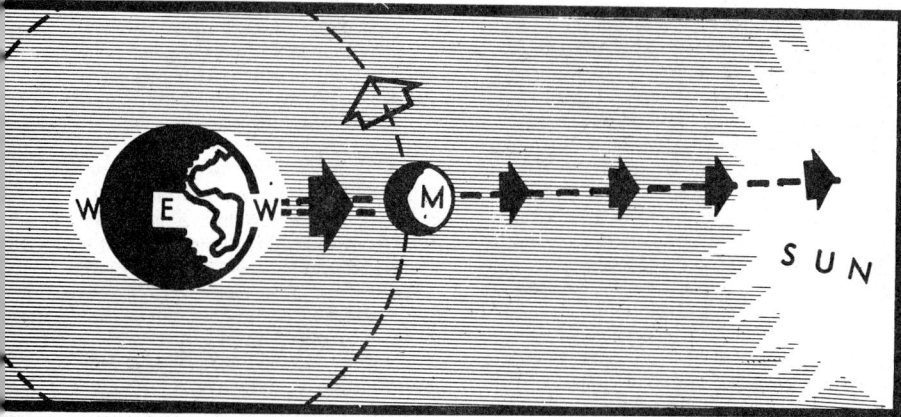

The gravitational attraction of the moon (*M*) causes every shore line (*W*) on earth (*E*) to have two high and two low tides daily. The moon attracts water facing it; at the same time it pulls the hard surface of the earth, thus causing a high-tide water bulge on the opposite side of the earth. Tides rise and fall as the earth spins. Twice a month the sun and moon combine their gravitational pulls to make a very high tide (as diagram shows).

large they are and how far apart they are. The larger they are, the greater the pull; the closer they are, the greater the pull. With the law of gravitation, many things can be explained. One of the most interesting is the rising and falling of the tides in the ocean. A tide is a movement of water in or out from the shore or beach. At high tide the water comes in toward the beach; at low tide it goes out from the beach. The law of gravitation tells us how this happens. The moon is constantly going around the earth, due to the earth's gravitational pull. But the moon is also pulling on the earth. It pulls on both the water and the land, but the water moves more easily than the land. The pulled-up water soon reaches the shore and makes a tide there. This is called high tide. When the moon has moved away from that part of the earth, the water settles back and we have low tide. The pull of the sun on the earth also causes tides.

Although Newton explained the way gravitation worked, he did not know how one body could pull another without touching it. This is called action at a distance. In 1916 the scientist Albert Einstein wrote a new explanation of gravity called the theory of relativity. He said that things did not pull on each other through a distance. The reason why a little body moves toward a heavy body, as do the planets toward the sun, is that the heavy body is in a downhill part of space. Because it is heavier it makes more of a dent in space than the lighter one. According to Einstein's theory, light would have to travel through these dents in space when it comes from the sun to the earth. This would cause it to be bent. In 1922, during an eclipse of the sun, scientists observed that light was bent, and part of Einstein's theory was proved. Thirty years later Einstein published another theory in which he tried to explain other kinds of motion, such as movement of electricity and light, by gravitation.

Gray, Asa

Asa Gray was an American botanist who was born in New York in 1810. A botanist is a man who studies plant life, but Asa Gray did more than this. He wrote about his work so clearly that his books are still of great value. He became

a professor of natural history at Harvard University, and became such an authority that the city in which he lived, Cambridge, Massachusetts, became a center for botanical study. He traveled a great deal and made friends everywhere. Charles Darwin was one of these friends. Gray died in 1888 after receiving many honors.

Gray, Elisha

Elisha Gray was an inventor with a sad story. He was born in Ohio in 1835, and he put himself through college by doing carpentry. His interest in electricity led him to make many inventions of telegraph equipment and appliances. He worked especially hard on a way of sending the human voice over wires from one place to another. When he succeeded, he went to the patent office in Washington to register this invention. But someone else had come there a few hours earlier with a similar invention; it was Alexander Graham Bell, and his invention was the telephone. Gray died in 1901.

Gray, Thomas

Thomas Gray was an English poet who lived about two hundred years ago. He was considered by some critics to be the greatest English poet of his century. He was born in 1716. His father was a cruel man, and finally Thomas's mother left him and supported her son by herself. She sent him to school and then helped him to travel to Europe. Gray was a very quiet and gentle man. He spent most of his life in Cambridge, England, where he went to school and later became professor of modern history. His most famous poem is the "Elegy Written in a Country Churchyard," but he also wrote many odes, and a number of poems that children like, such as the one about his favorite cat. Gray died in 1771. A famous story about the "Elegy Written in a Country Churchyard" is that the British commander James Wolfe recited the poem before the attack in which his army took the city of Quebec from the French. At the end of the poem Wolfe said to his men: "Gentlemen, I would rather have written those lines than take Quebec."

grayling

The grayling is a beautiful fish that lives in the cool rivers of Europe and

Alaska, and in the waters of Montana and Michigan, in the United States. The grayling has a slender, gracefully curved

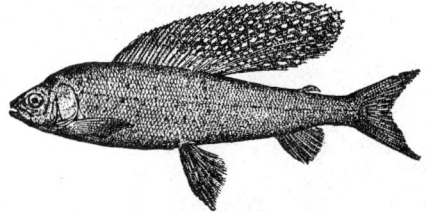

The grayling, an artful dodger of hooks and bait, challenges a fisherman's skill.

body and large fins. It is a bright blue, rose, and green color, though the graylings that are found in the United States are not as bright or as large as the European graylings. The American grayling weighs about two pounds, and the grayling of Europe weighs about four pounds. The grayling is a very lively fish. It has a small mouth, so it is difficult for fishermen to hook it. The meat of the grayling tastes very good, and people consider it a great delicacy.

greasewood

The greasewood is a plant that grows in the western part of the United States, where the soil is dry. The greasewood plant grows from four to eight feet tall, and it has deep roots that often reach far beneath the ground to buried streams. The greasewood can survive for very long periods without any rain at all. It has small, thick leaves that make a good food for cattle and sheep. The wood of the greasewood is hard and yellow. It is often used as firewood.

Great Barrier Reef

The Great Barrier Reef is the name of the largest coral reef in the world. A coral reef is built up by millions of tiny sea animals, and you can read about how it is formed in the article about CORAL. The Great Barrier Reef is off the northeastern coast of Australia, and it is more than 1,200 miles long. It ranges in width from less than one mile to several miles. At some places it is more than a hundred miles from the coast; at other places it may lie only ten miles from the coast. The Great Barrier Reef has rocky ridges that rise sharply from extremely deep waters. It is very dangerous to ships during a storm, because they may be blown onto the reef and break apart and sink. If a ship is able to pass into the water that lies between the reef and the mainland, it is then protected from the high waves and winds of the open ocean.

Great Basin

The Great Basin is a large area in the United States covering most of the state of Nevada and parts of the neighboring states of Utah, Idaho, Oregon and California. It is shaped like a triangle and is called the Great Basin because it has no rivers flowing out of it. It is rimmed by the Sierra Nevada Mountains on the west side and by the Wasatch Range of the Rocky Mountains on the east. In the Basin are mountains 5,000 to 7,000 feet high, and hundreds of broken ridges, some of which are 12,000 feet high. Death Valley, the lowest place in North America, is in the Great Basin,

as are the Great Salt Lake, near which the settlers called Mormons built homes, and the Mohave and Carson Deserts.

The climate is dry and few plants grow, but the Great Basin has rich mineral deposits. Many thousands of years ago, two great lakes called Bonneville and Lahotan covered most of the northern part of the Basin. The Great Basin was named by the explorer John Frémont.

Great Bear Lake

The Great Bear Lake is in northwestern Canada, near the Arctic Circle. It is 12,000 square miles in area. It is frozen over most of the year, and ships can sail there for a few weeks in August and September only. Pitchblende, an ore from which uranium and radium are taken, was discovered there in large amounts in 1930, and the largest town on the lake was named Port Radium.

Great Britain

Great Britain is one of the British Isles and by far the largest one. It has 88,619 square miles. Historically this is divided into England in the south (51,356 square miles), Scotland in the north (29,794 square miles), and Wales in a small southwestern section (7,469 square miles). From 1707 until 1927 Great Britain was the official name of the country that included these three sections of the island and that ruled the tremendous British Empire. Since 1927 the official name has been the United Kingdom of Great Britain and Northern Ireland. In speaking of either Great Britain or the United Kingdom, people ordinarily use simply the name Britain or the name England, which for two thousand years has been the most important of the British countries. The history of Great Britain is usually called English history, and you can read about it in the article ENGLAND.

Great Circle

A great circle is the largest circle that can be drawn around a sphere or any ball-shaped object. The equator, the imaginary line that runs around the "center" of the earth, is a great circle. Every point

on a great circle is exactly the same distance from the center of the sphere.

The great circle is extremely important in navigation. Though it is the longest line that can be drawn around a sphere, it is the shortest distance between any two points on the sphere. A navigator wanting to get from one place to another on a ship finds the great circle that runs through both of those points and follows that as his course.

Some great circles are already drawn on the globe so that you do not have to imagine them. The circles passing through the North and South Poles, called *meridians,* are great circles.

There are other circles that are drawn around the globe, passing through the meridians. These are called *parallels.* The equator is the only parallel that is a great circle.

In certain places a ship cannot follow a great-circle course because it may lead over land or into dangerous waters. In that case, it follows a course as close to a great circle as possible. This is called a *composite course* and is the one used by most ships.

Airplanes are usually able to follow a great-circle course without too much trouble. In flying from the United States to China, airplanes may soon be able to follow a great-circle course over the North Pole instead of flying over the Pacific Ocean. This great-circle course is really the shortest way, though it looks longer on a flat map.

Great Commoner

The Great Commoner was a name first given to William Pitt, who was Prime Minister of England about two hundred years ago. Before Pitt's time, most of the leaders of England had come from the House of Lords and were of noble birth. Pitt was called a "commoner" because he was a member of the House of Commons, or the elected body of the English Parliament, the lawmaking body of Great Britain. There is a separate article about William PITT.

William Jennings BRYAN, an American, was also called the Great Commoner. There is a separate article about him.

Great Dane

A Great Dane is a giant among dogs. It is one of the largest and most powerful breeds of dog in the world. Strangely enough, it did not come from Denmark but from Germany. The hunters who lived in Germany about four hundred years ago wanted a powerful, brave dog that had the strength and courage to hunt wild boars—the most dangerous of all game animals in Europe. The Great Dane was developed for that purpose, and it proved to be everything that the hunters had wanted in a dog. Today in both Europe and America great Danes are kept as watchdogs, as pets, and for hunting. They are good pets because they are usually gentle and affectionate.

A Great Dane stands between 28 and 34 inches high at the shoulders, and usually weighs between 120 and 150 pounds. The most common color is light tan, but Great Danes are sometimes also black, brindled (light tan with narrow black stripes), and white with black patches. Its coat is smooth and short and its tail is

long and thin. Its ears are long, but some owners clip the ears to make them stand up in sharp little points. The Great Dane has a large, noble-looking head, and a squarish muzzle.

Great Eastern

The *Great Eastern* was one of the most famous steamships ever built, and the largest of its time. It was called the "Great Iron Ship," and it was planned to be a luxury ocean liner; but from the day it was launched in 1858 until it was finally abandoned thirty years later, it had one misfortune after another. Men were killed in building it, it was damaged by storms at sea, and its owners lost great sums of money on it. The *Great Eastern* was almost 700 feet long, driven by sails, paddles (like the Mississippi river boats), and screws (under-water propellers such as modern steamships have). After its failure as a passenger ship, it was used for cable-laying and was the ship that laid the successful Atlantic cable, which you can read about in the article CABLE.

Great Lakes

The Great Lakes are a group of five large lakes in the central part of North America, between Canada and the United States. Ever since they were discovered by French traders nearly three hundred years ago, they have been very important to the commerce and trade of North America. Iron ore, coal, wheat and other foods are among the products carried in ships on the Great Lakes.

The Great Lakes are the largest group of lakes in the world. They are Lake Superior, Lake Michigan, Lake Huron, Lake Erie, and Lake Ontario. Some people remember these names by remembering that their initials spell the word HOMES. Lake Michigan is the only one that lies entirely within the United States; all of the others are partly in the United States and partly in Canada. On the Canadian side, all the great lakes are in the province of Ontario. The most important Canadian lake port is Toronto. On the American side the Great Lakes stretch all the way from Minnesota to New York. The most important ports are Duluth, Minnesota; Milwaukee, Wisconsin; Detroit, Michigan; Chicago, Illinois; Toledo and Cleveland, Ohio; Erie, Pennsylvania; and Buffalo, New York.

The total area of the Great Lakes is about 94,000 square miles, nearly as large as the state of Oregon. Lake Superior is the largest. It has an area of 31,820 square miles, about the size of North Carolina. Lake Ontario, with an area of 7,540 square miles, which is about the area of New Jersey, is the smallest.

The Great Lakes are all connected with each other, so that boats can travel all the way from Lake Superior in the west to Lake Ontario in the east. Some of the natural connections between the lakes were too shallow or too rough for ships to travel, so deeper channels or canals were built. The Sault Ste. Marie Canal connects Lake Superior to Lake Michigan and Lake Huron. Nearly all of the iron ore from the great Mesabi Range in Minnesota is shipped through this canal and across the Great Lakes to the steel mills of Indiana, Ohio, and Pennsylvania. Lake Erie and Lake Ontario are connected by

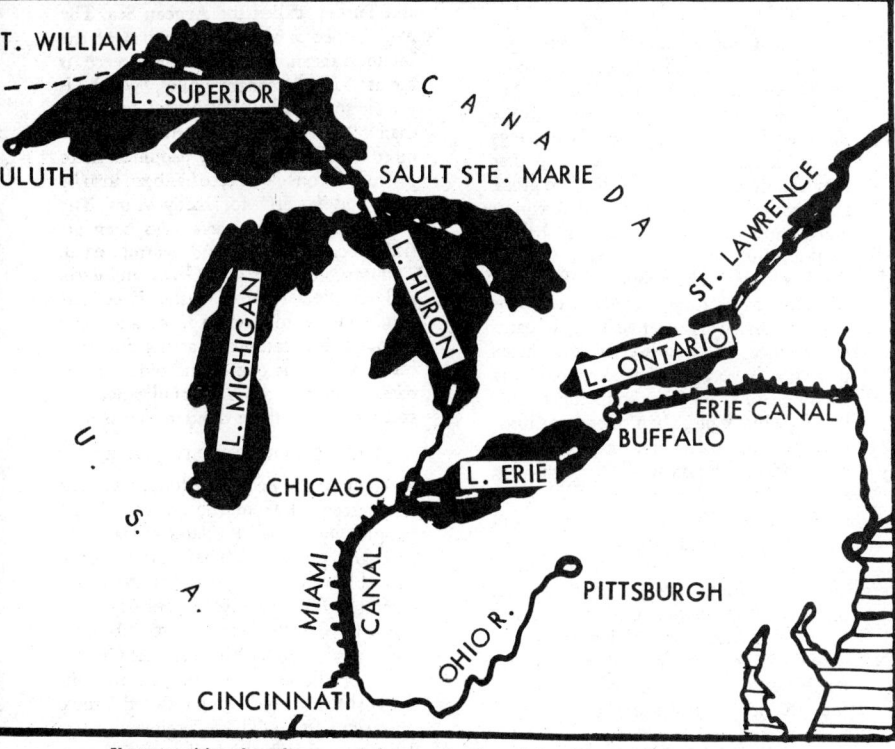

Vast quantities of goods are carried across the Great Lakes. The canal at Sault Ste. Marie carries more tonnage in a year than the Suez and Panama canals combined.

the great Welland Ship Canal, which by-passes Niagara Falls. The first of the Great Lakes canals was the ERIE CANAL, about which there is a separate article. It was built in 1825, to connect Lake Erie with the Hudson River. The Great Lakes are connected to the Mississippi River and the Gulf of Mexico in the south through the Chicago-Illinois River Canal.

The Great Lakes are connected with the Atlantic by the St. Lawrence Seaway. The Seaway makes it possible for sea-going ships from all parts of the world to sail all the way inland as far as Duluth, Minnesota. It was created by deepening the passageway from Lake Superior to the Atlantic. The work, a joint project of the United States and Canada, took five years and was completed in 1959.

From April to December there is heavy traffic on the Great Lakes. After that ice forms and navigation of any kind becomes impossible.

There are many summer resorts on the Great Lakes. The greatest inland naval training center in the world, the Great Lakes Naval Training Center of the United States Navy, is on the Illinois side of Lake Michigan, north of Chicago.

Great Plains

In the western half of the United States is a great stretch of level, treeless, grassy land that is known as the Great Plains. The Great Plains run from the Rocky Mountains in the west to the Missouri Valley in the east, and from Canada in the north to Texas in the south. Parts of ten states are in the Great Plains: Texas, North Dakota, South Dakota, Nebraska, Kansas, Oklahoma, Colorado, New Mexico, Wyoming, and Montana. Before the white men came, this area was the home of many American Indian tribes that came to be called the PLAINS IN-

DIANS. You can read about them in a separate article. There are a few rivers flowing eastward through the Great Plains, but there are not enough to irrigate the entire section, and therefore the Plains farmers depend a good deal on rain. When the summers are very dry, the wheat is very low.

The grazing lands of the Great Plains is called the *range*. This is a word that has been made famous in many American

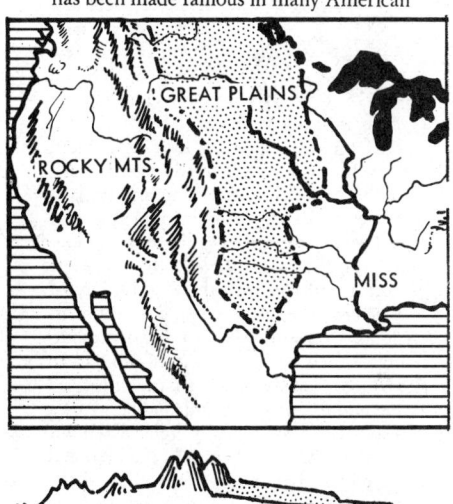

Much of the wheat and cattle in the United States come from the Great Plains. The dotted part of the section-through shows how the plains rise gently until they suddenly end in the great peaks of the Rocky Mountains.

cowboy songs such as "Home on the Range." On the range the cowboys live and work and have their rodeos, where they ride bucking broncos and rope wild steers.

During the days of the pioneers, more than a hundred years ago, people crossed the Great Plains in covered wagons look-

ing for places to settle and build their homes. They traveled for months over the flat, treeless country, enduring many hardships. Often they could not find water to drink. In summer they had no protection or shade from the burning sun, since there are no trees on the Great Plains. They were frequently attacked by bands of wild Indians. But the pioneers were brave people, and they kept on going until they found places to build their homes.

Great Pyrenees

The Great Pyrenees is one of the largest dogs in the world. It is a very old breed of working dog that has been known in Europe for nearly four thousand years. It is still used to pull sleds and dog-carts in Europe, to guard flocks of sheep, and as a watchdog in general. Long ago the shepherds of the Pyrenees Mountains, between France and Spain, had a saying that one Great Pyrenees was worth two men as protectors of a flock.

The Great Pyrenees has been called a "mat dog" because of its habit of curling up like a door mat outside its owner's home.

Few wild beasts dare to attack sheep guarded by a Great Pyrenees.

E. V. Crane

Great Pyrenees do not mind the cold, even in midwinter, because their coats are extremely thick and heavy. They stand about 27 to 32 inches high at the shoulders and weigh about 100 to 125 pounds. They are always white. They are shaggy-looking dogs and very much resemble St. Bernards in general size and shape.

Great Salt Lake

The Great Salt Lake is a shallow lake in Utah, near Salt Lake City. It is all that is left of an ancient inland sea called Bonneville Lake that gradually dried up. The lake varies in size from year to year, but it averages about 75 miles long and 50 miles wide, and its average depth is about 12 feet. The water of Great Salt Lake is more than five times as salty as ocean water; it is so salty that only one kind of animal, a small shrimp, can live in it. This is because the lake has no outlet, and as the water dries up, the salt is left behind. Because of its saltiness it is almost impossible for a swimmer to sink. This is one of the reasons that the summer resort of Saltair, on the northeast shore of the lake, is so popular. On the west side of the lake are flat, salt wastelands called Bonneville Flats, where many auto races

take place. These flats are like a great beach made of salt instead of sand. The salt in the Great Salt Lake is extracted from the water and used in industry.

Great Slave Lake

Great Slave Lake is one of the largest lakes in all of North America. It is in the Mackenzie District of the Northwest Territories of Canada, and it lies in a beautiful forest. Great Slave Lake is more than 11,000 square miles in area, or 1,000 square miles larger than Lake Erie. The two chief rivers that flow into Great Slave Lake are the Hay and the Slave Rivers. It is drained by the Mackenzie River at its west end. The lake is frozen over for nearly eight months of the year. From July to October, when the ice has melted, the great logs that have been chopped down by lumberjacks in the forests around the lake are floated down to the Mackenzie River. Then they are taken to sawmills, where they are cut into lumber. Great Slave Lake is a favorite spot for fishermen and for hunters and trappers of fur-bearing animals.

Great Smoky Mountains

The Great Smoky Mountains are a part of the North American range called the Appalachian Mountains. They lie on the border between North Carolina and Tennessee. The Great Smoky Mountains get their name from the fact that their peaks are usually hidden in a cloud mist. They are among the highest of all the Appalachian range. The highest peak of the Great Smoky Mountains is Clingmans Dome, which rises 6,642 feet. Part of the Great Smoky Mountains is a national park that is run by the United States government. It was established in 1930. More than one hundred kinds of tree grow on the Great Smoky Mountains. There is fishing for trout in the mountain streams and hiking along part of the famous Appalachian Trail. There are museums in which there are relics of the early pioneer days and of the Indians.

Great Wall of China

The Great Wall of China was a high wall of earth and stone that stretched from the northeastern coast of China on the Yellow Sea to the high mountains in the west. It was more than 1,500 miles long, and so wide that columns of soldiers could march on its top as if on an elevated highway.

The Chinese built most of the Great Wall during the reign of the powerful Chinese emperor, Shih Huang-ti, more than 2,500 years ago. He ordered the wall built to keep out the fierce horseback-riding tribesmen who were invading his country from the north. It was about 25 feet high, and every 200 to 300 yards there were towers as high as 40 feet. In these towers sentries were stationed. For many years this barrier kept the invaders from entering China. About seven hundred years ago, however, most of the tribes of the north had been united under the leadership of a great warrior named Genghis Khan. He was able to break through the wall with his army and soon conquered most of China. A large part of the Great Wall of China is still standing.

grebe

The grebe is an unusual bird that lives in many parts of Europe, the United States, and South America. Grebes are water birds, and they are excellent divers, but they are not strong flyers. Their legs are set far back on their bodies, so that they can dive swiftly and well. The grebe has webbed feet, short, rounded wings, and almost no tail. It is usually brown with a shiny white underpart. One of the kinds of grebe found in the United States has a long, slender neck. This bird builds a very strange nest. It gathers clumps of waterweeds and floats these on a lagoon or some sheltered body of water, and on this clump the female lays its white eggs. Then the parent birds cover the eggs with more weeds until they are hidden. The heat of the decaying weeds keeps the eggs warm until they are ready to hatch. The young birds come out of the shell covered with downy feathers, and they are striped with black and brown and white colors. The parent grebe will often carry the young bird on its back. When the parent senses danger, it will tuck the baby under its wing and dive beneath the water. During the mating season, the grebe grows a special tuft of feathers, and performs many complicated ceremonies. People use the feathers of grebes to decorate hats.

Greco, El

El Greco, which means "The Greek," was a great painter who lived more than three hundred years ago. His real name was Kyriakos Theotokopoulos.

 El Greco was born on the Greek island of Crete, probably in 1541. He went to Venice to study painting with the great artist Titian. After studying there for a few years he went to Spain in 1577 and stayed there until his death, in 1614.

El Greco's paintings look as modern as if they had been painted yesterday. All of the figures are very long and thin, as if they had been made in modeling clay and stretched. One of his most famous paintings is called *Toledo.* It is a scene from a hillside, with the Spanish city of Toledo in the distance and dark thunderclouds overhead. He also did two paintings called *St. Jerome as Cardinal.* In them St. Jerome has a small, thin head and a long, straggly beard, and he wears a heavy pink robe that weighs down his shoulders. One of them is in the National Gallery in London, in England, and the other is in the Frick Collection, in New York City.

There are several paintings by El Greco in the United States, including a beautiful picture of St. Francis in the museum at Detroit, Michigan.

Greece

Greece is a country in the southeastern part of Europe. It is a peninsula, that is, it is surrounded on three sides by water. It sticks out into the eastern end of the Mediterranean Sea, and there is another small sea that extends up the eastern shore of Greece, between Greece and Turkey, called the Aegean Sea. The Aegean Sea is almost like a bay of the Mediterranean. The area of Greece is about 51,000 square miles, which is a little smaller than Wisconsin, but more than 8,900,000 people live there, which is more than twice as many people as there are in Wisconsin. Greece has been torn by wars and poverty for many years. The people of Greece have always been artistic, beauty-loving, and warmhearted. Thousands of years ago, Greek architects and sculptors created masterpieces that have endured to modern times and have been an inspiration to artists for centuries. Greece is one of the oldest countries in the world. Greek civilization began more than three thousand years ago.

THE PEOPLE WHO LIVE THERE

Many of the people of today's Greece are descended from the ancient Greek people who settled the land at least five thousand years ago. These early people probably came from parts of Asia and migrated into the Greek peninsula and onto the Greek island of Crete. Besides these descendants of the original Greeks, some of the Greek people are the offspring of foreigners, who invaded Greece at various times. These foreign invaders have been absorbed into the general population. Despite this foreign influence, the Greek people of today have retained many traditions carried down from the original Greeks. For example, the Greek language is very similar to the language used in the 3rd century B.C. Also, today's Greek alphabet is the same alphabet used in ancient times. Many old ways of life, such as dress styles and family customs, are part of modern Greece.

HOW THE PEOPLE LIVE

Most of the people of Greece live in small villages and farming communities. There are only a few large cities in the entire country. Athens, Piraeus, and Salonika are the largest cities, and they seem very much like any large city in the United States or Canada. Athens and Piraeus are in the eastern central part, and Salonika is in the northeast.

Until recent years Greece had few modern conveniences. There is very little coal in the country, and coal used to be needed for nearly all electric-power plants. There were few paved roads, and travel inside the country was by donkey cart or on horseback. Since World War II, the Greeks have built several hydroelectric plants (which use water stored behind dams to turn electric generators). Now most places, even the villages, have electricity. Telephone and telegraph lines connect all parts of the country. Railroads connect all the cities except in the northwestern region, and many of the roads have been paved.

Most of the people make their living by farming, raising sheep, and quarrying marble. There is not much rain in most parts of the country, and sheep need less food and water than cows. The favorite meat of the Greek people is lamb, and the fleece of the animals provides wool for clothing.

Although the soil is poor, and there is very little rain, the farms of Greece produce enormous quantities of food. In the south there are all kinds of fruit and to-

bacco, grapes for wine, and olives. Greek olives and Greek olive oil are shipped all over the world. The farms of the northern part of Greece grow cereal grains and produce large quantities of wheat, barley, and maize. Greece also exports textiles, iron, copper, zinc, lead, and other minerals.

The Greeks have been seafaring men for thousands of years, and today Greece's merchant marine is one of the largest in the world and many of the men earn their livings as seamen.

Most village life centers around the church. The people are Christians, members of the Greek Orthodox Church. Whenever there is an important event in a village, you will find the people gathered around the church. It is the center of their social as well as their religious life.

· All children must go to school from the time they are six until they are twelve, even if they live in the very smallest of towns. After the age of twelve, they no longer go to school, but they can attend schools in the larger cities and towns if they want to. For many hundreds of years, Greek children did not have to go to school, and most people could neither read nor write. Today, however, four out of five people are literate (can read and write).

WHAT KIND OF PLACE IT IS

There are a great many mountains in Greece. Some are over 9,000 feet high. The most famous mountain is Mount Olympus in the northeast part of the country. The ancient Greek gods were supposed to live on Mount Olympus.

Greece has many rivers, but they are often too shallow for navigation. Many of the rivers in the southern part of the country are so shallow that in summer they dry up completely. There are many small lakes in the northern part.

Greece includes many islands in the seas that surround the peninsula. There is one large island, Crete, off the southeast coast. There are other island groups that are part of Greece in the Aegean Sea (the Dodecanese), others in the Mediterranean Sea, off the west coast (the Ionians), and still others around the southern tip of Greece, in the Aegean (the Cyclades, Lesbos, Samos, and Khios).

The mainland of Greece is divided by a natural channel called the Gulf of Corinth. The northern part of Greece is separated from the southern part (which is also called the Peloponnesus) except for a narrow strip of land called the Isthmus of Corinth.

Greece has a climate similar to other Mediterranean countries. Near the seashore the weather is mild, but in the mountains the winters are cold. About one-fifth of the land is covered with forests of fir, pine, and oak. They are used to produce turpentine and resin.

HOW THE PEOPLE ARE GOVERNED

Until 1973, Greece was a constitutional monarchy, at least in name. The monarch, King Constantine, had been in exile since the overthrow of the government in 1967. King Constantine had been unable to recover his power, and Colonel Papadopoulos had become Greece's premier. On June 1, 1973, Premier Papadopoulos declared Greece a republic and himself the provisional president. The republic of Greece is headed by the president, who is elected for a seven year term and has great power. The government also includes a 200-member parliament. Of the 200 members, 180 are elected and 20 are appointed by the president. All adults may vote.

CHIEF CITIES OF GREECE

The leading cities of Greece, with 1973 populations, are:

Athens, population 627,564 (with suburbs, 2,347,000), the capital and largest city.

Salonika, population 448,000, the second-largest city, in the northeast.

Piraeus, population 183,877, the third-largest city, often considered part of Greater Athens.

GREECE IN THE PAST

The history of Greece goes back for thousands of years. The earliest recorded history of Greece starts in 776 B.C., and the highest point in ancient Greek civilization came in about 450 B.C. After that, the expanding Roman Empire overshadowed Greece, and it finally became almost a minor Roman colony, or province. Greece was a part of the Roman Empire until the time of the Crusades in the 13th century. Then the Turks started their campaign to conquer smaller countries. By the beginning of the 1400s, Greece had been conquered by the invading Turks and remained under Turkish control for nearly four hundred years. Then a strong patriotism rose up in Greece, and in 1821 a revolution started,

very much in the same way that the American Revolution had started. England and France helped Greece to throw off the Turkish rule, and the war was over in 1829. Greece was once again a free country, and at that time the people decided they wanted to be ruled by a king. They did not surrender their love of personal liberty, and in 1844 they made the king agree to a constitution.

In the 1890s and early 1900s, Greece fought in the Balkan Wars (see the article on BALKANS) and won more territory. In World War I, from 1914 to 1918, Greece was on the side of the Allies (Great Britain, France, Russia, and later the United States), but there was not much fighting in Greece.

During World War II, Greece tried to remain neutral but the Italians invaded Greek territory. The Greeks fought with bravery that all the free world admired, but when the mighty German army joined the fight against Greece the Greeks were helpless. Their country was occupied by German troops until the end of the war.

After the war, Greece found itself surrounded by countries that had come under the control of Russia and were ruled by Communist governments. These countries tried to cause a revolution in Greece, but they were unsuccessful. The United States helped the Greek government with supplies and money, and by sending Army officers to advise the Greek Army.

In 1952 Greece joined the North Atlantic Treaty Organization (NATO), and in 1954 Greece, Turkey, and Yugoslavia formed a military alliance. From 1955 to 1959, however, relations with Turkey, and with the United States and Britain, were strained when Greek Cypriots on Cyprus, a British colony, demanded union with Greece and fought a guerrilla war. Peace was restored in 1959 and Cyprus was made a republic.

A time of rapid growth and development coupled with conservative governments led by Premier Constantine Karamanlis followed. George Papandreou became Premier in 1963 and then King Constantine succeeded his father in 1964. A series of military and political exchanges resulted in a military takeover on April 21, 1967 by Colonel George Papadopoulos. King Constantine attempted to stem off the harsh dictatorship imposed by Papadopoulos but failed and fled to Italy. Papadopoulos lost power in

The shaded section of the map shows the great empire conquered by the Greek soldiers of Alexander the Great. They brought civilization to the "outposts" of the old world.

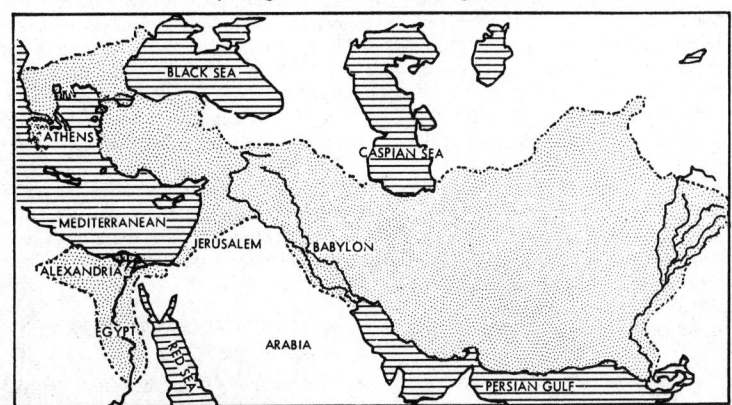

November of 1973 in a military coup. Greece then became involved in a coup on the island of Cyprus on July 15, 1974. Turkey followed a week later with an invasion of Cyprus. This conflict led to the collapse of the Greek junta (the ruling group of military men).

The military group then turned the charge of the government over to ex-Premier Karamanlis who returned from exile to assume command. He instituted a civilian cabinet, released political prisoners to settle the Cyprus issue and restored peace to Greece. On November 17, 1974 Karamanlis held public elections and won a large parliamentary majority in favor of his political party.

ANCIENT GREECE

The history of Greece goes back a very long time. There were civilized people and big cities there more than 2,500 years ago, long before there were any cities or civilized people in North America. At that time the Greeks did not have a single government, as a single nation. Instead they lived in separate city-states. A city-state was like a little country controlled by one powerful city. Each had its own kind of government, its own laws, and its own army. Sometimes one city-state would make war on another and conquer its people. In this way some city-states grew large and powerful. The Greek city-states also grew by sending out groups of pioneers to form settlements in new places. These new settlements were called colonies, and they were supposed to help their mother cities in war and in trading with other people; but sometimes a colony would revolt from its mother city and become independent. Greek colonies were started in places all around the Mediterranean Sea, and some grew into large and important city-states themselves. After a time there were Greek cities not only in Greece and on many islands in the Aegean Sea, but in Asia Minor (that part of Asia that is now Turkey) and in the lands we now call Sicily, Italy, southern France, and Spain. However, the two richest and strongest Greek city-states, Athens and Sparta, were on the Greek peninsula, the main part of the land we call Greece today.

WHAT THE CITIES WERE LIKE

The early Greeks lived in low houses made of mud brick. Most of the houses had no outside windows, and there was nothing along most of the streets but blank walls. The streets themselves were just wide enough for two or three people to walk between the houses. After a rain the streets would be full of mud, because there was no pavement. But the houses were very pleasant inside. They were built with their rooms arranged around courtyards open to the light and air. Most houses were only one story high, but the biggest had two stories and several courtyards, one leading into another. Often there would be one courtyard for the men and boys of a family and another one for the women and girls.

The public buildings in a Greek city were large and beautiful. Most of them

Remains of the great Greek past:
A sculpture of the Greek goddess Athena.

were temples to the gods. The Greeks worshiped many different gods, as you can read in the article on MYTHOLOGY. The articles on ATHENS and ACROPOLIS tell more about the Greek temples. Nearly every city had an acropolis, or fortified hill, to which all the people could go if they were attacked by an enemy.

Another kind of public building that you would have found in an ancient Greek city or near it was the open-air theater. The Greeks would build a theater by putting a stage at the bottom of a narrow valley and arranging stone benches in circles on hillsides surrounding the stage. The Greeks loved to go to their theaters to watch stage plays. At Athens the people held a big contest every year for authors and actors, and all the men of the city would spend several days watching and judging the plays. The winners of the contest would get valuable prizes and become famous all over Greece. AESCHYLUS, SOPHOCLES, EURIPIDES, and ARISTOPHANES were authors of prize-winning plays, which many people today think are some of the greatest plays ever written. You can read about these authors in separate articles.

In every Greek city you would have found a public market place, called the *agora,* where the people bought all the things they needed in daily life. Around the sides of the agora, which was a big open area, there were booths where craftsmen sold their wares and farmers from the countryside brought their produce. Here the citizens would come to meet their friends and to gossip, as well as to buy and sell. The agora was one of the most important places in an ancient Greek city, for it partly took the place of newspapers, radio, and television in our modern world. In the agora, an ancient Greek could hear the latest news or exchange opinions with his neighbors about political affairs.

ANCIENT GREEK ATHLETICS

The Greeks loved athletic contests of all sorts. Every four years the best athletes from all the city-states would meet at a place in southern Greece called Olympia. There the athletes competed against each other in many different kinds of contests. Today we call these contests the Olympic Games. The athletes who won in the Olympic Games were treated like heroes in their home cities. The Greeks considered the Olympic Games so important that they measured time in four-year periods between Olympic Games. They called these periods *Olympiads,* and they would say that something happened in the first year of the tenth Olympiad, or the second year of the eleventh Olympiad, and so on.

PHILOSOPHY, SCIENCE, AND LEARNING

Ancient Greece was the center of science and learning. Greek thinkers were the first to solve many of the mysteries of such sciences as mathematics, physics, and natural history. There is a separate article about the GREEK LANGUAGE AND LITERATURE, which in some ways has not been surpassed in 2,500 years. ARCHIMEDES, EUCLID, SOCRATES, PLATO, and ARISTOTLE are among the early Greeks whose wisdom gave the world much of what it knows today.

ANCIENT GREEK WARS

The ancient Greeks fought many wars. Sometimes the city-states fought among themselves, but the most bitter battles were against the Persians. Persia was then a great empire in Asia Minor, the territory across the Sea of Marmara and the narrow straits. Two great Persian kings, first Darius and later Xerxes, tried to conquer Greece but both failed. The Greeks are still proud to remember the battles of MARATHON and THERMOPOLAE, about which there are separate articles.

There is also a separate article about ALEXANDER THE GREAT, who spread the great learning and civilization of Greece to Asia and northern Africa. Alexander was a king of Macedon, a Greek country that had become so strong that it ruled all of Greece in the year 337 B.C. (about 2,200 years ago), when Alexander became king. Alexander set out to "conquer the world" and almost succeeded. Wherever his armies went, they taught the people Greek ways.

Less than two hundred years later, the Roman empire and not Greece had become the most powerful nation on earth. The Greeks were conquered by the Romans, and became a colony of Rome. Many of the best-educated men in Greece were captured in warfare and became slaves of the Romans. Yet in the long run Greece "won" over the Romans. They taught the Romans their skill in art and literature. When Rome fell to Germanic invaders, about 1,500 years ago, the capital of the Roman Empire moved to Greece and for a thousand years the Greeks kept Roman civilization alive in the BYZANTINE EMPIRE, which was actually a Greek empire. There is a separate article about it.

Finally, in the year 1453, the Byzantine capital, Constantinople, fell to the Turks and the history of ancient Greece was ended.

GREECE. Area, 51,843 square miles. Population (1973 estimate) 8,890,000. Language, Greek. Religion, Greek Orthodox. Government. Monetary unit, the drachma, 30 to $1 (U.S.).

Greek fire

Greek fire was a chemical mixture that burst into flames upon contact with water. It was first used in 673 A.D. by defenders of the Greek city of Constantinople, to destroy Moslem ships that sailed close to the city walls in an attempt to land troops. Constantinople (now called Istanbul) was a great center of Greek Christian civilization and was constantly being attacked by the Moslems. The Byzantine emperors kept the formula for Greek fire such a closely-guarded military secret that even today it is not known exactly what it consisted of, but it is thought that it was made of quicklime, sulfur and naphtha. The chemicals were placed in a tube, then water was pumped in to ignite the chemicals, causing extremely hot flames to spout from the tube, setting fire to everything they touched.

Greek language and literature

The Greek language belongs to the Indo-European family of languages, the same family that English and nearly all other European languages belong to. Among these languages, Greek is unique (the only one of its kind) in several ways. It was the first Indo-European language to produce literature, and though the early Greek literature was written thousands of years ago it remains among the greatest—perhaps it is the greatest—ever written. Greek was the first language in which there were words for the profound ideas of the greatest thinkers, and today we often use a Greek word to express an idea because no other language has such a word. Greek is the only one of the ancient languages that has lasted without great change into the present day. Old English, French, Spanish, German, and other languages have changed so much in a thousand years or less that speakers of the modern languages cannot understand them. Greek has changed so little in thousands of years that it can still be read by those who know modern Greek.

Greek today is the native language of only about ten million people, but in some ways it is more an international language than any other. Nearly all scientists and scholars use it. Through the Near East, people of different countries can speak to one another in a form of Greek that all of them know. For hundreds of years all well-educated men in England and other European countries learned Greek in school.

Greek had a great effect on modern English, because it had a great effect on Latin. Many words and forms in the Latin language were taken from the Greek. English, in turn, took these words and forms from Latin.

The ancient Greek language was quite complicated compared to English, or even compared to modern Greek. There were many inflections, or changes in the sound and spelling of a word depending on how it was used in a sentence. Differences in meaning were often shown by

The temple of Victory, a great classic building.

pitch accent (the tone in which the word was spoken) as well as by stress accent (pronouncing one syllable louder than others, as we do in English). Many of these complications have been dropped from modern Greek.

There are two forms of modern Greek. One is called Romaic, and is the usual spoken language. The other is called neo-Hellenic (new Greek) and is used more often in writing. It is more like the ancient Greek language, but is simplified.

According to the legends of the Greeks themselves, a king named Hellen founded the Greek people. He left his kingdom to his oldest son, Aeolus, while his son Dorus and his grandson Ion founded other kingdoms. The early Greek languages were accordingly called Aeolic, Doric, Ionic, and Attic (a branch of Ionic). Scholars recognize other branches of the Greek language, for example Achaean and Cyprian. The Minoan language, spoken on the island of Crete four thousand years ago, is now recognized as a form of early Greek.

The Greek alphabet is worth learning even by those who do not learn the language. It is much used in mathematics, physics, and other sciences. For example, the first two Greek letters, *alpha* and *beta,* are used to name the alpha rays and beta rays known to atomic science. The letter *pi* is important in mathematics. Most of the twenty-four letters of the Greek alphabet were developed into letters of the English alphabet that we use.

GREEK LITERATURE

Greek literature may be divided into three periods. The oldest period, which includes the classical Greek literature of the greatest writers, began almost three thousand years ago and lasted until about a thousand years ago. Then, about the year 529, the Byzantine period began. During the Byzantine period, the capital of the Roman Empire was the city of Constantinople, which formerly had been called Byzantium. The Byzantine period lasted until the year 1453, when Constantinople was captured by the Turks. After that the period of modern Greek literature began.

The first great Greek literature was the poetry of Homer. His great works were the long poems called the *Iliad* and the *Odyssey.* Homer is supposed to have lived sometime between 1044 B.C. and

850 B.C.—about three thousand years ago. No one knows if he ever actually lived, or if he wrote either or both of these poems, but they are as great as any poetry ever written.

Almost all of the early Greek literature was poetry. Sappho, a woman who lived on the Greek island of Lesbos, and Alcaeus, a man who lived on Lesbos at about the same time, wrote great poetry about six hundred years before the time of Christ. They wrote in the Aeolic branch of the Greek language. Pindar, who lived about a hundred years later in Boeotia, a region on the Greek mainland, wrote some of the greatest Greek poetry in the Ionic branch.

The greatest of the ancient Greek literature was the Attic literature. It was written in Athens, the city-state that was the center of the region called Attica. Between four and five hundred years before the time of Christ, Aeschylus, Sophocles Euripides and Aristophanes wrote their plays, and Herodotus and Thucydides wrote the first histories. In the next century, between 400 B.C. and 300 B.C., great scientific writing was produced. Plato and Aristotle wrote books of philosophy (general knowledge) and Euclid wrote his books on geometry. No other country or age has produced greater literature.

Greece was conquered by Rome in 146 B.C., but Rome adopted the Greek culture instead of replacing it. The greatest writers of Rome followed the Greek style in literature. The Roman emperor Marcus Aurelius wrote in Greek, and other great Greek literature was produced in Rome by Epictetus, a Greek slave.

During the Byzantine period there was a great deal of Greek literature written, but none of it did much more than imitate the literature of the ancients. Modern Greek literature, for some hundreds of years, also followed the ancient style. In the last fifty years it has become more like the modern literature of other countries.

The New Testament is one of the great works written in Greek. In the main it was written in the classical style, but parts of it use the conversational Greek used in the time of Christ.

Greek Orthodox Church

The Greek Orthodox Church is the church to which most Christians living in Greece belong. There are branches of this church in other countries near Greece, and in countries, such as the United States, where many people of Greek descent live. The church is also called the Eastern Orthodox Church.

In most of their beliefs, members of the Greek Orthodox Church agree with Roman Catholics, but they recognize the patriarch (archbishop) of Constantinople as their leader instead of the Pope of Rome. They usually say the Mass according to the Byzantine rite (which means the prayers are different from those used by the Roman Catholics, and that in Communion the communicants receive both bread and wine). Parish priests of the Greek Orthodox Church are allowed to marry, but there are many monks who never marry. The most famous Greek Orthodox monastery is Mount Athos, a picture of which is in-

cluded in the article on GREECE. A beautiful large church, the Saint Sophia Greek Orthodox Cathedral, was built in Los Angeles during the 1950s. The most important contributions for building this church were made by the Skouras brothers, motion-picture executives.

There are almost 2,000,000 members of the Greek Orthodox Church living in North and South America.

Greeley, Horace

Horace Greeley was one of the most famous American newspapermen of about a hundred years ago. He founded the New York *Tribune* and developed it into the leading paper of New York City.

Greeley was born in New Hampshire in 1811. His father was a farmer, and Horace did not get very much education. When Horace was about 20, he went to  New York City to seek his fortune. He arrived with only one suit of clothes and no money. He worked in the printing trade, and then began to write for weekly newspapers. In 1841 he started the New York *Tribune*, and he was its editor for thirty years.

Greeley also became active in politics. He was a good friend of Abraham Lincoln, and helped him to become President. Greeley wanted to be President but was unable to get the nomination. In 1872 he was nominated but was defeated in the election by Ulysses S. Grant. He died soon after the election.

Greeley lived in the days when the United States was growing up and spreading out, and advised, "Go West, young man, go West."

Greely, Adolphus

Adolphus Washington Greely was a great American explorer and soldier who made a famous expedition to Greenland and other arctic regions. He was born in 1844 in the little town of Newbury, Massachusetts. When he was seventeen years old, Greely enlisted in the army. He fought bravely during the Civil War and, though he was very young, he was made a major. In 1881, Greely was chosen to lead a government expedition to the Arctic. Greely set out with 25 men and provisions for three years. They made many valuable discoveries. The expedition set out for the return trip in 1883, but it was stranded for the winter. All but six men died before a relief ship arrived. Greely wrote an exciting book about his adventures in the Arctic. Greely also set up important telegraphic communications for the United States in Cuba, Puerto Rico, and Alaska. He spent most of his life in the Signal Corps of the Army, and he became a major general. Greely died in 1935. He received the Congressional Medal of Honor, which is the highest honor a military man can get.

Green, Hetty

Hetty Green was one of the world's richest women, but she hated to spend her money. She dressed very shabbily, and wore newspapers pinned around her instead of underwear to keep her warm in winter. She was born in 1835 in New Bedford, Massachusetts, where her father had amassed a great fortune. Her name was Henrietta Robinson, but she was always know by the nickname Hetty. She married Edward Green and had two children, but her chief interest was in managing and increasing her fortune. She was a very able trader in the Stock Exchange. She spent most of her time in Wall Street buying and selling stocks, and she had money invested in real estate and many other businesses. But rich as she was, she never got over her miserliness. She died in 1916 after a quarrel with a friend's cook over the price of the meat being served.

Green, William

William Green was an outstanding leader of United States labor organizations. Green was born in 1873, and went to work in the coal mines when he was quite young. He soon became interested in labor unions and became first a member and then an officer of the United Mine Workers. For a while he served in the senate of the state government of Ohio, but afterwards he returned to his union work. He became an officer of the AMERICAN FEDERATION OF LABOR (usually called the A.F. of L.), which is an organization of labor unions about which you can read in a separate article. In 1924, when the first president of the A.F. of L. died, Green was elected president. He was re-elected to that post many times, and held the office until he died. Green thought that the government should keep out of union affairs, but during World War II, he cooperated with the government by preventing strikes in war industries. He died in 1952.

Greenaway, Kate

Kate Greenaway was an English artist and writer who was born in London about one hundred years ago. Her father was an engraver. When she was still very young, he taught her to draw and also sent her to art school. When she grew up, Kate Greenaway began to draw pictures to go with stories for children. She is most famous for the pictures she made to go with "Mother Goose" and the "Pied Piper of Hamelin." Books that have Kate Greenaway drawings in them are very much valued now. Kate Greenaway also wrote many stories and poems for children. She was born in 1846 and died in 1901.

Greenback Party

A greenback is a piece of paper money. The paper in it has no value, so paper money is simply a promise of a government to pay. A government is supposed to have gold or silver with which it can redeem (buy back) its paper money when anyone wants it to, but during wars, when governments have to buy large quantities of war materials, a government often prints extra paper money as a way of borrowing from the people. Then, after the war, the government stops spending so much. It tries not to print more paper money than it can afford to.

During the Civil War, the United States government printed a lot of paper money, which people called "greenbacks." After the Civil War it stopped. This hurt many farmers who had been selling their produce to the government. For this reason the Greenback Party was formed in 1874, nine years after the Civil War ended. The Greenback Party wanted the government to keep on printing extra paper money and spending it so that they could get good prices for their crops. The party lasted only fourteen years, and did not succeed in electing a President or in persuading the government to print more greenbacks.

Greene, Nathanael

Nathanael Greene was an American patriot of the Revolutionary War.  Greene was born in Rhode Island in 1742. At that time the Colonies still belonged to England, but Greene was one of the people who thought they should be independent. As soon as the fighting began in 1775, he joined the army. He began as a private, but through his good work in every job, he rose to be a major general. Greene had many different assignments in the war. For a while he held the post of quartermaster-general, who is in charge of getting clothing and such things for the soldiers. He was president of the court-martial board that sentenced to death the British spy, Major John André. Later he was sent to the South, after the American army there had been defeated, and he managed to reorganize the broken army.

Greene did not win any great victories in the South, but he managed to drive the English out. Not long after the war was over, Greene died, in 1786.

Greenfield Village

Greenfield Village is a copy of an early American village. It was built in 1929 in Dearborn, Michigan, by Henry Ford. Some of the buildings are copies of buildings famous in American history. Others are the very buildings used by famous people and moved there especially for visitors to see. Thomas A. Edison's workshop is there, as are the house where Noah Webster lived, the house where Luther Burbank was born, Stephen Foster's home, the shop where the Wright brothers made the first airplane, and other old, interesting things. There are a number of shops, most of them working, that show early ways of making flour, cider, cloth, pottery, and many other things the early settlers made for themselves.

greenhouse

A greenhouse is a building that is mostly glass windows and a glass roof. Plants, fruits and vegetables are grown in it. The building itself is not colored green. The many green things that grow inside of it give it the name of greenhouse. The glass protects the plants inside from the cold and wind, and, at the same time, lets in the sunlight necessary for them to grow.

During the cold winter months a greenhouse is usually heated by a furnace. The temperature is checked carefully to see that it is not too hot or too cold. Care is also taken to see that there is enough moisture in the air inside the house so

that the plants do not dry up and die. The plants are watered and cared for just as if they were out in the open air. They are sprayed to protect them from bugs and other harmful insects and to guard them against plant diseases.

In a greenhouse plants can be grown during any season of the year. Some plants may be grown entirely in greenhouses, while others are begun there and then moved or transplanted outdoors during the warm months. Greenhouses may be small, with sides only a few feet long, or they may be so large that they spread over several acres. In large greenhouses, tractors and other farm machinery are often used to work the soil.

Many rich families have private green-

A greenhouse like the one above with an aluminum base is a great asset for any home gardener. Though small, it enables him to have cheerful flowers in his home all through the long winter months.

Lord & Burnham

houses. These are often called *conservatories.* Large cities also have greenhouses, in parks called botanical gardens. These greenhouses are often used to grow plants that would not ordinarily grow in cold climates. Such plants, called tropical plants, are raised in greenhouses called *hothouses,* where the temperature is kept very high.

One of the most important uses of a greenhouse is in growing plants out of season. This is called *forcing.* Many of the vegetables and fruits that you eat in the spring and summer were started in the winter in these forcing houses. Tomatoes, cauliflower, peppers, cabbages, sweet potatoes, cucumbers, grapes, and other fruits and vegetables are often planted in the winter in a forcing house. When spring comes, they are moved outdoors into the fields, where they are ready to be picked many weeks earlier than they would otherwise. Some vegetables, such as radishes, lettuce, and spinach, may be grown entirely in a greenhouse until they are ready to be picked.

HOTBEDS

Sometimes very small greenhouses, called *hotbeds,* are used by farmers and gardeners to start vegetables and fruits. A hotbed is a wooden frame set into a hole

in the ground. It is about two feet deep and about three feet square, and is covered with a glass window. Manure or some other fertilizer is put into the hole, about 20 inches high. Then a layer of soil is put over the top. Seeds are planted in the soil and are watered. The window lets in the sunlight and keeps the seedlings warm. Heat made by the decaying fertilizer also helps the seeds sprout faster. Soil is usually banked against the sides of the wooden frame to prevent the heat from escaping.

Greenland

Greenland is the largest island in the world, with an area of about 827,000 square miles. (Australia is more than three times as large but is considered a continent.) Greenland is a part of Denmark though it is 2,000 miles away. It lies almost entirely within the Arctic Circle, off the east cost of Canada. The interior of the island is covered by a sheet of ice more than 1,000 feet thick and is surrounded by high mountains, so the people of Greenland live along the coast. Greenland has a population of only about 37,000.

Most of the people in Greenland live on the west coast, which is divided into two provinces. Godthaab is the capital

The church in Godthaab, South Greenland's growing capital city, is still the community center.

of South Greenland and Godhavn is the capital of North Greenland. Each of these provinces has its own parliament, or ruling body, and Greenland sends its representatives to the Danish parliament which is headed by a Danish official.

Greenland is very important from a military point of view. It provides the shortest air route from North America to many parts of Europe and Asia. Planes can fly directly from Greenland across the North Pole. During World War II, the United States got permission from Denmark to build military and air bases in Greenland. It also set up weather stations, which proved to be very important.

Shortly after the end of World War II, the United States finished a great air base at Thule, a town on the northwest coast. The air base, which is called Blue Jay, cost more than three hundred million dollars to build. The United States has promised to help Denmark protect Greenland in time of war.

Since Greenland lies within the Arctic Circle, it is very cold. The temperature is below zero for more than half the year,

and during parts of the long winter there is almost no sunlight. The island was discovered by a famous Norse explorer, Eric the Red, nearly a thousand years ago. He founded a colony of Norsemen there, but they died or left. Most of the people today are either native Eskimos or Danish settlers who have gone to Greenland within the last few hundred years. The people speak Danish or a language called Greenlandic, which is an Eskimo dialect. Most of the people of Greenland make their living by fishing, sheep-herding, and growing vegetables in the summer. There are many minerals in Greenland. The most important are cryolite, which is used in making aluminum; graphite, which is used in the "lead" of pencils; and lignite, which is a fuel similar to coal.

GREENLAND. Area, 827,300 square miles. Population (1964 estimate) 37,000. Largest island on earth. Government, integral part of Denmark.

Green Mountains

The Green Mountains are a part of the great North American mountain range called the Appalachian Mountains. The Green Mountains stretch from Quebec in the north right through Vermont and into Massachusetts. Most of the Green Mountain range is in Vermont. The state called itself Vermont because *vert mont* means "green mountain" in French. We know Vermont as the "Green Mountain State."

None of the Green Mountains is very tall, but they are very rugged and not easy to climb. The highest peak of the Green Mountains is Mount Mansfield, in Vermont, 4,393 feet high. The Green Mountains are covered with fir and pine trees, and are green the whole year round. The Green Mountains are very beautiful and are popular with vacationists.

Marble and granite are dug from many quarries in the Green Mountains. Some Green Mountain farmers make maple sugar from the sap of the maple trees.

Before the American Revolution, a group of men who lived in the western section of what is now Vermont banded together under the name of the Green Mountain Boys to defend their territory against colonists in New York State, who wanted to make it a part of New York.

Later, the Green Mountain Boys fought against the British in the American Revolution. You can read about this in the article about their leader, a patriot named Ethan ALLEN.

Greenwich Observatory

The Greenwich Observatory was built in London, England, about three hundred years ago, to fix the exact time of day by observing the sun and stars. The purpose of the observatory was to help British ships at sea. It is extremely important for navigators to know the exact time, as you can read in the article on NAVIGATION. In 1954 the observatory was moved away from Greenwich, be-

British Inform. Service

Greenwich Observatory used to be in London, England, but was moved to this castle because the brightness of London's lights and the haze of industrial smoke hindered meteorological observation.

cause the smoke and the lights of London made it hard for the scientists to see the sky. The observatory is now in a castle about sixty miles from London.

The Greenwich Observatory has always been controlled by the British Navy. It was founded in 1675 and the first buildings were designed by the famous English architect Christopher Wren. In 1884 all the countries of the world decided to accept Greenwich time as the standard, but several of them, including the United States, now have their own observatories.

Greenwich Village

Greenwich Village is the name of a section in New York City. Many artists and writers have lived there. People who visit New York often like to walk through Greenwich Village, with its narrow winding streets, its many art and curio shops, and the outdoor art exhibits that are often held in or near "the Village." Washington Square, a small park where New York's famous Fifth Avenue begins, is considered the heart of Greenwich Village.

Gregory

Gregory was a name borne by sixteen Popes of the Roman Catholic Church. The last Pope Gregory died in 1846. Three of them were especially famous. Gregory I, known as Gregory the Great, was born about the year 540 in Rome. He came from a noble and rich family, and for a while he was a civil official of Rome. But Gregory decided to devote his life to religion, and he became a monk. In 590, all the people and priests of Rome chose Gregory to be Pope. He did not want the position, but finally he had to accept it.

As Pope, Gregory was a strong and powerful leader of the Roman Catholic Church. In the Church, he ruled with a strong hand, especially over the church-

es in Italy. He encouraged the growth and spread of monasteries, and sent a monk, Augustine, to England to convert people there, the Anglo-Saxons. He also insisted on reforms within the Church. The Gregorian chant, which is a form of church music, was developed in his time and named for him. Gregory was not only the head of the Church, but because of social and political conditions he was also in many ways the ruler of Italy. He was the first Pope to have great power outside the Church. Gregory I died in 604.

Gregory VII became Pope in 1073 and changed his name from Hildebrand to Gregory VII. He made many reforms in the Church and made the position of Pope more important than that of any other ruler. Once he forced the Holy Roman Emperor, who opposed him, to beg forgiveness. You can read about their quarrel in the article on HENRY, Holy Roman Emperor. In the end, Gregory lost his power and was forced to leave Rome. He died in exile, in 1085.

Gregory XIII became Pope in 1572. He is best remembered for having revised the calendar. The calendar we use today is called the Gregorian calendar. He was born in 1502 and died in 1585.

gremlin

A gremlin is an imaginary being, like a fairy or an elf. Gremlins are thought to be about a foot high and to cause much trouble. In World War II, when something went wrong with an airplane in a mysterious way, pilots jokingly blamed it on gremlins.

grenade

A grenade is a small bomb that is thrown by hand or fired from a rifle. The French first called the bomb *pomegranate*, because the first grenades looked like the pomegranate fruit. Grenades were first used more than three hundred years ago. Soon special groups of soldiers called *grenadiers* were formed to use them. The grenadiers wore high, brimless hats called *shakos*, which could not get in the way when the grenade was whirled about the head in throwing. After about a hundred years the grenade went out of use, and it did not reappear until World War I. Today the United States Army uses a grenade that is marked off into small squares. It is made to explode three to five seconds after a safety pin has been pulled out. The grenade can be fired from a rifle as far as two hundred yards, and when it explodes it bursts into pieces that act like bullets.

grenadier

A grenadier was originally a soldier who carried and threw grenades. He was chosen for his special strength. Because the first grenades were exploded by gunpowder fuses, the grenadier had to carry something to light the fuse. This was a piece of punk which held a spark for a long time, and was called a *slow-match*. When modern grenades were invented, there was little need for a special soldier because anyone could now throw grenades. The title of grenadier came to be used for members of certain special regiments of soldiers, such as "The Queen's Own Grenadiers" in England.

Grenfell, Sir Wilfred Thomason

Sir Wilfred Thomason Grenfell was a great English doctor who did more than any other person to help the fishermen and Eskimos of Labrador and Newfoundland, in Canada. He was born in 1865. Grenfell went to Labrador in 1892, and he spent more than forty years in this lonely country, where he worked to make life healthy and happy for the people who lived there. Grenfell traveled from

one place to another, taking care of the sick. He built hospitals and schools, and orphanages where children who had no parents could receive good care. He built libraries *Canadian Consulate* and stores and meeting halls. Every year, Grenfell traveled by boat to all the centers he had helped to set up. The ship he used was the first hospital ship, fully equipped to take care of sick people. Everyone loved and respected Grenfell, and the English government made him a knight in appreciation for his great work. Grenfell wrote many books about his experiences. One of them is called *Forty Years for Labrador*, and it is the story of his exciting life. Grenfell died in 1940.

Gretna Green

Gretna Green is a village in Scotland, just north of the English border. For more than a hundred years, many couples eloped, or ran away to be married, to Gretna Green. In England people who wanted to be married had to post a public notice of their intentions and then had to wait a certain length of time after that before the wedding ceremony could take place. These notices were called *banns* and were usually read in church. In Gretna Green no waiting period was necessary, and many couples who did not want to wait, or whose parents objected to their marriage, went across the border and were married there. In 1856 a law was passed that at least one member of the couple getting married had to live in Scotland for three weeks before the ceremony, so the runaway marriages were stopped. Any place where couples can get married quickly is sometimes called a "Gretna Green."

Grey, Albert

Albert Henry George Grey was a Governor-General of Canada. He was born in 1851. His grandfather, Earl Grey, had been Prime Minister of England, so it was quite natural for Albert Grey to go into politics. After he received his education in Trinity College, at Cambridge University, Grey was elected to Parliament, and he held many important positions in the English government. In 1895, Grey was given the responsible job of governing Rhodesia, a new British colony in Africa. Then, in 1904, he became Governor-General of Canada, and did many things to help the farmers and workers to have better working conditions. He died in 1917.

Grey, Edward

Edward Grey was the British foreign minister in 1914 when World War I broke out. Probably no man tried so hard to prevent the war as he did. Grey was born in 1862. He came from a famous family and was trained for government service.

Grey was a very sincere and honest man, and when it seemed to him that the Germans were preparing for war he tried to discourage them. He persuaded France and Russia to stand together with England, and he even tried to get the United States to join them. But the war began, and Grey resigned. He is remembered for his statement about World War I: "The lamps are going out all over Europe; we shall not see them lit again in our lifetime."

After the war Grey became ambassador to the United States, and he continued to fight for peace by helping the League of Nations. Grey was made a knight, and later Viscount of Fallodon, by the British government. He died in 1933.

Grey, Lady Jane

Lady Jane Grey was an English girl who for nine days was queen of England. This was about four hundred years ago. Jane Grey never wanted to be queen of England, but she was a great-granddaughter of King Henry VII and her ambitious father-in-law, the Duke of Northumberland, made her queen so that he could control England by controlling her. This was in 1553. The English Parliament would not let him do this, because Princess Mary was the oldest child of King Henry VIII. Mary became queen and Lady Jane Grey was beheaded in 1554, when she was only 17 years old.

Jane Grey's whole life was short and tragic. Her parents forced her to marry Lord Guilford Dudley, a man she did not love, before her sixteenth birthday.

Grey, Zane

Zane Grey was an American writer who wrote many popular stories about the days when men were settling the West and life was rugged and wild. Grey was born in Zanesville, Ohio, in 1875. He studied dentistry at the University of Pennsylvania, and became a dentist in New York City. Among his most popular novels were *Riders of the Purple Sage* and *The Vanishing American.* Many of his exciting books were made into movies. Grey died in 1939.

Gale Research Co.

Zane Grey, the American Novelist, was also a dentist.

greyhound

The greyhound is one of the oldest breeds of dog in the world. It can run faster than any other breed, and people have used greyhounds in hunting for over four thousand years. Although greyhounds are very gentle, even-tempered dogs, they are not usually kept as family pets, but more often are used for hunting hares or for racing. Many hundreds of years ago, only people with titles, such as princes, dukes, or earls, kept greyhounds. It is regarded as the dog of royalty.

A greyhound stands about 28 to 30 inches high at the shoulders, and it weighs about 65 pounds. It has a long, thin tail. The coat is short and smooth, and you can see greyhounds in almost any dog color. The name has nothing to do with the dog's color. You will recognize the breed by the fact that it appears gracefully curved on the underside. This is because the chest is roomy and powerful, and the hips are slender, with slim hindquarters that enable the strong legs to run swiftly without tiring quickly.

The swift and graceful greyhound is one of the few dogs that hunt by sight instead of tracking prey by smell.

Grieg, Edvard Hagerup

Edvard Hagerup Grieg was a Norwegian composer, or writer of original music. Grieg was born in the city of Bergen, Norway, in 1843. When he was a young man Grieg traveled in Germany, Denmark, and Italy, where he studied different kinds of music. Then he returned to his own country and wrote beautiful songs and pieces for the piano and violin. Grieg loved the folk music of the Norwegian people, and many of his compositions are based on their simple tunes. Henrik Ibsen, the great Norwegian playwright, asked Grieg to write some music to go with his play, *Peer Gynt.* The music that Grieg wrote, the *Peer Gynt Suite,* is among his most famous works. Grieg died in 1907.

griffin

The griffin was an imaginary monster in stories told by the Greeks and other ancient peoples thousands of years ago. The griffin had the body of a lion, the head and wings of an eagle, feathers all over its back, and a long, serpentlike tail. This monster was almost ten times as big as a lion. In the stories, the griffin drew the chariot that carried the sun across the sky. The griffin knew just where to find buried treasures, and it built its nests out of gold. Hunters were always fighting with the monster to reclaim the gold.

Griffith, D. W.

David Wark Griffith was one of the first men to make motion pictures. He was both a director and a producer. In 1915 he produced a full-length motion picture that set the standard for every motion picture that has been made since. This film was called *The Birth of a Nation* and was a story of the American Civil War and the years after it. It is considered to be one of the best motion pictures ever made.

Griffith was born in Kentucky in 1875. As a young man he acted in plays and motion pictures. He was rich and famous when he died in Hollywood in 1948.

King, a champion wire-haired pointing griffon, is lively and intelligent.

griffon

The griffon is a tiny dog with a turned-up nose and large, round eyes, kept as a pet both in Europe and America. There are different types. One is called the *Brabançon.* It has smooth, short hair like a Boston terrier. Another is called the *Belgian griffon,* and it has wiry hair, with a little, rough beard on its chin. Some puppies in a litter may be the smooth-haired type, and some may be the wire-haired type.

A griffon is a very small dog, standing only about 9 to 11 inches high at the shoulder. Some are even smaller. Usually they weigh about 9 pounds, but can weigh as little as 6 or as much as 12 pounds. Their tails are clipped short just after they are born.

The wire-haired pointing griffon is a hunting dog that has been known in the United States and Canada only since 1900. It was developed by a Hollander, E. M. Korthals, when he wanted to breed a new type of sporting dog.

It is a medium-sized dog, with extremely wiry hair that makes an effect of eyebrows and a mustache on the dog's face. It is about the size of a boxer, or slightly smaller. The color is usually gray and tan. The tail is usually clipped when puppies are a few days old.

Grimm, Jakob and Wilhelm

Jakob Ludwig Grimm and Wilhelm Karl Grimm were brothers who lived in Germany more than a hundred years ago. They are best known for the collection of folk tales, or stories that had been handed down among the German country folk for many years. This collection, now called *Grimm's Fairy Tales,* was first published in 1812. Both Jakob and Wilhelm Grimm were great scholars in the study of language. Jakob Grimm worked out a rule to determine the way in which sounds change from one European language to another. This rule is called Grimm's Law and is very important.

The Grimm Brothers, Wilhelm (*left*) and Jakob (*right*), wrote many delightful tales, but others were "grim" indeed.

Grimm's Fairy Tales was first written down in very scholarly language but it was later rewritten and became popular all over the world. Recently the stories have been criticized because some of the characters in them are so cruel, but they are still very popular with both children and adults. Wilhelm Grimm was born in 1786 and died in 1859. Jakob was born in 1785 and died in 1863.

grinding

Grinding is another name for rubbing or scraping. It is done with special materials called ABRASIVES, about which you can read in a separate article. Rubbing something with a piece of sandpaper is a kind of grinding.

Most grinding is done by machines. These have wheels that are made from abrasives or that have strips of abrasives cemented on their edges. The wheels are on a shaft, or long rod, which is turned by a motor. Pieces of a material are held against the turning wheels, to be smoothed, polished, sharpened, or made into different shapes. This is called turning. The earliest grinding machine was the grindstone, which is turned by hand. It is used to sharpen axes, knives, and other tools. The lathe was the first motor-driven grinding machine, and most grinding machines are patterned after it. (You can read more about the LATHE in a separate article.)

There are many types of grinding machines and each has a special use. They often are very large, the size of a large table or even larger, and must be securely attached to the floor so they do not move around and spoil the grinding operation. Some machines are able to grind off one-thousandth of an inch of surface or even less. These are called *precision grinders*. A *centerless grinder* is used to make perfect cylinders and ball-shaped pieces, such as billiard balls or the little metal balls that are used in ball bearings. Hollow cylinders can be smoothed and polished by grinders called *external* and *internal grinders*. An external grinder is a wheel that smooths the outside of the cylinder. The cylinder is usually placed on a turning shaft and automatically pressed against the revolving grinding wheel. Sometimes the grinding wheel is hollow so that the cylinder can be slipped inside of it and smoothed by the abrasive on the inside of the wheel. Internal grinders are wheels that smooth the insides of hollow cylinders. The grinding wheel is just small enough to slip inside the turning cylinder. Special grinding machines called *universal grinders* are used for both internal and external grinding.

Grinding wheels must often be cleaned and smoothed off. This is done by metal star-shaped wheels or by diamond stones. These remove pieces of metal dust and other unwanted material from the grinding wheels.

grippe, a disease that is like a very bad cold, and is very easy to catch from another person: see the article on INFLUENZA.

grits

Grits is ground-up kernels of corn that has been dried and bleached white. Throughout the southern part of the United States it is eaten as a vegetable in much the same way that potato is eaten in the North. Grits is usually boiled in water and looks very much like breakfast cereals such as Cream of Wheat. It may also be cooled until it hardens; it is then sliced and fried before it is eaten. Fried grits is usually eaten for breakfast, and is served with syrup and butter. Sometimes the corn is not ground up and the whole dried kernel is cooked and served. It is then called *hominy.*

grizzly bear, one of the largest and fiercest of all bears: see the article on BEAR.

grosbeak

The grosbeak is a bird. Its name means "heavy beak," and several birds with thick bills are known as grosbeaks, but the name is most often used for a kind of finch. The grosbeak is a small or medium-large bird. It is a singing bird and lives in pine woods in Europe and North America.

One kind is the cardinal grosbeak, which is also called the *Virginia nightingale.* It lives in the eastern part of the United States. The male bird, or cock, is bright red and has a beautiful song. The female is more modest in her coloring and her song is not as beautiful as the male's.

Grosbeaks have bills that are good for breaking seeds. They are helpful to man because they eat seeds of weeds that grow around gardens and crops.

Grotius, Hugo

Hugo Grotius was a great Dutch scholar who lived from 1583 to 1645. He  is best known as the author of the first book ever written on international law, which is the rules of conduct for countries in their dealings with one another. Grotius was an official of the Dutch government for a while but then he became involved in a religious quarrel that was going on in Holland and was sentenced to life imprisonment. With the help of his wife, he managed to escape by hiding in a trunk that was carried out of the jail. He made his way to France, and it was there that he wrote his famous book. It is called *De Jure Belli et Pacis,* which means "Concerning the Laws of War and Peace." Most people interested in systems of international law and world government have used many of Grotius's ideas.

Groundhog Day, February 2, the day on which the groundhog is supposed to come out of his burrow: see the article on CANDLEMAS.

ground squirrel

Ground squirrels are squirrels that live on the ground, and not in trees like other squirrels. Like all squirrels, the ground squirrels are rodents. Mice, rats, and other animals that have special teeth used for gnawing are called rodents. There are different kinds of ground squirrels, including the chipmunk and the prairie dog. Ground squirrels often live in large groups together in their underground burrows. When winter comes, they creep into their burrows and sleep until the warm weather returns. The animal that is usually called a ground squirrel has short legs and short ears. Its tail is bushy. Ground squirrels eat green plants and seeds and also many insects. They are found in most parts of the United States, except for the east coast.

ground water

Ground water lies below the surface of the ground and feeds all wells and springs. Solid rock is very rare below the ground; in most places the rock has openings in it ranging from tiny pores to enormous caverns. Water that falls on the ground drains into these openings in the rock. Ground water flows "downhill" underneath the surface of the earth, just as streams above the surface flow down mountainsides. Sometimes it can be gotten out by pumping. It also flows out from springs on hillsides. Sometimes water is forced out of the ground under great pressure, and it may furnish most of the water found in some brooks and rivers. A very large spring in the state of Florida, Silver Springs, gets its supply from ground water.

Ground water is very important in farming and also in industry. Farmers use it to water their crops during periods when no rain has fallen. It is used in industry because it is a fairly steady supply of water, and it is available even when there has been no rain. It is especially useful in industry for cooling machines, because it is cool when it comes from the ground. When it is used to cool things, the water is usually pumped out of the ground into the machine and back into the ground so that it may be cooled and used again.

grouper

A grouper is an ocean fish that is related to the sea bass family. It is a good food fish, and is very popular with sport fishermen. There are many kinds of grouper, ranging from small to very large. The most usual kind found in American waters is the red grouper, which is about two feet long and has a

red snout that blends into pink on the head. The red grouper is found in the Atlantic Ocean from Virginia to Brazil. Other kinds of grouper grow to be as much as twelve feet long and weigh up to five hundred pounds. Groupers of different kinds have different colors, usually greenish-gray or orange-brown. Even the smaller varieties have very large mouths, and they feed on shellfish and other fish.

grouse

A grouse is a wild bird that looks like a young hen. Grouse are game birds, that is, hunters shoot them because they are good to eat. The grouse has a plump body and a small head. It is chestnut-brown in color. Some species, called ptarmigans, turn white in the winter, making it difficult to see them in the snow. These grouse are found in Scandinavia and in other very cold parts of the world, such as Siberia, Alaska, and Newfoundland. Closely related to this kind is a red grouse that lives on the moors in the British Isles and feeds on heather, a bushy kind of flower. This is the kind that is hunted a great deal in England and Scotland. The ruffed grouse is found in America. The male bird can drum on a log, a sound that is heard in the woods in the spring. The sage grouse and the blackcock have drum "tournaments" in the spring. They have a special grounds for it and they all gather there to compete in the tournament. Still other kinds of grouse are the blue grouse or pine hen, which lives in forests of pine and other cone-bearing trees, and the sharp-tailed grouse and the prairie chicken, which live in the prairies.

growth

Any living thing, whether it is a plant or an animal, becomes larger as it becomes older, and this is called *growth.* A time comes when it stops growing but continues to become older, and then it is said to have reached *maturity,* or to have become *adult.* Many plants do not stop growing. They continue to grow throughout their lives, but they reach a point at which they grow more slowly. Some animals, too, continue to grow, but do so more slowly.

Scientists know a great deal about how things grow. They do not know why things grow. Especially they do not know why things stop growing.

In a separate article you can read about the CELL, the basic unit of life, of which all living things are made. Each type of living thing is made of cells of its own kind. Most cells have the ability to absorb food and turn it into other cells. As long as a living thing is growing, it is always making more cells than there were before. After it stops growing, it makes new cells to replace some of the ones that are constantly dying.

THINGS THAT AFFECT GROWTH

A living thing inherits from its parents the fact that it will grow to a certain size in a certain length of time. In human beings this means that tall parents are likely to have tall children. Members of certain races will be taller than members of other races. Men will usually be taller and heavier than women, but women are

likely to grow somewhat faster during their early years.

Certain GLANDS, about which you can read in a separate article, affect growth. The pituitary gland is sometimes called the "growth gland." If it is not working properly, a person may turn out to be a dwarf, and if it is doing too much work it may make a giant.

Good food and a proper amount of heat, as well as sunlight, are necessary to proper growth. A child who does not have a good nourishing diet may not grow as rapidly or as tall as he would if he were properly fed.

HUMAN GROWTH

It is not possible to say exactly how much a human child should grow in any particular year. Too much depends on how large the child will finally be, based on heredity and other things. It need not be a cause for worry if a child does not seem to grow rapidly. There are many cases in which rapid growth is delayed and then occurs during adolescence.

A girl will usually grow faster than a boy until she is 12 or 13 years old. At these ages she may be taller than a boy who is some day going to be considerably taller than she is. After the girl and boy are both 13 or 14 years old, the boy will grow faster than she does, and will overtake and pass her.

A baby will usually grow about ten inches in its first two years. It grows faster in its first years than it ever will again. During its third year a child will grow about four inches, or a little less, and for each of its next six years it will grow about the same. A girl's rate of growth will slow down when she is about 9 years old, and a boy's when he is about 11 years old.

Because they are eating better and more nourishing food, and are aided by scientific knowledge that tells what foods are best to eat and that also has stamped out many diseases, Americans are becoming taller in every generation. Between World War I and World War II the average height of men in the armed forces went up from a little under 5 feet 8 inches to a little under 5 feet 9 inches.

The mind grows along with the body. During the period when the body is growing, the mind becomes better able to understand. This ability in the mind does not depend on the size of the mind in the same way that the strength of the body depends on its size.

Because human beings are constantly learning, it is not possible to say how much of an increase in mental capacity is due to greater maturity and how much

is due to the person's increased knowledge. See also the article on INTELLIGENCE.

Gruenther, Alfred M.

Alfred Maximilian Gruenther, as general in the United States Army, held some of the most important positions in the defense of his country during World War II and since. He was born in Platte Center, a small town in Nebraska, in the year 1899, and was graduated from the United States Military Academy (West Point) in 1919. He was a regular army officer for nearly forty years. When he was promoted to major general during World War II he was the youngest man in the United States Army to have so high a rank. Later he was advanced to full general's rank. He was chief of staff under General Eisenhower and then under General Mark Clark in World War II. Then he was chief of staff to Eisenhower in the "SHAPE" organization (Supreme Headquarters, Allied Powers Europe) in Paris, France. In 1953, when Eisenhower was President of the United States, Gruenther became Supreme Commander of SHAPE. In 1957 Gruenther retired from the Army and became president of the American Red Cross. In 1965 he retired as Red Cross president.

grunion

A grunion is a small fish that is found in large numbers in the Pacific Ocean along the western shores of the United States. The largest grunion may grow to 7 inches, about the length of a pencil. The grunion's spawning, or egg-laying, habits are unusual. The female grunion lays its eggs only at high tide. Great schools of grunion rush in to very shallow water after the highest tide. The female wiggles backward into the sand, lays its eggs, and quickly moves out to sea. After two weeks, the eggs are hatched and the baby grunion are washed out to sea by the next high tide. When the fish come in to lay eggs at some beaches, hundreds of people gather to catch them and fry them for eating.

Guadalajara

Guadalajara is the name of a city in Mexico, and of a province and its capital city in Spain. The Mexican city of Guadalajara is the capital of the state of

The growth of most boys and girls follows this pattern, though there are many exceptions.

Jalisco, which is on the western coast of the country. It is the second-largest city in Mexico. About 1,196,000 people live there, or a little less than the population of Houston, Texas. Guadalajara is a very modern city, but it also contains many beautiful old buildings that date back more than three hundred years. There is a fine art museum and an excellent university in Guadalajara. The city is famous for the lovely pottery and glassware made by the people who live there. Guadalajara was first settled about four hundred years ago, in 1542.

The province of Guadalajara in Spain is in the central part of the country, not far from Madrid, the capital city of Spain. It is in the section of Spain called New Castile. More than a thousand years ago, most of Spain was controlled by Moslems from Africa, who were called Moors by the Spaniards. The Moors called this section *Wad-al-hejarra,* which means "valley of stones." One of Spain's most important rivers, the Henares River, flows through Guadalajara. The countryside is very fertile and good for farming, but is rocky and stony in parts. A great battle in the Spanish Civil War (which lasted from 1936 to 1939) was fought just outside of the city of Guadalajara, capital of the province.

GUADALAJARA, MEXICO. Population (1973 estimate) 1,196,218. Capital of Jalisco state.

Guadalcanal

The name of Guadalcanal has joined other names famous for American heroism, such as Valley Forge, Gettysburg, and Belleau Wood. Guadalcanal is one of the Solomon Islands in the southwest Pacific Ocean. Here, during World War II, the United States Army, Navy and Marine Corps fought a fierce and desperate battle with the Japanese. On August 7, 1942, twenty thousand Marines landed on Guadalcanal. They soon captured Henderson Airfield, but on August 9 the Japanese navy sank four cruisers that were protecting the landing of supplies and ammunition. For months the Marines, who were reinforced by the Army, fought the Japanese in the dense, steaming jungle. The Japanese put more troops on the island and counterattacked, but the Americans held on. In November there was another battle between the two navies near Guadalcanal. This time the United States won, and the Japanese were now no longer able to control the seas and land more men. In February 1943 the Japanese admitted that they were defeated and left the island. Guadalcanal was the first great American land victory of the war.

Guadalupe Hidalgo, Treaty of

The Treaty of Guadalupe Hidalgo was the agreement that ended the Mexican-American War in February, 1848. This war was fought principally over Mexico's refusal to let Texas join the United States. In the small town of Guadalupe Hidalgo, which is near Mexico City, it was decided that the United States would get the great piece of Mexican land out of which were made the states of California, Nevada, Utah, most of New Mexico and Arizona, and parts of Wyoming and Colorado. Texas was allowed to join the United States and its boundary was fixed at the Rio Grande. The United States paid Mexico fifteen million dollars, and agreed to pay claims that American citizens had against Mexico.

Guadeloupe

Guadeloupe is the name of a group of small islands in the West Indies, and is also the name of the largest island in the group. These islands belong to France. About 324,000 people live there, nearly all of them Negroes. Most of the people live on the largest island. The principal town of Guadeloupe is Basse-Terre, a city of about 15,690 on the western coast. The next largest island is called Grande-Terre, with the chief town of Pointe-à-Pitre, which has a population of about 29,538. The islands are fertile and the people grow sugar, coffee, cocoa, and bananas, and make rum. The climate is hot and damp, and often there are terrible hurricanes. Christopher Columbus discovered Guadeloupe in 1493 and the French settled it in 1635.

Guam

Guam is one of the Marianas Islands in the western Pacific Ocean. It is an important United States air and naval base because of its central location near Japan, China, the Philippine Islands, New Guinea, and Hawaii.

Guam is a small island with forest-covered mountains and fertile valleys. The climate is warm and pleasant, and many of the 85,000 people who live there work on coconut plantations or grow coffee, cacao, sugar, or rice. About a third of them are natives called *Chamorros,* and most of the others are of Spanish descent. The people speak English and Spanish.

Guam was discovered by the Spanish explorer Ferdinand Magellan in 1521, and it belonged to Spain until the Spanish-American War when the United States took it over. At the beginning of World War II it was attacked and captured by Japan. Near the end of the war the United States recaptured it and began to rebuild the ruined capital city of Agana, the naval base at Apra, and the airfield. Now the people of Guam are citizens of the United States and they elect their own government except for the governor, who is appointed by the President of the United States.

guan

A guan is a bird that looks somewhat like a turkey, but is smaller. It has a red throat without feathers and a fleshy red bag hanging at its throat. A guan is about thirty inches long, half of which is tail feathers. Its body is shiny reddish-green in color. The female guan has a border of white on the top of her head and along her chest. Guans are restless, noisy birds and fly up in the trees when they are alarmed. They roost in trees at night and make their nests on branches. Guans live in the American tropics, but some are found in Texas. In South America they have been domesticated for a long time.

guanaco

The guanaco is a wild animal that lives in South America. It belongs to the camel family, but is a good deal smaller than a camel and has no hump. It is related also to the llama, alpaca, and vicuña, which are other South American members of the camel family. The guanaco stands about four feet high at the shoulder. It has a curved neck and long slender legs. There are bare patches on the hind legs where the short tail curves down. The long beautiful hair of the guanaco is used to make a fine wool. It is fawn-colored on top of the body and white underneath.

Guanacos live in herds of from six to thirty. They are very shy and difficult to get near, although they can be tamed quite easily. The Indians of Patagonia in South America hunt them as food. The Indians also use the droppings of the guanaco for fuel, and its hide for clothing and tents. The puma, a kind of large wildcat, attacks the guanaco and feeds on it almost entirely. Guanacos live in the southern half of South America, from Peru to Cape Horn. The guanaco goes to a special place to die. There are great heaps of bones in these burial grounds of the guanaco.

guano

Guano is used by farmers as a fertilizer, which is a substance that keeps soil enriched. Guano is the waste matter of many kinds of sea birds, which leave deposits on the islands where they live. All the biggest deposits of guano are found in tropical areas, such as the west coast of South America and some islands in the South Pacific Ocean. The country of Peru was the leader in the production of guano and Peruvian farmers have used guano as a fertilizer for centuries. However, the best deposits have been used up, and guano has been replaced by synthetic, or man-made, fertilizers, or by fertilizer made from fish.

guaranty or guarantee

A guaranty is a promise to pay another person's debt, if he does not pay it himself. Suppose a person wants to borrow money from a bank, but the bank is not sure he will be able to pay it back. The borrower asks a rich friend to give the bank a guaranty. The rich friend then signs an agreement to repay the loan if the borrower does not. The person who borrows the money is called the *principal.* The rich friend who signs for him is called the *guarantor.* (In some cases he is called a *co-signer,* because he and the borrower both sign a note, or promise to repay the loan.) The bank cannot collect from the guarantor unless it has already tried to collect from the borrower and the borrower has failed to pay.

A guaranty is also spelled *guarantee,* but usually the word guarantee means a different kind of promise. This is a promise made by someone who manufactures or sells some kind of merchandise. A seller of vacuum cleaners may guarantee that the vacuum cleaner will work properly for at least a year. If it breaks down during the year, the seller will repair it or replace it without charge. A seller of cloth may guarantee that it will not fade. If it does fade, he will replace it or give back the money. Nearly all advertised merchandise has some kind of guarantee behind it.

A *title guaranty* is a special kind of

guaranty in real estate (lands and buildings). When you buy real estate, the seller gives you an official paper, called a *deed,* which you record in a town or county office. A title guaranty company will make a *title search* for you, tracing back all the deeds ever recorded on that land. The record may go back hundreds of years. If the company finds that everyone who ever sold the land had a legal right to sell it, the company will give you a *title insurance* policy, which assures you that you own the land.

guardian

When a child's parents are dead, or are unable to take care of him properly, a guardian may be appointed for him. A judge, in a court of law, appoints the guardian. The legal duties of the guardian are very much like those of parents. The guardian must make sure the child is properly fed and clothed and cared for in other ways, and the child must obey the guardian as he would his parents. The guardian manages any money or other property that belongs to the child, and must report regularly to the judge as to how he has managed it. The judge has the right to appoint a guardian for any child, even if its parents are alive, but this seldom happens unless the parents are neglecting or abusing the child. When the parents have died and have made a will asking that some particular person be appointed as guardian, the judge will usually appoint that person, but he does not have to. Usually the guardianship does not end before the child is 21 years old.

Guardians are sometimes appointed for persons who are mentally or physically unable to take care of themselves or to manage their own business affairs. This kind of guardian is called a *trustee.*

Guarnieri

Guarnieri was the name of a family of violin-makers who lived in the city of Cremona, in Italy, and made some of the finest violins of all history. Their violins are called Guarnierius violins. The first violin-maker in the family was Andrea Guarnieri, who was born about 1626. The greatest of all the Guarnieris was Giuseppe, who was born in 1683 and died in 1745. He was known as *"del Gesù"* (*Gesù* means Jesus) because he marked all of the violins he made with a cross and the letters IHS, which is a Greek abbreviation for Jesus. Three or four of the del Gesu Guarnierius violins are considered by experts to be the finest ever made.

Guatemala

Guatemala is a small country in Central America. It is about the same size as the state of Tennessee, but has more people than Tennessee. It has the largest population in Central America, with more than five million people. For a brief period in 1953 and 1954 Gautemala was often in the news because it fell under the control of a Communist government, but later in 1954 the Communist government was replaced by a more democratic one.

Guatemala extends through Central America, with a seacoast on the Pacific Ocean on the west and a shorter seacoast on the Caribbean Sea on the east.

Guatemala (black area on map) has many mountains, large farms, and cities.

WHAT KIND OF PLACE IT IS

A volcanic mountain range cuts through the center of Guatemala. This mountain area, called the highlands, covers most of Guatemala except for a strip of jungle about thirty miles wide on each coast, and a large plain in the north called El Petén.

Along the coast, where it is low and flat, the climate is uncomfortably hot and damp, and very few people live there. In the highlands it is cooler the higher you go, and the weather is usually like spring. The only seasons in Guatemala are the dry season from November to May and the rainy season from May to November. Because of the better climate in the highlands, only one Guatemalan out of every two hundred lives in the northern plain, though that region covers one-third of the nation.

There are more than thirty volcanoes in Guatemala, many of them more than 10,000 feet high. Some still erupt and spill their molten lava down the mountainside without much warning. Many cities and villages have been destroyed in this way. Earthquakes also occur often. However, the people come back to live in the highlands, because when the lava cools it makes excellent soil and fine coffee trees will grow there.

Many rivers flow down from the mountains, especially toward the Pacific Ocean. Ships cannot sail these rivers, but their waters are used to irrigate farm lands during the dry season. Ships can sail down the important Motagua River, which empties into the Atlantic Ocean. Guatemala has three large lakes, Izabal, Petén-Itza, and the beautiful Atitlán.

Many useful trees grow in the low jungle sections. Bananas are the most important, and the chicle, from which chewing gum is made, is widely grown. Mahogany for furniture, the huge ceiba for kapok to stuff mattresses, chinchona for the medicine quinine, and even camphor trees, are found in the jungle. In the Petén region there are jaguars, pumas (a kind of wildcat), crocodiles and many other wild animals. There are more than nine hundred kinds of bird. It is against the law to kill one kind, the quetzal bird. The quetzal has brilliant green and red plumage and a crested head. Guatemala has made this bird the national emblem,

like the eagle in the United States, and they call their dollar bills quetzals.

THE PEOPLE OF GUATEMALA

Guatemala was originally settled by the Mayas, one of the most intelligent and industrious Indian tribes in America. The Spaniards came, bringing with them European religon, art, styles of dress, and language. The Indians learned from the Spaniards but also kept their own customs. More than half the people in Guatemala are pure-blooded descendants of the original Maya race. The rest are either Spanish or a mixture of Spanish and Indian. A person having both Spanish and Indian blood is called a *ladino.* Wherever you go you will see both native Mayans and ladinos.

In the large cities, especially in Guatemala City, the capital, you may see men and women wearing the same style of clothing as in New York or Paris, but you will also see the bright-colored native dress. In the cities the people speak mostly Spanish and some English, but as you go to more isolated places you hear more of the native language spoken.

Almost all the people in Guatemala are farmers. On the cool mountain slopes they grow coffee, and in the coastal jungles they find chicle and grow bananas. The bananas are rushed to Puerto Barrios, where refrigerated ships wait to take them to the United States and Canada.

To the Guatemalan, the most important crop is corn, and it is grown everywhere. It is used in many tasty dishes, such as *tamales,* and to make corn meal. The people also raise and eat many strange fruits, such rhe mango, papaya, and anona.

The Guatemalans used to scoop out the fruit of a large gourd and use the shell to make a musical instrument called the marimba. Now the marimba looks like a large xylophone and it is the national instrument of Guatemala.

The schools in Guatemala are good, and all children must attend. After kindergarten there are usually separate schools for boys and girls, and sometimes the children wear uniforms. The excellent San Carlos University of Guatemala, founded in 1676, is one of the oldest in the New World.

HOW THE PEOPLE ARE GOVERNED

The Republic of Guatemala is divided into twenty-two departments, which are like states in the United States. Its government is similar to that of the United States, with a legislature to make laws and a President elected by the people. Citizens must be over 18 to vote. The judges are appointed by the legislature, and the governor of each department is appointed by the President. A new constitution adopted in 1956 guarantees freedom of the press, of speech and assembly, and the protection of workers. All men between 18 and 50 must serve in the army or air force.

CHIEF CITIES OF GUATEMALA

Guatemala City is the capital. It is the largest city in Guatemala and in all of Central America, with a population of about 374,000. It is the business, political, educational, and transportation center.

Quezaltenango, with 36,000 people, is the second-largest city. It is in the center of the important farming area.

Puerto Barrios is one of the most important ports on the Caribbean Sea, chiefly exporting bananas. Its population is about 20,000.

GUATEMALA IN THE PAST

The Mayan people probably settled in Guatemala about three thousand years ago. They went there from Mexico. They made a fine civilization, with great advancements in agriculture, astronomy, and arithmetic, but they were no match for the Spanish explorers in warfare. The first Spaniards, commanded by Pedro de Alvarado, arrived in the year 1523, not long after Columbus discovered the New World.

The Spaniards were greatly outnumbered, but they would help one tribe fight another, and by dividing the natives they weakened them. Finally, in a hand-to-hand battle between the great Indian chief Tecum Uman and Alvarado, the Spaniards won, and the Mayas became a conquered people.

One of the most dramatic episodes in Guatemalan history occurred after the death of Alvarado, who had become governor. His wife, Doña Beatriz, who called herself "The Unfortunate One" because of his death, wanted to become the new governor. On September 9, 1541, she became the first and only woman ever to head a government in the New World under the Spanish administration. That night a great flood of very hot water burst out of a nearby volcano, Agua, and swept over the capital, Ciudad Vieja, destroying the entire city and killing hundreds. One of those killed was "the unfortunate" Doña Beatriz. The city was never rebuilt.

Guatemala remained under Spanish rule until 1821, when most of Spain's American colonies rebelled. In the years that followed many men tried to seize power, but few were outstanding until Justo Rufino Barrios became president in 1873. He ruled for twelve years, in which time he established a department of education, built highways and railroads, encouraged the planting of coffee, cacao, and bananas, and tried to get all the Central American nations to unite into one country. Barrios is often called the Lincoln of Guatemala. There are statues of him everywhere and the seaport Puerto Barrios bears his name.

The government of Guatemala has had many changes and revolutions throughout its history. During World War II Guatemala fought on the side of the Allies.

GUATEMALA. Area, 42,042 square miles. Population (1974 estimate) 5,200,000. Language, Spanish. Religion, mainly Roman Catholic. Government, republic. Monetary unit, the quetzal, worth $1.00 (U.S.). Flag, a blue, a white, and a blue vertical stripe, with coat-of-arms in center stripe.

guava

Guava is a tree that bears a sweet-tasting fruit used in making jellies, jams, and preserves. It can also be eaten fresh. The guava fruit is shaped somewhat like a pear and is about the size of a hen's egg. The guava plant grows mostly in the West Indies, but it is cultivated by a few fruit-growers in the warm parts of the United States. It grows to a height of fifteen to thirty feet. It has smooth, light green, egg-shaped leaves, and fragrant white blossoms.

Guelphs and Ghibellines

The Guelphs and the Ghibellines were two opposing groups in Europe about eight hundred years ago. Each group was named for the family at the head of it. The Guelphs were named for a German family named Welf, from which came many later kings of European countries. The Ghibellines were perhaps named for Waiblingen, a possession of the Hohenstaufens, a German family from which came several emperors of the Holy Roman Empire. In Italy, these names were spelled Guelph and Ghibelline.

For several hundred years the two groups were rivals for power, and each group had its share of successes.

Guiana

Guiana is a stretch of land on the northeast coast of South America. It is between the two largest rivers of that continent—the Orinoco and the Amazon Rivers. It is also bordered by the countries of Venezuela and Brazil. The climate of Guiana is always extremely hot, although there is heavy rainfall throughout the year. Deeper inside the Guiana country there are hills and mountains. The highest mountain is Mount Roraima, 8,640 feet high. Many hundreds of years ago, the native Indian population of Guiana was defeated in a war with the Dutch. Later on, the French and English took over part of the land. See FRENCH GUIANA, BRITISH GUIANA (now GUYANA), and SURINAM (Dutch Guiana).

guided missile

A guided missile is a flying device, carrying an explosive charge, that is like an aircraft except that it carries no men but is steered by radio equipment that it carries and that can be controlled by ground crews or by automatic machinery inside the guided missile. In World War II there were no true guided missiles, though the German V-2, used in the last months of the war, was a forerunner of the guided missile (SEE FLYING BOMB). Since World War II every big country has developed guided missiles, most of them carrying "atomic warheads" (an atomic or hydrogen bomb as the explosive part of the missile) that can destroy big cities and kill all the people in them.

Guided missiles are grouped into classes, depending on how they are launched and what their targets are:

Ground-to-ground (or surface-to-surface). This type of missile is launched from the attacking country and is aimed and guided so as to hit a target on the ground, for example a city, in the enemy country. Guided missiles launched from ships or submarines are placed in this class.

Ground-to-air (or surface-to-air). A missile launched from the ground and designed to seek out and destroy an attacking aircraft or missile sent by an enemy.

Air-to-ground (or air-to-surface). A missile launched from an airplane toward targets on the ground or sea.

Air-to-air. A missile launched by an airplane toward an attacking airplane or missile.

BALLISTIC MISSILES

A true guided missile is distinguished from a *ballistic missile,* which is always of the ground-to-ground type and aimed when it is launched, just as a shell from a cannon is. Ballistic missiles are grouped in two classes, called by the initials of their names: The ICBM, or Intercontinental Ballistic Missile, which must be able to travel under its own power and strike a target 5,000 or more miles from its launching point; and the IRBM, or Intermediate Range Ballistic Missile, which is a similar device but is designed to strike targets only 800 to 3,000 miles from its launching point. An ICBM may have a speed ranging from 600 to 14,000 or more miles per hour. Nearly every artificial satellite has been developed from an ICBM. The Russian sputniks have resulted from their experimental ICBMs. In the United States, the Army, Navy and Air Force have independently developed guided and ballistic missiles, but since 1957 the Air Force has been given the chief responsibility and the Air Force base at Cape Canaveral, Florida, has been the chief base. Missiles developed in the United States have all been given names. The Army's ground-to-air "Nike" (named for the Greek goddess of victory) and ground-to-ground "WAC Corporal" missiles were the earliest put into operation. The Army's "Jupiter" and Navy's "Vanguard" powered the first successful American artificial satellites.

DESIGN AND OPERATION

Some guided missiles are called "glider" missiles, because they are launched from planes and depend partly on the power of gravity and the impetus given to them by the speed of the plane to carry them to their targets; but nearly all modern guided missiles are propelled by ROCKET power (about which there is a separate article) or have rocket boosters to start them, after which jet engines take over. The missiles may look like rockets or like medium-sized airplanes with short wings. Each missile carries, besides its warhead, electronic equipment by which it guides itself or can be guided by a control room on the ground. There are several methods of guiding the missile:

1. By radar, which registers in the missile the position of the target. The radar either guides the missile to the target or sends a radio message back to the control room, which then steers the missile by radio. But radio signals can be jammed by an enemy transmitter.

2. By an electric eye in the nose of the missile. This will guide the missile to anything that the beam of the electric eye strikes. However, enemy planes or missiles can drop obstructions that will meet the beam of the electric eye and send the missile astray.

3. By following a radar beam from the ground, which will intercept enemy aircraft or missiles. This is the favored method for ground-to-air missiles used in defense of cities and military targets.

4. By being preset so that a telescope takes bearings from the stars and sends back radio signals giving its position, so that a control unit can guide the missile by radio. This is the favored method for long-range missiles.

757

GUITAR

5. By a heat-seeker, an electronic device for measuring heat. There are devices so sensitive that they respond to the heat of planets or stars. A heat-seeker directs a missile to any source of heat; it may be the smokestack on a ship or factory.

All these methods have certain disadvantages. Radio signals can be jammed; radar signals end at the horizon; heat guided missiles may strike unintended targets.

USE OF GUIDED MISSILES

The guided missile is acknowledged to be the principal weapon of future warfare, and to be so deadly a weapon that it is hoped no major war can start because every country must fear total destruction from the guided missiles of its enemy. The United States has sought security by establishing throughout the world launching bases for guided missiles and by building aircraft carriers to carry planes capable of launching guided missiles, plus submarines and cruisers (some of them atomic-powered) that can approach an enemy coast by sea and launch guided missiles. In 1954, the U.S. Air Force spent only 10% of its procurement funds on guided missiles; in 1959 this had risen to almost 50%.

Missiles like the Titan and the Atlas have proved accurate within two miles at distances of 5,000 miles and can travel as far as 9,000 miles. Plans are on the drawingboard for super-rockets that will thrust 100-ton satellites into orbit or 50-ton satellites deep into space.

guild

Guilds were organizations of merchants and skilled craftsmen during the Middle Ages, hundreds of years ago. The labor unions of our time grew out of these guilds, and some unions, such as the Newspaper Guild, still use the name. The first guilds were formed by merchants in the cities of Europe. These guilds set the prices for which different merchandise could be sold, and established customs and rules for fair trade.

About seven hundred years ago, groups of these guilds in several European cities joined together in a league called the HANSEATIC LEAGUE, about which there is a separate article. About two hundred years later, the skilled workers or craftsmen, such as goldsmiths, weavers, and bakers, began to form similar guilds called craft guilds. The craft guilds became so important that in many places a person could not work at his trade unless he was a member of the guild. Each guild decided how its trade would be run, what materials should be used, and what things the workers should make. Anyone who wanted to become a member of a guild had to follow very strict rules. You can read more about them in the article on APPRENTICESHIP.

guillemot

The guillemot is a small sea bird about the size of a raven. It lives on fish and dives into the ocean to get them. Guillemots are numerous along rocky coasts of the northern oceans near the Arctic. They lay their eggs on ledges facing the sea. The egg of the guillemot is much thicker at one end than at the other, so that it cannot roll off the ledge. When the wind blows the egg it spins around instead of rolling. Each pair of guillemots produces one egg a year. The parents take turns lifting the egg onto their webbed toes and warming it with their feathered legs. Guillemots can be made into pets and become intelligent and entertaining companions.

guillotine

The guillotine is a machine for capital punishment, that is, for killing criminals who have been sentenced to death. It was invented in France but machines similar to it had been used earlier in other countries of Europe. In our time most countries use hanging, electrocution, or the gas chamber for capital punishment.

The guillotine is a high frame that holds a heavy knife blade. At the foot of the frame the condemned person places his head on a block. When a spring is released, the knife blade falls very fast and cuts off his head.

The first guillotine was built in 1792 by a French doctor, Joseph Guillotin. At that time the French Revolution was under way. The Revolution grew into a period called the Reign of Terror when noblemen, members of the royal family, and any real or imagined political enemies of the government were put to death, sometimes after an unfair trial, or even no trial at all. The king and queen of France, Louis XVI and Marie Antoinette, died on the guillotine.

Guinea

Guinea is a republic on the west coast of Africa. Formerly a part of French West Africa, it became an independent country in 1958. The name Guinea is also applied to the region in which this country lies, a vast area along a coastline of about 1,500 miles on the Gulf of Guinea, which is part of the Atlantic Ocean. A small part of this region is Portuguese Guinea, a possession of Portugal.

The Republic of Guinea has an area of 96,865 square miles, which is about the size of the state of Oregon. Its population is about 4,010,000. The capital is Conakry, an important seaport on the Atlantic, a city of about 197,267 people.

Almost all the people of Guinea are Africans of the Negro race. They speak a Sudan Negro language and, in the cities, French. Many of the people are Christians (chiefly Roman Catholics) but still more follow native religions. Most of the people are farmers, the soil being very fertile, and their principal crops are bananas and coffee; but there is mining of iron ore and bauxite (aluminum ore), about 1,500,000 tons of ores being shipped through Conakry each year. Nearly all the land belongs to the natives. The climate is tropical—hot all year around, with a rainy season in the summer. There are some mountains (the highest being 6,000 feet), in which are the sources of the Niger and Senegal Rivers.

The territory that is now the Republic of Guinea was claimed as a French colony in 1882. During the seventy-five years that followed, France did much to raise living standards in Guinea, which became one of the most prosperous parts of Africa. In 1958 the French premier Charles de Gaulle offered independence to any French overseas territory that wished it, and while all other territories chose to remain associated with France, the principal political leader in Guinea, Sekou Touré, favored independence and the people supported him by an overwhelming vote. Guinea then joined the United Nations. Touré became the first President of Guinea and followed a pro-Communist policy.

GUINEA. Area, 96,865 square miles. Population (1973 estimate) 4,010,000. Government, republic. Capital, Conakry. Monetary unit, Guinea franc. Flag, vertical bars of red, yellow and green.

guinea fowl

Guinea fowl are birds that are like chickens but smaller, and are considered very good to eat. Like chickens, they like to roost, that is, go to sleep on the branch of a tree or some other perch. They live in flocks, and they lay their eggs on the ground. Guinea fowl are usually black-and-white striped, but some of the males of the wild guinea fowl have long, colorful tails and fancy, bright-colored head feathers.

guinea pig

The guinea pig is a small rodent, or gnawing animal, related to the rat and the squirrel. The guinea pig is not a kind of pig at all. Another name for it is the cavy. It is about six to ten inches long, and it can be brown, black, white, or a mixture of tan and white.

Guinea pigs are very important to science. They are used for testing medicines and reaction to diseases. There are two reasons for this. The first is that the guinea pig breeds so fast. A female guinea pig gives birth to a new litter, or group of newly born animals, about every ten to twelve weeks, and there may be four to twelve animals in a litter. Another reason is that in many ways the guinea pig's reaction to drugs and bacteria that cause diseases is the same as the reaction of a human being.

guitar

A guitar is a stringed musical instrument. It is shaped somewhat like a violin but is much larger. It has six strings stretched over the sound box and up a long neck. Plucking these strings with the fingers or with a plectrum or "pick" produces the sound. Along the neck are steel ridges called frets. Holding any string down against a fret with the fingers will change the note it will play when plucked. The guitar has become one of the most important instruments in dance bands, where it has replaced the banjo.

The guitar most used today comes from Spain and has six strings. Three are silk covered with wire, and three are catgut, which is tough string made from the insides of certain animals.

The Hawaiian steel guitar is played by Hawaiian musicians. This guitar is not made of steel. It is called a steel guitar because a small steel bar is held

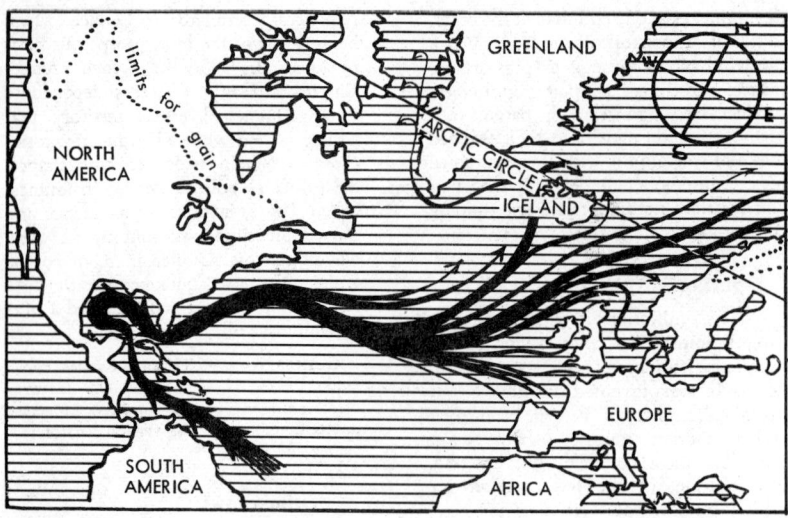

The Gulf Stream rises in the Gulf of Mexico from equatorial water drifts coming from South America. It flows around Florida, then north and east.

against the strings when the guitar is being played. The steel bar gives the music of the guitar a wailing sound.

Guiteau, Charles

Charles Guiteau was the man who killed President James A. Garfield. Guiteau was a lawyer in Chicago, and in 1880 he went to Washington, D.C. He spent a great deal of time trying to get himself appointed to a government job. He especially wanted the job of United State consul in Marseilles, France. But no one paid any attention to him, and this made him very angry. He shot President Garfield on July 2, 1881, in the waiting room of a railroad station in Washington. On September 19, the President died from the wound. Guiteau was hanged in June 1882, in the District of Columbia jail.

Gulf Stream

The Gulf Stream is like a river of warm water that flows through the Atlantic Ocean. The Gulf Stream is about fifty miles wide and about two thousand feet deep. It begins in the Gulf of Mexico and flows through the Florida Straits and up the east coast of the United States as far as Nantucket Island. Then the Gulf Stream heads east into the Atlantic Ocean, where it merges with another great current called the North Atlantic Drift. The Gulf Stream flows at a rate of about four miles an hour in the Gulf of Mexico. The temperature of the water in the Gulf of Mexico is about eighty degrees. The Gulf Stream cools off as it flows north and east, but its warm water helps to keep the land along the American shore much warmer than it would be otherwise and it also helps to keep the British Isles warm. In Florida the deep blue color of the Gulf Stream can be seen from the shore. Many large deep-sea fish live in the Gulf Stream, and it is a popular fishing ground.

gull

A gull is a long-winged, grey-white bird that lives at the seashore. Gulls sometimes float almost motionless in the air over harbors and along stretches of beach. With their powerful, graceful wings they use the least amount of motion to fly. Gulls can be seen in large num-bers along most shores, floating in the water as most ducks do. From a distance they look like ducks.

Gulls belong to the tern family. They are known all over the world, but they are most familiar in Arctic and temperate climates. There are a hundred different kinds of gull. Most of them live near the sea, and so are called sea gulls. In size gulls may be 20 to 30 inches long. In color almost all gulls are grey on top and white underneath, so that if you look up at them from the ground they are almost invisible against the sky. The young are usually brown, and some gulls remain brown, spotted with white. Others have large black markings. The roseate gull of the Arctic is a beautiful shade of

Margot L. Wolf

A soaring gull is one of the most graceful creatures in the world.

pink; it is sometimes called "the rose that blooms unseen," because so few people have come across it.

Sea gulls have many remarkable habits. They have almost unbelievable endurance and have been known to follow ships far out to sea and even cross oceans in flight. In some places they feed on clams, and since they cannot break the clam shell with their bills they fly up and drop it on a rock to break it open. Gulls breed in colonies on islands. When the young are hatched, they are covered with down. They are able to walk but they are dependent on their parents until they can fly. While gulls are breeding they feed on the young and the eggs of other birds that are nesting near them. A full-grown gull is a scaven-ger, which means it feeds on refuse cast off by ships or washed up on the shores by

the sea. This habit makes them useful to man.

gum arabic

Gum arabic is a kind of gum used in making perfumes, medicine, candies, and mucilage. The mucilage on postage stamps and envelope flaps is made from gum arabic, but it is mixed with sugar to prevent it from cracking. Gum arabic is very pleasant smelling and therefore it is used as a base for perfumes. Sometimes it is used on textiles to give them a sheen. Gum arabic comes from the sap of the acacia tree, which grows in the north-western part of Africa. For this reason it is sometimes known as *gum acacia.*

gum chewing

Chewing gum is a pliable substance that is given a sweet or other agreeable flavor and chewed for its taste and also be-cause it helps some people to be less nervous. Chewing gum as it is known to-day was first made in the United States, less than a hundred years ago, but chew-ing for pleasure had been known long before that, for hundreds or even thou-sands of years.

Many people had chewed the sap of the spruce tree and paraffin waxes in the same way that they chew gum today. Even the most primitive people chewed grasses, berries, and tree barks for pleasure. Although many people think that gum chewing is an unattractive habit, some doctors say that it is helpful be-cause it aids digestion, relaxes tension, and helps concentration.

Chewing gum is particularly popular in the United States, where the people spend $264,000,000 on gum each year. The making of chewing gum has become a major industry, and one of the tallest buildings in the United States, the Wrig-ley Building in Chicago, was built with the money earned from the sale of gum.

HISTORY OF CHEWING GUM

Chewing gum was first sold in 1869, in Jersey City, New Jersey. It was made by Thomas Adams, a merchant and inventor, and his son, Horatio. This gum was made from chicle, which is the latex from the sapodilla tree. This tree grows wild in southern Mexico and Central America.

Adams had been experimenting with chicle to see if he could use it as a sub-stitute for rubber, but he had had no success. One day he saw a little girl buying some paraffin chewing wax and remem-bered that he had chewed the chicle dur-ing his experiments with it. That night he and his son rolled the chicle into round balls, packed it in boxes, and put it on sale in a nearby drugstore. This first chew-ing gum was successful from the very start. Soon after this Adams started a large plant in Brooklyn, and within a few years several other companies built plants to make gum. The original Adams' Sons Chewing Gum Company later joined other companies and became the Ameri-can Chicle Company, one of the largest chewing-gum companies.

The first chewing gum was unflavored. The first flavoring to be used in it was licorice. Peppermint was used as a flavor soon after that. Dr. Beeman, a Cleveland pharmacist, started to put pepsin into gum

as an aid to digestion. As more and more companies began to make chewing gum, more and more flavors were used. The round balls of gum were replaced by pencillike sticks and finally by the flat slab form that gum is made in today.

Scientists working for the chewing-gum companies discovered that other gums added to the chicle made the gum smoother and finer. Most modern chewing gums are made from newly developed plastics, but some are made from a combination of several gums. Gutta siak, a sap obtained from trees that grow in Malaya, is one of the most commonly used gums. Bubble gum is made of a different plastic, one that is tougher and more elastic.

HOW CHEWING GUM IS MADE

Today chewing gum is made in modern factories with modern machines. If plastics are used, they are extruded, or forced through an opening, to form a long, flat bar that is cut into "sticks"; the flavoring is added when the plastic compound is mixed.

When gums are used, they are "cooked," or heated until they are "runny." Then the mixture is sweetened, usually with corn syrup, or sugar, and the flavors are added.

A machine called a kneader fixes the mixture into a velvety texture. Then the mixture is rolled on a rolling belt until it is the proper thickness. As the gum is being rolled it is sprinkled with powdered sugar.

Knives mark off widths and lengths in patterns, and then the gum is sliced into squares before it is cut down into individual sticks. Candy-coated gum, such as Chiclets, is rolled in thicker widths, broken into squares by machines, and coated. The coating is polished by another machine.

The wrapping and packing of chewing gum is also done by machine. The paper in which the gum is wrapped is moisture-proof and sealed airtight so that none of the freshness and flavor of the gum can escape. The individual packages are packed in boxes and shipped to all parts of the world.

USE OF CHEWING GUM

Most people like to chew gum. They feel that it makes them more relaxed, and they enjoy the taste. Some people are able to concentrate harder when they have gum to chew. Many students believe that they do better work on examinations if they chew gum.

During World War II many of the soldiers chewed gum to relieve the tension when they were on duty. The Army also found that gum chewing relieved the soldiers' thirst. Many athletes find that they are calmer if they are chewing gum during a big contest. Factory workers with dull jobs like to chew gum, too, for it relieves some of their boredom.

Many airlines give gum to their passengers to relieve the discomfort in their ears that is caused by varying air pressures. In the same way, the chewing of gum may relieve the temporary deafness that comes with a bad cold. People also chew gum, particularly chlorophyll gum, to make their breath sweeter.

There are certain rules that everyone who chews gum should follow. It is not good manners to chew gum in public places, such as in school or on the street. The person who chews gum should keep his mouth closed and should chew quietly. Most young children like to blow bubbles with bubble gum, but they have to learn to be careful that they do not get gum on themselves and on their clothing. Gum should always be thrown away wrapped in a paper of some sort so that it will not stick to anything, as it is very hard to remove from any surface.

gum tree, a tree that gives off a resin or gum of some kind: see the articles on EUCALYPTUS and SWEET GUM.

gun

A gun is a weapon that fires bullets or explosive shells. There are separate articles on the different kinds of gun. *Pistols* and *revolvers* are small guns that can be fired with one hand. *Rifles* are weapons that are fired from the shoulder. They have twisted grooves inside the barrel, so that the bullet spins as it flies through the air. This spinning keeps the bullet on a straight course, just as the spinning of a football does when it is thrown properly. *Shotguns,* which are also fired from the shoulder, shoot shells containing many tiny bullets that fly in many directions. Shotguns are often used for hunting animals. *Machine guns* fire a continuous stream of bullets. *Cannon* are large guns that are used by the artillery.

Most guns today are loaded with cartridges at the breech, which is the end where the trigger is. (See the article on AMMUNITION.) The first guns were invented about seven hundred years ago. Modern guns are of all sizes, firing bullets less than a quarter of an inch in diameter, or shells 18 inches in diameter. Big guns have been built to fire shells a distance of 75 miles.

gunboat

A gunboat is a small warship that is used for patrolling rivers and coasts. About 150 years ago, President Thomas Jefferson ordered the building of a fleet of gunboats for the navy, each carrying one large gun. These ships were not designed for sailing on the open sea, and they could not do much to protect the Atlantic coast from the British during the War of 1812. Gunboats were used by the North on the Mississippi River during the Civil War, and they helped capture control of this river for the Union. In 1937, there was a crisis between Japan and the United States, when Japanese planes sank the American gunboat *Panay* near Nanking, China. Gunboats are similar to the small cutters that are used by the Coast Guard.

guncotton

Guncotton is an explosive made by treating cellulose fibers, such as cotton, with nitric acid. It is a form of nitrocellulose. Guncotton was discovered during the 1890s and was one of the first materials used to make "smokeless powders," which replaced gunpowder as the principal explosive used in firearms. Guncotton looks like fine, very white, fluffy cotton such as that used to spin thread for cloth. Read also the articles on AMMUNITION, EXPLOSIVES, and NITROGEN.

gunpowder

Gunpowder is an explosive made of sulfur, saltpeter and charcoal ground up and mixed into the form of a powder. Its color is such a dark gray that it is almost black. When set on fire, it explodes and so can be used in firearms, as you can read in the article on AMMUNITION. It is believed that the Chinese were the first people to use gunpowder. They used it mostly in fireworks. When Europeans learned about it, they saw it could be used to fire missiles much harder than the catapults they had used before. The first cannons were used about 650 years ago. They changed the entire method of warfare.

The size and shape of the tiny grains of which gunpowder is made up are important, because space must be left between them so the fire can enter. For a long time no one knew much about this, and sometimes the guns loaded with gunpowder would burst. The gunner had to know just how to "ram" the powder into the gun so it would not go off too fast. This was hard to learn, and gunners who knew just how to pound the powder into the gun just right were highly paid.

HOW IT WAS MADE

When gunpowder was first made, it was ground in holes cut in logs. Then special machines were made to do this work. It was very dangerous because a small spark would cause the gunpowder to go off, killing the workmen. So many men were killed in England making gunpowder for use in hunting that a law was passed against this kind of factory. About three hundred years ago people learned to make gunpowder into a kind of cake by wetting it. After this it was ground, and the gunpowder worked better and was safer.

In those days guns were smooth inside. When it was learned that grooves inside the guns made them shoot straighter, a new kind of gunpowder was needed. This was because the grooves kept the cannon balls from being driven out of the gun as fast as before. The old kind of gunpowder exploded very fast and when the ball did not leave the gun quickly the gun would burst. General Thomas Rodman of the United States Army found a way to make a gunpowder that would not do this, and soon armies all over the world began using it.

In the early days of gunpowder not much could be made because it was hard to find enough saltpeter (which is also called niter).

Later large deposits of nitrate, which is used in making saltpeter, were found in Chile, but for most uses gunpowder has been replaced by smokeless powder and other explosives, as you can read in the article on EXPLOSIVES.

Gunpowder Plot, a conspiracy to blow up the British houses of Parliament in London, on November 5, 1605. See the article on Guy FAWKES.

guppy

The guppy is a tiny fish that is popu-

lar in home aquariums because it is an easy fish to breed. Male guppies grow to be about three quarters of an inch long, and their bodies have bright patches of red and yellow, violet, orange, and black. The female is about twice as large as the male, and it is a pale greenish-gray. The female guppy can have from fifteen to fifty live babies about once every month.

Guppies live in the warm waters of streams and ponds in South America, and they have been taken to almost every tropical part of the world. The little guppy is a very useful fish. It eats mosquito eggs, and for this reason it has been bred in many places. Scientists have learned many important new things from their study of the guppy.

The guppy was named in honor of Dr. R. J. Guppy, a scientist who lived in the West Indies and who first took guppies to the British Museum in London, England.

Gurkha

A Gurkha is a warrior of Nepal, a mountainous country in Asia between India and Tibet. Gurkhas are Hindus by religion.

The Gurkha regiments were part of the British Army in World Wars I and II and they were famous for their strength, bravery, and independence. In addition to a rifle, a Gurkha always carries a *kukri*, which is a heavy, curved knife. The Gurkhas used to say that when a kukri is drawn from its scabbard, it must draw blood before it is returned.

gurnards

Gurnards are small fish that seem to walk on the ocean floor. Actually, they are using their fins as legs. Other kinds of gurnard are flying fish that jump from the water and glide through the air for short distances. There are not many of the flying gurnards. Most kinds of gurnard are small, reaching a length of one foot. They are found mostly in the warmer waters, including some shores of the Atlantic Ocean. Other fish of the gurnard family are found in the Indian Ocean. The gurnard is also known as the *volanda*.

Gustavus

The name Gustavus has been borne by six kings of Sweden, and several of them were outstanding rulers and great leaders of their people.

Gustavus I, called Gustavus Vasa, was born in 1496. In his time, Denmark ruled Sweden, but some Swedish people wanted their country to be independent. Gustavus Vasa was a great leader in the war against Denmark, and when Sweden won its independence, he was elected its first king. He ruled until his death in 1560.

Gustavus II, known as Gustavus Adolphus, was a very great general. He was born in 1594. In his time, the countries of Europe were almost constantly at war, and Gustavus made his army one of the best in Europe and led it to many great victories. Gustavus II was also a great king at home. He reorganized the government, and helped

the country to grow more prosperous. Gustavus was killed in battle in 1632. He is still remembered as Sweden's greatest military hero.

Gustavus V was born in 1858, and became king in 1907. He was a very democratic king, and was always most interested in the welfare of his country. When he became king, he would not have any great coronation, or crowning ceremony, because he thought it would be a waste of the country's money. He managed to keep his country peaceful in both World Wars. Gustavus loved tennis, and even when he was past 80 he played a good game. When Gustavus died in 1950, he was 92 years old and had ruled for 43 years.

Gustavus VI, the son of Gustavus V, was born in 1882, and became king when his father died. Gustavus VI visited the United States twice before he became king, in 1926 and in 1938.

Gutenberg, Johannes

Johannes Gutenberg was a German printer who lived more than five hundred years ago in the city of Mainz. He was the first man to print a book from movable type. He was born about 1400. At that time books were printed by carving a complete page on a  block of wood and printing from it. The block of wood was useful only for printing that particular book. Gutenberg made movable type—each letter was a separate block. It could be rearranged any number of times for printing different books.

The first book Gutenberg printed was a Bible that came to be known as the Gutenberg Bible. He probably printed it over the course of several years between 1445 and 1455. Sometimes this Bible is called the Mazarin Bible, because the first one ever found was owned by Cardinal Mazarin of France, who died in 1611. Other copies have been found since then. The Gutenberg Bible is now the most valuable book ever printed, and one or two sheets from a Gutenberg Bible have been sold for hundreds of dollars. Gutenberg printed many other books before he died in 1468. There is a Gutenberg Museum in Mainz and many statues of him have been erected in Germany.

gutta percha

Gutta percha is a thick rubberlike substance that is used to protect submarine cables, and to coat electrical equipment. Dentists also use gutta percha, to make temporary fillings for cavities in teeth. At one time golf balls were made entirely of gutta percha, but now they are made of rubber with a covering of gutta percha.

There are two things that make gutta percha very useful in all of these different ways. It is waterproof, and when you heat gutta percha it becomes soft so that it can be easily molded into any shape. Then it hardens quickly as it cools.

Gutta percha comes from the trunk and leaves of large evergreen trees that grow in Malaya, other Asiatic countries and South Sea Islands, and some parts of South America. The natives gather the

thick green leaves and chop them to obtain the sticky juice. Sometimes they cut down the tree and make deep rings in the bark, and the gutta percha oozes from these rings. As it comes out, gutta percha looks like thick milk.

Guyana, formerly British Guiana: see the article on BRITISH GUIANA.

Gwyn, Nell

Nell Gwyn was an English actress who lived about three hundred years ago. She was born in 1650 and her parents died when she was very young, so she had to earn her own living. At first she did this by selling oranges near the theaters of London. A theater director noticed her beauty, her fiery red hair, and her good humor. He trained her for the stage when she was only 15. Her sense of humor and natural, unspoiled manner made her popular with audiences. She was a favorite of King Charles II, and though her behavior would not be considered moral today, she remained famous until her death in 1687.

gymnasium

A gymnasium is a place where people perform exercises and play certain games. It can be either indoors or outdoors. A gymnasium is built for such games and sports as basketball, handball, volleyball, boxing, wrestling, and badminton. Some gymnasiums are so large that they have room for tracks for races or for indoor baseball. Gymnasiums also have rings and bars and other equipment for gymnastics.

Gymnasium is from a Greek word meaning "to exercise," and gymnasiums existed as far back as ancient Greek times, when men used to go to a spacious arena for a variety of athletic games and contests. In Europe the word *gymnasium* is often used to mean a high school.

gymnastics

Gymnastics is a form of physical activity for developing the body by means of exercise. Another term for gymnastics is *physical culture*. People usually perform gymnastics in a gymnasium, a place for exercise. However, gymnastics can also be done at home.

There are many kinds of gymnastics. One kind is performed without the use of any equipment, or apparatus. This includes such body exercises as push-ups and sit-ups. However, most kinds of gymnastics are performed with the aid of light apparatus or fixed apparatus. Some forms of light apparatus are clubs, weights called dumbbells, and balls. Fixed gymnastic apparatus includes bars to swing on, and other equipment such as horses, bars, rings, ropes, and mats. All of these are used to strengthen the arms, legs, and the upper part of the body.

Gymnastics as a whole is used for the improvement of muscles, for physical coordination, and to keep the body fit. Most schools require a program of gymnastics and there are gymnastic contests where the performers compete for style and form.

gypsum

Gypsum is a mineral that is very important to man for a number of uses. Sheets of gypsum are sometimes used as ready-made walls for homes. Builders mix gypsum with cement so that the cement will not harden too quickly. Gypsum also is an ingredient of many kinds of plaster. In fact, gypsum is sometimes called *plaster rock.* When gypsum is heated to remove the water from it, it becomes *plaster of Paris,* a plaster that can be molded easily and is used by sculptors, and also by doctors to make plaster casts.

Gypsum is found all over the world in many forms. A fine, delicately col-

Gypsum is used in making the plaster that the worker is spreading on the wall.

National Gypsum Co.

ored gypsum is called *alabaster,* which is used to make beautiful statues and vases. It is translucent (light can be seen through it). Another type of gypsum is called *satin spar,* from which certain kinds of jewelry are made.

Gypsum is one of the softest minerals found in the earth. It is so soft that it can be scratched with the fingernail. It is usually white or gray. The United States is the leading producer of gypsum.

gypsy

Gypsies are a group of people who have wandered through parts of Europe for hundreds of years. Many of them now live in American countries. No one is sure just where the gypsies came from, but very likely they once lived in India, because their language, called *Romany,* is somewhat like the languages of northwestern India. They call themselves *Rom,* which in gypsy language means "man."

About a thousand years ago, gypsies began to appear in northern Asia, traveling on foot or in wagons. Later they spread to North Africa and Europe. More of them stayed in the Balkan countries, such as Rumania, Bulgaria, and Hungary, than anywhere else.

For hundreds of years almost no gypsies had any permanent home. They wandered in wagons and camped out. They are a colorful and interesting people. Most of them are rather small, with light-brown skin, very black hair, beautiful dark eyes, and extremely white teeth. Gypsies, especially the women, wear bright-colored clothes, and both men and women often wear large ear-

rings. Many of the women read palms, tell fortunes, and sell books on magic. Horse-trading used to be the main work of the gypsies, but they have had to change to other occupations, such as keeping stores in countries where they are allowed to own buildings and land. In Russia, Poland, and Hungary, many gypsies are musicians. They are especially good at playing the violin, and some great writers of music, such as Franz Liszt and Johannes Brahms, have used gay gypsy tunes in their compositions. The gypsies are known as good dancers, and gypsy girls used to be hired to entertain with their dances.

The gypsies' unsettled way of living has created prejudice against them in many places. In some parts of Europe they were driven out.

During the present century they have changed greatly. Many gypsies have settled in cities. They still keep to themselves, as they did earlier, but less than before. They still have their own language, but they also have learned the languages of the countries in which they have settled. Before World War II there were between two million and four million gypsies in the world. Since World War II there are fewer gypsies, because many were killed by the Germans when the Nazis controlled Germany.

gypsy moth

The gypsy moth is a destructive insect found mostly in the New England states of the United States. Its original home was Europe. While it is in the caterpillar stage and looks like a worm, it eats leaves and does great damage to trees. Many millions of dollars have been spent by the government in trying to wipe out or control the gypsy moth, but it continues to do great damage. It likes best to feed on the leaves of oak, birch, apple, alder, poplar and willow trees, but after such trees have been stripped of their leaves the gypsy moth caterpillars will feed on almost any tree.

gyroscope

The gyroscope is a kind of top. Like other tops, it spins. Originally, like other tops, it was only a toy. Then, because a man named Elmer Sperry had a brilliant idea for putting the gyroscope to practical use, it became one of the most important of all scientific instruments. Control of airplanes, bombsights and some kinds of guided missile are only a few of the scientific advances that have been based on the gyroscope.

Take any kind of top, and spin it in an upright position. As long as it is spinning fast, it will remain upright on its point, even though you know it would fall over if it were not spinning. As it begins to spin slower, it will lose its tendency to stand upright. It will gradually lean to the side until it topples over completely. Obviously, it stood upright because it was spinning and for no other reason.

Now spin a top in an upright position on a plank of wood that you can pick up and tilt to the side. While the top is spinning fast, pick up the plank and tilt it slightly. The top will not tilt with it. It will remain upright. If you tilt the plank enough the top will slide off, but it will

continue to spin in its upright position until it slides off, and if it falls to the floor and is still spinning fast it will still be upright.

The scientific principle behind this can be explained as follows:

Imagine a straight line drawn from the bottom point, or spike, of the top straight up through it. While the top is spinning, this line is the *axis* on which it is rotating.

A spinning object will resist any tendency to change the direction of its axis of rotation. The faster it is spinning, the greater its resistance will be.

Consider an aircraft instrument that is supposed always to show a line that is level with the surface of the earth. Connect this instrument with a top that is kept spinning at high speed. The nose of the plane may point up or point down; the wings may tilt to the left or tilt to the right; but as long as that top is spinning, the instrument will always be level because the spinning top will not permit its axis of rotation to be changed.

That is the principle on which "gyro-" instruments, such as the gyrocompass and the gyrostabilizer and others, are based.

HOW THE GYROSCOPE IS MADE

They used to sell gyroscopes in five-and-ten-cent stores for a quarter; they still sell them for a dollar or a little less. Any one of these ten-cent-store gyroscopes will show you how a gyroscope works.

There is a wheel, called the flywheel, and through the center of the wheel runs a shaft, or bar of metal. The ends of the shaft are mounted in a ring. The ring is attached to a base. The flywheel can spin on the shaft; the ring can turn on the base; the base itself can be put in any position.

Start the flywheel spinning, then turn the ring or the base, or both, in any direction. The shaft (which is the axis of rotation of the spinning flywheel) will continue to point in the same direction.

The first serious use of the gyroscope was in the year 1818, when a spinning gyroscope was used to show why the earth keeps the same position as it rotates around the sun.

One great bar to serious use of the gyroscope was that it was so hard to keep it turning. This problem was solved about a hundred years ago when the electric motor was invented.

In 1910, Sperry founded the Sperry Gyroscope Company in Brooklyn, New York, to make navigation instruments based on the principle of the spinning top.

USES OF THE GYROSCOPE

There is at least one gyrocompass on every ship of every navy in the world, on most commercial vessels, and on many airplanes. The gyrocompass makes use of the fact that a gyroscope always points very steadily in the same direction. The gyrocompass is more accurate than the magnetic compass, because anything made of iron or steel will cause a magnetic compass to be wrong, but nothing changes a gyrocompass as long as it is spinning properly.

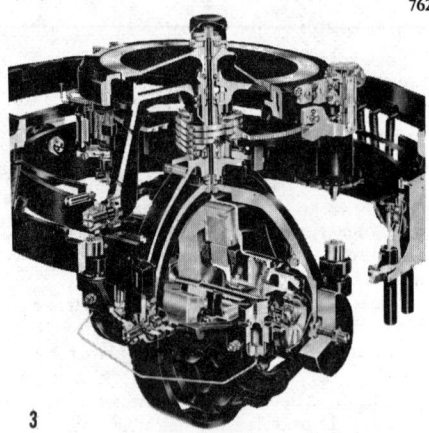

1. In its simplest form a gyroscope is a toy that tends to stay upright when it spins.
2. When the flywheel on the axle supported by the inner ring of the gyroscope is spinning,
3 The gyrocompass, shown with its housing removed, is a highly complex mechanism.

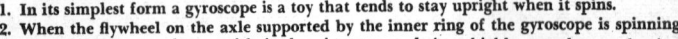

4. The air-driven Attitude Gyro is used in airplanes. The ball remains still. If the plane climbs, dives, or tips right or left, the markers on the gyro's face move around the ball, and show the plane's attitude or position.
5. Most airplanes have gyromagnetic compasses, which always point to the magnetic north.
6. The aircraft radio direction finder gives the pilot automatic compass readings. It also shows him the direction of north as recorded by a gyromagnetic compass.

Sperry Gyroscope Co. Photos

Some ships have their gyrocompasses connected to an electric motor that steers the ship. This arrangement is called a gyropilot. Whenever the ship veers a little off its course, the gyropilot causes the motor to turn the ship's rudder and steer it back onto its course.

The gyrostabilizer is a much larger instrument. One Italian ship has two gyrostabilizers that together weigh 660 tons. These devices make use of the steadying effect of the gyroscope. They are very heavy gyroscopes installed in the bottom of the ship to keep it from rolling. When a ship starts to roll in one direction, the gyrostabilizer shifts weight to the other side, making the ship stay level. This makes the voyage much more comfortable for the passengers and reduces strain on the ship.

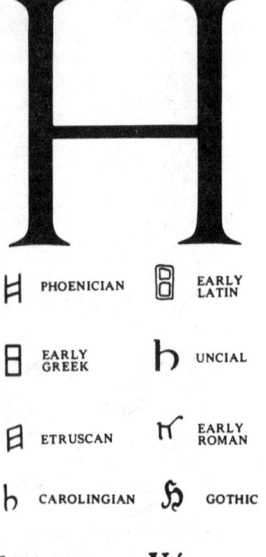

�H	PHOENICIAN	𐌇	EARLY LATIN
𐌇	EARLY GREEK	h	UNCIAL
𐌇	ETRUSCAN	ᴎ	EARLY ROMAN
h	CAROLINGIAN	ﬡ	GOTHIC
Hh	EARLY GERMAN	Hh	ALDINE
h	RENAISSANCE		

H or h

The letter H is the eighth letter of the alphabet. It can be traced all the way back to the earliest writing known to man, in Egypt thousands of years ago. In the Hebrew language, in which much of the Bible was written, the letter was called *cheth,* which means "fence." The ancient Greeks took the same letter and called it *eta.* At first the Greek eta was an *aspirate,* which means a heavily breathed sound used before or after another sound, as in the English word

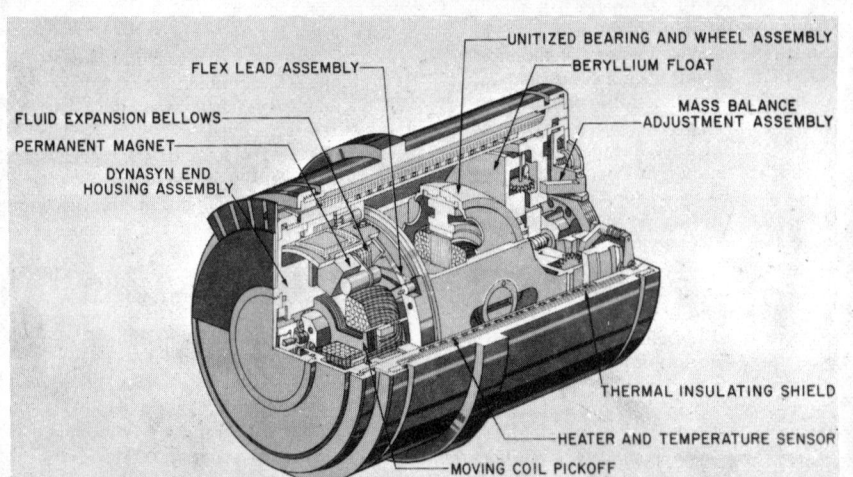

Sperry Gyroscope Company

This diagram reveals some of the parts in a special miniature gyroscope which is so advanced that it can enable a lunar landing vehicle to land within one mile of the predicted site.

hope. Later the Greeks expressed the aspirate, or rough breathing sound, by a sign somewhat like an apostrophe turned backwards. *Eta* then came to have a sound somewhat like the *a* in *fare.* The Romans, however, borrowed the earlier aspirate sound, and in English the H often has the rough breathing sound as in *hope,* but may have no sound at all, as in the word *hour.* In English the letter H can be joined with other letters to give sounds for which there is no single letter in our alphabet. We find these sounds in such words as *chop, shun, gherkin,* and *thin.*

On the opposite page, you can see what the Greek letter *eta* was like. If you leave off the top and bottom horizontal bars, it looks just the H we use today. When the Greeks reversed the letters in order to read from left to right, certain letters looked just the same, because they were symmetrical (same on both sides).

Read also the article ALPHABET.

Haakon

Haakon is a name of several kings of Norway. The one we know best is Haakon VII, who became the first king of Norway as we know it today. He was always well loved by his people, but especially so after his heroism in World War II. In 1940 Norway was one of the first countries attacked by the Germans. They struck without warning, and seized three seaports and the capital city of Oslo. Norway was unprepared and had no chance against the strong German armies, but King Haakon and his government refused to give in. They fled from the capital and declared war against Germany. At last Haakon was forced to flee from his country. He went to England and set up a government-in-exile there, working hard to encourage and help his people. As soon as the Germans were defeated, in 1945, Haakon returned to Norway.

King Haakon VII

For hundreds of years Norway was united with Denmark and Sweden, or sometimes with only one of these two countries. During this period Norway was independent but had no king of its own. In 1905, the Norwegian people decided to break off their union (at that time with Sweden) and elect their own king. They chose Prince Charles of Denmark, a son of the king of Denmark. Prince Charles was born in 1872 and was married to a daughter of the king of England. When Charles was elected to the throne of Norway, he chose for his official name an old Norwegian name and was crowned as King Haakon VII in 1906. He died in 1957, at the age of 85, and his son became king as Olav V.

habeas corpus

Habeas corpus are two words from the Latin language meaning "you may have the body." They have a legal meaning that is very important to liberty. Under the constitutions of the United States and other English-speaking countries, a person may not be imprisoned without a hearing before a judge. If a person is imprisoned without a hearing, his lawyer may get a writ of habeas corpus from the court. This writ, or order, means that the person must immediately be brought to court and unless the police can show good reason why he is being held he must be released.

The writ of habeas corpus has been a part of the law in England for hundreds of years. When the American colonies gained their freedom and wrote their constitution, the right of habeas corpus was put into the Bill of Rights, which is the first ten amendments to the Constitution.

habit

A habit is a need or desire to do something time after time, and to do it in the same way each time. A person may have a habit of rubbing his cheek when he thinks. Every time he is trying to solve a problem or decide something, he will rub his cheek. There are habits in speaking, such as saying "You see" many times when explaining something. *Doodling* is a kind of habit. A person doodles when he scribbles or draws with a pencil on paper while he is talking or thinking.

Habits that hurt the body, such as smoking too much or drinking too much, and habits that annoy other people, are called *bad habits* or *petty vices.* People who have them often try to give them up, but sometimes the desire to do them has become so great that this becomes very difficult. In these cases, the difficulty is in the mind and not in the body. That is, giving up the bad habit would not cause actual pain in the body. Dangerous drugs, however, can cause a kind of habit called *addiction.* When an addicted person stops taking the drug, he suffers actual pain and should be under a doctor's care. It is still necessary to give up the drug habit or die within a few years.

Certain habits become automatic. We do them without being conscious of it; that is, without thinking about it. Examples are swallowing when we eat and drink, and bending our knees when we walk. The special name for this kind of habit is *conditioned reflex.* There is a separate article on REFLEX.

hackberry

The hackberry is a tree of the elm family. It grows in North America. It is not as tall a tree as the elm, and has straighter branches and smaller leaves. The hackberry is sometimes called the *sugar-berry* or *nettle* tree. Its fruit is like a small black cherry, and it is good to eat. The wood of the hackberry is soft and coarse-grained; it is not strong enough to be very useful as lumber.

Hadassah

Hadassah is the name of a large organization of American Jewish women. It began in 1912 and was named for a Jewish heroine (see ESTHER). These women are Zionists; they believe that the Jewish people should have a homeland in Palestine. Both before and after 1948, when the state of Israel was founded in a part of Palestine, Hadassah did many things to help the people in that country.

Hadassah founded hospitals for the sick. It also started health centers and clinics, where mothers could learn how to take good care of their children. An important part of Hadassah's program is called Youth Aliyah. This works to give orphans and needy children a permanent family home and an education. It also sets up schools to help young people learn how to earn a living.

There are about 320,000 women in the United States who belong to Hadassah, and they have chapters in forty-eight states. The headquarters is in New York City.

haddock

The haddock is an ocean fish. It is one of the most important food fish along the eastern coast of the United States. The haddock is related to the cod, and it is caught by fishermen in the same places as cod, all along the New England coast, and along the Grand Banks of Newfoundland, off the northeast coast of Canada. It usually weighs three or four pounds, and rarely is found heavier than fifteen pounds. The fish is eaten fresh, or dried and smoked. Smoked haddock is called *finnan haddie,* which is what the people of Scotland called it when they invented this way of preparing and eating haddock. Haddock is also caught on the other side of the Atlantic Ocean, around Great Britain and in the North Sea.

Haddock swim in schools (in large groups). They feed on invertebrate, or spineless, animals on the bottom of the ocean. They lay their eggs in the late winter or early spring, depending on how far south they may be and how warm the water is.

Hades

Hades is a word now used to mean about the same thing as Hell, a place where the souls of bad people go after death. To the ancient Greeks, more than two thousand years ago, it meant a place where the souls of all dead people, good or bad, went. It was not especially a place of punishment, but it was very gloomy and unpleasant. The king of Hades was the god Pluto, or Dis. His kingdom was bounded by the river Styx and guarded by Cerberus, a fearful dog with three heads. The souls of the dead had to pass through Erebus, a place of complete darkness, on their way to Hades. In some stories, there was a god called Erebus who ruled over this gloomy place.

Hadrian

Hadrian was an emperor of Rome when it was the greatest empire in the world. He lived about a hundred years after the time of Jesus. Hadrian was a very good ruler, and during his reign he had many beautiful temples and palaces built. His villa near Rome was a magnificent place that covered several square miles. It included a theater, a stadium, a palace, several temples, and many other buildings. Its ruins can still be seen, and many of its fine statues

are now in museums in Rome. Hadrian visited Britain, which was part of his empire, and there he had built a fortification called Hadrian's Wall. This wall was almost 75 miles long, running across the narrow part of the island of Great Britain. It was built in the years 122 to 124. The bits of it that are left today show that it must have been six feet high and eight feet thick. Every mile or so there were towers built for lookouts. Along the wall were roads, and camps for soldiers. The whole defense system is considered one of the best of ancient times.

Hadrian also built a mausoleum, or tomb, which has since been rebuilt and is now called the Castle of Saint Angelo. It is 230 feet across and the ancient concrete foundations are 300 feet square. The burial room and passages underground are just as they were in Hadrian's time, but the rest of the building has been very much changed through the centuries.

Hadrian was born in the year 76 and died in 138.

Haeckel, Ernst

Ernest Haeckel was a German biologist, that is, a scientist who studies living things. He was born in 1834, and he lived and taught for most of his life in the city of Jena. In Haeckel's time, Charles Darwin had just developed his theory of organic evolution, which says that new kinds of animals develop from changes in older kinds. Haeckel agreed completely with this theory, but he carried it so far that not even Darwin would have agreed with a great many of the things he said. Haeckel wrote a great many books and scientific papers. He died in 1919.

Hagenbeck, Carl

Carl Hagenbeck was a German who had the most famous collection of wild animals of all time. He was born in 1844. He got the idea for his career from watching his father, who had made a hobby of collecting and training animals. Carl toured Europe with his animals and in 1893 he brought a collection of more than one thousand of them to the United States to be shown at the Columbian Exposition, or World Fair, being held at Chicago. The tricks he taught his animals were very popular with the people who came to his shows, and they gave American circus men many ideas for wild animal acts. Hagenbeck stayed for a while in the United States, and joined his show with that of another man, named Wallace, to make the Hagenbeck-Wallace Circus, which became famous throughout the country.

In Hamburg, a big city in Germany, Hagenbeck thought up and built a new kind of zoo, where the animals live in surroundings that are like their natural homes, and are kept in only by deep ditches instead of bars. This idea is now being used in some of the biggest zoos in the United States, such as the New York Zoological Gardens and the Brookfield Zoo in Chicago. Hagenbeck died in 1913, but other members of his family carried on his work.

Hague, The

The Hague is one of the most important cities of the Netherlands. Though the city of Amsterdam is the official capital, The Hague has long been the city where the principal government offices are, and the Dutch parliament meets there. The Hague is also famous as the seat of the INTERNATIONAL COURT OF JUSTICE, about which you can read in a separate article.

The Hague is the third-largest city in the Netherlands (after Amsterdam and Rotterdam). About 600,000 people live there. The city has many fine gardens and parks and is criss-crossed by many canals. It is close to the sea, and nearby are many popular seaside resorts. It also has many historic buildings that go back to important events in Dutch history.

The Hague was founded more than seven hundred years ago, in 1247, by Count William II of Holland. It was called 's-Gravenhage, which means "hedge of the counts," and that name is still used, even though the hedge that bounded Count William's castle and land is no longer there. Until 1948, The Hague was the home of the Dutch kings and queens.

Much of The Hague was destroyed by bombs in World War II, especially the remains of the great forest there in which the Dutch counts used to hunt. The people have since repaired much of the damage and have built new parks.

THE HAGUE, NETHERLANDS. Population (1976 estimate) 690,000. Founded in 1247.

Haig, Douglas

Douglas Haig was the highest-ranking officer in the British army at the end of World War I. He was born in 1861 in Scotland, and started his military career as a young man. In 1918, when the Germans started their last desperate drive and almost captured the city of Paris, Haig was commander of the British armies in France. Little by little he pushed the Germans back and finally won the last big battle of the war. At that time Haig was a field marshal, the highest rank in an army. After the war he was made an earl. He formed the British Legion, which is an organization of veterans somewhat like the American Legion. He also started the custom of selling poppies to raise money to help veterans. Haig died in 1928.

hail

Hail is little pebbles of ice that sometimes fall in showers from the clouds just before a thunderstorm, in very warm weather. Usually a shower of hailstones makes lots of noise, but does little damage. However, hailstones are sometimes as big as eggs, or even bigger, and then they can be very dangerous. The life story of a hailstone is interesting. It starts as a drop of ordinary rain water that is caught in a thundercloud blown up into the sky by a sudden blast of wind. The higher the raindrop goes the colder the air gets, until finally the raindrop is frozen into a tiny speck of ice. Now other blasts of wind catch the frozen raindrop and start blowing it up and down, all over the thundercloud. One moment it is whizzing through a pocket of warm, wet air, which coats it with water. The next moment it is zooming through another air pocket that is bitter cold and instantly freezes the water. In this way, little by little, a hailstone is built up. If the winds are fierce enough to keep the stone up in the air for quite a long time, it may grow as large as a baseball or a small grapefruit.

Haile Selassie

Haile Selassie is the name of a man who became emperor of Ethiopia, a country in Africa, in 1930. Five years later he became famous throughout the world because of his brave resistance to Italy's efforts to conquer his country. He personally led his armies in battle, even though they were armed only with swords and spears against the Italian cannons and tanks. In 1936 he made a very stirring speech to the League of Nations, begging them to help his country against the invaders. This speech was so moving that it was recorded, and many people have bought phonograph records of it.

The League of Nations would not help Haile Selassie, and the Ethiopians were defeated. Selassie escaped and fled to England. In 1941, after Italy had entered World War II as an ally of Germany, England flew Selassie back to Africa to encourage his people to fight the Italians. When World War II was over the Italians had lost and Selassie was emperor again. After the war Selassie continued his efforts to modernize and improve his country. He introduced schools, hospitals, electric lights, a European police sytem, and motion pictures. In 1954 Selassie came to the United States, where he was received by President Eisenhower and was a guest at the White House.

Haile Selassie traced his descent from King Solomon and the Queen of Sheba. His official title was the "Conquering Lion of Judah," and another of his titles was Negus, which means about the same thing as "emperor."

Ethiopia's capital city is ADDIS ABABA, about which there is a separate article.

hair

Hair is a thin, threadlike outgrowth of the skin. It is found on all mammals, which means all animals that (like human beings) bear living offspring and nurse them. No kind of animal except mammals has hair, but hair is more or less the equivalent in mammals of the feathers of birds and the scales of reptiles.

An ordinary hair consists of a *shaft* and a *bulb*. The shaft is the part we call the hair; that is, the part that grows outside the skin. This shaft is rooted deep in the skin in a tiny *follicle*, or hole in the skin. The bulb of the hair grows in this follicle, and is supplied with blood from blood vessels that grow around it.

The shaft of the hair is composed of a horny layer of scales, called the *cuticle*. You can feel these scales by pulling a hair the wrong way between your fingers. Under the cuticle there is another horny layer called the *cortex*, and in the center is a core called the *medulla*. The hair grows from the roots, not the ends. The individual cells of which the hair is made form at the root and push the older cells outward. A hair will live from two to four years. When an old one falls out, a new one grows from the same follicle.

Hair will continue to grow unless the follicle is destroyed.

Hair grows on all parts of the human body except for the palms of the hands and the soles of the feet. Mostly it grows on the scalp, the eyebrows, the edge of the eyelids, the pubic area, the chin, cheeks, armpits, chest, and entrance of the nose and ears. The hair generally grows in a slanting direction, because of the way the follicles are placed in the skin. Sometimes these follicles are placed differently in certain parts of the scalp, and then they form a "cowlick," in which the hair grows in a different direction from the rest of the hair on the scalp. This can usually be corrected with constant brushing. When we say that our "hair stood on end" with cold, or fright, or surprise, it can be literally true, because at such times tiny muscles in the skin may contract and cause the hair to stand up almost straight.

COLOR OF HAIR

Hair grows in different shapes. It is never really round, but straight hair is the most nearly round. Curly hair is slightly flattened. Kinky hair is very flat, like a ribbon, and has a groove along its length; it is believed that the tight twist of kinky hair is because the fibers are pulled tightly along this groove.

Hair also grows in different colors, and the color is determined deep in the root by an oil that is transmitted to the hair as it grows. The color also depends on many tiny air spaces in the hair. These reflect light and thus make the hair appear darker. Color and thickness of hair are related to color of skin and eyes. For example, blond hair is usually very thin, or fine, and people with blond hair usually have light skins and blue eyes; black hair is usually thicker, and people with dark hair usually have dark eyes and an olive skin. Gray hair is due to a lack of coloring pigment, which usually comes with age. But grayness of the hair has nothing to do with its health; gray hair is often stronger than hair that still has its color. Age and worry and illness can cut down the making of the coloring matter in hair and turn it gray. Since the nutrition of hair is provided through the blood, the general state of a person's health has a great deal to do with the condition of his hair. Persons who have been ill for a long time or who have had an improper diet will lose the shiny, healthy gloss of their hair. Baldnesss can be caused by poor circulation of blood in the scalp, or by neglect of the scalp, dandruff, and other conditions that reduce the nutrition of the hair; but there is evidence that the tendency to baldness is inherited.

ANIMAL HAIR

Animal hair is of even more varieties than human hair. There are the short, stiff bristle of the pig; the long, silky hair of the Persian cat; and the tight, curly hair of the Karakul sheep, from which fur coats are made. It may vary a little in structure, but it is all hair.

In animals the principal function of hair is protection from the weather. The long fur of many animals keeps them warm in winter, and in the hot weather

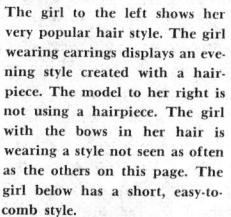

The girl to the left shows her very popular hair style. The girl wearing earrings displays an evening style created with a hairpiece. The model to her right is not using a hairpiece. The girl with the bows in her hair is wearing a style not seen as often as the others on this page. The girl below has a short, easy-to-comb style.

it insulates their bodies against the heat. As the warm season nears, most animals lose some of their fur. This is called shedding, and you have probably seen it happen to a dog or cat in the spring.

Animal hair is used for many things. The bristles of pigs are used to make brushes of all kinds. The pelts of many kinds of animal provide fur garments for human beings. The hair of rabbits, beavers, and other animals is used to make felt. Horsehair and the hair of oxen is used as stuffing for cushions and mattresses. Camel's hair makes fine cloth, and the hair of Angora goats is used for beautiful shawls and sweaters. Human hair is made into wigs, and into hairpieces for women to use if they want their hair to look longer for some particular new style.

HAIRDRESSING

Ever since prehistoric times hair has been considered an ornament to human appearance. The curl and the color of hair have always been important to people. The ancient Assyrians, a people who lived around the Mediterranean Sea in Biblical times, wore wigs if they were bald. They dyed their hair different colors, and wore ornaments in it. The men even curled their beards as well as their hair, and sometimes braided the hair and beard together. The Persians also dyed their hair, and used perfumed oils and ointments in it, but they preferred simple ways of wearing it. It was cut shorter and worn close to the head.

In ancient Egypt the ruling class wore their hair high on top of the head, combed straight back and held with a wide, stiff band. Later the Egyptians had

different styles. Cleopatra, the most famous queen of Egypt, wore her black hair in a long, simple frame about her face.

Greek women were the first to wear a hair style that has been popular from time to time ever since. This style frames the face with short curls and bangs across the forehead, and the long hair is gathered at the back of the head and worn in a tight knot high above the neck. Greek children wore their hair long until they were about 18; then they cut it off and sacrificed it to one of their gods, usually to Apollo. Young girls cut their hair off before they were married. The men of Greece wore their hair short, and slaves were not allowed to have long hair. The first known hairdressers were Greek. There was so much demand for their services that hairdressing became an industry.

Until about 2,200 years ago (about the year 300 B.C.) the Romans wore their hair long. Then a man named Ticinius Mena brought the first barber from the island of Sicily to Rome. Later, Roman women wore elaborate hair styles. They got false blond hair from captured women of the Germanic peoples, and braided it into their own. The North European races had long, coarse, blond hair, which they wore long and bound up behind the head. Short hair among these Celtic and Germanic peoples meant that the person was a servant, or was in disgrace for breaking a law, because criminals and slaves had their hair cut off.

During the Middle Ages, which lasted until about six hundred years ago, hair styles became simpler. Generally the men wore short hair and the women long

braids. About three hundred years ago, however, King Louis XIV of France changed this style. He was a very short man, and he wore a towering wig to make him look taller. The fashion spread to all the people, men and women, of the upper classes in France. Elaborate wigs were worn by all the people at the court. These wigs were built high in waves and curls, and powdered to give a soft effect around the face. This fashion continued until the Revolution in France, and finally disappeared. However, for women it returned about a hundred years later, in the reign of Queen Victoria of England, and elaborate structures of real and false hair again were worn, but without the powder. Today wigs are worn only by the higher members of a court of law in some European countries.

MODERN STYLES

After World War I, another big change took place. Women had worn their hair long, with or without wigs or false hair, for hundreds of years. In the 1920s they began to cut it off, and the fashion of bobbed hair began. Today most women wear their hair short.

Late in the 1920s, women started to have permanent waves in their hair. A permanent wave is a way of curling the hair so that it will stay curled for months or until it grows out. About the time of World War II, "home permanents" were developed. Women could give themselves permanent waves as easily as they could put their hair up in curlers. Ways were found to cut the hair so as to bring out even a slight natural wave.

Women have always known that it is important to care for their hair. They have treated it to keep it from becoming dry and brittle, and they have tinted or dyed it to hide the grayness that is a sign of age. Brushing and combing the hair regularly are aids to healthy hair.

Haiti

Haiti is a small American country on an island in the West Indies. The island is also called Haiti, though the present custom is to call it Hispaniola, and formerly it was called Santo Domingo (Spanish for Saint Dominic). The island is the first place Christopher Columbus landed when he discovered America in 1492.

Haiti is one of two independent republics on the island. The Republic of Haiti is on the western side. It is about the size of the state of Maryland, with an area of about 10,000 square miles, but its population of four and a half million is much greater than the population of Maryland. The other independent country on the island, the Dominican Republic, is about twice as large as Haiti. There is a separate article on the DOMINICAN REPUBLIC.

The Republic of Haiti is one of the most densely populated regions in the Americas. Most of the people live on small farms. Because of its steady climate, which is very pleasant, Haiti has become a very popular place for vacations.

Off Haiti's northwest coast is the island of Tortuga, which was once famous as a hideaway for pirates. Haiti has some mountains, and many fertile plains.

THE PEOPLE OF HAITI

When Columbus landed on Haiti in December, 1492, it was inhabited by Arawak Indians. The Spaniards enslaved them. The Indians could not stand the labor they were made to do, and soon died out. The Spanish then brought in African Negroes to be slaves. So many were brought in that today most of the people are Negroes or a mixture of white and Negro blood. Of course, slavery has been against the law for many years.

The official language is French, but most of the people speak a mixture of French with some African words and some Spanish words. Nearly all the people belong to the Roman Catholic Church.

The Negro people have also kept some of their African traditions and are said to

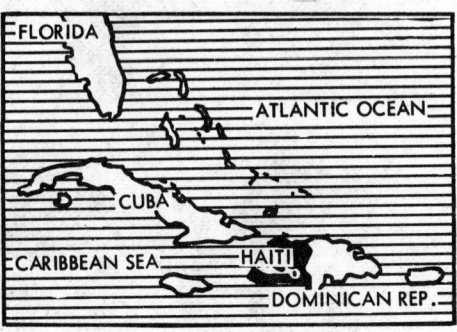

practice voodoo, which is a modified survival of some ancient African religion. Some of this has been made up just for the tourists.

WHAT THE COUNTRY IS LIKE

About four-fifths of the island of Haiti is covered by mountains with heavy forests. The most important ranges are the Massif du Nord, the Massif de la Sele, and the Massif de la Hotte. Between these are the fertile plains, such as the Plaine du Nord, Artibonite, Central, and Cul-de-Sac. The plains are watered by many streams. The most important river is also called the Artibonite. The climate is tropical (very hot and rainy) and changes very seldom. Trade winds from the northwest make the island a pleasant place.

The main crops of Haiti are coffee, cotton, and sugar. There are forests of very fine woods, such as mahogany, cedar, rosewood, and oak. Haiti has many minerals, including silver, copper, iron, sulfur, iridium, manganese, and bauxite (from which aluminum is made). Not much has been done to get them out of the ground, but bauxite is now being mined. Haiti has very few factories.

THE GOVERNMENT

According to its constitution, Haiti is a republic in which the people elect a president and a National Assembly of 67 members, which makes the laws. There is a cabinet (heads of departments) to conduct the government's affairs. But the way Haiti has really been governed is very different. For almost all its history as an independent nation, Haiti has been ruled either by a dictator or by a group (junta) of military men. There have been no really free elections. As a result, politicians and rich men who bribe them are very rich but most of the people of Haiti are very poor.

Education is free and children, according to law, must attend school. But this law is not enforced and almost 90 percent of the people cannot read or write.

The capital and largest city of Haiti is Port-au-Prince, population 200,000. It is also the chief seaport and has excellent natural harbors. The University of Haiti is located there.

The second-largest city of Haiti is Cap-Haïtien, called Le Cap by the people. It has a population of 25,000. Two interesting things to see there are the citadel La Ferrière, a huge fortress and the Sans-Souci palace.

Gonaïves is another port city, about 70 miles from Port-au-Prince. It is a historic town because the independence of the Republic of Haiti was proclaimed there.

HAITI IN THE PAST

Much of Haiti's history is made up of wars, revolutions, and assassinations. France gained control of the island in 1697. By 1789 there were many people who were free and who had money but who had no political rights. They asked for equality of political rights, and the French Assembly granted these, but the French landlords in Haiti did not like the grant and started trouble. These landlords, called colons, asked the English to help them against their mother country, France. In 1793, the English took possession of the island. It seemed that France had lost everything, because part of the island was held by the English and another part was held by the Spanish.

Then Haiti's most famous historical figure, Toussaint L'Ouverture, decided to help France. He was an amazing man with great personality. He was a Negro and had been a slave for forty years. Because of this he found it easy to enlist help from the natives. In a short time he drove both the English and the Spanish from the island. The French government rewarded him by making him a major general and appointing him governor of Haiti. In 1795, Spain gave its part of the island, called Santo Domingo, to France.

Later on, the French emperor Napoleon was afraid that Toussaint was becoming too powerful, and sent a Frenchman, General Leclerc, to be the new governor. A large army came with Leclerc in case of trouble. There were a few small battles, but Toussaint was tired of fighting and surrendered. He retired to one of his plantations, but Leclerc had him arrested and sent to France. Leclerc was afraid Toussaint might again rouse the natives. Arresting him was a mistake. The natives became very angry, and in 1802 they rebelled again, under the leadership of General Dessalines. They were successful, and on January 1, 1804, Haiti proclaimed its independence. One of the first laws passed by General Dessalines abolished slavery.

Since that time there have been many revolutions and assassinations. In 1915, United States Marines went in after the murder of President Guillaume Sam. The Marines remained in Haiti from 1915 to 1934, during which time the island received many benefits from the United States. There were revolutions in 1945, 1949, and 1956. The last revolution was followed by a period of chaos and a military junta took control. In 1957, François

Duvalier became president. In 1964, he was named President for Life. Upon his death in 1971, his son assumed the title.

HAITI. Area, 10,714 square miles. Population (1971 estimate), 4,960,000. Government, republic. Languages, French and Creole. Religion, Roman Catholic and pagan. Monetary unit, gourde (20 U.S. cents). Capital and largest city, Port-au-Prince.

hake

The hake is a fish that is valuable as a food. It is somewhat like the cod and the haddock. It is sometimes called a *codling* or a *whiting*. Hake fishing is an important industry. The hake can be eaten fresh or it can be eaten after it has been preserved by salting. The salted hake is called "boneless cod." The air bladders of hake are dried and used to make isinglass. The hake is found in the Atlantic Ocean along the eastern coast north of Virginia; it is also found in the Pacific Ocean. It lives in deep water and feeds on herring and other small fish.

Hale, Edward Everett

Edward Everett Hale was an American writer and clergyman who lived about a hundred years ago. He is best known for a story he wrote, "The Man Without A Country." He was born in Boston in 1822, and was the nephew of Nathan HALE and of Edward EVERETT, about whom you can read in separate articles. Edward Everett Hale entered Harvard College at the age of 13. After graduation he became a minister. For forty-five years he was pastor of the South Congregational Church in Boston. He spent much of his life trying to help others. He was opposed to slavery, and he believed that every American child should have the chance to be educated. Toward the end of his life he became chaplain of the United States Senate. Hale died in 1909.

Hale, Nathan

Nathan Hale, an American hero of the Revolutionary War, was executed  by the British as a spy. Hale was born in 1755 and was graduated from Yale College at the age of 18. He began a career as a teacher, but two years later the outbreak of the Revolution caused him to join the army as a captain. His first exploit was the capture, with only one other man, of a provision ship from under the guns of a British man-of-war. Hale divided up the prize goods among his fellow American soldiers.

In 1776 he was assigned to a dangerous spying mission. After the American retreat from Long Island, General Washington needed to know what the British were going to do next. Hale disguised himself as a Dutch schoolmaster, passed easily through the British lines, and made notes and drawings of the information Washington wanted. But he was seen and recognized by a relative who was a supporter of the British side. This relative betrayed him to the British, and he was seized and taken to the mansion where General Howe had his headquarters. There he was held all night in a greenhouse. Under questioning he freely ad-

mitted that he was an American officer and a spy. The next morning he was taken out to be hanged, without even a trial. He went to the gallows bravely, and just before he was executed he made a famous statement: "I only regret that I have but one life to lose for my country."

halftone, a method of printing a picture: see PHOTOENGRAVING.

halibut

The halibut is a large ocean fish. It is one of the most important food fish on the eastern and western coasts of the United States. At one time there were a great many of them off the east coast, but now the fishermen have to go up to the waters off Newfoundland and Iceland to catch them. Off the west coast halibut is very abundant, and there the halibut industry is second in importance only to the salmon industry.

The halibut is the largest of the flatfish. The flatfish swim flat in the water, and have both eyes on the upper side. The upper side of the halibut is grey-brown, and the underside is white. Halibut weigh as much as 400 pounds. One caught off the coast of Sweden weighed 750 pounds.

The meat of halibut is white, rather dry, and very good to eat. It is usually served in steaks. Halibut liver oil is rich in vitamins A and D. The fish are caught with hook and line. Fresh fish, often herring, are used for bait.

Halifax

Halifax is the capital and largest city of the province of Nova Scotia, in Canada. It is a peninsula (an arm of land sticking into the ocean) on the southern coast of Nova Scotia. Halifax is the most important seaport in Nova Scotia and has one of the finest harbors in the world. It is especially important during the win-

ter months, because the waters never freeze and ships can come and go easily.

More than 86,700 people live in Halifax. Many of them work in factories that build ships and make clothing and furniture. Some of them work in the large oil- and sugar-refining plants, and others are fishermen. Two Canadian railroads run to Halifax, and there is a fine airport.

Halifax has many historic buildings. One of them is St. Paul's Church, which was built in 1750 and is the oldest Anglican Church in Canada. There are three colleges. There is also a great fort, built about 150 years ago.

Halifax was founded in 1749 as a British naval base. This was very useful to the British during the Revolutionary War. During World War I and again in World War II, Halifax was a great naval base from which fighting men were sent to all parts of the world.

HALIFAX, NOVA SCOTIA. Population (1973 estimate) 86,792. Capital of Nova Scotia. On the Atlantic Ocean.

Hall, Charles M., an American inventor who developed a method of manufacturing aluminum, in 1886. See the article on ALUMINUM.

Hall of Fame

The Hall of Fame is a building on the grounds of New York University in the Bronx, New York City, in which are bronze busts (sculpture showing the head and shoulders) of great Americans. A tablet below each bust gives interesting words that were written or spoken by that person. The building itself is in the shape of a half-circle colonnade, or covered walk with pillars that support the roof. Anyone may suggest the name of an American to be included in the Hall of Fame, but the person must have been

MEN AND WOMEN IN THE HALL OF FAME

1900	John Greenleaf Whittier	James Monroe
John Adams	Emma Willard	James McNeill Whistler
John James Audubon	**1910**	Walt Whitman
Henry Ward Beecher	George Bancroft	**1935**
William Ellery Channing	Phillips Brooks	Grover Cleveland
Henry Clay	William Cullen Bryant	Simon Newcomb
Peter Cooper	James Fenimore Cooper	William Penn
Jonathan Edwards	Oliver Wendell Holmes	**1940**
Ralph Waldo Emerson	Andrew Jackson	Stephen Collins Foster
David Glasgow Farragut	John Lothrop Motley	**1945**
Benjamin Franklin	Edgar Allen Poe	Sidney Lanier
Robert Fulton	Harriet Beecher Stowe	Thomas Paine
Ulysses Simpson Grant	Frances Elizabeth Willard	Walter Reed
Asa Gray	**1915**	Booker T. Washington
Nathaniel Hawthorne	Louis Agassiz	**1950**
Washington Irving	Daniel Boone	Susan B. Anthony
Thomas Jefferson	Rufus Choate	Alexander Graham Bell
James Kent	Charlotte Saunders Cushman	Josiah Willard Gibbs
Robert Edward Lee	Alexander Hamilton	William Crawford Gorgas
Abraham Lincoln	Joseph Henry	Theodore Roosevelt
Henry Wadsworth Longfellow	Mark Hopkins	Woodrow Wilson
John Marshall	Elias Howe	**1955**
Horace Mann	Francis Parkman	Thomas J. Jackson
Samuel Finley Breese Morse	**1920**	George Westinghouse
George Peabody	Samuel Langhorne Clemens	Wilbur Wright
Joseph Story	James Buchanan Eads	**1960**
Gilbert Charles Stuart	Patrick Henry	Thomas Alva Edison
George Washington	William T. G. Morton	Edward A. MacDowell
Daniel Webster	Alice Freeman Palmer	Henry David Thoreau
Eli Whitney	Augustus Saint-Gaudens	**1965**
1905	Roger Williams	Jane Addams
John Quincy Adams	**1925**	O. W. Holmes, Jr.
James Russell Lowell	Edwin Booth	Sylvanus Thayer
Mary Lyon	John Paul Jones	Orville Wright
James Madison	**1930**	**1970**
Maria Mitchell	Matthew Fontaine Maury	Albert Abraham Michelson
William Tecumseh Sherman		Lillian D. Wald

dead for at least 25 years. Then a group of about one hundred outstanding men and women from all over the United States make the final choice. Elections are held every five years. The first one was held in 1900. There is room for 100 busts. By 1965, 93 men and women had been elected to the Hall of Fame.

Hallowe'en

Hallowe'en is the night of October 31. Traditionally it is a time for playing pranks, but actually it is the day before a holy day, All Saints' Day. This holy day was once called All Hallows or Hallowmas, because *hallow* meant "saint." Therefore Hallowe'en means the eve (night before) All Hallows day.

The legend of Hallowe'en is that the evil spirits and witches go out and celebrate that particular night because the next day, when the saints are honored, they had better be in hiding. In earlier times there were many superstitions connected with Hallowe'en. Robert Burns wrote a poem called "Tam o' Shanter," in which he describes the goblins and ghosts that travel about on Hallowe'en.

Modern children celebrate Hallowe'en with all sorts of pranks. They dress up in disguises and go about to neighbors' houses saying, "Trick or treat." This means that the householder must give them a treat of candy or cake, or the children will play tricks on him. The traditional colors of the day are orange and black, and Hallowe'en parties are decorated with witches flying on broomsticks, and black cats, and pumpkin jack o'lanterns. The children play special games such as bobbing for apples.

hallucination

A hallucination is imagining something that is not there. The most common kinds of hallucination are seeing or hearing things that are not present, but a person having an hallucination may feel sure that he is feeling, or smelling, or tasting something when he is not. Hallucinations occur in the mind. They are most common in persons who are mentally sick, but normal people who are under great strain or who have high fever may also have hallucinations. Hallucinations are different from mirages, which are caused by tricks of light. You can read about MIRAGES in a separate article.

halo

A halo is a ring of light around something. In painting, it is a bright circle that frames the head of Jesus or the Virgin Mary or the saints, and is put there to indicate their holiness.

The word *halo* is also used by astronomers to describe the bright circle that is sometimes seen around the sun or moon. This halo is usually reddish in color at the inner edge and violet on the outer edge. Sometimes long spokes of light can be seen extending out from the moon or sun to the circle of light; at other times two circles can be seen, one inside the other.

Halos are caused by ice crystals or other tiny particles in the earth's atmosphere that interfere with the light.

Hals, Frans

Frans Hals was a Dutch painter who lived about three hundred years ago. His most famous painting is *The Laughing Cavalier,* a portrait of a jolly Dutchman in the costume of the time. Hals was born in 1580, and lived at the same time as another great Dutch painter, Rubens.

Metropolitan Museum of Art

Frans Hals liked good food and good company, and often made them the subject of his paintings. *Merry Company* is a good example of his light-hearted work.

Hals painted rich merchants and influential ministers, but he also painted poor people, such as fishwives and wandering players.

Hals had a family of ten children, and he supported them very well until about 1652. Then things started going badly with him, and at last his possessions were sold at auction to pay his debts. Hals' paintings were not considered of much value until two hundred years after his death in 1666. Then they started to bring enormous prices at auction, and many of them are prized possessions of great museums. His painting *The Smoker* is in the Metropolitan Museum, New York City.

Halsey, William Frederick

William Frederick Halsey became famous in World War II as an admiral of the United States Navy. His doggedness in battle won him the nickname of "Bull" Halsey.

Halsey was born in 1882 in Elizabeth, New Jersey, and he graduated from the Naval Academy at Annapolis in 1904. When war broke out against Japan in 1941, Halsey was a vice-admiral. In October 1942 he was made commander of the Allied fleets in the South Pacific, and he won several victories over the Japanese near the island of Guadalcanal. In 1944 he became commander of the U.S. 3rd Fleet, and his aircraft carriers helped defeat the Japanese in the Battle of the Philippine Sea. He was promoted to admiral of the fleet, the highest rank in the Navy, in 1945, and he retired the same year. He died in 1959.

ham, the meat from the upper part of a hog's hind leg, that is eaten after it has been salted and smoked: see the article on MEAT.

Haman

Haman is a character in the Bible who is remembered mainly because he was hanged on the gallows he had intended for another man. His story is told in the Book of Esther. Haman was the favorite minister of King Ahasuerus of Persia at a time when the Jews were being kept in captivity by the Persians. Everyone used to praise Haman except a Jew named Mordecai, and in revenge Haman decided to have all the Jews in Persia killed. He persuaded the king to agree by telling him lies about the Jews. But the king's wife, Esther, was the niece of Mordecai. She told the king the truth about Haman's plot. Thus the Jews were saved, and Haman was hanged on the gallows he had built for Mordecai. Every year there is a Jewish festival, the festival of Purim, in memory of Esther's saving the Jews.

Hamburg

Hamburg is a city on the Elbe River, in West Germany. Seagoing ships sail up the Elbe and make Hamburg the largest port in Germany. Over 1,818,000 people live there. Many of them work in the great shipyards and docks, and others work in factories that make rubber, cloth, and chemicals.

Hamburg has a wonderful system of canals and bridges and tunnels that make it easy to travel from one part of the city to another. This is very important, because supplies must be carried to the warehouses and docks to be shipped to other places. Many young men and women go to the University of Hamburg, and others attend several technical and medical schools. There are also many concert halls. The great composers Brahms and Mendelssohn were both born in Hamburg, and the first German opera house was built there almost three hundred years ago.

Hamburg was founded more than one thousand years ago, when the great emperor Charlemagne built a mighty castle where the city of Hamburg now stands. In the year 1241, Hamburg and the port city of Lübeck made an agreement to help protect each other's business interests. This was the beginning of the famous HANSEATIC LEAGUE, which you can read about in a separate article. Hamburg became the most powerful city in the League. About four hundred years ago it was made a free city, with the power to make its own laws. Because it was such an important port, Hamburg was bombed very heavily during World War II. More than half of the city was destroyed, and many people lost their lives.

HAMBURG, GERMANY. Population (1973 estimate) 1,818,600. On Elbe River.

Hamilcar

Hamilcar was a great general of Carthage, a city that created a great empire more than two thousand years ago.

Carthage was on the coast of North Africa, near where the present city of Algiers is. At that time the Romans as well as the Carthaginians were trying to found great empires. They fought a series of wars against each other until the Romans finally won and destroyed Carthage.

In several of these wars Hamilcar was the leader of the Carthaginian forces. He failed to win the island of Sicily from the Romans, but he conquered all of Spain and made it into a province of Carthage. He was killed in battle in Spain when he was 42 years old. His campaigns were continued by his famous son HANNIBAL, about whom you can read in a separate article.

Hamilton

Hamilton is a city in the southern part of the province of Ontario, in Canada. It is on Lake Ontario, at the western end of the lake, and is built at the foot of a mountain. Over 309,000 people live in the city of Hamilton. They work in automobile and steel factories and in cotton and knitting mills, and some make typewriters and tobacco products. Hamilton was once separated from Lake Ontario by a sandbar, but more than a hundred years ago a channel was cut through the sandbar, making Hamilton a lake port. Hamilton has several beautiful churches and McMaster University. Dundern Castle, in Dundern Park, is a museum with exhibits of many things of interest in Canadian history.

HAMILTON, ONTARIO. Population (1971 census) 309,173. County seat of Wentworth County. Settled in 1813.

Hamilton, Alexander

Alexander Hamilton was one of the greatest of the early Americans. He served with distinction in the Revolutionary War as a fighter and as aide-de-camp and secretary to General Washington. He was one of the most active and successful supporters of the Constitution, and he became the first Secretary of the Treasury of the new United States.

Alexander Hamilton was born in the West Indies in 1757. He was sent to the Colonies in America at the age of 15, and later studied at King's College, which later became Columbia University. When he was only 17 he made a speech supporting the Colonies' cause against England.

Two years later, in 1776, Hamilton joined the army and was made captain of artillery. He served with such bravery that he came to the attention of General Washington, who made Hamilton his secretary, with the rank of lieutenant colonel.

After the fighting was ended, Hamilton left the army and became a lawyer. He built up a good practice in New York City, and became a member of the Continental Congress, which had been set up by the Articles of Confederation. He was a member of the convention that drafted the Constitution, and he did more than almost anyone else to get it accepted by the states. He did this especially by his writings in the Federalist Papers. These were a series of essays written by Hamilton, James Madison, and John Jay. Hamilton thought up the idea and wrote about fifty of the essays, which were published in New York newspapers and copied by papers in many other places.

Hamilton was appointed Secretary of the Treasury by President Washington, and when the first Congress under the new Constitution held its first sessions, Hamilton presented it with a complete program for the financial operation of the nation. He wanted the government to establish a national bank, to raise taxes, and to set up high tariffs, or duties, on goods imported from abroad.

A great many people did not like his program of strong Federal control, and this led to the formation of the first two political parties, the Federalists, led by Hamilton and John Adams, and the Anti-Federalists, led by Thomas Jefferson. Hamilton was able to achieve establishment of the Bank of the United States, but his other proposals on taxes and tariffs were strongly opposed. However, by the time he retired as Secretary of the Treasury in 1795 he had given the United States a very good financial (money) policy. Some experts think Hamilton was not only the first Secretary of the Treasury but the greatest.

After his retirement Hamilton returned to the practice of law in New York City, but he still held great political power. In 1796 John Adams was elected President, and Hamilton helped Washington to write his Farewell Address.

When the United States seemed on the verge of war with France in 1798, President Adams appointed General Washington commander-in-chief, and Hamilton as his second in command. On the death of Washington in 1799, Hamilton succeeded him as commander-in-chief, but the army was soon disbanded.

Hamilton and Adams had begun to disagree, chiefly over how much power Hamilton should have as leader of the Federalist Party. In the election of 1800, Hamilton's influence was responsible for the election of Thomas Jefferson as President and Aaron Burr as Vice President, even though Jefferson belonged to the opposite political party.

In 1804 Burr ran for the office of governor of New York. Hamilton had spoken against him in party meetings, calling him unreliable. When Burr was defeated in the election, he blamed Hamilton and challenged him to a duel. The two men met at Weehawken Heights, in New Jersey. Hamilton did not fire a shot, but Burr wounded Hamilton, who died the following day. He was only 47.

Hammarskjold, Dag

Dag Hammarskjold was the second Secretary-General of the United Nations, from 1953 until his death in an air crash in Africa in 1961. He was born in Sweden in 1905. He became an expert in the field of economics, dealing with problems of business, money, and trade. Hammarskjold held

many posts in the government of Sweden, and he represented his country in many international conferences. In 1952 and 1953, Hammarskjold was one of the Swedish representatives at the United Nations.

hammerhead, a fierce shark that has a hammer-shaped head: see SHARK.

Hammerstein, Oscar

Oscar Hammerstein is the name of two men who have contributed greatly to American music. The first Oscar Hammerstein was born in 1847 in Berlin, Germany. He came to America when he was 16 years old. He invented a machine for spreading tobacco leaves and this made him a fortune. Then he devoted his time and money to promoting music in the United States. He built several theaters and opera houses in New York City, and brought entire companies of singers from Europe to produce operas.

His nephew, Oscar Hammerstein II, became one of the outstanding American writers of the librettos (spoken words) of musical plays. He was born in New York City in 1895 and studied at Columbia University.

In several of the most successful musical plays since 1943, beginning with *Oklahoma!*, Hammerstein wrote the words and Richard Rodgers the music. These include *Oklahoma!*, *Carousel*, *South Pacific*, and *The King and I*. Previously, Hammerstein had written the words to music by Sigmund Romberg and Rudolf Friml, and to Jerome Kern's music for *Show Boat*. Hammerstein died in 1960.

Hammond

Hammond is a city in northwestern Indiana, on Grand Calumet River, near Chicago, Illinois, and near Lake Michigan. In 1960, the population of Hammond was 111,698. Hammond has factories that make soap, farm tools, and railroad cars. Printing also is an important industry. Hammond was founded in 1851.

Hammond, John Hays

Hammond is the name of two prominent Americans, father and son, both named John Hays Hammond. The first John Hays Hammond was a mining engineer who developed mines in many parts of the world. He was born in 1855. After working for the United States government as a mining expert, he went to Mexico and later to South Africa. During the Boer War in 1895, Hammond was captured by the Boers and sentenced to death. Later he was released upon payment of $125,000 to the Boers. Hammond was special ambassador from the United States when George V was crowned king of Great Britain in 1911. Later he returned to the United States and lectured at many universities. He died in 1936. His son, John Hays Hammond, Jr., was born in 1888. He became an electrical engineer and an inventor. Among his important devices was a radio-directed torpedo that he made for the United States Navy. He also invented devices to improve telegraph and telephone equipment, and was a pioneer in developing remote control for rockets and airplanes. He holds more patents than any other inventor of our time—about nine hundred, in the United States and other countries.

Hampton Roads

Hampton Roads is a channel, or water passageway, in Virginia. Three rivers—the James, the Nansemond, and the Elizabeth—meet there, and flow together through the channel into Chesapeake Bay. Hampton Roads is a very fine harbor, and the four cities on its shores are large and busy ports. These four cities are Newport News, Portsmouth, Hampton, and Norfolk. Hampton Roads and the city of Newport News are best known in the United States because one of the most important bases of the United States Navy is there. It is the headquarters for the Atlantic fleet.

Hampton Roads is famous in American history because of important events that took place there during the American Civil War. One was the battle between two warships, the *Monitor* and the *Merrimac,* in 1862. The *Monitor* fought for the North, and the *Merrimac* for the South. It was the first battle in history between two iron-covered ships. The other famous event was the Hampton Roads Conference, which took place in February, 1865. The North and the South were still fighting, but some people hoped that the leaders on both sides might be able to agree about ending the war. So President Abraham Lincoln met with some of the southern leaders on a ship in Hampton Roads. They talked for several hours, but the southern leaders would not agree to what Lincoln wanted, so the conference did no good. The South went on fighting a little longer but surrendered in April, 1865.

hamster

A hamster is a little animal that is related to the mouse. The hamsters that are kept as pets in the United States have furry brown or gray bodies about six inches long, and stubby tails only about half an inch long. They have broad heads and round ears, and in their cheeks are large pouches where they can hold food the way squirrels do. Other kinds of hamster grow as large as rats or guinea pigs.

Some hamsters are albinos, which means their bodies are almost pure white and their eyes are pinkish.

Hamsters build their homes underground and have several rooms for different uses. One room is used as a storeroom where the hamsters store corn for use during the winter. Animal homes that are dug in the ground like this are called burrows. In the winter, hamsters go into their burrows four or five feet deep in the ground, and close the entrance. They spend several months down there, sleeping and living on the food they have stored.

Hamsters are full of fight and can be quite ferocious for their size. The males fight for the females. Female hamsters have several litters of young during the year. There are about twelve baby hamsters in each litter. They are blind at birth. As soon as they are old enough they are turned out to build their own burrows. Hamsters feed on roots, fruits, and grains. They also eat lizards and insects. The hamster itself is the prey of foxes, dogs, cats, and other animals.

A small hamster makes a very interesting pet. It can be kept in a cage or box with enough earth and leaves in it so that the hamster can dig a hole and hide. The box should be kept very clean. Careful feeding is important.

Hamsun, Knut

Knut Hamsun was a Norwegian writer of novels. He was born in 1859, and he started writing stories while he was working as a shoemaker. When he was young he came to America, where he was a street-car conductor and a farm worker. He wrote mostly about poor people. His most famous book was *Growth of the Soil.* This book won him the Nobel Prize in 1920. After World War II the Norwegian government said Hamsun must go to prison for helping the Germans when they took Norway. But he was an old man then, and he was not sent to prison, but he had to pay a large fine. He died in 1952.

Hancock, John

John Hancock was an American patriot and one of the leaders of the Colonies' fight for independence. He was the first signer of the Declaration of Independence, and he signed with such a bold hand that we use his name to mean any signature. If someone says "I put down my John Hancock," he means he has signed his name to something important.

Hancock was born in 1737 in Massachusetts. He was graduated from Harvard College at the age of 17. His uncle was a merchant, and Hancock entered his business and later inherited it with a large fortune when his uncle died. Since he was a businessman, he was especially opposed to the Stamp Act and other taxes that the British levied on the colonies.

In 1774 a Continental Congress was called in Philadelphia, with representatives of eleven of the American colonies present. John Hancock was president of the Congress, and Samuel Adams was a delegate. You can read more about Samuel ADAMS in a separate article. Hancock and Adams worked so hard for the cause of freedom that they were called outlaws by General Thomas Gage, the commander of all the British troops in America.

General Gage was so eager to arrest Hancock and Adams that on April 18, 1775, he sent British troops out of Boston to look for them. Paul Revere's famous ride was made chiefly to warn Adams and Hancock that the British soldiers were coming to get them. A battle began at Concord, and it started the Revolutionary War. In the confusion of the battle, Hancock and Adams escaped. Later, when General Gage was still trying to make peace with the colonies, he offered a pardon to everyone but Adams and Hancock, whom he considered too dangerous to allow freedom. However, he never caught either of them.

Hancock was appointed the first major-general of the Massachusetts militia, and took part in much of the fighting in Rhode Island. He was a brave and clever officer. After the war he was elected the first governor of Massachusetts, and he was president of the state convention that ratified the national Constitution. Hancock remained governor of Massachusetts until his death in 1793.

hand

The hand, and especially the thumb, are among the greatest advantages besides the brain that human beings have over dumb animals. No other animal has a thumb that can be used with the fingers to form a sort of pincers. This makes the hand the most useful tool in nature. It enables men to do things that no other animal can do.

The human hand is composed of five digits, the four fingers and the thumb. The bones of the fingers are called *phalanges.* There are three phalanges in each finger and two in the thumb. There are five bones called *metacarpals* in the palm of the hand, and eight bones called *carpals* in the wrist. These bones are connected by muscles and nerves that get their directions from the brain. There are more nerves receiving messages from the brain in the tips of the fingers than anywhere else in the body. For this reason we think of the sense of touch as being centered chiefly in the fingers. Most of the movements of the hand are made without our

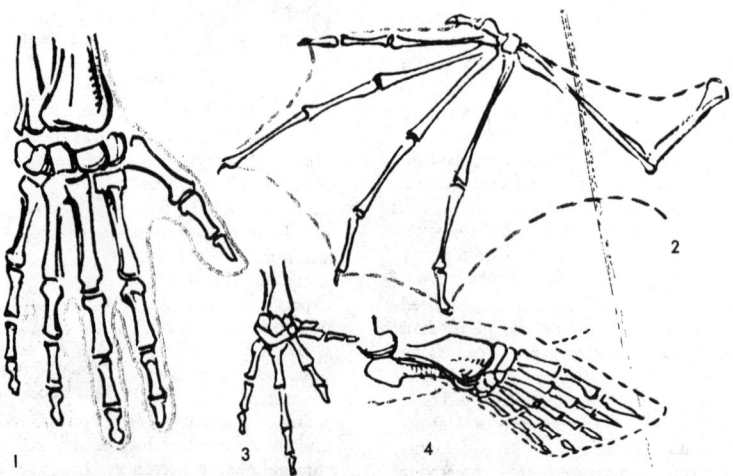

The human hand (1) is more highly developed than the "hand" of any other animal. But other animals do have similar bone structures at the lower end of their forelimbs. The bat's wing (2), the frog's forefoot, (3) which it often raises while sitting, and the seal's flipper (4) all resemble the human hand. But none of them has a thumb, the most important finger.

even realizing it. The hand and the brain work so well together that the hands' ordinary movements are almost automatic.

The right hand is operated by the left side of the brain, and the left hand is operated by the right side of the brain. Most people are right-handed, that is, they use their right hand with greater ease than their left hand. A few people are left-handed. There are different ideas about what causes left-handedness. Some say it is inherited. All agree that left-handed children should not be forced to use the right hand if it is difficult for them.

The hands show certain things about a person that make him different from any other person, even the members of his own family. Fingerprints, the marks made by the fingertips, are different in every person. Handwriting is also different with each person.

handball

Handball is a game played by hitting a small rubber ball with your hand. Your object is to hit it against a wall so that your opponent cannot return it (hit it back against the wall) on the first bounce at least. When your opponent has hit the ball against the wall, your object is to return it on the first bounce at least.

There are two forms of handball, one-wall handball and four-wall handball.

One-wall handball is played on a place, called a court, that is 20 feet wide and 34 feet long. A wall 16 feet high is at one end of the court. It is the same width as the court. A line 16 feet from the wall is drawn across the width of the court. This is called the *service line.*

One player stands by the service line, bounces the ball once, and hits it against the wall with the palm of his hand. He is called the *server.* On the serve, the ball must strike the wall without a bounce ("on the fly"). It must bounce back so that it passes over the service line on the fly. The other player must then hit it before it bounces, or after one bounce, so that the ball strikes the wall on the fly and stays within the court. The ball is hit by one player, then by the other, until one of them is unable to return it to the wall on the fly, or hits it out of the court. If the server does not return it, he loses the right to serve. If the other player cannot return it, the server gets one point. The first player to get 21 points wins the game. If the score is tied at 20 to 20, the first player to get two points more than the other wins the game.

In four-wall handball, the court is 46 feet long and 23 feet wide. It is surrounded by three walls 23 feet high and a back wall 10 feet high. The rules are the same as for one-wall handball, except that the ball may be hit off any of the walls or off a combination of them.

In one-wall handball, "first bounce" means a bounce off the floor. In four-wall handball it means a bounce off the floor or any wall.

When two persons play, it is "singles." When four play, two against two as partners, it is "doubles."

Handball may be played indoors or outdoors. It is a very strenuous game and helps to develop the muscles in your arms and legs. Thin leather gloves are often worn by the players to protect their hands. In the United States, there are handball courts in most playgrounds and gymnasiums. Men, women and children of all ages play the game. Tournaments are held to find out who is the best handball player. Once a year a tournament is held in the United States for the world's championship. People in the United States began to play handball in about 1882, but the game is very old and was first played eight hundred years ago in Ireland.

handcrafts

Handcrafts are the skills that we use in making things with our hands. Sometimes we call handcrafts "arts and crafts." Handcrafts often require the use of tools and other equipment. These tools may be as simple as the hammer and screwdriver or as elaborate as a workshop with electric drills and lathes. What is important about handcrafts is not the tools but the skill and imagination that are used in making things. The American Indians, who have made some of the best and most beautiful arts and crafts objects, had very few tools to work with.

Handcrafts, or arts and crafts, are taught in many schools and in recreation centers and summer camps. Doing handcrafts, of course, is quite different from doing arithmetic or spelling, and this is exactly why they are taught. They give children a chance to work with their hands and to make things from their imaginations. Handcrafts are also taught to people who are recovering from physical or mental illnesses because this gives them a chance to occupy themselves and take their minds off their troubles. This is called *occupational therapy.* Blind people are also taught some crafts, such as weaving and basketry. There are many grownups who do arts and crafts work as a hobby. They find it relaxing to work with their hands after spending their days at a business or profession.

Some of the most popular handcrafts are woodworking, leatherworking, metalworking, pottery, printing, bookbinding, weaving, basket-making, puppet making, making objects out of paper, and soap carving. Some of these crafts are discussed in separate articles (such as MODELMAKING). Here we will give a few simple projects to work at in some of the crafts.

MAKING A WOVEN BASKET

There is a separate article on BASKETS in another volume of this encyclopedia. Here is one way to make a woven basket:

A good material for weaving a basket is rattan. This comes from a vine which is grown in the Philippine Islands. Round rattan reed is graded by numbers ranging from 00 (very fine) to 9 (heavy).

In the weaving of rattan baskets the reeds that form the skeleton framework are called *spokes,* while those that pass in and out, thus filling in between the spokes, are called the *weavers.*

Rattan should always be moistened before it is used, but it should never be put into hot water and should not be soaked for more than half an hour. The reeds to be used as spokes should be cut to the proper lengths and tied together in bundles before wetting; those to be used as weavers should be coiled and tied before being wet. The basket-maker should keep his fingers moist by dipping them occasionally into water.

In making a rattan basket from five to eight inches in diameter, it is advisable to use No. 4 reed for the spokes and No. 2 reed for the weavers. The basket-maker takes four spokes in each hand, and, pressing these flat so that they lie beside one another, he places the four spokes held in the right hand upon the four held in the left hand. The groups of four reeds each are now made to cross each other at right angles, the point of intersection being midway from end to end on each group of reeds. A half-length spoke is now placed beside one group of four, and the weaving is begun. The weaver reed passes over and under each of the four groups of spokes in turn, until all the spokes are held securely in place. The next step is to separate the spokes and pass the weaver over and under each spoke in turn.

When the *start,* as this work is called, has reached a diameter of five or six inches, a new spoke is inserted beside each of those already in position except the last. The weaving of the basket is then carried on to completion. If the sides of the basket are to turn up abruptly the spokes will have to be bent. They may be tied together at their ends to keep them bent until the turn is made. To finish the rim, bring each spoke around the two following it and into the basket, moistening the reeds, pulling them into place, and pressing them tightly down upon the basket.

MAKING A CLAY BASKET

Pottery is the craft of making objects out of clay, which are then made hard by heat. There is a separate article on POTTERY in another volume.

Pottery objects can be made on a *potter's wheel,* or they can be made by the *coil method.* The project described here uses the coil method because it does not require much equipment. The clay for this project can be obtained from a craft supply shop.

FORMING THE VASE

The vase is made by building with clay coils rolled between the hands and the desk top. First protect the desk with a sheet of linoleum, a board, or a piece of heavy paper. A pasteboard disk having the same diameter as the base of the proposed vase is used as a guide in starting. This is covered with coils of clay wound around in a spiral and pressed firmly together to form a disk about one-fourth of an inch thick.

The building of the walls is also accomplished by this spiral arrangement of coils, which are welded together by being pressed firmly against the ever-growing wall. If the walls become unsteady because of their moist condition and the weight of the clay, the work should be set aside until it becomes leather-hard; then building may be continued. Before continuing, the rim formed by the last coil should be cut squarely off with a knife and a thick mixture of *slip* (clay and water mixed to the consistency of thick cream) should be applied with a brush.

When the vase has been entirely built it is allowed to dry out somewhat. Then it may be scraped and carefully "trued" with a knife and finally finished with sandpaper.

DECORATING

If you wish, you may add a decoration to the outside of the vase. The design is scratched on by means of the sharp point of a wire nail before the clay is thoroughly dry. The parts to be colored are brushed over with slip and the color is applied immediately. Colors may be obtained at a paint or drug store. Yellow ocher is used for yellow-red, red oxide of iron for red, and black oxide of copper for black. The colors, in powder form, are mixed with liquid glue and are painted upon the slightly moist clay in the form of a thick paste. It is a good idea to scratch the surface with a pin or piece of broken window glass before painting the clay. This will help the paint hold to the clay surface.

FIRING

In firing (baking) pottery it is not necessary to use a real kiln. An iron kettle placed in an open fire of wood can be used. This method is similar to that employed long ago by the American Indians. The kettle will keep the burning embers from falling upon and breaking the dishes. It should have an iron cover. The heating and cooling should be gradual; the kettle should be kept at a red heat for at least an hour.

MAKING A COPPER TRAY

A copper tray is easy to make. The only special equipment needed is a hammer with a ball-shaped striking end, which is called a *ball-peen hammer,* and a pair of metal snips or shears.

Cut out of sheet copper a circle ¼ inch larger in diameter than the plate is to be. Beat the edges of the tray with a hammer, causing the metal to become somewhat thicker at the edge. Beat down the depression in the plate using a block of wood as an anvil. To do this, first draw a line with compasses where the depression is to start; then hold the plate on the end of a block of wood and beat it down over the edge of the block with a hammer, along the pencil line.

If the plate is to have a deep impression, it will be necessary to "anneal" it, because it will become hard while being beaten. This is done by heating it to red heat in a gas or other flame, and then cooling it quickly in water.

If desired, the brim of the plate may have a border decoration etched on it. The design for this is painted on with asphaltum varnish, as are all parts of the plate that are not to be etched. The whole is placed, when the varnish is dry, in a solution of one part nitric acid and two parts water, in a stoneware or glass dish. The acid will, in a few minutes, begin to eat away or etch the metal that has been left bare.

After the metal has been etched deep enough (which will take anywhere from thirty minutes to three hours, according to the depth desired), take the tray out of the acid and remove the asphaltum varnish by soaking the tray for about an hour in turpentine or a solution of lye. Then the varnish can be wiped off.

Handel, George Frederick

George Frederick Handel was a famous composer who was born in Germany but made his biggest reputation in England. He wrote *The Messiah* and other great oratorios that lovers of music still know and hear every year. An oratorio is a sacred story with music, played by an orchestra and sung by soloists and a chorus.

Handel was born in Halle, Germany, in 1685. He became organist in the cathedral at Halle as a young man, and also played the violin in the Hamburg orchestra. When he was 20 his first two operas were performed in Hamburg with great success. He spent some time in Italy, and in 1710 became musical director to the elector, or king, of Hanover, which was a country in Germany. Four years later this elector became King George I of England. Handel went to England and lived there the rest of his life. He wrote many more operas, but the English people did not care much for them. Then he turned to writing oratorios, which became popular at once. Besides *The Messiah,* the story of the life of Jesus that he wrote in 1742, Handel is also known for the oratorios *Israel in Egypt* and *Samson.* Handel also wrote music for orchestras and an anthem for the coronation of George II. This anthem is played at the crowning of every English king and queen. Handel died in England in 1759.

handwriting

Handwriting is writing by hand with a form of letter called script. The word is not used for making capital letters, which we call printing, even when it is done by hand.

The script in which most people write developed long after the forms of the letters used for printing books and carved inscriptions, even though handwriting came long before mechanical printing. First there were capital letters only, but in the days before printing all books had to be copied by hand and the original capital letters were inconvenient, because before making each one you had to lift the pen from the paper. Therefore people gradually began to develop forms of the letters that would run together easily and could still be read. These letters are called *cursive,* which means "running along."

STYLES OF HANDWRITING

Most handwriting slants to the right. When instead it slants to the left it is called *backhand.*

Unless the letters are fairly carefully formed, they are hard to read. Many systems have been devised to make handwriting easier to do and at the same time easier to read. There are also many ways to teach handwriting. You can read about them in the article on PENMANSHIP.

The art of very beautiful handwriting is called *chirography.* Chirographers used to make up personal calling cards, wedding invitations, and many other forms that now are usually engraved or printed. Many diplomas and other such documents are still written by hand. Such a document is said to be *engrossed.*

Some people insist that you can tell about a person's character from his handwriting. They call this the art of *graphology.*

AUTOGRAPHS

A handwritten signature is called an *autograph,* and many people collect the autographs of famous persons. Usually they have the autographs written in autograph books, but sometimes they have them on cards that they trade with other autograph collectors.

Most genuine autographs are collected by young people who live in big cities where the stars actually appear. You can get autographs by writing for them, but there are so many requests that the celebrities do not have time to write them all and often the ones they send are printed or are signed by someone who imitates their signature.

There always have been collectors of the autographs of famous men and women of history. The most valuable autograph in the United States is that of Button Gwinnett. He was a signer of the Declaration of Independence from Georgia, but there are very few letters or other papers that he signed. Some people collect the autographs of signers of the Declaration of Independence, and they cannot complete their sets without one of the Button Gwinnett signatures. That makes a Gwinnett signature cost a lot.

Autographs of famous men and women are usually sold by the same dealers and stores that sell stamps to stamp collectors and coins to coin collectors. The values of various autographs are listed in catalogs.

HOLOGRAPHS

Handwriting sometimes has a special meaning in law. If a person writes a will in his own handwriting it is called a *holograph* will, and sometimes the courts will accept this will while they will not accept a will that was simply signed. Handwriting experts are often able to study handwriting and know definitely if a person did or did not write something, even if he tried to disguise his handwriting. Such experts have solved many crimes, including the crime of FORGERY, about which you can read in a separate article.

Handy, W. C.

William Christopher Handy is the name of one of the greatest American composers, or writers of original music. He is called the "father of the blues," and his most famous songs are of the type called blues. He also wrote down for the first time some of the Negro spirituals that are most popular today. In many cases he wrote the words as well as the music for his songs.

W. C. Handy, as he is usually called, was a member of the Negro race. He was born in Alabama in 1873, only a few years after the Negroes had been freed from slavery. His father had been a slave but became a preacher. W. C. Handy went through high school and attended

college, and then taught music in a southern college for blacks. When he was 35 years old he formed a band to play in Memphis, Tennessee. A few years later, E. H. Crump, who later became the most powerful political figure in Tennessee, was running for an office in Memphis and asked Handy to write a campaign song for him. The song Handy wrote, now called the "Memphis Blues," has since become famous.

Southern blacks had been singing *blues,* or sad songs, for many years, but Handy was the first man to use them as a serious musical form. His first song, the "Memphis Blues," was stolen from him by a southern publisher, because blacks still had few legal rights in the South, but later Handy regained ownership of it. His most popular song, written a few years later, is the "St. Louis Blues," and both the words and music are considered classic. After that song was published, Handy moved to New York City and founded his own publishing firm, which has been very successful ever since. He wrote down and published many spirituals that he remembered from his boyhood, among them "Steal Away to Jesus."

In middle age Handy lost much of the use of his eyes, and later he became totally blind, but he continued to write music and to manage his publishing business, which made him rich as well as famous. He died in 1958.

Hanging Gardens of Babylon

The Hanging Gardens of Babylon were a marvelous structure built in the ancient city of Babylon, more than 2,500 years ago. Babylon was the capital of a great empire in Asia. The Hanging Gardens were built by King Nebuchadnezzar, about whom you can read in the Bible, in the Book of Daniel. The land around Babylon was flat and dry. Nebuchadnezzar's queen, who came from a land of mountain scenery, was homesick. That is why the gardens were built.

The Hanging Gardens were really a kind of roof garden such as you might see on a penthouse in a modern city. They were laid out on a sort of square building that rested on arches and pillars. The pillars were hollow and filled with earth, so that the roots of the trees could have room to grow deep down into them. Masses of soil were laid on the flat roof and arranged into terraces one beneath the other. Waterfalls tumbled from one level to the next. The flowers and vines grew over the edges of the terraces so they seemed to be hanging there.

A force of men was at work constantly pumping water up to the gardens from the nearby Euphrates River. The gardens were threaded with walks, and people came to sit there in the coolness under the palm trees and enjoy the flowers, which were imported from foreign lands.

The Hanging Gardens could be seen for miles around the level countryside. From a distance they looked like a tower, narrow at the top and broad at the base. They were so wonderful that they are still called one of the Seven Wonders of the Ancient World. The ruins of the Hanging Gardens of Babylon can still be seen.

Hankow or Wuhan

Hankow, or Wuhan, formerly called also Wuchang, is a large city in the central part of China. It is situated on the great Yangtze River. Hankow is sometimes called the "Chicago of China," because, like Chicago, it is a very important manufacturing center and easy to reach by boat and train. Boats can sail from Hankow down the Yangtze River for six hundred miles, to the East China Sea. More than two million people live in Hankow. They make cloth and cement and chemicals, and they ship tea, cotton, and many other things from their city to many places in China and other countries. About one hundred years ago, a treaty was signed that stated that other countries could begin to trade in Hankow, and the city grew very fast. Most of the business was carried on in the European section of Hankow, where there were many banks. The Japanese held Hankow from 1938 until 1945; then in 1949 the Communists took control of the city, and renamed it Wuhan.

HANKOW, CHINA. Population (1972 estimate) 2,150,000. On Yangtze River.

Hannibal

Hannibal was the greatest general of Carthage, a city that created a great empire more than two thousand years ago. Carthage was on the coast of North Africa, near where the city of Algiers is today. At that time the Romans as well as the Carthaginians were trying to found great empires, and fought a series of wars against each other. Hannibal lived about two hundred years before the birth of Jesus. His father was HAMILCAR, another great general, about whom you can read in a separate article. When Hannibal was only 9 years old, he went with his father on an expedition to conquer Spain. Hannibal swore an oath that he would always fight the Romans, and when his father was killed he took up his campaign.

Hannibal's greatest campaign was an invasion of Italy, in which he almost conquered Rome. He marched his army and a big supply train, in which the heaviest loads were carried by elephants, across the Pyrenees Mountains. Then he faced the towering Alps, barring his way into Italy. He made this almost impossible crossing in fifteen days, battling all the way against barbarian tribes, snow, and storms. At first he won many victories in Italy. One of his most famous victories was the Battle of CANNAE, about which there is a separate article. But finally the Roman general Fabius defeated him. Hannibal had to give up and go back to Carthage.

The Romans continued to win battles from Carthage, and at last Carthage had to submit to a peace that included the payment of heavy taxes to Rome. Hannibal made reforms that enabled Carthage to pay these taxes, but the Romans still considered him dangerous and demanded that he surrender to them in person. Hannibal took refuge with the king of Bithynia, a country on the Black Sea, and when this king was about to turn him over to the Romans, Hannibal poisoned himself.

Hannibal was a just ruler, and was usually merciful to his enemies. He is still considered one of the greatest military leaders of all time.

Hanoi

Hanoi is the capital city of North Viet Nam, in southeast Asia. It is on the Red River, and it is a very busy port and railroad center. More than 414,000 people live in Hanoi. Many of them work in rice mills, and in factories where they make fine wool and beautiful silk cloth. Others make chinaware, matches, and leather products. There is a modern part of the city that has a large university, many fine buildings, and a beautiful park. In the old part of the city there are many ancient temples and narrow, winding streets. In 1954, the Communists in the northern part of Viet Nam took control of Hanoi from the French, who had made the city the capital of their colony, French Indo-China. Before that, the city had been occupied by Chinese, who ruled the country thousands of years ago.

HANOI, VIET NAM. Population (1973 estimate) 414,620. Capital of North Viet Nam.

Hanover

Hanover is the capital of the state of Lower Saxony, in West Germany. This territory was occupied by the British, after World War II. Hanover is situated on the Leine River. It is an important manufacturing center, and it has several large technical schools. About 519,700 people live in Hanover. Many of them work in factories, where they make automobile tires, machinery, and iron and steel. The city of Hanover is about eight hundred years old. During World War II more than half of the city was destroyed. Since then the center of Hanover has been completely rebuilt and is now one of the most modern cities in Germany.

There was formerly an independent German kingdom of Hanover, and the city of Hanover was its capital. The family of kings who ruled Hanover was called the House of Hanover. The official title of the king was *elector,* because he was one of the German kings who elected the Holy Roman Emperor. In 1714 the Elector of Hanover became also the king of England under the title of George I, and you can read about the Hanover kings of England in the article GEORGE, KING OF ENGLAND. In 1871, when the German Empire was formed, Hanover became part of it, and after World War II it became part of the province of Lower Saxony in West Germany. While West Germany was occupied by the Allied powers, Hanover was in the British zone.

HANOVER, GERMANY. Population (1973 estimate) 519,700. Capital of province of Lower Saxony. On Leine River.

Hanseatic League

The Hanseatic League was a group of cities in Europe that had an agreement to trade with one another, about seven hundred years ago. The agreement was made by the merchants in these cities.

At that time great changes were taking place in Europe. For hundreds of years, the noblemen in their castles had controlled all the European countries. Then cities began to grow, and as they became larger they also became more important and more powerful. The merchants began

to do business on a bigger scale, but they faced great obstacles, such as pirates at sea, and very high customs duties (or taxes on goods brought into other countries). So these merchants formed guilds, or trade associations, to protect themselves. As the merchant guilds grew stronger, they began to be competition for each other, and so groups of guilds joined together into organizations called *hanses*. At last the hanses joined together into a league, called the Hanseatic League.

The Hanseatic League at its strongest period included 85 towns. It made wars and dictated the terms of treaties. At one time, in 1370, it was so strong that Denmark agreed not to name any king without the consent of the Hanseatic League. The League owned and operated ships, and kept armed forces to protect the interests of its members. For many years it was the ruler of trade on the Baltic and North Seas.

The Hanseatic League was very powerful for about two hundred years. Then, as new nations arose, and the seas and roads were better protected, the League gradually lost its powers. Member groups dropped out, and during the 1500s the League went out of existence.

Hansel and Gretel

Hansel and Gretel is the name of an opera written for children, but people of all ages enjoy it. An opera is a play in which all the conversation is sung instead of spoken. *Hansel and Gretel* was written by a German composer named Engelbert Humperdinck. He based his story on the fairy tale of the same name. The opera is most often performed at Christmas.

STORY OF THE OPERA

The story is about a brother and sister named Hansel and Gretel who are sent into the woods by their stepmother to find strawberries. They lose their way and meet a witch, who persuades them to go with her to her house made of gingerbread. The witch tries to make them climb into an oven so that she can make gingerbread of them, something she has done to many other children. But Hansel and Gretel are too wise for the witch. They put her into the oven instead. The witch's spell is broken, and all the rows of gingerbread children turn back into living boys and girls, who go back to their homes singing happily.

Hanukkah

Hanukkah or *Chanukah* is a Jewish holiday that is observed about the same time as Christmas. It lasts for eight days and is a remembrance of the victory of the Maccabees over Antiochus IV, who had tried to suppress Judaism in the 2nd century B.C. Hanukkah is often called the Festival of Lights because candles are lit in Jewish homes and synagogues. The candles are held in a special candleholder called the Hanukkah Menorah, which holds a candle for each day plus a center candle. Gifts are exchanged during the eight days. Jewish people have observed Hanukkah for over 2,000 years.

Hapsburg

Hapsburg is the name of one of the most important royal families of Europe. For nearly seven hundred years they ruled various countries of Europe, including Spain, Holland and Hungary, but their principal possession was always Austria and later the combined country of Austria-Hungary. For many years members of the Hapsburg family were the Holy Roman Emperors. The emperors were elected, but it became a habit to elect a Hapsburg.

The name Hapsburg, which is also spelled *Habsburg*, comes from the name of the family's castle, Habichtsburg, meaning "hawk castle." This castle was in Switzerland.

harakiri

Harakiri is the name of a way of committing suicide, formerly used by the Samurai (warrior) class in Japan. When a Japanese man felt that he had been disgraced, or that he had failed to do his duty in some way, he used to believe that the only honorable way he could make up for his failure was by killing himself. This he did by committing harakiri, or stabbing himself in the stomach with a dagger. Years ago there were even special jeweled daggers for committing harakiri. The custom has been abandoned in recent years.

Harbin

Harbin is a city in Manchuria, which is a vast region in northeast China. Until about seventy years ago Harbin was an unimportant little village, but in 1896 China gave Russia permission to build up the town as a trade center, and it became one of the most important cities in eastern Asia. In 1924 China took control of Harbin again, in 1932 the Japanese captured the city, and during World War II the Russians took it from the Japanese and returned it to China. While the Chinese Communists were fighting their national government in 1948 they took Harbin and it was one of their most important cities until they finally gained control of the entire country. Today more than a million and a half people live in Harbin. It is the trade center of central Manchuria, and an important railroad junction.

HARBIN, MANCHURIA. Population (1965 estimate) 1,552,000. Capital of Singkiang Province.

harbor

A harbor is a sort of small bay into which ships can sail and be safe from winds and storms while loading and unloading goods. Some harbors are natural, and some are made by man.

A good harbor should be about fifty feet deep, so that ocean-going ships can sail in safely. The bottom must be hard and firm so that anchors can hold, even in storms. Usually an artificial, or manmade, harbor has two or more breakwaters, or sea walls. A breakwater breaks up heavy ocean waves. Most breakwaters are made of broken stone and concrete, which is dumped by the ton into the harbor until the wall is high enough. Some harbors have such natural breakwaters as sand bars, coral reefs, and islands.

Among the world's best natural harbors are those in New York City, San Francisco and Seattle in the United States. Important artificial harbors have been built in Los Angeles and in several cities on the Great Lakes.

THE NORMANDY INVASION HARBORS

The most unusual artificial harbors ever built were used by the Allied forces to invade Normandy, in northern France, during World War II. Huge, floating breakwaters were made in Great Britain, towed in sections across the English Channel, and put together on the French side. They turned open beaches into harbors where big ships could unload tanks, artillery, locomotives, and other heavy equipment.

Warren G. Harding

Warren Gamaliel Harding was the twenty-ninth President of the United States. He served from March 4, 1921, until his death in office on August 2, 1923. Calvin Coolidge, who had been Vice President, became President when Harding died.

Warren Harding was one of the most handsome presidents the country has ever had. He was a tall, well-built man, with gray hair that was almost white. He had a friendly smile and most people liked him. He enjoyed the social life of Washington and the interesting events that are part of a President's life.

As President he did not demonstrate a great deal of executive ability. After he had appointed a man to an important office, he usually paid no further attention to what that man did. This was unfortunate, because several of the people he put in office proved to be greedy and dishonest. Harding's administration earned the reputation of being one of the weakest in the history of the United States. Many people believe that when Harding finally realized how poorly he had controlled his appointed officials, the shock was too much for him and broke his heart with shame and disappointment. Some people thought that this had a great deal to do with the fact that he was unable to fight off the pneumonia that caused his death in 1923, when he had been President less than two and a half years.

HIS EARLY YEARS

Warren G. Harding was born near Corsica, Ohio, on November 2, 1865. His father was a farmer and a country doctor. Harding went to public school, and attended Ohio State Central College in Iberia, Ohio. He studied law, but after finishing college he taught school

for a time and then got a position on the *Daily Star*, a newspaper in Marion, Ohio. He married a young widow in 1891, when he was twenty-six years old. She was five years older than he was, and her maiden name had been Florence Kling. When Harding bought the Marion *Daily Star*, a few years later, his wife helped him run the paper.

Harding was a fine public speaker, and his friends urged him to go into politics where the ability to speak is important. Harding agreed to run for office, and in 1900 he was elected to the Ohio state senate, where he served for two terms. In 1904 he became lieutenant governor of Ohio, but was defeated when he ran for governor in 1910. In November of 1914 the people of Ohio elected Harding to the United States Senate. As a senator he voted for the bill that enforced the Prohibition Amendment. This was the law that made it illegal to sell or transport alcoholic liquors within the United States. He also voted for the "Woman's Suffrage" Amendment, which gave women the right to vote.

HOW HE BECAME PRESIDENT

In the Republican Convention of 1920, there were three powerful groups of delegates, each with its favorite candidate. One group wanted to nominate General Leonard Wood, one wanted Senator Hiram Johnson of California, and a third wanted Governor Frank O. Lowden of Illinois. Several ballots were taken and each of the three men received about the same number of votes on each ballot. Each man and his backers refused to drop out.

After the ninth ballot, a group of the top men in the Republican party left the convention hall and went to a hotel room to discuss what should be done. In this "small, smoke-filled room" they decided that they would use their influence to nominate Harding.

Very few people had ever heard of Senator Harding of Ohio. He had never done anything startling or unusual, but he at least had not done anything that made people dislike him. Also, he had always been a good, solid Republican. He spoke well, and he made a good appearance. The men in the hotel room knew they could get the tired convention delegates to nominate Harding instead of one of the three leading candidates.

Not only did the convention accept him, but the people of the country elected him with a large majority. The defeated Democratic candidate was James M. Cox, and Cox's running mate, as the candidate for Vice President, was Franklin Delano Roosevelt.

After Harding became President, he called the first great international conference of important representatives from countries all over the world to discuss the reduction of armaments. You can read more about this in the article on DIS-ARMAMENT.

In one of Harding's speeches, he advised a return to "normalcy." At that time, there was no such word in the English language. When Harding used the word, it was incorrect. He should have said "normality." However, the fact that a man who became president of the Unit-ed States had used the word made other people use it also, so Harding was responsible for adding a word to the English language.

During the Harding administration the Teapot Dome oil scandal made headlines, and his administration has always been associated with it in the memory of the public. The Teapot Dome oil fields near Caspar, Wyoming, were government property, but the Secretary of the Interior, Albert Fall, leased them to private operators. Several people were sent to prison for defrauding the government, which rightfully should have received all the profits from this oil land. The entire episode was a great scandal and it hurt the Republican Party.

Harding thought that he might help his party if he travelled about the country and talked to people everywhere, so he toured the United States, taking an extra trip up to Alaska at the same time. On the way back he became ill with pneumonia and died in San Francisco on August 2, 1923. He was buried in Marion, Ohio.

MRS. WARREN G. HARDING

Mrs. Florence Kling De Wolfe Harding was born in Marion, Ohio, on August 15, 1860. She was the daughter of a hardware merchant who later became a banker. She had been married once before, to Henry De Wolfe, by whom she had one son. At the time of her marriage to Warren G. Harding, she was 31. Mrs. Warren Harding died on November 21, 1924.

hardness

Hardness is a way of describing the degree to which a substance can resist being scratched by another substance. There is a scale for measuring how hard any particular material is. This scale is called Mohs' Hardness Test, and it rates the hardness of minerals by numbers from 1 to 10. The higher the number, the harder the substance. The scale is as follows:

1. talc	6. feldspar
2. gypsum	7. quartz
3. calcite	8. topaz
4. fluorite	9. sapphire
5. apatite	10. diamond

Any substance in the world can be rated by comparing it with substances on this scale. The numbers show where each one rates in hardness, but it does not show how much harder each one is than the next. The fact that apatite is rated 5 and diamond is rated 10 does not mean that diamond is twice as hard as apatite. The scale only shows that each substance is harder than the one before it, and provides a convenient way to express the hardness of all substances by comparing them with those on the scale.

Hardy, Thomas

Thomas Hardy was an English writer of novels and poems. He lived about a hundred years ago, having been born in 1840. His father planned for him to be a designer and builder of churches, so as a boy Hardy was apprenticed, or sent as a

Gale Research Co.

student, to an architect. He became quite successful in this work. When he was about 30, he decided that he preferred to be a writer, and this was his profession for the rest of his life.

Hardy's first successful novel was *Far from the Madding Crowd*, which was published in 1874. After that he wrote a series of books about the people of his native region, which was called Wessex. The most famous of these were *The Return of the Native* and *Tess of the D'Urbervilles*. Later Hardy turned to writing poetry and short stories. He came to be considered one of the greatest of English writers. Hardy died in 1928, when he was 88 years old. He was buried in Westminster Abbey, which is a mark of great honor in England.

hare

The hare is an animal that belongs to the same family as the rabbit and looks very much like a large rabbit, except that it has longer hind legs and ears. It is found in all sections of the world except Madagascar and Australia. There are many different kinds of hare. Its color depends upon the climate in which it is found. Its usual color is tan or gray, but in northern regions it is white so that it cannot be seen against the snow. The hare can run very fast. It is also a good swimmer. A hare may have several litters of young a year, and they are born covered with hair and with their eyes open. The hare is sometimes killed for its skin, which is used as a trimming on coats; it is also killed for its meat, which tastes somewhat like chicken. The most common hare found in North America is the jackrabbit.

harem

The Moslems, or people who follow the Mohammedan religion, believe that the women of a family should live separately from the men. The apartment for the women in a Mohammedan family is called the harem. Harem means "the prohibited," or "private," and no man except the husband or a near relative of the women is allowed to enter it. A Moslem is allowed to have more than one wife, and in his harem would live his wife, or wives, his mother and unmarried sisters if they live with him, his unmarried daughters, and all his female servants. Mohammedan boys live in the harem with their mothers until they are about twelve years old; then they move to the men's apartment. Harems have been used in all the countries where Mohammedan people live, and in other countries of Asia. In the last hundred years there have been fewer harems because the customs governing the separation of the women from the men have become less strict.

Hargreaves, James

James Hargreaves was an Englishman who invented a machine to spin thread. Before this machine was invented, about two hundred years ago, all thread had been made by hand on spinning wheels such as you may have seen in pictures or in museums. These spinning wheels spun one thread at a time. The thread was then woven into cloth. At that

time, in most households throughout the world the housewife made the clothes for the family, spinning the thread on spinning wheels and weaving the cloth on hand looms at home. Hargreaves' machine, which he called a *spinning jenny,* and the invention at about the same time of an automatic loom for weaving cloth, changed all this. English manufacturers became able to make cloth so cheaply that people could afford to buy it instead of making it themselves. This helped to make Great Britain the richest country on earth for more than a hundred years.

Hargreaves' neighbors destroyed the first jenny because they were afraid it would put many of the hand spinners out of work. They were wrong, because it finally turned out that the invention gave more people jobs. By the time Hargreaves died in 1778 there were thousands of jennies in England.

Harlem, a section of New York City, where many Negro people live: see the article on NEW YORK CITY.

Harlequin

Harlequin is a character you may have seen in children's plays or pantomimes or ballets. He is a kind of clown. His face is usually very white, and he often wears baggy trousers, a loose blouse with large buttons, and a two-pointed hat covered with bells and spangles. He sometimes seem sad because he cannot talk and has to express himself by hand movements and facial expressions. In the traditional, or very old, story he is always in love with Columbine, a lovely girl. He protects her until she is saved by the good fairy from another clown who tries to capture her. Harlequin is one of the oldest characters in stage history. In medieval times he was a demon, or evil spirit. Sometimes he was called the "Erlking." Later he became a kind of clown who was always lively and witty.

harmonica

The harmonica is a musical instrument. It is a mouth organ made of two short strips of metal and wood with small holes between them. When you blow through the harmonica, you produce different musical notes depending on which hole you blow through.

Another type of harmonica was very popular about 150 years ago. This instrument was made of several drinking glasses of different sizes and with different amounts of water in them. The player struck the glasses with his fingertips and each glass produced a different musical note. Benjamin Franklin made some improvements in this instrument, and two great composers, Mozart of Austria and Beethoven of Germany, wrote compositions for it.

harmony

Harmony is the study of how to make chords out of musical tones. A chord is a group of tones sounded at the same time. A melody, or tune, is said to be harmonized when other tones are sounded at the same time as the melody note, to give the whole a richer, fuller effect.

A melody is written in a certain key, or group of tones forming a scale. Each key has its own chords, which are built of notes a certain number of tones apart. The basic chord is called a *triad,* which means a group of three. Each tone in a chord is called a *voice.* In four-part harmony, the voices are called bass, tenor, alto, and soprano. The bass is the lowest, and the soprano is the highest. The soprano usually carries the melody, and the bass determines what the chord is. Since the chords are built in thirds, another tone is needed to make the fourth voice, and this is usually gotten by doubling, or repeating, one of the other tones.

Composers (writers of music) have been using harmony for only about 350 years, which makes it a recent development in the long history of music.

In ancient times music consisted only of melody. Then composers began to write two or more melodies to be played together. This is called *counterpoint,* and music written in this style is called *contrapuntal* or *polyphonic* ("many-voiced") music.

Since about the year 1750, most music has been *homophonic.* This means it is made up of one melody supported by chords, while polyphonic music is formed from two or more melodies going on at the same time. Homophonic music follows the rules and practices of harmony. Today, composers are showing an increased interest in music based on the rules and practices of counterpoint.

harness

Harness is equipment that makes it possible for an animal to pull a load. The most common harness is that used for horses. Years ago in the United States all the work on farms and most of the transportation depended on horses, and harness-making was a very important business.

A horse's harness is made mostly of leather, but has some metal or wood on it. It is made of many different parts and all parts work together so that the driver can direct the horse and so that the animal can pull a heavy load without injuring itself. Most harness has a padded collar made of leather that is fitted around the neck of the horse. When the horse is not pulling a heavy load the collar may be exchanged for a padded breastband. Strips of leather or metal chains called *traces* are attached to the collar by pieces of wood or metal called *hames.* The traces are connected to the wagon itself, or in some cases to shafts, which are pieces of wood coming out from a crossbar on the wagon. This is called the *whiffletree* or *swingletree.*

The horse is directed by the reins that the driver holds in his hands. The reins are leather straps, and they are attached to the bit, a piece of metal running across the back part of the horse's mouth. The bit is held in place by a part of the harness called a bridle. When the driver pulls the reins the horse feels the movement in his mouth and turns in the direction in which he feels the pull.

Harold

Harold was the name of two kings of England, but the more famous was Harold II, though he was king for only a short time. Harold was born in 1022. He was the son of one of the greatest English nobles and, next to the king, was the most powerful man in England. When Edward the Confessor, King of England, died in 1066, he said that he wanted Harold to be the next king. At that time the leading nobles chose the king. They followed Edward's wish and made Harold king. But William, the Duke of Normandy, who lived across the English Channel in what is now a section of France, said that Edward had promised him the throne. In October of 1066 he invaded England. At the same time Norwegian armies were invading England in the north. Harold defeated the Norwegian armies and then went south to meet William at the small English town of Hastings. The Battle of Hastings lasted all day. The English fought bravely but they were defeated by the Normans. Harold was killed in the battle and William became king. He is now known as William I, or William the Conqueror. His victory is called the Norman Conquest, and after it the Normans ruled England.

harp

The harp is a large musical instrument with strings. It is sometimes five or six feet high. It is shaped like a triangle, with three sides, and can stand alone. The player sits beside the harp and plucks the strings with both his hands. Because the harp is so large and because it has more than forty strings, it has a wide range of tone. It sounds a little like a piano.

The harp is a very old musical instrument. Some kind of harp has been played at some time in almost every part of the world. The Bible says that a man named Jubal invented the harp. One kind of ancient harp was called a *psaltery.* David, in the Bible, sang while he played the psaltery. His songs are called *psalms,* and there is a book of them in the Bible. At first, harps had to be rather small because they were carried by players on long journeys. About five or six hundred years ago, strolling minstrels in Europe told long and exciting tales while they played their harps.

harpies

Harpies are creatures in Greek mythology, the stories the ancient Greeks and Romans told of their gods and goddesses. The harpies are goddesses of the storms, which means they control the storm winds. Also they play mean tricks on men. They appear in the *Iliad* and the *Odyssey,* the two most famous long poems in Greek literature.

A harpy is described as a very ugly creature. Sometimes it has a human face with animal ears, but usually it has the head of a bird and its wings and body are covered with feathers. It has human arms and legs but has claws instead of hands and has the feet of a large and fantastic bird. Harpies in literature represent danger or forces of evil that must be overcome by the hero in the story.

harpy

The harpy or *harpy eagle* is a large bird of prey. A bird of prey feeds itself by attacking and eating other birds or animals. The harpy is found chiefly in Central America. It is sometimes three feet

long. It has a large bill and powerful talons, or claws. Its head and lower part are white, and its back is dark gray banded with black. It is different from other eagles because it has a double, rather than a single, crest on its head. The harpy hunts in the daytime, flying slowly until it sights its victim. It is named for the harpies, who were creatures in Greek mythology, the stories the ancient Greeks told about their gods and goddesses.

Harris, Joel Chandler

Joel Chandler Harris was an American writer. He was born in Georgia in 1848 and spent all his life in the South. He worked for the Atlanta *Constitution,* and it was in this newspaper that he first wrote about Uncle Remus. Uncle Remus was a kindly old Negro man who entertained the children by telling tales of Br'er (brother) Rabbit, Br'er Fox, and other animals. The tales became so popular that they were put into several books. Harris wrote other books, including a story of his own life called *On the Plantation,* but he is best known for the Uncle Remus stories. He died in 1908.

Harrisburg

Harrisburg is the capital of Pennsylvania. It is on the Susquehanna River, about a hundred miles west of Philadelphia, and it is surrounded by rich farms. Boats travel up the Susquehanna River to Harrisburg, and it is also a railroad center. The Enola railroad yards across the river are among the largest in the United States. About 68,000 people live in Harrisburg. Many of them work in iron and steel mills, and others make bricks, machinery, and clothing. Many books are printed in the city. Harrisburg is a handsome city, and the people are proud of their fine parks and beautiful public buildings. The state capitol is a magnificent domed building, with stately marble halls. There is an Education Building, with pictures on the walls that show the history of civilization, and a museum where there are many things recalling the history of the people of Pennsylvania.

Harrisburg was settled in 1712 by John Harris, and the city was named after him. His son built a ferry across the Susquehanna River, and for many years the town was called Harris' Ferry. In 1812, Harrisburg became the state capital.

HARRISBURG, PENNSYLVANIA. Population (1970 census) 68,061. Capital of Pennsylvania. County seat of Dauphin County. Settled in 1712.

Benjamin Harrison

Benjamin Harrison was the twenty-third President of the United States. He served from 1889 to 1893. He was defeated by Grover Cleveland when he ran for re-election to a second term.

Harrison was born in Ohio. His family for several generations had been prominent in the national affairs of the United States. His father was a member of Congress, his grandfather (William Henry Harrison) was President, and his great

grandfather was a signer of the Declaration of Independence.

Harrison was a distinguished-looking man. He was tall and well-built, with a full beard and thick white hair.

HIS EARLY YEARS

Benjamin Harrison was born on August 20, 1833, at North Bend, Ohio. He grew up on the family farm and at first attended a local log-cabin school. Later, however, he was instructed by a private tutor, and he was a good student. He next attended Farmers College, and he finally graduated from Miami University. He had studied law and was admitted to the bar when he was only 20 years old. A few years later, he was considered one of the most capable young lawyers in the state of Ohio.

The Civil War interrupted his career as a lawyer. He volunteered for the Union Army and was commissioned a second lieutenant. His loyal service and bravery in battle won him several promotions, and he was eventually given the rank of brigadier general. After the war he returned to his law practice. Although he was not actively a politician himself, he was always very much interested in the welfare of his country and in the activity of the Republican Party.

HOW HE BECAME PRESIDENT

The people of Ohio elected Benjamin Harrison to the United States Senate in 1881, and during his six-year term as senator he won the respect of both parties. His term expired in March, 1888. The following November the Republican Party nominated him for president, to run against Grover Cleveland, who was then seeking re-election. Harrison won the election and served for just one term.

During his administration, the first meeting of the Pan-American Congress was held in Washington. This was the first time the people of North, South, and Central America had ever sent representatives to talk over problems they all shared and to make suggestions as to how they could help each other. It was also during Harrison's administration that the Sherman Silver Act was passed. This law compelled the government to buy huge amounts of silver each year. This was very costly, and upset the financial standing of the country. It had a great deal to do with Harrison's defeat by the Democrat, Grover Cleveland, in 1892.

After Harrison retired from the presidency, he went back to his law practice and wrote several books on government. He was so highly respected as a lawyer that the government of Venezuela called upon him for help when they needed a representative in a hearing concerning a border dispute.

He died at Indianapolis, Indiana, on March 13, 1901, at the age of 67, and was buried there.

BENJAMIN HARRISON'S TWO WIVES

Mrs. Caroline Lavinia Scott Harrison was born in 1832 in Oxford, Ohio. She was the first head of the D.A.R.—the Daughters of the American Revolution. She married Benjamin Harrison when she was 21 years old. They had one son and one daughter. Mrs. Caroline Scott Harrison died in the White House in 1892.

Harrison's second wife was Mrs. Mary Scott Lord Dimmock, a widow. They were married in 1896 and had one daughter. Mrs. Mary Harrison died in 1948, at the age of 90.

William Henry Harrison

William Henry Harrison was the ninth President of the United States. He served only one month in office, from March 4, 1841, to April 4, 1841. It was the shortest term ever served by any president. He caught cold at his inauguration, and he died a month later of pneumonia.

William Henry Harrison was nominated by the Whig Party to run against the Democrat, Martin Van Buren, who was seeking re-election. Although Harrison was elected, almost all the presidential term was served by the man who was his Vice President, John Tyler.

HIS EARLY YEARS

William Henry Harrison was born in

Berkeley, Virginia, on February 9, 1773, before the Revolutionary War. His father, Benjamin Harrison, was one of the signers of the Declaration of Independence. His grandson, also named Benjamin Harrison, became the twenty-third President of the United States.

Young Harrison attended Hampden-Sidney College at Hampden-Sidney, Virginia, and later studied medicine at the

College of Physicians and Surgeons in Philadelphia, Pennsylvania.

His career plans changed when he was 19 years old. He could see how badly the country needed good soldiers. There was trouble with the Indians, and troops were short. Harrison volunteered for the army and was commissioned a lieutenant. In 1792, he fought under General Anthony Wayne. He continued in the service with frequent promotions for his skill and bravery.

HOW HE BECAME PRESIDENT

In 1800, President John Adams appointed Harrison governor of the Indiana Territory. Afterwards he was also governor of the Louisiana Territory. In 1811, an Indian chief of the Shawnees, Tecumseh, succeeded in uniting all the Indians of the West against the white man. There was a battle at a place called Tippecanoe, about seven miles north of what is now Lafayette, Indiana. Because of Harrison's able command, he defeated the Indians with a force of six hundred men, and he won for himself the nickname of "Tippecanoe," which lasted for the rest of his life.

He made his home in Ohio, finally, and in 1816 the people of that state elected him to the House of Representatives. From 1825 to 1828 he served as United States senator from Ohio, and in 1836 he ran for President on the Whig ticket against Martin Van Buren. He was defeated. Four years later, in 1840, with John Tyler as his running mate, he again ran for President. The combination of his nickname and the name of John Tyler fell naturally into a rhyming campaign slogan—"Tippecanoe and Tyler too." The people of the country elected Harrison by a large majority, because by this time they were tired of the Van Buren administration. Harrison was 67 years old, the oldest President ever elected.

Harrison caught cold during his inauguration and developed pneumonia. He was a very sick man all through the one month during which he was actually president, and he did not have a chance to do anything at all in that office. He died on April 4, 1841. He was buried in North Bend, Ohio, where he had his home. John Tyler succeeded him.

MRS. WILLIAM HENRY HARRISON

Mrs. Anna Symmes Harrison was born in Morristown, New Jersey, in 1775. She was the daughter of Colonel John Cleves Symmes, chief justice of the supreme court of New Jersey and a veteran of the Revolutionary War. President and Mrs. Harrison had ten children, six sons and four daughters. Mrs. Anna Symmes Harrison died in 1864.

harrow, a machine used to break and smooth farm land: see the article on FARM MACHINERY.

Harte, Bret

Bret Harte was an American writer who wrote many stories about the western part of the United States in the days when it was first being settled. His full name was Francis Bret Harte. He was born in New York City, in 1836, but he moved to California when he was only 16, and he worked there as a printer and editor. He wrote most of his stories there. His most famous one, called "The Luck of Roaring Camp," was published in 1871. Harte later moved to England, where he died in 1902. His other well-known stories include "The Outcasts of Poker Flat" and "The Twins of Table Mountain."

hartebeest

The hartebeest is a South African antelope. It is a graceful animal and runs very swiftly; it can easily outdistance a greyhound, one of the fastest racing dogs. Its front legs are much heavier than its hind legs. Both the male and the female hartebeest have horns shaped somewhat like a lyre, which is a harp-shaped instrument. The hartebeest is red and has a long face with a naked nose. Formerly great herds of these animals roamed Africa from Cape Colony to Rhodesia, but now there are only a few animals left, and they are found only in remote districts.

Hartford

Hartford is the capital and largest city of the state of Connecticut. It is on the Connecticut River. More than 158,-000 people live there. Several of the biggest insurance companies in the world have their main offices in Hartford. There are important factories that make typewriters and firearms, and in East Hartford, a city of about 57,583 across the Connecticut River, are some of the world's most important aviation factories.

The capitol of Connecticut is a domed building on the side of a hill. In the Supreme Court building hangs the most famous full-length picture of George Washington. This portrait was painted by Gilbert Stuart, a famous American artist. In Hartford is the place where the Charter Oak stood. This was an oak tree in which the early colonists hid an important document from the English governor, and you can read more about it in the article on CONNECTICUT. Trinity College for men was founded in 1823, and it has many fine old buildings. The home of Samuel Clemens (Mark Twain) is still used, as a library.

Hartford was an old Dutch trading post. In 1635 a group of colonists led by Thomas Hooker, a Puritan clergyman, settled there and called it Newtown. Two years later the name was changed to Hartford. In 1701, Hartford and the city of New Haven became the joint capital of Connecticut and remained so until 1875, when Hartford alone was made the capital. In 1814 the Hartford Convention took place in Hartford. Twenty-six delegates from New England met to discuss whether or not New England should continue fighting with the United States government in the War of 1812. Some of the delegates thought New England should secede (leave the Union) as the southern states did about fifty years later; but the war soon ended and New England did not secede. Also about this time Hartford was the center for a group of writers who were called the Connecticut Wits, or the Hartford Wits. They tried to create a literature that would be typically American, and also became interested in the political disputes of the time. Some of the Hartford Wits were Joel Barlow, John Trumbull, and Lemuel Hopkins, and they founded and wrote for a number of magazines.

HARTFORD, CONNECTICUT. Population 158,017 (1970 census). Capital of Connecticut. County seat of Hartford County. Settled in 1635.

Harun-al-Rashid

Harun-al-Rashid was the most famous caliph of Baghdad. He was born about 764 and died in 809. Caliph was the name given to the man who was the ruler of all the Mohammedan people. While Harun-al-Rashid was caliph, Baghdad, which is now the capital of Iraq, was the leading city of the Mohammedan empire. Harun-al-Rashid controlled all of southwest Asia as well as part of northern Africa. He lived in great splendor in Baghdad and was very generous to the poets and scholars of his time. Many of the stories told in the Arabian Nights are about Harun-al-Rashid, his wife Zobeide, and his vizier, or adviser, Graffir. Harun-al-Rashid is also spelled Haroun-al-Raschid.

Harvard

Harvard is the oldest university in the United States. The principal grounds and buildings are in Cambridge, Massachusetts. It was founded in 1636. In 1971 it had about 15,000 students, including those at Radcliffe College, and more than 7,000 members of its faculty, or teachers, by far the highest ratio of faculty to students in the world. Besides its college for undergraduates, Harvard has schools in law, medicine, dentistry, business administration, theology, architecture, and others. The university is named for John Harvard, an American clergyman who left his library of four hundred books to the University when he died in 1638.

The Harvard University Library has since become the world's largest college library, with more than 7,000,000 books. Harvard's property and endowment are more than 400 million dollars.

Until after World War II, Harvard was a college for men only, but Radcliffe College for women, also in Cambridge, had most of its courses taught by Harvard's professors. Since World War II, Harvard and Radcliffe have become almost the same as one coeducational university, and the men and women attend the same classes.

Five Presidents of the United States—John Adams, John Quincy Adams, Theodore Roosevelt, Franklin Delano Roosevelt, and John F. Kennedy—have been graduates of Harvard.

harvester, a machine that gathers grain and other crops: see the article on FARM MACHINERY.

Harvey, William

William Harvey was an English doctor who discovered that the blood circulates (moves around) the human body. He lived about 350 years ago. He was born in 1578 and studied in England and in Italy. At that time it was not known that the blood circulates. Harvey showed how the heart works and how the veins and arteries carry the blood to and from the heart. He died in 1657.

Hastings, Battle of

About nine hundred years ago, an English king called Edward the Confessor died without leaving an heir to succeed him on the throne. There were two noblemen, each of whom said Edward had promised the throne to him. One was Harold, an Englishman, and the other was William, Duke of Normandy, a region in the northern part of France.

William got together an army of about 10,000 men, made up of Normans and adventurers from all over Europe. They landed near Hastings on the southern coast of England. The Normans were cavalry troops who fought on horseback and with bows and arrows. The English under Harold were armed with spears, swords, and huge battle-axes. The English took up a position on a hill outside of Hastings, and William attacked with his cavalry. In between charges by the mounted Normans, they sent showers of arrows among the English troops, but the English stood firm most of the day. Then William used a trick to get some of the English down off the hill to a place where they would be easier to defeat. He had his horsemen pretend to run away. When the English left the hill to chase them, the horsemen turned and attacked. A small but strong group of English stayed on the hill around their king until evening, when Harold was killed by an arrow. One more attack by William killed most of the remaining English soldiers and put the rest to flight.

William became king of England as William I. In English history, William is known as William the Conqueror and his victory is called the Norman Conquest.

hat

A hat is a covering for the head. It may be made of felt, straw, silk, or fabric. A hat gives warmth, and it also protects the wearer from rain, snow, and the glare of the sun. Women often wear hats only to make themselves attractive or because they are going somewhere, for example to church, where it is customary to wear a hat. Men too may wear hats only so that they will be considered properly dressed. Hatmaking is a big business in the United States, where more than fifty million men's hats and even more women's hats are sold every year.

U.S. Air Force
Air Force General's hat

Algerian Ministry of Information
Algerian native's turban

Roy Stevens
Construction worker's helmet

STYLES IN HATS

Men's hats have changed less, through the centuries, than any other article of their clothing, but gradually the soft felt hat has replaced most other kinds of men's hats. The snap-brim fedora is the most popular hat for a man. It is a felt hat and has a brim about 2½ inches wide, which most men wear turned down in front. The straw hat is popular with men who live in warm climates. Another popular hat is the homburg, which has a stiff brim that is turned up all the way around. Most men's hats are brown, gray, blue, or black. A man seldom spends more than $5 to $10 for a hat, but a very fine hat for a man may cost as much as $200.

Women spend a great deal more money on their hats than men do, and the styles of their hats change often. There are many types of hat popular with women, and a woman's choice of hat often depends upon the way she fixes her hair, the rest of her clothes, and the occasion for which she is wearing the hat.

Women's hats are generally more complicated than men's. They are also more colorful. They may differ in size from the tight-fitting Juliet hat and cloche to the wide-brimmed picture hat. Added decorations, such as veils, flowers, sequins, or ribbons, may be put on a woman's hat.

Stetson
Western hat

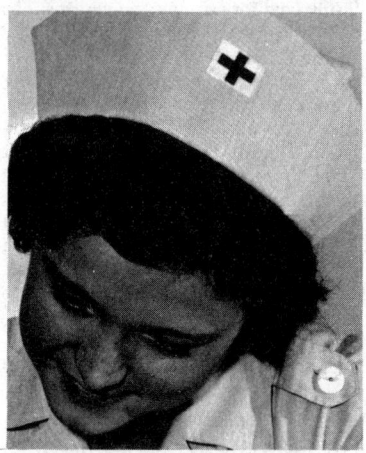
Nate Silverstein
Nurse's hat

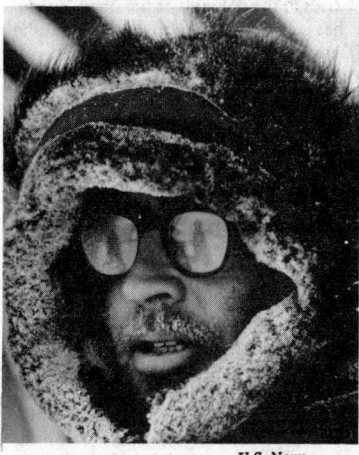
U.S. Navy
Antarctic explorer's hood

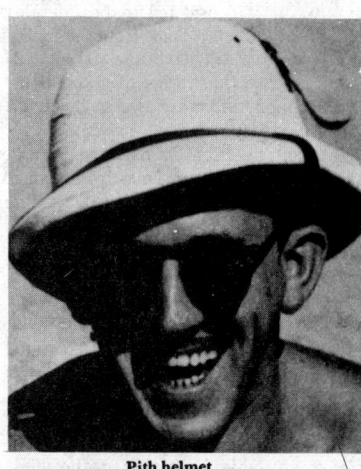
Pith helmet
National Archives

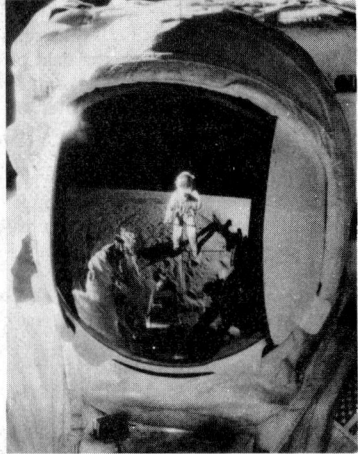

Space helmet

NASA

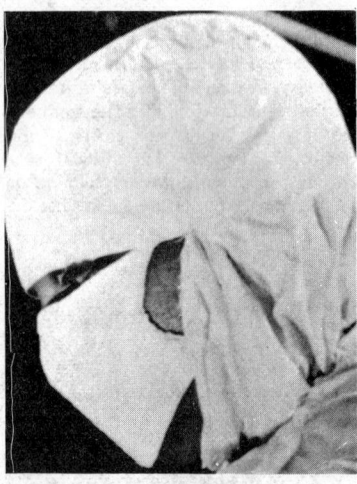

Sterile, lint-free hat
Chas. Pfizer & Co., Inc.

HAT MATERIALS

Most hats made in the United States are of felt. Also popular are hats made of straw, silk, and fabrics. In the ordinary felt hat, it is quite possible that the materials used were gathered from the far ends of the world. Most of the fur used for felt in the United States comes from the coney, rabbit, and hare. The fur is usually shipped from England, Scotland, Australia, Germany, France, and Austria. Sometimes the American rabbit is used, but its fur is considered to be inferior. Higher-priced felt is made from the fur of the beaver, which makes the softest and strongest felt. The skins of more than eight million rabbits are used each year in the United States.

The silk used for silk hats and for the silk band on felt hats comes from China and Japan, as does the silk that is used for the linings of these hats. The silk is usually woven in American mills. More than ten thousand yards of satin are used in the United States each year for this purpose. Artificial silk is also used for linings and bands.

In the brim of a felt hat, to give it stiffness, is embedded a shellac solution, made from the lac bug of India. The leather in the hat band, which makes the hat fit and feel comfortable, is made from the skins of sheep.

HOW HATS ARE MADE

The way the fur is made into FELT is described in a separate article. For felt hats, the felt is made in a cone shape somewhat like that of an ice-cream cone but much larger. This is stretched over a *block*, a piece of wood cut in the shape of the "crown," or rounded top part, of the hat. On this block the felt is *pounced*, that is, it is rubbed or pounded until it is smooth. The brim is flattened out and ironed. Finally the cloth parts, the lining and band, are sewed on.

Women's felt hats are made in much the same way as men's hats, but women's cloth hats are a different kind of manufacturing, related to the garment industry. The cloth for many hats is cut at the same time and the hats are sewed by workers at sewing machines.

STRAW HATS

Straw hats are made from rice straw grown in Japan or China, from Tuscan straw grown in Italy, from bamboo grasses grown in the Philippines, and from the leaves of the screw pine tree. The Panama hat is a straw hat made from the Jipijapa palm tree that grows in South America, in Ecuador. The Panama hat is woven by hand, from moistened fibers of the palm tree.

Most straw hats are made in factories. The material is woven into braids before it is sent to the factory. There the braid is bleached and cleaned. It is moistened again before it is ready to be sewn. The hat is started by hand at the tip of the center of the crown. It is then fitted to a block of the desired size and a machine weaves or sews it to fit this block. Gelatin is used to stiffen straw hats. After the hats have been stiffened, they are blocked, or steam-pressed, into the correct shape. Finishing steps include further moistening, blocking, and ironing.

HISTORY OF HATS

People have worn all kinds of amazing and unusual hats. The savage of olden times wore palm leaves and animal skins to protect his head. Later, the Greeks wore skull caps and metal helmets with horses' manes and tails for decorations. The art of making fur into felt and then trimming and shaping it to make a hat was practiced more than three thousand years ago.

Hatmaking was one of the early industries in the colonies of the New World. It has always been practiced along the Atlantic Coast of the United States. Important hatmaking cities are Danbury and Norwalk, Connecticut, and Newark, New Jersey. New York City is the center for women's cloth hats.

Havana

Havana is the capital of Cuba and the largest city in the West Indies. *Habana* means "harbor" in Spanish and Havana, on the Gulf of Mexico, has one of the most beautiful harbors in the world. Ships bring machinery, cloth, and food to Havana, and carry sugar, tobacco, and fruit to other world ports.

More than a million people live in Havana. They make cigars that are considered the best in the world, and also perfume and rum. Outside the city are great plantations where sugar cane is grown.

The climate in Havana is very fine, and even during the winter the temperature is about 75 degrees, which is like a pleasant spring day in the United States. The summers are quite hot. Sometimes Havana is hit by severe hurricanes.

Before the Cuban Revolution of 1959, thousands of people went to Havana for vacations. It is an interesting and attractive city, with fine old Spanish buildings. Some parts of the city are modern, and there are many handsome hotels and beautiful parks. The capitol is an impressive building, with a splendid gold dome. It cost $20,000,000 and is the most beautiful in Latin America. There are some fine churches, and a magnificent opera house. When people come to Havana by ship, they pass Morro Castle, an old fortress that guards the entrance of the harbor. Morro Castle was built by the Spanish almost four hundred years ago to protect Havana from enemies.

The Spanish people founded Havana in 1519, and it was made the capital of Cuba in 1552. A United States battleship, the *Maine*, was blown up in Havana harbor in 1898; this was one of the incidents that started the Spanish-American War.

HAVANA, CUBA. Population (1961 estimate) 1,158,203. Capital of Cuba.

Hawaii

Hawaii, the fiftieth state admitted to the United States, consists of a group of twenty islands in the northern Pacific Ocean. These islands are often called the Hawaiian Islands, since Hawaii, the name of the state, is also the name of the largest island of the group. The islands are 2,000 miles from the closest port on the North American continent—San Francisco—but jet airplane travel has reduced the traveling time to a few hours. The islands are about one-third of the distance from North America to Asia and so are a favorite place for ships to refuel and buy supplies.

All the people of Hawaii live on nine of the islands. These inhabited islands are beautiful places, with fine beaches, palm trees, gorgeous tropical birds, and fertile land for farming and gardens. The other islands are barren and rocky.

The Hawaiian Islands have an area of 6,423 square miles, ranking 47th among the states (only Connecticut, Delaware, and Rhode Island are smaller). In population Hawaii ranks 40th, with about 700,000 people living there; but since some of the islands are among the world's popular tourist resorts, visitors often swell the population to a million. Hawaii is the state most recently admitted to the Union, Congress having passed the law admitting it in 1959; before, Hawaii was a Territory (see TERRITORY).

Hawaii's importance to the defense of the United States is very great and includes the great naval base of Pearl Harbor, which was bombed by Japan on December 7, 1941, drawing the United States into World War II.

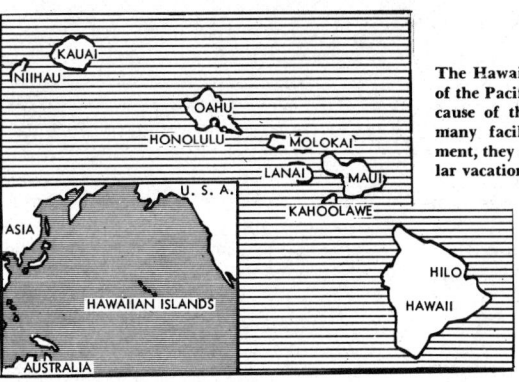

The Hawaiian Islands are at the crossroads of the Pacific Ocean (see insert on map). Because of their beautiful scenery and their many facilities for sports and entertainment, they are one of the world's most popular vacation spots.

THE PEOPLE OF HAWAII

The original people of the Hawaiian Islands were Polynesians. These people came from Asia long ago and settled on islands in many parts of the Pacific Ocean. Later, many Japanese and people from Europe and the United States came to the Hawaiian Islands to live, and there are also Puerto Ricans and Portuguese and people from the Philippines. Many Hawaiians are a mixture of some of these different peoples. There are still some pure Polynesians. They are handsome, brown-skinned people, who like to have a good time and enjoy life. Because they live surrounded by water, they are great swimmers and skillful divers and fishermen. All Hawaiians live and work peacefully together. Their songs and dances are famous all over the world.

Most Hawaiians are farmers. Some raise coffee or rice, and some work on sugar-cane plantations. Sugar is their main export to the United States. Near the plantations are mills where the sugarcane is made into sugar. Often the people who work in the sugar mills live in small villages that are owned by the mills. These workers do not have to pay any rent, and they can receive free medical care. There are playgrounds for the children and schools and churches.

Many farmers on the island of Lanai grow pineapples. Near the pineapple fields are canneries, where they can the fruit and the pineapple juice. In Honolulu there is a pineapple factory where you can drink pineapple juice from a drinking fountain. Most of the pineapple eaten in the United States comes from the Islands.

WHAT THE HAWAIIAN ISLANDS ARE LIKE

The Hawaiian Islands are really the tops of huge mountains that rise out of the ocean. These mountains were once volcanoes that belched fire and melted rock, called lava.

Hawaii is the largest of the islands. It has an area of 4,021 square miles.

Oahu Island is very small, with an area of only 589 square miles, but more than half the people of the Islands live there. Honolulu, the capital city of the Islands, is on Oahu. Most people who visit the Hawaiian Islands come to Honolulu first. It is a great port and air base. Pearl Harbor, the important naval base, is just outside the city. You can read more about HONOLULU and PEARL HARBOR in separate articles.

The five other important islands are Maui, 728 square miles; Molokai, 259 square miles; Lanai, 141 square miles;

Kauai, 551 square miles; and Niihau, 72 square miles. On Molokai there is a famous "leper colony" where people afflicted with the disease called leprosy live.

People say that the Hawaiians do not even have a word in their language for "weather" because they never have to think about it. The temperature is usually about 75 degrees. Showers are quite frequent, but they never last long, and the sun shines almost every day. There are very few wild animals in the Hawaiian Islands, but the forests are filled with brilliant tropical birds, and hundreds of different kinds of fish live in the waters around the Islands. Bananas, coconuts, tropical fruit called mangoes and breadfruit trees grow in abundance. There are forests of ferns that grow as tall as trees, and many rare and beautiful flowers. The Hawaiians make these flowers into wreaths that they call "leis." If you visit the Hawaiian Islands, you will be given a lei of blossoms when you arrive and another one when you leave. You will also hear the popular song, "Aloha Oe," which is sung both as an affectionate greeting and farewell, as your boat steams into or out of the harbor. The song was written by Queen Liliuokalani, the last queen of Hawaii.

THE GOVERNMENT OF HAWAII

Hawaii, like other states, has a governor who is elected by the people. The laws are made by a Legislature that has two houses, a Senate with twenty-five members and a House of Representatives with fifty-one members. Hawaii is entitled to elect two Senators and two Representatives in the Congress of the United States.

The capital is Honolulu. In Hawaii, as in all parts of the United States, education is free and all children must attend school. There is a large, modern university, the University of Hawaii, in Honolulu.

HAWAII IN THE PAST

People believe that the Polynesians first settled on the Hawaiian Islands about 1,500 years ago. In 1778, Captain James Cook, an English explorer, came to the Islands, and he called them the Sandwich Islands. When Cook arrived, the people were ruled by four kings. Then Kamehameha I became the only king, and he ruled until 1819. In 1829, a group of Americans from New England came to Hawaii, as missionaries, and they began to teach the people about the Christian religion. Very soon, most of them became Christians. The Hawaiians did not have

an alphabet, so the missionaries made up a special alphabet and taught the people to read and write. Now most of the people in Hawaii know how to read and write.

The people of the Hawaiian Islands were very much dissatisfied with their rulers, and finally, in 1893, the queen, Liliuokalani, was overthrown. The people then set up a republic. In 1900, the United States agreed to grant the request of the people of Hawaii to become a Territory. The residents long favored statehood and many bills were introduced in the Congress of the United States before it voted to admit Hawaii as a state.

PLACES TO SEE IN HAWAII

Hawaii National Park, about 220 square miles in the southern part of the island of Hawaii. Thousands of tourists visit the park each year to see the two great active volcanoes, Mauna Loa and Kilauea. The last volcanic eruption occurred in 1961, with an outburst of Kilauea accompanied by a series of small earthquake tremors.

Diamond Head, an inactive volcano that passengers arriving in the port of Honolulu see before they can identify any other landmark.

Waikiki Beach, a beautiful stretch of white sand near Honolulu. Waikiki is the favorite resort and bathing place for tourists. There are many modern hotels on the palm-fringed avenues along the beach. Waikiki is a fine place to see the Hawaiians riding their famous surfboards on the incoming waves.

Kalapana Beach, a marvelous stretch of black sand on the island of Hawaii. The sand is black because it comes from volcanic lava.

Mission House, in Honolulu, is the oldest wooden frame building in the islands.

Queen Emma Museum, where many of the treasures of Hawaiian rulers are kept.

HAWAII. Area, 6,423 square miles. Population (1970 census), 768,561. Capital, Honolulu. Nickname, the Aloha State. Motto, Righteousness Perpetuates the Life of the Land. Flower, red hibiscus. Song "Hawaii Ponoi." Annexed to United States, July 7, 1898. Admitted to Union, 1959. Official abbreviation, H.I.

hawk

"Hawk" is the name commonly given to several kinds of small birds of prey in the order *Falconiformes,* family *Accipitridae.* There are more than 270 species of hawk; some are as small as robins and some are two feet long. They all have strong, curved beaks, large powerful claws, and very keen eyesight. Most hawks are brown and white with dark brown, gray, or black markings. Some have a few bright tail feathers. There is not much difference in the appearance of the male and the female, except that the female is bigger.

Hawks prefer high, secluded spots for their nests, such as rock ledges, cliff embankments, and tall trees. The nests are built of branches and twigs, and lined with weeds, grasses, bark, or dead leaves. In these, from 2 to 6 eggs are laid in a "clutch". They are whitish, splotched with brown, lavender, and red.

Hawks hunt by daylight, either waiting on a high perch or soaring in the sky until they spot their prey. Then they swoop

down at great speed and seize the little animal in their talons (claws). Their strong beaks can kill in a single blow and then tear the prey to pieces. A few hawks habitually hunt other birds and therefore are nuisances to farmers who raise chickens. However, most hawks eat insects, reptiles and small rodents, and are beneficial to farmers. The Cooper's hawk is one of the few that prefers to eat birds. It rarely soars high in the air, but does most of its hunting in the woods. Unlike many hawks which are permanent residents in their areas, Cooper's hawk migrates.

Hawks and falcons were formerly grouped in the same family, but because hawks have shorter, broader, more rounded wings, they are now in a separate family.

The classification of hawks is sometimes complicated by the fact that many hawks have common or local names (such as the "chicken hawk") which have no scientific standing.

The regular hawks (that is, those other than eagles, kites, buzzards, and vultures) are classified into two categories: the *Accipiters* eat birds, which they catch by swooping at them from perches in the woods; the *Buteos* eat small rodents, which they spot by soaring over wide-open spaces for long periods of time.

Other well-known American hawks are the *red-tailed hawk*, the *red-shouldered hawk*, the goshawk, and *Swainson's hawk*.

Hawkins, Sir John

Sir John Hawkins was an admiral in the English Navy, almost four hundred years ago. He was one of the three admirals who saved England from being invaded by Spanish troops in the year 1588, when Spain sent the Armada, the greatest fleet that had ever been assembled, to attack England.

Hawkins was born in 1532 and went to sea as a young man. His early life would not be considered very respectable today. He was a slave trader, buying or capturing Negroes in Africa and carrying them across the Atlantic Ocean to be sold as slaves in America. He was also a privateer, a kind of pirate. When he was not quite 40 years old, a small fleet of ships that he commanded fought a fleet of Spanish ships and Hawkins' fleet was almost destroyed. He then retired from naval duty and became a Member of Parliament, but Queen Elizabeth I made him an admiral again to fight the Spanish Armada. After the battle was won, she knighted him (gave him the title Sir). He went to sea again in 1595, but died at sea.

hawthorn

The hawthorn is a small flowering tree or shrub. It has many branches and deeply cut leaves. At the end of the branches are sharp-pointed spines or thorns. The hawthorn blooms in May with clusters of sweet-smelling white flowers. The tree, if it is not trimmed, grows ten to twenty feet high. In Europe, especially England and France, it is used for hedges and forms what are called hedgerows. The wood of the hawthorn is very hard and can be used for such things as handles of hammers or cogs for millwheels.

Hawthorn has long been a symbol of spring in England, and the flowers were used as May Day decorations. Hawthorn is also the state flower of Missouri.

Hawthorne, Nathaniel

Nathaniel Hawthorne was one of America's greatest writers. He was born in Salem, Massachusetts, in 1804. His father was a sea captain who died when Hawthorne was young. The household of mother and son was one of gloom and solitude, and the boy grew up to prefer loneliness and silence.

He attended Bowdoin College in Maine, and there he made friends with Franklin Pierce, who later became President of the United States. After graduation Hawthorne returned to Salem and started writing. His life was a quiet one. He married Sophia Peabody and lived for a time in Concord, Massachusetts. Then he moved back to Salem, where he worked for the government in the Customs House (where taxes on shipping are collected). Later, through his friendship with President Pierce, he was appointed United States consul in Liverpool, England.

Hawthorne's books told the story of New England and its people. Because the early settlers were Puritans, men and women who spent much time thinking about religion and problems of good and evil, Hawthorne's books dealt with these problems. His first few books were made up of short stories, and they were not very successful. Then in 1850 he wrote the famous novel called *The Scarlet Letter*, which became popular immediately. This was followed by *The House of the Seven Gables*, which was equally successful.

Hawthorne also wrote books for children. His *Twice-told Tales* is a book of stories that have been enjoyed by readers of all ages, and he retold old Greek myths in *A Wonder Book* and *Tanglewood Tales*. He died in 1864.

hay

Hay is dried grass or other plants, cut as feed for farm animals. Several different grasses are grown for hay in the United States. Chief among them are timothy and orchard grass. Alfalfa and white and red clover are also grown and cut for hay.

Hay must be cut at a certain time to retain all the nourishment of the plant. If the grass is allowed to go to seed, the stem and leaves begin to rot. The hay should be cut when it is in flower, because then all the valuable food elements are still in the plant.

When the hay is cut it should be spread evenly on the field to be dried in the sun. On large farms this is done by machines that can do the work of twelve or fifteen men. Hay should be left to dry for three days.

Weather is very important when making hay because the hay can be easily spoiled. A scorching sun will burn the nourishment out of it; rain or dew will soak the salt and sugar out of it. Stacking hay must also be done with the weather in mind. Layers of straw put

in between the hay will absorb moisture and keep it from fermenting, or turning sour. Some farmers salt hay when they pile it in the stacks that stand in fields. Hay is very essential to the way we live. If hay could not be stored and kept for the livestock to feed on, people would not be able to survive in the winter. People would have to drive the cattle to grazing grounds. In some places in the world there are people who must travel with their cattle to find food. They are called nomads and have no particular home because they have no way of storing fodder for their animals. Haymaking in the United States has become a large industry. Hay is now pressed into bales, bound together in large bundles. These bundles are easily shipped to far-off places and livestock can be given food in parts of the country where it does not grow naturally.

Hay, John

John Hay was an American statesman who held several important offices. He was born in Indiana in 1838 and became a lawyer in Springfield, Illinois. There he met Abraham Lincoln, and when Lincoln was elected President in 1860 he made Hay one of his Secretaries. Later Hay and another of Lincoln's Secretaries, John G. Nicolay, wrote one of the most famous biographies, or stories, of Lincoln's life. Hay wrote several other books and became one of the best-known American writers.

In 1879 Hay was made Assistant Secretary of State, and in 1897 President McKinley appointed him ambassador to Great Britain. The next year McKinley made him Secretary of State, the highest-ranking office in the President's Cabinet. While Hay was Secretary of State, he and Lord Pauncefote, the British ambassador, made an agreement called the Hay-Pauncefote Treaty that led to the building of the Panama Canal. Until his death in 1905, Hay remained Secretary of State under President Theodore Roosevelt.

Haydn, Franz Joseph

Franz Joseph Haydn was a great Austrian composer, or writer of music, who is known as "the father of the symphony." A symphony is a long piece of music for a large orchestra. Though Haydn did not invent the symphony, he did a great deal to improve it and make it popular. Haydn was the leading musical figure of his time. He was so full of good

Haydn is buried in the little Chapel on the Hill in the town of Eisenstadt, Austria.

cheer and fatherly love to all that he was often called "Papa Haydn."

Haydn was born in Rohrau, Austria, in 1732. He was the second of twelve children of a poor wagon-maker. At the age of 5 he left home to study music with a relative. He sang in the choir of a cathedral in Vienna when he was 8.

In 1761 Haydn became musical director for a noble Hungarian family named Esterhazy. In those days rich and royal families often had their own orchestras. Haydn wrote much of his greatest music during his 29 years with the Esterhazys, including many symphonies, operas, and piano sonatas, and much church music. He wrote over a hundred symphonies in all. For several years he lived in England, and he dedicated his *London Symphony* to the English people. Two of his other famous symphonies are the *Clock Symphony* and the *Surprise Symphony*, in which a few bars of the opening melody are followed by a loud chord with which Haydn wanted to surprise his listeners.

When he was old Haydn wrote two of his greatest works, *The Creation* and *The Seasons*. These were oratorios, or religious stories sung by a chorus and soloists and played by an orchestra. Haydn died in Vienna, in 1809.

Hayes, Helen

Helen Hayes is one of the most beloved actresses of the American theater. She has played in many successful Broadway plays and occasionally has appeared in motion pictures, though she has preferred the stage. One of her most popular roles was Queen Victoria in the play *Victoria Regina*. Miss Hayes was born in Washington, D.C., in the year 1900, and her full name was Helen Hayes Brown. She first appeared on the stage with the Columbia Players in Washington when she was only 6 years old. In 1928 she married Charles MacArthur, an author and playwright, who died in 1956. They had two children, a son and a daughter, and their daughter, Mary MacArthur, died tragically of infantile paralysis when she was only 20 years old. Miss Hayes became active in many charitable organizations, especially those connected with the theater. Her autobiography, *A Gift of Joy*, was published in 1965.

Hayes, Patrick Joseph Cardinal

Patrick Joseph Hayes was a Roman Catholic priest who was made a cardinal by the Pope, the religious leader of the Catholic Church. Cardinals are called princes of the church, and the office is one of the highest honors that a Catholic priest can receive. Hayes was born in New York City in 1867 and later studied in Rome, Italy. When he was 25 years old, he became a priest. In 1919 he was made an archbishop, and only five years later he was appointed a cardinal. Cardinal Hayes organized the Catholic Charities of New York, an organization that helps people who are poor or sick or have other problems. He also did a great deal to bring about better working conditions and other changes that would help people to live better lives. Cardinal Hayes died in 1938, and he was buried in St. Patrick's Cathedral in New York City. People of

every religion, rich and poor, young and old, loved and respected Cardinal Hayes.

Rutherford B. Hayes

Rutherford Birchard Hayes was the nineteenth President of the United States. He served from 1877 to 1881, after an election so close that the final result was not official until two days before his inauguration.

Hayes was a distinguished-looking man, with a full, black beard and a high, broad forehead. He was habitually quiet and reserved.

HIS EARLY YEARS

Rutherford Hayes was born in Delaware, Ohio, on October 4, 1822, the son of a farmer who had died a few weeks before Rutherford was born. The boy was brought up by an uncle, Sardis Birchard, and attended schools in Connecticut and Ohio. After his graduation from Kenyon College in Gambier, Ohio, in 1842, he went to Harvard Law School, where he was graduated in 1845. He practiced law in Ohio for a time, but at the outbreak of the Civil War he volunteered for service in the Union army, and was made major of a regiment of volunteers. He was severely wounded during the war. He rose to the rank of major general, so he was one of the many American generals who later became President of the United States. After the war, he was elected to Congress by the people of Ohio, and served from 1865 to 1867.

Hayes was known as a hard-working, honest man, and the people of his state showed their belief in him by making him governor in 1867. He was re-elected in 1875, and his record made him a natural choice as Republican candidate for president in 1876.

HOW HE BECAME PRESIDENT

The Democratic candidate was Samuel Tilden, and the vote was extremely close. Hayes had 185 electoral votes and Tilden had 184. Tilden's popular vote, however, was 4,285,992, while Hayes's was only 4,033,768. The Democrats of South Carolina, Louisiana, Florida, and Oregon questioned the count, and accused the recorders of withholding votes on the Democratic side. Many people became dangerously angry at the suggestion of fraud. In

order to prevent real trouble, Congress created an electoral commission—a group of senators, representatives, and judges—to check the voting. The commission decided that Rutherford Hayes had actually won the election, and it gave its decision on March 2, 1877. He was inaugurated two days later. Some historians believe the commission was wrong, and that Tilden really won the election, but it is agreed that Hayes made a very good President.

During his term as President, Rutherford Hayes withdrew the occupation troops from the South, where they had been ever since the Civil War, and gave the southern states a chance to get on with their recovery program. He also tried to improve the regulations that controlled government employees, by changing the Civil Service laws. He had too much opposition in Congress, however, to succeed at this.

Hayes did not wish to run for a second term. He felt that there was a great deal to be done in private life, in trying to help others have a better life and a better chance at a good education. He retired to his home in Fremont, Ohio. He died in Fremont on January 17, 1893.

MRS. RUTHERFORD B. HAYES

Mrs. Lucy Webb Hayes was born in Chillicothe, Ohio, in 1831. She was the daughter of Dr. James Webb. She married Rutherford Hayes in December, 1852, and they had eight children—seven sons and one daughter. Both President and Mrs. Hayes were firmly opposed to all alcoholic beverages, and would allow no wines or liquors of any kind in the White House. Lucy Webb Hayes died in June, 1889.

hay fever

Hay fever is a sickness that many people have in the summer. It is called an ALLERGY, about which you can read in a separate article. Hay fever got its name because people used to think it was caused by hay. Doctors now know that dust and pollen from ragweed and other grasses and flowers cause hay fever. This pollen floats in the air and irritates the eyes and nasal passages of people who are sensitive to it. When a person has hay fever, his eyes itch and shed tears, his nose runs, he has violent sneezing attacks, and he feels very uncomfortable. There are two main seasons when people get hay fever. Some people have attacks in June, and others in late September. Some people get hay fever in both seasons.

There is no cure for hay fever, although doctors do know many things that can help. Some people are given injections before the hay fever season begins. There are drugs, such as antihistamine, that relieve some hay fever sufferers. Many people go away to the mountains or the seashore during the hay fever season.

The United States government has an agency that makes a check of the amount of pollen in the air in different areas. The pollen count in New York City is very high, which makes it a bad place for people who often get hay fever. Los Angeles, California, has a very low pollen count, which means that it is a good place for such people to live.

hazel

The hazel is a shrub or small tree that grows in many parts of the world. Its fruit, the hazelnut, is good to eat. Hazelnuts grow in clusters on the tree; they are green and look like leaf buds. Hazel wood is used for making furniture. When it is cut and polished, it has a veined pattern in it that is attractive as a veneer, or thin decorative layer of wood, on furniture. An extract of the hazel tree is used as a medicine to soothe and cool the skin.

head

The head is probably the most important part of the human body. In this one place are gathered a great many of the things that make the body work. First of all, there is the brain, which is the great nerve center from which go out the signals that control everything the body does. The head also contains the organs that we use to see, hear, smell, and taste. The nose and mouth are used to take in the air that we need to breathe, and the mouth also is the opening for the alimentary canal, which carries food down into the stomach.

The bony structure of the head is called the *skull*. It is covered by skin, called the *scalp*, and by hair. The bones of the skull that protect the brain are called the *cranium*. The cranium is much thicker on the top than it is on the sides. It is not one large bone, but is made up of a number of smaller pieces. When a baby is born, these small bones are separated, but they gradually grow together as it gets older.

The head is joined to the top of the spinal column, and to the collarbone and shoulder blades, by a very complicated system of muscles and tendons. These make it possible for the head to move around in almost every direction. Most of the head's weight presses down on the rear of the skull, where it is joined by muscles to the spinal column. These muscles keep the head erect, but if you begin to fall asleep they start to relax. That is why your head starts to nod as you get sleepy.

All of the mammals, birds, amphibians, reptiles and fish have heads, and many insects also do. Even an earthworm has a small section at one end that almost could be called a head.

headache

Any kind of pain in the head is called a headache. Headaches are not always sharp pains. They may be uncomfortable throbbing sensations. Along with a headache may go eye ache, dizziness, and vomiting. Even though they are unpleasant, many headaches are not serious. They can be caused by eyestrain, overwork, constipation, or too much excitement. If a headache continues for a long time, it may be a symptom of something more serious, such as sinus trouble, adenoids, fever, or one of the contagious diseases. There are many drugs, such as aspirin, that are often used to give temporary relief from headache.

health

A person is considered healthy when all the parts of his body function properly and there is no reason to think that his life expectancy (the number of years he will probably continue to live) is less than normal. A person who is not sick is generally said to be healthy.

Certain conditions are necessary for good health. These include proper food and care for babies both before and after they are born; proper diet for persons of all ages; and medical and dental care when needed. The right amount of sleep and exercise, proper clothing and good posture are also necessary for good health.

Maintaining good health is an important matter both for the individual and for the community (any group of people living together). You can read about how an individual should take care of himself in the article on HYGIENE. All of the people of a community must work together in certain ways to keep all of its members healthy, because disease spreads from one person to another. The principal ways this is done are sanitation, or keeping everything clean, and education, or teaching individual members of the community to keep themselves healthy by proper hygiene.

SANITATION

Good sanitation results from many things. It is a matter of proper disposal of garbage and sewage, draining swamps, and killing rats, insects and other pests that may spread disease germs. It means making sure that the community's drinking water is pure, and that the food sold in the community is properly inspected so it is fresh and clean and will not cause disease. It means protecting the members of the community against certain contagious diseases by vaccination, inoculation, and regular dental and physical examinations.

DEPARTMENTS OF PUBLIC HEALTH

Every city and state has a Public Health Department, and the United States government has several bureaus in the Department of Health, Education and Welfare, to guard the health of the public. A Public Health Department in a city is in charge of sanitation. It issues licenses to restaurants and grocery stores and can withdraw the licenses if the food they sell is not clean and pure. It inspects the water supply, and issues quarantines and makes other rules when disease occurs, to keep it from spreading.

A State Public Health Department advises the legislature on what laws to make that will help keep the people healthy, and it gives advice and instructions to local Public Health Departments.

In 1946 the United Nations formed the World Health Organization, with headquarters in Geneva, Switzerland, to help all the countries of the world in matters relating to health and hygiene.

Health, Education, and Welfare, Department of

The Department of Health, Education, and Welfare is one of the main divisions of the United States government. It helps the people to keep in good health and to improve their education. It helps take care of the very young and the very old who have no one to take care of them, and those who cannot earn a living because they are sick or crippled. The Department is quite new, having been founded in 1953. It replaced the former Federal Security Agency. Its head is the Secretary of Health, Education, and Welfare, one of the government's most important officials and a member of the President's cabinet. A woman, Oveta Culp Hobby, was the first Secretary.

More than 77,000 people worked in the Department in 1962. The Department also has more than 200 experts stationed abroad to teach foreign people how to keep healthy and to improve their schools and welfare systems. It also trains foreign people in the United States in health, education, and welfare methods.

WHAT EACH SERVICE DOES

The Department is divided into five main services.

The Public Health Service helps the states and other governments to fight disease and to develop good hospitals. It studies the causes of diseases and looks for better ways to fight them.

The Office of Education, founded nearly a hundred years ago, gives information and advice to schools and sees to it that money given to state schools by the Federal government is usefully spent.

The Social Security Administration manages the government's program for paying insurance money to older people. It helps the states in aiding mothers and young children. Its Children's Bureau helps about 200,000 crippled children yearly, and also puts out valuable pamphlets concerning children. Its booklet "Your Child from One to Six" has been very popular.

The Office of Vocational Rehabilitation helps the states in aiding crippled persons. It tries to get jobs for these people, and to get for them good artificial limbs, hearing aids for the deaf, and so on, so they can get along more easily.

The Food and Drug Administration sees to it that only pure food and drugs are sold and that labels on these products tell the truth.

The Department also operates or helps pay for the operation of several institutions. These are: Saint Elizabeth's Hospital in Washington, D.C., for people with mental illnesses; The American Printing House for the Blind, in Louisville, Kentucky; Gallaudet College, also in Washington; and Howard University, in Washington.

hearing

Hearing is the sense with which we receive sounds into the brain and can tell different sounds apart. SOUND is explained in a separate article; it is a kind of wave made by movements in the air and changes in the pressure of the air.

We hear through our ears. Sound waves enter the outer ear (the opening you can see) and travel down a passage called the ear canal until they reach a sheet of body tissue called the eardrum. The eardrum is connected by a chain of bones to the inner ear, or cochlea. Inside the inner ear are thousands of tiny hairs and a thick fluid. Sound waves strike the eardrum and make it vibrate (shake back and forth). The vibration is carried

through the chain of bones to the fluid in the inner ear. The movement of the fluid causes electricity to flow from the tiny hairs through a nerve (the auditory nerve) that leads to the brain.

When a person cannot hear as well as most people do, he is said to be deaf. There are some kinds of deafness that cannot be cured or helped, but many kinds can be helped by devices called *hearing aids.* (See also the articles DEAFNESS and EAR.)

HEARING AIDS

The louder a sound is, the more likely we are to hear it, so the earliest and simplest hearing aids were designed to make more sound waves enter the outer ear. The *ear trumpet* spreads out at one end like a horn. This causes it to collect more sound, which travels through a narrowing tube into the ear. Another hearing aid formerly used had a mouthpiece for the person talking, and a tube leading to the ear of the deaf person. The sound could not spread out, so all of it reached the ear.

All modern hearing aids are electrical. They amplify the sound (make it louder) in much the same way that radios and record-players do.

First the sound is changed into electricity by a kind of microphone made from crystals of Rochelle salt. Such crystals produce electricity whenever they are pressed or twisted. When sound waves strike the crystal in the microphone of a hearing aid, the crystal vibrates. This changes the sound into electricity.

A *diaphragm* (a thin, light piece of metal shaped like a cone) catches the sound waves and transfers their pressure to the crystal. The electricity from the crystal flows through wires to an electronic or vacuum tube, of the kind described in the article on ELECTRONICS, or to a *transistor,* as described later in this article. The tube or transistor increases (amplifies) this electricity by means of a low-voltage storage battery ("A" battery) and a high-voltage ("B") battery of 15 to 45 volts.

The electricity is then sent to a receiver, to be changed into sounds louder than those originally sent out. The receiver consists of a diaphragm with a magnet near one side of it and a coil or wire wound around the magnet. The electricity passes through the coil of wire in the receiver. Changes in the amount of electricity (caused by changes in the amount of sound reaching the microphone) changes the magnetic force of the magnet. These changes cause the diaphragm to vibrate. The vibrating diaphragm creates sound waves that act on the eardrum and result in hearing.

The receiver usually is attached to an eartip, made of a plastic material, that fits into the user's ear. The eartip has a hole in it through which the sound waves can flow.

Another type of receiver sometimes used with hearing aids contains a crystal similar to the one in the microphone. The electricity from the microphone makes this crystal change its shape slightly, and this change in shape causes another diaphragm to vibrate. The vibrations make sound waves. No coil of wire or magnet is needed.

DEVELOPMENT OF THE HEARING AID

One of the chief problems in the manufacture of a hearing aid is to keep it as small as possible. Dr. Ferdinand Alt of Germany is credited with producing the first electrical hearing aid, in 1900. It was a small model of a telephone and could pick up whispers two feet away, but it was too big for a person to wear. Many were used on desks of business executives and in churches.

In 1937, the first wearable vacuum-tube hearing aid was invented. It was about the size of a large folding camera, and was called the Stanleyphone. Hearing aids were gradually reduced in size until one could easily be carried in a man's "vest pocket." The size was further reduced in the transistor-type hearing aid, introduced in 1953. The transistor is a tiny sandwich of three thin slices of germanium, a rare metal. It takes the place

of vacuum tubes and also makes a "B" battery unnecessary. Unlike glass vacuum tubes, transistors cannot be damaged by shock and other accidents. The transistor lasts more than twenty years compared with a little more than one year for a vacuum tube. This cuts the cost of operating a hearing aid from $50 to about $5 a year.

BONE CONDUCTION

The hearing aids so far discussed all have been of the kind that uses air conduction. That is, the sound waves are carried by the air to the eardrums. Another kind of hearing aid uses bone conduction. The diaphragm, held by a headband, rests on the mastoid bone behind the ear. The movements of the diaphragm are transferred to the bony structure of the head. This causes the fluid in the inner ear to move, sending the sound through the auditory nerve to the brain.

heart

The heart is a hollow muscular organ that pumps blood to all the parts of the body. A man's heart is about the size of his fist, and weighs from ten to twelve ounces. A woman's heart weighs about two ounces less. The heart is shaped somewhat like a pear and is located to the left of the middle of the chest, slightly slanted. The widest part is on top and the narrower point—where you can feel it "beat" —is below and to the left.

The heart itself is divided into four sections, or chambers, two of which are called *auricles,* and two *ventricles.* The chambers are not all the same size, for each of them has a different job to do, and some must do harder work than others. The chambers are connected by valves, which keep the blood flowing in one direction. A wall called the *septum* divides the heart into the left and right sections, which are not connected but which operate together.

HOW THE HEART DOES ITS JOB

Hollow tubes called *veins* carry blood that is filled with waste products from the various parts of the body to the heart. The largest of these veins, the *vena cava,* brings the blood into the right auricle. When the right auricle has been filled, the blood enters the right ventricle which pumps it through the *pulmonary arteries* to the lungs. There, waste products (mostly carbon dioxide) are removed and replaced with oxygen. The blood then returns to the heart through *pulmonary veins* that lead into the left auricle. When the left auricle is filled, the blood enters the left ventricle. This is the largest of the four chambers of the heart, with walls three times as thick as any of the others. It provides the power that pumps the blood out through a main outlet, the *aorta,* to the arteries that take it to all parts of the body. This pumping process takes place from 70 to 80 times a minute in an adult, and more often in children. This is called the *pulse rate.*

Although it is made of strong muscles, the heart is a delicately adjusted instrument. If the valves do not work exactly right, blood will leak through and the heart will have to work much harder than

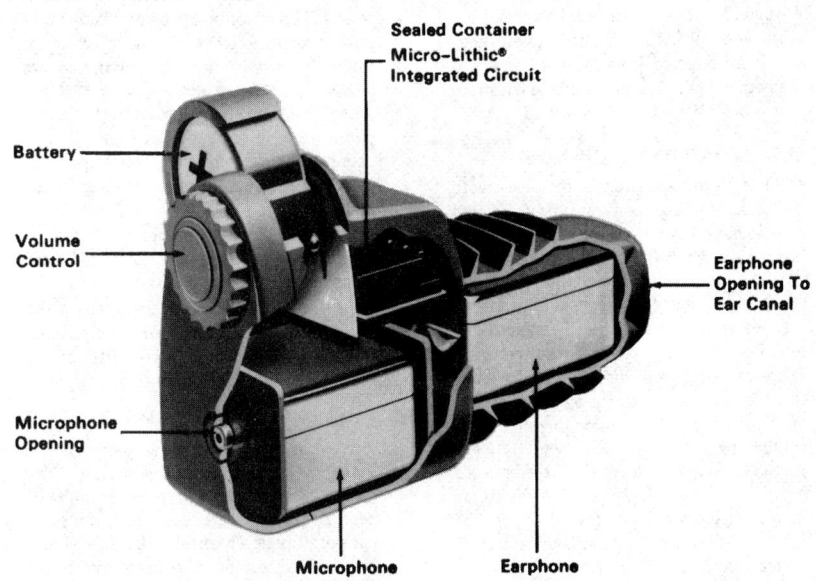

Sealed Container
Micro-Lithic® Integrated Circuit

Battery

Volume Control

Microphone Opening

Earphone Opening To Ear Canal

Microphone   Earphone

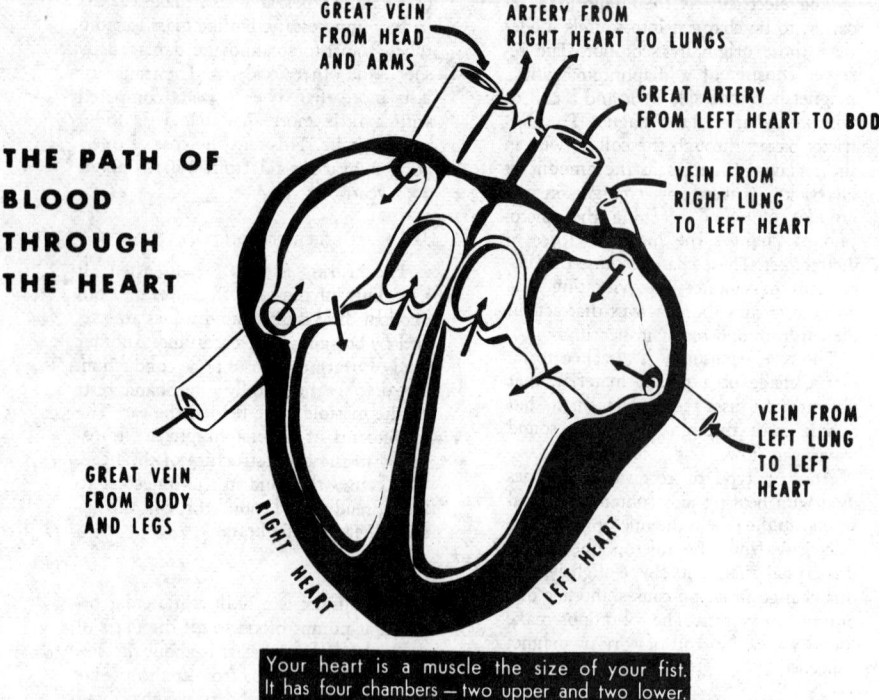

THE PATH OF BLOOD THROUGH THE HEART

GREAT VEIN FROM HEAD AND ARMS

ARTERY FROM RIGHT HEART TO LUNGS

GREAT ARTERY FROM LEFT HEART TO BOD

VEIN FROM RIGHT LUNG TO LEFT HEART

VEIN FROM LEFT LUNG TO LEFT HEART

GREAT VEIN FROM BODY AND LEGS

RIGHT HEART

LEFT HEART

Your heart is a muscle the size of your fist. It has four chambers—two upper and two lower.

it should. This may weaken it. Many children who have had rheumatic fever suffer from weakened heart valves. Proper care of the heart means following the usual rules of good health—getting enough rest and exercise, and taking care of colds.

HEART DISEASE

The heart is very strong, but if it becomes diseased so that it cannot do its work, a person dies. More people in the United States die of heart disease than from any other cause, but many people with heart disease live happy and useful lives.

There are many different kinds of heart disease. Two common types are hypertension and rheumatic heart disease, which comes from rheumatic fever. (There are separate articles about HYPERTENSION and RHEUMATIC FEVER.) The third most important kind is called *coronary* heart disease.

Coronary heart disease usually affects people over 40 years of age, and women do not get it as often as men. The heart must receive blood through the coronary arteries. (Arteries are hollow tubes.) As a person grows older the coronary arteries sometimes harden and the hollow space inside them becomes narrower. When this occurs the heart cannot easily pump the blood through the arteries. The arteries may grow so narrow that a clot of blood may form in the tube, preventing the blood from reaching the heart. If the blood supply is cut off, even for a short time, part of the heart muscle may die and a scar will form.

A person who develops coronary heart disease may have a severe pain in his chest. This is known as *angina pectoris*. The person cannot breathe easily. This is because the heart has not received oxygen which is brought to it in the blood.

Carditis is a disease in which the heart becomes inflamed or infected. The disease may be caused by bacteria ("germs"). *Endocarditis*, an infection of the inner lining of the heart, was once among the

most dangerous of all diseases and usually caused death, but the new "wonder drugs" (penicillin and other antibiotics) can now be used to control the bacteria and people with endocarditis usually get well.

Until recently doctors had never found safe ways to perform operations on the heart. Now they have many ways of operating on it. One development is the artificial heart. This is a device that pumps blood as the heart does. The patient is kept alive by an artificial heart while the doctor operates on his real heart. Doctors have machines that can tell whether a heart is working properly or whether it is diseased; see the article on ELECTROCARDIOGRAPH. They have medicines that keep the blood from clotting in a coronary artery, and others that help the heart to work faster, or to slow down. They have medicines that can make the arteries grow wider. The American Heart Association and the United States government spend millions of dollars on research so that doctors and scientists can learn more and more about heart diseases.

SYMBOLISM OF THE HEART

Though the workings of the heart were not understood until about 350 years ago, people have known its importance to the body for a much longer time. They knew that the heart was necessary for life, and they also believed that it was the seat of the emotions, or feelings. The emotions of love were supposed to come from the heart, and so people came to use the word heart as another word for love and liking and sympathy. The shape of the heart came to be a symbol of love, which means it stood for love just as a red traffic light stands for "stop." On St. Valentine's Day people still send Valentine cards in the form of hearts, and they still use terms of endearment such as "sweetheart." The quality of bravery was also thought to come from a person's heart, and some people still say "He has great heart," meaning "He has great courage."

hearts

Hearts is a popular card game, and a very easy one to play. It is good for any number of players from three up to seven or eight, but most people consider it best for four players. A regular pack of playing cards is used, and all of them are dealt out, one at a time. The player at the left of the dealer leads a card, and each player after him plays a card. He must follow suit (play a card of the suit led) if he can, but if he cannot follow suit he may play any card he has. The cards rank normally (ace is high, then king, queen, jack, ten, nine, and so on). When everyone has played a card, the player of the highest card of the suit led takes in the cards (the *trick*) and leads to the next trick. The object is not to win hearts. When all the cards have been played, each player loses 1 point for each card of the heart suit that he took in. In most games, the player who took the queen of spades loses 13 points for it. Some play with a "bonus card," which is usually either the jack of diamonds or the ten of diamonds. The player who takes in this card scores 10 points plus. If a player wins all thirteen hearts plus the queen of spades, instead of having them charged against him they count for him and he scores plus 26. At the end of a long game everyone will have a "minus" score, so the lowest score wins.

heat

Everyone has felt heat from the sun, from a radiator or fireplace, and from hot water in a bathtub. You can feel heat when you rub your hands together. You feel heat inside you when you are sick and have a fever.

Heat is caused by fast-moving particles, called molecules, striking against each other. As water becomes warmer, its molecules move around with greater speed. They strike one another and bounce around in the water. When the molecules reach a point where they cannot move any faster, they begin to knock each other out of the water into the air, where they become steam. This is called the boiling point. The motion of heated molecules pushes them farther and farther apart. Therefore, when a thing is heated, it grows larger. This is called *expansion*. Heat causes many things to expand. A gas expands when it is heated. A highway will expand during a hot day and sometimes you will even see bumps forming in the road.

When a gas is heated in a container, its molecules push against the sides. This increases the pressure of the gas. In the same way, an increase in pressure on the gas will make the molecules strike each other with more force. This will increase the heat and the temperature of the gas.

HEAT AND TEMPERATURE

Heat is not the same as temperature. Two things with the same temperature do not always have the same amount of heat. A glass of water may have the same temperature as a bathtub filled with water but it has less heat, because there are fewer molecules in the glass of water. The amount of heat depends on the number of molecules as well as on how fast they are moving.

Heat is measured in calories. (There is a separate article on the CALORIE.) It is also measured in British Thermal Units, abbreviated B.T.U. *Thermal* means "of heat." One B.T.U. is the amount of heat that is needed to raise the temperature of a pound of water one degree Fahrenheit.

Because the molecules of a hot body are moving faster than those of a cooler one, heat always moves from a body with a high temperature to one with a lower temperature. The molecules of the hot body strike those of the cooler one with a greater force and so speed them up. This slows down the faster molecules, raising the temperature of the cooler body and lowering the temperature of the hotter one. If you dip a hot piece of metal into a cold glass of water, heat will travel from the metal to the water, until their temperatures are about the same.

HEAT AND PRESSURE

An increase in pressure increases the boiling temperature, while a decrease in pressure lowers the boiling temperature. For this reason, if you try to heat water in a place where the pressure is low, such as on top of a mountain, you will find that the water boils at a lower temperature than at sea level. The additional pressure at sea level forces the molecules of water to strike each other more quickly than when the water is at a lower pressure on the mountain top. Pressure cookers are often used to cook food faster. The pressure cooker is a thick metal pot with a top that can be screwed on tight. This increases the pressure inside the pot so that the food in it can cook faster. A safety valve on the top prevents the pressure from becoming too great.

Heat has many uses. It is used to keep you warm and comfortable. It is used to cook your food. It is used in steam and gas engines to run motors and do work. It is important in helping to grow plants, fruits and vegetables.

HEAT EXHAUSTION

Heat exhaustion, or heat prostration, is an illness caused by too much exposure to heat. The symptoms are heavy perspiration, paleness, dizziness, and a feeling of being sick to the stomach. A person who does heavy outdoor work on a hot day, without being careful to protect his head and body against the sun rays, is likely to suffer heat exhaustion. But heat exhaustion also can strike a person working in a hot boiler room, or in front of an open furnace.

When a person is struck by heat exhaustion, a doctor should be called at once. Then the victim should be moved to fresh, cooler air, and stretched on the ground face down, with his head lower than his body. Keep his body warm, and give him tea or coffee to replace the liquid he has lost through perspiring. Then give him half a glass of water with half a teaspoonful of table salt in it, to replace the body salt lost through perspiration.

heat exhaustion, see HEAT.

Heath, Edward

Edward Richard George Heath served as Great Britain's 47th Prime Minister from June, 1970 to March, 1974.

Born in Kent in 1916, Heath was always a better-than-average student in the schools there. Later, he entered Balliol College at Oxford on a music scholarship and became a church organist. In World War II, he rose to lieutenant colonel in the Royal Artillery, afterward becoming a writer and a banker before being elected to Parliament. He rose rapidly thereafter, becoming, in turn, Minister of Labour, President of the Board of Trade, and Lord Privy Seal. In 1970, when political observers believed that HAROLD WILSON of the Labour Party would become the first Prime Minister to win an election three times in a row, Edward Heath won instead. In 1974, Heath's Conservative Party lost the election to the Labour Party and Wilson again became the Prime Minister.

heating

Heating is the method by which the inside air of houses and other buildings is kept warmer than the outside air. A single room can be warmed by a fire in a stove or fireplace, but most buildings in the United States and Canada have central heating. This means that the heat is produced in only one part of the building, for example, by a furnace in the cellar, and is then carried by pipes or by tubes called *ducts* to the different rooms.

In most countries, very few houses have central heating. The houses of rich people in ancient Rome often had central heating, but the people of Europe forgot how to build houses that way and even the palaces of kings and castles or mansions of noblemen were heated only by open fireplaces.

Heating is actually a matter of moving or transferring heat from one place to another. This is done in various ways.

HEATING BY CONDUCTION

One of the simplest and most common ways of transferring heat is by conduction. If you place a silver spoon in a hot cup of coffee, the handle of the spoon will soon get hot. The heat will be conducted from the bottom of the spoon in the hot coffee, along the handle to the top. When one part of the spoon gets hot, it heats the part of the spoon next to it. Silver, aluminum and copper are the best conductors of heat. Poor conductors of heat are called insulators. Liquids such as water and gases such as the air are poor conductors of heat.

Aluminum pots and pans are used for cooking because aluminum is a good conductor. The heat from the flame on the stove heats the bottom of the pan. The pan conducts this heat to the food. Aluminum is such a good conductor of heat that if you wrap some paper around an aluminum bar and hold it over a flame, the heat will be conducted so rapidly from the paper to the aluminum that the paper will not catch fire. Both the paper and the aluminum will have the same temperature. But if you touch them both, you will find that the aluminum feels hotter. The aluminum conducts heat more rapidly to your hand than the paper does.

While heating by conduction is a useful process, this method is not used to heat the insides of buildings.

HEATING BY CONVECTION

The most important way of heating is by convection. If you put a pan of water over a flame, the heat from the pan will be conducted to the water. The water at the bottom will be heated first. When it is heated, it begins to rise to the top of the pan. If you look closely, you will see bubbles of water actually rising to the top. The warm water is then replaced by the heavier cold water, which flows to the bottom and is heated until it begins to rise. This flow is called a *convection current*. In this way all the water in the pan is soon heated.

Most houses are ventilated and heated by means of convection currents of air. The air over a heater or radiator will be heated first. It will rise and be replaced by colder air until that is heated. After the warm air has reached the ceiling it will spread out over the room until it has cooled. Then it will sink downward again to be heated once more at floor level.

The air in your house can be heated in many different ways. One way is by a hot-air furnace. Cold outdoor air, mixed with cool air returned from the floor of each room, flows into a pipe and is circulated in a separate enclosed space around a *firebox* in which coal or some other fuel is burning. This heated air then rises or is blown out by a fan through pipes at the top of the furnace. From there it is spread through the house by means of ducts. It comes out in each room through an opening called a *register*.

In a hot-water heating system, water is heated in a boiler above a firebox enclosed in a furnace. The water is circulated, by convection or by a pump, through pipes that carry it to radiators in the rooms of the house. The room air is then heated by the convection currents set up by the heat from the radiator. When the water has passed through all the radiators and has given up most of its heat to the rooms, it returns to the boiler to be reheated.

In steam heating systems, the water is heated in the boiler until it changes into steam. The pressure from the steam forces it up into the pipes to the radiators. In the radiators, the steam gives up its heat to the room air. The steam then changes back to water and returns to the boiler.

The air in your home may also be heated by the heat from a fireplace. However, most of the heat will go up the chimney unless suitable arrangements are made for forcing it out into the room. For this purpose, a grill may be installed at the bottom and the top of the fireplace. Cold air enters at the bottom and is heated in the fireplace, while warm air is blown out through the top by a circulating fan.

HEATING BY RADIATION

We have spoken of radiators and how they may be used with different types of heaters to warm the air in a room. This is done by heat radiation. The heat is transferred from the radiator to the room by means of waves that travel at a rate of 186,000 miles per second. These waves are very similar to waves of light from the sun, and radio waves that you hear on your radio. The heat from the sun is radiated to the earth, where the soil absorbs it. Convection currents are set up as

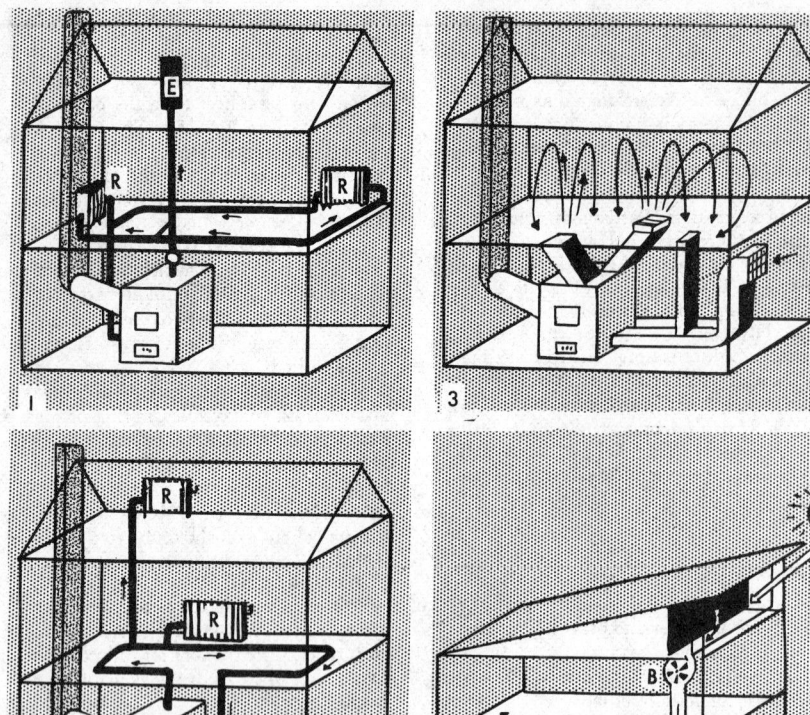

Different kinds of heating systems are used in modern homes. The chief ones are: 1. Hot-water heating sends hot water through the radiators (R). The expansion tank (E) keeps the water from boiling away. 2. Steam heating sends steam to the radiators; it returns as it cools. 3. Forced hot-air heating blows air from the furnace through the house. 4. Solar heating uses a black sheet to absorb the heat of the sun. The heat in the sheet is blown (B) to blocks of Glauber's salt, which melt. When they cool in the evening they release heat, which then enters the home. Daytime heat is direct from the sun.

the ground is heated, and the air that was next to the earth circulates so as to warm the air surrounding the earth much the same as a room is heated by a radiator.

Most of the heat rays from the sun cannot be seen by the eye. They do not affect the nerves of the eye as light rays do. For the same reason, the heat rays from a radiator cannot be seen, but you can easily feel them by placing your hand above the radiator.

ELECTRIC HEATERS

A single room, especially a small room, often is heated by an electric heater. Electric heating of a room is an example of heating by radiation similar to the way in which the sun heats the earth. Electric heaters are more expensive to operate than heaters that burn coal, oil, or gas, but they are cleaner and easier to work. They use a large amount of electricity, sometimes as much as 2,000 watts. (The light bulbs in your home rarely use more than 100 watts.) An electric heater has a long coil of wire wrapped around a fire-resistant asbestos tube. The coil is made of a metal called *nichrome,* in which there are nickel, iron, and chromium. Nichrome is a poor conductor of electricity, which means that electricity cannot flow through it easily. As large amounts of electricity try to flow through it, the friction between the electricity and the wire makes the wire grow red-hot. In some electric heaters there is a polished sheet of metal, called a reflector, behind the coils. When the nichrome gets red-hot,

waves of heat from the coil strike the reflector and radiate into the room, making it warm. In other electric heaters, an electric fan behind the coil blows the heat into the room.

Electric blankets and heating pads have coils of nichrome inside them. The coils heat an asbestos lining, which heats the woolen blanket or pad.

RADIANT HEAT

Many homes are now being heated by what is called *radiant heat.* The heat is furnished by hot water flowing through water pipes installed in the walls, floors, or ceilings. The pipes heat up the walls, floors, or ceilings, which radiate the heat to people and things in the room.

SOLAR HEATING

Another new form of heating is *solar heating,* in which the heat from the sun is used directly. A private house may be built with a large glass window, called a picture window, on the south side, and a large eave or section of the roof that sticks out over the window. In the winter the sun enters the window and warms the house. In the summer, when the sun is higher, the eave keeps it out of the house.

Another way of solar heating is to paint the top part of the picture windows black, so as to absorb some of the sun's heat. A black object will absorb more heat than a white or light-colored object, which explains why white clothes are often worn in hot climates. The heat absorbed by the top of the window is blown

down through a pipe to some blocks of Glauber's salt underneath the house. This melts the salt. In the evening, when the house begins to cool off, the salt begins to harden again. The heat given off by the salt as it hardens is then blown into the house by a blower, keeping the inside air warm in the evening.

heaven and hell

Heaven is the name for the place where good persons are rewarded after they die; hell is the name for the place where bad persons are punished. People may usually think of heaven as being "in the sky" and hell "below the earth," but in the Christian religion there is no exact place where heaven or hell is known or supposed to be.

Students of the Bible find evidence that heaven is not on earth. Jesus was taken "up" (away from earth) and so was the prophet Elijah in the Old Testament. The idea that hell is below the earth may come from old religions, such as the ancient Greek idea of HADES, about which there is a separate article.

Many religions besides Christianity have included the idea of a heaven. The American Indians called it a "Happy Hunting Ground." Mohammedans believe in seven heavens, through which the soul advances, one by one, to the Seventh Heaven where he sees God.

Hebe

Hebe was the goddess of youth in Greek mythology, the stories the ancient Greeks told about their gods and goddesses. Hebe was a lovely young goddess, the daughter of Zeus, the king of the gods, and Hera, his queen. Some stories said that Hebe could make old people young again. Hebe was the handmaiden, or helper, of the gods. At meals she filled their cups with nectar, which was the drink of the gods. She helped the god of war to put on his armor, and she helped her mother Hera to harness her horses to her chariot. When the great hero Heracles was made a god, Hebe married him. The Roman name for Hebe was *Juventas,* which means "youth" in Latin.

Hebrew

Hebrew is the language in which most of the Old Testament, in the Bible, was written. It was the language of the Jewish people after they left Egypt, where they had been slaves, and settled in the Land of Canaan, part of Palestine, on the eastern shore of the Mediterranean Sea. A somewhat different form of Hebrew is the language of the modern country of Israel.

The Hebrew language is one of the Semitic languages. These languages are spoken by Semitic peoples (those who trace their origin to Shem, one of the sons of Noah). The Arabs are Semites, and Arabic is one of the Semitic languages. Hebrew is one of the Canaanite forms of the Semitic languages.

The Hebrew alphabet was one of the alphabets from which the modern English alphabet was developed. In Hebrew, writing is read from right to left, and not from left to right as in English. The original Hebrew alphabet did not have any vowels (the letters A, E, I, O, U) but they

were added about a thousand years ago by Jewish scholars called Masorites. Hebrew written in this style is called Masoretic.

The greatest Hebrew literature of early times was the Old Testament. The Jewish rabbis, or teachers, later produced great writings in Aramaic, their spoken language. The Talmud, which is Jewish religious literature, is written in Aramaic. In recent years, there has been much Hebrew literature written in Israel.

Hebrews, Epistle to the, a book of the New Testament: see BIBLE.

Hebrides

The Hebrides are a group of many islands in the Atlantic Ocean. They are near the western coast of Scotland, and are part of Scotland. There are about five hundred of these islands, and they have an area of about three thousand square miles. About eighty thousand people live on the islands. The Hebrides are sometimes called the Western Islands.

Some of the islands are very small, and almost all the people live on only about a hundred of the islands. The people fish off the rocky coasts, and many of them are weavers who make a fine woolen tweed cloth, called Harris tweed, that is famous all over the world. Some of the people are farmers, and some raise cattle. Many people go to the Hebrides for vacations.

Long ago the people of the Hebrides spoke the language called GAELIC, about which there is a separate article. Some of them still speak this language.

Hecate

Hecate was a character in Greek mythology, the stories the ancient Greeks told about their gods and goddesses. Hecate was a goddess of the underworld, which was the Greek version of hell, and she ruled over the spirits of the dead, who lived there. She was the goddess of magic. Witches and sorcerers were believed to be taught by Hecate. At night, Hecate sent out demons and spirits, and sometimes she wandered about the world with them, haunting crossroads and graves. With Hecate went her dogs, and the Greeks thought that dogs howled at night when Hecate came near.

Hector

Hector is a character in the story of the TROJAN WAR, about which there is a separate article. The story is told in the *Iliad,* the famous poem of the Greek poet Homer. Hector was the eldest son of Priam, king of Troy, and Hecuba, his queen. Hector was the leader of the Trojan army, and he was the bravest and greatest of all the Trojans. It was said that Troy could not be defeated so long as Hector was alive. For ten years the war went on. Hector fought many great battles and killed many of the enemy Greeks, but finally he was killed by the great Greek hero Achilles. Achilles tied the body of Hector to his chariot, and dragged it behind him. Priam had to plead with Achilles and give him many gifts before Achilles would give up the body. Not long after, Troy was defeated.

hedgehog

The hedgehog is a small animal that lives in the woods of Europe, Africa, and Asia. There are no hedgehogs in the Americas or Australia. Because of the sharp stiff spines all over its back, the hedgehog looks a bit like a small porcupine, but these two animals are not related at all. Hedgehogs are up to 10 inches long, have small eyes, and hardly any tail. They have short legs, but are good climbers that can even get over wire net fences. When a hedgehog is attacked by another animal, it rolls itself into a ball so that the prickly spines stick out on all sides. Another unusual thing about the hedgehog is its great immunity to snake poison, which enables it to kill and eat many dangerous snakes. Its diet of insects, mice, and reptiles makes the hedgehog useful to farmers; on the other hand, its fondness for bird eggs makes it a pest in wildlife refuges. In countries where winters are cold, hedgehogs hibernate (go to sleep) until spring.

hegira

Hegira, or *hejira,* is from the Arabic and means departure, or flight. The word is particularly applied to the flight of the great religious leader, Mohammed, from the city of Mecca. Mecca was the holy city of the Arabian religion; when Mohammed began to oppose this religion, and to preach a new religion, the officials of the city opposed him. He was forced to leave Mecca and flee to another place, called Medina. His hegira, or flight, took place in our year 622. The Mohammedan calendar calls this the year 1.

Heifetz, Jascha

Jascha Heifetz, one of the world's greatest violinists, was born in Russia in 1901. Most children are still learning how to talk at the age of 3, but little Jascha was already playing the violin at that age.

Heifetz went to music school when he was 4, and at the age of 7 he was giving concerts. He traveled all through Europe, and the largest symphony orchestras were proud to have him give concerts with them. When he was 16 years old, Heifetz moved to New York, but he continued to travel all over the world, giving concerts everywhere.

Heine, Heinrich

Heinrich Heine was a German poet and newspaper writer. He was born in 1797 and studied law for several years. His first book was called *Poems.* His second book, *Book of Songs,* made him famous. The last part of his life was spent in Paris, where he wrote poems and newspaper articles. Heine was an invalid during the last eight years of his life; but he wrote his best poems at that time. Heine wrote many love poems and poems about the sea. Some of his writings were for a woman named Elise von Krientz, whom he loved very much. He died in 1856.

Helen of Troy

Helen of Troy was a character in Greek mythology, the stories that the ancient Greeks told about their gods and goddesses. She was supposed to be the most beautiful woman in the world. Helen married a Greek prince named Menelaus. She was loved by all the men because of her great beauty. Another prince, named Paris, stole her from Menelaus. Paris was a Trojan; that is, he belonged to the people who lived in the ancient city of Troy. Paris took Helen to Troy with him. An army of Greeks set out for Troy to rescue her. This started the Trojan War, the story of which is told in the *Iliad,* one of the greatest poems in Greek literature. The Greeks won the war, and the city of Troy was destroyed. Helen was rescued and returned home to her husband.

Helena

Helena is the capital of Montana. It is in Prickly Pear Valley, near the Missouri River. On either side of the valley rise the peaks of the Rocky Mountains.

About 22,000 people live in Helena. Many of them are miners because the land around the city is rich with gold, silver, and other valuable minerals. Some of the people are farmers, and they grow potatoes and grain, and raise fine cattle. There are many factories in Helena, which manufacture concrete, bricks, and machinery. There is a large veterans' hospital in Helena, and Carroll College, a school for men, is there.

Helena was founded about a hundred years ago by gold miners. They had been looking for gold in a stream, and had decided there was none to be found there. Then they took a "last chance" and found gold in the stream. They named the place Last Chance Gulch, and this is the spot where the city of Helena now stands. Helena became the capital of Montana in 1894, but even before Montana was a state, Helena was the capital of Montana Territory for twenty years. There have been some serious earthquakes in Helena, and in 1935 a very severe earthquake destroyed millions of dollars' worth of property, and many people lost their lives.

HELENA, MONTANA. Population (1970 census) 22,730. Capital of Montana. County seat of Lewis and Clark County. Settled in 1864.

Helgoland

Helgoland is a small island and popular seaside resort in the North Sea, about twenty-five miles away from the coast of Germany. It belongs to West Germany. The British owned it from 1807 until 1890, when the Germans took it over and built fortifications on it. In August 1914, less than a month after the beginning of World War I, the British won a naval battle near Helgoland and sank three German cruisers. The Allies captured Helgoland in May 1945, at the end of World War II, but it was returned to Germany in 1952. All buildings on the island were destroyed by bombs during the war, but they have since been completely rebuilt.

helicopter

A helicopter is an airplane that has no wings and no front propeller but instead has two propellers on top of the plane. The top propellers ("rotors") turn just like the propeller on most airplanes, except that instead of moving the plane forward, they lift it up into the air. Be-

Official U.S. Navy Photo

Helicopters can take off from a destroyer's deck, search out enemy submarines, and then direct the mother ship straight to her quarry. This is important in coastal defense.

cause of this, a helicopter can take off from the ground by going almost straight up into the air and can land by coming almost straight down. Unlike an airplane, it can fly backward as well as forward.

A helicopter can also stand still in midair, or come down very close to land or water and remain hovering in the air. This makes it useful for getting into places where most airplanes cannot land, as in jungles and on mountains. Helicopters are used for rescue operations, for fighting fires, and for landing supplies to people stranded in jungles, on mountain tops, on the water, and in other places that are hard to reach by other airplanes. Helicopters are used by the United States Coast Guard, by Forest Rangers, by police departments of most large cities, and by the armed services of the United States and other countries.

The idea of the helicopter was first used by the ancient Chinese, who made tops with feathers sticking out at the sides. When the wind blew against these tops, they would spin. Leonardo da Vinci, an Italian scientist, made models of helicopters about five hundred years ago. In 1921, Juan de la Cierva, a Spanish inventor, made the first *Autogyro* or *gyroplane*. The Autogyro looked like most airplanes except that it had another propeller on top. When the Autogyro got off the ground, the air blew against the top propeller and turned it as it does a windmill. This made the plane go higher into the air. The Autogyro could not take off from the ground by going straight up. It had to use a runway.

The first successful helicopter was made in Germany in 1936. The next year Igor Sikorsky, an American engineer born in Russia, made the first of many helicopters that he has designed. He started a company to manufacture helicopters, and soon he became known as the "father of the helicopter."

There are many kinds of helicopters. One kind has a rotor near the front and another near the back. Another kind has two rotors, one above the other, which turn in opposite directions. When the pilot wants to move this kind of helicop-

ter forward, he tilts the rotor blades forward. When he wants to move it backward, he tilts the blades backward.

heliograph

The heliograph is a signaling instrument that uses the sun's rays to flash signals over long distances.

Signals are sent by heliograph on a bright day by holding a mirror so the sun shines on it. When the mirror is covered, the flash is blocked. When the mirror is uncovered, the flash can be seen. The Morse code can be used with a long flash for dash and a short flash for dot.

heliotrope

Heliotrope is a flowering herb that is important for its fragrance. Its scent is used in perfumes and in many other beauty preparations. The plant is a small shrub, from which blue, violet or white flowers grow in small sprays at the end of forked stems. There are more than two hundred kinds of heliotrope. It grows in Europe, in South America, particularly Peru, and in the southern part of the United States. The Peruvian heliotrope is often cultivated in Europe and the United States.

helium

Helium is a gas. It is the second-lightest gas known (hydrogen being the lightest) and is very useful for balloons and blimps. Helium was first discovered in the sun. An English scientist named Norman Lockyer was examining the sun through a spectroscope, which is an instrument that shows a band of colored lines called a *spectrum*. Every chemical element has a pattern of lines all its own, and when Lockyer saw a new pattern of lines he knew he had found a new element.

Helium is very valuable because it will not burn or explode. The lightest gas known is hydrogen, but when hydrogen mixes with air it becomes explosive and is dangerous. Many balloons and dirigibles were filled with hydrogen, but they exploded and burned so often that people became afraid to use them. Helium will not explode or burn because it is chemi-

cally inert. This means that it will not form compounds with other chemicals. To burn or explode, a chemical must form a compound.

Helium is more expensive than hydrogen, but because of its safety it is more often used. It is found in natural gas wells, and it also can be made by heating a chemical called cleveite. The United States owns almost all of the world's supply of natural helium.

hell, see HEAVEN.

helmet

A helmet is a hat that is used to protect the head, and sometimes the neck and face. Metal helmets have been used by soldiers since the days of ancient Greece. During the Dark Ages, about 1,000 years ago, the usual kind of helmet was a round pot that protected the head and neck of the man wearing it. Sometimes a flat piece of metal was attached to the front of the helmet, to protect the man's nose. Gradually helmets became more elaborate, and some were made of bronze or gold.

Helmets of iron were made by expert armorers, who shaped them to fit the head exactly. A piece of metal called a visor covered the soldier's face. It was attached to the rest of the helmet by a hinge, and could be lifted over the helmet when the soldier was not actually in battle. It is said that the custom of saluting in the army comes from the habit of raising the right hand to lift the visor. This action showed that a man was being peaceful. About 250 years ago, soldiers stopped wearing helmets because they did not give much protection from bullets. But by the time of World War I all the troops had begun using steel helmets. A steel helmet will not stop a rifle bullet, but it will give protection from fragments of artillery shells. Until 1942, the United States Army used the same kind of flat helmets as the British, but then it changed to a deeper type of helmet that protected the neck as well as the head. Metal helmets are also worn by firemen and builders, to protect themselves from falling bricks and timber.

Heloise, a famous French woman, who lived about nine hundred years ago. The love of Heloise and Abelard is one of the great romantic stories of all time: see the article on ABELARD.

Helsinki

Helsinki is the capital and largest city of Finland. Helsinki is a peninsula (surrounded on three sides by water) on the Gulf of Finland. It is a very important port, but sometimes during the winter the water freezes so that ships cannot enter or leave the harbor. More than 529,000 people live in the busy city of Helsinki. Many work in shipyards, and in factories where they make paper, cloth, and machinery. Helsinki has the largest porcelain and ceramic factories in Europe. All these products are shipped to many parts of Finland and to other countries.

Helsinki is a very beautiful and extremely modern city. Many of the fine buildings are made out of a special light-colored granite rock that comes from the land near the city. The buildings look so clean and shining that Helsinki has the nickname "White City of the North."

There is an excellent university at Helsinki, and the railroad station is considered one of the most beautiful in the world. The city has a magnificent stadium that was used for the great Olympic games (the athletic contests in which many countries compete) in 1952.

Helsinki was founded by King Gustavus I of Sweden in 1550. About 150 years ago it was made the capital of Finland. Until rather recently the city was known in the United States by its Swedish name, Helsingfors. Helsinki was bombed during the war between Finland and Russia in 1939 and 1940, and also during World War II, but very little damage was done to this beautiful city.

HELSINKI, FINLAND. Population (1973 estimate) 529,090. Capital of Finland. Founded in 1550.

Hemans, Felicia

Felicia Dorothea Hemans was an English poet who is best known for her poem "Casabianca," which begins with the famous line, "The boy stood on the burning deck." She was born in Liverpool in 1794, and she began to write poems when she was a young girl. Some of them were published when Felicia was only 15 years old. When she was 18, she married Captain Alfred Hemans, but they were not happy together, and after a few years they separated. Felicia Hemans wrote many tender poems about love and courage, and many of them were quite popular. Felicia Hemans died in 1836.

hematite

Hematite is a mineral rock that is the most abundant source of iron. Large deposits of hematite are found throughout the world. The greatest deposits were found in the Lake Superior region of North America, around the states of Michigan and Minnesota in the United States. Hematite is bright red in color. So great is the coloring power of hematite that a small amount of it would redden a whole rock bed. There is also a hematite that is colored black, and known as *specular hematite*. Jewelers use this kind to make stones for rings or beads for black necklaces.

Hemingway, Ernest

Ernest Hemingway was a great American novelist and short story writer. Many people consider him the best writer in English of his time. Hemingway's work has influenced many other writers.

Charles Scribner's Sons Photo by Helen Breaker

Hemingway was born in Oak Park, Illinois, in 1898. His life was a very exciting one, and he used many of the adventures of his own life in his books. He was wounded in World War I, in which he served as an ambulance driver in the Italian Army. *A Farewell to Arms*, which most people consider his greatest novel, is a story about the war. After the war Hemingway continued to live in Europe. His first successful novel, *The Sun Also Rises*, published in 1926, tells about a group of Americans who are living in Europe. This is one of the several stories in which Hemingway discusses bullfighting, a sport that has always interested him. In 1937 and 1938 Hemingway was in Spain, where he covered the Spanish Civil War as a newspaper correspondent. From his experiences in Spain he got the material for another novel, *For Whom the Bell Tolls*. During World War II Hemingway was a newspaper correspondent in Europe, and in 1950 he published *Across the River and Into the Trees*, in which the main character is a colonel who fought in that war.

Hemingway always led an active life and did a great deal of hunting and fishing. In 1953 he received the Pulitzer Prize for his novel *The Old Man and the Sea*. This book describes the struggles of an old fisherman as he tries to catch a huge game fish. Hemingway spent much of his time after World War II in Africa and Cuba, where he owned a home. In 1954 a plane in which he was flying crashed in the jungles of Africa, and the whole world feared he was dead. He was not badly hurt, however, and continued to write and travel. In 1954 he received the Nobel Prize. He died in 1961.

hemisphere

A hemisphere is half a sphere. A sphere is a ball; the earth is called a sphere, because it is shaped like a ball. We use the word hemisphere to mean half of the earth, as though it were cut in half by a knife passing through its exact center.

In geography, we speak most often of the Western Hemisphere and the Eastern Hemisphere. The Western Hemisphere is the half of the earth whose surface includes North and South America. The United States and Canada are part of this Western Hemisphere, as are Mexico, Central America, South America, and all the islands near them. The Eastern Hemisphere includes Asia, Africa, Australia, and of course Europe (which is really part of the great land mass of Asia).

Astronomers speak more often of the Northern Hemisphere and the Southern Hemisphere. These two hemispheres would be formed if the earth were cut in half at the equator. The stars that can be seen in the sky are different in the Northern Hemisphere and the Southern Hemisphere. You may see the difference in the pictures that go with the article on CONSTELLATION.

hemlock

The hemlock is a tree that grows in Asia and North America. It is related to the pine tree, and has cones and needlelike leaves. It is sometimes called the hemlock spruce and it looks very much like some spruce trees. The tree has small leaves and small cones. It has a reddish bark.

The hemlock in the western part of the United States often grows to be a hundred feet high. The wood from this tree is used a great deal in building. The hemlock found in the southern part of the United States is smaller and is grown because it is so pretty.

There is also a shrub called hemlock. Its leaves resemble those of the hemlock tree; its root resembles a parsnip. This shrub grows throughout Europe and parts of Asia. It has been cultivated in North and South America because it has value as a medicine. All parts of this plant, including its roots, are poisonous. In ancient Greece, criminals condemned to death were often made to drink the juice of the hemlock. The great Greek philosopher Socrates was forced to commit suicide by drinking hemlock.

hemoglobin, a substance in the red corpuscles of the blood that carries oxygen from the lungs to the rest of the body: see the article on BLOOD.

hemorrhage

Bleeding in any part of the body is called hemorrhage. There are many different kinds. When an artery, which carries fresh blood from the heart, is cut, the blood is bright red in color and comes out in spurts. If the injury is in a vein, the blood is darker red and flows out evenly.

Bleeding also may occur from the body's openings or into the lungs, stomach, or other organs. Bleeding from a small cut will usually stop after a short while when the blood begins to harden or clot. But severe hemorrhage will bring on dizziness, weak and rapid breathing, and paleness. If serious bleeding is not stopped, it is possible for the victim to bleed to death.

A cerebral hemorrhage is the breaking of one of the small, delicate arteries next to the brain. Blood then escapes into the brain and damages it, causing what is called apoplexy, or "stroke." A stroke victim loses consciousness and, if he recovers, often suffers from paralysis of part of the body or a defect in his speech. Cerebral hemorrhages occur most often in men over forty who are suffering from hardening of the arteries.

hemp

Hemp is a plant that is important for its fiber, a slender, threadlike part of the plant. The fiber of hemp is used to make a kind of twine or rope that is itself sometimes called hemp. The fiber of the hemp must be taken from the stalk of the plant.

The hemp stalk grows to be three to eighteen feet high. The stalks are cut down and stripped of all leaves, roots, and tops. They are allowed to lie on the ground to be soaked by dew and rain, for this helps to separate the fiber from other woody substances of the stalk. Then the stalks are dried in the sun for a few days before they are taken to a mill, where the fibers are stripped clean of surrounding woody tissues.

Hemp was first used in China and India more than two thousand years ago, but its principal use there was for a drug it contains.

USES OF HEMP

The hemp plant was introduced into Europe about the time of Jesus, and in the Middle Ages it was grown in France, where its seed was used for food. The United States, Chile and many European countries cultivate hemp for its fiber. The fiber is coarse and dark and cannot easily be bleached. It is used for rope, coarse twine, sail cloth, and all other materials where strength and long wear are more important than appearance. The drug from Indian hemp, called *hashish*, is a strong narcotic. The hemp seeds provide

a valuable oil used in soap, varnish, and paint. The seed is also used as a bird food.

See also the article on SISAL.

Henley, William Ernest

William Ernest Henley was an English poet of about a hundred years ago. He was born in 1849. As a child he became ill with tuberculosis, and for the rest of his life he was never really well. He spent many months in a hospital after an operation to remove an infected foot, and while there he began to write poetry. He became a magazine editor, and was responsible for making known the names of such great writers as Joseph Conrad and Rudyard Kipling. Henley is best known for the famous lines from his poem "Invictus":

It matters not how strait the gate,
How charged with punishments the scroll,
I am the master of my fate;
I am the captain of my soul.

Henley died in 1903.

henna

Henna is a plant from which a dye is made. The plant is a small shrub that grows in India, Africa, and the West Indies. Natives of these countries have long used its leaves to make an orange-red dye for their hair and fingernails. In the United States, henna is most often used as a hair dye. A "henna rinse" gives the hair a reddish color that is admired by some women.

Henry, Holy Roman Emperor

The Holy Roman Empire, which was made up of the German countries in Europe hundreds of years ago, had seven emperors named Henry. The last of them was emperor more than six hundred years ago. The one best remembered is Henry IV, who was born in the year 1050 and was emperor from 1056 (when he was only 6 years old) until 1106, when he died. Henry IV fought against Pope Gregory VII of the Roman Catholic Church, and in 1076 the Pope excommunicated him—that is, declared that he was no longer a member of the Church. Henry went to the castle of Canossa, in Italy, where the Pope was living. It was midwinter, and there was snow on the ground, but for three days Henry stood outside the castle barefoot and wearing a coarse sackcloth dress until the Pope forgave him and took him back into the Church. Since then, when people humiliate themselves to be forgiven or to get something they want, they are said to "go to Canossa." Henry's entire reign was a series of fights with the German kings, with the Pope, and even with his own sons.

Henry, King of England

There have been eight kings of England named Henry. The first Henry was the son of William the Conqueror, who invaded England from Normandy, in France, in the year 1066. The other Henrys belonged to three different families, and three of them were founders of houses, or lines of kings. Here are all the English kings named Henry:

KING	BORN	DIED	REIGN
Henry I	1068	1135	1100–1135
Henry II	1133	1189	1154–1189
Henry III	1202	1272	1216–1272
Henry IV	1367	1413	1399–1413
Henry V	1387	1422	1413–1422
Henry VI	1421	1471	1422–1460
Henry VII	1457	1509	1485–1509
Henry VIII	1491	1547	1509–1547

Henry II was the first king of the PLANTAGENET family, about which there is a separate article. He married Eleanor of Aquitaine, who owned large possessions in France. Because of this, later kings of England fought long wars against France before they finally gave up their claims to French possessions.

Henry IV, Henry V and Henry VI were members of the House of Lancaster. Henry IV was the first Lancaster king. All three of these kings fought against France in the Hundred Years War, and Henry VI fought the House of York, in England, for the right to be king. He was murdered so that Edward IV, of the York family, could be king. It was in the reign of Henry VI that the English put Joan of Arc, the French heroine, to death. Shakespeare wrote plays about all three of these Henrys. You can read more about them in the articles on LANCASTER and WARS of the ROSES.

Henry VII was the first king of the TUDOR family, about which there is a separate article. Henry VII was a strong king, and during his reign the crown became more powerful than it had been for many years, and the great noblemen lost some of their power.

Henry VIII was perhaps the best-known of all English kings. This is partly because he married six times, and partly

Gale Research Co.

because he broke away from the Roman Catholic Church and made England a Protestant country. Henry VIII was a smart man, a scholar, and in many ways a good king, but he had absolute power in England and he often used it to put people to death unjustly. He was physically very strong and loved sports and fun. Most of the time he was very popular with the English people.

The first wife of Henry VIII was a Spanish princess, Catherine of Aragon. She had been married before to Henry's brother, who had died. Catherine had a daughter, who afterward became Queen Mary I, but she had no son. Partly for this reason, Henry wanted to divorce her and marry an English girl named Anne Boleyn. He asked the Pope to nullify his marriage to Catherine (declare that it never was legal) but the Pope refused. In 1529 Henry set up his own Church, which made him free to marry Anne.

Anne Boleyn had a daughter, who later became Queen Elizabeth I. After three years, Henry accused Anne of misconduct and had her beheaded. He next married Jane Seymour. She gave birth to a son (who became King Edward VI) but she died as a result of the childbirth. Henry next married Anne of Cleves, a German princess, but he found he did not like her and after a few months he had his Church nullify that marriage too. This was in the year 1540.

Henry immediately married another English girl, Catherine Howard. She was only 19 years old. Less than two years later he had her beheaded, as he had Anne

Boleyn, on a charge of misconduct. He then married Catherine Parr, the widow of an English nobleman, and seems to have lived quite happily with her, but he died a few years later, in 1547.

Henry, King of France

There were four kings of France who were named Henry. The last of them died about 350 years ago, in 1610.

Henry II, who ruled about four hundred years ago, was a cruel king. He persecuted the Huguenots, who were French Protestants. He also forced his people to go to war several times against other nations. Henry II was born in 1519 and died in 1559. His son, Henry III, who was born in 1551 and died in 1589, also persecuted the Huguenots, but he was soon forced to pass laws giving them certain privileges.

Henry IV, called Henry of Navarre, was born in 1553 and became king in 1589, when Henry III died. He was the most important of all the kings named Henry. He was the first king of the royal family called the Bourbons. He ended the war that had been going on between France and Spain, and he also

French Embassy Press

tried to stop the religious wars that were going on in France between the Catholics and non-Catholics. One of his most famous acts was the Edict of Nantes. The Edict of Nantes was a proclamation that gave civil rights to the Huguenots.

Henry IV did much to rebuild the country after the misrule of many of the kings who came before him. He was assassinated by a religious fanatic named Ravaillac in the year 1610.

Henry the Navigator

Henry the Navigator was a prince of Portugal who lived about five hundred years ago. He was given his surname, "The Navigator," because he was very interested in the sea and because he hoped to find new routes to the Orient.

Henry built a small castle and tower near a place called Sagres, on the southern coast of Portugal. Then he invited many explorers, mapmakers, geographers and sea captains from all over Europe to come to his castle, to study and exchange ideas and information. Prince Henry himself was a very hard worker, and often worked several days without sleep. Unfortunately

Henry died before his ships and the people he sent out had discovered a new route to the Orient. However, because of his work and advice to others, Portugal became one of the leading nations to discover and explore new lands.

Prince Henry was born in 1394 and died in 1460.

Henry, Joseph

Joseph Henry was an American scientist. He founded the United States Weather Bureau. He also is one of the scientists who discovered a way of generating electricity by means of electromag-

netic INDUCTION, about which there is a separate article. An electrical unit, called the henry, is named after him.

Henry was born in Albany, New York, in 1797. He became a professor at Albany Academy and later at the college that is now Princeton. He invented a kind of telegraph, but this idea was not made practical until Samuel Morse developed a system of dots and dashes, called the Morse code, for sending messages. Henry was the first secretary of the Smithsonian Institution in Washington, D.C., and helped found the National Academy of Science. He died in 1878.

Henry, O.

O. Henry was a "pen name" used by an American writer of short stories.

His real name was William Sydney Porter. He was born in Greensboro, North Carolina, in 1862. He did not go to school for very long, but he managed to learn a great deal by himself. When he was about 20 years old, O. Henry went to Texas. There he worked at many different jobs. One job was on a newspaper.

Another job he had was in a bank, and when some money was missing from the bank, O. Henry was accused of stealing it. He was sent to prison for more than three years. While he was in prison, he first began to write short stories. After he got out of prison, he went to New York and kept on writing. O. Henry was a very good story-teller. Usually he would tell a simple little tale, and then would finish with a surprise ending, a sudden unexpected change in the story at the very end.

Many of O. Henry's stories were about New York City and the life of the people there. He also wrote some stories about life in the Southwest. Some of O. Henry's books of short stories are *The Four Million, The Voice of the City,* and *Sixes and Sevens.* He wrote a novel—a long story—called *Cabbages and Kings.* He died in 1910.

Henry, Patrick

Patrick Henry was a great American orator and a leader at the time of the Revolutionary War. He is famous as the man who said, "Give me liberty, or give me death." Patrick Henry was born in Hanover County, Virginia, in 1736. He did not do very well in school or in business, but he was a great success as a lawyer. In 1765, he was elected to the House of Burgesses, which was the lawmaking body of the colony of Virginia. Henry became famous for the speeches he made in the House of Burgesses. Many people at that time thought that England was making harsh and unfair laws for the American colonies, and that England really had no right to rule over the American colonies. Patrick Henry was one of the first to say these things in public. He made stirring speeches about the rights of the colonies to rule themselves.

In his most famous speech, Henry was trying to persuade Virginia to get ready for war against England. Some people thought the colonies should try to get along with England, but Henry told them that they could never be free under an English government. He said, "Is life so dear, or peace so sweet, as to be purchased at the price of chains and slavery? Forbid it, Almighty God! I know not what course others may take, but as for me, give me liberty, or give me death!" Finally the colonies did go to war, and eventually they became independent.

When the colonies became independent, Henry was elected as the first Governor of Virginia. After the war, the Constitution was written to establish a government for the United States. Henry did not completely approve of this government. He thought it was too strong. He said that it was taking too much freedom and power away from the states. Patrick Henry was one of the men who fought to see that the Bill of Rights (which Virginia had already adopted as a state) was added to the Constitution. He always refused to accept any posts in the national government.

Patrick Henry died in 1799.

hepatica

Hepatica is a plant found all over North America, except in the Far West. It is usually found in woodlands. It is a very pretty member of the buttercup family of flowers. It is sometimes called liverleaf or liverwort because its leaves resemble a liver in shape. The plant does not die in the winter. You may find hepatica plants all year long. They may be recognized by their flowers, which look like buttercups, and their leaves, which are a deep olive green on top and a dark red underneath.

Hephaestus, the god of fire and metal in the stories of the ancient Greeks: see the article on VULCAN.

Hera, queen of the gods, in the stories of the ancient Greeks: see the article on JUNO.

heraldry

Heraldry is the decoration and design of family or organization seals, crests, and coats of arms. A coat of arms is a copy or drawing of a shield with the helmet and crest above it, like those carried by the knights of the Middle Ages. On the coat of arms are designs that tell something of the family history in pictures, or if it is of an organization, the designs usually represent the activity or products of the organization. The expression "coat of arms" came from the French words *cotte d'armes,* the name of a light coat worn over suits of armor by knights and soldiers during the Middle Ages. On this coat were symbols and designs like the ones still used in coats of arms today.

A crest, usually a picture of some animal's head, was worn on the helmet. Badges were heraldic designs worn by the warriors' followers, but were not placed on a shield.

Any badge worn by members of a certain group is a part of heraldry. A Boy Scout or Girl Scout pin is a badge that identifies a person as a member of the Scouts, and anyone who sees it knows immediately that the wearer is a Scout.

THE START OF HERALDRY

Seals with coats of arms on them were first used about eight hundred years ago, in the 12th century. Shortly afterward, warriors began to wear armor that covered the face, so it was impossible for anyone approaching them to know whether a knight was a friend or an enemy. Therefore they began to use designs on their shields, coats, and horses. At first these designs were very simple, a simple band of color or a cross, but they could be recognized at a distance. Each man had his own design, and soon all the members of one family would use the same design. Also all the knights who fought together would use the same design, and their leader would have an extra symbol painted on his shield so he could be recognized by his men.

During the Crusades, most knights belonged to one of five main groups, and each group had its own version of the cross as its shield design. All the knights in the group carried shields with that particular type of cross painted on them. One of these groups was the KNIGHTS TEMPLAR, another the TEUTONIC KNIGHTS. You can read about both in separate articles.

When knights and soldiers no longer carried shields in battle, their families began to use the designs and symbols on the shields as their family signs, or coats of arms. Not all families have a coat of arms. Probably the first families to use shield designs as coats of arms did so because they wanted everyone to know that they were descended from noble knights.

All coats of arms are designed in the shape of shields even today, because of the original painted shields from which coats of arms first developed. Although the first coats of arms as a general rule had only one symbol or design, the intermarriage of different families caused different designs to be combined. After

Coats of arms are often beautifully designed. The seal of the British queen is a fine example. Her motto, *Dieu et mon droit,* means "God and my right" in French.

several generations, the family coat of arms might have several symbols on it. Eventually many extra symbols were added to coats of arms, outside of the shield shape. As important events occurred in the family, it seemed a good idea to include something that would represent those events on the family coat of arms. Sometimes a family motto has been made part of the coat of arms, and a state, city, country, or institution usually has its motto on its coat of arms also.

The coat of arms of the royal family of England is an example of how events in history become part of a coat of arms. One of the symbols on the royal coat of arms is the lion, which is usually considered the king of beasts. This coat of arms also has a fleur-de-lys, the symbol of France, because many years ago the British conquered large parts of France. There is also a harp symbol on the royal coat of arms, which became a part of its design in honor of the addition of Ireland to the kingdom of England.

HERALDRY AND TOURNAMENTS

When a noble knight of the Middle Ages planned to hold a tournament, or contest, he issued invitations by sending his heralds or messengers to other knights and nobles with copies of his shield, painted or drawn on large cards or sheets of paper. This is how the name heraldry originated. The knights to whom he sent an invitation accepted by sending back copies of their own shields. In that way it was possible to know in advance how many knights, and which ones, would be present at the tournament.

During the period when knights held tournaments, shield designs became much more elaborate than they had been when a mere stripe or band of paint was the only ornamentation. Some knights chose to paint an eagle on their shields because the eagle is known to be fierce and powerful, and the knight wanted to use a symbol that would make people think of him as being fierce and powerful also. Some used lions for the same reason.

A full coat of arms includes a shield, helmet, and crest. From the helmet hang draperies, called *mantlings*, usually made of the main colors of the shield, and underneath on a ribbon is written the family motto. Sometimes a motto appears on the shield itself. A heraldry expert can tell the ancestry of a family from the combinations and positions of various symbols. Each symbol means a different branch or event in the family's history.

Not only do families have coats of arms, but cities, states, and countries have them also. Schools and colleges usually have their coats of arms, too, and the different branches of the armed forces are identified by heraldic symbols in shield-shaped shoulder patches on their uniforms.

The trademarks on products that are manufactured and sold everywhere grew out of heraldry and coats of arms. A company's trademark is as much a mark of identification as the design on the knight's shield used to be. Most automobiles today have their coat of arms as a means of identification, so that people will recognize the make of car when they see that identifying symbol.

THE LANGUAGE OF HERALDRY

The language of heraldry is a strange one. Many of the words used to describe

Many manufacturers use heraldic designs as trademarks of their products.

symbols and colors are French. For example, a heraldry expert would not say that the colors of a coat of arms are silver, blue, and black. He would say that its "tinctures" are "argent, azure, and sable." He would not say that one of the symbols is a lion standing on its hind legs. He would say instead that the symbol is a "lion rampant." He would not say that the figure was on the right or left side of the shield, but on the "dexter" or "sinister" side.

Not every coat of arms has a meaning. The earliest coats of arms are mostly geometric in design, that is, made up of bands of color across, up-and-down, or slanting, or crosses or chevrons (upside-down V-shape). Some designs were used because of their meaning; an example is the lion in the British coat of arms. A design often used an object that was a pun on the name of the bearer, such as three bows for the Bowes family. Such coats of arms are called *canting arms,* which means singing arms, because they chant the name of the family by means of a pun. Sometimes a symbol was added to a coat of arms in memory of some special event in the history of the family.

In order to know all the technical names for the hundreds of figures, marks and symbols used in heraldry, you would have to study for several years. Long ago there were many experts who kept up the study for a lifetime, either as a hobby or as a career. Today there is very little interest in heraldry except in Great Britain. The Herald's College in England has an official called the King-of-Arms who has charge of recording what coats of arms may be used, and by whom. This organization has existed since 1483.

There are very few people outside of England who are truly experts in heraldry, and there are thousands of combinations of symbols to be learned before anyone can become an expert. Heraldry is an extremely complicated study—the study that is indirectly responsible for modern trademarks, society seals, pins, and insignia, and for the official seals used to mark a legal paper.

herb

A herb is any plant that does not have a permanent stem and dies down to the ground after each growing season. There are many different kinds of herbs, most of which have certain properties that make them useful as medicines, as

garnishes or flavorings, or in perfume. Some are used fresh in cooking, such as mint, parsley, or chives, but most of them are dried. Different parts of the plant may be used—leaves, seeds, roots, buds, or fruit pods. Herbs have little or no food value, but they help make many foods tastier. Some of the more commonly used herbs in cooking are basil, chervil, marjoram, sage, rosemary, savory, tarragon, and thyme.

Many people raise their own herbs in small herb gardens. All that is needed is a small plot of good soil that has been well spaded and worked until the clods are very fine. The surface soil should be quite loose, and you should see that there is plenty of sun and that weeds are removed. Herbs should be picked for drying as they come into flower. They then can be washed and hung in bunches in a shady, airy room or dried in a very slow oven. When they are thoroughly dry, the herbs should be pulverized and kept in closed containers until used.

Herbert, Victor

Victor Herbert was a famous composer of charming light operas or operettas. His best-known operettas are *Naughty Marietta, Sweethearts,* and *Babes in Toyland.* His melodious tunes

are broadcast by radio and television almost as often as those of any other composer. Herbert was born in Dublin, Ireland, in 1859. He began his musical studies in the city of Stuttgart, in Germany, when he was only seven years old. Later he played the violoncello for the Stuttgart orchestra. Here he met and married Therese Foerster, a famous singer of that city. When she came to America to sing for the Metropolitan Opera in New York City, her husband came with her. He was given a position as violoncellist in the Opera's orchestra. At about this time he began his career as a composer. Though he was famous for his lighter works, he also wrote some music of a more serious type. This includes two symphonies and an opera called *Natoma.* Victor Herbert died in 1924.

herbivorous animals

Herbivorous animals are those animals that eat only plants and plant growth. These animals are found throughout the world. They include such animals as cows and sheep (called "grazers"). Grazers eat grass and small bushes. Rabbits are other herbivorous animals. Insects are, in the main, herbivorous, and some of them, like the grasshopper and Hessian fly, are very destructive to crops and plants. Mice, too, are herbivorous and sometimes are destructive. Some animals are called *carnivorous,* or meat-eating, animals. Others are *insectivorous,* eating insects. Still others are *omnivorous;* that is, they eat both plants and animals. Human beings are omnivorous.

Hercules

Hercules was a hero in Greek mythology, the stories the ancient Greeks told about their gods and goddesses. He was the strongest man in the world. His

father was Zeus, the chief god, and his mother was Alcmene, a human being, so Hercules was half a god, and sometimes the Greeks worshiped him and prayed to him. He was so strong that even when he was a baby he killed a great serpent that came into his cradle. By a trick of Hera, the wife of Zeus, Hercules was bound to perform certain very difficult tasks, or labors. These are remembered as the Twelve Labors of Hercules, and were:

1. To destroy a fierce lion that haunted a place called Nemea. Hercules strangled it with his hands.

2. To destroy the Lernean hydra, a nine-headed monster. Hercules cut off the heads while his servant burned their roots.

3. To capture the Arcadian stag, which was famous for its speed, its golden horns, and its bronze feet. After a year of pursuit Hercules caught it.

4. To bring back a wild boar that laid waste a whole countryside. He chased it through deep snow and caught it in a net.

5. To clean the stable of Augeas, King of Elis, where three thousand oxen had lived for thirty years. Hercules did this in one day by making two rivers flow through the stables.

6. To destroy the man-eating birds that lived near the city of Stymphalus. Hercules startled the birds by shaking a rattle, and shot them with his bow and arrows when they flew into the air.

7. To capture alive a beautiful bull, which the sea-god Poseidon had made mad. Hercules carried the bull back on his shoulders.

8. To capture the mares of Diomedes, King of Thrace, which fed on human flesh. Hercules tamed the mares by feeding them on the flesh of their master.

9. To obtain the girdle (belt) of Hippolyta, Queen of the Amazons. Hercules killed Hippolyta and took her girdle back.

10. To kill the three-bodied monster, Geryon, and bring his oxen to Argos. On his way to do this, Hercules built two pillars on the two sides of the straits of Gibraltar, which were then named the Pillars of Hercules.

11. To find and obtain the golden apples from the garden of the Hesperides. Hercules had the giant Atlas get the apples, and in the meantime took over Atlas' job of holding the world on his shoulders.

12. To bring the three-headed dog Cerberus from the lower world. Hercules accomplished this, and was freed from further duties and labors.

The ancient Greeks imagined Hercules as a great eater and drinker as well as a great fighter, and they thought of him as a kind man who could, however, be terrible when he was angry. They saw his outline in the stars of a big constellation that we still call Hercules. As they drew his picture in the sky, he was kneeling with his bow and arrows, and dressed in the skin of the lion he killed. Hercules was called *Heracles* by the Greeks.

heredity

Heredity is the process by which certain traits are passed on from parents to their children. People have always noticed that tall parents usually have tall children, and that red-headed parents quite often have children with red hair, but it was not until about a hundred years ago that it was discovered that there were scientific laws governing these facts. Gregor Mendel was the first man to find out how heredity works. We call some of the laws of heredity Mendelian laws after him. The Mendelian laws tell us that certain traits, such as the color of hair

or eyes, color blindness, prominent chins, easily tanned skin, and other physical characteristics are passed on from one generation to another. For more information about these rules of heredity, see the article on GENETICS.

Hermes, the messenger of the gods in the stories of the ancient Greeks: see the article on MERCURY.

hermit

A hermit is a man who lives alone, usually far away from other people. He often wears rough clothes and eats plain food; he may live in the mountains or out in the desert. Originally the word *hermit* was used to describe only men who lived alone to fast and pray. John the Baptist and St. Anthony were both hermits of this kind. Now anyone who lives away from other people is called a hermit, even if his only reason is that he wants to be alone.

hermit crab

The hermit crab is a kind of shellfish that is found along the shores of the ocean in most parts of the world. There are many species, or kinds, of hermit crab. Most of them are smaller than other crabs. The hermit crab that lives along the coast of southern New England is only one-half inch wide, but other kinds may grow to be a foot wide. The hermit crab is unlike other shellfish because it does not have a shell of its own. It protects itself by living in the discarded shells of other sea animals. It fastens itself to a shell that it finds along the shore, and it withdraws into this shell when there is any danger. When the crab outgrows one shell, it finds a bigger one and changes its home. Hermit crabs fight among themselves for the biggest and best shells. There are several kinds of hermit crab that can live on land as well as in the water.

hernia

When part of one of the body's internal organs pushes through the wall of the cavity in which it is located, we say that a hernia or rupture has been caused. The most common kind of hernia occurs when a small loop of the intestine bursts out through the front wall of the abdomen, so that it can be felt under the skin. Hernias can be caused by lifting heavy weights, overexertion, jumping off high walls, or fits of coughing. Men are more likely to get them than women. Small hernias can usually be eased by special appliances, such as trusses, but more serious cases require a surgical operation.

Hero and Leander

Hero was a young woman and Leander a young man in a very old Greek love story. They lived on opposite banks of a strait of water that separates Europe from Asia Minor. The Greeks called this strait the Hellespont; it is now called the Dardanelles. Hero served as a priestess at Sestos in the temple of Aphrodite, the goddess of love and beauty. Leander, who lived in Abydos across the Hellespont, met her at a festival in the temple and they fell in love. Every night Leander would swim the three or four miles across the Hellespont to visit Hero. She would light a lamp in her tower window to guide

him as he swam. But one night a storm blew out the lamp, and Leander, swimming in the dark, rough sea, could not find his way to the shore and drowned. In the morning Hero saw his body and, grief-stricken, leaped from her tower and was drowned.

Herod

There were several kings named Herod. They ruled in Judea and other lands of the Jews about two thousand years ago.

The first and most famous was Herod the Great, who lived in the century just before Jesus was born. He was a great builder. He did much for the city of Jerusalem, giving it a magnificent temple, a theater, and an amphitheater intended for games to honor the Roman emperor, Augustus. Herod the Great was an Idumaean, and the Jewish people looked on him as a foreigner, so he was always afraid he would be murdered. He became suspicious of his wife and her sons and he had them put to death. At his death he divided his kingdom among three sons by other wives.

One of these sons was King Herod Antipas, who executed John the Baptist, as told in the New Testament, in the 14th chapter of the Gospel of Matthew. It was to Herod Antipas, too, that Pontius Pilate sent Jesus, as told in the New Testament. Jesus came from Galilee, a region ruled by Antipas.

A third king Herod was a grandson of Herod the Great. His full name was Herod Agrippa. He was a friend of the Roman emperor Caligula and through his favor was made ruler of the old kingdom of his grandfather. He persecuted the Christians, as is told in the 12th chapter of the Book of Acts.

Herod Agrippa II, son of the first Herod Agrippa, is also mentioned in the Book of Acts, in the 25th and 26th chapters. St. Paul was brought before him, because Christianity was often against the laws of those times. Agrippa (as he is called in the Bible) was favorable to Paul and said, "You almost persuade me to be a Christian."

Herodotus

Herodotus was the first real writer of history. He lived about 2,400 years ago, about the year 450 B.C., in Asia Minor. As a boy Herodotus traveled to many countries, including Syria, Palestine, Babylon, Egypt, parts of Africa, Greece, Italy, and even parts of northern Europe. As an old man in Italy, he wrote his history of the wars between Greece and Persia and put into it everything he had learned of these countries and their neighbors. You can read more about Herodotus in the article on HISTORY.

heron

The heron is a bird that is found in many parts of Europe and in North and South America. There are more than one hundred species, or kinds, of heron. A heron has a thin body, a long, slender neck, a small head, and a narrow, pointed beak. Many herons have beautifully colored feathers on their heads. The heron is a "shore" bird and is found around

lakes, streams, and oceans. It wades in shallow water. It has long, slender legs on which it wades into the water. It then dips into the water with its beak and catches fish, which are its food. Usually it eats only in the morning or in the evening. Herons build their nests of twigs and sticks in the tops of high trees. The nesting places, which are called heronries, are used again and again by the birds.

The great blue heron is well known in North America. It is a beautiful blue color. It is about four feet long and has a wing spread of about six feet. The little blue heron, the little green heron and the egret are herons found in the eastern part of the United States. Many kinds of heron, including the egret, used to be killed in great numbers for their feathers, or plumes, which were used for hat decoration s. Today the laws protect herons from plume-hunters.

Herrick, Robert

Robert Herrick was an English poet who lived about three hundred years ago. Throughout much of his life the English king and Parliament were fighting about how England should be ruled. Those who supported the king were called Cavaliers, and those who supported the Parliament were called Roundheads. Herrick was the leader of a group of poets who were called Cavalier poets because they supported the king. These poets were lyric poets, which means that they wrote short poems that expressed their own feelings on such things as love and beauty and patriotism. His first book of poetry, *Hesperides,* is very witty. Herrick was a minister for many years, and he wrote some beautiful religious poetry, in a book called *Noble Numbers.* Two of his most famous poems are "To Daffodils" and "To the Virgins, to Make Much of Time." In both these poems Herrick advises us to enjoy all the beauty of life while we can. Herrick was born in 1591 and died in 1674.

herring

The herring is a valuable food fish. It is found in northern waters all over the world, but it is caught particularly in the North Sea in Europe and along the Atlantic coast of the United States, especially near Maine. A certain kind of herring is also caught along the Pacific coast of the United States. Herring travel in schools, or large groups, and are very easy to catch. They are usually caught in weirs or nets. Weirs are traps made of posts stuck into the water. The herring swim into these traps at high tide and are unable to escape when the tide goes out. Herring are usually packed in cans to be sold. The herring most often caught is 10 to 12 inches long. Small herrings are sometimes canned and sold as sardines, although the true sardine is a slightly different fish. Different kinds of herring are known as bloaters, kippers, and bismarcks.

Hesperides

The Hesperides were the four daughters of Hesperia and Atlas in Greek mythology, the stories the ancient Greeks told about their gods and goddesses. They were called Agle, Arethusa, Erytheia, and Hesperia. When Hera, the queen of heaven, married Zeus, the chief of the Olympian gods, they were given several golden apples by Gaea, who was goddess of the earth. It became the duty of the Hesperides to guard these apples. However, they were stolen from the Hesperides by Hercules, a great hero, as one of his twelve labors. See the article about HERCULES.

Hesse and Hessians

Hesse is one of the states in West Germany. It is about eight thousand square miles in size, about the same size as the state of Massachusetts, and about 4,700,000 people live there. Most of the people are farmers or work in iron and coal mines. The largest city in Hesse is Frankfurt-on-Main with a population of about 670,000. It is an important banking, business, and industrial center. See also article on FRANKFURT.

In former times Hesse was an independent grand duchy, a kind of kingdom. It is remembered by Americans because during the Revolutionary War the British hired soldiers from the duke of Hesse and sent them to America to fight against the colonists. After the war, many of the Hessians stayed to become citizens in the new republic.

Hessian fly

The Hessian fly is a tiny insect that feeds on cereal crops such as wheat, rye, and oats. Farmers try many methods to control the fly, since it can do great damage to these crops. One of the methods used is to plow the fields after the eggs of the fly have been laid. This may destroy the eggs. The Hessian fly is supposed to have come to the United States from Asia by way of Europe, during the Revolutionary War. It got its name from the Hessian soldiers, who were soldiers from Hesse paid by the British to fight against the American colonists during the Revolution, and who were thought to have brought the fly with them from Europe.

Hiawatha

Hiawatha was an Indian told about in the legends of the Algonquin Indians. The legends were made famous by Henry Wadsworth Longfellow in his epic, or long story-poem, called *The Song of Hiawatha.* Hiawatha was a great hero, almost a god, to the Indians, for he was supposed to have shown them how to grow maize, or corn, which was their most important food. According to legend, Hiawatha was the son of the West Wind. In Longfellow's poem, Hiawatha wrestles with his father and almost defeats him. Hiawatha was a great hunter and woodsman. He was supposed to have owned magic mittens and magic moccasins. His mittens made him stronger than any other man, and his moccasins made it possible for him to walk a mile at each step. Hiawatha married a beautiful Indian maiden named *Minnehaha,* which means "Laughing Water." Hiawatha was known by different names to most other North American Indian tribes.

hibernation

Certain animals spend the winter in a sleeping or inactive state. This state of sleep or half-sleep is called hibernation. During hibernation all the functions of the animal's body slow down, and the animal is able to live through the long, cold winter months when it would be hard or impossible for it to find food. Its heartbeat becomes slower, and its daily activities are stopped. Some animals may lie in a deep sleep during the whole period of hibernation; others may move around somewhat on warm days. They do not grow during hibernation and may lose as much as one-third of their weight.

Not many animals hibernate. Only those that are able to eat enough food before hibernation to carry them through the winter are able to hibernate. These animals are often those that feed on vegetables. Hibernation ends in the spring when the warm weather comes again.

The bear is often said to hibernate, because every winter it crawls into a cave and sleeps until the warm spring months arrive, but its body temperature does not go down as much as it does in a true hibernating animal.

Certain frogs and lizards bury themselves in the earth below the reach of frost. The horseshoe crab sinks into mud beneath deep water and does not awaken until May or June. Spiders and snails hibernate under stones and boulders. Caterpillars sleep under the bark of trees. One of the hibernating animals is the woodchuck, or groundhog. According to popular legend, the day the woodchuck comes out of hibernation is supposed to be the beginning of spring.

hibiscus

The hibiscus is a flowering tree or shrub that is found in warm climates in many parts of the world. A variety of hibiscus often grown in gardens in the United States is called rose of Sharon. This flower is also mentioned in the Bible. It grows to be eight or ten feet high and has pink or white flowers with many petals. It blooms in the summer. Another hibiscus, called the rose mallow, is a wild flower. It has bright pink blossoms. It is seen in marshes in the late summer.

In the tropical islands of the South Seas there are hibiscus trees that grow as high as twenty feet. Wood from these trees is light and wears well. It is used for many purposes.

The fruit of another hibiscus is used as an ingredient in food, particularly in soup. It is called *okra.*

Fibers from certain hibiscus plants are used for making rope. Musk seed, which is often used as a scent for perfume, also comes from hibiscus. In Egypt and Arabia the seed of the hibiscus is put in coffee to serve as a stimulant or to settle the stomach.

hiccup

A hiccup is a sharp sound that is caused when air is breathed in very sharply and hits against the glottis, a small section of the throat. The hiccup is usually caused by a spasm, or sudden movement, of the diaphragm, the large muscle that separates the chest from the abdomen. Hiccups usually continue for a few minutes and then stop, but sometimes they keep on for a long time. Everyone seems to have a pet remedy for hiccups—holding the breath, drinking water fast, and holding out the tongue are a few. The chief purpose of all these remedies seems

to be to put your mind on something else and forget about the hiccups, which will usually go away by themselves. If they do not go away they may be a sign of some more serious trouble.

Hickok, Wild Bill

Wild Bill Hickok was famous in the American West as a courageous and daring man and a great marksman. It was said that he could shoot his gun from the hip, not taking aim, and seldom miss a shot. One story about Wild Bill tells about how he fought alone against a gang of ten outlaws, and killed every one. We do not know how many of  the stories told about Wild Bill are true, but he lived in a time when the West was wild and lawless. He was on the side of law and order, and he had many fights with outlaws.

Wild Bill was born in Troy Grove, Illinois, in 1837. His real name was James Butler Hickok. Wild Bill spent most of his life in Kansas. During the Civil War, he was a scout for the northern side, and after the war he was a marshal, an officer of the United States government, in Kansas. For a while he toured around the country with Buffalo Bill's Wild West Show.

Wild Bill was a great hero to the Americans of his time, and everyone was very sad when he was treacherously shot in the back by a gambler, in 1876. When he was shot, Wild Bill was playing poker, and he had a pair of aces and a pair of eights in his hand. Ever since that time a poker hand with these two pairs in it has been called "dead man's hand."

Many of the stories about Wild Bill Hickok have in them another famous character, "Calamity Jane," who was his friend and was almost as good a shot as he was. Her real name was Martha Jane Burke.

hickory

Hickory is the name of 22 kinds of tree. All of them have branches that grow very high up on the trunk. They are found in the southern and eastern United States, eastern Canada, China, and Mexico. The nut from two kinds of hickory tree, especially from the one called shagbark hickory, is good to eat, but the tree is mainly important for its wood, which is strong and light and has a lot of elasticity. Horsedrawn carriages and wagons were made of hickory wood, and racing carts called sulkies are still made from it. Other things made from hickory wood are the handles for rakes, axes, and other tools. Hickory decays when it is exposed to the air, so it must be painted and varnished for protection. For this reason it is not used for building houses.

Hidalgo y Costilla, Miguel

Hidalgo is a great hero of the Mexican people because he was one of the leaders in their fight for freedom and independence. Hidalgo was born in 1753, and when he grew up, he became a priest. He did many things in the little parish of Dolores, where he lived, to help the na-

tives, and the Mexican government began to grow suspicious of him. In 1810, he led a revolt against the Mexican government, which was controlled by Spain. He spoke so sincerely that he convinced about fifty thousand men to join in this fight for freedom. They won several important victories, but finally Spanish soldiers crushed Hidalgo's army. Hidalgo escaped and started out for the United States to get help. On the way, he was captured and shot by the Spanish. This was in 1811. Later, when Mexico became a republic, the people built many statues of Hidalgo.

hieroglyphics

Hieroglyphics is a kind of writing with pictures (hieroglyphs) instead of with letters. The ancient Egyptians used hieroglyphs thousands of years ago. They used drawings of birds, men, trees and other objects in such a way that they gave a meaning. The word *hieroglyphics* means "sacred carvings" in Greek. The oldest hieroglyphics were carved on stone. These carvings were called sacred because they were done by priests and were found in holy places such as temples, monuments, and tombs.

At that time the priests were the only Egyptians who were taught to read and write the hieroglyphs. There were more than six hundred signs, and it took the priests many years to learn them all.

Of course, they could not draw pictures of words such as "quick," or "clever," or "love," so they used a picture of something to stand for an idea connected with it. If we wrote this way, we might draw a picture of a bird to mean "fly" or "quick." This kind of picture is called an *ideogram,* or "sense sign." Because each sign might have several meanings, the "sense signs" were very difficult to read.

The hieroglyphs could not be read for thousands of years. Then, in the year 1799, a *stele,* an engraved pillar of stone, was found at Rosetta in Egypt. This piece of stone, called the Rosetta Stone, had the same message written on it in Greek and in hieroglyphics. By comparing the two, a French scholar named Champollion was able to tell what the hieroglyphs meant. Even since then, scientists have been able to learn much about ancient Egypt by reading the hieroglyphics discovered in the ruins of ancient tombs and temples.

See also the article ALPHABET.

high school

In the United States a high school is a school for young people who have graduated from elementary, or grade, school. Its purpose is to turn out a person who is well enough educated for all ordinary tasks in life. High schools are often called secondary schools, and it is by that name that they are known in England and in Canada. Most boys and girls have the opportunity to go to high school, although this was not true even as recently as fifty years ago. In 1910 about one of every four boys or girls who finished elementary school went on to high school. Often others wanted to go, but their families could not afford to send them. Also they could get jobs without going to high school. Today it is very difficult to get any kind of good job without a high-school education.

High school is a preparation for college or for business school or for a trade. A high school offers many different subjects so that the student can study those things in which he is particularly interested. The student who enters high school is considered grown-up enough to choose the courses, or subjects, he wishes to study A student chooses these subjects with his future life in mind. If he is going on to college and wishes to be a teacher, a doctor, a lawyer, or some other kind of professional person, he takes a special group of subjects called a college course. These subjects are necessary for college entrance. The student who wishes to become a bookkeeper, a stenographer, a typist, or a secretary takes another group of subjects called a commercial course.

The student who wants to work in industry may choose to take an industrial arts course. This may be given in a separate high school, called a trade school, if the boy or girl lives in a large city. Usually the industrial arts courses teach boys to use the tools connected with many different trades and teaches girls all the skills relating to cooking, sewing, and home management. Many of the students who take college or commercial courses in high school take additional courses in the industrial arts.

Most high schools offer a four-year course. The four-year high school is entered after the boy or girl has finished eight grades in elementary school. About fifty years ago a new division of grades was started in the United States. A student finished six grades in elementary school, then went on to junior high school, usually for grades seven, eight, and nine. He then went on to senior high school, which consisted of grades ten, eleven, and twelve. Grade nine in a junior high school was the same as the first year of a four-year high school.

COURSES IN HIGH SCHOOL

Whether a student goes to junior high school and senior high school, or only to high school, he will study about the same subjects each year, depending upon the courses he takes. The following is a typical high-school curriculum, or course of study, for the college and commercial courses:

GRADE NINE—FRESHMAN

College	Commercial
English 1	English 1
Latin 1	General Science
General Science	Business Math
Ancient History	Ancient History
Algebra 1	

GRADE TEN—SOPHOMORE

College	Commercial
English 2	English 2
Latin 2	Biology
French 1 or	Civics
Spanish 1	
Biology	
Modern European	General Business
History	Training
Plane Geometry	

GRADE ELEVEN—JUNIOR

College	Commercial
English 3	English 3
Latin 3	Bookkeeping 1
French 2 or	Typing 1
Spanish 2	Shorthand 1
Physics	American History
American History	
Algebra 2	

GRADE TWELVE—SENIOR

College	Commercial
English 4	English 4
French 3 or	Bookkeeping 2
Spanish 3	Typing 2
(Latin 4)	Shorthand 2
Problems of	Business Principles
Democracy	Business Law
Chemistry	
Solid Geometry	
and Trigonometry	

You will notice that English is listed as a subject to be studied by both college and commercial students in each of the four years. In most schools the student is required to take English; in many states it is a law that every student graduating from a public high school must have taken and passed four years of English. Such courses are required because it is very important for everyone to speak good English and to write clearly and correctly.

It is also a law in most states that a student cannot graduate from high school until he has passed United States History. Many schools require every student to take a course in civics, which explains the working of the local, state and national governments and how the citizens should act to support them. Problems of Democracy is a course that is sometimes required. This subject discusses the way in which each citizen must act in order to keep his country strong.

More and more high-school teachers have realized that the courses offered in high school should be practical and of use to the student in later life. A student may go to the kind of high school where the "core" curriculum is offered. This means that he may study American literature, American history and the American language together as one subject. He will also probably do a great deal of experimenting so as to see the actual workings of the scientific facts taught in the chemistry and biology books. He will go on "field trips" to museums, newspaper offices, factories, and other places of interest to see how people put to use the things they learned in high school.

Many courses offered in high schools are *elective;* that is, the student may elect (choose) to take them. Such subjects are art and music. The larger city schools may offer additional courses in language and literature for the student who is interested in these subjects.

HIGH SCHOOL LIFE

The modern high school is not all study. Usually the school day starts at 8 or 8:30 and is over by 2 or 2:30. During the day the student moves from class to class. He usually has a different teacher for each subject, and has some time during the day to work on his assignments for the next day's classes. The high-school student often has to do part of his work at home, too, because he is expected to study ahead in all his subjects.

A high school usually has a newspaper and a yearbook that are written by students. In almost every high school there is a dramatic society for those students who like to act in plays. There are also many clubs formed by students who have hobbies such as photography, woodworking, or farming. Every high school has an athletic program, and the boy or girl can choose the game he wishes to play. Some high-school teams play games against the teams of other high schools; sometimes the sports are intramural, that is, teams within one school compete against each other.

Most high schools have a guidance program where the student can get help if he has any problems. The guidance teacher generally helps the student decide what kind of job he is best fitted for, and may assist the student in finding that kind of job. Usually the student helps to rule his own school by electing representatives to the student government or student council. The members of the student government work with the faculty, or teachers, to make the school a good and happy one. Most schools have many parties and dances during the school year; probably the boy or girl learns the latest dance steps in his gym class.

HOW HIGH SCHOOLS BEGAN

The first high school in America was started in Boston in 1635; it was called a Latin school because it emphasized Latin and the classics as preparatory for college. Somewhat more practical-minded were the academies, which were started by Benjamin Franklin in Philadelphia in 1749; they taught subjects such as embroidery, engraving, law, and music, in addition to the regular academic courses. Until 1821 parents had to pay for their children's high-school education, but in that year the first free public high school was established in Boston, and many others were soon opened throughout the country. At first high schools were for boys only. Then there were separate schools for girls. The first high school for boys and girls was established in Chicago, in 1856.

The most recent development of the high school in the United States is the adding of two extra years of study, grades 13 and 14, where the student takes courses similar to those that he would take in junior college. In Europe, where the high schools are called *gymnasiums,* or *lycées,* the student has for some time received an education that is comparable to the education received in a junior college in the United States. The larger cities have been the first to add these two new grades. More and more people wish to go to college, and few can afford it, but a free junior-college education may become possible for everyone who wants it.

hiking is taking a long walk in the country: see the article on CAMPING.

Hill, James J.

James J. Hill was one of the greatest of the men who built America's railroads. His greatest work was extending a railroad from St. Paul, Minnesota, to Seattle, Washington, on the west coast of the United States. Hill had to build the railroad across the Rocky Mountains, and he had no financial help from the government as so many other builders of railroads had. He is known as the Empire Builder because his railroads opened up so much undeveloped territory for settlement. Hill was born in Ontario, Canada, in 1838, but went to St. Paul, Minnesota, when he was only eighteen years old. There he became a clerk for the St. Paul and Pacific Railroad. Twenty years later he and a group of men bought the railroad. It was this railroad that Hill extended to the Pacific. Hill was helped by President Grover Cleveland and by J. P. Morgan, the banker. Hill was married and the father of ten children, seven daughters and three sons. He died in 1916, a rich and powerful man.

Hillel

Hillel was a Jewish rabbi, which means teacher. He lived in Jerusalem just before the time of Jesus. Some of his wise sayings are still known. Hillel was president of the Sanhedrin, a council that made all decisions about religious laws for the Jews. He was humble as well as wise, and was greatly respected.

Hilton, James

James Hilton was an English novelist. One of his best-known books is about an imaginary place called Shangri-La. The book is named *Lost Horizon.* In the book, an English flier finds a beautiful hidden monastery when his plane crashes in the mountains somewhere in Asia. Shangri-La became so well-known that President Franklin D. Roosevelt named his private vacation spot in the mountains for it.

James Hilton was born in 1900 and attended Cambridge University. He wrote many successful novels, and several of them have been made into motion pictures. These include *Lost Horizon, Random Harvest,* and *Goodbye, Mr. Chips.* Hilton died in 1954.

Himalayas

The Himalayas in central Asia are the highest mountains in the world. There are several chains of mountains running

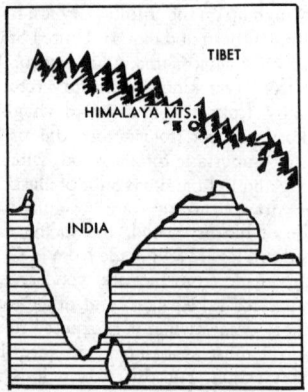

The snow-capped Himalayas reach their greatest height at Mount Everest. They stretch from Burma to Afghanistan, between India and Tibet.

side by side for 2,000 miles in a band sometimes 200 miles wide. They go from Afghanistan east to Burma and divide Tibet from India with the world's highest wall. There are about fifty peaks over 23,000 feet high. The highest, Mount Ever-

est, is 29,028 feet high. Mount Godwin-Austen is next highest, 28,250 feet. Mount Kailas is sacred to the Hindus and Buddhists, who call it "Mountain of Precious Snow" and believe it contains the thrones of their gods.

Himalayas in the old language of India meant "house of snow." Even though these mountains lie close to very hot lands, most of them are covered with snow all year round. The passes are so high and difficult to cross that the people who live in Tibet are almost entirely cut off from the rest of the world. The mountains also divide the climates sharply. The southern side gets heavy rain—100 to 900 inches of rainfall every year in the southern town of Darjeeling— while the northern side is very dry. This difference in climate causes differences in the things that grow. Some valleys are almost deserts, while others are thick with flowers. There are tropical forests in the Himalayas, with tigers and monkeys and elephants. There are cold forests where only pine trees grow, and other woods of oak and laurel. The Himalayas are so hard to cross, with no railroads or roads except dangerous foot trails, that it is almost impossible to send goods across these mountains.

Very few people can live in the Himalayas. Those who do live there are Tibetans who cluster in the high valleys where farming is easier. On the lower slopes, the people hunt animals, or cut timber, or graze their herds on the mountain meadows. They herd the yak. This is a useful animal that pulls their loads, draws their plows, and provides meat and milk. Its hair is made into cloth, and its skin is used to line boats.

On the southern slopes there are fig and palm trees and the people grow rice, corn, and tea.

Hindenburg, Paul von

Paul von Hindenburg was a German military leader and president. He was a hero to the German people because he was one of their most successful generals in World War I. When Germany was made into a republic, Hindenburg became the president. The "von" in his name means that he was a member of the nobility, one of the upper classes in Germany. He was born in East Prussia in 1847, and he was an army officer before he was twenty years old. During World War I he was in command of the armies fighting Russia, and he commanded the German army that won the famous battle of Tannenberg, where more than 100,-000 Russian soldiers were killed or taken prisoner. By the end of World War I Hindenburg and his second-in-command, General Erich von Ludendorff, commanded all Germany's armies, and had a great deal of power in the government as well. Hindenburg was elected as president of Germany in 1925, when he was 78 years old, and he remained president until he died in 1934. While president he made the bad mistake of allowing Adolf Hitler to gain control of the German government.

Gale Research Co.

Hindu

A Hindu is a person who follows a very ancient religion called Hinduism. There are about 472,000,000 Hindus, and most of them live in India. The Hindu religion was taken to India, more than 3,500 years ago, by people who came from eastern Europe. These people were called Aryans, and different tribes of them settled in various parts of Asia. In India they married into the families of the Dravidians and other people already living there and became Indians too.

The Hindu religion has changed a great deal in the course of the centuries. Today the beliefs of the many sects, or groups, of Hindus differ among themselves, but all members of the religion are known for the respect with which they treat the beliefs of others.

Most Hindus share certain beliefs. They believe that Brahma is the Supreme Being, or God, and that his spirit is everywhere, in everything, no matter how small. God also may have other forms. He appears as the god Vishnu, who saves and heals, and also as the goddess Siva, who destroys. The stories of the many Hindu gods are written in the books of sacred, or holy, poetry called the *Vedas*. Some of these poems were written more than a thousand years before the birth of Jesus.

The Hindus believe also that when a man dies his soul moves into another body, perhaps even into the body of an animal. This is called the transmigration of souls, and his new form is called a reincarnation. The Hindus do not believe that any living thing should be killed, not even an insect. They do not kill animals for food, and the cow is a particularly sacred animal. The Hindus believe that a man may avoid having to go through so many transmigrations if he lives according to the rules of Brahma and that his conduct in one body has a great deal to do with the next body that his soul inhabits.

The Hindus also believe in the caste system. They think that all persons are born belonging to one of four classes, or castes. The highest caste is the Brahman class, or the priests. Next comes the Kshatriya caste, or soldier. The Vaisya are the third caste, and they are farmers or tradesmen. The Sudra are the lowest caste and are laborers. Below these are people who have no caste at all; they are called untouchables or *pariahs*.

If a child is born a Sudra, he must always do hard work. His children must also be Sudras. He may not marry or eat with or even touch a person who is not also a Sudra. Hindus used to feel that just the shadow of someone from a lower caste, or the shadow of a European or an American without any caste at all, could make them dirty. The untouchables were not allowed to use the public roads or temples, and they had to live outside the Hindu villages and do unclean work. In 1947 the government of India declared that such treatment of untouchables was illegal. Today in India the untouchables are no longer forbidden to choose their work, and they may live where they please. Many people in India hope that in time the caste system itself will disappear entirely.

Hindustan

Hindustan is a name given to a region of northern India to distinguish it from the southern part of India. It is drained by the Ganges River and lies east of the Indus River. The name Hindustan is a Persian word that means "land of the Hindus." Since 1947, when India was divided into two countries, India and Pakistan, the term Hindustan has sometimes been used to mean the new Republic of India, since most of the people in India are Hindus and most of the people in Pakistan are Moslems, or followers of the religion of Mohammed.

hip is the place where the leg joins the rest of the body: see the article on JOINT.

Hippocrates

Hippocrates was a great Greek doctor who is called "the father of medicine." He lived in Greece, about 2,500 years ago. He was born in 460 B.C. and died in 357 B.C. In this period artists and philosophers and poets were working and studying in Greece as they never had before. Older doctors had tried to cure sick people with magic. Hippocrates was the first to study nature instead of magic, and the first to say the sick needed rest, fresh air, light, cleanliness, and proper food. He originated the Oath of Hippocrates, to which young doctors still swear today when they leave medical school. The oath binds them to honor their teachers, do their best for the sick, never give poisons, and keep the secrets of their patients.

hippodrome

A hippodrome is a large theater or arena where many people can watch plays, horse races, and other entertainments. The ancient Greeks, about 2,500 years ago, loved to watch horse races and chariot races, and they built huge hippodromes so that thousands of people could attend. Later, in Constantinople, racing became even more popular, and the ruins of a great hippodrome can still be seen there. In recent times hippodromes have been built in London and in New York, where they have been used as large theaters.

hippopotamus

Hippopotamus means "river horse." Hippopotamuses are huge animals that spend most of their time in water, usually living in lakes, rivers, and small streams. They are excellent swimmers and they can remain under water 8 or 10 minutes at one time.

The most familiar hippopotamus is found throughout Africa. It is a very large animal and weighs about 1,500 pounds, about as much as a jeep. It has a great square head, four short legs, and a short tail. Its thick skin is almost hairless and is dark grey. Its tusks, or upper front teeth, are very long. Hippopotamus tusks are considered valuable by the African people. The animal is also killed for its meat. The hippopotamus does not like trouble and it is quick to avoid a fight, but when it is cornered it can be very brave and fierce. It never travels alone. It can usually be found in herds of twenty or thirty hippopotamuses. It is a herbivo-

rous, or plant-eating, animal. It feeds on plants found in the water and along the shores. It often leaves the water after nightfall and goes to grassy pastures to eat some more. When this happens, natives set traps upon its path to capture it.

Hirohito

Hirohito became Emperor of Japan in 1926. At that time many people in Japan believed that the emperor was a god, so they thought Hirohito was a god. He was born in 1901, and became the 124th emperor in his direct family line. He was a quiet, studious man 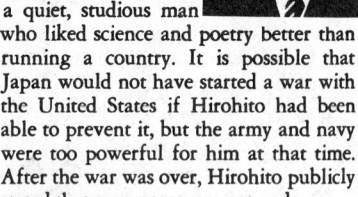 who liked science and poetry better than running a country. It is possible that Japan would not have started a war with the United States if Hirohito had been able to prevent it, but the army and navy were too powerful for him at that time. After the war was over, Hirohito publicly stated that emperors were not gods.

Hiroshima

Hiroshima is the name of a trading city and seaport in southern Japan. The city of Hiroshima is important in history as the first city to be hit by an atomic bomb. During World War II, on August 6, 1945, an American B-29 airplane dropped an atomic bomb over the center of the city. As a result of the terrible explosion, more than 4 square miles of the central part of the city were destroyed and many thousands of people were killed. Since the end of the war, Hiroshima has been rebuilt entirely, and in 1973 its population was 549,000 (compared to 225,000 in 1945).

Hispaniola, an island of the West Indies in the Caribbean Sea. It is often called Haiti. Over nine million people live there. See the articles on DOMINICAN REPUBLIC and HAITI.

Hiss, Alger

Alger Hiss was a United States government official who was found guilty of perjury (lying) when he denied he had ever been a Communist, and in 1950 was sent to prison for five years. Hiss was accused by Whittaker Chambers, a former Communist, of having given secret papers and information to the Russian government, and his trials were famous events of 1949 and 1950.

Hiss was born in Baltimore, Maryland, in 1904. He became a lawyer. In addition to his government positions, in 1947 he became president of the Carnegie Endowment for World Peace. When he was accused of being a Communist, in 1948, many prominent Americans could not believe it.

history

History is a record or report of what happened in the past. People study history for two reasons. One reason is that history is a fascinating story. The other reason is that knowledge of the past often helps a person to understand what is happening in the present and to know what will probably happen in the future. There is a saying that history repeats itself. This is not true, but it is true that many soldiers, statesmen and scientists could not do their work as well if they had not studied history. Many people particularly like to read the history of their own country, because the events of the past make them proud of their country and of the people who helped build it.

The past is divided into two main divisions, history and prehistory. Prehistory is the time before records were written down. Prehistoric times also include the period when there was some written history but not enough to tell us all we would like to know about the period. Most of our knowledge of prehistoric times comes from ARCHAEOLOGY and GEOLOGY, about which there are separate articles.

The earliest written history that has come down to us is the historical books of the Bible, such as 1 and 2 Kings and the Book of Judges. These books go as far back as a thousand years before the birth of Jesus. There are earlier records, but they are incomplete. Most of them tell only the names of a family of kings, or a king's achievements.

Herodotus, who lived in Greece about 2,400 years ago, is called "the father of history." He was the first man to write down the histories of other nations. He wrote nine books of history, mainly about the wars between Greece and Persia. In later centuries, Roman historians wrote the history of the past as well as the history of their own times. Two of the most important were Livy, who lived in Rome during the time of Christ, and Tacitus, who lived about fifty years later. At the same time Josephus, a Jewish scholar, wrote a history of the Jews from the time of creation to the time of the war with Rome. Too often, these historians set down legends as though they were facts.

The first writer to write history in the modern manner was the French writer Voltaire, who lived from 1694 until 1778. He tried to write about history as a whole and show its effect on the people. He did two important things that all historians have since adopted. Instead of depending upon what other historians said about things that had happened in the past, Voltaire read as many original papers and records as he could find. Such records are called original sources. Voltaire also documented his work, which means that when he stated a fact of history he told where he had found his information. All writers of modern history give documentation for the facts they include in their books.

The modern style of writing history began in England with Edward Gibbon, who in 1788 finished his six-volume work called *The Decline and Fall of the Roman Empire.* Gibbon, an Englishman, spent many years in Rome gathering material.

When the New World was discovered, many of the early settlers wrote about it. Of particular interest to Americans is the history of the Plymouth colony written by William Bradford, one of the early governors of the colony. George Bancroft's history of the United States was outstanding in the last century, as was Francis Parkman's *Oregon Trail.* the story of the settlement of the northwestern United States and of the Indians who lived there.

The present-day historian whose work has attracted the most attention is Arnold Toynbee, an Englishman. His chief work, *A Study of History,* began to be published in 1934.

It is usual to divide history into three periods, called ancient history, medieval history, and modern history.

ANCIENT HISTORY

Ancient history includes all written history from the beginning up until the fall of the city of Rome, about 1,500 years ago. It covers a period of about five thousand years. In ancient history is included the rise of the Egyptian and Hebrew civilizations. Some of this history goes back six or seven thousand years. It includes the rise and fall of great empires that grew up in Persia, Assyria, and many other nations on or near the Mediterranean. This includes the great Greek civilization, and the growth of the Roman Empire until it ruled nearly all the civilized world. In the year 455 Rome was finally overcome by German invaders, but the eastern part of the Roman Empire remained, with its capital at Constantinople, in Greece.

MEDIEVAL HISTORY

Medieval history covers a period of about a thousand years. Gibbon ended his history with the fall of Constantinople to the Turks in 1453, and some modern historians end medieval history there. Others think it ended in 1492, the year in which Columbus discovered America. Still others end it in 1648 when the religious wars called the Thirty Years War ended.

During the medieval period, or Middle Ages, Christianity spread throughout most of Europe, and the Roman Catholic Church became very powerful. A new religious leader, Mohammed, was born in Arabia, and founded a new religion. The Holy Roman Empire was founded. Soldiers from all over Europe organized crusades to recapture the Holy Land from the Mohammedans. Much of the learning of the Romans and Greeks was lost, and people later came to speak of much of this period as the Dark Ages.

During the period of medieval history new nations were born in Europe, and new feelings of nationalism, or patriotism, were built up. Great emperors, such as Charlemagne, lived. Near the end of the medieval period there came a new interest in the learning of the past, which people came to speak of as the Renaissance. New inventions were made, and explorers went out in search of new lands. It is at this point in history that we say the modern era began.

MODERN HISTORY

Modern history is only about five hundred years old. It is a short period compared to the other two divisions of history. Yet we know more about what has happened in the last five hundred years than we know about all the years of medieval and ancient history. Only in modern times has man been careful to keep a record of everything that happens.

Modern history has several divisions within itself. Some historians write social history, that is, history of the people themselves and the cultures in which they live and the ways in which these cultures change. Some write economic history, which tells how the wealth of the world influences the people who live in it. Some write political history, which tells of the governments of the world and the ways in which they change and what new ideas are used in them.

Much biography, the story of a man's life, is a kind of history, as is autobiography, the story a man writes of his own life. Biography and autobiography often tell a great deal about the conditions in which the subject of the book lived.

NATURAL HISTORY is a different kind of history. There is a separate article about it.

Hitler, Adolf

Adolf Hitler was Germany's fanatical dictator from 1933 to 1945. His actions resulted in the death of millions of people and plunged the world into

Gale Research Co.

World War II. He was born in 1889 in Austria, the son of Alois Hitler, a customs officer. Hitler's mother was a housemaid. Hitler wanted to study fine arts or architecture, but he had to go to

work as a day laborer before he was 20 years old. He moved to the city of Vienna, where he was very poor. He came to think that the world had treated him very badly, and for this reason he hated almost all the people around him and especially the Jews. He managed to live by doing odd jobs and by selling picture postcards that he painted himself. In 1913 he left Vienna and moved to Munich, the capital of Bavaria, part of Germany.

When World War I began, Hitler enlisted in the German army and became a corporal. In 1919, after the war, he joined a new political group called the German Workers' Party. At this time he discovered that by a certain kind of loud and excited speeches he could arouse many people to hate the things he hated himself. He talked to veterans of the war who were having a hard time getting back on their feet in civilian life. He ranted and raved against the unfairness (to Germany) of the Versailles Treaty that ended World War I, and against all Jewish people.

Hitler was a strange-looking man, with wild eyes, a lock of black hair that fell over his forehead, and a funny little mustache. He let it be known that he lived alone, ate a strict diet of vegetables and no meat, and never drank alcoholic liquors.

In 1920 Hitler formed his own political party and called it the National Socialist German Workers' Party, or, for short, the Nazi Party. Many prominent Germans joined this party, and Hitler organized his own little army and called them Storm Troopers. Three years later he felt strong enough to try to take over control of the city of Munich. He tried this in an attack that is now called the "beer hall putsch," because it started in a place where people went to drink beer. Hitler and his Storm

Troopers tried to scare the elected officers of Munich into surrendering. With him were Field Marshal Ludendorff, who had been one of Germany's principal military leaders, and Hermann Goering, who later became famous as one of Hitler's chief aides. The National Guard fired on the marchers, and fourteen Hitlerites were killed. Hitler ran away, but he was captured and sentenced to five years in prison. He served only about nine months of that sentence, but it was long enough for him to write a book, *Mein Kampf,* which means "My Fight." No one outside of Germany paid much attention to the book, though it contained the whole story of what Hitler planned to do to gain control of Germany and the world.

For the next five years Hitler had little success. Then, in 1929, business in Germany became very bad, and the Nazi Party began a propaganda campaign to win members by telling the working people that Hitler would bring them steady jobs by controlling big business, and that he was against Communism, which was then gaining some strength in Europe. Hitler became a German citizen, and he ran for the presidency of Germany. Although he lost, his Nazi Party soon became the strongest in the country. In 1933 Hitler was appointed chancellor, which was the highest office, next to president, in Germany.

Later in 1933, the Reichstag, or German parliament building, burned down. Hitler accused the Communists of burning it, though actually the Nazis had set the fire. The people believed Hitler, which gave his Storm Troopers a chance to spread terror across the nation while they arrested everyone suspected of being a Communist. In March, 1933, the Reichstag voted to give Hitler the powers of a dictator. He soon became both chancellor and president, and took the new title of *Führer,* or leader.

Although Hitler worked from the beginning by frightening and threatening the people, most of the German people approved of his rule at first. His propaganda chief, Paul Goebbels, pictured Hitler as a sort of superman to be worshipped by the German "master race." Everyone was obliged to give the salute "Heil Hitler."

In 1938, Hitler took control of Austria and made it part of Germany. Later that year he managed to get the big nations of Europe to sign the Munich Pact, giving part of Czechoslovakia to Germany. This was supposed to end Hitler's demands for territory, but in 1939 he signed a friendship treaty with his old enemy, Russia, and on September 1, 1939, he invaded Poland, and World War II had begun. At first this war went well for Germany, but in 1944 Germany suffered some serious losses, and a group of army and state officials tried to kill Hitler. Their plot failed, and the Nazis killed thousands of people in revenge.

Hitler is said to have suffered a nervous breakdown during the last months of the war, but he did not give up his power and he stayed in his Berlin headquarters, a bomb shelter under the chancellery, until Russian armies were in Berlin. Then he formally married Eva Braun, who for years had been his favorite but not his

legal wife, and shot his wife and himself to death.

During Hitler's twelve years in power, he was responsible for the most horrible crimes. Millions of people were tortured and slain, and those who lived in Germany and the conquered countries never could know a moment's peace or safety.

Hittites

The Hittites were a people who lived in Asia Minor about four thousand years ago. We do not know where they came from, but they founded an empire that lasted for several centuries. Their capital, which lay on the Halys River in Asia Minor, has been excavated and their records have been deciphered. The laws of the Hittites were strict but not so cruel as the laws of the other old peoples. The Hittites fought a great war with the Egyptians over the control of Syria and Palestine. There is a detailed account of the great Battle of Kadesh (about 1294 B.C.), in which the Egyptians narrowly escaped defeat. A great treaty of peace between the Egyptian and Hittite kings fixed the boundary between their empires on the northern border of Palestine. The Hittite empire collapsed at the time when western Asia was overrun by the migration of peoples coming from Europe and the Mediterranean islands. This was about 1200 B.C.

hives

Hives is a skin disease. It causes little spots in a red rash on the skin. It is very unpleasant because often the rash itches. Hives is caused by an allergy, a reaction to eating certain foods or to other things. There is a separate article on ALLERGY.

hobbies

A hobby is something a person likes to do in his spare time, apart from his regular business or school work. Hobbies in which you collect things are most popular. They include collecting stamps, coins, minerals, dolls, antiques, books, autographs (signatures) of famous people, phonograph records, and buttons. Some people even make a hobby of collecting such things as matchbooks, election campaign buttons, and theater programs. [There are separate articles on STAMP COLLECTING and NUMISMATICS (coin collecting)]

Then there are the model-building hobbies, in which the hobbyists build such things as model airplanes, ships, and railroad trains. Some model-building hobbyists specialize in building models that can actually operate.

Other popular hobbies are PHOTOGRAPHY (about which there is a separate article), arts and crafts (which are discussed in the article on HANDCRAFTS), painting, and sculpture. A favorite hobby of boys and girls is keeping pets such as tropical fish, parakeets, and hamsters.

In recent years there has been a great increase in the number of people who have hobbies. The reason is that people work fewer hours than they used to and so have more time for such activities as hobbies.

Although the main purpose of a hobby is recreation, some people make extra money from their hobbies. This is particularly true of those hobbies in which the people make things, as in photography and the arts and crafts.

There are special magazines and books devoted to particular hobbies. From these you can learn new and interesting things about hobbies. In some hobbies there are exhibitions of the work done. Sometimes there are contests for prizes, as in the case of the SOAPBOX DERBY, about which there is a separate article.

Hobby, Oveta Culp

Oveta Culp Hobby was the second woman in the United States ever to become a member of the President's cabinet. The cabinet members are chosen by the President to head the various departments within the government and to help and advise him. In 1953 President Eisenhower appointed Mrs. Hobby Secretary of the Department of Health, Education, and Welfare. The only other woman to have had a cabinet position was Frances Perkins, who was Secretary of Labor under President Franklin D. Roosevelt. During World War II Mrs. Hobby was director of the Women's Army Corps (WAC) of the United States Army. She held the rank of colonel.

Oveta Culp Hobby was born in Killeen, Texas, in 1905. Killeen is a small town that has only about twelve hundred people living in it. Her parents were very religious, and they brought her up very strictly. She was not allowed to play cards or to dance. Her father was a lawyer and was interested in politics. The young Oveta Culp spent much of her time with him. She spent hours in his office reading his law books or the Congressional Record, which reports everything that happens in the United States Congress. She also often went with her father to Austin, the capital of Texas, where the state's important political activities go on.

Mrs. Hobby went to public school in Texas and also had some private tutors. She studied at Mary Hardin Baylor College in Texas and at the Texas Law School. When she was only 20 years of age she became parliamentarian for the Texas House of Representatives. This means that she answered all questions about the procedure that the representatives should follow in making the laws. She ran for office in the Texas State Legislature three years later but was defeated.

In 1931, when she was 26 years old, Oveta Culp was married to William Hobby of Houston, Texas. He was a very rich and prominent man. He had also been governor of Texas, and he owned the Houston Post, a large newspaper. Mrs. Hobby helped her husband on the newspaper and later ran it alone when he became too busy with other duties. Governor and Mrs. Hobby had two children, a son and a daughter, but Mrs. Hobby continued to be very active in civic and political life. When the United States Army decided to enlist women, in 1942, it was obviously necessary to have one of the country's most prominent women as its director. The fact that Mrs. Hobby was selected is an indication of the respect in which she was held.

Hobson, Richmond Pearson

Richmond Pearson Hobson was an American naval hero of the Spanish-American War of 1898. Hobson was born in Greensboro, Alabama, in 1870, and was graduated from the United States Naval Academy at Annapolis. In the Spanish-American War, Hobson was a lieutenant in the United States Navy. The Americans wanted to keep the Spanish fleet from getting out of Santiago harbor, in Cuba. So Hobson took a coal boat, the *Merrimac,* to the entrance of the harbor, right in front of the Spanish guns, and sank it. Hobson and the men with him were taken prisoner, but they were set free again soon after, when the war ended. Thirty-five years afterward, in 1933, Hobson received the Congressional Medal of Honor for this act. He resigned from the Navy in 1903, and for some years he represented Alabama in the Congress, in the House of Representatives. He died in 1937.

Hobson's choice

This is an expression used when it seems that there is a choice between two things but when really you can take only a certain one or do without. It originated with a man named Tobias Hobson who lived in Cambridge, England, about four hundred years ago. He used to rent horses to the students of Cambridge University. Very politely he would ask them to choose the horse they wanted, but they soon found that if they did not choose the one nearest the door, they ended up with no horse at all!

hockey

Hockey is a game in which the players try to hit a small rubber disk or ball with sticks so that it will go into a goal at one end of the playing area. There are two kinds of hockey, field hockey and ice hockey. Field hockey is the original form of the game. It is played by both sexes, and in the United States it is the most popular sport in girls' schools and women's colleges. Ice hockey is a later development, played on ice by men and boys, and is very popular in winter in the northern parts of the United States and especially in Canada.

FIELD HOCKEY

Hockey gets its name from the word *hoquet,* which is French for "shepherd's crook." The game has been known for centuries, probably having been first played by the ancient Persians. The modern version of field hockey was begun in England in 1875 and was imported into America soon after. In 1922, the United States Field Hockey Association was formed, and it has been in charge of the game since then. Field hockey is played on a field that is 90 to 100 yards long and 50 to 60 yards wide, with goals at either end 12 feet wide and 7 feet high. There are 11 players on each team—5 forwards, 3 halfbacks, 2 backs, and a goalkeeper. The ball is made of cork and twine, covered with white leather, and is 9 inches in diameter.

A game, which consists of two 30-minute halves, is started by a *face-off* or *bully-off* between the two center forwards, after which the players dribble, drive, and pass the ball down the field, trying to put it into one of the goals. If an attacking player hits the ball out of bounds, a bully-off is held 25 yards in from where it went out; if a defender hits it out, it is put into play by the attackers by means of a *corner hit.* There are penalties for illegal use of sticks and for roughness. One point is scored for each goal that is made. In a number of foreign countries, especially India and Pakistan, field hockey is played by men. It is one of the games played in the Olympic Games.

ICE HOCKEY

Hockey was first played on ice in Canada, late in the 19th century. It was probably first played by students at McGill University in Montreal in the 1870s. The first set of rules was published in 1879, and the first league hockey game was played six years later. Hockey's popularity spread through Canada and into New England and other cooler parts of the United States. With the invention of artificial ice and the building of indoor rinks, the game spread to warmer sections of the country. In the North, children play hockey all winter on frozen streams and ponds.

HOCKEY LEAGUE

Professional hockey teams organized in leagues play games at indoor rinks, and they draw crowds as big as 20,000 people. The most important of the leagues is the National Hockey League, which was formed in Canada in 1908, and now is made up of six teams: the Boston Bruins, Chicago Black Hawks, Detroit Red Wings, Montreal Canadiens, New York Rangers, and Toronto Maple Leafs. Each team plays a season of 70 games, after which the four with the best won-and-lost records have a series of play-offs for the Stanley Cup, a trophy donated by Lord Frederick Stanley.

There are many colleges and high schools that have hockey teams, and in Canada there are a large number of amateur leagues sponsored by the Canadian Amateur Hockey Association. When a Canadian boy is 13 years old, he can begin playing as a Midget, and after that, if he is good enough, he can join a Juvenile, Junior, and finally a Senior league team. Then, if he has developed into a top-notch player, he may get a chance with one of the minor professional leagues or even a National Hockey League team. Most of the professional players in the United States and Canada are Canadians. In the United States, the National Collegiate Athletic Association sponsors a tournament each year among the best college hockey teams, and every four years a team of amateur players is picked to represent the United States in the Olympic Games.

HOW ICE HOCKEY IS PLAYED

The ice surface on which hockey is played is called the rink. It is rectangular in shape, with the corners rounded. Its length may be from 165 to 250 feet, with a width of from 60 to 110 feet, but the regulation size is 200 by 85 feet. The rink is surrounded by sideboards and endboards 3 to 4 feet high, and these are usually topped by a plastic or wire screen

to protect spectators. The goals are three-sided nets 6 feet long, 4 feet high, and 17 to 22 inches deep. They must be set at least 10 feet from each end of the rink so that there is room for a player to skate behind the net. Painted lines on the ice divide the rink into several playing areas. There is a red line that extends across the width of the ice, even with the mouth of each goal, and 60 feet out from these red lines are painted blue lines. An area of ice 8 feet wide and 5 feet deep in from each goal is outlined in red and known as the *crease*. The *puck* is made of vulcanized rubber, 1 inch thick and 3 inches in diameter. It is moved along the ice by sticks, which are about 4 feet long, with flat blades 3 inches high.

Each team has six players—three forwards (left and right wings and center), two defense men, and a goalie. Substitutions may be made at any time, and a team usually changes its forward lines and defense men frequently since the action is so fast and rough. A game is divided into three 20-minute periods. College teams play an overtime period in case of a tie; the National Hockey League uses overtime only in Stanley Cup play-off games. One point is scored for each goal that is made, and the scoring is never very high, four or five goals almost always being enough to win a professional game.

Play starts when the referee drops the puck on the ice between the sticks of the two centers, in what is called the *face-off*. The players then push the puck along the ice with their sticks, pass it to teammates, or shoot for their opponents' goal, all while skating along the ice at top speed. They are often knocked to the ice by *body checks*, and fights and injuries are not uncommon. There are many kinds of penalties. Players may be put off the ice for two, five, or ten minutes at a time for high sticking, interference, tripping, playing with a broken stick, arguing with the referee, and many other infractions of the rules. While any of its players are in the penalty box a team must play without them.

To be a good hockey player, you must be, first of all, a very good ice-skater. You must be able to start fast from a dead stop, turn quickly, stop in less than four feet of ice, and keep on your feet. You must be able to make short, quick, accurate passes, and be able to get the puck past the goalie. A forward should be a good stick handler and an accurate shot, and be able to get around the defense. A defense man should be able to body-check well, get the puck away from the attacking team, and recover rebounds. The goalie should have very fast reflexes and good eyes, and should know how to play the other positions, so that he can predict where shots are likely to come from.

Hoe, Richard March

Richard March Hoe was an American inventor whose ideas did a great deal to make possible the big daily newspapers of modern cities. Hoe was born in 1812. His father was the founder of a company that manufactured printing presses, and Richard Hoe entered the business at the age of 15. Hoe designed and manufactured a press in which the type was set in a flat bed and the paper was on a cylinder that rolled over it. Later he developed a rotary press, in which both the type and the paper were on cylinders. This press made it possible to print four times as many copies in the same length of time. Hoe also invented a folding machine to fold papers as they come from the press. He died in 1886.

hog, a domestic animal used for food: see the article on PIG.

Hogarth, William

William Hogarth was an English painter and engraver. He was born in 1697, and showed an interest in drawing even as a child. He did some illustrations for books and some portraits of famous people. But instead of painting only what was beautiful, Hogarth used his pictures to satirize, or poke fun at, those who pretended to believe one thing while they acted in a very different way. His most famous set of pictures is called, "Marriage à la Mode," or "Fashionable Marriage." It shows people who pretend to marry for love but really marry for money or position in society. Hogarth died in 1764.

Hohenzollern

Hohenzollern was the family name of many kings and emperors in Germany. The name means "high Zollern." Zollern was the family's castle in Germany more than seven hundred years ago. About the year 1400 the Hohenzollerns became the rulers of Brandenburg, a small kingdom of Germany. Later, in 1701, Frederick I, a Hohenzollern, became king of Prussia, the most powerful kingdom in Germany. In 1871 Prussia and other north German kingdoms joined together to form the German Empire, and a Hohenzollern, William I, became the German emperor, or Kaiser. The last Hohenzollern to rule in Germany was William II, who was German emperor during World War I and who lost his throne in 1918 when Germany was defeated.

Members of another branch of the Hohenzollerns were kings of Rumania. When Rumania became an independent nation, in 1878, a Hohenzollern prince was asked to become its first king. He accepted and in 1881 became Carol I of Rumania. After World War II the Communists gained control of Rumania, and in 1947 they forced Carol I's grandson, King Michael, to abdicate, or give up his throne.

Holbein, Hans

Hans Holbein was the name of two German painters, father and son. The father, called Hans Holbein the Elder, was a painter of religious subjects for church altarpieces. Very little is known of his life. He was born around 1460 and died, a poor man, about 1524.

Hans Holbein the Younger, his son, became famous as a portrait and religious painter. He was born in Augsburg, Germany, in 1497. He studied painting with his father and worked in many other fields of art, such as illustrating books and making woodcuts. He loved to paint, and he became famous throughout Germany and Hol-

land for his religious pictures. He went to England, where he spent most of his time painting pictures of the nobles at the court of King Henry VIII, and of Henry himself. The Holbein pictures you see today are usually these beautiful portraits. King Henry made him court painter, and in this position he painted many pictures, designed jewelry, painted scenery for plays, and designed furniture and decorations for houses. When Holbein died in England in 1543 he was rich and famous.

holiday

A holiday is a day on which people do not work. It is usually a day on which people celebrate in some way, often by having special ceremonies or parties. The word *holiday* comes from the words *holy* and *day,* and at one time holidays were days set aside for religious reasons. Now some holidays are religious but most are in memory of some important event in the history of a country.

LEGAL HOLIDAYS

In the United States legal holidays are the days on which all schools, banks and offices are closed. The government of each state decides which days will be legal holidays in that state, and the governor issues proclamations to the people that tell which days will be legal holidays and why. Not all states have the same legal holidays. The following days are legal holidays in all states: New Year's Day, January 1; Easter, a Sunday in March or April; Memorial Day, May 30; Independence Day, July 4; Labor Day, the first Monday in September; Veterans' Day, November 11; Thanksgiving, usually the last Thursday in November; and Christmas, December 25. There are other holidays that may be legal holidays in some states. These include Lincoln's Birthday, February 12; Washington's Birthday, February 22; Good Friday, the Friday before Easter; Columbus Day, October 12; and Election Day, usually during the first week in November. A state may have holidays celebrating the anniversaries of famous events in its history or the birthdays of famous Americans. Saturday is considered a half-holiday in most states, since most banks and offices are closed on Saturday afternoon.

Christmas and Easter are religious holidays and are celebrated by Christian people all over the world. In countries where the people are mostly Roman Catholics there are many more religious holidays. Other religions also have days set aside as holidays.

Canada celebrates many of the same holidays as the United States, as well as its own national holidays, which include Canada Day, July 1, and British Empire Day, May 24. Canadians celebrate Thanksgiving Day in October.

Holland is a small country in the northern part of Europe: see the article on NETHERLANDS.

holly

The holly, or *Ilex,* is a tree with shiny evergreen leaves and little bright berries. You have seen the kind with red berries at Christmas, but some have yellow or white or even black berries. Some have prickly leaves, and others not. There

are about three hundred kinds of holly, and it grows all over the world. About twelve kinds grow in the eastern United States. The American holly sometimes grows to be 50 feet high in moist regions along the coasts. The Virginia winterberry or black alder is a holly, and another kind, the cassena, was used by the Indians as a medicine.

The Indians of Paraguay still drink a kind of tea called maté, which is made from holly leaves. If people eat the berries they are made very sick, but birds like to eat them. The leaves are eaten by sheep and deer, and in parts of France the cattle are fed holly all winter. We also use the wood of the holly, which is hard and has a pretty white color like ivory. In Europe, the holly is a very old and famous tree that grows in groves and gardens. We still like branches of holly to decorate our houses at Christmas time. The ancient Romans also used it this way centuries ago at their rowdy festival called the Saturnalia.

hollyhock

The hollyhock is a flower that is very popular in gardens all over the world. It originally grew wild in China and India and in parts of Europe. The hollyhock may be anywhere from three to eight feet high. It has heavy foliage at its base and a tall, straight stem, along which the flowers grow close together, especially near the top of the stem. The blossoms are single or double and have five petals, which may be white, pink, yellow, scarlet, or purple. The hollyhock is either a perennial, which means that it comes up year after year, or a biennial, which means that it lives for only two years. It is often planted to make a border along a wall of a garden.

Hollywood

Hollywood is known throughout the world as the center of the American motion-picture industry. It was a separate city until 1910, when it became part of Los Angeles, California. Now almost 200,000 people live there. Many of them work in film studios and in offices connected with the motion-picture industry.

Because of the glamorous lives of film stars and the modern way of life shown in many films, the word Hollywood has been used to describe modern styles of clothing, architecture, and even ways of thinking. The corner where Hollywood's two main streets, Hollywood and Vine, meet is sometimes called the center of the motion-picture industry. Actually, many of the motion-picture companies now have their studios in other suburbs of Los Angeles, such as Culver City and Burbank.

Holmes, Oliver Wendell

There were two great Americans named Oliver Wendell Holmes. They were father and son. The elder Oliver Wendell Holmes was a doctor and writer. He was born in Cambridge, Massachusetts, in 1809, and was graduated from Harvard University, where he later taught medicine after studying in Paris, France. He was a very popular teacher and lecturer and wrote several important medical works, but he is best remembered for his humorous poems and essays. (An essay is a short article in which the author gives his thoughts on a certain subject.) Many of Holmes' poems and essays were published in the *Atlantic Monthly* magazine. Later they were collected in books, the best known of which is called *The Autocrat of the Breakfast-Table.* One very famous poem is "The Deacon's Masterpiece; or, The Wonderful One-Horse Shay." Another, which he wrote while he was studying at Harvard, is "Old Ironsides," about the warship *Constitution.* He died in 1894.

The younger Oliver Wendell Holmes was born in 1841. He also went to Harvard, where he studied law. Later he taught law at Harvard and wrote books and articles about law. In 1902, after having served as Chief Justice of the Supreme Court of Mas-  *Gale Research Co.* sachusetts, he became an Associate Justice of the United States Supreme Court. He was a great judge and was always interested in the problems of the people. He became known as the "great dissenter" because he disagreed with so many of the other judges when matters of the people's rights were concerned. Oliver Wendell Holmes died in 1935, when he was 94 years old.

Holy Alliance

The Holy Alliance was an agreement between Emperor Alexander I of Russia, Emperor Francis I of Austria, and King Frederick William III of Prussia. The alliance was made in 1815, shortly after Napoleon had been defeated at Waterloo. Europe was tired of the wars it had seen under Napoleon, and the alliance was supposed to bring lasting peace. The leaders of these three nations promised to follow Christian rules of conduct and not to fight any wars unless they had to punish nations that started them. Later most other European nations joined this alliance. Actually the alliance itself was not important, but it was made at a time when the strong rulers in Europe were dividing up some of the land that had been conquered by Napoleon, and it gave these rulers a chance to interfere in the affairs of other nations.

Holy City

Jerusalem is called the Holy City by three of the world's major faiths, Christianity, Judaism, and Islam. The Jews consider Jerusalem a holy city because the Temple of David, the most sacred shrine of the Jews, is there. Jews have always thought of Jerusalem as the city of peace and their real home. It is the capital of Israel. Mohammedans consider Jerusalem their third holy city, after Mecca and Medina, because so many of their saints, including Jesus himself, were Jewish. Christians consider Jerusalem the holy city because it was here that Jesus taught and near here that he was crucified.

Holy Cross

The College of the Holy Cross is a college for men in Worcester, Massachusetts. It is conducted by members of the Society of Jesus (the Jesuits), a Roman Catholic order. More than 1,500 men attend Holy Cross. It is on top of Mount St. James, which was once called the "Hill of Pleasant Springs." A student at Holy Cross can study many subjects, including business, education, sociology, and various sciences. The college has a fine library and a fully equipped astronomical laboratory. It also has its own radio station, run by the students. The College of the Holy Cross is more than a hundred years old. It became a Jesuit college in 1846.

Holy Family

The Holy Family is the family of Jesus. It includes Jesus, his mother Mary, and his earthly father Joseph. Mary's mother, Saint Anne, Jesus' cousin, John the Baptist, and John's mother, Saint Elisabeth, are sometimes considered part of the Holy Family. The Roman Catholic Church has a feast day in honor of the Holy Family. Artists all over the world have made paintings of the Holy Family. Usually such paintings show Jesus as a baby in his mother's arms.

Holy Grail

A grail is a cup, and the Holy Grail is the cup used by Jesus at the last supper. According to legend, this cup was given to Joseph of Arimathea, the man who gave up his own tomb so that Jesus could be buried in it. Because the Holy Grail had belonged to Jesus, it had magical powers. Joseph of Arimathea was supposed to have taken it to England, where members of his family guarded it for many years. However, when the Grail came into the possession of a man who was evil and unworthy of owning it, it disappeared. Legend said it would be found again only when a worthy descendant of Joseph went in search of it. For years many people searched for the Holy Grail, but no one could find it. According to the tales told of King Arthur and his knights, the Knights of the Round Table, the Holy Grail was found again by Sir Galahad, who was the purest of the knights and a descendant of Joseph of Arimathea.

Holy Land, see PALESTINE.

Holy Roman Empire

Holy Roman Empire was a name used for hundreds of years to describe the German countries of Europe. There were many of these countries—often thirty or more of them—and each had its own ruler, a king, a duke, or some lesser nobleman. Each country was independent, but the more powerful of the countries elected an emperor who was considered the most powerful of all and who settled arguments for the other rulers.

The name "Holy Roman Empire" was used for two reasons. The ancient Roman Empire had ruled the entire civilized part of Europe and Africa, so the word "Roman" seemed to stand for power. The word "holy" was used because the countries were all united in the Roman Catholic Church, of which the Pope was the spiritual head. But it has been said that the Holy Roman Empire was neither holy, nor Roman, nor an empire. The emperors often were unfriendly with the Popes. The Holy Roman Empire included much territory that had never been part of Rome. The word "empire" was wrong

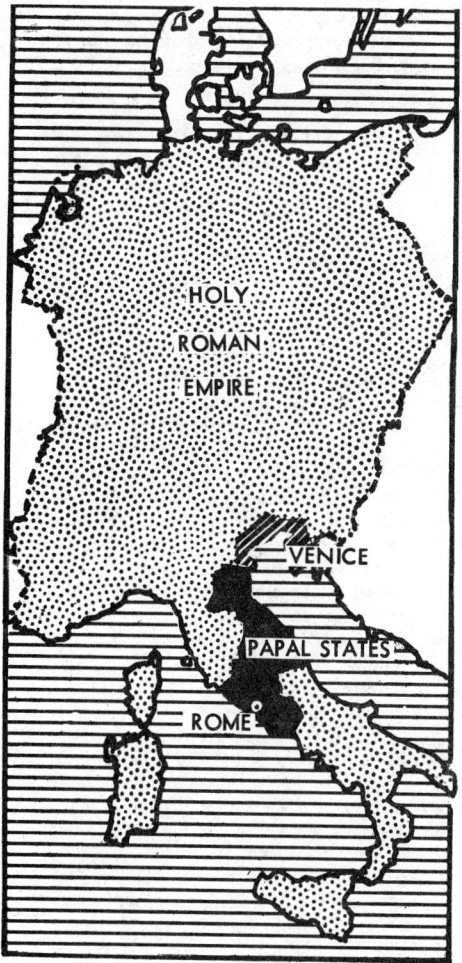

The dotted area shows the Holy Roman Empire in the year 1200. Compare it with the map of all Europe (see *Europe*).

because each part of it was independent, and the emperor had very little power except in his own country.

About a thousand years ago (in 962) the first Holy Roman Emperor was crowned by the Pope. He was Otto I, a descendant of the great French king Charlemagne. In 1273, Rudolf of Hapsburg was elected emperor, and after that the Holy Roman Emperors were usually elected from the HAPSBURG family (about which there is a separate article).

The German kings who had the privilege of voting in the election of the emperor were called *electors*. This was a more important title than king. King George I of England, before he became king of England, was the Elector of Hanover.

The Holy Roman Empire was never powerful or very important. At one time it included all of central Europe and north Italy, but France, the Scandinavian countries and southern Italy refused to join, and England and Spain paid no attention to it. In 1806 the emperor, Francis I, gave up the title of Holy Roman Emperor and instead used his title as Emperor of Austria.

Holy Week

Holy Week is the week that comes before Easter. Since this was the last week of Jesus' life on earth, it is a very solemn and holy period. Some people fast or do not eat anything on the Friday of that week, called Good Friday.

home economics

Home economics is the study of the ways to improve the home. Home economists work to discover new ways to better every aspect of the home environment. The field of home economics is divided into the five major aspects of the home: food and nutrition, clothing and textiles, family life and child development, management of the family income, and interior design.

Professional home economists are those people who have earned at least a college degree in this field. Everyone, however, who runs a home is a home economist. This person must know how to feed, clothe, and care for a family, budget the family income, and decorate the home attractively. A home is like a small business; it must be properly run in order to be successful.

Since home economics is so important, it is taught to students on a high school level. The students are given instruction in managing their future homes. For many years, home economics classes were taught only to girls; fortunately, today boys can also attend these courses. Everyone needs to know how to plan a budget so that all the needed things can be bought and all the bills paid without spending all the money. Also, everyone needs and wants an efficient, comfortable, and pleasant home.

HOME ECONOMICS AS A CAREER

Home economics is a fine career for many. Many colleges offer degrees in home economics, and courses that prepare people to be professional home economists. Home economics prepares you for two careers at the same time: earning a living and managing your own home. Today there are many worthwhile opportunities for those who choose this profession. Some manufacturers hire home economists to help in developing new products for the home. Others hire home economists to test recipes and foods before they are put on the market. Still other firms hire home economists to write booklets and articles about the many subjects that come under the heading of home economics.

Some home economists work for the government and prepare the many booklets distributed to housewives by the Department of Agriculture and other branches of the government. These booklets cover almost every subject that is in any way connected with home life and household management.

A professional home economist may also become a dietitian, which means that she would be qualified to plan well-balanced, tempting menus in a restaurant, hotel, school, hospital, or other institution. Training as a dietitian and the study of nutrition are also included in a college home economics course. There is a separate article about NUTRITION.

A person who has a college degree in home economics can choose from a wide variety of careers. As mentioned, a home economist can do research or become a dietitian. Teaching is another possibility. Many careers are available in the five different branches of home economics.

BRANCHES OF HOME ECONOMICS

1. FOOD AND NUTRITION

People who have specialized in this aspect of home economics are experts in buying, preparing, preserving, and storing food. They know that our bodies require certain elements, such as proteins and carbohydrates, for good health. Some foods provide these essentials better than other foods. Through research, they are constantly learning more about food and its nutritional value. Home economists have educated the public about the importance of a balanced diet.

Home economists have done many things to help women choose the right foods, save money in buying, and prepare nourishing, well-balanced and tempting meals. Buying meats is made easier for women by the United States Government inspection system. If a purple stamp is on the meat, the woman buying it knows that it came from a healthy animal.

Meat packers and good manufacturers publish hundreds of new and interesting recipes each year in free folders and booklets. The thrifty cook knows that she can make good use of inexpensive cuts of meat, as well as leftovers, by using the suggestions she will find in these folders.

An experienced housewife uses her knowledge of home economics when she goes to market. She knows that some foods may be cheaper at times than they are at other times. If she finds that lamb is a "better buy" than other meats, she will buy lamb. She also looks for the vegetables which are the best buys each day. By shopping in this way a housewife can save quite a bit of money over a year's time. The gadgets and appliances that make cooking and the preparation of food easier have been a great help to the housewife. Potatoes and carrots can be peeled with a special peeler, cake batters and mashed potatoes can be whipped up with an electric mixer, and a timer can automatically turn off the stove.

After a meal is over, the dishwashing can be made easier if the housewife takes advantage of things that home economists have learned. A most important point is the efficient arrangement and planning of the dishwashing process. An efficient homemaker washes her mixing bowls and utensils as soon as she finishes using them. Then they will not be piled up with the cooking pans and table dishes. It is efficient also to have the soap powder, scouring powder, dish drainer and towels all conveniently arranged, ready for use, and to have a table or counter beside the sink, where the clean things can be placed before they are returned to the cabinets.

2. CLOTHING AND TEXTILES

Clothing and textiles is another important branch of home economics. Home economists study different fibers used to make fabric and decide which fibers are best. A strong fiber is needed to make cloth for furniture upholstery, but a lightweight fiber may be better where strength is not important. Today many fabrics are synthetic or man-made, rather than coming from plants or animals. These new fabrics were researched by home economists to determine their proper use and care. A clothing and textile expert can design clothing and aid the home sewer.

Sewing is an important part of home economics, since most women have to do some mending and sewing. When a woman buys a sewing machine, she usually has the opportunity to take a course in dressmaking and sewing given by the manufacturer of the sewing machine. Many women make clothes for themselves and for their children.

Making draperies and slip covers is another part of the job of homemaking. A housewife can find many useful ideas and suggestions about this in books and magazine articles written by home economists.

3. FAMILY LIFE AND CHILD DEVELOPMENT

Family life and child development is the branch of home economics that works to improve the happiness and health of all those living in the home. They also study children at different age levels and provide information on the care and raising of children. This branch of home economics teaches methods of home health care and home nursing.

Parents must know how to take care of their children and themselves. They must be able to take temperatures and follow a doctor's instructions. In case of an emergency, they should know basic first aid until a doctor can be reached. Many children learn first aid in the Girl or Boy Scouts and can be very helpful in an emergency. All this is an important part of home economics.

4. MANAGEMENT OF FAMILY INCOME

Management of the family income is the branch of home economics that deals with the economics or the "business" of running a home. These home economists research the best ways to use money, time, energy, and talent in the home. They look for short-cuts in food preparation, housecleaning chores, and clothing care. They try to make budgets to suit families of different incomes. Few people can buy everything. Decisions must be made to determine what purchases are the wisest.

For example, a homemaker may decide that a new piece of furniture is needed. Plans then should be made to see how money can be put aside to make this purchase. The family could decide to eat less expensive foods. Whatever is done, the home should be a comfortable happy place. Every homemaker must face the challenge of providing a nice home, while still staying within the family budget.

In order to save the homemaker as much time and energy as possible, appliances should be kept up to date. Home economists test new appliances and gadgets to make sure that they live up to claims of the manufacturer.

5. INTERIOR DESIGN

This branch of home economics strives to learn more about the planning and designing of the home for beauty, comfort, and convenience. Everyone wants to create a home which fits the family's habits, pleases the eye, cleans easily, is comfortable, and uses space in the best way.

Through the efforts of interior designers, homemakers have learned how to combine colors, how to arrange furniture, and how to make the best use of the shape and size of a room. A homemaker must be aware of how long different fabrics can be expected to last and how to select the correct fabric to use. Choosing furniture that is attractive, is well made, and suits its purpose is not easy. Home economists try to help the homemaker with these problems. Magazines, books, and pamphlets put out by furniture manufacturers, textile firms, and paint companies often provide new ideas about interior design.

All of the five branches of home economics—food and nutrition, clothing and textiles, family life and child development, management of the family income, and interior design—work to create a home that does the most for its members. As more and more women combine a career with managing a home, the importance of home economics grows.

There are separate articles about many of the branches of home economics in other volumes of this encyclopedia. See the articles on COOKING, CROCHET, DRESSMAKING, EMBROIDERY, KNITTING, JAMS AND JELLIES, and SEWING.

Homer

Two of the world's greatest poems, the *Iliad* and the *Odyssey*, are said to be the work of a blind Greek poet and singer named Homer. They are exciting tales about the adventures of great warriors. We know little about Homer, and no one is sure that he wrote all of the poems. There is not even much proof that such a person ever lived, although it is known that some poems written by a man named Homer were read aloud in the Greek city of Sparta about 2,500 years ago.

One of the reasons why so little is known about Homer is that in those times most poets drifted from place to place singing and reciting poems for food or a little money. They did not often write down their poems; and sometimes they would borrow verses from other poets and add to them or change them. Often kings would listen to these poems, and it is said that Homer's poems were so much liked that the kings would take time from their war-making to hear them read aloud. Alexander the Great is supposed to have slept with Homer's poems next to him in a golden box.

Homer probably lived about a thousand years before the birth of Jesus. The style in which he wrote has been copied by many poets, and his works have been translated into most of the modern languages. Scholars consider the poetry of Homer as great as any ever written.

Homer, Winslow

Winslow Homer was an American artist. He painted scenes of fishermen and the sea. His pictures make you feel you are sailing in a boat with the salt water spraying in your face. Homer was born in Boston, Massachusetts, in 1836. He became the apprentice, or helper, of a printer. In this job he learned almost everything he knew about drawing. When he was 24 years old he fought in the Civil War, and as a soldier he made drawings of battles. He sent these to Boston to illustrate newspaper stories. After the war he went to live in Maine, where he painted beautiful seascapes. He died there in 1910.

homestead

A homestead is a house and the land around it. When a country has much unsettled land, the government sometimes passes laws to make it easy for people to buy land and build their own homesteads. The United States had an enormous amount of unsettled land in the West, about 150 years ago. At first the government sold this land for profit, but not enough people came to buy land and build on it, so the government passed the Homestead Act in 1862.

According to this law, any man could apply for a tract of 160 acres of land. If he lived there and farmed the land for five years he would become the owner of it. Men who took over the land in this way were called *homesteaders*. Later the law was changed to provide that men who served in the army could count that time as part of the five years. As good farm land became scarcer and the remaining land was useful only for raising cattle, the size was increased to 640 acres.

The size of these tracts of land was based on parts of a square mile. A tract of 640 acres, called a *section*, is equal to one square mile, and 160 acres, equal to a quarter of a square mile, were called a *quarter-section*. The farmers often further divided their land into 40-acre plots, which were a quarter of the quarter. For this reason farmers even today will sometimes talk about the crops on "the south 40," meaning the 40 acres in a certain section of the farm.

About 250,000,000 acres of land in the United States were given to settlers under the Homestead Act, or almost three times as much land as there is in the whole state of California. People who go to Alaska to settle can now get land under the Homestead Act. Each province of Canada has its own homestead law for the people who settle there.

homicide

Homicide is the term used to describe the killing of one person by another. Homicide is a crime unless it is done in self-defense or is permitted by law. A policeman, for example, is not punished if he kills a criminal who is trying to escape. Killing that is permitted by law is called *justifiable homicide*. There are two kinds of homicide that are crimes. They are called murder and manslaughter.

Murder is killing another person purposely. In most places in the world, a murderer can be punished by being put to death if he planned in advance to kill the person; this is called murder in the first degree.

Manslaughter is killing another person accidentally. The punishments for manslaughter differ in different parts of the world and often depend upon the kind of accident that caused the death.

hominy

Hominy is a word that came into our language from the Indians of North America. It means corn that has had the hulls, or hard outside part, removed. The Indians of this country were making

hominy and eating it long before this country was even discovered. Sometimes the hulls are removed with lye, which softens them so that they wash off. Hominy is a favorite dish in the southern part of the United States. It is often ground up, and in ground form it is called *grits*. There is a separate article about GRITS.

Honduras

Honduras is a small country in Central America. It has about 43,277 square miles, or somewhat smaller than the state of Louisiana, and its population of about 2,600,000 is smaller than Louisiana's. Honduras is on the Caribbean Sea, and a small part of it touches the Pacific Ocean on the west. Its name comes from a Spanish word, *honduras*, meaning "depth." There is a nearby British colony, BRITISH HONDURAS, about which there is a separate article.

THE PEOPLE OF HONDURAS

The people who live in Honduras come from three stocks: Indians, who lived there before any Europeans came; Spaniards, the first European settlers; and Negroes, who were originally taken to Honduras as slaves, though of course slavery has now been illegal for many years. These three peoples have often married with one another, so that most people in Honduras are a mixture of races.

Almost all the people speak Spanish, which is the official language of the country. Many people in the large towns and seaports can speak English because of the close ties between Honduras and the United States.

Most of the people are farmers. There is also a small mining industry. The farmers work on large plantations. The most important crop is bananas. Coffee, tobacco and coconuts are also grown, and Honduras supplies much of the sarsaparilla that is used in the world. Sarsaparilla

is a flavoring used in many soft drinks and other sweets.

Most of the people of Honduras are very poor. There is free education for everyone, and children are required by law to go to school, yet very few of the people can read or write.

Almost the entire population belongs to the Roman Catholic Church.

WHAT THE LAND IS LIKE

Honduras is a mountainous country, but there are many fertile lowlands that are good for farming. The important farm lands are near the Caribbean sea-

coast. Honduras also owns several tiny islands in the Caribbean Sea, just north of the mainland, where the people grow coconuts. The banana plantations of Honduras are on the level land near the Caribbean, and most of the people live there. The 1,100 miles of railroads in Honduras are in this region. The railroads do not reach the capital of Honduras, the city of Tegucigalpa, which is in the south. Most of the travel is by airplane, and there are many good landing fields in the country. There are also some good roads. The Pan-American Highway, which stretches from the United States to South America, goes through Honduras.

Honduras is rich in minerals but they are mostly undeveloped. Gold and silver have been mined most. Almost as important are the great forests, which provide many different kinds of wood, especially mahogany.

There are several small rivers in Honduras. The most important is the Ulua. Small boats can navigate the Ulua.

Near the two seacoasts the climate is hot and damp, but in the mountains and higher land in the interior of the country it is cooler and more comfortable.

HOW THE PEOPLE ARE GOVERNED

Honduras is an independent republic. The laws are made by the National Congress, which has about sixty-four members. The members are elected by the people every six years. There is also a president, elected every six years. No president is supposed to be elected for more than one term, but this rule has often been broken. The government of Honduras has often been very weak, and there have been several revolutions.

All men over the age of 18 must serve eight months in the armed services, and must then stay in the reserve forces until they are over 55. There are about five thousand men in the army, and there is a small air force.

HONDURAS IN THE PAST

Honduras was discovered by Christopher Columbus on his second voyage to America, in 1494. It was a Spanish colony, until it revolted and declared its independence in 1821. It has been involved in wars and national revolutions many times since then. The United States government twice sent troops to Honduras to keep peace, in 1903 and 1923. There were major revolutions in 1931, 1932, and 1937. In 1937, Honduras almost went to war against the neighboring country of Nicaragua because of a boundary dispute. Honduran exiles from Guatemala tried to invade the country and overthrow the government in 1945, but they were defeated. There have been several attempted uprisings in recent years, but the signing of an agreement with Nicaragua in 1959 not to allow their territories to be used to mount rebellions against each other will probably mean more stability.

HONDURAS. Area, 43,277 square miles Population (1973 estimate) 2,600,000. Government, republic. Religion, Roman Catholic. Monetary unit, lempira, worth 50 cents (U.S.). Flag, three horizontal bands, blue, white, blue, with five blue stars in center stripe. Capital, Tegucigalpa.

honey

Honey is the sweet substance made by bees from the nectar of flowers. It is composed mostly of sugar, with a little water, some minerals, and other substances. The flower nectar, or juice, is gathered by the bees and taken into a honey sack in the bee's body. There a substance called an *enzyme* turns it into honey. Scientists do not know exactly how enzymes work, but it is known that they can cause a chemical change such as the turning of flower nectar into honey. The bee takes the honey to the beehive and stores it in little wax cases called honeycombs, and the bees use it for food during the winter.

Honey is also a delicious and valuable food for human beings, and swarms of bees are kept by men for the purpose of getting the honey. Some people keep a few bees to get just the amount of honey they can use themselves. Other people are in the honey business, and they keep hundreds of swarms of bees. In either case, enough honey is left in the hive for the bees to live on, and the rest is taken out in the form of honeycombs. Sometimes it is packed and sold just as it is; sometimes the honey is strained from the honeycombs and packed as a clear, thick liquid.

The color and taste of honey depend on what kind of flower the bees have taken the nectar from. In the United States, most honey comes from alfalfa and clover. This honey is a pale, golden yellow and has a very delicate flavor. Other flowers from which bees make honey are buckwheat, which has a stronger flavor and a darker color, orange, palmetto, and sage. Some honey is imported into the United States, but honey is produced in large quantities in California, Florida, and New York, and in the midwestern states.

Honey has been used since ancient times. The Bible speaks about a rich and wonderful land and calls it "a land of milk and honey." In other olden times it was considered a sign of great wealth if people had honey in the house.

honeysuckle

The honeysuckle can be a shrub or a woody climbing plant, depending on the kind. There are more than a hundred kinds of honeysuckle. Most kinds are hardy plants and grow in many of the northern areas of the world. The bush honeysuckle, planted in a rich soil and given plenty of space, grows into a large shrub. The climbing honeysuckle, placed near a wall, fence, tree, or trellis, soon covers a large area. The small, sweet-smelling flowers of the honeysuckle are pink, white, yellow or orange in color. The most familiar honeysuckle in England, often called *woodbine* or *eglantine*, has larger, trumpet-shaped blossoms. The honeysuckle is one of the special flowers for people born in June.

Hong Kong

Hong Kong is the name of a small British colony on an island on the coast of southeastern China. The colony is made up of the island of Hong Kong, which is in the mouth of the Canton River; another tiny island called Stonecutters Island; and a small area of land on the mainland,

called the Kowloon Peninsula and the New Territories. The island of Hong Kong is a little larger than Manhattan Island, having an area of about 32 square miles.

The British have had this colony for more than a hundred years. They took the island of Hong Kong in 1841. The other parts of the colony were obtained from China several years later.

Hong Kong has a very good harbor, and was once an important trading center for southern China and the western Pacific. It was also a British naval base and military center. The Japanese captured it at once when they entered World War II in 1941. They had to give it back after they lost the war, but since China has had a Communist government the colony has been of little value to the British. The Chinese Communists do not allow much business to be done there.

The population of Hong Kong has almost doubled since World War II, because hundreds of thousands of Chinese have gone there to escape from the Communists. The population in 1973 was estimated at over four million. Most of the people live in two large cities, Victoria and Kowloon. Victoria is the capital and over 1,000,000 people live there. Kowloon has about 692,800.

The people are almost all Chinese. They work as farmers or fishermen, and some are employed in factories. Many of the fishermen, and also the people who work on the docks, live in boats called *sampans* or *junks*. Thousands of these boats, of all kinds and shapes, are usually lying close to one another in several of the harbors. Sometimes the boats are so close together that you can go from one boat to another without even seeing the water.

Honolulu

Honolulu is the capital of Hawaii, the United States state consisting of the Hawaiian Islands in the Pacific Ocean. Honolulu is on the island of Oahu. It is a famous seaport of the Pacific Ocean. It is a beautiful, modern city with excellent beaches near by, picturesque mountain slopes behind it, and a healthful, balmy climate. About half the people of Hawaii live in Honolulu. It has a population of almost 325,000, making it about the same size as Miami, Florida.

The people have come from all parts of the world, from China, Japan, Korea, the Philippines, Germany, Portugal, and the United States, and some are the original people of the Hawaiian Islands, who are Polynesians and who came from Asia in ancient times. Many of the people of Hawaii are mixtures of Polynesian and other races.

Tourists come from all over the world to spend their vacations in Honolulu. Waikiki Beach, near Honolulu, is one of the finest in the world.

The University of Hawaii is in Honolulu. In the Bishop Museum there are exhibits that tell about the people, history, and plant and animal life of the Hawaiian Islands. The government owns the royal palace of Hawaii where the original Hawaiian kings reigned when Honolulu was first built, more than a hundred years ago.

Near Honolulu, at Pearl Harbor, is the United States Navy's great naval base. It was here, on December 7, 1941, that Japanese airplanes attacked and badly damaged the United States fleet. This act led the United States into World War II.

HONOLULU, OAHU, HAWAII. Population (1970 census) 324,871. Capital of state of Hawaii. County seat of Honolulu County.

hoof and mouth disease

This is a disease that occurs among all animals with hoofs. It is also called foot and mouth disease. It raises blisters on the mouth and other parts of the body. It is usually so painful for the animal to eat that it may starve to death. If the disease is caught by one animal in a herd, this animal must be killed and buried immediately, for the disease spreads very rapidly.

Hoof and mouth disease was brought to the United States by cattle imported from Canada and England in 1870. The disease spread among American cattle and horses. Rigid laws were passed controlling animals coming into this country, and also controlling animals that came down with the disease in this country. These laws have been successful, and there has been almost no hoof and mouth disease in the United States since 1929.

hookworm

Hookworms are small animals with tiny teeth with which they can attach themselves to other animals. These animals can cause hookworm disease, or, as it is sometimes called, the "lazy disease." A person suffering from this has a pale face, pasty skin, and puffs under his eyes. He usually feels lazy and weak all the time. This sickness is very common in warm regions, especially where poor sanitary conditions are found. In some badly infected places, as much as 80 per cent of the population may have hookworm. The hookworm itself is a small worm which develops in warm, moist soil. If a person walks barefoot through soil in which the worm's larvae, or young, are breeding, they may begin burrowing through the skin of his feet. This is called "ground itch." The hookworms then follow the bloodstream of their victim to his lungs, from there to the throat, and then down into the intestines. When they reach the intestines (it takes them about a week to get there), the larvae develop into full-grown hookworms and attach themselves to the intestines' lining. They begin to suck blood and cause internal bleeding, and this produces a condition called anemia, where the number of red cells in the victim's blood is too low. The disease can be treated by taking one of several medicines that loosen the hold of the hookworms on the intestines, and then by eating plenty of foods containing proteins, vitamins, and iron to fight off the anemia.

Hoover Dam

Hoover Dam is the highest dam in the world. It is on the Colorado River, at a place called Boulder Canyon. For many years it was called Boulder Dam, but in 1947 President Harry S. Truman officially

changed its name to Hoover Dam in honor of Herbert Hoover, who was President when the dam was started. The dam is 726 feet high, and it stores enough water to cover 31 million acres a foot deep. This water is stored in a reservoir called Lake Mead; it is valuable for irrigation and is used all over the Southwest. Enormous generators are operated by water wheels turned by water flowing over the dam. The electricity they generate is used by many cities in the Southwest, especially Los Angeles.

Hoover, Herbert

Herbert Clark Hoover was the thirty-first President of the United States.

He served from 1929 to 1933. During these years, the nation suffered from a business depression and many people were out of work. Although this was the result of things that had happened before Hoover's election, many people thought Hoover was responsible for the bad times, and others felt that he did not do enough to improve conditions. But many other people thought he was a good President and would have improved conditions if he had been re-elected. Even the people who did not think he was a good President respected his honesty and intelligence.

Herbert Hoover was known as a fine mining engineer, an expert organizer, a good businessman, and a humanitarian.

HIS EARLY YEARS

Herbert Hoover was born August 10, 1874 in West Branch, Iowa. Besides his parents, he had a brother and a sister. All were Quakers, and later Hoover became the first Quaker President. (Richard Nixon was the second.) As a young child, Hoover lost both parents and lived with relatives.

He was an unusually good student, and very ambitious. He studied at night school to prepare for college, and earned the money to pay for his entire college education. He attended Leland Stanford University, in California, and specialized in engineering and geology, the study of the earth. While he was still a very young man, he became well known throughout the country as an expert on mining.

He was married when he was 25, and took his bride to China. They traveled for the next fourteen years on geological and mining expeditions. During this time they lived in all corners of the world, going from China to Australia, Russia, Burma, Italy, Central America, and Europe. Hoover was called upon as an expert engineering consultant by different companies in many lands. His two sons, Herbert Clark Hoover, Jr., and Allan Henry Hoover, were born during these fourteen years.

When World War I broke out, the Hoovers were caught in London, along with many other Americans, and at this time Herbert Hoover performed one of his first important public services. Thousands of Americans were stranded without money because banks would not cash their American checks after Europe went to war. So Hoover collected funds — using his own money and contributions from a group of other engineers whom he knew — and financed the food, lodging and transportation home for about 150,000 stranded Americans. The story of his skillful organization of this relief reached the ears of the Belgian government, and he was asked to take charge of a campaign to save the starving women and children of Belgium and France. He arranged this great relief program so well that he became world-famous.

When the United States entered the war, President Wilson asked him to serve as Food Administrator in the United States. Many people have said that mainly through his efforts the supply of food sent abroad helped to win the war. After the Armistice, he took charge of the American Relief Administration and sent more millions of tons of food to Europe.

When Warren Harding became President, he appointed Hoover as his Secretary of Commerce. Once more Hoover showed his ability as an organizer. He saved millions of people from starvation in Russia, when there was a famine in the valley of the Volga River, and later he took charge of the relief supplied to 700,000 flood victims on the Mississippi River in the United States.

HOW HE BECAME PRESIDENT

In the 1920s, while Harding and Coolidge were in office, the country had been reaching a serious financial condition. Farmers especially were suffering badly because there was no longer the large demand for farm products that had existed during the war years. At the same time, wild speculation and gambling were going on in the stock market. People who did not even know what a share of stock was were buying shares madly, and "playing the stock market" became almost a national hobby. You can read more about this in the article on STOCK EXCHANGE.

At the Republican convention of 1928, Herbert Hoover was nominated for President on the first ballot. In the election, he easily defeated the Democratic candidate, Alfred E. Smith of New York. Hoover's record of successful administration and organization made people feel that he could solve the problems of the country. He started his administration by proposing a bill that would regulate the production and sale of farm products at fair

prices. A Farm Board was established, but before it had time to get really under way, the stock market crash of October 1929 struck the country, and the great depression period began. More and more people lost their jobs and could not find work. Businesses failed, and the country was in a panic. Hoover thought it was the government's responsibility to help out, but he believed that the state governments should do most of the job themselves. He also believed that business would recover even without government help, and he kept telling the people of the country that things would soon be better. One of his phrases that became very famous was "Prosperity is just around the corner."

However, he asked Congress for public-works projects to provide jobs for as many people as possible. He also established a government corporation to help businesses that needed money to stay open, and another corporation to help people with homes on which they could not keep up payments. These were the Reconstruction Finance Corporation and the Home Owners' Loan Corporation. The first saved many banks and businesses from failure, and the second helped some people to keep their homes by lending them money to keep up the payments on their mortgages.

Although Hoover's administration was working constructively and was considering many projects for the future, the people of the country were discouraged with bad times and unemployment. As often happens in such cases, most people felt that to get rid of the party in power would cure everything. In 1932, Hoover was renominated by the Republican Party, but the Democratic nominee, Franklin Delano Roosevelt, was elected by a large majority on his promise to give the country a "New Deal."

HIS LATER YEARS

Herbert Hoover retired from public life after the election and lived for the next fourteen years at his home in Palo Alto, California. He did a great deal of writing on economics and current events, but he had nothing to do with politics. After World War II, President Truman appointed him honorary chairman of the Famine Emergency Commission, to help the starving people of Asia and Europe.

Still later, he was appointed chairman of the Committee on Reorganization of United States Executive Departments, to find out where government money was being wasted, where economy measures could be taken, and how the executive branch in general could be made more efficient. This report and the study that went with it covered every executive branch of the government and all its many departments. When it was finally submitted to the President, it included many excellent suggestions. It was generally agreed that it was the most complete and most detailed of any such report that had ever been made.

Herbert Hoover was always ready to serve his country in any way that was asked of him. He died Oct. 20, 1964.

MRS. HERBERT HOOVER

Lou Henry Hoover was born on March 29, 1875, in Waterloo, Iowa. Her father was Charles D. Henry, a banker. The family moved to Monterey, California, and she attended Leland Stanford University. A year after her graduation in 1898, she married Herbert Clark Hoover, and they had two sons, Herbert Clark Hoover, Jr., and Allan Henry Hoover. Mrs. Hoover died on January 7, 1944.

Hoover, J. Edgar

John Edgar Hoover became head of the Federal Bureau of Investigation, usually called the F.B.I., in 1924. He was only 29 years old at the time, having been born in Washington, D.C., in 1895. As head of the F.B.I., Hoover organized laboratories and special schools to train the men who worked for him, and under his direction it became one of the best police organizations of its kind in the world. Hoover had been a lawyer and had held several government positions before he entered the F.B.I. in 1921.

hop

The hop is a twining plant whose fruits (hops) are used to flavor beer and ale. Hop vines will grow as much as twenty-five feet in one season. The catkins or clusters of flowers are cone-shaped and hang from the ends of the branches. They are longish in shape, and the separate petals are very thin and yellow. The catkins are about two inches long and have a strong odor. When the catkins are dried, they form the hops that are used in brewing.

There are male and female hop plants. Four or five male plants to an acre will fertilize all the female plants. The hop plant is native to Europe and Asia, but it has been cultivated in North America since the 17th century. Large quantities of hops are raised in England. New York State and some western states lead in the production of hops in America. The meal left over from the hops after making the beer is sometimes spread in gardens to protect the roots of plants. See also the article on BEER.

Hopi

The Hopi are a tribe of Pueblo Indians. Pueblo Indians are those who have always lived in towns and made their living by farming. The seven small towns of the Hopi stand high above the sands of the desert on top of tall cliffs in northern Arizona. The Hopi are a small group of people. There are only about four thousand of them. They are called the "people of peace" because they have always been a gentle, peace-loving tribe. The Hopi "snake dance," which they do with live snakes, is still danced as it was hundreds of years ago.

hopscotch

Hopscotch is a game that boys and girls have played for many years. To play the game you need a space about twelve feet long and three feet wide, and a small piece of wood or a stone. The hopscotch court must be marked off into ten squares. Most players find that it is best to use a

There are several kinds of hopscotch court. The simplest consists simply of marked-off squares, but hopscotch stars like the young lady above prefer a fancy court that challenges their hopping skill.

piece of chalk to draw the hopscotch court on the sidewalk. A stick can also be used to mark the lines on hard earth. Any number of people can play hopscotch.

The first player begins at a starting point outside the court and tosses his stone into the first square. Then he hops into the square, throws his stone out over the base line, and hops out again. Then he tosses the stone into the second square. This time he must hop first into square No. 1 and then into square No. 2, where his stone lies. He again throws his stone out over the base line and hops back to the starting point. If a player hops on a line, or if his stone lands on a line, or if he tosses his stone into the wrong square, he must give up his turn and wait until all of the other players have taken their turns. The first person to toss his stone into every one of the ten squares wins the game.

Horace

Horace was one of the greatest Roman poets. His full name was Quintus Horatius Flaccus, and he lived just before the birth of Jesus. He was born in 65 B.C. A very wealthy man named Maecenas became his patron; that is, he supported Horace because Horace was such a great writer. Horace lived in a villa near Rome and wrote poetry that is still read. He wrote satirical poems, poems that poked fun at those who were proud and cruel; poems praising the simplicity of country life; odes, poems that were full of noble feeling; and poems of love. He wrote with such elegance and grace that even though we have to read his poems in translation, it remains sparkling and clear. He died in 8 B.C.

Horatius

Horatius was a Roman soldier who lived about 2,500 years ago. At that time the Romans owned only a small part of Italy. They were fighting the Etruscans, another people that lived in Italy. Horatius was famous for his bravery at a bridge across the River Tiber. The Etruscans were trying to cross the bridge so that they could go on to attack Rome. The Romans had to try to destroy the bridge. With two companions, Horatius crossed the bridge and held the Etruscans off while the Romans destroyed it. Just before the bridge came down, he sent his companions back over it. Then he himself plunged into the river and swam over to the Roman side. The state raised a statue in Horatius' honor and gave him a tract of land. Thomas Babington Macaulay, the English poet and historian,

wrote a famous poem about this incident, "Horatius at the Bridge."

horehound

Horehound is a plant that belongs to the mint family. Its dried leaves and flower tops are used in making horehound candy. The horehound is one to three feet high. It has many tiny, white, clustered flowers and woolly-white hairs. It is a native of Europe, but it now grows wild in almost all parts of the United States. The leaves, stems and flowers have a pleasant odor and bitter taste when dried, and syrup made from them is used for both hard candies and horehound tea, an old-time remedy for coughs and colds.

horizon

When you look into the distance as far as your eye can see, you will see a line where the earth and the sky seemed to meet. Such a line is called a *horizon*. You usually can see it much better if you are standing in an open field or are on a ship in the ocean.

Of course, the sky does not really touch the earth. It only looks that way. If you walked to where you thought the horizon was, you would not find a line. You would only see more land, and if you looked off into the distance again you would see another horizon. Each time you tried to reach the horizon, it would always seem to move on ahead of you.

The higher you are, the farther away the horizon seems to be. If your eyes are 6 feet above sea level, the horizon seems to be 3 miles away; at 50 feet above sea level it is 9 miles, and at 100 feet it is 12 miles.

When you can look all around, as you can on a ship in the ocean, the horizon seems to be a giant circle with you at its center. The circle is made by the curvature of the earth. Because there is not really a line between the earth and the sky, what you see is often called a "visible" or "apparent" horizon.

hormone

A hormone is a kind of chemical manufactured inside the body and usually carried by the blood to another part of the body. Nearly all hormones are manufactured by GLANDS, about which there is a separate article. Not much was known about hormones until recent years, but now it has been found that they have a great deal to do with health. Some of them are used in drugs, such as *cortisone,* that relieve diseases no other medicine has helped. Sometimes the male sex hormone (*testosterone*) and a female sex hormone, such as *progesterone*, are used as medicines and to help people have children.

Insulin is a hormone made by the pancreas. It is used as a medicine by persons suffering from the disease called diabetes.

Thyroxin is a hormone made by the thyroid gland. It can be used to help people whose thyroid glands are not working properly.

horn

Horns are hard growths that appear on the body or skin of an animal or human. There are two kinds of horn. One

is the continued growth of a bone, and one is a hardening of the skin.

The second group of horns, caused by the hardening of skin, are known as true horns. These horns are pliable, or easily bent, and they come in many different shapes. Examples of horny material on human beings are corns, fingernails, and toenails. These are made of the same kind of material as the claws of cats and the talons of birds. In animals except man, they are useful chiefly as weapons. Nails and claws begin at a spot called a *bed,* in the hand, foot, or paw. Just as skin is constantly growing, the nail or claw grows; but dead skin, being soft, flakes off and its loss is not noticed, while the nail or claw, being hard, is pushed outward as the new material grows.

Animals grow true horns in the form of scales that grow on snakes and lizards, birds' beaks, horses' hoofs, and the horns of sheep and cattle.

Bone outgrowth, the first kind of horn, can be seen by the deer's antlers. Such horns are solid and hard. The deer grows new antlers every year.

The horns of such animals as the giraffe and rhinoceros are hardened masses of hair and skin that cover bones. These horns are never shed. They may be solid or hollow. They are used as a means of protection against attackers.

Horn is used in the making of handles for umbrellas, canes, and eating utensils, for combs and buttons, and for other things.

When man first appeared on earth, he used horn for weapons, drinking cups, and handles. The musical instrument called a horn got its name because long ago men blew through the hollow horns of cattle to make musical sounds.

horn

The horn is a kind of musical instrument. Blowing into it produces a particular sound or sounds, depending on the shape of the horn and whether it is made of metal or wood. The earliest horns were actually made from the horns of cows and other animals that have hollow horns. Shepherds discovered that if they blew into a crooked or bent horn it made a louder and clearer sound, and that the sound depended on how much the horn was bent. You can read more about this in the article on MUSICAL INSTRUMENTS.

In olden days knights blew horns as a signal during battle or when they were hunting. They invented several different tunes for the horn. They played joyful tunes when they rode home after a successful hunt, and these were called *fanfares,* from the French word for "boasting." About 250 years ago, the Germans and Austrians began to use hunting horns in orchestras. All the wind instruments in the modern orchestra are descended from the ancient horn.

hornbeam, a tree that has a very hard wood: see the article on IRONWOOD.

hornbill

The hornbill is a bird related to the owl. It lives in Africa, India and Malaya. A South African ground hornbill is greatly respected by the natives because it at-

tacks snakes. It can overcome the largest and most poisonous snake found in that part of the world.

During the nesting season the female hornbill imprisons herself in the cavity of a tree where her nest is. She seals herself in by using her saliva and leaves only a small hole, through which the male bird feeds her. It is believed that the male bird throws up the lining of his gizzard in a kind of bag and the female hornbill and the young feed on it.

Hornbills are often large and bulky birds, some of them more than four feet long, but some are no larger than magpies. The hornbill has a large bill and a crest that varies in shape. The crest is full of air cells that make it lighter than it looks. Hornbills live chiefly on fruit but have been known to eat almost anything.

hornbook

The hornbook was a primer used by children in former times. It was made from a sheet of parchment on which were printed the alphabet, numbers up to nine, and the Lord's Prayer. This page was sometimes set in a frame but more often it was covered with a piece of transparent horn. It had a handle and could be tied around the waist. Some hornbooks were on slabs of wood. The same hornbook could be used by many children, so it saved the cost of printing. In the 19th century, when printing became cheaper, regular primers in book form replaced it. Hornbooks now are extremely rare.

horned toad

The horned toad is really a lizard, but it has a squatting position much like a toad's. There are about twenty kinds of horned toad, all of them found in the desert parts of the United States, Canada, and Mexico. They have spiny scales on their bodies and bony bumps on their heads.

Horned toads are often picked up as souvenirs in the deserts. Horned toads do not object to being captured and as pets they behave in unusual and entertaining ways. They like to lie in the sunshine and bury themselves in warm sand. They are quite inactive in cold weather and hibernate (sleep all winter).

Insects are the favorite food of horned toads. They hunt and catch insects during the warmest hours of the day. A female horned toad lays ten or twelve eggs, which hatch in about an hour.

hornet, a large, brightly colored flying insect closely related to the wasp. See the article on WASP.

hornpipe

The hornpipe is an English and Scottish dance that has been popular for hundreds of years. The dance was named after an old instrument like the clarinet. Sailors on shipboard liked the hornpipe because it could be danced in very small areas. Hugh Aston, a composer who died in 1525, wrote the earliest music for the hornpipe.

Horowitz, Vladimir

Vladimir Horowitz, a great pianist, was born in Kiev, Russia, in 1904. He began studying piano when he was only six, but his father insisted that young Vladimir should lead a normal life and continue with his regular education. He started giving concerts during the Russian Revolution, in 1917, and some of his listeners were so poor that they had to pay him in flour and butter. He first played in America in 1928 and within a few years he was considered by most authorities to be the best pianist in the world. Horowitz became a citizen of the United States. He married Wanda Toscanini, daughter of the famous conductor. In the 1940s he discontinued public performances but still did recording and some teaching. In 1965 he resumed giving concerts and proved to be more popular than ever.

horse

Throughout most of history the horse has been the most valuable animal that man has domesticated. This has changed a great deal since the invention of the automobile, but the horse is still very valuable. The horse used to do everything that the automobile and the tractor and even the railroads do now. It was also very important in warfare, in special units of mounted soldiers called *cavalry,* but now these have been replaced by tanks and trucks. The number of horses in the United States reached its highest point about 1918. In that year there were more than 21,000,000 horses on farms in this country. In the early 1960s the United States Department of Agriculture estimated that this figure had dropped to about 3,000,000 horses on farms, and perhaps another 200,000 used for other purposes.

HISTORY OF THE HORSE

The horse dates back some fifty million years. The ancient horse looked much like the horse we know today but it was a small creature, only 11 inches high. It had four toes on its front feet and three toes on its hind feet. This horse, which scientists called Eohippus, or "Dawn Horse," appeared at almost the same time in Europe and America. It had no horns or claws with which to protect itself, so it had to depend on speed. Its descendants became faster and faster at running, and their feet changed little by little until the toes became one large toe on each foot. They grew gradually in size and weight. Somewhere along the way the horse died in Europe, but the American horses gradually spread to Asia across a land bridge that used to connect the two continents at Alaska. Then the American horse died out, too, perhaps because of some sickness, so the modern horse originated in Europe and Asia.

Scientists have found horse bones along with the other refuse and garbage that the cavemen left in piles around their caves, so they know that horse meat was used as food long before men began to tame the horse. The first record of the horse as a domestic animal is about 2,500 years before the birth of Jesus. This first taming of the horse took place in Asia, but the horse was found to be so useful that the idea spread rapidly and soon the tamed horse was common in Europe, most of Asia, and parts of Africa.

The first important use of horses was in warfare. They were hitched to war chariots, and then later used as mounts for soldiers. It was the horse that made possible most of the great conquests of ancient history, such as those of Alexander the Great and Genghis Khan, because without horses the armies could not have traveled so far or so fast.

As the centuries passed, the horse was put to other work. It was used for farming, transportation, and sport, and the ownership of horses came to be a sign of high rank or wealth.

It was the Spanish who brought the horse back to America after it had disappeared so many thousands of years before. Although we may think of the Indians whom the settlers found in the New World as fierce men on swift horses, they had only learned the use of the horse in the hundred or so years before the coming of the British. When the Spanish came to the New World they brought many horses with them. When they left, they usually tried to load their ships full of gold and silver, so to make room they set their horses free. The horses ran all over North and South America, and the Indians rounded up herds of them and tamed them. Sometimes, too, the Indians stole horses from the corrals of the Spaniards.

BREEDS OF HORSES

Different kinds of horses are bred for different purposes. The work horse is generally the largest of all horses. The Shire horse of England is probably the biggest of all; it stands about 17 hands high, and weighs up to 2,400 pounds. Horses are always measured in *hands;* a hand is 4 inches, and therefore the Shire horse measures 68 inches high. In the United States the Clydesdale and the Percheron are favorite work horses. Both weigh about 2,000 pounds. The Percheron was the special horse for stagecoach travel, and later it was used for delivery wagons and fire engines. The Percheron is still very widely used in circuses.

For pulling light wagons and for horseback riding, lighter horses were needed. These were developed from the great Arabian horses, which had been bred in the East from about the year 800. The Arabian horse is famous for its strength and speed, and for the past four hundred years these horses have been bred with other kinds to get special characteristics for different uses. One of these is the Thoroughbred, a combination of the Arabian horse and the English horse. Many people think of a Thoroughbred as one that is purebred, but these two words mean entirely different things. A Thoroughbred is a special breed of horse, but a purebred horse is one born of two parents of the same breed. Thoroughbred horses were brought to America and became the greatest racing horses of the country.

Another breed that was developed from the Thoroughbred group was the Hackney horse. More than a hundred years ago the Hackney horse was used to pull hackney cabs, and that is where we get the nickname "hack" for a taxicab. Well-known American breeds are the Quarter horse, which is descended from horses brought to Virginia by the English settlers, and which became popular as a race horse, on cattle ranches, and as a saddle horse; the Morgan horse, which be-

gan as a farm horse but soon was used for riding and then as an Army and police mount; and the American Saddle horse, which was developed in Kentucky more than a hundred years ago and is the favorite horse for pleasure riding.

The modern cowboy's horse, or cow pony, is descended from the horses brought to America by the Spanish. These Spanish horses were called *mustangs,* which was an English way of saying *mesteno.* the Spanish word for "wild." Nowadays the mustang is crossed with horses of other breeds to increase its size and speed.

The pony is a small horse, but it is not necessarily a young horse. It is a special breed that you can read about in the article on PONY.

Other work animals related to the horse include the tame ass or *donkey,* the *burro,* and the *mule.* The burro of the western United States and Mexico is a very small ass that is used as a pack animal and as a pet. The mule is the offspring of a male donkey and a female horse. Usually, the mule is unable to reproduce itself.

COLORS OF HORSES

In ancient times it was believed that the color of a horse was important for various reasons. The Arabs used to believe that white horses could not stand heat, that bay horses were strongest, and that chestnut horses were hot-tempered. Now we know that the color of a horse makes no difference in its breed or in its quality. Nearly all colors can be found or bred into any particular breed of horse.

The principal colors of modern horses are as follows:

Black, which may include some white markings.

Brown, which includes some black horses with lighter markings.

Bay, in which the main coat color is brown, reddish-brown, or tan, with black mane, tail, and "stockings."

Chestnut, all-over brown, red-brown, or golden.

Sorrel, a lighter red or golden shade of chestnut.

Dun, grayish or yellowish, with points of black.

Cream, a very pale sorrel or yellow.

White.

Gray.

Roan, an effect produced by a sprinkling of white hairs among other colors.

Pinto, the popular name for various spotted patterns of white and any other color. This kind of horse with a patterned coat is also called paint (the famous cowboy-song name for a horse), calico, pied, piebald, and skewbald.

Palomino. which is really a color too, although horses of this color are so beautiful that many breeders are trying to make a special breed of palomino horses. They have golden coats that range from reddish or bronze to pale yellow or dark cream, with silvery manes and tails.

HORSEBACK RIDING

Horseback riding has been a very popular sport for centuries, and also for centuries it was the principal means of land transportation. In the United States it has become a city sport as well as a country one. There are many riding stables where horses can be rented by the hour, because city people have no way to keep horses of their own unless they are very wealthy. Most large parks have "bridle paths," which are unpaved roads for horseback riders.

Riding a horse is a skill that must be learned if it is to be done well. A horse has four principal gaits, or ways of walking and running. These gaits are the walk, trot, pace, and gallop. In each, the horse moves its feet differently, and the rider must adjust himself to the different motions of the horse. In a *walk,* the slowest gait, one foot at a time is placed on the ground. In the *trot,* the forefoot on one side and the hind foot on the other side touch the ground at almost the same moment, giving a two-beat rhythm. In the *pace* there is also a two-beat rhythm, but it is the two feet on the same side that touch the ground at the same time. The *gallop* is the natural top-speed run of horses. It has a three-beat rhythm that is slightly broken because once in each stride all four feet are off the ground at the same time. The *canter* is a slower form of the gallop.

Horseback riding is also part of a popular sport, POLO, about which there is a separate article. Horses have long been used in hunting, and the British "riding to hounds" means hunting on horseback with dogs to track down the game.

HORSE SHOWS

In countries where horses are bred for various uses, the horse show is an annual event at which the best horse in different classifications is chosen by judges. In the United States, horse shows include contests for harness horses, jumpers, saddle horses, and other groups. Many state and county fairs have horse shows for work horses such as the Percheron and Clydesdale.

HORSERACING

Horseracing has been a popular sport for almost as long as horses have been domesticated. In ancient Rome chariot races were held and drew great crowds, just as millions of people today go to horseraces in the United States and Europe. Horseracing was originally intended to improve the breed. The fastest horses were raced and the winners were crossbred to try to obtain even faster runners. You can read more about this in the article on BREEDING.

For the past hundred years horseracing has been interesting chiefly because so many people like to bet on which horse will win, although many people enjoy it simply for the pleasure of watching beautiful horses run. Betting on horseraces is legal in many states.

There are two main types of horseracing: running, and trotting or pacing. In *running* races, the horses gallop. They are ridden by jockeys, who must be very short men. Another form of the running race is the *steeplechase,* in which the horses jump over fences and other obstacles at intervals along the track. Trotting and pacing are two different gaits, but in both types of racing the horse pulls a light carriage called a *sulky.* The biggest trotting races are held in a group of cities called the Grand Circuit, but trotting races are held in many other cities and at state and county fairs.

CARE OF HORSES

A horse needs special care. It must be fed the right kind of food in the right quantity. It must be properly exercised. Its coat should be brushed or currycombed every day. Horses have very sensitive breathing organs. Care should be taken that a horse does not catch cold, because a cold will usually turn into pneumonia and prove fatal.

The weakest part of a horse is its legs. Although everything that a horse does depends on its legs, they are very thin in relation to the rest of the body. When a horse breaks a leg, it is usually necessary to kill the animal.

Most horses live to be 25 years old. When a horse is born it is called a *colt* or a *filly,* depending on whether it is male or female. After it is five years old it is called a *stallion* or a *mare.* A horse's birthday is considered to be the first of January in the year in which it was born. If a horse is born on December 13, for the record it is already a year old. This makes it easier to keep records when a person has many horses.

An adult mare may give birth or *foal* until she is about 20 years old. Usually only one foal is born at a time, but cases of triplets have been reported. When a mare has more than one foal at a time, the chance of a safe and successful birth is decreased, but is not impossible.

horse chestnut

The horse chestnut is a tree that grows in Europe and the United States. It is not related to the family of chestnut trees, but it gets its name from its large seed, which grows inside a burr and looks somewhat like a nut.

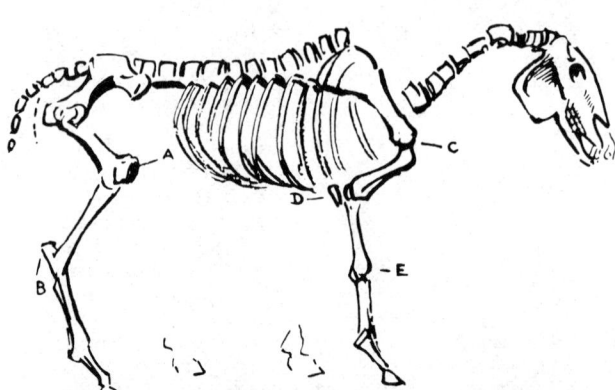

Left: The skeleton of a horse shows the animal's one great weakness: Its legs are thin and the bones are brittle, with the result that once it breaks a leg the horse loses its usefulness. Among the chief parts of the skeleton are the knee (A), the heel (B), the shoulder (C), the elbow (D), and the wrist (E). The modern horse developed from the much smaller Eohippus.

The horse chestnut that grows in the United States is called the *buckeye*. It has five leaflets, while the European horse chestnut has seven. So many of these trees grow in Ohio that they gave the state the nickname "Buckeye State."

The European horse chestnut grows mostly around the Mediterranean Sea. The seeds of the European horse chestnut, usually called nuts, are too bitter to be eaten, while those of the buckeye are poisonous.

The horse chestnut is very popular as a shade tree for parks and gardens. It has thick masses of dark-green leaves, and flowers that may be white or yellowish. The wood of the horse chestnut is rather soft, but it is used for wooden dishes and bowls and for boxes and some kinds of furniture.

horsefly is a large fly that annoys animals with its bite. It is also called a gadfly. See the article on GADFLY.

horse latitudes

The horse latitudes are areas of the ocean a little north and south of the tropical zone. In this part of the ocean the weather is always clear and calm and there is seldom much of a breeze. In the days of sailing vessels it was a terrible thing for a ship to get caught in the horse latitudes, because it could drift helplessly for weeks without a breeze to fill the sails. No one knows how the horse latitudes got their name. One story says that a sailing ship carrying horses once got caught in this windless sea, and that most of the horses died before the ship could get out.

horsepower

Horsepower is a word used to describe the rate at which different machines can do work. More than a hundred years ago, James Watt, the inventor of the steam engine, wanted to find out how much faster his engine could do work than horses could. He tested horses and found that one horse could raise 33,000 pounds to a height of one foot in one minute. The ability of a machine to do this is called one horsepower. Watt tested only strong, fresh horses; the average horse cannot do work at the rate of one horsepower.

horseradish

Horseradish is a herb that is grown mainly for its roots, which are used to make a strong, sharp relish that adds flavor to many foods. The root is whitish in color. It is ½ inch to 2 inches thick, and up to 3 feet long. If it is scraped or bruised, the root gives off a very strong, penetrating odor. Sometimes the odor is so strong it brings tears to your eyes. Horseradish root is grated and mixed with vinegar and salt to make the relish.

The horseradish plant grows about 2 feet high. It has small clusters of white flowers and small, narrow leaves. The plants do not grow from seeds but from small cuttings of the root.

horseshoe crab, a common name for a large sea animal: see the article on KING CRAB.

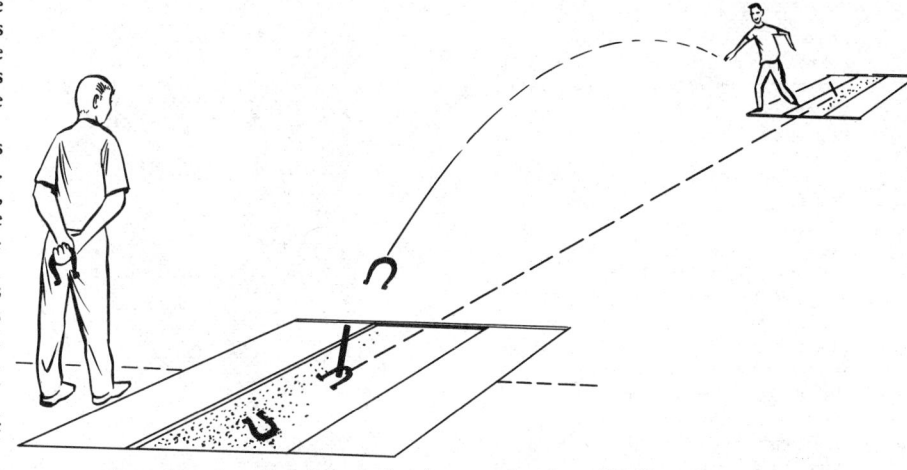

After missing the stake entirely, the first thrower made a ringer. Now his opponent tries to top it. The foot-high stakes are forty feet apart; the sand pit is 36 inches wide.

horseshoe pitching

Horseshoe pitching is a game that had its start at the time of the Revolutionary War. The object of the game is to throw horseshoes in such a manner that they land around a steel peg, or stake, or as close as possible to the stake. Quoits is a similar game played with metal rings.

The stakes are driven in the ground so that they extend 14 inches above the ground. They are 40 feet apart for men, and 30 feet apart for women or for children under 16 years of age. The court, or space in which the game is played, is 10 feet wide and 50 feet long. The players stand at one end of the court and throw (pitch) the horseshoes toward the stake at the other end. They take turns pitching until each has thrown two horseshoes. The horseshoes must not be heavier than 2½ pounds. The pitcher must stay within ten feet of the stake at his end.

The game is 50 points. If you throw a shoe closer to the stake than your opponent does, you score one point. A ringer (when the shoe encircles the stake) counts 3 points. Two ringers count 6 points. All equals count as ties, and no point is scored for either side. If a shoe lands so that it is leaning against the stake (a "leaner"), it does not count more than one that is merely touching.

The game may be played between individuals, or between teams of two members each. When teams play, one member of each side pitches from each end of the court. It is usually not convenient to have teams larger than two members.

horsetail

The horsetail is a plant with a slender, jointed stem and tiny leaves growing out of each joint. The horsetail stem contains so much silica (the chemical substance of which sand is formed) that it feels very rough to the touch. In ancient times people used the horsetail for scouring pots and pans. The horsetail now grows to only 2 or 3 feet in height, but millions of years ago there were horsetails as much as 40 feet high. They had huge leaves and were as big as trees. Three hundred million years ago they formed a large part of the world's vegetation. In the course of the ages they have changed to coal.

horticulture

Horticulture is the growing of fruits and vegetables for food and flowers for decoration. Science has done a great deal to improve the growing of fruits and vegetables by developing new fertilizers and discovering efficient ways of producing the most profitable crops. Chemistry and physics are the sciences that contribute. But in spite of the great contribution that science has made, horticulture is an art, and the best results are gotten by skilled horticulturalists who know and love plants. Horticulture can be broadly divided into four branches: fruit growing, vegetable growing, flower growing, and landscape art.

hosiery

Hosiery is a name given to all knitted garments used as coverings for the legs and feet—that is, stockings and socks. At one time hosiery meant any knitted garment at all, and most underclothing was also called hosiery. Today hosiery means the same thing as stockings because all modern stockings are knitted.

Leg and foot coverings were first used by men to protect themselves from the cold. They were long, loose coverings made of animal skins. Later woolen cloth was used. When soldiers wore armor their stockings and trousers were all one piece. Later the garment was cut into two garments, but the stockings were still bulky, ill-fitting, and uncomfortable. Men wore stockings of this kind long before women did. Women only started to wear stockings about six hundred years ago.

HOW HOSIERY IS MADE

For a short time hosiery was knitted by hand, but machine knitting as used to make hosiery today has been going on for nearly four hundred years. The first machine for knitting hosiery was invented by an English clergyman, William Lee, in 1589. Modern knitting machines are larger and have many improvements, but the basic idea of their design is the same.

In knitting it is necessary that a single thread be used for the whole process, and that the material formed be elastic and strong. All knitted garments are made with a looped stitch. Lee's machine, which is called a stocking-frame, mechanically produces the looped stitch. The stocking-frame is a series of long needles with

hooks at the end. Each loop has its own hooked needle. The thread is passed over the row of needles inside the open hooks, and thin plates of shaped metal, called sinkers, fall between each pair of needles to push the thread down in loops of uniform size. The size of the loops formed on the needles depends upon the depth of the fall of the sinkers. Then the points of the needle hooks are pressed to the needle itself by a pressure bar. The looped yarn is now inside the closed hook. The loops are then drawn over the hooks in much the same way in which a single stitch is knitted by hand, and a new series of loops is formed. The hooks open again, and the process is repeated again and again until the knitted material reaches its desired size. The material can be made wider or narrower by adding or taking away loops from the side of the frame.

MODERN HOSIERY

The great differences between modern hosiery and the first knitted hosiery are in the types of material used and in the fashions of the hosiery itself. For many years men's socks were made only of cotton, wool, and silk. More recently materials such as rayon came into use. Manufacturers call any thread made of artificial materials, such as rayon or nylon, fiber. Today many men's socks are made of one of these fibers, or a combination of fiber with silk, cotton, or wool.

The first women's stockings were made of cotton. Often these stockings were very thick and unattractive. When silk stockings were first made for women, they were considered a luxury. Many women felt that it was not quite proper to wear anything as fancy and as pretty as a silk stocking. About fifty years ago, silk stockings became more popular, though many women still wore them only "for best" because they were very expensive. In the course of the years silk stockings came to be made more and more sheer (which means thin).

Then, almost overnight, a remarkable thing happened. Nylon stockings for women were introduced in the early 1940s, and silk stockings almost completely disappeared. Women like nylon stockings better than silk because they are sheerer, fit better, wear longer, and dry much more quickly. Today nearly all women's stockings are made of nylon.

There have been many changes in the fashions of women's stockings. Stocking-makers design nylons in many colors and styles, and women often match their hose with their clothing. Today's women enjoy the convenience of pantyhose, a garment combining the stockings and the panty into one. The pantyhose are popular because they slip on easily and require no fasteners. Young girls, who once wore long cotton stockings, now wear knee socks or opaque (not transparent) tights. Both are available in many colors. College girls may wear knee socks, tights, or nylons depending upon their activities.

About fifty years ago, young boys wore knickerbockers (knee-length pants that were tight at the knee) and stockings that were long enough to fasten above the knees. Now even very young boys dress the same way as men and wear long pants and socks.

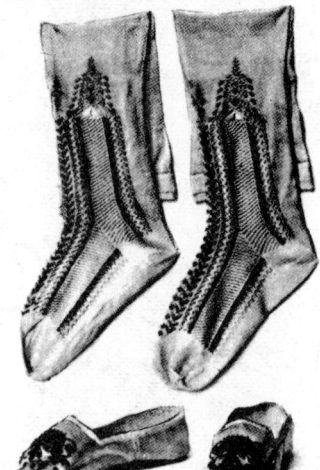

Medieval ladies wore hosiery decorated in silver and gold with clocking on the sides that shows great artistic skill.

In Colonial America, hosiery was not as sheer as women's stockings are today. But the workmanship was fine.

Fur-lined Eskimo stockings, called "mukluks," make up in warmth for their lack of beauty.

HOW TO BUY STOCKINGS

Stocking sizes are different from shoe sizes. For men, the shoe size is about the same as the length of the foot in inches, and the stocking size is two numbers higher. A man whose foot measures about ten inches wears a size 10 shoe and size 12 sock.

Women buy stockings of a certain gauge and denier as well as of a certain size. *Denier* is the measure of the fineness (thinness) of the yarn used in the stocking. The lower the number the finer the thread, so 12-denier hose is sheerer than

15-denier hose. The gauge tells how closely knitted the stocking is. The number of the gauge is the number of knitted loops, or stitches, there are in each inch and a half, going around the stocking. The more stitches there, the sheerer the stockings will be; 60-gauge hose is sheerer than 51-gauge hose. Women usually save their sheer hosiery for evening wear.

hospital

A hospital is a building that is specially equipped and managed to take care of people who are sick. Hospitals range in size from very small ones with only a few "beds" to enormous ones with thousands of "beds." (The number of beds is the number of patients the hospital can take care of at one time.)

A person may go to a hospital for *observation,* or for *diagnosis,* simply to find out if there is anything wrong; or for *surgery,* when he needs an operation; or when he is dangerously sick, so that there will be doctors and nurses on hand at all times; or for *emergency* treatment, when he has suffered an accident; or for *maternity* care, when a woman is about to have a baby; or for any other of several reasons.

A patient who stays in the hospital is called an *inpatient.* Most hospitals also have departments where people can be treated or examined (as they would be in a doctor's office) while they are living at home. These are called *outpatients.*

A big hospital will have separate floors or sections for the different kinds of medical care; for example, a maternity ward, a surgical ward, an emergency ward, and so on. Smaller hospitals use their rooms, or beds, for any patients that need them. Every hospital has at least one operating room, where surgery is performed; a laboratory, where blood and urine and other things can be tested for signs of disease; a nursery, where newborn babies are kept warm and clean; and rooms for X-ray and other special examinations.

THE HOSPITAL STAFF

Nearly every hospital has some *resident physicians,* who live in the hospital and receive salaries for their work, instead of charging fees to the individual patients. Often the resident physicians have private patients too, and charge them fees. One of the resident physicians is the superintendent. He is in charge of the entire hospital. Some of the resident physicians are *internes.* They are graduate doctors, but they are only recently out of medical school and their internship is a continued training for their profession.

There are also *staff physicians.* These are doctors who have their own offices. When a patient needs hospital care, the doctor will send him to a hospital where he is a member of the staff. In a big city, a doctor is likely to be on the staff of two or three or even more hospitals. A doctor cannot send a patient to any hospital where he is not on the staff. Staff physicians are expected to do some free work for the hospital, such as taking care of patients who are too poor to pay fees. If the hospital has a *clinic,* where outpatients are treated, the staff physician is supposed to work in it for a certain number of hours each week.

The *resident nurses* at a hospital receive salaries from the hospital and do not have any outside patients. They take care only of patients in the hospital. Many hospitals have nurses' training schools connected with them, and student nurses learn their profession by working in the hospital. A big hospital usually has a special building, or dormitory, where resident and student nurses live. These nurses are all women, but there are also some male nurses on the hospital staff.

Other members of a hospital staff include the dietitians, who are in charge of preparing the food for the patients (and also for the nurses and doctors who eat at the hospital); the housekeepers, or matrons, who keep the hospital clean and supply fresh sheets and towels and other bedroom supplies; pharmacists who prepare drugs needed by the patients; ambulance drivers and stretcher bearers, if the hospital has an ambulance service; engineers, porters, bookkeepers, and others who do the many kinds of work needed to keep a big building running smoothly.

When a patient is so sick that constant nursing is needed, nurses are brought in from outside. They are not members of the hospital staff, because a staff nurse cannot spend all her time on one patient. The outside nurse is paid directly by the patient and not by the hospital.

SERVICES AND RATES

A hospital usually has three kinds of service: private, semi-private, and ward.

A *private* patient has a room all to himself. In a modern hospital this room usually has a private bath and private telephone, just as a hotel room would. A private patient may have visitors at most hours of the day and at night until perhaps nine o'clock. The private patient pays by far the biggest price for the room and hospital care.

A *semi-private* patient usually shares a room with one other person. That is, there are two beds in the room. The care is just as good, but often there is no private telephone and visitors are permitted for only a few hours during the day (because the use of the telephone, or talking to visitors, might disturb the other patient in the room). Semi-private patients pay less than private patients.

Ward patients pay least of all. In a ward there may be any number of beds from four up to twenty or thirty. Visiting hours are usually limited to perhaps two or three hours a day, and on certain days no visitors are allowed.

Not only the cost of the room but also the hospital's charges for other services depend on whether the patient is private, semi-private, or ward. A private patient is charged more for the use of the operating room, for laboratory tests, and even for drugs. An injection of penicillin might cost a private patient four dollars, a semi-private patient two dollars, and a ward patient only one dollar, yet it is the same amount of penicillin, administered by the same doctor or nurse in exactly the same way.

Hospital charges always seem high, but it costs hospitals a lot of money to operate because they must be so careful about everything. The rooms and halls must be kept cleaner than in any other kind of building. Everything used in caring for patients has to be sterilized (made completely free of germs). The food has to be scientifically planned and specially cooked. Very careful records have to be kept, and nurses and doctors have to be on hand at every minute of the day and night. Most hospitals spend more money than they receive from their patients, and have to ask people for donations so that they can continue to give the finest service.

WHAT A PATIENT DOES

If you go to a hospital as an inpatient, you will first go to an office where you are *admitted*. At this office you will give your name, age, and other information about yourself and your family, and the name of your doctor. Your doctor will always have told the hospital to expect you, so a room will already be assigned to you. Next you will be led to this room. A nurse will come in and tell you to undress and get into bed. When you are in bed, the nurse will take your temperature and your pulse and make a record of it on your *chart,* a sheet of paper on which will be written everything about your condition and what treatment you receive, hour by hour and day by day, as long as you are in the hospital.

Your own doctor, who sent you to the hospital, may not come to see you for some hours, but one of the resident doctors will soon be in to see you. Your doctor will have given instructions as to what tests are to be made, or what medicines you are to be given, and the nurses and doctors at the hospital will take care of this.

Three times a day, your meals will be brought to you on trays and you will eat them in bed. A hospital bed is made so that the top of it can be tilted up by turning a crank, so that you can sit up in bed. A rolling table, which fits over the bed, will hold the tray. In between meals you will be given orange juice or milk or other things, depending on how sick you are and what your doctor thinks you should have.

If you have to go to the X-ray room or to other rooms for special tests, you will usually be put in a wheelchair and pushed along the halls, into and out of elevators, until you reach the room. When the tests are over, you will be wheeled back to your room. Hospitals often use wheelchairs even when you are strong enough to walk. They do not want you to become overtired when you are sick.

If you are to have an operation, it will usually be early in the morning. For an operation, you are put on a rolling bed, which is like a long table on wheels, and pushed to the operating room in that. In the operating room you will see your doctor, if he is going to operate on you; and an *anesthetist,* who will give you an anesthetic to put you to sleep during the operation; and two or three nurses who are specially trained to help the doctor during the operation. Everyone in the operating room will be wearing white clothes, masks over their faces, and gloves on their hands. Hospitals will not take any risk at all of letting germs get into the operating rooms.

In a big hospital, there may be a gallery, or balcony, built above the floor of the operating room. Here, behind glass windows, medical students and other doctors can sit and watch the operation, for that is one of the ways they learn.

The anesthetic will put you to sleep, and when you wake up you will be back in your own room, in your own bed. The operation will be over.

While you are recovering, you will probably be kept in bed nearly all the time. The nurse will bathe you and change the sheets on your bed without having to move you more than to roll you over once.

Just as you cannot be admitted to a hospital without having it arranged by a doctor, you cannot leave the hospital until your doctor signs a release that says you are well enough to go home. Hospitals try not only to cure people but to keep them well afterwards.

HISTORY OF THE HOSPITAL

The first hospitals were organized almost two thousand years ago, in the days of the Roman Empire. During the Middle Ages, the various religious orders founded places for the care of the sick. Most of these ancient hospitals, however, did not have any of the things which we think of as being necessary to a hospital. They were simply places where poor people went when they became sick because they could not be cared for at home. They were just left there to get better or to die. It was only during the 19th century that hospitals with scientific equipment and services were developed. The oldest hospital still in existence is the Hôtel Dieu in Paris, which was started in the year 660. The first hospital in the United States was organized, with the help of Benjamin Franklin, in Philadelphia in 1751. Today there are nine thousand hospitals of all sizes in the United States. About half of these are known as voluntary hospitals. They are not operated for a profit but are run by groups of private citizens, churches, or communities. Except for a few hospitals which provide luxury services and are run for profit, the other American hospitals are operated by cities and by various other branches of the government, such as the Veterans Administration and the armed forces. There are also special public hospitals which treat such illnesses as tuberculosis and mental diseases.

hotel

A hotel is a place where people can stay when they are away from home. Most hotels are big buildings with many rooms that can be rented for as short a period as one day. Each room in a modern hotel has a private bathroom, a private telephone, and usually its own radio or even a television set. Usually a hotel has more than a hundred rooms, and the world's largest, the Conrad Hilton in Chicago, has three thousand rooms.

When a hotel does most of its business with people who live somewhere else and stay for a day or a few days, it is called a *transient* hotel. There are other hotels called *residential* hotels, in which people can rent apartments in which they live all the time. Residential hotels are like apart-

ment houses except that they give some extra services and often they have some transient rooms in addition to their apartments.

Most hotels charge some regular price for the room, but meals cost extra and the guest may eat where he pleases, either in the hotel or in restaurants outside. This is called the *European plan*. Other hotels, especially resort hotels to which people go for vacations, operate on the *American plan*. The price the guest pays for his room includes three meals each day in the hotel dining room. He has to pay the same price whether or not he eats the meals. It is a standard joke that most hotels in America follow the European plan and most hotels in Europe follow the American plan.

In a hotel you may have a single room, for one person; a double room, for two persons; or a suite, which includes a parlor in which the guest can entertain friends or business visitors and a bedroom in which he sleeps.

WHAT A HOTEL IS LIKE

When you enter a hotel in which you are going to stay, you find yourself first in a big room called the *lobby*. This room is usually two stories high. Often there is a balcony running around the second-story level. This is called the *mezzanine*. In the lobby and on the mezzanine are sofas and chairs in which people can sit and wait for friends they are meeting in the hotel, or talk, or read.

Around the lobby there are several counters and shops for the convenience of the hotel's guests. There is a newsstand that sells papers and magazines and tobacco and candy; and a porter, a hotel employee who will buy you railroad or airline or steamship tickets for wherever you want to go, and will arrange to have your baggage picked up or delivered; and perhaps the entrances to one or more restaurants run by the hotel. Also in the lobby is the *desk*, which is a sort of hotel office. At the desk is a *room clerk*. The first thing you must do is to *register*, that is, sign your name and write your address on a card or book that the hotel keeps as a record. (The law requires you to register, and to sign your correct name and address.) When you have done this, the room clerk will assign a room to you, and will call a *bellboy*, who will carry your baggage and lead you to your room. You are expected to tip the bellboy for doing this. The tip may be 25 cents to a dollar or more, depending on how expensive the hotel is and how much luggage you have for the bellboy to carry.

At the desk, you will get mail addressed to you at the hotel; you can give the room clerk any money or jewelry or other valuables that you want to have kept in the hotel safe, so they cannot be lost or stolen; and you can leave the key to your room when you go out of the hotel and pick it up again when you come back, so that you will not lose it.

HOTEL SERVICE

Hotels are famous for the good service they give. A fine hotel usually has more employees to wait on the guests than it has guests.

When you leave your room, a maid comes in and cleans it thoroughly, put-

ting clean sheets on the bed and towels and soap in the bathroom. Bellboys will bring you anything you want to order from a drugstore or gift shop or newsstand or other shop in the hotel. Pick up the telephone in the room and call "Room service" and a waiter will bring any food or drinks you want to your room. In a hotel you are supposed to tip the person who performs each service. Bellboys and waiters are tipped at once. You do not tip the maid until you are leaving the hotel, and at that time you leave the tip in the room where she will see it when she comes in to clean.

Most hotels have big ballrooms in which organizations can hold meetings or give banquets. Some hotels have gymnasiums and swimming pools for their guests. Often a hotel has a garage attached to it. In a very big hotel there are several restaurants, and in one of them there will be an orchestra for dancing and various entertainers.

One of the newest kinds of hotel is called the *motel*, which means "motor hotel." The motel is for people who are making long trips by automobile. Each room is usually a little separate house with a covered space, or "carport," beside it for the automobile. Some motels have main buildings or rooms that are like the lobby of a city hotel. In many motels, each room or cabin has its own kitchenette so that guests can cook their own meals if they want to.

THE HOTEL CAREER

Hundreds of thousands of people work for hotels, and there are many schools at which people can get special training for hotel work. One famous school is

School of Hotel Admin., Cornell U
The hotel chef must have great skill. Correct seasoning is his treasured art.

part of Cornell University, at Ithaca, New York. The students in Cornell's School of Hotel Administration run a hotel themselves and learn many things by practical experience.

More than six thousand hotels in the United States are members of the American Hotel Association. This association has meetings at which hotel men and women can meet to discuss their problems. The association also gets information about hotel management and sends it to its members.

Many American hotels are owned by big chains that operate ten or more hotels. Since World War II these chains have bought hundreds of hotels that once were independently managed.

HOTELS IN HISTORY

The earliest hotels were called taverns, or inns. They go back in history for thousands of years—as long as people have traveled. Jesus was born in a barn because there was "no room in the inn" in Bethlehem. When big camel caravans used to cross the deserts in Asia, there were hotels called caravanserais at which the travelers slept and rested on their way.

During the Middle Ages, five hundred to a thousand years ago, there were few taverns except in the cities. Travelers were always welcomed at monasteries and castles. Then, as roads were built, and horsedrawn stagecoaches began to carry passengers between cities, hotels were built at points at which the stagecoaches stopped. The coming of the railroads, a little more than a hundred years ago, caused bigger hotels to be built along the railroad lines. Increased travel also caused the building of big luxury hotels at resorts such as Atlantic City, Miami, Palm Springs, and other places. Now millions of travelers and vacationists stay in hotels every year.

hot rod

A hot rod is an automobile that has had some of its parts changed, or has had special parts added to it, so that it will go faster. Usually, only an old car that has been fixed by a teen-ager is called a hot rod, but of course it does not really matter who fixed the car or who owns it. It is still a "hot rod" (usually shortened to "rod") if it has been changed in certain ways.

Here is how the hot rod got its name: One of the important parts of an automobile engine is the camshaft, about which you can read in the article on INTERNAL COMBUSTION ENGINES. The camshaft is a shaft, which means about the same thing as rod. In racing cars, the camshaft is made so that it will lift the valves higher than an ordinary camshaft will. This special kind of camshaft is said to be "hot"; that is, it is a "hot rod." When people put a hot camshaft, or hot rod, into an automobile they began to call the whole automobile a hot rod.

Usually the automobile that is called a hot rod has had other things done to it to make it go faster. This is called "souping it up." One of the ways is to put in a SUPERCHARGER (about which there is a special article) to supply more air and make the fuel burn better. Other ways are to use lighter flywheels, to change the gears, and to increase the power of the engine. A "hot rod" is usually very noisy and does not idle smoothly.

Hot Springs

Hot Springs is the name of several towns in the United States that have natural springs of hot mineral water.

The largest of these towns is Hot Springs, Arkansas, where almost fifty springs flow from the nearby Hot Springs Mountain. This water has many minerals dissolved in it, and sometimes it is very

hot. Many people bathe in this water for relief from such diseases as rheumatism and arthritis.

The Indians and the Spanish explorers knew about Hot Springs, but it was not settled until after the explorers Lewis and Clark passed through in 1804. Not long afterwards, in 1832, it was made a United States government reservation, and in 1921 it became the Hot Springs National Park. About 35,000 people now live in Hot Springs, Arkansas, and thousands more visit it each year. The city is also the site of an army and navy general hospital.

Hot Springs, Virginia, is a much smaller place, with a population of about 300, but it is well known because for many years it has been a favorite resort of America's richest men. Hot Springs, South Dakota, with a population of 4,434, is another popular resort.

Hottentots

The Hottentots are a group of people who live in the southwest part of Africa, mostly in the Kalahari Desert. They are members of the Negro race and are related to the Bushmen of South Africa. Hottentots are quite short—five feet or under—and very slender. Their skin ranges in color from yellow to yellow-brown. They have black, woolly hair and flat noses. The Hottentots used to live in better parts of Africa, but European settlers and stronger native tribes pushed them into the desert and mountain regions, where hardships and disease killed many of them. There are only about 15,000 Hottentots left and their number is declining. They do some farming, and know how to work with metals.

Houdini, Harry

Harry Houdini was one of the world's greatest magicians. He was born in Appleton, Wisconsin, in 1874, and his real name was Erich Weiss. He started to prepare for his life of daring when he was very young, learning to perform on a trapeze, working in a locksmith's shop, and training his toes to be as nimble as his fingers. There was no lock that he could not open and no knot that was too hard for him to untie. With his hands handcuffed behind his back he would be put into a chest that was sealed and then thrown into the water. In only a few minutes he was able to free himself and show himself to the amazed crowds. He collected a large library on magic, which he left to the Library of Congress. He died in 1926.

Houdon, Jean

Jean Antoine Houdon was a great French sculptor who carved many famous statues, including one of George Washington. This statue was carved in 1784 when Houdon visited the United States and was Washington's guest at his home, Mount Vernon. It is now in the state capitol in Richmond, Virginia.

Houdon was the finest sculptor of his time. He was born in France in 1741. After studying in France and Rome, he returned to Paris and began to carve "portraits," or busts. A bust is a statue of the head and shoulders of a person. Houdon carved busts of such great men as King Louis XVI of France and the French writer Voltaire. Later he did busts of Thomas Jefferson and Benjamin Franklin. When Houdon grew old, his hands weakened and he was unable to work, but he could still teach. He had many pupils when he died in 1828.

hound

A hound is a dog used for hunting. Hounds are noted for their keen sense of smell and their willingness to follow a trail. Hounds have been kept by man for more than five thousand years. Pictures of hounds have been found in ancient ruins, and hounds have been used by hunters in every period of history. Today they are kept in most sections of the world both as pets and to trail game. Some hounds are also used in police work, for trail following. You can read more about hounds in the separate article on DOGS. Among the many kinds are the Afghan hound, basset hound, bloodhound, Borzoi (Russian wolfhound), dachshund, foxhound, greyhound, and wolfhound.

hourglass

An hourglass is an instrument, made of glass, used for measuring time. It is made of two tubes or bulbs joined by a narrow neck. One of these tubes is filled with sand, and the hourglass is turned upside down so that the sand runs into the other tube. Time is measured by how long it takes all the sand to run through the narrow neck. Hourglasses can be made to measure different lengths of time by putting more sand in them or by making the neck smaller so that the sand goes through slowly. Small hourglasses that measure three minutes are used in many kitchens for timing soft-boiled eggs.

House of Commons, the lower house of the British Parliament: see the article on PARLIAMENT.

House of Lords, the upper house of the British Parliament: see the article on PARLIAMENT.

House of Representatives, the lower house of the Congress of the United States: see the article on CONGRESS.

housing

Housing is all the houses and apartments and other dwelling places where all the people of a country live. In a prosperous country such as the United States, most of the people can afford to have comfortable places to live in, but very few of the people have enough cash at any one time to buy land and build a new house. Therefore governments consider it their responsibility to furnish enough cash to build the houses, and let the people pay for them over the course of fifteen or twenty or more years.

There are three main cases when new housing is needed:

Population growth. As the population of a country, state or city grows, more houses are needed to make room for the greater number of people.

Replacement. Houses gradually wear out. From time to time, an old house should be torn down and a new house built in its place.

Slum clearance. All big cities and many smaller ones have sections where poor people live in houses without proper bathrooms, kitchens, or even windows for ventilation. The owners of these houses usually make a good profit on the rents they collect, and do not want to spend money to build new houses. The government wants to tear down the slum dwellings and build houses where people can live comfortably and yet pay low rent. Usually the government must lose money to do this, and the money comes from taxes that all the people pay.

HOUSING PLANS

Usually the government does not directly put up the money needed for new housing. Instead, it encourages banks and

WHAT REMAINS TO BE DONE?
A rough indication is provided by the number of dwelling units that in 1960 were dilapidated, deteriorating, or lacked basic plumbing facilities.

(Millions of Homes)

Dilapidated

NOT DILAPIDATED, BUT—

Deteriorating  8.3

No Private Toilet, Bath or Running Water  7.0

Housing Research

Bad housing is a problem in every nation of the world, including the United States. In 1960, the Bureau of the Census reported that more than eleven million homes were substandard. Congress passed the U.S. Housing Act of 1961 in an effort to remedy this situation.

private investors to lend or spend the money needed for new building. The government usually does this by guaranteeing, or insuring, mortgage loans made by banks to people who want to build new houses. This means that if the builder of the house does not pay the loan to the bank, the government will.

Often a family must put up as much as one-third of the total cost of its new house, but a special "G.I." law makes it possible for war veterans to put up only one-tenth of the cash needed.

Businessmen or construction companies that want to build houses for investment, and sell them to families who want to live in them, make complete plans for the houses they intend to build, how much they will sell them for, or how much rent they will charge if they rent them. If the proper government agency approves their plans, it will guarantee a loan at the bank that will give them the money they need and even assure them a profit. In many cases builders have made large extra profits from the borrowed money. This is called a "windfall" profit.

For slum clearance, a city usually buys the property on which slum dwellings stand and arranges with some company that has money to invest, such as an insurance company, to build apartment houses. The United States government will pay the city two-thirds of what it loses by doing this. Slum-clearance buildings are usually governed by rules that say no one can rent an apartment unless he has a certain income that is considered low. For example, the rule may say that no one can rent a certain apartment if he makes more than $85 a week.

Many U.S. government agencies were combined in 1966 under the new Department of Housing and Urban Development. Some of the important ones were:

Congress in 1947 created a Housing and Home Finance Agency responsible for giving the people better housing.

The Federal Housing Administration, or FHA, founded in 1934 to insure mortgage loans that are made to people who want to build or improve their houses. The bank or other institution that actually lends the money pays part of it to the FHA to pay for the insurance.

The Public Housing Administration, to provide low-rent housing (that is, for slum clearance).

Because substandard housing remained a problem, Congress passed the U.S. Housing Act of 1961 to help remedy the situation and to aid in urban renewal.

Housing and Urban Development, Dept. of

The United States Department of Housing and Urban Development was created by Congress in 1965. It is popularly called HUD. Since it is a U.S. Department, the Secretary at the head of the department is a member of the President's cabinet. In 1966 President Johnson appointed as Secretary Robert C. Weaver of New York, who became the first Negro to serve in a cabinet of the United States.

The new department was designed to combine many government agencies, and also create new ones, to solve problems that have arisen with the great growth of cities and industrial centers: decent places for people to live; slum clearance;

traffic problems; the pollution of rivers, lakes, and air; sewage disposal; and rapid transportation to the places where people work. By one estimate, the tasks assigned to the new department had previously been divided among fourteen government departments and agencies. See also the article CITY PLANNING.

Housman, Alfred Edward

A. E. Housman was an English poet who has been called the "poet of youth." He was born about a hundred years ago, in 1859. He became a Latin scholar and translated many great Latin works. He was a professor of Latin at Cambridge University in England. Housman is best remembered for *A Shropshire Lad* and other poems. He died in 1936.

Houston

Houston is the largest city in the state of Texas, with a population of about 1,230,000. Between 1960 and 1970 the population increased over 31 per cent or more than a quarter of a million people in ten years. Houston is an important seaport, though it is fifty miles from the water. The Houston Ship Canal connects it with Galveston Bay, a branch of the Gulf of Mexico. The important ports of Galveston and Texas City are also on this bay, near Houston.

Houston's nearness to the valuable Texas oil fields has made it one of the largest oil-refining centers in the world. It exports oil and petroleum products, and also a great deal of cotton and grain. Its factories make well-drilling machinery, cotton goods and cottonseed oil, furniture, chemicals, and other important products. Seventeen railroads run to Houston. Rice Institute and the University of Houston make it an important educational center. The climate is very hot in summer, but Houston is one of the richest cities in the world, and parks, swimming pools and much air conditioning add to the people's comfort. The Manned Space Flight Center, from which the Apollo moon missions were controlled, is near Houston.

HOUSTON, TEXAS. Population (in 1970) 1,232,802. County seat, Harris County. Founded, 1837; named for Sam Houston.

Houston, Sam

Sam Houston was a great hero of Texas, more than a hundred years ago.

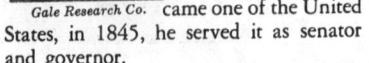

Before his time, Texas belonged to Mexico. Houston helped Texas to become an independent country, and he was its first president. After Texas became one of the United States, in 1845, he served it as senator and governor.

Gale Research Co.

Sam Houston was born near Lexington, Virginia, in 1793. When he was a boy his family moved to the new state of Tennessee. Sam did not like his new home and for a while he lived with the Cherokee Indians. When he was 20 years old he joined the United States Army, and fought under General Andrew Jackson in the War of 1812. After that, the gov-

ernment put him in charge of moving the Cherokees to a new home in Arkansas.

Houston became a lawyer in Tennessee, served as Representative in Congress, and was governor of the state for one term. In 1832 he moved to Texas and helped write a constitution for Texas that declared its independence. Mexico sent an army, under General Santa Anna, to subdue the Texans, but Houston led the Texas army and defeated Santa Anna in 1836, making Texas free. As president of the Republic of Texas, he favored joining the United States, though many Texans were against it.

When Texas did join the United States, Houston was sent to Congress as one of its first two senators. In 1859, he was elected governor of Texas, but he had to resign when the Civil War began and Texas joined the Confederate States of America, because he wanted it to remain in the Union. He died in 1863.

Howard University

Howard University is a large university in Washington, D.C. It is governed by the Office of Education, which is part of the United States Department of Health, Education, and Welfare. Howard was founded in 1867 by the FREEDMEN'S BUREAU, about which there is a separate article. Its purpose was to give educational opportunities to blacks, who had been freed from slavery only two years before. Now it has both white and black students. Both men and women may attend. In 1971 there were 8,200 students enrolled in the university's ten schools and colleges.

Howard University was named after General O. O. Howard, head of the Freedmen's Bureau.

Howe, Elias

Elias Howe is known for inventing the sewing machine. He did not invent the first one. Other men had had the same idea. This gave him a great deal of trouble in legally proving his own right to his invention. But he did succeed in bringing out the first practical sewing machine. This made possible mass production of clothing. Before then all sewing had been done by hand.

Gale Research Co.

Howe was born in 1819 in Spencer, Massachusetts. He was the son of a farmer. Because he was lame he could not do heavy farm work, so he went into a factory that made machinery for weaving cloth. This was when he first became interested in a machine that would sew. To continue with his mechanical training he worked in a watch factory. His early years were very hard because most of his money was needed to pay lawyers and other costs while he was fighting for a patent. He was finally successful and founded a factory to make sewing machines. He was awarded a gold medal for his invention at an exhibition in Paris, France, in 1867, and died later that year.

Howe, Joseph

Joseph Howe was an important citizen of Nova Scotia about a hundred years ago. At that time there was much argument about whether the Maritime Provinces (Nova Scotia, New Brunswick, and Prince Edward Island) should join Canada. Howe was against it, and many Nova Scotians agreed with him. Howe was born in 1804, and by the time he was 23 years old he was editor of a newspaper, *The Nova Scotian.* He held a number of important offices and in 1860 became premier (the highest office) in Nova Scotia. In spite of his opinions, Nova Scotia and the other Maritime Provinces voted to become part of Canada in 1867. Howe later changed his mind and decided it had been a good thing for them to join Canada. In 1873 he was appointed lieutenant-governor of Nova Scotia, but he died soon after in the same year.

Howe, Julia Ward and Samuel Gridley

Julia Ward Howe was an American woman who did much to end slavery. She wrote one of the most stirring and most famous poems of all time, the words of "The Battle Hymn of the Republic." The time and rhythm were taken from an old folk song, the same tune that was used in the song "John Brown's Body." Mrs. Howe's words, which inspired the Union army and people to fight against slavery, are familiar to almost everyone: "Mine eyes have seen the glory of the coming of the Lord . . ."

Mrs. Howe was born in New York City in 1819. She married Samuel Gridley Howe, a Boston physician, eighteen years older than herself (born in 1801), who founded the Perkins Institute for the Blind in Boston and

Gale Research Co.

who did as much as any other man of his century to help the blind. He educated Laura Bridgman, a girl who was deaf, dumb, and blind. It was the first time this had been accomplished.

Mrs. Howe helped her husband with his work and at the same time worked for the ABOLITION (anti-slavery) movement, about which there is a separate article. Early in the Civil War she went to Washington and spent much time talking with the troops stationed near there. It was then, in a soldier's tent, that she was inspired to write the Battle Hymn.

Dr. Howe died in 1876. Mrs. Howe wrote his biography and several books on social questions, and became a leader in the fight to give women the right to vote. She was a very beautiful and brilliant woman, and had five children. She died in 1910.

Howe, Richard and William

Richard and William Howe were brothers who commanded British forces against America in the Revolutionary War. Richard, the older brother, was born in 1726 and went to sea at the age of 14. At the age of 20 he commanded his own ship, and by the time the Revolutionary War broke out he had become a vice-admiral.

Soon after, Richard became commander of all the British ships in American waters. He and his brother William, who was a British army officer, helped each other in the fighting. After the United States won its independence, Richard Howe became chief commander of the entire British navy. He became a viscount and later an earl. He died in 1799.

William Howe was born in 1729. He too saw his first fighting at an early age, and by the time of the American Revolutionary War, he had become a major-general. He led the British soldiers to victory at the Battle of Bunker Hill and was put in General Gage's place as the highest officer of the British army in America. He won several battles, but unlike his brother, he was not considered a very good leader. Nevertheless, he was made a knight, and before he died in 1814, Sir William Howe was made a full general in the British Army.

Howells, William Dean

William Dean Howells was an American novelist who was born in Martin's Ferry, Ohio, in 1837. His father was a newspaper publisher, and young Howells got his start as a journalist, that is, a man who writes newspaper articles. He moved to New York and became editor of the magazine called the *Atlantic Monthly.* He started writing poetry and then novels. Howells wrote about the American people that he knew, their hopes, and their problems. His first book was called *Their Wedding Journey,* but his best-known novel is *The Rise of Silas Lapham.* In this book, Howells showed that even though a man becomes rich he is not necessarily happy. Silas Lapham was a poor boy who made much money by making paints. But he discovered that some people

Gale Research Co.

would have nothing to do with him because they had been born rich while he had been born poor and had to work hard for money. Even his daughters were ashamed of their father. In other books he wrote about America's growing industry and the troubles that were then developing between the employers and the workers.

In all of his novels Howells showed much sympathy for human problems. He died in 1920.

howitzer, a short cannon that fires shells in a high curve: see the article on ARTILLERY.

howler monkey

The howler monkey is a medium-sized monkey that lives in the jungles of South America. It has a peculiar appearance because its throat is enlarged and it looks as though it were wearing an old-fashioned ruffled collar. The enlargement is in the larynx of the monkey and enables it to make a loud and remarkable howling sound that is heard for great distances in the jungle. The howler has a long, strong tail that helps it to swing easily from one tree to another. It lives mostly in trees, but like most monkeys it

is curious and its curiosity will often bring it down to see something strange and interesting.

Hoyle, Edmond

Edmond Hoyle was an Englishman who lived about two hundred years ago and wrote rules for the playing of card games and other games. His books of rules were so popular that any book of rules for the playing of card games is still likely to be called a "Hoyle." Edmond Hoyle was born in the year 1679. Between the years 1742 and 1750, when he was already an elderly man, he wrote books that he called "short treatises" on five different games.

Hoyle's first treatise was on the game of whist, a card game from which we get the modern game of contract bridge. Later he wrote on the card game quadrille, which is no longer played; piquet, a card game that is still played; and chess and backgammon, which are "board games" and are still among the most popular games. He also wrote rules for the old game of brag, which was somewhat like the modern game of poker. Hoyle died in 1769, when he was 90 years old.

Edmond Hoyle *(left)* and Albert Morehead, who has been called "the modern Hoyle."

Hubbard, Elbert

Elbert Hubbard was a writer, editor, and printer. He is best known for his essay, "A Message To Garcia," about a message delivered to a Cuban general during the Spanish-American War. It showed how anything could be accomplished, no matter what the difficulties.

Hubbard was born in Bloomington, Illinois, in 1856. He founded the Roycroft Shop in East Aurora, New York, where he revived early handcrafts and printing, and published *The Philistine,* a magazine expressing his views. Other publications were *The Fra* and *Little Journies,* which were short biographical sketches. He had peculiar habits and was proud of them. He always wore a long flowing cape and a wide-brimmed hat. He and his second wife died on the *Lusitania,* a ship sunk by the Germans in 1915 during World War I.

Hubbard, Kin

Frank McKinney Hubbard, known as Kin Hubbard, was a cartoonist and humorous writer who created a popular character called Abe Martin. "Abe Martin's Sayings" appeared daily in many newspapers and were published also in a number of books. Hubbard was born in 1868 in Bellefontaine, Ohio. His father owned a small newspaper in Bellefontaine. Hubbard went from that to the *Indianapolis News,* where he remained on the staff for many years. He died in 1930.

huckleberry

The huckleberry is a small, purplish berry that is very good to eat. It grows on a bush that often grows wild but can also be grown in gardens in shady, sandy places where there is very little lime in the soil. Huckleberry bushes are usually three or four feet high but may grow as high as ten feet. Most people think huckleberries are related to blueberries, because they taste very much alike, though the huckleberries are usually much smaller; but actually they are two different plants. The blueberry has many tiny seeds, while the huckleberry has ten larger, nutlike seeds. Huckleberries can be found in almost any section of the United States east of the Rocky Mountains.

Hudson Bay

Hudson Bay is a big branch of the ocean. It is almost entirely surrounded by the land of northeastern Canada. It is nearly 600 miles wide and extends more than 1,200 miles in a north-south direction. Its shores are low and flat, except for the highlands to the east. The bay is connected with the Arctic Ocean by Foxe Channel and with the Atlantic Ocean by Hudson Strait.

During the cold winter months of December, January, February, and March, the water is almost completely frozen and navigation is not possible. Only in the spring, summer, and early fall, when the ice has melted and disappeared, can boats carry the farm products of the area to the other parts of the world.

Hudson Bay was discovered by Henry HUDSON, about whom there is a separate article. Following Hudson's discovery, in 1610, it became an important trading region for valuable furs.

In 1670, a group of English businessmen formed the Hudson's Bay Company, a fur-trading company that is still in existence. Large fur-trading posts were set up at the mouths of the many rivers that drain into Hudson Bay.

Hudson River

The Hudson River is the largest river in the state of New York. It serves as the natural boundary line between New York and New Jersey. It starts from a little pond called Lake Tear in the Cloud, in the Adirondack Mountains, a string of mountains in upper New York State. It is then fed by other mountain streams and flows past Troy, Albany, Kingston, Poughkeepsie, New York City, and into the Atlantic Ocean. The complete length of the river is 306 miles. At its mouth it is 4,000 feet wide, or slightly less than a mile. The tides of the Atlantic Ocean are felt in the Hudson as far north as Troy, New York, nearly 150 miles from the ocean. The Hudson cuts a deep undersea gorge in the Atlantic Ocean for a hundred miles. Once this was dry land and the Hudson flowed through it.

The Hudson has always been an important transportation route in New York. The land around the river mouth makes an ideal natural harbor for New York City, where the Hudson is often called the North River.

The Bear Mountain Bridge, set in one of the many scenic areas along the Hudson River, is one of the world's longest suspension bridges. Bear Mountain State Park is near by.

NYSPIX

The Lincoln and Holland Tunnels and the George Washington Bridge cross the river and connect New York City with New Jersey. The United States Military Academy is on the Hudson. In 1524, Giovanni da Verrazzano became the first white man known to have seen the river, although he did not explore it extensively. Eighty-five years later, Henry Hudson explored it all the way to the site of present-day Albany.

Hudson, Henry

Henry Hudson was an English explorer who is usually credited with the discovery of the Hudson River and Hudson Bay. Although it was Giovanni da VERRAZZANO who, in 1524, became the first white man known to have seen the river, it was actually Hudson who, in 1609, first explored it extensively. At the time, he was employed by a Dutch trading company called the Dutch East India Company. His assignment was to find a short passage to India.

In those days, Europeans thought that the land called North America was very narrow. They hoped to find a quick way to cross it to the Pacific Ocean so that they could easily reach India to get spices, rugs, and silks. While searching for such a route in 1609, Hudson sailed into New York harbor on his ship the *Half Moon*. He sailed up the river to the site of present-day Albany, hoping to find the Pacific Ocean.

Hudson failed to find a passage to India on this trip as he failed on two previous trips and as he failed on a trip the following year. However, during his fourth voyage (in 1610) on his ship the *Discovery,* he did discover Hudson Bay in northeast Canada.

Later in the voyage, the crew forced Hudson into a small boat to die in the Bay.

Hudson, W. H.

William Henry Hudson was a British novelist and naturalist. He was born in Buenos Aires, Argentina, of American parents in 1862. He later went to London to live. A naturalist is a student of nature, and so deep was Hudson's love and understanding of nature that his novels, as well as his scientific books, are full of wonderful and sympathetic descriptions of animals, birds, and plants. His best-known novel is *Green Mansions.* He also wrote scientific books about birds and animals. W. H. Hudson died in London in 1922.

Hughes, Charles Evans

Charles Evans Hughes was an American statesman who held many important positions and who almost became President of the United States, in 1916. During his lifetime he was Governor of New York State from 1906 until 1910, Associate Justice of the United States Supreme Court from 1910 until 1916, Secretary of State from 1920 until 1925, and Chief Justice of the Supreme Court from 1930 until 1941.

Gale Research Co.

Hughes was born in Glens Falls, New York, in 1862. He was a very good student and finished high school when he was only thirteen years old. He graduated from Brown University in Providence, Rhode Island, and from Columbia University Law School in New York City. He later taught law at both Columbia and Cornell Universiities.

In 1916 Hughes ran for the Presidency of the United States against Woodrow Wilson. It was one of the closest elections in history. Hughes went to bed on the night of the election thinking that he was the next President. The returns from the state of California, which came in later, gave the election to Wilson.

Charles Evans Hughes was respected and admired for his honesty, his dignity, and his great ability. He died in 1948 at the age of eighty-six.

Hughes, Thomas

Thomas Hughes was an English writer, lawyer, and judge. He wrote a book for boys, called *Tom Brown's School Days,* that has been read by millions of boys and girls.

Hughes was born in 1822 and was educated at Rugby, a famous boys' school in England, and at Oxford University. Many of his own experiences are told in his stories about Tom Brown, a typical English schoolboy of that time. The headmasters and teachers of English schools in those days were sometimes very cruel to the boys, and Hughes' account of these conditions led to many reforms in the school system. Hughes was also the principal of a school for working men who wanted to study in their spare time. He visited America a few times and started a model village in Tennessee called Rugby, but it failed. Hughes died in 1896.

Hugo, Victor

Victor Hugo was a French writer. He lived from 1802 until 1885, and throughout most of his long life he was the most important writer in France. He published his first book when he was only twenty-two years old, and he was still writing when he died at the age of eighty-three.

French Embassy Press

Victor Hugo wrote poems, plays, and novels, and he also wrote much about the political events of his time. Two of his dramas, *Ruy Blas* and *Hernani,* have always been favorites of the French people.

Two of Victor Hugo's novels, *Notre-Dame de Paris* and *Les misérables,* are known all over the world. *Notre-Dame de Paris* tells the story of a hunchbacked and ugly man named Quasimodo who lives in the cathedral of Notre Dame in Paris. He falls in love with a beautiful girl who has sought sanctuary, or safety, in the church, and protects her. She does not return his love, and Quasimodo dies an unhappy death. *Les misérables* means in English "The Unhappy Ones." When this novel was written, Victor Hugo's popularity was so great that it was translated into ten languages at the time of its first printing. *Les misérables* tells the story of Jean Valjean, an escaped prisoner; Cosette, a girl; and Monsieur Javert, a detective. Jean Valjean takes Cosette away from a home where she has been unhappy and brings her up as his own daughter. He goes to live in a town where he is not known and becomes a very successful businessman. He is finally discovered by Javert and has to run away. The most exciting part of the book tells of his flight from Javert.

When Hugo was almost 50 years old he was banished from France for opposing Napoleon III, who became the French emperor. Hugo lived on the island of Guernsey, just off the coast of France, until 1872, when Napoleon III was no longer in power. When Hugo returned to France, he was welcomed as a hero by the French people. He died a very famous and beloved man.

Huguenots

Huguenots was the name given to the earliest French Protestants, hundreds of years ago. Nobody is sure where the word came from, but it was first used in France about four hundred years ago. Many Huguenots were among the early settlers of America. Most of them settled along the Atlantic coast.

The leading Huguenot was John Calvin. Calvin left France to settle in Switzerland, where he became one of the leading teachers of Protestantism in the world.

At first Protestants were persecuted all over Europe. They were fought particularly hard in France. In fifty years there were eight Huguenot wars, which ended only with the Edict of Nantes in 1598. This edict, or proclamation, made in the French city of Nantes, gave freedom of worship to most Huguenots.

By this time the Huguenots had gained political power in many parts of France. Some of the leading thinkers of France, as well as many prosperous businessmen, were Huguenots. Later, after Louis XIV became king of France (in 1643), the Huguenots lost a great deal of political power, and also lost their religious freedom. It was at this time that many of them went to other countries to settle, especially to the New World. It was not until 1791 that the Huguenots were finally given full religious freedom again.

Hukbalahap

The Hukbalahap is the name of a group of Communists in the Philippine Islands who fought the Philippine government after World War II. Members of the Hukbalahap are called "Huks." Their leader was a Philippine peasant, or poor farmer, named Luis Taruc. In 1954 he surrendered to the Philippine government and was sentenced to twelve years in prison for fighting against the government of the country. The Huks fought by hiding in the hills where they could not be found easily. They killed many people and destroyed a great deal of property belonging to those who were loyal to the government. Jesus Lava became the new leader of the Huks in 1954. At that time there were about three or four thousand armed men in the Hukbalahap.

Hull, Cordell

Cordell Hull became famous as an American statesman who worked to bring about peace and understanding among the nations of the world. He was born in Overton County in Tennessee in 1871. He studied law and was later made a judge. For 22 years he served in the House of Representatives and in 1930 he was elected to the Senate. He resigned in 1933 when President Franklin D. Roosevelt appointed him Secretary of State. He used this important office to try to develop better relations between the United States and other countries. The "Good Neighbor Policy," a plan to have all the nations of North and South America think of one another as good friends, was one of his ideas. He also worked very hard to start the United Nations and is sometimes called the "father of the United Nations." Because of his work he was given the Nobel Peace Prize in 1945. He died in 1955.

human body

Your body is like a machine, because it has working parts that can do useful work if they are supplied with energy in the form of fuel (food, and oxygen from the air). But the human body is much more complex and much more remarkable than any machine that man could ever build. It has hundreds of different parts, and nearly every one of them does something that the body needs to make it work properly. There are separate articles describing different parts of the body, and this article will tell how they work together to accomplish the mysterious act called living.

First consider the body's structure (how it is built) and its composition (what it is made of). It is usually said that the body is made of "flesh, blood, and bones," and this is generally true, though there are many other things that go to make up the human body.

The bones form the skeleton, the

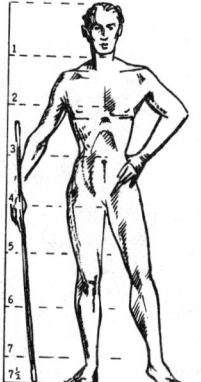
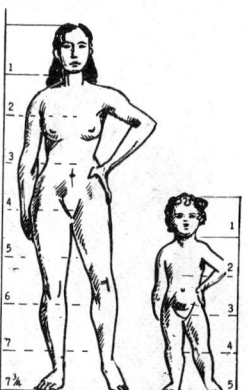

Artists drawing the human body use a scale that is based on the size of the head. A man's head is about one-eighth the length of his body. A woman's head is slightly smaller in relation to her body. A child's head, which is one-fifth the length of the body, is larger in relation to the body than an adult's head.

framework on which the body is built. The bones in the skeleton are joined together so that they can keep the body firm, but most of them are hinged where they meet so that the parts of the body can move.

Almost three-quarters of the human body is water. Other important substances in the body are calcium, phosphorus, and carbon. These substances are *elements*—they are among the hundred basic substances of which everything in the world is made. The following shows the percentages (parts in one hundred parts) of the various substances that make up the human body, and it also shows how much each substance would weigh in a man of average weight (154 pounds).

SUBSTANCE	PERCENTAGE	WEIGHT
Oxygen	65	100 lbs.
Carbon	18	28 lbs.
Hydrogen	10	15 lbs. 8 oz.
Nitrogen	3	4 lbs. 8 oz.
Calcium	1½	2 lbs. 5 oz.
Phosphorus	1	1 lb. 10 oz.
Potassium	⅓	8 oz.
Sulfur	¼	5 oz.
Others:	11/12	1 lb. 4 oz.
Sodium		
Chlorine		Cobalt
Iron		Iodine
Magnesium		and other trace
Manganese		elements

In the body of a person weighing 100 pounds, the skeleton would weigh 22 pounds and 4 ounces.

In a well-proportioned human body, the torso (from shoulders to hips) should be twice as long as the head and neck, and the legs should be three times as long as the head and neck.

The other proportions should be different in men and women. A man naturally has broad shoulders and narrow hips. A woman's hips are almost as wide as her shoulders. (See the article on GROWTH.)

THE DIGESTIVE SYSTEM

The body must have food and water. The food must be organic matter. That is, it must come from something that has once been alive, either vegetable or animal, and must contain the element carbon, which is present in all living things. The water is needed so that certain juices can be made to help digest the food (use

which carries them to all parts of the body. Some parts of the food are stored away as fat in various parts of the body. The rest of the food is not needed. It passes into the large intestine and finally is eliminated through the rectum.

THE RESPIRATORY SYSTEM

Meanwhile you are breathing, taking in air you can use and sending out air you cannot use. This is done by the lungs. From the air you breathe in, your lungs take oxygen. About one-fifth of the air is oxygen, but the lungs take only a small part of this. It is absorbed (taken in) by the blood. At the same time the blood gives off carbon that the body no longer needs, and this becomes part of the air that you breathe out.

The heart is a mighty pump that keeps the blood flowing through the tubes called arteries and veins. As the fresh blood passes different parts of the body,

The average temperature of a human being is 98.6 degrees on the Fahrenheit scale, but actually there is no "normal" temperature. Everyone changes temperature at various times during the day and night. When you have had some hours of sleep and are completely relaxed, your temperature is lowest. It will usually be 97 degrees or less. When you have taken violent exercise, your temperature may go above 99 degrees.

NERVOUS SYSTEM

Most animals can move voluntarily (because they want to) but none so completely as man. That is because man has a brain that is capable of reasoning. Your brain decides what you want to do. It then sends a message through a network of nerves, and this tells a certain muscle to pull a certain ligament, which in turn pulls a certain bone and causes your finger or hand or arm or leg to move as you

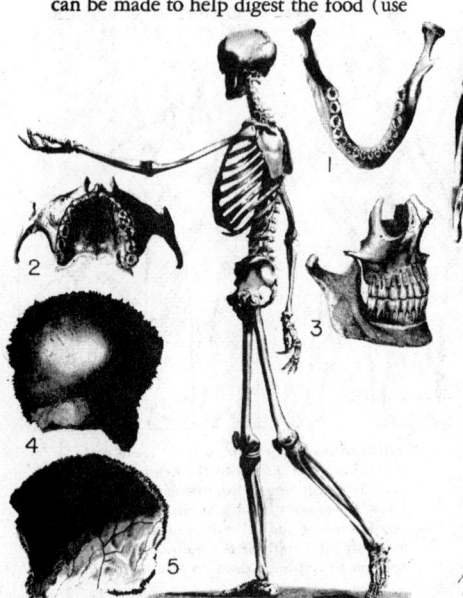

A side view of a skeleton shows the complex bone structure of the human body. The numbered parts of the skull show the bone structure of the jaw and front of the head (1, 2, and 3), and of the top and back of the head (4 and 5).

it in the body), and so that the blood will be liquid and can flow to all parts of the body, and so that the joints will be lubricated and can move easily, and for other purposes, including the carrying away of waste products in perspiration and urine.

The mouth is a wonderful machine for preparing the food. The teeth cut the food into pieces. Glands in the mouth pour out saliva that softens the food. The taste buds on the tongue often give warning when food is spoiled and not safe to eat.

From the mouth the food travels through the alimentary canal, an unbroken series of tubes that runs all the way through the body. First the food travels through the esophagus to the stomach. There it is dissolved in other digestive juices that are produced by the liver and other organs of the body.

The dissolved food passes into the small intestine, a tube that is porous (has tiny holes in it). Useful parts of the food ooze through these holes into the blood,

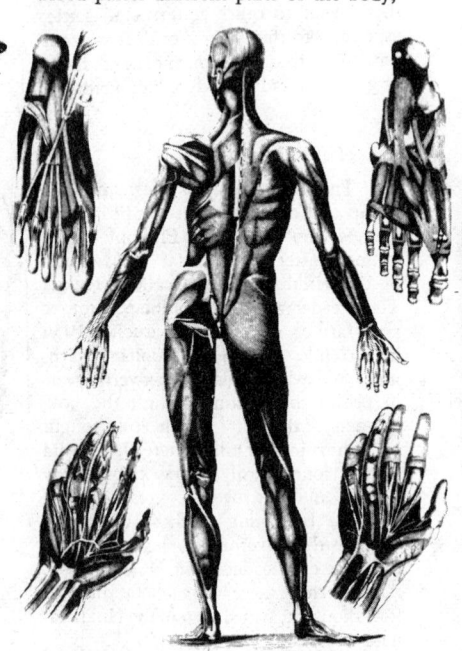

The muscles of the human body enable it to move and to exert power because they can be contracted at will. The muscular system of the hand is especially complex.

the nourishing parts of it seep into the tissues of the body and build them. The heart pumps five or more quarts of blood each minute, and all the blood in the body passes through the heart once every thirty seconds or even less.

BODY HEAT

The body is protected by an outside covering called skin. Under the skin is a layer of fat. Under the fat is the muscle, or red flesh.

The skin helps to keep the body warm. Human beings are warm-blooded animals and must remain warm to live, but they cannot become too hot without dying. When food is changed into energy inside the body, it creates a great deal of heat. The skin helps to keep this heat inside the body in cold weather. In warm weather, perspiration seeps through the skin and evaporates (is absorbed into the air). Evaporation makes things cooler. In both ways, the skin helps to keep the body at about the same temperature all the time.

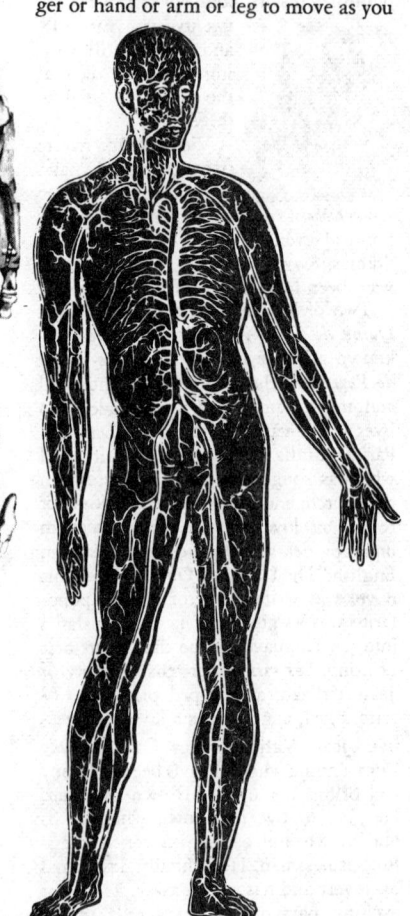

A system of arteries and veins carries blood through the human body. The blood is pumped by the heart (not shown here).

want it to. Your brain is helped by your senses. Your eyes, ears, and feelings of touch and taste and smell give information to your brain before it sends its messages through the nervous system.

The brain also controls many involuntary motions, the ones we cannot help making. We are not conscious of this, but we know when it happens.

One of the most valuable parts of the human body is the speech organs. Men can make more different sounds than any other animal, and can control them better. Many of these sounds are made in the larynx, which is sometimes called the body's sound-box. The larynx is in the

throat. It causes the air we breathe out to vibrate (shake) and this causes sounds. We control the sounds by holding our tongue and lips in certain positions. Without the power to make different sounds, men would not have languages and could not teach one another all the things they have learned.

REPRODUCTIVE SYSTEM

If men and women could not produce children, the race of man would die out. The ability to have children is called the ability to reproduce, and this is accomplished by the reproductive system. This reproductive system is the principal way in which men and women are different.

Every woman is born with about 70,-000 *ova*, or eggs, in two organs of her body called ovaries. About once in four weeks, one of those ova breaks loose and begins to travel out of her body.

Every man has special glands called the testes. These produce sperm—millions of tiny cells that carry new life. If sperm from the male meets the *ovum*, or egg, inside the woman, it fertilizes the ovum and a baby begins to grow. The baby grows inside a hollow, or pouch, called the uterus or the womb.

For a period of about nine months, the baby grows inside its mother. Then it is sent out of her body and becomes an independent living human being. There is a separate article about CHILDBIRTH.

The mother also has special glands, the mammary glands, in her breasts. These produce milk to feed the baby until it is old enough to take other food.

RESISTANCE TO DISEASE

The human body has remarkable power to overcome diseases and other things harmful to itself. When the body is cut or wounded, the blood coagulates (hardens) so that all of it cannot run out of the body, and the flesh grows together and forms new skin on top of it. When bacteria (germs) attack the body, the temperature rises, giving a person a fever, which kills some bacteria; and the blood produces special cells called antibodies that attack and kill the bacteria. The human body is not able to conquer all the wounds or diseases that may attack it, but it is able to cure many illnesses without help from drugs.

ENDOCRINE GLANDS

There are many other organs and working parts of the body. Some of them, the endocrine glands, are necessary to many of the processes of life and can control a person's height or weight or even his personality. There is a separate article about these GLANDS. See also the articles on the different parts of the body.

The scientific study of the form of the parts of the body is called ANATOMY, and the scientific study of how these parts work is called PHYSIOLOGY. There are separate articles about these.

humane societies, groups formed for the purpose of preventing cruelty to animals: see the article on the SOCIETY FOR THE PREVENTION OF CRUELTY TO ANIMALS.

humidity

Humidity is the measure of how much moisture (water) is in the air. At all times the air contains a certain amount of water in the form of a gas or vapor. Often this water turns into small particles of liquid, forming fog or clouds. When these particles condense (become more solid) rain falls, and when they freeze, snow or hail falls.

There is always some limit to the amount of moisture the air will hold. The limit depends on the temperature. When the temperature is high, the air will hold more water vapor than when it is cooler. If the air contains all the water vapor it possibly can hold, we say that it is saturated, or at the dew point; or that the *relative humidity* is 100 per cent. If the atmosphere holds half as much water vapor as it can, the relative humidity is said to be 50 per cent, and so on.

Relative humidity has much to do with how comfortable we feel. When the humidity is high in hot weather it takes longer for perspiration to evaporate and we draw less air into our lungs when we breathe. The most comfortable relative humidity is from 40 to 60 per cent. See the article HYGROMETER.

hummingbird

The hummingbird is a tiny bird with a long, slender bill, and wings that can support it while it remains almost stationary in the air. When a hummingbird holds itself in the air, its wings beat so fast they cause a humming sound.

Hummingbirds are beautifully colored. They are green with yellow and blue markings, and they are always iridescent, which means that their feathers reflect many colors like those of a rainbow.

The hummingbird has a long tongue, which it sticks deep into flowers to suck in nectar and catch the insects it eats. While feeding in this way the hummingbird picks up pollen on its beak and carries it to other flowers. Some orchids and other flowers are fertilized only by the hummingbird.

The hummingbird's nest is a small cup of some soft material. It rests on the limb of a tree. The female hummingbird lays two pure white eggs.

There are about five hundred kinds of hummingbird. Almost all of them live in South and Central America, but a few may be seen all over North America, even as far north as Labrador and Alaska.

humor

Only human beings laugh because something is funny. The ability to laugh at something funny is called a sense of humor. Different things seem funny to different people, but generally it is something strange that strikes people as being funny. Centuries ago, when the Norman conquest took place in England, the Normans invited some Saxon nobles to eat with them. Nightingale wings were served, and the Normans laughed at the Saxons because they did not know the proper way to eat nightingale wings. It seemed funny. At the same time the Saxons were laughing at the Normans because it seemed funny to the Saxons that anyone would think of eating nightingale wings.

The best sense of humor is the kind that makes it possible for a person to laugh at himself, when he says or does something that others laugh at. Anyone who can join in the laughter when the joke is on him is usually a popular person.

People like to laugh and to be amused. Since the beginning of history, the rich have hired entertainers to make them laugh, and court jesters are mentioned in many old novels, plays, and histories. Today comedians are popular because they appeal to humor, and make their audiences laugh.

There are as many kinds of humor as there are kinds of people, and everyone can find enjoyment in one kind or another.

Humperdinck, Engelbert

Engelbert Humperdinck was a German composer, or writer of original music. He is best remembered because he wrote the music for *Hansel and Gretel*, an opera (that is, a play in which the words are sung instead of spoken). *Hansel and Gretel* is very popular with children and is usually performed at Christmas time. Humperdinck was born in 1854. As a young man he studied under Richard Wagner, the greatest German composer of operas. He wrote several operas and much choral music (music to be sung by large groups). He also wrote the music for *The Miracle*, a play that was very popular in the United States. He died in 1921.

Humphrey, Hubert

Hubert Horatio Humphrey, Jr. was Vice President of the United States under Lyndon Johnson, from 1964 through 1968. He was born in Wallace, South Dakota, in 1911. As a young man he studied to become a pharmacist and then completed his education in Minnesota and became a permanent resident of that state. He taught in colleges for a few years, but was interested in politics and held several government jobs while teaching. In 1945 and again in 1947, he was elected mayor of Minneapolis. In 1948 he was elected United States Senator from Minnesota and was re-elected in 1954 and in 1960.

Humphrey was always among the leading liberals of the Democratic Party. He suported the policies of Presidents F. D. Roosevelt, Truman, and Kennedy, and of Eisenhower in foreign policy. In 1960 Humphrey tried to win the Democratic Party's nomination for the presidency but lost to Kennedy. In 1968 he did win the nomination but lost the race for the presidency to Richard Nixon.

humus

Humus is a dark, earthlike material found in the soil. It is very important because it makes the soil more fertile and helps the soil to hold water. Humus is one of the chief sources of nitrogen and other minerals used by plants. It is produced by the decay of insects, worms, grass, leaves, twigs, and other matter.

If soil does not have enough humus, farmers add fertilizers such as manure or grow certain plants, such as rye and crimson clover, that enrich the soil after they decay.

Hundred Years War

At many times in the past England and France were at war against each other. The longest of these wars started more than six hundred years ago and lasted more than a hundred years. For this reason it is called the Hundred Years War.

The chief reason for this war was that the kings of England claimed certain parts of France. One large part of France, the kingdom of Aquitaine, had come under English control when its ruler, Eleanor of Aquitaine, married King Henry II of England.

The first battles of the Hundred Years War started when the French king demanded that Aquitaine be given to him. At the same time King Edward III of England claimed the throne of France because his uncle had been the last king. In these first battles the English defeated the French. The English controlled most of France by the year 1360. Important battles were fought at Crécy, Calais, and Poitiers. In all of them the English king's son, Edward, who was called the Black Prince, fought with outstanding courage.

After ten years of peace the French started to fight again. This time they forced the English to leave most parts of France.

After this war there was another period of peace. Then King Henry V of England, helped by the French Duke of Normandy, won back much of the French territory. He fought the French at the famous battle of AGINCOURT, about which there is a separate article. The French promised to make Henry V king of France when their own king died, but Henry died before the French king did.

The great French heroine of the Hundred Years War was Joan of Arc, who in 1429 helped the French defeat the English at the battle of Orléans. Joan also helped to bring the separate parts of France together into a united nation. Soon after that, the French drove the English from their country.

Hungary

Hungary is a country in Central Europe. It is about the same size as the state of Indiana, with 36,000 square miles, but more than ten million people live there, which is more than twice as many as live in Indiana. Hungary has the best land in Europe for raising grain, and used to be called "the breadbasket of Europe." For hundreds of years it was allied with Austria by having the same king. After World War II, Communist Russia seized control of Hungary and put in a Communist government, so that the Hungarian people are no longer free.

THE PEOPLE WHO LIVE THERE

Most of the people who live in Hungary are Magyars, who were originally fierce tribesmen from Central Asia. More than a thousand years ago they settled in Hungary and formed a kingdom. Much later the Germans and Slovaks began to settle in Hungary, or were included within the Hungarian boundaries when small parts of other nations were joined to Hungary. The official language is Hungarian, the language of the Magyars. It is not a member of the same family of languages as most European languages, but it is related to one other European language, Finnish.

Two-thirds of the people belong to the Roman Catholic Church. There are other large groups that belong to the Greek Orthodox Church and to Protestant churches.

At one time there were about a million Jews in Hungary, most of them living in cities. During World War II Germany took control of Hungary, and since the German government, under Adolf Hitler and the Nazi Party, killed nearly all the Jews that came under its power, most of the Jews were killed or left Hungary to settle in other countries. In 1970 the Jewish population was only about 154,000.

HOW THE PEOPLE LIVE

Most of the people who live in Hungary are farmers. They raise chiefly grain—corn, wheat, and oats. They also grow potatoes and grapes. Livestock-raising is important in Hungary. Hungarian horses have been famous for many years, and before World War II were shipped to many other parts of the world. Under Communist control the country has very little trade with any foreign country except Russia.

There is much manufacturing in Hungary. Many of the industries have something to do with agriculture, such as canning food, milling flour, and sugar-refining. Hungary also has great factories for the production of railroad equipment and electrical machinery.

WHAT HUNGARY IS LIKE

The Danube River, the great river of southern Europe, flows south through Hungary, cutting it almost in half. East of the Danube Hungary is a low level plain.

In the west and north it is hilly. Some mountains of the Carpathian chain are in the north. The Danube River is important to transportation in Hungary. Another important river in Hungary is the Tisza River. The largest lake in central Europe, Lake Balaton, is in Hungary.

Hungary does not have many forests, and has to import wood. Mineral resources are also lacking, except that Hungary has very large deposits of bauxite, the ore from which aluminum is made.

Nearly one-fifth of the world's bauxite is in Hungary. Many of Hungary's fine roads and railroads were seriously damaged during World War II.

The capital and largest city is BUDAPEST, about which there is a separate article. Other important cities in Hungary are:

Miskolc, population 180,000, an important industrial center.

Szeged, population 119,000, an important manufacturing and flour-milling center.

Debrecen, population 160,000, an important agricultural center.

Pecs, population 146,000, in coal-mining section of southern Hungary.

HOW THE PEOPLE ARE GOVERNED

After the end of World War II, Hungary was occupied by Russian soldiers. The Russian officials who were in charge of the occupation forced the free political parties out of the government and set up a Communist dictatorship. The Communists turned Hungary into a so-called "people's republic" with a constitution like the Russian constitution. The people are governed by a presidium, which is made up of top Communists. There is a president, who is chosen by the presidium, but the real power in the government is the premier, who is elected by the presidium but actually is chosen under orders from Soviet Russia. There is also a parliament, whose members are chosen by the people, but the parliament is very weak and really has little to say about the governing of the people.

Children between the ages of 6 and 16 must go to school, and there are many schools and colleges.

HUNGARY IN THE PAST

West of the Danube, Hungary was part of the ancient Roman Empire, nearly two thousand years ago. The eastern part was roamed by barbarian tribes. The Huns, under the warlord Attila, lived in Hungary about 1,500 years ago and from them the country gets its name, though the Huns were eventually driven out.

About a thousand years ago the Magyars invaded Hungary and settled there. Descendants of their leader, Arpad, ruled Hungary for more than four hundred years. One of them, St. Stephen, brought Christianity to Hungary, about the year 1000. The family of Arpad and other Magyar chiefs became great noblemen whose families owned most of Hungary. Their huge estates lasted nearly a thousand years. They were partly broken up after World War I and the rest of them were seized by the Communist government after World War II.

Between the years 1200 and 1400 there were many invasions of Europe by Mongol hordes from Asia, and Hungary resisted these, but about four hundred years ago most of Hungary was conquered by the Turks. The western part of Hungary remained free of the Turks and came under the rule of the Hapsburg family, who were also rulers in Austria. Gradually the Turks were driven out and the Hapsburgs ruled all of Hungary.

In 1848, Hungary had a revolution because it did not want to be controlled by Austria. The leader of this revolution was Louis Kossuth. This problem was settled when it became a fully independent kingdom in the empire of AUSTRIA-HUNGARY, about which there is a separate article. As part of this empire, Hungary lost World War I and more than half its territories were taken away because the people in them were not Hungarians but were mostly Slavic or Rumanian people who had been cruelly ruled by the Magyar noblemen. These territories became parts of Czechoslovakia, Yugoslavia, and Rumania.

As early as World War I, the Communist Party was strong in Hungary. For six months, in 1918 and 1919, Hungary had a Communist government under a leader named Bela Kun. This government was unsuccessful and control passed to a royalist, Admiral Nicholas Horthy, who was the most powerful man in Hungary until World War II. Horthy called himself the regent (a person who acts for a king, but is not a king). During this period Hungary did not have a king.

During World War II Hungary fell under the control of the Germans and was an enemy of the United States and the other Allies. Russia invaded Hungary in 1945, put into power a Communist government, and controlled the country from the Soviet capital, Moscow. In 1956 the Hungarian people rebelled, seeking freedom and the right to elect their own government. Since nearly all the Hungarian people joined in the revolution, the Communist government fell; but Soviet troops and tanks were sent to Hungary and they massacred the rebelling people and restored a Communist dictatorship. In the meantime, nearly 200,000 Hungarians had escaped across the border into Austria, where the United States helped to take care of them and find them new homes in free countries.

HUNGARY. Area, 35,918 square miles. Population (1973 estimate) 10,360,000. Government, republic. Religion, Roman Catholic and Greek Orthodox. Monetary unit, the *forint*, worth about 8½ cents (U.S.). Flag, three horizontal bands, red, white, and green.

Huns

The Huns were a fierce people from Asia who invaded a large part of Europe about 1,500 years ago. They probably came originally from Mongolia. They pushed westward thousands of miles into what is now Russia, and southwest toward the country of the Germanic peoples.

Sometimes the Huns settled peacefully among the Romans, who then ruled southern and western Europe, but as their numbers grew they seized more power. By 445 they were strong enough to attack one of the greatest cities, Constantinople, the capital of the Eastern Roman Empire. Then under their most famous king, Attila, they stormed into Italy. Attila was called "the Scourge of God" by the frightened Romans, who saw him burn and plunder dozens of towns. Finally Attila reached the outskirts of Rome itself, but he turned back when Pope Leo I pleaded with him to spare the city.

After Attila died, his great empire was split among his sons, who fought against each other. Finally most of the Huns settled peacefully in the regions that are now Bulgaria and Hungary.

During World War I, the British called the Germans Huns, but this was intended as an insult. The Germans and Huns are not related peoples.

Hunt, Leigh

James Henry Leigh Hunt was an English poet, born in England, though his father was an American. Hunt was a tall, handsome man. He was a friend of the great poets of his day, Keats, Shelley, Byron, Browning, and others.

Because he insulted the Prince of Wales (later King George IV of England) in a magazine that he published, Hunt was put in jail for two years. This was in 1812. Later he and his wife and seven children lived in Europe, partly supported by Shelley and Byron.

Hunt wrote many poems, and he was generous in recognizing other men of talent, such as Keats and Tennyson. One of his best-known poems is "Abou Ben Adhem." Many people thought that one line in the poem applied to Hunt himself —"Write me as one who loves his fellowmen." Leigh Hunt was born in 1784 and died in 1859.

hunting

Hunting is looking for wild animals and killing them. The earliest men, thousands and tens of thousands of years ago, lived by hunting. It was their only way of getting meat. In the United States and Canada, within the last hundred years and even within the present century, men living on the frontiers (in regions not yet reached by civilization) have had to hunt for their meat, chiefly rabbits and squirrels, and deer and bison (buffaloes). Today hunting is a sport rather than a way of getting food.

Nearly all hunting is done with shotguns or rifles. A shotgun fires dozens of tiny balls of lead, brass, or steel. It is the gun used for killing birds and small game (small animals such as rabbits). A rifle fires a bullet. Some rifles are often used, instead of shotguns, for small game. Big rifles are used for large animals such as deer, moose, or elk, or bears, lions, and elephants. The most powerful hunting rifles will stop a charging elephant or rhinoceros.

There are special seasons for hunting in almost all states and countries, and in most places a hunter must have a license. See the article GAME AND GAME LAWS.

Since ancient times, men have trained dogs to help them hunt. Much hunting is still done with dogs that have been specially bred and carefully trained for particular kinds of hunting—birds, foxes, bears, and so on.

BIRD-HUNTING

Wild ducks and geese are hunted in many parts of the United States and Canada. The hunters usually go to the shores of a lake or river where the birds stop to feed and rest. The hunter usually puts out some wooden, duck-shaped *decoys* that float in the water, then hides in a *blind* on the shore. The flying birds see the decoys and think it is safe to come down on the water. This gives the hunter his shot. When a shot bird falls in the water, a dog of one of the breeds called *retrievers* swims out and brings it back. Such a dog holds the bird so gently in its mouth that the bird is not even bruised.

The shooting of pheasants is especially popular in Scotland, England, and Ireland, and the shooting of quail or partridge and related birds is especially popular in North America, but all these game birds are hunted in many parts of the world. Such birds nest on the ground, usually hiding in *coverts* (places hidden by bushes or underbrush). The dogs used in this kind of hunting are usually pointers, setters, or spaniels. They scent the bird, then stand motionless and point to where the bird is. When the bird flies from the covert, the hunter shoots at it. Many other kinds of game bird are hunted in this way. Often the hunter stays in a hidden place, called a *box,* while paid assistants *flush* the game (drive the birds from cover) so that he can shoot them.

Farmers often go crow-shooting both for sport and to protect their crops, which the crows eat.

BIG-GAME HUNTING

Most big game is not hunted with dogs. Packs of dogs are used to hunt bears. They may chase the bear into a tree, where it can be shot, and they may even fight the bear, but in this case the bear usually kills one or more dogs before it is killed by the pack. Packs of dogs are used also in hunting certain wildcats, such as the puma (mountain lion). The pack will usually kill the wildcat, but several dogs will be hurt and perhaps killed.

Hunting of the biggest game is done in Africa and parts of Asia, especially India.

In Africa, the hunter goes on a *safari,* a trip on which an expert "white hunter," one or more expert native hunters, and perhaps twenty other natives go along. The other natives are servants and assistants. The safari goes into the unsettled regions where wild animals are still to be found. Once safaris traveled only on foot, and most of the natives were *bearers*—they carried the food and supplies needed by the safari. Today safaris travel chiefly in trucks, and the hunter may have a trailer to live in. A safari lasts four to ten weeks and may cost ten or twelve thousand dollars. It hunts fierce animals that are dangerous, such as lions, leopards, elephants, rhinoceros, and hippopotamuses; and also animals that are swift and hard to shoot, such as antelopes, giraffes, and zebras.

In India, the most dangerous animal is the tiger. Elephants are used as domesticated animals in India, and shooting them is seldom allowed. The Indian people have a favorite kind of hunting called "pig-sticking." They hunt wild boars on horseback and kill them with spears. This sport requires the same kind of riding skill as the game of polo (which also originated in India).

In the United States and Canada, by far the greatest amount of big-game hunting is for deer and members of related families such as the moose and elk (which are found in the Northwest). The big problem in hunting these animals is to find them. They will run from the scent of a

man or from the slightest sound, and they are too fast to catch. Sometimes they can be attracted by special horns such as *moose-calls,* which give the sound of the animal. Such animals are hunted on foot and without dogs. Bears, wolves, and some other large wild animals are hunted, but bison were almost killed off by early hunters and are now protected by law. About three million Americans go hunting every year.

FOX-HUNTING

Fox-hunting is a special kind of hunting that is popular in the British Isles and in some eastern states of the United States, especially Maryland, Delaware, and Virginia. Hounds do the actual hunting and killing of the fox. The sport is in following the hounds on horseback when they chase the fox. Men and women alike go fox-hunting. In some other states, especially in the southern states, hunters often follow the hounds on foot.

Special kinds of hunting are done with FALCONS (hawks trained to hunt birds) and CHEETAHS (large, catlike animals trained to hunt fast-running animals). There are separate articles about these.

hurdy-gurdy

A hurdy-gurdy is a musical instrument that is hundreds of years old. At one time it was called an *organistrum.* The usual hurdy-gurdy has four strings that sound when a wheel is made to rub against them. The wheel is made of wood with a leather covering, well treated with rosin. It is turned by a crank. Two of the strings can be made to produce different pitches by pressing keys that touch the strings at different points. The other two strings are tuned five tones apart and can produce only one note each. The hurdy-gurdy is often mounted on wheels. See also BARREL ORGAN.

Huron, Lake

Lake Huron is the second-largest of the five Great Lakes. Lake Huron is about 200 miles long, and in some places it is almost 180 miles wide. Part of the lake is in the United States, and part is in Canada. The national boundary runs through the lake. Lake Huron has many islands. One of the most important is Mackinac Island, where people go for vacations, to enjoy sailing and other water sports. From December until the end of March Lake Huron is very often icebound, and there are severe storms. When the weather is good, boats carry iron, grain, coal, and other valuable products across the lake. People believe that a French explorer, Étienne Brulé, was probably the first white man to see Lake Huron.

hurricane

A hurricane is a big windstorm that begins in the Gulf of Mexico, Caribbean Sea, or Atlantic Ocean near the equator, and blows northward. When it blows over land it can do a great deal of damage, because the wind blows at a rate of about 100 miles an hour (sometimes considerably more). At sea, hurricanes are dangerous to ships.

The same kind of storm occurs in other tropical waters (near the equator) but is called by different names. In the China Sea it is called a *typhoon;* in the Philip-

pines, a *baguio;* and in the Indian Ocean, a *cyclone.*

WHAT CAUSES A HURRICANE

A hurricane begins with warm, moist air and frequent showers. Air begins gradually to flow into the region where the showers occur. This is usually in the part of the ocean called the *doldrums,* where ordinarily there are no strong winds. The hurricanes felt in America usually begin between June and September. As the air flows in, the rotation of the earth causes it to go around and around. It begins to blow faster and faster.

Next comes the *progressive movement* of the hurricane. That is, the whirling current of air begins to travel. Though the winds in the center of the hurricane may be going 100 miles an hour or even faster, the whole whirling mass travels slowly—perhaps at a rate of 10 miles an hour. Since hurricanes begin at sea, usually a thousand miles or more from shore, it takes five days or more for a hurricane to reach the American shores. Often they never reach land but continue to travel over the sea until they "blow themselves out."

THE "EYE"

At the center of one of these tropical storms there is an area called the "eye." Within this area, which may be about 15 miles across, it is very calm. All around the eye, the winds are whirling around and howling.

It is the "eye" that is said to travel. First comes a big, damaging windstorm. Next comes a calm period, when a region is in the eye of the storm. Next, as the eye moves on, there is another violent windstorm but the winds are blowing in the opposite direction. For example, if the

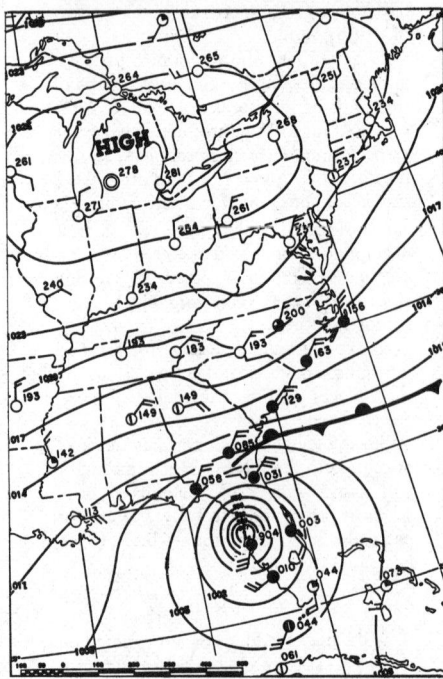

U.S. Weather Bureau
The weather map shows a hurricane centered near Tampa, Florida.

hurricane has approached from the east there will first be violent north winds, then the calm center, then violent south winds. Many people do not know this, and when the calm center is reached they

will leave safe places and go outside, thinking the storm is finished. This is likely to leave them unprotected when the second part of the storm begins. Many lives have been lost in this way.

In small hurricanes, the dangerous winds may whirl in a circle that is not more than 25 miles across. In the biggest hurricanes, it may be 400 to 500 miles across.

HURRICANE WARNINGS

Because it takes a hurricane several days to move from where it began to the shore regions and coastal waters where it can do the most damage, the United States Weather Bureau almost always has time to warn people whose boats or houses may be in danger.

There are various signs that a hurricane may be coming. One of the first is a *sea swell.* This is a long, unbroken wave at sea. Another sign is the appearance of cirrus clouds (high, feathery clouds). At sunset and sunrise the clouds on the outer border of the hurricane are highly colored. A brilliant red sky is sometimes a sign of an approaching hurricane.

In the North American area (North Atlantic Ocean, including the Gulf of Mexico and Caribbean Sea), the number of hurricanes in a year may range from one or two up to twenty-one. In 1953 there were twenty-one, in 1936 there were seventeen, and in a dozen or more recent years there have been at least ten.

Weathermen give girls' names to the hurricanes each season. The first hurricane of the season is given a girl's name beginning with A, such as Anne; the second has a name beginning with B, such as Betty; and so on, so that the fifth might be Edna and the ninth might be Irene. By counting which letter of the alphabet it is, you can tell how many hurricanes there have already been.

The word *hurricane* is used in other ways. A *hurricane wind* is any wind that blows 75 miles an hour or faster. A storm is said to be "of hurricane intensity" when the winds are more than 60 miles an hour and the air pressure, as shown on a barometer, is 29 inches or lower.

Hurst, Fannie

Fannie Hurst was a famous American novelist. She was born in Hamilton, Ohio, in 1889. After attending Washington University in St. Louis, Missouri, she moved to New York City and worked at many different jobs in order to see what life was like for different people. She worked in factories, stores, and restaurants, and even as an actress. Her first book was written in 1914, and she has written many novels since then. Most of her books are about unhappy and hardworking people, about whom she wrote with sympathy and understanding. Her novels include *Lummox, Imitation of Life, Back Street,* and *Great Laughter. Humoresque* is one of her famous short stories. Fanny Hurst died in 1968.

Huss, John

John Huss was a Christian religious leader. He lived more than five hundred

years ago, yet his teachings are still followed in several important Protestant Churches in the United States and in other countries.

Gale Research Co.

When John Huss was born, in the year 1373, the Roman Catholic Church was the official church in most of the countries of Europe, including Bohemia (now part of Czechoslovakia), where Huss was born.

Huss became a priest, and a teacher of religion at the University of Prague, the capital of Bohemia. At that time an English priest, John Wycliffe, who had translated some parts of the Bible into English, was questioning some of the beliefs of the Catholic Church. Huss agreed with many of Wycliffe's beliefs, and taught them to the Bohemian people.

The Catholic Church ordered Huss to stop his teaching of these beliefs. When he refused, the King of Bohemia put him in prison and later, in 1415, had him burned at the stake.

John Huss had thousands of followers, who were called Hussites. They adopted Huss's teachings, not only in religion but also in government. They wanted the peasants (poor farmers) of Bohemia to own more land and have more rights.

For about twenty years, there were crusades of Catholic armies against the Hussites. Finally the Hussites lost. They were not able to change the Church or the government, but those who lived joined the Moravian Church (named for Moravia, another part of modern Czechoslovakia), and several Moravian religious sects have survived to this day. There is a separate article about the MORAVIAN CHURCH.

Hutchinson, Anne

Anne Hutchinson was a religious leader in New England about three hundred years ago. She was born in England, about the year 1590. Her name was Anne Marbury, and when she grew up she married a man named William Hutchinson. The Hutchinsons were Puritans and left England in 1634, at a time when many other Puritans were seeking religious freedom in Massachusetts. Anne thought she had a special power to understand the Bible, and many Massachusetts people (including some ministers) believed her teachings. She was made to leave Massachusetts, and with some of her followers (who were called Antinomians) she moved to Rhode Island, and then to New York. In 1643 the Indians raided Anne Hutchinson's settlement and massacred almost everyone, including Anne.

Huxley

Huxley is a name of a family of English scientists and writers. The first to bring the name into prominence was Thomas Henry Huxley, who was born in 1825. He was a great thinker and scientist, and learned much that was new about animals, plants, and the earth. His writings attracted the attention of thinkers and scientists all over the world. He wrote many essays on Charles Darwin's theory of evolution so that it could be understood by most men and women. (You can read more about DARWIN and EVOLUTION in separate articles.) His interests spread into many fields of science. He wrote books on natural history, biology, geology, botany, and anatomy. His books and lectures were very popular and influenced the thoughts of many people.

During his later life, when he was a member of the board of education, Thomas Huxley suggested many improvements in English schools that helped raise the level of education in England. He died in 1895.

Huxley's grandson, Julian Sorell Huxley, also became a scientist and writer. He was born in England in 1887 and studied at Oxford University. After graduation, he taught in the United States for four years, and for the next twenty years in England. He is a popular lecturer and has written several books on biology. He was head of the United Nations Educational, Scientific, and Cultural Organization (UNESCO) from 1946 to 1948.

Julian Huxley's brother, Aldous, was born in England in 1894. He has written books poking fun at the way many people live and think, but he does it in a very clever and entertaining way. One of his most famous books, called *Brave New World*, describes a world in which people use all the newest inventions of science and are miserable and unhappy because they do not know how to love one another. Aldous Huxley went to Hollywood and wrote motion-picture scripts during the 1930s. He died in 1963.

Hwang Ho

The Hwang Ho, or Yellow River, as it is called in English, is the second-largest river in China. It is named the Yellow River because great quantities of yellow mud get mixed in with the water at its source, when it rushes down from high mountains in central China. As the Hwang flows 2,700 miles to empty into the Yellow Sea (or *Hwang Hai*), much of this yellow mud settles to the bottom, making the river very shallow. When there are heavy rainfalls, the shallow river cannot hold all the water, and it often overflows. Some of these floods kill thousands of people, and for this reason the Hwang Ho is often called "China's sorrow."

hyacinth

The hyacinth is a fragrant flower with a thick stem and small, waxy blossoms that point in all directions. Hyacinths can be white, pink, lavender, or blue. The leaves are straight and stiff, and they grow from twelve to fourteen inches high. Hyacinths are sold in flower shops in the spring and are especially popular for Easter. Hyacinths have been cultivated since very early times. They were introduced into Europe by the Dutch people in the 16th century. The fragrance of the hyacinth is strongest late at night.

hybrid

A hybrid is a plant or animal whose parents are two plants or animals that are different from each other in some way. The original pair may be of different races, species, varieties, or breeds. For example, a mule is a hybrid whose father is a donkey and whose mother is a horse. A mongrel dog is a hybrid of two different breeds of dog. Hybrids are also produced in many forms of plant life.

There is a good reason why men develop hybrids. It has been discovered that when two fairly pure strains of a plant are crossed, the first generation that is produced often will be sturdier and healthier than either of the original two strains. This quality is known as *hybrid vigor*. One plant that has been greatly improved by hybridization is corn. A number of varieties of hybrid corn have been bred that produce at least 15 to 20 per cent higher yields than either of the two kinds that were crossed to create them.

Hybrids are produced by CROSS-BREEDING, about which there in a separate article.

Hyderabad

Hyderabad is one of the largest cities in India. About 1,317,000 people live there, making it a little bigger than Houston, Texas. There are many beautiful old buildings in the city, as well as many factories where cotton textiles and tobacco products are made.

Hyderabad is located in the former Indian state of Hyderabad, which is now part of the state of Andhra Pradesh. When India became free from English rule in 1947, the Nizam (king) of Hyderabad wanted his state to be an independent country, but Indian troops invaded Hyderabad, and he had to agree to join the new union of India.

The former state of Hyderabad had an area of 82,698 square miles, and 18,655,108 people lived there. The area is in Central India and does not touch the ocean. It is one of the richest areas in the country, with excellent soil in which cotton and many other crops grow abundantly. It also has rich coal and iron mines and fine forests for timber.

HYDERABAD, INDIA. Population (in 1973) 1,316,802. Capital of state of Andhra Pradesh. Sixth-largest city in India.

Hydra

The Hydra was a ferocious, nine-headed water snake told about in the mythology of ancient Greece and Rome. It lived in the marshes in a part of Greece called Lerna, and its poisonous breath instantly killed anyone who happened to inhale it. Hercules was sent to kill it, which he did by a clever trick. The remarkable thing about the Hydra was that when a head was cut off, two immediately grew in its place. The ninth head was immortal. Hercules obtained a torch from Iolaus, his nephew, and as he cut off each head he burned the neck so that other heads could not grow. When he cut off the immortal head, he buried it under a gigantic rock. There is a separate entry on HERCULES in another volume.

Hydra is also the name given to a tiny freshwater animal that lives in lakes, ponds, and ditches throughout the world. It is an invertebrate (having no backbone) about one-half inch long or less, with a simple, tube-shaped body closed on one end. The other end is its mouth, surrounded by five or more stinging feelers with which it paralyzes its prey. The hydra can reproduce by eggs, or it can sprout a little "bud" that grows into another hydra, which detaches itself.

hydrangea

The hydrangea is a shrub that bears large, ball-shaped clusters of small pink or creamy white flowers on long, leafy stems. If the soil is treated with iron or alum, the flowers will be bright blue. Hydrangeas were originally grown in Japan and China, but are now cultivated in all parts of America. Their size ranges from 2 feet high to 12 feet high. Small ones are often grown in tubs. Wild hydrangeas grow in Asia, and in North and South America.

hydraulics

Hydraulics is the science that deals with liquids that are moving, and how these liquids can be made to do useful work. A person can press on a liquid with just a little force and the proper hydraulic machinery will turn this into a great force that will lift weights or apply pressure far beyond the strength of the strongest man. A barber chair is worked by a hydraulic pump. The barber very easily makes the chair lift a 200-pound man. Hydraulic brakes on automobiles make it possible to stop a speeding car with very little pressure of the foot on the brake pedal. Big freight elevators can be run by hydraulic pressure. Sometimes hydraulic pressure is made to lift loads as big as 20,000,000 pounds—as much as 150,000 people weigh. *Hydrodynamics* is another word for the science that deals with hydraulics.

Pressure is measured by pounds per square inch. Suppose you take a cylinder with a piston in it—the arrangement of an ordinary bicycle pump—and suppose the cylinder has an area of one square inch. Fill the cylinder with water and press down on the piston with a force of ten pounds, and the pressure of the water will be ten pounds per square inch. But if that water flows against another piston with an area of ten square inches, the pressure on the larger piston will be ten pounds on every square inch and the total pressure will be 10×10, or 100 pounds in all. With a force of ten pounds on the small piston you can make the large piston lift a hundred pounds. If the large piston had an area of 100 square inches, your ten pounds of pressure would produce 10×100 pounds, and could lift a 1,000-pound weight.

The illustrations show how hydraulic pressure is obtained. *Left:* In the cotton-bale press, pumping the handle (H) moves the small piston (S) down, forcing water through the tube into the tank and thus pushing up the large piston (P). Water returns to the small cylinder from the tank (L), when the handle is raised. *Right:* The car lift uses air pressure (A) pushing against oil (O) to raise the piston (P) and the platform on which the car rests.

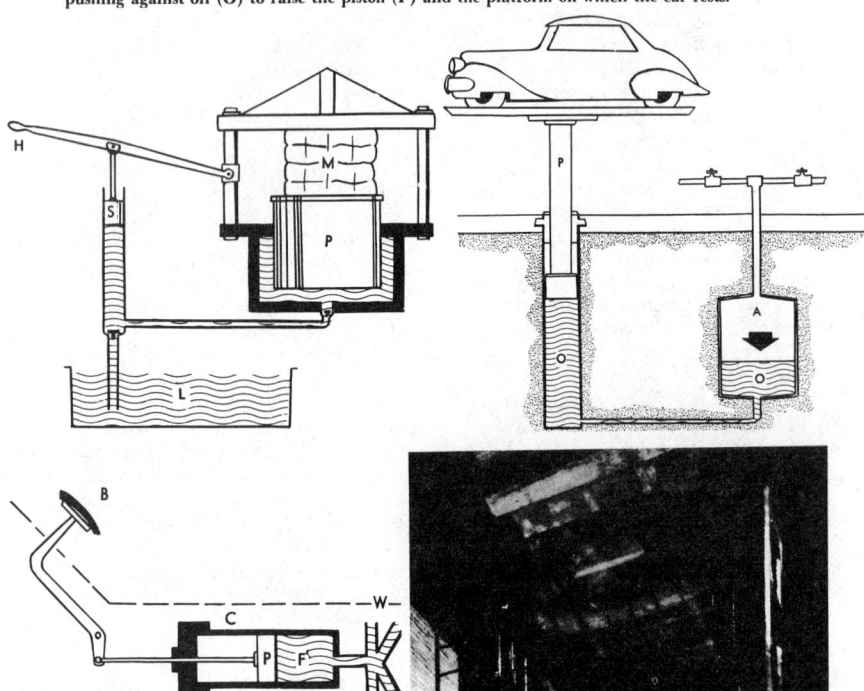

HYDRAULIC PRESS.

In a hydraulic press, a cylinder containing a piston is connected to two tanks of water, one on each side of the cylinder. At the bottom of the cylinder are two valves, called an inlet and an outlet valve. The inlet valve leads from one tank, called the reservoir tank, to the cylinder. The outlet valve leads from the cylinder to the other tank. A large piston is tightly fitted into the tank. On top of the piston is a large platform.

When the piston in the cylinder is pulled up, water enters the cylinder from the reservoir through the inlet valve. When the piston is pushed down, the water that has entered the cylinder is forced out through the outlet valve into the tank and against the platform piston. The area of the piston is always smaller than the area of the platform piston in the tank. A small downward force on the piston will produce a much larger upward force on the platform piston. The platform can be lowered by opening a valve in a tube connecting the tank and the reservoir. The water will flow back to the reservoir, reducing the pressure on the platform piston and allowing it to be lowered.

In most of the hydraulic presses used in industry, oil is used instead of water. In the hydraulic lift used in garages to raise cars so that mechanics can work more easily underneath them, a combination of air and hydraulic pressure is used to raise the platform. A compressed-air tank takes the place of the small piston in the hydraulic press. The air pressure in the tank may be as high as 135 pounds per square inch. The air pressure forces the oil into a tank that contains a plunger or shaft with a platform on top. The pressure of the oil is strong enough to raise a 3,000-pound car.

Other uses of hydraulic pressure are found in the hydraulic jack used for lifting up automobiles that have flat tires so that the tires can be changed. The hydraulic jack works very much like a water pump and the handles must be pumped up and down in order to lift the car. The same kind of device is used to raise and lower barber chairs.

Above: The hydraulic brake operates when the brake pedal (B) is pushed down. Then the piston (P) pushes the special fluid (F) through tubes to each wheel, where they force a brake shoe against the wheel, thus stopping its motion. *Below:* Engineering students experiment with hydraulic pressure. *Right:* Hydraulic machines are used to test the strength of metal objects under great pressure.

Northwestern University Photos

HYDRAULIC BRAKES

Another use of hydraulic pressure is in the hydraulic brakes used on most automobiles. When the brake pedal in a car is pressed down, it forces a piston against a liquid containing castor oil, ether, and glycerin. The liquid travels through tubes into brake cylinders inside each wheel of the car. The liquid pushes between two pistons in the cylinders and forces them apart. The pistons push curved metal bars called brake shoes against the sides of a metal drum called a brake drum. This keeps the drum from turning and stops the wheel. You can read more about the BRAKE in a separate article.

hydrocarbons

A hydrocarbon is a chemical compound, which is a substance consisting of two or more elements (basic substances). Hydrogen and carbon are the elements that make a hydrocarbon. Many hydrocarbons are found in natural gas, petroleum, asphalt, and coal tar. Most hydrocarbons burn easily and make good fuel for heating and lighting.

Most hydrocarbons contain more hydrogen than carbon. Some have the same amount of each. None has more carbon than hydrogen.

There are more than two hundred hydrocarbons. These are usually divided into four different families: methane, ethylene, acetylene, and benzene. Ethylene is used in "Ethyl" anti-knock fluid. There are separate articles about these families of hydrocarbons.

hydrochloric acid

Hydrochloric acid is a chemical compound, which is a substance consisting of two or more elements (basic substances). The elements in hydrochloric acid are hydrogen and chlorine. There is hydrochloric acid in your stomach, where it helps digest the food you eat. It causes the sour taste in your mouth when you have overeaten and have an upset stomach. If you are suffering from dyspepsia, another name for indigestion, your doctor might prescribe some hydrochloric acid to help you digest your food better. However, your dyspepsia might be caused by too much acid in your stomach, in which case your doctor will prescribe an antacid to reduce your stomach acidity.

Hydrochloric acid can be made in a laboratory by letting drops of sulfuric acid fall on some table salt. This forms a gas called hydrogen chloride. If the gas is dissolved in water, hydrochloric acid is produced.

Hydrochloric acid has many uses in industry. It is used to clean iron in the process called "pickling." For that reason, hydrochloric acid is sometimes called *muriatic acid*, from the Latin word meaning "pickling."

Hydrochloric acid is used also to make syrup from cornstarch, and to make glue from animal bones and tissues. The manufacturing of drugs and dyes also requires the use of hydrochloric acid.

hydrogen

Hydrogen is the lightest substance in the universe. It is an odorless, tasteless, and colorless gas, about fourteen times lighter than air. It was at one time used in balloons and airships, but it is dangerous because it catches fire easily. Yet hydrogen combined with oxygen makes water, which does not burn. Most of the hydrogen on earth is in water.

Hydrogen is a part of all acids. It is also a part of all plant and animal tissues. If you weigh 100 pounds, your body will contain 10 pounds of hydrogen. Natural gas and petroleum (oil) are mixtures containing compounds of carbon and hydrogen, called *hydrocarbons*.

An important use of hydrogen is the making of vegetable shortening, which is used instead of butter or lard in baking and frying. Hydrogen gas is forced through cottonseed oil, which is a liquid fat. This forms a solid fat, which is sold under various trade names, such as Crisco.

Blowtorches using hydrogen gas are often used for cutting and welding iron and steel. The heat from these torches sometimes is as high as 9000 degrees Fahrenheit.

Hydrogen can be combined with nitrogen to make artificial ammonia.

Two heavier kinds of hydrogen, called *deuterium* and *tritium*, are used in the manufacturing of HYDROGEN BOMBS, about which you can read in a separate article.

hydrogen bomb

The hydrogen bomb is the most powerful weapon ever made by man. Many scientists say it is the most powerful weapon man can ever make, because it creates heat in the same way that the sun does. We are ninety million miles away from the sun, yet its heat produces most of the energy on earth. The hydrogen bomb would bring the same kind of heat to the surface of the earth. It can destroy everything that lives. It can even level mountains and cause islands to sink into the ocean.

The atomic bomb, or A-bomb, when it was first used in 1945, was recognized as a weapon that could destroy any enemy and win any war. The hydrogen bomb, or H-bomb, can easily be made a thousand times as powerful as the A-bomb.

The first hydrogen bomb was built by the United States and was exploded, as a test, in the fall of 1952. It was the most powerful explosion ever known on earth. It took place on an island called Elugelab, one of the Marshall Islands near the middle of the Pacific Ocean. The test was called "Operation Ivy" because I is the ninth letter of the alphabet and this was the ninth big test of an atomic or hydrogen bomb. The explosion sent up a ball of fire more than three miles wide. After it was over, Elugelab Island had vanished. The only trace of it was a hole in the bottom of the ocean, 175 feet deep.

Yet the second test of a United States hydrogen bomb was even greater. This test, too, took place in the Marshall Islands. The explosion was 750 times as powerful as the explosion of the first atomic bomb used in warfare at the city of Hiroshima in Japan, nine years before. The hydrogen bomb explosion was so powerful that even the scientists who had made it were surprised. It was felt more than a hundred miles away and had

as much force as an explosion of fifteen million tons (30,000,000,000 pounds) of TNT.

Scientists tell us that it is possible to make H-bombs that will explode with any force we want. Unlike an atomic or A-bomb, there is no limit on the size or explosive force of an H-bomb.

HOW AN H-BOMB WORKS

An H-bomb works in a much different way from an A-bomb. In an H-bomb, atoms of hydrogen are *fused*, which means "joined together by melting." In an A-bomb, atoms are *fissioned*, which means "split apart." (You can read more about this in the article on ATOMIC BOMB).

To cause hydrogen atoms to fuse, millions of degrees of heat are necessary. The heat fuses the atoms together just like two pieces of metal that have been melted together to form one piece. That is why the H-bomb came after the A-bomb. The

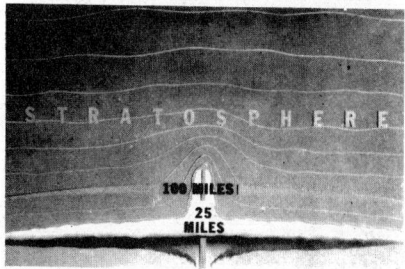

U.S. Air Force

The H-bomb's deadly mushroom cloud in twelve minutes is twenty-five miles high. The "umbrella" is ten miles high and spreads for one hundred miles.

U.S. Air Force

An H-bomb's fireball has a diameter of 3 1/4 miles. If an H-bomb hit the Empire State Building, most of Manhattan's business district would be destroyed.

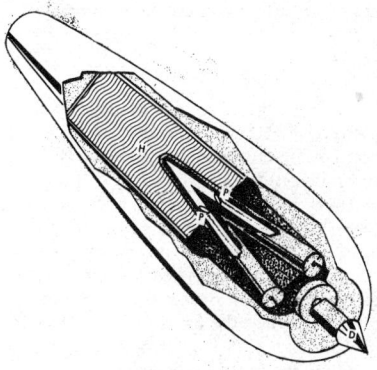

To explode a hydrogen bomb it is first necessary to explode an atomic bomb. The detonator (D) releases two pieces of plutonium (P) in V-shaped tubes. When they meet, the pieces form an atomic explosion. The heat of the explosion fuses the hydrogen (H).

heat that is released by the explosion of an A-bomb is often higher than 5,000,-000 degrees by the Centigrade scale, which means nearly 10,000,000 degrees in the Fahrenheit scale by which we measure the heat of the day. This great heat of the A-bomb is used to explode an H-bomb.

An H-bomb is actually an A-bomb surrounded by a mixture of two special kinds of hydrogen called *deuterium* and *tritium*. Deuterium is often called "heavy hydrogen," and is gotten from liquid hydrogen. Tritium, on the other hand, is so rare that it must be made in a special way. To do this, a plant costing more than a billion dollars was built near the Savannah River in South Carolina.

To explode an H-bomb, the A-bomb inside of it must first be set off. The explosion of the A-bomb releases enough heat to fuse the deuterium and tritium, producing an even more violent explosion. Once parts of the mixture of deuterium and tritium have begun to fuse, enough heat is produced to continue to fuse the rest of it. For this reason an H-bomb of almost any size can be made. There are no restrictions as to how large or small the pieces inside of it must be, as there is in an A-bomb. All that is necessary is enough heat to start the fusion, which will continue until the entire mixture of deuterium and tritium has been fused. The fusion makes it become helium gas, which rushes out in all directions with such great heat and force that it destroys everything in its path.

THE COBALT BOMB

As dangerous and destructive as the H-bomb is, it can be made more dangerous by placing it in a special container made of cobalt. Cobalt is a metal similar to iron and nickel. The explosion of a hydrogen-cobalt bomb would create a radioactive or "death" dust out of the cobalt container. The explosion of a hydrogen bomb with a steel container creates hardly any radioactive dust. For this reason, a hydrogen bomb can be tested, while a hydrogen-cobalt bomb cannot. The radioactive cobalt dust is three hundred times more deadly than any other radioactive substance so far discovered. It would be impossible to live with this dust in the air. Some scientists have figured that four hundred hydrogen-cobalt bombs would be enough to kill the entire population of the world.

THE HISTORY OF THE H-BOMB

Although the A-bomb was developed before the H-bomb, scientists knew about fusion even before they were able to split atoms for atomic energy. In 1938, Professor Hans A. Bethe, an atomic scientist of Cornell University, wrote a paper on how the hydrogen around the sun fuses to form helium. Other scientists had had the same idea for more than twenty years, but Professor Bethe was the first to write a clear explanation of how it happens. The fusion of the sun's hydrogen produces heat at the center of the sun as high as 20,000,000 degrees Centigrade. It is this heat that causes the fusion to continue. That may be the reason why the sun has been able to heat the earth for so many years without showing any signs of cooling.

Professor Bethe's explanation of how heat is made in the sun is called the *carbon cycle*. His explanation convinced many scientists that if they could fuse hydrogen atoms on the earth, they could make as much heat as the sun made. But to start the fusion, it was necessary to have almost as much heat as there is in the sun.

This the scientists did not have. It was not until the development of the A-bomb that such heat became available. The explosion of the first A-bomb made the hydrogen bomb possible.

The A-bomb brought World War II to an end. H-bombs have never been used in warfare, but several countries are testing or even manufacturing them in case another war should arise. It is difficult to imagine any country ever using an H-bomb against another. A war in which H-bombs are used could destroy most of the cities on the earth and kill hundreds of millions of people.

hydrometer

A hydrometer is a glass tube, large at one end, with a weight inside of it so that the tube will float straight up in a liquid. You can tell, by how far the hydrometer sinks into the liquid, if the liquid is heavier or lighter than the same amount of water. This measures the *specific gravity* of the liquid. When a hydrometer sinks far down into a liquid, the specific gravity of the liquid is low—it is lighter than water. When the hydrometer floats near the surface, it means that the specific gravity of the liquid is high—it is heavier than water. A scale is marked on the hydrometer to tell you the specific gravity of the liquid in which the hydrometer is floating.

Hydrometers are used very often to test automobile storage batteries, to check if they have enough electricity in them to start the car and to run the radio and headlights when the car is standing still. This is done by finding out how much acid the batteries have inside them. When a battery is discharging (giving out) electricity, the acid turns into water.

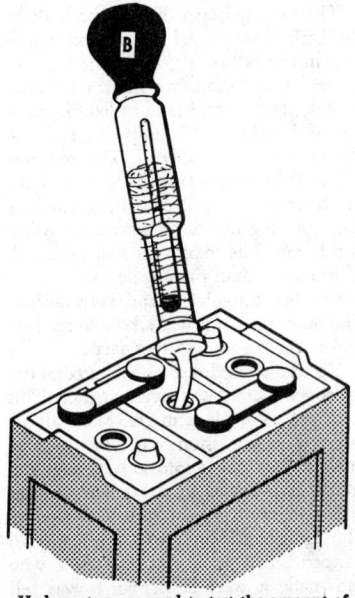

Hydrometers are used to test the amount of acid inside storage batteries in cars.

There is therefore more acid in a battery that is charged (with electricity) than in a battery that is discharged (without electricity.) Since acid is heavier than water, the specific gravity of the liquid in a charged battery is higher than in a discharged one. To test a battery, a large glass tube with a rubber bulb at the top is put into the liquid. The bulb is squeezed and then released so that some of the liquid comes up in the tube, as in an eye-dropper. Inside the tube is a hydrometer. If it sinks all the way down, the specific gravity is low, and the battery is discharged. If it floats near the surface, the battery is charged.

Hydrometers are also used to find out how much antifreeze there is in the radiator of an automobile and at what temperature it will freeze. An antifreeze such as alcohol or glycerin in the water keeps it from freezing. The more antifreeze in the water, the higher the specific gravity. Radiator hydrometers have a rubber tube through which some of the mixture of antifreeze and water is drawn into a special box. In the box is a hydrometer. The higher the hydrometer floats, the more antifreeze there is in the water, and the less chance there is of the radiator freezing.

You can make a simple hydrometer by using a pencil and an empty milk bottle. Fill the bottle near the top with water and see how far the pencil sinks into it. Empty the bottle and fill it again with salt water or alcohol or some other liquid. Then see how far down the pencil sinks this time. If it sinks further down, it means that the liquid is lighter than water. If it sinks less, it means that the liquid is heavier than water.

hydrostatics

Hydrostatics is the scientific name for the study of liquids that are standing still. It is especially the study of liquid pressure, and of how this pressure makes things float. Engineers must know hydrostatics in order to build dams, ships, and submarines.

Liquids such as water are pressing in all directions even when they are standing still. Take a container that is open at the top and fill it with water; the pressure of the water against the sides will be as great as the pressure of the water against the bottom. The pressure upward is equally great, though there is nothing to press against except the air.

The hydrostatic pressure on an object under water becomes greater as the object sinks farther. It will float if the pressure of the water underneath it is great enough to overcome both the pressure on top and the weight of the object.

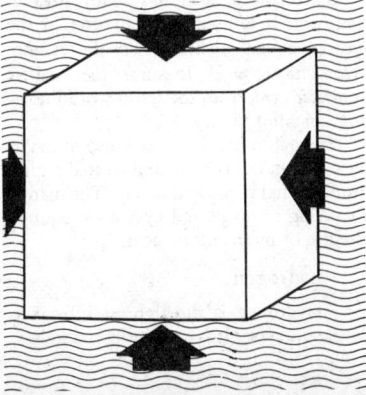

BUOYANCY

The upward force of a liquid on an object is what makes the object float. This upward force is called *buoyancy*. The downward force of any object is its weight. If this weight is greater than the buoyant force of the water, the object will sink. If it is less than the buoyant force of the water, the object will float.

The buoyant force of a liquid depends on its density. The more dense it is, the greater its buoyant force, or buoyancy. Since salt water has a greater density than fresh water, it is easier to float and swim in salt water than in fresh water. Because mercury is denser than any other liquid, most objects, including lead, are able to float in it. (There is a separate article on DENSITY).

The buoyant force of water is what

Hydrostatic pressure underneath the boat keeps it from sinking (1). But as the weight of the fisherman increases the pressure of the boat on the water (2) without increasing its volume, the rowboat is pushed farther down in the water.

makes you weigh less when you are weighed in water than when you are weighed in air. If you take an object weighing fifty pounds and attach it to a spring balance or scale, the reading on the scale will be fifty. If you lower the scale so that the object is dipped into a large tub filled to the brim with water, the object will sink into the water until the reading on the scale is zero. The reason is that the buoyant force of the water is equal to the weight of the object. When the object sinks, some water will overflow the tub. The object will sink until the weight of the water that overflows (is displaced) will equal the weight of the object. This is the same as the buoyant force of the water. This law was discovered by the Greek scientist, Archimedes, more than two thousand years ago.

When the weight of the displaced water is equal to the weight of the object, the object will float. A floating object will sink into a liquid until it displaces its own weight of liquid.

This is very important in building ships. A block of iron will sink in water if it does not displace an amount of water equal to its own weight. If it is hammered and shaped into a hollow form like a ship's, its volume will be increased so that it will displace its own weight of water and float. The larger the volume of the bottom of the ship, the more water it will displace and the higher it will float in the water.

For the purpose of submerging a submarine, sea water is pumped into the tanks inside the submarine so that its weight will be greater than the buoyant force of the water it displaces. To bring the submarine to the surface, the sea water is pumped out of the tanks, reducing the weight of the submarine until it is the same as the water it displaces.

In swimming, you can increase the volume of your body by filling your lungs with air and stretching out your body in the water. This will increase the amount of water you displace, and help you float and swim more easily.

hydrotherapy

Hydrotherapy means "water treatment." It is any way of treating disease by using water. To treat certain injuries, an arm or leg may be placed in special baths where water of different temperatures helps to repair muscles. Hydrotherapy is much used in the treatment of infantile paralysis (poliomyelitis). Persons with polio are given massages of the paralyzed limbs in water, and when they are recovering from the disease swimming is very useful to help restore the muscles. The National Foundation for Infantile Paralysis has a sanatorium at Warm Springs, Georgia, where patients are treated with spring water. This sanatorium was founded by President Franklin D. Roosevelt.

There are also many famous resorts, usually called mineral springs or spas, where people go to drink or bathe in water that contains a large amount of mineral salts. These are said to help in the treatment of such diseases as rheumatism, liver trouble, and gout.

hyena

A hyena is an animal that in some ways is like the bear and in other ways is like members of the cat family. It lives in Africa and southern Asia. A hyena is a large animal, weighing from 150 to 250 pounds. It has a doglike head, very strong forequarters, weak, drooping hindquarters, and a short tail. Its teeth are massive and, with the help of muscular jaws, can crunch the strongest bones of its prey. Its eyes are large, and the pupils are long and narrow. Its large ears stand straight up and are usually pointed forward. In color it is brownish-gray, with bands or spots of darker brown.

Hyenas are creatures of the night. They hide in caves during the day and go out to find food at night. The meat of dead animals is their usual food, and sometimes they have been known to dig up dead bodies. They also attack live animals, ravaging flocks of sheep. Goats are a favorite prey of hyenas. The cry of the hyena is weird and ominous. In ancient times it was believed to have a human voice.

hygiene

Hygiene is everything you do or should do to keep yourself in good health. The word "hygiene" comes from the name of the ancient Greek goddess of health, Hygeia. It is not very difficult to follow the simple rules for good hygiene, but very often we forget them in the rush

of the many things we have to do every day.

CLEANLINESS

One of the most important rules of hygiene is to keep clean. Bodily cleanliness is important because it helps to keep us free of disease-carrying germs. The hands should be washed before every meal. It is important to bathe frequently —every day if possible. The hair should be washed regularly and brushed every day. The nails of the toes and hands should be trimmed and clean.

REST

To stay healthy we must get enough rest. Most grownups should get at least eight hours of sleep, and children should have at least ten hours of sleep. A person who does not get enough rest is more likely to become sick than one who is well-rested. Also, when we have enough rest we can do things much better and more cheerfully during the day.

FOOD

Eating enough food (but not too much), and eating the proper food, are very important in good hygiene. From food your body gets the energy for living. Food also supplies the material for growth. The rules are: Eat a variety of foods. Eat at regular times. Chew your food well, since this gives the juices of the body a headstart in breaking up the food so that the body can use it for energy. (There is more about food in the article on DIET.) Mealtime should be a happy time. Talk, fun and laughter at mealtime make it easier for the body to digest the food you eat.

FRESH AIR

Air is necessary for breathing. The best kind of air to breathe is fresh, moving air that is free from dust and gases. In the warm seasons of the year, very few people have any trouble getting enough fresh air. But in the winter, some persons shut themselves up all day long in hot, stuffy rooms, and this is very likely to cause headaches and general sluggishness. Air-conditioning helps to ventilate, or air, rooms in the wintertime, and to keep them from getting too dry. If there is too little moisture in the air, the lining inside your nose may become dry, and you will be more likely to catch colds. In winter, some people place shallow pans of water on top of radiators if rooms seem too dry. The water will evaporate and change into water vapor in the air. The room in which you sleep in winter should be ventilated. You do not have to let an icy gale blow through the bedroom, but you should be sure to get some fresh air during the night.

PROPER CLOTHING

Human beings protect themselves from the cold, the sun, and the rain by wearing clothes. Today, people are much more sensible about clothing than they were years ago. Fashions do not force people to wear extremely unhealthful garments today, and most of our clothing is loose and light for easy movement. One should always dress according to the weather, not the time of year. Dress

warmly on a cold day, even if it happens to be in August. It is very important, too, to wear shoes that fit properly. Wearing the wrong kind or size of shoes can damage your feet permanently.

IMPORTANCE OF POSTURE

When a person stands and sits up straight he looks better and his health will be better. Here is an easy test for good posture. Stand up against the wall with both head and heels touching it; the hips, shoulders, and calves of the legs should all be touching the wall. If a person's posture is bad, the chest and abdomen will sag, and the weight of the organs inside the body will press down on the muscles and tire them out. The lungs will not be able to take in enough air. The digestive system will not be able to work properly.

DENTAL HYGIENE

Taking good care of the mouth and teeth makes for better health. This is called *oral hygiene*. The rules are: Brush your teeth morning and evening and, if convenient, during the day also. Use a toothbrush that is stiff enough to clear away food particles that get stuck between the teeth but not so stiff that it causes the gums to bleed. Visit the dentist at least twice a year so that he can take care of any cavities (holes) in the teeth.

CARE OF EYES

Proper care of the eyes is very important. Be sure that you have enough light when you read. Otherwise you may strain your eyes. Lamps should be placed so that most of the light comes from above, at the left if you are right-handed and at the right if you are left-handed. Keep your fingers and unclean objects such as soiled handkerchiefs away from your eyes. If you find you have trouble seeing things clearly, or if your eyes get tired quickly, be sure to see an eye doctor.

EXERCISE

Plenty of exercise and fresh air makes for better health. Out-of-door exercise, even a long walk, helps the circulation of the blood and the digestion of food and is relaxing to the nerves. When indoors, make sure that the room is properly aired and is not too hot or too cold. A temperature of 70 degrees for a room is about right.

See your doctor at least once a year for a thorough check-up. If you're in good health, so much the better. If there is something wrong, the doctor will know what to do.

Hygiene includes not only a healthy body but also a sound mind. This part of hygiene is called *mental hygiene*. One way of keeping in a good frame of mind is not to let yourself get upset at small things that go wrong. Try not to be irritable; an irritable person loses many opportunities to enjoy life. If you have any problems it is often a good idea to talk them over with parents or friends rather than let them build up inside you and make you unhappy.

hygrometer

A hygrometer is an instrument that measures how much moisture or water vapor there is in the air.

There are several different kinds of hygrometer. The most common kind is the *wet-and-dry-bulb hygrometer*. It is two thermometers filled with mercury, standing next to each other. One thermometer looks like the thermometer you use to measure the temperature of the air in your home. It is called a dry-bulb thermometer. The other thermometer has some cotton wrapped around the bottom. The cotton is dipped into a small tube of water. This thermometer is called a wet-bulb thermometer.

At different temperatures, air can hold different amounts of moisture. If there is less moisture in the air than it can hold, some of the water in the cotton on the wet-bulb thermometer will dry up by going off into the air. This is called *evaporation*. When you get out of a bath or a shower, some of the water on your body evaporates even before you have a chance to dry yourself. This makes you feel cool. The same thing happens to the wet-bulb thermometer. When some of the water

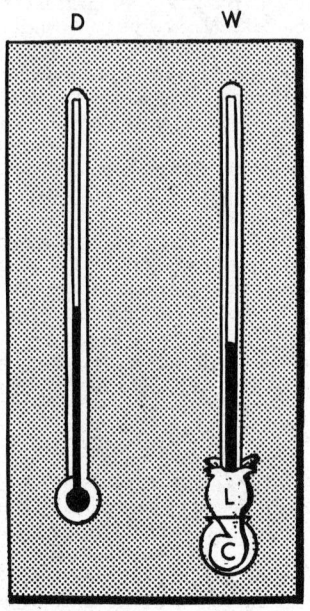

A hygrometer often uses dry-bulb (D) and wet-bulb (W) thermometers to measure the moisture in the air. By subtracting the temperature of the dry-bulb thermometer from the temperature of the wet-bulb thermometer, and looking up the differences on a special chart, you can find out how much moisture is in the air.

evaporates from the cotton, it cools the thermometer and lowers its temperature. The drier the air, the more water evaporates; and the more water evaporates, the lower the temperature of the wet-bulb thermometer will be. By subtracting the temperature of the wet-bulb thermometer from the temperature of the dry-bulb thermometer, and looking up the difference in a special chart, you can find out how much moisture there is in the air.

When the temperatures of the dry- and wet-bulb thermometers are the same, it means that the air has as much moisture as it can hold at that temperature. This is called the saturation point of the air. If the saturated air is suddenly cooled, dew, fog or rain will be produced.

DEW POINT

The temperature at which the moisture in the air will change into small drops of water or *dew* is called the *dew point* of the air. This temperature is found by using a *dew-point hygrometer*. The dew point can be used to find out how much moisture is in the air.

A dew-point hygrometer is very easy to make. Take a shiny metal can and fill it with water. Place a thermometer in the water. Then put some ice cubes in the water until little drops of water begin to form on the outside of the can. Look at the thermometer. The temperature of the thermometer is the dew point of the air. Most dew-point hygrometers use ether instead of water. Air is blown into the ether. This makes some of the ether evaporate. The evaporation cools the can and soon dew is formed on the outside.

The hygrometer used in most homes is the *hair hygrometer*. Hair can take in or absorb moisture from the air very easily. When it is moist it gets longer. When it dries it gets shorter. The hair in the hygrometer is connected to a pointer that moves along a dial as the hair changes its length. The numbers on the dial tell you how much moisture there is in the air.

The simplest kind of hygrometer is the *chemical hygrometer*. It is a piece of calcium chloride, exposed to the air. Calcium chloride is a substance that can absorb moisture from the air very easily. The calcium chloride is weighed before and after it is exposed to the air. The difference between the two weighings is the amount of moisture that the calcium chloride has absorbed. From this, you can find the amount of moisture in the air. See also the article HUMIDITY.

hymn

A hymn is a religious poem of praise or thankfulness. Usually a hymn is set to music and sung, but it may be chanted by a group of people together or recited aloud without any music. The Psalms in the Bible are hymns. In the early Christian church, people wanted to take a more active part in the services. Therefore, they were allowed to answer the priest in responses, which became quite elaborate hymns. An example is the *Gloria in Excelsis Deo* (which in Latin means "Glory to God on High"), often sung during the Easter services.

Most of the early Christian hymns were in Latin. Later many hymns were written in the language of the composer's native land. Martin Luther, the German religious leader, wrote hymns in German, and in England such men as Sir Isaac Watts and John and Charles Wesley, who lived about two hundred years ago, wrote hundreds of hymns in English.

hyperbola, a special kind of curve made by cutting through two cones lying upside down on each other: see the illustration and the article on CONE.

hypertension

Hypertension is a condition that is often called high blood pressure. Hypertension is not really a disease, but it can cause diseases of the heart and kidneys and other organs of the body. It occurs when the tiny branches of the arteries begin to tighten up. The arteries are tubes that carry blood through the body. The branches are called *arterioles*. When they tighten up, the heart has to work very

hard in order to push the blood through them. The heart muscle has to work so hard that it becomes thick. In time, the walls of the blood vessels also become thick, just as a person who uses an ax develops thick calluses on his hands.

Doctors do not know exactly what causes hypertension. Some believe that a person can inherit the condition from his parents. Others believe that nervousness and worry can cause hypertension. People who are very fat are likely to develop hypertension.

There is no complete cure for hypertension, but there are several ways to help a person who has it. Certain drugs and special diets can help. Sometimes an operation will help.

Hypertension most often occurs in people who are between the ages of 30 and 50 years.

hypnotism

Hypnotism is a method of causing a person to enter a sleeplike state. In this sleeplike state, which is called *hypnosis,* the person has control of most of his senses but what he does may be influenced by the suggestions of another person, called the *hypnotist.*

In *light hypnosis,* the subject (person who has been hypnotized) feels about the same when he is fully conscious. After he awakens he will remember what has happened. In *deep hypnosis,* the subject may do strange things at the suggestion of the hypnotist and have no memory of them when he awakens.

It is probable that nearly everyone can be hypnotized to some extent but that only about one person in five can go into the deep hypnotic state. Children between the ages of 5 and 12 are the easiest to hypnotize. Four out of five children of these ages can be placed in a deep trance (hypnotic condition) by a skillful hypnotist.

HOW HYPNOTISM WORKS

To be hypnotized the subject must want to be hypnotized. It is almost impossible to hypnotize anyone against his will. The hypnotist has his subject get into a comfortable position, usually in a place where it is very quiet so that the subject can concentrate. The subject is told to stare at a small object or light. The hypnotist talks to him in a low voice in a monotonous manner. He keeps repeating some simple phrase, such as "Your eyelids are getting heavy," over and over again. In a short while the subject's eyes do begin to tire, and soon, when the hypnotist suggests that he shut them, he does so, as if he were falling asleep. From then on until he is awakened, everything he does will be connected with suggestions from the hypnotist.

Hypnotism is not magic. It takes advantage of natural forms of human behavior. Everyone has a certain tendency to obey orders or to do things without thinking. This is called suggestibility. One or two persons can be standing staring at the roof of a building and soon a crowd will gather, all doing the same thing for no reason at all. One person may yawn, and soon a roomful of people may begin to yawn too. These are examples of suggestibility. The hypnotist simply makes use of this process to suggest to his subject that he appear to fall asleep.

Once in a hypnotized state, a person can be made to do some remarkable things. He will do things he ordinarily might consider foolish or embarrassing, but a person cannot be made to commit a crime or do anything that is opposed to his deep-seated feelings or beliefs. The subject may also be made to believe that an imaginary object is real, or that a real object does not exist. For example, the hypnotist may tell him to sit on an imaginary chair, and the subject will try to sit on an empty space. Or the hypnotist may tell him that a door that actually is closed is open, and he will try to walk through it. If the hypnotist tells him that the weather is hot, the subject will begin to perspire; if the subject is told that it has turned cold, he will start to shiver. While hypnotized, a subject may be able to do all sorts of feats of strength that he never could do before.

Hypnotism is sometimes used by doctors to study how the human mind acts. It is also sometimes used to treat or study certain kinds of mental illness. Some dentists and doctors have experimented in using hypnosis as an anesthetic, or painkiller, by telling patients that they are not able to feel any pain after they have been hypnotized. Hypnotism is often used as a stunt on the stage, but this is not allowed in some places. Hypnotism should be tried only by a trained psychologist or medical doctor. It may be very dangerous in the hands of an untrained person.

hypochondria

A person who has hypochondria is greatly worried about his health, usually for no good reason. Such a person is called a hypochondriac. A hypochondriac is constantly afraid that he already has or is about to come down with some terrible disease, and he spends a great deal of time going to doctors or dosing himself with all sorts of remedies and medicines. Many people worry about their health, but if this concern becomes so intense that the person spends almost all his time in such worry, the hypochondria probably is a sign of some more serious mental illness.

hypodermic

A hypodermic injection is a method of giving a drug by injecting it under the skin with an instrument called a hypodermic needle. This is a hollow needle attached to a container called a syringe, which holds a liquid solution of a drug and has a plunger on the end. When the plunger is pushed down, the liquid is forced out the end of the hollow needle into the patient's skin or blood stream. A hypodermic is used to give morphine, a drug that kills pain, and to give insulin, which is used to treat the disease called diabetes. A hypodermic is also used to give injections of penicillin and other drugs that combat infection. The "shots" a doctor gives you to keep you from getting certain diseases, such as typhoid fever and lockjaw, are also given with a hypodermic needle.

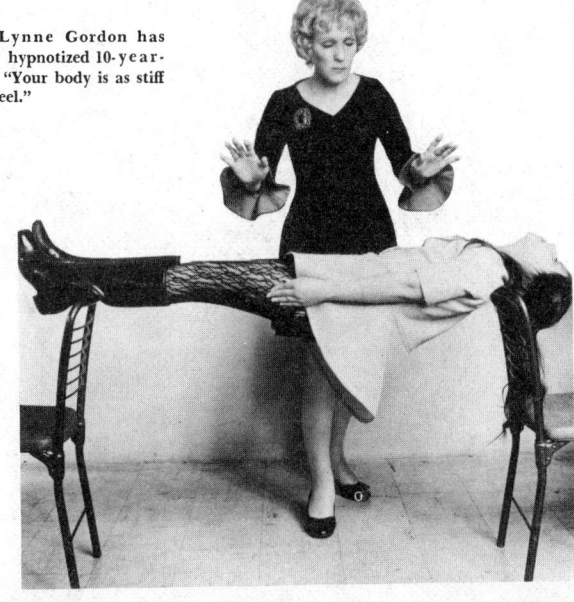

Hypnotist Lynne Gordon has told a deeply hypnotized 10-year-old subject, "Your body is as stiff as a bar of steel."

hysteria

Hysteria is a mild form of mental illness. The person who has hysteria is disturbed in some way that causes parts of his body or mind to work in a way that is not normal. He may lose his memory for a period of time, a condition called *amnesia.* He may lose sensation, such as the sense of touch, in any part of his body; or he may experience too much sensation, such as pain, in organs that have no real cause for such pain. He may be unable to walk, and, in some rare cases, he may become deaf, dumb, or blind, all temporarily. Doctors who know how to treat patients with mental diseases can help a person who has hysteria.

A person is often said to be hysterical if he finds it difficult to stop crying or laughing, or if he is very nervous. This is often called hysteria, but in its strict meaning hysteria is a disease that few adults and almost no children ever have.

Iberia

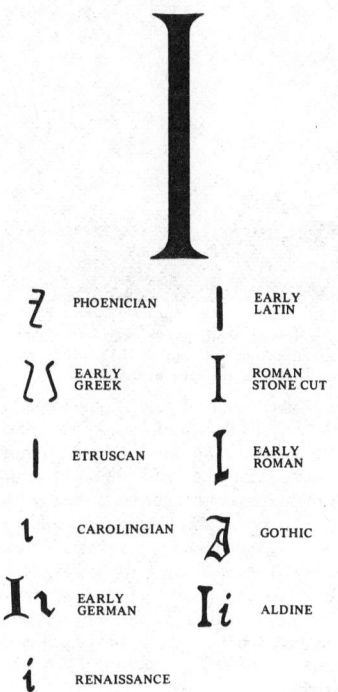

I | PHOENICIAN — EARLY LATIN

EARLY GREEK — ROMAN STONE CUT

ETRUSCAN — EARLY ROMAN

CAROLINGIAN — GOTHIC

EARLY GERMAN — ALDINE

RENAISSANCE

I or i

The letter I is the ninth letter of the alphabet. It can probably be traced all the way back to the earliest writing known to man, in Egypt thousands of years ago. In the Hebrew language, in which much of the Bible was written, the letter was called *yod*. The ancient Greeks took the same letter and called it *iota*.

The letter I was pronounced by the Greeks as we pronounce the *e* in *be*. The Romans also pronounced the "long i" sound this way, and added the "short i" sound that we use today, the sound of *i* in *fit*. Most other European languages still pronounce the "long i" as the Romans did. About four hundred years ago the "long i" in English came to have the sound of *i* in *ice*. The dot over the i appeared first in manuscripts about eight hundred years ago.

At the top of this page, at the far left, you can see the early Greek *iota* which looked something like a Z. In early times, writing was read from right to left, and in some of the old languages, such as Hebrew, it still is. But the Greeks changed and began to read from left to right, as we do today. When they made this change, they turned the letters around. So at the right of the early *iota*, in the illustration above, you will see the *iota* as it looked after being turned around. Through the years the letter became simpler and simpler in form until it became a straight line in the Roman alphabet. The Romans added the "feet" to the top and bottom of the letter; these feet are called serifs. Roman letters with serifs are the ones most used today in printing books and newspapers.

Read also the article ALPHABET.

Ibáñez, Vicente Blasco

Vicente Blasco Ibáñez was a Spanish author who wrote novels. He was born in Valencia in 1867, and as a young man he became interested in politics. He was against the government of Spain and he was put in prison and then exiled (made to live outside of Spain). His book about World War I, *The Four Horsemen of the Apocalypse,* made Blasco Ibáñez famous throughout the world. It was translated into many languages and made into a popular motion picture. Some critics say that his best works are his earlier ones about fishermen and peasants, especially one called *The Cabin.* He died in 1928.

Iberia

Iberia is the name of the peninsula, or body of land with water on three sides, that includes Spain and Portugal. Thousands of years ago people called the *Iberi* lived on this peninsula and the land was named after them.

Iberville, Pierre

Pierre le Moyne Iberville was a French-Canadian soldier and colonizer. He was born in Montreal, Canada, in 1661. He served for a while in the French navy and then came back to Canada and started fighting the British both on land and sea. He fought his way through the wilderness of Quebec to attack British trading posts on Hudson Bay. In 1690 Iberville was one of the leaders of French and Indian forces that burned Schenectady, New York. With a group of colonists he set out for the lower Mississippi Valley in 1698 and founded Old Biloxi, near the present city of Biloxi, Mississippi. He discovered the mouth of the Mississippi River. Iberville was all set to attack Boston and New York in 1706 when he became sick with yellow fever and died. His name is often spelled d'Iberville.

ibex

The ibex is a wild goat. There are several varieties, or kinds, of ibex, and they are found in mountainous regions in many parts of the world, including India, Arabia, Egypt, and northern Italy. The ibex is usually larger than most other goats. Its coat is coarse and is brown in summer and grayish in winter. Its horns are curved backwards from its face and are ridged in front. These horns grow from thirty to fifty inches long. The ibex can move very quickly and can jump very high. It likes to live on the steepest slopes of the mountains and only comes down where there are trees in order to eat. Often it will come down to feed at night and return to the barren slopes when morning comes. The ibex in the Italian Alps is now partly domesticated, or tamed. In the Himalayan Mountains in India, the ibex is hunted for sport because it moves so quickly that only an expert hunter gets close enough to shoot it.

ibis

The ibis is a water bird that is found in warm climates. It is about the size of a heron. It has long legs, webbed toes, and a long, but weak, bill. There are many different kinds of ibis, and they may be of many different colors. Some of them have a pretty, soft sheen, a sort of metallic glow. The ibis may build its nest with other birds of its kind, or it may breed alone. Its nest is a crude cradle of sticks built on a rocky ledge or in a tree. The eggs are usually green and may or may not have markings on them. The ibis has a coarse cry that it utters in flight. It wades in the water for much of its food, poking in the mud for insects and fish. On land it eats frogs and locusts. The ibis is found in Africa, Asia, Australia, and tropical America. At one time the plumes of the white and scarlet ibis found in America were used for decorations on hats, and this variety of ibis has almost entirely disappeared. The ibis was treated as a sacred, or holy, bird in ancient Egypt, probably because it appeared each year at the time when the Nile River began to rise. This meant a new farming season was beginning for the Egyptians.

Ibn Saud

King Abdul Aziz Ibn Saud united most of Arabia into one country, which is called Saudi Arabia after his family. As a young man, Ibn Saud had to fight to win his kingdom. When he was born, in 1880, his family had been driven out of its kingdom, but at the age of 21 Ibn Saud won part of it back in battles against Turks and other Arabs. During World War I, when Turkey was on the side of Germany, Ibn Saud helped the British fight the Turks, and after this war was won the British helped him to keep and enlarge his kingdom. In World War II he again helped the Allies, and once during the war President Franklin D. Roosevelt had a meeting with him. Ibn Saud was a very rich man because of the great oilfields in his country. Like his family before him, he supported the Wahabi sect of the Mohammedan religion, and he was himself a very religious man. He gave his country very honest government and was very generous with his wealth. He died in 1953, when he was 73 years old.

Ibsen, Hendrik

Hendrik Ibsen was one of the greatest writers of plays. He lived in Norway, almost a hundred years ago, and he wrote the first great plays about the problems people have in their everyday lives.

Norwegian Information Service

Ibsen was born in 1828. When he began writing, most plays were romantic stories written simply to entertain the audience. In almost all the plays, the characters spoke in poetry or in a way unlike ordinary speech. Ibsen himself, in his earlier plays such as *Peer Gynt,* uses a romantic folk story and poetic speech. In his later plays, such as *A Doll's House, Ghosts,* and *An Enemy of the People,* the speech seems as real as your own, and the characters' problems could be anyone's. In one way or another, all of these plays present a man or woman with ideas about what is true and good that are different from what most people believe.

Ibsen's plays are still performed. They

are especially important because they have influenced almost all later writers. Ibsen died in 1906.

Icarus, a character in the stories of the ancient Greeks, who escaped from the island of Crete on wings of wax that his father, Daedalus, had made. Icarus flew so near the sun that his wings melted. See the article on DAEDALUS.

ice

Ice is water that has frozen and turned into a solid. Water will usually freeze when its temperature goes below 32 degrees on the Fahrenheit thermometer, which is zero on the Centigrade thermometer. It takes lower temperatures to freeze salt water, or water in which there is sugar or alcohol.

About one-tenth of the surface of the earth is covered with ice. This is at and near the North and South Poles, where it is very cold. In earlier periods of the earth's history there was much more ice on earth. You can read about this in the next article, ICE AGE.

Ice is used to cool foods so that they will not spoil. Spoilage of food is caused by growth of bacteria in the food. Coldness does not kill all bacteria as boiling does, but bacteria do not grow when it is cold.

Ice is used also to make certain foods and drinks cool so that they will taste better. When ice is added to water, the ice melts until all the water is at a temperature of 32 degrees on the Fahrenheit scale. The water will remain at the same temperature, even when heated by the sun, until all the ice is melted.

The reason for this is that all the heat is used in melting the ice. Ice is made up of molecules, tiny particles of water, packed tightly together so they cannot move about as they do in water. The heat is used to pull these molecules apart, which melts the ice. After the ice has all melted, the heat will raise the temperature of the water by making the molecules move more rapidly.

When ice is added to water, the heat required to melt the ice is taken from the water. Ice melts very slowly because a great deal of heat is necessary to pull its molecules apart. The same amount of heat is needed to melt 10 pounds of ice as is needed to bring 8 pounds of water to a boil from the freezing temperature.

HOW ICE IS MADE

Most of the ice that is used for chilling or preserving food is made artificially. Artificial ice is made by freezing cans of water in brine (water containing as much salt as possible). The brine is kept cold, usually at 10 degrees Fahrenheit, by pipes containing ammonia gas. The very cold ammonia gas takes away heat from the brine, keeping the brine below the freezing temperature of water. This causes the water in the cans to freeze into cakes of ice. Different shapes can be gotten by freezing the water in molds, such as ice trays in a refrigerator, to form cubes, blocks, and tubes of ice.

In making ice, care is taken to freeze the water on the bottom and sides of the cans first. This prevents the cans from cracking due to the expansion of water as it freezes. (You can read more about

this in the article on EXPANSION and CONTRACTION.)

In northern parts of the United States and in Canada, blocks of ice often are cut out from frozen rivers and lakes in the wintertime and stored in special ice-houses until spring, when they are used in refrigeration.

The ice is usually scraped clean and then cut into blocks by a power saw or some other device. It is placed in an ice-house with specially insulated walls, or buried underground, to prevent heat from getting to it. Then it is covered with sawdust to insulate the ice further and keep it from melting.

Dry ice is frozen carbon dioxide gas. See the article DRY ICE.

Ice Age

The Ice Age is a period in geologic time when great mountains of moving ice, called glaciers, covered vast areas of the world. There have been several such periods in the earth's history, but the term "Ice Age" usually refers to the last one, which began about 3 million years ago and ended about 8,000 years ago when the glaciers disappeared from what is now the United States and Canada. The Ice Age in North America is usually divided into four glacial periods when the ice sheets grew and spread over the land, and three interglacial periods when the climate warmed up and the ice melted. During the glacial periods, the northern parts of Europe, North America, and Siberia were covered with moving ice. As the glaciers traveled slowly southward they gouged and tore up the earth beneath them, sometimes carrying huge boulders many hundreds of miles. Glaciers changed the directions of streams and rivers; the Mohawk Valley in New York was created by glaciers, as were the Great Lakes and thousands of small lakes throughout the northern part of the American middle west. There are many theories about the change in climate that brought on the Ice Age, but no one knows what caused it. There is a separate article on GLACIERS, describing the different kinds and how they are formed.

iceberg

Icebergs are great masses of ice that float in the oceans. The ice is extremely hard and rough. The iceberg has boulders, rocks and soil frozen in it. It can be of any size or shape. The walls, or sides, of an iceberg may be from fifty to a hundred feet high, and there may be spires, or projections, from them that stand as high as a thousand feet out of the water; yet most of the iceberg is under water.

Icebergs are formed when masses of ice break away from the front of a slowly moving glacier. Glaciers are huge rivers of ice that form in very cold regions. Most icebergs are found in the cold waters of the north. In the Atlantic Ocean they are found in the waters around Greenland, Labrador, and the Arctic regions. Icebergs slowly melt when they reach warm water. No icebergs are found more than four hundred miles south of Nova Scotia, in Canada, because the water becomes too warm. This point is called the "graveyard of the icebergs," and to get to this point an iceberg may have to travel

Coast Guard airplanes fly over icebergs to determine how fast and in what direction the "islands of ice" are moving.

nearly two thousand miles. Some icebergs melt farther north, and some of them become trapped or grounded by the many islands dotting the coast. Those that do not melt are very dangerous if they get as far south as the shipping routes, because they are a constant danger to ships. When the weather is foggy, an iceberg can hardly be seen, and many boats have been lost after crashing into one. The *Titanic*, a huge ocean liner built in 1910, sank on its maiden voyage because it ran into an iceberg.

ICEBERG PATROL

The United States Navy cooperates with other countries in maintaining an "iceberg patrol." Observers in ships and airplanes look for icebergs, and radio messages are sent out to tell where icebergs are likely to be at particular times. Any ship that sights an iceberg reports where it is, how fast it is traveling, and in what direction.

iceboat

An iceboat is a sort of sled with sails. It is sometimes called an ice yacht. It looks like an ordinary small sailboat except that it has runners. There is usually a runner at the rear of the boat and one runner on each side. Runners help the boat to glide over the ice, and they also help to balance the boat so that it will not topple over. The sails catch the wind and cause the boat to glide over the ice. They also help steer the boat. When the ice is hard and smooth, iceboats can go from 50 to 100 miles an hour.

Iceboats have been used for many years. On some early iceboats the runners were made from bone. The first man to use the iceboat for sport was a man from the Netherlands named Frederick Chapman. This was in 1778. Most iceboats used for sport are built to hold only one person. Iceboating is very popular in the Great Lakes region.

Large icebergs dwarf the tough icebreaker as it smashes its way through heavy ice.

837

icebreaker

An icebreaker is a ship that is especially designed to break up ice in frozen rivers, lakes, and seas, so that ships can travel on them. When the icebreaker hits ice it rides up on it. This brings the weight of the ship down on the ice and crushes it. When the ice is very thick, the icebreaker opens a channel by charging at the ice, then backing off and charging again. The hull of the ship is built so that if it gets caught in the ice the pressure will force the ship upward and not crush in the sides.

ice cream

Ice cream is a frozen food that not only tastes good but is also very nourishing. It is the most popular dessert in the United States, where the average person eats about half a pint each week. Ice cream is made mainly from milk products. It is a mixture of cream, milk solids, sugar, a stabilizer, and flavoring. The cream gives flavor and richness. The milk solids give a smooth texture. The sugar gives sweetness. Cane or beet sugar may be used, sometimes in combination with corn sugar, corn syrup, or honey. The stabilizer keeps the ice cream from turning to ice while it is stored; it is made from gelatin or vegetable gum. There are at least a hundred different flavors of ice cream, but vanilla, chocolate and strawberry have always been the favorites in the United States. Nuts, fruits and candies may also be added to ice cream for flavor.

HISTORY OF ICE CREAM

Ice cream was probably first made in France about three hundred years ago. It was introduced in the United States more than two hundred years ago by candy-makers and bakers. Unlike other dairy products, such as cheese and butter, which were first made in the home, most of the ice cream in the United States has always been made outside the home. By 1850 it was being produced commercially in Baltimore, Maryland, and the making of ice cream soon became a large industry in the United States. More than 700,000,000 gallons of ice cream are made each year in the United States. Almost six out of every hundred gallons of milk produced in the United States are used to make ice cream and other frozen dairy products.

Other frozen dairy products include frozen custard, parfait, mousse, milk sherbet, and ice milk, which are sold under various trade names. All these products are very much like ice cream and have about the same ingredients. Frozen custard, which is sometimes called French or New York ice cream, contains egg yolk solids; parfait is similar to frozen custard and has fruit or nuts in it; mousse is a frozen mixture that has whipped cream in it; and milk sherbet is the same as ice cream but has milk instead of cream. Ice milk is similar to ice cream but contains less milk fat and more milk solids, which are nonfat. About 180,000,000 gallons of these frozen products are made in the United States each year.

Many cities and states have regulations that say how much of each ingredient the ice-cream mix must contain.

Ice cream is often served in a cone.

There are several stories about how the ice-cream cone first came to be used. One story is that ice cream came to be served on waffles, and the waffles became thinner and thinner.

HOW ICE CREAM IS MADE

The basic mix is prepared first, then the cream, whole milk, and milk solids are added. After the mixture has been pasteurized, or heated to destroy all harmful bacteria, it is homogenized, which means that the fat is mixed with the other ingredients. It is then cooled and left for a short time at a temperature that is slightly above the freezing point. It is then whipped. Whipping adds air to the ice cream; it would be much too cold to eat if it were not full of air. Whipping also doubles the volume of the mixture. The ice cream is then frozen. The finished product is firm and smooth. When it comes out of the freezer the nuts or fruit are added by a special piece of equipment called a fruit injector. Large manufacturers use the continuous type freezer, in which ice-cream mix is fed into one end and is discharged partially frozen at the other end. The ice cream that is sold in packages is put into the packages by machine before it has fully hardened. Almost half of the ice cream made in the United States is packaged; the rest is put up in bulk, often in five-gallon containers.

ice hockey, a game of hockey that is played on ice: see HOCKEY.

Iceland

Iceland is an island in the northern Atlantic Ocean, between Greenland and Norway. Since 1940 it has been an independent republic with a government much like that of the United States, with a president and a Congress. Iceland has an area of about 40,000 square miles, about as much as the state of Virginia. Its population is about 210,000. This seems very small, but most of the island is covered with barren ice fields, and with volcanic mountains, some of which are still smoking. Everyone lives in a fairly

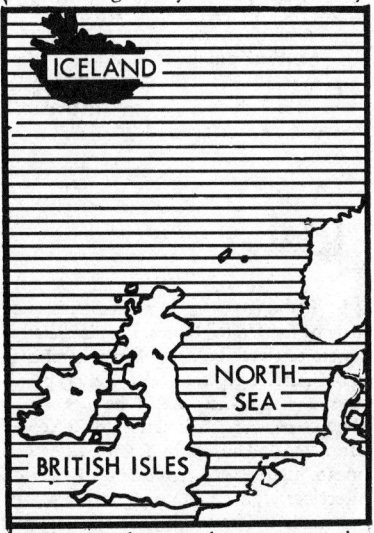

small area close to the ocean on the southern and western coasts, which are warmed by the part of the Gulf Stream called the Atlantic Drift.

Agriculture is not of great importance in Iceland, but potatoes and many other vegetables are grown. Many people raise

large herds of sheep that graze in the fields. Horses and cattle also are raised. Many people keep eider ducks, from which they get very soft feathers that are used to stuff pillows and mattresses. Foxes and reindeer are often hunted. Fishing is the biggest industry of Iceland. The fishermen go out in trawlers and catch huge amounts of cod, herring, and other fish, which are salted, smoked, canned or frozen in factories. Each year about seven thousand pounds of fish are caught for each person in Iceland. Most of this catch is sold to other countries.

HOT SPRINGS AND GEYSERS

One of the most unusual things about Iceland is the large numbers of hot springs and geysers there. The famous Great Geyser sends a column of boiling hot water as high as 150 feet into the air. There is so much of this natural hot water that pipes have been built to bring it into the capital city of Reykjavik, where it is used to heat houses and greenhouses. The hot springs create pools of water that are warm even in winter, and it is possible for people to go skiing or ice skating and then take a swim in these pools.

Another unusual thing about Iceland is that it is the only country in the world where all grown people know how to read and write. More books are written, printed and read in Iceland than by the same number of people in any other country. Some people explain this humorously, saying that because the winter nights there last from about four o'clock in the afternoon to about ten o'clock in the morning, they have plenty of time to read. But their long summer days, lasting from about two o'clock in the morning until eight in the evening, make up for this.

Children in Iceland must go to school until they are 15 years old.

THE STORY OF ICELAND

Iceland was settled more than a thousand years ago, about the year 870, when many Viking sailors went there from Norway to live. They soon formed the first republic in Europe, a government made up of men elected by the people to a general assembly which they called the Althing. In the following three hundred years, the most glorious in Iceland's history, Christianity became the people's religion, brave sailors explored Greenland, Leif Ericsson discovered America, and Icelandic authors wrote great tales called *sagas,* which told the stories of Icelandic heroes.

After Norway conquered Iceland, about seven hundred years ago, the glorious age ended. Denmark took Iceland from Norway a little later, and kept it until World War II. Since Germany had conquered Denmark then, Iceland declared itself an independent country. In 1944 almost every person in Iceland (98 percent) over 21 years of age voted to make the country a republic again. Iceland joined the United Nations in 1946 and the North Atlantic Treaty Organization in 1949.

ICELAND. Area, 39,758 square miles. Population (1973 estimate) 210,000. Language, Icelandic. Religion, Evangelical Lutheran mostly. Government, republic. Monetary unit, the krona, worth about 2.6 cents (U.S.). Flag, red cross on a white cross on a blue field.

ice skating: see the article on SKAT-ING.

ichneumon

The ichneumon is a small carniv-orous (meat-eating) animal found in India, southeast Asia, and Africa. In India it is called a mongoose. It is a brownish-gray animal that sometimes grows to a length of thirty inches, although it is often as small as a squirrel. Its tail is as long as the rest of its body, and it has a thin head that looks very much like the head of a weasel. It has short legs and short, rounded ears. The ichneumon eats snakes, rats, mice, and other vermin. In ancient Egypt the ichneumon was called "Pharaoh's rat," and was much admired because it destroyed crocodile eggs. It makes a good pet and is kept in many Indian and Egyptian households to de-stroy poisonous snakes. The ichneumon is not immune to the snake's poison, but it moves so fast that the snake is usually unable to touch it.

ichneumon fly

The ichneumon fly is a parasitic wasp that lays its eggs on the caterpillars and other larvae (young) of insects. It is called a parasite because it feeds on other living insects. There are more than ten thousand species, or kinds, of this fly, and they can be of almost any size. Some are so small that they can hardly be seen; others are an inch or more in length. One kind of female ichneumon fly has a bor-ing instrument somewhat like a needle. It is strong enough to go through the hard-est wood. With this the fly bores into the nests of other insects and deposits its eggs inside. There they hatch and feed on the larvae of other boring insects. Ichneumon flies also lay their eggs in caterpillars, but the caterpillar does not die immediately from this. It lives long enough to supply food for the ichneumon larvae, which then form little cocoons stuck to the back of the caterpillar. The ichneumon fly is very helpful to man because it destroys the larvae of so many insects that are harmful to crops.

ichthyology

An ichthyologist is a scientist who studies fish. Ichthyology is the science of fish, and it includes anything that con-cerns fish. It is a branch of another science called zoology, which is the science that studies all animals. Ichthyology is divided into several different branches. Some ich-thyologists classify the different kinds of fish. Others study the fossils, or skele-ton remains, of fish that existed many years ago. These fossils are found in many different parts of the world, and often ich-thyologists organize expeditions on which they go out to hunt for the fossils. They can tell from studying the fossils what the fish were like that lived in the ocean mil-lions of years ago. Petrus Artedi, a Swede, is called the "father of ichthyology," be-cause he was the first man to outline the way in which fish could be classified, or grouped. In a book published more than two hundred years ago, Artedi recorded 228 species of fish. Since then ichthyolo-gists have classified more than twelve thousand species and are constantly dis-covering and classifying more.

ichthyosaur

The ichthyosaur was a kind of rep-tile that lived in the ocean about 200 mil-lion years ago, in the age of the dinosaurs, or "terrible lizards." The ichthyosaur was much larger than lizards of later eras; it sometimes grew to be thirty feet long. It had a long body, a long head with a nose that looked like a porpoise's snout, a long tail, no neck, and very large eyes. Its legs were shaped somewhat like paddles, which aided it to swim; its teeth were set in grooves, which aided it to catch fish, its principal food. The ichthyosaur was different from other reptiles in that it did not lay eggs but bore its young alive. Scientists think it must have descended from some kind of land animal. They know about the ichthyosaur because skel-etons of the animal have been found in western and southern Europe.

icon

An icon is a picture of Christ, the Virgin Mary, an angel, or a saint. (The Greek word *ikon* means a likeness, or portrait.) Icons are used in Christian churches in Greece, Russia, and other countries in which most of the people be-long to Eastern Orthodox churches. In a Greek Orthodox church there are always at least two icons, an icon of Christ at the right of the doors and an icon of the Vir-gin Mary at the left. Most members of these churches also have icons in their homes.

The icons are considered sacred and are treated with reverence and adoration, but are not worshiped as God is. More than a thousand years ago, a strong party in the Christian Church objected to any use of icons, saying that the use of them violates the Ten Commandments (which forbid "setting up any graven image"). Christians who objected to icons were called iconoclasts (image-breakers). The Roman Catholic Church, in the west, op-posed the use of icons, while the churches of eastern Europe continued to use them. Protestant churches do not use icons. Religious pictures are not called icons unless they are considered sacred.

iconoscope, the tube in a television camera that changes the picture to electric current: see the articles on TELEVISION and ELECTRONICS.

Idaho

Idaho is a state in the northwestern part of the United States. People called it a gem of a state because of its magnificent mountains, high waterfalls, and deep val-leys, and so Idaho came to be nicknamed "the Gem State." The name Idaho comes from the Indian words *Edah hoe,* which mean "light on the mountain." This truly describes an early morning in Idaho, for the rising sun first lights the snow-topped peaks of the mountains.

In area, Idaho ranks 12th among the states, with 83,557 square miles. In pop-ulation it ranks 42nd, with about 713,-000 people living there. It became a state in 1890, as the 43rd state. The Capital is Boise.

THE PEOPLE OF IDAHO

More than half the people of Idaho are farmers and cattle ranchers. The soil is very dry, and the farmers must irrigate the land. Idaho has more irrigated land than almost any other state. The water for ir-rigation is provided by a fine system of dams and canals.

Many people in Idaho work in the large silver and lead mines. They also mine other precious metals, such as zinc, gold, and copper. Others work in the great pine forests, cutting down the valuable white pine.

About four out of ten people in Idaho live in the cities. Some work in offices and others in factories making beet sugar, flour, butter, cheese, and meat products.

The first permanent white settlers in Idaho were a religious group, known as Mormons, who settled in Idaho in 1860. You can read about the MORMONS in a separate article. In the same year, gold was discovered in the mountains, and people from all over the country rushed to the region in search of fortunes. Many of these Americans remained after the gold rush was over. Some Chinese also came at this time and settled there. Later, farmers from the Midwest were attracted by the vast stretches of land for cattle and sheep raising. After railroads were built, and irrigation made farming easier, many more settlers came, including people from England, Germany, and the Scandinavian countries. Today, most of the people of Idaho are American-born. There are sev-eral thousand Indians on reservations.

The Mormons have the largest church membership in Idaho. Other important religions include the Roman Catholic, Methodist, and Northern Baptist.

WHAT IDAHO IS LIKE

Idaho is shaped like a big L. The top of the state is like the handle of a pan, and so it is called the Panhandle region. Here the people do much mining and lumber-ing, and the largest lumber mill in the world is at Lewiston.

The central part of Idaho is a great mountainous region, with the Bitterroot, Sawtooth, Lost River and other ranges. Here you can see lofty, snow-capped peaks, deep valleys, and great forests. One of the most beautiful lakes in the world, the Coeur d'Alene, is in this region. There are little villages on the tops of some mountains, and many deserted mining towns, called "ghost towns." There are still parts of this wild section that have not been explored.

The southern part of Idaho was once a dry plain, formed long ago by hot lava that flowed from an erupting volcano. It has become a rich farming district through the use of irrigation. It is known as the Snake River Plain because the largest river in the state, the Snake River, runs through it. On the Snake River are the magnificent Shoshone Falls, which are higher than the Niagara Falls and are called "the Niagara of the West." Farm-ers in this area raise the large and delicious Idaho potatoes, as well as sugar beets and other crops. Cattle and sheep graze in the drier sections.

The mountain and plain regions are unconnected by railroads, so that people traveling from one part to the other have to go out of the state to reach their desti-

nation. The railroad lines in the state run mostly east and west rather than north and south. There are airports in the large cities. In the early days, one of the most famous roads was the OREGON TRAIL,

U.S. Forest Service

The Sawtooth Mountains in central Idaho are mined for gold, silver, lead, and zinc.

about which you can read in a separate article.

There are a great number of wild animals in Idaho, including bears, lynx, wolves, and moose, and many kinds of birds. The streams and lakes are filled with fish, and Lake Pend Oreille has the largest trout in the world. Every year the state issues thousands of hunting and fishing licenses to tourists.

Although Idaho is so far north, it is not all as cold as a person might think. It is very cold in the mountains in the winter, but in the plains and valleys it is much milder. It is extremely pleasant in the mountains in the summer, but in the

Sun Valley

A festoon of icicles frames skiers returning to Sun Valley after a day on the slopes, and ready for a dip in one of the warm-water, glass-walled pools.

plains the temperature can rise to 100 degrees.

GOVERNMENT OF IDAHO

Idaho, like most other states, is governed by a governor and a legislature. The governor is elected for a four-year term. The legislature is composed of two houses, the Senate and the House of Representa-

tives. The members of both houses are elected for a two-year term. Judges are elected for a six-year term. The capital is Boise. There are 44 counties in this state.

There are about 179,000 students enrolled in public elementary and high schools. Among the principal colleges and universities are:

University of Idaho, at Moscow. Enrollment, 6,007 in 1971 (co-ed)..

Idaho State College, at Pocatello. Enrollment, 7,554 in 1971 (co-ed)..

College of Idaho, at Caldwell. Enrollment, 850 in 1971 (co-ed).

Northwest Nazarene College, at Nampa. Enrollment, 1,079 in 1971 (co-ed).

CHIEF CITIES OF IDAHO

The leading cities of Idaho, with populations from the 1970 census, are:

Boise, population 74,990, the state capital and largest city. There is a separate article about BOISE.

Idaho Falls, population 35,776, third largest city, shipping center for farm products, in the eastern part of the state.

Pocatello, population 40,036, second largest city in Idaho, railroad and communication center, in the southern part of the state.

Twin Falls, population 21,914 fourth-largest city, trading center, in the southern part of the state.

IDAHO IN THE PAST

Until 170 years ago, Idaho was a wild territory, known only to the Indian tribes who lived there. In 1805 the explorers Lewis and Clarke became the first white men to see this part of the United States. They reported a vast region filled with fur-bearing animals, and this brought fur trappers and traders to the area. It was not until some fifty years later that the Mormons and the gold miners arrived. Later in the century, silver was discovered, and many more miners came into the region.

Idaho was part of the Oregon Territory until 1863, when it was made into a separate territory. At first it included Montana and most of Wyoming, but later these became separate territories.

For many years there was bitter fighting with the Nez Perce Indians, who did not want to be moved off their land. Finally they surrendered, and went to live on reservations. In 1890, Idaho came into the Union as the 43rd state.

Disagreements arose between the miners and the mine owners, and there were such fierce battles and strikes that troops had to be called out to restore order. The bitter feelings continued for a long time, and finally resulted in the assassination of an ex-governor of the state, Frank Steunenberg. Several mine union leaders were accused of murder, and put on trial. The trial was very dramatic and attracted the attention of people all over the world. At the end of the trial all but one of the men were freed.

After that, Idaho prospered peacefully. It was one of the earliest states to give women the right to vote. Its magnificent scenery has attracted many tourists, and Sun Valley is particularly popular for its winter sports.

PLACES TO SEE IN IDAHO

Craters of the Moon National Monu-

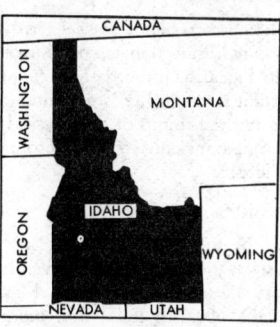

ment, 48,003 acres, in the southern part of the state, 70 miles from Idaho Falls, on U.S. Route 20. Fissure eruptions, volcanic cones, craters, and caves. Some craters are nearly a mile across and hundreds of feet deep.

Heyburn State Park, 7,838 acres, in the northwest, 9 miles east of Plummer, on U.S. Route 95, contains Indian cliffs, a pine forest, and wildlife. Excellent boating, fishing, swimming, and hiking.

Spalding Memorial State Park, 13 acres, in the northwest, 12 miles east of Lewiston, on U.S. Route 95. A collection of historic relics.

American Falls Dam, in the south, at American Falls, on U.S. Route 30 N. Nearly a mile long; the key reservoir for the largest continuous irrigated section in the United States.

Arrowrock Dam, in the southwest, 24 miles east of Boise, on U.S. Routes 20, 26, and 30. One of the highest irrigation dams in the world, 348 feet high. One may descend by stairs 230 feet into the dam and inspect the machinery.

Grand Canyon of the Snake River, in the west, in the Payette National Forest, west of U.S. Route 95. The deepest canyon in North America, 5,500 feet deep. Contains Hell's Canyon.

Sun Valley, in the south central part of the state, 4 miles north of Ketchum, on U.S. Route 93. One of the most popular winter and summer resorts in the West. Surrounded by mountains; skiing, hunting, ice-skating, swimming.

IDAHO. Area, 83,557 square miles. Population (1970 census) 713,008. Capital, Boise. Nickname, the Gem State. Motto, Esto Perpetua (Mayest Thou Endure Forever). Flower, syringa. Tree, white pine. Bird, mountain bluebird. Song, "Here We Have Idaho." Admitted to Union, July 3, 1890. Official abbreviation, Ida., or ID.

idealism

An *idealist* is a person who believes that everything can be ideal, or perfect, and who tries to make it so. His beliefs are called idealism. Often he thinks that things are better than they really are, and in this way he is the opposite of a *realist*, who tries to see things as they really are, no matter how unpleasant this may be.

Idealism has special meanings in art and in philosophy.

In art, idealism is the picturing of something as the artist feels it should look and not as it really does look. In idealistic painting or stories there is rarely anything unpleasant. All the men are handsome and good, all the ladies are beautiful and well-dressed, and the houses and worlds in which they live have no unhappiness or ugliness in them.

Idealism is also a special term in philosophy. Philosophers, or thinkers, are called idealists if they believe that the important thing in life is the mind or spirit and not the things of the physical world. Plato, an ancient Greek philosopher, was an idealist.

ides

In the calendar of ancient Rome, ides was the name of the thirteenth day of every month except March, May, July, and October. In those four months the ides was the fifteenth day of the month. When Julius Caesar was the most powerful man in ancient Rome, two thousand years ago, a soothsayer (fortune-teller) is said to have told him to "beware the ides of March," that is, watch out for March 15. On March 15, Caesar was killed.

idiom

Idiom is any special use of a language by the people of a particular country or region. Americans and British both speak the English language, but an American would say "I have a knife in my pocket" while an Englishman would say "I have got a knife in my pocket." It is American idiom to say "I have" and British idiom to say "I have got." Idiom is neither right nor wrong. It has nothing to do with the rules of correct grammar. Every country has its idiom, and people who live in that country learn the idiom as naturally as they learn the language.

A particular phrase or expression that is used by some groups of people is also called an idiom.

idiot

An idiot is someone with so little intelligence that he is not able to take care of himself in the simplest ways. He is not able to feed or dress himself, and his mental ability never gets to be more than that of a two-year-old child, no matter how old he may be. Idiocy may be caused by injuries to the brain, but most idiots have been that way since birth. There is not much that can be done to help these unfortunate people, except to place them in institutions where they can be cared for. According to law, an idiot cannot sign a contract or be blamed for a crime he commits.

idol, an object that people worship as a god: see the article FETISH.

I Doubt It

I Doubt It is the name of a card game. For years it has been popular with card players of all ages from nine to ninety.

The game may be played by any number of players from four to twelve. It is best for six to nine players. Four or five players may use one pack of fifty-two cards, but if there are six or more players you should shuffle together two full fifty-two card packs. No jokers are used. Very often two packs are used by four or five players, because it makes the game better.

The cards are dealt out one at a time, as far as they will go. It makes no difference if some players receive more cards than others. It is all right to deal more than one card at a time if the pack has been carefully shuffled.

The first player is the one who is at the left of the dealer. He begins by placing any number of cards from one to eight (or from one to four if only a single pack is used) face down in the center of the table. Then he announces, "These are three aces (or kings, sevens, fives, or any other rank)." Any other player may then say "I doubt it." If a player says that, the cards put down are turned face up. If they are what the player said they were, the player who doubted must take all the cards into his hand. If they were not exactly what was announced, then the player who put the cards down must take all the cards into his hand.

As long as no one doubts, the cards in the center pile up. Suppose the first player puts down three cards and says "Three tens." No one doubts it. The next player puts down five cards and says "Five kings." No one doubts it. At this point there are eight cards on the board. The next player puts down two cards and says "Two eights." Someone says "I doubt it." The last two cards are turned up. If they are both eights, then the doubter must take all ten cards in the center into his hand. If one of them is not an eight, then the player must take all the ten cards into his hand. Sometimes there are thirty or more cards that must be taken into the hand of a player when someone doubts the announcement.

When a player gets rid of all of his cards, the game ends. He wins one point from each other player.

idyl or idyll

More than two thousand years ago Greek poets began to write short poems called *idyls,* which meant "little pictures." The poet Theocritus wrote most of his idyls about country life and especially about shepherds out with their sheep in the pastures. For this reason idyls are often called pastoral poetry, which means "poetry about shepherds."

Typical idyls show how beautiful the country is compared with the city, or they compare childhood with springtime and old age with autumn.

The great Roman poet Virgil wrote many fine idyls. He called them *bucolics,* meaning poems about the country. Many English poets have written idyllic poems.

Tennyson's poem about King Arthur and the Knights of the Round Table, *Idylls of the King.* is an idyl only in the sense that it is a series of "little pictures."

Ifni

Ifni is a province of the African country of Morocco. It is on the Atlantic coast. In 1860, Morocco gave the area to Spain, but the Spaniards did not occupy it until 1934. In 1956, Morocco claimed Ifni for itself once more. Spain not only refused to give it up, but in 1958 made Ifni an overseas Spanish province. The entire area of Ifni is about 580 square miles, but Spain could effectively control only about 30 square miles, since most of Ifni is in the Sahara, the world's largest desert. Finally, in 1969, after 35 years of occupancy, Spain returned Ifni to Morocco.

About 52,000 people live in Ifni. They are mostly Berber tribesmen who practice the Moslem religion. Some of them raise sheep and cattle in the oases, while others have tiny farms where they raise just enough food for their own use. Some of the men who live along the Atlantic coast are fishermen. Others are craftsmen noted for making carpets, jewelry, and other hand-made items, many of which are exported. When the area was a Spanish province, it exported nothing at all. The main city and capital of the Moroccan province of Ifni, is Sidi Ifni. The population of the city is about 15,000.

igloo, a shelter built out of blocks of snow: see the article ESKIMOS.

igneous rock, a kind of rock that was formed by the cooling of hot liquid lava: see the article on ROCK.

ignition

The ignition, or ignition system, of an automobile supplies the spark necessary to explode the mixture of gasoline and air in the cylinders of a gas or internal-combustion engine. (You can read about the INTERNAL COMBUSTION ENGINE in a separate article.)

The ignition is run by a battery and a special device called an induction coil. These supply electric current to two pieces of metal in a device called a spark plug. The current makes a spark jump out of the spark plug, and the spark causes an explosion in the cylinder of the engine. Each cylinder of the engine has a spark plug. In the operation of the engine, the spark must occur at just the right time to ignite the explosive mixture. It must also occur in the proper cylinder. To accomplish this, a *timer* and a *distributor* are used. Both are connected to the engine in such a way that each cylinder will be fired at the right time.

The battery of the ignition system is connected to the induction coil. The induction coil is connected to both the timer and the distributor.

The timer is a special switch that breaks the circuit at just the right time. When the circuit is broken, it makes the induction coil deliver a large amount of electricity to the distributor.

The distributor is a small wheel with small pieces of metal along its edge. These are connected by wires to the different spark plugs. Inside the distributor is a piece of metal that turns like a dial on a clock. As it turns it touches the metal edges on the distributor and sends the electricity from the induction coil through the wires to the spark plugs, making them spark. (You can read more about the induction coil in the article on INDUCTION.)

Igorot, the name of a group of people who live on Luzon Island in the Philippines. These people were once savage head-hunters, but now they are more civilized. See the article on the PHILIPPINES.

iguana

An iguana is a lizard that is found in the tropical regions of Central and South America. It is greenish in color and blends with the tree on which it lives. Because of this, it cannot be seen easily. It often grows to be five or six feet long. The

iguana has a crest, or high ridge, that stands up along its back and tail. Its skin fits loosely and is covered with small scales that look somewhat like armor. It has large, powerful feet and a long, slender, sturdy tail. The iguana lays its eggs in a burrow dug along a stream or in the hollow of a tree. It lays twenty or thirty large eggs at a time. The iguana is a timid creature and will not harm humans. It is considered useful by the natives of Central and South America because it feeds on insects as well as on grass and leaves. Many of these natives eat the flesh of the iguana, which is tender white meat. The iguana is also found in the Fiji Islands and in Madagascar.

The village of New Salem, Illinois where Abraham Lincoln lived for six years has been authentically restored as a memorial to him.

Iliad

The *Iliad* is the name of one of the greatest stories of all time, a story that was told by the Greek poet Homer almost three thousand years ago. It is the story of how the Greeks went to war against the city of Troy, or Ilium, and of Achilles, the greatest of all the Greek warriors.

At the beginning of the poem, Achilles quarrels with Agamemnon, the leader of the Greek armies. Achilles becomes so angry that he swears he will not fight for the Greeks until Agamemnon apologizes for insulting him. Achilles keeps his promise and does not fight, even though the Greeks lose many battles. Achilles lends his armor to his friend Patroclus, who is soon killed by the Trojan champion, Hector. Finally, Agamemnon apologizes to Achilles and urges him to join the battle and avenge Patroclus. Achilles does, and he kills Hector after chasing him three times around the walls of Troy.

The Greeks bury the dead Patroclus and celebrate their victory over the Trojans. Priam, the old king of Troy, begs the Greeks to return the body of his dead son Hector. At last Achilles shows pity for the old man, and the *Iliad* ends with the return of Hector's body and the Trojan funeral.

See also the articles on HOMER and the ODYSSEY.

illegitimacy

A child is said to be illegitimate if its parents were not legally married when the child was born. In former times, illegitimate children (who are also called "bastards") could become noblemen and even kings, and some of the most famous men of history were illegitimate. Within the last two hundred years or more, there has been great prejudice against illegitimate children. In most states and countries a child's birth certificate showed when he was illegitimate, and this official record often made it impossible for a person to keep a good job or have a good reputation in society. Within the last forty years, many lawmaking bodies have recognized the unfairness of this and have passed laws that do not allow a birth certificate to show when a child is illegitimate. "Born out of wedlock" is another term that means illegitimate. In other uses, illegitimate simply means "against the law."

Illinois

Illinois is a state in the great midwestern plains of the United States. It is a large rolling prairie, which is level farmland with very few trees, and it is called "the Prairie State." The land in the central part is so flat that railroad tracks were laid many years ago without the workmen having to level the ground at all.

Illinois is named after an Indian tribe called Illini, who lived in that part of the country long before the white men came. Illinois is very proud of the fact that Abraham Lincoln came to the state as a young man, and rose to become a successful Illinois lawyer before he became President of the United States.

In area, Illinois ranks 24th among the states, with 56,400 square miles. In population it ranks 5th, with more than 11 million people living there. It was admitted to the Union in 1818, as the 21st state. The capital is Springfield.

THE PEOPLE OF ILLINOIS

At one time most of the people of Illinois were farmers. There are still many farmers, but many more people now work in the great meat-packing plants and the factories in Chicago and other cities. Three out of four of the people live in the cities. Others dig coal out of the rich mines in the state, and work in the important oil fields.

After the Revolutionary War, settlers began moving into this region from the eastern states. They were followed by settlers from Europe, who helped build the railroads and worked on the farms and in the mines. After the Civil War, many people from Germany, Poland, and other countries arrived to work in the growing cities. These families have lived so long in the state that today nine out of ten people in Illinois are American-born.

The leading churches of the state include the Roman Catholic and Methodist.

WHAT ILLINOIS IS LIKE

Illinois is a great level plain in the Mississippi Valley. Millions of years ago huge ice fields, called glaciers, pushed down across this part of America and, like an enormous piece of sandpaper, smoothed out the land. The glaciers missed the northwest corner of the state, leaving high hills with valuable lead and zinc mines.

The glaciers also missed the extreme southern part of Illinois, where there are valleys and hills covered with forests. Here the people mine coal and raise fruit. The southern tip of the state is a low, hot region in which the rich farming land lies below the level of the Mississippi River. This part of the state has been nicknamed "Egypt" because it looks somewhat like the region around the Nile River in Egypt, and because the chief city is called Cairo. Here the farmers grow tobacco, cotton, fruit, and vegetables.

In the rest of the state you may see field after field of corn and oats, which are the biggest crops the farmers raise. Illinois ranks second among the states in these products. Large quantities of apples, peaches, strawberries, pears, and plums are grown in Illinois. Millions of hogs, beef cattle, sheep and lambs are raised and shipped to the great stockyards in Chicago. Illinois leads all the states but Iowa in the raising of hogs. It is also an important producer of eggs and butter.

Illinois ranks third among the states in manufacturing. This is chiefly because Chicago, the second-largest city in the United States, is also the second-largest manufacturing city, after New York. Illinois manufactures more farm machinery, more food products, and more metal products than any other state. The largest glass bottle factory in the world is at Alton. More than half the pianos made in the United States are made in Illinois.

The climate of Illinois varies greatly because there are no mountains to stop the cold winds from the north or the warm breezes from the south. The temperature can change very rapidly. It has been known to go from 100 degrees to zero in a few weeks. Illinois usually has hot summers and cold winters, with an average temperature of 76 degrees in the summer, and 28 degrees in the winter. There is plenty of rainfall for the crops.

Railroads reach all parts of the state, and Chicago has twenty-two different railroad lines coming into the city. There are also many airports. The rivers, especially the Mississippi, Ohio, and Illinois, are important to transportation. The Illinois Waterway is connected to the Lakes-to-

Gulf Waterway, and makes it possible for barges filled with farm products to go from Illinois all the way down to New Orleans, or to Lake Michigan, where there are ships from all parts of the world.

GOVERNMENT OF ILLINOIS

Illinois, like most other states, is governed by a Governor and a Legislature. The Governor is elected for a four-year term. The Legislature, called the General Assembly, is composed of two houses, a Senate, whose members are elected for a four-year term, and a House of Representatives, whose members are elected for a two-year term. Judges are elected for a nine-year term. The capital is Springfield. There are 102 counties in the state.

There are about 2,325,000 pupils attending public elementary and high schools. Illinois is famous for its many fine colleges and universities, among them are:

University of Illinois, at Urbana. Enrollment, 31,267 in 1971 (co-ed).

Illinois State Normal University, at Normal. Enrollment, 14,230 in 1971 (co-ed).

Illinois Institute of Technology, at Chicago. Enrollment, 7,485 in 1971 (co-ed).

University of Chicago, at Chicago. Enrollment, 10,137 in 1971 (co-ed).

Northwestern University, at Evanston. Enrollment, 16,259 in 1971 (co-ed).

Wheaton College, at Wheaton. Enrollment, 1,842 in 1971 (co-ed).

Loyola University, at Chicago. Enrollment, 14,509 in 1971 (co-ed).

De Paul University, at Chicago. Enrollment, 8,581 in 1971 (co-ed).

Roosevelt University, at Chicago. Enrollment, 6,297 in 1971 (co-ed).

Southern Illinois University, at Carbondale. Enrollment, 33,035 in 1971 (co-ed).

Northern Illinois University, at De Kalb. Enrollment, 21,313 in 1971 (co-ed)

Illinois College, at Jacksonville. Enrollment, 802 in 1971 (co-ed).

Illinois Wesleyan University, at Bloomington. Enrollment, 1,588 in 1971 (co-ed).

CHIEF CITIES OF ILLINOIS

The leading cities of Illinois, with populations from the 1970 census, are:

Springfield, population 91,753, state capital and fourth-largest city. There is a separate article about SPRINGFIELD.

Chicago, population 3,366,957, largest city in the state. There is a separate article about CHICAGO.

Rockford, population 147,370, second-largest city, manufacturing center for farm tools, in the northern part of the state.

Peoria, population 126,963, third-largest city, trading and industrial center, in the central part of the state.

East St. Louis, population 69,996, fifth-largest city, manufacturing and railroad center, in the southwestern part of the state.

ILLINOIS IN THE PAST

When the French explorers Marquette and Joliet first entered the territory of Illinois, more than 280 years ago, they found the friendly Kaskaskia Indians living there. Father Marquette liked them so well that he returned a few years later and set up a mission for them. Some years later another French explorer, La Salle, came to the Illinois region and built a fort near where Peoria now stands. The

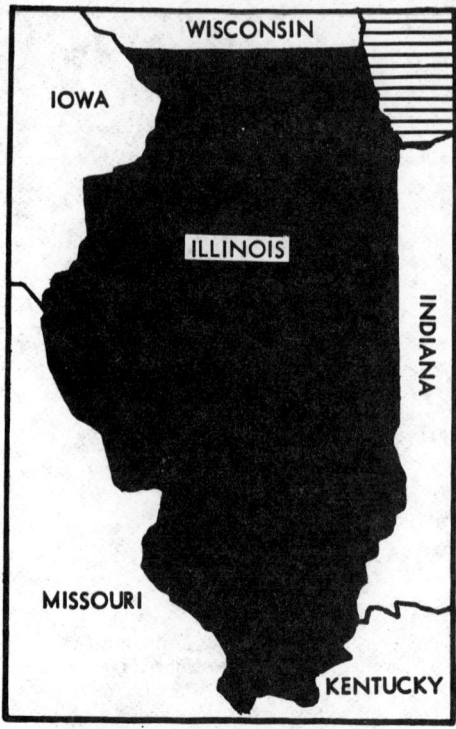

first permanent settlement was made by the French in 1699, at Cahokia.

After the French and Indian Wars, France gave the Illinois region to the English and some English settlements were started. During the Revolutionary War a group of frontiersmen called "the Long Knives," led by George Rogers Clark, captured several of the English villages, and the territory became part of the United States.

Settlers from the east began moving to Illinois, looking for new farm land. They found vast forests and great prairies covered with prairie grass that grew as high as a man's waist. The people thought this prairie land was not fertile, and they settled instead along the Ohio and Mississippi Rivers. It was left for later settlers to discover how rich the prairie was.

Illinois was part of the Northwest Territory until 1800, when it became part of the Indiana Territory. It became a separate territory in 1809. There were many fierce Indian raids, and in 1812 the Indians attacked Fort Dearborn (where Chicago now stands) and massacred the people there. Illinois became a state in 1818, but many people were afraid to go there because of the danger from the Indians. The Indians were finally driven out of Illinois in the Black Hawk War of 1832, and then the state began to grow more rapidly. One young American officer who served in this war was to become the most famous citizen of Illinois. His name was Abraham Lincoln.

In the Civil War, Illinois was loyal to the North, and sent more than 200,000 men to the Union forces. There were some people living in the southern part of the state who were sympathetic to the Confederates.

Illinois continued to grow at a rapid rate. In World War II, it contributed great quantities of ships, guns, ammunition and food to the war effort.

PLACES TO SEE IN ILLINOIS

New Salem State Park, 281 acres, in

the central part of Illinois, 2 miles south of Petersburg, on State Highway 97. An authentic restoration of the old town of New Salem, where Abraham Lincoln lived from 1831 to 1837.

Starved Rock State Park, 1,443 acres, in the north, 7 miles east of LaSalle, south of U.S. Route 6. The site of Fort St. Louis, built by La Salle in 1682.

Dickson Mounds, in central Illinois, 4 miles south of Lewiston, on U.S. Route 24. More than 230 skeletons of prehistoric people have been uncovered and left in their original positions, together with some of their possessions, tools, pottery, and weapons.

Ulysses S. Grant Home, in the northwest, in Galena, on U.S. Route 20. The house where General Grant lived for a time after the Civil War. It contains many of Grant's possessions.

Lincoln's Tomb and Monument, in central Illinois, in Oak Ridge Cemetery, at the northwest edge of Springfield.

Baha'i Temple, in the northeast, in Wilmette, on U.S. Route 41. A magnificent and interesting building with nine sides; the house of worship for the people of the Baha'i religion.

See also the article on CHICAGO.

ILLINOIS. Area, 56,400 square miles. Population (1970 census) 11,113,976. Capital, Springfield. Nickname, the Prairie State. Motto, State Sovereignty — National Union. Flower, native violet. Bird, cardinal. Song, "Illinois." Admitted to Union December 3, 1818. Official abbreviation, Ill.

illiteracy

An illiterate is a person who is more than 10 years old but who cannot read and write. Children under 10 years of age are not considered illiterates because they have not yet had the full opportunity to learn to read and write. Illiteracy is highest in the most backward areas of the world. In parts of Africa, Asia and South America about four out of five men and almost all the women are illiterate. The countries of western and northern Europe, North America, and Australia and New Zealand have the fewest illiterate people. More than half the people in the world are illiterate.

Compulsory education is the answer to illiteracy. When all children in a country must go to school and are given a good education, illiteracy will almost disappear. Only those people who have so little intelligence that they cannot learn will remain illiterate.

In World War II the armed forces found that more than a million men in the United States, who were otherwise fit for service, were illiterate. At first these men were rejected, but the services finally accepted them and taught them to read and write.

About five hundred years ago most people in the world were illiterate. Only the priests and a few other educated people could read and write. There were just a few handwritten books. The invention of printing provided more and more books, and gave more people a chance to read. As countries became more democratic, the common people were given the chance for an education. In some parts of the world all the people have been illiterate until recently because they had no written language. This was true of most of the

tribes in Africa. A missionary named Dr. Frank Lanback went to Africa and made up an alphabet and written language for the African tribesmen. He taught people to read and write, and organized the system called "each one teach one." This means that each person who learned to read taught at least one other person. Since Dr. Lanback began his great work, more than 60 million people who once were illiterate can now read and write.

illumination, bringing light to something: see the article on LIGHTING.

illustration

An illustration is a picture that helps to tell a story. The old saying "A picture is worth ten thousand words" may not be completely true, but it is a way of saying that pictures do help to make something more understandable than words alone can do.

The book you are reading now has many pictures that make it easier for you to understand many of the things described in the articles.

Illustrations are used to show what people, places and things look like. Words alone cannot do this. Illustrations also help make clear how some things are done and how other things work. In the separate article on VISUAL EDUCATION, you may read how illustration is becoming more and more important in teaching many subjects.

Ancient peoples used illustration even before there were any books. The Egyptians, Babylonians and Assyrians carved pictures on stone. The Greeks painted pictures on vases and plates. The first writing, in fact, was picture-writing. When real writing was developed men still used pictures to illustrate the writing. The monks who made handwritten copies of the early Bibles drew beautiful pictures to illustrate them. These pictures helped the people of older days to understand and love the Bible stories.

Modern book, magazine and newspaper illustration consists of pictures that are drawn or painted, and pictures that are taken with a camera. From the very time we begin to enjoy stories—even before we can read—we are helped by pictures. The books of nursery rhymes and other stories for little children contain as much illustration as they do writing. School textbooks are much more completely illustrated than they used to be.

Illustrations are also found outside of books. In an illustrated lecture, slides or even motion pictures are used to help the lecturer explain his material to his audience. The pictures may be of faraway places, or of things seen under a microscope. They often give people a clear understanding of things they had never seen before.

Il Trovatore

Il Trovatore is the name of a grand opera, which is a play in which all the conversation is sung, not spoken, and the music is classical, intended to be played by a symphony orchestra and sung by the greatest singers. The music for *Il Trovatore* was written about a hundred years

ago (in 1852) by Giuseppe Verdi, a great Italian composer. The libretto, or words, of the opera was written by Salvatore Commarano. *Il Trovatore* is in four acts, or parts. It is still often performed in the United States by both large and small opera companies.

THE STORY OF THE OPERA

Il Trovatore means "the troubadour." A troubadour is a wandering minstrel, or singer. In the opera the hero Manrico is a troubadour. He is believed to be the son of Azucena, a gypsy. Manrico and Count di Luna fight for the love of the countess Leonore. Count di Luna wounds Manrico in a sword duel but does not kill him. Leonore, however, thinks Manrico is dead and decides to enter a nunnery. A nunnery is a place where women spend their lives worshipping and working for God; no woman who lives in a nunnery is allowed to marry. Manrico finds' Leonore before she joins, and they plan to marry. The opera ends unhappily. Manrico and Leonore are captured by Count di Luna. In order to save Manrico's life Leonore marries the count, but she is so unhappy that she kills herself by taking poison. Count di Luna has Manrico killed, and then is told by Azucena, who was really not Manrico's mother, that Manrico was Count di Luna's long-lost brother.

imagination

Imagination is the ability we have to form pictures in our minds and see things differently from the way they appear to our eyes. When a small child sits on a chair and pretends it is a horse, he is using his imagination. As he gallops along, his imagination turns the rug into a stretch of ranchland, and the sofa becomes a steer. By using his imagination in this way the child is able to spend his time more pleasantly.

Everyone has imagination to some extent, but some people have much more imagination than others. Artists, writers, inventors and explorers are usually the most imaginative types of people. They combine imagination with talent and skill to accomplish their work.

The artist often uses imagination to show things in a picture or sculpture that are different from what we might ordinarily see. He also uses colors in an imaginative way. The writer uses imagination to create exciting and interesting stories and characters. The inventor uses imagination to make new products that did not exist before. He cannot make it unless he can first imagine what it will be like. The explorer uses imagination to picture what lies ahead of him.

Imagination is not always used for good purposes. Just as writers can create stories, other people can use imagination to tell lies. Just as one inventor can create a good product, another inventor can create a deadly weapon.

When you use imagination you can never really be bored, for you can make your life richer and more interesting.

Immaculate Conception

Immaculate means "without sin." or clean and pure. *Conception* is the beginning or creation of something. In some

Christian churches, the doctrine of Immaculate Conception is taught in this way: Ever since Adam and Eve disobeyed God in the Garden of Eden, all human beings have been born sinful creatures. But Mary, the mother of Jesus, was born free of sin, and when Jesus himself was conceived it was an immaculate conception. The Roman Catholic church has a holiday, the Feast of the Immaculate Conception, that celebrates God's choice of Mary to bear a holy child. Many Christian Churches teach that the Immaculate Conception applies only to Jesus, not to Mary.

immigration

An immigrant is a person who goes to a country where he was not born and settles in the new country. This moving permanently into a new country is called immigration. Usually the immigrant wants to become a citizen of his new country if the law allows him to. Throughout all of history people have been leaving old lands and moving into new ones. Whole families, tribes and races have crossed mountains, deserts, and seas to settle in new lands. Usually we speak of immigration as the moving of a person or a family into one country from another.

There are many reasons why people decide to leave their native lands to become citizens in another country. The reasons must be powerful ones, for it is a difficult thing to leave for a new country where you know almost no one and where the language and customs may be strange to you. In many cases, particularly in the cases of immigrants to America, hardship and poverty at home have been the causes. People leave their countries as a result of war, revolution, religious persecution, or natural catastrophes such as earthquakes, floods, plagues, or famines.

The Americas were settled entirely by immigrants from other parts of the world. Only the American Indian is not an immigrant. Sometimes you may hear a person spoken of as being an immigrant as if it were a bad thing to be, but that, of course, is silly. All Americans are immigrants or descendants of immigrants. The earliest immigrants came to America because it was a new world where there was plenty of land for everybody and where they could have religious fredom. Later immigrants came because there was so much opportunity to advance their standard of living in the New World. After the Civil War immigrants were brought into the United States because they would work for low wages. Before, during and after World War II many immigrants to the United States were political refugees, who left their own countries because they disagreed with the governments.

For a long time immigrants were welcomed to the United States. The new country had room and work for all who wanted to come. About sixty years ago the situation changed. By this time the United States had been settled from the Atlantic to the Pacific. Most of the good farm land had been settled. There were enough men to work in the factories, and sometimes during depressions there were not even jobs enough for the workers already in the country. The United States

The driver of this car is leaving Canada and entering the United States. A U.S. Immigration officer examines and returns the man's entry documents.

feared there might be immigrants who would not be able to earn a living. People in the United States objected to the immigrants brought in as cheap labor because they felt that these laborers would lower the living standards of the country. Congress decided to pass laws limiting the number and kind of immigrants that would be allowed.

Beginning about 1900 immigration laws began to be passed. By 1924 the present quota system had been adopted. This system allows a quota, or number, of immigrants from each country each year. The quota varies from country to country, and the countries from which the earliest settlers came have the largest quotas. In any case only desirable immigrants are accepted. In the 1950s laws were passed prohibiting Communists or members of political parties considered dangerous to the United States from entering the country. In 1953 the Congress of the United States passed a special law permitting people fleeing from Communist oppression or people who could not return to their homelands after World War II to enter the United States in larger numbers than the quotas of their countries allowed. The Migration and Refugee Assistance Act of 1962 permits the government to admit one refugee for every four accepted by the other countries of the world under the jurisdiction of the United Nations.

The United States Bureau of Immigration and Naturalization was established in 1891 to take care of all problems concerning immigration.

Emigration is the leaving of a country to settle in a new one, so every immigrant to the United States is also an emigrant from somewhere else.

immunity

When a person has immunity to a disease, he cannot get that disease. Certain things called "antibodies," which are in the blood stream, make immunity possible. These antibodies are produced by the body and they fight to kill germs that cause disease.

There are "natural" immunity and "acquired" immunity. Natural immunity is immunity with which a person is born, and which he has all his life. Different people are immune to different diseases. For instance, you may get the measles, and your mother may never get it. She may have natural immunity to measles.

Acquired immunity comes from having already had a disease or from being given medicines (called *vaccines*) that prevent it. When you have already had a disease, your body forms antibodies that will fight the germs and keep you from getting it again. When you are vaccinated against a certain disease, the vaccine causes your body to make these antibodies. There are vaccines to make people immune to smallpox, diphtheria, rabies (which people get if they are bitten by a dog who has the germs), typhoid fever, and other diseases.

The word *immunity* is also used when a person cannot be punished for breaking a law. Congressmen, when they speak from the floor of Congress, have "legal immunity." This means that a Congressman cannot be punished for anything he says. An ambassador or other diplomatic representative of a foreign country has diplomatic immunity and cannot be punished for any crime, except by being sent back to his country.

impeachment

Impeachment is the first step taken to remove a government official who has been dishonest, has used his position wrongly, or has committed a crime. When a government official is impeached, he is merely accused of having done something wrong. He must still be tried and found guilty before he can be removed from office.

In the United States, Congress is responsible for the impeachment and trial of Federal government officials. The state legislatures are responsible in the same way for officials in their states. The Constitution of the United States provides for the House of Representatives to impeach a Federal official, and for the Senate to try a person who has been impeached by the House. The House can impeach an official (even the President) by a ma-

jority vote. The Senate can find the official guilty only if two-thirds of the Senators vote against him. The state legislatures operate in a similar way—the lower house impeaches an official and the upper house acts as a court. In England and Canada the lower house of Parliament impeaches and the upper house acts as a court.

Impeachments are very rare. No one has been impeached in England for more than a hundred years. Only a few Federal officials have ever been impeached in the United States. The most famous impeachment in history was that of Andrew Johnson, 17th President of the United States. When Johnson was President, the nation was recovering from the Civil War and there was still much bitter feeling in the North against the South. Johnson tried to treat the southern states in a reasonable manner. His enemies hurled wild charges at him and said he was using his great office wrongly. The House of Representatives heard the accusations and voted to impeach Johnson. The Senate missed by one vote finding Johnson guilty. Thirty-five Senators voted to convict him and nineteen voted him innocent. If one of the nineteen had switched his vote, two-thirds of the Senate would have voted against Johnson and he would have been removed from office.

imperialism

Imperialism is the policy of a country when it tries to increase its territory by bringing other countries or territories under its control. In former times, when nearly every country was ruled by a king, an imperialistic country was one that tried to make itself an empire or a greater empire by conquering other countries and bringing the other countries' rulers under the control of its own, who was called an emperor. Today even a republic can practice imperialism.

Nations can form empires in various ways: by defeating other nations in war; by sending some of their people to begin colonies; or by obtaining special rights and favors from the governments of weaker countries.

Most of the famous empires throughout history have been based on victory in war. The Greek empire of Alexander the Great, the Roman empire, the French empire of Napoleon, and the recent German empire of Hitler are some examples of this kind of imperialism. These empires almost always kept their power with large armies, and when the army grew weak or was defeated the empire usually collapsed.

When Russia was ruled by the czars, or emperors, it was known as one of the most imperialistic countries. It was constantly trying to conquer and annex the small countries on its borders. When the Communist government came to power in Russia in 1917, its leaders Lenin and Trotsky said the country would not be imperialistic, but in spite of what they said, Russia has continued to seize control of weaker countries when it can.

The longest-lasting empires seem to be those that have begun colonies. The Spanish empire held most of South America for almost three hundred years

this way. The French and British colonial empires lasted a long time, but since the end of World War II, most of their colonies have been granted independence.

Countries try to explain their imperialism by saying that they need more "living room" because their country is too crowded, that they are bringing civilization to backward countries, or that they need to get raw materials from their colonies and have places to sell their manufactured goods. There is usually some truth in all of these claims, but they do not hide the fact that imperialism is usually greed, and undemocratic because it prevents other countries from running their affairs the way they want to. See also the article EMPIRE.

Imperial Valley, a section of the Colorado Desert in the southern part of California. It has been changed by irrigation to a rich farm country. See the article on CALIFORNIA.

impetigo

Impetigo is a skin disease. You can get it by touching someone who has impetigo, or the clothes or towels he has used. Impetigo sores appear on the exposed parts of the skin, such as your face, arms, and legs. When they first start, they look somewhat like blisters, but the sores are filled with a liquid that dries into a hard crust when the blisters burst. These crusts seem to be made up of many layers of dried material, and are hard to get rid of. They should be treated by a doctor, who may use one of the new "miracle drugs" (antibiotics) to cure them.

import, anything that is brought from a foreign country to be used or sold: see the article on FOREIGN TRADE.

Inca

The Incas are South American Indians who built a remarkable civilization more than five hundred years ago. They ruled the part of South America that now makes up the countries of Peru, Ecuador, and Bolivia. The achievements of the Inca nation during the one hundred years of its existence are probably equal to those of any nation in history.

The Incas were originally one tribe of the Quechua Indians. Gradually they fought and conquered neighboring tribes and increased their power. They persuaded other tribes to join them. The people of each tribe were ruled by their old leaders, but all the separate tribal leaders were ruled by the Inca chieftain. He was the king of the country and was also worshiped as the son of the sun god.

As the nation grew larger and stronger, many new arrangements were made to govern the people. Each family was allowed to own a small stone house and a garden where it raised corn, potatoes, lima beans, squash, tomatoes, and other fruits and vegetables. Apart from these small farms, however, everything belonged to the tribe or to the government, for whom the people had to work part of the time. Some tended the tribe's herds of llamas and alpacas, which were used for transportation and for their wool. Others worked for the government on farms and

A giant sundial near Cuzco, capital city of the Incas, who were also known as the "Children of the Sun."

in Cuzco, Peru, which was once the capital city of the Inca nation.

The Incas had wise and just rulers. They kept enough food in the storehouses to feed all the people for three years. They gave this food to the poor, to farmers whose crops were ruined by flood or drought, and to the Inca armies and government workers. They kept careful records by means of colored and knotted strings called *quipus,* and whenever the storehouses were too full everyone got an equal share of the extra food. Schools were started, and people learned to make metal tools and fine jewelry and to weave fine fabrics.

In 1525, when the Inca kingdom was larger and more powerful than it had ever been, its great chieftain Huayna

Ruins near Cuzco. Liquor was poured into the grooves on feasts and flowed like spring water to the celebrating people.

Capac died. Two of his sons, Atahualpa and Huáscar, divided the country, then began to fight each other. Just as Atahualpa triumphed, the Spanish explorer Francisco Pizarro led two hundred Spanish soldiers into the kingdom. In a short

in gold, silver, and copper mines, or they would help build the fine roads, storehouses for the extra food, temples, and fortresses. Some of these are still standing

time, the tiny band of Spanish soldiers armed with guns defeated the Incas and destroyed their kingdom. The conquerors killed Atahualpa, and showed great cruelty to the people. The great Inca civilization was destroyed in 1532.

incense

Incense is a kind of dried perfume that gives off an odor when it is burned. It is made from certain dried fruits, flowers, barks, woods, and gum resins. For thousands of years incense has been burned as a religious offering. The ancient Egyptians made a ceremony of burning incense in beautiful bowls, called *censers,* while priests chanted religious poetry. The Bible mentions the use of incense, and two of the gifts brought by the Three Wise Men to the infant Jesus were frankincense and myrrh—two kinds of incense. Incense is used in some services of the Roman Catholic Church and some other Christian churches.

inclined plane

An inclined plane is a board that has one end at a higher level than the other. The board is said to be slanted, or inclined, to the ground.

The inclined plane is a kind of machine. This means that it helps you to do work. With an inclined plane you can raise an object without lifting it straight up. You would need more effort to lift it straight up.

Inclined planes are used to roll heavy weights onto trucks or loading platforms. Workmen wheel wheelbarrows full of bricks up an inclined plane. Inclined planes are used in roads in steep mountain country, in ships' gangplanks, and in stairs.

An inclined plane has a *mechanical*

Inclined planes make it easier to lift objects. The worker uses one-third of the strength to roll the barrel up on the plane that he would have to use if he lifted it directly from the ground to the platform. He uses only one-third the strength because the plane (L) is three times as long as the height (H).

advantage. This advantage depends on the length of the board and on how much higher one end is than the other.

Suppose the board is 10 feet long and one end is raised 2 feet above the other. The mechanical advantage is 5; that is, 10 divided by 2. With such a plane, you would need only 20 pounds of force to raise a 100-pound weight from the lower end of the board to the higher end, because 100 (the weight) divided by 5 (the mechanical advantage) is 20. If you were to raise the 100-pound weight straight up from the ground, you would need a force of 100 pounds.

income tax

When a person pays a share of the money he earns as a tax, to help pay for the operation of the government, he is paying an income tax. Nearly every country and some states have income taxes. In the United States there has been an income tax since 1913, when the Constitution was changed by the 16th Amendment.

A person's income tax is based on the amount of money he receives in a year. The more he receives, the more tax he must pay; but also the person who receives more money must pay a bigger share, or percentage, of it than the person who does not receive so much. If a person does not make a great deal of money he may have to pay only about one dollar out of every five he earns, while a person who makes a great deal of money may have to pay $2.50 or more.

The income tax is based on a person's *net income*. He may receive a certain amount of money and not have to pay tax on it.

WHAT NET INCOME MEANS

Everyone needs a certain amount of money to live comfortably. The government does not tax anyone on that money, but anything over that amount is considered extra money and can be taxed. The government allows a certain amount, say $600, for each person that the head of a family has to support—himself, his wife, and each of his children. There are also certain deductions the head of a family can make from the money he earns before figuring out how much tax he must pay. These may be any business expenses he has to pay in order to make his money, any doctors' bills or other medical expenses over a certain amount, and money that he gives to his church or to charitable organizations.

Suppose a man makes $100 a week, and he has a wife and three children. His income for the year is $5,200. He spends a certain amount on doctors' bills and gifts to his church and to charity. He is buying his home and an automobile, and he can deduct the interest he pays on the money he borrowed to pay for them. He can deduct other taxes he has had to pay, such as a state income tax or sales tax. Suppose that these deductions add up to $500. If the allowance for himself and his family is $600 each, he subtracts $3,000 from his income of $5,200, leaving $2,200. Then he subtracts the $500 for other deductions, leaving $1,700 on which he must pay tax. This $1,700 is his net, or taxable, income.

WITHHOLDING TAX

For many years in the United States, each person paid his income tax in a lump sum at the end of the year. This was hard for many people, because they had to try to save enough through the year so they would have enough money to pay the tax all at once, and often they worried very much about it.

Then an economist, or financial expert, named Beardsley Ruml suggested that it would be easier if people could pay taxes on a "pay as you go" plan. Many ways of doing this were discussed, and finally a plan called the *withholding tax* was adopted, in 1943. Each week the employer takes a certain amount of each employee's pay, based on the number of people the employee has to support, and sends it to the government as a part of the employee's income tax. Then at the end of the year, the taxpayer figures out his tax just as he always did. Sometimes he finds that the withholding tax did not quite pay all of the tax he owed, and he has to send the government another payment. But sometimes the taxpayer finds that he has paid the government too much. In this case he sends in his tax return showing how he figures this, and the government checks his figures and sends him a refund to cover the overpayment.

TAX "BRACKETS"

The income tax is based on a percentage of the net income, or money that is left after the various deductions have been subtracted. Each $2,000 of income over a certain amount is taxed at a higher rate, and each extra $2,000 a person earns is said to put him into a higher tax bracket. For example, the tax law of 1954 provided that a person with a net income of $2,000 must pay a tax of 20%, or $400. If he had a net income of more than $2,000 but less than $4,000, he must pay $400 plus 22% of any amount over $2,000. To show how the percentage of tax rises as the net income goes up, suppose that the person had a net income of $9,000. He would have to pay $1,960 on the first $8,000 of his income, plus 34% of any amount over $8,000. In this that amount is $1,000, so his total tax would be $1,960 plus $340, or $2,-300. This goes up so high that a very, very rich person who makes a million dollars in a year finally has to pay as much as $9.10 on every $10. If he lives in a state where there is a state income tax, such as New York, his tax might take almost his entire income.

JOINT RETURN

Husbands and wives who both have some income are allowed to pay their taxes in one income-tax return. They may divide their income in half and each one pays the tax on one half of the total income. This usually puts them in a lower bracket and makes their tax smaller.

CORPORATE TAXES

A corporation is taxed in the same way that the individual taxpayer is, except that the rate of tax never goes quite so high. This is not favoritism to corporations. The reason is that the money the corporation makes is going to be given to the owners of the corporation, or stockholders, sooner or later and they will have to pay income tax on it, so that the government gets the same amount or even more.

In wartime there is usually an extra tax on corporations called an *excess profits tax*. The word *excess* means "too much." If a company makes a great deal more money than it does when the country is not at war, it has to pay a much higher tax, even up to 90 cents out of every dollar. This is done so that nobody can make a lot of money selling things to the government that it has to have to win the war, such as airplanes, guns, and tanks, or the materials with which to make them.

In Great Britain during World War II, the excess profits tax was 100%, which meant that no one could make any more money than he had made before the war began.

incubation

A newly born child is sometimes put in an incubator, which is a crib enclosed in glass. In the incubator the temperature is the same as the temperature within the mother's body where the child has been growing. This is called *incubation* and is an artificial way to keep babies alive. Ordinarily a baby should live in its mother's womb for nine months before it is born. If it is born too soon, it may die unless it is kept very warm and quiet and free from germs. The incubator has covered holes through which a nurse feeds and cleans the child. When the child has reached the stage in the incubator that it should have reached in its mother, it is taken out of the incubator and treated as any other newborn child.

Incubation is also used to hatch chickens. Incubation of eggs has been known since ancient times. The early Egyptians used to hatch millions of eggs each year by incubation. In order for eggs to hatch the mother hen sits, or broods, on them for a certain length of time to keep them warm. An incubator takes the place of the mother hen. Chicken incubators have large chambers with trays in them. The eggs are kept at an even temperature of about a hundred degrees. The chambers have plenty of air in them and enough moisture in the air so that the eggs will not dry out. The trays are made so that they can be turned, because the mother hen turns the eggs when she sits on them. Baby chicks may be kept in an incubator for a week after they are hatched.

The incubation period of a contagious, or catching, disease is the time between exposure to the disease and the time in which the first symptoms, or signs, of the disease appears. The incubation periods are different for different diseases.

Independence Day

Independence Day, or the Fourth of July, is celebrated as the day on which the United States declared itself an independent nation. This happened on July 4, 1776, and you can read about it in the article DECLARATION OF INDEPENDENCE. The Fourth of July is a legal holiday in every state. For many years the custom in the United States was to celebrate Independence Day by setting off fireworks. Usually people went on picnics, and there were parades, patriotic speeches, and band concerts. Some states have decided that fireworks are too dangerous, but families still have picnics and outings on July Fourth.

Independence Hall

Independence Hall is a building in Philadelphia. It was built in 1732, before the United States became an independent country, and was used as a statehouse by the colony of Pennsylvania. It is called Independence Hall because it was a meeting house for the leaders of the thirteen colonies before and during the Revolutionary War, and because the Declaration

of Independence was accepted there by delegates of the thirteen colonies. The Continental Congress also met there and chose George Washington to be Commander-in-Chief of the new United States Army. Independence Hall is a low, red-brick building with a white wooden tower in which hangs the Liberty Bell. You can read more about the LIBERTY BELL in a separate article. Independence Hall and the buildings around it were made a national park in 1948.

India

India is a large section, often called a subcontinent, in the south of Asia. India is also the name of the largest country on the Indian subcontinent.

A subcontinent is a part of a continent but is almost a continent in itself. India is called a subcontinent because it is so large, and also because it is separated, almost sealed off, from the rest of Asia by the Himalaya and other high mountain ranges that stretch along its boundaries. The subcontinent of India is about half as large as the United States, but it has almost three times as many people there. It includes more than 1,500,000 square miles of territory and has a population of about 600,000,000, mostly in the Republic of India.

For hundreds of years the subcontinent of India was considered one territory, but in 1947 it was divided into several different countries. Besides India, these are:

PAKISTAN, a large country in the northwest of the subcontinent. The majority of the people in Pakistan are Moslems, who follow the religion taught by Mohammed.

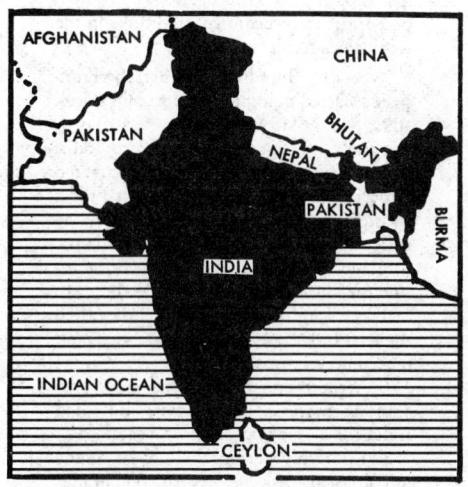

CEYLON, an island in the Indian Ocean, sixty miles off the southern tip of India. It is a fully independent nation in the British Commonwealth.

NEPAL, a small kingdom in the northern part of the subcontinent, along the southern slope of the Himalayas.

KASHMIR, or Jammu and Kashmir, in northern India, is claimed by both India and Pakistan and has been the subject of dispute since 1947. See KASHMIR.

BHUTAN, a semi-independent kingdom which is often considered part of India, and SIKKIM, a kingdom protected by India, are dealt with later in this article.

Government of India Information Service

The Taj Mahal, in Agra, was built in the 17th century by the Mogul emperor Shah Jahan as a tomb for his wife. (The Moguls were Mongolian Moslems who invaded India.)

THE REPUBLIC OF INDIA

The Republic of India includes five-sixths of the people and four-fifths of the territory of the subcontinent. It is the most densely populated big country in the world. Some of the world's richest people live in India, but millions simply are unable to obtain enough to eat; India has the world's finest palaces but also the world's worst slums.

THE PEOPLE WHO LIVE THERE

The people of India are of many races and religions. Most of the Indians are a mixture of two races, the Dravidians and the Aryans. The Dravidians are a dark-skinned people who have inhabited southern India since the beginning of history. The Aryans probably invaded India thousands of years ago and came from lands that lie west of India. The Aryans are light-skinned people with blue eyes, and they are related to most of the people living in Europe and America. In south India there are people that have Negroid features and whose ancestors came to India from Africa. In north India there are other people who have Mongoloid features and whose ancestors came to India from other parts of Asia.

More than two hundred different languages are spoken in India. Hindi, the language of most of the people, and English, the language of Indian businessmen, are the languages recognized by the central government of the Republic of India. Until 1966 twelve other languages were considered official for local use in states in which they are spoken by most of the people. After much rioting in 1965, Punjabi, the language of the Sikhs, was made a thirteenth official language in a new state created in northwest India. The thirteen languages are: Assamese, Bengali, Gujurati, Kannada, Kashmiri, Malayalam, Marathi, Oriya, Punjabi, Sanskrit, Tamil, Telugu, and Urdu. Many dialects of these languages, and other languages, especially of bordering countries, are also spoken.

The Hindu religion, which began in India, is very old. The Indian people belong to many different sects, or branches, of this religion. Buddhism, another great religion, was started in India, and there are many Buddhists in modern India. Members of other religions include Jainists, Parsee, and Sikhs. There are also some fifty million Moslems and ten mil-

lion Christians in the Indian Republic.

The crowded streets of the big cities present a picture of India in all its variety. Here Indians of all racial and religious backgrounds mingle. Some wear the long robes, called *saris,* which are the traditional clothes of India, while others wear modern Western dress such as is worn in cities of Europe and America. Some of the people may have very little clothing on, either because they are poor or because their religion teaches that clothing is not necessary. There are many beggars along the streets, too. Some of these are holy men called *sadhus,* to whom begging is a part of their religion. Others beg because they are poor and hungry. The very rich may wear costly jewels and yet be barefooted.

For hundreds of years many animals, especially cows, could be seen wandering freely about. The cow is a sacred, or holy, animal in the Hindu religion and is never destroyed. One of the things the new government has done is to get most of these animals off the streets.

HOW THE PEOPLE LIVE

Most of the people of India are farmers. Although India is a large country, there are so many people living there that often there is not enough food for all of them. The farmers have only recently begun to make use of modern machinery and methods of farming. Several of the Indian religions forbid the eating of meat.

Rice is grown in the great fertile plains south of the Himalaya Mountains. Other crops are cotton, wheat, flax, and jute.

India is receiving help from the United Nations and from independent nations in building railroads, roads, modern dams, and factories.

The Indian houses, even those belonging to the rich, are very simple and have little furniture in them. The people sit on the floor to eat. The food is placed in large shallow bowls and the Indians eat with their fingers, using only their right hands.

For hundreds of years the Indian people have followed the *caste system,* which is part of the Hindu religion. In the caste system people are divided into separate groups according to the families into which they were born. You can read more about the caste system in the article on HINDUISM. Members of the lowest caste were called "untouchables" and were not

allowed to live within the cities or to do anything except the most unpleasant work. The government has now made such things illegal, and the "untouchables" have equal rights with members of other castes.

Although there are several good universities in India, most of the Indian people have not gone to school at all. The government of India has now made it possible for Indian children to go to school until they are 14 years old.

WHAT KIND OF PLACE IT IS

India lies about the same distance north of the equator, the imaginary line that runs around the center of the earth, as North Africa or Central America. It is a large peninsula. A peninsula is land that is surrounded on three sides by water. The Arabian Sea is on the west, the Bay of Bengal on the east, and the Indian Ocean on the south. The northern part of India is bordered by the Himalaya Mountains, a chain of mountains that is more than 1,600 miles long.

There are four great divisions of land in India. The Himalayas in the north are the highest mountains in the world, and Mt. Everest, in the Himalayas, is the highest mountain peak in the world. It is 29,028 feet high. There are very few people living in this part of India, where there are forests on the lower slopes of the mountains and where there is always ice and snow on the highest peaks.

South of the mountains come the great central river valleys and fertile plains. Here most of the people of India live, and most of the important cities are found. Through this region flow the important rivers of India. These rivers all start in the Himalaya Mountains. The Ganges, the Indus, and the Brahmaputra are the most important rivers.

South of this is a high region, or plateau, called the *Deccan*. Much of it is thick forest. The fourth region is a narrow, sandy belt along the coasts.

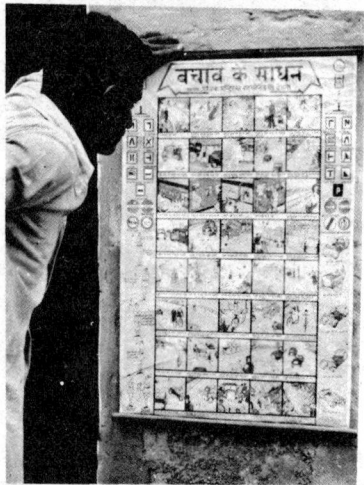

An adult learning to read by interpreting pictures.

The southern part of India, being close to the equator, has a tropical climate. In central and northern India it is cooler. Near the Himalayas there is sometimes frost, although the temperature seldom goes below freezing anywhere in India. The winds from the mountains make the plains region fairly cool even in summer.

India has three seasons. From October to March it is cool and dry. It begins to get hot in April; plants begin to wither and all the greenery dries up. India gets rain only three months each year; the rain comes in June and is called the *monsoon*. In some parts of India the monsoon rains are only showers; in other parts the water falls in torrents. If the rains come late or if they are not as heavy as usual, the farmers are not able to grow enough food. Then there is a famine in India, and many of the people starve. For many years India had a famine about once every ten years.

There are many minerals in India, including large deposits of iron and coal. Gold, manganese, copper, and asbestos are also found there. Many different trees grow in the forests. Many spices are grown in India; it was for these spices that Europeans first came to India.

CHIEF CITIES OF INDIA

There are many large cities in India. Benares is the holy city of the Hindus. It is on the banks of the Ganges, the Hindus' holy river. Each year millions of pilgrims go to Benares to worship. Some go there to die, so that their bodies may be burned along the banks of the Ganges and their ashes thrown into its sacred waters. Benares is more than 2,500 years old. There are 637,612 people living there.

Some other leading cities, with populations from the 1973 estimates are:

New Delhi, population 324,285, the capital of the republic of India.

Delhi, population 3,630,000, near New Delhi, and the former capital of India.

Bombay, population 5,700,358, an important seaport.

Calcutta, population 3,200,000 (with suburbs 8,200,000), also an important seaport.

Madras, population 2,086,036, fourth-largest city in India, known for its large artificial harbor.

There is a separate article about each of these cities.

HOW THE PEOPLE ARE GOVERNED

The constitution of India provides for a government much like the parliamentarian democracies of Europe. There is a president elected for a five-year term by the members of the parliament, or lawmaking body. The most important men in the government are the prime minister and his cabinet. The parliament is in two parts called the House of the People and the Council of State. The members of the House of the People are elected by the people; the members of the Council of State are appointed by the States. There are several political parties.

Before India became an independent country it was broken up into more than five hundred states headed by Indian princes, who acknowledged the British sovereign as emperor (or empress) of India. In 1947 Great Britain granted India its freedom, and after India became an independent country the princely states united to form the states (now sixteen) and territories (now eight) that make up the republic today.

The Indians had to work for many years to win their freedom. Their leader in the struggle was the Mahatma Gandhi,

a great religious leader. Jawaharlal Nehru, the first prime minister, was a follower of Gandhi.

INDIA IN THE PAST

There was a great civilization in India more than five thousand years ago. Scientists do not know exactly when it existed or for how long, nor do they know why it disappeared. They found out about it in 1925 when some workmen digging a road in the Indus valley discovered bits of pottery that were very old. Archaeologists, scientists who study ancient peoples, carefully dug in the same region and uncovered the ruins of a city called Mohenjo-daro. The streets were wide and straight and ran north and south, east and west, as do the streets in many modern cities. The houses were well built and several stories high. There were even bathrooms and a very advanced system of drainage. Fine jewelry was discovered in Mohenjo-daro, and even a piece of cotton cloth.

Many years later the Aryans came to India. They settled down and became merchants or farmers or workers. The early Aryans wrote the first books of the great Indian religious literature, which are called the Vedas. There are separate articles on HINDUISM and VEDANTA. The Aryans started both the Hindu and the Buddhist religions.

Many different peoples invaded India during its long history. First came the Persians, and then the Greeks led by Alexander the Great. About a thousand years ago the Moslems invaded India. They tried to persuade the Indians to change religions by burning the Hindu temples and killing the people. Gradually, they came to live peacefully with the Hindus.

Several hundred years later the Moguls invaded India, and they ruled there for more than two hundred years. One of the Mogul rulers built the Taj Mahal, one of the most beautiful buildings in the world, as a tomb for his wife.

About five hundred years ago the Europeans started going to India to buy spices, silks, and gold. Marco Polo was one of the early merchants who went to India. When Christopher Columbus discovered America he was really trying to find a shorter route to India; that is why he called the American natives "Indians." England, France and Portugal became influential in India through trade there. In 1612 an English trading company called the East India Company was founded, and it became very powerful. From 1746 until 1763 Britain and France fought for possessions in India. Britain won and ruled India for about two hundred years.

During this period there were many uprisings against the British, but gradually the Indian princes came to support British rule.

In 1915, during World War I, Mohandas Gandhi became the leader of the movement that finally led to Indian independence. Gandhi was killed by an assassin in 1948, shortly after India became independent. His successor, Jawaharlal Nehru, was prime minister from 1947 until his death in 1964. Then Lal Bahadur Shastri was prime minister until he died in 1966, immediately after settling a conflict with Pakistan over Kashmir. Nehru's daughter, Indira Gandhi, was made prime minister in 1966.

This lacy-looking screen inside the Taj Mahal is made of carved marble. The flowers surrounding the arched doorway and on the pedestal inside are made of thinly-sliced jewels embedded in marble.

When India and Pakistan became separate countries in 1947, most of the Moslems in India wanted to move to Pakistan and non-Moslems in Pakistan wanted to move to India. In the biggest movement of peoples in history, more than twelve million persons set out at about the same time. The two groups were unfriendly, and on the way they met, fought, and massacred one another. Hundreds of thousands died on their way to new homes.

The governments of India and Pakistan have never been far from a state of open warfare. Efforts by the United Nations to prevent fighting have been only partly successful. In 1956 India annexed Kashmir, defying the U.N. and also Pakistan, and in 1965 India and Pakistan had a brief war (see KASHMIR); Premier Kosygin of the Soviet Union arbitrated and succeeded in stopping the fighting but did not end the dispute. In 1961, India again defied the U.N. by invading and annexing the Portuguese enclaves (territories inside India) of Goa, Damão, and Diu. India's policy for years was to receive aid from both the United States and the Communist countries, but in 1962 Communist China occupied 12,500 square miles in the Ladakh area, on the India-China border but claimed by India and this ended the friendship between India and China. In a few cases Indian and Chinese troops fired at one another but not enough to start a war.

In 1971, India invaded East Pakistan and helped the people of that area free themselves from the rule of West Pakistan.

INDIA. Area, 1,221,880 square miles. Population (1973 estimate) 547,900,000. Language, Hindi (official), more than a dozen other main languages. Religion, mostly Hindu. Government, republic; member of British Commonwealth. Monetary unit, rupee, worth 21 cents (U.S.). Flag, wide saffron, white, and dark green horizontal stripes; wheel with 24 spokes (wheel of Asoka) in the white stripe.

SIKKIM

Sikkim, a tiny kingdom in the eastern Himalaya mountains, is surrounded by Nepal, Bhutan, Tibet, and India. It became a protectorate of India in 1950; until 1947 it was under British rule. In area, Sikkim is only 2,818 square miles, a little larger than Delaware. About 194,-000 people live there. The country is very mountainous. The people are chiefly farmers who grow corn, rice, and wheat. Buddhism is the official state religion but most of the people are Hindus. The capital is Gangtok, a city of about 10,000. In 1963 the rajah of Sikkim, Thondup Namgyal, married an American girl, Hope Cooke.

Indian

The Indians were the people who were living in America at the time that Columbus discovered the new continent. They were living not only in North America but also in Central and South America and on the islands near both continents and they had been doing so for thousands of years before Columbus arrived. When Columbus set forth from Spain in 1492, he was looking for a new, short route by water to India. When he reached land he thought he had come to a part of India, so he called the people he met Indians. Although Europeans soon realized that what Columbus had discovered was not a part of India at all, but a new world, they continued to call the natives Indians.

WHERE THE INDIANS CAME FROM

The question of how the Indians reached America and where they came from has long been a puzzle, but scientists who have studied the American Indian believe that he came from Asia. The Bering Strait, which connects the tips of Siberia and Alaska, is only about fifty miles wide. For many thousands of years this was dry land. The Indians passed over the dry land, and later over the water, which was frozen to solid ice in the winter. They spread out over all of North America, Central America, and South America. They did not come all at once, but probably came in several waves over a period of many years.

Scientists believe that one of the original homes of the Indians was the Gobi Desert, in northwestern China, close to the southern border of Siberia. In this desert explorers have found chipped stone arrow points and stone knives very much like the arrow points and knives that have been found in Alaska and places in North America farther to the south. Other origins may have been near Lake Baikal in Siberia, and in northern Siberia along the Arctic coast and elsewhere. These discoveries have led scientists to feel that the Indians crossed over into Alaska and then traveled southward through what is now the United States and down into Central and South America. Of course, many groups of Indians stopped off at places along the way and made their homes there.

Another reason why scientists believe that the Indians came from Asia is that they somewhat resemble the Mongols, the people who live in northeastern Asia. The Indian's skin ranges in color from yellow to red, the color of a copper penny. He has coarse, straight black hair and brown, almond-shaped eyes. Usually he is about the same height as the white man.

HOW THE INDIANS LIVED

The Indians of what is now the United States and Canada settled in six broad regions of these countries. The way of life of a people is called their *culture,* and we call a region a *culture area.* There were six great culture areas. The so-called Eastern Woodlands stretched all the way from the Atlantic coast to the Mississippi Valley. There was plenty of game here, such as deer and rabbits and other small animals, and the Indian man spent most of his time hunting. He was an expert hunter and got most of his game with the bow and arrow. Until the white man came, he had no metal, so arrowheads were made of stone. He also carried a stone knife. His only other weapon was a tomahawk, which was a hatchet with a stone head. The Eastern Woodlands were also very good for growing things, and while the Indian man was away hunting, the Indian woman took care of the crops, mostly corn, beans, and squash. The Indians had no plows, but used a stick to cultivate the ground. The corn and beans were carefully dried and stored away, for in the winter, when animals were scarce, they were the only foods that stood between the Indian and starvation. Some of the tribes and peoples in the Eastern Woodlands were the Algonquin, Iroquois, Chippewa, Cherokee, Choctaw, Creek, Ojibway, Mohegan, Sauk, Fox, Micmac, and Seminole. You can read more about the ALGONQUIN, CREEKS and IROQUOIS in separate articles.

THE PLAINS INDIANS

To the west of the Eastern Woodlands

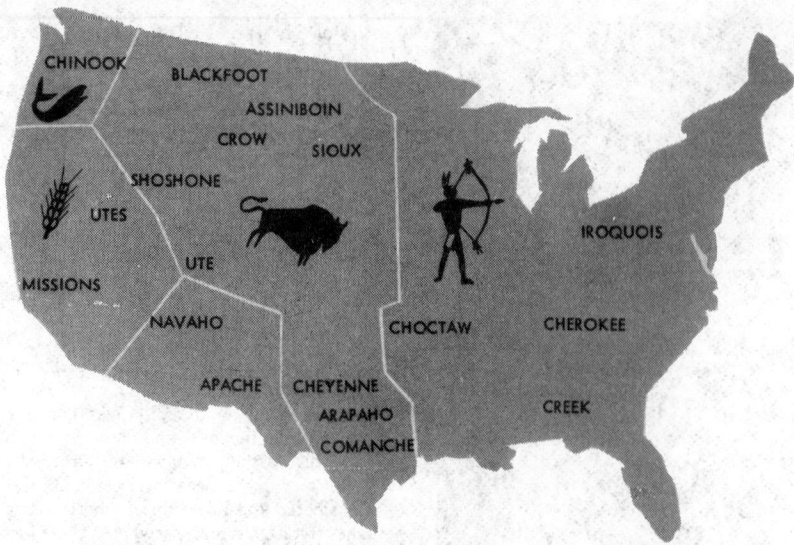

The map shows, looking from east to west, the areas of the United States occupied by the Indians of the Eastern Woodlands, the Plains Indians, the Desert or Pueblo Indians of the Southwest, the California Indians, and the Northwest Coast Indians.

were the great flatlands of North America, and the Indians who lived here are known as the Plains Indians. Before the arrival of the horse, the people farmed the valleys and hunted. When the Spanish introduced the horse, farming became less important and the chief occupation became hunting. The principal animal hunted was the great buffalo, or bison, which roamed the plains in great herds.

The buffalo's flesh was used for food, its horns were made into spoons and small containers, its ribs were made into knives, its hair was twisted into ropes and cords, its tendons were used for thread, and its skin was used for clothing and coverings for the Indians' tents.

Some of the tribes who lived in the Plains area were the Sioux, Assiniboin, Arapaho, Blackfoot, Cheyenne, Comanche, Crow, Ute, Apache, and Shoshone.

The third great culture area was the Southwest. This was a rather dry region, where little rain fell. Nevertheless the Indians managed to raise corn, beans, squash, and cotton. They also tended great herds of sheep after the Spanish settlers had arrived. Some of the tribes who lived there were the Apache and Navajo, the Hopi, the Zuni, the Pima, and the Papago- and Yuman-speaking tribes.

West of the Rocky Mountains, extending to the Pacific Ocean, was the California area, which included not only present-day California but also Nevada and Utah. This region too was very dry and not suited for farming, but there were enough nuts and fruits growing wild to support the Indians who lived there. They also got food from the small animals, like the rabbit, that lived on the land. The California Indians included the Missions, the Utes, the Paiutes, the Tulares, and others.

North of this region was the fifth culture area, which lay along the Pacific coast. The Northwest Coast Indians, as they are called, were mostly fishermen who found the waters of the ocean and of fast streams filled with salmon and halibut. Some of the Northwest Coast Indians were the Tlingit, the Chinook, the Haida, the Kwakiutl, the Bellacoola, and the Athapascan.

There was still another group of Indians, who lived in cold regions of northern Canada and Alaska. These were the Eskimos. While the Eskimos are true Indians, their way of life was so different from that of the other Indians that we usually do not include them in a discussion of the American Indian. There is a separate article on the ESKIMO.

AZTECS, MAYAS, INCAS

Large numbers of Indians also settled in Central and South America, and the chief peoples in these lands were the Aztecs of Mexico, the Mayas of Yucatan and Guatemala, and the Incas of Peru. They were much more advanced than the North American Indians and built great civilizations that died when the Spanish conquered them. You can read more about them in separate articles on AZTEC, INCAS, and MAYAS.

The clothing the Indians wore varied with the different parts of the country they lived in. It was almost always made of animal skins, except in the Southwest, where cotton clothes were worn as they were in Mexico and Peru. During the warm months they wore little clothing, usually only a breechclout around the loins. When it became cold, they added leggings and a leather robe. The Indian woman wore a skirt, a long jacket, and a robe when it was cold. Both men and women liked to wear a band of leather around the head, into which they sometimes stuck feathers. The big feathered headdress was worn only by the Sioux tribe of the western plains.

The Indian man of the east shaved his head, leaving only a ridge of hair from front to back. He dressed his hair with bear fat and mixed soot into it to make it look darker than it was. Like the women of today, the Indian woman had beauty aids to improve her appearance. She used fish oil or eagle fat to soften her skin and even mixed red color into the fat to make her cheeks look pink. Both men and women often painted pictures of birds and animals on their bodies.

WIGWAMS AND TEEPEES

Indians lived in many different kinds of shelters. The eastern Indians lived in a *wigwam,* which was a framework of poles bent into the shape of a dome and covered with tree bark in the summer and cattail stalks in the winters. Fires were built in the middle of the earth floor and a small hole in the roof allowed the smoke to escape. The Indians of the plains, who used to travel about a good deal, used a shelter that could be put up quickly. This was a *teepee,* which was made of three slanted poles tied together at the top and covered with buffalo skins. Some Indians of the Southwest had houses, called *pueblos,* somewhat like modern apartment houses. They were made of mud and stone.

For some reason, the Indians never discovered or invented the wheel, which has made it so easy to carry goods. The Indian therefore had to depend on other means of transportation. Where there were many streams and rivers, he used canoes. He made the canoe by digging out a large log or by building a frame of wood and covering it with birchbark. In traveling over land, the Plains Indians used a device called a *travois.* This consisted of two poles lashed to a dog, with a net spread at the wide end to hold goods. When the Indians learned to use the horse from the white man the horse replaced the dog to drag the travois, and the Indians also became expert in riding the horse bareback.

Although we speak of the Indians as being a primitive people, they were highly skilled at making many objects. They made beautiful and useful jars and pots out of clay. Some tribes of Indians wove baskets that were so expertly made that they could even hold water. If you visit the Southwest today you will see Indians stil making beautiful rugs, jewelry, pottery, and baskets.

THE INDIAN POWWOW

Each tribe had a chief, usually an outstanding warrior and hunter. Most often he was appointed by a council of the tribe, but sometimes the position was handed down from father to son. The council, usually made up of older men, really ruled the tribe, since they made the decisions that the chief was expected to enforce, or carry out. When the tribe was faced by a serious problem, a meeting was called that all men of the tribe attended. This was called a *powwow.* At the powwow, which is a word we use now in English to mean a meeting, a fire was lighted and everybody sat around it. Food was served, prayers were offered, sacred songs were sung, and there was much dancing and beating of drums. Between the dancing, singing, and praying, there were discussions of the problem. All of this might go on for many days, until a decision was reached.

All of the Indians were religious people, but their religion was quite different from ours. They believed in a great spirit who ruled the world that was called Manitou or Manibozo by some of the tribes. But they also believed that there were spirits in the things of nature—the trees, the rocks, the sun, and the winds. Many of the tribes had a favorite animal that they thought was a protective spirit for them, and the tribe adopted it as a sort of mascot.

This animal was called a *totem* and the Indians used to draw pictures of their totem animals as a way of bringing good luck. Some tribes also, particularly in the Northwest, used to carve images of the totem animal on poles that are called *totem poles*.

GOOD AND EVIL SPIRITS

The Indians believed that disease and weather were controlled by the spirits. When a person fell ill or when there was no rain for the crops they thought that evil spirits were the cause. They had a medicine man who used to lead the tribe in ceremonies to drive away these evil spirits. Almost all of the Indians' dances and music were religious, intended to drive away evil spirits or bring good spirits.

The Indians of North and South America spoke many different languages, and the tribes of one section could not understand the Indians of other sections, even though they might live fairly near. In North America there were about 56 languages. The Indians had no written language.

When tribes that could not understand

Santa Fe Railway Photos

The Pueblo Indians of Jemez, New Mexico, are famous dancers. Their dramatic dances, which are actually religious rituals, are much the same today as they were before the coming of the white men about four centuries ago.
1. A drummer in festival dress performs at the ceremonies that mark the opening of a pow-wow.
2. Eagle dancers seem actually to become giant birds swooping down on their prey.
3. Only a man gifted with perfect coordination can perform the fascinating Hoop Dance.

each other met they used finger signs to "talk" to one another. Or, if they had to communicate over long distances, they used smoke signals.

THE INDIAN AND THE WHITE MAN

Great changes began to take place in the lives of the Indians of North and South America when the white man came in the 16th century. The English and other colonists from northern Europe were interested mainly in making new homes for themselves, so they pushed the Indians off their lands and made them into farms and cities. It is no wonder that the Indians did not like this and often fought back fiercely. The Spanish, who came to the lands in the south, were mainly interested at first in getting great wealth out of the New World, so they enslaved many Indians or simply killed them when they stood in their way. But the Spanish, who did not bring their families with them, intermarried with the Indians, and today there are many people in Mexico and other countries of Latin America who are known as *mestizos,* or people of Spanish and Indian descent.

As the Indians were pushed farther and farther west, many of them died in the wars with the settlers. But many more also died because of the new diseases that the white man brought, since the Indians were not immune, or protected, against these diseases.

By 1840 almost all of the country east of the Mississippi had been taken from the Indians, but the land west of the great river was recognized as rightfully belonging to the Indian. However, with the discovery of gold in California in 1849, settlers began to pour across this western

territory. From 1851 to 1880 the bloodiest battles with the Indians took place, as the Indians tried, without success, to resist the white settlers.

Meanwhile, as more and more Indians gave in to the march of the settlers, they gave up their rights to large areas of land and agreed to live on much smaller territories. These smaller lands are called *reservations*. The reservations were set up by treaties, or agreements, between the Indians and the United States government. But even these reservations were made smaller in time as new treaties were written that allowed individual Indians to sell their shares of land for money, which they often needed to keep from starving. By the end of the 19th century the lands that remained to the Indian were only a very tiny portion of what had once belonged to him, and much of this land was very poor and could not be farmed or used for grazing cattle.

THE INDIAN TODAY

The fortunes of the Indians in the United States have improved greatly in recent years. Just a few generations ago it was thought that the Indians might die out as a people, but today their number is actually increasing. There are about half a million Indians in North America and it is believed that if they continue to increase at the present rate, by about 1980 there will be as many as there were at the time of Columbus.

Many Indians in the United States live on the hundred reservations where they may keep up their tribal life and customs if they wish. The Federal government runs schools on the reservations which the Indian children attend and the government also helps the Indians to improve their soil and use new and better ways of farming. But the Indians are not forced to remain on the reservations and many have left the lands of their ancestors and have gone into the cities or ranches to earn their living just as white men do. Those Indians who still live on the reservations have to abide by the laws of the tribe, which are recognized by the government and which are enforced by leaders of the tribes. There are still Indians on the reservations who speak nothing but Indian languages.

Indians are citizens of the United States. They may vote and hold office and are required to pay taxes, as all citizens are. In both World War I and World War II many Indians were drafted into the armed forces and served with distinction. Many others left the reservations to work in war plants, and after the wars some of them stayed on in the cities.

Many well-known Americans have been Indians or part Indian. The great humorist Will Rogers, and Charles Curtis, who was a Vice President of the United States, were part Indian. Jim Thorpe, who has been called one of America's greatest athletes, was a full-blooded Indian. Maria Tallchief, a leading ballet dancer, is of Indian birth.

Indiana

Indiana is a state in the great midwestern plain of the United States. It lies

directly in the path of the large flow of traffic across the country, and it is said that three-quarters of all motor cars driving east or west use one of the highways passing through Indianapolis. Indiana is nicknamed "the Hoosier State." There are several stories that tell how the state received this name. The most familiar story tells how the early settlers in Indiana had great curiosity and whenever they passed a house they would shout "Who's here?" —which sounded like "Hoosier." No one knows what the true story is.

Indiana means "land of the Indians," and was called that because of the many Indian tribes who went there to live after they were driven from their lands farther east.

Indiana ranks 38th in size among the states, with 36,291 square miles. In population it ranks 11th, with over 5 million people living there. It became a state in 1816, and was the 19th state admitted to the United States. The capital is Indianapolis.

THE PEOPLE OF INDIANA

Many of the people of Indiana are farmers on the fertile prairie. They raise more corn than any other state except Iowa and Illinois, and more tomatoes than any other state except California. They also raise valuable crops of fruits and vegetables and thousands of hogs and cattle.

Two thirds of the people of Indiana now live in the important industrial cities all over the state. They work in the great iron and steel mills, in automobile plants, and in other factories where they make articles such as furniture, refrigerators, and medicines. Many people also work in the state's quarries, which supply more than three-quarters of the limestone (used for buildings) in the United States. Still others work in the rich coal mines and oil fields. There is a large shipping industry in the lake cities.

The early settlers of Indiana were pioneers from New England and the South. They cut down the forests to build their cabins and cleared the land for farming.

Then, as the state grew, immigrants from Germany and Ireland came to work on the farms and in the expanding cities. Later many people from Yugoslavia, Czechoslovakia, Poland, and Hungary came to work in the factories and mills. These families have lived so long in the state that today most of the people of Indiana are American-born.

The Methodists have the largest church membership in Indiana. Other important churches are the Roman Catholic, Baptist, and Lutheran.

WHAT INDIANA IS LIKE

If you travel through Indiana, you will notice that, though it is generally flat like other Midwestern states, it differs in some parts. In the north are marshes and many lakes. The farmers cannot grow anything in the marshes except mint, which is used in large quantities to flavor chewing gum. Along Lake Michigan, in the northwest, are sand dunes and beaches, where many people spend their vacations. This section is also one of the most important steel centers in the United States. It is called the Calumet area. Such cities as Gary and

Indianapolis Chamber of Commerce

There are many beautiful buildings in Indiana. One of them is the state capitol building, which was built of Indiana limestone almost seventy years ago. The inset in the upper left shows the peony, which is the Indiana state flower.

East Chicago sprang up there because the Great Lakes ships could bring iron ore to them from the mines in Minnesota. Today, Gary has the largest steel plant in the world and Indiana ranks among the leading iron and steel states. If you visit the nearby city of Whiting, you will also see one of the largest oil refineries in the world.

Another interesting city in the northern part of the state is South Bend, where automobiles are made. One of America's great colleges, the University of Notre Dame, is in South Bend. This university has always been famous for its football teams.

The central part of Indiana is a level plain, smooth as a table for many miles. It is broken only by some river valleys and occasional low ridges. In this section the farmers grow large crops and raise cattle.

The Wabash River winds slowly through this part of Indiana. It is a broad, lazy river and has become famous through the song "On the Banks of the Wabash," written by Paul Dresser, who was born in the state.

The southern part of Indiana has beautiful scenery, with deep valleys, sharp ridges, and rounded hills. Here are the great limestone quarries and coal mines, as well as mineral springs and interesting caverns. Farmers raise tobacco and grain in the fertile land along the Ohio River.

The climate of Indiana is generally warmer in the southern part than in the northern part. The state sometimes has severe winters when the temperature goes down below zero. In the summer there are many hot days when the temperature goes up to 100 degrees. The average temperature in summer is 76 degrees, and in winter 29 degrees. Though the crops in some years get a great deal of heavy rain, there are years when there are droughts, especially in the southern hills, and then the crops suffer.

Railroads and highways reach all parts of the state. Indianapolis is one of the great railroad centers in the country. There are airports in all the important cities.

GOVERNMENT OF INDIANA

Indiana, like most other states, is governed by a governor and a legislature. The governor is elected for a four-year term. The legislature is composed of two houses, a Senate, whose members are elected for a four-year term, and a House of Representatives, whose members are elected for a two-year term. Judges are elected for a six-year term. The capital is Indianapolis. There are 92 counties in the state.

Everyone has to go to school between the ages of 7 and 16. Indiana has always been a leader in education. It had one of the first kindergartens, and it had the first classes where boys and girls were taught together. There are many colleges, universities, and other schools of higher learning. Among the principal colleges and universities are:

Indiana University, at Bloomington. Enrollment, 50,704 in 1971 (co-ed).

Purdue University, at Lafayette. Enrollment, 37,341 in 1971 (co-ed).

University of Notre Dame, at Notre Dame. Enrollment, 7,659 in 1971 (men only).

Indiana State College, at Terre Haute. Enrollment, 13,311 in 1971 (co-ed).

Ball State Teachers College, at Muncie. Enrollment, 14,446 in 1971 (co-ed).

De Pauw University, at Greencastle. Enrollment, 2,353 in 1971 (co-ed).

Butler University, at Indianapolis. Enrollment, 4,184 in 1971 (co-ed).

Valparaiso University, at Valparaiso. Enrollment, 4,281 in 1971 (co-ed).

CHIEF CITIES OF INDIANA

The leading cities of Indiana, with populations from the 1970 census, are:

Indianapolis, population 744,624, state capital and largest city. There is a separate article about INDIANAPOLIS.

Gary, population 175,415, second-largest city in the state, important steel center, in the northern part of the state. There is a separate article about GARY.

Fort Wayne, population 177,671, railroad and manufacturing center, in the northern part of the state. There is a separate article about FORT WAYNE.

Evansville, population 138,764, manufacturing center, in the southwestern part of the state.

INDIANA IN THE PAST

The first white men who entered the region of Indiana, more than 280 years ago, were French explorers and missionaries from Canada. They hoped to convert the Indians to Christianity. They were followed by fur traders, who gave the Indians trinkets and blankets in exchange for the furs. The first permanent settlement was made by the French at Vincennes, in 1732.

The English also came to this region, hoping to profit from the fur trade. France and England struggled for this part of the country until after the French and Indian Wars, when England gained control.

After the Revolutionary War, the United States controlled a large section known as the Northwest Territory, which included Indiana. People began coming from the East and the South to build homes and start farms; but the Indians became alarmed at this sudden arrival of so many settlers, and they attacked the pioneers again and again, hoping to drive them out. Finally General Anthony Wayne was sent by President Washington to crush the Indians. In 1795, after bitter fighting, he succeeded, and the Indians promised to stop their attacks.

In 1800, the Indiana Territory was formed. It was much larger than the state is now. It also included Illinois, Wisconsin, and Michigan. By 1809 Michigan and Illinois were made into separate territories, and Indiana became its present size.

Indiana became a state in 1816, and its population increased rapidly. Men, women and children went there on foot, on horseback, and in huge, creaking wagons drawn by ox teams or horses. For a long time they were forced to make most of the things they needed themselves, because transportation was so expensive. As roads and canals were built, the people prospered more. Log cabins disappeared, and brick or white frame houses were built. Clothes were imported from the East instead of being homemade. After the building of the railroads, the state grew even more quickly.

In the Civil War Indiana was on the side of the Union, but many of its people were sympathetic to the Confederates and formed a secret organization called the

U. of Notre Dame

Notre Dame is the school of the "fighting Irish." A statue of the Virgin Mary looks down over the campus from the golden dome of the administration building.

Knights of the Golden Circle, which was finally broken up when the government arrested the leaders. After the war the people were poor for some time, but then they began to prosper once again. The cities grew so rapidly that sometimes people moved into houses before they were finished. Stories are told of how workmen, going home along a dark path, would walk into a new house or toolshed that had not been there in the morning. More and more people left the farms and settled in these growing cities, and Indiana became a prosperous industrial state.

PLACES TO SEE IN INDIANA

Brown County State Park, 17,678 acres, in the central part of Indiana, south of Nashville, on State Highway 46. One of the most beautiful of the state parks; an 80-foot observation tower has a view of six counties; camping, swimming, hiking, and horseback-riding.

Spring Mill Village, a restored pioneer settlement, dating back to 1814, located in Spring Mill State Park, three miles east of Mitchell.

John Herron Art Institute in Indianapolis, where over 11,000 objects of art from ancient to modern times are shown in a museum.

Mesker Zoo, in Evansville, in the southwest, on U.S. Route 41. One of the most modern zoos in the United States; cages and bars have been done away with wherever possible, and the animals are kept in their quarters by wide, deep trenches.

Indianapolis Motor Speedway, in Indianapolis, in central Indiana, on U.S. Routes 52, 36, 40.

Santa Claus, tiny town in the south, 13 miles north of Tell City, south of U.S. Route 460. Has only 60 people living there; tons of mail are sent to the post office at Christmas time to be remailed with the Santa Claus postmark. The town has a huge statue of Santa Claus and a toy village where manufacturers display their products during the Christmas season.

Wyandotte Cave, in the south, 8 miles west of Corydon, on U.S. Route 460. One of the most wonderful caves in the world; 22 miles long; one of the rooms is large enough to set a church into it, steeple and all. Another room, called the White Cloud Room, has walls and ceilings covered with snow-white crystals.

INDIANA. Area, 36,291 square miles. Population (1970 census) 5,193,669. Capital, Indianapolis. Nickname, the Hoosier State. Motto, "the Crossroads of America." Flower, peony. Tree, tulip. Bird, cardinal. Song, "On the Banks of the Wabash." Admitted to Union, December 11, 1816. Official abbreviation, Ind.

Indianapolis

Indianapolis is the capital and largest city of Indiana. With a population of 744,000, it is one of the largest cities in the world that cannot be reached by water. However, Indianapolis is a crossroads through which many railroads, highways, bus lines and airlines pass. There are many factories where the people manufacture trucks, farm equipment, chemicals, and electrical appliances. Indianapolis has a very fine public-school system and an excellent public library. Butler University, and the law and medical schools of Indiana University, are in the city. Nearby is the Indianapolis Speedway, where the nation's most famous automobile race is held each Memorial Day (May 30).

If you visited Indianapolis you would be able to find your way around easily because most of the streets criss-cross like a checkerboard. In the center of the city, called the Circle, stands the impressive Soldiers' and Sailors' Monument, 285 feet high. Nearby is the state capitol. This has a high dome, and like many other buildings in Indianapolis is made of Indiana limestone.

Indianapolis was settled in 1821. It was made the state capital in 1825, although the capitol building was not finished for another ten years. The city has grown steadily in size. Because it has such excellent transportation, it gets coal from its neighboring eastern states and raw materials from its western neighbors. This situation is favorable to the growth of industry.

INDIANAPOLIS. INDIANA. Population (1970 census) 744,624. Capital of Indiana. Founded in 1821. Site of Butler University and Indianapolis Motor Speedway.

Indian Ocean

The Indian Ocean is the third-largest ocean in the world. It covers about 27,500,000 square miles. The largest are the Pacific and Atlantic Oceans.

The Indian Ocean lies south of Asia, east of Africa, and west of Australia. It forms one of the oldest trade routes in the world. Ships sailed across the Indian Ocean from Arabia to Hindustan (India) more than two thousand years ago.

In the Indian Ocean are thousands of islands. Most of them are very small, and are either coral reefs or of volcanic origin. Madagascar and Ceylon are the only two large islands in the Indian Ocean.

Most of the waters of the Indian Ocean are warmer than those of other oceans. This is because the equator crosses the ocean. In the northern part, the surface water temperature is usually about 80 degrees. There is a cold underwater current that comes from the Antarctic and cools the water in the southern part of the ocean to about 40 degrees.

The ocean has many currents, made by the winds that blow across it. The

monsoons of the northern section cause currents that change their direction twice a year. (There is a separate article about MONSOONS.) The northeast monsoon creates a northeast current, and the southwest monsoon creates a southwest current. Winds over the Indian Ocean are usually gentle, and there are often long periods of complete calm. Once in a while there is a hurricane.

The floor or bottom of the Indian Ocean has been well charted. The water near Java, in the northeast section of the ocean, is about 20,000 feet deep. This is the deepest section of the Indian Ocean. There is a huge basin, about 50,000 square miles in area, near the northwest shore of Australia. It has an average depth of 19,000 feet. An underwater ridge runs from east to west, slightly south of Australia, and here the average depth is only 12,000 feet.

Indian paintbrush

Indian paintbrush is a wild flower that is native to the New World. There are about 35 species of the plant found in North America. Indian paintbrush comes up each summer in the fields. The common eastern variety has orange and red flowers, but in the west the flowers can be of many different colors. It grows about two feet high. Indian paintbrush is a parasitic plant, which means that its roots feed on the roots of other plants.

Indian summer

Indian summer is the name given to a time of mild and lovely weather that comes in late October or early November. The days get warm again, and the sky is cloudless and blue. There is usually some haze in the air. Indian summer may last a few days or a few weeks, and in some years it does not come at all. No one is quite sure where the names comes from, but some people think that early settlers in North America thought that the haze in the air was smoke rising from the Indian camps on the prairies.

Indian Territory

Indian Territory was various western lands of the United States that were set aside for Indians to live in. Most of what is now the state of Oklahoma was once called Indian Territory. It was set aside in the early 1800s for the Five Civilized Tribes (the Choctaw, Creek, Seminole, Chickasaw, and Cherokee). Later, other tribes were allowed to settle in this region. From around 1840 to 1907 Indian Territory was governed by the tribes themselves. In 1890 the western half had become settled by whites and it was separated from the eastern half and called Oklahoma Territory. In 1907 the territories joined again to become the state of Oklahoma.

indigestion

Indigestion is an illness caused by the failure of some part of your body to work properly in digesting the food you have eaten. Indigestion often causes a headache and a steady, dull pain in the stomach. The pain may also be a sharp pain that comes every once in while. You may feel as if you had eaten too much, or you may feel very hungry. You may also feel sick to your stomach and dizzy. Indigestion is often caused by eating too much food too fast without chewing it properly. The digestive system cannot work fast enough to take care of all the food. You can usually avoid indigestion if you eat easily digested food slowly, taking care to chew it well. Indigestion may be a sign of more serious trouble, and, if you are bothered by it often, you should see a doctor. Indigestion may also be caused by nervousness, anger, or some other strong feeling.

indigo

Indigo is a small tree or shrub that is found in tropical regions. Several species, or kinds, grow in the southern United States. Indigo is important chiefly because it contains a substance, indogin, from which indigo dye is made. Indigo dye has been used for coloring fabrics for thousands of years. It has a beautiful blue color. The dyestuff has to be extracted from the plant. The plant is cut down just before it blossoms. It is placed in a container, where it is soaked in water and allowed to ferment for about twelve hours. A clear substance known as indigo white rises from the plant and mixes with water. When the water containing this substance is exposed to the air and shaken thoroughly, the indigo white becomes a substance called indigo blue, which will not mix with the liquid. It floats on the surface of the liquid for a time and then settles to the bottom like mud. The clear liquid is drawn off, and the indigo blue is collected and dried for use as a dye. About two hundred years ago the production of indigo dye was an important industry in South Carolina, and for hundreds of years before that it was important in Europe. Most indigo blue dye is now made synthetically (artificially).

Indo-China, see FRENCH INDO-CHINA.

Indo-European

The word Indo-European is applied to a "family" of languages that are spoken in Europe and parts of India. English, German, Italian, Russian, Greek, and most of the other languages of Europe are members of this family. These languages seem much different from one another, but scientists who study languages can tell that once they came from the same language. This was many thousands of years ago, and since tribes of men settled in different parts of the world they changed the language in different ways. There are a few languages spoken in Europe, such as Hungarian, Finnish, and Basque, that are not Indo-European languages. The principal branches of Indo-European languages are:

Germanic, which includes German, English, Dutch, and the Scandinavian languages (Swedish, Norwegian, Icelandic).

Slavic, which includes Russian, Polish, and the languages of various peoples of Czechoslovakia, Yugoslavia, and Bulgaria.

Italic, which includes Italian, Spanish, Portuguese, French, Rumanian, and other languages based on Latin (called *Romance languages*).

Celtic, which includes the original Scottish and Irish languages (called *Gaelic*) and languages still spoken in Brittany (in northwestern France) and in Wales.

Greek, spoken in Greece and used in many eastern countries.

Indo-Iranian (or *Aryan*), which includes most of the languages of India and the languages of Persia (Iran). Sanskrit is one of the old Indo-European languages.

Indo-European languages have also been called Indo-Germanic. Scientists are not sure where the Indo-European languages originated.

Indonesia

Indonesia is a nation made up of more than three thousand islands in the Southwest Pacific Ocean. The total area of these islands, about 735,000 square miles, is almost one-fourth as big as the United States, and more than 115,000,000 people live there. The islands stretch out from east to west for about 3,000 miles.

Most of Indonesia was controlled by the Netherlands when World War II broke out and the Japanese took over control. After the war ended in 1945, Indonesian patriots fought for independence and won it finally in 1949. But Indonesia has not had peaceful times since then. Socialists, Communists and military leaders have often fought for power.

THE PEOPLE AND HOW THEY LIVE

Most of the people of Indonesia are Malays, a brown-skinned people of the lands and islands in and around the southwest Pacific Ocean. There are smaller numbers of people from Europe and from the great nations of Asia.

The official language of Indonesia is a Malayan language, Bhasa Indonesia, but the different groups of people in the many islands of Indonesia speak a great many different languages.

Most of the people in Indonesia follow the Mohammedan religion. There are also some who follow the Christian, the Hindu and the Buddhist religions.

Most of the people are farmers. They live in small villages, in clearings in the great jungle forests, or in the swampy lowlands. On their own little farms they raise rice, which is their chief food, and some vegetables. Other farmers work on the plantations, which are huge farm estates. There they raise valuable crops of rubber, sugar, coffee, and many other products, which are shipped to other countries.

The homes of many of the people are simple huts, with grass roofs. Often the huts are built on stilts, to keep them above wet ground. The people have been living in the same way for hundreds of years. They do most of their work by hand, for they have very little machinery.

Some parts of the Indonesian islands have become more modern. Roads and some railroads have been built, connecting the larger cities.

Until recent years, very few of the people of Indonesia knew how to read and write. The government of the new republic has set up schools for children and also has classes for adults.

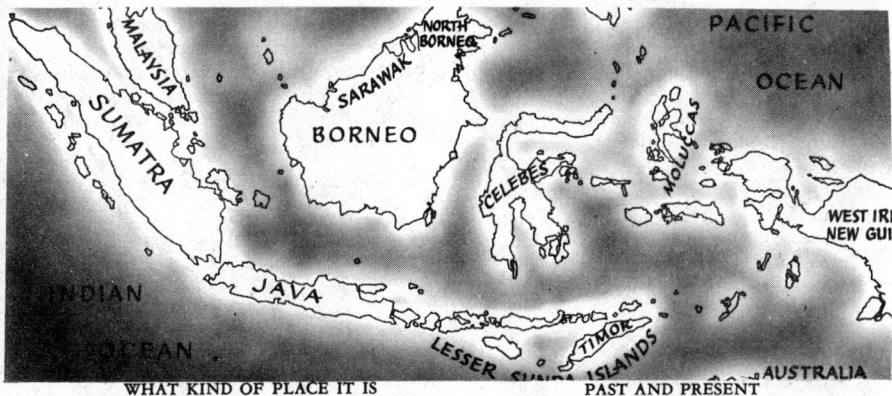

WHAT KIND OF PLACE IT IS

Indonesia lies on the equator, the imaginary line around the middle of the earth, and the hottest part of the earth. In the lowlands of the Indonesian islands the climate is very hot and there is a great deal of rain. A great chain of volcanic mountains runs through the islands, and in the higher regions the climate is cooler. Some of the mountains are active volcanoes; they rumble and belch forth smoke. Many of them have erupted in recent times.

Indonesia is very rich in resources. There is a great deal of tin, oil, and many metals. From the great tropical forests the people get fine woods, such as teak and ebony, and from the coconuts of the palm trees they produce oil, fibers that are used in rope, and many other things. There is not very much manufacturing in Indonesia, but in some places the people weave cloth with strange, beautiful patterns. Others work in the rubber industry, and in the factories that manufacture sugar from the sugar cane.

THE ISLANDS

Most of the Indonesian people live on the three big islands, Sumatra, Java, and Celebes. Indonesia also controls shares of two even bigger islands — the southern part of Borneo, and the western part of New Guinea (called West Irian), which Indonesia annexed in 1963. Some of the smaller Indonesian islands are very famous, especially Bali. There is a separate article about each of these islands.

CITIES

The leading cities of Indonesia, with populations as estimated in 1973 are:

Jakarta, or Djakarta, population 2,906,530, capital and largest city, in northwest Java, a commercial and industrial center. It was formerly called Batavia.

Surabaja, population 1,008,000, in east Java, commercial center.

Bandung, population 972,560, in west Java, an industrial center. It is 2,346 feet above sea level, cool and healthful.

Palembang, population 474,980, in southeast Sumatra, a trade and commercial center for the rubber and oil industries.

Makassar, or Macassar, population 384,160, largest city and chief seaport in Celebes.

Medan, population 479,100, in eastern Sumatra, seaport and tobacco exporting center.

Semarang, population 503,150, in central Java, a commercial center.

Surakarta, population 367,626, in south Java, a cultural and handicraft center.

PAST AND PRESENT

The islands of Indonesia were once called the East Indies. Men have lived there since earliest times (read about the Java Man in the article JAVA). Hundreds of years ago, big countries in Asia controlled the islands and the Asiatic civilization remains in temples still standing in parts of Indonesia.

In the centuries of exploration when European nations were forming empires, Portuguese, British and Dutch explorers landed in the East Indies. The Dutch won and the islands were called the Netherlands East Indies until World War II, when Japan captured them.

In 1945, when Japan surrendered, the Netherlands tried to control the islands again, but the Indonesians declared their independence. There was some fighting, but the United Nations helped to make peace and in 1949 the Republic of the United States of Indonesia was formed (in 1950 the name was changed to Republic of Indonesia) with a noted patriot, Dr. Sukarno, as the first president.

The Indonesian government of 1949 adopted a democratic constitution with a legislature elected by the people, but Sukarno became a dictator in 1959 and in 1960 he stopped elections to the legislature and appointed the members. Officially this was called a "guided democracy."

In world affairs Sukarno favored the U.S.S.R. and China, and he copied their aggressive policies: In 1964 Indonesia threatened war to prevent Malaysian annexation of the northern Borneo countries, and in 1965 Indonesia resigned from the United Nations, whose members favored Malaysia.

But under Sukarno's rule, Indonesia did not prosper. There was inflation and by 1965 it took 10,000 rupiahs to buy one United States dollar; before, it had been only 50 rupiahs. In October 1965, Indonesian Communists tried to take over the government. The Indonesian Army put down the revolt, but many thousands of people (mostly Communists or suspected Communists) were killed. Sukarno supported the Army, but later Sukarno was accused of encouraging the attempted Communist rebellion. President Sukarno retained his title, but lost all power to General Suharo, head of the army. Then in 1971, General Suharo was elected President by a popular vote.

INDONESIA. Area, 737,000 square miles. Population (1973 estimate) 115,000,000. Language, Bhasa Indonesia; also many dialects. Religion, Mohammedan. Government, constitutional republic. Monetary unit, rupiah (value uncertain). Flag, two horizontal stripes, one red, one white.

induction

Induction means "leading." It is the scientific name for leading electricity or magnetism from one object to another. When electricity is induced, it is called *electrostatic induction*. When magnetism is induced, is is called *magnetic induction*.

Induction is also the scientific name for using magnetism to make electricity, or for using electricity to make magnetism. This is called *electromagnetic induction*. An electric generator uses electromag-

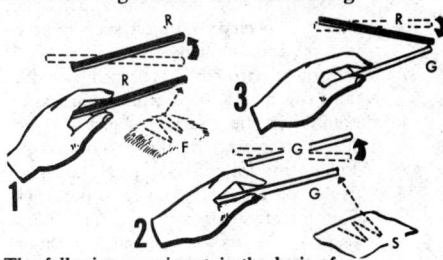

The following experiment is the basis of electrostatic induction. In 1, a rubber rod (R) that is given a negative charge by being rubbed with fur (F) will push away a second rubber rod with the same charge. Section 2 shows the same thing happening when a glass rod (G) rubbed with silk (S) is given a positive charge. But, as shown in 3, a glass rod will attract a rubber rod with an opposite charge.

netic induction to make electricity from magnetism. (See the articles on GENERATOR, ELECTRICITY, and MAGNETISM.)

ELECTROSTATIC INDUCTION

The simplest kind of induction is electrostatic induction. Electrostatic charge is another name for electricity that is standing still. There are two kinds of electrostatic charge, positive and negative. An object is electrostatically neutral when it has the same amounts of positive and negative charges. An object is positively charged when it has more positive charges than negative. An object is negatively charged when it has more negative charges than positive. Positive charges attract or pull toward them negative charges, and vice versa. Positive charges repel (push away) other positive charges. Negative charges repel other negative charges.

Negative charges are the only charges that can be removed or added to an object. In electrostatic induction, negative electricity is either removed or added to an object. This makes the object positively or negatively charged.

A special device is used for electrostatic induction. It is called an *electroscope*. It is a metal rod with a knob on top and two thin strips of gold or aluminum on the bottom. The rod is fitted in a glass jar to protect the metal strips from drafts of air.

When the electroscope is electrostatically neutral, the metal strips hang straight down from the rod. If the electroscope is negatively or positively charged, the metal strips will separate.

To induce a charge in an electroscope, a charged object must be held close to the knob. A glass rod that has been rubbed with silk will be positively charged. A rubber rod or hard rubber comb that has been rubbed with fur will be negatively charged. Either of these objects can be used.

If the glass rod is brought near the knob, the positive charge on the rod will attract the negative charges in the metal

strips and bring them up to the knob. It will also attract negative charges from the other side of the knob. This will leave only positive charges on the metal strips and the far side of the knob. Since both metal strips will be positively charged, they will repel each other and move apart. When the glass rod is taken away from the knob, the negative charges will return to the metal strips. This once again will make the metal strips electrostatically neutral and they will come together.

Exactly the opposite will happen when a negatively charged object, such as a rubber rod, is brought near the knob.

If the electroscope is charged by induction, the metal strips will remain apart even after the charged object is withdrawn from near the knob. This can be done in the following way: Hold a positively charged glass rod near the knob. The metal strips will separate. Now, keeping the rod in the same position, touch the knob with your finger. The metal strips will come together.

The reason is that when you touch your finger to the knob, you make a connection between the knob and the ground on which you stand. This is called *grounding*. It allows negative charges from the ground to pass up through your body into the electroscope, where they are attracted to the positively charged side of the knob as well as to the metal strips and they come together. When you remove your finger and the charged object, the negative charges on the knob repel the additional negative charges that have come from the ground. These charges are pushed down to the metal strips, charging them negatively. The metal strips once more repel each other and remain separated as long as the electroscope is charged. In this way the electroscope is charged negatively by induction. When a negative object is used to charge an electroscope by induction, the charge on the electroscope will be positive.

It is electrostatic induction that causes lightning to strike a building or a tree.

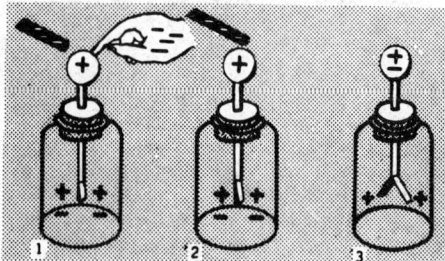

Using induction to charge an electroscope positively by means of a negatively charged rubber rod. The process is fully described in the text of the article.

The clouds in the sky are either negatively or positively charged. They are formed by small drops of water blown into the sky by warm breezes. These drops are either negatively or positively charged, and can be detected by an electroscope. The clouds that are formed by them often hang very low in the sky. In such cases they may be low enough to induce an opposite charge on a building or tree. When there is no more room for the charges, they are discharged in the form of a huge electrical spark called lightning. The lightning can go from the cloud to the building or from the building to the cloud.

ELECTROMAGNETIC INDUCTION

Electricity flowing through a coil of wire makes the coil into a kind of weak magnet. If a piece of iron is put into the coil it will increase the magnetism enough to attract nails and small metal objects.

It is easy to test this for yourself. Take a large nail and wrap some insulated wire around it. Connect the ends of the wire to a battery. If small tacks are placed near the nail, they will be attracted to it, showing that there is magnetism present in the nail. Such an arrangement is called an electromagnet. Scientists often speak of the *magnetic field* that is induced by an electric current flowing through a wire. This magnetic field can be used to make electromagnets that are strong enough to lift thousands of pounds.

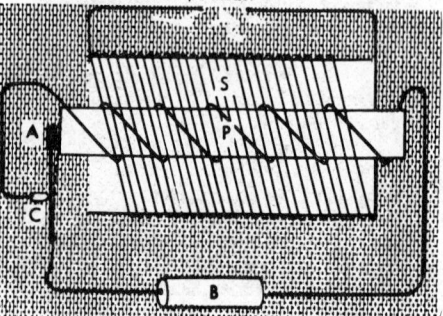

An induction coil is made up of a primary coil (P) placed inside a larger coil (S). The ends of the primary coil are connected to a battery (B), a switch (A) and a contact (C).

Just as an electric current can induce a magnetic field around a wire, so a magnet can induce a current in a wire. This was first discovered by the English scientist Michael Faraday more than a hundred years ago. It is the basis of the electric generator.

A magnet thrust up and down in a coil of wire will cause an electric current to flow through the wire. This can be tested by connecting the wire to a special instrument called a *galvanometer*. When the pointer moves along the dial of the galvanometer, it indicates that current is flowing through the wire. Scientists say that an electromotive force (EMF) is induced in the wire by the moving magnet.

It makes no difference whether the magnet or the coil is moved. In either case an electric current will be induced in the wire.

Scientists explain electromagetic induction by speaking of imaginary lines of force that surround every magnet or magnetic field. These lines connect one end of the magnet or coil of wire with the other. You cannot see these lines, but an easy way of finding out if they are there is to place a piece of paper on top of the magnet. Sprinkle some iron filings on the paper. The iron filings will arrange themselves in such a way that you will be able to see lines leading from one end of the magnet to the other.

When a magnet is thrust through a coil, these lines of force are cut by the coil. This induces an EMF. The same thing happens in an electric generator, except that a coil of wire is turned inside a magnetic field made up by several magnets surrounding the coil. As the lines of force are cut, current is induced in the coil.

INDUCTION COIL

The magnetic field induced around a current-carrying wire can be used to induce a larger current of electricity in another, near-by wire. This is called *mutual induction*. It is used to make an induction coil that is part of the ignition system of an automobile.

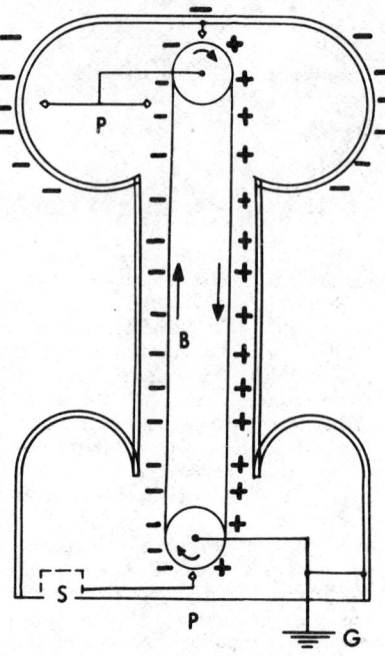

A Van de Graaf generator uses induction to induce electrostatic charges as high as five million volts. A source (S) of electricity supplies negative charges through the bottom contact point (P) to a belt (B) that revolves at about sixty miles per hour. Negative charges are taken off the belt at the top contact point (P) and are transferred to the outside of the generator. The belt returns with positive charges. The generator is grounded (G) to prevent overloading.

In an induction coil, one coil of wire, called the primary coil, is placed inside another, larger, coil called the secondary coil. The ends of the secondary coil are separated from each other by a narrow space. The ends of the primary coil are connected to battery and a switch. When the switch is closed, current flows through the primary coil. The current induces a magnetic field around the primary coil. The lines of the magnetic field are cut by the secondary coil as they move outward from the primary. This induces a current in the secondary coil. The current produces an electric spark between the ends of the secondary coil. If the switch is kept closed, the current will stop flowing through the secondary coil in the opposite direction.

Current will be kept flowing in an induction coil only if the switch is opened and closed rapidly. An EMF is induced in the secondary coil only when the lines of force of the primary coil are decreasing or increasing. The increasing and decreasing lines of force act in the same way as a magnet being thrust through a coil of wire. By putting more turns of wire on the secondary than are on the primary coil, it is possible to induce a 10,000-volt spark across the ends of the secondary coil from only 6 volts in the primary.

The transformer is a specially constructed induction coil used to increase or decrease the electricity from a generator. The electricity is then sent over special wires, called *transmission* lines, to homes,

factories and buildings. (There is a separate article on TRANSFORMER.)

There is another kind of electromagnetic induction. It is called *self-induction*. It is used in a special coil called a *choke coil*. This is a coil of wire in which there is a movable piece of iron. The coil is connected into a circuit with a series of lamps. When the lamp switch is closed, the lamps will flash brightly for a brief time and then become dim. When the switch is opened, the lamps will flash even more brightly and then grow dark. This is caused by the changing magnetic field around the coil. Such coils are used in theaters to dim the lights. Inserting the pieces of iron in the coils increases the magnetic field. The changing magnetic field caused by alternating current (AC), induces in the coil a current that flows in the opposite direction to the current already in the coil. This is called the *back EMF*. The back EMF reduces the total current and causes the lights to dim.

Indus River

The Indus is the largest river in Pakistan, a country in Asia. The Indus is one of the great rivers of the world. It begins high in the Himalayas, the highest mountains in the world, and flows about 1,800 miles before emptying into the Arabian Sea. Most of the way it flows very swiftly, and boats have a hard time sailing on parts of it. A great many bridges have been built to cross the river. The waters of the Indus are used to irrigate dry farm lands on which little rain falls. The government is doing much to irrigate more and more land. There are many kinds of fish in the river, but fishermen must always be on the lookout for vicious crocodiles.

Industrial Revolution

The Industrial Revolution was the beginning of the change from a world in which nearly everything was made by hand, to the world we live in today, where nearly everything is made by machines. The word *revolution* means a complete and sudden change from the usual way of doing things.

Before the Industrial Revolution, most people were farmers. They lived on their farms, grew their own food, and made their own clothes, furniture, and tools. They did not buy very much except iron for the plow, and salt. In the towns, some things were manufactured by men working in their own shops. These things included jewelry, swords, cloth, silverware, guns, and ammunition for the guns. These were bought by rich people, and sometimes were exchanged for food from the farms.

THE BEGINNING OF THE
INDUSTRIAL REVOLUTION

The Industrial Revolution began with the invention of machinery with which thread could be spun and cloth could be woven very cheaply and sold to people who had always before made their own cloth at home.

During the years between 1764 and 1800, machines were invented to spin thread, and the power loom was invented to make cloth cheaply and in larger quan-

tities than had ever been possible before. This led to the building of big factories in which many people worked at the same job. Before, people had worked at home or in small shops where everything was made by hand.

At first, water power was used to run the machines, and mills could be built only where rivers could be dammed. When James Watt perfected the steam engine, factories could be built anywhere, and cities began to grow larger. Other inventions that advanced the Industrial Revolution are told about in the articles on INVENTION and MASS PRODUCTION.

One of the most important things was the improvement of transportation when the railroads were begun in the 1830s. Another important factor was the quick exchange of information that was made possible by the invention of the telegraph and the telephone.

Two effects of the Industrial Revolution were the creation of a new kind of wealth and a new kind of rich man. Before then, the rich men had been the owners of the land, and they were principally the great noblemen. Now even richer men arose in the cities as the owners of factories and mills.

The Industrial Revolution increased the wealth of all the countries and distributed it better, which is generally a good thing. The bad effect was that the greed of the manufacturers led them to treat the working people very badly. They made young children work, and they made all their employees work very long hours under bad conditions that ruined their health. They paid them so badly that large parts of big cities were slums where nobody could live decently.

Gradually governments and businessmen both decided that the prosperity of the country was greatest if the factory workers were well paid, so that they could become customers for the merchandise that the factories made. That has been the greatest effect of the Industrial Revolution in this century.

See also the article on LABOR AND LABOR UNIONS.

industry

The industry of a country is all the businesses in which people work to make things. Industry also includes mining, for although the miner does not make a thing such as coal or gold or iron, he has to take it from the ground. In most cases, the metals must be further processed before they can be used. Transportation, which means moving people and things from one place to another, is also considered an industry. Many of the things needed in manufacturing must be transported from the place in which they are found to the factory or mill in which they are made into useful things.

There are three main classes of work: agriculture, which is farming; industry, which is the making of things; and services, which includes all the arts and sciences and all the professions, such as medicine and law. The wealth and power of a country are usually measured by its industry. Up until the time of the INDUSTRIAL REVOLUTION, about which you can read in a separate article, agriculture was more important than indus-

try. Most of the people in the world still earn their living by farming, but industry has become more important to most countries.

inertia

Nothing that is standing still would ever move, and nothing that is moving would ever stop or change direction, if some force did not make it. The tendency of an object to continue without change of motion or direction is called *inertia*.

On earth we cannot see the complete workings of inertia because there are always forces acting on everything we see. If you throw a ball, it cannot keep on going because gravity is pulling it to earth, and the resistance of the air is slowing it down. But if the ball were thrown out in

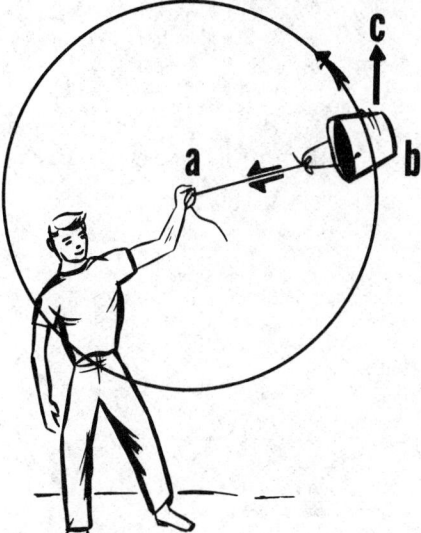

Because of inertia, a moving object always tends to follow a straight line. The boy who is swinging the bucket (b) in a circle feels a pull on his hand (a), because inertia tends to keep the bucket moving in a straight line (c). This is also called centrifugal force

space, where there is no air and where it is too far from the earth or any other body for it to be affected by gravity, it would keep going in a straight line and without ever slowing down. If it never came near any other object, it would keep going forever.

When the coal shoveler ends his swing, the coal's inertia moves it to the furnace.

We do see the effects of inertia all the time. When you are riding in an automobile and it stops suddenly, inertia makes you pitch forward. A coal stoker uses inertia to shovel coal into a furnace; he fills the shovel with coal, swings it toward the open door of the furnace, and suddenly stops the shovel. Inertia causes the coal to keep going, so it slides off the shovel and into the furnace.

People most often use the word inertia

only for the tendency of something to stand still unless it is pushed. It takes much more effort to push an automobile if it is standing still than if it is already rolling. The more an object weighs, the greater its inertia is, and the greater push or pull is needed to change its speed or direction.

Friction has an important effect on inertia. Give a sled a push and it will slide for a long way over ice or snow, where there is not much friction. It will not keep sliding on a living-room rug, where the friction is great.

Inertia is the subject of one of the Laws of Motion of Sir Isaac NEWTON, about whom there is a separate article. Read also the articles on MOTION, CENTRIFUGAL FORCE, and FRICTION.

infantile paralysis

Infantile paralysis is one of the most feared of all diseases. Its medical name is *poliomyelitis,* and it is often called "polio." It is a nerve infection that affects the nerves leading to some muscles. A person may become hopelessly crippled with infantile paralysis. Fortunately, many people have this disease in such a mild form that they do not even know they are ill; but in its worst form, infantile paralysis is a terrible thing.

Infantile paralysis begins with a headache and fever, and sometimes the person has a sore throat and vomits. He may have pains in his back and a stiff neck. The disease usually occurs in epidemics, which means that many people get it at the same time.

Most often infantile paralysis epidemics occur in the summertime. When there is an epidemic, it is important that people do not gather in groups, and that children stay away from theaters, beaches, and other places where there are large crowds of people.

Scientists do not know what causes infantile paralysis or how to cure it. They do know that infantile paralysis comes from a virus, a tiny germ that is so small it cannot be seen under most microscopes. In 1953 a vaccine called gamma globulin was tried, with some success, but in 1954 it was replaced by a new preventive medicine developed by Dr. Jonas Salk; and within the years that followed, the Salk vaccine was used to inoculate tens of millions of American children. The Salk vaccine reduced the number of infantile paralysis cases by about ninety per cent.

There is a great hospital at Warm Springs, Georgia, where people who have the disease can go for treatment. This hospital was visited very often by President Franklin D. Roosevelt, who was crippled by infantile paralysis. Though he could not walk, Roosevelt was able to become President, and this fact has given courage to many people who have had severe cases of infantile paralysis.

In 1938 President Roosevelt set up the National Foundation of Infantile Paralysis to fight this terrible disease. Each year, in January, this foundation conducts a campaign called the March of Dimes. Everyone is asked to give at least a dime, and as much more as he can afford. Millions of dollars are collected by the Foundation to do research that may prevent anyone

from getting infantile paralysis, and also to help people who have become ill with infantile paralysis.

In 1960 the Public Health Service approved a polio vaccine developed by Dr. Albert Sabin that can be taken orally.

infantry

The infantry are the men in an army who fight on foot instead of on horseback or in tanks. About six hundred years ago the most important men in an army were the knights, who wore armor and fought on horseback. The knights were attended by young boys who took care of their armor and weapons and acted as personal servants. These young attendants often followed their masters into battle and aided them when they were wounded or knocked from their horses. They were called infantry because the Spanish word *infante* means "young person."

In time these boys were replaced by strong young men, armed with swords and spears, who fought on foot. These foot soldiers tried to kill or cripple the horses of the knights and bring the armored horsemen to the ground. Although these foot soldiers were grown men, the word *infantry* came to be used for all men in an army who fought on foot.

The foot soldier of the great armies of the ancient Roman Empire was protected by a helmet and armor on the upper part of the body and on the front of the thighs and legs. He was equipped with a short spear for stabbing, a sword, and a shield. The modern infantryman or foot soldier wears no armor except a steel helmet, and he carries a rifle and hand grenades. Light machine guns are also carried by the infantry. Although tanks, artillery and aircraft are very important in today's armies, the largest part of any army is made up of infantry.

infection

When some part of the body is attacked by bacteria that cause disease, it is said to be infected and the condition is called infection. An infection can be very serious, or it can be just a cut that gets filled up with pus. The pus is made up of the bacteria and the white blood cells that attack the bacteria and try to kill them.

Most small infections can be cured by some chemical that kills bacteria, called a disinfectant or an antiseptic, such as iodine. Infections that cause serious diseases must be treated by a doctor. There are many drugs that fight such infections, such as the ANTIBIOTICS about which you can read in a separate article.

infinitive

The infinitive is the simple form of a verb. Usually the infinitive is expressed with the word *to* placed before it. We speak of the verb "to go," or "to be."

There are two kinds of infinitive, the present and the perfect. *Walk, play, run, go,* and *see* are all present infinitives. They name actions happening in the present. The perfect infinitives of these verbs would be *have walked, have played, have run, have gone,* and *have seen.* They name actions that have already happened.

For a long time it was believed that in good English writing nothing should come between *to* and the infinitive. Sep-

arating the *to* and the verb is called *splitting an infinitive.* Some people have even felt that in the perfect infinitive no other word should come between *have* and the infinitive. Some modern writers believe it is proper to split an infinitive if by so doing they can make the meaning clearer.

inflammation

An inflammation is a condition in which a part of a person or animal that has been hurt turns very red, swells up to be much larger than it should be, and sometimes hurts. It turns red because the blood rushes to the spot that is hurt, to carry white corpuscles there. The white corpuscles, which are tiny little cells in the blood, are very helpful in killing germs. During an inflammation, these white corpuscles travel through the blood vessels and into the part of the body which is hurt. There they kill many of the germs that are causing the trouble. You have probably seen "pus" coming from cuts or scratches that are infected. This pus, which is thick and yellow, runs out of the cut. It is really the white corpuscles and the germs, which are gathered in one place where the hurt is worst and are having a battle. The white corpuscles are trying to kill the germs. If they win, the hurt place will become well. If the germs win, then you will probably have to go to the doctor so that he can give you medicine to kill the germs.

inflation and deflation

Inflation is a condition in which the people of a country have a great deal of money but there is not a great deal they can buy with it. The value of money depends on what it will buy. If there are two men who want to buy an automobile, and each has a lot of money, but there is only one automobile for sale, they will bid against each other until one of them pays a lot more than usual for the automobile. After all, he can ride in the automobile and he cannot ride in the money.

It is the same thing when a lot of people have money and want to buy beefsteaks and eggs and washing machines and new clothes, but there are not quite enough beefsteaks and eggs and washing machines and new clothes to go around. Prices of all these things will go up. Prices of everything else will go up, too, because people will want to spend their money for something. Money will be worth less than it was before, because it will buy less. That is the condition known as *inflation.*

There are various reasons why inflation occurs, but the biggest inflation is the result of a war. The government has to spend a lot of money for arms and ships and munitions, and clothes and food and pay for the fighting men. This puts money into circulation—gives it to the people to spend. But the factories of the country are so busy producing war goods that they cannot produce many consumer goods (things for the people to buy). Soon there is too much money in circulation, and prices go up. World War II caused the prices of many things to double in the United States.

EFFECTS OF INFLATION

During a period of inflation, stock-market prices (the cost of shares of

ownership in companies) go far up. Banks lend a great deal of money to businesses, which puts more money in circulation. Salaries and wages go up for most people. Everyone seems to have a lot of money, but prices go up at the same time so it does not do them a great deal of good.

People who owe money are helped by inflation, because they pay their debts with money that is worth less than it was worth when they borrowed it. People who are owed money, or who live on the income from pensions or investments, or who work for the government and have salaries that are fixed by law, are hurt by inflation because they receive the same amount of money as before but can buy less with it.

When a government spends more money than it has in its treasury, it has to borrow. If a government has to borrow more than it can ever hope to repay, a condition known as runaway inflation is likely to result. The government prints paper money, but the paper money is only a promise of the government and that has stopped being worth much. Everyone tries to buy things that have practical or long-lasting value, for example real estate and furniture and jewelry. The price of everything goes up. The government has to print more and more paper money to buy what it needs, and the more money it prints, the less the money is worth and the higher the prices go. At last a time comes when the money is worth nothing at all. This happened in Germany after it lost World War I.

CEILINGS AND RATIONING

There are several things a government can do to prevent inflation from getting out of control. All these things were done during and after World War II.

One thing is to put *price ceilings* on the things people need most. The law fixes the highest price that anyone may charge for these things. The "ceiling price" on eggs may be 80 cents a dozen, and on the rent of a certain house it may be $80. Usually the ceiling is the highest price that had been charged on or before a certain date. People often get around this law by selling things "on the black market," which means that they break the law, and risk going to jail, by charging more than the ceiling price; but ceiling prices still help a lot.

Another way is by *rationing*. If gasoline, or coffee, or meat, or anything else is very scarce, the law says that no one may buy more than a certain quantity of it. For example, each person may be limited to five gallons of gasoline or a pound of coffee or two pounds of meat each week. Each person receives a "ration book" full of coupons. He must give up a coupon when he buys something. Then people with a lot of money cannot buy these things by paying more than others can afford to pay, and prices stay down.

Another way is by making people pay very high taxes. This takes a lot of money out of circulation and gives it back to the government.

DEFLATION

When people do not have as much money as they need to buy the things they want, the condition is called *defla-*

tion. It is exactly the opposite of inflation.

Usually inflation and deflation follow each other regularly. Inflation continues until prices are so high that people have to spend all their money just to live. Then they do not have enough money. In order to persuade the people to buy, businessmen have to reduce their prices. The value of money, based on what it will buy, goes up.

The 1930s, called the "depression," was a period of deflation in the United States. Fine automobiles were selling for less than $2,000. Ten years before they had cost as much as $5,000. Ten years later they cost as much as $4,000. People in the 1930s had very little money and would not pay high prices for anything.

Deflation can be just as bad for people as inflation. Millions of people are likely to be without jobs. People who owe money cannot pay it, and many businessmen become bankrupt. Deflation makes things better for only a very few people, those who are owed money and those who have fixed incomes.

In the best times, there is neither inflation nor deflation. Such times are called "normal." When there are many costly wars, as there have been in the twentieth century, there are no really normal times. Economists (scientists who study money and business conditions) are always trying to find ways to keep inflation or deflation from hurting the people very much.

influenza

Influenza is a contagious disease thought to be caused by a virus, a germ too small to be seen even through a microscope. Influenza is often called "flu," or "grippe." It is likely to spread rapidly from one person to another, causing an epidemic.

A person suffering from influenza usually has fever, chills, headache, aches in his back and joints, and inflamed nose and throat passages. Influenza itself is seldom serious but a person who has had it is likely to get a more dangerous disease, such as pneumonia, while he is recovering. A person who has influenza should get plenty of rest, drink much liquid, and call his doctor, who will usually give him penicillin or one of the antibiotic drugs.

Some influenza vaccines have been developed and they help prevent its spreading. In past years there have been many serious epidemics and pandemics (worldwide epidemics) of influenza, when as many as half of the people in an area were affected. The pandemic in 1918 and 1919 was one of the worst in the history of the world. Twenty million people died of influenza and its complications in just a few months, and it is estimated that fifty times as many persons had the disease —or a billion people in all.

inheritance tax

When a person receives a bequest, or an amount of money left to him by a relative or other person who has died, he has to pay a tax on it. This is called an inheritance tax. In the United States the inheritance tax may take nearly half of the amount of a large bequest. In Great Britain, inheritance taxes are called *death*

duties. They are so high that families that used to be very rich are not so rich any more. As each member of a family dies, some more of the family's money goes to the government in taxes.

Inheritance taxes must be paid in cash, and many estates are mostly in property. Therefore the heir sometimes has to sell a lot of property at much less than it is worth to pay the tax. For this reason rich men usually take out big insurance policies or keep a lot of cash when they are growing old, so as to have enough cash for their heirs to pay the inheritance tax. Sometimes they give a large part of their estates to their children and other heirs before they die. Although there are gift taxes to be paid on such gifts, they are not as high as the inheritance tax.

initiative

Initiative is a way in which citizens of a democracy have a chance to play a direct part in making their own laws. In the United States the law of initiative gives the citizens of a state the right to see that the elected state leaders make laws the people want. Any citizen may write a paper called a *petition,* in which he states any changes in the law that he wishes. If he can get enough other people to sign this paper, it can be presented to the governing body, or legislature, of the state, where it must be considered. This law is called initiative because the change is initiated, which means started, by the people themselves.

Usually a law that permits initiative also permits the *referendum,* which is an election in which all the people vote to decide whether or not a certain law should be passed, or money borrowed to build schools or roads, or the constitution changed. A referendum has the power to change or cancel a law passed by the lawmaking body of the state.

injunction

An injunction is an order from a court of law that tells a person he must not do something that he has been doing or may have planned to do. The court is said to *enjoin* the person from doing such a thing. Usually an injunction is issued by a court of equity, which is decsribed in the article on LAW. If a person disobeys an injunction he can be arrested for *contempt of court* and fined or put in prison.

As an example, if someone plans to put a public parking lot near a school and the parents of the school children think that this may be dangerous to the children, they may be able to get a court to issue an injunction that says the parking lot may not be opened.

Many famous injunctions have been issued to prevent a labor union from striking. In 1932 the United States Congress passed a law called the Norris-LaGuardia Act that made it much more difficult for employers to get this kind of injunction. The Taft-Hartley Act, passed in 1947, permits these injunctions in certain cases. There are separate articles on both of these laws.

ink

Ink is a liquid that is used for writing, drawing, or printing on paper or cloth. It may be dyed many colors. It is made from water and dyes, with a little

oil, carbon, and iron added. Throughout history, man has written down a record of his accomplishments in ink, and many of the records have remained to tell us of the past. More than four thousand years ago the Egyptians used a liquid for writing on parchment or papyrus, which was their paper. This liquid was made of water, powdered charcoal, gum, and other things, and it was not much different from the ink used in modern times. About three thousand years ago men in China used ink to print from woodcuts. They printed pictures and several thousand books, some of which can still be seen in libraries in China.

Inks may look alike, but they are often very different. We speak of ink as being either hard or soft. The soft ink is a thin liquid that runs easily; it is the type used in fountain pens. Hard ink is a very thick paste, sometimes so thick that you can hardly stick your finger into it. It is used for certain kinds of printing. This kind of ink is made from mineral oil, carbon, and special dyes. Banks and governments use special inks for records that must be kept a long time. These inks have iron added to them so they will not fade easily.

OTHER USES OF INK

Inks have been used for very different purposes. An ink was invented in China and Japan to use with brushes instead of pens. This ink is made in the form of sticks, which are rubbed down with the wet brush. Artists all over the world have used this ink. Another special kind of ink is used to print on metal. It contains much oil and is like paint. Indelible ink, which usually is purple or black in color, is used for marking cloth. It is made so it will not wash out. Other inks are intentionally made "washable," so that they will dissolve in water and cannot permanently stain clothes.

INVISIBLE INKS

One of the most unusual of all inks is secret, or invisible, ink. When it is used for writing it cannot be seen. Spies have often used secret inks, as have magicians and fortunetellers. In Arabia, priests used to go out at night and write the name of their religious leader, Mohammed, on rocks, and the heat of their bare backs against the rocks would make the words show.

Milk can be used as an invisible ink. It does not show on the page until some substance such as soot is dusted over it. The soot sticks to the paper where the milk has touched it, and the message becomes visible. Messages written in lemon juice are invisible until the paper is heated. Then the message will show. Scientists have invented many secret inks. Persons writing a message in invisible ink often write the secret message under another message written in ordinary ink.

Inness, George

George Inness was an American painter who liked to paint landscapes, or outdoor scenes. His pictures are filled with feathery-looking trees waving in golden afternoon sunlight; often cows are standing in the fields. Inness taught himself almost everything he knew about painting. He was born in Newburgh, New York,

and became an apprentice, or helper, to a map-maker. He went to Europe and saw many beautiful landscape paintings by the French artists Théodore Rousseau and Corot, and he began to paint as they did. Inness was very famous when he died in 1894.

Innocent, Pope

Innocent was the name taken by thirteen Popes of the Roman Catholic Church.

Innocent I, who later was declared a saint, was Pope from 402 until 417. He fought any heresies (false teachings) that threatened to break up the Church.

Innocent III was also a strong and active Pope. He ruled from 1198 until 1216. He became Pope when he was only 37 years old. He believed that the Pope should rule all earthly kings. He had great power in the governments of several countries, and he settled arguments between noblemen all over Europe. He put King John of England out of the church until John promised to reform and become a better ruler. Innocent III also wrote religious books and approved the organization of two religious orders, the Franciscans and the Dominicans.

Innocent XI, who was Pope from 1676 to 1689, tried to persuade Kings Louis XIV of France and James II of England not to persecute Protestants. If he had succeeded, many religious quarrels might have been prevented.

inoculation

Inoculation is a way of preventing certain diseases. A person is inoculated when he has serum put into his body or blood stream. The doctor penetrates his skin with a long, thin needle, through which he injects the serum. This serum is a liquid that contains the germs of the disease that is to be prevented. Actually, it gives the person who is being inoculated a very mild case of the disease. Scientists have discovered that once a person has had a disease, he is unlikely to catch it again. The person who is inoculated often feels no results from the inoculation, although he may have a slight fever and a headache for a day or so. Most people are inoculated for whooping cough, tetanus, and diphtheria. Nearly everyone is vaccinated, which is inoculation against smallpox. See the article on IMMUNITY.

Inquisition

The Inquisition was a court that the Roman Catholic Church set up about seven hundred years ago to prevent people from teaching things that were not approved by the Church. These unapproved teachings were called heresy, and the persons who taught or believed them were called heretics.

In those days the government of the Church and the government of the country were very closely connected in most European countries, and so it was against the law to believe in any religious teachings except the official ones of the Church. All punishments were very cruel, and the ones of the Inquisition were no exception. The actual punishments were carried out by the government of the country, not by the government of the Church. The most famous Inquisitor was

Tomas de Torquemada, who was a Spanish priest. He was put in charge of the Inquisition in Spain in 1483, and for more than ten years he had great power. The Inquisitors before and after him were so cruel that the Pope several times rebuked them for their severity, but it was under Torquemada that the Inquisition received a reputation for great cruelty, even though Torquemada himself may not have been the person to blame.

INSECT

An insect is a kind of small animal with certain features that make it different from every other kind of animal. It is an invertebrate animal, which means that it has no spine, or backbone. It is one of the four kinds of arthropods (animals that have jointed feet). Other arthropods are crustaceans (crabs, shrimps, and lobsters), centipedes, and spiders. Centipedes and spiders are not insects, though most people think they are.

Every insect has a body made up of three parts. These parts are the head, the thorax (chest), and the abdomen. An insect has only three pairs of legs. An insect has only one pair of antennae, the feelers that stick out from the head. Every insect has two pairs of jaws. These jaws vary a great deal among different kinds of insects. Biting insects have strong jaws; insects that live on fluids have the jaws joined in such a way as to make piercing and sucking organs.

INSECTS AND MAN

Everyone knows the housefly that gets on food, the mosquito that can ruin a night's sleep with its buzzing and stinging, and the "bug" that eats the leaves or fruit of plants. These pests sometimes make us forget the thousands of insects that are good friends to man. Many insects work for man by pollenizing flowers. Others help the farmer by eating and killing off weeds or feeding on insects that eat his crops. Most insects are food for birds and fishes that serve in turn as food for man.

Other insects have other important uses for man. The honeybee provides him with honey. The silkworm spins a valuable thread from which fine fabrics are made. The cochineal scale for hundreds of years provided the best red and orange dyes. The lac insects excrete, or give off, a gummy substance from which the best shellac is made. In the Far East a tiny insect called the tamarisk manna scale provides a substance that is used instead of sugar; it feeds on the tamarisk tree, and deposits on its leaves a layer of a sweet substance called manna. The Arabs of the Sinai Mountains collect this manna and use it for sweetening food.

Insects can be beautiful, and even the ugliest and most harmful can be interesting.

HOW MANY INSECTS ARE THERE?

No one knows exactly how many kinds of insect there are. More than 800,000 different species of insect have been described and named over the whole world, but scientists estimate there are millions

of species that are still unknown. Insects are believed to make up from 70 to 80 per cent of all animals.

About two-fifths of the known kinds of insect are beetles. Moths and butterflies, ants, bees, wasps and flies add up to another two-fifths. Each year, about 6,000 or 7,000 kinds are described and named for the first time.

Scientists can only guess how many kinds of insect there are. The guesses range all the way up to ten million kinds, but two million is the usual guess.

The total number of insects of all kinds is even harder to estimate. It is difficult even to estimate how many there may be in a given state, or on a single acre of land. In one summer season from April to August, the descendants of one pair of houseflies, if all lived and had young in the usual numbers would make a total of 191,000,000,000,000,000,000. Actually very few of these live, because they are killed by other insects, birds, diseases, man's insecticides, and weather.

Some insects lay eggs and produce young in even larger numbers than the housefly. Other insects have very few young, sometimes only one family each year, but even these may be very numerous. In Nebraska in the 1870s a swarm of locusts was seen that was half a mile high, a hundred miles wide and three hundred miles long. That single swarm was believed to contain more than 124,000,000,000 locusts.

HOW INSECTS GROW

Each of the three parts of an insect's body has very important functions. On the head are the jaws for biting and eating and the antennae, eyes and other sense organs. On the thorax are the wings and the legs. Each leg is divided into five parts, the last of which is the *tarsus*, or foot. The feet of insects vary greatly among different kinds. They may have

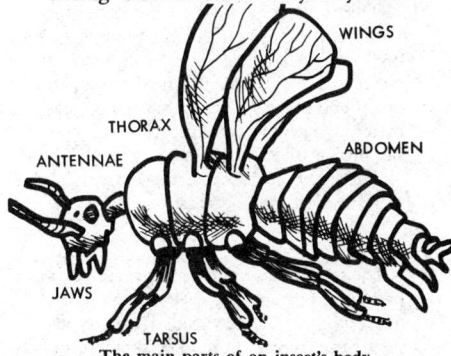

The main parts of an insect's body.

one to five sections. Usually they have claws at the tips, and they may be padded on the underside, as in some flies.

The largest section of an insect's body is the abdomen. It is divided into a number of ringlike segments. The insect breathes through special pores that are usually on the sides of the abdomen. Some insects have several bristles, or tails, at the end of the abdomen. A female insect usually has an *ovipositor*, or egg-laying organ, between two segments of the abdomen. All insects develop from eggs. A few insects carry the eggs inside the body until hatched, but most of them lay the eggs in a safe place. The eggs vary in size with different insects. Some are so small they can be seen only with a micro-

scope. Others may be a quarter of an inch long.

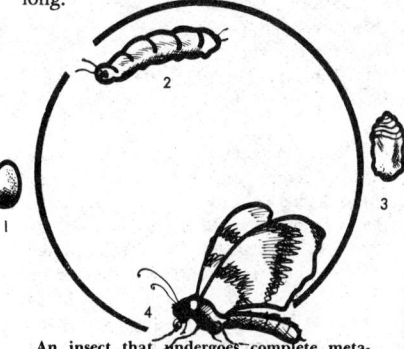

An insect that undergoes complete metamorphosis, or change, starts as an egg (1), becomes a larva (2), then a pupa (3), and finally emerges fully grown (4).

From the time the egg is laid until the adult insect is developed, a process called metamorphosis takes place. *Metamorphosis* means "change." There are two kinds of metamorphosis, complete and incomplete. An insect in incomplete metamorphosis goes through three forms: the egg, the young insect (or nymph), and the adult insect. The young insect looks much like the adult, but is smaller and usually wingless. In complete metamorphosis there are four changes, and the insect in the various stages may look very different. The egg develops into the *larva*, which is a wormlike form. The larvae of moths and butterflies are called caterpillars, the larvae of flies are called maggots, and the larvae of beetles are called grubs.

LIFE OF THE LARVA

The larva sheds its skin a certain number of times, depending on what kind of insect it is. Between sheddings there is an increase in size, until the larva is full-grown. At this time it stops eating and changes into a *pupa*. In most cases an insect makes a sort of container for itself before going into the pupal, or final growing, stage. Sometimes these cases are spun of a silklike material and are called *cocoons*. An insect such as a butterfly makes a hard case somewhat like parchment, which is called a *chrysalis*. The pupa remains in this case until it is fully developed as an adult insect.

KINDS OF INSECT

The *silverfish* or *bristletails* may have been on earth longer than any other insects, and probably are very much like the earliest insect life. These insects have no wings. The antennae are long and slender, and at the tip of the abdomen there are several tail-like parts that look like antennae, so it is sometimes difficult to tell which end of a silverfish is which. Most of the insects of this group are covered with scales so that they look silvery and feel slippery when you try to catch them. Most of them live under logs or in rotting plants, but two kinds have come to live with man. They eat starch and glue, and can do great damage to books and wallpaper.

The group of insects that includes the praying mantis, the cockroach, the grasshopper, the katydid and the cricket is called the *straight wings*. Most insects in this group have no wings at all. Some of them are so good at camouflage that they can make themselves look like green leaves, sticks, twigs, or stones. They are

found in every part of the earth, in hot and cold climates, and in high and low altitudes.

One of the most feared and harmful insects is the *termite*, but few people know that this wood-eating insect also does great good for man. Termites destroy whole buildings, and they eat the roots of trees and plants, but they help to keep forests growing by eating away fallen trees and actually cutting down trees that have died but are still standing in the way of new growth.

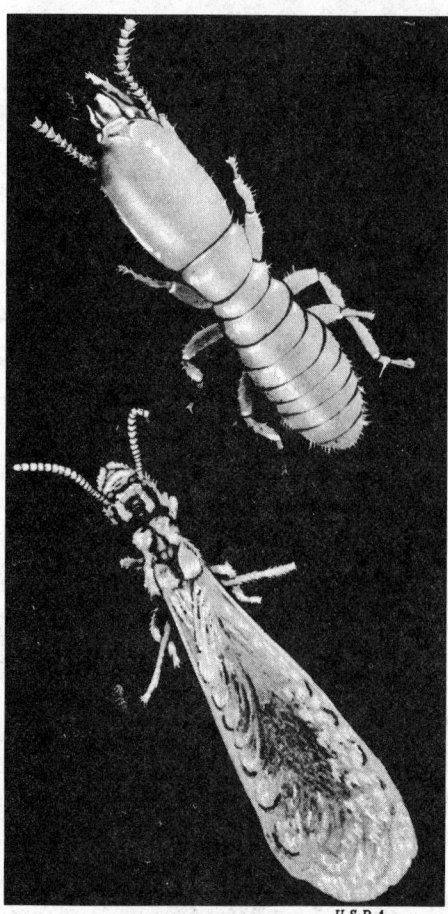

U.S.D.A.

Termites, which can undermine a house by eating away the wooden frame.

The *dragonfly* has been called the *devil's darning needle*, the *snake feeder*. and the *horse stinger*. It feeds chiefly on mosquitoes and also eats larger insects, such as honeybees and butterflies.

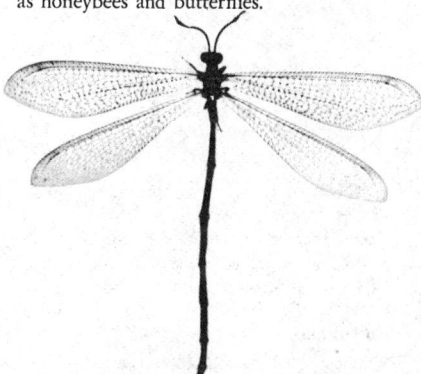

U.S.D.A.

The dragonfly, which eats insect pests.

Another large group of insects includes the *cicadas*, the *aphids*, and the *scale insects*. These vary greatly in size and shape. The tinier they are the more trouble they

cause. The aphid, which is also called the *plant louse,* feeds on nearly every kind of plant life.

Some of the scale insects are useful to man. Examples are the *cochineal scale,* which gives us dyes, and the *lac insects,* which give us shellac. Most of them do great damage to crops. Among these are the *cottony scale,* which is found on elm, maple, grape, and other plants; and the *San Jose scale,* which attacks fruit and forest trees.

BUGS

The word *bug* to most people means any ugly insect, but actually the true bugs are one large group of insects. They are called *half wings* because half of the wing is hard and horny and the tip is thin and filmy.

The horny parts of a bug's wings form a kind of shield, which makes it easy to recognize the bugs.

Many bugs are very beautiful, some are quite a nuisance to farmers, and one is the most hated bug of all, the *bedbug.* Other true bugs are the *stinkbugs,* which squirt a highly scented oil when they are frightened; the *shield bugs,* which have hard shields of beautiful colors under which their wings are hidden; the *squash bugs,* which feed exclusively on the squash plant; and the *chinch bugs,* which kill corn and grain by sucking out the sap.

Some bugs are swimmers, for example the *water scorpion* and the *back swimmer.*

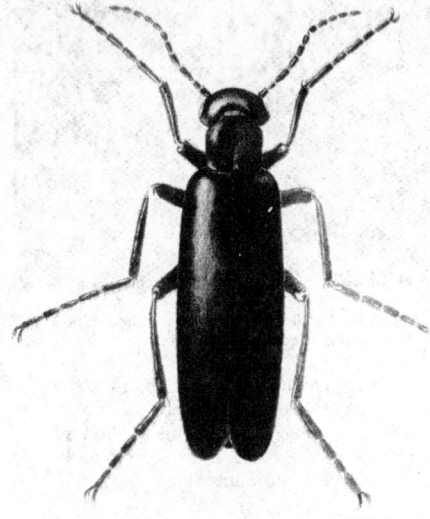

U.S.D.A.

A typical beetle. There are more than 250,-000 known kinds of this insect.

LICE

Next to the bedbug, the insects most hated by man are the *lice.* Of these insect pests there are two kinds, the *biting louse* and the *sucking louse.* The biting lice mostly infest birds and mammals, and the sucking lice infest men as well as other mammals.

BEETLES

The beetles are the most numerous of all insects. More than 250,000 different kinds of beetle have been described and named, and they vary widely in size and shape. There is a separate article about them.

BUTTERFLIES AND MOTHS

Because *butterflies* and *moths* are so beautiful and popular, we know more about them and their habits than most other insects. There is a separate article about them.

FLIES

Of all the insects that have the word *fly* in their names, only a few are true flies. Among these are the *housefly, bluebottle fly,* and *horsefly.* Other true flies are the *mosquito, midge,* and *fruit fly.* The chief difference between the flies and other insects is that a fly has only one pair of wings. All other insects have either no wings at all, or two pairs. Flies are found everywhere, and in all sizes. Some are very nearly invisible, some are very large. Some help man by acting as scavengers, or eaters of refuse; others bite painfully, or carry dangerous diseases.

The *mosquito* is probably the most harmful of all insects, both to human beings and to animals. It carries some of the most deadly diseases that affect man, such as malaria, yellow fever, filariasis, and a kind of paralysis called encephalomyelitis.

Other flies include the *midges* that can be seen in clouds of tiny flying particles around ponds and streams; the *sand flies* that can hardly be seen but inflict painful bites; other midges such as the *Hessian fly* that feed upon crops and do great damage; the *gadflies* and *horseflies* that torment animals and also carry the dangerous animal disease called anthrax; the *bee flies* that look like bumblebees; the *robber flies* that capture other insects in flight and carry their prey away to eat; and the common *housefly* that neither bites nor stings, but spoils our food and carries such diseases as typhoid fever, dysentery, cholera, and tuberculosis. One of the most dangerous of all flies is found only in Africa. This is the *tsetse fly,* which gives man the disease, often fatal, called sleeping sickness, and gives mammals several other dangerous diseases.

FLEAS

Another insect that is well-known because of its unpleasant habits is the *flea.* Adult fleas are bloodsuckers, and they can attach themselves either to animals or to man. The *dog flea* is very common in the United States.

BEES, WASPS, AND ANTS

A large group of insects that are often confused with the true flies is the group

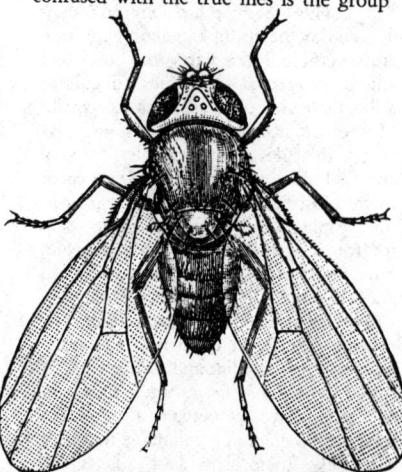

The fruit fly, one kind of true fly. Many insects called flies are not flies at all.

that includes *bees, wasps, and ants.* These insects have two pairs of wings, while the flies have only one pair. About 125,000 different kinds of insect have been de-

U.S.D.A.

The bee, which helps man by making honey.

The cicada killer, an example of a wasp. Like bees, wasps live in large groups.

scribed in this group, making it the second-largest order of insects after the beetles. The very smallest of all insects is in this group—a *chalcid fly,* so tiny that it lives on the body of another tiny insect called a book louse.

The *ants* form a big group of insects all by themselves. There is a separate article about them.

The *wasps* and *hornets* are close relatives; they are called social insects because they live in colonies or large families, although there are some kinds that live alone.

The third chief kind of insect of this group is the *bee,* and the most important bee is the *honeybee.* The honeybee has created a big industry in the United States and other countries, but many people enjoy keeping bees just to watch their fascinating lives and habits.

There are separate articles on these insects, and on many others.

FOSSIL INSECTS

The story of insects for millions of years past can be found preserved in the rocks of many parts of the world. The early insects were trapped in mud or sticky resin, where they died and remained imbedded for millions of years. A kind of huge dragonfly with a wing spread of 30 inches has been found as a fossil in rocks. The cockroach goes back some 250 million years, and the fossils differ very little from the cockroaches we know today.

Fossil records tell us that the earliest insects included creatures such as May flies, bugs, beetles, and bees, among others.

INSECT ODDITIES

In caverns deep inside the earth, there are snow-white, blind insects. One insect is able to live in the mud of hot springs where the water reaches a temperature of 120 degrees Fahrenheit, while another is

the ice bug that lives high up on mountains and is almost unable to move if the temperature gets as warm as 80 degrees. There is a species of beetle that gives out a little cloud of offensive gas when pursued. Many insects pretend to be dead when they are in danger.

insecticide

An insecticide is a poison used to kill insect pests. Though many insects such as the honeybee are helpful, many others are very harmful to man, animals, and plants. Some insects carry diseases. Others destroy crops. Farmers are constantly fighting insects that cause millions of dollars' worth of damage to crops every year. Flies, roaches, grasshoppers, aphids, corn borers, and beetles are some of the harmful insects.

People once used ordinary poisons against insects, but since these poisons also harm men and animals they were dangerous to use. Scientists set to work to find poisons that were useful against insects but that were safer to use. They had to develop many kinds, for some poisons kill one insect and have no effect on another. Some insects gradually build up an immunity against certain poisons. This means that the strongest insects are not killed and they pass on their ability to fight the poison to their children, so that after a while the poison has no effect on that kind of insect.

The poisons work in different ways. Some are taken in by insects when they eat, while others enter through the skin or the breathing tubes. They work on some important organ like the heart, or they stop a vital process such as breathing.

Insecticides are spread by machinery or by hand. They may be liquids that are sprayed on plants or powders that are dusted on. Airplanes are used to spread them. *Aerosols* are tiny drops of an insecticide in a sort of fog or mist. An aerosol is sprayed in one area and the wind helps to spread it over large distances.

Some of the insecticides used are arsenic, fluorine compounds, lead arsenate, and helleborine. The moth balls that are put in with woolens to protect them against moths contain a poison called naphthalene. One of the newest and most important insecticides is DDT. This is short for *d*ichloro-*d*iphenyl-*t*richloroethane. It is a combination of chlorine, benzene, and alcohol. A scientist named Paul Muller discovered in 1939 how useful DDT was, though it had first been made back in 1874. During World War II the army sprayed large areas with DDT to get rid of insects that might have caused many diseases. They even used it on people, for some insects hide in human skin and hair, and spread diseases from one person to another. DDT acts on the nervous system of insects. Some flies have become immune to DDT. They are somehow able to change it into a nonpoisonous substance.

Great care must be taken in the use of insecticides. Even though they are safer than the old poisons, most of them are still quite dangerous. Small children and pets should never be allowed near them. Instructions on the label should be carefully followed. Many insecticides catch fire easily, so they should be kept away from flames. Fruit should always be washed before being eaten as most fruit trees are sprayed with insecticides.

insignia

Insignia are marks, signs or badges used to identify a thing or a person—that is, to tell what the thing is or what the person has done. Insignia may be designs or pictures embroidered on cloth, painted on metal, stone, or wood, or stamped out of metal. A single one of these marks or badges is called an *insigne*.

The officers and men of all the armies and navies of the world wear insignia that tell what their rank is, what branch of the service they belong to, what honors they have received, and where they have fought. Boy Scouts wear many kinds of insignia on their uniforms.

Hundreds of years ago in Europe, all important families had their own family insignia, called a coat of arms. Today many societies, associations, sports, and social clubs have their own insignia, and the members of these organizations often wear a small emblem on the coat lapel. See also the article on HERALDRY.

installment buying

When a person wants to buy something that is very expensive and he cannot afford to pay for it all at once, he can usually buy it on the *installment plan*. An installment is a part payment. When a person buys something on the installment plan he makes a *down payment* at the time of the purchase, and a certain number of *installment payments* over a period of several months or years. In this way he gets the use of the expensive thing while he is paying for it.

A person who buys a house usually pays the owner a certain amount of money at the beginning, then pays the rest of the cost, a little at a time, over a period of as much as twenty or thirty years. Other things that are often bought on the installment plan are automobiles, furniture, refrigerators, television sets, and expensive jewelry.

The buyer must pay *interest* to the seller. That is, he pays an additional amount of money above the cost of the thing he bought to recompense the seller for waiting for his money. This interest is sometimes called a *carrying charge,* because the sale must be carried on the seller's business books until the final payment is made. Most installment sales of things that cost a great deal of money are financed by banks. The seller gets his money at once from a bank, the bank charges interest for the loan, and the interest is paid by the buyer.

Some people object to the idea of installment buying because it is really borrowing and owing money, but nothing has contributed more than installment buying to giving the American people their high standard of living. Because of installment buying, millions of people are able to have and enjoy things that they never could afford to buy if they had to wait until they could pay for them all at once. This is good for the people who sell things, too, because it enables them to do more business.

instinct

An instinct is a way of acting that does not have to be learned. Small animals may have many instincts, but large animals have fewer. Birds do not have to be taught to fly. Ducks do not have to be taught to swim. Fish do not have to learn to swim. Instinct tells birds how to build their nests and how to take care of their young.

Some instincts make animals work very hard. At one time of year salmon know that they must swim away from their homes in the sea. They must travel far up a river, past rocks and dams that men have built. They have to swim against the water that is running down the river. Finally, the salmon lay their eggs and return toward the sea. Instinct has made them swim up these long rivers.

Not all animals act because of instinct. Mother cats have to teach kittens to catch mice. Some dogs teach puppies to chase cats.

Human beings have some instincts, but experts disagree on what they are. Because human beings learn so much from their parents, it is hard to know what they do because they learned how and what they do because it is natural to them.

insulation

Any material that holds in or keeps out heat or sound is called insulation. Heat insulation is very important in keeping homes warm in winter and cool in summer. It also is used on steam and hot-water pipes, on furnaces, in refrigerators, and in other places where the transfer of heat is not desired.

Sound insulation is used in broadcasting studios, auditoriums, and homes to reduce the noise in rooms, eliminate echoes, improve the sound, and keep out unwanted noises.

Insulation of electrical conductors is explained in the articles INSULATOR and CONDUCTOR.

HEAT INSULATION

Many different materials insulate against heat. Asbestos, fur, glass, stone, wood and wool are some of the important ones. Dead air (air that is not moving) also makes good insulation. Moving air does not make good insulation because it transfers heat by its motion.

Air spaces are found in most heat-insulating material, such as asbestos and rock wool. Many houses are built with double walls that are separated by air or by other insulating material with air spaces in it. Many apartment buildings are built with bricks that have large holes in them, called insulating bricks. Bricks are also used to line furnaces and prevent heat from escaping through their walls. Furnaces are usually insulated with a special kind of material called magnesia, made from the metal magnesium and used to make special bricks called firebricks.

Because fur and wool make good insulation, they are used to make winter clothes to protect us from the cold. These materials also have many dead air spaces in them. Winter clothing made from them not only keeps the cold out but also keeps our body heat from escaping. People can keep warmer if they wear their coats with the fur inside and leather on the outside, as the Eskimos who live near the North Pole do. Leather is airtight

and keeps out the cold winds and air. When fur is on the outside, the winds blow out the warm dead-air spaces from between the hairs and lets the body heat escape.

Because dead air is such a good insulator, it is much better to sleep in winter with two thin blankets over you than one heavy one. The dead-air space between the two blankets increases the insulation.

The refrigerator in your home usually has two or even three walls in its sides, separated by mineral wool or cork board containing many dead-air spaces. This prevents heat from entering the refriger-

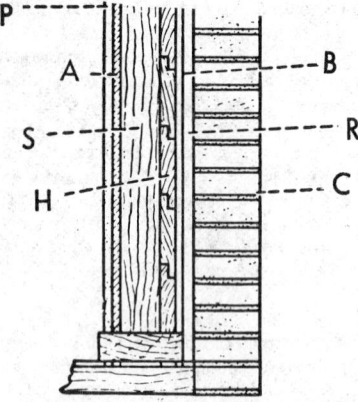

House walls are often insulated by leaving a space of "dead air" (R) between the bricks (C) and the building paper (B). Insulation is also given by the sheathing (H), studs (S), plasterboard (A), and plaster (P).

ator. Ovens are similarly insulated to prevent heat from escaping.

A vacuum (no air) is even better insulation than dead air. Such insulation is used in the familiar vacuum bottle (best-

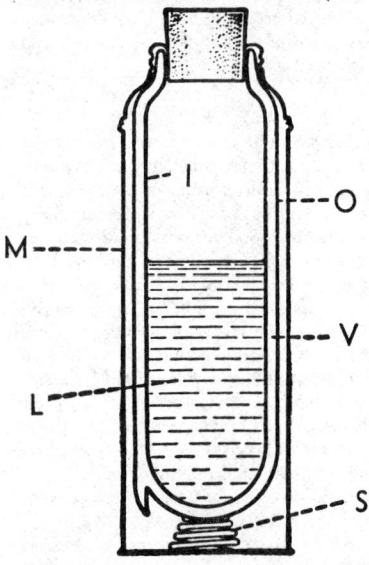

A thermos bottle uses a vacuum (V) to keep a liquid (L) warm. It is made up of a metal protecting case (M), an outside wall (O), an inner wall (I), and a spring (S) to protect the inner container.

known under the trade name "Thermos"), in which liquids such as coffee or tea can be kept hot or cold. The vacuum bottle is a metal container in which there are two glass containers separated from each other by a vacuum.

SOUND INSULATION

Special materials are used to deaden sound and keep it from getting out or into

a room. If you sprinkle sawdust on the floor, you will deaden the sound of footsteps. Rubber soles and heels accomplish the same effect. Rugs on the floor and curtains on the windows are used for both sound and heat insulation. Many churches and public places have inlaid cork floors to reduce echo and deaden unwanted noise. A material sold under such trade names as Celotex is often used to "soundproof" radio studios and lecture halls. This material has many small holes in it. The holes catch or absorb the sound so that it cannot bounce back into the room as a disturbing echo. Many modern broadcasting and recording studios have vacuum or dead-air spaces between the walls to eliminate outside noise.

A vacuum is useful for both heat and sound insulation, as sound cannot travel in a vacuum. (You can read more about sound in the articles on SOUND and ACOUSTICS.)

insulator

An insulator is any material that prevents the flow of electricity. Such materials as glass, porcelain, cotton, linen, rubber, wax, asbestos, and many plastics, are good insulators. Rubber and cotton are used to cover electric wires to prevent electricity from flowing out of them and shocking you when you touch them. Porcelain and glass rods are usually hung from the ends of high-tension wires carrying large amounts of electricity. You can see them out in the country on top of high steel towers, or in the city on top of the wooden transmission poles. These rods prevent electricity from seeping to the ground and causing serious injury and even death.

You can read more about insulators in the article on CONDUCTOR.

insulin, a substance that helps the body to use sugar: see the article on DIABETES.

insurance

Insurance is a method of making sure that no accident or other unfortunate happening can cost you more money than you can afford. Such an unfortunate happening might be the death of the person who supports a family; an accident or serious illness; the burning down of a house or factory; or any case in which you might unexpectedly owe much more money than you can pay.

The idea of insurance is based on this fact: such unfortunate things happen to only a few people, not to everybody. If everybody puts up a small amount of money that he can easily afford to pay, it will create a large fund (amount of money) from which the unfortunate few can pay their big losses. Such funds are held by companies called insurance companies.

TYPES OF INSURANCE COMPANY

There are two main types of insurance company. The *capital stock insurance company* is privately owned. If the company makes a profit, it goes to the stockholders who own the company. The *mutual insurance company* is owned by all the people who buy insurance from the company, and if the company makes a profit each of these people receives a share

(called a *dividend.*)

Before the formation of the big insurance companies that we know today, individual businessmen would take the risk of insuring people. Such men are called *underwriters.* A number of underwriters often band together to take the risk for an especially large policy. The most famous company handling marine insurance (the insuring of ships and their cargoes) is Lloyd's of London. This company began in 1690 with meetings of underwriters, shipowners, and merchants, in the coffeehouse of Edward Lloyd; in 1744 the underwriters formally banded together. But even today, Lloyds is only a large group of individuals, several of whom may share the risk on any policy.

HOW INSURANCE WORKS

When you want to be insured against some unfortunate accident, you buy a *policy* from an insurance company. The policy is a contract that tells how much you agree to pay to the insurance company, what they are protecting you against, and how much they will pay you for any one of a number of accidents. The amount you agree to pay for the insurance is called the *premium.* Premiums are based on a yearly figure, but usually they can be paid in several payments: monthly; quarterly (four times a year); or semiannually (twice a year). The amount the insurance company will pay if the accident happens is called the *benefit;* the person who will be paid is called the *beneficiary.*

There are three principal kinds of insurance used today: *life insurance, property insurance,* and *casualty insurance.* Each of these three kinds includes several subdivisions.

LIFE INSURANCE

Life insurance is the most common kind of insurance in the United States today. The *face value,* or total benefits promised, of all the life insurance policies now held amounts to about six hundred billion dollars.

A life insurance policy cannot insure that the holder of it will not die, but it does insure that his family will be taken care of financially if he does die. Anyone who has other people depending on him for support, especially the head of a family, usually takes out life insurance. If the policyholder should die his beneficiaries are paid the full amount of the insurance, either in one lump sum or as a regular income for a certain number of years or for the rest of their lives.

The amount of the premium that must be paid each year depends on the age of the person who buys the life insurance. The younger the person is when he buys the policy, the less he pays each year, because he is expected to live longer and pay more premiums over the years than an older person would. Once you have an insurance policy, the rate of premium never changes.

A person who applies for life insurance is given a thorough physical examination so that the company can decide whether he is a "good risk." Persons whose health is not good, or persons in dangerous jobs, often find it difficult to buy life insurance, or must pay higher premiums.

There are different kinds of life insurance. The simplest kind is called *term in-*

surance. It runs for only a short period of time, such as five years. If the policyholder survives this period, he receives nothing. If the policyholder should die within the term of the insurance, his beneficiaries are provided for. The insurance you can buy when you take an airplane flight is a form of term insurance, the term being only the length of the flight. Premiums are lowest on term insurance.

The most popular form of life insurance is called *ordinary,* or *straight life, insurance.* The premiums are higher than on term insurance, but the policy never expires. Straight life insurance is also a form of savings. It builds up a *cash value,* and the policyholder may borrow against it if he should need money badly. If the policyholder should die with a loan against his policy still unpaid, the amount of the loan is subtracted from the benefit of the policy before the beneficiary is paid. This cash value of the policy can be taken by the policyholder at any time he wishes, by surrendering the policy and asking that the cash value be paid him in a lump sum or in payments over a number of years.

Another kind of life insurance is the *annuity policy.* The annuity policy calls for payment of premiums over a certain number of years, perhaps twenty or thirty, and pays monthly benefits to the policyholder after the policy is paid up. The annuity is used by people who want to retire from work or business at a certain age.

Still another kind of insurance is the *endowment policy.* On this, premiums are paid for a certain number of years, usually twenty, and at the end of that time the face value of the policy is paid in a lump sum or as regular income.

PROPERTY INSURANCE

Property insurance protects policyholders from loss of money caused by damage to things he owns. You can protect your house, your jewelry, your automobile, your crops, your machinery or almost anything else you own by property insurance. *Fire insurance* is the most usual kind of property insurance. If a house burns down, the company must pay the cost of replacing it. A fire insurance policy may also include protection against other kinds of damage, such as windstorms, hail, hurricanes, floods, or falling aircraft.

Property insurance policies are usually made for short periods of time, such as three or five years. The premium depends on how much of a risk or loss there is. For example, if you live in a fireproof apartment house, your fire insurance premium will be less than if you live in an old wooden house. If you live on the Atlantic coast, hurricane insurance will cost more than if you live on the Pacific coast.

CASUALTY INSURANCE

Casualty insurance protects the policyholder from having to pay damages to another person who is injured through the policyholder's fault. If you are to blame for damaging someone else's car in an automobile accident, or if the driver of the other car is injured, you can be forced to pay for repairs or hospital bills. Casualty, or *liability,* insurance will provide the money you need for this. Almost all automobile-owners carry insurance of this

kind, and in some states they are required by law to do so. Liability insurance also protects you against claims for injury to another person while he is on your property, injury to another person by your dog or other pet, and many other kinds of personal injury. Another form of casualty insurance protects against loss of certain kinds of property by burglary or theft.

Accident and health insurance are also considered casualty insurance. These policies will pay the insured person if he loses time from work through accident or illness, and will pay a certain proportion of the hospital and doctor bills. Many people carry accident and health policies for themselves and their families. Some companies carry such policies for all their employees.

THE GOVERNMENT AND INSURANCE

The United States government and the governments of several other countries and of many states have insurance programs of their own.

Social Security is a form of insurance. It is a kind of annuity insurance that helps take care of people after they have passed working age. Under the social security system the employer and the employee share the cost of the premiums, and the employee's share is deducted from his salary by his employer, who turns it over to the government.

Unemployment compensation is another form of government insurance. A working person who loses his job may collect a certain amount of money each week for a certain number of weeks. The premiums for this insurance are paid entirely by the employer.

Workmen's compensation is a form of insurance that the employer is required to carry. The policy is usually bought from a private insurance company. It provides payment to any employee injured in the course of his work.

The laws of most states require insurance companies to have enough money on hand, called *reserves,* to pay any claims that might be expected. They also require insurance companies to take care of the money paid to them as premiums, and to invest it wisely.

HISTORY OF INSURANCE

Insurance is more than four thousand years old. Traders in ancient Babylonia had a kind of insurance to protect their caravans against robbers and other risks. Merchants have been insuring their goods in one way or another ever since then. Life insurance goes back to the Roman Empire, when men formed burial clubs that paid for their funeral expenses and made payments to their families. In the Middle Ages, the workmen's guilds protected their members against losses from fire, shipwreck, and pirates.

About 250 years ago, Edmund Halley (who is better known as an astronomer) compiled the first table of life expectancy. This made it possible for insurance premiums to be based on the age of the person to be insured. Before that time premiums were the same for persons of all ages, and this was unfair to the younger people.

Liability insurance was started in the 1880s, and the first Workmen's Compensation Act was passed in England in 1897. Other forms of insurance followed, to

meet the changing conditions of life and business. Today it is possible to get insurance against practically anything, from injury to a dancer's legs or a pianist's fingers to the possibility of rain on the day of an important ball game.

intaglio

Intaglio is a way of cutting a design into a stone, or a stone that has had a design cut into it. The pattern is "bitten" into the stone with acid, or it is carved out. If you try pressing something with a carved design onto a piece of soft wax or tallow, you will see that it leaves a raised pattern. In the days when people used their own seals or insignias for closing letters, they would have rings with initials in them. They would pour some hot wax on the back of the envelope and then press the ring against it to leave a pattern. Intaglios were used in ancient Egypt and Greece.

The word *intaglio* is also used to describe a method of printing. Engraved stationery is made by the intaglio process. The letters are cut or etched into metal. Ink fills the etched letters and is transferred to paper pressed against the printing plate. That is why the letters on engraved paper feel raised to the touch. You can read more about intaglio printing in a separate article on PRINTING.

intelligence and intelligence test

Intelligence is the ability to think, to learn, and to solve new problems. Just as different people are of different height, so people are of different intelligence.

Some people can learn many things well. When they are faced with new problems they can go right to work to find the answers. These people are said to have general intelligence. On the other hand, some boys and girls are quick about learning arithmetic but slow about learning spelling. Some are good in the use of words but not in the use of numbers. Because of these different abilities, some scientists have said that there are special kinds of intelligence for different things, and that people can be high in one kind and low in another.

The amount of intelligence a person possesses depends both on birth and on education. Every human being is born with a certain basic intelligence that will increase as he grows. It will increase to a greater extent in some than in others. How far each develops his intelligence depends on education and the opportunities that arise to use intelligence.

Very few people develop their intelligence as far as it can go. Low grades in school need not be a sign of low intelli-

Fitting differently shaped pieces of wood in holes, each of which fits only one piece.

:ːʿer	**ːʕʌ**
1. space around a fireplace	1. a bunch of flowers
2. a stream of water	2. business of printing magazines
3. a light flashes	3. one's reputation
4. note in the musical scale	4. a bird

Career Counseling Service—Richardson, Bellows, Henry and Co., Inc., N.Y.C.

Many sections of an intelligence test present interesting puzzles. One is the "broken-letter" section. When completed, the broken letters on the left spell "river," and the correct answer is therefore 2. Can you answer the question on the right? The answer is "raven," No. 4.

gence. There can be many other reasons. Some children have good intelligence but have trouble learning because they are unhappy and cannot think about their work. Others are slow to learn because no one has noticed that their eyes are bad and they need glasses.

When children are taken from poor schools or from crowded slums where no one had time to care for them and are given care and good educations, they usually develop their intelligence more than they were able to before.

INTELLIGENCE TESTING

Psychologists (scientists who study the human mind) have ways of testing intelligence. The first intelligence test was worked out in France by a French psychologist named Alfred Binet. With the help of an assistant, Théophile Simon, he tried to discover why some children had so much trouble with their school work. The two men examined hundreds of children and found that most children of the same age could do the same things. They then set up tests that most children of a certain age could pass. An American psychologist named Lewis Terman of Stanford University made changes in these tests. The test that he set up is called the Stanford-Binet Test.

Children are given the tests that are right for their age. A two-year-old child is asked to name certain things or do things with blocks. A ten-year-old child may be asked to name as many flowers as he can in one minute or to do simple arithmetic problems. If a child can work out all the tests of his own age, he is said to be of normal intelligence. Sometimes a six-year-old child can do the tests set up for nine-year-olds. He is said to have the intelligence or *mental age* of a child of nine. Thus a child's mental age can differ from his actual age. You may have heard of a person's Intelligence Quotient, or I.Q. To find it, we divide a person's mental age by his age in years and then multiply by 100. A child who has a mental age of nine and who is actually nine years old has an I.Q. of 9/9 x 100, or 100. A child of six who has a mental age of nine has an I.Q. of 9/6 x 100, or 150.

Most people have I.Q.s of 90 to 109. Those whose I.Q.s are much higher are called geniuses and those whose I.Q.s are much lower are called morons.

Psychologists have also given intelligence tests to animals. Usually the animals have to find their way through a twisting and turning path to a box of food. Many animals have some intelligence and can learn from their experiences. A grown-up chimpanzee is said to have the intelligence of a child of three.

APTITUDE TESTS

Aptitude tests are given to measure a person's ability to do certain jobs. We have seen that some people are especially good at one thing, such as learning languages, and slow at another, such as learning arithmetic. A person who wants a certain kind of job can take an aptitude test to see if he is suited for it. A girl might think that she would do well as a fashion designer, but an aptitude test might show that she did not have a good eye for color and that she could not draw well. Then the girl would know that she had better try to find a job for which she was better suited. There are many kinds of aptitude tests. Some measure how well a person can use his hands in putting things together. Some measure how well he can tell the difference between different sounds. Others measure how well he can write, how quickly he can read, or how well he can solve arithmetic problems. Many companies give aptitude tests to people who apply to them for jobs.

THE USE OF INTELLIGENCE AND APTITUDE TESTS

Intelligence and aptitude tests are used in many ways. Teachers can decide whether a child needs special training by his score on an intelligence test. Vocational-guidance counselors can help a boy or girl decide on the occupation for which he or she is best suited. The army uses tests to help decide the work men should do.

INTELLIGENCE AND RACE

For a long time it was thought that certain races were less intelligent than others. Some people also said that women were less intelligent than men. But psychologists showed that when boys and girls of different races were given the same chance for an education there were the same number of high, middle, and low I.Q.s in each group.

intelligence service

An intelligence service gathers information for an army, navy, air force, or government department. When the information is about an enemy's military strength, industrial strength, and future plans, it is called *military intelligence*. The intelligence men collect the information and then advise their commanding officers when and where to attack or where to watch for an enemy attack. For a war to be fought successfully it is as necessary to have this information as it is to have the right kind of fighting equipment. Governments also collect intelligence during peacetime, so that they can find out if a country is preparing

to attack them. A government wants to know about new factories that are being built in other countries and new scientific discoveries being made there. Friendly countries exchange such information with one another.

During a war there are intelligence officers assigned to each fighting unit. Some of these officers provide what is called *combat intelligence*. They send out patrols into enemy territory and try to capture prisoners. Any change that is reported behind enemy lines may lead intelligence officers to important information about troop movements. In the air force, intelligence officers tell pilots what to expect when they go out on bombing missions. They tell them about enemy planes that may attack them and about enemy antiaircraft guns that may fire on them. The intelligence unit of the air force also sends out men to photograph enemy territory from the air. Photo-intelligence officers study the photographs to find out what they can.

Armies also have a counter-intelligence section that works behind the lines trying to prevent the enemy from getting information. Sometimes they will give enemy spies false information to throw the enemy off the track. Some of this intelligence work is so secret that nothing can be reported about it.

The United States Army and Navy had separate intelligence units during World War II. The chief Army General Staff intelligence section was called G-2. Air Force General Staff was called A-2. Navy intelligence was called the Office of Naval Intelligence, O.N.I. for short. One department that did much good intelligence work during the war, especially in counter-intelligence, was the Office of Strategic Services, known as O.S.S. Many civilians worked for O.S.S. It was disbanded after the war and the Central Intelligence Agency took its place. You may read about this agency in a separate article.

Collecting military intelligence is a very old practice. The pharaohs (rulers) of Egypt sent spies ahead of their armies, and Greece and Rome also used spies. The embassies and consulates that countries set up in other countries to take care of their affairs are often used for collecting information about those other countries. People in the intelligence service must be carefully trained. You can read more about this in the article on ESPIONAGE.

interest

Interest is money paid for the right to use borrowed money. If you borrow $100 from a bank, you must usually pay back $106 or $107. The extra $6 or $7 is interest. Banks are in the business of lending money and charging interest for the use of it, just as a grocer charges a profit on the groceries he sells. Other businesses that make their profits by charging interest for the use of money are called "finance companies," or by other names.

Banks are not allowed to charge more than a certain rate of interest for the money they lend. This rate is set by state laws, and in most states the rate for ordinary loans is not more than 6 per cent. Any rate higher than the one set by law is called usury.

Even governments have to borrow money and pay interest. When a govern-

ment borrows money it usually pays less interest than you would, because lending money to a government is considered safe. A bank or a person who lends money to a government is almost certain to get the money back.

Some kinds of bank also pay interest to the people who deposit money with them. If you deposit money in a savings bank, the bank will pay you about four cents every year for each dollar you put in if you leave it for the whole year.

interior decoration

Interior decoration is the science that deals with the planning of the interior of a room, a home, an office, or a building. Modern interior decoration is not only a matter of good taste but is based on knowledge of mathematics and architecture, light and color, and the cultures and art of all ages.

An interior decorator starts with the floor plan. Next he plans the lighting, and only then does he choose the colors and fabrics to be used.

Color cannot be seen without light, and different kinds of light have different effects on colors. Under fluorescent light red looks purplish, while under ordinary light red appears as more of an orange color. That is why it is important to decide on the type of lighting before choosing colors.

The levels at which light is placed can change the appearance of a room. Eye-level light makes a room seem larger than it actually is. Light placed below eye-level makes a room more comfortable for resting or for having private conversations.

By selecting the right colors, an interior decorator can make a room seem smaller or larger. Light colors make a small room seem larger, while dark colors make a large room seem smaller.

STYLES IN DECORATION

There are many different styles in decorating rooms. Some of them copy styles that were popular long ago. Others have been designed by interior decorators in recent years and are called *modern*. Designs based on former times are called *period treatments*. The most important styles are given names that indicate the time in the history of a country when they first came into use. From France come styles named for the various kings named Louis, such as *Louis XIV* or *Louis XV*. *Directoire* is named for the period after the French Revolution when France was ruled by a group of men called the Directory; and *Empire* is named for the time when Napoleon Bonaparte was emperor of the French. In England the naming of styles has been very much the same. The *Elizabethan* style is named for the time when Queen Elizabeth I ruled England; the *Jacobean* style is named for the reign of James I (Jacobus is the Latin form of James); the *Georgian* style is named for the reigns of Kings George I, II, and III; and the *Victorian* style is named for the reign of Queen Victoria. The *Regency* style was named for a period when France was ruled by a regent who acted for the young Louis XV, and was later adopted for the period from 1811 to 1820 in England, when that country was ruled by a regent. Other well-known styles have

been named for men who were designers of furniture, about which you can read in the article FURNITURE. A popular style of decoration in the United States is *Colonial*, which originated in the days before the American colonies won their independence from England.

All styles of decoration are in use today, and often several styles are combined in one room. Modern backgrounds of wall treatment, windows, and lights are used to point up by their simplicity the elaborate beauty of period furniture. Even for period treatments, light, clean colors are preferred to the dusty, grayish colors of the periods.

The smaller the room, the more modern should be its treatment, because modern styles were designed for smaller houses. Modern furniture and materials are designed also to be very practical. Sturdy, rustproof, wrought-iron furniture is inexpensive and designed for today's use.

Plastic materials are often used for table tops and other surfaces, so that they will not be burned by carelessly dropped cigarettes or stained by food, drinks, or hot dishes. Tiles are used because they are easy to keep clean and are now made of inexpensive materials. Furniture is made to serve two or more purposes. Picture

The modern interior decorator has to make rooms and houses comfortable, even though today they are built much smaller than they were formerly. There-

fore many designs are made so as to save space. Modern designers find ways of keeping in the background little-used furniture, such as a dining table that is used for two hours a day while beds and chairs are used for much longer periods of time.

A bed that can serve as a sofa in the daytime is important in many small houses and apartments.

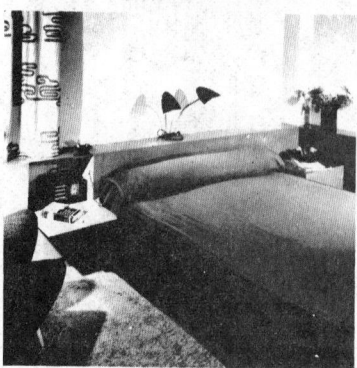

Another space-saving device is a storage wall that can be dismantled and moved but looks like part of the permanent wall. It provides space for books, dishes, linen, silverware, records and record-player, radio, television set, a typewriter desk and filing space, or a bar.

Designs and Illustrations, Courtesy of Kim Hoffmann—Stephen Heidrich, New York.

Designers have made desks that range from office-style units to simple planks of wood. There are even "dresks" (dressing-table-desks) that can be used both as a vanity-table and as a desk.

INTERIOR DECORATING AS A CAREER

Interior decorators plan the decorating scheme of homes and offices. Often they also buy the furniture, draperies and accessories for the places they plan. The decorator starts by learning how much his client wishes to spend and which style he prefers. Then the decorator makes a sketch of what he believes will

be suitable, showing the arrangement of furniture and the color scheme, and giving the cost. When the client approves the plan, the decorator proceeds to buy the furniture and other furnishings. The decorator buys at wholesale prices and may charge his client the retail price. The difference is what he gets for the job. Another way of charging is to set a flat fee in advance.

To be a decorator you must have a good sense of design and color and have a thorough knowledge of furniture styles, fabrics, lamps, and other accessories. If you want to become a decorator you can attend one of many special schools, but there are many good decorators who have never taken courses. They learn their profession simply by helping interior decorators until they learn enough to work for themselves. Many decorators are employed by department stores and furniture stores to help their customers plan

their homes. Interior decorating is a growing field and successful decorators are paid very well.

Interior, Department of

The Department of the Interior is one of the main divisions of the United States government. The purpose of the Department of the Interior is to take care of the land and natural resources that belong to the United States. It sees that the forests and parks and wild animals of the country are preserved, and it plans new parks and great dams, and many other projects that improve the country. The Department of the Interior is responsible for about 770 million acres of land in the United States, as well as the island territories and possessions.

The Department of the Interior was established more than a hundred years ago, in 1849. At first it was called the Home Department. The head of the department is called the Secretary of the Interior. He is appointed by the President and is a member of the President's Cabinet.

Altogether there were 63,353 people working for the Department of the Interior in 1962. There were 58,638 full-time workers and 4,210 part-time workers in the United States, 183 workers in United States territories and possessions, and 322 workers in foreign countries.

The Department of the Interior is divided into several large sections, and

each section does a special kind of work. The Bureau of Mines, for example, makes experiments to find better and safer ways to mine different minerals. The National Park Service and the Fish and Wildlife Service see to it that national parks are kept beautiful and that the animals are not harmed. The Bureau of Reclamation supervises the building of dams and other ways of getting and using water for irrigation and preventing floods. It decides how best to use the electric power that great dams produce.

The Bureau of Indian Affairs is concerned with the welfare of the American Indians who live in the United States and Alaska. This section makes it possible for the Indians to receive education and medical care. It helps them to improve their methods of farming and also assists them in money matters.

interjection

Interjections are words that show sudden or strong feelings. Sometimes interjections are also called exclamations. They may be the oldest form of speech. Early man used exclamations to show surprise, just as we do today. Some interjections are said or written alone without other words. We may cry out in a loud voice: *ah! oh! hurrah! hey! ssh! goody! alas! well! bravo! ouch! goodness!* If we wish to show excitement, we put an exclamation mark (!) after every interjection we write. Sometimes we use several words as an interjection, for example, *"What a lovely day!"* At other times we may start a sentence with an interjection such as "*Oh,* how late you are!" Here the interjection *oh* is an independent part of the sentence. That is the reason for its name. The word *interjection* means "something that is thrown in."

internal combustion engine

An internal combustion engine is a device for running automobiles, trucks, airplanes, motorcycles, motorboats, and many types of machine. When an internal combustion engine uses gasoline as a fuel, it is simply called a gasoline engine.

Most internal combustion engines work by burning a mixture of air and the fuel, such as gasoline or oil. This is caused by an electric spark from a special device called a spark plug. A diesel engine is an internal combustion engine that works without spark plugs.

Internal combustion means "inside burning," that is, the fuel is burned inside the engine. The burned fuel produces gases that push down a piece of metal called a *piston*. The piston is connected by a rod to a special shaft called a *crankshaft*. When the piston is pushed down it turns the crankshaft. The crankshaft turns a heavy metal wheel called a *flywheel*. In an automobile, the flywheel turns a long shaft connected to the rear wheels, which drive the car.

The piston of an internal combustion engine fits inside a hole called a *cylinder*. The hole is in a heavy block of metal. At the top of the cylinder are two openings. One opening is to allow air and gasoline to enter the cylinder. This opening is opened and closed by an *inlet valve*. The other opening is to allow the gases to escape from the cylinder after the air-and-

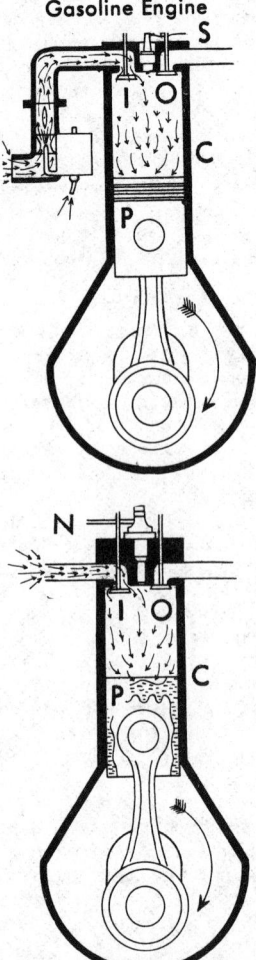

Gasoline Engine

Diesel Engine

General Motors Corp.

Both gasoline and diesel engines use internal combustion. In the gasoline engine, a mixture of air and gasoline enters the cylinder (C) through an inlet valve (I), and is exploded by a spark plug (S). This operates the piston (P), thus driving the engine. Vaporized gases left over escape through the outlet valve (O). The diesel uses fuel oil instead of gasoline. The fuel enters the cylinder at the proper moment through the injector (N). The heated air in the cylinder burns the fuel and drives the piston.

gasoline mixture has been exploded. This opening is opened and closed by an *outlet valve*.

Both the inlet and outlet valves are operated by two rods that rest on two lopsided disks called *cams*. The cams are on a special shaft called a *camshaft*. The camshaft is turned by a gear connected to the crankshaft. The camshaft turns at one-half the speed of the crankshaft.

When the camshaft turns, the cams raise and lower the rods that rest on them, opening and closing the inlet and outlet valves at exactly the right times.

STARTING THE ENGINE

To start the engine, the piston must be pulled down. Turning the crankshaft pulls down the piston. In old automobiles the crankshaft used to be turned by a hand crank in front of the car. In modern automobiles, it is done by pressing a *starter*. The starter turns an electric motor that turns the crankshaft.

Once the engine has started, the crank-

shaft will be turned by the up-and-down motion of the piston in the cylinder. Engines in which a piston moves up and down in a cylinder are called *reciprocating engines*.

As the piston moves down, the inlet valve opens and lets the air-and-gasoline mixture into the space at the top of the cylinder called the *combustion chamber*. When the piston has gone as far down

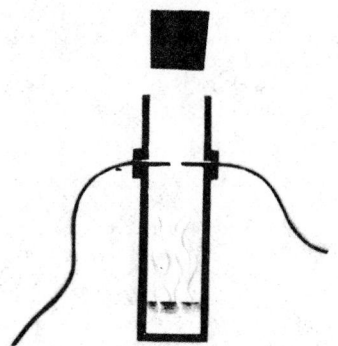

Copyright Curriculum Films, Inc.

An internal combustion engine uses air and fuel, ignited by a spark, to create an explosion inside a cylinder.

as it can, the inlet valve closes. The downward stroke of the piston is called the *intake stroke*.

The crankshaft keeps turning. The piston starts upward. As it does, it presses against the mixture of air and gasoline. In most internal combustion engines, this mixture is pressed into about one-seventh the space it originally occupied. (This is called a *compression ratio* of 7 to 1.) The upward motion of the piston is called the *compression stroke*.

IGNITION AND TIMING

When the piston reaches the top of the cylinder, an electric spark flashes from the spark plug. The tip of the spark plug is inside the cylinder. The back of the spark plug is outside the cylinder and is connected by wires to the *ignition system* of the engine.

The spark plug must shoot out its spark at just the right instant or the engine will not operate properly. For this purpose a special switch called a *timer* is used. The switch is closed by the cam underneath the inlet valve rod. When the switch closes, electricity flows from the ignition system to the spark plug and produces an electric spark. The spark should come at the end of the compression stroke of the piston.

The electric spark from the spark plug sets the air-and-gasoline mixture on fire. The burning mixture produces very hot gases that explode and give the piston a violent push downward. This is called the *power stroke*. The pressure of the gases against the piston is about 400 pounds per square inch.

When the piston reaches the bottom of the cylinder, the outlet valve opens. The flywheel and crankshaft continue to turn and by so doing they push the piston back up. The upward stroke of the piston is called the *exhaust stroke*. The moving piston forces the hot gases to shoot out of the open outlet valve and through an exhaust pipe to the back of the automobile. The hot gases shoot out of the ex-

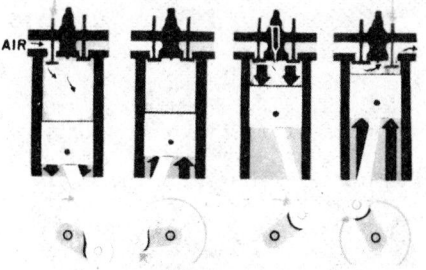

INTAKE   COMPRESSION   POWER   EXHAUST

Copyright Curriculum Films, Inc.

The four cycles of a diesel engine, using the principle of internal combustion.

haust pipe into the open air. A special device called a *muffler* usually is attached to the end of the exhaust pipe. The muffler allows the hot gases to expand and cool a little. Otherwise there would be a loud, popping noise made by the escaping gases.

After the gases have been pushed out of the outlet valve, the outlet valve closes. Then the whole process is repeated. It all happens so fast that the flywheel makes several thousand revolutions per minute.

CYCLES

The series of four strokes in which the piston goes up twice and down twice is called a cycle. Most gasoline engines are four-stroke cycle, or simply four-cycle, engines. Some engines used on motorcycles, outboard motorboats, washing machines and home electric-generating plants are two-stroke cycle (or two-cycle) engines. Every downward stroke is a power stroke.

In order to get more power a number of cylinders are usually operated together. The added power keeps the crankshaft and flywheel turning more smoothly. Most internal combustion engines have four or more cylinders. Six- and eight-cylinder engines are most commonly used in modern automobiles. Some airplane engines have thirty-six cylinders.

The pistons of all the cylinders are connected to the same crankshaft. The camshaft and the timer are so adjusted that the spark plugs in each cylinder fire one after the other. In an eight-cylinder engine each cylinder fires once for every two complete turns of the flywheel. In most automobiles, about five turns of the flywheel produce one turn of the wheels. When a car is traveling at sixty miles an hour, the wheels are making ten complete turns a second. This means that the flywheel must make fifty complete turns a second. In an eight-cylinder engine, this means that the cylinders must fire two hundred times a second. Each cylinder must fire twenty-five times a second.

Cylinders may be arranged on an engine in several ways. In six-cylinder automobiles, the cylinders are arranged one behind the other, called "in line." In most eight-cylinder automobiles, the cylinders are placed in two groups of four at an angle with each other. This engine is called a *V-8 engine*. In some airplane engines, the cylinders are placed in a circle, with the crankshaft turning inside the engine. The engine is called a *radial engine*.

The operation of an engine often produces temperatures as high as 4500 degrees Fahrenheit. Such temperatures are

sufficient to melt most parts of the engine. To prevent this from happening the cylinders usually are surrounded by metal pipes or jackets containing cool water. The jackets of water carry the heat away from the hottest parts of the engine to many copper pipes in the radiator at the front of the car. The water is pumped to keep it flowing continuously. A fan draws in air through the metal slats or fins of the radiator. The air serves to cool the water flowing through the pipes.

Many airplane engines, and some two- and four-cycle engines used in small machinery, are air-cooled. They use no liquid coolant.

All the moving parts of an engine must be well oiled to keep them from wearing out and keep them moving

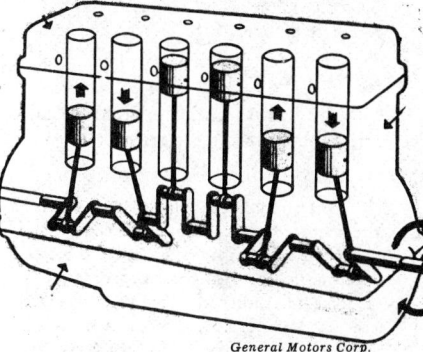

General Motors Corp.

Automobile and airplane gasoline engines use several cylinders to create internal combustion. As a result, the flow of power is smooth and there is less shaking. The engine shown here is that of "six cylinders in line."

smoothly. Oil is also very important in keeping the pistons fitting tightly in the cylinders. Unless the cylinders are airtight (no air allowed in except that mixed with gasoline from the inlet valve), the engine will not operate properly.

DIESEL ENGINE

A diesel engine is a special kind of internal combustion engine. It has no spark plugs and uses oil instead of gasoline. It is used in many heavy tractors, trucks, buses, locomotives, and ships.

The advantage of a diesel engine lie in the low cost of the fuel, the fact that the engine can start quickly, and its large power output. Because the pressure in a diesel engine is so much higher than in a gas engine, heavier pistons and cylinders are required. This added weight is one of the main reasons why diesel engines are not used in passenger cars.

In a diesel engine, air is compressed in the cylinder to a pressure of more than 500 pounds per square inch. The compression ratio is about 15 to 1 (compared to less than 8 to 1 in an automobile engine). This raises the temperature of the air to more than 1,000 degrees (on the Fahrenheit scale), making it hot enough to burn the fuel oil that is sprayed into the cylinder at the proper time. The mixture of air and oil burns without exploding, producing gases to drive the pistons.

A diesel engine may contain any number of cylinders, and is built for either two-cycle or four-cycle operation. It was invented by Rudolf Diesel, a German engineer, in 1892. Diesel's first engine used coal dust as the fuel, and many engines since then have been made to run on almost anything that will burn.

internal revenue

The money that a government raises inside its own borders is called internal revenue. The rest of its income comes from external revenue, the customs duties on goods that are imported into the country. Internal revenue today is by far the most important source of income for the United States government, amounting to more than nine out of every ten dollars the government receives. This has not always been true. In the early days of the United States, customs brought in nearly all the money. Most of internal revenue today comes from government taxes on personal incomes and the profits of corporations. The rest is produced by what are called excise taxes, which are taxes on the sale or use of such things as liquor, tobacco, gasoline, entertainment, transportation, telephones, furs, jewelry, and many other things. See the articles on TAX and INCOME TAX.

International Date Line: see the article on DATE LINE, INTERNATIONAL.

international law

International law is a name used for the methods that countries consider correct in dealing with one another. It is not like the law of a single country or state, because if a country does not want to obey the law there is no police force to make it do so. Most countries do follow the international law most of the time, because they do not want people all over the world to think badly of them.

Written international law consists of treaties, which are agreements signed by two or more countries. In a treaty, each country promises to do, or not to do, certain things. A treaty may deal with commercial (business) affairs, as when the United States and Canada make an agreement as to how the St. Lawrence Seaway is to be built and managed. Two countries may also make a treaty to be friends or allies, so that if one country is attacked the other will help it. Treaties are also called pacts, protocols, and by other names. The charter of the United Nations is a treaty.

Countries nearly always do what they agree to do in treaties dealing with commercial matters, unless they go to war against the country with which they made the treaty. In that case they cancel the treaty.

Countries seldom keep their promises in treaties dealing with war unless it pays them to do so. In World War I, Germany broke a treaty when it invaded Belgium. A country will sometimes "denounce" (call off) a treaty of friendship with another country, as a threat to that country. The Communist government of Russia did that to Turkey after World War II, because it wanted to demand more than the treaty gave it. Russia also violated many of its wartime treaties with the United States and its other allies, but pretended that it understood the agreements differently.

UNWRITTEN INTERNATIONAL LAW

Unwritten international law consists of customs that countries have followed for many years. Experts in this kind of international law know history thoroughly. When two countries have a dispute, they study past history to find out what other countries considered it right to do in the same circumstances. This is called *precedent*, which means "what happened before." Precedent gives certain rights to ambassadors and other diplomats, to neutral countries (countries that are not fighting) in time of war, to the rights of countries in their own territory and on the seas, and in hundreds of other cases dealing with both peacetime and wartime. Unwritten international law is very complicated but countries really get along very well by using it.

ENFORCING INTERNATIONAL LAW

It has always been very difficult and even impossible to enforce international law because there were no organizations that had enough power to enforce it. At the very end of the last century some organizations were set up which made a start in this direction. And in this century we have had first the League of Nations and then the United Nations to see to it that countries of the world work together to find ways to guarantee fair treatment of all countries by all other countries. One very important part of the United Nations is the International Court of Justice, in The Hague, in Holland. When two countries have a dispute, they can take their complaints to this court and have the dispute decided by a group of judges. They do not have to follow the decision of the judges, but they usually do.

See also GENEVA CONVENTION and UNITED NATIONS.

Interstate Commerce Commission

The Interstate Commerce Commission (ICC) is an agency of the United States Government. Its business is to make sure that common carriers (railroads, buses, shipping lines, and other companies that transport goods for anyone who pays their charges) are charging fair prices for their services and are giving good service. When passengers or freight are moved entirely within one state of the United States, only that state has the right to make laws controlling them, but when passengers or freight are carried across a state line, the Federal Government has the authority to make the laws concerning them. This means that the Interstate Commerce Commission controls nearly all the big railroads, bus lines and shipping lines in the United States. It has eleven members, who are appointed by the President to serve for seven years.

intestine

The intestine is a tube that forms the lower end of the digestive system and carries food from the stomach down to the rectum. It is divided into two sections, which are known as the small and the large intestines. The small intestine is a hollow tube about twenty-three feet long and one to one and one-half inches in diameter. It begins at the lower end of the stomach, and coils back and forth inside the abdomen. Contracting muscles move food along through this tube, where a number of different digestive juices act upon it and finish the digesting process that was begun in the stomach. The digested food is absorbed by the thousands of tiny, fingerlike projections called *villi* that line the wall of the small intestine. From these it is carried into the blood stream and the lymph vessels, which carry it to all parts of the body. At its lower end, the small intestine joins the large intestine. The place where the two intestines join is a small pouch called the *caecum*, to which the *appendix* is attached. The large intestine is divided into three parts, called the *ascending colon*, the *transverse colon*, and the *descending colon*. By the time food reaches these parts of the digestive system, about all that is left is indigestible matter. The large intestine absorbs water from this, and the body then eliminates the waste products that are left.

intoxication

Intoxication is a condition in which the body is poisoned by some toxin (a poison that is made by germs) or by a harmful drug. The poison gets into the blood stream and is carried to all parts of the body. Intoxication caused by toxins gives people headaches and makes them dizzy. Sometimes they throw up and get very sick and have to be put to bed and have a doctor. Intoxication that is caused by a harmful drug, such as alcohol, is very bad for a person's nerves and brain. Often a person who is drunk is said to be intoxicated.

invention

An invention is a new way of doing something. An invention can be a machine, such as the steam engine or the automobile, or it can be a useful method, such as a brand-new way of teaching languages. Inventions differ from discoveries and compositions. The inventor finds a new way of doing something. The discoverer finds something that was always there but that men did not know about before. The composer, the writer, and the artist create something different from anything else. Inventors get patents on their inventions so that no one else can use them for a certain length of time. Artists, writers, and composers of music get copyrights for the same reason.

Whether an invention is a machine or a method, the most successful ones are always those that answer the needs of millions of people. Thomas Edison once said, "I find what the world needs, then I go ahead and try to invent it."

INVENTORS WITHOUT NAMES

Many of our greatest inventions were developed so many thousands of years ago that today no one knows the names of their inventors. In the Stone Age, men learned that the fires that flared up when lightning hit a tree could be used to cook their meat and to heat their caves. Then they learned to make fire for themselves by rubbing together pieces of wood or by striking flint. The making of fire was man's first great invention. The second great invention was seed-planting, or agriculture. The development of farming meant that men could live in one place and grow their own food, instead of roaming around hunting for it.

Man's earliest manufacturing inventions were the chipping and grinding of tools out of hard stone, and the shaping and baking of clay to make pottery.

The next really great invention was a way to melt copper over a very hot fire

and shape it into any kind of tool. Soon men began mixing tin with the copper to form an alloy called bronze. This invention was so important that a great period in history is called the Bronze Age. Soon after this, the Iron Age began.

Meanwhile, other men were working on better ways of moving heavy loads such as the great stones used to build the pyramids of Egypt. Somewhere along the way they invented the wheel, which is another of civilization's greatest gifts. Without these three inventions—fire, the wheel, and seed-planting—our modern civilization would not have been possible.

Some other great inventions of ancient times are the sailboat, the windmill, the pulley for lifting heavy weights, and the plow. But great though these inventions were, we do not know the names of the men who developed them.

Nowadays the names of many great inventors are known to all of us. But even the greatest inventors depend heavily on the work of other inventors before them. Robert Fulton, for instance, did not have to invent a steam engine to drive his ship because James Watt had already invented it. The Wright brothers drove their airplane with a gasoline engine developed by Gottfried Daimler for use in his automobile.

Some of the great modern inventors, and their famous inventions, are:

Johann Gutenberg (Germany), movable type for printing, about 1436.

James Hargreaves and Richard Arkwright (England), machines for spinning thread, about 1765.

Edmund Cartwright (England), perfected the power loom, about 1785.

James Watt (Scotland) perfected the steam engine, about 1769.

Robert Fulton (United States) perfected the steamboat, about 1807.

Eli Whitney (United States), the cotton gin, 1793. Whitney also contributed greatly to MASS PRODUCTION, about which there is a separate article.

Cyrus Hall McCormick (United States), the reaper, in 1831.

Samuel F. B. Morse (United States), the electric telegraph, 1832.

Alexander Graham Bell (United States), the telephone, 1876.

Thomas A. Edison (United States), the incandescent lamp, 1879. He made many other inventions, including the phonograph and motion pictures.

Gottlieb Daimler (Germany) and many others made important contributions to the perfection of the automobile.

Guglielmo Marconi (Italy), the wireless telegraph, 1895.

Orville and Wilbur Wright (United States), the first successful power-driven airplane, 1903. Many other men, including Samuel P. Langley and Glenn H. Curtiss, made important contributions to the airplane.

THE FUTURE OF INVENTION

The 1900s have seen great changes in the way inventions are developed. There are no longer many inventors who work all by themselves. Today's inventions are being produced in huge research laboratories where dozens of brilliant men work together in teams, and no one man can say that he alone produced a great invention. This research laboratory idea was begun by Thomas Edison. Today many great corporations operate research laboratories. The atomic bomb was invented not by one man, but by at least a dozen top-flight thinkers plus hundreds of other physicists. So, like the ancient inventors without names, our Atomic Age inventors are little known to the public.

See also the article on PATENTS.

Io

Io was a character in Greek mythology, the stories the ancient Greeks told about their gods and goddesses. Io was loved by Zeus, the most important god. To save her from his wife's jealousy, Zeus changed Io into a white heifer, or young cow. Zeus' wife Hera found out who Io was, however, and sent a gadfly, or vicious stinging insect, to torment Io. The suffering heifer wandered through many lands. She came to rest on the banks of the river Nile and regained her form as a woman. Zeus and Io had a son called Epaphus. This story is very old. A later story tells that Io married the king of Egypt and was known as the goddess Isis. She was also called the goddess of the moon, the moon being seen as a woman with the horns of a heifer.

iodine

Iodine is a chemical element, which means that it is one of the hundred basic substances of which all materials in the universe are made. Pure iodine consists of grayish-black crystals.

A small amount of iodine dissolved in alcohol makes *tincture of iodine,* the dark-brown antiseptic (germ-killer) that is found in almost every home medicine cabinet, and is used on cuts and scrapes.

IODINE IN DIET

To keep healthy, all people must have a little iodine in their diet. Not quite one two-thousandth of an ounce is all that is needed. Lack of this little bit of iodine causes a disease called GOITER, about which there is a separate article.

IODINE AND CANCER

Iodine can be made radioactive, which means that it will continually shoot off X-rays and tiny particles that are smaller than atoms. A person who becomes sick with cancer of the thyroid gland is given radioactive iodine. Since the iodine goes directly to the thyroid gland, its X-rays get right in among the cancer cells and kill them.

IODINE IN INDUSTRY AND CHEMISTRY

Iodine combined with silver makes *silver iodide,* a material that is very important in photography. Iodine is used in making dyes, drugs and industrial chemicals from coal tar.

Iodine is important in food chemistry because when it is added to any solution that contains even a trace of starch, it turns the solution a deep blue color. This works the other way around, and chemists find as little as one part of iodine in three or four million parts of water by putting a little starch into the water.

When iodine crystals are heated, they *sublime.* This means that they do not melt, but change directly from solid crystals to a gas; and when this gas is cooled it becomes crystals again, without ever being a liquid.

IODINE IS POISONOUS

Iodine is a strong poison. Anyone who swallows iodine should immediately have his stomach pumped out, or he should be given something that will make him vomit. Then he must swallow starch dissolved in water. Laundry starch can be used.

WHERE IODINE COMES FROM

In each gallon of sea water there is a trace of iodine. Seaweeds take iodine out of the sea water and make it part of their tissues. Certain kinds of seaweed contain as much as ten pounds of iodine in every ton. When the seaweed is dried, then baked until it is charred, and then treated with chemicals, pure iodine is gotten from it.

In every ton of the mineral called Chile saltpeter there is a little more than one pound of iodine. This mineral is now the chief source of iodine.

The salt water that is found in oil wells contains about 1½ pounds of iodine in every 50 tons. It supplies much of the iodine for the United States.

Iodine was discovered in 1811, when Bernard Courtois, a French saltpeter manufacturer, noticed a purple vapor rising from the seaweed he was using as a raw material. He told a famous French chemist named Joseph Louis Gay-Lussac about it, and Gay-Lussac worked with the iodine to learn its properties. Because of its purple vapor he named it iodine, from the Greek word for violet.

ion

An ion is an atom or group of atoms that has gained or lost electrons. The article on the ATOM explains that it contains tiny particles called protons and electrons. Electrons can be removed or added to an atom. When electrons are added to an atom, the atom is called a negative ion or *anion.* When electrons are removed from an atom, the atom is called a positive ion or *cation.*

Ions are necessary for the flow of electricity. When electricity flows through a wire, electrons go in one end of the wire from one side of the battery or generator, and out the other end of the wire to the other side of the battery or generator. Work is done on the electrons in the battery or generator to carry them over to where they can again enter the first end of the wire, and so repeat their travels again and again until the "electrical connection" is broken by opening a switch.

Ions also conduct electricity through a gas. When a wire connected to the negative terminal of a battery or generator is placed in a gas, positive ions in the gas will be attracted to this wire. Another wire connected to the positive terminal of the battery or generator attracts the negative ions in the gas. These negative ions are mostly electrons. So the movement of the ions through the gas makes the electric current. When the positive ions reach the negative wire they get electrons from it and become molecules. When the negative ions, which are electrons, reach the positive wire they go into the wire and back to the generator.

Then how do we keep a supply of ions in the gas? The electrons in the gas move toward the positive wire with high enough

speed so that they knock electrons off the molecules of the gas, thus keeping up the supply of ions for passing the electricity through the gas.

Most substances are composed of ions. These substances are usually compounds, meaning that they are composed of more basic substances called elements. In many compounds, the atoms of different elements either gain or lose electrons, forming negative or positive ions. These atoms are held together by the attraction of negative ions for positive ions.

For instance, table salt is a compound formed by the combination of the elements sodium and chlorine. The sodium atoms give up an electron to the chlorine atoms. The atoms of sodium become positive ions, and the atoms of chlorine become negative ions. They attract one another, and so they stick together.

The number of electrons an atom can gain or lose is called the *valence* of the atom. The sodium atom in the salt has a positive valence of one, while the chlorine atom has a negative valence of one.

The ability of ions of a compound to break away from each other when in solution is what makes it possible for electricity to flow through liquids. Some ions can break away more easily than others, which is why electricity flows more easily in some liquids than in others.

Water is a poor conductor of electricity, because the hydrogen and oxygen ions that compose it do not break up easily. If two metal rods connected to an electric lamp and a source of electricity are dipped into a glass of water, the lamp will not light. The reason is that the water does not conduct the electricity well enough. But if some salt is added to the water, the lamp will light. The salt breaks up, or is ionized, into positive sodium ions and negative chlorine ions when it dissolves in the water. The sodium ions are attracted to the metal rod through which electrons are entering the water and take electrons from it. The chlorine ions are attracted toward the metal rod through which electrons are to be sent back to the source of electricity, and give electrons to it. An electric current can pass through a liquid only when ions are present.

There is enough salt in your body to make any water that is on you a good conductor of electricity. Therefore you should be extremely careful when in a bathtub or whenever you have any water on you *not* to touch an electric fixture. You will be very likely to get a dangerous shock of electricity through your body if you do.

You can read more about ions in the articles on BATTERY and ELECTROLYSIS.

Ionia

On a modern map you will find the Ionian Islands in the Ionian Sea off the coast of Greece. There are seven Ionian Islands, and for this reason they are also known as the Seven Islands. The largest is Cephalonia. The Ionian Sea is part of the Mediterranean Sea. It lies between Greece and Italy. Therefore these little islands are west of Greece. They have belonged to many countries, but now they are part of the kingdom of Greece. Although the islands have many mountains, the people who live there raise some

grain and fruits. They export large amounts of olive oil and a great number of currants every year.

A long time ago, there was a small region called Ionia, which was on the west coast of Asia Minor. It was settled by Greek sailors from Attica about three thousand years ago. These Greek sailors were called Ionians, and this name was sometimes given to all Greeks. The Ionians were fine sailors, and they frequently crossed the Mediterranean Sea, using the islands as steppingstones. When they found coastal islands or mainland ports that had good harbors and looked like good homes, they settled upon them. In this way, they founded about twelve Ionian city-states off the coast of Asia Minor, where Turkey is today. These city-states became a kind of bridge between the customs of the Greeks and the customs of Asia. Some of the greatest Greek ideas first came from these wealthy cities. Thales, one of the Seven Wise Men of Greece, came from Ionia. Thales studied the heavens and foretold an eclipse. Then he decided that the sun and moon were moved by certain laws and not because the gods were angry. Also, the greatest Greek poet, Homer, may have come from the Ionian island of Chios. Homer wrote the two Greek epics, the *Iliad* and the *Odyssey*.

In 1953 the Ionian Islands, particularly Cephalonia, Zante, and Ithaca, were stricken by earthquakes, causing many deaths and much damage. The other islands are Corfu, Leukas, and Paxos.

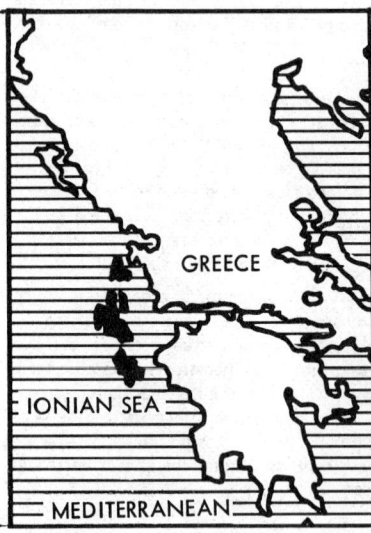

Iowa

Iowa is a state in the great midwestern plain of the United States. Its land is flat and its soil is very rich. Many westerners know the "Iowa Corn Song," in which people lustily sing, "That's where the tall corn grows." This is a true description of Iowa, for it grows more corn than any other state. It also is first in the raising of hogs and chickens, and in producing eggs. When the settlers first came to this region, they found a tribe of Indians known as *Ayuba*, or "sleepy people," and they called the territory Iowa, which sounds somewhat the same. Its nickname is "the Hawkeye State."

In area, Iowa ranks 25th, with 56,290 square miles. In population it ranks 25th, with nearly three million people living there. It became a state in 1846 and was the 29th state admitted to the United States. The capital is Des Moines.

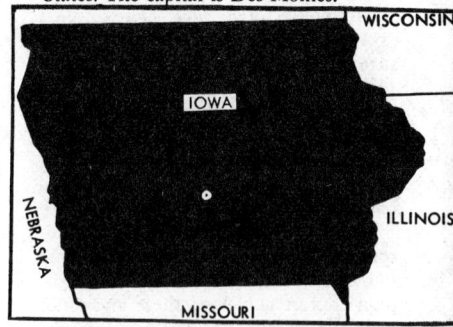

THE PEOPLE OF IOWA

More than half the people in Iowa are farmers. The rich black soil is ideal for growing crops, and the prairie makes excellent pasture for millions of cattle. However, many people have left the farms and gone to work in the big cities. This has not hurt the farms, because the farmers use more machinery to take the place of farm workers. Some people also work in coal mines. Although Iowa is a rich and beautiful state, three-quarters of the people who are born there leave it after they grow up, and live somewhere else.

The early settlers of Iowa were hardy pioneers from the eastern and southern parts of the United States. Later, many Irish, French, Norwegian and German people who had been driven from their countries settled there. They were followed by people from other European countries, who had heard about the wonderfully fertile Iowa land. Many of these foreign groups still celebrate festivals and holidays of their ancestors with songs and dances and colorful European costumes.

The churches are very important in the life of the Iowans. Nearly everyone goes to Sunday School and to church. The Roman Catholic, Methodist and Lutheran Churches each has about 300,000 members. There are also many Presbyterian and other Protestant churches.

WHAT IOWA IS LIKE

Visitors to Iowa see a great flat plain in the eastern part, and a rolling prairie in the western part. Millions of years ago huge ice fields, called glaciers, pushed down across this part of America and, like an enormous piece of sandpaper, they smoothed out the land. The glaciers did not flatten the northeastern part of the state, and here are beautiful deep valleys and cliffs covered with pine trees.

The most remarkable sight to a visitor are the fields of grain, which stretch as far as the eye can see. Sometimes whole miles of land are covered with a single corn field or oat field. Another sight is the great herds of grazing cattle, and the many horses. Iowa raises more horses than any other state.

All through Iowa are white farmhouses, big red barns, and tall, round silos, which are buildings in which the farmers store their grain.

The Des Moines River is the largest river in Iowa. It flows through the central

part of the state. On both sides of the river are large coal deposits.

Iowa has factories that make things eaten or used by people every day. In Sioux City are meat-packing plants where cattle are prepared as beef. In Cedar Rapids are factories where grain is made into cereals. There are factories that make many other useful products, such as butter, washing machines, fountain pens, and furniture. One of the most interesting cities is Muscatine, where people take clam shells from the Mississippi River and make them into pearl buttons and buckles.

The climate in Iowa varies greatly. The summers are hot, and the temperature may rise to 100 degrees and more. In winter it is very cold, and the temperature may drop below zero. Snowstorms and blizzards are frequent. In the growing season there is plenty of rain for the crops.

Railroads and highways reach all parts of the state. The people built the towns of Iowa near the railroads so they would have easy transportation, and today no town is more than twelve miles from a station.

There are airports at all the important cities.

A farm in Iowa, "where the tall corn grows."

THE GOVERNMENT OF IOWA

Iowa, like most other states, is governed by a Governor and a Legislature, called the General Assembly. The Governor is elected for a two-year term. The General Assembly is composed of two houses, a Senate and a House of Representatives. Senators are elected for four-year terms, members of the House for a two-year term. Judges are elected for four years or six years. The capital is Des Moines. There are 99 counties.

Students living on farms go to large consolidated schools, which combine public school and high school. Iowa has always taken a great interest in the education of its citizens, and 99 out of 100 people can read and write. There are about 660,000 pupils attending the public elementary and high schools. Among the principal universities are:

State University of Iowa, at Iowa City. Enrollment, 18,937 in 1971 (co-ed).

Iowa State University of Science and Technology, at Ames. Enrollment, 18,000 in 1971 (co-ed).

Drake University, at Des Moines. Enrollment, 6,958 in 1971 (co-ed).

St. Ambrose College, at Davenport. Enroll-

ment, 1,296 in 1971 (men only).

Marycrest College, at Davenport. Enrollment, 1,079 in 1971 (women only).

Coe College, at Cedar Rapids. Enrollment, 1,050 in 1971 (co-ed).

Grinnell College, at Grinnell. Enrollment, 1,127 in 1971 (co-ed).

CHIEF CITIES OF IOWA

The leading cities of Iowa, with populations from the 1970 census, are:

Des Moines, population 200,587, state capital and largest city. There is a separate article about DES MOINES.

Cedar Rapids, population 110,642, second-largest city, manufacturing center, in the eastern part of the state.

Sioux City, population 85,925, fourth-largest city in the state, manufacturing center, in the western part of the state.

Davenport, population 98,469, third-largest city, railroad and industrial center, in the eastern part of the state.

IOWA IN THE PAST

Iowa was visited by the French explorers Marquette and Joliet about three hundred years ago. At that time it was inhabited by friendly Illinois Indians. Later, the French explorer La Salle claimed the whole Mississippi Valley, including Iowa, for France, and in 1803 the United States bought it from France in the LOUISIANA PURCHASE, about which there is a separate article. The Iowa region was wild and unsettled, and as late as 1832 not more than fifty people lived there.

During the next eight years thousands of settlers came to Iowa on horseback and in large wagons, and farms began to grow. For a time Iowa was part of the Michigan Territory, then part of the Wisconsin Territory. Finally in 1838 it became a separate territory, and in 1846 it became a state.

In the years before the Civil War, the Iowans played an important part in the struggle over the slavery question. They were opposed to people owning slaves, and they helped many Negroes escape through the UNDERGROUND RAILROAD about which there is a separate article.

By 1870 the population of Iowa had risen to almost two million, and Iowa has been an important state ever since.

PLACES TO SEE IN IOWA

Effigy Mounds National Monument, 1,204 acres, in the northeast, 4 miles north of McGregor, on U.S. Route 52. Outstanding examples of Indian mounds in the shapes of birds and animals.

Lacey-Keosauqua State Park, 2,216 acres, in the southeast, 1 mile south of Keosauqua, on State Highway 1. The area is a wild-life sanctuary; ravines and cliffs; near by is a prehistoric Indian village.

Wild Cat Den State Park, 322 acres, in the east, 8 miles east of Muscatine, on U.S. Route 62. Noted for its rock formations and abundant wild flowers. Scenic attractions include Balanced Rock, Steamboat Rock, and the Devil's Punch Bowl. Camping and hiking.

Decorah Ice Cave, in the northeast, at Decorah, on U.S. Route 52. Ice forms on the walls of the cave even during the hot summer months.

Niagara Cave, in the north, 15 miles north of Cresco, on U.S. Route 52. A large

cavern containing a 60-foot waterfall at a depth of 200 feet; two underground streams and a lake.

Tulip Festival, at Pella, in the south, 16 miles west of Oskaloosa, on State Highway 163. Held in May every year.

Davenport Public Museum, contains exhibits on the life and cultures of the early American Indians.

Davenport Municipal Art Gallery, has paintings by notable American and European artists, including many old masters.

Championship Rodeo, at Sidney, in the southwest, 13 miles west of Shenandoah, on U.S. Route 275. Held in August; fancy and trick riding contests; calf-roping; Indian ceremonials.

IOWA. Area, 56,290 square miles. Population (1970 census) 2,824, 376. Capital, Des Moines. Nickname, the Hawkeye State. Motto, Our Liberties We Prize and Our Rights We Will Defend. Flower, wild rose. Bird, eastern goldfinch. Song, "Iowa." Admitted to Union, December 28, 1846. No official abbreviation.

Iran

Iran is a country in the Near East, the southwestern part of Asia. It has about 628,000 square miles, in which about twenty million people live. Before 1935, Iran was called PERSIA, about which there is a separate article.

The way of living in Iran has changed greatly during the last twenty-five years, but parts of the country are still quite backward and many Iranians are very poor.

THE PEOPLE OF IRAN

Different regions of Iran have violently contrasting climates, ranging from deserts where hot winds blow continually to steamy lowlands where crops grow well. Most of the Iranian people, who are still frequently called Persians, live in cities or villages near the best soil and water supply. In the mountains and on the deserts live a few nomads (wanderers), who earn a little money by herding sheep.

Persian is the principal language of Iran, but many of the educated people also speak French and English. Because the Arabs conquered Persia 1,200 years ago, there are many Arabic words in the Persian language.

Besides the Persians, there are many Arabs, Turks, Jews and Armenians in Iran. Some of these continue to live by themselves in separate villages. About one out of every four Iranians speaks Turkish.

Most Iranians follow the Mohammedan religion, but they belong to a branch of it that is called Shiah.

Most of the fields and villages of Iran are owned by a few hundred rich families. These families allow the Iranian farmers the use of the land, some seed, and enough water, in return for a large share in the crops.

Most Iranians look like people from southern Europe. Usually they have dark hair and eyes and olive-colored skin. They are very witty and love to talk.

HOW THE PEOPLE LIVE

Many Iranians live in towns of mud

huts. Each town has one public bath and a mill to grind wheat for the landlord

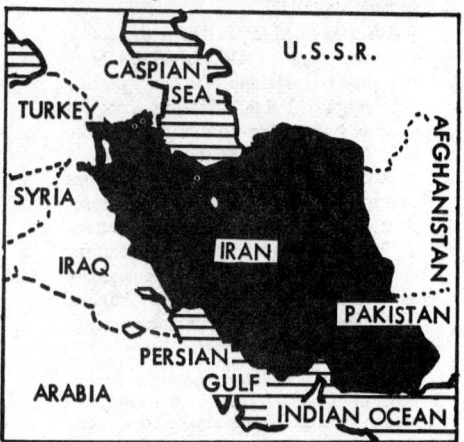

and the villagers. The nomads in the desert live in tents made of a goat hair cloth. They often use bright rugs for floors.

About thirty years ago Iranians began to give up their native costume and to wear Western clothing. Before that, most of the men wore white turbans, shirts, vests, and striped pantaloons. The women, who did not often leave their homes, wore veils and black cloaks that reached to the ground. All Iranian women have greater freedom now, and veils are seldom worn.

The principal foods of the Iranians are wheat bread, rice, cheese, fish, and mutton. They have as delicacies sweetened tea, pistachio nuts, almonds, and dried fruits such as dates and apricots.

In the cities and towns the bazaar is the center for trading and shopping. Here craftsmen display inlaid silver jewelry, brass and copper dishes, printed cotton cloth, and the famous Persian carpets. The Iranians also make beautiful handprinted books with delicate illustrations. American museums have a number of copies of the Koran, the Mohammedan holy book, handwritten and illustrated. Although much of Iran is desert or bare mountains, Iranian artists and writers deal only with the most beautiful portions. They show rows of graceful cypresses and mulberry trees, and blossoming fruit trees. The poets tell about gardens fragrant with thousands of roses. Even today, Iranian children learn the poems of the great Persian poet Hafiz, who lived about six hundred years ago.

Schools in Iran have improved in recent years, but only two out of every five Iranians can read and write. Most of the people learned what they know about their history and religion from a few wise men. The government now promises ten years of free education to all boys and girls, but there are not enough teachers or schools for all of the children. After six years of elementary school, children can enter other classes that are somewhat like American high schools, except that there are separate schools for boys and girls. The largest university is at Teheran, the capital, and there are a few other colleges that prepare students for special careers.

WHAT KIND OF PLACE IT IS

Two great mountain ranges run across Iran, separated by a plateau (a high, level region). Some of this plateau is covered by what used to be a salt swamp, in which the salt has hardened into a smooth surface. Desert covers the rest of the plateau. The summer temperature of the desert is one of the highest in the world. In the winter it is very cold.

Near the foot of the mountains, along the Caspian Sea and the Persian Gulf, are the farming centers of Iran. Irrigation permits the raising of wheat, barley, tea, tobacco, hemp, cotton, rice, and such fruits as melons and oranges. Because of the limited water supply, less than one-fifth of all the country is being cultivated. Many workmen earn their livings by digging great tunnels through which water is carried to farm lands. Not enough food is raised to feed all the people properly. Many children are underfed and suffer from diseases of malnutrition.

Iran had almost no industry up to twenty years ago. The last two shahs (kings) built factories that make silk and cotton cloth, glass, cigarettes, matches,

U.S. Army

Iran is famous for the beautiful jewelry made there, The jewel-encrusted pitcher and basin belong to the king.

leather goods, and cement. There are also sugar refineries and fish-canning plants. Iran has great mineral resources, but they have not been mined in large amounts.

Since 1910, Iran has been famous for its oil. An Englishman named William D'Arcy first received from the Persian government the right to search for oil. D'Arcy helped to form the Anglo-Iranian Oil Company, which built long pipe lines to carry the crude oil from the wells to refineries. The largest oil refineries are located in Abadan, a city on the Persian Gulf. From Abadan oil products are shipped to the rest of the world.

By 1960, Abadan was refining about 51 million tons of crude oil each year. More than a hundred thousand Englishmen and Iranians worked for the Anglo-Iranian Oil Company. In 1951 the Iranian government decided that Iran, not Great Britain, should control the company. The British were forced out, and the company was forced to close down because the Iranians were not able to run it by themselves. In 1954 Iran and Britain came to an agreement that permitted the reopening of the company.

Iran has few good roads. Most travel is by airplane, train, or animals such as horses, mules, and camels.

The mountains and forests of Iran are full of such animals as tigers, leopards, gazelles, foxes, wild pigs, and antelopes. The Caspian Sea yields sturgeon, caviar (eggs of sturgeon), salmon, and carp.

HOW THE PEOPLE ARE GOVERNED

Iran is a constitutional monarchy. It has a king and a parliament, but they must obey a constitution, or supreme law. The ruler of Iran is called the shah. In 1926 a sergeant in the Iranian army became shah. In 1941 he abdicated, and his son, Mohammed Reza Pahlevi, became shah.

Iran's parliament has two houses, or branches. One, called the *Majlis*, is like the United States House of Representatives, and the other is a Senate. The shah and the Majlis together select a prime minister who is head of the government, and a cabinet to help him. Members of the Majlis are elected every four years. All Iranian men and women over 21 may vote. The country is divided into ten provinces, each run by a governor.

CHIEF CITIES IN IRAN

The chief cities of Iran, with population figures from the first general census, held in 1970, or later estimates, are:

Teheran, population 2,719,730, the capital and largest city. There is a separate article about TEHERAN.

Isfahan, population 424,045, the second largest city, in the central part of the country. It is the center of the Persian rug-making industry.

Meshed, population 409,281, the third largest city, a religious shrine and trade center, in the northeast.

Tabriz, population 403,413, the fourth largest city, a center for trade, and an ancient meeting place for caravans. It is in the north, in the region of Azerbaijan, of which it is the capital.

Abadan, population 272,962, the fifth largest city, center of the greatest oil refineries in that part of the world, in the southwest, on the Persian Gulf.

Shiraz, population 269,865, the sixth largest city, in the southwest. It has one of the largest bazaars in that part of Asia, and is also a very beautiful city.

Most cities of Iran have been built on the buried foundations of ancient cities that date back thousands of years.

IRAN IN THE PAST

For more than 1,200 years, from the coming of Mohammedan invaders from Arabia about the year 640 to the present century, parts of the present country of Iran were ruled by foreign empires and other parts were independent, usually under local rulers. The Turkish, Russian and British empires each controlled parts of the country at the end of World War I, but in 1926 Iran became independent. In 1941, Russian and British troops occupied Iran to prevent its government from trading with Germany. They forced the shah, Reza Shah Pahlevi, to leave the country and put his young son, Mohammed Reza Shah Pahlevi (then 24 years old) on the throne. One of the important wartime meetings between President Roosevelt, Prime Minister Churchill and Premier Stalin was held at the Iranian capital, Teheran, in 1943. At this conference, Russia and Great Britain promised to remove their troops after the war and leave Iran independent.

The British did this, but the Russians tried to start a Communist revolution, especially in Azerbaijan, in 1946. The revolution failed and the Russian troops left.

In 1951, an Iranian statesman named Mohammed Mossadegh became Iranian

premier. His government was very anti-British and seized the oil refineries at Abadan. Since the shah opposed this, in 1953 Mossadegh forced him to leave the country. This proved unwise for Mossadegh, for the Iranian people favored the shah. They overthrew Mossadegh's government; Mossadegh was imprisoned and the shah returned triumphantly. The shah's new government improved the country's relations with Great Britain. Since 1950 the United States has given Iran grants and loans of money to build its economy. Defense assistance is provided under an agreement signed in 1959.

IRAN. Area, 628,060 square miles. Population (1973 estimate) 29,780,000. Language, Persian. Religion, Mohammedan. Government, constitutional monarchy.

Iraq

Iraq is a country in the southwestern part of Asia. Iraq is a little larger than California, having 172,000 square miles in which over nine million people live. Before 1921 Iraq was called Mesopotamia (which means "land between the rivers") because two long rivers—the Tigris and the Euphrates—flow through the country.

THE PEOPLE WHO LIVE THERE

More than half of the people of Iraq try to live close to the two rivers, in cities and towns, or on farms. The rest of the people are tribesmen, called Bedouins, who follow their camels, sheep, and horses to grazing places in the desert. Most of the inhabitants of Iraq are Arabs and speak Arabic, but there are a few Kurds, Turks, and Iranians who speak their native languages. There are also a few Christians and Jews in some parts of Iraq, but most of the people are Moslems, followers of the Mohammedan religion.

The article on ARABS tells about the way of life of many of the people who live in Iraq, but many of the old customs have changed in recent years. Many of the Iraqi men have stopped wearing their long robes and have begun to wear modern clothes. The women of Iraq no longer cover their faces with veils as they did until about forty years ago.

HOW THE PEOPLE LIVE

Most of the people of Iraq make their living from some kind of farming. They use some methods of farming that have not changed in many hundreds of years.

Iraq has minerals, such as copper, sulfur, coal, and iron, but the people have not been able to mine enough of these. Fortunately Iraq has great stores of oil, and many oil wells have been dug. The oil is pumped through pipelines across the country to ports on the Mediterranean Sea. There it is taken by tankers (large ships that carry oil) to European and American ports. Besides oil, Iraq sends products such as raw animal hides, raw wool, dates, and cement to other nations. There are not enough miles of railroads or paved roads, but there are railroads connecting the chief cities with one another and with Mediterranean seaports of other countries, and both the Tigris and Euphrates Rivers are used to carry people and goods toward the Persian Gulf.

Many of the older Iraqi cannot read or

write, and some children in the Bedouin tribes cannot go to school because they

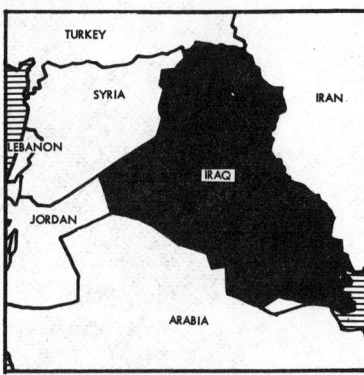

are always moving about. In the villages and towns all children can have twelve years of school, although there are not really enough teachers. Parents in the nomad tribes teach children how to care for and ride their horses, how to raise sheep and goats, and how to cook and sew.

Disease has not been conquered. There are not enough doctors, nurses, hospitals, or drugs, and malaria and hookworm disease take many lives each year.

WHAT KIND OF PLACE IT IS

Iraq has several different types of climate. In the north the summers are hot, with some rainfall. The south and central portions of the country are some of the hottest and driest parts of the world during both winter and summer. In most parts of the country only about ten inches of rain fall each year. Iraq has few trees except for poplars and dates along the canals and river banks or in a few oases (fertile places in the desert with springs and wells). For many miles the flat, treeless desert stretches across the nation. Few wild animals dare to live in the desert, but there are a few gazelles and antelopes, and some large birds such as ravens and vultures. All Iraqi are proud of the beautiful Arabian horses that they raise to sell abroad or to race in Iraq. These horses are very graceful, sturdy, and easy to train.

One of Iraq's greatest problems is the uncertain supply of water. For centuries the people have tried to force water from the large rivers into canals through the desert lands. Most of the farmers in Iraq have few of the machines that could be found on any American farm. The farmer must slowly plant and hoe by hand all his crops of barley, rice, or cotton. This takes a long time, and he often raises only enough for his own family. It is much easier to raise dates that need only some water at their roots and plenty of sunshine, which Iraq always has. Most of the world's dates are raised in Iraq. Date trees are used for fuel, and the trees' fibers are woven into ropes, mats, and roofs.

THE GOVERNMENT

From 1921 to 1958, Iraq was a constitutional monarchy. In July 1958, the nation's ruler, King Faisal II, was assassinated, the monarchy was overthrown, and the government became a republic. The nation's next leader was military commander, Abdul Kassem. Kassem was

executed in 1963, and a series of political revolts followed. In 1968 the Baath Arab Socialist Party gained control of the country. Major General Ahmed Hassan al Bakr became Iraq's leader. Under President Bakr, the government consists of a Revolutionary Command Council and a cabinet. The constitution, written after the 1958 revolution, remains in effect. Some constitutional changes were made in 1970 to appease the Kurds, a large minority group in northeast Iraq. Iraq has two separate court systems—one for legal matters and one for religious problems. Iraq is striving to bring education, modern agricultural techniques, and industry to its people.

CHIEF CITIES OF IRAQ

The principal cities of Iraq with population figures from 1973 estimates are:

Baghdad, population 1,745,328, capital and largest city, in center of Iraq. See the separate article on BAGHDAD.

Basra, population 313,327, a seaport near the Persian Gulf. It is on the Shatt-al-Arab,

Sheep are vital to Iraq's economy.

the river formed at the mouths of the Tigris and Euphrates.

Mosul, population 243,311, on the Tigris. It is north of Baghdad, near the ruins of ancient Nineveh. Mosul is a business center, close to the oilfields.

Kirkuk, population 167,413, in the northeast, an oil center with pipelines leading to the Mediterranean Sea.

HISTORY OF IRAQ

Even before written history, people were living in Iraq, then called Mesopotamia. The Tigris and Euphrates river valley was the site of ancient culture. The first recorded civilization was that of the Sumerians, who lived in 3000 B.C. They were taken over by two kingdoms, Babylonia and Assyria, in 2000 B.C. They became mighty empires by 1500 B.C. Under Hammurabi, a great ruler and lawmaker, Babylonia became a prosperous trading center. Then the Assyrians conquered the Babylonians and built their great city of Nineveh. Now only a few ruins lie there.

When the great religious teacher Mohammed died, about 1,300 years ago, the Arabs wanted to spread his teachings and came into Mesopotamia, the region between the Tigris and Euphrates. The leader of the Moslem religion after Mohammed's death was called a caliph. Under one of the caliphs, Harun al-Rashid, the country that is now Iraq lived through a golden age. The *Arabian Nights* are stories about the court of Harun al-Rashid at Baghdad. About 300 years ago, the Ottoman Turks conquered Iraq, which remained part of the Turkish Empire

until World War I. During this war, Iraq was able to free itself from the Turks, but it was placed under British control for a few years. When the country became entirely independent in 1921, the people chose the former ruler of Syria, Faisal, to be their first king. His grandson, Faisal II, ruled from 1953 to 1958. In 1958 a revolt against the monarchy led to the formation of a new government. Its leader, Kassim, stressed education and industrialization. The land, which was once owned by a few, was divided under Kassim's rule. Kassim held power until 1963, when a group led by Colonel Arif took over. Under Arif, Iraq improved its relationship with the other Arab countries. In 1968, Arif lost his power to General Bakr, a leader of the Baath Arab Socialist Party. Bakr has worked to improve the social and economic conditions of Iraq. President Bakr discourages contact with other Arab nations and dislikes political criticism.

IRAQ. Area, 172,000 square miles. Population (1973 estimate) 9,750,000. Language Arabic. Religion, Mohammedan. Government, Republic. Monetary unit, dinar, worth $2.80 (U.S.).

Delicious sweet dates are grown in Iraq, which produces most of the world's supply.

Ireland

Ireland is one of the two British Isles. It is also an independent country, the Republic of Ireland, or Irish Republic, which occupies somewhat more than three-quarters of the island.

The entire island has an area of about 32,000 miles and a population of slightly more than four million, so it is about the same size and population as the state of Indiana. Ireland is called the Emerald Isle because it is green and beautiful. An old Irish name for it is Erin.

The Republic of Ireland covers the southern part of the island. Its area is about 27,000 square miles and about three million people live there. It is usually called simply Ireland, and for some years it was called by the Irish name Eire. The section at the far north is called NORTHERN IRELAND, and there is a separate article about it. It is part of the United Kingdom of Great Britain and Northern Ireland.

King John's Castle on the River Shannon, in County Limerick.

In this article, only the Republic of Ireland is described.

THE PEOPLE WHO LIVE THERE

The present people of Ireland are descended from several different national groups who lived there in the past. The island was inhabited ten thousand and more years ago by Stone Age hunters and fishermen. Almost nothing is known about them. About 2,500 years ago a tall, blond race of invaders from the mainland of Europe entered Ireland. These were the Celts, and they remained almost undisturbed until another invasion took place about eight hundred years later. These new invaders were Danes and Norsemen. They introduced a strain of red-haired people into the blond Celtic group. In the 12th century and shortly after, numbers of brown-haired Normans, a French people, arrived from England, where they had conquered the English.

These three large groups of people, all with different types of complexions and different hair- and eye-coloring, blended to form the present-day Irish. This is why there are some Irish who have dark brown hair and blue eyes, some with red hair and either blue or brown eyes, and some with blond hair, fair complexions, and blue eyes.

There are two languages spoken in Ireland today—English and Irish, which is also called Gaelic. All school children are taught both.

HOW THE PEOPLE LIVE

Most of the people in Ireland work at farming, in one form or another. Agriculture and food processing made up the country's most important industry. Next in importance are tobacco production, weaving, clothing manufacture, and distilling whiskey. Many former agricultural workers have gone into manufacturing and shop work, but the most important concern of the Irish people still is keeping up farm production and keeping down the numbers of people leaving the farms for the cities. Modern farm machinery and scientific methods are used on the farms.

The largest city in Ireland is Dublin, the capital. It is about the same size as

Buffalo, New York, with a population of about 540,000. Other cities are Cork, Limerick, and Cobh.

There are not many railroads, modern highways, or telephone and telegraph lines, but these are being developed gradually. There are many hydroelectric plants where the natural waterpower of the country's rivers is used to produce electricity.

For generations, people in Ireland have been living in houses of stone and clay, many with thatched roofs. In larger cities there are many homes with the ordinary conveniences that are common in the United States and Canada, but in Ireland such modern household appliances as refrigerators, washing machines, and central heating are rare. In the villages in rural areas, many houses are still heated by peat from peat bogs throughout the country.

The life in Irish cities and towns centers about the church and local clubs. There are many organizations for both men and women. They conduct athletic contests, organize games of all kinds, hold dances, give concerts, and produce plays. These clubs also hold classes in all the different branches of farming and homemaking.

All children must attend school until they reach the age of fourteen. Grade school is free. High schools and colleges receive money grants from the state to help pay teachers and to keep the cost of tuition for students as low as possible. One of the best-known colleges is Trinity College, in Dublin. It was founded in 1591.

Nearly all the people are Roman Catholics, but there is freedom of religion for everyone.

WHAT KIND OF PLACE IT IS

Ireland is shaped roughly like a large bowl, with a rim of mountains all around the outside, near the coast. The coastline itself is jagged and irregular, and there are many bays and inlets. They go so deeply into the interior of the land that there is no point in the entire country more than 60 miles from the sea or some bay of the sea. The mountains range in height from about 500 to 3,000 feet. The highest peak is Mount Carrantuohill,

which is 3,414 feet high. It is in the Kerry Mountains, in the western part of the country.

There are large fertile plains in the

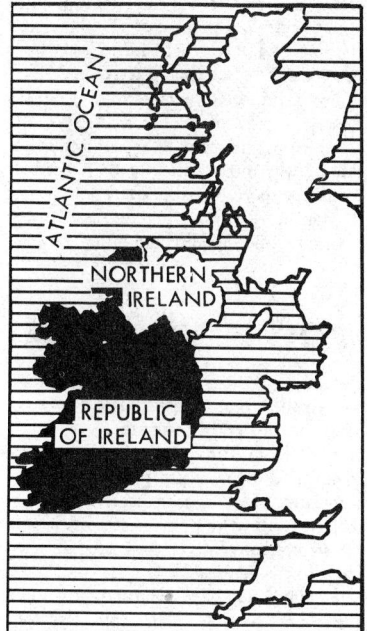

center of the country, and everywhere the visitor sees lakes, canals, and rivers. It is possible to go from the city of Sligo, on the northwest coast, to Dublin, on the east central coast, without ever losing sight of water. Altogether there are more than eight hundred lakes and inland rivers. The lakes are called "loughs," and the most famous of them is probably Killarney, in the southwest section.

The climate is mild. It is almost never hot in summer, nor very cold in winter. It is damp, and there is considerable year-round rainfall. There are also a great many fogs. The winter temperature averages between 40 and 44 degrees, with the lowest temperatures in the central part of the island. The average July temperature is between 58 and 60 degrees.

In some of the towns there are old castles and abbeys that have stood for hundreds of years, next door to modern factories and shops built since 1900. Landmarks known as the Round Towers mark places where universities stood a thousand years ago. The towers themselves were part of the original buildings; they are gracefully beautiful even today and almost as strong as when they were built.

PROVINCES AND COUNTIES

The Republic of Ireland is divided into four provinces, Ulster, Leinster, Munster, and Connaught. Each of these provinces is divided into counties. There are twenty-six counties altogether. Each has its own local government. The names of many of these counties are familiar, for Irish people often describe themselves or their families as being from a certain county, and many of the well-known Irish folk songs are about particular counties. The counties are: Carlow, Cavan, Clare, Cork, Donegal, Dublin, Galway, Kerry, Kildare, Kilkenny, Leitrim, Laoighis (Leix), Limerick, Longford, Louth, Mayo, Meath, Monaghan, Offaly, Roscommon, Sligo,

Tipperary, Waterford, Westmeath, Wexford, and Wicklow.

HOW THE PEOPLE ARE GOVERNED

Ireland is an independent democratic republic. It has a president, a prime minister and a cabinet, and a two-house parliament, with a house of representatives, called the Dail Eireann, and a senate. The president is responsible for the command of defense forces, but the prime minister is the actual head of the government. He is a member of the Dail Eireann and is elected by it.

The president is elected directly by the people, and serves for seven years. The senate has sixty members, of whom eleven are nominated by the prime minister and six by various universities, and the other forty-three chosen from people in five different lines of work. The Dail Eireann is elected by the people, and all grownups can vote.

IRELAND IN THE PAST

The recorded history of Ireland begins about the year 400. At this time Ireland had a complete body of laws. It covered almost every part of life, from the behavior of doctors, lawyers, and judges to the duties of foster parents toward adopted children. Irish culture was well developed and far advanced for that period.

Christianity grew and flourished in Ireland, and after the fall of the Roman Empire, while barbarians overran the continent of Europe, Ireland kept Western culture and learning alive. The teachings of the slave boy who became Ireland's patron saint, St. Patrick, were willingly received by the people. Missionaries from Ireland traveled as far north as Iceland and as far east as Kiev, in Russia; they founded monasteries in both England and Scotland. An Irish missionary, St. Aidan, taught the English to read and write. The only manuscript of *Beowulf*, the oldest known piece of English literature, is written in early Irish script.

This golden age of Irish culture ended when the Danes and Norsemen, who had invaded England, crossed over to Ireland. For the next five hundred years these invaders controlled the island. The Irish high king Brian Boru defeated them in the great battle of Clontarf in 1016, and became one of Ireland's great heroes, but his triumph lasted only until the Norman English began their invasions. This was about the year 1166, a hundred years after the Normans had invaded England from France.

For the next seven hundred years the Irish waged a constant struggle against the English for political and religious freedom. The English retaliated by forming "plantations" in which Scottish and English farmers were given large tracts of Irish land to farm. Scottish Presbyterians received a great percentage of the land in the province of Ulster, and that is one of the reasons why that part of Ireland is still primarily Protestant, while the rest is Catholic.

THE FIGHT FOR INDEPENDENCE

Starting about two hundred years ago, there was a series of bloody revolts of the Irish people against England. For a hun-

dred years England was successful in checking all of them. One of the leaders of the fight for independence in the 18th century was Wolfe Tone, who founded the Society of United Irishmen, composed of both Catholics and Protestants.

In the meantime, the population of Ireland was growing enormously. In 1800 there were about four and a half million people in Ireland. About fifty years later, the number had nearly doubled. With so many people in the country, the failure of a potato crop in 1849 had tragic results. A million men, women and children died in the famine that followed the crop failure, and another million and a half Irish people left the country, many of them emigrating to the United States.

From 1848 to 1922, underground conspiracies, open fighting, and agitation in the British Parliament all worked toward greater Irish independence. First the tenant farmers won the right to own their own land. One of the leaders at this time was Charles Stewart Parnell. Irish votes influenced the British Liberal Party to promise Ireland at least partial independence ("home rule"), but the promise was not kept, because the Liberals were pushed out of power.

During World War I, an organization in southern Ireland known as the Sinn Fein started a revolution on Easter Monday, 1916, and proclaimed an Irish republic. The British forces defeated the revolutionists, but two years later the Irish issued a declaration of independence and set up an Irish government, with Eamon de Valera as president. For the next three years, from 1918 to 1921, Ireland was at war with England. At the same time there was fighting among the Irish people, who disagreed on how complete they wanted their independence to be. People were murdered, buildings were burned, civilians were assassinated. The British sent soldiers called "Black and Tans" (from their uniforms) to put down the revolution, and these fought against the Irish patriots.

FOUNDING OF THE REPUBLIC

It was not until 1921 that the British offered a settlement, and in 1922 the Irish Free State was established, leaving the counties of northeast Ireland still under British rule. The Irish Free State was a dominion, like the Dominion of Canada, but the Irish people did not want even that much connection with Great Britain. In 1937, the people enacted a constitution that declared Ireland to be a "sovereign, independent, democratic State"— and the Republic of Ireland (its official name) finally gained international recognition in 1948. By the Republic of Ireland Act in the British Parliament, on April 18, 1949, and after centuries of struggle, Ireland became completely free. With independence Ireland lost much of its old bitterness against the English and, though Ireland was neutral in World War II, most of the Irish people supported the British and their allies.

REPUBLIC OF IRELAND. Area, 27,137 square miles. Population (1973 estimate) 2,971,230. Languages, Gaelic and English. Religion, Roman Catholic. Monetary unit, Irish pound, worth $2.80 (U.S.). Flag, ver-

tical bars of green, white and orange.

iris

The iris is a flowering plant that is grown in almost all countries north of the equator. Most irises grow from an underground horizontal root or *rhizome,* but a few kinds grow from a bulb. The flower's color varies from white, purple, yellow, to red. The plant is often two to three feet tall. Several flowers may appear on its straight thick stems. The leaves are swordlike and pointed. The iris has a faint, sweet perfume that is apparent in the air in the early morning or after a rain. There are over 300 species of iris. Cultivating and crossbreeding of the iris is carried on by amateur gardeners and professionals alike. It is native to Europe and Asia. It has been popular in China and Japan for centuries and is often represented in Japanese art. There are many wild species in North America, some of which do well under cultivation.

Irish Sea

The Irish Sea is a part of the Atlantic Ocean. It is between Ireland and England. It is only about 140 miles long from north to south, and at its widest point is a little less than 130 miles wide. It is important because of the large fishing industries that it supplies. It is a shallow sea, but is as deep as 850 feet at the far north end.

To reach the Atlantic Ocean from the Irish Sea, a ship must go through either the St. Patrick (or North) Channel between Ireland and Scotland or St. George's Channel between Ireland and Wales.

There are two important islands in the Irish Sea. They are the Isle of Man, in the north central part, and Anglesey, close to the northwest coast of Wales.

Irish setter, a large dog used in hunting. See the article on SETTER.

Irish terrier

The Irish terrier is a medium-sized dog that is at home in a city apartment or on a farm in the country. Children love Irish terriers because they are always willing to romp and play. Parents know that when the children are out with their Irish terrier, they have a brave and trustworthy

Though not large, the Irish terrier has hunted everything from rabbits to big game in the Arctic and the tropics.

guardian. In addition to being a fine pet and watchdog, an Irish terrier is expert at catching mice and rats.

An Irish terrier stands about 17 to 19 inches high at the shoulder, and is be-

tween 16 to 18 inches long from its chest to the base of its tail. It weighs about 25 to 30 pounds. People usually clip the tails of very young Irish terrier puppies. The Irish terrier has a wiry, thick coat that lies close to its body. The coat is reddish brown, golden red, or golden tan. Sometimes there is a white patch on the underside, but otherwise the color is solid.

Irish wolfhound

The Irish wolfhound is one of the oldest breeds of dog in the world, and it is one of the tallest dogs. It has been known for about two thousand years and came originally from Ireland. Many hundreds of years ago, the Irish wolfhound was used to hunt wolves and Irish elk, and today it is used in boar and lion hunting in Africa. The people of the western United States and Canada have found that the Irish wolfhound can track down, catch and kill huge and vicious timber wolves. With human beings the Irish wolfhound is an extremely gentle dog, with a good disposition.

The Irish wolfhound is about 32 to 34 inches high at the shoulder and about

The Irish Wolfhound Club of America

In the Middle Ages, feudal lords considered the handsome and strong Irish wolfhound one of the best hunting dogs.

the same length from chest to base of tail. It may weigh between 120 and 140 pounds. It has a long, curling tail, and small ears. Its coat is rough, thick, and hard, and it has longer hair over its eyes and under its jaw. Irish wolfhounds are usually gray mixed with black or reddish brown, or white, or tan.

Iron Age

The Iron Age is the time in any civilization's history when iron is the chief metal being used. Every group of human beings has developed its culture and civilization gradually. First, men knew nothing of metals and had to make everything out of stone; then they learned to use the softer metals, such as copper; finally they learned to use iron.

Men reach the Iron Age last because they must learn to build the hottest possible fires before they can get iron from its ore. Our modern world is in the Iron Age even now. This is because our most useful metal is iron (and steel, which is made from iron). Other metals are better for special purposes (for example, aluminum is lighter, and copper or silver conducts electricity better) but iron and steel remain the metals most used.

Different peoples have passed through the different ages at different times in history. In our civilization, which came from the Greek and Near Eastern civilizations, the Iron Age arrived about 1,100

years before the birth of Jesus. The Germanic tribes in the north of Europe did not begin to use iron until about 1,500 years later. Some primitive tribes in Africa and Asia did not reach the Iron Age until about a hundred years ago. The American Indians had not reached the Iron Age when the first Europeans arrived.

For a hundred years or more, during the early part of the Iron Age in the Western world, iron was so important that it was more valuable than gold. It would be more valuable than gold today, if men were forced to choose between giving up one metal or the other.

Iron and Steel

Iron is one of the oldest and most useful metals known to man. Steel, which is made from iron, is the most important metal used today. Both iron and steel became important to man because the materials from which they are made are found in many places and because they have so many uses.

Steelmakers have learned to make steel so strong that it can support bridges that carry heavy traffic; to make it springy enough for mattress springs; to pull it into fine wire; to mix it with other substances to make shining stainless steel.

Steel is used for many things in the home, from pins and scissors to kitchen stoves and refrigerators. It is used in transportation, for ships, trains, airplanes, and automobiles. Farmers use fences, tractors and tools made of steel. Builders use steel for bridges, buildings, tunnels, and dams.

HISTORY OF IRON AND STEEL

Early man first got iron from meteorites, which are metallic bodies that fall from outer space onto the earth. This did not give him very much of the metal. Then one day some early men probably built a fire on ground that was full of iron ore. When the fire went out they found lumps of iron in the ashes. At first iron was more precious than gold.

As early as three thousand years ago enough was known about making and using iron so that huge armies were equipped with iron weapons. That time in history began the Iron Age.

The early American colonists built furnaces and forges wherever they could get iron ore. The first successful American iron works was in Massachusetts on the banks of the Saugus River.

WHERE IRON ORE IS FOUND

Like other metals, iron is seldom found in its pure state. It is mixed in a kind of earth or rock called *ore.* One kind of iron ore has a rich red color. The best ore, called high-grade ore, is so rich in iron that it is nearly half iron. In the United States iron-ore deposits are found in northern Minnesota, Michigan, and Wisconsin. There are also many small deposits of iron ore in the Great Appalachian Valley, which extends from Pennsylvania to Alabama, and in California. The largest iron mine in the world is on the Mesabi range in northern Minnesota. More than two and a half billion tons of

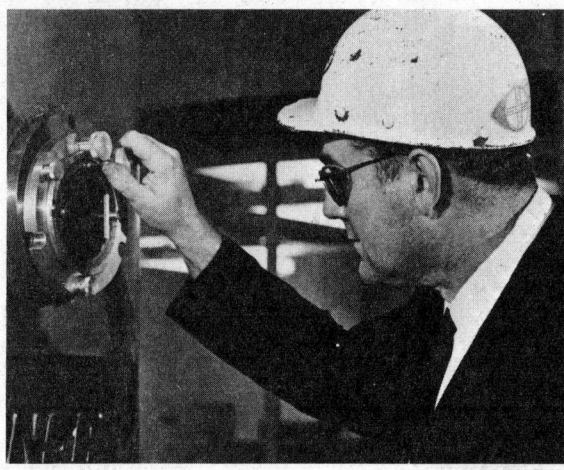

Republic Steel

The foreman of a large steel plant observes steel melting in a *vacuum melting furnace.*

high-grade ore have already been mined here, and about one billion tons remain. The Mesabi range produces more than half of all the iron ore mined in the United States. Canada is becoming more and more important in the production of iron ore. Great deposits have been discovered in many sections of the country and large mines have been opened. Iron ore is mined all over the world—in Europe, Asia and Africa as well as in America.

HOW IRON ORE IS MINED

Iron ore is mined in two ways. Where the layers of iron ore are near the earth's surface, the ore is mined by scooping it up. This is called *open-pit mining.* First the boulders, sand and gravel are scooped off the top. Then powerful electric shovels bite out the ore, sometimes taking as much as fourteen tons at once. An open-pit mine is made up of huge steps on which the electric shovels, and the railway cars and trucks that remove the ore, can travel. Some open-pit mines cover several miles of ground.

When the ore is below two hundred feet, *underground mining* is usually used. Shafts are sunk into the earth, sometimes as far down as three thousand feet. The miners dig passageways into the ore layers. They blast the ore loose with dynamite and send it up to the top in small cars called *skips.*

IRON SMELTING

Iron is extracted from the iron ore by a process called smelting. Iron ore contains iron minerals. During smelting the iron is separated from the minerals by a very hot gas that forms when coke is burned under special conditions. The separated iron then must be melted so that it can be readily removed from the smelting furnace.

Little by little, men discovered new ways of making their fires hotter. They used various devices, such as bellows, to make strong winds to fan the flames. They found that coke, made from coal, burns to make a hotter fire than either wood or coal. They finally developed the modern blast furnace to separate iron from iron minerals and other minerals in the iron ore.

The blast furnace that is used today is nearly a hundred feet high, as high as a ten-story building. It works twenty-four hours a day, seven days a week and month after month. It is a huge steel shell lined with bricks. Beside it are stoves that heat blasts of air to be blown into the furnace, near the bottom, to burn the coke and form the very hot gas. Layers of coke, iron ore and limestone are put into the blast furnace, and blasts of air, heated to about 1,250 degrees, are blown. The coke burns fiercely and produces the gas (carbon monoxide) that separates the iron from the iron minerals. The limestone combines with impurities in the ore to form a scum called *slag.* The slag is lighter than the iron and floats on top of it. Small railway cars (skips) add raw materials as they are needed. The red-hot melted iron hisses out of the furnace into large ladles. Some of the iron is made into *pigs,* which are small chunks of iron weighing fifty to one hundred pounds each. To make one ton of pig iron (also called *cast iron*) it takes two tons of iron ore, one ton of coke, and one-half ton of limestone. It also takes three and a half tons of hot air.

Pig iron is strong but very brittle. When most of the carbon is burned out of it we call it *wrought iron.* This can be heated and then hammered into any shape desired. Because it resists rusting, it is used to make some kinds of pipe and ornamental gates and garden furniture. Most of the iron produced in blast furnaces, however, is used for making steel.

TURNING IRON INTO STEEL

This is a good time to ask "what is steel?" and "Why is it different from iron?" Pig iron contains certain elements such as manganese, silicon, phosphorus, sulfur, and carbon. Pig iron is brittle because it contains a compound of carbon and iron in too great an amount. To make steel, the excess carbon must be burned out of the iron, and the excess of the other elements must be removed. Steel is really an alloy, or mixture, of iron and a very small amount of carbon. Most of the steel used is carbon steel. Sometimes other metals are mixed with steel to make other steel alloys.

There are three modern ways of turning iron into steel. The most important thing about all three ways is that tremendous heat is applied to the iron.

The first way is by using the Bessemer process. This was invented by an American and an Englishman, working independently of each other, between 1847 and 1856. William Kelly of Eddyville, Kentucky, began experimenting on the process in 1847. Henry Bessemer of England obtained a patent on the process in 1856. In this process steel is made by blowing air through molten pig iron. The oxygen in the air combines with most of the impurities in the pig iron and burns away the excess.

The melted pig iron is first poured into a large container called a *converter.* It is shaped like a huge pear and is made of steel plates lined with bricks that resist heat, and has holes in the bottom through which air is blown. The converter is tilted on its side and the pig iron is poured in. The blast of air is admitted at the bottom, and then the converter is turned up. The result is amazing. Long tongues of sparks and flame shoot out of the top. The brilliant sparks and the brown fumes show that the silicon and manganese are being burned out. Then the flames become longer and brighter as the carbon burns. A bright orange glow fills the sky, and it can be seen for miles around. This whole process takes about fifteen minutes. The flaming, bubbling metal is then iron containing an excess of oxygen and also very small amounts of other elements. Special compounds are added to remove the excess oxygen and to restore the correct amount of carbon

The blast furnace is a symbol of the steel industry. It consumes 1,253 tons of ore daily and yields 805 tons of iron.

U.S. Steel Corp.

FURNACE

STOVE

HEATED OPEN BRICK CHAMBER

SKIP CAR

SKIP HOIST

HOT BLAST ENTERS FURNACE

COLD AIR ENTERS STOVE

TAPPING HOLE

400°F

900°F

1800°F

2900°F

MOLTEN IRON

IRON ORE, COKE AND LIMESTONE IN FURNACE

GAS GOES TO CLEANING PLANT

SLAG GOES INTO LADLE

MOLTEN IRON FLOWS INTO LADLE

and other elements for the particular grade of steel being made. After those additions have reacted with the molten metal, it becomes steel. About five out of every hundred tons of steel are made by the Bessemer process.

The second way to make steel uses the open-hearth furnace. This is a long brick structure somewhat like a kitchen oven, except that the heat in it can go up to 3,000 degrees, while the heat in a kitchen oven goes up to only 550 degrees. The method is called open-hearth because the floor or hearth of the furnace is open to the flames that melt the metal.

Gas, powdered coal, oil or tar are used as fuels. There are fuel burners at both ends of the furnace. Then the heated air and the fuel are mixed and blown into the furnace first through one end, then through the other, but not through both

ends at the same time. Pig iron, scrap iron and limestone are pushed through doors in one side of the furnace. It takes about eleven hours for the materials to be put in and melted and the impurities driven out. Then a huge plug at the back of the furnace is knocked out and the metal flows into a huge ladle. The slag, lighter than the steel, floats on top and overflows into a smaller ladle called a *thimble.* About ninety out of every hundred tons of steel are made by the open-hearth method.

The third way to make steel uses the electric furnace. Because the heat can be controlled more exactly, these furnaces are generally used for making special kinds of steel, such as stainless steel, tool steel, bearing steel and some kinds of carbon steel. The electric furnace is a steel shell that looks like a large teakettle. It is lined with brick. Large sticks of carbon, called *electrodes,* point down through the roof of the furnace close to the metal. When the electric current is turned on, a steady spark flows between the electrodes and the metal, providing intense heat to melt the metal. The spark is so bright that special glasses are needed to look into the furnace. The metals that are mixed with the steel to make alloys, such as nickel, chromium, tungsten, and others, are then added. About five out of every hundred tons of steel are made in electric furnaces.

Most of the steel is poured into molds. When the steel cools it becomes solid and is then called an *ingot.* These ingots are great slabs that weigh up to 22 tons. Before the ingots can be used to make steel into many shapes and products, they must be reheated. They are put into soaking pits where they are soaked, not in water, but in heat. In about six hours they reach a heat of 2,200 degrees.

STEEL FINISHING

The white-hot ingots are then sent to a different kind of mill called a *semi-finishing mill.* Here they are passed between rolls just as wet clothes are passed between the rollers of a clothes wringer. They are shaped into bars or slabs and then sent to the finishing mills. Here some of these bars or slabs are made into rails and beams for buildings and bridges. Others are made into pipes, tubes, wire plates, or sheets.

STEEL ALLOYS

Certain elements are added to some of the steel to give it special properties. The skilled workmen follow recipes for mixing steel as carefully as a cook follows a recipe for cake. These added elements help the steel to stand up against heat, cold, acids, and weather changes.

When silicon is added, magnetic qualities of the steel are improved, making it useful for electrical equipment.

When copper is added, steel increases its corrosion resistance in air.

The stainless steel that you see in kitchen sinks, dishwashers, and pots and pans is made by adding chromium and nickel to the steel. Stainless steel is able to resist some kinds of acids. It is stronger than ordinary steel, even at high temperatures. Some stainless steel contains only

Am. Iron and Steel Inst.

One of the most dramatic sights in a steel mill is the giant ladle that pours molten metal into ingots. The pourer needs both skill and experience.

chromium. It is used for cutlery and surgical instruments because it can take and keep a sharp edge.

THE IMPORTANCE OF STEEL

The making of iron and steel has long been one of the greatest industries of the world. The small, privately operated furnaces and forges are things of the past. Today steel plants cover thousands of acres. Some plants were built near coal fields because coke (made from coal) broke into small pieces when transported over great distances. That is why so many iron and steel plants are found in Illinois, Indiana, Ohio, and Pennsylvania. The western part of Pennsylvania is an important steel-producing region because coal, coke, limestone and iron ore can be transported economically to that area. Great rivers provide a way of bringing all these materials together and shipping out the finished products. Northern Illinois and northwestern Indiana is another important steelmaking area. A third important iron- and steel-producing region is around Birmingham, Alabama.

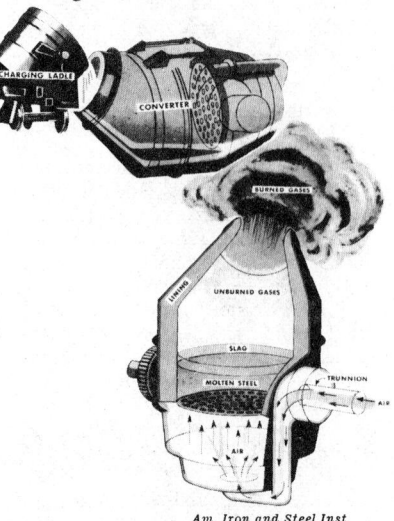

Am. Iron and Steel Inst.

The Bessemer process for converting pig iron into steel takes only fifteen minutes. The orange glow from the top of the converter can be seen several miles away.

The United States is the world's largest steel producer, making almost one-third of all the steel made in the world. In 1964, 126,800,000 tons of steel were made in the United States. The second-largest steel-producing country is the Soviet Union, which produces about 80,000,000 tons of steel a year. Canada has large iron mines in the great Ungava region of Quebec. Some experts have said that as much as three billion tons of ore lie buried there. The largest iron and steel industry in South America is northwest of Rio de Janeiro, Brazil. Chile and Venezuela have great deposits of iron ore, too. The most important iron region of Europe extends from the lower Rhine valley through Luxembourg into Belgium and northern France. Germany has much coal, and France has much ore. The coal and iron producers have arranged to trade French ore for German coal and so both countries can produce iron and steel.

The electric furnace, in which sparks shooting between electrodes heat the metal, is used in making stainless steel and steel alloys with other metals.

Am. Iron and Steel Inst.

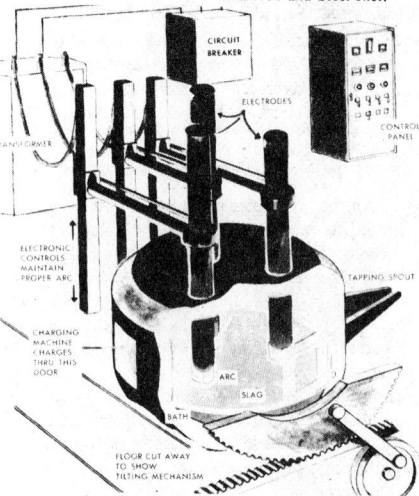

About 20,000 pounds of steel are used for every man, woman and child in the United States.

Molten steel being poured from the furnace is a beautiful sight. But the danger of being hit by one of the red-hot drops keeps observers at a distance.

Am. Iron and Steel Inst.

At the time of the Revolutionary War, most iron and steel came from single-furnace mills operated by one or two men. Today, a single large mill employs thousands of men. Most plants are built on rivers, where barges can provide cheap transportation of ore. Freight trains also come and go constantly, bringing ore and taking away finished iron and steel. The picture shows only a blast furnace and coke plant, but gives an idea of the mill's size.

The iron ore's journey from the mine or pit ends when the skip hoist dumps it into the furnace that separates iron from slag.

U.S. Steel Corp.

iron lung

When a person's lungs are paralyzed or weakened so that he cannot breathe, he may use a machine that is made to help him breathe. The real name of this machine is *artificial respirator*, but nearly everyone calls it an *iron lung*.

The iron lung uses air pressure to help the person breathe. (Breathing is explained in the articles BREATHING and LUNG.) The iron lung is often needed in cases of infantile paralysis, diphtheria, cerebral palsy, or serious injury.

The earliest type of iron lung is a steel cylinder that holds the patient's body while his head is on the outside. Air is pumped in and out of the cylinder. When air is pumped in, his chest contracts, forcing the lungs to exhale (breathe out). When air is pumped out, the chest expands, forcing the lungs to inhale (breathe in).

A later type of iron lung is a bowl-shaped device made of a plastic material. It fits around the patient's body. It is much more comfortable because plastics are so much lighter than metals. Patients wearing this respirator may remain sitting.

Another type of respirator is the *electrophrenic respirator*. It has two wires connected to the patient's phrenic nerve through a small cut in the neck. The phrenic nerve controls the muscles of the diaphragm. Electricity passing through the wires causes the nerve to move the diaphragm up and down. This makes the lungs breathe out and in.

ironwood

Ironwood is the popular name for many trees whose timber is very hard and heavy. The best known ironwood tree is the *hornbeam*, a tree that is very common in Europe and in some parts of the eastern United States. Hornbeam wood is white, tough, and hard. It burns as slowly as a candle. Its wood is mainly used as handles for tools such as the hammer, hatchet, and mallet. In certain parts of England, a hornbeam tree sometimes reaches a height of 100 feet. In the United States, the hornbeam is only about 40 feet high. Another American type of ironwood tree is found in isolated areas in Utah and Arizona. The ironwood tree is sometimes called the *hop-hornbeam*.

Iroquois

The Indians of North America belonged to many different small nations or tribes. Each tribe spoke a different language, but in some cases there were different tribes whose languages were much alike. These tribes were said to belong to the same "language group" or "family." The Iroquois were an important family. They were known as the Five Nations because about four hundred years ago five tribes joined together to form a very powerful group. These tribes were the Mohawks, Oneidas, Onondagas, Cayugas, and Senecas. In 1722, the Tuscaroras joined the Five Nations, and they became the Six Nations.

These six tribes lived in the state of New York. They were brave and cruel warriors, and defeated many other Indian tribes.

In the French and Indian Wars, when England fought to control America, the Iroquois fought on the British side. When the British fought the American colonists in the Revolutionary war, the Iroquois argued about which side they should take. All of the tribes except the Oneidas sided with the British. This argument broke up the great Six Nations of the Iroquois. After the Revolutionary War many of the Iroquois Indians were sent to reservations in Canada.

HOW THE IROQUOIS LIVED

The Iroquois tribes lived in villages that were surrounded by high fences made of strong wooden poles, pointed at the tops. These fences were called palisades, and they were built to protect the village and keep out enemies. Inside the village, as many as sixteen families lived together in a long house. The house was built on poles that were covered with bark and wood. In one large central room, the women built fires and cooked their meals in the middle of the floor. Raised platforms, like bunks, around the sides of the room, were used for sleeping and sitting. Smaller rooms in the long house were used for sleeping and storing food.

The clothing worn by both men and women was usually made from deerskins. The men and boys wore only a breechcloth during the summer months, or indoors in the winter time.

The Iroquois Indians worked very hard. The women raised corn and squash and beans in small forest clearings. The men were forest hunters. Deer supplied most of their meat and fine skins for cloth. The people made dishes out of elm bark and wood and clay. They made beautiful bows and arrows, and strong clubs with stone heads. The warriors wore helmets and armor made out of bark.

The women were very important in the Iroquois tribes. They elected the chiefs who ruled each tribe, and if the chiefs did not rule well, the women elected a new chief. All of the tribes met together for great national councils. Each tribe sent a certain number of people to represent it at these councils.

Irrawaddy River

The Irrawaddy is the longest river in Burma. It is 1,250 miles long and most people in Burma live in its big valley.

Two rivers called the Mali Kha and the Nimai Kha stream down from the mountains of northern Burma and join

to make the Irrawaddy River. North of the city of Mandalay the river is narrow and flows between cliffs of rock, but below Mandalay it spreads until it is between one and four miles wide. It has built a great delta of swamps and islands where some of Asia's richest rice fields are. Rangoon, the capital of Burma, is located in this delta.

irrigation

Irrigation is man's way of watering lands that do not receive enough natural water to make plants grow. Irrigation is a substitute for rain and snow, nature's way of watering the soil. If you have ever watered flowers in a garden with a watering can, you have applied one form of irrigation. With irrigation, dry lands such as deserts can become fertile and grow crops.

Arid (dry) or semiarid regions are found on all the continents of the world. In some regions, such as some islands off the Asiatic coast, rain falls heavily but not during the crop-growing season. These regions also need irrigation. Other regions go through drought periods (long spells without rain) and they, too, need irrigation.

BRINGING WATER TO THE SOIL

Water for the irrigation systems comes chiefly from lakes, ponds, and flowing streams—water on the surface of the earth. Irrigation water is also found underneath the ground, where it has collected in natural underground reservoirs, or pools of water.

Water is supplied for irrigation purposes in two ways. One method is called the *gravity method*. Water flows downward from its river or lake source to the fields to be irrigated. Channels or canals are built to direct the water to the fields.

When water is found in reservoirs or lakes that are lower than the fields that are to be irrigated, it must be raised. Farmers use pumps to do this job. Today, water pumps are able to raise water to a height of several hundred feet. These modern pumps are worked by gasoline, coal, oil, or electricity. A farmer can set up a pump himself at a nearby water source, or he can use water sent to his fields by large pumping plants that serve many farms.

Often the water source is miles away. There are many ways of transporting water to a field. Large canal systems are built to carry heavy volumes of water. The largest irrigation canal in the world is the All-American Canal in the United States. It carries the waters of the Colorado River, in Arizona all the way to the Imperial Valley in California, more than a hundred miles away. Water is also carried in pipe lines. Engineers even blast holes in mountain sides to create tunnels through which the water can flow.

Sometimes there is no steady supply of water. During part of the year, the water sources may dry up. In such cases it is necessary to store the water when it is most abundant, so it can be distributed to the fields when it is needed. Such water storage places are created by dams which form reservoirs, or artificial lakes.

IRRIGATING FIELDS

There are many methods of irrigation.

Bureau of Reclamation Photos

Siphon tubes bring water from a reservoir.

Since ancient times man has tried to make dry land useful by means of irrigation. Today, large projects have made many sections of the United States into rich farm regions.
The great Columbia Basin Project in Washington, opened in 1951.

One is the "furrow method." Crops that grow in rows, such as corn, potatoes, and cotton, are irrigated by this method. The farmers dig straight furrows (small trenches) in the soil about 2 to 4 feet apart. These rows are then flooded with water through pipes coming from nearby irrigating ditches. Another method of irrigation is called sub-irrigation, or irrigation from beneath the soil. In sub-irrigation, the water from under the soil's surface rises to the plant roots through tiny tubes placed in the soil. Sometimes farmers imitate a light rain through the spraying or sprinkling system of irrigation. Pipes laid on the top of the soil or beneath it let off a fine spray of water that covers the crops. The spraying of lawns is done in much the same way. For crops that grow under water, such as rice, the fields are completely flooded with water. Portions of the land called terraces, because they are like balconies one above the other, are flooded. The water overflows from one terrace to the next. This is one of the oldest methods of irrigation. The Chinese used it for hundreds of years.

HISTORY OF IRRIGATION

Irrigation is not a new method of bringing water to crops. It has been carried on in Egypt, Indian, Japan, China, and other countries for hundreds and even for thousands of years. The early farmers of these lands irrigated their fields by guiding water from streams flowing in the mountains. Bringing water from underground was done through wells and water wheels. A strong animal, such as the camel, pulled a shaft that worked a huge wheel. Upon the wheel were many buckets. As the camel turned the shaft, the buckets would dip into the water of a well beneath them. The ancient methods of irrigation taught a great deal to the farmers of later times. Today, irrigation improves by combining the old methods with the new.

Irving, Washington

Washington Irving was the first American who became famous as a professional writer. He also served the United States in its Embassy in Spain as a member of the diplomatic staff. He was born in New York City in 1783. He studied law and then traveled in Europe, where he got many ideas for stories. Irving was a very friendly person with a delightful sense of humor. He wrote many books and short stories. One of the first was written in 1809. It was called *Diedrich Knickerbocker's Comic History of New York*. Most of his best stories have their setting in New York State. Among the most famous are the *Legend of Sleepy Hollow*, the story of Ichabod Crane and the "headless horseman," and the *Story of Rip Van Winkle*, who slept for twenty years.

Sleepy Hollow Restorations

Irving became United States minister to Spain when he was 59. He wrote two books about Spain, *The Alhambra* and *The Conquest of Granada*.

When Irving was an old man he settled down near Tarrytown, New York. He died in 1859.

Isaac

The story of Isaac is told in the Bible. He was the son of Abraham and Sarah, and he was born to them when they were very old. The article on ABRAHAM tells about this, and also tells how Abraham was going to sacrifice Isaac when Isaac was a young boy, as an act of de-

votion to God, but an angel appeared and saved Isaac's life.

As told in the Bible, Isaac was one of the patriarchs, or fathers, of the Jewish people, and he was one of the first men to whom God spoke directly. He married Rebekah (Rebecca), and they had two sons, Esau and Jacob. Isaac preferred Esau, but Jacob was much smarter than Esau and he inherited Isaac's great wealth and power. You can read more about this in the article on JACOB. Isaac lived to be 180 years old.

Isaiah

Isaiah was one of the greatest prophets of the Jewish people. He lived in Jerusalem more than seven hundred years before the birth of Jesus.

Isaiah lived at a time when Judah, the land of the Jews, was invaded by many foreign conquerors, but he never lost faith in God or hope for the future. He explained to the Jews that their suffering was punishment for their sins, but that since God had promised to care for them, they would surely be saved as long as they continued to have faith in God. He predicted the coming of the Messiah who would save the people.

The book of Isaiah, in the Bible's Old Testament, is believed by most Bible scholars to have been written by two or three different prophets. Among the DEAD SEA SCROLLS (about which there is a separate article) there was an early copy of the Book of Isaiah, several hundred years older than any that had been available before.

Ishmael

Ishmael was the son of Abraham, the founder of the Jewish religion, and a young woman named Hagar. As told in the Bible, in the book of Genesis, Ishmael and his mother were driven from home by Abraham's wife, Sarah. They wandered over the country and Ishmael became an archer. An archer is someone who uses a bow and arrow. Meanwhile, the Lord came to Ishmael's father, Abraham, and told Abraham that Ishmael would have twelve sons who would found the twelve tribes of Ishmael. This happened and these twelve sons took the land, as the Bible tells, ". . . before Egypt as thou goest towards Assyria." Today's Arabs trace their descent to the Biblical Ishmaelite tribes.

isinglass

Isinglass is a gelatin or jelly used in the manufacture of adhesive tape, cement, and imitation pearls. It is prepared by boiling the swimming bladder of various fish, especially the sturgeon, cod, and hake. It has a strong, weblike structure and is white in color. The name isinglass is also given to transparent sheets of mica, a kind of stone.

Isis

Isis was a goddess worshiped by the ancient Egyptians. At first she was regarded as the goddess of the earth. She and her husband, Osiris, were the only gods worshiped by all the Egyptians. At a later time, in ancient Greece, she was worshiped as Demeter, the goddess of the earth. The ancient Romans built temples to Isis.

Islam

Islam is the name of a religion followed by many millions. The word is also used to mean all the people who follow this religion. The people who believe in Islam are followers of Mohammed, a great religious teacher, so the religion is often called Mohammedanism and the people who follow it are called Mohammedans. Another word for them is *Moslems,* which means "believers in Islam." *Islam* means "submission" (to the will of God).

Islam is the youngest of the great religions of the world. It began in Arabia about six hundred years after Christianity started with the birth of Jesus. Most people who believe in Islam live in Arabia, North Africa, and India, particularly in Pakistan. There are more than 433,000,000 Moslems.

In Islam, as in Christianity, the people worship one God. Their name for God is Allah. Islam also has a sacred book, as does Christianity. This book is called the Koran. It contains the words of Allah as taught by Mohammed. The Koran is written in Arabic and is the best-known and most-read book in Arabic literature. Islam also recognizes some parts of the Hebrew Torah as sacred, as well as the Psalms of the Old Testament and the teachings of Jesus.

Moslems consider that Mohammed is the last and greatest prophet of Allah, but they also number among their prophets many of the Hebrew prophets told about in the Old Testament of the Bible. Jesus and John the Baptist are also recognized as prophets in Islam.

Mohammed told his followers that Allah wished them to spread Islam all over the world, by peaceful means if possible, by force if necessary. From the time of its beginning, Islam has continued to spread. Within a hundred years after Mohammed died the religion had been spread to India, North Africa, southern Spain, and even parts of France.

To every Moslem, Mecca, the city in Arabia where Mohammed was born, is the chief holy city. Five times a day, a devout Moslem turns toward Mecca and prays. He is also supposed to visit Mecca at least once during his lifetime. This pilgrimage is called a *haj,* and a man who has made it can use *haji* as an honorary title before his name. There are other cities considered holy to Moslems. One of them is Jerusalem, which is also a holy city for both Christians and Jews. Medina is another holy city because it was there that Mohammed and his followers gained their first great success with their religion. The exodus of Mohammed to Medina is called the *Hegira* (really *hijra*) and from this event the Moslem calendar takes its beginning as Year One.

Each day every Moslem must say, in Arabic: "There is no God but Allah, and Mohammed is his prophet." The Moslem is also required to fast during one month of the year and to give alms to the poor. He may not drink alcoholic drinks. A man may have as many as four wives. Mohammed preached that Allah demanded complete obedience, and that he punished those who did not obey him. Much of the ethics taught in Islam is the same as what is taught in the Jewish re-

ligion and in Christianity. There are different sects in Islam, just as there are in Christianity.

island

An island is any body of land completely surrounded by water. Even a continent or great land mass is an island. The largest single island in the world that is not a continent is Greenland, far up in the northern waters of the Atlantic Ocean. Next to Greenland in size are such islands as New Guinea, Borneo, Madagascar, and Honshu (part of Japan), all of which are in the Pacific Ocean. Great Britain is also an island. It and the neighboring island of Ireland are sometimes called the British Isles.

Islands originated in many ways. Some islands were built up gradually by lava out of volcanoes. Some are themselves the tips of volcanoes that begin at the bottom of the sea and rise above the surface of the water. The Hawaiian Islands are such a group. Other islands were once part of a greater mass of land. However, water eroded, or ate away, the land between. Great Britain is such an island and it was once part of Europe. Other islands are coral islands, or islands formed from skeletons of sea life called corals. The Marshall Islands in the Pacific Ocean are coral islands.

In geography, islands are usually divided into two main categories (classes): continental and oceanic islands. Continental islands are those islands that have the same land and plant structure as a neighboring continent, while oceanic islands have their own land and plant structure. A group of similar islands is called an archipelago. There are great groups of thousands of islands in the South Pacific and Indian Oceans and north of Canada.

The largest islands in the world are:

ISLAND	OCEAN	SQUARE MILES
Greenland	North Atlantic	840,000
New Guinea	Pacific	316,861
Borneo	South China Sea	287,400
Madagascar	Indian	229,812
Baffin	Arctic	183,810
Sumatra	Indian	182,860
Honshu	Pacific	88,031
Great Britain	Atlantic	84,186
Ellesmere	Arctic	82,119
Victoria	Arctic	81,930

Australia, with 2,975,000 square miles, is so large that it is ranked as a continent.

isolationism

Isolation is being alone, or not connected with anything else. Some United States citizens say that the United States government should be interested only in affairs inside the country, and should pay no attention to whether foreign countries are rich or poor, or to any wars they may fight. This policy is called *isolationism.* When the United States was a young and weak country, its first President, George Washington, advised the people to keep the country out of any alliances with other countries. Isolationists think this policy should still be followed. Those who disagree are called *internationalists.* They say that conditions have changed so much since George Washington's time that the United States could not be safe if it did not work with friendly

countries to prevent war. Since the time of Woodrow Wilson, who was President during World War I, nearly all Presidents have been internationalists. These include Presidents Wilson, Hoover, F. D. Roosevelt, Truman, Eisenhower, Kennedy, and Johnson.

When a war is going on between foreign countries, those who think the United States should take sides have been called *interventionists* instead of internationalists.

isotope, see the article ELEMENT.

Israel Government Tourist Office
The John F. Kennedy Memorial in Jerusalem, Israel.

Israel

Israel is the name of a small republic in the Middle East, on the eastern end of the Mediterranean Sea. It occupies a large part of the ancient land of Palestine, which is the holy land of Christianity, Islam, and Judaism. The modern state of Israel is about as large as the state of New Jersey, having an area of about 8,000 square miles. About three million people live in Israel. Although the history of Palestine goes back many thousands of years, the modern state of Israel is very new, having become an independent nation in 1948.

THE PEOPLE WHO LIVE THERE

More than ninety percent of the people who live in Israel are Jews. There are a small number of Christians and a small number of Arabs who follow the Mohammedan religion. Many of the Jews who live in Israel today were not born there, but came to Israel from all over the world after Israel had become an independent state. The constitution of Israel states that "Israel is the national home for the Jewish people," and any Jew anywhere in the world who wishes to settle in Israel has the right to do so. The largest number came from Europe, where they had lost their homes before and during World War II.

Many of the newcomers to Israel were unable to understand one another because they spoke different languages. Soon, even the older people were going to school to learn Hebrew, the old language of the Jewish people and the language of Israel.

HOW THE PEOPLE LIVE

For many years agriculture has been the chief occupation of the people of Israel, but the many different people who have come to Israel have brought with them many new trades and professions that they learned in other lands.

A large number of the farmers of Israel live in large agricultural villages, and they work together farming large areas of land that a single family would be unable to take care of. This kind of farming is called collective farming, or cooperative farming.

The most important crops grown in Israel are citrus fruits, such as lemons and oranges. These fruits are sent to many different parts of the world. Other crops grown in Israel are olives, grains, tobacco,

and several kinds of vegetable.

Besides agriculture, many new industries have grown up in Israel. There are factories that make many kinds of manufactured goods. There is an important diamond-polishing industry. There are large factories that make cloth, and several large plants that preserve and pack foods.

There are several large cities in Israel.

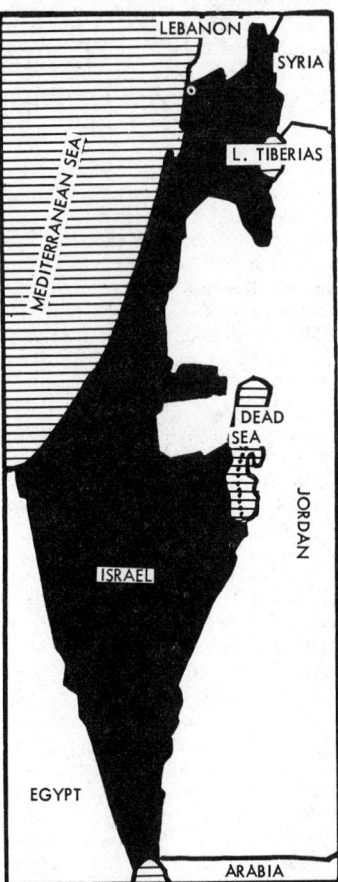

Jaffa-Tel Aviv, which is really two cities combined, is the largest, with almost 400,000 people. It is a large industrial city and an important seaport. Many of the buildings in Tel Aviv are very modern and the streets are wide and clean.

Haifa is the most important seaport in Israel. More than 174,000 people live there. Haifa is also located at the terminus, or end, of an important pipe line that carries petroleum from the oil fields in Iraq to a large refinery in Haifa.

The historic and holy city of Jerusalem has been divided into two parts. Part of the city is in Israel and the other part is in the part of Palestine that

now belongs to Jordan, but has been occupied by Israel since 1967. The part of Jerusalem that is in Israel was made the capital of the country.

There are two kinds of school in Israel. One school system is for the Jews and the other is for the Arabs. The schools for young children are free, but many of the secondary schools are private or semi-private. Children are required to go to school by law. Hebrew University, which was founded in Jerusalem about twenty years ago, is one of the best-known colleges in the Middle East. It has more than two thousand students.

WHAT KIND OF PLACE IT IS

Almost half of Israel is a large desert area that is very dry and hot. However, great progress has been made in developing the desert region of the Negev in the southern half of the country by irrigation. Water is piped in from the north, and a large desalination plant which will convert sea water to fresh water is being built on the Red Sea. The western part of Israel, along the Mediterranean Sea, is a very fertile plain about a hundred miles long and fifteen miles wide. This is where most of the people of Israel live today. The northern part of Israel is a low plateau and the central part of Israel is called the Plateau of Judea.

The only important river in Israel is the Jordan. This river begins in Syria, to the northeast of Israel, and flows along the Israel-Jordan border. It ends in the Dead Sea. The Dead Sea lies between Israel and Jordan, and each country controls half of it. It is a small body of water more than a thousand feet below sea level. It is the lowest point on earth. It is mostly important for the minerals that can be taken from its water. The people of Israel have also been able to develop other mineral resources of the country, such as copper, iron, phosphates, sulphur, limestone, rock salt, potash, and gypsum.

During the summers in Israel it is very hot and quite dry. Sometimes the temperature may go as high as 100 degrees. The winters are cooler, and there is some rainfall during the spring and fall months.

Israel has many good roadways and several hundred miles of railroads. Many of the large international airlines make stops at Tel Aviv airport, and Israel has its own airline which is called *El Al*. The people have also been building a small but well-run merchant marine.

HOW THE PEOPLE ARE GOVERNED

The people of Israel have a democratic

form of government. They have a president who is elected every five years by the Chamber of Deputies, the national law-making body. The 120 members of the Chamber of Deputies, which the Israelis call the *Knesset,* are elected by vote of all the people. Everybody over the age of 21 is allowed to vote. The government is run by a premier and a cabinet of ministers, selected from the Knesset.

Israel became a member of the United Nations in 1949. Aided by contributions from Jews all over the world, Israel maintains a modern air force and an army of about 100,000, with the best weapons.

HOW ISRAEL CAME TO BE

More than sixty years ago a group of Jewish leaders, calling themselves Zionists, set out to create a national home for the Jewish people in Pal stine, which the Bible calls the "promis d land" of the Jews. Zion is an old biblical name for Jerusalem. Chaim Weizmann, who later became the first president of modern Israel, was leader of the Zionists.

In 1917 Foreign Secretary Balfour of Great Britain, which then controlled Palestine, issued the famous Balfour Declaration, which said that Britain favored a Jewish national home in Palestine. But most of the people living in Palestine were Arabs and they were opposed to Jewish immigration. For twenty years there was steady Jewish immigration into Palestine, but the Jewish settlers had many fights with the Arabs. Jewish immigration grew during World War II, when Jews were being persecuted in Germany and in the European countries under German control. After World War II, Jews wishing to reach Israel were fought also by British warships and soldiers, in spite of the Balfour Declaration.

Britain turned the problem over to the United Nations, which decided to divide Palestine into two parts, one for Arabs and one for Jews, with the city of Jerusalem under U.N. administration. The Jews accepted this proposal but the Arabs said they would go to war to prevent it.

Nevertheless, in 1948 the Jewish settlers declared themselves the independent Republic of Israel, under the United Nations' partition plan. Armies of several Arab nations then attacked the new state of Israel. The Israelis (citizens of Israel) fought off the attacking forces and in 1949 the United Nations arranged for an armistice — that is, to have the fighting stop. But no general peace settlement was reached. The Arab countries continue to say that they are at war with Israel; they fire on Israeli ships at sea, and there are frequent "skirmishes" on the borders between Israel and its Arab neighbors, in which soldiers and others die.

In 1956, Britain and France joined in an attack on Egypt to avoid losing the Suez Canal. Israel promptly entered the fighting on the side of the attackers and its armies occupied Gaza and other parts of Egypt. However, the United States persuaded all three attacking countries to stop fighting and withdraw their forces from Egypt.

In June, 1967, President Nasser of the United Arab Republic, decided to send ships to block the Gulf of Aqaba, Israel's only water outlet to the Red Sea. He also persuaded other Arab nations to send soldiers to surround Israel with tanks, machine guns, and other weapons. The border skirmishes which had been going on for about 10 years suddenly broke into full-scale war. It was one of the shortest and most amazing wars in history. In only six days, Israel, with a population of fewer than 3 million, won a total victory over all the Arab nations having a combined population of 110 million. When both sides agreed to a cease-fire ordered by the U.N., 15,000 Arabs had been killed, 50,000 wounded, and 11,500 captured; but only 679 Israelis were killed, 2,563 wounded, and 16 captured.

Throughout the following three years gun-fire was exchanged almost daily across the Suez Canal. In addition, Israeli planes flew missions and raids over Egyptian borders. Reprisals on the part of Palestinian guerrillas occurred on the Jordanian, Syrian and Lebanese frontiers.

In June, 1970, peace negotiations sponsored by the United States resulted in a cease-fire agreement acknowledged by Israel, Egypt and Jordan. Palestinian guerrilla attacks continued, however, and hampered further attempts at reconciliation.

The "cease-fire" lasted from June, 1970 until March 7, 1971. This temporary "peace" was frequently violated by guerrilla raids against Israel by Lebanon and Syria.

Then, on October 6, 1973 (Yom Kippur—the most sacred day of the Jewish calendar) Egypt and Syria launched a surprise war against Israel.

Egyptian troops crossed the Suez Canal and Syrian forces pushed into the Golan Heights. Egypt and Syria were supported by massive Russian arms and airlifts. The United States offered airlifts to Israel in response. The Israelis fought the Syrians back to within twenty miles of Damascus. Then Israel surrounded the Egyptian Third Army.

A United Nations cease-fire went into effect on October 24, maintained by United Nations troops. Secretary of State Henry Kissinger negotiated the terms for a disengagement agreement which was signed on January 18, 1974. This called for Israeli withdrawals from territories captured in the "Yom Kippur War" (October 6, 1973).

Premier Golda Meir resigned on April 10, 1974. Thirteen days later, Yitzhak Rabin assumed the vacant post.

ISRAEL. Area, 7,993 square miles. Population (1976 estimate) 3,003,000. Language, Hebrew. Religion, Judaism. Government, republic. Monetary unit, Israeli pound, worth about 33 cents (U.S.). Flag, two horizontal blue bands on white field, with Star of David in center of field. Capital, Jerusalem.

Istanbul

Istanbul is the biggest city of Turkey and the only city in the world that is located on two continents. One part of Istanbul is in Europe, while the other part is in Asia, across the strait (narrow body of water) known as the Bosporus. Istanbul is the Turkish name for the city. Its ancient Christian name was Constantino-ple, and before that it was named Byzantium. As Byzantium, it was founded by wanderers from Greece hundreds of years before the birth of Jesus. Later it became the center of a great civilization that we call BYZANTINE.

In the year 328, the Christian emperor of Rome, Constantine the Great, captured Byzantium and rebuilt it, giving it the new name of Constantinople, which means "city of Constantine." As the capital of the Eastern Roman Empire it became a great center of art and learning, with many beautiful buildings. One of them is the Cathedral of Saint Sophia, which was built almost 1,500 years ago by the Roman emperor Justinian. It is now a mosque, or temple, of the Mohammedan people.

Constantinople was attacked many times in its history and in 1453 it was captured by the Turks. The sultans (kings) of Turkey made it their capital and so it remained until after World War I. In 1922 the capital of Turkey was moved to Ankara, but Istanbul remained the most important trading city.

Because Istanbul lies where Europe and Asia meet, it has always been a center for travelers from many different countries, many of whom remained to live there. Today its two and a half million people include not only Turks but also Greeks, Armenians, and other peoples. In addition to trading, the people make rugs, silks, embroideries, pottery, and leather goods.

The most important part of Istanbul is on the European side. Like Rome, it is built on seven hills on the two sides of an inlet of the Bosporus called the Golden Horn. From this part of Istanbul runs the important Baghdad Railway, which connects Europe with the Middle East. In Istanbul you may see parts of the ancient walls that the East Romans built around the city to protect it from invaders.

ISTANBUL, TURKEY. Population (1976 estimate) 2,600,000 including suburbs.

isthmus

An isthmus is a narrow strip of land that joins two larger areas of land. For example, the Isthmus of Panama joins the continents of North and South America. An isthmus is a favorable place for a city. It commands the only land route between the two larger land areas. Water is on each side of the isthmus, so it is very valuable for shipping and trading. For this reason, control of an isthmus usually gives a country great transportation power. Canals are constructed across isthmuses to connect the seas on both sides of it. Across the Isthmus of Panama is the Panama Canal. The Isthmus of Suez joins the continents of Africa and Asia, and its canal is the Suez Canal.

Istria

Istria is a small peninsula on the eastern coast of the Adriatic Sea. A peninsula is a body of land that sticks into the water. Istria was once part of the Roman Empire. Now it lies between the modern countries of Italy and Yugoslavia, and most of it belongs to Yugoslavia. Its biggest city is TRIESTE, about which there is a separate article.

Istria is a mountainous region. Its area is more than 1,500 square miles. Three

large groups of people live there, Croatians, Italians, and Slovenes. On the point of the peninsula, in the Adriatic Sea, lies the city of Pula (or Pola). This city was important in World War II when American planes flying from Italy used it as a guidepost on their way north to Germany.

Italian campaign

The Italian campaign was an important part of the fighting in World War II. In that campaign Allied troops, most of them from the United States, forced Italy to surrender. Italy was the first enemy country to surrender in World War II.

The Italian campaign began in 1943, after the United States and British troops had won control of Africa in the AFRICAN CAMPAIGN, about which there is a separate article. Before the Allies invaded Italy, they invaded and conquered Sicily, an island in the Mediterranean Sea that belongs to Italy. The Fascist government of Italy, which under the leadership of Benito Mussolini had led the Italian people to war against the Allies, fell soon after the invasion of Sicily. The new government wanted to make peace with the Allies, but the German army occupied Italy and disarmed the Italian army. The Italian Campaign was necessary in order to get control of Italy from the Germans.

The Fifth Army of the United States, led by General Mark Clark, with General Alfred M. Gruenther as chief of staff, and the British Eighth Army, led by General Bernard Montgomery, were the chief Allied forces in the Italian campaign. Later these forces were known as the Fifteenth Army group. Brazilians, Indians, Canadians and Free French troops also fought in the Italian campaign.

The Fifth Army landed first at Salerno, Italy, a small port south of the city of Naples, where they met fierce resistance. The Eighth Army landed first at Reggio, a coastal town much farther south, where the resistance was not as great. Four months later the Americans landed at Anzio, a town 30 miles south of Rome, to try to get behind the German lines. Some of the bloodiest fighting of the campaign occurred at Cassino and along the Rapido River.

The Allied forces captured Naples, the biggest city of southern Italy, without much trouble, but it took them months to capture Rome, which they took in June, 1944. They drove north but the German resistance was so strong that the Italian campaign lasted until May 2, 1945, only a few days before the end of the war in Europe.

Italian language and literature

The Italian language is spoken in Italy, on the island of Sicily (which is part of Italy), and on several other islands near Italy, such as Corsica. It is also spoken by many of the people of Switzerland, where it is one of the three official languages, along with French and German. Altogether more than fifty million people speak Italian.

Italian is one of the Romance languages, which means that it comes chiefly from the Latin language spoken by the ancient Romans. (The other principal Romance languages are Spanish, French, Portuguese, and Rumanian.) Italian is more like Latin than any of the others, chiefly because Italy was the center of the Roman Empire when it was the most powerful empire on earth.

In the course of the centuries, people living in different parts of Italy have made their own special changes in the language, so that now there are many different forms of the Italian language. Special forms of a language are called *dialects*. The dialects in Italy are so different that an Italian from the north can hardly understand people who speak a dialect of the south. The principal southern dialects are Sicilian and Neapolitan (the dialect of the region around the city of Naples).

It is only in the spoken language that the dialects are different. The pure Italian language, the language in which books are written, is known to all literate Italians (those who can read and write). This form of Italian is called Tuscan. It is the language of Tuscany, a region in central Italy, and of Florence, the principal city of Tuscany. The Tuscan form of Italian is closer to the original Latin than any other Italian dialect or any other Romance language.

Though Italian is like Latin, it is much simpler, for it does not have nearly as many inflections (changes in the sound and spelling of a word, depending on how it is used in a sentence). There are many more words in Italian than in Latin, for the people have been learning new things and finding words for them for two thousand years.

The Italian alphabet has only twenty-one letters. It does not use the letters *j, k, w, x,* or *y*.

ITALIAN LITERATURE

The ancient Roman empire whose capital was Rome, the present capital of Italy, came to an end nearly 1,500 years ago, but for hundreds of years after that the best Italian writers continued to write only in Latin. The first great writer in the Italian language was the poet Dante, who was born about seven hundred years ago. His *Divine Comedy* and other poems are still considered the best ever written in Italian and among the best ever written in any language.

For several hundred years the greatest Italian literature was almost all poetry. Exceptions were Giovanni Boccaccio, who lived about six hundred years ago, and who wrote great stories that are still read with pleasure; and Niccolo Machiavelli, who lived about 150 years later (from 1469 to 1527) and who wrote on politics. But Petrarch, who lived about fifty years after Dante and was the next great Italian writer, is remembered as a poet, though he also wrote some prose. Then came Lodovico Ariosto, who lived from 1474 to 1533, and whose great poem was *Orlando Furioso;* and Torquato Tasso, who lived from 1544 to 1595, and who wrote the greatest Italian poem of his time, *Gerusalemme Liberata* (Jerusalem Delivered, or set free), and also several other long poems and more than a thousand short ones.

In more recent centuries, there have been many Italians who were great scientists and thinkers, and Italy has produced some of the world's most important scientific literature.

One Italian poet was also among the country's principal political leaders. This was Gabriele D'Annunzio, who was born about a hundred years ago (in 1863) and was a hero in World War I. He had become famous as a writer of poetry, plays, and novels, and he used his popularity to help Benito Mussolini become dictator of Italy in 1923. D'Annunzio died in 1938.

Luigi Pirandello was the principal Italian playwright of the present century, and several of his plays have been translated into English and seen by many Americans, both on the stage and in motion-picture versions.

In the past twenty-five years, the works of many Italian novelists have been popular in English translations.

italics

Printed letters that slant to the right are called *italics*. The word "italics" in the last sentence is printed in italics.

Aldus Manutius, an Italian printer, invented italic type about 450 years ago in the city of Venice, Italy, where he printed many books in this style of type. Because straight type, called "Roman" type, is easier to read than italics, italics are seldom used except when a writer wished to emphasize or draw special attention to one or more words in a sentence.

Italy

Italy is a country in the southern part of Europe. It is a peninsula, a body of land surrounded on three sides by water. It is shaped like a boot that sticks out from the mainland into the Mediterranean Sea. On the north Italy is cut off from the rest of Europe by the Alps Mountains. The area of Italy is about 116,000 square miles, which is less than half the size of Texas. About 50,000,000 people live there, which is more than five times as many as live in Texas.

Italy has been torn by wars and poverty for many years, but the people are music-loving, gay, and warm-hearted. For centuries their art and music have been an inspiration to the world. The ancient Romans of Italy, two thousand years ago, built roads, aqueducts and temples that still stand. Italians are very proud of their past glory.

THE PEOPLE WHO LIVE THERE

The people of Italy are descendants of

many ancient tribes. Almost three thousand years ago a people called Etruscans, from the eastern shore of the Mediterranean, settled in Italy. The Greeks settled the towns along the southern coast about four hundred years after that. Several hundred years later people from Germany and France crossed the Alps to conquer part of northern Italy. Because so many different peoples have made up the Italian people, there is a considerable difference in the appearance of northern, central, and southern Italians. In the north many have light complexions and blond hair. In the central part of the country people have darker hair and darker skin. In the extreme south most of the people have jet black hair and still darker complexions, called "olive."

Though all the people speak Italian, a language that grew out of ancient Latin, there are many different dialects.

HOW THE PEOPLE LIVE

Although Italy is becoming more and more an industrial country, a large part of the population still works at farming. Many of Italy's farms are small, and a large number of them are in mountainous regions where farming is difficult.

Nearly half of the population of Italy lives in cities, some of which are over 2,000 years old. Rome, Italy's capital, for instance, was a capital and large city before Christ was born. In these cities, beautiful public buildings and churches that are hundreds of years old, and ruins of magnificent Roman structures, stand next to modern office and apartment buildings. Life in the cities offers almost all the modern conveniences, but in country towns houses often lack indoor plumbing and women cook over open fires.

Italians love grand opera as many people in the United States love the movies. Many famous composers and opera singers have been Italians.

Most of the people of Italy are Roman Catholics, although other religions are permitted. The world center of the Roman Catholic Church is in Rome, the capital of Italy.

All Italian children between the ages of 6 and 14 must go to school. They can also go to college without paying. Many towns and cities have colleges run by the government. As far back as the year 1500 there were ten colleges in Italy. It was the first country in Europe to have a university. More than three-quarters of the people in Italy can read and write.

INDUSTRIES IN ITALY

Some of Italy's industries are centuries old. Among these traditional industries, for which Italy is famous all over the world, are silk and cotton weaving, jewelry, furniture, glass, and ceramics. After World War II, great progress was made in developing other fields of industry, and today Italy is one of Europe's leading manufacturers of automobiles, heavy industrial equipment, machine tools, and office machines. Also, clothing industries have within the past years entered the world markets and Italian fashions are influencing styles in many parts of the world.

Italy's farms produce olives, wine, oranges, many other fruits, and a great variety of cheeses, much of which is exported.

The tomb of Dante in Ravenna is a beautiful monument to Italy's greatest poet.

On its long seacoast Italy has many busy seaports, among them Genoa, Leghorn, Naples, Palermo, Messina, and Catania. The country's large merchant fleet, a great part of which was lost during World War II, has been rebuilt in the post-war years.

Italy's railroads, which are almost entirely electrified, and also the telephone and telegraph systems, are owned by the government. Roads are not like the highways of the United States. Most of the highways, some of which date back to Roman days, are narrow and winding, and wide enough for only two cars. Although there are still many fewer people in Italy who own cars than in the United States, the number of Italians who own cars has increased sharply in the past few years.

WHAT KIND OF PLACE IT IS

More than a third of Italy is covered with mountains. The Alps at the north are met by the Apennines, which run straight down through the center of the Italian "boot" to the tip of the "toe." Below the southern tip of the peninsula is the island of Sicily, which is a part of Italy.

Siena's town hall and the surrounding buildings form an almost perfect circle.

The delicate mosaic of the Good Shepherd in Ravenna is about 1,500 years old.

Italy has several volcanoes. These are mountains that erupt fire and smoke. Two of them are very famous. An eruption of Mount Vesuvius, about two thousand years ago (A.D. 79), was so violent that it buried the entire city of Pompeii, which was built at its foot. Today a visitor to Italy can see the ruins of the ancient buildings of Pompeii, and can see the smoke swirling around inside the crater of the volcano. Another famous volcano is Mount Etna, in Sicily. This volcano is on a mountain peak 10,865 feet high.

The climate of the entire country is mild. Where the Alps Mountains extend into Italy, there are sections where winters are cold but there is snow in only a few places in the far north. The cold winds from the north of Europe are stopped by the Alps before they reach Italy.

The soil of the plains is generally rich. The valley of the Po River is especially fertile. This is in the northern part of the country. Another large Italian river is the Tiber, which flows through Rome. A third river of importance is the Arno, which flows through the city of Florence. Few ships use the rivers for commerce.

People who visit Italy like to stop in Venice. This is one of the most unusual cities in the world. Instead of streets and roads, Venice has a network of canals, on which boats called gondolas travel in the same way that taxis and automobiles travel on streets in other cities. Venice has been a port and a shipping center for hundreds of years.

Italy has not many minerals. There is a serious shortage of coal, which must be imported from other countries. Italy has valuable sulfur deposits near the bases of volcanic mountains.

The cities of Italy contain great art treasures and sights and buildings that are familiar all over the world. The Leaning Tower of Pisa, the Colosseum in Rome, the museums in Florence, and Vatican City, the seat of the Pope, are all places that tourists enjoy visiting. In the buildings of Vatican City there are beautiful decorations or paintings by Michelangelo, one of the world's greatest artists. The works of Leonardo da Vinci are also Italian treasures. There are many famous opera houses, especially La Scala in Milan.

CHIEF CITIES IN ITALY

The leading cities of Italy, with populations as estimated in 1973, are:

Rome, population 2,656,104, the capital and largest city, one of the historic cities of the world. There is a separate article about ROME.

Milan, population 1,687,264, second-largest city, industrial center in the northern part of Italy.

Naples, population 1,267,073, second seaport in importance and third-largest city. Industrial center, famous for its gayety and festivals. In southern Italy.

Turin, population 1,142,210, in northwest Italy. Industrial center; automobile factories.

Genoa, population 843,632, in northwest Italy, chief port. Center of commerce and shipbuilding.

Palermo, population 652,380, in Sicily, center of industry, agriculture, art.

Florence, population 456,370, in central Italy, center of industry, agriculture, art.

Bologna, population 486,973, industrial and historic educational center. In north central Italy.

St. Peter's in Vatican City is visited by thousands of pilgrims every year.

The buildings and statues of Rome make ancient history live once more.

Its ruined aqueducts and the Roman Forum recall "the grandeur that was Rome."

Venice, population 336,184, in northeast Italy, a city of canals built on 118 small islands. Center of art, industry, and commerce.

Catania, population 407,941, second-largest city in Sicily, transportation and industrial center, located near the foot of Mt. Etna.

HOW THE PEOPLE ARE GOVERNED

Italy is a republic. Before 1946 it was a monarchy, but in 1948, after World War II, Italy adopted a new constitution. It has a parliament that is like the British Parliament, with two houses, the Chamber of Deputies and the Senate. Members of the Chamber of Deputies serve for five years and Senators for six years. The President is chosen by the Parliament, and his term is seven years. After the President's term is over, he becomes a Senator. The actual head of the government is the Premier, or Prime Minister. The Premier has a cabinet to help him.

There are many small political parties in Italy, but only three parties are large. These are the Christian Democrats, the Socialists, and the Communists. Both men and women over 21 may vote.

ITALY IN THE PAST

The history of Italy goes back for thousands of years, but was most glorious in the time of the ancient Roman Empire, which had its center in Rome. This empire spread throughout Europe, North Africa, and parts of Asia. Under the Roman Empire, Italy was powerful and united, but the people of ancient Rome became soft and lazy, because they had conquered so many lands and captured so many slaves they no longer had to do any work.

By the year 476 Rome was so weak that German invaders conquered and ruled it. Italy was broken up into independent city-states, each with its own army, its own government, and its own ruler. These city-states were frequently at war with one another, and the strong ones gradually became small kingdoms. By the 15th century, about five hundred years ago, there were more than a dozen different countries on the Italian peninsula. The largest was the Kingdom of Naples, which included the island of Sicily. North of Naples were the Papal States, over which the Pope ruled. Still farther north were other individual countries, which included the Republics of Florence, Siena, Genoa, and Venice; the small duchies (ruled by dukes) of Modena, Ferrara, and Savoia; and several other independent districts.

Italy started to recover its strength at about the time of Columbus's voyages to America. This period was called the Renaissance, or "rebirth" of art and learning. There is a separate article about the RENAISSANCE.

Then for several hundred years Italy was a battlefield. Invasions from Austria, France, and Spain kept the land in constant state of war. This brought about a patriotic feeling and a unity among Italians. They grew more and more determined to throw out foreign rulers.

The Italian revolution finally started in 1848. A great soldier named Garibaldi led the revolution, with the help of the Kingdom of Sardinia, one of the divisions of Italy at that time. The revolution was a long one, and only in 1861 was Italy

Italian State Tourist Office Photos

From the time of the ancient Romans through the present day, Italy has been a great center of learning, culture, and art. People who visit Italy can see there many of man's great cultural achievements. Michelangelo, the Titan of the arts, created this powerful statue of Moses.

finally united as a single country. Victor Emmanuel II of Sardinia became the first king of united Italy, and Rome was made the country's capital in 1871.

In World War I Italy fought on the side of the Allies, and won, but nevertheless after 1918 poverty and unemployment kept the country in a state of unrest, and the people were sick and discontented. They were ready to listen to anyone who would promise them something better. A leader named Benito Mussolini formed the Fascist (united) Party in 1919, and many of the people were glad to join with him. Five years later in 1924, he was voted into power, and soon he became the absolute dictator in Italy. He took away the people's freedom of speech, freedom to vote as they pleased, and freedom to criticize the government.

Mussolini was very ambitious. In 1935 he sent Italian forces to invade and capture Ethiopia. This made the rest of the world angry, but no one stopped him. He went on to invade and seize Albania, a small, weak country in Europe. By this time, Adolf Hitler and the Nazi Party were in power in Germany, and Mussolini signed a treaty with Hitler, and later with Japan, in 1936. After that, those three countries (known as the Axis Powers) were lined up against Great Britain, France, and the United States, and other freedom-loving countries.

World War II eventually grew out of

this alliance, and Italy fought as one of the Axis Powers. Its armed forces could not resist the Allied attacks, and in 1945 Mussolini was killed by a firing squad of Italians. A year later the king was voted out, and the country became a republic. In 1957 Italy became a founding member of the European Economic Community.

ITALY. Area, 116,372 square miles. Population (1964 estimate) 50,955,000. Language, Italian. Religion, Roman Catholic. Government, republic. Monetary unit, the lira, worth 0.16¢ (U.S.). Flag three vertical stripes, dark green, white, red.

Ivan, Czar of Russia

There were six rulers of Russia called Ivan. The most important was Ivan IV, called the Terrible, who was the first Russian czar. He succeeded his father as grand duke of Moscow in 1533, when he was only 3 years old, and at the age of 14 he took over the actual government of the country. Three years later he was named czar.

Ivan's parents were both dead and he had grown up among cruel people, so it was natural that he too should be cruel. But he sided with the common people and hated the *boyars*, or aristocrats, whom he suspected of plotting to overthrow him. In 1570, he was told that a plot against him was being hatched in the city of Novgorod, and he massacred the people of that city. He even killed his own son. He carried on wars against Sweden, Poland, and the Crimea.

There was another side to Ivan that was more admirable, for he introduced self-government to parts of Russia and was interested in seeing his country grow not only in military strength but in the arts of peace as well. He died in 1584.

ivory

Ivory is the material of an elephant's tusks, or upper teeth. Since prehistoric times, ivory has been used for household and artistic objects. It has a creamy white color and though it is a solid, it is soft and can easily be sculptured or molded. The Bible tells us that King Solomon had a great throne of ivory. We have examples of ivory sculpture made a thousand years before Jesus. Ivory has long been used for household objects. The white strips on many piano keys are made from ivory.

The best ivory tusks are obtained from African elephants. Their tusks weigh about fifty to sixty pounds and are about six feet long. In addition to the elephant, there are other ivory-bearing animals, mainly the walrus and the hippopotamus. The narwhal, a kind of whale, also yields ivory. Killing elephants for ivory is now illegal in nearly all parts of Africa.

Ivory Coast, Republic of the

The Republic of the Ivory Coast is a country on the west coast of Africa, in size about the same as the state of New Mexico but with many more people living there. It was a territory of France until it became independent in 1960, and it is a member of the French Community and the United Nations.

The people are Negroes of several different tribes and most of them are farmers. Their chief products are coffee, cocoa, peanuts, bananas, palm oil, and wood from the big forests. Ores are produced in several big mines. The country is flat near the sea but rises to hills and mountains, from which many rivers flow through the coastal plains and empty into the Gulf of Guinea. The Ivory Coast is near the Equator and the climate is hot and damp all year. The capital is Abidjan, a city of about 300,000; it is an important seaport.

THE REPUBLIC OF THE IVORY COAST. Area, 127,520 square miles. Population, 4,-420,000 (1973 estimate). Capital, Abidjan.

ivory palm

The ivory palm is a palm tree from which is taken a substance that looks like ivory. The tree grows in the hot regions of South America and reaches a height of about thirty feet. On the underside of each leaf, a cluster of hard fruit grows. Each cluster contains about twenty-five nuts, called *coroza* or *tague nuts*. These nuts are white, like ivory, and the seeds are used in the manufacture of buttons.

ivy

Ivy is a name given to a number of different kinds of plants noted for their ability to creep or climb. Because it has this ability, ivy is often grown on walls, trellises, or the sides of houses.

The best-known kind is *English ivy,* which climbs by means of "air-roots" that grow out of the stem. The leaves of English ivy are somewhat triangular, are dark in color, and are evergreen. The small, yellowish flowers appear in late summer and are followed in autumn by purple-black berries, which birds eat.

Most of the other kinds of ivy are deciduous, that is, they shed their leaves in winter. One of the most popular of these is *Japanese* or *Boston ivy,* which is noted for its ability to climb on even the smoothest kind of wall. *Kenilworth ivy* is often planted on stonework or may be grown in hanging baskets. *Ground ivy* is frequently used as a ground cover in shaded places. One of the most unpleasant kinds of ivy is *poison ivy,* which contains a substance that is very irritating to the skins of many people. There is a separate article on POISON IVY.

Iwo Jima

Iwo Jima is a small island in the western Pacific Ocean. It is famous for a victory won there by the United States Marines in World War II. In February, 1945, the Marines attacked the island which was owned by Japan and used as an air base. After a hard, bitter fight during which thousands of lives were lost, the Marines captured the island. A combat photographer took a famous picture of a group of Marines raising the flag of the United States on Mount Suribachi, the highest point on Iwo Jima. The picture served as the model for the Marine Monument erected in Washington, D.C. in 1954. After its capture, the United States used the island, which has an area of about 8 square miles, as an American air base. Iwo Jima, which means "Sulfur Island" in Japanese, once contained sulfur mines. It is one of the three Volcano Islands. In 1968, the United States returned Iwo Jima to the Japanese.

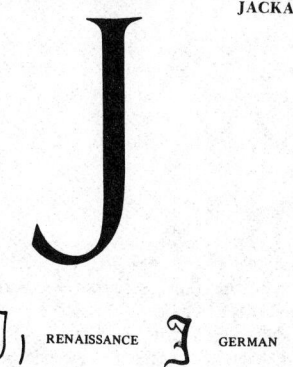

J J RENAISSANCE   GERMAN

J or j

The letter J is the tenth letter of the alphabet. Unlike most of the other letters of our alphabet, it did not exist in other older alphabets. It was first used, and only in its small form, during the Middle Ages, about eight hundred years ago. For centuries it was merely a form of the letter I, and the distinction between I and J in English was not regularly made until about three hundred years ago.

At first the small I was extended below the line whenever it came at the beginning of a word. At that time I sometimes had the sound that our letter Y has in the word *young.* Usually it had this sound only at the beginning of words, so the custom was established of drawing the I longer and below the line when it had a sound of Y, and drawing it shorter and on the line when it had a vowel sound. Later the sound of the longer I came to have the sound that J has today, as in *jump,* and became a new letter added to the alphabet. The sound of the J had already existed in our language, and was written as the letter G, which in a word such as *gem* has the sound of J.

Read also the article ALPHABET.

jabiru

The jabiru is a large bird belonging to the same family as storks and adjutants. It has a beak that curves slightly upward. Aside from that, it is almost exactly like a stork. The jabiru is found in South America, Africa, and Australia.

jacana

The jacana is a tall, slender bird that is found wading in tropical marshes. Because it spends most of its time in water, the jacana is also known as the *water pheasant.* It has extremely long legs and long, fingerlike toes with sharp claws. The jacana's unusual toes enable it to walk or even run on the large leaves of water plants, such as water lilies, that float on the surface. Its feathers make striking, beautiful patterns of such colors as black, white, yellow, and purple. The Mexican jacana is found in the southern part of Texas, as well as in Mexico.

jackal

The jackal is an animal that belongs to the wild dog family. It is usually in the company of another jackal or group of jackals. These groups are known as jackal packs. They are night scavengers; that is, they seek the remains of dead animals as their main food, and they look for them at night. Jackals occasionally hunt smaller animals, such as birds that live on the

ground, and mice. They are very sly and cunning. There are many kinds of jackal, most of them found in Africa. The best-known is an unattractive, drab-coated jackal called the yellow jackal. It is found in Africa and Asia.

jackdaw

The jackdaw is a small bird, slightly smaller than the crow, that is found mostly in Europe and in some parts of northern Asia. It is a very happy, sociable bird, and it is often seen in flocks of many jackdaws. This love of company is especially seen during its nesting season, when many pairs of jackdaws nest side by side in holes in trees and in such parts of buildings as church towers and castle turrets. The jackdaw is known as a thief because it sometimes steals food from other birds. It steals plants and some insects, which are its main food. It can easily be tamed. When it is in captivity, it can imitate the sounds it hears around it. The jackdaw is mostly black, but its sides and the back of its head are silvery gray.

jack-in-the-pulpit

The jack-in-the-pulpit is a plant that grows in deep, shady woods in the United States and Canada. It gets its name from the fact that a special kind of leaf (called the *spathe*), which is shaped like a hood, partly encloses the club-shaped stalk which bears the tiny, greenish flowers. This gives the appearance of a preacher in an old-fashioned pulpit. The plant grows from 1 to 2 feet high. In the late summer it bears brilliant scarlet berries. Its root, called a tuber, was once used in medicine; it is filled with tiny, needlelike crystals and has a biting taste.

jack rabbit

The jack rabbit is a member of the hare family, a family of animals that includes their relatives, the rabbits. The jack rabbit is larger than the rabbit. It is found throughout the continent of North America. In the United States, jack rabbits can be seen on the western prairies, both in the south and as far north as North Dakota. Over short distances, the jack rabbit is one of the swiftest four-legged animals known. It moves amazingly fast in short, quick hops, getting its spring and jumping power from its strong hind legs. Jack rabbits have offspring six or even more times each year. They multiply so rapidly that they sometimes overrun farms and eat the crops. When this happens, farmers go out and shoot them.

jacks

Jacks is a game played by children. They use five small metal objects called jacks, and a rubber ball. Jacks is a very old game, though it used to be called by other names—knucklebones, huckle-bones, dibs, chuckstones, and five-stones.

The metal jacks used today have six small arms. The jacks are somewhat like the old knucklebones, which once were really the knucklebones of sheep. To play the game one throws up the ball and must pick up the jacks before the ball can come down. On the first turn you pick up one jack at a time, then two at a time, and so on. The first person to pick up all the jacks in this way is the winner.

Andrew Jackson

Andrew Jackson was the seventh President of the United States. He served two terms, from 1829 to 1837. Before becoming President he had been a famous general. He was known as "Old Hickory," and there is a story about how he acquired that nickname. According to the story, two of his soldiers were talking together after a battle, and one of them remarked that Jackson certainly was tough. The other answered that he was as "tough as hickory."

Andrew Jackson was a man of the people, and a plain person who did not "put on airs." He was the first President elected from a "western" state. Tennessee, his home state, was then a part of the "new West."

A conflict between the North and South about slavery started to develop while Jackson was President. Some people thought that the governments of new states should decide whether or not their people could own slaves. Jackson argued against this idea. He thought the Federal government should decide this question, not the states. In other questions, too, he stood firm for the power of the nation rather than of the states.

HIS EARLY YEARS

Andrew Jackson was born in New Lancaster County, in South Carolina, on March 15, 1767. That part of South Carolina was a wilderness then and life was rough and hard. Growing up in a wilderness made Jackson understand the problems of frontier people. The pioneers were among his best friends and supporters throughout his life.

Jackson's parents and two older brothers came to America from County Antrim, Ireland, in 1765. Two years later Andrew was born. His father died at about that time, and his mother was left with the job of taking care of three children all by herself. The boys had to learn to be self-reliant and take care of themselves in the wild country where they lived.

The Revolutionary War started when Andrew Jackson was 8 and at 13 he took part in his first battle. He and one of his brothers were captured by the British and put in a prison camp. When young Andrew was ordered to clean an officer's muddy boots, he refused. The officer struck him across the face with his sword, making a scar that stayed with Jackson all his life.

Both boys caught smallpox at the prison camp. Finally their mother persuaded the British to release them so that she might take them home and nurse them back to health. Both of Jackson's brothers died during the Revolution. The death of his mother soon after left him alone in the world at the age of 16.

Andrew decided to become a lawyer. So hard did he work and study that he passed his examination and became a lawyer in North Carolina when he was only 20. He practiced law there for about a year, and then moved to a western district of North Carolina that later became the state of Tennessee. Jackson settled in Nashville, which became the capital of Tennessee. He dealt in real estate for a time, then raised cotton, and at last began his political career when he helped to write the constitution of Tennessee. During this time he was living in a house called "the Hermitage." It was a log house then, but later he built a beautiful mansion on the same plot of land, and the Hermitage became almost as famous as Mount Vernon, where George Washington lived, or Monticello, the home of Thomas Jefferson. It can be seen in Nashville today.

Andrew Jackson was elected in 1796 to serve as the one Tennessee member of the Senate in 1797, one year later, but gave up that post to become a judge of the Supreme Court of Tennessee. For six years he served as a judge. Then the War of 1812 started and the people called upon him to serve as a soldier.

JACKSON AS A SOLDIER

Although Jackson was well known in Tennessee, the rest of the country had not heard of him before the War of 1812. An Indian chief named Tecumseh had stirred up the Creek Indians in the Mississippi Territory. The American settlers there had the double problem of fighting both British and Indians. Jackson became famous all over the country when he led an attack against the Creek Indians and won the Mississippi Territory for the United States. This success earned him a promotion to the rank of major general in the United States Army. He went on to other important military victories. The most famous of them was the Battle of New Orleans, the last battle and greatest American victory in the War of 1812. There is a separate article about this war.

Jackson was a very competent general and he soon found other work to do. The Seminole Indians of Florida were making raids into the state of Georgia. Spain owned Florida at that time, and the Spaniards in Pensacola were supplying the Indians with guns and ammunition. Jackson led a small army against the Indians and captured Pensacola, so that there would be no more trouble from that quarter. The next year, 1819, the United States bought Florida from Spain. In 1821 Jackson became military governor of the Territory of Florida. Two years later he was elected to the United States Senate for the second time by the state of Tennessee.

HOW HE BECAME PRESIDENT

Jackson was asked to run for President on the Democratic ticket in 1824 and ac-

cepted the nomination. It was a strange election. There were four candidates for President. The Constitution says that the winner must receive a majority (more than half) of the electoral votes. In this election, the voting was split in such a way that no one received a majority. Andrew Jackson, a Democrat, received 99. John Quincy Adams, a National Republican, received 84. William H. Crawford, a Democratic Republican, received 41. Henry Clay, another Democratic Republican, received 37. Since no one had a majority, the members of the House of Representatives had to vote to decide the winner. They chose John Quincy Adams.

This was a bitter disappointment to Andrew Jackson, so he and his supporters started early to prepare for the next presidential campaign. In the election of 1828, Jackson defeated John Quincy Adams, who was up for re-election. This time Jackson had a clear majority.

JACKSON'S TWO TERMS

Andrew Jackson was a man of the people, and as President his slogan was "Let the people rule." He was not a quiet man, and he kept excitement running high throughout his administration by doing many things that caused violent debates in Congress.

One of the policies of Jackson caused a great deal of argument. He gave government jobs only to people who had been helpful to his party during the election campaign. This became known as the "spoils system," although Jackson called it "rotation in office." Under this system a person held his government job only as long as the party that appointed him was in power. The next election meant the end of the job, unless the same political party happened to stay in power. Thomas Jefferson had done the same thing in 1801, but for somewhat different reasons.

Another thing Jackson did was to surround himself with advisers whom he trusted but who had no official position. This was called his "kitchen cabinet" because people said it met informally, in the kitchen and not in the formal rooms of the White House.

The first national convention to select Presidential candidates was held in 1832, when Jackson was nominated for re-election. Before that, the Senate had chosen the candidates and put their names on the ballots. Jackson started the system of conventions, at which the important members of the political party chose the candidates. This system has been used by political parties ever since.

Jackson was re-elected in 1832. When his second term started, there was already considerable argument about states' rights, slavery, and the strength of the Federal government. Many people felt that the states should have the power to do as they chose, even though this did not fit in with laws passed by the national Congress. Other people felt that the Federal government should have greater power than the state governments, and that states should never attempt to overrule a national decision. Jackson was among those who felt that the Federal government was the more important.

South Carolina tried to ignore a Federal tariff bill, and refused to collect taxes on imports arriving at the harbor of Charleston. This was an example of a state government trying to disobey a Federal law. Jackson put a stop to it very quickly. He sent army and navy forces to Charleston, and there was no further trouble.

Another of Jackson's acts as President had lasting effects. At that time there was an official government bank, the Bank of the United States. When the Bank of the United States applied for a renewal of its charter to keep in business, Jackson refused the bank's application. He ordered the public funds in the bank transferred to local banks. He was suspicious of the people who controlled the Bank of the United States, and he was suspicious generally of people with large amounts of money, because he thought they had too much power. His actions ruined the bank and had a great deal to do with the financial panic that hit the country in 1837, soon after Jackson's second term ended.

HIS LATER YEARS

After the end of his eight years in the Presidency, Andrew Jackson retired to his home, the Hermitage, in Nashville. He lived there quietly, but never stopped taking an active interest in politics. His influence was a help in the election of James Polk, another Tennessean, as President in the 1844 election. Jackson died at the Hermitage in 1845, at the age of 78, and was buried there in the garden.

The state of Tennessee has made his home into a museum, and thousands visit it every year.

MRS. ANDREW JACKSON

Rachel Donelson Robards Jackson was born in 1767, the daughter of Colonel John Donelson, of Nashville. She was married before she met Andrew Jackson, to Captain Lewis Robards. The Jacksons had no children of their own, but adopted Mrs. Jackson's nephew and named him Andrew Jackson, Jr. Mrs. Jackson was ill at the time her husband was elected President, and died before his inauguration. She never lived in the White House, but died at the Hermitage in 1828. She is buried there, beside her husband.

Jackson, Robert H.

Robert Houghwout Jackson, an associate justice of the United States Supreme Court, was American prosecutor in the World War II war crimes trials. Jackson was born in 1892 in Spring Creek, Pennsylvania. Although he later gained world-wide fame as a lawyer, Jackson never took the time to get a law degree. He studied law, doing two years' work in one year at Albany Law School, but he did not get a degree because two years' attendance was required. He practiced law in Jamestown, New York, but had to get court permission to plead his first case because he was not yet 21 years old. Jackson made such a fine reputation that in 1934 he was appointed general counsel (lawyer) for the Internal Revenue Bureau of the United States government and in 1938 he was appointed Solicitor General, the government's lawyer in cases tried by the Supreme Court. In 1940 Jackson was appointed Attorney General, and President Franklin D. Roosevelt named him to the Supreme Court the following year. After World War II, President Harry S. Truman named Jackson to be United States prosecutor at the war crimes trials in Nuremberg, Germany. In this post he was credited with establishing a new theory of international law. Justice Jackson died in 1954.

Jackson, Stonewall

Thomas Jonathan Jackson was a great American general who fought for the South in the Civil War. He is usually called "Stonewall" Jackson. He won this nickname at the Battle of Bull Run, the first important battle of the Civil War, when the brigade he commanded  *Gale Research Co.* "stood like a stone wall," according to the Confederate General Hamilton Bee.

Jackson was born in what is now the state of West Virginia, in the year 1824. He went to the Military Academy at West Point. After he graduated, Jackson fought in the Mexican War. When this war was over, he resigned from the army and became a teacher at Virginia Military Institute, at Lexington, Virginia. He stayed there for ten years. Jackson was a shy and quiet man, and no one knew very much about him, or suspected what a great leader he would turn out to be.

When the Civil War began in 1861, Jackson chose to be loyal to his state, Virginia, and was made a brigadier general in the Confederate Army. He was a skillful soldier and a fine leader, loved by his men. He was very religious and often after a hard day of fighting Jackson and his soldiers would pray to God.

One May night in 1863, Jackson and some of his officers rode through the underbrush at Chancellorsville. They were mistaken for northern soldiers, and Stonewall Jackson was shot by one of his own men. He died a few days later.

General Robert E. Lee, the commander of all the Confederate armies, thought so highly of Jackson that when Jackson's left arm had to be amputated, because of a wound, Lee sent him a message saying, "You have lost only your left arm, I have lost my right." Jackson has been called the outstanding strategist in American history. His last, inspiring words were, "Let us cross the river and rest in the shade of the trees."

Jackson

Jackson is the capital and largest city of the state of Mississippi. It is on the Pearl River, about 45 miles east of Vicksburg. Several railroads go to Jackson and it is an important shipping center. It was named for the great American general and President, Andrew Jackson.

About 154,000 people live in the city of Jackson. They work in shops, cotton-processing plants, tobacco factories, and farm-machinery plants.

There are several beautiful public buildings in Jackson. The state library is known both for its appearance and for its fine selection of books. The people are proud also of the state capitol, the governor's mansion, and the monument to

Jefferson Davis, who was President of the Confederacy. During the Civil War, Jackson was the scene of bitter fighting, and was almost destroyed.

There are several colleges in Jackson, including Millsaps College, Jackson State College, and Belhaven College, all of which are co-educational. There is also a state college for the blind, and one for the deaf.

JACKSON, MISSISSIPPI. Population (1970 census) 153,968. Capital of Mississippi. One of the county seats of Hinds County. On the Pearl River. Planned as state capital 1821 on site of trading post (Le Fleur's Bluff), which was founded 1792.

Jacksonville

Jacksonville is one of the largest cities in the state of Florida. It is twenty-four miles from the Atlantic Ocean on the St. Johns River, in the northeast part of the state. Jacksonville was named for Andrew Jackson, the first territorial governor of Florida, and later President of the United States.

About five-hundred thousand people live in Jacksonville. It is the industrial and commercial center of the state and is an important port. The people of Jacksonville work in shipyards, cotton mills, lumber yards, citrus-fruit packing plants, and canning factories.

Many tourists visit Jacksonville each year for its fine hunting and fishing, as well as the beautiful beaches near by. There are many parks and scenic drives around Jacksonville. Several rail lines enter Jacksonville. It has a good airport.

Among the buildings that visitors notice especially are the Confederate Soldiers' Home, the Masonic Temple, the Federal Building, and the Church of the Good Shepherd.

JACKSONVILLE, FLORIDA. Population (1970 census) 528,865. County seat, Duval County. Laid out, 1822, on site of 1740 Spanish Fort St. Nicholas. Named for Andrew Jackson.

Jacob

The story of Jacob is told in the Bible, in the book of Genesis. He was the son of Isaac, and he had a brother, Esau. Esau was born before Jacob, and therefore was to become the head of the family when Isaac died. This was Esau's birthright. Jacob bought Esau's birthright by giving him "a mess of pottage" (a dish of food) when Esau was very hungry.

Jacob fell in love with Rachel, the younger daughter of Laban. Laban promised Jacob that he could marry Rachel if he would work for him for seven years. When Jacob had kept this bargain, Laban said he would have to marry Rachel's older sister, Leah, instead, and Jacob had to work seven more years before Laban would let him marry his first choice, Rachel.

Once God sent an angel to Jacob. The angel ordered Jacob to take the name Israel, which became a symbol of the Jews as the chosen people of God. Another time, when Jacob was fleeing from Esau, he had a wonderful dream about a ladder. In Jacob's dream God appeared standing beside a ladder, on which angels went up and down from Heaven, and God assured Jacob that he would return home safely.

Jacob had many sons, of whom his favorite was Joseph. Each of his sons founded a tribe of Israel, so Jacob is regarded as an ancestor of the Hebrew people. He spent his last years in Egypt, where he was highly regarded by the Pharaoh, or ruler. It is told that he lived to be 147 years old. He did not wish to be buried in Egypt, so his body was taken back to his home in Canaan by a caravan of Egyptian elders and given every honor.

Jacobins

The Jacobins were a group of members of the French National Assembly (the lawmaking body, like the United States Congress) during the French Revolution in 1789. This was a revolution in which the people of France overthrew their king and formed a republic. At first the Jacobins were loyal to Louis XVI, the king, but when he became frightened by the revolutionists all around him, and tried to run away from Paris, the Jacobins turned against him. After a long fight with another group called the Girondins, who wanted to spare the life of the king, the Jacobins succeeded in having the king executed in 1793. The Jacobins did not exist after 1794. Read the separate article about the FRENCH REVOLUTION.

Jacobites

The Jacobites were people who supported James II of England when he was trying to be king again after he had been forced to leave England. (The name James in English is the same as the name Jacob.) The Jacobites later supported the son and grandson of James II when they claimed the English throne. You can read more about this in the article JAMES, KING OF ENGLAND.

Earlier, when James I was the English king, the period was called Jacobean.

Jacquard, Joseph Marie

Joseph Marie Jacquard was a French inventor who lived almost two hundred years ago. He invented a new kind of loom that could weave cloth into patterns. Many of the designs and figures that we see woven into cloth now are possible because of this important invention. Jacquard was born in 1752, and when he grew up he became a weaver. He was a poor man, and worked very hard. He spent all his spare time working on his invention. Finally he was successful and became rich and famous. He also invented a special kind of loom that could weave nets. Jacquard died in 1834, when he was 82 years old.

jade

Jade is a fairly soft semiprecious gem or stone. It ranges in color from white to dark green. It is used for jewelry and carved ornaments. In China and Japan it is considered the most precious of all gems. (For more information about gems see the article GEM.)

The Chinese consider jade the symbol (sign) of justice, courage, wisdom, charity, and modesty. They also think that powdered jade, when mixed with wine or water, is a good tonic for the health.

There are two kinds of jade, nephrite and jadeite. The rarer and more costly stone is jadeite, and the best jadeite is emerald-green in color. Because it is an easy stone to cut and polish, the peoples who lived thousands of years ago in Mexico, Switzerland, France, Greece and ancient Egypt used to make arrowheads, spear points and knives out of jade.

jaeger

The jaeger is a large, swift-flying bird belonging to the gull family. It is very closely related to one of the fiercest of all birds, the skua, and it has many of the characteristics of the skua. The jaeger flies in the air almost all the time, searching for small birds from which it can steal food. The jaeger scares the smaller bird, causing it to drop its food. Then the jaeger swoops down to pick it up. It raids the nests of other birds to eat their eggs and the newly hatched little birds. Every part of the jaeger's body is a fighting weapon. It has a powerful beak and also fights with the tips of its wings and with its razor-sharp talons or claws. It lives mostly in the cold Arctic regions of the world.

jaguar

The jaguar is a big, spotted animal belonging to the cat family. It looks a great deal like the leopard. It is found in the hot, tropical areas of North and South America, and it is one of the most fearsome animals seen in those places. It is usually about seven feet long and weighs about two hundred pounds. In spite of its size, it can run very swiftly. Most of the time it travels alone, often covering several hundred miles in its travels. The jaguar is a very ferocious cat, and it will attack such farm animals as horses and cattle. If it is hungry, the jaguar will even attack a man.

Am. Mus. of Nat. Hist.

Ranchers in Central and South America fear the jaguar, which preys on their flocks and may attack an unarmed man.

jai alai

Jai alai is an athletic game that is very popular with the people of Central and South America. It resembles handball because it is played by hitting a ball against a wall.

The jai alai playing field, or cancha, is surrounded by three walls. The ball, called a pelota, is small and made of hard rubber. When it is hurled against a wall, it bounces back with extraordinary speed. A player wears on one of his hands a narrow, curved basket called a cesta. The player catches the pelota in his cesta and flings it back with great force against one of the walls. The ball shoots back from the wall and the opposing player catches it in his cesta. He then hurls it against the wall again. The ball may be played off any of the three walls.

A player scores a point when his op-

ponent cannot catch the ball or throws it out of the court's boundary lines. The game is extremely fast and strenuous because of the speed of the ball. A person has to be in fine physical shape to play it.

Jai alai is supposed to have been invented by the Basque people of Spain. In the Basque language, jai alai means "merry celebration." The game is also played in Florida.

jail, a building where a criminal is kept as punishment for a crime: see the article on PRISON.

Jakarta

Jakarta, or Djakarta, is the capital city of the country of Indonesia. The city is on the island of Java. For many years it was called *Batavia.* When Indonesia became an independent country, in 1945, the old Malayan name for the city, Jakarta, was adopted.

Jakarta lies on the northwestern coast of Java. It is the largest city and port in the country. It has two sections, the Old or Lower City and the Upper City. Lower Jakarta is like an old Dutch city, with odd old Dutch houses, shuttered windows, and brown tiled roofs. It is crossed by canals and by the Great River, or Tjiliwong. Most of the Javanese and Chinese people live in this part. Farther inland is the Upper City, which is more modern and has most of the government buildings, shops, and hotels.

This new section, which is called *Weltevreden,* was built about 1820. More than one hundred years before that an earthquake had ruined Jakarta and filled its river with mud from a volcano. The river then flooded the wrecked city with its mud and filth and even a century later it was still a dangerous, unclean place to live in. The Weltevreden was built to make a fresh start.

JAKARTA, INDONESIA. Population (1973 estimate) 2,906,533. Capital of Indonesia.

jam, fruit that is boiled with sugar until it becomes thick: see the article on JELLY AND JAM.

Jamaica

Jamaica, a large island in the Caribbean Sea—the largest in the group that made up the former British West Indies—is an independent nation in the (British) Commonwealth. In area it is about the size of the state of Connecticut, and nearly two million people live there.

One of the first parts of the Western Hemisphere to be developed, Jamaica was discovered in 1494 by Christopher Columbus, who named it St. Jago. But an older name, given the island by the American Indians who were already living there, was *Xaymaca,* or Jamaica, which means "well watered"—for the island has a heavy rainfall, about 70 inches a year, compared to 40 inches in the eastern United States. This makes Jamaica's trees and plants grow very fast.

Spain ruled Jamaica until 1655; Diego Columbus, Christopher's son, was the first Spanish governor. The Spaniards killed most of the American Indians, called Arawaks, who had lived in Jamaica and replaced them with African Negro slaves, whom they called maroons. More than nine out of ten of the people who live in

Jamaica today are wholly or partly Negroes, descendants of the maroons.

Britain captured Jamaica during a war against Spain in 1655 and ruled the island for more than 300 years. Then in 1958 Jamaica joined some nearby islands in the self-governing West Indian Federation, and in 1962 Jamaica withdrew from the federation and became independent.

Jamaica is officially a monarchy under the British queen, who is represented by a Governor General appointed by the Jamaican government (see BRITISH COMMONWEALTH). There are a Senate and a House of Representatives, and a Prime Minister is head of the government. The capital is Kingston, a city of about 117,400 and a seaport. Jamaica is a member of the United Nations.

Jamaica is warm all year around and is a popular vacation place, especially in the winter and especially with people who like yachting, for the island has a 500-mile seacoast, several fine harbors and river mouths, and beaches for swimming. The people of Jamaica export large quantities of sugar and bananas to Great Britain and the United States. Other crops are annotto, a dye for coloring oils and butter; cocoa, coconuts, coffee, and tobacco. An important industry is the mining of bauxite, the ore from which aluminum is taken.

JAMAICA. Area, 4,411 square miles. Population (1973 estimate) 1,900,000.

James, Saint

Two of the Apostles of Jesus were named James. James the Greater was one of Jesus' three favorite friends. With John and Peter, James stayed with Jesus in the Garden of Gethsemane the night before Jesus was put to death. After the Crucifixion, James boldly told King Herod that he was Jesus's friend, and he was condemned to death. The executioner who was to kill James was so moved by his courage that he too became a Christian and they were put to death together.

James the Greater is the patron saint of Spain. He was greatly revered in the olden days in England, and the king's palace was called St. James's Palace. Even though the kings and queens of England no longer live in this palace, their court is still called the Court of St. James's.

James the Less was also one of the Apostles. He is called "the Less" because he was younger, or perhaps shorter, than James the Greater. James the Less wrote the Epistle of James in the New Testament. It is believed that he was the brother of Matthew, who wrote the Gospel of Matthew.

James, King of England

There were two kings of England named James. James I became king of England after the death of Queen Elizabeth I in 1603. He was already king of Scotland, so this united the countries. James was the son of Mary Queen of Scots and was born in 1566. He was a member of the Stuart family. He was very unpopular in England because he believed in the divine right of kings. This means that he believed that a king's power came from God and not from the people, and so he could do whatever he liked.

During the reign of James I the Bible was translated in the beautiful form called the *King James Version.* James I married a Danish princess named Anne and they had three children, one of whom became King Charles I. James I died in 1625.

James II was the grandson of James I and the son of Charles I. He was born in 1633 and became king of England in 1685. While he was still a student, the people rebelled against his father, Charles I, and beheaded him. James and his brother Charles escaped to Holland, where he became a soldier. His brother Charles II was recalled to England in 1660 to become king. This was called the "Restoration." When Charles II died in 1685, James became king.

In those days in England there was much conflict between the Catholics and Protestants. Many of the people were dissatisfied with James II because he was Catholic and also because he had been unjust and cruel to those who rebelled against him in the early days of his reign. Also his Declaration of Indulgence in 1687, which granted freedom of religion to his subjects, served to heighten the tension among many Protestants who were afraid of increasing Catholic influence in England.

After James II was king for only three years, the people drove him out of England and sent for Mary, the daughter of James II, to become queen, with her husband, Prince William of Orange, as king. In 1688, after some fighting, James went into exile in France, where he died in 1701. For many years, followers of James II, of his son James (called "the Old Pretender"), and of his grandson Charles (called "Bonnie Prince Charlie" or "the Young Pretender") tried to make them kings of England. These followers were called Jacobites. They never succeeded.

James, Henry and William

James is the name of a family of American thinkers and writers. The first famous member of the family was named Henry James. He was born in Albany, New York, in 1811. He was a minister and wrote on religious subjects.

One of his sons, also named Henry James, wrote novels and stories. He was born in New York City in 1843, and studied in New York, Germany, and France. He decided to live in Europe, where he became friendly with some of the greatest writers of his time, men such as Robert Louis Stevenson and Emile Zola. He returned to America in 1904 for a long visit. Some of his best books are *Daisy Miller, Washington Square, The Portrait of a Lady,* and *The Awkward Age.* He became a British subject before he died in 1916.

His brother, William James, was one of America's greatest thinkers. He was born in New York City in 1842 and studied in New York, in Europe, and at Harvard. He spent some time on a trip of exploration in Brazil. He graduated as a medical doctor from Harvard, and for a while he taught medicine, but he was more interested in other problems. He studied psychology—the science of how people behave—and in 1891 he wrote one of the greatest books on that subject, *The Principles of Psychology.* Then he turned to religion and studied people who had had deep religious experiences. He published his findings in a book called *The Varieties of Religious Experience.*

William James

After this, James wrote books of philosophy, the study of knowledge. He originated the system of philosophy called *pragmatism.* He died in 1910.

James, Jesse

Jesse James was an American bandit and train robber. He became known all over the United States, in the years after the American Civil War, for his daring and cold-blooded crimes. He was born in 1847.

According to some stories, Jesse James began his life of crime because he wanted revenge against the North. His family had supported the South during the Civil War. Jesse James at the age of 15 joined a cavalry troop and became an excellent horseman, an excellent shot, and a man of cool nerve and steady courage.

When the war was over, Jesse James continued his own private war with the United States. It is said that in robbing trains he was just as interested in wrecking the mail system of the government as he was in the loot he took. He became the most feared bandit in the whole country, and the governor of Missouri offered $10,000 for his capture, dead or alive. To gain this reward, two members of his gang killed Jesse James in his home on April 3, 1882.

James, Will

Will James was an American artist who lived as a cowboy in the West. He wrote books about cowboy life and drew pictures of horses and cowboys and cattle ranches. He made some motion pictures about western life, in the early days of motion pictures. He was born in Montana in 1892 and died in 1942.

Jamestown

Jamestown in Virginia was the first permanent settlement of the English in America. The town was named after James I, who was king of England at that time.

In 1607, a group of 104 colonists sailed from London in a tiny ship. They landed months later on the banks of a river that they named the James, in honor of their king. Spanish ships were sailing the east coast of North America, and for fear of attack, the English settlers sailed 30 miles up the James River to found their settlement. The site they chose proved to be very unhealthful, and dozens of the colonists fell ill and died. The English sent supply ships, but when the first one arrived only a few months later, just thirty-eight of the colonists were still living.

The settlement would have failed entirely if it had not been for the brilliant leadership of Captain John SMITH, about whom you can read in a separate article. Smith was a strong and practical man. He made it a rule that "he who will not work shall not eat," so that everyone was obliged to do his share. He also persuaded the Indians to supply the colonists with corn.

The life was still hard, however, and the people were constantly sick, needy, and discouraged. In 1609, Captain Smith was recalled to England, and after that the Jamestown colony nearly starved. The few people still alive after two years of suffering decided to give up and go back to England. They were already on board ship when a British fleet at last appeared with enough supplies to save them.

In 1612 a system of land grants was begun, and the settlers gained a new interest in the colony since they could own their land. The growing of tobacco was introduced. Jamestown had the first representative government in the New World. It became the capital of Virginia, and remained so until 1699, when Williamsburg was named. Although the town was burned down three times, it was restored, and it lasted for almost a hundred years.

Jammu is part of a state in India: see KASHMIR.

January

January is the first month of the year. It has thirty-one days. January was named after the Roman god Janus. Janus was the god of doorways, and gradually came to be associated with the beginning of anything. January got its name because it is the beginning of the year. The first day of January is celebrated as an important holiday, called New Year's Day. Since 1937, Inauguration Day for a new President of the United States has been January 20th.

The birthstone for January is the garnet, a dark-red stone.

Janus

Janus was one of the gods in Roman mythology, the stories the ancient Romans told about their gods and goddesses. To the Romans Janus was a very important god, almost as important as Jupiter, who was the chief god in the Roman religion. Janus stood for the beginning of everything. January is named for him. He was the guardian of heaven and of all gates and doors. As doors face two ways, pictures of Janus show him with two faces.

Japan

Japan is a country that is part of Asia but consists of a group of islands and is not part of the continent of Asia. The islands are east of the mainland, in the Pacific Ocean. About four thousand of these islands make up Japan. The largest islands are Hokkaido, Honshu, Shikoku, and Kyushu.

The area of all Japan is 142,688 square miles. That is smaller than the state of California. Nearly a hundred million people are crowded on Japan's islands, about six times as many as in California. In the capital city of Tokyo there are more than ten million people. The country's Japanese name is *Nihon,* and in the United States it is often called *Nippon.* It is also called "The Land of the Rising Sun."

THE PEOPLE OF JAPAN

The Japanese people, who are called Orientals or Asiatics, belong to the Mongoloid race, one of the three great races of mankind. Many thousands of years ago they came to the Japanese islands from Asia and perhaps from islands in the South Pacific Ocean. There were some tribes living there already called the *Ainu,* about whom there is a separate article.

The Japanese are not very tall. They have black hair and a darker skin than most European and American people.

The Japanese have adopted more western (American and European) customs than have any other people of Asia. Large Japanese cities are like those in the United States.

Many Japanese people believe in the Shinto religion, which is a set of rules by which they live. There is no book, like the Bible, from which they learn Shintoism. They are taught by their families and by priests. There also are a great many Christians in Japan, but the largest religion is Buddhism.

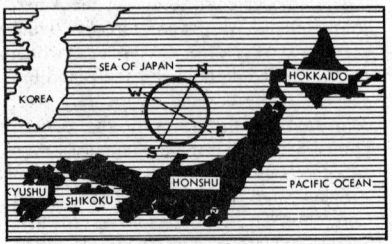

HOW THE PEOPLE LIVE

For many years the Japanese people were restricted by many rules about family life. Most of these laws and rules have

Osaka, Japan's second largest city.
Japan National Tourist Organization

Pine trees grow on the mountainsides in the north, while in the south there are palm trees and bamboo, from which furniture and many other things are made.

CHIEF CITIES OF JAPAN

The leading cities of Japan, with 1973 population estimates are:

Tokyo, population 8,840,942; with suburbs, 11,454,000. The capital and largest city, and the largest city in the world. A financial and manufacturing center.

Osaka, population 3,018,000, second-largest city and chief industrial center.

Nagoya, population 2,014,000.

Yokohama, population 2,144,000.

Kyoto, population 1,422,000, the ancient capital and cultural center.

Kobe, population 1,267,000.

There is a separate article about each of these cities. All of them are on Honshu, the largest Japanese island.

HOW THE PEOPLE ARE GOVERNED

The head of the government is the emperor. In English-speaking countries he is sometimes called the "Mikado." The Japanese used to think the emperor was divine, a kind of god, but after World War II the emperor himself told the people that this was not true.

The real ruler of Japan is the prime minister, who is like the prime minister of England. There is a cabinet, which helps the prime minister, and a parliament, called the Diet. The two divisions of the Diet are the House of Representatives and the House of Councillors.

A new constitution was put into effect in 1947 and since then there has been much more freedom for people in Japan than there used to be. The women have equal rights with men and are allowed to vote. Under the old system they were little better than slaves and had no rights. There are no longer any inherited titles of nobility. Japan is a constitutional monarchy and is more democratic than any other country in Asia.

now been removed. Old people were once very important in Japanese family life. The father, as head of the family, did everything first. He bathed first, was served his dinner first, and walked out of the door first. Under the new constitution there is a great deal more freedom. Some Japanese are not completely won over to the new way of living and still carry on the old ideas and customs.

Many people in Japanese cities today live in houses and apartments very much like ours, but even more people live in traditional wooden homes which are of light construction with inside walls consisting of frames covered with paper. These can be moved to change the layout of the rooms. The houses have little furniture. The floors are covered with mats and people squat on low cushions on the floor and eat from a low table not more than a foot and a half high. They sleep on thin quilts with wooden blocks for pillows. Like the Chinese, the Japanese eat with chopsticks, which are thin wooden sticks with which they pick up their food.

In the country many Japanese live as they did hundreds of years ago. The houses are very low. The roofs are made of sticks and grass and curl up at the corners. The Japanese are great lovers of flowers, rocks and trees, so there is always a garden near the house.

There are separate articles on various Japanese customs and traditions, such as GEISHA, HARAKIRI, JUDO, and others.

JAPAN'S FARMS AND FACTORIES

Only about one-sixth of Japan's land can be used for farming. This is partly because there are hundreds of mountains on the islands. The most famous one is Fujiyama (Mount Fuji), which is more than 12,000 feet high.

More than half of the available land is used for growing rice. It is grown in a field that is flooded with water. The farmers wade in the water to put in new plants. When the rice is ripe the water is drained from the fields and then it is harvested. Farmers also grow white potatoes, sweet potatoes, wheat, tea, barley, and rye. There are many fruit trees, including peach, cherry, pear, apple, and orange, and

grapevines. The average farm is very small, less than three acres, and provides a bare living for the farmer. The Japanese eat more fish than meat. There are large fleets of fishing boats that sail in the Sea of Japan and in the Pacific Ocean. Fishing is one of the largest industries of Japan.

Japan is one of the world's leading industrial nations. Its biggest industries are iron, steel products, chemicals, textiles, ceramics, precision instruments, cameras and other optical instruments, shipbuilding, fertilizers, electrical equipment, transportation equipment, and machinery.

Japan is relatively poor in minerals. In the mountains there are mines producing iron, coal, silver, gold, copper, lead, and salt, but all except copper are scarce. There is some petroleum, or oil.

WHAT KIND OF PLACE IT IS

In Japan there are many sights that seem strange to a visitor. One can see bridges that are built like half-moons and are very steep, or one might see what looks like a wooden gate sitting in the middle of a lake. There are beautiful gardens and large statues of Buddha. Some people still wear kimonos that touch the ground and large sashes called *obi*. There are temples that have roofs that curl up at the corners and are ornately carved with dragons and flowers. These temples are scattered all over the countryside.

In the north of Japan it is quite cold; in the south it is very warm. The islands are troubled by earthquakes and by windstorms called typhoons. They also have floods and tidal waves. These disasters kill thousands of people every year. In the early summer Japan has much rain. Winters are very cold along the west coast but mild in most other places.

Many thousands of years ago most of the Japanese islands were volcanoes (mountains that had fire and melted rock inside them). Most of these volcanoes have died out, but there are still about sixty that erupt, or overflow. An eruption can destroy houses and sometimes whole villages.

Japanese National Tourist Organization
Artistic flower arrangements have an important place in the Japanese home.

The snow-covered peak of Fujiyama is the highest point in Japan. The cone of this extinct volcano is perfectly shaped. It has long been considered sacred in Japan.

JAPAN IN THE PAST

Japan, compared to other Asiatic countries, is a "new" country. The first written history of Japan started about the year 500. Most of the history before that is based on old stories. One of the old stories is that the first emperor was descended from the Sun Goddess. He came to earth and became the ruler of Japan.

The Japanese people first came to the islands from the mainland of Asia. They split up into many clans, or groups, and each had its chief. About the year 600 one of the clans became very powerful and made its chief the emperor. The other clans became the nobles of the court and were ruled by the emperor. This was called the *Taika* (or *Taikwa*) *Reform* and was the first step toward making Japan a unified country.

The emperors did not keep control of Japan for very long. More than a thousand years ago, powerful warlords took control of the country. There were still emperors, but the warriors were actually the rulers. These warlords later took the title *shogun,* which means "great general." They kept their hold on Japan until less than a hundred years ago. Their system was like the feudal system of Europe during the Dark Ages. (There is a separate article on FEUDALISM.)

During a thousand and more years, Japan fought many wars with China and Korea but at the same time it adopted the Chinese and Korean civilization, which was very advanced. The Japanese wrote fine poetry and plays. These plays were of a kind that you can still see in Japan. They are called the "No" drama, and Kabuki, and are very beautiful. They are based on ancient legends and sometimes take seven hours to perform.

Christianity was taken to Japan by St. Francis Xavier about four hundred years ago, during the 16th century. He traveled all over Asia spreading Christianity, but his work in Japan did not last long. The Japanese lords began to kill Christians, just as the ancient Romans had. Christians were disliked in Japan until the end of the last century.

During this time no one was allowed to leave Japan and no one was allowed to enter. Occasionally a boat was sent to the Chinese mainland to find out what was happening in the rest of the world. Otherwise Japan became self-sufficient. The Japanese would not have known that guns had been invented in Europe if three Portuguese sailors had not been shipwrecked on the shore. After their guns were taken, the sailors were killed.

Japan remained closed until in 1854 the United States sent Commodore Matthew Calbraith Perry to Japan to open trade with the Japanese government. Perry succeeded in doing this. A few years later, in 1868, a new Japanese emperor named Meiji threw out the shoguns. He passed laws forbidding the killing of foreigners and made other efforts to get rid of old-fashioned ways. In 1869 the old system of keeping people at one job for all their lives was abolished. In 1872 the first railroad was built and public schools were opened.

The hundreds of years of rule by the warrior class had made Japan a warlike nation. First, Japan went to war against China in 1894, won the war, and took the island of Formosa. Ten years later, Japan declared war on Russia, won that war, and established itself on the mainland of Asia by taking part of Korea. During World War I, Japan was on the side of the Allies. It did little fighting but

Actresses telling a story of unhappy love, using gestures but no words.

received Germany's islands in the Pacific Ocean and holdings in China.

Still not satisfied, in 1931 Japan invaded China without provocation, fought a brief war, and took control of the rich industrial region of north China called Manchuria. The United States and European nations condemned this, so in 1933 Japan resigned from the League of Nations and in 1936 Japan became an ally of Germany and Italy as one of the "Axis powers," which were enemies of the Soviet Union and also of the United States.

In the name of "Greater East Asia Co-Prosperity," Japan threatened all British, French, Dutch and independent regions in East Asia, plus China, which Japan again attacked without any justification in 1937. This led to years of warfare in which Japan occupied more than a million square miles of Chinese territory, but the Chinese did not stop fighting. During the period 1932-1941 there was a struggle for political control of Japan between a "peace party" (which did not oppose limited warfare for new possessions but did oppose making the war bigger), and the "militarists," who thought Japan could beat the world. The militarists won and on December 7, 1941, they started a war against the United States by bombing the Pearl Harbor base in Hawaii, without warning. Japan won all the early victories. As conquerors they were usually cruel to their prisoners of war, including women and children, but did not murder them as the Germans and Russians did. After nearly four years of fighting, the U. S. ended the war abruptly by dropping atomic bombs on the Japanese cities of Hiroshima and Nagasaki in August, 1945. Japan surrendered promptly, having already lost the war anyway. China and Russia were given back territories Japan had taken from them in previous wars, and Korea became independent.

Japan Travel Bureau   *Margot L. Wolf Photos*

A sword hilt and a *netsuke,* or button, both beautifully carved.

An American occupation force under Douglas MacArthur took control of the Japanese government and insisted that democratic principles be adopted. The Japanese people cooperated. The United States spent more than three billion dollars helping Japan to become prosperous again, and Japan recovered prosperity faster than any other defeated country in history except perhaps West Germany. By 1953 Japan was a fully independent country again and in 1956 it joined the United Nations. There are anti-American groups in Japan, who enjoy freedom of speech as permitted and approved in the United States, but every Japanese election since the war has been won by groups who favor cooperation with the United States.

JAPAN. Area 142,688 square miles. Pop-

ulation (1973 estimate) 104,660,000. Language, Japanese. Religion, Shintoism and Buddhism; some Christians. Monetary unit, the yen, 360 to the U.S. dollar. Flag, red sun on white background.

Japan, Sea of

The Sea of Japan is a large body of water between the islands of Japan and the mainland of Asia. It is an arm of the Pacific Ocean. Many small Japanese islands lie in the Sea of Japan. Its area is about 400,000 square miles, and its greatest depth is about 10,000 feet. The Sea of Japan is dangerous because of frequent typhoons, sudden storms that wreck boats and destroy island property.

A scene from a Kabuki play, performed today just as it was centuries ago.

Japanese beetles

Japanese beetles are shiny, green-and-brown insects about half an inch in length. They came to the United States in the roots of shrubs that came from Japan. Since 1916, when they were first seen in New Jersey, they have become a pest in much of the eastern United States. They eat crops of all kinds, and while they are grubs (young) they live in the soil and feed on the roots of grass and other plants. Farmers kill the beetles with poison sprays. The beetles are attracted by the oil of geranium, which is put in traps to catch them.

The United States Department of Agriculture is using a wasp that eats the Japanese beetle grubs. The best time to kill them is while they are growing up as grubs in the ground, which takes about ten months. Poisons applied to the ground will kill them during this time.

Japanese language

The Japanese language is spoken by more than 104 million Japanese peo-

Pan American World Airways Photos
The art of the Japanese, like their manners, is very formal. At first their plays or paintings seem lifeless, but to one who knows them well they appear to have infinite gracefulness.
A giant bronze image of Buddha. The statue is three hundred years old.

ple. It is written in much the same characters as the Chinese language, but it is not like the Chinese language or any other language of east Asia. It probably originated somewhere in central Asia, thousands of years ago.

Japanese words are formed by combining syllables instead of by combining letters. Instead of an alphabet the Japanese have a *kana*, or list of syllables, such as *ro, ha, ni,* and so on. There are 45 sylla-

U.S.D.A.
Japanese beetles were not considered very harmful in Asia, but they became a terrible garden pest after establishing themselves in the eastern United States.

bles in the kana, and they can be combined in various ways to bring the number up to 110. Written Japanese can be very complicated, with thousands of different characters to learn. A simplified form of writing uses basic syllables only. This is called *hiragana.* A second system of basic syllables called *katakana* is used for foreign words. Many Japanese wish to adopt the Western style of writing.

There are some syllables that the Japanese do not pronounce as we do, but it is not very hard to learn to speak simple Japanese. Written Japanese is much harder to learn.

The Japanese language has adopted thousands of words from English and European languages.

jasmine

The jasmine is a beautiful plant of the olive family. It grows as a shrub or a climber with long, slender branches that bear fragrant, yellow flowers. It is a native of China and may be grown throughout most of the United States. It blooms in very early spring. The jasmine sometimes grows to 8 or 10 feet in height. The Carolina or yellow jasmine, with its trumpet-shaped flowers, grows in the southern United States. The fragrance of jasmine is delightful, and the oil of jasmine is used to make perfume. The flowers bloom from June to October.

Jason

Jason was a hero in Greek mythology, the stories the ancient Greeks told about their gods and goddesses. His father, Aeson, was a king. His uncle, Pelias, stole Aeson's kingdom and tried to kill the infant Jason, but Jason was saved and given into the care of Chiron, a centaur. (A centaur was an imaginary creature with the body of a horse and the head of a man.)

When Jason was grown up, he came to claim his father's throne. Pelias consented to surrender it if Jason would first bring him the Golden Fleece, which grew on a special ram in Colchis across the sea. Jason knew that the Golden Fleece was closely guarded by a dragon and would be difficult to get, so he gathered a band of Greek heroes, and they sailed for Colchis on his ship the *Argo.* From the name of the ship the adventurers became known as the ARGONAUTS, about whom there is a separate article.

After many adventures on the way, the Argonauts reached Colchis. While there Jason married Medea, a princess of Colchis, who helped him to get the Golden Fleece. They returned to Jason's home with the Golden Fleece, but Jason learned that his uncle, Pelias, had killed his father. Medea then tricked Pelias' daughters into killing their father, and for this deed, both Jason and Medea were driven away. They then went to live in Corinth, but there Jason fell in love with another princess, Creusa, and left Medea. In revenge, Medea killed Creusa and her own and Jason's children. According to some versions of the story, Jason then killed himself.

jasper

Jasper is a rock mineral often used for vases, seals, and paperweights. It is a type of quartz stone, and is either red, brown, black or blue in color. Its surface is so hard that it gives off sparks when rubbed by steel.

jaundice

Jaundice is a sign of disease. When a person has jaundice his skin, eyes and mouth lining take on a yellowish color. The yellow color comes from the bile, a digestive juice that is produced by the liver and stored in the gall bladder, and is supposed to help digest food in the small intestine. If something goes wrong somewhere along the line, the bile may be prevented from getting to the intestine. Then it will back up into the blood stream. This may carry the bile's yellow coloring to various parts of the body. Many things may cause jaundice: gallstones, or some other condition that blocks the bile ducts; infectious diseases, such as yellow fever or malaria; or sometimes some poisons such as snake venom. The best way to cure the jaundice is to treat the condition that is causing it. Until that is done, hot baths can help relieve the itching that often goes with jaundice.

Java

Java is a long, narrow island in the East Indies. It lies between the Sea of Java and the Indian Ocean. It is one of the largest islands of the Republic of Indonesia.

The island of Java has an area of 48,-763 square miles, which is about the size of the state of Louisiana. Though Java is not very big, it is one of the most crowded

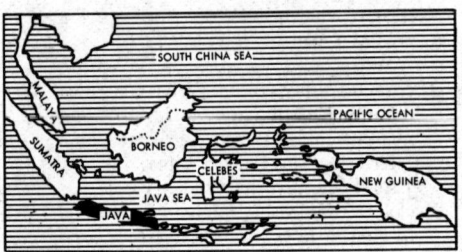

places in the world. Seventy-four million people live there, more than 21 times as many as live in Lousiana. Part of the island is too mountainous for people to make their homes, and near the coasts there are swamps and thick jungles, so that all of the people are crowded into a very small space.

THE PEOPLE OF JAVA

The people of Java are Malays. They are small and handsome. They have dark skin and eyes and straight black hair, and they are very graceful. Groups of dancers from Java have traveled all over the world and delighted thousands of people with their strange and exciting dances.

The Javanese people are also known for a special kind of shadow play in which they use puppets that they hold behind a screen, so that shadows appear on the screen. This is a favorite entertainment in Java.

There are many skilled artists in Java. They make beautiful jewelry of silver and gold. They also make a special kind of fine cloth that is called *batik*. It is dyed in patterns of bright colors.

Most of the people of Java are farmers. They raise rice, rubber, sugar, coffee, and many other crops. Things grow so well in Java that the people are able to grow more than enough food for themselves, so their crops help feed people of other countries. They also send quinine and teak wood to other parts of the world. The people of Java buy machines and iron and steel and cloth from other countries, and they use these things to build up their island.

Some people in Java work in coal and silver and gold mines. Others raise *kapok* trees. Pods from these trees contain a soft, fluffy down that is used to stuff pillows and mattresses, to make life jackets, and for other purposes.

Some Chinese people and some Arabs live in Java. Most of the people are members of the Mohammedan religion. They speak a Malay language called Bhasa Indonesia.

WHAT JAVA IS LIKE

The level lands of Java are very fertile and have a lot of rain. There are many volcanic mountains and some of these great volcanoes are still active. Sometimes they explode and send forth lava and fire and smoke. Many people of Java have lost their lives in these eruptions. The weather in Java is warm, with a temperature of about 80 degrees all year round, though high up in the mountains it is much colder.

Panthers, tigers and other wild animals make their home in the jungles near the coasts of the island. There are many enormous insects and gorgeous birds and flowers.

There are many small streams on the island. The Solo River is the most important waterway. Boats can travel on this river from one part of the island to another. Roads lead from Jakarta, the capital city of Indonesia, on Java Island, to nearly every part of Java, and there are several railroads and airports.

The people in most parts of Java live very simply, but the city of Jakarta is quite modern. The University of Indonesia is there. It includes colleges of law, medicine, and agriculture.

JAVA IN THE PAST

Men have lived on Java for many thousands of years. This was proved in 1891 and 1892 when Eugene Dubois, a Dutch scientist, discovered the bones of a primitive man believed to have lived between 300,000 and 500,000 years ago. Dubois named this early man *Pithecanthropus Erectus*, which means that he stood erect as men do today. This early man is usually called the *Java Man*.

Almost two thousand years ago, Java was occupied by Hindus from India. In Java you can still see the ruins of some of the magnificent religious monuments and palaces built by Indian princes.

About 550 years ago Mohammedan invaders conquered Java. Later it became the property of the Dutch. See the article on INDONESIA.

JAVA. Area, 48,763 square miles. Population (1973 estimate) 74,000,000. Part of the Republic of Indonesia.

javelin

A javelin is a light spear. It has a sharp metal point and a wooden shaft about five feet long. Javelins were used by the soldiers of ancient armies, thousands of years ago. About four hundred years ago, the aristocrats and nobility of Europe enjoyed the dangerous sport of hunting wild boars (pigs) on horseback and used javelins to kill these fierce animals. Javelins are still used by savage tribesmen in parts of Africa and Asia.

Javelin-throwing is one of the sports played by amateur athletes during track and field events. The athlete who throws the javelin farthest is the winner. The modern javelin used for sport is very accurately balanced and tapers to a point at each end.

jay

Jay is the name of many small, brightly-colored birds found all over the world. They belong to the crow family. Their feathers are attractively colored, ranging from gray and blue to black and white. The American jay is a bright blue and is known as the bluejay. The jay found in South America is a rainbowlike purple, blue, and yellow. Despite these bright colors, the jay is often hard to see in the woods because it blends almost perfectly with the shadows of the forest and the color of the trees.

On the ground, the jay moves about in a series of short, quick hops. In the air it flies swiftly but only for short distances. When it migrates, or moves from one region to another, it is capable of covering great distances. The jay's voice is a continuous chattering. It is noted for being a friend of the farmer because its main food consists of insects, such as ants and grasshoppers, that hurt the crops.

Jays have various nesting habits, varying with the areas in which they live. The Oregon jay, a relative of the bluejay, places its bulky nest of twigs high up on the branches of a tree.

Jay, John

John Jay was a great American statesman and the first Chief Justice of the United States Supreme Court. He was

born in New York City in 1745. When the Revolutionary War was over, Jay, more than any other person, brought about the treaty of peace between the United States and Great Britain. This was

Gale Research Co. in 1783. Then he fought for the adoption of the Constitution of the United States. Along with James Madison and Alexander Hamilton, he wrote the Federalist Papers, a series of articles that were very important in persuading the people to adopt the Constitution.

President George Washington was so grateful to John Jay for his services to the new country that he offered him any job he wanted in the government. Jay chose the office of Chief Justice of the Supreme Court.

In 1794 Jay went to England again and concluded a treaty that came to be known as "Jay's Treaty." Under the terms of Jay's Treaty, the British were to give up the forts they had continued to arm in the Northwest Territory. The United States was given equal trading rights with England in Great Britain and the East Indies, but not in the West Indies.

Since trade with the West Indies had been very important, American businessmen were bitterly opposed to part of Jay's Treaty. The treaty was finally accepted by the Senate, but only after John Jay had been accused of surrendering American rights.

John Jay retired from politics in 1801, but he devoted himself to anti-slavery and religious movements. He died in Bedford, New York, in 1829.

jazz

Jazz is a kind of music, and also a way of playing music. The first jazz music came from the United States, and was created by Negroes who lived in the southern states. Throughout the world, jazz is known as American music. Jazz is seldom considered "serious" music, though some fine composers (writers of music) have used features of jazz in their compositions.

There are different kinds of music called jazz, but all are alike in one way. Jazz music is different in rhythm and "beat" from other music. *Rhythm* is a pattern that sounds make when they are loud and soft, or long and short, at the same times over and over again. The *beat* is the time when the loud or long sound comes so regularly that the listener soon learns to expect it and wait for it. Jazz uses *syncopation,* which means making a loud sound even longer than it is supposed to be, so that the beat will be felt more strongly.

The first jazz was called *ragtime.* When a shoeshine boy in the South polishes your shoes with a rag, he snaps the rag in a rhythm like the beating of a

Trumpeter Ray Anthony leads one of the most popular modern dance bands.

drum. Syncopated music played in New Orleans and Memphis, more than fifty years ago, was called ragtime because it had the strong rhythm of the shoeshine boy's rag.

Then it was noticed that this kind of music makes people shake, or move their bodies, to the rhythm of the music. In the private language spoken by the Negroes of New Orleans and some other southern cities, a language called *jive,* this moving of the body could be described by the word *jazz,* so the music came to be called jazz music.

In the 1890s, there were ragtime bands. These were small groups of the kind that later came to be called *jazz bands* or *dance bands.* In the early 1900s, their

Assoc. Booking Corp.

Jack Teagarden has been called the greatest artist of the hot jazz trombone.

music came to be called jazz and a pioneer of the times, W. C. Handy, added another kind of music, called the *blues.* People who had been waltzing to the music of small orchestras in which the melody was played by violins soon found greater pleasure in dancing new steps— the one-step, the foxtrot—to music in which a saxophone or trumpet or clarinet played the melody, imitating wailing sounds or cries of joy that the human voice makes.

The capital city of jazz music moved from New Orleans, where it began, to Memphis, where W. C. Handy introduced the blues, to Chicago, where some of the all-time greats of jazz music played during and after the World War I period (1915 to 1925). Among these great jazz musicians were King Oliver, Bix Beiderbecke, Sidney Bechet, Louis Armstrong, and Jack Teagarden, but there were many others.

During the 1920s, jazz began to be noticed by audiences who liked serious music. Paul Whiteman built the small dance band into a large orchestra that could play in New York City's Carnegie Hall, where only symphony orchestras and classical musicians had played before. Duke Ellington made the small all-virtuoso band (in which every musician is good enough to give a solo performance) popular with large audiences.

In the 1930s, *swing music* was most popular. This manner of playing jazz music permitted any member of the band to break into a solo performance in which he might *improvise* (play whatever notes he wished, departing if he pleased from the written music). Benny Goodman, the best jazz clarinet player of his time, was the most popular swing musician. Woody Herman was another. During the same period, certain bands preferred to play "sweet" music, in which everyone played so as to emphasize the melody. Among the bands that played sweet music, Guy Lombardo's was the most famous.

The 1940s brought the widespread popularity of swing music to an end, but

there was a short period in which *bop* (or *bebop*) was popular. This was an even more extreme manner of playing swing music, and a bandleader named Dizzy Gillespie was the outstanding leader.

There are many thousands who collect phonograph records of the best performances of great jazz bands of past and present times. Artie Shaw, Bob Crosby, Raymond Scott, Stan Kenton, Tommy Dorsey and many others have led bands that made records of value to collectors. Glenn Miller led one of the most successful dance bands of all time. Ray Anthony, Harry James, Ralph Flanagan and

Assoc. Booking Corp.

Duke Ellington, the leader of one of the best large jazz orchestras and writer of many famous jazz compositions.

others have assembled bands that are much admired. See also the article on MUSIC.

jeep

Jeep is a name that American soldiers in World War II gave to a small military automobile. It is an open car and can carry four men. The jeep was used for many purposes, such as carrying messages, men, or supplies, and for scouting.

In most automobiles the engine turns only the rear wheels. A jeep has a four-wheel drive. This means that the engine turns both the front and rear wheels. The four-wheel drive gives the jeep amazing climbing power. It can ride over very rough ground, climb very steep hills, and pull out of soft mud or snow with ease. The jeep is built so that ordinary two-wheel drive can be used for riding on roads, and when additional pulling power is needed the driver can move a small lever and shift into four-wheel drive.

The jeep is still used by the United States Army, Navy, and Air Force, as well as by many foreign armies.

Jefferson, Joseph

Joseph Jefferson was a great American actor. He is best remembered because

he played the part of Rip Van Winkle for more than 30 years. Jefferson was born in 1829, in Philadelphia, and both his father and grandfather were actors. He began to act when he was a young boy, and he became successful quickly. He

formed a company of actors who traveled from one city to another, so that many people had an opportunity to see *Rip Van Winkle* and other plays. This was one of the first acting companies of this kind in the United States. It is called a road company. Jefferson was also a good painter. He wrote an autobiography, the story of his life in the theater. He died in 1905.

Thomas Jefferson

Thomas Jefferson was the third President of the United States, and one of the greatest American patriots. He was one of the first men to work for American independence. He wrote the Declaration of Independence. He served in the Continental Congress from 1775 on, as Vice President of the United States for one term, from 1797 to 1801, and as President for two terms, from 1801 to 1809. He was known as "The Great Democrat." He was responsible for many of the high principles that have made the United States a land where all men are free.

Jefferson was a violinist, a lawyer, a writer, an architect, a statesman. He did all things well. He was a truly democratic statesman. He had no use for pomp and ceremony, for so-called "upper-class" snobbery. He believed that there were only two things that made one man better than another. These two things were virtue and talents, and he thought they were the only foundations of a real aristocracy among men. Money, title or birth could not give a man virtue or talent, Jefferson believed. He dreamed of a democracy in which only true worth counted, and he labored all his life to build such a democracy. The phrase "Jeffersonian democracy," which has so often been used in political campaigns, refers to the type of government for which he fought.

Thomas Jefferson was an active man all his life. He was a fine horseman, and learned to ride expertly when a child. He was tall, straight, and well-built—a handsome man, with a kindly, gentle face. He was always busy, and once he remarked to his children, "Determine never to be idle. No person will have occasion to complain of the want of time, who never loses any. It is wonderful how much may be done if we are always doing."

Of all his accomplishments, he was proudest of three. He wrote the epitaph for his own tombstone, and it was found in his desk after he died. It said: "Here was buried Thomas Jefferson, Author of the Declaration of Independence, of the Statute of Virginia for Religious Freedom, and Father of the University of Virginia."

The political party of which Jefferson was a member used the name Republican at first, then changed it to Democratic-Republican, and finally to Democratic.

Jefferson lived to be 83, and until the end he wrote many letters. Among the best were those he wrote to another former President, John Adams. Sixteen thousand letters written by him have been preserved.

HIS EARLY YEARS

Thomas Jefferson was born on April 13, 1743, in the little town of Shadwell, in western Virginia. This region was almost a wilderness at that time. Jefferson's family owned great stretches of fertile farmland, but was not rich in the way that families of eastern Virginia were.

Thomas started school when he was 5, and was an earnest, eager student. When he entered William and Mary College his favorite subjects were mathematics, music, and architecture. He often spent fifteen hours a day working at his studies.

After his graduation from college Jefferson became a lawyer and practiced in Virginia for seven years. His first public office was as a member of the Virginia House of Burgesses. This group administered the affairs of the state under the control of the British Colonial Governor of Virginia.

In 1770, Jefferson's home at Shadwell burned to the ground. His violin was the only thing saved from the flames. Fortunately, he had already started to build another house that he himself had designed. As quickly as possible, the new mansion was completed. It was called Monticello, which is Italian for "little mountain." This was where Jefferson lived the rest of his life, except for the periods when he was away on official business, and except for the eight years when he lived in the White House in Washington.

Monticello is still standing, and it is one of the treasures of American colonial architecture. It is just a few miles from Charlottesville, Virginia.

Jefferson's originality and resourcefulness were shown in a clever kind of weathervane he invented and built. He ran a pole down through the roof to his study, and an indicator there showed the wind direction. Thus he could tell which way the wind was blowing without going outdoors. He also made an eight-day clock and a dumb-waiter.

Two years after he moved to Monticello, Jefferson was married to a young widow named Martha Wayles Skelton. They had six children, but only two daughters lived to grow up. The other four died while they were babies. Mrs. Jefferson herself died in 1782, ten years after her marriage to Jefferson, and he never remarried. His widowed sister and her six children became part of his official family. He cared for and educated all six children along with his own two daughters.

HIS FIGHT FOR INDEPENDENCE

The first Continental Congress met in 1774, and although Jefferson himself did not attend it, he wrote an important paper for the delegates. In it he made a list of the rights of the colonists. It was published later under the title, "A Summary of the Rights of British America," and many of the points he listed became part of the Declaration of Independence.

Jefferson represented Virginia at the Second Continental Congress in 1775, when he was 32 years old. One year later he was appointed chairman of the committee to write the Declaration of Independence, which was to state the reasons why the colonists wanted their independence from England. Jefferson asked John Adams to do the actual writing—perhaps out of respect for the older man. However, Adams replied that Jefferson wrote far better than he, and that Jefferson therefore should do the writing himself, as chairman of the committee. The Declaration of Independence was so well-written, and the words expressed each point so clearly, that many parts of it have been remembered and quoted by millions of Americans ever since.

From 1779 to 1781, Jefferson was governor of the state of Virginia. When the British entered the state, he was forced to leave his home. His two servants remained in the house, and managed to hide the family silver under the porch until the English soldiers had left.

The same year that Jefferson became governor, he presented to the legislature of Virginia his bill for religious freedom. It was officially adopted in 1786. This is believed to be the first time that a sovereign state passed a law that guaranteed religious freedom to every one of its citizens.

After the war, Jefferson was a member of the commission that went to France to establish friendly relations with that country for the new United States of America. The other men on the commission were Benjamin Franklin and Silas Deane. The following year Jefferson became sole minister to France.

Five years later, in 1790, President Washington appointed Jefferson as Secretary of State. At that time the national government had its capital in New York City, which was then a city of only thirty-five thousand.

When he returned from France to become Secretary of State, Jefferson observed that the people were not behaving in a democratic fashion. There was a great deal of ceremony in official circles, and many of the customs and formalities of the English nobility were still observed. In fact, some Americans wanted to have titles of nobility in the United States. Jefferson was violently opposed to this, and fought constantly to strengthen democracy in all its forms. He worked hard to eliminate unnecessary "fuss and feathers" and always served as a fine example of simplicity himself.

HOW HE BECAME PRESIDENT

When John Adams ran for President in 1796, Jefferson was also a candidate. Under the election laws of that time, the man who received the second-largest number of electoral votes for President became Vice President. Under this system, the President and Vice President were

usually of different political parties. John Adams and Thomas Jefferson disagreed violently on most subjects and became enemies, though years later they became good friends again.

Jefferson ran again for the Presidency in 1800, against Aaron Burr. The vote was a tie. The House of Representatives elected Jefferson, with Aaron Burr as Vice President. Jefferson was inaugurated in March, 1801. His was the first inauguration to take place in Washington, D.C.

Jeffersonian simplicity was illustrated by the manner in which he rode to the capitol for his inauguration. Before his time, incoming presidents had ridden in an elaborate coach, drawn by six horses, with footmen and guards in attendance. Jefferson rode to his inauguration alone on horseback, wearing plain, simple clothing. He walked quietly into the Senate Chamber and read his inaugural address.

HIS TWO TERMS AS PRESIDENT

Jefferson, as President, doubled the land area of the United States, added great natural wealth and resources to the nation, and greatly increased its strength. These things came as part of the Louisiana Purchase, one of the most important events of Jefferson's two terms. (There is a separate article on the LOUISIANA PURCHASE.)

The Louisiana Territory was the huge block of land west of the Mississippi, extending to the Rocky Mountains and running from what is now the border of Canada all the way south to the Gulf of Mexico. France owned this territory when Jefferson became President. In 1803 Jefferson sent a commission headed by James Monroe to see if the United States could buy at least a part of this great territory from France. Instead of just a part, the

Jefferson Memorial Found.

Jefferson invented many interesting gadgets. The clock in the reception hall at Monticello uses cannon-ball weights (*on the right*) to mark the days of the week.

commission bought the entire territory for $15,000,000 from Napoleon Bonaparte, who was then emperor of France. Napoleon was at war with England then. He was glad both to receive the money and to be relieved of the responsibility of the distant land holdings.

The territory eventually became the states of Louisiana, Arkansas, Missouri, Iowa, North Dakota, and South Dakota; most of Minnesota, Montana, Wyoming, Kansas, and Oklahoma; and part of Colorado.

Another important achievement of Jefferson during his administration was

Nat'l Park Service

The Jefferson Memorial in Washington, D.C. was opened in 1943, on the 200th anniversary of Jefferson's birth. The impressive white memorial is in the same classic style that Jefferson himself used when he built his stately home, Monticello.

the passage of a law that made people stop importing slaves. Jefferson was a slave-owner himself, but he thought slavery was wrong and knew that sooner or later the slaves must be freed.

One of Jefferson's strongest convictions concerned the importance of education for everyone. He had faith in the ability of the people to govern themselves, but he believed that only an educated people could select its government wisely. The public-school system of the present day, and the free education available to everyone in the United States, grew out of Jefferson's efforts.

During Jefferson's second term there was a great deal of trouble with piracy on the seas. Both England and France attacked American ships, because those two countries were at war and each feared that American ships were carrying supplies to the other side. Also, there was trouble with the Barbary pirates, and this made the seas dangerous for American vessels.

Because of the attacks on American shipping, Jefferson asked Congress to pass a law that was very unpopular. It was called the Embargo Act, and it forbade Americans to trade with either England or France. People who made their living by trading with these countries resented it very much.

The Embargo Act was not a success because the United States needed foreign trade. The problem was not solved until the War of 1812 was fought, and this took place after Jefferson's two terms were over.

At the close of Jefferson's second term he was offered the chance to run for a third time, but he refused. Like Washington, he did not think it wise for one person to remain in power for three terms.

HIS LATER YEARS

Thomas Jefferson now retired to Monticello. He was 65 years old. Although he had left public life, the next two Presidents, James Madison and James Monroe, often asked him for suggestions and advice.

In 1818, Jefferson founded the University of Virginia, one of the most advanced institutions of learning in the world. He not only planned the buildings but supervised their construction. When he was unable to ride his horse to the spot where the university was being built, he watched its progress through a telescope from the hill on which Monticello stood.

His hostess, and the mistress of his home during those later years, was his daughter, Martha, who had married Thomas Mann Randolph. She had eleven children, and the house was filled with young laughter and the voices of grandchildren, friends, and guests. Frequently as many as fifty people spent the night at Monticello. Jefferson's hospitality was famous.

Even though he had many guests, Jefferson always spent a certain number of hours a day in reading, and in work on his farm. He got up very early in the morning. On one occasion he remarked that the sun had not caught him in bed for fifty years.

Jefferson was vigorous and mentally alert to the very last. When he was 81 years old, he rode horseback every day, and mounted and dismounted without assistance.

Exactly fifty years to the day after the signing of the Declaration of Independence, Jefferson died. It was on July 4, 1826, the same day on which John Adams died. Although Jefferson died a few hours before Adams did, Adams on his deathbed believed that Jefferson was still alive, and his last words are said to have been "Thomas Jefferson still survives."

THE THOMAS JEFFERSON MEMORIAL

On the south shore of the Tidal Basin in Potomac Park, in Washington, D.C., there is a round, white stone building—the Thomas Jefferson Memorial. In the spring the pink-and-white cherry blossoms along the edge of the water provide a beautiful, colorful background to the graceful, simple lines of the memorial. The outside is of Vermont marble. Inside there is a round Memorial Room, lined

with white Georgia marble, with gray Tennessee marble for its floor. The domed ceiling is 92 feet high, and in the center of the room is a larger-than-life-size statue of Thomas Jefferson. It stands about 25 feet high, including the pedestal. It was carved by an American sculptor, Rudolph Evans. On the walls of the chamber there are four panels, inscribed with some of Jefferson's most famous words, including the Declaration of Independence.

The memorial was dedicated by President Franklin D. Roosevelt on April 13, 1943, on the 200th anniversary of Jefferson's birth. It was built at a cost of three million dollars, appropriated by Congress for its construction. The memorial is open to the public, and thousands visit it each year.

MRS. THOMAS JEFFERSON

Martha Wayles Skelton Jefferson was born in 1749, the daughter of a rich farmer. Her father's land and slaves became part of the Jefferson estate. Mrs. Jefferson was the widow of Bathurst Skelton. When she was 23, she and Thomas Jefferson were married. They had six children, but only two daughters, Martha and Mary, lived past infancy. Mrs. Jefferson herself lived for only ten years after her marriage. She died at Monticello in 1782.

Jefferson City

Jefferson City is the capital of the state of Missouri. It is on the Missouri River, in the center of the state. Jefferson City is the distribution point for a large farming area. Although only 32,407 people live in Jefferson City, it has a great many different industries. Factories produce shoes, furniture, machinery, bricks, paper, clothes, and dairy products.

The state capitol is an unusually beautiful building made of Carthage marble. Inside are murals and paintings by noted artists. The Supreme Court building has an extensive library. There are seventeen churches in the city.

Lincoln University was established in Jefferson City in 1866. It offers a four-year course, extension courses, and a summer school, and is coeducational. Originally it was for Negroes only and was called the Lincoln Institute.

JEFFERSON CITY, MISSOURI. Population (1970 census) 32,407. Capital of Missouri. County seat of Cole County. On the Missouri River. Laid out in 1822.

Jeffries, Jim

James J. Jeffries was heavyweight boxing champion of the world from 1899 to 1905. He was born in Carroll, Ohio, in 1875, and began fighting in California in 1896. Three years later he fought Bob Fitzsimmons, the heavyweight champion, and knocked him out in the eleventh round.

Jeffries actively defended his championship during the next four years, fighting all the leading contenders. In 1905 he retired undefeated, but five years later he returned to fight Jack Johnson for the title. In a very famous fight at Reno, Nevada, on July 4, 1910, Johnson knocked out Jeffries in the fifteenth round. This was the first time Jeffries had ever been knocked out and it was his last fight. Jeffries is said to be the first boxer to fight from a crouching position. He

Missouri's state capitol in Jefferson City is a handsome and dignified building.

Missouri Resources Div.

died in 1953.

Jehovah

Jehovah is a name for God. The name comes from the Hebrew language. In the Hebrew alphabet there are no vowels (*a, e, i, o,* or *u*). The people who read Hebrew made up these sounds as they read. The name of God was spelled YHWH or JHVH. The vowels that people should have put in would have made the name of God *Yahweh*. For hundreds of years people did not know this. They put in the wrong vowels and spelled the name Jehovah.

Jehovah's Witnesses

Jehovah's Witnesses are a religious group who believe that the second coming of Christ, promised in the Bible, has already occurred. The organization was founded in 1874 by Charles Taze Russell of Pittsburgh, Pennsylvania. Witnesses meet in buildings called Kingdom Halls.

Members believe exactly what the Bible says; they tell others of their belief by means of literature that they distribute widely. The most important publication of the group is *The Watch Tower Announcing Jehovah's Kingdom.*

The members of the group are pacifists, that is, they do not believe in fighting in a war for any reason. Many have refused to serve in armed forces because of their religious convictions. They will not take an oath of allegiance to anyone but God.

Jehovah's Witnesses believe that the second coming of Christ occurred in 1874. They think that since 1914 the world has existed in a state of social revolution that will eventually end with chaos. This will be followed by the Last Judgment, and after that the Kingdom of God will be established on earth.

jelly and jam

Jelly and jam are sweet foods made of fruit. They are put on bread or on other foods to make them taste sweeter. Many people make jams and jelly when they have more fresh fruit than they want to eat at once.

Jam is made by cooking fruit with sugar until a great deal of the water in the fruit has evaporated. When chilled, jam is thick and one can see and taste lumps of the fruit from which it was made.

Jelly is jam that has been strained. The little pieces of fruit and the little seeds, such as those of raspberries or black-

berries, are left out. While jam is thick, jelly is thin and clear. Most fruits contain a substance called *pectin,* which is a kind of gelatin. The pectin keeps the jelly from being liquid and too runny to spread on bread.

The fruits from which jams and jellies are made must be carefully cooked. If the fruit is boiled too hard or too long, the pectin is destroyed and the jams and jellies do not "jell" properly; if they are not cooked long enough, too much water remains in the fruit and the jam or jelly is likely to spoil.

There are artificial pectins that one can buy in the grocery store in bottles or packages. These help the jams and jellies to jell even if part of the pectin has been destroyed, or if the fruit itself does not contain enough pectin to "set" the jelly.

Various recipes show exactly how many pounds of sugar to use with a certain amount of fruit. The fruit must be washed, peeled, and cut up. The jelly jars must be prepared ahead of time. These must be carefully washed and then sterilized—placed in boiling water —so that no impurities are in the jars to cause the jam or jelly to spoil. Jams and jellies, if properly made and sealed, should last for years. People have been made quite ill by foods that were not properly sealed and were allowed to ferment or rot inside the jar. After sterilizing the jars and cooking the fruit with sugar for the proper amount of time (and straining the mixture if jelly is to be made), the cook pours the jam or jelly into the sterilized jars. These should then be allowed to stand and cool a few minutes. Then liquid paraffin, which is like melted wax, is poured on top of the jam or jelly to seal it. Paraffin can be bought in grocery stores. It keeps all air away from the jam or jelly and prevents spoiling. Jams and jellies not only taste good but provide energy and vitamins. They sweeten many foods and are even used with meats. Often little dabs of jelly decorate cakes and puddings.

jellyfish

The jellyfish is a very simple form of animal found in every sea of the world. It gets its name from the fact that it looks like a flimsy, transparent glob of jelly. The jellyfish's digestive system— the parts of its body that digest food— makes up almost all its insides, but it does not have any separate internal organs. The jellyfish usually is shaped like an umbrella, but some kinds are star-shaped. All around the center of a jellyfish's body there are arms, or tentacles, sticking out.

The tentacles of some jellyfish are like needles. If they touch you, they can sting very painfully. This stinging is the jellyfish's protection against its enemies and is also the way it gets the food it eats. It stuns or paralyzes its prey.

Most jellyfish eat by shoveling food into their mouths with their tentacles. Jellyfish will eat almost anything, from the eggs of other fish to seaweed.

There are many different kinds of jellyfish, in various sizes and weights. One kind of jellyfish, known as the Portuguese Man-of-War, is 8 to 10 inches long and its stinging tentacles droop several feet

below its head.

Jenner, Edward

Edward Jenner was an English doctor who discovered that people can be vaccinated against smallpox. He was born about two hundred years ago (in the year 1749). At that time smallpox was very common. It killed many thousands of people every year, and left other thousands badly scarred.

There was another common disease called cowpox. It was somewhat like smallpox but much less dangerous. Cowpox almost never killed anyone. Cowpox got its name because people caught it from cows. Farmers in Jenner's part of the country had noticed that milkmaids who got cowpox never seemed to catch smallpox afterwards. Jenner thought that if he could find some way of giving people a very small dose of cowpox, they would be protected against catching smallpox. He spent twenty-five years making experiments of various kinds, and finally he proved that this could be done. In 1796, when he was 37 years old, he took some infected matter from sores on a dairymaid who had cowpox, and injected it into cuts he had made in the hand of James Phipps, a healthy 8-year-old boy. He called the infected matter *vaccine*, which means "a substance from a cow." Two months later, he exposed the boy to smallpox. The boy never caught it.

At first, people did not think much of Dr. Jenner's new method of preventing smallpox, which he called *vaccination*. Dr. Jenner gave up his practice of medicine to spend all his time spreading the use of vaccination. Finally people were convinced of the value of his method, and before his death in 1823 Dr. Jenner was greatly honored. Today, almost everybody is vaccinated against smallpox, and the disease has all but disappeared in most parts of the world.

jerboa

The jerboa is a small, scrawny animal that belongs to the order of rodents, or animals that gnaw. The jerboa makes its home on the dry desert lands of northern Africa and Asia. The jerboa is a jumping mouse. It moves about by jumping, springing from its strong hind legs. It has a long snakelike tail that it uses for balance and steering. The jerboa is herbivorous, which means that it eats only plant food. It eats the few plants it can find growing on the desert. When it is attacked by a larger animal, the jerboa quickly digs a hole for itself and scurries into it to escape the attacker.

Jeremiah

Jeremiah was one of the great religious leaders, or prophets, of the Hebrew people in the times told about in the Bible.

Jeremiah was born more than 2,500 years ago, about the year 650 B.C. He was a member of the family of priests who served in the Temple. In Jeremiah's time the most powerful nations were fighting great wars against one another. Jeremiah believed in peace and warned the Jewish people not to take part in these wars. He told the Jews that if they did not worship God and obey His com-

mandments they would be destroyed. Many of Jeremiah's prophecies, or warnings of bad things to come, may be read in the Book of Jeremiah in the Bible. The Book of Lamentations gives more of Jeremiah's prophecies. Any sad, lamenting speech is called a *jeremiad* to this day.

The people did not follow Jeremiah's advice, and often he was persecuted for his unpopular teachings. It turned out that he was right, because the Babylonian empire conquered the Jews and destroyed their holy city, Jerusalem. Jeremiah was not killed in this war, but he had to leave his homeland and finally died, an unhappy man, in Egypt.

Jerome, Saint

The famous St. Jerome translated the Bible into the everyday speech or "vulgate" of the Latin-speaking people of Rome. He was born about the year 340 and became a priest in Antioch; then he moved to Rome, where he became the chief helper of Pope Damasus. Here he translated the New Testament and Psalms and wrote other religious books, for which he was made one of the four Doctors of the Church. After the death of Damasus he went to a monastery in Bethlehem. Here he translated the Old Testament and remained until his death in 420. The Vulgate Bible of St. Jerome is the official Latin version in the Roman Catholic Church. See BIBLE.

Jersey City

Jersey City is the second-largest city in the state of New Jersey. It is on the Hudson River, across from New York City, and it is the county seat of Hudson County. Almost 261,000 people live there.

Jersey City is part of the Port of New York. It is connected with New York City by the Hudson & Manhattan Railroad, which runs under the Hudson River in tunnels called the Hudson Tubes. Automobiles and other vehicles travel between New York City and Jersey City by means of ferryboats on the Hudson, or by the Holland and Lincoln Tunnels under the river.

Many railroads go through Jersey City. There are many factories in the city. Products include radios, asbestos products, drugs, waxes, paints, industrial chemicals, telephones, meat and macaroni products, soap, and toothpaste. Jersey City also is an important distribution center for livestock and farm produce.

Jersey City has several famous hospitals. Its Medical Center is one of the largest in the east. There are also a famous Tuberculosis Center and a Maternity Hospital. The Fourth Regiment Armory, the Hasbrouck Institute, the city hall, and St. Peter's College are among the other buildings of interest.

For many years Jersey City was controlled politically by Mayor Frank Hague, who became a highly controversial figure. He made many political friends but he also made enemies, and eventually a group was organized that took his power from him.

JERSEY CITY, NEW JERSEY. Population (1970 census) 260,545. County seat of Hudson County. Settled about 1660.

Jerusalem

Jerusalem is one of the world's oldest and most famous cities. It is built on a rocky plain in the desert mountains of Palestine. Jerusalem is a holy city to people of three religions, Jews, Christians, and Moslems. It is divided into two main sections, the Old City and the New City. The Old City of Jerusalem is built on two hills and is surrounded by a wall. Inside the wall are four sections: The Moslem quarter, which contains famous Mohammedan mosques, or places of worship, and the Jewish Wailing Wall; the Jewish quarter, much of which was destroyed in the Arab-Jewish fighting in 1948; the Armenian quarter; and the Christian quarter, in which stands the Church of the Holy Sepulcher on the site believed to have been that of Jesus' tomb. Most of the New City is only about a hundred years old. It has many modern buildings, schools, and museums.

The narrow streets of the Old City of Jerusalem are dark and shut in by high walls. Many of them are roofed-over entirely with low arches. The houses are square and have flat tops where families sometimes have little gardens in which they sit in the evenings. There are not many windows because in desert countries people like to keep their houses cool and dark and to keep out the sun.

Even in Jesus' time Jerusalem was very old. Fifteen hundred years before his birth, Jerusalem was a colony of Egypt, and the Egyptians left us the first definite record we have of the city. The Jewish hero, King David, took the city from a tribe of desert people called the Jebusites and made it the capital of his own kingdom, twelve hundred years before Jesus. Jerusalem is often called the City of David because he ruled there and built a holy shrine for the city. King Solomon also ruled in Jerusalem, and he made the city very rich and splendid, with a magnificent temple. The city was the capital of Judah until the Roman emperor Titus destroyed it 70 years after Jesus lived there. Later the Romans rebuilt Jerusalem under another emperor, Hadrian. When the Roman emperor Constantine became a Christian, he restored the holy places of the city, and once again pilgrims poured into it to worship. In the 6th century, Moslems captured Jerusalem, and it was five hundred years before the Christians recaptured it, in 1099, under a Crusader named Godfrey de Bouillon.

Since the Crusades, Jerusalem has been held by the Saracens, a Mohammedan people, and the British, who released it in the 1940s. The Arabs, who are Mohammedans, and the Jews of the new state of Israel both feel that they have ancient rights to Jerusalem, and they fought bitter battles over it after the United Nations divided Palestine into Jewish and Arab states in 1948. The following year the city was divided by an armistice agreement between Israel and the Arab country of Jordan. In the Arab-Israeli War of 1967, Israel captured the Jordanian sector and opened the entire city to Arabs, Jews, and Christians.

jester

A jester was a special servant of a

king or nobleman, in Europe hundreds of years ago. The jester's duty was to amuse his master. If a king was not in a good humor, he might call his jester and ask him to tell a joke that would make him laugh, or to perform some antic such as modern clowns do in the circus. But woe to the jester who failed to amuse when called upon to do so! He might be beaten, branded with a hot iron, or even put to death.

Jesters were generally dwarfs, or hunchbacks, or men deformed in some way. They wore checkered costumes of many colors, with pointed caps and shoes. Bells on their caps and shoes tinkled as they moved about.

If really clever and amusing, jesters often enjoyed privileges denied anyone else at court, no matter how powerful. The jester usually acted as if he was crazy, and people in those days were often afraid to hurt a crazy person.

Jesuit

Jesuits are members of the Society of Jesus, a religious order of the Roman Catholic Church. The order was founded by St. Ignatius Loyola about four hundred years ago, and its principal purpose is to teach the Roman Catholic religion both through missionary work and through schools. Among the Jesuit missionaries have been such famous men as St. Francis Xavier and the explorer Jacques Marquette. When St. Ignatius Loyola died in 1556 there were about a thousand Jesuits. Today the Society is divided into fifty provinces spread all over the world, including two in Canada and eight in the United States. There are almost eight thousand members of the Society of Jesus in the United States alone, and they operate ninety-nine schools including such universities as Fordham in New York City; Georgetown in Washington, D.C.; Marquette in Milwaukee, Wisconsin; and Boston College in Boston, Massachusetts.

It takes many years of study to become a Jesuit. Besides the years of spiritual training to become a priest, five years are required in study of the arts and sciences, and five years in teaching.

Jesus Christ

Jesus was the founder of Christianity, the religion of more than six hundred million people. The story of his life is told in the Gospels, the books of Matthew, Mark, Luke, and John, in the New Testament.

The Old Testament had promised a Messiah, or savior, who would come to earth to save the people. Christians for nearly two thousand years have recognized Jesus as this Messiah, and as the Son of God. Christ, in the Greek language (in which the New Testament was written), means the same as Messiah, or king. Jesus, too, is a Greek name; the Hebrew name is Joshua, meaning savior.

The life of Jesus on earth occurred a little less than two thousand years ago. Calendars in Christian countries are dated from the year in which Jesus was supposed to have been born. Actually, the men who made the earliest Christian calendars made a mistake, and Jesus was probably born four to nine years before they thought he was, so that the year

1955, for example, is not 1,955 years after his birth but 1,959 to 1,964 years after it. The day of his birth is not known, and December 25, the day on which his

Metropolitan Museum of Art
Giovanni Bellini's *Madonna and Child* shows Mary holding her infant son. Their faces seem to radiate spiritual peace.

birth is celebrated, was selected several hundred years later.

THE BIRTH OF CHRIST

The mother of Jesus was Mary, who lived in the town of Nazareth, in the province of Galilee, in Palestine, the homeland of the Jews. She was engaged to marry Joseph, a carpenter of Nazareth. Before their marriage an angel appeared to Mary and told her that she would have a son, whose father was not a man but the Holy Spirit (of God), and that this son would be the savior of mankind. This is called the Annunciation (the announcing).

Several months later, Mary went with Joseph to the town of Bethlehem, in Palestine, to be enrolled in a census being taken by the Romans who ruled Palestine. There was no room for them in the inn at Bethlehem so they spent the night in a stable. Here Jesus was born, and Mary used a manger—a feeding trough for cattle—as his crib. The birth of Jesus is called the Nativity. Miracles occurred when Christ was born. An angel of God told shepherds of his birth in a stable. The shepherds went to worship him; angels descended from the heavens and sang hymns of praise, saying, "Glory to God, and Peace on Earth." Priests, or wise men, called Magi, were guided by a star to Bethlehem to carry gifts to Jesus.

The king of Palestine at that time was Herod the Great. When he heard about Jesus, he was afraid that Jesus would be made king in his place. It had been prophesied that a descendant of David, the former great Jewish king, would become king. Joseph was a descendant of David, and that made Jesus a member of the house, or family, of David. Herod could not find Jesus, but he gave orders that all male children in Bethlehem under 2 years of age should be killed. Joseph had been warned by an angel that this would happen, and he took Mary and the baby Jesus to Egypt

until the danger was over. Then they returned home.

HIS BAPTISM AND TEMPTATION

Jesus grew up as a boy in Nazareth and learned to be a carpenter, as Joseph was. When he was 12 years old, Joseph and Mary took him to Jerusalem to be confirmed in the Temple, and the rabbis (teachers) in the Temple were astonished by his wisdom and his knowledge of the Bible.

The Gospels do not tell more of Jesus' life until he was about 30 years old. At that time, John the Baptist was baptizing people in the River Jordan and was promising that the Messiah would soon come. Jesus went to John and was baptized; and when he was baptized a voice from heaven said to him, "You are my beloved Son."

Then Jesus went into the wilderness (far from cities and houses) and for forty days he did not eat. During this time Satan (the evil spirit) tried to tempt Jesus to use his great powers for his own benefit, but Jesus could not be tempted.

THE MINISTRY OF JESUS

After this, the ministry of Jesus began. He performed many miracles, healing the sick, comforting those in distress, and even bringing the dead back to life, as in the case of Lazarus, who had been dead four days. Many disciples, or followers, believed in Jesus and followed him, and of these he selected twelve as his own Disciples, or Apostles, to teach his message to others.

As a preacher, Jesus followed the Jewish doctrine of the Old Testament but carried the messages of love and humility much farther, making them apply to all men and not only to the chosen people, the Jews. The greatest message of Jesus was in the Sermon on the Mount, when he preached to the plain people of Galilee. He used parables, or stories, to make his meaning understandable to these people. He used words they could understand, as when he called himself a shepherd who would care for them just as they cared for their sheep.

Jesus went to different cities in Palestine to preach. Finally he went to Jerusalem, the most important city. In Jerusalem was the Temple, in which the high priests Annas and Caiaphas were most powerful. The Temple had its own money, and those who went into the Temple had to change their Roman money for the Temple's money. The money-changers in the Temple made a large profit on this. Jesus drove the money-changers out of the Temple, and this made the priests fear him even more. They looked for ways to destroy him.

THE PASSION AND RESURRECTION

During the great Jewish feast of the Passover, Jesus ate with his twelve Disciples. This meal is called the Last Supper. At the Last Supper, Jesus broke bread for his Disciples to eat, saying that it was his body; and gave them wine to drink, saying that it was his blood. He told them that he must die, for it was prophesied in the Bible. He told them also that one of them would betray him, and that all of them would forsake him.

After the Last Supper, Jesus went into the Garden of Gethsemane, in Jerusalem, to pray. Meanwhile the high priests had arranged for the Roman soldiers to arrest Jesus. One of the Disciples, Judas Iscariot, betrayed Jesus by leading the Roman soldiers to him, in return for thirty pieces of silver. One of the Disciples, Peter, denied that he knew Jesus; he did this three times, as Jesus had said he would.

The chief priests and council of the Jews put Jesus on trial. They could not find witnesses against him that anyone would believe, but when they asked him, "Are you the Christ, the Son of God?" he answered, "I am." Then they accused him of blasphemy, which is disrespect toward God, and they went to Pontius Pilate, who was procurator, or representative, of the Roman Empire, and demanded that Jesus be put to death.

Pontius Pilate could find nothing wrong with Jesus, but when a large crowd of the people of Jerusalem, led by the priests, said they wanted Jesus put to death, Pilate was willing to do what they wanted. In those days, the worst criminals were crucified. They were nailed to a cross and left there to die. Jesus was beaten, then was made to drag a heavy wooden cross to a place called Golgotha, and there was crucified between two thieves. The Roman soldiers cast lots (gambled) to see which would get his clothes. When he was thirsty, they gave him vinegar. All this was prophesied in the Bible, in the 22nd Psalm. Finally, Jesus spoke the first words of that Psalm, "My God, my God, why has thou forsaken me?" and later he said, "Father, into Thy hands I commend my spirit," and gave up the ghost, which is to say that life left him. The sufferings of Jesus at this time are called the Passion.

Jesus was buried in a tomb of solid rock, and a heavy rock was rolled against the opening. Three days later, on the day celebrated as Easter, the heavy rock was rolled away but the body of Jesus was not in the tomb. He had risen to heaven. This is called the Resurrection.

For forty days after that, he came back to earth and appeared to his Disciples and to others. During this period he told the eleven remaining Disciples to go into other lands as Apostles (messengers) and preach Christianity to the people. After this, Jesus ascended into heaven, to sit at the right hand of God.

Some writers capitalize the pronouns He, Him, His, Who, and so on, when writing of Jesus, but neither the Protestant nor the Catholic Bible does, and most writers today prefer to follow their style and not use the capital letters.

Read also the articles CHRISTIANITY, CHURCH, MARY, JOSEPH, JOHN THE BAPTIST, and BIBLE.

jet engine

A jet engine is a device used primarily for propelling airplanes through the air at high speeds. The forward motion of an airplane so propelled is called *jet propulsion.*

Jet propulsion can be demonstrated by using a rubber balloon. Fill the balloon with air. Then, squeezing the mouth of the balloon between your fingers, release the balloon. The balloon will be pro-

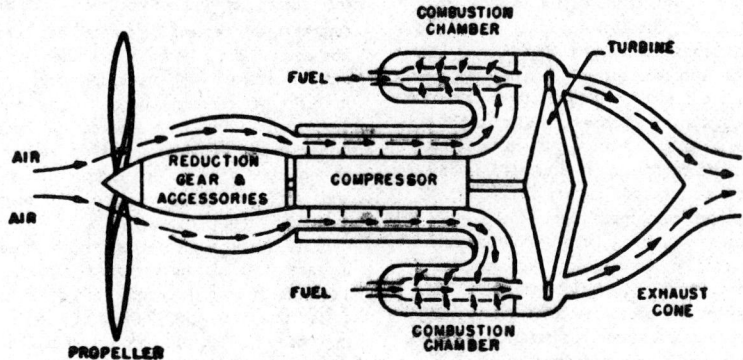

General Electric Co.

The turbo-prop has both a propeller and a jet engine. It was developed to drive high-speed military transports and bombers. Its operation is like that of the turbo-jet. The turbine spins more than ten thousand times a minute, operating the compressor and at the same time driving the propeller through reduction gears. Both the propeller and the jet engine drive the airplane.

pelled in one direction, while the air escapes from it in the opposite direction.

The explanation of this is simple. When the balloon is filled with air, the air is pressing against the inside of the balloon in all directions. When the balloon is released, air escapes from one end. The air pressing inside of the balloon at the other end propels it forward until all the air has escaped.

The escaping air is called the *action*. The air pressing inside the balloon at the other end is called a *reaction*. The forces of action and reaction are the same. The faster the air escapes from the balloon the faster the balloon will move in the other direction. It is for the same reason that a gun "kicks" backward when it is fired.

The law of action and reaction was demonstrated more than two hundred years ago by the English scientist Isaac Newton, and is known as Newton's third law of motion.

HOW A JET ENGINE WORKS

A jet engine works by forcing air and other gases out of an opening at the back of the engine. The reaction to this forces the plane forward. For the plane to travel forward at high speeds, the air must escape from the rear of the engine at high speeds. This is partly accomplished by giving the engine a wide opening to let the air in at the front and a narrow opening to let it out at the rear. The narrower the opening the faster the air will flow through it.

To increase the speed further, the air entering the front of the engine is compressed at a high speed by a rotating air compressor. The compressor acts like a fan. The air entering the engine is thrown back toward the rear by the turning blades of the compressor.

To increase the speed still further, the air is mixed with fuel, usually kerosene,

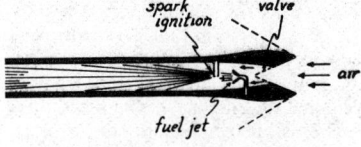

The ram-jet is the simplest of all the engines. Its top speed is in the neighborhood of one thousand miles per hour.

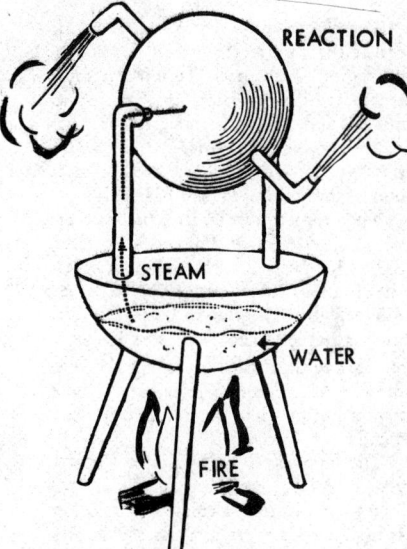

The first engine using the principle of jet propulsion was built by Hero of Alexandria more than two thousand years ago. Called an "aeoliphile," it spun a hollow ball by means of steam released through two bent nozzles connected to it. A lawn sprinkler works in a similar way.

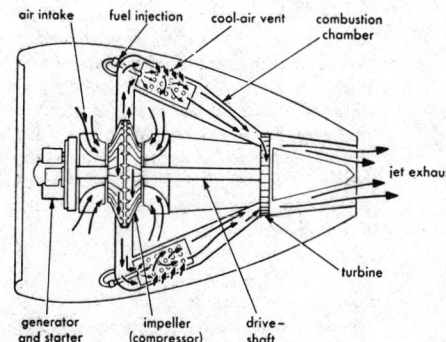

The turbo-jet engine is the kind that is used on most jet-propelled airplanes.

and is burned inside a combustion chamber. The gases that are formed exert a tremendous pressure inside the chamber on all sides. The hot gases are shot out through the back of the engine with a speed of thousands of miles an hour. At the same time there is an equal and opposite reaction of the gases against the front of the engine. This pushes the plane forward at a tremendous speed.

TURBO-JETS

The hot gases that escape through the back of the engine usually turn a *turbine* before they pass to the outside air. The turbine is a bladed wheel that turns like a windmill when the gas is forced against it. The turbine is connected to the com-

pressor at the front of the engine by a long shaft. The turbine spins the shaft, which spins the compressor and supplies the compressed air. Such a jet engine often is called a *turbo-jet*.

Because the temperature of the hot gases is extremely high, a jet engine must be made of special mixtures of metals, called alloys, that can withstand 2,000 or more degrees Fahrenheit.

Some propeller-driven airplanes have also carried jet engines, used to drive a compressor set near the propellers. This increases the pressure of the air striking the propellers. Such an arrangement is known as a turbo-supercharger.

RAM-JETS

There is a simple type of jet engine called the ram-jet or Athodyd (an abbreviation for Aero-Thermo-Dynamic-Duct), which has been used on guided missiles and similar weapons. It was originally devised in Germany in 1944 for the V-1 "buzz bombs" that were used to bomb cities during World War II.

The ram-jet must be launched into the air at speeds above 250 miles an hour. When it travels at such speeds, air enters the funnel-shaped nose. The air then mixes with a spray of fuel and the mixture is burned. The gases formed shoot out through the back, thrusting the missile forward. The ram-jet is hardly more than a hollow tube but can develop tremendous speeds.

The jet-assisted take-off units (abbreviated JATO), developed in the United States for assisting airplanes to take off at high speeds, were actually rocket-propelled units. You can read about the ROCKET in a separate article.

JET PLANES

Jet planes are designed to fly at speeds approaching or exceeding the speed of sound. This speed varies with altitude: At sea level it is 761 miles per hour and it decreases at higher altitudes to about 660 miles per hour at 37,000 feet. The speed of sound is called *Mach*, after the Austrian physicist Ernest Mach; Mach 1 is the exact speed of sound at the given altitude, Mach 2 is twice the speed of sound, Mach 1.5 is one and one-half times the speed of sound, and so on.

As an airplane approaches Mach 1, shock waves in the air buffet it severely. (Oddly enough, these effects disappear at speeds above Mach 1.) To smooth out the flow of air over the plane's surfaces, designers are now using sharply swept-back wings. They have also made wings thinner; for example, the wings of the B-47 jet bomber, in flight, flex as much as seven feet at their tips. Still another increasingly characteristic jet shape is a sharply pointed nose.

The jet engine's enormous potential power is best utilized only at high speed and high altitude. Jet fighter planes, as a result, can operate effectively all the way up to 50,000 feet or even higher, far higher than most piston-engined planes.

At that altitude, the air temperature is nearly 70 degrees below zero Fahrenheit. The air pressure, which normally measures 2,116 pounds per square foot at sea level, is a mere 280 pounds per square foot.

The jet is sluggish on take-off, because

the engine delivers only a part of its ultimate power before high speed has been attained. A land-based jet, loaded with every pound of fuel, armament and ammunition it can carry, needs a long runway or assistance from rockets mounted under its wings. A carrier-based jet must be launched with an acceleration of several "g's," a "g" being the acceleration of gravity, 32 feet per second.

Once the jet is air-borne at high speed, its rate of climb may reach 20,000 feet a minute. A jet fighter may thus get from a standing start to 35,000 feet in less than five minutes. Now in the reduced air pressure at 35,000 feet, some of the more volatile jet fuels, though not those of the kerosene type, will boil at a temperature of 70 degrees Fahrenheit. Since the temperature of the air at this altitude is about minus 60 degrees Fahrenheit, there would seem to be no danger of boiling.

But, when the plane has been on the ground in summer temperature only five minutes earlier, the fuel in its tanks has not had time to cool to the surrounding air temperature. A volatile (easily vaporizing) fuel will begin to boil somewhere around 27,000 feet. Before it cools and stops boiling, as much as 10 percent of it may have vanished in vapor through the tank vents.

The jet plane's flight is smoother than that of a piston-engined plane because

Lockheed

The "Shooting Star" was an early all-jet plane. Note the air intake where the wing meets the body of the plane.

Douglas

The Douglas X-3 is the last word in streamlining. Its wings are smaller than a normal plane's tail and its tapered body is shaped like a lance. Capable of flying at twice the speed of sound, it is one of the fastest of all jet airplanes.

the jet engine is nearly vibrationless. Its control is easier because there is no propeller torque, or yawing effect. The pilot can often perform normal maneuvers without touching his rudder pedals, using only the elevators for climb and descent and the ailerons for bank and turn.

The jet plane, because of its great speed, needs lots of room to maneuver. A turn, for example, takes longer to execute than in a slower plane.

It is one of the oddities of the jet engine, that its rate of fuel consumption per mile traveled does not decrease as the engine is throttling back. Instead, the fuel consumption goes up. To fly the greatest possible distance in a jet plane, you have to fly at almost full power.

Not only that—you also have to fly at relatively high altitude, somewhere above 35,000 feet. The thinner the air, the less resistance it offers to the plane and, therefore, the higher the plane's speed for the same power.

Of course, no engine can operate in a vacuum unless it carries its air supply along with it, like a rocket. Its fuel cannot be burned without air. This is spectacularly true of the jet engine, whose gaping air intakes suck in the atmosphere at an awesome rate. A jet engine developing 4,000 horsepower at 375 miles an hour would exhaust the air in a typical six-room house in about nine seconds. In those nine seconds, it would also burn more than a gallon and a half of fuel.

jetty

A jetty is a pier or wall that is built out from the shore into a river or the sea. Jetties may be used as breakwaters, to cut the force of rough waves and form smooth water for a harbor. Another purpose of a jetty may be to deepen the channel in a harbor or river, by making the current flow in a narrow path. This will make the water flow faster, and keep mud and silt from settling on the bottom.

Jetties are often built where a river enters a large body of water that does not have enough current or tide to carry away all the mud that the river carries down to its mouth. A jetty of this type was built at the mouth of the Mississippi River about a hundred years ago (in 1879). The longest jetty in the world, four and a half miles, has been built at the mouth of the Columbia River. Many of the world's most famous harbors, such as Dunkirk and Calais in France and Ostend in Belgium, depend on jetties. A jetty may be built of rows of braced timber-piles filled in with rubble, concrete, or mud; or it may be built in the form of a low, solid concrete or stone wall. Along the Atlantic coast of the United States, jetties slow down waves that might wash away the beaches.

jewelry

Jewelry includes any objects made of precious or beautiful materials, such as rare stones, rare metals, and ivory, worn to help a person's appearance. Bracelets, rings, beads, brooches, and pins are some of the kinds of jewelry.

Long ago, some sort of jewelry was probably worn to ward off "evil spirits," or to indicate a high position in society. The "jewels" may have been pebbles, shells, or even teeth, which might not seem very beautiful today.

With the discovery of metals such as bronze and gold three or four thousand years ago, men began to see that some metals were rarer and more beautiful than others. A metal such as gold was precious because it was so hard to obtain, but also because it would not rust or tarnish and so would remain beautiful. The same was true of certain stones, those we call pre-

cious gems, such as diamonds, rubies, emeralds, and sapphires, which are beautiful and are also hard, so that they cannot easily be scratched.

The ancient Egyptians, Greeks, and Romans all wore jewels thousands of years ago. The Egyptian jewelers are said to have been capable of doing anything with metal or stone that modern jewelers can do. The Greeks wore earrings so large that they had to be supported by headbands. Because of all their conquests, the Romans had much greater wealth than the Greeks and liked to show their wealth by wearing much jewelry.

From the western Roman Empire, Europeans learned how to set stones in metal; from the eastern Roman Empire they learned how to use enamel, that is, to bake paint onto metal so as to produce a more brilliant surface. About four hundred years ago, jewelry became part of dress in Europe and was fashioned into belts and hair nets and was sewn into garments. A rich European would often wear clothing completely embroidered with jewels. So great was the demand for jewelry that a new class of craftsmen appeared who made nothing but jewelry.

MODERN JEWELRY

Styles in jewelry change just as styles in dress do, though not so often. In our time, when a method of working with platinum was discovered, platinum became more popular than gold and silver as a metal in which to set stones. One result has been that stones have to be bigger and more brilliant than ever before, for platinum settings make the stones set in them seem smaller than they would appear in gold or silver. In modern times, too, diamonds have become more desired than any other precious stone.

One very great difference between the use of jewelry now and in the past is that jewelry is now worn chiefly by women. Men may wear rings, cuff links, scarf pins, watch chains, and wrist watches, but that is about all. Necklaces, brooches and bracelets are reserved for women.

COSTUME JEWELRY

"Costume" jewelry is one of the latest fashions. It was produced by modern science. Inexpensive metals have been developed that remain bright and unstained. Beautiful "stones" are made of glass and plastics. The result is sparkling jewelry that is worn by even the richest women, but that almost any woman can afford.

Some of the princes of India have the most famous collections of fine jewelry. An Indian princess often has her clothes embroidered with strings of precious stones.

There are separate articles about GEMS and about DIAMONDS, RUBIES, PEARLS, and other stones used in jewelry.

Jews and Judaism

The Jews are a people who are remarkable for the fact that they have kept their identity in many different countries and through many centuries when similar groups have become lost by merging with their neighbors. For nearly two thousand years the Jews were without a homeland of their own and were scattered through all parts of the world, yet they remained a separate people wherever they were. In 1948, the state of Israel was set up as a homeland for the Jews, but most Jews live in other countries. In 1961, there were about 12,926,180 Jews in the world, and nearly half of them were living in the United States and Canada. At that time about 2,000,000 had settled in Israel.

The thing that kept the Jews together as a people was, for the most part, their religion. They adopted the customs of the new lands, they spoke the languages of the new lands, they made many important contributions to the new lands, but their religion gave them a bond with Jews living everywhere else in the world. Until recent times, there was very little intermarriage between Jews and non-Jews, and this also helped the Jews to keep their identity.

THEIR HISTORY AND RELIGION

The history of the Jews began almost 4,000 years ago, when Abraham, who is considered the father of the Jewish people, settled in the land of Canaan (now Israel). The story of Abraham, his son, Isaac, and his grandson, Jacob, is described in the Old Testament. They are usually referred to as the Hebrew patriarchs.

Jacob's name was changed to Israel, and the ancient Jews were called *Israelites* or *Hebrews*. According to the Bible, the early Israelites moved to Egypt to escape a famine, and, after many years of slavery, were at last led to freedom by Moses and his brother, Aaron. For forty years, the people of Israel wandered through the wilderness of Sinai (between Egypt and Palestine). During this period the Ten Commandments were given to them by God, through their leader, Moses.

These commandments, and other laws described in the Bible, formed the basis of Judaism, the religion of the Jews. Its teachings included a love of God, respect for parents and the aged, a love of neighbor, including the stranger, just dealings, kindness to animals, and a love of peace.

The Jewish religion also taught the lesson of liberty. Taking as their inspiration the thrilling story of the Israelite march from Egyptian slavery to the land of freedom, the ancient Jews emphasized the importance of democracy. The words of Moses, "Proclaim ye liberty throughout the land to all the inhabitants thereof," was inscribed on the American Liberty Bell.

The ancient Jews were ruled by kings. Saul, the first king, was succeeded by David, and by David's son Solomon. King David, who was a shepherd as a boy, wrote some of the great Psalms of the Bible, the best-known of which begins with the words, "The Lord is my Shepherd, I shall not want." He also made Jerusalem the capital city, as it is today.

King Solomon built the first great Temple in Jerusalem, a beautiful house of God that stood on Mount Zion for many centuries. During the days of this first Temple, the Jewish people faced many difficult times. They were surrounded by mighty empires, whose armies constantly invaded Israel. They were not always faithful to their religion.

It was in these days of war and evil doings that the great prophets of Israel taught and preached. These prophets were not fortunetellers. They were men inspired by visions of God's love for mankind. Isaiah taught the lesson of peace on earth, predicting that some day men would not use arms against one another. Amos preached justice; Hosea reminded his people that God was forgiving; Malachi declared that all men were brothers because "have we not all One Father, has not One God created us all?"

Other important prophets included Jeremiah, Micah, and Ezekiel. These ancient teachers gave the world an understanding of God and His love for man through their addresses to the Jewish people, which are recorded in the Old Testament in what are called the Prophetic Books of the Bible.

The first Temple was destroyed in the year 586 B.C., but a new one was built seventy years later. However, many of the Jews settled in other countries, especially in Babylonia and Egypt. When the Romans destroyed the second Temple in 70 A.D., Jews moved to many lands. In place of the destroyed Temple, they built synagogues and houses of learning. These schools were organized by rabbis (meaning teachers). The outstanding rabbi of the ancient world was Hillel, who lived in Jesus' time. When asked about the Jewish religion, Hillel replied: "All of Judaism can be summed up in one sentence, Love thy neighbor as thyself, all the rest is commentary."

Out of Judaism grew two of the great historic religions, Christianity and Mohammedanism.

During the next centuries, Jews settled in Italy, France, Germany, North Africa, and Arabia. All the Jews not living in the homeland were called the *Diaspora,* which means "a scattering." They maintained their religion intact by emphasizing home life and family ties. Judaism came to be very largely a religion of the home and the synagogue school.

MODERN DEVELOPMENTS

In modern times, the Jewish religion developed into several branches. Reform Judaism began in Germany in the 1840s and spread to the United States and Canada.

Reform Jews believe that some of the ancient laws should be changed to fit the times. They are not so strict in observance of the Sabbath and the dietary laws mentioned in the Bible. They also believe that women should have a larger share in synagogue worship.

Orthodox Jews accept all the ancient laws, and are opposed to changes. Conservative Jews believe in some changes, but not as extremely as does the Reform group. Orthodox and Conservative Jews wear a head-covering at prayer; Reform Jews do not.

About a hundred years ago, many Jews began to work for the rebuilding of a Jewish homeland in Palestine. This movement was known as Zionism. In 1948, as a result of their efforts, the new state of Israel was born, and by 1962 almost two million Jews had settled there.

CUSTOMS AND CEREMONIES

The Jewish religion makes much use of rituals, or ceremonies, that dramatize

and make vivid a great ideal. For example, each of the holy days carries a moral lesson. *Passover,* celebrated every spring for a period of eight days, is the symbol of liberty, recalling the march to freedom of the ancient Israelites from Egyptian slavery. *Shevuoth,* in June, commemorates the giving of the Ten Commandments. *Rosh Hashanah,* the New Year, observed in September or October, when the ram's horn or *Shofar* is blown, is the time for examining one's deeds of the past twelve months, and resolving to live a better life. Nine days later, *Yom Kippur,* the Day of Atonement, is a solemn period for asking God's forgiveness. *Hanukkah,* in December, is the Feast of Lights. For eight days, candles are lit in reminder of the battle for religious freedom in ancient Palestine.

The Sabbath, too, which Jews observe from Friday at sundown until Saturday at sundown, has many rituals such as candle-lighting and a wine ceremony called *Kiddush.*

There are many family ceremonies. When a Jewish boy is born, he undergoes the rite of circumcision on the eighth day. On his thirteenth birthday, he celebrates his *Bar Mitzvah*—that is, his coming of age as a member of the congregation. Today the *Bas Mitzvah* ceremony has been added for girls. In their fifteenth or sixteenth year, Jewish boys and girls participate in a Confirmation ceremony, held in the synagogue at the *Shevuoth* festival in June.

Marriage is considered a sacrament. The wedding ritual includes a bridal canopy, a ring, and a cup of wine that the groom and bride sip together.

Mourning is observed elaborately. The immediate family remains at home for a week in a ritual called *Shivah,* which means seven days. A special prayer is recited for eleven months. It is called the *Kaddish,* and expresses the thought that God is just and man should trust in all His acts.

There are separate articles about the important ceremonies and holidays.

PERSECUTION OF THE JEWS

For many centuries the Jews suffered a great deal. They were always a minority, which means that they were smaller in numbers than other groups, and minorities are apt to be treated harshly by members of majority, or larger, groups. The Jews were not allowed equal privileges with other people for many years in most of the countries in which they settled. Sometimes they were forced to live in separate sections, called *ghettos,* and could only do certain kinds of work. Sometimes they were forbidden to settle in certain countries, or were forced out of countries in which they had settled. Gradually the Jews were given equal rights in most countries. The most recent, and the most terrible, persecution of the Jews occurred before and during World War II, when the German Nazis, led by Adolf Hitler, killed millions of Jews and drove millions of others from their homes to refuge in other lands.

jew's-harp

The jew's-harp is a small musical instrument. It has a little metal frame, usually shaped like a horseshoe, which the player puts between his front teeth. In the middle of this frame is a metal tongue, which the player hits with his fingers. He can change the sound or make it louder or softer by opening or closing his mouth.

The jew's-harp has been played for centuries in Asia and Europe. It has been given many different names, such as "buzzing iron," "mouth drum," "children's trumpet," and "drive-away-thought." Although children play it most frequently now, it was used by serious musicians in Germany and England about 150 years ago. They could make pleasing and varied music by playing several jew's-harps of different sizes at the same time.

jimson weed

The jimson weed is a coarse, poisonous plant. It first grew in the tropical (very hot) parts of the world, and spread to many parts of Europe and the United States.

The plant has broad leaves and large white or purple flowers that are shaped like trumpets. The fruit is prickly, and the plant has an unpleasant odor. The jimson weed, especially in its seeds, contains a drug called *stramonium.* This drug is smoked in a powdered form to relieve asthma. It is also a narcotic that can make a person sleep and have strange dreams.

The jimson weed is sometimes called the "Jamestown weed" because soldiers in Jamestown, Virginia, in the days of the early settlers of America more than three hundred years ago, ate the weed. It made them behave in strange ways.

jinrikisha

A jinrikisha is a small car with two wheels and with two long poles in front. These poles are pulled by one or more men. Pulling a jinrikisha is hard work, but the men who pull them are able to trot along between the poles for long hours every day, with one or two riders in the car. The jinrikisha was invented in Japan and has been used in various parts of Asia and Africa, especially in China. The inventor was not Japanese but an American, Jonathan Goble, a Baptist missionary. Since people in Asia do not have many automobiles, the jinrikisha is used there much as a taxicab is used in other countries. It is also called a *rickshaw.*

Joan of Arc

Joan of Arc was a young French heroine whose courage and daring gave inspiration to all France in its fight against the English. This was more than five hundred years ago, when the English kings claimed to be the rightful rulers of France. By 1422, the English had overrun most of northern France, including Paris, and they were attacking the city of Orléans. The Duke of Orléans fought bravely, although many French dukes were on the side of the English. But no help came to him. The old king of France died, and his son Charles was a coward who wanted to hunt and dance, not to fight wars. Just when the country was losing heart, when people felt they would never find a leader to help them fight the English, Joan of Arc appeared.

Joan was born in 1412 in a small town in France called Domrémy. In French, her name was Jeanne d'Arc. She was a peasant girl and spent her days spinning or caring for the sheep. She did not know how to read or write, but she was deeply religious and had a great love for France.

When she was 13 she started hearing voices that told her that one day she would lead France against the English. She said nothing about the voices for three years, but finally, when she was 16, she decided to obey them. She went to Vaucouleurs and persuaded the king's captain to take her to see Charles, who was called the *Dauphin,* or crown prince. At first everyone laughed at this peasant girl who had never even ridden a horse and who wanted to lead troops in battle, but she finally convinced them all, even the weak and frightened Charles.

Sitting on a fine black horse, dressed in white armor and carrying a white banner, she led an army of twelve thousand men to save the city of Orleans. She was always in the thick of the fighting, and her words of encouragement and her earnest and brave spirit led the French to victory. Then she led an army to Rheims, capturing forts and towns on the way and making it safe for Charles to follow. At Rheims he was at last crowned king.

Charles was never brave enough to help Joan fight, but he did persuade her to go on fighting for France. Finally she was captured by a French duke who was fighting for England. Heartsick, John learned that Charles would not help her. Instead, the English paid the duke to deliver her to them. They hoped to discourage France by killing Joan, and so they took her to Rouen, where a church court declared that she was a witch and must die. On May 30, 1431, dressed in flowing robes, she was led to the square of Rouen. Joan never lost her courage, even when she stood at the stake and watched the flames leap up at her. She clutched a cross and murmured the name of Jesus.

The world has never forgotten the heroism of Joan, the "Maid of Orleans". Three hundred years after her death, the Catholic Church proclaimed her a saint, and the brave, simple peasant girl had become Saint Joan.

Job

Job was a man whose story is told in the Book of Job, in the Old Testament of the Bible. Job lived in the land of Uz. He loved and feared God. He was a rich man and a happy man. He had seven sons and three daughters whom he loved.

God was pleased with Job because Job loved him, but Satan, the devil, said that Job loved God only because God had been so good to him. Satan said that Job would hate God if he were unhappy.

To prove to Satan that Job was a man who would always love God, no matter what, God sent great trouble to Job. All of Job's cattle were stolen, his servants destroyed, and his children killed. Job himself was given a horrible and painful skin disease.

Job's wife urged him to say that God was evil, but he would not. He prayed to God to tell him why these things had happened to him, and he argued with his friends about the reason for his troubles. For a short time Job doubted the goodness of God, but he repented and God forgave him. At the end of Job's life, God gave Job more than he had ever had

before, as a reward for his faith. Job lived happily for many years after that.

The writing in the Book of Job is considered by scholars to rank with the greatest poetry ever written.

Joffre, Joseph

Joseph Joffre was a French soldier and hero. He was born in 1852, and in 1914, when World War I broke out, he was the commander-in-chief of the French armies. He was the hero of the Battle of the Marne, the fighting along the Marne River when the German armies invaded France and almost captured Paris, its capital. The French under Joffre stopped this attack. But the war went badly for the French and Joffre was growing old, so he was replaced as commander-in-chief, and was made chairman of the joint war staff of the Allies (the nations fighting against Germany).

Joffre was very popular in France, where the people spoke of him as "Papa" Joffre. He became a marshal, the highest military rank. When Marshal Joffre visited the United States, in 1917, he was given an enthusiastic welcome. He died in 1931, when he was 79 years old.

Johannesburg

Johannesburg is the largest city in the Republic of South Africa. It is in the province of Transvaal. It is surrounded on three sides by the famous gold mines of the Witwatersrand, which are the richest gold mines in the world. The Witwatersrand (called the Rand Gold Reef) is a series of valleys and ridges about fifty miles long. When gold was discovered there in 1886, the Boers (Africans whose ancestors came from the Netherlands) began to build up the city. The city was named after Johannes Rissik, who planned it.

The climate of Johannesburg is mild, never too hot or too cold, though there is occasional snow in the winter. Sometimes there are strong winds that blow huge piles of white crushed matter from the mines about the city.

The people of Johannesburg have made it the educational and industrial center of South Africa. They have built colleges, including the University of Witwatersrand. Many of the people work in the gold mines; others make chemicals, explosives, iron and steel products, and textiles. Many tall buildings stand in the crowded city, but on the outskirts are fine brick or stone houses, with gardens and parks.

About two-thirds of the people who live in Johannesburg are African natives. Most of them are very poor. The native mineworkers who leave their homes to go to work in the mines for a few months out of the year live in quarters called "compounds," which are near the mines.

JOHANNESBURG, REPUBLIC OF SOUTH AFRICA. Population (1973 estimate) 1,309,-500. Gold and industrial center.

John, Saint

The most important Christian saint named John was an Apostle of Jesus. He was called St. John the Evangelist be-

cause he wrote one of the four Gospels, or accounts of the life of Jesus, in the New Testament. Other books of the Bible written by John are three Epistles, and the last book of the New Testament. This book is called the Revelation of St. John, or the APOCALYPSE, and there is a separate article about it. Here the author is called St. John the Divine, that is, the preacher.

John the Evangelist is sometimes called "the beloved disciple," because in one of the Gospels he is referred to as the disciple "whom Jesus loved." After Jesus' death, John became bishop of the city of Ephesus in Asia Minor. He is believed to have lived more than a hundred years. His feast day is December 27.

There are more than fifteen other saints named John. One of these is JOHN THE BAPTIST (see the next article).

John the Baptist

John the Baptist was the man who baptized Jesus. His story is told in the Bible, in the New Testament. He was born about the same year as Jesus. John was the son of Zacharias and Elisabeth, who was a cousin of Mary, the mother of Jesus. When he was grown he lived in the wilderness and baptized people in the River Jordan. People came to the river from long distances to hear his preaching. He wore rough clothing and ate nothing but locusts (a kind of grasshopper) and honey. It is said that he foretold the coming of Jesus. Jesus did come and was baptized by John.

At that time the king of the Jews was a man named Herod. Herod had married his brother's wife, Herodias. John went to Herod and told him that this was sinful. Herod threw John into prison. Herodias was very angry and demanded that John be killed, but Herod could not have John killed without greatly offending the people. Then Herodias's daughter, Salome, danced for Herod, and in return he promised to give her anything she wished. Obeying her mother, she asked for John's head. Herod had John killed and his head was brought to Salome. There is a separate article about SALOME.

John XXIII

John XXIII was Pope, or leader on earth of the Roman Catholic Church, from October 28, 1959, when he was elected, until his death June 3, 1963. Though he was the twenty-third Pope John, he was the first Pope to adopt that name since the year 1334.

John XXIII was born near Bergamo, Italy, November 25, 1881. His name was Angelo Giuseppe Roncalli and his parents were farm workers. He was ordained a priest in 1904 and, being an outstanding scholar, he was appointed to several important secretarial and diplomatic positions before he became an archbishop in 1925 and a cardinal in 1953. He was one of the most friendly and informal Popes of history, making many ppearances at schools, hospitals, and other public places; he was called "the Pope who always smiles." History will remember him for the ecumenical councils (meetings of high church officials) he assembled in 1962 and 1963, in an effort to bring all Christians closer together. He died during

the 1963 session.

John, King of England

John was a selfish, tyrannical, and unpopular English king. He was born about 1167. He first got power during the absence of his older brother, King Richard I (called the Lion-Hearted), who had gone off to Palestine on one of the Crusades. John tried to have himself made king but Richard returned safely and John had to wait.

John finally became king upon Richard's death in 1199, but his rule was a very bad one. He punished people who opposed him and showed no gratitude to those who supported him. Finally the nobles took action against him and in June 1215 forced him to sign the MAGNA CARTA, about which there is a separate article, guaranteeing them personal rights that no king since John's time has ever been able to take away. John died in 1216.

Johns Hopkins University

Johns Hopkins University is in Baltimore, Maryland. In 1876 a merchant in Baltimore named Johns Hopkins gave seven million dollars to found a college and hospital. In 1893 the Johns Hopkins Medical School offered its first courses, and no other medical school has ever had a better reputation.

Since then the university has opened schools of engineering, business, public health, and industrial relations (the study of how employees and their employers can best work together). In Washington, D.C., Johns Hopkins University has a branch called the School of Advanced International Studies.

About 7,000 men and women attend Johns Hopkins University.

Andrew Johnson

Andrew Johnson was the seventeenth President of the United States. He was Vice President under Abraham Lincoln and succeeded to office after the assassination of Lincoln in April, 1865. He served until March 4, 1869. Andrew Johnson had more opposition from the Congress than any other President before or since. He was the only President that Congress ever impeached (tried to put out of office by charging him with wrong behavior).

Johnson was a self-made man, and since his death it has been concluded that he was a badly misjudged and misunderstood man. Historians have found that the people of Johnson's day, who had suffered through the Civil War, were unfair to him. Johnson was innocent of the flimsy charges on which he was impeached, and even a hostile Congress was unable to obtain a two-thirds majority of the votes, which was needed for conviction.

HIS EARLY YEARS

Andrew Johnson was born of poor parents in Raleigh, North Carolina, on December 29, 1808. He did not even go to school, but managed to learn how to read and write through his own efforts. His father apprenticed him to a tailor when he was only 10 years old. He was the second President who rose from a tailor's apprenticeship to the highest office in the land. The other was Millard Fillmore. Andrew ran away from his apprenticeship when he was 18 years old, and went to live in Greenville, Tennessee.

There Johnson entered politics before he was 21. He married Miss Eliza McCardle, an intelligent young woman who realized the importance of education, and helped her husband to learn and study while raising a family. They had five children, three sons and two daughters.

Johnson's first political office was alderman of Greenville, and he rose gradually to become governor of the state of Tennessee. From this office, his next stop was membership in the National House of Representatives, and finally in the United States Senate. Johnson was a firm supporter of the interests of men who owned small farms. He opposed large plantation owners on many points. He was not opposed to slavery. He believed in allowing settlers of the West to have free land, and he wanted the United States to expand its territory as much as possible.

During the time Johnson was in the Senate as a member from Tennessee, that state seceded from the Union. Johnson refused to give up his seat in the Senate to join the Confederacy. He was opposed to secession and remained loyal to the Union throughout the Civil War. While the war was still going on, President Lincoln appointed Senator Johnson military governor of Tennessee. While Johnson was serving in that office, he set up complete plans for a non-military government of the state when the war should be over.

HOW HE BECAME PRESIDENT

In the fall of 1863 and the following spring of 1864, the Union forces under General Grant made great progress toward winning the war. In 1864 the people re-elected Lincoln. Andrew Johnson, a Democrat, had been made the candidate for Vice President, though Lincoln was a Republican. The purpose of this was to win the votes of both northern Democrats and southerners from states that had not left the Union. The party was called the Union Party.

One month and ten days after Lincoln's second inauguration as President he was assassinated, and on April 15, 1865, Andrew Johnson became President, to fill out the remainder of Lincoln's term. The Civil War had been over less than a week, and the postwar period was an extremely difficult one.

President Johnson, a Democrat and a southerner, had to deal with a Congress that was almost entirely Republican. The members of Congress did everything in their power to make Johnson's job difficult for him. Almost everything he proposed for repairing damages in the war-ravaged South was violently opposed. Johnson believed that the South should be given every chance to get back on its feet, as Lincoln had also believed.

In May, 1865, Johnson signed a broad proclamation. It restored the civil rights of all members of the Confederacy except certain leaders, on the condition that the states would ratify the 13th Amendment to the Constitution, give Negroes full rights of citizenship, and pledge their allegiance to the United States. But Congress was angry because the southern states refused to allow Negroes to vote, and representatives of southern states were not allowed to take their seats in the Senate and House. This angered Johnson, and he was further irritated by a law passed by Congress. This was called the "Tenure of Office Act," and it stated that the President could not remove from office any official who had been appointed or approved by Congress. Johnson wanted to dismiss the Secretary of War, Edwin M. Stanton, with whom he disagreed, and he decided to test the legality of the Act. He dismissed Stanton, and for this the House of Representatives impeached him (accused him of improper conduct and caused him to be tried by the Senate). The charges were flimsy, and the evidence was even flimsier. Under the Constitution, Johnson could be convicted only if two-thirds of the Senators voted against him. The count was 35 to 19, just one vote short of two-thirds, and Johnson was pronounced "Not guilty."

After Johnson's term was over he went back to Tennessee. He continued to fight for the measures helping the South that he had tried to have passed while he was President. In 1874 he was elected to the United States Senate, the only former President ever to serve in the Senate, but he had served only a few months when he died on July 31, 1875. He was buried in Greenville, Tennessee, and the little log cabin where he once worked as a tailor is now a museum, open to the public.

MRS. ANDREW JOHNSON

Eliza McCardle Johnson was born in Leesburg, Tennessee, in 1810. She was an invalid while her husband was President and her daughter Martha, one of their five children, served as White House hostess. Mrs. Johnson died in 1876.

Lyndon B. Johnson

Lyndon Baines Johnson became in 1963, after the assassination of John Fitzgerald Kennedy, the 36th President of the United States. He was the seventh Vice President to succeed to the presidency, and the fourth to reach that office as a result of the assassination of his predecessor. In his first public statement after becoming President, Johnson said, "I know the world shares the sorrow that Mrs. Kennedy and her family

bear. I will do my best. That is all I can do. I ask for your help—and God's." Later, while addressing Congress, Johnson pledged himself to continue the policies of the late President Kennedy. "This is our challenge — not to hesitate, not to pause, not to turn about and linger over this evil moment, but to continue on our course so that we may fulfill the destiny that history has set for us."

HIS EARLY YEARS

Lyndon Baines Johnson was born at Johnson City, Texas, on August 27th, 1908. His family was far from well-to-do. When he was nine years old, Lyndon Johnson worked as a shoe-shine boy in a Johnson City barber shop. But that did not interfere with his studies. He graduated from high school at the exceptionally young age of fifteen. Following his graduation, Johnson felt he should support himself. He worked first on a road-building gang; later, he had jobs as an elevator operator and a car washer. He regretted having discontinued his education, however, and many years later told an interviewer: "It became increasingly apparent to me that there was something to this idea of higher education."

In 1930 he graduated from Texas State Teachers College and for a brief period was a teacher of speech and debating in a Houston high school. Politics had greater appeal for him, however, and in 1931 he became secretary to a Texas congressman. In 1934 he met Claudia Alta (Lady Bird) Taylor. They were married within two months.

President Franklin Delano Roosevelt was impressed by the young congressional assistant and, in 1935, appointed him Texas state administrator of the National Youth Administration, whose purpose was bettering the economic opportunities of young people. Two years later, in 1937, after earning a reputation for great effectiveness as an administrator, Lyndon Johnson ran for Congress on the Democratic ticket and defeated nine other candidates.

World War II interrupted Johnson's career in Congress. A member of the Naval Reserve, he was called up by the U.S. Navy, and was the first member of Congress to enter active duty during World War II. He was awarded the Silver Star for gallantry in action during a flight over Japanese positions in

New Guinea. A year later, President Roosevelt ordered all congressmen serving in the armed forces to return to Congress. Johnson left the Navy as a lieutenant commander.

Johnson remained a Representative, until, in 1948, he ran for the U.S. Senate against a conservative politician who was then governor of Texas. Johnson won by less than one hundred votes. He rose rapidly to a position of power within the Senate. Four years after entering the Senate, Johnson, at the age of 44, became the Democratic leader of the Senate, the youngest man ever to take that post. As leader, Johnson was a Democrat serving under a Republican President, Dwight D. Eisenhower. Because of his skill in leading the Senate, many people regarded him as the second-most-powerful man in the United States.

HOW HE BECAME PRESIDENT

In 1960, Lyndon Johnson was nominated by the Democratic Party for the office of the Vice President of the United States. He had tried to obtain the Democratic nomination for President. John F. Kennedy won that nomination, however. To the surprise of many, who thought that the two men had become political enemies, Johnson, on the urging of Kennedy, accepted the nomination for the office of Vice President. Kennedy was elected in 1960, and Johnson became Vice President.

Johnson used his high office to become a politician of national importance. As Vice President he served on the National Security Council, the National Aeronautics and Space Council, the committee that advised the Peace Corps, and the President's Committee on Equal Employment Opportunity. While Vice President, Johnson traveled throughout the world, meeting leaders of other nations and learning about the problems that concerned the peoples of the various parts of the world.

When in 1963 an assassin's bullet struck down President Kennedy, Johnson was well prepared to assume the office. He followed the policies in which he had supported F. D. Roosevelt, Truman, and Kennedy. He advocated closer relations with other nations and strong armed forces to restrain communism. In domestic policy he favored medical care for the aged, federal aid to public schools, higher minimum wages for labor, government supports for farm prices, public power projects such as the TVA, and efforts to explore space.

As a senator Johnson had already steered through Congress the first important civil rights law in 75 years. In 1964, in his first year as President, Johnson persuaded Congress to pass an even stronger civil rights law. See the article CIVIL RIGHTS.

By the time he decided not to seek reelection in 1968, Johnson had become known for his support of strong civil rights laws, especially those which would prevent discrimination against Negroes in matters concerning their rights to vote and to rent or buy houses. President Johnson had also become known for using United States armed forces to combat the spread of Communism in the Dominican Republic and in the Republic of South Vietnam.

His attempts to end the fighting between North and South Vietnam were probably his most difficult tasks. He died on January 22, 1973.

MRS. LYNDON JOHNSON

Claudia Alta Taylor (Lady Bird) Johnson, the wife of Lyndon B. Johnson, was born at Karnack, Texas, in 1912. While she was a little girl, a servant said, "Why she's as pretty as a lady bird!" From that time on she was called *Lady Bird* by her family and friends. She graduated from the University of Texas in 1934 and married Lyndon B. Johnson in the same year. She soon became a valued adviser to her husband. At the same time, she entered various fields of business and, by the time her husband became President, had amassed for herself several million dollars. Two children were born to the Johnsons, Lynda Bird and Lucy Baines.

Johnson, Jack

Jack Johnson was heavyweight boxing champion of the world from 1908 to 1915, the first Negro to hold that title. He was born in Galveston, Texas, in 1878, and began boxing in 1899. In 1908 he knocked out Tommy Burns, the champion, in Sydney, Australia. Then he met Jim Jeffries, the former champion, who had retired, and knocked him out at Reno, Nevada, on July 4, 1910. Johnson held the title for five years more. He lost it to Jess Willard at Havana, Cuba, in 1915. Johnson died in an automobile accident in 1946.

Johnson, Samuel

Dr. Samuel Johnson was an English writer who lived about two hundred years ago. He wrote a very famous dictionary and many poems and books. He is most important for the influence he had on other writers and on the English language.

Until Johnson's time there had been no accepted rules for English spelling. Most of the spellings and meanings adopted by Dr. Johnson for his dictionary became standard.

Samuel Johnson was a big man and had a loud voice. He was often thought rude by people who met him. But he set up the standards for writing in his day and many people speak of his time as the "Age of Johnson." Johnson is described in a famous biography written by James Boswell; more people read Boswell's *Life of Johnson* than read Johnson's own work.

Samuel Johnson was born in 1709 and died in 1784. He was very poor as a young man and suffered many disappointments. At that time in England it was the custom for a rich nobleman to become the patron, which means financial helper, of a poor struggling writer. Early in his career Johnson tried to get help from the Earl of Chesterfield but received none. Later, when Johnson had become famous for his dictionary, the Earl of Chesterfield praised his work but Johnson refused Chesterfield's patronage in a famous letter.

Johnson, Walter

Walter Johnson was a great pitcher

in baseball. He could throw a baseball faster than any other pitcher. He was born at Humboldt, Kansas, in 1887, and from 1907 to 1927 he pitched for the Washington Senators. Though Washington usually had a very poor team, Johnson won as many as 36 games in a season and set several records. Johnson managed baseball clubs for a few years and became active in politics, in Maryland. He died in 1946.

Johnston, Albert Sidney

Albert Sidney Johnston was a Confederate general in the Civil War. Johnston was born in Kentucky in 1803. He graduated from the United States Military Academy at West Point in 1826. After fighting in the Black Hawk War, he left the United States Army to lead the forces fighting for the independence of Texas. When Texas became a republic, Johnston became its Secretary of War. Johnston later served the United States in the Mexican War. When the Civil War broke out, Johnston joined the Confederate forces and was made commander of the armies in the west. He was killed at the Battle of Shiloh in 1862, where he led an army of 40,000 men against the forces of General Grant.

Johnston, Joseph E.

Joseph Eggleston Johnston was a Confederate general in the Civil War. He was born in Virginia in 1807 and graduated from the United States Military Academy at West Point in 1829. In the United States Army he led campaigns against the Florida Indians and fought in the Mexican War. In the Confederate battle of Bull Run, which the Confederacy won. He was wounded at the battle of Fair Oaks in Virginia. He was the last Confederate general to surrender, in 1865. In later years Johnston served in Congress as a Representative from Virginia. He died in 1891.

Johnstown

Johnstown is a city in southwestern Pennsylvania. More than 42,000 people live there. Most of them work in coal mines in the region, or in steel mills and chemical, brick and lumber plants.

One of the worst floods in history occurred in Johnstown in 1889. After very heavy rains, a weak dam, 12 miles above the city, burst, releasing the water from Conemaugh Lake. The swirling flood waters completely submerged the city. More than two thousand people were drowned and $10,000,000 worth of property was destroyed. The city was rebuilt but in 1936 Johnstown had another flood, in which eight persons were drowned. Since then engineers have completed a program of flood control.

JOHNSTOWN, PENNSYLVANIA. Population (1970 census) 42,476. On the Conemaugh River. Settled in 1791.

joint

A joint is any place in the human body where two bones meet. A joint is sometimes called an *articulation*. Some bones meet in joints that cannot be moved at all, such as a tooth in the jaw. Other joints can be moved only slightly, such as the vertebrae in the spine.

The joints that we can move freely are usually divided into three groups. First, there are the joints known as *hinges,* which can move backward and forward in just one direction. The knee and the fingers are examples of hinge joints. A second group, called *pivots,* can be turned around in a circular fashion, such as the ankle and the wrist. The third kind of joint is known as the *ball-and-socket.* A round end of one bone fits into a hollow depression in another bone. Examples are the joints in shoulders and hips.

The ends of all the bones that move in joints are protected by a substance called *cartilage* or *gristle.* This is a smooth, elastic material that protects the bones from sudden jolts. The hollows between bones at joints are filled with a liquid called *synovial fluid,* which keeps the ends of the bones moist and lubricated. Bones that meet at a joint are fastened together by strong, flexible bands of tissue known as *ligaments.* If you tear or stretch one of these ligaments, it is a *sprain.* If the small end of one of the bones in a ball-and-socket joint slips out of the socket, it is a *dislocation.* These are painful injuries. Some diseases, such as arthritis, gout, and rheumatic fever, cause the joints to become sore or inflamed.

Joliet, Louis

Louis Joliet, a French-Canadian born in Canada in 1645, was a great explorer. With Father Marquette, another great explorer, he found and explored the northern Mississippi River, the territory around Lake Michigan, and other lakes and rivers. While Joliet was on his way home to Quebec his canoe overturned and he lost his written records, but his memory was so good that he could write most of them again. He did much more exploring in Canada. The city of Joliet, Illinois, is named for him. He died in 1700.

Jolson, Al

Al Jolson was for many years, from about 1920 to 1934, the most popular American singing entertainer on the stage, and he made the first talking picture *(The Jazz Singer,* 1928) and was a star in radio. His real name was Asa Yoelson and he was born in Russia in 1888 but was brought to America as a child. He made his first big success as a "blackface comedian" (see the article on the MINSTREL SHOW) 'with a song, still famous, called "Mammy." He died, rich and famous, in 1950.

Jonah

Jonah is the name of a book in the Old Testament of the Bible. It tells the story of Jonah, a Hebrew prophet who lived about eight hundred years before the birth of Christ. Jonah himself did not write the book. It was written hundreds of years after his death.

According to the book, Jonah disobeyed God and then tried to run away from Him. He went to sea, but God caused a great storm to come up. The sailors threw Jonah overboard so that God would end the storm. Jonah was swallowed whole by a big fish, and was inside the fish for three days and nights, praying for God's forgiveness. Because he was sorry that he had disobeyed God, Jonah was forgiven and God caused the fish to cast him up on dry land. People

usually speak of "Jonah and the whale," because the whale is the biggest animal in the sea, but the Bible does not mention a whale or any particular kind of fish.

Jonathan, the son of Saul in the Bible, who had a great friendship with David: see the article on DAVID.

Jones, Bobby

Robert Tyre Jones was the greatest golf player of the 1920s and 1930s. He was born in Atlanta, Georgia, in 1902, and studied to be a lawyer. Before he was 18 years old he was recognized as one of the finest golfers in the world. He remained an amateur throughout his career and was the only amateur in history who was always considered better than the best professionals. In 1930, Bobby Jones won all four of the biggest tournaments of the world, the British amateur and open and the United States amateur and open championships. It is the only time this feat, called "the grand slam," has been accomplished. After 1930 Jones retired from tournament play.

Jones, John Paul

John Paul Jones was the first and one of the greatest American naval heroes.

He was born in Scotland in 1747, and he became a sailor at an early age. In his youth he was first mate on a ship trading slaves and killed a man in self-defense during a

Gale Research Co. mutiny. He escaped to the American colonies, took the name Jones (he was born simply John Paul), and decided to help in the fight for American independence. He was given command of a ship, the *Ranger.*

Instead of waiting in American waters for a British warship to appear, Jones went to attack British ships in their own waters. He knew the British coast well, and captured the first British ship ever to be taken by an American man-of-war.

His next ship was the *Bonhomme Richard,* named to honor Benjamin Franklin, who sometimes wrote under the name "Poor Richard." It was in the *Bonhomme Richard* that John Paul Jones fought his most famous battle. In 1779, off the coast of England, he met the English ship *Serapis* early one evening. The *Serapis* was much larger than Jones' vessel and inflicted serious damage on it. When the *Bonhomme Richard* was sinking, the British admiral asked if Jones had had enough. But John Paul Jones answered stubbornly: "Sir, I have not yet begun to fight." Jones then fought his way onto the British ship, which he took over, letting his own ship sink.

After this great victory John Paul Jones became a hero in France, but the United States did not recognize his courage and military genius until much later. After the American states had won their independence, Jones served for a time in the Russian navy and won great battles for them in their war with Turkey. He died in Paris in 1792.

In 1905, the American minister to France found the grave of John Paul Jones and had his remains brought back to America. His body is now at the United

States Naval Academy at Annapolis, Maryland.

jonquil

The jonquil is a graceful yellow or white flower of the narcissus family. It grows in the warm climate of Central Europe near the Mediterranean Sea. In the United States and Canada it is best to grow jonquils in flowerpots indoors, though they will do well in gardens that get lots of sun. A jonquil bulb, which looks like an onion, is planted, and from it grow long narrow leaves. The flower part is a lovely cup surrounded by petals.

Jonson, Ben

Ben Jonson was one of the greatest of the English poets. We remember him

most for a few of his beautiful lyrics, especially the one called "To Celia," which begins: "Drink to me only with thine eyes."

Jonson was born in

National Portrait Gallery, London 1572. His stepfather was a bricklayer, and as a young man Jonson also was a bricklayer. Then he became an actor, before he started to write successful plays and poems. Among the most famous of his plays are *Every Man In His Humour, Volpone,* and *The Alchemist.*

During the years when he was most successful as a writer, Jonson was the leader of a group of younger poets and playwrights called the "Tribe of Ben." Jonson belonged to the group of writers that included William Shakespeare, and when Shakespeare died Jonson wrote a poem in his honor.

Ben Jonson died in 1637 and was buried in Westminster Abbey, where many great men are buried. The inscription over his tomb reads: *O rare Ben Jonson.* Scholars still do not know if this meant that Jonson was a rare poet, or if an ignorant stonecutter meant: "Pray for Ben Jonson." *Orare* in the Latin language means "to pray."

Jordan

Jordan is a country in the southwestern part of Asia. It has an area of 37,234 square miles, which is a little larger than the state of Indiana. Over two million people live in Jordan, far fewer than the five million who live in Indiana. The capital is Amman, a city of about 500,000.

Jordan was once called *Transjordan,* which means "across the Jordan," because it was separated from the country of Palestine by the JORDAN RIVER. The official name of the country is the Hashemite Kingdom of Jordan.

THE PEOPLE OF JORDAN

The people who live in Jordan are Arabs. Many of them are Bedouins, or wanderers, who do not have any permanent homes but travel from one place to another. They are shepherds and they move about in search of better pastures.

The people who live in the western part of the country are farmers. They grow wheat and barley and grapes, and many of them raise cattle. A few people work in factories, where they make soap, cloth, olive oil, and tobacco products. Almost all of the people are Moslems

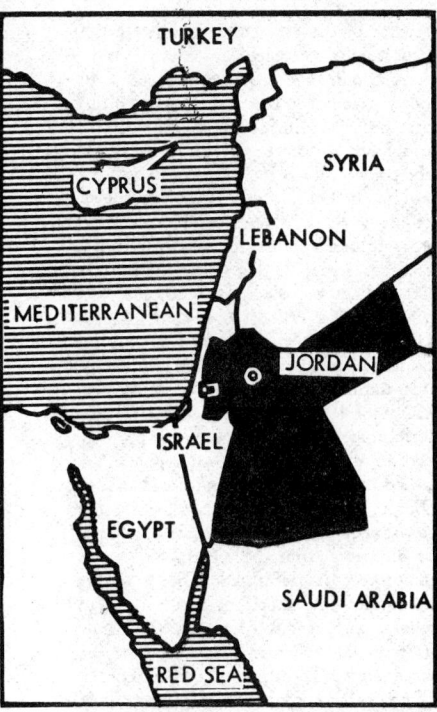

and follow the Mohammedan religion. They speak the Arabic language.

WHAT THE COUNTRY IS LIKE

Most of Jordan is desert land, with many hills and rugged mountains. There is very little rain. In the summer the days are hot but the nights are chilly. The winters are cool, and often there is snow on the mountains and plains. The western part of the country, near the Jordan River, is more fertile. Here the people are farmers, and some of them mine salt and other minerals found near the Dead Sea.

The people of Jordan work hard to irrigate their land, so that more crops will grow, and to develop new mines. They are proud of their good new highways and their railroad. Travelers now can go from Amman, the capital city, to many parts of Jordan, and to the neighboring country of Syria, by train.

HOW THE PEOPLE ARE GOVERNED

Jordan is a constitutional monarchy, which means that it has a king, a parliament that makes the laws, and a written constitution that protects the rights of the people. King Hussein became king in 1953.

Jordan's senate is called the House of Notables. The thirty members of this senate are chosen by the king. The people elect sixty members of the House of Representatives.

JORDAN IN THE PAST

Jordan is an old and important land. It is mentioned often in the Bible. The Children of Israel were led out of Jordan into the Promised Land (Palestine).

Many different peoples have ruled the land that is now Jordan. The ancient Greeks, Romans, and Egyptians all occupied this land at various times. About 450 years ago the country came under the control of the Ottoman Turks and it was part of Turkey until after World War I.

Then Jordan was controlled by the British until its independence in 1946.

Jordan's government opposed the formation of the new republic of Israel in 1948 and there is still some fighting along the Israeli-Jordan border, but not so much since 1950, when peace was made and the city of Jerusalem was divided between the two countries. In 1958, Jordan joined Iraq in the ARAB FEDERATION, but in less than a year, a revolution overthrew the government of Iraq and ended the alliance. In 1967, Jordan was defeated by Israel on the fourth day of a six-day war. See the article on ISRAEL.

JORDAN. Area, 37,500 square miles. Population (1973 estimate) 2,380,000. Language, Arabic. Religion, Mohammedan. Government, constitutional monarchy. Monetary unit, the Jordan dinar, worth $2.80 (U.S.). Flag, three horizontal bars, black, white, green; red triangle at staff with seven-pointed white star.

Jordan River

The Jordan is a very old and important river in Asia. There are many stories about the Jordan in the Bible. Jesus was baptized in the Jordan River.

The river rises in the mountains of Syria and Lebanon. It flows about 200 miles, runs through the Sea of Galilee, and finally empties into the Dead Sea. By the time it reaches the Dead Sea, it is 1,300 feet below sea level.

Few boats can travel down the Jordan River, because it is shallow and muddy and has many treacherous curves, but the Jordan is very useful to the people who live along its shores. Its waters irrigate their land. Since 1950 several dams and electric power plants have been built on the Jordan. When in 1963 Israel said it planned to take some of the Jordan's water for further irrigation, the nation of Jordan threatened war to prevent it.

Joseph

Joseph was a hero whose story is told in the Bible, in the Book of Genesis. The father of Joseph was Jacob, one of the great leaders of the Jewish people. Jacob had twelve sons, but he loved Joseph best. He gave Joseph a "coat of many colors," and this made Joseph's brothers jealous. The brothers were also jealous when Joseph had a dream that someday he would be more important than they were.

One day the older brothers were in the fields tending sheep and they saw Joseph coming toward them in his coat of many colors. They said, "Behold, this dreamer cometh." At first they planned to kill him, but they changed their minds and sold him as a slave to a group of merchants who were on their way to Egypt. The brothers soaked Joseph's coat of many colors in the blood of a lamb and took the coat to Jacob, telling him that Joseph had been killed by a wild animal.

Joseph was taken to Egypt and became the slave of Potiphar, who was an officer of Pharaoh, the ruler of Egypt. Joseph served Potiphar well, but he was put in prison because Potiphar's wife told lies about him. In prison Joseph met two of Pharaoh's servants and told them that he could explain the meanings of dreams.

Not long after this, Pharaoh had two dreams that troubled him. He heard about Joseph and sent for him.

Pharaoh had dreamed that seven fat cows were eaten by seven thin cows. Then he dreamed that seven good ears of corn had been eaten by seven thin ears of corn.

Joseph explained the dreams in this way: Egypt would have seven years of good crops, with enough food for everyone. Then Egypt would have seven years of famine, in which there would not be enough to eat. Joseph suggested to Pharaoh that he store food during the good years so there would be enough to eat in the bad years.

Pharaoh was very pleased with Joseph. He made Joseph the most important official in Egypt, next to himself. Joseph made all the farmers turn over part of the wheat they raised, and he stored it in great warehouses.

The famine arrived, as Joseph had said it would. In Egypt the people had enough to eat, because Joseph had stored the grain, but in neighboring countries the people were starving. Jacob's land did not have any food, so Jacob sent his sons (Joseph's brothers) to buy food in Egypt. At first Joseph did not let his brothers know who he was, and frightened them with threats, but finally he forgave them. He sent them to bring his father Jacob and his younger brother Benjamin to be with him in Egypt, and he gave food to all his family.

Joseph lived to be a very old man. He promised on his deathbed that someday the descendants of Jacob would return from Egypt to their homeland, Canaan (a part of Palestine). Many years afterward, this prophecy too came true.

Joseph, Saint

Joseph was the husband of Mary, the mother of Jesus. His story is told in the Gospels of Matthew and Luke, in the Bible. The Bible says God chose him to marry Mary because he was innocent and kind. Joseph was of the same family as David, the ancient king of Israel. He was a carpenter in the town of Nazareth, in Galilee, a part of Palestine. Joseph was with Mary when Jesus was born. He took her and the baby Jesus to Egypt to save them from King Herod's order that all Jewish boys under 2 years of age in Bethlehem and the surrounding country should be killed. God told Joseph in a vision when it was safe for his family to return to Palestine. Nothing is written of Joseph after Jesus was grown up, and he may have died in Jesus' boyhood. Joseph has been the patron saint of carpenters and woodworkers. St. Joseph's feast day is March 19.

See the articles on the Virgin MARY and on JESUS.

Josephine

Josephine was the first wife of Napoleon, who became emperor of France. For five years, from 1804 until 1809, Josephine had the title of empress of France. She was a beautiful, clever and popular woman, and she helped Napoleon a great deal in his rise to power.

Josephine was born in 1763 in Martinique, a French island in the West Indies. Her first husband, a nobleman named Alexandre de Beauharnais, was killed in the French Revolution. She had two children by this marriage, a son, Eugène, and a daughter, Hortense. Napoleon was fond of both these children and gave them important positions. Eugène de BEAUHARNAIS, about whom there is a

separate article, was a general in Napoleon's army and later became ruler of Italy. Hortense married Napoleon's brother and became Queen of Holland.

Napoleon and Josephine had no children of their own. Napoleon wanted a son who could become emperor of France when he died. He also wanted his son to have royal blood so that there would be no question of his right to be ruler of France. Napoleon himself did not have royal blood, and neither did Josephine. In 1809 Napoleon divorced Josephine so that he could marry Marie Louise, daughter of the empress of Austria. Josephine died five years later, in 1814.

Josephus

Flavius Josephus was a Jewish historian who was born in the year 37. His parents were noble, and Josephus grew up to be a powerful man in Judea. Once when some Jewish nobles were imprisoned in Rome, Josephus journeyed to ask the wicked Emperor Nero to set them free. He was impressed by the Roman power and learning. He went back to Jerusalem and joined a Jewish revolt against Rome, and even became a general in the war against the Romans, but after the war he moved to Rome and became a Roman citizen. He wrote a famous history of this Jewish war and also another book called *Antiquities of the Jews,* which tells Jewish history from the creation of the world to Josephus' own time. He died in the year 100.

Joshua

The story of Joshua is told in the Book of Joshua, in the Old Testament of the Bible. Joshua was a great prophet and was the leader of the Jews after Moses died. He was the son of one of Moses' advisers. Joshua, commanded by God, led the Jews to new lands across the River Jordan, and God stopped the waters of the river so they could cross on dry land.

Joshua was the leader who told the Jews how to capture the city of Jericho. He ordered seven priests carrying trumpets made of rams' horns to march around the city once each day for six days, and he had them followed by the Ark of the Covenant, the sacred chest in which the Ten Commandments of the Jews were kept. On the seventh day, the priests were told to march around the city seven times. On that day when the priests blew their trumpets, the people shouted, and the walls of the city of Jericho fell down. The Jews captured the city.

On another occasion Joshua commanded the sun to stand still so that the Jews would have time to defeat their enemies before it grew dark. The sun obeyed Joshua and the Jews won their battle.

Joshua tree, a plant that grows in the deserts of the southwestern part of the United States, and that looks like a huge cactus: see the article on YUCCA.

journalism

Journalism is the work of writing or editing for periodical publications. A periodical is reading matter that is published regularly under the same title, and not just once as a book is. Newspapers and magazines are periodicals. So are trade journals, which give news and other reading matter that will interest people in a certain line of work. Publicity, or public relations work, is a form of journalism.

Most often, journalism is thought of in connection with newspapers. There are several different kinds of journalistic work on a newspaper. Everything published in a newspaper (except the advertising) is classed as either news or features. A *reporter* writes news—stories of things that have just happened. A *feature writer* writes things that will teach or amuse or entertain the reader, even if it is not news. An *editor,* on a newspaper, is one of the executives, or managers. An *editorial writer* writes the editorials, articles in which the newspaper expresses the opinions of its publishers or editors. A *copyreader* actually edits (corrects) the news and feature stories, but he is not called an editor. The copyreader also writes the headlines that go over the news stories.

POLICY AND ETHICS

An honest newspaper or magazine, and an honest journalist who works for it, is supposed to follow certain "rules" in fairness to the readers. Very briefly, these are: Anything presented as news should be objective. That is, it should tell exactly what the facts are and should not express the opinion of the person who writes the story. Opinions are supposed to be expressed only in editorials and features, and even then, nothing should be stated as a fact unless it is true. It is all right for a newspaper to try to change the opinions of its readers, but it must not do so by telling them lies. Finally, there should be no advertising disguised as news. Reporters and copyreaders try to avoid mentioning commercial products in their news stories, and when an advertiser pays to have something published it should be obviously an advertisement. If it is printed in the same type as a news story, it should be marked with the word ADVERTISEMENT.

JOBS IN JOURNALISM

Usually, the first job a person gets on a newspaper is as a copy boy. (This job may be held by girls, too, and many girls have started newspaper work that way.) A copy boy runs errands. He carries "copy" (everything written for publication is called "copy") from the reporter to the copyreader and from the copyreader to the composing room, where the printing type is set. A copy boy learns a great deal. It is the best possible training for anyone who is interested in journalism.

A reporter must be able to write simply, so that any reader can immediately understand what he has written. A reporter must be able to typewrite at a fair rate of speed, but he does not have to be a scientific typist and his work does not have to look beautiful as a stenographer's letters must. A reporter should know a great deal about the city in which he works—how to get from one place to another, who the important people are, how the local government is run, and many other things. A reporter cannot be shy, because he must talk to complete strangers and ask them any questions at all if he thinks the answer will interest the readers of the newspaper or other publication he is writing for.

A copyreader has usually been a reporter. He has to be very good at spelling and punctuation. He has to know something about printing, because he marks the copy with instructions to the printers. He has to know the policy of the newspaper he works for—what kind of news its publisher wants to have published. Some newspapers like most to publish personal news, such as marriages and divorces and crimes and society news. Other newspapers like most to publish political news and other news of a serious nature. The copyreader must also know the laws about libel and other material that can cause a lawsuit.

The executives of a newspaper are called editors. The managing editor is in charge of everything that goes into the newspaper. The city editor is in charge of all news from the city in which the newspaper is published. The reporters are under his direction. He tells them what events to cover (report) and how to write about them. Most newspapers have telegraph editors who are in charge of news that comes in from out of town; the telegraph editor tells correspondents (out-of-town reporters) what events to cover and what length stories they should file (send by telegraph). Some newspapers have news editors who are in charge of all news.

There is a lot of difference between a metropolitan newspaper, published in a very big city, and a paper published in a smaller city. On the metropolitan paper, there are often "legmen" (outside reporters) who get the news and telephone it to *rewrite men* at the newspaper office. The rewrite man does the actual writing. Every reporter is likely to have a "beat," or a special type of news that he covers. On a small-city paper, a reporter gets the news and then goes to the office and writes it, and he is likely to cover any kind of story. Finally there is the "country weekly," a paper published once or twice a week in a very small place, and on this kind of newspaper everyone, including the editor, does every kind of work.

News magazines work very much as a metropolitan daily does. They have researchers who get the news and writers to write the articles.

Big newspapers and news magazines have offices in the capital of the country and in the capital of the state, province, or other division of the country, to cover political news. They also have *foreign correspondents* in other countries. Smaller newspapers depend on *news services,* which have these correspondents write a single story that is published in dozens or hundreds of different newspapers. The biggest American news services are the Associated Press, the United Press, and the International News Service.

Newspaper *syndicates* are companies that sell features to many different newspapers. Each newspaper may pay only a few dollars a week for a feature such as a comic strip or column of comment, but a hundred or more papers may use the same material and for that reason syndication is very profitable to a writer or artist.

Magazines have staffs of a different kind, because nearly everything pub-

lished in a magazine is bought from some writer who does not work for the magazine. The employees of a magazine are chiefly editors who select the stories and articles they want to publish, and other workers who are in charge of having it properly set in type and printed.

Every newspaper and magazine has special departments to take or get photographs and other illustrations.

TRAINING FOR JOURNALISM

There are more than thirty schools of journalism at which a student can get college training for journalistic work. Some of these schools accept only college graduates, but most of them accept high-school graduates and give a regular four-year college course. Students in schools of journalism usually put out a newspaper of their own, and they visit other newspapers to learn how the work is done professionally.

Almost all schools of journalism also offer courses in other kinds of writing, such as radio and television scripts. The first school of journalism in the United States was at the University of Missouri. It opened in 1908. The school of journalism at Columbia University, in New York City, opened in 1912.

The profession of journalism has an honor society, Sigma Delta Chi, and a labor union, the Newspaper Guild. There are two trade journals, *Editor and Publisher,* a weekly magazine, and the *Journalism Quarterly,* a magazine published every three months.

journeyman, a skilled worker who has completed his apprenticeship in a trade but has not yet become a master: see the articles on APPRENTICE and GUILD.

Joyce, James

James Joyce was one of the greatest modern writers, and his novels had a great influence on other writers. He was born in Dublin, Ireland, in 1882, and spent much of his life in Paris, France; Trieste, Italy; and Zurich, Switzerland. His most famous book, which took him seven years to write, is *Ulysses.* It was published in 1922, when he was 40 years old. It concerns most of the things that happen to a number of people in part of one day, about twenty hours, in Dublin. He describes all the thoughts and feelings of his three main characters, a method of story-telling often called the "stream-of-consciousness" or "interior monologue" method. This has been used by other writers since then.

After *Ulysses,* Joyce wrote another famous novel, *Finnegans Wake,* on which he worked for seventeen years. It was published in 1939. It is unlike any other book ever written before. The main characters seem to be asleep and dreaming when the book begins. Joyce tries to show the thoughts of his sleeping characters in a new kind of language he himself invented. It consists mainly of puns using many different languages.

His first novel, published in 1916, was *Portrait of the Artist as a Young Man.* It is much easier to read than the other two novels.

James Joyce was blind much of the time in his later years. He died in 1941.

Juarez, Benito

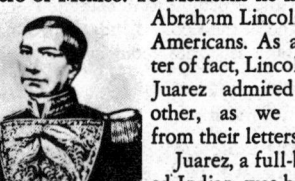

Benito Juarez is the great national hero of Mexico. To Mexicans he is what Abraham Lincoln is to Americans. As a matter of fact, Lincoln and Juarez admired each other, as we know from their letters.

Juarez, a full-blooded Indian, was born in 1806. He received a good education and while still a young man rose to an important position in the government of Mexico.

Benito Juarez was always a supporter of democracy and of the people's rights. When Santa Anna, the general who had fought the Texas army at the Alamo, tried to seize the government and make himself dictator, Juarez fought against him and was imprisoned for this. He escaped, went to New Orleans, and took part in planning a revolt against Santa Anna.

The revolt succeeded. As a reward for his efforts, Juarez was made minister of justice in the new Mexican government. While holding this position he issued a famous reform measure that limited the power of the generals and of the priests. After a civil war in Mexico, in May, 1858, he became head of the nation. His government was recognized the next year by the United States.

When Napoleon III, emperor of France, sent a French army to conquer Mexico and set up Maximilian of Austria as emperor of Mexico, Juarez declared war on France. After several years he defeated the French forces. He captured Maximilian and executed him.

This was not the end of Juarez's troubles. During the rest of his life, which he spent as head of the Mexican government, there was continual unrest in that land.

Benito Juarez died in Mexico City, in 1872, and his memory is honored to this day.

Judah

Judah was a kingdom told about in the Old Testament of the Bible. After the death of Solomon, the great king of the Hebrews, his kingdom was split into two parts. The northern part was called the kingdom of Israel and the southern part was called the kingdom of Judah.

The people of the kingdom of Judah were of the Hebrew tribes of Judah and Benjamin. The capital of the kingdom of Judah was the great city of Jerusalem. Judah was often at war with its northern neighbor, Israel. After some years, both countries were conquered by another greater power, Babylonia. First Israel fell, and then, about 150 years later, in 586 B.C., the kingdom of Judah was defeated and destroyed by King Nebuchadnezzar of Babylonia.

Judah was in the southern part of what is today the Republic of Israel. It is mostly a dry and hilly region.

Judaism, the religion of the Jewish people: see the article on JEWS AND JUDAISM.

Judas

Judas Iscariot was one of the twelve Disciples of Jesus. He was unfaithful and betrayed Jesus. "Iscariot" means that he came from a place called Kerioth, in Palestine.

There is an old story that says that before Judas was born, his mother, Cyborea, dreamed that he would murder his father and sell his God. She was so frightened by this that when Judas was born, she cast him into the sea in a chest, hoping to destroy him. But Judas lived and when he grew up he entered the service of the Roman governor of Judea, Pontius Pilate.

There he met his father and killed him so that his father could not tell who he was. Later, Judas joined Jesus's followers.

The life of Judas as a Disciple is told in the New Testament, in the Bible. A time came when the Roman soldiers were looking for Jesus, to arrest him. Judas told the soldiers he would show them where Jesus was if they would pay him thirty pieces of silver. That night, when Jesus was praying in a part of Jerusalem called the Garden of Gethsemane, Judas stepped forth and kissed him. That was the signal to the soldiers, and they appeared from all sides and seized Jesus.

Judas was so full of despair at what he had done that he killed himself. He did this in a field that belonged to a potter (a man who made pottery). The Romans took the thirty pieces of silver and used it to buy the field as a burial place for those who had no money. Ever since, such a burial place has been called a "potter's field." The word "Judas" is used for someone who betrays his friends, and a "kiss of Judas" is any act that betrays someone.

Judas tree

The Judas tree is a low, wide tree with pink flowers. Its odd name comes from the old fancy that Judas Iscariot hanged himself from the branches of such a tree, after he had betrayed Jesus to his enemies. The first Judas trees grew in southern Europe and Asia Minor, but there are some in America. These are smaller than the European kind. The American Judas tree is usually called the redbud. The pink flowers taste good in salads and can even be fried in fritters, or little cakes.

Jude, Saint

Jude was a cousin of Jesus and was one of his disciples. He was the brother of St. James, another disciple. The *Epistle of St. Jude* is one of the books of the Bible. After the death of Jesus, Jude preached in Mesopotamia. Some say that he was martyred in Persia, some that he died at Ararat in Armenia. The Armenians claim St. Jude and St. Bartholomew as the founders of their church. The feast of St. Jude is on Oct. 28.

Judea

Judea was the name given to the southern section of the country of Palestine when that country was controlled by the Romans. The Romans conquered Palestine about two thousand years ago, and ruled it for about seven hundred years. Judea was a mountainous section to the west of the Jordan Valley and the Dead

Sea. In the midst of these hills was the great city of Jerusalem. The town of Bethlehem, where Jesus was born, was also in Judea. This section is now a part of the Republic of Israel. Judea was named for the kingdom of Judah, which had been established in that region in more ancient times.

judge

A judge is the highest officer of a court of law. Most judges are appointed by a high government official; for instance, the judges of the United States Supreme Court, who are called justices, are appointed by the President with the consent of Congress. Judges of state supreme courts also are called justices. State and city judges may be either appointed or elected by the people.

The judge of a court usually sits at a high desk on a raised platform at the front of the courtroom. Usually he wears a long black robe over his street clothes. In Great Britain judges wear gorgeous scarlet robes trimmed with gold, and white curled wigs on their heads.

The duties of a judge depend on the court over which he presides. In a court that tries minor offenses, such as traffic violations, the judge has the power to decide whether a person is guilty or innocent, and how much fine must be paid or how much time the offender must spend in jail. If the crime is serious, it is not the judge who decides whether the accused person is guilty or innocent, but a jury of twelve persons.

In a trial by jury, the judge's principal duties are to see that the trial is conducted according to the rules of law, and to sentence the accused person if he is found guilty. In some cases a person may be tried by three judges, instead of by a jury and one judge. A judge must know the law, and also he must have good judgment and a high moral character.

Judges of some courts have special titles. A *magistrate* is the judge of a court that handles minor offenses. A *surrogate* is the judge of a probate court, which handles the settling of wills and the dividing of estates and all matters concerned with adoption and the care of orphans.

Judge Advocate General's Corps

The Judge Advocate General's Corps is the branch of the United States Army that is in charge of all the Army's legal matters. It is made up of a staff of Army officers who are also lawyers. They supervise the military justice system and review the decisions of military courts-martial to see that justice is done. They are also in charge of all other legal business that concerns the Army, and they give legal advice to the Secretary of the Army and to other high Army officials.

The head of this department is called the Judge Advocate General; he is a major general and is on the staff that advises the Army's Chief of Staff.

Judges, Book of

The Book of Judges is the name of one of the books in the Old Testament of the Bible. The Book of Judges tells what happened to the children of Israel after they escaped from Egypt and came to the Promised Land, which is now called Pal-

estine. Very often, the people of Israel sinned, and then they were attacked by enemies. Several great judges, or leaders, helped these people to defeat their enemies, and in the Book of Judges there are many famous stories about how they did this.

judgment

There are two different kinds of judgment. We speak of a person as having "good judgment" when we mean that he is able to come to a sensible decision after carefully looking at the facts in a given situation. Judgment can also refer to the decision of a court of law.

The simplest kind of judgment of facts is called *discrimination*. This means being able to arrange things in the right groups or classes, such as sorting things out according to color, size, or shape. Other kinds of judgment are much more complicated. A person's intelligence is often shown by the kinds of judgment he is able to make. As people become more familiar with certain subjects, they are able to make much finer and more exact judgments.

Judgment, in the legal meaning, is the decision that a judge makes after evidence has been presented at a trial. The evidence is first heard and then a verdict is given, either by a jury or by the judge. Then the judgment is made. If it is a criminal case and the verdict is "guilty," the judgment is called the *sentence*. Other cases that are brought to trial do not involve crimes. They come as a result of arguments between two parties, usually about money or property. These are known as civil cases. The judgment in a civil case often will award *damages* to one of the two parties. This means that his opponent is required by the law to pay him a certain amount of money. A judgment is the final decision in any case, unless a higher court later changes it.

Judith

Judith was a Hebrew woman whose story is told in the book of Judith, in the Bible. In Protestant Bibles this is part of the APOCRYPHA, about which there is a separate article. Judith lived about two thousand years ago, when a great king of the Assyrian empire, Nebuchadnezzar, was making war on Palestine, where the Jews lived. Holofernes, a general of Nebuchadnezzar, besieged Judith's city of Bethulia. Judith went to Holofernes' tent one night, waited until he was asleep, and then cut off his head with his own sword. After this her people attacked the invaders and drove them off, and Judith became a great heroine. The scene in Holofernes' tent has been the subject of many pictures and statues in which Judith is always shown as a very beautiful and commanding woman.

judo and jujutsu

Judo is a modernized form of jujutsu, practiced primarily as a sport. Jujutsu is an ancient form of wrestling used mostly in self-defense. The terms are very often used interchangeably. They are Japanese words, for judo and jujutsu are most popular in Japan.

The object of judo is to kill or so injure an attacker as to make him completely defenseless. Judo was taught to

men in the United States armed services during World War II so that they could defend themselves against enemy soldiers, especially the Japanese, in hand-to-hand combat.

A student of judo is taught how to press or strike various nerve centers and muscles of his opponent so as to temporarily paralyze him. Some of these centers are the solar plexus (just below the ribs), the Adam's apple, the area behind the ear, and the upper lip. These centers are struck with the side of the hand, stunning the opponent and leaving him open for more direct attack. Such attacks may often result in serious injury or even death due to damage of the nervous sys-

Official Marine Corps Photo

Marines are taught judo for hand-to-hand fighting. Knowing how to disarm a man with a knife could save the life of a Marine in time of war.

tem, brain, and other sensitive areas of the body.

Another important part of judo is to get your opponent off balance by striking or "clipping" him below the back of the knee with your leg, throwing him back and off his guard. There are various other ways of unbalancing him, such as grasping his hand and, quickly turning your back toward him, throwing him over your shoulder. This requires much practice and fast footwork. Such methods of attack make it possible for a small person to overcome a bigger person with little trouble. In fact, the weight of the bigger person is often a disadvantage to him, because the bigger he is the harder he falls.

Judo is often said to be a "dirty" form of jujutsu in which no holds are barred. Jujutsu was first developed by Chinese monks thousands of years ago to defend themselves against robbers. It was taken over by the warrior class of Japan, the *samurai*, who secretly passed it on from one generation to another. In modern Japan it is taught in schools to children in the form of physical training, and many Japanese soon become very good at it. The secrecy surrounding jujutsu has given many people the idea that it is the best method of defense and attack. However, a good wrestler can hold his own and even win over a jujutsu expert. Many jujutsu holds are used in modern wrestling.

Juggernaut

Juggernaut, or Jagganath, is a huge statue, or idol, that is supposed by Hindus to be one of the forms taken by Vishnu, an important Hindu god. The Juggernaut is one of several huge statues, representing various members of Vishnu's family, that are in a temple in Puri, India. Many Hindus make religious journeys, or pilgrimages, to Puri.

Every year there is an important ceremony in which Juggernaut and the other statues are removed from the temple, placed in a special cart, and dragged to the summer home of the god, about a mile away. The cart is very large, the statues are very heavy, and the trip takes several days. Thousands of Hindus help to pull the cart, and others act as servants for the idols, bathing them, dressing them, and preparing them for bed during the journey.

Many Hindus have been killed during this trip, because in their excitement they have fallen beneath the wheels of the huge cart and have been crushed to death. Some people used to think this was part of the religious ceremony, but it is not. Nevertheless, the word *juggernaut* is used to mean a force that keeps going straight ahead, not stopping or changing its course regardless of what may stand in its path.

juggling

Juggling means keeping several things, such as balls, dishes, or oranges, all flying through the air at once. A juggler throws a number of things into the air one after the other. Then, as each one comes down he catches it and throws it up again immediately before the next one comes down.

The juggler must be very quick. He must time his movements perfectly. A very expert juggler may be able to keep as many as ten things in the air at once. It takes a great deal of skill and long hours of practice.

A juggler is usually expert at balancing things. He may balance a stick or a sword on the end of his chin or nose, and balance a ball on the tip of the stick or sword.

Juggling probably goes back to ancient times, but it became prominent in the Middle Ages, when court jesters and others used their tricks to entertain the nobles.

jugular vein

The jugular vein is an important blood vessel through which all the blood returns from the head and neck back to the heart. Actually, there are four jugular veins. Two external ("outside") jugulars, one on each side of the neck, are small and are close to the surface of the skin. They carry blood from the outer parts of the head and neck, and may be seen close to the angle of the jaw. The two internal ("inside") jugulars are buried much deeper and carry the blood from the brain. They are much larger and are not visible. If one of these jugulars is cut, a person may die from loss of blood unless the flow of blood is stopped.

jujutsu, see the article JUDO AND JUJUTSU.

Cosmo-Sileo Assoc.

Eight tumblers at once. The juggler's quick hands and perfect timing make his art look easy, but actually it is very difficult.

Juliana, Queen

Juliana is queen of the Netherlands, or Holland. Her full name is Juliana Louise Emma Marie Wilhelmina. She is a descendant of the Dutch national hero, William the Silent of the House of Orange-Nassau. William, who lived about four hundred years ago, was called the "Father of His Country," like George Washington.

Consulate General of the Netherlands

Juliana's mother, Queen Wilhelmina, ruled Holland for fifty years. Another queen is expected to rule Holland after Juliana, because she and her husband, Prince Bernhard, have four daughters and no sons. The oldest girl is Princess Beatrix. The other princesses are named Irene, Margriet, and Marijke.

Juliana was born on April 30, 1909. She studied music, languages, religion, literature, and history. She went to Leyden University and earned the degree of Doctor of Literature and Philosophy.

In 1937 Juliana married Prince Bernhard of Lippe-Biesterfeld, a German state. Three years later German troops invaded Holland. Juliana and her children went to Canada to live, while Prince Bernhard joined the Allied armies in England. Several times Princess Juliana visited the United States. In 1945 the family returned to Holland. On August 31, 1948, Queen Wilhelmina retired and Juliana became queen.

As queen, Juliana always keeps in very close touch with her people. She frequently visits hospitals and places where poor people live, and helps with laws to aid those in need. She is quite religious, leads a simple life except for official affairs, and keeps close to her family. Her birthdays, and those of her husband and children, are gaily celebrated in Holland. In 1951 Juliana visited the United States as a guest of President Truman. She was cheered by crowds everywhere she went.

Julius, Pope

Julius was a name taken by three Popes of the Roman Catholic Church. Julius I was Pope about three hundred years after the time of Jesus. He was made a saint and his day is celebrated on April 12. Julius II lived about twelve hundred years later and helped many of the great Italian painters and architects, including Michelangelo, Bramante, and Raphael. Julius III was Pope from 1550 to 1555.

July

July is the seventh month of the year. It has thirty-one days. In ancient Roman times the year began with March, and the month now called July was the fifth month of the year and was called *Quintilis* (meaning "fifth"). About two thousand years ago, the Romans began to use the calendar we know today and July became the seventh month. It was named to honor Julius Caesar, who, in addition to having been a great conqueror and powerful ruler, started the reform of the ancient Roman calendar. The Fourth of July is one of the most important holidays in the United States, celebrated in honor of the Declaration of Independence on July 4, 1776. The birthstone for July is the ruby, a brilliant red stone of great value. Another birthstone for July is the onyx, a black stone.

junco

The junco is a small bird found in most parts of North America. It belongs to the finch family of birds. It is a constant friend and flying companion to the sparrow, another finch about its size. The junco is a very sociable bird, always flying in the company of flocks of other small birds. It can be seen in the wintertime hopping about in the snow. Because of this characteristic, the junco is also known as the *snowbird*. Its main food is insects in the summer and seeds during the winter. Its feathers are a drab blue-gray color, while its two outer tail feathers and breast are white. Its voice is gentle and sounds very much like a sparrow's chirping.

June

June is the sixth month of the year. It has thirty days. In ancient Roman times the year began with March, and the month now called June was the fourth month and was called *Iunius*. Some have said that Iunius was so called to honor part of the ancient Roman government, the Iuniores; others have said that the Iunius was named in honor of the goddess Juno. The birthstone for June is the pearl, a jewel of great value. Another birthstone for June is the moonstone, a less valuable stone.

Juneau

Juneau is the capital of Alaska. It

lies between the Taku River and Lynn Canal, and it is connected to Douglas Island by a bridge. There are two mountains behind Juneau, Mt. Juneau and Mt. Roberts. Back in 1880 prospectors found gold on Mt. Juneau, and people came rushing in to work the mines. That is when the city of Juneau was first started. One of the largest gold mines in the world, the Alaska Juneau mine, was on the slopes of Mt. Juneau.

Juneau became the capital of Alaska in 1900, and employment in the government offices is the chief occupation of a large part of the city's population. The city is quite small; the population in 1970 was 6,050.

Jung, Carl Gustav

Dr. Carl Gustav Jung was one of the co-founders of modern psychoanalysis. A student of Sigmund Freud, he later developed his own theories and coined the terms *introvert* and *extrovert*.

Dr. Jung was born in Basel, Switzerland in 1875, and studied medicine there. He lectured at the University of Zurich from 1905 to 1913, and became a professor at the Federal Polytechnic University, Zurich, in 1935. He was named a professor at the University of Basel in 1943. In 1948 he established the C. G. Jung Institute for research and the training of psychoanalysts. He died in 1961.

juniper

The juniper is a tall evergreen tree with leaves that are stiff and needlelike. The best-known juniper tree is the red cedar, which is found almost entirely in North America. The wood of this tree is used by builders for the interiors of houses and also for cedar chests, big boxes in which clothes and linens are kept because moths, whose larvae eat clothing, do not like the smell of cedar and will not try to lay eggs in cedar chests.

The berries of the juniper tree are almost completely hidden among the leaves. They are used in flavoring a liquor called *gin*.

The juniper tree also grows in Europe, where its bark is made into rope by the Laplanders, people who live in northern Finland, Norway, and Sweden. The wood is sometimes used in lead pencils, and the tannin in the bark is used to tan leather. The juniper holds and retains water a long time, and for this reason it is sometimes the only tree growing in the hot deserts of the American Southwest.

Juno

Juno was a character in the mythology or stories of gods and goddesses, in the religion of the ancient Romans, thousands of years ago. She was also a goddess of the ancient Greeks, to whom her name was Hera. She was worshiped as the queen of heaven both by the Greeks and the Romans. She was the sister and wife of the Roman god Jupiter, who was the Greek god Zeus. She was the most powerful of all the Greek and Roman goddesses. Even Jupiter or Zeus feared her. She watched over all women in every way from birth to death. She also was the goddess of money, and one of her temples contained the mint where coins were made. Here she was called *Moneta*. She is always pictured wearing a diadem or crown and carrying a scepter.

Jupiter

Jupiter was the most important god in the mythology, or stories of gods and goddesses, in the religion of the ancient Romans, thousands of years ago. He was also the chief god of the ancient Greeks, to whom his name was Zeus. The Greeks and the Romans believed in his absolute power and worshiped and feared him. To them he was immortal, but also a man with their own faults and standards of life. He was the husband of Juno. Jupiter had many children.

Jupiter, or Zeus, was the lord of heaven and the god of rain, storms, thunder, and lightning. He guarded law and justice. Nothing of importance could be undertaken without praying for his permission. The color white was sacred to him. His temple in Rome stood on a high hill and victorious generals always made a triumphal procession to it. In Greek and Roman art, he is shown as a tall, bearded man in flowing robes.

Jupiter

Jupiter is the largest planet in the sun's family. It looks like a very bright star, a little brighter than any of the real stars in the night sky. The diameter of Jupiter is 87,000 miles, nearly eleven times the diameter of the earth, and Jupiter weighs 318 times as much as the earth. Because Jupiter weighs so much, the pull of gravity there is stronger than on the earth. If you weigh 100 pounds on the earth, you would weigh 264 pounds on Jupiter.

Jupiter turns on its axis very fast. It has the shortest day of any of the planets. Day and night together are only ten hours long. It takes Jupiter twelve of our years to go once around the sun, because it is so far away—483,000,000 miles, more than five times as far from the sun as the earth is.

The air on Jupiter is very deep. It is composed of the gases methane and ammonia, so it would be poisonous to us. There are high winds and many clouds on Jupiter. The temperature of the air has been measured. It is 200 degrees below zero, Fahrenheit. This is colder than the polar regions on the earth. Because it is so cold, and because the air would be poisonous to us, we could not live on Jupiter.

Jupiter has twelve moons. Two of them are about as large as our moon, and two others are about as large as the planet Mercury. The other eight are very small. The four larger ones were among the first objects that Galileo saw with his little telescope in 1609.

See also the article on the SOLAR SYSTEM.

jury

A jury is a group of people who come together to listen to all of the known facts, and then decide whether a person is guilty or innocent of a crime. There are three main types of juries.

A *grand jury* is a group of twelve to twenty-three persons who must decide whether there is likely to be enough evidence so that a person should be tried for a crime he is accused of having committed. If the grand jury decides there should be a trial, it is said to *indict* the person.

A *trial jury*, also called a *petit* (little) *jury*, is a group of twelve people who hear all of the evidence that is presented by both sides in a trial and then judge whether a person is guilty or innocent.

A *coroner's jury* examines the circumstances of a person's death and decides if it was a natural death or if it resulted from a crime.

THE TRIAL JURY

A person must be 21 years old to serve on a jury. He must not have any knowledge or opinions about the case he is to judge. Every member of a jury receives a certain amount for each day that he serves on the jury. A juror should not be selected unless he is accepted by both of the parties that are opposed in the trial, and each side has a right to question each possible member of the jury. So that no one can delay a trial by refusing to accept jurors, the judge can finally decide on who shall be jurors.

After the jury has heard all of the evidence, it leaves the courtroom and tries to come to a decision, called a *verdict*. All the members of the jury must agree that a person is guilty or innocent. If they cannot come to an agreement, the jury is dismissed and there must be a new jury and a new trial. (This kind of jury is called a "hung jury"). The jurors choose one of their members to be the foreman. The foreman delivers the verdict (tells the judge what the decision is).

The idea that a person should be tried by a jury is a very old one. It is believed to have begun during the time of the ancient Greeks and Romans, more than two thousand years ago. The jury system as we know it began in England almost a thousand years ago. Most people believe that a trial by jury is the fairest way to judge whether a person is innocent or guilty. The Bill of Rights of the United States Constitution guarantees the right of an accused person to a trial by jury.

Justice, Department of

The Department of Justice is one of the main divisions of the United States government. Its purpose is to provide means of enforcing Federal laws, to represent (speak and act for) the government in legal cases, and to interpret the laws that control other divisions or departments of the Federal government. It was established as a department in 1870. At its head is the Attorney General, a member of the President's Cabinet.

Altogether, 32,056 people worked for the Department of Justice in 1962. There were 31,299 full-time workers and 416 part-time workers in the United States, 150 in the United States territories and possessions, and 191 in foreign countries.

The Department of Justice is divided into several different offices, divisions, and bureaus. The Office of the Attorney General is at the head. The Deputy Attorney General assists the Attorney General. The Office of the Solicitor General represents the government in cases that go to the Supreme Court; the Solicitor General may also represent the United States in any other court. The Office of Legal Counsel checks all proposed executive orders and proclamations to make sure they are legal.

The Office of Alien Property takes charge of any property or business owned by a foreign government, or by citizens of a foreign country. The Office of the Pardon Attorney deals with applications for pardons made to the President. The Antitrust Division of the Department of Justice investigates complaints about monopolies in business. (There is a separate article on MONOPOLY.)

The Tax Division represents the United States in all cases of unpaid or overpaid taxes that reach the courts. The Civil Division represents the government in all lawsuits for damages against the government.

The Lands Division is in charge of all suits dealing with land actions in which the government has an interest. This includes Indian affairs.

The Criminal Division watches how the Federal criminal laws are enforced. This includes trying to punish people for such crimes as counterfeiting, forgery, bribery, kidnapping, postal fraud, and many other kinds of offense covered by Federal laws.

The Federal Bureau of Investigation —the FBI—is a division of the Department of Justice. There is a separate article on the FEDERAL BUREAU OF INVESTIGATION. The Bureau of Prisons has general supervision of the country's Federal penitentiaries, prisons, reformatories, and correctional institutions, and the one Federal Prison Hospital in Springfield, Missouri. Immigration and naturalization of new citizens are also controlled by the Department of Justice.

justice of the peace

A justice of the peace is a kind of judge. In modern times, a justice of the peace is a judge in cases that are not important enough to go before a more important judge. A justice of the peace has the power to fine a person, and even put him in jail. The office of justice of the peace began in England, about six hundred years ago. Noblemen and big landowners were appointed to be justices of the peace in their localities. Today, a justice of the peace is usually elected. He is authorized to give out licenses and sometimes to collect taxes. He can marry people. He acts as judge in traffic cases, nuisances, and fights. Police courts in some places do the work that once was done by the justice of the peace.

Justinian

Justinian the Great was the most famous emperor of the Eastern Roman Empire, about 1,500 years ago. He was born in the year 483, and was only a poor peasant in a tribe of Slavs. When he died in 565 his generals had won many battles for the Roman Empire, his lawyers had arranged a famous code, or set of laws, for the empire, and he had caused whole cities and big churches to be built. One of these is the famous church of Saint Sophia in Constantinople, which is now called *Istanbul,* and which was Justinian's capital.

The taxes in Justinian's reign were cruelly high. The people of his empire had to pay for the new cities and for his expensive wars against Persia, Carthage, Italy, and Spain. His victories in war were due largely to the fine general Belisarius.

jute

Jute is a plant about ten feet in height. It grows well in damp heat. Some of the fibers, or threadlike pieces, of the jute plant are used in manufacturing coarse woven materials, especially burlap bags used to pack potatoes and many other heavy things. Stronger fibers of the plant are used for making ropes and rugs, and weaker fibers are used in the manufacture of paper.

Jute is planted in March or April and is cut down by August or September. The fiber comes from the outer layers of the slender stem. The fiber is separated from the stem by soaking in water for as long as three weeks.

Many people are employed in the jute industry. Farmers plant and cut down the jute. Others separate the fiber from the stem. Then it is woven onto a spindle, just as sewing thread is. Most of the world's jute comes from India and Pakistan.

Jutes, a tribe of people, possibly from Jutland, who settled in England in about the year 500: see the article on ANGLES AND ANGLO-SAXON.

Jutland

The biggest naval battle of World War I, and one of the biggest of all time, is called the Battle of Jutland. It was fought in 1916 between the British and German fleets, which were then the two largest in the world. Jutland is a section of Denmark, sticking into the North Sea, and the Battle of Jutland was fought in the North Sea near this section.

The main British fleet was called the Grand Fleet and was under the command of Admiral John Jellicoe. Part of the fleet was a squadron of battle cruisers under Vice Admiral David Beatty. Battle cruisers are ships as big as battleships but lighter and faster.

The main German fleet was called the High Seas Fleet and was commanded by Admiral Reinhard Scheer. It too had a battle-cruiser squadron, under Vice Admiral Franz von Hipper.

The battle was fought during the day and night of May 31, 1916. The British Grand Fleet received information that the German High Seas Fleet had put to sea, perhaps to raid British shipping. The Grand Fleet sailed out to meet the Germans. The battle-cruiser squadrons met first, and the Germans seemed to have the best of it, but Beatty was leading them northward to where the Grand Fleet waited. When the two main fleets met, the British lost more ships but they had more ships to lose, and the Germans had to break off the battle and try to return home. Night fell and the British could not find the German fleet. Though the British losses were much greater, the Germans learned from the Battle of Jutland that the British were stronger. The German fleet never left its base to seek battle again. Therefore the battle must be considered a British victory. Jellicoe, the British commander, was later said to be "the only man who could have lost the war in an afternoon."

juvenile court

A juvenile court is a place where children and young people in their teens appear when they get into trouble with the law. Also, children whose parents neglect them come to juvenile courts. A juvenile court is quite different from a court for grownups. The judge usually does not wear a robe. He sits with the child, his parents, and the law officers, and discusses the case with everyone in a friendly way. The purpose of a juvenile court is not so much to punish children who have done something wrong as to help keep them out of trouble in the future. To protect the children who come there, a juvenile court does not give their names to the newspapers.

juvenile delinquency

Juvenile delinquency is the breaking of the law by young people up to the age of about seventeen. Youngsters who break the law are called juvenile delinquents. Juvenile delinquency has probably always existed to some extent but there has been so much of it in the last fifty years that it is considered one of the most important problems facing many countries.

CAUSES OF JUVENILE DELINQUENCY

All sorts of reasons have been given for this increase in juvenile crime. There are some who say that the kinds of story children read and see in comic books, on television, and in the movies are the cause. Others are inclined to believe that while such things probably help to bring on juvenile delinquency they are not the most important reasons. They believe that children who commit crimes are unhappy children. The children may be unhappy because they are neglected at home, because their parents do not get along well together, or because they do not feel that their parents love them. Other reasons are that they may live in a bad neighborhood where committing crimes is the "smart" thing to do or where a grown-up criminal is admired by the children. Very important too is the fact that juvenile delinquents seem to have a kind of character that does not let them feel guilty or anxious about doing wrong. We call this a *psychopathic personality.*

KINDS OF JUVENILE CRIME

Juvenile delinquents commit almost all of the crimes that grown-up criminals commit—robbery, murder, setting fires, attacking people, to name only a few. Some crimes are actually committed more frequently by juveniles than by grownups. For example, by far the greater number of automobiles is stolen by youngsters in their teens. There are also some types of crime that are committed only by juveniles. Examples are being absent (truant) from school, running away from home, or disobeying one's parents over a period of time.

WHAT HAPPENS

When a boy or girl has committed a crime, in most states he is brought before a special court for juveniles called a juvenile court. (There is a separate article on JUVENILE COURT just before this one.) Here the judge will have information on his character and past life. This informa-

tion has been gathered by a court worker. If this is the first time that the young person has committed a crime, the judge may release him and have him meet with a social worker with whom he can talk over his troubles. If the boy or girl has committed a crime before, the judge may feel that he should be sent away to a training school or a reformatory. Here he will work and study until the authorities feel that he is ready to go back to a normal life. Unfortunately, not all of the training schools do what they are sup-

posed to do—help the juvenile delinquent. Instead many boys and girls who come out of them are bitter toward the grown-up world. When this happens there is a good chance that these boys and girls will grow up to be criminals.

PREVENTING DELINQUENCY

No one knows exactly how boys and girls can be prevented from becoming delinquents. It is known that if children who might become delinquents could have their difficulties discovered in time,

there probably would be fewer juvenile delinquents. Part of the job is up to the schools, for teachers see more of children than anyone else except their parents. Many schools recognize this and have special departments to help children with difficulties. Another way of preventing juvenile delinquency is to have what are called "child guidance centers," where specially trained doctors and social workers help boys and girls to get rid of the feelings of unhappiness that drive them to do criminal acts.

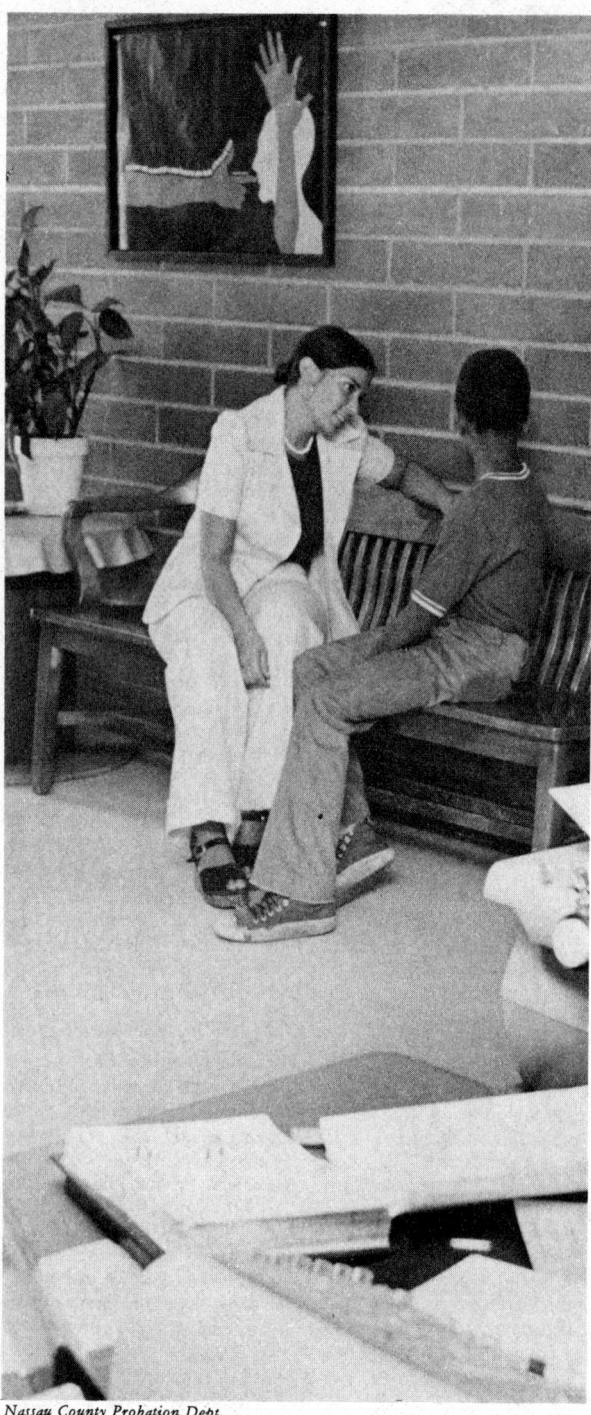

Nassau County Probation Dept.

In Nassau County, New York, most children who get into trouble are placed on probation instead of being "sent away" to institutions. Here, a probation officer and a young "client" talk things over in the Nassau County Probation Office.

Wiener Presse Bilddienst

Kaiser Karl I of Austria.

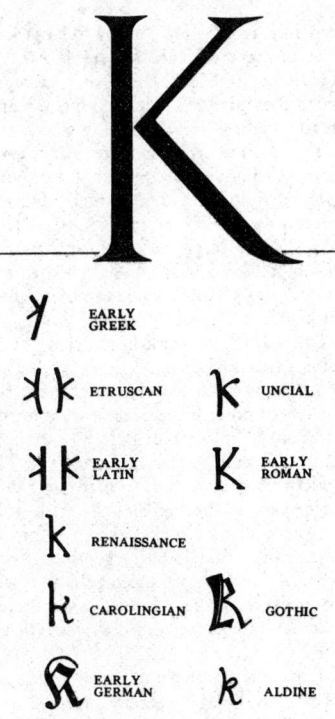

EARLY GREEK

ETRUSCAN · UNCIAL

EARLY LATIN · EARLY ROMAN

RENAISSANCE

CAROLINGIAN · GOTHIC

EARLY GERMAN · ALDINE

K or k

The letter K is the eleventh letter of the alphabet. Some say it goes all the way back to the earliest writing known to man, in Egypt thousands of years ago. In the Hebrew language, in which much of the Bible was written, the letter was called *kaph*. The ancient Greeks took the same letter and called it *kappa*.

At the top of this page, at the far left, you can see the earliest Greek *kappa*. In early times, writing was read from right to left, and in some of the old languages, such as Hebrew, it still is. But the Greeks changed and began to read from left to right as we do today. When they made this change, they turned the letters around. When the Greek *kappa* was turned around it looked almost like our own K. The Romans adopted the Greek alphabet and added the little "feet" or *serifs*. This Roman alphabet, with three letters added, became the ancestor of most western alphabets used today, including our own.

Read also the article ALPHABET.

Kaffir corn is a kind of grain sorghum: see the article on SORGHUM.

Kaiser

Kaiser means "emperor" in the German language. The word comes from the Latin word *Caesar*, because the first Roman emperor called himself Augustus Caesar. The Russian word *tsar* or *czar* means the same thing. The emperors of all German-speaking empires have been called Kaisers. William II, the German emperor during World War I, is usually meant when American or English people speak of "the Kaiser."

Kalb, Johann de

Johann de Kalb was a French soldier who helped America win its independence in the Revolutionary War. He was born in Germany and fought for his adopted country of France in several European wars. When the American colo-

nies rose against England, de Kalb became an officer in Washington's army. At the battle of Camden, de Kalb led his troops in four gallant charges. He was wounded eleven times, and died three days later, in 1780.

kale

Kale is a green leafy vegetable somewhat like cabbage. The kale leaves grow out from a thick stem. They do not form a tight head as cabbage does. Usually kale grows close to the ground, as does cabbage, but some kinds may grow to be seven feet high. The green kale leaves are used as food for human beings and for animals. Kale grows well in cool weather, so it is a good vegetable for wintertime, when many other vegetables do not grow. Kale provides vitamins that we need for health. It grows in the United States and in other parts of the world.

kaleidoscope

The kaleidoscope is a toy, but it can be useful. From the outside it looks like an ordinary cardboard tube with an eyepiece at one end. When you look through the eyepiece you can see beautiful colored designs that change with the slightest turn of the tube. Designers have used it to suggest patterns for fabrics and other things.

The bits of color you see in the kaleidoscope are tiny pieces of colored glass of various sizes and shapes. These pieces of glass are enclosed between two glass disks. The rest of the tube is taken up with two mirrors set at certain angles so that each piece of colored glass is reflected five times. When you look into the kaleidoscope, you see each piece of colored glass six times so that the original piece and its five reflections seem to form a full circle. Turning or jiggling the tube will shake and rearrange the pieces of colored glass,

thus forming a completely different pattern.

The kaleidoscope was invented by Sir David Brewster, a Scottish scientist who lived about a hundred years ago. Brewster was very much interested in the workings of light, and besides this fascinating toy he invented many important optical devices.

Kamchatka

Kamchatka is a province in the northeastern part of Asia. It is part of the Soviet Union. Kamchatka is a peninsula, or body of land surrounded on three sides by water. It is one of the most northern places that people live in, but its climate is like that of Scotland. On the west of Kamchatka is the Sea of Okhotsk, and on the east are the Bering Sea and the Pacific Ocean. The peninsula is about 750 miles long, and 80 to 300 miles wide. Down its center runs the Kamchatka River, between two mountain ranges.

Many of the people of Kamchatka are nomads, wanderers who do not try to settle down in villages or towns. There are about 58,000 people in Kamchatka. Most of them belong to tribes called Koryaks and Chukchis, who are related to the Eskimos, but there are also some Chinese, Koreans, and Russians. They hunt for animals in the dense forests and fish for herring and salmon in the rivers. There is also some lumbering done, and some of the people raise reindeer. The government of Russia has been trying to develop farming in the southern part of Kamchatka, but special seeds and farm equipment are needed because it is so cold.

The chief town in Kamchatka is Petropavlovsk, which is a seaport and is free of ice for about nine months of the year. Most of the people there work in the fish-canning industry.

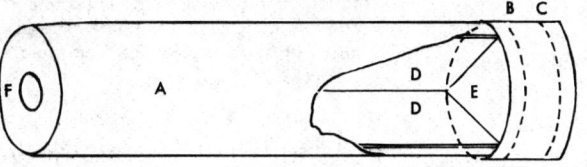

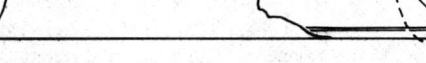

A—TUBE

B—CLEAR GLASS DISK

C—GROUND GLASS DISK

D, D—PLANE MIRRORS AT 60°

E— SECTOR OF VIEW INTO COMPARTMENT BETWEEN B AND C, HOLDING BITS OF GLASS

F—EYEHOLE

The kaleidoscope creates numberless lovely designs out of tiny pieces of colored glass.

Australian Inform. Office

Little Joey is ready for a ride in mother's pouch. Some kangaroos reach a speed of twenty-five miles per hour as they leap across the Australian countryside.

kamikaze

Toward the end of World War II, the Japanese fighting against the United States Navy in the Pacific Ocean sent out airplanes heavily loaded with explosives and ordered the pilots to dive into a United States aircraft carrier or other warship or crash into it. Of course, the Japanese pilot would have to die. These planes, sometimes called "suicide planes," were called *kamikaze* planes by the Japanese. There were thousands of kamikaze fliers who died for Japan. The word *kamikaze* means "divine wind" in the Japanese language. The Japanese used this word because more than seven hundred years ago a kamikaze (typhoon) saved the people of Japan when they were about to be attacked by enemies.

kangaroo

The kangaroo is a large jumping animal that is found mostly in Australia. It belongs to a group of animals called marsupials. A marsupial mother carries its young in a pouch, or bag, on its abdomen until they are strong enough to take care of themselves. The opossum, which is found in the United States, is another marsupial.

The largest kangaroo, called the gray kangaroo, is about seven feet tall and weighs almost 200 pounds. It has strong hind legs, and hind feet more than ten inches long, so that it can leap as far as twenty or thirty feet at a time. The front legs are very short. The tail is long and flat and is used for steering and balancing. This kangaroo is usually very gentle, but it can be dangerous if attacked, when it uses its tremendous kicking power and the sharp claws in its hind legs.

Another kind of kangaroo is the wallaroo, which is about five feet tall. Instead of the soft fur of the gray kangaroo, the wallaroo has a harsh, shaggy coat.

The wallaby is a smaller kangaroo and the most numerous of all. Some wallabies are about four feet tall, but others, called hare wallabies, are no larger than rabbits.

The tree kangaroo is a kind whose front and hind legs are more nearly equal in length. It is very much at home scampering about the branches of forest trees. It is found mostly on the island of New Guinea, in the Pacific Ocean.

All kangaroos are herbivorous (plant-eating) animals. They eat leaves, grass, twigs, and roots of plants, chewing them with very strong teeth.

kangaroo rat

The kangaroo rat is a small animal that is found in the deserts of western North America. It looks somewhat like an ordinary rat, but it has strong hind legs and a long tail, and it leaps as a kangaroo does. It can travel more than eight feet in a single jump. The kangaroo rat is a rodent, or gnawing animal, as the rat is.

The kangaroo rat eats seeds of plants. It drinks no water, getting all the liquid it needs from its food. It carries seeds back to its home in little pockets of skin on the inside of its mouth. The kangaroo rat lives in holes dug into the earth. These homes have many entrances and many rooms in which food is stored for the winter.

Kansas

Kansas is a state in the great midwestern plain of the United States. It lies exactly in the center of the country. Its nickname is the "Sunflower State," because of the great number of sunflowers that grow there. Kansas is an important farming region and produces more wheat than any other state. It is sometimes described as "First in freedom, first in wheat!"

Kansas ranks 14th in size among the states, with 82,264 square miles. In population it ranks 28th, with more than two million people living there. It became a state in 1861, and was the 34th state admitted to the United States. The capital is Topeka.

THE PEOPLE OF KANSAS

The early settlers of Kansas were hardy pioneers from other midwestern states, who came to start new farms. Later, many settlers came from New England and the South. As the state grew, people also came from Europe. Among the most important of these was a religious group known as the Mennonites. They were Germans but had lived for a hundred

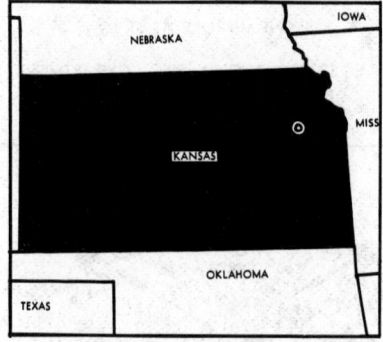

Kansas, whose state flower is the native sunflower, has rich fertile soil and an ideal climate for farming. It does not have many large cities, though industry is growing. The seat of the state government is the capitol building in Topeka.

years in Russia before coming to America. They brought with them a hardy variety of winter wheat called "red turkey," which they planted. It helped make Kansas the leading wheat-growing state.

Today most Kansans are American-born and there are more than a thousand Indians living on reservations. About half the people live in the big cities. They work in the large meat-packing plants and in food factories, making flour, butter and cheese, and ice cream. They also work in the important oil refineries.

Other Kansans work in the rich petroleum fields and in coal, zinc, and lead mines in the southeastern part of the state.

Once almost all the people were farmers. Today, fewer than half are, though farming is still the leading industry. With modern machinery, not so many workers are needed in the fields. The fertile soil in eastern Kansas makes the growing of corn, oats, fruits, and vegetables easy. Wheat flourishes in the central and western parts; and many farmers raise cattle on great ranches in the dry western region.

The churches of Kansas have been important in bringing about various reforms in the state. When the state was being settled, they helped make wild and dangerous towns safe for the citizens. The leading churches of Kansas are the Methodist, Roman Catholic, Baptist, and Presbyterian.

WHAT KANSAS IS LIKE

Kansas is a flat plain, like the other midwestern states. The eastern and western sections have such different soil that they are almost like two different states. The eastern part of Kansas is a fertile, rolling prairie, with rich grass, called bluestem grass. Here one can see many small farms, with gardens, chickens, and pigs. The Kansas or Kaw River flows through this part of the state.

The western part of Kansas is sandy and extremely dry. The grass there is short and fuzzy, and the soil looks barren, but it is excellent grazing land for cattle and rich in chemicals that make wheat-growing very successful.

Many important manufacturing industries are located in the large cities in eastern and central Kansas. Kansas City is part of the second-largest meat-packing center in the United States. Kansas ranks first in flour-making, with large flour mills at Topeka, Salina, and other cities. Wichita is one of the largest centers for the manufacturing of airplanes.

The winters in Kansas City can be very cold, with the temperature far below zero. In summer the temperature rises to above 100 degrees. The average temperature in July is about 80 degrees; in January it is about 30 degrees.

Like other prairie states, Kansas gets dangerous high winds, particularly in the western part. They cause great damage to buildings and crops and raise huge dust storms. Sometimes these winds come twisting across the country at a great speed, accompanied by a funnel-like cloud. When the people see this, they run into their strongly built cellars, for this is the terrible Kansas "twister," or tornado, which wrecks everything in its path.

Kansas has a great many railroads

reaching all parts of the state. All the large cities are important railroad centers. There are many airports in the state.

THE GOVERNMENT OF KANSAS

Kansas, like most other states, is governed by a Governor and a Legislature. The Governor is elected for a two-year term. The Legislature is composed of two houses, a Senate, whose members are elected for a four-year term, and a House of Representatives, whose members are elected for a two-year term. Judges are elected for six-year terms. The capital is Topeka. There are 105 counties in the state.

There are about 527,000 students attending public elementary and secondary schools. Among the principal colleges and universities are:

University of Kansas, at Lawrence. Enrollment, 18,064 in 1971 (co-ed).

Kansas State University of Agriculture and Applied Science, at Manhattan. Enrollment, 12,345 in 1971 (co-ed).

University of Wichita, at Wichita. Enrollment, 11,386 in 1971 (co-ed).

Washburn University, at Topeka. Enrollment, 4,251 in 1971 (co-ed).

Kansas State Teachers College, at Emporia. Enrollment, 6,798 in 1971 (co-ed).

Kansas State College of Pittsburg, at Pittsburg. Enrollment, 5,532 in 1971 (co-ed).

Below: A stone monument marks the exact center of the United States on a farm at Lebanon, near the junction of U.S. highways 281 and 36.

Fort Hays Kansas State College, at Hays. Enrollment, 5,261 in 1971 (co-ed).

CHIEF CITIES OF KANSAS

The leading cities of Kansas, with populations from the 1970 census, are:

Topeka, population 125,011, state capital and third-largest city. There is a separate article about TOPEKA in this encyclopedia.

Wichita, population 276,554, largest city in the state. There is a separate article about WICHITA.

Kansas City, population 168,213, second-largest city, industrial center, in the eastern part of the state. See separate article.

Salina, population 37,714, fourth largest city, trading and shipping center in the grain and livestock-raising section of the state.

KANSAS IN THE PAST

The first white people to enter Kansas were Coronado, a Spanish explorer, and his men, more than four hundred years ago. They were searching for a legendary rich kingdom of Quivira, where they hoped to find gold and other precious metals. They did not find these riches and moved on. Almost two hundred years later the French explored the Kansas region and claimed it as French territory. But they did not settle there, either. In 1803, the United States bought from France the great territory known as the Louisiana Purchase, which included most of Kansas. It was wild and unsettled Indian country, and no one knew how valuable it was.

The United States sent out an exploration party, headed by Lewis and Clark, to find out what this part of the country was like. They, like other American explorers after them, described Kansas as a useless desert, not fit for settling.

Kansas was included in the Missouri Territory in 1821. For the next thirty-three years it was unorganized territory that was left largely unsettled. In 1827, the first permanent settlement was made at Fort Leavenworth. In the 1840s many settlers traveled westward in large covered wagons, hoping to find gold in California. They passed through Kansas, and some decided to settle there instead of continuing the dangerous journey farther west. Finally, in 1854, the United States

Below: This building, called Hollenberg Station, was built as a ranch house in 1857 and later used as a Pony Express station. It is located in Hanover, Kansas.

Kansas Department of Economic Development

organized the Kansas Territory, which included parts of Colorado and was larger than Kansas is now.

Immediately, a bitter struggle began over the question of whether the people of Kansas should own slaves or not. People in New England sent settlers who did not want slavery; the South sent settlers who favored slavery. Serious fighting broke out, and Kansas became known as "bleeding Kansas." Finally the Free State party won out. In 1861, just before the Civil War, Kansas was admitted to the Union as a non-slave state. During the war, several struggles took place on Kansas soil.

The state began to grow and prosper after the Civil War. The new railroad to Kansas brought many settlers, and cattle were brought up from Texas to be shipped by railroad to the east. Towns sprang up along the railroad, Abilene, Dodge City, Wichita, and others, and became known as "cow towns." These towns were full of cowboys, gamblers, and cattle thieves, and there was little law and order. Men like Buffalo Bill Cody and Wild Bill Hickok went after the cattle thieves and bandits and made Kansas a safer place to live.

In 1912 women were given the right to vote. The discovery of large oil fields later brought new prosperity to the state.

PLACES TO SEE IN KANSAS

John Brown Memorial State Park, in the east, at Osawatomie, 48 miles south of Kansas City, on U.S. Route 169. Contains the log cabin that was once the home of John Brown, the anti-slavery fighter. The cabin is still furnished as it was when Brown used it.

Clark County State Park, 1,289 acres, in the southwest, 14 miles north of Ashland, on U.S. Route 160, 183. Beautiful scenery, with deep canyons; a dam holds back the largest and deepest lake in Kansas.

Lindsborg Music Festival, in central Kansas, at Lindsborg, 19 miles south of Salina, on U.S. Route 81. Held during Easter Week each year; a week of concerts, including the singing of Handel's *Messiah* by a chorus of 500 voices.

Indian Burial Pit, in central Kansas, 4 miles east of Salina, on U.S. Route 40. More than 145 skeletons of prehistoric Indians have been uncovered and left in their original positions, together with some of their tools, pottery, and weapons.

Reinisch Memorial Rose and Rock Garden, in the east, at Topeka, on U.S. Route 40. Contains thousands of roses of every variety and color.

Eisenhower Museum and Home, at Abilene. The home where former president Dwight D. Eisenhower lived as a boy. It contains trophies and medals.

Museum of Natural History of the University of Kansas, at Lawrence. Exhibits a panorama of North American mammals.

KANSAS. Area, 82,264 square miles. Population (1970 census) 2,249,071. Capital, Topeka. Nickname, the Sunflower State. Motto, Ad Astra per Aspera (To the stars Through Difficulties). Flower, native sunflower. Bird, western meadowlark. Song, "Home on the Range." Admitted to the Union, January 29, 1861. Official abbreviation, Kan., or Kans., or Kas.

Kansas City

Kansas City, Missouri, is the second-largest city in the state. It is at the north-western corner of the state, at the point where the Kansas and Missouri rivers meet. Kansas City is in the heart of the great wheat belt, and it is the site of the greatest winter-wheat market in the United States. More than 507,000 people live in Kansas City. Many of them work in oil-refining or flour-milling plants. Others manufacture steel products, especially farm machinery for the huge farming area that surrounds the city. It is one of the nation's biggest trade and transportation centers and a meeting point for eastern and western railroads.

Kansas City is very modern, with wide streets, excellent parks, and handsome buildings, such as the Board of Trade Building and the Livestock Exchange. There are more than a hundred public schools, several colleges including the University of Kansas City, museums, and an art institute.

Kansas City is known as the Gateway to the Southwest, because it was from there that the pioneer wagon trains of more than a hundred years ago left for the unsettled Southwest on the Santa Fe trail. A fur-trading post was established on the site of Kansas City in 1821. The town was incorporated in 1853.

KANSAS CITY, KANSAS

The city of Kansas City, Kansas, is the neighbor of the Missouri city, across the river that forms the state line. This Kansas City is the second-largest city and manufacturing center of Kansas. It is second only to Chicago as a meat-packing center. Other important products are soap, grain products, butter, bread and other bakery products, and oil. There are beautiful parks and playgrounds. Kansas City, Kansas, was incorporated in 1859.

KANSAS CITY, MISSOURI. Population (1970 census) 507,087. On the Missouri and Kansas Rivers, across from Kansas City, Kansas. Settled in 1821.

KANSAS CITY, KANSAS. Population (1970 census) 168,213. County seat of Wyandotte County. On the Missouri and Kansas Rivers. Settled in 1857.

Kansas-Nebraska Act

The Kansas-Nebraska Act was a law passed by the United States Congress in 1854 to settle a bitter dispute over the slavery question in Kansas and Nebraska. At that time, Kansas and Nebraska had not yet become states. The Kansas-Nebraska Act provided that when the two territories became states, the people of each could vote for or against slavery. The opponents of slavery protested that an earlier law, called the Missouri Compromise, barred slavery in Nebraska. The people who favored slavery argued that the Kansas-Nebraska Act repealed the Missouri Compromise.

Kansas became a battlefield, with the anti-slavery settlers fighting against the pro-slavery settlers. John Brown was one of the anti-slavery fighters. For two years, war and violence reigned there and the region became known as "Bleeding Kansas." The anti-slavery forces won, and Kansas was admitted to the United States as a "free" state.

Kant, Immanuel

Immanuel Kant was a German philosopher, or student of knowledge. He thought and wrote about how people learn, how much they can know, and how they know that they know. He also wrote  about ethics, the study of what is right and what is wrong. Kant said that people would lead good lives if they would follow one rule, which he called the *categorical imperative.* This rule is: Always act as you think anyone ought to act in the same situation, without thinking of your own wishes or interests. This means that you should never make an exception in favor of yourself, and comes very close to the Golden Rule.

Kant's personal life was a strange one. He was born in 1724 in Königsberg and never left that city. His life was so regular and methodical that his neighbors used to set their clocks by his goings and comings. Kant never married. He became a professor at the University of Königsberg and taught there for many years. He died in 1804, at the age of 80.

kaolin

Kaolin is a fine, white clay that is used to make porcelain. Kaolin is also used as a coating for shiny paper, in cotton goods, and as a base for paints. Kaolin is found in China, Europe, and Georgia, in the United States. It is mined dry with a shovel, or flooded loose with jets of water and then pumped out. After it has been washed and refined, it is molded into cakes and dried.

See the article on POTTERY, in another volume of this encyclopedia.

kapok

Kapok is the silky smooth fiber that lines the seed pods of the ceiba tree, which is also called the silk-cotton tree. The kapok fiber is a very thin, air-filled tube. This makes kapok useful in life belts used to keep people afloat in water, and in air-plane pilots' suits, because air weighs so little and it keeps heat and cold from passing through. A pound of kapok in a life belt can support twenty-five pounds. Kapok is also used to stuff cushions and mattresses. Kapok catches fire easily unless it is treated with chemicals to prevent it from doing so. Kapok comes from Java and Central America, where it is grown on plantations or gathered from wild trees.

Karachi

Karachi is the largest city and the former capital of Pakistan. It is in West Pakistan, on the Arabian Sea, and is the most important seaport in the country. About 3 million people live there. Most of them work in plants processing flour, cotton, and rice, and in factories that make chemicals, cement, leather goods, and glass. Many work in the large harbor of Karachi. Karachi is also the chief port for Afghanistan. The Karachi airport is one of the most important in Asia, and planes from all over the world land there. In 1947, when Pakistan was separated from India and became an independent

country, Karachi was made its temporary capital. In 1959 it was decided to build a new seat for the government near Rawalpindi in the north of the country, at the foot of the Himalaya mountains.

KARACHI. Population (1973 estimate) 3,060,000. In West Pakistan, on Arabian Sea.

karakul

The karakul is an animal of the sheep family. It is valued chiefly for its fur. It is raised mostly in Asiatic countries such as Afghanistan. The karakul lamb has a coat of tightly curled ringlets, usually black but sometimes brown or gray. These skins make the furs called broadtail, Persian lamb, and caracul.

Karelia

Karelia is an autonomous republic in the Soviet Union. The Soviet Union consists of fifteen constituent republics, which are like the states in the United States, and several autonomous republics. Karelia has an area of about 69,000 square miles, which makes it about the size of Oklahoma. It covers the northwestern part of Soviet Russia.

Almost three-quarters of Karelia is covered by dense forests of pine and fir trees. For this reason, lumber is the biggest industry of the country. Most of the people work in some branch of this industry, from the cutting of trees to the making of wood pulp for paper. Karelia is one of the main centers for the manufacture of paper in Soviet Russia. There are many lakes and marshes. Two of the largest lakes are Lake Ladoga and Lake Onega, both in the southern part of Karelia. The capital, Petrozavodsk, is on Lake Onega, and it is a port for lumber products coming down from the north. The Murmansk railroad crosses the country. The lakes abound in fish, and fishing is another major industry. There is little farming done in Karelia, because the soil is rocky and unfertile and the climate is cold and rather dry.

The population of Karelia is about 714,000. Most of the people are Russians, but there are many Karelians and Finns. Many hundreds of years ago, Karelia was part of a region that included Finland. For this reason the Karelians are very closely related to the Finnish people in language and culture.

Kashmir

Kashmir is the usual name of a state in Asia that is officially called *Jammu and Kashmir.* For hundreds of years Jammu and Kashmir were separate provinces. In 1846 they were joined under one ruler. **Today, Jammu and three-quarters of** Kashmir form one of the states of the republic of India and the rest is part of Pakistan. India and Pakistan have long disputed the right to govern Kashmir.

Kashmir covers 92,780 square miles (about the size of Oregon) and about 4,500,000 people live there. On its borders are five countries: the Soviet Union, Tibet (part of China), India, Pakistan, and Afghanistan. This is important because any of these countries can be invaded from Kashmir. The Himalaya mountains, highest in the world, form the northern border.

The English spelling of the name, Cashmere, is applied to the very soft and

fine wool from Kashmir's wild goats, used for sweaters, shawls, and fabrics. Kashmir's fertile valleys produce fruits, vegetables, grain, and beautiful flowers. In a famous poem ("Lalla Rookh") the Irish poet Thomas Moore wrote, "Who has not heard of the vale of Cashmere, with its roses the brightest that earth ever gave?"

The state of Kashmir has two capital cities. The summer capital is Srinagar, which means "Happy Valley." Srinagar is the largest city and is one of the most beautiful and unusual in the world. More than 200,000 people live in Srinagar. The winter capital is Jammu, an industrial city of about 60,000, where silk, rubber goods and pottery are made.

Because Kashmir's ruler is a Hindu, India claims it; but most of the people are Mohammedans, so Pakistan claims it. This resulted in open warfare in September 1965, when Pakistani troops invaded Kashmir and India then invaded Pakistan. The Soviet premier Kosygin, by brilliant diplomacy, persuaded the warring countries to agree to a truce after a few weeks of fighting, but neither of them gave up its claims to Kashmir.

Kattegat

The Kattegat is a channel between Sweden and Denmark. It connects the Baltic Sea and the North Sea, north of the continent of Europe. The Kattegat is 137 miles long. It is only about 37 miles wide in some places and more than 400 miles wide in other places.

The Kattegat is a dangerous place for ships. There are many large sand bars, and often there are severe storms. In the Kattegat there are a few small islands where people live. They make their living by farming and fishing.

Because shipping from the principal ports of Germany and Russia pass through the Kattegat to reach the Atlantic Ocean, the Kattegat was a favorite hunting ground for submarines in World Wars I and II.

katydid

The katydid is a small green insect related to the grasshopper. The ordinary grasshopper has short antennae, or feelers, growing out of its head, while the katydid has long antennae. Like the grasshopper, the katydid has strong hind legs that enable it to hop great distances at a time, and the katydid can also fly. Its large green wings look very much like leaves, making it very hard for enemies to see it.

The katydid makes its home on the branches and leaves of trees. The male katydid makes a noise that sounds very much like "Katy did, Katy didn't." On a quiet night this call can be heard for a long distance. It is made by rubbing one wing against the other. Although the katydid's chief food is plants, farmers do not find it a serious pest to their crops.

Kaunas

Kaunas is a city in Lithuania. It has been known for almost a thousand years as a trading center. Kaunas has been part of the Soviet Union since 1940, when the Communist government of Russia seized Lithuania by force of arms. The Russian name for Kaunas is *Kovno*.

About 214,000 people live in Kaunas. Many of them make iron and steel prod-

ucts or work in other factories. The city has a university, a school of music, and many old churches and monasteries.

kayak

A kayak is a long, narrow canoe used by Eskimo hunters and fishermen. Kayaks have light, rounded frames of bone or wood, pointed at each end. To make a kayak, the Eskimos chew animal skins, usually sealskins, to make them soft and easy to stretch. Then they sew the skins to the boat frame with large curved needles made of bone.

When an Eskimo goes out to hunt walrus or seal, or to fish, he climbs into the small round opening in the middle of the boat, which looks like the cockpit of an airplane, and laces himself in. The Eskimo fisherman wears a coat made of sealskin or sealgut, which is waterproof, and this coat fits over the sides of the round opening after he is seated, making the boat watertight.

A kayak is usually about fifteen to twenty feet long and just wide enough for one person. A double-bladed paddle is used to guide the kayak and to help balance it. When the waves are very rough, the boat and rider can roll completely over with the waves and bob right-side-up on top of the water again.

Keats, John

John Keats was an English poet, one of the greatest who ever lived. He was born in London in 1795. His father, who kept a stable, was killed in a fall from a horse when Keats was 8 years old. When Keats was 14 his mother died of tuberculosis, a disease that Keats himself later developed.

Keats learned to love the works of earlier poets, especially Spenser and Shakespeare, and to appreciate Greek art and literature. His guardians decided he should become a doctor and at 20 Keats entered medical school, but he was more interested in writing and in knowing such other writers as Charles Lamb, Percy B. Shelley, and Leigh Hunt.

Gale Research Co.

In 1816, when Keats was 21, he started publishing his poems. When his long poem "Endymion" was published it was harshly attacked, not really because the critics disliked it but because they hated Leigh Hunt, who had befriended Keats. Keats kept on writing.

Keats became engaged to a girl named Fanny Brawne, but he never married. The sickness that killed his mother and a brother was now beginning to weaken him. He had no money, his illness grew worse, and he moved to Italy because of its warm climate, but this did not help. In 1821 Keats died. He was only 26 years old, but he had written some of the finest of all English poems. He is buried in Rome and the epitaph on his grave is, "Here lies one whose name was writ in water."

The opening line of "Endymion" is, "A thing of beauty is a joy forever," and in another of his famous poems, the "Ode on a Grecian Urn," he wrote, "Beauty is truth, truth beauty—that is all ye know on earth, and all ye need to know." These

were the sentiments on which his life and poetry were based. Others of his best-known poems are "Ode to Autumn" and "Ode to a Nightingale."

Keller, Helen

Helen Keller, who became deaf and blind when she was only 19 months old, probably did more to help others like herself than anyone else who ever lived. She was born in 1880 in Alabama. When she was 7, she was put in the care of a great teacher named Anne Sullivan Macy. Mrs. Macy taught Helen to read with her fingers, using the Braille system of little raised dots to represent letters. She taught her to hear by feeling the vibrations of sound in the throat. She taught her to control the sounds of her voice in speech even though she could not hear. After graduating from Radcliffe College at the age of 24, Miss Keller became a lecturer and a writer, and raised money for the blind and deaf. She died in 1968, about a month before reaching the age of 88.

Kelvin, Lord

Lord Kelvin was a British scientist who supervised the laying of the first telegraphic cable under the Atlantic Ocean. His name was William Thomson, but for his scientific work he was awarded the title Lord Kelvin, in 1892. He also made discoveries about sound, light, heat, and electricity. Kelvin invented a scale of temperature that starts at absolute zero, which is the coldest cold possible. He was born in 1824, in Ireland, and died in 1907.

Kemal Ataturk

Kemal Ataturk was a great Turkish general and statesman. He was born in 1881, joined the Turkish army in 1904, and fought bravely against the Italians in the war of 1911 and 1912, and in World War I. After World War I, Kemal opposed the Allied plan to divide Turkey, and he won back many of his country's lost territories. In 1919 he organized the Turkish Nationalist Republican Party and set up a new government. He ousted the sultan and established a republican form of government, becoming its first president, in October, 1923.

For the next fifteen years Kemal devoted himself to making Turkey a modern, progressive country. He modernized the dress, laws and alphabet, established free schools, and did many things for the farmers of the country. He made the church (Mohammedan) and state separate, as in the United States. In 1934 the Turkish government gave him the name *Ataturk*, which in Turkish means "father of the Turks." He was re-elected president every four years until his death in 1938.

Kennedy, Jacqueline

"Jackie" Kennedy, the former Jacqueline Lee Bouvier, as the wife of President John F. Kennedy was acclaimed throughout the world as the youngest and most beautiful First Lady the United States has had.

Mrs. Kennedy was born in Southampton, N. Y. in 1929. She graduated in 1951

from George Washington University in Washington, D.C., where she became a journalist and met and married John Kennedy, then a Senator. In the White House, she advanced national culture by her interest in art, serious music, and history. She was only 34 when her husband was assassinated and she was admired for the courage and dignity she displayed and imparted to her children, Caroline (born in 1957) and John, Jr. (born in 1960). Five years after the death of John F. Kennedy, she married a multimillionaire Argentinean of Greek ancestry, Aristotle Onassis, who died in 1975.

John F. Kennedy

John Fitzgerald Kennedy, President of the United States from January 1961 to November 1963, was the youngest man and the only member of the Roman Catholic Church to be elected to that high office. He was the fourth President to be assassinated, and on his death he was mourned in his own country and in foreign countries as Abraham Lincoln had been 100 years before.

HIS EARLY LIFE

Kennedy was of distinguished American ancestry on both sides, though his forebears were comparatively recent settlers in the United States, having come to the U.S. from Ireland during the famines there in the 1840s. Kennedy's father, Joseph Patrick Kennedy, as a banker and investor, acquired one of the biggest American fortunes. He served from 1937 to 1940 as Ambassador to Great Britain, the highest U.S. diplomatic post. Kennedy's grandfather on his mother's side, John Fitzgerald ("Honey Fitz"), was a famous mayor of Boston.

Joseph and Rose Kennedy had nine children. John was the second. His older brother Joseph was destined for a political career but was killed in World War II. John took his place. The younger brothers, Robert (U.S. Attorney General 1961-64, elected Senator from New York in 1964) and Edward (elected Senator from Massachusetts in 1962) both succeeded in politics, although Robert was assassinated in California in 1968. Four of the daughters married distinguished men.

John F. Kennedy was born at Brook-line, Massachusetts, May 29, 1917. He had early training in private schools and when he was 14 he entered Choate Academy in Wallingford, Connecticut, graduating in 1935. After beginning his college education at Princeton, and dropping out because of illness, he transferred to Harvard, which his father had attended, and graduated *cum laude* in 1940, with government and political science his chief studies. The thesis he wrote at the time of his graduation, *Why England Slept*, was published as a book on the recommendation of one of his professors and became a best-seller.

When the U.S. was attacked at Pearl Harbor in 1941, Kennedy enlisted in the U.S. Navy as a seaman but was commissioned an ensign six months later. The PT boat he commanded was rammed and sunk by a Japanese destroyer in 1943. Kennedy towed a member of his crew three miles to shore and contrived the rescue of his crew; he received three medals and many stories and pictures have been based on this exploit. But Kennedy had contracted malaria and an ailment of his back and was retired from the service in 1945.

HIS CAREER IN POLITICS

Kennedy was elected to Congress from Massachusetts three times (1946-48-50) and to the U.S. Senate in 1952 and 1958. While he was a Senator his back ailment required that he have several operations and a long convalescence, in which period he wrote the book *Profiles in Courage* (1956) about unselfish acts in political life; the book won the 1957 Pulitzer Prize and is still a best-seller. Also while a Senator he met and married Jacqueline Lee Bouvier (see KENNEDY, JACQUELINE).

In the 1956 convention of the Democratic Party, Kennedy was a contender for the nomination for Vice-President but lost it to Estes Kefauver. In 1960 Kennedy, after campaigning vigorously and winning primaries in several states, became the Democratic nominee for President. With Lyndon B. Johnson of Texas as his running mate, he won the election by a small margin over Richard Nixon, the Republican nominee. An unprecedented series of public debates on television, in which Kennedy made a better appearance than Nixon, is credited with affecting or determining the result.

HIS PRESIDENCY

As President, Kennedy launched a plan that was widely called "the New Frontier." In the United States he asked for stronger laws to protect civil rights, especially of Negroes, and for more medical care to aged persons. Business conditions had fallen back slightly and Kennedy persuaded Congress to lower taxes so as to improve business. In foreign affairs Kennedy was firm in opposing the spread of communism. He visited Europe to meet the heads of the big countries. On these trips the popularity of Mrs. Kennedy helped him greatly.

When Kennedy became President, Fidel Castro was already heading a communistic government in Cuba. An early act of the Kennedy administration was to support an attack by Cuban refugees at Bay of Pigs, in Cuba, to start a revolution against Castro. The attack was badly planned and executed, and it failed. This was a black mark against the Kennedy administration, which then supported a gift of more than $60,000,000 worth of food and drugs to Castro to ransom some 1,200 prisoners taken by his forces. But when in 1962 Kennedy learned that Cuba with Russian assistance was setting up bases for atomic weapons aimed at the U.S. and other American countries, he acted with great bravery and forced Russia to withdraw the atomic weapons

On November 22, 1963, President Kennedy was killed by a bullet fired by an assassin, later identified as Lee Harvey Oswald, while riding through the streets of Dallas, Texas, on his way to deliver a speech. Not only in the U.S. but throughout the world there was mourning. Many geographical and place names were changed to "Kennedy" in honor of the martyred President. There were many books written about Kennedy's life.

A commission appointed by President L. B. Johnson and headed by Chief Justice Earl Warren decided in 1964 that Oswald, a former Communist but not at the time employed by any communistic country (or by any right-wing or segregationist group) had committed the crime without assistance. Oswald was never tried; on November 24, 1963, two days after the crime, he was shot and killed by a Dallas night-club proprietor, Jack Ruby. A Dallas jury convicted Ruby and he was sentenced to death.

Kennedy, Robert Francis

Robert F. Kennedy was the U.S. Senator from New York when he was shot by an assassin during a gathering of his supporters right after having won the Democratic Presidential primary race in California in 1968. Robert Kennedy was the younger brother of President John F. Kennedy. Born in Brookline, Massachusetts in 1925, Robert graduated from Harvard and received a law degree from the University of Virginia. He managed his brother John's campaign for the Senate in 1952 and for the Presidency in 1960. He became Attorney General in 1961 and U.S. Senator from N.Y. in 1964.

Kentucky

Kentucky is a state in the south central part of the United States. Its nickname is the "Bluegrass State," because the grass called bluegrass grows so well in parts of the state. It is here that the fine Kentucky horses are raised. Kentucky raises more tobacco than any other state except North Carolina. The state song, "My Old Kentucky Home," written by Stephen C. Foster, is known throughout the world. Kentucky ranks 37th in size among the states, with 40,395 square miles. In population it ranks 23rd, with about three million people living there. It became a state in 1792, and was the 15th state admitted to the United States. The capital is Frankfort.

THE PEOPLE OF KENTUCKY

The early settlers of Kentucky were courageous pioneers from states further east, such as Virginia and Maryland. They had to fight many bitter battles with the Indians, and Kentucky became known as

Kentucky Department of Information
The Governor's Mansion in Frankfort, Kentucky.

The leading cities of Kentucky, with populations from the 1970 census, are:

Frankfort, population, 21,356, state capital, in north central part of state. There is a separate article about FRANKFORT.

Louisville, population 361,472, the largest city, manufacturing center, on the Ohio River, in the northern part of Kentucky.

Lexington, population 108,137, the second-largest city, tobacco center, in the central area.

Covington, population 52,535, the third-largest city, commercial and industrial center, on the Ohio River, in the northern part of the state.

Owensboro, population 50,329, fourth-largest city, on the Ohio River, in the northwestern area.

"the dark and bloody land." As the state grew, people came from other countries, but today most Kentuckians are American-born.

More than half the people of Kentucky are farmers. Once they raised only tobacco and corn. Now they also raise many kinds of grain, fruits and vegetables. Many also raise dairy cattle and hogs. Others work in the rich coal mines and oil fields in eastern and western Kentucky. Two out of five people work in factories and stores in the cities.

The Baptists have the largest church membership in the state. Other important denominations are the Roman Catholic, Methodist, and Presbyterian, and the Christian Church, which was founded near Paris, Kentucky, in 1804 and has since spread across the nation.

WHAT KENTUCKY IS LIKE

A visitor to Kentucky finds that the eastern, central and western parts are quite different. The eastern region is mountainous. In the southeast are the Cumberland Mountains and the Kentucky Ridge. This is a beautiful and wild region, with deep valleys and valuable coal and oil deposits. It was through a natural gap in the mountains, known as the Cumberland Gap, that settlers came from the east. Later, herds of cattle and hogs were driven back through this gap to markets in the east. Many "mountaineers" live in these hills.

The central part of Kentucky is the bluegrass region. It is a rolling plain, known for its tobacco and livestock. Here the finest racing horses are raised on farms surrounded by white wooden fences. These farms are as carefully kept as city parks. The bluegrass provides such fine grazing for the horses that a baby colt reaches full size in 18 to 20 months. In the center of this region is Lexington, one of the greatest tobacco markets in the world.

The western part of Kentucky is generally rocky, with rich coal deposits. It has swamps, large forests, and many caves. The most famous is Mammoth Cave.

Although more people live in the country than in the cities, manufacturing is the largest industry in Kentucky. Most of the important factories are in cities in the Ohio River valley, which forms the northern boundary of the state.

Kentucky has a mild and even climate that is excellent for farming. The average temperature in July is 77 degrees. In winter, the average temperature is 36 degrees, and in the mountains there is often heavy snow.

Few states have such excellent river transportation as Kentucky. The Ohio, Mississippi, Tennessee, Kentucky and Cumberland rivers are the principal ones. Railroads and highways reach most parts of the state. There are airports in the principal cities.

GOVERNMENT OF KENTUCKY

Kentucky calls itself a "commonwealth" and not a state, but like the other states it is governed by a Governor and a Legislature. The Governor is elected for a four-year term and cannot succeed himself. The legislature is composed of two houses, a Senate, whose members are elected for a four-year term, and a House of Representatives, whose members are elected for a two-year term. Judges are elected for a six-year term, except on the Court of Appeals (Supreme Court), on which terms are for eight years. The capital is Frankfort. There are 120 counties.

In the past, many Kentuckians, especially in the mountains, could neither read nor write, but this has changed in the past eighty years. Among the principal colleges and universities are:

University of Kentucky, at Lexington. Enrollment, 27,920 in 1971 (co-ed).

Kentucky State College, at Frankfort. Enrollment, 1,600 in 1971 (co-ed).

University of Louisville, at Louisville. Enrollment, 8,780 in 1971 (co-ed)..

Western Kentucky State College, at Bowling Green. Enrollment, 10,148 in 1971 (co-ed).

Eastern Kentucky State College, at Richmond. Enrollment, 8,779 in 1971 (co-ed).

Murray State College, at Murray. Enrollment, 7,255 in 1971 (co-ed).

Berea College, at Berea. Enrollment, 1,303 in 1971 (co-ed).

KENTUCKY IN THE PAST

For a long time, Kentucky was a large unexplored part of the colony of Virginia. The most famous of the pioneers was Daniel BOONE, about whom there is a separate article. Other men followed Boone, and the first attempt at a settlement was made at Harrodsburg, in 1774. The following year, Boone was sent by a company that had purchased land in Kentucky to blaze a trail there. He did, and directed the building of a fort, which was the beginning of the first permanent settlement of Boonesborough, in 1775. Harrodsburg was made a permanent settlement later in the same year.

In spite of great danger from the Indians, Kentucky grew rapidly and was the first "western" state to be developed and the first to be admitted to the United States, which was in 1792.

In the War of 1812 against the British, Kentuckians played an important part. They were famous for being keen riflemen, and at the battle of Lake Erie Kentucky riflemen were stationed in the masts of the ships. Their marksmanship helped to win the battle.

Kentucky continued to prosper and to grow in population. It was a true "border state," partly like Ohio on the north and partly like Tennessee on the south. Kentucky was a slave state, but its cattle and grain did not depend on slave labor as did the raising of cotton farther south. At the outbreak of the Civil War Kentucky was sharply divided on the slavery question. Kentucky did not secede from the Union, but its people fought in both the Union and Confederate armies. Several battles were fought on Kentucky soil.

In the last fifty years, Kentucky has improved its farming and manufactures, and schools, railroads, and highways have been built.

PLACES TO SEE IN KENTUCKY

Mammoth Cave National Park, 51,-354 acres, in south central Kentucky, 20 miles northeast of Bowling Green, north of U.S. Route 68. The cave consists of a series of underground rooms and passages on five levels; covers an area ten miles around; includes three rivers and a lake. The temperature never varies, remaining at 54 degrees both in summer and winter.

Abraham Lincoln National Historical Park, 116 acres, in central Kentucky, 3 miles south of Hodgenville, on U.S. Route 31E. Contains a magnificent granite memorial and a restoration of the little log

cabin where Abraham Lincoln is supposed to have been born. The park includes 100 acres of the original farm of Lincoln's father.

"My Old Kentucky Home," in the central part, 1 mile east of Bardstown, on U.S. Route 62. A house that belonged to the Rowan family, cousins of Stephen C. Foster, though it is doubtful that he ever saw the house or that he wrote the song about it.

Pinnacle Mountain, in the south central part, 4 miles east of Middlesboro, on U.S. Route 58. One of the most beautiful peaks in the Cumberland Mountains. The Skyland Highway leads to the summit, 1,800 feet above the valley; a magnificent view of the region.

Fort Knox, in the north central part, 20 miles south of Louisville, on U.S. Route 31W. An army post of more than 106,000 acres. It includes a fortified building that holds the greater part of the gold reserve of the United States, the biggest quantity of gold ever assembled in one place.

Ancient Buried City, in the west, 5 miles south of Wickliffe, on U.S. Route 51. Once a city of the prehistoric Mound Builders. There are forty mounds, five of which have been excavated, including the Infant Burial Mound, with numerous child burials and toys.

Horse farms, in the bluegrass region in the central part, around Lexington, which is on U.S. Route 60. Some famous thoroughbred horses may be "visited" at these farms.

KENTUCKY. Area, 40,395 square miles. Population (1970 census) 3,218,706. Capital, Frankfort. Nickname, The Bluegrass State. Motto, United We Stand, Divided We Fall. Flower, goldenrod. Bird, cardinal. Song, "My Old Kentucky Home." Admitted to Union, June 1, 1792. Official abbreviation, Ky.

Kenya

Kenya is a nation in East Africa that became independent in 1963 after being controlled by Great Britain for more than 75 years. It has an area of about 225,000 square miles, almost as big as Texas, and, in 1973, nearly twelve million people. Nearly all of these were Africans of the Negro race, the largest group being the Kikiyu tribe, but there were 270,321 Kenyans who were white (Europeans) or from India. The capital is Nairobi, a modern city with a population of 535,200.

The central part of Kenya is high and level, 3,000 to 6,000 feet above the sea. Here the climate is cool and comfortable. The seacoast of Kenya is hot and damp. There are three big rivers, the Juba, the Tana, and the Sabaski.

Most of the people are farmers. In central Kenya they grow grains and bananas; along the coast they grow rice, coffee, cotton, tobacco, and many tropical crops such as coconuts, cinnamon, pineapples, sugar cane, vanilla, and dates. There are big forests, yielding rubber, timber, and olives, and the mountains produce gold, marble, and other stones. Many tourists go to Kenya for big-game hunting.

Great Britain took control of Kenya in 1886 and sent settlers there. In 1920 Kenya became a British colony. But the native Kenyans wanted independence and about 1950 a group called the Mau Mau, mostly Kikiyus, began a campaign

of terrorism to drive the British out. The Mau Mau killed not only British colonists but also any Africans who would not join them. For several years British armed forces fought the Mau Mau and by 1956 it seemed that the British had won, with Jomo Kenyatta, the Mau Mau leader, in jail; but in free elections in 1961 and 1962 the people decided to be an independent republic in the (British) Commonwealth. Kenyatta became prime minister in 1963 and president in 1964.

KENYA. Area, 224,960 square miles. Population (1973 estimate) 11,690,000.

Kepler, Johannes

Johannes Kepler was a brilliant German astronomer who was the first to explain how the planets move around the sun. This explanation is part of three statements known as *Kepler's Laws.*

Another astronomer, Nicholas Copernicus, who lived about fifty years before Kepler, had already said that the planets move around the sun, but Copernicus thought that the path or orbit in which

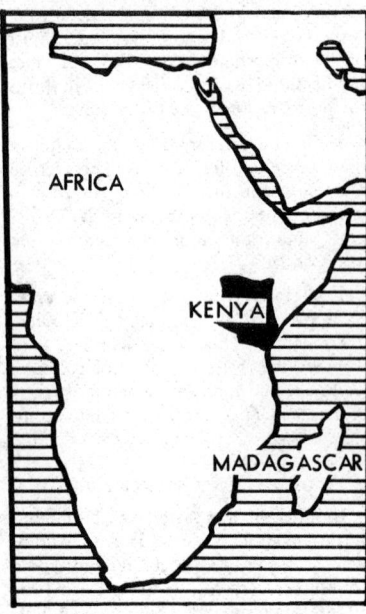

AFRICA

KENYA

MADAGASCAR

the planets move was a circle. This idea was disproved by Kepler, who showed that the orbits of the planets were not circles but ellipses (egg-shaped curves). He also disproved the idea that the planets always move around the sun with the same rate of speed. He showed that planets move faster when they are close to the sun, and slower when they are far away from it.

Kepler's Laws for a long time were considered heretical (contrary to the accepted opinions of the day) and many people refused to believe that they were true. The scientists GALILEO and Isaac NEWTON later proved that Kepler was right. There are separate articles about these men.

Kepler was born in 1571. At the age of 4, he was left crippled and nearly blind by an attack of smallpox. He spent most of his time studying, and when he was 22 he was made a professor of mathematics at the University of Graz. When he was 29, he was made assistant to the famous astronomer, Tycho Brahe, who was the royal astronomer of Bohemia, which is now part of Czechoslovakia.

Kepler helped Brahe make star charts

showing where the different stars were located in the heavens, and also to chart the positions of the planets in the heavens throughout the year. It was from these charts that Kepler got the information from which he developed his laws.

When Brahe died in 1601, Kepler took his place as royal astronomer. In 1609 he published a book containing information that he and Brahe had collected about the movements of the planet Mars. In this book were also contained the first two of Kepler's Laws, which explained these movements mathematically. The third law was contained in a book published ten years later. Kepler's Laws and Newton's Law of Universal Gravitation are the foundation of the modern science of astronomy. Most scientists consider Kepler to be one of the greatest scientists of all time. He died in 1630.

Kern, Jerome

Jerome Kern was the composer of many of America's most popular songs. Almost all his songs were written to be sung in musical shows. In 1927 Kern wrote the music for *Show Boat,* a musical show adapted from Edna Ferber's novel of the same name. It was one of the most popular musical shows ever written, and one of the songs Kern wrote for it, "Ol' Man River," is loved and sung everywhere.

Jerome Kern was born in New York in 1885. His mother gave him his first piano lessons, and later he studied music in New York and in Germany. He wrote successful songs for musical shows in London before he wrote them for the theater in the United States.

Among Jerome Kern's most successful shows were *Sally, Sunny,* and *Roberta.* Songs for these shows included "Look for the Silver Lining," "The Song is You," and "They Didn't Believe Me." Kern wrote many of his best shows with Oscar Hammerstein II, who worked with Richard Rodgers after Kern's death in 1945. Jerome Kern had one of the greatest collections of rare books in the world. It was sold at auction for more than a million dollars.

kerosene

Kerosene is a thin oil that is used as a fuel in lamps and stoves. In some cases it is used to run tractors and farm machinery, as gasoline is used to run automobiles. It is also used in jet engines.

Kerosene is almost colorless, and looks somewhat like water, but it has a strong smell and it catches fire very easily. Until about a hundred years ago, whale oil and candles were used for light, but then it was found that kerosene gave more and better light. Later, kerosene was found useful for cooking and heating also. Kerosene lamps with glass chimneys are still used in houses that have no electricity or gas.

Kerosene was once called coal oil, because it was made from coal. Now very little kerosene is made from coal. It is made from petroleum, the heavy crude oil that comes from oil wells. The crude

oil is put into a large tank and heated to the boiling point. This releases several gases, which are separated and cooled back into liquid form to make different oils such as gasoline and kerosene.

One of the big differences between gasoline and kerosene is that a gasoline and air mixture is usually too rich to burn at ordinary temperatures, while a kerosene and air mixture is explosive.

Kerry blue terrier

The Kerry blue terrier is a medium-sized dog that came originally from County Kerry, in Ireland. People in England and Ireland use Kerry blue terriers for hunting small game (animals and birds) and for retrieving. A Kerry blue will go and pick up game its master has shot, whether it is on the ground or in water. Kerry blues have also been used in the British Isles for herding sheep and cattle. In the United States and Canada, Kerry blue terriers are kept as pets and

American Kennel Club

The Kerry blue terrier, which originated in Ireland, is a fine hunting dog, a friendly pet, and a courageous watchdog.

watchdogs, because they are fine house dogs and gentle with children.

A Kerry blue terrier stands about 17 to 20 inches high at the shoulder, and it is about 16 to 19 inches long from its chest to the base of its tail. It usually weighs between 30 and 40 pounds. It is easy to recognize a Kerry blue terrier because it has straight, stiff-looking front legs, with hair clipped to look as if it were wearing chaps, and a bushy, squarish beard on the chin. The tails of the puppies are clipped short when they are a few days old. A Kerry blue terrier has a dark grayish-blue coat, with thick, wavy, soft hair. Sometimes the dogs are a light bluish-gray, and sometimes they are such a dark shade that they seem almost black.

kestrel

The kestrel is a small bird of prey that is found in Europe and Asia. A bird of prey is one that hunts other animals for food. The kestrel is a member of the falcon family and is related to the American sparrow hawk. The full-grown kestrel is about a foot long. The male is bluish-gray in color and the female is a reddish-brown. The kestrel has a powerful beak, which it uses to catch insects, other birds, and small animals such as field mice. It is very swift in flight, but it can also seem to hang motionless in mid-air. Actually it is far from motionless. It hangs in one spot by vibrating its wings so rapidly that they

cannot be seen to move. In this position it darts its head back and forth with amazing speed in search of prey on the ground. Because of this habit the kestrel is sometimes called the *windhover*.

The kestrel seldom builds its own nest. Usually it takes over the desert nest of another bird. The female lays from four to six spotted white eggs.

Key, Francis Scott

Francis Scott Key was the American poet who wrote the national anthem of the United States, "The Star-Spangled Banner." He was born in Frederick County, Maryland, in 1780, and became a lawyer.

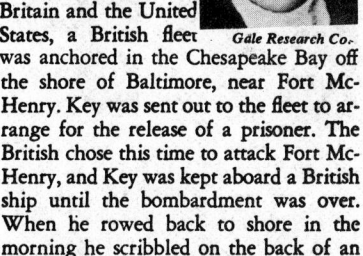

Gale Research Co.

On September 4, 1814, during the War of 1812 between Great Britain and the United States, a British fleet was anchored in the Chesapeake Bay off the shore of Baltimore, near Fort McHenry. Key was sent out to the fleet to arrange for the release of a prisoner. The British chose this time to attack Fort McHenry, and Key was kept aboard a British ship until the bombardment was over. When he rowed back to shore in the morning he scribbled on the back of an old letter a poem describing his feelings as he watched the attack. This poem was "The Star-Spangled Banner."

Key died in 1843. A monument to his memory stands at Fort McHenry. There is a separate article on the STAR-SPANGLED BANNER.

Kharkov

Kharkov is a city in the Ukraine, one of the constituent republics of the Soviet Union. It was once the capital of the Ukraine. It is the center of a wheat-producing region and is also an important railway center. About 1,223,000 people live in Kharkov. There are factories that make tractors and other farm machinery, locomotives, machine tools, and other metal products. Kharkov has a university and many scientific schools.

The city was founded more than three hundred years ago, about the year 1650, by the Cossacks, a tribe of horsemen who lived in old Russia. In the 1920s the Communists began to make Kharkov a beautiful modern city, with fine parks, wide streets, and handsome public buildings.

In World War II Kharkov was captured by the Germans, and more than half of it was destroyed. The damage has now been repaired.

Khartoum

Khartoum is the capital and main city of the Sudan, a nation in northeastern Africa. Khartoum is on the Blue Nile River. Mohammed Ali, an Egyptian ruler, conquered the Sudan in 1820 and founded Khartoum in 1823.

In 1882 a Mohammedan religious leader called the Mahdi led a revolt in the Sudan against the Egyptians and British. By 1885 the Mahdi had built up a huge army and attacked Khartoum. The city was defended by Egyptian troops under Charles G. Gordon, a British general known as "Chinese" Gordon because of his victories in China as the commander

of a Chinese army.

For ten months Gordon held off the fierce attacks of the Mahdi. His defense of Khartoum excited the imagination of all Europe. A British-Egyptian army was sent from Egypt to rescue him and his army, but the rescue force arrived two days after the Mahdi's troops had broken through the city's defenses. Gordon and his soldiers were all killed. Khartoum was reconquered in 1898 by another British general, Lord Kitchener.

KHARTOUM. Population (1973 estimate) 93,103, with suburbs 194,000. Capital of the Sudan.

Khrushchev, Nikita

Nikita Sergeyevich Khruschev was the most powerful man in the Soviet Union (U.S.S.R.) for about ten years, from 1954 to 1964. In 1939, under the dictator Josef Stalin, he became a member of the Politburo (the Soviet cabinet, now called the Presidium) and headman of the Ukraine. When Stalin died in 1953, Khrushchev took his place as Secretary of the Communist Party.

Khrushchev was born in a village in South Russia in 1894. As a boy he was a shepherd and as a young man he was a metalworker in a factory. He joined the Communist Party in 1918, gained much respect by improving agriculture in the Soviet Union when its people were in great need of food, and survived Stalin's "purges" of 1937-1939.

As Party Secretary, Khrushchev was able to oust the premiers Malenkov and Bulganin, who officially had more power, and also such prominent men as Molotov and Zhukov. In 1958 he became the premier and was thought to be a dictator with as much power as Stalin had before him. A jovial, earthy, and sometimes angry man, Khrushchev was liked in many countries where the people do not like Communism. He adopted the policy of getting along with the democratic countries and by so doing he caused the Soviet Union to become unfriendly with Red China, the other big Communist country. In October 1964 the world discovered to its surprise that Khrushchev was not so powerful as had been believed; he was abruptly dismissed from his positions as premier and Party Secretary and became just another unimportant citizen of his country. He died in 1971.

Khyber Pass

The Khyber Pass is a gap between mountains of the second-highest mountain range in the world, on the border between Afghanistan and India. No other pass has been more important to military history, because the Khyber Pass is the only place where an army from Europe can march through the mountains to invade India.

Today there is a modern road through the Khyber Pass. This road carries all the trade between Afghanistan and India. The pass is 33 miles long, and in some places it is only 20 feet wide. It is walled on each side by steep cliffs. The pass is open to travelers only two days a week; the other five days are set aside for traders, some of whom use camel caravans but most of whom use motor trucks.

Kidd, Captain

William Kidd was famous three hundred years ago as a daring and cruel pirate. He was born in Scotland about 1645. After serving well in the English Navy he settled in New York. He was given command of a ship and was sent out to defend shipping against pirates in the Indian Ocean. Captain Kidd returned to New York with a shipload of captured treasure, which he said he had brought back from captured pirate ships and meant to turn over to the British government. But the British authorities thought he had been a pirate himself. He was arrested and sent to England for trial as a pirate. He was convicted and hanged in 1701, though many people believed and many still believe that the trial was unfair.

In 1698, the year Captain Kidd brought his ship back to New York, a great treasure was found buried on Gardiner's Island, near Long Island. For hundreds of years afterward people dug all over the area for buried treasure.

kidnapping

Kidnapping is the crime of seizing and holding a person against his will either for the payment of money or for some other purpose. Kidnapping has been known almost throughout history. In olden days, slaves were gotten by kidnapping, and robber bands used to kidnap travelers on the highways and hold them for ransom. (Ransom is money that the family of a captured person has to pay to have him set free.) During the 1930s in the United States, gangsters used to kidnap businessmen or other gangsters and either kill them or hold them for ransom.

Today, the stealing of children is almost the only kidnapping. The first famous child kidnapping in the United States was that of Charley Ross, the son of a rich Philadelphia family, in 1874. No trace of the boy was ever found. In 1932, the most famous of all kidnapping cases occurred. It was the kidnapping and murder of the son of Charles A. Lindbergh, the great American flyer who made the first solo crossing of the Atlantic Ocean. This crime aroused the entire nation. A man named Bruno Hauptmann was convicted of the kidnapping and was executed. As a result of this case, a Federal law called the Lindbergh law was passed. This law makes kidnapping a Federal crime if the victim is taken across a state line or if a stolen automobile or other property used by the kidnappers is taken across a state line, or if United States property is involved. A Federal crime is one that national law-enforcement agencies, such as the Federal Bureau of Investigation, may take part in solving.

kidney

The kidneys are two organs of the body that remove waste materials from the blood. A kidney is shaped somewhat like a bean. The kidneys lie on each side of the spine, in the small of the back. They are reddish in color, and each one is about 4 inches long.

Some of the food digested in your body becomes dissolved and passes into the blood stream. Some of this dissolved food is not needed by the body and is carried by the blood to the kidneys. The kidneys are made up of many tubes, into which tiny blood vessels carry waste materials. These kidney tubes remove the waste materials from the blood. The purified blood goes on its journey through the body. The kidneys then transform the waste materials into a fluid called *urine*. Each kidney deposits the urine in a little pool, from which a tube called the *ureter* carries it to the bladder. From there the urine is passed out of the body.

Sometimes waste material in the tubes of the kidney solidifes into stony particles that are too big to pass easily through the tubes. This causes the painful condition known as *kidney stones,* and it takes medical treatment to relieve it. This condition seldom happens to children.

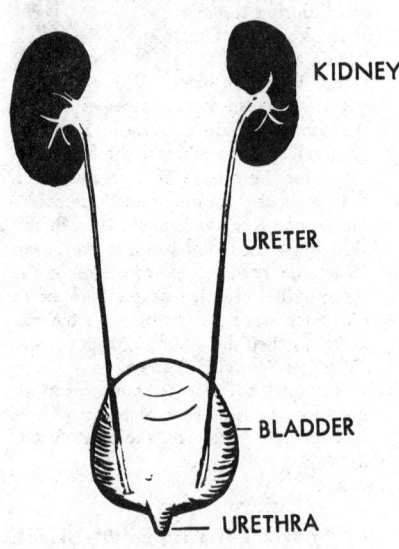

KIDNEY

URETER

BLADDER

URETHRA

The kidney, ureter, and bladder. The urethra carries urine from the bladder, thus passing off waste material.

Kiel Canal

The Kiel Canal is a waterway through which ocean-going ships may travel from the Baltic Sea on the eastern side of Germany to the North Sea, on the western side, and from the North Sea into the Atlantic Ocean. Without the Kiel Canal, these ships would have to go around Denmark, which would be several hundred miles farther.

The Kiel Canal is about 50 miles long. It was built in 1895 and at first it was called the Kaiser Wilhelm Canal, after the man who was then the German emperor. When Germany lost World War I and became a republic, the name was changed.

Kiev

Kiev is a city in Russia. It is one of the largest cities in the Union of Soviet Socialist Republics. It is the capital of the Ukraine, one of the Soviet republics. Before World War II, it was a beautiful city, with many historic monuments. The streets were wide and shaded, and there were many public gardens. Then Germany held the city for two years, and it was largely destroyed by bombs. Much of it has been rebuilt.

Kiev is the cultural center of the Ukraine, with museums, art galleries, a university, an academy of science, and a national gallery. Most of the city is surrounded by ancient walls.

About 1,632,000 people live in Kiev. The city is on the Dnieper River, and the surrounding countryside is excellent farm land. Many of the people work in the factories of Kiev, which include sugar refineries, tanneries, and flour mills.

Kiev has a long history. It is one of the oldest cities in Russia, where it is known as the "mother of cities." More than 1,500 years ago merchants sailed the Dnieper River with furs, honey, silk, and perfumes. They found the site of Kiev, at a place where three rivers flow into the Dnieper, ideal for a city. In the 10th century Kiev became Christian, and many magnificent churches were built. The city became so rich and famous that hordes of Mongol tribesmen from Asia invaded and robbed it, almost destroying it, but the people of Kiev rebuilt their city again and again. Later, Kiev was ruled by Lithuania, and then by Poland, and finally by Russia.

KIEV, U.S.S.R. Population (1973 estimate) 1,632,000. On the Dnieper River. Capital of the Ukraine S.S.R.

Kilauea is a large volcano on the island of Hawaii. See the articles on HAWAII and VOLCANO.

Kilimanjaro

Kilimanjaro is the highest mountain in Africa. It is in Tanganyika, a country in East Africa. Kilimanjaro means "Great Mountain." It has two peaks called Kibo and Mawenzi that are seven miles apart. Kibo, which is over 19,300 feet high, is the higher of these two peaks. People live on the southern slopes of Kilimanjaro below 5,000 feet. This region is called Chaga. It is so cold that the tops of the mountain peaks are always covered with ice and snow. Kilimanjaro is part of a chain of volcanoes, and its slopes are covered with deposits of volcanic rock. It was discovered in 1848 by Johannes Rebmann, a missionary.

Ernest Hemingway, the American writer, wrote a short story called "The Snows of Kilimanjaro," which was made into a successful motion picture.

Killarney

Killarney is the name of a district and a town in Ireland. The district is in County Kerry and is surrounded by the mountains of Kerry. It is known for the very beautiful Killarney Lakes that are found there. There are three of these lakes; they are connected and are called Lower, Middle and Upper Lakes. There are many small, wooded islands in each of them.

On an island in Lower Lake stand the ruins of an old fortress, Ross Castle, and on an island in Middle Lake are the ruins of a monastery built more than 1,300 years ago. Tourists come from all over the world to visit these lakes, and the town of Killarney is a tourist center. A poet once said that Killarney and its lakes are so beautiful that the angels fold their wings and rest there whenever they are tired.

killdeer

The killdeer is a bird that lives along seashores and in marshes in many parts of North America. It is a member of the plover family, and it got its name from its call, which sounds like "kill deer." It

is easy to recognize the killdeer because it has two black bands across its white breast. The back of the killdeer is reddish brown.

The killdeer is a strong flier, and each fall, when it migrates from its northern home, it flies for several thousands of miles to some place in the south where it spends the winter. When it returns north in the spring, it builds a nest in a hollowed-out place in sand or earth, and the female lays four tan speckled eggs that look very much like pebbles. The killdeer is quite tame and will sometimes build a nest on lawns or play fields. If you go near a killdeer's nest, the bird will often flutter along the ground and pretend it has a broken wing, so that your attention will be taken away from the nest.

Kilmer, Joyce

Joyce Kilmer was an American poet who wrote many well-known poems. His most famous is called "Trees." This poem begins, "I think that I shall never see / A poem lovely as a tree." The poem has been set to music and is a great favorite with many singers. Joyce Kilmer was born in New Brunswick, New Jersey, in 1886. He studied at Rutgers and Columbia Universities, and later worked on newspapers. He fought in the United States Army during World War I and was killed in action in France in 1918.

kiln

A kiln is a furnace or oven that is used for drying, baking or burning materials such as brick or pottery in order to make them hard.

A modern kiln in which bricks are made is a large ovenlike building with an arched roof and a tall smokestack for creating the necessary draft. It is built of brick and lined with fire brick. Fire brick is made from new clay mixed with clay that has been baked and then ground.

The bricks to be baked are piled in the kiln in such a way that the burning gases from the fire may move about among them. The fire is built under the bricks. Usually soft coal is used for fuel. There are two kinds of kiln, the up-draft kiln and the down-draft kiln. In the up-draft kiln the flames are allowed to pass through the bricks from the bottom to the top of the kiln. In the down-draft kiln, the flame does not reach the bricks until it has reached the top. Then it pours down through the bricks to the flues. A very high temperature is kept in the kiln, often more than 3,000 degrees Fahrenheit. Limekilns burn limestone and shells to make lime for cement, and pottery kilns harden clay objects by baking them.

kindergarten

Kindergarten is a school for children between the ages of four and six. Friedrich Froebel, a German educator, started the first kindergarten more than a hundred years ago. In the German language, *Kindergarten* means "garden for children," and Froebel gave his school that name because it was a place that helped children to grow. Later Maria MONTESSORI became a great kindergarten authority.

Froebel was at first a teacher of older children. Sometimes when he had trouble with a child he felt it was because the child had learned the wrong things when he was younger. He saw that it was important to teach little children so as to prepare them for further training later.

Froebel found that the best way to teach little children is by letting them do what they like best—play. In a kindergarten the children play games; they make things with blocks and clay and other things. They draw and paint, and learn to sing and dance to music. Though this seems like play, the children learn many things.

Before a child can learn to read and write, his hand and eye muscles must be well developed and he must learn to coördinate them—that is, learn to use them together. When he builds with blocks or draws something, he is learning to coördinate his actions.

One important thing children learn by going to kindergarten is to be away from their mothers for a while each day. A child must learn how to do things for himself and to solve his own problems when he can. If he stayed home where his mother did everything for him, he would never learn to depend on himself.

A child must also learn to play with other children. If you watch very young children playing you will see that even though they are in the same room they often play by themselves. In nursery school, in which the children are even younger than those in kindergarten, they usually play side by side but not with one another. At home the child may have played with his brothers and sisters, but he must also learn to play with children he does not know so well.

WHAT THE CHILDREN LEARN

There are usually rules a child must follow at home, such as when to eat and when to go to bed, but in kindergarten he learns to follow a regular routine in other things as well. He learns that he cannot do what he wants to whenever he wants to, and this is very good training for growing up.

The kindergarten teacher has an important job to do. She must be a friendly person who can help the child get along without his mother, but she must be sure to let the child try to solve his own problems before she comes to help him. She must be patient, because sometimes it takes a child a long time to learn to do something. Scolding may only make it harder for him. She must know each child very well, so that she can tell his mother how well he is getting along and report to his first-grade teacher what to expect from each child. The kindergarten teacher has the same training as other teachers. Since she loves children and wants to help them to get started in the right way, she is usually very happy in her work.

kinescope

A kinescope is a special kind of electronic tube, called a cathode-ray picture tube, which produces the picture you see on a television set.

The picture is first made in the television studio by a cathode-ray camera. The camera takes the picture and changes it into electricity. The electricity is sent through a cable to a high television antenna. The antenna then sends out waves of electricity that are picked up by the television antenna in your home. These waves are changed into beams of electrons (particles of electricity) by a device at one end of the kinescope called an *electron gun*. This gun sends a beam of electrons down the tube between two sets of metal plates called *deflecting* plates, which move the beam up or down and right or left depending on how the picture was taken in the television studio.

The beam falls on a special screen in front of the tube, producing a bright spot. This is called a *reproducing spot*. The reproducing spot moves rapidly across the screen from left to right, making lines as it moves. Each time the spot reaches the right-hand side it jumps back to the left and starts on the next line. The brightness of the different parts of the line depends on the strength of the electron beam. The strength of the electron beam depends on how bright the picture is that is being taken in the television studio.

In this way, the reproducing spot reconstructs the original picture on your television screen. (See also the articles on ELECTRONICS and TELEVISION.)

king, the ruler of a country that is a monarchy: see the article MONARCHY.

King, Ernest J.

Ernest Joseph King was the admiral who was at the head of the United States

Navy during World War II. He was the first naval flier to become commander-in-chief of the United States Fleet and, later, Chief of Naval Operations. He was born in 1878, in Ohio, and he was graduated from the United States Naval Academy at Annapolis. He served in many different positions in the Navy. He was the commander of the submarine base at New London, Connecticut, and captain of an aircraft carrier. When the rank of fleet admiral was created in 1944, Admiral King was one of the first men to receive it. He died in 1956.

King, Mackenzie

William Lyon Mackenzie King was prime minister of Canada for more than twenty years. He was born in Kitchener, Ontario, in 1874. His grandfather, William Lyon Mackenzie, after whom he was named, played a very important part in the history of Canada. King attended the University of Toronto, Harvard University, and the University of Chicago.

He worked in Chicago with Jane Addams, then he went back to Canada, entered politics, and in 1919 became the leader of the Liberal Party. He became Prime Minister in 1921, and except for a few months in 1926 and the years 1930-1935 he remained Prime Minister until 1948. He died in 1950.

King, Martin Luther, Jr.

Martin Luther King, Jr. was an American Negro civil rights leader who taught his followers not to be violent in protesting about the unfair ways in which Negroes are treated by many white people in the United States. He led marches, gave eloquent speeches, and made news in other ways to make the world aware of the discrimination against Negroes.

Martin Luther King, Jr. was born in 1929 in Atlanta, Georgia. Like his father, he became a Baptist minister, later receiving his doctorate degree in theology (the study of religion) at Boston University. In 1956, Dr. King led a Negro boycott of the bus lines in Montgomery, Alabama. The boycott ended when the United States Supreme Court ruled that segregation on the buses was illegal. In 1957, Dr. King founded the Southern Christian Leadership Conference, an organization whose members worked peacefully for civil rights.

Although often criticized and even arrested, he won the respect of educated and intelligent people throughout the world. In 1964, he won the Nobel Peace Prize. In 1968, he was assassinated in Memphis, Tennessee.

kingbird

The kingbird belongs to a group of birds known as flycatchers, or birds that catch all kinds of winged insects. The kingbird does a great service to farmers by eating insects that hurt crops. It is very brave and will fight bigger birds.

The kingbird is found throughout North America. It makes its nest out of grass and moss and places it high up at the end of a tree branch. It is blue-gray in color, and parts of its tail and breast are white. Some kingbirds have yellow breasts. The kingbird has a colored patch on top of its head. This has the appearance of a colored flower and attracts insects.

king crab

The king crab is an animal that lives in shallow sandy or muddy banks along the Atlantic coast from Nova Scotia to Florida. It has a shell-like covering on the outside that is shaped very much like a horse's hoof. For this reason it is often called the horseshoe crab. As the animal grows, it sheds this covering frequently and grows a new one.

Most scientists do not class the king crab with other crabs, but consider it more like a large spider. The king crab grows to be 2 feet long. It has six legs, and breathes through gills on certain of the legs. When it burrows into the mud or sand, it uses its head as a shovel. In the United States the king crab is used for fertilizer. Other kinds are found in China, the Philippines, and Japan, where they are used as food.

kingfisher

The kingfisher is a bird that gets its name because it truly is a king among the fish-catching birds. In catching fish it sits on a limb of a tree that hangs over a stream, looking into the water beneath. Then, as it sights a fish, it drops like a stone into the water. Seconds later, it pops up with the fish in its bill. In addition to fish, it eats worms, crabs, and shellfish. It is found mostly near the fresh-water streams of Europe and North America. The kingfisher's cry is shrill and piercing. The North American kingfisher, called the *belted kingfisher* because of a belt of blue feathers across its white breast, is larger than the European variety. There is a smaller kingfisher, green in color, that is found in Texas.

A kingfisher builds its nest at the end of a tunnel that it burrows into the bank of a stream. The nest is made out of old fishbones and other materials, and it may be used for several years. Young kingfishers are taught how to dive for fish by the parent kingfishers. The European kingfisher is a beautiful bird. Its feathers are bright blue, orange, deep red, pink, and green. The Australian kingfisher is called the KOOKABURRA. There is a separate article about it.

Kings, Books of

The Books of Kings are part of the Old Testament, in the Bible. There is a 1 Kings and a 2 Kings, but they are really a continuous story, and were divided only for convenience. They tell about the rule of the ancient Hebrew kings, from the time of the death of David, for about four hundred years. In the Roman Catholic Bible, there are four books called Kings. Two of these books are named 1 Samuel and 2 Samuel in Protestant Bibles. See the article on the BIBLE.

Kingsley, Charles

Charles Kingsley was an English clergyman and novelist. He was born in 1819 and was educated in private schools and then at King's College in London. He became chaplain to Queen Victoria and taught history at Cambridge University. Two of his best novels are *Westward Ho!* and *Water Babies. Westward Ho!* is an adventure story, full of pirates and great heroes such as Drake and Raleigh, and it tells about many sea battles between the English and the Spanish Armada. *Water Babies* seems to be a fairy story, but it is really an exciting lesson in the wonders of nature. The hero is a lonely chimney sweep named Tom who falls asleep and is turned into a water baby. Kingsley died in 1875.

king snake

The king snake lives in the eastern parts of the United States. It is about five feet long and is black or brown with yellow or white bands of color. The king snake eats birds' eggs, and frogs and mice, and also smaller snakes. A very unusual thing about the king snake is that it does not seem to be harmed by the poisonous bite of another snake. It will attack and eat poisonous rattlesnakes as well as harmless snakes. The king snake is not harmful to man, and scientists often use it for study purposes. When the king snake is captured it will become tame and friendly, and will live for many years. Some king snakes have white, black and red rings, the red bordered by black. They differ from coral snakes, which have red rings bordered by white or yellow.

Kings Point

Kings Point is a place on Long Island in New York State, only about 15 miles from New York City. The United States Merchant Marine Academy is there and this is usually called Kings Point, just as the United States Military Academy is called West Point. See the article on MERCHANT MARINE ACADEMY.

kinkajou

The kinkajou is a little animal that lives in the tropical jungles of South America, and in Mexico. Though the kinkajou is a member of the raccoon family, it is in some ways more like a monkey. The kinkajou has a tail that is about two feet long. It uses this tail to swing from tree to tree through the jungle to reach the figs and other fruits that it eats. The kinkajou can hold onto a tree so tightly with its tail and four feet that not even a strong wind can shake it loose. It sleeps in the treetops during most of the day and comes out at night to search for food. The female kinkajou has two or four babies at a time. They look like baby kittens when they are born. The babies have soft black fur that turns to a golden brown as the kinkajou grows. The kinkajou is a tame and friendly animal, and some people in South America and Mexico keep it as a pet. You can see kinkajous in zoos.

Kiowa

Kiowa is the name of an Indian tribe that lived in the Rocky Mountains of Montana about 250 years ago. The Kiowa wandered from place to place, and wherever they went, they made trouble. They were very fierce and warlike, and they had savage battles with other Indian tribes and with the white man. It is said that the Kiowa killed more white men than any other Indian tribe.

In 1867 the Kiowa were conquered and taken to a reservation in Oklahoma. The next year the Kiowa, along with other tribes, broke out of the reservation. It took General Custer a full winter of terrible fighting to bring them back to the reservation.

The Kiowa had a special language of their own. They also had a calendar on which they drew pictures to show things that happened. The Kiowa had a ghost-dance religion, and every year they held religious ceremonies that lasted for five days. There are now more than one thousand members of the Kiowa tribe. They live on a reservation in Oklahoma.

Kipling, Rudyard

Rudyard Kipling was one of the most popular English writers of his time, both with adults and with children. His

National Portrait Gallery, London

father was an artist and was in charge of a museum in Bombay, India. Kipling was born in Bombay in 1865. He went to school in England, then lived in India for about ten years. He wrote many stories and poems about life in India, and about British soldiers and civilians who were stationed there and in other Oriental or African countries. Some of his poems, such as "On the Road to Mandalay" and "Danny Deever," became popular songs when they were set to music.

Kipling married an American girl, and for a few years he lived in Brattleboro, Vermont. While there he wrote some of his best stories. Millions of children have enjoyed *The Jungle Book* and the *Just So Stories. Kim,* a story about a little boy who has many adventures, is one of Kipling's best-known books.

Kipling was the first English writer to receive the Nobel Prize for literature, which was awarded to him in 1907. He died in 1935.

Kitchener, Horatio

Horatio Kitchener was a great English soldier, the hero of many battles and conquests in Africa. He was born in 1850. In 1892 Kitchener became *sirdar,* or commander-in-chief, of the Egyptian army, which was controlled by Great Britain. With this army he conquered the Sudan, a large territory south of Egypt. Later Kitchener became the governor-general of the Sudan.

During the Boer War between England and the Dutch settlers of South Africa, Kitchener became commander of the British armies. He won the war, and for his victories he was given the title of viscount. He was then sent to India, to be commander of the British armies there. He was made an earl and given the rank of field marshal, the highest in the British army.

When World War I began, in 1914, Kitchener was made Secretary for War in the British government. He was one of the few leaders who knew then that the war would be a long one and that Russia, England's friend in the war, might not be able to hold out against the military might of the Germans. In 1916 he planned to visit the Russian ruler, Czar Nicholas II, to see what could be done to help the Russians. On the way, his ship was sunk by a mine and Lord Kitchener was drowned.

kitchen midden

A kitchen midden is a heap or mound of very old tools, bones, and shells. Some kitchen middens are many thousands of years old. The name comes from Danish words meaning "kitchen refuse or garbage." The peoples who lived long ago did not get rid of garbage as we do, but let it pile up around their villages. It may sound odd that anyone should be interested in old garbage, but scientists have been able to learn a lot about the people who lived long ago by studying these kitchen middens. The clam and oyster shells tell the scientists that the people must have been fishermen. The tools, mostly made of stone or bone, show that they knew how to make things. Most of the kitchen middens have been found in the Scandinavian countries, especially Denmark, but some have been found in Scotland, Ireland, and the United States.

kite

The kite is a long-legged bird, found throughout the tropical areas of the world. It is one of the most graceful birds in flight, and its long wings allow it to remain aloft for long periods of time. The swallow-tailed kite of North America glides over marshes in search of snakes, frogs, and insects, on which it feeds. All kites are birds of prey, which means that they eat other animals as a main source of food. There are about thirty different kinds of kite, ranging from the reddish-brown common kite to the light-colored white-tailed kite. The kite is a member of the falcon family.

kite

A kite is a device that is flown in the air at the end of a line. Kite-flying seems to be one form of recreation that knows no age limits. Both children and adults practice it. Kite-flying is an ancient custom, dating at least as far back as four hundred years before the birth of Jesus.

There are two general kinds of kite, the *plane surface kite* and the *box kite.* Each has several varieties, but both kinds of kite are usually made of a light wood framework over which paper or cloth is stretched. The line, usually string or twine, is attached to the stretched paper or cloth, and this line holds the kite as it

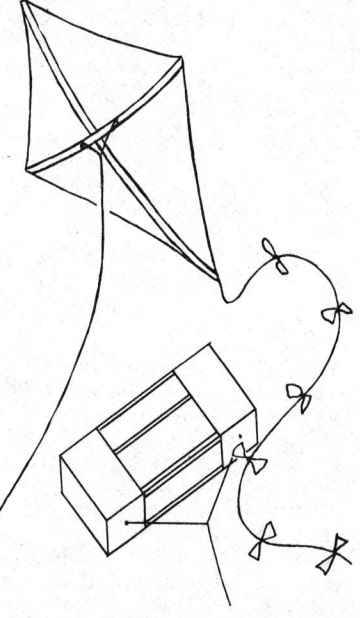

The two most popular kinds of kite are the "two-sticker" plane kite and the strong, high-flying box kite.

flies in the air. Wire should never be used as a kite line, because the wire may touch an electric power line and the holder of it might be electrocuted.

Kites come in various sizes and shapes, from a small two-foot kite to kites as high as a tall man. The most popular plane kite is called the "two-sticker," a diamond-shaped kite that is made of two crossed sticks. It has a tail, usually a long, narrow piece of cloth, that balances the kite and prevents it from tumbling through the air. Box kites, so called because they are shaped like boxes, are harder to make, but some kite-flyers find that they are much more fun than the plane kite. They say that the box kite is stronger than the plane kite, lasts longer, and flies higher. A box kite needs no tail.

WHY A KITE FLIES

A kite flies in the air because of the same scientific principle that makes an airplane fly. The air around us and in the sky has currents much like the currents of a river or stream. The air currents on the ground catch the front or "face" of the kite, forcing the kite back and off the ground. The wind continues to push up the kite, sending it gliding into the sky. If there is no ground wind, running with the kite will create enough wind to launch it. The best wind for kite-flying is a steady breeze.

In the countries of Asia, such as Korea, Japan, and China, kite-flying is a very popular pastime. In China, there is a national holiday called "Kites' Day," occurring on the ninth day of the ninth month of every year. On this day the Chinese people paint and shape their kites to look like birds, insects, flowers, butterflies, and dragons, and all along the countryside these fantastically shaped kites can be seen dotting the skyline. In Japan, there is a kite-flying holiday on May 5.

Kites are used not only for fun and recreation but for many practical purposes as well. In World War II, kites were used as targets in gunnery practice. Also they were part of the regular equipment of life rafts, serving as a guide for searching airmen and, by use of a metal line, as an emergency antenna.

Kitimat

Kitimat is a place in Canada, on the Pacific Ocean, where the world's largest plant for the manufacture of aluminum has been built. Kitimat, which is in the province of British Columbia, is a remarkable place because only a few years before 1954, when the plant opened, it was a wilderness where only a few Indians lived.

To supply the vast amounts of electrical power needed by the aluminum plant, a great power system was built far inland. The great Kenny Dam, 180 miles away, stores the water of a glacial lake and a river. From there the water runs 125 miles to Kemano, after passing through a 10-mile tunnel blasted through a mountain. At Kemano there is a power plant that generates electricity. This is then carried by wires 55 miles over high mountains to Kitimat. Kitimat is expected to turn out about one-fourth of all the aluminum made in the United States and Canada.

kittiwake

The kittiwake is a bird of the gull family. It gets its name from the sound of its call. The kittiwake lives along the coasts of both the North Atlantic and North Pacific oceans. It is about one and a half feet long. Its feathers are mostly white, but it has a gray back, called a mantle, and its wings are touched with black. Another kittiwake, which lives in the North Pacific, has red legs and a red bill. The kittiwakes are sociable birds and travel in large flocks. They build their nests of moss and seaweed in rocky crevices and cliffs. The female kittiwake lays three gray or tan eggs that are speckled with dark brown, and some people find these eggs very good to eat.

Kiwanis

The Kiwanis International is an organization of business and professional men. It has branches in many cities of the United States and Canada. There are other members of Kiwanis in Alaska and Hawaii. The members of Kiwanis meet on one day each week. They do many

kinds of useful work. They help improve business conditions in their communities and they support church and school projects. The Kiwanis Clubs sponsor vocational-guidance groups that help young people decide what kind of work they want to do.

The Kiwanis International was started in 1915, and there are now more than 260,000 members in about 4,000 clubs. The headquarters is in Chicago, Illinois.

kiwi

The kiwi is a strange, shy bird that cannot fly. It lives in New Zealand. During the day it hides in rocky crevices and holes and at night it comes out to hunt for worms and insects. The kiwi is about the size of a hen. It has long brown feathers that hide its small, undeveloped wings, and it has very strong legs. The kiwi has a powerful kick, which it uses to defend itself against enemies. It is a very fast runner. With its long, curved bill it pulls worms out of the ground. The kiwi, unlike most birds, has an excellent sense of smell, and this is a big help when it searches for food.

The kiwi lays the largest eggs, considering its size, of any bird. A kiwi's egg usually weighs about a pound, while the full-grown bird weighs only about four pounds. It takes more than two months for a kiwi egg to hatch, and the male sits on the nest.

kleptomania

Kleptomania is a mental disturbance that gives a person an uncontrollable impulse to steal. Such a person is not really a thief. He is sick and cannot help himself. All small children act on impulse, and as they grow up they normally learn to control their impulsive desires. The kleptomaniac, for certain psychological reasons, has failed to grow up with respect to developing control over his impulse to take things that do not belong to him. Often the things that a kleptomaniac steals are trifles of no great value, and seldom things that he really needs. Kleptomaniacs often give away what they have stolen, or hoard a collection of stolen objects without using them. More women seem to suffer from this sickness than men.

Klondike

The Klondike is a section of northwest Canada, in the Yukon Territory. It is best remembered because gold was discovered there in 1896. In the Klondike the winter temperature is often as low as 24 degrees below zero, yet thousands of people came pouring into this frozen region after 1896. They were willing to endure the hardships for the chance to find gold.

In 1896 a prospector named George Carmack discovered gold in Bonanza Creek, a small river in the Klondike. The whole town of Bonanza started digging for gold. The next summer a ship pulled into Seattle, Washington, carrying the gold they had mined. The word spread like wildfire, and the gold rush was on. So many people went to the Klondike that Dawson City, which had only one hut in 1896, held more than nine thousand people by 1901. Altogether, thirty thousand people poured into the Klondike between 1896 and 1901. They did not find gold easily, for the gold was deposited in gravel and the gravel was frozen seven months of the year. The miners had to thaw the gravel with fire. Later, special steam equipment was used.

After 1910 the gold rush started petering out, but between 1885 and 1929 the total value of the gold mined in the Klondike was $176,000,000.

knee, a joint at the middle of the leg: see the article on JOINT.

knife

A knife is a cutting instrument with a short blade and a handle. Men have used it as a tool or weapon for thousands of years.

Ancient men made knives out of animal bone or stone. American Indians on the western plains of North America used to make knives out of the ribs of the bison. The stone knives made by ancient man were made of flat slivers of flint, a very hard stone. They heated the stone in a fire and let drops of cold water fall on the edges, which caused little flakes of stone to chip off. The chipping continued until a sharp edge was formed. The handle was wrapped in animal hide or skin, or was

wound with leather strips to make a good grip for the hand. The ancient Egyptians made knives out of hardened copper, which they fitted with wooden handles. Later, man learned to make harder metals, bronze and then steel, and knives were made from them.

In the days when all writing was done with goose-quill pens, a small knife was used to sharpen the quill when the point became dull. This knife became known as a penknife.

The pocketknife with a blade that folds into the handle was invented in Europe about the year 1600. Most pocketknives of the folding variety have steel blades two to three inches long. Some of these knives have little bottle openers, scissors, and files that fold into the handle along with one or two blades.

Hunting knives are usually carried by sportsmen. A hunting knife usually has a steel blade with a single edge and is four to six inches in length. It is carried in a leather sheath. The handle may be made of wood, bone, or another material.

The bowie knife was used by soldiers and frontiersmen for camping and hunting in the American Southwest about a hundred years ago. This knife is about ten inches long. It has a single edge and a hilt that protects the hand. It was invented by Rezin P. Bowie, brother of James Bowie, the great Texas hero who fought against Mexico for the independence of his state.

See also the article MACHETE.

knighthood

Knighthood was a name given to a certain way of life in the Middle Ages. In those days there were no powerful nations with large armies as there are today. In Europe the land was owned by a great number of powerful noblemen. (You can read more about this system in the article on FEUDALISM.) Each nobleman, or lord, had his own band of warriors who fought on horseback. These warriors were called knights.

BECOMING A KNIGHT

Only the sons of noblemen could become knights, and they had to go through a course of training before they could be admitted to the rank of knighthood. When a nobleman's son was about 7 years old, he went to live in the lord's castle, as a page. There he attended the lord, and helped to serve him. He was taught to be courteous and well-mannered. Also, he began his training for knighthood, by learning horsemanship.

When the young page was about 14, he became a squire. He attended his lord on hunts, and carried the lord's armor in battle. He continued his training for knighthood by learning how to use his weapons, the sword and the lance. He took part in practice fights, where he had to ride at a dummy hanging in the fields and hit it with his lance. This is a little like the way boys today practice football by tackling a dummy.

When the squire was about 21 years old and could prove his skill, he was ready to be admitted to knighthood. Through a whole night he stood watch over his armor and weapons in the chapel of the castle, praying, and thinking about the honors

The bleak, stormy Klondike was the scene of a gold rush about seventy years ago. The Yukon River runs through the region, which is still mostly unsettled.

and duties of a knight. The next day he was dressed in the armor of a knight. He knelt before his lord and swore to be loyal to the lord and to the rules of knighthood. (You can read more about these rules in the article on CHIVALRY.) The lord touched him on the back of the neck or on his shoulder with a sword, and said, "I dub thee knight." Then the lord would say, "Arise, Sir Charles," or whatever the new knight's name happened to be. All knights bore the title "Sir."

THE LIFE OF A KNIGHT

The first duty and interest of a knight was fighting. When the lord went to war, his knights fought with him. When there was no war, the knights took part in tournaments, which were mock battles. These were very gay affairs. All the lords and ladies sat in the stands around the lists, the field where the knights fought. Flags fluttered and trumpets sounded. The knights were dressed in their shining armor, carrying lance and sword and shield. Sometimes they wore ribbons and handkerchiefs given them as favors by the ladies.

Sometimes only two knights fought, and at other times whole groups of knights fought. At a signal, they began to ride down the field towards each other. The idea was to unseat the opponent from his horse.

A knight was not only expected to be brave. He was also supposed to be pious and polite and helpful to people in need. The code of knighthood was usually applied only to noblemen—to lords, and knights, and their ladies. The knights were often unkind to the ordinary people.

Most knights lived in their lords' castles. They had farmers, called *serfs*, living on their land. The serfs did the work and paid a good share of what they produced to the knights, as taxes.

Some knights, called *knights errant*, spent their lives roaming around the country, seeking adventures. Many knights joined the armies of the Crusades, which were wars of the Christian peoples to try to recapture the Holy Land from the Moslems. Some of these knights banded together into groups. You can read more about them in the articles on KNIGHTS TEMPLARS and TEUTONIC KNIGHTS.

Many stories and poems were written to celebrate the brave deeds of the noble knights of the Middle Ages. These include the legends about King Arthur and the knights of the Round Table, and the story of Roland.

After the Middle Ages, knighthood became less and less important. Gradually large, strong nations began to grow up, and they used armies of foot soldiers instead of horsemen. The foot soldiers began to use a new weapon, called the longbow, which could shoot metal-tipped arrows with such force that they could pierce the steel armor of the knights. When gunpowder was invented, the new firearms could do the same thing. The heavy metal armor of the knights could not protect them any more.

Today, knighthood is an honorary award, given to outstanding people in some countries, such as England, in recognition of some special work that they have done.

Knights Templars

The Knights Templars were a large and powerful group of knights who fought in the Crusades. (The Crusades were wars fought hundreds of years ago by Christians who tried to recapture the Holy Land from the Mohammedans.) The complete name of the organization was the Order of the Knights of the Temple of Solomon. Each knight who belonged to this group promised to fight for the Cross, which was the symbol of Jesus, and each knight promised to remain poor and unmarried.

The order of Knights Templars was started in the year 1118 by Hugh de Payens. The order grew to be the largest order of knights. Its sign, which was a red cross on a background of white, became known as a symbol of bravery.

After about two hundred years the Knights Templars lost their power in Europe when they were accused of heresy. Heresy means preaching a religion other than the recognized religion, and at that time heresy was a crime. Many of the Knights Templars were persecuted and killed.

The last leader of the Knights Templars was a Frenchman named Jacques de Molay. When he died in 1314, the organization came to an end.

In modern times the Knights Templars are a branch organization of the Masons. The Knights Templars began in the United States about three hundred years ago. They have chapters in every state in the United States. There are more than 400,000 members. The ritual of the order, which is based on the life of Jesus, goes back to the ritual used by the original Knights Templars of the Middle Ages. The Knights Templars wear black uniforms and red hats with large white plumes.

knitting

Knitting is a method of making a kind of cloth. It is not woven as most cloth is, but is made by interlocking rows of loops. Each interlocking of loops is called a stitch. Usually one continuous strand of thread or yarn is used. The yarn

HOW TO KNIT

The simplest kind of knitting is done on two straight knitting needles. A knitting needle is about six inches to a foot or more long, and about as thick as string or cord. It must bend easily, and may be made of bone, a plastic, wood, steel, or some other metal. A knitting needle usually has a button or knob on one end, to keep the stitches from slipping off.

The yarn is wound into a ball. One end of the yarn is taken and looped over one of the needles any number of times —the more loops you make, the wider the knitted piece will be. Making these loops is called *casting on.* Now the point of the other needle is stuck through one of the loops. The yarn is thrown over this needle, and is pulled through the loop so that the entire loop, or stitch, is transferred to the other needle. When all the loops have been taken off one needle and transferred to the other, one row of knitting is completed. Now the first needle has no stitches on it, and it is used to take the loops off the second needle. Each row adds to the length of the knitted piece.

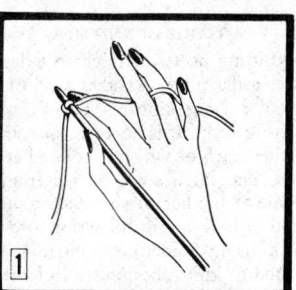

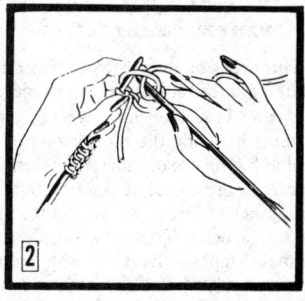

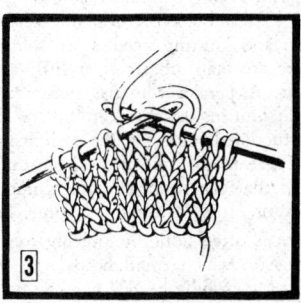

J. & P. Coats—Clark's Diagrams

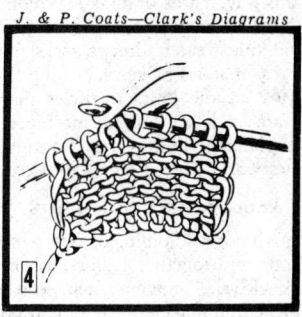

In knitting stockingette stitch, the way the thread is thrown over the needle is important. Also important is how the needle point is inserted.
1. To keep correct tension, the yarn leading to the ball should be held with fingers in this position.
2. When actual knitting begins, a loop of yarn is pulled through each stitch on the needle.
3. When the needle is inserted from the front of the loop, the side toward the knitting looks this way.
4. When the needle is inserted from the back of the loop, the side toward the knitter looks this way.

When the piece is long enough, the knitter *casts off*—closes up the stitches—and the knitting is complete.

The appearance of the knitted piece will depend on the way the yarn is thrown over the needle. One kind of stitch is called *knitting,* another kind *purling.* Purling makes a rough surface, knitting a smooth surface. The stitches can be mixed in various ways. If you knit a few stitches and purl a few stitches, you produce *ribs.* If you knit one row and then purl one row, you produce a piece that is rough on one side and smooth on the other.

TUBULAR KNITTING

Knitting on two straight needles produces a flat piece. Another kind of knitting is *tubular* knitting. This is used in knitting socks. It is done on four straight needles, each of which is pointed at both ends. The stitches are carried from one needle to another, around and around, instead of back and forth across rows as in flat knitting. Sometimes a circular needle is used to knit tubes, instead of the four straight, double-pointed needles. A circular needle is often used to knit skirts.

MANY DIFFERENT PATTERNS

Hundreds of different patterns can be made by knitting. Experts can product effects that look like fancy weaving, with patterns made by the threads or yarns as well as by the use of different colors. This requires a great deal of practice, but even a beginner can make many useful and attractive articles. There are simple tricks to make fancy effects. In any knitting pattern book several of these are usually described and explained simply. Knitting pattern books are available wherever yarn and knitting needles are sold, and there are many that cost as little as ten cents. A person who has mastered the basic knitting stitches can follow these instruction booklets without difficulty.

There is no limit to the beautiful designs that can be made by learning one trick of fancy knitting at a time. Beadwork is often done by knitting together yarns on which small beads have been strung. A solidly beaded bag can be knit in this way. Yarns of different colors can be used to make any kind of pattern. Hand-knit sweaters, dresses, socks, gloves, scarves or stoles make beautiful gifts.

Most of the knitted articles that we buy are made on knitting machines. For an explanation of how these knitting machines work, see the article on HOSIERY.

knots, hitches, and splices

A knot is a joining of two pieces of rope or cord together. Sailors, fishermen, truck drivers, moving men, cowboys, farmers, shipping clerks and many others must know how to tie knots skillfully. Those whose hobby is boating, climbing, camping, or hiking, also find knots important.

There are many different ways of tying a knot. Usually a particular kind of knot will best suit the purpose.

The *hitch* is a knot used to fasten a rope to a log or post. There are four main types of hitch, the *half-hitch, timber hitch, clove hitch,* and *tautline hitch.* The half-hitch is sometimes doubled and is used for fastening a boat to a dock. The timber hitch is used for stringing a bow or hauling lumber. The clove hitch is used for fastening something to a stationary object, for example, for tying a horse to a tree. The tautline hitch is best for fastening a rope to a hook, because the main rope will jam tightly against the hook and cannot slip.

The loose ends of two ropes are best joined by the *square knot* or the *reef knot.* These are both better knots than the "granny," which often slips or jams.

The *fisherman's knot* also is used for joining two ropes. It is very strong, yet easily comes apart when the short end is pulled.

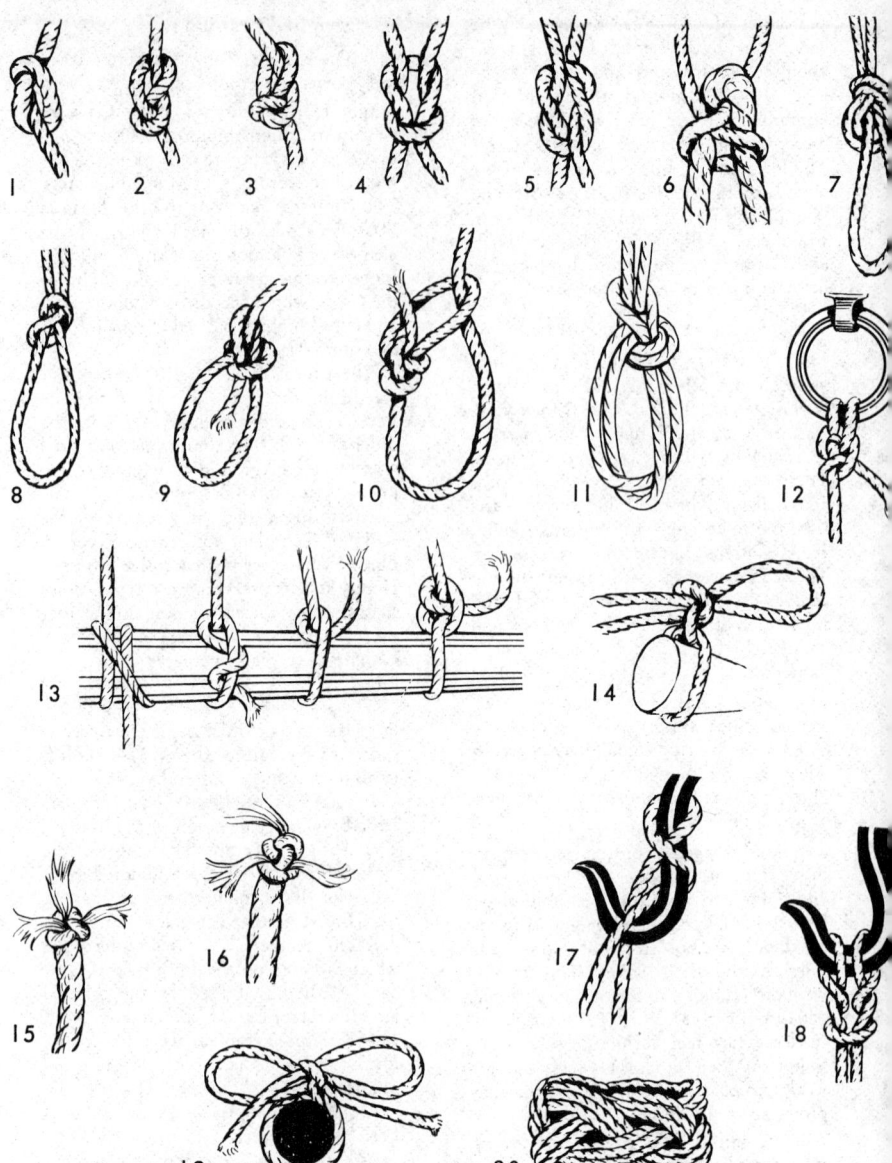

The art of tying knots probably dates back to primitive man's first ropes. Over the centuries knots have been devised to meet a great variety of needs. Sailors, especially those who work on sailboats, probably know how to tie the greatest number of knots. Trick knots are a specialty of magicians. And firemen can often tie a series of knots that make a rope into a chair in which people can be lowered from a burning building. Every one should know how to tie at least some of the basic knots. Learning all of them can be a useful hobby. The main kinds are: 1. The overhand knot. 2. The figure-eight knot. 3. The stevedore's knot. 4. The square knot. 5. The granny knot. 6. The weaver's knot. 7. The loop knot. 8. The slip knot. 9. The bowline. 10. The running bowline. 11. The double bowline, or bowline on a bight. 12. The anchor knot. 13. The clove, timber, half-, and two half-hitches. 14. The slip knot. 15. The wall knot. 16. The wall and crown. 17. The blackwall hitch. 18. The cat's-paw. 19. The bowknot. 20. The Turk's head.

SPLICING

Ropes should be spliced when the thickness of a knot would get in the way. The four types of splice are the *short splice, long splice, back splice,* and *eye splice.* The general principle in splicing is that two parts of rope are joined together by interweaving the strands. Splicing is important for lengthening ropes, repairing broken ropes, forming eyes at the ends of ropes, and eliminating fraying at the ends of ropes.

The short splice is used to join frayed or broken ropes. The strands of each end are separated and then twisted together with strands from the other end. In the *long splice,* strands from one piece of rope replace strands in the other piece, so that the area where the rope is joined is no thicker than any other part of the rope. The *back splice* finishes off the end of a rope so it will not fray. The *eye*

splice is used to form a loop or eye. The rope is bent back into itself, forming a loop, and the strands of the end are spliced into the body of the rope.

OTHER KNOTS

Other valuable knots are the *sheet bend,* which is used for joining two ropes of unequal thickness; the *sheepshank,* which is used for taking up the slack in a rope; and the *bowline,* which is used to make a lifeline to save people from drowning or to rescue people who have fallen into a hole.

Lashing is a type of knot work that was used by the early pioneers of America in building their homes. It is a substitute for hammer and nails. Posts or poles are lashed together where they must join tightly, instead of being nailed together.

Know-Nothings

The Know-Nothings were a political party in the United States about a hundred years ago. They wanted control of the United States to be held by people whose families had lived in the United States at least fifty years. They called themselves the American Party, or the Star-Spangled Banner Party. Their beliefs were contrary to the American tradition that people are equal. According to this tradition, a naturalized citizen is as good a citizen as a person who is born in the United States.

The Know-Nothings were formed in secret groups, and when the members of these groups were asked questions they said they knew nothing. That is how the party got its name.

There have been other groups and political parties since the Know-Nothings who have believed things that are against American tradition, but none of them has been very successful. After a few years, the Know-Nothings passed out of existence.

Knox, John

John Knox was the leader of the Protestant Christian movement in Scotland more than four hundred years ago. He was responsible for many of the beliefs of members of the Presbyterian Church. The Presbyterians believed that the church should not be governed by clergymen but by members of the congregation or their representatives. In many ways the Presbyterians follow the teachings of John Calvin. (You can read about CALVIN in a separate article.)

Knox was born in Scotland in 1505. When he grew up he preached and wrote about the teachings of Calvin. He was sent to prison because of his beliefs, and several times his life was in danger. Finally Knox had to flee from Scotland. In the long run John Knox succeeded, because the Presbyterian Church is the most important church in Scotland. John Knox died in 1572.

koala

The koala is a small animal that looks like a teddy bear. It is found in the

Australian News & Information Bureau

forests of Australia. It is not really a bear at all; it is a marsupial, one of the animals that carry their young in pouches of skin attached to the mother's abdomen. (You can read more about MARSUPIALS in a separate article.)

The koala grows to be about 2½ feet tall. It has large, floppy ears and bright black eyes. The koala has no tail. It has thick, dark gray fur and a white stomach. It is a good climber and spends most of its time high up in the branches of the

eucalyptus trees. The thick, tough leaves of the eucalyptus are the koala's main food.

For a long time people killed the koala to make warm coats out of the thick fur. Now the Australian people have made it a law that no one can shoot the koala. Some koalas have been captured and are raised in zoos and parks. They are friendly and tame.

Kobe

Kobe is a big city in Japan. It is on Honshu Island and is the capital of Hyogo Prefecture. (Japan is divided into forty-six prefectures or sections.) Kobe is on Osaka Bay, and it is one of the most important seaports in Japan.

Until about a hundred years ago, Kobe was a small fishing village. Then the harbor was opened and ships from many countries sailed to Kobe. The city grew quickly and now it is a busy place. Over 1,288,000 people live in Kobe, a little more than live in the city of Houston, Texas, in the United States.

Many of the people of Kobe are shipbuilders. Some of the people work in factories, where they make machinery and rubber goods and chemicals. Others work in sugar-refining plants and flour mills.

Kobe is surrounded by high mountains that protect it from the cold north winds. This makes a very good climate, and people come from other places in Japan to spend vacations at Kobe, where they enjoy winter sports on Rokko Mountain. There is also a popular bathing resort at Kobe.

Kobe is a modern city with large warehouses and office buildings, a subway, and a railroad terminal. People who go to Kobe may visit the ancient Buddhist temples and shrines. There are also Christian churches. Kobe is such a large industrial center and seaport that during World War II the city was bombed very severely.

KOBE, JAPAN. Population (1973 estimate) 1,288,937. On Honshu island. Sixth-largest city of Japan.

Koch, Robert

Robert Koch was a great German scientist. He is often called the founder of the science of BACTERIOLOGY, about which there is a separate article.

Koch was born in 1843, and when he grew up he became a doctor. He began to study bacteria, which are among the simplest forms of life known and are so tiny that you cannot see them without a microscope. Koch worked out ways that enabled him to separate different kinds of bacteria from one another, and proved beyond question that bacteria were the cause of infectious diseases of men and animals. Then he looked for ways to kill these particular bacteria.

Koch traveled all over the world to study various diseases. He studied malaria in New Guinea, sleeping sickness in West Africa, rinderpest in South Africa, and the plague in India. He discovered the bacteria that cause tuberculosis and cholera, two diseases that had taken many lives. Robert Koch was awarded the Nobel Prize in medicine in 1905. He died in 1910.

Kodiak

Kodiak is the largest island off the Pacific coast of Alaska. It is about a hundred miles long and ten to sixty miles wide, and has an area of 3,670 square miles. The land is very rocky, but there are several good harbors. About nine thousand people live on Kodiak, and most of them are Eskimos. Many are fishermen who make their living by catching salmon in the Kurluk River. Some of the people work in fish-canning factories, and others are fur traders. The largest settled place is the village of Kodiak, which in 1973 had a population of about 3,800.

There are many wild animals in the fine forests. The largest breed of bear on earth, the Kodiak bear, lives on the island.

Kodiak was settled by Russians, about two hundred years ago, and it was the first Russian settlement in Alaska. Now the United States has a large naval and submarine base, called Womens Bay, on Kodiak Island.

kohlrabi

Kohlrabi is a member of the cabbage family. It grows in England, Sweden, and some parts of the United States. The leaves of the kohlrabi plant grow out of a thick rounded stem that is about as big around as a baseball. People eat the stem and not the leaves. When the stem of the kohlrabi is cooked, it tastes like turnips. In Europe it is a popular vegetable. People also feed kohlrabi to cows.

The kohlrabi is a hardy plant that can stand very cold weather. It grows best in a rich soil.

kola

Kola, or cola, is the name of a tree that grows wild in tropical Africa and in the West Indies. The seeds of the tree are called cola nuts, and they are chewed as a delicacy by natives. The seeds are reddish in color, and have a scent like that of roses. They contain some caffeine, as coffee does.

The cola tree grows to a height of 50 to 65 feet. It has been cultivated in several countries, since the great growth in popularity of the commercial beverage made from cola-nut syrup. See the article on COCA-COLA.

kookaburra

The kookaburra is a bird with a funny name, a funny look, and a funny voice. It lives in the forests of Australia. The kookaburra is a brownish bird, about one and a half feet long. It has a long bill and a very large mouth, and a crest that sticks up on the top of its head, giving it a very saucy look. The kookaburra is the largest member of the kingfisher family, but it does not eat fish. It lives on mice and small snakes and insects. Often the kookaburra will steal the eggs from the nests of smaller birds. The kookaburra is sometimes called the laughing jackass because it has a loud, sharp cry that sounds somewhat like a laugh.

Kootenai or Kootenay

The Kootenai River, a branch of the mighty Columbia River, rises in the Rocky Mountains of Canada and flows through the states of Montana and Idaho, in the United States. The Kootenai then

turns back into Canada, where it forms Kootenai Lake and then joins the Columbia. The Kootenai is about four hundred miles long. It flows through wild and beautiful scenery, but it is dangerous to travelers. There are many rocky places and rapids.

Near Libby, Montana, the United States government has built a great dam on the Kootenai River. This dam helps to control floods and supplies power for electricity. The Kootenai River was first explored by David Thompson, an English traveler, in 1807.

In Canada the name is spelled Kootenay.

Koran

The Koran is the holy book of the Mohammedan religion. The people who practice this religion are called Moslems. According to many Moslems, the Koran has always existed and was written by rays of light on stone tablets in heaven, then was told by God and the angel Gabriel to the Prophet Mohammed during his life on earth, from 570 to 632. Mohammed's follower, Zaid ibn Thabit, copied it down as the prophet spoke it, and the caliph ("successor to Mohammed") named Othman had an edition put out soon after Mohammed's death.

There are 114 chapters, called *suras*, in the Koran. The chapters are named according to the subjects they deal with. Some chapter names are "The Cow," "The Fig," "The Poets," "The Stars." The main belief expressed in the Koran is that there is only one God. This is also the main belief of the Hebrew and Christian religions.

Moslems memorize as much of the Koran as they can, and some of them know the whole book by heart. It is the book by which they live. When a Moslem wants to know what to do in a certain case, he always looks for the answer in the Koran. Rich Moslems have beautiful copies of the Koran, written in gold and covered with silk and precious jewels.

The Koran is written in the Arabic language. For more than a thousand years Moslems said that the Koran must not be translated into any other language, but in this century it has been translated into English by scholars who are pious Moslems.

The name is also spelled *Alcoran,* which simply means "the Koran."

Korea

Korea is a small peninsula on the east coast of Asia, nearly halfway around the world from the United States. Its area is about 85,000 square miles, about the size of the state of Kansas. The forty million people who live in Korea are descended from one of the oldest civilized peoples on earth. Koreans were writing books, learning about the stars and making beautiful pottery and gold jewelry while most European people were leading primitive lives, and long before America was discovered. The Koreans were the first to invent a way of printing

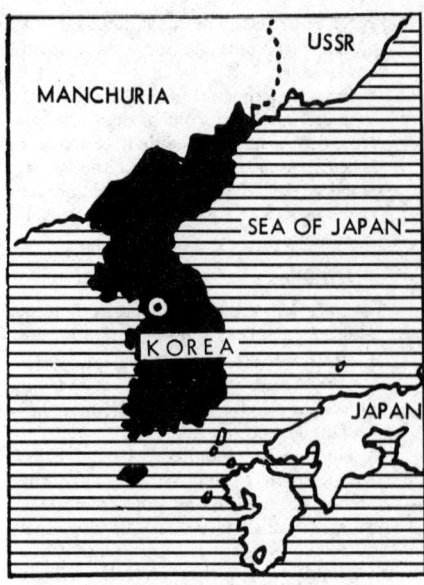

books with separate pieces of metal that could be easily changed; the first to build warships protected by armor-plating; the first to build a suspension bridge (that is, a bridge that hangs from heavy ropes or cables); and the first to use a magnetic compass in steering a ship.

There was fighting in Korea from 1950 to 1953. United States armed forces took part, with other soldiers in the United Nations army. The trouble started when Communist soldiers from North Korea tried to conquer South Korea, invading the land without any warning. The Communists were beaten back and Korea remained half Communist (the North) and half free (the South). The official name of the southern part is the Republic of Korea. The northern part calls itself the Korean People's Republic but is actually a dictatorship. Neither North Korea nor South Korea is a member of the United Nations.

THE PEOPLE OF KOREA

Like the Chinese and Japanese, the Koreans belong to the Mongolian race. These people have skins of a yellowish color, and narrow, heavy-lidded eyes that look as though they were slanted. Most Koreans are a little taller than the Chinese, and they have brown rather than black hair, flat noses, and high cheekbones. They speak a language that is a little like both Japanese and Chinese. The Koreans have invented a way of writing their language that makes it easy to spell words, even for young children in school. They call this writing *onmun.*

Most Koreans are poor and wear very simple clothes. Both the men and the women work in large, baggy-looking pants, and shirts or warm jackets. Sometimes the women wear long, flowing white gowns, somewhat like heavy nightgowns. They "iron" the gowns by spreading them on the ground and beating them with flat sticks. Not many Koreans can afford finery, but once in a while one might see a man wearing a top hat. This means that he belongs to an aristocratic, or noble, family.

The oldest religions in Korea are Buddhism and Confucianism. There are also many Koreans who are Christians and a few who have adopted Shintoism, the re-

ligion of the Japanese.

HOW THE PEOPLE LIVE

The Koreans work very hard to earn a living. Korea is a mountainous country with a very large population, so that every bit of ground on which rice or vegetables or fruit can be grown must be carefully tended. The Korean farmers and their wives and children spend long hours up to their knees in water cultivating the flooded rice fields (called *paddies*), which must be covered with water for the tender rice shoots to grow. Many of the people also raise silkworms, from which fine silk thread is obtained.

In the southern part of Korea most of the people are farmers or fishermen. In northern Korea, where gold, iron, coal, copper, silver, and other minerals are mined, many of the people work as miners or in factories and cotton mills. The making of cotton goods and silk fabrics is an important industry.

WHAT KIND OF PLACE IT IS

Considering how small it is, Korea is a very fortunate land. It is very mountainous, but it also has many wide valleys and coastal plains where the soil is very rich and the climate is well-suited to the growing of rice and other food crops. Winters in Korea are cold and wet, but the summers are long and pleasant. Swift rivers flow down to the sea from the mountains and these are more and more being used to drive hydroelectric generators to create electric power. Many bays and inlets ring the coastline, so that there are plenty of good harbors for the fishermen's boats and for seaports for large ships. The Japanese built good railroads across the country, as well as roads, bridges, and docks for the seaports.

CHIEF CITIES OF KOREA

The leading cities of Korea, with population estimates are:

Seoul, population (1961 estimate) 2,444,883, the capital and largest city of the Republic of Korea (South Korea). It was badly damaged by bombs and gunfire during the Korean conflict.

Pusan, population (1961 estimate) 1,162,614, a modern city on the southeast coast of Korea, the chief seaport and fishing center of the Republic of Korea (South Korea).

Pyongyang, population (1961 estimate) 285,965, the capital of the (Communist) People's Republic of Korea (North Korea). It is very old, dating back almost three thousand years, and was the capital of the ancient Korean kingdom.

HOW THE PEOPLE ARE GOVERNED

At the end of World War II, Korea, which had been a Japanese territory for nearly forty years, was divided into two halves at the 38th parallel of latitude, which is a straight line almost exactly across the middle of Korea from east to west. Russian soldiers occupied the northern half, and American and Allied soldiers controlled the southern half. Free elections were supposed to be held in both sections of the country within a few years. The Communists never allowed these elections to take place in North Korea, so in 1948 the United States allowed the Koreans in the south to elect their own government in 1948 and to establish

the Republic of Korea.

There are therefore two forms of government in Korea. North Korea has a parliament and holds elections, but the people have no real say in their own government. South Korea is a democratic republic, in which the people are encouraged to vote for whatever leaders they want. They elect representatives to the National Assembly, which makes all the laws, just as Congress does in the United States. The people also elect a president, who serves for a term of four years. However, a miltary junta seized control in 1961 to solve the nation's economic problems. Military government continued until 1963, when free elections were held.

KOREA IN THE PAST

According to the legends told in Korean storybooks, Korea was founded as a nation by an imaginary king, called *Tan'gun,* in 2333 B.C., more than four thousand years ago. Historical records, however, show that about 1100 B.C., more than a thousand years later than the storybooks have it, a powerful leader named Kija came to Korea with his followers from somewhere in China and established the kingdom of *Chosen,* as Korea was then called. This kingdom flourished for nearly two thousand years, but then it was destroyed by cruel Mongol conquerors, Genghis Khan and then Kublai Khan, whose soldiers brought death and destruction to almost all of Asia.

With the help of the Chinese, the Koreans rebuilt their country and established a new kingdom. This was the period of their great glory, when writing and the arts were at their highest and when the Koreans made notable scientific discoveries.

In 1592 the Japanese invaded Korea and tried to capture the country. After seven years of bitter fighting, the Japanese were driven out. The Koreans owed their victory partly to the armored boats they had invented.

This experience made the Koreans very angry and for the next three hundred years they sealed off their country completely, allowing no one to come in and sharing none of their knowledge with other people. During this period Korea was known as the "Hermit Kingdom." In 1876 the Koreans finally agreed to let foreign ships come into their harbors and buy Korean goods. Soon the Japanese tried again to conquer the country. This they easily succeeded in doing in 1910, because the Koreans were now much weaker than they had been once. The Japanese called the country by its old name, *Chosen.* The Koreans never stopped hating the Japanese conquerors, and resisted them as much as possible, but they were powerless.

After Japan was defeated in World War II, Korea was occupied by Russian and American soldiers, and divided into two countries.

THE WAR IN KOREA

The dividing of Korea into two halves pleased almost no one. The people in South Korea wanted the whole country to be a free republic, and the Communists wanted to control the whole country. The Communists built up a powerful

army in North Korea, and in June, 1950, they sent their tanks and soldiers across the 38th Parallel into South Korea, hoping to conquer that country very quickly and force the South Koreans to join their Communist government.

But they did not count on the United Nations and President Harry S. Truman of the United States. President Truman called the invasion of South Korea a case of "unprovoked aggression," meaning an attempt by one country to rob another of its territory and freedom. He ordered the United States fliers, sailors and soldiers who were in Korea to help the South Koreans defend their country. The United Nations immediately supported President Truman's action, and many of the free countries of the world, including Great Britain, Turkey, Canada, New Zealand, France, the Netherlands, and others, sent soldiers to Korea too. It was the first time in modern history that the free nations of the world had gotten together to stop a country from starting a fight. The fighting in Korea was called a "police action," rather than a war. General Douglas MacArthur was named commander of the United Nations army.

At first things went badly for the United Nations and South Korea, but more soldiers arrived and pushed the North Koreans far back into their own country. By Christmas of 1950 the United Nations had clearly won. Then the Chinese Communist government decided to help North Korea. They sent huge Chinese armies into North Korea and easily pushed the smaller United Nations army back to the 38th parallel again. There the war continued for another two years, with both sides facing each other more or less across the middle of the Korean peninsula.

It was a terrible war for American soldiers and other United Nations soldiers in Korea, and also for the people of South Korea. The bombing of their cities and the bitter fighting brought death and destruction to their land. It took many years before their ruined cities could be rebuilt and before their rutted fields once again grew enough food to support the Korean people.

At the end of three years, in July 1953, an armistice was signed and the fighting stopped. The frontier between North and South Korea remained in about the same place after the war as it had been before the war.

SOUTH KOREA (Republic of Korea). Area 37,427 square miles. Population (1964 estimate) 27,633,000. Language, Korean. Religion, Buddhist, Confucianist, Christian. Government, republic.

NORTH KOREA (People's Republic of Korea.) Area 47,858 square miles. Population (1964 estimate) 11,800,000. Language, Korean. Religion, Buddhist, Confucianist, Christian. Government, republic.

Kosciusko, Tadeusz

Tadeusz, or Thaddeus, Kosciusko was a Polish soldier who helped the American colonies win their independence in the Revolutionary War. He was born in Lithuania in 1746 and fought for America from 1776 to 1783. (He was one of two great Polish commanders in the Revolutionary War. The other commander was PULASKI, about whom you

can read in a separate article.) After the Revolutionary War, when the United States had become an independent country, Kosciusko returned to Poland. In 1794, he became commander-in-chief of Poland's army, which was fighting Russia for Polish independence, but Russia won, and Kosciusko was wounded and taken prisoner by the Russians. When he was freed, he again visited the United States. This was in 1797. He was received as a hero and Congress gave him a pension (a regular income) for the rest of his life. With this he went to Switzerland, where he died in 1817.

kosher

Kosher is a Hebrew word that means lawful or clean. In the Jewish religion, kosher describes food that is prepared according to certain laws, called the *dietary laws.* The dietary laws say that Jewish people should not eat milk and meat together; they should not eat pork, or fish without scales and fins (which means they do not eat lobsters, clams, or oysters); all meat must be slaughtered in a special way, under the supervision of a rabbi. Very religious Jews prepare their food according to these rules, which were set down in the Talmud, the Jewish holy law, long ago.

Kossuth, Louis

Louis Kossuth was a Hungarian statesman who led a revolution in 1848. At that time the emperor of Austria, one of the largest European empires, was also king of Hungary. Many Hungarians, who wanted their country to have as much power in the government as Austria, rebelled against the emperor's government. Kossuth was their leader.

It seemed at the time that Kossuth's revolution failed. He and many of his followers had to leave Hungary and settle in the United States and other places. In 1867 it became apparent that his revolution had been successful after all, because Hungary was given equal rights in the Austro-Hungarian government. You can read more about this in the article on AUSTRIA-HUNGARY.

Kossuth was born in 1802 and lived to be a very old man. He was 94 years old when he died, in 1896.

Kosygin, Alexei

Alexei Nikolayevich Kosygin became the premier of the Soviet Union (U.S.S.R.) in 1964, when Nikita Khrushchev was removed from that position. Kosygin was born in Russia in 1905, was a factory worker as a young man, but became mayor of Leningrad when he was 33 and a cabinet minister when he was 41, the youngest man in the cabinet. He achieved the Presidium, the governing council, in 1957. Kosygin was known to be an influential man in the Soviet government but still it was a surprise to the world when he was selected to succeed Khrushchev.

Krakatoa

Krakatoa is a tiny group of islands in the Indian Ocean, between the islands of Java and Sumatra. Krakatoa is also the name of one of these islands, about three miles wide.

In August 1883, a volcano on Krakatoa erupted. It was the most tremendous natural explosion of modern times. People in Japan and Australia, hundreds of miles away, heard the explosion. The particles of lava and ashes and dust shot up more than seventeen miles into the air and were carried over thousands of miles. Scientists believe that these particles caused the particularly beautiful sunsets that appeared for several months afterwards in many parts of the world. The volcano made a gigantic tidal wave that was more than fifty feet high. This tidal wave swept away entire villages, killing more than thirty-five thousand people, on the island of Java and on other islands. No human beings live on Krakatoa at present. There have been several recent eruptions.

Kreisler, Fritz

Fritz Kreisler, one of the greatest violinists of his time and a composer of music, was born in Vienna, Austria, but later became a citizen of the United States. He was born in 1875.

Kreisler began to play the violin when he was very young. He knew how to read music before he could read words. When he was 14 years old, he made a concert tour of the United States and everyone said he would be a great musician, but he gave up music to study medicine and art. He served in the Austrian army in World War I. After the war, he began to play the violin again, and after that he never followed any other profession. Kreisler wrote one of the most popular operettas, *Apple Blossoms,* and many other compositions. He died in 1962.

Hugo Kreisler was the brother of Fritz. He was a great cellist; some considered him the world's greatest. The cello is not as popular an instrument as the violin, so Hugo Kreisler never became as well known as Fritz. Hugo Kreisler was born in 1884 and died in 1929.

Kremlin

The Kremlin is a walled-in section in the center of Moscow, which is the biggest city in Russia and the capital of the Union of Soviet Socialist Republics. The Kremlin is in the shape of a triangle, and it covers about thirty acres, which is about the same as ten to fifteen big city blocks. In this section there are several churches, a palace, and other buildings.

The Kremlin contains a great many relics and souvenirs of Russia's history. For hundreds of years the czars (emperors) who ruled Russia lived in the Kremlin. Then they moved to the city that is now Leningrad. When the Communists came into power in Russia, they moved back to the Kremlin and it held their government offices for more than twenty years. People often speak of the entire Russian government as "the Kremlin."

Moscow is a very old city, and the Kremlin is the oldest section in it. The pink brick walls of the Kremlin were built about five hundred years ago. At that time the entire city was within the walls.

Later the merchants and working people began to move outside the walls. The churches and palaces within the Kremlin have been built at different times. The Great Palace was not completed until about a hundred years ago, while the Cathedral of the Assumption, in which all the Russian monarchs since Ivan IV have been crowned, was completed about five hundred years ago. This cathedral has many icons decorating its walls. An icon is a painted image of Christ or a saint. These icons are covered with precious jewels.

Many Russian rulers are buried in the Cathedral of St. Michael the Archangel. This building is more than four hundred years old. It is decorated with pictures of the rulers who are buried there. The churches are built around Cathedral Square. At the edge of this square is the Tsar (Czar) Cannon, the largest cannon in the world. This cannon was built almost five hundred years ago to protect the city. It was never fired. The largest bell in the world, called the Tsar Bell, is in the Kremlin. Because a piece of it broke off when it was made, it has never been rung. You can read more about this in the article on BELL. The tower of Ivan the Great, a Russian ruler, is one of the most impressive buildings in the Kremlin. It is 322 feet high and has a gilt (gold-covered) dome. Until modern times this tower was the highest building in Moscow.

In the Ordnance Palace, or armory, the crowns, robes, thrones and other possessions of the czars are kept. Among other relics are weapons and beautifully decorated armor used by Russian noblemen hundreds of years ago.

In 1954 parts of the Kremlin were opened to sightseers for the first time in many years.

Kruger, "Oom Paul"

Stephanus Johannes Paulus Kruger was an important South African statesman more than fifty years ago. He was one of the leaders of the Boers (people of Dutch ancestry) who fought against Great Britain in the BOER WAR, about which there is a separate article.

Kruger was born in 1825. As a boy he took part in "the Great Trek," when the Dutch people of South Africa moved to territories farther to the north. Kruger's family settled in a new state called Transvaal. Many years later, in 1883, Kruger became the president of Transvaal. He was very popular with the Boers, who called him "Oom Paul," which means Uncle Paul.

During the war between the Boers and Great Britain, Kruger went to Europe to seek help for his country. Since the British won the war, he could not safely return and he died in Switzerland in 1904. There are many statues and parks in memory of Paulus Kruger in South Africa.

Krupp

Krupp is the name of a German family that has owned the biggest steel mills in Germany, and some of the biggest in the world, for more than 150 years. They have manufactured the guns and other weapons with which Germany has fought a series of wars.

Friedrich Krupp began to manufacture steel in a new way in 1810. Soon the Krupps owned many mines and factories. They supplied armies all over the world with guns and cannons.

When Adolf Hitler became dictator of Germany, in 1933, the Krupp works became the center of German armament manufacture. After World War II, Alfred Krupp von Buhler und Halbach, the head of the Krupp industry, was tried on a charge of helping to cause a war in which millions had died. He was found guilty and sentenced to twelve years in jail. Some people thought this might end the long line of power of the Krupp family, but after about five years Alfred Krupp was released from jail. He was again allowed to operate the Krupp business and his property was given back to him, so that once again he and his family were among the richest people in the world.

krypton

Krypton is a very rare gas that is used in photographic flash lamps. Krypton is found in the air in very small quantities. (Only about one-millionth part of the air is krypton.) Krypton was discovered about fifty years ago. It was difficult to discover krypton because it has no color and no smell. Krypton is an inert gas, which means that it will not combine with any other substance to form a different substance.

Kublai Khan

Kublai Khan was the ruler of a great empire that the Mongol people formed more than seven hundred years ago. This vast empire was begun by Kublai's grandfather, Ghengis Khan. After many years of war, Kublai Khan conquered all of China and set himself up as emperor. His territories included other parts of Asia and parts of Russia. He was a good ruler. He did not try to change the people but accepted most of their customs and introduced some useful reforms. Kublai Khan made Buddhism the state religion, and he encouraged an interest in art and literature among the people. The capital of the empire was where the city of Peiping, China, now stands.

Men from all over the world came to live at the magnificent court of Kublai Khan. The famous Venetian traveler, Marco Polo, spent about seventeen years at the court. He wrote about Kublai Khan's love for beautiful things. He described the magnificent summer and winter palaces, filled with precious jewels and costly tapestries. He wrote about the thousands of servants who waited on the emperor, and he told of gorgeous entertainments where lovely women danced, and the air was filled with perfume.

The English poet Samuel Taylor Coleridge wrote a poem called "Kubla Khan" that is considered one of the great poems of the English language.

Ku Klux Klan

The Ku Klux Klan has been the name of two secret organizations of men in the southern part of the United States. The first Ku Klux Klan was formed soon

after the Civil War, nearly a hundred years ago, in 1886. It was somewhat like the vigilantes that were formed in the western United States before there was any government there to enforce laws. The South had just lost the Civil War. Its army disbanded, and control of the state governments was usually in the hands of criminals or ignorant men.

Since the early members of the Ku Klux Klan wanted to frighten Negroes, who were often uneducated and superstitious, they dressed themselves in white sheets to make themselves look like ghosts. They wore masks so no one could know who they were. They burned huge wooden crosses, and "the fiery cross" became their symbol.

The headquarters of the Ku Klux Klan came to be Nashville, Tennessee, and their leader was General Nathan Bedford Forrest, who had been a cavalry leader in the Civil War. He was called the "Grand Wizzard of the Empire." The Klan was divided into *realms*. Each realm was headed by a "Grand Dragon." Other members of the Klan with important positions were called "Goblins" and "Ghouls" and the "Grand Cyclops."

When order was restored in the South, the first Ku Klux Klan ended. The second Ku Klux Klan was formed in 1915. Unlike the first Klan, it spread to northern states, and was very strong in Indiana, Illinois, New Jersey, and some other states. The purpose of this second Klan was to advance citizens who were white, members of Protestant Christian churches, and born in the United States. This Klan reached its peak in the 1920s. It died finally in the years just before World War II. It favored the Nazis of Germany, who were enemies of the United States.

When Supreme Court decisions made integration of schools and public places the law (see CIVIL RIGHTS) the Ku Klux Klan became active again in opposing Federal law-enforcement officers, journalists and photographers, and Civil Rights advocates both Negro and white, by violence that included homicide with bombs, gunshot, and beatings. The Klan defended persons accused of murder in the courts. In 1965 President Lyndon Johnson condemned the Ku Klux Klan and advised all well-meaning members of it to resign their membership. In 1966 a United States Senate committee investigated the Ku Klux Klan and learned that many of its leaders favor violence to accomplish their purposes. There are at least three separate Ku Klux Klan organizations.

kumquat

The kumquat is a tree, 10 to fifteen feet high, that grows in China. Its fruit, called the kumquat, is one of the CITRUS FRUITS about which you can read in a separate article. The kumquat fruit has a skin that tastes sweet, while the inside of the fruit is juicy and sour. The Chinese people cook the kumquat fruit in sugar and make a delicious candy of it. Kumquat trees are also grown in Japan and Florida and California. The leaves are dark green, and they stay green all year around. The tree has a lovely white flower that smells very sweet. Florists grow dwarf kumquat trees in greenhouses, and many people like to have this kumquat plant in their homes.

Kurdistan

Kurdistan is a region in southwestern Asia. Parts of it are now in the countries of Turkey, Iran, and Iraq. The boundaries of Kurdistan are not definite, but it has an area of about 75,000 square miles, which is about the size of the state of Nebraska. Some of the land is a plateau (high like a mountain, but flat like a plain), but most parts are mountainous.

About three million people live in this land. Most of them are Kurds, a handsome people with dark skin and eyes. They are excellent fighters, and though foreign conquerors have often ruled the Kurds, they have always given these conquerors a great deal of trouble.

Some of the Kurds are nomads (wanderers) who live in tents and move from place to place. All of these nomads are shepherds. In the summer they live high in the mountains, and when the cold weather comes they travel down to the valleys to search for better pastures. Other Kurds live in villages. They build low wooden houses with flat roofs. Some of the Kurds make beautiful rugs. Some of them are farmers and raise wheat, vegetables, cotton, and tobacco.

The Kurds follow the Mohammedan religion. Very few of them can read or write, but they speak many languages because they travel so much.

The Kurds were most powerful about eight hundred years ago. Since that time they have not been independent, but they have often revolted against their rulers, especially since World War I. None of these revolts has been successful.

Kurile Islands

The Kurile Islands are forty-seven islands in the North Pacific Ocean. They stretch out in a string or chain from the northern tip of the Japanese islands to the southern tip of Kamchatka, which is connected to the eastern end of Asia. The Kuriles all together have only 3,944 square miles, which is smaller than any United States state except Delaware and Rhode Island. All the islands have volcanoes on them, but most of them are dead. About 16,000 people live on the Kuriles. Some of them are Japanese or related peoples, and some are Ainus, who were the people who lived in Japan before the Japanese went there. The people farm and fish.

Russia explored and owned the Kuriles until 1905, when the Japanese took them as a result of the Russo-Japanese War. After World War II, Russia took them back.

Kuwait

Kuwait is a small country in the northeast part of Arabia. A former British Protectorate, it declared its independence in June, 1961. However, it has continued to rely upon Great Britain for military protection.

Kuwait is ruled by an amir (king), who until recently was an absolute ruler. In 1962 Kuwait received its first constitution, which provided for a Council of Ministers chosen by the king and an elected National Assembly.

In area, Kuwait is about 6,200 square miles, less than the state of New Jersey. More than 830,000 people live there, most of them Mohammedans. Most of the

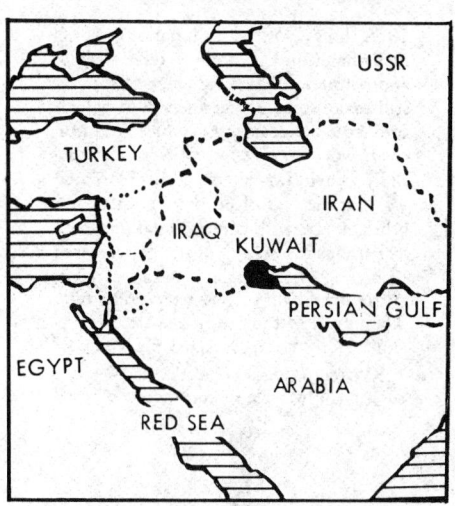

people worked as farmers in the country districts and as shipbuilders and traders in the cities until oil was discovered in 1938. Since then, many of the workers have been employed by oil companies.

Kuwait is an important seaport area on the northern part of the Persian Gulf. At one time its capital city, also called Kuwait, was the principal port for trade between Arabia and India. Today, while trade is still important, most of Kuwait's revenue comes from oil. In fact, Kuwait is one of the world's leading producers of oil. Most of the money made by selling the oil has been used to benefit the people of Kuwait and other Arab peoples.

KUWAIT. Area, 6,200 square miles. Population (1973 estimate) 830,000. Capital, Kuwait (99,609). Language, Arabic. Religion, Moslem. Monetary unit, Dinar.

Kyoto

Kyoto is the fifth-largest city in Japan, with a population of about 1,419,000, making it almost as big as Detroit, Michigan. It was the capital of Japan for more than a thousand years; in fact, its name in Japanese means "capital city." The emperor lived there in a magnificent palace, and the city became the center of

Japan Travel Inform. Off. Photos

For almost 1,100 years Kyoto was the capital of Japan. Its original name meant "city of peace and tranquillity," a phrase that well describes this city of lovely old temples and castles.

Japanese religion and culture.

The capital was moved to Tokyo in

1868, but Kyoto is still famous for its many handsome palaces, pagodas, shrines, and temples. Native craftsmen of the city still make some of the finest pottery, embroidery, woodcarvings, statues and other art work in the country. Kyoto is especially noted for its beautiful cloisonné work, a method of decorating vases and other objects with colorful inlaid enamel.

Perhaps the setting of the city inspired its artists, for it lies on a beautiful plain surrounded by a ring of steep green hills. The city is in the southern part of Honshu Island, the main island of Japan.

KYOTO, JAPAN. Population (1973 census) 1,419,165. On southern Honshu Island.

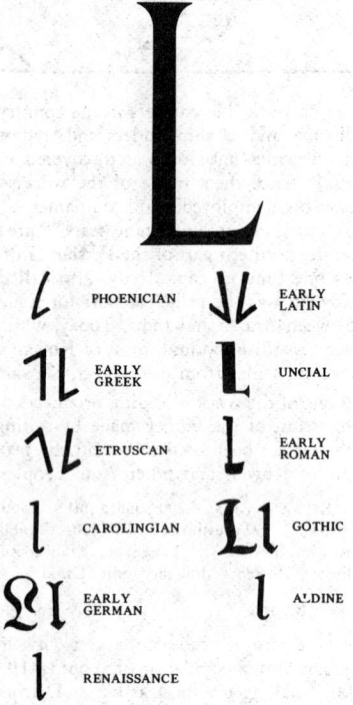

PHOENICIAN
EARLY LATIN
EARLY GREEK
UNCIAL
ETRUSCAN
EARLY ROMAN
CAROLINGIAN
GOTHIC
EARLY GERMAN
ALDINE
RENAISSANCE

L or l

The letter L is the twelfth letter of the alphabet. It can be traced back to the earliest writing known to man, in Egypt thousands of years ago. In the Hebrew language, in which much of the Bible was written, the letter was called *lamed,* a word that meant "ox goad." (A goad is a long stick with a pointed end, used for prodding animals.) The ancient Greeks took this same letter and called it *lambda.*

At the top of this page, at the far left, you can see the Phoenician form of this letter which the Hebrews adopted for their own written language. Below that can be seen the two forms of the Greek lambda that were used in the classical Greek language. In early times, writing was read from right to left, and in some of the old languages, such as Hebrew, it still is. But the Greeks changed and began to read from left to right as we do today. When they made this change they turned most of the letters around. Before this change was made, the later Greeks had progressed to the point of using a form which looked like an upside-down v. (This form is still used in modern Greek.) When the shift in reading direction was finally put into effect, this "upside-down v" came to look like the letter L tilted slightly to the left.

Read also the article ALPHABET.

labor and labor unions

All people who work for wages, that is, for payment by the hour or the day of actual work, are spoken of as *labor.* Those who own or manage the companies that labor works for are called *capital* or *management.* In previous years there were other distinctions. For example, the word labor was used to mean only union labor for a while, and did not include clerical workers who work in an office for a fixed weekly salary. Now some of the clerical workers are organized into unions too, and such people as actors and writers and artists often are members of unions. So labor has come to mean almost anyone who works for pay.

A labor union is an organization that is a sort of club, but its purpose is to represent all the workers in a particular trade or kind of job. Its principal duty is to make agreements with the management of the company or industry on how much the workers are to be paid and under what conditions they are to work. This is called COLLECTIVE BARGAINING, and there is a separate article about it.

In modern times labor is one of the most powerful forces in almost any country, and from time to time it has been the most powerful force in one country or another. For hundreds of years laborers had no power and they had to accept whatever wages the employers offered them. These wages were often too low to enable the workers to live decently, and workers were often made to work under conditions that were bad for their health and happiness. Now all this is changed in nearly every country. Labor is usually protected by law from being underpaid or treated as badly as it used to be. But the laws are not actually necessary because nearly all employers now believe that the prosperity of everybody in the country, including themselves, depends on paying as much as they can afford and making working conditions as good as they can make them. Then the working men will have money with which to buy things and enough leisure time to enjoy them, and this keeps the nation's industry going at full speed, which is good for management too. Also, it has been found scientifically that anyone who works will turn out more and better work if the conditions are healthful and pleasant. In the United States about 60,000,000 men and women are considered labor, and more than 18,000,000 belong to labor unions.

HOW A LABOR UNION IS ORGANIZED

The basic group in a labor union is the *local.* This is a group of people who do the same work, or sometimes related work, in the same city or for the same employer. In the newspaper industry, for example, the typesetters are members of one union, the men who run the printing presses are members of another union, the reporters, the photographers, the drivers of the trucks, and other workers, are members of still other unions. This includes the men who run the elevators in a big newspaper office.

All the locals belong to a national or international union. Most of the big American unions are international because they include locals in both the United States and Canada. The local be-

longs to the national or international voluntarily, that is, it can withdraw if it wants to. In most cases the local has the power to fix wages and working conditions for its own members. But usually locals feel they are better off by belonging to a national or international union that can help the local in its bargaining.

The local collects dues from its members to pay its expenses and the salaries of its officers, and some part of the dues money is sent to the national or international union. Every local and every big union tries to build up as big an amount of cash as possible to help its members if they go on strike.

Most of the large unions belong in turn to federations, or organizations of many unions. In the United States the big federations are the American Federation of Labor and Congress of Industrial Organizations, and the Railway Brotherhoods (which include the four big railroad unions of locomotive engineers, conductors, firemen, and trainmen). There is a separate article about each of these federations.

Each national and international union is a voluntary member of the federation and can withdraw at any time. Usually, like the locals, the unions feel they are better off remaining members of a federation, and they send some small part of the dues they receive to pay the expenses of the federation. The federation represents them by speaking for labor as a whole in political matters and by trying to get laws passed that are good for labor. Labor federations do not take part in such things as collective bargaining or the running of a union.

In some countries labor is organized as a regular political party. This is especially true in Great Britain, but in the United States labor has never formed a big political party. There is a separate article on LABOR PARTIES.

HOW THE LOCAL WORKS

Local unions have any one of several arrangements with employers about the workers in particular plants or companies. One is the *closed shop,* which means that the employer can hire no one who is not a union member in good standing. Another is the *union shop,* in which the employer can hire nonunion men but they must join the union within a certain period after being hired. *Maintenance of membership* is an arrangement whereby everyone who belongs to the union at the time of signing of an agreement, or contract, with the management must remain a member in good standing during the life of the contract. Many employers also have agreed to the dues *checkoff,* under which the employer deducts each union member's dues from his pay and turns it over to the union. All of these arrangements are designed to keep the union strong and to prevent workers from getting the benefits of the union without taking part in it.

Members of the local meet at intervals to discuss problems and to vote on such things as admission of new members and what they are going to ask of their employers in the way of wages and working conditions in the next contract. Occasionally when the officers of the union have not been able to reach agreement

with employers, the union members take a strike vote. You can read more about this in the article on COLLECTIVE BARGAINING.

Each plant or shop elects a group of members who act as *shop stewards*. Individual members take their problems to their shop stewards, and if they cannot easily be settled they are referred to a grievance committee. This elected committee is in charge of taking up more serious problems directly with the management.

Each local sends a delegate or delegates to meetings of the national or international union, and each national or international union sends delegates to meetings of the federation. In this way unions conduct their affairs by representative government, just as the United States does.

STRIKES

The great weapon of labor always has been the threat to strike, or stop working, if they could not receive the wages or the working conditions they thought they should have. If the employer cannot get enough workers he cannot manufacture his product and cannot stay in business. Everyone agrees that a strike is a very poor method of settling a disagreement. The men who go on strike cannot make the money they need to buy food or pay living expenses, the employers cannot make any money, and everybody suffers. However, most of the advances that labor made until very recently were gained by means of strikes.

For a long time employers opposed strikes by violent means. Sometimes they would hire private armies, or bring in nonunion workers called strikebreakers. Often the strikers and the company police or strikebreakers would fight. There were some very bloody battles in which many people lost their lives.

The employers also fought back by refusing to hire men who had been leaders in the strike and sometimes refusing to hire anybody who had ever struck or even joined a union. This was called a *lockout*.

Famous strikes of the early days of unions in the United States were at the McCormick Harvester Works in Chicago, when strikers and their families who had assembled in Haymarket Square were fired upon by police and two hundred of them were killed; the strike against Carnegie Steel at Homestead, Pennsylvania, when the Pennsylvania National Guard was called in and smashed the union so completely that the steel industry was not organized again for more than forty years; and the strike against the Pullman Company, when United States soldiers broke the strike.

Most of these strikes were fifty or more years ago. Strikes continue to take place, but they are becoming fewer and there is seldom violence.

LABOR LEGISLATION

In the early days of labor organization there were almost no laws to protect labor. In 1913 the United States Congress set up a national Department of Labor to look out for labor's interests, and the following year the Clayton Anti-Trust Act included several clauses favorable to labor, such as limiting the use of the injunction, or court order not to strike. The Railroad Brotherhoods were the first unions to win important gains by law, among them the eight-hour day, which was granted in 1916. In 1934 the Railway Labor Act was passed, and it gave railroad workers many protections that workers in other industries still do not have.

The National Labor Relations Act, also called the Wagner Act because it was introduced by Senator Robert Wagner of New York, was the greatest advance that labor as a whole had made in the United States. This law, passed in 1935, set up a National Labor Relations Board to regulate dealings between employer and labor. It ensured the right of

U.S. Department of Labor
Employees who belong to a labor union conduct a peaceful strike for higher wages and better working conditions.

working people to belong to unions and to bargain collectively. Under this law employers could no longer oppose unions. At about the same time the Wages and Hours Act was passed, which set minimum wages—the least pay any worker could receive. You can read more about this law in the article on WAGES.

The most recent major labor law is the Taft-Hartley Act, which was passed in 1947 to revise the National Labor Relations Act. This act prohibited *jurisdictional strikes* (those called by one union because an employer deals with a rival union). It reduced *featherbedding* (the forcing of an employer to pay for work not actually done, to meet a union's requirements), and it forbade the closed shop (not the union shop). It required a "cooling-off" period of sixty days before a strike could be called.

Although the Taft-Hartley Act retained most of the advances made by labor, it was bitterly opposed by almost all unions. Many efforts were made to change it because of labor's objections, but it appeared that most parts of it would remain United States law for some time.

Labor Day

Labor Day is a holiday on which people celebrate the important part that workers play in the country. It is celebrated in most states and in Canada on the first Monday in September. The day was chosen because an early labor union, the Knights of Labor, used to parade on that day in New York City, back in the 1880s. On June 28, 1894, Congress passed a bill making it a legal holiday. On Labor Day there are parades and picnics, and meetings and speeches praising the importance of the labor movement.

Labor, Department of

The Department of Labor is one of the main divisions of the United States government. Its purpose is to look after the welfare of workers in the United States. It was established as a separate department of the government in 1913, and it was the ninth United States Department to be formed. Its head is the Secretary of Labor, one of the government's most important officials and a member of the President's cabinet. The Department of Labor was the first department ever to have a woman at its head. Frances Perkins was appointed Secretary of Labor in 1933 by President Franklin D. Roosevelt.

Altogether, 8,951 people work for the Department of Labor. There are 8,252 full-time workers and 608 part-time workers in the United States, 54 people in United States territories and possessions, and 37 in foreign countries.

The Department of Labor has many duties. Everything concerned with the employment of workers comes under the jurisdiction of the Department of Labor if the firm that employs them is engaged in any form of interstate commerce. This includes checking the working conditions of apprentices or beginners at a trade, so that they are given fair pay and working hours and so that they do not run unnecessary risks while learning. It also includes checking to be sure that workers are protected by insurance for any accidents that may happen on a job; the supervision of unemployment insurance; the protection of the workers' health by maintaining good working conditions on the job; and the regulation of working hours per week for employees of firms doing government contract work.

The Bureau of Labor Statistics is a part of the Department of Labor. This is the bureau that keeps track of the cost of living, the number of people working throughout the country, and the average pay rates.

Labor Party

A Labor party is a political party in which workingmen, especially members of unions, join to vote together for what is best for them. The most powerful Labor Party is in England.

Labor Parties began to grow when the workingman acquired the right to vote. Many years ago in most countries one had to own property, usually land, in order to vote. This restriction made it impossible for most workingmen to vote. Gradually this restriction was dropped. Many workingmen were dissatisfied with the older parties and felt that they could get the things they wanted only by having their own political party.

In England, the Labour Party—with "*labour*" spelled the English way—grew out of the trade-union movement and was formed in 1900. Its leaders promised, if elected, to increase the wages of the workingman; to shorten his hours of work; and to guarantee him a job. The Labour Party was first elected to run the government in 1924. Since that time the Labour Party and the Conservative Party have been the two major political parties in England. After World War II the Labour Party was elected by a great majority and remained in power for more than six years. Clement Atlee was head of the government. During this period free medical and dental care for everyone was established and some important industries were nationalized (made the property of the government): coal mining, steel, transportation, and national banking. After the Conservative Party had regained and held power for ten years, in 1963 the Labour Party won a bare majority of 4 votes in the House of Commons. Its leader, Harold Wilson, became Prime Minister. In the elections of 1966 Labour increased its majority to 97 votes.

In the United States Labor Parties have not had as much success as in England. The Socialist Party, which stands for about the same things as the English Labour Party, has elected very few men to office. The American Labor Party was fairly strong in the 1930s and 1940s, but only in New York State. The reason why a strong labor party has not developed in the United States is probably that many of its ideas have been taken over by Democrats and Republicans.

Labrador

Labrador, at the northeastern tip of Canada, is part of the province of Newfoundland and Labrador. It has an area of 112,000 square miles, about the size of the state of Nevada. Labrador is a rich country, but it is very cold and wild, and fewer than 15,000 people live there.

THE PEOPLE OF LABRADOR

Most of the people who live in Labrador are white. A few hundred Eskimos, who live along the northern coast of Labrador, make their living by catching fish. Small bands of Algonquin Indians live in the interior. They hunt for reindeer, bears, and wolves, and sell the fur. In the spring, many fishermen from Newfoundland come to Labrador and spend the summer fishing for herring, trout, cod, and salmon. In the fall, when the cold weather begins, they return to their homes in Newfoundland. Some of the people of Labra-

dor work in logging camps. There are many forests of spruce and pine and other valuable timber.

Sir Wilfred Grenfell, an English doctor who went to Labrador in 1892, did a great deal to help the people improve their country. You can read about GRENFELL in a separate article.

WHAT LABRADOR IS LIKE

Labrador has a steep and rocky coast on the Atlantic Ocean. In many places the cliffs are more than four thousand feet above the sea. There is no soil along the coast, so trees and plants cannot grow, and the view is dreary.

It is very difficult to travel inland from the coast of Labrador, because much of the country is still unsettled. There are huge forests and lakes and rivers, and in warm weather you can travel to many parts of the country by small boat. In the river valleys, some people grow potatoes and cabbage and other vegetables. Labrador has rich zinc and iron-ore deposits, and people are working to develop mines.

The climate in Labrador is very cold. Often during the long winters the temperature drops to 20 degrees below zero. This is because of the Labrador current, a current of cold water that flows through the North Atlantic Ocean from the Arctic regions. For about seven months of the year, the lakes and rivers of Labrador are frozen and the coastline is blocked with ice. The summers in Labrador are cool and pleasant, and people go there for summer vacations.

HISTORY OF LABRADOR

Labrador was first visited by the Vikings, more than a thousand years ago. John Cabot, a Venetian explorer, sailed under the English flag to Labrador in 1497, and about forty years later, Jacques Cartier, a French explorer, reached the coast. People did not begin to settle in Labrador until about 150 years ago, when fishing villages and religious missions were set up. Both Quebec and Newfoundland claimed Labrador until 1927, when it became a territory of Newfoundland; then in 1964 it was incorporated into the province. To read about how Labrador is governed, see NEWFOUNDLAND.

LABRADOR. Territory of Newfoundland. Area, 112,000 square miles. Population (1961 census) 13,534.

laburnum

The laburnum is a small tree that grows in the Swiss Alps and in other mountainous parts of Europe. People raise the laburnum because its shiny, dark green leaves and graceful sprays of yellow flowers, which blossom in May and June, make it a decorative tree in gardens and parks. Many laburnum trees grow to be about 40 feet high. The wood is dark brown or dark green and it is very hard, so that it can be polished well. Cabinetmakers often use laburnum to make fine furniture. The leaves and seeds of the laburnum are poisonous.

labyrinth

In the stories told by the ancient Greeks, the labyrinth was a large tunnel built by Daedalus, a great inventor, in ancient Crete. It was built for the Minotaur, a fierce and cruel monster with a bull's

head and a human body, whose favorite food was young men and girls. The labyrinth was a long path with so many twists and turns that no one who entered it could ever find his way out again.

The Greek hero Theseus was sent to Crete to kill the Minotaur. He persuaded Ariadne, the daughter of the king of Crete, to give him a long thread. He tied one end to the entrance of the labyrinth and then entered and killed the Minotaur. He was able to find his way out by following the thread.

Any passageway that is full of twists and turns is still called a labyrinth.

lac

Lac is a sticky substance that comes from the bodies of certain female insects in India and parts of Asia. These insects feed on the sap of twigs from certain trees. As the sticky substance comes out of the female's body it hardens, and the female and her young get stuck to the tree. People then scrape this hard stuff, called *stick-lac*, from the tree. They prepare the stick-lac to make shellac, sealing wax, and some dyes.

lace

Lace is a decorative material made of thread. It has an openwork pattern, which means that there are many holes, or open places, in the pattern. It may be woven, netted, crocheted, or twisted thread. The thread may be linen, silk, cotton, nylon, or other materials. Lace garments and cloths have been found on mummies thousands of years old, excavated from ancient Egyptian tombs, and it is known that the ladies of ancient Greece and Rome also wore laces.

Laces are made by machine as well as by hand, but the most valuable lace is handmade. Lacemaking is an art. There are many ways to make lace.

HOW LACE IS MADE

Needlepoint lace is made with a needle and thread. It is very closely related to embroidery, but the stitches are made without cloth underneath them. They are simply woven and twisted on each other and on loops of thread held by the lacemaker, using fine buttonhole stitches.

Irish lace is made with a fine crochet hook. Raised patterns are worked into the design, with such details as separate flower petals. Both the crochet needle and the thread are very thin and fine. More than three hundred separate stitches may go into a flower figure that is only three-quarters of an inch across. Lacemaking of this kind is very fine, delicate work, and good Irish lace is expensive.

Another type of costly lace is *Valenciennes*. This lace is often used for wedding veils. It is woven in a mesh or net with a figure or pattern that is part of the mesh itself. *Chantilly* is another kind of handmade lace that can be made into veils, gowns, blouses, or shawls.

There are many other laces, some of which developed as variations of older styles, and some of which are totally different from the types already mentioned. An English lace called *Honiton* is made on a foundation of net. Fine braid is placed on the net in graceful patterns and woven in place.

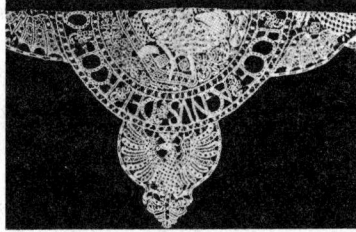

Needlepoint lace is typical of French and Italian work. The design is formed by making a network of looped or buttonhole stitches. Like making lace with bobbins, needlepoint lacemaking exhausts the eyes, and many of the women who make lace for a living go blind. *Above:* A design made in Venice 250 years ago. On the top is the coat of arms of the family for which it was made. *Right* and *below:* Two fine examples of 18th-century French lace.

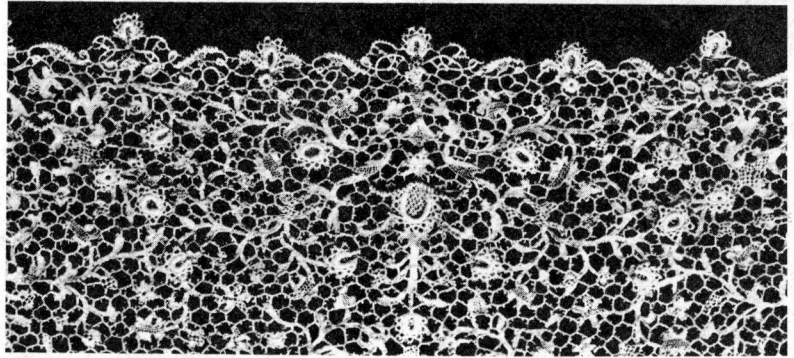

Machine-made lace can be made by weaving with bobbins on a loom. The kind of lace of which lace curtains are made is of this type, and so is the lace that is used to trim lingerie and is sold in department stores.

Tatting is a kind of lacemaking. This makes a kind of knotted lace. The knots are made by catching loops of thread and forming them into rings. It is done with a single thread wound on a bobbin, and it is one of the many forms of lacemaking that require great skill and much practice.

Laces are sometimes made with gold or silver threads instead of plain fibers. It is possible to obtain lace for hundreds of different uses, from ornamentation of upholstery to trimming baby clothes. Simple lacemaking is a pleasant hobby. It can be learned in handcraft classes in many cities, or from the instruction booklets available wherever crochet hooks, tatting bobbins and crochet yarns are sold.

lacewing

The lacewing is an insect with delicate wings that look like lace because of many veins in them, and with golden eyes. The lacewing lays its eggs on a leaf, and out of the eggs hatch the larvae, which are like little worms. The lacewing larva is one of the greediest and hungriest of all insects. It destroys other small insects by sucking the juices out of their bodies. This larva, called the *aphid lion,* is a friend to farmers because it devours many aphids, small insects that are harmful to plants.

When the aphid lion is grown it spins a cocoon, or shell, around itself. Later, out of the cocoon comes the lacewing. It is about half an inch long. There are many different kinds of lacewing, and they are found throughout the world, but only a few kinds are found in the United States.

lacquer and lacquer ware

Lacquer is a kind of varnish or paint used to protect or to decorate things made of metal, wood, or paper. The first lacquer was made in China more than three thousand years ago from the sap of a tree that grows in China and Japan. This lacquer can be mixed with many lovely colors, and it is very hard, smooth, and shiny, when it dries. Artists in ancient China, and later in Japan, learned to make beautiful objects, called lacquer ware, by applying many coats of lacquer to a surface. Then the artist made a picture or a design by setting many tiny pieces of gold, silver, seashells, or precious stones in the lacquer. The boxes, bowls and furniture made by these artists are prized for their beauty. Some can be seen in museums. The Japanese artists became so famous for their work that decorating with lacquer is sometimes called *japanning.*

Modern lacquers are made of the same materials as plastics. They are used on nearly all metal products, such as automobiles, machines, and toys, and on many wood products. Most of these lacquers are made so thin that they can be sprayed on. Some articles are dipped in the lacquer. The lacquered articles are then baked until the lacquer hardens.

The first modern lacquers were made from nitrocellulose, in a form called *pyroxylin.* By the 1930s lacquers were being developed from other plastics. Many of these lacquers are even harder than the lacquers made from nitrocellu-

lose, or have such properties as being fireproof or stainproof.

lacrosse

Lacrosse is an outdoor athletic game. It is played by two teams of ten players each, on a field somewhat larger than a football field. There are two goals, 80 yards (240 feet) apart, which is closer together than the goals are on a football field. The goals are posts 6 feet high and 6 feet apart, with a crossbar on top. Each player has a *crosse,* which looks like a big, loosely strung tennis racket. There is a rubber ball about 8 inches around (a little smaller than a baseball).

The object of the game is to throw the ball through the opponents' goal. The ball is caught in the net of the crosse and is thrown from player to player. A player may not touch the ball with his hands. Each goal scores one point.

Lacrosse was played by American Indians before white men reached America. It is very popular in Canada and in some of the northern states of the United States.

Ladoga, Lake

Lake Ladoga, in the western part of Russia, is the largest lake on the European continent. It covers an area of about seven thousand square miles and is fed by more than seventy streams. The lake is not very deep, so men have dredged parts of it and made canals, permitting boats to go from one city to another on the opposite shore. The water is clear and cold and contains many fish.

From October until April, the waters of the lake are frozen solid. The Russian people, during World War II, built a railroad across the ice so that they could carry supplies to the city of Leningrad when it was attacked. The Germans held the south part of the lake from 1941 until 1944, when the Russians took it again.

Half of Lake Ladoga was in Finland, but the Russians took it away from Finland in World War II. A people called the Karelians live around the lake.

ladybird or ladybug

The ladybird is a pretty little beetle that is found in almost every part of the United States and Europe. Most ladybugs are bright red or yellow with black spots, but some are black with red or yellow spots. If you hold a ladybird, it will give off a yellow liquid that has an unpleasant odor. Most ladybirds are very useful, because they eat insects that destroy fruit trees and other plants that farmers grow. There is one kind of ladybird that eats the bean plant and is a great pest to farmers. Many people think of the ladybird in connection with the verse:

Ladybird, ladybird, fly away home,
Your house is on fire, your children
will burn.

lady's-slipper

The lady's-slipper is a beautiful flower, a member of the orchid family, that grows in many parts of Europe, Asia and the United States where the weather is mild. The flower got its name because its petals are shaped like slippers. It is sometimes called the *moccasin flower.* There are about thirty different kinds of

lady's-slipper. Many of them grow to be about two feet high. Some of these plants have yellow flowers, others are white, pink, violet, or these colors lined or spotted with another color. The lady's-slipper is easy to grow. Girls of some American Indian tribes used the lady's-slipper to make wreaths for their hair.

La Farge

La Farge is the name of a family of American artists and writers.

John La Farge, an American artist, was born in New York City in 1835. His grandfather taught him to draw, and then he studied art in Paris. He painted landscapes, figures, and murals, and later became most famous for his work in stained glass. John La Farge also wrote about his work and his travels, and all of his books have beautiful pictures that he himself drew. He died in 1910.

Three sons of John La Farge were prominent. Christopher Grant La Farge, born in 1862, was one of the most famous American architects. He designed many churches and public buildings, but is best remembered for the Cathedral of St. John the Divine in New York City. He died in 1938. His brother Bancel La Farge was a painter and his brother John La Farge became a Catholic priest and author.

Two sons of C. Grant La Farge were prominent writers. Christopher La Farge, born in New York City in 1897, wrote novels and poems, and he also painted watercolors that are much admired. He died in 1956. Oliver La Farge, born in New York City in 1901, studied anthropology (the study of men and how they live) and wrote many books. He lived among American Indian tribes in Arizona and other parts of the Far West and he knew their customs and beliefs. One of his books about the Indians (*Laughing Boy*, a story about a young Navaho man) won the Pulitzer Prize as the best American novel of 1929. He died in 1963.

Lafayette, Marquis de

When the American people were fighting for their independence from the British in the Revolutionary War, one of the men who helped them most was a young French nobleman named Marie Joseph Paul Yves Roch Gilbert du Motier, the Marquis de Lafayette. Lafayette was born in 1757, and at the age of 20, while

he was training to be a soldier in France, he became so excited at the idea of American independence that he crossed the Atlantic and joined Washington's army. Soon he was made a major general and became a friend of Washington's. He was with Washington at Valley Forge and was one of the commanders at the Battle of Yorktown, the battle that won the war for the Americans.

When the war was over Lafayette returned to France, which was soon to have a revolution of its own. Lafayette believed in liberty and human rights for all and was on the side of the people in the French Revolution, even though most of the noblemen were against the revolution. In 1789 Lafayette gave to France the tri-

color, the red, white, and blue flag that is still used by France. Lafayette served as a commander, but when the extremists gained control of the revolution, he fled the country and did not return until Napoleon came to power.

In 1824 Lafayette visited the United States and was given an enthusiastic welcome by the grateful people, who remembered what an important part he had played in the Revolution. When his carriage appeared in the streets, the horses were removed and men pulled his carriage. To show him gratitude, the United States made Lafayette's children and their descendants, members of the Chambrun family, honorary citizens of the country. Lafayette died in 1834.

Laffite, Jean

Jean Laffite was a pirate and a smuggler who lived about 150 years ago. He was born in France, but he went to the United States shortly after it became independent. He carried on his piracy in the Gulf of Mexico. At first he was a privateer, that is, he had been given permission by France to attack ships of its enemies. Later he began to attack and rob all ships.

During the War of 1812 Jean Laffite learned that the British planned to attack New Orleans. The British offered him a high position in their navy if he would help them. He refused and turned over the information to the United States government. He offered to fight for the United States if he and his men were pardoned for their acts of piracy. The United States government agreed, and he and his men fought with General Andrew Jackson at the Battle of New Orleans, at which the British were defeated.

After the war, Laffite and his men returned to piracy, operating out of what is now the city of Galveston, Texas. When Laffite attacked an American ship his headquarters were raided by an American warship, but he escaped. He continued to be a pirate and smuggler until his death. He probably died at sea about 1825.

La Follette

La Follette is the name of a Wisconsin family that became important in American political life. Robert Marion LaFollette was born in Dane County, Wisconsin, in 1855. He studied law, served in Congress, and in 1901 became governor of Wisconsin. At that time the lumber and railway corporations were so powerful in Wisconsin that they almost controlled the state. As governor, La Follette fought the large companies and ended this control. In 1905 he was elected to the United States Senate. He was opposed to World War I, not because he thought the Germans were right but because he thought all war was wrong. In 1924 he was the Progressive Party's candidate for President of the United States. He was defeated, but he received five million votes. His life was so full of work and action for what he thought was right that he was called "Fighting Bob." He died in 1925.

His son, Robert Marion La Follette, Jr., followed his father in his political career. "Young Bob" was born in Madison, Wisconsin, in 1895. He became his father's

secretary and was appointed to his father's seat in the Senate in 1925, when his father died. He was re-elected in 1928, 1934, and 1940. As chairman of the Civil Liberties Committee of the Senate, he investigated the wages and working conditions of workers, and their standard of living, and did much to help workers better their conditions. He was not in favor of the United States becoming entangled in foreign affairs, and he tried to keep the United States from getting into World War II. He was defeated for re-election in 1946 and died in 1953.

Another of Fighting Bob's sons, Philip La Follette, who was born in 1897, was governor of Wisconsin from 1931 to 1933, and from 1935 to 1939. He later served in World War II under General Douglas MacArthur.

La Fontaine, Jean de

Jean de La Fontaine was a French writer of stories and fables. A fable is a short story that teaches a lesson. La Fontaine was born in 1621. In his fables, many of which were about animals, he gently poked fun at the stupid things people often do. He himself was very absent-minded, and his friends loved to tell stories about things he did, such as wearing his stockings wrong side out. He died in 1695.

Lagerlöf, Selma

Selma Lagerlöf was a Swedish novelist and short-story writer. In 1909 she won the Nobel Prize for literature, which is the most important prize a writer can receive. Selma Lagerlöf was born in 1858. Her first recognition as a writer came when one of her stories won first prize in a

newspaper contest. In 1891 she published one of her best-known novels, *The Story of Gösta Berling*, which was translated into many different languages.

Many of Selma Lagerlöf's short stories are about the problems of growing up; her main characters are often teenagers. Her book *The Wonderful Adventures of Nils* is particularly popular with young readers. Selma Lagerlöf died in 1940.

LaGuardia, Fiorello H.

Fiorello Henry LaGuardia was an American Congressman and for twelve years was mayor of New York City. He was born in New York City in 1882, as a young man held several United States government jobs, then studied law and became a lawyer in New York. He was in

the Army Air Force in World War I and rose to the rank of major. After the war he returned to New York, entered politics, and was elected to Congress. While he was a Congressman (more than ten years) he and Senator George W. Norris of Nebraska introduced the Norris-LaGuardia act, a law that helped labor unions by giving them greater legal right to strike.

In 1933, after the public had been given proof that there was much dishonesty in the government of New York City, LaGuardia ran for mayor with the backing of the Republican Party and of many independent voters who grouped together as the Fusion Party. LaGuardia was elected and was re-elected twice, remaining mayor from 1934 to 1946. He was a very honest mayor and improved New York City's government a great deal. He was popular with people. He was a small man with a very expressive face, and his speeches entertained millions.

Once when New York's newspapers were not being published because of a strike, he read the "funny papers" on the radio so that children did not have to miss them. He was not in good health when he retired as mayor in 1946, and he died the next year, in 1947, at the age of 65.

lake

A lake is a body of water that is surrounded by land on all sides. A lake does not flow as a river does, and it is larger than a pond. Usually a lake has fresh water, while a sea or ocean has salt water.

Most of the lakes in the world were made about twenty thousand years ago, by GLACIERS, great sheets of ice, about which you can read in a separate article. At that time glaciers covered large parts of the earth. When the glaciers began to melt, some of the waters formed rivers to the sea, and some filled hollows in the land to form lakes.

Some lakes were formed by dams. At various times in the earth's history, huge landslides of mountainous rock and lava would block the course of mountain streams and rivers, and the dammed-up water formed lakes. Today there are many man-made lakes, formed by the huge lams that have been built to supply water power and control floods.

Other lakes were formed by tremendous volcanic explosions. Crater Lake, in the state of Oregon, was made in this way. About twenty thousand years ago, after a great explosion, the top of the volcano caved in and formed a huge hollow bowl. Snow and rain and the water from streams gradually filled the bowl, so that now Crater Lake is almost two thousand feet deep.

Some lakes grow deeper and change their shapes as they are fed by springs and rivers and underground streams. Some lakes grow shallower as they fill up with mud, rocks, and dead trees carried to the lakes by streams and rivers, and in time they may disappear altogether. In some places, the weather becomes much warmer, and there is not enough rain to fill up the lake. GREAT SALT LAKE, about which there is a separate article, is a lake that is gradually drying up.

There are separate articles on the GREAT LAKES and other important lakes in the world.

lake dweller

Lake dwellers were early men, before the time of written history, who lived in houses built on log stilts near lakes or over the waters of lakes. Sometimes they built small islands called crannogs. They made the crannogs of large baskets of tree branches that they filled with stones and sod. They sank many of these baskets close to one another in the water, and then built their houses on them. Many houses were built close together to make small towns above the water. The towns often were connected to the shore by narrow wooden bridges

When we speak of lake dwellers we mean those who lived in Europe many centuries ago, but there are still lake dwellers in New Guinea and in the swamps of the Amazon River.

No one knows exactly why lake dwellers built their houses over the water. Some anthropologists, scientists who study different civilizations, think that the lake dwellers built their houses over water to protect themselves from wild beasts and from enemy tribes. Other anthropologists think that the lake dwellers were weak tribes who were driven from good rich farmland by stronger tribes. So, to save for planting every inch of what little land they had, lake dwellers built their small towns over water.

In 1854, when a long rainless period lowered the level of Lake Zurich, in Switzerland, the first ancient European lake dwellings known to modern man were uncovered. Every once in a while more lake dwellings are found. In 1954, scientists drained an Irish lake and found lake dwellings under its waters.

From things found in lake dwellings, ranging from crude stone tools to ornaments of bronze, silver, and gold, scientists know that the dwellings were built as long as ten thousand years ago.

lamaism

Lamaism is a religion practiced in the country of Tibet, in Asia, and in a few other parts of Asia. It is a form of BUDDHISM, about which there is a separate article. The *lamas* of the religion are monks or priests, and their monasteries are called *lamaseries*. Followers of lamaism believe in *reincarnation;* that is, they believe the soul of a dead person comes back to earth in a new body. They also believe in numerous gods or spirits.

The most important lama is the DALAI LAMA, who is traditionally head of both the government and the religion (see the separate article); but in 1959 the Chinese Communists drove the Dalai Lama out of Tibet, so that they could rule the country without opposition, and he took refuge in India. The active head of the Tibetan religion, and next in importance to the Dalai Lama, is the Tashu Lama (so called because he is head of the great Tashu, or Teshu, lamasery). He is also called the Panchen Lama ("the lama of the court, or council").

Lamb, Charles and Mary

Charles Lamb was an English writer who lived about 175 years ago. He became famous for his essays (short compositions in which the author expresses his personal opinions). Lamb's best essays are collected in a book called *Essays of Elia.* Elia is a name under which he wrote.

Charles Lamb was born in 1775. His older sister Mary, who was born in 1764, had attacks of insanity, and when Charles

Charles Lamb

was 21 years old she had a terrible fit and killed their mother. This tragedy changed Charles' whole life. He gave up all ideas about getting married, and promised to take care of his sister for the rest of her life. Lamb had a job as a clerk and he worked at this job for thirty-three years, while he and Mary lived quietly together.

Charles and Mary Lamb wrote the stories of Shakespeare's plays, in a book called *Tales From Shakespeare,* and other stories that children have enjoyed.

The Lambs were liked by most of England's great writers who lived at the same time. They were friends of the "Lake Poets" (Wordsworth, Southey, and Coleridge), especially of Coleridge. Lamb died in 1834, when he was 59 years old. Mary Lamb died in 1847, when she was 83.

lamprey

The lamprey is a strange kind of fish that does not look very much like other fish.

The lamprey's mouth is a round hole designed for sucking; the lamprey does not have any jaws, as other fish do. It has many sharp teeth, all around its mouth, and its tongue is rough and sharp. With this mouth, the lamprey attaches itself to other fish and sucks out the blood and juices from their bodies. Sometimes the lamprey fastens onto boats and even to people swimming in the water, but it cannot harm people.

The lamprey is long and narrow, like an eel, and it has no scales on its body. It has two fins on its back and one on its tail, but it does not have the two side fins that most other fish have. Some kinds of lamprey live in the ocean, but they swim up rivers to lay their eggs. They can move stones with their round sucking mouths to build nests for their eggs. The young lampreys that hatch from the eggs live in the mud and sand of the river bed for four or five years, then they usually go back to the ocean or lake for two or three years, and then they return to fresh-water streams to lay their eggs. They may grow to be as much as three feet long.

Some scientists think that the lamprey is the oldest kind of animal with a backbone that is still living. Lampreys are found in many parts of the world where the climate is moderate. The small, baby lampreys are useful as bait for fishermen, but the full-grown lampreys are harmful, because they destroy many fish.

Lancaster

Lancaster was the name of a famous English house, or family, about five hundred years ago. Three members of the Lancaster family were kings of England. The first was Henry of Lancaster, also called Bolingbroke. He was born in 1367. In 1399 he led an army against Richard II, who was king at that time. He forced Richard to give up the crown and made himself King Henry IV of England. Henry IV died in 1413.

Henry IV was followed by his son Henry V, and then came Henry V's son,

Henry VI. But while Henry VI was king, another English family, the house of York, claimed the right to rule England. This was the beginning of a war between the House of Lancaster and the House of York. The war, which lasted from 1455 to 1485, was called the War of the Roses, because the special badge of the House of Lancaster was a red rose, and the special badge of the House of York was a white rose. Finally, in 1485, Henry Tudor, who was one of the Lancaster family, managed to make himself King Henry VII of England. The next year he married Elizabeth of York, and so the two families were united.

Lancelot

Sir Lancelot was the finest knight in the court of King Arthur, about whom many old stories are told. Sir Lancelot was the bravest, and the best fighter. Often he fought in disguise, but he was always recognized because no other knight had as much strength and skill as he. Lancelot was brought up by Vivianne, a fairy known as the Lady of the Lake, and so he is often called Sir Lancelot of the Lake.

When Lancelot was 18 years old he was taken to Arthur's court, where he proved his courage and was made one of the Knights of the Round Table. He was loved by Arthur's queen, Guinevere, and for her sake he did many daring deeds. He was also loved by Elaine, the fair maid of Astolat, but he did not return her love and she died of a broken heart. After Arthur's death, Lancelot hoped to marry Guinevere, but she became a nun and so he entered a monastery and lived a holy life until his death. In some of the stories, Lancelot marries Elaine, the daughter of King Pelles, and their son is another famous knight, Sir Galahad. Lancelot's name is sometimes spelled Launcelot.

landing craft and ships

Landing craft and ships are special warships that were developed during World War II to land men, equipment, and supplies on enemy shores. Landing craft were used in the invasions of North Africa, Sicily, Italy, France, and many of the islands of the Pacific. They were also used during the Korean War.

At the end of World War II, the United States and Great Britain had 25,000 landing craft. Many of these were being prepared for the invasion of the home islands of Japan, which never was necessary. The Axis (enemy) forces also used landing craft in their capture of Crete and the Pacific islands.

The main job of landing craft is to get men and equipment ashore in places where there are no regular ports or harbors where full-sized transport vessels can land. Landing craft are designed with very shallow bottoms so that they can go into water only a few feet deep, or directly onto the beaches. Many landing craft have large hinged doors in the front. The doors swing down to form ramps, across which men can walk and trucks and tanks can be driven.

The United States Navy used designations beginning with the letters "LC" for smaller landing craft, such as the LCM (landing craft-mechanized), LCI (landing craft-infantry), LCVP (landing craft-vehicles, personnel). For larger vessels, known as landing ships, the designations begin with "LS"—such as LST (landing ship, tanks), and LSD (landing ship, dock). The LST, one of the largest and most used landing ships, displaces 4,000 tons and can carry several tanks, trucks or large guns onto a beach. The use of landing craft with air and sea support is called AMPHIBIOUS WARFARE, about which there is a separate article.

Landon, Alfred M.

Alfred Mossman Landon was an American political leader who ran for the office of President of the United States in 1936, but was defeated by President Franklin D. Roosevelt. Landon was born in 1887, at West Middlesex, Pennsylvania. For a while he was in the oil business in Kansas. He became a leader in the Republican Party in his state, and in 1933 he was elected governor of Kansas. As governor he was outstanding for running the government of the state in a very economical way; that is, he was very careful and did not waste the state's money. In 1936, Landon was chosen by the Republican Party to be its candidate for President. But at that time the people were very much in favor of the Democratic Party, and Landon was badly defeated. Only two states, Maine and Vermont, voted for him.

landscaping

Landscaping is changing outdoor surroundings to make them prettier and more pleasant to be in. Planting a flower bed or sowing grass to make a good front lawn is landscaping on a small scale. Landscaping can mean planting or removing trees, pulling up weeds, making a road, filling a ditch, building a swimming pool or a golf course, putting a statue in a garden, or doing anything to add beauty or usefulness to the scenery.

Landscaping goes far back in history. The Hanging Gardens of Babylon, one of the seven wonders of the ancient world, more than 2,500 years ago, were a famous example. Other examples are the gardens of Versailles in France, the gardens of the Taj Mahal in India, and the gardens of Vatican City in Rome, Italy.

Landscaping has been developed to its highest point in the United States in the last hundred years. Most of the landscaping is planned by men and women who have studied at college to become landscape architects. A landscape architect draws up plans for landscaping and sees that these plans are carried out by the workmen. A landscape architect plans the landscaping to suit the needs of the people who will use the grounds. A landscape architect must know botany, the science of plants, so that he will plant flowers that will grow easily in the places planned for them. In the United States, the landscaping of most public parks, public beaches, housing developments, public buildings, schools and colleges, and parkways is done by landscape architects.

Landseer, Edwin

Edwin Henry Landseer was an English painter and sculptor. He is best known for his paintings of animals and for the great sculptured lions in Trafalgar Square in London. Landseer was born in 1802. He was first taught to draw by his father, who was an engraver, a person who makes plates that are used to print pictures. When Edwin Landseer was only 13 years old, one of his pictures was exhibited at the Royal Academy of Arts, an English organization that runs an art school and exhibits paintings. In addition to his many animal pictures, Landseer painted portraits of some famous people,

There are many styles of landscaping. Lambert Gardens in Portland, Oregon, has ten beautiful gardens, each in a different style. Above is the formal Spanish garden.

Oregon State Highway Comm.

including Queen Victoria and Sir Walter Scott. Queen Victoria honored his work by making him a knight in 1850. He died in 1873.

Lands End

Lands End is the westernmost tip of England. It is a promontory, or little point of land, that juts out into the Atlantic Ocean from Cornwall. It is one of the first thing that travelers see when they sail across the Atlantic to England, and one of the last things they see when they sail away.

Lands End promontory is made up of great cliffs of granite rock, some of them as much as a hundred feet high. These rocky cliffs are very dangerous to ships, and so, on the rocks near the promontory, the Longships Lighthouse has been built to guide ships safely past.

Langley, Samuel

Samuel Pierpont Langley was one of the early experimenters with airplanes. Some of his experiments worked, and he did build a small model that could fly; but his full-sized plane crashed on both launchings when trial flights were attempted in 1903, so the first powered flight by a human being in a flying machine was made by the Wright brothers, that same year. Langley's work was very important in the development of the airplane. The first aircraft carrier of the United States Navy and Langley Air Force Base, near Hampton, Virginia, were named for him.

Samuel Langley was born in 1834, in Roxbury, Massachusetts. He went through high school, then continued to study by himself and became a scientist. Besides working on flying machines, Langley was interested in astronomy and made many important observations. In 1887 Langley was appointed head of the Smithsonian Institution, an organization of laboratories and museums that is run by the United States government, and he held this post until his death in 1906.

language

A language is any system by which human beings or animals use signs or sounds to tell one another what their thoughts are. The song with which a male bird calls a female bird, a nod of the head to mean "Yes" or a shrug of the shoulders to mean "I don't care," or the sending of roses to a girl to mean "I love you" are all parts of languages if they always mean the same thing. When we think of language, we usually think of the spoken or written sounds by which human beings express their thoughts.

All men have developed spoken languages, and wherever there has been any kind of civilization a written language has finally developed too. Linguists (scientists who study languages) have compared the languages spoken by different races and nations of men and have divided them into families, most of which go back many thousands of years to times long before men had taught themselves to write.

Languages change gradually over the course of the years. Any group of men who live together will invent new words that no other group knows. They will also change the way they pronounce spoken words and the way they spell written words. Two groups living apart, and speaking the same language at the start, after a few hundred years will probably be speaking languages that sound quite different. After thousands of years the languages will be so different that only a scientist can tell that they were once the same.

Linguists use the *comparative method.* They compare the words and meanings of many different languages. They find certain languages in which the words seem to be related, even though they have changed enough to seem different. For example, the modern Italian language came from the old Latin language, but words that began with *fl-* in Latin begin with *fi-* in Italian. By studying several related languages, linguists work out a "parent" language from which these languages developed. This parent language is *hypothetical;* that is, the linguists suppose that it once existed, but they cannot prove that it did because it goes back too far to have had any written form.

Two German brothers named Grimm (the same ones who wrote Grimm's Fairy Tales) were famous scientists in this field. One of them, Jacob Grimm, formulated the "law" that came to be called *Grimm's Law.* This law has helped to prove that English and German and Greek and Latin and most of the other languages of Europe belong to the same family of languages. This family is called the INDO-EUROPEAN family, and there is a separate article about it. Linguists have worked out a large number of original words, or *roots,* that must have been used in the parent language from which all the Indo-European languages came. In the Indo-European parent language there must have been a root *ed-* that meant eat." From this came a root *edont-* that meant a tooth, something one uses in eating.

As the various languages developed, the *d* in the original Indo-European roots always remained *d* in Greek and Latin but always changed to *t* in English and later always changed to *z* (pronounced *ts*) in German, so in English we have the word *tooth* beginning with *t* while the Germans have the word *Zahn* (meaning "tooth") beginning with *z* (*ts*). In the same way the English word "to" is the German word "*zu*" and the English word "two" is the German word "*zwei.*"

When linguists cannot find this kind of connection between languages, they say that the languages belong to different families. There are many families, of which Indo-European is only one. The Hebrew language, in which the Old Testament was written, and Arabic and other languages, belong to the Semitic family. There are several different families of languages in Asia, including the Chinese and the languages related to it, and the Mongolian languages. The peoples of the islands in the Pacific Ocean speak languages belonging to still other families. The American Indians, though they are all believed to be related in some way, have several quite different families of languages.

Within each family of languages there are different branches. For example, Italian and Spanish and French are all members of the same branch of the Indo-European family of languages. German and English and Dutch and Norwegian are all members of another branch.

Within each branch there are different national languages (such as Italian and Spanish), and within each national language there are almost always special ways of speaking in different regions. These are called *dialects.*

The study of the older periods of literature of different languages is called *philology,* but today that is considered much the same as the science of *linguistics,* or of languages in general.

Lanier, Sidney

Sidney Lanier was an American writer best known for his poems. He also wrote a book about King Arthur and the Knights of the Round Table, and other books for boys.

Lanier was born in 1842, in Macon, Georgia. During the Civil War he fought in the Confederate Army. At that time he developed the serious lung disease that troubled him for the rest of his life. He traveled to many places, trying to find one that would be good for his health, and he worked at different jobs, but he kept on writing.

Many of his poems describe the beauties of nature. One of the most famous is "Song of the Chattahoochee," in which a river tells what it sees as it rushes along from the hills down to the plain. Other of his famous poems are several that he called "Songs of the Marshes," and a poem about the mocking bird.

Lanier was also a fine musician. He played the flute well enough to be a member of several symphony orchestras. Sidney Lanier died in 1881.

lanolin

Lanolin is the fat from sheep's wool. The fat is taken from the wool as it is being prepared for spinning. The fat is then purified. Lanolin feels creamy to the touch and is used in many medicines and ointments for the skin. It is supposed to make the skin softer. It is also used in many shampoos and other preparations for the hair. It makes the hair smooth and soft but not greasy. Lanolin is different from most oily substances because it can take up large amounts of water and does not separate from the water for a long time. Lanolin can be dissolved in alcohol, ether, or benzene.

Lansdowne, Henry Charles

Henry Charles Lansdowne was an English nobleman and statesman. He was born in 1845. In 1883 Lansdowne was appointed governor-general of Canada, representing the British queen. He held this post until 1888. During the time when Lansdowne was governor-general, a disagreement between Canada and the United States about who should control the fisheries at Newfoundland was settled. Lansdowne also held other posts in the government of England. He was viceroy of India, the representative of the British queen in India. Later he held the post of foreign secretary in the British government.

Lord Lansdowne died in 1927.

Lansing

Lansing is the capital of Michigan. It is on the Grand River, about eighty-five miles from Detroit. There are several railroads, fine highways, and a good airport, and farmers from many parts of Michigan send their crops to Lansing for shipment.

About 131,000 people live in Lansing. Many of them make automobiles, trucks, and buses. Every year Lansing has an exhibition of new improvements and latest developments in the manufacture of automobiles.

The state capitol is a fine building with a large dome. It stands in a huge park, through which runs the Grand River. There are many other parks, and shady streets in Lansing. The State Historical Museum contains things that have to do with the early history of the people of Michigan.

Outside the city, in East Lansing, is Michigan State University of Agriculture and Applied Science, which is attended by about 24,000 students. Many of them study new and better methods of farming. This university was started in 1855, and was the first school of its kind in the United States. The city of Lansing was founded in 1836, and it became the capital of Michigan in 1847.

LANSING, MICHIGAN. Population (1970 census) 131,546. Settled in 1836. Capital of Michigan.

Laocoön

Laocoön was a character in the stories the ancient Greeks told about the Trojan War, a war between Greece and the city of Troy. Laocoön was a priest of Troy. He was very wary of the Greeks. After many years of war, the Greeks suddenly sailed away, leaving behind a huge wooden horse. Laocoön warned the Trojans that this might be a trick. He advised them to distrust everything about the Greeks, even their gifts. But just then two huge serpents rose up from the sea. They glided up the shore and twined themselves around Laocoön and his two sons, killing all three. The Trojans thought that this was a sign from the gods that Laocoön had been wrong. So with great rejoicing they pulled the great horse into the city. However, the horse was hollow, and inside it was a band of the bravest Greek warriors. At night the Greek ships returned. The men in the horse opened the gates of the city for them, and the sleeping Trojans were overwhelmed. Troy was soon defeated because the Trojans had ignored the warning of Laocoön. There is a famous statue in Rome, Italy, that shows Laocoön and his sons entangled in the coils of the great serpents

Laos

Laos, one of the states that formerly made up French Indo-China, is a kingdom in southeastern Asia. The capital is Vientiane, a city of about 132,253. Laos is 91,429 square miles in size, which is a little smaller than Oregon, and more than three million people live there.

Most of the people in Laos are farmers. They raise rice, corn, cotton, vegetables, and tobacco. Like the Chinese, they live mainly on rice. There are few modern industries, and many people work in their homes weaving baskets and making cloth and dyes. There are rich mineral deposits, but except for the mining of tin they have not been developed.

Most of the people belong to the Buddhist religion, but some still worship gods of their own. Many uncivilized tribes still live in the hills of Laos.

Laos is a mountainous country that is cut by narrow valleys. The hot, rainy season lasts from May until October, and the rest of the year is dry and cooler. There are valuable forests of teak in Laos. The people cut the teakwood into logs and float them down the Mekong River to Saigon. The Mekong River is the chief means of transportation because there is no railroad and only a few good roads. The chief cities of Vientiane and Luang Prabang are on the Mekong River.

More than a thousand years ago, Laos was a powerful kingdom that often made war on its neighbors. About six hundred years ago it was taken over by Siam, which ruled it until 1893. Then France controlled the country until 1947, when it became a constitutional monarchy. However, the transfer of sovereignty was not completed until 1954. Since then Laos has been troubled by conflicts among neutralist, Communist, and anti-Communist factions. Peace was temporarily restored by the formation of a coalition government in 1962, but bitter fighting broke out again in 1963.

LAOS. Area, 91,429 square miles. Population (1973 estimate) 3,030,000. Government, constitutional monarchy.

Lao-Tse

Lao-Tse was a wise man of China. His teachings became the basis of Taoism, which is the religion of many people of China. (There is a separate article about TAOISM.) Lao-Tse lived more than 2,500 years ago, and we do not know very much about his life. He was the friend of another wise man, CONFUCIUS, about whom you can read in a separate article. Lao-Tse's real name was Li Urh.

Lao-Tse was born in a small village called Kiuh-jin. Later he went to the city of Loyang and worked in the king's library there. In his old age, Lao-Tse went away by himself and wrote a book called the Tao. Many years after his death, certain people in China began to follow the teachings of Lao-Tse's book.

La Paz

La Paz is the chief city of Bolivia, one of the countries of South America. It is not really the capital of Bolivia. The capital, by law, is supposed to be at Sucre, a small city about 250 miles south of La Paz, but Sucre is so far away from all the important things happening in the country that the government prefers to do most of its work in La Paz. Only the Bolivian Supreme Court meets at Sucre. La Paz is therefore called the seat of government, though it is not the capital city of Bolivia.

About 525,000 people live in La Paz, about as many as there are in Jacksonville, Florida.

La Paz is the highest big city in the world. It is in a valley 12,000 feet above sea level. This is even higher than Mount Hood, in Oregon, one of the highest mountains in the United States. Up that high there is less oxygen in the air and a person who is not used to this gets tired very quickly if he walks too fast. The streets of the city are steep and winding, so that it is very easy to get tired.

High as the city is, there are even higher mountains towering above La Paz and protecting it from the winds. These mountains are part of the great Andes range of South America. From the city can be seen the great Illimani Mountain, more than 18,000 feet high and always covered with snow.

In the center of the city is a big square, or park, called the Plaza Murillo. Around this square stand the most important government buildings and a beautiful cathedral. Although La Paz is more than four hundred years old it is quite a modern city, with streetcars, parks, and new houses.

Alonzo de Mendoza, a Spanish explorer, first (in 1548) built a city where La Paz now is. He named it La Ciudad de Nuestra Senora de La Paz, which in Spanish means "The City of Our Lady of Peace." Later the city's name was changed to La Paz Ayacucho, in honor of a battle that freed Bolivia from Spanish rule. The people of Bolivia call the city La Paz for short.

LA PAZ. Population (1973 census) 525,000. Seat of Bolivian government. In West Bolivia.

lapis lazuli

Lapis lazuli is a stone that is used in jewelry. It is a semiprecious stone, which means that it is valuable but not nearly as valuable as a precious stone like a diamond or a ruby. Lapis lazuli is a beautiful deep-blue color, often with tiny specks of a kind of iron mineral. These specks sparkle like stars in a blue sky.

Lapis lazuli is found in the western part of the United States and also in South America. There is some lapis lazuli in Siberia and in other parts of Asia. The ancient Egyptians used lapis lazuli to make necklaces and to decorate shields and vases, and sometimes they used it as a good-luck stone, thinking it would keep away evil spirits. People once powdered lapis lazuli to make a blue paint called ultramarine. Now they have found ways to make paint of this color chemically.

Lapland and Lapps

Lapland is the northernmost part of Europe. It is not an independent, separate country, but a section of land, parts of which are in Sweden, Norway, Finland, and Russia.

The people who live there are called Lapps, or Laplanders. The Lapps moved into Europe from Asia, hundreds of years ago. They speak a language like that of the people of Finland. Lapland has an area of about 95,000 square miles, which is nearly as large as the state of Oregon. About 30,000 people live there, which is not as many as live in Salem, Oregon.

Lapland has two seasons, known as day and night. The night season is about nine months long. All that time it is dark and very cold. The day season is only three months. During that time it is al-

ways daylight, and the weather is mild and pleasant. Because of the long season when it is cold and dark, very few plants can grow in Lapland. There are some trees, and many mosses. The Lapps keep reindeer for milk, meat, and hides. They live in huts or tents of reindeer hide, and dress in furs.

Most Lapps fish and hunt throughout the short summer, and store up food to last through the winter. Many different dialects are spoken. Half of the Lapps are Finnish, but still they are called Lapps.

The people are rather short as a general rule, but they are very muscular. Until very recently, it was the custom for a man to buy a wife by giving her father a certain number of reindeer. Most Lapps are members of the Lutheran or Greek Catholic Churches.

lapwing

The lapwing is a bird about the size of a pigeon. It is noted for the crest of feathers on its head. The head is black, the back is green, and the crest feathers are a greenish-black color. The lapwing is sometimes known as the *peewit*, or *pewit*, because that is what it seems to say when chirping.

The lapwing is found in many parts of Europe and Asia in the summertime, but in the winter most lapwings travel southward to warmer lands. The lapwing is not native to the United States or North America, but lapwings have been known to fly all the way across the Atlantic Ocean to North America. The lapwing usually lives in open fields or marshy places. It lays its eggs in a hollow in the ground. To protect the eggs or young birds from other animals, the lapwing hops about and flies as if it were lame, so that the animals will follow it and leave the nest alone. Both the bird and its eggs are good to eat.

larceny

Larceny means stealing, but in law it makes a difference whether a person steals a lot or a little. Stealing something of great value is called *grand larceny*. Stealing something of small value is called *petty larceny*. The punishment for grand larceny is greater.

Grand larceny is a *felony*, or serious crime. For hundreds of years it was punishable by death, but today the worst punishment for grand larceny is long imprisonment. Petty larceny is a *misdemeanor*, or minor crime, and is usually punishable by a fine and by imprisonment for less than a year.

The legal meaning of larceny is taking property without the owner's consent but without force or threats. Burglary is larceny because it means breaking into someone's house or building with the intent to steal. Robbery is not larceny, however, because the robber uses force or threats. The pickpocket commits larceny, but the holdup man commits robbery.

larch

Larch is the common name of a group of trees that bear cones, but it is different from other cone-bearing trees because it sheds its needles in the fall. The needles grow in clusters on the branches. The larch is native to the United States, Europe, and Asia.

The larch is a straight and beautiful tree, and may grow as high as 100 feet. Sometimes this kind of larch is planted in the United States for decoration.

A kind of larch that grows wild in the northern parts of North America is sometimes called the *tamarack* or the *hackmatack*. This American larch has very small cones, usually half an inch in length. It grows in cool swamps in the northern United States and Canada.

The wood of the larch tree is useful for many purposes. It is used for telegraph poles and fence posts, and is very good for shipbuilding. The bark of the larch tree is used in tanning leather, in dyeing, and in the making of some medicines.

lard

Lard is fat that comes from a hog. It is a pure white substance. Bakers use lard in making cakes and pies, and some lard is used to make candles. Some ointments, which are used to treat skin troubles, contain lard.

The best lard is called *leaf lard*. It is made out of the fat that surrounds the hog's kidneys. Fat from the back and other parts of the hog's body is also used to make lard. The fat must be rendered (melted) and then strained to remove any dirt or impurities that may be in it.

Lardner, Ring

Ringgold Wilmer Lardner was an American writer. He was best known as a humorist, but experts consider his short stories among the finest ever written. Ring Lardner was born in Niles, Michigan, in 1885. He worked as a sportswriter for newspapers in Chicago, St. Louis, and Boston. Many of his short stories are about sports, or about the people who play them. Lardner also helped write a successful Broadway play, *June Moon*. He died in 1933. Two of his sons, John and Ring, Jr., also became professional writers.

lares and penates

The Romans, like other ancient people, worshiped little statues, or idols, that represented gods. Little statues of the lares and penates were kept by each family for household worship. Lar was believed to be the ancestor of the family, and so was a god that watched over the family and protected it. The penates were gods that watched over the family's goods and protected them from thieves. It was customary to have a statue of the lar placed between two statues of the penates. All war camps and even the state itself had their own lares and penates to bring good luck. On feast days, especially on New Year's Day, when Vesta, the goddess of the home, was honored, each little statue was given gifts and food to make it happy so that the family would have good luck in the coming year.

lark

The lark is a bird that is famous for its sweet song. Many poets have written of how the lovely song pours from the throat of the little bird as it flies high in the air. Larks live in the open country and build their simple nests out of grass, in hollows on the ground. They lay their eggs, which are gray with darker spots, in the nest. Their feathers are of quiet, dull colors— usually tan and brown. The lark is often the same color as the ground it lives on; this helps the lark, by making it harder for its enemies, such as the hawk, to see it. Larks are small birds, about seven or eight inches long.

The skylark is the sweetest singer among the larks. Most kinds of lark live in Europe, and only one kind is usually found in the United States. This kind is called the *horned lark,* because it has two tiny tufts of feathers on its head.

larkspur

The larkspur is a popular flowering plant. Its flowers are usually blue, but there are also white, purple, and pink larkspur. Some kinds of larkspur are annuals, and have to be planted every year. Other kinds are perennials, which means that once they have been planted, they will grow and bloom again every year without being replanted. Larkspur is found in the northern half of the world, where the climate is moderate or cool.

The kinds of larkspur usually grown in gardens in the United States come from Europe. The larkspur that is native to North America may poison cattle if they eat it. Larkspur plants are usually from one to four feet high, and some even grow to be six feet high. They get their name from the little spur, or pointed projection, on each flower. The seeds of one of the European kinds of larkspur is useful in making medicine.

larva is the young of animals which undergo METAMORPHOSIS. Also see INSECTS.

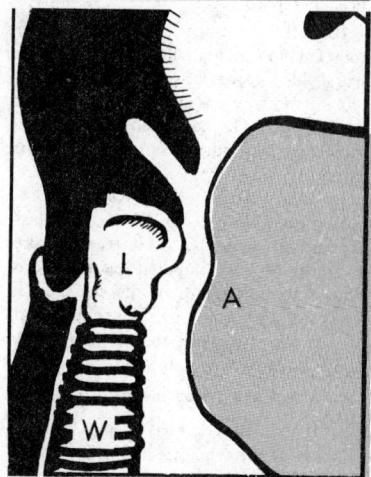

The larynx (L) is located just above the windpipe (W). Its front part is often called the "Adam's apple" (A).

larynx

The larynx or voice-box is the part of your body that allows you to make sounds when you speak or sing. It is located just above your windpipe or *trachea*. The front part of the larynx often is called the "Adam's apple."

The larynx consists of two bands of tissue called *vocal cords*. They are separated by a long, narrow slit. When you breathe the slit opens to admit air to your windpipe. When you speak, the slit becomes very narrow. The air goes through the narrow slit and causes the vocal cords to vibrate, or ripple like waves in the ocean. This vibration sends out sound

LA SALLE, RENE ROBERT

952

waves.

If you stretch a rubber band tightly so that its two sides are very close together, and blow between them, you will hear a sound produced by the vibrating rubber. This is similar to the sound produced by your vocal cords. By loosening or tightening your vocal cords, you can produce different sounds. When the vocal cords are loose, air will easily pass between them, producing a low, deep sound. When the vocal cords are tight, the sound will usually be higher and finer. The vocal cords of a young child are usually tighter than those of an adult, which is why a child's voice is often so much higher.

When you have used your voice too long or have been attacked by a germ, your larynx will usually swell up. This is called *laryngitis*. During laryngitis, the voice is hoarse and often so low that it can hardly be heard. It is hard to swallow and the throat is very dry. The doctor usually will give you some medicine to relieve the swelling and will tell you not to talk until the swelling has gone down.

La Salle, René Robert

René Robert La Salle was a French explorer. His most famous expedition was the one in which he traveled the length of the Mississippi River. He claimed the entire valley of the Mississippi for France, and named it Louisiana in honor of King Louis XIV. The present state of Louisiana is one small part of this old French territory.

La Salle was born in France in 1643 and came to Canada when he was only 23 years old. He was interested both in exploring new regions and in setting up new trading posts. He made many expeditions, some of which turned out very unfortunately.

La Salle found the Ohio River and explored the valley of the Illinois. His last expedition was in 1687. He tried to take a group of two hundred people from France to the mouth of the Mississippi River to start a colony. The expedition lost its way, however, and on March 19, 1687, La Salle was murdered.

Las Casas, Bartolomé de

Bartolome de Las Casas was a Spanish priest who was a missionary in America only a few years after it was discovered by Christopher Columbus. He taught Christianity to the Indians and set up schools for them in Mexico and the West Indies. One of his pupils is said to have translated the Bible from Latin into an Indian language. Although Las Casas was made a bishop and offered a great church, he stayed with the poor Indians in Mexico. He was later forced to return to Spain, where he died at the age of 92.

laser

Laser stands for "Light Amplification by Stimulated Emission of Radiation." It is a device that can shoot light beams out in nearly parallel rays and with great intensity. It was developed by Charles H. Townes in 1960. Laser beams are so powerful they can penetrate steel,

or be used for surgery or radar.

Lassen Peak

Lassen Peak is a mountain in northeast California. It is the only active volcano in the United States. It began erupting in 1914, and between 1914 and 1921 there were several hundred eruptions. There are holes in the sides of the mountain from which come steam and boiling water. Lassen Peak is 10,500 feet high. It is at the southern end of the Cascade mountain range. It was named for Peter Lassen, who was an explorer and guide in the West about 100 years ago.

Lassen Volcanic National Park, a national park of the United States government, surrounds the peak. The park has an area of about 160 square miles and contains beautiful drives and trails. It also has places for skiing, camping, and fishing.

Las Vegas

Las Vegas is a city in Nevada that has become famous as a resort with many fine hotels and amusements. It is closer to Los Angeles, California, than any other city in Nevada, and many rich people like to go to Nevada because gambling is not against the law there. The big Las Vegas hotels pay high prices to motion-picture and television stars, and other performers, to entertain their guests. Even before Las Vegas became so popular as a resort, it was the principal manufacturing and railroad center of southwest Nevada. It is only 20 miles from the great Hoover Dam. The population in the 1970 census was 125,787, almost double what it was in 1960.

Lateran

The Lateran is a great palace in Rome, Italy. The palace was built on the spot where another palace once stood that belonged to a great Italian family named Laterani. More than eight hundred years ago, the Popes made their homes in the Lateran Palace, and they held important church meetings there. These meetings were called Lateran Councils. The palace burned down in the year 1308, but about 250 years later it was rebuilt. Connected with Lateran Palace is St. John Lateran, the first-ranking Roman Catholic church in the world.

In 1929, the Roman Catholic religious leaders met with Benito Mussolini, who was then the dictator of the Italian government. They signed an important treaty at the Lateran Palace. This treaty,

called the Lateran Treaty, gave back many rights and powers that other Italian governments had taken away from the Roman Catholic Church. It made the Vatican City an independent state, with the power to make its own laws.

latex is a thick white juice that comes from the bark of rubber trees. See the article on RUBBER.

lathe

A lathe is a machine that is used for cutting wood, metal, or other material. Ordinarily, to cut something you hold it still and move a knife against it. A lathe works in the opposite way. It has a motor that makes the material revolve while the knife stands still. The knife, or cutting tool, is pressed against the turning piece. Cutting or shaping a piece in this way is called *turning it*.

The wood is held or gripped by clamps or chucks at both ends of the lathe, while the cutting tool is held in the hand. Several tools can be held in a revolving tool holder or turret, which can be turned to bring any particular cutting tool against the wood.

With a lathe, it is possible to change a rough, irregularly-shaped piece of wood into a smoothly shaped cylinder. For this reason lathes are used in making furniture, especially the legs of tables and chairs, gateposts, pegs, and many other objects that must be shaped.

Lathes also can be used for shaping and cutting metal. A lathe for shaping wood is called a wood-turning lathe. A lathe for shaping metal is called an engine lathe. Candlesticks, bolts, and many machine parts are made on engine lathes, which for that reason often are called machine tools.

Lathes can be used for many purposes. They are used for cutting the threads in screws and bolts, for drilling holes, for grinding, polishing, and all types of wood and metal finishing.

KINDS OF LATHE

There are many types of lathe. A gun lathe or gun-barrel lathe is used for boring holes in long solid pieces of metal for the manufacture of cannon and guns. A precision lathe is used by watchmakers to grind and polish metal that must be within one-thousandth of an inch of the desired size. A mandrel or spinning lathe is used to make hollow circular shapes out of sheet metal. A potter's wheel is a kind of lathe used in pottery factories to

The first method of shaping wood (*above*) was awkward and tiring. A modern lathe (*left*) shapes either wood or metal in much less time and is accurate to within a few hundredths of an inch.
American Tool Works Co.

953

Lathes come in many different sizes, some small enough to carry and place on a table, others as large as a room and weighing several tons.

Lathes are classified according to the size of the work they can handle. For example, a 10-inch by 40-inch lathe (10″ x 40″) is one that will handle wood or metal work 10 inches wide and 40 inches long.

Latimer, Hugh

Hugh Latimer was a priest who lived in England about four hundred years ago. At that time there was a great deal of argument between Catholics and Protestants. Latimer sympathized with the Protestants. King Henry VIII of England made Latimer Bishop of Worcester, but later the Catholics accused him of heresy, which is preaching a religion other than the official religion. In those days heresy was a crime. Latimer was tried and found guilty.

In 1555 Latimer and Nicholas Ridley, another man convicted of heresy, were put to death by burning. The last words of Hugh Latimer were: "Be of good comfort, Master Ridley, and play the man. We shall this day light such a candle, by God's grace, in England, as I trust shall never be put out."

Latin

Latin was the official language of the Roman Empire when it was the most powerful nation on earth, two thousand years ago. Originally the language was spoken in Latium, a region in central Italy. Rome, the capital of Latium, became the capital of the Roman Empire, and Roman soldiers and colonists spread the language.

Today Latin is often called a "dead language" because it is not the native language of any people; but it is not really dead. Many Latin words are used in medicine and other sciences and professions. Latin literature of the highest quality is still written in the official letters of the Pope and other men of high rank in the Roman Catholic Church.

From Latin grew the modern Romance languages, which are Spanish, French, Portuguese, Italian, Rumanian, and some others.

Latin is a highly inflected language. That is, the words are often changed in sound and spelling, depending on how they are used in a sentence. Latin does not use articles (*a, an, the*) nor does it always use prepositions (such as *of, to, for*) as we do in English. For example, *puer* means "boy"; *pueri* means "of the boy"; *puero* means "to the boy"; and so on.

The Latin language was different in different ages, as most languages are. *Classical Latin* was used over a period of some 250 years, from about 80 years before the time of Christ to about 150 years after it. *Late Latin* was the language for three or four hundred years after that. It added many words, and built new words from the classical Latin words. *Medieval Latin* came next, and was filled with slang and new words. It gradually turned into the Romance languages.

The pure Latin was the language in which books were written. At all times there was a *vernacular,* or language spoken by most of the people in ordinary conversation, which was not as careful in words or grammar as the language used in literature and in formal speeches delivered by Roman senators in the Forum.

LATIN LITERATURE

The literature of ancient Rome is among the greatest ever written. It began more than two hundred years before the time of Christ. Great writers of this *ante-classical* period were Plautus, who was born about 250 B.C. and who wrote plays and poems; and Terence, born about fifty years later, who was also a playwright, one of the greatest writers of comedies.

There were many great writers during the classical age. The greatest poet was Virgil, whose *Aeneid* is considered one of the four or five greatest poems ever written. Other poets were Horace, Catullus, and Ovid. Livy was one of the first great historians. The masters of prose writing were Julius Caesar, who was not a professional writer but whose history of his military campaigns is written in nearly perfect Latin; and Cicero, a senator whose orations (speeches) are other examples of fine Latin writing.

For more than a thousand years after Rome fell to invading Germanic peoples, about 1,500 years ago, serious writing in nearly every western European country was in Latin. The "Dark Ages" were on in Europe and learning was kept alive by Christian monks and priests who wrote in Latin. Even within the last few hundred years, scholars have done some of their writing in Latin. Sir Francis Bacon, the great English scientist who lived about four hundred years ago, wrote his most serious books in Latin. Every scholar of two hundred and even one hundred years ago learned to read and write Latin almost as easily as he could his own language.

Latin America, the countries of North and South America where the people speak Spanish, French, or Portuguese, languages that came from Latin. There are ten Latin-American republics in North America and the West Indies: COSTA RICA, CUBA, DOMINICAN REPUBLIC, EL SALVADOR, GUATEMALA, HAITI, HONDURAS, MEXICO, NICARAGUA, and PANAMA. There are also ten in South America: ARGENTINA, BOLIVIA, BRAZIL, CHILE, COLOMBIA, ECUADOR, PARAGUAY, PERU, URUGUAY, and VENEZUELA.

There are separate articles on all these countries.

latitude, a means for reckoning the angle from the equator of a point on the earth's surface: see the article on MAP.

Latvia

Latvia is a country in the north of Europe. In 1940 it was invaded and taken over by the Communist government of Russia, and it is now called the Latvian Soviet Socialist Republic. When Latvia was seized by Russia, it had about two million people, about as many as Mississippi. Today the population is slightly larger, but we don't know much about what goes on in Latvia. The United States has never officially recognized the country as part of Soviet Russia. Free countries do not trade much with Latvia or get much news from there.

Latvia is a small country, about as large as West Virginia. It lies on the Baltic Sea and is one of the "Baltic States." The other two are Estonia and Lithuania. Both of these countries were conquered by Soviet Russia at the same time as Latvia. Latvia is a land of low rolling hills, great forests, gentle valleys, and many lakes, swamps, and rivers. The largest river is the Dvina, which flows into the Gulf of Riga.

THE PEOPLE OF LATVIA

Most of the people of Latvia have blue eyes and blond hair. Their religion is largely Protestant Christian. Their language is related to the old Sanskrit, the language spoken in India in early times. Most Latvians are farmers, raising oats, rye, barley, flax, and other grains, and potatoes. They keep large herds of cows and produce milk, butter, and cheese.

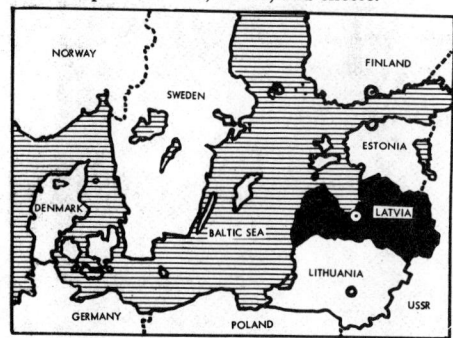

The capital of Latvia is Riga, a city of about 733,000 people.

The people of Latvia, called Letts as well as Latvians, have had many rulers. About eight hundred years ago they were conquered by the Teutonic Knights, bands of German soldiers returning from the Crusades. Later Latvia was conquered and taken over in turn by Poland, Sweden, and Russia. It became free after World War I, and for 22 years it was an independent country. After Russia took it in 1940, the Germans came in 1941 and drove the Russians out. In 1944 the Russians again took over Latvia.

LATVIA. Area, 24,695 square miles. Population (1973 estimate) 2,365,000. Language, Lettish. Religion, mostly Protestant; Roman Catholic, Russian Orthodox, and others. Monetary unit, the ruble. Flag, three horizontal stripes, red, white, red.

Lauder, Sir Harry

Harry Lauder was a great Scottish entertainer who traveled all over England, Scotland, and the United States, and delighted many people with his lively songs and funny stories. Harry Lauder's real name was Harry MacLennan. He was born in Scotland in 1870. When he was a boy he worked in a cloth-spinning factory and as a miner. He liked to sing and tell stories, so he soon gave up this kind of work and went into vaudeville. (Vaudeville is a kind of stage show where different entertainers sing and dance and tell stories.) Lauder also wrote songs. One of the most popular

was called *Roamin' in the Gloamin'*.

The British king made Harry Lauder a knight in 1919, to show appreciation for the pleasure he had given to millions of people. Lauder died in 1950.

laundry

A laundry is a place where clothing, bed and table linens, and other things are washed. The word *laundry* may also mean the things that are washed.

The modern commercial laundry is a big business. It grew from the small hand laundry, where the washing and ironing were done by hand in the shop itself. Now even the so-called hand laundries often send clothing and linens out to be washed in a huge laundry plant. When

The young woman in this picture is demonstrating a clothes washer and clothes dryer designed to save space by fitting one on top of the other, rather than side by side.

Westinghouse

the clean laundry is returned to the shop it is pressed or ironed before delivery to the owner.

Most laundry is now done by machines. The first of these is the *washing machine,* which is a big watertight drum with a door in the flat side. Inside the drum is a cylinder, usually made of metal such as aluminum, with many holes in it. The drum is filled with water and soap, and the cylinder spins around, whirling and tumbling the clothes. After a certain period of time the soapy water is drained off, and several rinsing waters are run through.

The second important machine is the *flatwork ironer,* which is made of two or more long rollers that press sheets and other large flat surfaces between them. There are also machines for shirts and wearing apparel and other special jobs. Some of the work, such as women's dresses, is hand-finished with steam irons. Modern laundries provide a number of different services, such as wet- or damp-wash that will be ironed at home, rough dry, and finished laundry.

LAUNDRY PROBLEMS

An important part of the laundry business is the study of materials and the best ways to handle them in washing, the study of soaps and other cleansers, and other improvements in the washing of clothing and linens. The American Institute of Laundering has a big laboratory for research on these problems. In the laboratory, certain kinds of fabric are put through tests to determine the best methods of washing and how many times they can be washed without showing wear.

In recent years shops, sometimes called "launderettes," have been established where housewives can wash, dry, and sometimes iron their laundry themselves in automatic machines. Many apartment-house basements have automatic washing machines that residents can use at small cost.

laurel

Laurel, or sweet bay, is a tree that grows in the Mediterranean region of Europe. In the wild it may be as high as 40 or 60 feet, but when cultivated it is usually clipped so that it forms a small tree or rounded shrub. It is often grown in tubs or large pots. The plant has small yellowish flowers and purple, cherrylike fruits. The leaves of laurel are stiff, leathery and dark green. Among the ancients laurel was sacred to Apollo and laurel wreaths were used to crown heroes and the victors in games of skill. It was also, like the olive, used as a symbol of peace. Laurel belongs to the same family as sassafras, spice-bush camphor, cinnamon, and avocado or alligator pear.

The name *laurel* is also given to a number of other plants with thick, evergreen leaves. Among these are: mountain laurel, an American shrub belonging to the heath family; cherry laurel, which is related to the cherry and plum; and spurge laurel, which is native to southern Europe.

Laurentian Plateau

The Laurentian Plateau is a huge region in Canada. It covers nearly 2,000,000 square miles, or more than half of Canada. The Laurentian Plateau is the eastern part of Canada. A small part of it is in the United States (in upper Michigan and in the Adirondack Mountains of New York State). The Laurentian Plateau is also called the Canadian Shield.

A plateau is a region that is high, like a mountain, but more or less level, like a plain. Most parts of the Laurentian Plateau are not really a plateau. They are mountains that have been worn down, in the course of billions of years, by rain and ice and rivers. Some of the oldest rocks of the region are three billion years old. For long periods they were covered by great sheets of ice. As the ice melted and moved, it carried away most of the good soil. It also left tens of thousands of lakes, large and small. There are now vast forests in the region, and valuable minerals, but in most places the soil is too poor for farming and very few people live there.

Most of the Laurentian Plateau is one to two thousand feet above sea level. In Labrador it is a genuine plateau. Around the Hudson Bay it slopes down to sea level. It takes its name from the St. Lawrence River at its southern edge.

Laurier, Sir Wilfred

Sir Wilfred Laurier was Prime Minister of Canada for fifteen years, from 1896 until 1911. The Prime Minister of Canada is the most important official in the government. He has much the same power as the Prime Minister of Great Britain or the President of the United States. Canada prospered greatly during the years that Sir Wilfred Laurier was premier. His motto was "Canada First." He wanted his country to

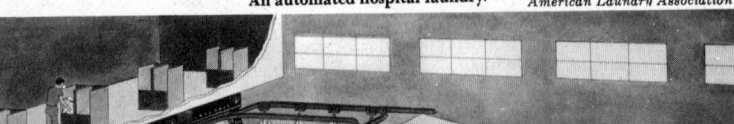

An automated hospital laundry. *American Laundry Association*

be strong and prosperous in its own right. He founded the Canadian navy, built another railroad across Canada, encouraged new settlers to come to Canada, and won the right for Canada to make its own trade treaties.

Laurier was also popular in Great Britain. He sent Canadian soldiers to help the British in the Boer War in South Africa. He also signed a trade agreement with the British that made it easier for the British to ship their goods into Canada.

Laurier was the first French-Canadian ever to become Prime Minister. His family was of French origin and lived in the province of Quebec, where Laurier was born in 1841. As a boy Laurier stayed for a time with an English-speaking family. He came to understand the problems of both the English- and the French-Canadian. The English- and French-Canadians often disagreed strongly about political matters, and Laurier was famous for his ability to please both groups.

Laurier became a lawyer and soon was very interested in politics. In 1874 he was elected to the Canadian Parliament. Several years later he became the leader of the Liberal Party. He became Prime Minister in 1896, and in 1897 he was knighted by Queen Victoria, which meant that he was allowed to put "Sir" before his name. Even after he was no longer Prime Minister, Laurier continued to be the leader of the Liberal Party until his death in 1919.

Lausanne, Treaty of

The Treaty of Lausanne was a treaty of peace between Turkey and the Allies after World War I. During the war Turkey fought on the side of the Germans and against the United States and the Allies. Turkey was defeated and through the Treaty of Sèvres, which it was forced to accept soon after the war, Turkey was severely punished. A great deal of its land was taken away, it was required to pay reparations—large sums of money—and its waters were occupied by foreign warships. After this treaty had been forced on Turkey, there was a revolution in its government, and the new government, under the leadership of Mustafa Kemal, refused to accept the Treaty of Sevres. Three of the countries that had defeated Turkey and Germany in the war—England, France, and Russia—agreed to meet again and give Turkey a new treaty. They met in Lausanne, in Switzerland, in 1922 and 1923. Here Turkey was given back most of its lost territories, the foreign warships were withdrawn, and it was decided that Turkey would not have to pay reparations. Turkey had to promise to protect the groups of foreign peoples living on her soil.

lava

Lava is melted rock that flows out of volcanoes or out of cracks in the earth. When the lava pours out upon the ground, it is red-hot and thick, and runs like melted tar. The heat of lava is between 1,800 and 2,300 degrees Fahrenheit, which is about the heat of melted glass. It runs over the ground very slowly. As it moves, the lava cools and soon forms a hard crust on its upper side. The lava underneath is still hot enough to flow, and it pushes the whole mass forward, so that sometimes lava creeps onward for years. Sometimes the hot liquid lava underneath breaks through the crust, and then itself crusts over. This happens again and again, and jagged sharp-edged blocks of lava are carried as a tumbling jostling mass on the surface of the slowly moving flow. In the southwest part of the United States, land covered by this kind of lava is called *malpais*. This is a Spanish word that means "bad country." If lava does not break up, but hardens into long ropelike sections or billows with a satiny surface, it is called *pahoehoe*, a Hawaiian word meaning "smooth." When lava cools and is changed into soil, it can become very fertile. Some of the richest farm land in the United States was made from lava.

No one knows just what causes lava to pour suddenly out of the earth at certain times. Some scientists believe that when the earth's crust is slowly folded by the great forces that build mountains, the melted rock that seems to be everywhere beneath the crust is squeezed out through weak places in the rocky crust—just as you would squeeze toothpaste out of a tube. Other scientists believe that water seeping down to the layer of melted rock forms steam and other gases that have so much pressure that holes or cracks are blown through the earth's crust, and the escaping steam and gas carry lava along with them.

lavender

Lavender is an evergreen shrub that grows to about two feet in height. It now grows in the gardens of all countries, but its native home is the Canary Islands, eastward along the Mediterranean shores, and on to India. The flowers grow on the end of a long stalk and are a pale violet color.

Shiny oil glands grow on the flower and produce a fragrance used in perfumery. The flowers are dried and put in little bags called *sachets*. Women use these sachets to perfume handkerchiefs and linen. In England lavender is sold on the streets by sellers who call out, "Sweet lavender for sale!"

law

A law is a statement of what a person must do or must not do. All laws together, and there are many thousands of them, are often spoken of as "the law."

Laws are made for two purposes. One purpose is to protect every citizen from being hurt. A law may say, "If you take something valuable that belongs to another person, you can be put in jail for a year." The purpose of that law is to protect citizens against having their property stolen. Or a law may say, "If you throw old papers on the streets, you will have to pay a fine of two dollars." The purpose of that law is to protect the community (all the people who live in the same place) from having dirty, littered streets.

Another purpose of the law is to let people know exactly what their rights are when they make contracts, or agreements, with each other. This helps them to avoid arguments and misunderstandings. Suppose one man says to another, "Mow my lawn every Thursday and I will pay you two dollars." A few weeks later, he wants to stop having his lawn mowed; but the other man says, "You made an agreement, and I insist on the right to mow your lawn and get two dollars." The law prevents such misunderstandings by saying, "Every contract must state a definite time when it begins and when it ends."

There are thousands of laws of both kinds. They are different in all different countries, states, and cities. Because there are so many different laws, and because they are so complicated, hundreds of people make their livings by studying and knowing the law. These people include lawyers, who advise people on the law, and judges, who decide what is right or wrong according to law. Such men are called the *legal profession*. There are other workers in the lawyers' offices, and officials in the judges' courts, not to forget the legislators, or people who make the laws in the first place.

Yet civilization, many people living together, would be impossible without the law. No one would be safe.

WHO MAY MAKE A LAW

A law is no good unless it is made by someone who has the right to make it. The right to make laws is called *sovereign power*. In former times, the king was thought to have special power, given to him by God, to make the laws for everyone in his kingdom. He was the only sovereign. In modern times, all the people of the community have the sovereign power. They cannot all get together and write laws, so they elect representatives to meet in a legislature and make laws for all of them. The legislature (which may be called a Congress, or Parliament, or City Council, or by any other name) has the sovereign power because it was given that power by the people.

In most countries there is a higher law than any legislature can make. The higher law is called the constitution. It does not deal with minor things like stealing or throwing trash in the streets. It only tells what kind of laws the legislature may make and what kind of laws it may not make. For example, the United States Congress could not make a law against any particular religion, because the Constitution guarantees to every citizen the right to follow whatever religion he wishes.

STATUTORY AND COMMON LAW

In the English system of law, which is followed in the United States and other English-speaking countries, there are *statutory law* and *common law*.

A *statute* is a written law made by a legislature. Statutes usually say very clearly what is legal and what is not legal, and what the punishment is for doing something illegal.

The *common law* is harder to understand. It is a combination of all the customs and ideas of justice that the English-speaking people have had for many thousands of years. The common law gives the judge in a court the right to interpret (understand and explain) a statute in a way that fits those customs and ideas of justice.

Suppose there are a husband and his

wife. The wife owns an automobile; it is her property and not her husband's. They have a quarrel, and the husband gets into his wife's car and drives away. The wife goes to court and says that the husband has taken his wife's valuable property; but the judge says, under the common law, "It is quite usual for a husband to use his wife's car without asking her permission. This is not considered stealing, so the man cannot be punished."

Every decision of this kind, made by a judge, becomes part of the common law in the future. In settling disputes at law, lawyers and judges go far back into the past to find out how other judges have interpreted laws. These past decisions are called *precedent,* and in many cases they

LEGAL PROCEDURES IN CRIMINAL SUITS

CRIMINAL (FELONY)
(State vs. Defendant)

GRAND JURY VOTES INDICTMENT

WARRANT OF ARREST SERVED; PERSON IS TAKEN INTO CUSTODY

IF PERSON PLEADS NOT GUILTY TO CHARGE, TRIAL BY JURY

IF CONVICTED, RIGHT TO APPEAL

FINE AND/OR IMPRISONMENT IF GUILT UPHELD (Trial Judge may suspend execution of sentence)

Graphics Institute, N.Y.C.

are just as important as a written law. The reason for this is that a citizen has a right to know what the law is. He has the right to expect that if one judge made a certain decision, the judge was correct and other judges will decide in the same way.

TRIALS AT LAW

The law is used in *courts,* in cases in which two persons have a dispute or one person has a complaint against another. There are two sides, or parties, to every case. One is called the *plaintiff.* He is the one who is complaining, and who began the case. The other party is called the *defendant.* He defends himself against the plaintiff's charges or claims. The plaintiff and the defendant are both represented by *counsel,* professional lawyers who advise them and speak for them.

The head of the court is the judge. He listens to the arguments of both sides and then decides what law applies to the case and how it applies. When the parties cannot agree on what the facts are, there is usually a jury that hears the case. A jury is usually twelve people, but it may be more or less. If the two parties tell different stories, the jury decides which should be believed. The jury decides only what the facts are. The judge alone decides what the law is.

To begin a case, the plaintiff has a written document called a *summons* handed to the defendant. The summons tells him to appear in court at a certain time. Handing him the summons is called *serving him.* Men called *process-servers* make a business of finding people and serving the "papers" on them.

At the time set, the two parties appear in court and the *trial* begins. Strict and complicated laws and customs control the way a trial is held. Both parties bring witnesses to prove they are right. What the witness says in court is called *testimony* and is subject to the rules of evidence. A witness may tell only what is directly connected with the case and only what he knows because he saw it himself. Information he got from other people is called *hearsay* and cannot be used in court.

In the course of the trial the lawyers may file *briefs* with the judge. These are written arguments and usually they mention similar cases in other courts, which are precedent they want the judge to follow. A party that loses in one court can usually appeal to a higher court, which may either *sustain* (agree with) or *reverse* (change) the decision of the first court.

LAW AND EQUITY

There are three main kinds of cases in court. Special laws apply to each kind, and there are lawyers that specialize in each kind.

Contract law deals with cases in which the two parties disagree about what their rights or duties are.

Torts are cases in which one party says he has been hurt in some way by the other. He wants to *recover damages* (be paid) for his loss or suffering. When someone is run over by an automobile, and sues the driver of the car, the case is a tort.

Criminal law deals with cases in which

LEGAL PROCEDURES IN CIVIL SUITS

CIVIL
(Between persons, incl. corp's and partnerships)

SUMMONS AND COMPLAINT SERVED

INTERCHANGE OF PLEADINGS TO DEFINE ISSUES

TRIAL BY JURY
(in some cases before Judge alone)

JURY VERDICT; JUDGMENT AND RIGHT TO APPEAL

IF CLAIMANT PREVAILS, DEFENDANT MUST PAY DAMAGES AND COSTS

Graphics Institute, N.Y.C.

laws made for the public safety have been broken. In such cases, the plaintiff is all the people of the state or other community, represented by an official called a *district attorney,* or *attorney general,* or *public prosecutor.* The defendant may have robbed a particular house or person, but the idea is that if people are permitted to do such things no one in the community is safe, so all of them have a complaint. A serious criminal case cannot begin, in the United States, unless a special jury called a *grand jury* has investigated the complaint and decided that there is enough evidence against the defendant to justify having a trial. The grand jury then issues an order, called an *indictment,* that the suspected person be brought to trial.

There are also courts of *equity*, which are considered different from courts of law. *Equity* means "fairness." A court of equity hears cases that are not clearly covered by law, or in which the written law would be unjust. Courts of equity are called courts of *chancery* in some countries and states; and the judge who presides in such a court is called the *chancellor*. In some states there are no courts of equity, but the principles of equity are followed in certain cases in the courts of law.

A person who refuses to obey the order of a court can be cited for contempt of court and fined or put in jail. The decisions of a court of equity are usually enforced by punishing a party for contempt of court if he refuses to obey them.

After a court has given its decision, or judgment, there has to be some way to enforce the judgment—to make the parties obey. The right to judge and enforce the law is called *police power*. Policemen or other law-enforcement officers carry out the judgments of the court.

PRACTICE OF LAW

A person educated and trained to try cases in court and to give advice on the law is called a *lawyer* or by other names such as *attorney* and *counselor*. In British countries a lawyer who speaks for a party in court is a *barrister* and a lawyer who gives advice is a *solicitor*.

The education of a lawyer usually includes a two- or three-year course at a law school. To get into most law schools you must be a college graduate. After graduation from law school, a lawyer must usually pass a difficult examination called a *bar examination*. If he passes this, he is *admitted to the bar* (licensed to practice law) and can become a professional lawyer and charge fees for his services. See the article on BAR.

OTHER LEGAL SYSTEMS

The English legal system, described in this article, is different from the systems in most other countries. In Europe, most of the countries use a system that goes back to the Roman Empire of two thousand years ago. While Napoleon I was ruling France, about 150 years ago, a revised set of laws was prepared. This is usually called the *Code Napoleon* and most countries use it. The same principles govern English and European law, but the trials do not follow the same rules.

SPECIAL COURTS OF LAW

There are many different sets of laws covering particular branches of business or human affairs, and there are special courts that deal only with particular branches of law. *Maritime law* deals with ships, shipping, the men who sail the ships, and things that happen at sea. An example is the law governing FLOTSAM AND JETSAM, about which there is a special article. *Patent law* deals with disputes about patented inventions. *Tax law* deals with disputes between citizens and the government about how much tax the citizen should pay. *Military law* deals with members of the armed services and its special courts are called *courts-martial*. (Martial law, however, is a different thing. It is government enforced by the military rather than the police forces, in a time of emergency.)

There are in addition various agencies that are called *quasi-judicial*, which means they are almost but not quite courts. The Federal Trade Commission is an example. It is a group of commissioners who can issue certain orders that have almost as much force as if a court had issued them. Fortunately for the public, one can appeal from such orders to the genuine courts. See also the article on COURTS.

Lawrence, Gertrude

Gertrude Lawrence was an English actress. She was born in London, England, in 1901. She started to take dancing lessons when she was very young. She loved the theater and would stand around stage doors to see the stars. By the time she was 22, she too was a popular star in London. In 1924 she went to New York and made a great success. She acted in many plays, but was most famous for her singing and dancing in musical comedies such as *Lady in the Dark* and *The King and I*.

Gertrude Lawrence died in 1953.

Lawrence, James

James Lawrence was an American naval hero of the War of 1812. He is remembered for having said, "Don't give up the ship!" Lawrence was born in Burlington, New Jersey, in 1781, and joined the United States Navy at the age of 17. In 1802 he became a naval lieutenant. He saw much service in the wars against Tripoli in 1804 and 1805, when he was second in command to Stephen Decatur.

In 1813, during the War of 1812 against England, Lawrence was promoted to captain and placed in command of the *Chesapeake*.

Lawrence sailed out of Boston harbor to attack British supply ships headed for Canada, but met the *Shannon*, a British frigate blockading the port. The *Chesapeake's* crew was poorly trained and not ready for battle, and the fight soon became hopeless. Lawrence was so badly wounded that he had to be carried below, but he shouted, "Don't give up the ship!" But the *Chesapeake* was captured, and Lawrence died in Halifax four days later. The Navy took his words as a slogan, and Captain Oliver Hazard Perry used them on his flag at the Battle of Lake Erie. They have stood as a symbol of naval courage ever since.

Lawrence of Arabia

Thomas Edward Lawrence was one of the most famous yet mysterious persons of this century. He was a British explorer, fighter, and scholar. He was born in Wales in 1888 and studied at Oxford University. He spent the years between 1911

and 1914 exploring Palestine, Syria, and Mesopotamia, and studying ancient ruins.

When World War I broke out in 1914 he tried to enlist in the British Army, but he was turned down at first because he was too short. Then he was made a British secret agent in the countries of the Near East that he knew so well. It was his job to help the Arabs organize their army to fight against the Turks who ruled over them. He could speak Arabic, and he quickly won the confidence of the Arabian leader Feisal al Hussein of Arabia. Dressed in flowing Arabian robes, he rode and fought with the Arabs, blowing up bridges, wrecking trains, joining raiders in guerrilla attacks against the Turks, and pushing behind enemy lines to discover their secrets. He was once captured, but he escaped by pretending to be someone else.

Stories of his daring excited the whole world. He became known as "Lawrence of Arabia," and the British and French governments offered him many decorations for his brave work, but he turned them all down. He had lived and fought with the Arabs for so long that he had come to think like one, and he felt that the British government had not treated the Arabs properly. He wrote a book describing his adventures, called *The Seven Pillars of Wisdom*. When it was finished, the manuscript was lost and he had to write it all over again from memory.

Everywhere he went people recognized him, but he was a shy person and tried to escape from publicity. He changed his name, first to Ross and then to T. E. Shaw. He had been an officer, but he joined the British Air Force as a mechanic. He was killed in a motorcycle accident in 1935, at the age of 47.

laxative

A laxative is a medicine that you take when you are constipated, which means it is hard for you to have a bowel movement. Your body does not use up all the food that you eat. This unused food changes in your intestines into waste matter that your body must get rid of. When you eat a lot of vegetables and fruits and drink a lot of fruit juices and water, the waste matter is soft and your intestines can easily push it out. Sometimes the waste matter is hard and then you become constipated. A laxative will help your intestines to push the waste out.

It is a very bad idea to use laxatives too often. If you do, your intestines may become used to being helped and then you will have to use laxatives all the time. When laxatives are used too often, they sometimes irritate the delicate lining of your intestines and cause real trouble.

It is best to relieve constipation by eating the proper foods. Prune juice, raisins, and various dried fruits are very helpful. You should see your family doctor if you become constipated too often. Let the doctor tell you if you should take a laxative and which laxative is best for you.

Lazarus

The story of Lazarus is told in the Bible, in the eleventh chapter of the Gospel according to St. John. He was a friend

of Jesus, and when he died Jesus raised him from the dead. The Bible tells how Lazarus died and lay in his tomb for four days. Then his sisters, Mary and Martha, sent for Jesus, who called him back to life. The miracle Jesus had worked made many people believe in him, but it so angered his enemies that they decided to arrest him and have him killed. Later accounts say that Lazarus lived for thirty years longer and traveled far and wide. According to legend, he became the first bishop of the French city that is now called Marseilles.

Leacock, Stephen

Stephen Butler Leacock was a Canadian writer and teacher who wrote many books that made people laugh. Leacock was born in England in 1869. He went to school in Canada and became a professor of economics and head of the Department of Economics at McGill University, in Montreal. Leacock taught for more than thirty years. He wrote several serious books about economics, the study of money and other valuable things. He also wrote books about the lives of two great writers, Mark Twain and Charles Dickens.

Leacock is best known for his humorous writings. These were published in several books, two of which were *Literary Lapses* and *My Remarkable Uncle.* Stephen Leacock died in 1944, when he was 75 years old.

lead

Lead is a heavy, silvery-blue metal. It is a chemical element, which means that it is one of the hundred basic substances of which the world is made. Lead is useful in many ways. The type used in the printing of this book was made of a metal alloy that was mostly lead. Lead is so soft that you can easily scratch it with your fingernail, bend it with your bare hands, or cut it with a knife. Plumbers and electricians bend lead pipes around curves in buildings and under floors. Lead can be easily formed into almost any shape by bending and pressing, but it cannot be drawn out into wire because it is not a strong metal. Toothpaste and shaving-cream tubes, and foil made of lead, show how easily it will bend.

Lead melts at a very low temperature for a metal. A thin piece of lead can be melted in the flame of a match. Because it has such a low melting point, it is made into the metal called solder, which plumbers use to join pipes and electricians use to join wires.

Lead is one of the heaviest metals. You can probably lift a bucketful of water, but it takes a strong man to lift a bucketful of lead. Lead is about eleven and a half times as heavy as water. A bucketful of water weighs about 21 pounds and a bucketful of lead weighs about 237 pounds. Because it is so heavy, lead is used for boat keels, bullets and shot, and fishing-line sinkers.

LEAD POISONING

Lead may be poisonous if taken into the human system in sufficient quantities. It is much less dangerous when it enters the system through the mouth than when it is inhaled in the form of dust or fumes. Seventy-five to ninety percent of lead taken through the mouth passes completely through the system. While many paints contain lead pigments, most of those used for children's toys and furniture and interior surfaces contain little or no lead. Nevertheless, it is not wise to chew painted objects, not only because of the lead that might be in the paint but because other paint ingredients may also be poisonous. Lead that is inhaled is generally only a hazard in industry where lead is used in molten form or in lead compounds in the form of fine dust or powders. In industry, however, precautions are generally taken so that workers do not inhale the dust or fumes.

LEAD SMELTING AND REFINING

Lead, like most metals, is found in rocks called ores. The lead is combined chemically with sulfur and is called galena or lead sulfide. These ores are mined, that is, dug out of the earth. After lead is dug out of the mine, it is crushed. Then it is churned in water to which have been added certain chemicals and an oil called pine oil. Air is blown through this mixture, and the bubbles form a froth. The part of the ore that contains the lead and the other metals collects in the oily froth, which is skimmed off. The rock and waste material in the ore sink to the bottom and are thrown away.

After the ore is removed from the froth, it is roasted in a large furnace to burn away the sulfur and change the metal sulfides in the ore to oxides. These are then put in another furnace called a blast furnace along with coke and limestone. With the help of the air-blast the coke burns and melts the limestone and the metal oxides. The oxides then give up their oxygen to the coke and become molten metal. This collects at the bottom of the furnace where it can be drawn off for further refining. Other waste materials or "slags" combine with the limestone, are lighter, and float on top of the melted lead where they can be drawn off.

The lead at this point still contains small amounts of copper, antimony, arsenic, silver, and gold. The first three of these are removed by transferring the molten metal to a large "drossing" or "softening" kettle where air can be bubbled through it. The copper, antimony and arsenic combine with the oxygen in the air and float as oxides to the top, where they can be skimmed off.

REMOVING SILVER AND GOLD

Now we have lead that is almost pure, but it still may contain silver and gold. To remove the silver and gold, a small amount of zinc is added to the lead-silver-gold mixture. The mixture is well stirred. The zinc hardly dissolves in lead, but the silver and gold easily dissolve in melted zinc. When this has happened, the mixture is allowed to cool. A solid scum forms on top of the lead. This scum is made up of zinc, silver, gold, and a little lead. It is skimmed off, leaving almost pure lead behind. If very pure lead is wanted, it can be obtained by means of electrolysis. (There is a separate article that explains ELECTROLYSIS.)

COLOR OF LEAD

You may have been surprised to read in this article that lead is silvery blue, when all the lead you have ever seen is dark gray. But the dark gray color you see is really a thin film made by the oxygen in the air combining with the lead to form a black substance called lead oxide. The shiny lead seen through the black film looks gray.

OTHER USES OF LEAD

In the United States, most lead goes into making storage-battery plates and grids. Another important use of lead is in gasoline. Here lead is in the form of a chemical compound called tetraethyl lead. When gasoline with tetraethyl lead in it explodes in automobile engine cylinders, the engine will not make the rattling bang that is called a "knock."

The electric power and telephone cables seen strung on poles throughout the country are covered with lead. The lead forms a sheath that keeps moisture away from the wires and insulating material inside. Most underground cables in cities are sheathed with lead.

Because of lead's great durability and resistance to attack by chemicals, it is used extensively in the construction of equipment for the manufacturing, transportation and storage of such corrosive chemicals as sulfuric acid and in the plumbing systems of buildings and chemical laboratories.

WHITE AND RED LEAD

Much lead is used in making white lead. This substance is a chemical combination of lead, carbon, oxygen, and hydrogen. It is a bright white color, and since Roman times it has been used for white paint. Red lead, one of the many different substances that result when lead and oxygen combine, makes a paint that is excellent for preventing rust in bridges, storage tanks, ships, and other iron and steel structures.

LEAD AS AN INSULATOR

Lead can stop x-rays, so the walls of x-rays rooms in hospitals are lined with lead. This keeps the x-rays from getting out of the x-ray room and doing harm. The operators of x-rays always wear protective clothing that is made of cloth with some lead in it. Lead is also widely used to guard against gamma rays from radium and other atomic radiations and is of great importance in the growing use of atomic energy. When uranium or radium or any of the other radioactive elements finally run down and can give off no more rays, they have turned to lead.

Lead does not ring when struck, as other metals do. Because it has this property, lead is used to cover the doors and walls of broadcasting and recording studios, to deaden the sound and prevent unwanted noises from coming in from the outside.

A lead pencil has no lead in it. See the articles on PENCIL and GRAPHITE.

leaf

A leaf is a flat green blade that grows from the stem and branches of a plant. The green material of a leaf is called *chlorophyll.* Chlorophyll helps the leaf manufacture food for the plant.

The leaves breathe in the gas called

carbon dioxide and breathe out the gas called oxygen. (Human beings breathe in oxygen and breathe out carbon dioxide.) The leaves of plants are useful to men because they take from the air carbon dioxide, which is poisonous to men, and supply the air with oxygen, which men need. In the country, where many leafy plants grow, the air is said to be *fresh*.

The sun shining on the leaves helps the chlorophyll change the carbon dioxide and water into sugar. This process is known as PHOTOSYNTHESIS, and there is a separate article about it. The sugar is stored in the leaves in the form of starch. Both sugar and starch are *carbohydrates*. At night some of the starch is changed back into sugar to feed the stem, roots, and seeds of the plant.

Many of the foods you eat contain carbohydrates manufactured by the leaves of plants. Green peas, beans, potatoes, carrots, beets, and parsnips contain large amounts of carbohydrates. Tomatoes, oranges, bananas, prunes and pears also contain carbohydrates. Other sources of carbohydrates are cereals such as rice, wheat, barley, and corn.

HOW LEAVES GROW

Leaves grow out of the stem from small *buds*. The leaves are attached to the stem, and the place where each is attached is called a *node*.

There are three common ways in which leaves are arranged on a stem, namely *spiraled*, *opposite*, and *whorled*. In a *spiral* or *alternate* attachment, each leaf is arranged on the stem like a wound spring. The leaves grow that way on elm, apple and oak trees. In an *opposite* arrangement, there are two leaves at each node, growing on opposite sides from each other. This is true of leaves found on ash, maple and walnut trees. In a *whorled* arrangement, three or more leaves grow out from the same node. Leaves grow like that on the aster, the milkweed, and the pogonia plant. The system of leaf arrangement on a stem is called *phyllotaxy*.

Leaves are arranged on the stem in such a way that they will get as much sunlight as possible. If the sun does not fall on the leaves, the leaves will often bend toward the sun. Leaves growing on vines on the walls of buildings are arranged so that the sun will fall on every one of them.

In the evening, when there is no longer any sunlight, the leaves of some plants droop down and fold together. These movements are called *sleep movements*. That is the way such leaves protect themselves from the cold when there is no sun.

The leaves of some plants will close at the slightest touch even in the daytime. An example of such a plant is the Venus' flytrap. Its leaves close like the covers of a book when touched by anything. Insects are often caught between the leaves and eaten up by the juices in them.

FORM OF A LEAF

A leaf usually consists of a broad green part called the *blade* to which a stalk or *petiole* is attached. Often there are two small leaflike flaps of plant tissue called *stipules* at the bottom of the petiole

where it is attached to the stem. Some leaves do not have petioles, and these are called *sessile* leaves.

The blade of a leaf usually is flat and thin, making it possible for light and carbon dioxide to get to all parts of the blade. The blades have many different sizes and shapes. A blade may be less than an inch long, like those on many herbs, or it may be more than ten feet long, like those of the banana plant. On some palm trees the blade may be as long as sixty feet. Some blades are long and thin, like those of grass, while others are almost entirely round, like those of the nasturtium.

The edge of a blade, called the *margin*, can be *entire*, *toothed*, or *lobed*. An *entire* margin is completely smooth, with no rough edges. The dogwood and corn leaves have entire margins. A *toothed* margin has little rough teethlike edges that appear either singly or in pairs. Apple and elm leaves have toothed margins. A *lobed* margin has curved edges that seem to be cut out from the blade. When the edges curve toward the middle of the blade, it is a *pinnate* leaf. The oak leaf is pinnate. When the edges curve toward the bottom of the blade, it is a *palmate* leaf. The maple leaf is palmate.

A leaf that has one blade is called a *simple* leaf. Elm, oak, and apple leaves are examples of this type. They are called *compound* leaves. When the leaflets are all attached to the top of the petiole, it is a *palmately compound* leaf. When they are attached at different points along the stalk like a feather, it is a *pinnately compound* leaf.

The *veins* of a leaf are narrow tubes leading from the petiole into the blade. They branch out into all parts of the blade, carrying water and mineral salts to the leaf and carrying food downward from the blade through the petiole to nourish the rest of the plant. There usually is a large vein running through the center of the leaf. This is called the main vein or *midrib*.

The arrangement of veins in a leaf is called *venation*. There are two types of venation: *parallel* and *net*. In *parallel* venation, the veins usually start at the bottom of the blade and go to the top, always running in one direction and remaining at the same distance from each other. The veins in an iris or corn leaf are parallel. In *net* venation, the veins branch out from each other many times

The parts that make up a typical leaf.

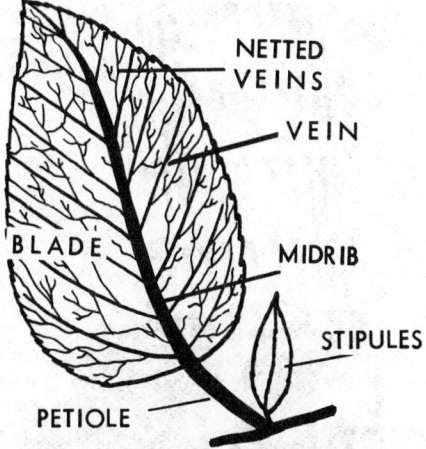

and form a complete network over the blade.

In *pinnate venation*, there is only one midrib from which the smaller veins branch out. Such venation is found in the elm and oak leaf.

In *palmate venation*, there are several midribs from which the smaller veins branch off. Such venation is found in the maple and geranium leaf.

WHAT THE LEAF IS MADE OF

Every blade has a single layer of plant cells called *epidermis* on its upper and lower surfaces. The epidermis, which is colorless, protects the inside of the leaf from injury. Light can shine through the cells of the epidermis into the inside of the leaf.

On the outside of the epidermis is a layer of waxy material, called *cutin*, that is waterproof. This layer of material helps to keep the water inside the epidermis.

Beneath the epidermis are the veins and the food-making material of the leaf, which is called *mesophyll*. Mesophyll is composed of layers of plant tissue that are rich in chlorophyll. There are many air spaces in this tissue, which make it possible for carbon dioxide to reach all parts of the leaf.

In the epidermis on the under part of the leaf are thousands of little openings called *stomata* (from the Greek word meaning "mouth"). The upper layer of the epidermis of some kinds of leaf also has some stomata, but there are many more on the lower layer. In a leaf two inches long, there are about 500,000 stomata.

The stomata can be opened and closed by pressure from special cells that surround them, called *guard cells*. Through the stomata pass oxygen, carbon dioxide, and water vapor. This is part of the breathing process of the leaf. The stomata are opened widest during the day, and are almost entirely closed at night. Sunlight increases the pressure of the guard cells on the stomata, causing them to open quickly.

League of Nations

The League of Nations was an organization of most of the nations of the world. It was like the United Nations, but it was founded after World War I.

Woodrow Wilson, who was then President of the United States, had the idea for a League of Nations when the United States entered World War I, in 1917, and helped England and France defeat Germany. President Wilson felt, as have many others since that time, that World War I would never have been fought if all the nations involved had had a chance to sit down together and talk about their problems; if all the talk that led up to the war had been public, instead of secret; and if each country had understood the problems of the other. The League of Nations was set up to represent all the nations of the world. It was to provide a meeting place where each nation would discuss its problems publicly.

HOW THE LEAGUE WAS FORMED

The Covenant (constitution, or agreement) of the League established two

main bodies, the League Council and the League Assembly.

The Council was a small group, with one member from each of the big and powerful nations, and several representatives of smaller nations, who took turns being represented on the Council. The League Council was to decide when a situation existed that was a threat to the peace of the world. It was then to call the threatening nation before it, listen to the problems, discuss them, and recommend what should be done. The Council could and did decide, for example, when Italy invaded Ethiopia in 1936, that a nation had started a war, and that all other nations were to stop sending it materials that might help it in the war.

The League Assembly was a large body, with one representative from every member nation. At one time or another every nation in the world, except for the United States and Saudi Arabia, was a member of the League of Nations. The Assembly could discuss any problem that any member thought was important enough to bring before a forum representing almost the whole world. But the Assembly could not make a final decision; it could only recommend what it thought should be done. The Council, on the other hand, could issue an order, and all the nations had promised, in advance, to obey certain decisions of the League Council.

The League of Nations also had a court. Its judges were to decide, on the basis of international law, any questions which were brought before it. This was the Permanent Court of International Justice. It was composed of leading judges from all over the world. They were to make recommendations to help the League Council arrive at its decision.

There were several other parts of the League of Nations that did not have to do with preventing war. It was their object to improve the conditions of peace, so that nations would not feel they had to resort to war to solve their problems. The International Labor Organization, composed of representatives of workers from all over the world, was to improve working conditions. The Economic and Financial Organization was to arrange loans of money to poor countries. The Mandates Commission was established to run, for the League itself, certain countries that did not seem educated or strong enough to govern themselves at that time. Sooner or later these mandated countries were to become independent states. The actual control of these mandates was given to countries that had wanted to annex them —England, France, and Belgium, among others. Parts of Palestine, Syria and Iraq did achieve independence after being mandated.

FAILURE OF THE LEAGUE

The League of Nations failed in its primary purpose of maintaining the peace of the world. Many said that it failed because the United States, its original sponsor, later refused to join it. At that time (in 1920) many people in the United States wanted to leave Europe and Asia to solve their own problems. They voted against President Wilson's desire to join the League.

Others feel that the League of Nations failed because of the way it was set up. The League idea (which is substantially the same as the idea behind the United Nations today) was that in order for any action to take place, all nations must agree to it. This is the idea of unanimous consent, in which, when one nation vetoes, there can be no action. Japan, Germany and Italy simply resigned from the League when other nations objected to their warlike acts. Then nothing could be done to stop them.

Leahy, William D.

William Daniel Leahy is the name of an American admiral who served as Chief of Staff to President Franklin D. Roosevelt during World War II. The Chief of Staff is a high government official who advises the President about problems of war. Leahy was born in Hampton, Iowa, in 1875, and attended the United States Naval Academy at Annapolis. He was made an ensign in the United States Navy in 1899, and he rose finally to the rank of fleet admiral, the highest possible rank. He served in the Spanish-American War and in World War I. In 1937 Leahy became the Chief of Naval Operations, a high post in the U.S. Navy. Leahy retired from the Navy in 1939, when he was 62 years old, but he continued to serve his country in other ways. He served as governor of Puerto Rico and as United States ambassador to France before the United States entered World War II. He died in 1959.

Leaning Tower of Pisa

The Leaning Tower, in the city of Pisa, Italy, is one of the most unusual structures in the world. It leans so much that the top of the tower is more than fourteen feet to the side of the base.

The tower is a circular building that

Visitors come from every country of the world to see the marvelous Leaning Tower of Pisa, which has been "falling" for more than seven hundred years.

Cultural Div. of the Ital. Embassy

has eight stories and is 179 feet high. It is made of white marble. It is a bell tower, called a *campanile,* and it stands next to the great cathedral of Pisa. The tower was begun in the year 1170, but the people of Pisa had to stop work on the tower after three stories had been completed. The land was sandy and the tower had begun to lean. Later it was considered safe to complete the tower, even though it slanted at so great an angle. About thirty years ago the Italian government made sure that the tower would be safe by pouring tons of cement around the base.

According to legend, GALILEO dropped two iron balls of different weights from the top of the Leaning Tower. The balls hit the ground at the same time, proving that objects of the same shape and material fall at the same rate of speed. During World War II the Germans used the Leaning Tower as an observation post, and the Americans feared they might have to destroy it, but fortunately this did not happen. People who visit Pisa can still climb the narrow circular stairway to the top of the tower, where they get a very fine view of the city.

leap year

Every fourth year is called leap year. It has 366 days instead of 365. The calendar year is supposed to measure the time it takes the earth to go once around the sun. This takes the sun about 365¼ days, so the extra day makes the calendar come out even. When Julius Caesar revised the Roman calendar, about two thousand years ago, he put the extra day at the end of the month of February. The Roman year began with the month of March, and he was adding the day at the end of the year. We still put the extra day at the end of the month of February, even though our year ends in December. In a leap year February has 29 days instead of 28.

If a year can be evenly divided by 4, it is a leap year; 1964 is a leap year, 1966 is not. When the year ends a century, it is not a leap year unless it can be evenly divided by 400; therefore 2000 and 1600 are leap years but 1800 and 1900 are not.

There is an old legend that during leap year a woman may ask a man to marry her, instead of waiting for him to ask her. This has never been more than a joke, of course, but more than seven hundred years ago, in Scotland, a man who refused a leap-year proposal had to pay a fine.

Lear, Edward

Edward Lear was an English landscape painter and writer of "nonsense" poetry. He is particularly famous for his LIMERICKS, a kind of humorous poem about which there is a separate article. One of his best-known poems is "The Owl and the Pussycat." Lear gave drawing lessons to Queen Victoria of England. During his lifetime, his paintings of birds and landscapes were well-known. Lear was born in 1812, one of fifteen children. He received very little education because his parents, who had been rich, lost most of their money while he was still a boy, so they could not afford to send him to school. Lear spent much of his later life

traveling in Europe, Asia, and Africa, and he wrote several accounts of his travels. He lived for many years in Italy and died at San Remo, Italy, in 1888.

leather

Leather is the skin of animals, reptiles, or birds, used to make shoes, gloves, belts, upholstery, balls for various sports, and many other things. An important use for leather in the United States for many years was in the making of harnesses, until the horse was replaced by the automobile as the principal means of transportation.

Men have made and used leather since prehistoric times. Examples of Egyptian leather three thousand years old have been found in very good condition. The ancient Hebrews discovered a method of preparing hides with oak bark. This method, which is still used, is called *tanning*.

Tanning in America goes back to the days before the white man settled in the New World. Settlers arriving here found that the Indians already had primitive tanning methods. The Indians taught the early colonists how to make the famous buckskin tans that American frontiersmen used for shoes and clothes.

The first tanner to set up shop in the colonies was Experience Miller, who arrived in 1623. Peter Minuit, who later became governor of New Amsterdam, built the first machine used in tanning—a horse-driven stone mill for grinding oak bark to get tanning liquid. The tanners of Salem used sea water for soaking hides. They spread thousands of dry hides on flat barges, weighted them down with stones and left them to soften with the ebb and flow of the tide.

The principal use of leather has always been for shoes. The United States produces and uses more leather than any other country in the world, though a large part of the raw hides are imported. In the early 1960s, the manufacturing of leather was a billion-dollar industry and employed almost four hundred thousand people. About 125,000,000 hides and skins are processed in United States tanneries every year.

KINDS OF LEATHER

Cattle hides make up more than half of the skins used in leather. Cowhide, as these skins are called after tanning, is very heavy and thick, and is used chiefly for the soles and upper parts of shoes. Cowhide is also used for upholstery on big chairs and sofas, for belts, and for some leather garments. Horsehide is similar to cowhide; it is used in making the covering of baseballs. The hides (called kips) of young cattle are used for the upper parts and lining of shoes, and for luggage, handbags, gloves, and garments. Sheep and lamb skins are used mostly for gloves and garments, and shoe linings, but they are also important in the manufacture of handbags, bookbindings, sporting goods, and other articles. Sheepskin can be made into a paperlike sheet called parchment that is used for diplomas, very fine books, lampshades, and drumheads. Kidskin makes an even softer sheet of this kind, called vellum, which is also used for fine books. Goat and kid skins

The Leather Zoo

CATTLE, raised largely for beef, are a major source of sole leather and shoe upper leather. Tough and long-wearing, cattle hides are also used for machine belting and harnesses. Thinned down hides are used for luggage, gloves, clothing, innersoles, upholstery and hundreds of other items.

GOATSKIN and kidskin, imported largely from abroad, make fine women's shoes. Goatskin is also used in garments. One of the sturdiest leathers, kid is also one of the softest and most pliable. It is one of the best materials for suede leathers, used mainly for shoes & handbags.

PECCARY, a kind of wild hog found in Latin America, is our main source of pigskin. The pores or tiny holes, left by the removal of bristles, give pigskin its unusual texture. It is used for gloves, saddle seats, wallets, sport shoes, luggage, bookbinding, upholstery, innersoles and razor straps.

ALLIGATOR skins come from Latin America, Florida, and Louisiana. The beautifully textured skins are made into shoes, handbags, luggage, belts, and billfolds. Water-snakes, lizards, pythons and cobras furnish skins of many colors and designs for shoes, handbags and accessories.

CALF leather has a fine grain and is very good for shoes because it withstands scuffing, knocks and hard wear. Calf skin is also used for handbags, purses, gloves, garments, bookbinding, luggage and other articles.

SHEEP and lambskins are used for shoe uppers and linings, gloves, garments, handbags, chamois, parchment, textile mill rollers, hat sweat bands and piano parts. Lambskins with the wool on — called sherlings — are used for coats, boots, slippers and other cold weather garb.

BUCKSKIN, largely used for gloves and the upper parts of good quality shoes, comes from deer almost entirely imported from abroad. Latin America and Canada are chief supply sources. An abundant supply of unusual leathers is obtained from seals, sharks, whales and water buffalos.

KANGAROO is an inch long when it is born, and seven feet when fully grown. It provides a strong, flexible leather for shoe uppers. The ostrich is the only bird from whom we get leather. Its pinkish-colored skin is used for fine handbags and wallets.

are used in shoes, gloves, and garments.

The shoe industry uses more than four-fifths of all the leather used in the United States. Most of it is cowhide, calfskin, and goatskin, but deer, alligator, reptile and kangaroo leather also are used. Pigskin provides a strong, handsome leather used for sport shoes, gloves, wallets, luggage, and other things. Its unusual marking of tiny holes is caused by the removal of bristles from the hides. The only bird from which we commonly get leather is the ostrich, whose skin makes fine wallets and handbags. Among the unusual leathers are seal, shark, whale, and water buffalo. There are also a number of specialty leathers, such as capeskin, which is sheep or lamb skin prepared in a special way. It was first produced in the Cape Colony in South Africa. A weak and cheap leather, called skiver, is a skin split into thin layers.

THE TANNING PROCESS

The preparation of leather from hides is called *tanning*. There are various methods of tanning, but all of them are intended to preserve the skin and make it tough yet flexible. The two principal methods of tanning are the vegetable process, which uses tannin or tannic acid, and the chrome method, which uses chemicals called chromium or aluminum salts.

The first step in tanning is to clean and soften the hides by soaking them in water or caustic soda. Then the hair is removed by soaking the skins in a lime preparation. In this step the skins soften and swell up and the hair and outer skin can be scraped off easily. Most big tanneries now use machines to do this scraping. The hides are then ready to be tanned.

Vegetable tanning uses liquids made by boiling or soaking the wood, bark, nuts or leaves of certain plants and trees. This releases the substance called tannic acid, which preserves the hides. Different plants and trees produce different tannins, and each has a different effect and produces a different color in the leather.

The hides then go through several tanning tanks, each stronger than the one before it. This step may take from three to sixty days, depending on the weight of the skin. Usually the heavy leathers such as cowhide are tanned with vegetable tannin because the process produces a firmer leather. After the tanning, oil and grease are worked into the leather to make it more flexible and stronger. The leather is then stretched on a frame to dry, after which it is ready for use.

Some lighter leathers such as calf, sheep and goat skins are also tanned by this method, but they are not left in the various solutions for as long a period. Goat leather tanned in this way is usually finished as *morocco*, which is a way of graining. Graining gives the leather a pattern. It is done with a special tool while the leather is still moist. Morocco has a fine pebbled grain, and it is used for making wallets and fine bookbindings.

The *chrome tanning* method is a faster process, taking only hours instead of days, and it produces a very strong leather. After the hides have been cleaned and the hair removed, they are turned in a drum containing a chemical called

Skins and hides used in making leather come from the four corners of the earth.

chrome alum, and other chemicals. After about eight hours the skins are ready for washing and drying.

After tanning, leathers can be treated by dyeing, calendering, graining, and other processes to produce special effects. Calendering, or glazing, is rolling the leather to give it a high gloss. Graining brings out the natural pattern of the skin. Artificial graining (for instance, making cowhide look like seal or reptile skin) can be done by embossing, or stamping, the leather. Patent leather is made by applying several coats of enamel or lacquer to produce a high gloss.

Lebanon

Lebanon is a small country in the part of Asia that is called the Near East. It is a long and narrow country, lying along the eastern shores of the Mediterranean Sea. In area, the whole country is only about half the size of the state of New Jersey. It is very mountainous. There are 2,870,000 people. Lebanon has wild and beautiful scenery, snow-capped peaks, and fertile valleys. It is hot during the summer, except in the mountains. The name, in Arabic, means "white."

As an independent nation, Lebanon is very new, for it did not become a free republic until 1943. But the Lebanese people have been there for many centuries, ruled by one foreign power or another. The great Phoenician empire, which established colonies all along the Mediterranean two thousand years before the birth of Christ, had its beginnings in Lebanon. The Bible tells how King Solomon sent to Lebanon for its great cedar trees, from which was made carved paneling in his temple.

THE PEOPLE WHO LIVE THERE

Most of the people of Lebanon belong to the Arab family of peoples. They speak the Arabic language. About half of them follow the Mohammedan religion and about half are Christians.

Most of the people are farmers, growing fruits and vegetables or tending small flocks of sheep and perhaps a few cows. Where it is not too mountainous, the soil is very rich. Most of the farmers use old-fashioned methods of agriculture.

CHIEF CITIES OF LEBANON

The leading cities of Lebanon, with populations from 1973 estimates, are:

Beirut, population about 700,000, the capital and largest city. It is a very important seaport, on the Mediterranean Sea. There is a separate article on BEIRUT.

Tripoli, population about 127,611, a seaport in northern Lebanon. A pipeline for oil, extending to the rich oilfields of Iraq almost 300 miles away, leads to the docks of Tripoli.

HOW THE PEOPLE ARE GOVERNED

Lebanon is a republic, which means that it has no king. It has a constitution, a parliament that makes the laws, and a president who is elected for a term of six years. The parliament is called the Chamber of Deputies and it has 99 members. These are not members of political parties but represent different religious groups. The Mohammedans and the Christians are equally represented. The president must be a Christian and the prime minister a Mohammedan. Lebanon was one of the original members of the United Nations.

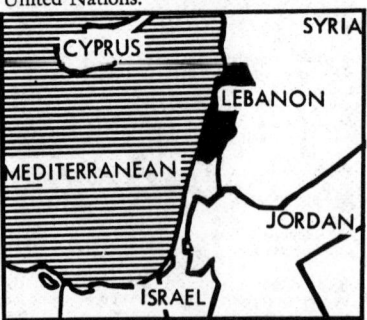

LEBANON IN THE PAST

Until about a hundred years ago, Lebanon was a part of Syria and was included in the great Ottoman Empire of Turkey. Lebanon was ruled by the Turks for hundreds of years.

When Turkey was defeated by the Allies in World War I, Lebanon became a French mandate—that is, France was to control the country until the Lebanese could take over their own government. France clung to control as long as possible, but losses in World War II left France so weak that Lebanon became independent in 1943. The new Lebanese government was torn by quarrels between

religious groups and by efforts of Communists and pro-Nasser Moslems to gain control. As Arabs, the Lebanese fought against the new nation of Israel and Lebanon has continued to support the Arab enemies of Israel. In 1958 there was danger of a Communist-inspired revolution to prevent free elections; 10,000 United States Marines were landed in Lebanon, and while they did no fighting, their presence prevented an armed uprising against the government. In 1967, Lebanon played a minor role in the Arabs' war with Israel. The main Arab nations involved were Egypt, Syria, and Jordan. On December 28, 1968 an Israeli raid on Beirut's airport left 13 Lebanese planes demolished in retaliation for Palestinian commando raids into Israel from Lebanon. Since then, a continued conflict between Israel and Lebanon over the Palestinian commandos (accused of repeated acts of terrorism) has resulted in reprisals by both countries. This tension has been felt world-wide, particularly since 1970.

Internal strife between Moslems and Christians erupted into civil war in 1975 after years of tension between the two factions. The Moslems, who are in the minority, had been demanding equal rights with the Christian majority. In the early weeks of 1976 the capital city of Beirut was partially destroyed and almost wholly evacuated after terrible bloodshed and violence. Later in the year, Syrian government officials helped both sides. In spite of the efforts, fighting has continued.

LEBANON. Area, 4,015 square miles. Population (1973 estimate) 2,870,000. Language, Arabic. Religion, Mohammedan and Christian. Monetary unit, the (Lebanese) pound, worth about 32 cents (U.S.). Flag, three horizontal bars, red, white, and red, with green cedar in center.

Lee

Lee is the name of a famous American family in the state of Virginia.

Richard Henry Lee was one of the signers of the Declaration of Independence and a member of the first Congress. He was born in 1732, in Virginia, and he went to school in England. Lee did a great deal to persuade the American people to seek their independence from England. He introduced the motion in the Continental Congress that led to the adoption of the Declaration of Independence. As a United States senator, he was one of the most active supporters of the first ten amendments to the Constitution, which we now call the Bill of Rights. Richard Henry Lee died in 1794, at the age of 62.

Henry Lee was a cousin of Richard Henry Lee and the father of Robert E. LEE, about whom there is a separate article. He was born in 1756, and when he was only 20 years old he became the captain of a cavalry company that served as bodyguard to George Washington in some of the important battles of the Revolutionary War. Lee was so daring and successful as a scout against British positions that he won the nickname "Light-Horse Harry." After the war, Henry Lee became a member of Congress. He was elected governor of Virginia, and later returned to Congress, where he held office

at the time of Washington's death. In a speech to Congress on that occasion, Lee coined the famous phrase, "First in war, first in peace, and first in the hearts of his countrymen," a tribute to Washington that is still quoted. Lee died in 1818, when he was 62 years old.

Lee, Robert E.

Robert Edward Lee is ranked among the greatest generals. He was one of the best-loved and respected men in American history. During the Civil War he commanded the Confederate army. Though defeated, he became a symbol of the highest courage and devotion.

Lee was born in Virginia, in 1807, a member of one of the South's leading families. His father, called "Lighthorse Harry" Lee, had been a general in the Revolutionary War, and several other members of his family were important in government. Two of them had signed the Declaration of Independence. See the article LEE.

Lee was raised on a large plantation called Stratford. When he was 11 his father died; Lee decided that he wanted to be a soldier, too. He went to West Point Military Academy, when he was 18 years old, and during the fifteen years after his graduation he had many different assignments as an army officer. In the Mexican War, in 1846, Lee did so many brave and useful things that his commander, General Scott, said that the success of the war was due largely to the bravery and skill of Robert E. Lee.

Lee had married Mary Custis, the great-granddaughter of Martha Washington (George Washington's wife). They had seven children and were a very happy family.

After the Mexican War, Lee was appointed commandant of the Military Academy at West Point, and served there until 1855. Then he was made a lieutenant colonel and had many adventures while he patrolled the borders of Texas. In 1861, he was promoted to colonel.

THE CIVIL WAR

In 1861, some of the southern states had left the Union, and it looked as if there might be war. Lee was very much against this, but he saw that war was inevitable, and he had to make the hardest decision of his life. Abraham Lincoln offered Lee the position of commander of the Union forces. Lee loved his country, but he decided he could not lead the northern soldiers to fight against his own people and the state of Virginia. He refused President Lincoln's offer and gave up his commission in the United States army. Two days later, Virginia decided to leave the Union. When the governor of Virginia asked Lee to take command of its soldiers, Lee accepted.

In less than two months, Lee raised an army of nearly fifty thousand men. Jefferson Davis, the president of the Confederacy, made Lee his military adviser. Lee's rank rose to lieutenant general. Some of Lee's achievements as a general were the start of modern warfare, but even his military genius could not win the war. In 1865, Lee had to surrender. He met General Grant, the commander of the Union armies, in a farmhouse in a Virginia vil-

The Lee Mansion in Virginia, now a national memorial, was the Southern general's home before the Civil War. During the Civil War the stately home was used as a hospital for wounded soldiers.

Nat'l Park Service—Sukert

lage called Appomattox Courthouse. It was a friendly meeting, and Grant accepted Lee's surrender with generous terms. When Lee returned from this historic meeting, his men met him with tears in their eyes. They all wanted to touch the hand of their beloved leader, and many men patted Traveller, Lee's big gray horse, which had been with him through the long and terrible years of the war.

LEADER IN PEACE

After the war, Lee worked as hard for peace as he had in war. Though he had lost his citizenship, no other man had a greater influence for friendship between the North and the South.

Lee was offered many important jobs, but late in 1865 he accepted an offer to become the president of a small college in Lexington, Virginia, called Washington College. He said, "I have led young men of the South in battle; I have seen many of them die on the field; I shall devote my remaining energies to training young men to do their duty in life." For five years he served as president of the college. In 1870 he had a stroke of paralysis and died. The college later changed its name to Washington and Lee.

leech

A leech is a kind of worm that lives in muddy ponds and swamps and lakes in many parts of the world. The body of the leech is divided into segments, and the leech has a sucker at each end of its long body.

The leech attaches itself to an animal and sucks its blood. Leeches suck the blood of turtles and fishes, and they also like to suck the blood of dogs, cows, and human beings. A person who goes swimming in fresh-water lakes may sometimes find a leech attached to his arm or leg when he comes out of the water.

The leech has tiny teeth with which it bites into the skin and then sucks the blood. The leech gives off a special substance that keeps the blood from clotting, or growing hard, at this time. That is why a place bitten by a leech may bleed for some time after the leech is removed. The leech does not digest all of the blood it sucks. It stores up some blood and may save it for months.

The leech is usually about two inches long, and it can stretch itself to twice that size. Some leeches are larger. Most leeches are greenish black, and they have dark brown spots.

Though it is not pleasant to be bitten by a leech, a leech bite is not very painful or serious. For a long time, doctors believed that when a person was sick it would help him to let out some of his blood, and the medicinal leech was used to do this. This is still done in some parts of the world.

Leeds

Leeds is a city in the northern part of England. About 500,000 people live in Leeds. It is on the Aire River, and is connected by canals with the eastern and western coasts of England. The city is also a railroad center.

The people of Leeds make woolen cloth that is very famous, for they have been spinning wool for six hundred years. In other factories they make leather goods, machines, and furniture. Farmers live near by, in the fertile valley of the Aire River, and miners who work in iron mines near Leeds.

In the Leeds town hall a music festival is held every three years. It attracts people from all parts of England Leeds has a museum, an art gallery, and the University of Leeds. Near the city is an abbey that was built about a thousand years ago.

During World War II, the Germans bombed Leeds severely and destroyed a great aircraft plant and other buildings. It has since been rebuilt.

LEEDS, ENGLAND. Population (1973 estimate) 506,100. Location, West Riding, Yorkshire, on Aire River.

leek

The leek is a plant that grows very well in many parts of Europe and the United States. The leek is a member of the onion family, and it tastes very much like an onion, except that it is not so strong. The leek has thick green leaves around a white stem. Both the leaves and the stem are good to eat. People make soup out of leeks. Sometimes leeks are creamed and eaten on toast, as asparagus is. The ancient Egyptians, Greeks and Romans were fond of leeks.

The leek is a hardy plant. It grows best in a rich garden soil. It should be planted in the spring. The leek is the national

flower of the Welsh people, and on certain holidays many people in Wales wear leeks in their hats.

Leeuwenhoek, Antonius van

Antonius van Leeuwenhoek was a Dutch scientist who was famous for his improvement of the microscope, which is a scientific instrument that magnifies things and makes them look much larger than they are. Leeuwenhoek was born in Holland, in 1632. He was not educated to be a scientist, but he became interested in microscopes and decided to leave the business he was working at and spend all his time in scientific studies. He became a lens grinder, a person who makes magnifying glasses. His microscopes were so much better than others of that time that he could see very small things that had never been seen before.

Leeuwenhoek used his better microscopes to study many parts of the human body—blood, and hair, and skin—and he learned many new things about them. He was the first person to see bacteria, which are little plants so tiny that a great many of them can live in one drop of water. Many years later, scientists learned that some of these bacteria that Leeuwenhoek discovered are the causes of disease. Leeuwenhoek died in 1723.

Leeward Islands

The Leeward Islands are a chain of islands in the Caribbean Sea, between North and South America. These islands are part of the Lesser Antilles. They are colonies of England, and form part of the British West Indies, the name given to all islands in the Caribbean Sea belonging to Great Britain.

If they could all be lumped together, the British Leeward Islands would be only about a third as big as Long Island, in New York State. The islands were first discovered by Christopher Columbus in 1493, on his second voyage to the New World, but nobody paid much attention to them until about two hundred years later, when Dutch, English, French and Danish settlers began to come there to make money growing sugar, cotton, and tobacco. The British Leeward Islands have a population of about 135,000 and a total area of about 423 square miles.

During World War II the United States built an air base on Antigua, one of the Leeward Islands.

legacy

A legacy is a gift of property that a person receives from someone who has died, according to that person's will. (A will is a paper that a person writes telling how he wants his property divided after his death.) A legacy may be money or something else that belonged to the dead person, such as a watch or a library of books.

Sometimes the will gives a person a legacy only under certain conditions. A will may be written so that a person will receive a legacy only if he marries, or on some other condition. You can read more about legacies in the article WILL.

legend

A legend is an ancient story of something that probably did happen, but so long ago that the story has been changed many times in the telling. Legends are different from myths, because myths are imaginary stories of things that never happened.

Some legends go back to ancient times, before men knew how to write down the history of their times. It is difficult to know what really happened and what was made up in legends that have been passed from generation to generation for thousands of years.

The ancient Greeks and Romans and the people of China and Scandinavia and other parts of the world have had legends. Many of them are very exciting stories, and they help us to understand how those people thought and felt.

Long ago, legend meant a written story. One of the earliest of these written legends was an account of the lives of saints, called *The Golden Legend.* This was written about 750 years ago. Sometimes a motto or a short title on a coin or shield is called a legend.

Léger, Cardinal

Paul-Émile Léger is a Roman Catholic priest who was made a cardinal by the Pope. Cardinals are called princes of the Church. Paul-Émile Léger was born in Valleyfield, in Quebec, Canada, in 1904, and went to school in Montreal and in Paris, France. When he was 25 years old he was made a priest, and in 1950 he became Archbishop of Montreal. In 1953 he was appointed cardinal. Cardinal Léger is known as a powerful public speaker. He has worked hard to improve education in Montreal and throughout Canada. He died in 1975.

Leghorn

Leghorn is the English name for the Italian city of Livorno. Leghorn is on the Tyrrhenian Sea and is the third most important seaport on the west coast of Italy. It is also a railroad center. About 174,000 people live in Leghorn. Many of them are shipbuilders. They also manufacture chemicals, soap, and cement. Some of them make straw hats. The Leghorn hat is famous.

At the naval academy at Leghorn young men study to be officers in the Italian navy.

Leghorn is a very old city. During the Middle Ages it was a great castle and then, about five hundred years ago, it came under the control of the powerful Medici family. They improved the town and built many fine buildings.

During World War II Leghorn was heavily bombed, and many of the fine old buildings including a great cathedral, were destroyed. United States troops liberated the city in 1944.

LEGHORN, ITALY. Population (1973 census) 174,134. Capital of Livorno Province, on Tyrrhenian Sea, on west coast.

legislature

A legislature is a group of men and women who are elected by the people to make the laws of a state or country. The Congress of the United States and the Parliament of Great Britain and other countries are legislatures. In the United States, the name Legislature is usually given to one of the two branches of the lawmaking department of a state, the other being called the Senate.

A branch of the legislative, or lawmaking, department of a government is also called a *house,* or a *chamber.* When a department has two of these houses, or chambers, it is said to be *bicameral.* The Congress of the United States is an example of a bicameral legislature. Its two houses are the Senate and the House of Representatives. The British Parliament has two branches, the House of Commons and the House of Lords. All but one of the states of the United States have bicameral legislatures. The other, Nebraska, has only one lawmaking body. This form of legislature is called *unicameral.* A few countries, such as Greece, have unicameral legislatures.

The articles on CONGRESS and PARLIAMENT describe the workings of a legislature. See also the article GOVERNMENT.

leguminous plants

Leguminous plants are an important family of flowering plants. They include such different members as peas, beans, peanuts, clovers, the wisteria vine, the locust tree, and many others. There are nearly 13,000 known kinds of leguminous plants. Next to the cereals, they are the most important sources of human food, and they contain more protein than any other vegetable product.

Many of the leguminous plants are especially important to farmers as a crop because their roots contain a kind of bacteria that can turn the chemical element called nitrogen in the soil into nitrates, which enrich the soil and make the next crop that is planted grow better. (See the article on NITROGEN.) Other leguminous plants provide substances that are used in industry and in medicines.

The fruit of a leguminous plant is called a legume. It is a pod that opens lengthwise when the seeds are ripe. The leguminous plants that are most widely grown in the United States are the various kinds of bean. The family of leguminous plants also includes several poisonous weeds, such as the loco weed and the wild lupine. Others are plants used for dyes, and for ornamental garden purposes, such as the sweet pea.

Leipzig

Leipzig is a large and very old city in Germany. It is famous as a trade center, and throughout the world it is known for the many books that have been printed and published there, more than in any other city in Germany.

Almost 600,000 people live in Leipzig. The city is almost in the middle of Germany, in the former state of Saxony. This is now a part of East Germany, which is dominated by Communist Russia. Until World War II, there was a big trade fair in Leipzig every year. Farmers and merchants brought their goods into town to display them in the big market place in the center of the city. Since World War II, the Communist government of East Germany has conducted the fair at Leipzig each year.

Leipzig is famous for the many great writers, musicians, scientists and artists who have lived or studied there. Johann

Sebastian Bach, the great composer, was organist in one of Leipzig's churches; Felix Mendelssohn, Richard Wagner and other composers lived there; Johann Wolfgang von Goethe, perhaps Germany's greatest writer, studied at the University of Leipzig.

In parts of Leipzig the streets are very narrow and paved with cobblestones, and the houses have tall, pointed roofs, just as they had in medieval times, nearly a thousand years ago. Around the edges of the city there are modern factories where electrical machinery and scientific instruments are made. There are also modern apartment houses where factory workers live. Since Leipzig is now a part of East Germany, life in the city is not as gay as it used to be.

LEIPZIG, GERMANY. Population (1973 census) 587,761. Location, former state of Saxony in German Democratic Republic.

lemming

The lemming is a small animal, about the size of a rat, that lives in the mountains of Norway and Sweden and in the cold parts of Canada. The lemming has a very strange custom. Every few years, when the lemmings can find no more food, great swarms of them begin to travel from their homes to the sea. They travel at night, and as they go they eat all of the grain and other crops in their path. Many are killed by larger animals on this journey. When the lemmings reach the sea, they plunge into the water and swim until they drown. The lemmings that do not go on this journey catch a disease, so that almost all of them are wiped out anyway. It takes about four years for the lemmings to become plentiful once more, and eventually they will again make this tragic journey that ends in death.

lemon

The lemon is a juicy, oval, yellow fruit that belongs to the same family as the orange and the grapefruit. All of these are called CITRUS fruits, and you can read about them in a separate article. The lemon grows in tropical parts of the world, where the climate is warm and the soil is moist. The Italians grow more lemons than any other people in the world. Many farmers in California also raise lemons. The lemon tree cannot withstand frost, and sometimes the farmers build small fires or place smudge pots among the lemon trees to make certain that they are not injured by frost.

The lemon tree grows to be about fifteen feet tall. It has tough green leaves and sharp, thorny branches. Its pink blossom has a very sweet smell. The lemon tree is an attractive plant, and some florists grow lemon trees in large pots for people to keep in their houses or gardens.

Lemons are very useful in many ways. The sharp, sour flavor of lemon juice improves the taste of fish and seafood and certain kinds of meat. Lemonade is a very popular cooling drink. It is made of lemon juice, sugar, and water. The juice of the lemon is also canned and frozen. Many people are fond of lemon peel that has been candied. The oil from the lemon skin is used to make drinks and as a flavoring for cakes. Lemon juice is useful as a

bleach to remove stains. The lemon contains vitamins that are healthful, and many doctors advise people to have some lemon or other citrus fruit in their diet.

lemur

The lemur is an unusual animal that belongs to the same order as monkeys and apes, the primates. It lives on the island of Madagascar, in the Indian Ocean, off the coast of Africa. "Lemur" means ghost, and the lemur is a weird-looking little creature, with long arms and legs, a foxlike face with large, staring eyes, and a bushy tail. It is about the size of a cat.

Some lemurs walk upright, while others walk on all fours. Lemurs, like monkeys, spend most of their time in trees. At night they travel through the forests in groups, and from time to time they let out shrill cries. Lemurs are shy and gentle animals. They eat fruit and insects.

There are several different kinds of lemur. The indri is a large lemur that has no tail. It has a very striking black-and-white fur. The people of Madagascar believe that the indri has magical powers and that the leaves and bark of the trees in which the indri lives will cure sick people.

The lemur that people see when they visit the zoo is most often the ring-tailed lemur, which has a gray coat and a long tail with black-and-white rings on it.

The female lemur has one baby at a time and is a very good mother.

Lena River

The Lena River is one of the longest rivers in the world. It flows through the lonely forests and the empty, frozen wasteland of Russian Siberia, which covers the northern half of Asia. The Lena is 2,680 miles long, which is almost the distance from New York to San Francisco, California. Rain water from an area of land twice as big as Alaska flows into it through hundreds of smaller streams.

Few people ever see the Lena River, for it flows through one of the coldest and unfriendliest regions of the world. The river rises near Lake Baikal, in eastern Asia, flows toward the North Pole, and empties into the Arctic Ocean. The river is frozen over most of the year, so that the few Asiatic natives who live near it can use their boats and fish in it for only two or three months in the summer.

Lend-Lease

The Lend-Lease Act was a law passed by the United States Congress on March 11, 1941. At that time Great Britain was fighting alone in World War II, against Germany and Italy. The United States and Russia had not yet been drawn into the war. The United States wanted to help the British by giving them war materials and food, but the British could not afford to buy these things. President Franklin D. Roosevelt asked Congress to pass the Lend-Lease Act, saying, "When your neighbor's house is on fire and he wants to borrow your hose, you do not make him pay for it." Under the Lend-Lease Act, the United States "lent" some materials to the British, for the British to pay back when they could, and "leased" other materials and services, for which

the British paid by "reverse lend-lease," that is, they gave certain materials and services to the United States. After June, 1941, when Germany attacked Russia, the United States gave lend-lease help to Russia also, and later China and other countries received it. Altogether, the United States spent about fifty billion dollars on lend-lease. The British Prime Minister, Winston Churchill, called the law the most unselfish one in the history of dealings between nations. Less than ten billion dollars was repaid to the United States by reverse lend-lease.

Lenin, Vladimir Ilyich

Vladimir Ilyich Lenin was the leader of the Russian revolutionists who seized power in 1917 and turned Russia into a Communist country. He was the dictator of Russia until he died seven years later, and he is considered one of the great heroes of the Union of Soviet Socialist Republics.

Vladimir Lenin was born in Simbirsk, Russia, in 1870. His real name was Vladimir Ilyich Ulyanov. He was known by several names during his lifetime, and he is often called Nikolai Lenin. When Lenin was a boy, his brother took part in a plot to murder the czar, Alexander II. (The emperors of Russia were called czars.) Lenin's brother was caught and executed. At this time Lenin made up his mind that he would spend the rest of his life trying to overthrow the Russian government.

After Lenin had graduated from law school, he began to study the writings of Karl Marx, a German philosopher, or thinker. Marx had written that one day the workers of the world would all unite and overthrow all governments and all the wealthy and powerful people. Lenin believed that Marx was right, and he later put into practice many of Marx's ideas.

Lenin formed a workers' group called "Union for the Liberation of the Working Class." He was arrested for this and sent to Siberia, a cold, lonely region in northern Russia where prisoners of the Communists are still sent. Later Lenin returned to St. Petersburg, as the capital of Russia was then called, and married N. Krupskaya, who also believed in Marx and who helped Lenin for the rest of his life.

Lenin then went to Switzerland to organize all the revolutionaries, or people who were plotting a revolution. This organization had to be secret, for plotting a revolution was illegal. Lenin printed a newspaper that was also illegal. In 1903 the revolutionists divided into two groups, the Bolsheviks, which means "majority," and the Mensheviks, which means "minority." Lenin was the leader of the Bolsheviks, and he led them to power in Russia in 1917.

Before the Bolsheviks gained power, they suffered many defeats. In 1905 they started a revolution, but they were defeated by the czar's police. Lenin was forced to leave Russia, and he did not return again until 1917.

In World War I, Russia lost land and many soldiers. The people would no longer support the czar, and a republican group led by a man named Alexander Kerensky came into power. When Kerensky's government was not able to end the war and improve conditions immediately, Lenin, with a very few men, was able to take over the government. His new government asked Germany for peace. Russia lost a great deal of Russian territory to Germany at this time, but the war did stop.

In spite of all he had said about human rights, Lenin proved to be just as cruel and unjust as any other dictator. All the people who opposed Lenin, the wealthy people who owned land, and many members of the czar's government, were shot or sent out of the country. The land was taken over by the government and was supposed to be given to the poor farmers to keep for themselves, but actually the farmers found themselves with no more rights than they had had under the czars.

When Lenin died, in 1924, the Communist Party was in control of all of Russia.

See also the article on COMMUNISM.

Leningrad

Leningrad is the second-largest city in the Union of Soviet Socialist Republics, which is the official name of Russia. Leningrad was built more than 250 years ago by the Russian czar Peter the Great to be his capital. Before that Moscow had been the capital, as it is again today. Peter called his new city St. Petersburg, in honor of his patron saint, and he made it a beautiful modern city of stone. It was laid out at the mouth of the Neva River on the Gulf of Finland. In the Gulf, on an island called Kotlin, Peter had built a great fortress called Kronstadt; to defend his capital. During World War I when Russia went to war against Germany, the name St. Petersburg was changed to Petrograd, because St. Petersburg was a German name. Petrograd means "City of

Peter" in Russian. After the Communist revolution the name was changed again to Leningrad, in honor of one of the leaders of the revolution, Nikolai Lenin. At the same time Moscow was again made the capital of Russia.

Leningrad is an important seaport, for it is the only Russian port that ships can reach without going all the way up around Norway to the Arctic Ocean, or through the Mediterranean Sea and into the Black Sea. But it is very cold in Leningrad during the winter, and sometimes there is too much ice in the harbor for ships to enter it.

More than 3,950,000 people live in Leningrad, about half a million more than there are in Chicago, Illinois, the second-largest city in the United States. A great many of the people of Leningrad are highly skilled factory workers, for the city has a large number of factories where electrical machinery, delicate scientific instruments, chemical products, and many other things are made. Leningrad also has many beautiful public buildings, wide avenues, and lovely parks. The palace in which the czar used to live was once the largest royal palace in the world. It has seven hundred rooms, and it is now used as a museum. The libraries, schools and art galleries of Leningrad, which were considered among the best in Europe, were greatly damaged in World War II when the Germans bombed and shelled the city, but the Germans were never able to capture Leningrad and most of the art treasures were kept safe. The biggest museum of Leningrad, the Hermitage, is still one of the three greatest in the world, along with the Vatican and the Louvre. The city has been rebuilt and remains very beautiful.

Leningrad was one of the principal centers of the revolutions that made Russia a Communist country. Mutinies by the sailors stationed at the fortress of Kronstadt, and uprisings of the workers and soldiers of Petrograd, began the successful revolution of 1917.

LENINGRAD, U.S.S.R. Population

(1973 estimate) 3,950,000. Second-largest city in U.S.S.R.

lens

A lens is a curved piece of glass or glasslike material so made as to bring closer together or send wider apart the rays of light passing through it. All rays of light passing through a lens are refracted (bent) except those passing through a point in the center of the lens called the optical center.

Lenses that bend rays of light toward each other are called *convex* lenses. Those that bend rays of light away from each other are called *concave lenses*. Convex lenses are thicker in the middle than at the edges. Concave lenses are thicker at the edges than at the middle. A magnifying glass is a convex lens, and so are the lenses in microscopes, binoculars, telescopes, cameras, and motion-picture projectors.

A convex lens brings rays of light together at a point called a *focus*. A line joining the focus to the optical center is called the *principal axis* of the lens. The distance between these two points is called the *focal length*. This distance de-

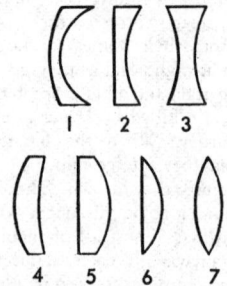

The three types of concave lens (1, 2, 3) all are thicker at the edges than they are in the middle. The four types of convex lens (4, 5, 6, 7) all are thicker in the middle than they are at the edges.

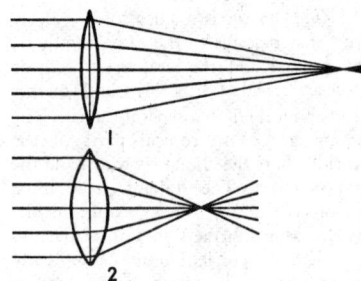

The convex lens (1) is thinner and therefore weaker than the convex lens (2). A stronger lens focuses light nearer to itself than a weaker lens does.

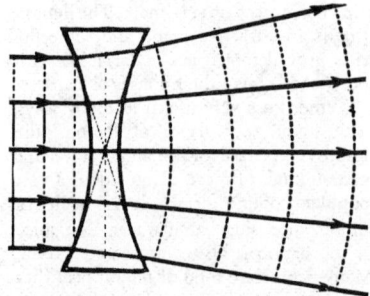

A concave lens spreads out, or diffuses, light that passes through it.

A canal runs through the heart of Leningrad. In the distance is the beautiful Russian-style Church of the Resurrection.

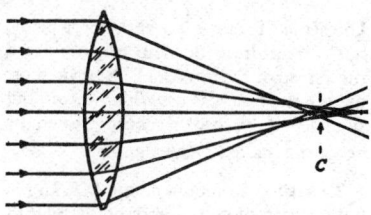

If a lens has been poorly ground, light rays passing through it come together at different points instead of at the focus (C). This is called spherical aberration.

pends on the curvature of the lens. The greater the curvature, the shorter the focal length of the lens.

A lens refracts light in such a way as to form a picture, or image, of an object in front of it. An image may be *virtual,* in which case it cannot be projected onto a screen; or it may be *real,* in which case it can be projected onto a screen. Only convex lenses can form real images.

Sometimes the image may be larger than the object, and sometimes it may be smaller. The image may be erect (right-side up) or inverted (upside down). It all depends on what kind of lens is used and the distance of the lens from the object.

A lens may focus light improperly, causing what is called *spherical aberration.* This occurs when rays of light are focused at several points instead of at one point. Someone looking through such a lens will see a blurred object. To correct this, the lens must be reshaped.

Sometimes a lens will break up white light into different colors, which then are focused at different points. This is called

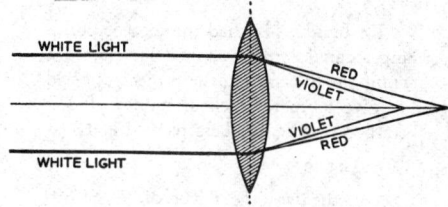

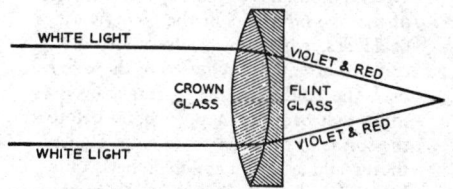

White light that passes through a lens sometimes is separated into different colors, all of which focus at different points (1). This is called chromatic aberration. In order to correct this, a combination of two lenses, called an achromatic lens, is used (2).

chromatic aberration. To correct chromatic aberration, two lenses are used. One is a convex lens made of crown glass and the other is a concave lens made of flint glass. Such a combination is called an *achromatic lens.*

Most lenses are made by cutting blocks of special glass called optical glass. After the blocks have been cut, the pieces are shaped by grinding, and then smoothed and polished. Many lenses are made from special plastics.

Each lens is given a special number, called its *refractive index,* that tells how much it bends the light passing through

it. A number called the *radius of curvature* also is used, to tell how curved the lens is.

Lent

Lent, in many Christian Churches, is a time of fasting—giving up certain food, or eating no food at all, as a religious duty. Lent lasts about forty days, as a reminder of the forty days when Jesus fasted. Lent begins on Ash Wednesday and lasts until Easter Sunday.

Lent used to be more strictly observed than it is today. People used to eat no meat at all during Lent. Some sort of sacrifice is still encouraged by many Christian Churches. In some Churches, the Catholic and Episcopal especially, there are special services and prayers during Lent.

See also the articles CARNIVAL, MARDI GRAS, and EASTER.

lentil

The lentil is a plant that grows in many parts of Europe and Asia and in the United States. The seeds of the lentil plant are eaten. They are very nourishing, and they are used as a vegetable like peas or beans. The seeds are green, reddish, gray, or brown. They are small and flat. They grow in pods, like peas, except that there are only two seeds in each pod.

The lentil plant grows from 6 to 20 inches high, and it has pale blue or white flowers that bloom in July. Lentils are easily grown. They are used to make a thick soup, or they can be ground into meal. People in Europe use them in stews, and also feed them to cattle. The lentil is a very old plant. It is believed that Esau, in the Bible, who sold his birthright for "a mess of pottage," really sold it for a dish of lentils.

See the article on LEGUMINOUS PLANTS.

Leo, Pope

Thirteen Popes of the Roman Catholic Church have been named Leo. The first, Leo I, was called Leo the Great. He was born about the year 390 and lived at the time when savage people from Asia, called the Huns, were invading Europe. When the Huns approached Rome, Leo went out to meet them dressed in his finest robes and gave their general, Attila, so solemn a warning not to attack Rome, the Holy City of the Christians, that Attila obeyed him. Attila is supposed to have said that a vision of St. Peter and St. Paul, "two noble old men," appeared at Pope Leo's shoulder and threatened Attila with their ghostly swords unless he spared Rome. Pope Leo the Great was made a saint. He died in 461.

Another Pope, Leo X, was a prince of the famous Medici family. He was born in 1475 and became a cardinal when he was only 13 years old. He became Pope in 1513. He was very fond of rich or beautiful things, which shocked many plain, religious people, and he had trouble when he tried to raise money to rebuild St. Peter's Cathedral in Rome. Leo X died in 1521.

Leo

Leo is the name of a constellation, or group of stars, whose pattern in the sky is supposed to resemble the shape of a lion.

Leo is the Latin word for "lion." It is said that this constellation was named by the ancient Egyptians, thousands of years ago. The summer, when Leo is brightest, was the time when lions would come from the jungles to drink from the Nile River. To honor the lions, the Egyptians called the bright pattern they found in the sky Leo.

This constellation has one of the twenty brightest stars in the sky, Regulus, which is the heart of the lion. You can find this star and the constellation Leo if you follow with your eyes an imaginary line from the bottom of the Big Dipper straight down to the bright Regulus. Leo is one of the signs of the ZODIAC, about which there is a separate article. Leo is often represented by the sign ♌.

Leonardo da Vinci

Leonardo da Vinci was one of the greatest painters and sculptors of all time, and was also a man with a keen scientific mind. He was an Italian, born in the village of Vinci, in the Tuscan region of Italy, about five hundred years ago, in 1452. This was during the period called the Renaissance, or rebirth of learning and the arts. When Leonardo was 8 years old he was made an apprentice (a student and helper) to a painter in the city of Florence. This began his career as an artist.

Very little is known about Leonardo's work as a boy, except that he was found to be astonishingly talented and had made a reputation before he was out of his teens. When he was about 25 years old he won the patronage of Lorenzo de'Medici (called Lorenzo the Magnificent), the richest and most powerful man in Florence. During the five following years he painted pictures of many subjects, but especially of religious subjects. Unfortunately, almost nothing that is still in existence is known surely to be the work of Leonardo during that period.

Sometime during the 1480s, Leonardo moved to Milan to do painting and sculpture for Duke Ludovico, ruler of Milan. Leonardo stayed in Milan almost twenty years. There he painted the picture that is considered his greatest work. It is named "The Last Supper" and shows Jesus and his disciples at the table. "The Last Supper" was a mural (a painting on a wall), done in a monastery in Milan. It was not an oil painting but was done in tempera, a kind of watercolor. Unlike many of the great paintings of hundreds of years ago, "The Last Supper" has not lasted. It has chipped and faded away, and during World War II the monastery was hit by a bomb and the painting was left exposed to rain and wind for nearly three years. There is a famous copy of the painting in the Louvre, in Paris, France.

Also in the Louvre is Leonardo's most famous portrait, called the Mona Lisa. It is a painting of a woman named Lisa del Gioconda, and for that reason is often called "La Gioconda."

Leonardo was known during his lifetime to be a talented engineer, but his

genius in this field was not fully appreciated until after his death, when his *Notebook* was published. This was composed of thousands of pages of notes and sketches he had made over a course of some fifty years. The *Notebook* shows that Leonardo had worked out the theory of flight hundreds of years before airplanes were actually flown. Two of his ideas for flying resembled the modern airplane and helicopter. He also worked out plans for a submarine. He had advanced ideas on many phases of science and astronomy, and he wrote one of the greatest of all books on the art of painting. Leonardo da Vinci had a great influence on artists for hundreds of years after his death, which was in 1519.

Leonidas

Leonidas was a king in ancient Greece, nearly 2500 years ago. He was the king of Sparta, one of the Greek city-states. King Xerxes of Persia attacked Greece, and Leonidas was sent to defend a mountain pass called Thermopylae against the advancing Persian army. Leonidas had six thousand soldiers, of whom three hundred were his own Spartans, and they stopped the Persians. Then a Greek spy showed the Persians a path by which they could attack Leonidas from the rear. Leonidas and his men fought to the death. Their heroic resistance inflamed the Greeks with patriotic fervor and the example of their bravery has inspired men through the ages.

leopard

The leopard is a fierce and dangerous animal that lives in parts of Asia and Africa. Leopards are sometimes called panthers. The leopard is a beautiful animal, with soft yellowish fur that has clusters of black spots on it. These clusters are known as *rosettes*.

The leopard is usually about eight feet long and weighs about a hundred pounds. Though it is smaller than a lion or a tiger, it is a more savage fighter. The leopard is so powerful that it can leap more than ten feet into the air, and it can run up and down a tree as easily as a small cat can.

Leopards eat deer and sheep, and also monkeys and other small animals. They like to sleep in the daytime, and at night they come out to hunt for food. The leopard is a very patient and crafty animal, and it will lie in wait for many hours for its victim. Leopards sometimes go into African villages and kill dogs, but they do not often attack men unless they are provoked.

One of the most beautiful of all the leopards lives in Siberia, where it is very cold. This leopard has soft gray fur.

Leopold, King of Belgium

There have been three Belgian kings named Leopold. Leopold I was the first king of the Belgians. He was born in 1790, when Belgium did not exist as a separate nation. Leopold was one of Napoleon's officers, and he also fought for a while in the army of Russia. He married a British princess, Charlotte, and was made a duke in England. Leopold was asked to become king of Greece, but refused because not all the people wanted him to be their king. Later, when Belgium was first separated from Holland, the Belgians chose him to be their first king. He proved to be a very wise and careful ruler, and when he once offered to give up his throne, the Belgians insisted on keeping him as their king. He died in 1865.

His son was Leopold II, who was born in 1835 and succeeded his father as king. Under Leopold II Belgium acquired territory overseas, and it was he who added the Belgian Congo in Africa to Belgian rule. Leopold II died in 1909.

Leopold III, grandson of Leopold II, was born in 1909 and became king in 1934. In World War II his army was defeated after a campaign of eighteen days. He was taken prisoner by the Germans. After the war the Belgian people voted to put him back on the throne, but it was by only a slight majority, and in 1951 he gave up the throne in favor of his son, Baudouin.

Leopoldville

Leopoldville is the former name of the capital city of the Republic of Zaire. In 1966, the city was renamed Kinshasa. It is located on the Zaire River about 240 miles from the Atlantic Ocean. Although many waterfalls prevent ships from reaching this city from the sea, the Zaire and its tributaries do provide 7,000 miles of navigable rivers from Kinshasa to the inland areas of the country. A modern city of over a million people, it is a trade and railroad center. Several violent riots which erupted in Leopoldville in 1959 led to the withdrawal of the Belgians and to the country's independence. The city had been named for King Leopold of Belgium. The country has been called Belgian Congo, Democratic Republic of the Congo, and is now Zaire.

leprosy

Leprosy, or *Hansen's disease,* is one of the oldest diseases known to man. It is caused by bacteria, or germs, that attack the skin, nerves, and mucous membranes of the body in one of two ways. One form of leprosy causes open infected sores and lumpy ulcers that spread rapidly on the skin and in the nose, throat, and eyes. This form of leprosy usually results in death. In the other form of leprosy, the germs gather in the nerve endings in the skin, and the victim gradually loses feeling on patches of the skin. These patches turn red or brown, and they spread very gradually. Over several years' time, they may eventually cause the sufferer's fingers or toes to drop off.

In ancient times, lepers (people with leprosy) were greatly feared. Lepers were made outcasts and were forced to wear bells, to warn people from coming close. Their property was taken away from them and they were herded into miserable leper colonies. This was because men thought that leprosy was very contagious. Now we know that leprosy is one of the least contagious diseases. You can get it only by living for a long time in close contact with someone who has leprosy.

Leprosy is most common in tropical regions that have poor sanitary conditions. There are only about two thousand lepers in the United States. Most of the more serious cases in this country are treated at the National Leprosarium at Carville, Louisiana. There is no cure for leprosy, but certain drugs do help to slow down the spread of the infection. The drug most used in the past was *chaulmoogra oil,* but since 1942 leprosy has been treated by new drugs called *sulphones.*

Lesotho, an independent African republic, completely surrounded by the Republic of South Africa. See BASUTOLAND.

Lesseps, Ferdinand de

Ferdinand de Lesseps was a clever, determined man who organized the building of the Suez Canal. He was born in France in the year 1805. He became French consul, a representative of France, in Egypt. While in Egypt he found a note written by Napoleon that told of the French emperor's interest in the idea of a canal through the Isthmus of Suez, the strip of land that divides the Mediterranean Sea from the Red Sea. For almost two thousand years people had felt the need of a waterway between these seas so that ships sailing between the East and West could shorten their journey, instead of traveling around the tip of Africa, far to the south.

De Lesseps persuaded the French and Egyptian governments to help him, and he gathered a group of workers to build the canal and raised the money to pay for it. The Suez Canal, more than a hundred miles long, was opened on November 17, 1869.

De Lesseps also had the idea of building a canal across Panama. He started a company to carry out the project, but had to give it up for lack of money after a start was made. De Lesseps died in 1894.

Lethe

Lethe was the River of Forgetfulness, in the stories told by the ancient Greeks, thousands of years ago. It was one of the five big rivers of the Underworld, or Hades, where the souls of the dead traveled after death. One sip of the water of Lethe could make one forget everything that had ever happened. So before the spirits of the dead could enter Hades, they would taste of it and then they would forget all about their life in the world. Sometimes spirits that were going to live again would drink of Lethe to forget about the Underworld before returning to earth.

letter-writing

A letter is a written message sent to someone else. The word is used mostly for a message of some length, put in an envelope and mailed. A shorter message is often called a *note.*

Letters may be either typewritten or handwritten. A business letter sent by a business house is always typewritten. A personal letter may be either typewritten or handwritten. In a few cases it is usually considered more polite to write the letter by hand, as explained in the article on ETIQUETTE.

The ability to write good letters is valuable in business life and makes a person

more respected in social life. The important thing about a letter is that it should say what the writer means, as briefly and as simply as possible, but there are some customs connected with letters that every letter-writer should know something about.

FORMS OF LETTERS

A letter has six parts: 1, heading; 2, address; 3, salutation; 4, body; 5, complimentary close; 6, signature. The following shows the six parts:

512 Oak Avenue
Preston, S: C.
March 18, 1955

Mr. Robert Jones
15 South 6th Street
Capital City, Ohio
Dear Mr. Jones:

I have been told that you are selling part of your stamp collection, and I may be interested in buying some of the stamps. Do you have a list you can send me? I will appreciate it very much.

Yours sincerely,
WILLIAM SMITH

The address and date in the upper right-hand corner are the *heading*. Business houses use printed *letterheads* giving their names and addresses, and need to fill in only the date. Personal letter paper often has the name and address, or the address only, printed on it.

The name and address of Mr. Jones are grouped together as the *address*. This should seldom be permitted to occupy more than three lines, but sometimes it will require four in a business letter: Name of person, name of firm, address, and city and state.

The "Dear Mr. Jones" is the *salutation*. In the salutation you should call the person whatever you call him when you speak to him. If you call him Bob, you should say "Dear Bob," even in a formal business letter.

It is considered more formal, in the salutation, to say, "My Dear Mr. Jones." British people use this in all letters, so they would write, "My Dear Bob," even in an informal letter. A formal business letter to a man may begin, "Dear Sir," and to a business house it should begin, "Dear Sirs," or "Gentlemen." The colon (:) always comes after the salutation. Except for Mr. and Mrs., the title of the person should be spelled out: "Dear Doctor Jones," not "Dr. Jones"; but in the address this is abbreviated, as "Dr. Robert Jones."

The paragraph under the salutation is the *body* of the letter. This is the message you want to send.

The "Yours sincerely" is the *complimentary close*. There are many forms of this. In a formal business letter it is usually "Yours truly," or "Yours very truly." In a letter to a person it is more often "Yours sincerely," or "Sincerely yours," or just "Sincerely." To a government branch or official it is usually "Yours respectfully," or "Respectfully." To a close friend or a member of the family it may be "With love." It is mostly a matter of preference. The complimentary close is followed by a comma.

In a typewritten letter, the name of the writer should be typed about four lines below the complimentary close, and the signature of the sender, in ink, should be written just above that. In a handwritten letter, the signature is enough. A married woman should usually sign her first name or names, then give her married name, like this: "Cecilia C. Smith (Mrs. William D.)."

LESS FORMAL LETTERS

A letter to a personal friend or relation never has the "address" on it. Instead of the three lines beginning "Mr. Robert Jones," you would simply start the letter, "Dear Bob."

Even in business letters, many men and companies now put the "address" in the lower left-hand corner instead of at the top. Such an arrangement of the letter looks like this:

512 Oak Avenue
Preston, S. C.
March 18, 1955

Dear Mr. Jones:

I have been told that you are selling part of your stamp collection, and I may be interested in buying some of the stamps. Do you have a list you can send me? I will appreciate it very much.

Yours sincerely,
WILLIAM SMITH

Mr. Robert Jones
15 South 6th Street
Capital City, Ohio

THINGS TO REMEMBER

Most people could write good letters if they would remember to write them just the way they talk. The best rule is to imagine the other person is sitting across the table and you are talking to him. Put down the words you would say. Avoid using long words just because you are writing and not talking. If in talking you would say, "I bought some new stamps," do not say in the letter, "I purchased some new stamps."

When you have said everything you have to say, put on the "complimentary close" and end the letter. It is not necessary to write something like, "Must close now."

When someone you like receives an honor or a promotion, you should write him a letter of congratulation. This may be very brief—as brief as, "I was very happy to hear of your promotion. Congratulations."

When there is a death in the family of someone you like, you should write a letter of condolence. Most people consider this a difficult kind of letter to write, but it too may be very brief. It does not have to say more than, "I was very unhappy to hear of your brother's death, and I sympathize with you very much."

The article on ETIQUETTE tells of other occasions on which letters should be written.

lettuce

Lettuce is a small plant that grows in Europe, Asia, and the United States. The lettuce plant grows close to the ground, and it has clusters of large green leaves. The plant has small white or blue or yellowish flowers.

The lettuce plant is hardy, and it grows well in any good garden soil. In the United States some varieties of lettuce, such as the prickly lettuce, are weeds that grow wild in fields and are a great pest to farmers.

There are many different kinds of lettuce, but three kinds are most popular for use in salads. The cabbage lettuce is the kind you most often see in grocery stores. It has a tight head of pale green leaves. Another kind, called leaf lettuce, has loose, curling leaves that are a darker green color. Romaine or cos lettuce has tall leaves that are pointed at the tips.

There is a great deal of water in lettuce, and it does not have much food value, but crisp lettuce tastes good in a salad or sandwich. Some people cook the leaves to make soup. Lettuce is a very old plant and was raised by the ancient Romans and Greeks.

leukemia

Leukemia is a disease of the blood. Few people ever get leukemia, but if and when they do, they become very dangerously ill. There still is no real cure for leukemia. Doctors are not even sure how leukemia starts.

Leukemia is sometimes called cancer of the blood. Your healthy blood has a certain number of red blood cells and white blood cells. (Read about them in the article about BLOOD.) Your white blood cells are produced mostly from the bone marrow that is found inside some of your larger bones, such as the long, round arm and leg bones. When people get leukemia their bone marrow begins to manufacture too many white blood cells. These many white cells crowd the blood stream. The overcrowded blood begins to break through the various parts of the body. People who have leukemia lose a lot of blood. Doctors may inject blood from healthy people into the people suffering from leukemia, but usually it helps for only a short while.

levee, a structure that keeps the water of a river from overflowing its banks: see the article on DIKES AND LEVEES.

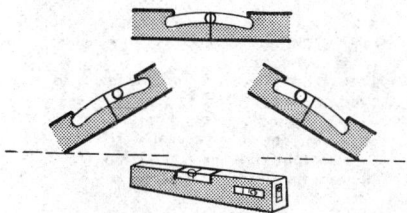

When the level is exactly horizontal, the bubble moves to the center of the tube. But if either end is higher, the bubble moves toward that end. A carpenter's level also has a vertical tube.

level

A level is an instrument used to check whether something is exactly parallel with the surface of the earth. Masons, carpenters and other construction workers use a level for testing the trueness of walls and other surfaces. Levels are used by surveyors, engineers, and astronomers as one of their most important instruments. The usual kind of level is the *spirit level*, which consists of a small glass tube filled with alcohol or ether that has a small bubble of air in it. When the surface being tested is exactly level, the bubble moves to the exact center of the tube. The tube is built into a wooden or metal bar

to protect it. Most levels have two of these tubes, one to check horizontal (level) surfaces, the other for vertical (upright) ones.

The spirit level was invented in France in the 17th century. Before that, builders used a *plumb line*, a line with a pointed weight, attached to the cross-bar of a T-square. The plumb line is still used sometimes by masons and some other construction workers.

lever

A lever is a simple machine that makes it possible to do a lot of work with comparatively little effort. Many of the tools and appliances that are used every day to move or lift objects are based on the idea of the lever. A crowbar is a lever, but so are shovels, pliers, nutcrackers,

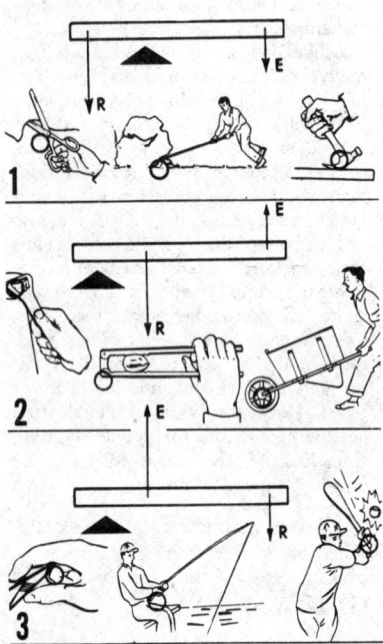

A lever is a simple machine that makes work easier. Many tools used every day employ the idea of a lever.
1. In a first-class lever, the fulcrum is between the effort (E) and resistance (R).
2. In a second-class lever, the resistance (R) is between the fulcrum and effort (E).
3. In a third-class lever, the effort (E) is between the fulcrum and resistance (R).

pump handles, and fishing rods.

If there is a heavy rock in your garden, the best way to lift it out of the ground is by using a crowbar. Place one end of the crowbar under one side of the rock, and a small stone under the bar near the rock. When you push down at the other end of the crowbar you will find that the rock can be lifted out of the ground with little effort on your part.

The small stone on which the crowbar rests is the *fulcrum* or *pivot*. The distance from the rock to the fulcrum is called the *weight arm*. The distance from the end on which you press down to the fulcrum is called the *force arm* or *lever arm*. When the lever arm is longer than the weight arm, it will take less effort to lift the rock than would be needed if you did not use the lever.

When a machine such as the lever makes it possible for you to do some sort of work with less effort, it is said to have a *mechanical advantage*. The amount of this advantage in a lever depends on the lengths of the long arm (lever arm) and the short arm (weight arm). If the long arm is four feet long and the short arm is one foot long, the mechanical advantage of the lever is four. This means that you can lift a weight of four pounds by pressing down on the end of the lever arm with a force or weight of only one pound.

KINDS OF LEVER

There are three kinds of lever. A *first-class lever* is one in which the fulcrum is between the weight and the force. A crowbar and a seesaw are first-class levers. In a *second-class lever*, the weight is between the fulcrum and the force. A wheelbarrow and a nutcracker are second-class levers. In a *third-class lever*, the force is between the fulcrum and the weight. Fire tongs, a baseball bat, a broom, a shovel and even your forearm are third-class levers.

In first- and second-class levers, the weight is usually greater than the force needed to raise it. In the third-class lever, the force is usually greater than the weight.

The purpose of a third-class lever such as a fishing rod is not to raise a heavy object through a short distance, but to raise a comparatively light object through a long distance. In the fishing rod, the fulcrum is at the end of the rod near your body. You apply a force with your hand only a short distance away from the fulcrum. The fish on the line at the other end of the rod is the weight. Although the force of your hand is greater than the weight of the fish, the fish will move a greater distance than your hand. A pull of a few inches on the rod sometimes will raise the fish several feet out of the water. The fish will also rise much faster than your hand.

The Greek scientist Archimedes is supposed to have said, "Give me a lever long enough, and something to rest it on, and I can lift the world." He meant there is no limit to the amount of work it is possible to do with the lever.

Levite

A Levite was a member of one of the twelve tribes of ancient Hebrews that are told about in the Bible. The Levites were all descended from Levi, one of the sons of Jacob. When the land of Canaan was settled, the Levites were the only tribe that did not receive any land. Instead, they were supported by various cities, and they were given the honor of taking care of the temple. This task was handed down from fathers to sons, and only Levites could become priests. The founder of the Levite priests was AARON, the brother of Moses, about whom there is a separate article. The Levites were also teachers of the law, and the book of Leviticus in the Old Testament is a book of laws. You can read more about the book of Leviticus in the articles on OLD TESTAMENT and PENTATEUCH.

Lewis, Sinclair

Sinclair Lewis was a great American writer of novels. He was the first American to win the Nobel Prize for literature. He was born in 1885 in Sauk Centre, Minnesota. After several novels that were not very successful he wrote *Main Street,* published in 1920, which made him famous. In this book Lewis describes middle-class life in a mid-western small town. *Babbitt,* Lewis's next novel, describes a typical American businessman as a self-satisfied person without much imagination; "Babbitt" has come to be used as a word to describe such a businessman.

Some of Lewis's other novels are *Arrowsmith,* the story of a medical scientist, for which he won the Nobel Prize, in 1930, and *Dodsworth,* the story of a rich but unhappy American couple in Europe. Several of Sinclair Lewis's novels have been made into motion pictures. He died in 1951.

Lewis and Clark Expedition

The Lewis and Clark Expedition was the first trip ever made across the United States over land to the Pacific Ocean. It opened the way for colonists to settle in the western part of the United States. This was about 160 years ago. President Thomas Jefferson had bought the vast Louisiana territory from France in 1803. The territory took in the valley of the Mississippi River and today would cover a part of thirteen states. Jefferson hoped the men and women of America would settle in this unknown territory and make the United States stretch from the Atlantic Ocean to the Pacific Ocean.

Later, in 1803, Jefferson appointed Captain Meriwether Lewis, his private secretary, to lead an expedition to explore the Louisiana territory, and appointed Lieutenant William Clark to assist him. They bravely set out, going to the Mississippi River and choosing volunteers from military posts along the way to accompany them. When they got to their first winter camp they had twenty-three soldiers and three Indian interpreters.

They set out in May of 1804 up the Mississippi River, and in October they reached their second winter camp, among the Mandan Indians, near what is now Bismarck, North Dakota. The journey was a hard one, for they had to fight their way through the swift currents and rapids of the river. Lewis went much of the way on foot, hunting, collecting interesting specimens of plants, and making notes on the country. By April 1805 they had reached the mouth of the Yellowstone River.

To guide them through the difficult trip across the Rocky Mountains, they were lucky enough to find a young Indian girl named Sacajawea who knew the country. With her help they fought the dangers of the rest of the journey. They followed the Columbia River down to where it enters the Pacific Ocean, and on November 15, 1805, they at last reached the Pacific after traveling more than four thousand miles. They spent the winter on the coast and

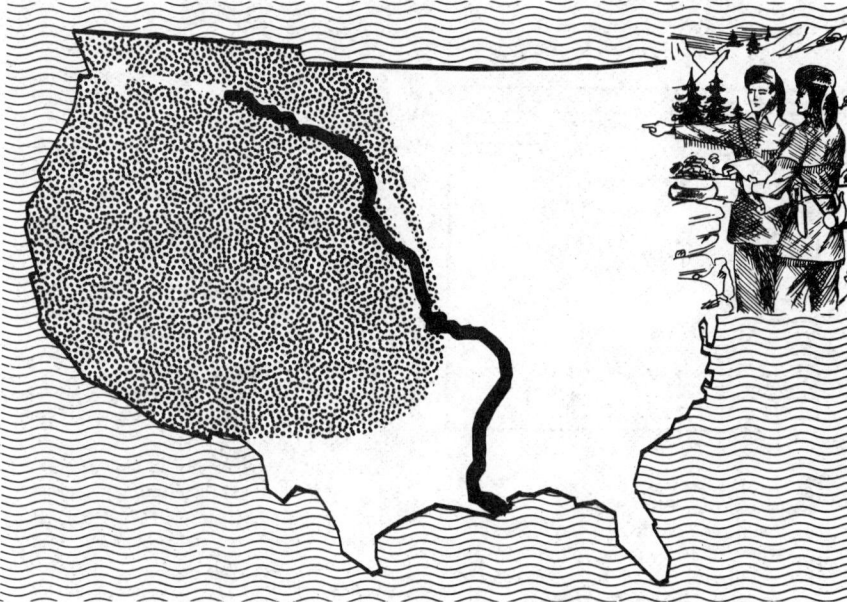

Captains Meriwether Lewis and William Clark led an expedition up the Missouri River and explored a great part of what is now the western half of the United States.

large country in central Asia that once was independent but now is controlled by the Communist government of China. The city is sometimes called the *Forbidden City,* because very few people from other countries have ever visited it. About twenty thousand people live in Lhasa. They are followers of the Buddhist religion.

Lhasa is on the Kyi Chu River. It is about 12,000 feet above sea level and is surrounded by much higher mountains.

On a hill in the city stands the palace of the Dalai Lama, whom Tibetans recognize as their supreme leader, though in 1959 Chinese Communists drove him into exile. The hill on which the Dalai Lama's palace stands is called the *Potala.* The palace is a group of buildings that are made of red and white stone. The buildings are built in tiers, with terraces and majestic towers that make the palace a very impressive sight. Some parts of the palace are more than 1,000 years old.

There are several great monasteries and temples in Lhasa. It is the sacred city of Tibet. People from many parts of Tibet come to the city to worship, and great religious festivals are held there.

The people of Lhasa live quite simply. They do not have many of the things that make modern life easy and comfortable. Until about fifty years ago almost no Europeans or Americans were permitted to visit Lhasa. Since then many have visited Lhasa and have written about it.

LHASA, TIBET. Population, about 20,000 (1950 estimate). Location, on Kyi Chu River.

liberal

A liberal person believes that everyone has the right to act and think according to his conscience; but a liberal also believes in protecting the rights of those who have other ideas or who are too weak to protect themselves.

More than a hundred years ago men who were against any government interference in business—a policy called *laissez-faire*—were called liberals. Liberals throughout the years have been against slavery; they have favored letting all the people vote; they have worked for social reforms such as public schools and public housing; they have been for freedom of religion and for civil liberties such as freedom of speech.

Liberals have usually wanted change of some kind, but they have usually been against change by force or revolution. In England about one hundred years ago, a political party called the Liberal Party was developed to vote for liberal beliefs against the Tory (later called the Conservative) Party, which favored control by privileged classes. For almost fifty years England was led by great men of the Liberal Party, the foremost of whom was William Gladstone. Gladstone was first elected Prime Minister, or head of the government, in 1868. Under the Liberal Party, the English Parliament passed laws that freed businessmen from many of the anti-industry laws that the landowning Conservatives had passed.

About the beginning of the 20th century, the Liberal Party began to decline and the Labour Party began to grow. The

then started the long trip back. They wanted to explore as much of the country as they could, and so they split into two groups for the trip back. They met again on the Missouri River in August, and on September 23, 1806, they arrived back in St. Louis. Despite the hardships of the journey and the length of time they were gone, they had lost only two men.

Both Lewis and Clark were given grants of land, and in March 1807 Lewis was made governor of a part of the Louisiana Territory. Both Lewis and Clark had kept notebooks in which they wrote down all that they found interesting about the land, the animals, the plants, and the Indians. Their journals were later published and were very useful to explorers and colonists.

lexicography

Lexicography is the work of writing dictionaries. (*Lexicon* is another word for dictionary.) It is a lexicographer's job to put in the dictionary the way a word should be spelled, pronounced, and used. Many people make the mistake of thinking that a lexicographer decides what is right and what is wrong, but he does not. He makes a record of how educated people usually spell and pronounce and use each word. If he thinks a word should be spelled in a certain way, but most people spell it in a different way, he puts it into his dictionary in the way most people spell it.

The first great English lexicographer was Dr. Samuel Johnson, who wrote a dictionary nearly two hundred years ago. The first great American lexicographer was Noah Webster, who wrote a dictionary more than a hundred years ago. The National Lexicographic Board, which wrote this encyclopedia, is a group of experienced lexicographers who got together to write dictionaries and encyclopedias. Writing dictionaries and encyclopedias is very hard work, but those who do it like it very much.

Lexington, Battle of

The Battle of Lexington was the first battle of the American Revolutionary War. It was fought in the center of the village of Lexington, Massachusetts, about six miles from Concord, Massachusetts.

On the night of April 18, 1775, some Americans had heard that the British commander, General Gage, planned to attack at Lexington, capture the American leaders John Hancock and Samuel Adams, and then move on to take Concord and destroy the store of guns that the Americans had collected there.

Paul REVERE, an American patriot, about whom you can read in another volume, spread this information. A small group of farmers got together to defend the village of Lexington against the British army. The farmer-soldiers were called Minutemen, and today a famous statue of a Minuteman marks the place where the battle of Lexington was fought. The Americans were defeated, but they had served their purpose, which was to give the citizens of Concord time to prepare for the British attack. Concord was ready when the British arrived, and the British were driven back.

Leyte

Leyte is one of the islands of the Philippines. It lies north of the large island of Mindanao and has an area of 2,785 square miles. Leyte is a very mountainous island. About one million people live there. Off the island, to the east, lies an arm of the Pacific Ocean called Leyte Gulf. In Leyte Gulf in October, 1944, was fought one of the greatest naval battles in history, between the Japanese and United States fleets. This battle, which lasted for four days, from October 23 to October 26, broke the naval power of the Japanese and opened the way for Allied victory in the Pacific.

Lhasa

Lhasa is the capital city of Tibet, a

LABOUR PARTY (about which you can read in another article) attracted the working classes, while the richer people supported the Conservative Party. The Liberal Party had been made up of people from both groups, but lost them to both the Conservative and the Labour Parties. David LLOYD GEORGE, about whom you can read in a separate article, was the last Liberal Prime Minister.

Although the Liberal Party has not won a national election in England since World War I, it is still important, because the Conservative and Labour parties are so nearly equally divided in Parliament that both try to win the votes of the Liberals.

In American politics there is also a Liberal Party, in New York State. It was organized in 1944. It sponsors its own candidates for some elections, but it usually has the same candidates as the Democratic Party, especially in national elections.

Liberia

Liberia is a small country in Africa. It was founded about 130 years ago by Negroes who had been slaves in the United States. They settled on the southwestern corner of the big bulge on the west coast of Africa. Liberia is about the size of Tennessee, having an area of 43,-000 square miles, and about a million people live there, which is about one-fourth the population of Tennessee.

THE PEOPLE WHO LIVE THERE

The descendants of the original settlers, called Americo-Liberians, form a small part of the population of Liberia. There are only about fifteen or twenty thousand of these people. Most of them live in the coastal regions of Liberia. These people and others living along the coast speak English, which is the official language of Liberia. Most of them follow Protestant Christian religions.

The great majority of the people in Liberia are members of the African tribes that were living there when Liberia was founded. There are more than twenty-five different tribes, and they speak different languages of their own. Some of them are Christians and others follow the Mohammedan religion. Some follow the old African religions of their ancestors. The chief tribes in Liberia are the Kru, the Mandingo, and the Gola.

HOW THE PEOPLE LIVE

Most of the people in Liberia are farmers. They raise rice, coffee, and sugar cane. From the palm trees they gather the coconuts, from which they make oil and fibers used in rope. The soil of Liberia is good for farming, but the farmers have a hard life. They do not know much about modern methods of farming. They live in clearings in the jungle, and they must constantly struggle to keep their lands clear. The jungle grows very fast, and the farmers must burn away the bushes and plants that threaten to overrun their land.

This jungle could be very valuable to the Liberian people if they could develop it, but they do not have the money to build up lumbering industries. Also, they do not have a good transportation system. There are few roads in Liberia, and almost no railroads. The people must travel on foot, and everything has to be carried through the jungle by porters on foot.

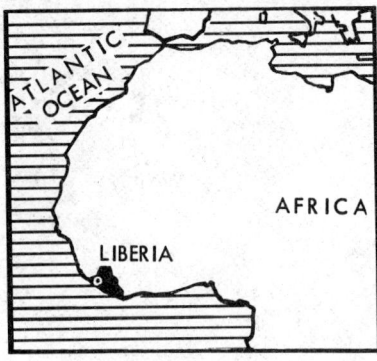

The few cities of Liberia are on the coast, and the people who live there understand more of modern ways. They are the educated people, who run the government. The government is trying to spread education in Liberia. There are free public schools that are open to everyone. There are some colleges, including one named for a great American Negro leader, Booker T. Washington. This college was built by and is supported with the help of money given by people of the United States.

WHAT KIND OF PLACE LIBERIA IS

Liberia is a tropical country, which means that it is very hot and damp. This kind of climate nourishes the great tropical forests that cover most of the country. The only part of Liberia that has been much cultivated and developed is the narrow strip along the 350-mile Atlantic coast.

The capital city is Monrovia, which was named for James Monroe, who was President of the United States when Liberia was founded. About 53,000 people live in Monrovia. The city has been developed as a harbor with the help of the United States. Other cities in Liberia are Harper and Robertsport. Neither of these are very large.

Liberia has many resources. The great jungle could provide much lumber. Iron ore, gold, and some diamonds have been found in the country. The United States is providing technical and financial aid to speed the development of these resources. The country also has about 80,000 acres of rubber plantations. The principal exports are iron ore and rubber. There is one railroad line, which connects the iron mines with Monrovia at the coast.

Most of Liberia is fairly low, but there are some areas of low mountains. The country is crossed by many rivers, including the Cavalla and the St. Paul.

HOW THE PEOPLE ARE GOVERNED

The founders of Liberia formed a government like that of the United States. Their constitution, which is like the Constitution of the United States, provides for a president and for a legislature, or lawmaking body. The president is elected for eight years, and he may be re-elected for another four years. To help him in his work he has a group of men called a cabinet, like the Cabinet that assists the President of the United States. The same party, representing the descendants of the original settlers, has been in continuous power since 1878. W.V.S. Tubman was president from 1943 until his death in 1971. The Liberian legislature, like the Congress of the United States, has a Senate and a House of Representatives. To vote, a person must be over 21 years old, must be a Negro, and must own some land.

The native tribes still follow their own customs, and have their own kind of local government. Most of these people do not vote, but each province sends a representative to the House of Representatives.

LIBERIA IN THE PAST

In the early years of the last century, there were many American Negroes who had been freed from slavery. An organization called the American Colonization Society was formed to help these Negroes find a country of their own. The Congress of the United States gave them the right to found a new settlement, or colony, for themselves. In 1822, the first group of freed Negroes settled at Monrovia. The American Colonization Society sent men to govern the new settlement until 1847, when the people of the new country declared that they were independent. They elected as their first president Joseph J. Roberts, who had once been a slave in Virginia.

In World War I, Liberia went into the war on the side of the United States. It did not enter World War II, but the Liberian government allowed the United States to set up bases in Liberia. When the United Nations was formed, in 1945, Liberia was one of the original members.

LIBERIA. Area, 43,000 square miles. Population (1973 estimate) 1,570,000. Language, English, African dialects. Religion, Protestant Christian, Mohammedan, and others. Government, republic. Monetary unit, Liberian dollar (equal to U.S. dollar). Flag, 11 stripes, alternating red and white; in the upper corner near the flagstaff, a blue square with one white star.

liberty

Liberty is being free—not ruled or enslaved by anyone else. The word *liberty* may be seen on coins of the United States, because the country and its citizens value liberty above all else. See the articles on FREEDOM, CIVIL LIBERTIES, and BILL OF RIGHTS.

Liberty Bell

The Liberty Bell, in Independence Hall, Philadelphia, Pennsylvania, is one of the most familiar symbols of freedom in the United States. This bell was rung for the first time in Philadelphia at the first public reading of the Declaration of Independence, on July 8, in 1776. The bell was cast in England in 1753 and inscribed on it are these words: "Proclaim liberty throughout the land unto all the inhabitants thereof." The words come from the book of Leviticus in the Bible. Shortly after it was hung it was cracked during a test and had to be recast. The bell was cracked again in 1835 while tolling for the death of Chief Justice John Marshall. The Liberty Bell has not again been recast, nor has it been rung since, although it was lightly sounded in honor of the Allied victory in Europe in World War II, in 1945.

Liberty, Statue of

The Statue of Liberty stands in New York harbor to welcome ships coming to the United States. It is a statue of a woman, more than 150 feet high, that stands on a pedestal almost 150 feet high, so the top of the statue is more than 300 feet above the waters of the harbor. Liberty wears a crown. She holds in one hand a tablet, and her other hand holds aloft a torch that is lighted at night. At night, the statue is lit by floodlights.

The full name of the statue is *Liberty Enlightening the World*. It represents the American spirit of freedom and liberty for all people. The statue was made by a French sculptor, Frederic A. Bartholdi, and it was given to the United States by

Nat'l Park Service

Ever since 1886, when the Statue of Liberty was unveiled, the flame of her torch has stood for the American ideal of freedom and opportunity for all who arrive there.

the French government in 1884. The money to build the huge concrete pedestal was given by thousands of Americans.

The statue is made of copper plates fastened onto an iron framework. The inside of the statue is hollow, and visitors can climb an inner staircase to the crown of the statue and look out over the harbor. The statue was made in France and shipped to the United States in parts. It was put together in 1886.

The Statue of Liberty stands on an island of 13 acres, formerly called Bedloe's Island but now called Liberty Island.

Libra

Libra is the name of one of the groups of stars in the sky, called constellations. It was given this name thousands of years ago, and in the Latin language *libra* means "pound" or "balance." The sign that stands for the constellation Libra is ♎, which looks like a balance scale. Libra is one of the signs of the zodiac. There are separate articles about CONSTELLATION and ZODIAC.

Library

A library is any collection of books, however few or many. If you own this book you are reading, then you have the beginning of a library. Wherever people gather they collect books in some central place where others may come to read them. Schools need libraries so that both teachers and children can find the things they need to know, and some of the best libraries in the world are in universities and colleges. Cities and countries have public and national libraries where anyone may go to find what he wants to know or simply to read for fun. Business firms, scientific laboratories, art galleries, and many other special groups have libraries.

If you can write your own name and know how to keep books clean then you are probably old enough to borrow books from the public library. Children's libraries also have story hours when the librarians tell stories to the children. Often there are interesting things to see in your children's library, such as doll shows, model airplane exhibits, collections of old-fashioned toys or valentines, or paintings made by children. Some libraries also lend phonograph records for use at home.

ANCIENT AND MODERN LIBRARIES

There were some wonderful libraries in the world long before books were printed. More than six hundred years before Jesus was born the ancient city of Nineveh had a library with more than ten thousand "books." These were not books at all but big tablets of baked clay with writing carved on them. This was one of the oldest "public" libraries, although it belonged to the king, Assurbanipal. Noblemen of Egypt had palace libraries two thousand years before Jesus, and the temples of ancient Egypt had their libraries of books written on papyrus, a kind of paper made from reeds, and some also on baked clay. The philosopher Aristotle is said to have been one of the first Europeans to collect a private library. King Ptolemy of Egypt founded a great library at Alexandria, which was one of the most famous in the ancient world, with perhaps as many as four hundred thousand volumes, but it was destroyed in the year 394 by order of the Roman emperor, Theodosius the Great, who also closed the Roman temples and their libraries with them.

Modern libraries grew much faster than the largest libraries of the ancients. Books are printed all over the world every day and the national libraries try to gather everything that seems of lasting interest. The biggest libraries in Europe are the library of the British Museum in London, England, founded in 1753 and the Bibliothèque Nationale in Paris, France, which is at least six hundred years old. They each have more than six million printed books and hundreds of thousands of pictures and manuscripts. The American national library is the LIBRARY OF CONGRESS, about which you can read in another article.

The oldest European library is probably the Vatican library in Rome. No one knows exactly when its basic collection was begun, but Pope Boniface VIII catalogued it in the early 14th century, and the present Vatican library was founded by Pope Nicholas V between 1447 and 1455. Another great European library is the Saltykov-Shchedrin Public Library in Leningrad, Russia, which had ten million books in 1961. This library was begun by Peter the Great in 1714, and contains the personal libraries of the French philosophers Voltaire and Diderot, as well as many documents relating to the French Revolution. In Italy the sculptor Michelangelo designed a marvelous library building in Florence, the Laurentian Library, which was opened to the public in 1571. It is not very large but it owns many rare and beautiful books. In the Middle Ages and the Renaissance, books, being quite scarce and valuable, were chained to the shelves of a library to prevent their being stolen, and the Laurentian Library still has some of its treasures chained in this fashion.

Books can usually be borrowed from modern public libraries free of charge, but for hundreds of years even "public" libraries were really open only to scholars or to rich persons. Of course, comparatively few people knew how to read until recent times, but now that we try to teach every child how to read, we also try to bring books within easy reach. Even out-of-the-way places have their public libraries, and there are loan systems by which country libraries may borrow books from the bigger libraries. Also, there are bookmobiles, little traveling libraries, which drive from place to place in the country areas around the big cities. And the county or regional libraries often have collections established all over their country areas, sometimes in a post office or a store or even in a filling station. However, although so much has been done to give people the pleasure of books, and almost every state has passed laws and assigned money for libraries, there are still 30,000,000 people in the United States who do not have library service.

PEOPLE WHO WORK IN LIBRARIES

The people who work in libraries are called librarians. They get their training in special schools for librarians. There are both men and women librarians in most public, school, and college libraries. One of the most important things that librarians do is to choose books that they think their readers will be interested in or that they feel are important. They also see that new books are listed in the catalogs, and decide in which part of the library they belong. Librarians also have the job of attracting new readers. Some of the ways they may do this is by arranging interesting displays of books or by giving talks about new and interesting books. Librarians may arrange for lectures and discussions in their libraries and then encourage the people who attend to learn more about the subjects by reading books in the library. Librarians who work in children's libraries must be good storytellers.

In the larger libraries, librarians who are expert in some one subject are needed. For instance, the reference department of the New York Public Library operates special collections that require experts in books about music, art, the theater, Slavonic languages, economics, science, and other subjects.

A librarian must be interested in many different things, and he must like people and enjoy helping them. In their work

librarians meet dozens of people every day, and they should be able to make everyone feel at home and free to ask for help.

Many of the routine jobs in a library do not require people with special library training. Clerical workers type the cards for the books and catalogs, register new borrowers, and keep the library records. Boys and girls often work in the public library after school hours as pages, getting books for readers, shelving them correctly, and stamping borrowers' cards.

USING THE LIBRARY

You can learn many things for yourself if you can use the library tools properly. The most useful tool is the alphabetically-arranged card catalog, which lists every book the library owns, just as an index lists the contents of a book. Each book is usually represented in the catalog by at least three cards: one for the book's title, one for the name of the author, and one for the subject with which the book deals. On each card you will see a number, which helps you know where to find the book. In a big library you may have to copy the number with the book's author and title on a slip of paper and wait for a few minutes while the librarian sends someone to find the book for you. If you need to ask the librarians to explain anything about the library they will be glad to answer your questions.

Library of Congress

The Library of Congress is the national library of the United States. It occupies two buildings in Washington, D.C. Although it is only about 150 years old, the Library of Congress is the largest library in the United States and one of the largest in the world. It has more than eleven million books. It is also a treasure-house of maps, pictures, music scores, films, phonograph records, and motion-picture reels. It has the world's best collection of books printed before the year 1500. Such books are called *incunabula*. They are very rare and many of them are extremely valuable.

The first Library of Congress was opened in 1800, but in 1814, in the War of 1812, the British burned the Capitol in Washington, and all the books with it. The next year Congress bought the private library of Thomas Jefferson and started all over with his collection of more than 6,000 books.

Now the Library of Congress, as the agency that issues copyrights in the United States, receives two copies of every book copyrighted, as well as plays, music, and other works to be copyrighted. It collects many thousands of books every year from all over the world as well.

The Librarian of Congress is appointed by the President, with the consent of the Senate. Although students may use the Library, it is really intended to help Congressmen make our laws. There is a tunnel connecting the Library with the Capitol and an "endless-chain system" carries back and forth books that Congressmen may need in their work. The Law Library of Congress alone has more than 2,000,000 books. The collection of books and papers about airplanes and flying is the world's largest. The Library of

Congress is also in charge of the Books for the Blind program, through which thousands of talking-book machines have been distributed in the United States.

Libya

Libya is a country on the northern coast of Africa, with a long seacoast and several seaports on the Mediterranean Sea. In 1969 the monarchy was overthrown and the country became the Arab Republic of Libya, ruled by the Revolution Command Council, which appoints the cabinet. Libya is very large in area—679,378 square miles, almost as big as Mexico—but most of it is part of the Sahara Desert, where nothing can grow. By a 1964 estimate, only 1,559,000 people lived in Libya. However, the population grew rapidly, due to the discovery (since 1959) of vast oil deposits in the Libyan deserts. This has brought businessmen, technicians and laborers to Libya in large numbers. The population is now over 2 million.

THE PEOPLE WHO LIVE THERE

Most of the people of Libya are Berbers, descended from a people that has

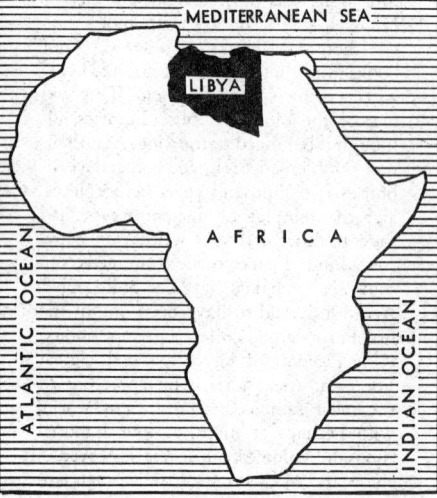

lived in North Africa for thousands of years, or Arabs, descended from Arabians who settled there hundreds of years ago. All these are Mohammedans and speak the Arabic language. In the western province of Tripolitania there are thousands of Italians, who settled there when Italy controlled Libya (from 1922 until World War II).

Throughout the centuries, some of the Libyan people have been nomads, wanderers who do not live in any one place but roam the country with their camels and their herds of goats, sheep, and cattle. Others have been farmers in the few parts of the country that have enough rainfall to make farming possible; the crops are wheat and barley, peanuts, and olive, date and fig trees. On the coast, fishermen draw sponges and tunny (tuna) fish from the sea. There are no big industries, but there are craftsmen who make carpets, other woven goods, and fine products of leather and metal.

Since 1961, when the oil industry became big and many laborers were needed, tens of thousands of the nomads, farmers, fishermen, and even craftsmen have left their ancient occupations and gone to the

cities to seek jobs with the oil companies. Now Libya does not produce enough meat and farm products to feed its people and must import food in exchange for oil.

But Libya, formerly one of the poorest countries on earth, has become one of the richest because the oil production (more than a billion barrels in 1971) has raised the average income per person from about $35 to over $900 a year and geologists predict that even larger oil deposits will be found.

WHAT THE COUNTRY IS LIKE

Except along the coast, Libya is desert land with only a few fertile oases (places where there are springs and wells). The only railroads and good roads are along the coast. Travel inland is by camel caravan. The climate is hot and dry, and the temperature in Libya once reached 136 degrees, the highest ever recorded in the world. In the winter the country is comfortably cool.

The oil prosperity has affected chiefly the cities, where many new buildings and fine hotels have been built, there are many new automobiles on the streets, and the shops have expensive merchandise for sale.

The chief cities are the seaports of Tripoli and Bengasi (or Benghazi), each with a growing population of about 250,000. Each is one of the two capital cities, but a new capital, Baida, has been partly built on the highlands near the coast. Another seacoast city is Tobruk, in the east.

The oil fields are in the desert, in the southern part of Libya, in the regions of Tripolitania, Cyrenaica, and Fezzan.

THE GOVERNMENT OF LIBYA

King Idris (Mohammed Idris al Sanusi) became king with the independence of Libya in 1951. He was a generous, progressive king who used Libya's new oil wealth to build schools, hospitals, roads, factories, and low-cost houses for the poor. In 1969 a group of military officers deposed the king and proclaimed a republican government ruled by the Revolution Command Council (RCC) of 12 members. They appointed a prime minister and 12 ministers. There are no political parties in Libya.

LIBYA IN THE PAST

Although Libya has had people living in it for thousands of years, it was never an independent country before 1951. Ancient Rome took over control from Carthage before the time of Christ; Vandals from Germany ruled Libya after Rome fell; then conquering Arabs and Turks ruled the country and introduced the Mohammedan religion. At one time during the Turkish rule, Tripoli was a base for pirates — see the article on the BARBARY STATES. Italy took Libya away from Turkey in 1922 and Italians did much to modernize the country and develop its desert territories. During World War II Libya was a battleground—see the article AFRICAN CAMPAIGN—and finally the British occupied the country but the United Nations decided in 1949 that Libya should be independent. In 1951 the Libyan people decided to have Idris as their king and in 1952 they elected their first legislature. Idris licensed American and British military bases in exchange for

Unations Photos

Despite the many changes brought by the discovery of large quantities of oil, some aspects of Libya remain unchanged. This shepherd watches his sheep graze as he always has; his life has not been greatly affected by his country's sudden prosperity.

gifts and loans until oil made the country rich, then he withdrew these privileges. Libya is a member of the United Nations.

In 1971, Libya, Syria, and Egypt formed the Federation of Arab Republics.

LIBYA. Area, 679,358 square miles. Population (1973 estimate) 2,010,000. Language, Arabic, and a little Italian. Religion, Mohammedan. Government, constitutional monarchy. Monetary unit, Libyan pound (100 piastres), worth $2.80 (U.S.).

lichen

Lichens are a group of plants that grow mostly in the northern and arctic regions, though some are found in tropical regions. The lichen is really made up of two plants, an alga and a fungus. An alga is a plant like seaweed, and fungus is a plant like a mushroom or toadstool. The alga manufactures the food and takes up water and minerals from the surface the lichen is growing on.

Lichens are not like other plants, for they do not have stems, leaves, or flowers. Some lichens are much thinner than moss and look like lace growing over rocks, tree stumps, and posts. Some lichens are several inches long and stand erect, looking like tiny shrubs. They grow in many different colors; some are gray, others green, blue, violet, rust, brown, or black.

Many lichens are important to man and animals. In northern regions called the tundra, reindeer moss, which is a lichen and not a moss, is used as food by reindeer and cattle. Another lichen called Iceland moss is eaten by Eskimos and other northern peoples. Ancient people used to obtain dyes from lichens. There is an acid in lichens that eats into the rocks on which it grows and gradually turns the rocks into soil.

Portions of the lichen break off and are carried by the wind to other places, where they form new plants. They also produce tiny spores or seeds that are carried by the wind and grow wherever they land.

licorice

The licorice is a plant that grows mostly in the southern part of Europe, and in Asia. Some licorice plants also grow in the United States, especially in California, where the climate is warm. The root of the licorice plant contains a very sweet substance that is used to make candy and to flavor medicines, tobacco, and sometimes beer. The licorice plant grows to be about three feet high. It has pale blue flowers. The roots are dark brown outside and yellow inside.

Lie, Trygve

Trygve Lie of Norway was the first Secretary General of the United Nations. He served from 1946 until 1953. As Secretary General, Lie had the power to recommend for study or action to either of the two most important bodies of the United Nations, the Security Council and the General Assembly, any problems that in his opinion represented a threat to the peace of the world. Lie is best remembered for his action at the time of the Korean War.

In June 1950 the Communist country of North Korea attacked South Korea. At Lie's request, the United Nations sent troops to protect South Korea against the Communist invasion. For the first time in history an army fighting in behalf of an international organization defended the land of a nation that had been attacked.

Trygve Lie, born in Norway in 1896, was foreign minister of that country before becoming Secretary General of the United Nations. He died in 1968.

Liechtenstein

Liechtenstein is one of the smallest independent countries in the world. It is on the Rhine River in Europe, between Austria and Switzerland. Its area, about 62 square miles, is a little bigger than the District of Columbia. Its population is about 21,350.

Most of Liechtenstein lies in the Rhine valley, between the Rhine River and the Tyrolean Alps. The climate is mild. Most of the people are farmers who grow cereals, flax and fruits, but some of them make their living raising livestock, weaving, and carving wood. There is some small industry, mostly the manufacture of delicate instruments such as calculating machines and measuring devices.

There are two main sections in Liechtenstein: Vaduz includes the mountainous area, and Schellenberg makes up the lowlands. The capital is the city of Vaduz. Liechtenstein is a constitutional principality, which means that a prince is head of the government and there is a parliament that operates under a constitution. Prince Franz Joseph II became prince in 1938. The Diet, or parliament, has 15 members who are elected for four-year terms. Everyone is allowed to vote. Liechtenstein has almost no taxes, because the government income comes chiefly from the sale of postage stamps and from taxes on corporations. Many foreign firms are incorporated in Liechtenstein.

Liechtenstein is closely allied to Switzerland, which operates its postal and telegraph services, its customs, and its foreign affairs. There is no army, and the police force has only fifty members.

LIECHTENSTEIN. Independent principality. Area, 62 square miles. Population (1973 estimate) 21,350. Language, German. Religion, Roman Catholic. Government, constitutional principality. Monetary unit, Swiss franc, worth 23 cents (U.S.). Flag, blue and red bars.

lie detector

The lie detector is a machine used to try to tell whether or not a person is telling the truth. When you tell a lie, your face may not show it, but certain other changes in your body take place that would give you away if they could be measured. Your pulse would beat faster, your breath would come in gasps, and your blood pressure would change. The lie detector measures these changes and makes a record of them.

The most frequently used kind of lie detector is called the *polygraph*. It consists of a kind of bandage that is placed around the subject's right arm to measure his pulse and blood pressure; a large rubber tube that goes around his chest to

record his rate of breathing; and a metal plate that is placed on his left hand to measure the electrical changes that take place on his skin. All four measurements are recorded by pens on a moving sheet of paper.

The subject usually is asked several innocent questions, and the pens go along in a fairly regular way as he gives his answers. When he gives an untruthful answer, they usually make a sharp jump, showing that he is not able to control his emotional reactions to the question. Lie detectors do not work absolutely correctly—they are right only about eight times out of ten—so their results cannot be used to convict a person of a crime. Very nervous and emotional people and hardened liars are not good subjects for lie-detector tests. Lie detectors are often valuable in clearing innocent people, in detecting a guilty person, or in making guilty criminals confess.

Liège

Liège is a city in eastern Belgium, on the Meuse and Ourthe Rivers. It is the fourth-largest city in Belgium and the capital of the province of Liège. It is the seat of the University of Liège. More than 150,000 people live in Liège. Its main industries include the processing of metals, the making of munitions and machinery, brewing, and flour-milling.

Before World War I, Liège was strongly fortified. Its location commands the entrance from Germany into the heart of Belgium, and in both world wars the city was the scene of fighting. In World War I its fortifications fell to the Germans, but the heavy bombardments did little damage to the city itself. In World War II, almost half of the city was destroyed by bombs, but the principal historic buildings escaped serious damage.

LIÈGE, BELGIUM. Population (1960 estimate) 156,362; with suburbs, 607,117. Capital of the province of Liège. Province: area, 1,118 square miles; population, 1,010,611.

life

Life is something that plants and animals have and nothing else on earth has. It is the ability to grow and to reproduce—that is, to have children or to have seeds or in some other way to create others of the same kind. The study of life and of living things is called BIOLOGY, and there is a separate article about it.

Scientists know a great deal about life, yet they do not know how it began or why it exists. They do know how it works. All living things are composed of tiny particles, or CELLS, about which there is a separate article. Each cell is a living thing itself, but millions or billions of cells combine to form a particular kind of animal or plant.

There are a hundred different elements, or basic substances, of which everything (all matter) is composed. Four of these are necessary to life as it is known on earth. The four are hydrogen, oxygen, carbon, and nitrogen. All living things contain carbon; they require air and water, which are composed of hydrogen and oxygen; and they require nitrogen as part of themselves and in the making of their food. Most living things require

other elements, but not all living things require the same ones.

Another requirement of life is that the temperature should not go above the boiling point of water and should not stay for too long periods below the freezing point of water. Life is possible at higher and lower temperatures, but (so far as is known) reproduction is not, so even if there were living things they would soon die out.

These requirements for life cause scientists to doubt that there can be living things on the other planets in our solar system. On every other planet there is not enough oxygen, or enough water, or it is too hot or too cold. Some forms of plant life may exist on some of the planets, most likely on Mars and Venus, but not the kind of animal life there is on earth. However, there is the possibility that life may exist in other solar systems.

The course of life with most living things is: A seed, or germ, comes from a living plant or animal; it takes in food, and grows until it reaches a stage that is called maturity; then it stops growing but continues to live; and eventually it weakens so that it dies. According to this, there can be no life without death. Actually, the cells in living things die rapidly and constantly, but new cells replace them for a certain period of time. It cannot be proved that everything must die naturally sooner or later. Many things die from disease or accident or a change of conditions. There are trees that have continued to live and even to grow for as long as men have been able to study them or their history, and it cannot be proved that every one of them would finally have to die of "old age," but scientists believe they would have to die like everything else.

lifesaving service

In almost all countries that border on the sea there is some kind of lifesaving service for the shipwrecked. In the United States this service is a part of the United States Coast Guard. The Coast Guard maintains lifesaving stations all along the coast. Each station has such equipment as lifeboats and life preservers, flag and rocket signals, and guns that shoot lifelines out to ships in distress. Each station also has a lookout or observatory where crew members keep constant watch for trouble at sea. The station is connected by radio and telephone with other stations and with the central Coast Guard office of the district.

The first organized attempt at a lifesaving service in the United States was begun in the early 1800s by the Humane Society of Massachusetts, which built huts on the shore for the use of victims of shipwreck. In 1848 the United States government organized a Life Saving Service that operated along the New Jersey and Long Island coast, and in 1915 this was merged with the Revenue Cutter Service to form the present Coast Guard. By 1938 transatlantic airplane flights were being put on a regular basis, and the Coast Guard took over air-sea rescue work. In 1961 it operated more than 40,000 aids to air and sea navigation, including lightships, lighthouses,

buoys, day marks, fog signals, and radio and radar beacons. It also uses boats called cutters, airplanes, and helicopters.

Canada has a similar service run by the government, with about fifty rescue stations on seacoast and Great Lakes.

See also ARTIFICIAL RESPIRATION and FIRST AID.

ligament

A ligament is a short piece of tissue in the human or animal body. It looks like a tough, white tape or cord. Ligaments connect the various bones at the joints. Each ligament has a specific name. There are some ligaments that hold organs of the body in place, and some that form coverings for the joints. Others hold the tendons that run through the joints themselves, and some ligaments hold muscles fast to the bones.

light

Light is as important as anything else in our lives. This is not only because we need light to see. Sunlight provides the energy with which green plants manufacture food for animal life; if we did not have light we would not have food.

Objects that give off light are said to be luminous. Stars give off light. Metals give off light when they are made hot enough. Substances that give off light when they are heated are called incandescent substances. Insects such as the firefly, and many deep-sea fish, give off small amounts of light because of certain chemicals in their bodies.

WHAT IS LIGHT?

Light is a kind of energy because it makes things happen. It makes your eyes able to see, makes plants able to manufacture food, changes the color of cloth, sunburns your skin, and makes pictures appear on photographic film.

Light from the sun or an electric light bulb moves out or radiates in all directions. For that reason, light is called a kind of radiant energy. It can change into other forms of energy, and other forms of energy can change into light. When light causes sugar to form in green leaves, some of the light energy is changed into chemical energy and stored in the sugar. Light falling on a dark object is absorbed and changed into heat energy. In an "electric eye" (photoelectric cell), light falling on a metal is absorbed and changed into electrical energy.

Light moves in large numbers of small particles called photons. These photons move in a kind of wave and their path is usually a straight line. This explains why we cannot see objects that are around a corner, although we sometimes can hear their sounds. You cannot see an object unless you are in the path of a ray of light that comes from the object.

Albert Einstein, the greatest scientist of this century, showed that light can sometimes be bent by the force of gravity of large objects such as the sun. Scientists have been able to observe this during eclipses of the sun. The light coming from a star is bent by the gravity of the sun and makes the star appear in a different position in the sky from where it actually is.

THE SPEED OF LIGHT

Light travels through air at a speed of about 186,300 miles a second. This speed was first accurately measured by an American scientist, Albert A. Michelson. It takes about one ten-thousandth of a second for the light from a lightning flash twenty miles away to reach our eyes. The sun is about 93,000,000 miles away so it takes the light from the sun a little over eight minutes to arrive on the earth. It would take an airplane traveling at 300 miles an hour 35 years to cover the same distance.

However, even with the tremendous speed of light, it takes about four years for the light from the nearest star, Alpha Centauri, to reach the earth. The light that we see coming from some distant star groups called galaxies actually started out on its journey more than 100,000,000 years ago. The distances of these star groups from the earth are measured in units called light-years. A light-year is the distance traveled by light in one year's time. It is equal to about six trillion (six million million) miles.

Light does not travel with the same speed through all substances. The speed of light through glass is about 124,000 miles a second. In water its speed is about 140,000 miles a second. Lights of different colors also have different speeds. The speed of blue light through glass is faster than the speed of red light through glass.

LIGHT WAVES

Because light moves in waves, it is very similar to radio waves, heat waves, X-rays, and ultraviolet and infrared rays. However, these waves cannot be seen because they are either too long or too short, and vibrate too quickly or too slowly. Radio waves may be miles long. Infrared, or heat, waves are longer than visible light waves. The ultraviolet rays are shorter than visible light waves, and X-rays and gamma rays are still shorter. However, all of these waves travel at the same speed, 186,300 miles a second.

The method of producing light by

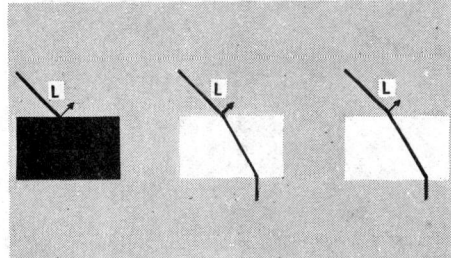

The object at the left is *opaque;* no light (L) can pass through it, and little is reflected, or bounced off it. Most of the light is absorbed in the object. The material in the middle is *translucent;* some light passes through it, some is absorbed, but most of it is reflected. The object on the right is *transparent;* most of the light passes through it.

heating a metal wire in a light bulb is to get it hot enough so it will radiate light waves. As the wire is heated, it begins to radiate the long, invisible, infrared heat waves. As it gets hotter, it begins to produce the long light waves— red. As it becomes still hotter the waves become shorter and the light changes to yellow and then to white.

White light is really a mixture of all the different colors. Each color is made by a light wave of a different length. They are roughly divided into the colors of red, orange, yellow, green, blue, indigo, and violet. All these colors taken together are called a spectrum. Red light has the longest light waves of the spectrum, violet the shortest.

THE MOVEMENT OF LIGHT

An object must send light to our eyes before we can see it. Objects that do not send out light of their own must be lighted by some source of light. If we are to see an object, light from the luminous source must be reflected from the object to our eyes. Light is reflected from objects in about the same way as a ball is bounced off a building. Light from the sun or from a lighted lamp travels to an object and bounces off the object.

We see more reflected light than we do light from a luminous source. In reading this page, you are depending upon the reflection of light from the paper.

Light is reflected better by a smooth surface than by a rough one. A mirror

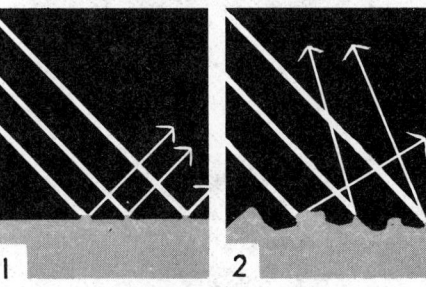

A smooth object (1) reflects light evenly or regularly, whereas a rough object (2) reflects it unevenly or diffusely.

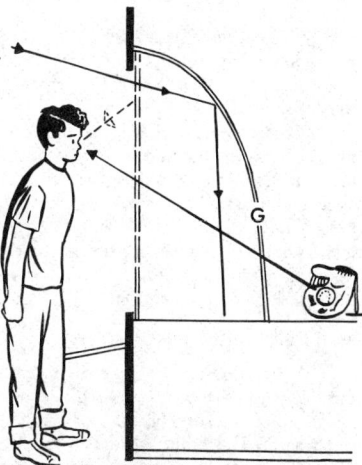

Because the curved glass (G) in the store window reflects light (L) down and away from the boy, he cannot see the glass. He would see a straight pane of glass (*dotted line*) because it would reflect light back to his eye.

reflects light better than a piece of paper. A mirror gives regular reflection, which means that it reflects a whole beam of light together. A piece of paper gives diffuse reflection, which means that it scatters the beam of light in different directions. For that reason, you can see yourself in a mirror, but not in a piece of paper.

Diffuse reflection is very important in lighting. Painting the walls and ceilings so as to give rough surfaces causes diffuse reflection. If the walls are too smooth, beams of light will be reflected by them, causing glare and eyestrain. If the pages of this book were too smooth,

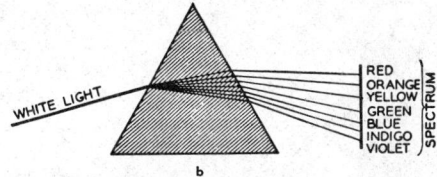

White light is actually composed of different-colored lights, which together are called a *spectrum.* These lights can be separated by passing the white light through a glass prism (b).

you would see a reflection of light from a window or lamp instead of seeing the words on the page.

Some materials, such as glass, allow light to pass through them instead of reflecting it. We say that a material such as glass is transparent. Air and cellophane are two other transparent materials.

Some materials such as paper allow some light to pass through them but not enough to enable us to see objects clearly on the other side. Such materials are called translucent. Ground glass, frosted glass, oiled paper, thin silk and parchment are other translucent materials.

There are some materials that do not allow light through at all. They are called opaque. Metals are opaque. So are pieces of wood and many thick substances. Opaque substances reflect and absorb light. Dark substances absorb more light and reflect less light than light substances.

Some substances reflect only some light waves and absorb others. A dress appears green because the dye in the dress absorbs all of the colors in the sunlight except green. The green is reflected to your eye, and you see the dress as green. If the green dress is held in a red light, it will look black, because there is no green light to reflect. A white dress will reflect all colors equally and therefore appear white.

REFRACTION

Although light usually travels in straight lines, it can be bent. Usually, a light beam passing from air into water is bent. This is called *refraction.* The refraction of light from water into air is what makes a stick placed in water appear bent. Refraction, or bending, is necessary for sight. Without it, our eyes could not focus light coming to them and we would not be able to see.

Refraction also takes place when light passes through one substance into another because light travels at different speeds in different substances. The number we use to describe the amount of bending for each substance is called the index of refraction of that material. The higher the index of refraction, the greater the bending of light that takes place.

In winter when you look at objects above a hot stove or radiator they appear to shimmer. This is because the light as

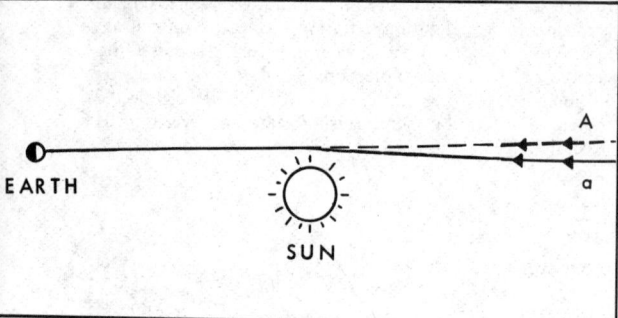
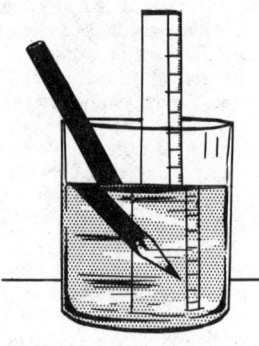

Left: The tremendous pull of the sun causes light from a nearby star (a) to bend as it passes near the sun. To an observer on the earth it seems to be at point (A) in the sky. *Right:* Light is also bent, or refracted, as it passes from one substance, such as air, to another, such as water. This is why the pencil and ruler appear to be broken.

it passes from cold to hot layers of air is refracted. Cold air is denser and has a higher index of refraction than warm air.

The bending of light is similar to what happens when a line of marchers turns a corner in a parade. To hold the line together, the man on the inside must walk more slowly while the men on the outside swing the line around. When light travels through glass, a part of the beam of light strikes the glass first and is slowed down before the rest of the beam reaches the surface. The whole beam swings around to permit the part that is traveling faster to remain with the rest of the beam, which is traveling slower. This shifts the direction of the beam and bends the light entering the glass.

HOW LIGHT IS MEASURED

Light is measured by the candlepower. One candlepower is the amount of light given off by a standard-size candle when it burns. Light is measured in a device called a photometer. This is a box about

Another device, called a light meter, is used by photographers to measure the brightness of light. Light falling on an electric eye moves the pointer.

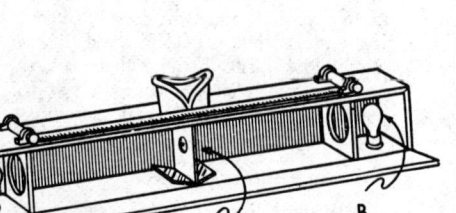

Light is measured by a photometer. This device is made up of bulbs (B) placed at both ends, and separated by a piece of oiled paper (P) in the center.

three feet long. Suppose you want to find out how many candlepower there are in a certain electric light bulb. At one end of the box you put a burning candle, and at the other end you put the light bulb. Between the two you put a piece of white paper. You move the paper back and forth between the two lights until there is exactly the same amount of light on both sides of the paper. At this point suppose the paper is twenty inches away from the light bulb and only one inch away from the candle. That means the light bulb is 400 candle-

power (20 times 20 candlepower). The photometer has mirrors in it that make it easy to see both sides of the paper at the same time.

Light is also measured by the foot-candle. That is the amount of light produced on a surface by one candlepower one foot away. Photographers measure light by foot-candles when they use exposure meters to find out how to set their cameras for taking pictures. This is explained in the article on PHOTOGRAPHY.

lighthouse

A lighthouse is a tower that sends out large beams of light to guide and warn ships entering harbors or dangerous waters. The light, located in the top of the tower, flashes every few seconds and usually can be seen for about twenty miles. Each lighthouse has its own system of flashes by which ships can tell where they are.

Lighthouses may be built on large rocks in the ocean, or on piers sunk into the ocean bottom, or on the shore. Lighthouses usually are made of stone and concrete, but some are made of iron and steel, or of brick. They may be as high as 200 feet, but most of them are about 150 feet high.

Inside the lighthouse there are several rooms, one beneath the other, connected by a spiral staircase. In these rooms, the

person who takes care of the lighthouse, called a lighthouse-keeper, lives, eats, and sleeps. His job is to see that the light is flashing properly. Ships usually bring him food and other supplies about once a month, and he can get in touch with the mainland by wireless or radio.

Most lighthouses also have foghorn signals to warn ships lost in the fog that they are near the coast. Many lighthouses are equipped with radar units that can be used both for airplane and ship guidance and detection.

The lantern in the top of the lighthouse is operated by oil, gas, or electricity. In most modern lighthouses electricity is used. Large light bulbs, of about 3,000 watts, flash their light beams into the night. The flashes are caused by a lens, shaped like a barrel, that revolves around the bulbs. Part of the lens is blackened. Each time the black part of the lens passes in front of the light, it cuts out the beam. When the clear part of the lens is in front, the beam flashes on again. The lens may be as large as 8 feet high and 6 feet wide. It may be turned on rollers or floated in a tank of mercury. An electric motor or weight is connected to a clock attached to the lens, causing it to revolve slowly.

Many lighthouses are operated automatically and therefore do not require a keeper. The light is automatically turned on at night and turned off during the day. Many lighted buoys are used along the coastline of the United States. These are made of metal and float on the water. The light is made by burning acetylene gas. The sun operates a thermostat valve in the buoy during the day, preventing the light from turning on. At night, when the sun goes down, the thermostat cools and turns the light on. Special lightships—ships that flash lights—also are used along foggy coastlines to mark off danger points in the water.

U.S. Coast Guard

The lighthouse keeper leads a lonely life on his tiny rock island open to the winds and the waves. Today, most lighthouses are automatic and need no keeper.

Lighthouses are thousands of years old. The most famous lighthouse was the one on the island of Pharos, near Alexandria, Egypt, built more than two thousand years ago. It was considered one of the seven wonders of the ancient world. Light was furnished by burning coal or wood in metal baskets hung from poles on top of the tower.

lighting

Lighting is a way of providing light to enable people to work, play, and do many other things at night. Until recently all light at night came from fire. Many different kinds of fuel were burned —candlewood, oils, waxes, fats, and illuminating gas.

Then, in 1879, Thomas Edison announced his invention of the incandescent filament electric lamp. The light of the Edison lamp came from electricity flowing through a small thread of carbon wire called a filament. The electricity caused the filament to become white-hot and give off light. To prevent the filament from burning, Edison sealed it inside a glass bulb and pumped the air out of the bulb.

Today electric light bulbs have filaments of tungsten, a metal which can be drawn into very thin wires, with a melting point of about 6,000 degrees on a Fahrenheit thermometer. Some bulbs are filled with argon and nitrogen gas to help the tungsten last longer. Sizes up to 60 watts last about 1,000 hours, and the larger sizes 750 hours. Modern bulbs give about twelve times as much light as Edison's original type for the same amount of electricity. Two feet of coiled tungsten wire are used and heated to about 5,000 degrees Fahrenheit when the bulb is lighted. Approximately two billion light bulbs are used in the United States each year.

Another type of light source is the fluorescent tube. In fluorescent tubes the electricity goes through a gas instead of a metal wire. This produces light with much less waste in the form of heat. (See the article on FLUORESCENCE.)

Electric lighting has many applications in many forms—indoors, on automobiles and streets, in baseball and amusement parks, and in outdoor advertisements, to name only a few.

LIGHTING PLANS

Indoors there are two major types of lighting. *General lighting* lights a whole room or section of a room. *Local lighting* is used to give extra light on objects that we want to look at closely or for long periods of time. It is uncomfortable to read for long periods of time with light only on the book to be read and the rest of the room in darkness; therefore reading requires general lighting, and local lighting if there is not enough general lighting.

The closer an object is to the source of light, the more light will fall on it. However, a floor or table lamp should be far enough away (behind and to one side) from you to light your entire work. To get more light use a larger light bulb (one with a greater number of watts marked on it).

All electric bulbs (including fluorescent tubes) should be shaded to keep the direct light from your eyes. Some lighting fixtures have a means for breaking up the light into many separate rays. This results in fewer or lighter shadows, since if something gets in the way of one ray there are still many others shining from the same fixture. In indirect lighting the light is directed first against a white ceiling or walls from which it is bounced back to all parts of the room. This pro-

duces excellent, almost shadowless lighting, but some light is wasted because it is absorbed by the room surfaces.

lightning

Lightning is a discharge of electricity through the air. It is a gigantic electric spark, often a mile or more in length, that passes between two clouds, or between a cloud and the ground.

The voltage of electricity in a flash or *bolt* of lightning often is as much as 100,000,000 volts, or about fifty thousand times more electricity than will kill a person. The electricity you use in your home is usually only 120 volts.

The electricity in a cloud is formed by small drops of water that are blown up into the air by warm air currents. The warm air currents give these drops of water a small charge of electricity. Some drops are charged with positive electricity, others with negative electricity. The drops rise into the air and form clouds. Some clouds are charged positively, others negatively.

Low-hanging clouds often can charge a house or a tree with electricity. This is done by INDUCTION, about which you can read in a separate article. A low-hanging cloud with positive electricity will charge an object on the ground with negative electricity. If the cloud has negative electricity, it will charge an object with positive electricity.

When the charges on the clouds or on the ground become powerful enough, a flash will leap from one cloud to another, or from one cloud to the ground. The

Westinghouse Electric Co.
There are millions of volts in the "fingers" of this wild flash of lightning.

lightning flash will go from the negative electricity to the positive electricity.

The passage of the lightning heats the air along its path and makes it expand (grow larger) suddenly. This starts large waves of air moving through the sky and makes the sound of *thunder*. When the lightning is several miles away, the waves of air will bounce off nearby hills and buildings, making echoes and rolling sounds of thunder.

LIGHTNING RODS

Lightning, like any other form of uncontrolled electricity, is dangerous. It can kill, destroy, and start fires. To protect buildings against lightning, a metal lightning rod is often placed at the top

of buildings. The rod is connected to pipes and wires that lead to the ground. In this way, if lightning should strike, it will be conducted through the rod to the ground without damage to the buildings.

Lightning rods usually have sharp points on their ends. This is so the electricity that is given them by induction can leak off into the air more easily. This prevents the electricity from building up and violently discharging as lightning.

Lightning may be a release of electricity either between two oppositely charged clouds or between opposite charges on the earth and in a cloud. The lightning hitting the barn is striking a lightning rod, which prevents damage by conducting the charge into the ground.

lignum vitae

The lignum vitae is a tree noted for its very hard, heavy, tough wood. It is the hardest wood known to man. This tree is also called the *guaiacum*. The wood of the tree is greenish-brown in color. It is useful for such things as mallets and bowling balls, and it is used by sculptors. An oily, gummy substance called resin can be collected from the tree. The resin, the bark, and shavings of the wood are used in medicines for rheumatism and some skin diseases. The lignum vitae grows in the West Indies and in the jungles of some northern parts of South America. It is sometimes grown in the United States, in Florida and California. The tree has a furrowed bark and many twisted branches. It is usually twenty to thirty feet high but sometimes grows higher. The leaves are smooth and oval in shape, and they grow in pairs. The flowers are a pale blue color.

lilac

The lilac is a shrub or tree with clusters of purple or white flowers growing on slender stalks. It grew originally in southwest Asia and in parts of Europe, and then it was brought to the United States. Now it grows well almost everywhere. The flowers of most kinds of lilac appear in May and June. The scent of lilac is a welcome sign of spring to many people. Because lilacs grow so well and are so beautiful, they are planted in gardens and parks all over the country.

There are many different kinds of lilacs. They may have clusters of single or double flowers, and they appear in all shades of purple. Lilac trees may grow as high as twelve feet. Each year many cities in the United States have a lilac festival at which many different kinds are shown.

Lille

Lille is an important manufacturing city in northern France. About 195,000 people live in Lille, which is about the same as the number of people living in Flint, Michigan. It is the capital of the department of Nord. (A department is like a large county.) Lille is especially noted for its textile mills, where cotton, wool, and other kinds of thread and cloth are produced. A special kind of thread, called *lisle,* was first produced in Lille (which used to be spelled Lisle). There are many other industries in Lille, and it is also an important trade center.

Lille is only a few miles from the Belgian frontier. The city was founded about nine hundred years ago, and because of its location near the border of France it has often been overrun by invading armies.

There are many interesting sights to be seen in Lille. The citadel, or fortress, was built almost three hundred years ago. There are churches four and five hundred years old, and a museum with a fine collection of old paintings.

LILLE, FRANCE. Population (1973 census) 194,948; with suburbs, 431,148. Capital of Nord Department, northern France.

lily

The lily is the name of a family of plants that includes both flowers and a few vegetables. As a flower it is very popular in gardens, and about sixty different kinds are grown. The flower of the lily is trumpet-shaped, round or hanging. It usually grows out of a bulb. This fleshy bulb can sometimes be eaten. The onion is a kind of lily bulb.

One of the most glamorous lilies is the tiger lily. It has a long orange tube with a speckled throat and grows to about three feet in height. The gold-banded or Japanese lily is a large white flower with a yellow band and red or purple spots. The white lily that we think of as the Easter lily comes from Bermuda, though originally it grew in Japan.

The lily has been known for thousands of years. It is thought of as a sign of purity, and we say "pure as a lily." The Greek poet Homer mentions the lily in his writings. One Greek legend says that lilies grew out of the milk of Hera, the chief goddess. The Bible also mentions the lily, although some think that not the white lily we know but a red flower is meant in the lines, from the Sermon on the Mount in the Gospel of Matthew, about the lilies of the field that "toil not, neither do they spin."

lily-of-the-valley

The lily-of-the-valley is a tiny and delicate member of the lily family. It grows well in many climates, in Asia, Europe, and the United States and Canada. Tiny white bell-shaped flowers grow on a slender stalk almost hidden by broad green leaves. The scent is delicate and appealing. The lily-of-the-valley is one of the signs of spring. It is often used in bridal bouquets or for decorations.

Lima

Lima is the capital and the largest city of Peru. It is on the Rímac River, and the name Lima is a changed form of Rímac. The Lima bean is also named for this river; it originated in the river valley. Lima is eight miles up the Rímac from the Pacific Ocean, and its seaport is Callao.

About 3,317,000 people live in Lima. There are American Indians, mestizos (mixtures of Spanish and Indian), Italians, and Chinese. Most of the people work in factories that make cotton and woolen cloth, and in factories that make sugar, cocaine, and marble products. Lima has a pleasant climate, with an average temperature of 66 degrees the year round. During the winter months there are heavy fogs and mists, but there is almost no rain.

Lima is considered one of the most beautiful cities in the world. The old buildings are of Spanish architecture, built of adobe (sun-dried brick). The walls are very thick to withstand the earthquakes that are common in the region. Among the beautiful historic buildings are the cathedral, the University of San Marcos, and many mansions and churches. During this century many modern buildings, spacious avenues and parks have been built.

Lima was founded in 1535 by Francisco Pizarro. He made it the capital of the Spanish colony of New Castile. Two years later the King of Spain gave it the name of City of Kings because its site was chosen on the feast of the Three Wise Men, or Kings. For years Lima was the principal stronghold of the Spaniards in South America. When the South American colonies began their movement for independence from Spain, Lima was the headquarters of the Spaniards. In 1821 General José de San Martín entered Lima and proclaimed the independence of Peru.

LIMA, PERU. Population (1973 census) 3,317,648. Capital of Peru and Peru Department. On Rimac River.

Lima bean, a bean that originated near Lima, Peru. See the article on BEAN.

lime

The lime is a juicy, egg-shaped, greenish fruit that belongs to the same family as the orange, lemon, and grapefruit. All of these are called CITRUS fruits, about which you can read in a separate article. The lime grows in parts of Asia where the climate is very warm, and also in Mexico, the West Indies, and southern Florida.

The lime tree is more easily hurt by frost than any of the other citrus fruits, and this makes it very difficult to raise. Lime growers in Florida often build small fires or put smudge pots in the lime-tree orchards to make certain that the blossoms, fruit and trees do not freeze.

The lime tree grows to be about fifteen feet high. It has shiny green leaves and tough, thorny branches. The tree bears beautiful white flowers.

The fruit is about two inches long. It has a thin green skin. The juice of the lime is used to make drinks and for flavoring. Sometimes it is frozen and canned. The lime contains healthful vitamins.

lime

Lime is a cream-white solid substance that is obtained when limestone is heated to a very high temperature. The separate article on limestone tells how limestone is made partly of a gas called *carbon dioxide,* that comes from the air. When limestone is heated strongly, carbon dioxide gas leaves it and goes back into the air. The solid substance that is left behind is lime. It is also called *quicklime.*

If lime is put into water, it makes the water boil. While this is happening, the lime combines with the water and *hydrated lime* or *slaked lime* is formed. Hydrated lime is a powder; slaked lime is a wet mass like putty. If hydrated lime is stored in airtight containers, it remains a powder and can easily be shipped. If slaked lime, or hydrated lime, is left in the open air, it takes water and carbon dioxide from the air. When this is done it becomes a hard substance just like the limestone from which it was made. The fact that it can harden like this gives lime its chief use—as *mortar.* Mortar is the tough rocklike material that holds bricks and plaster together in buildings and walls.

Lime has other uses. A weak clear solution of lime called *limewater* is used in medicine. A thick solution of slaked lime in water is called *milk of lime* or *whitewash,* and is used to whiten fences or to make the white lines on baseball and football fields. Lime is used to make bleaching powder for making laundry very white. It is also used in leather tanneries to remove the hair from animal hides. Lime is frequently added to soils that are too acid, thus producing better yields of crops.

limerick

A limerick is a short humorous verse. It is always five lines long. The first, second, and fifth lines rhyme, and the third and fourth lines, which are shorter, rhyme with each other. No one knows how the limerick got its name or where it first was started. One of the first men to write limericks that became well known and loved was Edward Lear. He published books of poems for children, and many of these poems were limericks. Here is one of Edward Lear's limericks:

There was an old man with a beard
Who said, "It is just as I feared:
Two owls and a hen
Four larks and a wren
Have all built their nests in my beard!"

limestone

Limestone is a kind of rock that is very much like chalk. In fact, chalk is one kind of limestone. Limestone is usually grayish or white, but it may have in it coloring matter that makes it yellow, brown, red, blue, or black. It is softer than most rocks. You can scratch it with a penny. Limestone is found in every part of the world.

Limestone is very useful. Certain kinds are tough enough to be used for building, especially in dry climates where there is not enough rain to make it crumble. The Egyptian pyramids were made of huge blocks of brownish limestone. When farmers have trouble with soil that is too acid, or "sour," for crops to grow in it, they spread powdered limestone on it. Limestone is an alkali and makes harmless the acid in the soil. (There are sep-

arate articles on ACIDS *and* ALKALIS.) Limestone helps make foundations for roads. It is also used in blast furnaces that heat the iron ore, and it helps to change iron to steel. When it is heated to a high temperature, it forms LIME, about which there is a separate article.

When you hear people complaining that it is hard to make soapsuds with certain kinds of water, they are usually talking about water that has limestone in it. Such water is called *hard water*, or *limestone water*.

Limestone is formed in two ways. Much of it comes from the hard parts, or skeletons, of billions of tiny animals called *foraminifera* and other sea animals with shells. They live in seas and lakes. Their shells and skeletons are made of a substance called *calcium carbonate*. When these shelled animals die, they sink to the bottom of the sea or lake, and the water presses down upon them. After millions of years, they form solid beds of limestone. At Dover, England, the famous chalk cliffs, which are more than three hundred feet high, are made of limestone.

Many rocks have in them a substance called *calcium*. This substance can be dissolved out of the rock by rain water. Rain water has dissolved in it a gas that comes from the air and is called *carbon dioxide*. In the water, the carbon dioxide gas and the dissolved calcium form *calcium carbonate*. Sea shells, eggshells, and skeletons of foraminifera are formed of this substance. If water with calcium carbonate in it is suddenly chilled, it can no longer hold its calcium carbonate. Then the substance sinks to the bottom. After millions of years, it too, like the tiny skeletons, becomes hardened into limestone.

Sometimes, when hot springs flow out of the earth, they leave behind them a very soft, flaky limestone that is called *Travertine* or *tufa*. The iciclelike stones that hang down from the roofs and stick up from the floors of caves are made of limestone that was dissolved in dripping water.

Under continued heat and pressure within the earth's crust, limestone sometimes changes to marble. Limestone is composed chiefly of the mineral *calcite*.

limitations, statute of

A statute of limitations is a law that says a person may not be sued for a debt, or prosecuted for an offense, after a certain number of years have passed. If there were no statutes of limitations, a person might be arrested for something that happened so long ago he could no longer remember the circumstances and know how to defend himself. A statute of limitations may set any limit the lawmakers wish. Sometimes the period is only one year and sometimes it is as much as twenty years. For most debts, it is five to seven years. There is no statute of limitations on serious crimes, such as murder. If a legal action is begun before the time limit has expired, it may be carried on beyond the end of the time limit.

limpet

The limpet is a small mollusc or shellfish that is related to the snail. Limpets live in the ocean. They are found along the shores of North America and on every other seacoast in the world except the very cold regions close to the North and South Poles.

Like the snail, the limpet has only one shell, on the upper side of its body. The shell is cone-shaped; usually it is rounded at the bottom and rises to a point in the center. The limpet has a large flat organ called a "foot," which it uses for clinging to rocks and for moving about. On the head of the limpet are two feelers, or tentacles.

Limpets eat plants that grow in the sea, such as seaweeds. Fishermen use limpets as bait. Certain kinds of limpet are used as food in Europe.

Lincoln

Lincoln, located in southeastern Nebraska, is the second-largest city in Nebraska, and is the state capital.

Lincoln was first settled in 1859. Many of the first settlers came from Lancaster, Pennsylvania, and the town was originally called Lancaster. When Nebraska became a state, in 1867, the name of the new capital was changed to honor President Abraham Lincoln.

Lincoln is noted for its beautiful, modern state capitol building. This building was completed in 1934. It has a great tower 400 feet high that can be seen from a distance of several miles. Lincoln is an important trade center, and many bus lines, highways and railroads run through the city. There are three airports. The people of the city work in food-packing houses, and manufacture farm machinery, machine parts, and many other things.

There are several colleges in the city, including the University of Nebraska and Nebraska Wesleyan University. There is the State Historical Society Museum, and there are many lovely parks. Every year people from all over the state go to Lincoln for the Nebraska State Fair.

LINCOLN, NEBRASKA. Population (1970 census) 149,518. Capital of Nebraska. County seat of Lancaster County. Settled in 1859.

Abraham Lincoln

Abraham Lincoln, the sixteenth President of the United States, stands in world history as one of the greatest men who ever lived. He took office on March 4, 1861, and served until his assassination on April 14, 1865, one month and ten days after his second inauguration. His honesty and humanity have earned him the respect and affection of millions of people since his time. Early in life he won the nickname of "Honest Abe," and as a President he became known as the "Great Emancipator," because of the part he played in setting free millions of Negroes who were slaves in the southern states of the United States before he took office.

Abraham Lincoln was the tallest President the country ever had. He was six feet four in his stocking feet, and his arms and legs were unusually long. His hands and feet were extremely large, and he was a rangy, thin man with deep, kindly eyes, and a firm chin. His face was touched with a sadness of expression that was accentuated by his hollow cheeks and dark beard.

As an orator, Lincoln had the power to hold his hearers spellbound. His language was both simple and forceful. He wrote some of history's greatest English prose for his speeches and other state papers. He also had such a genius for witty remarks and joke-telling that people still chuckle over some of the things he said.

HIS EARLY YEARS

Abraham Lincoln was born on February 12, 1809, in a log cabin on his father's farm in Kentucky. The cabin is now a national shrine.

That part of Kentucky is now part of Larue County; at the time of Lincoln's birth it was backwoods country. His father, Thomas Lincoln, was a farmer, and very poor. He provided his family with only the barest necessities. Lincoln's mother, Nancy Hanks Lincoln, was a frail, gentle, religious woman who lacked the strength necessary for the rough frontier life she led.

When young Lincoln was seven, his family moved to Indiana, and for the first winter there they lived in a three-sided shed, with only a buffalo skin hung over the open side to keep out the winter winds. The next year Lincoln's mother died, and later a log cabin was built to house the family.

Lincoln taught himself to read and write and to do simple arithmetic. He had no pencils or paper, but used a wooden shovel as a slate and charcoal for chalk. Later, when he was able to obtain paper, he wrote his compositions with a pen made from a wild turkey feather and ink made of blackberry roots.

He studied by the light of the fire in the evening, after working hard all day helping his father in the fields. He also did odd jobs for neighboring farmers, but still found time to walk miles for books. He commented once that he had "read through every book that he had heard of within a circuit of fifty miles."

He was popular among his neighbors because he was good company and an excellent speaker and storyteller. It was partly his gifts as a speaker and partly his sense of justice that made him decide to study law. This was difficult because he had neither law books nor money to buy them. Often he walked 12 miles to the

office of a lawyer friend to read a law book.

By the time he was 19, Abe Lincoln was a faster runner and a better wrestler than any other man or boy in the region. His strength and physical endurance proved useful to him when the family moved to Illinois, in 1830. He and his father built another log cabin, and young Lincoln split enough rails to make a fence around the entire ten-acre plot on which the cabin stood. On another occasion he paid a woman for making him a pair of trousers by splitting fourteen hundred rails for her. It is easy to understand why one of his nicknames was the "Rail Splitter."

Among the many other odd jobs that Lincoln did was to sail a flatboat down the Mississippi River to New Orleans with a load of vegetables and bacon. In New Orleans he saw chained Negro slaves sold on the auction block to the highest bidder. The sight touched his heart, and he never forgot it.

After his return from New Orleans, Lincoln settled in New Salem, Illinois. For a time he worked as a clerk in a store. There is a story that he won the nickname of "Honest Abe" when he walked two miles to repay a customer six cents because he had made an error in giving the man his change.

Business was not good in the store and Abe had plenty of chance to keep up his studies. After a year the business failed, and at the age of 22 Lincoln was out of a job. At this time, the Black Hawk War was going on, and a troop of volunteers from New Salem chose him to serve as they got into action. (There is a separate article about the BLACK HAWK WAR.)

THE START OF HIS POLITICAL CAREER

Lincoln decided to enter politics in the spring of 1832 and announced that he would be a candidate for the Illinois legislature. By this time he was well-known in his own part of the state. He received a great many votes, but they were not enough to elect him.

The next year he went into business with a man named Berry, and the partners bought three small stores in New Salem. The business failed, leaving them with a debt of $1,200. When Berry died, Lincoln assumed the debt and eventually paid it off. This was extremely difficult, and it was fifteen years before the last dollar was paid. The determination to pay this debt was another indication of Lincoln's honesty, because he could legally have declared himself bankrupt, and in that case would not have had to pay anything.

Shortly after this unfortunate investment, he found a job as an assistant surveyor of the county. Lincoln also held the position of postmaster at this time, but the mails were so light that he laughingly said that he "kept his office under his hat." He could tuck the few letters in his pocket, and deliver them personally with very little trouble.

Lincoln ran again for the state legislature in 1834, and this time he was elected. During his first term in the legislature he met Stephen A. Douglas. It was the beginning of a rivalry between the two men that lasted for years.

At the same time Lincoln became a lawyer and moved to Springfield, the state capital. He served in the legislature for four consecutive terms. During those eight years he began to show signs of his greatness. His law practice grew at the same time, and by 1842 he was known throughout Illinois. He was a familiar sight as he rode from courthouse to courthouse with the district judge.

In 1842, Abraham Lincoln married Mary Todd. Both Stephen A. Douglas and Lincoln had courted the attractive young woman from Kentucky, and Lincoln won.

A year later, Lincoln entered another partnership. This time it was a law partnership, with a man named William Herndon. Lincoln took only cases that he believed to be honest and fair. There is a story that he dropped a case while testimony was being given in court because he suddenly realized that his client was in the wrong.

Lincoln had a habit of illustrating his points with stories that not only made his case clear but also spread good humor in the courtroom. It was not long before he became one of the best known and most competent lawyers in Illinois.

The people of Illinois elected Lincoln to the House of Representatives in Washington in 1846, but after serving one term he was not re-elected.

In 1856 the Republican Party was started. The first Republican National Convention was held in Philadelphia in that year, and although Lincoln was mentioned as a possible candidate for the vice-presidency, he was not nominated. Two years later Lincoln ran for the United States Senate. In the campaign he carried on a series of debates with his Democratic opponent, Stephen A. Douglas, over the question of slavery in the new territories of Kansas and Nebraska. Douglas believed that when these two territories became states, each should have the right to decide for itself whether it would be a free state or a slave state. Lincoln disagreed with this; he thought that the United States government should decide the question before admitting the new states. At one of these debates Lincoln made one of the many statements that we remember him for. He said, "A house divided against itself cannot stand. I believe that this government cannot endure permanently half slave and half free." Although Lincoln lost the election, these Lincoln-Douglas debates made him known throughout the country.

Two years later, in 1860, Lincoln's fame and reputation won him the Republican nomination for President, and he was elected. But he faced an extremely difficult task. Great bitterness over the question of slavery had developed between the North and South, and even before Lincoln took office, seven southern states had left the Union.

Lincoln's first inaugural address made his position clear. He said, "The Union of these States (United States) is perpetual. No State upon its own mere motion can lawfully get out of the Union." When the Civil War started just a little more than a month later, on April 12, 1861, Lincoln emphasized the fact that

the issue was the preservation of the Union—not slavery. The fact that slavery was a second great issue became clear to Lincoln within the next year.

The hardships, tragedy, and bitterness of the war touched Lincoln closely. He shared the suffering of those who were injured and of those who lost husbands, sons, and brothers. The death of his own small son, Willie, in the darkest of the war years, added to the sympathy and grief he felt for the others whom the war had hurt. He once said, "I feel as though I shall never be glad again."

The Union forces suffered many severe defeats, and the outlook was grim when Lincoln issued his famous Emancipation Proclamation on January 1, 1863. Four million slaves became free men on that day, but the war dragged on.

Later that same year Lincoln spoke at the dedication of a national cemetery at

Springfield, Ill., Chamber of Commerce

Lincoln's tomb and monument are in Oak Ridge Cemetery in Springfield. Members of his family also are buried there.

Gettysburg, at which he made his justly famous Gettysburg Address. The words of that speech, beginning "Fourscore and seven years ago . . . ," have been enshrined in the hearts of Americans ever since.

The tide turned in favor of the North in 1863, and Lincoln's faith in General Ulysses S. Grant was justified. Victory followed victory, and the people expressed their love and trust of Lincoln by electing him in 1864 for a second term as President. In his second inaugural address Lincoln urged a lenient attitude towards the South, again in words that have been long remembered: "With malice towards none, with charity for all . . . let us strive on to finish up the work we are in; bind up the nation's wounds . . ."

In the spring of 1865, the terrible war was over, and Lee surrendered to Grant at Appomattox Courthouse in Virginia. Lincoln and his cabinet knelt and gave thanks to God when news of the surrender reached Washington. This was on April 3, 1865, and eleven days later, on April 14, Lincoln's last official action was to sign a pardon for a soldier sentenced to death for desertion.

That night President and Mrs. Lincoln

attended the Ford Theater in Washington to see the play *Our American Cousin.* It was a festive occasion. The war was over, everyone was celebrating the coming of peace, and the presidential box was gaily decorated with flags. As everyone's attention was focused upon the action of the play, a shot rang out, at twenty minutes past ten, and Lincoln slumped forward in his seat, mortally wounded. His assassin, John Wilkes Booth, escaped in the confusion, but was pursued and killed later as he tried to evade capture. The stricken President was taken to a house across the street, and although doctors did everything in their power to save him, he never regained consciousness. All Washington prayed for him throughout the terrible night, and he died the next morning, surrounded by his devoted friends. Among them was his Secretary of War, Edwin M. Stanton, who whispered to the others at the bedside, "Now he belongs to the ages."

The entire nation mourned Lincoln's death and his body was taken reverently to Philadelphia, New York, Chicago, and other northern cities so that a grieving people might pay him the tribute of funeral honors. The sad procession finally reached Springfield, Illinois, where Lincoln's body was buried, and where a monument to the Great Emancipator stands today. Lincoln was just 56 years old when he died.

MRS. ABRAHAM LINCOLN

Mrs. Mary Todd Lincoln was born in Lexington, Kentucky, in 1818. She was the daughter of a pioneer and frontiersman, Robert Smith Todd, and married Abraham Lincoln on November 4, 1842. The Lincolns had four sons, only two of whom lived past childhood. Mrs. Lincoln died in 1882. The Lincoln's oldest son was Robert Todd Lincoln. He served as Secretary of War under Presidents Garfield and Arthur, and was president of the Pullman Company. At his death in 1926 he left an important collection of his father's papers to the Library of Congress with instructions that they were not to be opened until twenty-one years after his death. The papers were opened in 1947 and revealed many important facts about the life of the great President.

THE LINCOLN MEMORIAL

The Lincoln Memorial in Potomac Park, Washington, D.C., is one of the unforgettable sights of the capital. A great statue of Lincoln seated in an armchair 12½ feet high is the central point of interest. Over all, the statue is 19 feet high, and it is made of Georgia white marble. Daniel Chester French designed and modeled this majestic statue, and it has held visitors spellbound by its beauty since its unveiling in 1922. The statue is placed so that the seated figure of Lincoln faces the Capitol and the Washington Monument.

The Lincoln Memorial contains three chambers, each of them with a memorial tribute to him. In addition to the great statue of Lincoln in the giant armchair, there is an inscription of the Gettysburg Address on one wall and of the Second Inaugural Address on another. Outside the Memorial is a reflecting pool, almost

National Park Service

The Lincoln Memorial in Washington, D.C., is the nation's way of honoring one of its greatest men and most beloved leaders.

a third of a mile long, and at its end is another pool with a huge fountain of two hundred sprays.

Thousands of people visit the Lincoln Memorial each year. It is a sight of imposing majesty, set upon a terrace that makes it tower over the surrounding land.

Lincoln Highway

The Lincoln Highway is a road stretching across the United States from New York on the Atlantic Ocean to San Francisco on the Pacific Ocean. It goes through the most thickly settled parts of the eastern and central United States and some of the most beautiful parts of the West.

Before 1912 there was no continuous road across the United States. In that year a small group of men in the automobile industry started to work on a plan to build such a road. Through their efforts the governments of towns and states, as well as the Federal government, became interested in the plan and supported it. The route was laid out, state and national funds were given, and fifteen years later, in 1927, the road was ready for use. Since that time many changes have been made to improve the road and shorten its distance.

Today the Lincoln Highway is known as U.S. 30 from Philadelphia to Salt Lake City and as either U.S. 40 or U.S. 50 from there to San Francisco. In many places, especially in New Jersey and Pennsylvania, new turnpikes have taken much of the traffic away from it, but it is still one of the backbones of the road system of the United States.

Lind, Jenny

Jenny Lind was one of the greatest singers of all time. She was born in Stockholm, Sweden, in 1820, and started training for the stage when she was still a child. Her teachers soon discovered her singing voice, and she took singing lessons as well. She was a rare combination of a fine actress, excellent singer, and beautiful woman, and she met with tremendous success on her tours. P. T. Barnum, the great

circus manager and showman, sent her on a triumphant tour through the United States in 1850. She was called "the Swedish nightingale." She was a generous, warm person, and was greatly loved by those who knew her. She died in 1887.

Lindbergh, Charles A.

Charles Augustus Lindbergh was an American aviator who was the first man to fly solo nonstop across the Atlantic Ocean. He was born in Detroit, Michigan, in 1902, but spent his boyhood in Little Falls, Minnesota, from which state his father was a Congressman. In 1927, when he was 25 years old, he flew alone in his plane, *The Spirit of St. Louis,* from New York to Paris. The trip covered 3,600 miles and took 33½ hours. He was given a hero's welcome in Paris and London, and later in New York and other American cities.

Lindbergh was made a colonel and toured Latin American countries for the United States. While in Mexico he met Anne Morrow, whom he married. She was the daughter of the American ambassador to Mexico, Dwight Morrow. Together they made trips to many parts of the world.

In 1932 the world was shocked when the Lindberghs' two-year-old baby, Charles, Jr., was kidnapped. The Lindberghs paid the $50,000 ransom that the kidnappers demanded, but their baby was found dead. After a dramatic trial, a New York carpenter named Bruno Hauptmann was found guilty of the crime, sentenced to death, and executed.

After this the Lindberghs went to live in England. Before World War II, Charles Lindbergh made several statements and speeches that advised the American people not to fear the Nazi government of Germany and not to be interested in European quarrels. This angered the United States government and Lindbergh resigned his commission in the Army Air Force. When the United States entered World War II, Lindbergh worked as an adviser to the United States government, and also flew as a technical observer. More than once he fought against Japanese planes. In 1953 President Eisenhower made him a brigadier general in the Air Force. Lindbergh died in 1974.

Charles Lindbergh was the author of *We* and *The Spirit of St. Louis,* books that tell about his history-making flight. He wife, Anne Morrow Lindbergh, has written several books, including *North to the Orient; Listen, the Wind; Wave of the Future;* and *A Gift from the Sea,* a bestseller that was a poem in prose.

linden, a tree that is also called basswood. See the article on BASSWOOD in another volume of this encyclopedia.

Lindsay, Vachel

Nicholas Vachel Lindsay was an American poet. He was born in Springfield, Illinois, in 1879. He became a

wanderer and went through many states, singing and reciting his poetry to anyone who would listen. Sometimes he would stop long enough to give a lecture in return for some food and a place to sleep.

Lindsay wrote poems of different kinds. Some, such as "Abraham Lincoln Walks at Midnight," were about America's heroes. Some were about the poverty and despair in which so many Americans were forced to live. Many, such as "The Congo," are full of unforgettable power and rhythm. A number of books of Lindsay's poetry have been published. He died in 1931.

linen

Linen is a fine cloth made of thread woven from the fiber of the flax plant. Linen was one of the first cloths made by ancient man. It is mentioned frequently in the Bible. The Egyptians and Hebrews used linen four thousand years ago. In the great Greek civilization linen was used for the clothing of the very rich. Flanders, which is now part of Belgium, became famous for its linen nine hundred years ago. The manufacture of Irish linen began as early as the year 1200. Irish linen is still considered among the finest in the world. The United States has never been an important linen-making country because the best linen yarn is made by hand and the high wages paid to American workers make its manufacture by hand unprofitable. Most of the linen used in the United States is imported from Great Britain and Europe.

Flax for the making of linen was brought to the New World by the first settlers. Later the colonists grew their own flax and wove their own linen. Linen was for many years the fabric most often used in the United States for men's shirts and men's and women's underwear. For this reason these garments are still often called "linen," although few of them are made of linen any more. The invention of the cotton gin led to the wide use of the cheaper cotton fabrics. Nowadays fine linen is used principally for tablecloths and napkins, women's dresses, and handkerchiefs.

There are many heavier kinds of linen, used for various purposes. Among them are: canvas, used in making tents and such things; sailcloth; duck, used for sports clothes; and ticking, used for covering mattresses and pillows. The fine linens include: lace; lawn, the filmy material used in women's blouses and children's clothing; Jacquard, a fine linen with a pattern woven into it; and damask, a heavier patterned linen used for fine tablecloths.

Linnaeus

Linnaeus was a Swedish scientist who lived about 250 years ago. He was born in 1707, and his name was originally Karl von Linné. He is especially famous for his classification of living things, that is, the arranging of plants and animals in different groups. Plants or animals that are alike are

grouped together.

Linnaeus was the first to use in all his work the system of giving every living thing a scientific name, made up of two Latin words. Linnaeus himself classified and named thousands of living things, and scientists have continued to name and classify plants and animals by a method developed from Linnaeus' system. When a scientist in one country writes about a plant, using its Latin names, scientists everywhere else in the world know what he means, even if they cannot read his native language.

Linnaeus died in 1778.

linnet

The linnet is a small bird that has a very sweet song. It sings happily, even in a cage, and for that reason many people like to keep it as a pet. The linnet is a member of the finch family. It is found in the northern parts of Europe and Asia. It is about six inches long and has a forked tail and a short pointed bill. Its wings are quite long.

Linnets are usually brown with markings of grayish white, but in the spring, when the birds mate, the breast and the crown of the male linnet turn a bright crimson color.

The linnet builds its nest in trees or bushes. The nest is very neatly made of twigs and grass, lined with something soft, such as hair or wool. The linnet lays four or five eggs, which are pale bluish-white with dark spots. The linnet eats oily seeds, such as the seed of the flax plant, from which linen cloth is made, and this is how the linnet got its name. In the United States the name linnet is sometimes given to other members of the finch family.

linoleum

Linoleum is a smooth, waterproof covering for floors, walls, tabletops, and many other flat surfaces. It is made from a mixture of linseed oil, powdered cork, and resin, spread on a backing of the coarse cloth called *burlap*.

HOW IT IS MADE

The original formula for linoleum was made up by Frederick Walton in Yorkshire, England, in the 1860s, and the linoleum we use today is not much different from Walton's first product. Here is how it is made: Raw linseed oil, which comes from the plant called flax, is purified in a refining tank, and then mixed with air in an agitator to produce a rubbery film called *linoleum cement*. The linoleum cement goes to a steam kettle, where gums and resins are added to make it tough and waterproof. Then the cement is aged for several weeks in storage bins to make it even tougher and doughlike. After this aging, the linoleum cement goes to a mixer, where ground cork, wood flour, and a pigment to color it are added. Then this mixture is dropped onto a strip of burlap and is sent to a machine called a *calender*, which has large rollers to press the cement and burlap together and make it the right thickness. It is finally dried in an oven, inspected, and tested.

Linoleum is sold in several forms. Plain linoleum comes in one solid color. Printed linoleum has gone through a printing press and received a design in oil paints. Inlaid linoleum is made up of separate pieces, usually square blocks, of different-colored linoleum pressed together onto the burlap. Linoleum tiles have a raised surface like tiles and are without burlap backing.

Most linoleum is one-eighth inch thick, but some kinds are only half that thick. Double-thickness linoleum is called "battleship linoleum" because it was first used to cover the decks of battleships.

Linotype, a typesetting machine. See the article on PRINTING.

linseed oil, an oil made from the seed of the flax plant. See the article on FLAX.

lion

The lion is one of the largest and fiercest members of the cat family. Because of its strength, its cleverness at stalking prey, its terrifying roar, and its royal-looking head and mane, it is called "the king of beasts," though the tiger is even greater in size and fierceness.

Male lions grow to be as tall as four feet, and up to ten feet in length. The female is usually a foot shorter. Large lions may weigh as much as 500 pounds. The lion has a coat of short hair that is usually tawny (yellowish-brown), to blend with the desert country in which it lives, but sometimes is reddish or nearly black.

The tail is sometimes three feet long and ends in a tuft of bushy hair. The male lion has a mane, or large brush of hair, growing about its neck. This mane does not appear until the lion is about three years old. The lioness (female) never has it.

Lions are good hunters. They eat whatever game is easy to find. Usually they hunt at night. They know the habits of their prey and can either stalk them silently or lie in wait at their favorite feeding or drinking places. Lions will attack men, but not often. Usually it is the old or weak lion that will attack humans, because it is no longer able to capture the faster animals.

The lion's front legs are tremendously strong and the claws are huge and sharp. Small animals can be killed by a single blow from one of the lion's paws. To catch and kill a larger animal, the lion may grab the animal's throat in its teeth, and break its neck. Usually the lion carries its prey away to a quiet place to eat. If other lions have helped in the hunt, they join in eating first. Then the young lions and the lionesses get their share of what is left.

Lions usually mate for life, after the male has fought off other contestants for the lioness of its choice. They seldom have more than two young, called cubs or whelps, at a time. The cubs are born with their eyes open. Their fur may be spotted or dimly striped. Both parents care for the young until they are able to shift for themselves. Lions are among the easiest animals to keep in captivity, because they breed easily. The cubs are appealing and playful, but they soon become dangerous to handle.

Lions have been known since the earliest days of man's history. In prehistoric

times they roamed over all of southern Europe, Germany, France, and the British Isles.

In modern times lions are found in much of Africa and in parts of Asia, though in Asia most of them have been wiped out by tigers. In 1954 it was estimated that there were only 50 to 100 lions left in India, and the Indian government ordered tiger hunts organized to try to save the lions.

The lion has long been one of the favorite game animals of hunters, because it is one of the most challenging and dangerous. The usual method is to drive the lion into the open and shoot it as it charges the hunter, but one shot seldom kills a lion and it becomes more ferocious after it has been hit.

The lion is mentioned in the Bible more often than any other animal. There are many fables about lions, such as the one about the Roman slave Androcles who removed a thorn from a lion's paw and later was rewarded for his kindness when the animal refused to attack him in the Roman arena. The lion is the emblem of Great Britain and appears on the British flag. It is also used as a symbol of courage, though some people say that the lion is not as brave as it has been made out to be.

Lions Clubs

The Lions Clubs are clubs of business and professional men. Their purpose is to help and improve their towns and cities. There are Lions Clubs in many cities of the United States and in 117 other countries of the world.

The first Lions Clubs were started in the United States in the year 1917. These clubs joined together to form the International Association of Lions Clubs. The organization has grown steadily in the years since then. In 1962 there were 16,500 clubs, with about 660,000 members. The clubs send representatives to an international meeting held every year. At this meeting officers for the whole organization are elected. In each district, members from different clubs meet to choose the governor, or head, of that district.

The members of the Lions Clubs do many kinds of useful work. They help to improve business conditions in their communities, and they support many worthwhile community activities. Among these activities is scouting, and the Lions support many Boy Scout and Girl Scout troops all over the world.

Lippi

Lippi was the name of two great artists who lived in Florence, Italy, between the years 1400 and 1500. Filippo Lippi, born about 1406, was known as Fra Lippo Lippi. *Fra* means "brother," and Lippo Lippi was so called because he was a monk or *fra*. He painted religious subjects. He had great skill in painting drapery and clothing. Today many of his famous paintings can be seen in art museums of London, Paris, Berlin, Florence, Rome, and New York. He died in 1469.

Filippino Lippi was the son of Filippo. He was born in 1457, and he too was a great artist. Like his father he painted re-

ligious subjects. His paintings can be seen in art museums throughout Europe. Filippino Lippi died in 1504.

lip reading, a method used by deaf persons to understand speech: see the article on DEAFNESS.

Lipton, Thomas J.

Thomas Johnston Lipton was a British merchant who started out with one small grocery store and gradually built up a huge chain of stores, farms, and factories.

Thomas Lipton was born in 1850, in Glasgow, Scotland, and he opened his first store there in 1871. His business was very successful, and soon he had many more stores. Lipton bought tea plantations in Ceylon and started the Lipton Tea Company. He made a great fortune, and he used much of his money to help other people. The British king honored him by giving him the title of baronet.

Lipton was also interested in yacht racing. He wanted very much to win the America's Cup, which is a prize in international yacht racing, and he spent a huge amount of money for ships. He entered ships in the race five times. But he was not so successful in sports as he was in business, and he lost every time. He was, however, much admired for his sportsmanship and good humor in accepting defeat even when he wanted so much to win.

Sir Thomas Lipton died in 1931.

liquid

A liquid is one of the three kinds of matter. The other two are gas and solid.

A liquid such as water differs from a solid such as ice in that a liquid does not have any definite shape, while a solid does. A liquid will take the shape of whatever container it is poured into.

However, a liquid does have a definite size. No matter what kind of container it is poured into, it will always take up the same amount of space. This is what makes a liquid different from a gas. A gas does not have any definite size.

A liquid can be changed into a solid by cooling it below a certain temperature, called its *freezing point*. A liquid can be changed into a gas by heating it above a certain temperature, called its *boiling point*. When water is heated above its boiling point, it increases in size. If the entire liquid is boiled away into a gas, it will become 1,700 times larger than it originally was. This means that the gas can fill a space 1,700 times larger than the space originally filled by the liquid.

USES OF LIQUIDS

There are many different liquids, and these have many different uses. The most common liquid is water, which we use to wash ourselves and to quench our thirst. Alcohol is another common liquid, used in medicines, in certain drinks, and in many other products. Turpentine is a liquid often used in paints. Gasoline is a liquid used as a fuel to run automobiles, trucks, and airplanes. Carbon tetrachloride is a liquid used as a cleaning fluid and to help put out fires. Ether is a liquid made from alcohol and is used as an anesthetic to put people to sleep during surgical operations.

Not all liquids act in the same way. Ether will change into a gas at only 34 degrees on the Centigrade scale, while water must be heated to 100 degrees Centigrade (which is 212 degrees on the Fahrenheit thermometer). Gasoline can be easily set on fire, while water will put out a flame. Oil is often put on metal parts to keep them from rusting, while water causes metals to rust.

SOLUTIONS

Liquids are often mixed with gases, solids, and other liquids to form *solutions*. If a solid, such as a lump of sugar, is placed in water, it will separate or *dissolve* into smaller pieces. After a while you will no longer be able to see any of the pieces. They will have dissolved into even smaller pieces, called *molecules*.

All matter is made up of molecules separated by air spaces. The molecules of a solid are closer together than the molecules of a liquid, and the molecules of a liquid are closer together than the molecules of a gas. In a solution of a solid in a liquid, the molecules of the solid go into the spaces between the molecules of the liquid. This is called *diffusion*. It also explains how a gas such as carbon dioxide can be dissolved in water to make the "soda water" used in many drinks.

Liquids can be dissolved in other liquids. Alcohol can be dissolved in water. Liquids that can be dissolved in each other to form solutions are called *miscible*. When one liquid cannot be dissolved in another, the two liquids are *immiscible*. Ether will not dissolve in water but will form a layer on top and on the bottom; ether and water, therefore, are immiscible.

EVAPORATION

The molecules of a liquid are always moving about. They move more slowly than the molecules of a gas, but faster than the molecules of a solid. As they move about, these liquid molecules strike one another and bounce away. Sometimes they strike so hard that they bounce off into the air. This is called *evaporation*, and the liquid molecules become molecules of a moist gas or *vapor*.

A liquid is constantly evaporating. The speed of evaporation depends on how large the surface of the liquid is, the temperature of the liquid, and the speed of the air around it. The larger the surface of the liquid, the more molecules there will be to go off into the air, and the greater the evaporation. A higher temperature speeds up the movement of the molecules in the liquid. This causes them to strike one another harder so that more of them bounce off into the air. Air blowing over a liquid also speeds up the molecules. In drying wet clothes, it is most effective to spread them out on a line in a place where the sun and the wind will be most likely to strike them. This will speed up the evaporation and dry the clothes more rapidly.

OTHER PROPERTIES OF LIQUIDS

The molecules of a liquid are constantly attracting or pulling on one another. This is called *cohesion*. The cohesion between the molecules on the surface of the liquids as well as the cohesion

between the surface molecules and the molecules inside the liquid causes a kind of membrane or skin to form on the surface of the liquid. This is called *surface tension*. The surface of the liquid acts as though it were being pulled from both sides as well as from underneath. The surface membrane often is so strong that insects can walk on it and a steel needle will float on it.

The molecules of a liquid not only cohere, they also attach themselves or *adhere* to molecules of other substances. The water on your body after you have taken a bath is an example of adhesion. However, liquids do not adhere to all solids. Water will not adhere to fat or wax.

liquid air

Liquid air is a pale blue liquid made by cooling air to about 197 degrees below zero on the Centigrade scale. If the temperature of liquid air is then raised, the liquid will boil and change back into the gas we call air.

Liquid air is used to make pure oxygen, nitrogen, and argon. These gases are part of the air we breathe, and therefore, in their liquid form, are also part of liquid air. Liquid oxygen boils at 183 degrees below zero, liquid nitrogen at 196 degrees below zero, and liquid argon at 185 degrees below zero.

If liquid air is boiled, the nitrogen will boil off first, then the argon, and finally the oxygen. Each of these can be separated from the others and collected as a gas in large steel tanks.

The process for making liquid air was first discovered by two German-born English engineers, Sir William Siemens and his brother Frederick, about a hundred years ago. Large-scale production of liquid air was not begun until about fifty years ago.

The process for making liquid air depends on two important facts. The first one is that when a gas is compressed (is pressed into a small space), it gets hot. The second one is that when a gas expands (enters a large space), it gets cold. This last fact is known as the *Joule-Thomson* effect, named after two English scientists, James Prescott Joule and William Thomson (Lord Kelvin), who discovered it about a hundred years ago.

The process for making liquid air on a large scale is called the Linde process, named after a German scientist, Karl R. von Linde. The air first is cleaned, and the dust, water and carbon dioxide gas are removed. Then it is compressed by a pump. The pressure on the air usually is about 3,000 pounds per square inch. The air is pumped through a metal tube, or cooling coil, where the heat caused by compression is removed from the air by cold water flowing over the tube.

The air then flows out of the tube, through a narrow opening, into a closed chamber. There it expands and cools some more. The cold air then flows back to the pump, where it is again compressed and the entire process repeated. This goes on until the air is so cold that it changes into a liquid. It is collected in special insulating bottles called Dewar or "Thermos" bottles, invented by Sir James Dewar, a Scottish scientist, about 50 years ago. (See the article on INSULATION.)

Lisbon

Lisbon is the capital and largest city of Portugal. It is in the southwestern part of the country, on the banks of the Tagus River, about ten miles from the Atlantic Ocean. The city spreads out over a considerable area, and almost a million people live there.

Lisbon is a beautiful city, built partly on the shores of the Tagus River, and partly on seven hills that overlook the port. Many different things are manufactured in Lisbon. The city is an important seaport, with a fine large harbor along the Tagus River, which is about six miles wide at this point. There are several railroads.

A notable attraction in Lisbon is the 18-mile-long aqueduct that brings in the city's water supply. It is the most remarkable example of bridge architecture in the world, according to many experts. Other interesting structures in the city are the custom house, the Monastery of the Jerónimos, with its marble cupola, the National Library, and the royal palaces, a reminder of the days before Portugal became a republic. The University of Lisbon was founded in 1910.

Near the city is a famous resort town, Estoril. It is about twelve miles west of Lisbon, on the Portuguese Riviera. Estoril is known for its colony of exiled European royalty. At various times there have been former kings of Denmark, Italy, Hungary, Rumania, and Austria there. Many children and relatives of former kings and queens have permanent homes in Estoril. The climate is mild and pleasant, with much sunshine.

LISBON IN THE PAST

Lisbon is a very old city. It was once the capital of ancient Lusitania. At that time it was called *Olisipo*.

When the early Romans first invaded Portugal, Olisipo (Lisbon) was a flourishing city. This was in the early days of Christianity. Later the Moors captured most of Spain and Portugal, and they called Lisbon *Lishbuna*, which is like *Lisboa*, its present Portuguese name. It has been the capital of modern Portugal since 1422. In 1755 much of the city was destroyed by an earthquake.

During World War II, Lisbon was the most important port of entry to Europe, because Portugal was neutral. The city was filled with people of all nationalities, and spies from the various warring countries made Lisbon a city of international intrigue and espionage.

LISBON, PORTUGAL. Population (1973 census) 830,600; with suburbs, 962,761. Capital and chief seaport.

Lister, Joseph

Joseph Lister was an English surgeon who lived about a hundred years ago.

He was the first man to use antiseptics to prevent infection from setting in after a surgical operation. Lister was born in 1827 and studied medicine. Before his time, many people died after their operations. The French scientist Louis Pasteur showed, in the 1870s, that many diseases were caused by the tiny living things called bacteria. After learning about this, Lister began to use antiseptics (germ-killers) when he operated. He prevented bacteria from entering open wounds, and after that people seldom died when he operated on them. The methods used in operations today are based on Lister's discoveries. Lister was made a baron, an English nobleman, and received many other honors. He died in 1912.

Liszt, Franz

Franz Liszt was a great Hungarian pianist and composer. He was the fa-

ther-in-law of Richard Wagner, the great German operatic composer. Liszt was born in Hungary in 1811 and began to study music when he was 6 years old. His first concert was given when he was only 12, and it was a great success. His talent was such that several Hungarian nobles offered to pay for his musical studies, and he became the greatest concert pianist of his day. His own compositions were written after he had established himself as a performer.

Among the most famous of Liszt's works were his *Hungarian Rhapsodies,* based on Hungarian folk tunes. A series of thirteen symphonic poems are believed by many critics to be his greatest compositions.

Franz Liszt was a man of humor. Once one of his pupils noticed that he had written a chord that contained eleven notes. Since a pianist has only ten fingers, she wondered how the eleventh note could be played. Liszt demonstrated by striking five of the notes with his left hand, another five with his right hand, and the eleventh with his nose.

Franz Liszt was a deeply religious man, and at the height of his success he decided that he would withdraw for a time from worldly things, devoting himself to his religion. Some of his finest compositions were of a sacred nature.

During the last year of his life, Liszt made a concert tour in which he was acclaimed as the greatest master of his time. He died in 1886, a few months before his 75th birthday.

litany

A litany is a kind of prayer or song. It is a series of invocations (or petitions) by the leader, each followed by the same refrain, or answer, by the people. Litanies were once sung by groups of people in times of disaster or public mourning. There are several litanies that are still chanted in Christian churches, all beginning with the Greek phrase *Kyrie eleison,* which means "Lord have mercy," and ending with a plea to "the Lamb of God who taketh away the sins of the world."

litchi

The litchi is a large evergreen tree that is grown for its fruit. It grows in China and on the Malay Peninsula. Some attempts to grow litchi trees in other warm regions, such as California and Florida, have succeeded.

The litchi fruit, or nut, is about the size of a walnut. It has a thin, brown, brittle shell. There is a hard core, but the fruit itself is very soft and sweet. It is a great favorite of the Chinese, who eat it fresh, dried, or as a preserve. Sometimes the name is spelled in other ways, such as *leechee, lichee,* and *lichi.*

literature

Literature is fine writing that can be read for pleasure as well as for information. A catalog or a signboard contains writing but is not literature.

The two main forms of literature are *poetry* and *prose.* Poetry may be called music in words. By using rhythm (a pattern of sounds) and rhyme (words that sound alike), poetry makes a pleasing sound. Prose is any writing that is not poetry. Of course, prose should sound good, but not in the same way as poetry. The important thing with prose is to make the reader understand clearly what the writer is trying to tell him.

Fiction is prose writing about things that did not actually happen. All other prose is *nonfiction.* It may be *history,* or *biography,* or *essays,* or instruction (as in textbooks), or any other kind of message from the writer to the reader. Another kind of literature is *drama,* or plays to be acted on the stage. At one time drama was usually written in poetry, but now it is written in prose.

Every civilized country has its own literature in its own language. There are separate articles in this encyclopedia about the literature of important countries and languages. This article deals with literature written in the English language.

ENGLISH LITERATURE

There has been English literature for more than a thousand years, but the English language has changed so much since then that a modern reader could not understand any part of the early literature. The Anglo-Saxon, or Old English, language was spoken and written in England until the year 1066. The famous poem BEOWULF, about which there is a separate article, was written in this language. King Alfred the Great, about the year 900, had many books translated into Anglo-Saxon, and for several years a history called the Anglo-Saxon Chronicle was written year by year, but most writing in those days was done in Latin.

In the next period, from about 1100 to about 1500, Middle English was the language. One very great poet, Geoffrey Chaucer, wrote in Middle English. There were several other fine poets in the same period, the years around 1400. In this period John Wycliffe made the first English translation of the Bible, and Sir Thomas Malory wrote the first book in English about King Arthur and his Knights of the Round Table. A king of Scotland, James I, who was murdered in 1437, wrote a poem called "The King's Quhair." Middle English is not much easier to read than Old English.

The 1500s saw the beginnings of modern English and began a great period in English literature, perhaps the greatest of all time.

In the early years of the century, William Tyndale made a great translation of the Bible; later his translation was revised to form the "King James" Bible of 1611, one of the greatest examples of English literature. The first plays were written in English in the middle of the century. The first comedy was *Ralph Roister Doister,* written by Nicholas Udall in 1552. The first tragedy was *Gorboduc,* written by Thomas Norton and Thomas Sackville and first acted in 1561. *Gammer Gurton's Needle,* the second comedy, was written in 1566. These were not great literature, but they encouraged others to write plays and the greatest English writers began to appear.

The greatest of these was William Shakespeare, whose first plays appeared in 1591 or 1592. Others were Christopher Marlowe, Beaumont and Fletcher, and Ben Jonson. Shakespeare and Edmund Spenser were the greatest poets of the century and among the greatest of all time. Sir Philip Sidney was another leading poet. Sir Francis Bacon wrote books of philosophy and wise essays that rank with the best of all time.

John Milton was the great poet of the 1600s, and John Dryden was the great literary figure. Dryden wrote poetry, plays, and prose. This was a time of political turmoil, when England beheaded one of its kings (Charles II) and exiled another (James II), and much of the writing was on politics. It was also a time when men were beginning to think about and learn about the facts of life and science, and among the greatest English literature were the books of philosophy by John Locke, especially his *Essay on the Human Understanding,* published in 1690, and the scientific books of Sir Isaac Newton, published at about the same time.

In the 1700s, English literature included important works of nearly all kinds. Early in the century, Joseph Addison and Richard Steele wrote their essays and set the standard for magazines. Jonathan Swift, best known as the author of *Gulliver's Travels,* was also a noted essayist and the leading Irish writer of the time. Daniel Defoe wrote books that led the way to the modern novel, the most famous being *Robinson Crusoe.* The greatest poet of the century, Robert Burns, was Scottish. Leading English poets were Thomas Gray, William Collins, and William Cowper. Adam Smith, whose *Wealth of Nations* and other works were fine literature as well as noteworthy scientific writing, was another Scottish writer. Edward Gibbon wrote the first great history with his *Decline and Fall of the Roman Empire.* Toward the end of the century, the first true English novelists appeared. Henry Fielding, whose best novel was *Tom Jones,* was outstanding among them. So were Oliver Goldsmith and Laurence Sterne. Samuel Richardson and Tobias Smollett were famous novelists at that time, but their books seem overlong and dull to most readers of today. Dr. Samuel Johnson, who wrote the first worthy English dictionary, was the leading literary man of the late years of the century.

In the 1800s the writers were literally too numerous to mention. It was especially a century of poets. William Wordsworth, Samuel Taylor Coleridge, Lord Byron, Percy Bysshe Shelley and John Keats were the greatest poets of the early years, but there were many others. Later in the century the principal poets were Robert Browning and Lord Tennyson, and again there were many others. Sir Walter Scott wrote romantic poems and novels that are still much read. The greatest novelist of the century was Charles Dickens, but William Makepeace Thackeray was also very popular. Outstanding novels were written by Charlotte Brontë, Emily Brontë, and George Eliot. Thomas Carlyle and Thomas Babington Macaulay are notable among the historians, and John Ruskin and Matthew Arnold as essayists.

The present (twentieth) century has produced many fine English writers, but it is always more difficult to judge writers of the present time than writers of past times. Some of the outstanding writers of the 1900s began writing in the previous century. Thomas Hardy was foremost among the novelists. Others include Arnold Bennett, John Galsworthy, and W. Somerset Maugham. Galsworthy and Maugham were also successful playwrights, but the outstanding playwright was George Bernard Shaw. Sir James Barrie wrote plays and stories that are enjoyed by children as well as by adults. Rudyard Kipling's poems and stories also are popular with children. H. G. Wells wrote a tremendous number of books, novels and histories and science stories. John Masefield and Robert Bridges were noted poets. Some of the leading English writers of this period were not born in England: Shaw and the poet William Butler Yeats were Irish, the poet Dylan Thomas was Welsh, the poet T. S. Eliot was born in the United States, and the novelist Joseph Conrad was Polish.

The great English historians of this century have been Sir Winston Churchill, who wrote histories of both World Wars, and Arnold Toynbee, author of *A Study of History.*

AMERICAN LITERATURE

American literature started much later than English literature. In the early years, before the United States became an independent country, there were no fine professional writers in America except Benjamin Franklin, and in his later years he was a statesman rather than a writer. Thomas Jefferson and other early patriots wrote beautifully (in such documents as the Declaration of Independence) but they too were statesmen rather than writers.

The first important professional writer in the United States was Washington Irving, whose stories of old New York include the "Legend of Sleepy Hollow" (the story about the headless horseman) and "Rip Van Winkle." Other early writers were James Fenimore Cooper, who wrote exciting novels of Indians and pioneers, and Edgar Allan Poe, who is ranked near the top among all American writers. Poe wrote poetry, stories (including the first "mystery" stories), and essays.

In the middle of the nineteenth century, beginning about the 1840s, a group of great writers appeared in New England, especially around Boston. The leading figure in this group was Ralph Waldo

Emerson. Others were the poets Henry Wadsworth Longfellow, John Greenleaf Whittier, and James Russell Lowell, and the novelist Nathaniel Hawthorne. Herman Melville, whose novel *Moby Dick* is among the world's greatest, was a New York man but lived part of the time among the New England writers, and William Cullen Bryant, one of the greatest poets, was born in Massachusetts but later moved to New York.

The great writers of the second half of the century were Samuel Clemens (Mark Twain) as a novelist and essayist, and Walt Whitman as a poet. Whitman inspired many of a new group of poets that wrote in the early years of the twentieth century. Henry James was a leading novelist of the late nineteenth and early twentieth centuries. Bret Harte and O. Henry were much admired as writers of short stories.

During the twentieth century, Americans began to produce literature that was at least as important as the literature being produced in England.

Early in the century a group of American poets began to write "modern" poetry that was different in several ways from the style of the earlier English poets. These new poets included Vachel Lindsay, Amy Lowell, Carl Sandburg, and Ezra Pound. A few years later, the outstanding poets Robert Frost, Edna St. Vincent Millay, and Edwin Arlington Robinson wrote poetry that was more traditional in form.

The novels of Theodore Dreiser and Upton Sinclair, published in the early 1900s, were "realistic" and exposed social conditions that needed correction. Three great novelists of this period were women —Edith Wharton, Willa Cather, and Ellen Glasgow. The greatest group of American novelists appeared in the 1920s. They were Sinclair Lewis, Ernest Hemingway, James Farrell, William Faulkner, Thomas Wolfe, and several others whose novels were nearly as important. H. L. Mencken, as a critical essayist, did much to win recognition for the new group of writers. Eugene O'Neill was the outstanding American playwright of the century, but many others became deservedly famous. One of the most popular books of the century, and one of the greatest, was *Gone With the Wind,* written by Margaret Mitchell; it was the only book she ever wrote.

Since the 1920's, eight to twelve thousand new books have been published in the United States every year. The quality of the writing is so high, and there are so many fine writers of all kinds, that an article on American literature cannot even begin to tell about it. The librarian at your public library can give advice on selecting books that meet nearly any taste in reading.

BOOKS FOR CHILDREN

Until less than a hundred years ago, there were few good books that were written especially for children. Writers of former years believed that children should read only what would educate them.

The famous books of Lewis Carroll, *Alice in Wonderland* and *Through the Looking Glass,* published in 1865 and 1872, were among the first books written merely as enjoyable reading for children. Since that time, tens of thousands of children's books have been published. The most popular ones include:

For children: the original "Oz" books by L. Frank Baum; the "Pooh" books by A. A. Milne; *The Wind in the Willows* by Kenneth Grahame; the "Dr. Dolittle" books by Hugh Lofting; Rudyard Kipling's story books.

For teen-age readers: *Tom Sawyer* and *Huckleberry Finn,* by Mark Twain; Louisa May Alcott's books, especially *Little Women;* Robert Louis Stevenson's *Treasure Island;* Rudyard Kipling's *Jungle Book, Kim, Captains Courageous,* and others; many dog stories, including Eric Knight's *Lassie Come-Home,* Jack London's *Call of the Wild,* and the books of Albert Payson Terhune.

For very young children, the Mother Goose rhymes, Grimm's and Andersen's fairy tales, the humorous poems of Edward Lear and Eugene Field, and many picture books are among the classics.

Schools and libraries have lists of books recommended for young readers. There are several good magazines and encyclopedias for ages from elementary school through high school.

lithography

Lithography is a method of printing. It is based on the same principle as blotting. If you write with ink on paper, and then press a clean sheet of paper on the ink while it is still wet, some of the ink will come off on the clean paper. To make a lithograph, you draw a picture on a flat, smooth stone. You draw the picture with a chemical that ink will stick to. Then you coat the stone with water. You roll an oily printing ink over the entire stone. The ink will stick to the chemical with which you drew the picture, but it will not stick to the rest of the stone, which is coated with water, because oil and water do not mix. Next you press blank paper down on the stone. The ink will come off on the paper, making a printed copy of the picture. By continuing to roll on ink and press on paper you can make many copies of the same picture.

Lithography was invented by Alois Senefelder, a printer who lived in Bohemia (now Czechoslovakia), in 1796. George Bellows, an American artist famous for prize-fight drawings, and James A. McNeil Whistler, another famous American artist, were among many who made fine lithographs. Diplomas and scrolls were often printed by lithography, but the words had to be put on the stone backwards (as you would see them in a mirror) so that they would read in the right direction when they were printed.

Printers later found that zinc and aluminum, and even some plastics, made better plates for lithography than Senefelder's limestone had. This led to the development of offset printing, which is one of the principal modern forms of printing. Offset printing is based on the same principle as lithography, but the plates are prepared by a photographic process instead of by drawing or writing directly on the printing plate. (*Offset* is a printer's term for "blotting.") The process is often called offset lithography.

You can read more about it in the article on PRINTING.

Lithuania

Lithuania is a small country in the north of Europe. It has a population of about 3,129,000. In 1940 it was taken over by the Communist government of Soviet Russia, and it is now called the Lithuanian Soviet Socialist Republic. It was occupied by German troops during World War II, but then was retaken by the Russians. However, the United States, and most of the western countries, have never officially recognized the country

Consulate General of Lithuania

Kaunas, Lithuania's chief port, has many beautiful old buildings. The 17th-century convent was designed by Italian architects and took fifty years to build.

as part of the Soviet Union. Free countries do not trade much with Lithuania or get much news from there.

Lithuania is about as large as West

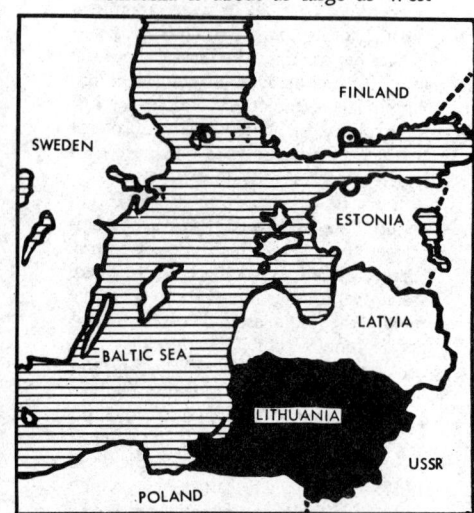

Virginia. It lies on the Baltic Sea and is one of the three Baltic States. The other two are Estonia and Latvia. Both of these countries became part of the Soviet Russia at the same time as Lithuania. Lithuania is a flat plain, with more than two

thousand lakes and many swamps and marshes. It has many large forests. The most important river is the Niemen.

Most of the people of Lithuania have blond hair and blue eyes. Their religion is chiefly Roman Catholic. They speak a language that is very old and is a branch of the Indo-European group of languages. Most Lithuanians are farmers. They raise oats, rye, barley, and other grains, and potatoes. They keep large herds of cattle, and produce milk, butter, and cheese. The capital of Lithuania is Vilnius (Vilna), a city of 235,000. Other cities are Kaunas, with 214,000 people, and Klaipeda (formerly Memel), with about 89,000.

The Lithuanian people settled in Lithuania more than a thousand years ago. Some four hundred years ago, the country became part of Poland. Two centuries later, Poland was divided up, and part of Lithuania went to Russia and part of it to Prussia After World War I, Lithuania became an independent country. In 1940, Russian troops entered Lithuania and forced the country to become a Soviet republic. The following year, the Germans occupied the country and held it until 1945, when the Russians drove them out. Lithuania has been a Soviet republic ever since.

LITHUANIA. Area, 26,173 square miles. Population (1973 estimate) 3,129,000. Language, Lithuanian. Religion, mostly Roman Catholic. Monetary unit, the ruble. Flag, three horizontal bars, yellow, green, and red.

litmus paper

Litmus paper is a kind of colored paper that is used in chemistry to test liquids. The litmus paper turns red when it is dipped into any solution that is acid, and it turns blue when it is dipped into any solution that is basic, or alkaline. Because it does this, it is called a chemical indicator. Litmus paper contains a dye called litmus, and it is really this dye that makes the color of the paper seem to change. Litmus is the oldest acid and base indicator known.

For many years most litmus was made in Holland from lichens, which are plants that look like moss and grow on rocks, tree trunks, posts, and walls. Certain kinds of lichens have litmus dye in them. The Dutch would mash, dry, and powder the lichens, then make them into a blue paste by adding a solution of ammonia, potash, or lime. They let this paste ferment, and then they got it ready for sale by adding chalk to make it solid enough to press into cakes. Today litmus is made synthetically, which means that certain chemicals are combined to make exactly the same kind of dye as the Dutch used to get from the lichens. The paper used to soak up the litmus dye is like thin blotting paper. Litmus paper is used in thin strips about two inches long and a quarter inch wide. You can use litmus paper over and over again if you wash it in running water after each time you use it. Sometimes the litmus dye is used without the paper. It is dropped into the solution that must be identified.

Little America

Little America is a place on an ice sheet near the continent of Antarctica, which lies around the South Pole. The ice lies over a part of the ocean called the Ross Sea. It is several hundred feet thick. Richard Evelyn Byrd, a United States admiral, led four expeditions to Antarctica and explored about a million square miles of territory.

You can read more about the Antarctic continent in the article on ANTARCTICA. It is very cold, and the land is covered with ice most of the year. There are high mountains where the ice never melts. Plants that are useful to man cannot grow there. But there are valuable minerals in the mountains, and several nations have considered it worthwhile to explore Antarctica and claim part of the land for future use.

Admiral Byrd's expeditions were made in 1929, 1933, 1939, and 1946. Each time he had ships and airplanes. He built small houses in Little America and each time he went back he found them still there. Food that had been left there was still edible. On his first trip, in 1929, he stayed more than a year and flew over the South Pole.

In 1955 an American expedition to Little America found that most of the ice on which the settlement was built had broken off and floated away. In 1958 it was decided to abandon Little America.

Little Rock

Little Rock is the capital and the largest city of the state of Arkansas. It is in central Arkansas, on a low, rocky cliff by the Arkansas River. Little Rock was named by a French explorer, Bernard de la Harpe, who saw the cliff as he was traveling up the Arkansas River and called the place "the little rock."

Little Rock is the leading center of trade and industry in the state. In the country around Little Rock, the farmers grow a great deal of cotton, and the people in the city use the cottonseeds in manufacturing such products as cottonseed oil and fertilizer. Furniture and other lumber products are also manufactured in Little Rock.

Among the sights of Little Rock are the building that was the capitol of the Territory of Arkansas (before Arkansas became a state in 1836); this building has been restored to its original condition. Since 1911 there has been a new capitol building, with a large dome. General Douglas MacArthur was born in Little Rock and there is a fine park named for him.

From 1957 to 1959, Little Rock—under orders from Governor Orval Faubus of Arkansas—defied the ruling of the U.S. Supreme Court that public schools must be integrated, that is, that white and Negro children must attend the same schools. In 1957 airborne troops of the U.S. Army were stationed in Little Rock to enforce the court order. In 1958 two Little Rock high schools were closed to evade compliance with the order.

LITTLE ROCK, ARKANSAS. Population (1970 census) 132,483. Capital of Arkansas. County seat of Pulaski County. Settled about 1815.

liver

The liver, the largest of all the organs in the body, is sometimes called the storehouse of the body. One cannot live without the liver.

The liver is flat and wide. It is dark red in color because an enormous amount of blood flows into your liver every minute. The liver of a grown-up person weighs about 3 pounds. It lies just under the chest in the upper-right side of the abdomen. (See the separate article about ABDOMEN.) The liver is made of a great number of tiny compartments called *lobules,* and each lobule is made of many tiny cells. The liver cells are the machines that make the liver work.

WHAT THE LIVER DOES

The liver manufactures a great number of things for your body. One of its products is a sticky, greenish-brown liquid called *bile.* Food material and broken-down blood cells are used in making bile. There are special pipes in your liver, called *bile ducts,* which collect and carry bile to your intestines, where it helps you to digest, or mash up finely, all the fatty foods that you eat so that they can be easily dissolved in your blood and be ready for use. Part of the bile is stored away for later use, in a small reservoir called the *gall bladder.* You can read more about BILE and the GALL BLADDER

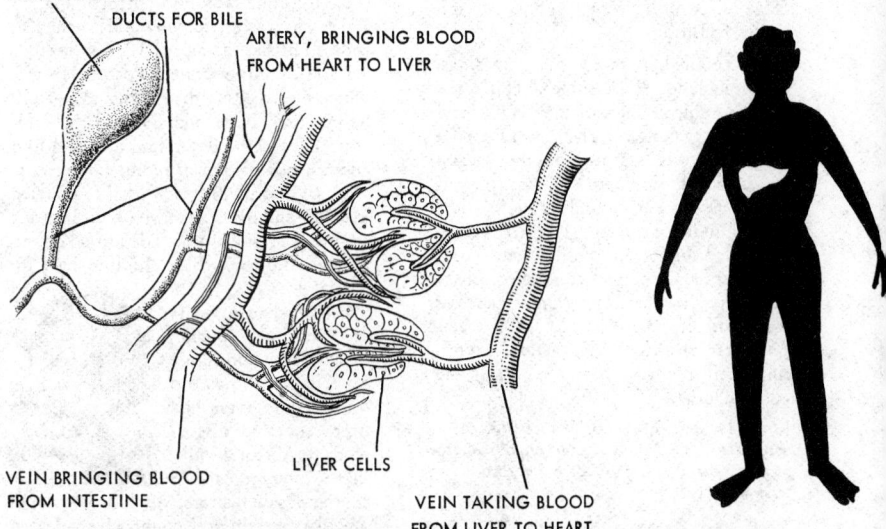

GALL-BLADDER
DUCTS FOR BILE
ARTERY, BRINGING BLOOD FROM HEART TO LIVER
LIVER CELLS
VEIN BRINGING BLOOD FROM INTESTINE
VEIN TAKING BLOOD FROM LIVER TO HEART

The liver, which lies just beside the stomach, is a storehouse for extra food. The blood takes food from the liver, and carries it to the cells when they need additional food.

in special articles about them.

The liver also manufactures a material that makes your blood clot or dry up, when you cut yourself. Your liver also gives your blood a certain material without which you would become anemic. (Read the article about ANEMIA.)

The liver is not only a factory but also a storage center. When you eat a lot of sweets, you have more sugar dissolving in your blood than your body can use. But your liver stores some of that sugar until your body needs sugar for energy.

The liver has another very important job to do for you. Some of the food that you eat may not be very healthful for you. Sometimes you may even eat foods that would be poisonous if allowed to stay in your body. Most such materials are made harmless and stored in liver cells until a blood vessel carrying blood from your liver to your kidney picks them up. Your kidney will take over from there, and it will help you get rid of these now harmless, but still unwanted, particles.

Sometimes the liver becomes overworked and weakened. Disease germs may take advantage of it and attack the liver. Many liver cells then become hurt and do their job badly. They often put the coloring that makes bile greenish-brown into the blood instead of putting it into the bile. The blood with the bile coloring in it makes people's eyes and skin yellowish, and when that happens people have a sickness called jaundice. Jaundice may also be caused by clogged bile ducts.

Liverpool

Liverpool is a large city in England. It is a seaport on the west coast of England where the Mersey River enters the Irish Sea. It is one of the busiest ports in the world and second only to London as an English seaport. The Liverpool docks, one of the great sights of the city, stretch for nearly eight miles along the Mersey River. Goods for all of northern England and parts of Scotland are landed at Liverpool, but especially cotton for the textile mills. Cloth made in England is shipped from Liverpool to other countries, as are metal wares, machinery, and chemicals. Although the city owes its importance to trade, many of its people work in its large flour mills, sugar refineries, and candy factories.

Liverpool has many fine buildings. They include St. George's Hall, the Town Hall, Philharmonic Hall, and Walker Art Gallery. The new Liverpool Cathedral was planned as the largest church in all England.

Liverpool was founded more than seven hundred years ago, in 1207, but remained unimportant until about 1715, when its first dock was completed. Liverpool merchants first became active in trade with the Americas. By 1800 Liverpool was already a very active seaport, importing raw cotton and exporting cotton cloth.

LIVERPOOL, ENGLAND. Population (1973 estimate) 688,000. Location, on the Mersey River near the Irish Sea, in Lancashire, on the west coast.

liverwort

The liverwort is a kind of plant that lives along the banks of streams, in damp woods, and in other shady, damp places. It is found all over the world where the climate is moderate. The liverwort is a very simple plant. It has no flowers and no real roots. Usually the liverwort grows flat along the ground. It looks like a group of thin, flat leaves, shaped like strips of tape or ribbon. The ribbonlike strip is about half an inch wide and about three inches long.

The liverwort does not produce seeds like the flowering plants. New liverworts grow from simple little formations, called *spores,* that are blown by the wind to new spots where they can grow. The liverwort is related to moss, and some kinds of liverwort look much like moss. The liverwort is a very primitive plant, which means that it appeared on the earth quite early in the history of the plant world.

Livingston, Robert

Robert Livingston was an American patriot and statesman. He was born in New York City in 1745, went to King's College (now Columbia University), and became a lawyer. He worked with John Jay, about whom you can read in another volume, in fighting some of the British practices in the American colonies. Robert Livingston worked on the committee that wrote the Declaration of Independence and on the commission that wrote the Constitution of the United States. He also helped write the constitution of the state of New York. As chancellor of New York he inaugurated George Washington as the first President of the United States, in 1789, and he was the United States representative in France in 1803, when the Louisiana Purchase was made, giving the United States ownership of the vast central part of the country. After he returned from France, he worked with Robert Fulton and helped to make the first steamboat. Livingston died in 1823.

Livingstone, David

David Livingstone was a physician and a missionary who lived about a hundred years ago. He was one of the first men to go into the unknown wilds of central Africa.

Livingstone was born in Scotland, in 1813. He was a poor boy and worked in cotton mills at the age of 10, but he studied and finally became a doctor. He was sent as a missionary to Africa, and in 1840 he explored Bechuanaland and the Limpopo River. One day a lion attacked him and crushed his left arm, but Livingstone went right on with his work. He married in 1844 and his wife stayed with him for a while, but when he decided to go on exploring she took their children back to England.

After sixteen years in Africa, during which Dr. Livingstone saw many things no other white man had ever seen and discovered the Victoria Falls, in 1856 he returned to England, saw his family again, and wrote a book describing the country he had been through. Then he went back to Africa.

Dr. Livingstone saw and reported the cruelty of the Arabian and other slave traders, how they captured the defenseless natives, often killing them for no reason. His reports helped to stop the slave trade.

The whole world was excited by the travels of Livingstone. When he went on an exploring trip and no word was heard from him for many years, people everywhere were greatly worried. A New York newspaper, the *New York Herald,* sent a reporter named Henry Stanley to find him. Stanley found him at a village called Ujiji on Lake Tanganyika, and is supposed to have said, when they met, "Doctor Livingstone, I presume?"—words that have been much quoted ever since. This was in 1869.

Livingstone and Stanley together explored the north end of Tanganyika. Stanley left Livingstone the next year. Livingstone was worn out by his hard years, and though he tried to keep on going, on May 1, 1873, his men found him dead in his tent. His body was taken to England and buried in Westminster Abbey, where many other great Englishmen are buried.

Read also the article on Sir Henry STANLEY.

Livy

Livy was a Roman historian who lived about two thousand years ago. His full name was Titus Livius, and he was born in Padua, a city in what is now Italy, about 59 B.C. Little is known of his personal life, but his *History of Rome* is highly praised by scholars. It tells about the city of Rome from the time of its founding in 753 B.C. to 9 B.C. Originally there were 142 books in this history, but all but 35 have been lost. Livy died in the year 17 A.D.

lizard

The lizard is a reptile that has dry scales, claws, and movable eyelids. Like all reptiles, the lizard is cold-blooded, which means that its blood is the temperature of the air around it. Thus, the lizard cannot survive extreme heat or cold and is found in the tropical and temperate climates throughout the world. Lizards have lungs and breathe air. The lizard group includes 3,000 varieties, ranging in size from 3 inches to 10. The lizard is like the bird in its bodily

Am. Mus. of Nat. Hist.
The "dragon of Komodo" is the largest member of the lizard family. It grows to be about ten feet long and weighs 150 pounds.

structure. The skeleton of a lizard is much like the skeleton of an ostrich. Like birds, most lizards lay eggs. Some lizards live on the ground, some burrow under the ground, and some live in trees. Many lizards live near water, and all lizards can swim, but no true lizard lives in the water.

Some of the most familiar members of the lizard family are chameleons, skinks, Gila monsters, horned toads, and glass snakes.

llama

The llama is an animal that lives in the Andes Mountains of South America. It is related to the alpaca, the guanaco, and the vicuña, which also live in South America. These animals are all members of the camel family, but they do not have humps, nor are they as large as camels. The llama looks very much like a sheep with a long neck. Its color varies from brown or black to white. It has a short bushy tail and a thick woolly coat.

The llama is a very strong animal and is very good at climbing mountains. For these reasons it is useful as a beast of burden, especially in rough mining country. It can travel from twelve to fifteen miles a day, carrying a load as heavy as two hundred pounds.

A llama that thinks it is carrying too much will grumble, lie down, and refuse to budge, no matter how hard the driver beats it. It will even spit and try to bite. The Incas, an ancient people of Peru, made much use of the llama.

Lloyd George, David

David Lloyd George was a British statesman who served his government for more than fifty years. He was born in Wales in 1863, and was elected a member of Parliament in 1890. Lloyd George had a fiery personality and rapidly rose to a position of leadership in the Liberal Party. He was against the British policy of conquest in Africa and violently opposed the Boer War in that country.

The British Parliament, which makes the laws of the country, is composed of two parts: the House of Commons, to which members are elected by the people, and the House of Lords, whose members are there because they were born into noble families. In 1910 the House of Lords refused to agree to a law passed by the House of Commons. Lloyd George insisted that a body of men who were not elected by the people should not be permitted to veto laws passed by the House of Commons. So he took the issue to the people of England, who voted for it over the veto of the House of Lords. Since that time the House of Lords has had no veto power.

During World War I Lloyd George became Prime Minister, or head of the British government. He represented Great Britain at the peace conference after the war. He was the last member of the Liberal Party to lead the British government. In the years before World War II Lloyd George was opposed to the policy of giving in to Germany and its warlike behavior. In recognition of his service to his country Lloyd George was offered an earldom, which meant that he would have a seat in the House of Lords, which he had fought so long. For many years he refused, but finally he accepted and became the Earl of Dwyfor. He died in 1945.

Lloyd's

Lloyd's is one of the world's oldest and most famous insurance organizations, with headquarters in London, England. It handles all sorts of insurance, and, with certain exceptions, will insure anybody or anything against almost any kind of misfortune. A large part of its business is in insuring ships and their cargoes.

The company had its beginnings in 1688, when a number of shipowners and merchants met in Edward Lloyd's coffee-house to do business. Lloyd's is not an insurance company but an association of individual underwriters of insurance who are grouped into syndicates. Several of these syndicates usually share the risk of any large insurance policy.

Lloyd's publishes a daily bulletin, *Lloyd's List,* which gives shipping information. Another famous publication, *Lloyd's Register of Shipping,* is now put out by another firm not connected with the original Lloyd's. It gives complete descriptions of every merchant ship in the world of 100 tons or more. Lloyd's London building is famous for its bell, which tolls once if a ship the firm has insured is lost at sea and twice if an overdue ship reaches port safely.

lobbying

Many people in business or other kinds of work can be helped or harmed by the laws that Congress and other law-making bodies pass. Farmers, for example, want laws that will give them a bigger price for their crops. Suppose the farmers get together and pay someone to try to persuade the lawmakers to pass such laws. The person they pay is known as a *lobbyist,* and what he does is called *lobbying.*

There are many lobbyists in Washington and in state capitals. They may work for manufacturers, farmers, labor unions, or any other group that is interested in laws that would affect it. Lobbyists who work in Washington are required by law to register; that is, to say who employs them and for what reason.

Many people believe that lobbying is bad and should be against the law, but there are usually lobbyists on both sides of every question, and the system often helps to explain both sides to the lawmakers.

lobelia

The lobelia is a plant that many people grow in their gardens for its bright red or blue flowers. There are many different kinds of lobelia. Some kinds are annuals, which means they must be planted every year. Others are perennials, which means that once they have been planted they will bloom every year without replanting.

Lobelia plants are found in many parts of the world where the climate is warm or hot. Usually they grow in shady places where there is plenty of moisture. Many kinds of lobelia grow in America and in northern India. The kind of lobelia that is best known in the United States is called Indian tobacco, because the Indians put

Fish and Wildlife Service

Lobster is known as a very delicious food, but only half the grownups in the United States have ever eaten it.

it in the mixtures they smoked in their pipes. It grows to be a foot or more high. The leaves and tops of these plants were once used in many kinds of medicines, and they are still used occasionally to cause people to sweat a great deal or to vomit. The plant or its whitish juice can be poisonous.

lobster

A lobster is a member of the animal group called crustaceans, and is related to shrimp, crayfish, and crabs. Lobsters are prized throughout the world for their delicious meat.

The lobster's body is in two parts. The head and thorax are fused together, forming the front part, called the *cephalothorax,* made up of 14 immovable parts. The second part consists of the abdomen with 7 segments joined by a flexible membrane, and the tail, which fans out from the last segment. The lobster can swim or crawl forward slowly, but when he flips the abdominal section under his body, the movement propels him backwards very rapidly. Four pairs of little paddles called *swimmerets* attached to the underside of the abdomen aid in the lobster's forward motion. The female attaches her eggs to the swimmerets and carries them around with her until they hatch, about a year later.

The lobster's entire body is covered with a thin shell or crust called an *exoskeleton.* (*Exo-* means "outside.") This exoskeleton does not grow as the lobster becomes larger, but must be shed. A new and larger shell then develops, and the lobster's body grows to fit it. The shell of a live lobster is dark green mottled with darker spots, and the underside is yellowish. When the lobster is cooked, the shell turns bright red.

A lobster is a *decapod* ("having ten legs.") The two front legs are large pincher claws used in fighting or capturing food, but they are not identical.

One claw is long, narrow, and has small sharp teeth along its inner edges. It is used to cut food. The other front claw is much larger, but its teeth are dull and are used to crush food. These two front claws can make up half the lobster's total weight. The other eight legs are used for walking. The "spiny lobster" of southern waters is not a true lobster, and does not have the big pincher claws of the northern lobster. The so-called "rock lobster" is a crayfish, and only the tails are eaten.

A lobster has two pairs of *antennae,* or "feelers," a short pair pointing forward, and a long pair that move in any direction. In addition, there are sensitive, hairlike projections on its legs. All these structures are used to detect the presence of food or enemies. The lobster's compound eyes are on stalks, and are movable. The mouth is on the underside of the body, behind the antennae, with six pairs of toothed parts that help push food into the esophagus. From there the food goes into the stomach where it is ground up by little stonelike patches of stomach lining called *ossicles.* Lobsters eat small animals such as worms, fish, molluscs, larvae, and other lobsters.

In winter, lobsters live in deep water, moving into the shallows in warm weather, at which time they spawn. The female lays about 15,000 eggs. The newly hatched larvae look somewhat like transparent fleas. Only about one-tenth of one percent survive the larval stage, as they are quickly eaten by other sea creatures. Most lobsters sold in stores are from 1 to 5 pounds, but if one is lucky enough to escape capture, it can grow to a size of 40 pounds or more.

lock

A lock is a device for fastening a door, drawer, or box. It consists of a bar or bolt that is moved back and forth by turning a key. The bolt slides into a hole or staple. While it is there, the door or other opening is locked and will not open.

There are two main kinds of lock: the *warded* lock and the *tumbler* lock. In warded locks, there are special wards or ridges inside the keyhole, which are intended to prevent any other key but the one made for the lock from releasing the bolt. Warded locks are not considered very reliable and for that reason are used mostly on clothes closets and on doors separating rooms.

The tumbler lock is a much more secure lock. It has a tumbler, or lever, that must be raised to release the bolt. This is done by the end of the key, which raises the tumbler and moves the bolt at the same time.

TUMBLER LOCKS

The *pin-tumbler,* or *cylinder,* lock is probably the most secure key-operated lock ever invented. It was invented in 1861 by Linus Yale, Jr., an American locksmith. He took the ancient Egyptian locks and improved on them. These locks had wooden pegs in the staple that fell into holes in a hollow bolt, preventing the bolt from moving. The only way the bolt could be moved was by inserting a special key (actually a wooden stick with pegs sticking out of it) in the bolt and raising out the pegs of the staple. The

Modern banks use time locks with complex combinations to safeguard their vaults.

A burglar would have to spin a new combination every minute for 380 years to try all the possible combinations of this thirty-ton vault door. It is seven feet in diameter and sixteen inches thick but can be swung with one finger.

pin-tumbler lock is based on the same idea. It contains a *key plug,* into which the key is fitted. The plug turns inside a hollow cylinder. The plug and the cylinder have holes that line up with each other. There are a pair of pins for each pair of holes. These pins fall into the holes and prevent the plug from turning in the cylinder. When the proper key is inserted in the plug it raises each pair of pins, allowing the plug to turn and release the bolt.

In a *disk-tumbler* lock, disks in the cylinder fit into slots in the key plug, preventing the plug from turning. The correct key pulls the disk out of the plug so that it can turn.

COMBINATION LOCKS

The keyless or *combination* lock is a kind of disk-tumbler lock. The disks all have slots in them. When the disks are lined up, the bolt can pass through the slots, opening the lock. A number dial is turned to line up the slots. Each lock has a special combination of numbers to which the dial must be turned to line up the slots and open the lock.

A *time lock* is a combination lock in which a clock prevents the combination from being operated until the time for which it is set. This type of lock is used on all modern bank safes. It is burglar-proof, in that the only way to open it ahead of time is to blow up the door to the vault.

locomotive

A locomotive is a powerful engine on wheels. It runs on railroad tracks and has so much power that it can pull a whole train. Most locomotives make their own power. This is the case with steam and Diesel locomotives. Electric locomotives have big electric motors that use electricity taken from an overhead wire or a third rail.

Modern passenger-train locomotives weigh from 125 to 400 tons and are capable of pulling a 20-car passenger train at speeds as high as 100 miles an hour. A freight-train locomotive may weigh as

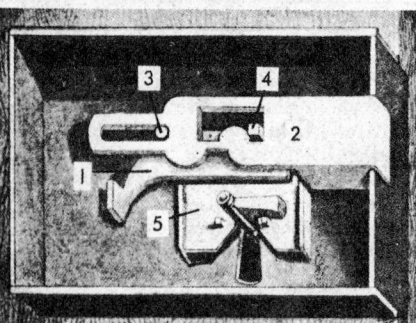
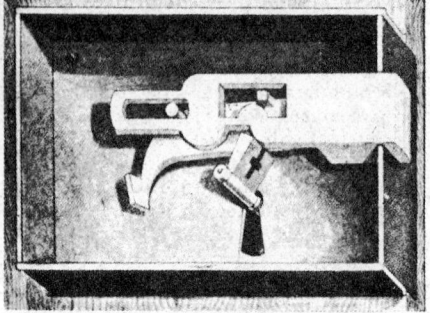

N.Y. Public Library

The common tumbler lock is made up of a tumbler (1), bolt (2), pivot (3), stud (4), and wards (5). At the top, the key is shown passing the wards. Below (with wards removed), the key lifts the tumbler and stud, at the same time pushing the bolt forward and locking the door.

much as 600 tons and pull a 190-car freight train, but at a lower speed.

A steam locomotive is operated by an engineer in the back part called the cab. In a steam locomotive, a car called a tender is pulled behind the locomotive. It carries coal and water. Heat from burning coal in a furnace causes water to boil in a boiler and change into steam. The boiler is the big, long tube, the largest part of the locomotive. The furnace or firebox is located between the engineer's cab and the boiler. Most steam locomotives burn coal, but some are oil-burners.

The steam from the boiler drives the pistons of two steam engines at the sides of the locomotive near the front. The pistons are fitted tightly into steel cylinders. The pistons are connected by rods to the large driving wheels of the locomotive. Sometimes there are two sets of pistons and cylinders on each side of the locomotive. One piston drives the front wheels, the other drives the rear wheels.

THE CHOO-CHOO

The puffing of the so-called "choo-

Baldwin-Lima-Hamilton Corp.

Matthias W. Baldwin (*inset*) produced one of the first successful American steam locomotives, *Old Ironsides,* completed in 1832.

choo" train comes from the fact that after the steam has forced down the pistons, it leaves the engine through the smoke-stack. The smokestack lets out both the smoke from the furnace and the steam from the engine. Every time a valve lets the used steam out of one end of the cylinder, there is a puff of steam in the stack. This helps the smoke escape more rapidly and makes the coal burn more readily. The steam pressure is about 250 pounds per square inch.

Besides the driving wheels, a locomotive has several pairs of smaller wheels. Those in the rear are called trailing wheels and those in the front are called called pilot wheels. The pilot wheels guide the locomotive along the tracks. The driving wheels may be 7 feet high.

Locomotives often are classified according to the arrangement of their wheels. A 442 or Atlantic type locomotive has 4 pilot wheels, 4 driving wheels, and 2 trailing wheels. A 462 or Pacific type locomotive has 6 driving wheels. A 482 or Mountain locomotive has 8 driving wheels.

In order to develop a greater pull, a freight-train locomotive may have as many as 16 driving wheels, which usually are smaller than those on a passenger-train locomotive. The smaller wheels give a greater pull but a slower speed. Sometimes a freight train is pulled by two locomotives, one in back of the other. This is called a *doubleheader* locomotive. Often a locomotive also may be placed at the rear of the freight train and is called a *pusher* or a *helper* locomotive.

In operating the locomotive, the engineer can increase or decrease its speed by pulling a lever that opens and closes a throttle valve. This regulates the amount of steam entering the engine. The engineer also can feed water into the boiler by operating a lever leading to the water tender. The air-brake controls for stopping the locomotive also are in the engineer's cab.

A steam locomotive can also be constructed so as to develop electric power to drive the wheel axles. Such locomotives are already in operation. They are called steam-turbine-electric locomotives. The steam generated by the boiler at about 600 pounds per square inch is used to drive a turbine in the same way as in an electric power plant. The turbine turns an electric generator that supplies electricity to motors between the driving wheels of the locomotive. The motors are mounted on the driving axles and, through a system of gears, they turn the wheels.

In Diesel-electric locomotives, which are used on most streamliners and many other trains as well, electricity is produced by an electric generator turned by a Diesel engine. (You can read more about the DIESEL ENGINE in a separate article.) In a Diesel-electric locomotive the engineer rides in a cab at the front, giving him a clear view of the track ahead. The locomotive is carried on 8 to 32 driving wheels and is powered by three or four 16-cylinder engines.

The electric locomotive gets its power from overhead transmission lines or third rails, which supply electricity to motors attached to the driving axles. They are

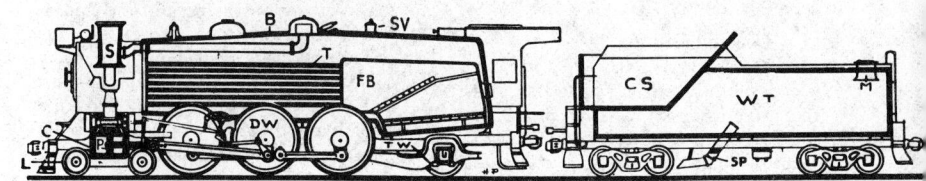

The Parts of a Steam Locomotive and Tender

S—Smokestack	B—Boiler	WT—Water tank
C—Cylinder	DW—Driving wheels	FB—Firebox
P—Piston and piston rod	T—Tubes	
L—Leading truck wheels	SV—Safety valve	TW—Training wheel
		CS—Coal space
SP—Scoop	M—Manhole	

used mostly in cities where smoke from steam or Diesel locomotives is undesirable. There is a separate article on ELECTRIC RAILWAY.

ATOMIC-POWERED LOCOMOTIVE

A locomotive driven by atomic energy will resemble the steam-electric-turbine locomotive except that the heat for boiling the water will be made by a steam-generating atomic reactor surrounded by a 200-ton shield of lead to keep the deadly radioactive gases from escaping. The first experimental locomotive has been designed to cost more than one million dollars.

locoweed

Locoweed, or *crazyweed* is a plant that is poisonous to animals. *Loco* is a Spanish word that means "crazy." The locoweed got its name because if animals such as sheep, cattle, and horses eat the green part or the dried tops of the plant, it gives them a disease that makes them behave strangely. They cannot use their muscles very well, and they sometimes go around and around in circles for no reason. At such times they will not eat anything but the locoweed, and finally the loco disease kills them.

The flowers of the locoweed may be purple or white in color. They are perennials, which means that they will grow again year after year. Farmers and ranchers must take great care to get rid of them, because of the harm that they do to animal herds. Locoweed grows in the western parts of North America, in open fields and pasture lands.

locust

The locust is an insect of the same family as the grasshopper. In many parts of the world grasshoppers that travel in swarms are called locusts. In the United States only a few kinds of grasshopper are called locusts. Two of these are the Carolina locust and the pygmy locust. The Carolina locust is about two inches long and has yellow-banded wings. The pygmy locust is short-horned and only about one inch long. It lives near streams and ponds, and, though it does not usually swim, it can swim out if it should happen to fall into the water.

The cicada is not really a locust, though it is often called the "seventeen-year locust." It gets its name from the fact that it lives seventeen years, most of them underground.

The female locust lays from 20 to 100 eggs, in the ground or on rotted wood.

The young locusts, called *nymphs,* emerge from these eggs. They grow rapidly, shedding their scaly covering about five times.

Locusts have long back legs with strong muscles that are used for jumping. Locusts and grasshoppers are very destructive. They have destroyed crops in every continent of the world. Locusts are so bad that, the Bible tells us, when God wanted to punish the Egyptians for making slaves of the Israelites, he sent swarms of locusts into Egypt, so thick that they blotted out the sky.

locust tree

The locust is a tree or shrub with very lovely flowers. It grows in the United States and Mexico and is often called the *false acacia*. A tree very much like it grows in Europe and is called the *acacia*. Because of its clusters of delicate flowers, it is used to beautify gardens and parks. It is often planted in hedges. The wood is very hard and durable and is used in shipbuilding and for fence posts. The tree grows especially well in the southern United States, as high as seventy or eighty feet. Many locust trees have been destroyed by insects, especially by one called the locust borer.

Lodge, Henry Cabot

Henry Cabot Lodge was an American statesman who was active in law-making bodies for more than forty years. He was born in Boston, Massachusetts, in 1850. From 1887 to 1893 he was a Representative in Congress and for thirty years after that, until he died in 1924, he was United States Senator from Massachusetts. When President Woodrow Wilson wanted the United States to join the League of Nations, in 1920, Lodge led the opposition to it. Some say that he was chiefly responsible for the United States' not joining the League of Nations.

Lodge's grandson, Henry Cabot Lodge, Jr., was United States Senator from Massachusetts from 1937 until 1942, when he resigned to serve in the United States Army in World War II. He was elected to the Senate again in 1946, but was defeated for re-election in 1952, by John F. Kennedy. In 1953 President Eisenhower appointed him chief United States delegate to the United Nations. In 1960 he was the Republican candidate for Vice President of the United States, but was not elected. President Kennedy in 1962, and again President Johnson in 1965, asked him to serve as ambassador to Vietnam during the most difficult

times there, and each time he agreed to serve his country.

Lofoten Islands

The Lofoten Islands are a group of islands off the northwest coast of Norway that were used as a base for British airplanes and small warships during World War II. Some of the islands are within one mile of the mainland; others are nearly fifty miles away. An ocean current called the North Atlantic Drift, which comes from the warm Gulf Stream, helps make the islands warmer than other places so near the Arctic Circle.

There are really two groups of islands: one called the Lofoten and the other the Vesteraalen Islands. The islands are full of fiords (narrow inlets). The herring and cod fisheries are the largest in the world. Though the waters are full of treacherous tidal currents, thousands of brave fishermen go out to sea. Some of the people raise cattle and sheep. The total area of the islands is about 2,000 square miles, and about eighty thousand people live on them.

Lofting, Hugh

Hugh Lofting was an author of children's books. He was born in England in 1886 and moved to the United States in 1912 to study engineering. During World War I he was in the British army, and he wrote many letters to cheer up his children while he was gone. These letters amused his children so much that he turned them into a series of books for children. The books are about Dr. Dolittle, a funny, kind little man who knew how to speak animal-language and who lived with his parrot Polynesia and other pets in a town called Puddleby-on-the-Marsh. Dr. Dolittle and his animals had many wonderful adventures. Hugh Lofting wrote twelve books about Dr. Dolittle, and drew pictures for them as well. He died in 1947.

log

A log is a device that shows how fast a ship is moving. Most modern ships can measure their speed by counting the revolutions of the propellers, but many things, such as the weather and the condition of the ship's bottom, may make this inaccurate. The *Forbes log,* which is much used today, has a small tube that projects out from the bottom of the ship. Water flows into the tube and turns a small propeller. This small propeller is attached to an electric measuring instrument that records the ship's speed on a dial.

Another similar type of log is the *pitometer,* which measures speed by recording water pressure. A small rod, called a Pitot tube, sticks out from the ship's bottom. It has small openings on its front and sides. The front opening gets pressure from both the weight of the water and speed of the ship, while pressure on the side openings comes only from the water's weight. The difference between these two pressures is measured and translated into the speed of the ship, which is recorded on dials like those of the Forbes log.

The old kind of ship's log, known as the *common log* or *chip log,* was first used more than three hundred years ago. A small chip of wood, shaped like a tri-

angle, rounded, and weighted on the bottom, was cast off the back of the ship. It was attached to a long rope called a *log line.* Knots were tied in this line every 47 feet, 3 inches. A small sand glass like an hour glass was turned over. It took 28 seconds for the sand to run out, and in 28 seconds the number of those knots that came off the reel of line was counted. From this, we get the term *knot,* which is still used to measure the speed of a ship. When we say a ship is going at a certain number of knots, we mean that it is traveling at a rate of that many nautical miles an hour. (A nautical mile is 6,080 feet.)

A later development of this log was the *taffrail,* or *patent log.* It consists of a small propeller that is towed through the water behind a ship. As the propeller's spiral fins turn, they turn a wire or chain connected with a dial on the deck. The dial shows the distance traveled and the speed, just as an automobile's speedometer does when the automobile's wheels turn. A ship's *log book* is a sort of diary. It is the official record of the voyage. In it, the navigating officer puts down the speed, distance traveled, weather, and anything unusual that happens.

Logan, Mount

Mount Logan is the second-highest mountain in North America, and the highest mountain in Canada. It is in the southwestern corner of the Yukon region, quite close to Alaska. It is part of the St. Elias mountain range. Mount Logan is 19,850 feet high. Mount McKinley is the only mountain in North America that is higher.

Mount Logan is covered by a great glacier, which is a huge river of ice. There is snow on top of the mountain all year. Mount Logan was named for Sir William Logan, a Canadian scientist who made a survey of Canada about one hundred years ago. Only one mountain-climbing expedition has succeeded in getting to the top of Mount Logan. That was in 1925.

loganberry

The loganberry is a kind of blackberry. The berries, however, instead of being black, are a dark red in color. They are shaped like blackberries and taste a little like raspberries. The loganberry plant is a trailing vine that grows along the ground. This plant was first discovered in the garden of a California judge named J. H. Logan, and the plant was named for him. Now it is grown in many places along the Pacific Coast. The berries are eaten fresh, canned, and made into jellies, jams, and juice.

logarithms

Logarithms are a system of numbers used to simplify multiplication, division, and other operations of arithmetic. Many scientists work with very big numbers, and logarithms save many hours of their valuable time. Mathematicians consider logarithms to be one of the greatest inventions in the history of mathematics. Some of their many uses are understood only by skilled mathematicians, but other uses of logarithms are quite easy to learn.

When it is necessary to multiply big numbers, for example $35,763 \times 84,312$,

it would obviously be a great help to have "multiplication tables" like the ones that go $2 \times 2 = 4$, $2 \times 3 = 6$, and so on. But such multiplication tables would fill so many books that it would not be practical to use them. Logarithms serve the purpose even more easily. They reduce multiplication to simple addition, and division to simple subtraction.

To understand logarithms, you must know the meaning of an *exponent,* so it will be explained first.

EXPONENTS

Each number used in multiplication is called a *factor.* In $7 \times 9 = 63$, the 7 is a factor and so is the 9. When every factor is the same number, an *exponent* can be used to show how many factors there are. You can write $3 \times 3 = 9$, but you can also write $3^2 = 9$. The little 2 is an exponent. It means there are two factors and each of them is 3. This is a great simplification when there are many factors. It is much simpler to write 3^5 than to write $3 \times 3 \times 3 \times 3 \times 3$.

The product, or result, of multiplying a number by itself is called a *power.* When you read the number 3^5 aloud, you call it "three to the fifth power." The product of 3^5 ($3 \times 3 \times 3 \times 3 \times 3$) is 243, and 243 is one of the *powers* of 3. Here are some of the powers of 3:

$$3^1 = 3$$
$$3^2 = 9$$
$$3^3 = 27$$
$$3^4 = 81$$
$$3^5 = 243$$
$$3^6 = 729$$
and so on

Therefore 3, 9, 27, 81, 243 and 729 are powers of 3.

ADDING AND SUBTRACTING EXPONENTS

Suppose you have to multiply $3^2 \times 3^4$. You know that 3^2 is the same thing as 3×3, and 3^4 is the same thing as $3 \times 3 \times 3 \times 3$. Therefore $3^2 \times 3^4$ is the same as $3 \times 3 \times 3 \times 3 \times 3 \times 3$, and this is the same as 3^6. It is clear that you could arrive at the same thing by adding the exponents: $3^2 \times 3^4 = 3^{2+4}$, and that is 3^6. The list of powers of 3, shown earlier in this article, tells you that $3^2 = 9$ and $3^4 = 81$, so you could have gotten the answer by multiplying 9×81, but it is much easier to add $2 + 4$, then look at the list, or table, and find that $3^6 = 729$.

Just as you can multiply by adding exponents, you can divide by subtracting them. If your problem is $3^4 \div 3^2$, you subtract 2 from 4 and your answer is 3^2, or 9.

The larger the numbers, the more time this saves. Suppose you had to multiply 243×729. This would take you a while, and you might make a mistake. But you look at the table, you see that 243 is 3^5 and 729 is 3^6, you add $5 + 6$, and then you look farther down the table to where 3^{11} is given. The power of 3^{11} will be your answer.

But you cannot add exponents that apply to different numbers. You cannot get the answer to $7^6 \times 8^4$ by adding $6 + 4$, because they do not apply to the same numbers.

HOW LOGARITHMS ARE USED

In the logarithmic system, the factor 3

in the example above, or any unchanging factor, is called the *base*. The exponent is called the *logarithm,* and the power is called the *antilogarithm.* In $3^4 = 81$, the base is 3, the logarithm is 4, and the antilogarithm is 81. The number 4 is called "the logarithm of 81 to the base 3," and this is written, $\log_3 81 = 4$.

A logarithmic system selects one number as the base. In "common logarithms," the base is 10. In a table of logarithms you can look up every factor in your problem of multiplication and the table will tell what exponent, applied to 10, would produce that number. Since these exponents (now called logarithms, or *logs*) apply to the same number, or base, you can add or subtract them and thus simplify your problem as we did in the examples above.

Suppose you want to multiply 4,216 × 6,593. First you look up 4,126 in the table of logarithms. You find that the log is 3.62490. Then you look up 6,593. The log is 3.81910. Add the logs together:

$$3.62490$$
$$3.81910$$
$$\overline{7.44400}$$

The number to the right of the decimal point, or dot, is called the *mantissa.* In this case, the mantissa is 44400. That is the number you will look up to find your answer. The number to the left of the decimal point is called the *characteristic.* In this case, the characteristic is 7. The characteristic tells how long a number the answer will be.

You look up the mantissa in the table of logarithms. You find this:

NUMBER	LOG
2779	44400

The digits in your answer, when you use a table of common logarithms, must be the characteristic plus 1. In this case the characteristic was 7, so the answer must be 8 digits long. The number 2779 gives you your answer, but you must add four zeros to it to make it the right length. This makes the answer 27,790,000. By adding two logarithms and looking up three numbers in the table of logarithms, you have learned that 4,216 × 6,593 is about 27,790,000.

This is not an exact answer. The exact answer is 27,796,088. But in most practical problems involving such large numbers it is seldom necessary to be accurate beyond the first few figures. It *is* important to be sure those first few figures are correct. For example, there is a number that is very important in designing airfoils used on airplanes. It is a small number, 1.06. But finding this small number required the multiplication and division of more than two hundred 10-digit numbers.

Logarithms were invented in 1614 by a Scottish mathematician named John Napier. Other mathematicians had the general idea of logarithms before him, but he first showed how to use them.

logic

Logic is the study of how man can use his power of reasoning to learn new truths from truths he already knows. It is a branch of philosophy, which is the study of all knowledge, and great philosophers for thousands of years have written about logic.

A simple example of logic is the *syllogism,* in which you take two true statements, called *premises,* and learn from them a third true statement, called a *conclusion.* For example:

Premise: Wood floats in water.
Premise: Pine is wood.
Conclusion: Therefore pine floats in water.

If the premises are true, the conclusion must be true. We use this kind of logic every day, usually without knowing we are doing it.

In the example given, we took a general truth, one that applies to a whole class or group, and drew a conclusion from it. (The general truth was, "Wood floats in water.") This kind of reasoning is called *deduction,* or *deductive reasoning.*

Sometimes we take a number of related facts and from them we learn a general truth. If every dandelion we have ever seen or heard about has a yellow flower, we can draw the conclusion "All dandelion flowers are yellow," and be fairly sure it is correct. This is called *induction,* or *inductive reasoning.*

logistics

Logistics is the process of seeing that an army gets enough equipment and supplies, and gets them at the right time. A great many men in the United States Army work at logistics. See the article on ARMY, U.S.

logwood

The logwood is a tree whose wood is very valuable for making dyes. The logwood is found in Central and South America and in the West Indies. It grows in flat regions, in very wet soil. It is usually between 30 and 45 feet high, and it bears yellow flowers. The logwood is a dark red color. To make logwood dyes, chips of wood are soaked in boiling water and the wood is treated with chemicals to make dyes of different colors—black, red, and purple. These dyes are used for coloring cloth and for making ink.

Lohengrin

Lohengrin is a grand opera that tells a story about a knight of King Arthur's court. (An opera is a play in which all the conversation is sung, not spoken.) The music for Lohengrin was written by Richard Wagner, a great German composer. The famous "Wedding March" is the most familiar of the tunes in *Lohengrin.*

Franz Liszt, a noted composer and father-in-law of Richard Wagner, directed the first performance of *Lohengrin,* which took place in Weimar, Germany, in 1850. It was first produced in New York in 1871, and has been sung hundreds of times since.

THE STORY OF THE OPERA

Lohengrin, the Knight of the Swan, is the son of Parsifal, one of an order of knights to whom has been entrusted custody of the Holy Grail. Their home is on Mount Monsalvat. In the opera Lohengrin is sent, in a boat drawn by a swan, to do battle for the Princess Elsa of Brabant. He wins her, but tells her she must never ask where he came from. But Elsa cannot contain her curiosity and finally asks where he came from. He answers her, but then the swan reappears. Lohengrin sails away forever, to the castle of the Grail.

Loire River

The Loire River is the longest river in France. It starts in the southeastern part of France, in the Cévennes Mountains, and winds northward and westward for 625 miles. Finally it flows into the Atlantic Ocean on the west coast of France. The river runs through fine farm land. There are many magnificent royal residences, called *châteaux,* in the beautiful Loire valley.

At times the river fills up and overflows its banks. In many places the people living along the river have built dikes, or high embankments, to keep the Loire from flooding their lands. They have also built canals to connect the Loire with other rivers of France. Many fine cities, including Orléans, Tours, and Nantes, are situated on the Loire River.

Loki

Loki was a great godlike giant in Scandinavian mythology, the religion of the ancient Germanic peoples. By his trickery, he got into the company of the gods, where he was known as the "spirit of evil." He pretended to be a friend of the gods and, when he wanted to, he could really do good things. But somehow he always ended up doing cruel and destructive things. He tricked another god into killing Balder, the god of light. For that terrible deed, the other gods tied him to a rock with ten chains, with a snake hanging right over his head. Loki had three children. They were the serpent Fenris, the wolf Midgard, and Hela, death.

Lombards and Lombardy

The Lombards were a Germanic people who played an important part in the history of Europe more than a thousand years ago. For hundreds of years, the Lombards had lived on the border of the Roman Empire, on the Danube River. About 1,300 years ago they invaded and conquered the northern part of Italy. This region is still called Lombardy.

The kingdom of Lombardy became one of the wealthiest and most powerful in that part of the world. The laws of the Lombards later became the model for the laws of the Germanic kingdoms during the Middle Ages. But the nobles of Lombardy fought many little wars among themselves, which prevented the kingdom from becoming very strong.

The great French king, Charlemagne, married a daughter of the Lombard king, but later he sent her back to her father. This insult started a war with Charlemagne, in which the Lombards were defeated. In the year 774, Charlemagne invaded Italy, and in the following year the kingdom of Lombardy was overthrown.

The region called Lombardy today is more than 9,000 square miles in size, and more than six million people live there. It is the most important industrial

section of Italy and produces large quantities of wine, silk, and cheese. Milan is the most important city. Because of its large industries, Lombardy was heavily bombed during World War II.

London

London is the largest city and the capital of England, of the United Kingdom, and of the British Commonwealth of Nations. It is in southeastern England, on the River Thames. It is one of the largest cities in the world. London has been a political, cultural, and commercial center since the Middle Ages. London began as a Roman fort called Londinium and was built along the Thames in 43 A.D. By the 11th century London was a large and important city. In 1973 about 7,400,000 people lived in London and its boroughs.

Until 1963 when a new London Government Act was passed, London's government had been patterned after a law made in 1888. The new act has changed the government's structure and the political divisions within the city. London has been enlarged to include suburban areas and now has 32 boroughs instead of 28. The central authority for the boroughs is the Greater London Council, which includes a Chairman, councillors, and aldermen. The Council governs an area of 610 square miles.

The oldest part of London is known as the City of London and has an area of one square mile. Its government is separate from the Greater London Council and is called the Corporation of the City of London. Its officials include the Lord Mayor, the aldermen, and the councilmen. The Corporation of the City of London and the Greater London Council have similar powers.

WHAT LONDON IS LIKE

London is about sixty miles from the mouth of the Thames, on the North Sea. The river channel is kept deep by dredging, and large ships can use it. London is one of the world's greatest ports and has nearly seventy miles of docks along the river. It manufacturers many things and ships many of them abroad. It imports much food and other supplies for all of England.

London is the center of the United Kingdom's national government. It is also the center of business management, and of the banking and financial activities of the country and to some extent of the Commonwealth. London banks have branches all over Great Britain. London has a stock exchange like those in New York and Toronto.

The Thames divides London into a northern and southern half. The northern half is divided again at Charing Cross into the West End and the East End. Wealthy people have homes in the West End. Business buildings crowd into the East End. The dock area is in the East End; this was badly bombed in World War II. The old City is in the East End. All of London is also divided into districts, such as Dulwich, Battersea, and so on.

London provides much entertainment, especially during "the season" from May to early July. It has five permanent orchestras, large halls for concerts and ballets and operas, fifty theaters, and many motion-picture houses. Its theaters are large and have big, comfortable seats, and prices for tickets are reasonable. The Sadler's Wells Ballet and Old and Young Vic companies are known over most of the world. In or near London, in season, one can see horse racing, tennis, cricket, and soccer and rugby football. In London are noted museums, libraries, art galleries, and universities. The city has many rail lines running to all parts of Great Britain, and a large airport.

GOVERNMENT

The ancient City has the same sort of government it did in the Middle Ages, and this, it is said, was based on Roman customs. There are a Lord Mayor, a council, and a police force just for the City. Only taxpayers may vote. The Mayor lives at the Mansion House and has offices in a famous old building called the Guildhall.

The rest of London is divided into 32 boroughs and is governed by an overall authority called the Greater London Council. The Greater London Council oversees the functions of all boroughs, although each borough looks after itself. A borough operates as a small town and is responsible for its own programs of housing, education, health, welfare, local roads, and garbage collection. The Greater London Council provides services that affect all boroughs such as major housing, environmental, and transportation programs.

HOW LONDONERS LIVE

London's climate is mild, with temperatures running from 40 degrees in winter to about 64 degrees in summer. The average temperature is around 50 degrees; the city does not often get very cold or hot. London was once noted for its heavy fogs. Due to a successful cleanup of the city's air and the Thames River, London rarely has dense fog.

People in London live in flats, for the most part. A flat is usually a complete floor in a building that houses three to six separate families. There are very few large apartment buildings.

In the suburbs there are many semi-detached houses. These are double houses attached to each other on one side only, so that the family on each side has its own lawn and back yard.

At one time, the rich had homes set back from the edge of the River Thames with huge lawns that extended to the river banks. Only one of these mansions remains and it is a public building. Buckingham Palace, the residence of the kings and queens of England, is in the West End, and because of that the West End is the fashionable part of town. Buckingham Palace overlooks Hyde Park. In this park is a famous bridle path called Rotten Row.

The richest Londoners have homes in the country and "town houses" in the city. They live in these town houses during the social season, in the spring. Many years ago, a group of bachelors would maintain one town house together. This is how some of the finest men's clubs originated.

When people in London want to go from one part of town to another, they can ride on the Underground, a subway system that covers many miles in all directions. Passengers buy tickets for just the distance they want to go. Many bus lines criss-cross the city and all its suburbs. Most buses are double-deckers.

PLACES OF INTEREST

Visitors to London can arrive by air, car, or train. London is the center of a major transportation system of roads and railways. London's two main airports are Heathrow and Gatwick.

The places that visitors want to see are easily accessible by bus. A few of them are: Fleet Street, where newspapers are published; Regent and Oxford Streets, where the fashionable shops of London can be seen; Trafalgar Square, with its Nelson Column (statue of Lord Nelson) and its famous lion statues; Westminster Abbey, where kings and queens of England have been crowned, and where the great of English history are buried; and the British Museum, with its collection of treasures from all the ages in history.

There are beautiful parks in all sections of the city. Among the most famous are Hyde Park, St. James Park, Kensington Gardens, Hampstead Heath, and Lincoln's Inn Field.

Some of London's streets are narrow and winding, especially those in the old City. The Bank of England is named the "Old Lady of Threadneedle Street" from the narrow lane on which it stands. In contrast, the beautiful, wide Victoria embankment runs along the bend of the Thames from Birdcage Walk to Blackfriars Bridge. Along it are many interesting attractions, among them Cleopatra's Needle, an old obelisk that is the twin to one in New York City's Central Park.

Piccadilly Circus is a bright and busy crossing with shops, hotels, theaters, and restaurants. The Strand, Pall Mall, Paternoster Row, Cheapside and Holborn are all names of business streets in London.

No visit to London would be complete without watching the colorful ceremony called the Changing of the Guard. It takes place in front of Buckingham Palace every day at 10:30 A.M., when the queen is living there, and at St. James's Palace when she is away from London.

The famous churches of London are St. Paul's Cathedral, Westminster Abbey, St. Bartholomew, St. Giles's, and St. George's.

The River Thames is crossed by many bridges, but most Americans think first of the London, Tower and Westminster Bridges. The Tower Bridge has twin bascules, which are raised many times daily to let big ships pass under it. In the Tower of London, at one end of the bridge, are historical relics and uniforms, armor, and instruments of torture. Here royal and noble prisoners were once confined. The Tower is about nine hundred years old.

LONDON IN THE PAST

In the days of the ancient Roman Empire, nearly two thousand years ago, the

soldiers of Rome founded a city about where London is today. The Latin name for the city was Londinium. About three hundred years after that, to Londinium's name was added the word Augusta and it was made the capital of Britain. Its real development as an English city, rather than Roman, began with King Alfred the Great, who lived 1,100 years ago. During the Middle Ages London had the standing of a county, self-governing and free.

Two serious calamities hit London about three hundred years ago. In 1665, there were 68,000 people killed by the plague, and the next year a great fire destroyed 13,200 houses and 89 churches. London quickly recovered, and in the 1800s it became the biggest and richest city on earth.

World War II brought devastation to many large areas. Thousands of buildings were destroyed by bombs. For years following the end of the war, Londoners were busy with the task of clearing and rebuilding their bomb-torn city. In 1954, during the process of removing rubble and digging out the wreckage, the remains of an ancient Roman temple were uncovered. It had been buried for many years. The ruins were removed, to be set up in another place.

London has a spirit all its own. The people of London never gave up when the war was at its worst, and they entered into the business of repairing their city with vigor and determination.

LONDON, ENGLAND. Capital of United Kingdom and of British Commonwealth of Nations. Population (1973 estimate) City of London, 5,000; including boroughs, 7,400,000. Area, including boroughs, 610 square miles. On River Thames. Founded 43 A.D.

London, Jack

Jack London was an American adventurer and writer. His full name was John Griffith London. He was born in San Francisco, California, in 1876, and from the time he was a boy he lived an exciting and adventurous life. At 17 he became a sailor. Before he was 21 he had taken part in the gold rush in the Klondike. Then he tramped across the United States and Canada. Whatever Jack London saw, he wrote stories about. Japan and Russia were at war in 1905, and he was sent to Japan as a foreign correspondent to write about the war. Later he was sent to Mexico to write about the daring bandit Pancho Villa. In 1906 Jack London and his wife made a trip around the world on a small yacht.

Jack London wrote many exciting adventure books. Three of the most popular were *Call of the Wild*, *White Fang*, and *The Sea Wolf*. He wrote some books that told about his own life; the best-known is *Martin Eden*. And because he himself suffered when he saw people living in misery and poverty, he wrote several books describing their unhappiness, such as *The Iron Heel*. His books were translated into many languages and read everywhere. Jack London died in 1916.

Long Beach

Long Beach is a city in southwestern California, on the Pacific ocean. It has a fine harbor, and many of the 358,000 people who live there work at the docks or in the shipbuilding industry. Others work in the oil fields and the oil refineries, in aircraft factories, in fish- and fruit-packing plants, or in lumber mills.

Because of its beautiful seven-mile beach and its warm, sunny climate, Long Beach has become very popular as a vacation resort the year round. Each year beautiful girls are chosen from many countries to go to Long Beach for the Miss Universe Beauty Pageant, where one of the girls is chosen as the most beautiful in the world.

There are many beaches and towns called Long Beach. Another one that is very well known is in New York State, on Long Island.

LONG BEACH, CALIFORNIA. Population (1970 census) 358,633. In southwestern California, on the Pacific Ocean. Settled in 1887.

Longfellow, Henry Wadsworth

Henry Wadsworth Longfellow is one of America's most popular and beloved poets. He was born in Portland, Maine, in 1807. His family encouraged him to read, and he started reading and writing poetry as a young boy. He went to Bowdoin College at the time another great American writer, Nathaniel Hawthorne, was there. After college he traveled through Europe, meeting many people, learning new languages, and reading the literature of many countries. He came back to teach at Bowdoin College. Then,  after another trip to Europe during which his wife died, he started teaching at Harvard College in Cambridge, Massachusetts. His house in Cambridge, called Craigie House, is still standing and can be visited.

Longfellow married again, in 1843, and was very happy with his wife and children, but in 1861 tragedy struck him again when his wife was burned to death.

Longfellow had many friends. His desire to help young writers made his home a place full of visitors looking for advice and friendship. He was as well known for his gentleness and thoughtfulness to these young writers as for his poetry. He died in 1882.

Longfellow wrote many short poems that told dramatic stories, such as the "Wreck of the Hesperus" and "Paul Revere's Ride." His children loved to play with him and pull his long white beard, and in one poem, "The Children's Hour," he wrote about his happy family. Some poems are about familiar American characters, for example, "The Village Blacksmith" who stands "under the spreading chestnut tree."

Longfellow's longer poems include *Evangeline*, about the Acadians of Canada; *Hiawatha*, about an Indian hero; and *The Courtship of Miles Standish*, about the Pilgrim Fathers and especially John Alden, who was one of Longfellow's ancestors. (See the articles on ACADIA, HIAWATHA, and ALDEN.) Longfellow also wrote about his travels, and translated a great deal of Italian and German poetry, including the *Divine Comedy*, the principal work of Dante, Italy's greatest poet. Few Americans have written as much as Henry Wadsworth Longfellow did.

Long Island

Long Island is a large island that is part of the state of New York. More than half the people of New York City live on one end of it, in the parts called Brooklyn and Queens. The East River separates these sections, or boroughs, from the parts of New York City called Manhattan and the Bronx. A narrow strip of water called Long Island Sound separates the island from other parts of New York State and from Connecticut and Rhode Island. On the south side of Long Island is the Atlantic Ocean. Altogether, almost six and a half million people live on Long Island. Two or three million more go there for summer vacations.

Long Island is 120 miles long and 12 to 20 miles wide. Along the south coast of the island there are several long, narrow sandbars. Fire Island and Coney Island are the names of two of these bars. They are popular summer playgrounds. Both the north and south coasts of Long Island have many inlets and bays, and this makes the island a very good place for yachts and fishing boats. The northern coast of Long Island has many hills and forests. The southern part of the island is flat.

Some of the world's richest people have summer homes on Long Island. There are many fine estates and golf courses and attractive parks.

Many of the people who live in the eastern part of Long Island are farmers. They raise potatoes and cauliflower and other vegetables and fruits. Long Island is known also for the fine ducks that are raised there. Fishermen catch many varieties of fish and clams and oysters off the coasts of Long Island.

People can travel to Long Island on the Long Island Railroad, and there are many good highways. New York City's two great airports are on Long Island. They are La Guardia Airport and John F. Kennedy International Airport.

Long Island was settled more than three hundred years ago. Both the Dutch and the English had colonies on the island. The Battle of Long Island, fought in August 1776, was one of the great battles of the Revolutionary War. It was fought in what is now Brooklyn Heights, and more than a thousand American soldiers lost their lives. George Washington and most of his men escaped to Manhattan Island, but the battle was a great defeat for the Americans.

LONG ISLAND, NEW YORK. Area, 1,401 square miles. Population (1970 census) 7,-115,137.

longitude a means for reckoning the angle of a point on the earth's surface from the chosen prime meridan: see the article on MAP.

Lookout Mountain, a mountain and a town near Chattanooga: see the articles on BATTLE ABOVE THE CLOUDS and CHATTANOOGA.

loon

The loon is a water bird. It is the most expert swimmer and diver in the

bird kingdom. It lives in cold climates and is a great traveler. Loons can swim under water fast enough to catch fish, which they eat. Loons have been caught in fish nets as deep as 175 feet below the surface of the water. They can swim very fast on the surface of the water, and can sink below without causing a ripple. When they are in danger of capture, they usually try to escape by diving under water rather than by flying away.

Because of their shape, loons are often mistaken for ducks or geese. A loon, however, is clumsy on land because its legs are set far back on its body. To walk on land, it must use its wings and beak for support. The common loon cannot even take off into flight from land, but must make its "take-off" run on the water's surface.

A full-grown common loon is about three feet long, with black-and-white checked markings on the back, a greenish-black head and neck, and a white underside. It nests on low coastal lands in northern America, Europe, and Asia. A loon lays two spotted, greenish-brown eggs each year, and the young swim away with their parents immediately after they are hatched.

The call of the loon sounds like insane, wild laughter, and gave rise to the expression "crazy as a loon."

loran

A loran is a kind of radio station that sends out special radio signals to airplanes and ships to guide them to their destinations. Loran is an abbreviation for Long Range Navigation. It was first used during World War II on warships that convoyed freighters across the Atlantic Ocean (went with them to guard them). Today there are loran operators on many airplanes and ships. Special radio signals produced by loran transmitters (sending sets) give them readings on their loran oscilloscopes (similiar to television receiving sets). They use these readings to plot their position on a special loran chart.

High-powered, land-based loran transmitters are kept in operation twenty-four hours a day. In sending signals to ships and airplanes, two loran stations work together. One is called the *master station,* the other the *slave station.* They are usu-

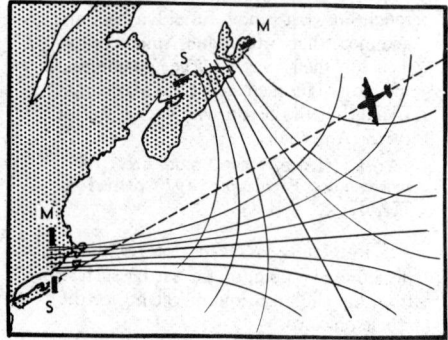

Signals sent out by two pairs of master (M) and slave (S) stations enable the loran operator in the plane to determine the plane's exact position. The dotted line shows the plane's path of flight.

ally located about 300 to 400 miles apart. This distance is called the *base line.*

The master station sends out its signal first, and the slave station sends its signal a fraction of a second later. This time difference makes it possible to identify the signals.

This idea is similar to dropping two pebbles in a pond, one slightly after the other, and a few feet apart in the pond. The ripples of water made by these pebbles will meet at a certain point, depending on the time difference between the two drops. This point will be closer to where the last pebble was dropped.

The time difference between the signals of one pair of master and slave stations gives one line on the loran chart. To determine his exact position on this line, an operator must have the time difference between another pair of stations. The point where the two lines cross is the position of his craft. Other readings, taken later, show the direction in which he is traveling.

The range of loran in the daytime is about 700 miles over water, and about 250 miles over land. At night, because of increased noise in the air, the range is shorter.

Lords, House of, one of the two parts of the British Parliament. See the articles on PARLIAMENT and ENGLAND.

Lord's Prayer

The Lord's Prayer is the most widely used prayer in the Christian religion. It was taught by Jesus to his followers in the Sermon on the Mount, as an example of the best form of prayer. Matthew quotes it in his Gospel in the New Testament, as follows:

"Our Father which art in heaven, Hallowed be Thy name. Thy kingdom come. Thy will be done in earth, as it is in heaven. Give us this day our daily bread. And forgive us our debts, as we forgive our debtors. And lead us not into temptation, but deliver us from evil. Amen." Because the first words are "Our Father," the prayer is sometimes called the *Pater Noster* from those words in Latin.

Luke also quotes the Lord's Prayer in his Gospel in the New Testament, but his version is a little shorter, and instead of "forgive us our debts," it says "forgive us our sins." This difference arises because of different translations of the original writings.

DIFFERENCES IN TEXT

In saying this prayer, Roman Catholics and some Protestants say "forgive us our trespasses as we forgive those who trespass against us," instead of "forgive us our debts." The Bible most Protestants use has an added sentence at the end of it: "For Thine is the kingdom, and the power, and the glory, for ever." This version appears too in some other Bibles, but apparently it was not part of the original text. In the days before printing, when monks wrote all the Bibles laboriously by hand, some monk made a little note in the margin while thinking about the meaning of the prayer. This note was the phrase that begins "For Thine is the kingdom," and it was picked up as part of the original and used in all Protestant Bibles for hundreds of years. When scholars discovered how it first appeared, later Protestant Bibles omitted the ending.

Lord's Supper

The Lord's Supper is a ceremony that is celebrated in nearly all Christian churches as a way of uniting Christians with Jesus and with one another. The supper was the last time that Jesus ate with all of his disciples. They were celebrating the Jewish feast of the Passover, which occurred on the night that Jesus was arrested. At this supper Jesus predicted that Peter would deny him and that Judas would betray him. The Apostle John tells in his Gospel how Jesus had promised his flesh to eat and his blood to drink. At the Lord's Supper, Jesus took bread and wine and made them represent his flesh and blood. He passed the bread and wine among his disciples.

The ceremony of the Lord's Supper is also called the Eucharist, or Communion, in various Christian churches. The priest or preacher distributes consecrated, or blessed, bread and wine among the congregation.

Lorelei

The Lorelei is a very famous huge rock on the banks of the Rhine River in Germany. The people tell a story about a beautiful young girl who threw herself into the river from the Lorelei because her sweetheart left her. The story tells how fishermen thought they heard her voice when they reached the rock. The fishermen would look up to the top of the Lorelei to try to see the girl and while they were looking the swift current of the river dashed their boats on the rocks, and the men were drowned. The German poet Heine wrote a poem about the Lorelei, and it became very popular as a song.

loris

The loris is a small animal related to the lemur and distantly related to the monkey. The loris is somewhat smaller than a cat. It has a round head, very long legs, a short muzzle, large eyes, and no tail. Its fur is thick and soft. The loris is a nocturnal, or night, animal. It spends the day sleeping in a tree, where it grips a branch with all four feet, rolls its body into a ball, and buries its head among its legs. The loris moves very slowly and creeps up on the creatures it catches for food.

There are two kinds of loris, the slender loris and the slow loris. The slender loris is about five inches long, and its fur is brown. It has beautiful eyes that shine with a golden glow at night. The slender loris eats insects and lizards, and likes the slow-moving snail that it can catch easily. It is found in southern India and in Ceylon.

The slow loris is about ten to twelve inches long. It is even slower than the slender loris. It has thick gray fur. The slow loris eats fruits and insects. Sometimes it creeps along branches hanging upside down, as a sloth does. This loris is found in the islands of the southwest Pacific Ocean and in southern Asia.

Los Alamos

Los Alamos is a town in New Mexico. It is famous as the place where the first atomic bombs were designed and assembled. The United States government

chose this isolated place in the desert, about thirty miles from Santa Fe, for making the bombs. The town was not founded until 1942. Scientific equipment was set up there, and a whole town was built for the scientists and their families. During World War II, the exact location of the town was a secret. The area is 7,500 feet above sea level. After the war, the United States Atomic Energy Commission took over the town. The population in the 1970 census was 11,310.

Los Angeles

Los Angeles is the biggest city in California and the third-largest in the United States. New York and Chicago have more people, but Los Angeles is the largest in area. For years it has been the fastest-growing city in the country. In 1970 there were nearly 3 million people living there, which is about thirty times as many as there were in 1900. Today the city is continuing to grow as fast as ever.

Los Angeles lies along the southern coast of California. It is about fifty miles long and about thirty miles wide. It includes more than 450 square miles. The city itself is a few miles from the coast, but an artificial harbor was dug about fifty years ago and Los Angeles is now an important seaport. Its chief industries are airplane manufacture, oil-refining, motion-picture production, and food production and food processing.

WHY THE CITY GREW SO FAST

There are several reasons for the growth of Los Angeles. One of these is the climate. It is almost never too hot or too cold there. Almost every day is bright and sunny, although the mornings are sometimes cloudy. The cloudiness in Los Angeles is called *smog*, because it is a combination of smoke and fog that hangs over the city.

Another reason for the rapid growth of Los Angeles is the beauty of the city and the surrounding country. It is ringed with hills on which the many surrounding towns, or suburbs, were built. These suburbs include such towns as Beverly Hills, Glendale, Pasadena, and Hollywood. Many of the suburbs have become part of the city itself. People have built fine houses on the hillsides, where there are beautiful views of the city.

Los Angeles does not have nearly as many skyscrapers (high buildings) as other big cities. This is because there is more space for building. Because of Los Angeles' history, there is much Spanish architecture. The different parts of the city are connected by long, straight boulevards, and it is easy to drive from one end of the city to the other.

Many older people retire to Los Angeles because of its warm climate. There are many beautiful beaches near by, and the swimming is good most of the year.

Los Angeles is the center of one of the richest areas in the world. The finest gardens in the United States for raising fruits and vegetables are found in Southern California. Many of these fruits and vegetables are shipped out of Los Angeles, or canned or prepared in its factories. Near Los Angeles are very rich oil fields,

Beautiful palm-bordered MacArthur Park in Los Angeles is one of the city's famous places. Visitors ride on the lake in little electric boats, bask in the warm sunshine, or take a ride along lovely Wilshire Boulevard.

and the city has big oil refineries. Thousands of people work in the airplane factories, which are among the largest in the world. Los Angeles weather plays an important part in this industry. The planes can be tested as soon as they are built, for generally the weather conditions are favorable for flying.

The weather was also the reason that Los Angeles became the center of the motion-picture industry, one of the most important in the city. About fifty years ago the motion-picture companies filmed nearly everything out-of-doors. They chose the area around Los Angeles, particularly nearby Hollywood, because of the bright sunlight.

Los Angeles is also a center of education. There are many colleges, including the University of California at Los Angeles, the University of South California, Occidental College, and Loyola University of Los Angeles.

HISTORY OF LOS ANGELES

The Spaniards first settled Los Angeles, almost two hundred years ago. The name they gave to the city was *El Pueblo de Nuestra Señora la Reina de Los Angeles,* which in the Spanish language means "The Village of Our Lady, the Queen of the Angels." People soon shortened the name to Los Angeles. Until 1847 California was ruled by Spaniards and Mexicans.

In 1847 the United States took over California. Los Angeles became important about twenty years later when two great railroads, the Southern Pacific and the Santa Fe, reached Los Angeles, for then the city was easy to reach from the east.

In the 1890s oil was discovered nearby, and about 1913 the motion-picture industry began to move there.

LOS ANGELES, CALIFORNIA. Population (1970 census) 2,816,061. County seat of Los Angeles County. Settled in 1781.

Lost Colony

The Lost Colony was a group of people who settled on Roanoke Island, Virginia, in 1587 and then vanished so that

four years later there was no trace of them.

Sir Walter Raleigh, who had explored Virginia before, sent a group of English colonists to Roanoke in 1587, with John White as their leader. They built houses and planted crops and were delighted when one of their families had a child, the first English child to be born in America. She was named Virginia Dare, and John White was her grandfather.

Food supplies began to run low, and John White went back to England to get help for the struggling young colony. England and Spain were at war when he got back to England, so his return to Roanoke was delayed. When he returned, in 1591, no trace was left of the colony or its people. It is thought that some were killed by disease or Indians and that others escaped and moved elsewhere.

Lot

Lot is a character in the Bible. He was the nephew of Abraham. His life is described in the book of Genesis, in chapters 11 to 19. Lot and Abraham journeyed together to Canaan and Egypt, and finally to the town of Bethel. They grew rich, but their servants quarreled and they separated. Lot crossed the Jordan River and settled near a wicked city called Sodom. That city was destroyed because of the sins of the people who lived there. Lot had been warned by the Lord about this coming disaster, and he fled to another city. He and his wife were warned not to look back as they left Sodom, but she disobeyed and was turned into a pillar of salt. Lot himself was not a good man. He was greedy and selfish.

lottery

A lottery is a way of deciding who should get some prize or reward. In a simple form of lottery, everyone is given a number. A slip of paper or card is marked with each number. All the slips of paper are put into some kind of container and mixed. Then a blindfolded person reaches into the container and takes out one slip of paper. This is called a *drawing,* because he draws the number out of the container. The person who has the number on that slip wins the prize.

Lotteries have been popular throughout history. In the United States and many other countries they are against the law, though they used to be legal. In some countries lotteries are still legal and huge prizes are put up and tickets bearing numbers are sold for as much as several dollars apiece. The prizes are never as much as all the people together have paid for their tickets, so lotteries make large amounts of money for those who run them. Some countries run lotteries and use the profits for government expenses, just as governments use money they get from taxes.

A raffle is a kind of lottery. The prize is always something besides money, for example, a turkey or even an automobile. People buy tickets and the lucky number wins the prize. Some organizations conduct raffles to get money for their expenses or to give to charity.

lotus

Lotus is a name given to several kinds of water plant. The true lotus is an

Egyptian water lily. It grows in still or slowly running water, and its roots spread out in the soil. Its large, blue-green leaves float on the surface of the water, and above them on a tall stem are large, beautiful flowers, which may be either blue or white. The lotus was considered a sacred flower by the Egyptians, and it is the national emblem of Egypt. It is one of the principal designs used in Egyptian decoration and architecture.

The Indian lotus, also called the sacred bean, is a tall water plant with round leaves and pink flowers. This lotus also is important in the religion and art of India. It is often seen in pictures and statues of ancient gods.

In the United States the water plant called lotus, or water chinquapin, is similar to the Indian lotus except that it has yellow flowers. Its seeds, which have a nutlike flavor, were cooked and eaten by the American Indians. The American lotus flower varies in size, from very small to as large as twelve inches.

The name lotus has been given wrongly to other plants in the past. The ancient Greeks had a legend about a people who lived on the northern coast of Africa and ate nothing but the lotus plant. They were called the "lotus eaters," and the lotus was supposed to make them forget all their troubles and live happy and lazy lives.

Louis, King of France

Louis was the most popular name among kings of France. In the thousand years that France was a kingdom, there were seventeen kings named Louis. They numbered from one to eighteen (I to XVIII) because one of them, Louis XVII, never really became king. Only a few of the kings named Louis were very important.

Here is a list of all of them:

		Born	Died	Reigned
Louis	I	778	840	814–840
Louis	II	845	879	877–879
Louis	III	863	882	879–882
Louis	IV	921	954	936–954
Louis	V	966	987	986–987
Louis	VI	1078	1137	1108–1137
Louis	VII	1120	1181	1137–1180
Louis	VIII	1187	1226	1223–1226
Louis	IX	1215	1270	1226–1270
Louis	X	1289	1316	1314–1316
Louis	XI	1423	1483	1461–1483
Louis	XII	1462	1515	1498–1515
Louis	XIII	1601	1643	1610–1643
Louis	XIV	1638	1715	1643–1715
Louis	XV	1710	1744	1743–1774
Louis	XVI	1754	1793	1774–1789
Louis	XVII	1785	1795	
Louis	XVIII	1755	1824	1814–1824

Louis I was the son of Charlemagne, the great king who made France a kingdom in the first place. The kings who followed Louis I were usually quarreling. Brothers fought each other, sons fought their fathers, and one king, Louis V, was poisoned in 987 by his own mother because she wanted someone else to have the throne.

One of the best of the early kings of France was Louis IX, who is called Saint Louis. Louis IX was a bold knight who fought in the Crusades, and he was just and firm in his treatment of people. He was killed on a Crusade in 1270, and

the Catholic Church later canonized him (declared him a saint).

Louis XIV, who was born in 1638, became king when he was only 5 years old. He ruled France for 72 years. He was powerful, ambitious, and extravagant. One of his famous sayings was "L'état, c'est moi," which in French means "I am the state." He built himself a huge palace at Versailles. The French nobles flattered him, calling him the Sun King and the Great Monarch. The people were heavily taxed, not only for the luxuries that Louis loved, but also to support several wars. More powerful than many of Louis' ministers were three women he loved, Louise de La Vallière, Madame de Montespan, and Madame de Maintenon.

Louis XIV was the most popular king in Europe, and during his reign France established colonies in the New World from Canada to Louisiana, developed its industries, and built a powerful navy. Nevertheless, Louis XIV did much that eventually hurt France, because he spent so much of the people's money on wars.

Louis XV became king in 1715, when Louis XIV died. He was Louis XIV's great-grandson, and he too was only 5 years old when he became king. He reigned for fifty-nine years, and during the first years of his reign the people liked him and called him Louis the Well-beloved. But he was a weak and timid man, and things became much worse in his reign. Instead of ruling the country himself, he usually took the advice of two women that he loved, first Madame de Pompadour and later Madame du Barry. He fought a losing war against England, and France lost many of her colonies in America. The whole country, from the people to the nobles, had become disgusted with Louis XV by the time he died in 1774. Louis XV had said, "Après moi, le déluge," which in French means, "After me, the flood will come," because he knew there was danger of a revolution.

Louis XVI, grandson of Louis XV, was the next king, and the French Revolution did come. Louis XVI and his queen, Marie Antoinette, lived a life of luxury and splendor while the people were often hungry. In the French Revolution, which broke out in 1789, Louis XVI was tried for treason and beheaded on the guillotine in 1793. His son was called Louis XVII, but he died in 1795, at the age of 10, and never became king.

Louis XVIII, the last Louis of France, was king for a few years, from 1814 o 1824, when the Revolution was over and Napoleon, who had been emperor, was exiled. He was Louis XVI's brother. Louis XVIII was a clever king and did not make the mistakes of his ancestors. At his death in 1824 France was again a prosperous country.

Louis Philippe

Louis Philippe was king of France from 1830 to 1848. He was born in 1773. His father, though a member of the French royal family, had taken sides against King Louis XVI in the French Revolution, and Louis Philippe fled to

America to get away from the anger of the other nobles. He went back to France and pretended that he believed that the people of France had been right in starting the revolution. Then as soon as he became king, he showed himself to be a vain and selfish man. In 1848 the people of the French capital, Paris, rebelled against him. He and his queen were smuggled out of the country to England, where Queen Victoria gave them a home. He died in England in 1850.

Louis, Joe

Joe Louis was heavyweight boxing champion of the world from 1937 to 1949. His real name was Joseph Louis Barrow, and he was born in Lexington, Alabama, in 1914.

Louis began boxing in Detroit, Michigan, where his family had moved when he was a child. He won the championship when he knocked out James J. Braddock on June 22, 1937. So powerful was he as a fighter that he became known as the "Brown Bomber." He defended his title against many challengers, including Max Schmeling, the German boxer, who was the only man who had ever knocked him out. He served in the United States Army for three years during World War II. Louis announced his retirement in 1949, but a year later he came back to fight Ezzard Charles, who had been recognized as champion in most states. Louis lost a fifteen-round decision to Charles. Louis tried another comeback in 1951, but was knocked out by Rocky Marciano and retired again.

Louise, Lake

Lake Louise is a beautiful lake in western Canada. It is in Banff National Park, in the province of Alberta. Lake Louise is about a mile and a half long and three-quarters of a mile wide. Magnificent mountains rise steeply from the shores of Lake Louise, and the snowy peaks, the sky, and the surrounding forests are reflected in the blue waters of the lake. Many people spend their vacations there.

Louisiana

Louisiana is a state in the "deep south" of the United States. Its nickname is the "Pelican State" because many pelicans live along its marshy coast. It is sometimes called "the nation's sugar bowl" because it produces more sugar cane than any other state. It also leads all other states in the production of shrimp and ranks second in the growing of rice. Louisiana was named after Louis XIV, the king of France, almost 300 years ago, when this region was claimed as French territory

Louisiana ranks 31st in size among the states, with 48,523 square miles. In population it ranks 20th, with more than 3,600,000 people living there. It became a state in 1812, and was the 18th state admitted to the United States. The capital is Baton Rouge.

THE PEOPLE OF LOUISIANA

About one-quarter of the people are farmers. They raise large crops of sugar-cane, cotton, rice, and tobacco, as well as cattle, fruits, and vegetables. Many of the farmers still work their fields with horses and mules.

More than half the people live in large cities such as New Orleans, Shreveport, and Baton Rouge. They work in big canning and petroleum plants, and in factories, making lumber products, paper, turpentine, and many other useful things.

Other Louisianians work in the important oil and natural gas fields, and many are fishermen for fish, shrimp, and oysters.

There are many different kinds of people living in Louisiana. More than one million are Negroes, whose ancestors were shipped to this part of the country as slaves. Many Creoles live in Louisiana. They are the descendants of the early French and Spanish settlers. Another interesting group is the Acadians, called "Cajuns," whose French ancestors fled from Nova Scotia and settled in Louisiana nearly two hundred years ago. There are also several Indian tribes, but only about

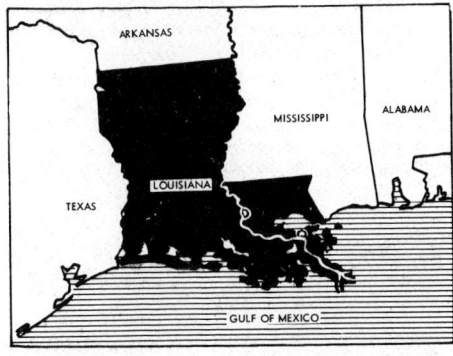

3,500 Indians still live in the state of Louisiana.

The earliest settlers in Louisiana were the French, who came to Louisiana almost three hundred years ago. Later the Spanish came and intermarried with the French. British colonists settled there after the Revolutionary War, and many Americans came to the territory after Louisiana was bought from the French in 1803. Today, almost all the people of Louisiana are American-born, but many of the French customs and traditions remain.

Most of the people in the southern part of the state are Roman Catholics, while many of those in the northern part are Protestants.

WHAT LOUISIANA IS LIKE

Louisiana is shaped like a boot. The toe of the boot is the rich, fertile delta of the Mississippi River, which extends out into the warm Gulf of Mexico. The whole southern and eastern sections of the state are low and very flat, and are the finest farming region. This part of the state is so low that it would be flooded every year by the Mississippi if people had not built strong *levees*, or high banks, to keep out the water. This large region also has many lakes, marshes, and picturesque slow-winding streams called *bayous*. The people who live along the bayous talk a mixture of French, English,

and Indian. For generations, these bayou people have managed to make a small living as farmers, fishermen, and fur trappers.

The northwestern part of Louisiana has beautiful scenery along the Red River, with many forests that cover low, rolling hills. Men cut down the shortleaf pine, oak, gum, and hickory trees, and ship the wood to factories to be made into wood pulp and furniture. Many of the important oil and natural gas fields are situated in this part of the state. The soil is fertile here, too, and farmers grow peanuts, pecans, and cotton. Dairy farming is an important industry around the large cities of Shreveport and Monroe.

As in other southern states, there are many small fur-bearing animals in Louisiana. The marshes supply most of the country's muskrat furs, and there are also raccoons, mink, coypu, and opossums.

Louisiana has a semitropical climate with a heavy rainfall that makes the plant life thick and green. Hardly anyone living in the southern part of the state ever sees snow. The average temperature in winter is 52 degrees, while in summer it is about 82 degrees. Louisiana's warm climate makes it a place where people can go to enjoy winter vacations.

The people have always found the many rivers and streams the best means of transportation. Louisiana has nearly five thousand miles of navigable waters, particularly on the Mississippi River, with steamboats and barges carrying vast quantities of products down to New Orleans and Baton Rouge. There are also thousands of miles of good railroads and highways, as well as airports in the important cities.

THE GOVERNMENT OF LOUISIANA

Louisiana, like most other states, is governed by a Governor and a Legislature. The Governor is elected for a four-year term. The Legislature is composed of two houses, a Senate and a House of Representatives. The members of both houses are elected for a four-year term. Judges are elected for a fourteen-year term. The capital is Baton Rouge. There are 64 parishes or counties.

There are about 853,000 pupils enrolled in public and elementary schools. Among the principal colleges and universities are:

Louisiana State University and Agricultural and Mechanical College, at Baton Rouge. Enrollment, 15,873 in 1971 (co-ed).
Louisiana Polytechnic Institute, at Ruston. Enrollment, 6,670 in 1971 (co-ed).
Loyola University of the South, at New Orleans. Enrollment, 4,736 in 1971 (co-ed).
Southern University and Agricultural and Mechanical College, at Baton Rouge. Enrollment, 6,776 in 1971 (co-ed).
Tulane University, at New Orleans. Enrollment, 7,115 in 1971 (co-ed).
University of Southwestern Louisiana, at Lafayette. Enrollment, 2,002 in 1971 (co-ed).
Northwestern State College of Louisiana, at Natchitoches. Enrollment, 5,151 in 1971 (co-ed).

The leading cities of Louisiana, with populations from the 1970 census, are:

New Orleans, population 593,471, the largest city in the state. There is a separate

article about NEW ORLEANS.
Shreveport, population 182,064, the second-largest city, industrial and financial center, in the northwestern part of the state.
Baton Rouge, population 165,963, the state capital and third-largest city. There is a separate article about BATON ROUGE.
Lake Charles, population 77,998, the fourth-largest city, commercial center, in the southwestern part of the state.

LOUISIANA IN THE PAST

More than four hundred years ago, Spanish explorers, led by Hernando de Soto, first saw the Louisiana region. They were searching for gold, and when they did not find any they moved on. In 1682 La Salle, the French explorer, sailed down the Mississippi River and claimed the large region around it for France. Eighteen years later a group of Frenchmen established Fort Iberville, the first settlement in Louisiana. The French tried unsuccessfully to encourage people to settle in Louisiana, but finally they gave the territory to Spain. The French people living in Louisiana did not like Spanish rule, and they rebelled, but the Spanish sternly put down the rebellion.

Gradually, more Spaniards came to Louisiana and built it up. But Spain was growing weaker, and finally Napoleon Bonaparte, who was then ruling France, forced Spain to return the territory to France, in 1800. Napoleon dreamed of building up a great French colonial empire that would bring France large sums of money and many products, but his plan failed. In 1803 he sold the territory to the United States. This became known in American history as the LOUISIANA PURCHASE, about which you can read in the next article.

In 1812, Louisiana was admitted as a state to the United States. People from other parts of the country came to settle there, and Louisiana soon became an important sugar-cane and cotton-growing state. In it were large plantations, whose rich owners lived in fine mansions and owned hundreds of slaves who worked the fields. When Abraham Lincoln was elected President in 1860, and it appeared that the slaves would be set free, Louisiana was one of the states that seceded from the Union.

In the Civil War, Louisiana suffered much destruction. For much of the war it was in the hands of the Union Army. When the war was over, the people of Louisiana were very poor, with no money to rebuild their state. "Carpetbaggers," outsiders who came with nothing but carpetbags, controlled the state government and robbed it of millions. However, the people finally got back control of the state.

Instead of the old plantation system, farms were now worked by tenants called sharecroppers, who shared in what they produced. Trade with other nations grew, and manufactures quickly developed because of the many raw materials and cheap labor in the South. Modern Louisiana is a flourishing farm and industrial state.

PLACES TO SEE IN LOUISIANA

Chalmette National Historic Park, 82 acres, in New Orleans, in the southeast, on U.S. Route 90. Scene of part of

the Battle of New Orleans.

Vieux Carre, old French quarter of New Orleans, with many picturesque houses.

Avery Island, ten miles south of New Iberia, in the south, west of U.S. Route 90. On this island are the beautiful Jungle Gardens, containing many rare plants, and Bird City, a sanctuary established in 1893 especially for herons and egrets, but now a haven for all birds.

Longfellow-Evangeline Memorial State Park, 157 acres, at St. Martinville, in the south, on U.S. Route 90. The region made famous by Henry Wadsworth Longfellow's poem *Evangeline*.

Natchitoches, in the west, west of U.S. Route 74. The oldest town in Louisiana, settled in 1714. Still has its French customs, and beautiful old houses built before the Civil War.

Mardi Gras, at New Orleans, in the southeast, on U.S. Route 90. The famous carnival time, with parades and colorful balls, on Shrove Tuesday before Lent.

LOUISIANA. Area, 48,523 square miles. Population (1970 census) 3,641,306. Capital, Baton Rouge. Nickname, the Pelican State. Motto, Union, Justice and Confidence. Flower, magnolia. Bird, pelican. Song, "Song of Louisiana." Admitted to Union, April 8, 1812. Official abbreviation, La.

Louisiana Purchase

In the earliest days of the United States, more than 150 years ago, the large territory in the middle of the country, reaching from the Mississippi River westward to the Rocky Mountains, was called the Louisiana Territory and belonged to France. In 1803, the United States under President Thomas Jefferson bought this vast territory from Napoleon. This was the Louisiana Purchase. Its acquisition doubled the size of the United States.

This territory had first belonged to Spain. In 1801 Spain had to give it to France. At that time Napoleon was the French emperor. The United States Government did not want to have such a powerful neighbor as France.

President Jefferson wrote immediately to Robert Livingston, the United States minister in France, asking him to tell the French that if they took over the Louisiana Purchase, the United States would ask for Great Britain's help in keeping the French out. This might mean war for France against the English and Americans. Jefferson sent his friend, James Monroe, later the fifth President of the United States, to help Livingston. Napoleon offered to sell Louisiana for fifteen million dollars. Livingston and Monroe were astonished. They had no authority to buy an empire—for this truly was what Louisiana was—a tract of land far larger than most European countries. Napoleon needed the money, for he was about to start a war with Britain, and he would not like to see the United States as an ally of Britain. Livingston and Monroe knew this was a wonderful bargain, and most Americans agreed. Only the Federalists, the political party that represented eastern business, were angry. They were afraid that the new farming states which would be created out of the territory would control Congress. But the fears of the Federalists were not justified. Other problems

—such as the issue of slavery—were to become far more important than that of farming states as against industrial states. The Louisiana Purchase was a stroke of great fortune for the United States and one of the most important events in the history of the United States.

Louisville

Louisville is the largest city in Kentucky. It is on the Ohio River. It was founded in 1778 by George Rogers Clark, an American army officer, and was named for King Louis XVI of France, who had sent help to the United States in the Revolutionary War.

About four hundred thousand people live in Louisville. It is a very important center of trade on the Ohio River, and many railroads pass through it. Farmers from Kentucky and other parts of the South send their products, especially tobacco, to Louisville for sale and shipment. The people work in factories that turn out cigarettes, alcohol, lumber products, textiles, and many other things.

Louisville has many schools and colleges, including Louisville University and Southern Baptist Theological Seminary. Every spring many horse-racing fans travel to Louisville for the famous Kentucky Derby, which is run at the Churchill Downs racetrack near by. In the fall, the Kentucky State Fair is held in Louisville.

LOUISVILLE, KENTUCKY. Population (1970 census) 361,472. County seat, Jefferson County. On the Ohio River. Settled, 1778.

Lourdes

Lourdes is a town in southwest France. In that town, in 1858, a young peasant girl reported that she had seen a vision of the Virgin Mary in a grotto (a cavelike place). The girl's name was Bernadette Soubirous, and she later was canonized as Saint BERNADETTE by the Roman Catholic Church. There is a separate article about her. About two million pilgrims visit Lourdes every year to see the grotto. A large church has been built on the spot, and a statue of Mary has been placed on a rock above the grotto. Many sick people have come here to be cured, and there are piles of canes and crutches that were left behind by crippled people who were·able to leave without them. About sixteen thousand people live in Lourdes.

louse

A louse is a small insect without wings. It is a parasite; that is, it depends on other animals for its food. Lice live on birds and other animals, including human beings. The animal a louse lives on is called its "host." A louse either eats its host's hair or feathers, or bites it and sucks its blood.

There are five main kinds of louse. The largest is the hog louse, which grows to be about a quarter inch long. The other kinds are the bird louse, body louse, crab louse and head louse. Body lice, crab lice and head lice live on human beings. They are unclean insects and are known to carry disease from one person to another.

Lice have existed for thousands of years, but they can be eliminated from in-

dividuals by the use of certain insecticides (chemicals that kill insects). When people or animals are completely clean they are seldom bothered by lice.

In the time of ancient Greece, there was a riddle about the louse. The riddle goes: "Those I find, I throw away. Those I cannot find, I keep. What are they?" The answer, of course, is "lice."

Louvre

The Louvre is the national art gallery of France. It is on the north bank of the Seine, in the city of Paris. No one knows exactly when it was first built, but it was started about 750 years ago. At one time it was the palace of the kings of France. They brought their art treasures there and kept adding galleries to the old building. King Louis XIV added a beautiful section, and the Emperor Napoleon completed the building. It was set apart as a museum in 1793, after the French Revolution, and ever since it has been one of the most famous art museums in the world.

The Louvre contains paintings, drawings, sculpture, furniture, bronzes, tapestries, and every other kind of work of art. There are beautiful gardens around the buildings, with fine statues in them. The Louvre's collection of paintings is the largest in the world. In addition to the works of French painters, it has the paintings of many of the masters of other countries. Many old masterpieces are found here, including the *Winged Victory of Samothrace,* a marble statue from ancient Greece, and the *Mona Lisa,* a famous painting by Leonardo da Vinci.

Lowell

The Lowells are a distinguished Massachusetts family that has given to the United States prominent writers, ministers, statesmen, lawyers, and businessmen. The following four are the most famous members of the family:

James Russell Lowell was a writer of poetry and essay. He was born in 1819 in the Lowell family home, "Elmwood," in Cambridge, Massachusetts. He studied to be a lawyer, but soon gave this up in favor of writing. He married Maria White, who was an abolitionist, a person who wanted to end slavery. (In those days Negroes were slaves in the southern states.) Lowell felt the same way, as is shown by the many abolitionist editorials and articles he wrote. Lowell wrote many popular poems, including "A Vision of Sir Launfal." He was the first editor of the *Atlantic Monthly,* an important magazine, and he was a professor at Harvard. He served the United States government as an ambassador. He died in 1891.

Percival Lowell was an astronomer. He was the grand-nephew of James Russell Lowell. He was born in 1855, in Boston, Massachusetts. His greatest achievement was saying that a planet existed beyond Neptune, which was then thought to be the planet farthest from the sun. This planet, Pluto, actually was not seen until fifteen years after his death. He built an observatory at Flagstaff, Arizona, from which he made extensive studies of the planet Mars. He died in 1916.

Abbott Lawrence Lowell was president

of Harvard University from 1909 to 1933. He was born in Boston in 1856. He practiced law in Boston and was also a professor of political science at Harvard. Percival Lowell was his brother, and Amy Lowell his sister. He died in 1943.

Amy Lowell was a poet. She was born, in Brookline, Massachusetts, in 1874, sister of A. Lawrence and Percival Lowell. She was one of the leaders in a group of poets called Imagists. The Imagists chose words to describe their feelings rather than their meanings. Amy Lowell's home was a center for poets and writers. She was a very unusual woman. She smoked big black cigars, had a large number of dogs about her all the time, and seemed unfriendly to those who did not know her well. One of her best books was a biography of the English poet John Keats. She died in 1925.

Loyola, Saint Ignatius of

St. Ignatius of Loyola was the founder of the religious order known as the Jesuits. He was born in Spain, of a noble family, in 1491. He first became a courageous and enthusiastic soldier. He was severely wounded in battle, and in the course of his recovery he happened to read a book on the lives of saints.

The stories of the saints so inspired him that he renounced his profession of soldier and became a humble pilgrim. He walked barefoot from Spain to Rome, where he received the Pope's blessing, and from there to Jerusalem in the Holy Land. He wanted to preach, but was not allowed to, for he did not have the proper education.

To prepare himself, Loyola went to several universities, including the great University of Paris. There he gathered around him a group of followers which was the beginning of the Catholic order called the Society of Jesus, or JESUITS (about which you can read in another volume). Loyola wrote the strict rules of the order, including the Spiritual Exercises, a book of prayers and devotions.

The Jesuits, like their founder, are known for their learning, their selfless devotion to their ideal of improving not only their own souls but the condition of humanity.

Ignatius of Loyola died in 1556 and was proclaimed a saint in 1622.

Luke, Saint

St. Luke was one of the evangelists, or preachers of the Gospel, of the early Christian Church. He wrote the Gospel according to St. Luke, the third book of the New Testament. This Gospel was the first part of a two-part history of Christianity and the Church. The second part is the Acts of the Apostles, also in the New Testament. St. Luke was a close friend of the Apostle Paul, with whom he made trips to spread the gospel after the death of Jesus. Luke was probably a Greek doctor, and he is the patron saint of doctors. Many hospitals and medical societies are named for him. Luke is also the patron saint of painters. He is believed to have been a painter himself, and he is often represented with a brush and palette in his hands. St. Luke's feast day is October 18.

lumbago

Lumbago is a pain in the lumbar region, the lower part of the back. It is sometimes called "muscular rheumatism," and is usually a sharp, sudden pain. Lumbago may be brought on by exposure to a draft, by some unusual exercise, or by sudden strain. It is often a symptom of a muscle injury or of a trouble in the intestines, kidneys, or some other internal organ. Lumbago is usually treated by resting in bed, keeping warm, and using liniment, a mustard plaster, or a heating pad.

If back pains disappear after such treatment, the patient probably had lumbago. If the pain continues, they may show the presence of a more serious back injury or disease, and a doctor should be called.

Lumber

Lumber is timber (wood suitable for building purposes) that is cut and sawed into boards or planks. Lumber is used in more than four thousand ways in our daily lives. The lumber industry has been important in the United States ever since the earliest colonists started to clear the land. About 644,000 people work in the lumber industry in the United States, where almost half of the world's lumber is produced.

There are about 1,100 different kinds of tree in the United States, but only about 100 of them are used for lumber. Most of our lumber comes from 35 of these kinds. Lumber-producing trees are about evenly divided into two different kinds of wood, the *hardwood* and the *softwood*. Most softwoods are *conifers*, or trees bearing needles and cones, such as pine, cedar, fir, and hemlock. Building and construction lumber is made mostly from softwood lumber. Most hardwoods are *deciduous*, or trees that shed their leaves each year, such as ash, birch, cherry, gum, maple, oak, mahogany, and walnut. Most hardwood lumber is used for interior trim in houses, and for flooring, furniture, and cabinets.

LUMBERING

Lumbering begins in the woods. More than half of the lumber in the United States comes from privately owned forests, including farm wood lots. The rest of the lumber comes from public lands, largely national forests. Scientifically trained foresters select the trees to be cut, leaving seed trees and young growing trees for use in the future.

The cutting of trees for lumber is called a *timber harvest*, just as the collecting of crops in the fall is called a harvest. After the foresters have marked the trees to be harvested, the trees are cut by men called *fallers*. Two fallers work together. They use cross-cut or power saws to cut the trees close to the ground. The limbs of the trees are then removed and the trunks are cut into lengths suitable for lumber. This process is called *bucking*.

The logs are then dragged out of the woods, by tractors or draft animals, and

HOW WOOD IS CONSUMED

FUEL WOOD 17 %

LUMBER 49%

11 % LOST TO FIRE AND DISEASE

PAPER AND PAPER PRODUCTS 9 %

ALL OTHER 14%

are loaded onto trucks or railroad cars to be taken to the sawmill. For many years logs were rolled into nearby rivers and floated downstream to the mill, and in some areas this method is still used. Most sawmills are built on rivers or lakes so that the logs can be floated in a "log pond" near the mill until they are ready to be sawed. Storage in water protects the wood from insect and fire damage.

THE SAWMILL

Logs are pulled lengthwise into the mill by a conveyor chain called a *bullchain* or *jackladder*. There they are lifted onto the *sawing deck*. The logs move sideways on the sawing deck, one at a time, to the carriage, which carries them to the saw. Here the *sawyer* takes over. The sawyer is one of the most important men in the mill. He knows how to cut the lumber so that the largest amount of high-quality lumber can be secured from each log. He regulates the cutting of the lumber by controlling the *headrig*, which is the name of the carriage and the headsaw where logs are squared and cut into timber. These cuts are called *cants* or *flitches*. The carriage, mounted on wheels, rolls on a metal track back and forth past the headsaw.

The headsaw in most of the larger mills is an endless steel belt called a bandsaw. It runs on two large wheels. As the carriage moves forward the bandsaw's sharp teeth bite through the log. When the saw has passed through the log's length, the carriage shoots back and the position of the log is shifted for a second cut. Smaller mills usually use a circular headsaw.

Large mills have saws called *resaws* that cut the larger timber into boards of regulated thickness, but in smaller mills the entire log is cut into standard sizes by the headsaw.

Farther along the production line, *edger saws* rip off bark and rough edges from boards and reduce them to standard widths. Then the boards move sideways into a row of *trimmer saws*. These square the ends of the boards, cut out defects, and saw the boards to the desired lengths.

Lumber may be sawed in either of two ways. In the flat-, or "slash," grain cut, the lines (rings in the trees) run in the same direction as the surface of the board. In the edge-, or "vertical," grain cut, the lines run at right angles to the surface of the board. (The picture shows the two cuts.) Flat-grain boards are cheaper because

Principal Timbered Regions of the United States

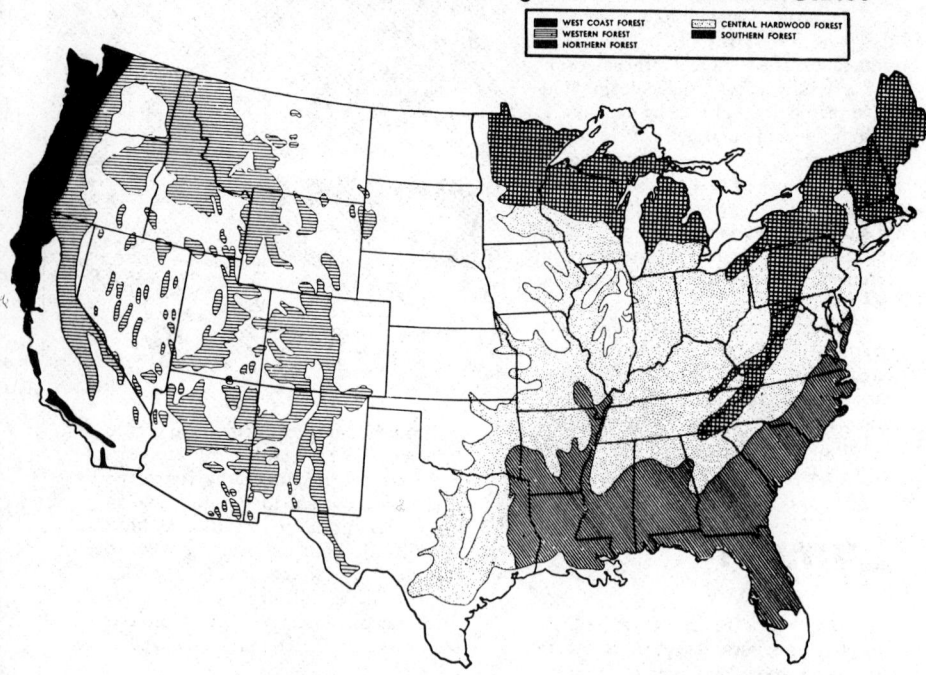

WEST COAST FOREST
WESTERN FOREST
NORTHERN FOREST
CENTRAL HARDWOOD FOREST
SOUTHERN FOREST

American Forestry Assn.

The United States is the second-largest lumber-producing nation in the world. The leading states are Oregon, Washington, Alabama, Georgia, North Carolina, and Mississippi.

they are milled in less time and with less labor, but they have more defects and warp more quickly. The edge-grain cuts will not swell, shrink, or warp, and will wear more evenly and hold paint better.

After the lumber is sawed, it goes to a long *sorting shed,* where each board is graded and marked for price and use. This lumber is called *green* lumber, not because of its color but because it is freshly cut and needs to be seasoned and dried before it is used for building. The lumber is dried outdoors in the air, or in kilns (ovens).

GRADES OF LUMBER

Common lumber, which you will see stacked outside a lumber yard or any place where lumber is sold, is a cheap grade of lumber used for certain kinds of building. It is less than five inches thick and may have defects such as knots, splits, and the like. This common lumber is graded 1, 2, 3, 4, and 5. Number 1 Common lumber is the best of this kind.

Select lumber, which is usually stacked under cover for protection, is a better grade of lumber. It has fewer defects and is used for interior finishing and for furniture. Select lumber is graded A, B, C, and D. The Grade A Select lumber is the best of these.

Structural lumber is a kind of lumber that is much heavier than the other kinds.

CUTS AND SIZES OF LUMBER

Lumber that is less than two inches thick is usually called boards. When boards are less than eight inches wide, they are often called *strips.* Thicker and wider lumber is called *planks.* Some of the special kinds of lumber cuts are illustrated on these pages. The 8-inch *shiplap* or 6-inch *D&M* (dressed and matched) is used for sheathing the side walls

of a house and roof, also for rough flooring. *Flooring* is used for finish flooring and may be either hardwood or softwood. The 5/8-inch *beaded ceiling* is used chiefly for porch ceilings. *Drop* and *bevel sidings* are used for outside wall coverings of a building. The *moldings* are used for trim both inside and outside.

Lumber is sized according to its rough-cut, or original, size, that is, its size when it comes from the sawmill. A 1" × 8" board, for example, actually measures one inch by eight inches when it comes from the sawmill. When it has been dressed (dried and planed) it is thinner and less wide.

LOGGING AND LUMBERJACKS

Until about fifty years ago, logging,

which means cutting down trees and preparing them to be sent to sawmills, was one of the most exciting and dangerous jobs a man could have. Logging was done by men called lumberjacks. For several months of the year the lumberjacks lived in rough camps in the forests of the West. Logging camps were usually set up near a river. During the winter the lumberjacks felled the trees, stripped them of branches and leaves, and piled them up near the river. In the spring, when the ice on the river melted, the current carried the logs downstream to the sawmill. Often the lumberjacks had to ride downstream on logs, so that they could make sure the logs did not pile up and stop moving in some narrow part of the river.

The lumberjacks lived a rugged, outdoor life. No women were allowed in the camp, and the men lived in rough barracks and had to work very hard.

One of the lumberjacks' popular sports is called *birling.* This is standing on a log in the water and making it revolve rapidly by treading it with the feet. Newsreels often show birling contests in which the winner is the man who can keep the log whirling longest without falling off into the water.

Logging today is an industry using modern machines. Trees are cut down by huge, power-driven chain saws instead of by hand. They are loaded by cranelike equipment onto trucks, which take them to the river. Machines join the logs together into rafts that are driven downstream to the sawmill. When logs pile up, they are blasted loose by dynamite or other explosives.

The life of the lumberjack has changed too. Most lumberjacks live in houses with their families and are picked up by buses every day to take them to their work. There are still some logging camps, but they have been modernized, and the men live much more comfortably.

lungs

The lungs are the organs of your body with which you breathe. The lungs supply oxygen from the air to the blood and take away carbon dioxide and water vapor from the blood, delivering it to the outside air.

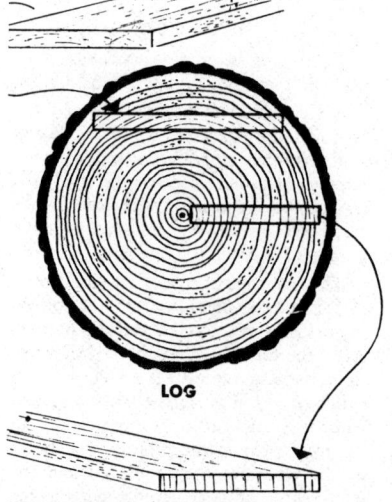

FLAT- OR SLASH-GRAIN BOARD

LOG

VERTICAL-GRAIN OR QUARTER-SAWED BOARDS

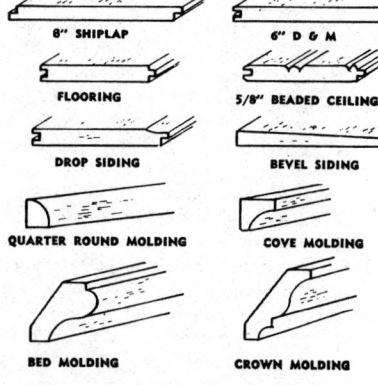

10 TYPES OF FINISH LUMBER

8" SHIPLAP

6" D & M

FLOORING

5/8" BEADED CEILING

DROP SIDING

BEVEL SIDING

QUARTER ROUND MOLDING

COVE MOLDING

BED MOLDING

CROWN MOLDING

American Magazine—Walt Durbahn's TV Workshop

Flat-grain and vertical-grain lumber come from different parts of the log. Finished lumber is cut in a specific shape, so that it will be suited for a specific purpose.

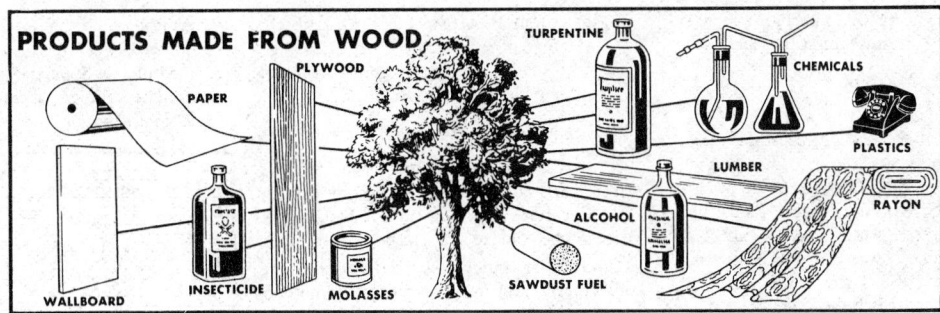

PRODUCTS MADE FROM WOOD

TURPENTINE • CHEMICALS • PLASTICS • RAYON • LUMBER • ALCOHOL • SAWDUST FUEL • MOLASSES • INSECTICIDE • WALLBOARD • PLYWOOD • PAPER

Wood is used chiefly for lumber, but also for many by-products of the lumber industry.

The lungs are the most important part of the body's *respiratory* (breathing) system. The other parts are the nose, throat, trachea or windpipe, and bronchial tubes. (There is a separate article on BREATHING.)

The lungs are very light, spongy organs. They are connected to the throat by the trachea and by two bronchial tubes or bronchi. One bronchial tube is connected to the right lung, the other to the left lung. These tubes branch off into smaller tubes called *bronchioles* that lead to all parts of the lungs. At the ends of the bronchioles are millions of tiny air sacs or *infundibula*. Scientists believe that the lungs contain about six million of these air sacs. If they all were flattened out and placed next to each other, they would cover half of a football field.

Surrounding the air sacs are thousands of very tiny tubes called *capillaries*. The capillaries carry blood to and from the larger tubes, called veins, that lead to the heart. The walls of the capillaries are thinner than anything man has yet been able to make. Because of this oxygen can pass from the air sacs through the capillary walls into the blood, and carbon dioxide and water vapor can pass from the blood into the air sacs. The breathing movement of your chest gets the carbon dioxide out of the air sacs of your lungs and fills the lungs with fresh air.

HOW THE LUNGS WORK

Your lungs are inside your chest. They are surrounded on both sides by the ribs and chest muscles and separated from the abdomen by a strong, movable, dome-shaped muscle called the *diaphragm*. When you breathe in, or inhale, the chest muscles cause the ribs to move up while the diaphragm moves down. This increases the size of the chest so that the lungs can expand (grow larger) and take in fresh air, filling the air sacs. When you breathe out, or exhale, the chest muscles move the ribs down while the diaphragm goes up to its original position. This decreases the size of the chest, and carbon dioxide is forced out of the lungs into the outside air.

The movements of the lungs are like those of a sponge. When you inhale, your lungs absorb air as a sponge absorbs water. When you exhale, your lungs squeeze out the carbon dioxide as a sponge squeezes out water.

Sometimes the chest muscles cannot move the ribs up and down. This may happen when a person has drowned or has contracted infantile paralysis. In such cases, the lungs cannot breathe in or breathe out. Artificial respiration must be given either by hand or by the use of a special device called an iron lung. (There are separate articles on IRON LUNG and ARTIFICIAL RESPIRATION.)

DISEASES OF THE LUNGS

Sometimes the lungs are attacked by an illness known as *pleurisy*. Each lung is surrounded by two smooth shining membranes called *pleura*. One pleura covers the lungs, the other lines the inner surface of the chest wall. During breathing, the pleura of the lungs slides over the pleura on the inside of the chest. When you cough a great deal or have a bad cold, the pleura often become rough and do not slide smoothly over each other. Breathing becomes difficult and there are pains in the chest. This is pleurisy. If care is not taken, pus will form in the space separating the two pleura, and a disease known as *empyema* will result. Penicillin and other antibiotic drugs have almost ended deaths from pleurisy, but King George V of England died of it. Sometimes a needle or tube must be put in the chest wall to drain off the pus.

Emphysema, which sounds the same, is a different lung disease. The lungs become stretched and do not take in enough air to give a person the oxygen he needs. A person suffering from emphysema might die of a common cold or a stopped-up nose, when an oxygen tent could save his life.

TUBERCULOSIS, also called consumption or phthisis, has always been the most deadly lung disease. See the separate article.

Lung cancer has become an increasing cause of death and studies have indicated that it may be caused by smoking cigarettes.

lungfish

The lungfish of Africa is a strange animal. It lives in the water, like any other fish, but it must breathe air. It comes to the surface occasionally to breathe, and then goes back under water. It buries itself in the mud at the bottom of tropical streams when they start to dry up, keeping a tiny air hole through which it can still breathe. The lungfish sleeps until the fall rains soften and moisten the mud in which it is sleeping.

A lungfish grows to a length of three feet or more. It is considered a great delicacy by many African natives who use it for food. It is strange-looking, with four fins toward the front and center of its body that look like small ribbons or tails, rather than like fins. The female lays eggs about ⅛ inch in diameter, and the male guards them until they hatch.

The lute was the favorite musical instrument in Europe during the Middle Ages and the Renaissance. But the simpler guitar replaced it in the 18th century.

lute

The lute is an old-fashioned stringed musical instrument that looks like a mandolin. It is shaped like a giant pear cut in half, and it has a long neck. The strings run down this neck. On the neck are crosspieces called *frets*, and the fingers of the left hand are pressed down between the frets to make different notes, as in playing a banjo, mandolin, or ukelele. The right hand plucks the strings. Lutes originally had one single and five double strings, but the number was gradually increased until there were 24 strings, which made the lute more like the zither or harp. The lute came originally from Asia, but it was very popular in Europe in the late Middle Ages, between the

years 1300 and 1700. Lutes can sometimes be seen in museum collections.

Luther, Martin

Martin Luther was a German religious reformer who lived more than four hundred years ago. He was first a priest of the Roman Catholic Church. He founded the Protestant faith, and the Lutheran Church was named for him.

Martin Luther was born in Eisleben, Germany, in 1483. He was the son of a poor miner, and his father had great difficulty in saving enough money to send young Martin to school. Even then there was so little money that the boy often sang in the streets to get money for food. One day his singing was heard by a kindly woman, Madame Conrad Cotta. She took Martin into her home and cared for him until he went to the University of Erfurt.

Luther had always been a religious young man, but became a priest for an odd reason. One day there was a bad electrical storm, and lightning was striking on all sides. Badly frightened, Luther swore that if he was not struck he would become a monk. He kept his vow. At the age of 22, he joined the Augustinian Monastery at Erfurt, Germany, and studied hard there. By the time he was 25 he was a professor at the University of Wittenberg.

In 1517, Martin Luther openly stated certain objections to some teachings of the Church. He did this by writing ninety-five *theses,* or statements, and nailing them to the door of the Church at Wittenberg. Many people agreed with him and became his followers. The Church demanded that Luther take back his words, but Luther said, "It is neither safe nor right to go against conscience. There I take my stand. I cannot do otherwise. So help me God. Amen." These words were quoted by President Woodrow Wilson, 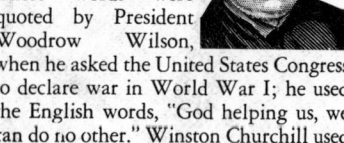 when he asked the United States Congress to declare war in World War I; he used the English words, "God helping us, we can do no other." Winston Churchill used a similar phrase during World War II.

THE START OF PROTESTANTISM

After Luther's defiance of the Church, his friends hid him in an old castle, where he stayed for nearly a year. During that year he began the first German translation of the New Testament. Previously it had always been printed in Latin or Greek.

The Holy Roman (German) emperor, Charles V, ordered all of Luther's books to be burned, which only made the people more eager to read them.

The rulers of some German kingdoms agreed with Luther, while others insisted that the Roman Catholic faith should be the only religion in Germany. Finally the emperor ordered that there should be only the Catholic religion. The other rulers protested, and from this they got the name *Protestants.* Luther, with the help of Philipp Melanchthon, then wrote a statement of his beliefs. This was called the Augsburg Confession. He published it in the year 1530. It later became the basic statement of the Lutheran Church.

Martin Luther died in 1546, at the age of 63, but the Protestant faith continued to spread for hundreds of years.

Lutheran

A Lutheran is a person who follows the Christian religion founded by Martin Luther more than four hundred years ago. It is the oldest and largest Protestant Church. It quickly spread throughout Germany, and north to the Scandinavian countries. Today it is the official religion of Denmark, Norway, Sweden, Finland, and Iceland, as well as the religion of most of the people in Germany.

Many Lutherans came to the New World before the Revolutionary War, but the greatest number came about a hundred years ago, when many German and Swedish Lutherans moved to the United States and settled in the Midwest.

Each Lutheran church is called a *congregation.* Congregations are governed by *synods,* which are councils whose members include both ministers and laymen. In the United States the synods are organized into two main groups: the National Lutheran Council and the Lutheran Synodical Conference. Since World War II, most Lutherans have joined the Lutheran World Federation, which today can be said to speak for most Lutherans.

There are about 90 million Lutherans throughout the world. Of these, nearly 9 million live in the United States. The United States has 17,909 Lutheran congregations, as well as many schools, hospitals, and welfare institutions. Lutheran churches and missions are very active all over the world.

Luxembourg

Luxembourg is a country in Europe. It is one of the smallest nations in the world. It is 999 square miles in size, which is smaller than the state of Rhode Island, and about 345,000 people live there.

Most of the people are of German descent and belong to the Roman Catholic religion. Their own language, *Letzeburgesch,* is like German, but with many French and Dutch words in it. French is the official language of the court.

A large number of the people work in the very valuable iron mines in the southwestern part of the country. Many are farmers. They raise oats, potatoes, and fruits, especially grapes, which are made into Moselle wines. The people who live in the cities work in large pig-iron and steel mills. Although Luxembourg is very small, it is a leading steel-producing country.

Everybody has to go to school until the age of 15. There are a number of technical and commercial schools in Luxembourg.

WHAT THE COUNTRY IS LIKE

Luxembourg is a country of steep hills and narrow valleys. Old castles and fortresses are perched on its hills, making Luxembourg look like a fairyland country. It is covered with oak and pine forests. In most parts, the soil is not very fertile. The Ardennes Mountains and forests cross the northern region. Some peaks rise to more than 1,700 feet. The southern part of Luxembourg is a pleasant and very fertile region. Most of the farming is done there.

The climate of Luxembourg is quite cold in winter and hot in summer. The

Sauer and Mosselle are the most important rivers.

The city of Luxembourg is the capital and largest city. It is an important manufacturing center, with a population of 78,032. Esch-Alzette is the second-largest city, with 27,539 people. It is a mining center.

THE GOVERNMENT OF LUXEMBOURG

Luxembourg is a constitutional monarchy, called a grand duchy. The head of of the state may be a grand duke or grand duchess; the Grand Duchess Charlotte, after reigning for forty-five years, in 1964 gave up the throne to her son, Grand Duke Jean.

Laws are made by the Council of State, with 21 members chosen for life by the grand duke, and the Chamber of Deputies, with 56 members elected for five-year terms by the people.

LUXEMBOURG IN THE PAST

Luxembourg became a duchy in the Holy Roman Empire more than six hundred years ago. In 1815 Luxembourg became a grand duchy, but it was ruled by the king of the Netherlands until 1890, when it became independent.

Although Luxembourg was neutral in World War I, the Germans marched through the country to invade France. In World War II, the Germans occupied Luxembourg and made it part of Germany. The Grand Duchess Charlotte fled with her government to Montreal, Canada, and conducted her government from there. The people of Luxembourg tried to oppose the Germans, but all resistance was brutally put down by the Germans. Part of the Battle of the Bulge in the Ardennes was fought in Luxembourg. Many Allied soldiers, including General

George S. Patton and nine thousand men of his Third Army, were buried in the United States Military Cemetery at Hamm.

Luxembourg has many castles hundreds of years old. The one shown below once belonged to an ancestor of U.S. President Franklin D. Roosevelt. It was heavily damaged in World War II, after this picture was taken.

Luxembourg Nat'l Tourist Office

After the war, the Grand Duchess Charlotte returned to her throne. The country entered into an economic agreement with Belgium and The Netherlands. These countries are known as the BENELUX countries, about which there is a separate article. Luxembourg joined the United Nations in 1947.

LUXEMBOURG. Area, 999 square miles. Population (1973 estimate) 345,000. Languages, Letzeburgesch, German, and French. Religion, principally Roman Catholic. Government, constitutional monarchy. Monetary unit, the Luxembourg franc, worth about 2 cents (U.S.). Flag, three horizontal bars, red, white, and blue.

Luzon

Luzon is the largest and most important island in the Philippines, and it is the most northern of the Philippine islands. Luzon is about 41,845 square miles in size, which is about the size of Kentucky, and about ten million people live there, which is nearly half the population of the Philippines. Most of the people are farmers. They raise almost half the rice grown in the Philippines, as well as sugar cane, Manila hemp, tobacco, coffee, and coconuts. Most of the farming is done in the large and fertile Cagayan Valley in the central part of the island. In the cities, people work in factories making leather, embroidery, and cordage.

Luzon has high mountain ranges, and some of the mountains are active volcanoes. Mt. Mayon erupted violently in 1947. The Sierra Madre range is in the northeastern part of the island, the Cordillera Central is in the northern part, and the Caraballo range is in the southern part of Luzon. There are mines in these mountains, producing manganese, copper, gold, and iron.

Luzon has several large rivers. The Cagayan is the largest river in the Philippines.

On the coasts of the island there are many large bays. The most important ones are Manila Bay and Lingayen Gulf. Manila, the largest city in the Philippines, is on Manila Bay. Some ten miles away is Quezon City, the capital of the Philippines. Many people go to Baguio on their summer vacation. During World War II, Luzon was occupied by the Japanese for more than three years. See the article on the PHILIPPINES.

lye

Lye is a chemical called an alkali. (There is a separate article on ALKALIS.) Lye is always used "in solution," that is, dissolved in water. One of its uses is for making soap. In the United States the name lye usually refers to a solution of a chemical substance called *caustic soda* (or *sodium hydroxide*) or to *caustic potash* (*potassium hydroxide*). The wives of pioneers made lye for soap-making by running water slowly through ashes obtained by burning logs of hard wood. The water running out of the ashes contained an alkali called *potassium carbonate*. Lye is then produced by reacting the potassium carbonate with quick lime.

Because lye is so strong an alkali, it will burn one badly if it touches the skin. If it does get on the skin it should be washed off with running cold water, and vinegar or lemon juice should be put on it. If a person swallows some lye, he should swallow lemon juice or weak vinegar. A doctor should be called quickly.

Although lye is a dangerous poison, it is also very useful. It is used in making rayon and for removing grease and oil from metals just before they are electroplated. Housewives use lye to dissolve hardened fats that have stopped up the drainpipe of the kitchen sink. One should never put lye into aluminum pans, pots, or cans, because it will eat holes in them.

lymph

Lymph is a watery, colorless liquid that flows inside your body in thin tubes called *lymphatics*. Lymph brings food particles from your blood to the tissues of your body and takes waste products back to the blood.

Lymph is made from the liquid part of the blood, called *plasma*. Lymph contains mostly water, some sugar and salt, and some protein, which is necessary for the nourishment of your body tissues. It also contains colorless little bodies called *lymphocytes,* which are similar to the white corpuscles of the blood. Like the white corpuscles, the lymphocytes kill germs in your body and prevent them from getting into your blood stream.

Germs also are prevented from getting into your blood by small fleshy lumps in your body called *lymph nodules*. These nodules often are called lymph glands, but they are not glands like the adrenal, thyroid and pituitary glands. The lymph nodules are in your body to catch germs. They are located at various points along the lymphatics and act as small strainers.

The most noticeable lymph nodules are those in your neck. They catch the germs that have entered your body through your tonsils, nose, throat, and teeth. Sometimes the germs are so powerful that they make the lymph nodules swell up and form pockets of pus, called abscesses. These are very painful and usually must be cut or lanced by a doctor so that the pus can be removed.

Sometimes when you have a sore throat or an infected finger you can feel two small lumps under your jawbone or under your armpits. These are the lymph nodules that have been swollen by the infection-carrying germs. Your doctor may give you some medicine or an injection to help destroy the germs and reduce the swelling in your lymph nodules.

lynching

Lynching is a way of taking the law into your own hands and punishing someone when you feel that the regular authorities will not or cannot do the job. Of course, lynching itself is a violation of the law and no respectable person approves of it. No one knows for certain how the word *lynch* originated, but it probably comes from the name of Charles Lynch, a Virginia planter in the days of the Revolutionary War. He felt that some Americans who were loyal to the King of England should be punished, and held his own court to decide on a punishment for them.

Lynchings have been held in many parts of the United States. In the old days of the West, when the law-enforcement authorities were weak and not respected, citizens often got together and decided who was guilty and gave out their own punishments.

In the South after the Civil War blacks were frequently lynched. A group of citizens who thought a black had committed a crime might carry him away and punish him, even possibly hang him. Or, if some people thought a black had been convicted of a crime but had not received a stiff enough sentence, they might break into the jail and carry him off to punish him in their own way. There have been some lynchings even in recent years, but they have become very rare.

lynx

The lynx is one of the smaller wildcats. It lives in the forests and mountains, generally in northern countries. The Canadian lynx and the bobcat, or wildcat, or red lynx, live in the United States and Canada. (There is a separate article about the BOBCAT.) The European lynx lives in wooded regions of Europe and Asia. Lynxes are usually between 30 and 40 inches in length, and weigh about 60 pounds. Their fur is thick, and is grayish or reddish-brown with white spots. A lynx has side whiskers and tufts on the ears. It has extremely long rear legs and a bobtail. Its feet are large and broad, so it can walk easily on snow. It kills and eats small animals, especially rabbits.

Lynx is a popular fur for women's coats. It is warm and light in weight.

Lyon, Mary

Mary Lyon was a famous American educator who lived more than a hundred years ago. She was born in 1797 in Buckland, Massachusetts. She became a schoolteacher, and became very interested in higher education for women. During her time, very few women went to colleges and universities, which were mainly attended by men. Mary Lyon founded Mt. Holyoke Female Seminary (which later became Mt. Holyoke College for women). She served as its principal until her death and made it famous throughout the world. Mary Lyon died in 1849. She was elected to the Hall of Fame in 1905.

Mary Lyon, who lived from 1797 to 1849, founded Mount Holyoke College in Massachusetts.

Lyon

Lyon is the third-largest city in France. It is in the east central part of France, at the point where the Rhone and Saône Rivers meet. Over 527,-000 peole live there. Many of them work in the great Lyon textile (cloth) industry, which has produced fine silks and beautiful embroideries for five hundred years. Today the largest mills produce rayon, nylon, and other synthetic fabrics. There are also large chemical plants, metal foundries, and automobile factories.

Lyon is a lovely city. The two rivers divide it into three sections. The central part has most of the textile mills. The "new city" on the east has many modern factories and homes. On the west is the old city, where many beautiful old buildings still stand. The medieval Cathedral of St. Jean attracts many visitors, though its stained-glass windows were shattered during World War II. The textile museum shows the history of that industry. The oldest stock exchange in France, *la Bourse de Lyon,* is also in Lyon. It was founded about 450 years ago.

Lyon is about two thousand years old. It was the first city in France to follow the Christian religion. It has always been important because it is at the hub of roads leading to Paris, Italy, and Switzerland.

LYON, FRANCE. Population (1973 estimate) 527,800. Capital of Rhone department.

lyre

The lyre is among the most ancient of stringed musical instruments. It consists of a sound box, and curved side pieces and crossbars to which strings are attached. It is played by plucking the strings. Ancient Greek and Egyptian mythology mention the lyre, and there is one legend that Mercury invented the instrument, using the dried shell of a tortoise as a sounding board.

The first lyres had three strings, but later instruments had seven, eight, eleven, and thirteen strings. The lyre was played while resting on the ground, as the player sat cross-legged. Today in Ethiopia there is a seven-stringed instrument that is very similar to the ancient lyre.

lyrebird

The lyrebird is a native of Australia. It is so named because the tail plumage of the male is shaped like a lyre, with two long curving feathers that look like the lyre's curved side pieces. The lyrebird is small—about the size of a large pigeon—but it looks much larger because of its tail, which is about four times the height of the bird's body. The tail feathers are brilliantly colored, but the body is an olive-brown color. The lyrebird is a weak flier. It lives on insects, especially beetles, and snails.

A single egg is laid each year in a nest of moss, sticks, and fibers, lined with a wiry kind of native tree-fern. The egg is pale buff-colored, and looks as though it had been smudged with ink. Young lyrebirds stay in the nest longer than most other young birds.

Lysenko, Trofim

Trofim Lysenko is the name of a Russian student of plant life. He was born in 1896. He became famous for saying that "acquired traits can be inherited."

Lysenko soaked spring wheat in water and froze it, a process called *vernalization.* Now, he said, the wheat seeds or kernels from the spring wheat produced winter wheat.

Then Lysenko said that his ideas could be applied to heredity in people as well as in plants. It is known that people can be changed by their surroundings; Lysenko said that these changes or *traits* could be inherited by their children.

Scientists outside of Russia did not agree with Lysenko. Scientific laws uncovered by the work of the great scientists Thomas Hunt Morgan and Gregor Mendel had shown that children will inherit certain traits from their parents, but that these cannot be changed by what happens to the parents. Lysenko said that this is not so, but no proof of his claims was ever shown to any scientists outside of Russia.

The Communist government of Russia made it a crime for any scientist to disagree with Lysenko. For political reasons, the Communist dictator, Joseph Stalin, wanted people to believe that a Communist country could breed better men and women than any other country. Some Russian scientists lost their jobs and were even put in prison for disputing Lysenko's claims.

After Stalin died, in 1953, the Russian government gave Russian scientists some freedom to say what they really thought and most of them said they had never agreed with Lysenko. Lysenko lost his great power and held unimportant jobs for several years. In 1961 he was again given an important position but other Russian scientists were no longer required to agree with his theories.

EARLY GREEK   ETRUSCAN

UNCIAL

EARLY ROMAN

CAROLINGIAN   RENAISSANCE

GOTHIC

ALDINE

M or m

The letter M is the thirteenth letter of the alphabet. It can be traced all the way back to the earliest writing known to man, in Egypt, thousands of years ago. In the Hebrew language, in which much of the Bible was written, the letter was called *mem*, a word that meant "waves." The ancient Greeks took the same letter and called it *mu*.

At the top of this page, at the far left, you can see the early Greek form of the letter M. The later Greeks eliminated the "tail", and in this form it was adopted by the Romans who modified it into the M we use today. The Uncial form of M is a development from the rounded written Roman m, which is the basis of our modern small m, both in printing and in handwriting.

Read also the article ALPHABET.

macaroni

Macaroni is a food usually made of wheat flour. It consists of a soft dough made of flour and water, which is formed into any desired shape and then dried. The dried macaroni is boiled in water and served with many different kinds of sauces. Macaroni first became popular in Italy several hundred years ago, but similar pastes made of wheat or rice flour were made in Asia thousands of years ago.

Macaroni originally was a general name for any such product of flour and water, including spaghetti, noodles, and all the other shapes in which it was made. In the United States, however, macaroni has come to mean particularly the long, thin tubes with a hole down the center that are so popular as "macaroni and cheese." Spaghetti is also made of long, thin, tube-shaped strands, but without the hole. However, all the different forms are made in more or less the same way.

To make macaroni, wheat is ground into a coarse meal, and the bran, or outer coating of the grain of wheat, is removed. Various kinds of wheat are used, but the best is a hard variety called durum wheat. The flour is then kneaded, or squeezed, with water to make a dough. If the macaroni is to be the long thin kind, the dough is forced through a mold into a tube shape. To make other varieties it is stamped into little squares or shell shapes, or cut into short pieces called elbows. The shaped dough is then dried in special rooms where the temperature, moisture, and circulation of air can be carefully controlled.

Other forms of macaroni include vermicelli, which consists of very thin strands or strings of dough; noodles, which are made by adding a certain quantity of egg to the dough and rolling it into flat ribbons; and spaghetti, which is made in thin rods that are somewhat thicker than vermicelli. In the United States macaroni is also made of soy flour, obtained from soy beans, and of whole wheat, which is wheat flour from which the bran has not been removed. Sometimes one of several vegetables is added to macaroni products, especially to noodles, such as spinach, tomato, or carrot. This colors the noodles and adds a slight extra flavor.

Several hundred years ago macaroni was so especially an Italian and European food that the British used the word as a teasing name for any young man who traveled abroad and then came home to England with fancy, affected ways. This is how the word *macaroni* got into the Revolutionary War song, "Yankee Doodle." The British sang about the colonial soldier as a "Yankee doodle dandy," who "stuck a feather in his hat and called it macaroni," meaning to make fun of the poorly dressed, untrained American soldiers. But the American soldiers were proud of themselves, and they took the song over and made it their own.

MacArthur, Douglas

Douglas MacArthur, a General of the Army ("five-star general") in the United States Army, was one of America's greatest military heroes in World War II. He was commander of all United States forces in the Pacific campaign against Japan. When early Japanese victories forced him to leave the Philippine Islands in 1942,

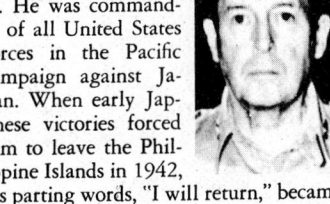

his parting words, "I will return," became a rallying cry for all the Allied peoples.

Douglas MacArthur was born in 1880 in Arkansas, where his father, Arthur MacArthur, was stationed at an Army post in Little Rock. Arthur MacArthur was also a noted military man. He was born in 1845 and served in the Civil War at the age of 17, for which service he was given the nickname of "the boy colonel of the West" and was awarded the Congressional Medal of Honor. He became the eleventh lieutenant general in the history of the United States Army. Later he was appointed military governor of the Philippines. He died in 1912.

When Douglas MacArthur was 13 his father was stationed at Fort Sam Houston, Texas, and Douglas attended the Texas Military Academy. His father was assigned to the Philippine Islands, and during this time Douglas and his mother lived in Milwaukee, Wisconsin, which city MacArthur made his official home for many years. He entered the United States Military Academy at West Point at the age of 19, and scored one of the best scholastic records ever made there. He served in the Philippines and in Japan, and then was appointed aide to President Theodore Roosevelt.

When World War I began, MacArthur was a staff officer in Washington, D.C. He was the first member of the famous 42nd Division that was the first combat unit to reach France, and he gave it the nickname Rainbow Division. He was sent to France in 1917, was wounded twice, and was decorated thirteen times. The following year he was promoted to brigadier general by General John J. Pershing.

After the war MacArthur was superintendent of West Point for three years, and then spent three years in the Philippines. In 1930 he became Chief of Staff, the highest Army position. In this post he made many enemies because he was sure that Germany and Japan were arming to attack the United States, and he said so. He helped to prevent the Army's strength from being cut down, and he did a great deal to bring the service up to date.

In 1935 the President of the Philippines, Manuel Quezon, asked that General MacArthur be sent to his country to help build up the army there. MacArthur made up a ten-year plan for Philippine defense that included the establishment of a Philippine Military Academy and the training of 40,000 men a year.

MacArthur retired from the Army in 1937, at the age of 57. Four years later, in 1941, he was recalled to active service, and shortly after the Japanese attack on Pearl Harbor he was back in the Philippines. There he led his small force with little equipment until he and his men were bottled up by the Japanese on Bataan peninsula. President Franklin D. Roosevelt ordered MacArthur to leave Bataan with his staff officers and his wife and four-year-old son. It was then that he made his famous promise to return, and three years later he did return to liberate the Philippines from the Japanese.

In 1945 MacArthur was put in command of all United States forces in the Pacific, and in August of that year he received the surrender of Japan on the battleship *Missouri*. MacArthur was made Supreme Commander in Japan after the war, and he is credited with making that nation a democratic country. When fighting broke out in Korea in 1950, MacArthur was head of all United Nations forces. In 1951, President Harry S. Truman relieved General MacArthur of his command. A great many people disapproved of this action, but a Senate inquiry decided that it was done because the general had disregarded President Truman's request that MacArthur get approval from the Department of Defense for any

statements he wanted to make on United States policy.

MacArthur returned to the United States in 1951. He was mentioned as a candidate for President of the United States at the Republican national conventions of 1948 and 1952, but both times he insisted that he sought no public office. Later he accepted a high position in private industry. He died in 1964.

Macaulay, Thomas Babington

Thomas Babington Macaulay was an English historian and writer of essays and poems. He was born in 1800 and learned to read by the time he was 3 years old. As a schoolboy he could read in eight languages, and his friend Sydney Smith once said he was like "a book in breeches."

When Macaulay was 25 he had an essay published in a magazine called the *Edinburgh Review*. For the next twenty years he wrote essays that made the *Review* famous in England. He began a history of England that was so interesting its volumes were sold out almost as fast as they could be published, and it was translated into all modern languages. He left it unfinished at his death. Macaulay wrote a book of poems about old Roman heroes. The book is named *Lays of Ancient Rome*. Millions of boys and girls have enjoyed its exciting poems, especially one called "Horatio at the Bridge."

Macaulay held various positions in the English government, and in 1857 he was made a baron. When he died in 1859 he was buried in Westminster Abbey, with England's most famous writers.

macaw

The macaw is a large parrot that lives in the jungles of Central and South America, where the climate is hot. The macaw is one of the most beautiful of all parrots. It grows to be about three feet long, and it has brilliant red, yellow, green and blue feathers and a long graceful tail. The macaw eats fruit and seeds. It uses its strong, curved beak as a nutcracker. The macaw usually builds its nest in the hollow of a tree. Sometimes it will build a nest in a hole in a cliff. The female macaw lays two white eggs. Many people admire the macaws that are kept

The macaw is the largest and most brightly colored member of the parrot family. It is often seen in the Brazilian jungle.

in zoos in large cities. The macaw is not a very talkative parrot, but it is friendly and affectionate.

Macbeth

Macbeth was a king of Scotland who ruled from 1040 until his death in 1057. He is best remembered by the great play that William Shakespeare wrote about him. Macbeth was an ambitious Scottish general who longed to be king. He killed the king, Duncan I, and took the throne himself. But a Scottish nobleman by the name of Macduff, rose up against Macbeth and killed him in battle.

Maccabees

The Maccabees were a heroic Jewish family who became prominent about two hundred years before the birth of Jesus. At that time, the Jews were ruled by Syrian invaders, under the king Antiochus IV. When Antiochus commanded the Jews to worship foreign gods and to burn a sacrifice to the god Zeus on the Jews' own temple altar in Jerusalem, one old Jewish priest, Mattathias of the Maccabee family, refused to obey. He killed the king's messenger and fled with his own five sons to the mountains. Then he began to urge the Jews to revolt against the Syrians.

When Mattathias died, his son Judah became leader of the group fighting for Jewish liberty. He was a great soldier and defeated three Syrian generals. Because the temple had been dishonored by the enemies of the Jews, Judah purified and re-consecrated it in the year 165 B.C. This is still celebrated by Jews at the festival of Hanukkah.

Judah and his brothers Jonathan and Simon went on fighting to free the Jewish people. Simon at last accomplished this and was made leader and high priest of his countrymen. The Maccabees ruled in Judea until 37 B.C.

There are two books about the Maccabees as part of the APOCRYPHA (about which there is a separate article).

Mack, Connie

Connie Mack, whose real name was Cornelius McGillicuddy, was one of the great figures in the game of baseball. He was born in Massachusetts in 1862, was a big-league catcher and then a manager for 66 years, and died in 1956. He helped found the American League, in which his Philadelphia Athletics team won nine pennants and five world series.

McClellan, George B.

George Brinton McClellan was an outstanding general in the Union (northern) army during the Civil War in the United States. For almost a year he was commander-in-chief of all the Union armies. McClellan was particularly known for his ability to organize men into fighting groups and for his personal popularity with the men who fought under him.

McClellan was born in Philadelphia in 1826 and was graduated from the United

States Military Academy (West Point) in 1846. He took part in the Mexican War before he was 21 years old. At the beginning of the Civil War, in 1860, he was made a major general and put in command of the Union troops in Ohio. He led a campaign into northern Virginia and drove out the Confederate troops, making it possible for this region to become the new state of West Virginia. This was the first Union success of the war and made McClellan a hero to the people living in the North. President Abraham Lincoln then appointed him commander in chief of the Union armies, although he was only 35 years old. He led the Army of the Potomac, the chief Union army in the east. Though he was in command at the battle of Antietam, a great Union victory, he was removed as commander-in-chief because he did not pursue the retreating Southern troops. In 1864 McClellan ran against Abraham Lincoln for the Presidency, but was defeated. Later he served as Governor of New Jersey. He wrote several books on the Civil War. He died in 1885.

McCloskey, Cardinal

John McCloskey was a Roman Catholic priest who was made a cardinal. Cardinals are called princes of the Church.

John McCloskey was born in Emmitsburg, Maryland, in 1810, and went to school in Rome, Italy. When he was 24 years old he became a priest. In 1864 he was made Archbishop of New York, and eleven years later he was made a cardinal. Most of St. Patrick's Cathedral, the biggest Catholic church in New York City, was built while he was cardinal. Cardinal McCloskey died in 1885.

McCormick, Cyrus Hall

Cyrus Hall McCormick was an American inventor. His invention, the McCormick reaper, was the first of the great farming machines and it revolutionized farming. He was born in 1809 in Walnut Grove, Virginia. His father was a farmer, and had tried for years to make a grain cutter, or reaping machine. Young Cyrus became interested in the idea, and worked for several years to finish what his father had started. In 1834 he obtained a patent on his reaper, and it was so successful that he soon opened a large factory in Chicago to make harvesting machines. McCormick received many honors for the help his invention gave to agriculture. He became a very rich man, and the heirs to the fortune he left have become famous themselves in many ways. Some entered the publishing field and owned large newspapers. Some married members of other famous American families and became important in the field of politics. Cyrus Hall McCormick died in Chicago in 1884, at the age of 75. You can read more about him in the article on FARM MACHINERY.

Macdonald, Sir John Alexander

Sir John Alexander Macdonald was a Canadian statesman. He was responsible for a large part of the organization

of the Dominion of Canada, the building of the great Canadian Pacific Railway, and the opening of the Canadian northwest territory. He was born in Glasgow, Scotland, in 1815, and when he was 5 years old he moved with his family to Kingston, Ontario. He became a lawyer in 1836. The people of Kingston elected him to the Canadian Parliament in 1844, and later he became Premier of Canada. He held this office for nineteen years, and for the last thirteen years of his life he had more influence in Canadian politics than any other single person. He died in 1891, at Ottawa, while still in office.

MacDonald, Ramsay

James Ramsay MacDonald was Prime Minister of the first Labour Party government in England. The Prime Minister of England is the head of the government, and the Labour Party is one of the two big political parties. MacDonald was born in Scotland in 1866 and began his career as a writer for Socialist publications. He helped to organize the Labour Party and was its secretary for many years. In 1911 he became the leader of the party, but he resigned in 1914 because Great Britain had entered World War I and MacDonald was a pacifist, a person who does not believe in the use of force.

In 1924, when the Labour Party first was elected to run the government, MacDonald became Prime Minister. He did a great deal to make England's finances more secure and to relieve unemployment. However, the Labour Party was defeated that same year because MacDonald had tried to be more friendly with the Communist government of Russia. In 1929 MacDonald and his party were reelected. To remain in power he had to join forces with the Liberal Party, whose policies he had long considered wrong. This lost him the support of his own party, and in 1935 he was defeated. He retired unhappily, having lost the confidence of both sides in English politics. He was offered a title of nobility by the king, but he refused, saying that he was still a Socialist and could not accept a title. He died in 1937.

MacDowell, Edward

Edward MacDowell was an American composer, or writer of original music. He was born in New York City in 1861, and he studied music in France and Germany. In 1896, when he was only 35, he became the first professor of music at Columbia University. MacDowell is best known for his two concertos for piano and orchestra, and for his *Indian Suite*, which uses melodies of the American Indians. He also wrote the very popular *Woodland Sketches*. MacDowell died in 1908, at the age of 47. His widow, Marian Nevins MacDowell, founded the MacDowell Colony for composers of music, artists, and writers, at their summer home in

Peterborough, New Hampshire. This was a plan that MacDowell had not lived long enough to accomplish himself.

Macedonia

Macedonia is a section of Greece that in ancient times was a powerful and important kingdom. Under one of its kings, Philip II, who reigned more than 350 years before the birth of Jesus, Macedonia controlled all of Greece. Under his son, Alexander the Great, it controlled most of the civilized world. After the death of Alexander, the great Macedonian Empire was divided by the fighting of his generals. The Romans conquered Macedonia and made it a Roman province. When the Roman Empire fell, Macedonia was broken up. For more than a thousand years, part of southern Macedonia has been part of Greece. The other sections have belonged at different times to Turkey, Greece, Austria, Serbia, and Bulgaria.

During World War II, when Greece and Yugoslavia were occupied by Germany, most of Macedonia was made part of Bulgaria. After the war the region was divided among Greece, Yugoslavia, and Bulgaria.

Greek Macedonia is an important part of Greece. Salonika, the second-largest city and harbor of Greece, is in Macedonia. There is little industry in this section of Greece, but fishing and tobacco farming are important.

Yugoslavian Macedonia is a republic (similar to a state in the United States) of Yugoslavia. It is a poor section, with few roads and railroads, and little industry. In the mountains, sheep and cattle are raised; in the fertile river valleys, fruits and silkworms are grown.

Bulgaria has only a small strip of Macedonia, which lies along its southwestern frontier.

McGill University

McGill University is one of the largest universities in Canada. Its main campus of about 50 acres is in the city of Montreal. It was founded in 1821 with money left by James McGill, a prosperous merchant who had come to Canada from Scotland as a poor boy. McGill University is one of the few universities in Canada that gets most of its money to run the school from funds left to it by private individuals. The men and women who attend McGill University can study to be scientists, teachers, engineers, architects, physicians, dentists, lawyers, and members of other professions. In 1975-76, McGill University had 17,971 men and women students. There were about 2,200 faculty members. Distinguished graduates from McGill University live all over the world.

McGraw, John J.

John Joseph McGraw is considered the greatest manager in the history of the game of baseball. He was born in New York in 1873, was a star third baseman on the famous Baltimore Orioles team of the 1890's, and from 1902 to 1932 made the New York Giants the most successful of all teams. He won ten pennants, was second eleven times, and third four times. He died in 1934.

McGuffey, William Holmes

William McGuffey was an American teacher and a writer of schoolbooks from which millions, of schoolchildren learned. He was born in Pennsylvania, in 1800, and when he was 2 years old his parents moved into the wild forests of the Ohio Territory. Although McGuffey had very little chance to go to school, he learned for himself the things that most children were taught, and he became a teacher in the country schools of Ohio when he was only 13 years old. In 1826 he was graduated from Washington College in Pennsylvania.

McGuffey wished to make better schoolbooks for children and to plan better ways to teach. He set up a model school for the children of his neighbors, and he wrote a set of books that became amazingly popular. These "McGuffey Readers" for the rest of the century were almost the only readers used in the schools of the Midwest and the South. At least 122,000,000 copies were sold. When McGuffey died, in 1873, he was a professor of philosophy at the University of Virginia.

McGuigan, Cardinal

James Charles McGuigan is a Roman Catholic priest who was made a cardinal. Cardinals are called princes of the Church.

James McGuigan was born on Prince Edward Island, Canada, in 1894. He went to school at Laval University in Quebec, Canada. When he was 24 years old he became a priest. In 1930 he was made Archbishop of Regina, Canada, and four years later he was made Archbishop of Toronto. He was appointed cardinal in 1946. Cardinal McGuigan is known throughout Canada for the many things he has done to help the poor, and for greatly improving education.

machete

A machete is a long, straight-bladed knife used in the West Indies and South America. One kind of machete is used as a weapon. It has a narrow blade sometimes as much as three feet long. A shorter-bladed machete is used for cutting sugar cane and clearing away underbrush. Machetes are used also in the southwestern United States.

Machiavelli, Niccolo

Niccolo Machiavelli was a political writer, historian and statesman who lived in Italy almost five hundred years ago. He is best known for teaching that the head of a government must be ruthless and even dishonest.

Machiavelli was born in 1469. In his day there was great unrest in Italy. There was no single government; each city had its own leaders, its own soldiers, its own laws. It was unsafe to travel, even during the day, because bands of outlaws roamed freely. Most people were very poor.

Machiavelli wrote two great books, *The Prince* and the *Discourses*. *The Prince* was dedicated to Lorenzo de' Medici, and it was written to teach him how

to become an all-powerful ruler and unite Italy. According to Machiavelli, the Prince must do whatever is necessary to become an all-powerful ruler. If it is a help to appear to be a good man, he should appear to be a good man; if it is a help to lie, steal, cheat, then he may do so. Results are what counts.

MACHINE

Today people use the word *machiavellian* to describe a shrewd, scheming, cynical person. But Machiavelli was not simply a ruthless man. He believed in the republic, a form of government in which many people have a voice. The *Discourses* tell about such a government, and describe the methods of ruling once the ruler has become powerful. In this book, Machiavelli writes of modern, humanitarian ideals. Machiavelli died in 1527.

machine

A machine is any device or tool that helps you do work. There are thousands of different kinds of machine. Each of them is made to do a different job. Our lives are made easier and more comfortable by the hundreds of machines that help us to do work every day.

We usually think of engines, sewing machines, printing presses, and similar complicated devices as machines, but when scientists talk about machines they usually mean simple machines. The complicated machines are special ways of using the simple machines.

There are six kinds of simple machine: LEVER, WHEEL AND AXLE, INCLINED PLANE, WEDGE, PULLEY, and SCREW. There are separate articles that tell you how these simple machines work.

We use machines every day. We use so many machines that the time in which we live has often been called the Machine Age. A bicycle is a machine that uses the lever and the wheel and axle; so is a door knob. A pencil sharpener uses an additional machine, the screw. A knife combines the wedge and the lever.

The more complicated machines, used in industry, may combine four or more of the simple machines. When a machine becomes as complicated as a printing press that takes a roll of blank paper at one end and turns out a complete printed and folded newspaper at the other end, it may be hard to recognize the "simple" machines, but they are there. Without them, there would be no big machines.

USES OF ENERGY

Sewing machines, automobiles, and washing machines are some of the modern machines that work with little or no help from us. Many of the machines used today are run by electricity, steam, water, and air. These are called sources of energy. This energy is actually what does the work in the machines.

To do work, a machine must move something. That is what work means. It means moving something with a certain force over a certain distance. The force is supplied by our own bodies, as when we press down a can opener or push the pedals of a bicycle. What a machine usually does is to increase the size of this force.

For example, when we use a pulley to help us lift heavy weights, we exert a force at one end of a rope, by pulling on it. This is called the *work input*. It creates a force at the other end of the rope, a force that can be used to lift something. This is called the *work output*.

The *efficiency* of a machine is found by comparing the work output to the work input. It is found by dividing the work output by the work input. Since some of the work input is always wasted in overcoming resistance or friction, the efficiency is usually multiplied by 100, which gives the *percent of efficiency*. The efficiency of a machine is always less than 100 percent (100%).

machine gun

A machine gun is a gun that will fire a continuous burst of bullets as long as the trigger is pressed or until there are no more bullets left. It is a small-arms weapon, which means that it can be carried from place to place by one or two men. It usually is mounted on a tripod (three-legged stand). Lighter machine guns, which can be fired from the shoulder or the hip, are called machine rifles or automatic rifles.

The first machine gun was invented by Richard Gatling, an American inventor, in 1862. It had six to ten barrels arranged in a circle. One barrel after another was moved into firing position by an operator turning a crank. The shots were fired as fast as he turned the crank. The Gatling gun was used by the United States Army shortly after the Civil War (1866), and was used by many other countries from 1870 on.

The first really automatic machine gun was invented in England in 1884 by Sir Hiram Maxim, an American from Sangerville, Maine. Each time the gun was fired its backward force, or recoil, caused another piece of ammunition or cartridge to drop into the barrel. To keep firing the gun, all the operator had to do was to press the trigger. The gun would fire eleven bullets a second.

As the gun was fired, the barrel grew very hot. To prevent overheating, Maxim placed a metal tube filled with seven pints of water around the barrel.

The machine guns now used by the United States Army were developed about 1895 by an American gunsmith named John Moses Browning. They operate in almost the same way as the Maxim machine gun, but are simpler and easier to manufacture and use. The Army uses a heavy and a light machine. The heavy one is water-cooled and weighs about 33 pounds, while the light one is usually air-cooled and weighs several pounds less.

The heavy machine gun can fire 550 rounds of ammunition in a minute at objects 2,000 to 6,000 yards away (one to three miles).

The Thompson gun, or Tommy gun, invented just before World War I by an American army officer named John T. Thompson, is a portable machine gun. It is usually called a submachine gun, and is not much heavier than the automatic rifles used today. See the article RIFLE.

machine tool

A machine tool is any machine that grinds, shapes, drills, or polishes metal in the manufacture of tools and parts for other machines. The most common of all machine tools is the *engine lathe*. See the article on LATHE.

McIntyre, Cardinal

James Francis McIntyre is a Roman Catholic priest who was made a cardinal. Cardinals are called princes of the Church.

James McIntyre was born in New York City in 1886. He was a poor boy and had to go to work when he was 13 years old to support his sick father. He went to school at night, because he wanted to become a priest. He was very successful in business, but left it when he was 30 years old to study at Cathedral College and St. Joseph's Seminary, New York. When he was almost 35 years old, he became a priest. In 1948 he was made Archbishop of Los Angeles, and only four years later he was appointed a cardinal.

Mackenzie River

The Mackenzie River is the second-longest river in North America. It is in the Northwest Territories of Canada and is 2,514 miles long. It rises near Mount Brown in the Rocky Mountains and flows north to the Arctic Ocean. Where it rises it is called the Athabasca River. After flowing about six hundred miles it becomes the Slave River, and after reaching the Great Slave Lake it becomes the Mackenzie River. The river is navigable in summer from the Great Slave Lake to the Arctic Ocean and steamers travel up and down this part of it. The river is also navigable farther south, but there are also rapids that make it dangerous.

The mouth of the Mackenzie at the Arctic Ocean is closed by ice from October to June. Further south, the river is filled with trout and whitefish. The Mackenzie River was named after Sir Alexander Mackenzie, who discovered it and sailed to its mouth in 1789.

Mackenzie, Sir Alexander

Alexander Mackenzie was a Scottish explorer who traveled across thousands of miles of unexplored country in Canada's Northwest Territories with only six canoes and a party of twelve. He was born in Scotland, about the year 1770, and moved to Canada when he was very young. He worked for eight years in the fur-trapping country of Saskatchewan near the shore of Lake Athabasca. His employers then decided to send him on a journey of exploration.

In six weeks, Mackenzie worked his way along rivers and through lakes until he reached the Arctic Ocean, at the spot where the northeast border of Alaska meets Canada. Mackenzie Bay and the river leading into the bay were named for him. A later exploration took him west to the Pacific Ocean. As a reward for his perilous journeys, he was made a knight, becoming Sir Alexander Mackenzie. He died in 1820.

mackerel

The mackerel is a fish that lives in the warmer waters of the ocean. It is usually about a foot long and weighs be-

tween 1 and 6 or 7 pounds. Its long, sleek body is a bluish-green color, with tiny black markings on the back. The mackerel looks like a torpedo as it glides through the water. Thousands of mackerel swim together in what are called *schools*. At night the schools break up, and the mackerel come together again when it is daylight.

One of the interesting things about the mackerel is that it must constantly keep moving. If the mackerel stops swimming, it will not get enough oxygen from the water to breathe and it will die. Mackerel eat almost every kind of small fish, and sometimes a mackerel will eat smaller mackerel. The female mackerel lays its eggs in the spring, many miles from shore. It takes about a week for the eggs to hatch. The young fish are quite helpless for several weeks after they are born, and many young mackerel die during this period.

The mackerel is a very tasty fish. The mackerel that lives in the Pacific Ocean is usually canned, while the Atlantic Ocean mackerel is most often eaten fresh or frozen. The people in the United States eat about thirty-five million pounds of mackerel every year.

William McKinley

William McKinley was the twenty-fifth President of the United States. He served from March, 1897, until September 14, 1901. He was elected for two terms, but before his second term was finished he was assassinated at a reception held in his honor at Buffalo, New York. His Vice President, Theodore Roosevelt, then became President.

McKinley was friendly to all and very popular. He worked hard to help American business and industry. He was a kindly, religious man, and his last words, when he knew he was dying, were, "It is God's way. His will, not ours, be done."

William McKinley was born in Niles, Ohio, on January 29, 1843. His father was an iron manufacturer, and William was the seventh of nine children. He attended local schools until he was 16. Then he entered the junior class of Allegheny College in Meadville, Pennsylvania. His health was not good and he returned to Ohio, where he taught school for a time. He enlisted as a private in the Union Army at the outbreak of the Civil War. His record was excellent and he was promoted to the rank of major. After the

war, McKinley returned to Ohio making his home in the town of Poland. He became a lawyer in 1867 and opened an office in Canton, Ohio.

HOW HE BECAME PRESIDENT

McKinley soon became a prominent member of the Republican Party, and he was elected to the House of Representatives in 1876. This was the beginning of a long service in Congress. It lasted fifteen years, until 1891.

In those years United States business was growing rapidly and new industries were being started. Working people in Europe received lower pay than working people in the United States, therefore European manufacturers could sell their goods cheaply. For that reason, United States businessmen feared that European goods would pour into this country and keep them from selling their own goods at a profit. To guard against this, they wanted a "protective" tariff, or tax, put on imported goods, to make them cost more so that people would buy American-made goods.

McKinley believed in a protective tariff. Some people said this was needed to protect the "infant industries" of the United States against the "pauper (poorly paid) labor" of Europe. So McKinley wrote the McKinley Tariff Bill, which became a law in October, 1890. Many people did not like this bill, feeling that it raised prices for the consumers, the people who used the goods. The bill cost McKinley his seat in Congress in 1890 and it also helped to defeat him when he tried to be the Republican candidate for President in 1892. Benjamin Harrison won the nomination.

But McKinley, defeated for Congress, had a powerful supporter in Senator Marcus A. Hanna, chairman of the Republican National Committee. With Hanna's help, McKinley served two terms as Ohio governor, 1891 to 1895.

McKinley ran for President in 1896 against the Democratic candidate, William Jennings Bryan. The campaign issues had to do with the use of silver and gold in United States currency. Bryan wanted "free silver," while McKinley wanted the gold standard. (There are separate articles on BRYAN, FREE SILVER, and the GOLD STANDARD). McKinley won the election of November, 1896, and was inaugurated President in 1897.

Two years later the United States battleship *Maine* was blown up in Havana harbor. There had been much resentment in the United States about Spain's treatment of the Cubans. For these reasons, McKinley asked the Congress to declare war against Spain. The United States quickly won the Spanish-American War.

During McKinley's administration another tariff law, the Dingley Bill, was passed. This also protected business. McKinley was considered a businessman's President, and was very conservative. The country was prosperous.

McKinley was unanimously nominated for a second term as President in 1900, and again he defeated Bryan. Six months after his inauguration, on September 6, 1901, he was shot by a terrorist named Leon Czolgosz. He died eight days later, on September 14. He was buried in Canton, Ohio.

MRS. WILLIAM MCKINLEY

Mrs. Ida Saxon McKinley was born in Ohio in 1847. She was the daughter of a banker in Canton, Ohio. When she was working as a cashier in her father's bank she met, and later married, William McKinley. They had two daughters, both of whom died in infancy. Mrs. McKinley was present at the reception at which her husband was shot. She died six years after her husband, in 1907, and was buried next to him in Canton.

MacMillan, Donald

Donald Baxter MacMillan, an American explorer, was born in Provincetown, Massachusetts, in 1874. He settled in Maine and became a teacher, but in 1908 he joined the explorer Robert E. Peary on an expedition to reach the North Pole. He then made several expeditions on which he was the leader. In 1913 he was sent on an expedition to find a place that Peary had supposed to exist and had called Crocker Land; the expedition lasted four years and MacMillan and his party were finally rescued by a relief ship in 1917, after concluding that Crocker Land was probably a mirage seen by Peary.

MacMillan served in both World Wars. He made many other trips to the Arctic, bringing back rare plants and birds. He also wrote many books.

Macmillan, Harold

Harold Macmillan became British Prime Minister in January 1957, when Anthony Eden resigned. Macmillan is a member of a family that is famous in book-publishing. He was born in 1894, attended Oxford University, and in 1924 was elected to Parliament as a member of the Conservative Party. He served in several cabinets and was Chancellor of the Exchequer (similar to the U.S. Secretary of the Treasury) at the time that Eden resigned.

As Prime Minister, Macmillan adopted the policy of close friendship with the United States but tried also to reduce international tension. In 1959 he visited Moscow to confer with Soviet Premier Khrushchev and then Washington to confer with President Eisenhower. In 1963 he resigned the Prime Ministry, though the Conservative Party was still in power, because of ill health.

McNair, Lesley

Lesley James McNair was an American general who was in command of all United States Army Ground Forces in World War II. He was born in 1883 in Minnesota, and was graduated from the United States Military Academy at West Point in 1904. He served in France in World War I, and was promoted to brigadier general. In 1940 he was put in charge of the Army's training program for tactical forces. In 1942, shortly after World War II began, General McNair was made responsible for training and preparing for combat all ground forces in the United States. He was promoted to lieutenant general in 1941. In 1944, while in the front lines in France, he was killed by a bomb dropped by an Allied plane.

McNaughton, Andrew

Andrew McNaughton is the name

of a Canadian military leader of both world wars. He was born in 1887, and was educated at McGill University. In World War I he served in France and Belgium. He was made a major general in 1929, and for six years was chief of the general staff of the Canadian Army. In World War II he commanded Canadian forces in Great Britain. He became a full general in 1944, and was appointed minister of national defense, but he was defeated in an election the following year. He served for two years as president of the Canadian Atomic Energy Control Board, and in 1948 was appointed Canadian representative to the Security Council of the United Nations. Since 1949 he has been Canadian chairman of the International Joint Commission, which settles questions that concern the territory that lies along the boundary between the United States and Canada and the people living in this territory.

Madagascar

Madagascar, a former French colony, achieved its independence on June 25, 1960 and became known as the Malagasy Republic. The fourth-largest island in the world, it is located in the Indian Ocean, off the eastern coast of Africa. It is 227,800 square miles in area and more than six million people live there. Most of the people are farmers. They produce more than half the world's supply of vanilla. Other crops are coffee, rice, potatoes, and sugar.

The people of Madagascar belong to many different tribes. Some are related to the Malay, or brown-skinned, people of the islands of the Pacific Ocean. Others are related to the Negro people of Africa. There are seventy-four thousand Europeans, most of them French. The main languages of Madagascar are Malagasy (a kind of Malay language) and French. Most of the native people follow the Mohammedan religion. There are still some savage tribes on Madagascar.

Eastern Madagascar is mountainous, with dense forests. The central part is a plateau, a high, level area. It contains valuable minerals, including gold, mica, and agate, but the people have little modern machinery and have not been able to mine much of it. Western Madagascar is a coastal plain that receives less rain than the rest of the island and is less fertile. Most of the island is tropical, hot and rainy, but in the mountains and the plateau it is pleasantly cool.

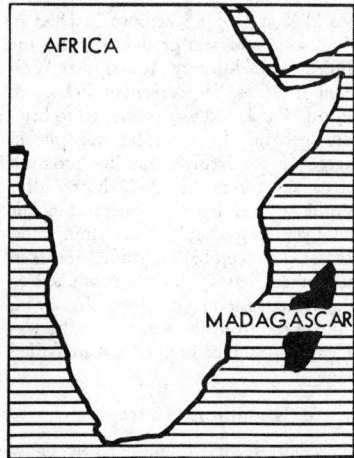

AFRICA

MADAGASCAR

Ewing Galloway

The market place in Tananarive, capital of Madagascar, is crowded with farmers selling fruits and vegetables, and merchants selling silks and cotton goods.

Madagascar became a French colony in 1896, when French troops took control. During World War II, British soldiers occupied the island to prevent the Japanese from using it to attack Allied ships. Madagascar became a fully independent republic within the French Community in 1960. The capital is Tananarive, a city of about 339,233. Other important cities are Antsirabe, Majunga, and Tamatave.

MADAGASCAR (MALAGASY REPUBLIC). Area, 227,800 square miles. Population (1973 estimate) 6,750,000. Languages, Malagasy and French. Religion, Mohammedan. Capital, Tananarive. In the Indian Ocean.

Madame Butterfly

Madame Butterfly is the name of a grand opera, which is a play in which all the conversation is sung instead of spoken. The music was written by Giacomo Puccini, a great Italian composer of operas. The story is taken from a book by an American writer named John Luther Long. *Madame Butterfly* was first presented in 1904 in Milan, Italy, but it was not very well received. Later it became very popular.

Madame Butterfly is a very unhappy love story. It tells about a young Japanese girl, Cho-Cho-San, who falls in love with an American naval officer named Lieutenant Pinkerton. They are married and have a short honeymoon, and then the lieutenant sails away from Japan, promising to return soon. But Lieutenant Pinkerton has been told that Japanese marriages do not really mean much, and he returns to the United States and marries an American girl. The next year he comes back to Japan and Cho-Cho-San sits up all night waiting for him. When he does not come, she weeps bitterly, and the American consul tells her that Pinkerton has married another girl. Pinkerton's new wife comes to see Cho-Cho-San, and in a very sad scene the Japanese girl promises to give her baby son to the American. Then Cho-Cho-San kills herself, just as Lieutenant Pinkerton comes rushing in to beg her to forgive him.

Madeira Islands

Madeira Islands are a group of islands in the North Atlantic Ocean, west of Morocco in North Africa. They belong to Portugal. People live on only two of the islands, most of them on Madeira, the largest island, and some on Porto Santo. Madeira is 240 square miles in area, and more than 280,000 people live there. Most of the people are farmers. They

Embroidery is the chief industry of Madeira. The island has few factories.

raise bananas, sugar, and grapes that are made into Madeira wine, a famous sweet wine. The island is mountainous, and its beautiful scenery and pleasant climate have made it a popular resort. The capital and chief seaport is Funchal, a city of about 100,500.

The Portuguese discovered the Madeira Islands in 1419. They have been ruled by the Portuguese ever since, except, briefly, by Spain more than three hundred years ago and by Great Britain about a hundred years ago.

MADEIRA ISLANDS. Area, 308 square miles. Population (1971 estimate) 283,000. Capital, Funchal. In the North Atlantic Ocean.

Madison, Wisconsin

Madison is the capital of the state of Wisconsin. It is about eighty miles west of Milwaukee and is the center of a rich farming region and the state's big dairy industry. Madison is also an important manufacturing center.

Many Madison people work in factories making machine tools, medical supplies, and automobile parts. Others work in large meat-packing plants and in tobacco markets.

Madison is a very beautiful city. It is famous as the home of the University of Wisconsin, one of the largest universities in the United States. Almost 30,000 students go to school there, and the university has a campus of about a thousand acres.

The state capitol building, made of white granite, rises three hundred feet above the city. In 1836 Madison was named the capital of the Territory of Wisconsin, though it was then a wilderness and not a single white family lived there. The following year the first settlement was made at Madison. The city was named after President James Madison.

MADISON, WISCONSIN. Population (1970 census) 173,258. Capital of Wisconsin. County seat of Dane County. On an isthmus between Lakes Mendota and Monona, in the southern part of the state. Site of University of Wisconsin. Settled 1837.

James Madison

James Madison was the fourth President of the United States. He served two terms, from 1809 to 1817. It was Madison who planned the form of the United States Congress as it is now. Just after the Revolutionary War, and many years before he became President, he set up the system of having an equal number of

Senators from each state, and the members of the House of Representatives according to the state's population.

Madison was a calm, quiet man. He was not physically powerful, but he had the endurance that many thin, wiry peo-

ple appear to have. Throughout his public life, which began in 1776 when he was only 25 years old, he always delivered his speeches in a logical, unexcited manner. He did not shout or wave his arms about, but depended on the common sense of what he said to convince his hearers, rather than the dramatic effects that many other orators have used.

He was one of the group called the "Founding Fathers" of the United States. Madison himself has often been called the "Father of the Constitution," because of the hard work he did in helping to prepare it, and in writing the final draft that was sent to the states for approval and ratification by the voters.

HIS EARLY YEARS

James Madison came from a family of rich landowners in Virginia. He was born on March 16, 1751, at Port Conway, Orange County, Virginia. He was the eldest of twelve children. Madison grew up with all the advantages of wealth. He attended the College of New Jersey—which later became Princeton University—and was graduated in the class of 1771. For about a year after that he continued to study, but politics started to interest him and he was elected to the Virginia Convention in 1776. The Convention was the group of lawmakers that took the place of the Virginia House of Burgesses after the Declaration of Independence. The House of Burgesses had been under the control of the British.

Madison served his state for many years. He represented Virginia as a delegate in the Continental Congress, and he remained in office during the last part of the Revolutionary War and for a time after the war was over. When his term expired in 1783 he went back to Virginia to study law. Soon he was elected to the Virginia legislature, and in 1785 he helped Thomas Jefferson put through a bill that guaranteed religious freedom to all people in Virginia. It had been voted down several times before, but Madison was able to convince the other members of the legislature that the idea was a good one.

The new United States of America held its Constitutional Convention in Philadelphia in 1787, to frame the constitution by which the country would be governed. Madison was a delegate at the convention and made many notes about each day's speeches and activities. Though he could not have known it at the time, these notes proved to be the only record there ever was. The convention was held in great secrecy, and if it had not been for Madison's many pages of notes, no one would know today how the Constitution came into being. The notes were published after Madison died.

James Madison did a great deal of the actual writing of the Constitution. He also wrote most of the amendments that became our Bill of Rights. In 1789 he was elected to the House of Representatives and served for eight years.

HOW HE BECAME PRESIDENT

In 1797 James Madison retired from Congress and became active politically in his home state of Virginia, where he was a member of the state legislature. Four years later, his friend, Thomas Jefferson, became President of the United States and appointed Madison his Secretary of State. For eight years Madison served in this position, and worked very closely with Jefferson. The two men thought alike about most things, and both had deep feelings about the people's right to liberty.

When Thomas Jefferson refused to accept the nomination for a third term, James Madison was placed on the Democratic-Republican ticket to run for President. In the election of 1808, Madison defeated Charles Pinckney, a Federalist, and became the fourth President of the United States.

The first Presidential Inaugural Ball was held at Madison's inauguration, and with it his famous wife, Dolly Madison, began her career as the most popular first lady to live in the White House for many years.

MADISON'S TWO TERMS

When Madison took office as President, in 1809, the United States had been having difficulties with England and France. The ships of both countries had interfered with American vessels on the sea, kidnapped American sailors, and seized American property. Each day the problem seemed to grow worse. Jefferson had put through the Embargo Act, which forbade all trade with both England and France, but this did not help. It just made a great many Americans angry, because they lived by trade.

The government of France finally agreed to stop interfering with American shipping, but England persisted, and relations between the United States and England grew steadily worse. The country was drifting toward a second war with the British.

Madison was a peace-loving man and did not want war, but in the country as a whole many people thought it was the only thing to do. Madison in time gave in to them. In June 1812 the United States declared war against Great Britain. This was the WAR OF 1812, about which there is a separate article. A few months later Madison was re-elected for a second term, which began in 1813.

In 1814, with the war going badly for the United States, a group of five thousand British soldiers sailed up the Chesapeake River and marched into Washington. There were no defense forces in the city, and almost without resistance the British set fire to the Capitol, the White House, the Library of Congress, and several other buildings. The President's wife, Dolly Madison, bravely rescued Gilbert Stuart's portrait of Washington and President Madison's official papers.

The country came out of the War of 1812 stronger and more honored than before, and President Madison shared in the general rejoicing that the fighting was over. Peace came on December 4, 1814, and the remaining part of Madison's term was quiet. In 1817 he retired to his farm at Montpelier, Virginia, and spent the last twenty years of his life there. He did a little farming and enjoyed the company of his friends.

Madison was a man of dignity, honesty, and calm wisdom. He died on June 28, 1836, at the age of 85, and was buried near Montpelier.

MRS. JAMES MADISON

Mrs. Dorothy Payne Todd Madison was born in 1768 in North Carolina, the daughter of a Virginia Quaker. She has always been known as Dolly (or Dolley) Madison. Dolly Payne Todd was a widow when she married Madison. Her first husband, John Todd died in 1793, and she married James Madison in 1794. She was 26 and Madison 44 at the time.

Her fame and popularity as a hostess began during Jefferson's administration and continued throughout her life. Her parties were famous, and she is credited with being the first American hostess to serve ice cream. She died at the age of 81, in 1849, and was buried beside Madison near Montpelier, Virginia.

Madonna

Madonna means "My Lady" in the Italian language. Usually a painting of Mary, the mother of Jesus, is called a Madonna, and if the baby Jesus is in the painting it is called "Madonna and Child."

Thousands of artists have painted Madonnas. The Italian painter Raphael painted more than fifty Madonnas. Mary is usually shown as a young woman with her baby in her arms, as in Raphael's round picture *The Madonna of the Chair*, but sometimes she is the aging mother grieving for Jesus killed, as in a wonderful marble statue by Michelangelo, his *Pietà*, in St. Peter's Cathedral in Rome.

There are modern Madonnas from Mexico, Japan, Italy, the United States, and other countries. These do not always follow all the old traditions. Once Mary was always dressed in red, white, or blue ("red for love, white for purity, blue for truth" in the old color-language of the painters). Often she would appear with a moon at her feet (as she is described in the Book of Revelation, in the Bible) or with a crown of twelve stars.

Madras

Madras is the capital city of the Indian state of Tamil Nadu in India. Until 1968, the state of Tamil Nadu was called

Madras. Tamil Nadu is located in the southern part of India and has a coastline along the Bay of Bengal. The population is about 14,103,125 (1973).

Most of the people of Tamil Nadu are farmers. They grow rice, sugar cane, cotton, and indigo, and raise cattle. Others work in gold and iron mines in the mountains. In the cities there are food-processing plants and silk and cotton mills. Most of the people follow the Hindu religion. Although few are well educated, many have begun to go to school in recent years. Tamil Nadu has been a battlefield for the British, French, and Dutch. The British finally won control of it more than 150 years ago.

The city of Madras is the capital of the state and the third-largest city in India. More than 1,700,000 people live there. Madras is an important seaport and industrial center, and is the religious center of southern India. It has many important buildings, including Madras University. It was founded in 1639 by the British, as a fortified trading post.

Madrid

Madrid is the capital and largest city of Spain. It is on the Manzanares River. It is Spain's chief railroad center, and its principal financial and cultural center. About two million people live in Madrid. They work in factories making leather goods, jewelry, fans, and wine. One of their favorite sports is bullfighting. Every week during the warm months, thousands go to watch the bullfights at the large Atocha arena, which seats as many as 28,000 people.

Madrid is built on a plateau, a high, level place. Its climate is very severe, with sharp changes in temperature. The weather is bitterly cold at times, then terribly hot.

Madrid is a beautiful city with many fine buildings and boulevards. A noted boulevard is the Prado, which is several miles long. Along the tree-lined Prado are many fountains and statues. In the Royal Palace, where the kings of Spain lived until Spain became a republic in 1931, there are many works of art, and Madrid has fine museums. One of the largest universities in Europe is the University of Madrid. Its library contains more than two million books, and scholars from all over the world have studied there.

Madrid was settled more than a thousand years ago by the Moors, a Mohammedan people who then ruled much of Spain. The architecture of some of its buildings shows the Moorish influence. The Spaniards made Madrid their capital about four hundred years ago. From 1936 to 1939 Madrid was the scene of bitter fighting during the Spanish Civil War. Much of Madrid was reduced to ruins, and men, women, and children were killed by bombs.

MADRID, SPAIN. Population (1973 estimate) 3,146,071. Capital of Spain.

Maeterlinck, Maurice

Maurice Maeterlinck was a Belgian writer who wrote in the French language. He was born in 1862. He wrote many gentle, rather dreamlike plays and a wonderful book about bees, called The

Life of the Bee. His play The Blue Bird is a favorite with children, for it is a fairy tale about the search for the blue bird of happiness, in which all familiar things come alive. Sugar, Bread, Light, the Cat and the Dog, Water, Fire, and Night are characters that follow two children looking for the blue bird. Maeterlinck also wrote a series of little plays for the puppet theater. Besides his book about the bees he wrote other books of nature study, such as The Life of the Ant and Pigeons and Spiders. In 1911 he won the Nobel Prize for literature. He died in 1949.

Mafia

The Mafia was a secret society of outlaws in Sicily. It was first started about a hundred years ago. For many centuries it was the custom for rich Sicilian noblemen to hire ruffians who would protect them and their property. The nobles kept these men from being prosecuted for their other lawless activities. The Mafia grew from bands of ruffians and outlaws that were not attached to any specific noblemen. They lived in the hills of Sicily and stole from travelers, farmers, and townspeople. In many cases their power was so great that the police could do nothing against them.

Each band of the Mafia operated under its own leader. Some people think that the leader of each band was under one powerful overlord, but this was probably not so. The Mafia gained more and more power in Sicily, until Benito Mussolini became dictator of Italy (in 1923) and broke up the society.

Some Sicilians who came to the United States were probably members of the Mafia. In New Orleans, in 1891, members of the Mafia killed the chief of police. A similar group of criminals called the "Black Hand" was powerful about fifty years ago, and it terrorized many Italians who came to the United States. In 1950 and 1951 a committee headed by Senator Estes Kefauver investigating crime in the United States found that organized crime is controlled by the "Mafia" but probably not by the Sicilian Mafia. Testimony in 1964 indicated that underworld leaders call their organization cosa nostra, an Italian phrase meaning "our affair."

magazine

A magazine is a kind of book that is not published just once, as a book is, but every week or every month or perhaps every three months. Usually a magazine has paper covers. It may contain only a few pages or as many as three hundred pages. Its contents are stories, articles, and usually advertising.

POPULARITY OF THE MAGAZINE

Next to the newspaper, the magazine is the favorite reading of the American people. During the 1950s more than two billion magazines were sold in the United States and Canada every year, which means that an average of twenty magazines were read by every American who was old enough to read.

KINDS OF MAGAZINE

There are general magazines and special magazines. The general magazines have information that might appeal to almost anyone. The publishers try to make them interesting to both men and women, and they are likely to have stories and articles that both sexes and all ages would like. General magazines are of two kinds, slick and pulp. The slick magazine is one that is printed on a good grade of paper that is smooth and shiny. The pulp magazine is printed on cheap, rough paper. There are not many pulp magazines any more. Most of them nowadays are the comic books that are read mostly by children and young people.

Most magazines today are special magazines, designed to appeal to some particular group of readers. The biggest group of special magazines are the women's magazines, which are primarily for housewives. They print instructions on cooking, sewing, and other household matters, and stories and articles that the editors think women would want to read. The second-biggest is the group of magazines that tell people how to plan and care for their homes and gardens. The children's magazines have stories, articles on how to make things, puzzles, and other things of interest to children. There are trade journals that appeal mostly to people in particular lines of business; farm journals that tell the farmer about the newest machines and methods of raising fine crops; house organs, which appeal mostly to employees of one particular company, or members of one organization; and scientific journals for such specialists as doctors, dentists, chemists, and others.

Another type of magazine that has become popular in recent years is the digest magazine. "Digests" reprint entire articles from other magazines. Some digests do not publish any advertising.

Some magazines are devoted entirely to news. These usually call themselves newspapers because this permits them to pay lower postage rates for mailing, but they are actually magazines.

Another group is called "little magazines." These are devoted to publishing new and experimental literature. They usually have very small circulations, but they have done a great deal to encourage better writing.

SALE OF MAGAZINES

Usually a magazine is sold for less than it actually costs, so it is a great bargain to the public. This is possible because most of the money the magazine makes comes from payment for advertising. Advertising rates depend on circulation, or the number of copies sold, and this may be anywhere from a few thousand up to several million copies of every issue. You can read more about this in the article on ADVERTISING.

Magazines call themselves weeklies, bi-weeklies, or monthlies, depending on the frequency with which they are published. The weekly comes out the same day every week; the bi-weekly comes out every two weeks; and the monthly comes out every month. A few magazines are quarterlies, which means they are published only four times a year.

Magazines are sold in two ways: by subscription and on the newsstands. When a person becomes a subscriber, he pays in advance for all the issues for a year or more, and he gets a special price that is lower than the regular price. The newsstands sell single copies and charge the full price. The total number of people who buy the magazine in either of these two ways is called the *net paid circulation.*

DEPARTMENTS OF MAGAZINES

The preparation of a magazine begins in the editorial department. In this department, editors buy stories and articles, usually from writers who do not work for the magazine. The editors prepare the stories and articles for publication, making corrections if necessary. The art department is in charge of getting illustrations for the stories and articles. This may be done by staff artists or photographers, or drawings and photographs may be bought. The advertising department persuades business firms to buy advertising space and helps prepare the advertising copy for publication. The production department gets the stories and articles and advertisements set in type and the illustrations ready for printing.

The department of a magazine that tries to get people to subscribe is called the circulation department. The department that takes care of circulation mailing lists and the sending out of magazines to subscribers is called the fulfillment department.

HISTORY OF MAGAZINES

Magazines began more than three hundred years ago. A magazine containing articles on literature and science began publication in France in 1665. In England in the early 1700s Richard Steele and Joseph Addison were largely responsible for introducing the magazine with articles on various subjects when they wrote and published first *The Tatler* and later *The Spectator.* The word *magazine* was first used by the *Gentleman's Magazine,* published in England in 1731. In America the early magazines lasted only a few years. The first weekly to survive was the *Saturday Evening Post,* which was started in 1821 as an outgrowth of a magazine founded by Benjamin Franklin in 1729. It was a very different magazine then, however, from the one that is published today.

About a hundred years ago the publication of fine magazines began in the United States with such magazines as the *Century* and the *Atlantic Monthly.* The popular magazine started with *Leslie's Weekly* in 1855 and the monthly *Munsey's Magazine* in 1889.

The great growth of the modern magazine became possible when huge circulations became possible with improved printing and transportation methods. The *Ladies' Home Journal* was founded in 1883, and six years later Edward W. Bok became its editor. The *Saturday Evening Post* was bought by Cyrus H. K. Curtis in 1897, and edited from 1899 to 1937 by George Horace Lorimer. These two magazines were published by the Curtis Publishing Company, and within a few years they

built up circulations in the millions. This encouraged many other publishers to go into the magazine field. Notable among them was William Randolph Hearst, whose magazine *Good Housekeeping* introduced the idea that the publisher of a magazine should stand behind every product advertised in it. This appealed to the advertisers and to the readers, and now many magazines and newspapers make such guarantees.

The next big developments were both made by the publishing house headed by Henry Luce. In 1923 he and his associates brought out *Time,* a weekly magazine of news. Now there are a number of such news magazines. Later the Luce organization brought out *Life,* which gives the news mostly in pictures. This idea proved so popular that *Life* grew to a circulation of more than seven million every week. *Look,* a magazine modeled on *Life,* has been as great a success.

The digest magazines began with the *Reader's Digest,* founded by DeWitt Wallace and his wife Lila Wallace in 1922. It has been the most successful magazine of any kind in history. Its circulation has reached fifteen million monthly in the United States alone and it is published in many countries and languages, including Arabic and Chinese, and in an edition in Braille for the blind.

Another type of publication that most people do not usually think of as a magazine is the magazine section of a newspaper. For some years big newspapers published their own magazine sections, and some still do. But nowadays most of them are put out by big independent publishers and are distributed to ten, twenty, or even a hundred newspapers, which publish them as part of their Saturday or Sunday papers. Although the newspapers buy these magazine sections from the publisher, they get a part of the income from the advertising in them, so actually they make a profit by carrying the magazine section.

Magellan, Ferdinand

Ferdinand Magellan was a Portuguese explorer and sea captain. He organized the first voyage around the world. He was born around 1480 in Portugal, the son of a nobleman. When he was  about 25 years old he sailed to India, and he spent seven years in India, the East Indies, and East Africa.

In 1517 he offered to find a western route to the Indies for King Charles of Spain. Portugal controlled the eastern route, and Charles, jealous of the wealth pouring into Portugal, accepted Magellan's offer.

In August 1519, in command of a fleet of five ships and 270 men, Magellan sailed from Seville, Spain. During his first winter on the wild coast of what is now Argentina he had to put down a revolt of his frightened men. In October 1520, he discovered the passage now named after him, the Strait of Magellan, at the tip of South America. From here he entered the Pacific Ocean.

By this time Magellan had only three ships left. In three months he reached the

Marianas Islands, the first place in the Pacific where he and his men could rest and get food and drink. The men suffered terribly during this part of the trip and they were forced to eat leather and sawdust. In March 1521 the group reached the Philippine Islands. A few weeks later Magellan was killed in a battle with some native tribes. Several of the other leaders were killed a short time later, and two more ships were lost.

The only remaining ship, after sailing around the Cape of Good Hope, reached Seville in September 1522 with a load of spices and only 18 men. Though Magellan did not live to finish his voyage, it proved that it was possible to sail around the world. It also opened the Pacific Ocean to the ships of the Europeans.

Magi

The priests in the religion of ancient Persia were called *magi,* but we think of the word chiefly in connection with the Three Wise Men who came from the East and followed the Star of Bethlehem to the place where Jesus lay in the manger. These three men took gifts of gold, frankincense and myrrh to Jesus.

In legends, the Three Wise Men were called Magi and their names were supposed to be Melchior, Gaspar, and Balthazar.

The magi or priests of Persia had knowledge of all the sacred rituals. They were wise men, but they also were diviners and astrologers who pretended to foretell the future. It is from the magi that we have our word *magic.*

magic

Magic is the art of doing wonderful things in a mysterious way. It has been practiced by every race and nation since long before history began. In ancient times, long before the birth of Christ, magic was connected with the beginnings of religion and of medicine. The word *magic* comes from the *magi,* who were the priests of ancient Persia, but there is really little connection between them and what we call magic.

For thousands of years most people believed that remarkable things could be done by influencing spirits of mysterious powers to carry out one's desires. There were various names for the men who were supposed to be able to do this. They were called magicians, sorcerers, witch doctors, medicine men, or conjurors.

There were various beliefs as to how a spirit or other agency could be influenced. Knowing a spirit's name already gave a person some power over him. A trace of that old belief is found in the fairy tale about Rumpelstiltskin. He loses his power over the queen when she learns his name. But usually a proper ritual or "incantation" was necessary to influence the spirits. Certain words such as abracadabra, and some numbers, too, were supposed to have magical powers. In the story of Aladdin there is another of the many methods of summoning spirits: Aladdin rubs the lamp and the genie appears to obey him. The particular lamp he had possessed magic qualities.

With the aid of magical powers, the magicians could supposedly make people sick, or cure them; bring rain to help the

crops; make fire (which at one time was thought to require magic). We know now, of course, that these magicians were victims of superstition or fakers.

ASTROLOGY AND OMENS

Gradually the art of magic became more elaborate and was called a "science." In ancient Babylon, five thousand years before the birth of Jesus, the priests were magicians and they had worked out a whole system of evil spirits and ways of getting rid of them.

Astrology was invented by the Babylonians, and of all the magical arts it has lasted the longest. Some people today believe that one's fate and fortune can be told by the stars. There is a separate article on ASTROLOGY.

The Greeks and Romans, thousands of years ago, also made magic part of their religion. They consulted their gods about various problems through oracles in the temples. An oracle was a mysterious voice. No one knew where it came from. People believed that the oracles could give them answers straight from the gods. In Rome, sorcery had a high official place in the government. The people believed that the gods sent secret signs, called omens, to tell their wishes and intentions. The rulers never made any important decision without consulting the oracle to find out if the omens were good. You can read more about this in the article on AUGURS. The augurs were the priests who read the omens.

MAGIC IN CHRISTIAN TIMES

Though the Christian Church was opposed to magic it was not able to exterminate it. That sort of thing always went on, if not openly, then in secret. Magic power used for a good end was known as white magic, and the power of the sorcerers was believed to come from the devil or the underworld and was known as black magic. Severe punishments were decreed for persons who practiced black magic. A legendary sorcerer of Europe was Dr. Faust, hero of a famous poem and of an opera. Three hundred years ago, in Massachusetts, people believed in the existence of witches who were "in league with the devil." Magic began to decline when science began to rise.

Magical beliefs still exist in our day in the form of superstitions. When a person spills salt and then throws some over his shoulder, or when he knocks on wood, he is trying to avoid evil magic—although he may not know it. Pulling petals off a daisy to see whether "he loves me, he loves me not" is a superstitious way of consulting an oracle or spirit to foretell the future. Another belief in magic that goes on is the practice of spiritualism, or calling up the spirits of the dead. Persons who do this are called mediums, and they hold séances at which spirits are supposed to appear or speak.

MAGIC FOR ENTERTAINMENT

Most magic today is an entertainment. It is performed by highly skilled magicians on the stage and is also one of the most popular hobbies. There are two kinds. In one kind, the magician uses paraphernalia or devices called illusions. These may be worked by machinery, or they may be elaborate devices with mirrors set at different angles to deceive the eye. The ancient Greeks and Romans knew about optical illusions, in which the watcher is made to believe he sees something that is not there. The modern use of optical illusions for entertainment began in the 1800s, when a jeweler named John Maskelyne invented a wood cabinet in which people were made to vanish and reappear. This trick was done with mirrors, but they were so cleverly placed that they could not be seen even under careful examination. Another famous illusion is the box in which the magician "saws a woman in half." This is done by having two women curled up in the box, one with her head showing at one end, and the other with her feet showing at the other end.

Sleight-of-hand, also called *legerdemain* or *prestidigitation*, is the art of deceiving the eye without the help of mechanical illusions. Such a trick is called a *sleight*. Tricks with cards and coins are examples of this.

The secret of many magical tricks is that the magician draws attention away from the place where the "magic" is being done by calling attention to a place where nothing special is being done.

There are many devices sold to help you do feats of magic, but there is no substitute for hours and hours of practice. The great magicians have made a career of their art, and they work constantly practicing old tricks and inventing new ones. Among the greatest early magicians were the Italian Joseph Balsamo, known as Count Cagliostro, and the Frenchman Robert Houdin. Both lived almost two hundred years ago.

Houdin was famous for his optical illusions, and he was one of the first stage magicians to tell the public that his "magic" was done by natural means instead of by real magic. Harry Houdini, the best-known of all American magicians, took his stage name from that of Houdin. Other famous American magicians include Harry Blackstone and Howard Thurston.

Magna Carta

The Magna Carta is a historic English document that was written more than seven hundred years ago. It is very important to the English because it took away from the king some of the rights that the kings of most countries had then and in European countries held for hundreds of years longer. However, the Magna Carta did not give these rights to the serfs, or working men, but only to the nobles and the freemen who owned their own land and homes.

In 1215 the king of England was John, who was very unpopular and was considered to be a tyrant. The barons, who owned the castles, the land, and for all practical purposes the workers, prepared a charter called the Magna Carta, which means "great charter." This stated that every freeman had a right to a trial before being imprisoned or executed; that property could not be taken or destroyed without legal procedure; that justice must not be sold, denied, or delayed. The Magna Carta established that the law was greater than any single person, even the king.

The Magna Carta has been considered the basis of English, and therefore of American, liberties.

magnesium

Magnesium is a bright silvery metal that is very light in weight. It is a chemical element, which means that it is one of the basic substances that make up the world. Most magnesium that is used is obtained by electrolysis of sea water. (There is a separate article on ELECTROLYSIS in another part of this encyclopedia.)

Magnesium is a very useful metal. It is one of the five elements that make up chlorophyll, the green matter of the leaf of a plant that produces sugar and starch necessary for all life.

Magnesium weighs a little more than half as much as aluminum and a little less than one-fourth as much as iron. So it is used wherever it can replace heavier metals and make things easier to carry and move. For instance, in the building of airplanes, sheets of magnesium have taken the place of sheets of heavier metals. Railroads save coal and oil when they haul lighter passenger cars made of magnesium. Industry lightens its burdens with magnesium truck and trailer bodies, wheelbarrows, hand trucks, ladders, and tools. In the home, magnesium chairs and tables, sewing machines, washing machines, vacuum cleaners, electrical appliances, and ladders make housework easier because they are so easy to move or carry.

Magnesium burns with an extremely bright flame, so it is used in photographic flash bulbs. Magnesium powder is used in skyrockets to make white bursts of light in the sky. The flares that are used as distress signals by survivors of wrecked ships or planes also get their bright light from burning magnesium powder. In war, it is used in star shells to light up enemy territory. Since magnesium burns so easily, it is used in wartime in incendiary bombs, those bombs whose purpose is to start fires. (There is more about incendiary bombs in the article on BOMBS.)

MAGNESIUM ALLOYS AND COMPOUNDS

Actually, pure magnesium is used to make very few things because it is soft and not strong enough. But when it is mixed with aluminum, copper, and sometimes manganese, it becomes a strong, tough alloy. (An alloy is made by melting two or more metals together and allowing them to harden.) Two of the most important magnesium alloys are *magnalium* and *Dow-metal*. When a little magnesium is added to cast iron, it changes it from a very brittle metal to one that is ductile, so that it can be drawn out into thin wire.

Magnesium also forms compounds with several other substances. (A compound is a combination of two or more elements.) When magnesium burns, it combines with the oxygen in the air to form a white powdery substance called *magnesium oxide*, or *magnesia*. Magnesia does not allow heat to pass through it readily, so it is used to cover pipes that carry hot water and steam. Since magnesia can stand extremely high heat without melting, it is made into bricks that line the inside of electric furnaces. Your

doctor uses magnesia when he wants a medicine that will cancel out the acid in the body. He also uses it as a laxative in the form of *milk of magnesia* or *citrate of magnesia.*

Magnesium combined with the elements sulfur and oxygen is called *magnesium sulfate.* It is very useful in the dye industry to make colors that will not run. Magnesium sulfate is also called *Epsom salts,* which are used in medicine as a laxative.

When magnesium combines with the element silicon, it forms many things, including ASBESTOS, TALC, MEERSCHAUM, and SOAPSTONE. You can read more about these substances in separate articles.

The first form in which magnesium was found was Epsom salts, so called because it was first mined at Epsom in England. The first scientist to obtain it in the laboratory was Sir Humphry Davy, the English chemist, in 1808.

magnet and magnetism

A magnet is any substance, usually a metal, that attracts other substances (also usually metal) through space. Magnetic substances often are found in the ground. They are special kinds of iron ore called *magnetite* or *lodestone.* These are natural magnets.

Magnets can also be made by a special process called electromagnetic induction, about which you can read in the article on INDUCTION. Iron, nickel and cobalt are the metals most often used in the making of magnets. Such a magnet is usually in the form of a bar or a horseshoe. It acts in exactly the same way as a natural magnet.

A magnet dipped into a dish of iron filings will attract the filings. The filings will hang on to the ends of the magnet. These ends of the magnet are called *magnetic poles.*

A magnet is often used to find direction. In this form it is known as a compass. A compass is a magnet that is free to turn in a circle. When it does, one pole points to the north, while the other pole points to the south.

The reason for this is that the earth itself is a huge magnet. Its poles are in the far north and the far south. The magnetic pole of the earth that is in the north attracts the north-seeking or north pole of the compass. The magnetic pole of the earth that is in the south attracts the south-seeking or south pole of the compass.

When two magnets are brought near each other, the north poles of each magnet will repel (move away from) each other. The same thing will happen with the south poles. However, the north pole of one magnet will attract or be attracted by the south pole of the other magnet. Scientists call this attraction the law of magnetic attraction and repulsion. The law states that like poles (either two north or two south poles) repel each other, while unlike poles (a north and a south pole) attract each other.

POLES OF THE EARTH

It is sometimes confusing to think of the magnetic North Pole of the earth attracting the north-seeking pole of a compass. Actually, in terms of magnetism,

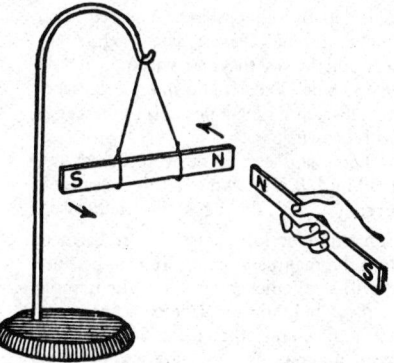

A north pole repels another north pole.

the magnetic pole of the earth that is near the North Pole is really a "south" pole, and the magnetic pole of the earth near the South Pole is really a "north" pole. This must be so if we call the pole of the compass that points north a "north" pole.

The earth acts as if it had a giant magnet inside of it. This is what makes a magnetic compass point toward the north.

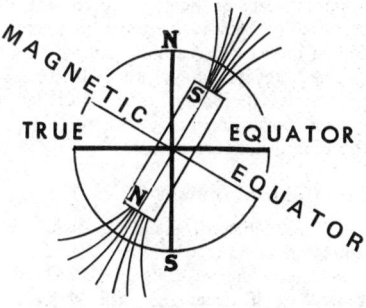

MAGNETIC FORCE

Magnetism is the force with which a magnet repels or attracts an object. This force cannot be seen, heard, or felt. We know it is there because we see how it pulls or pushes objects when a magnet is held near them.

Scientists use another name for the magnetic force. They call it a magnetic *field.* This field surrounds all magnets. It is made up of invisible lines of force that pass from the north pole to the south pole. There are many more lines of force at the magnetic poles than at any other part of the magnet. The poles are the spots on the magnet where the force is strongest.

Place a piece of paper over a bar magnet and sprinkle iron filings on the paper, tapping the paper gently as you do. The filings will form a series of lines going from the north to the south pole of the magnet. These are the magnet's lines of force. The more lines of force, the stronger the magnet.

It is very easy to magnetize a piece of iron. Take a magnet and slide one of its poles along a nail. Always slide the magnet in the same direction. When you take the magnet away, and hold it near the nail, you will find that the nail is repelled by the end of the magnet with which it was stroked. The reason is that the nail has been magnetized. The end of the nail that was stroked with the north pole of the magnet becomes a south pole.

The small magnetic particles that are

contained in all metals are the source of magnetism. These particles are really atoms of metal. The atoms contain tiny particles called electrons, which revolve around the center or nucleus of the atom. As it revolves, the electron also spins. Scientists believe that the spin of the electrons makes every atom into a small magnet with two poles.

In a piece of ordinary unmagnetized iron these atomic magnets are not arranged in any special way. In this arrangement there is no magnetic force. When a magnet is brought near the iron, the atomic magnets line up in an orderly arrangement. When these atomic magnets are so arranged, they all pull together. This causes the iron to become magnetic.

If a magnet is cut in half, two smaller magnets will be formed, each with a north and a south pole. This is caused by the arrangement of atomic magnets inside the magnet. All that is necessary to destroy this magnetism is to disarrange the atomic magnets. This can be done by heating the magnet, or striking it hard with a hammer.

Since all matter is made up of atoms, all matter also contains atomic magnets. Some atoms make stronger atomic magnets than others. The reason is that some atoms have electrons that spin in only one direction, while other atoms have electrons that spin some in one way and some in another. Atoms that have electrons that spin in only one way make strong magnets. Such atoms are contained in iron, cobalt, and nickel. Weak atomic magnets are contained in wood, paper, glass, and rubber. These substances show very little attraction for magnets.

Substances such as pure iron are often used to make temporary magnets. In such magnets, the atoms are easily lined up by a magnetic field brought near them. Once the magnetic field has been withdrawn, they become easily disarranged and lose their magnetization.

Steel is often used to make permanent magnets. The atoms in steel are difficult to line up and therefore it is much harder to magnetize steel, but once they are lined up they stay put.

Wrapping a wire that carries electric current around a magnet increases the magnetism. Such magnets are called *electromagnets.* Electromagnets are used to lift scrap iron, steel beams used in construction work, and other metal objects that cannot otherwise be easily lifted. Electromagnets are also used in atom smashers such as cyclotrons and betatrons.

The substances that are attracted or repelled by a magnet fall into three classes. Those substances that point in the direction of the lines of force are called *paramagnetic.* Those substances that cut through the lines of force are called *diamagnetic.* Substances that are attracted or repelled by a magnet more strongly than others are called *ferromagnetic.*

The lines of force of a magnet are very important in producing current in an electric generator and in turning a motor. Cutting magnetic lines of force generates electricity. (There is a separate article on GENERATOR.)

magnifying glass

A magnifying glass is a piece of glass that is shaped or ground so that it will make things look larger. The glass is thicker in the middle than it is at the edges. It is curved outward on both sides. This is called a double convex lens.

People use magnifying glasses for reading small print in newspapers and books. Jewelers use them to examine gems. Many scientists use magnifying glasses to help them see small details that they could not see so well with the naked eye.

A combination of two magnifying glasses is used in the compound microscope with which scientists examine small objects such as bacteria, amebas, and plant and animal tissue. A single magnifying glass by itself often is called a simple microscope.

A combination of magnifying glasses also is used in telescopes.

To magnify an object, the magnifying glass must be held at just the right distance from the object. If it is held too close or too far away, the object will appear blurred or smaller and upside down.

The amount by which a magnifying glass makes an object seem larger is called the magnifying power of the glass. When a magnifying glass makes an object seem three times larger, it is said to be a three-power glass, written $3\times$.

magnolia

The magnolia is a tree that grows in the southern part of the United States, in Asia, and in Central America, where the climate is warm and· moist. Magnolia trees grow best along the banks of rivers and near swamps. Sweet bay and the cucumber tree· are types of magnolia that people most often plant in parks and along the sides of roads in southern cities of the United States. Some kinds of magnolia are large shrubs and some grow to be about eighty feet high. The magnolia is an evergreen, which means that it does not lose its green leaves in the fall. The magnolia is a beautiful tree, with shiny green leaves and white, rose and yellow flowers that have a very sweet smell. The magnolia has an unusual fruit that is shaped like a cone, and pretty red seeds hang from the cone by slender threads.

The hard wood of the magnolia tree is used to make furniture, boxes, and venetian blinds.

The magnolia is the state flower of Louisiana and Mississippi. Each spring many people visit Charleston, South Carolina, and places near it, to see the magnolia trees in bloom.

magpie

The magpie is a large, handsome bird that lives in many parts of Europe. Some magpies are found in the western part of the United States. The magpie is a member of the crow family. It is about a foot and a half long. It has a white breast, and its head and tail feathers are black. When the sun shines, the feathers of the magpie gleam with green and purple colors. The magpie usually builds its nest high in a tree, but some magpies make their nests in low bushes. The magpie's nest is very remarkable. It is a strong basket made of sticks and earth. The top of the basket is covered with fine twigs and leaves. The magpie enters and leaves the nest through a hole in the side. The female magpie lays between six and nine pale bluish-green eggs with brown spots.

The magpie is a noisy, mischievous, bold bird. It is known as a thief because it likes to steal the eggs of other birds. Sometimes it kills small birds. Farmers find the magpie a great nuisance because it will steal chicken eggs, but the magpie is also a help to the farmers because it attacks mice and other pests. Some people keep magpies as pets. The magpie, like the parrot, can also learn to say a few words.

Magyars

The Magyars are the people who live in the country of Hungary, in central Europe. The ancestors of the Magyars came from central Asia. They began to invade central Europe more than a thousand years ago. They were savage fighters and conquered many people. The Magyars settled in Hungary. At first they were not Christians, but after about one hundred years St. Stephen taught them Christianity. Most of them became members of the Roman Catholic Church.

The Magyars' language is called Hungarian. It is different from most languages spoken in Europe. It is related to the Finnish language.

Mahican Indians

The Mahican Indians are a tribe of American Indians who were found by Dutch settlers in the early 1600s in New York State. Their enemies, the Mohawk Indians, defeated them. Some of the Mahicans sold their land to the Dutch settlers, and later to English settlers. More than a hundred years later, in the 1730s, some of the Mahicans moved west to Indiana, while others moved to Stockbridge, New York, and came to be called the Stockbridge Indians. The Mahicans are remembered mainly because (with their name spelled *Mohican*) they are the subject of a famous novel, *The Last of the Mohicans,* by the American writer James Fenimore Cooper. About a thousand Mahicans are still living.

mah jongg

Mah jongg is a game that has been played in China for hundreds of years. In the early 1920s it became the most popular game in the United States for a few years, and there are still many Americans who play mah jongg. Mah jongg is played with pieces called *tiles.* They are usually made of plastic materials that look like ivory and are marked with Chinese characters and pictures. Like playing cards, the tiles are divided into suits and are numbered. Mah jongg is played like the card game of rummy, and some experts believe that rummy is based on mah jongg, which is a much older game. In mah jongg, the object is to form sets of tiles of the same kind and sequences of tiles of the same suit.

mahogany

Mahogany is a tree that grows in the West Indies, Mexico and in some parts of South America and Africa. Some mahogany trees are also found in Florida, in the United States. The tree grows to be about seventy feet high. It is an evergreen, which means that it does not lose its leaves in the fall. The leaves of the mahogany are tough and leathery, and they grow in clusters. The tree has small white flowers.

The wood of the mahogany is very valuable. It is a fine wood that is hard and strong, and when it is polished it gleams. It comes in many shades of brown, from a light golden brown to a deep reddish brown. Mahogany is used to make fine furniture and musical instruments and is also used in shipbuilding.

Mahogany became very popular in England about 250 years ago when Thomas Chippendale, a famous English furniture-maker, began to use it.

mail order

Mail-order selling is done by sending circulars or catalogs to customers. The customer selects what he wishes to buy from the printed description and pictures. He does not actually see the goods he buys until after ordering them.

Hundreds of thousands of people in the United States buy billions of dollars worth of goods by mail each year.

Some mail-order companies are huge businesses that sell hundreds of different kinds of merchandise, including clothing, books, machines, furniture, and almost anything that a family needs. The biggest of these companies, called mail-order houses, are Sears Roebuck and Montgomery Ward. Each issues one large catalog and several smaller catalogs or "flyers" each year. These are mailed to

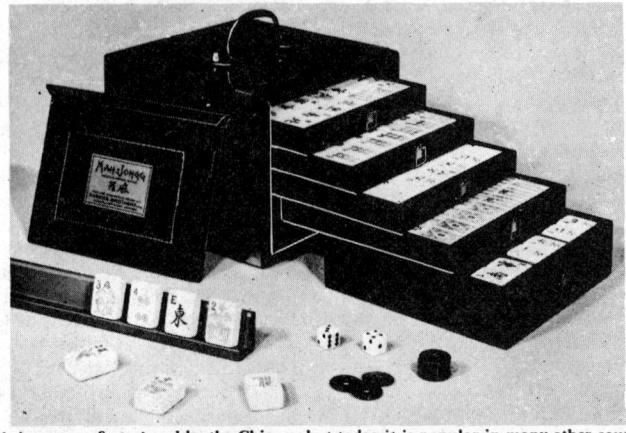

Mah jongg was first played by the Chinese, but today it is popular in many other countries.

thousands of customers. The big catalogs may have as many as 1,400 pages. They are filled with attractive pictures and descriptions of the goods offered.

The first big mail-order house was founded in 1872 by Aaron Montgomery Ward. Sears Roebuck was started in 1886 by Richard W. Sears. Sears was a railroad station agent in Minnesota. A shipment of watches arrived at the station, addressed to a jeweler who had gone out of business. Sears bought the watches at a low price and wrote dozens of letters offering to sell them to other railroad employees. He was so successful that in a short time he gave up railroading and devoted his full time to mail-order selling.

For a long time the chief customers of the mail-order houses were farmers, who lived far from shopping centers. They found it convenient to order what they needed from catalogs. When farmers began to have automobiles and could travel to the cities, they did not have to depend on catalogs for their goods. Realizing this, in the 1920s the big mail-order companies began to open retail stores. Now the mail-order companies sell both by catalog and in their stores.

DIRECT MAIL

Similar to mail-order selling is selling by *direct mail,* also called *direct-by-mail advertising.* The main difference is that in direct mail a company offers only one article, or a few articles, in a letter or circular. This usually brings only one sale at a time. A mail-order company expects many sales to be made from each catalog.

Direct mail is used not only to sell goods but also to ask for contributions to charities, to get votes for political candidates, and for similar purposes.

Maine

Maine is the largest and most northern of the New England states in the United States. Its nickname is the "Pine Tree State" because of its magnificent evergreen forests. These and its beautiful mountains and fine lakes and beaches make Maine one of the most popular vacation places in the country. It is noted for its seafood, especially lobsters. Maine is believed to have received its name from an ancient province in France.

Maine ranks 38th in size among the states, with 33,215 square miles. In population it ranks 38th, with about a million people living there. It became a state in 1820, and was the 23rd state admitted to the United States. The capital is Augusta.

THE PEOPLE OF MAINE

The earliest settlers in Maine were the English and Scotch-Irish. French Huguenots, who fled from religious persecution in their own country, also went to Maine, about three hundred years ago. In later years many Germans and Scandinavians settled in Maine. Most of the people who live in Maine are American-born. The largest religious group in the state is Roman Catholic, but there are almost as many Protestants.

The people of Maine are sturdy, independent and hard-working. Almost half the people of Maine are farmers. The most important crop they raise is the famous Maine potato. Tons of them are shipped every year to all parts of the country. Maine supplies three-quarters of the nation's blueberry crop. The farmers also raise oats, corn, and juicy apples.

In the cities are great paper and wood-pulp factories, shoe shops and textile plants. There is a big lumbering industry in the forests of pine, spruce, balsam, and hemlock. People of Maine have been fishermen and shipbuilders for several hundred years.

One of the most important things the people do is to take care of the thousands of vacationists who go to Maine every summer. There are also winter resorts for those who like to ski and ice-skate.

WHAT MAINE IS LIKE

Maine has great, dark forests that cover more than three-quarters of the state, and magnificent mountains in which there are thousands of sparkling blue lakes.

The highest mountain in the state is Mount Katahdin, 5,267 feet high. Most of the state is a plateau, a high but level region. The Aroostook Plateau in the north is one of the most fertile sections in the country for raising potatoes.

The other outstanding thing about Maine is its long, jagged coastline, with many deep harbors and hundreds of islands. These islands are the tops of hills that were pushed down millions of years ago by a great glacier, or sheet of ice, that moved over this part of North America. This rugged coastline is one of the most beautiful in the world.

Hunters in Maine will find deer, grouse and black bears. For those on a fishing holiday, there is an abundance of salmon, brook trout, bluefish, tuna, and herring sardines.

The climate of Maine is very pleasant and cool in the summer, which is one reason it is so popular with vacationists. The average temperature in July is 60 degrees. The winters are very cold, with sharp winds and deep snow. The average temperature in January is about 23 degrees.

The swift rivers in Maine are very important. The Penobscot, St. John and Kennebec rivers are some of the most useful for floating logs down from the forests to the lumber mills. The rivers are also used to supply water power for the factories. In the past, traveling by boat was the best means for getting from one place to another. The rivers are still an important means of transportation, but there are now almost three thousand miles of railroads and more than ten thousand miles of improved state highways. Maine built one of the country's first "thruways." There are airports in the important cities.

THE GOVERNMENT OF MAINE

Maine, like most other states, has a Governor and a Legislature. The Governor is elected for a four-year term. The Legislature is composed of two houses, a Senate and a House of Representatives. The members of both houses are elected for a two-year term. Judges are elected for a seven-year term. The capital is Augusta. There are 16 counties.

EDUCATION IN MAINE

There are about 240,000 pupils attending public elementary and high schools. Among the principal colleges and universities are:

University of Maine, at Orono. Enrollment, 16,226 in 1971 (co-ed).
Bates College, at Lewiston. Enrollment, 1,100 in 1971 (co-ed).
Bowdoin College, at Brunswick. Enrollment, 947 in 1971 (men only).
Colby College, at Waterville. Enrollment, 1,450 in 1971 (co-ed).

Ram Island Lighthouse at Boothbay Harbor, Maine.

Wooden lobster traps, such as these in Stonington, are often seen along the coast of Maine.

The leading cities of Maine, with populations from the 1970 census, are:

Portland, population 65,116, the largest city in the state. There is a separate article about PORTLAND.

Lewiston, population 41,779, the second-largest city, important textile and shoe manufacturing center, in the southwestern part of the state.

Bangor, population 33,168, the third-largest city, commercial and industrial center, in the southern part of the state.

Augusta, population 21,945, the state capital and fifth-largest city. There is a separate article about AUGUSTA.

MAINE IN THE PAST

The first white men to land on the shores of Maine were probably the Norsemen, more than nine hundred years ago. They visited the New World from time to time, but never made any settlements there. About five hundred years later John Cabot, the English explorer, investigated the coast of Maine, and after that the Frenchman Samuel de Champlain explored the region. In 1607, English settlers started a colony, but it did not last very long because of the very cold weather and hard conditions. It was not

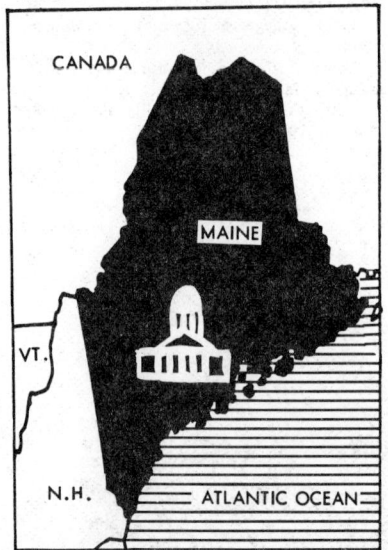

The pine cone (*right*) is a good choice for Maine's state flower, because much of the state is covered by vast pine forests. When people think of Maine, they usually recall its hardy fishermen, beautiful countryside, and lovely small villages.
1. The sketch on the map represents the state capitol, built of Maine granite, in Augusta.

Maine Department of Economic Development
Tuna fishing, as seen in this picture taken at Booth Bay, Maine, is an important source of income for the state.

The world's smallest church is located in the town of Wiscasset, Maine.

Maine's cold winters enable sports-lovers to enjoy activities such as snowmobiling.

until 1623 that the first permanent settlement was made on the Saco River by the English. After that, other English settlements grew up.

The French claimed part of Maine, and they encouraged the Indian tribes to attack the white settlers. The English people lived in constant terror of Indian raids until after the French and Indian Wars, which ended about two hundred years ago.

In 1677, the Massachusetts colony bought the Maine territory from the Gorges family, which had obtained it under a charter from the Plymouth Colony. During the Revolutionary War, the colonists living in Maine suffered from attacks by the British, but they loyally supported the colonies. In 1820, Maine was admitted as a separate state of the United States.

The people were always strongly opposed to slavery, and Maine sent almost 73,000 men to fight against the South in the Civil War. The people of Maine also opposed alcoholic liquors, and more

than one hundred years ago they passed a "dry" law. In 1934 the law was repealed.

Maine has always been considered an important state politically. There is an old saying, "As Maine goes, so goes the nation," though this has not been true for years. The people have usually voted for the Republican candidates, but in 1954 they elected a Democratic governor for the first time in twenty years.

PLACES TO SEE IN MAINE

Acadia National Park, 41,965 acres, off the southern coast, on Mount Desert Island, just south of Bar Harbor, on State Highway 3. The highest elevation on the Atlantic Coast, with spectacular cliffs.

White Mountain National Forest, 49,-245 acres, in western Maine, about 20 miles southwest of Rumford, on U.S. Route 2. Beautiful scenery and recreational facilities.

Fort William Henry Memorial, 3 miles south of Pemaquid, on the southern coast, south of U.S. Route 1. A British fort built almost three hundred years ago against Indian attacks.

Wadsworth Longfellow House, in Portland, in the southwest, on U.S. Route 1. The home of the poet Henry Wadsworth Longfellow when he was a boy.

MAINE. Area, 33,215 square miles. Population (1970 census) 992,048. Capital, Augusta. Nickname, the Pine Tree State. Motto, *Dirigo* (I Guide). Flower, pine cone and tassel. Bird, chickadee. Song, "State of Maine Song." Admitted to Union, March 15, 1820. Official abbreviation, Me.

maize is another name for the corn that is raised mostly in the United States: see the article on CORN.

Malagasy Republic, the former French colony of Madagascar, achieved its independence on June 25, 1960. It is an island in the Indian Ocean off the eastern coast of Africa. See MADAGASCAR.

malaria

Malaria is a dangerous disease that is caused by a tiny parasite, an organism that lives in the blood of human beings. A certain kind of mosquito, the anopheles mosquito, carries these malaria parasites from one person to another. Anopheles mosquitoes are found in many parts of the world where the climate is very warm.

When a person gets an attack of malaria he has severe chills and a high fever. These attacks may occur only once, but in severe cases they may come many times. After an attack the person is very weak.

Some people get very light cases of malaria and others have severe cases. There are some people who have malaria parasites in their blood and never feel sick at all. People who have the parasites are called "carriers." If an anopheles mosquito bites a carrier, then bites another person, it can carry malaria to the other person. A person who has had malaria must be careful when he has an operation or another illness, because if he is weak and run down he may get malaria again.

Malaria is a serious disease, but it would be much more serious if it were not for the drug QUININE, about which

there is a separate article. If a person takes quinine regularly he is unlikely to get malaria, so people living in the tropics where there are anopheles mosquitoes take it every day. Atabrine is a newer drug that has the same effect. These drugs also control an attack of malaria, though they do not prevent other attacks if a person already has the disease.

Since mosquitoes breed in water, one way to control malaria is to drain the swamps where anopheles mosquitoes live and spray open water with chemicals that kill their eggs.

Malawi

Malawi is the national name adopted by the new African country, formerly the British colony called Nyasaland and after that part of the Federation of Rhodesia and Nyasaland, when it became independent on July 6, 1964. Malawi is a member of the United Nations. See the articles on NYASALAND and RHODESIA.

Malay

The Malay people belong to the brown-skinned race, one of the giant races of mankind. The people who live in Malaya are called Malays, but they are related to the people of the Philippine Islands, the islands of Indonesia, and thousands of other islands in the Pacific Ocean, as far east as Hawaii. The languages spoken by these many peoples are also related. See the article on the RACES OF MAN.

Malay Archipelago

The Malay Archipelago is the largest group of islands in the world. They are in the Pacific and Indian Oceans between Asia and Australia. The equator crosses them. There are thousands of islands in the archipelago. A few are large. Many are small but fertile. The most important are the Philippine Islands and the Malaccas, Borneo, Sumatra, and Java, which are part of Indonesia. New Guinea is sometimes included. About 104,000,-000 people live in the Malay Archipelago. These islands were once the tops of volcanic peaks, and there are still many active volcanoes in this region. The bones of the Java Man, believed to have lived as much as a million years ago, were discovered in the Malay Archipelago.

Malay Peninsula

The Malay Peninsula is a long arm of land that stretches from the southeastern tip of Asia down toward the islands of Indonesia. The peninsula is about 700 miles long and 50 to 200 miles wide. The north of it is mostly a part of Thailand (Siam), though a small strip belongs to Burma. The southern part is in the Federation of MALAYSIA, about which there is a separate article.

More than 10,000,000 people live on the Malay Peninsula. Most of them live in the southern part. In the mountains they work in mines. The Malay Peninsula produces one-third of the world's tin and also has valuable deposits of gold and other minerals. In the lower sections the people are farmers. They work on the rubber farms and plantations, and also they grow coconuts, rice, coffee, and fruits, especially pineapples.

High mountain ranges run the length of the Malay Peninsula, some of them

rising to more than 7,000 feet. It is pleasantly cool in the mountains, but the peninsula is generally a hot, damp region with dense jungles and swamps. Even in winter the temperature seldom falls below 71 degrees. From 100 to 200 inches of rain fall every year—about four times the United States average. Many wild animals live in the jungle, including the elephant, rhinoceros, tiger, jungle cat, monkey, ape, and black panther. The jungles also have many beautiful wild birds and bright-colored tropical flowers.

Malaya, states on the Malay Peninsula and nearby islands, formerly British colonies or protectorates, then an independent country called Federation of Malaya, now part of MALAYSIA.

Malaysia

The Federation of Malaysia is an independent country, founded in 1963. It includes the part of the Malay Peninsula that was formerly called the Federation of Malaya, and also parts of some islands in the Malay Archipelago. About nine million people live in Malaysia and the area is about 130,000 square miles. The capital is Kuala Lumpur, a city of about 316,000 people in the state of Selangor on the peninsula.

The part called Malaya includes nine States that have their own rulers, formerly called sultans or kings. Four of these, once called the Unfederated Malay States, are Selangor, Pahang, Negri-Sembilan, and Johore. The other five, once called the Federated Malay States, are Kedah, Perak, Kelantan, Treng-Ganu, and Perlis. These are on the peninsula, as is Malacca, a former British colony. Another former British colony is Penang, a small island (400 square miles) near the west coast of the peninsula, but Penang includes the city George Town with a population (in 1957) of 234,930. These colonies plus Singapore were called the Straits Settlements until 1946 and were under British control.

In 1957 Malaya became independent; in 1963, Singapore, and two sections of the big island of Borneo, North Borneo or Sabah, and Sarawak, joined Malaya to create Malaysia. In 1965 Singapore left the federation and became independent.

In Malaya, the people of Malaysia are Malays, who are members of the brown-skinned race. On Borneo they are mostly Dyaks, a dark-skinned people akin to the Australian aborigines. Many of these are primitive people, still living much as men did thousands of years ago.

WHAT KIND OF PLACE IT IS

See the articles on MALAY PENINSULA and BORNEO. Except around the big cities the country is underdeveloped, with few railroads and highways.

In government, Malaysia is a kingdom —but unlike any other kingdom in the world. The king is elected from among the nine rulers of the Malay states for a five-year term. He is aided by a cabinet headed by a Prime Minister. The laws are made by the Parliament, consisting of a 38-member Senate and a House of Representatives of 100 members.

When Malaysia expanded, in 1963, to take in parts of northern Borneo, Indonesia objected and threatened war. Most

members of the United Nations approved the formation of the new Federation of Malaysia, and this led Indonesia to resign from the United Nations in 1964. Indonesia did not declare war but did make many attacks which led to much fighting in 1964 and 1965 on the borders between parts of Borneo controlled by Malaysia and Indonesia.

MALAYSIA. Area, 130,000 square miles. Population (1973 estimate) 10,876,982. Religions, Mohammedan, Buddhist, and Hindu. Government, constitutional elective monarchy. Flag, jack of crescent and star with seven red and seven white stripes. Monetary unit, dollar (former Straits dollar) at par 33 cents (U.S.).

Maldive Islands

The Maldive Islands became an independent nation on July 26, 1965. They are a chain of small coral islands, or atolls, in the Indian Ocean 400 miles southwest of Ceylon. The total land area is only 115 square miles, and the population is about 95,000. The Maldivians, whose main occupation is fishing, resemble the Singhalese people of Ceylon in both appearance and language. They follow the Mohammedan religion. The capital and largest city is Malé, with about 10,000 people. The Maldive Islands were formerly a British Protected State. They are ruled by a sultan (king), a prime minister, and a parliament.

MALDIVE ISLANDS. Area, 115 square miles. Population (1973 estimate) 115,000. Government, constitutional monarchy.

Malenkov, Georgi

Georgi Maximilianovich Malenkov was premier, or official head, of the government of the Union of Soviet Socialist Republics (the Soviet Union) from 1953 to 1955. Malenkov was born in 1902 in the town of Orenburg in the Ural Mountains of Russia. His ancestors were Cossacks. Malenkov joined the Communist Party after World War I and rose slowly in power. He became premier after Josef Stalin but was forced to resign when he was accused of opposing the policy of the Communist Party.

Mali

The Republic of Mali, one of the newest of the African nations, achieved full independence on June 20, 1960. For many years it was part of the French West Africa and was called the French Sudan. In 1958 its name was changed to the Sudanese Republic and in 1959 it joined with neighboring Senegal in the Mali Federation. When Senegal withdrew from the Federation in August 1960, the Sudanese Republic changed its name again to the Republic of Mali.

Mali has an area of about 460,000 square miles and more than four million people live there. A railroad connects the capital, Bamako, with Dakar at the Atlantic coast in Senegal. The north of Mali is part of the Sahara desert. Further south are semi-arid grasslands where large herds of cattle, sheep and camels are raised. Mali's principal crops are peanuts, corn, rice, sesame, and cotton.

REPUBLIC OF MALI. Area, 464,874 square miles. Population (1964 estimate) 4,485-000. Capital, Bamako, population 69,000.

The mallard is a duck that lives in many parts of Europe, Asia, and the United States, where the climate is not too warm. Mallards make their homes near lakes and marshes. The male mallard, or drake, is a handsome bird about two feet long. It has a shiny green head. The back of its neck and breast are a chestnut color, and it has a bright and white collar. The tail feathers are black and curly. On each wing the drake has a patch of bright blue that is surrounded by white. This patch is called a window. The female mallard is a plain brown color but also has a window on each wing.

The female builds a nest on the ground near the water. After the female lays her eggs, the drakes disappear. They gather together in a marsh nearby. In midsummer the mallards shed their feathers. This is called *molting*. For a few weeks, while the ducks are molting, they cannot fly.

There are domesticated types of mallard, raised for eating. The wild ducks are hunted in special "seasons."

mallow

There are almost a thousand different kinds of herbs and shrubs and trees that belong to the mallow family. They grow in almost every part of the world where the climate is not very cold. All plants of the mallow family have flowers that grow in five parts. Some of the mallow plants are very valuable, and some are bad weeds. The plant from which cotton comes, for example, is a mallow. The hibiscus plant that grows in the warm parts of the United States is also a mallow. It is noted for its gorgeous white, yellow, and rose blossoms. Okra also is a kind of mallow.

Malory, Sir Thomas

Thomas Malory was an English writer who lived about five hundred years ago. He wrote one of the first books to be printed in the English language. It was called *Morte d'Arthur*, which means *Death of Arthur* in French, and it was about King ARTHUR and his knights of the Round Table, about whom there is a separate article. Almost nothing is known about the life of Malory.

malt

Malt is barley or oats or other grain that has been treated in a special way so that the starch in the grain is changed into sugar. It usually comes as granules or in a dry powder. Malt is used in making beer. People have made malt since ancient times. To make malt, large fresh grains of barley are soaked in water for several days. Then the grains are piled together and grow for a certain length of time. Then they are spread out and kept warm, at a temperature of about 60 degrees. The grains must constantly be turned during this time. Then the barley sprouts are dried in an oven for about twelve hours. The dried grains of barley are called malt. Today malt is made by huge machines. Malted milk is made of dried milk, barley mash, and wheat flour. This is mixed with milk to make a nourishing drink.

Malta

Malta became an independent nation on September 21, 1964. It is composed of the island of Malta (95 square miles) and several smaller islands in the Mediterranean Sea. The total area is 122 square miles and about 330,000 people live there. The capital and chief city is Valletta, with about 20,000 people.

Many of the Maltese people work in the shipyards of the British Navy, which still has a base on the island. Others are farmers or work in factories that make lace, textiles, buttons, and shoes. They speak the Maltese language (which resembles Arabic) and English. Almost all of them belong to the Roman Catholic Church.

Malta (once called Melita) has always been important because if a nation with a strong navy held Malta it could control shipping in the Mediterranean Sea. St. Paul was shipwrecked on Malta. In the year 1530, Malta was given to a group called the Knights Hospitalers, who later were called the Knights of Malta. They built a powerful fortress on Malta from which they opposed the Turks. They also built many beautiful buildings and a famous hospital.

For a long time Great Britain and France fought over Malta, but in 1800 it became the property of the British. During World War II, the Germans bombed Malta more than 1,200 times. The entire population was so brave that the king of England, George VI, awarded everyone on Malta a medal.

Malta is governed by a House of Representatives, headed by a Prime Minister and his cabinet. It is a member of the United Nations and the (British) Commonwealth.

MALTA. Area, 122 square miles. Population (1973 estimate), 330,000.

Malthus, Thomas

Thomas Robert Malthus was an English writer who studied the growth of population (number of people) in the world and wrote a famous book on the subject. He was born about two hundred years ago, in the year 1766. When he was 32 years old, his book *Essay on the Principle of Population* was published. In this book Malthus said that populations grow so fast that the world would soon run out of food, if it were not for diseases and wars that kill many of the people. He showed that the population of the world would double at least once in every twenty-five years if this were not so. Events since his time have proved him right. Malthus wrote other books on economics, which is the study of man's possessions and needs. He died in 1834.

mamba

The mamba is a poisonous snake that is found in Africa. It is one of the most dreaded of all snakes, and the people who live in Africa tell many stories about the miraculous powers of the deadly mamba. Most of these stories are not true. The mamba is a slender, black snake that grows to be about 14 feet long. The mamba can travel very fast. It has sharp, thin fangs and its venom is poisonous. People believe that at the time the female mamba lays its eggs it is more dangerous than at other times because it will fight to protect its nest.

Mamelukes

The Mamelukes were a group of

about twelve thousand Turkish slaves captured in a war on their country and taken to Egypt more than seven hundred years ago. The Sultan (king) of Egypt trained them as soldiers. They were very intelligent and capable men, and gradually many of them were freed and appointed to high positions in the government. When the Egyptian sultan died, the Mamelukes took control of the country and elected one of themselves sultan. From that time, for more than two hundred years, Mamelukes were sultans of Egypt. They fought bitterly against one another; there was much plotting for power and most of the Mameluke sultans were assassinated by rivals. Despite this they did a great deal for Egypt, and increased its possessions by conquering new lands. They built beautiful buildings and some of the finest mosques in Cairo. In 1517 they were defeated when the Sultan of Turkey invaded and conquered Egypt, but more than two hundred years later there were still Mamelukes governing some of the provinces of Egypt. When Napoleon I invaded their country in 1798 they raised armies and tried to stop him, but Napoleon conquered them. In 1811 most of the remaining Mameluke leaders were tricked into meeting in a fortress, where they were slain by orders of the governor of Egypt, Mohammed Ali. He then ordered all Mamelukes in the country massacred.

mammal

The mammals are a large group of animals. There are about fifteen thousand different kinds of mammal, and they live in every part of the world. A great many more have become extinct. There are mammals in hot deserts, in frozen arctic regions, in jungles, and in cities. Some mammals, for instance the bat, fly in the air. Other mammals, such as the mole, burrow underground. Whales and seals are mammals that live in the sea. Some mammals are very small and others are huge. Human beings are mammals.

The thing that all mammals have in common is that the mother nurses her babies with milk that is produced by glands in her body. (You can read about how this happens in the article on BREAST.) The Latin word for breast is *mamma,* and that is why this group of animals is known as "mammals."

All mammals have backbones, and all breathe air. All mammals have front limbs, although they may look very different. Man has hands and a bat has wings and a whale has flippers. No mammal ever has more than two pairs of limbs, unless the grasping tail of certain kinds of monkey is regarded as an extra limb.

Mammals are warm-blooded animals. They have special glands in their bodies, called sweat glands, that help keep their body temperature the same in hot or cold weather. All mammals have some hair, but there are some mammals, such as the whale, that have almost no hair at all. Almost all female mammals give birth to live babies, but a very few mammals such as the platypus, lay eggs.

The mammals are the most complicated and intelligent forms of life in the world. In world history this is the "age of mammals." For the last fifty or sixty million years mammals have been the domi-

nant (most important) animals on earth. See the article on ANIMAL LIFE.

man

The word *man* is used to describe all human beings. The scientific name for man is *Homo sapiens,* Latin words meaning "man who can think." The science that studies man is called ANTHROPOLOGY, and there is a separate article about it. Anthropology is a new science compared to many others. It is not much more than one hundred years old. During that period anthropologists have learned a great deal about man, but there is still much to learn.

Man is an animal. He is a *mammal,* one of the animals that bring forth their young alive and nurse them. He is a *primate,* one of the group of animals that includes also the apes and monkeys. Human bodies and the bodies of other mammals are very much alike in the way they breathe, eat and digest food, see and hear, grow and live and die. Men and other primates even look somewhat alike. Yet between man and any other animal there is such a wide difference that it can hardly be described in words. Some other animals can reason in simple ways, but their reasoning cannot be compared to man's reasoning power. Man is the only living thing that can feel responsibility and humor and grief, that can understand science and religion and enjoy beauty. Man is the only living thing that can make a record of knowledge and experience and so pass it along to the next generation.

ADVANTAGES OF THE HUMAN BODY

The anatomy of man (the form of the parts of his body) gives him certain advantages over other animals. There are also disadvantages (man is not so strong as most other animals, compared to his weight and size, and he has no fur to protect him against cold and heat), but man's advantages outweigh these.

One of man's advantages is that he can make more different sounds than any other animal. This has helped greatly in developing speech.

Man's hand is the most valuable tool in the world. This is because of the *opposed* thumb, which makes it possible to grasp things between the thumb and the fingers.

Altogether, man has keener senses than other animals. Different animals can smell better, hear better, or see better, but none combines all the senses (smell, sight, hearing, taste, and touch) so well as man.

Man lives longer than most other animals. This gives him a greater opportunity to learn from experience and to use his knowledge.

Nevertheless, the important difference is man's intelligence, which is the ability to learn from experience. The size of man's brain may have something to do with this. A man's brain is much larger than the brain of even the largest ape, the gorilla. A man's brain weighs about 35 ounces and a gorilla's brain only about 18 ounces, though the gorilla as a whole may weigh two or three times as much as the man. However, scientists do not believe the size of the brain is very important to man's intelligence.

OTHER QUALITIES OF MAN

Man is a social animal, which means that he lives and cooperates with other men, and he is a gregarious animal, which means that he enjoys the company of other men.

The combination of intelligence and a social nature has helped man greatly. When a man cannot do something alone, he can get other men to help him. The company of other men encouraged early man to develop speech, and the use of speech allowed men to share their knowledge so that what one man knows, all men may know.

DEVELOPMENT OF MAN

The article on ARCHAEOLOGY tells how scientists have traced man's progress from primitive life to modern civilization, over a period of tens of thousands of years. During this period man has made unbelievably great progress in knowledge, but there is no scientific reason to believe that man's mental ability has increased.

The different races and nations of men, though they lived far apart from one another, invented the same tools and methods and even the same stories and beliefs. No particular race has been found to have any mental superiority over any other. Some nations would get a few thousand years ahead of others in the discovery of metals or machines, but this is a very short time compared to the life of man on earth, and the faster progress of any particular people has probably been due to accident or good fortune.

In addition to the article on ARCHAEOLOGY, the articles on RACES OF MAN, INVENTION, and LANGUAGE tell of man's development through the ages.

Man, Isle of

The Isle of Man is an island in the Irish Sea, about halfway between northern Ireland and England. It is 227 square miles in area, and more than 48,000 people live there. The people are descended from the Celts, who lived in England more than two thousand years ago. Some people on the Isle of Man can still speak a Celtic language, called Manx, as well as English. Many of the people are farmers. They raise fruits, grains, and vegetables. Others take care of the visitors who come every year on their vacations. The Isle of Man is noted for its beautiful scenery and mild climate. The capital is Douglas, a town of about 20,000. The island became a British possession in 1827. It has its own legislature, but the governor is appointed by the British government.

The Isle of Man is famous for the Manx cats, which come from there. The Manx cat looks like an ordinary house cat except that it has six toes on each paw and it has no tail. Actually, many Manx cats have very tiny tails, but some are bred to have no tails at all. The Manx cat hops somewhat like a rabbit, and is often called a "rabbit cat."

ISLE OF MAN. Area, 227 square miles. Population (1973 census) 56,289. Capital, Douglas. In the Irish Sea.

management

Management is the name given to the owners of a business or the people

who run a business and represent the owners. It is used in talking about the dealings between the owners of a business and the workers, or the unions that represent the workers. For that reason you may find the terms management and labor in articles dealing with industry. You can read more about management in the articles on CAPITAL and COLLECTIVE BARGAINING.

Managua

Managua is the capital city of Nicaragua. It is on the southern shore of beautiful Lake Managua. More than 300,000 people live in Managua. Many of them work in factories that produce soap, cement, candles, textiles, and canned goods. Managua is a railroad terminal, has a large airport, and is joined by highway to Puerto Somoza, a port on the Pacific Ocean. Near the shore of Lake Managua is Central Park. Around the park are many beautiful buildings, including the National Palace and the impressive cathedral. Managua has an unhappy history. Once it was flooded and twice earthquakes almost destroyed it. The worst disaster was an earthquake and fire in December, 1972.

MANAGUA, NICARAGUA. Population (1973 estimate) 318,000. Capital of Nicaragua. In the southwest.

manatee

The manatee is a large clumsy animal that lives in the waters off the coasts of South America, Africa, and the West Indies. Some manatees are found off the eastern coast of the United States, especially in Florida.

The manatee is a mammal, which means that the mother bears live babies and nurses them. It lives in the water but must come to the surface very often because it needs air to breathe. The manatee is from seven to twelve feet long and weighs from 400 to 2,000 pounds. It has a small head, tiny sunken eyes, and whiskers. It has flippers and a huge flat tail that looks like a paddle. There are six teeth on each side of its upper and lower jaws. When a tooth becomes worn, it falls out. Then all of the teeth move forward and the manatee grows a new back tooth to replace the old one.

The life of the manatee is filled with danger because it cannot defend itself very well against crocodiles and sharks and other enemies. The manatee has a large appetite and may eat as much as one hundred pounds of seaweed each day.

The female has one or two babies in the spring. The male and female manatee are excellent parents and take very good care of the babies until they are full-grown. Manatees are playful animals and like to dive and chase each other. They become very friendly when they are captured and kept in aquariums. In Florida people are forbidden to hurt manatees.

People in South America eat the flesh of the manatee. It is somewhat like beef or other red meat.

Manchester

Manchester is the largest city in New Hampshire. About 88,000 people live there. It is in the southern part of New Hampshire, and the Merrimack River flows through it. Manchester is an industrial center and manufactures textiles, shoes, machinery, and other products. The Amoskeag textile mill in Manchester was founded 150 years ago and became the largest cotton textile mill in the United States. During the depression of the 1930s, the mill was closed and hundreds of people were put out of work. The mill was bought the next year, in 1936, by a group of Manchester businessmen and operated so that the people would have work. Grenier Air Force Base, which was used during World War II, was built in Manchester in 1941.

MANCHESTER, NEW HAMPSHIRE. Population (1970 census) 87,754. County seat of Hillsboro County.

Manchester, England

Manchester is the fourth-largest city in England. It is one of the great manufacturing centers of the world. It is on the Irwell River, about thirty miles northeast of Liverpool. More than 660,000 people live in Manchester, and it is the center of an area in which more than two million people live. Many work in cotton mills and in factories that make machinery, airplanes, locomotives, trucks, cars, chemicals, rubber goods, and paper products. One of the world's most famous newspapers is the *Manchester Guardian*.

Manchester is one of the chief ports in England, even though it is more than thirty miles from the Irish Sea. The Manchester Ship Canal, built in 1894, allows ocean vessels to reach Manchester's busy docks.

Manchester is more than six hundred years old. In World War II it was heavily bombed because of its important factories and mills.

MANCHESTER, ENGLAND. Population (1971 estimate) 603,000. In Lancashire, on the Irwell River.

Manchu

The Manchus are a people whose leaders ruled China for hundreds of years. The Manchus are a Mongolian people. Their original home was probably in the part of Asia that is just north of Korea. They are closely related to the Tungus, people who live in Siberia. For many years before the Manchus became rulers in China, they fought the Chinese, conquering the Chinese in Manchuria first. In 1644 the Manchus established the Ch'ing dynasty, or ruling family, in China. There were ten Manchu rulers, and their control of China lasted until 1912. The Manchus adopted many Chinese customs, but they also brought many customs of their own into China. Many of these customs are now thought of as being Chinese.

Most of the Manchus intermarried with the Chinese and lost their identity as a separate people. The Manchu language, a type of Mongol language, has almost entirely disappeared. See the article on MANCHURIA.

Manchukuo, a name used at one time for Manchuria: see the article on MANCHURIA.

Manchuria

Manchuria is a region in northeastern China. It is separated from the rest of the country by mountains. Manchuria has been very important in modern times, and it has had a stormy history. It has an area of about 400,000 square miles, which is almost twice the size of Texas. About 44,000,000 people lived there in 1948, which is almost a quarter of the population of the United States. Manchuria is named after the Manchus an Asiatic people who ruled China for almost three hundred years until 1912. The capital of Manchuria is MUKDEN (now called Shenyang), about which there is a separate article.

Most of the people of Manchuria are Chinese, but there are many Mongols, Japanese, and Russians. Most of the people are farmers. They grow soybeans and haoliang (Manchurian corn), also wheat, rice, tobacco, and fruits. In recent years, manufacturing has increased. Many people work in large steel, aircraft, and cement plants. Others work in the rich coal and iron mines. Most of the people of Manchuria cannot read or write, but more are going to school now than in the past. The religion of most of the Chinese in Manchuria is a combination of the teachings of Buddha, Confucius, and Lao-tze.

Most of Manchuria is a vast plain, surrounded by mountains. In the south is fertile farm land where the important cities are located; in the north is rolling grassland, good for cattle, and large forests filled with fur-bearing animals. The winters in Manchuria are very cold, and the temperature often falls far below zero. Farmers have to build strong stone houses to keep out the bitter winds. The summers are mild and pleasant, with a temperature of about 75 degrees.

MANCHURIA IN THE PAST

Manchuria was settled more than three thousand years ago by an Asiatic tribe known as the Tungus. The Mongols later won control of the region, and more than three hundred years ago it came under the rule of the Manchus.

Both Russia and Japan wanted control of Manchuria. In 1905 they went to war and the Japanese defeated the Russians. They took over the Kwantung Peninsula in Manchuria, which the Chinese had leased to Russia. The Japanese then controlled the trade of Manchuria, and they built railroads and factories there. When the Chinese people finally drove the Manchu rulers out in 1912, they began to organize China and build up a strong government. The Japanese were afraid that they would lose their influence in Manchuria, and in 1931 they invaded Manchuria and won complete control of it. The Japanese combined Manchuria with Jehol, another large Chinese province that they captured at the same time, and in 1932 established what they called the kingdom of Manchukuo, which means "land of the Manchus." Henry Pu-Yi, a member of the Manchu family that had ruled China until 1912, and previously China's "boy emperor" (from 1908 to 1911), was named Manchukuo's emperor. Actually, Manchukuo was not an independent kingdom but was completely under the control of Japan. For that reason its government was called a "puppet" government, which meant that Japan "pulled the strings" as a puppeteer does. Many countries, including

Dairen, a port on the Bay of Korea, is one of Manchuria's modern cities. The Japanese built most of the large buildings in its business district.

the United States, protested at the way in which Japan took over Manchuria, and refused to recognize the Manchukuo government. Japan built large munitions factories in Manchuria, which were bombed by the United States forces during World War II. At the end of World War II, Manchuria was occupied by the Russian Army. In 1949, when the Russians withdrew, the Chinese Communists took over the control of Manchuria. During the Korean War the Chinese Communists used Manchuria as a base for their attacks on United Nations forces.

Mandalay

Mandalay is the second-largest city in Burma. It is on the Irrawaddy River. More than 360,000 people live there. Most of the people are silk weavers, and they sell the silk at open stalls along the streets. Mandalay has beautiful old pagodas, monasteries, and temples. Many people come to the city on pilgrimages. Colorful street fairs and bazaars have been built along the river. There are also many modern buildings that were built after a great fire destroyed much of the city in 1892. Mandalay was occupied by the Japanese during World War II, and was heavily bombed by the Allies. Rudyard Kipling wrote a poem called *Mandalay* that later became the words of a well-known song.

MANDALAY, BURMA. Population (1973 estimate) 360,000. On Irrawaddy River.

mandarin

The mandarins were officials of China for more than three hundred years, during the Ch'ing dynasty that ended in 1912. A dynasty is a royal family whose members rule in turn. The word *mandarin* is not Chinese, but Portuguese. The Chinese called these officials *kwan*. The mandarins were of nine ranks, and each rank had its own elaborate robe. Members of the different ranks wore buttons of special colors on their caps to distinguish them. The mandarins were governed by very strict rules planned to keep them honest in their work. They were not allowed to serve in the province where they were born. In the province where they held office they were not allowed to marry or to own land. No mandarin served more than three years in office.

Mandarin Chinese was the language of the court, and it became the official language of most of China. It is still spoken by most educated Chinese.

mandolin

The mandolin is a pear-shaped stringed musical instrument of the lute family. Different kinds of mandolin have different numbers of strings, but the mandolin that was developed in Naples, Italy, had four, and this is the one most often used today. The strings are plucked with the fingers or with a *plectrum*, which is a little pick made of ivory, wood, or a plastic material. The mandolin is not much used in orchestras, but Beethoven wrote several pieces that included it. The mandolin is played a great deal in South America, and it is quite popular in the United States.

mandrake

The mandrake is a plant that grows in Europe. In the United States the May apple, a different plant, is sometimes called mandrake. The mandrake is a herb, which means that it does not have a woody stem. It has a very large root, usually more than three feet long, and sometimes this root is shaped somewhat like a human being. The root is poisonous but is used in some medicines that are used as laxatives. In the past, many people believed that the mandrake root had strange magical powers and could make a person fall in love.

mandrill, a brightly colored baboon that lives in Africa: see the article on BABOON.

Manet, Edouard

Edouard Manet was a French artist who lived about a hundred years ago. Today his paintings are very famous and hang in many of the best American and European art galleries. During Manet's lifetime, most people disliked his paintings.

Manet was born in 1832. As a young man he went to sea. Later he returned to France to study painting. Many of his paintings show the influence of impressionism, a kind of painting that was popular at the time. An impressionist paints things as he sees them and not necessarily as they actually are. Many of Manet's impressionistic paintings are of out-of-door scenes. Manet has had a great deal of influence on other painters. He died in 1883.

manganese

Manganese is a gray metal with a pale reddish tinge. It is very much like iron, but it is harder and more brittle. It is a chemical element, which means that it is one of the hundred basic substances that make up the world. When manganese is added to steel, the steel becomes so hard that it can be used to make saws that cut other metals and chisels that cut stones. The edges of these tools will stay sharp for a long time.

One very important alloy of manganese is *spiegeleisen*. (An alloy is made by melting two or more metals together and allowing them to harden.) Spiegeleisen is made of four parts iron and one part manganese. When steelmakers want to remove sulfur and oxygen from the iron that they are making into steel, they put fourteen pounds of spiegeleisen into the molten iron for every ton of steel.

When manganese combines with oxygen, it forms a substance called *manganese dioxide*. This is the black, powdery stuff that you find inside a dry-cell battery. It is put there to keep gas from forming inside the battery. The ore from which manganese comes is really impure manganese dioxide. It is called *pyrolusite*. The U.S.S.R. mines the most manganese ore. India, South Africa, the Gold Coast, French Morocco, and the United States also have valuable manganese mines.

Manganese combined with the elements potassium and oxygen makes *potassium permanganate*. This is in the form of purple crystals. They are dissolved in water and used in treating athlete's foot, poison ivy, and other ailments.

mange

Mange is a skin disease of some animals, especially dogs. Usually it is caused by tiny mites that eat into the skin. This causes itching and also makes the skin form scabs and the hair fall out. There are special soaps and medicines that kill the mites. An animal is less likely to get mange if its skin is kept clean. Cows often get a kind of mange that is somewhat like the mange that dogs get. To cure or prevent this mange, the cows are "dipped"—made to walk through a bath of chemicals that kill the mites.

mangel-wurzel

The mangel-wurzel is a kind of beet. People in Europe have raised mangel-wurzel for more than four hundred years, and some farmers grow it in Canada and the United States. It is a hardy plant with a thick lower stem and a root that is a reddish color. This root is an important food for cows and sheep. It is very nourishing and has a sweet taste. Farmers pick the mangel-wurzel in the fall, before it is ripe, and store it during the winter. By spring the mangel-wurzel is ripe and supplies the cattle with food during the summer. Its rather odd name comes from two German words that mean "beetroot."

mango

The mango is a tree that grows in warmer parts of the world. People in southern Asia, Africa, and South America grow mango trees, and there are also mango trees in Florida and California, in the United States. There are more than five hundred different kinds of mango tree, and some grow to be about 90 feet tall. It is an evergreen tree, which means that it does not lose its leaves in the fall. The mango is a beautiful tree with long

The mango has a delicious, spicy flavor. It is very popular in Florida, where the warm climate makes the tree easy to grow.

shiny leaves and clusters of pink flowers. It has a soft gray wood that is used to build canoes and other light boats.

The fruit of the mango tree is also called mango. It is oval-shaped and may be about the size of a plum or as large as an apple. The skin is thick and has a yellowish-red color. The flesh of the mango is yellow in color and very juicy. It has a large seed. The taste of the mango is sour and sweet at once and it is very delicious. Mangoes are as important a food for the people who live in tropical parts of the world as apples are to people who live in colder climates. Most people eat mangoes fresh. Some of the fruit is canned and dried and made into sauces and jellies.

mangrove

The mangrove is a strange tree that grows in the tropical parts of the world, where the climate is hot. The mangrove is usually about forty feet high. It is an evergreen, which means that it does not lose its leaves in the fall. The mangrove grows along the shores of swamps and muddy rivers. To grow, it must have its roots in shallow salt water. The leaves of the mangrove tree are shiny, and it has light yellow flowers that bloom all year around. The fruit is a berry.

The mangrove is unusual because its roots grow from the branches and stem of the tree. They anchor themselves in the muddy ground. The mangrove trees then form a kind of thicket. The mangrove trees help keep the soil firm so that water will not wash it away. A group of mangroves make a fine home for many different kinds of water birds, and certain shellfish attach themselves to the trees.

The bark of the mangrove tree contains tannin, a substance that is used in making leather. The wood of the mangrove tree is strong and hard, but it is not used very often because the bark is more valuable and taking the bark from the tree destroys the wood.

Manhattan

Manhattan Island is the busiest and most important part of New York City. It is a real island, lying between the East River on the east, the Hudson River on the west, the Harlem River and Spuyten Duyvil Creek on the north, and New York harbor on the south. It is only 22 square miles in area, but almost two million people live there. When people say that they are going to visit New York City, they usually mean they are going to visit Manhattan. On Manhattan Island are Wall Street, the financial center of the nation; Times Square, the great entertainment district; and more skyscrapers than there are in all other places in the world put together, including Rockefeller Center and the Empire State Building, the highest building in the world.

Manhattan Island was settled by the Dutch in 1626. In that year Peter Minuit, the first Dutch governor, bought the island from the Manhattan Indians for $24 worth of beads, blankets, and other goods. Today Manhattan Island is the most valuable piece of land of its size in the world. See NEW YORK CITY.

MANHATTAN ISLAND. Area, 22 square miles. Population (1970 census) 1,524,541. Borough of New York City; constitutes New York County in the State of New York.

Manila

Manila is the largest city in the Philippine Islands. For many years it was also the capital of the country, but in 1948 Quezon City became capital of the Republic of the Philippines. Manila is on Luzon, the largest Philippine island. It is a great port, with a fine harbor on Manila Bay, which is sheltered from ocean storms. About 1,500,000 people live there. Most of them work in plants where farm products are processed. They produce sugar, hemp products, and canned goods, and work in many other kinds of factory.

Before World War II Manila was called the "Pearl of the Orient" because of its many beautiful Spanish-style buildings. The Japanese occupied the city in 1941, when they entered World War II, and when they were defeated in 1945 they left the city a heap of smoking ruins. The industrious people rebuilt dam-

Manila's City Hall is unusually graceful. To the right of its tower is the Legislative Building, and to the left is the campus of the Normal School.

aged buildings and built new ones over the ashes of the old. Today, Manila is a modern metropolis.

Manila is the cultural center of the Philippines, with beautiful parks and museums, a well-known theater, and several colleges and universities. The University of Santo Tomas, which was founded in 1609, is the oldest in the Philippines. Others are the University of the Philippines and the Philippines Women's University.

Manila was founded by the Spanish in 1571. It was taken by the United States after the Battle of Manila Bay in 1898, during the Spanish-American War. In 1954, the Manila Pact was signed there. In this pact, or treaty, the United States, Australia, New Zealand, the Philippines, Pakistan, Thailand, Great Britain, and France, agreed to help one another in case of war in the Far Pacific.

MANILA, REPUBLIC OF THE PHILIPPINES. Population (1971) 1,500,000. On the island of Luzon. Seaport on Manila Bay.

Manila Bay

Manila Bay is a gulf, or large body of water, that forms the harbor for Manila, the capital and largest city in the Philippine Islands. It is about thirty miles long and about thirty miles wide. Manila Bay is remembered mostly because of a great American victory in a

battle fought there during the Spanish-American War. When war broke out between Spain and the United States, the strongest fleet of the United States Navy was at Hong Kong, China. This fleet, under the command of Admiral George Dewey, sailed to Manila Bay and attacked a Spanish fleet there. The American fleet destroyed every ship in the harbor and all the coastal guns protecting the city. More than 350 Spaniards were killed or wounded, while only seven of the Americans were injured. It was at this battle that Dewey spoke the words that have since become famous. As the fleet sailed up the harbor, Dewey said to Charles Gridley, commander of the flagship of the fleet, "You may fire when you are ready, Mr. Gridley." The Battle of Manila Bay destroyed Spanish naval power in the Pacific, and Dewey became a popular hero. Corregidor, the scene of heavy fighting during World War II, is an island at the entrance to Manila Bay. There is a separate article on CORREGIDOR.

manila, a kind of yarn, cloth or paper made from hemp grown near Manila in the Philippine Islands. See the article on HEMP.

Manitoba

Manitoba is one of the provinces of Canada. It is in the central part of the country and is one of the three important Prairie Provinces. The rich black soil of Manitoba is so fertile that farmers there raise the finest wheat in the world. Manitoba ranks sixth in size among the Canadian provinces, with 251,000 square miles, which makes it almost as big as Texas. In population Manitoba ranks fifth among the Canadian provinces, with more than 1,014,000 people there. The name Manitoba comes from an Indian word meaning "strait of the spirit." It became a province in 1870. The capital is Winnipeg.

THE PEOPLE OF MANITOBA

The earliest white settlers in Manitoba were British and French fur-traders. They found many Indian tribes living there. Later people came from Scotland, England, the United States, and other parts of Canada.

Most of the people of Manitoba

are of English descent. About 15,000 Indians live on reservations.

More than half the people of Manitoba are farmers. They raise large crops of wheat and other grains, and also potatoes, beets, and soybeans. Many farmers raise beef and dairy cattle, and some keep bees for their honey.

Many people live in the cities and work in dairy plants, meat-packing plants, and flour mills. Others work in large factories that make railroad cars, lumber and wood products, and paper.

People also work in rich mines that produce gold, copper, zinc, and other valuable minerals. Others are fishermen who catch whitefish, pickerel, pike, and the Winnipeg goldeye. Still others work in the spruce forests, cutting down the timber that is used to make lumber products and paper. One of the important jobs in Manitoba is fur-trapping. Men catch muskrats and other fur-bearing animals in the forests, while some raise minks on farms.

Most of the people of Manitoba are Protestants, but there are also many Roman Catholics.

WHAT MANITOBA IS LIKE

The northeastern part of Manitoba, along Hudson Bay, is a cold, rocky region where the soil is not very good for farming. Few people live there. The central part of Manitoba is a large plateau, a high, level place, covered with forests. The important minerals are in this region.

The southern part of Manitoba is a rich prairie region. It is part of the very fertile Red River Valley that extends down into North Dakota in the United States. This region is fertile because millions of years ago it was the bottom of a large lake called Lake Agassiz. When the water drained off it left a rich black soil. The grass makes excellent grazing pasture for cattle. Persons traveling through this part of Manitoba will see great fields of grain like those in the Middle West of the United States. Most Manitoba people live in this part of the province. The important cities are there.

There are three lakes in the prairie region, filled with fresh-water fish. They are Lake Winnipeg, Lake Winnipegosis, and Lake Manitoba, and they are so large that they are called "Manitoba's Great Lakes."

The winters in Manitoba are long and the temperature often drops far below zero. The summers are short and warm, and there is much rain during the growing season.

The rivers and lakes are important for transportation in Manitoba, but railroads reach many parts of the province. Most of the highways are in the southern region, and there are airports in the important cities. Airplanes carry supplies to the northern mining and lumbering camps.

THE GOVERNMENT OF MANITOBA

The head of the government of Manitoba is a lieutenant governor, who is appointed by the British queen on the recommendation of the Canadian government. The province is actually run by a Premier. He is appointed by a legislature,

which is elected by the people. The Premier has a cabinet, just as the President of the United States has. He stays in office as long as he can keep the confidence of the majority of the legislature. The legislature is elected for a five-year term. Judges are appointed by the Canadian government in Ottawa, and hold office permanently. The provincial government is in the capital, Winnipeg.

Everyone has to go to school between the ages of 7 and 14, and there are grammar schools and high schools throughout the province. The University of Manitoba, at Winnipeg, had 4,369 students in 1961.

CHIEF CITIES OF MANITOBA

The leading cities of Manitoba, with populations from the 1967 estimate, are:

Winnipeg, population 257,005, the capital and largest city. There is a separate article about WINNIPEG.

Saint Boniface, population 37,600, the second-largest city, a meat-packing and grain center, in the southern part of the province.

Brandon, population 28,166, the third-largest city, a railroad divisional point, in the southwestern part of the province.

Portage la Prairie, population 12,388, fourth-largest city, a railroad center and grain market, in the southern part of the province.

Winnipeg, largest city of Manitoba, is one of the world's great wheat markets. Because many rail lines meet there, Winnipeg is called the "Canadian Chicago."

MANITOBA IN THE PAST

The first white man to visit the region of Manitoba, more than three hundred years ago, was the English explorer Sir Thomas Button. British fur-traders of the Hudson's Bay Company followed him and began trading with the Indians. Later, French-Canadian fur-trappers from the North-West Company established trade with the Indians, and there was bitter rivalry between the two companies.

Almost 150 years ago, the Red River Valley Colony was settled by Scottish Highlanders, who had been driven off their land. Sir Thomas Douglas (Lord Selkirk) felt sorry for them and induced

the Hudson's Bay Company to give them land along the Red River where they could live. The farmers had a very difficult time because the North-West Company objected strongly and tried to drive them off the land. The company burned the houses and destroyed the crops, and finally the colony was disbanded. In 1817 it was reëstablished, again with the help of Sir Thomas Douglas.

Manitoba became a province of Canada in 1870. After a railroad was built, extending from the United States, the province grew more rapidly.

PLACES TO SEE IN MANITOBA

Riding Mountain National Park, 1,148 square miles, 50 miles north of Brandon, in the southwest, on Highway 10. Beautiful scenery; bird and wildlife sanctuary; a popular vacation spot.

International Peace Garden, partly in North Dakota, on the southern border, on Highway 10. Beautiful garden commemorates the lasting peace between Canada and the United States.

Duck Mountain Provincial Park, 1,246 square miles, 70 miles northwest of Dauphin, in the west, on Highway 31. Vacation spot; excellent boating, fishing, hiking, and camping.

Baldy Mountain, 2,727 feet high, 40 miles northwest of Dauphin, in the west, west of Highway 10. The highest point in Manitoba; beautiful view.

Old Trading Post, 43 miles west of Brandon, in the southwest, on Highway 1. One of the old fur trading stations of the North-West Company.

MANITOBA. Area, 251,000 square miles. Population (1967) 961,000. Capital, Winnipeg. Coat of arms, a buffalo standing on a rock; above it is the Cross of Saint George. Flower, prairie crocus. Admitted to Dominion in 1870. Official abbreviation, Man.

Mann, Horace

Horace Mann was an American who did a great deal to improve schools and ways of teaching in the United States. He lived more than a hundred years ago. He was born in Franklin, Massachusetts, in 1796. When he was 23, he was graduated from Brown University, in Providence, Rhode Island, with the highest honors possible. Afterward he studied law and became a lawyer.

All his life, Horace Mann worked to improve conditions everywhere he possibly could. He was especially interested in making the schools better. Once he traveled to Europe at his own expense to find out if anything in the European school system might be used to improve schools in the United States. He was often called upon to give legal advice to schools, and he never charged them a fee. He was strongly opposed to slavery, and both wrote and lectured on the evils of such a condition.

For many years Horace Mann served in the Massachusetts State Legislature, and was responsible for the founding of many teachers' colleges, which at that time were called "normal schools." In 1837 he became secretary of the Massachusetts State Board of Education. As secretary he was responsible for improving

public schools in that state to such an extent that he has since been considered the father of the American public school. He served also in the House of Representatives in Washington.

Horace Mann's last years were spent as president of Antioch College in Yellow Springs, Ohio. He died in 1859 at the age of 63.

Mann, Thomas

Thomas Mann is the name of a German writer who is considered by many to be the greatest novelist of this century. He was born in 1875. As a young man he worked for a time as a clerk until his first great writing success came with the novel *Buddenbrooks,* a story about a family of merchants. It was published in 1900 when Mann was only 25. Mann's stories and books were widely read from then on. In 1924 he published *The Magic Mountain,* which had taken ten years to write. Four years later he received the Nobel Prize for literature, largely because of this book. Next he started on a four-volume work about the Biblical story of Joseph. The four books together are called *Joseph and His Brothers,* and Mann spent sixteen years on them. The first one was published in 1934.

When Adolf Hitler became dictator of Germany in 1933, 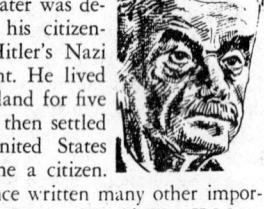 Mann left his homeland and later was deprived of his citizenship by Hitler's Nazi government. He lived in Switzerland for five years, and then settled in the United States and became a citizen. He has since written many other important books. During World War II Mann made many radio speeches to his former countrymen in Germany, urging them to help the Allies free Germany from the Nazis. He died in 1955.

manslaughter is the illegal but accidental killing of a human being: see the article on HOMICIDE.

mantis

The mantis is an insect related to grasshoppers. It is from 1 to 5 inches long, and has big, bulging eyes. There are about 2,000 species of mantises, but only a few kinds live in the United States. They were brought here early this century to combat the Japanese beetle, a garden pest. Unfortunately, the mantis also eats useful insects. It sits very still in the foliage until an insect approaches, then suddenly seizes the insect with its powerful front legs. While waiting, the mantis folds its front legs in such a way that it appears to be praying, hence its common name, "praying mantis," and its scientific name, *Mantis religiosa.* It is a fierce fighter, and will attack insects larger than itself, including other mantises. It is the only insect that can turn its head and look over its shoulder. It also has binocular vision (focusing both eyes on one point). The female mantis lays about 200 eggs in the autumn. They stick together and harden into a case about the size of a large grape. When the young hatch in the spring, they scatter quickly to avoid being eaten by the other young ones. Mantises are good flyers and are sometimes found on window sills of high buildings. A large mantis can jump about three feet. It may bite you if you try to pick it up. Some people catch mantises and keep them for pets.

manufacturing, the making of useful products: see MASS PRODUCTION.

Manx cat, a tail-less cat bred on the Isle of Man: see MAN.

Maori

The Maoris are the natives of New Zealand, a group of islands in the South Pacific that form an independent nation in the British Commonwealth of Nations. The Maoris belong to the Polynesian race, which also includes the natives of Hawaii and Samoa. Most Maoris are tall and strong. Their skin color may be anything from a dark white to a dark brown, but light brown is the usual color. Their hair is black, and may be straight or wavy.

Maoris have always been daring and skillful sailors. In dugout boats and canoes they used to sail hundreds of miles out to sea. After white men settled in New Zealand more than two hundred years ago, the number of Maoris declined for many years, but recently it has increased again. In 1972 it was estimated that there were about 225,000 Maoris in New Zealand. They enjoy full political rights as citizens, and Maoris have been members of the New Zealand parliament. Maori music and customs are taught in the public schools. Read also the article on NEW ZEALAND.

Mao Tse-tung

Mao Tse-tung led the Communist revolution in China and became the most important government official there in 1949. He was born November 19, 1893, in the south of China. His father was a poor peasant, and Mao had to do farm work before he was seven. Later he studied to be a teacher, but while he was at a university in Peking he became a Communist. He helped form the Communist Party of China in 1921, and soon he became one of its top men. He quarreled with other top men over how to take over China, but went ahead with his plans and became so powerful that in 1934 all the other Communists in China agreed that he should be their leader. Mao fought the national government of China, which was headed by Chiang Kai-shek. Mao set up a Communist government in North China, and after a few years he had a strong army there and controlled much territory.

Then, in 1937, Japan made war on China. Mao did not help the Chinese government, but he had his soldiers make raids on the Japanese troops and trap them in ambushes whenever they could. Many Chinese people joined Mao's army because it fought the Japanese very cleverly. In 1945 the Japanese had to leave China because they lost World War II, and Mao again began to fight the regular government of China. He got modern weapons from Russia for his soldiers. By 1949, Mao's armies controlled all of China and he was head of the government that ruled "Red China." His gov-

ernment was very unfriendly to the United States and fought against the United Nations in Korea. President Nixon met Mao in China in 1973 to start normalizing relations. When Mao died in 1976, Hua Kuo-feng became China's new leader.

map

A map is a picture of some part of the earth, drawn on a flat surface. There are many kinds of map. Some show geographical features of a country or region, such as mountains, rivers, and valleys. Some show cities, roads, and railways. Others show what the earth is like at the bottom of the ocean, or how the ocean currents flow. Still others show the positions of the stars and planets in the sky. No matter what kind of map it is, its purpose is to show certain things about an area too large to be seen at one time by the human eye.

Maps are made by surveyors, who determine the size and shape of areas by actual measurement and by mathematics. A great deal of this work is now done by aerial photography. The science of map-making is called *cartography.*

Since the earth is shaped like a ball, the only accurate map of the world or any part of it is the GLOBE, about which there is a separate article. But globes cannot always show the world or small areas of it in sufficient detail, and the globe is not very handy for many uses to which maps are put. Therefore some way had to be found to show on a flat surface the same relation of sizes and distances that the globe can give.

PROJECTIONS

Suppose you peel an orange, taking all the skin off but keeping it in one piece. Next you try to lay the skin out so that it is perfectly flat. You will have to stretch the skin quite a bit to flatter it. Wherever you stretch it, different points on the skin will become farther apart than they actually are when they lie on the surface of the orange. The smaller the piece of skin, the less you will have to stretch it to make it lie flat.

Every map shown on a sheet of paper represents some sort of stretching of the surface of the earth. This stretching, or flattening out, of the earth's surface onto a flat map is called a projection. There are many kinds of projection. Some are useful for some purposes, some for other purposes. None is entirely accurate, but it is possible to read them with great accuracy because of the lines you can see crossing each other on every map. These lines are called *parallels* and *meridians.*

PARALLELS AND MERIDIANS

For making a projection, the globe is divided up by a series of horizontal and vertical lines that form what is called a geographic grid. Starting with the equator, which is an imaginary line that circles the earth about halfway between the North Pole and the South Pole, we draw a series of circles above and below the equator until we reach the smallest circle at each of the poles. These lines are called parallels of latitude, so that latitude tells how far north or south of the equator any given spot is. Then a

set of lines is drawn from pole to pole, making a division of the earth somewhat like the segments in an orange. Each of these lines is called a meridian of longitude. These meridians are numbered to the east and to the west of the zero meridian.

Every circle, no matter how large or small, is measured in degrees, from zero to 360 degrees. The parallels are numbered from zero at the equator to 90 de-

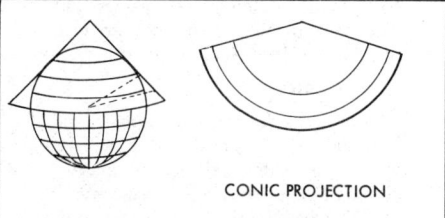

CONIC PROJECTION

In making a conic-projection map, a cone of paper is placed over a globe so that it touches one of the lines of latitude on the globe. The lines of latitude are then projected on the paper in the form of circular arcs. Such a projection gives the least distortion, and shapes are almost the same as on the globe.

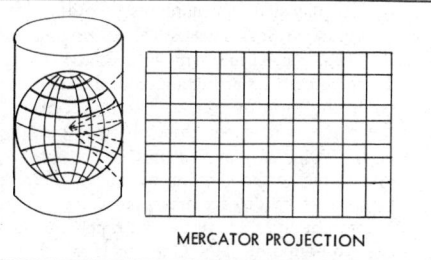

MERCATOR PROJECTION

The Mercator projection, as explained in the article, is used mainly by air and marine navigators for plotting courses.

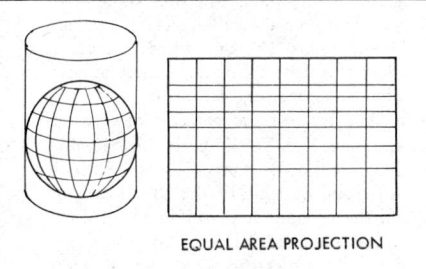

EQUAL AREA PROJECTION

In an equal-area projection, the map is made by drawing lines straight out on paper rolled into a cylinder around a globe. Lines going straight across the map are projections of lines of latitude. Distances between them get smaller as they get farther from the equator. But the areas in each of the boxes on the map are the same as they were on the globe.

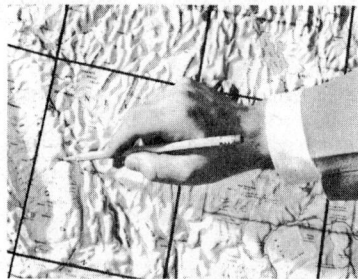

A relief map of the western United States shows the different levels of land. The black horizontal lines are lines of latitude; the black vertical ones are lines of longitude. The pencil is at 119 degrees longitude and 37 degrees latitude.

grees at each pole. The meridians are measured from the zero meridian to 180 degrees going east and 180 degrees going west.

The zero meridian, called the prime meridian, can be placed wherever people want to place it. In modern times, most nations of the world have accepted the Greenwich meridian, which puts zero meridian in a part of London, England, called Greenwich. You can read more about this in the article on NAVIGATION.

If a place lies at the spot where a certain parallel crosses a certain meridian, we can know exactly where that spot is because two lines can cross at only one point.

CONIC PROJECTIONS

When you see a map of the United States, or a single state, or a continent such as Europe, it is usually a conic projection. For a small part of the earth's surface, it shows territories just about as big and places just about as far apart as they actually are.

MERCATOR'S PROJECTION

For a larger area, and especially for the entire surface of the earth, "the skin of the orange" would have to be stretched much farther than is possible in a conic projection. The usual method of showing the entire surface of the earth on a flat map is technically called a *cylindrical projection,* and one kind of it is called the *Mercator projection.*

Mercator was a Flemish map-maker who lived about four hundred years ago. His projection was the first important change in map-making for 1,400 years, and he was the first to use the name atlas for a book of maps. Mercator's real name was Gerhard Kremer. It was the fashion in his day to translate one's name into Latin; *Kremer* means "trader," and so does *Mercator* in Latin.

CYLINDRICAL PROJECTIONS

A cylindrical projection is made by taking a cylinder, or straight-sided tube, of paper, and laying it around the globe with the paper touching the equator. At the equator and for a tiny distance north and south of it, the map will be accurate. However, on the globe the meridians are farthest apart at the equator and they meet at the two poles. On the cylinder they could not be made to meet because the tube of paper was as big at the top and bottom as in the middle. But the parallels were still equally distant from one another. Mercator decided that for every bit that the meridians were farther apart than they had been on the globe, he would make the parallels that much farther apart. That meant that a place on the map near either the North or South Pole would look much larger than a place of the same size near the equator.

You might think this would make the map useless, because there would be no way of telling what size a place really was. That is where the parallels and meridians become important. No matter what size the place may look, the parallels and meridians measure it exactly. The Mercator projection is used chiefly for navigation charts for sailors.

HOW TO READ A MAP

To read a map accurately, one must know scale and direction. Direction is indicated by an arrow pointing north. Scale is always given in a corner of the map. The scale is the size of a place represented on the map in relation to its true size. The scale may be 1 inch = 10 miles, which is a fairly large-scale map, or it may be 1 inch = 100 miles, which is a smaller scale. Large-scale maps are easier to read, and are used mostly in road maps and maps of small areas.

Each map has also a legend, which tells what signs and symbols it uses for different things on the map. A map of the United States will have certain symbols to represent the cities of various sizes. A road map will have special symbols to indicate highways, paved roads, and other things that will help travelers.

A map of a large part of the earth, such as a map of Europe and Asia, will be divided into countries. This is called a political map. Each country will be printed in a certain color, and the territories or possessions of that country will be printed in that color too.

A relief map shows natural features of the earth, such as mountains and rivers. It uses various colors and shadings to show the height of mountains and the steepness of their slopes.

There are many other kinds of map for different purposes, such as weather maps, navigation charts, political maps that show voting trends, business maps that show buying habits in different places, and any number of maps for other special purposes.

maple

The maple is a fine large tree that grows in the midwestern and eastern parts of the United States and in some parts of Canada. There are more than seventy-five different kinds of maple. Those that are best known are the sugar maple and the black, silver and red maples. Many maples grow to be more than a hundred feet high. The maple is a deciduous tree, which means that it loses all of its leaves in the fall. The leaves begin to come out in early spring, along with tiny, bell-shaped, pale green flowers. In the fall the maple leaves turn beautiful shades of red. The seeds of the maple tree have little wings that are easily blown by the wind to new places where other maple trees begin to grow.

The maple is a very useful tree. Maple sugar comes from the sugar maple tree. The wood of the maple is hard and strong and takes a polish well. It is used to build floors that must be very strong, such as dance floors and bowling alleys, and for furniture, musical instruments, boxes, spools, and automobile parts. Maple wood is also used to make charcoal, wood alcohol, and paper.

maple sugar

Maple sugar is a delicious brown sugar that comes from the sugar maple tree. The Indians were the first people to discover that the sap of the sugar maple was sweet and good to eat. In the northern parts of the United States the sap of the sugar maple tree is used to make maple syrup and maple sugar.

In early spring, when the days are

warm and the nights are cool, the sap begins to flow. Men cut the bark of the sugar maple trees about 4½ feet from the ground. (This is called "tapping" the trees.) They attach buckets to the trees and the sap flows out of the bark into the buckets. The sap is then treated in machines that turn it into maple syrup and maple sugar. A single machine can make about four hundred gallons of maple syrup in one hour.

The Indians had no machines. They dropped hot stones into the containers filled with sap. This made the sap boil. Then they froze the sap and it turned to sugar. The early settlers in America cooled the sap by dropping it in the snow. They then poured the sugar into molds and let it harden. Though people now make maple sugar in machines, the method is very much the same.

One maple tree produces about one gallon of maple syrup, or up to eight pounds of sugar. A maple tree lives to be about three hundred years old, and it can produce a great deal of sugar in that time.

When people began to use cane and beet sugar, maple sugar became less important. It is still eaten as a candy, and the maple syrup made from it is used on waffles and pancakes and in many other ways. Most of the maple sugar in the United States comes from the states of Vermont and New York.

marabou

The marabou is a bird that is a member of the stork family. It makes its home in Africa. The marabou is a strange-looking white bird. It has greenish-gray wings and long, thin legs. The marabou has a pouch that hangs from its neck that it can fill with air, like a balloon. The marabou eats tortoises, lizards, and other small animals. It is easily tamed, but it can be a great nuisance because it is fond of chickens and turkeys. The beautiful white feathers of the marabou are used to make scarves and shawls, and people decorate hats with marabou feathers. The marabou is related to the ADJUTANT BIRD, about which there is a separate article.

Marat, Jean Paul

Jean Paul Marat was a leader in the French Revolution, the time when the French people overthrew their king and noblemen and set up a republic, more than 180 years ago. Marat was a "terrorist." He had hundreds of people put to death, often for no good reason.

Marat was born in France in the year 1744, and started out in life as a physician. He did not get along well with other people, and became bitter and cruel, perhaps because of his unhappy experiences. When the French Revolution started in 1789, he joined in with wild enthusiasm, and was one of the most bloodthirsty of the revolutionist mob. He wrote pamphlets and articles that demanded the execution of thousands of people. He had great power in France, but many people hated him for the things he had done. He was assassinated by a young woman named Charlotte Corday on July 13, 1793. Many people thought that she did France a great service, but Marat's powerful political supporters condemned her to death on the guillotine.

marathon

The Battle of Marathon was fought in ancient Greece, almost 2,500 years ago. The Greeks were fighting the Persians on the plain of Marathon, about twenty-five miles from Athens. The Greeks won the battle and a Greek athlete named Pheidippides ran twenty-five miles to Athens to carry the good news. He arrived and proclaimed the victory in the market place, and then fell dead.

In the first modern Olympic games in 1896, there was a "marathon" race of about 25 miles. It was won by a Greek in 2 hours, 55 minutes and 20 seconds. In 1908 the Olympic games were held in London and the course for the marathon was laid out over 26 miles of roads. At the last minute it was decided that the finish line should be in front of the royal box, where the king was to sit, and this added 385 yards to the course. The distance of that race, 26 miles and 385 yards, was then set as the standard marathon course. In 1960 the marathon was won by Abebe Bikila of Ethiopia, who ran the course in 2 hours, 15 minutes and 15.2 seconds.

In the United States a marathon race is held every year in Boston, on Patriots' Day, April 19, the date of the first battles of the Revolutionary War. The Boston course is the same distance, and it is run through the city streets, which are lined with thousands of watchers as the runners go by.

The word *marathon* also was given in the 1920s to a succession of endurance fads in the United States, such as the "dance marathon" in which couples danced continuously, with only brief intervals of rest, until they were exhausted. In the 1950s a new kind of marathon was devised, the "telethon," which was a continuous television program put on for the purpose of getting contributions to charity.

marble

Marble is a kind of rock that is used for decorating buildings and for statues. It is used for these two purposes because it is tough and wears well, because it can be given a high polish, and because its many different colors are in beautiful swirls, waves, layers, and other pleasing designs. When marble is pure, it is snow white, but it may be pink, yellow, brown, gray, blue, black, or mixtures of two or three of these colors. You have seen marble lining the walls and floors of banks, office buildings, libraries, museums, city halls, and other public buildings. Marble statues should be protected from rain because water will wear away their high polish. Marble statues that the ancient Greeks and Romans placed outdoors were badly crumbled by rainwater after many centuries.

Sometimes from deep down in the earth, a large amount of rock so hot that it is melted to a liquid is pushed up into the earth's crust. If the melted rock happens to push up into beds of limestone rock or dolomite rock, the great heat and pressure that are created change these two kinds of rock into marble.

The name *marble* comes from the ancient Greek word meaning "sparkle." If you look closely at marble, you will see right below its polished surface many sparkles. Some may be as big as an inch across and some may be so small that you cannot see each one separately. The sparkle comes from the many crystals that marble is made of.

Very beautiful marble comes from Vermont and Georgia. The finest marble comes from Carrara in Italy. The wonderful statues carved by the ancient Greeks were made of an especially fine marble from the Isle of Paros in the Aegean Sea.

Marble used to be carved into little balls that children played games with. The marbles you play with now are made of glass that looks like real marble.

marbles

Marbles is a game popular with boys and girls the world over. It is played with small, shiny balls called marbles, although they are no longer made of marble. The best marbles are made of the fine stone called agate. Most marbles today are made of glass and are called aggies, immies, or nibs. They are made to look like marble. Marbles have also been made of stone and clay.

Marbles can be played in several ways, but there is only one form of the game that is played in tournaments according to regular rules. This is called *ringer*. Ringer is played in a ring 10 feet across. Thirteen marbles are arranged in the center in the form of a cross. The object of the game is to shoot these marbles out of the ring. A player scores one point every time he shoots a marble out of the ring. From two to six may play.

Straight lines are drawn to touch the circle on opposite sides. One line is called the *lag line,* the other the *pitch line.* To decide the order in which the players shoot, they lag. This means that they stand at the pitch line and shoot their shooting marbles, called *shooters,* toward the lag line. The one whose shooter is closest to the lag line goes first, the next-closest, second, and so forth.

The play of the game is made from the pitch line. To shoot, the players must knuckle down; that is, shoot with at least one knuckle of the shooting hand on the ground. A player knuckles down at any point on the pitch line and shoots into the ring to knock one or more marbles out of the ring.

A player continues to shoot when he knocks one or more marbles out of the ring, provided his shooter remains inside the ring. When his shooter goes outside the ring, he has to stop and the next player shoots.

If a player misses, he picks up his shooter and the next player shoots. When his turn comes again, he takes *rounders;* that is, he shoots from any point on the ring line.

The game ends when one player has knocked seven marbles from the ring. If no player has scored seven points when all the marbles have been knocked out of the ring, the player having the largest number of points wins.

march

A march is a musical composition that is written to be played while soldiers are marching, so that they can keep time to the music. Usually a march is played by a military BAND, about which there

is a separate article. A *military march* is played in quick time. It usually has three parts. John Philip Sousa's march, *The Stars and Stripes Forever,* is a popular military march. A much slower march is a *funeral march,* or *dead march,* which used to be played in funeral processions. There are also *wedding marches,* played while the bride and her attendants walk to the altar during a wedding. One of the most popular of these is popularly called "Here Comes the Bride."

March

March is the third month of the year. It has thirty-one days. In ancient Roman times the year began with the month of March. About two thousand years ago the Romans began to use the calendar we know now, and March became the third month. In the Latin language the month was called *Martius,* after Mars, the Roman god of war. People who were born in March have the aquamarine, a bluish-green stone, as their birthstone. Another birthstone for March is the bloodstone, a green stone with small red spots on it. The flower of March is the daffodil, because it is one of the first flowers to bloom in the spring.

March, Peyton C.

Peyton Conway March was a general in the United States Army. He was chief of staff in the last year of World War I. He was born in 1864 in Easton, Pennsylvania, and was graduated from Lafayette College and the United States Military Academy at West Point. In 1917, when the United States entered World War I, March commanded the artillery forces of the American Expeditionary Forces. In May, 1918, he was recalled to the United States to be chief of staff. In this post he was successful in improving the Army's efficiency and bringing about a quick victory.

March retired from active service in 1921 and died in 1955. His 1932 book *The Nation at War* caused a great deal of discussion because it criticized General John J. Pershing, the commander of the American Expeditionary Forces, who had been the chief American war hero.

Marconi, Guglielmo

Guglielmo Marconi was an Italian scientist who invented the wireless telegraph. From this grew both radio and television. Marconi was born in 1874 and began his experiments with electrical waves while still studying at the University of Bologna. In 1895, when he was only 21 years old, he succeeded in sending signals more than a mile. The next year he patented his system in England and organized a wireless telegraph company. In 1899 he set up a wireless telegraph system to cross the English Channel, and in 1901 he sent the first message across the Atlantic Ocean.

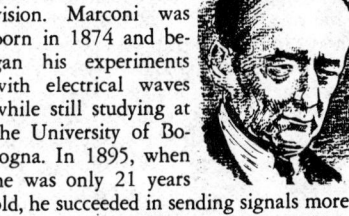

The use of wireless telegraph quickly spread around the world. In 1909 Marconi was awarded the Nobel Prize in physics for his achievement, and he received high honors from many countries.

During World War I, he demonstrated the value of wireless telegraphy in warfare. Marconi died in 1937, at the age of 63.

Marcus Aurelius

Marcus Aurelius Antoninus was a Roman emperor and a great philosopher. He was born about the year 120 and died about 180. He was adopted by his uncle, the Emperor Antoninus Pius, and took the name Antoninus from him. Marcus Aurelius studied philosophy and became a Stoic. There is a separate article about the STOICS.

While Marcus Aurelius was emperor he did many things to improve the life of the people. He established funds for orphans, reduced taxes for poor people, and eliminated much of the brutality of gladiator contests. In one way he was not kindly at all. He persecuted Christians. He thought that Christians were dangerous to the empire because they believed in a God more important than the state.

He wrote a famous book called *Meditations* that is still read. In this book he wrote many proverbs, or brief sentences giving good advice. Among them are:

"Nothing is made better or worse by being praised."

"What is not good for the swarm is not good for the bee."

"Do everything as though it were your last act."

Mardi Gras

Mardi Gras is a day of fun and merrymaking just before the period in spring called Lent. Lent is the forty days before Easter, when many people are very serious and give up many things they like. Mardi Gras is the last day of carnival week, which is a whole week. In England Mardi Gras is called Shrove Tuesday. In French the name Mardi Gras means "fat Tuesday." The day after Mardi Gras is called Ash Wednesday, and it is the first day of Lent. There are separate articles about LENT and about CARNIVAL.

margarine

Margarine is an artificial butter. The first margarine was made in 1870 by a French chemist named Mège-Mouriès. He made it from oleo oil, which comes from beef fat, and from this oil it got the name *oleomargarine.* Later, vegetable oils were added. Now, in the United States, margarine is made from vegetable oils only.

Margarine is very much like butter; it gives the same amount of nourishment and body heat, and it is easily digested. It can be spread on bread or used in cooking, just as butter can.

Vegetable margarine was once made chiefly from cottonseed and soybean oils, but now corn oil is equally important. Peanut and other seed oils often are added. All these are like salad oils, but when they are hydrogenated — when hydrogen gas is forced into them — they become solid fats. The fats are churned with skim milk and become homogenized (made the same throughout), producing a smooth, butterlike material. This is chilled, salted, and churned again to remove water left over from the skim milk. Usually Vitamin A is added.

At this stage, margarine is like pure white butter. A harmless coloring matter can make it yellow like butter, but some "dairy states," where much real butter is made, have passed laws against putting artificial coloring in margarine.

Marianas

The Marianas are a group of islands in the western Pacific Ocean about six thousand miles from the west coast of the United States. There are fifteen islands in the group, of which the best known is the island of Guam. Guam and several of the other islands were the scene of much fighting during World War II.

Until 1899 the Marianas were ruled by Spain. Then Guam came under the control of the United States and the rest of the islands under the control of Germany. In 1919, after World War I, the German islands came under the control of the Japanese, who had fought on the side of the Allies in that war. In December, 1941, at the beginning of World War II, the Japanese seized the island of Guam, which they used for a naval and air base. The Marianas Islands were captured by the American forces between June and August of 1944. In 1947 the United Nations placed the Marianas under the protection of the United States.

Maria Theresa

Maria Theresa was an important queen in Europe about two hundred years ago. She was arch-duchess (queen) of Austria and queen of Hungary and Bohemia. She was born in Vienna in 1717. Her father, Charles VI, belonged to the Hapsburg family and was the Holy Roman Emperor. Because he had no sons to whom he could pass on his vast lands, he arranged with the various kings of Europe for Maria Theresa to inherit these lands.

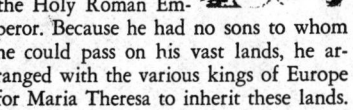

When Charles died in 1740, most of the countries lived up to this agreement, and Maria became ruler of Austria, Hungary, and Bohemia. But Frederick the Great, king of Prussia, refused to recognize the agreement and seized the part of Austrian lands called Silesia. This started a great war, called the War of the Austrian Succession, that involved many of the countries of Europe. When the war ended in 1748, Maria Theresa agreed to let Frederick the Great keep Silesia, but in return it was agreed that her husband, Francis I, would be elected Holy Roman Emperor.

One daughter of Maria Theresa and Francis was Marie Antoinette, who became the wife of Louis XVI and queen of France. Maria Theresa died in Vienna in 1780, at the age of 63.

Marie Antoinette

Marie Antoinette was a queen of France who was put to death by revolutionaries. She was born an Austrian princess, the daughter of Maria Theresa,

the Austrian empress and queen of Hungary.

Marie Antoinette was born about two hundred years ago, in the year 1755. When she was 14, she was married to Louis XVI, who became king of France in 1774. As queen, she was gay and lighthearted, frivolous and extravagant. Marie Antoinette was beautiful, blonde, slender, and graceful, and set the fashion for all of France for many years. At a time when the people of France were grumbling about their poverty and misery, the French court was a place of gaiety, rich parties, and great luxury. At the royal palace of Versailles Marie Antoinette had some farmers' cottages built, where she could play at being a milkmaid.

When one of her advisers tried to explain that the people were dissatisfied because they had no bread, she is supposed to have remarked, "Let them eat cake." She probably did not actually say this, but the story was told to show how little she understood the misery of the people.

The French Revolution started in 1789, and the revolutionists won complete power. They executed first Louis XVI, and then, a few months later, Marie Antoinette, on the guillotine, a machine that cuts off the head. She died in 1793.

marigold

The marigold is a bright yellow or orange flower that first grew in Mexico and South America and is now found in many parts of Europe and the United States. The marigold is an annual plant, which means that it must be planted every year. It blooms in late summer and early fall. The marigold is a hardy plant and grows best in a soil that is not too rich.

There are several different kinds of marigold. The Aztec or African marigold is two to three feet high. It is often used to make a border in flower gardens. The French marigold is a little smaller. It has a small yellow flower. The marsh marigold, which belongs to the buttercup family, grows wild near ponds. Several small yellow flowers bloom on one stalk in the spring. Sometimes people eat the leaves of the marsh marigold.

marihuana is a drug that is made from the dried flowers of the hemp plant and is smoked in cigarettes. In Arabia it is called hashish. See NARCOTICS.

Marine Corps, United States

The Marine Corps is one of the five armed services of the United States. It is that nation's force-in-readiness—ready to fight, anywhere, on short notice. Marines also are trained for special duties in almost any part of the world. They fight on land, like the soldiers of the Army; at sea, like the sailors of the Navy; and in the air, like the Air Force men. Before air-fighting was added to their duties, Marines were called "soldiers of the sea." They are nicknamed "Leathernecks."

The first Marines were formed by a resolution of the Continental Congress on November 10, 1775. These first American Marines were required to have a "knowledge of the sea," and Marines

ever since have had that knowledge. The first Marine group numbered only 300. They wore green coats, green shirts, and breeches of light-colored cloth. The Continental Marines of 1775 were replaced by the Marine Corps as it exists today on July 11, 1798, by an Act of Congress.

The Marine Corps expands quickly when war seems near, and shrinks in peacetime. In World War I there were 75,101 officers and enlisted men, including nearly 300 women, in the Marine Corps. In World War II the Corps grew from 70,425 at the beginning of the fighting to a peak of 485,052, including 18,224 women. By 1950 it had been reduced again, to only 74,279 officers and men. It rose during the Korean fighting to 261,343, including 2,787 women. In 1965 it numbered about 214,000, including some 1,600 women. A law passed by Congress in 1947 requires the Corps to maintain always three combat divisions and three air wings. A division ranges from 17,000 to 22,000 men. There are about 12,000 men in a Marine air wing.

WHAT THE MARINES DO

Marines are called on to do many different jobs in many parts of the world, both in war and in peace. Their most important wartime duty is to capture, from the sea or the air or both, shores occupied and fortified by enemy troops. They drive out the enemy and establish *beachheads* there. These are strong points that soldiers of the Army can occupy later and from which they can join the advance against the enemy. This kind of fighting, largely done by Marines, is called AMPHIBIOUS WARFARE, and there is a separate article about it.

Marines have other regular duties. They guard naval bases in the United States and abroad. Also, they guard United States property all over the world. In peacetime they often are sent to far places to keep order, especially when American people and property need protection. They parade on special occasions, and they furnish escorts, as when important visitors come to the United States. The President may call on the Marines at any time for almost any kind of duty.

Here are some examples of the different kinds of job the Marines have done in their 180 years of existence. Marines fought with General George Washington on land, and with Captain John Paul Jones at sea, in the Revolutionary War. They have made nearly three hundred landings on foreign soil. They fought Barbary pirates in the Mediterranean Sea in 1803. They stopped a Massachusetts State Prison riot in 1824. They battled Indians in Florida in 1836. They helped stop the reckless and illegal killing of seals in the Bering Sea in 1891. They rode camels in the country of Ethiopia, in Africa, while guarding American diplomats in 1903. They protected San Francisco from looting after its great earthquake and fire in 1906. They guarded the United States mail all over the country against robbery in 1921 and 1926.

HOW THE CORPS IS ORGANIZED

The Marine Corps is a part of the Department of the Navy, which is one of the three branches of the Department of Defense. The Marine Corps and the Navy

are considered "partners" in the Department of the Navy, working together. For example, the Navy lets the Marines use its dentists, doctors, and chaplains, and the Marines guard Navy bases. The Marines capture places on land that the Navy wants, using special landing ships furnished by the Navy.

The Marine Corps is divided into two main forces: operating or fighting forces, and supporting forces. The supporting forces include men who furnish ammunition and supplies, and who work to keep the operating forces ready for action. In 1965 the Marine Corps had three active divisions and three air wings. The Marine Corps Reserve (described on page 3291) made a fourth division. In 1966 a fifth division was put into action. Three battalion landing teams were on sea duty.

MARINE AVIATION

The squadron is the basic Marine aviation unit. It is made up of planes, men who fly them, and others who service the planes and keep them ready for flying. Some Marine planes are the same as those used by the Navy. Marines fly the latest jets, and are assigned to duty aboard aircraft carriers. They also fly giant transport planes, and are specialists in the use of helicopters.

The Marines are proud of their progress with helicopters. The Corps sent the first transport helicopter squadron in history to Korea in 1951. In October of that year the squadron, in "Operation Bumblebee," lifted an entire battalion of 958 troops and their equipment and carried them fifteen miles into battle. The squadron used twelve Sikorsky HRS helicopters, each carrying six Marine riflemen. These helicopters also performed wonders in picking up wounded men and flying them to hospitals. Since then many new helicopters, able to carry more men and equipment, have been developed. These proved very effective in Vietnam.

RANKS AND PAY

Although the Marine Corps is a part of the Navy, its ranks and pay scales follow those of the Army. When a man enlists in the Marines he is a private and gets $87.90 a month. After four months this is raised to $93.90. It is raised to $97.50 when he becomes a private first class. He can rise to corporal and sergeant and, becoming an officer, to lieutenant, captain, and so on, as in the Army. Each grade draws higher pay than the one below.

The head of the Marine Corps, called the Commandant, is a general who wears four stars. That is the highest rank a Marine may attain. In the article about the U.S. ARMY, there is a chart listing ranks and pay.

TRAINING AND CAREERS

Marines must undergo long and exacting training. For enlisted men there are two Marine Corps Recruit Depots, at Parris Island, South Carolina, and at San Diego, California. These are called "boot camps," probably from the first article of clothing issued to recruits years ago—boots. The course at boot camp lasts eight weeks.

Recruits first get tests to find out where they will best fit in and what schools they

1. This memorial in Virginia celebrates the flag-raising by the United States Marines after the capture of the island Iwo Jima in the Pacific Ocean from the Japanese during the Second World War.

2. Firing from a concealed position is one of the skills learned during basic training.

3. These special landing craft are designed so that Marines can reach shore quickly and efficiently.

All photos: U.S. Marines

With his white silk parachute like a giant mushroom above him, a Paramarine drops to earth during jump practice.

ris Island. Here they are instructed in military customs and courtesies, administration, drill, Marine Corps history, and other subjects. There are 26 occupation fields and 87 specialties for women in the Marines. Among them are: secretary, typist, job analyst, bookkeeper, draftsman, teletype operator, cryptographer, and others.

MARINE CORPS RESERVE

The Marine Corps Reserve was formed to help expand the service rapidly in time of war. It was created by law in 1914, but little was done about it until the United States entered World War I in 1917. In late 1918 it had 463 officers and 6,773 enlisted men, including 250 women.

The Reserve was reorganized in 1925. In 1962 there were more than 200,000 men and women in the Reserve.

In 1953 the Reserve was classified into three branches: Ready (organized); Standby (volunteer); and Retired. In an emergency the Ready would be called first, then the Standby, then the Retired.

Ground Reserves train at local centers, and take two weeks of active duty each year at a regular Marine Corps base. Marine Air Reserve members are trained in forty-two fighter squadrons and Marine ground control intercept (radar) squadrons at twenty-five Marine and Navy air stations. Volunteers are mostly specialists and technicians.

HISTORY OF THE MARINES

The history of the Marine Corps follows closely the military history of the United States, or the history of the Navy and the Army. (See the separate article on the U.S. NAVY.)

Some of the jobs done by the Marines through history have already been mentioned. Their first amphibious landing was made in the Bahamas in the Revolutionary War, when the men rowed ashore in whaleboats. Marines have fought both at sea and on land in every war since.

will later attend. They learn about military courtesy and discipline. (These are described in the article about the U.S. ARMY.) At boot camp there is recreation as well as hard work. Marines have thirty days of vacation each year. From boot camp Marines go to specialist schools, posts, and stations, or to the operating fleet marine force.

Young men in the Marine Corps, as in other service branches, may learn how to do many special jobs and work at special trades. The Corps lists 43 occupational specialties, or major job fields, with 470 specialist jobs. There are 140 specialist schools that Marines may attend. A Marine may become an expert in electronics, utilities, photography, motor transport, radar, surveying, engineering, hydraulics, and many other fields. But always, basically, he is a rifleman. He may retire with an income for life after twenty or more years of service.

Many Marines, after completing boot camp, go to the Marine Corps schools at Quantico, Virginia, or to Camp Lejeune, North Carolina. There they take advanced training.

At Quantico there is an Officer Candidate School Course (OCC), which trains promising enlisted men for commissioned rank, and a Platoon Leaders' Course (PLC), which instructs college students during their vacation months. At both Quantico and Lejeune Marines study and practice for the infantry, artillery, ordnance, and so on.

WOMEN IN THE MARINES

Women who are between 18 and 30 years of age, are single, and have a high-school education or its equivalent, may enlist in the Marine Corps. They first undergo eight weeks of training at Par-

Some major Marine actions include the Naval War with France, 1798–1801; the war against Tripoli, 1801–05; the War of 1812 against England; the Florida Indian War, 1835–42; the Mexican War, 1846–48; the Civil War, 1861–65, where the Marines fought at Bull Run; the Spanish-American War, 1898; the Philippine Insurrection, 1898–1902; the Boxer Rebellion in China, 1900; the two World Wars; and the United Nations action in Korea.

In World War I, Marines gained glory at Belleau Wood and other places. France renamed Belleau Wood the *Bois de la Brigade de Marines.* In World War II the Marines, after heroic stands at Wake, Bataan, Corregidor, and Midway, started the first American offensive against the Japanese at Guadalcanal. They followed this with island warfare right up to Iwo Jima and Okinawa. In Korea, they were prominent in the Inchon landing operation of September, 1950.

The Marines became a major force in active fighting again when war broke out in Vietnam.

MARINE CORPS TRADITIONS

Marines are very proud of their traditions and their heritage of two centuries of service. They are usually the first ashore on hostile territory, whether in the hot tropics or the cold Arctic. There is an old saying of which they are especially proud: "The Marines have landed and the situation is well in hand." It is believed to have been said first by the author Richard Harding Davis. Marines have fought almost everywhere, from the "Halls of Montezuma" in Mexico, to "the shores of Tripoli" on the Barbary coast, as sung in the *Marines' Hymn.* The first verse of this in the 1960s has been changed from earlier versions to fit the growing duties of the Marine Corps:

From the Halls of Montezuma
To the shores of Tripoli,
We fight our country's battles
In the air, on land and sea;
First to fight for right and freedom
And to keep our honor clean;
We are proud to claim the title of
United States Marines.

The tune of the *Marines' Hymn,* first sung after the Mexican War in 1847, occurs in an old Spanish folk song and in the French comic opera *Geneviève de Brabant,* by Jacques Offenbach.

The Marine colors are scarlet and gold. The Marine insigne, adopted in 1858, is a globe showing the Western Hemisphere, an eagle, and an anchor, with a motto at the top, *Semper Fidelis,* Latin words meaning "Always Faithful."

MARINE BAND

When Congress authorized the Marine Corps on July 11, 1798, at the same time it voted enough money for "musick" by thirty-two drummers and fifers, with a drum major. There has been a Marine Band ever since. It is said to be the oldest band in the United States. Today it is a full concert band, with about eighty-five members and with every band instrument.

The Marine Band has been called "the President's Own." It has entertained every President of the United States since George Washington. The most famous Marine Band leader was the "March King," John Philip SOUSA, about whom there is a separate article. Sousa was leader from 1880 to 1898, and he took the band on nationwide tours. The leader in 1962 was Albert Schoepper, with the rank of lieutenant colonel.

The Marine Corps library of music and arrangements is valued at more than two million dollars.

Marion, Francis

Francis Marion was an American patriot who led a band of South Carolina colonists against the British during the Revolutionary War. Marion had only sixteen men in his band when he first formed it, but later he received the rank of brigadier general from the governor of South Carolina and formed a larger force, called a brigade. Marion's brigade was poorly clothed and underfed, but it was very successful in fighting the British in South Carolina. At one time, the brigade was the only force fighting the British in the South. Marion's brigade made many daring raids against the British. William Cullen Bryant, an American poet, wrote a well-known poem called "Song of Marion's Men," which describes these raids. Francis Marion was born in 1732 and died in 1793.

Maris, Roger

Roger Maris has hit more home runs in a single season than any other major-league baseball player. He was born in Hibbing, Minnesota, in 1934 and played football and baseball in high school. He began his major-league playing career with the Cleveland Indians in 1957, but was traded to the Kansas City Athletics in 1958 and to the New York Yankees in 1960. In 1961 he hit 61 home runs in 162 games. This broke the record for a single season established by Babe Ruth in 1927. But Ruth had hit 60 home runs in only 154 games. Maris played a longer season, and did not hit his sixtieth home run until after 154 games. He was voted the Most Valuable Player in the American League in 1960 and in 1961.

Maritime Provinces

The Maritime Provinces are the three eastern provinces of Canada. They are NOVA SCOTIA, NEW BRUNSWICK, and PRINCE EDWARD ISLAND. There is a separate article about each. Most of the people living there are fishermen or farmers. The beautiful scenery along the Atlantic coast has made these regions popular vacation spots.

Mark, Saint

St. Mark was an early Christian who wrote the second Gospel of the New Testament. His full name was Mark John. He was a friend of St. Peter, one of Jesus' beloved Apostles. St. Mark probably wrote his Gospel from things told to him by St. Peter. He tells the life of Jesus in a very moving way. The story is fast-moving and the reader sees Jesus as a great preacher and man of action.

St. Mark's mother was named Mary. She let St. Peter come to her house after he had been released from prison. St. Mark went with St. Paul to Antioch and Cyprus, where they converted many people to Christianity. Later he did missionary work in Rome, where he saw St. Peter, who was a prisoner there. A very old tradition says that St. Mark died after starting the Christian Church in Alexandria, Egypt. He is the patron saint of the Italian city of Venice, where there is a beautiful cathedral named for him. Artists often use a lion to stand for St. Mark because of the strong picture St. Mark gives of Jesus in the second Gospel. His feast day is April 25.

Markham, Edwin

Edwin Markham was an American poet. His most famous poem was "The Man with the Hoe." He was born in Oregon City, Oregon, in 1852. When he was only 5 years old his father died and he was taken to California, where he grew up working on cattle ranches and studying in country schools. He became a teacher and superintendent of schools, and wrote verse for California newspapers. In 1899 the San Francisco *Examiner* published "The Man with the Hoe," and Markham was famous almost overnight. The poem tells how working people were badly used by rich and powerful rulers for thousands of years. Markham was inspired by a famous painting by the French painter Jean Millet. After this success Markham moved to New York City. One of his best-known later poems is "Lincoln, the Man of the People." Markham died in 1940, at the age of 88.

Mark Twain, a name under which Samuel Clemens wrote. See CLEMENS.

Marlborough, Duke of

John Churchill, Duke of Marlborough, was one of England's greatest military commanders. He was born more than three hundred years ago, in the year 1650. When he was 16 years old he became an officer in the guards of the Duke of York (who later became King James II). The British Prime Minister and World War II commander, Winston Churchill, was descended from the Duke of Marlborough.

John Churchill was not born a duke, or any kind of nobleman. He rose to the rank of general in the British Army, and became first a baron, then an earl, and finally a duke. During his military career, he fought under four different British rulers. The first was Charles II, when England and France were at war against Holland. Then came James II, and then William and Mary. It was William who made him an earl.

Churchill's greatest military successes came during the reign of Queen Anne, who became queen in 1702. At that time the British were fighting against France in the War of the Spanish Succession. Marlborough and his ally, the Austrian Prince Eugene, won important victories, including a famous one at Blenheim, in Bavaria. Queen Anne made Marlborough a duke

and had the finest private palace in England built for him. It is called Blenheim Palace in honor of his victory, and the Dukes of Marlborough, descendants of John Churchill, still live there.

Churchill's wife, the Duchess of Marlborough, was Sarah Jennings Churchill, a woman of unusual talent and intelligence. For many years she was Queen Anne's dearest friend, and this had a great deal to do with the Duke's success, as you can read in the article about Queen ANNE. Later Anne and Sarah stopped being friends, and Marlborough lost his power, but when George I became king after the death of Queen Anne, the Duke recovered his influence. He remained active in Parliament and public life until his death in 1722.

marlin

The marlin is one of the most beautiful and most powerful of all fishes. It lives in the warmer oceans of the world. The marlin got its name because of a long pointed "sword" that extends from its upper jaw. This sword looks like a tool called a marlin-spike that sailors use to separate strands of rope. The blue marlin is found in the Atlantic Ocean from the coast of Florida to New York. It is dark blue in color, with a silver underside. It is about twelve feet long and usually weighs about two hundred pounds, although some marlins weigh much more. The marlin is a fierce fighter. Marlin fishing is a popular sport requiring skill and strength. Marlins sometimes travel in large groups, but often they are found alone or in pairs. The marlin eats other fish.

Several kinds of marlin live in the Pacific Ocean. The black marlin is about fifteen feet long and often weighs more than a thousand pounds.

Marlowe, Christopher

Christopher Marlowe was one of the greatest English playwrights of the Elizabethan period, nearly four hundred years ago, when Shakespeare was also writing plays. Marlowe was born in 1564, and attended Cambridge University. His writings caused a great deal of comment and much criticism, because of the bold way in which he wrote. Christopher Marlowe is the only Elizabethan playwright, other than Shakespeare and Ben Jonson, whose plays are still performed today. *Tamburlaine* and *Dr. Faustus* are two of Marlowe's plays that are still performed. Some people have believed that Christopher Marlowe wrote some things that Shakespeare is supposed to have written, but it is impossible to prove or disprove this. Marlowe died in 1593, as the result of a wound received in a violent quarrel.

Marmara, Sea of

The Sea of Marmara (or Marmora) is part of the important water route that connects the Black Sea and the Mediterranean Sea. It lies between Europe and the westernmost part of Asia, called Asia Minor. The Sea of Marmara is connected to the Black Sea on the north by the Bosporus, and with the Aegean Sea on the south by the Dardanelles. Both of these are narrow straits, passages of water only a few miles wide. The Sea of Marmara is 4,500 square miles in area and more than

4,000 feet deep at its deepest point. The city of Istanbul, in Turkey, is its most important seaport. There are several islands in the Sea of Marmara. The most important is the island of Marmara, which is famous for its marble quarries.

marmot

The marmot is a little animal that lives in the Alps mountains and in other parts of Europe where the climate is cool. It is about as large as a rabbit, with short legs and a long tail. Its fur is gray. Marmots live in burrows, holes that they dig in the sides of hills. Sometimes a burrow has several rooms and two entrances and a large group of marmots lives together in it. When the weather grows chilly in autumn, the marmots retire to their burrows and sleep through the long winter months. They do not come out again until the spring. Marmots eat grass, roots, and insects. The marmots that live in the United States are called *woodchucks*.

Marne

The Marne is a river in northeastern France. It is about 325 miles long and flows into the River Seine near Paris, the chief city and capital of France. The Marne River is not an important river and is remembered mostly because it was the scene of two battles during World War I. Some experts think that these two battles were the most important of the war, because if the Germans had won them they could have occupied the city of Paris.

The first battle of the Marne took place in September, 1914, a month after the beginning of World War I. The Germans crossed the Marne, and the French were so sure that Paris would be defeated that they moved the government to Bordeaux, a city farther south. The Germans were turned back at the Marne because of the courage and determination of the soldiers fighting under the British commander, Field Marshal Sir John French, and the French commander, General Joseph Joffre. They were told that they must not retreat, and they did not. Help for these soldiers at the front came from the soldiers stationed in the city of Paris, who were moved to the front lines by the French General Joseph Gallieni. He seized every taxicab, private car, bus, and any other kind of transportation in Paris and sent his soldiers to the front, leaving Paris undefended. Finally the Germans retreated, and Paris was saved. This broke the first German offensive of the war.

The second battle of the Marne took place in 1918 near the end of the war. The Germans realized that they were losing the war and decided to try one last major attack on Paris. This time, too, the French thought the Germans might take the city, and had even prepared a public statement titled "When Paris Falls." But Paris did not fall because the Germans were weaker than the French had expected.

In this second battle troops from the the United States under the command of General John J. Pershing drove back the Germans when they crossed the Marne at Chateau-Thierry. Two days later Allied forces, commanded by the French commander, Marshal Foch, attacked the German armies along the Marne. The Ger-

mans were driven back, and about 100,000 German soldiers were killed or wounded. The German army's failure at the second battle of the Marne was actually the end of the war for Germany.

Marquesas Islands

The Marquesas Islands are a group of nine islands in Oceania in the south Pacific Ocean. They belong to France. Altogether they are 492 square miles in size, and their population is 4,200. The islands were originally volcanoes that rose all the way from the floor of the Pacific. The largest island is Nuku Hiva. The capital, Atuona, is a tiny town on Hiva Oa, the second-largest island. The Marquesas Islands are fertile. Fruits grow wild on them, and the people grow copra and vanilla.

Marquette, Jacques

Jacques Marquette was a French priest who came to the New World about two hundred years ago to teach Christianity to the Indians and to explore the new country. He and a French trader named Louis Joliet were the first men to explore the Mississippi River. In 1673 they led a small party of men from Mackinaw, Canada, down the Mississippi as far as the mouth of the Arkansas River. Marquette wrote an account of this journey for France. This was a journey of more than 2,500 miles, and the men traveled in open canoes.

Marquette was born in France in 1637. He became a Jesuit, or a member of a special order of teachers in the Roman Catholic Church. He sailed to Canada when he was 29 years old. For almost ten years he worked with the Indians there, learning their languages and setting up missions. He explored much of the region around the Great Lakes at the same time. He died in Canada in 1675.

marriage

When a man and a woman agree to live together, to become husband and wife and have a family, their agreement is called a marriage. In law marriage is an act, or ceremony, in which the bride and groom agree to do certain things. They agree to stay together and to love each other. If they cannot live up to this agreement, in many countries they are allowed to be divorced. (There is a separate article on DIVORCE.) In most religions, marriage is also a religious ceremony and the marriage is performed by a minister and takes place in a church or other place of worship. Roman Catholics consider marriage one of the seven sacraments, and do not allow divorce. Christians consider marriage holy because St. Paul compared the relationship between a husband and wife to the relation between Jesus and the Church.

The marriage of one man to one woman is called *monogamy*. If a man marries more than one woman, or a woman marries more than one man, it is a *polygamous* marriage. Most people think that men have been monogamous since the earliest times, but many ancient civilizations permitted polygamy. It was recognized by the Jewish religion and is still recognized by followers of Mohammed. In the United States, the Mormons under

Brigham Young permitted polygamy about a hundred years ago, and many people persecuted them because of it. Polygamy has never been very widespread because, beside the religious and social customs forbidding it, few men have enough money to support several wives and few people can love more than one wife at a time.

An important purpose of marriage is to enable the husband and wife to have children whom they can love, shelter, and educate in the proper way. This means that the family is the foundation of society. Because of this, governments make regulations concerning marriage. For example, some states do not permit first cousins to marry.

MARRIAGE LAWS AND CUSTOMS

In the United States, no one may be married against his will. Usually a girl has to be 18 years old and a man 21 years old before they may marry. If they are younger, they must have the consent of their parents before they may marry.

In many countries, marriages are arranged by the couple's parents. In some the bride has to bring a dowry, or sum of money, and in others the groom has to "pay" for his bride. Most people who get married in the United States decide for themselves whether they will marry, without any dowry or payment. Each state has its own marriage laws, but most of them contain the same basic features. There must be one or more witnesses to the marriage ceremony, the couple must have a license to marry, and they must pass a blood test that shows they have no dangerous disease.

About seven out of every ten people in the United States 14 years of age or over are married. Only five out of every 100 people have been divorced. Most people get married between the ages of 20 and 24. Because men do not usually live as long as women, and usually marry women younger than themselves, there are about 8,064,000 widows (women whose husbands have died) and only 2,112,000 widowers (men whose wives have died) in the United States.

Marriage of Figaro

The Marriage of Figaro is an opera by the Austrian composer Mozart. An opera is a play in which all the words are sung instead of spoken. The story of *The Marriage of Figaro* is based on a play of the same name by the French playwright Beaumarchais, and the words for the opera were written by Lorenzo Da Ponte. This was Beaumarchais' second play about the character Figaro. The first was called *The Barber of Seville,* and the Italian composer Rossini later made an opera of it. *The Marriage of Figaro* was first presented in 1786.

The story of the opera is gay and very complicated. It concerns the Count Almaviva, who is bored with his wife Rosina and has fallen a little bit in love with Susanna, who is engaged to marry Figaro, the barber of Seville. Figaro suspects Susanna of flirting with the count, and the count suspects his wife Rosina of flirting with a handsome young page named Cherubino. After many mix-ups in which even the characters hardly know what is happening, the countess wins back the

love of the count and Figaro is again happy with his Susanna.

Mars

Mars was the god of war in the religion of the ancient Romans, more than two thousand years ago. The Romans built many temples to Mars. They thought he would help them to win their battles if his temples were beautiful and imposing. Next to Jupiter, whom the Romans regarded as king of the gods, Mars was the most important Roman god.

In Greece, the god of war was called Ares. He was much more savage than the Roman Mars. Ares was supposed to delight in the horror and bloodshed of battle, while Mars was supposed to stand for the triumph of victory rather than the killing and cruelty of war itself.

The month of March is named for Mars. So is the planet MARS—see below.

Mars

Mars is the fourth planet from the sun. In our solar system, it is the second lightest in weight (Mercury is lighter) and the third smallest (Mercury and Pluto are smaller). Its diameter is 4,220 miles, about half the size of Earth's; its density (how tightly the matter is packed) is about three-fifths as great as Earth's; and its volume (the amount of space it occupies) is about eleven hundredths of Earth's. An object on Mars weighs only about two-thirds as much as it would on Earth. A day on Mars lasts about half an hour longer than a day on Earth, and a Martian year lasts about ten months longer than an Earth year.

The distance from Mars to the sun varies greatly during the course of its revolution, from 129 million miles at the least, to 155 million miles at the most. The distance from Mars to Earth varies

NASA

The surface of Mars with a light sky in the distance, photographed by a camera aboard the Viking I Lander.

from 34 million miles at the least, to 250 million miles at the most.

Scientists think that Mars is the most likely planet in our solar system on which life might have evolved, although they no longer believe, as they once did, that complex or intelligent beings might live there.

In 1969, United States scientists sent two unmanned spacecraft, Mariner 6 and Mariner 7, to the vicinity of Mars. Photographs were radioed back from an altitude of about 2,200 miles above Mars, revealing that the surface is covered with many deep craters, like those on the moon.

In 1976, United States scientists sent two more unmanned spacecraft, Viking 1 and Viking 2, to the Martian surface. Extremely clear photographs showed a reddish, rocky desert with wind-swept sand dunes and a light pink sky. Martian soil was tested for the presence of life which might exist despite the thin Martian atmosphere and despite the fact that the temperature on Mars can vary during a single day from about 100 degrees below zero Fahrenheit at night, to over 70 degrees above zero Fahrenheit in the daytime. No definite proof was found.

Marseillaise

The *Marseillaise* is a lively, stirring song that is the national anthem of the French people. The song was written in 1792 by Claude Joseph Rouget de Lisle, a French officer, during the French Revolution. The mayor of the town of Strasbourg gave a banquet for a brave group of volunteers who were about to leave for battle. The mayor asked de Lisle to write a song for the occasion. He wrote the words and selected an old tune as the music. The song was first called *Battle Song of the Army of the Rhine.* People in Paris did not hear the song until a few months later. Then a group of soldiers from the town of Marseilles, in southern France, sang it in Paris. The people were thrilled by its music and words and they called it the *Song of the Marseillais,* that is, the song of the men of Marseilles.

Marseilles

Marseilles is the second-largest city in France. It is in the south, an important port on the Mediterranean Sea. The harbor is a colorful and busy place because ships from every part of the world dock there. More than 893,000 people live in Marseilles. They work on the docks and also in many factories that make steam engines, automobiles, soap, oil, and other products.

The original harbor at Marseilles is called the Old Port. A new, bigger and deeper harbor was built more than a hundred years ago. More than four thousand ocean vessels go in and out of the harbor every year.

The old part of the city was noted for its narrow, winding streets. This old part of the city was destroyed by the Germans during World War II. The modern city of Marseilles is built around the old district. It is surrounded by hills covered with vineyards. The Church of Notre Dame de la Garde is one of the most famous buildings in the city. It is on a high hill, and a huge statue of the Virgin Mary stands on top of its steeple. It can be seen far out at sea and serves as a landmark for sailors. It is also considered a shrine by the seamen of Marseilles.

The city of Marseilles was founded by Greeks more than two thousand years ago.

MARSEILLES, FRANCE. Population (1970 estimate) 893,111. In the department of Bouches-du-Rhône. On the Mediterranean Sea.

Marseilles is the chief French port on the Mediterranean. One of the most colorful sights of Marseilles is the fishing fleet anchored in the Old Port.

French Gov't Tourist Office

marshal

Marshal is the title given to the highest-ranking military officers in many countries in which there is or has been royalty. A marshal ranks as though he were a prince of the royal house of the country. He is called "Your Excellency." The only other nonroyal title that ranks as high as marshal is cardinal. A cardinal also ranks with princes of the royal family and is called "Your Eminence." Princes are addressed as "Your Highness." Until about 75 years ago, the English simply gave their highest-ranking military officers titles of nobility; for example, the Duke of Marlborough and the Duke of Wellington. In modern times they have adopted the rank field marshal. Napoleon I, the French emperor, gave many of his officers the title of marshal. Germany's leading officers in World War II held the rank of field marshal. The United States never had any regular rank higher than general until 1945, when it created the rank General of the Army, which is usually known as "five-star general." A United States General of the Army ranks as high as a marshal from any other country. A marshal carries a baton (a small, short wand) as a sign of his high rank, but a General of the Army does not.

Certain law-enforcement officers of the United States government are also called marshals. It is a position like that of a sheriff.

Marshall, George C.

George Catlett Marshall is the name of the United States Army officer who was chief of staff of the United States Army during World War II. After the war he became even more noted as a statesman, especially as Secretary of State. He was appointed chief of staff in 1939 over the heads of thirty-four higher-ranking generals. In 1944 he was the first man to be given the

new rank of General of the Army, or "five-star general." As Secretary of State, Marshall proposed the MARSHALL PLAN (about which there is a separate article) to help the countries of Europe.

Marshall was born in 1880 in Uniontown, Pennsylvania. From early boyhood he had planned to be a soldier, and in 1897 he entered Virginia Military Institute. When he was 22 he was commissioned a second lieutenant in the United States Army. In those days it was a handicap for an officer not to be a West Point graduate, and for this reason promotions came slowly to Marshall. He served in various posts in the United States and the Philippines until World War I, during which he served in France. Under General John J. Pershing, Marshall was assigned to move 500,000 troops and 2,700 guns within two weeks and secretly. Pershing later had high praise for Marshall's successful plan. Marshall was aide-decamp to Pershing from 1919 to 1924, and the two worked together to convince Congress that the country must be prepared for war at any time. By this time Marshall had moved up to the rank of lieutenant colonel.

From 1924 to 1938 Marshall served in China and in various posts in the United States, and rose to the rank of brigadier general. In 1939, when he became Chief of Staff with the rank of general, he began a difficult campaign of building up American armed forces. He was a member of the policy committee that guided development of the atomic bomb. Marshall took part in most of the important diplomatic conferences of the war years, attending the Atlantic Charter conference, and the meetings of Presidents F. D. Roosevelt and Harry S. Truman with foreign leaders abroad.

In 1945, Marshall resigned as chief of staff and was immediately appointed special representative of President Truman to China. In 1947 he was recalled to become Secretary of State. He was responsible for the United States plan of aid to Greece and Turkey to forestall Commu-

nist Russia's moves to take over those countries, and he then proposed the Marshall Plan to head off Russian aims in other countries. Marshall resigned as Secretary of State in 1949. The following year he was appointed Secretary of Defense and held that post for exactly a year, resigning in 1951. He died in 1959

Marshall, John

John Marshall was the fourth Chief Justice of the United States Supreme Court. He was probably the most important Chief Justice in American history. He made the Court a strong branch of the government and made decisions about the meaning of the Constitution that have been followed ever since. When the United States was first made a country, many people thought that each state should have a great deal of power to decide its own affairs and that the central government should not be very strong. Marshall believed that the power of the Federal government should be much stronger in some matters than that of the states, and many of the decisions he made while he served as Chief Justice helped establish that power.

John Marshall was one of the most important of the early Americans who helped form the United States. During his lifetime he served in many positions. He was a lieutenant during the Revolutionary War and was Washington's aide, was one of the men who supported the new Constitution, was a special envoy to France for President John Adams, and served as Secretary of State and Secretary of War as well as a member of Congress.

John Marshall was born at Germantown, Virginia, in 1755. After serving in the army he practiced law and quickly became well known. George Washington offered him the position of Attorney-General in his first Cabinet, but Marshall refused. President John Adams appointed Marshall Chief Justice in 1801, and he served for 34 years, until his death in 1835. He wrote a biography of Washington and a history of the colonies, but his best writings are the legal opinions that he handed down while he served on the Supreme Court.

Marshall, Thomas

Thomas Riley Marshall was an American lawyer who became Vice President of the United States when Woodrow Wilson was President. Marshall was born in North Manchester, Indiana, and was a descendant of the famous Marshall family of Virginia to which John Marshall, Chief Justice of the Supreme Court, belonged.

Thomas Marshall was born in 1854. He practiced law for 33 years in Columbia City, Indiana. He became known as an orator who spoke with a great deal of humor. In 1908 he was elected governor of Indiana, and in 1912 and 1916 he was elected Vice President.

Marshall is especially remembered for a remark he made while he was presiding at a dull session of the United States Senate: "What this country needs is a good five-cent cigar." Marshall died in 1925.

Marshall Islands

The Marshall Islands are a group of

thirty-two islands in the western Pacific Ocean, about five thousand miles from the west coast of the United States. They were the scene of heavy fighting during World War II. Before World War I the islands belonged to Germany. At the end of the war, they were given to the Japanese, who had fought on the side of the Allies. During World War II the United States forces carried out the war in the Pacific by a policy that is known as "island hopping." They attacked and captured one group of Japanese islands after another, each time coming nearer and nearer Japan itself. Early in 1944 they attacked one of the Marshall Islands, Kwajalein, which they captured after fierce fighting. The rest of the Marshall Islands were taken from the Japanese very shortly after this. After the war was over, the United States kept control of the Marshall Islands.

The most famous of the Marshall Islands today is Eniwetok, where the United States tested the hydrogen bomb. The force of the bomb was so great that it destroyed the island and made the waters around it radioactive and extremely dangerous.

Marshall Plan

The Marshall Plan was the popular name of an offer made by the United States to help other countries become prosperous again after they had spent most of their money fighting World War II. The plan was named for General George C. Marshall, who was the highest-ranking army general in the United States Army during the war, and who was appointed Secretary of State in 1947. In a speech at Harvard University that year, Marshall suggested that the United States would be willing to help the countries of Europe return to good financial condition and rebuild their business and industry. Many European countries immediately accepted this offer, and the United States set up the Economic Recovery Program to work out the details of how the help was to be given. In 1948 President Harry S. Truman signed an act setting up the Economic Coöperation Administration to put the program into effect.

The United States did not actually give money to the people of these countries. The people bought and paid for many things made in the United States that were not available in their countries, such as tractors, machinery, food, drugs, and chemicals. They paid in their own money, but the United States made available to their governments enough United States dollars to pay American manufacturers for these products. The whole idea was that the United States would help them to buy American goods if the countries would help themselves by putting people to work using these goods.

Only the democratic countries of Europe benefited by the Marshall Plan. Czechoslovakia and some other countries under the control of Communist Russia wanted to join the Marshall Plan, but Russia immediately forbade them to take any part in it.

marsh hawk

The marsh hawk is a bird that lives in many parts of the United States. It has a white patch on its lower back that makes it easy to recognize. The wings and tail are long and narrow. The male marsh hawk is pale gray in color, and the female is dull brown. The marsh hawk builds a nest on the ground and carefully hides it in tall marsh grass or under low bushes. The female lays four or five white eggs. The marsh hawk flies close to the ground in order to spot the frogs and mice that it eats. During the mating season, the male marsh hawk flies in graceful circles and power dives to attract the attention of the female marsh hawk.

marsh mallow

The marsh mallow is a plant that grows in Europe and the eastern parts of the United States. The marsh mallow is a perennial, which means that it grows up from the same roots every year. The plant grows best in wet swampy places. It grows to be about three feet high. It has large pink flowers, and its stems and leaves are soft and fuzzy. The roots of the marsh mallow contain a valuable sticky substance. The roots are collected in the fall and dried. Then people scrape the roots to collect the sticky substance, which is used in cough drops and in candy marshmallows, though people have discovered other and better ways to make the candy.

marsupial

A marsupial is an animal that carries its young in a pouch, a fold of skin that is attached to the mother's abdomen. Long ago, these animals lived all over the world. Gradually they died out, and now almost all of the marsupials make their home in Australia. The only marsupial that does not live in Australia is the opossum. It is found mostly in Central and South America, but one variety of opossum lives in the forests of the southeastern part of the United States.

The best-known marsupial is the kangaroo. It grows to be about seven feet high and weighs more than two hundred pounds. The wallaby is a smaller kangaroo. Other marsupials, such as the marsupial mice and moles of Australia, are tiny creatures less than a foot long. There are marsupials that live in trees and others that live on the ground. The marsupial wolf is a fierce animal that eats meat. The wombat, which looks like a small, fat bear, is a shy animal that hides during the day and comes out at night to search for grass and leaves to eat. One marsupial that lives in the jungles of Australia flies through the air; it is called a flying phalanger and it looks like a flying squirrel. Another marsupial swims in the rivers of South America; it is called a yapok and is a member of the opossum family.

The marsupials are very helpless when they are born. All a tiny marsupial is able to do is to crawl into its mother's warm pouch. There it nurses and quickly grows big and strong. When the babies grow too large for the cozy pouch, they climb out. Often they spend some time after that clinging to their mother's back. In case of danger the young marsupial will return to the pouch for safety.

Marsupials are not intelligent animals and they have many enemies. Man hunts some marsupials, and dogs and cats and owls and other creatures often attack them. Some people believe that these animals may slowly die out altogether.

marten

The marten is a small animal about the size of a cat. It lives in the forests of Europe, Asia, and the United States. The marten has a soft, golden-brown fur, with a patch of cream color at its throat. It has a long, bushy tail. The marten is prized for its beautiful fur, and coats made from it are very expensive.

The marten is a member of the weasel family, and like most weasels, it is a fierce and brave little animal that will attack animals many times its size. The marten is such a savage fighter that few animals other than man can kill it. It is very swift and can run up a tree more quickly than the fastest squirrel. Martens eat squirrels, rabbits, and mice. They also eat fruit and berries. The marten usually builds its nest in a hollow tree. Sometimes it builds a burrow in the side of a hill. The marten lines the nest with moss and soft grass. The female marten has four babies at a time.

Martens are not very sociable animals, and they usually live alone. The marten is very curious, and when it sees a trap that hunters have set, its curiosity leads it to investigate, so that it is easily captured.

So many people have hunted the marten because of its valuable fur that now there are not very many martens left.

martial law

The word *martial* is connected with "war." The word comes from Mars, the name given by ancient Romans to the god of war. When a place is under martial law, it is no longer controlled by the usual peacetime government but by the army or some other military group. Martial law is often declared during a war, but it is also put into effect when there is a riot or a disaster, such as a flood or an earthquake. Martial law is necessary for the protection of life and property during a period of disaster and conflict. It is also needed when the usual police force cannot deal with the situation.

In the United States the President or the Governor of a state announces martial law at such a time, and the highest-ranking army officer in the area takes complete control.

martin

The martin is a friendly, sociable bird that lives in almost every part of Europe and the United States. It is a member of the swallow family. It is a graceful flyer and is well-known for its lovely song. The purple martin is a handsome, dark purple bird that is about 8 inches long. In the autumn, when the first signs of winter appear, the martins begin their journey south. People build large houses where many families of martins live together and they wait for the martins to return in the spring. Martins will return to the same house for many years. Martins eat flies and other insects. They have large mouths, and as they fly they keep their mouths open so that they can catch insects. The female martin lays about

eight shiny white eggs.

The martins that live in England are called house martins. They build their nests on the sides of houses. The nests are made of mud and twigs, with an opening in the side of the nest so that the martins can fly in and out. The house martin is a black bird with white underfeathers.

The sand martin is smaller than other members of the martin family. It gets its name because it hollows out long tunnels in sandbanks to build its nest. At the end of the long tunnel it makes a nest of soft grass and leaves lined with feathers.

Martinique

Martinique is one of the Windward Islands in the West Indies. It belongs to France. It is 425 square miles in size, which is less than one-half the size of Rhode Island, and about 300,000 people live there, which is about one-third the population of Rhode Island. Its capital city is Fort-de-France, a city of about 60,650, which is also its chief port.

The island is really the top of a volcanic mountain that reaches all the way down to the bottom of the ocean. Martinique itself has several mountain peaks. Between them are fertile valleys where the people grow great quantities of sugar cane. Sugar and rum produced on the island are sent to other countries.

The people are often troubled by hurricanes, earthquakes, and volcanic eruptions. In 1902, Mont Pelée, a volcano about 4,500 feet high, erupted violently and destroyed Saint-Pierre, a town that was then Martinique's leading city.

Martinique is an Overseas Department of France, which means that it can send two senators and three men to represent it in the French National Assembly in Paris. French is the official language, but most of the people speak a "creole" language that mixes French and other languages.

MARTINIQUE. Island in the West Indies. Area, 425 square miles. Population (in 1964), 310,000. Overseas Department of French Community. Chief city and capital, Fort-de-France.

martyr

A martyr is a person who gives his life for what he believes in. Most often the word applies to someone who suffers or dies rather than give up his religion. The spirit of martyrdom pervades the book of Daniel, written at a time when the Jewish religion was being persecuted, in the second century before Christ.

The first Christian martyr was St. Stephen, who was stoned to death for defending his Christian belief. (This is described in the Bible, in the Acts of the Apostles, Chapter 7.) St. Paul, who was then persecuting the Christians, was present and the event probably helped him become a Christian.

The Romans demanded that everyone participate in the state religion. This meant worshiping the emperor. One could worship as many other gods as one chose. Christians could not join in emperor worship. They could only worship one Lord, Jesus Christ. In the eyes of the Roman authorities all such people were disloyal and deserved death. When they were brought to the attention of the police they were given a chance to do what they required. If they bore witness

that Christ was the only one whom they would worship they were sentenced to die. The word *martyr* is Greek and means "a witness." Some were taken into a crowded arena to be killed and eaten by lions; others were burned to death. Later many martyrs were recognized as saints, and received a day in the calendar. The stories of their martyrdom were then considered good reading for their particular days. There is a great collection of these stories in many volumes.

Men who have died for other beliefs are also called martyrs. Very often they become symbols of that belief, and their courage inspires others to risk their lives in order to make the belief known and accepted by others. Real and supposed martyrs have played an important part in politics. Often a government will refuse to punish a criminal for fear he will be treated as a martyr and in this way awaken revolt.

Marx, Karl

Karl Marx was a German writer and thinker who lived about a hundred years ago and who had many original ideas about how people should live and how they should be governed. The ideas of Karl Marx, which are now called Marxism, led to the development of the system of government that is now called communism, so it may be said that very few men have had a greater influence on today's world than Karl Marx.

Because communism is an enemy of liberty and religion, and most of the people of the world value their liberty and their religious freedom higher than anything else, it is usual in free (democratic) countries today to disapprove of everything Karl Marx said. This is not a very scientific way to look at it. Karl Marx did not suggest the cruel kind of government that Communists have today. Much of what he taught was wrong, but in some ways he was a brilliant thinker.

Karl Marx was born in Prussia, the largest German kingdom, in the year 1818. As a young man he published a magazine that criticized the government of Prussia. In those days most countries were governed in about the same way, so Marx was actually criticizing nearly all governments. Countries were run by the "upper classes," who were rich and who lived on the work of the "lower classes," who were very poor. Karl Marx wrote that this was wrong. Most people today agree with him, but strangely enough it is the democratic countries, which do not follow Marx's teachings, that have corrected it, and the Communist countries, which say they follow Marx's teachings, that have not corrected it.

The Prussian government made Marx stop printing his magazine and made him leave the country. He went to Paris, France, but after 1849 he was not allowed to live there either. So Marx went to England, where (as in other English-speaking countries) everyone has freedom of speech. Though Marx attacked the British government as much as he did other governments, he was permitted to live and write in London the rest of his life.

In London Marx was very poor. He was married and had several children, and they had to live in the slums. Here Karl Marx wrote his most famous works. The ideas of Karl Marx are explained in the article on COMMUNISM. With another German writer, Friedrich Engels, he had already published a brief document called the *Communist Manifesto,* in 1848, and in England Engels helped him to write his longest book, *Das Kapital* (which in the German language means "capital" and is about the systems known as CAPITALISM and SOCIALISM, both of which are explained in separate articles).

During Marx's lifetime, an International Workingmen's Association was formed (in 1866) to follow Marx's teachings. Marx died in 1883, at the age of 65, with *Das Kapital* not quite finished, but Engels finished it for him.

Mary, the Virgin

The Virgin Mary was the mother of Jesus. Her story, as told in the Gospels, the first four books of the New Testament, is:

Mary was a young girl of Nazareth, a town in Palestine, the land of the Jewish people. She was engaged to marry a carpenter, Joseph. Before they were married, the archangel Gabriel came to her and told her that she would be the mother of Jesus. This was the *Annunciation,* which means "announcing." When Jesus was conceived (began to grow) in Mary, she was still a virgin, which means that she had not known or been married to a man.

Mary then went to see her cousin, Elisabeth, who was also expecting a child (who grew up to be John the Baptist). This is called the *Visitation.* Mary visited her cousin Elisabeth for three months, then returned to Nazareth. Some months after that, she went with Joseph to the city of Bethlehem, where the law required them to go to pay their taxes. There was no room in the inn, so they put up for the night in a stable, and there Mary gave birth to Jesus.

After the birth of Jesus, Joseph, Mary, and Jesus had to flee to Egypt to escape Herod, the king in Palestine; for Herod had heard the prophecy that Jesus would be king, and he was seeking to kill Jesus. When Herod died, they returned to Nazareth. Jesus grew up in the home of Mary and Joseph. He performed his first miracle (changing water into wine) because Mary asked him to; this was at a wedding in the nearby village of Cana, when there was not enough wine for all the guests.

Mary was present at the Crucifixion of Jesus. He told the Apostle John to take care of her, and from then on she lived in John's house. Mary was with the disciples when they were waiting, after Jesus was risen, for the Holy Spirit to come and give them the wisdom and courage to preach the Christian faith; this is told in the first chapter of the Book of Acts of the Apostles.

BELIEFS ABOUT MARY

There are many accepted traditions about the Virgin Mary, and some or all of them are taught in the churches of the various Christian denominations.

Almost all Christians believe that Mary was a virgin, and for that reason she is often called merely the Virgin or

the Blessed Virgin. The article on the IM-MACULATE CONCEPTION describes the belief that she was conceived without original sin (the sin inherited from Adam's fall). Another belief, called the *Assumption*, is that she was taken up to heaven, body and soul, by God. Another is that Mary was the daughter of Saints Anne and Joachim.

Many people, especially Roman Catholics, pray asking Mary to seek graces for them from God. There are separate articles about the AVE MARIA and the ROSARY. There is a beautiful litany, the Litany of Loreto, that describes her.

There are famous shrines to Mary at Lourdes, in France, and Fátima in Portugal. A new Roman Catholic cathedral in Washington, D.C., is dedicated to Mary, who is the Catholic patron saint of the United States.

Among the hymns to Mary are *Stabat Mater Dolorosa,* telling of her sorrow as she stands near Jesus during his Crucifixion, and the *Salve Regina,* which addresses her as the queen of heaven.

There are many feasts celebrated in honor of Mary. They are celebrated by Catholics and in many cases by Protestants. December 8 is the feast of the Immaculate Conception; February 2, of the Purification of Our Lady; May 31, the Queenship of Mary; July 2, the Visitation; August 15, the Assumption; September 8, the Birthday of Our Lady; November 21, the Presentation of Our Lady in the Temple.

Mary Magdalene

Mary Magdalene was a saint who lived in the time of Jesus. Her story is told in the New Testament. She was a bad woman until she met Jesus. Then she repented and became one of his followers. She was present at the Crucifixion and the Resurrection of Jesus (about which you can read in the article on JESUS). Her name means that she came from the town of Magdala, in Palestine.

Mary, Queens of England

There have been two queens of England named Mary who were rulers in their own right. Others have become queen by being married to a king. The first to become queen by inheritance rather than by marriage was Mary I, or Mary Tudor, the daughter of Henry VIII and Catherine of Aragon. She was born in 1515 and was trained to be a queen from her early childhood. Her father had his marriage to Catherine of Aragon anulled and married Anne Boleyn, who was the mother of Elizabeth I, Mary's sister. Later he married Jane Seymour, who was the mother of Henry's only son, Edward VI.

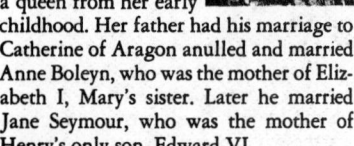

While Henry VIII was alive, Mary's life was very sad. Her father favored her sister Elizabeth. He treated Mary cruelly and did not want her ever to become queen. After the death of Henry VIII, Mary's brother Edward VI became king; but Edward died while he was still a boy, and Mary was next in line. Though she had many enemies, she became queen. This was in 1553. She was 37 years old.

When Mary I became queen, some of the people of England were Catholics and some were Protestants, and they were very unfriendly toward one another. Mary was a Catholic, as her mother had been. Her father, Henry VIII, had been a Protestant.

Both Catholics and Protestants suffered persecution during that period. Sometimes Protestants were in power and persecuted Catholics. Sometimes Catholics were in power and persecuted Protestants. There was no such thing as religious freedom. Many people were executed for their religious beliefs. Because of the things that happened during her reign, she was nicknamed "Bloody Mary."

Mary I married Philip, a Spanish prince, but they had no children. This disappointment, and the fact that she was sick much of the time, made her a very unpleasant person. She died in 1558, when she was 43, and her sister Elizabeth became queen.

MARY II

The second queen of England named Mary was born in 1662, about 150 years after the first Mary. The father of Mary II was James II, who was king of both England and Scotland.

When Mary was only 15 years old, she married William, Prince of Orange, who was a Dutch prince. In 1688, when Mary was 26, revolution forced her father to give up the throne and William and Mary became king and queen together. They were crowned in 1689.

This was the only time two persons of equal rank ever shared the British crown. William was often away at wars, and while he was gone Mary II was a wise and popular queen. She died of smallpox in 1694, when she was 32, and her husband continued to reign as William III until he died in 1702. William and Mary College in Virginia was named for them.

MARY OF TECK

The best-known Queen Mary of modern times was the wife of King George V of Great Britain. Her full name was Victoria Mary. Her father, the Duke of Teck, was a German, and her mother was a British princess, Mary Adelaide.

Mary of Teck was born in 1867, and in 1893, when she was 25 years old, she married the man who was then the Duke of York. In 1910 he became King George V of England and Mary became his queen.

Queen Mary always put her duty as queen before her own desires. She felt very strongly that kings and queens are different from other people and should always be very formal and dignified. Queen Mary never used a telephone, because she felt it was not dignified.

King George V and Queen Mary had four sons and one daughter. Two of them became kings—Edward VIII and George VI. Mary had tried to give her children the same strong sense of duty that she had, but her eldest son, Edward VIII, gave up the throne so that he could marry as he wished; he became the Duke of Windsor. Queen Mary lived to see her granddaughter, Elizabeth II, become the reigning queen in 1952. In 1953, two months before Elizabeth was crowned, Queen Mary died at the age of 85.

Mary, Queen of Scots

Mary Stuart, who was Queen of Scotland about four hundred years ago, was one of the most tragic queens in British history. She was born in 1542. Her father died when she was a baby, and she was crowned queen of Scotland when she was less than a year old. When she was 16 she married Francis, son of Henry II, king of France. After about a year, Henry II died, and for nearly two years Francis and Mary were king and queen of both Scotland and France, but Francis died in 1560.

Mary returned to Scotland and immediately encountered difficulties because she was a Catholic and the people of Scotland were mainly Protestant.

Four years after the death of Francis, Mary married Henry Stuart, Lord Darnley, an English nobleman. They had one son who was later to become James I of England. After a blast intending to take his life failed, Darnley was strangled as he attempted to escape. Many people suspected that Mary had known about the plot to kill Darnley and had done nothing about it. Another Scottish nobleman, the Earl of Bothwell, was suspected of causing the explosion, and when Mary married him the people became very angry and turned against her. She fled to England, where she hoped that Queen Elizabeth I would help her. Instead, Elizabeth threw her into prison. Elizabeth thought Mary had ambitions to become Queen of England.

For the next eighteen years, Mary plotted to escape from prison. Finally, she was charged with being part of a plot to kill Elizabeth. Tried, convicted, and sentenced to death, she was beheaded at Fotheringay Castle, in February 1587, at 44.

Maryland

Maryland is one of the South Atlantic states of the United States. It was one of the thirteen original colonies. Its nickname is the "Old Line State" because Maryland soldiers showed great bravery fighting in the front lines during the Revolutionary War, and received special praise from General George Washington. Maryland is named after Queen Henrietta Maria, the wife of King Charles I of England.

Maryland ranks 42nd in size among the states, with 10,577 square miles. In population it ranks 18th, with more than three and a half million people living there. It was the seventh of the thirteen colonies to become a state, in 1788. The capital is Annapolis.

THE PEOPLE OF MARYLAND

The English were the earliest and largest group of Maryland settlers. Most of them were Roman Catholics. They went to Maryland about three hundred years ago because their religion was not the official English religion. Later, many French, German and other European people went for the same reason, religious freedom. Most of these people started farms on the rich Maryland soil, and they brought in Negro slaves to work the plantations. As factories were built in the cities, other immigrants settled in Maryland from Russia, Poland, Italy, and other European countries. Today, most of the people in Maryland are American-born.

Many people in Maryland are still farmers, but even more now work in the large cities, especially in Baltimore, where almost one-third the people live.

The early settlers in Maryland were determined that it should be a place where people of all religions could worship as they pleased, without fear of persecution. They passed such a law more than three hundred years ago. Today, the largest religious group is the Methodists.

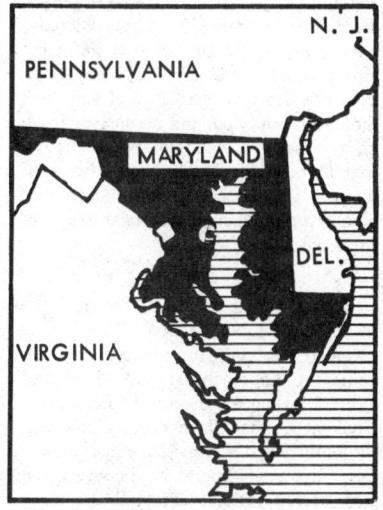

WHAT MARYLAND IS LIKE

Maryland is divided into two parts by the Chesapeake Bay. The region around the bay is called the coastal plain, and it is very flat. There are many fine harbors along the jagged coastline. There is fishing for bluefish, oysters, bass, and many other fish, both in Chesapeake Bay and in the Atlantic Ocean. The soil of the coastal plain is very fertile.

In the north central part of the state is the Piedmont Plateau, a high, level region. It is one of the best dairy-farming regions in the country.

The western part of Maryland is the Appalachian Plateau. Here are high mountain ridges of the Allegheny and Appalachian mountains, with narrow, fertile valleys in between. The Potomac River runs through this part of the state, and it has cut many deep gorges in the mountains.

The climate of Maryland is varied. In the eastern and southern parts of the state the winters are mild and the summers hot. In the mountains the summers are cool and the winters very cold. The average temperature in winter is 34 degrees, and in summer about 75 degrees.

Hunting is a favorite sport with people in Maryland. There are many small fur-bearing animals such as the squirrel, raccoon, and fox. There are also bears and deer in the woods.

Because so much of Maryland faces the water, transportation by boat has always been important to the people. Shipbuilding became an important industry in colonial days, and ships built in Baltimore became famous all over the world. Today, Baltimore is one of the great ports for world trade, and the Chesapeake and Delaware Canal was built to provide a short cut for ocean vessels. It connects an arm of Chesapeake Bay with the Delaware River. Railroads were built to reach parts of the state where there

Johns Hopkins University

Beautiful Johns Hopkins University is one of the best-known schools, not only in Maryland but in the entire country.

were few rivers, and now Maryland has about 1,500 miles of railroad. The state is crossed by many roads and highways, and many of the old roads in Maryland are historic. The famous Cumberland Road, which today is a big highway, was the route many pioneers took as they went west. Maryland also has many airports, including the Friendship International Airport, which covers 3,200 acres in Baltimore.

THE GOVERNMENT OF MARYLAND

Maryland, like most other states, has a Governor and a Legislature. The Governor is elected for a four-year term. The Legislature is composed of a Senate and a House of Representatives. The members of both houses are elected for a four-year term. Judges are elected for a fifteen-year term. The capital is Annapolis. There are 23 counties.

There are about 892,000 students attending public elementary and high schools. Among the principal colleges and universities are:

University of Maryland, at College Park. Enrollment, 48,740 (co-ed).

Johns Hopkins University, at Baltimore. Enrollment, 9,373 (men only).

Goucher College for Women, at Baltimore. Enrollment, 1,085 (women only).

Morgan State College, at Baltimore. Enrollment, 3,817 in 1971 (co-ed).

United States Naval Academy, at Annapolis. Enrollment 4,094 in 1971 (men only).

University of Baltimore, at Baltimore. Enrollment, 4,587 in 1971 (co-ed).

The United States Naval Academy is located at Annapolis, Maryland.

Official U.S. Navy Photo

CHIEF CITIES IN MARYLAND

The leading cities of Maryland, with populations from the 1970 census, are:

Baltimore, population 905,759 the largest city in the state. See separate article.

Hagerstown, population 35,862 manufacturing center, in the northern part of the state.

Cumberland, population 29,724 a railroad and industrial center, in the northwestern part of the state.

Annapolis, population 29,592 the state capital. There is a separate article about ANNAPOLIS.

Bethlehem Steel Co.

The Havre de Grace Bridge over the Susquehanna is part of the chief highway route between north and south Maryland.

MARYLAND IN THE PAST

The first permanent settlement in Maryland was made by the English, who set up trading posts on Kent Island more than three hundred years ago. In 1632, King Charles I of England gave the Earl of Baltimore a large grant of American land that included Maryland, and in the following years many English colonists settled in the region. These colonists were gentlemen who were used to living comfortably, and they built beautiful houses and had slaves to serve them. They also brought many English customs with them, and one could often see Maryland gentlemen going fox-hunting in their scarlet costumes and celebrating Christmas with large parties, much as they had done in England.

About two hundred years ago Maryland had a disagreement with Pennsylvania, its neighbor to the north, about its boundary. The disagreement was finally settled by the famous Mason and Dixon's Line, which came to be considered the dividing line between the North and the South.

Maryland soldiers fought bravely in the Revolutionary War and the War of 1812 against the British. It was while watching the attack on Fort McHenry near Baltimore, during the War of 1812, that Francis Scott Key was inspired to write "The Star-Spangled Banner," the national anthem of the United States.

At the time of the Civil War, Maryland was in an important position because it lay on the boundary between the North and the South. The Maryland plantation-owners owned slaves, but Maryland, unlike other slaveholding states, did not secede from the Union, though many of its people wanted to.

After the Civil War, Maryland expanded rapidly. Its cities grew and big factories were built. Baltimore became one of the large industrial centers in the country. In both World War I and II,

Maryland contributed to the war effort with large supplies from its farms and factories.

PLACES TO SEE IN MARYLAND

Fort McHenry National Monument and Historic Shrine, in Baltimore, on U.S. Routes 1 and 40. The successful defense of this fort in 1814 inspired the writing of "The Star-Spangled Banner."

Antietam Battlefield, near Sharpsburg, in the northwest, west of U.S. Route 40. The scene of one of the bloodiest battles during the Civil War, in 1862.

Annapolis National Cemetery, at Annapolis, in the central part of the state.

The United States Naval Academy, at Annapolis. Visitors are usually permitted to enter the grounds and buildings.

Great Falls of the Potomac, north of Bethesda, on U.S. Route 240. Spectacular cataracts made by the Potomac River.

The State House in Annapolis, completed in 1774 and the oldest capitol in the United States that is still in daily use.

MARYLAND. Area, 10,577 square miles. Population (1970 census) 3,922,399. Capital, Annapolis. Nickname, the Old Line State. Motto, *Scuto Bonae Voluntatis Tuae Coronasti Nos* (With the Shield of Thy Goodwill Thou Hast Covered Us). Flower, black-eyed Susan. Bird, Baltimore oriole. Song, "Maryland, My Maryland." Admitted to Union, April 28, 1788. Official abbreviation, Md.

Masaryk

Masaryk was the name of two Czechoslovakian statesmen, father and son.

Thomas Garrigue Masaryk is called the "father of Czechoslovakia" and is considered its greatest statesman. In 1850, when he was born, Austria-Hungary controlled the territories that later became the nation of Czechoslovakia. Thomas Masaryk was born in Moravia, one of these territories. The Moravians are a Slavic people. Along with the Czechs, Slovaks, and other Slavs, they had tried for years to become independent of their Austrian and Hungarian rulers.

Masaryk became a professor at the University of Prague. He was interested in politics and was elected to the Austrian parliament, which governed Moravia and the other territories. He headed a party that wanted complete independence from Austria. In 1914, when World War I broke out, Masaryk fled to Paris to avoid being on Austria's side. There he formed an organization called the Czech National Council to work for Czech independence. During the war Masaryk went to the United States to raise money for his organization. When the Allies won World War I, in 1918, they made Czechoslovakia an independent nation. Masaryk's organization became the new Czech government and Masaryk became its first president. He served from 1918 until 1935. When he was 85 years old, he resigned because of his age, and he died two years later, in 1937. He was greatly loved by the people of his country.

Jan Masaryk, his son, was born in 1886. He served as his country's minister to Great Britain from 1925 to 1938. Germany took over Czechoslovakia in 1939 and during World War II Czechoslovakia set up a government-in-exile. Jan Masaryk was the foreign minister of this government. In 1945, when the Allies won World War II, he returned with the government to his country, but then in 1948 the Communists took over Czechoslovakia. Masaryk remained in the cabinet, even though he was not a Communist. A few days later, in the spring of 1948, he died as a result of a fall from a window. It was announced that he had committed suicide, but some believe he was murdered by being forced out of the window.

Masefield, John

John Masefield is the name of an English poet who became poet laureate of his country. The poet laureate is appointed by the king or queen to write poems for special occasions and to commemorate great events. Masefield was born in 1878. His father was a lawyer, but John was too restless for an office career. At the age of 14 he went to sea, and later he worked for a few years in New York City. In 1897 he returned to England and became a newspaperman, writing poetry at the same time. His first books of poems showed the influence of his experiences at sea. One of these was *Salt-Water Ballads,* which contained a famous poem named "Sea Fever."

In 1911 Masefield had published a long story-poem, *The Everlasting Mercy.* This was compared with Chaucer's *Canterbury Tales,* and it was said to bring back to poetry a life and strength that had been missing for hundreds of years. It was followed by three other narrative poems, *The Widow in the Bye Street, Dauber,* and *The Daffodil Fields.* Masefield also wrote adventure stories for boys, and various other books. He was made poet laureate in 1930.

masks

Masks are made of cloth, paper, rubber, wood, or some other material and are worn over the face or head. In primitive religions, witch-doctors or "medicine men" have worn masks to make themselves look like gods or spirits. They believe that if they have the appearance of gods they will also have the powers of gods and will be able to cure diseases, protect their people, and punish their enemies. Children often wear masks, par-

Masks first were used in religious ceremonies, and then by actors in plays. Today, they are most commonly worn at festivals when people are making merry.

ticularly on Hallowe'en, for amusement. The catcher on a baseball team wears a mask to protect his face, and people who work in certain industries also wear masks for protection. In wartime soldiers and sometimes civilians wear gas masks for protection against poison gas. Sometimes criminals wear masks so that they cannot easily be recognized.

Another kind of mask is a death mask. For many hundreds of years death masks were made whenever a famous person died. The face of the dead person was covered with wax or plaster that hardened into a mask that looked like the person. This practice was carried on at least two thousand years ago, and because of it we know what many famous people of the past looked like. Masks have also been worn by actors in certain kinds of dramas. You can read more about these masks in the article on MASQUE.

Mason and Dixon's Line

Mason and Dixon's Line, or "the Mason and Dixon Line," is the name given to the boundary between Pennsylvania on the north and Maryland and West Virginia on the south. Before the Civil War, when slavery was allowed in the United States, the Mason and Dixon Line was the boundary between the free states in the north and the slave states in the south. Long before this time, when the United States belonged to Great Britain, the colonies of Pennsylvania, Maryland, and Virginia had argued about the exact boundaries separating them. Two English surveyors named Charles Mason and Jeremiah Dixon had settled the dispute. Both before and during the Civil War, "below the Mason and Dixon Line" was used to mean the southern, or slave holding, states of the United States. We use this term today to refer to the South in general.

masque

A masque is a kind of dramatic entertainment that was popular in England about four hundred years ago and is seen occasionally in modern theaters. The masque is a play in which there is a great deal of music and dancing. Often the characters in the masque are allegorical, that is, they represent thoughts or emotions rather than human beings. The masque gets its name from the word "mask." At first all actors who appeared in this kind of play wore masks. The actors did this because it was the custom in the early Greek theater to have the actors wear masks representing the emotions of the characters in the drama, and the first masques were presented by the Greeks. In England the masques were private entertainments put on at court or at the homes of noblemen. They were in imitation of masques performed in the Italian and French theatres. The best-known writer of masques in English literature is Ben Jonson, but the best-known masque is *Comus,* written by John Milton, one of England's greatest poets.

masquerade

A masquerade is a fancy-dress party or dance at which people wear masks in order to disguise themselves. Masquerade balls have been popular for hundreds of years, but especially in France and England about three hundred years ago. Be-

fore that time, masquerades were often part of religious festivals, but many such masquerades were later forbidden by the Church. In the United States masquerade parties are popular, especially around Hallowe'en. The Mardi Gras, a celebration held each year in New Orleans on Shrove Tuesday, the day before Lent begins, is a religious festival that has a masquerade connected with it. At most masquerade parties, people remove their disguises at midnight.

Mass

The Mass, in the Roman Catholic and Eastern Orthodox Churches, is a public religious ceremony. This means that it is a way of praying in public together with other people. The prayer is always performed in a certain way. Many people compare the Mass to a play or drama, because it combine words and actions. It is a way of praising God, like the Sunday services in a Protestant church.

The Mass recalls the Last Supper, when Jesus said to his disciples "This is my body"—giving them bread—and "This is my blood"—giving them wine—as Chapter 22 of the Gospel of Luke tells the story. Catholics believe in *transubstantiation,* that is, when a priest repeats these words at the Mass the bread and wine actually become the body and blood of Jesus, though they continue to look like bread and wine. (See the article on COMMUNION.)

HOW THE MASS IS SAID

Only a priest ordained by a bishop can say Mass. He is usually helped by altar boys, who say the responses to prayers. When there is a high Mass, there may be a deacon and subdeacon. Usually they are also priests. A high Mass is one in which many of the prayers are sung or chanted. Most Masses are low Masses, in which the prayers are spoken.

Most people who go to Mass in the United States or Canada go to one in a Roman Catholic church. For many hundreds of years the Mass was always said (or sung) in the Latin language. The Mass is considered very beautiful and a person who does not understand Latin can follow the words by using a MISSAL, about which there is a separate article.

In 1962 and 1964, the greatest priests of the Roman Catholic Church met in ecumenical councils (meetings for the purpose of bringing different churches together), in Rome, and they decided that it was not necessary to use the Latin language for the Mass, but that the language of any country could be used, for example English in the United States. This was like a-rule made by a similar meeting more than 1,500 years ago, when it was first decided that Latin could be used in the Mass. After 1964 most priests changed to the language of the people in reading the Mass, but there were some who complained that the change from Latin reduced the beauty of the Mass.

THE PARTS OF THE MASS

The Mass is divided into two parts: the Mass of the Catechumens, and the Mass of the Faithful. In early Christian times no one who had not been baptized could attend the second and more important part of the Mass. People who had not yet been baptized, but were studying for baptism, were called catechumens.

The Mass of the Catechumens is also divided into two parts: the introductory prayers, when the priest and people speak to God, and the instructions, when God speaks to them. The instructions include the epistle, gradual, gospel, and creed. The introit states the main idea of the Mass for the day, and the epistle and gospel are taken from the New Testament. The instructions change daily and are included in the movable parts of the Mass.

The Mass of the Faithful is also divided into two parts. In one part the priest and people make their offering to God through Jesus. This includes the offertory and the canon of the Mass. In the second part God's love descends through Jesus. This is the communion. In the offertory, the priest offers up bread and wine.

An altar boy rings bells at the end of the offertory. This begins the canon of the Mass. It opens with prayers for all the members of the church. Then the altar boy rings the bell once as the priest spreads his hand over the bread and wine. The priest takes the bread and wine and repeats the words of the Last Supper. This is called the consecration. After consecrating the bread, he raises it for all to see. He does the same with the wine in the chalice. The consecration is the most important part of the Mass, because it is the part recognized as changing bread and wine into the body and blood of Jesus.

The communion comes next and the Mass ends with prayers of thanksgiving.

Massachusetts

Massachusetts is one of the New England states in the United States. It was one of the thirteen original colonies, and the place where the Pilgrims landed more than three hundred years ago. The nickname of Massachusetts is the "Bay State" because the early settlers lived along Massachusetts Bay. The people of Massachusetts played important parts in the founding of the United States. You can see some of the most important historical landmarks in American history in

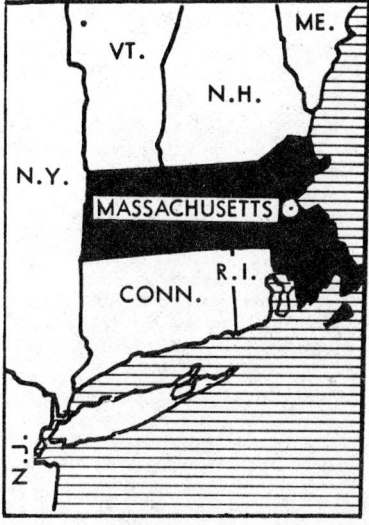

Massachusetts. Today, Massachusetts is one of the great manufacturing states and is also a favorite vacation place. It takes its name from the Indian tribe that lived there before the Pilgrims arrived.

Massachusetts ranks 45th in size among the states, with 8,257 square miles. In population it ranks 10th, with more than five million people living there. It joined the Union in 1788, the sixth of the original colonies to become a state. The capital is Boston.

THE PEOPLE OF MASSACHUSETTS

The first settlers in Massachusetts were English. They were the Pilgrims, who sailed from England in the *Mayflower* and landed at Plymouth Rock in 1620. (You can read about the PILGRIMS in a separate article.) The Pilgrims and later English settlers became farmers and fishermen like the Indians who had lived there before them. It was difficult for farmers to earn a living from much of the rocky New England soil, so many of them turned to manufacturing and started small factories.

As the state grew, immigrants arrived from Ireland, France, and Germany, and later many Italians, Russians, and people from other European countries came to work in the growing factories and mills.

Most of the people of Massachusetts live in the large manufacturing cities and work in factories making shoes, cotton and woolen goods, rugs, electronic equipment, twine, and many other products. Others work in the large fisheries for which Massachusetts is famous. It leads all other states in the value of the fish caught by its fishermen.

Massachusetts farmers produce dairy products, corn, onions, and poultry. They also grow a large part of the country's cranberries, and delicious apples and strawberries. Some of the people work in granite, marble and sandstone quarries.

The largest number of people today are Roman Catholic, but Massachusetts is the original home of the Congregational, Unitarian, Christian Science and other Churches.

WHAT MASSACHUSETTS IS LIKE

The eastern part of Massachusetts, on the Atlantic Ocean, is low and sandy, with several large bays, including Boston Bay and Cape Cod Bay. Cape Cod, which juts out into the ocean like a big hook, is a famous vacation place, with summer theaters and artists' colonies. In this section most of the Massachusetts cranberries are grown. Off the sandy coast are popular vacation islands, including Martha's Vineyard and Nantucket.

From this low region, Massachusetts rises to a plateau, or high, level region, in the central part of the state. Here the factories are supplied with water power from the swift streams and rivers.

Farther west is the very fertile Connecticut Valley, where most of the farming is done. The Connecticut River runs through this section. The western part of the state is another popular place for vacations, with the Berkshire Hills rising to their highest point at Mt. Greylock, 3,497 feet high. Thousands of people every summer attend the musical festival

New buildings of Harvard University stand on the Cambridge side of the Charles River. Harvard, founded in 1636, is the oldest college in the United States and is famous throughout the world.

Harvard University

Modern dormitories of M.I.T., famous engineering school, in Cambridge.

at Tanglewood. In this part of the state there are also many summer camps for boys and girls.

When the early settlers lived in Massachusetts, it was filled with many wild animals. Today there are only foxes, deer, and rabbits.

The climate along the eastern coast is mild in the summer. In the winter it is cold and damp. In the hills of the Berkshires the winters are very cold, with heavy snow, but in summer it is pleasantly cool. The state's average temperature in summer is 69 degrees. In winter it is about 23 degrees.

Massachusetts has many railroads and highways reaching all parts of the state and there are airports in all the important cities.

THE GOVERNMENT OF MASSACHUSETTS

Massachusetts calls itself a "Commonwealth" and not a state, but like the other states, it is governed by a governor and a legislature. The governor is elected for a two-year term. The legislature is called the General Court, and is composed of two houses, a Senate and a House of Representatives. The members

Mass. Dept. of Commerce

Paul Revere's home was already a hundred years old when the famous patriot and silversmith lived there. It is kept just the way it was when he was alive.

of both houses are elected for a two-year term. Judges are appointed for life or until they retire. The capital is Boston. There are fourteen counties.

Some of the oldest schools in the country are in Massachusetts, and it has always been a leader in education. About 1,148,000 students attend public elementary and high schools. There are many colleges, universities, and other schools of higher learning, some of which are among the most famous in the world.

There are separate articles about HARVARD, RADCLIFFE, MOUNT HOLYOKE, SMITH, AMHERST, HOLY CROSS, WELLESLEY, and the MASSACHUSETTS INSTITUTE OF TECHNOLOGY. See the article on BOSTON for Boston College and Boston University. Other important colleges include the following:

University of Massachusetts, at Amherst. Enrollment, 18,378 in 1971 (co-ed).

Northeastern University, at Boston. Enrollment, 42,149 in 1971 (co-ed).

Tufts University, at Medford. Enrollment, 4,810 in 1971 (co-ed).

Clark University, at Worcester. Enrollment, 3,091 in 1971 (co-ed).

Brandeis University, at Waltham. Enrollment, 2,171 in 1971 (co-ed).

CHIEF CITIES OF MASSACHUSETTS

The leading cities of Massachusetts, with populations from the 1970 census, are:

Boston, population 641,071, the state capital and largest city in the state. There is a separate article about BOSTON.

Worcester, population 176,572, the second-largest city. There is a separate article about WORCESTER.

Springfield, population 163,905, the third-largest city, manufacturing center for machinery, in the southwestern part of the state.

Cambridge, population 100,361, fourth-largest city, educational and industrial center, in the eastern part of the state.

MASSACHUSETTS IN THE PAST

More than nine hundred years ago, it is believed Norsemen visited the shores of Massachusetts. Later it was explored by John Cabot and John Smith. The first

settlers did not arrive until 1620, one of the important dates in American history, when the Pilgrims landed at Plymouth Rock. Many others later joined these settlers at Plymouth Colony, which grew into a prosperous community. A group of Puritans from England started the Massachusetts Bay Colony farther north. The Puritans were a strict people, and dealt harshly with those who did not agree with them. You can read about the PURITANS in a separate article.

The Massachusetts Bay Colony and the Plymouth Colony were finally joined and given a charter by the English king. The colony prospered but as more and more taxes were placed on them by England, the people protested, and finally they became leaders in the struggle for freedom and independence. John Adams, Samuel Adams and John Hancock were the Massachusetts leaders. The Boston Massacre and the famous Boston Tea Party were two of the important events that led to the Revolutionary War. The first battles of the Revolutionary War were fought at Lexington and Concord in Massachusetts, in 1775.

Massachusetts continued to grow as a manufacturing state and also as a cultural center. Some of the great American writers and thinkers lived in the state about a hundred years ago. They included Emerson, Longfellow, Hawthorne, and many others. The Massachusetts peo-

Massachusetts is the center for the New England style of architecture. The interior of Christ Church in Cambridge is a fine example of its simple elegance.

ple were also very much against slavery. The ABOLITION (anti-slavery) movement, about which there is a separate article, was most important in Massachusetts.

In the Civil War, Massachusetts sent more than 150,000 men to fight in the Union Army. In World Wars I and II, it contributed many men and important supplies to the armed forces.

PLACES TO SEE IN MASSACHUSETTS

Adams Mansion National Historic Site, at Quincy, in the east, on State Highway 135. The home of Presidents John Adams and John Quincy Adams.

Salem Maritime National Historic Site, at Salem, in the northeast, on State Highway 114. Contains the Old Custom House where Nathaniel Hawthorne worked, and other places associated with New England's history.

Plymouth Rock, at Plymouth, in the east, on U.S. Route 44. The place where the Pilgrims probably landed in the *Mayflower* in 1620.

Minuteman Statue, at Lexington, in the northeast, on State Highway 25. A statue dedicated to the Minutemen who fought in the Battle of Lexington, the first battle in the Revolutionary War.

Old North Church, in Boston, in the east, on U.S. Route 20. The famous church from which Paul Revere received the signal that the British soldiers were going to attack Lexington. The tower from which the signal was given was blown off by a hurricane in 1954.

Bunker Hill Monument, in Boston, in honor of the men who fought so bravely at the Battle of Bunker Hill in the Revolutionary War.

Charlestown Navy Yard, in Boston. The famous warships *Constitution* and *Constellation* can be seen here.

Sleepy Hollow Cemetery, at Concord, in the northeast, on State Highway 126. Some of the most famous American writers are buried here: Emerson, Thoreau, Hawthorne, and the Alcotts.

MASSACHUSETTS. Area, 8,257 square miles. Population (1970 census) 5,689,-170. Capital, Boston. Nickname, the Bay State. Motto, *Ense Petit Placidam Sub Libertate Quietem* (By the Sword We Seek Peace, but Peace Only Under Liberty). Flower, May flower. Bird, chickadee. Song, "Massachusetts." Admitted to Union, February 6, 1788. Official abbreviation, Mass.

Massachusetts Institute of Technology

Massachusetts Institute of Technology is one of the most important universities in the United States. It is located in Cambridge, Massachusetts, and was founded in 1861. Many of the leading engineers, architects, and scientists in the United States and other countries have been graduated from M.I.T. This school also has done outstanding research in many branches of science. Much work on the development of the electronic brain was carried on here. The students at M.I.T. are mostly men, but some women attend the advanced schools. In 1971 8,024 students were enrolled at the school, nearly all of them men. There were 1,811 teachers on the faculty.

The Massachusetts Institute of Technology is one of the greatest engineering schools in the world. The massive dome is the Institute's main architectural feature.

massage

Massage is a method of rubbing or kneading (pinching) the body. This makes blood and lymph (another fluid in the body) flow more freely. Certain pains in the muscles, such as backache, are relieved when the circulation of the blood is greater. Heat also increases the circulation of the blood and other body fluids, and rubbing always produces greater heat in the muscles. Massage is good for certain diseases, such as infantile paralysis (poliomyelitis) and cerebral palsy. A man skilled at giving massages is called a *masseur,* and a woman is called a *masseuse.* A machine such as an electric vibrator can produce some effects that are the same as a massage by hand. Massage cannot remove fat from overweight persons.

Massasoit

Massasoit was the sachem, or king, of the Wampanoag Indians who were living in the lands around Plymouth, Massachusetts, when the Pilgrims landed there in 1620. Massasoit had once been a very powerful sachem, with more than thirty thousand Indians in his tribe. Shortly before the Pilgrims came, all except three hundred of the tribe had died from a terrible disease. Massasoit and the Pilgrims signed a peace treaty in 1621 that was not broken by either the Indians or the Pilgrims during Massasoit's lifetime. The settlers helped Massasoit when he was sick and hungry, and he was so grateful that he warned them of a plot that unfriendly Indians had made to destroy them. Massasoit gave up many of his lands to the new settlers, and went to live in what is now the town of Warren, Rhode Island. He died in 1661, when he was about eighty years old.

Massey, Vincent

Vincent Massey, a Canadian statesman, served as the first native-born Canadian to be Governor-General of Canada. In Canada the Governor-General acts in place of the British queen, who is also Queen of Canada. Massey was born in 1887. He was graduated from the University of Toronto in Canada and from Oxford University in England. He taught history at the University of Toronto from 1913 to 1915, was chancellor of the university from 1947 to 1953, served on the military staff of Canada during World War I, was the Canadian minister to the United States from 1926 to 1930, and was a delegate to the United Nations Assembly in 1946. He was appointed Governor-General in 1952 and retired after 1959 but continued to be prominent in Canadian political life. His brother Raymond Massey achieved fame as a motion-picture actor.

mass production

Mass production is the making of many manufactured products of the same kind at the same time. For thousands of years, such products were made one at a time, by hand, and no two were exactly alike. In mass production they are all exactly alike.

The two most important things in mass production are *interchangeable parts* and the *assembly line.*

Eli Whitney, the American inventor who is best remembered because he invented the cotton gin, also was the first man to use interchangeable parts. This was more than 175 years ago. In the year 1798, the United States gave Whitney a contract to manufacture some muskets for the army. He took so long to deliver the muskets that the government was going to cancel the contract. But in the meantime Whitney had made tools that could turn out the separate parts of a musket very rapidly. When all his tools were completed, a worker could take one of each part and put a musket together a hundred times as fast as it had ever been done before. In modern mass-production manufacturing, "tooling up" to make the separate parts may take many months, but once the tools are finished the parts can be made and put together so rapidly that each worker can make thousands of finished products in the time that a worker once would have needed to make one.

The assembly line is a moving belt or chain that carries an unfinished product from one worker to another. Each worker puts on one part or does one particular job on the product, such as polishing or painting it. The worker stays in one place, which saves time. He has only one part to reach for and only one operation to learn. After the moving belt has passed all the workers, the product is completed and drops off the line, ready to be shipped to the user.

Assembly-line production was tried in France and other countries nearly a hundred years ago, but most of the credit for it is given to Henry Ford. By using the assembly line to make automobiles, beginning in 1913, Ford was able to make several thousand cars a day and sell them at very low prices. Other manufacturers learned from him and soon the assembly line was being used in nearly all modern factories.

AUTOMATIC MACHINERY

Mass production depends also on automatic machinery that does many jobs that once were done by hand. Many automatic machines are actually assembly lines in which the work is done mechanically instead of by hand.

For example, in a plant that makes soft drinks there are machines that mix the drink in big vats, automatically pour exactly the right quantity into each bottle, put a cap on the bottle, pack the bottles into cartons or boxes, and deliver them to a loading platform where a truck is waiting for them. A chewing-gum machine automatically mixes the gum, chops it into sticks of the right length, wraps it, counts out the right number of wrapped sticks and wraps them together as a package, counts the right number of packages and puts them in a carton, packs the cartons in a box for shipment, and even addresses the box. Such machines take in rolls of paper, print it, cut it into the right lengths, and deliver it to the place where the gum is to be wrapped. At another place in the machine, rolls of cardboard go in and printed cartons come out at the right spot.

The first automatic machines were mostly made for the textile industry (the industry that makes cloth and other fab-

rics). A knitting machine was invented more than 350 years ago. Machines to spin thread and to weave cloth automatically were invented almost two hundred years ago. The first machines of this kind were invented in England and the textile industry that grew out of them made England the richest country on earth. During the 1800s, dozens of automatic machines were invented, and in the 1900s there have been many more. Mass production is practiced more in the United States than in any other country. In some countries, manufactured products are made cheaply because of "cheap labor": The workers are paid so little that they cannot live comfortable lives. In the United States, manufactured products are made cheaply because of mass production, and the workers are paid more instead of less. This has given the United States the highest living standard in the world. It is the same in Canada. Several European countries are almost as far advanced in mass production, but most countries of the world are far behind.

Masters, Edgar Lee

Edgar Lee Masters was an American poet who became famous for one book of poems, *Spoon River Anthology*. He was born in 1869 in Kansas, but he grew up in Illinois in a town on the Spoon River. He became a successful lawyer in Chicago, and wrote poetry under an assumed name for fear that being known as a poet would hurt his law practice.

Spoon River Anthology was published anonymously (that is, without any name signed to it), but Masters became known and famous as the author. The book is a collection of epitaphs for the gravestones of a small-town cemetery. The 250 epitaphs are supposed to have been written by the dead persons whose graves they mark, and each one reveals his secret hopes and fears, good and bad deeds, joys and sorrows. The book was a sensation when it was published in 1915. Masters also wrote novels, a biography of Abraham Lincoln, and the story of his own life, *Across Spoon River*. Masters died in 1950, at the age of 81.

mastiff

The mastiff is a giant of a dog. It has been known for two thousand years in England, and there were mastiffs in ancient Egypt as long ago as 3000 B.C. They are heavy, powerful dogs, and long ago they were used as fighting dogs in competition with bulls and other animals. They are kept today mainly as watchdogs and pets, but they are so large they are seldom seen in the city. A mastiff usually has a gentle, friendly disposition, but if anyone threatens a member of the family it will quickly become angry. It is strong enough to knock down a man with a single leap.

The mastiff is about 30 inches high at the shoulder and about 33 inches long from the chest to the base of the tail. It may weigh as much as 150 or 160 pounds. It has strong, straight legs, a square muzzle, and a long, straight-hanging tail. Its coat is short and thick, with the hair lying flat against the skin. It is usually light in color, either tan or golden brown, and sometimes it has dark stripes over the entire body. The nose and head are usually quite dark, almost black.

The *bull mastiff* is another kind of dog, bred from the mastiff and the bulldog. It was originally intended to be a game-warden's assistant and its job was to keep off poachers (hunters who were after animals belonging to the landowner). It is slightly smaller than a mastiff, and its muzzle is like that of a bulldog.

mastodon

The mastodon was an animal that lived in many parts of the world thousands of years ago. The mastodon looked very much like an elephant, but there were some important differences between the mastodon and the elephant that we know. The mastodon had a much flatter head, and its jaws were longer. The mastodon was about 10 feet tall, and it had long shaggy hair to keep it warm. It ate leaves and roots and branches. The teeth of the mastodon were not as complicated as the teeth that elephants have now.

People in the United States have discovered the bones of many mastodons, especially in New York State. Scientists believed that when the first men lived in North America, mastodons roamed the country. Now people who visit large museums can see the bones of these animals.

Matanuska Valley

The Matanuska Valley is a fertile region in south central Alaska. It is about one thousand square miles in size, and only about three thousand people live there. In 1935 the United States government sent 208 families from Michigan, Minnesota, and Wisconsin to start a farming project there. These people were farmers who were suffering from the depression and droughts and had to give up their farms in the United States. The government gave them loans and sent men to help them clear the land and build houses. Many of these families left, but still the community grew. The farmers raise grains, vegetables, berries, poultry, and dairy products. They ship their products by the Alaska Railroad and by a highway that runs through the valley.

match

Matches are sticks of wood or cardboard tipped with a chemical that bursts into flame when rubbed against a rough surface. The most important chemical used in matches is phosphorus, which bursts into flame very easily.

Three main kinds of match are made today. The wooden, "strike-anywhere" match ignites (begins to burn) when it is rubbed against any rough surface. Wooden matches used to cause fires because rats used to nibble at them until they ignited. They are now made with a substance that is distasteful to rats.

A second kind of match is the wooden *safety match*. This is ignited by striking it on a special strip on the side of the box in which the matches are packed. Some of the chemicals needed to create fire are in the head of the match and some in the striking strip on the box.

The third kind of match is the *book match*. Book matches are similar in principle to the wooden safety match, but they are made of cardboard. In the United States book matches are the ones most used. About 250 billion of them are made each year. Few people pay for book matches, for they are given away with cigarettes and cigars and are used as souvenirs by hotels, restaurants, and other companies. The United States is the only country in which most matches are free. Most match books contain advertising, and the advertiser pays the cost of the matches.

HOW MATCHES ARE MADE

Matches are made in huge machines, 60 feet long and as high as a two-story house. A machine changes a small stick of wood or cardboard into packaged matches in sixty minutes, and turns out 1,125,000 matches an hour.

The machines that make wooden matches begin the process by taking blocks of pine wood and cutting them into *splints* (little sticks). These splints are held in a chain of metal plates, each with twelve rows of holes. The splints then ride through a series of five dips and baths in chemicals that treat the wood to prevent afterglow, provide a collar of paraffin to speed burning, put on the heads, or tips, and finally dip the heads into a chemical that protects them from changes in the weather. Thirty-two different chemicals are used. The matches are then dried and pour down a trough to drop into endless chains of boxes waiting for them.

THE STORY OF MATCHES

Matches are so much a part of our everyday lives that it is hard to believe that the match as we know it is little more than a hundred years old.

The story of matches begins in 1668, when a German alchemist named Hennig Brandt discovered phosphorus. A few years later a British scientist, Robert Boyle, coated paper with phosphorus and splinters of wood with sulfur. When the splinter was drawn through the paper, it burst into flame. But in those days phosphorus cost about $250 an ounce, so not many of these early matches were sold.

Beginning about 1781, a number of more practical matches were invented. They bore such odd names as the phosphoric candle or ethereal match, the pocket luminary, and the instantaneous light box. The phosphoric candle consisted of paper tipped with phosphorus and sealed in a glass tube. When the glass was broken, air rushed in and set the paper flaming.

The first true match was invented in 1827 when an English druggist, John Walker, tipped small sticks of wood with chemicals that ignited when they were drawn over sandpaper. An improvement was made a few years later when Charles Sauria of France first used phosphorus as an ingredient for match heads. But phosphorus was a dangerous chemical for match workers to handle, for it attacked their bones and gave them a deadly disease known as *necrosis*, or "phossy jaw." Matchmaking was not made safe until 1911 when William A. Fairburn found a way of making phosphorus harmless by mixing it with another chemical.

Wooden safety matches were invented in Sweden in the middle of the 19th century. In 1892 the book match was in-

vented by an American lawyer, Joseph Pusey. Since then the chief improvements in the match have been the invention of matches without an afterglow and matches that have no disagreeable smell.

During World War II, a waterproof match was invented that will light after it has been in water for eight hours.

The United States leads the world in the production of matches. Other large manufacturers are Great Britain, Russia, and Sweden.

mathematics

Mathematics is most familiar to us as the study of numbers. We use numbers every day of our lives, in counting, measuring, and computing. But there is much more to mathematics than that. It is the study of relations, or proportions—how different things compare with one another. Every natural science has a mathematical side, which tries to discover general "laws," or truths, with which we can discover new facts, predict future events, and make useful inventions.

The mathematics taught in elementary schools and high schools deals with operations that are useful in every field, including everyday life.

In *arithmetic* we study the operations of addition, subtraction, multiplication, and division as applied to the simplest numbers. We have to understand arithmetic to buy and sell goods, invest money, read clocks or thermometers, measure land, lumber, cloth, gasoline, groceries and other things, make plans for houses, bridges, airplanes, and so on.

Algebra includes more complicated numbers. It introduces letter symbols such as x, a, p, to stand for these numbers. It studies the relations that hold true whatever the numbers may be. It uses such symbols as $=$ (equals), $<$ (is less than), and many others. The field of algebra is so large that it is divided into at least two parts: elementary algebra, taught in high schools, and advanced algebra, taught in college.

Geometry deals with measurements and relations in space, with distances, sizes and shapes. *Trigonometry* deals with the properties of triangles and provides important methods of measurement used in surveying, engineering, astronomy, and many other fields.

Calculus is the "arithmetic of higher mathematics." It deals with quantities that change continually, such as the speed of a bomb falling to earth from an airplane. It is the basis of much of the mathematics dealing with the physical world—light, heat, sound, gravity, electricity, magnetism, and other things.

Knowledge of arithmetic is necessary in our everyday life. High-school students are required to study also elementary algebra and geometry. They may not need to use this knowledge in later life, but it teaches them the mathematical way of thinking. Anyone who intends to make a career in a science such as physics, astronomy, chemistry, electricity, or electronics, or in engineering, must continue the study of mathematics in college.

There are separate articles on the different branches of mathematics.

THE NEW MATHEMATICS

"The new mathematics" is a term used to describe a system of teaching some branches of mathematics, especially arithmetic. This system became popular in many elementary schools a few years after World War II ended. Unlike non-Euclidean geometry, which teaches that certain former ideas about geometry were wrong and should be replaced by new ideas, "the new mathematics" does not seek to change former ideas but only the methods by which those ideas are calculated or expressed.

Here are some of the things you will learn about when you study "the new math."

SETS

A set is nothing more than a collection of objects. Any collection can be a set—the objects need not have any special properties in common. For example, we might talk about "the set of all objects on the desk." This set might consist of a pencil, a pen, an eraser, and a paper clip. It would be written thus:

$$\{ \text{pencil , pen , eraser , paper clip} \}$$

Sets are measured by the number of objects in the collection. Thus, the set of all objects on the desk, described above, could be considered a "size four" set. Sometimes it is said that the set has cardinal number four.

Some sets are very large, others very small. The largest set is the collection of everything, and is called the universal set. Of course, we cannot fit this set onto a desk top, but we can imagine it so. The smallest set is the unusual set with nothing in it. If we sweep the desk top clean of all objects, "the set of all objects on the desk" will not have any objects at all! Such a set with no objects is called the empty set.

Sometimes we wish to combine two (or more) sets to produce some new sets. There are two basic ways to do this. First, we can take our two sets and make one big set out of everything from the two sets. This is called taking the union (written $\cup$) of the two sets. Second, we can check lists of the objects in each set and make up a new set of those objects which are on both lists. This is called taking the intersection (written $\cap$) of the two sets.

Another way to construct a new set from an old one is to take the objects which are not in a certain set and make a new set out of these. This is called taking the complement (written $'$) of a set.

For example, let us suppose we are considering all the objects in a room and certain special collections of these objects. (A collection that is part of a larger set is called a subset.)

The study of sets leads to many important applications which include determining whether or not an argument is logical, whether or not certain statements are true or false, and how likely it is that certain events will occur.

This method of studying sets and their properties is called Boolean algebra. It is named for George Boole, an English mathematician. Boolean algebra is of great value because there are many different things that behave in the same manner as sets. Thus, by studying sets, we are really learning about several different things all at once.

NUMBERS

We have just used numbers to describe the size of a set. Since the same number is used to describe different sets of the same size (such as three oranges, three apples, three monkey wrenches, etc.) we can see that a number is not a thing, but an expression of a quantity.

Arithmetic uses numbers to save space. Instead of saying that if we have four apples and find another three apples we then have seven apples, we say "$4 + 3 = 7$." All of arithmetic is therefore nothing more than a restatement (in shorthand) of facts about the sizes of sets.

The particular system of notation which we use to write numbers (called the decimal system because it is based on the number ten) has no relationship to the meaning of the numbers themselves. We write the numbers 0, 1, 2, and so on to stand for certain quantities. These quantities remain the same whether we write 0, 1, 2, ... or zero, one, two, ... The form of the number does not alter its basic meaning.

The decimal system uses the figures 0, 1, 2, 3, 4, 5, 6, 7, 8, and 9. When a set is so large that we require a number higher than nine to describe it, we use the symbol 10 to stand for ten. Broken down, the symbol 10 stands for one quantity of ten and zero quantities of one. Similarly, 11 abbreviates one quantity of ten and one quantity of one—and is thus larger than 10 by one unit. The need to use two symbols arises because no single symbol represents ten objects.

Just as our ordinary numbers depend on the number ten, we could use a number system which hinges on some other number in the same way. The binary system (based on the number two) is the most important of these because of its application to electronic computers. In the number system based on two, there is no single symbol which represents two objects. Thus, the only symbols are 0 and

Universal set (all the objects in a room)	$\left\{\begin{array}{l}\text{Desk , chair , lamp , bookcase , rug} \\ \text{pencil , pen , eraser , paper clip}\end{array}\right\}$
Set of all objects on the desk	$\left\{\text{pencil , pen , eraser , paper clip}\right\}$
Set of all green objects in the room	$\left\{\text{lamp , rug , pencil , pen}\right\}$

Then we would have

$$\left\{\begin{array}{l}\text{Set of all objects} \\ \text{on the desk}\end{array}\right\} \cup \left\{\begin{array}{l}\text{Set of all green} \\ \text{objects in the room}\end{array}\right\} = \left\{\begin{array}{l}\text{pencil , pen , eraser ,} \\ \text{paper clip , lamp , rug}\end{array}\right\}$$

$$\left\{\begin{array}{l}\text{Set of all objects} \\ \text{on the desk}\end{array}\right\} \cap \left\{\begin{array}{l}\text{Set of all green objects} \\ \text{in the room}\end{array}\right\} = \left\{\text{pencil , pen}\right\}$$

$$\left\{\begin{array}{l}\text{Set of all} \\ \text{green objects in the room}\end{array}\right\}' = \left\{\begin{array}{l}\text{desk , chair , bookcase ,} \\ \text{eraser , paper clip}\end{array}\right\}$$

1. Two objects are represented by the number 10 which stands for one quantity of two and zero quantities of one; three is represented by 11—one quantity of two and one quantity of one. We cannot represent four with two symbols, so we must use three symbols: In binary, what would be 4 in the decimal system is written 100 (one two-times-two, no two, no one), just as 100 in the decimal system represents one ten-times-ten, no ten, no one. The binary system continues:

101—one two-times-two, no two, one one; what in the decimal system we would write as 5.

110—one two-times-two, one two, no one; what in the decimal system we would write as 6.

111—one two-times-two, one two, one one; what in the decimal system we would write as 7.

1000—one two-times-two-times-two, nothing in the other columns, what in the decimal system we would write as 8.

ALGEBRA AND LAWS OF NUMBERS

Algebra goes one step farther and sets up laws that all number systems must obey. An algebra is a system that does in fact obey these laws. Our number system is one example of an algebraic system.

Some of the basic algebraic laws that govern our numbers are the following:

The commutative law of addition: Numbers may be added in any order. Example: $4 + 5 = 5 + 4$

The commutative law of multiplication: Numbers may be multiplied in any order. Example: $3 \times 6 = 6 \times 3$

The associative law of addition: It does not matter which of a series of additions is performed first. Example: $(3 + 5) + 7 = 3 + (5 + 7)$

The associative law of multiplication: It does not matter which of a series of multiplications is performed first. Example: $(2 \times 3) \times 4 = 2 \times (3 \times 4)$

The distributive law: Multiplication may be performed separately over each part of an addition. Example: $2 \times (3 + 4) = (2 \times 3) + (2 \times 4)$

The law of zero: Adding zero to any number does not change it. Example: $361 + 0 = 361$

The law of one: Multiplying any number by one does not change it. Example: $564 \times 1 = 564$

From our basic numbers (called integers), other, more complicated number systems can be developed. These include negative integers, fractions (called rational numbers), all quantities used in measurement (called real numbers), and even some numbers called imaginary which do not really exist but which serve a function in mathematics nonetheless.

This list is by no means a complete account of the new mathematics. The new mathematics presents more advanced work from the same point of view: an emphasis on understanding rather than memorization.

Mather

Increase Mather and his son Cotton Mather were two important American clergymen in Massachusetts in colonial times. In those days, clergymen had a great deal to say in the governing of Massachusetts. Both Increase and Cotton Mather were PURITANS, about which there is a separate article.

Increase Mather was born in 1639 and at the age of 17 was graduated from Harvard College. He was pastor of the North Church in Boston for 62 years, and for a time was also president of Harvard College. He went to England and from King Charles II obtained a charter that joined the Plymouth Colony with the Massachusetts Bay Colony. He died in 1723, at the age of 84.

Cotton Mather was born in Massachusetts in 1663 and entered Harvard when he was only 12 years old. At the age of 17 he became his father's assistant at the North Church, and four years later was ordained a minister. Cotton Mather is best remembered for his activities in the witchcraft trials in Salem. He believed there were evil spirits that made people act strangely, against the forces of good, and he wrote several books on the subject. (See the article on WITCHCRAFT.) Cotton Mather helped to found Yale University. His ideas about witches seem strange to us today, but in some ways he was a forward-looking man and was one of the first people to approve of inoculation against smallpox.

Cotton Mather died in 1728, at the age of 65.

Mathewson, Christy

Christy Mathewson was a pitcher in professional baseball. Some experts have considered him the greatest pitcher of all time. His full name was Christopher Mathewson, and he was born in Factoryville, Pennsylvania, in 1880. He was graduated from Bucknell University in 1902 and became a member of the New York Giants, at a time when it was very unusual for a college graduate to be a professional baseball player. During his career, which lasted until 1918, he won 373 games. He joined the United States Army in 1918 and fought in France, where he was injured by poison gas. He died in 1925.

Matisse, Henri

Henri Matisse is the name of a great French painter and sculptor. He was one of a group who called themselves Fauvists, from the French word for "wild beast." They used this name because their painting was so new and violent, full of strange shapes and strong colors. Matisse was born in 1869. While he was still studying painting in Paris he was such a fine artist that he got a job copying the paintings of old masters for the French government to sell. He painted in the classic style until about 1900, when he began to develop his new method. Many of his paintings can now be seen in museums in the United States. One of Matisse's greatest achievements was the designing of the chapel Ste. Marie du Rosaire at Vence, France.

Matisse died in 1954.

matter

Matter is anything that takes up space and has weight. The air around you is matter; so is the water in the ocean and the ground under your feet. In fact, you cannot go anyplace on the earth without coming upon some sort of matter.

Of course, there are places where there is hardly any matter at all. Hundreds of miles above the earth, the air becomes very thin, much too thin to breathe. But there is some matter even there, even though it is a very small amount.

There are three different kinds or states of matter: liquid, solid, and gas. Water is a liquid form of matter. Air is a gaseous form of matter. The ground under your feet is a solid form of matter. (There are separate articles on LIQUID, SOLID, and GAS.)

Liquids and gases are often called *fluids* because their parts can flow or move and can be separated from one another. Solids cannot flow and must be

Museum of Modern Art

Oil painting, "The Red Studio," by Henri Matisse (1911)

The three different kinds or states of matter are: liquid (1), solid (2), and gas (3). Liquid and gas are called fluids because their parts can flow or move.

heated or struck hard to split them up into separate parts. Solids always have a definite shape. Liquids and gases change their shape whenever their parts move from one space to another.

When people speak of empty space, they usually mean a space that does not contain either a liquid or a solid. However, the space usually does contain air or some other gases. Most of the time, these gases cannot be seen. That is why the space is often said to be empty. But to be truly empty, the space must contain no matter at all, not even a gas. A space that contains no matter whatsoever is called a *vacuum*.

Volume is the amount of space filled by matter. Volume is measured in cubic inches and cubic feet. (You can read more about cubic measurements in the article on CUBE.)

Mass is the amount of matter filling a space. Mass is measured in several different units, such as ounces, pounds, and tons. In most cases the mass of an object is measured by weighing it. Therefore most people confuse the mass of an object with its weight. But the mass and weight of an object are not always the same. The weight of an object is the amount of force with which it is being pulled or attracted to the earth by gravity. Matter has mass even when it is not being pulled to earth by gravity.

Since all matter has volume and mass, we say that all matter also has *density*. The density of matter is found by dividing the mass by the volume. This gives the amount of mass that is contained in a particular space. Density is measured in pounds per cubic foot, as well as in several other units of measurement.

All matter is made up of very tiny particles called *molecules*. Different substances have different kinds of molecule. These molecules are made up of even smaller particles called *atoms*. Atoms were once thought to be the smallest units of matter, but today we know the atom is composed of even smaller units called *positrons*, *electrons*, *protons*, and *neutrons*. When the atom is "split" (divided), tremendous amounts of energy are released and the atom itself is changed into atoms of other elements. The discovery of how to do this has led to the development of the atom bomb and the development of atomic energy that can be used for industrial or other purposes. See also ATOM and MOLECULE.

Matthew, Saint

St. Matthew was one of the twelve Apostles sent out by Jesus to preach the

The generation   Chap. j.   of Christ.

THE GOSPEL ACCORDING to S. Matthew.

CHAP. I.

1 The genealogie of Christ from Abraham to Ioseph. 18 Hee was conceiued by the holy Ghost, and borne of the Virgin Mary when she was espoused to Ioseph. 19 The Angel satisfieth the misdeeming thoughts of Ioseph, and interpreteth the names of Christ.

THE booke of the generation of Iesus Christ, the sonne of Dauid, the sonne of Abraham. 2 Abraham begate Isaac, and Isaac begate Iacob, and Iacob begate Iudas and his brethren.

3 And Iudas begate Phares and Zara of Thamar, and Phares begate Esrom, and Esrom begate Aram.

4 And Aram begate Aminadab, and Aminadab begate Naasson, and Naasson begate Salmon.

5 And Salmon begat Boos of Rachab, and Boos begate Obed of Ruth, and Obed begate Iesse.

6 And Iesse begate Dauid the King, & Dauid the King begat Solomon of her that had bin the wife of Urias.

7 And Solomon begat Roboam, and Roboam begate Abia, and Abia begate Asa.

8 And Asa begate Iosaphat, and Iosaphat begate Ioram, and Ioram begate Ozias.

9 And Ozias begat Ioatham, and Ioatham begate Achas, and Achas begate Ezekias.

10 And Ezekias begate Manasses, and Manasses begate Amon, and Amon begate Iosias.

11 And Iosias begate Iechonias and his brethren, about the time they were caried away to Babylon.

12 And after they were brought to Babylon, Iechonias begat Salathiel, and Salathiel begate Zorobabel.

13 And Zorobabel begat Abiud, and Abiud begat Eliakim, and Eliakim begate Azor.

14 And Azor begat Sadoc, & Sadoc begat Achim, and Achim begat Eliud.

15 And Eliud begate Eleazar, and Eleazar begate Matthan, and Matthan begate Iacob.

16 And Iacob begate Ioseph the husband of Mary, of whom was borne Iesus, who is called Christ.

17 So all the generations from Abraham to Dauid, are fourteene generations: and from Dauid vntill the carying away into Babylon, are fourteene generations: and from the carying away into Babylon vnto Christ, are fourteene generations.

18 Now the birth of Iesus Christ was on this wise: when as his mother Mary was espoused to Ioseph (before they came together) shee was found with childe of the holy Ghost.

19 Then Ioseph her husband being a iust man, and not willing to make her a publique example, was minded to put her away priuily.

20 But while hee thought on these things, behold, the Angel of the Lord appeared vnto him in a dreame, saying, Ioseph thou sonne of Dauid, feare not to take vnto thee Mary thy wife: for that which is conceiued in her, is of the holy Ghost.

A 2   21 And

Christian faith. In the Bible, the first book of the New Testament, which is a Gospel or story of Jesus' life on earth, is titled "the Gospel according to St. Matthew." The Gospel of Matthew gives a beautiful picture of Jesus as a teacher.

Matthew, who was also called Levi, was a publican. A publican was a man who collected taxes for the Roman emperor. The people in Palestine at the time of Jesus hated publicans. Many of the people were shocked when Jesus made Matthew his friend. But others, who had faith in Christ, saw in this a lesson: That a man's past is not the important thing. The New Testament tells us very little about Matthew. We do know that he probably was richer than the other Apostles. He had enough money to give a big dinner for Jesus at his house. The last time the New Testament speaks about him is when the Holy Spirit comes to the Apostles, as told in chapter 13 of the Acts of the Apostles. There is a very old story that Matthew was killed while preaching in Ethiopia. Artists often use a young man or angel to picture St. Matthew. His feast day is September 21.

Maugham, W. Somerset

William Somerset Maugham is the name of an English writer of plays, novels, and short stories. He was born in 1874 in Paris, France, where his father was a member of the British Embassy. Maugham studied medicine and spent a year as an intern at a hospital in London. From this experience he wrote his first novel, *Liza of Lambeth*. His most famous novel, *Of Human Bondage*, is partly the story of his own early life. One of his short stories, "Miss Thompson," was made into a play and later into motion pictures under the titles *Rain* and *Sadie Thompson*. Several other of his books became successful motion pictures, including *The Razor's Edge* and *The Moon and Sixpence*. His successful plays include *The Constant Wife* and *The Letter*. Groups of his short stories also were made into films, called *Quartet* and *Trio*, with Maugham himself introducing them on the screen. Maugham died in 1966.

Mauldin, William

William H. Mauldin is an American author and cartoonist who became well known during World War II for his cartoons of the American soldier. He signed these "Bill Mauldin." In 1944 he won a Pulitzer Prize for these cartoons. Mauldin was born in New Mexico in 1921. He served in the United States Army during World War II in Italy, in France, and in Germany. He received the Purple Heart and the Legion of Merit. During that time many of his cartoons were published in the Army newspaper *Stars and Stripes*, for which he also wrote many articles, Mauldin wrote several books, of which the most famous are *Up Front* and *Back Home*. After World War II Mauldin wrote magazine articles and became a political cartoonist.

Mauna Loa is a large volcano on the island of Hawaii. See the articles on HAWAII and VOLCANO.

Maupassant, Guy de

Guy de Maupassant was a French writer, considered by many to be the greatest writer of short stories. He was born in 1850, served in the French Army for a time, and then studied literature with another great French writer, Gustave Flaubert. De Maupassant's style of writing has been imitated by thousands of writers since his death. His stories have been translated into many different languages, and are still read throughout the world. Toward the end of his life he suffered from a mental illness. He died in 1893, at the age of 43.

Mauritania

The Islamic Republic of Mauritania is a country in northwest Africa. It is a former French Overseas Territory which became fully independent on November 28, 1960. Mauritania has an area of more than 416,000 square miles, which is almost twice the size of Texas. About 1,200,000 people live there, most of whom are Moors. The predominant religion is Islam. The chief products of Mauritania are dates, palm oil, grains, tobacco, iron and copper. The capital is Nouakchott, with a population of about 15,000. Mauritania is administered by a Prime Minister, a cabinet, and a parliament, called the National Assembly, which has 34 members.

ISLAMIC, REPUBLIC OF MAURITANIA. Area, 418,810 square miles. Population (1974 estimate) 1,200,000. Capital, Nouakchott. Government, republic. Languages, French, Arabic, and African languages. Religion, Moslem. Monetary unit, franc C.F.A.

Mauritius

Mauritius, a new republic to which Great Britain agreed to grant full independence in 1966, is an island in the Indian Ocean off the east coast of Africa. Its area is about half that of Long Island and it is quite densely populated. Many of the people are Indians, and many are Creoles, whose ancestors were Europeans and Africans. A number of British and French people also live on the islands. Most of the people are farmers who raise sugar cane in the fertile central plateau. In the cities people make rum, perfume, and drugs. Port Louis, a seaport city of about 142,300, is the capital.

Mauritius has a warm climate, and in the summer the temperature around Port Louis can go up to 95 degrees. The island was first settled by the Dutch more than three hundred years ago and was named for Maurice of Nassau. It came under British control in 1810.

MAURITIUS. Area, 720 square miles. Population (1973 estimate) 830,600. Capital, Port Louis.

Maury, Matthew Fontaine

Matthew Fontaine Maury was an American naval officer and scientist who lived more than a hundred years ago. He was an oceanographer, which is a scientist who studies tides and currents and winds and other things that affect the ocean.

Maury was born in Fredericksburg, Virginia, in 1806. He went to sea when he was only 19 years old, but fourteen years later he was in a bad accident that left him lame. He was then put in charge of the Navy's Depot of Charts and Instruments, and later of the Naval Observatory. He made studies of the winds and currents of the Atlantic Ocean that proved to be very valuable to seamen.

When the Civil War broke out, in 1860, Maury resigned from the United States Navy and helped the Confederates, first in the United States and later in England. After the war he became a professor of meteorology (the study of weather) at the Virginia Military Institute, where he remained until his death in 1873. A building at the United States Naval Academy at Annapolis is named in his honor, and his birthday, January 14, is a school holiday in his native state of Virginia.

Maxim

Maxim is the name of an American family of inventors. The most famous member of the family was Sir Hiram Stevens Maxim, the inventor of the Maxim machine gun, about which you can read in the article on MACHINE GUN. Hiram was born in 1840 in Sangerville, Maine. He worked in machine shops and iron works in New England and New York. At the age of 27, he invented a device for making cheap gas with which to light homes. In 1877, he invented an electric light bulb. This was two years before Thomas A. Edison invented his light bulb, but Maxim's proved too expensive to manufacture.

Maxim soon directed all his attention to the making of guns, and in 1884 he invented the first fully automatic machine gun. He then went to England, where he formed a company to manufacture his new invention. He remained in England until his death in 1916, working on such inventions as a smokeless powder and an airplane powered by steam engines. He was knighted by the King of England in 1901. This made him Sir Hiram Maxim.

Hudson Maxim, the brother of Sir Hiram, was a chemist who developed the first smokeless powder used in the United States. He also developed an explosive called *maximite* that could smash the strongest armor plate. The explosive *motorite*, later developed by him, was used to shoot torpedoes through the water. Hudson Maxim was born in Orneville, Maine, in 1853, and died in 1927.

Hiram Percy Maxim, the son of Sir Hiram, was a mechanical engineer. He was born in Brooklyn, New York, in 1869. He is best known for his invention of the Maxim silencer. This is a device used on guns, in automobile exhausts, and in ventilating machines, to reduce noise. You can read more about the silencer, or *muffler*, in the article on INTERNAL COMBUSTION ENGINE. Hiram Percy Maxim died in 1936.

Maximilian

In the early 1860s, the United States was so occupied with the Civil War that

it could not pay much attention to other American affairs. The French emperor, Napoleon III, was a very ambitious man and he thought this would be a good time for him to seize control of Mexico.

He decided to do this by putting in a Mexican king, or emperor, that he could control. For this purpose he chose a young Austrian archduke (prince) named Ferdinand Maximilian Joseph, and made him the Emperor Maximilian of Mexico.

Maximilian was born in Vienna, the capital of Austria. In 1857 he married Princess Charlotte of Belgium, who was afterward known as Carlotta (the Austrian spelling of her name). Maximilian and Carlotta set sail for Mexico in 1864.

Part of Mexico was then under the control of France, and part was independent, with its own government under President JUAREZ, about whom there is a separate article. From the start, Maximilian had an impossibly difficult time. Juarez and his supporters were violently opposed to the idea of having a foreign ruler. As soon as the Civil War was over, in 1865, the government of the United States told Napoleon III that it was opposed to the presence of a foreign emperor in Mexico—and that there were two million United States soldiers to back this up. Napoleon III quickly decided to inform Maximilian that he must abdicate —give up his crown.

The Empress Carlotta went to France in an attempt to persuade Napoleon to help her husband, but she was unsuccessful. The worry and disappointment affected her mind, and she became insane.

Maximilian refused to give up, and attempted to fight it out with Juarez. He was badly defeated, was captured, and was sentenced to death.. He was shot in Querétaro, Mexico, in 1867, when he was only 35 years old. Carlotta remained insane, but lived for sixty years more. She died in Belgium in 1927. Maximilian's brother, the Austrian emperor Francis Joseph, had his body buried in the imperial vault in Vienna.

Maxwell, James Clerk

James Clerk Maxwell was a Scottish scientist who lived about a hundred years ago. He was a physicist, which means that he studied matter (anything that has weight and takes up space). He is best known for his idea that light is a form of electricity and magnetism. This is called the electromagnetic theory of light.

Maxwell was born in Edinburgh, Scotland, in 1831, and attended the University of Edinburgh and Cambridge University in England. After graduating, he set out to investigate many of the things that interested him. He examined the planets in the sky and was the first to explain the rings around the planet Saturn. He showed that almost all colors can be made by combining three primary colors: red, blue, and yellow. Before he was 35, he had devel-

oped the electromagnetic theory of light.

He was asked to set up an experimental physics laboratory at Cambridge University. He did and was head of the laboratory until his death in 1879. See also the article on INDUCTION.

May

May is the fifth month of the year. It has thirty-one days. In ancient Roman times the year began with March, and May was the third month of the year. It was called *Maius*. It is believed that the month was named after Maia, the Roman goddess of earth and growth, since May is the time when things begin to grow. About two thousand years ago the Romans began to use the calendar we know now, and May became the fifth month.

People who were born in May have the emerald, a very valuable green stone, as their birthstone. The flower of the month of May is the lily of the valley.

Maya

The Mayas were American Indians who lived thousands of years ago in parts of the present countries of Mexico, Guatemala, and Honduras, in Central America. They lived on the Yucatan peninsula (a piece of land surrounded on three sides by water). There the Mayas built a great civilization that lasted for thousands of years. At one time it had a population of several million.

Scientists have spent much time studying the civilization of the Mayas, but no one knows very much about their early history. Some believe that their history goes back more than two thousand years before the time of Christ. Usually the Maya civilization is divided into two periods that are called the Old Empire and the New Empire. The mighty Mayan civilization died out several hundred years ago. There are different ideas about why this happened. Some think it was caused by wars. Others blame it on disease, or on the fact that the Mayan people could no longer raise crops on the land because the soil became poor.

WHAT THE MAYAS WERE LIKE

The Maya Indians were dark-skinned people. They were not tall but they were strong. Some of them lived in high mountains where the weather was very cold; others lived in warm valleys. The Mayas were farmers. They raised corn and beans and pepper. They also raised bees.

The Mayas were skillful weavers and made beautiful cloth that they dyed in rich colors and decorated. They were fine artists and carved figures and designs out of wood, stone, and jade. They made jewelry out of gold, silver, and copper. They used copper for money. The Mayas did not know how to make tools out of metal, but made them out of wood and stone.

The Mayas built their houses of mud and branches, and they lived in villages. Each village was ruled by a chief. They also built great ceremonial centers of stone and plaster.

The Mayas achieved three remarkable things. They developed a system of mathematics, a calendar, and a system of writing. They knew much about astron-

Near Copán in Honduras there are ruins of an old Mayan city. The stone carving was made before the birth of Jesus.

Mexican Gov't Railway System

The ruined Mayan city of Chichén Itzá in southern Mexico contains many examples of handsome Mayan-style building.

omy, the study of the stars. They made their hieroglyphics (written symbols and pictures that stand for things) on the walls of temples and palaces, and they wrote on sheets of paper that were folded and looked very much like the books we have now. When the Spaniards came to the cities of the Mayas, about four hundred years ago, they destroyed many of the books. Fortunately several books remained and these have been studied and translated. From these writings we have learned many important things about the Mayan religion and way of life.

The Mayas were great builders. They used limestone and mortar to make temples and flat-topped pyramids. Their buildings were grouped around a plaza (an open place) and the temples were built on terraced hills that they made. The Mayas put carvings and decorations on the walls of their buildings. The ruins of some of these buildings still stand in Mexico and Central America.

In war, the Mayas used bows and arrows, stone-edged wooden swords and spears, slings, and armor of thick cotton. They tried to capture enemy prisoners, to use as slaves. The Mayas worshiped four gods whom they called "Lords of the Forest." They also believed the sun and the moon were gods.

By the time the Spaniards landed in Central America the great Maya civilization had almost died out and the people were scattered all through the jungles.

May apple

The May apple is a plant that grows in many parts of the United States where the climate is not too hot or too cold. It grows best in shady woods. The plant is about one foot high and has large flat green leaves. Many May apple plants grow together, so that their leaves make a kind of awning that covers the ground. The plant bears one white waxy flower, shaped like a cup. In late summer, after the white flower dies, an egg-shaped yellow fruit appears. The fruit has many seeds. It does not taste sweet, and most people do not eat it, but some people make jelly from it. The May apple is sometimes incorrectly called the mandrake.

Mayflower

The *Mayflower* was a ship that carried the Pilgrims to America in the year 1620. The Pilgrims were the first English settlers of what is now Massachusetts and some other parts of New England. They left England because their religion was not the same as the official English religion, and they hoped to find religious freedom in the New World. There is a separate article about the PILGRIMS.

The *Mayflower* actually sailed from Leyden, a city in Holland (The Netherlands). The Pilgrims had gone there first from England. They had planned to use two ships for their trip to America but one of the ships, the *Speedwell*, was not in good condition and had to be left behind. Altogether, 102 Pilgrims were on the *Mayflower*. It was a three-masted wooden ship, driven by sails as all seagoing ships were in those days, and displacing 180 tons. The Atlantic crossing took it sixty-three days. First it anchored in Cape Cod Bay, on November 21, 1620. Then it sailed again and anchored in Plymouth Harbor on December 21, 1620. During the first winter it served as headquarters for the Pilgrims while they were building houses on land. The following spring the *Mayflower* sailed back to England.

In 1897 the Society of Mayflower Descendants was founded in the United States. Any person who is 18 years of age or older and a descendant of one of the signers of the Mayflower Compact may belong to this society. The Society was formed to honor the memory of the Pilgrim Fathers, to preserve things and places connected with the Pilgrims, and to defend the freedoms for which the Pilgrims founded the Plymouth Colony. In 1963 the Society had more than eleven thousand members.

May fly

The May fly is an insect that makes its home near fresh-water lakes in many parts of Europe and the United States where the climate is not too cold. There are many May flies, especially around the Great Lakes in the United States. The May fly has two sets of delicate wings that you can see through. The back wings are much smaller than the front wings. There are two or three long feelers that are attached to the end of the May fly's body. As the insect flies, these feelers stream out behind it.

The May fly has an unusual life. In the spring the female drops clusters of thousands of eggs into the lake. These eggs hatch, and little brown creatures called *naiads* begin their underwater life. It may take as long as three years for a naiad to become full-grown. Then it rises to the surface of the lake, sheds its skin, and flies to a place nearby where it again sheds its skin and emerges as a beautiful May fly.

The fully grown May fly lives only a few hours or a few days. The May fly is useful to man because it is one of the most important foods of fish.

Mayo

Mayo is the name of a family of American doctors and surgeons. They are remembered for having founded a great center for medical research, the Mayo Clinic in Rochester, Minnesota.

William James Mayo was born in Le Sueur, Minnesota, in 1861; his brother Charles Horace Mayo was born in Rochester, Minnesota, in 1865. Both studied medicine and entered practice with their father, William W. Mayo, who was a pioneer doctor. The two young surgeons, in their constant search for new methods of curing disease, made the clinic their father had founded in 1889 the most famous in the world. Both died in 1939 but the clinic continues.

The Mayo Clinic today consists of several buildings for research and for diagnosis (finding out what illness a person has). Each year some 140,000 patients visit the Mayo Clinic, which has a staff of more than 300 doctors and scientists. In 1915 the Mayo Foundation for Medical Education and Research was endowed by the Mayo brothers as a branch of the University of Minnesota.

Mazarin, Cardinal

Jules Mazarin was an Italian cardinal of the Roman Catholic Church who became Prime Minister of France, about three hundred years ago. He was born near Naples, Italy, in 1602. His family name was originally Mazarini; his first name in Italian was Giulio. He went to France when Cardinal Richelieu was Prime Minister, during the reign of Louis XIII. At that time he changed his name to its French form, Mazarin. When Richelieu died, Mazarin became Prime Minister.

At the death of Louis XIII, the young king, Louis XIV, was only 5 years old. Mazarin practically ruled the country, and Louis XIV's mother was completely under his control. The people of France resented him, because he was an Italian. A civil war broke out in 1648, and Mazarin was banished to Germany for a while. In 1654 he returned to France and took control again. He died in Paris in 1661, at the age of 58.

Mazzini, Giuseppe

Giuseppe Mazzini was an Italian patriot who worked for years to make Italy a united nation and a republic. He was born in Genoa in 1805. Italy had been divided into small kingdoms for hundreds of years. The American and French revolutions, which had been successful a few years before, inspired him. He came from a rich family but believed in the ideals of democracy. His efforts attracted many enthusiastic supporters, some of whom were imprisoned for their violent revolutionary efforts. The unification of Italy as a single kingdom under the first King Victor Emmanuel encouraged him somewhat, but he still worked to have the kingdom become a republic. He was imprisoned for his opposition to the king's government, but was soon released. When Mazzini died at Pisa, in 1872, he was so loved that more than fifty thousand people attended his funeral.

Meade, George Gordon

George Gordon Meade was a general in the Union, or northern, army during the Civil War in the United States. He was in command of the northern forces that defeated the forces of the southern General Robert E. Lee at the Battle of Gettysburg, the most important battle of the Civil War. Meade was born in 1815. He was born in Spain but his parents were Americans. He was graduated from the United States Military Academy at West Point and served in the war against the Seminole Indians in Florida and in the Mexican War. He was made a general in command of volunteers in the Union Army when the Civil War broke out in 1861. He was in command of forces at the second Battle of Bull Run and at the Battles of Antietam, Fredericksburg, and Chancellorsville. He was placed in command of the Army of the Potomac, the chief Union army in the east, just three days before the Battle of Gettysburg, and he remained in command of it until the end of the war. He served as commander of various military districts after the war. He died in 1872.

meadowlark

The meadowlark is a pretty bird that lives in many parts of the United States. It got its name because it builds its nest on the ground in meadows and fields. The meadowlark can hide very well in the tall grass because its back feathers are brown and tan. The meadowlark has a bright yellow breast, and the male has a black bib. The short outer tail feathers are white, and when the meadowlark flies they flash in the sun. The female meadowlark is not as brightly colored as the male. The female lays several spotted eggs.

The meadowlark builds its nests on the ground instead of in a tree. Its melodious song is delightful to hear.

The meadowlark that lives in the western part of the United States is especially noted for its lovely song. It is very useful to farmers because it eats insects that destroy crops and the seeds of weeds.

measles

Measles is a disease that most children get between the ages of 5 and 10 years. When a very young child or a baby gets measles it is serious, but for most children measles is not a dangerous disease. It is important for a child who has measles to receive very good care, because measles can lead to pneumonia and other serious complications.

If you have been near someone who has measles, and you have never had measles, you are likely to catch it. Measles is a contagious disease; you can catch it very easily from someone who has it. Often in the spring there are epidemics of measles and many children get the disease.

You will not know whether you have been infected with measles for about ten days. The disease begins like an ordinary cold. The person has a fever and a cough and has to blow his nose frequently. His eyes may be red and watery. Peculiar spots appear inside his mouth. About three days later slightly raised red spots appear on the face and neck. The rash spreads to the arms and legs and the rest of the body. The rash itches and is uncomfortable. The person's eyes ache. He should not look into a bright light when he has measles. After about a week the rash begins to fade, and the person feels better. It is very important to stay in bed and be careful at this time so that there will be no serious complications.

In 1962 medical researchers succeeded in isolating the virus that causes the disease, and a vaccine was developed that can now be used to prevent measles.

measurement

Measurement is a way of finding out distances, weights, temperature, time, and other information of the same kind. Accurate measurements are necessary in nearly all branches of manufacturing and building, and in many other kinds of work.

All measurements depend on some standard unit. In the United States and in British countries, the standard unit of length is the *foot,* the unit of time is the *second,* of weight the *pound,* and of temperature the *degree* (on the Fahrenheit or Centigrade scale). In most other countries the METRIC SYSTEM is used; it is described in a separate article.

The usual way of measuring anything is to compare it with a standard. To measure the length of something we lay a ruler beside it. When we say that something is 6 feet in length, we mean that the object is six times as long as a one-foot ruler. Anyone else who measures that object will find that it is 6 feet long because he will be using the same standard.

Measurements have not always been based on standards of this kind. Early units of length were taken from parts of the human body, and the length of these parts was different in different persons. The Egyptians used the length of the forearm, from the point of the elbow to

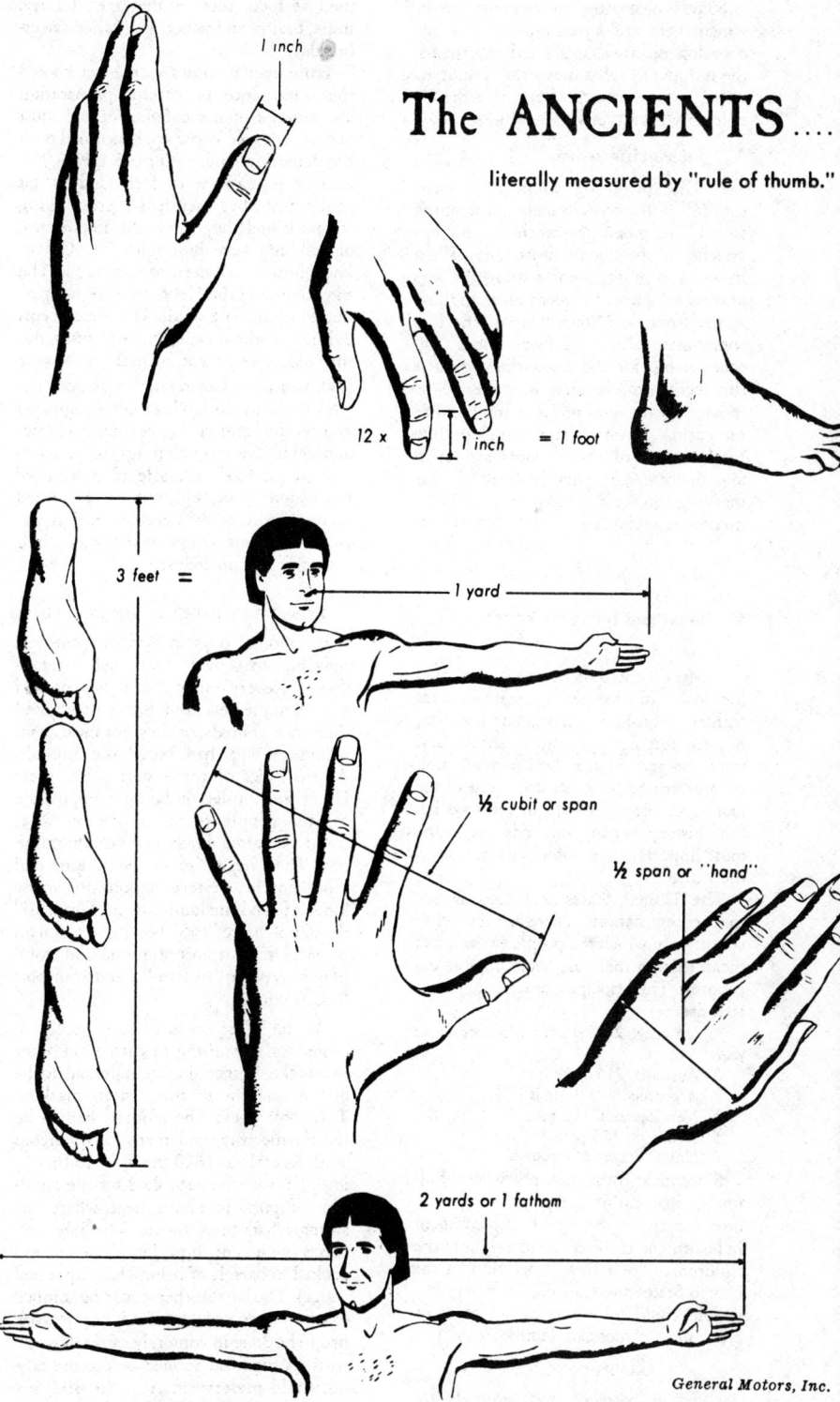

The ANCIENTS....

literally measured by "rule of thumb."

1 inch

12 x ‖ 1 inch = 1 foot

3 feet = 1 yard

½ cubit or span

½ span or "hand"

2 yards or 1 fathom

General Motors, Inc.

the end of the middle finger as a unit of measurement. It was called a cubit and was about 20 inches long. The Greeks used the width of a man's thumbnail. This became the unit we now call an inch. The hand opened flat was a unit of measure. It is still used to measure horses, who are said to stand so many hands high, a hand equaling about 4 inches. The human foot used as a unit of measurement has come to mean 12 inches. Three times the length of a foot was about the same as the distance from the tip of a man's nose to the end of his outstretched arm. This distance is very close to what we now call a yard.

The old units of weight were not much

better, but the Babylonians compared the weights of objects with a set of stones they kept just for that purpose. In digging through the ruins of Babylonian cities, archaeologists have found some of these stones all nicely shaped and polished. These probably were the world's first weight standards.

The Babylonians used different stones for weighing different objects. This later was carried over to England, where stone weights have meant different things. One stone weight is still used. It is a 14-pound weight. An Englishman will say, "I weigh ten stone," when an American would say, "I weigh 140 pounds."

Some measuring instruments about which there are separate articles in this encyclopedia are CLOCKS AND WATCHES, the BALANCE, THERMOMETER, MICROMETER, and BAROMETER. See also the article on WEIGHTS AND MEASURES.

measuring worm

The measuring worm is a small caterpillar that lives in many parts of the world. The measuring worm has no legs attached to the middle of its body. When it wants to move, it must bring the legs at the back part of its body close to those at the front, in a loop. This is why it is sometimes called the loop worm. Another name for the measuring worm is the inchworm, because it seems to be measuring the ground as it moves. The measuring worms later develop into moths. Most of these moths are small and delicate, and they have many fine markings on their wings. For more information, read the article on CATERPILLAR.

meat and meat packing

Meat is the flesh of any animal used for food. In this sense meat includes poultry and fish, but in ordinary use meat is only the flesh of cattle, sheep, and swine, or pigs. That is, beef or veal, lamb or mutton, and pork. Meat was one of the first foods eaten by man in the days before history began, and today it is the most important and widely used food in the world.

The United States and Canada are meat-eating nations. There are few other countries in which the people eat so much meat, though there are some notable exceptions. The principal meat-eating countries are:

1. Uruguay, 248 pounds per person per year
2. Australia, 215 pounds
3. Argentina, 191 pounds
4. New Zealand, 180 pounds
5. Denmark, 175 pounds
6. United States, 161 pounds

Since meat is the most nutritious of all foods, meat-eating habits have contributed greatly to the steady improvement in health and the increase in height of the children of each new generation in the United States and Canada. Once very few people could afford to eat meat daily. Now most American families can.

KINDS OF MEAT

Different parts of meat animals are called by different names when they are used for food. The meat of swine (that is, hogs and pigs) is called *pork*. Among the more important pork products are ham, pork chops, shoulder butts, bacon, and sausage. The meat of steers, or male cattle, is called *beef*, and it provides various cuts of steak and roasts. The meat of calves, called *veal*, is prepared as chops, shoulder of veal, and breast of veal, among other cuts. The meat of sheep is called *mutton*. It is very popular in England and eastern countries, but is little used in the United States. *Lamb*, the meat of young sheep, is more widely used in the United States, in the form of chops, leg of lamb, and breast of lamb. Some of the organs of all these meat animals are

used as food, such as the liver, kidney, heart, brains, and pancreas, (called sweetbreads).

From ancient times men have known the importance of careful preparation and storage of meat. Some of the most ancient laws we know are concerned with the handling and eating of meat. The ancient Romans were forbidden to eat goat's meat, but they had a great liking for pork and they knew the importance of cooking it very thoroughly. The Greeks knew how to salt meat to preserve it. The Egyptians and the Hebrews were not permitted to eat pork at all. The Phoenicians did not eat the meat of cows or hogs, but they did eat dog meat. As early as the year 700, Germany had regulations about the use of meat. As civilization progressed and nations and cities grew up, the laws and regulations concerning the preparation of all foods for sale became more strict and more efficient. The United States developed the handling and preparation of animals to be used for food into a science and an industry.

HOW MEAT-PACKING DEVELOPED

In colonial days in America, the settlers had to provide their own meat as they did every other thing they needed for life in the new land. Either they raised their own animals, or they got meat from neighbors who had raised the animals. As the cities of the eastern coast grew larger and busier, it became impossible for the people there to live on what could be raised in their own communities. They began to depend more and more on the western regions for many kinds of food, including meat. Gradually the supplying of food became a problem of large-scale transportation, and companies grew up to handle and transport food products.

As the West opened up, it became a center for the raising of cattle and other livestock. At first the animals had to be driven on foot to the eastern markets. This took weeks, the animals had to be fed on the way, and many of them ran wild. As early as 1820 the first meat-packing plants were established for the handling of pork in places near where the animals had been raised. The hog carcasses were cut into large pieces and packed in barrels of brine (heavily salted water). The barrels then could be shipped east by wagon or by boat. All of this work had to be done in winter, because in warm weather the meat spoiled before the salting could preserve it. Also, transporting the meat by rivers had to be done in spring, when floods made the water high.

In the early days the biggest meat-packing center was Cincinnati, Ohio, which was nicknamed "Porkopolis." In the 1840s other river cities had meat-packing plants. Then, as the railroads moved west, plants sprang up in cities that were rail terminals. In the 1850s the principal center of the industry shifted to Chicago. It is still there, although other midwestern cities such as St. Louis and Kansas City are important meat-packing centers.

The canning of meat began about 1870 with corned beef, and later included other canned-meat products. The original purpose was to preserve the meat.

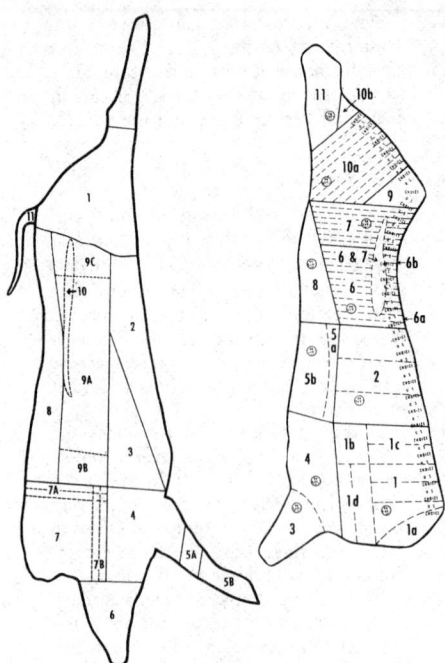

After an animal has been slaughtered, its carcass yields many different cuts. The cuts of pork (*left diagram*) are: 1. Ham. 2. Bacon. 3. Spareribs. 4. Picnic. 5. Hock (A) and foot (B). 6. Boned rolled butt. 7. Boston butt and shoulder steak (A, B). 8. Fat back salt pork. 9. Center loin roast (A), rib chop (B), and loin chop (C). 10. Tenderloin. 11. Tail. The cuts of beef (*right diagram*) are: 1. Neck (a), Boston cut (b), bladebone chuck (c), round-bone chuck (d). 2. Standing or rolled rib roast. 3. Shank. 4. Brisket. 5. Plate. 6 & 7. Tenderloin. 6. Short loin, club steak (a), and porterhouse and T-bone steak (b). 7. Sirloin steak. 8. Flank. 9. Rump. 10. Round steak (a) and heel of round roast (b). 11. Hind shank.

Later "meal in a can" dishes such as beef stew, corned-beef hash, chili, and many others became popular because they were easy to prepare.

MEAT-PACKING IMPROVEMENTS

The greatest development in meat-packing was refrigeration. This was needed in the processing plants so that work could be carried on in summer as well as in winter. It was also needed in transportation so that fresh meats as well as salted ones could be sent to market. The first refrigerator railroad cars were hardly more than iceboxes on wheels. With the invention of mechanical refrigeration fresh meats could be shipped long distances with complete protection all the way.

As improvements were made in refrigeration methods, freezing came into use. For many years certain cuts of meat were frozen in the fall and winter when supplies were plentiful, and used in the summer when meat was harder to get. Shortly before World War II, "quick-freezing" was invented, and frozen meats packaged for individual use began to be sold in stores. Certain meats are better suited to quick-freezing than others. The most popular are pork chops, veal cutlets, cube steaks, and hamburger. The more expensive cuts such as steaks and roasts can be frozen, but the cost of the process makes them more expensive.

HOW MEAT-PACKING IS DONE

The meat-packing industry is one of the most carefully operated and most

carefully inspected food industries in the United States. From the raising of the animals to the labeling of the meat and its sale in neighborhood stores, every precaution is taken to see that the buyer gets fresh, pure meat and knows exactly what quality he is buying. Meat inspection and grading is handled by the Meat Inspection Division of the Bureau of Animal Industry, which is part of the Department of Agriculture.

The inspections begin with the arrival of the animals at the slaughterhouse, or *abattoir*. They are herded into holding pens while an inspector watches their movement into the pens and their condition while at rest. Any animal whose condition seems doubtful is removed and tagged "U.S. condemned," which means that the animal cannot be used for food, or "U.S. suspect," which means that further examination is required.

The animals are slaughtered quickly and almost painlessly, and the second inspection takes place. This is the examination of certain glands and organs to detect possible disease. The carcass is then handled in one of several ways, depending on whether or not the hide is to be used for leather or for its wool. When the hair or hide has been removed, the carcass is sent to the chilling room, where it remains for 24 to 48 hours until it is thoroughly cooled. The meat is then divided into the various cuts that will be shipped to wholesale or retail markets throughout the country.

An assembly-line method is used, with the carcass passing by a succession of butchers and inspectors. The cuts of pork that are to be cured and smoked go to curing cellars. The cuts of beef that are to become "aged beef" go to special chilling rooms, where they are kept at even temperatures for two to three weeks. The fat is trimmed off and processed to make lard and other shortenings.

BY-PRODUCTS OF MEAT-PACKING

Some of the by-products of the meat-packing industry have become almost as important as the meat itself. The by-products are things made from parts of animals that otherwise would be thrown away. These are some of the principal by-products of the meat-packing industry:

The first by-product of meat was soap. Most of the inedible parts of the meat animals are placed in tanks and put under high steam pressure until the fat comes to the surface. The fat is then drawn off and used to make soap. In the soap-making process, glycerine is obtained. There are more than 1,500 uses for glycerine, from medicines to automobile polish.

One of the newer by-products is drugs. Doctors have found that from some parts of healthy animals they can obtain substances to help human beings who are ill. One of these drugs is a "wonder drug," ACTH, which is used in the treatment of rheumatic heart disease, asthma, burns, and many other ailments. ACTH is made from the pituitary gland found in the heads of all animals. Other medicines obtained from the meat-packing process are insulin, liver extract, and thyroid.

Leather is another major product that is really a by-product of the meat-packing industry. There are all colors, textures

and weights of leather, from rough sole leather to fancy kid and pigskin glove leathers. The hair from the hides is processed and used in mattresses and upholstery.

About 15 percent of all the wool produced in the United States is *pulled* wool, that is, wool removed from the sheep carcass instead of being sheared before the animal is sold for slaughter.

Glue is one of the oldest and still one of the most important meat by-products. Different kinds of glue are made from bones, hides, and other inedible portions of animal carcasses. Sheep intestines are used to make the catgut that surgeons use to sew up wounds and surgical incisions. Intestines of other animals form the casings for sausages.

The parts of meat animals that cannot be used for any other purpose are prepared by heat and pressure into *tankage*. Most tankage was once sold as fertilizer, but modern methods have improved the quality and now most tankage is used as livestock and poultry feed.

Mecca

Mecca is the most famous city of Arabia. It is the birthplace of Mohammed, founder of the Mohammedan religion, and to Moslems, those people who believe in the religion of Mohammed, Mecca is a holy city. It is in a rocky valley where few things can grow. Few things are manufactured there. The 300,000 people who live in Mecca mostly make their living by selling goods to pilgrims who visit the holy city. The temperature of Mecca is often far above 100 degrees. Many pilgrims faint from the heat, and every year some of them die.

Any Moslem who can, makes a pilgrimage to Mecca. There he visits the great mosque. (A mosque is a building in which Moslems pray.) In the middle of the courtyard of the mosque is the Kaaba. This is a block-shaped building. In it is the Black Stone, recognized by Moslems as the most holy object in the world.

The most important part of the pilgrimage to Mecca is when the Moslem kisses the stone. After kissing it, he walks around the Kaaba seven times. About one hundred thousand Moslems make this pilgrimage every year. The pilgrimage is called a *Hajj*, and a person who has made it is addressed with the honorary title *Hajji*.

People who do not belong to the religion of Mohammed are not allowed to visit Mecca. Some men have done it. One of these was Richard Burton, who made the pilgrimage to Mecca about 75 years ago, disguised as a Moslem. He wrote a famous book about his experiences on the way to Mecca, and at the shrine.

mechanics

A mechanic is a man who works on machines, but mechanics is the name of a science. It is the study of how various forces can produce motion or change motion.

There are various branches of mechanics. The study of how forces affect moving objects is called *dynamics*. The study of how forces affect objects that are standing still is called *statics*. Then there

are special names that depend on what substance is affected by the forces; the following are some of them:

Aerodynamics is the study of how forces affect the air or other gases. This study is of the utmost importance in aviation.

Hydraulics is the mechanics of liquids that are moving, and *hydrostatics* is the mechanics of liquids that are standing still.

Pneumatics is the mechanics of gases.

Mechanics itself is one of the branches of the science of PHYSICS, about which there is a separate article.

FORCES STUDIED IN MECHANICS

Most of the forces that are studied in mechanics are produced by machines: the lever, the pulley, the inclined plane, the screw, the wheel and axle, and the wedge. Many other forces are produced by our own bodies, as when we dive into a pool of water, or open a door, or even walk along the ground. Mechanics studies how these forces are produced and how they act on different objects.

Another force that is studied in mechanics is the force of gravity. It is the force that pulls things down toward the center of the earth and gives them weight and that causes objects to fall to earth.

Read also the articles CENTRIFUGAL FORCE and FORCE.

Medea

Medea was a woman in Greek mythology, the stories the ancient Greeks told about their gods and goddesses, thousands of years ago. Medea was the daughter of the king of Colchis, and she was supposed to have magic powers. She married Jason, and helped him capture the Golden Fleece. (There are separate articles about JASON and the GOLDEN FLEECE.) Later when Jason left Medea to marry Creusa, Medea killed both Creusa and her own children in order to pay Jason back for the suffering he had caused her. Great playwrights of many countries and ages have written dramas about Medea. They include the Greek playwright Euripides, the Roman playwright Seneca, and the French playwright Corneille. In the 1940s Robinson Jeffers, an American poet, wrote a poetic drama about Medea, based on the drama by Euripides. Judith Anderson played the part of Medea when this drama was produced on Broadway.

Medes

The Medes were an ancient people who lived in the western part of present-day Iran. Their country was called Media. The name Mede was given them by the Romans; the Medes called themselves Arii, which means noble.

Media was a fertile country. In ancient times it was famous for the wine, figs, oranges, and honey produced there. The people followed the Magi religion, which was the religion of the three Wise Men who journeyed to visit Jesus at his birth.

In the early period of their history, the Medes were greatly feared as fighters. They had developed strong, swift horses, and were fine horsemen. Mede soldiers could shoot arrows very accurately while riding. But a long period of peace,

coupled with wealth and luxurious living, left the Medes weak. About 2,500 years ago the great ruler of the Persian Empire, Cyrus the Great, easily conquered the Medes. The Medes were afterwards considered examples of the weakness that follows too much luxury and love of pleasure.

Medici

Medici is the name of a family that was rich and powerful in Italy hundreds of years ago. They lived in Florence, which was then an independent republic.

The first Medici to become well-known was Giovanni de' Medici, who saved a fortress in Florence from attack by soldiers of Milan in the year 1351. Salvestro de' Medici, a few years later, gained popularity with the people by resisting the tyranny of the nobles, and he was chosen chief magistrate of Florence.

The family engaged in commerce and banking, and grew rich. The second Giovanni de' Medici was the most successful of all the Medici. He died in 1429 and left an immense fortune to his sons. The family coat of arms had three balls on it, and this has remained the symbol of a pawnshop because the Medici were bankers and moneylenders.

The Medici were important in the Roman Catholic Church. Two Popes and two cardinals were members of the Medici, but one of the Medici, Lorenzo I, who lived from 1449 to 1492 and was known as Lorenzo the Magnificent because of his hundreds of great public works, was an enemy of Pope Sixtus IV. Lorenzo's troops and the Pope's troops fought several battles.

A great-granddaughter of Lorenzo the Magnificent, Catherine de' Medici, became a powerful queen of France. There is a separate article about CATHERINE.

medicine

Medicine is the science and study of diseases and the ways to treat or cure them. A man trained in this science is called a *physician* or (usually) a "doctor," because he holds the degree M.D., which means "doctor of medicine." Medicine is a profession, which means that it requires knowledge and skill that can result only from training. When a doctor works at his profession he is said to "practice medicine."

Medicine is one of the oldest of the professions. It may be the oldest. More than four thousand years ago, when nearly everyone was superstitious and believed that disease was a punishment from one of the many gods that were worshiped, some men were studying disease in a scientific way and had also learned ways to make splints for broken bones and tourniquets to stop bleeding. About 2,500 years ago, a Greek physician named Hippocrates studied the causes of disease and made records of them for the benefit of other physicians. He also wrote a statement of what a doctor should and should not do, and this statement (called the Hippocratic Oath) is still followed by doctors.

The Greek god of medicine was called Asclepius (the Romans called him Aesculapius), and the "priests" of this god were running hospitals two thousand

years ago, treating diseases in ways they had found to be best by actual practice, and keeping records of what happened.

In spite of its early start, the science of medicine advanced very slowly through the centuries. There has been more progress in the last two hundred years than in all the ages before. Great forward steps were made when the English physician William Harvey discovered the circulation of the blood, when the French chemist Louis Pasteur proved that bacteria can cause disease, and when the English physician Edward Jenner discovered the principle of vaccination, the English physician Joseph Lister developed the use of antiseptics, and the German chemist Robert Koch founded the science of bacteriology. Hundreds of other physicians have made important contributions to medicine.

SPECIALIZATION

Today so much is known about different diseases and the working of different parts of the body that many doctors *specialize*. That is, they treat only certain diseases or parts of the body.

A doctor who does not specialize is called a *general practitioner,* or "G.P." Some of the kinds of specialist are:

A *surgeon* operates—cuts into the body to remove diseased parts or to repair damaged ones. Many specialists are surgeons who usually operate only on particular parts of the body.

A *pathologist* studies the causes of disease.

A *diagnostician,* or "internal medicine man," treats diseases that do not require surgery.

A *pediatrician* treats diseases of children.

An *obstetrician* takes care of childbirth, and a *gynecologist* treats diseases of women. Most often a doctor specializes in both these fields at once.

A *psychiatrist* treats mental diseases.

An *ophthalmologist* treats diseases of the eye.

There are dozens of other fields of specialization.

THE MEDICAL CAREER

A young man or woman who wants to be a doctor must give up years of study and hard work to the career.

First, it is necessary to take a full four-year college course. This should be a "premed" course, which includes certain subjects important to medicine (such as chemistry, which is later helpful in understanding drugs, and Latin, the language in which much medical information is written). After this, the student attends a medical school for four years. Upon graduating from medical school, the student has his M.D. degree but must still be an *intern* for one or two years. An intern lives in a hospital, receives very little pay (seldom enough to live on), and works very hard treating patients in the hospital.

Finally, after these nine or ten years, a person can begin to practice medicine; but it still takes some money to buy the equipment needed in a doctor's office. Some doctors start in salaried jobs, working for hospitals or helping established doctors, until they save enough to "hang

out their own shingles" (open their own offices).

Even after he is practicing on his own, a good doctor must continue to study nearly every day, because the science of medicine is moving forward so fast that there is always something new to learn.

Because it takes so long and requires so much hard work, medicine as a career appeals only to those who are so interested in medicine that they do not want to do anything else. Fortunately, there are many of these.

MEDICAL ETHICS

A doctor is not allowed to solicit business. That is, he must not advertise and must not ask anyone to become his patient. When a doctor sends a patient to another doctor (for example, to a specialist), he is not supposed to receive any commission. This would be "fee-splitting," which is considered wrong by the members of the medical profession. A doctor must treat anyone who needs his help, even if the person is poor and cannot afford to pay a satisfactory fee. (See also the articles on HOSPITALS, ANATOMY, DISEASE, and DRUGS.)

AMERICAN MEDICAL ASSOCIATION

The American Medical Association is a national organization of doctors in the United States. It publishes magazines and booklets of interest to doctors, its committees decide on what is ethical or proper for doctors to do, and it helps to spread new information among doctors everywhere. Each state of the United States has a state medical association that is associated with the national organization. Usually the legislature (lawmaking body) of a state consults with the state medical association before making laws that have to do with the practice of medicine.

GROUP MEDICINE

Group medicine is a form of insurance that has become very popular within the last thirty years. A person pays so much per month, and if he or any member of his family gets sick the group organization pays all or part of the expense. One form of group medicine is called "hospitalization." This pays hospital expenses only. The biggest hospitalization group is known as the Blue Cross. Allied to it is the Blue Shield, which pays doctors' bills for its members.

The American Medical Association and most of its members have opposed group medicine plans that pay doctors' bills. They and others have attacked such plans as "socialized medicine." In Great Britain, real socialized medicine was put into effect in the late 1940s. The government paid the cost of all medical care for everyone, including dental care and such things as glasses and hearing aids. Many people in the United States favor a similar plan for this country. President Harry S. Truman proposed such a plan in 1948, and in 1962 President John F. Kennedy proposed a plan that would provide medical care for the aged, but Congress failed to make them into law.

medicine man

A medicine man, or "witch doctor,"

is a kind of priest that some primitive or uncivilized tribes have. His job is to treat diseases, but he does not do this scientifically as physicians do. He does it by appealing to the sick person's superstition, which is a kind of belief in things that do not exist. For example, the medicine man wears fierce-looking masks to frighten away "evil spirits" that are causing the disease, and he makes up drugs, or potions, that are based on strange mixtures (of lizards' tails, and frogs' teeth, and such things) instead of on chemistry. Many primitive tribes still believe in medicine men.

Medina

Medina is a city in Saudi Arabia. It is built on an oasis in the middle of the desert. About 60,000 people live there. Medina is important because it is a holy city of the Moslems (followers of the religion of Mohammed). Mohammed is probably buried in the great mosque that is the chief building of Medina. Moslems making the pilgrimage to Mecca, the Moslem holy city, also stop at Medina.

Mediterranean Sea

The Mediterranean Sea is a large body of water lying between Europe, Asia, and Africa. It is the world's largest inland sea and is one of the most important shipping routes in the world. The Mediterranean is about 965,000 square miles in size, or about a third the size of the United States. It is more than 14,000 feet deep at the deepest point. It is connected to the Atlantic Ocean by the Strait of Gibraltar; to the Red Sea by the Suez Canal; and to the Black Sea by the Dardanelles, the Sea of Marmara, and the Bosporus.

The Mediterranean has several "arms" that are small seas in themselves. The Tyrrhenian, Adriatic and Ionian Seas are off the coasts of Italy. The Aegean Sea is off the east coast of Greece. There are several important islands in the Mediterranean, including CORSICA, SARDINIA, SICILY, CRETE, and CYPRUS (about which there are separate articles).

The Mediterranean is filled with hundreds of different kinds of fish, and the finest sponges in the world grow there. Its water is salty. The people who live along the Mediterranean enjoy a warm, sunny climate. Thick evergreens and shrubs grow along the coasts, and farmers grow tropical fruit trees, grapes, and olives. The winters are mild and dry. Sometimes a hot, dry wind filled with dust blows across the region from the Sahara Desert. This is called a sirocco. Along the shores of the Mediterranean and some of the islands are several of the most famous volcanoes in the world, such as Mt. Vesuvius and Mt. Aetna.

THE MEDITERRANEAN IN THE PAST

In ancient times, three thousand years ago and more, the Phoenicians used the Mediterranean as a trade route. Later, Greece, Rome, and Carthage fought for control of it. The Roman Empire, two thousand years ago, called the Mediterranean *mare nostrum,* meaning "our sea." In the Middle Ages, the Mediterranean was the greatest trade route in the world,

but it grew less important as shipping on the Atlantic Ocean was opened to ports in Spain, France, and England.

After the Suez Canal was opened in 1869, the Mediterranean again became one of the great shipping routes and a region of great political importance. Many countries have wanted control of it. The British have powerful military bases at Gibraltar, Malta, and Cyprus. Control of the Mediterranean during World War II was so important that the United States sent large armies into North Africa and Italy.

Some of the most important Mediterranean ports today are Barcelona, Spain; Marseilles, France; Genoa and Naples in Italy, and Algiers in North Africa.

Medusa was one of the three hideous sisters known as the GORGONS, about whom there is a separate article.

meerschaum

Meerschaum is a very light, creamy-white mineral that is highly prized for making the bowls of pipes and the tips of cigarette holders. Some meerschaum has a yellow or red tinge. It is translucent. This means that you can see light through it, but you cannot see things on the other side of it as you do when you look through glass. When meerschaum is mined it is soft and can be easily carved to whatever shape is wanted. The name meerschaum is the German word for "sea foam." It is a good name for this mineral because, besides being white like foam, dry meerschaum is full of tiny bubbles that make it light enough to float on water as sea foam does. Scientists call meerschaum *sepiolite.* This is from a Greek word meaning "stone like cuttlefish bone," and it was given because cuttlefish bone is light and full of pores, too.

When meerschaum pipes and cigarette holders have been used for a while, the tobacco tars enter the pores and color the meerschaum golden brown. Smokers who have colored their meerschaum pipes brown are very proud of them.

The best meerschaum comes from Asia Minor. Meerschaum is also found in Greece, Czechoslovakia, Spain, and Morocco. In the United States it has been found in Pennsylvania, Utah, New Mexico, and California.

Meighen, Arthur

Arthur Meighen is the name of a Canadian political leader who was twice Prime Minister of Canada. He was born in Ontario, in 1874, and attended Toronto University. He became a member of the Canadian House of Commons in 1908, and held several government posts until 1920, when he was chosen Prime Minister. The following year his administration was defeated, and Meighen resigned. In 1926 he was again Prime Minister, but resigned within the year. He was appointed to the Senate in 1932 and remained there for ten years. In 1942 he was defeated in a contest for a seat in the House of Commons, and he retired from public life. He died in 1960.

Meistersinger, Die

Die Meistersinger von Nürnberg ("The Mastersingers of Nurenberg") is

an opera by the German composer Richard Wagner. An opera is a play in which all the words are sung instead of spoken. Wagner wrote both the libretto (the words) and the music of *Die Meistersinger.* It was first produced in the city of Munich in 1868. It is the only one of Wagner's many operas that is a happy story instead of a tragedy, and also is the only one that is based on actual history instead of on legend.

The Mastersingers were a group of musicians and poets in Germany, four to six hundred years ago. Each person who wanted to become a Mastersinger had to write a song according to very strict rules. One of the best poets among the Mastersingers was a shoemaker named Hans Sachs, and Wagner put this real man into his opera.

The story of *Die Meistersinger* concerns a young man named Walter who is in love with Eva, the daughter of a goldsmith. Eva's father had promised his daughter to the winner of a song contest to be held by the Mastersingers. Although Walter is not a Mastersinger, he composes a song to sing in the contest. The song does not meet all the strict rules of the Mastersingers, but Walter hopes it will win him membership anyway. The "villain" of the opera, Beckmesser, knows every tiny bit of the rules, but still he cannot write a good song and cannot even properly sing Walter's song, which he has stolen. Then Hans Sachs reveals that it is Walter's song and after Walter has sung it, Sachs persuades the Mastersingers that the beauty of the music should outweigh the technical flaws. Although Sachs himself is in love with Eva, he gives up his hopes to help Walter win admittance to the Mastersingers and thus marry Eva.

The most frequently played music of *Die Meistersinger* is the "Prize Song" itself, and also the overture, which contains an orchestral version of this song.

Mekong River

The Mekong River is the largest river in southeast Asia. It is about 2,800 miles long, which is somewhat longer than the Mississippi River in the United States. The Mekong rises in Tibet, flows between Burma and Thailand, crosses Cambodia and Vietnam, and empties into the China Sea. The name of the river changes at various points along its course. At the mouth of the river is the large Mekong delta, a great rice-growing region. Ships cannot go very far up the Mekong because of rapids and sandbars.

Melanesia

Melanesia is the name given to a large division of the islands of the South Pacific Ocean, including New Guinea, the Solomon Islands, New Hebrides, New Caledonia, the Bismarck Archipelago, and the Admiralty and Fiji Islands. The natives of these islands are called Melanesians. The Melanesians are scattered over so many thousand of miles of ocean that they differ widely in appearance and customs. Most Melanesians are dark-skinned. Many Melanesians are highly skilled in such arts as the making of masks, wood carvings, and shell and stone ornaments. Some early Melanesians were cannibals, but this practice has

largely disappeared. Farming, fishing and livestock-raising are the principal ways of life in Melanesia. There are more than a hundred Melanesian languages.

Melbourne

Melbourne is the second-largest city in Australia. It is also the capital of the state of Victoria. It is on the Yarra River and is an important railroad and commercial center. More than 2,503,000 people live in Melbourne. They work in mills, factories, and offices. Many work in the big port at Melbourne. This is more than two miles away but large vessels can go up the Yarra River to the city's center. A large part of Australia's exports is shipped through Melbourne.

Melbourne is a beautiful, modern city, with wide streets, fine parks and gardens, and high buildings. It is noted for its water sports. The University of Melbourne is one of Australia's great universities.

Melbourne was settled in 1835, and was named after Lord Melbourne, the British Prime Minister. The city was scientifically planned, and the streets were named after important people in history.

MELBOURNE, AUSTRALIA. Population (1973 estimate) 2,503,500. Capital of Victoria. On the Yarra River.

melon

There are several kinds of large, juicy fruit called melons. They are grown in many parts of the world where the climate is warm. Some people who live in places with a cold climate grow delicious melons in greenhouses. The melon is an annual plant, which means it must be planted every year. The round fruit grows on vines, and melons taste best when they ripen on the vine.

The melon that is most often grown in the United States is the muskmelon, also called the cantaloupe. The muskmelon is about the size of a grapefruit. It has a grayish skin with pockmarks in its surface. The flesh of the melon is a golden orange color, and it has a sweet smell and taste. Melons in the United States were first grown in Colorado. Now people in many parts of the country raise melons.

The Persian melon and the honeydew melon are two popular melons. Both of them are larger than the cantaloupe. The Persian melon has a rough skin and, like the cantaloupe, has flesh that is golden-orange in color. The honeydew has a smooth green skin, and its flesh is pale green. The Persian melon and the honeydew are winter melons. They take longer to ripen than the other muskmelons and keep very well.

People in Europe grow a cantaloupe that has a harder skin than the muskmelon. The flesh is a dark yellow color. People believe that this melon first grew wild in the southern parts of Asia. The ancient Egyptians and Romans were fond of this fruit.

Watermelon is a melon that grows in Africa, and it is raised in Europe and the United States, in places where the climate is warm. The watermelon is a large juicy fruit that is egg-shaped. It often weighs more than 50 pounds. It has a smooth dark green skin. The flesh of the watermelon is a deep pink, and it has oval-shaped slippery black or white seeds. The sweet and juicy fruit of the watermelon is a very refreshing food on a hot day. Some people pickle and candy the skin of the watermelon.

Watermelon was eaten by people in India and in Egypt thousands of years ago. The early Egyptian artists drew pictures of watermelons in their paintings.

melting point

The melting point of a substance is the temperature at which it changes from a solid into a liquid. A substance usually will melt if it is heated to a high enough temperature. Most solid substances have a definite temperature at which they suddenly melt. For example, aluminum melts at 660 degrees on the Centigrade scale (1220 degrees on the Fahrenheit scale). Some substances do not have such a definite melting temperature. Sealing wax and glass are two substances that change gradually from a solid to a liquid. For this reason, glass is easily shaped. It becomes softer and softer as it is heated instead of changing suddenly from a solid to a liquid.

Ice changes to water when its temperature is brought to zero Centigrade, or 32 degrees Fahrenheit. That is its melting point.

WHY SUBSTANCES MELT

When a solid changes into a liquid it is because it has been given more heat and the molecules of the substance move faster. This means that the molecules no longer just vibrate, but must move about in the substance. In this way the substance melts, becoming a liquid.

Most substances increase in volume when they melt, because of the greater activity of the molecules. However, this is not true of water and some other substances. Water at zero degrees on the Centigrade scale has only about nine-tenths the volume of ice at the same temperature.

The melting point of a substance can be changed by increasing or decreasing the pressure on the substance. For some substances, an increase in pressure lowers the melting point. For others, an increase in pressure raises the melting point.

A combination of two metals usually has a lower melting point than either of the metals heated separately.

Melville, Herman

Herman Melville was one of America's great writers. His best-known novels are about sailing ships and sailors. He was born in New York in 1819 and ran away to sea when he was 18. His first voyage gave him a lasting interest in sailing. In 1841 he shipped aboard a whaler and sailed to the South Pacific. The cruelty of the ship's captain disgusted him so much that he deserted when the ship docked at the island of Nukahiva in the Marquesas. He lost his way and was captured by natives who were cannibals, and they held him for four months until he was rescued by an Australian ship. He returned to the United States on an American naval vessel. The flogging and other harsh treatment of the sailors that he had seen on the sailing ships infuriated Melville, and when he got home he wrote a novel about it, *White Jacket*. This book aroused so much protest that the treatment of the men was improved. Melville became a farmer in Pittsfield, Massachusetts, and divided his time between writing and farming. His most famous book is *Moby Dick*, the story of a sea captain's search for a white whale, Moby Dick, that had bitten off one of his legs. Other stories by Melville describe life aboard ship and among the natives of the South Seas. For more than ten years he lived in Massachusetts and was a friend of Nathaniel Hawthorne and other great New England writers. He died in New York in 1891, at the age of 72.

membrane

A membrane is a tough, skinlike tissue that covers organs or bones inside the body. It may be seen on some of the meat that you eat. Membrane looks somewhat like a thin film, and is translucent (light shines through it) but is not transparent. *Mucous membrane* is membrane from which flows a thick liquid called *mucus*, which keeps it moist. The eyes, stomach and lungs are lined with mucous membrane, as are some other parts of the body.

Memel

Memel is a city in Lithuania. It is a port on the Baltic Sea. In 1962 there were 89,000 people living there. The Lithuanian name of the city is Klaipeda or Klaypeda. It is a manufacturing city.

Memel was once part of Prussia, but after World War I Germany had to give it up and in 1923 Lithuanian troops seized it. Almost half of the people were Germans, however, and in 1938 Adolf Hitler, the German dictator, threatened war unless Lithuania gave up Memel. In 1939 Lithuania surrendered Memel to Germany. At the end of World War II Russia took Memel and incorporated it into the Lithuanian Soviet Socialist Republic.

Memnon

Memnon was a character in Greek mythology, the stories the ancient Greeks told about their gods and goddesses. He was a king of Ethiopia who brought an army to help the Trojans fight the Greeks. Memnon killed the Greek Antilochus but almost immediately afterward was himself slain by Achilles. (See the article on the TROJAN WARS.) A large statue of Memnon, about sixty feet high, was one of a pair in Thebes, Egypt. It was called "the vocal Memnon" for many years, because sounds were reported to come from it at sunrise. Some people thought that the sound was produced by a trick, with someone hidden inside the pedestal, but actually the sound was caused by the expanding of the stones in the heat of the morning sun.

Memorial Day

Memorial Day, sometimes called Decoration Day, is a holiday set aside in honor of United States servicemen who gave their lives for their country. It is usually May 30. It was established in 1868 by General John A. Logan, commander-in-chief of the Grand Army of the Republic (an association of United

States veterans), in remembrance of soldiers who died in the Civil War. General Logan set May 30 as Memorial Day, but because there was still great bitterness between the North and the South, the Confederate states refused to recognize this day. The southern states set their own days and these are still observed, although more and more the South is coming to recognize May 30 also. The Confederate Memorial Days are variously set on April 26, May 10, and June 3.

Observances of Memorial Day include military parades and the placing of flowers and wreaths on the graves of soldiers and sometimes civilians. There are special services at the battlefield at Gettysburg, Pennsylvania, and the Arlington National Cemetery in Washington, D.C.

memory

Memory is the mind's ability to retain past experiences and to recall them (bring them to mind again). The brain retains everything it experiences, but it can recall only certain ones. All memories fade gradually as time passes. Those experiences that have pleased us, or that have had the strongest immediate effect on us, are remembered longest. Some people deliberately forget unpleasant things, though they may not know they are doing so. Psychologists assure us that these memories are retained in the brain and can be recalled under some kinds of treatment for mental disturbances.

Sometimes experiences are recalled wrongly, and there are several reasons for this. Most people have a tendency to exaggerate or improve on an experience in telling about it, to make a good story. Sometimes people remember things not the way they happened, but the way they think the events should have happened. Sometimes a person intends to do a certain thing, and the intention is so strong that the memory takes hold of it and the person "remembers" having done it although he never did. These are only a few ways in which the memory can play tricks on people.

There are some people who have remarkable memories for things they have seen or read only once. You may have heard people say "I never forget a face," and this may be perfectly true. Such people have what is called a "photographic" memory. Ability to remember things is not necessarily a sign of superior intelligence.

Memory is sometimes divided into two kinds, visual and auditory. A person with visual memory is able to remember best things that he has seen. A person with auditory memory remembers best things that he has heard.

People in general remember best the things that interest them, or that have an important part in their lives. For example, a great baseball pitcher such as Bob Feller may remember years later the details of a game. He can remember the order of batters that faced him, each ball he pitched, his reasons for choosing those particular pitches, and what happened to the ball. A good golf player can tell you about every stroke on every hole in a game played years before.

The study of ways to train the memory is called *mnemonics.* Mnemonics teaches ways of training the memory by associating things or events with other things. The verse that begins "Thirty days hath September" is a mnemonic method of aiding the memory.

Loss of memory is called AMNESIA, about which you can read in a separate article.

Memphis

Memphis is the largest city in the state of Tennessee. It was named after Memphis, the capital of ancient Egypt, about which you can read in the article on EGYPT. Memphis, Tennessee, is on the Mississippi River, and is one of the greatest cotton markets, hardwood-lumber markets and mule markets in the world. About 623,000 people live in Memphis. They work in the important freight yards and in iron and steel foundries, machine shops, chemical plants, and rubber factories. Memphis is the most important distributing or shipping point on the Mississippi River between St. Louis and New Orleans. Farmers in the fertile region around the city send their cotton, corn, sweet potatoes, tobacco and soybeans to Memphis for shipment.

Memphis has many places of historical interest, as well as museums and universities. Every year thousands of people go to Memphis to enjoy the colorful Cotton Carnival. It is a gay celebration that lasts for five days, beginning on the second Tuesday in May. A King and Queen of Cotton are chosen to rule the carnival.

The French and the Spanish were the first white people to come to the place where Memphis now stands. The first permanent settlement was made in 1819, by Andrew Jackson and several other men. It became a city in 1849.

MEMPHIS, TENNESSEE. Population (1970 census) 623,530. County seat of Shelby County, on the Mississippi River. Founded in 1819.

Mendel, Gregor

Gregor Johann Mendel was an Austrian priest and a student of plant life. He lived about a hundred years ago. His experiments with plants were very impor-

Gale Research Co.

tant to our knowledge of how different characteristics or traits of plants and other living things are passed on through the seeds to their off-spring. The facts he discovered are called Mendel's law.

In one experiment Mendel used two kinds of garden pea. One was very small, the other very tall. He kept these plants covered so that the pollen (the small grains that help make plant seeds) from other plants would not fall on them.

First he put some pollen from the very small plant onto the very tall plant. Then he put some pollen from the very tall plant onto the very small plant. This is called *cross-breeding.*

When the seeds had developed, he planted them in the ground, and expected that the plants grown from them, called the *first generation,* would be of medium height, not too tall or too small. Instead, all of the plants that grew from the seeds were very tall. Because tallness had shown up in all of the plants, Mendel called it the *dominant* trait. Because shortness had receded or withdrawn from all the plants, he called it the *recessive* trait.

Mendel next planted the seeds made by using only the pollen of first generation plants. Some of the plants that grew from these seeds, called the *second generation,* were tall and some were small. About three times as many plants were tall as were small. This showed that the seeds from the first-generation plants had contained both traits, even though all the plants had been tall. Such plants are called *hybrids.*

A hybrid will always breed or produce mixed offspring, some of which will have the dominant trait and some the recessive trait. Plants whose seeds contain only one kind of trait are called pure breeds. They will always breed plants that have the same trait. This is called *breeding true.*

Mendel's ideas have been very important to the science of GENETICS, about which there is a separate article.

Mendelssohn, Felix

Felix Mendelssohn was a German composer, or writer of original music, who lived more than a hundred years ago. Although he lived to be only 38, he wrote a great deal of music. Mendelssohn was born in 1809, in Hamburg, Germany, of a wealthy and cultured family. He is one of the few great composers whose lives were not filled with hardship. As a child, he was composing music almost before he could talk, and at the age of 6 he played the piano well. When he was 9 he gave his first public concert in Berlin. His father was not sure whether to let Mendelssohn devote his life to music, and he took him to Paris to see the composer Cherubini and other musicians. They all predicted a brilliant future for the boy, whose career was then decided. Mendelssohn gave many successful concerts. By the time he was 15 he had written his first symphony. In 1827, when he was only 18, his *Overture to A Midsummer Night's Dream* was performed and won him tremendous popularity.

Mendelssohn traveled widely and found inspiration for many of his works in foreign lands. Among his most famous works are two great oratorios (musical stories), *St. Paul,* and *Elijah.*

Until 1845, Mendelssohn taught music, conducted orchestras, and gave concerts. Then he resigned all his positions to devote himself to writing music. His favorite sister, Fanny, died in 1847, and Mendelssohn never recovered from his grief. He died less than six months later. His full name was Jakob Ludwig Felix Mendelssohn-Bartholdy.

menhaden

The menhaden is a fish that lives in the Atlantic Ocean, near the eastern coast of the United States. It is a greenish-brown fish that has a black spot

behind each gill and a silver underpart. The menhaden is about a foot long. Although many people have never heard of the menhaden, fishermen catch over a billion of these fish every year in huge nets. People do not eat the menhaden (some people do eat the eggs), but the fish is very useful in other ways. The menhaden is made into feed for hogs, cattle, and chickens. It is also used for fertilizer to make the soil rich so that better crops will grow. The oil of the menhaden is used to make soap, paint, and insecticides.

meningitis

Meningitis is a serious disease in which the membranes (linings) that cover the brain and spinal cord become inflamed. The disease is caused by a germ called *meningococcus*. The germ enters the body through the nose and throat. Meningitis is very infectious, which means that a person can easily catch it from someone else. Sometimes a person is infected with meningococcus germs and although he does not feel ill himself he spreads the disease to other people. Such a person is called a "carrier." Meningitis usually occurs in the winter and early spring. It is most likely to occur in barracks and schools and other places where many people crowd together.

A person who becomes ill with meningitis develops a fever and a severe headache. It often becomes painful to bend the head forward. Sometimes the person develops a skin rash. Until recently people who had meningitis usually died. Now the antibiotics, or "wonder drugs," help cure the disease. A person who gets meningitis should receive treatment from a doctor immediately and should be kept away from other people as much as possible.

Mennonite

Mennonites are Christians who follow the teachings of Menno Simons, a Dutch reformer who lived about four hundred years ago. Menno believed that people should live very strictly, and should follow closely the teachings of the Bible. He recognized two sacraments, baptism (but of adults, not babies) and communion or Lord's Supper. His followers were persecuted for a long time after he died in 1559.

The Mennonites first came to colonial America in 1683. Today many Mennonites live in Pennsylvania, Ohio, Indiana, and Illinois. They refuse to go to war or to take oaths, because of their religion. Most Mennonites are farmers and people enjoy visiting Mennonite communities because of the simple, pious way the Mennonites live. Their cooking is famous. There are several branches of the Mennonite church; a separate article tells about the members of one of these, the AMISH.

Menotti, Gian-Carlo

Gian-Carlo Menotti is an American composer, or writer of music. He is best-known for the operas he has written. Operas are plays in which the words are sung rather than spoken. Menotti writes both the libretto (words) and the music. Menotti was born in Italy in 1911, but became a citizen of the United States. His most successful operas include *The Medium, The Telephone, The Consul,* and *The Saint of Bleecker Street.* In 1951 Menotti wrote an opera, *Amahl and the Night Visitors,* especially to be performed on television at Christmas. It has been performed every Christmas since then.

mental illness

A person is mentally ill when his mind does not work properly. Such a person may imagine that things are so when they are not, or may have impulses (desires to do things) that he cannot control and that cause him to do unnatural things. Mental illness may be caused by damage to the brain, for example by a hemorrhage (bleeding) inside the head or a severe blow on the head; but most often the principal causes of mental illness are disturbing experiences that a person has had during his life. Such a disturbing experience is called a *trauma.* Extreme worry or fear are examples of disturbing experiences, but many people can have such experiences without suffering any permanent effects, while some other people can be made mentally ill by experiences that they seem hardly to notice at the time.

In the 1950s mental illness cost the United States more than a billion dollars a year, and this amount was increasing each year by $100,000,000. A million persons each year were being treated in mental hospitals and 100,000 more were receiving treatment elsewhere for mental illness. About half the hospital beds in use throughout the United States were occupied by mentally ill persons. During World War II four of every ten men discharged for reasons of health were mentally ill.

There was a time when mental illness was considered disgraceful, something to be ashamed of; but modern science has brought most people to realize that a mental disease is simply a matter for medical treatment, just as pneumonia or appendicitis or any other serious disease is.

The serious kind of mental disease is called *psychosis.* A less serious mental illness or disturbance is called *neurosis,* or *psychoneurosis,* and a person who is suffering badly from neurosis is often said to have a "nervous breakdown."

Mental illness is treated by doctors, called *psychiatrists,* who are specialists in mental cases. *Psychologists* who are scientists but are not medical men, also are trained to help in the treatment of people who are suffering from mental troubles.

NAMES OF MENTAL ILLNESSES

One of the words most often heard in connection with serious mental illness is *schizophrenia* (which means "split personality"). Nearly one out of every four persons suffering from psychosis is found to have schizophrenia. A person suffering from another mental disease that is as common as schizophrenia is called a *manic-depressive.* A manic-depressive person will be extremely cheerful and active, and then for no apparent reason he will feel very depressed (unhappy) and may want to kill himself. More depressives commit suicide than any other group of mentally ill persons. There are many other kinds of mental illness and some of these, such as AMNESIA, HYSTERIA, and PARANOIA, are described in separate articles in this encyclopedia.

A person suffering from a serious mental illness, or psychosis, is said to be "insane," but insanity is not a name for a form of mental illness. Insanity is a term used mostly in courts of law, where a person is said to be insane if his mental condition is such that he cannot tell the difference between right and wrong and is not responsible for his actions. A psychiatrist who specializes on deciding whether or not a person is legally insane is called an *alienist.*

There are other words, such as *madness, lunacy, craziness,* and others, that are often used to describe mental illness, but these are not scientific words and may mean almost any kind of mental illness.

MENTAL DEFICIENCY

Some persons are born without normal intelligence, or lose some or all of their normal intelligence because of an injury or illness that affects the brain. There are special words for deficiency (lack) of intelligence. An *idiot* has only the intelligence of a two- or three-year-old child. He cannot dress himself or carry on a conversation (if he can talk at all). A *cretin* is a special kind of idiot. An *imbecile* is one grade above an idiot. Mentally he is no better off than a little child. A *moron* has a low "I.Q." (about which you can read in the article on INTELLIGENCE TESTS). He is often said to be "dull" or "mentally retarded," but he can learn to read and write (with difficulty) and live a more or less normal life.

TREATMENT OF MENTAL ILLNESS

When mental illness is caused by damage to the brain, it is sometimes possible to cure it by an operation. In other cases in which the brain is damaged, a person may be able to learn again the things that the injury caused him to forget. For example, a person may forget how to write, due to a brain injury, but he can learn again.

Some mental diseases are caused by bacteria that attack the brain and nervous system. These are treated by destroying the bacteria. Penicillin and other antibiotic drugs are effective against most of these bacteria.

When mental illness has psychological causes, the cure is not so easy. The best-known treatment is PSYCHOANALYSIS, about which there is a separate article. In psychoanalysis, the patient is helped to find out what experiences in his previous life were so disturbing that they led to the mental illness. The psychiatrist can usually make the patient feel better by various forms of treatment, such as changing the patient's living habits and actions to reduce the sources of his worry.

MENTAL HOSPITALS

There are hundreds of public and private hospitals for the care of people who are mentally ill. There was a time when these were called "lunatic asylums" and were classed with prisons, but modern science has progressed and mental hospitals are now like other hospitals.

A person may become a patient in a mental hospital in one of two ways. In many cases the person realizes he is suf-

fering from a mental illness and volunteers to enter a mental hospital for treatment. Once he is in the mental hospital, he may leave whenever he wants to, unless the doctors in charge of the hospital think it would be unsafe to release him.

The other way in which one enters a mental hospital is by *involuntary commitment*. In such a case, the person may not want to go to the mental hospital, but doctors who have examined him certify that he is too ill mentally to know what is good for him and that he requires hospital care. A person cannot be committed to a mental hospital against his will except by a court of law after two psychiatrists have examined him and have certified that he would not be safe outside of a mental hospital.

A mental hospital always has a staff of psychiatrists and trained psychiatric nurses who understand the problems of those who are mentally ill. The mental hospital also has special equipment for the several different methods of treating those who are mentally ill. Because little was known about mental illness until the last fifty years or so, and the building of hospitals is seldom fast enough to keep up with new medical knowledge, there are not enough mental hospitals in any part of the world to take care of all the patients who need treatment. Mental hospitals in the United States are the finest in the world, but even they are often crowded and do not have enough doctors and nurses to take care of all the patients. This has led to many reports of bad conditions in mental hospitals, especially in those that are supported by state governments. Some of these reports have been exaggerated and some have been true, but nearly every state and country is making efforts to improve the treatment of those who are mentally ill.

NATIONAL INSTITUTE OF MENTAL HEALTH

The National Institute of Mental Health was set up by the United States government in 1946 to promote mental health throughout the nation. The Institute awards money to local institutions for training psychiatrists, social workers, nurses, and other staff members. It awards money to students who want to follow careers in mental health and conducts training programs for persons already in that field. It also assists the states in conducting their mental health programs by helping them to establish clinics and programs in the schools, and by other activities. It conducts research in the problems of juvenile delinquency and in the special problems of older people as well as studying the causes and cures of mental diseases. It also helps spread information on mental health throughout the country.

menthol

Menthol is a substance that will give you a cool feeling if you put some of it on your skin or on your tongue. It is very useful in medicine. Menthol not only cools but it also relieves pain in those parts of your body—the skin and mouth and the inside of the nose and throat—where it can touch the endings of nerves. This is why doctors put it on itching and burning skin. If you have a sore throat, the doctor may spray it with

menthol dissolved in alcohol, or he may give you cough drops that have menthol in them. Menthol is mixed with wax to rub on chapped lips. Menthol is also a mild germ killer, but it is not much used for this purpose by itself.

Menthol is made by freezing peppermint oil. When the oil becomes cold enough, colorless crystals of menthol separate from it. Menthol is sometimes called peppermint camphor.

Mercator, Gerardus

Gerardus Mercator was a Flemish geographer and mapmaker who lived about four hundred years ago. He is best remembered for a kind of map that he invented, called Mercator's projection. It is explained in the article on MAP. Mercator was born in 1512. His real name was Gerhard Kremer. In those days it was the fashion to use the Latin spelling of one's name. The German name *Kremer* means "trader," and so it became Mercator (Latin for "trader"). Mercator surveyed and made a map of his native country, Flanders. He made maps of the world and of the skies. His first map using Mercator's projection was published in 1569. In 1585 Mercator began to put together a book of maps, which he called an atlas. He was the first to use this term for a collection of maps. In 1594 Mercator died before finishing the atlas. His son completed it and published it that same year.

merchant marine

The merchant marine of a country consists of all its ships that carry goods and passengers over oceans, rivers, and other water routes. In peaceful times a country carries on much of its foreign trade with its merchant marine, and few countries can prosper without foreign trade. When war threatens, all ships in a country's merchant marine are usually taken over by the government and many of them are used for carrying troops, ammunition, equipment, food, and other supplies to the battle area. In war the merchant marine is called a "second line of defense." To keep this line of defense strong, governments encourage and help shipbuilders, and often *subsidize*, or help with money, operators of large ships.

TONNAGE

A country's merchant marine is measured by the number of ships in it, and their total *tonnage*. Tonnage is a ship's carrying capacity, or the weight of the cargo it can transport, expressed in tons. There are several ways to figure tonnage. It is generally estimated that each 100 cubic feet of space inside a ship can carry a *long ton*, which is 2,240 pounds. Figuring this way, the entire space inside the *Queen Mary* of the Cunard White Star Line can carry 80,773 long tons. Its *gross tonnage* is therefore 80,773. *Deadweight tonnage* is the officially estimated weight of the cargo a ship normally carries. Another term is *displacement tonnage*, which is the weight of sea water that a ship displaces when it floats. The *America* of the United States Lines has a displacement of 35,440 tons.

These two ships are passenger vessels, although they usually carry a small

amount of goods or cargo. There are also general cargo vessels, or *freighters*, which carry only a few passengers if any. The usual cargo ship has a displacement of about 12,000 tons. Some of these are on regular schedules, going to and from certain seaports at specified times. Others, called *tramp ships* or *tramps*, go to almost any port at which they may pick up a cargo going to almost any destination. These have no definite time of sailing; they simply leave when they are fully loaded. A merchant marine also includes *tankers*, which carry liquids such as oil; and *colliers* or *ore ships*, which take coal, iron ore, and so on. There are also *tugs*, *icebreakers*, *fishing trawlers*, and many types of smaller vessels.

SHIP REGISTRY

Ships must register under the flag of some country. If the United States has helped to build or operate a ship, its owner must register under the United States flag. Some countries, including the United States and Canada, have strict laws regarding taxation, ship insurance, and the health, wages and living conditions of crews. Some shipowners transfer their ships to the flag of a country that does not have such strict laws, such as Panama or Liberia. Many ships owned by United States and Canadian citizens are registered under those flags. Liberia in 1962, for example, had the fourth largest merchant marine in the world, largely for that reason.

Through the centuries, various countries have risen to power by the strength of their merchant fleets. For a while Holland ruled the oceans, with 3,000 ships against England's 300, and Dutch was the language of the admirals. Then for more than two hundred years, up to World War II, Britain's merchant marine was the largest. Britain's fleet was badly hurt by German submarines in World War I.

In World War II, the United States built a huge merchant fleet. In 1946 it had more than half of the world's total tonnage, with about 5,500 ships totaling 40,000,000 tons. In 1962, the United States still had the world's largest merchant fleet of 2,733 ships, with 30,975,000 deadweight tons. However, a considerable number of these ships were part of a large government-owned "mothball" or reserve fleet. The United Kingdom had the largest active, privately-owned merchant marine, with 25,685,000 deadweight tons. In 1962 Norway was third, Liberia fourth, and Japan fifth.

Merchant Marine Academy, United States

The United States operates several academies, or colleges, that teach young men to be officers in its armed forces: at West Point, New York, for the Army; at Annapolis, Maryland, for the Navy; at New London, Connecticut, for the Coast Guard; at Colorado Springs, Colorado, for the Air Force. There is a similar academy, the United States Merchant Marine Academy, at Kings Point, New York. This trains young men to serve as officers on ships carrying goods and passengers, not warships of the Navy. These ships, which in peacetime are not fitted out with guns but which are useful in

wartime for carrying men, food, and other supplies, form what is called the Merchant Marine. When war comes, the Merchant Marine is under orders of the government.

The United States Merchant Marine Cadet Corps was started on March 15, 1938. The Academy was dedicated in 1943. In World War II there were 2,670 men at the Academy; in peacetime about 700 are enrolled, with 200 more in training at sea.

Young men study at the Academy for four years. They are members of the Merchant Marine Cadet Corps, also Mid-

An officer swears in members of the graduating class at the United States Merchant Marine Academy at Kings Point, N.Y.

The United States Merchant Marine Academy trains the young men who will eventually command the ships of the merchant marine.

shipmen of the Naval Reserve, so they are called Cadet-Midshipmen. They study either Nautical Science to become Deck Officers, or Marine Engineering to become Engineering Officers. Men who graduate become Third Mates or Third Assistant Engineers, and earn about $500 a month aboard ship. They become Ensigns in the United States Naval Reserve, and in wartime serve in the Navy. They also receive degrees of B.S., or Bachelor of Science, as do graduates of technical colleges.

The first year at the Academy is for basic training, when the student learns military customs and discipline and also takes study courses. First-year men are officially Fourth Classmen, but are nicknamed "plebes" as at West Point. The entire student body is trained as a regiment, which is divided into battalions and companies. The second year is spent at sea, and the Cadet-Midshipman may

sail 40,000 miles on several ships, visiting far-off countries. During this "sea year" men are paid $82.50 a month by the shipowner. In the last two years, special studies are taken, such as electronics, astronomy and engineering, as well as languages, history, economics, and other college subjects. The Academy has athletic teams as do most colleges. Its campus, which occupies sixty-five acres facing Long Island Sound, has good equipment for sports.

To enter the Academy, one must be between 16 and 21 years of age, a United States citizen, unmarried, and physically sound. He must have a high school education or its equivalent. He must pass competitive examinations held each April. Students receive tuition, room, board, uniforms like those of Navy men at Annapolis, textbooks, and medical and dental care, at government expense. They have thirty days' leave a year and vacations at Easter and Christmas. Incoming Cadet-Midshipmen have certain expenses, but in later years these are made up to them.

Mercier, Cardinal

Désiré Joseph Mercier was a Roman Catholic priest who became a cardinal, the highest Church office next to that of the Pope. He was born in Belgium in 1851 and was ordained a priest in 1874. Eight years later he became a professor of philosophy at the University of Louvain, in Belgium. In 1906 he was made Archbishop of Malines, and the next year the Pope appointed him to be cardinal. Cardinal Mercier became famous in World I for his bravery in defying the Germans. When the king of the Belgians was separated from his people, Cardinal Mercier became spokesman for the Belgians. His letters to his countrymen did much to help them resist the invaders. He also wrote letters abroad telling the world what the Germans were doing to his country. After the war Cardinal Mercier visited the United States and Canada. He died in 1926.

mercury

Mercury is a silvery metal that is a liquid at ordinary temperatures. Mercury is also called *quicksilver* because it slides very quickly over surfaces. In fact, it got the name mercury from the Roman god Mercury, who was a very swift runner. Mercury is a chemical element, which means that it is one of the more than one hundred substances of which the world is made. It is the only element that is usually seen in liquid form.

In a thermometer the silvery line whose height you read to tell the temperature is a thin column of mercury. Mercury is also used in other scientific measuring instruments, such as BAROMETERS and HYGROMETERS, about which there are separate articles. Mercury is very good for this purpose because it does not rise as high up into a tube as water does. A mercury barometer is only 30 inches high, while a water barometer would have to be about 34 feet high.

If you cool mercury to 76½ degrees below zero Fahrenheit, it will freeze solid. Mercury is nearly as heavy as lead. If you filled a quart milk bottle full of

mercury it would weigh 28 pounds. Mercury is a very good conductor of electricity, and it is used in many electrical appliances.

Some mercury is found in the ground in tiny droplets, but there is very little of it in this pure form. We get most of our mercury from a red mineral called *cinnabar*. Cinnabar is a combination of mercury and sulfur. To separate these two elements, you heat the cinnabar in a vessel that is open at the top. The sulfur will combine with the oxygen gas of the air to form a gas called *sulfur dioxide*. The sulfur dioxide rises out of the vessel and leaves mercury behind. Cinnabar is mined chiefly in Spain, but also in Austria, Italy, Mexico, Texas, and California. Mercury is sold in iron flasks, each one of which holds 76 pounds. Mercury has been known since ancient times.

USES OF MERCURY

You can combine mercury very easily with other metals, except iron and platinum, to form substances called *amalgams*. This fact is used to separate gold and silver from the rock of their ores. The ore is crushed with mercury. The grains of silver and gold amalgamate or combine with the mercury, but the other elements in the rock do not. The mercury in amalgam form is poured off, leaving the rock behind. Then the mercury is boiled away and what remains is silver or gold.

MERCURY COMBINATIONS

There are many useful combinations of mercury and other elements. For instance, mercury and chlorine form *mercuric chloride*, also called *bichloride of mercury* or *corrosive sublimate*. It is a very powerful germ killer, but only doctors should use it, for it is also a dangerous poison. If you combine mercury and chlorine in a different way, you get a substance that is called *mercurous chloride* or *calomel*. It is used in medicine as a laxative and as a way of killing worms that live inside the intestines of people with certain diseases. Mercury and oxygen combine to form *mercuric oxide*, a substance used in ointments, and in paint that keeps sea water from eating holes in the hulls of ships. A very pure combination of mercury and sulfur is used to make the artists' paint called vermilion. Mercury combined with nitrogen and oxygen forms a substance called *mercuric nitrate* or *fulminate of mercury*. If you strike it, it will explode. It is used to set off other explosives, such as dynamite and the high explosives packed into bullets, shells, grenades, and torpedoes.

When mercury is placed into a bulb from which the air has been pumped, and an electric current is passed through the bulb, the mercury takes on a glow that gives off the very valuable *ultra-violet rays*. These bulbs are called mercury-arc lamps.

Mercury

Mercury was a god of the ancient Romans, two thousand and more years ago. To the Greeks he was known as Hermes. The Greeks considered him a messenger of the gods, as well as a patron of music, astronomy, military tactics, and gymnastics. The Romans be-

Mercury, the messenger of the gods, wore a winged cap and sandals. His staff, the *caduceus*, is the symbol of medicine.

lieved that he was the god of trade and profits, and the merchants of Rome celebrated his feast day to insure their own business success. He is supposed to have invented the lyre and the flute. Mercury, or Hermes, is usually shown in statues wearing a cap with wings, with wings on his heels, carrying a winged staff with two snakes winding around it. With these he flew rapidly to carry messages from the gods. The winged sandals are still used as a symbol of speed, and Mercury's staff, called the *caduceus*, is used as a symbol of doctors and the practice of medicine. Ancient Greek and Roman statues of Mercury are still in existence.

Mercury

Mercury is the smallest of the nine planets (which include the Earth) that revolve around the sun. It is the one closest to the sun, about 36,000,000 miles away from it. Mercury is less than half the size of the Earth. The Earth weighs twenty-five times as much as Mercury does. Because Mercury is so much lighter, its force of gravity is much less than the Earth's. A person weighing 100 pounds on the Earth would weigh only 26 pounds on Mercury.

It takes Mercury about 88 days to make one complete turn about the sun, compared to 365 days for the earth. The speed of Mercury as it travels through the skies is about 30 miles a second. Mercury takes about 88 days to make one complete turn on its own axis, compared to 24 hours for the earth. One side of Mercury is always light, while the other side is always dark. Because Mercury is so close to the sun, the light side has a temperature of about 770 degrees on the Fahrenheit thermometer. The dark side is about 500 degrees below zero. Mercury has the hottest and the coldest places of all the planets.

Mercury and the moon are about the same size and seem to have the same appearance when viewed with a telescope. Like the moon, Mercury has very little air surrounding it, so it is unlikely that any plant or animal lives on it.

The surface of Mercury has a reddish-yellow color. Every two months, starting at the beginning of each year, Mercury can be seen in the sky as a morning and evening star. For about two weeks of each of the two months Mercury appears in the morning for about an hour and in the evening for about an hour.

Meredith, George

George Meredith was an English writer. He is best known for his novels, but he also wrote fine poetry. He was born in England in 1828. As a young man he planned to become a lawyer, but found he preferred to be a writer. He wrote many novels. The best known are *Diana of the Crossways*, *The Egoist* and *The Ordeal of Richard Feverel*. Meredith died in 1909, at the age of 71. Because he lived in a time when there were many very great poets, he was not given as much credit for his poetry as he might have received if he had lived in another period.

merganser

The merganser is a duck that makes its home in many parts of the United States and Canada where the climate is not too warm. It is also called the *shelldrake*. It dives into deep water to catch the fish it eats. The merganser has a bill with sharp edges that are like teeth, and it can hold a slippery fish very tightly. Its contrasting colors, of black, reddish-brown, and white, make it a beautiful bird. Some mergansers are two feet long.

Mergansers make their nests among grasses and rocks on the ground. Sometimes they build their nests in hollow trees. They line the nests with soft feathers. The female lays several light-colored eggs. Mergansers are strong fliers and they make long journeys to warm climates for the winter. The flesh of the merganser has a fishy taste.

The hooded merganser is a handsome black-and-white bird that is about 18 inches long. The red-breasted merganser has a speckled, brownish-red breast. It is not good to eat.

mermaid

A mermaid is an imaginary creature who lives in the sea. Her upper part looks like the body of a beautiful woman, but her body ends in the tail of a fish. There are also stories of *mermen*, but mermen are not heard of so often. The folk tales and legends of many countries tell of mermaids who sit on a sandy shore holding mirrors and combing their long golden hair. In some of the stories mermaids take on completely human shapes, and they often lure mortal men to live in the sea with them, or even stay to live on land. No one is sure where the idea of mermaids and mermen began. It is believed that sailors in ancient times may have seen seals or other sea mammals in the distance and mistaken them for half-human beings.

mesa

In the southwestern desert of the United States, especially in Arizona and New Mexico, there are many flat-topped mountains and hills rising steeply up from the surrounding desert. These are called mesas. *Mesa* is the Spanish word for table. It is used because the tops of mesas are flat, as tables are.

Mesas are the remains of plateaus (high, level regions) that have been worn down by erosion, the destroying action of water and wind. The top of a mesa is usually a kind of rock that is hard and can stand the erosion better than the ground around it.

Most mesas extend for only a few hundred feet, but there are larger ones, such as the Mesa Verde of Colorado, which is fifteen miles long and eight miles wide and rises two thousand feet above the lowland. Very small mesas are called buttes.

Mesabi Range

The Mesabi Range is a chain of high hills in northern Minnesota. Originally it was the most important iron-ore mining region in the United States and in the world. More than half the iron ore used in the United States was dug from the mines in the Mesabi Range. Much of the ore has now been used, but the mines are still very rich. The ore is so near the surface that the miners do not have to go underground, but work out in the open, digging out the ore with steam or electric shovels. This is called open-pit mining. The chief mining centers are at Hibbing and Virginia. The iron ore is shipped by freight cars to ports on Lake Superior, then it is carried in big ships across the Great Lakes to steel-producing cities.

The great iron-ore deposits in the Mesabi Range were first discovered in 1887.

Mesopotamia

Mesopotamia was an ancient country in western Asia. It was in the region between the Tigris and Euphrates rivers, the region of the modern country Iraq. The region is often called "the cradle of civilization" because many of the first known cities of the world were located there. There are separate articles about two of these cities, Ur and Babylon.

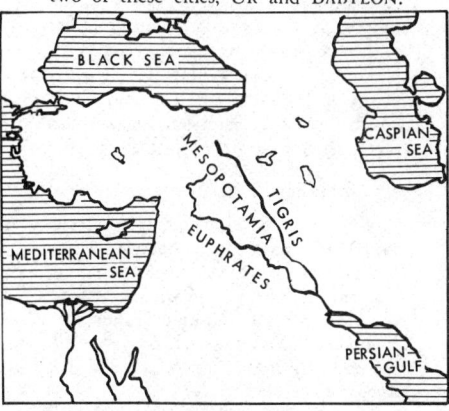

The region of ancient Mesopotamia is often called the "cradle of civilization."

Later, Mesopotamia fell under the Assyrian, Babylonian and Persian empires. The land of Mesopotamia is very dry, and one of the earliest irrigation systems was built there in ancient times. Today this

region has many important oil fields, and is also visited by scientists who study ancient peoples.

mesquite

The mesquite is a small tree or shrub that grows in Mexico, in parts of the West Indies and South America, and in the western part of the United States. The mesquite also is one of the most valuable trees on the Hawaiian islands, to which it was taken from America. The mesquite needs very little water and can grow well in deserts. It has a few scrubby leaves, sharp thorns, and pods that contain its seeds. The pods and seeds of the mesquite shrub are sweet and make a good food for cattle. A gum that comes from the mesquite is used to make candy.

When the mesquite shrub grows in a place where it gets plenty of water, it becomes a tall tree. The wood of the mesquite tree is hard and strong. It is used to make fences and railroad ties.

Messiah

In the Old Testament, there are many predictions that God will send a king who will save the Jewish people both from their sins and from those who oppress them. This king is called the Messiah or "anointed one." This refers to the Jewish custom of anointing a king by pouring oil over his head. The Messiah will be anointed, that is, made king, by God. The prophets of the Bible describe the Messiah as a king and ruler. He will be a descendant of King David. He will suffer for the people, but also bring them power and wealth. Pious Jews still wait for the Messiah. Christians recognize Jesus as the Messiah, and give him the title of Christ, which is the Greek word for Messiah.

metabolism

Metabolism is the process by which the body uses food and water and air to make its flesh, bones and other tissues and to stay alive. The body does this by a kind of burning process, and like any burning it produces heat.

Nearly all parts of the body take part in the metabolic process. If some of the parts of the body are not working properly, a person may become too fat or too thin, even though he is eating properly; or he may not have enough energy or strength. Doctors test this by giving a person a BASAL METABOLISM test, about which there is a separate article. See also the article on the HUMAN BODY.

metal and metallurgy

A metal is a substance that is solid, shiny, and hard. It is opaque, which means that you cannot see through it. You can hammer it into whatever shape you want and you can draw it into wire. It conducts heat and electricity very well. It melts at a high temperature, and it is usually quite heavy.

Not all of these things are true of all metals. Mercury is a metal but it is a liquid, not a solid. Sodium and potassium are metals but they are quite soft. Bismuth and vanadium are very brittle, tin, lead and zinc melt at temperatures that are not very high, and there are other exceptions.

Some metals, such as silver, gold, iron, and aluminum, are chemical *elements*. That is, they are among the more than one hundred basic substances of which everything in the world is made. Other metals are *compounds* or *alloys*. That is, they are made by combining two or more elements. Brass, copper and steel are examples of alloys.

PROCESS METALLURGY

The study of metals, how to get them from their ores, and how to use them, is called *metallurgy,* and the people who study metals for these purposes are called *metallurgists* or *metallurgical engineers*.

The first problem in metallurgy is to get metals from their ores. This is usually done by smelting the ores—heating them to a high temperature in a furnace, so that the metal will melt and separate from the rest of the ore. Along with the ore, certain materials called *fluxes* are put into the furnace. The fluxes combine with the nonmetallic part of the ore, leaving the metal free. Iron is smelted.

In other cases an electric current is used to separate the metal from a solution of the ore by means of the process called ELECTROLYSIS, about which there is a separate article. Aluminum is obtained by electrolysis.

Once the metal is free of its ore and melted, it is poured into molds, where it cools into rough, thick bars called *pigs*. The pigs are shipped to the users of the metal.

This work is called *process metallurgy*. There are two main branches of process metallurgy. *Ferrous* process metallurgy deals with the production of iron, steel, and their alloys. *Nonferrous* process metallurgy deals with the production of all other metals (the ones containing little or no iron) and their alloys. Chief among the nonferrous metals are copper, lead, zinc, aluminum, magnesium, chromium, tin, mercury, nickel, platinum, gold, and silver.

PHYSICAL METALLURGY

The user of a metal must know many things about it before he is certain he can use it. He wants to know how pure the metal is, how strong it is, whether it is as hard or soft as he wants it, whether it can be bent and shaped easily, whether it can be forged or machined. A metallurgist makes tests of all these properties of a metal and many others besides. For instance, he might find out how many hundreds or thousands of pounds of power are needed to pull apart a metal bar of a certain thickness. This would be testing the metal for its *tensile strength*. He might test a piece of metal for its hardness. To do this, he puts the metal in a Brinell machine, which presses a very hard steel ball into the metal. Then, with a microscope, he measures how big a dent the ball made in the metal being tested. All of this work is called *physical metallurgy*.

When metals are cast into different forms they sometimes have air bubbles in them. These weaken them. Physical metallurgists called *metallographers* examine castings (metal poured into molds to harden) with X-rays and microscopes to find the bubbles and to learn how to

prevent bubbles from forming in castings. Metallographers also examine metals to learn why they crack in places where they get a lot of bending or bumping. Such metal is said to be "fatigued."

TEMPERING AND ANNEALING

Tempering is treatment of metal by heat, to harden it or make it resist corrosion. Metallurgists heat the metal to a temperature they have found best for the hardness they want to get. They control the temperature by watching the changes in color as the metal is heated. First it becomes cherry red. Then, as it becomes hotter, it turns orange, yellow, and finally white. When the metal is the right color, the metallurgist suddenly cools it by plunging it into cold oil or cold salt water. Tempering may make the metal too hard or the sudden cooling may set up strains inside the metal. To avoid this, metallurgists heat the metal slowly to a temperature well below the tempering heat; then they cool it very slowly, sometimes taking days to do so. This process is called *annealing*.

A physical metallurgist also studies ways of putting protective surface coatings on metals by means of plating, galvanizing, or burnishing. *Powder metallurgy* is the making of articles by heating and pressing metal powders to the shape wanted, until the powder grains combine into a single piece of metal. One of the most important tasks of physical metallurgists is the planning, making, and testing of alloys to fit thousands of special requirements.

IF YOU WANT TO BE A METALLURGIST

If you want to become a metallurgist you should study scientific subjects, especially chemistry, physics, and mathematics.

To qualify as a metallurgist you will need at least a four-year college course leading to a Bachelor of Science (B.S.) degree in metallurgy, metallurgical engineering, or sometimes in chemical engineering. The first job you will get when you are just out of school will probably be that of laboratory assistant in testing or research, or an assistant in the operation of furnaces or electrolysis equipment, or an observer in smelting and refining operations.

metamorphosis

Metamorphosis is a change in the form of certain animals, especially insects and amphibians. It includes changes in habits. Many insects and animals change their habits as they grow older. Dragonflies live in water when they are young, and begin to fly only after they have grown larger. Butterflies and moths change from caterpillars, which eat solid food, into insects that suck juices from plants. The metamorphosis of many insects is very complicated and may have as many as six different stages as they change from eggs into full-grown insects. (Read also the article on BUTTERFLIES AND MOTHS.)

meteor

There are countless little pieces of iron and stone that move in the space between the planets. These pieces are called *meteorites*. Most of them are no bigger

than peas.

When one of the meteorites comes close to the earth, it falls to the ground. It comes in at a speed of about 30 or 40 miles a second. This is so fast that friction with the air makes the meteorite so hot that it burns. We see the burning as a *meteor*.

About 25,000,000 of these meteors fall every day, but they burn up while they are still 50 or 60 miles high. Bigger meteorites are closer to the earth when they burn up. The largest ones burst and drop fragments (little pieces) on the earth, usually in the woods or in a field or in the ocean. If a big piece fell on a person it would kill him, but so far it is not known that any person has been killed by a meteorite.

A meteor is sometimes called a *shooting star* or a *falling star*. Of course, it is not really a star falling. Stars do not fall.

Meteors can be seen on any clear evening. More can be seen on moonless nights, and there are more after midnight than before. Sometimes meteors come in great numbers. People call this a "meteor shower." These showers come every year. Most of them are in the fall, but the best one comes on August 11 each year.

meteorology

Meteorology is the scientific study of how and why the weather changes. People who study the weather are called *meteorologists*. They collect information, such as the changes in atmosphere (air) pressure, temperature, direction and strength of the wind, the amount of moisture in the air, and so on. From this, they sometimes can tell how the weather will change. For this reason, a meteorologist is often called a "weatherman."

methane

Methane is a gas that burns well and for this reason is an important fuel. It is a very important part of the mixture of gases burned in the gas furnaces that heat houses, cook foods on kitchen gas ranges, and make power for industrial plants.

If you stand in a marsh on a warm sunny day, you probably will see bubbles rising through the water from the mud.

The bubbles are methane. This explains why methane is sometimes called marsh gas. Methane is being made beneath the mud by the dead plants as they decay and have no contact with air. Plants and trees that died and were buried millions of years ago went on decaying and making methane. They formed pockets of gas that have become gas wells. Pipes are put down to these gas wells, and the gas is brought up to the surface of the ground and stored in tanks for use. When a gusher oil well spouts oil high in the air, the pressure that pushes the oil upward so hard is provided by methane gas that has formed above the underground pool of oil.

Methane is found deep in coal mines. Miners call it *firedamp*. To a miner, "damp" means gas or vapor, so firedamp means a gas that will catch fire. There is a separate article on FIREDAMP.

Methodist

A Methodist is a person who belongs to one of the Protestant Christian churches that grew out of the movement started by John Wesley. John Wesley was a minister in the Church of England about 225 years ago. With his brother, Charles Wesley, and a friend, George Whitefield, he resolved to lead a very strict life and to preach wherever he could find people to listen. All three lived a life of "rule and method." Their followers came to be called Methodists.

The special quality of Methodist preaching was enthusiasm. The Methodists lived strict lives and tried to follow the teaching of Jesus closely. Many of them became missionaries and preached their religion all over the world.

The first Methodists came to the United States before the Revolutionary War. In 1784, the Methodists left the Church of England and formed a separate Church. Francis Asbury was in charge of this Church in the United States. It was called the Methodist Episcopal Church of the United States of America. An episcopal church is one that has bishops. Many Methodists did not want bishops and broke away to form the Methodist Protestant Church. Several other Methodist churches were formed. In 1939, the

Methodists decided that they should unite again. They formed the Methodist Church, to which most Methodists now belong. The Methodist Church is the second-largest Protestant body in the United States, with nearly 13 million members. (The Baptists have the most members: over 25 million.) Methodists believe in one God; that Jesus was the son of God and died for men's sins; that each man must be saved by Jesus; and that the basic religious truths are found in the Bible. Methodists have built many homes and hospitals for orphans. They also have missions and they publish newspapers and magazines. The Methodist commission on world peace has worked hard to find ways to prevent wars.

Methuselah

Methuselah is the oldest man named in the Bible. He lived to be 969 years of age. His was one of the first names in the recorded history of man. Adam was 930 years old when he died. Noah, who was Methuselah's grandson, was 950 years old when he died. Historians and scholars of modern times have attempted to explain these figures, but do not agree. Today we speak of very old persons as "Methuselahs."

metric system

The metric system is a system of measurement based upon a unit of length called the *meter*. It was adopted by the French government in 1793, and is now used by nearly all scientists throughout the world.

A meter is about 39 inches long (more exactly, 39.37 inches). It was supposed to take ten million meters to cover the distance from the North Pole to the Equator when measured along a line running along the surface of the earth through Paris, France. A standard meter bar made of platinum-iridium alloy is kept under carefully controlled temperatures and pressures in a laboratory in Paris and serves as the standard for the entire world. Accurate copies of this standard meter are kept in other countries for use by scientists.

The metric system is a decimal system, which makes it possible to change one unit into another of the same kind by moving the decimal point a certain number of places. All units can be found by multiplying or dividing by 10. There are ten *decimeters* in a meter, 10 *centimeters* in a decimeter, and 10 *millimeters* in a centimeter. If we wish to change 52,624 centimeters to meters, we move the decimal point two places to the left, giving 526.24 meters, there being 100 centimeters in a meter.

There are 10 meters in a *dekameter*, 100 meters in a *hectometer*, and 1,000 meters in a *kilometer*.

The metric system also has volume and weight measures. The *liter* is the basic measure of volume. It corresponds roughly to our quart. For weight, the basic unit in the metric system is the *gram*. This is a very small unit, for it takes a thousand grams, called a *kilogram*, to balance with a little less than 2¼ pounds.

At first the metric system proved difficult to adopt. In France, just as in other countries of Europe, people were accustomed to think in terms of yards and

Left: The stone meteorite which fell in Arkansas is the largest that scientists have observed while it was falling. It weighs 845 pounds. *Right:* As the meteor enters the atmosphere, it begins to glow. When it reaches the denser atmosphere, friction makes it burn at a white heat. In most cases it breaks and burns up before it reaches the ground.

inches and pounds and quarts. The metric system did not fit in with the customs of the people. After nineteen years, during which most of the French people still used the old familiar weights and measures, Napoleon, who was then the French emperor, had to give up the metric system.

In 1837 France went back to the meter, this time to stay. Today, much of Europe and South America uses the metric system. The United States, as well as Great Britain, Canada, and Australia, uses the foot and pound system.

metronome

A metronome is a device used by musicians to help them keep time while playing a piece of music. It is a kind of pendulum or swinging clock that can be set in motion at any desired speed. A flat metal rod is held by a spring at the bottom of a wooden box. The spring causes it to move from side to side at a speed that does not change. Each time the rod completes one swing, it makes a clicking noise by which a musician can tell if he is playing too fast or too slow. The speed of the metronome can be changed by sliding a weight up or down on the rod. In an electric metronome, an electromagnet varies the speed. Often a sheet of music may have 100 MM written at the top, indicating that the metronome should be set for 100 clicks a minute.

Metternich, Prince von

Prince Clemens von Metternich was an Austrian statesman who was one of the most important men in Europe for a period of nearly fifty years. His career began about 150 years ago, when the French Revolution had begun a series of changes that were to throw Europe into a turmoil. Metternich was born in 1773 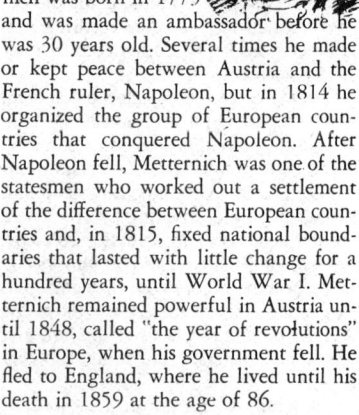 and was made an ambassador before he was 30 years old. Several times he made or kept peace between Austria and the French ruler, Napoleon, but in 1814 he organized the group of European countries that conquered Napoleon. After Napoleon fell, Metternich was one of the statesmen who worked out a settlement of the difference between European countries and, in 1815, fixed national boundaries that lasted with little change for a hundred years, until World War I. Metternich remained powerful in Austria until 1848, called "the year of revolutions" in Europe, when his government fell. He fled to England, where he lived until his death in 1859 at the age of 86.

Mexican War

From 1846 until 1848 the United States and Mexico were at war. The main reason for this war was that part of Texas was claimed by both Mexico and the United States. In 1837 Texas had become independent from Mexico, and in 1845 it had become part of the United States. The disputed territory was between the Nueces and Rio Grande rivers in what is now southern Texas. When Texas became part of the United States, Mexico announced that it would fight to keep this territory.

President James K. Polk sent United States troops to Texas to defend this territory. General Zachary Taylor, who later became a United States President, was in charge of these troops. Taylor had about 1,500 men under his command. He went first to Corpus Christi and then to the border of the Rio Grande, both places in the disputed territory. The Mexican government said he was in Mexican territory and warned him to leave. Instead Taylor built a fort there, which he called Fort Brown.

The Mexican forces attacked the fort, and in May, 1846, the Congress of the United States declared that a state of war existed between Mexico and the United States. The government called for 50,000 volunteers to fight the war, and raised $10,000,000 to pay for the war.

Mexico was not as strong as the United States and it had fewer good generals. Also it was having trouble with the people in its own country. Two United States armies, led by General Taylor in the north and General Winfield Scott in the south, fought the Mexicans in many battles, most of which the United States won.

In September of 1847 about 13,000 men under General Scott started a march against Mexico City, the capital of Mexico. Several fierce battles were fought before the United States forces finally captured the city. More than 2,000 Americans and about 7,000 Mexicans were killed in these battles. The capture of Mexico City, was the last important battle of the war, but it was not until February of 1848 that Mexico and the United States signed a peace treaty.

RESULTS OF THE WAR

While these battles had been going on, smaller United States forces had marched through other territories belonging to Mexico and had claimed them for the United States, particularly the territory that is now the state of California. The Mexican War was ended by a treaty signed at Guadalupe Hidalgo, a town in Mexico, and by this treaty these territories became the possessions of the United States.

The United States government paid Mexico $15,000,000 for what is today the states of California, Nevada, and Utah, and parts of New Mexico, Arizona, Colorado and Wyoming. The United States also agreed to withdraw its troops from the rest of Mexico's territory and to pay certain debts that Mexico owed to individual United States citizens. The boundary of Texas and Mexico was also decided upon.

The Mexican War was bitterly opposed by many people in the United States. Some people believed that the United States had deliberately gone to war with Mexico in order to win the valuable western territories, and that the United States had been wrong to fight such a weak country and take away so much of its territory.

Mexico

Mexico is a country in North America, on the southern border of the United States. It is more than 760,000 square

miles in area, almost three times as large as Texas, and over fifty million people live there, over four times as many as live in Texas. Many of the people of Mexico live and work as their ancestors did, in sleepy little villages. Visiting these villages is like going back many centuries in time. But parts of Mexico, for example the capital, Mexico City, are very modern. Many people go to Mexico for vacations because of the beautiful scenery, the fine vacation resorts, and the ancient remains of the highly civilized Maya and Aztec Indians who lived there long before the white men came.

THE PEOPLE WHO LIVE THERE

Almost two-thirds of the Mexican people are a mixed race. They have some ancestors who were American Indians and some who were Europeans from Spain. These people are called *mestizos*. A smaller group are pure-blooded Indians. They have not intermarried with the Spanish and have kept their own customs and ways of living. A still smaller group are those with no Indian blood. These are members of families that came from Spain, the United States, and Canada.

Most of the Mexican people belong to the Roman Catholic Church. They speak Spanish, but it is mingled with many Indian dialects. Many Mexicans also speak or understand English, especially in northern Mexico.

There is a great difference in the way various groups of Mexicans live. Some of the people are very rich. They live in beautiful Spanish-style houses. Usually such a house has white columns in front, an open balcony on its second story, and an inner courtyard, or *patio*, where flowers and vines grow, and where the family can gather to eat and entertain guests.

Most of the Mexicans, however, are very poor and don't live quite so well. But in recent years the life of the poor people has improved and there has been an important growth of a middle class, that is, of people who are in between the very rich and the very poor.

Outside the cities the houses are made of sun-dried bricks or of mud and straw, called adobe. These houses usually have no windows and are not very comfortable. The people have little furniture and sleep on the floor or on straw mats.

The Mexican farmer most often wears a pair of cotton trousers, a shirt, a wide-brimmed straw hat, and a pair of sandals called *huaraches*. A Mexican farm woman wears a blouse and a full-length skirt, with a shawl, called a *rebozo*, on her head. She usually goes barefooted.

In the large cities, such as Mexico City, however, many of the people live and dress much the same as they do in the United States.

The Mexicans love highly seasoned food. The most popular food in the country is the *tortilla*, a kind of dumpling made of corn. With it they eat boiled black beans, called *frijoles*. They rarely eat meat, though on holidays they celebrate with turkey, cooked with a highly spiced sauce.

The Mexicans love holidays and celebrations, and there are many festivals, called *fiestas*, during the year. For these celebrations, the people dress in bright-

A rodeo in Mexico.

colored costumes, and there are singing, dancing, and fireworks.

The famous Mexican *siesta*, or afternoon nap that everybody used to take after lunch, has almost vanished in the cities, where the people now have a workday more like the one in the United States, but many people still take their siesta in the afternoon.

HOW THE PEOPLE LIVE

More than half of the people in Mexico are farmers. Many of them still use methods and equipment like those of their ancestors. In recent years farmers have improved their land by using irrigation, and they now raise enough corn, sugar, and rice to feed the country. They also raise beans, tomatoes, and coffee, which are important parts of a Mexican's diet. Many of the farmers raise cattle.

Many people work in the valuable Mexican mines, which are among the richest in the world. Mexico produces more silver than any other country, and ranks second in the production of lead. There are also zinc, copper and gold mines. Mexico ranks seventh in the production of petroleum.

Some of the most popular products made by Mexicans are their beautiful silver jewelry, pottery, and leather goods. These are made by hand.

Children have to go to school in Mexico up to the age of 15. Fifty years ago, most of the people could not read or write, but now more than half the people have had some education.

WHAT KIND OF A PLACE IT IS

The northern part of Mexico is mostly a desert. Not many people live there. The central region is a high, level region. It is surrounded by the Sierra Madre mountain ranges, with their valuable mineral deposits. Most of the people in Mexico live in this region. The soil is fertile and the climate is healthful and cool because it is so high up. Mexico City, the capital of Mexico and one of the biggest cities in the world, is on the highest part of the plateau. It is noted for its beautiful scenery. People visiting Mexico City can see the towering snowcapped peaks of Popocatepetl and Ixtaccihuatl, two famous volcanoes.

The southern part of Mexico consists of low plains that are very hot and damp. Few people live in this region. A great deal of rain falls there and it is swampy and filled with tropical vines and underbrush. This region is infested with mosquitoes.

There are many wild animals in Mexico —wolves, bears, coyotes, and mon-

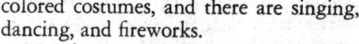

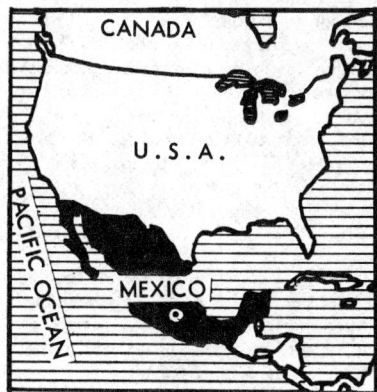

1. The ancient cathedral of Mexico City, off El Zocalo (the Square), nerve center of the city.

2. The Pyramid of the Sun, a monument of Aztec civilization.

3. The white houses and cobblestone street of a typical small Mexican village.

4. The 57,000-pound stone Aztec calendar in the National Museum. The Aztecs, who were skilled astronomers, made it in 1479.

5. The brilliantly decorated University of Mexico.

Pottery is one of the treasured handcrafts of Mexico. Skilled artists shape and decorate their work with colorful designs. Like many Mexican arts, the pottery combines Spanish and Indian styles in a very distinctive way.

keys, as well as many small fur-bearing animals. Mexico is also famous for its many bright-colored birds, many of which fly to Mexico from the north during the winter months.

Mexico has few navigable rivers, but there are many railroads and highways. Also there are many seaports, and steamships travel from Mexico to all the important ports in the world. A great river, the Rio Grande, is a boundary between Mexico and the United States.

THE GOVERNMENT OF MEXICO

Mexico is a republic. It has a President, who is elected for a six-year term. It also has a Legislature (like the United States Congress) composed of two houses, a Senate and a Chamber of Deputies. The Legislature makes the law. Members of the Senate are elected for a six-year term. Members of the Chamber of Deputies are elected for a three-year term. Mexico is divided into twenty-nine states, and each has its own government as do the states in the United States. All married citizens over 18 and all unmarried citizens over 21 have the right to vote.

CHIEF CITIES OF MEXICO

The leading cities of Mexico, with 1973 population estimates, are:

Mexico City, population, 8,541,070, the capital and largest city in Mexico. There is a separate article about MEXICO CITY.

Guadalajara, population 1,196,218, the second largest city. There is a separate article about GUADALAJARA.

Monterrey, population 1,177,361, the third-largest city, industrial center in the north.

Puebla, population 521,885, the fourth-largest city, railroad and commercial center, in the central part of the country.

Ciudad Juarez, population 436,054 fifth-largest city, on Rio Grande River.

IN THE PAST

When the white men came to Mexico, more than four hundred years ago, Mexico was ruled by the Aztec Indians. Their capital was where Mexico City now stands. The Aztecs had high buildings of beautifully carved stone, and they made beautiful sculpture and pottery. It is believed that about 100,000 Aztecs lived in the capital and more than six million Indians lived in Mexico.

The Spanish conqueror Hernando Cortez landed with his men in Mexico in 1519, and within two years he had conquered the country. He destroyed the Aztec temples and brutally put down all resistance. For the next three hundred years Mexico was ruled by the Spanish. Most of the people suffered under this rule because the Spanish were interested only in getting the mineral wealth from the country. The people were heavily taxed and had nothing to say about the making of the laws. The people grew more and more dissatisfied and wanted to be independent. Finally, in 1810, the first attempt to break away from Spain occurred. It was led by Miguel Hidalgo. The uprising was put down, and it was some years before Mexico became an independent country, but Hidalgo is considered the George Washington of his country, and the day of the uprising that he led on September 16 is still celebrated as a national holiday.

Other uprisings followed, and in 1821 Mexico was recognized as an independent country. The people did not know very much about ruling themselves, and there were many revolutions and continual unrest in the country. In 1846 Mexico had further trouble when it became involved in the Mexican War with the United States. As a result of the war, Mexico had to transfer to the United States a large territory, which became the states of California, Nevada, and Utah, and parts of Colorado, Wyoming, and New Mexico.

In 1860, Benito Juarez became the President of Mexico and he tried to improve the country. (There is a separate article about JUAREZ.) For many years afterward, Mexico was ruled by a powerful dictator, Porfirio Diaz. The people suffered under Diaz, though he improved the country in some ways. In 1910, the people overthrew Diaz, but again the country was in great confusion. Leaders rose and fell and no one was able to establish a strong and peaceful government. From 1934 to 1940 Lazaro Cardenas was President. He made many changes in the government and life of the Mexican people. It was the most successful and peaceful time Mexico had known.

During World War II, Mexico fought on the side of the Allies. It joined the United Nations after the war. Mexico is one of the countries toward which the United States is most friendly.

MEXICO. Area, 758,259 square miles. Population (1973 estimate) 50,830,000. Language, Spanish. Religion, chiefly Roman Catholic. Government, republic. Monetary unit, the peso, worth about 8 cents (U.S.). Flag, three vertical bands, green, white, and red; coat of arms on white band.

Mexico, Gulf of

The Gulf of Mexico is a large body of water along the southern coast of the United States and the eastern coast of Mexico. It is an "arm" of the Atlantic Ocean. Its waters are about 9 degrees warmer than those of the Atlantic Ocean because the Gulf Stream enters the Gulf of Mexico by way of the Yucatan Canal and raises the temperature of the water. The Gulf of Mexico is about 700,000 square miles in size, and is more than 12,000 feet deep at the deepest point.

The low, curving coastline of the Gulf of Mexico is smooth and has few good harbors. The most important ports are New Orleans, Mobile, Tampa, Galveston and Houston in the United States, Vera Cruz and Tampico in Mexico, and Havana in Cuba.

Mexico City

Mexico City is the capital and the largest city in Mexico. It is the highway, railroad and airline center of the country, and in recent years it has become an important manufacturing city. More than 8,000,000 people live in Mexico City. Many of them work in factories that make cigars and cigarettes, jewelry, textiles, and machinery. Many work in the big markets, to which products are shipped from other parts of the country.

Many of the people of Mexico City are Indians and mestizos (people who are of Indian and Spanish blood). They work in the factories and on the farms in the surrounding region. Many people from other countries live in Mexico City, and they manage businesses.

Mexico City is set in a beautiful region. It is built on a plateau, or high, level region, more than 7,000 feet high, surrounded by mountains. Because of this altitude, the climate of Mexico City is extremely pleasant and cool all year round, unlike many other parts of the country, which are very hot. The city is surrounded by fertile farm land and rich mines. In the distance are the famous snow-capped volcanoes of Popocatapetl and Ixtaccihuatl.

The city itself is a mingling of the old and the new. They are beautiful modern buildings and shops, tree-lined avenues, and parks filled with flowers. The most popular entertainment is the bullfights. There are ancient buildings and palaces. Mexican Indians sell their wares in open markets and on the streets as their ancestors did. One of the interesting but confusing things about Mexico City is that the streets change their names at almost every block, according to Spanish custom.

Mexico City is quite old and is believed to have been settled by the Aztec Indians more than six hundred years ago. It grew into an important Aztec city where many thousands lived. The Spanish, under Hernando Cortez, conquered the city in 1521, after much bitter fighting in which the Spaniards destroyed a large part of the city. Cortez rebuilt it and made it the capital of Mexico. Today Mexico City is the oldest capital in the Western Hemisphere. It is a popular vacation place, and thousands of people visit it every year.

MEXICO CITY, MEXICO. Population (1973 estimate) 8,541,070. Capital of Mexico. In the Federal District.

Miami and Miami Beach

Miami is the largest city in the state of Florida. It is on Biscayne Bay. It is one of the most popular vacation resorts in the United States. Some three million visitors go there each year to enjoy the sun, the white beaches, and the many outdoor sports.

Over 334,000 people live in Miami all year around, and many of them take care of the vacationists. Many of the people also work in factories making airplane parts, canned fruits and vegetables, and furniture. Miami is an important railroad and airline center, and the people ship large quantities of oranges, lemons, and other citrus fruits. It is a beautiful modern city, with skyscrapers, luxurious hotels, shops, and theaters. Tall palm trees grow along the wide boulevards. Miami was first settled in 1870, and became a city in 1896.

Miami Beach is an island that lies across Biscayne Bay from Miami. It is connected with Miami by several causeways, or roads across the water. Like Miami, it is a popular resort and has beautiful hotels, shops, and boulevards lined with palm trees. More than 87,000 people live there, but many thousands more go there each year on their vacations. Sixty years ago, Miami Beach was a wilderness with swamps and sand dunes. The swamps were filled in and the land area made larger. In 1917 it became a city, with a tiny population of 300. Today it is the eighth-largest city in Florida.

MIAMI, FLORIDA. Population (1970 cen-

sus) 334,859. County seat of Dade County. Founded in 1870.

MIAMI BEACH, FLORIDA. Population (1970 census) 87,072. Located on an island across Biscayne Bay from Miami.

mica

Mica is the name for a group of minerals that can be split into thin sheets that you can see through. Before the days of window glass, mica was used for windows. Because it is also fireproof, mica is still used for windows in stove and furnace doors. Valuable papers are covered with thin sheets of mica to protect them from loss by fire. Mica is an insulator; it can stop the passage of electric current better than any other material. It is used in all kinds of electrical, radio, and television apparatus to shield certain parts from the flow of electricity. Small flakes of mica are the "snow" you see under Christmas trees. If you see wallpaper with a sparkly sheen, it probably has powdered mica on its surface. Mica is elastic; you can bend it easily and it will snap back.

About four out of every hundred rocks have mica in them. The different kinds of mica and their colors are: muscovite (colorless), phlogopite (brown), biotite (black), lepidolite (violet), and fuchsite (yellow or green). Only muscovite and phlogopite are of much value. Muscovite is best because it is clear like glass, and it can be split into the largest sheets. Some muscovite sheets are as much as two feet long and two feet wide. Mica is sometimes called *isinglass*.

When mica is taken out of the ground, any rock attached to it is knocked off with a hammer. Then it is split with a hammer into thick slabs called *books*. The books are split into thin sheets with a knife. In the United States, mica is mined in the Appalachian and Rocky Mountains. Two other countries that mine much mica are India and Brazil. In 1960 the United States mined 119,929 tons of mica, more than any other country produced.

Michael, Saint

St. Michael is an angel described in the Bible as a great fighter. Artists have painted him as a prince with a great sword, with which he fights against and conquers Satan. The French warrior and saint, Joan of Arc, saw a vision of St. Michael. St. Michael's feast day is called Michaelmas in England, and is celebrated on September 29. See the article on ANGELS.

Michael, King of Rumania

Michael is the name of the last king of Rumania, before it was taken over by a Communist government in 1947. In Rumanian, his name is Mihai. Twice Michael was king as a boy. He was born in 1921 and became king at the age of 6 because his father, Carol II, had given up his right to the throne. Three years later, Carol reclaimed the throne, but in 1940 Carol gave up the throne again and Michael became king at the age of 19. It is difficult to say how good a king Michael was, because he did not have much power. From 1940 to 1944, Rumania was controlled by a fascist party allied with Nazi Germany, and after 1944 the Communists of Russia controlled the country. In 1947 the Com-

munists made Michael abdicate (resign as king) and he left the country. In 1948, Michael married Princess Anne, a descendant of a branch of the Bourbon family, which also was a royal family without any country to rule over.

Michelangelo

Michelangelo was an Italian sculptor, painter, poet, and architect who lived more than five hundred years ago. He was the most famous artist of his time, and even today there is no greater figure in the history of art. Popes, kings and princes begged for the honor of having work done by his hand. His poetry, much of which was deeply religious, was greatly admired. Michelangelo felt himself to be first of all a sculptor.

His full name was Michelangelo Buonarotti. He was born in Caprese, a town in Italy, in 1475. He was the son of a public official in Florence. As was the custom in those days, the baby was given

In his self-portrait, Michelangelo captured his own deep vision, which enabled him to create many of the most beautiful paintings and statues the world has known.

to the care of a nurse. This nurse was the wife of a stonemason, and Michelangelo said he drank in his love of sculpture with his milk. At the age of 13 he was apprenticed (sent as a pupil) to the Ghirlandaio brothers, who were noted artists, and in their studio the boy painted his first picture. When he was 15, some of his early sculptures came to the attention of Lorenzo de' Medici, a great patron of art who was practically the ruler of Florence. Lorenzo invited Michelangelo to live in his house, and there the young man became acquainted with most of the leading men of literature and art. He lived there for two years, until the death of Lorenzo. Only two works of these student days survive, but they show his genius.

In 1496 Michelangelo went to Rome, where he stayed five years. During this period he created the *Pietà* in St. Peter's Church, which immediately brought him fame as the greatest sculptor of his day. The *Pietà* is a sculpture of the dead Jesus in the arms of his sorrowful mother Mary at the foot of the cross.

When Michelangelo returned to Florence he was commissioned to carve a

On one of the walls of the Sistine Chapel in the Vatican is Michelangelo's conception of the Last Judgment. This detail from the painting gives an idea of the great power of his work.

huge statue 18 feet high from a single block of marble, to commemorate a military victory of the city. This was a statue of David from the Biblical story in which David slew the giant Goliath. It was the last work of Michelangelo's early style, in which he depicted all his subjects with great realism and naturalism. From that time he drew on his vivid imagination as much as on life.

PAINTING THE SISTINE CHAPEL

In 1508 Michelangelo began what was to be his greatest work of painting. He was ordered by Pope Julius II to decorate the ceiling of the Sistine Chapel in the Vatican. He did the painting almost without help and it took four years. A large part of the time he worked lying on his back on the scaffolding. The great painting is divided into many sections, showing scenes from the Bible such as the creation, the fall of man, the deluge or flood, and many other subjects.

After the death of Julius II, Michelangelo carved a great statue of Moses, perhaps one of his most famous sculptures, for the Pope's tomb.

When he was 60 years old, another Pope, Paul III, commissioned him to paint more frescoes in the Sistine Chapel. The greatest of these was a painting to cover the entire altar wall. It was called *The Last Judgment,* and it contained more than a hundred figures, all larger than life.

The last years of Michelangelo's life were mostly devoted to architecture. In 1546 he was appointed chief architect of St. Peter's Church in Rome. He designed the dome of St. Peter's. He took no pay for this position, believing it his religious duty to devote himself to the Church. Michelangelo died in 1564.

Michigan

Michigan is one of the north central states in the United States. Its nickname is the "Wolverine State." The reason for this is not known. Wolverines were never found in this region.

Michigan is a big and busy state on the Great Lakes. Three-fifths of all the

automobiles in the world are manufactured in Michigan, and it is the leading state of the United States in furniture-making. Michigan also ranks first in the production of cherries and second in the production of iron ore. The state gets its name from Lake Michigan, which comes from an Indian word meaning "great water."

Michigan ranks 22nd in size among the states, with 56,818 square miles. In population it ranks 7th, with more than 8,875,000 people living there. It became a state in 1837, and was the 26th state admitted to the United States. The capital is Lansing.

THE PEOPLE OF MICHIGAN

The first settlers in Michigan were French fur trappers and traders, who came there almost three hundred years ago. Much later, people from England, Scotland, and the eastern United States settled in the region. As the lumber and mining industries grew, immigrants from

all over Europe came to work there. In the past forty years, many more people from Italy, Russia, Poland, and other European countries, and many Negroes who had been farmers in the South, came to work in the automobile industry and other factories. About half the people in Michigan are American-born.

Almost three-quarters of the people live in big cities and work in huge automobile factories and factories that make iron and steel, machinery, furniture, chemicals, and breakfast foods. Many people are farmers and produce dairy products, cattle, and large crops of cherries, apples, pears, and grapes. Others work in the rich iron and salt mines, and many earn their living by catching lake trout, whitefish, herring, and many other kinds of fish in the Great Lakes.

The Roman Catholics are the largest religious group in Michigan. There are also many Methodists, Baptists, and Lutherans.

WHAT MICHIGAN IS LIKE

Michigan is divided into two parts by Lake Michigan and Lake Huron, so that it forms two peninsulas (land almost, but not wholly, surrounded by water). The Upper Peninsula is low in the east, but rises to beautiful mountains, covered with pine forests, in the western part. There are many fine lakes and rivers, and valuable iron and copper mines in this part of the state. The Lower Peninsula

is where most of the farmers raise their crops. Most of the important industrial cities are in the Lower Peninsula.

More than a hundred years ago, Michigan had many beavers, otters, and muskrats, but they were hunted so greedily for their furs that today hardly any remain.

The climate of Michigan is very pleasant on the whole, since the state is surrounded by four of the Great Lakes. Many summer resorts have been built along the lakes because of the cool breezes, and in winter the lakes keep the region from getting too cold. In the Upper Peninsula the winters are more severe. The average temperature in Michigan in winter is 20 degrees and in summer is about 69 degrees.

The lakes and many rivers in Michigan have always provided excellent transportation. The Grand River in the Lower Peninsula is the longest in the state. The Great Lakes have long been the great waterway to the west. Railroads and highways reach almost all parts of the state, and there are airports in all the big cities.

THE GOVERNMENT OF MICHIGAN

Michigan, like most other states, is governed by a Governor and a Legislature. The Governor is elected for a two-year term. The Legislature is composed of two houses, a Senate and a House of Representatives. The members of both houses are elected for a two-year term. Judges are elected for an eight-year term. The capital is Lansing. There are 83 counties.

Everyone has to go to school between the ages of 6 and 16. There are about 2,165,000 pupils enrolled in the state's public elementary and high schools, and many more in the colleges, universities and other schools of higher learning. Among the principal colleges and universities are:

University of Michigan, at Ann Arbor. Enrollment, 38,328 in 1970 (co-ed).

Michigan State University of Agriculture and Applied Science, at East Lansing. Enrollment, 44,274 in 1970 (co-ed).

University of Detroit, at Detroit. Enrollment, 8,350 in 1970 (co-ed).

Wayne State University, at Detroit. Enrollment, 34,924 in 1970 (co-ed).

Western Michigan University, at Kalamazoo. Enrollment, 19,247 in 1970 (co-ed).

CHIEF CITIES OF MICHIGAN

The leading cities of Michigan, with populations from the 1970 census, are:

Detroit, population 1,511,482, the largest city in the state. There is a separate article about DETROIT.

Grand Rapids, population 197,649, the second-largest city, manufacturing center known for its furniture, in the southern part of the state.

Flint, population 193,317, the third-largest city, automobile-manufacturing center, in the southern part of the state.

Lansing, population 131,546, the state capital and fifth-largest city. There is a separate article about LANSING.

MICHIGAN IN THE PAST

The first white man to visit the Michigan region was probably Étienne Brulé, a French explorer, who went there more than three hundred years ago. He found vast forests filled with fur-bearing animals, and soon French fur-trappers and

traders followed him. The first permanent settlement was made by Father Marquette at Sault Sainte Marie, in 1688. Detroit was founded in 1701 by Antoine Cadillac. Other villages soon grew up.

After the French and Indian Wars, about two hundred years ago, the Michigan territory was given to the British. The Indians living there were not friendly to the British settlers, and they attacked the British forts and often massacred the people.

Michigan was given to the United States after the Revolutionary War, but the Indians continued to attack the settlements until the warlike tribes were defeated by General Anthony Wayne.

For a while Michigan was part of the NORTHWEST TERRITORY, about which there is a separate article. Then it became a separate territory, and in 1837 it finally became a state.

The people of the state discovered the great wealth they had in the woodlands and mountains. They rapidly cut down

Coast Guard Photo

Michigan is bordered by four of the Great Lakes. The lighthouse at Spectacle Reef in Lake Huron warns lake boats of danger.

the valuable forests with no thought to the future, and they mined the copper and iron ores. Industries thrived and the population of Michigan grew enormously, but about forty years ago the state realized it had not been wise to use up its natural resources so thoughtlessly. Forests had been stripped and the wild life had almost entirely disappeared. Now there is a program of conservation to protect Michigan's natural resources.

PLACES TO SEE IN MICHIGAN

Hiawatha National Forest, 882,013 acres, near Shingleton, in the northwest, on U.S. Route 2. Beautiful woods and scenic spots.

Isle Royal National Park, 133,838 acres, a forested island, the largest in Lake Superior; distinguished for its wilderness and great moose herd.

Fort Custer, six miles northeast of Battle Creek, in the south, on State Highway 89. An important military camp.

Automobile plants in Detroit, Dearborn, and other cities. Tours are conducted through these big plants where automobiles are made.

Sparks Illuminated Cascades, at Jackson, in the south, on U.S. Route 12. A group of waterfalls beautifully lighted at night.

Greenfield Village, at Dearborn, in the east, south of U.S. Route 12. An "old American" village, built by Henry Ford, containing many historic buildings, including the laboratory where Thomas A. Edison worked.

Pictured Rocks, about 8 miles northeast of Munising, on State Highway 28. Magnificent cliffs, beautifully colored and in strange shapes.

Dutch settlements, one named Holland, along Lake Michigan. People have continued the Dutch tradition; farming carried on in typical Dutch style; tulip festival held each year.

MICHIGAN. Area, 56,818 square miles. Population (1970 census) 8,875,083. Capital, Lansing. Nickname, the Wolverine State. Motto, *Si Quaeris Peninsulam Amoenam Circumspice* (If You Seek a Pleasant Peninsula, Look Around You). Flower, apple blossom. Bird, robin. Song, "Michigan, My Michigan." Admitted to Union, January 26, 1837. Official abbreviation, Mich.

Michigan

Michigan is the name of one of the most popular card games played in the United States. It is played also in many other countries. There are several other names by which the game is known: Stops, Boodle, Newmarket, Saratoga, and Chicago.

The game is played with a standard pack of 52 cards. There is a *layout* on the table, made of four cards taken from another pack of cards: any ace, king, queen and jack, but they must be of different suits. These are called the *boodle* cards. Each player uses chips or matches as counters. Three to eight players may play. Before the deal, the dealer puts two chips on each boodle card and each other player puts one chip on each boodle card.

The dealer deals the cards one at a time, face down, to each player and to one extra hand called the *widow*. The widow belongs to the dealer. If he does not like his hand (the cards dealt to him) he may throw it away and take the widow instead. If he wants to keep his hand, he may sell the widow to the highest bidder. A player who owns the widow must throw his own hand away before looking at the widow.

The player at the dealer's left then puts down a card from his hand. This is called a *lead*. He must lead the lowest card in the suit he selects, but may select any suit. Any player who holds the next-higher card of the same suit must then play it, and so on. The player must announce the card he plays. For example, the leader puts down the three of spades, saying, "Three of spades." Whoever holds the four of spades must then play

it and say, "Four of spades." The same is true for the holder of the five, the six, and so on. When nobody has the next card in order, it means that the missing card is in the widow or dead hand. The player who played the last card then leads.

When a player plays a card that matches one of the boodle cards, he takes all the chips on that boodle card. When a player gets rid of his last card, play ends. Each other player pays him one chip for every card that player has left in his hand.

Michigan, Lake

Lake Michigan is the third-largest of the Great Lakes, which lie between the United States and Canada. It is the only one of these lakes entirely within the United States. It is 22,400 square miles in size, and 923 feet deep at the deepest point. Lake Michigan borders most of the state of Michigan, and part of the states of Wisconsin, Ilinois, and Indiana.

Lake Michigan often has sudden and dangerous storms, but a great deal of shipping is carried on there. Boats bring huge amount of iron ore, coal, grain, and lumber to ports along its shores. The southern ports are open all through the year, but the northern ports are closed with ice for four months in the winter. The most important port on Lake Michigan is Chicago, on the southwest shore. Other important ports are Gary, Indiana, and Milwaukee, Wisconsin. Lake Michigan is part of the vast waterway system in the United States that links the lake with the Atlantic Ocean and the Gulf of Mexico.

microfilm

Microfilming is a way of photographing important papers so that the pictures can be used in place of the originals. A number of photographs are recorded on one long strip of film. The pictures on the film are too small to read, but they are projected onto a screen, or viewed in a special device called a *reader,* and are magnified so that they can be read easily. The film can also be developed as a photograph of the original paper.

Microfilming is used to make a permanent record of many important historical documents. Often these are on paper that

is so old it will fall apart if handled. Students look at the micrbfilm picture instead.

Many business firms save space by microfilming important letters, contracts, checks, and other papers. Hundreds of such papers, which would occupy a whole file drawer, can be microfilmed on a strip of film that takes up only a few inches of a desk drawer. Librarians save a great deal of valuable space by microfilming newspapers.

Engineers microfilm plans to save the space that the bulky original drawings take up. The microfilm can be kept for protection against possible loss of the originals by fire.

micrometer

A micrometer is an instrument for measuring objects as thin as a ten-thousandth of an inch. The word means "measurer of small things."

The idea for the micrometer was first thought of by a French astronomer, William Gascoigne, in 1638. He was interested in measuring the size of the sun, the moon, and various planets. To do this, he placed two metal bars, or indicators, outside the eyepiece of the telescope. By turning a screw connecting them, Gascoigne could move the indicators nearer together or farther apart until they just enclosed the image of the planet he saw in the eyepiece of his telescope. Then he would measure the distance between the indicators, and, using other information, could figure out the width of the planet.

However, to do this properly Gascoigne had to measure the distance between the indicators very accurately. This could not be done by an ordinary ruler. In fact, no ruler could be made with marks fine enough to give him the accurate measurements that he needed.

Gascoigne then came up with the idea that is the basis of the micrometer. He counted the number of times he had to turn the screw to open the indicators from a fully closed position. First he counted the number of threads or cuts in the screw in a distance of one inch. By dividing this number into one inch, he found out the distance between threads. In this way, he knew how far the indicators would move for every complete turn of the screw. If the screw was given only part of a turn, the indicators would move only a fraction of this distance.

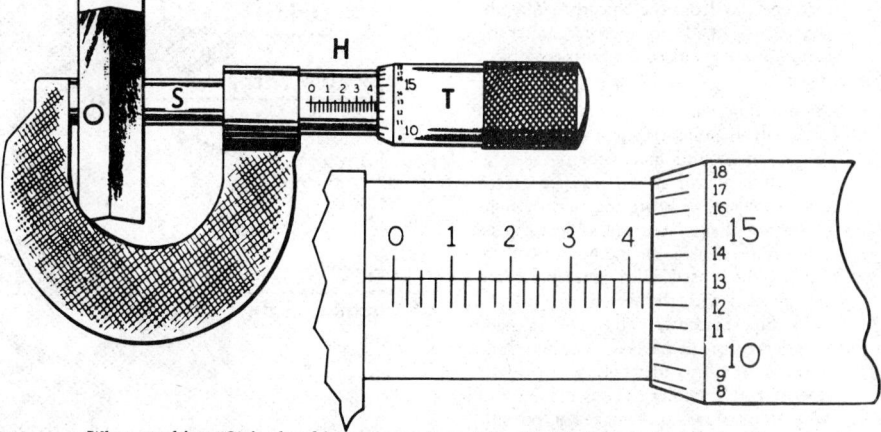

When an object (O) is placed in a micrometer and the thimble (T) is twisted so that the object is held between the ends of the spindle (S), the markings on the hub (H) and thimble give the exact thickness of the object. Each small division on the hub represents 25 thousandths of an inch, and each small division around the thimble represents one thousandth.

Gascoigne's idea was improved upon by another Frenchman, several hundred years later, so that distances could be measured quickly and easily without figuring out the distances between screw threads. The screw has 40 threads to an inch and the barrel that turns the screw has 25 evenly spaced marks around it. Turning the barrel to one of the marks moves the screw one-thousandth of an inch.

The object whose width is to be measured can be clamped in the micrometer as in a vise, and its width can be read directly off the barrel.

microscope

A microscope is an instrument that is used to help see things that are too small to be seen with the naked eye. With the microscope, scientists can see tiny organisms that cause diseases, examine the structure of metals, observe the behavior of small insects and plants, and so on. This has helped them to make many important discoveries in science.

A simple microscope is a single magnifying glass. The microscopes used by scientists in the laboratory contain two or more magnifying glasses in a tube, and are called *compound microscopes*. They can magnify things (make them appear larger) as much as 1,000 times. The microscope that is bought for use in the home usually can magnify 50 to 100 times.

The glass at the top of the tube into which you look is called the *eyepiece*. The glass at the bottom of the tube, directly above the object to be observed, is called the *objective*. The object is placed on a glass *slide*, which rests on a platform below the objective and above a small movable mirror. The mirror directs light onto the object.

The object is magnified by the objective and then further magnified by the eyepiece. The magnifying power of the microscope is the magnifying power of the objective multiplied by the magnifying power of the eyepiece. If the objective makes an object seem 6 times larger, and the eyepiece makes it seem 3 times larger, the magnifying power of the microscope is said to be 18 diameters, written 18✕.

You can make an object appear larger in a microscope by turning the barrel of the eyepiece so that the eyepiece is moved farther away from the objective. The object can be made to appear smaller by bringing the eyepiece closer to the objective.

Sometimes an object is stained with dyes, which helps brighten certain parts of the object and makes them easier to see. Often a drop of oil may be placed on the object, to bring the rays of light closer together so that the object can be seen more clearly. In many cases ultraviolet light is used. Ultraviolet light cannot be seen with the naked eye. In such cases the eyepiece and objective are made of quartz instead of glass, because glass absorbs the ultraviolet light while quartz does not. Ultraviolet light is made up of very short waves and makes it possible to see objects too small to be seen in ordinary light.

The *resolving* power of a microscope is its ability to make the fine details of an object show up clearly upon magnification. Occasionally an object may be magnified so much that its details appear fuzzy. This is called *empty magnification* and occurs when the magnification has gone beyond the resolving power of the microscope. The magnification must be reduced until the object is clear (*in focus*). This point is called *useful magnification*.

Sometimes a microscope may have two and even three objectives in the bottom of the tube. These have different magnifying powers and can be swung into position above an object when desired. Only one objective can be used at a time.

A *binocular microscope* has two eyepieces side by side, so that it is possible to look at an object with both eyes. Such microscopes are constructed in much the same way as BINOCULARS, about which there is a separate article.

THE ELECTRON MICROSCOPE

An *electron microscope* is a very high-powered microscope. Instead of glass lenses, it uses magnets. Also, special waves of electrons (particles of negative electricity), called *DeBroglie waves*, are used instead of ordinary light. These waves are focused by the magnets in the same way as light is focused by the objective and eyepiece in the optical microscope. The object then appears on a special screen, or is made to fall on a photographic plate. About 30,000 volts of electricity are required to operate an electron microscope. A modern electron microscope is about the size of a desk and is operated by a control panel set into the top. It can magnify objects as high as 100,000 times, so it is about 100 times as powerful as most optical microscopes.

The electron microscope is mostly used in medical and biological research. It has been very useful in understanding the causes of many diseases such as influenza and the common cold.

Midas

Midas was a king in the legends, or stories, told by the ancient Greeks thousands of years ago. He was king of a Greek country called Phrygia. In return for a favor to the god Bacchus, or Dionysus, he was told that any wish he made would be granted. Midas asked that everything he touched might turn to gold. He was granted his wish, but found he could no longer eat, because even his food

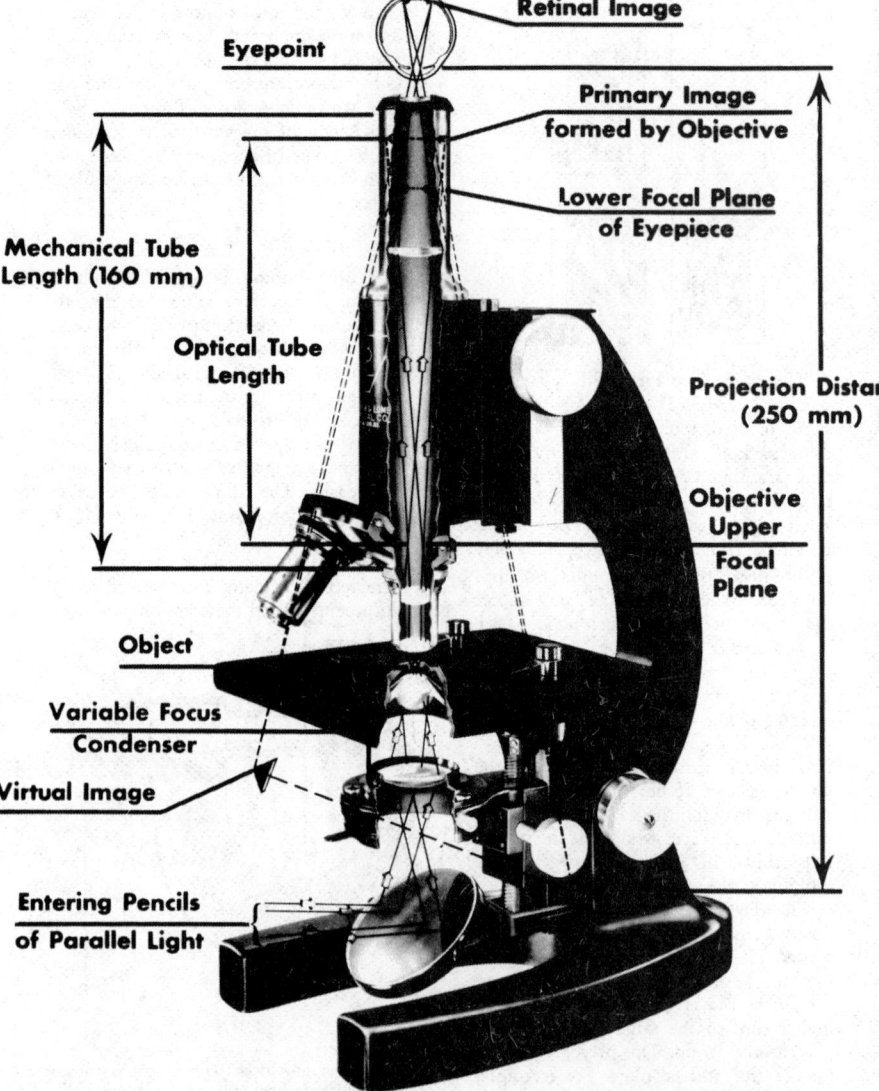

Bausch & Lomb

The diagram shows the path of light from the point where it enters a dynoptic microscope through the eyepoint to the retina, where the mental image of the object is formed.

turned to gold. He almost starved, and begged Bacchus to take back his power. Bacchus instructed him to bathe in the waters of the River Pactolus. This removed the power, and made the sands of the river turn to gold.

In another story, Midas judged a musical contest between the gods Pan and Apollo. Midas decided in favor of Pan. This made Apollo so angry he turned Midas's ears into the ears of an ass (donkey). Midas wore a cap to hide his ears, but the servant who cut his hair saw them. The servant was afraid to tell any one, but he dug a hole in the ground and whispered into it, "King Midas has ass's ears." Reeds grew up there, and legend says that whenever the wind blew over the reeds they whispered those words.

Midas is supposed to have killed himself by drinking the blood of an ox.

Middle Ages

The Middle Ages were a period of about a thousand years in the history of the world. This period began at about the time when the city of Rome, capital of the mighty Roman Empire, fell to Germanic invaders. This was in the year 476. The period ended at about the time that Columbus discovered America, in 1492.

While the Romans ruled most of the civilized part of Europe, laws were enforced and art and literature were active. During the Middle Ages, there was no strong government in many parts of Europe and the strongest fighters could rob or rule their neighbors. People were so busy protecting themselves that few of them had time for learning. For this reason the Middle Ages are often called the Dark Ages. Only the Christian Church, in its abbeys and monasteries, kept learning alive.

The Middle Ages were the time of the CRUSADES, and of FEUDALISM and KNIGHTHOOD, about which there are separate articles.

The Middle Ages ended with a new birth of learning, called the RENAISSANCE, about which there is a separate article.

midnight sun

Near the North Pole, the sun shines all day during the summer. The "land of the midnight sun" is a region in the far northern part of Norway and Sweden, so near to the North Pole that in summer the sun may still be shining at midnight. You can read more about this region in the article on LAPLAND. Because of its pleasant summer climate, the land of the midnight sun attracts many tourists.

Midway

Midway is the name of two tiny islands in the central Pacific Ocean, about four thousand miles from the western coast of the United States. The islands are known mostly because the United States Navy won a great victory in a sea battle off Midway early in World War II. Some experts think this was the most important battle of the war.

The Midway Islands came to belong to the United States after the Spanish-American War in 1898. Early in World War II Japan tried to capture Midway but failed. At Pearl Harbor the Japanese

had almost destroyed American naval power in the Pacific, and the American Navy did not have enough strength left there to defend Hawaii or even the Pacific Coast of the United States. Japan sent a large fleet to take advantage of this weakness. What the Japanese did not know was that United States naval cryptographers had broken the Japanese code and knew exactly what the Japanese were going to do. When the Japanese fleet approached Midway it was heavily bombed by American torpedo bombers. At the same time Japanese aircraft bombed the small American fleet that had been gathered together and sent out to meet the Japanese. For three days this air battle continued, until finally the Japanese fleet was forced to turn back, without having exchanged a single shot with the American fleet. In this battle the Japanese lost four carriers, one cruiser, three destroyers, 275 planes, and about 5,000 men. The Americans lost one carrier, one destroyer, 150 planes, and about 300 men.

mignonette

The mignonette is a plant that first grew in the northern part of Africa. It is now raised in gardens in Europe and the United States. The mignonette is an annual, which means that it must be planted every year. It is a hardy plant and grows best in a cool soil that is not too rich. It grows to be about one foot high. The plant has thick, dark green leaves and lovely sprays of greenish, white, or pale yellow flowers. The flowers have a very sweet smell. The mignonette usually blooms in June. Some people plant seeds again in July and then the mignonette blooms a second time before the first frost in the fall.

migration

Migration is the traveling of a large group of animals from one place to another. In the early times of men's life on earth, thousands of years ago, entire tribes of men would leave the place where they were living and travel to find a new home where it might be easier to raise vegetables for food and kill animals for meat and skins. Such migrations sometimes took many years, in which the people who began the migration would die and their children and grandchildren would be the first to reach the new home. The American Indians probably populated the entire Western Hemisphere by great migrations from Asia. The Germanic peoples spread over Europe by the migrations of their tribes from one part of the continent to another.

Animals of many kinds migrate. Grasshoppers or locusts by the millions leave one place and fly to another. Fish in large numbers leave a river in which they are born, swim hundreds of miles through the ocean to a new home, and later return to the same spot in the same river to lay eggs and produce a new generation of fish that will migrate just as they did. Birds migrate when they change their homes from a northern land to a southern one in the winter and from the southern one back to the northern one in the summer. Scientists have not found the reason for the migration of many insects and fishes, and not even the migration of

the birds can be explained by their change to a warmer climate.

Milan

Milan is the second-largest city in Italy. It is in northern Italy, and is the most important commercial city and the largest railroad and financial center in the country. About 1,680,000 people live in Milan. They work in big factories that make automobiles, furniture, musical instruments, and textiles. Many also work in publishing houses. Like most Italians, the people of Milan love music, and the La Scala Opera House in Milan is the most famous in the world.

Milan has many beautiful buildings and churches, though during World War II many of them were destroyed by bombings. The great cathedral of Milan

Italian State Tourist Office

Milan has many beautiful buildings built hundreds of years ago. The General Hospital, with its arched columns and delicate sculptures, dates back to the Renaissance.

was only slightly damaged. Milan has wide, modern streets, fine libraries and schools, and valuable collections of paintings and sculpture that attract visitors every year. The most famous work of art is Leonardo da Vinci's *The Last Supper*.

Milan is an ancient city, more than two thousand years old. It became a powerful and wealthy city under the Romans, and in later centuries was ruled by the Huns, Germans, Spaniards, and Austrians. It became part of Italy in 1859. In 1945, during World War II, Benito Mussolini, the dictator of Italy, was executed in Milan.

MILAN, ITALY. Population (1973 est.) 1,687,265. Capital of the province of Milan. On the Olona River.

mildew

Mildew is a fungus, or simple kind of plant, that feeds on dead matter or on other plants. When it eats other plants it causes a disease that often destroys the plants. (You can read more about this in the article on FUNGUS.)

There are two kinds of mildew. Downy mildew feeds on the leaves of grapes, lettuce, onions, and other plants. It forms white patches on the leaves of these plants and they shrivel up and die. Powdery mildew makes a kind of cobweb

growth on the leaves and sometimes on the stems of many different flowers and fruit plants. Roses, lilac bushes, and cherry and peach trees are some of the plants that are often attacked by mildew. Tiny rootlike threads pierce the leaves of the plant and gather the food.

Housewives know that mildew also attacks cloth, paper, and foods. Mildew grows best in places where there is very little sunlight and where it is damp. People do not store books and papers and clothes in damp, dark places for this reason. There are many poisonous sprays and powders that people now use to protect plants and kill mildew. The tiny organisms from which mildew grows are carried from place to place by the air.

Military Academy, U.S.

The United States Military Academy is a special college where young men study to become officers in the United States Army. It is located high above the Hudson River at West Point, New York, and is generally referred to simply as "West Point." West Point graduates are commissioned as second lieutenants, and receive a degree of B.S. (bachelor of science). Enrollment in the spring of 1962 was 2,444, and there were 433 teachers, most of whom were officers.

Men between 17 and 22 years of age, unmarried, with a good school and character record, of sound body, and between 5 feet 6 inches and 6 feet 4 inches in height, are eligible to enter West Point. The course is four years, and students—who are called *cadets*—do 'not have the usual college summer vacations. They have occasional "leaves," or short vacations, but are under strict discipline all the time. A cadet receives an allowance of $111.15 per month plus $1.35 a day for rations. From their pay cadets are required to buy their uniforms, textbooks, and some incidental items. Entering cadets must deposit $300 to cover the initial cost of uniforms and equipment.

To get into West Point, a youth must first receive an *appointment*. These are allotted as follows: eight from each state; four from each Congressional district and from Puerto Rico; six from the District of Columbia; two from the Panama Canal Zone; 172 from the United States at large; and 180 from the regular Army and Air Force and Reserves. Others may be appointed from among sons of men who won the Medal of Honor, and from foreign countries.

HOW APPOINTMENTS ARE MADE

Various officials, governmental bodies and military organizations have the privilege of making appointments, or naming candidates, for West Point. There are also *competitive* nominations, given to those who do best in certain tests. All persons named must pass regular examinations to become cadets. These are mental, medical, and physical.

Noncompetitive nominations are made by: Members of the House of Representatives, four each; Senators, four each; the Vice President, three; District of Columbia, six; Panama Canal Zone, two; and Puerto Rico, four. For each West Point vacancy four men may be named, a *principal,* and a *first, second* and *third*

alternate. If the principal fails to qualify, the first alternate tries, followed by the others in order. Young men seeking appointments should apply to their own Senators or Congressmen, or to their territorial government.

The competitive appointments are awarded to youths who make the best scores in the West Point Achievement Tests in Mathematics and English and the West Point Aptitude Test. These tests are held on the first Tuesday in March, when all other West Point examinations begin. Enlisted men in the Army

U.S. Army Photo

Cadets at the United States Military Academy, wearing full-dress uniform, march with sharp precision. The future officers receive very strict training.

and Air Force, regular and reserve, may win 180 such appointments. The President makes 89 other appointments from among the sons of military men. For sons of deceased veterans, forty appointments are reserved. Forty others go to Honor military and naval schools. Up to twenty may go to Latin American youths, and one to a Filipino. Information about these may be obtained from The Adjutant General of the United States Army, Washington 25, D.C.

During the first or freshman year, cadets are called *plebes*. Then they become third (sophomore) year, second (junior) year, and first (senior) year men. They live in dormitories, which they must keep clean and neat. They study hard, drill, and also have strenuous gymnastics plus the choice of seventeen sports. In studying, science takes up more than half of the curriculum. West Point uses the "honor system," under which the cadets themselves make sure all rules are obeyed.

WEST POINT IN THE PAST

The Academy was officially established on March 16, 1802, at the key military fortress of West Point. It was opened on July 4, 1802. There were two reasons why it was considered necessary. During the Revolutionary War the colonists had depended largely on foreigners to drill and lead many of their soldiers. They had also been obliged to use foreign engineers and artillerymen. President Washington wrote in his 1797 message to Congress: "However pacific

(peaceful) the general policy of a nation may be, it ought never to be without a stock of military knowledge for emergencies.... The art of war demands much previous study." The second reason was that the foreign situation at that time was threatening, because of the Barbary pirates, frontier battles, and boundary disputes.

The site of West Point had been occupied by the Army since 1778. The first Superintendent was Major Jonathan Williams. He had ten cadets. When the War of 1812 began, the strength of the Corps of Cadets was increased to 250.

From 1817 to 1833 Colonel Sylvanus Thayer was Superintendent. He was called the "Father of the Military Academy." He had one ideal: to produce men who would be trained and worthy leaders. He demanded excellence of both character and knowledge. He increased the study of civil engineering, made every cadet pass his courses or drop out, and permitted no classes larger than 10 to 14 members.

From time to time the Academy has changed its course to keep up with trends in modern warfare. General Douglas MacArthur, who became Superintendent in 1919, emphasized physical fitness, and also taught lessons learned in World War I.

Most of the great United States military leaders have been West Point graduates.

Young men serving in the armed forces who wish to enter West Point may get special instruction at the United States Military Academy Preparatory School at Stewart Air Base, Newburgh, New York. This school is maintained by the Army and is supervised by the West Point Commandant. It helps candidates pass the entrance examinations to West Point. Classes begin in September and last the usual school year.

military police

The military police of an army keep order among the soldiers and arrest soldiers who break the army's rules, just as a police force does in enforcing the laws of a city or state. The United States Army has a branch called the military police, under the command of an officer called the Provost Marshal General. When large numbers of soldiers are in a city, military police patrol the city streets to make sure the soldiers do not get into trouble and that they return to the army post safely, but if soldiers break the laws of the city it is the city police and not the military police who arrest them. Like other police forces, military police are on hand to help the soldiers. Military police also do other kinds of police work, such as directing traffic. The United States Navy has a similar branch called the Shore Patrol.

milk

Milk is a fluid made by the bodies of most female mammals for the feeding of their young. Mammals are animals whose young are born alive and nursed by their mothers. For thousands of years man has used as food the milk of cows, goats, ewes (female sheep), asses, camels, buffaloes, reindeer, and other animals. The word milk, as most often used, means the milk of cows.

Milk is the most nearly perfect of all human foods. Besides its use as a drink it is also the basis for a number of other foods, such as BUTTER, CHEESE, CREAM, and ICE CREAM, about which there are separate articles. It is important in the preparation of various foods in the home and in factories.

Fluid whole milk supplies almost all the food needs of babies, and it is very valuable in the diet of children and grownups. In the United States, every man, woman and child consumes an average of nearly three quarts of milk a week. Even more is consumed in other forms of milk and milk products.

WHAT MILK IS MADE OF

Milk contains proteins, fats, carbohydrates, and minerals, all of which are necessary for health. The principal milk proteins are *albumin, globulin,* and *casein,* which are made up of amino acids and are substances needed by the human body for the building of muscle tissue and blood.

Of the minerals found in milk, calcium is the most important. It is needed by children to build bones and teeth, and by persons of all ages to keep these parts of the body strong and healthy. Milk also contains phosphorus, iron, potassium, and magnesium, all of which the body must have.

The fats in milk are an important source of energy. The milk fats contain substances that give milk its odor and flavor. They also contain the pigments found in the green plants eaten by cattle. These give milk its color. Milk also contains all known vitamins but it is principally a source of Vitamin A and riboflavin.

HOW MILK IS PRODUCED

The production, processing, distribution and marketing of milk has become a huge industry in the United States. The various levels of government, from national down to state, county, and city, have set up many regulations to insure the purity and good quality of the milk supply.

The United States leads the world in the production of milk, with a total of more than 120,000,000,000 pounds every year. About half of this is sold as whole milk and cream. About a quarter is used to make butter, about one-tenth to make cheese. Ice cream and other frozen dairy products take up a small percentage, and the rest goes to make evaporated milk, powdered milk, and other products.

Since fluid milk spoils easily, it must be handled carefully and quickly. The milk is collected from farms and taken to receiving stations where it is inspected, weighed, and chilled. It is then transferred to a pasteurizing plant in special tank trucks or railroad cars. Pasteurizing is required by the United States government for most milk. It kills all dangerous bacteria in milk and makes it safe to drink. The milk is heated to at least 143 degrees Fahrenheit for 30 minutes, or to 161 degrees for 15 seconds. At the pasteurizing plant some of the milk is *homogenized,* which means it is treated to break down the fats so that the cream stays distributed throughout the milk and

does not rise to the top. Some of the milk is made more nourishing by adding Vitamin D. It is then cooled quickly, is bottled and capped, and is ready for distribution.

Milk for home use is distributed mainly through retail stores in paper cartons or bottles, or by delivery in bottles to homes.

SPECIAL KINDS OF MILK

Certified milk is a trade name for milk produced under special regulations and guaranteed pure by a medical commission. Certified milk may be sold raw or pasteurized.

Evaporated milk is useful where refrigeration is not available. It is whole milk that has been homogenized, boiled to remove about half of the water, sealed in cans, and sterilized. In this form milk will keep for long periods. Condensed milk is evaporated milk with a certain amount of sugar added to make it keep longer. Condensed milk was invented by Gail BORDEN, about whom there is a separate article.

Skim milk, sometimes called fat-free milk, is milk from which most of the fat has been removed. It retains most of its food value, and is useful in special diets. Dried skim milk is a powder produced by removing nearly all of the water from skim milk. It is used by bakers, candy and ice-cream manufacturers, and other food industries. Recently it has been sold for use in homes.

milkweed

Milkweed is the name of a group of plants that contain a milky juice. Milkweed grows in many parts of the world where the climate is warm. The milkweed is a perennial plant, which means that it grows up from the same roots every year. Milkweed grows best in a damp soil.

There are many different kinds of milkweed. The butterfly milkweed has attractive orange flowers and it is sometimes planted in flower gardens. Other

Standard Oil Co.

Milkweed is sometimes called silkweed because of its silky seed, which is carried by the wind. The plant is found in many parts of the United States.

milkweeds have pale lavender flowers and are not so handsome. Some milkweeds have crimson flowers. There are milkweeds that have a sweet smell and others that have an unpleasant odor.

The milkweed has pods that contain small seeds with soft tufts of hair attached to them. These soft hairs are used to stuff pillows and mattresses. Some milkweed plants that grow in the deserts in the western part of the United States contain latex, a valuable substance that is used in making rubber.

Milky Way

The Milky Way is the name given to the more than one hundred billion stars and cloudlike patches of matter called *nebula,* that can be seen from the earth. Such a collection of stars and nebula is called a *galaxy,* which comes from the Greek word meaning "milk." The Milky Way is just one of a million galaxies that make up the universe. The sun is part of the Milky Way, and so are all the stars and constellations described in other articles in this encyclopedia.

The Milky Way is shaped like a large wheel, and is believed to be about six million million million miles wide, and about six hundred thousand million million miles thick. Traveling at the speed of light, 186,300 miles a second, it would take about 100,000 years to go from one end of the Milky Way to the other.

The center of the Milky Way is near the constellation Sagittarius. The sun is about eighteen thousand million million miles away from it. The entire Milky Way is turning about its center at a speed of 150 miles a second. Because of its tremendous size, it takes the Milky Way two hundred million years to make one complete turn.

The Milky Way was first closely examined by the German-born English astronomer, Sir William Herschel, in 1784. Most of our knowledge of the shape and structure of the Milky Way has come from the work of Harlow Shapley and Bart J. Bok of Harvard University.

Millay, Edna St. Vincent

Edna St. Vincent Millay was an American poet, by many critics considered the greatest of this century. She was born in Rockland, Maine, in 1892, and graduated from Vassar College. Her first long poem, "Renascence," was written when she was only 19. It is so good that at first people could hardly believe anyone so young had written it. It is still among the best she ever wrote. It was published in 1917 as the title poem in her first volume of verse. Two more volumes followed, and then in 1922 came the *Ballad of the Harp-Weaver,* for which Miss Millay won the Pulitzer prize for poetry in 1923. She also wrote three poetic plays, and the libretto (or story) for Deems Taylor's opera *The King's Henchman.* Miss Millay was married in 1923 to Eugen Jan Boissevan. She died in 1950.

millet

Millet is the name of a large group of grasses that have small seeds. The seeds are used as food. Millet grasses are grown in many parts of the world where the climate is not too hot or too cold. Some millet, such as the foxtail millet, grows in about two months. It is an important food for cattle. The foxtail millet

is a very old grass that was one of the sacred plants of the Chinese people about three thousand years before Christ.

The people of India, China, and Japan eat millet as a cereal and use it to make bread and cake. People in the United States do not eat millet.

Millet, Jean François

Jean François Millet was a French painter who lived about a hundred years ago. He came of a poor farming family and he gained his fame as the painter of scenes of peasant life. Millet was born in 1814. As a boy he worked in the fields, but he was always sketching and drawing.

Millet's father sent him to Cherbourg to study painting, and later the town of Cherbourg gave Millet an award so that he could study further in Paris. There he painted the pictures that made him famous, among them *The Gleaners, The Angelus,* and *The Man with the Hoe.* This last painting was the inspiration for a poem, "The Man with the Hoe," by the American poet Edwin Markham. Millet never made much money with his painting, and he died a poor man in 1875. Very soon after his death his work became highly prized. Many of his pictures now hang in museums in the United States and Europe.

Millikan, Robert

Robert Andrews Millikan was an American scientist who won the Nobel Prize in Physics in 1923 for finding the amount of electricity in an electron (a small particle found in all atoms of matter) and the amount of energy in a photon (a small bundle of light).

He was born in Morrison, Illinois, in 1868, and attended Oberlin College in Ohio and Columbia University in New York City. He was professor of physics at the University of Chicago for twenty-five years and head of the research laboratory at the California Institute of Technology for thirty years. He died in 1953.

millinery, the business of making hats for women and the materials used in them: see HAT.

Milne, A. A.

Alan Alexander Milne is the name of an English writer who has written famous stories for children. Milne was born in 1882, and he first wrote plays and stories for grownups. When his son Christopher Robin was 3 years old, Milne wrote a book of verses for him and put Christopher Robin himself into most of them. Then followed *Winnie-the-Pooh* and *The House at Pooh Corner,* stories that were peopled with many of the child's stuffed animals. Pooh himself is a "bear of very little brain," and there are Piglet, Kanga and Little Roo, Rabbit and all his relations, and many others. *Now We Are Six* is another book of verse.
Milne died in 1956.

Milton, John

John Milton was one of the greatest of all English poets. Some consider him

the greatest. He was born in London in 1608, and when he was very young he began to study Latin, Greek, and Hebrew. He also learned to play the organ. He was a handsome slender young man, with gray eyes and light brown hair that fell in curls to his shoulders. He decided early to be a writer.

It is difficult for modern readers to appreciate some of Milton's poems. They are filled with names and statements taken from the ancient Latin, Greek and Hebrew literature. In Milton's time, all educated men studied the Latin and Greek classics, because they were considered a necessary part of a good education.

Among Milton's earliest well-known poems were *L'Allegro, Il Penseroso,* and *Lycidas.* Experts have said that *Lycidas* is the most nearly perfect poem in the English language. Milton wrote it when he was 29 years old, to mourn the death of a man named Edward King who had been his friend at Cambridge University. Milton wrote many sonnets, short poems of fourteen lines each. No one except Shakespeare ever wrote them so well. His most famous sonnet is about his blindness. He became blind when he was 46.

Milton's life was eventful. He lived during a time when England was in the midst of a religious and political revolution. Most of the writing he did for twenty years was of a political nature. He was on the side of the Puritans, the religious group that opposed the English king.

Milton's greatest work was his long poem, *Paradise Lost.* It is about the original sin of Adam and Eve in the Garden of Eden. He started it after he became completely blind, and dictated most of it to his daughters. *Paradise Lost* was finished in 1663. Milton received only twenty-three pounds for it; this was English money worth about $115, though it was actually worth more than $600 is worth today.

Paradise Regained, another long poem, appeared in 1671. It is about the temptation of Christ in the wilderness, as told in the Bible.

Milton wrote constantly for more than fifty years, and never stopped studying. He often declared that he wrote well only from fall till spring. The work he did during the summer months never pleased him.

John Milton died in London in 1674, after a long illness. He was 66 years old.

Milwaukee

Milwaukee is the largest city in Wisconsin. It is on Lake Michigan and has the most beautiful harbor on the lake. It is one of the most important ports in the Middle West. About 700,000 people live in Milwaukee. They work in large factories that make hosiery, heavy machinery, automobiles, tractors, and many other things. Milwaukee is famous for its great brewing plants, which are among the largest in the world. Milwaukee ranks tenth in the United States in the value of its products.

Milwaukee has many fine avenues and parks. Lake Park and Juneau Park, along Lake Michigan, are noted for their beauty. There are beautiful beaches along the lake. Milwaukee has many colleges, and it has one of the largest zoos in the world.

Milwaukee was founded by Solomon Juneau in 1818, when he built a trading post where the city now stands. In 1835 the town was laid out. It grew rapidly. It was largely settled by German immigrants. For a long time the people spoke German more than they did English, and more German newspapers were published than English newspapers. There was a theater where plays were given in German. This gradually changed, and today Milwaukee is like any large American city.

MILWAUKEE, WISCONSIN. Population (1970 census) 717,099. County seat, Milwaukee County. On Lake Michigan. Settled in 1818.

mimosa

Mimosa plants grow in parts of the world where the climate is warm. Some mimosa plants grow as tall as trees, while some are small and are grown as ornamentals in greenhouses. The mimosa plants are perennial, which means that they grow from the same roots every year.

One kind of mimosa that is sometimes called the "sensitive plant" is a pretty plant with light purple flowers. It grows to be about two feet high. It gets this name because when a person touches its dark green leaves they close up.

The mimosa is a legume; like the pea and bean plants, it has pods that contain the seeds.

Mindanao

Mindanao is the second-largest island in the Philippine Islands. It is at the southern end of the islands in the Pacific Ocean. It is 36,537 square miles in size, which is about the size of Indiana, and about three million people live there. Most of the people are farmers. They grow coconuts, corn, Manila hemp and rice in the fertile Cotabato and Agusan valleys. The Cotabato Valley is the largest farming region in the Philippines. There are iron, coal and gold mines in the mountains, which are the highest in the Philippines. These mountains are covered with dense forests and some of them are active volcanoes. Mount Apo is the highest point in the Philippines. It is 9,690 feet high. The most important rivers in Mindanao are the Rio Grande de Mindanao and the Agusan River. In the central part of the island there are many wild sections where nobody lives. In this region there are forests of valuable woods.

The largest city of Mindanao is Davao, a city of about 337,000. Cagayan and Cotabato are other principal cities.

During World War II, the Japanese occupied Mindanao, and several battles were fought there. See the article on the PHILIPPINES.

mine (see also MINING)

A mine is a container with a heavy explosive charge in it. Mines are used in warfare. They are like bombs, except that they are not dropped on the enemy.

They are put in the sea where enemy ships may come, or on land and bridges over which enemy tanks and troops may pass. When the enemy reaches the mine, it explodes.

NAVAL MINES

The mine used at sea is tub-shaped and large, containing several hundred pounds of an explosive (usually TNT). It is called a submarine (underwater) mine because it remains below the surface of

Minesweepers perform valuable service by destroying enemy-planted submarine mines and keeping sea lanes open. The men are lowering an orapesa float. The cable attached to the hook in its nose traps moored mines, which are then drawn into a device that cuts the mooring gear. The mine rises and is exploded by gunfire.

the water so that approaching enemy ships cannot see it. A special ship called a *minelayer* places the mines in the water. Most mines are moored (attached by a cable) to the bottom of the ocean so that they will stay in one place and their location will be known. As it lays the mines, the minelayer makes a chart of where they are. Then the ships of the minelayer's country can steer clear of the mines, while enemy ships, not knowing where they are, may run into them.

During wartime, thousands of mines are laid in this way to protect harbors and trade routes that are much traveled. One purpose of mines is to keep enemy warships, especially submarines, from attacking a country's ships or coasts. Another purpose of mines is to sink the enemy's merchant ships. Mines are so powerful that the explosion of a single mine will usually sink a merchant ship or small warship.

MAGNETIC MINES

During World War II, magnetic mines were much used. The mine was magnetized so that it would be attracted to the steel sides of a ship. After magnetic mines were used for a while, ships began to protect themselves by carrying a magnetized metal band, all around the ship, that would repel the magnetic mine instead of attracting it. (The principle of this is explained in the article on MAGNETISM.) This device was called a *para-*

vane, but actually a paravane is a cutting device used by special ships called *minesweepers.* As the minesweeper moves through the water, the paravanes in front of it cut the cables by which the mines are moored to the bottom. The mines then float, and guns are shot at them to explode them at a safe distance. When a fleet moves through mined waters, minesweepers go ahead to clear out the mines. Then the fleet follows safely.

Mines were once very good protection against submarines, but radar and similar detecting devices have made it easier for submarines (and other warships) to avoid them.

When a war ends, all the warring nations sweep out the mines they have laid, so that the shipping lanes will be safe again. Even so, some mines are overlooked and can cause damage to shipping years later.

LAND MINES

Land mines are usually much smaller than naval mines. They are buried underground, and are built so that when anyone steps on the ground overhead they explode. Ground troops, like minelaying ships, carefully chart the places where they put mines, so that friendly troops can avoid them. A mined place is called a "booby trap" by soldiers.

When an army goes forward through territory that the enemy may have mined, men go first with *mine detectors.* A mine detector has a long handle so that a soldier can hold it out in front of him. When the mine detector passes over a spot where there is metal, it gives an electrical signal. This warns that there may be a mine there, and no one ventures on the spot until the mine has been exploded.

CONTROLLED MINES

Controlled mines are often used to prevent the enemy from passing over a bridge or similar narrow passage. The mines are laid and are connected by wires to a switch at some point at a distance. Stepping on the bridge or on the mined spot will not set off the mine. The mines can be made to explode at a particular moment by use of the switch.

During World War I and other wars in which there was much fighting in trenches, troops called *sappers* would dig long tunnels underground to lay mines under the enemy trenches or near them. These also were usually controlled mines, exploded by a fuse or by an electric current.

mineral

A mineral is a natural substance that is taken out of the earth. Gold, silver, iron, diamond and sulfur are only a few of thousands of minerals. Next to crops, minerals are the things in nature most useful to mankind.

All minerals are taken out of the earth, but not all things in the earth are minerals. Nothing that ever grew—that is, nothing that is animal or vegetable—is a mineral. Bones or tree roots are not minerals even if they are buried in the ground.

HOW TO TELL A MINERAL

People who study minerals are called *mineralogists.* They have made very defi-

nite rules as to what a mineral is and how you can tell it from a rock or something buried in the ground.

First, a mineral is a natural substance; this means that it is not made by anyone, but is found in nature.

Second, all of each mineral is composed of the same substance. This means that no matter how many pieces you divide a mineral into, all of them will be made of the same substance.

Third, all pieces of the same kind of mineral are made up of the same chemical elements. For instance, all nuggets of gold that are dug up anywhere in the world are made of the same element—gold. Mineralogists make a distinction between minerals of this kind and rocks. Rocks are mineral matter, but they are composed of pure minerals plus impurities.

Fourth, any piece of the same kind of mineral always is formed in the same way as any other piece of the same mineral.

These four rules make it possible always to tell one mineral from another.

WHERE MINERALS COME FROM

Some minerals are formed when melted rock from deep in the earth pushes up to the surface of the earth, where it cools and hardens. Quartz is a mineral formed this way. Seas drying up leave behind all the minerals that were dissolved in them.

There is a separate article on ROCKS.

mineral water

Mineral water is water that comes from underground springs and has minerals dissolved in it. Ever since ancient times people have drunk it and have bathed in it because they believed it would cure gout, rheumatism, liver trouble, diseases of the blood, and many other kinds of sickness. Some people still use mineral water as a cure, but doctors do not think it will help many diseases. Mineral springs do have their uses. Some mineral springs are hot, and when people with rheumatism bathe in the warm water they get relief from their pains. Some mineral waters have Epsom salt in them and this makes them very good as laxatives.

SPARKLING WATERS

Certain mineral waters have gas dissolved in them. Like carbonated water, they are full of bubbles. These are the "sparkling waters," that are used in mixing drinks.

Many kinds of mineral water are put in bottles and you can buy them at drugstores.

WHERE THE SPRINGS ARE

Among the most famous American mineral-water springs are those at Saratoga Springs, New York; White Sulphur Springs, West Virginia; Hot Springs, Arkansas; and French Lick, Indiana. Some of the ones in Europe are at Bath, England; Aachen, Germany; and Aix-les-Bains, France.

Some mineral waters have been carefully analyzed by chemists to learn what minerals are in them. Then these waters are made artificially in a factory by putting the same minerals into pure water.

Minerva

Minerva was one of the goddesses who were worshiped by the ancient Romans, thousands of years ago. The ancient Greeks called the same goddess Athena, or Pallas Athena. According to the legend, she was not born in the usual way but sprang full-grown from the forehead of Jupiter (or Zeus), the chief god. She was goddess of heroism among men, and patron of all the womanly arts, such as sewing, weaving, and spinning. In addition, she was the goddess of wisdom and the symbol of thought. The Greeks of Athens built their most beautiful temple to Athena. It was called the Parthenon, and was on the ACROPOLIS, about which there is a separate article.

mining

Mining is finding useful minerals, digging them out of the ground, and getting them ready for market. All metals come from minerals that are mined. Many gems, except pearls, are mined. Many other things such as asbestos, marble, granite, gypsum, salt, and sulfur, are mined.

MINERAL DEPOSITS

A quantity of mineral that is underground in one place is called a *deposit*. If the deposit is in thin branching sheets enclosed in rock, it is called a *vein*. When a group of veins are so close together that they and the rock enclosing them can be mined together, the deposit is called a *lode*. Deposits that are hundreds of thousands of feet thick are called *beds*. Thinner beds, especially when they are of coal, are called *seams*. Deposits of sand and gravel that contain valuable minerals are called *placer deposits*. The worthless rock, sand, and earth with which a mineral may be mixed, and which is thrown away, is called *gangue*. This word is pronounced just like "gang."

PROSPECTING

Before you can dig for minerals, you must find them. Searching for the places where minerals are buried is called *prospecting*. In ancient times, chunks of minerals that were found lying on the ground told miners that they might find more if they dug nearby. Miners sometimes found mineral deposits by coming upon breaks in the earth's crust, called *faults*, that exposed the minerals to plain view. In the early days of the United States, especially in the western states, lone prospectors and their burros wandered in the wilderness for months at a time, seeking silver, gold and other minerals.

GEOLOGISTS AND GEOPHYSICISTS

Prospecting is done by two kinds of scientists. They are called *economic geologists* and *geophysicists*. The economic geologists know what kinds of land and what kinds of rock are most likely to contain valuable minerals. This saves a lot of useless searching. Geophysicists locate deeply buried minerals. They fire a charge of explosive on the ground, and then they measure how fast the shock of the explosion travels through the ground. They know that the shocks will move through certain minerals at certain speeds. When they get measurements, they make calculations that tell them at just what place and how far below ground the mineral deposits lie.

SAMPLING AND ASSAYING

After a deposit has been found, mining engineers dig up small pieces of it, called *samples*, from different parts of the deposit. They send these pieces to a chemist who analyzes them in order to tell how much of the deposit is valuable mineral and how much is gangue. The job the chemists do is called *assaying*. When you see the report of the assay, you can tell whether your mineral deposit contains ore.

ORE

Ore is a mineral deposit that contains enough of the valuable part of the mineral so that you can sell it at a profit. It is not always easy to say just what is or is not ore. For example, before the first atomic bomb was made, almost the only use for uranium was to make a dark greenish glaze on chinaware. Very little uranium was needed and the price paid for it was low. So, if you had a uranium deposit, it had to be very pure in order to be called an ore deposit. But when the invention of the atomic bomb was followed by so great a need for uranium, deposits containing even very small amounts of uranium along with much gangue became very valuable ores.

If you owned an iron deposit in Minnesota, it need not contain rich samples, because you could easily, quickly, and cheaply send your ore over water to iron foundries and steel mills in Chicago. If you owned an iron deposit in the frozen ground of northern Canada, no matter how rich the deposit, it would not be ore. Even if you could find ways to mine it, without railroads or highways it would cost you so much to ship it that you would lose money.

CLAIMS

Once you have located your mineral deposit and have decided it contains ore, you will probably file a *claim*. In the United States, this means that above the deposit you must measure off a piece of land not more than 1,500 feet long and 600 feet wide, and then you must place at the corners wooden stakes with your name on them. Then you tell the United States government just where your land is, how large it is, and what you want to use it for. This is your claim. You must also advertise your claim in a nearby newspaper. After you have done these things, and if no one has done them before you, you pay the government a small amount of money for each acre of your land. The land now becomes your claim, and is yours as long as you work on it.

MINES AND QUARRIES

Once you are ready to dig your ore, you must decide how to do this so that it will cost the least. Suppose you know that you have a seam of coal a thousand feet underground. If you just start to dig a big hole to get at the coal, you will spend so much time and money in removing the earth above it (called the *overburden*) that you will never be able to sell the coal for enough to get back the money you spent digging down to it. Therefore you must dig a narrow hole, or *shaft*, down to the coal. Once you have reached the coal, miners can go down the shaft and start to dig tunnels, or *stopes*, sidewise into the coal. Most mines, not only coal mines, are shaft-and-tunnel mines.

If you have an iron deposit like those of the Mesabi district of northern Minnesota, you could just use steam shovels to dig up the ground and dump it into freight cars, because there is no overburden here—the ore comes right up to the surface. Mines like this soon become vast holes and are called *open pit mines*.

If you want to mine stone, such as marble or granite, you drill and split the stone in an open pit called a *quarry*.

If you have a placer deposit that contains grains and flakes of gold, you will use powerful hoses, like fire hoses, to wash the gravel into a line of long wooden boxes called sluice-boxes. The gravel will wash away and leave the heavy gold behind in the sluice-boxes. This kind of mining is called *hydraulicking*.

MINING FOR OIL

Getting oil out of the ground is a kind of mining. Of course, you do not dig for it. Instead, you drill a narrow hole down to the pool of oil. If there is natural gas stored above the oil pool, the pressure of the gas will push the oil out in a gusher, and you have to get a pipe over the gushing oil so that you do not lose your oil all over the landscape. If the well is not a gusher, you have to pump the oil out of the well.

ORE CONCENTRATION

People who buy ore from mines pay for it by the ton. So, of course, they want as much useful ore and as little gangue as possible. Getting all the ore together and getting rid of the gangue is called *ore concentration*. This is usually the job of scientists called metallurgists. You can learn about how they do this job by reading the separate article on METALS AND METALLURGY.

MINING LONG AGO

Mining began long before history was first written. It began when first man figured out that he could get more pieces of flint by digging than just by searching on top of the ground. Places have been found where flint was being mined as long ago as 125,000 years. In Egypt and Mesopotamia, 3,500 years ago, men were digging copper and tin out of the ground to make bronze. They were also mining turquoise and other stones they prized for their beauty. When Egyptian miners wanted to get at valuable minerals in rock, they heated the rock with fire and then threw cold water on it to make it crack. They learned how to run water through gravel so as to wash away the lighter material—the stones and sand—and leave the heavy gold.

The Greeks and Romans were very skillful miners. They showed much engineering skill by working large underground mines. They had no machinery; their mines were worked by slaves who were treated very cruelly.

After the end of the Roman Empire,

people in Europe forgot how to mine. But mining was one of the first industries to be started up again during the late Middle Ages. In the 16th century in Europe, none of the miners were slaves. They had three shifts a day—early morning, noon, and evening. And they worked only five days a week. They were known by the job they did. They were miners (who used pick, wedge, hammer, and crowbar), shovelers, carriers, and windlass men (who turned a big crank that wound up rope and pulled buckets of minerals up from the mine). They broke rock with fire and water, just as the ancient Egyptians did. They had ventilators to get fresh air into the mines and pumps to remove underground water that seeped into their mine tunnels. Still their job was not easy. Mines were cold, dark, and wet, and like all miners, they had to face the danger of cave-ins.

minister

To minister to someone is to help him or serve him. Many clergymen are called ministers, or ministers of the Gospel, because of their work of caring for the people and trying to save their souls. The period in which Jesus preached to the people and cured or helped them is called the period of his ministry.

Certain government officials are called ministers in many countries. They are the most important assistants to the head of the government and are heads of the chief government departments. In the United States, men holding the same positions are the heads of the government departments and are usually called secretaries, such as the Secretary of State. In other countries the man holding the same position would be called the Minister of Foreign Affairs. Ministers are members of the cabinet, which in most countries is a committee that decides government policies. The head of this committee is called the Prime Minister or Premier, and the other members are called *cabinet ministers* or simply ministers. A member of the cabinet who is not the head of a department of the government is called a *minister without portfolio*.

mink

The mink is a small fur-bearing animal that lives in many parts of Europe, Asia, and the United States. The mink makes its home near marshes and streams, and it is an excellent swimmer. It has a soft, deep brown fur with long black hairs that protect its coat when it is in the water.

The mink is a member of the weasel family. It is only about two feet long, but like most weasels it is a brave fighter and will attack a fox or any other animal that threatens it. The mink has glands in its body that give off a certain odor that keeps some of its enemies away.

The mink usually makes its home in a hollow tree. Sometimes it digs a burrow in the side of a river bank. Here the mink stores fish, muskrats, and other food. The female mink has between four and eight babies in the spring. The mink family stays together during the summer months. Minks are playful and often have wild roughhouse games. When autumn comes the young minks go off to make new homes.

The mink is prized for its beautiful fur and coats made from it are very expensive. People in the United States now raise minks for their fur, but the fur of the mink raised on farms is not considered as fine as that of the wild mink.

For information on how mink is used as a fur, see the article on FUR.

Minneapolis

Minneapolis is the largest city in the state of Minnesota. It is built on both sides of the Mississippi River, near a waterfall called the Falls of St. Anthony. The waterfall supplies the city with power. Minneapolis is so close to the city of St. Paul that the two cities are called the "Twin Cities."

Almost 435,000 people live in Minneapolis. Many of them work in flour and lumber mills. Minneapolis is an important center for both these products. Others make butter. Minneapolis is sometimes called the "Butter Capital of the United States." Some of the people who live in Minneapolis make cloth and jewelry, and work in printing plants. Minneapolis is a railroad center and has a large airport.

Minneapolis is a very attractive city, with wide streets and handsome public buildings. In it are more than twenty lakes and many fine parks. Minnehaha Falls is in one of the parks in Minneapolis. The heroine of Longfellow's poem *Hiawatha* was named Minnehaha. The climate of Minneapolis is clear and cool.

The University of Minnesota is built on a hill that overlooks the Mississippi River. Minneapolis has an art school, a music school, a fine art museum, and the Minneapolis Symphony Orchestra, which is one of the finest in the United States.

The Falls of St. Anthony were discovered by a French explorer, Father Hennepin, almost three hundred years ago. A military fort, Fort Snelling, was built there in 1823. It is now a military training center just outside the city.

MINNEAPOLIS, MINNESOTA. Population (1970 census) 434,400. County seat of Hennepin County. On the Mississippi River. Incorporated in 1856.

Minnesota

Minnesota is one of the north central states of the United States, on the Canadian border. Its nickname is the "Gopher State" because of the number of gophers that have been found there. The Minnesota region was the setting of

Henry Wadsworth Longfellow's poem *Hiawatha*. Minnesota has rich rolling farm land. Its dairies produce more butter than any other state. It also ranks first in the production of oats, sweet corn, and turkeys, and is second in the raising of flax. The state gets its name from an Indian word meaning "sky-colored water," and Minnesota is often called "the land of the sky-blue water."

Minnesota ranks 12th in size among the states, with 84,068 square miles. In population it ranks 19th, with more than three and a half million people living there. It became a state in 1858, and was the 32nd state admitted to the United States. The capital is St. Paul.

THE PEOPLE OF MINNESOTA

The first settlers in the Minnesota region were English and French, but about a hundred years ago large numbers of people from Norway, Sweden, and Denmark came to Minnesota and settled on the fertile farm land. Later, people from many parts of Europe came to work in

the iron mines and factories. Today most Minnesotans are American-born.

More than half the people of Minnesota live in the cities and work in factories that make food products, machinery, and chemicals. Many also work in printing and meat-packing plants. Minneapolis is famous for its flour mills, and Duluth has large iron and steel mills.

Although more people work in cities than on farms, farming is still the largest industry in the state. The farmers living in the fertile Red River Valley in the western part raise large crops of potatoes and wheat. In other sections are big cooperative dairies. Minnesota is a leading producer of milk and eggs, and its

Duluth, Minnesota.   *Duluth Convention and Visitors Bureau*

farmers also raise large crops of corn, hay, soybeans, and barley.

Many people work in the rich iron mines in the northeastern part of the state. The mine at Hibbing is the biggest man-made hole in the world. Minnesota is the leading iron ore state, furnishing about sixty-five per cent of the country's supply. A number of people also work in the forests, cutting down the large trees for lumber.

One of the biggest industries of the state is taking care of the many vacationists who come to Minnesota each summer to enjoy the beautiful scenery and outdoor sports. There are many fine resorts along the state's thousands of blue lakes.

The two largest religious groups in Minnesota are the Roman Catholics and the Lutherans.

WHAT MINNESOTA IS LIKE

Most of Minnesota is a rolling prairie, but in the north there are rocky ridges that are part of an old mountain range. The beautiful pine forests and the valuable iron mines are in this part of the state.

Hunters in Minnesota will find many fur-bearing animals in the woods— mink, muskrat, and red fox, as well as black bear, deer, and moose, and game birds including the duck and pheasant.

Minnesota is very cold in the winter, but the air is very dry. Summers are pleasant, though near Lake Superior it is very hot during the day. The average temperature in summer is 70 degrees and in winter about 10 degrees.

Minnesota has many rivers that have been used for transportation since the time of the Indians. The great Mississippi River starts in this state, as does the Red River of the North. These rivers with their many tributaries also furnish valuable water power. The Minnesota River, the St. Croix, and the Rainy River are among the navigable rivers in the state. Lake Superior carries a large portion of the water traffic. There are railroads and highways that reach almost every part of the state, and airports in all the big cities.

THE GOVERNMENT OF MINNESOTA

Minnesota, like the other states, is governed by a Governor and a Legislature. The Governor is elected for a four-year term. The Legislature is composed of two houses, a Senate and a House of Representatives. Members of the Senate are elected for a four-year term. Members of the House of Representatives are elected for a two-year term. Judges are elected for a six-year term. The capital is St. Paul. There are 87 counties.

There are about 914,000 pupils attending the public elementary and high schools. Among the principal colleges and universities are:

University of Minnesota, at Minneapolis. Enrollment, 50,686 in 1971 (co-ed).

College of St. Thomas, at St. Paul. Enrollment, 1,946 in 1971 (men only).

St. Olaf College, at Northfield. Enrollment, 2,550 in 1971 (co-ed).

Morehead State College, at Morehead. Enrollment, 5,260 in 1971 co-ed).

Hamline University, at St. Paul. Enrollment, 1,270 in 1971 (co-ed).

CHIEF CITIES OF MINNESOTA

The leading cities of Minnesota, with populations from the 1970 census, are:

Minneapolis, population 434,400, the largest city in the state, and St. Paul, population 309,980, the state capital and second-largest city. These are called the Twin Cities. See the articles on MINNEAPOLIS and ST. PAUL.

Duluth, population 100,578, the third-largest city, iron and steel center, in the northeastern part of the state.

Rochester, population 53,766, the sixth-largest city, seat of the Mayo Clinic, one of the most famous medical centers in the world, in the southeastern part of the state.

MINNESOTA IN THE PAST

French fur-traders were the first white men to visit the region of Minnesota three hundred years ago. Other French traders came and set up trading posts. The first permanent settlement was made at Grand Portage, in 1731. After the French and Indian Wars, about two hundred years ago, a large region that included Minnesota was given to the British, who set up fur-trading companies. The eastern portion of Minnesota was given to the United States in 1783, and the western part was included in the Louisiana Purchase from France, in 1803.

The Minnesota region grew slowly. For many years it remained a place for fur-trading, and large sections were still held by the Indians. After the Indians finally gave up millions of acres west of the Mississippi River, settlers from the eastern part of the United States moved in. By 1858, Minnesota was large enough to be admitted as a state.

Out of these early pioneering days, grew the famous story of Paul Bunyan and his blue ox, Babe. This mythical figure was made up by boasting lumbermen, who told how there was nothing Paul Bunyan could not do. He was so strong he could uproot trees with his bare hands, and his footprints were said to form Minnesota's many lakes. There is a separate article about Paul BUNYAN and some of the feats he was supposed to have performed.

Minnesota continued to grow into an important industrial and farming state, particularly after the iron mines were opened up about seventy years ago.

PLACES TO SEE IN MINNESOTA

Pipestone National Monument, 115 acres, at Pipestone, in the southwest, on U.S. Route 75. Quarry from which Indians obtained materials for making peace pipes used in ceremonies.

Grand Portage National Historical Site, 660 acres, in the northeast, 5 miles north of Portage, on U.S. Route 61. Nine-mile portage on a principal route of Indians, explorers, missionaries, and fur traders into the Northwest interior.

Itasca State Park, 31,976 acres, 20 miles north of Park Rapids, in the central part of the state, on U.S. Route 71. Beautiful forest area, noted for its wild animals and lakes. Lake Itasca is the source of the Mississippi River.

Misquan Hills, 2,230 feet high, in the northeast, in the Superior National Forest, north of U.S. Route 61. The highest point in Minnesota.

Lake of the Woods, on the Canadian

border, in the north. A beautiful boat trip can be taken here in summer; excellent hunting and fishing.

MINNESOTA. Area, 84,068 square miles. Population (1970 census) 3,804,971. Capital, St. Paul. Nickname, the Gopher State. Motto, L'Etoile du Nord (The Star of the North). Flower, moccasin flower. Bird, American goldfinch. Song, "Hail! Minnesota." Admitted to Union, May 11; 1858. Official abbreviation, Minn.

minnow

Minnows are the largest group of fish that live in the fresh waters of Europe and the United States. People usually think of minnows as being the tiny brightly colored fish that swim in home aquariums. But there are hundreds of different kinds of minnow; some of them are less than an inch long, while others are several feet long.

There are important differences between minnows and other fish. A minnow does not have teeth in its jaw as most fish do. Instead, a minnow has a few large teeth in its throat. The minnow also has a special network of tiny bones that connects the ear with the air bladder.

Some minnows hollow out places in the sand to lay their eggs. Other minnows do not build any nest at all. Minnows are very useful to man because they eat mosquitoes and other insects. They also eat many water plants. When people want to catch fish they often use minnows as bait, because minnows are one of the most important foods of other fish.

Minoan civilization

The Minoan civilization was part of the Bronze Age culture that began on the island of Crete before 4,000 B.C. and spread to surrounding islands and mainland Greece. This era is known as the Aegean phase of Greek civilization. The ruler of the Aegean people was called Minos, a title like that of the Pharaohs of Egypt, which is why the civilization is called Minoan. Early in the 20th century, Sir Arthur Evans, a British archeologist, found the remains of the palace of Knossos on Crete, and spent the rest of his life unearthing evidence of the life and times of the Minoan people. We know from this evidence that by 1600 B.C. the Minoans had attained an amazingly "modern" stage of civilization. They were skilled craftsmen and artists; they traded extensively with other peoples, especially Egyptians and mainland Greeks; their homes were colorfully decorated and had almost modern plumbing systems; they had factories that turned out pottery, cloth, and metal goods. Women were highly respected in Minoan life, and enjoyed complete equality in all affairs. None of the towns or palaces was fortified, so we can assume they were peace-loving people. This great civilization came to an abrupt end some time around 1100 B.C. The palace was destroyed by fire and earthquake, and there may have been an invasion of Greek warriors, but no one knows for sure what happened.

minor

A minor is a person whom the law does not consider old enough to make decisions for himself. Such a person is said

to be in his *minority*. He does not have ful legal rights until he *attains his majority*, or becomes "of age." In the United States, each state decides the age at which a person attains his majority; in some countries, the national government decides. In most states, a person is a minor until he is 21 years old. Until then, the law gives him certain protection. He cannot be forced by law to fulfill an agreement or contract or to pay a debt. In some cases, his parent or guardian is responsible for what he does. Separate laws usually state the age at which a person can get married without his parents' consent. In most states the age is 21 for men and 18 for women.

Minotaur

The Minotaur was a monster told about in Greek mythology, the stories the ancient Greeks told about their gods and goddesses. The Minotaur had the head of a bull and the body of a man. It belonged to Minos, the king of Crete. Each year Minos forced the people of Athens, whom he had conquered, to send him seven young men and seven young girls to be sacrificed to the Minotaur. The Minotaur lived in a labyrinth, a strange and complicated place full of winding paths from which no one ever escaped. At last the Greek hero Theseus entered the labyrinth, killed the Minotaur, and was helped to escape by King Minos' daughter Ariadne. See the article on THESEUS.

minstrel

The minstrel was the musical entertainer of England in the Middle Ages, five to seven hundred years ago. Such entertainers were known in many countries and called by many different names. In Germany they were the minnesingers, in the northern countries they were the skalds, and in Ireland they were the bards. In France, the men who wrote their own verses and songs were usually noblemen and were called troubadours. The men who accompanied them on musical instruments, or sometimes were hired by noblemen to sing and play, were called jongleurs. The French took this idea to England about nine hundred years ago, and the jongleurs provided the principal entertainment of the country. In addition to singing and playing musical instruments, the jongleurs danced, performed acrobatics, and did juggling acts (from which fact we get our word *juggler*). They were mostly people of the poorer classes, and they were considered untrustworthy wanderers.

After several hundred years the jongleurs were taken up by the noblemen of the feudal castles, and they received a new name and a new position. They became minstrels, a name that came from the Latin word for court attendant. They became more highly respected and had an easier life.

It is not known exactly how many of the ballads and songs of the Middle Ages were composed by the minstrels. Many of the most famous ones were, and the minstrels were responsible for keeping alive and passing along others that they did not write themselves. Minstrelsy flourished for a long time, but it began to die out when printing became more and more widespread. When that hap-

pened people could read books and no longer had to depend on personal entertainers.

THE MINSTREL SHOW

In the United States in the middle of the 1800s, a kind of musical show called a minstrel show became popular. It did not disappear until early in the 20th century, with the coming of radio and the motion picture.

The minstrel show consisted of three parts. In the first part the company of men called minstrels paraded around the stage in a song-and-dance act, then marched to their places in a semicircle of chairs facing the audience. One was called the interlocutor. He always sat in the center of the semicircle. He would then give the order, "Gentlemen, be seated." After this he would go into an act of funny conversation and jokes with the end men, who sat at the ends of the semicircle. The end men were always in blackface, that is, had their faces blackened with burnt cork to make them resemble Negroes. An end man was usually called Mr. Bones, or Sambo, or Rastus. The end men were the real stars of the show. In the second part, or *olio*, various specialty acts, such as songs and dances, were presented by different members of the company. This was followed by either a burlesque making fun of a popular play or opera, or a singing and dancing number by the whole company.

The first minstrel show was presented in 1843 by a company headed by Daniel D. Emmett, who is best remembered as the writer of the song "Dixie." By the time of the Civil War the popularity of the minstrel show was well established, and companies were appearing in cities all over the country. Some of the famous comedians of the 1900s got their start in minstrel or "blackface" shows, including Al Jolson, Eddie Leonard, George Jessel, Eddie Cantor, and others.

mint

A mint is a place where metal coins are made. The manufacture of coins is known as *minting*.

There are three mints in the United States: in Philadelphia, Pennsylvania, in San Francisco, California, and in Denver, Colorado. They produce all the coins used in the United States. They are controlled by the Bureau of the Mint in Washington, D.C., a part of the Treasury Department.

The Mint of the United States was established by Act of Congress, April 2, 1792. The first mint was set up in Philadelphia and in 1793 produced the first United States coin, the copper cent or penny. Silver, then gold coins followed in 1794 and 1795. Until 1966 silver coins of the United States were made of the pure metal, although other countries had adopted cheaper alloys such as stainless steel. The use of gold coins was discontinued in the United States in 1933.

When a coin is made of pure gold or silver, the metal is first *assayed* (tested for purity); then *refined* (melted so that less valuable metals can be removed); then *cast* into ingots or bars and pressed into thin strips. These strips are cut into coin blanks or *planchets*, just thick enough to make coins, and the planchets are

weighed to make sure they are not too light or too heavy. Planchets of the correct weight are stamped into coins between dies, or hard-metal stampers, under pressure of as much as 150 tons, in enormous presses. After being baked, hardened, and cleaned, the coins can be put into circulation. In a mint about a hundred coins are produced each minute.

Shortage of gold and silver caused the adoption of laminated coins in the United States in 1965. One-cent pieces (pennies) made of bronze, and five-cent pieces (nickels) made of copper plus some nickel, remained the same; but the silver pieces, the 10-cent coin (dime), 25-cent coin (quarter), and 50-cent coin (half-dollar), have a disc of alloy in the center and thin slivers of silver on the outsides. The silver dollar is not made. The new coins look almost like the solid metal ones.

mint

Mint is a plant that grows in almost every part of the world where the climate is not too hot or too cold. Mint is a perennial plant, which means that it grows from the same roots every year. The mint is a hardy plant and can grow in almost any climate, but it grows best in a damp soil. There are many different kinds of mint.

The most useful mints are peppermint and spearmint. They grow to be two or three feet high and have purple flowers. The stems of the plants are square and the leaves are small. The leaves of the mint contain a sweet-smelling oil that has a pleasant flavor. The oil from the mint plant is used in many ways. Ice cream, chewing gum, tobacco, and drinks are flavored with mint. Mint is used in tea and as a seasoning for meat and cake. People make mint jelly and a candy that is flavored with mint. Mint is also used in many medicines and toothpastes, and in soap and perfume.

Minuit, Peter

Peter Minuit was the first governor of the Dutch colony of New Netherland, an area in the New World around the mouth of the Hudson River. In 1626 Minuit bought Manhattan Island from the Manna-hatan Indians for about $24 worth of trinkets, hatchets, and knives. The village founded on this island as a trading post was first called New Amsterdam. It is now New York, the largest city in the world. Peter Minuit was born in 1580 and died at sea while setting out for a new colony in the West Indies in 1638.

minuteman

Minuteman was a name given to many American colonists who were soldiers in the Revolutionary War. These colonists were called minutemen because they declared they were ready to fight for their independence from Great Britain at a minute's notice. Minutemen was a name used particularly to describe the farmers in Massachusetts who fought against the British at the Battles of Lexington and Concord, the first battles of the Revolutionary War. There is a famous statue of a minuteman in the town square at Lexington, Massachusetts.

Mirabeau

Gabriel, Count of Mirabeau, was a

French statesman who was one of the leaders in the French Revolution, when the people threw out their king and noblemen and France became a republic. Mirabeau helped the revolutionists though he was a count, one of the noblemen against whom the people were fighting.

Mirabeau was born in 1749 in Paris, and was an unusually ugly child. One foot was twisted, he was tongue-tied, and smallpox disfigured him with scars. His father was so ashamed of him that he was sent to a school far from home, under a false name. He was a brilliant student, and became extremely popular in spite of his appearance. He spent several years in prison for debt because his rich father refused to help him.

Mirabeau became interested in politics, and when the French Revolution started in 1789 he was one of its eloquent spokesmen. He had mastered his tongue-tied condition and was a superb orator. He fought for the rights of the people, but he insisted that the royal family also had the right to just treatment. Mirabeau died, after a long illness, in 1791.

miracle

A miracle is something that happens by a special act of deity (God), when it could not possibly happen by the usual processes of nature. The Bible tells of many miracles, including a number of miracles performed by Jesus. The first miracle of Jesus was at a marriage at Cana, a town in Palestine, when he turned water into wine; later he healed the lame and blind and made dead persons live again. Miracles have occasionally been reported since the time when Jesus was on earth.

miracle play, an old form of drama: see MYSTERY PLAY.

mirage

A mirage is a trick that light plays on people's eyes, making them see images of things that are not really there.

Most mirages are made by the peculiar way in which light behaves in hot, dry places such as deserts, or in cold, damp places such as the ocean. In a desert, the air close to the sand is much hotter than the air above it. Sunlight is reflected off

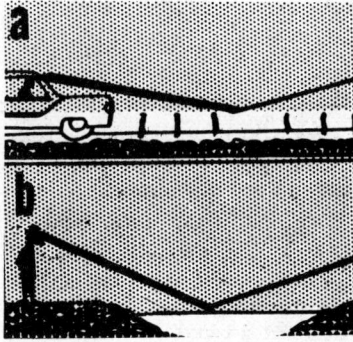

MIRAGE. The man driving across a south-western desert (a) "sees" a pool of water. It is a mirage. The light passing through the cool air has bounced off the warm air near the ground without ever really touching the ground, and looks as if it is reflected by a pool of water. The light reflected in a real pool of water (b) looks very much the same.

the layer of warm air, as shown in the picture on the preceding page.

This reflected light fools people, especially those who are very thirsty, into thinking that the light is coming from water. You may have seen these "pools of water" on a highway when you have been riding in a car on a summer day. In many cases, trees and other objects that are several miles away are reflected in these "pools" in the same way they would be reflected by real water.

On the ocean, mirages of ships are formed in the sky by light passing from a ship through the cold air above the water into the warmer air higher up. The mirage often looks like an upside-down ship sailing in the sky. The bending of light in the air above the ocean also explains why ships often seem to be closer than they really are. This mirage is known as *looming*.

A remarkable mirage known as the *fata morgana* makes it appear that ships, houses, or men are floating in the sky above the water. There usually are two mirages, one right-side up, the other upside down. These mirages were first seen in the Straits of Messina, a body of water separating Italy from Sicily. They gave rise to many legends of ghosts and spirits that were believed to haunt the straits.

Many mirages have been photographed and examined by scientists.

mirror

A mirror is a highly polished surface off which rays of light are bounced or reflected in such a way as to give a picture or image of objects in front of it.

Pools of water were the first mirrors. Later, polished metals were used, and then glass, blackened on one side and coated with silver or tin and mercury.

There are three kinds of mirror: plane (flat); concave (curved inward); and convex (curved outward). Convex and concave mirrors often are called *spherical* mirrors.

PLANE MIRRORS

A plane mirror is the one commonly used in the home as a wall mirror or a looking-glass. When you stand in front of such a mirror, your image appears to be coming from behind the mirror. Such an image is called a *virtual* image. The image also appears to be reversed. The right side of your body will appear on the left side of the image. If you put your finger over your right eye, it will appear over the left eye in your image.

A plane mirror will regularly reflect light. That is, a beam of light striking the mirror will be reflected as a beam of light, instead of being broken up or diffused into separate light rays. Light falling straight on the mirror will be reflected straight back. Light falling on the mirror at an angle, called an *angle of incidence*, will be reflected in another direction at the same angle, called an *angle of reflection*.

Plane mirrors often are used in periscopes, devices used in submerged submarines to see what is happening on the surface of the water. A periscope has two mirrors, one at the top and one at the bottom. Light strikes the top mirror, which is set in a tube at an angle, and is reflected down to the bottom mirror, set

in the tube at the same angle. A person looking into the periscope through a slit near the bottom can see what is happening several feet above and in front of him.

Plane mirrors also are used in carnivals to create what are called *optical illusions,* or tricks of the eyes. One of the most familiar is the "headless" man or woman.

This optical illusion is created by mirrors placed in front of the head of a man or woman sitting in a chair. The mirrors are placed at an angle to each other and so arranged that they reflect the images of the walls on both sides of them. A person looking at the mirrors does not see them but only what he thinks is a wall behind the shoulders of a headless man or woman.

The spherical mirror (S) brings light to an approximate focus (F), but a parabolic mirror or reflector brings the light to an exact focus (F) and thus gives a more concentrated beam of light.
The headless man is easy to create. All it takes is an arrangement of mirrors so that they reflect opposite walls.

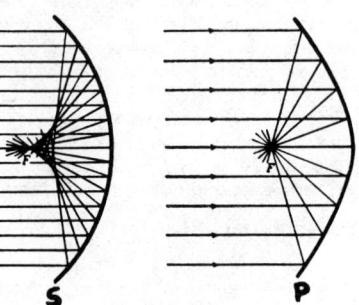

The one-way glass is a type of mirror that partly reflects and partly lets through light. A person looking at the polished side of the glass can see only his own reflection. A person on the other side can see through the glass without being observed.

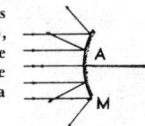

As convex mirror (M) is bent back on its axis (A), it reflects light from more directions than a plane mirror does, and gives a wider view.

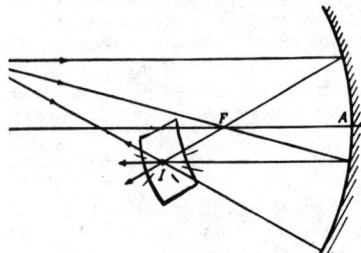

The concave mirror (M) is bent forward on its axis (A). Light from the bulb is brought to a focus at the focal point (F) and is reflected on the paper in the form of a spot of light, or image (I).

SPHERICAL MIRRORS

Spherical mirrors have many important uses, one of the most important being to spread out a beam of light or bring it to a smaller point or focus. A concave mirror brings light to a focus and the spot can be thrown onto a screen. Such a spot is called a *real* image. Concave mirrors also can make virtual images

1085

that are larger than those made on a plane mirror. For this reason, a dentist uses a small concave mirror on a long handle placing it behind your teeth to make them appear larger so that he can examine them more closely.

Almost all large telescopes use large concave mirrors to gather the light from near stars so that distant stars can be seen more clearly or photographed.

The largest concave mirror of this kind is in the Mount Palomar Observatory located in southern California. It is 200 inches in diameter.

A special kind of concave mirror, made of polished metal and called a *parabolic reflector,* is used in automobile headlights. The mirror is placed behind the light and is shaped in such a way that the light rays come out as a straight beam. Parabolic reflectors are used also in search lights and in photoflash attachments to a camera.

Metropolitan Museum of Art

In ancient times mirrors were made of highly polished metal. The elaborately decorated Etruscan mirror (made of bronze) is between 2,300 and 2,400 years old.

Convex mirrors are used often as rearview mirrors on trucks and automobiles. The image is smaller in a convex than in a plane mirror, making it possible to see more of what is behind you.

Both convex and concave mirrors are used in amusement parks. A person looking into one of them sees himself all out of shape. The reason for this is that light is reflected differently from a curved surface than from a plane surface.

misdemeanor

A misdemeanor is an act that breaks the law but is not considered important enough to call for severe punishment. Examples are parking overtime, littering the streets with trash, or creating a nuisance by making loud noises. A person who commits a misdemeanor usually has to pay a fine but is seldom sent to jail. A more serious crime is called a FELONY, about which there is a separate article.

missal

The missal is a prayer book used by priests in the Roman Catholic Church when they say Mass, and by people who are present at Mass. (There is a separate article about the MASS). All missals are taken from the Roman missal, which is in the Latin language. The missal used by the priest is in Latin, but the missal used by the people usually has a translation of the Mass into the language of their country. It has all the prayers of the Mass and directions telling how the Mass should be said. Some missals give the different Masses for every day of the year. Others are called "Sunday missals" and they have only the Masses for Sundays and holy days when all Catholics have to go to Mass.

missions and missionaries

A missionary is a man who leaves his own home to preach his religion in distant places. He goes where his religion is not yet known or established, and afterwards stays there to help it grow among the people. Most missionaries are Christians, though other religions such as Islam (the religion of Mohammed) have also had missions.

The first Christian missionaries were the Apostles whom Jesus told to go and preach to all nations. The New Testament of the Bible tells about their missionary work in the "Acts of the Apostles" and the Epistles, especially the Epistles of St. Paul. St. PAUL, about whom you may read in a separate article, is often called the greatest of the missionaries. His journeys took him as far away from Palestine as Greece and Rome, where he brought many people into the Christian faith. The missionary work of the early Christians was quite successful. About four hundred years after the birth of Jesus, the Christian faith was spread throughout the known world.

During the Middle Ages, which began about five hundred years after Christ's birth, missionaries moved north to central Europe and northwest to the British Isles. The great missionaries of this period included St. Patrick, who brought the Christian faith to Ireland, St. Augustine of Canterbury, who was an important founder of Christianity in England, and St. Boniface, who is often called the Apostle of Germany.

ROMAN CATHOLIC MISSIONS

During the second part of the Middle Ages, when most of Europe was Christian, missionary activities were not widespread. Then, when the great explorers began to discover new lands, missionaries again began to be numerous. There were several earlier Roman Catholic missionary *orders.* An order is a group of monks, priests, or nuns, who follow certain special rules and live very simply, away from other people. Among the orders were the Dominicans, the Benedictines, the Franciscans, and the Carmelites.

The greatest of the Roman Catholic missionary orders during the period of discovery and settlement was the Jesuits. This order was started in 1534, soon after the voyages of Columbus. They traveled to the New World and to the Far East, the Orient. St. Francis Xavier, the best known of the Jesuit missionaries, preached in India, and Japan. St. Isaac Jogues was killed by Indians at Auriesville, New York. Many early missionaries explored the rivers of America and were the first to learn Indian languages and to write books about them. There is a Roman Catholic organization called the Society for the Propagation of the Faith. It is in charge of the work of Catholic missionaries all over the world.

PROTESTANT MISSIONARIES

At first, Protestant churches did not have many missionaries. Later, when Protestantism had grown, Protestant missions were started all over the world. The first Protestant missionaries came to the New World in the 16th century, but they could not survive. There were several later missions, both in America and in other newly discovered places.

The great period of Protestant missionary work resulted from the deep faith of the founder of Methodism, John WESLEY, and his good friend Charles WHITEFIELD. (There are separate articles about both men). Societies were formed to send missionaries to India, Africa, and the Orient. During the 19th century every Protestant country had missionary societies. The people gave generously to pay expenses. Missions were founded all over the world. The missionaries helped to educate people and cure them when they were sick.

This work has been continued in the present day. During World War II, in spite of hardships, missionaries helped those who lost their homes or families. Hospitals, orphanages, and churches destroyed in the war were rebuilt.

There are separate articles on two famous Protestant missionaries, David LIVINGSTONE and Albert SCHWEITZER.

Mississippi

Mississippi is a state in the "deep south" of the United States. Its nickname is the "Magnolia State" because of the many beautiful magnolia trees that grow there. Mississippi is one of the leading cotton states and visitors can see large plantations and fine mansions that remind one of the Old South in the days before the Civil War. Mississippi is named for the Mississippi River, which runs along the state's western boundary.

Mississippi ranks 32nd in size among the states, with 47,716 square miles. In population it ranks 29th, with more than two million people living there. It became a state in 1817, and was the 20th state admitted to the United States. The capital is Jackson.

THE PEOPLE OF MISSISSIPPI

The earliest settlers in the Mississippi region were French and Spanish explorers. Later many more English and Scotch-Irish came and started large farms. These families have lived so long in the state that almost all the people of Mississippi are American-born.

Visitors to Mississippi will see almost as many Negroes as white people. The Negroes were brought as slaves from Africa about 200 years ago, to work on the large cotton plantations. Now there are almost a million Negroes living in the state, and they make up almost half the population. Most of the Negroes work on the farms or in factories.

Most of the people of Mississippi are farmers. Cotton is still their most important crop, as it was before the Civil War, but farmers have learned also to grow many other crops, such as peanuts, sugar cane, rice, sweet potatoes, and corn. They also raise dairy cattle and large

quantities of fruits and vegetables. In the past fifty years farmers have raised tung trees. The nuts from these trees produce an oil that is used in paints and varnishes. More than half the tung trees in the United States are grown in Mississippi.

Many people also work in the large pine forests in the southern part of the state. They also cut down other valuable timber that is used for lumber products.

A number of people live in the cities and work in factories, making cottonseed oil, textiles, and paints. Some work in natural gas fields and in the recently discovered oil fields in the southern part of the state.

For a long time, the people of Mississippi were very backward, and there were many who could neither read nor write, particularly among the Negroes. This situation has gradually improved.

The churches are very important in the social life of people in Mississippi. Nearly everyone goes to Sunday School and to church. In the smaller towns especially, people have their clubs and give parties and picnics through their churches. The largest religious group in the state is the Baptists. There are also many Methodists.

WHAT MISSISSIPPI IS LIKE

Mississippi is a state of rolling prairies and hills. The most fertile section is the Mississippi Delta in the western part, between the Mississippi River and the Yazoo River. It is one of the greatest cotton-producing areas in the world. This part of the state is very low, and the Mississippi River would flood it constantly if the people had not built a series of strong walls called *levees*. Even so, sometimes there are serious floods that smash the levees and cause great loss of life and property.

In the central part of the state are the North Central Hills, where the farmers grow peanuts and fruit. This region was once more fertile than it is now. It was ruined when the people cut down the forests, letting the rich soil be washed away. This washing-away is called *erosion*. New forests have been planted to remedy this situation.

In the extreme northeast are the Tennessee Hills, the highest point in the state. Farther south is a fertile, grassy section that is excellent for cattle-raising. In the southern part of the state is the Piney Wood region, with fine forests that produce large quantities of lumber, turpentine, and tar.

Along the Gulf of Mexico, the southern boundary, are the sandy Coastal Meadows. This section has inlets and islands that are ideal for fishing. Many vacation resorts have been built along the coast, which includes the longest man-made beach in the world—26 miles of gleaming white sand.

As in other southern states, there are many small fur-bearing animals. Hunters will find raccoon, squirrel, and opossum.

The climate of Mississippi is subtropical, with long, hot summers and short, mild winters. Flowers bloom almost all year long in the southern part of the state, though in the northern part it is somewhat colder, and there is occasional snow. The summers are hot and damp, but they are made somewhat more pleasant by the breezes from the Gulf of Mexico. The average temperature in summer is about 81 degrees, and in winter about 47 degrees.

The Mississippi River has always been the most important means of transportation. The important Mississippi River ports are Natchez and Vicksburg. Railroads and highways now reach to almost all parts of the state. There are airports in the important cities.

THE GOVERNMENT OF MISSISSIPPI

Mississippi, like all of the other states,

The majestic state capitol building in Jackson was built in 1903 in American classic style.

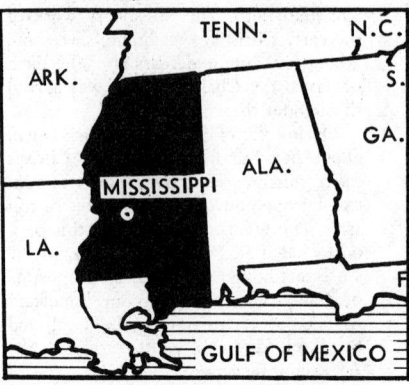

is governed by a Governor and a Legislature. The Legislature has two houses, a Senate and a House of Representatives. Their members, and the Governor, are elected for four-year terms, judges for eight-year terms. There are 82 counties. The capital is Jackson.

Mississippi has resisted integration of its schools, perhaps more than any other state, by law and by violence. In 1971 there was still great resistance to integration. In 1962, U. S. Government marshals were sent to Oxford, Mississippi, to force the University of Mississippi to admit Negro students. There was rioting and two persons were killed, but the Negroes were admitted and some Negroes (though very few) have since attended Mississippi's "white" colleges and a small number of its schools. Mississippi's colleges and universities include:

University of Mississippi, at University. Enrollment, 6,205 in 1971 (co-ed).

Mississippi State University, at State College. Enrollment, 8,607 in 1971 (co-ed).

Mississippi Southern College, at Hattiesburg. Enrollment, 8,000 in 1971 (co-ed).

Jackson College (for Negroes), at Jackson. Enrollment, 4,541 in 1971 (co-ed).

Delta State College, at Cleveland. Enrollment, 2,582 in 1971 (co-ed).

Alcorn Agricultural and Mechanical College, at Lorman. Enrollment, 2,290 in 1971.

CHIEF CITIES OF MISSISSIPPI

The leading cities of Mississippi, with populations from the 1970 census, are:

Jackson, population 153,968, the state capital and largest city in the state. There is a separate article about JACKSON.

Meridian, population 45,083, the third-largest city, railroad center, in the eastern part of the state.

Biloxi, population 48,486, the second-largest city, fishing resort, on the southern coast of the state.

Greenville, population 39,648, the fourth-largest city, cotton center, in the western part of the state.

Hattiesburg, population 38,277, the fifth-largest city, industrial and railroad center, in the southern part of the state.

Also the sea resort Gulfport (40,791) and the river ports Vicksburg (25,478) and Natchez (19,704).

MISSISSIPPI IN THE PAST

More than four hundred years ago, Hernando De Soto, the Spanish explorer, was the first white man to visit the region of Mississippi. More than one hundred years later the French explorer La Salle claimed the entire Mississippi Valley as part of France. The first permanent settlement was made at Old Biloxi by the French in 1699.

The French settlers had several fierce wars with Indians. The French were not very successful at starting new settlements, and about two hundred years ago part of the region was given to the British. A section of this was later conquered by Spain. After the Revolutionary War, all of it finally became part of the United States. In 1798 the Mississippi Territory was formed. This territory then included part of Alabama. In 1817 Mississippi became a state and the rest of the territory became the Alabama Territory.

The population grew and Mississippi soon became one of the most important cotton-growing states. There were large plantations, where hundreds of Negro slaves worked in the fields. When Abraham Lincoln became President in 1861, and it appeared that the slaves would be set free, Mississippi was one of the states to secede from the Union. The most important battle of the Civil War fought on Mississippi soil was the Battle of Vicksburg in 1863.

When the Civil War was over, Mississippi was very poor and in a state of disorder. "Carpetbaggers" (northerners who came with their suitcases and nothing else) controlled the state government and robbed it of millions. The people finally got back control of the state and began to rebuild and prosper, but only in the last fifty years has manufacturing become important in Mississippi. Since then, factories have sprung up rapidly, helped by the building of dams and electric-power lines.

PLACES TO SEE IN MISSISSIPPI

Ackia Battlefield National Monument, 49 acres, at Tupelo, in the northeast, on U.S. Route 78. Site of a Chickasaw Indian village, where the Chickasaws, aided by British troops, repulsed an attack of French and their Choctaw allies, in 1736.

Brices Cross Roads National Battlefield Site, 1 acre, at Baldwin, in the northeast, on U.S. Route 45. Scene of a battle in 1864, in which Confederate cavalry was employed with extraordinary skill.

Like most southerners, Mississippians are especially proud of their history and their famous men.

Jackson's historic City Hall.

A memorial at Vicksburg, where the Union won an important victory.

Vicksburg National Military Park, 1,649 acres, at Vicksburg, in the west, on U.S. Route 61. Remarkably preserved fortifications of the 47-day siege of Vicksburg in 1863, during the Civil War.

Delta Plantation, 38,000 acres, five miles east of Scott, in the west, on State Highway 1. The largest cotton plantation in the world.

Natchez, in the southwest, on U.S. Route 61. Has many beautiful, old houses built before the Civil War.

MISSISSIPPI. Area, 47,716 square miles. Population (1970 census) 2,216,912. Capital, Jackson. Nickname, the Magnolia State. Motto, *Virtute et Armis* (By Valor and Arms). Flower, magnolia. Bird, mockingbird. Song, "Mississippi." Admitted to Union, December 10, 1817. Official abbreviation, Miss.

Mississippi River

The Mississippi is the most important river in the United States. It is 2,348 miles long. If the Missouri River, which flows into the Mississippi, is considered part of the Mississippi, the combined river would be 3,860 miles long. That would make it the second-longest river in the world. The Nile River in Egypt is thought to be the longest.

The Mississippi flows through the Great Plains of the United States, one of the most fertile farming regions in the world. The Mississippi and its many tributaries (the rivers that flow into it) drain more than one million square miles between the Appalachian Mountains and the Rocky Mountains.

ITS COURSE

The Mississippi rises near Lake Itaska, in Minnesota, as a stream about ten feet wide and less than two feet deep. As it flows south through Minnesota, it is joined by the Minnesota River and becomes deep enough for boats to travel on. The Mississippi continues to widen and

deepen as it flows south between high hills. It forms part of the boundary between Minnesota and Wisconsin, and the boundary between Iowa and Illinois. Along this part of the river there are swift rapids. Many dams and locks have been built to let ships through, and the rapids supply useful water power. At Keokuk, Iowa, there is one of the largest power dams in the world and a hydroelectric plant.

Just above St. Louis, Missouri, the Mississippi is joined by the great Missouri River, known as "Old Muddy." For some distance, a person can distinctly see the two rivers as they flow along together. The Mississippi is very clear and the Missouri is a reddish, muddy color. Then the Mississippi becomes muddy.

At Cairo, Illinois, the Mississippi is joined by the Ohio River. Here the river reaches its greatest width, and is almost a mile wide. It winds on past rich and fertile farm land, and forms the boundaries between Arkansas on the west and Tennessee and Mississippi on the east. It then flows into Louisiana and past the city of New Orleans.

Below Baton Rouge is the large Mississippi delta. The river splits into several branches. Between them are deposits of soil brought down by the river over the course of centuries. This lower part of the river winds through swamps and bayous, and finally empties into the Gulf of Mexico. The Mississippi carries more than 600,000 cubic feet of water into the Gulf of Mexico every second.

LEVEES AND FLOOD CONTROL

The Mississippi deposits a great deal of sand, mud and gravel along its banks. This has built up walls, or natural levees, and the river flows between them. In some places the level of the river is higher than the land. These regions are very fertile, but heavy spring rains can make them dangerous. The rushing waters have often burst their banks, flooding cities and farms.

To prevent these terrible floods, men have built high banks of earth and stone, held together with asphalt. These are called levees. The levees usually hold back the waters during flood time, but sometimes the river rises above the levees, and sometimes it breaks through them. The United States government has helped by building canals and channels into which some of the water can go.

NAVIGATION

Most of the year the Mississippi is a peaceful river. Important industrial cities are situated along its banks, and dams on the river provide electric power for many factories. Some of the big cities are: St. Paul and Minneapolis, Minnesota; Dubuque and Davenport, Iowa; St. Louis, Missouri; Memphis, Tennessee; Vicksburg and Natchez, Mississippi; and Baton Rouge and New Orleans, Louisiana.

Tugboats go up and down the river every day, carrying important products. These tugboats can push a long line of barges loaded with cargo. The Mississippi is part of the great waterway system in the United States. It is connected with the Great Lakes in the north by the Illinois Waterway, and ships can sail from Chicago all the way down the

Mississippi to New Orleans. The Intracoastal Waterway crosses the Mississippi delta near New Orleans, connecting the river with the Atlantic Ocean.

THE MISSISSIPPI IN THE PAST

Mississippi is an Indian name meaning "Big River." The river is often called the "Father of Waters." More than four hundred years ago, the Spanish explorer Hernando de Soto first discovered the Mississippi near where Memphis, Tennessee, now stands. Later it was partly explored by Marquette and Joliet. Exploring the river, from its mouth almost to its source, was not completed until one hundred and forty years after de Soto by Robert La Salle.

The most important and colorful period of the Mississippi began after 1803, when the United States bought much of the Mississippi Valley in the Louisiana Purchase. Pioneers paddled down the river on rafts and flatboats to settle in the fertile region. A few years later, the first steamboat sailed down to New Orleans, and the Mississippi became one of the most important means of transportation in the country. Large plantations grew up in the south, and huge bales of cotton were carried down the river to the growing port of New Orleans.

Life on the Mississippi a hundred years ago was full of excitement, with its big paddle-wheel steamboats going back and forth. One of the most colorful things to see was the gaily decorated showboats, which would stop at towns along the river and put on plays. Mark Twain wrote several famous books about the river as it was then.

After railroads were built in the West, the Mississippi became less important, but it has continued to be the most important waterway in the United States.

Missouri

Missouri is a state in the great midwestern plain of the United States. Its nickname is the "Show Me State" because of an old belief that the people of Missouri have to be shown something before they believe it. When a person says "I'm from Missouri," he means he is doubtful of what has been said, and wants it proven to him. Missouri is famous for its folk tales, told among the people in the Ozark Mountains, and for the river stories that grew up along the Mississippi River, on the state's eastern boundary. Missouri gets its name from an Indian tribe that lived in the same region.

Missouri ranks 19th in size among the states, with 69,674 square miles. In pop-

ulation it ranks 13th, with more than four million people living there. It became a state in 1821, and was the 24th state to be admitted to the United States. The capital is Jefferson City.

THE PEOPLE OF MISSOURI

Americans from the eastern part of the United States were the first large group to settle in Missouri. Most of them became farmers. Later, people from Germany, Ireland, England, and many other European countries came and worked on the farms and in the growing factories. Most of these families have lived so long in the state that almost all Missourians are American-born.

A large group of people from Tennessee and Kentucky settled in the Ozark Mountains, in the southern part of Missouri. Their ancestors were English and Scottish. They still keep many of their old customs, and they even talk differently from the people in the rest of Missouri. These mountain people live in cabins and love to hunt and to tell stories. They are very suspicious of strangers, but once they accept a new person they are very hospitable.

More than half the people of Missouri live in the big cities and work in large factories. St. Louis is one of the largest manufacturers of shoes in the country. It is also one of the big meat-packing centers. In fact, St. Louis has so many important manufactures that it ranks seventh among the manufacturing cities in the United States. Many people work in the flour and meat-packing plants in Kansas City, which is the second-largest meat-packing center in the country (next to Chicago). The people of Missouri also make more corncob pipes than any other group in the world.

The farmers raise large crops of corn, wheat, oats, and barley. Others raise cattle and produce dairy products. The state is famous for the mules bred there.

There are rich lead mines in the southeastern and southwestern parts of the state. They produce more lead than any other state. Valuable timber is cut in the hardwood forests in the Ozarks.

The people of Missouri belong to many different churches. The largest groups are the Roman Catholic, Baptist, and Methodist. There are over 480,-000 Negroes in the state.

WHAT MISSOURI IS LIKE

The northern and southern parts of Missouri look very different. In the northern half of the state is a large rolling prairie, with many rivers. Here farmers raise corn, fruits and vegetables, and cattle.

In the southern half of Missouri are the rugged and beautiful Ozark Mountains, a favorite vacation area. Thousands come every year to enjoy the fine scenery and to fish in the lakes and streams. Between the high hills are deep valleys where there are flourishing apple orchards and vineyards. The important lead, coal and iron mines are in this part of the state. Hunters will find rabbits, foxes, opossums and other small fur-bearing animals in the woods.

The southeastern corner of Missouri, on the Mississippi River, is one of the most fertile regions. The land is very low and was once covered with thick forests. Now it is a rich farming and dairy section.

The climate of Missouri is quite varied. In the northern part of the state it is fairly cold, but the southeast has a warm climate like that of the "deep South." The Ozarks have mild summers and winters. The average temperature in Missouri in the summer is about 78 degrees; in winter it is about 31 degrees.

The people of Missouri use their many rivers for transportation. The Mississippi and Missouri rivers are most important. Railroads and highways reach almost all parts of the state, and there are airports in the important cities.

THE GOVERNMENT OF MISSOURI

Missouri, like most other states, is governed by a Governor and a Legislature. The Governor is elected for a four-year term. The Legislature is called the General Assembly, and is composed of two houses, a Senate and a House of Representatives. The members of the Senate are elected for a four-year term. Members of the House of Representatives are elected for a two-year term. Judges are elected for a ten-year term. The capital is Jefferson City. There are 114 counties.

There are more than 1,077,000 pupils enrolled in the public schools. Among the colleges, universities and other schools of higher learning, the principal ones are:

University of Missouri, at Columbia. Enrollment, 19,828 in 1971 (co-ed).
University of Kansas City, at Kansas City. Enrollment, 8,798 in 1971 (co-ed).
St. Louis University, at St. Louis. Enrollment, 10,890 in 1971 (co-ed).
Washington University, at St. Louis. Enrollment, 10,497 in 1971 (co-ed).
Lincoln University, at Jefferson City. Enrollment, 2,068 in 1971 (co-ed).

CHIEF CITIES OF MISSOURI

The leading cities of Missouri, with populations from the 1970 census, are:

St. Louis, population 622,236, the largest city in the state. There is a separate article about ST. LOUIS.

Kansas City, population 507,087, the second largest city. There is a separate article about KANSAS CITY.

Springfield, population 120,096, the third-largest city, trade and industrial center.

St. Joseph, population 72,691, the fourth-largest city, railroad and industrial center, in the northwestern part of the state.

Jefferson City, population 32,407, the state capital and twelfth-largest city. There is a separate article about JEFFERSON CITY.

MISSOURI IN THE PAST

The French explorer La Salle claimed the entire Mississippi River Valley for France almost three hundred years ago. His claim included the region of Missouri. The first permanent settlement in Missouri was not made until 1735, at Ste. Genevieve. Some years later the French gave their land west of the Mississippi River to the Spanish. The settlers in Missouri were ruled by Spain until 1800, when Spain gave the territory back to France. The region came under the control of the United States three years later as part of the Louisiana Purchase.

In 1812, the Territory of Missouri was formed. Many settlers from the East poured into the region and towns and farms quickly grew. The Indians did not like all these white settlers coming to their land, and they frequently attacked the settlements and killed the people. Finally peace treaties were signed with the Indian tribes and the territory grew even larger. Many southerners came to Missouri with their slaves and started large farms.

When Missouri asked to be admitted to the United States as a state, there was a question of whether it should be admitted as a slave state or as a free state. Northerners and southerners all over the country argued bitterly about Missouri, and finally it was settled by the Missouri Compromise in 1820, and Missouri came into the Union as a slave state. (There is a separate article about the MISSOURI COMPROMISE.)

Although many people were for slavery, many were opposed to it. When the Civil War broke out, Missouri decided to remain with the Union, but many Missourians joined the Confederate Army, and the state was very divided in its loyalty. After the Civil War the big plantations were broken up, and tenant farmers began to work the land instead of slaves.

Cities like St. Louis and Kansas City grew into important manufacturing and transportation centers, and mining developed and attracted workers from other countries. In both World War I and II, Missouri's prosperous farms and factories contributed greatly to the war effort. Today, the Missouri Valley Development is building many dams and reservoirs for flood control, and large power plants to supply electric power.

PLACES TO SEE IN MISSOURI

George Washington Carver National Monument, 210 acres, ten miles south of Joplin, in the southwest, on U.S. Route 71. Site of the birthplace and childhood home of the famous scientist.

Jefferson National Expansion Memorial, 82 acres, in St. Louis, in the east, on U.S. Routes 61 and 67. To commemorate the territorial expansion of the United States.

Mark Twain Home, in Hannibal, in the northeast on U.S. Route 36. The home where the author of *Tom Sawyer* and *Huckleberry Finn* grew up; now a museum.

Pony Express Monument, at St. Joseph, in the northwest, on U.S. Route 36. A statue to honor the riders who carried mail through dangerous Indian territory between St. Joseph, Missouri, and Sacramento, California, in 1860.

Lake of the Ozarks, 16,500 acres, north of Camdenton, in the central part of the state, on U.S. Route 54. Beautiful scenery and an excellent vacation spot for fishing, boating, and swimming.

Ste. Genevieve, in the east, on State Highway 25. The oldest town in Missouri; many historic buildings and a museum containing old relics.

MISSOURI. Area, 69,674 square miles. Population (1970 census) 4,676,501. Capital, Jefferson City. Nickname, the Show Me State. Motto, *Salus Populi Suprema Lex Esto* (Let the Welfare of the People Be the Supreme Law). Flower, hawthorn. Bird, bluebird. Song, "Missouri Waltz." Admitted to

Union, August 10, 1821. Official abbreviation, Mo.

Missouri Compromise

In the early years of the United States, Negroes were slaves in the southern states but not in the northern states. The rich southerners, whose wealth came from cotton and other crops raised by their slaves, constantly worried for fear the northern states would try to pass laws to do away with slavery. Whenever a new state was admitted to the United States, there was an argument over whether it should be a "free" state or a "slave" state.

That was the situation in 1819, when Missouri asked Congress to admit it as a state. Missouri had been settled by southerners, and it wanted to enter as a slave state. The northern members of Congress were against admitting another slave state; but at the same time they wanted to admit Maine, and of course Maine, the most northern of the states, would be a free state. The southerners did not want to admit Maine unless at the same time Missouri came in as a slave state.

In 1820 and 1821 the problem was solved by the "Missouri Compromise." In a compromise, each side gives up part of what it has been asking for. Maine was admitted as a free state. Missouri was admitted as a slave state, but it was agreed that from that time on no other state as far north as Missouri could be admitted as a slave state. Henry Clay, the statesman from Kentucky who came to be known as "the great compromiser," was given most of the credit for the Missouri Compromise. He did not propose it, but he supported it in Congress.

The Missouri Compromise was the first of many arguments that arose over the admission of states, and in the end all the compromises failed and the question of slavery was settled by the CIVIL WAR, about which there is a separate article.

Missouri River

The Missouri River is the longest river in the United States. It is 2,466 miles long and is the chief tributary of the Mississippi River. It is called the "Big Muddy" because of the muddy waters along much of its course. The Missouri River rises in Montana and flows southeast through North and South Dakota. As it continues southward, it forms parts of the boundaries between South Dakota and Nebraska, Nebraska and Iowa, Nebraska and Missouri, and Kansas and Missouri. It then winds across the state of Missouri and joins the Mississippi River, which flows down to the Gulf of Mexico. As the Missouri River flows along its long course it gathers a great deal of sand, gravel, and very fine earth, called silt. Every year it carries millions of tons of silt into the Mississippi River. Much of the Missouri is navigable for large boats.

The Missouri River is an important waterway, but the river and its many branches have often overflowed their banks and caused millions of dollars' worth of damage. Sometimes the vast Missouri Basin has also had severe droughts (dry spells) that killed the cattle and crops. This is because the upper part of the valley usually gets too little water, while the lower part of the valley gets too much. In 1944, the United States government started the Missouri River Basin Project. Its purpose was to provide a system of flood control and to build many new dams and reservoirs that would store up water in flood time and use it to provide irrigation in dry periods. Fort Peck Dam in Montana was built as part of the project. It is one of the largest earth dams in the world.

It is not known who were the first white men to explore the Missouri River, almost three hundred years ago. French fur traders followed them and explored the river farther north. About 1804, Lewis and Clark explored the river up to its source. A steamboat first sailed up the river in 1819. River traffic grew, and many pioneers going west traveled on the Missouri. After the railroads were built the Missouri became less important, but it may still become one of the chief sources of transportation and water power.

mistletoe

The mistletoe is a plant that grows in many parts of the world where the climate is not too cold. The mistletoe is a parasite, which means that it lives by getting its food from other plants. There are many kinds of mistletoe and many of them live on trees that are deciduous, which means they lose their leaves in the fall. The mistletoe itself is an evergreen plant; it does not lose its thick yellowish-green leaves in the fall. The common American mistletoe has small white berries. It is an attractive plant that is popular for decorating homes during the Christmas season. There is a custom in many countries that anyone who stands under a piece of mistletoe can be kissed. The Druids (ancient Celtic people in England) believed that the mistletoe was sacred. Mistletoe is the flower of the state of Oklahoma.

Mitchell, Margaret

Margaret Mitchell was an American writer. Her novel, *Gone with the Wind*, was one of the most successful books of this century, and one of the most successful of all motion pictures was made from it. Margaret Mitchell was born in Atlanta, Georgia, in 1900. As a young woman she wrote for newspapers there. She married John R. Marsh, an Atlanta business executive, when she was 25. She worked for years on her long novel, which was a story of the South at the time of the Civil War. Margaret Mitchell received many honors and could have sold another novel for a tremendous price, but refused. In 1949 she was killed in an automobile accident.

Mitchell, Maria

Maria Mitchell was an American astronomer, or scientist who studies heavenly bodies. She lived more than a hundred years ago. She was born in Nantucket, Massachusetts, in 1818, and later taught school there. She became interested in astronomy, and in 1847 she discovered a comet, for which she was rewarded by the king of Denmark with a gold medal. Maria Mitchell then became a professor of astronomy at Vassar College, where she remained until her death in 1889. She was the first woman to be elected to the American Academy of Arts and Sciences, and in 1905 she was elected to the Hall of Fame.

mite

The mite is a tiny animal resembling a spider that lives in almost every part of the world.

The mite has an egg-shaped body and four pairs of legs. It has sharp pincers that it uses to pierce its prey. Many mites are parasites (they live on other plants or animals). Some mites are useful because they feed on insects that are pests to man. Other mites feed on cattle, horses, and dogs and also on human beings. The mites that live on people are hard to find because they are so small, and they are a whitish color. When a human being or an animal is bitten by a mite it causes an unpleasant itch. Some mites feed on plants, such as fruit trees and evergreens. Farmers have poisonous sprays that they use to kill mites. Some mites infest cheese and other foods.

Mites are usually thought of as insects, but to scientists they are a different kind of animal. Mites are *arachnids*, as are spiders.

moa

The moa was a strange bird that lived in New Zealand long ago. There are no moas in existence now, but men have discovered traces of them in rocks that make it possible to tell what they looked like. The moa was a huge bird that weighed about five hundred pounds and was about nine feet high. With its long, thin legs, it probably looked somewhat like an ostrich. The moa could not fly.

Am. Mus. of Nat. Hist.

The New Zealand moa was a strange and interesting bird. Unfortunately, it became extinct in the 17th century because tribesmen killed it for food.

Scientists believe that the early people who lived in New Zealand hunted the moa, and it was such a fat and lazy bird that it could not protect itself, so gradually it died out.

Mobile

Mobile is the second-largest city in Alabama and its only seaport. About 200,000 people live there. The port is on Mobile Bay, part of the Gulf of Mexico. Four rivers flow through the city and empty into the bay.

Many of the people of Mobile work in shipyards. Others work in factories that manufacture railroad equipment, aluminum, concrete, and chemicals. Many ships sail from Mobile to South America. They carry cotton, metals, metal equipment, and corn and other grains, and bring back rubber, bauxite (aluminum ore), man-

ganese, bananas, and other South American products.

The area around Mobile was first settled by the French, more than 250 years ago. Later, Mobile belonged to the British and after that to the Spanish. In 1813, it was taken over by the United States. During the Civil War, Mobile was an important Confederate harbor, and was blockaded by Union ships. The Battle of Mobile Bay, in which the Confederate fleet was defeated, is described in the article on Admiral David FARRAGUT. For pictures of Mobile see the article on ALABAMA.

MOBILE, ALABAMA. Population (1970) 190,026. On Mobile Bay, on Gulf of Mexico.

moccasin

The moccasin is a poisonous snake that lives in swamps and along the banks of streams in the warm parts of the United States. The moccasin often reaches a length of 5 feet. The young snake is light brown or olive green in color, with clear black bands that circle its body. As the snake grows older, these bands fade. The fully grown moccasin snake is a grayish black color.

The moccasin is a greedy eater. It will devour birds, fish, frogs, eggs, and almost anything else it can find. When it is angry the moccasin will shake its tail and open its mouth very wide. The inside of the moccasin's mouth is white. For this reason people in the southern part of the United States sometimes call the moccasin by the nickname "cottonmouth." The bite of a moccasin is very dangerous.

mocking bird

The mocking bird lives in the southern part of the United States, where it is a great favorite because of its beautiful song. The mocking bird is very skillful at imitating the songs of other birds and it can also imitate the sound of a hen or frog. It is about the size of a robin, and is quite plain in appearance. It is a slender bird with short wings, and its feathers are dull gray and white.

The mocking bird builds its nest in a low tree. The female lays pretty green eggs with reddish brown spots. The male is a brave defender of the nest and will

Am. Mus. of Nat. Hist.
The mockingbird is able to imitate the calls of as many as thirty other birds.

fight any enemies that come near. The mocking bird eats insects and sometimes it eats fruit.

mock orange

The mock orange is a shrub that grows in Europe and the United States and in some parts of Asia where the climate is not too warm. The mock orange is sometimes known as syringa. It is a deciduous plant, which means that it loses its leaves every fall. It is a hardy plant that can grow well even in places where there is very little sunlight. There are several different kinds of mock orange, most of them growing to be more than six feet high. The mock orange is a very attractive shrub. It has shiny green leaves and beautiful sprays of white sweet-smelling blossoms that appear in early summer. People often grow mock orange shrubs in their gardens and in parks. It gets its name from the fact that its blossoms resemble the blossoms of the real orange.

models and model-making

A model is a small-scale likeness or copy of something. The models most frequently made are those of airplanes,

Tomorrow's pilots learn much about airplanes by making model planes.

ships, trains, houses, and people. Models are made both for study and for enjoyment. Engineers and architects first make models (or "mock-ups") of ships, planes, and buildings they have designed. They check these for weaknesses in proportion and construction, improvements in design.

Youngsters and grownups of all ages make model airplanes and ships, many of which actually work, for the pleasure of building and operating them. Many inventions are developed through the use of models of devices thought up by their inventors.

Clay modeling by hand is very popular. It is a form of sculpture in which models of people and things are made from clay. The clay is then baked, to harden it. It may be painted and decorated in all sorts of ways to make it as lifelike as its original.

MODEL AIRPLANES

The most popular form of model-making is the building of model airplanes. Millions of dollars each year are spent by model-airplane enthusiasts on balsa wood, tissue paper, razor blades, glue, waterproofing material, and other items necessary in building model planes. Special kits containing blueprints and all the necessary material are sold.

Model planes may contain a small gas, jet, or rocket engine or a rubber band to drive the propeller and enable the models to fly. Each year contests or meets are held

throughout the United States to determine the best model. Some model planes have flown as high as 2 miles for a distance of 50 miles.

MODEL SHIPS

Of interest too is the building of model ships inside narrow-necked bottles or jars. Such work takes patience and extreme care. Most of the construction is done outside the bottle. Holes are made in the hull (bottom of the ship) so that pieces of wood can be placed in them once the materials are inside the bottle. The sails and other movable parts are collapsed and held together by thread before the ship is inserted through the neck. When the ship is placed entirely inside the bottle, the threads are pulled tight and the ship is drawn up to its full size. A great deal of the work is done with long tweezers that are inserted in the bottle to put the various parts of the ship in place.

mohair

Mohair is a fine cloth that is made from the hair of the Angora goat that lives in Asia, South Africa, and Australia. Some Angora goats are now raised in the United States, in Texas. The goat has long silky hair, usually pure white. In the spring its hair is clipped. It is woven into a cloth that is strong and smooth. Mohair cloth does not collect dust and it lasts a long time. It is used to cover couches and chairs, and to make drapes. Mohair has also been used for making wigs and switches.

Mohammed

Mohammed was the founder of the great religion called Islam, or Mohammedanism. His name was formerly spelled Mahomet. He lived almost 1,400 years ago. The followers of Mohammed are called Mohammedans or Moslems, and they live in many parts of the world, particularly in Arabia, North Africa, Pakistan, and other parts of Asia. Although Mohammed never learned to read and write, he is considered one of the greatest religious leaders of the world. He brought the idea of one God and of right conduct to many people who before his time had worshiped many gods.

Mohammed was born in Mecca, a city in Arabia, in the year 570. His father died before he was born, and his mother died when he was a young child. He was brought up by his grandfather and his uncle. His uncle had many children of his own and was very poor. Mohammed had no schooling and as a young boy tended sheep. Later he became a camel driver and a caravan leader for a rich widow named Khadijah. When Mohammed was 25 years old he married Khadijah. They were married for many years and she helped him with his religious work.

At the time Mohammed was born, re-ligions such as Christianity, Judaism, Hinduism, and Buddhism had become strong in other parts of the world. But in Arabia, people of different tribes and cities had their own private gods. They did have a word, *Allah*, that stood for any god. Mohammed later

used this word to stand for the one and only God that he told his followers to worship.

Several years after Mohammed married, he became very interested in religion. He joined a group of people who called themselves *Hanifs,* or "penitents." He went often to a cave on Mount Hira, where he fasted and prayed. Here, he reported, the Angel Gabriel appeared to him in a vision, holding a scroll on which was written a message that Mohammed understood clearly as coming from Allah, even though Mohammed could not read. At first, Mohammed said, he could not believe that Allah had chosen him to lead the people, but when two years later he had another vision he was convinced, and from that time Mohammed never doubted that he had been chosen to bring the law of Allah to the people. The messages from Allah that Mohammed taught are recorded in the KORAN, the holy book of the Moslems, about which there is a separate article.

At first Mohammed's followers were few. They were mostly his own relatives and friends. Mohammed did not think he was starting a new religion, but reminding the people of an old one that had been forgotten. When Mohammed began to criticize the lesser gods of the people, saying that Allah would punish anyone who believed in them, many people became angry. Finally, after his wife had died, Mohammed had to flee from Mecca north to Medina. This flight, which took place in 622, is called the Hegira. The year 622 marks the beginning of the Mohammedan era in the Moslem calendar. The people of Medina listened to Mohammed's message, and many joined his religion.

Mohammed lived only ten years after he went to Medina. He died in the year 632, when he was 62 years old. During that time he gained more and more people to his religion and trained many of the prophets who spread his faith after he died. There is a separate article on ISLAM that tells more about the religion Mohammed preached.

Mohican, another spelling of the name of the Mahican Indians. James Fenimore Cooper wrote a famous book called *The Last of the Mohicans.* See the article on MAHICAN.

Mojave Desert

The Mojave Desert is part of the Great American Desert. It is in California, south of Death Valley. The Mojave Desert is a hot, dry region of mountains and plains, about 15,000 square miles in size. Few plants can grow there because of the dryness, but there are important deposits of borax, salt, gold, and tungsten. Farmers can grow crops in only a few places where there is irrigation. There are some cattle ranches. The Mojave River is the only river in this region. It flows mostly underground.

mold, a plant that feeds on other plants: see the article on FUNGUS.

mole

The mole is a small animal that lives in many parts of Europe, Asia, and the United States, where the climate is neither too hot nor too cold. Very few people have ever seen a mole because it spends almost all of its time underground. The mole is about seven inches long. It has powerful front claws and a long snout. The mole is so blind that it can hardly tell the difference between day and night, but its very sensitive snout partly makes up for its poor eyesight. The mole is a very hard worker. It spends all of its time digging long tunnels several feet beneath the surface of the earth. As it digs the mole eats the insects and worms that it finds in the ground. It makes a nest in its underground tunnel, and the female mole has five or six babies. The baby moles are almost completely helpless when they are born, but two months later they are fully grown and ready to join in the work.

The mole is useful to man. It has a thick, soft, gray or black fur that is made into fine fur coats. It eats harmful insects, and as it plows the earth to build tunnels it helps the farmers to keep the soil soft and rich.

molecule

A molecule is the smallest particle into which a substance can be divided without being changed into a different substance. Molecules are so small that they cannot be seen by the naked eye. Molecules are smaller than the finest grain of sand. In fact, a grain of sand contains millions of molecules. The air that you breathe is made up of molecules. In one breath of air you breathe in more than a million, million, million molecules.

All matter that is found in nature is made up of molecules. The basic substances of the earth, called *elements,* are made up of molecules. The combinations of these elements, called *compounds,* also are made up of molecules.

WHAT IS IN A MOLECULE

A molecule is not the smallest particle of matter. Molecules are made up of even smaller particles called *atoms.* The atoms in a molecule are arranged in a special way. If this arrangement is changed, the molecules will change into molecules of a different kind, and the substance made up of these molecules will also be changed.

Most molecules contain two or more atoms. A molecule of oxygen contains two atoms of oxygen. A molecule of hydrogen contains two atoms of hydrogen. Molecules that contain two atoms are called *diatomic* molecules. There are some molecules that have only one atom each. A helium molecule contains only one helium atom. Such a molecule is called a *monatomic* molecule. Some molecules contain more than fifty atoms. Such molecules are called *giant molecules,* or *macro-molecules.* The molecules of many viruses that cause sicknesses such as colds, influenza, and pneumonia are giant molecules. So are the molecules of substances such as sugars and starches, called carbohydrates.

All molecules of a particular element or compound have the same size, shape, and weight. All the molecules of an element are made up of the same kind of atoms, and the same number of atoms. Every oxygen molecule contains two oxygen atoms.

The molecules of a compound are made up of two or more different kinds of atoms. They all have the same number and arrangement of atoms. A molecule of water, which is a combination of hydrogen and oxygen, contains two atoms of hydrogen and one atom of oxygen.

CHANGES IN MOLECULES

When two or more elements combine to form a compound, the atoms of their molecules break away from each other and regroup themselves to form new and different molecules. This is known as a *chemical change.*

When one form of matter, such as a solid, changes into a different form of matter, such as a liquid (for example, ice into water), the molecules are unchanged. This is known as a *physical change.* The molecules of water are the same as the molecules of ice. The grouping of the atoms in these molecules is also the same.

SPACES BETWEEN MOLECULES

The molecules that make up all matter are separated by very tiny spaces. The smaller the spaces between the molecules, the more the molecules pull on each other. The pull between molecules of the same substance is called *cohesion.* The pull between molecules of different substances is called *adhesion.*

The spaces between molecules are smallest in solids, where cohesion is therefore greatest. In liquids the spaces are larger, and in gases they are still larger. The cohesion of molecules of a gas is much less than the cohesion of molecules in a liquid or solid.

It is hard to believe that a solid substance such as gold or iron really has spaces between its molecules. However, if a piece of iron is placed in a dish of mercury, the mercury will go in between these spaces and be absorbed by the iron.

BROWNIAN MOVEMENT

Because there are spaces separating the molecules, the molecules can move about. Molecules of matter are constantly moving. The molecules of a gas move about more than the molecules of a liquid or solid. Gas molecules move about in different directions, striking one another and bouncing away. Such motion is called Brownian movement, because a Scottish scientist named Robert Brown discovered it, more than a hundred years ago. The smaller the molecule the faster it moves about.

MOLECULAR WEIGHT

The weight of a molecule is given by a number that compares it to the weight of an atom of oxygen. The weight of an oxygen atom is represented by the number 16. Therefore, the weight of a molecule of oxygen, which contains two atoms of oxygen, is 16 plus 16, or 32. A molecule of carbon dioxide, a gas that is in the air you breathe out, contains one carbon atom (weight 12) and two oxygen atoms (16 each). The weight of a carbon dioxide molecule is therefore 12 plus 16 plus 16, or 44.

Molecular weight is also expressed in grams. For this purpose scientists use a quantity called a gram-molecule, or *mole.*

A mole of oxygen weighs 32 grams or a little more than an ounce. A mole of carbon dioxide weighs 44 grams. The number of molecules in a mole of a substance is the same for all substances. The number of molecules in 32 grams of oxygen is the same as the number of molecules in 44 grams of carbon dioxide. The number, 603,000,000,000,000,000,000,000 molecules (six hundred and three thousand million, million, million'), is called Avogadro's number, named after an Italian scientist who first discovered this law almost 150 years ago.

Molière

Molière was a great French writer of plays who lived three hundred years ago. He has been called the Shakespeare of France.

His real name was Jean Baptiste Poquelin, and he was born in Paris in 1622. His father and grandfather were servants of King Louis XIII, and young Jean Baptiste at first expected to follow in their footsteps but soon he developed a powerful interest in the theater.

After attending school he became the leader of a small band of traveling actors, and took the name of Molière. He was actor, company manager, and writer while he was traveling with this group. During this time he wrote many short plays and sketches that he afterward expanded into full-length plays.

He published his first play in 1653 and quickly became famous as a writer of comedy. One critic has said that though Shakespeare was a greater genius, Molière was better than Shakespeare at writing comedy. Molière's plays were witty and made fun of the small shortcomings and habits of people in general. They often expressed his scorn and contempt for the foolishness, snobbery and hypocrisy of the social and political life of the time. *Le Tartuffe, le Misanthrope,* and *le Bourgeois Gentilhomme* are among his most famous plays. In 1673, while acting in one of his own plays, he had a stroke and died an hour later.

mollusc or mollusk

A mollusk is an animal that has a soft body and no bones. There are more than seventy thousand different kinds of mollusk and they live in almost every part of the world. Most mollusks live in the water. A few make their homes on land. A mollusk usually has a hard shell that covers its soft body, but there are some mollusks, such as the octopus, that do not have shells. Many kinds of mollusk have a long thin foot that sticks out from the shell. The mollusk finds this foot helpful when it digs and crawls and swims.

The largest mollusk is the giant squid, which has a body about 19 feet long. This squid lives in the sea and few people ever have a chance to see it, although sometimes a dead giant squid is washed up on the beach, especially in Newfoundland. Some mollusks, such as the snail, are very small. Clams, oysters and scallops are mollusks that are good to eat. There is

more about mollusks in the article on ANIMAL LIFE.

Molotov, Vyacheslav

Vyacheslav Mikhailovich Molotov, once premier and at other times foreign minister of the Soviet Union, became prominent there soon after the Communists gained control in 1917 and was the only Soviet statesman who remained prominent in the government throughout the periods in which first Lenin, then Stalin, had power. Soft-spoken but firm, Molotov more than any other Soviet statesman has resembled the leading statesmen of the Western European and American countries.

Molotov was born in 1890. His real name was Skriabin, and he was the son of a shopkeeper. As a boy of 12 he joined a Communist group. In those days it was dangerous to be a Communist and young Skriabin changed his name to Molotov (which means "hammer" in Russian) to escape arrest. After the Communists began to rule Russia, Molotov rose rapidly in the government. In 1930, when he was 40 years old, he became premier. This was the highest office in the government, but actually Russia was controlled by Josef Stalin. However, from 1930 on Molotov was one of the chief spokesmen of Russian policy toward other nations. When Stalin died in 1953, Molotov was appointed again to be foreign minister, which he had been from 1939 to 1949. Then Molotov joined with some other leading officials in an attempt to prevent Nikita Khrushchev from becoming a dictator as Stalin had been. Khrushchev won, and in July 1957 Molotov lost his high position and after that served in minor diplomatic posts.

molting

When a living creature loses its skin, hair, feathers, or other outside covering, and replaces this covering with a new growth, it is said to *molt*. Many animals molt. Birds lose their feathers and grow new ones after their young birds are born. Some birds grow feathers that are particularly bright and beautiful before the mating season. Young birds often molt several times before they finally develop the feathers they will have during their adult lives.

Some birds, such as the pelican and the puffin, have bills with an outer covering and they molt these outer coverings. Grouse molt their long, sharp claws in the spring.

Animals molt their fur. Deer shed their antlers in the spring or the fall. Shellfish, such as lobsters and crayfish, shed their shells and develop new ones. Lizards and snakes lose their skins and grow new ones.

Many insects molt. The caterpillar changes its skin five times before it becomes a chrysalis. Scientists have discovered that insects that live longest seem to molt most often.

molybdenum

Molybdenum is a hard metal with a bright silvery luster. It has a very high

melting point. It is a chemical element, which means that it is one of the basic substances that make up the world. Molybdenum added to steel makes the steel very hard. Molybdenum steel tools are used to cut other metals. Cutting tools move at very high speeds and become very hot, but because of the high melting point of molybdenum they do not melt and lose their sharp edges. The turbine blades of turbo-jet airplane engines are made of molybdenum because it will not melt from the extremely hot gases that turn the turbine. Molybdenum is used in radio, television and X-ray tubes, and in the tips of the wires across which the sparks jump in spark plugs.

By combining molybdenum with other chemical elements, dyes can be made for coloring wool, leather, and silk. When molybdenum is combined with lead, it makes a bright orange-red dye that is used to color paints.

Molybdenum comes from the ore named *molybdite*. This ore is found in many parts of the world, but there is not very much of it. The United States mines more molybdenum ore than any other country. Utah leads in molybdite production, followed by Colorado, New Mexico, Arizona, Nevada, and California. These states mine about 70,000,000 pounds of molybdite a year. Molybdite is also mined in Canada, Chile, Finland, Norway, Yugoslavia, and other countries. A less important molybdenum ore is called wulfenite.

momentum

Momentum is the ability of a moving thing to overcome resistance. The momentum depends on the mass, or weight, of the thing, and on the velocity, or speed, with which the thing is moving.

You find out the momentum by multiplying the mass by the velocity. If a rock that weighs ten pounds falls off a ledge and hits the ground at ten miles an hour, its momentum is 10 times 10, which is 100. If a rock that weighs only two pounds falls off a higher ledge and hits the ground at fifty miles an hour, its momentum is also 100, because that is the result of multiplying 2 times 50.

You can feel the effect of momentum when any moving thing strikes against you. Suppose you stretch your arm out and someone lays a baseball in your hand.

The heavy car will strike the fence with a momentum more than a thousand times as great as that with which the ball hits the fence—even though the ball is traveling much faster than the car.

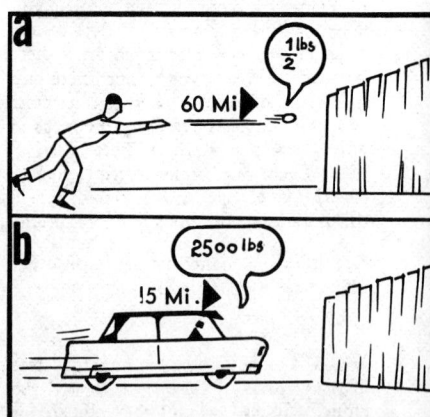

This will not cause your hand to move downward. But suppose the baseball were dropped into your hand from high above. It would be moving so fast that its momentum would cause your hand to move downward several inches. If a fifty-pound weight were laid in your hand, no matter how gently, it would cause your hand to move so far down that you would drop it.

Very heavy objects need not move at high speed to have a large momentum. An automobile that bumps into a wooden fence will smash the fence even though the automobile is moving slowly. A base-ball thrown against the fence with the same speed will do hardly any damage. A bullet, weighing only an ounce or so, will go all the way through the wood because of its great speed.

The momentum of an object can be transferred to another object. This is the basis of the game of billiards. If a billiard ball that is moving strikes squarely against a billiard ball that is not moving, the first ball will slow down or stop and the second will roll along with the momentum not used up by the first.

Monaco

Monaco is a tiny country in Europe on the Mediterranean Sea. It is nine miles from Nice, in France, near the border between France and Italy. It has an area of only 368 acres, which is smaller than the area of any other independent country except Vatican City. A little more than 20,000 people live there. They speak French. The capital, Monaco, is on the sea, and 2,000 people live there.

Monaco is famous because it is the location of the Casino of Monte Carlo, to which people go from all over the world to gamble at games, especially one called roulette. Citizens of Monaco are not allowed to play.

Monaco is a principality, which means it is ruled by a prince. The prince is assisted by a cabinet and National Council. Everyone is allowed to vote. The people are not taxed because the tax on gambling and the tourist trade pay the government's expenses. The French government controls Monaco's foreign affairs.

In 1956 the American people were thrilled when Grace Kelly, a beautiful Philadelphia girl who had become a famous motion-picture star, married Prince Rainier, the reigning prince of Monaco, and became a princess.

Monaco is a very popular winter resort. The capital has a museum and an Institute of Oceanography, at which scientists study the ocean and ocean life.

MONACO. Area, 368 acres. Population, 22,500. Language, French. Religion, Roman Catholic. Government, principality. Monetary unit, French franc. Flag, two horizontal bands, red and white. Capital, Monaco.

monarchy

Monarchy is a form of government in which a king is the head of the country. The king is said to be the *sovereign*, which means that he has the power to rule. There are other titles that mean about the same thing as king: monarch, emperor, prince, and many others. A country ruled by any one of these, or by a queen, may be called a kingdom, an empire, or by other names, but in any case it is a monarchy.

In a monarchy, when the king dies his oldest son or closest relative (if he has no son) becomes the next king. This is *hereditary monarchy*. In early times, kings were often elected, but for hundreds of years all monarchies have been hereditary. There are two ideas behind hereditary monarchy. One is the *divine right of kings*. It was once believed by many people that God had appointed the kings, and that disobedience to the king would be defiance of God. The other idea was that *royal blood* was different and better than the blood of all other people and that no one could become a king unless he was descended from kings. In modern times, almost no one believes this.

In an *absolute monarchy*, the king has power to make laws, and to put people in prison or have them executed. The king owns everything in the country, and can take it whenever he wants to. In ancient times there were many absolute monarchies, but for several hundred · years there have been few. Some countries have been called absolute monarchies, but actually the king had to keep on good terms with the most powerful noblemen or they would kill him and get a new king. A *limited monarchy* is one in which the king has some powers and the people or their representatives have other powers. The people in a limited monarchy have the most important powers, which include the right to make the laws and decide what the taxes will be. One kind of limited monarchy is called a *constitutional monarchy*. This means that there is a written constitution to say what powers the king has and what powers the people have.

The first kings, many thousands of years ago, were either war leaders or high priests who became so powerful that they were able to make their sons kings after them. This created *dynasties*, which are long lines of kings in which the *succession* (passing on of the king's power) is from father to son. In ancient Egypt and Rome, and until recently in modern Japan, kings taught the people to worship them as gods, to increase their power.

Most European countries have followed the *Salic law*. Under this law, a woman cannot become the ruler and the succession cannot pass through a woman. In England, which does not follow the Salic law, if a king has no son but does have a daughter she becomes the *queen regnant*, which means that she reigns (has a king's powers). There have been several reigning queens in England, beginning with Mary I, more than four hundred years ago. Elizabeth II is a *queen regnant*. In a Salic-law country, the former king's closest male relative would become the king.

A king's wife also is a queen but is a *queen consort*. The king or queen is addressed as "Your Majesty." Sons of a king are *princes* and daughters of a king are *princesses*. They are addressed as "Your Highness." The oldest son of a king is the *heir apparent*. Unless he dies, he is sure to become the next king. He is usually called the *crown prince*, but in England he is called the Prince of Wales and when France was a monarchy he was called the *dauphin*. When the king has no son, his closest relative is called the *heir presump-*

tive. An heir presumptive loses his place whenever the king has a son.

When a king is officially using his powers, he sits on a big chair called a *throne* in a room called his *court*. He wears a *crown* on his head, and may hold a gold, jeweled rod called a *scepter*. The throne, crown and scepter are said to be symbols of the king's rights and powers, so a new king is often said to inherit the throne, or the crown, or the scepter. A person is officially recognized as king or queen by having the crown placed on his head for the first time. This ceremony is called a *coronation*. When a king or reigning queen signs an official paper, the Latin word *rex* (meaning "king") or *regina* (meaning "queen") is used, so that George VI of England signed his name "George R." to stand for George Rex, and Elizabeth II signs her name "Elizabeth R." to stand for Elizabeth Regina.

When a king is too young or too sick to reign, one or more other persons are usually appointed to act for him. These persons are called *regents*, and the government is called a *regency*. It is still a monarchy, but its monarch is not reigning in person. England last had a regency from 1811 to 1820, when King George III was insane and the Prince of Wales was regent.

See also the article EMPIRE.

monastery

A monastery is a place where religious men live strictly regulated lives dedicated to their religion. Most monasteries are Christian, but the Buddhist and Moslem religions also have monasteries. Most Christian monasteries are Catholic. Among Protestant churches, only the Church of England has many monasteries.

Men who live in monasteries are called *monks*. They may be priests, or laymen (ordinary men) who have taken vows to remain poor, not to marry, and to be obedient to the man who is in charge of the monastery. The article on ABBEY describes one kind of monastery. Another kind is the *priory*. Sometimes a priory is ruled by an abbey. Convents, in which nuns live, are also called monasteries.

Many early Christians became hermits. They lived alone and spent most of their time praying. About 1,700 years ago, when many hermits lived in the deserts of Egypt, other religious men began to build their huts or "cells" near them. They would try to find a hermit who was very holy and then ask him to instruct them. That is how monasteries began.

Monasteries grew rapidly. In the Middle Ages, many monasteries were like small towns. They had their own farms and businesses. Some became famous for one product, such as a wine. For example, the Carthusian monks still have a secret formula for making a liqueur, or sweet alcoholic drink, called *chartreuse*.

Monasteries were also important as places of learning, for the monks would spend much time copying manuscripts. This was before the printing press had been invented, so books had to be copied by hand. The learning of the monks and the care with which they copied books preserved many great works that might otherwise have been lost forever. The monks also drew pictures to illustrate the books. Illustrations in a manuscript

are called *illuminations*. Many of these are very beautiful. The monks often used gold ink, and even now, many centuries later, the illuminations are bright and attractive. One of the most famous of these is the *Book of Kells,* which is kept in Ireland.

During the Reformation, when the Protestant Christian churches were formed, many monasteries were taken over by kings and other nobles. Their great holdings in land and buildings were used for the state.

The Benedictines and Trappists are two of the best-known Catholic religious orders that have monasteries. Many people of every faith visit the Trappist monastery at Gethsemane, Kentucky.

Monday

Monday is the second day of the week. Its name comes from a word meaning "moon's day," or the day sacred to the goddess of the moon. Monday is the first day of the working week in most Christian countries, coming after Sunday, the day of rest. In the United States, most national holidays that fall on Sunday are celebrated on Monday so that working people will have the additional day of leisure.

Labor Day is always observed on the first Monday in September.

Monet, Claude

Claude Monet was a French painter who lived about a hundred years ago. He was a leader of the Impressionist school of art, which took its name from a critic's comment on one of his paintings, *Morning, Rising Sun*. Monet was born in 1840. As a young man he studied the classical style of painting, but he soon felt he could not express himself in the formal traditions and he began to paint things as he saw them. He paid little attention to the details of his subject, but tried to picture the effects of light and air. His works were laughed at for many years, but gradually they won recognition and Monet became prosperous and well known. Among his famous paintings are *Rouen Cathedral, Water Lilies,* and *Fontainebleau Forest*. Monet was nearly blind for the last ten years of his life, and he died in 1926.

money

Money is anything that people will accept in payment for goods or services, and that can *circulate*—pass from one person to another many times without losing its value. We think of money as being coins or paper money, but actually people have used many different things for money. Fish, stones, corn, skins, cattle and sheep have all been used as money. The American Indians of New England used beads called *wampum* as money. An American farmer of today would not sell his coin for wampum, but neither would an Indian farmer have sold his corn for a printed piece of paper. What makes a particular article money is the fact that the people living in a community are willing to accept it as payment.

BARTER

At one time, long ago, there was no need for money. If a fisherman wanted some vegetables, he found a farmer and exchanged a certain number of fish for a certain number of vegetables. This method of trading one product for another is called *barter*. Barter still exists among certain peoples.

The difficulty with barter was that it was not always convenient. Suppose the fisherman could not find a farmer who happened to want fish at the moment. He would have to do without vegetables. Besides, if the fisherman wanted to exchange his fish for many different products, he would have to make many individual visits and perhaps have little time left for fishing.

HOW MONEY IS USED

Sooner or later, all groups of men found barter very inconvenient. Suppose the fisherman wants corn, but the farmer does not want fish. The fisherman must find someone who wants fish and who is willing to trade something that the farmer wants. He may have to trade several times before he can get his corn. When there is one thing that everyone wants—money—no one has to trade more than once.

Money also makes possible *savings*. A fisherman cannot wait to trade his fish, even if there is nothing he wants at the moment. The fish would spoil. Money, which does not spoil, can be saved until there is use for it.

In order for a certain material to be used as money, it must have certain qualities. It must be durable so that it does not wear out. It must be able to be carried without too much trouble. It must be able to be divided into smaller units in case goods of different values are traded. It must have a steady value so that people will know from one day or month to the next just what their goods are worth in terms of the money.

Not all things that have been used as money had all of these qualities, which is why some of them were abandoned. Stone was too heavy to carry about. Beads tended to get broken. Cattle and sheep might die. In time it was found that the best material for money was metal. In the beginning many metals were used as money, but gradually gold and silver became the most used metals, although some small coins are made of copper, nickel, tin, and other metals.

PAPER MONEY

About three hundred years ago another advance was made. Gold and silver coins are convenient for exchanges of small and medium values, but for large exchanges it was very cumbersome to carry about many heavy coins to make payment. So paper money (first used in China a thousand years ago) came into use in nearly all parts of the world. Paper money differs from other money because it has little or no value in itself. The paper of a hundred-dollar bill is not worth a penny. What gives the hundred-dollar bill its value is the fact that the government agrees to pay to the owner a hundred dollars' worth of gold or silver, or something of equal value. People accept a small slip of paper as money because they have confidence in the government.

Another name for paper money is *legal tender*. This means that when anyone tenders (offers) paper money in payment of a debt, the law requires that it be accepted. Coins such as fifty-cent pieces, quarters, nickels, and pennies are also legal tender, because the value of the metal they contain is not as great as the amount stamped on the face of the coins.

UNITS AND STANDARDS OF MONEY

The money of a country is made and controlled by its government. It decides which metals, and how much of the metals, are to be used for money. The United States uses silver and copper in coins worth ten cents or more, nickel and copper in five-cent pieces (nickels), and bronze in pennies (cents). Before 1933 the United States also had gold coins in various values, or denominations, from one dollar up to one hundred thousand dollars. Coins are made in government mints. The United States government has mints in Philadelphia, Denver, and San Francisco. Its paper money is made by the Bureau of Engraving and Printing, in Washington, D.C.

A government also decides what the unit of money should be. In the United States and Canada it is the dollar; in England, the pound sterling; in France, the franc; in Italy, the lira; in Mexico and other Latin-American countries, the peso.

But deciding on a monetary unit means more than giving it a name. More important it means deciding how much the unit is worth. A monetary unit is fixed by law as being a certain quantity of a certain metal. In the United States a dollar is worth $15\frac{5}{21}$ grains of a kind of gold that consists of nine parts of gold and one part of copper. Until 1933, anyone who wanted to could exchange his money, coins or paper, for gold and get

Unless you are a weight-lifter, shopping with the stone money of Yap is difficult.

Silver money used in Laos is designed to look like the tongue of a native tiger.

$15\frac{5}{21}$ grains of gold for each dollar. When a country's money is exchangeable for gold in this way, it is said to be on the *gold standard*. Some countries have based their monetary units on silver of a certain quantity and these countries are said to be on a *silver standard*.

In the past, some countries, including the United States, have used two metals for their standard. Until 1873 a person in the United States could get either silver or gold for his money. He could exchange a dollar either for a certain amount of gold or for about fifteen times as much

The *assignat* of the French Revolution had lands taken by the state as security.

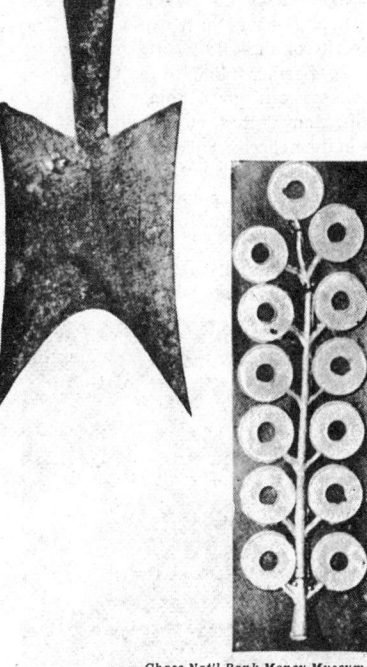

Chase Nat'l Bank Money Museum

The spade coin of China is the earliest known metal money. It was probably used in 2000 B.C. Below it is a tin tree coin of Malacca. It was cast in this form, and the "leaves" were broken off for use.

balances with other countries. (See the article on FOREIGN TRADE.)

money order

A money order is a paper issued by the Post Office Department. It is like a check on a bank, and makes it possible for people to send money safely through the mail. It is not safe to put bills or coins in a letter that is to be mailed, because the letter may be lost or stolen. A money order guarantees that only the person or business to whom the money is sent will be able to get the money.

An application for a money order must be made on a blank provided in all post offices. When the application has been filled out, giving the name of the sender of the money order, the name of the person who will receive the money, and the amount of money that person is to receive, a post-office official makes out a money order that includes all this information. The person sending the money order gives the official the money he wishes to send, plus an additional small charge, and he receives a receipt for his money. Then he encloses the money order in an envelope and mails it. When the person for whom the money is intended receives the money order, he can exchange it for money at any post office.

Money orders can be for any amount up to a hundred dollars, and charges for sending them depend upon their amount.

For many years the Post Office Department also sold postal notes, which were somewhat like money orders. Postal notes were discontinued in 1951.

Mongolia

Mongolia is a large region of east central Asia, between China and Soviet Russia. It includes the great GOBI DESERT, about which there is a separate article. It is about one million square miles in area, which is almost four times the size of Texas. More than 7,000,000 people live there, which is less than the population of Texas.

Mongolia is divided into two main parts. *Inner Mongolia* is an autonomous region of Communist China. The Chinese government has repeatedly altered its boundaries by adding other areas to it. The population in 1953 was 6,100,104. Outer Mongolia, also called the *Mongolian People's Republic,* is supposed to be an independent country but is controlled by Soviet Russia. It is 625,495 square miles in size, with a population estimated in 1961 to be 954,000.

THE MONGOL PEOPLE

The people of Mongolia are called

Bronze currency in the form of knives was used as money in ancient China.

During the Civil War the Confederate government of Missouri issued war scrip.

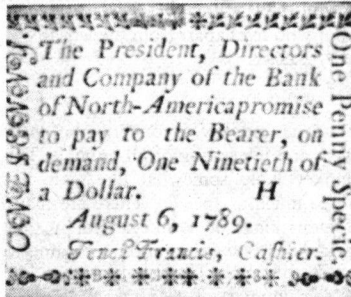

The first United States chartered bank issued paper money worth 1.1 cents.

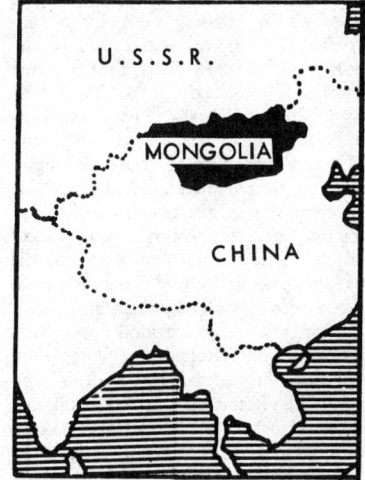

silver as gold. This system is called *bimetallism.* Bimetallism did not work out very well and was abandoned by the United States and the other countries that used it.

When a country has silver or gold, or both, as its money standard, it makes coins of these metals and must keep on hand a supply of the metals for people who wish to exchange their money for the standard metals. Until the early 1930s, most countries of the world were on the gold standard and had reserves of gold. But those were depression years and the governments had to use much of their gold reserves. In order to keep as much of the gold as possible, they called in all their gold coins and declared that their money could no longer be exchanged for gold. This act is known as going off the gold standard. In 1933 the United States joined the other countries of the world and went off the gold standard. Even though the world got over the depression and built up the gold reserves again, the countries have not gone back to the gold standard.

At the present time, there are no gold

Wampum made from mollusc-shell beads was used as money and jewelry by Indians.

coins in circulation in the United States. The dollar cannot be exchanged for gold, and anyone who has gold must sell it to the government (unless it is used in manufacturing, as in jewelry, or in dentistry). Nevertheless, the dollar still has a value of a certain amount of gold. The United States government maintains a large supply of gold at Fort Knox, Kentucky, which it uses to settle foreign trade

The pine-tree shilling minted in Boston by John Hull is a noted Colonial coin.

Mongols. They have yellowish skin, straight black hair, and rather square faces with prominent cheekbones and wide noses. Many Mongols are nomads. That is, they seldom stay in one place for long, but constantly move to new homes with their families and flocks. Most of them raise livestock, and a man's wealth is judged according to the number of sheep, cattle and goats that he owns. Most of the people are Lamaists. Lamaism is a form of the Buddhist religion.

Mongols are famous camel-drivers. Marco Polo and other early European travelers to China crossed the Gobi Desert and the rest of Mongolia under their guidance. For hundreds of years, large camel caravans driven by Mongols took goods from north China to Russia and Europe. Roads in Mongolia still follow the routes of the ancient caravans.

In recent times the Mongols have become less nomadic. Their farms produce millet, barley, and wheat. They work at mining iron, coal, gold, lead, zinc, and copper. The Chinese Communist government has built steel mills at Paotow, an important city of Mongolia.

WHAT IT IS LIKE THERE

Mongolia is a high, level region, more than a mile high and bordered on the east, north and northwest by very high mountains. These include the ALTAI MOUNTAINS, about which there is a separate article. The Gobi Desert in the center separates Inner from Outer Mongolia. Mongolia runs as far south as the ancient Great Wall of China.

Most of Mongolia is a very flat country, though it is high above sea level and rises to mountains as high as 12,300 feet in the central part. The region is very dry, and in most spots the only plant is short, tough grass. In many parts, the only buildings are the monasteries belonging to the Buddhist monks. Many of the people live in tents that they can take with them when they move. Only in the north, near Soviet Russia, are there any large rivers. Mongolia is very cold in winter and hot in summer.

MONGOLIA IN THE PAST

People have lived in Mongolia for many thousands of years, but the Mongols did not arrive until about six hundred years ago, when GENGHIS KHAN (about whom there is a separate article) established the heart of his great empire in Mongolia. His sons and grandsons increased the empire he founded. In the year 1240 the Mongol empire reached from the Pacific coast of China all the way to the frontiers of Poland and Germany, and included parts of Russia and Hungary, and much of Asia. This empire broke up, but about a hundred years later another Mongol warrior, Tamerlane, or Timur, again established a vast Mongol empire. After Tamerlane's death the Mongol empire declined. There is a separate article about TAMERLANE.

Mongolia never regained importance. The Soviet-style Republic of Outer Mongolia was formed in 1924, with its capital at Ulan Bator, a city of about 160,000. Inner Mongolia fell to the Chinese Communists in 1947. The capital is Huhehot (formerly Kweisui), a city of about 110,000.

MONGOLIA. Area, 1,000,000 square miles. Population about 7,000,000. Vast, flat region in east central Asia.

mongoose

The mongoose is a fierce little animal that lives in Asia, Africa, and in Spain, where the climate is warm. The mongoose is about 2 feet long. It has a sharp, pointed face with bright eyes. The fur of the mongoose is brown or black, and it has a long, bushy tail. The mongoose is a skillful fighter and it can kill a snake many times its size. Most often the mongoose is the winner in these savage battles, and then it settles down to eat the snake. The mongoose also eats rats, mice, birds, and many other small animals.

The mongoose has great curiosity, and if it spies some interesting object it will go right into a person's house to have a better look. People took the mongoose to Hawaii in order to kill rats. But they discovered that it is fond of killing chickens, and it has become a great nuisance to the farmers. The great English writer, Rudyard Kipling, wrote a popular story about a mongoose named Rikki-tikki-tavi.

Monitor and Merrimac

The *Monitor* and the *Merrimac* were both American warships. During the Civil War they fought against each other in a battle that is famous in naval history. It was the first battle ever fought between ironclad ships; that is, ships covered with iron. The *Merrimac* had belonged to the United States Navy, but it had been scuttled when the Union forces had to leave their naval yard at Portsmouth, Virginia, at the beginning of the Civil War. The Confederates raised the sunken ship, changed it into an ironclad, and renamed it the *Virginia*. The rebuilt *Merrimac* defeated several Union ships before it finally met the *Monitor* at Hampton Roads, Virginia, on March 9, 1862. The *Monitor* was a heavy iron ship just built by the Union navy. It was much smaller than the *Merrimac* and had a very peculiar shape. The Confederates made fun of it and called it a "cheesebox on a raft." It looked like a platform with a round tower as it floated in the water. Actually it was so well protected that the *Merrimac* could not hurt it. The battle between the two ships lasted over three hours. Neither ship won a decisive victory, but the *Merrimac* fled to Norfolk and never fought the *Monitor* again. Later the navy made many more ships like the *Monitor*.

monk, a member of a religious order who lives apart from the world. See MONASTERY.

monkey

The monkey is one of the most lively and interesting of all animals. The monkey looks somewhat like man, but not so much as apes do. There are many different kinds of monkey. Usually they are divided into two groups, according to where they live. The monkeys that live in the jungles of Central and South America and Mexico are called the New World monkeys. The monkeys that live in Asia and Africa are called Old World monkeys. There are some important differences between these two groups.

The New World monkeys have more teeth. Their noses are flat, and the nostrils are much farther apart. Almost all of the New World monkeys have tails (called prehensile) with which they can grasp things. This tail is very handy when a monkey wants to travel quickly through the forest. It can use its tail as another arm to swing from one tree to the next.

The monkeys of the Old World have four fewer teeth than the New World monkeys. (The Old World monkey and man both have thirty-two teeth.) The nostrils of the Old World monkey are closer together. None of the Old World monkeys can grasp things with their tails. Many of these monkeys have pouches in their cheeks. They use these pouches to store the fruit, nuts, small birds, and eggs that they eat. Some Old World monkeys eat leaves, and they have no cheek pouches.

Monkeys usually like to sleep at night and are wide awake when the sun comes

Am. Museum of Nat. Hist.

The colobus monkey from Africa seems to think that its white beard requires it to act in a quiet and dignified manner.

up. Most monkeys live in trees, although some monkeys, such as the Old World baboon, make their homes on the ground. There are tiny monkeys, like the capuchin of South America, which are about as large as a cat. There are large monkeys, like the Old World baboon, which is as tall as a Great Dane dog and very heavy and powerful. Some monkeys are dull brown in color and others are bright yellow. There are monkeys that are covered with hair and monkeys that have no hair. There are friendly, sociable monkeys, such as the rhesus of the Old World, and angry, mean monkeys such as the New World howler.

Monkeys have long been one of man's favorite animals because they are usually full of tricks and have hundreds of funny expressions. Monkeys are intelligent and can be taught to do many tricks. The stunts of monkeys in the circus and in zoos are amusing, and many people have been pleased by the little monkey that the organ grinder has. Some people keep monkeys for pets. You can read about the RHESUS, the CAPUCHIN, and the HOWLER monkeys in separate articles. See also the article on the BARBARY APE.

Monmouth, Duke of

James, Duke of Monmouth, was an Englishman who insisted that he was the son of King Charles II of England and who claimed the right to be king after Charles II died. Monmouth was born about three hundred years ago, in the year 1659. Most of the influential Englishmen did not believe Monmouth was the son of Charles, and when Charles died in 1685, James II, the brother of Charles, was made king. Monmouth found enough supporters to raise a small army in Hol-

land. He landed in England, where he hoped the people would support him and add to his army. He did not get enough support and was defeated by the king's forces. Monmouth was captured and put to death in July, 1685, only six months after the death of the man he said was his father.

monopoly

When different companies are struggling against one another for customers, it is called *free competition,* and it is very good for the public. If one company tries to charge too much, people can buy from another company. But if a single company controls the entire supply of something, it can charge what it pleases and people have to pay the price or do without. This is called a *monopoly.*

In the years after the Civil War in the United States, companies in the same business began to get together and make secret agreements that they would all charge the same high prices. This was a new kind of monopoly, and was called a *trust.* A "Board of Trustees," representing all the companies, would decide what the prices should be. If some small company outside the trust would try to charge fair, low prices, the trust would set its own prices very low and drive the small company out of business. Then the trust would raise prices again.

The American people became frightened because so many trusts were springing up and were growing very rich and powerful. To prevent this, Congress in 1890 passed a law, called the Sherman Anti-Trust Act because it was introduced by Senator John Sherman of Ohio, to break up these trusts. A newer and stronger law introduced by Henry Clayton, a Congressman from Alabama, and called the Clayton Anti-Trust Act, was passed by Congress in 1914. Today, if a company becomes so big that it can control prices, or if several companies get together to do that, the Department of Justice will use the Anti-Trust laws o stop them.

When big companies in different countries (such as Great Britain, France, Germany, and the United States) make an agreement to control markets, they are called a *cartel.* There is a separate article about CARTELS.

When one person owns or controls the entire supply of something, he is said to *corner the market.* There are many stories about men who have tried to corner the wheat market; that is, to own or to have the only right to buy all the wheat in a country. Since everyone eats bread, a person who could control the price of wheat could make the world's biggest fortune. No one ever succeeded in cornering the wheat market, and today a person would be prevented by law from doing so.

James Monroe

James Monroe was the fifth President of the United States. He served for two terms, from March, 1817, until March, 1825. His administration was known as the "era of good feeling," because there was almost no major political disagreement or financial distress during these years. Monroe became famous for

the Monroe Doctrine, the statement in which the United States said it did not want European countries to interfere in the affairs of any country of North, Central, or South America.

Monroe was so popular that he was re-elected without opposition. One member of the electoral college cast his vote against Monroe, although he too wanted Monroe to be elected. He voted against him because he believed that the honor of a unanimous election should be reserved to Washington, who had been re-elected unanimously.

HIS EARLY YEARS

James Monroe was born in Westmoreland County, Virginia, on April 28, 1758. His father was a planter and the family had been in America since 1652. Young James first attended a private school in the county. At the age of 16 he entered William and Mary College. Two years later the Revolutionary War started and he enlisted in the Continental Army. He rose from private to major during the war.

After the fighting was over, he became a member of the Virginia State Legislature, and from 1783 to 1786 he was a member of the Congress of the Confederation (of American states). This was before the formation of the permanent Congress of the United States, which first met in 1789. Monroe was elected to the United States Senate in 1790.

After his term as Senator, he represented the United States in France, Spain, and England. During his time in France he displeased the government of the United States by showing great friendship toward France. This was considered unwise, because at the same time another representative, John Jay, was in England attempting to negotiate a treaty with Great Britain. At that time, Britain and France were not on friendly terms. It was feared by some Americans at home that Monroe's extreme friendliness toward French officials might cause the British to distrust the intensions of the United States. The United States was trying to keep on equal terms with both, without showing any favor in either direction.

Three years later, in 1799, Monroe was elected governor of Virginia. It was at this time that he proposed settling freed Negro slaves in Africa. Later these freed slaves formed a new country, Liberia, and its capital was named Monrovia in his honor.

Thomas Jefferson was President of the United States in 1803 and wanted to buy the vast territory, then called the Louisiana Territory, which is now the central part of the United States. Jefferson sent Monroe to buy it from Napoleon, the French emperor. Monroe succeeded, as you can read in the article on the LOUISI-ANA PURCHASE. Monroe himself said that he was more proud of his contribution to this purchase than of any other thing he had done in his entire public life.

HOW HE BECAME PRESIDENT

James Madison was the next President after Jefferson. At that time England and France were quarreling and in the course of their warfare American ships were captured and American sailors kidnapped by the British. Madison was elected in 1808, and in 1811 he made Monroe his Secretary of State, which is the most important position in the President's cabinet. Therefore Monroe was in charge of the country's foreign affairs during the War of 1812, and after the capture of Washington by the British, in 1813, Monroe took over the office of Secretary of War.

Monroe found both these departments of the government badly disorganized. With great energy and vigor he set to work and made them orderly and efficient in a short space of time. He used his own money to support the city of New Orleans so that it could set up a defense against the British, who were preparing to attack. The Americans won the Battle of New Orleans in 1815.

Monroe had served so well that he was nominated for the Presidency, and elected in the fall of 1816. During his administration he did much to develop the resources of the United States. Florida was bought from Spain, the Missouri Compromise was reached, and the famous Monroe Doctrine was stated.

The Monroe Doctrine was part of Monroe's annual message to Congress in the year 1823. It outlined the policy of "neither entangling ourselves in the broils of Europe, nor suffering the powers of the Old World to interfere with the affairs of the New." Monroe added that any attempt on the part of the European powers to "extend their system to any portion of this hemisphere" would be regarded by the United States as "dangerous to our peace and safety," and would accordingly be opposed. The Monroe Doctrine has been an important part of the foreign policy of the United States ever since. President Kennedy followed it in 1962 when he forced Soviet Russia to remove its nuclear missiles from Cuba.

HIS LATER YEARS

After the end of his second term as President, Monroe retired to his estate in Oak Hill, Virginia. There he served as a justice of the peace and presided over the county court. He also served as a member of the board of the University of Virginia, and later took part in the revision of the Virginia State Constitution. Ill health compelled him to resign from this position, and he retired again to his estate at Oak Hill. Soon afterward he moved to his daughter's home in New York, where he spent the rest of his life.

Like John Adams and Thomas Jefferson, Monroe died on the anniversary of the signing of the Declaration of Independence. He died on July 4, 1831, at the age of 73. His body is buried in Hollywood Cemetery, Richmond, Virginia.

MRS. JAMES MONROE

Mrs. Eliza Kortwright Monroe was born in New York, in 1768. Her father

was a former British army officer. Eliza Kortwright and James Monroe were married in 1786. They had two daughters. Mrs. Monroe was responsible for the pardon and release from prison of Madame de Lafayette, who had been sentenced to the guillotine during the French Revolution.

Mrs. James Monroe died in 1830, at Oak Hill, Virginia.

Montaigne, Michel de

Michel, Seigneur de Montaigne, was a French writer whose essays are still read throughout the world. He was born in France, in 1533, of a noble family. His education was remarkable. He spoke nothing but Latin until he was 6 years old and had completed a college course at the age of 13.

Montaigne was a brilliant student, but once he had learned a subject he seldom troubled to remember it. He was famous for his bad memory. He could not remember the names of his own servants, often read books he had read before, under the impression that they were new, and forgot the purpose of an errand before it was done. He was also famous for his laziness. His one important work was the writing of the *Essays*. A translation of Montaigne's essays is believed to have been the only book possessed by William Shakespeare. Montaigne died in 1589, at the age of 56, in the chateau in which he was born.

Montana

Montana is a state in the United States. It is in the northern part of the Rocky Mountains and its nickname is the "Treasure State" because of its rich mineral deposits, especially its vast copper mines. The largest copper mines in the country are in Montana. The state is also famous for its great herds of cattle and sheep and its magnificent mountain scenery. Montana gets its name from a Spanish word meaning "mountainous country."

Montana ranks 4th in size among the states, with 147,138 square miles. In population it ranks 44th, with about 700,000 people living there. Although Montana is three times as large as New York State, its population is only one-twenty-fifth as large as New York's. Montana became a state in 1889, and was the 41st state admitted to the United States. The capital is Helena.

THE PEOPLE OF MONTANA

The first settlers in the Montana region, more than two hundred years ago, were French fur-trappers and traders. Later, when gold and silver were discovered, American settlers came in large numbers. They were joined by people from Germany, Ireland, and other European countries. Scandinavians came and settled on farms, and Russians, Italians and English were among the many immigrants who came to work in the growing cities. Today most of the people of Montana are American-born. Thousands of Indians live on large reservations.

More than half the people of Montana live on farms or ranches and raise some of the finest beef cattle and sheep in the country, and large crops of wheat, corn, and other grains. The soil in Montana is so dry that most of the farmers have to use irrigation. Large dams have been built for this purpose on the Missouri and Madison rivers. The Fort Peck Dam on the Missouri River is the largest earth-filled dam in the country and has the third-largest reservoir.

Many people work in the rich mines in the mountains of western Montana. They mine not only copper but also coal, zinc, gold, and silver. Montana leads all other states in the production of manganese, an important mineral in the making of steel. Some of the people work in the large oil and natural gas fields that have been discovered in the past fifty years. In the cities people work at smelting and refining metals, in fruit- and vegetable-canning plants, in flour mills, and in factories that make lumber products. The forests of Montana supply these factories with much yellow pine and Douglas fir.

The largest religious group in Montana is the Roman Catholic, but there are also many Methodists, Lutherans, and Episcopalians.

WHAT MONTANA IS LIKE

Montana is divided into two regions. The eastern two-thirds of the state is part of the Great Plains. It is a farming region that is excellent for the grazing of cattle and sheep. There are wide river valleys and high hills called *buttes* that have been worn down by the wind into strange and beautiful shapes. In the southeastern part of the state are the Montana *badlands* that many people come to see for their remarkable rock formations. In these rocks scientists have found fossils

(old skeletons) of animals that lived millions of years ago.

The western part of Montana is rugged and mountainous. These high ranges of the Rocky Mountains are part of the Continental Divide, sometimes called the "Great Divide." The mountains are very beautiful, and people go there on their vacations to enjoy fishing, hunting, and mountain-climbing. Between the high mountain ranges lie fertile valleys where the farmers grow fruits and vegetables. Many of these valleys contain lakes.

The great mining region of Montana is in this western section. In its center is the important city of Butte, which has been described as "a mile high and a mile deep" because there are more than two thousand miles of tunnels, made by miners, under the city. More than two and a half billion dollars worth of copper and silver have been mined in this region since 1864. Butte is said to be built over "the richest hill in the world."

The climate of Montana is dry and healthful. West of the Continental Divide the winters are milder and the summers cooler than east of the Divide. In the eastern part the summers are often very hot and the winters very cold, with blizzards and heavy snowfalls. Montana has been known to have hailstorms in which the hailstones were big enough to kill barnyard animals. The average temperature in winter is about 18 degrees and in summer about 68 degrees.

Many wild animals live in the dense forests of Montana. Hunters have found deer, moose, grizzly bears and many small fur-bearing animals such as the muskrat, beaver, mink, and fox.

For many years the people used the Missouri and Clark Fork rivers, with their many tributaries, as the chief means of transportation. It took the people a long time to build good roads because of the great size of the state and because it was so difficult to get through the mountains. Today there are thousands of miles of paved roads and railroads to almost all parts of the state. There are airports in the important cities.

THE GOVERNMENT OF MONTANA

Montana, like most other states, has a Governor and a Legislature. The Governor is elected for a four-year term. The Legislature is composed of a Senate and

Montana Chamber of Commerce
The Montana state capitol in Helena is the headquarters of the state government. It also houses many historical paintings of the old West.

a House of Representatives. The members of the Senate are elected for a four-year term. The members of the House of Representatives are elected for a two-year term. Judges are elected for a six-year term. The capital is Helena. There are 56 counties.

Bill Browning, Montana Chamber of Commerce
A stage coach on a Montana dude ranch.

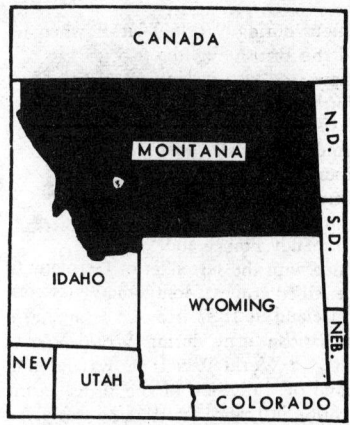

There are about 175,000 pupils attending the public elementary and secondary schools in the state, and several thousand more attending the colleges, universities and other schools of higher learning. Among the principal colleges and universities are:

Montana State University, at Missoula. Enrollment, 7,586 in 1971 (co-ed).

Montana State College, at Bozeman. Enrollment, 6,843 in 1971 (co-ed).

Montana School of Mines, at Butte. Enrollment, 793 in 1971 (co-ed).

Eastern Montana College of Education, at Billings. Enrollment, 3,250 in 1971 (co-ed).

CHIEF CITIES OF MONTANA

The leading cities of Montana, with populations from the 1970 census, are:

Great Falls, population 60,091, the second-largest city in the state.

Helena, population 22,730, the state capital and fifth-largest city. There is a separate article about HELENA.

Billings, population 61,581, the largest city, trading and shipping center for livestock, in the south central part of the state.

Butte, population 23,368, the fourth-largest city.

Missoula, population 29,497, the third-largest city.

MONTANA IN THE PAST

The first white men to enter the Montana region, more than two hundred years ago, were French fur-trappers and traders. They found many Indian tribes living in the plains and the mountains. In 1805, Lewis and Clark crossed Montana. In the next few years fur-trading posts were established but the region remained mostly uninhabited for a long time. In 1852 gold was discovered, and miners began coming from all over the United States. Other rich mines were discovered, and the population grew rapidly.

For a time Montana was part of the Idaho Territory, but in 1864 it became a separate territory and in 1889 it became a state.

During these early years the people had many bitter encounters with the Indians. One of the historic battles was in 1876, at Little Bighorn, where General George Custer of the United States Army and his 226 men were wiped out by Sioux Indians.

Since World War II, Montana has built new electric power plants and has continued to expand its program for more irrigation and water conservation.

PLACES TO SEE IN MONTANA

Glacier National Park, 1,013,129 acres, in the northwest, on the Canadian border, on U.S. Route 2. Superb Rocky Mountain scenery forms part of the Waterton-Glacier International Peace Park.

Yellowstone National Park, 151,624 acres, in the southwest, on the Wyoming border, on U.S. Route 89. Most of this park is in Wyoming. Spectacular falls and canyons made by the Yellowstone River.

Big Hole Battlefield National Monument, 200 acres, about 60 miles west of Butte, in the southwest, on State Highway 43. Site of an important battle along the route of the famous retreat of Chief Joseph and his Nez Percé Indians, in 1877.

Custer Battlefield National Monument, 765 acres, about 55 miles east of Billings, in the southeast, on U.S. Route 87. Site of the famous Battle of the Little Big Horn.

Granite Peak, 12,850 feet high, 30 miles west of Red Lodge, in the south, west of U.S. Route 12. The highest point in Montana, with a beautiful view for hundreds of miles around.

Fort Peck Recreational Area, 18 miles south of Glasgow, in the northeast, south of U.S. Route 2. A beautiful vacation spot, with boating, fishing, and swimming.

MONTANA. Area, 147,138 square miles. Population (1970 census) 694,409. Capital, Helena. Nickname, the Treasure State. Motto, *Oro y Plata* (Gold and Silver). Flower, bitterroot. Bird, meadowlark. Song, "Montana." Admitted to Union, November 8, 1889. Official abbreviation, Mont.

Montcalm, Louis Joseph de

Louis Joseph de Montcalm was the commander of the French forces during the French and Indian Wars. In these wars, the French, who had many possessions in the northern United States and in Canada, joined with the Indians to drive the English out of this territory. The French lost the wars and lost most of their territories. Montcalm was killed during the most important battle of the war, the battle of Quebec in 1759. Wolfe, the head of the English armies, was also killed during this battle.

Montcalm was born in France in 1712. He was a marquis, a nobleman. He was only 14 years old when he entered the French army. He had become well known as a soldier before he was appointed the commander of all the troops in Canada in 1756. He was skillful and courageous in the three campaigns at Fort Ontario and Fort William Henry before he was finally defeated at the battle of Quebec.

Monte Cassino

Monte Cassino is a hill, or low mountain, in southern Italy. It is the site of a famous monastery, also called Monte Cassino, that was built more than 1,500 years ago (in the year 529) by St. Benedict. The hill overlooks the town of Cassino, which has a population of about 11,500.

Monte Cassino and the town of Cassino were very important and much talked about in World War II, during the ITALIAN CAMPAIGN (about which there is a separate article). Allied forces had landed in Italy and were trying to move north. German forces were opposing them. The Germans established themselves on the hill, which gave them such an advantage that the Allies could not get past. The Allies wanted the Germans to stop using the monastery as a defense post, so that the historic building could be spared, but the Germans would not leave it. The Allies then drove the Germans from the hill with bombs and artillery, but in doing this they damaged the monastery severely.

Montenegro

Montenegro is a small state, called a constituent republic, in southern Yugoslavia. It has many mountains. Its area is 5,343 square miles, which is a little larger than Connecticut. More than 500,000 people live there, which is only about one-sixth the population of Connecticut. The capital of Montenegro is Titograd, a city of about 54,500. Formerly this city was called Podgoritsa. Its name was changed in honor of Tito, the Yugoslavian dictator.

The people of Montenegro have to work very hard to make a living. In most parts it is difficult to grow crops. Nevertheless farmers there grow wheat and corn in the plains and some barley and rye in the mountains. Most of the people raise sheep and goats, which they let graze in the mountains. There are hardly any factories, but the industrious people make many things at home. In the large forests of eastern Montenegro many people work as lumberjacks.

From 1910 to 1918 Montenegro was an independent kingdom. After World War I it became part of Yugoslavia. Italian soldiers occupied it during World War II.

MONTENEGRO. Area, 5,343 square miles. Population (1971 census) 531,213. Capital, Titograd. In southern Yugoslavia.

Montessori, Maria

Maria Montessori was an Italian teacher and doctor who devised a system for teaching small children. She believed that children from 1 to 5 years of age could be best taught by giving them freedom of action and through games and exercises designed to develop their senses of touch, sight, and hearing. The teacher in her system acts mostly as a guide, and the children learn through trial and error. The Montessori method is widely used in European and American nursery schools or kindergartens. Maria Montessori was born in 1870. She founded a school for mentally retarded children, and her success with them led to her ideas on the training of normally intelligent children. The first Montessori nursery school was founded in Rome in 1907. Maria Montessori died in 1952.

Montevideo

Montevideo is the capital and biggest city of Uruguay. It is on the La Plata River, and is the most important port in the country. The busy docks handle most of Uruguay's trade with other nations. About one million people live in Montevideo. Most of the people work in the

large slaughterhouses and meat-processing plants. Farmers ship their cattle, sheep, and hogs from the plains of Uruguay to Montevideo. The meat, wool, and many by-products that are prepared in Montevideo are then shipped to countries all over the world. About one-third of the

Moore-McCormack Lines

Montevideo, capital of Uruguay, is a modern city. It has many public parks, as well as a fine beach on Horseshoe Bay.

people of Montevideo are French, Spanish, or Italian.

Montevideo is one of the most beautiful and modern cities in South America. It has many fine boulevards, parks, and buildings, and it is well-known for its clean appearance and excellent methods of sanitation. Montevideo is sometimes called the "City of Roses" because of the hundreds of varieties of beautiful roses that bloom late in autumn. The city also has many fine beach resorts, and it is one of the most popular vacation places in South America.

Montevideo was settled by the Spanish in 1726. When Uruguay won its independence in 1828, Montevideo was made the capital.

MONTEVIDEO, URUGUAY. Population (1973 estimate) 1,154,465. Capital of Uruguay. Capital, department of Montevideo. On the La Plata River.

Montezuma

Montezuma was the name of rulers of the Aztec people, a group of American Indians who lived in ancient Mexico. Montezuma I was born about the year 1390, and became emperor about 1437, when he was nearly 50 years old. During his reign he waged many wars on neighboring tribes and succeeded in making the Aztec Empire large and powerful. It extended throughout the central and southern part of Mexico, from the Gulf of Mexico to the Pacific Ocean. (There is a separate article on the AZTECS.) Montezuma I reigned for about 35 years, dying about the year 1470.

Montezuma II was born about 1480 and became the Aztec emperor in 1502. Under him the Aztec Empire reached its greatest size. His campaigns extended as far as Nicaragua and Honduras. In 1519 there were about five million people in his empire.

At that time Spaniards, commanded by Hernando Cortez, began an invasion of Mexico. Montezuma decided to greet the Spanish invaders as friends. At first Cortez treated him with respect, but later there was a battle between Spaniards and Mexicans and Cortez arrested Montezuma and put him in prison. After his release, Montezuma was humble and beaten. He tried to make an address to his people and tell them they should try to get along

with the Spaniards, but an angry Mexican threw a rock at him. It struck him in the temple and a few days later he died, in 1520, the last of the Aztec emperors.

Montfort, Simon de

Simon de Montfort was an English statesman who lived about seven hundred years ago. He is given credit for having originated the idea of the House of Commons in the British Parliament. Montfort was born about the year 1208 in France.

Montfort inherited an English title and when he was about 20 years old he went to England and was recognized as Earl of Leicester by King Henry III. Montfort married the king's sister Eleanor and became one of the king's advisers. Later he lost favor with the king and was dismissed.

At this time Henry was being very harsh with the barons and nobles of England. Montfort led them in a protest to the king and forced Henry to turn the government over to a committee of fifteen noblemen. Several years later, the king went back on his agreement and the barons took up arms against him. In a great battle at the town of Lewes, Montfort captured the king and thus became so powerful that he was really the ruler of England.

Montfort called together a Parliament that for the first time included not only representatives of the nobles but also knights and citizens from counties and towns. The Great Parliament has been called the first House of Commons. The fighting went on, however, and in 1265 Montfort was killed in a battle against forces that were trying to restore the king to the throne.

Montgomery

Montgomery is the capital and third-largest city of the state of Alabama. It is on the Alabama River in the "Black Belt" section, which is one of the most fertile regions in the United States. Montgomery is an important manufacturing center, and one of the biggest cotton and cattle markets in the South. More than 130,000 people live in Montgomery. Many of them work in factories that make canned goods, cottonseed oil, candy, and lumber products.

Many people of Montgomery are proud that they are Southerners and that their city played an important part in the Civil War. The state capitol building was the first capitol of the Confederate States of America. Jefferson Davis, the President of the Confederacy, lived in a house in Montgomery that is called the "First White House of the Confederacy." It is now a museum that people may visit.

Montgomery was settled in 1817, and was first called New Philadelphia. Two years later it was given its present name. In 1846, Montgomery was made the capital of Alabama. Today Montgomery is the most important railroad center in the state. Maxwell and Gunter United States Air Force bases are there.

MONTGOMERY, ALABAMA. Population (1970 census) 133,386. Capital, Alabama. County seat, Montgomery County. On the Alabama River. Settled in 1817.

Montgomery, Bernard

Bernard Law Montgomery became

famous during World War II when he led the British Eighth Army to victory in North Africa. Later he was for a time commander of all the ground forces in the campaign that began with the invasion at Normandy, France, and ended with the surrender of Germany to the Allied armies. Montgomery was born in Ireland in 1887. He was a captain in the British army during World War I. Early in World War II he was in command of a division of the British army fighting in France. In 1944 he was given the rank of field marshal, the highest military rank possible. In 1946 he was given the title of Viscount Montgomery of Alamein, which made him a member of the nobility and of the House of Lords in the British Parliament. After the war Montgomery became the commander of the British zone of Germany and then the head of the staff of the British army. He died in 1976.

month

A month is one of the twelve parts of a year. The twelve months, in order, are JANUARY, FEBRUARY, MARCH, APRIL, MAY, JUNE, JULY, AUGUST, SEPTEMBER, OCTOBER, NOVEMBER, and DECEMBER, about all of which there are separate articles. These names were used by the Romans two thousand years ago, but the length and order of the months have been changed several times since then.

A month originally was the time it takes the moon to make one complete turn around the earth. This is 27 days and almost 8 hours, called a *sidereal* month. Later, a month was the period of time from one new moon to another. This is called a *synodic month.* This time is about 29½ days and is closer to the length of the *calendar,* or *civil,* month fixed by law.

January, March, May, July, August, October and December each has 31 days. April, June, September and November each has 30 days. February usually has only 28 days, but every leap year it is given an additional day, making it 29 days long.

The following verse is the usual way of remembering the number of days in the months:

Thirty days has September,
April, June, and November.
All the rest have thirty-one,
Save February, which alone
Has twenty-eight, except the time
When leap year gives it twenty-nine.

Montpelier

Montpelier is the capital city of the state of Vermont. It is in the valley of the Green Mountains in the center of the state, on the Winooski River. Almost nine thousand people live in Montpelier. Many of them are in the insurance business. Some of them make granite memorials and others work in factories where they manufacture machinery, plastics, and wood products. There are several railroads that go to Montpelier, and there is

an airport. Vermont Junior College is at Montpelier.

The capitol is a fine-looking granite building with a dome-shaped top. It was rebuilt about a hundred years ago after the old capitol was destroyed by fire. In the capitol building there is a museum showing things that have to do with the history of the people of Vermont.

Montpelier was settled in 1787. It was named after a city in France. Montpelier was the birthplace of George Dewey, a great admiral in the United States Navy.

MONTPELIER, VERMONT. Population (1970 census) 8,609. Capital, Vermont. County seat, Washington County. On the Winooski River. Settled in 1787.

Montreal

Montreal, in the province of Quebec, is the largest city in Canada. It is on Montreal Island in the St. Lawrence River. More than one million people live in Montreal. Most of them are of French descent and speak Canadian French as well as English. This large French population makes Montreal the world's largest French city outside of France.

Montreal is the leading business city of Canada. Railroads from all over Canada and steamers that come down the St. Lawrence from the Great Lakes take goods to Montreal. Many of these goods are then put into ocean-going vessels bound for other major ports of the world. Montreal is farther inland than any other major ocean port in the world.

Many of the people of Montreal work in factories, where they make railroad cars, chemicals, paper, electrical equipment, aircraft, clothing, and other products. There are large food-processing plants. The Montreal Stock Exchange is important throughout the world, and the Bank of Montreal, which opened in 1817, is one of the largest in the world.

Montreal is an interesting place to visit. Though most of the city is very modern, there are some old sections that resemble a French city of a hundred years ago. Mount Royal, 869 feet high, overlooks the city. There is a lookout station near the top where visitors can go and look down over the entire city to the St. Lawrence beyond. Horse-drawn carriages carry people to the top of the hill. Montreal has several large parks, including one with a "flower" clock. The hands, numerals and face of the clock are planted with different-colored flowers, and when they are in bloom the clock is very beautiful.

In Montreal there are a fine art gallery and a museum of Canadian history, and also McGill University and the University of Montreal (where courses are given in French). There are many churches, including St. James Cathedral, which is built to look like St. Peter's in Rome. Many pilgrims visit St. Joseph's Oratory, which is one of the best-known Catholic shrines in America.

The French explorer Jacques Cartier visited the site of modern Montreal in the year 1535, when it was an Indian village. The first settlers came about a hundred years later. Most of them were fur traders, and the settlement grew as trade with the Indians expanded. Montreal remained a French possession until 1760, when it surrendered to the British. During the Revolutionary War, American forces occupied Montreal for a short time. In 1832, it became a city.

MONTREAL, QUEBEC. Population (1967 estimate) 1,222,255 (with suburbs, 2,418,984). In Hochelaga County. Founded, 1642.

moon

A moon is any heavenly body that revolves around a planet. A moon is also called a satellite. The most familiar moon is the one that revolves around the earth. Many other planets have moons. The planet Jupiter has thirteen moons. Mars has two, Uranus, five, Saturn nine (and millions more in its surrounding rings), and Neptune two.

The earth has only the one moon. It is about 2,100 miles wide, and about eighty times lighter than the earth. For that reason, the moon's force of gravity is much less than the earth's. A person who weighs 100 pounds on the earth would weigh only 17 pounds on the moon.

The moon makes a wonderful subject for the astronomer's telescope. On most nights it can be seen very clearly with the naked eye. One reason is that it is the heavenly body nearest to the earth, about 240,000 miles away. Another reason is that the moon has no atmosphere. There are no gases surrounding it to block out the light from the sun. It is this light that causes the moon to shine. The moon has no light of its own.

At certain times of the month, spots can be seen on the moon. Occasionally these spots seem to form the face of a smiling "man in the moon." In spite of many stories written about the strange people on the moon, there is no life on the moon. There is no air, water or soil to support life if it somehow did get on the moon. During the day, the temperature on the moon reaches as high as 212 degrees on the Fahrenheit thermometer, and during the night, it drops to 240 degrees below zero. If there were no other reason, the extreme temperatures on the moon would be enough to make life unbearable.

THE CRATERS

The spots seen on the moon are really large chains of mountains, deep holes or craters, and long stretches of flat plains. There are about 30,000 craters. Many of them have been named after famous men such as Copernicus, Plato, and Galileo. The craters are huge pits, some a hundred miles across. The sides rise straight up like walls many miles high. On the outside of the holes the ground usually drops away sharply.

Scientists have many theories about how these craters were made. One theory is that the craters were made by bubbles bursting in the hot melted rock of the moon when it was first created. Another theory is that after the moon cooled, huge pieces of rock, traveling at great

Montreal, Canada's largest city, is an important business and transportation center. It is a busy but friendly city visited by vacationists from the United States and Canada.

Canadian Pacific Railway

The diagram shows how the sun's rays hit the moon as it travels around the earth (E). The outer circle shows the eight phases of the moon as seen from the earth.

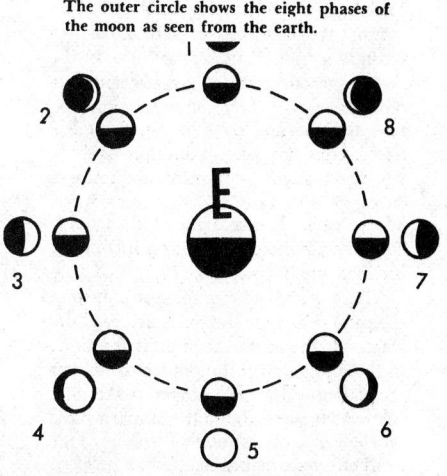

speed through space, may have hit the moon so hard that they left holes, just as a stone does when it is thrown into the sand.

The moon turns on its axis in the same way as the earth turns on its axis. It takes the moon about the same time to make one complete turn on its axis as it does to make one complete turn about the earth. For this reason, the moon keeps the same face toward the earth at all times. We always see the face of the man in the moon but never the back of his head.

PHASES OF THE MOON

Always one half of the moon is lighted by the sun, but we do not always see this lighted half, because the moon is moving around the earth at about 2,300 miles an hour and changing its position. It takes the moon about 27 days and 8 hours to go once around the earth. This is called the *sidereal period*.

Sometimes we can see all of the lighted half of the moon. Then we have a full moon. When we seen no moon at all, the moon is almost between the earth and the sun. We cannot see the moon then because its dark side is turned to us. The sun's light is so bright that the unlighted moon is lost in its brightness. We call this the new moon. The time between new moons is called the *synodic period* and is about 29½ days. This is the basis for the month.

When we see only a thin moon, then we are looking at it from away off on one side. This thin part is called a *crescent,* which means "increasing." When we see only a half moon, the moon is on one side of the earth. When we see the moon full-faced, it is almost behind the earth and the sun is in front of the earth. The different positions of the moon are called its phases.

ECLIPSES

Sometimes the earth gets between the sun and the moon, and the sunlight cannot shine on the moon. So the moon's light gets very dull, until we can scarcely see it. This is an eclipse of the moon. An eclipse means that something is shutting off the light from something else. The earth keeps the sun from shining on the moon for about two hours during an eclipse of the moon.

There can be an eclipse of the sun, too. This happens when the moon gets between the earth and the sun. Then the sunlight is shut off from part of the earth.

At a certain time of the year the full moon rises at nearly the same time for several nights and keeps shining for many hours. This happens in autumn, or harvest time, when the farmers take in their crops. At this time many farmers work late at night by the light of the moon. That is why the early autumn full moon is called the harvest moon.

There is a much more important thing the moon does for the earth. It keeps the waters of the earth moving all the time, in the rising and falling movements that are called tides. The moon makes the tides. As it goes around the earth, it pulls on the earth by its force of gravity. This pulls the waters back and forth.

The moon is of great interest to astronomers because it is so close to the earth that it can easily be studied.

1. The old moon in the arms of the new. The slender crescent seems to embrace the earth-lit night portion.
2. In 1969, these U.S. astronauts accomplished the first lunar landing. They are (left to right) Neil A. Armstrong, commander; Michael Collins, command module pilot; and Edwin E. Aldrin, Jr., lunar module pilot.
3. The still, dead surface of the moon. Some craters are almost 150 miles across.
4. An artist's idea of the moon's landscape. Mountains rise to 20,000 feet.

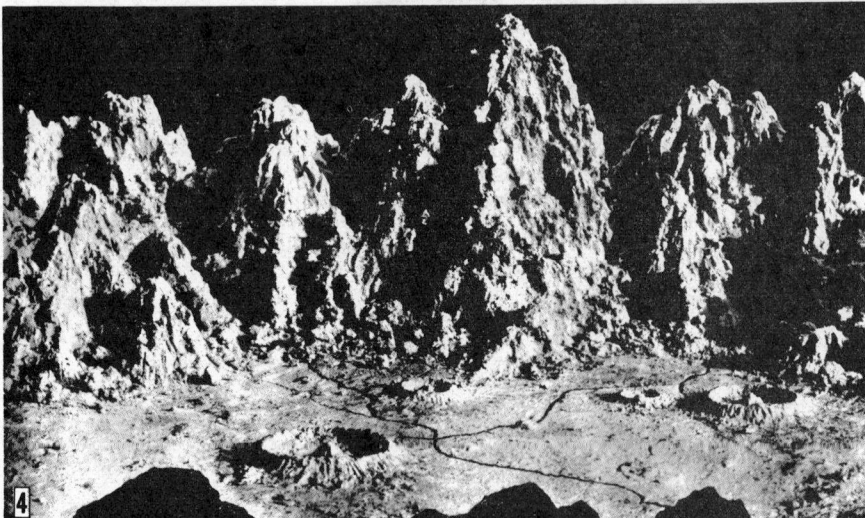

NEW KNOWLEDGE OF THE MOON

The launching of spacecraft, powered by rockets, added greatly to man's knowledge of the moon in the years from 1959 to 1965. Russians and Americans made many new discoveries.

Since the moon rotates "over and over" and not from side to side, men using telescopes can never see more than one side of the moon from the Earth. In October 1959, a Russian spacecraft went around the moon and sent back photographs of its "dark side" by television. These showed astronomers that the side we cannot see is about the same as the side we can see.

Several times Russian and American craft have landed on the moon, sending back television pictures until the moment they crashed on the moon. The Russians did this first, in September 1959, and the Russians also were first, early in 1966, to make a "soft landing" on the moon—a landing in which the spacecraft is not destroyed by crashing but lands without damage to itself, as an airplane does. In 1969, the United States sent three Apollo 11 astronauts to the vicinity of the moon. While Michael Collins remained in the *command module* orbiting the moon, Neil A. Armstrong and Edwin E. Aldrin, Jr. flew to the surface of the moon in the *lunar module* which had been attached to the command ship. They landed safely and became the first men ever to set foot on another world. They later flew the lunar module back into orbit around the moon, linked with the command ship, and blasted out of orbit and back to a safe splashdown in the Pacific Ocean.

moonflower

The moonflower, a climbing plant, is a member of the morning glory family. It is a perennial, which means that it grows from the same roots each year. The moonflower vine, found in the warm parts of America, grows almost twenty

feet high. The moonflower has large, heart-shaped leaves. The plant gets its name from the fact that its flowers open at night and close during the day.

moonstone

A moonstone is a kind of jewel. It has a bright, milky, bluish color much like the full moon's and a white line seems to glow in it. Some people have believed that this glow grows brighter as the moon becomes fuller and dies out as the moon wanes. Of course, this is really not true. In ancient India, people believed that if a man put a moonstone in his mouth he would speak beautiful words to the woman he loved.

A kind of rock called satin spar looks very much like moonstone. It is much softer than real moonstone, and soon loses its polish. An ancient Roman naturalist named Pliny complained that dishonest jewelers sold satin spar for real moonstone.

Moore, Thomas

Thomas Moore was an Irish poet who lived more than 150 years ago. He was the most popular of all poets of his period, with the possible exception of Lord Byron. Moore was born in Dublin in 1779, and attended Trinity College in that city. He started to study law, but at the age of 21 he published a volume of poems entitled *Anacreon,* and thereafter earned his living as a writer. His best-known works include a long romantic poem called *Lalla Rookh,* and shorter poems called *Irish Melodies,* many of which were written to fit Irish tunes that he knew. One of the most famous is known and sung today as *Believe Me If All Those Endearing Young Charms.*

Moore was a fine singer, and often entertained his friends with his own songs.

Moore died in 1852, at the age of 72.

Moors

The Moors are a people who now live along the Mediterranean coast of North Africa, chiefly in Morocco. They are of Arab and Berber ancestry, speak the Arabic language, and follow the religion of Mohammed. Othello, the hero of Shakespeare's famous tragedy, is a Moor. From this play, many people get the idea that the Moors are Negroes. Actually they are not.

The religion of the Moors is very important in their history. They first became followers of Mohammed about 1,200 years ago. Soon they were the fiercest fighters in the holy wars against the Christians, whom they called infidels (non-believers in Mohammedanism). In the year 711, the Arabs and Moors invaded Spain, and soon they occupied most of the country. At the same time the Moors also became more and more powerful in North Africa, until finally they ruled both Spain and Morocco.

In Spain, the Moors founded a great civilization. The most powerful Moorish state was at Cordoba. They built beautiful buildings and opened fine universities. Other Moorish cities were Toledo and Seville. Then, gradually, the Moors began to lose power. The Caliphate (state) of Cordoba fell to Spanish forces in 1031. In 1212, the Spanish broke the Moorish

Spanish Tourist Inform. Office
There are many examples of Moorish architecture in Spain. The Alcazar at Seville is one of the finest.

hold on Spain and only the Moorish kingdom at Granada remained. About 280 years passed before King Ferdinand was able to defeat the Moors completely. This took place in 1492, the same year that Columbus discovered America.

The Moors were given the choice of either being driven out of Spain or of becoming Christians. Many of them became Christians, and were called Moriscos. The Spanish government never trusted them, and they were often persecuted. In the late 16th century the Moriscos revolted and most of them were forced to leave Spain.

Anyone who visits Spain is impressed with the great influence of the Moors on that country. Many of the most beautiful buildings are of Moorish origin and have a very distinctive style. Just as important was the learning that the Moors brought to Spain, and therefore to Europe. They knew a great deal about science, and this helped modern Europe to develop.

moose

The moose is a large member of the deer family. It makes its home in Europe, the United States, and parts of Canada. The moose is a strange-looking animal with great hunching shoulders, a short neck, and long skinny legs. It has long, shaggy, brown hair and a grayish face and stomach. Its antlers are flat and very large, sometimes spreading six feet across. Hanging from its throat is a loose fold of skin covered with long hair; this is called a *bell.* It has a large underlip that sticks out. The moose is about six feet high at the shoulder and weighs more than a thousand pounds. The moose eats grass and leaves and tender branches. It cannot bend its short neck down low enough to eat grass or drink water, but must get down on its knees to eat. Usually the moose prefers to reach up and eat the leaves that grow on small trees. It is fond of water lilies and in the summer will wade out into ponds to get them.

The moose is usually a timid animal, but in the autumn, during the mating season, the males become fierce and fight savage battles for the females. The female moose most often has one calf in the spring, although sometimes two or three are born. There were once thousands of moose but so many of them have been killed that there are very few now, and they are protected by law.

Moose, Loyal Order of

The Loyal Order of Moose is a fraternal organization, or a kind of club, for men. Members join to enjoy one another's company, but also to take part in the charitable work of the organization. Members over 65 who have been members for a certain length of time may wish to live at the old folks' home called Moosehaven in Orange Park, Florida. The Moose also supports the orphaned children of its former members at a childrens "city" in Mooseheart, Illinois. The Loyal Order of Moose has about 1,159,090 members, who are organized in about 3,951 individual lodges throughout the United States. Wives and daughters of members may join the women's auxiliary, known as the Women of the Moose, which has about 300,000 members. Headquarters of both organizations is in Mooseheart. The head of the Moose is known as the director general. At meetings of the lodges the officers wear special collars, with a moosehead insignia, to designate their office, and there are special passwords.

Moravia

Moravia is an area in central Europe that is now part of Czechoslovakia. A former province, it covered about 8,000 square miles and had a population of more than 2,000,000. It is a beautiful and fertile region, surrounded by mountains. Most of the people follow the Roman Catholic Religion, and there are also many Lutherans. Many of them are farmers who raise grain, flax, and sugar beets. Others work in cities manufacturing cotton and woolen goods, leather goods, and machinery. The main city is Brno. (There is a separate article about Brno.)

Moravia was given its name by Slavs who settled there more than a thousand years ago. More than four hundred years ago Moravia, then connected with Bohemia, became part of the Austrian Empire. In 1918 it became part of the newly formed Republic of Czechoslovakia. During World War II Moravia was a protectorate of Germany, but after the war it was restored to Czechoslovakia. It was a province until 1949 when Czechoslovakia abolished its provinces and replaced them with administrative units.

Moravians

Moravians are members of a Christian church, called the Moravian Church, or the Renewed Church of the Brethren. Moravians recognize Jesus as the source of all truth, and imitate the forms of worshiping God used by the Apostles, as told in the New Testament. The first Moravians were followers of John Huss, about whom there is a separate article. They lived in Moravia and Bohemia, in what is now Czechoslovakia. This was five hundred years ago. They were persecuted for

a long time. After the Thirty Years' War, few Moravians were left. They were called the "hidden seed" and secretly kept the Moravian Church alive. As their numbers grew, the Moravians sent missionaries all over the world. Many Moravians came to colonial America, and settled in Pennsylvania. There they founded many cities, including Bethlehem and Nazareth in Pennsylvania. Many people visit Moravian churches to hear the singing. Moravian hymns are popular with people of all religions.

More, Sir Thomas

Sir Thomas More was an English statesman and writer. He is best known for having invented the word "Utopia" as a term for an ideal country. He used the word as the title of one of the books he wrote. More was born in London in 1480 and attended Oxford University. He became a lawyer and was a very successful one. His skill as an orator won him many political positions, and eventually he became a Member of Parliament.

At one time, More was a friend of King Henry VIII, but he disapproved when Henry divorced his first wife, Catherine of Aragon, and married Anne Boleyn. Because he refused to acknowledge this second marriage, More was charged with treason, and in 1535 he was condemned to death. He was beheaded on July 6, 1535. His last act was to move aside his beard before the executioner struck, saying: "Pity that should be cut; that has not committed treason."

Sir Thomas More was a very pious man, and in 1935 the Roman Catholic Church proclaimed him a saint, so he is also St. Thomas More. His feast day is July 9.

Morgan, Henry

Henry Morgan was a pirate who lived about three hundred years ago. Later he became a respectable and important man, and eventually was made lieutenant governor of Jamaica. He was born on a farm in Wales about the year 1635. He was of an adventurous nature, and farm life was too quiet for him. He went to sea, and for many years he was a professional pirate. The island of St. Catherine in the West Indies was his headquarters for some time, and much of his piracy was done around the Caribbean Sea. He had a large crew of pirates, adventurers from all parts of Europe. He made a fortune over a period of years, and was finally satisfied that he had treasure enough to live in luxury the rest of his life. He settled in Jamaica, and King Charles II of England appointed him lieutenant governor of the island and gave him a knighthood, which made him Sir Henry Morgan. He died in 1688.

Morgan, House of

One of the most famous banking firms in the world is called the "House of Morgan." The first member of the Morgan family to become a banker was Junius Spenser Morgan, who was born in Springfield, Massachusetts, in 1813. He went into the dry-goods business in Hartford, Connecticut, and later in Boston, and made large profits. When he was about 40 years old he became a banker and was even more successful. At his death in 1890 he was worth about ten million dollars.

John Pierpont Morgan, the son of Junius, was the most famous member of the Morgan family. He is usually called Pierpont Morgan. He did not enter his father's banking firm but formed a different one, whose chief office came to be in New York City. He was born in 1837 and became active in the banking business during the period following the Civil War, when great industrial and railroad firms were being formed. J. Pierpont Morgan persuaded rich men in England and European countries to invest in these firms, and he made big commissions. He found the investors needed to supply the money to found the United States Steel Corporation, which for many years was the biggest company in the world. He died in 1913.

The son of J. Pierpont Morgan, who had the same name but was always called J. P. Morgan, carried on the work of his father's banking house, which was called J. P. Morgan and Company. He was born in 1867 and died in 1943.

Both J. Pierpont Morgan and his son J. P. Morgan were interested in art and literature. They had famous collections of paintings and they supported a fine library in New York City.

Mormon

A Mormon is a person who belongs to the Church of Jesus Christ of Latter-Day Saints. This Church, a Christian sect, was founded about 125 years ago by Joseph Smith, in Palmyra, New York. In 1827, he reported that an angel had appeared to him and had given him a mission to found a Church; and had led him to gold plates on which was written the Book of Mormon, or Golden Bible. Smith said the book was written by the prophet Mormon, who lived in New York 1,550 years ago, and that Mormon had hidden the Golden Bible so that it was unknown until Joseph Smith found it.

By 1831, Joseph Smith had many followers. He moved to Kirtland, Ohio, and soon new believers joined him from all over the United States. These people had very deep faith, but their beliefs were different from those of their neighbors and the Mormons were often attacked and made the butt of jokes. Other Mormon settlements were opened in Missouri. People there were also unfriendly, and Joseph Smith and many others were put in jail. Finally, the Mormons left Missouri and moved to Illinois. There they founded a city called Nauvoo. Though they were admired for the way they built the city, their customs made many people angry. The governor of Illinois put Joseph Smith and his brother in jail. A lawless mob broke into the jail on June 27, 1844 and shot and killed both of them.

Brigham Young was chosen to be the new leader. He decided to move beyond the already settled parts of the United States and chose what is now Utah as a place where the Mormons could live in peace and not be troubled by neighbors. The Mormons made the long journey and settled in what is now Salt Lake City.

They used the name Deseret, or "land of the honeybee," for their new territory.

Under the leadership of Brigham Young the Mormons were very successful, but many people still disliked them and the Mormons in turn did not trust outsiders, whom they called "Gentiles." Much of the early trouble came from "forty-niners" going to California for gold. Later there were fights between the Mormons and the judges and troops sent to Utah by the Federal government. These conflicts did not stop until after Utah became a state in 1896.

MORMON BELIEFS

Mormons believe that God has an invisible body, and that He was once a man, but became perfect in both mind and body. There are two kinds of priest in the Mormon Church. Church business is under the priests of Aaron, while spiritual matters are under the priests of Melchizedek. The Council of the Twelve Apostles rules the church and is important in the business as well as the religious life of Mormons.

One Mormon teaching was that one man may have many wives at the same time. Such a practice is called *polygamy*. Since 1890, however, polygamy has been

Chicago Historical Soc.

The Mormons built a handsome temple in Nauvoo, Illinois, in 1846. But they were forced to leave the state in the same year and the temple was completely destroyed by fire a few years later.

forbidden by the Mormon Church and members who marry several wives are excommunicated (excluded) from the Church. Polygamy is now forbidden because the Mormon Church believes and teaches that its members should obey the laws of the land, and polygamy is illegal in all parts of the United States. Most Mormons still live in Utah, although many have moved elsewhere in the United States. Mormons also have foreign missionaries.

morning glory

The morning glory is a climbing plant that grows in the warm parts of South America and United States. Morning glories also grow in Japan. Some morning glories are perennial, which means they grow up from the same roots every year. Others are annual and have to be planted each year. Many

people grow morning glory plants in their gardens. It is a hardy plant that grows quickly and reaches a height of about fifteen feet. It climbs over porches and fences and garden trellises. It has trumpet-shaped, purple, blue, and white flowers. Most morning glory flowers close during the day.

Some morning glory plants are dwarf, that is, they grow only about one foot high. The dwarf kinds are popular for planting in hanging baskets. They produce many blossoms that do not close during the day.

Morocco

Morocco is a kingdom in northwest Africa, across the Strait of Gibraltar from Spain. Because of its location, which is important in wartime, many countries have sought control of Morocco and for many years it was controlled mostly by France and partly by Spain. In 1956 Morocco became an independent country. Morocco is about 172,000 square miles in size, about the size of California, and over fifteen million people live there, somewhat less than there are in California. During World War II, many American soldiers were in Morocco.

The capital of Morocco is Rabat, but Fez, where the king makes his headquarters, is also considered a capital.

THE PEOPLE OF MOROCCO

Most of the people in Morocco are Berbers. They have lived there longer than any other race of people. They speak their own language, which is very old and which has in it many words taken from the languages of other peoples who settled in Morocco. One of these peoples were the Arabs, who speak Arabic. Many Arabs are nomads, or wanderers, who have no permanent homes but live in tents. Moroccans are often called Moors, a name used chiefly for people of mixed Arab and Berber descent.

About 200,000 Europeans, mostly French and Spanish, live in the cities of Morocco. There are also about 100,000 Jews. Most of the people of Morocco, except the Europeans, are Moslems (follow the Mohammedan religion).

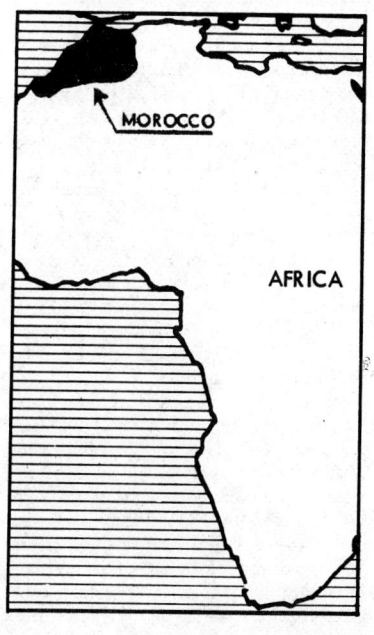

Most Moroccans are farmers. They raise wheat, barley, olives, and citrus fruits. City people work in factories that make building materials, textiles, shoes, and soap. They also weave carpets. Some Moroccans live and dress like city dwellers in the United States and Canada, but many of them still wear their native dress, with the Mohammedan women wearing veils over the lower part of their faces. Most of the poorer people lead simple lives and few can read or write.

WHAT KIND OF A PLACE IT IS

Morocco is a country of mountains, fertile plains, and deserts. The Atlas Mountains stretch across the country from southwest to northeast, and in some places rise more than 13,000 feet. Along the Mediterranean are the Riff Hills. Between these hills and the Atlas Mountains are fertile plains for farming. South of the Atlas Mountains is the Sahara Desert. Morocco has a number of small rivers that flow into the Sahara and dry up. The Moulouya, the most important river, flows north into the Mediterranean.

The climate of Morocco along the coast is warm but is made comfortable by the breezes from the sea. In the interior of the country, especially in the desert, the summers are extremely hot.

The principal cities of Morocco, with populations from the 1971 census, are:

Casablanca, the largest city, an important seaport, population 1,719,421. (See CASABLANCA.)

Marrakesh, an inland city, population 1,558,541.

Fez, one of the capitals, an inland city, population 1,071,416. Seat of a large Moslem university.

Rabat, the official capital, a seaport on the Atlantic, population 641,174.

Tangier, on the Strait of Gibraltar, a historic city in international affairs, population 215,502. (See TANGIER.)

Meknes, an inland city near Fez, population 753,117.

HOW THE PEOPLE ARE GOVERNED

Morocco is ruled by a king (formerly called sultan) in national affairs and by the heads of the many tribes and communities in local affairs. The people had little voice in their government. But the king, Hassan II, and his advisors promulgated a new Fundamental Law in 1961, and in 1962 voters approved a constitution which would give the country its first parliament.

MOROCCO IN THE PAST

Morocco was settled more than two thousand years ago as a province of the Roman Empire, and later was conquered by the Arabs. More than two hundred years ago, the coast of Morocco on the Mediterranean was part of the famous Barbary Coast. Fierce Mohammedan pirates used to attack ships and capture Christians to be held for ransom or sold as slaves. European countries became interested in Morocco about a hundred years ago, and several countries tried to get control of it for political reasons. Several times the struggle for Morocco almost brought about a war. In 1912, the French were given control of part of Morocco and Spain was given smaller parts.

After World War II, the people of Morocco rebelled against foreign rule and

independence was granted to them by France in 1956 and Spain in 1957. Tangier, an international zone since 1923, became part of Morocco in 1956.

MOROCCO. Area, 166,000 square miles. Population (1971 census) 15,379,259. Capital, Rabat. Languages, French, Spanish, Arabic, Berber, and others. Religion, chiefly Mohammedan. Government, kingdom. Monetary unit, the Dirham, worth 20 cents (U.S.). Flag: Red with green, five-pointed star.

Morris, Gouverneur

Gouverneur Morris was one of the men who helped write the Constitution of the United States. He was a great lawyer and statesman and helped with many of the problems that the new United States faced. He was the American minister to France from 1792 until 1794, and in 1800 he became a member of the United States Senate. Gouverneur Morris was born in Morrisania, New York, in 1752, and died there in 1816. His family had been among the earliest settlers in New York and were rich and aristocratic. His brother, Lewis, was a signer of the Declaration of Independence.

Morris, Robert

Robert Morris was a signer of the Declaration of Independence. He has been called the "financier of the Revolution" because he managed the financial affairs of the colonies during their fight for independence. Morris not only borrowed money for the colonies, but he also gave money of his own for the support of their armies. He and other citizens founded a bank in Philadelphia that paid the expenses of the armies, and in 1781 Morris supplied almost all of the money necessary to carry on the campaign against Cornwallis, the leader of the British forces. Robert Morris served as secretary of finance and secretary of the treasury under the Confederation, the government used in the colonies before the present Constitution was adopted. Later he helped write the Constitution and was a senator from Pennsylvania in the first Congress of the United States. Robert Morris was born in England in 1734, and came to the United States when he was 13 years old. He settled in Philadelphia, where he became a wealthy businessman. In his old age, Morris lost his fortune. He died a poor man in 1806.

Morris, William

William Morris was an English poet and artist who lived about a hundred years ago. He was born near London in 1834 and attended Oxford University, where he studied architecture and painting. He was interested in the design of furniture, wallpaper, art fabrics, and stained glass. He invented the Morris chair, a kind of big armchair that was popular for many years.

Morris is best remembered as a poet. His most popular poems are based on myths and legends, such as *Sigurd the Volsing, Defense of Guinevere,* and *The Life and Death of Jason.* Morris died in 1896, at the age of 62.

Morse, Samuel F. B.

Samuel Finley Breese Morse was an American artist and inventor. His portraits were among the best that were painted by American artists of his time,

but he is remembered chiefly because he invented the telegraph.

Morse was born in Charlestown, Massachusetts, in 1791. His father was Jedidiah Morse, who wrote the first geography ever published in the United States. Samuel F. B. Morse was graduated from Yale in 1810 and the next year went to England to study art with the American painter, Washington Allston. Morse became well known as an artist in the United States and was the first president of the National Academy of Design.

In 1829 he went back to Europe and stayed for three years, traveling and painting. It was aboard ship on his way home that he conceived his idea for the telegraph. He heard a discussion of how someone had produced a spark from an electromagnet, and this gave the idea for the telegraph. Several years later, in 1835, he ran half a mile of wire around a room and proved to his own satisfaction that his invention worked. Two years later he gave a public demonstration of the telegraph.

Morse persuaded Congress to run a telegraph line between Baltimore and Washington. Many people then sued him, claiming that he had stolen their inventions, but he finally won full credit. In his later years, nearly every country in the world bestowed honors on him. He was 81 when he died, in 1872.

See also the Morse Code, in the article on the TELEGRAPH.

mortgage

A mortgage is a kind of contract by which a person borrows money and gives some kind of property (usually real estate) as security. This means that if he does not pay back the money, the person who lends it may take his property instead.

The person who borrows the money is called the *mortgagor*. The person who lends the money is called the *mortgagee*. The contract itself is a *mortgage deed* or *bond*.

Usually a person puts a mortgage on a new house that he is buying, because he does not have enough cash to pay for the house in full. This kind of mortgage is called a *purchase-money mortgage*. Mortgage loans are usually made by banks, and they will usually lend one-half to two-thirds of what they consider to be the full value of the property. The mortgagor pays interest on the money lent by the bank, and also makes regular *amortization* payments. For example, a person owns a house worth $10,000. He borrows $5,000 on a mortgage. The first year he pays $300 in interest (which is at the rate of six per cent) and also pays $500 as amortization. At the beginning of the second year he owes $4,500 on the mortgage. During this year he will pay only $270 in interest, and again he will pay $500 to amortize or reduce the loan. At the beginning of the third year he will owe $4,000, and pay $240 interest that year; and so on.

Most mortgages on new houses in the United States are repaid in monthly payments, which are about the same as would be paid in rent for the same house. The monthly payments go on for fifteen to thirty years. Each payment includes part for interest and part for amortization, but it is worked out in advance so that the same amount is always paid each month. The loan is usually made by a bank but guaranteed by the Federal Housing Administration (FHA) or another branch of the United States government. In return for this guarantee, the bank pays a small part of the interest to the FHA.

When a mortgagor fails to make his payments, the mortgagee can *foreclose*. This means that he takes the property. Every state and country has very strict laws to control mortgages and foreclosures.

If a person owns a house that can be sold for $20,000, and cannot pay a $5,000 mortgage, the mortgagee cannot foreclose and own the house. He must put the house up at auction to be sold. Suppose the house is sold for $20,000 at the auction. The mortgagee can take the $5,000 he lent, plus all interest that is due to him, plus whatever it cost him to foreclose the mortgage. Everything else goes back to the mortgagor. This amount is said to be the mortgagor's *equity* in the property.

Morton, William

William Thomas Green Morton was an American dentist who lived about a hundred years ago. He was one of the first men to use anesthesia successfully. During his time, most people had to undergo operations while they were awake, and they suffered great pain. William Morton began to practice dentistry in Boston, Massachusetts, in 1842. One of his friends, a chemist named Charles T. Jackson, interested him in using a gas called sulfuric ether as an anesthetic. A patient inhaling sulfuric ether would fall into a deep sleep and would feel no pain during the operation. Morton first tried this gas on animals, then on himself, and finally on a patient. He was so successful that many other dentists and doctors began to use anesthetics. Morton was born in 1819 and died in 1868. Read also the article ANESTHESIA.

mosaic

Mosaic is a decoration made by fitting together pieces of colored stone, glass, tile, or other material, into a design or picture. The making of mosaic is ranked as a fine art because a *cartoon,* or colored design, must first be made and this requires the skill of an artist. In making mosaic, the area to be decorated is covered with a special cement. When this has hardened slightly, the colored pieces, or *tesserae,* are set in place according to the prepared design. Since the pieces are never perfectly flat, they reflect light differently and this adds greatly to the effect of the mosaic.

Mosaic is one of the most ancient arts. Mosaic designs on ivory were made in Egypt and Mesopotamia thousands of years ago. Mosaic was adopted by the Greeks, and later by the Romans, who used it not only for pavements but also for pictures such as landscapes, battle scenes, and portraits of great men. In the early days of Christianity, mosaic came to be used for the inside walls and ceilings of churches.

Ravenna, a city in Italy, became the world's center of mosaic work, and some examples of the art found there have never been surpassed. Oil paintings by such artists as Raphael have been copied in mosaic, the work sometimes taking as long as twenty years and requiring fifteen thousand different colors of stone and glass. Some mosaic has been made of precious stones.

Moscow

Moscow is the capital of the Soviet Union, or the Union of Soviet Socialist Republics (Russia). It is on the Moscow (Moskva) River. Moscow is the largest city in the Soviet Union and one of the world's largest cities. About seven million people live there. The people work in factories that make textiles, machinery, foodstuffs, leather, and many other things. Most of the people live in apartment houses, but many live in the suburbs and travel to work in Moscow every day. Moscow is very overcrowded, even though many new apartment buildings have been built in recent years. The government has even had to build new stories on top of old buildings to give the people more space to live in. The tallest building is Moscow University, which has 32 stories and is 720 feet high.

The people in Moscow love music, ballet, and plays. The Moscow Art Theater is widely known. Moscow also has many theaters. Few of the people in Moscow have automobiles. They travel on buses, on streetcars, and on a big subway that was built about twenty years ago. The subway stations have marble walls with murals painted on them. The shops, factories, and office buildings are all owned by the government. There are many libraries, museums, youth clubs, stadiums, and schools, which are also run by the government.

THE KREMLIN AND RED SQUARE

Moscow has very old churches and palaces with high domes, but it also has big modern buildings and parks. In the center of Moscow stands the Kremlin, the most important structure in the city. It has walls of pink brick. The Russian czar (emperor) and his court once lived there. Since 1918 it has been the headquarters of the Communist government of Russia. In 1954 part of it was turned into a public museum. There is a separate article on the KREMLIN.

The Kremlin faces Red Square. This huge square is more than a half-mile long, and the people hold national parades and important celebrations there. In Red Square is the Lenin Mausoleum, built of many different colored granites. In this tomb lies the body of Nikolai Lenin, the founder of Communist Russia, in a glass-covered coffin.

Moscow was founded more than eight hundred years ago. About four hundred years ago, Czar Ivan the Terrible made Moscow the capital of Russia. Moscow was the scene of much fighting through the centuries. In 1703, Peter the Great moved the capital to St. Petersburg (now Leningrad, but Moscow remained an important city. In 1812, Napoleon captured Moscow with his French army.

Much of the city was destroyed, but the Russians finally won the war. In the Russian Revolution in 1917 there was much fighting in Moscow. The Soviet government moved to Moscow in 1918, and it again became the capital of Russia. During World War II, the Germans tried to capture the capital, but the Russian Army drove them back. Since the war, the city has been rebuilt.

Moscow, U.S.S.R. Population (1973 estimate) 7,300,000. Capital of U.S.S.R. On the Moscow River.

Moses

Moses is called the "liberator of the Jews," for the Bible tells us that he led them from slavery in Egypt to the Promised Land in Palestine. He was a great law-giver who gave his people the rules (the Ten Commandments) that have guided them and millions of other people for the last 3,100 years. It is believed that Moses wrote the first five books of the Old Testament, which are also called the *Pentateuch* and the *Books of Moses.*

The Book of Exodus, the second in the Bible, tells the story of Moses. He was born in Egypt at a time when the Egyptians were treating the Jews very cruelly. The pharaoh (king) of Egypt was afraid there were getting to be too many Jews, so he passed a law saying that all Jewish male children were to be killed. At this time Moses was only three months old. His mother, whose name was Jochebed, put him in a basket woven of bulrushes and put the basket in the Nile River, hoping he would not be found and killed. Moses was found by an Egyptian princess. She pitied him and took him home. By chance, she asked Jochebed, Moses' own mother, to care for him.

When Moses grew up to be a young man, he heard a voice coming from a burning bush. He recognized it as the voice of God, and it told Moses that he would free his people from slavery. Moses could not talk without stammering, and he thought this would prevent him from being a forceful leader. But God appointed Aaron, Moses' brother, to be Moses' helper. He would speak for Moses, whose stammering made talking before an audience difficult. They went to

Michelangelo portrays Moses as a man of great strength and dignity. In his right hand are the tablets of the Ten Commandments, the foundation of moral law.

Pharaoh and demanded in the name of the Lord that the Jewish people be set free. Pharaoh refused.

Then God sent nine plagues, or misfortunes, to Egypt, but still Pharaoh refused to let the Jews go. Then, in the tenth plague, God killed the oldest male child in every Egyptian house but he passed over (spared) the houses of the Jews, and this is told about in the article PASSOVER, in another volume of this encyclopedia.

Now Pharaoh was very much afraid, and he let the Jews leave Egypt. Moses led them out of the hated country. Then Pharaoh was sorry that he had been so frightened and sent Egyptian soldiers out after their former slaves. Moses guided his people across the Red Sea, whose waters rolled aside to let them through. When the Egyptians followed, the waters rolled back, and the Egyptians were drowned.

MOUNT SINAI

Moses and his people stopped at Mount Sinai. Moses went alone up the mountain. God appeared to him there. To Moses God renewed the covenant, or promise, that He had made to Abraham and the Jewish people. Then the Lord gave Moses the Ten Commandments. They were written on stone tablets.

When Moses went down from Sinai, he found the people worshiping an idol, a golden calf. In anger, he broke the tablets containing the commandments. But then he made a great sacrifice, and offered himself to the Lord to make up for the sins of the people. The Lord spared Moses. After a year at Sinai, Moses commanded the people to follow him again.

THE FORTY YEARS

The next part of the journey took forty years. The Jews set out. Moses sent spies into Canaan, a country to the north, to find out about it. When the Jews reached the River Jordan, they were afraid of the people who lived on the other side. Even Aaron and Moses lost courage. The Lord punished the people for their lack of faith by sending fiery serpents that killed many of the people.

Finally, the country across the Jordan was divided among the tribes of the Jewish people. In the Book of Deuteronomy, the fifth book of the Bible, Moses again told about the laws that were first described in the books of Numbers and Leviticus. He was permitted by God to look down from Mount Nebo at the Promised Land, the goal of his hopes. But he died without entering the land. After his death, the people mourned him for thirty days, because he had delivered them from slavery. Through Moses, God had established His law for the Jewish people. They reached the Promised Land and the forty years of wandering were over.

Moses was the great law-giver. Before him there were many systems of law, but none lasted very long. The Mosaic law has never been weakened since the time of Moses. It has been the foundation on which the laws of all great religions of the Western world have been built. Christians and Mohammedans, as well as Jews, still honor its principles.

Moses, Grandma

Grandma Moses is the popular name of an American farm woman who began to paint when she was 78 years old and became famous throughout the world for her pictures. Her full name is Anna Mary Robertson Moses, and she was born in New York State in 1860. As a child she loved to draw, but she grew up like any farm girl, married, and had ten children. She worked on the farm, and after the death of her husband in 1927 she ran the farm herself.

When Grandma Moses was in her seventies, the farm work became too hard for her. One of her daughters suggested that she embroider pictures in wool to amuse herself. Then her fingers became too stiff to hold a needle, and Grandma Moses began to paint in oils. Her fame began in 1939, when an art collector saw some of her paintings and bought all he could get. Since that time she has painted about 800 pictures. Mostly she paints landscapes in a style called *primitive.* Primitive art is done by persons who need not have training but who have natural talent. Grandma Moses' pictures are full of tiny details that make a farm scene look alive and familiar. Her colors are sharp and bright, and all of her paintings are cheerful and happy in mood. Among the best are *From My Window* and *The Old Oaken Bucket.* Grandma Moses died in 1961.

Moslem, a follower of Islam, the religion of Mohammed: see ISLAM and MOHAMMED.

mosque

A mosque is a Moslem house of prayer. (Moslems follow the religion of Mohammed.) From the outside, a mosque is most easily recognized by the four *minarets,* which are towers at each corner of an open courtyard. The call to prayer is given from the top of the minarets. The courtyard has walls on three sides. The fourth is open and usually has several pillars.

The main building is the prayer hall. There are no chairs or benches in the prayer hall. Rugs, on which the Moslems kneel to pray, cover the floor. On one wall there is a prayer niche, which shows the direction of Mecca. This is necessary because Moslems, when they are praying, always face Mecca, the city where Mohammed was born. Next to the prayer niche is the *mimbar,* or pulpit, and near the mimbar is the *cikka,* a raised platform from which the prayers and services are read.

Many mosques, especially those in Persia, have bulb-shaped domes on top of the minarets and the main building. These are often very beautiful, but are not a necessary part of a mosque. There are famous mosques in Mecca and Medina. One of the most famous in Istanbul, Turkey, was formerly the famous Christian church of St. Sophia.

mosquito

The mosquito is an insect that lives in many parts of the world. It grows best in places where the climate is warm and moist. Mosquitoes are also found in cold parts of the world, such as Alaska. The

mosquito is a great pest to man and animals.

The bite of a mosquito itches and is very annoying. Some mosquitoes carry very tiny organisms called viruses, which cause dangerous diseases. The *aedes mosquito* carries the virus that causes yellow fever, and the *anopheles mosquito* carries the virus that causes malaria. There are separate articles on MALARIA and YELLOW FEVER.

Although the mosquito can be dangerous and is a nuisance, it is a beautiful insect. The female has a long delicate beak that it uses to pierce the skin and suck the blood of its prey. Only the female mosquito bites. The female lays its eggs in ponds, and still water that collects in swamps or drainpipes or even in buckets. The eggs hatch quickly. Some mosquito eggs hatch in only a few hours. When the eggs hatch they are *larvae* (often called "wigglers"). They feed on water plants. After a while the larvae turn into mosquitoes. Mosquitoes do not fly long distances but often they are carried for miles by the wind. Man has developed many poisons and other ways to get rid of mosquitoes.

moss

Moss is an important group of plants that grow in almost every part of the world. There are thousands of different kinds of moss, and some of them are very beautiful. Most moss grows best in places where the climate is moist and warm and the soil is damp. In places where the climate is cold and dry, moss shrivels up and looks as if it were dead. When the weather grows warmer and there is rain, the moss comes to life again. Moss is found on tree trunks, on logs, on rocks, and on objects in rivers. Some moss is pale green, some is dark green, and there is moss that is almost black.

Moss has a soft stem and many tiny green leaves. It does not have regular roots, but clings to the ground or the trunk of a tree or a rock by tiny threads on its underside. Instead of seeds, moss has spores, tiny powdery structures that make it possible for new moss to grow. (You can read about spores in the article on PLANTS.) Moss does not have any flowers.

Moss is useful to other plants because it keeps their roots warm. People who grow flowers often use moss for this purpose. Moss also provides a home for many different kinds of insects. Reindeer and cattle eat some kinds of moss.

moth, a kind of insect: see BUTTERFLIES AND MOTHS.

Mother Goose, an imaginary author of nursery rhymes: see the article NURSERY RHYMES.

mother-of-pearl

Mother-of-pearl is the smooth inside layer of the shells of certain shellfish, especially oysters, mussels, and abalones. It is usually whitish or grayish and seems to have the colors of the rainbow just below its surface. Cameos are cut from mother-of-pearl, and brooches, buttons, letter openers and knife handles are made from it. It is also used for inlaying musical instruments and furniture. It is an important by-product of pearl fisheries.

Mother-of-pearl is made of the substances called *aragonite* and *chonchiolin,* which are manufactured by the body of the shellfish. These are the same substances that pearls are made of. Mother-of-pearl is sometimes called *nacre.*

Mother's Day

Mother's Day is a holiday that has been observed in the United States since 1914. Before that it had been observed in certain cities for several years. It was first observed in Philadelphia in 1910. Mother's Day is the second Sunday in May. Unlike most holidays, which are proclaimed by the governors ot the separate states, Mother's Day is declared by a proclamation of the President of the United States.

On Mother's Day all mothers are honored, whether living or dead. There are special services held in most churches to do honor to the mother and to the home. Many people buy their mothers presents on this day. In some parts of the United States it has become the custom to wear a red carnation if one's mother is living, and a white carnation if she has died.

motion

Motion is the act of going from one place to another. The famous English scientist, Sir Isaac Newton, who lived about three hundred years ago, explained motion in terms of three laws, known as Newton's laws of motion.

The first law of motion states that an object will move only if there are forces on it that do not balance each other (are not equal and opposite in direction). Thus we say that motion can take place only if an unbalanced force acts on a body.

A book will remain motionless (at rest) on a table top unless it is pushed or pulled. The book is at rest because its downward force (weight) on the table is balanced by the upward force of the table top. The two forces are equal and opposite.

When objects are acted on by an unbalanced force, their motion may be one of two kinds: *rectilinear* (motion in a straight line), and *rotational* (motion in a curved line). Newton's first law also says that a body set in motion will move in a straight line unless acted on by an unbalanced force. When a ball rolled along the floor moves in a curved line, it is because the force of friction between the floor and the ball moves it off its normally straight path. Friction is the unbalanced force. (There is a separate article on FRICTION.)

Newton's second law states that if an object is acted on by an unbalanced force, its speed will continue to increase (called *acceleration*) as long as the force continues to act on it and remains unbalanced. The direction of motion will always be in the direction in which the force is acting. The greater the force, the greater the acceleration.

The third law of motion states that for every action there is an equal and opposite reaction. This law is the explanation of jet propulsion. Gases leave a jet engine with great force. This causes an equal and opposite force in the engine, which drives the jet plane forward. See

the articles on JET ENGINE, FORCE, and INERTIA.

motion pictures

Motion pictures, usually called "the movies," are the most popular form of entertainment that has ever been invented. Millions of people the world over see motion pictures every week in theaters, and in their homes many people show family movies that they have made themselves. In recent years television has taken many people away from movie theaters, but television is another form of motion pictures and many of the programs shown on television are produced on film.

HOW THE MOVIES DEVELOPED

For hundreds of years men tried to invent a way of recording action in permanent form, but no practical way was found until Thomas Edison invented a motion-picture camera, about 1893. The Lumière brothers, two Frenchmen, may have invented the first movie camera some years earlier, but Edison's was the first practical one. The pictures taken with Edison's camera were shown in penny arcades, in a machine that the viewer turned with a crank. Later, movies began to be shown on screens in stores and halls where seats had been installed. The admission price to these places was a nickel, so they were called *nickelodeons.*

The movies shown at this time were very short and had almost no stories. They just showed some kind of interesting action, and people went to see them because of their novelty. Some wise movie men believed that people would be interested in movies that told stories. They wrote simple stories to be acted out and photographed. Their studios were in open lots and even on the roofs of buildings. In those days all scenes, even those supposedly taking place indoors, had to be shot in full sunlight. No artificial light was bright enough.

It was not long before people began to go to the movies regularly. As the producers (the men who were in charge of making the pictures) saw that they could make a great deal of money from the movies, they made longer and more elaborate pictures. Regular theaters that had live stage performers added movies to their shows and found their business improving. Many theaters gave up the stage shows and showed only movies.

In a short time audiences began to find favorites among the actors and actresses who appeared on the screen. At first, the names of the players were not even mentioned, but when the producers realized that audiences were interested in the movie actors, they began to feature their names. Actors and actresses who were particular favorites were given bigger parts, and their names were advertised more than the pictures they played in. They became known as movie stars, and the star system has continued to this day. Some of the early movie stars were Mary Pickford, Douglas Fairbanks, Charlie Chaplin, Francis X. Bushman, Maurice Costello, and William S. Hart. Movie stars are probably the best-known people in the world today, and audiences know more about them than they do about presidents and kings.

The first motion picture to tell a com-

plete story was *The Great Train Robbery,* made in 1903. It was one of the first movies in which the camera photographed scenes from different positions instead of remaining fixed in one spot. An equally important movie was *The Birth of a Nation,* a story of the Civil War, made by D. W. Griffith in 1915. This was the first long, expensive movie of the kind made today. In one part of this story, Griffith put the camera on a truck and, as a group of soldiers rode their horses at breakneck speed, the camera kept pace with them, making a very exciting effect that people had never seen before. Griffith also introduced other uses of the camera that we see in almost every movie today. One of them was the *close-up,* which is a picture of a person or an object taken from so close that you can see every detail of it.

By the time of World War I, movies were being made in large studios especially built for the purpose. Most of the studios, which had been in New York, moved to Hollywood, California, where there was plenty of sunshine. Hollywood was also near many different kinds of natural settings that could be used for pictures — mountains, deserts, seashores, farm country, or almost any other scene. The movies by this time were a big business, and stars and producers made enormous amounts of money.

Until 1927 the movies were "silent." Conversation appeared in printed form, called *subtitles,* that appeared on the screen between scenes. In 1927 the first talking picture was introduced. Al Jolson sang and the actors talked in *The Jazz Singer.* The next year the first all-talking picture was made, and within a very short time all movies were being made with sound.

Not long after the introduction of sound, a good way of making movies in natural color was found. The most effective method was called *Technicolor.* The use of color has increased gradually ever since, but it is expensive and most movies are still made in black and white.

Up to the end of World War II, movies drew enormous audiences. As many as ninety million people went to the movies in the United States every week. After the war, a great new rival came into being. This was television. Instead of going to the movies, people sat at home and watched television. Desperately, the motion-picture industry tried to find a way to get people back into the theaters. They found a partial answer in making longer, more expensive and more spectacular pictures than ever before and by using a wider screen than before, to make the actors appear more lifelike. They also made plans to show the new films on home television sets, through a system by which viewers can pay to see them.

HOW MOVIES ARE MADE

The motion-picture camera is very much like a still camera, which is described in the article on PHOTOGRAPHY; but, unlike the still camera, the movie camera rapidly photographs many individual pictures, or *frames,* on a strip of film. For sound pictures, the camera photographs twenty-four frames each second. Each frame is a photograph of a part of the action. The strip of film is then run through a projector, which casts one

frame at a time onto a screen. A *shutter* passes in front of the projector's lens and blocks out the picture between each two frames. It does this so fast that the audience is not aware of it. The audience sees the frames, one after the other, so fast that the people and things in them seem to move as they do in real life.

Motion-picture film used for professional movies is 35 mm. (millimeters) wide (about 1⅜ inches). Home movie film is 16 mm. or 8 mm. wide.

The sound portion of a movie is recorded on a separate strip of film, which runs at the same speed as the photographic film (and is said to be synchronized with it). Sound is picked up by a microphone and then changed by an electronic system into light that is printed on the film in the form of different patterns or lines. Usually more than one sound strip, or sound track, is used in the making of a film: one for the dialogue (the actors' words), one for the sound effects (noises and other natural sounds), and one for the musical background. When the picture is finally assembled, all the different tracks are made into one and are printed at one side of the picture strip. Until recently it was very difficult for home movie makers to add sound to their pictures, but a new process, magnetic sound recording, makes it easy to do this.

A professional motion picture is the work of many skilled persons. Writers produce a *shooting script* that details all of the film's action and dialogue. A picture may be made of hundreds of different scenes or shots, and each one is described and numbered in the script. When the script is approved by the *producer,* who is in complete charge of the picture, actors are chosen, a *director* is selected to give instructions to the actors, and the shooting begins. This may be in a studio or *on location.* A location is a place outside the studio that has been chosen because it provides a good background for the story.

When you enter a studio where a movie is being made, all may seem to be confusion, but actually everyone is busy at his job. In preparation for shooting, the cameraman is telling a group of electricians high up on a scaffold just how he wants the many lights placed. In a corner, the stars are rehearsing their dialogue as the director listens. The sound man, seated at a control panel, is testing his equipment. An assistant director is placing chalk marks on the floor of the set to guide the actors in their movements before the camera so that they will remain in focus and within the picture frame. A cameraman's assistant is putting film in the camera and placing the camera in a "blimp." A blimp is a covering for the camera that deadens the noise of its mechanism so that it will not be picked up by the sound recorder. If the camera is to be moved during the scene, it will be placed on a truck called a *dolly.* Or it may be placed on a *boom* that can carry the camera high into the air or move it about wherever the director wishes.

"TAKING" A SCENE

When all is ready, the director calls for a rehearsal of the scene. The scene may last only a minute or less on film, but he

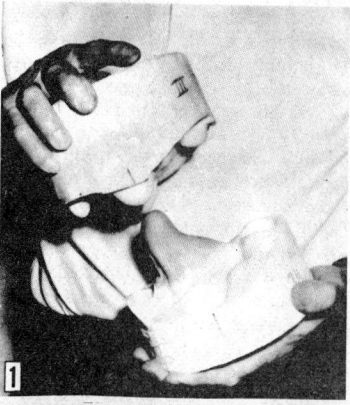

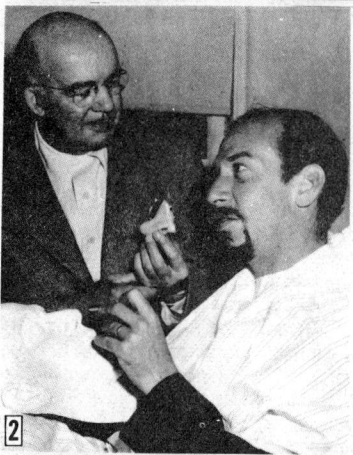

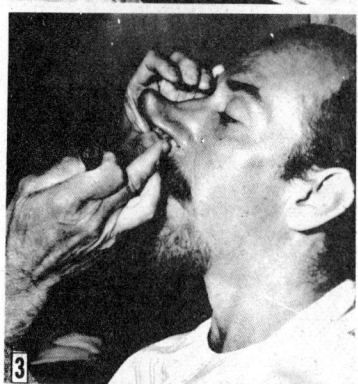

One of the most important jobs in a motion-picture studio is that of the makeup man. It is his task to make over the face of an actor so that it fits the part he is playing. For example, when José Ferrer played the part of Cyrano de Bergerac he had to be given the long, ugly nose for which Cyrano was most famous.

1. After a cast had been made of Ferrer's face, a nose was modeled to fit his features.

2. Holding the plaster cast, the actor looks over his new nose before trying it on.

3. When it is put in place, it is almost impossible to tell that the fake is not the real thing.

goes over it many times. He must make sure that the actors do their parts properly, that the camera is photographing it exactly as he wishes, and that the microphone, which usually is hung on a boom or arm just out of view of the camera, is picking up the sound clearly. When the rehearsal is completed, the director orders a "take." This means that the scene will be recorded by the camera and sound apparatus. Often several takes are made before the director is satisfied. When the scene is finished, the technicians prepare for the next one.

The scene that is taken next may or may not be one that follows in order in the shooting script. Very often scenes from the beginning and end of the picture are shot together. The reason is that they may take place in the same setting, and it is cheaper for the company to shoot all the scenes that take place there at the same time than to leave the set standing until it is needed again.

When the day's shooting is finished, the film is developed and looked at by the producer and director to make sure that the scenes are just right. The developed scenes of a day's work are called *rushes* or *dailies*.

When all the shooting is completed the film passes into the hands of the *editor*. His job is to fit together all the individual shots, trim bits of the scenes if they are not good or are too long, and arrange to have certain special effects made. These special effects include fade-ins, fade-outs, dissolves, and wipes. In a *fade-in*, a scene gradually appears on the screen. A *fade-out* is the reverse; it makes one scene disappear. A *dissolve* makes a scene gradually melt into another. A *wipe* removes one scene from the screen, meanwhile replacing it with another.

When all the scenes of a picture are assembled, the background music is recorded. Then a *print* of the picture (a film that can be put through a projector) is made and shown to a preview audience at some out-of-the-way theater. The audience is asked to write its reaction to the picture. Sometimes changes are made as a result. Then more prints are made, sent out to theaters, and *released* (shown to the public).

From the start of shooting to the end may take twelve weeks or even longer. It is not unusual for a motion picture to cost a million dollars, and some cost several million.

WIDE-SCREEN MOTION PICTURES

Most important movies today are made by one of the wide-screen systems. They are called wide-screen systems because the picture they show is wider than the one for a regular screen. One of these systems, CINERAMA, is described in a separate article.

A regular screen is about 1⅓ times wider than it is high. (This relation, called the *aspect ratio,* is written 1.33 to 1.) Other systems use aspect ratios of 2 to 1, 1.85 to 1, or 2.66 to 1.

Wide-screen movies have become popular because their scenes have almost a three-dimensional effect. Actually three-dimensional ("3-D") pictures have been popular from time to time, but they require the audience to wear special glasses and their popularity has never lasted long.

In the wide-screen system known as CinemaScope, a special camera lens, called an *anamorphic lens,* is used in front of the regular lens. This squeezes onto a regular 35-mm. film frame a picture that is twice as wide as usual. Then, when the picture is projected, another anamorphic lens is placed on the projector, and this spreads the image out again, to fill a screen that is 2.66 to 1 instead of 1.33 to 1. A slightly curved screen is used.

Another wide-screen system is Vista-Vision. This uses a regular lens, but it runs the film through the camera sideways and photographs two frames at once. This makes each picture almost twice as wide as the regular 1.33 to 1.

Home movies can also be made in wide-screen proportions by using a Vistascope attachment in front of the camera and projector. The Vistascope attachment is available for both 16-mm. and 8-mm. cameras.

The Todd A-O process, introduced in 1955, uses a curved screen that extends for 128 degrees (about one-third of a full circle, and more than three-quarters of what the eye normally sees). Cinerama also uses a curved screen, but while Cinerama uses three cameras, Todd A-O uses only one camera, which has several lenses. The Todd A-O camera uses 65-mm. film, almost twice as wide as regular film. The screen is 50 feet wide and 25 feet high.

Motley, John Lothrop

John Lothrop Motley was an American historian and statesman who lived more than a hundred years ago. He was born in 1814. After his graduation from Harvard, in 1831, he went on a long tour of Europe and became very interested in the history of the Netherlands. He wrote several important books about the Netherlands, the most famous being *The Rise of the Dutch Republic.* In 1841 Motley was made secretary of a United States legation in the capital of Russia. Twenty years later he served for six years as United States minister to Austria, and shortly afterward President Grant appointed him minister to Great Britain. However, Motley quarreled with other United States statesmen, particularly with the Secretary of State, Hamilton Fish, and Grant had him recalled. Motley died in 1877.

motorboat (SEE BOATING)

A motorboat is a boat driven by an INTERNAL COMBUSTION ENGINE, about which there is a separate article. The engine is connected to a propeller by means of a shaft. The turning of the propeller in the water at the rear drives the boat.

The size of a motorboat ranges from 15 to 50 feet, from a small speedboat carrying one or two people to the large motor yacht, driven by twin engines and carrying as many as 15 people, with kitchen and sleeping space. Motorboats of various constructions and sizes are used for racing, fishing, or cruising, and even as a temporary summer home.

Most motorboats are equipped with an engine located inside the boat, near the middle. Such boats are classified as *inboard* motorboats.

The bottom of a motorboat may have various shapes, depending on what the boat is used for. *Speedboats* usually have a V-shaped bottom to allow them to move through the water more easily. A *hydroplane,* or highspeed racing boat, has less of a V-shape. It is so constructed that the front of the boat rises up from the water when the boat is moving at high speed. This enables the boat to move along on top rather than through the water, reducing the friction between the water and the boat and bringing it to speeds as great as 160 miles an hour. Large boats, which are not designed for high speeds, have rounded bottoms.

Motorboats usually are made of hardwood such as oak, pine, and teak wood. Steel is too heavy. Many boats are made of an alloy of aluminum.

A small boat can use a portable engine, weighing twenty pounds or more, that can be carried and attached to the stern of the boat. Such boats are classified as *outboard* motor boats. Although usually used on boats that do not require speeds greater than 35 miles an hour, some outboard motors can develop speeds as great as 70 miles an hour.

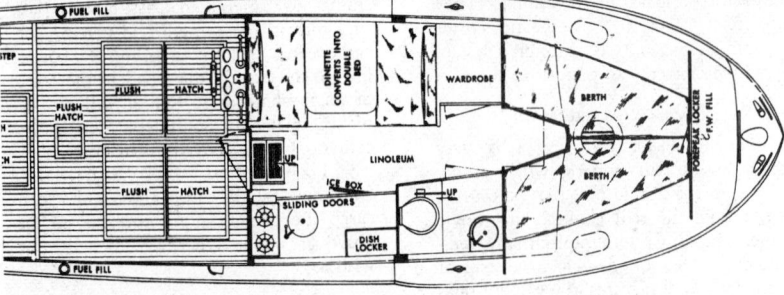

Chris Craft

A good motorboat can be used for fishing, cruising, or racing. The diagram above shows the various parts of the trim 32-foot cruiser.

motorcycle

A motorcycle is a kind of bicycle that is driven by an INTERNAL COMBUSTION ENGINE, about which there is a separate article. The engine is located under the driver's seat. On some motorcycles, a chain from the engine drives the rear wheel. On others, the engine turns a shaft that serves as the rear wheel's axle.

Motorcycles are used for police patrol, pleasure riding, and racing. They can travel at speeds as great as 150 miles an hour, using about one gallon of gasoline for every 60 miles. The American Motorcycle Association conducts races every year, including hill-climbing, cross-country racing, and track racing.

A motorcycle is fast, maneuverable, and inexpensive to operate. Many motorcyclists form clubs and go on trips together.

Harley-Davidson

The speed of a motorcycle is controlled by turning one of the grips on the end of the handle bars. It works like the accelerator pedal of an automobile. Transmission gears enable the driver to run the motorcycle at different speeds.

A motorcycle is heavier and longer than a bicycle. The seat is lower, giving the driver greater control. There are footstands on both sides for the driver's feet. Often there is a seat in back of the driver for another passenger. A motorcycle may be equipped with a sidecar, supported by an extra wheel and attached to the side of the motorcycle, in which a passenger sits.

A *motorbike* is a regular bicycle with a small engine attached to the rear wheel. When the engine is running, it turns the wheel. When the engine is off, the rider can pedal as on a regular bicycle.

A *motor scooter* has only two wheels, as a motorcycle or bicycle has, but between them it has a board on which the driver can place his feet while he rides. The rear wheel is driven by a small engine under the driver's seat. A motor scooter can go as fast as 40 miles an hour.

motor vehicles

Automobiles, trucks, buses, and certain tractors are called motor vehicles. They carry their own engines and go wherever they are steered instead of being confined to tracks as streetcars and trains are. There are literally thousands of ways in which one motor vehicle can be different from another, yet there are other ways in which all motor vehicles are alike.

The vehicle begins with a steel frame, two long pieces of steel that run the length of the vehicle and two crosspieces at the front and rear. These are securely fastened together in the shape of a rectangle. At each corner there is a wheel. Each pair of wheels, front and rear, is fastened together on a crosspiece called an *axle* and are attached to the frame by springs. When a wheel passes over a rough place it moves the spring rather than the frame, which reduces jolting of the frame. Each wheel is also attached to a device called a *shock absorber*. This is a hydraulic device similar to the one that closes doors automatically and keeps them from slamming. The shock absorber helps the springs to prevent jolting.

In the front of the vehicle the frame supports an engine. This is almost always an INTERNAL COMBUSTION ENGINE, described in a separate article. The engine turns a long rod called a *driveshaft* that leads to the rear axle. The driveshaft is attached to a gear that turns the rear axle. The turning of the rear axle turns the rear wheels and this makes the vehicle move. Nearly every motor vehicle is driven by its rear wheels. The machinery where the driveshaft meets the rear axle is called the "rear end."

There is always a universal joint on the shaft. This keeps it from bending if bumps in the road cause the rear axle to move up and down.

One of the gears is in the rear end and is called a *differential*. It permits either rear wheel to turn over more slowly than the other. If the vehicle goes around a corner, the inside wheel must turn more slowly than the outside wheel, because it has a shorter distance to go.

FRONT-WHEEL AND FOUR-WHEEL DRIVES

When a vehicle is driven by its rear wheels, the front wheels are used only for steering. Each front wheel is hung on a sort of pivot so that it can move from left to right. Bars attached to these pivot devices lead to a steering wheel above the frame. The driver of the vehicle sits behind the steering wheel. By turning the steering wheel he guides the vehicle.

There are certain advantages to having a vehicle driven by its front wheels instead of by its rear wheels. Some of the power is lost in turning the long driveshaft. (Some automobiles have their engines in the rear for this reason.) The vehicle is less likely to skid on the road if the driving wheels are always pointed in the direction in which it is going. With rear-wheel drive, the driving wheels are always pointed forward. Some automobiles have used front-wheel drive. The difficulty has always been that it requires more complicated machinery to drive wheels that can constantly change direction.

Automobiles that must run in heavy sand and mud are sometimes built with four-wheel drive. This means that the power from the engine goes to the front wheels as well as to the rear wheels. The same kind of driveshaft and "rear" axle is used. The jeep used by the United States armed forces has four-wheel drive.

Heavy buses and trucks often have a "gas-electric" or "diesel-electric" drive. The engine does not turn a driveshaft. It turns an electric generator. This produces electricity, and the wheels are driven by electric motors run by this electricity.

TORQUE

Torque is twisting action. As the rear wheels turn, they try to turn the rear axle along with them. Therefore the rear axle must be held so that it cannot move. This is done by a torque tube, a tube fastened from the rear axle to a crossbar in the center of the frame, and also by rods that run from the rear axle to the sides of the frame. The driveshaft runs through the torque tube. The tube protects it against dirt and rocks thrown up from the road.

TRACTORS AND TRAILERS

Tractors are used on farms to pull farm machinery. The kind of truck that pulls a trailer is also called a tractor. The semi-trailer is most used. The front end of the trailer rests on the rear of the tractor (truck); the back on the trailer has its own wheels. The trailer is attached to the tractor by a big disk that is mounted at the back of the tractor. This disk is called a "fifth wheel," but it is nothing like the wheels that motor vehicles ride on. The fifth wheel permits the trailer to turn from side to side as the tractor turns.

In a separate article on the TRACTOR, the crawler-type tractor is described. This kind of tractor is driven by a moving tread, of which the best-known make is called *caterpillar*. Some trucks are driven by similar treads. They have wheels in the front, for steering, and the tread in the back. They are called *half-tracks*.

CONTROLS AND BODIES

Behind the engine of nearly any motor vehicle there is a seat for the driver, where he can use the steering wheel and other controls such as the brakes and can see an instrument panel that shows how the engine is operating, how much fuel he has, and so on. The frame, wheels, and driver's equipment are called the *chassis*. There is almost no limit to the number of different bodies or types of equipment that can be mounted (put on top of) the chassis. See the articles on AUTOMOBILE, BUS, and TRUCK.

Nassau Cycle Center
This "snowmobile" has a 40-horsepower engine and automatic transmission.

mound builders

Mound builders is the name given to certain American Indians who built mounds of earth in the Ohio and Mississippi valleys, long ago. Most of the mounds were places where the Indians buried their dead, and so were like our cemeteries. Sometimes the buried Indians had been sacrificed to spirits worshiped by the mound builders. Other mounds were the walls of forts.

The mound builders put the dead person's tools, weapons, household articles and religious articles into the mound along with the body. They believed that the dead person's spirit would need these

Ohio Development Comm.

The mound builders were American Indians who built mounds of earth as fortifications and places of worship throughout eastern and central North America. Scientists are still trying to find out exactly who they were and why their civilization disappeared.

things in the land where his spirit would go. Burial mounds often were in the shape of snakes, birds, and other animals. The animal mounds represented animals that each Indian tribe worshiped. They wanted the animal's spirit to guard the tribe from evil. In Adams County, Ohio, there is a great snake-shaped mound that is nearly a quarter of a mile long, 30 feet wide, and 5 feet high. It is 75 feet across its wide-open jaws.

On the prairies, the mound builders made mounds that looked much like the pyramids of Egypt, except that they were cut off flat about three-quarters of the way to the top. On the tops of these pyramid-mounds the Indians built houses of worship, so the mounds are called *temple mounds.*

The first mounds were built about three thousand years ago, and the last were still being built four hundred years ago when the first Europeans were exploring North America. Scientists used to believe that the mounds were built by people who lived in America before the Indians, but they now believe that the Indians themselves built the mounds.

People in several other parts of the world also built burial mounds and temple mounds.

mountain

Mountains are places that are considerably higher than the land around them. If they are only a little higher, they are called hills. A mountain must stand up sharply from the surrounding land, and usually it must taper from a wide bottom to a narrow top. The plateau or high level region, called the Great Plains, between the Missouri River and the Rocky Mountains is as high above sea level as the peaks of the Appalachian Mountains, but because it is flat we do not call it a mountain.

WHY MOUNTAINS ARE IMPORTANT

Mountains play an important part in the lives of people. It is hard to climb over them, so they have always been a protection against invading armies. That is why mountains form the boundaries of many countries.

Mountains that stand crosswise to the direction from which the wind usually blows are very important in making the climate of a country. The side of the mountains that faces the wind—the windward side—is likely to have heavier rainfall, because the wind drops the moisture it carries before it moves over the mountain tops. The other side—the lee side—is likely to have a drier climate. The western part of the states of Washington and Oregon is on the side of the Cascade Mountains, which face the moist wind blowing off the Pacific Ocean, and so it has a heavy yearly rainfall. The eastern side of these mountains is dry and desertlike.

Mountains may shield valleys from cold winds in winter and from hot, dry, crop-killing winds in summer. Rain running off mountain slopes forms rivers in the valleys and provides the water needed to grow crops.

MOUNTAIN GROUPS

A mountain range is a chain or closely set group of mountain ridges that stretches across the land. The Sierra Nevadas of California are a mountain range. Rising above the range may be individual mountain peaks.

A group of mountain ranges that are close together and were formed together form a mountain system, such as the Rocky Mountains and the Alps of Europe.

HOW MOUNTAINS ARE MADE

There are several ways in which mountains are made.

From deep in the earth a great mass of melted rock may slowly push its way upward. Taking thousands of years, it slowly bends the crust up into a dome, and then it has formed a *dome mountain.* The Black Hills of South Dakota are dome mountains.

Cracks, called faults, in the earth's rocky crust may mark the boundaries of the slow sinking or rising of great blocks of rock. When this happens, mountains are formed with steep slopes or sharp cliffs. These are *fault-block mountains.* The Sierra Nevada Mountains were formed in this way.

The great forces that are always changing the shape of the earth's crust sometimes fold the crust in the same way that a tablecloth pushed across a table becomes folded. The tops of the folds are *fold mountains;* the troughs of the folds are *valleys.* The Appalachians in Pennsylvania are fold mountains.

When a high plateau has been worn down by erosion for millions of years, the parts of the plateau that resist erosion best stand high and are called *residual mountains.*

German Tourist Office

The Alps are the greatest mountain chain in Europe. High on the slopes of the Alps are many winter resorts and tiny villages where livestock is raised. The Alps form a great natural barrier between several countries of Europe, but the many passes make crossing easy.

The kind of mountains called volcanoes belch out great amounts of cinders and even greater amounts of melted rock, called lava. Some volcanic mountains have built themselves up from their own cinders and lava. There is a separate article about VOLCANOES.

WORLD'S HIGHEST MOUNTAINS

The highest mountains of the world are in Asia, chiefly in the Himalaya Mountains. The Himalayas have about forty peaks that are over 20,000 feet high. The highest of these, and the highest mountain in the world, is Mount Everest, which rises to 29,028 feet. Next is Mount Godwin-Austen, also called K-2, which is 28,250 feet high, and Mount Kanchenjunga, 28,146 feet high. The highest peak outside of Asia is Aconcagua, in the Andes Mountains in Argentina; it is 23,081 feet high. Almost as high is Illampu, in the Bolivian Andes, which rises to 22,703 feet. South America has many other peaks higher than 20,000 feet. The only mountain in another continent that rises so high is Mount McKinley, in Alaska, 20,269 feet high, the highest in North America. The highest mountain in Africa is Mount Kilimanjaro, in Tanganyika. It has two peaks, the higher of which is 19,340 feet high. Mont Blanc is the highest peak in Europe; it is in the Swiss Alps, and is 15,781 feet high. The highest peak in Canada is Mount Logan, 19,850 feet high, in the Yukon Territory. Mount Whitney, in California, is the highest peak in the United States. It is 14,495 feet high.

mountain ash

The mountain ash is a slender tree that grows in many parts of Europe and the United States where the climate is not too warm. It grows best in damp places and on rocky hillsides. It grows to be between thirty and fifty feet high. It is deciduous, which means that it loses its leaves in the fall. The leaves of the mountain ash have jagged edges and there are many small leaflets on one stalk.

People plant the mountain ash in parks and in their gardens. In May it bears lovely clusters of white flowers, and in the fall it has bright red berries. Its wood is not very valuable.

Some people in Europe long ago believed that the mountain ash had magical powers. They thought that if a person put a branch of the tree above his bed it would keep away evil spirits.

mountain climbing

There are many kinds of mountain climbing, almost as many kinds as there are mountains. When people are very young, a hill only a few hundred feet high seems like a mountain. When they clamber to the top they feel like mountain climbers, which they are. Some years later, perhaps at a summer camp or on vacation, the same boys and girls, who are older now, go on organized hikes into the woods, perhaps climbing a fair-sized mountain. They may even spend a night on or near its summit. They have become mountain climbers.

Young people in the United States and Canada do not do much mountain climbing. Most of them prefer to get their exercise in other sports. But some people, especially Europeans, think mountain climbing is the greatest sport in the world. They go at it slowly, first climbing the "easy" peaks, then trying ones a little harder, until they can go up the highest and most difficult ones.

There are many thrills in mountain climbing, partly because it is so dangerous. Climbers may slip and fall; they may be hit by falling rocks, or be swept down by an avalanche, which is a big slide of snow, ice, rocks, or other material. More than a hundred climbers are usually killed every year in the Alps. Few climbers can give a logical, sensible reason why they want to fight their way up a high, snow-capped peak. Some simply give as a reason, "Because it's there."

At one time men climbed mountains for scientific reasons, to survey the surrounding land, or to find out about the climate, the winds, and so on. Now mountain climbing is more of a sport. Men always want to be the first to climb a certain peak and they spend much time, effort, and money doing it.

CLIMBING EQUIPMENT

The lower slopes of a mountain are usually easy to climb. But near the top of high mountains may be steep, rocky cliffs, often covered with snow or ice. For rock climbing or ice climbing, special equipment and climbing aids are needed. Climbers wearing ordinary shoes would slip, so they use *crampons*. These are metal frames with spikes, and they are attached to the shoes. Climbers carry *pitons,* which are short iron rods. Each has a sharp point at one end, and a ring at the other. The piton is hammered into ice or into cracks in rocks. Then it can be used to step on or to hold onto by hand, or its ring can hold tight one end of a rope. Climbers also need plenty of rope which must be light but strong. They need ice axes, warm clothing, and goggles and face cream to prevent dangerous sunburn.

When climbing up steep cliffs, the climbers are usually roped together, from 20 to 40 feet apart. The best climber goes first. He chops out a path, hammers in pitons, climbs up a short distance, and then helps the others up by pulling on the rope. They follow in his very footsteps. If one man slips, the others hold tight and pull him to safety.

For long, difficult climbs, mountaineers take sleeping bags, lamps, tents, oxygen masks, food supplies, scientific instruments and many other things. For climbing high, snow-capped mountains, elaborate preparations are made and many people take part. In fact, a mountain-climbing expedition is like a small army attacking a fortified camp.

FAMOUS ASCENTS

For example, early in 1953 a group set out to climb Mount Everest in the Himalayas, in Nepal-Tibet north of India. Everest, whose native name is *Chomolungma* or "Goddess of the Snows," is the highest peak in the world, 29,028 feet high. In the expedition were 14 Europeans, 20 native helpers, and 362 porters. They took 10,000 pounds of baggage. First they set up a base camp;

from it they had to travel eighty days to reach the foot of Mount Everest. As they climbed, they set up other camps. Many of the climbers became exhausted or sick, and dropped out as others went higher. The cold was intense, snow and sleet storms almost blew the climbers away, the air had little oxygen, and the climbing became very difficult. Only two men reached the top. The date was May 29, 1953. The men were Edmund Hillary, a New Zealand beekeeper, and Tensing Norkey, a native guide. Since then, Mt. Everest has been scaled by the Swiss, in 1956, and by the Americans in 1963.

Other famous climbs have been made in the Himalayas. The second-highest peak, Mount Godwin-Austen (also called K-2), was conquered by Italians on July 31, 1954. Kanchenjunga, the third-highest, was scaled by a British expedition on May 25, 1955. Lhotse I, fourth-highest, was conquered on May 18, 1956.

The highest peak in North America is Mount McKinley in Alaska, 20,320 feet. It was climbed in 1913. In the Western Hemisphere, the highest is Mount Aconcagua in Argentina, 23,081 feet. It was first climbed in 1897.

See the articles on ANNAPURNA, EVEREST, and ACONCAGUA.

mountain lion, a fierce, wild member of the cat family: see the article on COUGAR.

Mount Vernon

Mount Vernon is the name of the beautiful house and large estate in Virginia where George Washington lived. Both George Washington and his wife are buried at Mount Vernon. About a hundred years ago an organization called the Mount Vernon Ladies' Association bought Mount Vernon and opened it to the public. The Mount Vernon Ladies' Association has furnished the main house with much of the furniture that George Washington himself used, has restored many of the other buildings to look much as they did in Washington's time, and has made one small building into a museum in which many of the things owned by Washington and his family can be seen.

Mount Vernon is a few miles south of Washington, D.C. The main house is a white building that stands at the top of a hill. The hill is a rolling lawn that goes down to the Potomac River. The gardens on the estate are beautiful. Each year thousands of visitors walk through the shaded paths from the main house to George Washington's tomb near the river and back to the many other buildings that make up the estate.

George Washington inherited Mount Vernon from his half-brother, Lawrence Washington, in 1752. He lived there all the rest of his life, except when he was serving his country in its army or as its President.

mouse

The mouse is a small animal that lives in almost every part of the world. Most people think of the mouse as a great pest and some people are even afraid of mice, although they do no serious harm and are not dangerous. There are many different kinds of mouse and

some of them are very attractive and interesting. The ordinary house mouse is usually less than 6 inches long. It builds its nest in walls. During the day it hides and at night it comes out to search for food. The house mouse is especially fond of cheese and sweet foods. It is not a very smart animal, so it is easy to catch a house mouse in a trap. The female has from four to nine young about once every month or two.

The field mouse lives in meadows and fields. It eats grass and weeds. The field mouse needs to eat its own weight in food each day, and this means it has to spend almost all of its time searching for food. The field mouse is surrounded by enemies. So many animals eat mice that although the female field mouse has about 120 babies a year, not many of them live to reach the grown-up stage.

There are many stories and superstitions about mice. For example, many people believe that mice can sing. This is not true. Scientists have found that some mice have a kind of asthma that makes it difficult for them to breathe, and they make a strange noise in breathing. Though so many people dislike mice, white mice are often kept as pets and they are lively and interesting animals. Scientists have used mice in their experiments and have discovered many valuable things from their study of the bodies and behavior of mice.

Moussorgsky, Modeste

Modeste Moussorgsky was a Russian composer, or writer of music, who lived more than a hundred years ago. He was born in Russia in 1839. He earned his living as a government official, but devoted himself to the study of music. His greatest work is the opera *Boris Godunoff*, about which there is a separate article.

Moussorgsky died in 1881. His name is sometimes spelled Musorgski.

mouth

The mouth is the opening in an animal's body through which food is taken in. Most mammals (animals that bring forth their young alive, and nurse them) have mouths very much like the human mouth except in outer appearance. There are upper and lower jaws, with which the mouth is opened and closed; there are teeth, and there is a tongue that can be moved.

The human mouth is also called the *oral cavity*. The roof of the mouth is formed by the hard palate in front and the soft palate farther back. The bottom of the mouth is formed by the tongue. Tongue, palates, and the insides of the lips have glands from which comes saliva, the fluid that softens food in the mouth and makes it possible to swallow. Also on the tongue and linings of the mouth are taste buds with which we taste food. The mouth is important in speech. The position of the tongue, teeth, and lips controls many of the sounds we make. In the back, the mouth has two openings, one into the esophagus, or passage that leads to the stomach, and the other into the windpipe, or passage that leads to the lungs. We learn to control those openings without thinking about it, so that when we breathe through the

mouth we open the way into the windpipe and when we eat or drink, we open the way into the stomach.

Mozambique

Mozambique is a territory belonging to Portugal, on the southeastern coast of Africa. Its area is about 300,000 square miles, which is bigger than Texas, and about seven million people live there, fewer than live in Texas. The capital and largest city is Lourenço Marques, a city of about 100,000, which has one of the best harbors in southern Africa.

Most of the people are Negro. Only about one of every two hundred is white. Most of the Negro people in Mozambique belong to various Bantu tribes. Every year almost 100,000 of them go to South Africa, where they work in mines. Many of them own small farms where they grow cotton, rice, corn, and beans. Others work on large plantations owned by Europeans, most of whom are Portuguese. Sugar cane, coconuts and peanuts are grown on these plantations.

One of the large cities is also called Mozambique. It is on a small island on an inlet of the Indian Ocean and has a fine harbor.

Portuguese settlers first went to Mozambique about three hundred years ago. For a long time they carried on slave trade, but this was outlawed in 1878. Mozambique is ruled by a governor-general appointed by Portugal.

MOZAMBIQUE. Area, 302,329 square miles. Population (1964 estimate) 6,872,000. Capital, Lourenço Marques.

Mozart, Wolfgang

Wolfgang Amadeus Mozart was a great composer, or writer of original music, who lived in Austria about two hundred years ago. He started to play the harpsichord (an instrument somewhat like the piano) when he was only 3 years old, and by the time he was 5 he was composing music.

Mozart was born in Salzburg, Austria, in 1756. His father was a musician, and his older sister had musical talent also. When she was 10 and young Mozart was 6 they gave concerts in Munich and Vienna.

Mozart's first published work, four sonatas for harpsichord and violin, were

brought out when he was only 8 years old. Three years later the Holy Roman Emperor, Joseph II, paid him to compose a light opera and the Empress Maria Theresa asked him to compose a mass for her. He did so, and conducted it himself in her presence in Vienna the following December.

After this, Mozart was appointed concert master of the cathedral at Salzburg. He was unhappy in this position when a new archbishop was appointed; but according to the customs of the times he could not get another job if he quit that one before he was of age. When he reached the age of 21, in 1777, he resigned his position. At this point he had composed more than two hundred works, including grand operas, masses, and symphonies. He was considered the finest pianist in Europe, one of the first organists, and in the highest rank of violinists.

After he left Salzburg in 1777, he went to Munich, then Mannheim, and finally Paris. He found it difficult to earn money. Musicians in that period were seldom paid enough to live on. He returned to Salzburg in 1779, and obtained a new and better contract with the archbishop.

Between 1780 and 1791, the year of his death, Mozart composed six operas. His best-known operas today are *The Marriage of Figaro, Don Giovanni,* and *The Magic Flute.* In only three months, in 1788, he wrote his three greatest symphonies, the thirty-ninth, fortieth, and forty-first (called the *Jupiter Symphony*).

In 1782 Mozart married a young woman named Constanza Weber. They had several children, but only two of them lived past infancy.

When Wolfgang Amadeus Mozart died in 1791, after a long period of overwork and poor health, he left more than eight hundred compositions for the piano, for orchestra, and for singers. He lived to be only 35.

Mukden

Mukden, or Shenyang as it is now called, is an important industrial city in northern China in the former province of Manchuria. About 2,500,000 people live there. They work in factories making steel, oil, flour, soap, and soybean products. Most of the people are Chinese,

Mozart wrote the beautiful hymn "God Is Our Refuge" in 1765. He presented the manuscript (reproduced here) to the British Museum a short time later.

but there are many Russians. Part of Mukden is very old and is surrounded by high walls. The most beautiful building is the Imperial Palace. A few miles away is the modern part of the city. Here there are schools, department stores, parks, and wide roads. There are also many factories. The people travel about the city on buses and trolley cars. The city is on the South Manchurian Railroad.

Mukden is more than eight hundred years old. Long ago it became one of the important cities of China, though people in the western world knew little about it. The city was the scene of bitter fighting during the Boxer Rebellion in 1900. During the Russo-Japanese War, five years later, the Battle of Mukden was fought there. When the Japanese invaded Manchuria in 1931, they moved the capital from Mukden to Changchun (Hsinking). In 1948, after World War II, the Chinese again made Mukden the capital of Manchuria until that province was dissolved as an administrative unit.

MUKDEN (SHENYANG), CHINA. Population (1957) 2,411,000. On the Hun River.

mulberry

The mulberry is a tree that grows in Asia and Europe and in the United States where the climate is not too hot or too cold. There are several kinds of mulberry tree. The black mulberry tree grows to be about fifty feet high. It is deciduous, which means that it loses its leaves in the fall. The fruit is dark red or black and grows in a cluster. It looks somewhat like a blackberry. It is very sweet and makes a delicious dessert. People use the fruit to make jam and a fine wine.

The red mulberry is grown in the eastern part of the United States. It is taller than the black mulberry, growing to sixty feet or more. People find the fruit too sour, but birds are very fond of the red mulberries. The wood is hard and strong and is used to make furniture.

Another important mulberry is the white mulberry. This tree first grew in China. Many people in Europe and the warm parts of the United States and Central and South America raise the white mulberry. Its leaves are a favorite food of the valuable silkworm. The fruit of the white mulberry is white or pale pink, and it is not good to eat. People in Europe make a yellow dye from the roots of the tree. The white mulberry is not so large or strong as the other mulberry trees.

mule

The mule is a strong, intelligent animal that men have raised since ancient

times. The father of a mule is a jackass (donkey) and the mother is a mare (a female horse). Female mules do not have any young of their own. The mule is about the size of a horse, but has more endurance and usually more strength. It has long ears and a short tail. Its voice is a bray, like that of the ass. The mule is very useful to farmers because it can work very hard and is sure-footed and steady, but most of the mules once used have been replaced by tractors and trucks.

Mules in South America are sometimes led by an old female horse with a bell tied to its neck. The mules will obediently follow the horse and can learn to recognize the sound of the bell. Although mules are intelligent, they have a reputation for being very independent. For that reason, people sometimes say that a person is as stubborn as a mule.

When a male horse and a female ass are bred, their offspring is called a hinny, a smaller animal than a mule.

mullein

Mullein is a plant that grows in Europe and along the side of roads and in fields in parts of the United States, where the climate is not too hot or too cold. The mullein is a biennial, which means that it has flowers only every second year. The mullein is a hardy plant and does not need a great deal of rain. It may grow to be between three and six feet high. It has spikes of yellow flowers. The mullein is sometimes called the velvet plant because its leaves are covered with a soft downy fuzz that feels like velvet.

mummy

A mummy is a dead body that has been preserved so that it will keep for a long time. When people talk about a mummy, they usually mean just one kind of mummy: a dead body that has been made ready for burial by embalming it as the ancient Egyptians did, thousands of years ago. (There is a separate article on EMBALMING.)

The Egyptians had different ways of embalming a body, depending on how much money was to be spent for the job. The body of a rich and important Egyptian, such as a pharaoh, was first washed. Then the brain, liver, and other internal organs were taken out. The body and the removed organs were soaked for seventy days in a liquid called *natron,* which includes the chemical elements sodium and carbon. Then the body was filled with perfumes and oils and wrapped in hundreds of yards of linen bandages that had been soaked in balsam or a tarry substance such as asphalt.

After the body was embalmed, it was put inside a mummy-case that had been made to fit the outlines of the body. This case was put inside another one. Both cases were made of wood, usually from a cedar tree. The inner mummy-case was plain. The outer one was covered with pictures and writing that told the deeds in the life of the dead person. The two mummy-cases were put inside a wooden coffin, and the coffin was put inside a sarcophagus, which is a stone coffin on a pedestal. The organs were put into jars of perfumed oil and placed in the sarcophagus along with the coffin.

The Egyptians went to all this trouble because they believed that a dead person's soul would some day return to the body, and they wanted the soul to be able to recognize the body it came from.

mumps

Mumps is a disease that many children are apt to get. Very few people get mumps after the age of 15. Mumps is not usually a dangerous disease, though when an adult gets mumps it can be very unpleasant.

Mumps is infectious, which means that you can catch it from someone who has it. If you have been near someone with mumps who coughs and sneezes, or if you have touched the person or kissed him or even used the same drinking glass, you may catch the mumps. You will not know whether you have been infected for about three weeks.

The first sign that you have mumps is a pain under your ear. Then there may be fever and a headache, and in a day or two the glands in the neck or throat will begin to swell. Usually these glands are just in front of the ear, and a person with mumps has a very fat face that looks funny. Mumps is quite painful and it hurts to laugh or swallow. Most cases of mumps last for about one week.

Mumps is caused by a tiny germ, called a virus, that is so small it cannot even be seen under a microscope. This virus is present in the saliva (the fluid) in a person's mouth when he has the disease. A person who has had mumps will almost surely never get it again; see the article on IMMUNITY.

Münchhausen, Baron

Baron Hieronymus Karl Friedrich von Münchhausen was a German soldier known for his exaggerated stories. He was born in Germany in 1720 and served as a cavalry officer in the Russian army. After his army service was over, he returned to Germany and told exciting stories of his adventures as a soldier. His tales were so wild and improbable that the name of Münchhausen (or Munchausen, as it is usually spelled in English) eventually was used to describe anyone who told impossible tales of adventure that could never have occurred.

One of the classic Münchhausen stories concerns the time he tied his horse to a post after a heavy snowstorm. He lay down in the snow to sleep, and during the night a warm breeze melted away the snow. In the morning he found that he was lying on the bare ground at the side of a church, and his horse was suspended high on the steeple. The snow had been so deep that he had tied the horse to the tip of the church steeple, the only part of the church that was not completely buried in snow.

Baron von Münchhausen was a real person, but the stories that have been told about him were usually the product of other writers' imaginations. He died in 1797, at the age of 57.

Mundelein, Cardinal

George William Mundelein was a Roman Catholic priest who was made a cardinal. Cardinals are called princes of the Church.

George Mundelein was born in New York City, in 1872 and went to school at Manhattan College and in Rome, Italy. When he was 23 years old he became a priest. In 1915 he was made Archbishop of Chicago, and nine years later he was appointed a cardinal.

Cardinal Mundelein did much work to help the poor find better housing and earn better salaries. He was a good friend of President Franklin D. Roosevelt, who dis-

cussed many problems with him. In 1937 Cardinal Mundelein publicly condemned the Nazis who controlled Germany under Adolf Hitler. Cardinal Mundelein also built many churches and schools. His seminary (a school where young men study to be priests), called St. Mary's of the Lake, is one of the biggest in the world. It is in Mundelein, Illinois, a village named for the cardinal. The Catholic Youth Organization (CYO), a club that offers boys and girls a chance to play sports and organize teams, was started with the cardinal's help. Cardinal Mundelein died in 1939.

Munich

Munich is the capital of the state of Bavaria in West Germany, and is the largest city in the southern part of the country

Munich is on the Isar River at the foot of the Bavarian Alps. More than one million people live there. The most famous product of Munich is its beer. It is exported to all parts of the world. There are also factories producing heavy machinery, automobiles, and food products.

The city of Munich is very beautiful and is one of the most important German educational and cultural centers. It has two opera houses, many art galleries and museums, the State Theater, and an important university. There are many book-publishing houses.

Every year there are many festivals. Among them are the Munich Carnival, the Strong Beer Festival in the spring, and the October Festival. The city is an international air, rail, and highway center.

Munich was the first headquarters of Adolf Hitler and his Nazi Party, who later became supreme rulers of Germany. They first met in the Bürgerbrauhaus, or beer hall (a place where beer and food are served and there is music for entertainment), in Munich. From there they started a minor revolution, later called the "beer hall putsch," in 1923. It was unsuccessful. (See the articles on HITLER and NAZISM.) Later, in 1938, a meeting in Munich led to the MUNICH PACT, about which there is a separate article.

Munich was greatly damaged by Allied bombers during World War II, but in less than ten years the people repaired nearly all the damage and the city was prosperous again.

MUNICH, WEST GERMANY. Population (1976 estimate) 1,330,000. Capital of Bavaria, in West Germany. On the Isar River.

Munich Pact

The Munich Pact was an agreement made by the European countries of Germany, Italy, Great Britain, and France, at a meeting in the city of Munich in September, 1938. By the agreement, the Sudetenland, or Sudetes Mountain region of Czechoslovakia, was taken away from Czechoslovakia and given to Germany.

At that time, Adolf Hitler was the dictator, or absolute ruler, of Germany. He had built up a powerful army and air force and he threatened to start a war if necessary to seize territories that Germany wanted. One of these territories was the Sudetenland, where most of the people were of German origin. France was an ally of Czechoslovakia, and Great

Britain was an ally of France. Both France and Great Britain were afraid of Germany and were not willing to go to war to save Czechoslovakia. Italy was an ally of Germany, and Italy was not ready for war.

In September, 1938, just when it seemed that Hitler was going to send his army into Czechoslovakia, his ally Benito Mussolini, the dictator of Italy, suggested a meeting in Munich. Hitler and Mussolini met there with Neville Chamberlain, who was British Prime Minister, and Edouard Daladier, who was French premier. Chamberlain and Daladier agreed that Hitler could take the Sudetenland. The government of Czechoslovakia was not given any voice in the matter, but Czechoslovakia was too weak to fight Germany alone and had to give in. The Munich Pact was dated September 29, 1938, and signed on September 30.

The Munich Pact is a famous example of *appeasement*—giving in rather than fight when threatened. Like most appeasements, it did not succeed. Five months later, Hitler seized all of Czechoslovakia and less than a year later he started World War II. But many people believe the Munich Pact was necessary because it gave Great Britain and France an extra year in which to rearm.

mural

A mural is a picture that is part of a wall. It may be a painting, a mosaic, a sculpture in marble or some other stone, or a carved wooden paneling. The decoration of walls goes back thousands of years to cavemen who drew or carved pictures on the rock walls of the caves in which they lived. The earliest true mural painting is probably that of Egypt. Paintings have been found on the walls of tombs that were built as much as four thousand years ago. The ancient Greeks and Romans, more than two thousand years ago, used mural paintings, and the Romans developed mosaic murals to a great art. (A mosaic is a picture made up of tiny pieces of stone or glass fitted carefully together.) Mural paintings represent much of the work of the greatest painters of all time. Leonardo da Vinci, Raphael and Michelangelo became famous for the murals they painted for churches and museums in Italy.

In the modern world, mural painting and mosaic are used to decorate many churches and public buildings. Great mural paintings were created by the Mexican artists Diego Rivera and Jose Orozco, who became famous throughout the world. In the United States, notable murals were painted by the French artist Puvis de Chavannes and the Americans John Singer Sargent and Edwin Austin Abbey. In 1934 the United States government set up an official organization for the decoration of public buildings. See also the articles FRESCO, MOSAIC, and PAINTING.

murder

Murder is the crime of intentionally killing a human being. It is *first-degree* murder if it is done *with malice aforethought* (that is, if the murderer planned in advance to kill his victim), and it is *second-degree* murder if it was not planned in advance.

First-degree murder is punishable by death in most states and countries, but may also be punished by imprisonment for life. Second-degree murder is never punished by death. See the articles on HOMICIDE and CAPITAL PUNISHMENT.

Murillo, Bartolomé

Bartolomé Esteban Murillo was a great Spanish painter. He was born in Seville, probably in 1617, and began to study painting as soon as he could read and write. He soon painted as well as his teacher. His first works were paintings of the ragged, sunburnt children and peasants of the Spanish countryside. Later he devoted himself mainly to Biblical scenes and characters, and painted many murals in churches. One of his paintings, *The Immaculate Conception,* was once the highest-priced picture in the world, and many of his paintings hang in the art galleries of the world's chief cities. In 1682 he fell from a scaffolding in a church in Cadiz while he was painting a picture on the wall, and died as a result of the accident, at the age of 64.

Murray, Philip

Philip Murray was an American labor union leader. Murray was born in Scotland in 1886, the son of a coal miner who himself was a union president. At the age of 10, after only a few years of school, Murray went to work in the mines. His family moved to the United States when he was 16, and he at once got a job in the Pennsylvania coal mines. Two years later he was involved in his first labor dispute. He won the fight, but he lost his job and 550 men went on strike to support him. The strike failed, but Murray was elected president of the local union.

In 1911 Murray became a citizen of the United States and took the first of a series of jobs in labor unions. By 1919 he was vice-president of the United Mine Workers, a large international union. In 1936 he became president of the United Steel Workers of America and remained its head until his death. In 1940 he was elected president of the Congress of Industrial Organizations and led it through the difficult years of World War II. He fought hard to get rid of Communists in the C.I.O. Murray died in 1952.

Muscat and Oman

Muscat and Oman is the former name of an independent country on the southeastern end of the Arabian Peninsula. Its name was changed to the Sultanate of Oman by Sultan Qabus bin Said who overthrew his father's rule on July 23, 1970. The sultan is an absolute monarch who governs with the help of a personal adviser and a minister of interior. Governors are appointed by the sultan for all of the principal towns and districts in the country.

The Sultanate of Oman is bounded on the north by the Gulf of Oman; on the east and south by the Arabian Sea; on the southwest by Southern Yemen; on the west by Saudi Arabia; and on the northwest by the Trucial States. It has an area of 81,979 square miles and a population of about 750,000. The capital city, Muscat, where about 5,500 people live, is a seaport on the Gulf of Oman. The largest city

is Matrah, with a population of over 14,000. Oil has recently been discovered in the sultanate.

Muses

The Muses were the ancient Greek goddesses of music, poetry, and the arts. There were nine of them, supposed to be the daughters of Zeus, the chief god, and Mnemosyne, the goddess of memory. They played and sang at the banquets of the gods, with Apollo their leader. They inspired poets, musicians, and artists.

Their names were Calliope, the muse of epic poetry (poetry that tells a great story); Euterpe, the muse of lyric poetry; Erato, the muse of love poetry; Clio, the muse of history; Melpomene, the muse of tragedy; Thalia, the muse of comedy; Terpsichore, the muse of dancing; Urania, the muse of astronomy; and Polyhymnia, the muse of oratory and solemn song.

museum

A museum is a place where valuable and interesting works of art and scientific objects can be seen. Art museums have collections of paintings, sculpture, and other works of art such as costumes, prints, musical instruments, and photographs. Science museums, which often call themselves museums of natural history, display scientific instruments, old objects that show how primitive man used to live, models of animals and plants, and maps and charts of the stars.

The first places called museums were temples to the Muses. Later a museum became a kind of study or library. The first museums of the modern kind were established at the time of the Renaissance, about six hundred years ago, when people revived their interest in art and learning. Noblemen used to store their collections of ancient statues and paintings in special buildings called museums. Later more of them were taken over by the government and opened for everybody to see. Today almost every large city has at least one museum.

MUSEUMS IN THE UNITED STATES

A few of the most famous museums in the United States are:

American Museum of Natural History, in New York City. Has collections on the natural sciences and anthropology with many prehistory displays. The Hayden Planetarium is a feature.

Art Institute of Chicago, in Chicago, Illinois. Has fine collections of paintings, sculpture, and prints. Also has a theater and a library.

Chicago Natural History Museum, in Chicago, Illinois. Has exhibits dealing with anthropology, botany, zoology, and geology. A feature is the realistic animal exhibits.

Cleveland Museum of Art, in Cleveland, Ohio. Has collections of the art of all ages, from Europe, the East, the Americas, and the Pacific.

Detroit Institute of Arts, in Detroit, Michigan. Paintings, sculpture, and examples of other arts, from prehistoric times to the present day. Owned by the city of Detroit.

Metropolitan Museum of Art, in New York City. Has the largest collection of paintings, sculpture, and other arts in the Western Hemisphere. Covers five thousand years, from the ancient world to the present. The Cloisters, a museum of medieval art, is a branch.

Museum of Fine Arts, in Boston, Massa-

chusetts. Has large collections of paintings and the other arts. Well known for its collections of art objects from the East and Egypt.

Museum of Modern Art, in New York City. Has paintings and sculpture from the late 19th century to the present day. Its theater has daily showings of famous American and foreign movies.

Museum of Science and Industry, Chicago, Illinois. Has hundreds of exhibits on industrial and scientific processes, with many devices that the visitor himself can operate.

National Gallery of Art, in Washington, D.C. Many fine paintings, sculpture, and prints, donated by Andrew W. Mellon, Samuel H. Kress, and other collectors. The gallery is run by the United States government.

Philadelphia Museum of Art, in Philadelphia, Pennsylvania. Has many fine examples of art from the time of Jesus to the present.

Smithsonian Institution, in Washington, D.C. See the separate article.

FAMOUS FOREIGN MUSEUMS

Ashmolean Museum, at Oxford University, in England. The oldest museum in England. It has collections of objects from ancient times and natural history objects.

British Museum, in London, England. In its Department of Antiquities it has many outstanding treasures from the ancient world, including the famous Elgin Marbles and the Rosetta Stone. (There is a separate article on the ROSETTA STONE.) The library of the museum is one of the largest in the world.

The Hermitage, in Leningrad, Russia. Has one of the greatest collections of European painting and sculpture. Also many fine examples of ancient sculpture.

Kunsthistorisches Museum, in Vienna, Austria. Is well known for its collection of ancient Egyptian, Greek, and Roman art. Has a fine collection of great masters of painting.

The Louvre, in Paris, France. See the separate article.

Museum of Natural History, in Paris, France. A very large museum, with a zoo and botanical gardens and a fine natural history collection.

National Gallery, in London, England. Has more than 1,500 paintings, many of them the finest works of the old masters. It includes the Tate Gallery.

National Museum of Canada, in Ottawa, Quebec. Its exhibits illustrate the natural history of Canada—its biology, geology, and anthropology.

Pinakothek, in Munich, Germany. Its Old Collection has fine examples of European painting, particularly of German masters. The New Collection has the works of contemporary artists. The Pinakothek buildings were destroyed in World War II.

Pitti Gallery, in Florence, Italy. In the Pitti Palace. Has one of the world's finest collection of paintings, and is especially rich in the paintings of the Italian masters of the 16th century.

The Prado, in Madrid, Spain. The Spanish national museum of painting and sculpture. Its collection of 2,500 paintings is especially noted for its works of the Spanish masters.

Ryks-museum, in Amsterdam, the Netherlands. Known for its collection of paintings and engravings. Rembrandt and other Dutch and Flemish masters are well represented.

Uffizi Gallery, in Florence, Italy. In the Uffizi Palace. It is rich in antique statues. Its fine painting collection is noted particularly for the works of the Renaissance masters, especially Titian and Raphael.

Vatican Palace, in Vatican City, Rome, Italy. Parts of the palace have been turned into galleries and museums. Probably most noted for the wonderful ceiling and *The Last Judgment* by Michelangelo in the Sistine Chapel. Also has many fine antique sculptures.

Victoria and Albert Museum, in London,

England. Its art division has paintings and drawings. The science division has a survey of transportation and a collection of scientific instruments.

mushroom

The mushroom is a fungus that grows in Asia, Europe, and the United States. Like other fungus plants, the mushroom has no roots, stem, or leaves. It does not have any chlorophyll, with which most plants make their own food out of air, soil, and sunshine. The mushroom must get its food from other plants or from dead matter. (You can find out

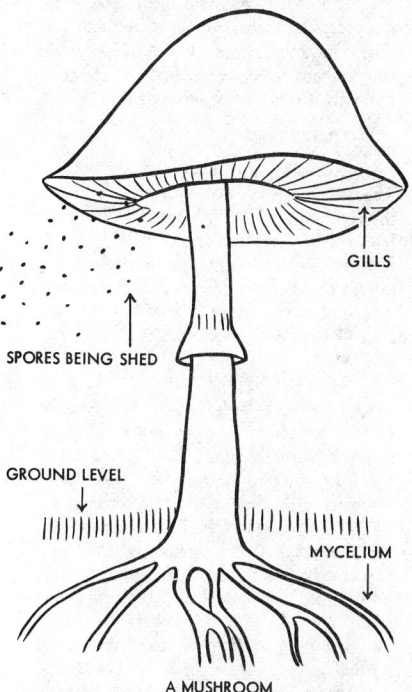

GILLS

SPORES BEING SHED

GROUND LEVEL

MYCELIUM

A MUSHROOM

Spores shed from the gills of a mushroom grow into new plants under favorable conditions. A single mushroom will often produce more than a billion spores.

more about this in the article on FUNGUS.)

Mushrooms grow best in dark, damp places. They grow in woods and fields and are usually found under logs and stones. Some mushrooms grow in grassy meadows and gardens. People raise mushrooms in cellars, and in some places they grow mushrooms in abandoned mines. There are many different kinds of mushrooms. Some of them are good to eat. Others are poisonous. The mushrooms that are poisonous are called toadstools. It is very important to know which mushrooms are safe to eat and which ones are poisonous. No one should ever pick wild mushrooms and eat them.

The meadow mushroom is an interesting pale tan plant with a cap at the top that looks like an umbrella. The underside of the cap has little pink ridges. These ridges are called gills. As the mushroom grows, the pink gills turn to a dark chocolate-brown. This is where the spores are (tiny, powdery structures that make it possible for new mushrooms to grow).

Under the ground the mushroom plant sends out thin threadlike fibers that are called *mycelium*. The mycelium of the mushroom is like the roots of other plants. New mushrooms spring up from

the mycelium. The tiny mushrooms are called buttons. They grow quickly and in a few weeks they are full-grown.

Many mushrooms are very beautiful. Some of them are white and others are black. There are pale pink mushrooms and rare blue and purple mushrooms. The puffball is a mushroom that is good to eat. It is brownish white and looks like a ball growing close to the ground.

People have eaten mushrooms for thousands of years. The ancient Greeks and Romans were very fond of them. People now fry and stew and broil mushrooms. They taste very good when they are eaten with eggs and meat, and some people put mushrooms in soups and salads. The mushroom is a delicious food that is sometimes eaten instead of meat, but it is not as nutritious as meat.

music

Music is the language of sound. The language of words expresses ideas; the language of sound expresses feelings. Its "words" are tones and chords; its "sentences" are melodies and harmonic sequences; its "stories" and "essays" are songs, dances, fugues; its "books" are suites, sonatas, symphonies.

TONES AND THE GAMUT

Our music is based on the use of only certain tones. Each tone has a different *pitch*, making it "higher" or "lower" than the tone next to it. All the "permitted tones, taken together, are called the *gamut*. The gamut is well represented by the notes of a modern piano, which cover practically the whole range through which the ear can hear differences of pitch.

The white notes of the piano are named A, B, C, D, E, F, G, going upward from the lowest. The note above G is in *octave* with the first note, A; that is, the vibrations that cause it are just twice as fast. It is called A also; the next is the octave of B, and so on. Seven letters are enough to name all the white notes.

In musical notation (the method by which music is written), the white notes are represented by the lines and spaces of the *staff*. A black note is indicated by a white note with an *accidental* before it: a *sharp* (♯) for the black note above the white; a *flat* (♭) for the black note below. A *natural* (♮) means that the white note should be played, even if the music previously called for a sharp or flat.

Between any two adjoining notes of the piano, black or white, the difference of pitch is a *semitone,* also called a *half-tone* or *half-step.* Two semitones make a *whole-tone* or *whole-step.* These intervals came originally from *natural harmonics,* in which they are not all the same.

About three hundred years ago, *equal temperament* was adopted. This meant that all the semitones of the gamut were made equal. The octave is now the only natural interval that we tune "true." To tune a piano, we actually put all other intervals "out of tune" with the natural harmonics—but only gifted or trained ears can detect the difference.

SCALES AND TONALITY

Play the white notes upward from A to A; these form the natural *minor scale.*

Play from C to C and you will hear the *major scale.* Most of our music is based on these scales, though there are a few others. Each scale includes two half-steps and five whole-steps. The only difference in the scales is the order of these steps.

The first (lowest) note of a scale is called the *tonic,* or *keynote.* The scales are named from the keynote, such as "the key of B-flat minor." *Tonality* is the name for the feeling of being in a certain key. This feeling is given when the melodies and chords are composed chiefly of notes of the chosen scale.

Tonality is found in most of the music written in the last five hundred years, but in the present century there have been experiments in *atonality*—music written deliberately to avoid any feeling of key.

ELEMENTS OF MUSIC

In listening to music we recognize certain elements of which it is made up: melody, harmony, rhythm, dynamics, and tone color.

A *melody* is a succession of notes that "go together" as the words of a sentence go together—with a sense of "meaning." In songs, the melody is often called the *tune* or *air.*

Two or more tones sounded together form a *chord.* The structure and sequence of chords is *harmony.* Melody usually needs harmony to bring out its meaning and also to keep it from becoming monotonous. That is why a recital by a melody instrument, such as a violin or the human voice, is almost always accompanied by a piano, organ or harp to supply harmony.

Rhythm is a regular pattern based on how long the tones last and how loud each is played. Throughout a composition we hear a regular *beat* of primary accents (the tones that are longer or louder), like the beating of the heart or

N.Y. Public Library

Church music of the Middle Ages—called Gregorian chant—used an early system of notation called *neume.* The neumes showed the rise and fall of the melody, which earlier had usually been learned by ear.

the ticking of a watch. The rate of the beat is called *tempo.* Different patterns of

rhythm are made by arrangements of primary and secondary accents, such as

P s / P s / etc.	*duple time*
P s s / P s s / etc	*triple time*
P s s s / P s s s / etc.	*common time*

Dynamics refers to loudness and softness. Some percussion instruments, such as drums, are used solely to give rhythmic and dynamic emphasis. Others, as the triangle, are used for tone color.

Tone color refers to all those effects that arise from the *timbre,* or quality, of instruments and voices. The quality of sound of a violin is very different from that of a clarinet. The same melody may have different "meaning" on the two instruments. Also, each has marked differences of timbre in its low, middle, and high ranges. A melody effective at one level may be dull or harsh at another.

MUSICAL GROUPS

The only instruments commonly heard in *solo recital* (playing alone) are the piano, organ, and harp. Occasional concerts are given by xylophone, marimba, or harmonica. All these instruments can play harmony as well as melody. The melody instruments commonly heard in recital are the human voice, the violin, cello, and clarinet, and sometimes others, such as the flute or viola. Almost always the soloist is accompanied by a piano or other harmony instrument.

Of *ensembles* (groups of musicians playing together), the largest is commonly the symphony orchestra, numbering about 50 to 120 players. It has four sections: strings, woodwinds, brass, percussion. Many smaller and more limited groups are called orchestras. This usually means that some strings are included, whatever else is omitted.

The military band has no stringed instruments. It uses a larger woodwind section, especially the clarinets, to take the place of strings. It often has brass instruments unusual in an orchestra, for example saxhorns, saxophones, and sousaphones.

The concert band, a relatively modern creation, is a cross between the orchestra and the band, with stringed instruments but with a larger brass section than the orchestra.

Any group that plays popular music, regardless of its size, is usually called a band. The modern "name band" (in which the band or its leader has a big name, or reputation) has about 20 to 50 players. Its melody instruments are saxophones and trumpets, backed by trombones and the sousaphone or tuba. The large percussion department is helped by double basses, playing almost always *pizzicato* (plucking the strings). There is also a sprinkling of violins and woodwinds—clarinet, flute, oboe—and a piano, sometimes two pianos. Additional instruments sometimes featured are the guitar, xylophone, or marimba.

In small dance bands of three to a dozen players, the backbone is the piano. The most frequent melody instruments are saxophone, trumpet, and clarinet.

Chamber music is instrumental music for small groups. A favorite ensemble is the string quartet: first violin, second violin, viola, cello. Another is the piano trio: piano, violin, cello. Music has been written for many other combinations.

A large group of singers is called a *chorus*. It includes sopranos (high female voices), altos (low female voices), tenors (high male voices), and basses (low male voices). A male quartet of first and second tenor, baritone (between tenor and bass), and bass is a popular feature of glee club recitals.

VOCAL FORMS OF MUSIC

The late Middle Ages saw the rise of wandering minstrels (called by various names, such as *troubadour, bard, jongleur, minnesinger*)', who played on the old stringed instrument called the lute while singing or chanting poems of war, love, or adventure. A minstrel usually played the same tune for each verse, and sometimes each verse ended with a refrain in which the audience joined in. This form of song is called a *ballad*. It has remained the form most used in popular songs and hymns. Early jazz songs had parts labeled "verse" and "chorus" (refrain). Many people would learn the chorus, few the verse. Later songs therefore omitted the verse and provided merely a chorus.

Another form is the *art song* or (in German) *Lied*. Here the music is written to fit the sense of the words. The tune does not repeat the same phrases over and over, but varies according to the words.

The chanting of religious services grew gradually into *part-singing* during the Middle Ages. The chorus or choir was divided into sopranos, altos, and so on, and a separate part (*melodic line*) was written for each group. Secular (nonreligious) music also experimented with part-singing, in simple songs called glees, madrigals, and by other names. One of the problems of part-writing is to make each part interesting to the singers and the hearers. A device developed early was *imitation*, of which the simplest form is the round, such as "Three Blind Mice" and "Frère Jacques." All voices sing exactly the same tune, but they begin at different times. Another form, in which the imitation need not be exact, is the *canon*. In the *fugue*, the same *theme* (series of notes) occurs often but there are also *episodes* from which the theme is absent.

From liturgical music (music written to accompany church services) was developed the *oratorio*, a choral work on a religious subject. An oratorio is presented apart from church services, and usually lasts two to five hours. It includes choruses, solos, and often duets, trios and quartets of solo voices. An oratorio usually tells a story from the Bible. The *cantata* is a simpler and shorter work of the same kind, with choruses and solos.

The combination of music with dramatic action gave rise to several kinds of *opera*. In *grand opera* the words are accompanied by music throughout, and the subject is usually tragic. Dramatic comedies become *comic opera* or *light opera*, and here some of the dialogue may be spoken instead of sung. A *folk opera* is put together from popular songs of the day, fitted to a story. A *musical comedy* has a story but also has many acts of a vaudeville kind—comedians, dancers, and singers—and introduces new popular songs.

INSTRUMENTAL FORMS

Instruments were used from earliest times to mark the beat in dancing and marching. From this came many rhythmic patterns that composers have used. Long-forgotten dances such as the *allemande, pavane, sarabande*, and *gigue*, and later ones such as the *minuet* and *waltz*, are found in the music of many of the great composers. The *passacaglia* and *chaconne* are no longer used as dances but they survive as musical forms in which the same melody or harmonic sequence is repeated again and again, with changes and transformations. These gave rise to the even more elaborate *theme and variations*. Early instrumental compositions also borrowed forms from choral music, the canon and fugue.

A *suite* is a group of unrelated pieces, grouped together to make a single concert piece.

The name *sonata* was originally given to any instrumental piece, to distinguish it from a vocal piece. Later it became a series of two, three or four pieces called *movements*, forming an artistic whole but not necessarily using the same themes. Finally a sonata came to be a particular form (also called *sonata-allegro*) in which composers from Beethoven to Rachmaninoff cast the first movements of their sonatas.

The term *concerto* had a somewhat similar history. At first it meant a "sounding together" of two or more instruments. Today it means a composition in several movements (three to four) played by a solo instrument with an orchestra. The piano and violin (or cello) are the popular solo instruments. Occasionally there are two or even three soloists.

A *symphony* is a sonata for orchestra. Like the sonata, it has come to have certain traditional features. The first movement is in *sonata-allegro* form and is the most complex in structure. The second is slow and lyric or solemn. The third is a minuet, waltz, march, scherzo (a fast playful piece), or other form in relaxed mood. The last is fast and brilliant or grandiose.

Orchestral compositions in one movement have been given various names—*overture, fantasia, rhapsody,* and *tone poem*.

musical instruments

Musical instruments fall into three great classes. Each class uses a different method of causing the air to vibrate, or move in waves. (All sound is caused by vibrations in the air.)

The three classes are:

(a) *strings:* the air is set in motion by vibrating strings.

(b) *wind:* vibration is produced by a current of air, from the player's lips or from a bellows.

(c) *percussion:* sound is produced by striking a resonant body—one that will ring with sound.

Within each class there are different *kinds*, according to the mechanics of the instruments. Thus, stringed instruments include the *plucked* kind and the *bowed* kind. Within each kind, we find many *families*. Thus, the *viol family* includes the violin, viola, cello, and double bass; these instruments are all built on the same plan but differ in size. The members

of a family are commonly designated as treble (or soprano), alto, tenor, and bass.

STRINGED INSTRUMENTS

1. *Plucked.* Examples of stringed instruments that are plucked are the guitar, the ukelele, the banjo, and many others. All such instruments have four or more strings stretched along a long "neck" and over a hollow body that makes the sound waves resound. The strings are plucked with the fingers or with a *plectrum*, or "pick," which is a small piece of metal, bone, or shell. With his other hand the player holds down one or more strings at places along the neck. On some instruments these places are marked by ridges called *frets*. Holding down the string shortens it and changes the pitch.

2. *Bowed.* All bowed instruments are members of the violin family, except for some ancient instruments that are no longer played or are played only in some foreign countries.

3. *Struck.* The harp is the largest instrument that is plucked. It is so large that the player's hand cannot stretch to as many strings as he wants to sound at the same time. This problem is solved by *keyboard instruments* such as the piano. Keys that the hand can reach cause hammers to strike strings that the hand could not reach.

WIND INSTRUMENTS

1. *Reedless.* Blowing across the end of a narrow tube causes the air in the tube to vibrate, producing a musical tone. The pitch of the tone depends on the length of the tube. In instruments such as the flute or piccolo, there are holes in the tube, called *stops,* that change the length of the tube and so change the pitch.

2. *Reed instruments.* A *reed* is a thin strip of metal or wood. Blowing across it makes it vibrate and produces sounds. Most reed instruments are called *woodwinds* (because they used to be made of wood, though they no longer are). There are *single-reed* instruments, such as the clarinet and saxophone, and *double-reed* instruments, such as the oboe, English horn, and bassoon.

3. *Brass instruments.* The typical brass instrument, such as the bugle, has a mouthpiece into which the player blows, and the pitch is controlled by the tension of his lips. Since the pitch is also controlled by the length of the tube, such instruments as the trumpet and cornet have *valves* that close sections of the tube and shorten its length, while in the trombone the length of the tube is controlled by sliding a section of the tube in and out.

PERCUSSION INSTRUMENTS

1. *Melodic.* The xylophone, marimba and glockenspiel are played by striking resonant strips of wood or metal with hammers. The length and shape of the strip determines the tone it will sound.

2. *Drums.* A drum is made by stretching a piece of parchment (a kind of leather) over a frame. This forms a *drumhead.* When the drumhead is struck, it vibrates to produce a tone of definite pitch. Kettledrums (shaped like hollow balls cut in half, with the drumhead over the open end) and various flat drums such as the bass drum are used in most orchestras.

3. *Other instruments.* Ringing sounds

or noises are made by striking two cymbals (brass plates) together, or by striking metal forms such as the triangle, gong, and castanets.

There are articles about most of the musical instruments, and see also MUSIC and ORCHESTRA.

Muskhogean, see CREEKS.

musk ox

The musk ox is a clumsy-looking animal that lives in the cold regions of Canada and the Arctic islands. The musk ox is not really an ox at all, but is related to the sheep. It is about 4 feet tall. The male weighs about 800 pounds. The female is a little smaller. The musk ox has a long, shaggy coat that is dark brown in color. This thick hair makes it look much larger than it actually is. Underneath the hair the musk ox has a fine coat of thick, soft wool that keeps it warm in the coldest weather. Its horns are peculiarly shaped and cover its head like a helmet. It has short legs and looks awkward, but it is a swift runner and is very sure-footed when it climbs the high rocks.

The musk ox is a sociable animal. Groups of about 40 musk oxen often travel together. The musk ox eats leaves, branches, and grass. The musk ox gives off a strong, unpleasant odor, called musk, during the mating season.

muskrat

The muskrat is a small animal that lives near swamps and lakes in many parts of the United States. The muskrat is a member of the rodent order of animals, which are gnawing animals and include the rat, the beaver and the squirrel. It is a very valuable animal because of its fine, soft, brown fur. More than ten million muskrats are killed every year, and the fur is used to make coats. The muskrat looks like a large field mouse. It is almost a foot long and has a broad flat tail.

The muskrat is a good swimmer and builds its nest with an entrance underwater. Sometimes it makes its nest out of grass and twigs in shallow water. The muskrat may also dig a hole in the side of the riverbank and make its nest there. The female muskrat has from two to six babies. One muskrat may have as many as thirty babies during one year. The muskrat eats tiny animals that it finds in the water. It also eats grass and seeds. During the long winter months, when food is scarce, the muskrat begins to eat the walls of its nest.

The muskrat got its name because it has glands in its body that give off a substance that has an unpleasant, strong odor that is called musk. This substance is sometimes used to make perfume.

mussel

A mussel is an animal that lives in water. The mussel is a member of the mollusc family, which includes also oysters and clams. (You can read about MOLLUSCS in a separate article.) Its shell consists of two parts called valves. The valves are held together by special muscles, which open and close the valves on a hinge. Mussels are found along the shores of oceans in all parts of the world where the climate is neither too hot nor too cold. Some mussels live along the shores of fresh-water lakes. They are

Musical instruments are as different as the kinds of sound men wish to make in playing music. For example, one modern symphony uses bottles as musical instruments: different sizes and shapes are struck to produce different sounds. It is easy to see relationships between several of the instruments shown above, and how one instrument, such as the harp, developed from an earlier one, such as the lyre. 1. A lyre. 2. A modern concert harp. 3. A grand piano. 4. A Jewish shofar or ram's horn. 5. A French horn. 6. A pipe organ. 7. A syrinx or Panpipes. 8. An ocarina or "sweet potato." 9. A calabus. 10. A Russian balalaika. 11. A violin. 12. A mandolin. 13. A double bass (the bow is not in scale).

Percussion instruments: 1. A tam-tam, or gong. 2. Cymbals. 3. Castanets. 4. A tambourine. 5. A snare drum. 6. A kettledrum. 7. An African tom-tom. 8. A primitive marimba.

sometimes found by the hundreds attached to the side of wharves and pieces of wood.

The oval shell of the mussel is about three inches long. The mussel has a small foot that sticks out of the shell and it uses this foot to drag itself along the shore until it finds a suitable place to rest. Then it attaches itself very firmly by a thin, fiberlike thread. In Europe, mussels are a very popular dish, and some people in the United States also like to eat them. The shells of the mussels have a smooth, white lining, and they are used to make buttons.

Mussolini, Benito

Benito Mussolini was dictator of Italy for about twenty years before and during World War II. He made Italy a Fascist country, which means that the political party in power was the only party permitted and the people lost their personal freedom.

Mussolini was born in 1883. His father was a Socialist and Mussolini became a member of the Socialist Party too. He held several jobs on newspapers but lost them because he was always calling for revolution. When World War I broke out, however, Mussolini thought Italy should join the Allies against Germany. He founded his own newspaper, Il Popolo d'Italia, in which he tried to bring people to his opinion. He joined the Italian Army and was wounded.

After the war Mussolini organized a group of veterans into the first Fascist Party in Italy, and they opposed both Socialism and Communism. Times were very bad in Italy after the war and many people believed that Mussolini could bring back order and prosperity. He was elected to the Italian Parliament and his party spread through Italy. (There is a separate article on FASCISM.) In 1922, the king, Victor Emmanuel III, asked Mussolini to become the head of the government and from then on Mussolini took increasing control of Italy. He built up a strong secret police, permitted the newspapers to print only what he wanted, and exiled, imprisoned, tortured or killed those who opposed him. He was ambitious to restore Italy as the empire it had been in ancient times. Nearly all the Italian people followed him enthusiastically. He was called Il Duce, or "the leader." The king approved of his rule, and they got on well together.

In Germany Adolf Hitler used Mussolini as a model and became the dictator, setting up a fascistic government, but Mussolini at first had little use for the German dictator. Then Mussolini invaded and conquered Ethiopia because he was greedy for more territory. This made most of the world very angry, and Mussolini found Italy without friends. He had to take Hitler as an ally. Soon Hitler was the master and Mussolini was just a follower.

The two dictators helped General Francisco Franco take control of Spain. In 1936 they formed an alliance called the Rome-Berlin axis. From this point on, Mussolini began to lose his popularity at home, because the Italian people did not like the Germans or their unfair measures, such as discrimination against the Jews.

Mussolini kept Italy out of World War II until Germany had already beaten France, in 1940; then he had Italy declare war. When Italy did join the fighting the Italian armies met with several defeats. By 1943 they were beaten and Mussolini's own Fascist Party revolted against him. The king dismissed Mussolini and he was put in prison. Two months later he was freed by a German rescue party, but when the Germans were defeated by the Allies in 1945 Mussolini was captured by the Italian underground fighters and put to death in the streets of the north Italian city of Milan.

Benito Mussolini was a powerful speaker who could create great enthusiasm in crowds. In many ways he was a skillful ruler, but he was dishonest in dealing with other countries and he almost ruined his own country.

mustard

Mustard is a plant that grows in Europe, China, Japan, South America, and the United States where the climate is not too warm or too cold. Mustard is an annual plant, which means that it must be planted every year. There are two important kinds of mustard plant.

White mustard grows to be two to six feet high. It has large, fuzzy, green leaves and a yellow flower. It has pods that contain small round yellow seeds that are white inside.

Black mustard plants are smaller, and have dark brown seeds that are yellow inside. The seeds contain a valuable oil that is used in medicines. People use both the black and white mustard seeds as a spice to make food tasty. Sometimes the black mustard, which is sharper than the white mustard, is mixed with the white mustard to make a seasoning.

Mustard is a very old plant. It is mentioned in the Bible and was known to the ancient Greeks and Romans. It is often a bad weed and is found growing in fields, gardens, and along the roads and railroads.

mutiny

Mutiny is refusal of soldiers or sailors to obey their superior officers. Mutiny by sailors at sea, or by soldiers at the front (the battle area) in time of war, is considered the most dangerous kind, and in former times was usually punished by death. The law still calls for the death penalty in such cases, but a long term of imprisonment is a more usual punishment. The superior officer has the right to shoot mutinous men if he finds it necessary. The most famous mutinies of history were one on the English ship BOUNTY (about which there is a separate article), more than 150 years ago, and the Sepoy Rebellion in India about a hundred years ago, when native troops rebelled against their British officers.

myrrh

Myrrh is a resin (an oil that hardens after it comes from the tree) of a small tree that grows in Arabia and parts of Africa. The tree has a grayish-white bark and small leaves. Its bark contains an oil that is thick and yellow. When the bark is cut, the oil oozes out. Gradually the oil hardens and becomes a dark reddish-brown color. This hard oil is called myrrh. Myrrh has a sharp but sweet smell and a bitter taste. It is used in perfume and in some medicines. The ancient people valued myrrh very highly. It was one of the presents that the three wise men, or Magi, brought to the infant Jesus, according to the Bible.

myrtle

The myrtle is a shrub or small tree that grows in Europe and Asia near the Mediterranean Sea, where the climate is warm. Some people in Europe and the United States grow myrtle plants in pots. The myrtle is an evergreen, which means that it does not lose its leaves in the fall. There are a number of different plants that belong to the myrtle family. The best known is a beautiful shrub that grows to be about ten feet high. It has shiny leaves that are dark green in color. The white flowers of the myrtle have a sweet smell, and the plant has small, bluish black berries. People use the leaves of the myrtle to make perfume.

The myrtle was sacred to the ancient Greeks and Romans. The plant was often used by artists in religious paintings, and there are many pictures of the Virgin Mary and the baby Jesus that have some myrtle in the background.

Crepe myrtle and ground myrtle (or periwinkle) are kinds that belong to different families of plant.

mystery play

The mystery play was a drama based on a story from the Bible or from the life of a saint. It was also called a miracle play. Mystery plays were first presented in the churches of Europe almost a thousand years ago, at Christmas and at Easter. They were a part of the church service and were religious and serious. Later they became less religious and even humorous. Then they were no longer performed in the church by the priests but outside on the church steps or on special wagons made to resemble stages. They were particularly popular in England about five hundred years ago. By that time the actors in the plays were no longer priests but members of guilds, or groups of organized tradesmen. On holidays and special occasions the guilds presented a series of plays, one after the other, in different places in each town. As one play finished, the wagon, or movable stage, moved on to another place, and the next play took its place. The series of plays could be very long. The guild at the city of York had 48 plays in its series.

mystery story

A mystery story is a story or novel that tells about a crime and the detection or punishment of it. The crime is usually murder, but it may be any of several others. The mystery story used to be called detective story, and some people still think that is a better name.

Mystery stories probably started with Edgar Allan Poe, who has been called the father of the mystery story. His story "The Murders in the Rue Morgue," pub-

lished in 1841, introduces the first fictional detective, C. Auguste Dupin, who solves the crimes. The English writer Wilkie Collins may have written the first book-length detective novels, *The Woman in White* (published in 1860) and *The Moonstone*. The mystery story really came into its own in 1887, when Sir Arthur Conan Doyle began to write about Sherlock Holmes.

Most successful modern mysteries are laid in interesting or familiar surroundings. The characters are introduced and each is given a motive for the crime, which soon takes place. Then we meet the detective, who quickly eliminates the innocent characters and, usually very dramatically, traps or confronts the guilty person.

There have been well-known writers of mysteries in several countries, notably Emile Gaboriau and later Georges Simenon of France. Detective stories about Nick Carter sold by the millions in the United States from the 1880s to the 1920s. The modern murder mystery in the United States began with Willard Huntington Wright. In 1925 Wright suffered a severe illness, and while he was recovering he wrote mysteries to amuse himself. He wrote under the name S. S. Van Dine, and he created the detective Philo Vance. The first of these books appeared in 1926. They were so popular that hundreds of American writers turned to the mystery story field. Perhaps the most popular have been Erle Stanley Gardner, who created the lawyer-detective Perry Mason, and Ellery Queen (the pen-name of two men, Frederic Dannay and M. B. Lee, who devised a style in which the reader can solve the mystery from clues given in the book).

Since the 1940s paperbound editions of mystery novels, selling for 25 to 50 cents, have had by far the largest sale.

myths and mythology

Myths are stories that people of ancient times told about their gods and heroes. They differ from legends, which are stories of actual people and events, though perhaps altered in many tellings. Mythology is the whole group of these stories or myths. Taken together, the myths formed the religion of ancient peoples.

In the days before written history began, man was just beginning to look at the world around him and wonder what made things work the way they did. Language had not developed very far, and there were no words to express ideas or feelings. Every name meant a particular object, and therefore it was impossible to speak of any object without giving it an individual and personal character. For example, the sun had a personality, and at sunset men thought of it as growing old, or dying. Rivers, forests, mountains, rain, the ocean, fire, thunder and the stars in the sky all had personal characteristics.

Since man could see that all these natural things or events had great effects on his life, he believed they did things on purpose and that they could help or hinder him in his daily living. He thought these natural elements were gods who had power over all that man did. When there was a great tidal wave or a flood, he thought the god of the sea was angry.

In this way he explained natural events to himself, so the myths were also his science.

Students of mythology have noticed that almost all countries and races have myths that are very much alike. They explain this by saying that myths had grown up before there were separate nationalities such as Indian, Greek, Roman, Slavic, Teutonic, and Celtic. As man moved to many parts of the world, he took these primitive myths with him. Over the course of centuries the myths changed, but some traces of their original sameness remained.

GREEK AND ROMAN GODS

The earliest written record of the gods worshiped by the Greeks and Romans is probably the poems by the great Greek poet Homer, the *Iliad* and the *Odyssey*. These poems constantly refer to the gods but they do not tell their full stories. According to the myths of the Greeks, the first rulers of the earth were great giants, called Titans. The Greek gods fought and conquered the Titans, and then set up their home on Mount Olympus and chose the god Zeus to be their king. There were twelve chief gods, as well as many lesser ones. The Romans later adopted some of the Greek gods, whom they usually called by different names. In some cases the Romans combined Greek gods with other gods they had worshiped before, so the Roman gods are not always exactly the same as the Greek.

GREEK NAME	ROMAN NAME	GOD OF
Zeus	Jupiter	Chief god
Poseidon	Neptune	Sea
Ares	Mars	War
Hephaestus	Vulcan	Fire
Hermes	Mercury	Messenger
Hera	Juno	Chief goddess
Athena	Minerva	Wisdom
Artemis	Diana	Hunting
Aphrodite	Venus	Love
Hestia	Vesta	Hearth-fire
Demeter	Ceres	Agriculture
Apollo	Apollo	Sun

Among the lesser gods and goddesses were Pluto, god of the underworld, whom the Romans called Dis or Dis Pater; Dionysus, god of wine, whom the Romans called Bacchus; Persephone, goddess of the underworld, whom the Romans called Proserpine; Pan, god of shepherds, whom the Romans called Faun. There were also monsters who were children of the gods, such as the Harpies, Pegasus, and Cerberus.

NORSE MYTHOLOGY

The Germanic tribes of northern Europe, who lived in the regions that are now Scandinavia, Germany, and countries near-by, had another set of myths. It is usually called Norse mythology, and is told about in the Norse *sagas* (stories about heroes) and in the EDDA, about which there is a separate article. In this mythology there were four chief gods. They lived in Asgard, a city of palaces. The greatest of these palaces was Valhalla, where the chief god, Odin (also called Woden), received the spirits of heroes slain in battle. Norse mythology is very warlike, full of tales of battle and heroism.

The chief god was Odin and the chief goddess was his wife, Frigga (later called Freya).

Frigga was goddess of the household and of marriage, and later became, as Freya, goddess of the earth. Their first son, Thor, was the strongest of the gods, and also was god of thunder. Their second son, Balder, was the fairest of the gods.

Other important gods were Loki, a fickle, mischievous god; Tyr, a brave daring god; Ragnarok, Hoenir, Vidharr, and Vali, all very brave gods. Odin's battle maidens were called the *Valkyries;* they protected his favorite warriors and granted them victory. A group of operas by the German composer, Richard Wagner, tells some of the stories about the Norse gods.

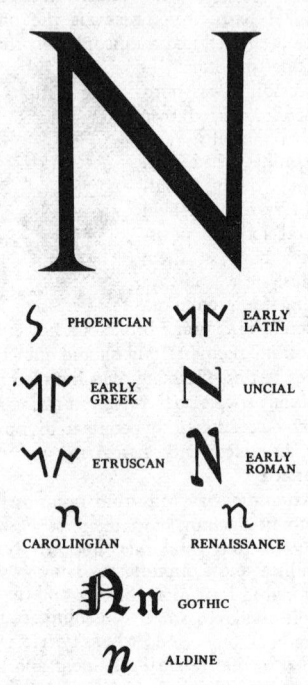

PHOENICIAN		EARLY LATIN	
EARLY GREEK		UNCIAL	
ETRUSCAN		EARLY ROMAN	
CAROLINGIAN		RENAISSANCE	
GOTHIC		ALDINE	

N or n

The letter N is the fourteenth letter of the alphabet. It can be traced all the way back to the earliest writing known to man, in Egypt, thousands of years ago. In the Hebrew language, in which much of the Bible was written, the letter was called *nun,* a word that meant "fish." The ancient Greeks took the same letter and called it *nu.*

At the top of this page, at the far left, you can see the Phoenician N. Below it is the early Greek *nu.* In early times, writing was read from right to left, and in some of the old languages, such as Hebrew, it still is. But the Greeks changed this and began to read from left to right, as we do today. When they made this change, they turned the letters around. The Etruscans and early Latins used the same form, which gradually became modified by the Romans into the N you see at the left of the large letter in the center, above. This was further modified during medieval times into the familiar forms you see on the right.

Read also the article ALPHABET.

Nagasaki

Nagasaki is a city in Japan. It is on the island of Kyushu. It has been one of

Japan's most important ports for hundreds of years, and until 1945 it was one of the most important shipbuilding centers in the country. On August 9, 1945, during World War II, the Allies dropped an atomic bomb in Nagasaki that killed or wounded about 75,000 people. In 1940, more than 252,000 people lived there. In 1947 only 198,642 people lived in Nagasaki. Since then the population has grown to almost 350,000.

NAGASAKI. Population (1960 census) 344,079. Seaport on island of Kyushu, Japan.

Nagoya

Nagoya is one of the most important industrial cities in Japan. It is on the island of Honshu, and is the third-largest city in the country. More than 1,500,-000 people live there. They work in textile mills, chemical plants, and in factories that make beautiful porcelain and pottery. Nagoya is also one of the big railway centers in Japan. During World War II, the city was heavily bombed, and many of the factories were destroyed.

In Nagoya is a beautiful medieval castle, built more than three hundred years ago. It is five stories high, with high granite walls. At the top of the castle are two golden dolphins. Another famous building in Nagoya is the Atsuta Shrine that guards one of the three imperial treasures. There are also beautiful Buddhist temples. Some of these were damaged during World War II.

NAGOYA. Population (1960 census) 1,591,-914. Capital of Aichi Prefecture. On Ise Bay.

Naguib, Mohammed

Mohammed Naguib was the President and Premier of Egypt from 1952 until 1954. He was one of a group of Egyptian soldiers who forced King Farouk I of Egypt to give up his throne, in 1952, and who made Egypt a republic.

Naguib was born in 1901, so he was 51 years old when he became head of the Egyptian government. He had become an officer in the Egyptian army at 19. After that, he joined the group of army officers headed by Lieutenant Colonel Gamal Nasser, about whom there is a separate article. In 1952, they dethroned the king and Naguib became President and Premier. While in office, he was friendly to the United States and worked hard to persuade the British to declare Egypt a republic.

In 1953 Naguib declared Egypt a republic. However, Nasser felt that Naguib was trying to take too much power, and in 1954, he removed Naguib from office.

naiad

In the stories of the ancient Greeks, thousands of years ago, the naiads were lovely young maidens, with long flowing hair, who made their homes in freshwater lakes and in rivers and fountains. They were the favorites of poets and soothsayers because they could inspire a person who drank from the waters where they lived. The naiads also had the power to cure people who were sick.

nail

Nails are pointed pieces of metal that are used to fasten things together.

Most nails are made of steel, but some are made of other metals (such as brass, which resists rust better than steel). A nail is usually a length of wire with one end pointed and the other end having a flat surface called a *head*. A hammer is struck against the head to drive the pointed end into a piece of wood or other material.

Nearly all nails are made from rolls of wire. The wire runs through an automatic machine that shapes one end into a point and hammers or *upsets* the other end into the round, flat head. Such machines can make more than a thousand nails in a minute.

The size of a nail is expressed by the word "penny." A fourpenny nail is about one and one-half inches long; a tenpenny nail is about three inches long; a sixtypenny nail is about six inches long. Anything bigger than sixtypenny is usually called a spike and not a nail. Nails are sold to hardware stores in kegs (small barrels) by the pound. The hardware stores sell small nails by the pound and big nails by the dozen.

Some nails are cast or forged. These are more expensive than the nails that are upset from rolls of wire.

nail, one of the horny pieces at the ends of the fingers and toes (*fingernail* or *toenail*): see the article HORN.

Nanking

Nanking is a city in China, on the Yangtze River. It used to be the capital of China. About 1,500,000 people live in Nanking. They make silk and cotton goods, fans, paper flowers, and porcelain. The city has been famous for centuries as the center of learning in China, and there are many schools there. The University of Nanking is the best known. Nanking also has many beautiful temples, and tombs of ancient Chinese emperors. It has modern government buildings and shops that were built after Nanking became the capital of China. The city is surrounded by thick walls that are more than five hundred years old.

Nanking was founded more than two thousand years ago. Many battles have been fought there. It has been the capital of many different governments. About a hundred years ago, Nanking was captured by revolutionaries who destroyed the most famous building in the city, a beautiful porcelain tower, nine stories high.

In 1928 Chiang Kai-shek took control of the Chinese government and made Nanking the capital. The Japanese captured Nanking in 1937, and the Chinese government moved its capital to Chungking. After World War II, Nanking again became the capital, but in 1949 the Chinese Communists seized control and moved the capital to Peking.

NANKING, CHINA. Population (1957 estimate) 1,419,000. Former capital of China. On the Yangtze River.

Nantes, Edict of

For many years, beginning nearly five hundred years ago, France was torn apart by Wars of Religion between the Protestants (who were called Huguenots) and the Roman Catholics. Finally, in 1598, the French king Henry IV signed a decree, or official paper, that said everyone in France could belong to any church he wanted to. This decree was called the Edict of Nantes, because it was signed in the French city of Nantes. The edict was repealed (called off) by King Louis XIV of France, about seventy years after it was issued. Then fighting broke out again, and Protestants suffered greatly. Many of them left France and settled in America. Of course, there is full religious freedom in France now and has been for more than two hundred years.

naphtha

Naphtha is a colorless liquid that is very useful in dissolving fats, oils, paint, lacquer, varnish, and rubber. There are different kinds of naphtha. Petroleum naphtha is made by distilling petroleum, coal-tar naphtha by distilling coal tar, and wood naphtha by distilling wood. When these substances are distilled, the liquid that boils off at about 175 to 250 degrees Fahrenheit is naphtha.

Because naphtha dissolves fats and oils so well, it is used by dry-cleaners to take grease spots out of suits and dresses. Soap-makers put naphtha into laundry soaps to help get greasy and oily stains out of clothes and linens.

Naphtha looks and smells somewhat like gasoline. When the automobile was still a new invention, people sometimes used naphtha instead of gasoline to run their cars. You could still run a car on naphtha, but it would take a long time to get it started and you would get much gummy carbon in the engine's cylinders.

Naples

Naples is the third-largest city in Italy. It is one of the most important ports and manufacturing cities in the country. More than a million people live in Naples. They work in large shipyards and in factories that make locomotives, machinery, and canned goods. The people of Naples manufacture most of the gloves produced in Italy.

Naples is a crowded, noisy city, and the people are known for their gaiety and colorful festivals. Many visitors go to Naples to see the fine works of art and interesting old castles and churches. The San Carlo Opera in Naples is one of the most famous in Europe.

Part of Naples is very old, with old, ugly houses, but part of the city, along the bay, is modern and beautiful. Looking out on the Bay of Naples, the city has one of the finest views in the world. The bay is an inlet of the Mediterranean Sea, and the water is a beautiful deep blue. There is a picturesque drive along the curving shore of the bay. In the distance can be seen the famous volcano, Mount Vesuvius.

Naples is more than two thousand years old. During the Middle Ages it was the capital of the kingdom of Naples. Over the centuries, Naples has been the scene of much fighting and was ruled by various countries. In 1861, Naples became part of Italy. The city was severely bombed during World War II, and many buildings and part of the harbor were destroyed or badly damaged.

NAPLES, ITALY. Population (1961 census) 1,179,608. Capital of the province of Naples. On the Bay of Naples.

Napoleon

Napoleon Bonaparte was one of the great men of history. He was a hero of France and became the French emperor under the name of Napoleon I. He was one of the most skilled military leaders of all times, a great conqueror, and an extremely efficient ruler. People are still not agreed whether this man, who lived more than 150 years ago, is a hero or a villain, but no one denies that he changed the course of history.

NAPOLEON'S EARLY LIFE

Napoleon Bonaparte was born on the island of Corsica in the Mediterranean Sea, in 1769. From his earliest boyhood he wanted to become a soldier, and at the age of 10 he was sent to military school in France. When he was in the military school in Paris, his friends called him the "Little Corporal" because he was so short, and later many people called him this.

When he was graduated from military school Napoleon was filled with the ideas of revolution that filled the air in those days, and when the French Revolution broke out he went to Corsica to help in a democratic movement. Then he returned to France to take part in the Revolution there.

In 1793 he was made a captain in the army and in the same year he commanded the artillery that forced the British to withdraw from the Mediterranean port of Toulon. Within a short time he was made a brigadier general.

Two years later Napoleon, back in Paris, was ordered to put down an uprising against the government. He took a force of men and ordered them to fire "a whiff of grapeshot," as he described it, into the crowd. They killed a hundred persons, and the uprising was ended. Word of this bold action spread quickly and the name of Napoleon became known to the public for the first time.

In March 1796, Napoleon married Josephine de Beauharnais, a widow of a French nobleman. She had been born in the West Indies, and she had two children by her first marriage.

NAPOLEON'S RISE TO POWER

Within two days of his marriage Napoleon was off to command a French army that was invading Italy. In this first big assignment Napoleon proved himself a brilliant soldier who could inspire his troops with his own enthusiasm and make them willing to die for him. This ability was to prove important in his many later successes. Also he showed that he was a successful diplomat, for he negotiated a treaty of peace, even though he had been told not to do so by his government. But he calmed his superiors by sending back to Paris large amounts of art treasures and other booty.

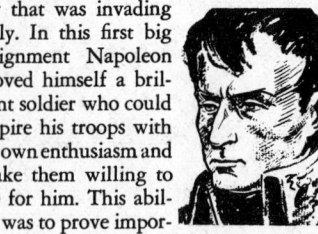

In this conquest and in later ones, Napoleon was welcomed by the people of the conquered lands because they believed he was overthrowing the old oppressive rulers and bringing the new freedoms of the French Revolution. For some years this seemed to be true, and the governments installed by Napoleon were better for the people. But after a time, Napoleon forgot about his revolutionary ideas and conquered only for more lands to rule and to make himself a more powerful man.

In 1799, Napoleon, the Abbé Sieyes and Roger Ducos, calling themselves "consuls," set up a new government. Within a short time, though, Napoleon alone was in control and had himself named First Consul. For the next fifteen years Napoleon was to be the strong, dictatorial ruler of France.

Napoleon saw that many changes were needed in the government of France. He improved the educational system, started the metric system of weights and measures, and placed many local governmental offices under the central government of France. Perhaps most important, he drew up a code, or set, of laws that France and some other European countries still use. This is often called the Napoleonic Code.

THE NAPOLEONIC WARS

Meanwhile Napoleon was carrying on the NAPOLEONIC WARS, about which there is a separate article. He had himself proclaimed emperor of France in 1804. The Pope went from Rome to Paris to crown him, but at the moment of crowning, Napoleon took the crown from the Pope's hands and placed it on his head himself. By this gesture Napoleon was telling the world that although the Pope approved his becoming emperor, it was he himself who was making it possible.

Napoleon quickly spread his power to other countries. By treaty he gained control of Germany and Italy. By force he conquered the Netherlands and the kingdom of the Two Sicilies. Then followed victories over Austria, Prussia, and Russia. One of his greatest victories was at Austerlitz, in 1805, over Austria and Prussia.

By 1807 Napoleon was in control of almost all of Europe and was at the height of his power, but England was still his enemy, and quietly Prussia, Austria, and Russia were arming themselves.

Meanwhile Napoleon became dissatisfied with his wife Josephine, who was unable to have children to whom he could pass on his title. In 1810 he divorced her and married Marie Louise, an archduchess (princess) of Austria, and a son was born to them.

THE DECLINE OF NAPOLEON

Napoleon's downfall came after he decided to attack Russia, in 1812. He had a more powerful army than Russia's, but he let his army be caught deep in Russia in the winter of 1812–13. They did not have food enough and they could not return home. Nearly the entire army was lost.

Napoleon's defeat in Russia was a signal for other countries to attack. Austria, Russia and Prussia sent huge armies against him. They invaded France and captured Paris in April, 1814. This was the end of Napoleon's dream. He was forced to abdicate (resign as emperor) and was sent to the island of Elba, in the Mediterranean, as a prisoner.

Early in 1815 Napoleon made a last attempt to return to power. He escaped from Elba and landed in southern France with a thousand supporters. He gathered an army as he marched north to Paris. Louis XVIII, who had been placed on the French throne, fled. England and its allies hastily assembled their armies.

In June, Napoleon attacked the allies near Waterloo, a town a few miles south of Brussels, Belgium. The allied armies under the English commander, the Duke of Wellington, and the Prussian commander, von Blücher, defeated him decisively.

Napoleon then abdicated again and fled to the city of Rochefort, in France, where he gave himself up to the commander of a British ship. This brief return of Napoleon to power lasted only three months and is called "The Hundred Days." This time Napoleon was exiled on the island of St. Helena in the Atlantic Ocean, about a thousand miles off the coast of Africa. Here, with a few followers, he spent his last days. He died May 5, 1821, at the age of 51.

Napoleon was buried on St. Helena, but in 1840 his body was removed to Paris and placed in a tomb in a magnificent building called the Invalides.

NAPOLEON II

Napoleon's son was born in 1811. His father called him the King of Rome. He was also called *l'Aiglon*, which in French means "the little eagle." His father abdicated in his favor in 1814 but the allies never accepted him. Nevertheless, he was known as Napoleon II. After 1814 he lived in Vienna, where he had the title Duke of Reichstadt. He died in 1832.

See also the article about the BONAPARTE family.

Napoleon III

Napoleon III was emperor of the French, about a hundred years ago. He was a nephew of the first Napoleon, who had failed in his effort to control all of  Europe but who was still a great hero to the French people. The father of Napoleon III was Louis Bonaparte, the first Napoleon's brother, and the mother of Napoleon III was Hortense de Beauharnais, daughter of the French empress Josephine. At first Napoleon III was known as Louis Napoleon. He was born in 1808. In 1848, when France threw out its previous king and became a republic, he became its president. In 1852 he was made emperor. His wife was Empress Eugénie, a beautiful and fashionable woman.

As emperor, Napoleon III was a strong ruler but very ambitious. France was very prosperous under him and seemed very strong, but after he had been emperor eighteen years he led France into a war against Prussia, the strongest German kingdom. This war is called the Franco-Prussian War. Prussia won the war easily and even captured Napoleon. As a result of losing the war he lost his throne and died in exile in England in 1873.

France became a republic and has been a republic ever since.

At one time the ambition of Napoleon III led him to try to control Mexico, in which he set up as emperor MAXIMILIAN, about whom there is a separate article. Threats from the United States, in 1866, forced him to give up the hope of creating a French stronghold in America.

Napoleonic Wars

The Napoleonic Wars were a series of wars fought in Europe, somewhat more than 150 years ago, between France under the leadership of Napoleon and other European countries including chiefly Great Britain, Russia, Austria, and Prussia. The wars began during the period of the French Revolution, when the French people had overthrown their king and made France a republic. The kings of the other European countries were afraid that they might lose their thrones too, so they were unfriendly toward France. But France was the strongest country on the continent of Europe, and in Napoleon Bonaparte it developed the greatest general, so during most of the Napoleonic Wars the French were successful. The Napoleonic Wars lasted from 1796 to 1815. At the end of them Napoleon could not hold out against the combined strength of all the other countries.

The Napoleonic Wars began when Napoleon was a very young general, only 26 years old. In the spring of 1796 he led a French army into Italy and won a series of victories over Austrian and Italian armies, so that by 1797 France controlled most of Italy (which was then divided into several small kingdoms and other states).

Next Napoleon persuaded the French government to let him take an army and try to conquer Egypt. By controlling Egypt, he wanted to make possible a campaign against India, which was the richest British possession. Napoleon was very successful with his army in Egypt, but his plans were wrecked when the great British naval hero, Horatio Nelson, defeated the French fleet in the Battle of the Nile, in August, 1798. Without naval control the French could not send supplies across the Mediterranean Sea to Napoleon's army in Egypt, so Napoleon gave up that plan and returned to France.

When Napoleon returned to France, in 1799, he gained control of the government. In 1800 he invaded Italy again and defeated the Austrians, who had seized control during his absence. This brought peace in Europe, but Napoleon continued to fight the British for overseas colonies. His greatest ambition was to invade and conquer England, and several times he assembled fleets of ships for the invasion, but he never succeeded.

In 1805, after several years of peace in Europe (while Napoleon made France an empire with himself as emperor), war broke out again in Europe. The French forces invaded Austria and Napoleon won a series of victories, including the Battle of Austerlitz, which was his greatest triumph. The following year he defeated Prussia. Russia, which had helped both Austria and Prussia, now came to terms with Napoleon and in 1807 there was again a general peace in Europe. But

Great Britain had kept command of the seas by a great victory of Admiral Nelson at the Battle of Trafalgar, in which the French fleet was again badly defeated, and the British remained Napoleon's undefeated enemy.

THE CONTINENTAL SYSTEM

Napoleon set up in Europe the "Continental System," an agreement by which European countries were to trade with one another but not with England. This was good for France, which was at war with England, but not for the other countries, which could profit from trading with the British.

From 1808 to 1814, the Peninsular War was fought between Great Britain and France. This war was fought in Spain and Portugal. During the Peninsular War, Arthur Wellesley (later the Duke of Wellington) became recognized as the greatest British general. Napoleon had tried to capture Portugal (because it was trading with the British) and to control Spain. The British fought to prevent him from doing either. The Peninsular War did not bring victory to either side for years, but finally it helped to defeat Napoleon.

The Russian ruler, Czar Alexander I, gradually came to disregard the Continental System and to trade with Great Britain, and in 1812 Napoleon decided to invade Russia. With the most powerful army in history, numbering more than half a million men, Napoleon marched into Russia in June, 1812. The Russian armies were smaller and much weaker, and without much trouble Napoleon captured the Russian capital, Moscow. The Russian general, Kutuzov, destroyed everything in Napoleon's path that might provide food for the French army, and had Moscow burned. As winter approached, Napoleon's army found itself without food or fuel enough to withstand the extreme cold of the Russian winter. Napoleon's "Grand Army" retreated, trying to return to France, but in the march across Russia most of the French troops died.

Napoleon never recovered from this defeat. Austria and Prussia joined Russia in the war, and the British were already at war against France. In 1814 Napoleon had to abdicate (resign as emperor). In 1815 he returned to France and led a brief battle for control, but the British and Prussians beat him at the Battle of Waterloo where he was finally defeated, ending the Napoleonic Wars.

narcissus

The narcissus is a flower that grows in many parts of the United States, Canada, and other countries where the climate is not too hot or too cold. The narcissus grows from a bulb, which is a stem that develops underground. You can read about BULBS in a separate article. The narcissus is a perennial plant, which means that the flowers bloom every year. Most kinds bloom in early spring.

The narcissus plant has narrow green leaves and lovely white or yellow flowers that have a sweet smell. Many people like to grow the plant in their gardens or in pots in their homes. Popular types of narcissus are *jonquils* and *daffodils*. One unusual kind of narcissus plant will

Margot L. Wolf

The daffodil is one of the most popular flowers of the narcissus family. It is a familiar sight during the springtime.

grow in a jar of water without any soil at all.

The narcissus plant is sometimes used to make perfume.

Narcissus is also the name of a beautiful young man in Greek mythology. Although many nymphs fell in love with Narcissus, he did not love any one. (The beautiful nymph Echo loved Narcissus so much that she pined away until there was nothing left of her but her voice.)

One day Narcissus saw his face reflected in a pool, and he thought he was so beautiful that he fell in love with himself. He pined away and died of love. Some legends say that the sweet flower narcissus sprang from his body. Like Narcissus, it blooms for a short while and then fades.

Psychiatrists (doctors who study minds) say that a person who is too much interested in himself is "narcissistic."

narcotics

We use the word *narcotic* for a number of drugs that seem to make people feel better for a short period but that are very dangerous and illegal unless they are used under a doctor's orders. A person who uses narcotics regularly will usually form the habit of using them and cannot easily rid himself of the habit. He is then said to be *addicted*. An addict comes to depend so much on the drug that if necessary he will commit a crime to get it.

Narcotics are often called "dope," or simply "drugs." Strictly speaking, a narcotic is a drug that produces *narcosis,* a condition in which a person loses most or all of his power of feeling and may lose consciousness (fall into a deep sleep from which he cannot awaken until the effects of the drug are ended). However, there are other drugs that produce the opposite effect—make a person more wideawake than ever—and some of these drugs also are called narcotics.

Doctors can make good use of narcotics, to relieve patients who are suffering great pain, but in some ways narcotics are a danger to the entire world. This is because of the way they are used by certain criminals. The criminals encourage young people to try narcotics, hoping to make addicts of them. Once a person is an addict, the criminal can control him by

threatening to shut off his supply of the drug.

HABIT-FORMING DRUGS

A person can be addicted in either of two ways. Certain narcotics cause *bodily addiction*. This means that the victim's body will become dependent on the narcotic, and he will suffer great agony if he cannot get it. Furthermore, the victim's body will build up a *tolerance* for the drug, which means that every day he will need more and more of it to satisfy him. Since every narcotic is poisonous, an addict of this kind will soon die unless he can be taken to a hospital in time and cured.

A drug that causes this kind of addiction is said to be *habit-forming*. Most of the habit-forming drugs come from opium, and opium comes from the poppy plant, which has beautiful flowers. Drugs taken from opium are called *opiates*. One of them is morphine, which doctors use as a pain-killer. Another is heroin, which is favored by drug addicts. Codeine, used in many cough medicines, is another. It is not as quickly habit-forming as morphine or heroin, but it is still dangerous.

Other habit-forming drugs are taken from the coca plant, which is grown in South America and southern Asia. The principal drug taken from coca is cocaine. Cocaine was once used in many medicines, and many people became addicted without knowing what was happening to them. Now safe substitutes have been found.

The other kind of addiction is mental. Some drugs are said not to be habit-forming, because a person's body does not suffer when he cannot get the drug, but a mental habit can be almost as bad. For example, marihuana does not build up a tolerance in the body, but a person who is used to it will often have an uncontrollable desire for it if he cannot get it. In the same way, an alcoholic has an uncontrollable desire for liquor, which is not "habit-forming." Such an uncontrollable desire can lead to crime or to the ruin of a life or career.

STIMULANTS AND DEPRESSANTS

Narcotics may be either *stimulants* or *depressants*.

A stimulant steps up all the activities of the human body. The heart beats faster, the lungs take in air faster, and the person feels stronger. If he was tired, the tired feeling passes. If he was unhappy, he may feel happy (but also he may feel more irritated than ever). Cocaine is a stimulant. So is benzedrine, which is much less dangerous unless overdoses are taken.

A depressant slows down bodily activities. A person who has taken a depressant feels calm and relaxed. If the drug was strong enough, he goes to sleep. Most of the opiates, such as morphine and heroin, and the barbiturates (used in many "sleeping pills") are depressants.

OPIUM DRUGS

Opium, made from the poppy plant, is usually pressed into a pill that will burn and can be smoked in a pipe. The smoke puts the person to sleep.

Morphine and heroin (diamorphine) are usually injected into the veins with a hypodermic needle. They are very strong and anything but a tiny dose will put a person to sleep—unless his body has built up a tolerance to it. Heroin is used by most addicts because it is about four times as strong as morphine.

These drugs come in the form of a white powder that looks like sugar. It is dissolved in water for an injection, but some addicts sniff it up the nose, much as tobacco snuff is taken.

COCAINE

Cocaine used to be sniffed up the nose, but most addicts now inject it. Unlike the opiates, cocaine causes hallucinations. This means that the person thinks he sees or feels things that are not there, such as tiny people running on the walls or insects crawling on his body. In trying to fight against these imaginary things he may attack a real person.

MARIHUANA

Marihuana (also spelled *marijuana*) is a form of *cannabis*, a drug made from the hemp plant. In the United States, the leaves are dried and smoked in cigarettes called "reefers." The smoke is very sharp and must be taken in small puffs. Smoking marihuana makes a person feel happy and gay. He may find everything exciting or amusing. Later he will feel drowsy and probably fall asleep. Part of the danger of smoking marihuana is that it leads to taking more dangerous drugs. Marihuana smokers usually say they are not going to take the habit-forming drugs, but sooner or later many of them do.

In some countries hemp is used to make *hashish*, a cake of resin taken from the hemp plant. This can be chewed and swallowed for the narcotic effect. Like cocaine, it often makes a person dangerous.

BARBITURATES

Millions of people have taken barbiturates in sleeping pills. They are *sedatives*, drugs that quiet the nerves and permit a person to go to sleep when he is worried or suffering mild pain.

For a long time it was believed that barbiturates were harmless unless overdoses were taken. Now it is known that barbiturates are habit-forming, and a person who develops enough tolerance for them and then is deprived of them may suffer as great torture as a person who is addicted to morphine and cannot get it. Some addicts take barbiturates by injection into the veins, and this causes infections, or ulcers, on the skin. It may also cause heart disease.

TREATMENT OF ADDICTS

Any dependence on narcotics or on any stimulants or depressants, no matter how mild they are, is now treated as an illness. Treatment is possible only in hospitals that are specially equipped.

The United States government operates two hospitals for drug addicts. One is at Forth Worth, Texas, and accepts most of its male addicts from states west of the Mississippi. The other is at Lexington, Kentucky, and accepts both men and women addicts, most of them from states east of the Mississippi. A patient pays five dollars a day if he can afford to, but if he has no money he is treated free. Every patient must stay in the hospital at least four and a half months. When he is cured, he is allowed to return to his home and friends.

At these hospitals, and at various private hospitals, methods are used to make it as easy as possible for the person who is ridding himself of dependence on drugs. However, a person who has been dependent on drugs will lose his dependence on them even if no treatment is given. After he is deprived of the drugs for some weeks or months, his body will no longer need them.

narwhal, a small member of the whale family: see WHALE.

Nashville

Nashville is the capital city of the state of Tennessee. It is on the Cumberland River in the central part of the state. Nashville is the second-largest city (Memphis is the largest) in the state, and is a business, manufacturing and educational center.

About 447,000 people live in Nashville. They make shoes, cloth, cellophane, and stoves and heaters. Nashville is the most important center for the publishing, recording and broadcasting of folk music in the United States. There is a fine airport at Nashville, and three railroads come to the city. Boats sail up the Cumberland River from Nashville to the Ohio River and then by the Mississippi River to the Great Lakes or to the Gulf of Mexico.

Nashville has many fine parks, handsome public buildings, and fine houses. The state capitol is built to resemble a temple of ancient Greece and its stately columns and high tower make it an impressive sight. In one of the parks there is a copy of the ancient Greek temple, the Parthenon.

Nashville is sometimes called the "Athens of the South," because of its many schools and libraries. There are fifteen colleges and universities in Nashville. Vanderbilt University, Fisk University, schools of law and religion, and George Peabody College for Teachers are there.

Near Nashville is the estate where Andrew Jackson, the seventh President of the United States, lived about 150 years ago. Jackson's home is called the Hermitage. It is now a museum and many people visit it.

Nashville was founded in 1779. During the Civil War the city was captured by the Union soldiers, who made it their headquarters. After the war the people of Nashville rebuilt their city.

NASHVILLE, TENNESSEE. (1970 census) 447,877. Capital of Tennessee. County seat, Davidson County. On the Cumberland River. Founded in 1779.

Nasser, Gamal Abdel

Gamal Abdel Nasser was the head of Egypt and the most important Arab leader, from 1952 to 1970. Born in 1918, he became head of the Egyptian government in 1954 and President of the United Arab Republic in 1958.

Nasser spent most of his early life fighting for Egyptian freedom. Though Egypt supposedly became independent after World War I, Great Britain still had great

power there. When Nasser was 16, he led a group that protested against the British. In 1952 he was leader of the Egyptian Army group that dethroned King Farouk I and made Mohammed Naguib President and Premier. After a struggle for power, Nasser forced Naguib to resign as Premier in 1954, and later, as President. Nasser took both offices.

At first, Nasser was friendly toward the United States and its allies, but later became closer to the Soviet Union and Communist China. In 1958, he united Syria, Yemen, and Egypt as the United Arab Republic, but this union lasted only until 1961.

Although greatly admired by fellow Arabs for his strong and handsome appearance, personal charm, and an ability to influence crowds by speechmaking, Nasser accomplished relatively little for his country. This was partly due to his inability to pay much attention to social problems since he was almost constantly preoccupied with war or preparation for war. He led his country into humiliating defeats by Israel in 1948, 1956, and 1967.

Nasser died of a heart attack in 1970 and was replaced by his Vice President, Anwar Sadat.

Nast, Thomas

Thomas Nast was an American cartoonist. He was born in Germany, in 1840, but was taken to New York City when he was 6 years old. He began to draw cartoons for a newspaper when he was only 15.

Nast invented the donkey to represent the Democratic Party and the elephant to stand for the Republican Party. He pictured Tammany Hall, the Democratic headquarters in New York City, as a tiger. He also painted pictures, and one of his paintings is in the Metropolitan Museum of Art in New York City. Nast died there in 1902.

nasturtium

The nasturtium is a plant that was first found growing in South America and is now raised in gardens in many parts of Europe, the United States, and Canada. It is an annual plant, which means that the seed must be planted every year. Some nasturtiums are climbing plants that grow to be between 5 and 10 feet tall and that grow well over trellises and fences. Other nasturtiums are dwarf plants.

The nasturtium has gay yellow, red, or orange blossoms that are shaped like a funnel. They have a sweet smell. The leaves of the plant are flat and the stem is thick and fleshy.

Some people eat nasturtium leaves in salads, and soak the flower buds and seeds in vinegar for use as a spice. The nasturtium is also called *Indian cress*.

Nation, Carry

Carry Nation was an American woman who was a leader in the temperance movement in the United States. A temperance leader believes that no one should drink alcoholic liquor. Carry Nation became famous because she went around her native state of Kansas preaching against the evils of alcohol and wrecking the saloons where liquor was

sold. At first she broke bottles and smashed beer kegs, but later she took a hatchet and chopped up furniture and smashed windows. She said God had directed her to see that all saloons and taverns were destroyed.

Carry Nation was born in 1846. Her first husband was a drunkard. After he died, she married David Nation, a minister and lawyer. She left him to begin her campaign for temperance. Carry Nation was arrested many times because of her activities, and once served seven weeks in jail. Later she lectured to groups all over the United States and Europe. With the money she earned she set up a home for the wives of drunkards. She died in 1911, nine years before the Eighteenth Amendment to the Constitution, which prohibited the making or selling of liquor in the United States, was passed.

National Education Association

The National Education Association, or N.E.A., is an organization of people who are interested in improving and furthering public education in the United States. It tries to get more support for public education and to get better salaries and working conditions for teachers. Most of its members are teachers and others who work in education, especially in elementary schools and high schools. It was established in 1857 and has more than 800,000 members organized in 2,100 state and local associations. Its headquarters is in Washington, D.C. The N.E.A. has done a great deal for education in the United States.

national forests

The national forests of the United States are large regions of forest lands that are owned by the Federal government and are used for the benefit of the people as a whole. There are about 185,-000,000 acres of national forests in forty-four states of the United States. Most of this land is in the western states, although some eastern states also have national forests, chiefly in the Green Mountains, the White Mountains, and the Alleghenies. There are also national forests in Puerto Rico.

The resources of the national forest lands are put to good use, under the careful control of the Forest Service of the Department of Agriculture. The Forest Service allows private lumber companies to cut down trees, but only in certain numbers and in certain places. Livestock grazes in the national forests, but the Forest Service makes sure that the grazing does not take too many plants from the soil. The areas drained by rivers and streams, called watersheds, are carefully supervised to protect the free flow of water. Water-power sites are leased to private companies. Regions that are rich in metals are mined. There are many trails and camps that are open to thousands who visit the national forests each year. The wildlife that lives in the national forests is protected.

The national forest system was set up at the end of the last century and was enlarged by President Theodore Roosevelt, who was a great believer in conservation.

National Guard

The National Guard of the United States is made up of men who take military training and drill in peacetime, to be ready for action in times of war or during other emergencies. Its members are called "spare-time" citizen-soldiers. They meet regularly and drill in large armories or school gymnasiums. In the summer most of them spend two weeks in regular military camps. No one is forced to join the National Guard. It is made up entirely of volunteers.

Each state organizes its part of the National Guard, with the governor as commander in chief. The Federal government provides guns and equipment, and pays members for drilling and for their retirement pensions. The Guard can be called on by the governor of the state in case of any local emergency. This might be a natural disaster, such as a flood, fire, or earthquake, or man-made trouble such as rioting, prison breaks, and so on. In wartime the Guard is called out by the Federal government and its members join the armed forces. At the beginning of World War II, many Guard units, including 18 divisions and totaling 300,-034 men, were in active service with the Army. There are now both an Army National Guard and an Air National Guard.

Voluntary military groups, or *militia,* have existed in the United States since the 1600s. In 1824, the New York state militia took the title "National Guard" in honor of General Lafayette, who had commanded the *Garde Nationale* in France and who was then visiting the United States. The name was soon adopted by the militia of other states.

nationalization, the act of a government in taking over ownership and operation of businesses or industries. See the article on GOVERNMENT OWNERSHIP.

national parks and national monuments

National parks and monuments are places of interest in the United States that are owned and protected by the Federal government for the use of the people. The national parks attract thousands of visitors each year. They go to see the

National parks and monuments are places set aside for the benefit and enjoyment of the people of the United States. Some are in honor of historic events. Others have notable scenic features. Shown below is a famous balanced rock in Chiricahua National Monument in Arizona.

Nat'l Park Service

scenery, the wildlife, or the natural and historical objects.

There are 38 national parks in the United States and the Virgin Islands. The largest one by far is Yellowstone National Park. Because the western states have the most spectacular scenery, most of the national parks are in that part of the country, but some of the most interesting ones are east of the Mississippi, such as Everglades National Park, in Florida, and Mammoth Cave, in Kentucky.

The national monuments of the United States were set up to preserve places of historical and scientific interest. There are almost a hundred national monuments, and they include such places as the Petrified Forest, in Arizona; the Statue of Liberty; and Fort Sumter, in South Carolina, where the Civil War began.

Both national parks and national monuments are supervised by the National Park Service in the Department of the Interior.

natural gas

Natural gas is gas that is found deep in the earth, in hollows called gas pockets. This gas is burned in furnaces and in kitchen ranges.

Underground gas probably was formed by decaying plants. Millions of years ago, vast numbers of plants grew in marshes, lakes, and fresh-water inland seas. These bodies of water dried up, became muddy swamps, and eventually were covered over by earth. The decaying plants were buried deeper and deeper until some were miles deep. Gas was formed as they decayed. When it could no longer bubble up through the water or mud, it was trapped in underground hollows.

To get at the gas, holes are drilled down to the gas pockets, and pipes are put into the holes. The gas is led through the pipes to storage tanks, and then from the tanks through other pipes to places far across the country. Natural gas wells in Texas may supply gas for cities as far

away as St. Louis or Cleveland. Natural gas may be put under pressure in small steel cylinders. This "bottled" gas is used in houses in country areas that are not reached by gas mains, the big underground pipes that supply cities with gas.

Some gas wells contain helium, a gas that cannot burn. It is used in lighter-than-air craft and in other places where a burnable gas would be dangerous. Another natural gas is methane, which does burn. (You can read more about HELIUM and METHANE in separate articles.)

Much natural gas lies above the oil in oil wells. It is the pressure of this gas that may cause a newly-drilled oil well to spout oil high into the air.

In the United States, gas wells are found in Texas, Oklahoma, Arkansas, California, and other places where there are oil wells.

naturalization

Naturalization is the process by which a person who was born in one country becomes a citizen of another country. In most countries, a naturalized citizen has all the rights of a native-born citizen. In the United States, a naturalized citizen has all the rights of a native-born citizen except that under the Constitution he may not become President or Vice President of the United States.

Every country has special rules and regulations for naturalization. In the United States for many years, persons wishing to become citizens had to file a declaration of intention, which was usually called "first papers." This is no longer required, but a person may file such a declaration if it will help him prove to an employer or other person that he has taken steps to become a citizen.

An applicant for naturalization must be at least 18 years old, and he must have been a lawful resident of the United States for five years. For husbands or wives of United States citizens, this period is usually only three years, and there are

special provisions for members of the armed forces. Applicants must take a test to prove that they can read and write English and that they have a general knowledge of the history, principles, and form of government of the United States. They must be of good moral character. Two witnesses must swear to the applicant's character, residence, loyalty, and other qualifications. When the five-year waiting period is up, a Federal Court will grant naturalization, at which time the applicant takes an oath of allegiance to the United States, renounces his former country, and promises to fight for his new country, or to perform noncombatant service in the armed forces, or to perform work of national importance. (Read also CITIZENSHIP and IMMIGRATION.) Full details on becoming a citizen can be obtained from the Immigration and Naturalization Service, a branch of the Department of Justice, in Washington, D.C.

natural history, the study of things in nature: see ANIMAL LIFE, MINERALS, and PLANTS.

Nauru

Nauru is one of the world's smallest independent countries. It is an island in the Pacific Ocean, located 1,300 miles north-east of Australia. Since 1920, it had been under a trusteeship of Australia, Britain, and New Zealand. (See the article on TRUSTEE.) On January 31, 1968, Nauru became an independent republic. It has only 5,263 acres. (Monaco, the smallest country, has 370 acres.) In 1968, the population was 3,100, of which 1,100 were Chinese.

nausea

Nausea is an unpleasant feeling a person gets when his stomach is upset. Often when a person has nausea he vomits and this relieves the discomfort. Nausea may be caused by riding in a car, boat, or airplane. Sometimes, it is the sign of an illness like appendicitis, so it is important to see a doctor when nausea continues.

nautilus

The nautilus is a shellfish that lives in warm ocean waters. There are several different kinds. The largest is the *pearly,* or *chambered, nautilus* of the deep waters of the South Pacific and Indian oceans. Its shell looks like the shell of a giant snail, with coils that wind in spirals to the front opening. The shell may be as large as ten inches across. The animal

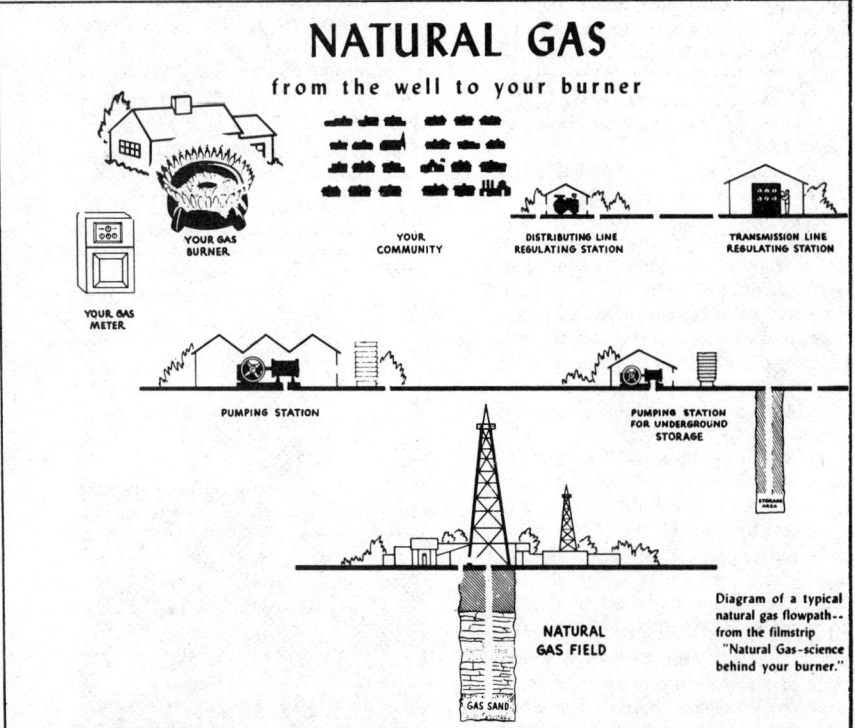

NATURAL GAS
from the well to your burner

YOUR GAS BURNER

YOUR GAS METER

YOUR COMMUNITY

DISTRIBUTING LINE REGULATING STATION

TRANSMISSION LINE REGULATING STATION

PUMPING STATION

PUMPING STATION FOR UNDERGROUND STORAGE

STORAGE AREA

NATURAL GAS FIELD

GAS SAND

Diagram of a typical natural gas flowpath-- from the filmstrip "Natural Gas-science behind your burner."

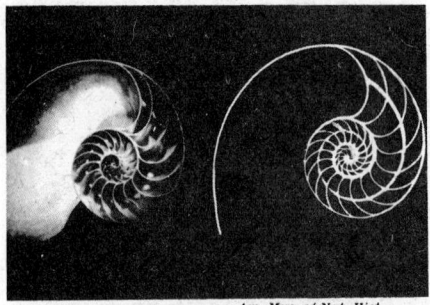

Am. Mus. of Nat. Hist.

The young nautilus lives in a small shell, but as it grows the nautilus draws itself inward and closes a door behind it. The chambered spiral on the left results. On the right is a cutaway of the shell that shows the chambers.

itself is only about six or seven inches long, and it lives in the chamber nearest the front opening. There are several other "rooms" or chambers behind this one. Each time the nautilus needs larger living quarters, it builds a new shell over the old one. Its head sticks out of the front of its portable home, and there are about ninety tentacles arranged about its mouth. They collect food and also serve as "feet" to help the nautilus move along the floor of the ocean.

The *paper nautilus,* or *argonaut,* found in the Mediterranean Sea, is different. It is not a true nautilus. Only the female builds a shell, and this is merely to contain her eggs. The shell is very thin. The animal and shell together are about eight inches long. The male is only one inch long, and resembles a small octopus.

Naval Academy, U.S.

The United States Naval Academy is a college where young men learn to become officers of the United States Navy or Marine Corps. The Academy is on the Severn River at Annapolis, Maryland, and is usually referred to simply as "Annapolis." Annapolis graduates are awarded a B.S. or Bachelor of Science degree, and are commissioned Ensigns in the Navy or Second Lieutenants in the Marine Corps. Annapolis enrollment in the spring of 1962 was 3,772; its faculty numbered 505, many of whom were Navy officers.

Young men between 17 and 22 years of age, unmarried, with a good educational and character record, and sound body, are eligible as candidates for the Academy. The course is four years, without the kind of summer vacations that other colleges have. The students, called *midshipmen,* have occasional *leaves* (short vacations), but are under strict discipline all the time.

Every accepted candidate must deposit $300 on entering. He also receives a loan of $600, and the $900 is used to buy books, uniforms, and so on. He must pay back the loan from his own pay of $111 a month plus $1.35 daily for rations.

OBTAINING AN APPOINTMENT

To enter Annapolis, a young man must first obtain an *appointment.* Appointments are made by high officials. The President may appoint seventy-five midshipmen a year from the sons of men in the armed forces. The Vice President, and each Senator and member of the House of Representatives, may have five midshipmen in the Academy at any one time. Each member of Congress names six candidates, a *principal* and five *alternates,* for each vacancy. If the principal fails to qualify, the first alternate tries, followed in turn by the others.

Appointments go to 320 men from the Navy and Marine Corps, regular and reserve. Sons of persons who have received the Congressional Medal of Honor may be appointed. Forty men may be appointed from the sons of deceased veterans of World War I and II. Twenty appointments go to "honor schools" and to the 52 colleges having Naval Reserve Officers Training Corps units. Five go to the District of Columbia, six to Puerto Rico, one to the Panama Canal Zone, twenty

to other American nations and four to the Philippines. The Secretary of the Navy may appoint additional midshipmen.

Information regarding these appointments may be obtained from one's Senator or Representative.

ANNAPOLIS EXAMINATIONS

After a man receives an appointment, he must qualify by passing examinations. Except for those appointed by the Vice President and members of Congress, and for sons of Medal of Honor holders, candidates take competitive examinations. These examinations are held in July of the year before one wishes to enter the Academy.

Regular Annapolis examinations are held in April of the year in which one wishes to enter.

The Annapolis scholastic examinations are much like college entrance examinations. They emphasize English, mathematics, and American history. In some cases, a high-school or preparatory-school certificate may take the place of an examination in American history. A physical examination and a physical aptitude test are necessary.

Information regarding these examinations may be obtained from the Academic Board, U.S. Naval Academy, Annapolis, Maryland.

ACADEMY WORK AND PLAY

The midshipmen are organized into a brigade of two regiments. The Academy grounds occupy more than 365 acres along the Severn.

There are many fine playing and athletic fields, tennis courts, a golf course, a gymnasium, and swimming pools. Many small boats are kept on the Severn for recreation and training.

A midshipman's day begins at 6:15 in the morning. Classes end at 3:55 in the afternoon, and "taps" or "lights out" is 10:15 P.M. The work week ends Saturday at noon. There are frequent "hops" or dances for the three upper classes. Many midshipmen go in for music, hobby clubs, and theatricals.

There are strong athletic teams, which in intercollegiate athletics are known simply as "Navy."

Summers are busy. In the first summer the *plebe* or fourth classman studies small boats, including how to row a whaleboat, tie knots, signal, and so on.

The next summer, as a third classman (called a *youngster*), he takes a cruise on a warship, usually to a foreign port. In the third summer, as a second classman, he learns about aviation, aircraft carriers, and amphibious warfare. In his final year he is a first classman.

ANNAPOLIS IN THE PAST

The Naval Academy was established in 1845 by Secretary of the Navy George Bancroft. It has remained in session at Annapolis since then except for a few Civil War years, when it was moved to Newport, Rhode Island. In 1899 Congress voted $10,000,000 for rebuilding all structures in French Renaissance style (see ARCHITECTURE). The largest building is Bancroft Hall.

Other buildings are named after Navy heroes. In the Chapel is the sarcophagus

(stone tomb) of John Paul Jones, early hero of the Navy.

navigation

Navigation is the art of guiding a ship over long ocean distances so that it reaches its final destination. Once a ship leaves a harbor and goes out beyond sight of land there is nothing to be seen but the sky and the vast, endless waters of the ocean. It took thousands of years for man to learn how to find his way across the seas. Five hundred years ago European sea captains did not dare sail very far into the Atlantic Ocean. Like the sea captains of ancient Rome, Greece, and Egypt, they followed the coastline of Europe or Africa and seldom ventured far from sight of land.

USE OF THE STARS

These mariners did not rely only on the landmarks of the seacoast they were following. They knew in what direction they were heading during the day by the position of the sun in the sky. Since the sun rises in the east and sets in the west, it was easy to know north and south also. If you stood with your right side to the east and your left side to the west, you were facing north and south was behind you.

At night mariners could find north by looking in the night sky for a star called Polaris or the North Star. It is always due north. South of the equator, a group of stars called the Southern Cross always points to the south.

THE COMPASS

Unfortunately, on cloudy days or nights it was difficult to see either the sun or Polaris. The invention of the magnetic compass made it possible for mariners to know in what direction to steer their ships even on cloudy days or nights. The needle of a compass always points to the north, no matter which way the ship turns. The Chinese are said to have invented some sort of compass more than four thousand years ago. Europeans began using the compass much later.

LATITUDE AND LONGITUDE

While the compass showed the mariner his direction, it could not tell him just where his ship was located on the ocean. To know the exact position of his ship on the sea, the mariner needed accurate maps and charts and instruments that would tell him his longitude and latitude.

If you look at a map you will notice that it has lines across it from side to side (east and west) and from top to bottom (north and south). The east-west lines show *latitude,* distance north or south of the equator, which is an imaginary line around the middle of the earth. The north-south lines show *longitude,* distance east or west of an imaginary line called the Prime Meridian, which runs through Greenwich, a suburb of the city of London, England.

The Prime Meridian runs through Greenwich because in 1675 the English government had an observatory built there. In this observatory, with its large telescope, astronomers (scientists who study the heavens) observed the movements of the sun, moon, and stars, and

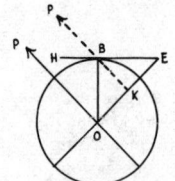
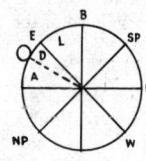

Left: Determining latitude by geometry from Polaris. The navigator at B sights Polaris (P) and takes its altitude, that is, the angle between the line from him to Polaris and the horizon line (HB). OP represents the axis of the earth, and OE the equator. *Right:* Determining latitude by geometry from the sun. The axis and the equator are lines NP-SP and E-W. The navigator at B has his horizon line at H, perpendicular to the line connecting B to the center of the earth O. The small circle is the sun, and its altitude is the angle A. D is the sun's declination for the day, which is found in the Nautical Almanac. The navigator's latitude is 90 degrees minus A plus D.

did complicated mathematical calculations to figure out for a year in advance just where in the sky the sun and stars would be on each day or night. All this information they arranged in easy-to-read tables in a book called the *Nautical Almanac.* Such books are now published by many countries for the officers of their naval and merchant fleets.

Soon it became customary for navigators everywhere to use Greenwich as the dividing line on the globe from which distances are figured eastward or westward.

Longitude and latitude are all imaginary lines, yet navigators can locate the exact position of their ship at sea by finding the point on a map where two of these lines cross each other. Suppose you had to meet a friend "on Main Street." If Main Street is several miles long, you might never find him. But if you were to meet him at "the corner of State and Main Streets," it would be easy to find him. Latitude and longitude are the Main and State Streets of the globe.

The lines of latitude are numbered from 0 at the equator to 90 at the North Pole. South of the equator the lines are numbered in the same way, with 90 at the South Pole. To avoid having too many lines on the map, only every tenth *degree.* as the lines are called, is shown. Each degree of latitude is divided into 60 lines called *minutes* and the space between the minute lines is further divided by another 60 lines called *seconds.* On a large navigation chart all these degrees, minutes, and seconds are shown as small marks along both sides or edges. Each two degrees of latitude are 60 miles apart.

USE OF THE SEXTANT

To find his latitude the navigator must measure the angle of elevation or height of the sun above the horizon at noon. He does this with an instrument called a *sextant.* Long ago astronomers discovered that the sun at noon stands at a different height above the horizon on each day of the year. They also found that the height of the sun above the horizon is different at each degree of latitude. If the navigator knows the angle of elevation, or the height of the sun on a particular day, he can easily discover his latitude by looking in his *Nautical Almanac.* In this

book he turns to the tables on the sun and looks for the date of that particular day. Under this date he goes down a column of figures until he finds the angle of elevation that he has just measured. Like latitude and longitude this is written in degrees, minutes, and seconds. The same table will now tell him on what degree of latitude his ship is.

The sextant used by navigators is a triangular instrument. It is usually made of brass and is about nine inches tall. At the bottom of the sextant there is a curved strip of brass marked off in degrees, minutes, and seconds. A movable metal arm pivoted at the top of the sex-

U.S. Coast Guard

A U.S. Coast Guardsman "shoots" the sun with his sextant. An experienced navigator can quickly find his location in this way.

tant reaches down to the curved strip and rides along it. A small telescope, about six inches long, is mounted on this movable arm. There are also two small mirrors on the instrument. To measure the sun's elevation or height above the horizon, the navigator moves the arm to which the telescope is fixed and adjusts the two mirrors until he can see the sun and the horizon at the same time. Then he reads the numbers on the curved strip. This is the sun's elevation above the horizon.

At night, latitude is obtained (north of the equator) by measuring the elevation of the North Star with a sextant. It is easier to obtain latitude from the North Star than from the sun, because it is not necessary to use the *Nautical Almanac.* If your sextant reads 40 degrees after measuring the North Star's elevation, then your latitude is 40 degrees. If the sextant reads 30 degrees, then latitude is 30 degrees, and so on.

FINDING LONGITUDE

There are twenty-four *meridians,* or longitude lines. On a globe it is possible to see that these lines are really circles that go completely around the earth, each one passing through both the North and South Poles. There are really 360 longitude lines, or degrees of longitude, as navigators call them. Daily radio signals from Greenwich tell every ship at sea when it is exactly noon in Greenwich, England. To find longitude, the navigator merely has to look at the chronometer when it is noon on the ship. Suppose the chronometer says that it is 2 p.m. in Greenwich. The navigator then knows that he is two hour-circles or meridians away from Greenwich. If he happens to be sailing in the Atlantic

Sperry Gyroscope Co.

Once the navigator decides on the course to be taken, the gyropilot, known as "Iron Mike," steers the ship automatically, freeing the helmsman for other duties.

Ocean he knows he is west of Greenwich. Since each meridian is equal to 15 degrees, he is 30 degrees west of Greenwich. Our navigator has then found the point "where State Street crosses Main Street," and knows his exact position and marks it on his map.

DEAD RECKONING

Navigators also use dead reckoning to keep on their course or path to their destination. This is a method of figuring how far and in what direction the ship has traveled in a certain amount of time. It is used when cloudy weather makes it possible to get latitude from the sun or North Star. Using the last position on the map made with the sextant and chronometer, the navigator draws a line from this point with a ruler and pencil in the direction the ship is going. He knows this direction by looking at his compass. Certain instruments tell him the speed of the ship. If the vessel has been steaming at 10 miles an hour for the past 10 hours, he is 100 miles from his last position along the line he has drawn on the map. The ship's new position is marked on the map every hour. In case of emergency the ship's wireless operator can radio its exact location to all nearby ships, so that they can come to its rescue.

MODERN INSTRUMENTS

In addition to the magnetic compass, most ships today carry a *gyrocompass.* This is a compass whose needle points to the true geographic north, that is, the North Pole as we see it on a map. The magnetic compass does not point to the geographic north but to the magnetic north, which is a place about 138 miles south and west of true north and is located on the Boothia Peninsula and in northern Canada. The gyrocompass is explained in the article GYROSCOPE.

Another important device used by the modern navigator is RDF (radio direc-

tion finding). This is a special type of radio. It has a tubular ring about 15 inches in diameter, which serves as an antenna. Around the base of this antenna there is a circle of metal marked off in 360 divisions or degrees. The antenna is turned slowly until the signal from a radio broadcasting station comes in loudest. The scale of degrees on the metal circle at the base of the antenna tells the direction from which the signal comes. The location of the radio station on land is known and a line is drawn on the map, with a ruler and pencil, from its position in the compass direction shown on the scale of degrees. This procedure is repeated with three other broadcasting stations. The point on the map where all the lines cross each other is the location of the ship. RDF is used for distances up to about 400 miles and is accurate to within a mile.

AIR NAVIGATION

Air navigation is very much the same as navigation at sea. The navigator in a large plane uses a sextant, chronometer, nautical almanac, magnetic compass and gyrocompass, and dead reckoning. Air navigators usually use what is known as a bubble sextant. This has an artificial horizon that acts like the bubble in a carpenter's level. By merely holding the sextant straight when he looks through the little telescope, the air navigator need only make an observation of the sun, the North Star, or any other star, and it is not necessary to see the horizon at the same time. An air navigator makes his observations of the sun or stars through a large plastic turret or dome that can be raised or lowered through the top of the plane.

Navigators on planes usually make more use of RDF than those on ships because an airplane moves so quickly and this is one of the fastest ways of getting a "fix" or position. Dead reckoning in a plane must take careful account of helpful or contrary winds. A plane's *tachometer* or speedometer may show that it is flying at 200 miles per hour but a tailwind of 50 miles an hour will raise its speed to 250 while a headwind of 50 miles per hour will cut its speed to 150 miles per hour. Special instruments tell the air navigator the speed and direction of winds outside the plane.

RIDING THE BEAM

Planes that fly on regular scheduled flights from city to city do not need to make use of special navigation instruments (except for a compass) because they "ride a radio beam" that keeps them on their course. The "beam" is made up of a long line of automatic radio broadcasting towers spaced many miles apart along the course the plane must follow. These towers operate day and night and broadcast certain signals. They are maintained by the United States government. These signals are picked up by a special radio receiver and are shown on a dial in front of the pilot. When the plane veers off course to the right, the arrow on the dial points right. If the plane veers left, the arrow points in that direction. When the plane is on course, the arrow points straight up.

USE OF RADAR

Both ships and planes make use of radar when a harbor or airport is fogged in. Radar is simply a short-wave radio sender and receiver. The radio wave from the sender goes out in a straight line until it strikes a solid object. Then it bounces back like an echo. This "echo" is received by the receiver part of the radar. The returning signal is shown on a glass screen. Radar waves go through darkness and fog and show the location, shape, and distance of an object beyond the plane or ship. At sea, ships use radar to avoid collision with other vessels during a fog and to find a coastline at night.

Planes use radar to land at an airport during a fog. In one system called Ground Control, the radar operator spots the plane while it is approaching the airport and tells the pilot at what speed to come in, whether to move left or right, and the angle or slant toward the earth the plane must take to descend to the runway. In the Instrument Landing Approach the pilot has radar instruments that give him all this information on their dials, so that he can land safely even though he cannot see a foot in front of him.

navy

A navy is a nation's organization of ships and men used in fighting a war at sea. The ships include not only warships such as battleships and submarines but also supply ships, transports to carry ground forces, and many other kinds of ship. The men include not only the crews of the ships but also large numbers of men and women on land who help to direct and supply the forces at sea. A modern navy includes many airplanes, aircraft carriers to carry them, and aviators and mechanics to fly and service them.

In time of war, a nation's entire merchant marine (ships used in commerce) comes under the control of its navy.

EARLY NAVIES

The first organized navies were formed by people living along the Mediterranean Sea. The Egyptians and Phoenicians had armed ships, organized for warfare, as many as four thousand years ago. The Greek countries had powerful navies, and in 480 B.C. the Greeks under Themistocles defeated the Persians under Xerxes, at the battle of Salamis, and saved Greece from invasion. In 31 B.C. the battle of ACTIUM, about which there is a separate article, won control of the Roman Empire for Octavian.

Early navies, like modern ones, were used to protect their country's trading ships and colonies from attack.

The early warships were mostly *galleys,* long, low vessels driven by oars. The oars were manned by slaves, who were either prisoners of war or convicted criminals. Sails were used too, but sailors had not yet learned to sail into the wind, so oars were necessary. Oar-driven ships became bigger and bigger: A *unireme* had only one bank of oars, but there were *biremes* with two banks, *triremes* with three, *quadriremes* with four. A fleet might consist of hundreds of these ships. They fought chiefly crashing into enemy ships and boarding them for hand-to-hand combat.

The Norsemen, or Vikings, used long, low boats with one bank of oars. Small fleets of these boats would raid the coasts of European countries, and sometimes they supported large-scale invasions, as when the Angles and Saxons and later the Danes invaded England.

During the Middle Ages, six and seven hundred years ago, oar-driven ships gradually gave way to sailing ships, and cannons came into use. In the 1500s Spain and England grew to be the greatest naval powers, and the English kept that position for hundreds of years. From time to time France was a great naval power, but never so great as England.

The biggest warships of the days of sailing vessels were called *ships of the line.* They are described in the article on BATTLESHIP. There were great fleet battles between these ships, supported by smaller warships. Much of naval warfare, however, was fought by a single ship or two that roamed the seas to raid the enemy's commerce. Some of these were *privateers*—ships that were privately owned but were licensed by the government to capture enemy ships for profit. Such a license was called a *letter of marque.*

MODERN NAVIES

Modern naval vessels may be said to date from the American Civil War, when both sides built armored ("ironclad") ships and the north built a ship, the *Monitor,* on which the guns were mounted in a revolving turret and could be pointed in any direction. Both were steam-driven. The old, wooden, sailing ship was quickly abandoned by all navies. Boarding parties became a thing of the past. In naval battles, ships fired at each other from distances of miles.

In 1890 there was published a book called *The Influence of Sea Power Upon History, 1660–1783.* It was written by an American naval officer, Captain Alfred T. Mahan. In the book he showed that a strong navy was necessary to a nation that wanted to be important. This book convinced several countries, including the United States, that they should build powerful navies.

When World War I began in 1914, Great Britain was the strongest naval power, Germany was second, and the United States and Japan had strong fleets. During this war the Germans made very effective use of submarines, and almost won the war simply by destroying British merchant ships. Submarines have been recognized ever since as an important part of a great navy.

After World War I, the German Navy was destroyed. All others were much weakened except those of Great Britain, the United States, and Japan. In Naval Disarmament Conferences held in 1921 and 1922, these countries agreed on a "5-5-3 ratio," which meant that Great Britain could have five ships and the United States could have five ships for every three Japanese ships. (Of course, the size of the ships was controlled by the agreement.)

During World War II, the United States built the greatest navy in history. Most of the Japanese navy was destroyed. After World War II, Soviet Russia began to build a big navy, including the world's biggest fleet of submarines.

Much of the most recent developments in navies is secret. The aircraft carrier may still be the most important warship, but atomic-powered submarines and other ships, carrying guided missiles with atomic explosives, now seem even deadlier than aircraft.

Navy, U.S.

The United States Navy is the organization of sailors and naval aviators trained to defend the United States and fight its battles on sea wherever the enemy may be. The United States Marine Corps is a part of the Navy, and the United States Coast Guard is put under Navy command in wartime. There are separate articles about the MARINE CORPS and COAST GUARD.

The first American navy was born in the early days of the Revolutionary War. It was called "The Navy of the United Colonies." It was created in October, 1775, when the Continental Congress voted $100,000 (a huge sum in those days) to fit out four ships. They were cargo vessels, crudely made into warships. The flagship was a tea-carrying ship named the *Alfred*. One of its officers was John Paul JONES, who became the great American naval hero of that war, and about whom there is a separate article. The other ships were the *Columbus*, the *Andrew Doria*, and the *Cabot*. General George Washington was in command of this navy. When the war ended a few years later, these ships were sold. The Navy that exists today was born on April 30, 1798, when Congress voted to have a Navy Department.

In times of war the Navy greatly expands; in peacetime it is much smaller. In 1965 the Navy had nearly 900 combatant vessels (including more than 50 nuclear-powered ships) and about 9,000 aircraft. More than 720,000 people were serving in the Navy, plus more than 214,000 in the Marines. This was the most powerful navy in the world. But in World War II the United States Navy was far stronger. Near the end of that war, in 1945, it had nearly four million men and women serving in it, with 8,400 warships and many other service ships, and about 20,000 planes.

To join the Navy, a man must be between 17 and 30 years of age, a woman between 18 and 25. The applicant must be in good physical condition, a citizen of the United States, able to read, write, and think clearly, and of good character. Those who pass these tests are *recruits*. They enlist for terms ranging from two to six years. Their pay begins at $87.90 a month, and all living expenses, including dental and medical care, clothing and so on, are free. Pay is raised at regular intervals, and also when a recruit wins promotion. Extra pay is given for sea and foreign duty, also for hazardous duty including flying, submarine service, parachute jumping, diving, and handling of explosives. Recruits have thirty days of *leave*, or vacation, a year. After twenty years of service, one may retire with a monthly income for the rest of his life.

RECRUIT TRAINING CENTERS

New recruits are sent, at government expense, to a Recruit Training Center either at San Diego, California, or at Great Lakes, Illinois. Here they are nicknamed "boots," or "bluejackets" (a term used for all enlisted men). They receive uniforms, shoes, and other equipment. They live in barracks with other recruits, and all of them sleep, eat, march, work and play together. They are divided into small groups called *companies*, and into larger groups called *regiments*.

Recruit training lasts nine weeks. Then there are two weeks of leave. At the Center they learn about Navy pay, allowances, and insurance, customs and courtesies, naval history and traditions. They practice military drill, handling small boats, and firefighting and signaling. They learn to swim, which is a "must" in the Navy. They find out that "swabbing" must be done to keep the barracks "shipshape." When work is done, recruits may play baseball, football, and other sports, and may go to movies or to smokers and parties in the recreation rooms.

CHOOSING A NAVY CAREER

Early in recruit training, each bluejacket has a *classification review*. During this an expert finds out what a recruit likes to do, what he does best, and for what he is best fitted. His record and aptitudes show whether the bluejacket will make an expert mechanic, an electronics specialist, a flier, an accountant, or simply a good fighting sailor.

After recruit training, recruits may be assigned to one of four duties. Some may be sent aboard ships on sea duty, for sailors "see the world." Some may go to a Navy shore station in a foreign land, others to a post in the United States. Still others may go to special schools, to learn to become petty or commissioned officers.

In the special schools Navy men learn to act as petty officers, to handle deep-sea diving equipment, to operate machines or drive engines, or to do any one of the many jobs in the Navy. The Navy is a huge outfit and many skills are needed to keep it going. If a man learns a trade in service, he can continue at that trade, earning a living at it, when he leaves the Navy. There are 62 major job fields in the Navy. A few of them are aviation, photography, clerical work, hospital service, radar, pipefitting, and communications. In these 62 fields there are about 1,100 special jobs such as steelworker, bookkeeper, gyroscope expert, parachute rigger, dental technician, and so on.

Life in the United States Navy is much like that in the Army, especially in regard to hours of duty, kinds of service, telling time, bugle calls, saluting, military justice, and so on. The article about the United States ARMY describes these.

RANK IN THE NAVY

The Navy, like the Army, divides its service people into two groups, *officers* (also called *commissioned officers*), and *enlisted men*. The officers are either graduates of the United States Naval Academy at Annapolis, Maryland, or of special training courses in colleges, or they have become officers by working their way up from the enlisted men's ranks. In each group there are grades, or ranks, as follows (from highest to lowest):

ENLISTED MEN	OFFICERS
Master Chief Petty Officer	Fleet Admiral
Senior Chief Petty Officer	Admiral
	Vice Admiral
Chief Petty Officer	Rear Admiral
Petty Officer First Class	Commodore
	Captain
Petty Officer Second Class	Commander
	Lieutenant Commander
Petty Officer Third Class	Lieutenant
Seaman	Lieutenant Junior Grade
	Ensign
Seaman Second Class	Warrant Officer 4
Seaman Recruit	Warrant Officer 3
	Warrant Officer 2
	Warrant Officer 1

All officers rank above the enlisted men. The two groups do not eat or live together, and they are not supposed to get too friendly. This is considered necessary to keep strict discipline, so that an enlisted man will promptly obey an officer's command without thinking him "unfriendly."

The USS Bainbridge, DLG(N), cruising in the Mediterranean Sea.
U.S. Navy Photos

Pay in the Navy is like that in the Army, and women get the same pay as men. There is a chart showing pay scales in the article on the United States ARMY. An Admiral in the Navy receives the same pay as a General in the Army, a Navy ensign the same as an Army second lieutenant. Enlisted men's pay, as well as that of officers, is the same for the corresponding rank in all services.

BRANCHES OF THE NAVY

The Department of the Navy, or the Naval Establishment, is one of the three divisions of the United States Department of Defense. It is directed by a non-uniformed civilian, the Secretary of the Navy, appointed by the President. The Navy consists of two main parts: the *Operating Forces* and the *Shore Establishment.*

The Operating Forces are composed of several fleets, sea frontier forces to defend United States borders, Fleet Marine forces, and other groups. In the Operating Forces are the big Atlantic Fleet and Pacific Fleet. There are also special naval forces, or subfleets, in the Eastern Atlantic, in the Mediterranean Sea, in the Far East, in the Caribbean Sea, and in Alaskan waters. Naval forces are sent all over the world, often simply as a good-will gesture to foreign friends, or to be on hand where trouble may start. A fleet may remain in an area such as the Mediterranean for months, then it might be sent to another part of the world. Such changes are determined by the President and his foreign policy planners in Washington.

The Navy Department is located in Washington, D.C. It is the headquarters from which all Navy operations are directed. In it are the Secretary and many other high officials.

In the Shore Establishment are *naval bases,* as at Norfolk, Virginia, and at San Diego, California; also naval air bases, and stations that guard the defense of the United States, its ships, sea lanes, and so on.

TYPES OF NAVY SHIPS

In World War I, the *battleship* was the "queen bee" or spearhead of the United States Navy. In World War II this was changed and the *aircraft carrier* ("flattop") became the most important front-line ship. (There is a separate article about the AIRCRAFT CARRIER). A special kind of ship grouping and arrangement was used by the United States in World War II. This was called a *fast carrier task force.* A big carrier was in the center of a large group of ships. From the carrier, planes flew off to attack the enemy. Other ships were stationed in circles around the carrier, guarding it. The task force carried ammunition, food, and other supplies, and could stay away from home bases for months at a time. It was a complete "floating city."

There are many types of ships in the Navy. Carriers are the largest. (In 1965, the carrier U.S.S. *Enterprise* was the world's largest ship.) Next come the *cruisers,* which are fast, hard-hitting, and long-cruising. *Destroyers* are small and fast and have varied equipment. They are used to fight submarines, airplanes, and surface vessels. *Escort destroyers* are used chiefly against enemy submarines. *Submarines* also are of many types. Some carry guided missiles, others fight enemy submarines and surface ships. There are cargo and transport submarines. There are separate articles about all these warships.

The Navy also has special vessels to use in capturing an enemy shore. (There is a separate article about AMPHIBIOUS WARFARE). They are of many types. A few are: *infantry landing ships, large* (LSIL), *tank landing ships* (LST), and big *dock landing ships* (LSD). There are also *minelayers,* ships that plant mines in the water, and *minesweepers* that get rid of enemy mines. There are patrol vessels, and many types of auxiliaries such as repair ships, floating drydocks, oilers, gasoline tankers, and cable-laying ships. There are hundreds of service craft, such as barges, tugs, dredges, ferry boats, and so on.

NAVY PLANES AND FLIERS

The aircraft carrier is the spearhead of the fleet, and its airplanes are the carrier's weapons to strike the enemy. Naval aviation is thus an important part of the Navy. Naval aviators have to be physically fit, of better-than-average education, with quick minds and muscles. They have to pass very strict tests. Men found eligible are sent to the headquarters of the Naval Air Training Command at Pensacola, Florida, on the Gulf of Mexico. This is for their primary training. They then go to Corpus Christi, Texas, for advanced training. Training at these two centers lasts eighteen months. The battle operations of naval aviators is described in the article on AIRCRAFT CARRIERS.

Since World War II, jet planes have been built for the Navy with more than double the speed of the World War II planes and going faster all the time. Among the newer Navy planes are the A-6 attack aircraft, the F-8 and F-4 fighter planes, all of which may be carrier-based, and the P-3 Orion, a land-based plane designed to locate and destroy enemy submarines. The Navy abandoned its lighter-than-air program in 1961. It makes much use of helicopters. In the Korean conflict these were used often in rescue work. The Navy also has GUIDED MISSILES, about which there is a separate article.

RESERVE FORCES

If war should come suddenly, none of the military services would have enough trained men and women. So they all have *reserves,* people who have some skills and training and who can be called on in an emergency. The Navy has a Ready Reserve numbering about 342,321, and a Standby Ready Reserve of about 29,203 members. The Organized Reserve members train regularly at Navy centers, and each year take cruises of two weeks. They receive pay while training. In this Reserve are aviation pilots, who are expected to fly about four hours a month, and who train for two weeks at a naval station or on a carrier. There is also a Fleet Reserve of those who have been honorably discharged from the Navy after at least four years of service. There is a Submarine Reserve of men who train regularly.

Young college or university students can become officers in the Navy without leaving their campuses. They enroll in the NROTC, or Naval Reserve Officers' Training Corps, and take special courses and drills. On graduating one may be appointed an ensign in the Navy.

WOMEN IN THE NAVY

Many Navy jobs can be handled by women. The Navy first used women in 1908, when it organized the Navy Nurse Corps. Later came the "Yeomanettes," officially *yeomen F (female),* who served in World War I. Some, assigned to the Marine Corps, were called "Marinettes."

In 1942, early in World War II, the Navy organized the WAVES (Women Appointed for Voluntary Emergency Service). About 85,000 served in that war. In 1948 this group was disbanded, but many women transferred to the regular Navy.

NAVY HISTORY AND TRADITIONS

History calls John Adams, Massachusetts patriot and second President, the founder of the American Navy. He was on the Marine Committee organized by the Continental Congress on October 13, 1775, to handle naval affairs. Adams prodded the Congress to take the action that resulted in the little Navy of John Paul Jones.

The first sea battle had already been fought. It took place off Machias, Maine, in May, 1775, and was won by Jeremiah O'Brien and about forty lumberjacks. Seizing a lumber sloop, they attacked a British schooner. Armed only with muskets against cannon, they boarded the English ship like timber wolves. They tore down King George's flag and ran up a white flag on which a green pine tree stood above the legend, "An Appeal to Heaven."

The flag of the *Alfred,* which was raised by Jones in the absence of Captain Dudley Saltonstall, was "a Union flag with thirteen stripes in the field emblematical of the Thirteen United Colonies." Later, Jones became captain of the *Providence,* and in 1777, of the *Ranger.* His daring exploits during the war were remarkable and greatly heartened the colonists.

Navy men remember best a letter Paul Jones wrote to Congress. It became sort of a blueprint, or pattern, for future Navy men. In part it reads:

"It is by no means enough that an officer of the Navy should be a capable mariner. He should be as well a gentleman of liberal education, refined manners, punctilious courtesy, and the nicest sense of personal honor. When a commander has by tact, patience, justice, and firmness, each exercised in its proper turn, produced such an impression upon those under his orders in a ship of war, he has only to wait the appearance of his enemy's ship topsails upon the horizon. When this moment does come, he may be sure of victory over an equal or somewhat superior force, or honorable defeat by one greatly superior."

Jones took his Ranger into enemy waters and captured many valuable prizes. Later, in the *Bonhomme Richard* he defeated the *Serapis* in a memorable battle. Seemingly beaten badly, he called when asked if he had surrendered, "I have not

yet begun to fight!" He won the battle. But by 1779 most of the tiny Continental Navy was gone. The British were far too strong.

WARS THE NAVY FOUGHT

For some years there was no United States Navy, and the Barbary pirates in the Mediterranean knew about this. They seized United States ships and held the sailors for ransom. Finally Congress voted to build six frigates. Two of them became famous, the *Constellation* and the *Constitution* (later called "Old Ironsides"). They forced the pirates to stop their attacks.

The present Navy was then begun, in 1798. When the War of 1812 against Britain took place, the British had a huge navy, but the United States won a few notable victories. The *Constitution* beat the *Guerriere,* and Commodore Oliver Hazard Perry defeated the British on Lake Erie.

In the Mexican War, in 1846, the Navy was used to blockade Mexican ports. In 1854 Commodore Matthew Calbraith Perry sailed to Japan and persuaded the Japanese to trade with the Western World.

During the Civil War, fought from 1861 to 1865, the Union Navy blockaded the Confederate ports and had a great deal to do with the victory of the North, but both North and South made naval history, for both produced the first warships with metal armor. The most famous were the *Monitor* and the *Merrimac.*

About twenty years after the Civil War ended, warships began to be made of steel, with engines rather than sails. That was the start of the modern navy. In World War I, the Navy was used mostly to guard transports carrying United States soldiers to Europe and to fight German submarines, but before the war ended the United States had built the biggest fleet in history. After that war, the big nations agreed to cut the size of their navies. Some big United States ships, such as the battleship *Washington,* were purposely sunk.

In World War II, the United States found it had to have two navies, one for the Atlantic and one for the Pacific. The Atlantic fleet carried soldiers overseas and fought submarines. The Pacific fleet defeated the Japanese and helped carry the war right to Japan. The United States Navy became by far the strongest in the world and in the history of the world.

In the Korean War, the United States Navy carried soldiers overseas and bombarded the enemy along the coasts. In both Korea and Vietnam it provided carriers from which many air strikes were flown.

Nazareth

Nazareth is a town in Lower Galilee, in Palestine. It is the town where Jesus Christ lived, and because of this Jesus was sometimes called the Nazarene. In ancient times Nazareth does not seem to have been greatly admired, for in the first chapter of the book of John in the New Testament, one of the disciples who has not yet met Jesus asks, "Can there anything good come out of Nazareth?"

Many Christians make pilgrimages to Nazareth, which today is in the country of Israel and is the home of about 23,000 people. The town is on a hill, and looks down over the Jordan Valley. Nazareth has many churches and shrines. One of the most beautiful is the church and convent on the spot where the Annunciation is traditionally thought to have taken place (when the angel Gabriel announced the coming of Jesus to the Virgin Mary). There is a separate article about the ANNUNCIATION.

Nazism

Nazism, or National Socialism, is a form of government. Germany had a National Socialist government from 1933 until 1945, when it lost World War II. In several other countries there have been political parties that were in favor of this form of government, but none of them became very powerful except in countries that Germany controlled during the war.

The National Socialist movement began in Germany in 1919, soon after Germany had lost World War I. A political party was formed with the name "National Socialist German Workers Party." A member of the party named Adolf Hitler became its leader. The party was called the *Nazi* party because the first two words of its name, in German, are *Na-tional-sozialistische.* The Nazis were organized in Munich, the leading city of southern Germany.

In the early days of the Nazis, the German people were poor and discouraged, and many of them were out of work. They were looking for a strong leader. Gradually, more and more of them came to believe that Hitler could lead them back to the prosperity and power their country had before World War I. They were so anxious for this that they were willing to give up their personal rights and liberties.

THE NAZI POLICIES

Here are the principal things that the Nazis put into effect in their government of Germany:

1. The state (that is, the country itself) was more important than the people who lived in it. In a democratic country the government is run for the benefit of the people, but in a Nazi country everyone must do whatever the government demands.

2. Only one political party (the Nazi Party) is allowed. Anyone who opposes this party is imprisoned or killed.

3. The "leader principle" means that the *Führer* (leader) has complete power over the party, the government, and everything and everybody in the country. Under him are other leaders who control their own groups or districts. When Germany was ruled by the Nazis, Hitler had supreme power.

4. The government controls schools, and brings up the children of the country to believe in Nazism. It controls newspapers, all other reading matter, and radio, so that people can read and hear only what the government wants them to believe.

5. The lawmaking bodies of the country can pass only the laws that the government tells them to pass, and the judges in the courts must make the decisions the government tells them to make, whether these decisions are right or wrong.

6. The government opposes religions, labor unions, and all other organizations in which a person can be loyal to anything except the state. In Germany, one of the important policies of the Nazi government was anti-Semitism (enmity toward Jews), and during their rule the Nazis murdered millions of Jews.

7. Since the Nazis believe that anything is "right" if it helps the state, a Nazi government has no honesty in dealing with other nations. It tries to build up its military power so that it can conquer other countries and enrich itself. Even schoolchildren in Nazi Germany were trained to become soldiers, and as soon as Germany had built a powerful fighting force it started World War II, in hope of conquering the world.

RISE AND FALL OF NAZISM

In its first few years, the Nazi Party grew slowly. In 1923, Hitler and some of his followers tried to seize control in Munich, but they failed and Hitler was imprisoned. While in prison, Hitler wrote a book, *Mein Kampf* (My Struggle), in which he explained his plans for Germany. He was helped, in writing the book, by Rudolph Hess, who was one of the earliest and most prominent Nazis. Hitler's book was very successful in Germany and won many followers for the Nazi Party. The Nazis also organized private fighting forces, the "brown shirts" or "S.A." and the "elite guard" or "S.S.," and these men brought terror to those who opposed the party.

By 1933 the Nazis were so powerful in Germany that the German president, Paul von Hindenburg, made Hitler the chancellor, or head of the government. Once in power, the Nazis crushed all opposition and within a year they were in complete control. Some of Hitler's early followers seemed likely to become too powerful, so Hitler organized a "blood purge" and killed them. His principal assistants after that were Hermann Goering, who began at once to build up a powerful air force, and Joseph Goebbels, who was in charge of propaganda (the spreading of news that would make people believe what the Nazis wanted them to believe).

The Nazis enforced their power through the Gestapo, or secret state police. It was dangerous even to whisper anything that criticized the government. The Gestapo made neighbors spy on each other and even made children spy on their parents. A person who criticized the government would be seized by the Gestapo and put in a concentration camp, a large prison camp far from any city. There were many of these concentration camps in Germany. An accused person had no right to a trial, and suspected people were often tortured.

The German Nazis tried to build up Nazi parties in other countries, especially among the people of German descent in those countries. In many countries, including the United States, these small Nazi parties carried on propaganda for the Germans.

One of the Nazi beliefs, which is often called *racism,* was that a group of European peoples whom they called the "Aryan race" are better than other peo-

ples and ought to rule the world. They thought that people of German descent were superior to all other peoples. This is scientifically untrue, but it pleased many people to believe it.

The articles on HITLER, GERMANY, and WORLD WAR II tell how the Nazis seized and terrorized other countries, started World War II, and finally lost to the Allies. The Nazi movement then died out in most parts of the world, including Germany. Some people continued to believe in it, and their effort to bring back Nazi rule is called *neo-Nazism* (new Nazism).

See also the article on FASCISM.

nearsightedness, see the articles on EYE and GLASSES.

Nebraska

Nebraska is a state in the great midwestern plain of the United States. It lies just north of the geographical center of the country. Its nickname is the "Cornhusker State" because of its great crops of corn. Nebraska ranks fourth in the nation's production of corn. Nebraska is sometimes called the "Tree Planters' State" because of the great interest the people have taken in planting trees, which help to keep the soil from washing away. The first Arbor Day in the United States was celebrated in Nebraska. The state gets its name from an Indian word meaning "shallow water," which was first given to the Platte River in Nebraska. This river is so shallow that parts of it are sometimes completely dry in the summer.

In area, Nebraska ranks 15th among the states, with 77,227 square miles. In population it ranks 35th, with about a million and a half people living there. It became a state in 1867, and was the 37th state admitted to the United States. The capital is Lincoln.

THE PEOPLE OF NEBRASKA

The earliest settlers of Nebraska were Americans who came from the eastern part of the United States. They were later joined by many Germans, who were attracted by the fertile farm land. Today, about one-third of the population is of German descent. Many people also came

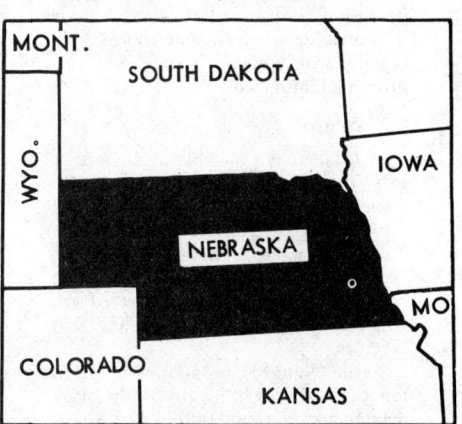

from the Scandinavian and other European countries.

A large portion of the people in Nebraska are farmers since the basic industry in the state is agriculture. The land can be divided into three major areas, the Loess region, the Sand Hills, and the High Plains.

The Loess region which is the eastern one-third to one-half of the state is fertile, deep soil on which is grown corn, wheat, oats, barley, rye, sorghum, potatoes, hay, soybeans, clover, alfalfa, fruit, and vegetables. Cattle, hogs, sheep and poultry are also important agricultural products.

The Sand Hills in the north-central part of the state are covered with a rich grass that is excellent feed for the state's famed range cattle.

The High Plains in the western section of the state respond to irrigation and produce large yields of corn, sugar beets, potatoes, and vegetables.

Many people work in meat-packing plants in the cities. Omaha is the second-largest meat-packing center in the United States, next to Chicago. Many work in huge flour, feed and grain mills, and in important food-processing plants.

There are many religious groups in Nebraska. The largest are the Roman Catholic, Lutheran, and Methodist. The Presbyterian, Baptist and Protestant Episcopal Churches also have large followings.

WHAT NEBRASKA IS LIKE

Nebraska is mostly a rolling plain. The eastern part of the state is made up of fertile farms like those in Iowa, Illinois, and other Corn Belt states. The western half of Nebraska is more like the western states. It has big cattle ranches where cowboys ride over the plains, taking care of great herds of grazing beef cattle.

The northern, eastern and western borders of the state are broken by hills. In the northwest are beautifully wooded buttes and hills.

Nebraska is famous for its fossil, or skeleton, remains. Millions of years ago, prehistoric animals roamed the plains of Nebraska. In recent years, scientists have dug up some of the skeletons of these huge animals. They found the bones of a pig six feet high, a dog as big as a bear, and prehistoric elephants and horses. The skeleton of one mammoth was discovered that was more than fourteen feet high—the largest ever found.

The winters in Nebraska are very cold, and blizzards can cause much damage to the herds of cattle on the open plains. The summers are very hot, but the air is so dry that the climate is most healthful. The average temperature in summer is about 76 degrees and in winter about 14 degrees, though it can often drop below zero.

The plains of Nebraska were once filled with buffalo. These animals disappeared long ago because of wasteful killing for their skins and meat. Now there are only small wild animals such as the muskrat, badger, and squirrel.

Railroads and highways reach all parts of the state, and there are airports in the important cities and in many smaller towns. The Missouri River is an important means of transportation.

THE GOVERNMENT OF NEBRASKA

Nebraska, like most other states, has a Governor and a Legislature. The Governor is elected for a two-year term. The Legislature is composed of one house, the only one of its kind in the United States. This is called a *unicameral* legislature. The members are elected for a two-year term. Judges are elected for a six-year term. The capital is Lincoln. There are 93 counties.

There are about 330,000 pupils enrolled in the public elementary and high schools. Among the principal colleges and universities are:

University of Nebraska, at Lincoln. Enrollment, 19,019 in 1971 (co-ed).

Creighton University, at Omaha. Enrollment, 3,896 in 1971 (co-ed).

Municipal University of Omaha, at Omaha. Enrollment, 10,880 in 1971 (co-ed).

Nebraska Wesleyan University, at Lincoln. Enrollment, 1,200 in 1971 (co-ed).

Hastings College, at Hastings. Enrollment, 844 in 1971 (co-ed).

Union College, at Lincoln. Enrollment, 1,018 in 1971 (co-ed).

CHIEF CITIES OF NEBRASKA

The leading cities of Nebraska, with populations from the 1970 census, are:

Omaha, population 347,328, the largest city in the state. There is a separate article about OMAHA.

Lincoln, population 149,518, the state capital and second-largest city. See separate article on LINCOLN.

Grand Island, population 31,269, third-largest city, railroad center, in the south central part of the state.

Hastings, population 23,580, fourth-largest city, manufacturing center, in the southern part of the state.

NEBRASKA IN THE PAST

About two hundred years ago two Frenchmen, Pierre and Paul Mallet, traveled across the Nebraska region, and were probably the first white men to do so. Nebraska was a vast wilderness where many Indian tribes lived and hunted. For a time this region was part of the land claimed by France. Later it belonged to Spain. Finally it became part of the Louisiana Purchase, in which the United States bought a vast midwestern territory from France in 1803.

Nebraska remained unsettled for many years, except for fur-traders. The first permanent settlement was made by Americans at Bellevue in 1823. Others followed, but the region did not grow quickly because there were reports that the land was not fit for cultivation. It was known as "the Great American Desert."

Nebraska belonged to the Missouri Territory. When Missouri became a state, Nebraska was left without a government for many years. In 1854, Nebraska and Kansas were made into separate territories. Before this happened there were bitter quarrels in Congress about whether slavery should be permitted in the new territories. Finally Congress let the territories choose for themselves. Nebraska finally became a state in 1867, when slavery had been ended.

The building of the Union Pacific Railroad across Nebraska brought thousands of settlers, called "homesteaders," eager to start farms. About seventy-five years ago there was an even greater rush of people. Many people left the state because of a bad drought (dry spell) but

gradually the state became prosperous and cities grew into important industrial centers.

PLACES TO SEE IN NEBRASKA

Homestead National Monument of America, 162 acres, 4 miles west of Beatrice, in the southeast, on U.S. Route 77. Site of the first claim under the Homestead Act of 1862.

Scotts Bluff National Monument, outside Scottsbluff, in the west, on U.S. Route 26. Landmark on the Oregon Trail, used by thousands of settlers moving west.

Boys Town, ten miles west of Omaha, east of U.S. Route 6. The famous community for homeless boys founded by Father Flanagan. There is a separate article about BOYS TOWN.

The Badlands, near Crawford, in the northwest, on U.S. Route 20. Famous for its strangely shaped rock formations. Prehistoric monsters roamed through this region millions of years ago.

Chimney Rock, 2 miles south of Bayard, in the west, on U.S. Route 26. A well-known landmark on the Oregon Trail. A jagged mound of red sandstone that rises to a spire 350 feet high.

NEBRASKA. Area, 77,227 square miles. Population (1970 census) 1,483,493. Capital, Lincoln. Nickname, the Cornhusker State. Motto, Equality Before the Law. Flower, golden rod. Bird, western meadowlark. Song, none officially. Admitted to Union, March 1, 1867. Official abbreviation, Nebr. or Neb.

Nebuchadnezzar

Nebuchadnezzar was the name of two kings in the ancient country of Babylonia.

Nebuchadnezzar I ruled about three thousand years ago, but we remember the name chiefly for Nebuchadnezzar II, who ruled about five hundred years after that. Under him the old city of Babylon was rebuilt, and recently archaeologists (men who study ancient peoples) have dug up many of its palaces and temples. Nebuchadnezzar was a very religious man, and he had his people make many religious inscriptions (writings on stones, walls, and so on). These have helped scientists to learn the language of those times.

The Bible tells us more about what Nebuchadnezzar did. He twice besieged the city of Jerusalem, which had promised to be friendly to him and then had rebelled. The first time, in 597 B.C., he carried off the king and many leading citizens as prisoners. Ten years later, when Jerusalem rebelled again, he destroyed the city and deported (sent out of the country) all its people. Most of the stories about Nebuchadnezzar are in the Bible, in the books of Ezekiel, 2 Kings, Jeremiah, and Daniel. Nebuchadnezzar ruled from 605 to 562 B.C.

nebula

A nebula is a cloud of dust and gas located among the stars. Astronomers believe that there are about two million such clouds in the heavens. Those that are in the Milky Way are called *galactic nebulae;* those outside the Milky Way are called *extra-galactic.* The extra-galactic nebulae are believed to be other galaxies of stars as numerous as those in the Milky

The spiral nebula of Ursa Major looks much like a Fourth of July pinwheel.

Way. A few seem to be masses of hot gases that may be developing into clusters of stars.

There are two types of galactic nebulae: *planetary,* and *diffuse* (spread out). A planetary nebula is shaped like a large planet. It is really a large mass of gas with a bright star in the center. There are about 130 such nebulae now known, many of them trillions of miles wide and much larger than our solar system. The diffuse nebulae have irregular shapes and look like hazy patches in the heavens. Some are very bright, getting their light from near-by stars. The gases are believed to be hydrogen and helium. Some diffuse nebulae are very dark and were once thought to be holes in the sky in which there were no stars. It is now believed that these nebulae are dense areas of gas hiding millions of stars behind them. Some nebulae are so dark that they are called coal-sacks. The most famous coal-sack is one near the SOUTHERN CROSS, about which there is a separate article.

Extra-galactic nebulae are made up of tens of thousands of millions of stars so far from the earth that if you were traveling with the speed of light (186,300 miles a second) straight out into space without stopping, it would take you a million years to reach them. As a result, most of these nebulae can be seen only with the most high-powered telescopes.

Some nebulae have round shapes and are called *spherical nebulae.* Others are egg-shaped and are called *elliptical nebulae.* Still others are spiral-shaped. The spiral nebulae are often called *island universes* because they are similar to our own universe in their make-up. The Great Nebula near the constellation of Andromeda, in the northern skies, is the only spiral nebula that can be seen with the naked eye. Astronomers believe that it is traveling out into space at millions of miles an hour.

The *nebular hypothesis* is an idea thought of by the famous German philosopher Immanuel Kant and the French mathematician Pierre Simon de Laplace. According to this idea, the planets (such as our earth) were formed by the cooling of the hot nebulae given off by the sun. This idea is no longer held by astronomers. Instead it is believed that the sun, by its motion and gravitational attraction, caused large pieces of matter to fall off another body similar to the sun. This is known as the "hit-and-run theory"

and is accepted by most astronomers.

nectar

Nectar was the drink of the gods, according to Greek mythology. It was supposed to be a delicious drink that had wonderful powers. It made the gods immortal (able to live forever), and kept them always young and beautiful. Sometimes, in the stories that the Greeks told, nectar and *ambrosia* were the same thing. (Usually *ambrosia* meant the food that the gods ate.)

Nectar also refers to the sweet substance formed in flowers that the bees use to make honey.

nectarine

The nectarine is a kind of peach that has a smooth skin. It is sometimes called a smooth-skin peach. It grows on trees very much like peach trees, in the United States, Canada, and other lands. The nectarine is a very old fruit that the people of Asia enjoyed many hundreds of years ago. Now it is popular in many countries. The flesh of the fruit is juicy, and it may be reddish-yellow, white or yellow in color. You can read about the way the nectarine grows in the article on PEACH.

needle

A needle is a sharp-pointed piece of a hard material that is used to pull a softer material, such as thread, through a hole. Modern needles are made of steel wire, sharpened at one end and punched at the other end to form a hole (called the *eye*) into which the thread goes. In very ancient times, thousands of years ago, men made needles of bone, sharp thorns, and other things that were provided by nature.

The making of needles has been an important industry for about two hundred years. Until about fifty years ago, most needles were made by a process in which many things had to be done by hand. Now needles are made by automatic machines. The manufacture begins with a roll of steel wire. The machine cuts the wire into short lengths and a cutting tool comes down on each piece and stamps the eye through it. The piece then passes between grinding wheels that sharpen and polish it. At this stage it is a needle, but it must be heat-treated to harden it. It is heated in an oven and cooled very rapidly, which makes it hard and also gives it a bluish color.

Negro

A Negro is a member of the race of man that has the darkest skin color. (There are three great races of man, the Caucasoid or "white" race, the Negroid or "black" race, and the Mongoloid or "yellow" and "brown" race.) The home continent of the Negro race is Africa, where there are more than 150,000,000 Negroes.

In the United States about one out of ten persons is wholly or partly black making about 20,000,000 in all. (A person with one or more Caucasian or Mongoloid ancestors and one or more Negro ancestors is said to be partly a black). On some American islands, such as Haiti and Jamaica, most of the people are wholly or partly blacks.

Most of the blacks who live in the Uni-

ted States and in other American countries are descended from men and women who were brought to America as slaves. (see the article on SLAVERY).

About a hundred years ago, there were more than three milion black slaves in the southern states of the United States. In the northern states, slavery was not allowed. The United States split into two sections, the slave and the free states, and finally they settled their differences by fighting a great war, called the Civil War. As a result of that war, the blacks in the United States stopped being slaves, but there were still many problems to be solved before blacks could be truly equal with the white people of the United States in either capability or opportunity.

As slaves, blacks had not been given any education; in fact, several southern states had laws against teaching a black to read or write. Therefore, when they became "free," most blacks were not as well equipped to support themselves as white citizens were.

Also, as slaves the blacks had been deprived of the privilege of "selective breeding" (see EVOLUTION), so a natural upper class of aptitude and education among blacks has had to be developed in little more than 100 years as compared with thousands of years for white people. Anthropologists and other scientists have never found any evidence that the color of the skin affects a person's natural ability, and many geniuses have risen in the Negro race, but children whose parents are poverty-stricken and uneducated, as many black families in the United States are, start life under a severe disadvantage.

Prejudice has also hampered the advancement of blacks. To excuse their institution of slavery, persons in the South were taught for hundreds of years that blacks are inferior to whites, and this belief (though it has no scientific support) has continued.

Despite all these handicaps, blacks

UPI

Dr. Martin Luther King, Jr. leads the historic 1965 civil rights march from Selma to Montgomery, Alabama.

have made great advancements in the United States during the hundred-odd years since the Civil War. Thousands of blacks have become eminent as professional men — teachers, doctors, lawyers, scientists, statesmen. Many of the most prominent athletes are blacks.

In Africa, since World War II, more than twenty new nations whose people are almost wholly of the Negro race have achieved independence and self-government. The leaders of these new nations are mostly men of education and ability, but the populace is uneducated and backward compared to Europeans.

American blacks have shown increased impatience with the rate of their progress toward equality with the white majority. During the 1960s and 1970s they have usually pursued their aims peaceably and legally, through organizations dedicated to their purpose, but from time to time they use violent means, such as riots, to express their resentment.

NEGRO ASSOCIATIONS

The National Association for the Advancement of Colored People (NAACP, pronounced "N—double-A—C—P") is the oldest and largest of several organizations in the United States that try to protect the Negro. It was founded in 1909 and has about 500,000 members. The NAACP defends Negroes whose race may prevent their getting a fair trial and its lawyers have argued many cases involving Negro rights before the Supreme Court. The National Urban League, founded 1910, has tried to improve living conditions and job opportunities for Negroes in cities. The Southern Christian Leadership Council, founded in 1955 by Martin Luther King, has followed principles used in India by Mahatma Ghandi and demonstrates without violence. CORE (Congress on Racial Equality) and SNCC (Student Nonviolent Coördinating Committee) have somewhat younger members. The Black Muslims, who adopt the Mohammedan religion, say that Negroes and Whites should be enemies and should not be integrated.

Nehru, Jawaharlal and Indira

Jawaharlal Nehru helped India win independence from Britain in 1947 and was prime minister, or head, of the Indian government until his death in 1964.

Jawaharlal Nehru was born in 1889 in Allahabad, a city in north India. He was of a wealthy family and grew up with many advantages that most boys in India did not have. He was educated at first by private tutors, but when he was 16 his family took him to  England, where he attended Harrow school, one of the most famous boys' schools there. Later he went to Cambridge University and to the most famous law school in England, the Inner Temple.

He went back to India in 1912 to become a lawyer, and he traveled all over India making speeches and stirring up the people to resist the British government. Because of this he was put in jail by the British government in 1922, 1930, 1932,

and 1934. Meanwhile he became a close friend of Mahatma Gandhi, who was the leader of India's largest political party, called the Indian National Congress. This party was working for Indian independence, and Nehru was elected its president in 1929 and several times later.

During World War II, Nehru went to jail again for resisting the British government, but he was released in 1945. As head of the Indian government, he was often unfriendly toward Pakistan, and at times war seemed possible. Nehru called himself "neutral" in the quarrels between the Communist countries and the democratic countries.

Nehru wrote many letters to his daughter, Indira, when he was in jail and she was a little girl. Some of these letters were collected and published in 1936 in a book entitled *Glimpses of World History*. In 1966, Indira Nehru Gandhi, 48 years old and the widow of Feroze Gandhi, unrelated to the mahatma, became prime minister of India, the first woman to head so large a nation.

Nelson, Horatio

Horatio Nelson was an English admiral, the greatest naval hero of England. He was born in 1758, entered the British Navy when he was 12 years old, and was made a captain at the age of 21.

Nelson was a man of great ability and daring in the series of wars that followed the French Revolution, beginning in 1793, and the Napoleonic Wars. Nelson was placed in command of the British warship *Agamemnon* in the Mediterranean Sea. He fought an engagement at Calvi and lost his right eye. After that, he wore a black patch over the eye.

Nelson sometimes achieved victory by acting independently of his superiors. This happened in a battle with the French and Spanish off Cape St. Vincent. As a reward for the victory, he was made an admiral and given the Order of the Bath. Not long after, in 1797, he fought an engagement off Santa Cruz, Spain, in which he lost his right arm.

One of Nelson's greatest victories over the French took place in 1798 at the Battle of the Nile, which was fought off Aboukir, Egypt, at the mouth of the Nile River. The French fleet lay at anchor in the harbor and was protected by shore guns. Any ships that wished to attack had to pass by dangerous rocks in the harbor. Nelson skillfully led his fleet into the harbor during the night, and although outnumbered, beat the French force of seventeen ships severely. Only two French ships escaped. Nelson was made Baron Nelson of the Nile in recognition of this victory. After that he was Lord Nelson.

In Naples, Italy, Nelson met Emma, Lady Hamilton, wife of the British ambassador there, and even though he was married, he fell deeply in love with her. Later, Nelson separated from his wife and Lady Hamilton from her husband.

In 1801, Nelson was second in command of an attack on the Danish fleet off Copenhagen. The battle was not going well for the British and Nelson was signaled to break off the action. The story is told that Nelson, putting his telescope to his blind eye, said that he could not see the signal, and then proceeded to continue the battle, which he won. Actually,

Nelson had the right to make this decision. For this victory Nelson was made a viscount.

In 1803, Nelson was in charge of a fleet that had been ordered to keep the French bottled up at Toulon, in France. He succeeded in doing this for almost two years, but in March, 1805, Admiral Villeneuve, the French commander, managed to get his fleet out. Nelson chased him back and forth across the Atlantic and finally caught up with him and the Spanish fleet in October off Cape Trafalgar, Spain, in the Atlantic. Nelson ordered his flagship, the Victory, to run up the signal, "England expects that every man will do his duty." His fleet won a great victory that probably forced Napoleon to cancel plans to invade England. But the battle was a costly one, for Nelson was mortally wounded. As he lay dying, with the thought of Lady Hamilton on his mind, he said, "Poor Emma, what will become of her now." Then, turning to his second in command, he said, "Kiss me, Hardy," and died.

All England went into mourning for its hero, and he was buried in St. Paul's Cathedral, in London. Later, in London, a statue of him was placed on a column, called Nelson's Column, in Trafalgar Square, named for the great battle.

Even today, over one hundred and fifty years later, this eighteen foot high statue serves as a memorial to one of the most famous of all British naval heroes. In England today, the people still celebrate Trafalgar Day in honor of Admiral Nelson's last victory at sea.

Nemesis

Nemesis was the ancient Greek goddess who punished those who made the gods angry.

neon

Neon is rare gas that is found in the air. It is a chemical element, which means it is one of the 103 basic substances of which the world is made. Neon is used in the glass tubes that make the letters and numbers of advertising signs. It conducts electricity seventy-five times as well as air, and when an electric current is sent into one of the neon-filled glass tubes, the neon glows with a bright orange-red color. The other colors that you see in the glass tubes of signs are made by mixing neon with small amounts of other gases. The orange-red light of neon can be seen through fog better than light of any other color, so glass tubes of glowing neon are used at airports as markers and guides for pilots when they take off and land their planes in the fog.

Of every million parts of air, only eighteen parts are neon. It is obtained by distilling liquid air. Neon is an inert gas, which means that it cannot be made to combine with any other chemical element. It is also called a "noble" gas because, just as nobles at one time held themselves apart from the rest of the people, neon remains apart from the other elements. Neon was discovered in 1898 by the English scientists William Ramsay and M. W. Travers. A French scientist, Georges Claude, was the first man to use neon in an advertising sign, in 1913.

Nepal

Nepal is a small kingdom in the Himalaya Mountains in south central Asia. It is about 54,000 square miles in size, about the size of Iowa, and about ten million people live there, which is more than three times the population of Iowa. The capital is Katmandu, a city of about 200,000, in which there are several beautiful Buddhist temples.

Most of the people of Nepal follow the Hindu religion, though many follow Buddhism. They speak the Nepali language, which resembles languages of Tibet and Burma and is related to Chinese. Very few can read and write, but education is increasing. The largest group of people is the GURKHAS, about whom there is a separate article.

Nepal has many mountains, and on the border between Nepal and Tibet is Mount Everest, the highest mountain in the world.

Most of the people of Nepal are farmers. They live on the lower parts of mountains and in the Nepal Valley, which runs through the center of the country. They grow rice, jute, oranges, and potatoes, much of which is sent to India. Timber is taken from the great forests, and many visitors go to Nepal to hunt the wild animals found in its jungles. These include elephants, tigers, leopards, rhinoceroses, and other big game animals. In recent years Nepal has built some factories that produce textiles, soap, chemicals, and other products. The mines yield quartz, mica, salt, and graphite.

Railroads, airlines and a highway link Nepal with India, with which it has close ties. Nepal was formerly governed by a parliament and prime minister, but in 1960 the king seized the reins of power and the country is now ruled by a Council of Ministers with the king as its chairman. In 1962 a new constitution provided for a National Assembly. Nepal is a member of the United Nations.

NEPAL. Area, 54,054 square miles. Population (1964 estimate) 9,900,000. Language, Nepali. Religion, principally Hindu. Government, constitutional monarchy. Monetary unit, Nepalese rupee, worth about 14 cents (U.S.).

Neptune

Neptune was the god of the sea in Roman mythology, the stories told thousands of years ago about gods and goddesses. In Greek mythology his name was Poseidon. Although he was very powerful, Neptune was not as mighty as his brother, Jupiter, the king of all the gods. Sometimes Neptune and Jupiter had terrible battles and sometimes they helped each other.

Neptune made his home in the sea and was the special ruler of the Mediterranean. He controlled the clouds and could make terrible storms and earthquakes. Neptune watched over ships and sailors, and he ruled all of the gods and goddesses who lived in the sea. Neptune was married to Amphitrite and they had three sons.

Neptune created the horse and taught the art of horsemanship. He is usually shown in pictures holding a spear with three points, called a *trident*. He rode in a chariot that was pulled by sea monsters. The ancient Romans held horse and chariot races in honor of Neptune, and horses were sometimes sacrificed in his honor.

Neptune

Neptune is the fourth-largest planet in the solar system. The planets, including the earth, revolve around the sun. Neptune is approximately 17 times heavier than the earth and about 4½ times wider, with a diameter of 33,000 miles.

It takes Neptune nearly 165 years to make one complete turn about the sun, compared to 365 days for the earth. However, it takes Neptune only 15 hours and 48 minutes to make one complete revolution on its axis, compared to 24 hours for the earth.

Neptune is almost 2,800,000,000 miles away from the sun, more than thirty times as far as the earth is. This explains why the temperature on Neptune is 350 degrees below zero on the Fahrenheit scale. Large amounts of methane (a gas found in swamps on earth) surround Neptune. The low temperatures and lack of oxygen are the reasons why scientists believe it impossible for life as we know it to exist on Neptune.

Neptune has two moons, or satellites, that revolve around it as the moon does around the earth. They are called Triton and Nereid, which were names in Greek mythology.

Neptune is the only planet whose position in the heavens was predicted even before the planet itself was discovered. In 1781, astronomers accidentally discovered the planet Uranus. They observed that Uranus was not moving around the sun according to the laws of planetary motion. They guessed that there was another large body near Uranus that was causing this disturbance. Two astronomers, John Couch Adams of England and Urbain J. Leverrier of France, predicted the path of this unobserved body. In 1846, Neptune was finally located in the heavens on the basis of these predictions.

Nero

Nero was a powerful and wicked emperor of ancient Rome. He was born  almost two thousand years ago, in the year 37. His full name was Nero Claudius Caesar. When he was 17 years old, Nero became emperor. For a few years, things went well because Nero's teacher, Seneca, a great Roman philosopher and writer of plays, guided him. After that, Nero began to do many evil things. He put his wife Octavia and his mother to death. He then married Poppaea, who is said to have encouraged him to do many of the wicked things he is remembered for.

One of the best-known stories about Nero tells that he set fire to the city of Rome, and played the violin while it burned ("fiddled while Rome burned"), but scholars now do not believe that Nero did either of these things. However, there was a great fire in the year 64. When the great fire was over almost the whole city was destroyed. Nero blamed this disaster on the Christians and he had many of them put to death, in very cruel ways. Nero then built up the city of Rome again.

Finally people could not stand the wickedness of Nero and formed a plot to

overthrow him. Nero discovered the plot and this gave him an opportunity to kill more people. He ordered his old teacher, Seneca, put to death, along with other great Romans.

After this Nero, who was fond of sports and music traveled to Greece to enter contests there. He won many prizes.

When Nero returned to Rome, the people of Gaul, Spain, and Rome revolted and Nero had to flee from the city. The Roman Senate condemned him to death, and soldiers were sent to arrest him. When the soldiers arrived, Nero ordered one of his former slaves to kill him. He died in the year 68, when he was 31 years old.

nervous system

The nervous system is the control and message system of the human body. It is like a great telephone network. The central switchboard of the network is the brain and the spinal cord that runs through the backbone. The nerves are the telephone wires that run from the brain and spinal cord to all parts of the body, and carry messages to and fro.

Man has a more complicated and highly developed nervous system than any other animal.

NERVE CELLS

The nervous system, like other parts of the human body, is made up of millions of tiny cells. These cells are the building blocks of the human body. Nerve cells are like other cells in the body—blood cells, muscle cells, skin cells—because they have a central part called a nucleus and an outer very thin covering called a membrane. But they differ from other cells in the body, because they look different and because they do a different job. Unlike other cells, a nerve cell has several whip-like arms growing out from its center.

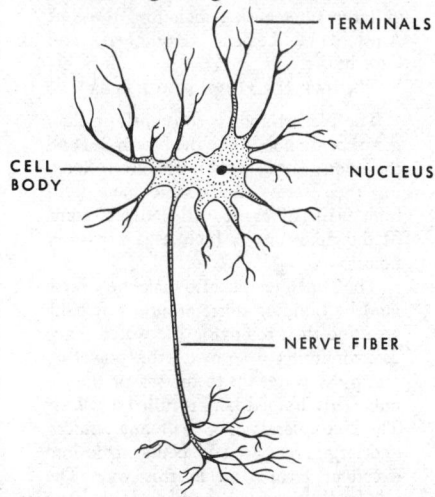

NERVE CELLS (NEURONS)

The nerve cell, or neuron, is the basic unit of work in the nervous system. The terminals pick up messages from other neurons, and pass them along the nerve fiber to the next nerve cell. In this way the messages are transmitted to the brain. It sounds like a long process, but takes only a small part of a second.

One of these arms is usually much longer than the others, and in some nerve cells this threadlike extension may be two or three feet long. This long nerve thread is actually the message-carrying wire of a nerve cell. Millions of nerve cells, joined together in a connecting chain, carry mes-

sages from the brain and spinal cord to all parts of the human body.

HOW THE NERVOUS SYSTEM WORKS

If you come near or touch a plant, nothing will seem to happen. If you come near or touch an animal, the animal will move or show some sign of irritability. Irritability is a word scientists use to describe what happens when something that has life in it becomes bothered by something that happens or is done to it. Irritability is present in animals and not in plants, because an animal has a nervous system and a plant does not.

The nervous system works because the irritability produced in one nerve cell is almost immediately transferred to its neighbor and so on down a whole chain of nerve cells. Scientists have not yet found out everything about the workings of the nerve cells and the nervous system, but they do know that something very much like electricity passes through the nervous system. A tiny electrical charge is passed from the long thread of one nerve cell to one of the shorter threads of the next nerve cell, and so on.

TWO KINDS OF NERVE

When you talk with someone on the telephone, your voice and the other person's voice travel on the same wire, but this is not true of the wires or nerves in your body. The nerves in your body are

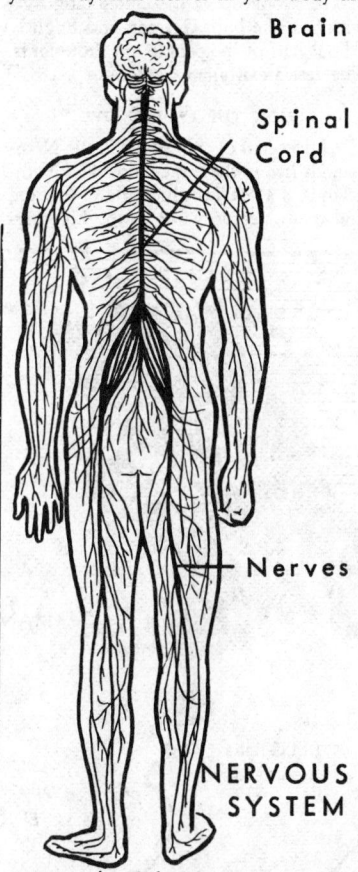

one-way wires—they can carry a message only in one direction, either to the brain or spinal cord or from the brain or spinal cord. Since the brain and spinal cord are connected by nerves with all parts of the body, it is necessary that there be two different nerves connecting the brain and spinal cord with each different part of the body. The nerves that carry the messages from a part of the body to the brain

are called *sensory nerves*. The nerves that carry a message from the brain and spinal cord to other parts of the body are called *motor nerves*. Sensory nerves tell the brain what is going on inside and around the body. Motor nerves from the brain and the spinal cord tell the different parts of the body what to do. Everything you see, hear, feel, taste or smell is carried to the brain by sensory nerves. Every movement you make, no matter in what part of your body, is caused by a message carried to your muscles by motor nerves.

Suppose your finger accidentally touched a hot pot on the stove. Immediately the sensory nerve leading from your finger to your spinal cord would send a message. At the spinal cord, the message would jump over to the motor nerve leading to the muscle nerve of your hand and your hand would jerk away from the hot pot. This is a very simple action called a *reflex,* but other things would probably happen at almost the same time. Through the marvelous network of nerves you would almost immediately bring your other hand over to grab the burned hand, you would probably cry out in pain, and perhaps tears would come to your eyes.

TWO NERVOUS SYSTEMS

Just as there are two kinds of nerve, motor and sensory, there are two kinds of nervous system in your body. One is a *voluntary* nervous system that controls all the actions of which we are conscious —that is, those actions which we are able to control. These include most of the movements of our hands and legs and mouths. The second system operates within our bodies without our even knowing about it. This system is called the *involuntary,* or *autonomic,* nervous system. This system controls the beating of our hearts, our breathing, and our digestion. Most of the voluntary nervous system is controlled by the spinal cord, plus some parts of the brain. The higher parts of our body, such as our mouths, are controlled high up in the spinal cord. Thus when we chew we are under the control of a high point on the spinal cord. Our feet, on the other hand, are controlled by the lowest control point on the spinal cord.

The involuntary nervous system is mostly controlled by that portion of the brain called the *brain stem,* or *medulla oblongata,* which leads from the base of the brain itself to the top of the spinal cord. This part of the nervous system, like the brain and the spinal cord, is very well protected. Only a severe blow at the back of the head or neck can damage this brain stem. Sometimes a person who falls backward and strikes his head on a sharp point or object will die instantly because the brain stem has been severely injured, thus stopping breathing and the motion of the heart.

DEVELOPING THE NERVOUS SYSTEM

We are born with complete nervous systems, but the nervous system must grow and develop just as bones and muscles do. As a baby grows, things that were very difficult for him to do become easier. This is because the nervous system has become trained to do and understand different things. The brain begins to develop and to store up information and memories and begins to be able to make more and

more decisions and judgments. In some ways, training the nervous system is like beating a path through a field or a forest. The more you walk along a certain path, the smoother it becomes. The same sort of thing happens when you learn to play the piano. At first it seems almost impossible; your fingers are not used to striking the keys, you cannot remember the notes, everything seems to be jumbled up. The more you study, the more you practice, the more you play, the easier it becomes. This is because you are training the part of the nervous system that controls the many movements of your fingers and the memory of the notes to be played. Every skill that a person has comes because he has practiced and trained his nervous system to do the same thing over and over until it becomes almost an automatic and simple act.

DISEASES OF THE NERVOUS SYSTEM

Most people are never troubled by any disease or injury to their nervous system. Some older people develop painful conditions caused by irritation of some part of the nervous system. One such disease is called *sciatica*. This is a very painful condition of the leg caused by an injury or irritation to the large sciatic nerve that runs down through the leg.

When a nerve is injured, pinched, or cut entirely, something very serious happens to the part of the body through which the injured nerve runs. Feeling in a particular part of the body may be lost because the sensory nerve from that part of the body to the spinal cord is either damaged or destroyed by injury. Control of some part of the body may be lost because the motor nerve in that case is damaged or destroyed. What we call *paralysis* is the result of damage to a motor nerve or to that part of the spinal cord to which the motor nerve runs.

Doctors know what causes the various nerve diseases and injuries, and the different kinds of paralysis, but they do not know how to repair or replace injured or destroyed nerves. Perhaps someday they will be able to do even this, and then persons whose lives seem hopelessly affected by paralysis will be able to move around freely and do all the things that a normal person is able to do.

nests are the homes that some animals build: see the article BIRD.

Netherlands

The Netherlands is a small but rich country in northwestern Europe. It is on the North Sea. Most people in other countries call the country Holland, and the people who live there are known as the Dutch. The people of the Netherlands refer to themselves as Hollanders or Netherlanders.

The Netherlands is part of the Low Countries, which include Belgium and Luxembourg. The Netherlands is a flat country with no mountains and only a few hills, in the southeast. More than half the country is below sea level. Once in a while the Netherlands suffers from great floods.

In both area—15,450 square miles—and population, about twelve million people, the Netherlands is just about twice as large as the state of New Jersey.

WHAT THE PEOPLE ARE LIKE

The Dutch people are serious and hard-working. They have had to be, to make their country prosper as it has. If they had not worked and built to keep out the sea, much of the country would have become a great swamp.

The Dutch people are known for their cleanliness and neatness. In the cities, the people dress very much like people in America. In the country, some people wear a kind of costume that has been worn in their villages for centuries. Many farm people wear wooden shoes, called *klompen,* which make walking in the muddy Dutch soil easier. They do not wear their wooden shoes indoors. They leave them outside the door when they come into the house.

The Dutch are a strong and healthy people. They are hearty eaters and love food. Thick pea soup is a favorite dish, and so is meat. Vegetables are usually served mashed together with potatoes. The milk, cheese and butter of the Netherlands are noted for their excellence.

The Dutch people also love flowers, and keep them in vases and pots all through the house.

The people speak the Dutch language, which is like both German and English. About half of the people are Protestants. The rest are Roman Catholics.

HOW THE PEOPLE LIVE

Almost half of the people in the Netherlands live in the large cities. The Netherlands is a leading shipbuilding nation, and many people work in the big ship-

building yards at Amsterdam and Rotterdam. Others work in factories that make steel products, electrical products (especially radios), chemicals, textiles (cloth), and ceramics (pottery and dishes). One of the most important industries in the

Netherlands is food-processing, the making of dairy products and the canning of meats, vegetables, and fruits. The Netherlands is famous for its Gouda, Edam and Leiden cheese.

Many of the people are farmers. They make good use of land reclaimed from the water, and grow potatoes, grains, vegetables and fruits in large quantities. Many raise fine dairy cattle. Their Frisian cattle are famous. Farmers also grow large crops of tomatoes, grapes, cucumbers, and lettuce, in hothouses.

The flower-growers of the Netherlands are world-famous. They grow tremendous quantities of bulbs, particularly tulip bulbs, and ship them to countries all over the world. A most beautiful sight each spring is the flowering bulb fields between the cities of Haarlem and Leiden. Aalsmeer is a famous auction center for hothouse flowers.

A number of the people are fishermen. They catch herring and oysters. Others work in the coal and salt mines.

Although the Dutch people are serious, they also have many holidays and celebrations. The *kermis* is a carnival at which the people can enjoy games and rides as Americans do in an amusement park. One of the favorite sports in the Netherlands is ice-skating. A favorite team sport is soccer.

Almost everybody in the Netherlands has a bicycle. Children go to school on them and women go shopping on them. Even a bank president may step out of his office and go off on his bicycle to make a call. The Dutch are very skillful riders, and often two or three couples can be seen riding along the street on their bicycles, with their arms linked.

Everyone has to go to school between the ages of 6 and 15. There are a number of large universities, including those at Amsterdam, Leiden, Groningen, and Utrecht.

WHAT KIND OF A PLACE IT IS

The Netherlands is constantly in danger of being flooded by the North Sea and the rivers. To keep the water from flooding their farms, the people have built high walls of earth, called dikes. Some of the dikes are as high as a two-story house.

The Dutch people also make new farm land by building dikes around a marshy area and then removing the water. They use windmills to provide the power to pump the water up to the sea or the canals. This drained land is called a *polder*. The Netherlands now has many polders, and large areas are still being made into excellent farm land in this way. The windmills have been replaced in many regions by large electrical pumping plants.

Windmills can still be seen all through the Netherlands. They are used not only for pumping water, but also to grind grain and to saw timber.

The Netherlands has many rivers and canals. Many ships sail on them, carrying goods from one town to another. This is much cheaper than sending things by train or by truck. The country is crossed by the Rhine, Meuse (Maas) and Waal rivers. The Netherlands also has many railroads and good roads. Schiphol Airport near Amsterdam is one of the busiest in Europe.

Netherlands Inform. Service

More than three hundred bridges cross the canals of Amsterdam, capital of the Netherlands. Small boats move along the canals while cars drive on either side.

Some of the cities of the Netherlands are among the most important ports in Europe. Millions of tons of goods are handled in the harbors of Amsterdam and Rotterdam, as well as in smaller ports.

The climate of the Netherlands is damp and chilly. The temperature in winter is about 35 degrees, and in summer about 70 degrees.

CHIEF CITIES IN THE NETHERLANDS

The leading cities of the Netherlands, with 1960 estimated populations are:

Amsterdam, population 869,602, the capital and largest city in the Netherlands. There is a separate article about AMSTERDAM.

Rotterdam, population 729,852, the second-largest city. There is a separate article about ROTTERDAM.

The Hague, population 606,110, the third-largest city and seat of government. There is a separate article about The HAGUE.

Utrecht, population 254,186, the fourth-largest city, a railroad center, in the central part of the country.

Haarlem, population 169,215, the fifth-largest city. Center of largest bulb-growing area.

HOW THE PEOPLE ARE GOVERNED

The Netherlands is a constitutional monarchy, which means that it has a king or queen, a parliament that makes the laws, and a written constitution that protects the rights of the people.

The ruler of the Netherlands is Queen Juliana. The parliament is composed of two houses, the First Chamber and the Second Chamber. The First Chamber is like the United States Senate. It has 75 members who are elected for a six-year term. The Second Chamber is like the United States House of Representatives. It has 150 members who are elected for a four-year term. Judges are appointed for life by the Queen. The country is divided into 11 provinces. The capital is Amsterdam. The Netherlands is a member of the European Economic Community.

THE NETHERLANDS IN THE PAST

More than a thousand years ago, the Low Countries, which included what is now the Netherlands, were ruled by the French emperor Charlemagne. Five hundred years later it became part of Burgundy. The Dutch merchants grew wealthy and powerful at this time, as shippers and traders. But then the Netherlands came under the stern and harsh rule of the Spanish. The people, led by William of Orange, revolted, and after a struggle of eighty years they finally won their independence. In 1648, the Republic of the United Provinces was established.

In the 17th century, the United Provinces grew in power and in wealth, and Dutch trading ships visited all parts of the world. They founded rich colonies in the East Indies and other parts of the world. This period is known as the "Golden Age" because some of the great Dutch painters lived and worked at that time, and because the nation was rich and powerful. Among the painters were Rembrandt, Frans Hals, Vermeer, and Ruysdael. Craftsmen of this period also produced beautiful china and glassware.

In the years that followed, the power of the Netherlands declined. The country fought several wars and finally came under French rule in 1795, when it was conquered by Napoleon. After Napoleon's downfall in 1815, the Kingdom of the Netherlands, which included Belgium, was created. In 1830, Belgium set up its own government.

In World War I, the Netherlands remained neutral. After that war, one of the most important projects was begun when the government decided to drain the water from the large Zuider Zee and make it into farm land. (There is a separate article about the ZUIDER ZEE.) Thousands of acres, once under water, have been turned into farm areas.

During World War II, the Netherlands was invaded and occupied by the Germans. The people formed an underground movement and in many ways quietly fought the Germans. The Dutch underground was of great help to the Allies when they finally liberated the country in 1945. The country was badly damaged in the war, and afterward lost its empire in the East Indies. (See the article on INDONESIA.)

In 1948 Queen Wilhelmina retired from the throne, in favor of her daughter JULIANA, about whom there is a separate article.

THE NETHERLANDS. Area, 15,765 square miles. Population (1964 estimate) 12,127,000. Language, Dutch. Religion, Protestant and Roman Catholic. Government, constitutional monarchy. Monetary unit, the guilder, worth 27½ cents (U.S.). Flag, three horizontal stripes, red, white, and blue.

nettle

Nettles are weeds that grow wild in most parts of the United States, Canada, and other countries. Some kinds grow on waste land or rocky soil; others grow in the woods. Nettles have rough, hollow hairs over the surface of their stems and leaves. When a passerby brushes lightly against these spiny hairs, the tips break and release a stinging fluid called formic acid that irritates the skin. This causes a burning rash that lasts for several hours. If a nettle is grasped firmly, pressing the spiny hairs flat so that the ends do not pierce the skin, it does not cause any irritation. Wilted nettles are often used as fodder for cattle, and some can be eaten cooked, although few people like the flavor.

neuritis

Neuritis is a disease in which one or more of the nerves in the body become inflamed. It is very painful, but with proper treatment it may not be very serious. The inflamed nerve causes a burning sensation and the skin often becomes reddened. This may cause the part of the body supplied by the nerve to become numb. A common form of neuritis is called *sciatica,* an inflammation of the nerve that runs along the back of the leg.

There is one form of neuritis in which all of the nerves become inflamed. This is not common but it is very serious. The fingers and feet become numb and tingle. The person may feel hot, and then suddenly cold. He may have a slight fever and may begin to feel pain in his muscles. This type of neuritis is called general neuritis. If the person does not receive proper treatment he may become paralyzed.

Doctors do not know exactly what causes neuritis. It seems to occur when a person has been ill and is weak and run down, or when he does not eat enough of the proper foods, especially foods that contain vitamin B. (Vitamin B is in meat, eggs, cheese, and bread.)

The countryside in the Netherlands is quite flat, and windmills frequently stretch across the horizon.

People who work in jobs where they are exposed to certain chemicals, such as lead and arsenic, may develop neuritis.

Sometimes a nerve causes severe pain although it is not actually inflamed. This condition is called *neuralgia*. Neuralgia can be very painful but it is not so serious. Doctors have many drugs that can help relieve neuralgia and neuritis.

neurosis or **psychoneurosis**, a kind of mental disturbance: see the article MENTAL ILLNESS.

neutrality

When a war is going on, a country that is not taking part in the war is said to be *neutral*. A neutral nation is supposed to be impartial—is not supposed to help either side.

A neutral nation may continue to trade with a warring nation, but it is not supposed to sell the warring nation any weapons or munitions or other war supplies. Such supplies are called *contraband of war*. If a ship of a warring nation stops a neutral ship on the seas, and finds contraband on the neutral ship, it may take the contraband without paying for it. In modern warfare, almost anything is considered contraband because food and clothing and other peacetime supplies are almost as important as munitions to a nation at war. Sometimes a warring nation declares a BLOCKADE (about which there is a separate article). This means it will consider anything shipped to its enemy as contraband, and will also seize the neutral ship that carries the contraband.

If a warship of a warring country enters a neutral port, or if a plane of a warring country lands on neutral territory, the neutral country is supposed to keep the ship or plane and its crew under guard so that they cannot reënter the war. This is called *interning* them.

During World War II, some countries stayed out of the war and still were not neutral, because they favored one side or the other. Such countries called themselves nonbelligerent, which means "not fighting." Italy did not enter the war during the first few months, but was on the side of Germany. Spain never entered the war, but was on the side of Germany. Both these countries called themselves nonbelligerents.

Nevada

Nevada is a state in the Great Basin of the United States. Its nickname is the "Silver State" because of rich deposits of silver in the mountains. It is also called the "Sagebrush State" because sagebrush is one of the most familiar sights in the Nevada deserts. The state gets its name from a Spanish word meaning "snow-clad." The name was first given to the Sierra Nevada Mountains because of their beautiful snow-capped peaks.

In area, Nevada ranks 7th in size among the states, with 110,540 square miles. In the 1960 census Nevada had only 285,000 people, the smallest population of any state except Alaska. Since then its population has been growing, and in 1970 it had 488,738 people and ranked 48th in population.

Nevada became a state in 1864, and it was the 36th state to be admitted to the United States. The capital is Carson City.

Las Vegas News Bureau

Red Rock Canyon recreation area, just west of Las Vegas, Nevada.

THE PEOPLE OF NEVADA

The first white settlers in the Nevada region were the Mormons, a religious group. They started farms and trading posts over a hundred years ago. After the rich silver and gold mines were discovered in 1859, people from all over America and Europe flocked to the region. Miners came from England, Ireland, and Scotland. People from Germany, France, Italy, and the Scandinavian countries came later to work in the forests and to start farms and ranches. Today most of the people are American-born, and about five thousand Indians live on reservations.

Mining used to be the main occupation of the people of Nevada. Many people still are miners, though the mining of silver is no longer so important. The people now mine chiefly copper, zinc, gold, and tungsten. One of the most valuable minerals found in Nevada is uranium.

Many people are farmers, but the land is so dry that almost all of it has to be irrigated for any crops to grow. The Nevada soil is best suited for growing hay and alfalfa. It is better for cattle-raising than for crops. There are huge cattle and sheep ranches in the mountain valleys, where the bunch grass is excellent for grazing.

Only a small number of people work in the cities. There are few important manufactures in Nevada. Nevada is the only state in which it is legal to gamble with dice and other gambling implements, and there are many "gambling houses" where this is a business. The state taxes gambling houses, but most people think the gambling has done the state more harm than good. Nevada laws also make it very easy to get a divorce there, and this attracts many visitors. Many people work in hotels, resorts, and dude ranches to which the visitors go.

The largest religious groups in Nevada are the Roman Catholics and the Mormons (Latter Day Saints).

WHAT NEVADA IS LIKE

Nevada lies almost entirely in the Great Basin, where there is very little rain. Nevada is the driest state in the country. It is a mountainous region, and is covered with deserts, large mountain ranges, and valleys. There are many beautiful canyons and lakes, but some of the lakes are so shallow that they dry up in

Nevada State Highway Dept.

Above: The Nevada capitol in Carson City. *Below:* Hoover Dam on the Arizona-Nevada border.

the hot summer sun, leaving hard, sun-baked mud. Lake Tahoe, on the border beween Nevada and California, is one of the most beautiful lakes in the United States. Most of the rivers have no outlets to the sea, and flow only during the rainy season.

In the western part of Nevada are the beautiful Sierra Nevada Mountains, the highest part of the state. The beautiful mountain scenery, and the many dude ranches and hot springs have made Nevada a very popular vacation place. Las Vegas, with its many resorts and hotels, has become important as a place of entertainment.

The temperature varies greatly. In the mountains, the winters are long and cold. In the deserts and low valleys, the winters are short and mild, and the summers long and hot. The average temperature in winter is about 31 degrees, and in summer about 73 degrees.

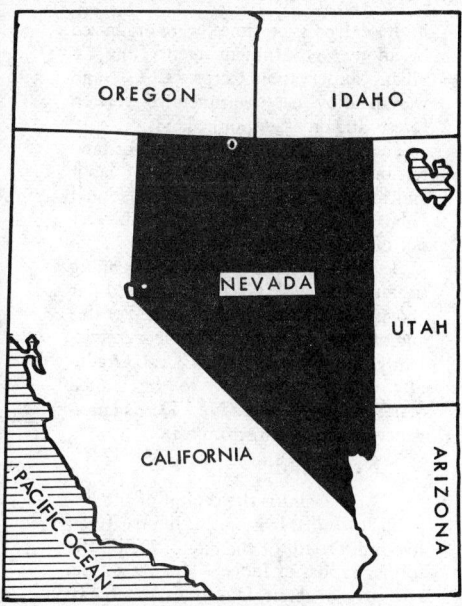

Many hunters go to Nevada. There are deer, beavers, muskrats, and raccoons, and many wild game birds.

Transportation in Nevada was difficult for a long time because it was so hard to cross the deserts and mountains. Today railroads and paved roads reach most parts of the state, and there are airports in the important cities.

THE GOVERNMENT OF NEVADA

Nevada, like most other states, has a Governor and a Legislature. The Governor is elected for a four-year term. The Legislature is composed of two houses, a Senate and an Assembly. It meets in Carson City, the capital. The members of the Senate are elected for a four-year term. The members of the Assembly are elected for a two-year term. Judges are elected for a six-year term. There are 17 counties.

There are about 123,000 pupils enrolled in the public elementary and high schools. There are several universities including the University of Nevada, at Reno, with an enrollment of 6,682 in 1971.

Reno Chamber of Commerce

Chief Thunderface, a full chief tribal medicine man of the Paiute Indians, is from Nevada's Pyramid Lake reservation, which is thirty miles from Reno.

CHIEF CITIES OF NEVADA

The leading cities of Nevada, with populations from the 1970 census, are:

Las Vegas, population 125,787, the largest city, resort center in the southeastern part of the state. There is a separate article about LAS VEGAS.

Reno, population 72,863, second-largest city in the state. There is a separate article about RENO.

Sparks, population 24,187, third-largest city, railroad division point, in the western part of the state.

Carson City, population 15,468, the state capital and seventh-largest city. There is a separate article about CARSON CITY.

NEVADA IN THE PAST

Only occasional fur-trappers and travelers on their way west had entered Nevada until 1843, when an expedition led by John C. Frémont surveyed Nevada and mapped out the region. His information was of great use to the Mormons, who made the first permanent settlement in the Carson River Valley in 1849.

In 1859 silver was discovered in the famous Comstock Lode. Almost overnight, miners poured in from all over the country. Virginia City became a booming mine town. Immigrants from Europe swelled the population, and within two years Nevada became a separate territory. For many years the Comstock Lode was the richest silver-mining center in the world.

During the Civil War, the Union needed another anti-slavery state to support certain amendments to the Constitution urged by President Abraham Lincoln, so in 1864 Nevada was made a state. The wealth from the Comstock Lode was also of great use to the Union during the Civil War.

As the output from the Comstock Lode declined, many people left Nevada. In the early 1900s many new and valuable mines were discovered and the state again prospered. Cities grew and farmers learned to use irrigation to help them grow crops. In World Wars I and II, the minerals from Nevada mines were of great importance to the armed forces. The southern Nevada deserts have been used for atomic bomb experiments.

PLACES TO SEE IN NEVADA

Lehman Caves National Monument, 640 acres, about 45 miles southeast of Ely, in the east, on U.S. Routes 6 and 50. Caverns with many tunnels and strange formations.

Death Valley National Monument, of which 115,240 acres lie in Nevada, 105 miles northwest of Las Vegas, on U.S. Route 95. Vast desert, extensive salt beds, strange and beautiful scenery.

Boulder (Hoover) Dam Recreational Center, 679,000 acres, 20 miles east of Las Vegas, in the southeast, on U.S. Route 95. Popular vacation spot; includes Hoover Dam, beautiful Lake Mead, and the gorges of the Colorado River.

Pyramid Lake, 31 miles long, 7 to 10 miles wide, 30 miles north of Reno, in the northwest, on State Highway 33. The largest body of water entirely inside Nevada; rocky peaks that look like the ancient pyramids of Egypt rise out of the water.

Copper Pit, at Ruth, in the east, on U.S. Route 6. One of the largest open-pit copper mines in the world.

NEVADA. Area, 110,540 square miles. Population (1970 census) 488,738. Capital, Carson City. Nickname, the Silver State. Motto, All for Our Country. Emblem, sagebrush. Bird, mountain bluebird. Song, "Home Means Nevada to Me." Admitted to Union as 36th state October 31, 1864. Official abbreviation, Nev.

Newark

Newark is the largest city in the state of New Jersey. It is on the Passaic River and Newark Bay, eight miles west of New York City. Newark is one of the most important industrial centers in the United States, and nearly 400,000 people live there. The people make a great many different products, including electrical equipment, paint, machinery, leather goods, chemicals, and food products. Newark is also one of the biggest insurance centers in the country.

Newark is an important port, with a fine harbor. It is connected to New York City by bus, railroad, and a subway, known as the Hudson Tube. Newark has several important colleges; the best-known is a branch of Rutgers University. Many people live in beautiful suburbs surrounding the city. Among the most famous of these suburbs are the ones called "the Oranges."

Newark was settled in 1666 by Puritans who came from Connecticut. During the Revolutionary War, General George Washington used Newark as a supply base. In the past hundred years, Newark has grown rapidly into one of the most important commercial cities in the United States.

NEWARK, NEW JERSEY. Population (1970 census) 382,417. County seat of Essex County. Airport, seaport on the Passaic River and Newark Bay. Settled in 1666.

New Brunswick

New Brunswick is one of the maritime provinces of Canada. It is on the eastern coast. It ranks eighth in size among the provinces, with 28,354 square miles. In population it also ranks eighth in Canada, with more than six hundred thousand people living there. New Brunswick became a province of the Dominion of Canada in 1867. The capital is Fredericton.

A large number of the people of New Brunswick are French Canadians, and they still speak French. Many others are of English and Scottish descent. About half the people belong to the Roman Catholic Church, and most of the others

belong to the United Church of Canada.

About half the people of New Brunswick are farmers living in the fertile central and southern regions. They grow grain, potatoes, and apples, and raise cattle and sheep. In the vast forests, men work cutting down spruce, birch, cedar, and oak trees. Most of it is used to make woodpulp and paper. Many of the people catch fish off the coast of New Brunswick. The waters there are filled with herring, lobsters, cod, and smelts. New Brunswick ranks third among the provinces in the value of its fish products. In the cities, men work in large fish-canning plants, in lumber mills, and in shipbuilding yards.

WHAT NEW BRUNSWICK IS LIKE

New Brunswick is generally a rolling plain. The western part is covered with forests. In the northwest are high ridges that are part of the Appalachian Range. There is a low, sandy coast along the Gulf of St. Lawrence in the east. The coast along the Bay of Fundy in the south is rocky.

New Brunswick has great extremes of climate. The winters are very cold, and in the northern part there are heavy snowfalls. It is milder along the Bay of Fundy. The summers may be very hot, and the temperature often rises to more than 90 degrees. New Brunswick has several navigable rivers and many beautiful lakes. The St. John River is the most important in the province. Railroads and highways connect the cities and towns, and there are airports in the chief cities.

THE GOVERNMENT OF NEW BRUNSWICK

The head of the government of New Brunswick is a lieutenant-governor. He is appointed by the British queen with the consent of the Canadian government. The province is actually run by a premier. He is appointed by the legislature, which is elected by the people. The premier stays in office as long as he can keep the confidence of the majority of the legislature. The legislature is elected for a five-year term. Judges are appointed by the Canadian government in Ottawa, and hold office permanently. The provincial government is in the capital, Fredericton.

All children between the ages of 7 and 16 must go to school. There are several universities in the province. The one which is both the oldest and the largest is the University of New Brunswick. It is located in Fredericton.

St. John is the largest city in New Brunswick, with a population of 101,100 in 1967. It is the chief port and an important manufacturing center. Fredericton, the capital, has a population of 22,-460, and is the third-largest city in the province.

NEW BRUNSWICK IN THE PAST

The first white settlement in New Brunswick was made more than three hundred years ago by Samuel de Champlain, the French explorer. Other settlements grew up, and the region became known as Acadia, which included the present-day provinces of New Brunswick and Nova Scotia and part of the state of Maine, and Prince Edward Island. The English also settled in this region, and fought the French fiercely for Acadia. In

1713, the region was won by the English. Many settlers from England and Scotland came to Acadia, and many more came from the New England states in the United States after the Revolutionary War. In 1784, Acadia was made into the two separate provinces of New Brunswick and Nova Scotia. In 1867, New Brunswick was admitted into the Dominion of Canada.

NEW BRUNSWICK. Area 28,354 square miles. Population (1967) 619,000. Capital, Fredericton. Coat of arms, an ancient galley, with the British lion above it. Flower, purple violet. Official abbreviation, N.B.

Newcastle

Newcastle, also called Newcastle-upon-Tyne, is an important manufacturing and shipping city in England. About three hundred thousand people live there. It is on the Tyne River, about ten miles from the North Sea. So much coal used to be shipped from Newcastle that when someone does something unnecessary he is said to be "carrying coals to Newcastle."

New Deal

The "New Deal" was the administration of President Franklin D. Roosevelt in the United States, from 1933 to 1945. The name came from a speech made by Roosevelt in 1932, when he was a candidate for President. In this speech, he promised "a new deal for the forgotten man."

When Roosevelt was inaugurated as President in March, 1933, the United States was suffering from a great depression (bad business condition) in which millions had no jobs and nearly everyone was poor. Roosevelt surrounded himself with advisers who came to be called the "brain trust." Many of them were college professors and others who had studied economics (the science of money and trade) and political science.

One New Deal policy was called "pump-priming." The United States government spent a great deal of money to build public works and to buy things, just so that people would have jobs. The purpose of this was to put more money in the hands of the people so that they could buy things and get business started again. The Works Progress Administration (WPA) and the Public Works Administration (PWA) were two government agencies that were established to spend the money.

Another New Deal policy was to increase the prices that farmers and manufacturers got for their products. Business had been so bad that everyone had cut prices in desperate efforts to sell things. Congress passed laws to raise the prices. The National Industrial Recovery Act set up an agency called the National Recovery Administration (NRA), and this agency called businessmen together and got them to agree to keep prices at a reasonable level. The Agricultural Adjustment Administration (AAA) paid farmers to raise smaller crops, because when there is less food on the market the price of the food goes up. This plan was called "creating an artificial scarcity." The United States Supreme Court later found that these laws were not permitted by the Constitution of the United States.

Young men, who could not find jobs

in those depression times, were organized by another government agency, the Civilian Conservation Corps (CCC), and were paid by the government to work in forests and on other public lands.

The New Deal passed important laws for the protection and benefit of labor and labor unions. It set up the National Labor Relations Board (NLRB) to carry out these laws.

Because the government was spending so much money, taxes were raised far above what they had been before. For this and other reasons, many people were violently opposed to the New Deal. Gradually prosperity returned to the United States and most of the New Deal's emergency measures were dropped.

New Delhi

New Delhi is the capital of the Republic of India. It is on the Jumna River, five miles south of the city of Delhi, the former capital of India. (There is a separate article about DELHI.) About two million people live in New Delhi, and many of them work in the many government offices. The city is very beautiful, with modern buildings, shops, and homes for government officials. There are wide streets and many historic monuments. The president of India lives in a beautiful building of red sandstone and marble that was formerly a palace. Another fine building is the National Sports Stadium, which seats thirty thousand people. The first Asian Olympic Games were held there in 1951.

New Delhi is a new city, completed in 1929. The old capital of Delhi was very crowded, and the government decided to build its new public buildings several miles away. In 1931, New Delhi became the capital of India, which was then under British control. After India became an independent republic, in 1947, New Delhi remained the capital.

New Delhi in the summer is very hot, with the temperature often rising to more than 110 degrees. During these hot months the government moves to the town of Simla in the Himalayas, where it is much cooler.

NEW DELHI, INDIA. Population (in 1961) 2,000,000. Capital of India.

New England

New England is a name given to the northeastern tip of the United States. It includes six states, Maine, New Hampshire, Vermont, Massachusetts, Rhode Island, and Connecticut. New England looks very small on a map, and its area (66,608 square miles) is less than a fiftieth of the whole United States, while its population (10,509,367 in the 1960 census) is almost exactly the same as New York City and its suburbs; but New England has been of tremendous importance in American history and is still of great importance in American life and business.

The name "New England" is a proper one, because the section was first settled almost wholly by English people. The first of them were the Pilgrims, who arrived at Plymouth, Massachusetts, in 1620. Sir Francis Drake, the English explorer, had already sailed along the Pacific Coast in 1577, and had called the region New Albion. (Albion is a name sometimes used for England.)

Boston, Massachusetts, is called "the cradle of liberty" because so many things happened there to help make the United States an independent country. The first battles of the Revolutionary War were fought near Boston. Four of the six New England states were among the original thirteen states, and a fifth, Vermont, was the first state admitted after the United States was formed.

For many years, New England was the principal manufacturing section of the United States. Until recent years, nearly all of the country's textiles (thread and cloth) and nearly all of its shoes were made in New England. The many streams and rivers that rise in the New England mountains provided water power to run the mills.

New England has also been a center of education and the arts throughout the history of the United States. During the last century, most of the great American literature came from a group of writers centered around Boston and Concord, Massachusetts. These included Ralph Waldo Emerson, Henry Wadsworth Longfellow, John Greenleaf Whittier, James Russell Lowell, Nathaniel Hawthorne, and many others. Harvard and Yale, two of the oldest American colleges, are in New England.

Nearly all of New England is beautiful in the spring and summer, and nearly all parts of it are popular vacation resorts. Some of the soil is fertile, but some of it is rocky and hard and the pioneers had trouble making it yield a living. In the winter, New England is cold but this only makes it more suitable for winter sports. The mountains of New England —the Berkshires, Green Mountains, White Mountains, and others—are high enough to be cool and low enough to attract tourists and vacationists.

New England Confederation

The New England Confederation was a union of the early colonies in New England. The Confederation was formed by the colonies as protection against the Indians and against the Dutch colony south of New England, in what is now New York. In 1643 delegates from the Connecticut, New Haven, Massachusetts, and Plymouth colonies met at Boston and formed this Confederation. It lasted for more than forty years, until 1686.

Under the New England Confederation each colony made its own laws and kept its own independence. Two members from each colony formed a board of commissioners who met at least once a year and made suggestions. Then each colony decided for itself whether or not to follow them. Rhode Island, another New England colony, was not allowed to join the Confederation at all. The New England Confederation was also known as the United Colonies of New England.

Newfoundland

Newfoundland is an island that is part of Canada. It is in the Gulf of St. Lawrence, with the Atlantic Ocean on its east. It is 43,359 square miles in size, a little larger than the state of Ohio.

With LABRADOR (about which there is a separate article) the island of Newfoundland forms the Canadian province of Newfoundland and Labrador.

The capital is St. John's, a city on the island of Newfoundland and the largest city in the province, with a population of about 100,000 (1967 estimate).

THE PEOPLE WHO LIVE THERE

The people of Newfoundland are mostly of Irish and British ancestry. They must get used to cold weather, because the temperature averages about 20 degrees in winter and rises to only 55 degrees in summer. About half of the people live on Avalon Peninsula, which is in the south and is warmer than the rest of the province.

The Grand Banks off Newfoundland is a famous fishing region. Newfoundland's fishermen catch salmon, cod, herring, and lobsters, in great quantities. These are canned or frozen in factories on the island. Other Newfoundland people are hunters who catch seals and other fur-bearing animals and sell their skins. Some of the people have "farms" on which they raise mink and fox and sell their fur. There are few real farms on Newfoundland, because the soil is poor and the climate is too cold. Berries are

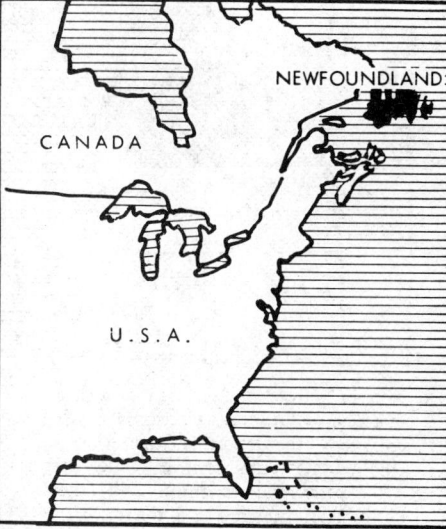

grown on Avalon Peninsula and shipped to other parts of Canada.

Newfoundland has many natural resources. Its pine and spruce forests, which cover much of the island, are cut down and made into paper, which is sent to Great Britain and the United States. It has mines that produce zinc, iron, lead, copper, and gypsum. Newfoundland's many rivers produce electric power.

A visitor to Newfoundland first notices the cold, and then the fog that blankets the island almost all the time. The coast is rocky and has many steep cliffs descending into the sea. Most of Newfoundland is flat, though there are low mountains in the northwest. It has many lakes, some of which are large and quite beautiful.

THE GOVERNMENT OF NEWFOUNDLAND

The head of the government of Newfoundland is a lieutenant-governor, who is appointed by the British queen with the consent of the Canadian government. This province is actually run by a premier. He is appointed by the legislature, which is elected by the people. The premier stays in office as long as he can keep the confidence of the majority of the

legislature. The legislature is elected for a five-year term. Judges are appointed by the Canadian government in Ottawa, and hold office permanently. The provincial government is in the capital, St. John's.

Everyone has to go to school between the ages of 6 and 14, and there are elementary schools and high schools throughout the province. Memorial University, Bishop Field College and St. Bonaventure's College are in St. John's.

NEWFOUNDLAND IN THE PAST

Newfoundland was the first British colony. John Cabot discovered it in 1497 and called it "new-founde-land," the name it has kept ever since. At first no one lived there but fishermen, who spent only part of the year there. Many settlers came from Ireland in the 1840s, when there was a potato famine in Ireland.

Airplane travel made people realize the importance of Newfoundland. It is an ideal stopping-place for planes flying between Europe and North America. There is a great airport at Gander, a town of about 7,000 in the northeast. In World War II, Newfoundland became an important base for Allied airplanes. There are still important air bases there, including one belonging to the United States in Argentia on the Avalon Peninsula.

In 1949, the people of Newfoundland voted to become a province of Canada. Since then, many new houses and factories have been built.

NEWFOUNDLAND. Province, including Labrador, of Canada. Area, 156,185 square miles, including the island of Newfoundland (43,359 square miles). Population (1967 estimate) 500,000, including the island of Newfoundland.

Newfoundland dog

The Newfoundland is one of the largest of all dogs. It is a working dog, strong enough to pull carts. It is a tireless swimmer and has a heavy coat that protects it from the cold on land or in water. It stands 26 to 29 inches high at the shoulder and is 30 to 33 inches long from the chest to the base of the tail. It weighs 120 to 150 pounds. The Newfoundland is usually black, but is seen in other colors including white.

New Guinea

New Guinea is the second-largest island in the world. (Greenland is the largest.) New Guinea is in the Pacific Ocean, at its nearest point about a hundred miles north of Australia. It is 316,-861 square miles in area, twice the size of California, and about 2,500,000 people live there, which is about as many as live in the state of Connecticut.

THE PEOPLE WHO LIVE THERE

Most of the people of New Guinea are Papuans and Melanesians. They speak their own language and have a very primitive civilization. In some parts of New Guinea there are pygmies. Some of the natives in remote areas may still be headhunters. This means that they cut off the heads of their enemies because they think in this way they get the strength that the enemy had while alive. There are many tribes about which little is known. Some of New Guinea has never been explored.

Recently tribes who had never before seen people from the outside world were discovered in mountain areas.

Most of the people of New Guinea have small garden plots on which they grow enough to feed themselves and their families. Those who live along the coast also fish. Others work on large plantations that grow coconuts, coffee, rubber, cocoa and hemp.

WHAT IT IS LIKE THERE

In some ways New Guinea is like America when it was found by Columbus. It is a country that has great deposits of minerals and many villages where agriculture could prosper. The big difference is that the climate is very hot and wet and the tropical jungles are very dense. As a result it is hard to make use of the wealth New Guinea offers. High mountain ranges run the entire length of the island. Its swamplands are the home of poisonous snakes and crocodiles. There are many beautiful flowers, butterflies, and a great variety of bright-feathered birds, including the Birds of Paradise.

DIVISIONS OF NEW GUINEA

New Guinea is divided into three parts: West New Guinea, formerly Netherlands New Guinea, which passed to the control of Indonesia in May 1963. (The Indonesian name for New Guinea is Irian.) In the northeast is the U.N. Trust territory of New Guinea, which is administered by Australia. Papua, in the southeast, became independent in 1975.

Port Moresby, a city of 66,000 in Papua, and Hollandia (now called Sukarnapura) in West New Guinea, are the chief cities.

The Japanese wanted Port Moresby in World War II, as a possible base for an invasion of Australia. There was fighting on New Guinea throughout the war, mostly in the jungles. The last Japanese surrendered when the war ended in 1945.

New Hampshire

New Hampshire is one of the New England states in the United States. It was one of the thirteen original colonies. Its nickname is the "Granite State" because of its large deposits of granite. The state gets its name from the county of Hampshire in England.

In area, New Hampshire ranks 44th among the states, with 9,304 square miles. In population it ranks 42nd, with more than 700,000 people living there. It became a state in 1788, and was the 9th of the thirteen original states. The capital is Concord. There is a short seacoast on the Atlantic Ocean.

THE PEOPLE OF NEW HAMPSHIRE

The early settlers of New Hampshire were English. They left their country more than three hundred years ago to escape religious and political persecution. Later the Scotch-Irish came. They planted the first potato in the United States, and brought with them the art of linen-weaving. Since then, textiles have been outstanding among the manufactured goods of the state. People also came from all over Europe to work in the growing cities. Today most of the people are American-born.

The people of New Hampshire are considered typical Yankees, thrifty, hard-working, and independent. More than half the people live in the cities. Many

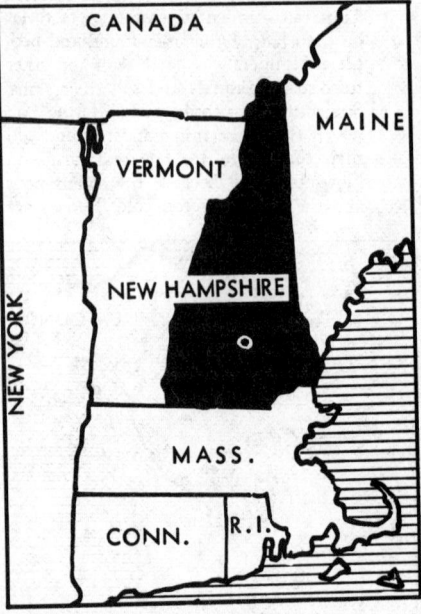

work in factories that make shoes, textiles, machinery, furniture, electronic devices and many other products. Others work in shipbuilding yards and in plants that make paper and woodpulp. Still others cut lumber in the forests in the north.

Many New Hampshire people are farmers. Much of the soil is rocky and poor and they have found it more profitable to raise cattle and poultry. Farmers in the fertile Connecticut Valley raise apples, strawberries, and other fruit.

Some people work in the large granite quarries around Concord. The mines of New Hampshire also supply a large part of the country's mica and feldspar.

The largest religious group in New Hampshire is the Roman Catholics. There are also many Congregationalists, Methodists, and Baptists.

WHAT NEW HAMPSHIRE IS LIKE

New Hampshire is a land of mountains, forests, and swift rivers. Its fine scenery has made it a popular vacation place both in summer and in winter.

In the extreme north are great forests. A little farther south are the beautiful White Mountains with their snow-capped peaks. Mt. Washington, 6,288 feet high, in the White Mountains, is the highest point in the northeastern United States. The swift Merrimack River rises in these mountains. It is an important source of water power for factories that have been built along its banks. Lake Winnepe-

saukee, a lake of more than 100 square miles in the center of the state, is a vacation spot and it is also used for transportation.

In the western part of New Hampshire is the fertile Connecticut Valley, the best farming region in the state. The Connecticut River supplies much of the electric power for the state. In the south is the Merrimack Valley, which is an important manufacturing region.

The summers in New Hampshire are cool, and people go there to escape the heat of the cities further south. There are also many summer camps for boys and girls. The long winters are very cold, but the clear air and deep snow make New Hampshire mountains ideal for winter sports. The average temperature in winter is about 23 degrees. In summer, it is about 69 degrees.

Hunters and trappers can find many small fur-bearing animals, such as the rabbit, fox, mink, and raccoon. There are also bears and deer in the woods.

Railroads and paved roads reach almost all parts of the state. There are airports near the important cities.

THE GOVERNMENT OF NEW HAMPSHIRE

New Hampshire, like other states, has a Governor and a Legislature. The Governor is elected for a two-year term. The Legislature is composed of two houses, a Senate and a House of Representatives. The members of both houses are elected for a two-year term. Judges are appointed by the Governor for a life term. The capital is Concord. There are ten counties in the state.

There are about 1,500,000 pupils enrolled in the public elementary and high schools. Among the principal colleges and universities are:

University of New Hampshire, at Durham. Enrollment, 9,900 in 1971 (co-ed).

Dartmouth College, at Hanover. Enrollment, 3,759 in 1971 (men only).

St. Anselm's College, at Manchester. Enrollment, 1,587 in 1971 (men only).

CHIEF CITIES OF NEW HAMPSHIRE

The leading cities of New Hampshire, with populations from the 1970 census, are:

Manchester, population 87,754, the largest city, manufacturing and industrial center, in the southern part of the state. There is a separate article about MANCHESTER.

Nashua, population 55,820, second-largest city, industrial center, in the southern part of the state.

Concord, population 30,022, state capital and third-largest city. There is a separate article about CONCORD.

Portsmouth, population 25,717, fourth-largest city, seaport, U.S. Navy submarine base, on the Atlantic Ocean.

NEW HAMPSHIRE IN THE PAST

The first white man to explore the New Hampshire region was probably Martin Pring, an Englishman, who is believed to have landed there more than 350 years ago. Some years later, Captain John Smith surveyed the region. The first permanent settlement was made at Dover by the English in 1623, and several other settlements were started. Some of the people came from England and some

Fort Point Lighthouse at New Castle is one of the best spots to view New Hampshire's short but fascinating seacoast.

from the Massachusetts colony. Most of these early settlers were fishermen and traders.

In 1629, John Mason was given a grant of land that included New Hampshire. When he died, the colony was put under the rule of Massachusetts. It was not until 1679 that New Hampshire got its own charter and became a royal province of Great Britain.

Indian tribes made many attacks on the English settlements and this discouraged other people from coming there to settle.

The colony fought loyally in the Revolutionary War, and was the first of the colonies to form a government entirely independent of England. As a state it began to develop its industries from the beginning. By the time of the Civil War, New Hampshire was a leading manufacturing state.

The people of the state were strongly against slavery and had passed a law freeing the slaves as early as 1783. When the Civil War broke out, New Hampshire sent many thousands of men to fight on the side of the Union.

After the Civil War, New Hampshire continued to expand. Many more factories were built, and cities grew rapidly. In World War II the big textile and leather factories supplied large quantities of uniforms and shoes for the fighting men.

PLACES TO SEE IN NEW HAMPSHIRE

Cannon Mountain, 8 miles north of Lincoln, in the north, on U.S. Route 3. A great natural stone profile on the mountain, called "The Old Man of the Mountain." It was made famous in a story by Nathaniel Hawthorne called "The Great Stone Face."

Daniel Webster's Birthplace, 4 miles west of Franklin, in the central part of the state, west of U.S. Route 3. Many souvenirs of Webster, the famous statesman, are there.

Mount Sunapee State Park, 1,600 acres, 6 miles east of Newport, in the southwest, on State Highway 103. Winter and summer vacation spot, with picnicking, skiing, hiking, and a chairlift 3,200 feet long.

Mount Washington, 6,288 feet high, 9 miles southwest of Gorham, in the north, west of State Highway 16. The highest point in northeastern U.S. A beautiful trip to the top by cog railway or by automobile toll road.

Crawford, Franconia, Pinkham and Dixville Notches, in the White Mountains, places where the highway passes between high, steep peaks.

White Mountain National Forest, 1,055 square miles in the north central part. Tent camping areas and hiking trails.

NEW HAMPSHIRE. Area, 9,304 square miles. Population (1970 census) 737,681. Capital, Concord. Nickname, the Granite State. Motto, Live Free or Die. Flower, purple lilac. Song, "Old New Hampshire." Admitted to Union, June 21, 1788. Official abbreviation, N.H.

New Haven

New Haven is the third largest city in Connecticut. It is on Long Island Sound, an arm of the Atlantic Ocean, and is about 72 miles northeast of New York City. More than 137,000 people live there. Most of them work in factories that make clocks, electrical equipment, machine tools, toys, guns, and many other things. New Haven is also an educational center. It is best known as the home of Yale University, one of the oldest colleges in the United States.

The streets of New Haven are wide and many of them are lined with tall elm trees. There are many parks and many old buildings that were built before the Revolutionary War, 175 years ago and more.

New Haven was founded in 1638 as a separate colony and became part of the colony of Connecticut in 1664. It became a city in 1784. For a time it was an important port, and New Haven clipper ships brought riches from the Indies. It became a manufacturing city after the Civil War. Many famous Americans are buried in New Haven, including Eli Whitney, Samuel F. B. Morse, and Noah Webster.

NEW HAVEN, CONNECTICUT. Population (1970 census) 137,707. County seat of New Haven County and home of Yale University. On Long Island Sound.

New Hebrides

The New Hebrides are a group of islands in the southwest Pacific Ocean, about one thousand miles east of Australia. The islands form a chain about four hundred miles long. They are about 5,700 square miles in size, and about 70,000 people live there. The capital is the city of Vila on the island of Efate, the most important island in the New Hebrides.

The islands are actually volcanoes that rise from the floor of the ocean. Coconut palms, sandalwood and orchids grow wild on the islands. The inhabitants are Melanesians, a people of the South Pacific. Many of them are farmers and they grow coffee, copra (a product of the coconut tree), and cocoa.

The New Hebrides belong to the British and the French, who have ruled the islands since 1906. During World War II, they were the location of an important naval base belonging to the Fighting French. The people of the New Hebrides continued to fight against Hitler after Germany had forced the French government to surrender.

New Jersey

New Jersey is one of the Middle Atlantic states in the United States. It was one of the thirteen original colonies. Its nickname is the "Garden State" because of the large crops of garden vegetables the farms grow. New Jersey was named after the island of Jersey in the English Channel.

In area, New Jersey ranks 46th among the states, with 7,836 square miles. In population it ranks eighth, with more than seven million people living there. It became a state in 1787, and was the third of the thirteen original states. The capital is Trenton.

THE PEOPLE OF NEW JERSEY

The first settlers in New Jersey were the Dutch, more than three hundred years ago. They were followed by large numbers of English, both from England and from the New England colonies. French and Scottish people came to escape religious persecution. As the factories and mills of New Jersey grew, people came from Germany, Ireland, and eastern Europe to work in the cities. Today more than three-quarters of the people live in the large industrial cities.

Most of the people in New Jersey work in large factories making products that are used all over the United States. They manufacture more chemicals than any other state. They are also among the leading producers of electrical machinery and equipment. Many people work in huge petroleum-refining plants, in paint and varnish factories, and in food-canning and dyeing plants. Others work in the busy shipyards. New Jersey is the nation's center for scientific research and development, having more than four hundred laboratories.

Only a small number of people are farmers, but they produce large quantities of vegetables and fruits in truck gardens. A person traveling through New Jersey can see truck farming going on in all parts of the state. The farmers are famous for their sweet potatoes and tomatoes. They also grow large crops of asparagus, beets, beans, and cauliflower. Many farmers raise dairy cattle and produce eggs, butter, and milk. All of these products are shipped to markets in the large eastern cities.

There are important zinc mines in northern New Jersey. New Jersey is one of the leading zinc-producing states in the country. There are also many fishermen. The state ranks high in oysters, clams, bluefish, and sturgeon.

The largest religious group in New Jersey is the Roman Catholics. There are also many Jews, Methodists, and Presbyterians.

WHAT NEW JERSEY IS LIKE

New Jersey is divided into two large regions: the coastal plain on the east and south, bordering the Atlantic Ocean, and the Kittatinny Mountains area in the northwest. The northern region has beautiful hills and many lakes, and farmers grow fruits and vegetables in the fertile valleys. Cattle graze on the green slopes.

Along the northeastern boundary, between New Jersey and New York, is the Hudson River. Along the Jersey shore of the Hudson River are the famous Pali-

sades, which rise several hundred feet above the water. Most of the important industrial cities are in the northeast. Other industrial cities are along the Delaware River in the west, which is the boundary between New Jersey and Pennsylvania.

The coastal region is low and sandy, and much truck farming is carried on here. Along the coast, with its many bays and beaches, are some famous resorts, such as Atlantic City, Asbury Park, and Cape May. Thousands of people come to New Jersey every summer to the many seaside resorts.

The climate of New Jersey is mild along the Atlantic coast, but it is colder in the mountains. The average temperature in winter is about 31 degrees, and in summer about 74 degrees.

New Jersey is so close to the big cities of New York and Philadelphia that thousands of people travel to work in these cities every day. Many important bridges and tunnels have been built.

The George Washington Bridge connects New Jersey with New York City, as do the Lincoln and Holland tunnels for motor vehicles and three railroad tunnels under the Hudson River. The Delaware River Bridge connects Camden, New Jersey, with Philadelphia. The New Jersey Turnpike, which was opened in 1951, is 118 miles long, and runs the length of the state. It has two extensions and a connection with the Garden State Parkway, a scenic highway that New Jersey first put into use in 1954. New Jersey was the first state to use elevated highways. The best-known of these, the Pulaski Skyway, connects New York City with the eastern New Jersey cities. One of the busiest airports in the country is at Newark.

THE GOVERNMENT OF NEW JERSEY

New Jersey, like the other states, has a governor and a legislature. The governor is elected for a four-year term. The legislature is composed of two houses, a Senate and a General Assembly. It meets at Trenton, the capital. The members of the Senate are elected for a four-year term. Judges are appointed by the Governor for a seven-year term.

There are about 1,500,000 pupils enrolled in the public elementary and high schools. Among the principal colleges and universities are:

Rutgers, the State University, at New Brunswick. Enrollment, 30,017 in 1971 (co-ed.)
Fairleigh Dickinson University, at Rutherford. Enrollment, 18,000 in 1971 (co-ed).
Seton Hall University, at South Orange. Enrollment, 9,713 in 1971 (co-ed).
Newark College of Engineering, at Newark. Enrollment, 3,900 in 1971 (co-ed).
Princeton University, at Princeton. Enrollment, 4,983 in 1971 (men only).
Montclair State College, at Upper Montclair. Enrollment, 8,452 in 1971 (co-ed).
Upsala College, at East Orange. Enrollment, 1,811 in 1971 (co-ed).
Newark State Teachers College, at Union. Enrollment, 7,850 in 1971 (co-ed).
Drew University, at Madison. Enrollment, 2,366 in 1971 (co-ed).

CHIEF CITIES OF NEW JERSEY

The leading cities of New Jersey, with populations from the 1970 census, are:

Newark, population 382,417 the largest city in the state. There is a separate article about NEWARK.
Jersey City, population 260,545, the second-largest city. There is a separate article about JERSEY CITY.
Paterson, population 144,824, third-largest city, silk-manufacturing center, in the northern part of the state.
Camden, population 102,551, the fifth largest city, port on Delaware River.
Trenton, population 104,638 the state capital and fourth-largest city. There is a separate article about TRENTON.
Atlantic City, population 47,859. There is a separate article about ATLANTIC CITY.

The metropolitan area including Newark, Jersey City, Elizabeth, and adjoining cities is one of the largest in the world. In an area comparable to that of New York City it has a population of more than two million.

NEW JERSEY IN THE PAST

The first white man to visit the region of New Jersey was probably Giovanni da Verrazano, an Italian navigator, who sailed along the coast more than four hundred years ago. Nearly a hundred years later the Dutch arrived and made the first permanent settlement, at Bergen, in 1618. Many Dutch settled on farms in the eastern part of New Jersey. Swedish settlers came and settled in the western part along the Delaware River. The Dutch ruled over all of the New Jersey territory until the English conquered the Dutch in 1664. The Quakers started their first settlement in America in the western part of New Jersey in 1674. New Jersey became a British colony in 1702.

New Jersey played an important part in the Revolutionary War. Some of the most important battles were fought there. General George Washington crossed the icy Delaware River in 1776, and won the Battle of Trenton. This was a turning point in the war for the American colo-

nists. The battles of Princeton and Monmouth were other important ones fought in New Jersey.

During the Civil War, most of the people were on the side of the Union. There was also a strong and active group, known as "Copperheads," who favored the South.

After the Civil War, New Jersey be-

A surfer in the Atlantic Ocean off Island Beach State Park in Ocean County, New Jersey.

gan a period of great prosperity. Cities grew rapidly and farming developed. The state became one of the great manufacturing and truck-farming centers. Later it became an important place for scientific development. Samuel F. B. Morse and Alfred Vail tapped out their first message on the telegraph near Morristown. Thomas A. Edison, in his laboratories at Menlo Park and later at West Orange, invented the electric light, the phonograph, and the motion-picture camera. At the Institute for Advanced Study at Princeton, Albert Einstein and other physicists and mathematicians made essential contributions to the development of atomic energy.

PLACES TO SEE IN NEW JERSEY

Morristown National Historical Park, 958 acres, 3 miles south of Morristown, in the north, on U.S. Route 202. Site of General Washington's winter headquarters during the Revolutionary War.

Edison State Park, 30 acres, at Menlo Park, in the northeast, on State Highway 27. Contains the Edison Memorial Tower, where a light burns continually. A museum there contains some of Edison's inventions, but more are to be seen in the Edison Museum at West Orange, in the northeast, near Newark.

Delaware Water Gap, about 10 miles west of Blairstown, in the northwest, on U.S. Route 46. The Delaware River flows through a break in the Kittatinny Ridge; the water is more than 1,500 feet below the top of the mountain.

Walt Whitman House, in Camden, in the west, on U.S. Route 130. The house where Walt Whitman, the poet, lived during the last part of his life; contains many things belonging to him.

NEW JERSEY. Area, 7,836 square miles. Population (1970 census) 7,168,164. Capital, Trenton. Nickname, the Garden State. Motto, Liberty and Prosperity. Flower, purple violet. Bird, eastern goldfinch. Song, "New Jersey Loyalty Song." Admitted to Union, December 18, 1787. Official abbreviation, N.J.

Newman, Cardinal

John Henry Newman was a Roman Catholic priest who became a cardinal, the highest rank in the church, except for the Pope.

Cardinal Newman was born in England in 1801. He studied at Oxford University and became a priest in the Church of England. Then he became a teacher at Oxford, and he and two other teachers, Edward Pusey and John Keble, wrote pamphlets that tried to make people more devoted to the Church of England. Their work became popular and was called the Oxford Movement.

In 1845, Cardinal Newman left the Church of England and joined the Roman Catholic Church. A year later he became a priest, and in 1879 he was made a cardinal. Although many people in the Church of England had been disappointed when he left their Church, he remained a beloved figure throughout England. He died in 1890.

During his lifetime, Cardinal Newman wrote many books. His book *Apologia pro Vita Sua*, which in the Latin language means "A Defense of His Life," is a very moving story of his own life. He also wrote several hymns, including "Lead, Kindly Light."

New Mexico

New Mexico is one of the Rocky Mountain states in the United States. Its nickname is the "Land of Enchantment" because of its beautiful and varied scenery. It is also called the "Sunshine State" because of its hot, sunny climate all year round. New Mexico was named by the Spaniards who came from Mexico. The word Mexico comes from the name of the Aztec war god *Mexitli*.

In area, New Mexico ranks fifth among the states, with 121,666 square miles. In population it ranks 37th, with more than a million people living there. It became a state in 1912, and was the 47th state admitted to the United States. The capital is Santa Fe.

THE PEOPLE OF NEW MEXICO

Persons traveling through New Mexico will find three different groups of people living there. Each has its own customs and culture.

Pueblo Indians live in ancient villages along the Rio Grande Valley, and are famous for their pottery. The Navajo Indians live on reservations in the northwest, and are known all over the world for their colorful blankets and silver jewelry. Smaller groups of Apaches also have reservations in New Mexico.

The Spanish-Americans make up one-third of the population. They are the descendants of Spanish settlers who came over 350 years ago. They live in adobe (sun-baked brick) villages throughout the state, and most of them still speak Spanish. They have kept many of their colorful ceremonies and customs.

The Anglo-Americans are the people who came from other parts of the United States about a hundred years ago to start cattle ranches and work in the mines. More and more have come to New Mexico in recent years to work in the oil fields and to live in the healthful dry climate.

About half the people in New Mexico are farmers. Most of them raise cattle and sheep that graze on huge ranches. The soil is so dry that for a long time little could be grown, but the farmers now produce cotton, wheat, peanuts, and fruits and vegetables. New Mexico is noted for its beans, peppers, apples, and melons.

Many people work in the valuable mines in the mountains of New Mexico. The mines produce more potash than any other state. They also produce large quantities of zinc, copper, coal, and lead. There are great oil and natural-gas fields in the southeastern and northwestern parts of the state.

The people who live in the cities work in oil-refining plants and in factories that make lumber products, chemicals, and textiles. New Mexico blankets, pottery, and jewelry are made for sale to the many tourists who visit the state.

Most of the people are Roman Catholic. Other religious groups include Baptists and Methodists.

WHAT NEW MEXICO IS LIKE

New Mexico has wild and beautiful scenery. There are plains, high mountains, and deserts covered with desert flowers. There are also many strangely shaped rock formations that are a big attraction to tourists.

The large eastern part of the state is called the Great Plains. Here big herds of cattle and sheep graze, and farmers grow fruit in the fertile Pecos Valley. The Pecos River is used by the farmers for irrigation.

In the north central part of the state are the high Rocky Mountains, with their lofty peaks. This part of New Mexico has some of the most beautiful scenery, and is a favorite vacation spot. Dense forests of fir and pine cover many of the mountains and supply much of the lumber for the state.

In the south and southeast are scattered mountain ranges with broad desert plains between. The northwest is particularly notable for its deep canyons, steep cliffs,

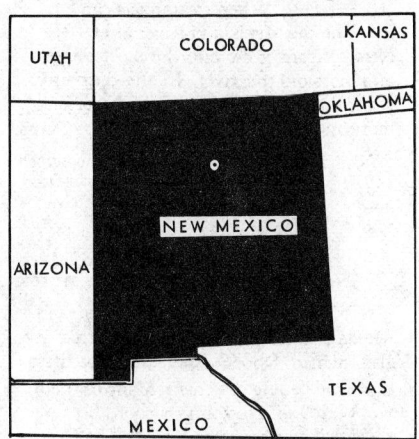

and mesas or plateaus of red rock.

Cutting through the center of the state from north to south is the Rio Grande, the "big river." It forms a belt of green through the unbroken brown stretches of the desert, for where the river passes there is water to irrigate the fields.

The climate of New Mexico is warm and very dry. In the mountains, the winters are cold and snowy. The average temperature in winter is about 34 degrees, and in summer about 73 degrees.

There are many wild animals in New Mexico—the bobcat, bear, deer, mountain lion, and coyote. There are also fur-bearing animals, such as the mink, rabbit, and beaver.

Railroads and highways reach most parts of the state. There are airports in the important cities.

THE GOVERNMENT OF NEW MEXICO

New Mexico, like most other states, has a Governor and a Legislature. The Governor is elected for a two-year term. The Legislature is composed of two houses, a Senate and a House of Representatives. The members of the Senate are elected for a four-year term. Members of the House of Representatives are elected for a two-year term. Judges are elected for an eight-year term. The capital is Santa Fe. There are 32 counties.

In 1970 there were more than 275,000 students in public elementary and high schools. Among the principal colleges and universities are:

University of New Mexico, at Albuquerque. Enrollment, 14,940 in 1971 (co-ed).

Eastern New Mexico University, at Portales. Enrollment, 3,622 in 1971 (co-ed).

New Mexico Highlands University, at Las Vegas. Enrollment, 2,300 in 1971 (co-ed).

CHIEF CITIES OF NEW MEXICO

The leading cities of New Mexico, with populations from the 1970 census, are:

Albuquerque, population 243,751, the largest city in the state. There is a separate article about ALBUQUERQUE.

Roswell, population 33,908, fourth-largest city, in the southeast.

Santa Fe, population 41,167, the state capital and second-largest city. There is a separate article about SANTA FE.

Las Cruces, population 37,857, third-largest city, in the southwest.

Carlsbad, population 21,297, center of important potash mines, in southeast.

NEW MEXICO IN THE PAST

Many centuries before the white men came to New Mexico, the cliff dwellers and Pueblo Indians lived in this region. The remains of the cliff dwellers' villages can still be seen. They are one of the attractions for tourists today.

The first white men to visit the region of New Mexico were the Spaniard Cabeza de Voca and three of his followers, who came in search of gold more than four hundred years ago. The first permanent settlement was made at San Juan in 1598, by Juan de Oñate. Many missionaries came to the region and set up missions. The Pueblo Indians were friendly but other tribes were not, and this discouraged settlement. For two hundred years New Mexico was hardly settled at all.

New Mexico became a province of Mexico about 150 years ago, but after the Mexican War in 1848 New Mexico became a possession of the United States. Two years later it was made a territory. Miners began coming to New Mexico in search of gold. Others came and started large cattle ranches.

After the railroad was built through New Mexico, the population grew rapidly with miners and ranchers. In 1912 New Mexico finally became a state. Since

A Taos Indian's blanket contrasts with the brown pueblo walls.

then the state has grown and prospered. During World War II, Los Alamos became an atomic energy center. The first atomic bomb was tested near there.

PLACES TO SEE IN NEW MEXICO

Carlsbad Caverns National Park, 49,-447 acres, 20 miles southwest of Carlsbad, in the southeast, on U.S. Routes 62 and 180. Largest underground chambers yet discovered; a series of connected caverns with magnificent and curious formations.

Aztec Ruins National Monument, 27 acres, at Aztec, in the northwest, on State Highway 44. Ruins of a prehistoric American Indian town.

Bandelier National Monument, 27,103 acres, about 20 miles west of Santa Fe, in the north central section, north of U.S. Route 85. Ruins of prehistoric Indian homes of the later Pueblo period.

Capulin Mountain National Monument, 680 acres, 5 miles northeast of Capulin, in the northeast, on U.S. Route 87. A symmetrical cinder cone; an interesting example of an extinct volcano.

El Morro National Monument, 1,278 acres, at El Morro, in the west, on State Highway 53. "Inscription Rock," a soft sandstone monolith, or pillar, covered with inscriptions carved by Spanish explorers and early settlers.

Chaco Canyon National Monument, 21,478 acres, in the northwest, north of U.S. Route 66. Thirteen major Indian ruins, representing the highest point of Pueblo prehistoric civilization.

Gila Cliff Dwellings National Monument, 160 acres, 30 miles north of Silver City, east of U.S. Route 260. Well-preserved cliff dwellings in face of overhanging cliff.

Gran Quivira National Monument, 610 acres, 50 miles southeast of Belen, south of U.S. Route 60. Old Spanish mission and Pueblo house mounds.

White Sands National Monument, 146,535 acres, 12 miles west of Alamogordo, in the south central section, on U.S. Route 70. Glistening white gypsum sands and dunes.

NEW MEXICO. Area, 121,666 square miles. Population (1970 census) 1,016,000. Capital, Santa Fe. Nickname, the Land of Enchantment. Motto, *Crescit Eundo* (It Grows As It Goes). Flower, yucca flower. Bird, road runner. Song, "O Fair New Mexico." Admitted to Union, January 6, 1912. Official abbreviation, N.M.

New Orleans

New Orleans is the largest city in the state of Louisiana. It is on the Mississippi River, and is one of the most important ports in the South. Almost 600,-000 people live in New Orleans. Many of them work at shipping sugar, cotton, rice, and lumber. Many also work in sugar-refining and seafood-packing plants, and in factories that make clothing, meat and dairy products, and cottonseed products.

New Orleans is also one of the gayest and most interesting cities in the United States. The old part of the city, along the waterfront, is called the French Quarter. This section is famous for its quaint buildings and delicious food. The people who live there are called Creoles, which means that they are of French and Spanish descent, and they have kept many of the customs of their ancestors. Many of the people speak French as well as English. Every year in February or March they have a Mardi Gras celebration, on the day before the Christian season of Lent begins. This is one of the most colorful carnivals in the world, and it is seen by thousands of visitors each year.

The northern part of New Orleans is more modern. There are fine houses and gardens, wide residential streets, and parks filled with flowers. New Orleans has several universities. The best-known is Tulane University.

New Orleans was settled by the French in 1718. Later, it was ruled by Spain. In 1803, it became part of the United States when President Thomas Jefferson bought the huge territory known as the Louisiana Purchase. When steamboats came into use on the Mississippi River after 1812, New Orleans grew into the most important port on the river. In the past fifty years the port has been made larger and more modern.

NEW ORLEANS, LOUISIANA. Population (1970 census) 593,471. Parish seat, Orleans parish. On the Mississippi River. Settled, 1718.

Newport, Rhode Island

Newport is an important city in Rhode Island. It is on an island that is also named Rhode Island. About fifty thousand people live there. Many of them work around Newport harbor, because the city is an important seaport. The United States Navy has important naval stations there, including a naval war college. Newport also has many interesting old buildings, because the city was founded more than three hundred years ago, in 1639. Until 1900 it was one of two capitals of Rhode Island, the other being Providence, the present capital. About a hundred years ago, Newport became the most fashionable summer resort in the United States, and rich people built great mansions there. Polo, tennis, boating and

other sports meets are still held there every summer.

NEWPORT, RHODE ISLAND. Population (1970 census) 94,559. County seat, Newport County. Settled, 1639.

newspaper

Newspapers are publications that give the latest information to their readers, and also print "features" that are intended to instruct, amuse, or inform. The news stories inform people of what is going on in the world, either next door or on the other side of the globe. The special features and editorials are often educational, telling readers how to bake a cake, how foreign peoples dress, or what certain political events may mean to the average reader. Some features and editorials are meant to entertain. These may be comic strips, funny stories, poems, puzzles, or articles by amusing writers.

Newspapers also carry advertisements that inform readers about something offered for sale, generally with arguments to persuade people to buy. (There is a separate article about ADVERTISING). No newspapers could pay their way without advertisements. The advertiser pays large sums of money to get his message in a big newspaper. The small sum of 5 or 10 cents paid for a paper at a newsstand does not nearly pay for the cost of that paper, which is likely to be several times higher. The difference is made up to the newspaper publisher in the money received from advertisers.

DEPARTMENTS OF A NEWSPAPER

A large newspaper generally has four main divisions: editorial (see JOURNALISM); printing or mechanical; circulation; and advertising or business.

The editorial department takes care of all stories, including pictures and everything printed except the advertisements. In the editorial department are reporters who go out and get stories; rewrite men who put the news in correct form; copyreaders who correct the stories and write headlines for them; and editors who direct all operations, deciding what stories are important and where each one should be placed in the paper.

The article on JOURNALISM tells more about newspaper editorial work.

When the editorial department finishes with a story, it sends it to the composing room, which is part of the mechanical department. There it is set into type, a proof (hand-printed copy) is made from the type and is corrected, and printing plates are made. (This is explained in the article on PRINTING.) All newspapers except the very smallest are printed by huge rotary printing presses. Some presses can turn out 50,000 papers in an hour.

The circulation department delivers the papers to homes and to newsstands. This is generally done by huge, fast trucks. If papers are to be sold in distant cities, "mats" (molds) of the complete type pages are usually flown to that city and copies are printed there. For example, The New York Times daily is printed from plates flown to Amsterdam, in the Netherlands, and copies are sent from there to other European cities.

The business department directs the sale of advertising. It usually also has charge of hiring, accounting, and other

general operations. Most large papers also have promotion departments that try to stir up public interest in buying the paper.

Small papers do not have all these departments. Often the editor, who is also the publisher, does much of the reporting, copyreading, headline-writing, and proofreading. There are many "one-man" newspapers, or papers with very small staffs.

NEWSPAPER CIRCULATION

There are about 2,300 newspapers in the United States, not including the weekly and semi-weekly newspapers of small towns. Of the big papers, about 1,760 are printed every day, and 560 on Sundays. The daily papers have about 59,000,000 readers; the weeklies about 22,000,000. In recent years the number of newspapers has declined. This is because many big papers have consolidated; that is, one paper has been bought by another and a single paper formed out of the two. Also, a number of newspapers have been linked to form what is called a "chain." This has brought less expensive operation.

The United States newspaper with the largest circulation is the New York Daily News. It prints about two million copies daily and more than three million on Sundays. It is a "tabloid," a smaller size than most papers. Several papers in London, England, have larger circulations.

newt

The newt is a small animal that looks somewhat like a tiny lizard, but unlike the lizard it has a smooth, moist skin. The newt is an amphibian, which means that it lives part of its life on land and the other part in the water. (You can read more about AMPHIBIANS in a separate article.) There are several different kinds of newt. Newts are found in almost every part of the world. They are born in ponds and quiet streams. When a newt is a few months old it leaves the water and begins its life on land. For about three years the newt lives in shady forests. It makes its home under logs and stones. During this period it is called an *eft*. Then it returns to the water, and the female newt lays its eggs there.

The baby newts are tadpoles. They look very much like baby frogs, but the newt does not lose its tail as it grows, as frogs and toads do. Newts grow to be three to six inches long. The newt that lives in the United States is a light yellow or green color. When it leaves the water it changes to red.

During the time that the newt lives in the water it eats leeches, water insects, and worms. When it lives on land it eats spiders, insects, and worms. The newt is useful to man because it is fond of mosquito eggs and destroys many other insect pests.

New Testament

The New Testament is the part of the Bible that tells of the life of Jesus, his teachings, the reasons why Christians should follow them, the ways in which Christians can live according to his teachings, and the acts and deeds of his early followers. The first part of the Bible is the Old Testament, which is a holy book to Jews as well as to Christians.

The twenty-seven books of the New Testament can be divided into three parts:

The Gospels are the four books (Matthew, Mark, Luke, and John) that tell about Jesus' life and teachings. They are sometimes called the most influential books ever written because through these writings most people in the Western World have become and remained Christians. They are recognized as great models of narrative writing and describe Jesus in such a way that people who read the Gospels are able to feel that they have actually met him. To these four books is added The Acts of the Apostles, a book that tells the story of the early Christian Church. The Acts tells how, after the departure of Jesus, his Apostles went about converting others to Christianity and establishing the Christian faith. The Gospels and the Acts are historical books and tell a vivid and stirring story.

The Epistles of St. Paul are fourteen letters written by St. Paul (or maybe in some cases by his close followers) to the newly formed Christian Churches, and also to other apostles and ministers of the Christian faith. These letters or epistles contain the first great descriptions of Christian beliefs after the departure of Jesus. Besides giving advice on how to act in accordance with the teachings of Jesus, they are beautiful literature.

The General Epistles are seven letters written by James, Peter, John, and Jude, and addressed to Christians everywhere. Like the Epistles of St. Paul, they give practical advice for Christian life and describe Christian belief.

The last book of the New Testament is the Revelation of St. John, or the Apocalypse. It is a prophecy of what will happen when the end of the world occurs, but at the same time it describes the difficulties, sufferings and great hopes of the early Christians. There is a separate article about the APOCALYPSE.

Newton, Sir Isaac

Isaac Newton was an English mathematician and scientist, one of the greatest who ever lived. His discoveries and ideas have guided other scientists for nearly three hundred years.

Isaac Newton was born in England on Christmas day in 1642. He studied at Cambridge University and was graduated in 1665. Between 1665 and 1686 he made his most important discoveries. He invented the calculus (a branch of higher mathematics), discovered that white light was really made up of six basic colors (red, orange, yellow, green, blue, and violet), and developed the idea of universal gravitation. His most famous books are the *Principles of Natural Philosophy,* which explains his ideas on motion, and *Optics,* which explains his ideas on light.

When he was 50 years old, Newton had a nervous breakdown. From that time until his death he did very little scientific work. He became very absent-minded and short-tempered, and was even careless about the way he dressed. He was president of the Royal Society of London, an organization of scientists, for 25 years. Also he was a member of the English Parliament. In 1705, he was made a knight by Queen Anne of England, after which he was known as Sir Isaac Newton. He always remained a very modest and religious man. Although other scientists considered him a genius and the greatest thinker of his time, he is said to have remarked on his deathbed: "If I have seen farther than others, it is by standing on the shoulders of giants." He died in 1727.

Read also the articles GRAVITATION and MOTION.

New Year's Day

New Year's Day is January 1, the first day of the year. It is a legal holiday in all the states of the United States and in many other parts of the world. New Year's Day and also the night before, called New Year's Eve, are celebrated in special ways. There are services in the churches, and on New Year's Eve many churches have "watch parties" as people wait for the New Year, which begins at midnight, and pray for a good year. On New Year's Day many people make lists of resolutions, good things they will try to do during the year to come.

Many people have gay parties on New Year's Eve. At midnight everyone shouts, cheers, or blows a horn to say goodbye to the Old Year and to welcome the New Year. Usually everyone kisses everyone else as a sign of friendship and joy. Often people sing "Auld Lang Syne," which is the New Year's song.

New York

New York is one of the Middle Atlantic states in the United States. It was one of the thirteen original colonies. Its nickname is the "Empire State" because it is a leading state in wealth and population. New York ranks first in manufacturing, is among the leaders in many farm and mineral products, and is one of the most popular vacation places in the country. New York City is the largest business and entertainment center in the United States. New York was named for the English Duke of York, who later became King James II.

In area, New York ranks 30th among the states, with 49,576 square miles. In population it ranks second, with about eighteen million people living there. It became a state in 1788, and was the 11th of the thirteen original states. The capital is Albany.

THE PEOPLE OF NEW YORK

New York was first settled by the Dutch, almost 350 years ago. Then came many French, Germans, Irish, Scandinavians, and settlers from the New England colonies. The English settled in New York in large numbers after 1664. Two hundred years later as New York grew into an important manufacturing state, thousands of people from all over Europe came to work in the cities, particularly in New York City. No other region of the world has people of as many different national origins as New York.

Most of the people in New York live in the large industrial cities and work in

factories. More than half of the people live in New York City.

Few of the people of New York are farmers, but they raise large and important crops. New York ranks second in the country in dairy products, and in apples, hay, grapes, onions, beets, cabbages, and cauliflowers. Many farmers have large truck gardens and duck farms on Long Island.

Some people work in valuable salt, iron, and gypsum mines. Others work in forests in the northern part of the state, cutting timber to be made into paper and pulpwood. Others fish in Long Island Sound, Lake Ontario, and Lake Erie.

One of the most important things the people of New York do is to take care of the thousands of visitors and vacationists who go every summer to the mountain and beach resorts, and to New York City. People also go to northern New York State for winter sports.

There are many different religious groups in New York. The largest are the Roman Catholic, Jewish, Methodist, and Episcopal.

Nyspix—Commerce

New York State's capitol at Albany is built in cathedral-like fashion.

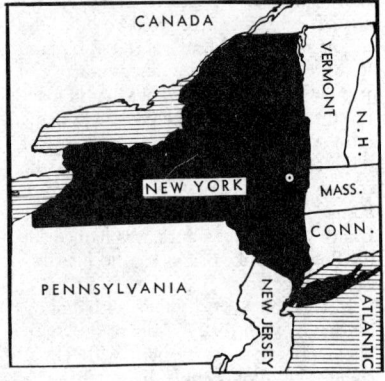

WHAT NEW YORK IS LIKE

New York is mostly a hilly and rolling region, with beautiful mountains, fertile valleys, and fine lakes. In the north are the Thousand Islands, a beautiful area and a fertile dairy-farming region. Also in the north are the Adirondack Mountains, with forests and wild scenery. This is one of the most popular vacation places in the eastern United States. In the southeast are the Catskill Mountains, with many historical spots and fertile valleys. This is also a favorite resort region.

The Hudson River flows through the eastern part of the state. It is the most important river on the Atlantic coast, and there are several important manufacturing cities along its banks. Off the southeast coast of New York is Long Island, with many farms and beach resorts.

The central and western parts of New York are made up of fertile plains and valleys, where cattle graze and farmers grow many crops. In the west, along Lake Erie and Lake Ontario, are orchards and truck farms.

The climate of New York is varied. In the mountains the winters are cold, with heavy snowfalls, but the summers are cool and pleasant. Along the southeastern coast and in the plains the summers are long and often very hot. The average temperature in summer is about 70 degrees, and in winter about 23 degrees.

The rivers and canals in New York carry large quantities of freight. The rivers furnish water power to generate electricity for factories and cities. Niagara Falls is a mighty generator of electric power. The state has about 75,000 miles of highways and almost 7,000 miles of railroads. There are more than 285 airports. The John F. Kennedy International Airport is the largest in the world.

There are many wild animals in the forests of upper New York, and the state is important in fur-producing. Trappers can find the muskrat, fox, raccoon, beaver, and mink.

THE GOVERNMENT OF NEW YORK

New York, like most other states, has a Governor and a Legislature. The Governor is elected for a four-year term. The Legislature is composed of two houses, a Senate and an Assembly. The members of both houses are elected for a two-year term. Judges are elected for a fourteen-year term. The capital is Albany. There are 62 counties.

About three and a half million children are enrolled in public schools. There are 218 colleges, universities and other schools of higher learning, among them some of the most famous in the country. There are separate articles about COLUMBIA, CORNELL, the United States MILITARY ACADEMY, and VASSAR. Others are described in the articles on New York City and the other large cities of New York. Other important colleges include:

State University of New York, with branches throughout the state. Enrollment, 136,721 in 1971 (co-ed).

Adelphi College, at Garden City. Enrollment, 7,925 in 1971 (co-ed).

Alfred University, at Alfred. Enrollment, 1,876 in 1971 (co-ed).

Clarkson College of Technology, at Potsdam. Enrollment, 2,525 in 1971 (men only).

Colgate University, at Hamilton. Enrollment, 2,075 in 1971 (men only).

Hamilton College, at Clinton. Enrollment, 864 in 1971 (men only).

Hofstra College, at Hempstead. Enrollment, 11,535 in 1971 (co-ed).

Niagara University, at Niagara. Enrollment, 2,803 in 1971 (co-ed).

Rensselaer Polytechnic Institute, at Troy. Enrollment, 5,977 in 1971 (co-ed).

Rochester Institute of Technology, at Rochester. Enrollment, 10,776 in 1971 (co-ed).

St. Bonaventure, at St. Bonaventure. Enrollment, 2,456 in 1971 (co-ed).).

Sarah Lawrence College, at Bronxville. Enrollment, 725 in 1971 (women only).).

Skidmore College, at Saratoga Springs. Enrollment 1,568 in 1971 (women only).).

Syracuse University, at Syracuse. Enrollment, 22,667 in 1971 (co-ed).

Union College and University, at Schenectady and Albany. Enrollment, 1,764 in 1971 (co-ed).

CHIEF CITIES OF NEW YORK

The leading cities of New York, with populations from the 1970 census, are:

New York City, population 7,867,760, the largest city.

Buffalo, population 462,768, the second-largest city.

Rochester, population 296,233, the third-largest city.

Syracuse, population 197,208 the fifth-largest city.

Yonkers, population 204,370 the fourth-largest city.

Albany, population 114,873, the state capital and sixth-largest city.

There is a separate article about each of these cities.

NEW YORK IN THE PAST

New York was inhabited by two powerful Indian tribes, the Algonquin and the Iroquois, when the first Europeans arrived. The first European explorer was an Italian, Verrazano, sailing for the French. In 1609, Henry Hudson sailed up the river that was later named after him, while Samuel de Champlain, representing France, entered the state from the north. In 1614 the Dutch made the first permanent settlement, Fort Nassau (now Albany). In the next few years other people from the Netherlands settled on Manhattan Island, which they called New Amsterdam.

The Dutch controlled the region until 1664, when the English took it and renamed it New York. The French also claimed New York, and assisted by the Algonquin Indians they went to war against the English, who were helped by the Iroquois Indians. The long and bitter French and Indian Wars kept the region from being settled for a long while.

New York played an important part in the Revolutionary War, and the region has many historic spots. Many of the battles of the Revolution were fought on New York soil, including the Battle of Saratoga, in 1777, an important American victory.

After the war, New York City became the first capital of the United States, and it was there that George Washington was inaugurated as the first President of the United States. Gradually people began settling on the fertile land. The state was again the scene of much fighting during the War of 1812. In the next ten years, thousands settled in regions farther west. After the Erie Canal was opened and a railroad was built, the state grew rapidly into the leading manufacturing state as well as an important farming state.

PLACES TO SEE IN NEW YORK

Father Millet Cross National Monument, near Niagara Falls, in the west, on U.S. Route 62. Memorial cross to Father Pierre Millet, who erected a cross on this site in 1688.

Saratoga National Historical Park, 5,500 acres, ten miles southeast of Saratoga Springs, in the east, on U.S. Route 4. Scene of the American victory over the British in 1777; turning point of the Revolutionary War.

White Plains National Battlefield Site, at White Plains, in the southeast, on State Highway 22. Memorials showing the positions held by Washington's army at the Battle of White Plains in 1776.

Trophy Point, on the grounds of the
United States Military Academy at West Point,
overlooks the Highlands section
of the Hudson River.

New York State Department of Commerce

Albright-Knox Art Gallery, designed in the style of Greco-Roman architecture, is located in
the city of Buffalo.

Home of Franklin Delano Roosevelt, at Hyde Park, in the east, on U.S. Route 9. Birthplace, home and "Summer White House" of the President.

Jones Beach, 2,413 acres, on Long Island, on Sunrise Highway. Largest waterfront park on the Atlantic Ocean.

Niagara Falls, at Niagara Falls, in the west, on U.S. Route 104. Magnificent spectacle, famous throughout the world.

Fort Ticonderoga, off Lake Champlain, at Ticonderoga, in the northeast, on State Highway 22. The old colonial fort where Ethan Allen and his "Green Mountain Boys" forced the British to surrender.

National Baseball Hall of Fame, at Cooperstown, in the east, on State Highway 28. Museum commemorating the birthplace of modern baseball.

See also the article on NEW YORK CITY.

NEW YORK. Area, 49,576 square miles. Population (1970 census) 18,190,740. Capital, Albany. Nickname, the Empire State. Motto, *Excelsior* (Higher). Flower, rose. Bird, none. No official song. Admitted to Union, July 26, 1788. Official abbreviation, N.Y.

New York City

More people live in and around New York City than in any other place in the world. It is the largest city in the United States and with its suburbs it is the largest in the world. It is in the southeastern corner of New York State, on the Hudson and the East rivers and on New York Bay. It is made up of five boroughs: Queens, Brooklyn, the Bronx, Manhattan, and Richmond (Staten Island).

New York City is about 323 square miles in size, and almost eight million people live there. About sixteen million people live in New York's metropolitan or urbanized area, which extends for a radius of fifty miles. New York is one of the great seaports of the world. It is the financial and entertainment center of the United States and one of its biggest manufacturing, educational and cultural centers. Millions of people visit New York City every year.

THE PEOPLE OF NEW YORK CITY

People from all over the world live in New York. More than half were born in the United States, but nearly half are foreign-born. Large numbers of immigrants have settled in certain sections of the city, where they have kept their native languages and many of their old customs. There are an Italian section known as "Little Italy," a Jewish section on the Lower East Side, and a Negro section in Harlem. There are also Chinese, Spanish, Irish, German and other neighborhoods.

Most of the eight million people in New York work in the busy borough of Manhattan, although many of them live in other boroughs. They travel to work by subway and automobile. Many people who work in Manhattan live in the nearby states of New Jersey and Connecticut. In New York are some of the largest industries in the country. More women's clothing is manufactured there than in any other city. People make many other products, including hats, fur goods, cosmetics, lace, and baked goods and other foods. There are large printing and publishing industries. Banking, brokerage, and insurance, in the "downtown" district around Wall Street, and advertising and selling, in the "midtown" district, employ hundreds of thousands.

WHAT THE CITY IS LIKE

Although Manhattan is next to the smallest of the boroughs in size, it is the most important. When people say they are going to visit New York City, they usually mean they are going to Manhattan. Here visitors can see the world's tallest skyscrapers, which make up the impressive New York skyline. Skyscrapers can safely be built on Manhattan because much of the island is solid rock, which makes a strong foundation for building supports. Manhattan is the city's shopping center. On Manhattan are most of the city's theaters, museums, and other places of interest.

More people live in Brooklyn than any other borough. Brooklyn is sometimes called the "borough of homes." The Bronx, Queens, and Richmond are also residential, though there are many factories, stores and businesses there. The city has a number of beautiful parks and historic buildings.

New York City has one of the world's largest transportation systems to take care of all its people. Bridges, bus lines, subways, tunnels and parkways connect the boroughs. The city is connected to the state of New Jersey by tunnels, the George Washington Bridge, ferries, and railroads. New York City's two largest railroad terminals are the Grand Central and Pennsylvania Stations. Hundreds of trains from all parts of the country enter and leave these stations every day. The John F. Kennedy International Airport, in Queens, is the largest airport in the world. LaGuardia Airport, also in Queens, is another of the world's busiest airports.

GOVERNMENT OF THE CITY

New York City is divided into five boroughs, each of which is a county of New York State. The state legislature has some control over how much money the city can spend, for the legislature decides how large a part of the state's tax income will be spent in the city, and the city cannot collect any taxes of its own without the legislature's consent.

At the head of the city's government is a mayor, elected by the people who live in the city. His acts are subject to the decisions of a committee called the Board of Estimate, which has eight members.

The city's laws are made by a City Council, which consists of a president and 25 members. Each borough has a borough president, who is a member of the Board of Estimate. The mayor and all other elected officials serve four-year terms.

The police, fire, and other departments of the government are headed by commissioners appointed by the mayor. New York City has its own courts, with judges or magistrates elected by the people.

The principal income of New York City is from a tax on real estate. In 1963 the land and buildings in New York City were assessed at about $27,000,000,000, which is far more than in any other city of the world. The city's income and budget was close to $3,000,000,000.

COLLEGES AND UNIVERSITIES

New York City has many large colleges and universities. Two of the largest, Columbia and Fordham, are subjects of separate article. Others are:

City University of New York, with a total enrollment in 1971 of 117,786 includes among others, Brooklyn, City, Hunter and Queens colleges.

Brooklyn College. Enrollment, 27,510 in 1971 (co-ed).

College of the City of New York. Enrollment, 19,286 in 1971 (co-ed).

Hunter College. Enrollment, 19,666 in 1971, (co-ed).

Queens College. Enrollment, 23,541 in 1971 (co-ed).

Cooper Union. Enrollment, 1,161 in 1971 (co-ed).

Juilliard School of Music. Enrollment, 1,005 in 1971 (co-ed).

Long Island University. Enrollment, 7,339 in 1971 (co-ed).

Manhattan College. Enrollment, 4,497 in 1971 (men only).

New York University (not a state institution). Enrollment 44,401 in 1971 (co-ed).

Polytechnic Institute of Brooklyn. Enrollment, 4,413 in 1971 (men only).

Pratt Institute. Enrollment, 4,333 in 1971 (co-ed).

St. John's University. Enrollment, 12,800 in 1971 (co-ed).

Yeshiva University. Enrollment, 7,829 in 1971 (co-ed).

NEW YORK CITY IN THE PAST

The first white settlement on the island of Manhattan was made by the Dutch more than three hundred years ago. The island was bought from the Indians for $24 by the first Dutch governor, Peter Minuit, in 1626. The Dutch called their colony New Amsterdam. When the British conquered the Dutch colony in 1664, they renamed it New York.

The English settlement grew rapidly, and from the beginning people came from many countries to live there. Most of the people lived on the lower end of the island, but there were villages to the north and east. These villages grew into cities that later became the other boroughs of New York City. In 1898, all the five boroughs were joined into the city of Greater New York. New York soon grew to be the largest city in America.

Among the important events held in New York have been two World's Fairs, one in 1939–40 and another in 1964–65.

PLACES TO SEE

Times Square at Broadway and 42nd Street, and "the Great White Way," Broadway north of 42nd Street in Man-

hattan. A famous entertainment section, with many theaters, restaurants, night clubs, and hotels. At night this part of the city blazes with lights and huge electric signs.

Fifth Avenue, in Manhattan. A noted shopping district. St. Patrick's Cathedral and the New York Public Library (containing about seven million books) are on Fifth Avenue.

Coney Island, in Brooklyn. A popular beach, with a large and colorful amusement park, and an aquarium.

Museum of Natural History, and Hayden Planetarium, in Manhattan. Notable exhibits of natural science, and of wonders of the heavens.

Empire State Building, in Manhattan. The highest building in the world, 1,250 feet high, with 102 stories. A famous view from its observation tower.

Radio City Music Hall, in Manhattan. The most famous motion-picture theater in the world; seats 6,200 people.

Bronx Zoo, in the Bronx. One of the biggest zoos in the country, with animals that live in their natural surroundings.

Central Park, in Manhattan, 840 acres, in the heart of the city. Contains two lakes, a zoo, an outdoor concert stadium,

The Metropolitan Opera House at Lincoln Center for the Performing Arts in New York City.

Empire State Bldg

A fairyland of lights greets the gaze of evening visitors to New York City. The Empire State Building dominates the scene.

and beautiful wooded scenery.

Statue of Liberty, in New York Harbor (see LIBERTY, STATUE OF).

United Nations Headquarters, on the East River, in Manhattan. Officially this is an independent territory.

NEW YORK CITY. Population (1970) 7,867,760. Settled in 1626.

New Zealand

New Zealand is a country in the South Pacific Ocean, about 1,200 miles east of Australia. It is an independent, self-governing member of the British Commonwealth of Nations. New Zealand is made up of two large islands and many smaller ones. The three main islands are North Island, South Island, and Stewart Island. Altogether, New Zealand is 103,736 square miles in size, which is a little smaller than Colorado. More than 2,800,000 people live there.

WHAT THE PEOPLE ARE LIKE

Most of the people in New Zealand are of British descent, but more than 223,-

New York State Department of Commerce

The "Lady with the Torch" dominates the New York harbor scene as she has done since 1886. The Statue of Liberty National Monument on Liberty Island is under the jurisdiction of the National Park Service. Tour boats to the monument leave the Battery daily on the hour.

000 Maoris live there. They are a brown-skinned people who were the original settlers of New Zealand. (There is a separate article about the MAORI people).

The New Zealanders are a progressive people, using modern machinery and methods on their farms and in their factories. New Zealand was the first country in the world to give women the right to vote and the first to give all its people social security and old-age pensions.

The people of New Zealand speak English. Most of them belong to the Church of England or to the Presbyterian, Roman Catholic and Methodist Churches.

HOW THE PEOPLE LIVE

More than half the people of New Zealand live in towns and cities. Since World War II, manufacturing has grown rapidly, and many people have moved to the cities to work in factories that make machinery, clothing, furniture, leather goods, and canned foods. No New Zealander in the cities is without a job; in fact there are thousands of jobs waiting for workers. For this reason, New Zealand welcomes settlers from Great Britain and Europe.

Although more people live in the cities than in the country, dairy farming and the raising of cattle and sheep are the

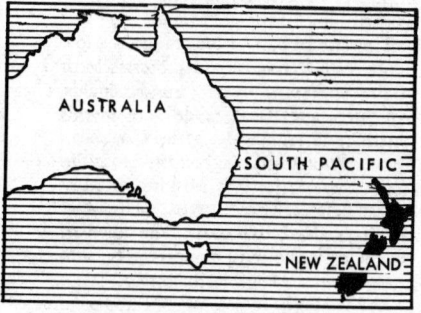

largest industries in New Zealand. The dairy farmers send large amounts of butter and cheese to Great Britain in refrigerator ships. Ranchers raise sheep not only for their wool but also for their meat, which is called mutton. New Zealand exports more mutton than any other country. Other farmers in New Zealand raise wheat, oats, barley, and fruits.

Most New Zealanders live in small, modern bungalows. There is usually a flower garden in front and a vegetable garden behind the house.

Everyone has to go to school between the ages of 6 and 15. There are many excellent elementary schools and high schools, six universities, nine teachers' training colleges, and 114 Maori schools.

WHAT THE COUNTRY IS LIKE

The three main islands of New Zealand are mountainous. In South Island, the Southern Alps stretch almost the full length of the island. In these mountains is Mount Cook, 12,349 feet high, the highest peak in the country. There are large grazing areas for sheep on South Island. North Island also has mountain ranges and several active volcanoes. Two-thirds of New Zealand is covered with dense forests called the "bush," where men cut timber for furniture, paper pulp, and other products. Natural steam occurring in the volcanic areas is used to provide

power for industry. New Zealand also produces coal, iron, oil, and natural gas.

Stewart Island is much smaller than North and South Islands. It is 670 square miles, and is a popular summer resort.

New Zealand has 59,012 miles of roads and 3,336 miles of railroads. It is connected to other countries by ship and air lines.

New Zealand has a pleasant and moderate climate, though the high mountains have snow on them all year round. When it is winter in Europe and the United States, it is summer in New Zealand. Visitors to New Zealand enjoy its hot springs and geysers, caves and waterfalls. Sportsmen call its big-game fishing the best in the world.

CHIEF CITIES IN NEW ZEALAND

The leading cities of New Zealand, with populations, including suburbs (1971 estimate), are:

Auckland, population 640,000, the largest city in New Zealand, the chief port and a manufacturing center, on North Island.

Wellington, population 320,000, the capital and second-largest city, on North Island.

Christchurch, population 270,000, the third-largest city, an industrial center, on South Island.

Dunedin, population 150,000, the fourth-largest city, a manufacturing center, on South Island.

HOW THE PEOPLE ARE GOVERNED

The head of the government of New Zealand is a Governor-General, who represents the British queen. He is appointed by the queen for a five-year term. The country is actually run by a Prime Minister. He is appointed by the legislature, which is elected by the people. The Prime Minister stays in office as long as he can keep the confidence of the majority of the legislature. The legislature is composed of one house. It has 84 members, four of whom are Maoris. The members are elected for a three-year term. The capital of New Zealand is Wellington.

NEW ZEALAND IN THE PAST

More than six hundred years ago, the Maoris came in open canoes and settled in New Zealand. They lived there undisturbed by white men until the Dutch explorer Abel Tasman tried to land on the coast more than three hundred years ago. He and his men were driven back by the Maoris, and no settlement was made. The first settlement was made by Captain James Cook, a British explorer, in 1769.

For a time the country was without real law and order, and the people had trouble with the Maoris. Finally, in 1840, New Zealand became a British colony. Settlement was still slow until 1861, when gold was discovered on South Island. Many more settlers arrived in the 1870s. New Zealand became known all over the world for its progressive laws, many of which were later adopted by other countries. In 1907 New Zealand became an independent British dominion. In both World War I and II, New Zealand soldiers were greatly praised for their courage. Along with the Australian forces, they were called *Anzacs*. Since World War II, New Zealand has continued to grow and prosper.

NEW ZEALAND. Area, 103,736 square miles. Population (1971 census) 2,860,475. Language, English. Religion, principally Protestant. Government, self-governing member of the British Commonwealth of Nations. Monetary unit, the New Zealand dollar worth $1.15 (U.S.) Flag, blue background with Union Jack and four five-pointed red stars with white borders.

Ney, Marshal

Michel Ney was one of the bravest and most skillful officers who fought under Napoleon, the French emperor and military leader. Ney was born over two hundred years ago, in 1769. His family was not a rich or important one. When he was 18 years old he rose to be commander of his regiment. He fought for Napoleon in Germany and in Switzerland, and was honored for his bravery by being made a marshal, which is the highest rank for an army officer. When Napoleon was defeated and sent into exile in 1814, Ney was honored by the new French king, Louis XVIII, by being made a nobleman. In 1815 Napoleon escaped from exile and tried to rule France again. Ney was put in command of soldiers sent to stop Napoleon, but instead he decided to join Napoleon. Napoleon was defeated, and Ney was arrested, found guilty of treason, and executed later in 1815.

Niagara Falls

Niagara Falls is one of the famous natural wonders of the world. It is on the Niagara River, at the city of Niagara Falls, on the border between New York State and Ontario. It is one of the most popular tourist attractions in North America, and is famous as a place where couples go on their honeymoon.

Niagara Falls is about halfway along the Niagara River, which flows from Lake Erie to Lake Ontario. The river flows along quietly until about half a mile before the falls. There it changes into swift and swirling rapids. Just above the falls is Goat Island, which divides the river as it plunges down a steep precipice into a gorge through which the river flows. The river falls in two mighty falls. The larger of the two is on the Canadian side, and is called the Canadian, or Horseshoe, Falls. These falls are 158 feet high and almost 3,000 feet wide at the widest point. The smaller falls are called the American Falls. They are 167 feet high but only about half as wide as the Horseshoe Falls. People can take a sightseeing trip in a boat around the bottom of the Falls, or they can get excellent views of the plunging water from a bridge that crosses the steep canyon. At night the falls are lit up with colored lights.

Five hundred thousand tons of water plunge over the edge of Niagara Falls every minute. The water has been gradually wearing away the edge of the falls, and sometimes pieces fall off. Portions fell off in 1931 and 1934. In 1954 the largest section broke off, and 185,000 tons of rock fell into the river below. The edge of Horseshoe Falls is being worn away at the rate of about 3 feet a year, while the American Falls move back about 5 inches a year. The water and the

Buffalo Chamber of Commerce
Beautiful Niagara Falls is visited by thousands of sightseers every year. The American Falls are on the left, and the Canadian Horseshoe Falls are facing the camera.

strong spray have also worn caves in the rock just below the ledge of the falls. One of these is called the Cave of Winds and it is possible for people to get into the cave and watch the tremendous falls thundering by.

In winter, Niagara Falls can look like a white wonderland. Often the water freezes and huge icicles hang from the edge of the falls. But usually the falls continue to fall with tremendous force. The falls are not only very beautiful but also very useful, for they supply water power that runs the important hydroelectric power plants nearby. These plants supply electricity to large parts of New York State and Pennsylvania, as well as to parts of Canada.

Nibelung

The Nibelungs were imaginary dwarfs in the myths and literature of the German people, hundreds of years ago. The Nibelungs were supposed to possess a great treasure in gold, but there was a curse on the gold. A group of Germanic legends grew up around the imaginary group, and a German poet wrote a long song about these people, including the Icelandic legends. This was called the *Nibelungenlied,* which in German means "Song of the Nibelungs." In this poem, or song, the hero Siegfried steals the gold and marries a girl named Kriemhild. She is the sister of King Gunther of Burgundy. Siegfried kidnaps a Frankish maiden, Brunhild, for Gunther. Brunhild hates Siegfried for this, and persuades another man, Hagen, to kill Siegfried. Hagen obtains the treasure of the Nibelungs and hides it by burying it in the Rhine. The widow of Siegfried, Kriemhild, determines to get revenge for the murder of Siegfried, and she marries the Hun king, later known as Attila, with the result that there was general killing on all sides, and only a few survived.

Richard Wagner, the German operatic composer, wrote a series of operas about these legends. The series is called *Der Ring Des Nibelungen,* and it is usually called the Ring Operas. The four operas in the Ring are *Das Rheingold, Die Walküre, Siegfried,* and *Götterdammerung.*

Nicaragua

Nicaragua is the largest country in Central America. It has shores on the Caribbean Sea and the Pacific Ocean. Nicaragua is 57,145 square miles in size, which is a little smaller than the state of Michigan. About one and a half million people live in Nicaragua. Although the country has valuable resources, such as fertile soil, valuable forests, and rich mineral deposits, it has not developed them thoroughly. Nicaragua is becoming a modern nation, but slowly.

THE PEOPLE WHO LIVE THERE

Most of the people of Nicaragua are of mixed Spanish and Indian descent. Some are pure Spanish, some pure Indian. Many Europeans have settled on the eastern coast, where they have developed large banana plantations. There are also many Negroes who came from the West Indies to work on the plantations.

Most of the people are Roman Catho-

lic, once the state religion, but there is complete freedom of worship. The Nicaraguans speak Spanish, but everyone who goes to school must study English. More than half the people cannot read or write, but education is now being encouraged. Everyone has to go to school between the

ages of 6 and 14, and there are a number of high schools, colleges, professional schools, a school of engineering, and a university located at León.

HOW THE PEOPLE LIVE

Most of the people of Nicaragua are farmers. They grow large crops of bananas, coffee, cotton, and sugarcane, but most of them do not have modern farming machinery.

Nicaraguans also work in valuable gold mines in the northwestern part of the country. Nicaragua exports more gold than any other country in Central America. Many people who live in the cities work in sugar-refining and coffee-processing plants. Some work in small factories making soap, cigarettes, and cotton goods. Most people in Nicaragua are poor.

WHAT KIND OF PLACE IT IS

The Cordillera, a range of mountains, runs through the central part of Nicaragua. In these mountains is perhaps the greatest mineral wealth in Central America, consisting of rich deposits of gold, silver, copper, iron, zinc, and lead. Most of the minerals have not been mined because of the lack of modern machinery and good transportation. Some mining companies from the United States have installed modern equipment and have worked some of the gold mines.

The eastern part of Nicaragua is a low plain, with dense tropical forests. Most of the important rivers (the Bluefields, San Juan, and Rio Grande) are in this region. The region along the Caribbean Sea is swampy and is called the Mosquito Coast, named after the Miskitto or Mosquito Indians. There are sandy beaches and bays along this coast. The town of Bluefields is the most important Nicaragua port on the Caribbean.

The western region of Nicaragua is also a low plain. Here farmers grow tropical fruits, corn, and rice. There are two large lakes in this part of Nicaragua. Lake Nicaragua, about 3,100 square miles in size, is one of the largest lakes in North America. In the west along the Pacific Ocean are ranges of mountains that contain a number of volcanoes. There are several important harbors on the Pacific coast. The most important one is Corinto.

The climate of Nicaragua is hot, except in the central mountain region, where it is cool. The eastern coast has very heavy rainfalls. There the temperature is about 80 degrees in summer and only a few degrees cooler in winter. The western region also has a tropical climate, and in summer it is very hot and damp.

Transportation in Nicaragua is very poor. There are few good roads or railroads. There is little travel between the eastern and western parts of the country, which are separated by mountains.

CHIEF CITIES OF NICARAGUA

The leading cities of Nicaragua, with latest estimated populations, are:

Managua, population 183,783, the capital and largest city of Nicaragua. There is a separate article about MANAGUA.

León, population 46,321, the second-largest city, an educational center, in the western part.

Granada, population 30,158, the third-largest city, a railroad and industrial center, in the southern part.

Masaya, population 28,208, the fourth-largest city, an Indian handicraft center, in the southern part.

HOW THE PEOPLE ARE GOVERNED

Nicaragua is a republic, which means that it has a president, a legislature that makes the laws, and a constitution that protects the rights of the people. The president of Nicaragua is elected for a six-year term. The legislature is composed of two houses, a Senate and a Chamber of Deputies. The members of both houses are elected for a six-year term. Nicaragua is divided into sixteen departments. The capital is Managua.

NICARAGUA IN THE PAST

The first European to explore the coast of Nicaragua was Christopher Columbus, more than four hundred years ago. Some years later, the Spanish arrived and made several settlements. Under Spanish rule these settlements were made part of Guatemala. The Spaniards were stern rulers and in 1821 the colonies in Central America revolted. Nicaragua declared its independence in that year.

Two years later Nicaragua joined the Central American Federation. When this federation was dissolved in 1839 Nicaragua became an independent republic.

The history of Nicaragua since then has been filled with wars, revolutions, and much unrest among the people. On several occasions the United States, Great Britain, and Mexico have intervened.

Since 1850 or before, Nicaragua has been considered a good place for a big ship canal joining the Atlantic and Pacific Oceans. Panama instead was selected (see PANAMA CANAL), but Nicaragua is still being considered for a second and larger interocean canal.

In 1941, during World War II, Nicaragua joined the Allies. After the war, in 1945, Nicaragua was the first country to approve the United Nations Charter.

NICARAGUA. Area, 57,145 square miles. Population (1964 estimate) 1,597,000. Language, Spanish. Religion, mostly Roman Catholic. Government, republic. Monetary unit, the cordoba, worth about 14 cents (U.S.). Flag, three horizontal bars, blue, white, and blue.

Nice

Nice is a city in southeastern France. It is on that part of the Mediterranean coast known as the Riviera, and it is a noted winter resort. People go to Nice to enjoy its beaches and gay festivals. Nice has factories that make perfume, olive oil, and soap.

Nice is a beautiful city with many fine hotels and private houses, called villas. Part of the city is very old, with narrow, crooked streets, but the part of the city where visitors stay is quite modern. Nice is known for its colorful flowers and gardens. Its climate is pleasantly warm even in winter, because the high Alps mountains cut off the cold north winds.

Nice was ruled by the Romans more than two thousand years ago. Through the centuries, it was controlled by other rulers, but in 1860 it was finally given to France. During World War II, it was occupied by the Germans.

NICE. Population (1973 estimate) 325,400. Capital of the department of Alpes-Maritimes in France. On the Mediterranean Sea. Sixth-largest city in France.

Nicholas, Saint

St. Nicholas lived about the year 300. He was a real person, the bishop of Myra, an ancient section of Asia Minor. He is the patron saint of boys and sailors, and of Greece and Sicily. In the Netherlands, St. Nicholas Day (December 6) is a children's holiday, a time for giving presents. In the early days of New York, the English settlers took over the Dutch settlers' observance of St. Nicholas, but eventually the English name became Santa Claus. There is a separate article about SANTA CLAUS.

Nicholas

Nicholas was the name of two czars, or emperors, of Russia. Nicholas I was  born more than 150 years ago, in 1796, and became czar in 1825. Some of the Russians wanted his brother to be czar and started a revolt, which is called the Decembrist Revolution, but this revolt was put down. Nicholas became the most powerful ruler in Europe, but he was feared and hated by his subjects. He was defeated in the CRIMEAN WAR, about which there is a separate article. He died in 1855.

Nicholas II, the great-grandson of Nicholas I, was the last czar of Russia. He was born in 1868 and began to reign in 1894. In 1904 he tried to conquer Japan in the Russo-Japanese War, in which Russia was badly defeated. The people were angry and discontented, and held strikes and other uprisings against the government. Nicholas was dominated by  his wife and her adviser, the monk RASPUTIN, about whom there is a separate article. Toward the end of World War I, in 1917, the Russian people forced Nicholas to abdicate (resign as emperor). He and his family were imprisoned, and when the Communists came into power a few months later they were executed.

nickel

Nickel is a tough white metal with a slightly yellow tinge. It is a chemical element, one of the more than one hundred basic substances of which everything in the world is made.

Nickel can be polished so that it shines very brightly, and it tarnishes so little that polished nickel stays bright for a long time. Many things made of other metals, especially of brass and iron, are nickel-plated (covered with a coating of nickel) to keep them from rusting.

NICKEL ALLOYS

When only a small amount of nickel is melted along with steel, it keeps the steel from rusting. When three parts of nickel and one part of copper, along with a very little amount of iron and manganese, are melted together, they make Monel Metal, an alloy almost impossible to corrode. Monel Metal is used for ships' propeller blades, restaurant kitchen equipment, and tanks and pipes in the chemical industry. Three parts of nickel and two parts of chromium make an alloy called by the trademarked name Nichrome. Wire made of Nichrome becomes red-hot when an electric current passes through it, so Nichrome is used for the heating coils in electric toasters, broilers, hot plates, electric irons, electric furnaces, and other kinds of electric heater. Nickel, copper and zinc combined make

Nickel Co. of Canada

Streams of molten nickel pour from a four-lipped ladle onto high-pressure jets of water.

German silver, an alloy that is used to make knives, forks, spoons, and cheap jewelry. Permalloy and Alnico are two alloys of nickel that can be made very highly magnetic. These alloys are used in many electrical instruments. A one-ounce piece of Alnico can be made into so strong a magnet that it can pick up a 281-pound piece of iron. Invar is a nickel alloy that expands and contracts so little with changes in temperature that it is used in delicate scientific instruments.

The United States five-cent piece—the "nickel"—is made of only one part nickel and three parts copper.

Powdered nickel is used as a catalyst in the chemical process called hydrogenation. (A catalyst is a chemical that brings about a change in other chemicals, but is not affected itself.) In this process, hydrogen gas is combined with oils to make them into solid fats; fish and whale oils become soap, vegetable oils become margarine, coal oil becomes lubricating grease. The powdered nickel causes the hydrogen and oil to combine, but the nickel itself remains unchanged.

THE STORY OF NICKEL

In the 17th century, metallurgists—men who work with metals and metal ores—were puzzled by a rock that looked very much like copper ore but from which they could get no copper. They thought that Satan had made the rock to bedevil them, so they named the ore Kupfernickel, which is a German word meaning "Old Nick's (Satan's) copper." In 1751, the Swedish chemist Axel Fred-

ric Cronstedt found a white metal in Kupfernickel, and realizing it was not any kind of copper, he just kept the "nickel" part of the name.

Nickel ore is mined in large quantities in Canada, the island of New Caledonia, Soviet Russia, and Finland. The metal is taken from the ore by ELECTROLYSIS, about which there is a separate article.

nicotine

Nicotine is a very powerful poison found in the tobacco plant. It is a colorless, oily liquid which turns brown when exposed to air. Less than a drop of pure nicotine taken into the body will kill a person.

Because nicotine acts directly on the central nervous system, people who smoke cigarettes or chew tobacco may find that their hearts beat faster, blood pressure rises, food seems harder to digest, and breathing becomes more difficult. Heat from burning tobacco destroys some of the nicotine, but 1 to 2 milligrams are absorbed by inhaling one cigarette.

Nicotine was named after Jean Nicot, the man who introduced tobacco into France.

Nietzsche, Friedrich

Friedrich Wilhelm Nietzsche was a German philosopher whose ideas had a very important influence on many people. Nietzsche was born in 1844. He was a brilliant student and when he was only 25 years old he became a professor of classical literature at Basle University in Switzerland. After about ten years he had to stop teaching because of poor health. When he was 45 years old he became mentally ill. His sister took care of him for the next eleven years, until he died in 1900.

Nietzsche wrote that Christian ideals of humility and sacrifice are false. He said that a really great man is proud and knows that he is superior to everyone else. These ideas are expressed in one of Nietzsche's best-known books, *Thus Spake Zarathustra*. It gives Nietzsche's ideas about what he called the *Ubermensch*, which means "superman" in German. The Nazis under Adolf Hitler adopted this idea.

Niger, The Republic of the

Niger is a republic in northeast Africa. It became independent in 1960, after having been a colony of France since 1920. Niger is almost twice as big as Texas in area but only about a third as many people live there. This is partly because much of the country is in the Sahara Desert, too dry for farming. Niger has no seacoast but it touches on Lake Chad and some of the people are fishermen, but mostly they are farmers, since the land in the south of the country and along the Niger River is fertile. The principal products are peanuts, cotton, gum arabic, and tin.

The people are Negroes of several tribes, the largest being the Hausa. Niger is governed by a president and a National Assembly, elected by the people for five-year terms.

THE REPUBLIC OF THE NIGER. Area, 490,000 square miles. Population (1971 estimate) 3,800,000. Capital, Niamey, population about 70,000.

Niger River

The Niger River is the third-largest river in Africa. It is about 2,600 miles long. The Niger River rises in the mountains of Guinea, flows north through Mali, then curves and flows south through Niger and Nigeria, emptying into the Gulf of Guinea on the Atlantic Ocean. The central part of the river is navigable, but in many places there are rapids. The Benue River is the chief tributary of the Niger. It is navigable for about half the year. At other times the river is not high enough. The large, marshy delta formed by the Niger River covers about 14,000 square miles along the coast of Nigeria.

The Niger River was first explored almost two hundred years ago by Mungo Park, who died in its dangerous rapids when his party was attacked by natives.

Nigeria, Federal Republic of

The Federal Republic of Nigeria, a country in western Africa on the Gulf of Guinea, became independent in 1960. The new nation included all of the former British colony of Nigeria and a small part of the former British Cameroons. In area Nigeria is about twice the size of California and its population, more than fifty-six million, is the largest in Africa.

The people of Nigeria are divided into about 200 different tribal groups. The most numerous are: the Hausa and Fulani in the north (the region that has the most people); the Yoruba in the west; and the Ibo in the east. In the north almost all the people follow the Mohammedan religion. In other sections of the country the people are Mohammedans or Christians, or follow tribal religions. There are many native languages, but the official language is English. Most of the people are farmers who grow cacao, cotton, palm, and peanuts. Nigeria's rich natural resources include oil (the leading export), tin, and columbite. The capital and chief seaport is Lagos. (Other major cities are listed at the end of this article.)

In 1966, the Ibos of the east grew uneasy over the North's control of the government and army. The Ibos overthrew the government but the Northerners, led by Yakubu Gowan, soon regained control. Gowan tried to limit Ibo power and to deprive them of control of oil land, by dividing the eastern region into three states, two of which had more non-Ibos than Ibos. But the Military Governor of the eastern region, General Ojukwu, defied Gowan and declared in 1967 that eastern Nigeria would thereafter be the independent state of "Biafra". This was the start of a civil war which lasted over two and a half years. About two million Biafrans died in the war, mostly by starvation, since they were surrounded by Nigerian troops during most of the war and had little or nothing to eat. On January 14, 1970, Biafra formally surrendered.

FEDERATION OF NIGERIA. Area, 356,669 square miles. Population (1973 estimate), 56,510,000. Principal cities (1973 estimate), Ibadan (745,756), Lagos, the capital (875,477), Ognbomosho (380,239), Kano (351,175), Monetary unit, pound worth about $2.80 (U.S.).

nighthawk

The nighthawk is a bird that seems to have the wrong name. It is not a hawk and it does not fly only at night. The nighthawk is a member of the *nightjar* family, a group of about seventy different kinds of bird. They have a call that is so sharp and loud that it jars the listener.

The nighthawk makes its home in many parts of the United States. It grows to be about nine inches long and is of a brownish color, with white markings. During the mating season the male nighthawk likes to show off for the female. It circles gracefully high above the earth and then swoops down in a swift dive. Suddenly it changes direction and as the air rushes through the nighthawk's wings. it makes a booming noise.

nightingale

The nightingale is a bird that has been a favorite of poets since ancient times because of its beautiful song. The nightingale lives in Europe, Asia, and Africa. It is not an especially handsome bird. It is rather small and slender and is of a dark brown color with a grayish-white breast. The nightingale makes a rough nest of leaves and twigs in a small bush or even on the ground. The female lays four or five greenish-brown eggs. Nightingales eat caterpillars and the eggs of insects.

The nightingale sings mostly at night. Sometimes people catch nightingales and keep them in cages in their homes to hear them sing. Nightingales that are captured during the mating season will not sing in cages and often they grow so lonesome for their mates that they die.

Nightingale, Florence

Florence Nightingale was an Englishwoman who founded the profession of modern nursing for women.

Though she was English, Florence Nightingale was born in Florence, Italy (in 1820). Her parents were rich and expected her to be a society woman only, but from the time she was a little girl Florence Nightingale wanted only to help people who were sick. When she grew up she visited hospitals in many parts of Europe. Then she went to Germany and studied nursing in a hospital.

In 1854 British soldiers were fighting in the Crimea, where there was a war (the Crimean War) between Russia and Turkey. Great Britain and France were on Turkey's side. The English newspapers told how English soldiers were dying in the hospitals because they did not receive proper care. Florence Nightingale organized a group of about forty women and set out for the Crimea to care for the soldiers.

From the time that Florence Nightingale arrived, things changed and fewer soldiers died from wounds. She stayed in the Crimea for two years. Living conditions were very bad there and often Florence Nightingale was sick herself, but she never deserted her patients. The soldiers loved this brave and gentle woman and gave her the name "the lady with the lamp."

When Florence Nightingale returned home the English people raised about $200,000 and gave it to her so that she could open a school to train nurses. This school was called the St. Thomas School

of Nursing, and Florence Nightingale was in charge of it.

Florence Nightingale was honored by people all over the world. During the Civil War the people of the United States consulted her about the best nursing methods. In 1907 the English government awarded her the Order of Merit. She was the first woman ever to receive it. Florence Nightingale died in 1910, when she was 90 years old. There is a statue in London in her honor.

nightshade

Nightshade is the name of a large group of plants that grow in many parts of the world where the climate is warm. Some of the most important plants that man uses for food belong to this family. The potato, tomato, egg plant, and pepper are all members of the nightshade family. (You can read about these plants in separate articles.)

Many members of the nightshade family have small white flowers and black berries. These plants usually have a weak stem and grow along the ground. Some of them grow to about 2 feet.

The *deadly nightshade,* or *belladonna,* contains poisons. The leaves of this plant are used to make medicines.

Nijinsky, Vaslav

Vaslav Nijinsky was a Polish ballet dancer. Many consider him the greatest who ever lived. He was especially famous for his leaps, during which he seemed almost to be suspended in midair. Nijinsky was born in 1890, the fifth generation in a dancing family. At the age of 9 he was a fine dancer, and when he was 17 he made his first public appearance as a soloist. He was chosen by the great ballet producer Sergei Diaghilev to head a new Russian ballet, and he was the first to dance some of the modern ballets, then considered sensational. Nijinsky retired from dancing in 1917 because of mental illness. He died in 1950.

Nile

The Nile is the longest river in Africa and one of the world's most important waterways. It is 3,485 miles long from its source at Lake Victoria, in eastern Africa, to the point where it empties into the Mediterranean Sea near Alexandria, Egypt. (Some people trace the source of the Nile farther back, and make it 4,150 miles long. In this case, the Nile is the world's longest river.)

The Nile is formed by two headstreams, the Blue Nile and the White Nile. Both of these are part of the Nile River system, but the point where they join near Khartoum, capital of the Sudan, is the beginning of the Nile proper. From Khartoum, the Nile flows north between vast deserts. After passing the deserts it flows through the famous valley of the Nile, which grows wider and wider. Finally the Nile forms a delta and empties into the Mediterranean in two main streams with several branches.

The importance of the Nile to civilization has been great. Throughout the centuries Egyptian farmers have depended on it to make the soil fertile and give them abundant crops. The reason for this is the yearly flood, which reaches its height in late August. The flood deposits

fertile soil from Ethiopia along the valley and in great quantities throughout the delta. This yearly flood made possible the wealth of the great Egyptian civilization, more than six thousand years ago.

Six thousand years ago men first tried to harness the Nile's power during the flood, but they were not successful. In 1902 the Aswan Dam (also spelled Assuan Dam) was started in southern Egypt. The dam is more than a mile long and about 176 feet high. It helps to prevent floods in the waters farther north, and to regulate irrigation. Work on a new and larger Aswan Dam was begun in 1960. It will provide needed electrical power for Egypt's industries as well as irrigation for its farms. For this project Egypt needed large loans from the United States and other countries, and the refusal of these loans in 1956 caused Egypt to seize the SUEZ CANAL (see the separate article).

BATTLE OF THE NILE

The Battle of the Nile was a naval victory of the British admiral Horatio Nelson over the French fleet, at the mouth of the Nile, in 1798.

Nimitz, Chester William

Chester William Nimitz was an American naval officer who became famous in World War II, during which he was commander-in-chief of all naval forces in the Pacific. He was an admiral during most of this war and in 1944 was made a fleet admiral, or "5-star admiral," the highest rank in the United States Navy. Nimitz was born in Texas in 1885. He was graduated from the United States Naval Academy at Annapolis in 1905. During World War I Nimitz was chief of staff to the commander of the submarine forces in the Atlantic Fleet. He served in various naval jobs between the two World Wars. Nimitz received many medals and decorations for his leadership during World War II, from both the United States and other countries. After the war, Nimitz became Chief of Naval Operations. He retired from the Navy in 1947 but acted as an adviser until his death in 1966.

Nimrod

Nimrod was a great warrior who is told about in Genesis, the first book of the Bible. Nimrod was the great-grandson of Noah and the son of Cush. He lived about four thousand years ago. The Bible says that Nimrod was "a mighty hunter before the Lord." People who study the Bible believe that Nimrod was a great military chief who conquered other lands and ruled them by force. They are not sure what land Nimrod ruled. Some think it was the land where the ancient city of Babylon stood.

Nineveh

Nineveh was the capital of the ancient Assyrian Empire that came to an end about 2,500 years ago. It was one of the great cities of the ancient world, but it was completely destroyed.

Until recent years, most of what men knew about Nineveh came from the

Bible. It tells us that Nimrod came from Babylon to Assyria and built Nineveh. It mentions some of the Assyrian kings—Tiglath-pileser, Shalmaneser, Sargon, Esarhaddon and Phul (Ashurbanipal). It tells of the prophet Jonah's preaching at Nineveh, and the book of the prophet Nahum describes the feelings of the downtrodden peoples when Nineveh was facing destruction.

All this made men curious about Nineveh, and some decided to look for it. An English scientist, Sir Austen Henry Lazard, digging in the great mounds of a ruined city near Mosul on the Tigris River, rediscovered Nineveh about a hundred years ago.

We now know that Nineveh had some wonderful palaces. These were decorated with the type of sculpture called *relief.* Relief sculpture is the carving of partially raised figures from a flat surface. Most of the relief sculpture found at Nineveh shows scenes of war or hunting. It was found mostly in the palaces of Sennacherib and Ashurbanipal. In Ashurbanipal's palace was also found part of a great library, containing thousands of baked tablets of clay on which were written the histories of the kings, religious texts, laws, letters, and business documents. The writing was what we call *cuneiform,* or wedge-shaped. It was made by pressing small wedges into wet clay. From the cuneiform tablets we know that the Assyrians wrote about mathematics, astronomy, geography, and chemistry, and even had their own folk tales and poetry.

Nineveh was destroyed by the enemies of Assyria, the Medians from the north and their allies the Babylonians, in 612 B.C. The conquerors divided the realm between them. The Babylonians took over the western provinces, Syria and Palestine. That is how Judah's capital city, Jerusalem, came to be destroyed by the Babylonians when it rebelled against the Babylonian rule, as told in the Bible.

Niobe

Niobe is a character in Greek mythology, the stories the ancient Greeks told about their gods and goddesses. She was the daughter of Tantalus, king of Lydia. Niobe married Amphion, who was king of Thebes. They had six sons and six daughters. Niobe was very proud of her children. She boasted that she had more children than Leto, who was the mother of the god Apollo and the goddess Artemis. When Apollo and Artemis heard how Niobe had insulted their mother, they killed all of Niobe's children, one by one, and Niobe was turned to stone. So great was her sorrow that the stone statue wept silent tears. Many poets have written poems about Niobe. In Florence, Italy, there is a famous sculpture of Niobe and her children.

nitrogen

Nitrogen is a gas that has no color, odor, or taste. It is an element, one of the hundred or so substances of which the world is made. Pure nitrogen has only a few uses. It is put into electric light bulbs to make the wires in them last longer. It is put into thermometers that are used to tell high temperatures, because it keeps the mercury in them from boiling.

Once nitrogen is combined, or "fixed," with other elements, it can be used to make many useful substances. It is used in making explosives, such as dynamite and nitroglycerine, and in combination with other chemicals it is used as a fertilizer to help plants grow.

Nitrogen is the most plentiful gas in the air. Almost four out of every five ounces of air are nitrogen. It takes 52 quarts of nitrogen to weigh an ounce. Yet, light as it is, there are more than twenty million tons of nitrogen in the air above every square mile of the earth's surface. There are also billions of tons of nitrogen locked up in the minerals of the earth's crust. Chief among such minerals is niter, or saltpeter. Chile and South Africa have vast beds of saltpeter, some of which are as much as 200 miles long, two miles wide, and five feet thick.

THE NITROGEN CYCLE

Nature combines nitrogen with other elements to make proteins. Protein is part of all plants and animals. Certain plants called legumes, such as clover, alfalfa, and cowpeas, have on their roots lumps that are caused by bacteria. These bacteria can take the nitrogen out of the air and turn it into proteins in the soil. The proteins go into plants. The plants are eaten by animals, and the plant proteins become part of the animals' proteins. When plants and animals die, they decay. Of the many kinds of bacteria that cause decay, some break up proteins so that nitrogen is freed and goes back into the air. The same thing happens to animals' waste matter, such as manure, that lies on the ground or is buried. This is why manure is used as a fertilizer. The nitrogen that has been returned to the air is ready to be fixed into plant proteins again by the bacteria on the roots of legumes. Because this process happens over and over again, it is called the nitrogen cycle.

The most important way of making nitrogen into a useable form is the Haber Process. By mixing hydrogen and nitrogen in a tank containing powdered platinum and applying heat and pressure, ammonia is formed. The nitrogen in ammonia can easily be removed.

Richard M. Nixon

Richard Milhous Nixon was elected the 37th President of the United States in November, 1968 and took the oath of office in January, 1969.

HIS EARLY YEARS

Richard Nixon was born in Yorba Linda, California in 1913, the second of five sons of Francis and Hannah Nixon. His Irish Quaker mother came from Pennsylvania and his father from Ohio. Francis Nixon was a citrus farmer and later owned a grocery store where Richard worked after school. Richard's older brother died of meningitis at 18, and a younger brother died of tuberculosis at 7.

HIS EDUCATION

Nixon attended high school in Whittier, California and went on to Whittier College from which he graduated second in his class in 1934. In 1937, he graduated from Duke University Law School and returned to Whittier to practice law.

In 1938, Nixon met Patricia Ryan, a teacher of commercial courses at Whittier High School. They were married two years later.

After the attack on Pearl Harbor in 1941, Nixon joined the Navy and served in the Pacific. He received two South Pacific Battle Stars and two commendations before being honorably discharged with the rank of Lieutenant Commander in 1946.

POLITICAL CAREER

Nixon's first political campaign resulted in his election to the House of Representatives in 1946. As Congressman from the 12th Congressional District of California, Nixon assisted in the drafting and passage of the Taft-Hartley Act (concerning labor-management relations) in 1947. In the same year, he went with the Herter Committee to assess the ability of the European States to resist Communism and, upon his return, fought for the passage of the Marshall Plan to give economic aid to foreign nations. He was re-elected to Congress in 1948.

As a member of the House Un-American Activities Committee, Nixon won national acclaim for his role in the investigations of Soviet espionage in the State Department. These investigations led to the conviction of Alger Hiss for perjury. Hiss, a State Department employee, was believed to have falsely denied that he had given secret information to the Communists. Although the Committee was often accused of intimidating witnesses, Nixon was noted to have kept the proceedings legal and to have insured that the witnesses were treated fairly.

In 1950, with tremendous support from both the Democrats and the Republicans, Nixon was elected to the United States Senate. As a Senator, he openly opposed, in 1951, President Truman's decision to remove General Douglas MacArthur from his command in Korea.

Richard Nixon had become a celebrated national figure whose work attracted the attention of General Dwight D. Eisenhower. At the Republican Convention of 1952, Eisenhower selected Nixon as his Vice-Presidential running mate. The landslide Republican victory that year made Nixon, at the age of 40, the second youngest Vice-President in the history of the United States.

During his two terms as Vice-President, Nixon visited 56 countries and 5 continents as the personal emissary of President Eisenhower. In December, 1956, he went to Hungary, where thousands of refugees were crossing the border to escape the Russians who had crushed their rebellion. He returned to the United States and obtained clearance for these victims to enter the country.

In 1958, Nixon went to Latin America on an 18-day "good-will" tour, and faced several anti-American demonstrations, the most violent of these occurring in Venezuela. In spite of the incidents, Nixon said later, most of the people were friendly to the United States, and he urged that Latin America be given more attention in United States' foreign policy decisions.

The following year, Nixon went to Russia where he engaged in the famous "Kitchen Debate" with Premier Khrushchev inside the American exhibit in Moscow. On this occasion, Nixon told Khrushchev that "no nation . . . is strong enough to issue an ultimatum to another without running the risk of self-destruction."

DOMESTIC ACHIEVEMENTS

Among Nixon's notable domestic accomplishments were his direct intervention (representing the Government) in the settlement of the Steel Strike of 1959, and his use of executive powers in the legislature to secure civil rights for American Negroes. In addition, Nixon became "acting" President three times because of major illnesses that had stricken President Eisenhower. Each time, Nixon received praise from the press and publicly-acknowledged gratitude of the President and his Cabinet.

In 1960, Nixon was nominated as the Republican candidate for the Presidency. He lost the election by two-tenths of 1% to Democratic candidate John F. Kennedy. Two years later, Nixon was defeated in his campaign for Governor of California. He then retired from public life, joined a New York law firm, and worked for six years as a private lawyer. In 1968 Mr. Nixon made an astonishing comeback. He was nominated and elected to the office of President. Mr. Nixon and his running-mate Spiro Agnew defeated Democratic candidate Hubert Humphrey and his running-mate Edmund Muskie.

As he took office in 1969, Nixon's most difficult problem was the unpopular war in Vietnam. During his next four years in office, the war continued. U.S. troops, however, were slowly removed from South Vietnam. In 1973 a peace settlement was reached. Nixon and Agnew ran against George McGovern and his running-mate Sargent Shriver to win a landslide victory in the 1972 presidential race. After the election, Nixon's administration was accused of using illegal tactics to obtain political and personal gains. Vice-President Agnew resigned and was replaced by Gerald Ford who became President when Nixon resigned in 1974. See WATERGATE.

President Nixon attempted to fulfill his duties as chief executive of the United States in spite of the ever-growing complications and problems with the Watergate scandal. On February 21, 1973, Nixon arrived in Peking for his historic "peace journey." His trip opened the way for new relations with China. He continued his diplo-

matic advances with a trip in June of the same year to the Mid-East where he tried to temper tensions between Egypt and Israel.

Despite these important foreign accomplishments, discontent at home with domestic affairs quickly lessened the President's popularity. His involvement in the Watergate episode became more and more evident to the American public and on May 9, 1974 impeachment proceedings were begun by the House Judiciary Committee. In an attempt to allow the constitutional impeachment process to runs its course, President Nixon encountered increasing pressure from both close friends and the public to resign. And so, with tremendous emotion and an uncertainty for his political future, President Nixon resigned from office on August 8, 1974. He claimed that he was not resigning because of any guilt in association with the Watergate crimes, but because of the critical state of the American government.

Vice-President Gerald Ford became the 38th President. (See GERALD FORD). On September 6, 1974 President Ford declared an unconditional pardon for ex-President Nixon for all federal offenses that he "committed or may have committed" while in office.

MRS. RICHARD NIXON

Thelma Catherine "Pat" Ryan was born in Ely, Nevada on March 17, 1912, the daughter of William and Kate Ryan. Orphaned at the age of 17, Pat managed to finance her own education and eventually to graduate from the University of California at Los Angeles. She later taught commercial courses at Whittier High School in California. In 1938, she met Richard Nixon who proposed on their first date. They were married in 1940 and had two daughters, Patricia and Julie.

Mrs. Nixon, an attractive woman, radiates warmth and charm in public.

Noah

The story of Noah is told in the Bible, in the book of Genesis. It tells how God decided to rid the earth of wicked men by drowning them in a great flood. But God also decided to spare Noah and his family. He told Noah to build an ark, a kind of ship, and to gather in it his wife and his three sons, Shem, Ham, and Japheth, and their wives. (There is a separate article about the ARK that Noah built.) God also told Noah to take into the ark two of every living thing, one male and one female. Then God caused a great flood that lasted for forty days, and at the end of it Noah and his family and the beasts they had taken into the ark were the only living things on the earth. A rainbow appeared in the sky, and God told Noah that this was a sign that there would never again be a flood that would cover the earth.

Then God told Noah and his sons to live in peace and grow fine plants on the earth, and have many children. Noah became a farmer and planted a vineyard.

Ham became the ancestor of a people called the Canaanites, Shem the ancestor of a people called the Semites, and Japheth the ancestor of the Gentiles.

Nobel, Alfred B.

Alfred Bernard Nobel was a Swedish inventor. He is best remembered for his invention of dynamite and for the large amount of money he left to give prizes to leading persons in various fields. These are now known as Nobel Prizes.

Nobel was born in Sweden in 1833. His father went to work in Russia as an expert in the manufacture of weapons and farm tools. Young Nobel was sent to study in the United States and later returned to Russia to work in his father's factory. In experimenting with the powerful explosive nitroglycerin he caused an explosion that destroyed the plant and killed his younger brother, Emil. Nobel then tried to find a mixture that was less dangerous, and in 1866 he made his first dynamite, which was much less dangerous but almost as powerful. He continued his experiments with explosives, and was given a total of 129 patents. Nobel died in 1896, and most of his fortune went to establish the fund from which the Nobel Prizes are awarded.

Nobel's will provided that prizes were to be awarded to persons who had rendered the greatest service to mankind in the following fields: medicine or physiology; physics; chemistry; literature; and peace. The value of the prize depends on how much money the trust fund has earned. In 1962 a prize was worth about $50,000. It is not necessary that each prize be awarded each year, but each must be awarded at least once every five years. The prizewinners are chosen by different groups of experts in the several fields. Among noted persons to receive Nobel prizes are: Rudyard Kipling, the first English-language writer to win the prize in literature; Theodore Roosevelt, the first American to win the peace prize; and Sinclair Lewis, the first American to win the prize in literature. Since that time many Americans who have made outstanding contributions to science, literature, or peace have received awards.

Norfolk, Virginia

Norfolk is the largest city in the state of Virginia. It is on one of the finest harbors in the United States, Hampton Roads, on the Atlantic Ocean. Norfolk is one of the most important ports in the country and is also a manufacturing city. More than three hundred thousand people live there. Many work in the port, shipping oil, coal, tobacco, and cotton. Others work in factories that make canned foods, cotton goods, machinery, and chemicals. There are also important shipbuilding yards.

Norfolk is the headquarters for the United States Navy's Atlantic Fleet and for the largest naval supply station, Langley Field. One of the largest Air Force bases in the country is in Norfolk. Many people go to Norfolk every summer to spend their vacations at the fine beaches along the coast.

Norfolk was founded in 1682 and was an important naval station even in Colonial days. During the Civil War, a famous sea battle between the Monitor and the Merrimac was fought off the shore of Norfolk. In World War II, Norfolk was

one of the busiest cities in the country, building ships and shipping men and supplies overseas.

NORFOLK, VIRGINIA. Population (1970 census) 307,951. On Hampton Roads. Settled in 1682.

Normandy

Normandy is a coastal region in northwestern France, on the English Channel. Late in World War II it was the region where the Allies landed to invade Europe. (There is a separate article about the NORMANDY INVASION.) William the Conqueror, who founded the present line of English kings in the year 1066, was Duke of Normandy.

More than two million people live in Normandy. Most of them are farmers and are known for their dairy products. Many of the farmers still use old-fashioned methods of farming and live in houses that have few modern appliances.

The Normandy countryside is noted for its apple orchards and its many hedgerows. The hedgerows are embankments of earth that have shrubs and even trees

French Government Tourist Office
The 13th-century monastery, Mont-Saint-Michel, is just off the coast of Normandy.

growing from them. They were built and planted by the Normandy farmers as boundaries for their fields.

The people in the cities of Normandy are more modern. They work in large textile mills and in the important ports at Rouen, Le Havre, and Cherbourg. The Norman cities are very old and are famous for their beautiful churches and castles. Many people visit Normandy's seaside resorts along the English Channel.

Normandy is named after the Normans, or Norsemen, who ruled the region more than nine hundred years ago. For a time Normandy belonged to England. The English and French fought over the region until about 1450, when it again became part of France. Almost two hundred years ago Normandy was divided into the French departments (counties) of Manche, Orne, Calvados, Eure, and Seine-Inferieure.

Normandy invasion

Late in World War II, on June 6, 1944, Allied troops (chiefly American and British) crossed the English channel from British ports and fought their way onto the coast of Normandy in France. This was the beginning of the campaign that freed France from German rule and that later conquered Germany.

The Normandy invasion had been planned under the leadership of General Dwight D. Eisenhower. Tremendous supplies of ships, planes, ammunition and equipment were made ready for the attack. The exact spot where the Allies were going to land was kept very secret

so that the Germans would not know where to expect the attack. The date of the invasion, known as "D-Day," was also a secret, and few men in the Allied forces knew when it was going to start until the very last minute.

The night before the Normandy invasion, hundreds of planes bombed the French coast. Parachute troops were dropped behind the Normandy beaches to destroy bridges, to block roads, and to cut railroad lines. Early on the morning of June 6th, which was called "D-Day," Allied warships opened up a tremendous attack on the coast of Normandy with their big guns. Planes dropped many tons of bombs on the German fortifications. Then the Allied troops, waiting on invasion barges, waded bravely ashore under fire from German guns. The British and Canadians landed on beaches near Caen. United States troops landed on "Omaha Beach" and "Utah Beach." Wave after wave of troops and equipment came ashore. Artificial harbors were towed across the channel and set up on the beaches, so that big ships could unload heavy equipment. Within five days, the Allies had captured eighty miles of the coast of Normandy.

As the Allies moved inland, they found fighting difficult because of the hedgerows throughout the Normandy countryside. Hedgerows are high embankment of earth with shrubs and even trees growing from them. The Germans could easily defend themselves behind these hedgerows, and they even dug holes in them, in which they could hide and shoot at the Allied soldiers. But the troops moved ahead and after fierce fighting, on June 18, United States troops captured Saint-Lo, an important communication center. On June 25, a tremendous offensive was started, known as the "breakthrough." Planes bombed the German lines and prepared the way for the troops. British and Canadian troops joined in and the forces completely trapped thousands of German soldiers. The Allied troops then raced toward Paris, which was liberated on August 25 by French forces.

In the Normandy campaign more than 400,000 Germans were either captured or killed. The German army was not through fighting, but the success of the Normandy invasion played an important part in the final defeat of the Germans.

All through the rest of the war in Europe, the Normandy beaches were an important supply center, and ships went back and forth across the English Channel to carry food, ammunition and other supplies to the fighting forces.

Norsemen or **Northmen,** Scandinavian warriors in Europe about a thousand years ago: see VIKINGS.

North, Lord

Lord Frederick North was the Prime Minister, or head of the government, in England both before and during the American Revolutionary War. For many years before that he had been a member of the English Parliament, or lawmaking body. He was hated by many of the colonists living in America because he supported the Stamp Act, which the colonists said was unfair to them. He thought England had the right to tax the colonies as it wished. This attitude caused the colonists to fight and win their independence from England. Lord North was born in 1733 and died in 1790.

North America

North America is the third-largest continent in the world. It is in the northern part of the Western Hemisphere, and it extends from the Atlantic to the Pacific Oceans. At the far north it reaches the Arctic Ocean. The southern tip of the mainland tapers down to a small strip of land known as the Isthmus of Panama. When people speak of North America, they usually mean only Alaska, Canada, Greenland, the United States, and Mexico. The countries between Mexico and the Isthmus of Panama, as well as the islands of the Caribbean Sea, are considered part of Central America, but this is really part of the same continent. Sometimes Mexico and the Central American countries are grouped together as "Middle America."

North America has an area of about 9,300,000 square miles. It is more than twice as large as Europe, and half as large as Asia. There are about 300,000,-000 people living in North America.

North America has been settled by white men for only about four hundred years. Before that, only Indians and Eskimos lived there. When people in Europe started moving to the Americas, they called them the "New World." Europe was known as the "Old World."

THE COUNTRIES OF NORTH AMERICA

There are three independent countries in North America: Canada, the United States, and Mexico. A fourth large territory is Alaska, which is part of the United States. Canada is a member of the British Commonwealth of Nations, and Mexico is an independent republic. Greenland belongs to Denmark.

There are some sections of North America where very few people live, others where there are no houses at all for many miles, and other places—such as New York City—where tens of thousands of people are crowded into a few square miles.

THE PEOPLE OF NORTH AMERICA

The people of North America, or their ancestors, came from all parts of the world. European, Oriental and African Negro people moved to North America in great numbers, joining the Indians who were already there, and today the population is a mixture of all these races. In Mexico, the majority of the population are of Indian and Spanish ancestry. In Canada, most people are of British descent, but many are French. Alaska's population is Indian, Eskimo, Scandinavian, Russian, and people from the United States and Canada. In the United States, there are more white people of western European descent than any other single group. This includes English, Scottish, Irish, German, Dutch, Scandinavian, French, Italian and Spanish groups.

WHAT THE CONTINENT IS LIKE

North America extends from the Arctic Ocean to the Torrid Zone. There are as many different kinds of climate as there are anywhere in the world.

In the far north, where Canada and Alaska reach up into the Arctic Circle, there is snow all year, and great glaciers cover large areas. The mountains and lakes in Canada and Alaska are rich with wild life. There are deer, caribou, elk, moose, bears, wolves, and other animals in the unsettled or thinly populated areas. Lakes and streams are full of fish. The salmon fisheries of Alaska and of eastern Canada are enormous industries. Furtrapping is another important industry in the wild northern country. Each year thousands of pelts brought out by trappers supply a large part of the world's fur market.

Farther south, North America is a rich agricultural continent. Its climate and soil vary in different sections, and nearly everything grown in Europe or Asia can be grown somewhere in North America.

U.S. Army Photo

The Normandy invasion was one of the great Allied triumphs of World War II. Members of the second wave of troops wait patiently as their landing craft approaches Utah Beach on D-Day.

Union Pacific Railroad Photo

A view of the Grand Canyon in northern Arizona.

North America comes closer than any other continent to supporting completely the people who live there. From the precious gold, fur, fish and timber of the far north to the great oil deposits of the south that help to power industry and transportation, North America is truly a continent of abundance. The people who live there are fortunate indeed.

Scenically, there is much variety in North America. The Canadian and American Rockies are unexcelled for beauty and majesty. The broad Mississippi that divides the East, from the West is one of the world's greatest rivers. The grassy, fertile plains of the central section is a rich farming region. The prairies of the West are similar to the pampas of South America, or the steppes of Russia. There are deserts and jungles.

The natural wealth of the continent is almost limitless. There are vast deposits of coal, iron, bauxite, gold, silver, and other minerals, and rich oil fields. The rivers are a source of water power, and thousands of square miles of forest provide plenty of timber. Grains are raised in large quantities, and the great grasslands have made much of the continent a fine stock-raising land.

North America still has thousands of square miles that are undeveloped and almost unpopulated. There is room for expansion, room for growth, and room for millions more people for years to come. It is still the "New World."

North Atlantic Treaty Organization

The North Atlantic Treaty is an agreement among member nations to defend one another against armed aggression by any nation. The treaty was signed in 1949 by Belgium, Canada, Denmark, France, Iceland, Italy, Luxembourg, the Netherlands, Norway, Portugal, the United Kingdom (Great Britain), and the United States. In 1952 Greece and Turkey joined, and in 1954 West Germany, making fifteen members.

The treaty says that an armed attack against any of the member nations will be considered an attack against them all, and that in case of such an attack the members will go to war if necessary to protect every member. The members agreed to support the charter of the United Nations.

The treaty is administered by the North Atlantic Treaty Organization, called NATO. The controlling body is the North Atlantic Council, whose members are the foreign ministers of all member nations plus a secretary general and an international staff. The headquarters of this body was placed in Paris, France, as also was the principal military command, called SHAPE (Supreme Headquarters, Allied Power Europe).

Other important NATO bodies are the Military Committee, made up of military officers from the member nations, with headquarters in Washington, D.C.; the Supreme Allied Command for the Atlantic (Ocean), the naval branch, with headquarters in Norfolk, Virginia; the NATO Defense College; the Military Agency for Standardization (to make weapons and equipment interchangeable among the member nations); and an advisory group for aeronautics research.

In 1965 President de Gaulle of France announced that France would withdraw from NATO and in 1966 he demanded that foreign forces that had been stationed in France be withdrawn by April 1, 1967. President Johnson of the U.S. said that the other member countries would continue NATO without France.

The treaty and NATO were strongly opposed by Communist groups in most of the member nations, and the government of Soviet Russia tried in various ways to weaken or wreck the program, but NATO proved effective against Communist expansion in Europe.

North Carolina

North Carolina is one of the South Atlantic states in the United States. It was one of the thirteen original colonies. Its nickname is the "Tarheel State" because North Carolina once produced large quantities of tar from its pine forests. During the Civil War, the soldiers from North Carolina were called "Tarheels." Carolina was named after Charles I of England.

In area, North Carolina ranks 28th among the states, with 52,712 square miles. In population it ranks 12th, with about five million people living there. It became a state in 1789, and was the 12th of the thirteen original states. The capital is Raleigh.

THE PEOPLE OF NORTH CAROLINA

The earliest white settlers to come to the region of North Carolina, almost four hundred years ago, were the English. Later many Scots, Irish, Germans and French Huguenots came there. Today most of the people are American-born.

More than one million Negroes live in North Carolina. Most of them are descendants of slaves who once worked on the large plantations. Most of them now work on farms and in the large tobacco factories. More than 3,000 Indians live on a large reservation in the western part of the state.

About a third of the people of North Carolina are farmers. They grow more tobacco than any other state. The farmers also raise cotton, corn, and peanuts. Many raise dairy cattle and produce dairy products.

In the cities are some of the largest factories and mills in the world. The biggest cigarette factories in the United States are in North Carolina. The people of North Carolina make most of the cigarette paper used in the United States, and make more furniture and textiles (cloth and other woven products) than are made in any other state.

North Carolina fishermen catch more fish than those of any other state on the South Atlantic coast. The North Carolina mica and feldspar mines produce more of these minerals than any other state. North Carolina has big forests in which lumbermen cut the timber used for furniture.

The largest religious group in North Carolina is the Baptists. Other large groups include the Methodists and Presbyterians.

WHAT NORTH CAROLINA IS LIKE

The eastern part of North Carolina is a broad coastal plain, where the farmers grow tobacco, cotton, and peanuts. It is

a low, sandy region with many rivers. Along the coast are bays, seaside resorts, and sandbars that extend far out into the ocean. These sandbars, particularly at Cape Hatteras, are very dangerous, and many ships have been wrecked on them. So many shipwrecks occurred at Cape Hatteras before radar was invented that it became known as the "graveyard of the Atlantic." A large, dark swampland covers a large area of this coastal region. It has high trees covered with moss, and mysterious, winding streams. The largest of these swamps is called the Great Dismal Swamp.

The central part of the state is a fertile and rolling plateau, a high, level area. More people live in this region than in any other part of the state. Some of the largest cities are in this part of the state, including the important tobacco centers of Durham, Winston-Salem, and Reidsville.

Also in the central part are the Sandhills, a famous golfing and horseback-riding resort. Two towns there are Pinehurst and Southern Pines.

The western part of North Carolina has very beautiful mountains, the highest in the Appalachians. The Blue Ridge Mountains and the Great Smoky Mountains are favorite summer and winter vacation places. Asheville is the center of this region. Visitors may see fine waterfalls, swift streams, deep ravines, and beautiful flowers growing on the mountain slopes.

Hunters can find many wild animals in North Carolina, including the deer, bear, raccoon, and opossum.

The climate of North Carolina is varied. Along the coast and in the south, the summers are hot and the winters are mild. In the mountains the winters are quite cold but the summers are pleasantly cool. The central part of the state has a moderate and even climate. North Carolina's average temperature in winter is about 42 degrees and in summer about 77 degrees.

The rivers of North Carolina are important for transportation. Railroads and highways reach almost all parts of the state. There are airports in the important cities.

THE GOVERNMENT OF NORTH CAROLINA

North Carolina, like most states, has a Governor at the head of the government, and a Legislature that makes the laws. The Governor is elected for a four-year term. The Legislature is composed

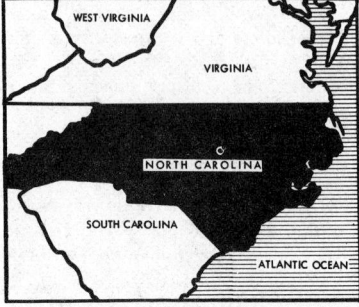

of two houses, a Senate and a House of Representatives. The members of both houses are elected for a two-year term.

Judges are elected for an eight-year term. The capital is Raleigh. There are 100 counties.

There are more than a million pupils enrolled in the public elementary and high schools. Among the colleges, universities, and other schools of higher learning are:

University of North Carolina, at Chapel Hill. Enrollment, 37,724 in 1971 (co-ed).

North Carolina State College of Agriculture and Engineering, at Raleigh. Enrollment, 11,792 in 1971 (co-ed).

North Carolina College, at Durham. Enrollment, 3,350 in 1971 (co-ed).

Duke University, at Durham. Enrollment, 7,961 in 1971 (co-ed).

Agricultural and Technical College of North Carolina, at Greensboro. Enrollment, 6,062 in 1971 (co-ed).

Wake Forest College, at Winston-Salem. Enrollment, 3,083 in 1971 (co-ed).

CHIEF CITIES OF NORTH CAROLINA

The leading cities of North Carolina, with populations from the 1970 census, are:

Charlotte, population 241,178. The largest city in the state. There is a separate article about CHARLOTTE.

Greensboro, population 144,076, the second-largest city, textile center, in the north central part of the state.

Winston-Salem, population 132,913, third-largest city, tobacco center, in the northern part of the state.

Raleigh, population 121,577, the state capital and fourth-largest city. There is a separate article about RALEIGH.

Durham, population 95,438, the fifth-largest city, a tobacco center.

High Point, population 63,204, the sixth-largest city, a furniture-manufacturing center, in the central part of the state.

Asheville, population 57,681, the seventh-largest city, center of the resort area in the western part of the state.

NORTH CAROLINA IN THE PAST

The first white man to visit the region of North Carolina, more than four hundred years ago, was Giovanni de Verrazano, an Italian explorer. In 1585, Sir Walter Raleigh made the first English settlements in the New World on Roanoke Island; one of these became famous as the LOST COLONY, and there is a separate article about it.

The first permanent settlement was made by the English at Albemarle, in 1650, and in 1729 North Carolina became a province of Great Britain. Later the freedom-loving colonists protested strongly at their unfair treatment by England. North Carolina was the first colony to instruct its delegates to the Continental Congress to vote for independence.

During the Revolutionary War, some of the North Carolina people moved across the mountains and settled in the west, where they organized a new state. They called it Franklin. The state was not recognized by the Continental Congress. At the end of the Revolutionary War, North Carolina gave this land to the new government. It was admitted to the United States in 1796 as the state of Tennessee.

At the outbreak of the Civil War, most of the people were for the South, though there were many who favored the North.

North Carolina was one of the last states to secede from the Union and fight on the side of the Confederacy. After the war the state had a difficult time. "Carpetbaggers," outsiders who had nothing but a carpetbag, controlled the state government and robbed it of millions. Gradually the citizens of the state got back control.

The state then began to grow and prosper. Not only did farming increase, but big factories were built. In the past fifty years North Carolina has become one of the most prosperous of states.

PLACES TO SEE IN NORTH CAROLINA

Great Smoky Mountains National Park, 508,446 acres, 25 miles west of Asheville, in the northwest, partly in Tennessee, on U.S. Route 441.

Wright Brothers National Memorial, 314 acres, 3 miles south of Kitty Hawk, on the Outer Banks in northeast, on U.S. Route 158. Site of the first airplane flight made by Wilbur and Orville Wright, in 1903.

Guilford Courthouse National Military Park, 224 acres, 6 miles north of Greensboro, in the north, on U.S. Route 220. Commemorates an American victory in the Revolutionary War.

Moore's Creek National Military Park, 49 acres, 22 miles northwest of Wilmington, in the south, on State Highway 210. Scene of a battle in the Revolutionary War in 1776; the first American victory in North Carolina.

Tobacco markets, at Durham, in the north central part of the state, on U.S. Route 70. Tourists may watch tobacco being sold, and may also see the great tobacco factories.

Ocracoke Island, off the eastern coast, south of Cape Hatteras. An isolated island where the pirate Blackbeard hid out, and where he was killed in 1718. Noted for its wild ponies.

NORTH CAROLINA. Area, 52,712 square miles. Population (1970 census) 5,082,059 Capital, Raleigh. Nickname, the Tarheel State. Motto, *Esse Quam Viveri* (To Be Rather Than to Seem). Flower, dogwood. Bird, cardinal. Song, "The Old North State." Admitted to Union, November 21, 1789. Official abbreviation, N.C.

North Dakota

North Dakota is a state in the Great Plains of the United States. Its nickname is the "Flickertail State" because of the many flickertails (ground squirrels) found there. It is also known as the "Sioux State" because it was once the home of the Sioux or Dakota Indians.

In area, North Dakota ranks 17th among the states, with 70,665 square miles. In population it ranks 46th, with more than 617,000 people living there. It became a state in 1889, and was the 39th state admitted to the United States. The capital is Bismarck.

THE PEOPLE OF NORTH DAKOTA

The first white settlers in the region of North Dakota, more than a hundred years ago, were Scottish people who had been living in Canada. About 85 years ago, immigrants from northern Europe flocked to its fertile farmland. They were from Norway, Russia, Germany, and other countries. Today most of the people

of North Dakota are American-born. More than ten thousand Indians still live on reservations.

Most of the people of North Dakota are farmers. They have large farms and use modern, power-driven machinery. They grow more spring wheat than farmers in any other state, and are among the biggest producers of barley, rye, and flaxseed. There are many dairy farmers, and in the western part of the state there are large cattle ranches.

In the cities there are meat-packing plants, plants that make butter and other dairy products, and large flour mills. Many people now work in the rich oil fields that were discovered only a few years ago in the western part of the state.

WHAT NORTH DAKOTA IS LIKE

Persons visiting North Dakota will see a vast rolling prairie with very fertile soil. It is one of the most important farming regions in the United States. Most of the soil is so fertile because millions of years ago it was covered by glaciers, or sheets of ice, and when the ice melted it left rich black soil.

In the eastern part of North Dakota is the low Red River Valley. It is the richest wheat-growing section in the country. Farmers also raise large dairy herds there. More people live in the Red River Valley than in any other part of the state.

The central part of North Dakota is a rolling plain that is also a fine farming and grazing region. On the western border of this plain is the Missouri River, which was once an important route for explorers and traders.

The western part of the state is a plateau, a high, level region. This region is less fertile than the rest of the state, and is very dry, but farmers irrigate the soil and grow wheat there. The western section is excellent for cattle-raising. There are more than 600 billion tons of lignite (a kind of coal) not far below the surface of the soil.

In the western part of North Dakota are the famous *Badlands*. They were given this name by early travelers, who found the section very difficult to cross. The Badlands have many beautiful canyons and strange-shaped rock formations.

Many wild animals live in the woods of North Dakota, including the white-tailed deer, beaver, muskrat, coyote, and mink.

North Dakota has long, cold winters and short, hot summers. The air is very dry and summer days are long and sunny. The average temperature in summer is 69 degrees and in winter about 7 degrees.

Railroads and highways reach most parts of the state. There are airports in the important cities.

THE GOVERNMENT OF NORTH DAKOTA

North Dakota, like most states, has a Governor to head the government, and a Legislature that makes the laws. The Governor is elected for a two-year term. The Legislature is composed of two houses, a Senate and a House of Representatives. The members of the Senate are elected for a four-year term. Members of the House of Representatives are elected for a two-year term. Judges are elected for a ten-year term. The capital is Bismarck. There are 53 counties.

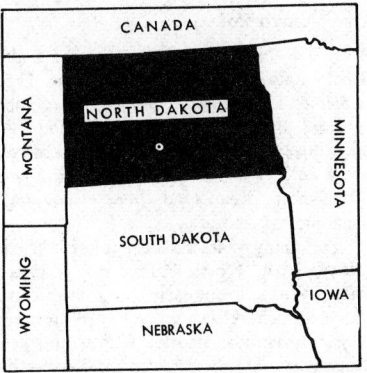

About 150,000 pupils are enrolled in the puplic elementary and high schools. The principal colleges and universities are:

University of North Dakota, at Grand Forks. Enrollment, 7,925 in 1971 (co-ed).
North Dakota Agricultural College, at Fargo. Enrollment, 6,228 in 1971 (co-ed).
Jamestown College, at Jamestown. Enrollment, 605 in 1971 (co-ed).

CHIEF CITIES OF NORTH DAKOTA

The leading cities of North Dakota, with populations from the 1970 census, are:

Fargo, population 53,365, the largest city in the state. There is a separate article about FARGO.
Grand Forks, population 39,008, the second-largest city, a railroad and industrial center, in the eastern part of the state.
Minot, population 32,290, the third-largest city, a railroad center, in the north central part of the state.
Bismarck, population 34,703, the state capital and second-largest city. There is a separate article about BISMARCK.

NORTH DAKOTA IN THE PAST

The first white man to explore the Dakota region, more than two hundred years ago, was the French-Canadian Sieur de la Vérendrye (Pierre Gaultier de Varennes). Fur-traders came there and set up trading posts. The first permanent settlement was made at Pembina by Scottish settlers from Canada in 1812.

The territory was settled very slowly because transportation was poor and because the Sioux Indians were unfriendly. The Dakota Territory was formed by the United States in 1861, but the Sioux wars kept settlers away. It was not until about 85 years ago, after a railroad was built, that the Dakota Territory began to grow.

After 1870, many people came to start farms in the fertile regions. The western part of North Dakota was settled by ranchers. In 1889 the Dakota Territory was divided into North and South Dakota and both were admitted as states to the United States.

The Homestead Laws, which gave land to settlers, brought more people to North Dakota. The state prospered, more railroads and roads were built, and cities grew. The last wars with the Sioux Indians ended in 1890 when their leader, Sitting Bull, was killed

Heavy droughts and dust storms in the 1930s caused great suffering for the farmers. It was also a time of very low prices. Many farmers gave up their farms and went to other states. In more recent years, heavy rainfall and higher prices have helped the farmers.

Bald Hill Dam is one of the irrigation projects that protect farms against drought.

North Dakota is a state of open spaces: the cities are small and the farms are large, with the houses built far apart. It produces many crops and minerals needed by the nation. In the fertile eastern and central region, there are large dairy and wheat farms, like this.

PLACES TO SEE IN NORTH DAKOTA

Vérendrye National Monument, 253 acres, south of Sanish, in the west, on State Highway 23. Commemorates the Vérendrye explorations in North Dakota and along the upper Missouri River.

North Dakota Travel Dept.

The original cabin once belonging to Theodore Roosevelt when he ranched in the North Dakota badlands during the 1880's.

Theodore Roosevelt National Memorial Park, 71,181 acres, 28 miles west of Dickinson, in the west, on U.S. Route 10. Located in the heart of the scenic Badlands; includes part of Theodore Roosevelt's Elkhorn Ranch.

Turtle Mountain, on the border between the United States and Canada, in the north central part of the state, on State Highway 3. Noted for a great variety of songbirds. Contains the beautiful International Peace Garden, which commemorates the long peace between the United States and Canada.

The Center of North America, 7 miles west of Rugby, in the north central part of the state, on U.S. Route 2. Stones mark the spot that is considered the geographical center of North America.

Devils Lake, in the east, on U.S. Route 2. The largest of several glacial lakes; the second-largest salt lake in the United States.

NORTH DAKOTA. Area, 70,665 square miles. Population (1970 census) 617,761. Capital, Bismarck. Nickname, the Flickertail State. Motto, Liberty and Union, Now and Forever, One and Inseparable. Flower, wild prairie rose. Bird, western meadowlark. Song, "North Dakota Hymn." Admitted to Union, November 2, 1889. Official abbreviation, N.D.

Northern Ireland

Northern Ireland is part of the United Kingdom of Great Britain and Northern Ireland. It is about one-seventh of the entire area of Ireland, its size being 5,451 square miles, which is a little larger than the state of Connecticut. About 1,500,000 people live there, more than half the population of Connecticut. The capital and chief city is BELFAST, about which there is a separate article.

About two-thirds of the people of Northern Ireland are Protestants, and that is a principal reason why they have not joined the Republic of Ireland, in which nearly all the people are Roman Catholics.

There are linen mills near Belfast and Lisburne, and there are shipyards and aircraft factories in Northern Ireland, but most of the people are farmers. They grow potatoes and flax, which is used in making linen. They also raise sheep, cattle, and poultry. Eggs and dairy products produced in Northern Ireland help feed the people of Great Britain.

There are many mountains in Northern Ireland. Among the most beautiful are the mountains of Mourne, which sweep down to the sea. In the center of Northern Ireland is Lough Neagh, the largest lake in the British Isles. The coast is rocky and windswept and noted for its dramatic scenery.

Northern Ireland was established in 1920, when the Republic of Ireland became independent. See the article on IRELAND.

NORTHERN IRELAND. Political division of the United Kingdom of Great Britain and Northern Ireland. Area, 5,451 square miles. Population 1,458,000. Capital, Belfast.

Northern Lights are discharges of electricity resembling yellowish searchlight beams that appear from time to time in the northern sky. See the article on AURORA.

North Pole

The North Pole is one of the ends of the axis on which the earth spins. The other end is the South Pole. The region around the North Pole is covered by floating ice, and the climate is always very cold. The North Pole is a point in the Arctic Ocean, and there is no land near it.

For many years Arctic explorers tried to reach the North Pole. Many expeditions were sent out early in the 20th century, and there was great rivalry among different explorers to see who would get there first. The honor went to Robert E. Peary of the United States. He tried to reach the North Pole six times before he finally succeeded, on April 6, 1909.

After that, more explorers reached the North Pole. The development of the airplane after World War I allowed men to fly over the pole. In 1926 Richard E. Byrd and Floyd Bennett first flew an airplane over the pole. Airplanes traveling between certain parts of North America and Europe now pass over the regions near the North Pole, because that is the shortest route. In 1954 the Scandinavian Air System started a regular airline over the Arctic Region between Los Angeles, California, and Copenhagen, Denmark. See also the articles about the ARCTIC OCEAN and the ARCTIC REGION.

MAGNETIC NORTH POLE

The magnetic North Pole is the place where the needle of a magnetic compass points straight down, and toward which the needle points when the compass is in other parts of the world. The magnetic North Pole is located at 73 degrees north latitude and 100 degrees west longitude, about 1,200 miles from the North Pole, on Prince of Wales Island, which is part of the Canadian Northwest Territories, in the Arctic Ocean. Its position changes from time to time. Formerly it was located at Boothia Peninsula, about 1,100 miles from the North Pole. The magnetic North Pole is also discussed in the article about MAGNETISM.

North Sea

The North Sea is a large arm of the Atlantic Ocean between the island of Great Britain and the northern part of the continent of Europe. The sea is 222,000 square miles in size, which is almost the size of the state of Texas. It is shallow, with an average depth of 180 feet. Near Norway it is 2,165 feet deep, which is its greatest depth. Rain and fog are very frequent on the North Sea, and often there are violent northwest storms that endanger small boats.

Despite the rain and fog, the North Sea is one of the most heavily traveled waterways in the world. Several important rivers empty into it—the Elbe, Weser, Ems and Rhine from the continent and the Thames and Humber from Great Britain.

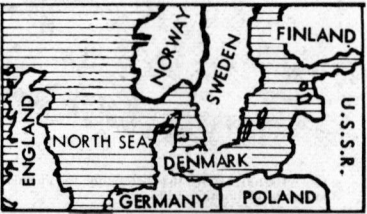

The floor of the North Sea has many banks. These are the home of great schools of codfish and herring. Many of the people who live along the coast make their living as fishermen.

In some places, as in Norway and Scotland, there are many small bays lined by rocky cliffs. In Denmark, Germany, Belgium, and the Netherlands, the coast is very low and smooth.

Several of the world's greatest ports are on the North Sea, or joined to it by river or canal. They are London, England; Antwerp, Belgium; Rotterdam and Amsterdam, the Netherlands; and Bremen and Hamburg, Germany.

North Star

The North Star is the star that seems to hang directly over the North Pole. It is the biggest star in that region. Because of the rotation of the earth about the sun, all the stars seem to rotate around the North Star, which seems to stand still in the sky but which actually makes a small circle about the North Pole, once every 24 hours.

The position of the North Star is a great help to navigators of airplanes and ships. It is one of the oldest known stars, appearing in records dating back more than three thousand years.

The North Star is part of the constellation known as Ursa Minor, the Little Bear, or the Little Dipper. The technical name for the North Star is Polaris. It is also called the Pole Star. In the Little Dipper it is the star at the very end of the handle.

The position of the North Star depends on where on the earth an observer is located. A person in New England will find the North Star halfway up the northern sky. A person at the North Pole will find it directly overhead. A person at the equator will see the North Star just above the horizon. A person south of the equator will not be able to see it at all.

Because of the pull of the moon upon the earth, the axis of the earth is tilting more and more away from Polaris, so that in several thousand years another star will be called the North Star. This will be the star Alpha Cephei, the brightest star in the constellation Cepheus. About five thousand years ago, Thuban, the brightest star on the constellation Draco, was the North Star, and the Pyramid of Cheops in Egypt was built directly beneath it.

Northwest Passage

Ever since the continent of North America was discovered, more than 450 years ago, explorers have looked for a sea route from the Atlantic to the Pacific Ocean.

The sea route they hoped to find was called the Northwest Passage, because the shortest way to the Pacific Ocean from Europe would be by sailing up the Atlantic coast toward the North Pole and then steering westward to the Pacific—if there was a way through the continent by water. The overland route across the continent took many months and involved many hardships.

In the 16th century, many famous explorers tried to find the Northwest Passage. These included Jacques Cartier for France, Sir Martin Frobisher for Eng-

land, and Henry Hudson for Holland. The Hudson's Bay Company, one of the largest and most important trading companies of early American times, was formed mainly to find the Northwest Passage, but it was not successful.

Many discoveries were made during the search for the new route, including William Baffin's discovery of Baffin Bay. No one knew for certain that such a route even existed until 1854, when Robert J. Le M. McClure sailed on the ship Investigator to a point that had been reached from the east by a land expedition. The Northwest Passage was finally completed by a Norwegian explorer, Roald Amundsen, in an expedition that lasted from 1903 to 1906, but the expedition had to make a detour around McClure Strait. In August, 1954, two United States Navy icebreakers cut through ice from 4 to 10 feet thick to cross McClure Strait, the final link of the Northwest Passage.

Northwest Territories

The Northwest Territories is a large region in northern Canada. More than half of it lies north of the Arctic Circle. Though it covers well over a million square miles, twice the size of Alaska, only about 29,000 people live there, largely because it is so cold and icy.

Most of the people are Eskimos and Indians. The Eskimos are fur trappers. They catch mink, beaver, muskrat and fox, whose fur is very valuable. They get their own clothing from the skins of the caribou, and musk oxen provide them with food.

The Indians also are fur trappers and hunters. Most of the other people who live in this region are miners. They produce gold, lead, and copper, and work in the rich uranium mines around Great Bear Lake. This section has one of the largest uranium deposits in the world. There are also valuable oil fields.

WHAT THE REGION IS LIKE

The Northwest Territories make up nearly one-third of the area of Canada. It is mostly a rocky plateau (a high, level place) with many rivers and lakes. In the western part are the Mackenzie Mountains, which rise to a height of more than 9,000 feet. These mountains

Eskimos of the Northwest Territories do not mind the cold. The woman on the left wears the costume of the eastern Arctic; her companion's parka shows that she is a native of the western Arctic.

Dept. of Northern Aff. & Nat'l Res.

are the northern range of the Rocky Mountains, and contain valuable minerals. East of the mountains are two of the largest lakes in Canada, Great Bear Lake and Great Slave Lake. The Mackenzie River Valley has valuable forests. Many fur-bearing animals live in these forests.

The central part of the Northwest Territories is a vast plateau, while in the east, toward Hudson Bay, the land is level and has many lakes. The southern part of the region is called the Barren Grounds. It is an Arctic prairie where hardly anything grows.

There are many islands in the northern part of the Northwest Territories. They are always covered with snow and ice. The largest are Baffin Island, Victoria Island, Ellesmere Island, and Devon Island. These islands extend to within 500 miles of the North Pole. Eskimos live on them.

The Northwest Territories has no large cities. The largest town is Yellowknife, with some three thousand people. It is a gold-mining center. Most of the other towns are trading posts. There are schools in the larger towns.

There is only one paved road and no railroads, but minerals mined in the Northwest Territories are shipped on the Mackenzie River in the summer when it is not frozen. Planes are often used to carry supplies and equipment to workers in the mining camps and oil fields that are difficult to reach.

The average temperature in winter is about 18 degrees, but it can drop as low as 70 degrees below zero in some places. The summers are cool and vary from 40 to 60 degrees.

HOW IT IS GOVERNED

The government of the Northwest Territories is headed by a Commissioner, who is appointed by the Canadian government at Ottawa. His offices are at Fort Smith. The Royal Canadian Mounted Police enforces the law in the region.

Alexander Mackenzie was the first explorer of the Northwest Territories, more than 150 years ago. In 1870 Canada bought the region from the Hudson's Bay Company. Parts of it later became the provinces of Manitoba, Alberta, and Saskatchewan, and the Yukon Territory. In 1905 the Northwest Territories got its present form of government.

NORTHWEST TERRITORIES. Area, 1,-304,903 square miles. Population (1967 estimate) 29,000.

Northwest Territory

The Northwest Territory was a region of the United States two hundred years ago, before the United States became an independent country. The territory included the present states of Ohio, Indiana, Illinois, Michigan, and Wisconsin, and part of Minnesota.

Much of the land of the Northwest Territory had once been claimed by France. In 1763, at the end of the French and Indian War, which was fought between England and France, the lands were given up to England by the French. At the end of the Revolutionary War, when the colonies became independent, England gave up this land to the colonies. At first the land was claimed by the colonies of Massachusetts, Virginia, and Connecticut, because their original char-

ters had given them all the lands from the Atlantic to the Pacific, but by 1786 these colonies had given up most of their claims. The Continental Congress then passed a law called the Ordinance of 1787, which opened the Northwest Territory to settlement and allowed the settlers later to form new states.

Norway

Norway is a country in northern Europe. It is on the North Sea and the Atlantic and Arctic Oceans. It forms a narrow strip on the western side of the Scandinavian Peninsula. Its jagged coast line is 1,700 miles long Its northern tip is the northernmost tip of Europe. About one-third of Norway lies in the cold Arctic Circle, and this region is known as the "Land of the Midnight Sun" because from the middle of May to the end of July the sun never entirely sets there.

Norway is 125,064 square miles in size, which is more than twice as large as the State of Georgia. More than four million people live there, almost as many as live in Georgia, but for its size Norway has a smaller population than any other country in Europe.

THE PEOPLE OF NORWAY

Most of the Norwegians are descended from the Norsemen, who lived on and near the Scandinavian Peninsula more than a thousand years ago. These early Norsemen, who were known as the Vikings, sailed in fast oar-driven ships to raid the coasts of Britain and continental Europe. A small number of Lapps and Finns live in the northern part of Norway.

The Norwegians are sturdy and industrious. They have been known for centuries as skillful sailors. The Norwe-

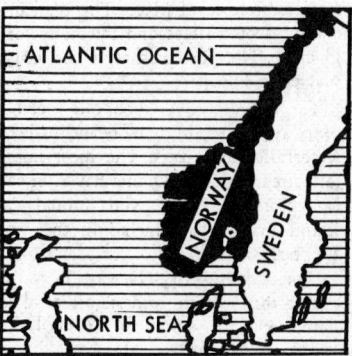

gians are a very democratic and intelligent people, and among them have been many fine writers of books and composers of music. They are great readers of books and magazines. Although the people are up-to-date, they have kept

many of their old customs and colorful costumes. Visitors can see these during festivals and celebrations. The Norwegians are famous for their skill in skiing and ice skating.

Norwegian, the language spoken by the people of Norway, closely resembles the languages of Sweden and Denmark, and is a Germanic language related to German, Dutch, and English. Most of the people in Norway belong to Lutheran churches.

HOW THE PEOPLE LIVE

About one-fifth of the Norwegians are farmers, though only a small part of Norway can be used for raising crops. Most of the farms are quite small. The farmers grow oats, hay, barley, and potatoes. Many of them raise cattle on the high mountain pastures. In the north, the Lapp people raise reindeer, and get from them milk, meat, and skins for clothing.

A large number of Norwegians are sailors and fishermen. Fishing has always been one of the most important industries in Norway. Herring, cod, haddock and mackerel are caught. Norwegian fleets search the North Atlantic for whales. Norway's merchant fleet is third largest in the world.

Many Norwegians work as lumberjacks in the great pine forests in southeastern parts of the country. Others work in the iron mines in the north. About one-third of the people work in the cities, in factories that make paper, wood pulp, iron products, and chemicals. A large industry is the canning of fish

The Norwegians live simply but well. Most Norwegian houses are well-built, roomy, and very clean.

Everyone has to go to school between the ages of 7 and 16. There are many excellent, modern elementary schools and high schools. There are universities at Oslo, Bergen, and other cities.

WHAT THE COUNTRY IS LIKE

Most of Norway is mountainous, with snow-capped peaks. The highest ranges are the Jotunheim Mountains. Along the western coast are thousands of islands and long bays, called *fiords*. These fiords are valleys that have become flooded by the sea. (There is a separate article about FIORDS.) Most of the Norwegians live along the coast.

In the central part of Norway is a plateau, a high, level place. The plateau is cut by deep valleys and by many large glaciers. The Jostedalsbre is the largest glacier in Europe.

Large forests cover about one-fourth of Norway. There are many beautiful lakes, waterfalls, and rivers. The most important stream is the Glomma River, in eastern Norway. Many wild animals are found in Norway, including the wolf, fox, bear, and deer.

The climate of Norway is varied. Along the coast the winters are mild and damp and the summers are cool. The country is warmed by the Gulf Stream, a current of warm water in the Atlantic Ocean. The summers are short, but during that time the air is very clear and the sun shines brightly. In the plateau and mountain regions the winters are very cold, with heavy snowfalls.

Norway does not have many good roads, and its railroads are mostly in the southern part of the country. Much of its transportation is carried on by water, on the ocean, rivers, and fiords. Norway has many fine harbors and important ports, such as Oslo, Bergen, and Trondheim. There are several airports in the chief cities.

CHIEF CITIES OF NORWAY

The leading cities in Norway, with populations as estimated in 1975, are:

Oslo, population 464,900, the capital and chief city. There is a separate article about OSLO.

Bergen, population 213,992, the second-largest city, important seaport, in western Norway.

Trondheim, population 134,037, the third-largest city, shipping center, in western Norway.

Stavanger, population 85,613, the fourth-largest city, shipping center, in southwest.

HOW THE PEOPLE ARE GOVERNED

Norway is a constitutional monarchy, which means that it has a king, a parliament that makes the laws, and a written constitution that protects the rights of the people. Haakon VII became king in 1905. He was succeeded by Olav V in 1957.

The parliament is called the Storting, and is composed of 150 members. They are elected for a four-year term. When the Storting meets, it divides into two groups. One group, called the Lagting, has 38 members. The other group, called the Odelsting, has 112 members. The country is divided into twenty counties. The capital is Oslo.

Every man over 20 years of age must serve in the army for 16 months, or in the navy or air force for 18 months. The navy and air force are small but modern. Everybody 21 years old or older has the right to vote.

NORWAY IN THE PAST

More than one thousand years ago, Norway was a group of small kingdoms ruled by chieftains. The people, called Vikings, were a bold, seafaring people. They explored and conquered many parts of the world. It is believed that one of the Vikings, Leif Ericsson, discovered America more than nine hundred years ago.

About six hundred years ago Norway was united with Denmark, but as Norway grew into an important trading country through the centuries, the people wanted to be independent. In 1814, Norway was united with Sweden. In 1905 the Norwegians declared their independence and elected Haakon VII king of Norway.

Norway grew and prospered, and became an important shipping nation. During World War I Norway, along with Sweden and Denmark, remained neutral. Norway continued to develop peacefully until World War II, when the Germans invaded and occupied the country. Norway was unprepared for war, and the Germans were helped by people within Norway who worked with the Germans. The Norwegian politician Vidkun Quisling helped the Germans to conquer his own country, and the Germans made him head of the Norwegian government. The word "quisling" was used after that for any person who was a traitor to his country. The king and his government refused to give in, and set up their government in England to resist the Germans. Many Norwegians formed a secret underground movement and fought the Germans as well as they could until 1945, when Germany was defeated by the Allies. After the war Norway joined the United Nations. It began to rebuild its shipping industry and has prospered peacefully.

NORWAY. Area, 125,064 square miles. Population (1964 estimate) 3,695,000. Language, Norwegian. Religion, Lutheran. Government, constitutional monarchy. Monetary unit, krone, worth 14 cents (U.S.) Flag, a white-bordered blue cross on red background.

nose

The nose is the most important feature of the human face. Its size and shape have much to do with how a person looks. The nose is most important, however, because the sense of smell is located there and because it is wonderfully constructed for taking in and cleaning the air we breathe into our lungs.

The framework of the nose is a notched bone that grows out of the brow or forehead of the skull. Below this bone is a piece of cartilage, which is not quite as hard as bone. This cartilage makes the ends of our noses flexible (easy to move).

A wall inside the nose separates it into two channels. These channels begin at the nostrils and go up through the nose and become one channel again at the top of the throat. The inside of the nose is lined with a tissue called *mucous membrane,* much like the tissue that lines the mouth and throat. This mucous membrane gives off a watery, sticky substance. This substance traps the dust in the air we breathe and helps keep it from entering our throat and lungs. Larger pieces of dust are screened out of the air by the hair in the nostrils. The membranes inside the nose have thousands of tiny whiplike projections, which help to sweep the dirt in the air away.

In the membranes of the nose are many tiny blood vessels. These blood vessels lie close to the surface of the membranes and give off heat, helping to warm the air that is breathed in. The air is also moistened by the mucous surface of the nasal membranes. Thus you can see that the nose does three important things for the air breathed in: 1, it cleans it; 2, it warms it; 3, it moistens it. All these things are very important because if the air breathed into the lungs were not clean, warm, and moist, the lungs would not remain healthy and in good condition. When people breathe through their mouths, their throats may become dry and dusty and their lungs may receive impurities that the nose would have shut out.

THE SENSE OF SMELL

As odor-carrying air passes through the nose, it is examined by many extremely sensitive nerve endings inside the membranes of the nose. These nerve endings are the outposts or sentries of a pair of important nerves called the *olfactory nerves,* which lead to the brain. Whatever is smelled by the nose is passed along on the olfactory nerves like messages on a telephone wire. When these messages get to that part of the brain that

understands, sorts out, and identifies all the many smells, the brain then tells us that this is such-and-such a smell.

NOSE TROUBLES

Today doctors are able to do much to help people who have nose trouble of one kind or another. Sometimes a person has what is called a *deviated septum*. This means that the wall separating the two channels inside the nose is off to one side and makes one channel much too small. Surgeons not only can straighten out a deviated septum, they also can practically rebuild a broken nose, or give people who have large and unlovely noses rebuilt and handsome ones. This is part of what is called plastic surgery. There are even cases where people have had their noses cut off in accidents. Doctors have sewn them back quickly and so skillfully that one could hardly tell that there had been so serious an accident.

notary public

A notary public is an official of a state or other government. In the United States his main duty is to be present when someone signs an official paper (such as a deed when a house is sold). The person who signs the paper takes an OATH (about which there is a separate article) and the notary public signs the paper to show that he was present when the oath was taken. Usually the notary public has to stamp the paper with his official seal. In some states a *commissioner of deeds* has most of the powers of a notary public. In France a notary represents the government in various business transactions.

Notre Dame

Notre Dame is the name of a famous cathedral in Paris, France. Its full name is *Notre Dame de Paris*, which means "Our Lady of Paris," and it was built more than 750 years ago, from 1163 to 1230. It is one of the finest examples of Gothic architecture, a style of building that uses high, pointed arches and towers. It has many beautiful sculptures, both outside and inside, and fine stained-glass windows.

UNIVERSITY OF NOTRE DAME

Notre Dame is also the name of a large university for men in Notre Dame, Indiana. It is run by members of the Congregation of Holy Cross, a Roman Catholic order, and about 6,400 students go there. It has schools for arts and sciences, law, engineering, and business. Notre Dame's football team, nicknamed "the Fighting Irish," is one of the best-known in the United States. The University of Notre Dame was founded in 1842.

noun

A noun is the name of something—a person, a thing, or simply an idea. A noun is one of the parts of speech. A part of speech is a word that has a particular duty when you say it or write it. The duty of a noun is to tell what something is.

John (a person), New York (a place), table (a thing), and happiness (an idea) are all nouns. John and New York are called *proper nouns,* because they are names of particular things that cannot be anything else. Table and happiness are called *common nouns* because they might

be used for any of millions of different tables or for almost any kind of happiness.

A noun is also called a *substantive,* a word that means "something that exists." It is not only a thing you can touch or feel, or an idea that you can understand, that can be said to exist. Many words or combinations of words can be used as substantives even when they are not really names. You may say, when someone asks you to do him a favor, "To say yes would cause me a lot of trouble." The three words "to say yes" are a substantive, because together they stand for an idea that makes sense even if there are no other words to go with them.

Nouns have *singular* and *plural* forms. A noun "in the singular" means just one of the person or thing it names. A noun "in the plural" means more than one. Usually a noun is made plural by adding *s* to the singular form; *table* means one table and *tables* means more than one table. If the noun ends in such a sound as *s* or *ch,* you add *es* to make the plural; *buses* are more than one bus, and *matches* are more than one match.

Nouns also change to show a *possessive* form, a form that shows that something is owned. Usually the possessive is made by adding an apostrophe and *s,* so that *John's hat* means "the hat owned by John." When the noun stands for more than one person or thing, the apostrophe is put after the *s;* so if you have more than one table, and all the tables have black tops, you would write, *All the tables' tops are black.*

Many nouns are *irregular,* meaning that the usual rules do not apply to them. One example is *man,* of which the plural is not *mans* but *men.* The possessive of *men* is formed as though it were a singular noun. You would write, *The men's clothes were hung in the closet.* The apostrophe comes before the *s,* even though *men* is a plural noun.

Nova Scotia

Nova Scotia is a province of Canada. It is one of the Maritime (seacoast) Prov-

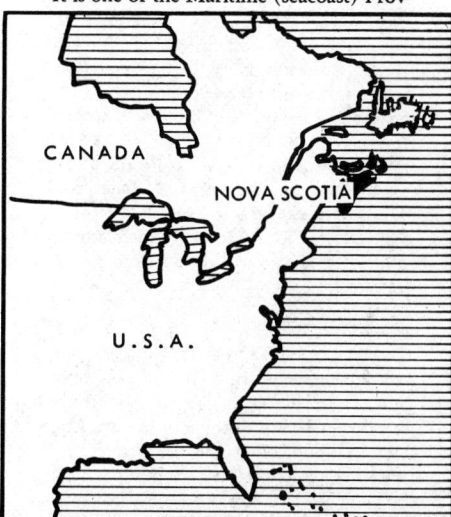

inces, on the Atlantic Ocean. It ranks ninth in size among the provinces, with 21,425 square miles, which is almost three times as large as the state of Massachusetts. In population it ranks seventh, with more than seven hundred thousand people living there. Nova Scotia became

a province of the Dominion of Canada in 1867. Its capital is Halifax.

Most of the people of Nova Scotia are of English and Scottish descent. More than half of them belong to the Roman Catholic Church or to the United Church of Canada. The people work at various industries. Many of them are farmers who raise grain, potatoes, and fruit. Nova Scotia is famous for its apples. Many people fish off the coast of Nova Scotia, where the waters are filled with cod, lobsters, haddock, and herring. Nova Scotia ranks second among Canadian provinces in the value of its fish products. A large number of the people work in coal mines and in the large forests, where men cut spruce, balsam, and pine. In the cities, the people work in large steel mills, furniture factories, and food-processing plants.

WHAT NOVA SCOTIA IS LIKE

Nova Scotia is a peninsula that sticks out into the Atlantic Ocean. To the north of this peninsula is Cape Breton Island, which is part of Nova Scotia. Most of the province is made up of fertile valleys and low hills. On the Atlantic coast are many excellent harbors. This area is often foggy in the winter and spring. In summer it is a favorite vacation spot. The western region has fertile river valleys, crossed by the low mountains. Cape Breton Island is noted for its beautiful scenery, and many people go there on their vacations. There are valuable coal mines on the island.

Nova Scotia does not have extremes of heat and cold as some Canadian provinces do. Though the winters are fairly cold the summers are pleasantly cool, with an average temperature of about 65 degrees. Nova Scotia has many short rivers and beautiful lakes. Popular with visitors is the large Bras d'Or Lake on Cape Breton Island. There are many wild animals in the province, including the deer, moose, wildcat, and bear.

Railroads and paved roads connect most parts of the province. There are airports in the important cities.

THE GOVERNMENT OF NOVA SCOTIA

The head of the government of Nova Scotia is a Lieutenant-Governor, who is appointed by the British Queen with the consent of the Canadian government. The province is actually run by a premier. He is appointed by the legislature, which is elected by the people. The premier stays in office as long as he can keep the confidence of the majority of the legislature. The legislature is elected for a five-year term. Judges are appointed by the Canadian government in Ottawa, and hold office permanently. The provincial government is in the capital, Halifax.

Everyone in the cities has to go to school until the age of 16. In the country, children have to go to school until they are 14. There are elementary schools and high schools throughout the province. Nova Scotia has 10 colleges and universities which grant degrees. The largest is Dalhousie University in Halifax.

Halifax is the capital and largest city in Nova Scotia, with a population of 99,372 in 1967. It is an important port and manufacturing center. Dartmouth is the second-largest city, with a population of 58,745.

NOVA SCOTIA IN THE PAST

Nova Scotia was settled by the French more than 350 years ago. They called the region Acadia. (There is a separate article about ACADIA.) There were fierce struggles between the French and English over possession of this region. In 1713, Acadia was given to England, and the English drove out the Acadians from their land because they refused to swear allegiance to the British king. In 1776 Nova Scotia had a difficult choice between joining the other colonies in the Revolutionary War and remaining loyal to the British king, but it decided to remain British. It became a province of the Dominion of Canada in 1867.

Since then, Nova Scotia has prospered and grown. Halifax has become one of the most important ports in Canada, and Nova Scotia's manufactures have increased rapidly.

NOVA SCOTIA. Area, 21,425 square miles. Population (1967 estimate) 756,039. Capital, Halifax. Coat of arms: at the top, the Royal Arms of Scotland; in the center, the cross of St. Andrew; left, a British royal unicorn, and right, an American Indian. Flower, trailing arbutus. Admitted to Dominion, 1867. Official abbreviation, N.S.

novel, a long work of fiction: see the article on LITERATURE.

November

November is the eleventh month of the year. It has thirty days. In ancient Roman times the year began with March, and November was the ninth month. It was called "Novembris," which means ninth in the Latin language. About two thousand years ago the Romans began to use the calendar that we know now, and November became the eleventh month. People who were born in November have the topaz, a pale yellow stone, as their birthstone. The flower of the month of November is the chrysanthemum.

Noyes, Alfred

Alfred Noyes is the name of an English poet whose work became very popular in the United States. He was born in 1880, and attended Oxford University. He visited the United States several times, and from 1914 to 1923 he was professor of English literature at Princeton University. Noyes' first book of poems, *The Loom of Years,* was published in 1902 when he was only 22 years old. Other well-known works include *The Forest of Wild Thyme,* and *Tales of the Mermaid Tavern.* Among his most famous poems are "The Highwayman" and "The Barrel Organ." He died in 1958.

numismatics

Numismatics is the study of coins and medals. The hobby of coin- and medal-collecting is also called numismatics. Thousands of people collect coins. Coin collectors are interested in certain coins because of their rarity and their condition, and not so much because of their original value. For instance, a fifty-cent coin used by the Confederate States, during the Civil War, is such a rare coin that it is worth hundreds of dollars to a coin collector.

Another thing that affects the value of a coin is its physical condition. A coin that has not been used is usually worth more than one that has. A coin is said to be in mint condition if it is just as new and fresh as it was when it first came from the mint, the factory where coins are made.

Sometimes a coin will have a very high value because some mistake was made when the coin was minted. For example, a word on the coin may be misspelled, or part of the design may be wrong. Perhaps a few coins were issued with these mistakes, then the mistakes were discovered and the coin taken out of circulation. Those few coins that remained in circulation would have a high value for the collector because there would be so few of them.

A collection of really rare and unusual coins can be very expensive, but collectors can enjoy the hobby even when they do not have very much money. Some collectors specialize in the regular coins of their country or in the coins of a particular denomination (value), such as pennies or dimes. Perhaps a collector builds a collection of dimes of certain years. He gets these dimes from the change that passes through his hands in everyday business. Collecting Indian-head pennies is another specialty of coin collectors. At one time many of these pennies could be found in the change that one got every day; now an Indian-head penny is seldom seen. It should be remembered that the fun of collecting coins is not so much in the value of the coins as in the work of gathering the collection.

You can learn a great deal about a country, its customs, and its ideas from examining its coins. On some coins there are mottoes that give an idea of what the country believes in. For example, suppose a person two thousand years from now saw a United States coin with the words "In God we trust" and "Liberty" on it. He would know immediately that in the United States the ideas of freedom and religion were very important.

From the pictures that are stamped on some old coins, we can get a good idea of what clothes the people wore, who their rulers were, what animals were known to them, and many other things.

Coin collectors have their own magazines, which tell about interesting coins, outstanding collections, and places where coins can be bought and sold.

Many museums have collections of coins. The museum of the American Numismatic Society, in New York City, is famous for its collection, which comes from all over the world and from every time in the history of man.

nuns and sisters

Nuns and sisters are women who dedicate (give) themselves to their religion. They belong to groups called religious orders. Most of these orders are Roman Catholic, but some are Protestant. Nuns belong to a religious order in which they take solemn vows (promises) to own no property, to obey their superiors, and never to marry. These vows are expected to last for their lifetime. Sisters belong to an order in which they take simple vows. This means that they can own property but cannot use it, and that they can leave the order if they wish. Orders for women are either *contemplative* or *ac-* *tive.* Contemplative nuns spend most of their time in prayer. Active nuns do such work as teaching or nursing. Each order wears a particular style of clothing, called a *habit.* Mostly, the habits are the same as the clothes worn hundreds of years ago, but in recent years some of the orders have changed to more modern dress.

Nuremberg

Nuremberg is a city in West Germany, the second-largest city in the German state of Bavaria. It has a population of more than 460,000, which makes it almost as large as Columbus, Ohio. Nuremberg is a very old city. It was an important trade center as long as seven hundred years ago. In the years that followed it became a great center of art and culture. Nuremberg is famous for the toys made there. It also manufactures machinery and precision tools, and it has plants where fine printing is done.

Nuremberg was the favorite city of Adolf Hitler, who ruled Germany from 1933 until the end of World War II, in 1945. Hitler's Nazi Party held its biggest meetings there. At the Nazi meeting of 1935 the Nuremberg Laws were passed, depriving the Jews who lived in Germany of most of their rights as German citizens.

After Germany had been defeated in World War II, the Allied countries charged the leaders of the German government with crimes against humanity. Most of those leaders were proved to have been guilty of such crimes. The chief American prosecutors were Robert H Jackson, General Telford Taylor, and Dr. Robert M. W. Kempner. See also the articles on Robert H. JACKSON and on NAZISM.

nursery rhymes

Nursery rhymes are the first rhymes that are taught to children when they are learning to talk. There are hundreds of nursery rhymes that have been used by English-speaking peoples for hundreds of years, and they have a great appeal to children. Many nursery rhymes do not seem to make sense, but they may have when they were first written. Tiny children like certain sounds and rhymes, such as are found in "Hickory, Dickory, Dock":

Hickory, dickory, dock,
The mouse ran up the clock;
The clock struck one,
The mouse ran down,
Hickory, dickory, dock.

Many of the nursery rhymes have some connection with English history and were written to make fun of political figures.

When a German, George of Hanover, became King George I of England in 1714, many people thought he was a foreigner who should not be their king. Their feelings went into a nursery rhyme:

Hark, hark, the dogs do bark,
The beggars are coming to town,
Some in rags, and some in tags,
And some in velvet gowns.

Many of the favorite nursery rhymes are published under the name "Mother Goose," although there may never have been such a person. The name "Mother Goose" may have been taken from the first nursery rhyme in an old book.

nursery school

A nursery school is a school for children from 2 to 4 years of age. It is very much like KINDERGARTEN (about which there is a separate article), and it is intended for children whose parents believe a child should begin even younger than 4 or 5 years to learn how to get along with other children.

nursing

Nursing is the work of taking care of people who cannot take care of themselves. Nurses take care of people who are sick or recovering from illness, or care for babies or very old people.

Almost anyone who does this kind of work can be called a nurse, but there are three different groups of people who are trained for it in different ways. These are the *nurse's aide,* the *practical nurse,* and the *professional nurse.* The nurse's aide is trained while she is working. The practical and professional nurses go to schools where they are especially trained to care for the sick and to teach people how to get well and to prevent illness. The practical nurse works under the direction and supervision of the professional nurse. This article tells about the professional nurse, who is also called a *registered nurse.*

Professional nurses work in hospitals and in people's homes. They assist doctors in offices. Many large factories employ nurses to care for workers who become ill. There are nurses in schools and hotels and large department stores. Nurses work on trains and boats and airplanes. Nurses work closely with doctors in time of disaster, such as flood or fire or accident. Nurses have been very important during wartime. In World War II more than 60,000 nurses served with the United States Army and Navy.

Most nurses are women, but there is a great need for more male nurses and many young men now are beginning to consider nursing as a career. A person who wants to become a professional nurse must receive special education and training.

THE EDUCATION OF PROFESSIONAL NURSES

If you want to become a nurse you must go to high school for four years. You should take courses in English, mathematics, social studies, and science. After you have graduated from high school you may go to college and take a special degree in nursing. Many students prefer to go directly to the hospital nursing school.

There are more than a thousand accredited schools of nursing in the United States. ("Accredited" means that they are recognized by the state.) Most schools of nursing are owned and operated by hospitals. The length of time you spend in such a school varies from two to five years; the average time is three years.

As a student, you will study the human body and chemistry and biology and many other scientific subjects. A great deal of your time will be spent in the hospital. As a nursing student you will have an opportunity to try many different kinds of nursing. You will work in the pediatrics department of the hospital, where you will take care of children who are sick. You will work in obstetrics (with newborn babies and their mothers). You will take care of people who are mentally ill and you will assist in the operating room.

When you graduate from nursing school, you must take an examination given by the state in which you live. When you pass this examination, you receive your license. You are called an R.N., which stands for "registered nurse."

THE WORK OF NURSES

There are several different fields of work included in nursing.

Many nurses work in hospitals. Those who take care of the sick are called *staff nurses.* A nurse in a hospital has many duties, in addition to caring for patients. Those who supervise the wards and operating rooms and special departments are called *head nurses* and *supervisors.* Nurses also work on research projects.

Many other nurses specialize in taking care of patients who are ill with tuberculosis or infantile paralysis or some other disease. A nurse who works in a hospital takes care of many patients.

Some nurses are *private-duty nurses.* A private-duty nurse is responsible for the care of one patient in the hospital or at home. The private-duty nurse cares for the patient until the doctor decides that the person no longer needs the attention of a special nurse.

Public-health nurses work outside of hospitals. Many of them are employed by the United States government or private organizations. The chief work of public-health nurses is to prevent illness. They visit homes and teach families how to discover when a member of the family has some sickness and how to care for the patient. They inform people about where to go to receive good medical care. They work with doctors to discover cases of illness in schools and factories. Public-health nurses cooperate with teachers and social workers in programs to reduce illness and prevent accidents.

Some nurses are *teachers.* They work in nursing schools, teaching students to become nurses. They also give advanced courses in new methods to nurses who have already graduated and are working.

Some nurses work in the military services. They help take care of soldiers and sailors during peace and war. They serve in all parts of the world where servicemen go. Nurses also work in factories. These nurses are called industrial nurses. They give first aid to factory workers and also teach them how to keep well.

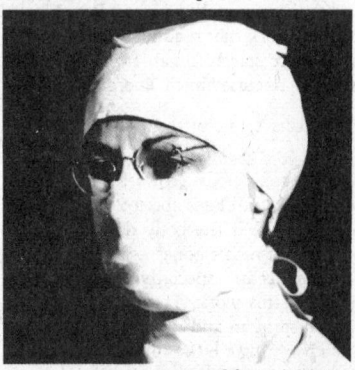

Johnson & Johnson
A surgical nurse wears a cap and gauze mask while assisting at an operation.

THE HISTORY OF NURSING

Professional nursing is a new field of work. Less than a hundred years ago there were no official nursing schools in the United States. Florence Nightingale, the founder of modern professional nursing, built up a fine system for training nurses in England and in 1873 the first American school of nursing, founded on the Florence Nightingale principles, was established in New York City. Now there are about 815,000 registered nurses in the United States. Many of them belong to such organizations as the American Nurses Association and the National League for Nursing.

WHO SHOULD BECOME A NURSE

A person who wants to become a nurse must be friendly and sympathetic. A sense of humor and a calm disposition are very helpful qualities. A nurse must be able to follow instructions because it is necessary to carry out the doctor's orders exactly. A nurse must be in good health. She is often exposed to disease, and may be required to work under great strain. A nurse must do many things, from a simple task, such as giving a patient a bath in bed, to a complex one, such as injecting a drug into a vein. Her work requires some highly specialized skills and much patience.

Nursing is not easy work, but it is a profession that has many rewards. A person who becomes a nurse is doing something that is necessary and useful to others.

nut

The nut is a kind of dry seed or fruit. It grows inside a wooden shell. The shell does not split open when the fruit is ripe.

The seed of this fruit is good to eat. Many different kinds of trees that grow in all parts of the world bear nuts. Some things we call nuts, such as the peanut, and the coconut, are not true nuts, although they are grouped with the acorn, the chestnut, the hazelnut, and other true nuts.

Nuts contain fats, starches, proteins, and these substances when eaten give us energy. People have sometimes thought that nuts were not healthful, but this is not true. People in many parts of the world eat nuts as part of their diet instead of meat. In the United States, Canada, and other countries where the supply of meat is plentiful, people eat nuts as a dessert. Nuts are used in making cake, candy, and bread. They are used in soup and salads and in many other ways. Many nuts contain a valuable oil that is used for cooking. Some nuts, such as the peanut, are ground to make peanut butter and other spreads. Nuts are sometimes used to make a substitute for coffee.

Nut trees are hardy and the crop of nuts is plentiful. Nuts keep well for a long time in a cool place, and they will not spoil when they are shipped. Thousands of tons of nuts are grown in the United States each year. They are sent to countries all over the world, and other nuts are brought to the United States from other countries.

nuthatch

The nuthatch is a friendly little bird that makes its home in many parts of Eu-

rope and the United States. It has gray feathers and its underparts are white. The nuthatch can cling to the bark of a tree with its feet and run quickly up and down the trunk to search for insects, on which it feeds. The nuthatch is also fond of nuts. It places a nut firmly in a crack in a tree and then pecks at it with its sharp bill until the shell breaks and opens. This is how the nuthatch got its name.

The nuthatch builds its nest in a crack in a tree. Sometimes it plasters mud around the entrance so that squirrels cannot enter. The female bird lays five to seven eggs. The eggs are white with patches of red on them. The nuthatch does not sing.

The red-breasted nuthatch has a red breast and white stripes on its head. It lives in evergreen forests in places where the climate is quite cool.

nutmeg

Nutmeg is a spice that comes from a tree that was first grown in the Molucca Islands in the Pacific Ocean. (These islands are sometimes called the Spice Islands.) Now it grows in many places where the climate is warm and moist, and the soil rich.

The nutmeg is a handsome evergreen tree, which means it does not lose its leaves in the fall. The tree grows to be between 30 and 60 feet tall. It has small, pale yellow flowers and a golden fruit that looks like an apricot. When the fruit dries, the skin splits open. There is a shiny brown seed inside, and the kernel of the seed is the nutmeg. The brown seed has a red cover that makes another spice called *mace*.

Nutmeg is a delicious spice with a sweet smell. It is used to flavor cakes and puddings, and tastes very good in some drinks. The oil of nutmeg is used to make perfume and to flavor tobacco. Nutmeg also contains a valuable thick yellow fat that is called *nutmeg butter*. Nutmeg butter is used to make candles and is important in certain salves and medicines.

nutrition

Nutrition is the science and study of the foods that make the body strong and healthy. The body gets the nourishment it needs from raw materials that are contained in foods. Starch, sugar, fat, protein, minerals, vitamins and water are all raw materials. From these raw materials the body builds bones and muscles, and makes blood.

Chemists and nutritionists have studied almost every kind of food. They know that a person must eat enough food, and different kinds of food. Some foods nourish the body better when they are combined with other foods. For example, the body can use cereals better when they are combined with milk.

The body gets the energy it needs from food. The amount of fuel or energy that food contains is measured in CALORIES, about which there is a separate article. Some foods contain more calories and can supply more energy to the body than others.

FOODS THAT SUPPLY ENERGY

Certain foods contain large amounts of sugar, starch, or fat, and all of these supply the body with energy.

Bread, cereals, potatoes, peas and beans are all foods that have much starch. Sweets such as jelly, honey, cake, and candy contain sugar. Cream and butter, nuts and fat meat contain fat. A person who does not get enough sugar, starch and fat in his diet may not be healthy. He may be too thin. He may get tired easily and feel hungry all the time. People who do hard work that requires a lot of energy need more starch, sugar, fat than people who do not use much energy.

FOODS THAT BUILD AND REPAIR THE BODY

A person's body grows from the time he is born until he is about 23 or 24 years old. After that the body does not grow, but it must repair bones, skin, and tissues. Some foods are especially valuable to the body for this work. These are foods that contain protein and iron. Meat, fish, eggs and cheese have large amounts of protein. Some meats, such as liver and kidney, contain iron. Spinach and other leafy green vegetables contain iron and so does the yolk of an egg. A person who does not get enough protein and iron may feel tired and is more likely to catch diseases. A young person who does not get enough protein and iron in his food may not grow properly.

FOODS THAT MAKE STRONG BONES AND TEETH

The material that helps build bones and teeth is calcium. Milk is one of the most important calcium foods. Cheese, lettuce, cabbage, and other leafy vegetables also contain some calcium. A person who does not get enough calcium in his diet may have weak teeth. A young child who does not have enough calcium may develop bowlegs, or his body may not grow properly in some other way. When people do not drink enough milk and other calcium foods, they may have to take pills containing calcium.

FOODS THAT HELP THE THYROID GLAND

The thyroid gland controls the way the body uses food. Fish and salt are the most important sources of iodine, which is needed by the thyroid gland.

NUTRIENTS WE NEED

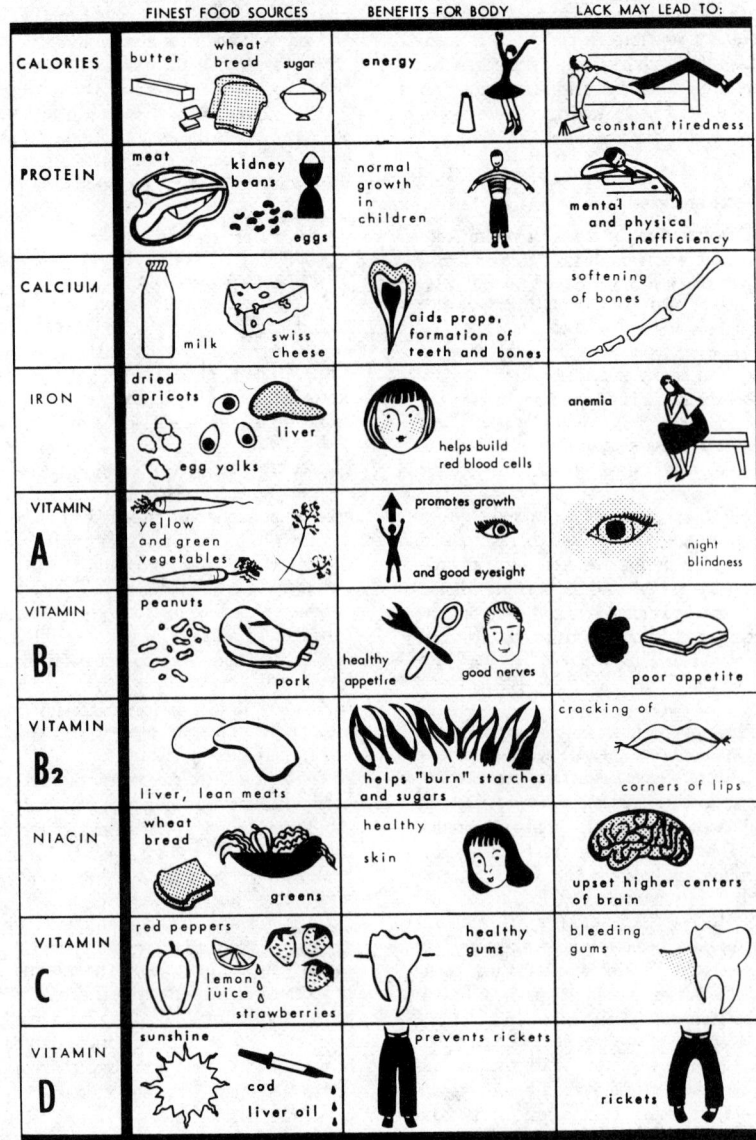

	FINEST FOOD SOURCES	BENEFITS FOR BODY	LACK MAY LEAD TO:
CALORIES	butter, wheat bread, sugar	energy	constant tiredness
PROTEIN	meat, kidney beans, eggs	normal growth in children	mental and physical inefficiency
CALCIUM	milk, swiss cheese	aids proper formation of teeth and bones	softening of bones
IRON	dried apricots, liver, egg yolks	helps build red blood cells	anemia
VITAMIN A	yellow and green vegetables	promotes growth and good eyesight	night blindness
VITAMIN B₁	peanuts, pork	healthy appetite, good nerves	poor appetite
VITAMIN B₂	liver, lean meats	helps "burn" starches and sugars	cracking of corners of lips
NIACIN	wheat bread, greens	healthy skin	upset higher centers of brain
VITAMIN C	red peppers, lemon juice, strawberries	healthy gums	bleeding gums
VITAMIN D	sunshine, cod liver oil	prevents rickets	rickets

HOW VITAMINS HELP GROWTH

Vitamins are important materials that help a body to grow. Some foods contain more vitamins than others. There are several different kinds of vitamin and each has its particular use. Vitamin C, for example, is found in oranges, grapefruit, and other citrus fruits. It helps build bones, teeth, and muscles, and helps the body to heal when it has been wounded. A person who does not get enough vitamins may have poor eyesight, rough skin, or sore gums and weak teeth. People who are too thin or feel tired much of the time often need more vitamins. Sometimes doctors give people vitamins in the form of pills.

DEFICIENCY DISEASES

There are some diseases, such as pellagra, scurvy, and beriberi, that occur when the body does not receive enough vitamins. These diseases are called deficiency diseases. You can read about them in separate articles. Even if a person does not get a deficiency disease he may not be really healthy. He may not feel as energetic as he wants to, he may have poor eyesight, or his skin may break out in pimples, because he is not eating the proper foods.

A WELL-BALANCED DIET

A person should enjoy the food he eats, and he should eat the foods that contain the raw materials needed by his body. Scientists have figured out a certain number of what are called "basic foods." Every person should eat these foods every day. Fortunately there are enough foods in each group so that a person can find some that he likes.

A person should eat one leafy green vegetable each day. Lettuce, cabbage and spinach are leafy green vegetables. A person should have a tomato, some raw cabbage, or an orange or other citrus fruit each day. He should have two servings of potatoes or other vegetables or fruit. Fruits and vegetables can be eaten fresh, dried, canned, or frozen.

Children should drink from one half to one quart of milk each day. Adults should drink about two glasses of milk a day. Milk can be eaten in puddings, soups, or ice cream. Cheese can be eaten as a substitute for some of the milk that a person needs. The body grows best if a person eats one serving of meat, chicken or fish each day. Dried peas or certain kinds of beans or peanut butter can sometimes be substituted for meat, because these foods contain many of the same important raw materials.

A person should have a slice of bread, or a portion of noodles, spaghetti, or rice, at each meal. He should eat one to three tablespoons of butter or margarine each day.

The body needs water and a person should drink four to eight glasses of water a day. Milk or fruit juice can be substituted for water.

Studies are still being made to find out more about how food affects the body.

Nyasa, Lake (Lake Malawi)

Lake Malawi is a large lake in east Africa, between Malawi on the west and south and Mozambique and Tanzania on the east and northeast. Before 1964, it was called Lake Nyasa. It is the third-largest of the great lakes of east Africa. The lake is about 11,000 square miles in size, which is a little larger than Lake Erie. It is 360 miles long and from 15 to 50 miles wide. It is in a deep valley and is lined by high mountains. Steamers take passengers from one settlement to another along the shore of the lake. It was first sighted by Portuguese explorers in the 17th century, but was forgotten until it was investigated by David Livingstone in 1859.

Nyasaland (Malawi)

Nyasaland, in southeast Africa, has been called Malawi since becoming independent in 1964. It was a British colony from about 1890 to 1953 and then a member of the Federation of Rhodesia and Nyasaland, which ended in 1963. As Malawi it is a member of the (British) Commonwealth.

The country runs along the southern and western shores of Lake Malawi and is noted for its beautiful lakes and mountains. Almost four million people live there. Most of them are blacks of Bantu stock. Farming is the main occupation, with large crops of tobacco, cotton, and tea.

NYASALAND (MALAWI). Area 47,200 square miles. Population (1975 estimate) 5,040,000. Capital, Zomba.

nylon

Nylon is a plastic substance that is made from coal, air, and water, and is used instead of silk or other materials in hundreds of useful articles. Most nylon is made into thread and then is woven into many kinds of cloth, ranging from sheer women's stockings to heavy cloth that is like canvas.

Nylon is cream white. It is translucent, which means that you can see light through it, though you cannot see things on the other side of it. By using the proper dyes you can give nylon any color you want.

Nylon fibers have great strength and toughness, and they can stretch very far without breaking. This makes nylon a good material from which to make rope and cord that must stand very great pulls. Nylon is twisted into glider tow-ropes, mooring ropes for ocean liners, fishing line, tennis racquet strings, parachutes, and the cords that make up the inner walls of automobile tires.

Nylon absorbs very little water when you wet it, so it is practically waterproof. Clothes made from nylon dry very quickly after washing. Nylon fibers are made into mosquito nets and window screens that will not rot in wet weather and besides are almost as strong as copper screens.

NYLON AS A PLASTIC

You can give nylon a certain shape by using heat, moisture, and pressure. Then, no matter how much it is stretched, it always comes back to the shape you made it in. The only way to change the shape is to put it under heat and pressure again. Plastics that can be treated this way are said to be *thermoplastic*, a word that means "shaped by heat." Because of its ability to hold the shape it is given, ny-

Surrounded by the nations of Tanzania, Mozambique, and Zambia in southeast Africa, lies the Republic of Malawi. Along most of Malawi's eastern border runs Lake Malawi, the southern end of which forms Monkey Bay, shown in this photograph.

lon is made into women's stockings that never lose their shape. Clothes such as men's shirts made of nylon straighten themselves out after washing and so they need little or no ironing. Moths will not eat nylon as they eat wool.

NYLON MOLDING

Nylon in the form of powder is used by manufacturers to make many plastic objects. The powder is put into a mold. It is heated until it is soft and is then pressed into all parts of the mold. When it cools it keeps the shape of the mold. Toothbrush handles and bristles, combs, watch straps, and belts, are some of the things made of nylon.

Nylon is an insulator against electricity. Dissolved in a suitable liquid, it becomes a kind of enamel that is put on electric wires to cover them so that anyone touching them will not get a shock, and there will be no short circuits.

nymph

The nymphs were lovely maidens in Greek mythology, the stories the ancient Greeks told about their gods and goddesses. They were young and beautiful. They had long flowing hair, and they wore light graceful robes. The nymphs were the goddesses that were most like human beings, and a nymph could even marry a man.

Nymphs lived in the oceans, forests, rivers, and mountains. They were fond of dancing and hunting and were the special guardians of the beautiful things of nature. Some stories said that when a nymph deserted a tree, the tree would die. The nymphs did not live forever, but they never grew old.

Dictionary of American Portraits

Marksman and circus performer Annie Oakley traveled with Buffalo Bill's Wild West Show.

Israel Government Tourist Office

The green foliage of this oasis near Jericho, Jordan stands in marked contrast to the sandy wastes of the nearby Judean Desert.

Oak Ridge National Laboratory

An aerial view of the Oak Ridge National Laboratory, where experiments in atomic physics are conducted for the United States government.

U.S. Forest Service

Spanish moss drapes a live oak forest on Jekyll Island, Georgia.

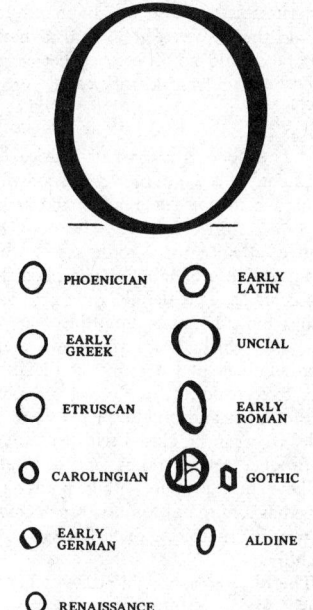

O PHOENICIAN   O EARLY LATIN

O EARLY GREEK   O UNCIAL

O ETRUSCAN   O EARLY ROMAN

O CAROLINGIAN   O GOTHIC

O EARLY GERMAN   O ALDINE

O RENAISSANCE

O or o

The letter O is the fifteenth letter of the alphabet. It can be traced all the way back to the earliest writing known to man, in Egypt, thousands of years ago. In the Hebrew language, in which much of the Bible was written, the letter was called *ayin,* a word that meant "eye." The ancient Greeks took this same letter and called it *omicron.*

The Greeks used omicron to indicate the "short o" sound, such as we use in the word *olive.* They developed another letter, called *omega,* to indicate the "long o" sound, such as we use in the word *pole.*

The Romans took over the *omicron* to indicate both the long *o* and the short *o.* In the English language the letter O is used for both the long *o* and the short *o* sounds as well as many others. The principal other sounds are: *o* followed by *r,* as in *glory;* a double sound indicated by a single letter, as in *do;* the *u* sound, as in *money;* and the sound that *o* has after the letter w, as in *word.*

The shape of the letter O has changed very little since earliest times.

See also the article ALPHABET.

oak

The oak is a tree that grows in many parts of the United States, Canada, and other lands where the climate is not too cold. Some oaks are large and magnificent, others small and scrubby. There are about three hundred different kinds of oak trees. Some of them are *evergreens,* which means that they do not lose their leaves in the fall. Most oak trees are *deciduous,* which means that they do lose their leaves in the fall.

Many oaks grow to be more than 100 feet tall. It takes an oak tree about 150 or 200 years to become fully grown, and some are more than one thousand years old. It is a stately tree, with large spreading branches and dark green leaves that turn to brilliant scarlet, gold, and deep red colors in the fall. The flowers of the oak appear in early spring. They are graceful drooping yellow tassels. The fruit of the oak is a small nut that is called an acorn.

Some of the best-known oak trees are the *white oak* and the *red oak.* These great trees grow in many parts of the United States. People plant oaks in cities and parks, and there are also huge forests of oak trees.

The wood of the oak is very useful. The white oak tree has a strong hard wood that takes a polish very well. This wood is used to build bridges, houses, and handles of tools. Fine floors and furniture are made of oak. The *live oak* that grows in some states has the hardest wood of all the oak trees. It is used to make farm machinery. The live oak is an evergreen.

The bark of some oak trees contains a valuable substance called *tannin* that is used to treat leather. The American Indians made a meal from acorns and in many parts of the world people still eat them. The acorn is a favorite food of squirrels and other animals.

Oakland

Oakland is the fourth-largest city in California. It is on the east shore of San Francisco Bay, and is joined to San Francisco by the beautiful San Francisco-Oakland Bridge, the longest bridge in the world.

About 360,000 people live in Oakland. Many of them work in the transportation industry. There is a fine harbor on the bay, including a port used by troop transports taking soldiers to army bases in the Pacific. There are many factories, among which are fruit and vegetable canneries, automobile and truck plants, and lumber mills.

Oakland has several beautiful parks and a fine museum. Mills College and the College of the Holy Names are there. Oakland was founded in 1850 and became a city four years later. It grew with San Francisco, and after the San Francisco earthquake and fire in 1906 many people from San Francisco moved to Oakland.

OAKLAND. Population (1970 census) 361,561. County seat, Alameda County. On San Francisco Bay. Founded, 1850.

Oakley, Annie

Annie Oakley was an American woman who could shoot a rifle better than anyone else of her time. She was born in Ohio, in 1860. Her real name was Phoebe Anne Oakley McGee. When she was 4 years old, her father died. Annie began to help the family get food by shooting rabbits and other animals. She became a fine shot when she was still a little girl. When she grew up she had a contest with Frank Butler, one of the greatest shots of the time. Annie Oakley beat Butler in the contest. They fell in love and were married. Annie Oakley was a better marksman than her husband, so he became her manager. She could shoot a cigarette out of Butler's mouth at thirty paces. In one contest she shot 943 out of 1,000 glass balls that were tossed in the air. She could slice a playing card that was held with the thin edge of the card towards her. For many years, Annie Oakley traveled with Buffalo Bill's Wild West Show and with other shows. She performed in both America and Europe. Everywhere she went, people marveled at her skill. Free tickets to a theater or other performance have come to be called "Annie Oakleys" because holes are punched in free tickets and one of Annie Oakley's feats was to shoot the spots out of a playing card. Annie Oakley died in 1926, at the age of 66.

Oak Ridge

Oak Ridge is a city in eastern Tennessee that is the location of an installation of the Atomic Energy Commission. It is run by the commission for the United States Government. The government took over Oak Ridge in 1942 for the "Manhattan District" project, which developed the atomic bomb. Scientists worked here in secrecy until 1945, when they made the first atomic bomb.

In 1946, all of Oak Ridge was placed under the Atomic Energy Commission. The Oak Ridge National Laboratory and other agencies there work for the commission. Huge plants have been built, employing thousands of workers. There is also an Institute of Nuclear Studies at Oak Ridge. Its members, thirty-one southern universities, cooperate in studying atomic science. Oak Ridge in 1970 had a population of 28,319.

oasis

An oasis is any spot where there is a spring or well or other source of water in a desert. A desert is a place where it almost never rains. The soil is sandy and almost no plants will grow. But where there is any water, the soil becomes fertile. Trees and other plants will grow.

In the world's biggest desert, the Sahara, there are many places where a spring bubbles up out of the ground and forms a spot of green in the midst of hundreds of miles of barren sand. Through the ages, caravans (parties of travelers) have stopped at these oases to rest, to give water to the camels who carried them, and to fill their water bags for the next step of the journey across the desert.

The banks of rivers flowing through barren land are often considered oases.

oath

An oath is a solemn promise to tell the truth, or a statement that you have said or written is true. The person who makes the promise or statement calls on God to witness the truth of what he says. To take an oath and then say or write something untrue is a crime. This crime is called *perjury.*

Witnesses in court trials are required to take an oath that their testimony will be true. Before a witness testifies, he is asked to place his left hand on a Bible and raise his right hand. The clerk of the court asks, "Do you solemnly swear that the testimony you are about to give is the truth, the whole truth, and nothing but the truth?" The witness replies, "I do," and he is then bound by his oath.

Members of some religions will not take an oath. They believe that it is taking the name of the Lord in vain, which is forbidden in the Ten Commandments. The law does not require anyone to take an oath when it is against his religion. Such a person must say, very seriously, that he has told the truth or will tell the truth. This is called *affirming,* while taking an oath is called *swearing.*

See also the article on NOTARY PUBLIC.

oats

Oats are an important food crop that is grown in many parts of the world where the climate is not too warm. Like wheat, barley, and rice, oats belong to the family of plants known as "cereal grasses." Oats have been known for thousands of years. They seldom grow wild. Oats are food for both men and animals. They are made into oatmeal, a nourishing breakfast food, and into flour from which cookies and cakes are made. Oats form a fine food for cattle and horses. (When we want to say that a horse is feeling frisky we may say that the animal is "feeling his oats".) The leaves are a bluish-green color. The grain or kernel, which is the part we eat, grows at the top of the plant and is covered by a hull that is white, red, yellow, or black. Oat plants are hardy; they will grow in almost any soil, but need much water. Farmers in Scotland and Ireland grow fine oats.

obelisk

An obelisk is a four-sided stone monument that rises to a point at the top. The ancient Egyptians, thousands of years ago, used to place a pair of obelisks at the entrance to a temple. Each obelisk was carved out of a single piece of stone, usually granite or marble. Its sides were carved with hieroglyphs (picture-writing) telling of the wonderful things one of their rulers had done. Often an obelisk was more than a hundred feet high.

Two obelisks that were made about 1,500 years before the birth of Jesus may now be seen in England and the United States. They are made of red granite, and they are called Cleopatra's Needles because of their long, thin shape. One is 68½ feet high and stands in London,

Mass. Dept. of Commerce

Millions of Americans are as familiar with this 220-foot marble obelisk as with their ABC's. It is in Charlestown, Massachusetts, and commemorates the stand of raw American troops against the British in the Battle of Bunker Hill.

England. The other is 69½ feet high and is in Central Park, in New York City. The United States has built obelisks too. The Washington Monument in Washington, D.C., and the Bunker Hill Monument, near Charlestown, Massachusetts,

are obelisks in shape, but they are not carved out of single pieces of stone.

Oberammergau

Oberammergau is a village in southern Germany, high in the Bavarian Alps. About five thousand people live there. Every ten years for more than three hundred years—since the year 1633—a Passion Play has been performed at Oberammergau. A PASSION PLAY is a play that shows the Crucifixion of Jesus; there is a separate article about it.

obesity

Obesity means "fatness." A person who weighs more than the proper amount for his height and the structure of his body and his age suffers from obesity. Doctors have estimated about how much a person should weigh and they have charts that show this. A person who weighs more than fifteen pounds above his normal weight is said to be obese.

Obesity is never a healthy condition, but as a person grows older it is more serious. A person who weighs too much needs a lot of energy to move around. His heart has to work harder than it should, and fat people are likely to develop heart trouble and high blood pressure and other diseases. A fat person cannot stand an operation as well as a person of normal weight. He cannot resist infections so easily. All medical studies show that overweight people do not usually live as long as people of normal weight. Yet millions of people are too fat.

There are several reasons why a person might be overweight. A few people are overweight because their glands do not work properly. They are not able to use up the energy they get from the food they eat and so it is stored in the body as fat. Doctors usually know how to treat a person who has gland trouble.

Most people are fat because they eat too much. A person may not eat large quantities of food but he may have poor eating habits. He may eat the wrong kinds of food. Fats such as butter and nuts, and starches such as bread and potatoes, and sweets such as candy and ice-cream and cake, all have many calories. (A calorie is a measure of the amount of heat, or energy, that the body gets from a certain amount of food.) Foods with many calories cause a person to gain weight.

People often eat more food than their bodies need. They eat even when they are not hungry. Some people get into the habit of eating many times every day and they find it hard to cut out these extra meals. Sometimes when people are unhappy or bored they eat because they cannot think of anything else to do. When someone feels that other people do not like him or things are not going well in his life he may want to eat sweet things to comfort himself. It is necessary for a person who eats because he is unhappy to find out why he feels unhappy before he will be able to stop eating too much.

A person who wants to lose a few pounds can eat plenty of fresh fruit and vegetables and cut down on rich desserts and between-meal snacks and he will lose weight. Obesity is unhealthy but people

sometimes try to lose weight in a hurry and do themselves a great deal of harm. No one should go on a strict diet except when he is under a doctor's care.

oboe

The oboe is a kind of musical instrument. It is a double-reed woodwind, about which you can read in the article MUSICAL INSTRUMENTS. The oboe has been used since the Middle Ages, when it was called a Schalmey. The oboe that is used today is a slender tube about 21 inches long. It has a mouthpiece at one end, into which the player blows, and a small, bell-shaped opening at the other end. It is made in three pieces, or joints. In the upper and middle pieces there are holes that can be closed with the fingers to produce certain notes, and a number of keys that produce other notes. The oboe has a range of almost three octaves. Its tone is penetrating and somewhat melancholy.

The oboe is used widely in orchestral music, and a number of composers, including George Frederick Handel, have written solo compositions for the oboe.

observatory

An observatory, or astronomical observatory, is a special building containing telescopes, clocks, mirrors (called *reflectors*), spectroscopes, and other instruments with which astronomers can investigate the sun, stars, planets, and other heavenly bodies.

Some observatories have special instruments for getting information about the

Astronomers at an observatory use the reflecting telescope to observe stars that are very far from earth.

Harvard University

earth's magnetism, earthquakes, or the weather.

Most astronomical observatories are dome-shaped. An observatory may be as high as 150 feet. The dome can be turned in a circle to provide the astronomers with a view of all the visible heavens.

The telescope is the most common instrument used in an observatory. It may be a reflecting, or mirror, telescope, which

reflects light from the stars to a photographic plate or to an eyepiece through which the astronomer looks; or a refracting, or lens, telescope, much like the small telescopes that can be bought in optical shops.

The oldest observatory on record was built by the king Ptolemy I in Alexandria, Egypt, more than two thousand years ago. Lacking telescopes, ancient astronomers relied on information gained by the use of the *astrolabe,* an instrument with which they could determine the position of the stars in the sky.

Many of the first observatories were used to provide information for navigators of ships. Among the more famous observatories built for this purpose, and still in existence, are the Paris Observatory in France, built in 1667, and the Greenwich Observatory in England, built in 1675. The Harvard Observatory, in Massachusetts, with a branch in South Africa, has become famous for its cataloguing of the stars in the Milky Way. Mt. Palomar Observatory in California has the largest reflecting telescope, a mirror 200 inches in diameter, with which valuable information about the heavens has been discovered. Other notable observatories are the Yerkes Observatory at the University of Chicago, which has the largest refracting telescope, 40 inches in diameter, and Mt. Wilson Observatory near Pasadena, California, which until the completion of Mt. Palomar Observatory possessed the largest reflecting telescope.

A complete catalog of all the active observatories is published by the Naval Observatory in Washington, D.C.

ocean

The ocean is the great body of water that surrounds the continents and covers almost three-quarters of the surface of the earth.

The ocean has an area of 142 million square miles. The average depth of the ocean is a little more than two miles, but in many parts it is much deeper. The deepest place is the Marianas Trench, near the island of Guam in the central Pacific. It is nearly seven miles deep.

When you compare the depth of the ocean to the whole earth, it can be seen that the ocean is really just a thin film of water on the earth's surface. It may be compared to the water that sticks to the surface of a wet orange. The oceans are

only one-thousandth of the total volume of the earth but they contain 98.4 percent of the earth's water.

Geographers usually divide the ocean into the Atlantic, Pacific, Indian, Arctic, (and sometimes, the Antarctic) oceans.

THE OCEAN LONG AGO

A very long time ago—perhaps more than three billion years—the surface of the earth was soft because the rocks of which it was made were so hot they were melted. At this time there could be no ocean—or any other water—on the surface of the earth, because as soon as rains fell on the hot rock, they boiled up into the air as steam to form clouds.

The earth gradually cooled and its rocky crust began to wrinkle, just as the skin of an orange or apple wrinkles when it dries out. The biggest folds of the wrinkles formed the high places that are the continents, and the downfolds formed the deep hollows. Finally, the earth became cool enough for water to remain on the surface. Down it poured into the deep folds, where it formed hot, steaming oceans.

Although the oceans have not moved away from the places where they first formed, many times they have spread across the lands, as the running water of streams and rivers wore the continents down to sea level. Then the earth's crust folded some more, the continents were pushed up again, and the oceans retreated to their deep basins. More than once, half of North America was under the ocean. Fossils of fish and rocks made of seashells may be found high in the Appalachian Mountains. Today, because the climate of the earth is growing warmer, the ocean water frozen into the vast ice caps at the

earth's poles is melting. This makes the amount of water in the ocean greater, and the ocean is rising. On the east coast of North America the ocean is rising about one foot every hundred years. About 1,500 years from now, some of the streets in the great cities on the east coast of the United States may be covered by the Atlantic Ocean.

THE FLOOR OF THE OCEAN

The bottom of the ocean is a place that looks much like rough mountainous land.

The submerged "Washington Monument" of the ocean is a rock pinnacle that rises 650 feet from the ocean floor near Alaska. It was found by a wire-drag in 1915. It is actually 95 feet higher than the real Washington Monument in Washington, D.C.

U.S. Coast & Geodetic Survey

There are three different kinds of underwater "lands."

From the shore, the ocean bottom runs gently downward in a long slope called

U.S. Coast & Geodetic Survey

A wire-drag is used to find underwater rocks and other menaces to navigation. The wire-drag is made up of a cable whose depth is controlled by buoys. It is towed by two boats. Sonar is now often used to detect underwater dangers.

the *continental shelf.* In the Atlantic Ocean, the continental shelf slopes gently downward for 40 to 60 miles from the shore until it reaches a depth of about 600 feet. In the Pacific, the continental shelf is only about 10 miles wide. The continental shelf is cut by valleys and canyons, some of which are as deep and wide as the Grand Canyon of the Colorado River. These deep cuts were made at times when a large part of the water of the oceans was frozen into glaciers, and the continental shelves were dry land that was being deeply cut by great rivers. One great submarine canyon is off the harbor of New York. Before the ocean rose and drowned it, it was a river valley. It is twenty-five miles long, three miles wide, and half a mile deep.

A view of the ocean at sunset.

Orville Andrews

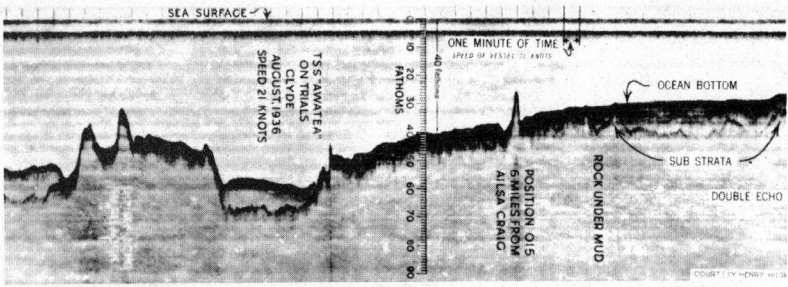

As the survey ship moves along the surface of the ocean, the fathometer automatically records depths on paper tape. This gives an accurate "profile" of the ocean floor.

U.S. Coast & Geodetic Survey

Where the continental shelf ends, there begins a steeper slope called the *continental slope.* This drops downward at the rate of 100 to 200 feet in every mile. It, too, is cut by deep canyons, but how they were made no one is certain. The continental slopes form the walls of the great depths of the ocean basins. Nowhere on land are there such high cliffs, for in some places the edge of the continental slope drops downward a steep 30,000 feet.

The *ocean basin,* or *deep sea,* is as rugged as the roughest and most mountainous land, and includes most of the area of the ocean bottom. Here there are great chasms into which Mount Everest, the highest mountain on earth, could be sunk without a trace showing above the surface.

Much of the rough surface of the ocean basins is made of lava that has been poured out by underwater volcanoes. Sometimes volcanoes have poured out so much lava that they have built themselves into peaks that reach above the surface of the ocean. The Hawaiian Islands and many other islands are the tops of active or extinct volcanoes.

The continental shelves are covered by sand and other sediment that have been carried out to sea from the land. There is also mud from decaying seaweed and from broken corals.

On the continental slope and on the floor of the ocean basin, where no seaweed grows and which are too far out for sediment to be carried, the whole ocean bottom is covered with a soft ooze. On the continental slope the ooze is made of the skeletons of tiny sea plants, such as those called diatoms, which lived in the upper layers of water in untold billions and sank to the bottom where they died. In the ocean basin, the ooze is made of volcanic dust that has settled to the bottom, and also of dust from outer space that the earth has swept up in its whirling course through the universe.

HOW THE OCEAN BECAME SALTY

Ocean water carries in it about 3½ pounds of solid matter for every 100 pounds of water. More than two pounds of this solid matter is salt, just like table salt. How did it get into the water? The first hot seas that formed upon the earth had no salt in them. But the rains slowly dissolved the rocks of the land, and from them it brought to the ocean much of the chemical element sodium. Volcanoes on land and below the ocean poured out great amounts of chlorine gas, and this was dissolved in the ocean water. The coming together of the sodium and the chlorine made the chemical called *sodium chloride,* which is the scientific name for table salt.

There are many other chemicals dissolved in the ocean. Chemical companies take the liquid element bromine and the metallic element magnesium from ocean water. Shellfish remove the element calcium from ocean water to make their shells. There is far more gold dissolved in the ocean than men have ever found on earth.

OCEAN CURRENTS AND WAVES

The water of the ocean is in constant motion. Great wide "rivers" of water called ocean currents slowly circle between the continents. The surface of the ocean moves in waves, and rises and falls in tides.

The warm ocean waters from the regions near the Equator move on the surface slowly toward the poles, while the cold water from the polar icecaps sinks and flows toward the Equator to be warmed and circle back to the poles again. The paths taken by the moving water are called *currents.* Most ocean currents are only faint drifts that move no more than ten miles a day; a few move as much as a mile an hour. They touch the ocean floor only on the continental shelves. Rarely do they pass over the bottom with even enough force to stir up the sediment.

Ocean currents are of great importance in making the earth's climate. The warm Gulf Stream is the one we know best. It flows from the equator northward along the eastern shore of the United States as far as the mouth of the Delaware River, between the states of Delaware and New Jersey. Then it turns northeastward, crosses the Atlantic Ocean, and takes warm air to Norway, England, France, and other European countries.

The Japan Current, which runs from the southwestern Pacific along the shore of Japan and then turns eastward just south of the Aleutian Islands, keeps the coasts of the states of Oregon and Washington warmer in the winter.

Ocean currents are of great importance to the life of the ocean. Some plants and animals are born and live all their lives in the area swept by a single current. Remaining within the current is a matter of life or death to them. There have been times when a warm ocean current has temporarily shifted a few miles from its regular course, and millions of fish and other ocean life have been killed by the colder water that flowed in.

TIDES

The sun and the moon, pulling on the earth by the force of gravity, cause the ocean to bulge up. The coming and going of this bulge of water upon the shores of the continents causes the rise and fall of the tides. Usually, there are two high tides and two low tides every day, but in parts of the world where the coastlines are very irregular, or where there are many islands in the way, the time between the tides may be so far off schedule that there seems to be only one tide a day.

The average tide raises the water on an exposed coast about five or ten feet. In landlocked bays, where the wind helps to pile up the water, the tide may rise 50 feet, as it does in the Bay of Fundy.

WAVES

Winds blowing over the surface of the

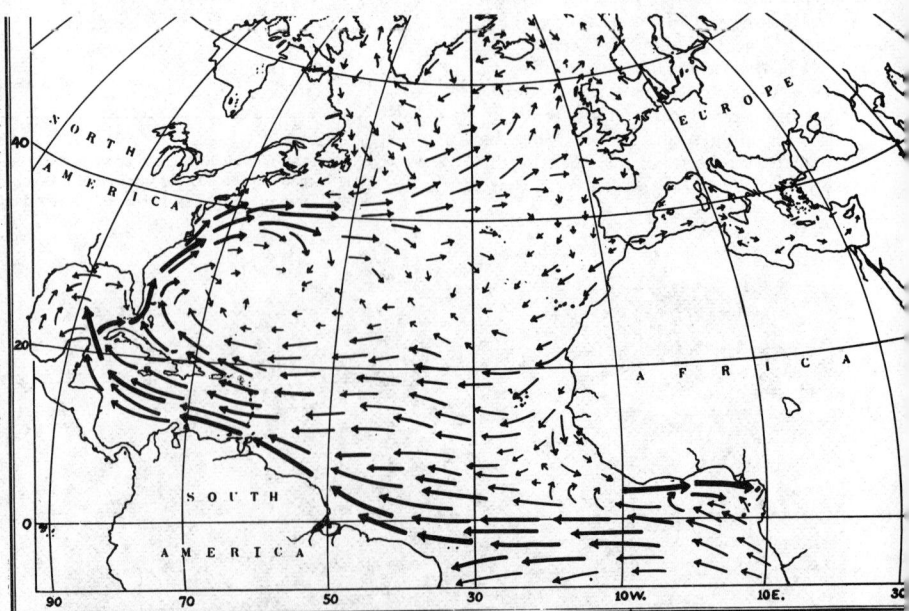

The arrows show the paths of the major currents in the North Atlantic Ocean. Accurate navigation is virtually impossible without knowledge of ocean currents.

U.S. Coast & Geodetic Su

ocean cause the water to move in the same direction as the wind. The swells that the wind pushes up on the surface are called *waves*. The longer a swell is pushed by the wind, the bigger it becomes. The distance the waves run before the drive of the wind is called the *fetch* of the wave. It takes a fetch of 600 to 700 miles to raise great 40- to 60-foot-high storm waves. When a wave becomes one-seventh as high as it is wide, its crest topples over, and the form it makes causes it to be called a *whitecap*. After the wind has stopped pushing on a wave, it gradually becomes smaller in size until it disappears. If a wave runs into crosswinds or rain or snow, it becomes smaller.

Waves are an important force in shaping the coastlines of the continents. The waves carry sand, stones, and boulders, and pound the shore with them, so that even rocky coasts are worn down.

A tidal wave does not have anything to do with the tide. It is a great wave that is caused by the sudden movement of the ocean floor in an earthquake. The right name of such a wave is *tsunami*. In April 1946, an earthquake on the floor of the Pacific Ocean near the Aleutian island of Unimak caused a tsunami that traveled 2,300 miles to the Hawaiian Islands at the rate of 450 miles an hour, and then piled up on the shores of the islands, causing much damage and loss of life. The same tsunami reached the city of Valparaiso, in Chile, 8,066 miles from the Aleutians, within 18 hours.

OCEAN LIFE

The ocean is full of living things. Light penetrates ocean water down to a few hundred feet; below this depth, it is always dark. In the upper part of the sunlit zone there live both plants and animals. Below this zone, only animals live.

The upper waters of the ocean are called the *pelagic zone*. Here live all the swimming and floating animals and plants. The swimmers include fish, squid, whales, porpoises, seals, and sea lions. The floaters include certain kinds of seaweed and tiny plants, such as diatoms, and also the eggs of plants and animals. In the *benthic,* or bottom zone, live the *sessile* plants and animals. These are the ones that are attached to rocks or to the ooze of the bottom by stems or by immovable feet. Here are sponges, mussels, barnacles, oysters, corals, and seaweeds. Other benthic living things are the creepers: lobsters, snails, crabs, and certain fish, such as flounders.

The animals that live in the ocean make use of body colors and shapes to hide from their enemies or their prey, in the same way as land animals do. In the upper levels of the ocean, where the light is blue, fish, jellyfish and other swimming animals are blue or blue-green. In the shallow waters of the continental shelves, the fish, crabs, lobsters, and shellfish mimic the sand and the abundant seaweed, so that they are as hard to see as a tiger in the shadows of the jungle. In deeper water where the faint light is a pale blue, the fish are silvery or colorless. In the deep sea, where it is always black, the fish are black, dark purple, or dark brown. Some of these deep-sea fish carry lights with them. (See the article on ABYSS.)

People used to talk about the silence of the depths of the ocean, but since they have lowered sound-recording devices into the ocean they have learned that the ocean bottom is as noisy as a barnyard. Fish called croakers make not only croaking sounds but also noises like a compressed-air drill digging up a pavement. Porpoises whistle and squeal, tick and cluck, and sometimes mew and chirp. Beds of shrimp, constantly snapping their claws together, sound like dozens of sizzling frying pans.

OCEANOGRAPHY

The study of the ocean, the ocean bottom and the living things in the ocean is called *oceanography*.

Samples of ocean water are taken in different places and chemical analyses are made of them. Tide gauges measure the height of the tides. Instruments called *wave dynamometers* measure the force of waves.

To map the bottom of the ocean, sound waves or radar waves are sent down to echo, or bounce back from the ocean floor. The depth is shown by the length of time it takes for the bounce. Coring tubes, instruments that are dropped to the bottom of the ocean to bring up samples of the ooze, tell oceanographers about the composition of the ocean bottoms.

Marine biologists collect animals and plants from the ocean in much the same way as do land biologists. They use nets, traps, guns, harpoons and their hands to get living specimens.

Underwater television has been used to study ocean life to a depth of several hundred feet. Oceanographers use special equipment, such as the BATHYSPHERE and Bathyscaph, to descend far lower.

ocelot

The ocelot is a small, handsome member of the cat family. It makes its home in the jungles of South America and Mexico. The ocelot is usually two to four feet long. It has a fine coat of soft, tan-colored fur that is marked with black stripes and spots and circles. The fur of the ocelot is used to make coats and other furpieces for women. The ocelot does not like the sunshine and comes out at night to hunt for its food. It eats snakes, birds, and small animals. The ocelot is a good climber and often robs the nests of birds and eats the eggs. Sometimes the ocelot will climb a tree to escape from its enemies, although it is a swift and clever runner and can backtrack and run in circles so that it fools its enemies.

The ocelot makes its den in a rocky cave or the hollow of a tree. It lines the den with grass and twigs that it first chews so that the den will be soft and comfortable. The female ocelot has two young in the fall.

Ochs, Adolph S.

Adolph Simon Ochs was a great newspaper publisher who made *The New York Times* one of the most famous papers in the world. He was born in 1858 in Cincinnati, Ohio, and began his newspaper work as a boy of 11 in Knoxville, Tennessee. He bought *The Times* in 1896 and gave it its slogan, "All the News That's Fit to Print." He died in 1935.

O'Connell, Cardinal

William Henry O'Connell was a Roman Catholic priest who was made a cardinal. Cardinals are called princes of the Church.

William O'Connell was born in Lowell, Massachusetts, in 1859. He went to school at Rome, Italy. When he was 25 years old he became a priest. In 1907 he was made Archbishop of Boston and four years later he became a cardinal. Cardinal O'Connell was a very forceful leader. Many new churches, schools and hospitals were built while he was Archbishop. He wrote frequently for newspapers and composed beautiful hymns. Many of his sermons and other speeches were collected in a book in 1934.

Cardinal O'Connell died in 1944.

O'Connell, Daniel

Daniel O'Connell was a great Irish statesman who lived in the early part of the last century. He was called the "Liberator" by the people of Ireland.

Daniel O'Connell was born in County Kerry in 1775. When he grew up he became a successful lawyer and then began to take part in politics. At that time the British ruled Ireland. He insisted that Ireland should have its own government. Also, the British law allowed only members of the Church of England to hold high government positions, and nearly all the people of Ireland were members of the Roman Catholic Church. O'Connell wanted Catholics to have just as much power as the Protestants. In 1828 O'Connell was elected to Parliament, but he could not accept because he was a Catholic. A year later a law was passed that allowed Catholics to be members of Parliament, and then he accepted.

O'Connell made many speeches to arouse the people of Ireland. For this, he was arrested but he appealed to the British Parliament and was finally pardoned. O'Connell died in 1847, when he was 72 years old. Ireland did not become independent for another seventy-five years, but Daniel O'Connell had helped to start it on its way.

October

October is the tenth month of the year. It has thirty-one days. In ancient Roman times the year began with March, and October was the eighth month. It was called "Octobris," which means eighth in the Latin language. About two thousand years ago the Romans began to use the calendar that we know now, and October became the tenth month. People who were born in October have the opal, a stone that shines with red, blue, gray and green colors as the light changes, for their birthstone. The flower of the month of October is the calendula.

octopus

The octopus is a sea animal that is one of the molluscs, a group of animals that have no backbones. The octopus lives in the warm oceans of the world. It has a soft, pear-shaped body and eight tentacles, which are like long arms. It has large eyes that bulge out of its head and look very much like human eyes. Some octopuses grow to be about 28 feet long, but others are as small as an inch long. The octopus that lives in the North

Atlantic Ocean is bluish in color, with brown spots. The Pacific Ocean octopus is gray. Both of these are small octopuses, about three inches long.

When the octopus is frightened, it often changes color. It also gives off a black, inky liquid that clouds the water and hides it from its enemies.

On the undersides of the tentacles are rows of little suckers that the octopus uses to gather up the molluscs and fish that it eats and put them into its mouth. These suckers are also useful when the octopus wants to crawl over the rocks at the bottom of the ocean.

The octopus is such a fierce-looking creature that there are many stories about how monster octopuses attack men. The great French writer Victor Hugo tells about a very exciting battle between an octopus and a man in his book *Toilers to the Sea.* None of these stories about the octopus are true. The octopus is a peaceful creature and will not bother a person. But when it is attacked or frightened it will fight back and its eight arms make it a dangerous enemy.

Odd Fellows

The Independent Order of Odd Fellows, or I.O.O.F., is an organization of men and women who meet to enjoy one another's company, and also to receive certain practical benefits. These benefits include payments when they are sick and burial expenses when they die. The Odd Fellows also support many homes where old members can live if they wish.

The Odd Fellows have lodges throughout the world, but most of them are in the United States. There are about 9,400 lodges for men, with about 1,300,000 members, and about 8,500 lodges for wives of Odd Fellows, called Rebekah lodges, with 814,000 members. There are also some lodges for the children of members. The headquarters of the order is in Baltimore, Maryland. The head of the order is called the Sovereign Grand Master.

The Odd Fellows began in England in the late 1700s. First their official name was the Manchester Unity. They started as the Independent Order of Odd Fellows in the United States in 1819. The members were called Odd Fellows probably because people considered them "odd" for giving help to members who were in need.

Odessa

Odessa is one of the most important seaports in Soviet Russia. It is in the southwest Ukraine, on the Black Sea. It is also an important industrial center. About 670,000 people live in Odessa. Many of them work in factories that produce machinery, oil, flour, sugar, and chemicals. Others work near the port, through which grain, lumber, sugar and many other products are sent all over the world. Odessa has a university and several other schools, an opera house, and a marine academy. The city is built from a hill down to the Black Sea. It has many fine buildings.

Odessa was built more than 150 years ago as a port and naval base. It soon became the chief center for sending grain from Russia to other countries. In 1917, at the beginning of the Russian Revolu-

tion, the city was occupied in succession by troops of different countries and sides, until it was finally taken over by the Communists in 1920. During World War II Odessa was taken in 1941 by German troops and was held by their allies, the Rumanians, for two years. During that time many of its buildings were destroyed, and many of its people, mostly those of the Jewish religion, were killed or deported (sent out of the country).

ODESSA, U.S.S.R. Population (1959 census) 667,000. Seaport on the Black Sea.

Odin

Odin was the chief god in Scandinavian mythology, the religion of the ancient Germanic peoples of northern Europe. Odin created the world, and he was the god of war. He was usually pictured with a raven upon each shoulder. These birds were called Hugin and Munnin. Hugin stood for mind and Munnin stood for memory. They whispered into Odin's ear all of the things that they saw and heard in their flights around the world. Odin had only one eye. It was thought that he had given up one of his eyes to gain more knowledge.

Odin and his wife, Frigga, lived in Asgard. Frigga was next to Odin in power. They had many children. One of the greatest of their children was Thor, the defender of gods and men. In some legends Thor became even more powerful than Odin. Odin held his court at Valhalla, the name of his palace. This was the place where all brave warriors went when they died.

The German people called this chief god Woden. In the great operas of Richard Wagner, he is called Wotan. The fourth day of the week, Wednesday, is named for him.

See also the article on MYTHOLOGY.

Odyssey

The *Odyssey* is the name of one of the greatest stories of all time. It was told by the Greek poet Homer about three thousand years ago, and it is the story of Odysseus, or Ulysses, a Greek hero who fought in the war against Troy. The story of the Trojan War is told in the ILIAD (see the separate article).

The *Odyssey* begins at the end of the Trojan War, when Odysseus and his men are sailing back to their homes in the Greek kingdom of Ithaca. They have many adventures and face many dangers on the way. They land in a country called Ismarus, which was the home of the Ciconians. They plan to capture some of the wealth of the country to take back to Ithaca. The Ciconians attack them and kill many of Odysseus' men before they can escape to their ship. Then they are driven by a storm to the land of the Lotus-Eaters, who eat the lotus plant's fruit and juice to make themselves happy and forgetful of trouble. Odysseus has to force his men back to the ship.

Their next adventure is with the Cyclops, a great one-eyed giant who lives on the island of Sicily. The Cyclops eats several of the men before Odysseus puts out the giant's one eye and helps his sailors to escape. Next they come to the island where the enchantress Circe lives. Trying to make Odysseus and his men stay with her, she changes many of them

into pigs. The god Mercury helps Odysseus avoid this fate, and he stays for a time with Circe.

In various other adventures all the men but Odysseus are killed. Odysseus sails alone to the island where Calypso, a daughter of the god Atlas, lives. His ship has been wrecked and he has to stay there for seven years. At last, with Mercury's help, he returns home to find his wife Penelope almost convinced that he is dead. Several young men of Ithaca have been trying to marry her, but Odysseus soon gets rid of them. There are separate articles about most of the people mentioned in the *Odyssey*. See also the article on HOMER.

Oedipus

Oedipus was a character in Greek mythology, the stories the ancient Greeks told about their gods and goddesses. When Oedipus was born, it was foretold that he would one day kill his father, Laius, the king of Thebes. Laius had his son put on a mountain to die, but Oedipus was saved and was brought up by the king of Corinthia. Oedipus thought he was this king's own son. When Oedipus grew up, it was foretold not only that he would kill his father but also that he would marry his mother. To stop this from happening, Oedipus left Corinthia. By chance he traveled toward Thebes, and on the way he met Laius, who blocked his way. Oedipus killed Laius in a fit of temper. He went to Thebes and fell in love with Jocasta, the widow of Laius, and married her. Later he discovered that he had killed his real father and married his mother, as had been foretold. Then Oedipus punished himself by putting out his own eyes, and Jocasta killed herself.

The story of Oedipus has been the subject of many plays, the most famous of which is *Oedipus Rex* (*rex* means "king") by the great Greek writer Sophocles. Psychologists use the term "Oedipus complex" when they talk about someone who is so fond of his mother that he is jealous of his father.

Offenbach, Jacques

Jacques Offenbach was a French composer, or writer of music, who lived about a hundred years ago. He wrote more than a hundred operettas (gay musical plays to be acted and sung on the stage), but he is best remembered for his only serious opera, *The Tales of Hoffmann*. Offenbach was born in 1819 in Germany. He studied music at the Paris Conservatory in France and later became a French citizen. Among his most popular operettas are *Orpheus in the Underworld, La Vie Parisienne,* and *La Belle Hélène.* Offenbach worked for many years on *The Tales of Hoffmann,* and it was not produced until after his death in 1880

Oglethorpe, James E.

James Edward Oglethorpe was an Englishman who settled the present state of Georgia. He was a great military leader, with the rank of general, and also a Member of Parliament, the lawmaking body of England. While he was serving in Parliament, he received a charter from King George II permitting him to establish a colony in the New World. He first went to this new colony in 1733. He

named it Georgia in honor of the king. For ten years he worked to make the colony successful. At the end of that period there were many settlements in the colony, including Augusta and Savannah, and Oglethorpe had successfully defended the colony against the Spanish living in Florida. During the Revolutionary War, Oglethorpe refused to take command of the English troops fighting against the colonists, and was one of the first Englishmen to offer congratulations to the colonists when they had won their independence. Oglethorpe was born in 1696 and died in 1785.

O'Higgins

O'Higgins was the name of two important South American statesmen. Ambrosio O'Higgins was viceroy (the representative of the Spanish government) in Chile and later in Peru. His real name was Ambrose Higgins. He was born in Ireland in 1720. When Higgins was a boy he was sent to live with his uncle, a priest, in Spain. When he grew up he traveled to South America to seek his fortune. Higgins joined the army and fought so bravely against the Indians that he was made a brigadier-general. When he became viceroy of Chile, Higgins changed his name to O'Higgins. He received the honor of being made a marquis before he died in 1801.

Bernardo O'Higgins was the son of Ambrosio. He was born in 1780 and went to school in England. He then returned to Chile, where he led a revolution against Spain. He became known as the liberator of the people of Chile. He was made dictator in 1817. O'Higgins did many good things for the people of Chile. He succeeded in forcing the Spanish soldiers to leave the country and reduced the amount of money that Chile owed to other countries. After six years, O'Higgins was forced out of power and he retired from public life. He died in 1846.

Ohio

Ohio is a state in the north central part of the United States. Its nickname is the "Buckeye State" because of the large number of buckeye chestnut trees that once grew there. Ohio is named after the Ohio River, which got its name from the Iroquois Indians, who lived in that region before the white men came.

Ohio is one of the most important manufacturing and industrial states in the country. It produces more rubber tires, cash registers and pottery than any other state. It is also famous for the number of important men who were born there. Ohio is sometimes called the "mother of

presidents" because seven presidents of the United States were born there— Grant, Hayes, Garfield, Benjamin Harrison, McKinley, Taft, and Harding. The famous inventors Thomas A. Edison and the Wright Brothers also came from Ohio.

Ohio ranks thirty-fifth in size among the states, with 41,222 square miles. In population it ranks sixth, with more than ten million people living there. It became a state in 1803, and was the seventeenth state admitted to the United States. The capital is Columbus.

THE PEOPLE OF OHIO

The earliest settlers in Ohio were the Scotch-Irish. Later, they were joined by pioneers from many states farther east. Many of these were from the New England states, because northern Ohio was the "Western Reserve" (extra territory) of the state of Connecticut, and other New Englanders settled in the southern part of the state, in the valley of the Ohio River. About a hundred years ago, many immigrants from Ireland, Germany, and Switzerland settled in Ohio. After the cities began to grow, people from many parts of Europe went to Ohio to work in the factories. Today most of the people in Ohio are American-born.

Most of the people in Ohio live in the large cities and make a great many important products. They work in huge iron and steel mills and in factories that make heavy machinery, rubber tires, automobiles, clay products, electrical equipment, glass, paper, meat products, flour, and hundreds of other things.

Many other Ohioans are farmers. They raise corn, wheat, hay, and fruits, especially grapes, apples, and peaches. A number of farmers raise cattle, sheep and hogs, and many produce dairy products. One of the important farming industries is hatching baby chicks, which are shipped to many parts of the country. Ohio also has valuable coal mines that supply the large industries in the cities. There are oil and natural gas fields and important clay pits.

The largest churches are the Roman Catholic, Methodist, Lutheran, and Presbyterian.

WHAT OHIO IS LIKE

Most of Ohio is a region of wide valleys, hills, and plains. The eastern section is part of the Alleghenies and is hilly, rising to mountains in some places. Large herds of cattle and sheep graze there. This section contains the valuable coal, oil and clay deposits. It has some of the most beautiful scenery in the state. The

industrial cities of Akron, Youngstown, and Canton are in this eastern section.

The western and southwestern part of Ohio is a rolling plain that joins the central prairies of the United States. It is one of the world's best farming countries. The farmers grow many crops and raise large herds of cattle and hogs. The industrial cities of Cincinnati, Dayton, and Columbus are in this plains region.

Along the northern border of Ohio, on Lake Erie, is a flat, narrow section where farmers grow large quantities of fruit. This section is the center of the grape-growing industry. It is also one of the busiest shipping and manufacturing centers. The largest cities, Cleveland and Toledo, are on Lake Erie. There are many summer resorts along the lake shore.

The winters in Ohio are cold and the summers hot, though along Lake Erie the climate is milder. The eastern part of the state gets heavy snowfalls. The average temperature in Ohio in summer is about 74 degrees and in winter about 25 degrees.

Ohio has many rivers. The most important is the Ohio River, which is an important water transportation route that connects the state with the Mississippi River and the Gulf of Mexico. Cincinnati is the chief port on the Ohio River. Lake Erie also carries large quantities of freight and passenger traffic. It connects Ohio with the other Great Lakes and with the Atlantic Ocean. Railroads and highways reach all parts of the state. There are many large airports.

THE GOVERNMENT OF OHIO

Ohio, like other states, has a governor at the head of the government. He is elected for a four-year term. The laws

are made by a legislature composed of a Senate and a House of Representatives. Half the senators are elected for four-year terms, half for two-year terms. Representatives are elected for two-year terms, judges for six. The capital is Columbus. There are 88 counties.

Everyone has to go to school between the ages of 6 and 18. There are more than two million pupils enrolled in public elementary and high schools. The five state universities are:

Ohio State University, at Columbus. Enrollment, 44,463 in 1971 (co-ed).

Miami University, at Oxford. Enrollment, 14,350 in 1971 (co-ed).

Ohio University, at Athens. Enrollment, 16,500 in 1971 (co-ed).

Bowling Green State University, at Bowling Green. Enrollment, 14,110 in 1971 (co-ed).

Kent State University, at Kent. Enrollment, 25,256 in 1971 (co-ed).

Cincinnati, Ohio.

Among the principal private colleges and universities are:

Western Reserve University, at Cleveland. Enrollment, 9,334 in 1971 (co-ed).

University of Cincinnati, at Cincinnati. Enrollment, 29,410 in 1971 (co-ed).

University of Toledo, at Toledo. Enrollment, 9,871 in 1971 (co-ed).

University of Akron, at Akron. Enrollment, 15,022 in 1971 (co-ed).

University of Dayton, at Dayton. Enrollment, 8,900 in 1971 (co-ed).

Xavier University, at Cincinnati. Enrollment, 6,072 in 1971 (men only).

Oberlin College

Hall Auditorium of Oberlin College in Ohio.

Oberlin College, at Oberlin. Enrollment, 2,593 in 1971 (co-ed).

Youngstown University, at Youngstown. Enrollment, 14,762 in 1971 (co-ed).

CHIEF CITIES OF OHIO.

The leading cities of Ohio, with populations from the 1970 census, are:

Cleveland, population 750,903, the largest city in Ohio.

Cincinnati, population 452,524, the second-largest city in the state.

Columbus, population 539,677, the state capital and third-largest city.

Toledo, population 383,818, the fourth-largest city.

Akron, population 275,425, the fifth-largest city.

Dayton, population 243,601, the sixth-largest city.

Youngstown, population 139,788, the seventh-largest city.

There are separate articles about these cities.

OHIO IN THE PAST

For thousands of years, Indians lived in Ohio. They built mounds as burial places and as fortifications, and these mounds can still be seen in many parts of the state.

The first European to explore Ohio, more than three hundred years ago, is believed to have been Robert La Salle, a Frenchman. The French claimed the Ohio region along with other parts of north central America, which at that time was known as the Northwest. The English also claimed this region, and in the French and Indian Wars, about two hundred years ago, the Northwest Territory was won by the British. Then in the Revolutionary War the Americans won the Northwest Territory through the victories of George Rogers Clark. The first settlement by Americans in the Ohio region was made at Marietta, in 1788.

The settlers had difficulties with the Indians for some years, but peace was finally established in 1794 and the Indians gave up much of their land to the Americans. In 1803, Ohio became a state.

As railroads and canals were built, Ohio prospered and cities began to grow up. By the time of the Civil War, Ohio was a leading manufacturing state. In the Civil War, Ohio fought on the side of the Union, though many people in the southern part of the state were sympathetic to the South. After the war, Ohio continued to grow as an industrial state. This was possible because of its rich coal fields, which supplied fuel, and its excellent land and water transportation. In both World Wars I and II, Ohio contributed large quantities of materials to the war effort.

PLACES TO SEE IN OHIO

Mound City Group National Monument, 57 acres, in south central Ohio, outside Chillicothe, on U.S. Route 23. Famous group of prehistoric Indian mounds.

Perry's Victory and International Peace Memorial National Monument, 14 acres, in northern Ohio, on Put-in-Bay Island, 15 miles northwest of Sandusky. Memorial to the greatest naval battle of the War of 1812 and also to a century of peace between the United States and Canada.

Old Man's Cave, in southern Ohio, 23 miles northeast of Chillicothe, on State Highway 56. One of many interesting caves in this region.

Buckeye Lake, 4,000 acres, in central Ohio, 9 miles south of Newark, on U.S. Route 40. One of the largest summer resorts.

Lake St. Mary's, 15,500 acres, in western Ohio, 4 miles southwest of St. Mary's, on U.S. Route 33. Many summer resorts and summer camps along its shores; beautiful wooded trails and scenery.

Birthplace of Thomas A. Edison, at Milan, in north central Ohio, on U.S. Route 250. The small brick house where the inventor Thomas A. Edison was born.

Blue Hole of Castalia, in northern Ohio, 6 miles southwest of Sandusky, on State Highway 101. One of the largest springs in Ohio, pouring forth about seven million gallons of water a day.

OHIO. Area, 41,222 square miles. Population (1970 census) 10,652,017. Capital, Columbus. Nickname, the Buckeye State. Motto, With God, All Things Are Possible. Flower, scarlet carnation. Bird, cardinal. No official song. Admitted to Union, February 19, 1803. Official abbreviation, O.

Ohio River

The Ohio River is one of the biggest and most important rivers in the United States. It is formed when two other rivers, the Allegheny and the Monongahela, come together at Pittsburgh, Pennsylvania. The Ohio then flows 981 miles westward, to Cairo, Illinois, where it enters the Mississippi River.

Some important cities are on the Ohio River; in addition to Pittsburgh, they include Wheeling, West Virginia; Cincinnati, Ohio; and Louisville, Kentucky.

The territory through which the Ohio flows is called the Ohio Valley. It has some of the richest farming country in the world, and is also an important manufacturing section. Several of the main Atomic Energy Commission installations east of the Mississippi are in the Ohio Valley, at Portsmouth and Miamisburg, Ohio, and Paducah, Kentucky.

The Ohio has long been used for transportation, because barges or river boats can carry heavy cargo for its entire length. Traffic on the Ohio is almost twice as great as on the Panama Canal. It has been dredged to a depth of 9 feet, and a series of 46 dams and locks aid navigation. The river boats carry their cargo cheaply. Among the main goods transported are coal, coke, iron, steel, sand, oil, gravel, cement, and heavy machinery.

The Ohio drains a great area, more than 200,000 square miles in size. This means it carries excess water off the land, making the land better for farming and for building. Dams on the Ohio produce electric power for these regions.

Early settlers moving to the Midwest traveled on the Ohio. After the railroad was built the river became less important for passenger transportation, but in recent years it has carried more and more freight.

Many times the Ohio Valley has suffered from bad floods in the spring, when melting snows from the mountains have caused the level of the Ohio to rise as much as 60 feet above its low-water mark. Whole cities along its shores have been covered by water. The danger from floods has been made much less by setting aside certain fields into which the river waters can be allowed to flow when they are too high.

oil

An oil is a greasy liquid that feels slippery and is usually thicker than water. Oil cannot dissolve in water, but does dissolve easily in alcohol or ether. All oils will burn. Some oils are solid at ordinary temperatures and must be warmed to make them liquid.

One of the most important uses of oil is that of a lubricant. A lubricant is a material that forms a thin slippery film over moving parts of machines, so that the parts will move smoothly over one another. Oils are also important in foods and as fuels.

KINDS OF OILS

There are three kinds of oil: mineral, animal, and vegetable.

Mineral oil is another name for PETROLEUM, about which there is a separate article. Mineral oil gets its name because it is found deep in the earth like other minerals. All mineral oils are *hydrocarbons,* which means that they are made up of the chemical elements carbon and hydrogen. Gasoline is just one of the hundreds of useful things that are made from mineral oil.

Animal and vegetable oils are called fatty oils. Lard, tallow, suet, butter and blubber are animal oils that are solid at ordinary temperatures, and are usually called fats. Fish-liver, neat's-foot, seal and porpoise oils are animal oils that are liquid at ordinary temperatures. Examples of vegetable oils are olive, coconut, corn, walnut, palm, cottonseed, linseed, castor, mustard, croton, sunflower, and poppyseed. Both animal and vegetable oils are made up of chemical substances called *glycerides.* Almost all of these oils can be

eaten without harm, but some should not be taken into the body except on the recommendation of a doctor. Fatty oils are used in large amounts to make soaps.

Animal oils are gotten by boiling, or heating with steam, the fatty parts of the bodies of animals. This process is called *rendering.* The tissues that hold together the tiny globules of fat or oil are broken down by the heat, causing the oil to separate from them. Vegetable oils are gotten in either of two ways: They may be dissolved in chemicals, which are later separated from the oil; or they may be *expressed* in an oil press. A first, gentle pressing yields a light, pure grade of oil. If there is a second pressing, it is accompanied by heat and gives a heavier, less pure oil.

DRYING OILS

Certain vegetable oils will harden when exposed to air. Such oils are called *drying oils.* They are used in making paints, lacquers, varnishes, and printing inks. When we say that paints have been dried, we really mean that the drying oils have hardened. Among the drying oils are linseed, tung nut, walnut, castor, sunflower, poppy-seed, fir, and menhaden. (You can read more about drying oils in the article on PAINT.)

ESSENTIAL OILS

Oils that quickly evaporate in the air and that have a strong aroma are called *essential,* or *volatile, oils.* The odor of flowers is due to the essential oils they contain, so these oils are dissolved out of flowers or leaves and are used in perfumes. Examples of essential oils are geranium, spearmint, peppermint, lavender, camphor, laurel, coriander, celery, anise, fennel, gardenia, jasmine, carnation, carrot, and sunflower.

Essential oils come from many different parts of plants. Mint oil comes from the leaves, ginger from the roots, spice oils from the seeds and fruits, camphor from the wood, cinnamon from the bark, and flower oils from the petals.

Essential oils are removed from the different parts of plants by dissolving in ether, alcohol, or other liquids that will dissolve them, and sometimes by gentle pressing. Many essential oils can be made from coal tar and petroleum. This means that chemists, using substances found in coal tar and petroleum, can make certain essential oils in a laboratory, without using any part of the plant in which the oils are found in nature. Essential oils are made up of chemical substances different from those in either mineral oil or fatty oils.

okapi

The okapi is a four-legged animal that lives in the deep forest country of central Africa. It is related to the giraffe, but has a much shorter neck. Its long, "donkey" ears and its stripes are like those of a giraffe. An okapi is about 5 feet high at the shoulder. The female bears one calf at a time. Okapis are leaf-eaters and live where foliage is plentiful. The okapi was not known to naturalists until 1900, but now okapis may be seen in zoos in most parts of the world.

Okefenokee Swamp

Okefenokee is a large swamp, or wet, marshy piece of land, in southeastern

Georgia and northeastern Florida. In size it is 660 square miles, more than half the size of the state of Rhode Island. Okefenokee has not been fully explored, but it contains many wild animals, including the alligator, bear, deer, wildcat, raccoon, opossum, and many kinds of bird. Throughout most of the swamp the water is too shallow for boats and the mud too soft for automobiles or other vehicles. The swamp contains some open forests, some large treeless areas, and several lakes, in some of which are floating islands. Very few people live in the swamp, and most of them live in the eastern part, where there are twenty-five large islands of sand. A large part of Okefenokee was taken over by the United States government in 1937, for use as a game preserve. The name *Okefenokee* comes from an Indian word meaning "trembling earth."

Okinawa

Okinawa is the largest of the Okinawa Islands, which are in the Ryukyu Islands group in the Pacific Ocean. Until World War II, Okinawa belonged to Japan. One of the fiercest battles of World War II took place on Okinawa, and more men lost their lives there than on any other island in the Pacific.

Okinawa is 467 square miles in size, which is about the same as the city of Los Angeles. More than 500,000 people live on Okinawa. Most of the people are farmers. They raise sugar cane, rice, bananas, and sweet potatoes. The people in the cities work in factories that make textiles, dyes, and metal products. Most of the people are of Japanese ancestry or belong to races related to the Japanese.

Okinawa is generally mountainous, but there are level plains in the southern part of the island. The coast has many bays, and Buckner Bay on the eastern coast is the largest harbor. Naha is the capital and largest city of Okinawa. It was almost completely destroyed during the war but is being gradually rebuilt. The climate of Okinawa is hot and damp, and typhoons often cause much destruction.

THE BATTLE OF OKINAWA

During World War II, the Allies wanted to use Okinawa as a base from which they could attack the main islands of Japan. On April 1, 1945, after United States planes and battleships had bombed Japanese air bases and ships, invasion troops under General Simon Bolivar Buckner, Jr., landed on the coast. About 120,000 Japanese defended the island, and for more than a month there was violent fighting. The Japanese hid in deep caves where bombardments could not reach them, and after each attack they came out and fired on the attackers. The naval ships, which continued to bombard the island, were attacked from the air by "kamikaze" planes, in which the Japanese pilots, sacrificing their own lives, crashed into United States warships. **Thousands of sailors were killed in this way, and many ships were sunk or damaged.**

On May 19, after terrible fighting, Sugar Loaf Hill, which defended Naha, was taken. The most serious fighting was over by May 30, but groups of Japanese

soldiers continued to fight. By June 21 Okinawa was safely in the hands of the Allies. In the battle of Okinawa more than 100,000 Japanese and about 12,000 United States troops were killed. Much of the island was in ruins, but after the war rebuilding began under the United States Military Government.

OKINAWA. Area, 454 square miles. Population (1960) 758,100. Capital, Naha, population about 218,000.

Oklahoma

Oklahoma is a state in the Great Plains region in the midwestern United States. Its nickname is the "Sooner State" because many settlers claimed land in the Oklahoma Territory before the law permitted them to do so, and they were called "Sooners." Oklahoma means "red people" in the language of the Choctaw Indians who lived there before the white men came.

Oklahoma ranks 18th in size among the states, with 69,919 square miles. In population it ranks 27th, with about 2,500,000 people living there. It became a state in 1907, and was the 46th state admitted to the United States. The capital is Oklahoma City.

THE PEOPLE OF OKLAHOMA

Most of the people who live in Oklahoma are descended from settlers who went there from southern and midwestern states in 1889 (when Oklahoma was first opened) and in the following fifteen or twenty years. Others came from Germany, Russia, and other European countries.

Nearly half the people in Oklahoma are farmers. Many raise cattle and sheep on the broad, grassy plains. Once Oklahoma was mostly made up of large cattle ranges, but farmers called "homesteaders" came to the territory and fenced off more and more sections for farms. Farmers now raise large crops of cotton, corn, wheat, and potatoes.

Although Oklahoma is an important farming state, it is even more important for its rich oil deposits. Many people work in the oilfields, where thousands of wells have been drilled. People also work in the important natural gas fields and in zinc and lead mines.

Almost 65,000 Indians live in Oklahoma, more than in any other state except Arizona. For many years the Oklahoma Territory was set aside as a region for Indian tribes who had to give up their land farther east. It was the home of the Five Civilized Tribes—the Cherokee, Choctaw, Chickasaw, Creek, and Seminole Indians. Today the Indians in Oklahoma dress and live much like the white people. Many are well-educated and some hold political offices. Many are rich because of the oil that was discovered on their land. But the Indians still have their colorful ceremonies each year.

About half the people of Oklahoma live in the busy cities. They work in the large oil-refining plants that make kerosene, gasoline and other products from crude oil. Tulsa, the oil center of Oklahoma, is one of the richest cities in the United States. Oklahoma people also work in flour mills, meat-packing and food-processing plants, and in factories that make aircraft, machinery, paints, and

Oklahoma City Chamber of Commerce
The State Capitol Building in Oklahoma City.

electrical equipment.

The people of Oklahoma belong chiefly to the Baptist, Methodist, Christian (Disciples of Christ) and Roman Catholic Churches.

WHAT THE STATE IS LIKE

Oklahoma is mostly a rolling prairie, but in the eastern part of the state are the low Ozark and Ouachita mountains. These are covered with dense forests of hickory, walnut and pine trees. West of these mountains is the valley of the Arkansas River. This is very fertile land and has great oil deposits.

The rest of the state is made up of high plains and fertile prairies. Most of the men who raise cattle have their large ranches in the western region. In the northwestern part of Oklahoma is a plateau (a high, level region). This plateau is called the Panhandle because it is shaped like the handle of a frying pan. It is an important wheat- and cattle-raising region. Along the southern border of the state is the Red River Valley, a rolling prairie that has the richest farm land

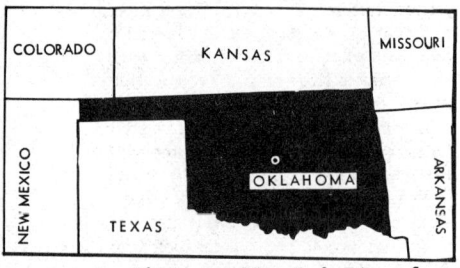

in Oklahoma. The Red River flows through this region.

Oklahoma has a warm, dry climate, with very hot summers. It is somewhat cooler in the western half of the state, where the land is higher. Parts of Oklahoma suffer from droughts in summer and from severe tornadoes that cause great damage. The average temperature in summer is about 82 degrees, and in winter about 38 degrees.

On the plains of Oklahoma are small wild animals, including the coyote, prairie dog, and rabbit. In the forests there are deer, raccoons, mink, and squirrels. Seventy-five years ago Oklahoma was covered with Indian and buffalo trails. These have disappeared, and today there are thousands of miles of railroads and paved highways that reach most parts of the state. There are airports in the large cities.

THE GOVERNMENT OF OKLAHOMA

Oklahoma, like most states, has a Governor at the head of the government. He

is elected for a four-year term. The laws are made by a Legislature, composed of two houses, a Senate and a House of Representatives. The members of the Senate are elected for a four-year term. The members of the House of Representatives are elected for a two-year term. Judges are elected for a six-year term. The capital is Oklahoma City. There are 77 counties.

Everyone has to go to school between the ages of 7 and 17. There are more than 500,000 students enrolled in the public schools. There are 34 colleges, universities, and other schools of higher learning. Among them are:

University of Oklahoma, at Norman. Enrollment, 21,540 in 1970 (co-ed).

Oklahoma State University of Agriculture and Applied Science, at Stillwater. Enrollment, 17,320 in 1971 (co-ed).

University of Tulsa, at Tulsa. Enrollment, 856 in 1971 (co-ed). l).

Oklahoma City University, at Oklahoma City. Enrollment, 2,256 in 1971 (co-ed).

Phillips University, at Enid. Enrollment, 1,283 in 1971 (co-ed).

Oklahoma College for Women, at Chickasha. Enrollment, 859 in 1971 (women only).

Langston University, at Langston. Enrollment, 1,069 in 1971 (co-ed).

CHIEF CITIES OF OKLAHOMA

The leading cities of Oklahoma, with populations from the 1970 census, are:

Oklahoma City, population 366,481, the state capital and largest city. There is a separate article about OKLAHOMA CITY.

Tulsa, population 331,638, the second-largest city. There is a separate article about TULSA.

Lawton, population 74,470, the third-largest city, in the southwestern part of the state, in a farming and oil-producing area on Cache Creek.

Enid, population 44,008, the fourth-largest city, a trade and processing center, in the northern part of the state.

Muskogee, population 37,331, the fifth-largest city, a railroad and trading center, in the eastern part of the state, near the Arkansas River.

OKLAHOMA IN THE PAST

The first European to enter the Oklahoma region, more than four hundred years ago, was Francisco Coronado, a Spanish explorer. He and his men were searching for gold, but found nothing but Indian tribes there. More than a hundred years later the French explored the region, and the first permanent settlement was made by them in 1796 at Salina. In 1803, the United States bought from France a large region known as the

Louisiana Territory. This region included Oklahoma.

Oklahoma was not settled by white men for many years. After 1825, Indian tribes who had been forced to give up their lands to the United States traveled west and settled in the Oklahoma area. It was then known as the Indian Territory. The Indian tribes in Oklahoma were quite civilized. They set up their own governments, and many became prosperous farmers and merchants. White settlers were forbidden by the United States to settle in this region.

In 1879, many people demanded that the Indian Territory be opened up to white settlers. These people were known as "boomers." After ten years the United States finally gave in to these demands and bought two million acres from the Indians. Pioneers and their families, eager to get a portion of this fertile land, lined up on April 22, 1889, the day the territory was opened. At the sound of a pistol, they raced in their wagons, loaded with all their belongings, to claim the best farm land or the best spots where towns could be built. Within one day, this new territory in Oklahoma had about fifty thousand settlers. A few settlers who had claimed land sooner than they should have were called "Sooners."

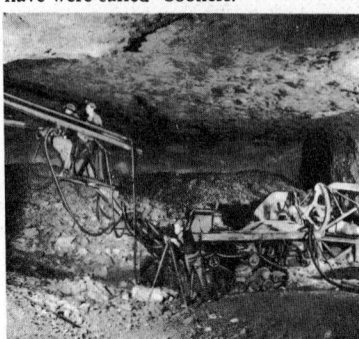

Miami, Okla., Chamber of Com.
Oklahoma is one of the leading lead- and zinc-mining states. The underground mine near Miami is the largest in the world.

More and more sections of Oklahoma were opened up to settlers, and the territory grew very rapidly. In 1907, Oklahoma became a state, and the Indian Territory was admitted as part of it. Oklahoma grew faster than any other state. Its rich oil deposits, first discovered in 1888 but developed mostly in the 1900s, did much to make it very prosperous.

In the early 1930s a great drought, or dry spell, ruined thousands of farms in Oklahoma. The soil turned to dust and blew away. Oklahoma is in the center of the region called the DUST BOWL, about which there is a separate article. Between 1933 and 1936 many Oklahoma farmers, who could no longer raise anything on their farms, packed up everything they had and went to California and other states of the Far West to find jobs on the farms and orchards there. These people were called "Okies," and they had a very hard time. The United States Department of Agriculture did many things to make their farms fertile again so that they could return to Oklahoma.

PLACES TO SEE IN OKLAHOMA

Platt National Park, 911 acres, in the south, at Sulphur, on State Highway 7.

Sulfur and other cold mineral springs.

Quartz Mountain State Park, 11,500 acres, in the west, 18 miles north of Altus, on U.S. Route 283. Mountain views; red granite and quartz hills.

Lake Texhoma and Grand Lake, in the south central part of the state.

Southern Plains Exhibit and Craft Center, at Anadarko. Shows life of Southern Plains Indians.

Cherokee Sacred Fire Ceremony, held on the top of Black Gum Mountain, in the east, between Gore and Sallisaw, on State Highway 1. Held on July 19 each year; a colorful Indian ceremony to celebrate the giving of fire by the Great Spirit to the Cherokee Indians.

Will Rogers Memorial, 40 acres, in the northeast, near Claremore, on U.S. Route 66. A museum filled with many relics of the Indians and pioneers. One room contains mementos of Will Rogers, the humorist, who was born near by.

OKLAHOMA. Area, 69,919 square miles. Population (1970 census) 2,559,229. Capital, Oklahoma City. Nickname, the Sooner State. Motto, *Labor Omnia Vincit* (Labor Conquers All Things). Flower, mistletoe. Bird, scissortailed flycatcher. Song, "Oklahoma." Admitted to Union, November 16, 1907. Official abbreviation, Okla.

Oklahoma City

Oklahoma City is the capital of the state of Oklahoma. About 500,000 people live in the city and its suburbs. Many of them work in the oil industry, and

Oklahoma Chamber of Commerce

Oklahoma City is the capital and largest city in the state. Gas is almost the only fuel used in the city, and buildings stand for years without becoming discolored.

others in meat-packing plants and factories that make iron and steel, furniture, clothing, and electrical equipment. The city has many parks and fine buildings, including the capitol and a civic center.

Oklahoma City was founded when Oklahoma was opened to homesteaders in 1889. It was made the state capital in 1910. During World War II, Oklahoma City had an important air base.

OKLAHOMA CITY, OKLAHOMA. Population (1970 census) 366,481. Capital of Oklahoma. County seat of Oklahoma County. On the North Canadian River. Settled, 1889.

okra

Okra is a food plant that first grew in Africa and is now raised in most parts of the world where the climate is warm. Okra is particularly plentiful in the southern parts of the United States.

The okra is an annual plant, which means that it must be planted every year. The plants grow to be between 3 and 6 feet tall. They have large green leaves.

The okra is a member of the mallow family, which are plants with splendid large flowers. The flower of the okra is yellow, and it has a red center. The plant is often used in gardens and parks because of its striking appearance.

The okra has greenish pods that grow to be about 6 inches long. The young pods are cooked as a vegetable and are used to thicken soup and stews. Many people know okra by the name *gumbo*. The stems and ripe pods of the okra plant are sometimes used to make paper and cloth.

Old Testament

The Old Testament is the first part of the Christian Bible. It is the Jewish Holy Book, or Scriptures. It is more than three times as long as the New Testament. The word Testament means the same as covenant, an agreement or promise made by God to man. The earliest parts of the Old Testament were written more than three thousand years ago. The latest parts were written more than two thousand years ago, about 150 B.C. Hebrew was the original language of the Old Testament, but it has been translated into nearly every known language.

The individual books of the Old Testament are given in the article on BIBLE. There are 64 books in the Old Testament in most Protestant Bibles, and 71 books in the Catholic Bible.

oleander

The oleander is a shrub that grows in Asia and in parts of Europe and the United States where the climate is warm. Oleander grows best in damp places and it is often found near streams. People who live in cool climates often raise oleander in large pots because it is a beautiful shrub. The oleander grows to be about 10 feet high. It has thick green leaves and large flowers that are pink or white. The oleander contains a milky juice. People sometimes use parts of the oleander to make medicines, but no one should ever taste the leaves or stem of the oleander because it is a poisonous plant.

The English people call this shrub the *rose bay*, and in France it is called the *rose laurel*.

oleomargarine, an artificial butter: see the article on MARGARINE.

olive

The olive tree grows in many warm parts of the world. Its fruit, the olive, is a nourishing food, and the oil made from this fruit is important in cooking.

Since ancient times the olive tree has been grown in southern Asia and in lands around the Mediterranean Sea such as Italy, Spain, Syria, and North Africa. About two hundred years ago people began to grow it in Southern California, and now olives and olive oil are valuable products there.

The olive is a small, pretty evergreen tree, which means that it does not lose its long thick leaves in the fall. It grows to be between 25 and 40 feet tall. It has white flowers and a small, shiny fruit that is purplish-black when ripe. Some olives are picked before they are ripe,

or when they have developed a dull or yellowish green color. These olives are treated with special preparations and are sometimes pickled. Both ripe and unripe olives are popular and healthful foods.

To get the olive oil, unripe olives are pressed by machine. The clear, yellowish oil is used as a dressing for salads, and for cooking.

Many medicines contain olive oil. It is used in salves that soothe cuts and burns. It is valuable as a laxative, to cure constipation. Olive oil is also used in making soaps and dyes.

The olive branch has for centuries been used to mean peace. Ancient peoples crowned their heroes with leaves from the olive trees as a special mark of honor. Kings in olden days prized the oil highly. They rubbed it on their bodies, and sometimes offered it to their gods as a present.

Olympia

Olympia is the capital of the state of Washington. It is in the western part of the state, at the southern tip of Puget Sound. Olympia is not a big city as many state capitals are. About 23,000 people live there. Many of them work near the harbor, because Olympia is an important seaport and has a big shipping industry. Others work in lumber mills and in factories that make mineral and food products. Olympia has a beautiful old capitol building, built in 1893. St. Martin's College, a Catholic college for men, is there. Olympia was settled about 1846, and seven years later, in 1853, was made the capital of the newly created Washington Territory.

OLYMPIA, WASHINGTON. Population (1970 census) 23,111. Capital of Washington. County seat, Thurston County. Settled about 1846.

Olympic Games

The Olympic Games are a series of sports events in which the best athletes of many nations take part, competing either as individuals or as team members, in feats of speed, strength, and skill. The Games are held every four years in various cities throughout the world. The site is chosen by an International Olympic Committee, which also establishes the rules and regulations of the games. The modern Olympics are patterned after the Olympic games of the ancient Greeks, which were held on the great plain near Mount Olympus, believed to be the home of the gods.

The modern Olympics, though based on the original Greek games, are much bigger and include more contests. The young Greek athletes competed against one another in foot-racing, jumping, throwing the javelin and the discus (a large pancake-shaped piece of stone or metal), wrestling, boxing, and racing on horseback or in chariots. Today's Olympics have these events, except for chariot-racing, and many others. In the Summer Games are also contests in swimming, diving, canoeing, cycling, fencing, gymnastics, rowing, boxing, shooting, soccer, judo, water polo, and so on. There are about fifty events. Women take part in some of them. Winter Games were established in 1924, and are contests in skiing, figure skating, speed skating, bob-sledding, ice hockey, luge

(small sled or toboggan), and biathlon (cross-country skiing and rifle shooting).

Athletes who plan to compete usually travel in a group to the place where the games are to be held. The Olympic Oath is pronounced by an athlete from the host nation, who speaks for all the participants, saying "In the name of all the competitors I promise that we will take part in these Olympic Games, respecting and abiding by the rules which govern them, in the true spirit of sportsmanship, for the glory of sport and the honor of our teams."

The Games are opened with an impressive ceremony. A lighted torch is carried by hand all the way from Olympia, Greece, and from it the Olympic Flame at the Games is lighted. Whenever a contest is completed, the flag of the winner's country is displayed. Although there are no really official contests between nations, unofficial scores are kept. In this scoring, winning an event counts 10 points; second place, 5; third, 4; fourth, 3; fifth, 2; and sixth, 1. By this scoring, the U.S.S.R. (Russia) won the 1960 Games with 807½ points, and the United States was second with 564½.

OLYMPIC GAMES IN THE PAST

The first events resembling Olympic Games were probably memorial services held nearly 3,400 years ago, about the year 1453 B.C. They took place to honor heroes who had died during the previous "Olympiad," or four-year period. The Greeks kept track of periods of time by olympiads. Little is known of these ancient services, but accounts of the Games from 776 B.C. have been dug up by archaeologists. In these Olympics, Greek cities sent not only athletes, but also orators, poets and musicians to compete. Women were not even allowed to watch these early Games. Only free-born Greek men of good character could take part. Each winner received a palm branch and a crown of leaves from sacred olive trees. Winners became heroes and received valuable gifts from their home cities.

After Rome conquered Greece in 146 B.C., the Romans took part in the Games. This led to quarrels, and in A.D. 394 Emperor Theodosius stopped the Games.

The ancient stadium at Olympia was ruined about 1,500 years ago by an earthquake. It was dug up in 1881, and much was learned of the ancient Olympics. Some years later a French baron, Pierre de Coubertin, worked to revive the Games. Money was raised and a stadium built near Athens, Greece. The first modern Olympic Games were held there in April, 1896. The American Olympic Committee, which organizes the United States teams today, had not been formed, but athletes from Boston and from Princeton, Harvard and other colleges competed and made fine records. In Olympic games from 1900 through 1952, United States teams always won the most medals. Then in 1956 and 1960 teams from the Soviet Union won, partly because they had better athletes with their women's teams and performers in winter sports. In the 1964 games, held at Tokyo, the U.S. did best but the U.S.S.R. had won in the winter sports at Innsbruck, Austria. The 1968 Olympic games were awarded to Mexico City.

The chariot race was an important part of the Olympic Games held in ancient Greece.

The ideal of the Olympic Games is one of international good sportsmanship: *Above:* The ideal is well stated in the motto of the Games. *Right:* The torchbearer lights the Olympic flame.

Olympus, Mount

Mount Olympus is a peak in the Olympus Mountains of Greece. It is the highest mountain in Greece, rising more than 9,000 feet. It is on the coast of the Aegean Sea. In Greek mythology, the stories the ancient Greeks told about their gods and goddesses, Mt. Olympus was the home of the gods. Its summit is usually hidden by clouds.

In modern times, the Olympus Mountains have been very important in warfare because they stand on the border between Greece and Macedonia and block entrance to Greece. In World War II these mountains were a stronghold of the Greek guerrilla fighters.

Omaha

Omaha, the largest city in Nebraska, is in the eastern part of the state, on the Missouri River. Wheat, corn, oats, rye, and barley produced in the surrounding farm region are marketed in Omaha and shipped all over the United States. Omaha is the world's leading producer of butter and has the second-largest cattle market in the world.

More than 300,000 people live in Omaha. Almost 20,000 of them belong to an order called the Knights of Ak-Sar-Ben (Nebraska spelled backwards.) This organization has built a beautiful athletic field, where an annual rodeo is held. The Joslyn Memorial art museum and the Union Pacific Museum, with an authentic display of life in the early West, are in Omaha. Colleges include Creighton University, Omaha University, and the Nebraska University Medical College. BOYS TOWN is near Omaha.

Omaha was founded in 1854 and became capital of the territory of Nebraska in 1855. It is near the site of the winter camp built by the Mormons on their journey to Utah in 1846-47. Though Lincoln became the capital when Nebraska became a state in 1867, Omaha grew as a river port and railroad junction.

OMAHA, NEBRASKA. Population (1970 census) 347,328. County seat, Douglas County. On the Missouri River. Founded, 1854.

Omar Khayyam

Omar Khayyam was a great Persian poet and mathematician who lived more than nine hundred years ago. Not very much is known about his life. The name *Khayyam* means "tentmaker" in the Persian language, so it is believed that his father was a tentmaker. Omar Khayyam was famous as a scientist. He wrote an important book about algebra and was one of the men who worked out a new kind of calendar for the people of Persia.

Omar Khayyam's poems are called the *Rubaiyat*, which means that they are written in stanzas of four lines each. The poems are about love, the beauties of the world, and sadness. The most famous translation of the *Rubaiyat* was made by Edward Fitzgerald, an English writer, about a hundred years ago.

onager

The onager is another name for the Persian wild ass. It lives in desert country from Persia and Syria to the northwest

part of India. In summer the onager's coat is a cinnamon brown, but it becomes a yellowish brown in winter time. Foals are born in May or June, and are usually born singly, although twins sometimes occur. The onager is a very fast runner. Onagers usually travel in herds.

O'Neill, Eugene

Eugene Gladstone O'Neill is by most people considered the greatest American writer of plays. All but one of his best-known plays were tragedies, or stories of unhappy and dreadful things that happen to people. O'Neill used many different devices to put across the meaning of his plays. In *The Great God Brown*, the characters wear masks to show the difference between their real selves and the selves they pretend to be. In *Strange Interlude*, O'Neill used *asides,* in which the characters speak aloud things that they are supposed to be saying to themselves.

O'Neill was born in 1888, the son of a well-known actor. He studied for a year at Princeton, attended Harvard, and then lived a wandering life for some time. He worked at all kinds of jobs, including hunting for gold in Central America, sailing on a cattle boat, and newspaper reporting in Connecticut. When O'Neill was 24 years old he became ill, and while he was recovering he began to write. His first full-length play, *Beyond the Horizon,* won the 1920 Pulitzer Prize for drama, and he won this prize twice more, with the plays *Anna Christie* and *Strange Interlude.* He also was awarded the 1930 Nobel Prize in Literature. Among O'Neill's other successful plays were *Mourning Becomes Electra, The Hairy Ape,* and *The Iceman Cometh.* His one notable comedy, *Ah! Wilderness,* was especially popular.

Eugene O'Neill died in 1953.

onion

The onion is a very old food plant that was probably first raised by people who lived in Asia several thousand years ago. Onions are grown in many parts of the world where it is not too hot or too cold. They grow best in cool, damp places. Onions are hardy and will grow in almost any soil, although they like a sandy soil best.

The onion is an unusual plant because most of the food is stored in the bulb (the bud that develops at the surface of the ground). It is a *biennial,* which means that it has flowers only every second year.

Onions may be grown in several different ways. Most of those raised for market are grown from seeds. Others are grown from small bulbs. Some onions have bulbs that break up into separate bulbs and continue to grow after they are planted. These are called *multipliers.*

Most onions have small white flowers and long, cylinder-shaped green leaves. The bulbs may be white, red, or yellow. Most onions have a sharp taste and smell. The mildest and best onions are large Bermuda and Spanish onions. LEEKS, SHALLOTS, GARLIC, and CHIVES are types

of onion that you can read about in separate articles.

Ontario

Ontario is one of the provinces of Canada. It is sometimes called the "Garden of Canada" because it is the richest of all the provinces. From Ontario come more farm, mineral and manufactured products than from any other province. It ranks second in size among the provinces, having 412,582 square miles, and though this includes about 70,000 square miles of lakes, the land area of Ontario is still considerably larger than that of Texas, the second-largest state in the United States. In population Ontario ranks first in Canada, with over seven million people living there; this is about one-third of Canada's population. The name *Ontario* comes from the Iroquois Indian language. Some people say it means "beautiful lake," but others say it means "rocks standing by the water," which refers to the famous Niagara Falls there.

THE PEOPLE OF ONTARIO

The first people found living in Ontario were tribes of American Indians, mainly the Iroquois and Huron tribes. French fur traders and settlers entered the region about 350 years ago, in the 1600s. They were followed by settlers moving westward from Quebec, most of whom were of English, Scottish and Irish descent. Some married Indians. Later, people from Germany and other European nations settled in Ontario. Today most of the people of Ontario are of British and French descent.

The earliest European settlers were fur traders. The Indians had been making their living by hunting, fishing, and raising such crops as corn. The settlers soon turned to farming, also to raising cattle and cultivating fruit trees. In the sandy soil near Lake Erie tobacco and flax are the principal crops grown. In the central section, oats, wheat, barley, corn and vegetables are raised. In the eastern and western sections fine cattle, sheep, hogs, horses and poultry are raised. In the south fruits and vegetables are the main farm products.

In the far northern parts of Ontario, logging, mining and fur trapping are the main industries. The nickel deposits there are the largest in the world, and also

platinum, copper, gold and other minerals are mined. In the southwest there are oil wells. Ontario shares with the United States the right to fish in all the Great Lakes except Lake Michigan, and fishing is an important industry.

More than six out of every ten persons in Ontario live in the cities. These include Ottawa, the capital of the Dominion of Canada and Toronto, the capital and largest city of Ontario and the second-largest city of Canada. In the cities there are factories that make farm machinery, automobiles, food products, paper, steel, and many other products.

When the French first came to Ontario they established many Roman Catholic missions. The British who came next were members of the Church of England. Later a number of other Protestant churches were built. Many of the Protestants joined with people in other provinces and formed the United Church of Canada, which became the largest religious group of Ontario.

WHAT ONTARIO IS LIKE

Ontario lies between Hudson Bay on the north and Lakes Superior, Huron, Erie and Ontario on the south. Most of Ontario is a low plateau (high, level land). The plateau is crossed by two groups of hills. The highest point is Tip-Top Hill, north of Lake Superior, which is 2,120 feet high.

Ontario has several important rivers and waterfalls, and thousands of lakes. The most important rivers are the St. Lawrence, the Ottawa, and the Niagara. The waterfalls include the world-famous Niagara Falls, and Kakabeka Falls, on the Keministiquia River. Important lakes (besides the Great Lakes) are Lake of the Woods, on the United States border; Lake Nipigon, north of Lake Superior; and Lake Nipissing, east of Georgian Bay. In addition Ontario has the Thousand Islands, a famous group of islands in the St. Lawrence River.

Southern Ontario has a pleasant climate, especially in summer, when the average temperature is about 68 degrees Fahrenheit. In winter it drops to about 18 degrees. In northern Ontario the climate is much more severe, with an average temperature of about 63 degrees in summer and about 6 degrees in winter. In the far north it is even colder, dropping 10 degrees below zero in winter.

Both Canadian and some United States railways serve Ontario, which has more than ten thousand miles of railroads. Fine roads, several airlines, and river and lake transportation make it easy to get to places throughout the province.

THE GOVERNMENT OF ONTARIO

The official head of the government of Ontario is a lieutenant-governor, who represents the British Crown. He is appointed by the Canadian government. The province is actually run by a Premier. He is usually the leader of the majority party in the legislature, which is elected by the people. The Premier has a cabinet, just as the President of the United States has. He stays in office as long as he can keep the confidence of the majority of the legislature. The legislature is elected for a five-year term. Judges are appointed by the Canadian govern-

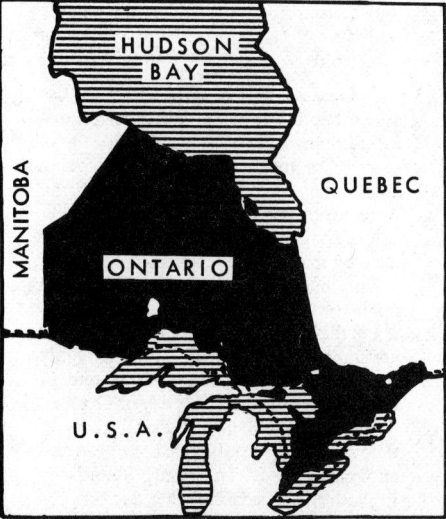

ment in Ottawa, and hold office permanently. The provincial government is in the capital, Toronto.

Everyone has to go to school between the ages of 8 and 18, and there are many fine elementary schools and high schools throughout the province. There are twelve colleges and universities in Ontario.

CHIEF CITIES OF ONTARIO

The leading cities of Ontario, with populations as estimated in 1967, are:

Toronto, population 664,584 (with suburbs, 1,881,691), the capital and largest city. There is a separate article about TORONTO.

Hamilton, population 298,121, second-largest city, a port on Lake Ontario, steel-making center of Canada and important producer of cloth, clothing, tobacco, shoes, and glass.

Ottawa, population 294,377, third-largest city, capital of Canada. There is a separate article about OTTAWA.

London, population 194,416, fourth-largest city, manufacturing center in south.

Windsor, population 211,000, fifth-largest city, across the border from Detroit, Michigan, sometimes called the "Detroit of Canada" because of its large automobile and farm-machinery manufacturing plants.

ONTARIO IN THE PAST

Ontario was first explored by Europeans in the early 1600s. In 1613 the French explorer Samuel de Champlain sailed up the Ottawa River, and two years later he explored the region farther south. He was soon followed by French fur traders and missionaries. Their coming was resented by the Iroquois Indians, who raided their settlements and massacred many of the settlers. Canada came under the control of Great Britain in 1763, but Ontario was not widely settled by the British for some time. After the American Revolutionary War, many of the colonists who had sided with Great Britain fled to Ontario and settled there. In 1791 the settled part of Canada was divided into two provinces, Upper Canada, or Ontario, and Lower Canada, or Quebec. The new province was soon involved in a war with the United States, the War of 1812, during which American forces invaded Ontario and Canadian troops took Detroit, Michigan.

During the 1800s Ontario became involved in a number of quarrels with other parts of Canada and with Great Britain. These were peaceably settled, and later, when Canada became a British Dominion, Ontario became one of the provinces.

In the 1870s valuable minerals were found in north Ontario and its industrial importance grew rapidly from that time. More territory was added to Ontario in 1912.

PLACES TO SEE IN ONTARIO

Point Pelee National Park, 6 acres, on Lake Erie in southern Ontario. A forest park with camping facilities, lovely beaches, and a recreation area.

St. Lawrence Islands National Park, nearly 186 square miles on the mainland and 13 of the Thousand Islands in the St. Lawrence River. Camping and recreation facilities, including boating and fishing.

Georgian Bay Islands National Park, 30 islands in Georgian Bay. Camping, recreation area, fishing.

Bell Memorial, at Brantford, home of Alexander Graham Bell, the inventor of the telephone.

Eliza's Cottage, at Amherstburg, a refuge for runaway slaves from the United States during the days of the Underground Railroad.

Fort Sainte Marie, ruins of a Roman Catholic mission dating from 1639.

Fort Wellington National Historic Site, at Prescott, a British defense post built on the St. Lawrence River during the War of 1812. A nine-acre park and a museum.

Niagara Falls. See the separate article on NIAGARA FALLS.

ONTARIO. Area, 412,582 square miles. Population (1974) 8,031,000. Capital, Toronto. Coat of arms, a shield showing the cross of St. George and three maple leaves surrounded by a bear, a moose, and a deer. Flower, trillium. Admitted to Dominion in 1867. Official abbreviation, Ont.

Ontario, Lake

Lake Ontario is a large lake in the north of the United States. It is one of the Great Lakes that lie between the United States and Canada. Ships from cities along the Great Lakes sail through Lake Ontario and then down the St. Lawrence River to the Atlantic Ocean. The ships carry iron ore, wheat, coal, and heavy machinery. Traffic is very heavy, except for the period from the end of December to the end of March, when much of Lake Ontario is frozen over. The lake is 193 miles long and 53 miles wide. Its area is 7,600 square miles, which is about the area of the state of New Jersey. Its average depth is about 700 feet. All the other Great Lakes overflow into Lake Ontario, which in turn is drained by the St. Lawrence River. Lake Ontario was first explored by the French explorer Samuel de Champlain, in 1615. See also the article GREAT LAKES.

onyx

Onyx is a semiprecious stone. It is a kind of agate. The colors of onyx are usually white and black, but sometimes onyx is red and white, yellow and white, or green and white. Penholders, desk-lamp bases, handles for letter-openers, and many ornaments are carved from onyx. The only difference between onyx and other kinds of agate is that the bands of color in onyx are straight while those of most other agate are curved or wavy.

opal

Opal is a kind of stone that is used as a gem because it has hundreds of beautiful rainbow-colored specks in it. These specks are made by thousands of tiny cracks that have water in them. If the water dries out of an opal, the rainbow colors disappear, but they may be brought back by soaking the opal in water.

For many years people believed that opals brought misfortune and disaster upon their owners. No one believes this any more, and the opal is now a highly prized semiprecious stone. It is one of the birthstones for the month of October.

Opal is found in almost all parts of the world, but the kinds that are beautiful enough to use in jewelry are found only in Australia, Czechoslovakia, Mexico, the

Honduras, and the states of Idaho and Nevada in the United States.

open shop, a factory or plant where non-union workers may be hired: see the article on LABOR AND LABOR UNIONS.

opera

An opera is a play in which all the conversation is set to music and the actors sing the words instead of speaking them. In *grand opera*, all the words are sung and the music is supposed to be of the finest kind, to be played by large orchestras and sung by the best singers. In *light opera*, or *operettas*, some of the conversation is spoken and some is sung. The songs are of the kind that become "popular songs." Grand operas are usually tragedies (with unhappy endings) and light operas are usually comedies (with happy endings), though this is not always so.

In grand opera, the leading members of the cast sing a certain number of *arias*, which are solo songs. There are *recitatives*, which are spoken words set to music but not actually songs. Usually there are large choruses that accompany (sing with) the leading singers. Many operas have *ballets*, or dancing acts that are made part of the story. Before the opera begins, the orchestra plays an *overture* that is made up of the best melodies used in the opera.

The most popular writers of opera were an Italian, Giuseppe Verdi, whose operas include *Aida, Rigoletto, Il Trovatore, La Traviata*, and several others that have remained popular for a hundred years or more, and a German, Richard Wagner, whose operas include *Lohengrin, Tristan*, the four operas called the "Ring" (based on old Germanic legends), and others that also have remained popular for a hundred years or more. The most popular single opera is *Carmen*, by Georges Bizet, a Frenchman. Nearly all great composers (writers of music) wrote operas. The music is the important thing in an opera; the writer of the words (*libretto*) is seldom remembered.

There are many famous "opera houses," or theaters where operas are presented, throughout Europe and the Americas. Among the most famous are La Scala, in Milan, Italy; the operas of Paris, Rome, Berlin, and other great European cities; and the Metropolitan Opera House in New York City. The most elaborate scenery and costumes are used in presentations at these opera houses.

There are separate articles on most of the great composers and the most popular operas.

opium, a drug taken from the poppy: see NARCOTICS.

opossum

The opossum is a small animal that lives in Mexico and South America. One member of the opossum family makes its home in the United States. The opossum is a marsupial, an animal that carries its young in a pouch on its abdomen.

The Virginia opossum lives in the woods in the eastern part of the United States. It is a small animal, about the size of a domestic cat. It has a long coat of rough, grayish-white fur, and its face is

white. It has a pointed nose and sharp eyes. The tail of the opossum is *prehensile,* which means it can be used to grasp things. When a light is flashed at the opossum, it becomes so frightened that it faints and seems to be dead. People sometimes say that a person is "playing 'possum" when he pretends to be asleep or not aware of what is being said or done.

The opossum eats mice and other small animals, and it also likes to eat insects, fruit, birds, and eggs.

The opossum makes its den in a hollow tree or rocky place. The female opossum has about twenty young once a year. She cannot feed all of them inside the pouch, so some of them die. Those that survive grow quickly. When they are strong enough to crawl out of the warm pouch they cling to the mother's back until they are able to get along by themselves.

Several different kinds of opossum live in South America. One of the most unusual is the yapok. It is the only marsupial that is at home in the water. The yapok is a skilled swimmer and diver.

The most handsome opossum is the woolly opossum. It has beautiful reddish-gold fur. Its tail is about twice as long as the rest of its body.

Opossums are useful to man because they kill rats, mice, and cockroaches. Sometimes they become a nuisance because they also eat chickens and eggs.

optical illusion

In an optical illusion the eyes are made to see things that seem different from what they really are. Lines may seem longer than they really are. Objects may seem nearer than they really are, and so on.

An optical illusion actually is a trick played on the eyes. This can be done either by the special shape or arrangement of objects or by the peculiar way in which light sometimes behaves.

Many optical illusions are made by drawing lines on paper in certain ways. Other optical illusions are made by specially-curved mirrors that cause a person

to see himself all out of shape. The way the moon seems to move rapidly through the sky on some nights is an optical illusion. It is caused by the clouds drifting over it. A straight stick placed in water often will look bent when observed from above.

A MIRAGE is a special type of optical illusion. There is a separate article about it. See also the articles on MIRROR and LIGHT.

optics

Optics is the scientific study of light, its composition, how it travels, its effects on objects, and how it enables us to see. Optics is a branch of physics, the scientific study of matter (anything that has weight and takes up space). Physicists who study optics study such things as the measurement of light, how it is produced, how it travels, the various sources of light, and the construction of optical instruments such as microscopes, telescopes, and glasses.

Optics is usually divided into two branches. *Geometrical optics* is the use of geometry, a branch of mathematics, to explain how mirrors and lenses form pictures or images of objects by the refraction (bending) and reflection (bouncing off) of light.

Physical optics is the study of the causes and effects of light.

Formerly, a person who studied optics was called an optician, but that word has since come to mean one who makes glasses and a person who studies optics is now called an *opticist.* There are articles on LIGHT, GLASSES, LENS, and MIRROR.

optometry

Optometry is the measurement of eyesight. A person who studies optometry is called an *optometrist.* He examines your eyes and prescribes or tells you the kind of glasses you need, if any. An *optician* is one who makes up the glasses according to the prescription of the optometrist.

An optometrist does not treat diseases of the eye. This is done by an *oculist* or *ophthalmologist,* a doctor who studies

ophthalmology, a branch of medicine dealing with the eye and its diseases. See the articles on the EYE, BLINDNESS, and GLASSES.

oracle

An oracle, in the ancient Greek religion, was a means by which the gods were believed to speak to human beings. At first the god's message itself was called an oracle. Later the oracle meant the place at which the message was given. There were oracles at different places, and each was supposed to be a means of communicating with a particular god. The oracle was usually attended by a priest, who explained the meaning of the god's message. A person would consult an oracle for advice on how to handle his personal affairs. A government might consult an oracle in times of national emergency, when the country was threatened with war or wished to make war.

The message of the oracle was given in various ways. Sometimes it came through a person in a trance. Sometimes the message was given in a dream. Sometimes a message was read in natural occurrences such as the rustling of leaves. Usually the message was received by the priest in very mysterious words, which he then interpreted, or explained, and put into verse.

There were many oracles in ancient Greece. The most famous one was the Delphic oracle of the god Apollo. In the temple of Apollo, at Delphi, there was a crack in the floor just over a stream of water called the Cassotis. A woman prophet seated herself over this crack, from which steam rose. The vapors were supposed to send her into a trance, during which she spoke the words of Apollo. The priest took down her words, and then interpreted them.

orange

The orange is a juicy round fruit that belongs to the same family as the grapefruit and the lemon. These are citrus fruits, and you can read about them in separate articles. Oranges first grew in Asia, and now they are raised in many parts of the world where the climate is warm. Orange trees cannot stand cold or frost. Farmers often build small fires in orange groves to make certain that the

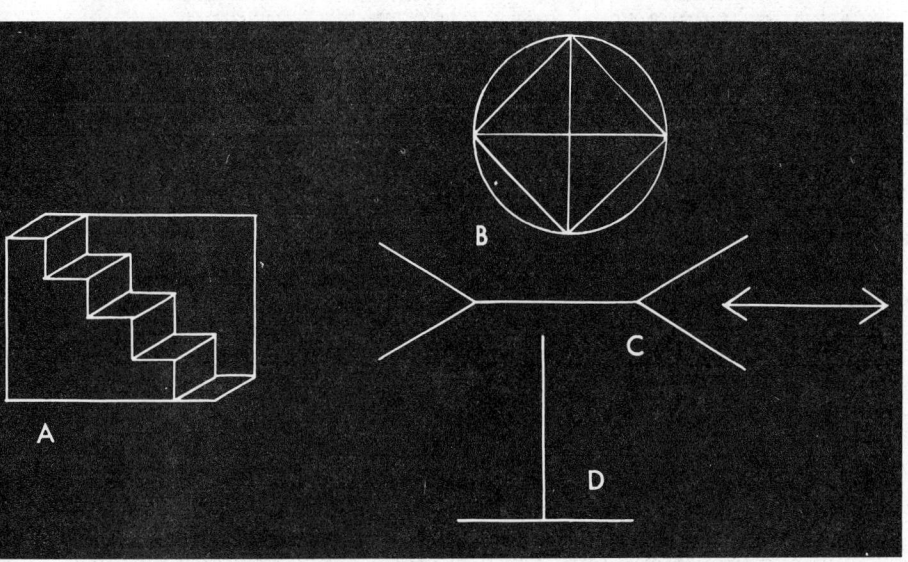

An optical illusion makes things look different from what they are: A. Put this book flat on the table. Lean forward, then backward, and watch the "front" wall of the flight of stairs change. B. The circle is perfect, though it looks flattened. C. The lines between the arrow heads are the same length. D. The horizontal and vertical lines are the same length.

Sunkist

Whether squeezed for their juice or peeled and eaten in sections, oranges are among the most healthful and delicious fruits.

trees are kept warm enough. The trees are *evergreens,* which means that they do not lose their leaves in the fall. Most American oranges are raised in California and Florida.

There are several different kinds of orange tree. The sweet orange tree grows to be more than 20 feet high. The flowers are white and have a very sweet smell. Some sweet oranges have seeds; others do not. Blood oranges have a reddish flesh. Navel oranges have a small bump at one end.

The king orange is another variety of orange tree. It includes the popular *tangerine,* a small orange with a loose skin.

Oranges were once considered a great delicacy but now they are plentiful in most places. They are a very healthful fruit because they contain much Vitamin C. Oranges are eaten fresh, and the juice is canned and frozen. The skin is used to make candy and marmalade, and as a flavoring. The skin contains an oil used in making perfume and soap.

The lovely orange blossom is a flower that brides carry on their wedding day. It is the flower of the state of Florida.

Orange Free State

The Orange Free State is a province of the Republic of South Africa. It is 49,866 square miles in size, about the size of North Carolina, and the population in 1960 was 1,373,790. Most of the people are farmers. They grow corn and wheat and raise cattle and sheep. Others work in diamond mines, and more and more people are working in gold mines. The Orange Free State has the world's richest known gold field. It is believed to contain more than $12,000,000,000 worth of gold. Uranium, the mineral most important for developing atomic energy, is also mined in the Orange Free State.

The Orange Free State was settled by Dutch people and became an independent republic in 1854. During the BOER WAR, about which there is a separate article, the people of the Orange Free State sided with the people of the Transvaal Republic against the British. It became a province of the Republic of South Africa in 1910. See SOUTH AFRICA.

orang-utan

The orang-utan is an ape that lives on the islands of Borneo and Sumatra in the Pacific Ocean. It has no tail and is more like a man than like a monkey. It is about 4½ feet tall and weighs between 150 and 200 pounds. The orang-utan can spread its long arms more than 7 feet. It is covered with long, shaggy, dark red hair. It often walks about on its two feet, instead of going on all fours.

The orang-utan lives in the thick jungle. It spends most of its time in the tree tops, where it swings from branch to branch. The orang-utan must test each branch to make sure that it can hold its weight. It builds a nest of boughs in the trees. It is fond of comfort, and when it rains the orang-utan covers itself with leaves. The female orang-utan has one baby at a time and is a good mother. The orang-utan eats fruit. It is especially fond of the sour taste of unripe fruit.

Chicago Park District

Tong licks his chops and Tanga looks on with interest as bananas are unloaded from a delivery truck. Their keeper has a hard time holding the orang-utans back.

The orang-utan is very intelligent. It can learn to dress itself, to use a hammer, and to ride a tricycle. It has a cheerful disposition and likes to entertain people who come to visit it in zoos. Some orangutans in captivity live to be about 25 years old. Orang-utans that live in the jungle probably grow to be even older.

See also the article on APES.

oratorio

An oratorio is a long musical composition. It has words and music, and is sung by solo singers supported by large choruses. An oratorio tells a story on a religious subject and usually is based on the life of Christ or something else from the Bible.

The oratorio was originated about four hundred years ago by Saint Philip Neri, an Italian priest, who gave lectures on Bible history and with them used music and hymns written specially to go with the subject. The first oratorios, like operas, were presented in costume, with scenery, acting, and sometimes a ballet. Later the oratorio became strictly a musical performance, with orchestra or organ accompanying the singers. The oratorio took its name from the prayer hall (oratory) of a church, in which it was usually presented.

The most popular of all oratorios in England and the United States, by a wide margin, is Handel's *The Messiah,* which is sung every year by thousands of choral societies. It was written in 1742. Others much favored are Bach's *St. John Passion* (1720), *St. Matthew Passion* (1729), and *Christmas Oratorio* (1734); Mendelssohn's *Elijah* (1836); Brahms' *German Requiem* (1868); and Haydn's *The Creation* (1796) and *The Seasons* (1800). The only American oratorio that has survived more than a few years is Horatio Parker's *Hora Novissima.*

oratory

Oratory is public speaking before an audience. It usually means a very persuasive kind of speech, with fine choice of words and a method of delivery (or way of saying the words) that pleases people and convinces them that the speaker is right in what he says.

In ancient Greece, more than three hundred years before the birth of Jesus, one of the greatest orators was Demosthenes. When he first appeared to speak at the assembly, Demosthenes spoke so badly that he was laughed out of the hall. This made him angry, and he studied and practiced for seven years until he was able to speak so well that he could sway the whole country. Cicero was one of the greatest orators in ancient Rome, about two thousand years ago.

For many years in the British Parliament, and then in the United States Congress, oratory was very important. Patrick Henry was a great American orator whose speeches had a great deal to do with persuading the American colonies to fight the Revolutionary War.

After the United States was founded, Daniel Webster and Henry Clay won fame as orators. William Jennings Bryan won the nomination for the Presidency with a great speech at a Democratic Party convention in 1896, and for a long time he was considered the finest American orator. The success of Franklin D. Roosevelt in being elected President four times was credited in part to the fact that he was considered the best American orator. Winston Churchill's great prominence in England is also credited partly to his ability as an orator. This does not mean that an orator may not be a great statesman, but oratory helps him explain his ideas to the people.

orchard, a group of fruit trees: see the article FRUIT.

orchestra

Any group of musical instruments playing together may be called an orchestra, a permanent organization that gives regular concerts.

The first orchestras were small bands, or groups, of musicians hired specially for an occasion, which might be a dance, a fair, a concert, a church service, or an opera. Four or five hundred years ago, such groups consisted chiefly of wind instruments, such as the shawm, bombard, and sackbut (which later became the oboe, bassoon, and trombone). In the 17th century (about three hundred years ago), the improvement of stringed instruments (violin, viola, cello) brought them into the bands. The string choir became the basis of the indoor orchestra, which then began to grow in size and variety of instruments.

Sometime before the year 1770, permanent orchestras were established in the famous Italian opera houses, La Scala in Milan and San Carlo in Naples. Other pioneers were the opera houses in Paris, Berlin, and Dresden.

The first orchestral works were written to accompany operatic or choral singers. Then composers began to write instrumental works for their own sake, and nonoperatic orchestras were organized to play these works.

The opera orchestra of the 17th century consisted of perhaps a dozen strings (violins, violos, cellos), 2 oboes, 2 bassoons, 2 trumpets, and kettledrums. In 1777, the Austrian composer Mozart visited Mannheim, a city in Germany, where there was a flourishing orchestra of forty to fifty players. Mozart wrote to

his father: "The orchestra is excellent and strong. On either side there are ten or eleven violins, four violas, two oboes, two flutes and two clarinets, two horns, four violoncellos, four bassoons and four double-basses, also trumpets and drums."

The following table shows the kinds and approximate numbers of instruments with which the up-to-date symphony orchestra is equipped. Of course, almost no composition uses all of these instruments.

STRINGS	BRASS
16 first violins	5 horns
12 second violins	3 trumpets
10 violas	3 trombones
8 cellos	tuba
8 double-basses	
harp	
piano	PERCUSSION
	3 kettledrums
WOODWINDS	bass drum
piccolo	snare drum
3 flutes	cymbals
3 oboes	chimes
3 clarinets	tam-tam
English horn	gong
3 bassoons	tambourine
bass clarinet	celeste
contrabassoon	triangle, etc.

THE CONDUCTOR

The Conductor. Small groups in the 18th century, as today, were led by the most experienced member, at the same time that he played his own instrument. In early orchestras the task of leading fell by tradition to the chief violinist. He was called the *Concertmeister.* This title is still used, though the duties are no longer very great. Presently his job was shared by the *Kapellmeister,* who played the clavichord and served as a time-beater. Neither was a conductor in the modern sense.

The nonplaying conductor with authority over the orchestra came about early in the 19th century, through the force of personality of certain composers who conducted their own works. Later in the century another composer-conductor, Richard Wagner, established the position of the conductor as an interpretive artist. The composers had outstripped the players. Such works as Beethoven's *Ninth Symphony* were regarded as "incomprehensible," if not unplayable. Wagner wrote an essay explaining how this symphony should be conducted. He drew attention to the need of more thorough training of players, and also the need of more active guidance of the orchestra by the conductor.

ORCHESTRAS IN THE UNITED STATES

The oldest orchestra in the United States is the New York Philharmonic Society, founded in 1842. The Boston Symphony Orchestra was organized in 1881. These and the Philadelphia Orchestra, founded in 1900, have been generally considered the leading American orchestras. Other leading orchestras have been established in Chicago, Cincinnati, and many other American cities.

orchid

The orchid is one of the most highly prized of all flowers. It grows in almost every part of the world, except in the cold regions near the Poles. Orchids grow best in tropical places where the climate is warm and damp. There are thousands of different kinds; many of them are magnificent flowers of brilliant purple, rose, yellow, white, or green colors.

The orchid has a very unusual appearance. The flower always has three petals. One of these petals is called the lip. This petal is often a different color and shape from the other two petals. The lip may be flat and wide, or it may be shaped like a small sac. The *lady's slipper* is an or-chid that grows in the United States. It got its name because the lip looks like a woman's shoe.

The roots of some orchids grow underground. Other orchids that grow in the tropics have roots that grow in the air. These orchids are called *epiphytes.* You can read more about them in the article on AIR PLANTS. Most orchids have green leaves. Some varieties do not have any chlorophyll, the agent which most plants use to make their own food out of air, soil, and sunshine. These orchids must get their food from decayed matter in the earth. They are a yellow or brown color. Some orchids have a very sweet smell.

Margot L. Wolf

The *Cypripedium* orchid has distinctive spots and a lovely shape. It is raised in Great Britain and North America.

One type of orchid that grows in the tropical parts of North America is valuable because it produces pods that are used to make vanilla, a flavoring.

Many people raise orchids in greenhouses. It is easy to develop new kinds of orchids, and some people belong to clubs of orchid-growers. Some orchids have been sold for many thousands of dollars.

ordeal

Ordeal was a way of trying a person accused of a crime. It was used by Germanic peoples, many hundreds of years ago. That was before these people became Christians, and they believed in many gods.

The person who was accused might be made to walk through fire, and if he was not burned it was thought that the gods were showing that he was innocent. Another ordeal was to put the person in water, and if he did not drown he was considered innocent. Ordeal was one of several forms of TRIAL, about which there is a separate article.

Order of the Eastern Star

The Order of the Eastern Star is an association of women who are wives, daughters, or other relatives of Master Masons. There are about 11,000 local chapters (separate clubs) of the Eastern Star in the United States, and they have about 3,000,000 members. The women of the chapters have meetings much like those of the MASONS, about whom you can read in a separate article. The Order

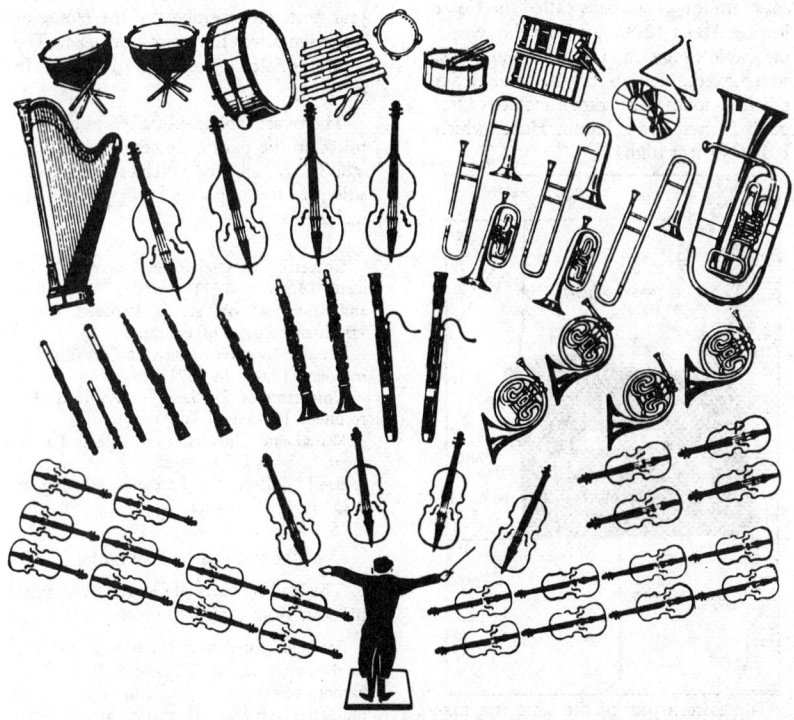

The symphony orchestra has four main sections: the strings, the woodwinds, the percussion and the brass. The sections are arranged so that they resemble a fan with the conductor as hinge. Thus, he remains in view of all the members of the orchestra.

of the Eastern Star was founded in the year 1876. The headquarters is in Washington, D.C.

Ordinance of 1787

The Ordinance of 1787 was one of the most important documents in United States history. It provided for the government and organization of the Northwest Territory, a region around the Great Lakes. The states of Ohio, Indiana, Illinois, Michigan and Wisconsin were formed from this territory.

The Ordinance of 1787 prohibited slavery in any part of the Northwest Territory. In the Ordinance the government promised to support schools in the territory and guaranteed freedom of religion to everyone living there. Most important, the Ordinance provided for new states from the Northwest Territory to be the full equals of the thirteen original colonies that formed the United States.

ordnance

The ordnance branch of any army deals with weapons, ammunition, tanks, and other vehicles, and bombs, mines, and other explosives. In the United States Army the Ordnance Department develops and tests new weapons, works with industries that make military supplies, and stores, repairs and issues weapons and supplies to troops in the field. Sometimes people speak of ordnance when they mean artillery weapons, about which you can read in the article ARTILLERY.

ore is a mineral or rock that contains metal; see the article on MINING.

Oregon

Oregon is a state in the northwestern United States. Its nickname is the "Beaver State," because so many beavers used to be trapped there. It was named for its greatest river (now the Columbia), which was called the Ouragan by the Indians. The name *Ouragon* was first used by Jonathan Carver, an early explorer, and the spelling *Oregon* was immortalized when William Cullen Bryant used it in his poem "Thanatopsis."

In population, Oregon ranks 31st in the United States, with over two million people living there. In area it ranks 10th, having 96,981 square miles. It became a state in 1859, and was the 33rd state admitted to the United States. The capital is Salem.

THE PEOPLE OF OREGON

As late as 1805, when explorers Lewis and Clark went to Oregon, most of the people living there were Indians, including the Chinook, Calapooia, Coquille, Cayuse and Shoshone tribes. French-Canadian fur traders went there early in the 1800s. In the 1840s American pioneers crossed the continent in search of furs, lumber, and later gold. Many of them came along the OREGON TRAIL, about which there is a separate article. The building of railroads, about twenty years later, brought many Chinese workers from California, and then people came from such European countries as Finland, Norway, and Spain (especially Basque shepherds). Today there are only about 8,000 Indians in Oregon, and most of them live on government reservations. About 92 out of every 100 persons in

Oregon today are native-born Americans.

A little more than half of the people in Oregon live in cities. Some work in shipyards, others in factories that produce steel and aluminum products, twine and thread, woolen products, flour, and dairy products. There are also large lumber mills and fish canneries.

Fishing, lumber, mining and farming are the main occupations of people who live in the country. The most important kind of tree used for lumber is the Douglas fir, which is the second most important tree in the United States (after the yellow pine). Young Douglas firs are very often used as Christmas trees. Raising livestock is the main farming activity. Beef cattle, sheep, hogs and poultry are raised. Hay is an important farm product. It is used to feed the livestock. The most valuable fish caught in Oregon is the salmon, which is found in huge quantities at the mouth of the Columbia River. Millions of pounds are canned and sent to all parts of the country each year. Other fish found include the albacore tuna, trout, halibut, shad, herring, and sturgeon. In the north, fur trappers catch many minks, foxes, bobcats, and muskrats.

The miners of the 1840s and 1850s struck rich deposits of gold in eastern Oregon. They also found such minerals as quartz, copper, silver, and cinnabar ore (from which mercury is taken). Other minerals found are coal, chromite, manganese, and platinum. The shale, limestone and gypsum found in Oregon are used to make Portland cement, which is used in construction all over the country.

Among the leading Churches are the Roman Catholic, Presbyterian, Methodist, and Congregationalist.

WHAT THE STATE IS LIKE

The western part of Oregon extends about four hundred miles along the Pacific Ocean. Directly on the coast are sandy beaches and dunes. Very near the coast are low mountains called the Coast Range. About 120 miles from the coast a mountain range, the Cascade Mountains, stretches the length of the state from north to south. This range includes Oregon's highest peak, Mount Hood, which is 11,245 feet high.

The eastern part of the state is a plateau (high, level land) that is crossed by another mountain range, the Blue Mountains. The plateau is from 2,000 to 5,000

feet high, so the Blue Mountains, with their average height of 7,000 feet, do not seem very high. There are several fertile valleys in this region.

There are many rivers in Oregon, but by far the most important is the Columbia, which flows for about 300 miles along the state's northern boundary. Important rivers that flow into it are the Willamette, Deschutes, and John Day. In the south there are several lakes, the most interesting of which is Crater Lake. It lies in the crater of a volcano, Mount Mazama, and its blue waters are thought to be the deepest in the United States, with a depth of about 2,000 feet. In the south are the Rogue and Umpqua Rivers.

Oregon has two very different climates. Near the coast the climate is mild and moist, and on the slopes of the Cascades it is very wet, with an average rainfall of 75 to 100 inches a year. East of the Cascades the climate is colder and very dry, with as little as 8 to 22 inches of rainfall a year. The average temperature is about 50 degrees Fahrenheit.

Transportation in most of Oregon is not very advanced, mainly because most of the people live in the western part. In this part there are many railroads, and the ports are served by steamship lines. In the eastern part of the country people travel mostly by highways. Oregon has about 5,000 miles of railroads, and nearly 7,500 miles of hard-top state roads. The Columbia and Snake Rivers are navigable for 570 miles from the ocean.

THE GOVERNMENT OF OREGON

Oregon, like the other states, has a governor at the head of its government and a legislature that makes the laws. The legislature is made up of a Senate and a House of Representatives. The governor is elected for a four-year term, but he may serve only two terms within a twelve-year period. Senators are elected for a four-year term, and members of the House of Representatives for a two-year term. The capital is Salem. There are 36 counties in the state.

There are about 400,000 pupils enrolled in the public elementary and high schools. Among the colleges and universities, six are supported by the state. They include:

University of Oregon, at Eugene. Enrollment, 14,298 in 1971 (co-ed). The medical and dental schools are at Portland. There are three colleges of education.

Oregon State University, at Corvallis. Enrollment, 14,000 in 1971 (co-ed).

University of Portland, at Portland. Enrollment, 1,743 in 1971 (co-ed).

Willamette University, at Salem. Enrollment, 1,534 in 1971 (co-ed).

Reed College, at Portland. Enrollment, 1,251 in 1971 (co-ed).

CHIEF CITIES OF OREGON

The leading cities of Oregon, with populations from the 1970 census, are:

Portland, population 382,619, largest city in the state, on the Willamette River. Fine harbor, center of shipbuilding and lumber industries. There is a separate article about PORTLAND.

Eugene, population 76,346, second-largest city, with important woolen mills.

Salem, population 68,296, third-largest city and state capital. There is a separate article about SALEM.

Medford, population 28,454, fourth-largest city, center for a fruit-growing region.

OREGON IN THE PAST

The first explorers of Oregon landed in 1788, from a boat commanded by a Bostonian, Robert Gray. Three years later Gray discovered the Columbia River, and in 1805 Lewis and Clark reached its mouth. Few settlers came until the 1840s, when the gold rush and the opening of the Oregon Trail brought many more. The Indians, who resented their coming, raided settlements and killed many of the settlers. Wars with the Indians continued until the late 1870s, when the last strong tribes were subdued.

The old territory of Oregon included also the present states of Washington and Idaho and parts of Montana, Wyoming, and the Canadian province of British Columbia. Though no one settled there, it was claimed first by Spain, since Spaniards had sailed down its coast in the 1500s. The English claimed it too, since Sir Francis Drake and others had sailed the coast, and Russia wanted it. But the United States claimed Oregon as part of its rightful territory, and in the early 1800s the other countries ceded Oregon to the United States.

The first real settlement was established at Astoria by John Jacob Astor's fur-trading company in 1811. Rival companies soon followed. The first permanent settlement was made by Methodist missionaries in 1834. Many more Americans came during the gold rush of 1849 and the following years. In 1848 Oregon was made a territory, with the capital at Oregon City. Land grants from the government encouraged more settlers. Oregon became a state in 1859. The building of dams made it possible to farm the great river valleys, and shortly before World War II the greatest public project, the Bonneville Dam on the Columbia River, was finished.

PLACES TO SEE IN OREGON

Crater Lake National Park, in the southern Cascades, including Crater Lake, one of the scenic wonders of the United States. Includes Phantom Ship and Wizard Island, small volcanic islands.

Oregon Caves National Monument, in Josephine County, in the southern Cascades. Underground limestone formations.

Mount Hood National Forest, in the Cascades, including Mount Hood, Oregon's highest peak. National forest with recreation area and outdoor sports facilities. Includes Lost Lake and many other lakes and waterfalls.

Silver Falls State Park, near Silverton. Trails along the scenic little river, which includes some 10 waterfalls.

Oregon Trail, U.S. highway No. 30 from Ontario to Seaside, and U.S. 197 and 26, around Mount Hood. At some points wagon tracks can be seen on this historic route. Columbia River Gorge allows transportation at water grade on U.S. 30.

Astoria, site of first permanent settlement (1811) and Oregon's fishing center.

OREGON. Area, 96,981 square miles.

Population (1970 census) 2,091,385. Capital, Salem. Nickname, the Beaver State. Motto, The Union. Flower, Oregon grape. Bird, western meadow lark. Song, "Oregon, My Oregon." Admitted to Union, February 14, 1859. Official abbreviation, Oreg.

Oregon Trail

The Oregon Trail is a route that was used by American pioneers going westward. It is about two thousand miles long, beginning at Independence, Missouri, crossing the Rocky Mountains, and ending at what is now Vancouver, in the state of Washington. The beginnings of the Oregon Trail were blazed by Indians and fur-trappers.

The first explorer to travel over the whole trail was Nathaniel J. Wyeth, in 1832. He left Boston, Massachusetts, in April and arrived in Vancouver in October. After that time many settlers passed over the trail, especially when gold was discovered in California in 1848 and 1849.

Orestes

Orestes is a character in Greek mythology, the stories the ancient Greeks told about their gods and goddesses. Clytemnestra was his mother and Agamemnon was his father. Clytemnestra was in love with another man, Aegisthus, and together they murdered Agamemnon. They planned to murder Orestes too, but his sister Electra saved him. She sent him to the king of Phocis, and he was brought up there. Orestes and Pylades, the son of the king of Phocis, became close friends.

When Orestes grew up, he returned to his home and avenged his father's murder by killing his mother and Aegisthus. After this, Orestes was pursued by the Furies and wandered from one place to another.

Several ancient Greek dramatists, including Euripides, wrote plays about the story of Orestes.

organ

The organ, or pipe organ, is the largest of musical instruments. It consists of many pipes in which sound is produced by a blast of compressed air. The pipes vary in length from a few inches to about 32 feet. Some organs have as many as 7,000 pipes.

The organ pipes are placed out of sight in a room or loft. The row of handsome gilt pipes often seen in front of the organ loft, in a church or theater, is just for show; these pipes are dummies.

Air to play the organ used to come from a *bellows,* a large box with flexible sides, that could be squeezed together. The bellows was pumped by an assistant, often a small boy. In the modern organ, the bellows is a series of tanks filled by an electric air-compressor.

Like the piano, the organ is played from a keyboard; but the organ has several keyboards, from two to six. The keyboards for the fingers, called *manuals,* are arranged one above and behind the other. The *pedal* is another keyboard, played by the feet. The pedal keys are long, thick, wooden levers. The assemblage of keyboards is called the *console.*

In the modern organ, each key closes

an electric circuit, which opens a valve and lets air into the pipes.

Besides the manuals and pedals, the console includes many push buttons or hinged pallets for *stops* and *couplers,* and a special *swell pedal.* It has been said that not even the instrument panel of a modern airplane has surpassed the organ console in the number of "gadgets" available to the performer.

The *pitch* of a tone produced by air vibrations in a pipe depends mostly on the length of the pipe.

The organ produces four broad classes of tone quality: 1, *organ tone,* the full round tone, sometimes called *diapason,* which only the organ can produce; 2, *flute tone,* like that of a flute; 3, *string tone,* like that of the violin or cello; 4; *reed tone,* which can produce a variety of sounds. The reeds include pipes that imitate the oboe, clarinet, bassoon, and other woodwinds; the trumpet, trombone, tuba, and other brasses; the human voice; bells, chimes; and others.

A stop is a group of pipes that produce the same tone color, one pipe for each note throughout all or part of the range of the organ. The entire stop can be turned "on" or "off" by a knob at the side of the keyboard. The average church organ today may have 40 stops; a theater organ may have 80 to 100 stops.

Each stop is played from a separate keyboard (though it can be coupled to others). In a large organ there may be five manuals, named from top down: *echo, solo, swell, great,* and *choir.* The most important is the *great organ,* which provides diapason and flute tones throughout the manual and pedal range. These are often called *foundation* stops.

The organist cannot, like the pianist, vary the loudness of tone by the pressure on the key, but any number of stops, from one to all, can be turned "on" at once.

OTHER ORGANS

The *harmonium* is a small portable organ built in a cabinet. Its range is only two or three octaves. There can be no pedal keyboard, because the performer pumps the bellows with his feet. The pipes are all reeds, and because of its tone the instrument is commonly known as the "squawkbox." It was once widely used but has been replaced in nearly all cases by the electric organ.

The *electric organ* (not to be confused with a pipe organ run by electricity) likewise uses any of several other ways of producing sound. One method is a disk rotating at high speed—the same principle as is applied in the siren. Electric organs were first introduced in the early 1930s and have made organ music available to thousands of public places and private houses that could not afford the cost or the space for a pipe organ.

oriole

The oriole is a very pretty bird that lives in Europe and the Americas. There is a separate article about the BALTIMORE ORIOLE, which makes its home in the eastern United States. In the western states are found the Arizona hooded oriole, the orchard oriole, Scott's oriole, and a Mexican form of the bird.

The oriole is a rather small bird. The male is about eight inches long and the

female is somewhat smaller. The female is usually a pale yellow color with greenish-black markings. The female oriole is a fine architect. It builds a beautiful nest that gracefully hangs from the bough of a tree. The elm is a favorite tree. The female lays between four and six small white eggs that have black or brown markings on them. The Baltimore oriole has a clear, sweet whistle. Some of the European orioles have lovely songs.

Orion

Orion is a constellation (group of stars) that lies partly in the northern and partly in the southern skies. In the mythology (stories about gods and goddesses) of the ancient Greeks, Orion was a mighty hunter. The stars in the constellation seem to show him standing with shield held in front of him and sword raised, awaiting the charge of Taurus, the bull.

Orion is one of the brightest constellations in the heavens and can be seen with the naked eye from almost any part of the earth. The sword and belt of Orion have been adopted as the insignia of the 27th division of the United States Army.

Orléans

Orléans is an important city in the central part of northern France. About 80,000 people live there, and many of them work in factories that make clothing and metals. The history of Orléans goes back to the time of the ancient Romans. Julius Caesar burned the city about two thousand years ago, in 52 B.C. It was rebuilt by the Roman emperor Aurelian, for whom the city is named. Several hundred years later, Orléans became one of the favorite residences of French kings. During the Hundred Years War, in the 1400s, the city was besieged by the English and was saved from them by Joan of Arc. The feast of St. Joan is still celebrated by the citizens of Orléans every May. During World War II much of Orléans was destroyed by fire, but a few of its fine old buildings are still standing.

ornithology is the scientific study of birds. It is a branch of biology. See the articles BIOLOGY and BIRD.

Orpheus

Orpheus was a musician in Greek mythology, the stories the ancient Greeks told about their gods and goddesses. His father was the god Apollo and his mother was Calliope, one of the nine Muses. (The Muses were goddesses of music, poetry, and art). Apollo gave Orpheus a lyre and the Muses taught him how to play it. His music was so beautiful that when wild beasts heard Orpheus play they became tame.

Orpheus married the nymph Eurydice. She died from a snakebite and Orpheus was filled with sorrow. He journeyed to Hades (the place where the souls of the dead went) to find Eurydice. Orpheus played such beautiful music that Pluto, the ruler of Hades, agreed to send Eurydice back to earth on one condition. He made Orpheus promise that he would not look back at Eurydice until they reached the upper world. Just before they reached the upper world, Orpheus broke his promise and looked back. Eurydice vanished and was lost to Orpheus forever.

He was so sad because of this that Orpheus treated the women of Thrace cruelly, and they killed him. It was said that when Orpheus was buried, a nightingale sang over his grave.

Ancient Greek poets wrote many beautiful poems about the sad tale of Orpheus. The German composer Gluck wrote an opera, *Orpheus and Eurydice,* and the German composer Offenbach wrote a comic opera, *Orpheus in the Underworld.*

orthodontia, the branch of dentistry that deals with straightening teeth: see the article on DENTISTRY.

Osaka

Osaka is the second-largest city in Japan. It is in southern Honshu (the chief Japanese island), and is an important port on Osaka Bay, part of the Inland Sea. About three million people live in Osaka. Many of them work in shipyards, and in the shipping industry, which is very large because railroads bring many goods to be shipped from Osaka's port. Others work in steel mills and in factories that produce metal and chemical products.

Osaka has many buildings that interest visitors. Most popular is the palace built almost four hundred years ago by the Japanese general and ruler, Hideyoshi. It was a great fortress and one of the most impressive buildings in Japan. It was destroyed by fire about a hundred years ago, but much of it has been rebuilt. There are also a park with beautiful flower displays and a museum of art and science. Several colleges and universities are in Osaka, including the Osaka University.

Osaka is an ancient city. It was the capital of Japan about 1,500 years ago. Much of the city was destroyed by a terrible fire in 1909, and during World War II its factories and harbor were heavily bombed by Allied airplanes. By 1955 this damage had been repaired.

OSAKA. Population (1960 census) 3,011,563. Capital of Osaka prefecture.

Osiris

In the religion of ancient Egypt, thousands of years ago, Osiris was the god of the underworld, to which the spirits of the dead went. He was also the god of fertility, or growth, and he was believed to have brought agriculture and civilization to Egypt.

Osiris was the husband of Isis and the brother of Set, the evil god of the night. Osiris is usually pictured wrapped in mummy cloths and wearing an Egyptian crown.

Oslo

Oslo is the capital of Norway and its largest city. It is in the southeastern part of the country. Much of the city is built on a hill that slopes down to Oslo fiord, an inlet from the ocean.

Almost half a million people live in Oslo. Many of them work in factories whose chief products are machines, electrical equipment, chemicals, clothing, paper, and food products. Ships come to Oslo from ports all over the world, and many people work in the transportation industry.

Oslo is the chief cultural and religious center of Norway. Visitors who arrive by train can take a taxi down the beautiful Karl Johans Gate, which is the main street of Oslo. On their ride they pass the stately parliament building, the beautiful University of Oslo, the National Theater, and the Royal Palace, which is the home of the king. Oslo has many museums, including the well-known Ski Museum and the Nobel Institute. The 650-year-old Askershus fortress overlooks Oslo fiord. Near Oslo is the town of Bygdoy, which is a popular resort. At Bygdoy there is a display of ships that were used by the Vikings when they sailed the North Atlantic more than 1,100 years ago.

Oslo was founded near its present site about the year 1050, and three hundred years later it became the home of the Norwegian king. It was an important port under the German merchants of the HANSEATIC LEAGUE, about which there is a separate article. A terrible fire destroyed almost the entire city in 1624, and it was rebuilt on the Oslo fiord. During World War II, Oslo was occupied by the Germans.

For pictures of Oslo, see NORWAY.

OSLO. Population (1960 estimate) 471,310. Capital of Norway. Port on Oslo fiord.

osmium

Osmium is a gray metal. It is the heaviest substance known. A baseball weighs five ounces, but if it were made of osmium it would weigh ten pounds. Osmium is a chemical element, one of the more than one hundred basic substances of which everything in the world is made. It is found in river sands in North and South America and in the Ural Mountains in the Soviet Union.

When combined with iridium, osmium makes *osmiridium,* an alloy that is very hard and tough. This alloy is used on the tips of expensive fountain pens, and bearings for machinery are made from it.

Osmium will not dissolve in acids, so it is used to make certain instruments used in chemistry. Osmium is also used in the manufacture of ammonia.

osprey

The osprey is a large bird that lives near coasts and on the shores of lakes and rivers in many parts of Europe and the United States. The osprey is about two feet long. It has dark brown feathers, with a white head and breast. The osprey is sometimes called the *fish hawk,* because it is a very skillful fisherman. It flies gracefully above the water and when it spots a fish it swoops down to catch it. The osprey's thick feathers keep it from hurting itself when it hits the water. The osprey spears the fish with its sharp claws. Sometimes a lazy eagle, rather than catch its own dinner, forces the osprey to give up the fish it has caught.

osteopathy

Osteopathy is a branch of medicine that was founded in 1874 by Andrew T. Still, who was a regular physician. Still's belief was that the living body makes all the substances necessary to prevent or cure disease, and that it is only when the body is out of mechanical adjustment that it cannot make these substances. His treat-

ment consisted of manipulating bones and muscles to restore them to proper adjustment. Andrew Still opened a college of osteopathy in 1892, at Kirksville, Missouri.

Several other colleges have been established since then. The course of study requires four years, after which the student is graduated as an osteopath with the degree of Doctor of Osteopathy. These colleges do not give the degree of Doctor of Medicine. The individual states require licenses for the practice of osteopathy, and in most states osteopaths are permitted to prescribe drugs and perform surgery.

ostrich

The ostrich is the largest of all birds. It makes its home in Africa and Asia. The ostrich cannot fly. The male ostrich is about 8 feet tall and weighs almost 200 pounds. The female is a little smaller. The ostrich has long, thin legs, a long, thin neck, and a small head. It has beautiful black and white feathers.

Many people believe that the ostrich is a timid bird that hides its head in sand when it sees enemies coming near. This is not true. Although the ostrich lives surrounded by fierce lions and other unfriendly beasts, it is very well able to take care of itself. The ostrich can run about 40 miles an hour on its long legs. It also has keen eyesight and can see its enemies when they are far away. The ostrich is so well able to sense when danger is near that zebras and gnus often keep the ostrich company. They know that if there is any danger the ostrich will find out very quickly. When an ostrich is cornered it can kick very hard.

The feathers of the ostrich are very beautiful. People have used them for fans and as decorations for hats. In South Africa there are ostrich races, run like trotting-horse races in the United States.

Ottawa

Ottawa is the capital city of Canada. It is a beautiful city at the meeting of the Rideau and Ottawa Rivers in the province of Ontario.

About three hundred thousand people live in Ottawa. Many of them work in Ottawa's thriving industries, which produce paper, woodwork, and watches, but most of them are employed in the offices of the government of Canada.

Ottawa is a city of great beauty and has many fine houses and buildings. The streets are wide and straight and are lined with trees. Several of the government buildings are on top of Parliament Hill, which looks down over the Ottawa River. The Parliament buildings burned down in 1916 but were rebuilt in the same style as when they were first built, about a hundred years ago. They are made of sandstone in the Gothic style of the Middle Ages. One of the features is the Peace Tower of the Parliament buildings, which represents Canada's love of peace.

Ottawa is an important cultural and religious center. The Anglican Christ Church Cathedral and the Roman Catholic Cathedral of Notre Dame are among its loveliest buildings. Its colleges and universities include the University of Ottawa, St. Patrick's College, and Carleton University. It has many libraries and museums, including the National Museum of Canada (the Victoria Royal Museum) and the great Parliamentary Library with more than 500,000 volumes.

The scenery around Ottawa attracts many visitors. There are waterfalls on the Ottawa River and hillside resorts with facilities for sports and relaxation.

Ottawa was founded in 1827 by Colonel John By, who was an engineer in charge of building the Rideau Canal. At first it was called Bytown and was used simply as a home for By and his workers. In 1854, its name was changed to Ottawa and four years later Queen Victoria made it capital of the colony of Canada. When Canada gained self-rule, Ottawa continued as the capital. It is the residence of the Governor-General, who represents the British queen in Canada.

OTTAWA. Population (in 1973) 302,341. Capital of Canada. On the Ottawa and Rideau Rivers, in the Province of Ontario.

otter

The otter is an animal that lives near lakes and rivers in many parts of the world. Some otters make their home in the Pacific Ocean. The otter is the fastest swimmer of all the land mammals. (A mammal is an animal that bears live babies and nurses its young.)

The otter that lives in North America is an attractive animal that is about 2½ feet long and weighs about 20 pounds. It has a flat head and tiny ears. Its legs are short and its hind feet are webbed. The otter has a powerful tail, about one foot long, which helps it to swim. The otter has beautiful, thick, dark-brown fur. Otters are great underwater swimmers and skillful fishermen. They can kill a fish that weighs as much as 20 pounds, although most of the time they eat smaller fish that are easier to catch.

SEA OTTER

The sea otter that lives in the Pacific Ocean is larger than other otters. It weighs as much as 80 pounds. The sea otter spends almost all of its time in the water.

The female sea otter has one baby, and she is a very good mother. It is believed that otters mate for life and a family of otters will stay together, even after several babies have been born. If a mother and baby otter are separated both will cry in a pitiful way.

The sea otter was so much prized for its fur, used for fur coats, that nearly all of the sea otters were killed. Now the few remaining ones are protected by law.

Ovid

Ovid was a great Roman poet who lived two thousand years ago. He is especially remembered for the love poems he wrote. Ovid was born in the town of Sulmo, near Rome, in the year 43 B.C. His full name was Publius Ovidius Naso.

Many fine writers have translated the poems of Ovid. His best-known works are *The Art of Love*, the *Amores*, love poems, and the *Metamorphoses*, which are poems about the Roman gods and goddesses. Ovid died in the year 18.

owl

Owls are birds that live in almost every part of the world. Most of them leave their nests only at night. There are hundreds of different kinds of owl. Some of them make their homes in deserts. Others live in the cold Arctic regions. Many owls live in deep forests, far from men. Others are more sociable. They live in barns and church steeples, in towns and villages.

From early times man has considered the owl a very wise and mysterious bird. The owl has a round face and large, saucerlike eyes that give it a solemn, thoughtful appearance. It has a weird hooting or screeching call that sounds very ghostly in the silent night. The owl is actually not a particularly intelligent or frightening bird. It is a very useful one, because it is an excellent hunter and kills many rats and mice and insect pests.

The owl sleeps during the day. It comes out at night to hunt for food. The owl cannot see well in the dark, but it hunts on moonlit nights. The owl's soft, downy feathers make no sound as the owl swoops down on its victim. It swallows rats and mice whole. Later it brings up the fur and bones in the form of little pellets.

ox

An ox is the bull, or male, of cattle. It is called an ox when it is fixed so that it cannot produce offspring. Oxen are used mostly for pulling heavy loads. They are slow but gentle and can pull heavy loads. Oxen are the most powerful of the domestic animals used in the United States. Usually two oxen are stood side by side and fastened together by a piece of wood called a *yoke* that fits over their shoulders. The pair of oxen is referred to as a yoke of oxen. The oxen pull carts, plows, wagons, or other equipment by pushing their weight against the yoke, which is hitched to whatever is to be pulled. The oxen learn to follow simple commands. When the farmer says, "Gee," the oxen turn to the right, and when he says, "Haw," the oxen turn to the left. All domestic cattle, including cows, bulls, and steers, are sometimes referred to as members of the ox family.

Oxford

Oxford is a city in south central England. It is known throughout the world as the site of Oxford University, the oldest in England. More than 100,000 people live in Oxford. Many of them are connected with the university, but most of them work in Oxford's large factories, which make automobiles, electrical equipment, and paper.

The town of Oxford was a Roman Catholic shrine more than 1,100 years ago. The University opened about seven hundred years ago. The town grew rapidly and the university became the leading one in England.

Today, Oxford University is made up of 23 colleges. Both men and women study there. The organization is different from that of American universities. Each of the colleges governs itself. The same subjects may be taught in several colleges in Oxford, but many of the colleges are known for excellence in a particular subject such as mathematics or history. Teachers may teach in several of the colleges. The university awards degrees in many subjects.

Among the oldest colleges of Oxford

University are University College (the first college, founded in 1249), Balliol, Merton, St. Edmund Hall, and Exeter. Originally, only such subjects as literature and philosophy were taught, but today instruction is also given in science. The libraries of Oxford are among the best in the world.

Oxford University has a very important place in British life. Many of Great Britain's intellectual and political leaders have received their training there. In the 19th century it became famous as the center of the Oxford Movement, whose most famous member was Cardinal NEWMAN, about whom there is a separate article.

OXFORD. Population (1960) 106,124. Seat of Oxford University. Capital of Oxfordshire County. On the Thames River.

oxygen

Oxygen is a colorless, tasteless, odorless gas. It is a chemical element; that is, it is one of the 103 basic substances of which everything in the world is made. Oxygen is the most plentiful of all elements. One-fifth of the air is oxygen, nearly half the weight of all minerals and rocks of the earth's crust is oxygen, and eight-ninths of all water is oxygen. More than half of the human body is made of oxygen. Of all this oxygen, only that which is in the air is a gas. The rest is combined with other elements in solids and liquids.

OXIDATION

Oxygen combines very easily with many other elements. This combination of oxygen and another element is called *oxidation*. When oxidation is so rapid that it gives off heat and light, it is called *burning*, or *combustion*. Since air is only one-fifth oxygen, materials will burn more rapidly and brilliantly in pure oxygen than in air. A piece of wood that is only glowing in air will burst into flame if it is put into a jar of oxygen. Extremely rapid oxidation may result in an explosion, as when gunpowder burns in the barrel of a gun. Sometimes oxidation is very slow, as when iron rusts or when dead plants or animals decay.

OXYGEN AND BREATHING

For human beings, the most important kind of oxidation is that which takes place in the bodies of all animals. This is called *respiration*. Oxygen breathed into the lungs is picked up by the red corpuscles of the blood. The corpuscles carry this oxygen to food stored up in the tissues of the body. When the oxygen and the stored food combine, oxidation takes place and the body gets energy to move its muscles and heat to keep it warm. When a person is ill of pneumonia, and his inflamed lungs are clogged with pus, he cannot get enough oxygen from ordinary air. Then he may be put in an "oxygen tent," where he can breathe a mixture that is half pure oxygen and half air. (He cannot be given pure oxygen, for this would actually burn up his lungs.) When a person is rescued from drowning, a mixture of air and extra oxygen is pumped into his lungs in the hope of starting his breathing again. When fliers and mountain climbers go up so high that the air is thin, they take tanks of compressed oxygen.

PLANTS AND OXYGEN

Plants manufacture starch by the process called PHOTOSYNTHESIS, about which there is a separate article. In this process they use carbon dioxide gas from the air. This carbon dioxide, which is formed by a combination of the elements carbon and oxygen, comes from oxidation of one kind or another. It comes from the burning of wood, coal, and oil, and from the breathing of animals. In making starch, the plants take the carbon from the carbon dioxide and return the pure oxygen to the air. In this way the oxygen of the air is renewed over and over again.

oyster

The oyster is a sea animal with a double shell. It is a member of the mollusc family, which includes clams and mussels. (You can read about MOLLUSCS in a separate article.) The oyster is different from other molluscs in several ways. The two parts of the oyster's shell are not the same size and shape. One side, the left or lower side of the shell, is larger than the other side. The left side is thick and flat. The outside of the shell is rough. The oyster has no foot as the clam does, and it cannot move from one place to another.

Oysters are found off many coasts where the climate is not too cold. The best oysters are found at spots where streams flow into the ocean waters and carry plants and animal food to the oysters, which cannot travel about and search for food.

The female oyster lays as many as nine million eggs. These eggs are so tiny that altogether they would take up only about an inch of space. The eggs hatch in a few hours, and in about a day and a half the young, or tiny larvae, begin to develop shells. After about three weeks a young oyster settles at the bottom of the ocean. It attaches the large left side of its shell to a stone or to another shell, and there the oyster remains.

Oysters are an important food and many people in the United States and other parts of the world fish for oysters. Some fishermen gather oysters and take them to new places so that they can start new oyster beds. Oysters are raised the way farmers raise chickens or sheep. Oysters can grow to be about 18 inches long, but most are caught when they are only about 4 or 5 inches long. People eat oysters raw, and they also fry them and cook them in many other ways.

A special kind of oyster that lives off the coast of Australia and the East Indies is called a pearl oyster. Sometimes valuable pearls are found in the shells of these oysters.

Ozark Mountains

The Ozark Mountains are a plateau, or section of high land, that lies between the Arkansas and Missouri rivers. The plateau is about 50,000 square miles in size, about the size of the state of New York. Most of it is in Missouri, but parts of it are in Arkansas, Oklahoma, and Kansas. Its average height is about 2,000 feet, and the highest section, called the Boston Mountains and lying in Arkansas, is about 2,400 feet high. Lead and zinc are mined in the Ozarks. There are good

fruit-growing areas along the slopes, and some mineral springs. The Ozarks are a popular vacation spot.

ozone

Ozone is a pale bluish gas. It is a form of oxygen, a gas that is part of the air and that we need to stay alive. If you have ever been around a large electric motor or generator, you may have smelled a sharp odor. The odor was ozone that was being made from the oxygen of the air as electric current jumped from the armature to the brushes of the motor or generator. Ozone can be smelled when there is only one part of ozone in half a million parts of air.

Ozone is used to purify water, since it kills any bacteria or tiny animals in the water. It is used to bleach oils, waxes, starch, and flour. When ozone is bubbled through fish oils, rancid butter, or other fats, it removes their unpleasant odor and helps to keep them from spoiling.

OZONE IN AIR

Many people think that ozone is good for the health and that the air at the mountains or the seashore has more ozone in it than the air in the city. Actually there is no more ozone in one part of the world than in another. Lightning flashes make a little bit of ozone in the air, but not even enough to measure. Even if there were some extra ozone in the country or seashore air, it would not necessarily be healthful, for more than two parts of ozone in a million parts of air is poisonous.

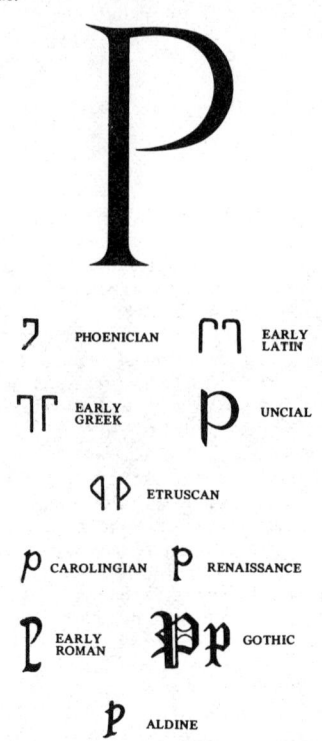

Ɂ	PHOENICIAN	⌐Ꞁ	EARLY LATIN
⊤Ͳ	EARLY GREEK	ρ	UNCIAL
९ Ρ	ETRUSCAN		
ρ	CAROLINGIAN	Ρ	RENAISSANCE
Ρ	EARLY ROMAN	𝔓p	GOTHIC
ρ	ALDINE		

P or p

The letter P is the sixteenth letter of the alphabet. Some scholars think that it can be traced all the way back to the earliest writing known to man, in Egypt, thousands of years ago. In the Hebrew language, in which much of the Bible was written, the letter was called *pe,* a word that meant "mouth." The ancient

Greeks took this same letter and called it *pi*.

On the opposite page, you can see some early forms of the letter P. In those days writing was read from right to left, and in some of the old languages, such as Hebrew, it still is. But the Greeks changed this and began to read from left to right, as we do today. When they made this change they turned the letters around. On the far left, above, are the two forms of *pi* used by the Greeks, before and after it was turned around. Later they changed it still more, and by the time of the classical Greeks it looked like this: π Our own letter P was made by curving the small hook around until it joined the stem of the letter. The Etruscan P is very much like ours, but angular instead of curved. The Uncial and later styles were the bases of our own printed and written letters.

Read also the article ALPHABET.

Pacific Ocean

The Pacific Ocean is the largest and the deepest ocean in the world. It covers 64,000,000 square miles. With its adjoining seas the area is 70,000,000 square miles, which makes it about twenty times as large as the United States and almost twice as large as the Atlantic Ocean. The Pacific Ocean covers about one-third of the earth's surface. Its average depth is about 14,000 feet, though at its deepest point the Pacific is more than 35,000 feet deep. The ocean was named in 1520 by the explorer Ferdinand Magellan, who called it the Pacific, which means "calm" or "peaceful." But the Pacific can get just as stormy as the Atlantic, particularly in the hurricane and typhoon belts.

The Pacific extends from the Arctic Ocean in the north to the Antarctic Ocean in the south. On its eastern boundary are North and South America, and on its western boundary are Asia and Australia. The part above the Equator is called the North Pacific. The part below the Equator is called the South Pacific, or the South Sea. Near the equator the Pacific reaches its widest point—almost 11,000 miles wide.

The Pacific has a number of adjoining seas, or arms. The most important are the Bering Sea, Sea of Okhotsk, Sea of Japan, Yellow Sea, China Sea, and Coral Sea. There are separate articles about the principal seas.

The Pacific is linked to the Atlantic Ocean by the Panama Canal and by Drake Passage below South America. It connects with the Indian Ocean in the south through Bass Strait, and with the Arctic Ocean in the north through Bering Strait.

CURRENTS AND WINDS

The tides of the Pacific Ocean produce several currents that are like great rivers flowing through the open sea. One such current is the Japan Current. It begins in the Philippine Sea, where the water is warm, and carries the warm water past Formosa, the Aleutian Islands, and along the North American coast.

The Pacific also has a cold current called the Humboldt, or Peru, Current. It flows north from the Antarctic Ocean along the coast of South America. In general, the Pacific Ocean is colder than the Atlantic.

Some of the winds of the Pacific are warm and dry, and they take definite paths. They are known as *trade winds,* and they flow toward the equator. Certain regions of the Pacific are noted for their storms and fierce winds, called *typhoons.* Some of the worst typhoons occur in the China Sea. Hurricanes frequently rage off the Pacific coasts of Central America and Mexico.

WHAT THE PACIFIC IS LIKE

The floor of the Pacific is not level. It consists of plateaus (high, level places), volcanic peaks, and coral reefs, most of which are covered with water. Those that stick out of the water form islands. The largest plateau, an island, forms the continent of Australia. The deepest place in the Pacific (such ocean spots are called *deeps* or *trenches*) is the Marianas Trench near Samoa, discovered in 1952. It is 36,-198 feet deep. Other deep trenches include the Mindanao Trench near the Philippines, which is 34,578 feet deep, and the Ramapo and Tuscarora, off the coast of Japan.

The Pacific is filled with plants, fish, and tiny shelled animals. These live in the greatest abundance in the colder waters, which hold large amounts of oxygen. One of the greatest fishing areas in the world is in the North Pacific.

THE PACIFIC ISLANDS

In the Pacific are about 15,000 islands that together are called Oceania, or the South Sea Islands. These are divided into three groups, the Polynesian, the Melanesian, and the Micronesian.

The Pacific islands are either volcanic or coral islands. The volcanic islands are often mountainous, and have dense forests, rivers, and sandy beaches. The coral islands are sometimes sandy banks, called *atolls.* They are very low and flat, and most of them are fertile. The islands, particularly those in the South Pacific, have a tropical climate and are very beautiful. Coconut-palm trees grow nearly everywhere. Plants and birds are brightly colored.

There are other island groups of great importance, such as the Aleutians, the Philippines, Indonesia, and Japan.

IN THE PAST

The American coast of the Pacific Ocean was discovered in 1513 by the Spanish explorer Balboa. He called it the South Sea. Seven years later, Magellan crossed the ocean on his way to the Philippines. He renamed it the Pacific. Other important explorers of the Pacific included Sir Francis Drake, Captain James Cook, Vitus Bering, and George Vancouver. By 1800 all the major Pacific islands had been discovered. Various countries have controlled islands in the Pacific, including England, the Netherlands, France, Russia, Germany, Japan, and the United States. Many of the islands were of great importance during World War II.

The first airplane flight across the Pacific took place in 1931, and today there are regular flights across the ocean.

See also the article on OCEAN.

pack rat

The pack rat is an interesting little animal that makes its home in many parts of the United States, particularly in the Rocky Mountains. The pack rat is about as large as a squirrel and has a bushy tail. It has thick, soft, brown fur. It is sometimes called the "trade rat" because it likes to steal nails, coins, pieces of cloth, and other things. It will even rob a person's pockets while he is asleep. In place of the objects it has stolen, it leaves some nuts or leaves or twigs.

The pack rat builds its nest in a hollow tree or in the branches of a tree. Sometimes it builds its nest on a rocky hillside. The nest is a large structure, five or six feet high. It is made of branches and is lined with soft grass. The nest sometimes has two rooms. The pack rat stores leaves and nuts in its nest for eating during the winter. The female pack rat has from two to six babies. The pack rat is a good mother and takes care of the young even after they are old enough to search for their own food. Pack rats stay in their nests during the day and come out at night to search for food.

Paderewski, Ignace Jan

Ignace Jan Paderewski was a Polish statesman and one of the greatest pianists who ever lived. He was born in 1860, and began studying the piano at the age of 7. He made his debut as a pianist in 1887 and quickly became world-famous. In 1891 he visited the United States for the first of many highly successful concert tours, during which he became the highest-paid concert artist in history, earning as much as $2,500 for a single concert.

When World War I broke out in 1914, Paderewski abandoned his career and devoted himself and his fortune to work for Poland. He gave concerts to raise funds, and he returned to the United States to recruit men of Polish descent for the war against Germany. Paderewksi represented Poland at the Versailles Peace Conference and at the League of Nations. When the Polish republic was established in 1919 Paderewski was the first premier, holding office for ten months. In 1922 he resumed his concert career and continued to play to vast audiences everywhere until 1939, when he was 79 years old. When Germany invaded Poland in that year, Paderewski became president of the Polish government in exile. In 1940 he returned to the United States to live in California, and the following year he died.

Paderewski composed much music, but little of it is played today. His most famous piece is the *Minuet in G.*

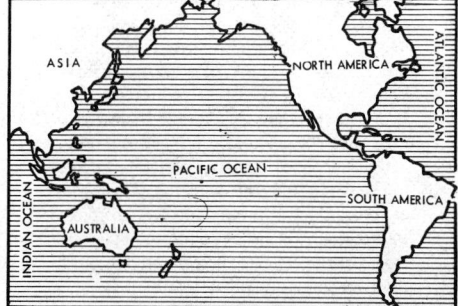

ASIA · NORTH AMERICA · ATLANTIC OCEAN · PACIFIC OCEAN · SOUTH AMERICA · INDIAN OCEAN · AUSTRALIA

Paganini, Nicolo

Nicolo Paganini was a very great Italian violinist. He was born in 1782 in the city of Genoa. He began to play the violin when he was only 6 years old, and he made his first public appearance when he was 11.

Paganini's father was a poor man and he hoped to make some money from his son's talent, but Paganini ran away when he was 15 years old, and began to give concerts. He made a great deal of money and began to gamble and lead a wild life. Soon he settled down and gave concerts in all the important cities of Europe. He was given titles and presented with medals, and poems were written about him. Paganini died in Nice, Italy, in 1840, when he was 56 years old. He wrote many compositions for the violin and some are still played.

pageant

A pageant is a dramatic show that has a special meaning. Some pageants are plays celebrating events of history, other pageants are processions with floats representing special scenes and with actors in costume. The actors on a float may form a *tableau*, which is a dramatic scene, or picture, in which the actors stand still in certain poses. Many communities and schools present pageants on holidays such as the Fourth of July or Christmas.

The most famous pageants in the United States are the Mardi Gras in New Orleans, the Mummers' Parade on New Year's Day in Philadelphia, and the Tournament of Roses on New Year's Day in Pasadena. These are all parades, with fantastic and beautiful floats and persons dressed in strange costumes.

Pagliacci, I

I Pagliacci is an Italian grand opera by the composer Ruggiero Leoncavallo. It was first presented in 1892 in Milan, Italy. Leoncavallo wrote both the music and the words. The name means "The Clowns" in Italian.

The story of *I Pagliacci* concerns a group of strolling actors who go from town to town putting on harlequin shows. The chief actor, Canio, is afraid that his wife Nedda has fallen in love with a young villager named Silvio. Canio's suspicions have been aroused by Tonio, who has been treated rudely by Nedda and wants to cause her trouble. During the play Canio forgets all about the scene he is supposed to be acting with his wife, and angrily demands to know whether it is true that she is in love with Silvio. When she does not answer, Canio kills her there on the stage, and when Silvio tries to come to her rescue, he also is killed. The most famous aria of the opera is the prologue, a song sung by Tonio before the curtain rises on the opera itself, in which he tells how a clown must laugh even though his heart is breaking.

pagoda

A pagoda is a towerlike structure built in the Far East, usually connected with a temple or serving as a shrine or memorial. In India the pagoda is a stone tower of pyramid shape built above the entrance to a temple and having no inside space. In China the pagoda is often a memorial building. Most of these are eight-sided towers with many stories, each of which has an upward-curved veranda roof. Most Chinese pagodas are of brick, sometimes faced with colored tile. The pagoda was taken to Japan along with the Buddhist religion. There it is usually built in the Chinese style, except that it is often made of wood. Pagodas are common in other countries of Asia, such as Burma, Tibet, and Korea.

pain

Pain is a feeling of being hurt. It can be either physical or mental, but usually when we speak of pain we mean physical pain. Pain is a warning signal that some part of our body is injured or diseased.

We feel pain because in all the parts of our bodies there are sensitive nerve endings. If you read the article on NERVOUS SYSTEM you will see how messages are sent to and from the brain over the wonderful pathways called nerves. One of these messages is the sense of pain. The sensitive nerve endings tell the brain what is going on in different parts of the body.

Nerve endings that can feel pain are present throughout the body, especially in the skin, but there are more in the face, hands, and feet than anywhere else. The eye is probably the most sensitive place. A tiny speck of dust in the eye can be very painful.

Pain is very important. If we did not suffer from pain we would not be warned to do something about what causes the pain. Our pain also helps a doctor to locate the trouble. If you did not feel pain from very hot water you might step into a tub full of it and your skin could be severely burned.

The best way to end pain is to get rid of its cause, whether it is a disease or an injury. Sometimes pain is so unbearable that a doctor has to give a narcotic (a drug that deadens the nerves that carry the message of pain). In this way he cuts off the pain signal from the brain.

Paine, Thomas

Thomas Paine was a writer who greatly influenced the American colonies to fight against Great Britain for their independence in the Revolutionary War. His pamphlet, "Common Sense," which he wrote in 1775, inspired the people with a desire for independence. Much of Paine's other writing has been widely read, particularly *The Age of Reason*.

Thomas Paine was born in England in 1737. In England he met Benjamin Franklin, one of the early leaders in the colonies, who persuaded him to go to America. He arrived in Philadelphia in 1774 and became the editor of a magazine. In his articles he wrote that the colonies should be independent and that they should not allow slavery. Thomas Paine was against any form of government that did not allow all men to be free and equal.

During the Revolutionary War Paine wrote a series of inspiring pamphlets called *Crisis*. He also served in the American army and helped collect money to form a bank that supplied money for the army.

Later Thomas Paine went to France, where he helped the French in their fight for independence. He helped write the constitution for the new French republic formed at the end of the war. Because Paine did not believe that the French king should be killed, he was put in prison by the leaders of the revolution. While he was in prison he wrote *The Age of Reason*.

James Monroe, the American minister to France, who later became President of the United States, managed to have Paine freed from prison in 1794. Eight years later Paine returned to the United States, where he died in 1809. Although Thomas Paine is admired by most freedom-loving people for many of his ideas, he has been criticized for many of the ideas expressed in *The Age of Reason*, particularly those having to do with religion.

paint

A paint is a colored liquid that is put on surfaces in order to protect or decorate them. Paints may be brushed, sprayed, or spread with rollers. When they dry they become thin, tough films, or *coats*. Paints are made to form many different kinds of coat, smooth and glossy, satiny, or flat (dull and rough).

WHAT PAINT IS MADE OF

Every paint has three parts: the *body*, the *vehicle*, and the *pigment*.

The *body* of a paint is a very fine powder, usually white, which is the main substance that forms the protective film when the paint dries. White lead is the most widely used paint body, but it loses its white color after a few years of exposure to air. Zinc oxide and lithopone are two other substances much used for paint bodies. The clay called kaolin and the chemical sulfate are used as bodies for cheaper grades of paint.

The *vehicle* is a liquid in which the other two parts of the paint are mixed. The vehicle enables the paint to run so that it can be spread on the surface to be painted. One type of vehicle is oil mixed with a *thinner*, which is a liquid that evaporates quickly. Turpentine is one kind of thinner. The oil used is of the kind that is known as a *drying oil*. This kind of oil does not actually dry. As soon as the thinner evaporates, the oil begins to combine with the oxygen of the air to form a tough, hornlike film. The oil is sometimes called a *binder*, because it holds the body and pigment of the paint together. Paints that use an oil and thinner mixture for a vehicle are called *oil paints*. Most house paints and artists' paints are oil paints.

Another type of vehicle is simply a mixture of water and glue or some other resin. The body and pigment are mixed in the water and glue solution. The water evaporates, and the glue acts as a binder. Paints using this type of vehicle are called *water paints*. Such paints are often used for covering plaster walls.

The *pigment* is a very finely ground

powder of a colored substance. It is used to give a paint its color. For example, powdered titanium dioxide makes white paints brilliantly white. Red lead is the orange-red pigment in the paint that is used on iron bridges and girders. Dyes that will dissolve in water are used as pigments in water paints.

ENAMELS AND LACQUER

An *enamel* is a colored varnish, which means that it is an oil paint in which the body is one of the chemical substances called resins.

A *lacquer* is a paint made with a vehicle that dries very quickly and results in a very hard, glossy coat. Most of the paints used on automobiles are lacquers.

Printer's inks, calcimine or *kalsomine,* and *whitewash* are also considered paints.

Paint was being used before history was first written. The first paints were simply colored clays and were applied to the bodies of people during religious ceremonies, or when the men went on the warpath. In a cave in southern France, twenty thousand years ago, artists painted many beautiful pictures on the walls, using clay pigments. The colors of these pictures are still bright.

painting

Painting is a way of making a picture. It is done by applying pigments, or colors, on a surface, usually with a brush but sometimes with a pencil, a knife, or the fingers.

Prehistoric men made the earliest paintings known, perhaps as many as fifty thousand years ago, on the walls of caves. During the period of history called the Renaissance, about six hundred years ago, such men as Leonardo da Vinci and Michelangelo did paintings that have never been surpassed.

For hundreds of years there have been many different groups, or schools, of painting, in many different countries, such as Holland, England, France, Spain, and Italy. Some of these schools produced great artists for periods of a hundred years or more. The schools of painting, which are often named for the city or country in which they were popular, differed from one another in their choice of subjects as well as in their methods of painting. For example, painters of the Renaissance often chose religious subjects or painted characters from the stories told by the ancient Greeks and Romans about their gods and goddesses. Some schools are named for their aims, or for their methods. The Impressionist school, which arose in France a hundred years ago, was so called because its painters preferred to have their paintings give a general idea of a subject rather than give an exact likeness of it (as a photograph does).

For about four hundred years after the Renaissance, the most popular kind of painting was the painting of portraits—pictures of individuals or groups of individuals. Like the photographer of our time, the artist painted pictures of people so they would be remembered by those who loved or admired them. There were many different ways of doing this. Some artists, such as the Dutch painter Rembrandt, tried to show their subjects exactly as they were and tried also to bring out the important elements of the subject's character, such as kindness, greed, vanity, sadness, and so on. Others, such as the English painter Thomas Gainsborough, usually flattered their subjects by making them look more beautiful or handsome than they really were.

Today painting is more important than ever, both as an art and as a hobby. Even people without great talent, or without the ability to improve their work by study and practice, can enjoy painting as a hobby.

THE MATERIALS OF PAINTING

The kind of paint depends on the material with which the pigment, or color, is mixed. *Oil paint* is pigment mixed with oil; *water color* is pigment mixed with water; *tempera* is pigment mixed with a sticky base, such as thin glue or albumen; *fresco* is paint applied to wet plaster; *pastel* is pigment mixed with chalk and gum water into a dry paste, usually in the form of crayons. The surface to which paint is applied may be canvas, paper, wet or dry plaster, silk or some other cloth, wood, and so on. The appearance of a picture varies according to the kind of

The Metropolitan Museum of Art, Rogers Fund, 1951; from The Museum of Modern Art, Lizzie P. Bliss collection.

This portrait done in 1923 by the Spanish painter, Pablo Picasso, is called *Woman in White*.

paint and the kind of surface used. According to the surface used, a painting is *mural* (painted on a wall, ceiling, or other stationary surface) or *easel* (a movable panel of canvas or paper).

THE SUBJECTS OF PAINTING

Certain types of subjects have been used so widely that paintings are often classified according to them. The principal forms of paintings are: *portrait,* a painting of an individual or a group of people; *genre,* a scene from everyday life; *historical,* a scene of historical interest or importance; *landscape,* a picture of a countryside; *animal,* a picture of one or more animals; *figure,* or *abstract,* a geometrical pattern or design; and *still life,* a motionless object or group of objects, such as a vase of flowers on a table.

Until about a hundred years ago, artists painted their subjects as they appeared. Though each artist had an individual view of his subject and had his own way of putting it down, the painting looked enough like the subject to be recognizable. When a subject was imaginary or historical, and therefore could not be painted at the time and place to which it belonged, the artist often used living persons for models or painted from his memory.

The main purpose of the artist has always been to create something beautiful. During the last hundred years there have been many changes in ideas of what is beautiful. Different schools of painting have appeared, each with its own idea. One of the principal new ideas of beauty was that geometrical forms and designs (such as circles, cubes or blocks, and so on) were beautiful. Artists of this school of thought, called *cubism,* would paint portraits in which their subjects were arranged into geometrical forms that seldom resembled the real appearance of the subject at all. From painting in which the real-life subject could not be recognized, many artists went one step further and painted purely abstract designs, using no model at all.

Today two opposite views still exist: one, that a painting should resemble its subject just as a photograph does; the other, that the resemblance of a painting to anything in real life is completely unimportant. Modern painting includes examples of both these views, as well as all the degrees between them.

MAKING AN OIL PAINTING

Most painters begin by making some sort of sketch, or rough drawing of the scene or person they intend to paint. This sketch is made on the canvas with charcoal. Usually it shows only the barest outline of the main figures that are to be painted. When the sketch is made, it may be sprayed with a liquid called a fixative, for example shellac. This keeps it from smearing.

The oil paints usually come in small tubes. A small amount of paint is pressed from the tube onto the palette, the flat board that the artist holds as he paints. All required colors can be mixed from red, blue, and yellow, so these three colors plus white are enough; but there are dozens of other colors that can be bought at artists' supply stores.

The painter uses a kind of dull knife, or spatula, for mixing different colors on the palette and making a new color from them (as, for example, mixing blue and yellow to make green). Then, with his brush, he takes a bit of paint from the palette and daubs it on the canvas.

Many painters advise painting the large and dark shapes first, then the medium dark ones, and finally the light tones and colors. Oil paints are opaque (you cannot see through them), so if a painter makes a mistake or wants to change anything he simply paints over what he did before and nobody can see the difference. This is often necessary because the appearance of a color may change as other parts of the canvas are filled in. For example, a tree may look unnaturally green against a white background but when the background is filled in with a color the tree may appear just as it does when it grows naturally.

There are many different kinds of brush and also there are different strokes of the brush—crosswise, or up-and-down,

In Italy and other countries of Europe, some of the greatest paintings are in the vast medieval cathedrals. This Madonna is part of a painting that hangs above a church altar.

The Greeks excelled at decorative painting. This wedding procession dates from 540 B.C.

This etching is by the great Rembrandt.

or daubing—and the finished appearance of the picture depends greatly on what brush and stroke are used for each part of it. As a simple example, crosswise strokes with a coarse brush might give the appearance of log in a log cabin when up-and-down strokes or a finer brush might not.

A water color is painted in much the same way except that it is not so easy to correct mistakes, because when you try to paint over one color with another color the water will make the colors mix together.

PAINTING AS A HOBBY

Many famous men have adopted painting as a hobby. President Dwight D. Eisenhower and the British statesman Winston Churchill are among them. Thousands have learned that a person does not have to be a good painter to enjoy the hobby, and some who begin as "amateurs," as did Grandma Moses, discover such skill that they become famous and highly paid professionals.

Pakistan

Pakistan is a country in southern Asia on the subcontinent of India. In 1947, Pakistan became a separate country when the British Empire of India was divided into two countries, India and Pakistan. Pakistan declared itself a republic in 1956, although it remained a member of the British Commonwealth. Pakistan was a country consisting of two parts, East Pakistan and West Pakistan. These two land areas are on opposite sides of India and are over a thousand miles apart. In 1971, however, East Pakistan became a separate nation and is called Bangladesh. Bangladesh was formed as a result of rebellion in the country of East Pakistan and as a result of the war between India and Pakistan. West Pakistan is now just called Pakistan.

Pakistan, formerly West Pakistan, is located between the countries of Iran, India, Afghanistan, and the disputed area of Kashmir. Its southern border extends to the Arabian Sea. Pakistan's area is 310,403 square miles, which is about the size of Texas and New York combined. Since 1967, the country's capital has been Islamabad. The previous capitals were Rawalpindi and Karachi. Pakistan is no longer a member of the British Commonwealth.

THE PEOPLE OF PAKISTAN

Most of the people speak Urdu, which is the official language. Since only a minority of the people are literate, the government is strongly urging educational and vocational programs. Nearly all the people are Moslems, followers of the Mohammedan religion.

Although the land is mountainous and dry, 80% of the people are farmers. Irrigation is used to make the land more cultivable. Fortunately, Pakistan has several rivers from which to get water. Crops include rice, wheat, maize, cotton, tea, and citrus fruits. Sheep, goats, horses, and camels are raised.

Industry is important in Pakistan, especially in the cities. The manufacture of cotton cloth is Pakistan's largest industry, and many people work in cotton textile factories. Factories also produce wool, silk, rayon, cement, leather goods, sugar, chemicals, and dyes. Pakistan is admired for its beautiful fabrics, which are often hand woven.

WHAT PAKISTAN IS LIKE

The geography of Pakistan consists of mountains and hills in the north and deserts and dry plains in the south. The Indus River is most important and flows for about 1,000 miles. It starts at the foot of the Himalaya Mountains and ends at the Arabian Sea. The Indus and other rivers provide Pakistan with a water supply, hydroelectric plants, and canals.

Pakistan has a harsh climate. Winters are cold and dry. Summers begin in April, and temperatures may reach 120 degrees by June. The rainy or monsoon season begins in July and ends in September.

Railroads and highways reach many parts of Pakistan and there are airports in the important cities. Some of the important cities, besides Karachi, are Lahore and Peshawar in West Pakistan, and Dacca and Chittagong in Bangla Desh.

A view of the Alfala Market section of the city of Lahore, Pakistan.

Pakistan is governed by a president and a one-chamber national legislature, under a constitution adopted in 1962. The previous constitution was annulled in 1958 because the government was not being run right, and reforms were made.

Pakistan has about 250 colleges and 6 universities, including Punjab University at Lahore, and Sind University at Karachi.

PAKISTAN IN THE PAST

Pakistan has an old history, dating back about 5,000 years. The Indus Valley was the site of one of the earliest civilizations in the world. It was there that cotton was first woven and spun. Bronze, an alloy of copper and tin, which is hard enough for making useful tools, was first made there. About 330 years before Jesus was born, Alexander the Great, a famous Greek king and founder of a mighty empire, with his armies reached the Indus River, and for long afterwards Greek culture and

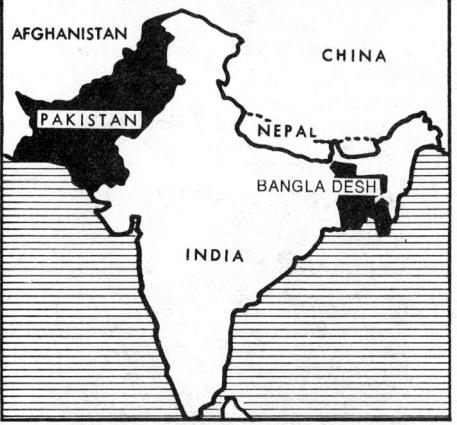

art influenced the culture of the people living in the area of present-day Pakistan. About a thousand years ago, this area was ruled by Arabs who introduced the Moslem religion there. In the centuries that followed, the people were ruled by the Mongols, the Hindus of India, and then the British as part of British India. When Britain agreed that all of India could be independent, in 1947, religious differences had made the Moslems of India and the Hindus of India so unfriendly that they would not be part of the same nation; yet in many places they all lived together. Pakistan and India were formed as separate na-

tions; then millions of Moslems moved to Pakistan and millions of Hindus, Buddhists and others moved to India. As they passed one another on the roads, they often fought and tens of thousands were killed. In 1965, a short war broke out over

A Chitrali tribesman of Pakistan.

the ownership of KASHMIR, but no definite settlement was reached. In 1971, the government of Pakistan sent troops to what was then East Pakistan to crush a rebellion over the lack of concern which the government displayed for the needs of the Bengali people of Pakistan. Instead of merely stopping the rebels, the troops killed and tortured millions of innocent men, women, and children, as millions of others escaped into India. At that point, India invaded East Pakistan and forced the Pakistani troops to surrender. The East Pakistanis immediately declared themselves independent from West Pakistan, and named their new country Bangla Desh, meaning "The Bengal Nation."

PAKISTAN. Area, 310,403 square miles. Population (1973 estimate) 60,000,000. Capital, Islamabad. Religion, Moslem. Monetary unit, Pakistan rupee.

paleontology

Paleontology is the study of plants and animals that lived long before history was first written. It is chiefly the study of *fossils*, the skeletons, footprints, or other traces left in rocks and soil by living things of long ago. Since fossils are found in rocks, paleontology is really a branch of the science of geology, the study of the earth, especially rocks.

Often geologists can tell how old the rock is, and the fossil can be dated by that. Paleontologists also get information from biologists, who study all living things. From what they learn in these ways, paleontologists have pieced together a story of how life has developed.

EARLY LIVING THINGS

The oldest fossil that has been found was made by a small jellylike plant of a single cell, much like modern algae, a form of seaweed. This fossil was found in rocks that were formed not quite two billion years ago. For 700 million years these algae floated in the hot seas that covered most of the earth. This great stretch of time is called the Archaeozoic Era, which means "age of first life."

In the next 350 million years, seaweeds, bacteria, and finally sponges, developed in the warm seas. During the 200 million years after that, while great chains of volcanoes poured out lava that built the continents higher, and glaciers (rivers of ice) formed in Africa and Asia, coral plants appeared in the warm shallow southern seas and built coral reefs. All these 550 million years together are called the Proterozoic Era, which means "age of early life."

PALEOZOIC ERA

During the 90 million years that followed, the seas covered most of the earth at one time or another. The first animals whose fossils have been found are small shellfish called trilobites. They appeared in the seas and grew to such large numbers and so many kinds that they dominated all other kinds of life. Sea snails came into being, too, and there appeared the first plants to live on land, plants like those called lichens today. The climate was warm and very damp. This was the Paleozoic Era, or "age of ancient life."

It took another 85 million years for the land to rise enough to roll back the seas. Sometime in this period vertebrates (creatures with backbones) began to swim in the seas. These creatures looked very much like fish. In the same period there grew up on land the first plants that had stems and spore-pods (but no leaves). Toward the end of this period, sea-scorpions ventured out on land and became air-breathers.

During the next 40 million years, fishes became more numerous than any other animals and dominated the seas. There appeared the first amphibians, animals that hatch from eggs in the water but later can live on land. Forests began to cover the continents. These forests consisted of ferns and horsetails as big as trees, club mosses, and trees that were the ancestors of modern evergreens. Within these forests, the first spiders and insects lived.

During the next 75 million years, while most of the coal of the world was

being made from the great swamp forests growing in the warm, moist climate, sharks dominated the seas, and the trilobites died out. Reptiles appeared and were born on land. Insects grew to the greatest size they have ever reached. There were dragonflies with a wingspread of three feet. There were more than a thousand kinds of cockroach. At the end of this period, the first plants to make seeds appeared.

Then followed 40 million years of cold weather, during which glaciers (rivers of ice) spread over almost all the earth. The cold killed off great numbers of animals, plants, and insects. Low-slung four-legged reptiles, beetles, small dragonflies, evergreen trees and ferns were among the living things that survived the cold dry weather.

MESOZOIC ERA

For the next 50 million years, the climate very slowly grew warmer and damper. This was the Mesozoic Era, or "age of middle life." Reptiles increased in numbers and size until, by the middle of this period, they dominated the earth. Some reptiles, called dinosaurs, grew larger than any other land animals have ever been. The dinosaur called Diplodocus was 87 feet long and weighed 35 tons, or about seven times as much as an elephant. Butterflies, moths, locusts, termites, cicadas and grasshoppers became abundant as the climate became warmer. Toward the end of this period, birds appeared.

During the next 25 million years, small mammals developed from certain small reptiles. At the end of this period the lands rose high and the climate became cold again. The dinosaurs disappeared, because they could not survive the cold or for some other, unknown reason. Many new kinds of bird appeared.

CENOZOIC ERA

Next came the Cenozoic Era, or "age of mammals." It designates the era of geological history extending from the end of the Mesozoic Era to the present day. During the first 30 million years of this era, the climate slowly became milder and also drier than it had been in previous eras, and mammals became the dominant animals. The first horses, cats and dogs appeared. Modern grasses and cereals began to grow.

Then, for 18 million years, as the climate became cooler and the Rocky, Sierra, Himalaya, Andes and Alps mountains rose, and a great chain of volcanoes formed the Cascade Mountains, modern types of furry mammals and heavily feathered birds appeared, while some mammals—whales, seals, and sea lions—came to live in the oceans. Modern trees and flowers covered the continents.

For the next 10 million years, as the worldwide rise of the land and the cooling of the climate continued, mammals reached their greatest development, and wandered from continent to continent over "bridges" that existed because much of the earth's water supply was frozen in the ice of glaciers.

In the last two million years, several glaciers advanced and retreated. Large, fierce mammals, such as the mastodon, the mammoth, and the saber-toothed tiger, appeared but soon vanished. Human beings began to kill off all other animals that threatened them.

Fifty thousand years ago, the last of the glaciers began to melt. They are still melting as they retreat toward the poles.

There is a separate article on GEOLOGY that tells about the changes in the earth.

Palermo

Palermo is the capital and most important city of the island of Sicily, which is part of Italy. About 600,000 people live there, making Palermo about the same size as Pittsburgh, Penna. Palermo is a manufacturing city, has big shipyards, and is the chief seaport of Sicily. It is a very ancient city, and many of its fine cathedrals and palaces are more than eight hundred years old. The city was founded by the Phoenicians more than 2,500 years ago and later became an important Roman city. During World War II, Palermo was badly bombed.

PALERMO. Population (1973 estimate) 652,380. Capital of Sicily and of Palermo Province. Seaport on the Gulf of Palermo in the Mediterranean Sea.

Palestine

Palestine is a region on the eastern shore of the Mediterranean Sea. It is part of the continent of Asia. It is the Holy Land of Jews, Christians and Moslems: of Jews, because it is the Promised Land of the Old Testament; of Christians, because Jesus was born and lived there; of Moslems, because their founder, Mohammed, recognized the kinship of his religion to Judaism and Christianity.

During its history, Palestine varied in size. It occupied much the same region as the modern countries of Israel and Jordan, and the articles on these countries tell what it is like today.

EARLY HISTORY

The Old Testament book of Exodus

Israel Inform. Office

Bethlehem, a tiny town in Palestine, was the birthplace of Jesus. The Church of the Nativity is built over the spot where he is thought to have been born.

tells how Moses delivered the Jews from slavery in Egypt, and God promised them a land of their own. This land was then called Canaan, and after forty years of wandering the Jews conquered the land of Canaan under their great general, Joshua. They divided the area among their twelve tribes and named it Israel. (The name Palestine was not given to the region until much later.)

For many years each tribe ruled its own territory, but about a thousand years before Jesus was born, Saul was made the first Jewish king. He was followed by the two greatest Jewish kings, David and Solomon. Under Solomon, Palestine grew, though it still had many enemies among neighboring peoples, such as the Philistines.

JUDAH AND ISRAEL

After Solomon died, in 933 B.C., Palestine was split into two kingdoms, Judah and the Northern Kingdom of Israel. They were ruled by different kings, and often were at war with each other as well as with other countries. However, both nations were closely tied to the Jewish religion, and Jerusalem, capital of Judah, remained the center of the Jewish faith.

About seven hundred years before the time of Jesus, Assyria conquered the Northern Kingdom of Israel. Judah lost its independence when the Babylonians overran the territory a little more than a hundred years later. Jerusalem was destroyed, and the people were taken into exile. Later, Palestine was ruled by Persians, Macedonians, Egyptians, and Syrians.

LATER HISTORY

Palestine had one more period of independence. This was under the Maccabees, a family of Jewish kings. They led a revolt against the Syrians and defeated the Syrian armies. The new Jewish state lasted for less than a hundred years. Then the Romans conquered Palestine and ruled it for about seven hundred years. The southern section of Palestine was called Judea, and it was in this province that Jesus was born.

Nearly seven hundred years after the time of Jesus, Palestine fell under the control of Moslems. When Moslems destroyed many of the Christian holy places

The winding Jordan River was crossed by Joshua when he led the Jewish people for the first time into the region of Palestine. The river is mentioned frequently in both the Old and the New Testament.

in Palestine, the Christians of Europe decided to take Palestine from the Moslems. Off and on during three hundred years, Christian armies made a series of campaigns called Crusades to win back the Holy Land. The Crusades never won all of Palestine, and for four hundred years, ending with World War I, the region was ruled by Turkey.

About 90 years ago, many Jewish people started to settle in Palestine. Most of

them went there from countries in Europe where Jews were not given full freedom. Then began the Zionist movement, which had the purpose of establishing a Jewish state in Palestine. The article on ISRAEL tells how this was finally done, after many troubles and much bloodshed.

Palisades

The Palisades are a long cliff of gray rock rising 350 to 500 feet above the west bank of the Hudson River, near New York City. The Palisades are about thirty miles long. Many sections of the Palisades are set aside by the states of New Jersey and New York for a park, which is called Palisades Interstate Park.

The Palisades were formed from rocks that were pushed up from deep in the earth more than two hundred million years ago. They attained their present form, however, only within the past two million years, when great glaciers advanced and retreated.

palm

The palm is a tree that grows in many parts of the world where the climate is warm. There are more than a thousand different kinds of palm tree. Some kinds grow to be more than 100 feet high. Others are only about 3 feet high. Some have enormous greenish yellow leaves that are as long as 50 feet. Palms may have huge seeds that are larger than a grapefruit, or tiny seeds that are only about the size of a pea. Many palm trees have flowers that hang in huge clusters.

Some palm trees grow near coasts, others grow in thick inland forests, and still others grow in open spaces. Palm trees can grow in places where no other trees grow. The palm trees that are found in the United States are mainly the COCONUT, DATE, and PALMETTO PALMS about which there are separate articles.

Palm trees are very useful, for their stems, leaves, and fruit. People eat coconuts and dates. The stem of the date palm and the flowers of certain other palms contain sugar. The stem of the sago palm contains starch that is made into flour. The seeds of some palms contain a hard substance called vegetable ivory, from which such things as buttons, knobs, and chessmen are carved.

The leaves of palm trees contain wax that is used to make candles. The leaves of palm trees that grow in Central America are woven into Panama hats. The fibers of palm leaves are used to stuff pillows and to make brooms and brushes.

The palm branch stands for joy and victory. The branch or leaf was given to military and athletic heroes in ancient Greece, as an honor. See also the article on PALM SUNDAY.

Palmer, Alice Freeman

Alice Freeman Palmer was an American educator who lived almost a hundred years ago. She was born in 1855 in Colesville, New York. Her maiden name was Alice Freeman. When she grew up she taught history at Wellesley College and later became its president. When she was 32 years old she married George Herbert Palmer, a professor at Harvard University. Later, Mrs. Palmer served as dean of women at the University of Chicago. She died in 1902.

palmetto

The palmetto is a palm tree that grows in the United States, Mexico, and Central America, where the climate is warm. It is a beautiful tree about 50 feet tall. It has a long, straight trunk and its top is crowned with large green leaves that are one to five feet long. The palmetto is an evergreen, which means that it does not lose its green leaves in the fall. It bears small, greenish flowers that hang in clusters. The fruit is black, about as long as a pea pod. It is not good to eat. Some people cook the buds, and the tree is sometimes called the cabbage palmetto because the buds taste somewhat like cabbage.

The palmetto has a strong wood that is used to build docks and wharves. The tree is so handsome that it is used to line the streets of some southern cities. It is the tree of the state of South Carolina, which is nicknamed the "palmetto state."

palmistry

Palmistry is a form of fortunetelling that is based on the idea that the lines in the palm of the hand show what sort of person you are and what your fortune is going to be. The life line is the curved line that surrounds the thumb. If it is long and unbroken the person is supposed to have a long life. The heart line stretches across the palm just below the fingers. If this line is long and unbroken, the person is supposed to have a warm, affectionate nature. The head line is just below the heart line. If the head line is strong, it is supposed to indicate high intelligence; if it goes almost to the outside of the palm, it indicates imagination.

Almost nobody takes palmistry seriously, but it is often fun to use as a sort of parlor game.

Palm Sunday

Palm Sunday is a feast celebrated by Christians on the Sunday before Easter. It is in memory of the time when Jesus entered Jerusalem, riding on an ass, and the people honored him by throwing palm branches and leaves in his path. In many churches it is the custom to give palm leaves to people who come to church on Palm Sunday. Many people make the palms into crosses and pin them on their clothing. The palm leaf is often kept in the house throughout the year, until a new one is given on the next Palm Sunday.

Pan

Pan was a god in Greek mythology, the stories the ancient Greeks told about their gods and goddesses. He watched over shepherds and their flocks, and he was also the god of fishermen and hunters. Pan was a strange-looking creature. He had a man's body and head, but he had a beard and horns and his feet were like those of a goat. He also had a goat's tail. Pan lived in rocky caves. He liked to dance with the wood nymphs and play lovely songs on his shepherd's pipe (a kind of horn). Pan had a very loud voice and frightened travelers who met him in the woods on a dark night. Pan was a favorite of all the gods and the special pet of Dionysus, the god of wine. Many

artists have painted pictures of Pan, and great poets have written poems about him.

Panama

Panama is a small country in Central America. It is on the Isthmus of Panama, the narrow section of land that connects Central and South America. The building of the Panama Canal, almost fifty years ago, connecting the Atlantic and Pacific oceans, made Panama important in world trade. Panama is 28,575 square miles in size, which is about half the size of Illinois, and more than one million people live there. The strip of land through which the Panama Canal runs is called the Canal Zone. This zone, about 10 miles wide, is governed by the United States. More than 40,000 people live there, most of whom work for the United States government. The capital of Panama is Panama City.

THE PEOPLE WHO LIVE THERE

People of different races and countries live in Panama. Spaniards settled in Panama more than five hundred years ago and many married Indians who already lived there. Today more than half the people are of Spanish and Indian descent. When the Panama Canal was being built, many people came from North America, Europe, and the West Indies to work on it.

More than half the people of Panama live in the country and are farmers. Many of them work on the large banana plantations, which are owned by United States

companies. More bananas are exported than any other crop. Other people have small farms. The people in the cities make a few important products, such as Panama hats.

Most of the people in Panama speak Spanish, but English is spoken by many in the cities. Most of the people belong to the Roman Catholic Church.

WHAT PANAMA IS LIKE

Panama is largely a mountainous country, much of it covered with forests of rubber trees and palms. Some peaks rise to more than 11,000 feet. Between the mountain ranges are fertile valleys for farming. In the eastern part of Panama are dense jungles, and along the coast are swamps. The coasts of Panama are irregular and have many gulfs.

Panama has a tropical and rainy climate. It is cooler in the mountains than along the coast. The average temperature is about 80 degrees. The best time to visit Panama is between December and May, when it is not so rainy.

Panama has a number of railroads, highways, and airports, but the Canal is the most important transportation route.

HOW THE PEOPLE ARE GOVERNED

Panama is a republic, with a president, a legislature that makes the laws, and a constitution that protects the rights of the people. The president is elected for a four-year term. The legislature is called the National Assembly and is composed of one house. The members of the Assembly are elected for a four-year term. The country has neither an army nor a navy.

Everyone has to go to school between the ages of 7 and 15. There are several colleges and universities, including the University of Panama, in Panama City.

CHIEF CITIES OF PANAMA

The leading cities in Panama, with populations as estimated in 1960, are:

Panama City, population 270,000, the capital and largest city in Panama.

Colón, population 59,360, the second-largest city, one of the two Atlantic ports of the Panama Canal, a commercial center, in the north-central part of Panama. Cristobal, the other Atlantic port, adjoins it.

Balboa, population 3,139, in the Panama Canal Zone, the Pacific port of the Panama Canal, a United States naval station.

PANAMA IN THE PAST

The first white men to land on the coast of Panama were the Spaniards, more than four hundred years ago. In 1513, the Spanish explorer Balboa crossed the Isthmus and discovered the Pacific Ocean. The Spanish colony of Panama was an important stopover point for the expeditions the Spaniards made into Peru to capture the treasures of the Incas. They shipped these riches to Panama, then back to Spain. The old city of Panama was famous for its wealth. It was attacked and burned by the British buccaneer, Sir Henry Morgan, almost three hundred years ago.

In 1821 Colombia won independence from Spain, and Panama was part of Colombia (then called New Granada). This did not satisfy the Panamanians and there were frequent revolutions. In 1903 the United States (which had been unsuccessful in making a satisfactory treaty with Colombia for a Panama Canal), supported one of these revolutions, recognized Panama as independent, and almost immediately made an agreement with the new government for the canal. The canal brought prosperity to Panama, but in the 1960s there were anti-U.S. riots because the government and people of Panama did not consider that they were profiting enough and the annual rental paid by the U.S. (originally $250,000 a year and gradually increased to about twice that) had become unrealistic in terms of money's value today. In 1963 the U.S. agreed to negotiate a new treaty.

PANAMA. Area, 28,576 square miles (excluding the Panama Canal Zone, 553 square miles). Population (1964 estimate) 1,210,-000. Capital, Panama City. Language, Spanish. Religion, Roman Catholic. Government, republic. Monetary unit, the balboa, worth $1.00 (U.S.). Flag, rectangle of four quarters: white with blue star, blue, white with red star, and red.

Panama Canal

The Panama Canal is one of the most important waterways in the world. It crosses the Isthmus of Panama in Central America, so that ships that once had to go all the way around South America to get from Atlantic to Pacific ports can save nearly 8,000 miles by going through the canal.

The Panama Canal is a little more than 40 miles long from its Atlantic ports at Colón and Cristobal to its Pacific port at Balboa. Measured from its channel entrances—from Limon Bay in the Atlantic to the Bay of Panama in the Pacific—the Canal is a little more than 50 miles long. It was completed in 1914, and cost more than $365,000,000. Nearly half a million men worked seven years to build the canal.

HOW THE CANAL WAS BUILT

For centuries men had dreamed of a waterway that would connect the Atlantic and Pacific oceans. Many plans were made but it was not until almost a hundred years ago that the French began building a canal at Panama. Lack of proper digging equipment, tropical diseases that caused many deaths, and lack of money prevented the French from continuing. They sold their rights in the Panama region to the United States.

The United States and Great Britain had made a treaty, the Clayton-Bulwer treaty, under which the British were to have some rights in the canal. Before the United States could build the canal alone, this treaty had to be changed. The American Secretary of State, John Hay, and the British ambassador, Lord Pauncefote, made a new treaty in 1901. It is called the Hay-Pauncefote treaty. It gave the United States control of the canal but required the United States to permit all nations to use it.

Work on the Panama Canal began in 1907, after several years of planning. The work was done under United States Army engineers, headed by Colonel George Goethals. The difficult problem of fighting malaria and yellow fever was under the direction of Colonel W. C. Gorgas, whose heroic work has become famous in medical history.

Digging the Panama Canal was a tremendous job. The men had to cut through mountains, drain swamps, and dig huge ditches through jungles. To do this job hundreds of locomotives, barges, steam shovels and dredgers were used. Sometimes there were cave-ins and work was slowed up. In 1914 the first ship passed through the canal.

WHAT THE CANAL IS LIKE

The Panama Canal is made up of a series of locks through which ships pass. (There is a separate article about LOCKS.) The locks are in pairs so that ships can pass in both directions. There are six pairs of locks, each 1,000 feet long, 110 feet wide, and 70 feet deep. In the middle of the canal is Gatun Lake, an artificial lake formed by Gatun Dam. There are several other dams and lakes, including Miraflores Lake. It takes seven to eight hours for a ship to make the entire trip through the Panama Canal. More than ten thousand ships pass through the canal each year. See also CANAL.

Pan American Highway

The Pan American Highway is an automobile road that runs from Texas in the United States through Mexico, Central America, and South America. The entire route is about 15,000 miles long, but there are long stretches in Central America where no road has yet been built because of mountains and jungles.

The United States and other countries in the Americas began to plan the Pan American Highway in 1923. Each country agreed to pay for building the highway in its own territory, but the cost was so high that the United States gave millions of dollars to some of the poorer countries to help them build their parts of the highway. Mexico would not take any money from the United States, and it built its part of the highway without help.

The north end of the Pan American Highway route, called the Inter-American Highway, runs from El Paso and Laredo, Texas, through Mexico, and other sections have been built between Mexico and Panama City, Panama. In South America the highway runs from Venezuela to Ecuador, stops because of mountains, and begins again in Peru. It runs between Peru, Chile, Bolivia, and Argentina.

Most of the highway is paved, but there are places in high mountains where the road is blocked by snow in winter, and other places where mud and rivers block the way in rainy weather. Even so, automobiles can travel over the Pan American Highway for thousands of miles across mountains and through deserts and jungles, where people could travel only on foot or horseback a few years ago.

Pan-Americanism

Ever since the countries of North America, Central America and South America became independent states, most people have believed that all American countries should coöperate. The United States gave several South American countries help in winning their liberty from Spain, and by the Monroe Doctrine in 1823 the United States announced that it would not permit any European country to conquer and rule any American country. However the American countries were not always friendly with one another. In the last sixty years or so a greater effort has been made to bring representatives of all these countries together so that they could coöperate in matters that interest all of them.

PAN-AMERICAN UNION

Representatives of these countries had met at various times for many years, but in 1889 the first official Pan-American Conference was held in Washington, D.C. At this meeting was founded the American Republics Bureau. In 1910 its name was changed to Pan-American Union. The prefix Pan- means "all," so it was like saying "All-American." The day of the founding of the Union, April 14, was made Pan-American Day.

From that time on, meetings were held every few years in a different country. There were still difficulties, and sometimes wars, among nations of the Union, but as time passed coöperation became more frequent than disagreement.

In 1945 the Inter-American Conference on Problems of War and Peace was held in Mexico City, Mexico. This conference adopted the Act of Chapultepec,

by which twenty American nations agreed to take joint action in case of attack on any of them. At the 1948 conference the Organization of American States was established, and the Pan-American Union became the administrative agency for the larger body.

See also the article on the AMERICAS.

pancreas

The pancreas is a part of the body that is important in the digestion of food. The pancreas is about 5 or 6 inches long and an inch thick. It is in the abdomen. It is connected to the small intestine by a tube through which it pours the digestive juices that it manufactures. The juices help break down the starches, sugars, fats and proteins that enter the digestive system, so that they can be used by the body.

The juice called *insulin* is made by a part of the pancreas called the *Islets of Langerhans*. You can read more about insulin in the article DIABETES. The pancreas of some animals, such as the calf and lamb, is used as a meat. It is called *sweetbreads*.

panda

The panda is a large, attractive animal that looks like a bear but is really a member of the raccoon family. It makes its home high in the lonely mountains of China and Tibet. Although very few people have ever seen a panda in its natural home, it is one of the most popular animals in zoos. The panda was first brought to the United States about thirty years ago.

The panda is about six feet tall and weighs almost 200 pounds. It has white fur with black on its shoulders. The panda's legs are black. It has tiny black ears and two black cirles around its eyes. The panda is a good climber. It eats bamboo stalks and leaves and sometimes smaller animals. The female panda has one or two babies, called cubs, in the winter.

The lesser panda is a small panda that lives in the mountains of northern India and in some parts of China. It is about the size of a cat. It has beautiful dark red fur and a white head with a dark stripe that runs from its eyes to its mouth. It has a long, bushy tail. The lesser panda is a skillful climber. It makes its den in hollow trees.

Pandora

Pandora was the first woman, according to Greek mythology, the stories the ancient Greeks told about gods and goddesses. Zeus, king of all the gods, created Pandora and sent her to Prometheus and his brother Epimetheus. Pandora became the wife of Epimetheus, and she brought him great misfortune. Some legends say that Pandora was sent by Zeus as a punishment because Prometheus had stolen fire from heaven and given it to man. Another version of the story says that Zeus sent Pandora to earth to bless man. All of the gods had given wonderful gifts to Pandora. Epimetheus had a box that contained disease and envy and hatred and all of the evils of the world.

Pandora was curious, and she opened the box and all of the evils flew out.

The only thing that did not escape from the box was hope. After that mankind had to suffer many terrible things, but hope was left to him.

pansy

The pansy is a flower that grows in many parts of the world where the climate is not too hot or too cold. It was developed from the violet, and is sometimes called *heart's-ease*. The pansy's flowers form all season if the old blossoms are not allowed to go to seed. It is a perennial plant, which means that it grows from the same roots every year, but it is best to grow new plants each spring.

The flower of the pansy has a long, thin stem, and the leaves are green and oval-shaped. The flowers have large petals of yellow and white and many shades of purple and soft violet.

pantheon

In ancient Greece, a pantheon was a temple to all of the gods. The Romans took over the idea and the word, and one of the most famous Roman buildings still standing is the Pantheon in Rome. It was built in 27 B.C. by the Roman general Agrippa and rebuilt a hundred years after the birth of Jesus. Several hundred years later the Pantheon was made into a Christian church.

Another well-known pantheon is the one in Paris, France. This Pantheon was built in the 1700s as the Church of St. Genevieve. The French Revolutionists called it the Pantheon (meaning "of all the gods") to show their contempt for religion. Later the Pantheon was used as a burial place for many great Frenchmen, including Voltaire, Rousseau, Hugo, Zola, and others.

panther

A panther is a big wildcat—almost as big as a tiger or a lion. It lives in Asia from India to Siberia, and in most parts of Africa. The leopard and panther are the same, and the name panther is used chiefly for the black panther, which lives in Ethiopia and the East Indies. It is a solid jet black. See also the article LEOPARD.

pantomime

A pantomime is a play without words, acted out by gestures, bodily movements and facial expressions. Pantomime was very popular in ancient Rome, and it has been known among such peoples as the Chinese, Persians, Egyptians, and Hebrews. Traditional pantomime in England in the 1800s always had the same characters, which were taken originally from Italian comedy. They were Harlequin, Clown, Pantaloon, Scaramouche, and Columbine. The silent motion pictures required skill at pantomime, and Charles Chaplin was a master of the art. Modern ballet also depends largely on pantomime. The circus clown uses pantomime to create his character and make us laugh.

Papal States

The Papal States were lands in Italy ruled by the Pope, the religious leader of the Roman Catholic Church. They included much of Italy south of the Po River.

About a thousand years ago, it was a custom among noblemen to leave some of their land to the Church. The Papal States grew in size, but they were so far from Rome that few Popes ever completely controlled them. In 1796, Napoleon's French army invaded the Papal States, which the French then governed for about twenty years. They were then given back to the Pope, but in 1870 the king of Italy declared that they were part of Italy. There were many disputes between the Church and the Italian government over the Papal States. Finally, in 1929, the Pope and the Italian government led by Benito Mussolini agreed to establish Vatican City as the Pope's independent state, and in return the Pope gave up the Church's claims to the old Papal States.

papaya

Papaya is a sweet fruit that grows on a tree in the warm parts of South and Central America. The tree is also raised in southern California and Florida in the United States and on the Hawaiian Islands.

The papaya tree grows to be about 25 feet high. It is a deciduous tree, which means that it loses its leaves in the fall. The tree has yellow flowers, and the oval-shaped papaya fruit grows in clusters. The papaya fruit looks somewhat like a melon. It has a yellowish-orange color and a sweet taste. Papaya is eaten raw in salads and as a breakfast fruit. It is cooked in pies and in jams and preserves. The juice is used to make drinks. The fruit and other parts of the papaya tree contain a substance called latex that is used in chewing gum and in certain medicines.

paper

Paper is a thin, flexible material that is made from the fibers of wood or other materials pressed together. Paper is one of the most widely used products in the world today. Not only printed matter but boxes and packing materials, roofing and building materials, toys and games, and thousands of other things are made of paper or have some paper in them. Enough paper is made in the United States to give every person four hundred pounds of it each year.

HOW PAPER IS MADE

A sheet of paper is made up of thousands of tiny fibers that are about one-eighth of an inch long and about the thickness of a human hair. The fibers stick together because the outsides are rough. If you want to see these fibers, tear off a small piece of newspaper and look at the torn edge. The little white hairs that stick out are the fibers.

Almost all of the paper we use today is made of wood fiber. Rag fibers are used in the manufacture of fine writing paper, paper used for currency, and some special papers used in industry. Straw is also used, to make paperboard.

The story of paper made from wood begins in the forest where pine, spruce, fir, hemlock and poplar trees grow. These are cut down and the logs are cut into five-foot lengths for shipment to mills. These mills make pulp, which is a mixture of wood fibers and water. There are two ways of making pulp.

In one method the logs are ground in a machine with a rotating stone grinder that shreds the wood into very small particles. This pulp is called *groundwood* and is used to make newsprint (the paper on which newspapers are printed) and other cheap kinds of paper. Because groundwood contains many impurities, paper made from it yellows very quickly and does not last long.

Better kinds of paper come from pulp that is made by a chipping process. The wood is cut into chips about half an inch square and one-sixteenth of an inch thick. The chips are cooked with various chemicals that soften and separate the wood fibers, and the impurities are strained out.

From here on both the groundwood pulp and the chemical pulp follow the same steps to turn them into paper. The pulp is fed into a huge machine called a *Fourdrinier machine.* When pulp enters the Fourdrinier machine it consists of 99 parts of water to 1 part of fiber. When it comes out of the machine the paper consists of 96 parts of fiber and only 4 parts of water. So one of the most important jobs of the machine is to get rid of the water in the pulp and press the fibers together into sheets. This is done by rolling the pulp onto fine screens. The water runs through the screen and the fibers stay on top. A Fourdrinier machine can turn out newsprint 24 feet wide at rates up to 2,000 feet per minute. A big Fourdrinier machine is about as long as a city block and can cost well over a million dollars.

In the paper machine the pulp goes through various sets of rollers and drying compartments that get rid of the water and give the paper a firm finish. At the end of the dryers the roll of paper goes between revolving polished steel rolls, called *calenders,* which smooth and polish the surface of the paper so that it will have a good printing surface. If the paper is to be used for certain special printing or for photographs, it goes through another step called *coating.* Here a mixture of clay, casein and other materials is applied to the paper so that it has a very smooth, almost mirrorlike surface.

Some kinds of paper get a watermark in the paper-making machine. The watermark can be seen by holding the paper up to a light; it appears to be lighter than the rest of the paper. Watermarking is put into the paper by a pattern in the screen.

When the paper comes off the machine it is rolled onto a great spool and sent to another department of the paper factory where it is inspected and cut into flat sheets or smaller rolls.

SIZE AND WEIGHT OF PAPER

Paper is sold by the number of sheets, size of the sheet, and weight of the paper. When you buy a package of typewriter paper, which usually comes in the size 8½ by 11 inches, you may notice that the package will give the weight of the paper, usually 16 or 20 pounds. But, if you weigh the paper, you will find that it weighs much less than the pounds stated. Your stationer has not tried to cheat you. Paper weights are given for a ream (500 sheets) of a certain size, bigger than 8½ by 11. This is the paper's *basis weight.*

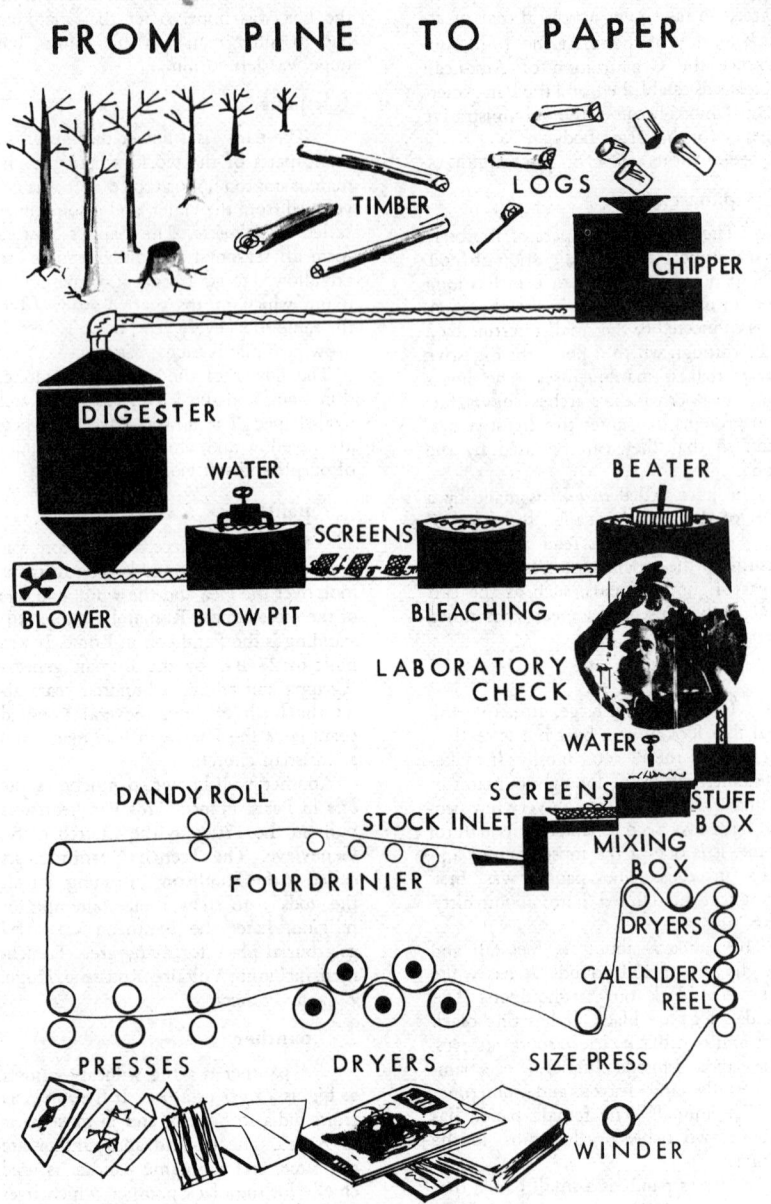

FROM PINE TO PAPER

TIMBER · LOGS · CHIPPER · DIGESTER · WATER · SCREENS · BEATER · BLOWER · BLOW PIT · BLEACHING · LABORATORY CHECK · WATER · DANDY ROLL · STOCK INLET · SCREENS · STUFF BOX · MIXING BOX · FOURDRINIER · DRYERS · CALENDERS · REEL · PRESSES · DRYERS · SIZE PRESS · WINDER

Basis weight is the weight of a ream of paper of a certain size. The standard size is usually a number of times larger than a popularly used page size. In the case of typewriter paper, the standard size sheet is 17 by 22 inches. Out of this standard sheet, four pieces of typewriter paper 8½ by 11 can be cut. This means that if your package says the basis weight is 20 pounds, 500 sheets of the 8½ by 11 paper will weigh 5 pounds (one-fourth of 20 pounds).

Other kinds of paper have different standard sizes on which the basis weights are computed. The standard size of many book papers, for example, is 25 by 38 inches. Actually the paper may be bought in any size the publisher wants, but its weight is figured on the 25 by 38 size. Most book paper comes in weights of 50 and 60 pounds.

THE STORY OF PAPER

When man first began to write, he used stone or clay to record his message. Then he began to use boards of wood, bamboo, and the skins of animals. The first use of anything at all like paper was by the Egyptians, who wrote on papyrus. Papyrus is a plant. The Egyptians split thin strips from the papyrus plant and glued them together. We get our word *paper* from papyrus.

The Chinese first invented paper, about the year 105. Their method of making paper was brought to the Western world by the Arabs in the year 751 and gradually spread to Europe, England, and North America. The first paper mill was opened in North America by William Rittenhouse in Germantown, Pennsylvania, in 1690.

Until the middle of the 19th century almost all paper was made of rag fibers. The idea of making paper from wood originated with a French scientist named René de Réaumur. He got this idea from watching a wasp. He saw the wasp take slivers and other small bits of wood, chew them to a pulp, and make his nest of the

pulp. In 1850 a machine was made that ground wood into fibers, and in 1865 an American, Benjamin Tilghman, invented a way of preparing pulp by a chemical method. The Fourdrinier machine was introduced in 1800.

Papermaking has developed into one of the world's most important industries. About 70 million tons of paper and paperboard are made each year. The leading pulp-and paper-producing countries are the United States, Canada, Sweden, Germany, England, Norway, Finland, and Japan. The United States manufactures and uses more paper than all the rest of the world put together. It uses so much paper that much of the wood for the pulp has to be imported from Canada. The leading papermaking states are New York, Wisconsin, Ohio, Louisiana, Maine, Pennsylvania, and Michigan. The states of Washington, Florida, Georgia, Louisiana, and Maine together make about 42 per cent of the wood pulp produced in the United States.

papier maché

Papier maché is a material that looks and feels much like cardboard, but instead of being in smooth sheets it is molded into different shapes and thicknesses. Papier maché is used to make simple toys such as party hats, false faces, and horns. The big figures of people, animals, and trees that decorate parade floats are usually made of papier maché. Much of the scenery used in stage plays is made of papier maché.

Papier maché is made of old newspapers, ground to a pulp and soaked in water. The resulting soft mush is mixed with glue and blown by compressed air into molds made of a fine wire mesh. The compressed air also blows the water out of the mush, and when the papier maché is dry it holds the shape of the mold.

The printing industry uses a kind of papier maché to make type matrices (called *mats*), but the pulp used has stronger fibers than common papier maché has. The mats are flat pieces of papier maché into which are pressed the type and engravings that are to be printed. This makes a mold. Hot metal is poured on the mat and takes the shapes that have been pressed into the mat. When the metal has cooled and hardened, the mat is removed and a metal plate remains that can be used directly in a printing press.

paprika

Paprika is a tasty, bright-red spice that comes from the seeds and fruit of a plant of the pepper family. The plant grows in many parts of Europe where the climate is not too cold. Hungarian paprika is one of the best-known of these plants. It has long, pointed fruits. The seeds and skin of the fruit are ground into a powder, which is the spice.

papyrus

Papyrus is a water plant that grows along the Nile River. It was used by the ancient Egyptians for many purposes. The roots were burned as fuel, and other parts were used for making sandals, boats, boxes, sails, and cloth. Its most famous use was as one of the first writing papers. Much that we know of ancient Egypt has been learned by deciphering the writing on ancient rolls of papyrus.

All kinds of documents have been found written on papyrus, rolled into thin tubes, stored in pottery jars and placed in the tombs of great Egyptians. One of the oldest bits of writing in the world is the *Presse Papyrus*, which is in a museum in Istanbul, Turkey. It is more than six thousand years old, and the first sentence reads: "Alas, times are not what they used to be. Everyone wants to write a book and children are no longer obedient to their parents."

parable

A parable is a story that is told to teach a lesson. Many of Jesus' teachings, in the New Testament, are in the form of parables.

Here is one of the parables that Jesus used when he was asked, "Who is my neighbor?" It is called the parable of the Good Samaritan, and it is repeated here as it is retold in the book *Hurlbut's Story of the Bible:*

A certain man was going down the lonely road from Jerusalem to Jericho; and he fell among robbers, who stripped him of all that he had and beat him; and then went away, leaving him almost dead. It happened that a certain priest was going down that road; and· when he saw the man lying there, he passed by on the other side. And a Levite also, when he came to the place and saw the man, he too went by on the other side. But a certain Samaritan, as he was going down, came where this man was; and as soon as he saw him, he felt a pity for him. He came to the man and dressed his wounds, pouring oil and wine into them. Then he lifted him up, set him on his own beast of burden, and walked beside him to an inn. There he took care of him all night; and the next morning he took out from his purse two shillings and gave them to the keeper of the inn and said, "Take care of him; and if you need to spend more than this, do so; and when I come again, I will pay it to you."

"Which one of these three do you think showed himself a neighbor to the man who fell among the robbers?"

The scribe said, "The one who showed mercy on him."

Then Jesus said to him, "Go and do thou likewise."

The Samaritans, the people who lived in Samaria, were looked down on by the Jews of Jesus' time. This story was meant to teach the lesson that every man is your neighbor, even a member of a hated people.

parabola

A parabola is a curve made by cutting a cone with a plane or knife along a line that is always at the same distance (parallel to) from the side or element of the cone, as shown in the diagram. Such curves are called *conic sections.* The path of a bullet, called its *trajectory,* and the cables of a suspension bridge are shaped very much like a parabola. There is a separate article on CONE.

Paracelsus

Paracelsus was a Swiss physician who lived more than 450 years ago. He was born in the year 1493. At that time, many people thought diseases were caused by certain conditions in a sick person's body that could not be changed by medicines or other treatment. Paracelsus studied both medicine and chemistry, and investigated especially the diseases of miners. He found that certain remedies did cure certain diseases. He introduced new medicines, including sulfur, opium, arsenic, and mercury. Many people opposed his teachings, and once they made him leave the university where he taught. Paracelsus died in 1541. Though some of his ideas have been proved false, Paracelsus made many valuable contributions to the science of medicine.

parachute

A parachute is a device that is used to slow down a fall from great heights. If you open an umbrella and try to run with it, you will notice that you are slowed down because the umbrella seems to pull against you. This is because the air rushing into the cup or canopy of the umbrella offers resistance to it. The same thing happens when a parachute is used. The parachute, being much bigger than an ordinary umbrella, is filled with much more air, and offers more resistance.

The parachute was first used about 180 years ago, in France, but did not become important until World War I. At that time the airplane became an important instrument of warfare. Many pilots were lost in airplane crashes before parachutes were used.

The standard parachute is 24 feet in diameter (across the bottom of it when it is open). It is made of silk or nylon and is extremely fine and light in weight. The main part of the parachute is called the canopy. It is made of 24 triangular pieces, so that if a tear occurs in any part triangular piece is made up of smaller pieces, so that if a tear occurs in any part it will be limited to a small piece.

The canopy is folded into a small bundle, or *pack,* and is attached by 24 long cords (*shroud lines*) to a harness worn by the aviator. There are three ways to wear a parachute: the seat pack, the back pack, and the chest pack. A pilot usually uses a seat pack or back pack, using either as a cushion to sit on or rest his back against. A paratrooper usually wears both a chest pack and a back pack, so if one fails to open he can use the other.

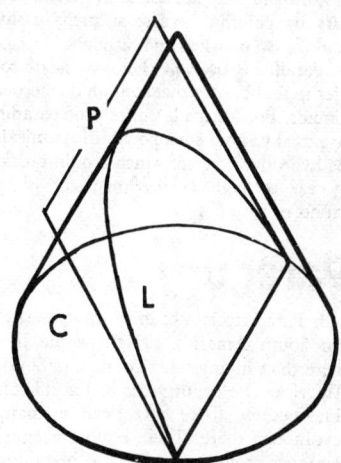

The plane (P) cutting a cone (C) forms a parabola (L). Note that the plane is parallel to one side of the cone.

A parachute opens when a ripcord is pulled by a handle on the pack. This opens the heavy cloth covering of the pack and allows the parachute silk to spill out and catch the air. Usually a small pilot 'chute is attached to the top of the main parachute. As this small 'chute catches the air, it pulls out the silk of the main parachute and makes it more certain that the main parachute will open.

A person wearing a parachute drops through the air at about 15 feet a second, which is 10 to 12 miles per hour. He can guide himself by pulling on the cords or shroud lines, that lead from the harness to the parachute. By pulling on the shroud lines on one side, the parachutist can make the parachute drift toward that side.

A parachute harness is made so that a person can get out of it quickly. This is important because sometimes a parachutist may land in water or in a high wind that would drag him across the ground.

Parachutes are also used to drop many types of equipment in wartime, including such heavy things as tanks and trucks. Of course, much larger parachutes are necessary for this work. Parachutes are used in peacetime to drop supplies and medicines to people in distress areas, places where there have been floods, fires, and earthquakes. They are also used as brakes on jet airplanes. The pilot of such a plane releases a parachute in the tail of the plane as he lands. The parachute helps to pull the plane to a stop.

paraffin

Paraffin is a colorless, odorless, tasteless substance. It is sometimes called mineral wax because it comes from mineral oil, or petroleum, and it looks and acts very much like wax. It is waterproof.

There are many uses for paraffin. It is used to make candles and tapers. When paraffin is worked into certain fabrics they become waterproof. It is also used as a sizing, which means that it is spread on wood or other materials before they are painted in order to fill and seal up the tiny cracks and holes. It is also used to make wrapping paper water- and moisture-proof, as in the lining of cereal and cracker boxes. Wood and the paper from which matches are made are often dipped into paraffin to make them burn steadily.

Jam and jelly are sealed in glasses and jars by paraffin because it melts easily and is also odorless and tasteless.

Paraffin is used in chemical laboratories to seal bottles that contain dangerous liquids. Bottles made entirely of paraffin are used to hold such powerful chemicals as hydrofluoric acid, which would quickly eat through bottles made of glass, stone, or metal.

Paraguay

Paraguay is a country in southeastern South America. Fewer people live there than in any other country in South America. The country has had a difficult time because there have been so many revolutions there. These have prevented Paraguay from prospering and becoming more modern. Paraguay is 157,647 square miles in size, which is about the size of California. About two million people live there, which is about one-ninth as many as live in California.

Most of the people are of mixed Spanish and Indian descent. Many people of Spanish descent live in the cities. There are also several thousand Indians, many of whom live as their ancestors did.

The people speak Spanish and an ancient Indian language called Guarani. Most of them belong to the Roman Catholic Church.

Most of the people are farmers and they are very poor. They grow cotton, sugar cane, rice, and tobacco, they also raise cattle. A much smaller number of rich people own great stretches of land and rent out small portions to farmers. Some people work in the forests, from which various products come, such as maté or Paraguay tea, vanilla, and cinnamon. The people who live in the cities work in meat-packing and sugar-refining plants, and in factories that make molasses, rum, tea, and cigars.

Although there are some free elementary schools, many children do not go to school. In some parts of the country there are no schools at all.

WHAT PARAGUAY IS LIKE

The eastern part of Paraguay is a fertile lowland with dense forests. Most of the people live in this eastern section. The capital, Asunción, and other large cities are on the Paraguay River. The region west of the Paraguay River is made up of large grassy plains, with forests and several rivers. Cattle are raised in the western region. In the northwest is a region called the Chaco, where the Indian tribes live. Part of this grassy region has still not been explored.

The Paraguay and Paraná Rivers are the most important in the country. Ships can travel on the Paraguay from the Atlantic Ocean to Asunción. Part of the Paraná is navigable, but in many places it has rapids and very beautiful waterfalls.

Many wild animals wander through the forests of Paraguay, including the jaguar, puma, and deer. There are also many alligators and poisonous snakes.

The climate of Paraguay is subtropical, which means it is like that of Florida. In summer (which is when Florida is having winter), the temperature may go as high as 100 degrees. In winter, the temperature is a pleasant 65 degrees.

Paraguay has few railway lines, but new roads through the western region and to the Brazilian port of Paranagua have improved transportation. Before they were built, the rivers were the best means of transportation.

HOW THE PEOPLE ARE GOVERNED

Paraguay is a republic, with a president, a legislature that makes the laws, and a constitution that protects the rights of the people. The president is elected for a five-year term, but various presidents have taken away many of the rights of the people and have become dictators. The legislature is composed of one house. Asunción, the capital, is the largest city. There is a separate article about ASUNCION.

PARAGUAY IN THE PAST

The first white man to explore the region of Paraguay was Sebastian Cabot, more than four hundred years ago. Soon afterward, Spain sent men who claimed the region as a Spanish colony. When Jesuit priests were influential in the colony it grew, but when they were forced to leave by order of the Spanish king, about two hundred years ago, Paraguay made no further progress. It has remained a backward and poor country.

Under various dictatorships the army of Paraguay was made extremely powerful, and in 1865 the country went to war against Brazil, Argentina, and Uruguay. The war lasted for five years and left Paraguay ruined. More than half the people of Paraguay were killed. Since then Paraguay has fought other costly wars against Bolivia, as told in the articles GRAN CHACO and BOLIVIA. During World War II Paraguay helped the United States. Afterwards it joined the United Nations.

PARAGUAY. Area, 157,647 square miles.

Cultural Institute of Paraguay

La Amistad ("Friendship") Bridge over the River Parana in Paraguay.

Population (1973 estimate) 2,680,000. Capital, Asuncion. Language, Spanish and Guarani. Religion, Roman Catholic. Government, republic. Monetary unit, the guarani, worth about 1 cent (U.S.) Flag, three horizontal bars, red, white, and blue; also the republic's coat of arms; on the back of the flag a lion and the inscription *Paz y Justicia* (Peace and Justice).

parakeet

The parakeet is a small bird that is a member of the parrot family. It can be trained to talk, as a parrot can, and to do many tricks. It makes its home in many parts of the world where the climate is hot.

One kind of parakeet used to live in the southern part of the United States. It was called the Carolina parakeet. It was a beautiful little bird with bright yellow-and-green feathers and a long tail. It made its nest in hollow trees. The female parakeet laid between three and five white eggs. These birds were hunted for sport and also because their feathers were very popular as decorations for women's hats and fans. Parakeets eat fruit, and farmers often shot them because of this. So many Carolina parakeets were killed that they are no longer seen. The last ones were seen in Florida 60 years ago.

Many parakeets now are brought to the United States from other parts of the world, and they are very popular as household pets.

paralysis

Paralysis means loss of movement. The normal, healthy human body is able to move in many ways and in many directions. When something happens to part of the body and it is unable to move in a normal way, paralysis has occurred.

Movement is possible because the bones are jointed, because muscles are attached to the bones, and because nerves cause the muscles to act. If something happens either to the joints, to the muscles, or to the nerves, paralysis will result.

Paralysis can also be present in parts of the body that are not jointed. Our lungs can become paralyzed, or even our digestive system. This is because the muscles that cause the chest to move and make breathing possible, or the muscles that cause the stomach to churn our food, lose their ability to act properly. This may be because the muscles themselves are damaged or because the nerves connected with these muscles are damaged or destroyed.

Paralysis may be temporary or it may be permanent. Temporary paralysis is usually caused by some disease or injury that for a short time affects nerves or muscles. Permanent paralysis is the result of a disease or an injury that completely destroys or injures nerves or muscles. If you read the article on the NERVOUS SYSTEM you will see how the brain and the spinal cord control movement. If anything happens to a part of the brain or the spinal cord, paralysis in some part of the body may result. Thus there are certain nervous-system diseases that cause paralysis. Among the better-known of these diseases are infantile paralysis, multiple sclerosis, and cerebral palsy.

CEREBRAL PALSY

Cerebral palsy is not a disease, but it is a condition in which some part of the brain is damaged. This usually happens at birth, and as a result the person having cerebral palsy is unable to do some of the normal things that we all do. A person with cerebral palsy may have complete intelligence but find it difficult or impossible to make certain movements or do certain things such as talk.

MULTIPLE SCLEROSIS

In the disease called multiple sclerosis, the paralysis occurs because damage is done to the covering of the nerves. The damage is somewhat like a short circuit in the wires of an electrical system. It makes it impossible for the messages to be sent along these nerves that control the action of muscles in various parts of the body.

PARAPLEGIA

A person who is paralyzed in both legs is called a *paraplegic*. Most often this is the result of injury to the spinal cord. It is usually an injury in the lower part of the spinal cord, which controls the movements of the legs. Many men who have been in war and have suffered an injury to their spinal cords are paraplegics.

There is a separate article on INFANTILE PARALYSIS, or poliomyelitis.

Paraná River

The Paraná River, the second-largest river in South America next to the Amazon River, is 2,025 miles long. It starts in Brazil and flows south along the border of Paraguay. This part of the river has some of the highest and most beautiful falls in South America. The current is so swift here that ships cannot travel on it. The Paraná is joined further on by the Paraguay River, its largest branch, and continues its course through dense jungles and through part of Argentina. There it joins the Uruguay River. It finally empties into the Atlantic Ocean through Rio de la Plata estuary. Ocean vessels can travel up the lower part of the Paraná. Some of its most important ports are Rosario, Paraná, and Santa Fé.

paraplegia, the condition in which the lower half of the body is paralyzed: see the article PARALYSIS.

parasite

A parasite is an animal or plant that receives food or shelter or some other benefit from another animal or plant, which is called the *host*. The parasite gains from its relationship with the host, and the host always suffers. Some parasites take advantage of their hosts only for a short time. The pesty bedbug, which lives on the blood of human beings, is an example of this kind of parasite called a *temporary parasite*. Other parasites, such as tapeworms, are called *stationary parasites* because they live off the host for a long time. Some parasites live on the skin of other animals. Lice live on the skin of birds and other animals, including men. Some parasites live in the intestines of animals. Many of these are worms.

Some plants are parasites and live on the roots, leaves, stems and fruit of other plants, or on animals. Many kinds of fungus and mold are parasites. Bacteria are parasites and some of them cause serious diseases. Some pretty plants such as the mistletoe are also parasites.

paratroops

Paratroops are army forces that are dropped by parachute behind enemy lines, to surprise the enemy from the rear or to prepare for the coming of ground forces. Paratroops are also called *airborne forces,* and a soldier trained for this work is called a *paratrooper.* Paratroopers are very proud of their assignments and often consider themselves the elite, or best men, of the army. Usually they wear special emblems and dress. The French paratrooper wears a red beret, and the American paratrooper wears highly polished boots and a patch on his cap.

The use of paratroops was first thought of during World War I. The United States planned to use them against Germany, but the war ended before this plan was carried out. The first big maneuvers with paratroops were made by Russia in 1931, and nine years later paratroops were used by the German army when it invaded the Netherlands. During World War II the United States trained large numbers of paratroops, or airborne forces, and several divisions of them took part in the war in Europe and later in the Korean War. Today most of the paratroopers of the United States Army belong to the 18th Airborne Corps.

All paratroopers in the United States Army are volunteers, which means they choose to be trained for this work. First they must pass a difficult physical examination. Then they are sent to the Airborne School at Fort Benning, Georgia, where they learn how to jump with parachutes and also receive special physical training. First the student jumps off a platform a few feet high. When he has learned the correct way to land or fall on the ground, he learns how to jump from a tower thirty feet high. In this exercise, the student wears a harness that is attached to a guide rope. When he jumps off the tower his fall is stopped by a sharp pull from the rope, which is like the pull of a parachute as it opens, and he lands on the ground safely. Finally he must learn to jump from a tower 250 feet high. He is pulled to the top of the tower by cables attached to a frame that holds his parachute. His parachute is open. When he reaches the top of the tower, the parachute is released, and he drops down with it. When he has learned how to do this correctly, he is ready to jump from an airplane.

Paratroops have become very important in modern warfare, because of the increasing importance of air power. Some military experts have said that the armies of the future will be made up mainly of paratroopers.

parchment

Parchment is animal skin prepared for use in writing. Originally all parchment was made of sheepskin, but later the skins of goats and calves also were used. *Vellum* is a finer grade of parchment, made from the skins of calves or kids. Parchment and vellum are made by soaking the animal skins in water, treating them with lime to remove the hair, and then washing and stretching them. After the skins are dried they are rubbed with pumice stone to make them smooth.

Fine parchment and vellum still are

used for college diplomas, fine books, lamp shades, and other things. Heavy parchment is used for such things as drumheads.

parent-teacher association

Parents of children in grammar schools and high schools are encouraged to join the parent-teacher associations of these schools. These associations, often called PTA's, help the parents to learn what is being taught to the children and how the school is run. The parents meet their children's teachers, and at regular meetings held in the schools they discuss various school problems. Often the parent-teacher associations raise money to buy things for the schools that are not supplied by the Board of Education. In the United States, about ten million parents and teachers are members of the 47,000 local parent-teacher associations. These belong to the National Congress of Parents and Teachers, which has its headquarters in Chicago, Illinois.

Paricutín

Paricutín, in Mexico, is the youngest volcano in the world. Until 1943, it did not exist. On February 20, 1943, steam began coming out of a cornfield. The volcano kept erupting and building up a cone of cinders. By the end of a year, Paricutín was more than 1,500 feet high. It has been growing at a slower rate since then. Many people have visited Mexico to see Paricutín.

Paris (prince)

Paris was a handsome young man who is told about in Greek mythology, the stories the ancient Greeks told about their gods and goddesses. Paris was the son of Priam, king of Troy. Because it was predicted that Paris would cause the ruin of Troy, when he was a baby his parents left Paris on a lonely mountain. Fortunately, a shepherd found him and brought him up.

The goddesses Athena, Hera and Aphrodite had a quarrel about which of them was the most beautiful. (In Roman mythology these goddesses are called Minerva, Juno, and Venus.) The most beautiful goddess was to receive a golden apple. They agreed to let Paris settle their quarrel. Each of the goddesses promised Paris wonderful presents if he chose her. Aphrodite promised him the most beautiful woman in the world for his wife. Paris decided in favor of Aphrodite.

Aphrodite sent Paris to the home of the Greek prince Menelaus, because his wife, Helen, was the most beautiful woman in the world. Paris stole Helen and took her away with him to Troy. Because of this, the Greeks attacked Troy, and the TROJAN WARS (about which there is a separate article) were fought.

Paris, France

Paris is the capital and largest city of France. It is on the Seine River. It is one of the best-known and most beautiful capitals in the world, and people go there to see its sights, to study, and to enjoy its gay life. It is called the "City of Light." Many writers and painters have gone there to study or live. Paris is also a great fashion center, and some of the world's most famous designers of women's clothing are in Paris.

French Gov't Tourist Office

The Eiffel Tower is a symbol of Paris to people the world over. It is on the left bank of the Seine, and has been visited by many millions of people since it was built.

About three million people live in Paris. There are factories that make women's clothing, perfume, hats, and jewelry, for which Paris is famous. There are big plants that make automobiles, machinery, chemicals, and dyes. Paris prints more books, magazines and newspapers than any other city in France.

WHAT PARIS IS LIKE

A person visiting Paris can spend months enjoying all its sights. The city is known for its wide, tree-lined boulevards, its gardens and fountains, and its sidewalk cafés, where people may sit at tables outdoors in the warm weather.

Perhaps the most famous sight in Paris is the EIFFEL TOWER, the tallest structure in Europe. With its TV antenna, it is 1,056 feet high. One of the best-known streets is the Champs Elysées. At one end of this boulevard stands the Arch of Triumph (about which you can read in the article on ARCH). Another noted street is the Rue de la Paix, where people shop in luxurious stores as they do on Fifth Avenue in New York City.

Paris has many historic churches, museums, and buildings. Every year thousands visit Notre Dame Cathedral, a splendid example of Gothic architecture. It is on a little island in the Seine called the *Ile de la Cité* (Island of the City). Many also visit a building with a high dome called *Les Invalides*, where the body of Napoleon rests. Few leave Paris without seeing the world-renowned museum, the Louvre, or the magnificent Opéra. Another popular place is Montmartre, the colorful entertainment section of Paris, with its steep, narrow streets. Montmartre is a hill, the highest point in Paris, and at the top stands the Sacré Coeur, a beautiful white church from which a person can get a wonderful view of the entire city. All through Paris are monuments to French patriots and heroes.

Paris has a number of important colleges and universities. The University of Paris is one of the oldest in the world. One of its schools, the Sorbonne, is more than 750 years old. Students from many countries study there. The University of Paris is on the side of the Seine River called the Left Bank. Many painters live in the section called the Left Bank, and

visitors may see some of them painting out-of-doors and selling their works on the sidewalks.

Paris is one of the communications and travel centers of Europe. Railroads and highways branch out into all directions to other capitals and large cities. Airplanes from Britain, North America, the Middle East, North Africa and from other European cities land at its big airports. Paris is an inland port, and ships can travel on the Seine River to the English Channel. Paris has a large subway system called the Métro. The Paris stock exchange, called the Bourse, is one of the most important in the world.

PARIS IN THE PAST

Paris is a very old city. It was a little fishing village in ancient Roman times, two thousand years ago. Eight hundred years ago it had already become a great center of learning and was the capital of the kings of France.

During World War I, the Germans came close to capturing Paris but never took it. In World II, the Germans did take the city and occupied it until 1944. All during the war, many of the people of Paris worked in underground groups and fought the Germans as best they could. Paris was not damaged much during the war except in the suburbs where the large factories stood.

THE TREATIES OF PARIS

Many important treaties in history have been signed in Paris. In 1763, the treaty ending the French and Indian Wars between the French and the British was signed in Paris. The signing of the treaty that ended the Revolutionary War between Great Britain and the American colonies, making the United States an independent nation, was signed in Paris in 1783. The defeat of Napoleon in the Na-

French Gov't Tourist Office

Napoleon is buried under the gilded dome of Les Invalides. The group of buildings was a hospital for disabled soldiers when it was built by Louis XIV in 1671.

poleonic wars ended in a treaty signed in Paris in 1814. In the following year, a second treaty was signed after Napoleon's final defeat at Waterloo. The Crimean War, between Russia on one side and France, England, Turkey and Sardinia on the other side, ended in a treaty signed in Paris in 1856. In 1898 Paris was chosen as the place to sign the treaty between the United States and Spain after the Spanish-American War. After World War I, the Peace Conference met in Paris and in nearby places where treaties with the various countries were signed. The fa-

mous treaty with Germany in 1919 was signed at Versailles, outside Paris. After World War II, several treaties were signed in Paris.

PARIS, FRANCE. Population (1969 estimate) 2,607,625. Capital and largest city of France. On Seine River.

Parkman, Francis

Francis Parkman was an important American writer and historian. He was born in Boston in 1823. After he was graduated from Harvard University, Parkman went to the West to study the Indians. His health was never good, and the hard life on the frontier was too much for him. After two years he returned to Boston in a very weak condition. His eyesight was so poor that he could not see to write. He dictated his best-known book, called *The Oregon Trail*. It was published in 1849 and told the exciting story of his adventures in the Far West. The book is still very popular. Parkman also became an authority on flowers. He died in 1893, when he was 70 years old.

parliament

Parliament is the name of the British law-making body and the law-making bodies of many other countries, such as Canada and France, which are based on the English Parliament.

The British Parliament dates from the year 1295, but its nature has changed quite a bit in the six hundred years since then. The parliamentary system, which is used by most countries, is quite different from the United States system. Parliament is the law-making body, as Congress is, but it has both legislative and executive powers. The President of the United States and the Prime Minister of England are different because the President is not a member of Congress, while the Prime Minister is a member of Parliament and is the chairman of its executive committee.

There are two branches of Parliament, the House of Lords and the House of Commons. The head of any family that has a title of nobility, from baron up, is automatically entitled to be a member of the House of Lords. Such members are called hereditary peers. Only men can be hereditary peers. Additional members of the House of Lords are the archbishops and most important bishops of the Church of England, the principal judges of the courts of law, and—since 1957—a new class of members called "life peers," who may be either men or women. Life peers have titles of nobility but their children do not inherit these titles.

Anyone who is not a member of the House of Lords can be elected to the House of Commons. He becomes a Member of Parliament and uses the initials M.P. after his name.

Either house of Parliament may pass a law. The law does not become effective until it is passed by both houses except that after one year the House of Commons can make a law final even if the House of Lords voted against it. This makes Commons so much more powerful than the House of Lords that many English statesmen have refused titles of nobility rather than give up the right to be members of the House of Commons. In 1963 it became legal for a lord to give up his title so that he can be eligible for election to the Commons.

The leader of the political party that has a majority in the House of Commons is the head of the British government and is called the Prime Minister. He is appointed by the king or queen, but actually the king or queen cannot refuse to appoint anyone that this majority party wants. The Prime Minister could be a member of the House of Lords, and at one time he often was, but today this is almost impossible. When no party has a majority in the Commons, two or more parties may agree on a Prime Minister and form a *coalition government*.

The Prime Minister has a cabinet of chief government officials who assist him, and they also are chosen by the majority party. The Prime Minister and his cabinet are called "the government" or "Her Majesty's Government." Members of the cabinet can be members of either the House of Commons or the House of Lords. Members of the minority party are called Her Majesty's Loyal Opposition.

The two houses meet separately. They debate questions and vote just as any other law-making body does. For hundreds of years they had a most unusual method of voting. When a question was put to a vote, "the house divided." All of the members would walk out of the meeting room. Those in favor of the question would enter a room on one side and those against the question would enter a room on the other side. Then the members in each room were counted to find out which had a majority. Seats for the members are divided so that all the members of one of the principal parties sit on one side of the room and the members of the other party or parties sit on the other side. The members of the government, that is, the cabinet, sit on a bench facing the other members. Each party chooses a member to be party *whip*. The whip's job is to make sure members of his party are present for important votes and that they vote the way the majority wants them to.

The cabinet, through the Prime Minister, usually suggests whatever laws Parliament is asked to pass. If Parliament fails to pass an important law proposed by the Prime Minister, he is supposed to resign. Then if any other person can get a majority, the king is supposed to appoint him Prime Minister. If not, the entire House of Commons is dissolved (ended) and a national election is held to elect a new House of Commons. Even if the Prime Minister continues to have the support of Parliament, which is called "having its confidence," there is supposed to be an election at least once every five years. The Prime Minister may call for an election at any time. There is no limit on the number of terms a member may serve, and prominent members almost always are elected time after time.

TRADITIONS OF PARLIAMENT

The debate or argument in both Houses of Parliament is likely to be very loud and angry, with the members hurling insults at one another. They are not permitted to use personal insults, but they can attack the ideas of the other members. Usually the debates do not lead to hard feelings outside, but sometimes they do. The king or queen is never permitted to enter the House of Commons. This is a rule that was adopted many years ago to keep the king or queen from using personal popularity to influence the voting of the members.

At the opening of each session of Parliament, the king or queen addresses the Parliament. Today Queen Elizabeth II would go to the House of Lords, and a messenger would be sent to summon the House of Commons. All the members of the House of Commons would walk into the House of Lords to listen to the queen outlining what kind of laws she expects the government to propose. Even if she disagrees with these proposals, if the Prime Minister and the cabinet want them she must propose them herself.

The House of Commons has 630 members. Of these, 511 are for England, 36 for Wales and Monmouth, 71 for Scotland, and 12 for Northern Ireland. Most of these members are usually present when Commons is in session. The House of Lords had 915 eligible members in 1962, but very seldom do that many choose to take part in the work of the House. The Prince of Wales and other princes of the royal family are usually made members of the House of Lords, but the king or queen does not have to make them members. The two archbishops and the bishops of the Church of England are always members. In 1958 women became eligible for the House of Lords as well as Commons.

Both houses of Parliament meet in Westminster Palace, which used to be the home of the kings of England. In World War II the meeting room used by the House of Commons was almost completely destroyed by German bombs. The British considered this almost a blessing, because the room had become much too small. The House of Commons met in the quarters of the House of Lords until their quarters could be rebuilt.

Before any new Parliament meets, the palace is searched for bombs or explosives. This is because of the Gunpowder Plot in 1605, an attempt to blow up both houses of Parliament, about which you can read in the article on Guy FAWKES.

A member of the House of Lords, if accused of crime, can be tried only by the House of Lords. A member of the House of Commons has even more immunities than a member of Congress in the United States. There is almost nothing for which he can be sued, and he cannot be held accountable for libel for anything he says in Parliament.

OTHER PARLIAMENTS

The Canadian Parliament is based on the English Parliament, except that the Governor General exercises the functions of the king or queen. The upper house is called the Senate instead of the House of Lords, and its members are appointed by the cabinet.

When France formed the Third Republic in 1871 it based its parliament on the British Parliament, except that it had no king or queen. The Parliament elected a president who was not supposed to be a member of, or to favor, any party. The members of the Senate were appointed for life by the president so that they could not lose their seats. The Chamber of Deputies was elected by the people as the House of

Commons is. The French Parliament now works about the same, but a few changes were made in the constitution adopted in 1958. See the article on FRANCE.

The Australian Parliament is more like the United States Congress in that members of both houses are elected by the people. Most of the countries of Europe have some form of parliament that works like the British or French parliament.

parliamentary law

Parliamentary law is the special set of rules that governs behavior and procedure in any law-making body or in any meeting of an organization or group that has the power to make decisions, such as a club. The word comes from the English Parliament, and most parliamentary law is based on rules originally established in that Parliament. Every important law-making body makes special rules of its own or changes the rules as it pleases. Most groups and organizations follow rules of parliamentary law written about seventy years ago by either of two men, Luther S. Cushing, who wrote *Cushing's Manual*, or Henry M. Robert, who wrote *Robert's Rules of Order*.

Under parliamentary law, a meeting goes like this: One person is the presiding officer, called the *president* or *chairman*. All members have an equal right to speak, but the chairman decides who "has the floor," or has the right to speak at any particular time. When the chairman gives a person permission to speak, he is said to "recognize" him.

In order for the meeting to take action on any question, one member must make a proposal in the form of a *motion*. He asks the chairman for the floor and then says something like this: "I move that the club do so and so." If he wants the meeting to make a formal statement of what it thinks about something, his motion may begin "Resolved, that so and so," and if this kind of motion is approved it is called a *resolution*. Before any motion can be discussed and voted upon, it must be *seconded* by another member, who may merely say "I second the motion." Then the chairman opens the floor for debate.

If another member thinks the motion is a good one but has a change he wants to make in it, he will move to *amend* the motion, and his *amendment* must be voted upon before the motion itself can come to a vote.

After everyone has had a chance to speak for or against the proposal, and when no one else wants the floor, the chairman will ask the members if they are "ready for the question." A member may "call for the question" at any time during the debate, and if two-thirds of the members agree with him the debate ends and the question is voted upon immediately. In a voice vote all those in favor of the question say "Aye," and then those opposed say "No," and the chairman decides whether more members were for or against the motion. Sometimes it is impossible to be sure, and a standing vote is taken. Those in favor stand up and are counted, and then those against stand up and are counted. In large bodies such as the United States Congress, and on important questions, each member votes separately and publicly announces whether he is for or against the question.

Parliamentary law is extremely complicated. There are dozens of rules as to who is entitled to speak, what should be voted on first, when a motion may be amended or tabled (postponed for discussion at a later meeting). Many organizations and legislatures have special rules governing debate. For example, in the United States Senate when a man gets the floor he may speak as long as he wants, even for days at a time, and no one can stop him. In the House of Representatives, and in most other organizations, there is some definite limit on how long a member may speak.

One motion takes precedence over all others. That is the motion to adjourn, or end the meeting. If two-thirds of the members vote to adjourn, the meeting must be ended at once.

Parnell, Charles Stewart

Charles Stewart Parnell was a great Irish statesman who lived about a hundred years ago. He was born in 1846. He went to school at Cambridge, England, but then returned to Ireland. In 1875 he was elected to Parliament. For the rest of  his life he fought very hard to help the people of Ireland become independent of England. Parnell had many enemies and finally he was put in jail. While he was in jail he wrote a famous letter to the Irish people that was called the "No Rent Manifesto." Parnell told the people not to pay any rent to the English landowners.

Parnell was so popular with most of the Irish people that he was called the "uncrowned king of Ireland." The last few years of his life were sad. He had many difficulties in his personal life. When these became known many of his supporters turned against him. In 1891 he married Katherine O'Shea, but he died a few months later.

parole and probation

Parole means "word of honor." It is used in the case of people who have been convicted of crimes and put in prison but are let out before they have finished their full prison term. They are let out on the condition that they will lead good and useful lives. During the period between the time they are let out and the time that their prison terms end they are said to be "on parole."

Every state in the United States has a parole board. Usually it is made up of citizens who are not police officers or prison officials. After a prisoner has served part of his time he can apply for parole. The parole board studies his case, and if the members think he will be a useful citizen he is allowed to appear before them. Then they make their final decision.

While a person is on parole he is supposed to have a regular job, and he is not allowed to do certain things that are considered to lead to bad companionship, such as drinking and gambling. He has to report once a week or once a month, depending on the law in his state, to an official called the parole officer.

Probation is like parole except that a person is put on probation when he is not in prison but when he has committed some crime for which he could be sent to prison.

Parole is also used in warfare and is recognized in international law. When a military officer becomes a prisoner of war he is permitted to give his parole, or "word of honor," that he will not try to escape. If he does this, he is often given a great deal of personal freedom and can come and go as he pleases within the enemy country where he is imprisoned.

parrot

The parrot is the most popular of all birds that are kept as pets. There are more than three hundred different kinds of parrot. Most of them are found in parts of the world where it is very warm.

There are parrots that are only about the size of a bluebird, and others, such as the great macaw, that are about three feet long. One kind of very small parrot is called the lovebird, because the male and female are so faithful and affectionate to each other. A kind of medium-sized parrot called the parrakeet is a popular pet because it is easy to tame. Most parrots are brilliant birds with gorgeous green feathers that have touches of blue, red, yellow, or black or white color. Parrots have large heads and small, bright eyes. They have strong, curved bills. Their claws are powerful and they are able to grasp a tree or hold a nut in their claws. Parrots are strong fliers. They often travel in flocks.

Most parrots make their nests in a hollowed-out place on the ground or in the side of a cliff. Sometimes a parrot will rob the nest of another bird. The female parrot lays two or three white eggs. Smaller parrots lay as many as twelve eggs. Parrots eat nuts, fruit, and seeds.

Parrots are able to copy the sounds of other animals. They can imitate the sound of laughter and crying, and many parrots can be taught to talk. Many people keep parrots as pets. Parrots sometimes carry the germs of a serious disease called psittacosis that people can catch, so for some time it was against the law to take parrots into the United States. Then doctors found a cure for the disease and now parrots are allowed into the United States.

Parsees

The Parsees are a religious group that live in India. They are descendants of people who went there from Persia more than 1,200 years ago. These people were followers of a man named Zoroaster. They believed and still believe in the worship of fire. The name Parsee comes from the name Persian. These people pray at altars where a sacred fire is kept burning constantly.

parsley

Parsley is a herb that grows on the rocky coasts of the Mediterranean Sea in Europe and in many other parts of the world where the climate is cool. Parsley plants usually have curled fernlike leaves. Parsley is a biennial, which means that it grows the leaves we eat the first year, then produces flowers and seed the next year, and then dies.

Parsley leaves are used to decorate meat dishes. The leaves are often cooked with meat or eggs and are used to flavor soups and in stuffing for chickens and

turkeys. Some people cook the thick roots of a kind called Hamburg parsley that is raised in Germany. They eat these white roots as a vegetable.

parsnip

The parsnip is a plant that first grew in Europe. It is now grown in many parts of the world where the climate is not too warm. The leaves of the parsnip plant grow two or three feet long. The plant has thick white roots. The root of the parsnip contains sugar, and many people cook and eat the parsnip root as a vegetable.

Parthenon

The Parthenon was a temple to the Greek goddess Athena. It was built in Athens, Greece, 2,500 years ago, on the ACROPOLIS, about which you can read in a separate article. The Parthenon is now in ruins, but it is considered the finest example of Greek architecture and the ornamentation was planned by the greatest Greek sculptor, Phidias.

partnership

A partnership is formed by two or more people who own a business together. They may select some name, called a firm name, under which they do business; or they may use the names of the partners. Large businesses usually are not partnerships but corporations. A part-owner of a corporation is not personally responsible for debts of the corporation, but in a partnership each partner is responsible for the debts of the partnership, even if it was one of the other partners who caused the debt. Firms of lawyers are always partnerships, and some other professional men, such as accountants, form partnerships and not corporations. A "silent partner" is a person who owns part of a partnership but does not do any of the work of running it. A "limited partner" is a person who owns part of the business but who is not responsible for all the debts of the partnership.

part of speech

A word becomes a part of speech when it is used in a sentence. A sentence tells about, or asks about, something that happens. Part of the sentence must say what makes it happen; another part of the sentence must say how it happens. Different parts of speech have different uses in making the sentence complete.

In English, the parts of speech are: noun, verb, adjective, adverb, pronoun, preposition, conjunction, and interjection. There is a separate article about each of these parts of speech.

The same word may act as more than one part of speech, depending on how it is used in the sentence. For example, "The fly is walking on the wall, but it can fly through the air." The first time, *fly* is a noun; the second time it is a verb.

partridge

The partridge is a bird that lives in Europe, Canada, and the United States. The partridge is a member of the pheasant family. It is a bird for which hunters go hunting. Some partridges are called *quails*. The most common partridge in the United States is the BOBWHITE, about which there is a separate article.

The European gray partridge is an attractive gray bird with a reddish-brown tail. It is an important bird in Canada.

passionflower

The passionflower is an unusual plant that grows in Central and South America and in the southern parts of the United States where the climate is warm. There are many plants that belong to the passionflower family. They are climbing plants. The flowers are about two inches across. The petals are white or purple. Over the petals there is a circle of tiny stalks (called filaments). Out of this circle rises a stalk with five seed pods.

When the early Spanish explorers first saw the passionflower in South America, they made up stories connecting its parts with events in the life of Jesus. The leaves, for example, they said were the hands of the people who persecuted Jesus, and the circle of tiny stalks was the crown of thorns. It got its name from the suffering, or passion, of Jesus.

Passion Play

A Passion Play is the acting out of the passion, or suffering and death, of Jesus as told in the New Testament. Six or eight hundred years ago, *Passion Plays* were put on by many groups of actors and in many cities and towns. Today the most famous performance of the Passion Play takes place once every ten years, at Easter, in the village of Oberammergau, Germany. It was first given there more than three hundred years ago, in the year 1634. At that time there had been a terrible plague, a disease that had killed millions. Then the plague ended. The villagers of Oberammergau were so thankful that they vowed to give the Passion Play every ten years. The play is put on outdoors and takes a whole morning and afternoon to perform. More than seven hundred villagers take part in it, and many of the parts have been passed on from father to son for hundreds of years. Several towns in the United States also hold Passion Plays. One version is called *Veronica's Veil*, and it has been given every year since 1914 in Union City, New Jersey.

Passover

Passover is one of the greatest yearly festivals of the Jewish religion. It begins on the fourteenth day of the Jewish month Nisan, and lasts for eight days. This is in late March or early April.

The feast of Passover is celebrated in memory of the time when the Jews escaped from Egypt, where they had been enslaved. This is told in the Bible, in the Book of Exodus.

During Passover the Jews eat only matzoth, or unleavened bread. Unleavened bread is bread in which no yeast has been used. It is eaten during Passover in memory of the fact that the Jews had no time to leaven their bread when they hurried away from Egypt.

On the first, or first and second, nights of Passover a supper called a *Seder* is served. At this meal there are special foods that are not eaten at any other meal during the year. The story of the Exodus is recited, usually in the Hebrew language. Orthodox (strict) Jews also have a special set of dishes that they use only during Passover.

passport

When a person wants to travel outside his own country, he receives from his government a booklet or official document called a passport. The passport contains a statement from the Secretary of State (if the person is a citizen of the United States) or the Foreign Minister (if he is a citizen of another country) that the bearer is a citizen of his country and it asks foreign governments to give the traveler every courtesy.

The passport also contains a picture and a specimen signature of the owner, and a description of him (such as where he was born, how tall he is, and the color of his hair and eyes) so that nobody else can use the passport. Before a person can travel abroad, he is usually required to have inoculations against some diseases.

In addition to his passport, a traveler usually has to have permission from the countries he plans to visit. This permission is called a *visa*. When a person plans to visit a foreign country, he goes to the embassy or consulate of that country and has a visa, or permission to travel, stamped on a blank page of his passport. However, many countries, especially in Europe, have dropped the visa requirement in recent years because of the large number of people traveling from one country to another.

Except in time of war, or in countries ruled by dictators, passports are usually easy to obtain. However, you may be denied a passport to a country where, because of strife or other reasons, your country does not feel it can protect you.

pasteboard

Pasteboard is the name most often given to heavy paper products that are stiff and strong enough to make boxes, cards, and various kinds of container. Often this material is called *cardboard*, and the paper industry groups all kinds of it together as *paperboard*. The making of paperboard is one of the most important industries of the world.

Some pasteboard is actually made by pasting together thinner sheets of paper. Cheaper paperboards may be coarse wood fibers pressed together (this is often called *chipboard*) but then a glossy paper may be pasted over the cheaper board to give it a fine appearance. *Corrugated* board is made of heavy paper in crinkled form, glued onto flat sheets of heavy paper; the cartons made from these corrugated sheets can hold weights of hundreds of pounds. The original manufacturing process of all kinds of paperboard is basically the same as described in the article on PAPER.

Pasternak, Boris

Boris Leonidovich Pasternak was a famous Russian poet, translator and novelist. He was born in Moscow in 1890. His father was a well-known painter and his mother was a concert pianist. Pasternak wanted to be a musician when he was young, but gave this up to become a poet. He is also noted for his many translations, particularly of Shakespeare. In 1957 the publication of *Doctor Zhivago* brought him world-wide fame. He was

awarded the Nobel Prize for Literature in 1958, but declined to accept it for political reasons. He died in 1960.

Pasteur, Louis

Louis Pasteur was a French scientist who founded the science of bacteriology (the study of bacteria, or germs) and invented one of the most important methods for the prevention of disease, out of which grew inoculation and vaccination. Pasteur was born in 1822. He studied to be a chemist, and while still a student made several important chemical discoveries that resulted in his being appointed a professor at a government school. Later he became professor at other colleges. In 1888 the Pasteur Institute was founded in his honor, and he was its director for the rest of his life.

Pasteur early began studies to find out what causes fermentation. These studies led to many improvements in the quality of French wine and beer. In 1862 the French silk industry was threatened by a mysterious disease that attacked the silkworms. Pasteur studied the problem for five years and succeeded in discovering a parasite that was causing the disease.

Although Pasteur had proved that fermentation and rotting are caused by living organisms, the world still believed that these organisms, or bacteria, were spontaneously generated (that they sprang from nowhere). Pasteur proved that they were carried by the air, and this discovery led to the use of antiseptic (germ-killing) methods in surgery.

PASTEURIZATION

Pasteur's studies led to the invention of a process that now bears his name, pasteurization. This is a process of treating foods, especially milk, with heat to kill harmful bacteria and make the foods last longer and be safer to eat. When milk is pasteurized, it is heated to about 147 degrees Fahrenheit for at least 30 minutes. The milk is then chilled and kept cold until it is used.

Another of Pasteur's achievements was the development of a serum to prevent rabies, the disease carried by mad dogs. Pasteur proved his method on animals, but he was afraid to try it on human beings. When a young boy was near death from rabies after having been bitten by a mad dog, Pasteur consented to try his serum and the boy recovered. Pasteur also did important research leading to eventual control of such other diseases as tuberculosis, cholera, diphtheria, and tetanus (lockjaw).

Pasteur received many honors from his native France and from other nations during his lifetime. France gave him an annual pension and the Legion of Honor, and he was awarded medals by most of the countries of Europe. He died in 1895, at the age of 73.

Patagonia

Patagonia is a region in the southern part of South America, between the Andes Mountains and the Atlantic Ocean. Part of it belongs to Chile but most of it belongs to Argentina. It makes up about one-third of the country, but not many of the people live there.

Patagonia is also the name of a province of Argentina, but it covers only part of the region of that name. Most of the region is a dry, grassy plateau (high, flat land). Most of the rivers there cannot be navigated by boats because they are too shallow or dry out from time to time. There are a few fertile valleys, and there are several large lakes in the west.

The people of Patagonia include native Indians, especially of the Tehuelche tribe, Argentinians, Chileans, and people from European countries, especially from Great Britain. Most of them raise sheep, but in the western sections near the Andes they also raise cattle and some crops. Oil has been found in Patagonia, and the oil industry is growing there. Tourist resorts have been built near the large lakes.

patent

A patent is an official paper given to an inventor of a new thing or way to do something. In the United States, the patent is issued by the Patent Office, a branch of the Department of Commerce. For seventeen years after he is given his patent, the inventor is the only person who has a legal right to use the invention (or to give others permission to use it). After that, anyone may use it. Other countries have somewhat different laws.

It does not cost a great deal of money to apply for a patent, but many people who try to get patents are not entitled to them. You cannot patent an idea. You may think it would be fine to have a special machine to turn off the radio when you fall asleep, but you cannot get a patent unless you have actually built or designed such a machine and it works.

Among the inventions that can be patented are machines, chemical formulas, and new plants made by breeding other plants together. Before the Patent Office issues the patent, it will examine previous patents for inventions of the same kind, and if it finds that your invention is not really new and workable, it will not give you the patent. Even if it does give you the patent, the patent may not be valid —that is, you may not have the right to keep someone else from using it. If someone else can go to court and prove that your idea was not new when you patented it, your patent loses all its value.

PATENT ATTORNEYS

Patent attorneys are professional men who specialize in helping inventors to get patents and in defending those patents in court. First the patent attorney makes a patent search. That is, he has the files of the Patent Office examined to see if anyone else patented the same kind of invention before. If the search shows that the invention is patentable, the attorney makes out an application in which he lists certain *claims*—statements of what he thinks is new and patentable about the invention. The application is sent to the Patent Office in Washington, D.C., with the fee required by law. The *examiners* in the Patent Office then make their own search, and they may write many letters back and forth with the patent attorney before they decide to issue the patent.

Most inventors are unwise to spend money getting patents, for the patent is not worth having unless the product can actually be made and sold. Profitable patents are almost all owned by professionals, many of whom work for big companies and transfer ownership of the patent to the company as soon as it is issued.

Trademarks, which are designs and emblems used to mark a particular product, also are issued by the Patent Office. See also the article on COPYRIGHT.

pathology

Pathology is the branch of medicine that studies the changes in the body brought about by disease or injury. A pathologist studies the changes in the structure, or anatomy, of the body, and he also studies the changes in the operation, or physiology, of the body. By knowing what changes have occurred in the structure or operation of the body, a pathologist is able to tell in what stage of disease or injury the patient is.

A pathologist is a great help to other doctors. He usually does not see patients himself, but works in laboratories in hospitals and clinics. When a doctor suspects that a patient has a certain disease, he sends specimens of one kind or another to a pathologist to be examined. The specimens may be blood specimens, skin or tissue specimens, or even X-rays. By examining a blood specimen, for instance, a pathologist can tell what disease has caused certain changes in the blood. By examining small slices of tissue, a pathologist can tell whether cancer is present.

patriarch

A patriarch is a father considered as the head of a family, household, or government. In a patriarchy, the father is the head of the family and all the fathers together are the heads of the community.

A patriarch is also a person who founds something, and is thought of as its father because he is responsible for its being. In the Bible, the patriarchs were the early leaders of the Jewish religion. Abraham, Noah, Isaac and Jacob were among the patriarchs.

In the Orthodox Catholic Church, which is also called the Eastern or the Greek Catholic Church, the most important priests are called patriarchs. The patriarch of Constantinople is the leader of the Church, in somewhat the same way that the Pope is the leader of the Roman Catholic Church.

patrician

The patricians were the noble families of ancient Rome, more than two thousand years ago. Only the patricians could be members of the governing body, the Senate, and only they could own land in Rome and its colonies. The common people, who were called the plebeians, did not have these rights. In time of war the plebeians had to fight for the patricians, and in time of peace they had to work for them. After the year 133 B.C., the plebeians were allowed to own some land, but most of the land remained in the hands of the patricians. Long after the fall of Rome, until three hundred years ago, the name *patrician* was used for the noble families of Italy.

Patrick, Saint

St. Patrick is the patron saint of Ireland. He lived about 1,500 years ago, and

he was the first man to spread the Christian faith throughout Ireland.

St. Patrick was probably born in the year 389. When he was 16 years old, he was stolen from his home in Britain by Irish outlaws and was sold as a slave in Ireland. After six years as a slave he escaped, but he was sure that he could bring Christianity to the pagan Irish. The Pope, the religious leader of the Catholic Church, made him a bishop and sent him to Ireland. In Ireland, St. Patrick opposed the pagan priests called druids. He converted many people, both rich and poor, to Christianity. He founded many churches and monasteries, and by the time he died, in 461, Ireland was well on the way to being a Christian nation.

There are many legends about St. Patrick. One says that he used the three leaves of the shamrock to explain the idea of the Blessed Trinity; that is, that there are three persons—the Father, Son, and Holy Spirit—in one God. For this reason, the shamrock is often used to stand for St. Patrick and Ireland. Another legend tells that he drove the snakes out of Ireland, but though it is a good story, it is not true because there were none in Ireland at that time. His feast day is on March 17 and on that day the Irish people of New York City parade up Fifth Avenue past St. Patrick's Cathedral in his honor.

Patton, George S.

George Smith Patton was an American general who became one of the best-known commanders in World War II, both for his aggressive and able behavior in battle and for his free-spoken, reckless behavior in other matters. Patton was born in 1885 in San Gabriel, California. As a boy he was a fine athlete, and as a member of the American Olympics team in 1912 he took honors in track events, swimming, and target shooting. He was graduated from the United States Military Academy at West Point in 1909, and served in France in World War I until he was seriously wounded in 1918. In World War II, he was a leader of the triumphant Allied march across France and into Germany.

In 1943 occurred an incident that almost ended Patton's military career. It was revealed in a newspaper article that General Patton, while inspecting an army hospital, had slapped a soldier who was suffering from a mental illness due to combat fatigue. General Eisenhower, the Supreme Allied Commander, rebuked Patton and ordered him to apologize to all concerned in the incident.

General Patton explained his behavior by saying that he thought the man was pretending to be ill to escape further fighting. Patton was criticized for several other actions, but his reputation as a first-class soldier was never seriously harmed. He was called "Old Blood and Guts" by his men, and he never lost their admiration and respect. Many people were surprised to learn that this tough soldier spent much of his free time writing poetry, which he planned to have published after the war. Patton died in Germany in 1945, as a result of injuries suffered in an automobile accident.

Paul, Saint

St. Paul was one of the greatest men of the early Christian Church. He wrote more of the New Testament than any other man. He was not one of the original Apostles of Jesus, but he traveled farther to preach the gospel and won more converts to Christianity than any of the others, and he is called St. Paul the Apostle.

Paul was born about fifteen years after Jesus was born. His birthplace was Tarsus, a city in Asia Minor, which then belonged to Rome. Paul's family were Pharisees, strict members of the Jewish religion, but were Roman citizens. Paul was actually given the name Saul, but later he used his Roman name, Paulus, instead of his original name.

As a young man Saul went to Jerusalem, where he learned to be a tentmaker and a rabbi (teacher of the Jewish religion). Jesus had been crucified a short time before. His disciples and a few others in Jerusalem and Damascus, a nearby city, were the only Christians. Saul was a leader in persecuting the Christians in Jerusalem, and then he was sent to Damascus to persecute the Christians there. While Saul was on the road to Damascus, Jesus appeared to him in the heavens and said, "Saul, Saul, why do you persecute me?" From that time on, Saul recognized Jesus as his master. When he reached Damascus, he preached Christianity instead of persecuting the Christians. He was almost captured and put to death in Damascus, but he made a dramatic escape from the walled city and returned to Jerusalem to join the Christians there as Paul the Apostle.

PAUL'S MISSIONARY JOURNEYS

Much of Paul's life is told in the book, Acts of the Apostles, in the New Testament. He made several journeys to cities on and near the Mediterranean Sea, and everywhere he helped the people to become Christians and to set up churches. At first Paul was accompanied by an apostle named Barnabas. On later trips he took with him other apostles named Silas, Timothy, and Luke (who wrote one of the gospels and also the book of Acts).

Paul was often persecuted. Five times he was flogged with the maximum of thirty-nine lashes given under Jewish law. He was imprisoned for two years at the city of Caesarea, and would have been put to death except that he was a Roman citizen and had the right to appeal to Caesar (the emperor). Festus, the Roman governor at Caesarea, had him put on a ship and sent to Rome. On the way, the ship was shipwrecked and Paul finally reached Rome by land. The journey of a few hundred miles took almost two years. He spent another two years in jail before he came to trial before the emperor Nero.

The Bible does not carry the life of Paul any farther, but tradition of those times has led many writers to believe that Paul was released in Rome, preached Christianity there for a short time, but was put to death in one of the frequent persecutions of Christians that occurred in the reign of Nero. His death, then, would be sometime around the year 60, when Paul was about 50 years old. The traditional date is the year 67.

THE EPISTLES OF PAUL

Fifteen of the twenty-eight books of the New Testament were written by Paul. They were epistles (letters) written to members of Christian churches in cities that Paul had visited. In these letters Paul explains the teachings of Jesus, advises the congregations on the duties of Christians, and encourages them to practice Christianity in spite of the dangers of being Christians in those times.

See also the articles on BIBLE and NEW TESTAMENT.

Paul, Pope

Six popes of the Roman Catholic Church have been named Paul. The last, Paul VI, was crowned Pope on June 30, 1963, succeeding Pope John XXIII. The former Cardinal Montini, Archbishop of Milan, was 65 years old at the time. He was the 262nd Pontiff (leader) of the Church. As a close friend of Pope Pius XII and Pope John XXIII, he was expected to continue many of their progressive policies. Paul II, who was Pope from 1464 to 1471, started many reforms in the governing of the Church. Paul III became Pope in 1534. In 1545 he called the first meetings of the Council of Trent. He died in 1549.

Paul of Russia

Paul was czar (emperor) of Russia more than 160 years ago. He was the son of Catherine the Great. His mother tried to keep him out of public affairs and tried to prevent him from becoming czar, but after her death in 1796 Paul did become czar. He ruled Russia tyrannically, and his people feared and hated him. He was called "the mad czar," because he was thought to be insane. He was murdered by a group of his courtiers. Paul was born in 1754 and died in 1801.

Pavlova, Anna

Anna Matveyevna Pavlova was a Russian ballet dancer. She was born in 1882. When she was 10 years old she entered the Imperial Ballet School in St. Petersburg, Russia, and when she was 14 she made her debut as a solo dancer. She gained fame after 1906 when she began tours that took her all over the world, including the United States. Her dancing technique was perfection in the classic style, and her beauty endeared her to a huge public. Pavlova died in 1931.

pawnbroker

A pawnbroker is a person who lends money and as security takes some small object of value that he can sell if you do not pay back the money. If he has a store it is called a pawnshop. The objects most often pawned are jewelry, musical instruments, cameras, furs, and so on. They are small and easy to sell.

Most states have laws that tell very exactly what a pawnbroker may do and what he may not do. They say how much interest he may charge, which may be as

much as 2 or 3 percent a month on a small loan ($5 or $10) but much less on a large one ($100 or more).

When you pawn something you get a piece of paper called a pawn ticket. This ticket has a date on it, usually one year from the day you got it. If you pay the loan or the interest on it within a year, the pawnbroker cannot sell the valuable thing you pawned. In some states, if you do not redeem the pledge (pay back the loan and get back the thing you pawned) within a year, the pawnbroker has to sell it at auction, and if he sells it for more than the amount of the loan plus the interest plus the cost of the auction, you get the difference.

Pawnshops often use a special sign made of three balls. This sign used to be part of the coat of arms (special sign) of a famous Italian family, the Medici, who were among the first bankers in Europe.

pawpaw

The pawpaw is a tree that grows along the eastern coast and also in the central parts of the United States. It grows to be only about 40 feet high. The pawpaw is a deciduous tree, which means that it loses its leaves in the fall. In the early spring, light green flowers appear. These flowers later become a dark reddish-purple in color. Each flower grows by itself on a twig. The pawpaw fruit appears in the fall. It looks like a short, plump banana. The skin of the fruit is green and the flesh is a yellowish-orange color. The pawpaw has many brown seeds. People eat pawpaw fruit, but they cause the inside of your mouth to pucker.

Payne, John Howard

John Howard Payne was an American actor and playwright, but he is best known because he wrote the popular song "Home, Sweet Home." Payne was born in New York City in 1791. When he was only 18 years old he became successful as an actor. Payne went to England, where he acted in many plays. He also wrote many plays himself. The song "Home, Sweet Home" was sung in his opera *Clari, or The Maid of Milan.* Payne wrote poems and articles about poetry and literature. He was made the representative of the United States government in Tunis, in Africa. He died in Tunis in 1852, when he was 61 years old.

pea

The pea is a very important food plant that grows in many parts of Europe, Asia and the United States where the climate is not too warm. The pea is a legume, one of the plants whose seeds grow in a pod. Usually, only the seeds are eaten, but some pea plants have tender pods that are good to eat.

The pea is an annual plant, which means that the seeds must be planted every year. It is a climbing plant. Some varieties grow to be more than six feet high. Others grow close to the ground.

The garden pea has white flowers. The seeds are usually smooth. When the seeds are dried they become yellow or white.

The chick pea is a special kind of pea that is an important food plant for people in Asia, Africa, and Central America, especially in places where meat is not plentiful. The leaves of the chick pea plant are poisonous.

Peace Corps

The United States Peace Corps was established by executive order of President John F. Kennedy on March 1, 1961. It is a semi-independent agency within the U.S. Department of State. Its members are mostly young men and women who volunteer to serve in underdeveloped countries overseas. They help the peoples of these countries learn the latest ways of doing things, and so improve themselves, in the areas of health, education, agriculture, and industry.

To become a member of the Peace Corps, you must be at least 18 years of age and a citizen of the United States, and be willing to serve for two years. At the end of 1962 there were 3,650 Peace Corpsmen serving in forty countries all over the world, and another 1,100 in training in the United States. It was hoped to increase the number serving overseas to 13,000 by the end of 1964. A presidential committee, appointed in 1962, recommended that a domestic Peace Corps be established.

peach

The peach is a sweet fruit that grows on trees in many parts of Europe, Africa, South America, and the United States. The peach tree grows to be about 20 feet high, though some peach trees are much smaller. It is a deciduous tree, which means that it loses its leaves in the fall. Before the leaves appear in the spring, the peach tree bears beautiful pink blossoms.

The fruit is covered with a soft, downy fuzz and the flesh is juicy. Inside the fruit there is a hard, wrinkled "stone," and inside the stone there is a nut somewhat like an almond but more bitter. This is the seed. The seeds of the peach contain valuable oils that are used to make perfume. In *clingstone* peaches, the flesh of the fruit is hard to remove from the stone; in *freestone* peaches the flesh pulls away easily.

peacock

The peacock is one of the most gorgeous of all birds. It is a member of the pheasant family. It lives in the East Indies and some parts of Asia. A few peacocks have also been discovered in Africa. The male peacock has a blue neck, and its body is different shades of green and purple and black. The male peacock has a splendid "train" of gold and green rear feathers with blue spots that look like eyes. For this reason they are called eye-spots. When the male wants to attract the female peacock it struts in front of her, raises its train, and spreads it like a magnificent fan. People feel that the peacock is a vain bird because it shows off in this manner and we sometimes say that a person is as "proud as a peacock." The female peacock is smaller than the male and does not have a beautiful train.

The ancient people of Greece and Rome were fond of peacocks and often ate them at great banquets. The bird was brought to the banquet table decorated

with its own feathers. The people of India considered the peacock a sacred bird.

peanut

The peanut is a tasty and nourishing food that is really not a nut but a legume. Legumes are plants with pods that split open when the seeds are ripe. The British name for peanut is groundnut.

Peanut plants first grew in Brazil, but they are now raised in Europe, the United States, and Africa. The plant grows to be between one and two feet high. It is an annual, which means that the seeds must be planted every year. The plant has a thick green stem that is covered with a soft fuzz. The peanuts develop underground.

The peanut pods are a pale yellowish color. They are wrinkled and slightly curved. Each pod contains two or three seeds.

The pods and the green parts of the plant are nourishing food for cattle. The seeds are eaten roasted and salted, and they are ground into a paste that is known as *peanut butter.*

Peanuts contain a valuable oil. It is used for cooking and is often one of the ingredients in margarine. Peanut oil is also used to make soap, and sardines are packed in peanut oil. When all of the oil has been pressed out of the peanut, the part that remains, called the cake, is fed to pigs and other animals.

pear

The pear is a sweet fruit that grows on a tree in orchards in many parts of the world. Some pear trees grow to be about 60 feet high, but growers often prune the trees so they will not grow more than 20 to 25 feet high. The pear tree is deciduous, which means that it loses its leaves in the fall. The tree bears white blossoms that appear with the green leaves in the spring.

The fruit may be roundish or round at one end and pointed at the other end, depending on the variety. It has a yellowish-green skin. Pears are eaten raw or cooked. People in Europe make a drink called perry out of pears. Perry is like apple cider.

pearl

A pearl is a beautiful gem that is made by certain shellfish, especially oysters and mussels. It has a shimmering rainbow color and a velvety-smooth surface. Pearls are used in pins, rings, necklaces, tiaras, and bracelets.

The best pearls are those that are nearly perfect spheres (balls) and are free from dull-colored patches or lumps on their surface. White pearls are most valued, but fine black pearls are valuable also.

Pearls that are irregular in shape are called *baroque pearls.* If they are of good color, they are valuable. *Button pearls* are those that are only half round, having one flat side. *Blister pearls* are those that have grown attached to the shell of the oyster or mussel.

HOW PEARLS ARE MADE

Pearls are made of thousands of tiny crystals of a substance called *aragonite.* These crystals are held together by a sticky, horny substance called *conchiolin.* No one knows exactly why shellfish

make pearls. Some people think that a sharp grain of sand gets inside the shell and irritates the shellfish. In trying to get rid of the irritation the shellfish gives out the pearl-making substance that covers over the grains of sand. Most scientists believe that it is not a grain of sand but a very tiny worm that gets into the shell.

Oysters and mussels are raised for their pearls, just as sheep are raised for their wool. Places where they are raised are called pearl fisheries. There are pearl fisheries on the coasts of countries on the Pacific and Indian Oceans and in some other warm seas. There are fresh-water pearl-mussel fisheries on the Mississippi River, and pearl-bearing fresh-water mussels are found in many rivers.

CULTURED PEARLS

If a small sharp object is placed inside the shell of an oyster or mussel, and the shellfish is then returned to the water, it will, in three or four years, grow a pearl. Pearls made this way are called *cultured pearls*. In Japan, in 1920, a way was discovered to make really fine cultured pearls. The shell of a live oyster is opened and a little piece is cut out of the part of the oyster that makes pearls. This piece is tied as a sack around a small ball of mother-of-pearl, about the size of a BB shot. Then the sack and the ball are sewn into the part of a second oyster that makes pearls. After the wound has been treated, the second oyster is put back into the water. The oyster begins to cover the ball of mother-of-pearl with layers of aragonite and conchiolin, and in three or four years a fine round pearl is formed. Such pearls are called *Mikimoto pearls*, after the Japanese inventor of the method. It is very hard to tell a good cultured pearl from a completely natural one.

Pearls are soft and can be easily scratched. The luster can be returned to a pearl by peeling off the outer layers, but this makes the pearl smaller.

Pearls can be imitated by coating the inside of a thin-walled sphere of glass with a solution made from fish scales, and then filling the rest of the sphere with wax.

Pearl Harbor

Pearl Harbor is an inlet on the south coast of Oahu Island in the Hawaiian Islands, about six miles west of the city of Honolulu. Though the harbor is as deep as sixty feet in some places, its entrance is blocked by a coral reef. About fifty years ago, in 1908, the United States set up an important naval base there. On December 7, 1941, Japanese bombing planes suddenly attacked the naval base at Pearl Harbor, and the following day the United States entered World War II on the side of the Allies. "Remember Pearl Harbor!" became an American battle cry.

The attack on Pearl Harbor had been planned by the Japanese for some time, though at the same time representatives of the Japanese government were making statements about peace and cooperation with the United States. The Japanese attack lasted about two hours, during which ships and naval installations and nearby airfields were bombed. About 2,400 persons were killed in the attack, and nearly 1,200 were wounded. Six battleships and several smaller vessels were sunk, and

many others were seriously damaged. It took about a year for the United States Navy to recover from the attack on Pearl Harbor, and during this period the Japanese won many victories in the Pacific Ocean area.

Peary, Robert E.

Robert Edwin Peary was an American explorer who is best remembered as the first person to reach the North Pole. Peary was born in 1856 in Cresson, Pennsylvania. After graduation from Bowdoin College, in Maine, he joined the United States Navy as a civil engineer. He became interested in Arctic exploration, and in 1886 he led an expedition that brought back a great quantity of new geographical information, including the fact that Greenland is an island. He made several other trips to the Arctic. By 1898 he had determined to find the North Pole.

On his first try he came within four hundred miles of the Pole but had to turn back because of severe hardships and shortage of supplies. He had been gone for four years and had reached a point farther north than any man had ever been. In 1905, in a ship called the *Roosevelt* that had been built especially for the purpose, Peary made another attempt to reach the Pole and this time managed to get within two hundred miles of his objective.

On the third try, in 1908, Peary sailed the *Roosevelt* to Grant Land and spent the winter there preparing for the dash over the ice to the North Pole. On April 6, 1909, Peary finally reached the North Pole. With him were his servant, Matthew Henson, and four Eskimos. The rest of his large party had turned back one by one as supplies ran out.

When Peary returned home his triumph was dimmed by the claims of Frederick A. Cook, who claimed to have reached the Pole the year before. After great controversy, the United States Congress proved that Cook's claim was false, and in 1911 it gave Peary a vote of thanks as the discoverer of the North Pole. In that same year Peary retired from the Navy as a rear admiral. He died in 1920.

peat

Peat is a combination of leaves, moss, ferns and other kinds of plant material that have decayed. Peat is found in marshy places that are called bogs. There are peat bogs in many parts of the world.

Some peat bogs are only a few feet deep, while others are as much as 30 feet deep. The color of peat depends on how far the process of decay has gone. When there has not been very much decay the peat may be a light yellow color. Peat that has decayed a great deal is almost black.

Peat is a very useful substance. People who live in countries where there is not much wood use peat as fuel, after it has been dried. Peat that has not decayed very much is sometimes used as bedding for cattle. Plants are sometimes packed in peat when they are shipped from one place to another. A good peat bog is a very good place for planting a vegetable or flower garden.

pecan

The pecan is a nut that grows on

large trees in the southeastern part of the United States. The pecan tree is a member of the hickory family. It is deciduous, which means that it loses its leaves in the fall.

The pecan tree grows to be over 100 feet tall, and some trees reach a height of 170 feet. It takes about ten years for a pecan tree to begin to produce enough nuts to make it a valuable tree to the farmer. One cultivated pecan tree can produce up to 600 pounds of nuts each year.

The pecan nut is oval-shaped. It has a dark, reddish-brown shell. Some pecans have a very thin shell that is easy to crack. They are called paper-shelled pecans, and they are especially popular as a food. The pecan contains more fat than any other vegetable, and it is a very nourishing food. Pecan wood is used to make furniture, floors, and boxes.

peccary

The peccary is a small, wild relative of the pig. It lives in the forests and brush country of southern United States, Central and South America. It has a scent gland near the tail, and only three toes on its hind feet instead of four, as true pigs have.

The peccary is about two feet high and weighs about fifty pounds. It has coarse, brownish-black hair. One kind of peccary has a stripe that runs around its neck. It is called a *collared peccary*. Another kind has a white face and is called a *white-lipped peccary*.

The peccary eats fruit and roots and leaves and it also eats small animals. The peccary can be a savage fighter. It makes its den in a hollow tree or in a thick bush. The female usually has two babies.

The skin of the peccary is used to make fine gloves and belts and wallets and handbags. See LEATHER.

pectin

Pectin is a sticky, jellylike substance that is found in most plants, especially in fruits and vegetables. It can easily be dissolved in water and can be used as a food by both plants and animals. Pectin becomes solid when taken out of the plant, and it is used to make jellies and jams.

pedigree

A pedigree is a record of the ancestors of a person or an animal. The pedigree of a human being would give the names of his parents, grandparents, great grandparents, and so on, back as far as they were known or could be traced. A person's pedigree is also called his lineage, and the work of tracing it is called GENEALOGY, about which there is a separate article.

Pedigree is especially important for livestock and animals that are exhibited in shows, such as cats and dogs. In breeding such animals, pedigree is taken into account so that animals with certain traits can be bred to produce finer, stronger, more beautiful or more useful examples of the breed. You can read more about this in the article on BREEDING. Pedigree is so important that associations have been formed to keep such records. The American Kennel Club registers pedigreed dogs, and other associations do the same for various kinds of livestock.

Peel, Sir Robert

Robert Peel was an English states-man. He was born in 1788, attended Oxford University, and was then elected to Parliament. For more than forty years he played an important part in English politics. He became Prime Minister twice.

One of the important things that Peel is remembered for is the Catholic Emancipation Act. This act entitled people who belonged to the Roman Catholic Church to hold positions in the government. Another important thing that Peel did was to carry through the repeal of the Corn Laws. The Corn Laws were taxes on breadstuffs that raised the price of bread, making it hard for poor people to buy it. Peel had first been against both of these important changes, but when he saw that the people wanted them he changed his mind.

Peel established a police force in London, and the policemen were called "Peelers" or "bobbies," after him. Policemen in England are sometimes called "bobbies" even now. In 1850 Peel fell from a horse and died of injuries he suffered in the fall. He was 62 years old.

Pegasus

Pegasus was a winged horse that is told about in Greek mythology, the stories of the gods and goddesses of the ancient Greeks. Pegasus was caught and tamed by the goddess Athena. (In Roman mythology, Athena is called Minerva.) Athena gave Pegasus to the Muses as a present. Pegasus pawed at the earth, and from the cleft sprang the fountain of inspiration, which was called Hippocrene. For this reason Pegasus was connected with poetry and carried poets to the land of inspiration on his back.

Pegasus belonged to the Greek hero BELLEROPHON, about whom there is a separate atricle.

Peiping

Peiping is the capital and the second-largest city of the People's Republic of China, or Communist China. For more than five hundred years the city was known as Peking or Pekin, but its name was changed to Peiping in 1928. It is an important railroad and trading center. More than four million people live there. Many of them work in iron and steel plants and in factories that make woolen goods, leather, matches, and glass. Peiping publishes more books than any other city in China. It has several colleges and universities.

Peiping is a beautiful and interesting city. It is divided into two parts. In the northern part of Peiping is the Inner City. It is surrounded by high walls and was used in the past by the Manchu emperors. It has wide streets and many beautiful temples and palaces. Within the Inner City are two walled areas. The first is the Imperial City, where the government buildings stand. The second, which is within the Imperial City, is the Forbidden City, where for a long time no one was allowed to enter except the members of the emperor's family.

In the southern part of Peiping is the Outer City. This is where the business section is. The most beautiful building in this section is the Temple of Heaven, which is set in a large park.

Peiping is a very ancient city. It was first made the capital of the Mongols some seven hundred years ago by the great conqueror Kublai Khan. He built many of the city's beautiful buildings. In 1421 it was named Peking.

In 1928, when China became a republic, the capital was moved to Nanking and the name Peking was changed to Peiping. During World War II, the city was occupied by the Japanese. In 1949 the city was taken by the Chinese Communists and was made their capital.

PEIPING, CHINA. Population (1961 estimate) 4,140,000. Capital of (Communist) People's Republic of China.

Pekingese

A Pekingese is a small dog that came originally from Peking (now Peiping), China. The Chinese people for hundreds of years thought that Pekingese dogs were sacred. Only royal families were allowed to keep them. The dogs are now kept as pets in many parts of the world. They are quiet and dignified, and not usually very playful.

A Pekingese stands about 8 to 10 inches high at the shoulder, and it is slightly longer than it is tall. It weighs between 7 and 15 pounds. It has a small short nose, and many people think that it looks "pushed in." A Pekingese's eyes are big, round, and black. It has a bushy tail that curves up over its back. Its coat is very thick, with long, straight hair that looks a little like a lion's mane around the neck. A "Peke" may be almost any color, from a light tan to a dark reddish-brown or black, and sometimes it has two colors combined in its markings. It is also called a Pekinese.

pelican

The pelican is a large, odd-looking bird that lives along the coasts of the southern United States and South America, and near rivers and lakes in many parts of the world.

The pelican grows to be about five feet high. It has webbed feet and a remarkable bill that is more than a foot long. The pelican has a large pouch of skin under its bill that makes a handy bag to carry fish.

Even though the pelican is such a large bird, it is a strong flier.

The brown pelican makes its home on the coasts of Florida and California in the United States. It skims over the water and when it spots a fish it swoops down and catches it in its great bill. When it comes to the surface, the water runs out

Walt Disney Prod.
The pelicans seem to be laughing at a good joke, which gives the observer a chance to look inside the large pouches in which they carry their catch of fish.

of its bill and the pelican eats the fish. Sometimes it carries fish to its babies in its convenient pouch.

The white pelican lives mainly on islands in lakes in the western part of North America. Instead of diving for fish, it swims in the water and scoops them up.

Pelicans are sociable birds and make their nests in huge colonies on the ground. Pelican Island in Florida is the home of about two thousand pelicans.

pellagra

Pellagra is a disease that attacks people who lack B complex vitamins in their diet. These vitamins are present in lean meat, eggs, milk, cheese, and leafy green vegetables such as spinach and lettuce. Pellagra was once common in the southern states of the United States and in India, China, and parts of South America.

When a person gets pellagra he develops a red rash on the inside of his mouth and on his tongue and skin. He has diarrhea and headaches, and cannot sleep; he feels nervous and loses weight. For a long time almost every person who had pellagra died. Now doctors have discovered a vitamin called nicotinic acid that cures pellagra.

Peloponnesus

The Peloponnesus is a section of Greece. It is south of the mainland of Greece, and is connected to the mainland by an isthmus, or narrow strip of land (the Isthmus of Corinth, about ten miles wide). The area of Peloponnesus is 8,350 square miles, which is about the size of the state of Massachusetts. More than a million people live on the Peloponnesus.

About 2,400 years ago, from 431 B.C. to 404 B.C., two great Greek nations, the Spartans and the Athenians, fought each other to see which would have the best territory and dominate the other. Sparta was on the Peloponnesus and Athens was on the mainland. The war was won by the Spartans. It is known in ancient history as the Peloponnesian War.

pelvis

The pelvis is one of the important bones of the body. It is the foundation bone for the entire upper body, and serves as strength and support for the parts of the body that lie inside the abdomen. The pelvis is a broad, thin bone, shaped somewhat like a saddle. Its outer sides form the hips. The leg bones are joined to it at the hips. The bottom of the spine, or backbone, is attached to the back of the pelvis.

pemmican

Pemmican was a dried food used by North American Indians, principally when they were traveling. To make pemmican, deer or buffalo meat was dried and pounded to a paste, made into cakes, and then packed with fat in rawhide bags. Sometimes dried berries were added. Although pemmican was not very pleasant to eat, it was useful because it supplied quick nourishment, was easy to carry, and would not spoil over long periods. Indians who lived on the Pacific coast used fish to make a similar mixture. A form of pemmican made of beef with raisins and sugar is still used by explorers and army expeditions.

pen

A pen is an instrument for writing with ink. The earliest writing implement was probably the *stylus,* a pointed tool made of metal or bone, but this was used to cut or engrave letters in a hard wax surface. The true ancestor of the pen was the *calamus,* a hollow reed that was frayed or slit at the end and dipped into some kind of ink. The calamus was used in ancient times in Asia.

The quill, a large feather from a bird, usually a goose, first came into use about 1,500 years ago and was the principal writing instrument up until the 1820s. Many improvements were devised in the quill to make it more efficient. The most important of these improvements was made in 1809, when a machine was invented to cut up the quill into separate *nibs,* or points, to be held in a handle, called a penholder. The penholder with separate nibs was in standard use until the invention of the fountain pen.

Quill pens were sharpened by hand, and this was the origin of the penknife, a small knife carried in the pocket or sometimes on a watch chain. Every desk also had its little box of sand for blotting a page of writing. For many years quills were gilded to make them last longer. Then fine pen nibs began to be made of horn or tortoise shell, and sometimes tiny bits of diamond or ruby were set into the points to make them harder. The metal pen nib, with a hole and slit to make the ink flow freely, came into wide use in the 1820s. Many metals were used, including silver, zinc, aluminum, and bronze, but the great majority of pen nibs were made of steel.

The penholder and nib are still much used but have been largely replaced by the FOUNTAIN PEN and ball-point pen, about which you can read in a separate article.

pencil

The pencil is the instrument for writing that is most used today. There are many different kinds of pencil, but the most common is the general writing pencil. It consists of a long, slender piece of wood (usually painted) that surrounds an even thinner stick of "lead." This stick is not actually the mineral called lead, but a mixture of clay and a soft, black substance called graphite. The wood is shaved away at one end so that a small piece of lead sticks out beyond it. This is the pencil's point, the part that makes marks on paper or wood or other materials. The shaving-away is called "sharpening the pencil."

Pencils are used everywhere by almost everyone. Twelve pencils are used each year for every person in the United States.

Special pencils are made for special purposes. There are drawing pencils used by draftsmen and artists. There are special pencils to mark china, glass, cellophane, film and other materials on which ordinary pencils leave no mark. Pencils such as eyebrow pencils and pencils to whiten the fingernails are used as beauty aids by millions of women. Colored pencils are used by artists and businessmen and students.

There are also mechanical pencils, which are metal or plastic holders for short pieces of lead. The lead is the same kind that is used in ordinary pencils, but it is usually thinner.

THE HISTORY OF PENCILS

The pencil that is used by most people today began to be made about 150 years ago. Before that time most people wrote with pen and ink. However, the ancient Romans had discovered nearly two thousand years ago that lead (the metal) would make readable marks. For this reason we still refer to the writing part of pencils as "lead."

About four hundred years ago, in 1564, a new substance, graphite, was discovered at the town of Barrowdale, England. Graphite alone was too soft and crumbly. It required a binder (something to hold it together). About two hundred years after the discovery of graphite, the first important pencil factory was established. It was founded by Casper Faber near the town of Nuremburg, in Bavaria (which is now part of West Germany). Faber used sulfur for a binder. He poured powdered graphite and melted sulfur into molds, and when it cooled the material was used in pencils. A few years later, in 1795, a Frenchman named Conté mixed the graphite with clay, and this mixture proved to be so successful that the method was adopted by all pencil makers and is still used by them.

In 1856 the first pencil factory in the United States was built by descendants of Casper Faber. The company is now the Eberhard Faber Pencil Company.

HOW PENCILS ARE MADE

Pencils are usually made of three main substances—graphite, clay, and wood. The wood that is preferred is red cedar, but there were not enough red cedar trees. Then it was found that another kind of cedar, incense cedar, which grows in the far West, can be used.

Graphite and clay and water are mixed together. The kind of pencil depends on this mixture. If more clay is used, the pencil will be *harder*—that is, it will make a finer line and more pressure will be needed to make the line blacker. If more graphite is used, the pencil will be *softer*—that is, it will make thicker, blacker lines with less pressure. The mixture is then put into molds that form it into strings. They are dried, packed into metal molds, and heated in ovens to a very high temperature. Then the "leads" are cooled and put for a time into a bath of melted wax. This will make them write more smoothly.

The wood for the pencil is bought by pencil manufacturers in the form of thin, slatlike pieces. The slats are dried, stained and soaked in a wax bath. Then grooves are cut in the slats and a special kind of glue is applied. The leads are placed in the grooves and another grooved slat is put on top. The glue holds the slats together. Everything has to fit very exactly. If the lead is too loose in the groove, the pencil will not write well; if the lead is too tight, it will break.

The pencils are smoothed with sandpaper and coated with lacquer (a kind of paint). Then they are stamped with the maker's name and a number showing how hard or soft they are. Usually metal bands to hold erasers and the erasers themselves are added.

The steps in making a pencil were formerly all done by hand. Today pencils are made almost entirely by machines.

KINDS OF PENCIL

Manufacturers usually grade pencils—that is, give them numbers to show their hardness or softness. The usual numbers are No. 1 (soft), No. 2 (medium), No. 3 (firm), and No. 4 (hard). The No. 2 grade is preferred by most people for general writing. Some manufacturers also give grades between No. 1 and No. 4, such as No. 2B or No. 2½.

There are also *indelible* pencils. This means that the marks they make cannot be erased. Other pencils made of a white pigment are used to cover mistakes made by other pencils.

pendulum

A pendulum is any object that swings back and forth repeatedly, following the same path. A simple pendulum can be made by hanging a weight on a string and letting it swing.

The time it takes the weight to make one swing back and forth is called the *period* of the pendulum. The period depends only on the length of the string. Once the pendulum has been started, the period will remain practically the same even though the length of the path, called the *amplitude,* becomes smaller and smaller. For this reason, pendulums have been used for almost three hundred years to keep time.

The operation of a pendulum was first explained by the famous Italian scientist, Galileo. However, it was a Dutch scientist, Christian Huygens, who first used a pendulum to regulate the movement of clocks. He used a *compound pendulum* —a rod suspended at one end and allowed to swing back and forth at the other. Compound pendulums are still used on some clocks and on metronomes.

Penelope was the good and faithful wife of Odysseus (or Ulysses), king of Ithaca, according to the legends of ancient Greece and Rome. See the article about ODYSSEUS.

penguin

The penguin is one of the best-known and most popular birds. They live in the lonely Antarctic regions, where the climate is very cold. Some penguins live in New Zealand and Australia, and on the Galápagos Islands.

The Australian penguin is called the *little blue penguin.* It is only about a foot high. The *emperor penguin,* which lives in the Antarctic, is more than 3 feet high and weighs about 90 pounds.

The penguin is a clumsy bird on land, but it is very agile in water. It cannot fly. It has a wide body and flat feet, and it stands upright. When it walks it has an odd waddle and a curious stare that makes it a most amusing bird to watch. It has a black and a white or pale yellow front.

Penguins are very sociable birds and sometimes as many as a hundred thousand penguins live together in a colony.

The male penguin wins a wife in an unusual way. It presents pebbles, one by one, to the female. A male who has no

pebbles will steal some pebbles from another penguin. The penguin build foundations for their nests out of pebbles.

The female penguin lays one egg. It carries this egg around on its feet. It has a kind of awning of skin that covers the egg and keeps it warm. When the baby penguin is born it stays in this pouch until it grows too large for it.

penicillin

Penicillin is a drug that cures many kinds of infection and disease. It comes from a green mold of the kind you see on stale bread and cheese. This mold is formed by tiny living creatures (microbes, or germs). The mold stops the growth of bacteria that cause certain infections, such as a boil or ear abscess, and many other diseases including pneumonia, scarlet fever, and tonsilitis. Penicillin was the first of the "wonder drugs," about which you can read in the article on ANTIBIOTICS.

Penicillin was discovered accidentally in 1928 by a Scottish scientist, Sir Alexander Fleming. Fleming was studying many different microbes that cause disease. He was growing these microbes in flat glass dishes. One morning he noticed a green mold in the middle of a dish in which he was growing staphylococcus bacteria, a kind of germ that causes many different diseases. He did not know how the green mold got there. It was probably started by a speck of mold blown in from the air. He saw that around the mold all the other germs had been destroyed. This seemed to show that something in the mold could kill the bacteria.

Finding the chemical that did this, and learning how to make it in quantities, took almost twenty years. The man who first did this was another British scientist, Howard W. Florey.

On February 12, 1941, a drop of penicillin extracted from mold was tried for the first time on a human being. A London policeman was dying of staphylococcus germ infection of the blood, picked up by cutting himself during shaving. His fever was 105 degrees, his face was covered by pussy sores, and all medicines had failed to help him. The penicillin brought his fever down in a few hours. He seemed to be getting better, but when there was no more penicillin to give him, the infection spread again and he died.

Growing molds and getting penicillin out of them was very hard to do at first, so that in the early part of World War II all supplies of the drug were reserved for fighting forces. In 1943, the entire world supply of penicillin was only enough to treat four hundred people. Now the drug is made in huge fermentation tanks, and by the 1950s there was enough of it to treat more than thirty million patients each year. Penicillin has saved hundreds of thousands of persons from dying of infections from wounds and from diseases that a short time ago were deadly.

Some people, about six out of a hundred, are sensitive or allergic to penicillin. When it is given to them, they break out in a rash or develop a fever. But other drugs, called antihistamines, help to overcome this sensitivity.

Penn, William

William Penn was the founder of Pennsylvania. He was also an important preacher and writer in the Society of Friends, or Quakers.

Penn was born in London in 1644. His father was an admiral in the British navy. When Penn was only 15 years old, he became a Quaker. This was not respectable at the time, because the Church of  England was the only official church. His father tried in many ways to get his son to change his mind and at one time he even turned the boy out of his home, but Penn never changed his mind about his religion.

In 1681, King Charles II of England gave Penn land in America in payment for a debt that he owed Penn's father. Penn was given about 45,000 square miles of land, for which he agreed to pay the king two beaver skins a year. Penn at first wanted to call his land New Wales. Later he decided to call it Sylvania, meaning a woodland. King Charles insisted that the land be called Pennsylvania in memory of Penn's father.

Penn wanted to form a colony where people would work together in love and friendship. He advertised for settlers to go to this colony and promised them that there would be freedom of religion for everyone and that the government would be set up for the good of the people. Penn urged that people of the Quaker faith join him in this colony, and many Quakers, from both Germany and England, were among the first settlers.

One of the first things Penn did in his colony was to buy land from the Indians and to sign a peace treaty with them. Penn promised to deal fairly with the Indians and the Indians promised to live in peace with them. Both the Indians and the settlers kept the peace. No Quaker was ever harmed by an Indian in the whole history of the colony.

Later in Penn's life he had a great deal of trouble with the English government. At one time he was not allowed to govern the colony of Pennsylvania for two years. He died in England in 1718.

Pennsylvania

Pennsylvania is one of the Middle Atlantic States in the United States. It was one of the thirteen original colonies. Its nickname is the "Keystone State" because it was in the middle of the thirteen original states that extended from New Hampshire to Georgia. (A keystone is the center stone that holds an arch together.) Pennsylvania got its name from William Penn, who called the region Sylvania, meaning "woodland." King Charles II of England added Penn's name to it, and so the region became known as Pennsylvania.

Pennsylvania is one of the most important industrial and mining states in the United States. It produces more iron and steel than any other state, and Pittsburgh, one of its cities, is the greatest steel center in the world. Pennsylvania is also the greatest coal center, and produces almost all the anthracite or hard coal in the country. The state ranks second in the manufacturing of textiles and clothing, and it produces more than half of the nation's tin plate.

Pennsylvania is also one of the most historic states. Some of the most important events in American history took place there, including the signing of the Declaration of Independence and the Constitution of the United States.

Pennsylvania ranks 33rd in size among the states, with 45,333 square miles. In population it ranks third, with more than eleven million people living there. It became a state in 1788, and was the second to join the United States. The capital is Harrisburg.

THE PEOPLE WHO LIVE THERE

The earliest white settlers in the Pennsylvania region, more than three hundred years ago, were Swedish and Dutch people.

These settlers were followed by people from many nations and of many religions because Pennsylvania was known for its political and religious freedom. Pennsylvania is sometimes called the "Quaker

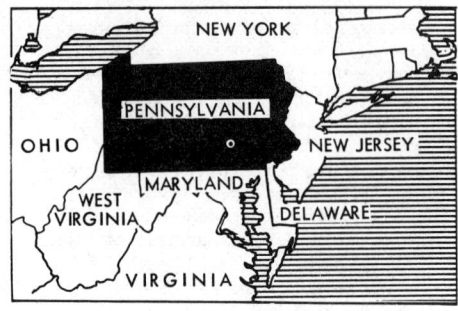

State" because many Quakers, who came from England, were important in settling it. Germans, Irish and Scots were important settlers. After the great coal mines began to be developed and the large cities grew, many people came from Italy, Poland, and other European countries. Most of the people of Pennsylvania are American-born.

About two out of three of the people of Pennsylvania live in the busy cities. They work in the large steel and iron mills, and in factories that make thousands of important products. Many work in big shipbuilding yards.

Large numbers of people in Pennsylvania are miners. They work in the valuable bituminous (soft) and anthracite (hard) coal mines, and in the iron mines and the rich oil fields.

Although Pennsylvania is a very important mining and manufacturing state, many of its people are farmers. More than half of the state has rich farm land. The farmers raise grain, hay, and potatoes, and cattle and poultry. They also produce large quantities of dairy products.

The people belong to many religious groups. The largest are the Roman Catholic, Lutheran, Methodist, Presbyterian, and Jewish.

WHAT THE STATE IS LIKE

Pennsylvania is a mountainous state with many beautiful valleys. The western and northern parts of the state are called the Allegheny Plateau. Many peo-

ple spend their vacations there in the Allegheny mountains. Coal mines and oil fields are in this region. The Allegheny and Monongahela rivers meet in this section at Pittsburgh to form the Ohio River. The place where they meet is called the "Golden Triangle."

East of the Allegheny Plateau are the Appalachian Mountains, with high ridges and wide and beautiful valleys, such as the Cumberland Valley and the Lebanon Valley. The famous Delaware Water Gap, noted for its fine scenery, is on the eastern border.

In the southeastern part of the state is a rich farming region, where most of Pennsylvania's crops are grown. Philadelphia, with its many industries, is in this section. There is another fertile farming region in the northwestern corner of the state, along Lake Erie.

Pennsylvania has a varied climate. In the southeast, around Philadelphia, it is mild. In the valleys in the central part of the state the summers are hot and the winters cold. In the mountains the winters are very cold, the summers pleasantly cool. The state's average temperature in winter is about 29 degrees, and in summer 71 degrees.

Many wild animals are found in Pennsylvania, including the deer, mink, beaver, and opossum. In the Pocono Mountains are black bears.

The rivers in Pennsylvania are important to the state. The Ohio River, which pioneers once used in traveling westward, now links Pittsburgh with the Mississippi River and the Gulf of Mexico. The Delaware River, along the eastern border of the state, is deep enough for ocean vessels to travel on it to Philadelphia. Other rivers, such as the Susquehanna, form fertile valleys as they flow through the mountains, through mountain gaps of great beauty. Besides its many navigable rivers, Pennsylvania has thousands of miles of railroads and highways that reach nearly every part of the state. There are airports in the large cities.

THE GOVERNMENT OF PENNSYLVANIA

Pennsylvania is called a commonwealth instead of a state, but there is no real difference. Like other states, it has a Governor at the head of the government. He is elected for a four-year term. The laws are made by a Legislature, composed of two houses, a Senate and a House of Representatives. The members of the Senate are elected for a four-year term. The members of the House of Representatives are elected for a two-year term. Judges are elected for a 21-year term. There are 67 counties.

There are about two million students in the public schools. Among the colleges, universities and other schools of higher learning are:

University of Pennsylvania, at Philadelphia. Enrollment, 18,767 in 1971 (co-ed).

Pennsylvania State University, at University Park, with other campuses throughout the state. Enrollment, 49,759 in 1971 (co-ed).

Bucknell University, at Lewisburg. Enrollment, 2,763 in 1971 (co-ed).

Franklin and Marshall College, at Lancaster. Enrollment, 2,576 in 1971 (men only).

Dickinson College, at Carlisle. Enrollment, 1,536 in 1971 (co-ed).

Lafayette College, at Easton. Enrollment 1,002 in 1971 (men only).

Lehigh University, at Bethlehem. Enrollment, 4,850 in 1971 (men only).

Muhlenberg College, at Allentown. Enrollment, 1,505 in 1971 (co-ed).

Washington-Jefferson College, at Washington. Enrollment, 813 in 1971 (men only).

University of Scranton, at Scranton. Enrollment, 2,745 in 1971 (men only).

University of Pittsburgh, at Pittsburgh. Enrollment, 25,260 in 1971 (co-ed).

Other important colleges and universities are listed in the articles on PHILADELPHIA and PITTSBURGH.

CHIEF CITIES OF PENNSYLVANIA

The leading cities of Pennsylvania, with populations from the 1970 census, are:

Philadelphia, population 1,948,609, the largest city. There is a separate article about PHILADELPHIA.

Pittsburgh, population 520,117, the second-largest city in the state. There is a separate article about PITTSBURGH.

Erie, population 129,231, the third-largest city, a shipping center, in the northwest.

Scranton, population 103,564, the fifth-largest city, the industrial center for the anthracite coal region, in the northeast.

Allentown, population 109,527, the fourth-largest city, and Bethlehem, population 72,686, which adjoins it, steel center, in the east.

Reading, population 87,643, the sixth-largest city, a manufacturing center, in the east.

Harrisburg, population 68,061, the state capital and eighth-largest city. There is a separate article about HARRISBURG.

PENNSYLVANIA IN THE PAST

The first permanent settlement in Pennsylvania was made by Swedes at Tinicum Island, in 1643. About forty years later, the large region that is now Pennsylvania was given to Sir William Penn of England by King Charles II, in payment of a debt the king owed Penn's father. William Penn was a Quaker, and with a large number of Quakers he arrived in Philadelphia and began to build the English colony. Penn made friends with the Indians, built schools, and made the colony known for its religious freedom. After Penn's death, for many years the settlers were troubled by Indian uprisings.

The people of Pennsylvania played an important part in the Revolutionary War, and many important events took place there. The colonists met in Philadelphia and wrote the Declaration of Independence. Several important battles were fought in Pennsylvania, and Washington had his headquarters at Valley Forge, in southeastern Pennsylvania, during the hard winter of 1777–1778. In 1787 the Constitutional Convention met in Philadelphia and wrote the Constitution of the United States. It was adopted by the colonies at Independence Hall, the most historic building in the state. From 1790 to 1800, Philadelphia was the capital of the United States.

During the Civil War, Pennsylvania fought on the side of the Union. Perhaps the most important battle of the war was fought at Gettysburg, a town in southern Pennsylvania.

After the Civil War, western Pennsylvania began to prosper as eastern Pennsylvania already had. The first important oil fields in the United States were in the region around Titusville and Oil City,

Below: The Colonial American flag flies in front of Betsy Ross House in Philadelphia, home of the woman commissioned by the Continental Congress to make the American flag.

in the northwestern part of the state. The rich coal and iron mines around Pittsburgh made it the greatest steel center in the world.

Pennsylvania has had several serious floods. The worst one was the famous Johnstown flood in 1889, when two thousand people were drowned. The state has done many things to prevent floods, but there was another serious one in 1936, when 430,000 people were made homeless and millions of dollars' worth of property was damaged. Many steps toward flood control have been taken since.

PLACES TO SEE IN PENNSYLVANIA

Gettysburg National Military Park, 2,534 acres, in the south, at Gettysburg, on U.S. Route 15.

Fort Necessity National Battlefield Site, 2 acres, in the southwest, ten miles southeast of Uniontown, on U.S. Route 40. Scene of a battle between colonial troops led by George Washington and French troops assisted by Indians, July 3, 1754; the opening battle of the French and Indian Wars.

Hopewell Village National Site, 848 acres, in southeastern Pennsylvania, 12 miles southeast of Reading, east of U.S. Route 122. The village was built more than two hundred years ago, and in it cannons were made for the Revolutionary War.

Valley Forge State Park, 2,033 acres, in southeastern Pennsylvania, 7 miles southeast of Norristown, on State Highway 23.

Betsy Ross's House, in Philadelphia. The small brick house where Betsy Ross lived. She is said to have made the first flag of the United States.

Independence Hall, in Philadelphia. Historic building where the Declaration of Independence and the Constitution were written; contains the famous Liberty Bell.

Washington Crossing State Park, 1,000 acres, in the southeast, 8 miles north of Morrisville, on State Highway 39. The place where General Washington and his men, on Christmas night in 1776, crossed the Delaware River and successfully at-

tacked the British in Trenton, New Jersey.

PENNSYLVANIA. Area, 45,333 square miles. Population (1970 census) 11,793,909. Capital, Harrisburg. Nickname, the Keystone State. Motto, Virtue, Liberty and Independence. Flower, mountain laurel. Bird, ruffed grouse. Song, none officially. Admitted to Union, December 12, 1787. Official abbreviation, Penna.

pension

A pension is a regular income, like weekly or monthly pay. It is given to a person for something he did in the past. A person who works at a job many years may receive a pension when he grows too old to work. A soldier receives a pension if he is wounded in a war and is no longer able to earn a living. Pensions probably began hundreds or even thousands of years ago when old soldiers or wounded soldiers were given money by their government.

Almost all the people in the United States and many other countries are now covered by some form of pension that will take care of them in their old age.

The oldest form of pension in the United States is the military pension. In 1776, when the American army was first formed, there was a provision made for pensions for wounded and disabled soldiers. Today there are pensions for any member of the armed services who has put in twenty years or more in active service.

Pensions are also given to government employees in what is called the Civil Service. These include policemen, firemen and teachers who have served the proper number of years or who have reached the retirement age, usually somewhere over the age of 60.

In 1935 the United States started the Social Security System which provides pensions for millions of workers in American business and industries. Many employers make contracts with labor unions to pay pensions to retired workers. In most cases, workers contribute to their own pension funds.

Pentagon

The Pentagon is the immense headquarters of the U.S. Department of Defense and is located in Arlington, Virginia near Washington, D.C. Named Pentagon for its five-sided shape, it is the world's largest office building. The Pentagon has over three times as much floor space as the world's tallest building, the Sears Tower in Chicago.

The Pentagon covers 34 acres and the total area of its five floors is more than six million square feet. The building was built during World War II in the record time of sixteen months. At first it was used by the United States Army only. It was completed on January 15, 1943, and it cost about $83,000,000.

The Pentagon is like a small city in itself. About 27,000 people work there. In it are stores, a post office, chapels for religious services, a dispensary and a dental clinic, and a bank, as well as restaurants and cafeterias. There are 3,000 clocks, 550 water fountains, and 240 rest rooms. The building is surrounded by 204 acres of lawns and terraces, of which 67 acres are reserved for parking 9,300 cars.

Though the Pentagon is so huge that people often joke about getting lost in it, the greatest distance between any two rooms in it is only 1,800 feet, or about a six-minute walk.

F.C.D.Y.

The vast Pentagon, so called because the building has five sides, is the military nerve center of the United States.

Pentateuch, a name given to the first five books in the Old Testament of the Bible: see the article BIBLE.

Pentecost

Pentecost is one of the most important feasts celebrated in Christian churches. It occurs fifty days after Easter. It is in memory of the descent of the Holy Spirit on the Apostles, as it is recorded in the Bible, in the second chapter of the Acts of the Apostles. In England, it is called Whitsunday. Pentecost is also the Greek name for the Hebrew Shevuoth or Feast of Weeks, which was celebrated in Palestine at the end of harvest time. It occurs fifty days after the Passover. It was on this Hebrew holiday, the New Testament says, that the Holy Spirit came to the Apostles in the form of tongues of fire.

peonage

Peonage is a system by which many people through the ages have become slaves or servants. Peonage makes people pay off debts by working for the person to whom they owe the debt. In Central and South America a peon was a poor farmer who was little better off than a slave, because he could not get his debt paid. While he was working off his debt, he still had expenses for food and shelter, and these would be added to his debt, which became larger and larger.

In the 1800s peonage was used on some farms and in some factories in the United States. In the South, after slavery was made illegal, the peons were poor farm workers. They were not called peons but *sharecroppers.* They lived and worked on the land of an owner. In return for his work, the sharecropper would receive a certain share, or part, of the money the owner got when the crops were sold. But by that time he was usually so much in debt to the owner that he received little if any cash from the sale, because the money he owed was subtracted from his share.

peony

The peony is a flower that grows in many parts of the world. Peonies are perennial plants, which means that they grow up from the same roots every year. Most peony plants grow to be one or two feet high. The blossoms are very large. They are white, pink, or purple,

The tree peony originally came from China. Its beautiful red and white blossoms make it a favorite with home gardeners.

A. Boutrelle

but there are a few peony varieties that have yellow flowers. Some peonies have a very sweet smell.

Pepin

Pepin was the name of three men who were very powerful in France and Germany more than a thousand years ago. Their title was "mayor of the palace" (*major domo*) of the French kingdom, but in reality they were more powerful than the kings. Pepin I, of Landen, died about the year 639, and Pepin II, of Herstal, died about the year 714. Pepin III was the father of CHARLEMAGNE, about whom there is a separate article. Pepin III, also called Pepin the Short, was the first mayor of the palace to become actual king. This began the Carolingian dynasty, or line of kings. He also did a great deal to help religion and education. Pepin III died in 768.

pepper

Pepper is a very valuable spice. It is the fruit of a plant that grows in India and other parts of the world where the climate is very hot.

The pepper plant is a climbing plant that grows to be about 50 feet high. It has a weak stem but will climb up a post or small tree. It has tough, green leaves and small flowers. The plant is an evergreen, which means that it does not lose its leaves in the fall.

The fruit of the pepper plant is a small berry that is about as large as a pea. The berries grow in clusters. As they ripen, they change from a bright green to red and finally to yellow.

Black pepper is made from berries that have turned red. White pepper is made from yellow berries, which means that the berries are riper. The berries are soaked in water and the skin and pulp are removed to make the pepper. White pepper is milder than black pepper.

Pepper has a sharp taste and stimulates the appetite. It is used in many kinds of cookery and is also an ingredient in some medicines. During the Middle Ages pepper was considered so valuable that people paid tribute to their rulers in pepper instead of gold.

peppermint

Peppermint is an important herb that grows wild in many parts of the world. People in Europe and the United States raise peppermint because it con-

tains valuable oils. The plant is a perennial, which means that it grows from the same roots every year. It grows to be about three feet high and has small purple flowers.

The leaves of the peppermint are used to flavor drinks and sauces. The oil from the peppermint plant is used to flavor candy and chewing gum. Oil of peppermint is used in certain medicines and in soap and perfume.

pepsin

Pepsin is an enzyme found in the gastric juices in the stomach. Enzymes are chemical substances that make digestion possible by changing the chemical composition of food. Pepsin acts on proteins, changing them into peptones, which are soluble and can be assimilated by the body. Pepsin can act only when acid is present, which the stomach supplies in the form of hydrochloric acid. Pepsin is sometimes used as a medicine to aid digestion. It is obtained from the stomachs of sheep, calves, and hogs.

Pepys, Samuel

Samuel Pepys was an Englishman who became famous because he kept one of the best diaries ever written. Pepys was born in London in 1633. He went to Cambridge University and then worked for the government in the naval department for many years. He knew many of the most important people of his time.

When he was 27 years old, Pepys began to keep a diary. For nine years he wrote about the people he knew and important events such as the great London fire, and he described the plays he saw and the entertainments he attended. He also wrote about his own feelings and opinions. The diary was written with so much humor and honesty and is so lively that it has given pleasure to thousands of people. The diary was written in a kind of shorthand that was not deciphered until a hundred years after Pepys' death. Pepys died in 1703, at the age of 70.

percentage, a special way of working with fractions: see the article FRACTIONS.

perch

The perch is a fish that lives in many fresh-water lakes and rivers. Some perch live in the salt water of the oceans. Sportsmen enjoy catching perch.

There are many different kinds of perch. All of them have spines in their fins. The yellow perch that is found in Canada and around the Great Lakes in the United States is a very valuable food fish. It is usually a little more than a foot long and weighs about a pound.

perfume

Perfume is a substance that is used for its pleasant odor. It may be used directly to scent the body, or in soaps, cosmetics, and other products. Perfume is of two types: *natural,* and *synthetic* or artificial. The natural perfumes are obtained from various plants, and almost every part of the plant may be used to obtain special odors. Artificial perfumes are made by combining the chemicals found in the natural perfumes to give the same, or almost the same, odor.

NATURAL PERFUMES

When we speak of perfume, we usually mean the liquid product that is applied directly to the skin and is sold under various brand names. Most of these perfumes are composed of the essential oils of plants, which are dissolved in a solvent such as alcohol and combined with a *fixative,* a substance that helps make the odor last.

Essential oils are the chemical substances that give plants their distinctive odor. They are obtained from the plant by various methods, depending on the part of the plant that yields the oil. The essential oil of mint is found in the leaves of the plant; of cinnamon and cassia, in the bark; of cedar and sandalwood, in the wood; of orange, in the petals of the flower and the rind of the fruit; and of camphor and myrrh, in the resinous gum from the tree.

Givaudan-Flavors, Inc.

The oil for floral perfumes, such as rose and violet, is obtained from the petals of the flower. This is done by one of two methods, *distillation* and *enfleurage.* In distillation the petals are boiled in water, turning the essential oil into a gas. This gas is caught in another container and cooled, when it again becomes a liquid. In enfleurage, the petals are placed on glass trays and covered with fat, which absorbs the essential oil. To recover the oil from the fat, it is mixed with alcohol and heated. The essential oil dissolves in the alcohol and rises to the top of the container, where it can be skimmed off.

Extracting essential oils is a very tricky and delicate job, and it cannot be done on a mass-production basis. This is the principal reason for the very high cost of fine perfumes.

1. The control panel of a perfume distillation and purification system.

2. High-vacuum distillation stills are used in the manufacture of aromatic chemicals.

3. These are some of the substances used in the manufacture of perfumes: (a) *cinnamon bark* (b) *civet* (secreted from a civet cat's scent glands; seen stored in a horn) (c) *musk* (from the glands of a musk deer; one gland is shown) (d) *ambergris* (from a whale's intestines) (e) *sandalwood* (f) *vanilla* (the seed pod of a vanilla plant is shown).

4. The numerous fragrances which the perfumer works with make it difficult to create the exact scent each time. It is an art and a skill to combine the right perfumes to achieve the desired scent.

FIXATIVES

Many of the natural perfumes are highly *volatile,* which means that they disappear easily and quickly. To make the perfume last, both in the bottle and when in use, fixatives are added. Some fixatives are themselves pleasantly scented, others have very unpleasant scents, and still others have no scent at all. The best fixatives are obtained from animals: *Ambergris* is a substance made in the body of the sperm whale; *musk* is a substance found in the musk deer; *civet* is found in the civet cat; and *castor* is found in the beaver. Certain chemicals and plant substances have also been found to have the power to fix scents.

The combination of a fixative with a natural perfume usually changes the scent to some degree. Other perfumes are made by combining natural perfumes in a *bouquet.* The formulas of most famous perfumes are jealously guarded secrets of the people that invented them.

PERFUME IN THE PAST

Perfume has been used from the earliest days of history. The incense mentioned in the Bible, and still used in some religious services, is a kind of perfume, and the ancient Egyptians used perfume in the substances with which they embalmed their dead. In ancient Rome and Athens, perfume was used at feasts, at funerals, and in theaters.

The art of perfume-making was lost in Europe until about eight hundred years ago, when the Crusaders brought it back from their travels to Asia. Later, the growth of the science of chemistry enabled men to analyze the essential oils of flowers and make them in the laboratory.

Pericles

Pericles was a great statesman of ancient Greece. He was born in Athens nearly 2,500 years ago, about the year 500 B.C. Pericles came of a noble family

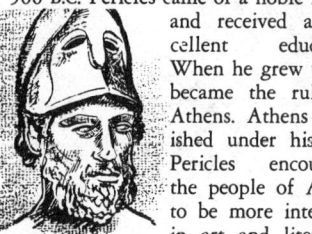

and received an excellent education. When he grew up, he became the ruler of Athens. Athens flourished under his rule. Pericles encouraged the people of Athens to be more interested in art and literature. He built many splendid buildings, including the famous Parthenon, which many people believe is the most beautiful building of all time. This period of Greek history is one of the most brilliant of any in the world, and we call it the Age of Pericles.

Pericles hoped that all of the Greek states would become united, but this did not work out. A terrible war broke out between Athens and Sparta. This is called the Peloponnesian War. After this war had gone on for about a year, a fearful plague broke out in Athens. Thousands of people died. Pericles was one of those who became ill, and he died in 429 B.C. His wife Aspasia was one of the most beautiful and intelligent women of ancient Greece.

periscope

A periscope is an instrument used to see objects that are above and in front of a person. The most familiar use of a periscope is in a submarine. A tube about 30 feet long and 6 inches wide extends from a submerged submarine to the surface of the water. At one end of the tube is a mirror set in an angle, and at the other end is another mirror set at the same angle but with its surface facing in the opposite direction. Both ends also contain lenses through which light can pass and be magnified.

Light entering the top of the periscope is reflected by the mirror and is sent to the lower mirror by means of prisms similar to those contained in binoculars. A person looking through the lens at the bottom of the tube thus can see what is happening above the water,

peritonitis

Peritonitis is an infection of the lining that covers the inside of the abdomen and surrounds the stomach, kidneys, and other organs inside a person's body. Peritonitis occurs when bacteria or germs get into the abdomen. The most common cause of peritonitis infection is an infected appendix that has burst. This causes germs and pus to be dropped into the abdomen. A festering sore (ulcer) in the stomach or intestines may cause peritonitis.

Until about twenty years ago almost every person who got peritonitis died. Now doctors have penicillin and other "miracle" drugs that can kill germs and stop infection. Today most people who get peritonitis are cured. Sometimes doctors operate on people who have peritonitis.

Perkins, Frances

Frances Perkins became famous as the first woman to be a member of the President's cabinet in the United States. She was born in 1882 in Boston, Massachusetts. After being graduated from Mt. Holyoke College and Columbia University, Miss Perkins became a citizen of New York State and interested herself in the problems of making factory work safe and healthful. In 1913 she married Paul C. Wilson. When Franklin D. Roosevelt was governor of New York, he appointed Miss Perkins industrial commissioner of the state, in charge of enforcing factory and labor laws. When Roosevelt became President in 1933, Roosevelt named Miss Perkins to his cabinet as Secretary of Labor. It was her responsibility to put into effect many of the President's New Deal policies. During her term of office, the National Labor Relations Act and the Fair Labor Standards Act were passed. Miss Perkins was always proudest of her work in originating the Social Security system. In 1945 Miss Perkins resigned as Secretary of Labor, and in 1946 President Truman appointed her to the Civil Service Commission. She served until 1953.

Perón, Juan and Eva

Juan Domingo Perón is the name of an Argentine army officer who became president and dictator of his country. When he ran for the office of president, in 1946, the United States opposed him, but he used this opposition to convince the people of Argentina that the United States wanted to interfere with their government. This won him many supporters.

Perón was born in 1895. When he grew up he joined the army, and he soon became a high-ranking officer. In the 1940s he was a leader in a group that supported the Axis (Germany and Italy) during World War II. In 1943 he helped this group overthrow the government, and the next year he became minister of war and secretary of labor in the new military government. Next he rose to the office of vice-president, and in February, 1946, he was elected president. As president Perón tried to strengthen Argentina's army and navy, and to build up its trade and industry. Those who opposed Perón's ideas were imprisoned or driven out of the country. In 1949 Perón had the constitution changed so that he could be re-elected. Perón was re-elected in 1951, but in 1955 he was overthrown by a revolution and fled to Paraguay.

EVA PERÓN

Perón was greatly aided in his work by his wife, Eva Perón. Maria Eva Duarte Perón was born in 1919. Before she mar-

ried Perón, in 1945, she was a well-known actress. She had great influence with Perón, and did a great deal of work to improve the conditions of the working classes of Argentina. She was very popular with the people, who called her "Evita," and her death in 1952 was mourned by the whole country. The city of La Plata was renamed Eva Perón in her honor, but in 1955 the name was changed back.

perpetual motion

A "perpetual motion" machine would be one that would keep running forever, without getting power from anything outside the machine. For centuries, people have tried in many ways to make perpetual-motion machines, but no one has succeeded. According to science, such a machine is impossible. One reason is that no machine can create its own power. It must have some outside source to supply it with this, such as a waterfall, coal, oil or steam power, or sunlight. Another reason is that every machine wastes some power in overcoming friction (the rubbing together of its parts).

The closest that anyone has come to perpetual motion is a machine (such as a clock) that gets its power from changes in temperature or from sunlight, but such machines are not truly perpetual (everlasting) because sooner or later they must wear out.

Perry

Perry was the name of two brothers who were officers in the United States Navy.

Matthew Calbraith Perry was born in 1794. He joined the United States Navy when he was 15 years old. His greatest feat came in 1854, when he was 60 and had risen to the rank of commodore. He was put in charge of an expedition to Japan. At that time the Japanese did not like foreigners, and there was only one port in Japan that was open to foreign ships. Instead of going to this port, Perry sailed into Tokyo Bay and asked that he be allowed to speak to the rulers of Japan. These rulers were very impressed with Perry, particularly because of the ceremony with which he carried out his duties, and he was able to arrange several treaties between the United States and Japan. These treaties opened Japan to influences from the outside world. Matthew Calbraith Perry died in 1858.

Oliver Hazard Perry was born in 1785. He entered the United States Navy when he was 14 and also rose to the rank of commodore. He became a national hero in the War of 1812 when he defeated the British at the battle of Lake Erie. After the battle was over he wrote a short report to General William Henry Harrison. The report began, "We have met the enemy and they are ours." These words have become very famous. Later Perry headed an expedition against the pirates in the West Indies. He died in Trinidad from yellow fever on August 23, 1819.

Perseus

Perseus was a hero of Greek mythology, the stories the ancient Greeks told about their gods and goddesses. His father was the chief god, Zeus, and his mother was named Danae. Perseus had several great adventures. The one best known is his killing of the monster named Medusa. She was one of three sisters, called Gorgons, whose hair was made of snakes and who were so hideous that anyone who looked at one of them was turned to stone. Perseus killed Medusa by looking at her reflection in his polished shield and chopping off her head. Another of his deeds was the rescue of a maiden named Andromeda from a sea monster. He then married Andromeda.

Pershing, John J.

John Joseph Pershing was the United States Army officer who commanded the American Expeditionary Force, the United States troops who fought in France during World War I. He is credited with making a first-rate fighting force out of the unseasoned recruits that had been sent 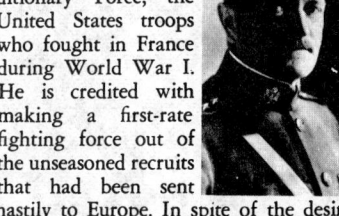 hastily to Europe. In spite of the desire of other Allied commanders to put the Americans into the front lines to replace tired soldiers of other countries, Pershing insisted on keeping the Americans as a solid unit. After the war Pershing was given a military rank created for him by Congress, that of General of the Armies of the United States.

Pershing was born in 1860 in Linn County, Missouri. He had finished school and had become a schoolteacher when he saw a notice of an examination for entrance to the United States Military Academy at West Point. Pershing took the examination and was accepted. In 1886 he was graduated as a second lieutenant. Pershing saw service in the Spanish-American War and in the Philippines, where he gained fame for defeating the Moro tribesmen who had never before been conquered.

In 1915 Pershing's wife and three of his four children were burned to death in their home in San Francisco.

Pershing's nickname was "Black Jack." The story is told that Pershing was very bad at remembering names, but he had the reputation of being very good at it. The explanation was his aide-de-camp, a young man who later was to become General of the Army George C. Marshall, who always stood by and whispered the names of visitors to Pershing.

In 1924 Pershing retired from the army. For a time he served as ambassador to Peru. Pershing's book *My Experiences in the World War* won the 1932 Pulitzer Prize for history. He died in 1948.

Persia, a country in southwestern Asia: see IRAN.

Persian Gulf

The Persian Gulf is an arm of the Arabian Sea. It is about 600 miles long and about 200 miles wide and is very shallow—less than 100 feet deep in most places—but is an important shipping route. It is so shallow because it has been filled in with soil and other matter carried by the many rivers flowing into it, the most important of which are the Tigris and the Euphrates.

The principal countries on the Persian Gulf are Iran, Iraq, and Saudi Arabia; but there are also the small countries of Kuwait, Qatar, and the Trucial States, which are ruled by sheiks (Arab chieftains) under British protection. There are many islands, of which the Bahrein Islands are the largest. The Persian Gulf is in one of the richest oil-producing regions on earth, including the countries on its shores and the Bahrein and other islands. Bahrein also has pearl fisheries. Abadan, in Iran, is the chief port. In World War II, the United States shipped supplies to Russia by way of the Persian Gulf and Iran.

persimmon

The persimmon is a tree that grows in China and the eastern part of the United States. It has been raised in many parts of the world where the climate is not too cold. The people in Japan raise more than eight hundred different kinds of persimmon tree.

The persimmon tree grows to be more than 50 feet high. It is deciduous, which means that it loses its leaves in the fall. It is a handsome tree and has many small tube-shaped white blossoms in the spring. The fruit is a reddish-orange berry. It has a smooth skin, and its soft flesh is sweet and delicious when it is fully ripe.

The wood of the persimmon tree is hard and strong, and it shines when it is polished. The wood is used to make fine floors, golf club heads, billiard cues, and mallets.

personality

Personality is everything that makes one person different from every other person. It is the way he acts and how he feels about things.

Some characteristics, or ways of acting and feeling, are called *personality traits.* Cheerfulness, or optimism, or carefulness, would be an example of a personality trait. Very often a personality stays with a person all his life. Sometimes it changes, not because the person tries to change it but because of experiences that he has.

There are so many different meanings that the word *personality* might have that not even scientists can agree on exactly what it should mean. Most people say a person has a "good" personality if other people like him and enjoy being with him.

Good health may contribute to a good personality. Included in this are good posture and cleanliness—including clean hands, fingernails, and hair. Proper rest and exercise and a good diet also contribute to good personality, because they make you energetic and lively.

perspective

Perspective is a particular way of looking at something. When you look at an automobile from the front it seems wide but not very long. When you change your position and look at the same automobile from the side it now looks quite long but not very wide. The automobile looks different to you in the two cases because you changed your perspective.

Artists have to understand perspective to make their pictures look natural. An example is a set of railroad tracks that go off into the distance. We know that the railroad tracks are the same distance apart all along their length. Yet as we look at them, they seem to grow closer and closer together until at a point in the distance they seem to join. An artist drawing railroad tracks in a picture would have to show them joining in the distance, or else his picture would lack the proper perspective.

Perspective is important in television. As different cameras are used to photograph a scene, different perspectives are shown on the screen of your set. Television cameras often are used to show things from a ground view, or a level view, or a view looking down from above.

HISTORICAL PERSPECTIVE

Just as different perspectives make things look different to the eye, so do things seem different at different times. That is what is called historical perspective. It means simply that what may seem important to us today may seem unimportant to us at some time in the future.

When you were very young and you received a slight cut or bruise it seemed terribly important and you may even have cried over it. As you grew older, tiny cuts and bruises seemed less important, and instead of crying you may even have been able to laugh about them. Older people often laugh at some of the

things that seemed very serious and important in their younger days, because they have gotten a different perspective on their own lives. News that makes headlines today may be forgotten tomorrow—but other news may seem more important than ever.

perspiration

Perspiration, the moisture given off by the body through the skin, is very important to good health. It not only aids the body in getting rid of some of the waste materials that collect in the body, but it also serves to air-condition the body. The body is always giving off some moisture or perspiration through the skin, but much of the time we are not aware of this because perspiration evaporates or passes into the air so quickly. At other times, perspiration pours down the skin in little rivers.

Perspiration comes from many tiny sweat glands that are located in the skin. These millions of sweat glands lie below the outer surface of the skin. They are all over our bodies, but are most heavily concentrated in the soles of the feet, in the palms of the hands, and in the armpits. These sweat glands lie next to many small blood vessels. The blood vessels give off waste liquids and other impurities to the sweat glands. The sweat glands have coiled little tubes that lead to the pores or openings in the skin. Through these tubes the waste moisture is carried to the surface of the skin.

Along with the waste matter the sweat glands also carry extra heat from the blood. In hot weather this helps to keep the body at a normal temperature, because the perspiration evaporates and evaporation causes cooling. This is why on humid or damp days we may feel much more uncomfortable than we do on dry, hot days. When the air is humid, it cannot absorb the perspiration and evaporation is slowed down.

Much of the waste matter carried by perspiration is left on the skin when the moisture evaporates. That is why it is necessary to bathe more frequently in warm weather.

Peru

Peru is the third-largest country in South America. It is on the western, or Pacific, coast, and much of it is high in the Andes Mountains. Peru was the center of the powerful Inca civilization more than five hundred years ago. It was very rich and had vast treasures of gold and silver, but when the Spaniards conquered the Inca Indians they destroyed the great empire.

Peru is 514,059 square miles in size, which is about twice as large as Texas; over fourteen million people live there, slightly more live in Texas. Peru is making progress toward modern industrialism and better living for its people.

THE PEOPLE WHO LIVE THERE

Almost half the people of Peru are Indians. They speak Indian languages called Quechua and Aymara. Long ago many Indians intermarried with Spaniards, and today many Peruvians are of mixed Indian and Spanish descent. In the

last fifty years many of these people have gone to the cities to work in industry. They speak Spanish.

Most of the other people are of Spanish descent. Some of them own vast plantations and estates. A number of people from European countries and North America live in the cities in Peru. Most of the people of Peru are Roman Catholics.

About a third of the people in Peru cannot read or write, and for that reason they are not permitted to vote. There are no schools in many parts of the country, and it is only in the large cities that children can get an education.

HOW THE PEOPLE LIVE

Most of the Indians live in old villages on the slopes of the Andes Mountains. They live very much as their ancestors did. They follow ancient customs, observe old ceremonies, speak their own Indian languages and wear clothing like that worn long ago.

Most of these Indians are farmers. They are poor and uneducated, and they make barely enough to live on. Some work as paid laborers on the large plantations of the Spaniards; others have small patches of land of their own. On the big plantations they raise cotton, sugar cane, coffee, and rubber. Many people take care of large flocks of sheep, alpacas and llamas, whose wool is used for clothing and blankets. The llama also carries heavy burdens and is a familiar sight in Peru.

The Indians live in houses of unburnt brick or clay called adobes. The houses usually have only one room and have

little furniture. In the fields the farmers use crude equipment, with oxen pulling the plows. An Indian woman usually walks behind the plow, breaking up the clods of earth with a stone that is attached to a stick. The children help by taking care of the few pigs or sheep that they own. The Indians have few amusements except for religious festivals, dances, market days, and celebrations.

Many people work in the mines. Peru produces silver, gold, copper, lead, zinc, and oil.

The people in the large cities live much like people in cities in the United States. Many work in factories. The people in large cities such as Lima, the capital, enjoy bullfighting, horse racing, tennis, and other sports.

WHAT KIND OF PLACE IT IS

The great mountain ranges of the Andes extend all along Peru. Some of the peaks are more than 19,000 feet high. In the valleys between the mountains there is excellent farming and pasture land. The great mineral wealth of Peru is in the Andes, but much of it has not been mined because the people do not have modern machinery or good transportation. In the Andes the temperature averages about 50 degrees, but at night it drops and it gets very cold. In the deep valleys between the mountains it is much hotter.

West of the Andes, along the coast, is a narrow, dry plain. Crossing it are many short streams used to irrigate the land. Cotton, sugar cane, fruits and vegetables will grow there. These strips of irrigated land are called oases, and most of the important cities are there. It is the wealthiest region in Peru. In this region there are important oil fields. Severe earthquakes frequently shake the west coast.

Although the coast of Peru is near the equator, the temperature is mild and pleasant. The average temperature around Lima is about 67 degrees.

There are more than forty small islands off the coast of Peru. Millions of birds live on these islands and feed on the swarms of small fish that live in the cool ocean waters. The waste matter from these birds has formed thick layers of a substance called guano, which makes excellent fertilizer. For years, men dug up the guano and sold tons of it to other countries. Most of the guano deposits on these islands are now used by farmers within the country.

The eastern part of Peru, on the other side of the Andes, is very different from the dry western region. It is a wet, tropi-

The Government Palace in Lima, Peru.   *Peruvian Embassy*

cal region, covered with thick jungles and crossed by many rivers. Few people live in this region, although it covers more than half the area of Peru. There is one important city, Iquitos, on the Amazon. Lumber and rubber from the jungle is shipped from this port.

The most important rivers in Peru flow through this eastern region into the Amazon River. The Marañón and Ucayali are the largest. Lake Titicaca, on the border between Peru and Bolivia, is the largest lake in South America.

Peru has a number of railroads and highways that reach many parts of the country. The Pan-American highway crosses the country. There are airports in the important cities.

HOW THE PEOPLE ARE GOVERNED

Peru is a republic, which means that it has a president, a legislature that makes the laws, and a constitution that protects the rights of the people. But many of the presidents have been dictators, who took away many of the rights of the people. A military group or junta seized control in 1968, and selected a president and an all-military cabinet.

All men and women between the ages of 21 and 60 must vote if they can read and write.

The capital of Peru is Lima.

CHIEF CITIES OF PERU

The leading cities of Peru, with populations (including suburbs) from the 1973 estimates, are:

Lima, population 2,415,700, the capital and largest city in Peru. There is a separate article about LIMA.

Callao, population 321,700, the second-largest city, chief seaport of Peru, in the west-central part.

Arequipa, population 194,700, the third-largest city, a commercial center, in the southern part.

Cuzco, population 105,400, the fourth-largest city, famous for its Inca ruins, in the south-central part.

PERU IN THE PAST

Long before Europeans came to Peru, highly civilized Indian tribes lived there. They were finally united into one great empire under the Incas more than seven hundred years ago. Peru was the center of this empire, which covered almost half of South America. The Inca empire flourished until 1532, when the Spanish under Francisco Pizarro entered the country and conquered the people. They wrecked the Inca capital at Cuzco, greedily gathered the treasures they found, and marched to the coast, where they founded the city of Lima. The Indians were made slaves and were brutally treated.

Peru's great mineral wealth made it the most important possession of Spain. The Indians revolted several times, but these uprisings were put down with great cruelty. The Peruvians continued to struggle for independence, and they finally declared their freedom in 1821, but it took them three years more to drive the Spaniards out.

Like many other South American countries, Peru did not find peace or prosperity in its freedom. The country had a number of dictators at the head of the government, and Peru was constantly

fighting wars and revolutions. Almost a hundred years ago Peru went to war against Chile and was defeated in the War of the Pacific. Some of the presidents of Peru tried to improve the conditions of the people and to make the country less backward, but the people continued to be discontented because of poverty and poor working conditions. During World War II Peru sided with the Allies, and in 1945 it became a member of the United Nations. In the same year, it peacefully elected a genuinely democratic government, which collapsed in 1962.

PERU. Area, 514,059 square miles. Population (1973 estimate), 14,010,000. Capital, Lima. Language, Spanish and Indian languages. Religion, Roman Catholic. Government, republic. Monetary unit, the sol, worth 2.6 cents (U.S.) Flag, three vertical bars, red, white, and red, with coat of arms on white.

Petain, Marshal

Henri Philippe Petain was a French marshal, which is the highest military rank. When he was quite an old man, he became a statesman also. He now is remembered mainly as a leader of the "Vichy government" in France, the government that was set up after France's surrender to Germany during World War II.

Petain was born in 1856. He was educated at the French military academy, Saint-Cyr. By 1916, during World War I, he had been made general of a division, and he led the French troops that held off the Germans' greatest attack, at Verdun. This made him a national hero. In 1918 Petain was made vice-president of the French War Council, and in 1934 he became the Minister of War. In 1925 he had gone to Morocco, where he led combined French and Spanish troops to victory over the rebel leader, Abd-el-Krim. Francisco Franco, who later became the Spanish dictator, served under Petain in this campaign, and in 1939, when Franco headed the government in Spain, France made Petain its ambassador to Spain.

In 1940, when France was suffering heavy losses to Germany in World War II, Petain was recalled by the French premier, Paul Reynaud, and was made vice-premier. In June of that year, Petain recommended that France surrender. Reynaud resigned and Petain became premier. He signed an armistice with Germany, by which half of France was occupied by German troops. The French capital was moved to Vichy, a city in the southern part of France, which was not occupied by the Germans.

The Allies invaded France in June, 1944. Petain told the French people they should support the Germans, and then he fled to Germany. In April, 1945, he returned to France and faced trial for treason. He was found guilty and sentenced to death, but General de Gaulle (who had been his greatest political enemy) had the sentence changed to life imprisonment.

In 1951, Petain was released from imprisonment because he was very sick, and he died a month later.

Peter, Saint

St. Peter was the chief of the twelve Apostles sent by Jesus to preach the Christian faith. Roman Catholics recognize him as the first Pope.

Peter's real name was Simon, but Jesus called him *Cephas,* which means "rock" in the Aramaic language spoken by Jesus and his followers. The name *Peter* is a Greek translation and also means "rock." Jesus told Peter that he was the rock upon which he would build his Church.

Peter was married, and was a fisherman with three men who later became Apostles like himself—Andrew, who was his brother; James, and John. He was brave, and when Jesus was arrested Peter cut off the ear of one of the soldiers. But later, during Jesus's trial, Peter became afraid, and three times told people there that he was not a friend of Jesus. After he denied Jesus for the third time, a cock crowed, and Peter remembered that Jesus had foretold these denials. He was sorry, and later preached far and wide, despite great danger and attempts to kill him.

Peter made the first speech calling on people to become Christians. He made many journeys on which he preached the gospel. The Gospel of St. Mark is probably taken from the sermons of St. Peter.

The last place St. Peter preached was in Rome. He was crucified there during the reign of Nero, who hated the Christian religion. A very old story says that this took place about sixty-seven years after the birth of Jesus, and that St. Peter asked to be crucified with his head pointing down to show that he was less important than Jesus.

In 1947, scientists digging under the Church of St. Peter on Vatican hill in Rome found remains of an ancient burial place. Pictures carved on the wall make many think that this is the place where St. Peter is buried.

There are several feast days celebrated by Christians in honor of St. Peter. One is the feast of St. Peter in Chains, which is called Lammas Day in England. It is celebrated on August 1. Another is the feast of Sts. Peter and Paul, which is celebrated on June 29.

The New Testament includes two Epistles of St. Peter.

Peter the Great

Peter the Great was a czar (emperor) of Russia about 250 years ago. He was the first man to introduce the science and learning of western Europe to his

country. Peter was born in 1672. At that time, most of Russia was overrun by barbaric tribes. Though the country was very large, its government was weak and disorganized. As a young man Peter traveled to the countries of western Europe and visited factories and museums and schools. He studied mathematics and military science. When his half-brother, Feodor III died in 1682, Peter was proclaimed czar. At first he ruled together with his half-brother, Ivan, and his half-sister, Sophia, but in 1696 he became sole ruler.

As czar, Peter hired men from other

countries to come to Russia and train his people. He tried to gain more seaports for Russia by fighting the Swedes in the north and the Turks in the south. He founded a new Russian capital, the city of St. Petersburg (which is now called Leningrad). His desire to make Russia a modern, powerful nation was so great that when his son Alexis opposed his reforms, Peter had him killed. Peter died in 1725. He is also called Peter I.

Petrarch

Francesco Petrarch was a great Italian poet who lived six hundred years ago. He was born in 1304. His parents wanted him to become a lawyer, but he loved poetry and became a writer instead.

When Petrarch was 23 years old he met Laura de Sade, a beautiful woman who was married to someone else. He fell hopelessly in love with her and wrote many beautiful poems to her. Petrarch's great ability was appreciated by the people of his time and the senate at Rome crowned him poet laureate when he was only 37 years old. Petrarch died in 1374, at the age of 70.

petrel

The petrel is a lonely bird that makes its home in all the oceans of the world, but especially in the Antarctic seas. The petrel has webbed feet and appears to be able to walk on water by patting the water with its feet. There are many different kinds of petrel. Some of them, such as the giant petrel, are large birds that have a wingspread of almost two feet. Others are small birds no bigger than a robin.

The petrel is brown and gray and dull white. Its feet and bill are black. It has a strong, hooked bill, and its nostrils are joined together in a kind of tube. Petrels build their nests on lonely islands far from any people, in a rocky cliff or on the ground.

The female lays one white egg. Petrels eat shellfish and other tiny animals that live in the sea.

Petrels often stay at sea for many months, and they are well-known to sailors, who have given nicknames to different kinds of petrel. The giant petrel is sometimes called "Nelly." The tiny stormy petrels are called "Mother Carey's chickens."

petrified wood

Petrified means "turned to stone." Petrified forests are places where the trees have turned to stone. This came about because the living forest was buried many millions of years ago under silt or clay, or under ashes from volcanoes. After the trees were buried, hot mineral water seeped through the ground and replaced the wood, cell by cell, leaving in its place the mineral silica, which was carried in the water.

Eventually the wood of the whole tree became silica, which is a kind of stone. Weather wore away the ground that covered the forest and exposed the stone trees to view.

THE PETRIFIED FOREST

In southwest Arizona there is a large petrified forest, protected by the United States government under the name of The Petrified Forest National Monument. The trees in this forest were buried more than 200 million years ago. They had probably been killed by a forest fire. Now they are beautiful brown, yellow and red stone.

Some of the tree trunks are as much as 6 feet in diameter and 100 feet long. The stone distinctly shows the fibers and the grain that once were part of the wood.

In Yellowstone National Park there is a place where seventeen forests, one after the other, were killed by volcanic ashes. Some of the buried tree trunks are still standing upright. A river has cut through the ground and has exposed the petrified forests to view along the steep sides of the river gorge.

Petrograd

Petrograd is an old name for the city in Soviet Russia that is now called Leningrad. The city was originally named St. Petersburg, but during World War I the Russians changed its name to Petrograd, because St. Petersburg is a German name. See the article on LENINGRAD.

petroleum

Petroleum is an oily liquid that may be dark brown, golden brown, dark green, or black in color. Because petroleum is found in pools buried deep in the earth, as other minerals are, it is called "mineral oil." It is most often called simply "oil," even though there are other kinds of oil besides petroleum. When people talk about oil wells, oil fields, crude oil, and so on, the oil they are talking about is petroleum.

Petroleum is one of the most valuable and useful of all minerals. It is a mixture of hydrocarbons, which means that the substances that make up petroleum are themselves made up of the chemical elements hydrogen and carbon. The petroleum mixture is divided up according to the boiling points of the different hydrocarbons it contains. Starting with the one that boils at the lowest temperature, the parts, or "fractions" of the mixture are: 1, naphtha and petroleum ether; 2, gasoline; 3, kerosene; 4, gas oil (to be "cracked" into gasoline); 5, lubricating oil; 6, greases and petrolatum (vaseline); 7, paraffin; 8, asphalt and petroleum coke. From these fractions come thousands of products, such as plastics, lubricating oils and greases, fertilizers, detergents, waterproofing materials, drugs, insect powder and sprays, dyes, perfumes, and photographic chemicals.

THE STORY OF PETROLEUM

No one knows exactly how petroleum was formed in the earth. Most scientists think that hundreds of millions of years ago tiny plants and animals lived in shallow seas in numberless billions, and when they died their dead bodies piled up in deep layers on the ocean bottom. Then they were covered over with sand or mud and were eventually buried deeply. Far underground, they decayed to form petroleum.

Mankind was using petroleum even before history was first written. Later, the Egyptians and Babylonians used tar to make the seams of their ships waterproof, and they made walls and roads of asphalt.

The greasy part of petroleum was used by the Greeks, Romans and American Indians to rub on sprains and bruises. Some of the lighter parts of petroleum were burned in lamps and used for cooking. It was not until 1859, in Titusville, Pennsylvania, that the first oil well was drilled so that petroleum could be obtained on a large scale.

PROSPECTING FOR OIL

Finding just where petroleum is hidden underground is a very difficult task. At first, it was easy. Some oil was so close to the surface of the ground that it seeped up to the surface and made little pools. Often it stained the soil black, and men knew that a little distance beneath the oily ground was petroleum. The oil well at Titusville was only 69 feet deep. But soon the petroleum close to the surface was used up, and deeper wells had to be drilled.

To find out where to drill for petroleum, oil companies have to call in scientists called *geologists*. Geologists know what kinds of rock are most likely to cover pools of petroleum. To prove their guesses, they may drill down to bring up pieces of rock and send these to a laboratory to see if they contain fossil remains of the tiny petroleum-making sea plants and animals. Or geologists may explode dynamite in holes in the ground and make records of the shock waves the dynamite causes. They know what the record of shock waves passing through an oil pool should look like.

In another method, geologists measure very carefully the force of gravity in different parts of an area, because they know just how this force should change in the rocks around oil wells. Not only do they search under different kinds of land, but also under swamps and even under the ocean floor.

They work very carefully at prospecting, because the oil pools may be very far underground—as much as four miles—and drilling down that far is a very expensive undertaking. Even with the best efforts of the geologists, one out of every three wells drilled is a dry well that never produces any petroleum.

DRILLING

Once the geologists have decided where they believe a petroleum pool to be, the drilling crew begins to drill down to it. Over the spot where the hole is to be, they erect a four-sided steel tower, 125 feet high. This tower, called an *oil derrick,* is narrower at the top than at the bottom, and about halfway to the top it has a platform called a *monkey-board.* Most of the drilling crew works at the bottom of the tower, but one man works on the monkey-board. The drilling crew puts a hard steel drill-bit with even harder diamond teeth in it on the end of a 50-foot length of iron pipe. The pipe is connected to a powerful engine that spins the drill around. As the well grows deeper, more 50-foot pipe lengths are added until the string of pipes may be more than three miles long. It is to handle these long joints of pipe that the derrick is built.

Drilling is a very difficult job. Sometimes the hole has to be drilled in a curve, in order to avoid extra-hard rock. Other

Huge pipelines are used to transport crude oil to pumping stations and refineries, and to carry petroleum products across the nation.

times, the rock cannot be avoided, and a drill may grind for ten hours and move down only six feet before it wears out its diamond teeth. Then the drill has to be hauled up and a new drill-bit put on the end of the pipe. A whole day may be spent in hauling the drill up.

Sometimes the drill-bit becomes loosened or the pipe breaks. When this happens, the drillers have to send down special tools that fish for the lost or broken parts, catch them, and haul them up.

Drilling is very expensive. If the drill does not strike oil, as much as a million dollars may have been wasted in drilling the dry well. But the geologists know their job well enough so that two out of every three wells "come in," which is an oil man's way of saying that the well produces oil.

GUSHERS AND WELL SHOOTING

If the oil pool has above it a pocket filled with natural gas, the pressure of the gas may make the oil shoot high in the air, making a *gusher*. It is another tough job to get pipes over the gushing well so that the oil stops spouting all over the landscape. Most oil wells are not gushers, but have just enough gas pressure to make them flow gently.

Every well sooner or later stops flowing by itself and must be pumped. Still later, the well runs dry. When this happens, petroleum geologists "shoot" the well. This means that they send down into the well cans filled with the powerful explosive nitroglycerine. The nitroglycerine is exploded, in the hope that it will crack or break up any sand or rock that may separate the bottom of the well from a neighboring pool of oil. Sometimes this works, sometimes it does not. If it works, then more than one underground oil pool may be tapped without the trouble and expense of drilling new wells.

Although the great demand for oil has caused many fields to be pumped dry, the new methods of prospecting developed by geologists have uncovered enough petroleum in the world to last more than a hundred years at the present rate of use. Also, in many places, there is much petroleum in the soft, spongy rock called *shale*. There is even more petroleum in shale than in underground pools. But it is expensive to get the oil out of the shale.

TRAP FARMS AND REFINERIES

Usually there is salt water beneath the oil pool, just as there may be gas above it. The oil coming from the well may be a mixture of petroleum, salt water, and gas. This mixture is pumped through pipes to a *trap farm*. This is a place with thousands of different pipes and hundreds of tanks. When the oil is pumped into this maze of pipes, the salt water and gas are trapped and separated from the oil. The gas is stored in tanks and used later.

To transport the oil, pipes big enough to crawl through are buried in long ditches that run thousands of miles across the country, and the petroleum is pumped through these pipes to refineries. Or the oil is pumped into railroad tank cars or into ships called *tankers* which carry it to the refineries.

The refinery is a small city made of hundreds of huge tanks and thousands of miles of pipes. Here the petroleum is separated into its different fractions, and the fractions themselves are divided into many different products.

Gasoline is the biggest single product of an oil refinery. Simply boiling off the second petroleum fraction to get natural gasoline would not supply half the demand. Therefore heavier fractions are made into gasoline by boiling them under great pressure. This is called *cracking*. Modern refineries crack their heavy fractions in huge fourteen-story-high pressure tanks called *cat crackers*. The name stands for the words "catalytic cracker" and means that the cracking process is helped along by substances called *catalysts*.

PETROLEUM PRODUCTION

In 1965 the world produced about ten billion barrels of petroleum, with each barrel containing 42 gallons. Of this total, the United States produced three billion barrels of oil, or nearly one-third. The states that produced the most oil, in order of the amount they produced, are Texas, Louisiana, California, Oklahoma, Wyoming, and Kansas. Next to the United States, the largest oil-producing countries, in order of amount produced, are the Soviet Union, Venezuela, Kuwait, Saudi Arabia, Iran, and Iraq.

petunia

The petunia is a flower that first grew in South America. It is now raised in gardens in many parts of the world. There are petunias of almost every color except yellow, and they are very cheerful and pretty flowers.

Some petunias are perennials, which means that they grow up from the same roots every year. However, people have found that if they grow the petunia as an annual and plant new seeds each year,

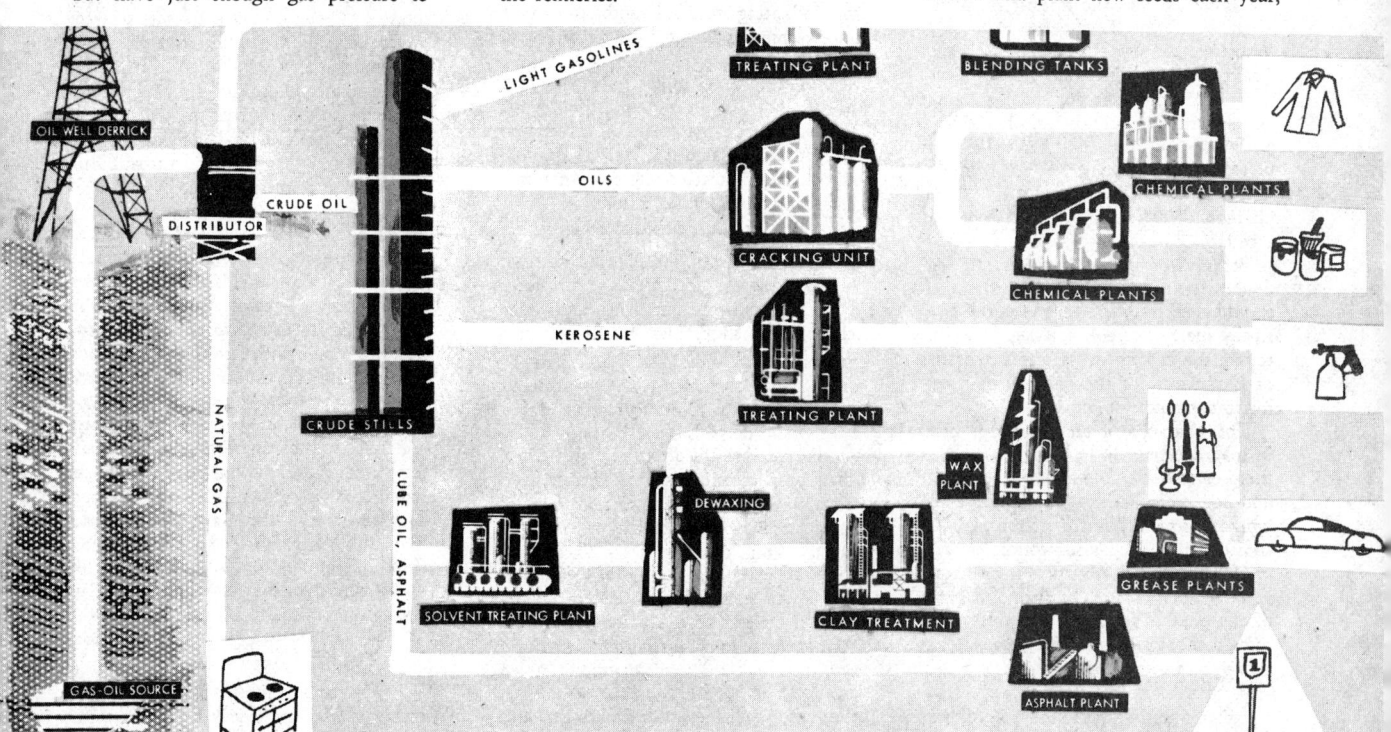

Crude petroleum and natural gas are brought from the well to a distribution point. From there, the oil goes through its first refining. Since it may finally be used for anything from powering an airplane to making paint or plastics, the oil then goes to various plants where it is treated in special ways. The products at the right show a few of the ways petroleum is useful to man.

the blossoms will be larger and more beautiful. Petunia plants grow to be one to two feet high. They have thick green leaves. Some kinds of petunia have a strange unpleasant odor, while others smell very sweet.

Many people grow petunias in flowerpots and window boxes. The petunia is a hardy plant that will bloom all winter.

pewter

Pewter is a soft, silvery metal. It is an *alloy*, or mixture of metals, and is usually made of four parts of tin and one part of lead. Sometimes copper, antimony or zinc is used in place of the lead, or along with it. Pewter is soft enough to be scratched with a penny, and it melts at a low degree of heat, so it is easily shaped into any desired form. In ancient times, dishes were made of pewter. Up to about a hundred years ago it was used to make such things as dishes, candlesticks, and ornaments. Cheap ways to make chinaware and the art of silver-plating put an end to most uses of pewter.

Phaeton

Phaeton was the son of Helios, the god of the sun, in Greek mythology, the stories the ancient Greeks told about their gods and goddesses. Phaeton begged his father to let him drive the chariot of the sun through the sky for one day. Helios did not want to grant this request but finally he agreed. Phaeton discovered too late that he was not strong and powerful enough to control the chariot, so it plunged to earth. Rivers dried up, and great deserts were created where there had been fertile land. It seemed that the whole earth would be destroyed. Then Zeus, king of all the gods, sent a bolt of lightning that killed Phaeton, and the earth was saved.

pharaoh

Pharaoh was the title of the kings of ancient Egypt. They began to rule the country about seven thousand years ago. The ruling families were called dynasties. The word pharaoh means "great house," and the king owned all the land of Egypt. The ancient people believed that the pharaoh was descended from the sun god, whom they called Re. After a pharaoh died he too was worshiped as a god.

Because the pharaohs supposedly had divine blood, it was believed that they should keep this sacred blood in the family by marrying their relatives. For this reason the custom in the great dynasties of Egypt was for the pharaoh to marry his sister or aunt or cousin.

The pharaohs of ancient Egypt lived in magnificent palaces. They surrounded themselves with splendid works of art and had every luxury. All of the people worked to make the life of the pharaoh comfortable. They also worked to prepare the mighty tomb where the pharaoh would be placed when he died. The tombs of the pharaohs were in the great pyramids that are still seen in Egypt.

Pharisees

The Pharisees were a group of Jews who lived in Palestine during the time of Jesus. They were very pious and wished to give religion a place in the state. They wanted the Jews to follow strictly the law of Moses and all traditional Jewish practices. During the lifetime of Jesus, the Pharisees were very powerful. Jesus opposed them because they preferred the letter of the law to its spirit; that is, they were more concerned with observing the law than with loving God and their neighbors. Most of the Pharisees were very learned men, and their arguments with Jesus are recorded in the New Testament. Even after Jerusalem was destroyed, seventy years after the birth of Jesus, the Pharisees continued to be an important means for preserving Jewish tradition.

pharmacy

Pharmacy is the science of making medicines and drugs. A person who is trained in this science is called a *pharmacist*. Pharmacy is very important to the science of medicine. Doctors know what medicines and drugs to prescribe or give to their patients, but pharmacists make the medicines that the doctors order.

Modern pharmacy is only about four hundred years old. There were very few medicines and drugs known to mankind before that. Pharmacy probably originated in the most ancient times when witch doctors, or medicine men, found that certain herbs and plants could help to cure sick people. Many of these herbs and plants actually did nothing to help make people well again, but modern science has found that some of the early witch-doctor remedies actually did have great value.

THE STUDY OF PHARMACY

It is only in the last hundred years or so that pharmacists have been required to have a special college education before they could practice their science. Now, just as in many other fields, a person has to take four years of college training in the special field of pharmacy. Upon graduating from college he must pass an examination given by a State Board of Pharmacy.

The principal things a pharmacist studies in college are chemistry, botany (the science of plants), and mathematics. He learns to use a microscope and many special instruments for weighing, measuring, and mixing drugs.

MODERN PHARMACY

In former times, the pharmacist (also called an *apothecary*, or *chemist*, or *druggist*) sold nothing but drugs and medicines in his shop. Nearly all medicines were made by individual pharmacists in their own drug stores. The pharmacist would carefully mix the medicine, following the doctor's prescription.

Pharmacists still do exactly this work. They prepare millions of prescriptions in their own stores. But more and more of the medicines prescribed by doctors are made by large manufacturers. These medicines are packaged and sold to the pharmacist, so he has them already prepared when the prescription is presented to him. A pharmacist keeps a record of every prescription he fills. The prescription is given a number in his file. If you want more of the same medicine, the pharmacist looks up the number and fills the same prescription, so you do not have to go back to the doctor for another prescription. However, there are some prescriptions that the law does not permit to be refilled. A new prescription is required each time. Narcotics and other dangerous drugs come under this law.

PHARMACY STANDARDS

There are international standards set for the drugs (called *pharmaceuticals*) with which a pharmacist works. Each nation also has its own standards. These standards control the purity of drugs, the naming of them, and the labeling of them. The standards are listed in a book called a *pharmacopoeia*.

In the United States, standards are set by the Federal government. Whenever a new drug is discovered and prepared for public use, it must be approved by the Food and Drug Administration, which is part of the Department of Health, Education, and Welfare, before it can be put on the market.

WHERE PHARMACISTS WORK

Pharmacists work not only in drug stores but also in many other institutions. There are pharmacists in every hospital. They prepare the drugs used in the hospital. Pharmacists work for large manufacturers of drugs and medicines. There are many pharmacists who work for the government. They study drugs and decide whether they are useful and where they should be used.

In 1962 there were 123,997 registered pharmacists in the U.S., both men and women. About 36,500 belong to the American Pharmaceutical Association.

pheasant

The pheasants are a large group of birds that include partridges and quails and beautiful peacocks. Pheasants live in Europe, China, India, and the United States. Most pheasants are good to eat. They have large, fat bodies and small wings and strong legs. Pheasants are fast runners. They use their feet to scratch in the ground for the insects and plants that they eat.

The male pheasant is a handsome bird with a long, pointed tail and usually a crest on its head and a loose fold of bare skin that hangs at the throat. This fold of skin is called a wattle, and it is bright in color. Many pheasants have brilliant red, blue, green and gold feathers that gleam in the light. The female is a smaller bird and is duller in color.

The golden pheasant that lives in the lonely parts of China is one of the most beautiful of all pheasants. It has gorgeous scarlet, gold, green, and black feathers.

The ring-necked pheasant was introduced into the United States from Europe and Asia. It is a handsome bird with red, purple, and yellow feathers. It gets its name from a ring of white feathers on its neck. Around its eyes the ring-necked pheasant has bright red circles of bare skin. Its tail feathers are marked with white bars, and they have been used to decorate women's hats.

Phi Beta Kappa

Phi Beta Kappa is the oldest honorary society and Greek-letter fraternity in the United States. It was founded at the College of William and Mary at Williamsburg, Virginia, in 1776, as a secret social club. It soon became an honorary

society, that is, it was an honor or distinction to become a member of it. In those days its members wrote stories and poetry and scholarly papers on philosophy and other subjects. Today Phi Beta Kappa has chapters, or branches, in many colleges and universities in the country. Its members are usually picked during their last, or senior, year at school, for their excellent scholarship and service to the school. A few members are chosen during their next-to-last, or junior, year. The members are admitted during a secret ceremony, and are allowed to wear a Phi Beta Kappa key. This is the sign of the organization, shaped like a key and inscribed with the Greek letters for P, B, and K. The society has a magazine, *The American Scholar.* See also the article FRATERNITIES AND SORORITIES.

Phidias

Phidias was a great sculptor of Athens, in ancient Greece, about 2,500 years ago. One of his most famous statues was a figure of the goddess Athena, whom the Romans called Minerva. The statue of Athena was about 50 feet high. It was placed inside the Parthenon, a temple to Athena. Another great statue was the seated figure of Zeus, king of all the gods. It was about 60 feet high and was made of ivory and gold. This great statue was considered one of the Seven Wonders of the World. Unfortunately, it was carried to Constantinople, where it was destroyed in a fire almost five hundred years after Phidias died. Phidias was accused of having stolen the gold from some of his statues. He was also accused of having offended the gods by carving his own head on one of his masterpieces. For these crimes he was put into prison, where he died about 432 B.C.

Philadelphia

Philadelphia is the largest city in Pennsylvania and the fourth-largest city in the United States. It is on the Delaware and Schuylkill rivers and is one of the busiest ports in the country. It is in the extreme southeast corner of Pennsylvania, about 90 miles from New York City. From it extend many railroads, highways, and airlines. Philadelphia was founded by the Quakers, and its name means the "City of Brotherly Love." It is often called the "Quaker City."

WHAT PHILADELPHIA IS LIKE

More than two million people live in Philadelphia. Many of them are of English, Irish, German, Russian, and Italian descent. There are more than 300,000 Negroes. Philadelphia is one of the biggest manufacturing cities of the country. The people produce large amounts of silk, hosiery, woolen and cotton products. They make about one-third of all the rugs and carpets made in the United States. There are also large shipbuilding yards and factories that make heavy metal products. Philadelphia is a great publishing center.

Philadelphia has many famous historic buildings, for its people played an important part in early American history. One of the best-known buildings is Independence Hall, where the Declaration of Independence was signed. Another important building is Congress Hall, where

the first Congress of the United States met and where George Washington was inaugurated for his second term as President. Many people also visit the house of Betsy Ross, who has often been credited with making the first American flag.

Philadelphia has many museums and parks. The Philadelphia Museum of Art ranks among the outstanding art collections in the world, with thousands of paintings by famous masters of all centuries and periods. There are thirty colleges and universities in Philadelphia. Among the principal ones are:

University of Pennsylvania. Enrollment, 17,894 in 1962 (co-ed).

Bryn Mawr College. Enrollment, 1,019 in 1962 (women only).

Drexel Institute of Technology. Enrollment, 9,095 in 1962 (co-ed).

La Salle College. Enrollment, 4,509 in 1962 (men only).

Swarthmore College. Enrollment, 960 in 1962 (co-ed).

Temple University. Enrollment, 16,232 in 1962 (co-ed).

Villanova University. Enrollment, 5,962 in 1962 (co-ed).

PHILADELPHIA IN THE PAST

Philadelphia was founded in 1682 by William Penn as a Quaker colony and was known as Penn's "holy experiment." Penn wanted the colony to be a place of religious freedom. He also encouraged the people to make Philadelphia a healthful, beautiful place. It grew rapidly into one of the most important colonial cities. One of its most prominent citizens was Benjamin Franklin.

During the Revolutionary War, many events took place in or near Philadelphia. It was the capital during most of the war, and the capital of the United States from 1790 to 1800. Later, the city continued to grow as a port and manufacturing center. Many celebrations, such as world's fairs, have taken place in Philadelphia.

PHILADELPHIA, PENNSYLVANIA. Population (1970 census) 1,948,609. On the Delaware and Schuylkill rivers. Settled, 1682.

Philip, Saint, one of the Disciples of Jesus: see APOSTLE.

Philip, Duke of Edinburgh

Philip, Duke of Edinburgh, is the husband of Elizabeth II, Queen of England. He is not a king, though he is a queen's husband. Before he became a British duke he was called Prince Philip, because he was a Greek prince, grandson of King George I of Greece, but he was brought up as an Englishman.

Philip was born on the Greek island of Corfu in 1921. When he was a boy, he went to England and was brought up by his uncle, the Earl of Mountbatten. He used the name Philip Mountbatten, his mother's family name. He was a naval lieutenant during World War II. In 1947 he married Elizabeth. He has been one of England's best amateur athletes in several sports. He is very popular with the British people. See the article on ELIZABETH.

Philip, King

King Philip was the chief of a tribe of American Indians, the Wampanoag, about three hundred years ago. Under the leadership of Philip's father, who was named Massasoit, the Wampanoag lived

in peace with the English settlers in New England. When Philip became chief, he began preparations for war. He said his preparations were against another tribe of Indians, but the English became suspicious. Then a Christian Indian who had been acting as a spy for the English was found dead. Three Wampanoag were accused of the murder and executed by the English.

This was the beginning of a war between the Indians and English settlers that is called King Philip's War. The Indians raided settlements and burned towns, and many men, women and children were killed. The English tried to draw the Wampanoag and the other tribes assisting them into open warfare, but they finally had to use Indian methods of fighting—secret attacks and raids. Gradually the settlers subdued the Indians. They captured Philip's wife and son, and then another Indian betrayed Philip's hiding place and Philip was captured and executed.

The result of King Philip's War was that most of the remaining Indians of that region fled to Canada and their territory was open to settlement by the British.

Philip, King of France

Philip was the name of six kings of France, but today only two of them are considered important. They were Philip II, who was called Philip Augustus, and Philip IV, called Philip the Fair.

Philip II lived more than 750 years ago. At that time the nobles in France were very powerful, and often had more power in the government than the king. Philip II made war on several of these nobles, and brought France under control of the crown (the king). He joined Richard I of England in a Crusade to win the Holy Land from the Saracens, but soon afterward made war on Richard and won more land for France. Philip built many churches and schools, and made France an important world power. He was born in 1165 and died in 1223.

Philip IV ruled France about a hundred years later. He is remembered mainly for his quarrels with the Roman Catholic Church. He quarreled with Pope Boniface VIII, and was responsible for establishing Avignon, France, as the seat of Pope Clement V. Philip IV was born in 1268 and died in 1314.

Philip of Macedon

Philip was the name of six kings of Macedon, or Macedonia, a country in the northeastern part of Greece. They lived more than two thousand years ago. The most famous was Philip II, who made Macedon an important empire of the ancient world. Philip was born in 382 B.C. He spent his childhood in Thebes, then the leading city of Greece, where he studied Greek culture, politics, and military science. When he was 23 years old he returned to Macedon, seized the throne, and built up a strong army, with which he conquered and ruled all of Greece. He was king for twenty-three years. Then, in 336 B.C., Philip was assassinated by an officer in his army. Philip II was the father of ALEXANDER THE GREAT, about whom there is a separate article.

Philip of Spain

Philip was the name of eight kings of Spain, who ruled over a period of some four hundred years. During that time Spain was divided into a number of smaller kingdoms, which included Navarre, Castile-León, and united Spain.

The most famous Spanish king named Philip was Philip II,  who was king of united Spain more than 350 years ago, from 1566 to 1598. During that time he was the most powerful ruler of western Europe. He was born in 1527. Before he became king of Spain, he had already been made ruler of Milan, Naples and Sicily, and the Netherlands. For a time he lived in the Netherlands, where he waged a successful war against France. Philip tried also to conquer England. He was a powerful supporter of the Roman Catholic Church and supported the INQUISITION, about which there is a separate article. He sent a great fleet, the Spanish Armada, against England, but it was badly defeated by the English. At his death, in 1598, Philip left his country exhausted and nearly bankrupt from the many wars during his reign.

Philippians, a book of the New Testament, written by St. Paul when he was a prisoner in Rome: see EPISTLE.

Philippines

The Philippines is a group of about seven thousand islands in the Pacific Ocean, off the southeast coast of Asia. Since 1946 it has been an independent country called the Republic of the Philippines. More than thirty million people live in the Philippines, most of them on about four hundred of the islands. The total area of the Philippines is 115,707 square miles, about as large as the state of New Mexico. The largest of the islands

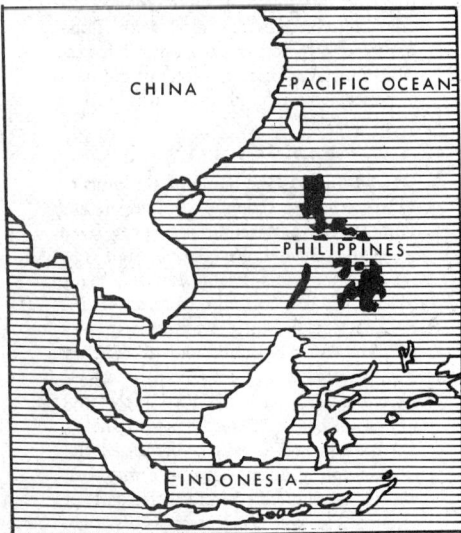

are LUZON and MINDANAO, about which there are separate articles. Others include Samar, Negros, Palawan, Panay, Mindoro, Leyte, Cebu,. Bohol, and Masbate. The most important cities are: on Luzon,

Quezon City (the capital of the Republic), Manila (the largest city), and Baguio; Cebu on Cebu Island; Bacolod on Negros; Iloilo on Panay; and Zamboanga and Davao on Mindanao.

THE PEOPLE WHO LIVE THERE

Most of the people of the Philippines, who are called Filipinos, are descended from the Malays, a light-brown-skinned people of Asia and the Pacific islands. Over a period of hundreds of years, the Malays moved from southeast Asia through Indonesia to the Philippine Islands. During this time they married with several other peoples, including the Indonesians and the Chinese.

In 1521 the Portuguese explorer Ferdinand Magellan discovered the Philippines in the name of King Philip of Spain, and the country was ruled by Spain for nearly four hundred years after that. During this time a new type of Filipino arose, the *mestizo,* who was a mixture of Spanish and Filipino blood. Under Spanish rule most of the people became members of the Roman Catholic Church.

There are some other peoples on the islands. These include the Moros, who are descended from natives that were converted by Mohammedan traders about five hundred years ago. Most of the people, however, are of the Roman Catholic and other Christian faiths, and the Philippines today is considered the only Christian nation in the Far East.

The official national language is Filipino, a new language based on Tagalog, a Malayan dialect. There are about eighty-seven different dialects spoken, but most of the educated people know Spanish and English.

WHAT THE COUNTRY IS LIKE

Most of the Philippines is mountainous, and much of the highland is covered by jungles. Mt. Apo, 9,690 feet high, is the highest peak. There are also thick forests, wide valleys and plains, mineral and hot springs, and many volcanoes. On Luzon and Mindanao there are many lakes. Of the many rivers, the Cagayan, on Luzon, is the largest.

The climate is hot and moist. There are two main seasons, the dry season from November to June and the rainy season from July through October.

The soil is very fertile, and farming is the main occupation of the people. Rice, corn, coconuts, sugar cane and tobacco are the main crops. Fishing is another important occupation. There is much diving for pearls. The Philippines is rich in many minerals, including gold, silver, iron, copper, manganese, asbestos, and gypsum, and the forests have many valuable kinds of wood.

THE PHILIPPINE GOVERNMENT

The government of the Republic of the Philippines was modeled after that of the United States. There is a Congress, which is divided into a Senate of 24 members and a House of Representatives of 120 members. Senators are chosen for a six-year term, and Representatives for a four-year term. There is a President, who is elected for a four-year term of office, and he is aided by a Cabinet of 20 members. The Supreme Court consists of a chief

justice and 10 associate justices. The Philippines is divided into 55 provinces, and each of them elects its own governor. The official capital is Quezon City, but some government offices are in Manila.

HISTORY

The Philippines was named for King Philip II of Spain. The country was ruled by Spain from 1521 to 1898. The Spaniards introduced not only their religion but also their language and their ideas of government, education, and art. In 1898 the United States won the Philippines in the SPANISH-AMERICAN WAR, about which you can read in a separate article. Several years earlier, the Filipinos under such leaders as Emilio Aguinaldo had begun a strong movement for independence. When the United States got possession of the islands, Aguinaldo led a revolt (called the Philippine Insurrection) against the new governors, but the revolt was suppressed in 1901. During the next forty years, the United States helped build up the Philippines, and gave the people more and more self-government. In 1935 the Philippines was given a new form of government, called the Commonwealth of the Philippines. This was to last for ten years, with the United States having less and less control. The plan was carried out, and on July 4, 1946, the Philippines became an independent nation, the Republic of the Philippines.

The Philippine Commonwealth began in its first year, 1935, to prepare for the defense of the country. It was clear that Japan wanted to seize as much territory as it could. General Douglas MacArthur was given a leave of absence from the United States Army to serve as military adviser to the Philippines. Japan's attack on the United States (at Pearl Harbor) in 1941 was followed within hours by an attack on Manila and other parts of the Philippines. The Philippine army fought beside the American troops at Bataan and resisted the Japanese invasion at other places, but the Japanese were too strong and during most of the war the Philippines was under Japanese control. However, guerrilla or underground warfare continued all over the islands during the entire period of enemy occupation. In late 1944 and early 1945, United States forces led by MacArthur returned and drove the Japanese out of the Philippines, though some Japanese troops on Luzon continued to fight until August, 1945.

PHILIPPINES, REPUBLIC OF THE. Area, 115,707 square miles. Population (1964 estimate), 31,270,000. Government, republic (since 1946). Total, about 7,000 islands and islets. Most important islands, Luzon, Mindanao, Samar, Negros, Palawan, Mindoro, Leyte, and Cebu. Capital, Quezon City, suburb of Manila. Language, Filipino (national), English, Spanish, and many local dialects. Religion, chiefly Roman Catholic. Monetary unit, the peso, worth about 26 cents (U.S.). Flag, a blue and red horizontal stripe; a large white triangular field on the left containing a golden sun with three gold stars.

Philistines

The Philistines were an ancient people who lived in Philistia, a country on the Mediterranean Sea southwest of Judea. Their chief town was GAZA, about which there is a separate article. The Old Testament records many battles between

the Hebrews and the Philistines. The articles on DAVID and SAMSON tell the stories of those two Jewish heroes against the Philistines. The Philistines were never fully conquered by the Hebrews. Later, they were overcome by the Egyptians. The Philistines were enemies of the Jewish religion; for this reason the term "philistine" is often applied to anyone who cannot or will not appreciate high ideals or works of art.

philosophy

A philosopher, in ancient Greece (where the word came from), was a "lover of wisdom." In those ancient times, little was known about the world. A philosopher studied any and every branch of knowledge—what made plants grow, how the planets moved through the heavens, the workings of animal bodies, mathematics and chemistry and religion, and everything else that could add to man's knowledge.

Philosophy is still the study of all knowledge, but it has changed greatly. Most of the matters that were studied by ancient philosophers have become separate sciences.

The modern philosopher no longer searches out the reasons for things by performing experiments in chemistry or physics or other sciences. He leaves that to the chemists and physicists and astronomers and other scientists. Philosophy is more the study of everything that cannot be proved by experiment.

Philosophers study what the great philosophers of past ages have thought and written. They study what scientists in special fields have learned and are learning constantly. They put all this knowledge together and try to find the meaning and the explanation of the world as a whole.

BRANCHES OF PHILOSOPHY

Philosophy includes several branches, though not every philosopher agrees on exactly what these branches are. They include:

Logic, the study of reasoning. There is a separate article on LOGIC.

Ethics, the study of what is right and what is wrong.

Aesthetics, the study of beauty and what makes things seem beautiful.

Epistemology, the study of human knowledge—how much man is capable of knowing.

Metaphysics, the study of the meaning of life and nature and the world in general.

PHILOSOPHERS OF THE PAST

The first written philosophy of any importance that has survived the ages came to us from Greece and dates back about 2,500 years. There were thinking men, "lovers of wisdom," long before that, but not enough is known of them to call them philosophers.

Thales was the first of the important Greek philosophers. He was active about 585 B.C. Pythagoras, who came about a hundred years later, made important contributions to mathematics and astronomy, and some of his teachings have been followed as a religion. The three greatest Greek philosophers were Socrates, his pupil Plato, and Plato's pupil Aristotle.

Though they lived so long ago, some of their philosophy has never been surpassed and still has many followers.

The great philosophers of the Middle Ages were concerned with religion. Many were Christian philosophers, but some were followers of the Mohammedan religion. All these philosophers thought deeply about the relationship of man to God, and about ethics, how man should behave and what he should believe. The study of God is *theology,* a branch of philosophy.

Modern philosophy is generally said to have begun with the French philosopher, René Descartes. He founded a type of philosophy known as *rationalism,* which holds that there are some ideas that are simply in our minds and that do not have to be learned from experience. Also, the test of our ideas is whether they are clear and distinct. Spinoza and Leibnitz belonged to this school. In England, Bacon Locke and Hume developed a school known as *empiricism,* which held that we get our ideas and test them by experience. A German, Immanuel Kant, tried to work out a compromise that included religious faith.

A recent American philosopher was John Dewey, who died in 1952. He taught that philosophy, like other sciences, should be studied in such a way that ideas can be proved and not merely treated as opinions. Dewey has had great influence on many modern students.

phlox

The phlox is a popular flowering plant. There are many different kinds of phlox, but the most popular bloom in the summer and are annuals, which means that they must be planted every year. Phlox often grow to be more than three feet high. Their blossoms may be rose, lavender or white in color.

phobia

Phobia is the scientific name for an unreasonable fear. A person who has a phobia has a fear of a particular thing, person, or situation. He may be a calm, relaxed person except at those times when he is faced by the object he fears, and then he becomes very anxious.

One of the best-known phobias is called *claustrophobia,* the fear of small and enclosed places. A person with claustrophobia becomes very anxious and fearful in a small room, and often will refuse to use a telephone booth or to ride in an elevator. Other phobias are fear of high places, of crowds, of water, of tunnels or bridges, of animals, and so on.

Almost everyone has gone through a period in childhood when he has had one or more phobias, such as fears of being alone, or of darkness, or of lightning and thunder. Most children outgrow these phobias gradually. Psychiatrists, doctors trained in problems of the mind, can help to clear up the causes of unreasonable fears that continue into adulthood.

phoebe

The phoebe is a small bird that lives near lakes and rivers in many parts of the United States. Its call sounds like "fee-bee." It is also called the *water peewee.*

It is about as large as a sparrow. It is a brownish-black color with a black head and white underneath its body. The phoebe is a member of the flycatcher family, birds that eat flies and other insects.

The phoebe builds a very fine nest of mud and twigs and attaches it to a rocky cliff or steep river bank, or sometimes to a bridge or a building. The female bird lays four or five white eggs with brownish spots. The phoebe migrates to warm parts of South America for the winter.

Phoenicia

Phoenicia was an ancient country on the Mediterranean Sea, in what is now western Syria and Lebanon. More than 2,500 years ago, Phoenicia was composed of a number of city-states (cities that governed themselves). The most important ones were Tyre and Sidon.

The Phoenicians were a Semitic people. They called themselves Canaanites and their language was spoken throughout Palestine. Hebrew, in which much of the Bible was written, was a Canaanite language. The Phoenicians were the greatest sailors and traders among the Mediterranean peoples. The cedar wood of Lebanon was in demand everywhere for building temples and palaces.

The Phoenicians founded many colonies along the coast of North Africa, including the great cities of Carthage and Utica. To these places they took their learning, which included an alphabet they devised. The Greek alphabet (from which we get our alphabet) came from the Phoenician. The Phoenicians made fine glassware, metal articles, and cloth.

Phoenicia's power and importance gradually grew less when the empires of Persia and Greece became stronger. Later, Phoenicia became a Roman colony.

Phoenix

Phoenix is the capital and largest city of Arizona. It is on the Salt River, and in the center of the Salt River Valley, a rich farming region. It is an important shipping center for fruits, farm products, and cattle. It is growing very rapidly. Almost 600,000 people live there. They work in food-packing and fruit-canning plants and in flour mills and breweries. The climate of Phoenix is very warm and dry and many people go there for their health and for winter vacations. The desert scenery is very striking.

Phoenix was once the home of several Indian tribes. Today the Heard Museum and the Arizona Museum have many relics of these people. Visitors to Phoenix can also see ruins of ancient Indian dwellings, called *La Ciudad* (meaning "the city" in Spanish). Every February the city has an exciting rodeo, and in March there is a colorful Indian celebration called the Festival of the Sun. There is an Indian school in Phoenix, and several Indian reservations are near the city.

Phoenix was founded in 1871 and became the capital of the Arizona Territory in 1889. The city was named after a mythical bird called the phoenix, which according to the Greek legends was born out of fire.

PHOENIX, ARIZONA. Population (1970 census) 581,562. Capital of Arizona. Coun-

ty seat of Maricopa County. On the Salt River. Settled, 1871.

phonograph

A phonograph is a machine that will play music or other sound that has been recorded on a round, flat disk called a record. A phonograph is also called a record-player, and in England it is called a gramophone.

All sound is caused by vibrations, or shaking movements. These cause waves, or ripples, in the air, and these sound waves falling on our ears are what make us hear. In a phonograph, it is a needle that vibrates. Its vibrations are carried to a loudspeaker, which sends out the sound waves. A phonograph record is cut with grooves that have tiny irregularities in them. The record revolves on a turntable that is turned by a motor. The needle travels along the grooves. Each irregularity makes it vibrate in a different way, making a different kind of sound wave.

The first phonograph was invented by Thomas A. Edison, in 1876. At first he used a cylinder wrapped in tinfoil for his record. Then he used hard wax. Gradually the disk instead of the cylinder was adopted for phonograph records, and the material changed from wax to hard rubber and then to shellac and various plastics. During the 1920s, when radio had come into existence and the radio tube was being used to amplify sound (make it louder), record-players came to be made like radios, with the sound produced by the needle amplified with tubes and sent out through a loudspeaker.

In the 1930s, the "juke box" became popular. This is a big phonograph that automatically plays records when you put a coin in a slot and press a button to choose the record you want. After World War II, record-changers came to be used on many phonographs used in homes.

The records used for many years revolved on the turntable at a speed of 78 revolutions per minute and the usual record, which measures 10 inches across, would play for about three minutes. In the 1930s, "long-playing records" began to appear. They run at a much slower speed, 33⅓ revolutions per minute, and a 12-inch long-playing (LP) record may play for as long as 30 minutes. A third speed, 45 revolutions per minute, is used on some records. Records that spin at 16 revolutions per minute have also been produced, but have not been too popular. The sound on these records is not as accurate as on the other records. They have been used on phonographs installed in automobiles. Radio stations use records (called *transcriptions*) that measure 16 inches across.

Three developments of the 1950s that have greatly affected the phonograph are magnetic tapes, "hi-fi" sets, and stereophonic sound. Magnetic tapes are long ribbons of plastic that have been treated chemically so that they can record sound through magnetic impulses. They are wound on spools and played on tape-recorders. Tape recorders are very different from the phonograph invented by Edison. Sometimes it is possible to record whole symphonies or other long works on a single tape.

Hi-fi (high fidelity) sets are phonographs that reproduce sound with the utmost fidelity (faithfulness) to the original. Usually they consist of components (parts) that are bought separately and linked together by the owner. These usually consist of a turntable and arm, with stylus (needle), an amplifier, and two or more loudspeakers. Owners try to buy components that work well together, and they install them in such a way as to produce the best sound.

Stereophonic sound is a way of reproducing sound so that it has "depth" or dimension to it. When you hear it, you feel as if you are right in the studio or concert hall where the sound is being produced. It requires a special phonograph to play "stereo" records, but most phonographs today are made so they can play these new records as well as the older (monaural) records. Stereo records accounted for about 40 per cent of the more than $600,000,000 in recordings sold in the United States in 1962.

See also the article on RECORDING.

phosphorescence

Phosphorescence is the ability of certain substances to glow in the dark after being exposed to light. Phosphorescence is similar to FLUORESCENCE, about which there is a separate article, except that fluorescent substances will glow only as long as they are exposed to light.

When light shines on phosphorescent materials, it changes the shape of the tiny particles, called molecules, of which they are made. When light stops shining, the molecules return to their original shape and in the process give off a light of their own.

Phosphorescence should not be confused with the ability of substances such as phosphorus, and objects such as glow worms, fireflies, and plants, to give off light by themselves without any light falling on them from the outside. Such ability is called *luminescence*.

phosphorus

Phosphorus is a soft solid substance that glows in the dark. It is a chemical element, which means that it is one of the basic substances of which everything in the world is made. There are three kinds of phosphorus: white (or yellow), red, and black.

White phosphorus is extremely poisonous. It should never be allowed to touch the skin, nor should its vapors ever be breathed. When exposed to the air, it combines with the oxygen gas in the air and may catch fire. (For this reason, it must always be kept and handled under water.) It is used in tracer bullets, in incendiary bullets, bombs, shells, and hand grenades, and in other weapons.

Red phosphorus is used on that part of matchboxes or book matches on which safety matches are struck. It is not poisonous.

Black phosphorus is a scientific curiosity that probably has not existed outside of one laboratory where it was prepared for scientific study.

Phosphorus combined with other elements has hundreds of uses: as a fertilizer, water softener, rust-proofing agent, bronze hardener, and metal cleaner; as an ingredient of toothpaste, toothpowder, and baking powder; as a detergent (soap); as an aid to the fermentation of liquors and beer; in the refining of sugar, the tanning of leather, and the dyeing of cloth; and as an addition to foods in order to make them bone- and muscle-builders.

PHOSPHATES

Phosphorus is present in a number of compounds that are called *phosphates*. The most important of these is calcium phosphate. Phosphorus is a necessary element for growing plants. If the soil is lacking in phosphorus, it needs fertilizers that contain calcium phosphate. From the plants this compound finds its way into the body. Almost a third of the weight of the teeth and bones is calcium phosphate.

FINDING PHOSPHORUS

Phosphorus is contained in many different rocks. The most important mineral it forms is a rock called *apatite*. When a mixture of apatite (or burnt bones), sand and coke is heated in an electric furnace at a very high temperature, white (or yellow) phosphorus is separated from the mixture. Red and black phosphorus can be made from this.

photoelectric cell, see the section on the *electric eye* in the article ELECTRONICS.

photoengraving

Photoengraving is a way of making printing plates through the use of photography. Plates made by the photoengraving process are used for printing drawings, photographs, and paintings.

There are two types of photoengravings, *line cuts* and *halftone* engravings. A line cut is used to reproduce artwork that consists only of lines. This includes pen-and-ink drawings, hand lettering, and letters set up in type. A halftone will reproduce a photograph or painting.

LINE CUTS

When a line cut is made, the artwork is photographed by a special camera onto a negative. Then a sheet of copper or zinc is covered with a substance that is sensitive to light. The negative is placed on this plate and exposed to light. The plate is bathed in a chemical acid that eats away all parts of the metal except those that form a picture of the original artwork. This leaves the lines from which the plate will print standing higher on the plate than the parts that do not form the picture. In printing, these higher parts receive ink and, when the plate is pressed onto paper, leaves a picture of the original.

HALFTONES

A photoengraving that reproduces shades of gray is called a halftone. It is made in about the same way as a line cut except for one very important difference. When the original artwork is photographed by the camera, a screen is placed in front of the negative. This screen has crisscrossed lines that break up all the tones of black and gray into very small dots. Very dark parts have larger dots, and gray parts have smaller dots. If you examine a photograph printed in a newspaper carefully with your naked eye, or, better yet, with a magnifying glass, you can clearly see these little dots. When

you look at the photograph very closely, these dots are annoying, but from ordinary reading distance you hardly notice them.

In making halftones, screens with different numbers of lines to the inch are made, according to the kind of paper that will be used in printing the engrav-

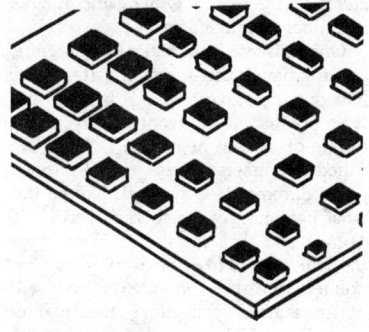

The photoengraver's halftone engraving looks like a waffle iron when enlarged. Small, wide-apart dots produce printing that looks gray, the larger ones black.

ings. Newsprint, the paper used in newspapers, absorbs ink readily and lets it spread, like a blotter, so coarse screens with about 65 lines to the inch are used. In most magazines and books, photographs are printed on smoother paper that does not let the ink spread, so finer screens are used, up to 150 lines to the inch. The finer the screen, the clearer the reproduction.

In both line cuts and halftones, the engraving can be made either larger or smaller than the original artwork.

Sometimes a piece of artwork will have both a line drawing and a photograph. To reproduce this properly, part of the photoengraving will have to be a line cut, for the drawing, and part halftone, for the photograph. A cut like this is called a combination plate.

COLOR ENGRAVINGS

Engravings that will reproduce colored artwork in their original colors are more complicated. When colored artwork is to be reproduced by a line cut, a separate line cut must be made for every color. If a line drawing of a person has a black outline, dark red lips, a green

A line cut gives a sharp reproduction, but there are no shades of gray and black.

A halftone is really a mass of dots. *Left:* A fine-screen halftone makes the picture clear, and the dots are not noticed. *Right:* The dots are seen easily when the screen is coarse.

suit, and blue eyes, four different cuts must be made, one showing the outline, one the lips, one the eyes, and one the suit. The paper goes through the printer's press once for each color.

Halftones can reproduce any color by mixing three or four colors. The colors of even the most complicated painting or colored photograph can be reproduced from four separate halftone plates, a black plate, a blue plate, a yellow plate, and a red plate. Sometimes the black plate is omitted.

In making a set of four-color halftone plates, the original artwork is photographed first as for a regular engraving. This makes the black plate. Then a colored filter is placed over the camera lens to strain out all colors except red. For the blue plate a filter of another color is used, and for the yellow plate a filter of still another color is used. When we say that these plates are yellow, red, and blue. we do not mean that the plates themselves are of these colors. If you were to look at these plates you could not tell them apart by color, for they are all the same color, that of copper. By yellow, blue, and red, we mean that these are the colors of the inks that are used in printing each plate. Four-color halftones, like four-color line cuts, require that the sheet go through the printer's press once for each plate.

photography

Photography is a way of recording a scene by means of an instrument known as a camera. Millions of people have found photography a fascinating pastime and hobby. They take pictures during vacations, of birthday parties, of their friends, of their children as they grow up, and have a record to look back to as the years pass. Photography is also a good career. Photographs are also used widely in newspapers and magazines as part of the news or in advertisments. About two and a half billion photographs are taken each year in the United States alone.

The picture-making process is simple. You decide on what you want to photograph, focus your camera on the subject, then snap the shutter. This permits the light from the scene to pass through the lens of the camera to the film at the back of the camera. When this is done, a chem-

ical change takes place on the film. You then develop the film or send it out to be developed. In the process of development the image on the film is brought out and you get what is called a negative. On the negative the tones of the original subject are reversed; that is, what was black on the subject is white on the negative and what was white on the subject is black on the negative. To get a picture just like the original subject, light is allowed to shine through the negative onto a special kind of paper. This now becomes a "positive" view, with the black and white shown just as they were in the scene that was photographed.

HOW A CAMERA WORKS

To take good photographs you do not need very expensive equipment. As a matter of fact, it is better to start with a simple camera because it has fewer gadgets that can be used incorrectly. There are satisfactory cameras that cost only a few dollars.

Whether a camera costs much or little, it works on the same principle. You can get a good idea of how a camera works by making a pinhole camera. Take a cardboard box and punch a hole with a pin in the front end. Then cut the back end out and in its place put a sheet of tightly stretched tissue paper. Direct this at a brightly lighted object and you will see the image on the tissue paper. If you replace the tissue paper with film, you have a workable camera. To take a picture with the pinhole camera, you expose the film by uncovering the pinhole, holding the camera steady while the image is recorded on the film, and then covering the pinhole.

Every camera is just an advance on this simple pinhole camera. Instead of just a hole, a lens is used. The lens gives a sharper image and permits a shorter exposure. Also, in most cameras there is a diaphragm inside or next to the lens that allows you to adjust the amount of light that passes through the lens. Instead of having to uncover and cover the lens by hand to permit light to reach the film, a mechanical shutter is included that does this when you press a button or a lever. To help you aim the camera at the subject, you have a glass *finder* in which you see what you want to photograph. A

Inside a camera

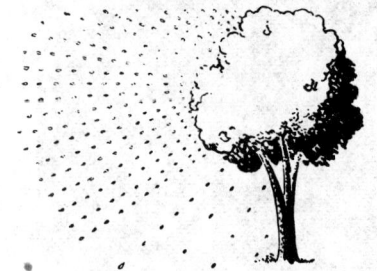

1. This small character is a photon, a unit of light. He and his innumerable brothers move in straight lines at 186,000 miles a second.

2. When light units hit something, they bounce back — or are absorbed. If they bounce back to your eye, the object looks bright . . . If they are absorbed, the object looks dark.

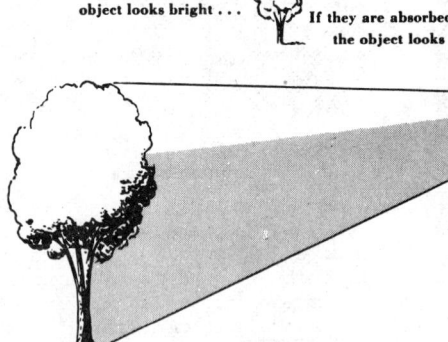

3. From every bright part of a scene, many units of light radiate to the lens of your camera — and the lens lines them up and passes each unit along to the proper point on the film.

4. A large-aperture lens cannot focus sharply the light units from both very near and very far objects. Therefore, it's mounted so it can be moved forward or back, until it's set for the objects you want sharpest.

5. The film at the back of your camera is a sensitive silver screen. Units of light strike it and leave an invisible record, a "latent image." Each unit, sent to its proper spot by the lens, adds a little to the pattern of light — thus reproducing the scene the lens sees. (Later on, chemical development makes the "latent image" visible.) To measure out exactly the right number of units from the available light, your camera has two "front gates" (see below).

6. Your camera's shutter is a gate which opens and closes quickly (unless you've set it for "bulb" or "time" exposures). When it's shut, no light passes through. The shutter (below) always opens fully and closes completely. But the other gate (the diaphragm, on facing page) is always partly open or wide open, to admit more or fewer units of light.

holder in the back of the camera keeps the film in place and allows you to turn the roll of film to the next position after you have taken a snapshot.

ƒ NUMBERS

On simple cameras all you have to do to take a picture is to point the camera and press the button. Other cameras have a number of refinements.

One of these is a device that permits you to change the *aperture* (size of the lens opening). You do this by setting a little pointer on the front of the camera to one of a series of numbers. These are called ƒ numbers. Every ƒ number gives you a different lens aperture. To see just what happens, set the shutter speed to T (time) and click the shutter. This keeps the lens open. Now move the ƒ number pointer to various numbers. You will notice that as you move this pointer toward the higher numbers, such as 8, 11, 16, 22, the diaphragm makes a smaller and smaller opening. This means that less and less light will be able to go through the lens. When you turn the pointer in the opposite direction, the hole gets larger and more and more light can go through. In other words, the higher the ƒ number the less the amount of light that will reach the film. An ƒ 8 opening will give you more light than ƒ 11, and ƒ 11 will give you more light than ƒ 16. By using different lens openings, or ƒ numbers, you can take pictures in weak light or cut down on the light if it is too strong.

A lens is rated according to its ƒ number when it is completely open. The commonly used lenses are ƒ 1.5, 3.5, and 4.5.

Another important thing happens when you change the aperture of a lens. The higher the ƒ number, the greater the depth of field. Depth of field means the distance in front of the lens that it will photograph in sharp focus. For example, when a lens is set at ƒ 22 everything from seven feet in front of the camera and beyond may be in focus. Then, as you open the lens to ƒ 16, ƒ 11, ƒ 8, and so on, this in-focus area gets narrow, so that by the time you get to ƒ 4.5 the depth of field may be only a few feet. This means that when you use the lens at its wide openings you must be careful that what you are photographing is in focus.

There is another quality of lenses that helps you to take better pictures. This is the focal length of a lens. Focal length means the distance from the lens to the point in the camera where the rays of light passing through the lens gather to make a clear picture. When a lens has a short focal length, you can get some very peculiar effects. For example, if you ask a person who is sitting at a desk to place his feet on the desk top and you photograph him with his feet close to the camera, his feet in the picture will look several times bigger than his head and you will have a very comical picture.

Sometimes you get this same peculiar effect when you do not want it. This happens when you take a photograph of a person's face and stand too close to him. In the picture his nose will appear very large. To correct this, simply step back from the subject a bit.

The "telephoto" lenses that you see

7. When the light is strong, as in bright sun, many units can crowd quickly through the shutter. But when light is dim, with units scattered and few the shutter must remain open longer, so enough units can straggle through and impress the picture image on the film.

8. Instead of leaving the shutter open longer, you can open the camera's other "front gate"— the lens diaphragm — to a wider setting. The wider it's open, the more light passes through in a given time. In dim light, a wide-open lens setting may permit you to take snapshots at 1/25 or 1/50 second, instead of making "time" exposures. In bright light, you may often close your diaphragm down to a small opening — such as *f*/11 or *f*/16 — and your lens will then focus a deeper zone, helping you get both near and far objects sharp. The reserve lens speed, adjustable diaphragm, focusing movement, and shutter with a choice of speeds, all enlarge the picture capacity of a fine camera.

ground-glass focusing screen at the top of the camera, which permits you to see the subject almost exactly as it will appear on the photograph.

One of the most useful and compact cameras of all is the 35 mm. camera, or miniature camera. The film it uses is 35 millimeters wide, which is much smaller than the film used in most other cameras. Most miniature cameras have very fast lenses and very high shutter speeds. They are excellent for taking candid pictures, or pictures made when the subject is unaware that he is being photographed. They are also popular for taking color

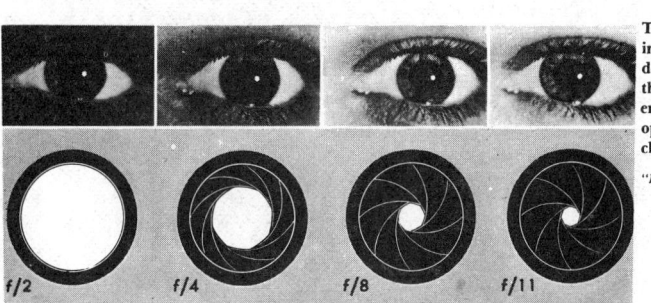

The iris of the eye opens in dim light and closes down in bright light. In the same way, the camera's diaphragm should be opened in dim light and closed in bright light.

"How to Make Good Pictures"

newspaper photographers use at baseball games are actually lenses with very long focal lengths. The long-focal-length lens magnifies the subject and makes subjects taken from a distance seem very close.

LENS AND SHUTTER

The lens is usually made of glass. In simple cameras it is one piece of glass. Finer lenses are made of several pieces of carefully ground glass. The pieces may be cemented together or have air spaces between the parts or elements. Some cameras are so made that the lens can be removed and other lenses, of different focal lengths, can be inserted.

Most good lenses today are *coated.* Coated lenses pass more light through than uncoated lenses and also permit you to photograph a light or a bright reflection without flare. Flare is the objectionable spreading of light.

The shutter of a camera determines how fast the picture is taken, or how long the film will be exposed to light. If your camera has no marking on the outside for the shutter speed, its speed is probably about one-fiftieth of a second. Some cameras have shutters that will keep the lenses open for as long as one whole second or for as little as $\frac{1}{1200}$ of a second.

You may often see the letters T and B marked on the outside of the camera. T means time exposure. B means bulb exposure. To make a time exposure you click the shutter to open the lens and click it a second time to close it. For a bulb exposure you push the shutter down to open the lens and then push it up to close the lens.

KINDS OF CAMERA

The camera department of your photography shop may display a bewildering variety of cameras, but actually there are only a few basic kinds of cameras. The simplest is the box camera. It is just a box with a simple lens and shutter. Another simple type of camera is the folding camera. It has a *bellows,* a device that folds back into the body for ease in carrying. Both box and folding cameras are good for beginners.

The reflex camera is popular with more advanced photographers. This usually has a good lens with various speeds and a special viewing device. This is a

John's dad wants to take a picture of John. Little children are difficult to pose, so he focuses the camera, adjusts the lens, and waits for the right pose while John is playing. The image of John inside the camera is upside down, just as it actually is when seen by the eye.

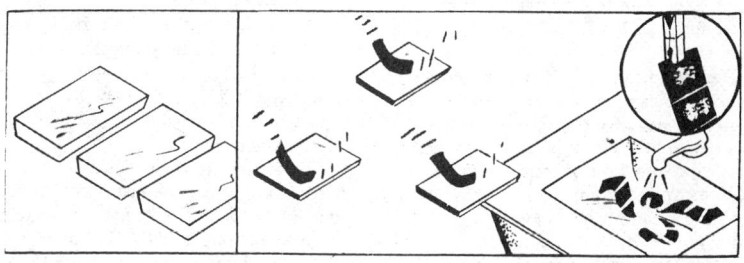

Above: The roll of film is developed, fixed, washed, and dried. *Below:* Then a contact print or **an** enlargement is made on photographic paper. The paper is developed in the same way that **the** film was, though it takes less time. It may be finished with a dull or glossy surface.

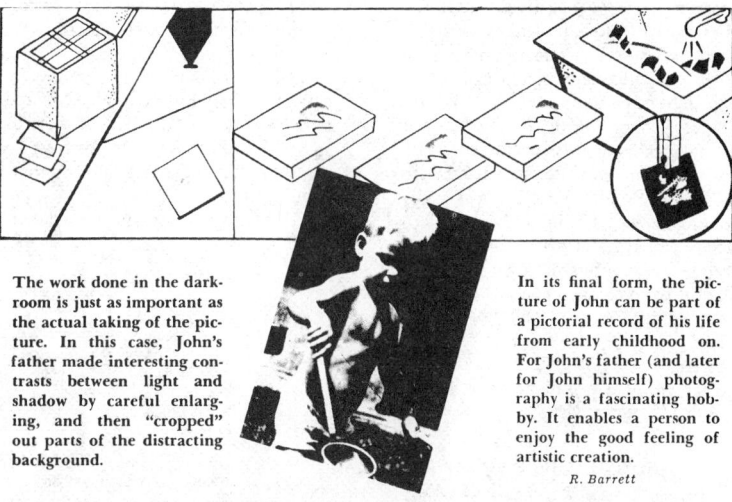

The work done in the darkroom is just as important as the actual taking of the picture. In this case, John's father made interesting contrasts between light and shadow by careful enlarging, and then "cropped" out parts of the distracting background.

In its final form, the picture of John can be part of a pictorial record of his life from early childhood on. For John's father (and later for John himself) photography is a fascinating hobby. It enables a person to enjoy the good feeling of artistic creation.

R. Barrett

1. When the subject is moving and the shutter speed is too slow, the subject is blurred, although the background is clear.

2. When the photographer's hand is not steady, the camera moves. This causes the entire picture to look blurry, almost as if the lens were not focused.

3. Since the viewfinder is a few inches away from the lens, it does not "see" exactly the same picture the lens does. This often results in "chopped off" heads, especially in close-ups. (This problem is eliminated by using a camera which enables the photographer to view his subject through the same lens that "sees" the final picture, rather than through a viewfinder.)

4. Letting too little light reach the film causes underexposure, and the picture will be too dark.

5. Sunspots are caused by reflections of the sun's rays on the camera lens.

All photos: Eastman Kodak

pictures because the individual picture or frame is so small that it is quite inexpensive.

The favorite camera of newspapermen is the press camera. This is a large camera with a negative 4 inches by 5 inches. Newspapermen like it because it is good for almost any kind of photograph, from portraits to fast-action sports shots. It has two shutters and both an eye-level finder and a ground-glass focusing screen.

If you have your portrait taken in a photographer's studio, you will probably see him use a big studio camera held securely in place on a tripod. The studio camera takes large negatives, usually 8 inches by 10 inches. Its lens is very fine but not very fast, but it doesn't have to be fast because the photographer can add as much light as he needs.

There is one kind of camera that has become popular with snapshooters in recent years. This is the Polaroid Land camera. The Polaroid Land camera is really a folding camera, but in the back it has a special compartment where the picture is developed right after you take it. With a Polaroid Land camera, you get a finished print (no negative, though) in sixty seconds.

Of course, there is also the motion-picture camera, which is discussed in the article on MOTION PICTURES.

PHOTOGRAPHIC FILM

When you look at a piece of photographic film, you will see that one side is shiny and the other is dull. The dull side of the film is called the *emulsion* side. This side contains a chemical emulsion, or coating, that changes its property when light strikes it. It consists of many thousands of tiny particles of silver bromide that are sensitive to light.

Films differ in their sensitivity to light. One film is said to be faster than another when it needs less light to record a scene. When you buy a roll of film its sensitivity or speed is given on a printed slip enclosed in the package. If one film is rated as twice as fast as another, it needs only half the exposure of the other film.

The best way to decide on what exposure a particular scene needs is to use an *exposure meter*. An exposure meter is a little instrument with a photoelectric cell or electric eye (explained in the article on ELECTRONICS) that measures the light of the scene and translates it into the shutter speed and f number that you should use.

Another quality of film is color sensi-

tivity. Except in color photography, film does not reproduce actual colors but renders them in different shades of gray. Most films are insensitive to blue. The type of film called *orthochromatic* is very sensitive to red. This means that red photographed with this film will appear much darker in the print than it is in the subject. The film called *panchromatic* (which means "all colors") renders colors in shades of black and white and gray in much the same relationship as they are in real life.

DEVELOPING AND PRINTING

After a roll of film is exposed (that is, after you have taken pictures with it) it must be processed or developed. Whether you process your film yourself or send it to a professional photofinisher, it goes through the same steps.

Three separate steps are necessary to develop the film. In the first step, the film is placed in a mixture of chemicals called a *developer* for ten to twenty minutes. The developer separates the silver bromide crystals of the exposed film into silver and bromide. The silver remains on the film, while the bromide is washed out into the developer. Then the film is placed briefly in water or in a weak solution of sodium bisulfate, called a *stop bath,* to stop the developing. Finally it is placed in a solution called *hypo* for about five minutes to fix the image on the film and harden the film. Then the film is washed in clear running water for about half an hour and hung up to dry.

Developing must be done in a completely dark room, for any light that strikes a film before it is developed will ruin it. There are "safe lights" that give some light to work by and do not spoil the film.

One step remains before we get our final picture. This is called *printing.* In printing, we press the negative tightly against a sheet of sensitized paper and expose it to light. Then the paper is developed, fixed, and washed in trays in much the same way as the film. A print obtained in this way is called a contact print.

ENLARGING

Sometimes, if our final print is small, we may wish to enlarge it. Good clear negatives as small as a postage stamp can easily be enlarged many times to the size of your television screen and larger. This is done in a photographic enlarger. An enlarger is a device for projecting the negative through a lens that enlarges the picture, just as a movie projector enlarges a film when it projects it on a screen. The enlarger throws the magnified picture onto a sheet of photographic paper, on which it is printed.

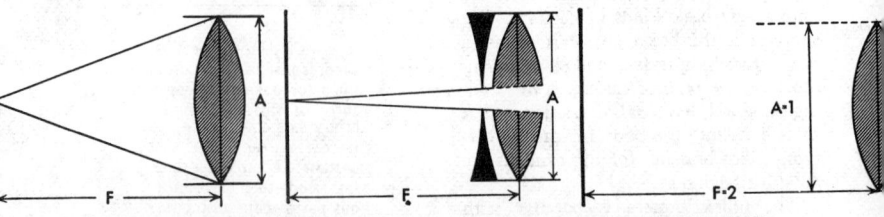

Left: A cross-section of a very fast lens. Note the ratio of aperture (A) to focal length (F). *Center:* The same lens closed down to a small aperture. It is now a low-speed lens. *Right:* The numbers seen on a fine lens, such as f/2 or f/4, show the relative speed of the lens. Actually, f/2 means that focal length (F) is twice aperture (A).

COLOR PHOTOGRAPHY

Color photographs are of two types, transparencies and prints. A color transparency is a sheet of film on which your picture appears in color. In order to see it you must hold it up against the light, look at it in a special machine called a viewer, or project it onto a screen by means of a projector. This last method is best, because in projecting your transparency, you enlarge it many times and make it seem more real and lifelike.

Other kinds of film are made to give you color prints. When you use such a film you get a color negative. When the negative is printed on paper, you see the original colors of the scene you photographed.

THE STORY OF PHOTOGRAPHY

Photography is so popular and is used so widely—in newspapers, magazines, books, in motion pictures—that it is hard to realize that it is only a little more than a hundred years old. In the form in which we now use it, it is even younger than that.

The first true photograph was made about the year 1822 by a Frenchman named Joseph Nicéphore Niepce. Some fifteen years later, another Frenchman, Louis Daguerre, invented a kind of photograph that was named the daguerreotype in his honor. This was made on a thin sheet of copper coated with a light-sensitive chemical. The daguerreotype required an exposure of about six minutes in strong sunlight. Despite this, daguerreotypes became very popular for portraits. Many daguerreotypes are still considered beautiful photographs.

Photographs that could be made by a negative did not come until 1841, through a process invented by William Henry Fox Talbot. Even after this, taking photographs was a cumbersome job. Cameras were very big and clumsy, but worse, glass negatives were used that had to be coated in the dark with a chemical liquid just before being exposed. This meant that every photographer had to travel with a large tent where the coating could be done. Nevertheless, many fine photographs were made in those days. Some of the best were the work of Mathew B. Brady, whose many photographs of the American Civil War are still admired.

The man who was responsible for making photography practical for the average person was George Eastman, an American inventor. In 1888 he invented roll film and a small hand camera that he called the Kodak. Since then, many refinements have been made, but the basic tools and equipment remain the same.

The principal advancements have been:

Flash bulbs, perfected in 1929 (but they were not widely used until, in 1942, a mechanical method of synchronization also was perfected).

Color photography. Excellent motion pictures and still prints in "full color" (three or four colors) were made in the 1920s, but much hand work was required in the development. The producing company, Technicolor, was owned jointly by the big motion-picture producers, had no competition, and made little effort to improve its expensive procedure. In 1935 Leopold Maness perfected Kodachrome,

Trick photography often uses montages for humorous effects and to disprove the saying that a camera never lies.

making color photography available at low cost to the masses. In 1942 Kodacolor made "color movies" similarly available.

Electronic flash, or speedlight, invented by Harold E. Edgerton about 1940, permitting pictures to be taken at speeds as high as $1/10,000$ of a second.

Printing in the camera, invented by Edwin H. Land in 1947 and incorporated in the Polaroid-Land camera, which produces a photograph in a few seconds and a color print in less than one minute.

Photomicrography, by which objects can be magnified or reduced by factors in the hundreds or thousands. This has practical value chiefly in scientific work but in some cases is usable by business firms.

PHOTOGRAPHY AS A HOBBY

About twelve million persons in the United States are interested in photography as a hobby. Some hobbyists concentrate only on taking good pictures. Others have their own darkrooms and develop and print their pictures. Quite a few hobbyists belong to camera clubs. These clubs have regular meetings, hear talks by experts, and often have exhibitions of members' work. If these pictures are good enough they may be sent out on traveling exhibits sponsored by the Photographic Society of America, a national organization to which many camera clubs belong.

There are newspaper columns and magazines devoted to photography.

PHOTOGRAPHY AS A CAREER

Photography offers many opportunities to people who want to work at it for a living. The most interesting job in photography is that of the photographer himself. If he works for a newspaper or magazine, he will be sent out on many challenging assignments. Many photographers work as free-lancers and sell pictures to periodicals and business firms. A familiar member of the profession is the portrait photographer who operates a neighborhood studio.

To qualify for a job as a photographer, you must have great skill in your field and be ready to take good pictures under any circumstances. You should have some artistic aptitude and know what goes into making a good picture. Imagination is another important requirement.

Photographers get their training in many ways. Some professional photographers learn their work by starting as amateur photographers. Others pick up

their skill by working at minor jobs in a photographic studio. Courses are also given in photography at special schools and in some public schools.

There are many other kinds of jobs in photography. Darkroom workers process film for a studio or work for photo finishers who handle the film of amateurs. Photographic retouchers spend their time fixing up negatives and correcting small defects in photographic prints, mostly portraits.

Photostat

A Photostat is a copy of written, drawn or printed material made by a photographic process. Photostat is a trade-marked name for the camera used, but it is applied by most people to any copy made with this kind of camera.

A Photostat differs from a photograph in that there is no negative made. This is its principal advantage over photography, because it makes possible quick copying. In photography the camera makes a film negative, on which light colors show dark and dark colors show white. Also the image is reversed, or turned around, so that when writing is photographed it will appear backward on the negative. To get a true copy of the original, this negative must be developed by having light shone through it onto paper. In Photostats, light is shone directly onto sensitized paper, and therefore the paper itself becomes a kind of negative; the colors are reversed, but the image is not, so that writing reads properly when copied in the Photostatic process.

For most purposes these "negative" copies can be used as is. To make Photostatic copies that are like the original in black and white areas, the Photostat process must be done twice. The second time the black and white areas are restored to their original form. See the entries on DUPLICATING MACHINE and XEROGRAPHY.

photosynthesis

Photosynthesis is the process by which green plants make sugar and starch from water and carbon dioxide, with the help of sunlight and the green material in their leaves, called chlorophyll. Photosynthesis is the basic process of sugar manufacture in nature.

In the process of making sugar, plants give off oxygen to the air. Each year all the plants of the earth produce about 400 billion tons of oxygen from the water they absorb through their roots.

The fact that green plants can produce oxygen was first discovered by Joseph Priestley, an English scientist, in 1772. Seventy years later a German doctor, Julius Robert Mayer, discovered that light was a necessary part of photosynthesis.

Scientists do not yet know the whole story of photosynthesis, but many significant discoveries were made by U.S. scientists in the 1950s and 1960s that may soon provide the key to this process of nature. When that happens, man may be able to make simple carbohydrates, the basic compounds which compose all food.

phrenology

Phrenology is a so-called science based on a study of bumps on top of the head. These bumps (according to be-

lievers in phrenology) show how the brain is divided into sections that control a person's emotions and abilities. This theory, which almost no one believes any more, was invented in 1764 by an Austrian named Franz Gall. He said he could tell whether a person was a musician, a poet, a businessman, a murderer, or anything else, simply by feeling the bumps on the person's head.

Phyfe, Duncan

Duncan Phyfe was a great designer and maker of fine furniture. He was born in Scotland, about 1768. When he was about 15 years old he traveled to the United States and settled in Albany, New York, where he became an apprentice to a cabinetmaker. In his early twenties, Phyfe moved to New York City and opened his own shop. For more than thirty years he designed and made fine sofas, tables, sideboards, and other furniture.

At various times Phyfe's brother and two sons worked with him. They made their furniture out of the finest mahogany wood. The furniture was so well designed and beautifully decorated that it soon became very popular. Many furniture makers have imitated the style. An original Duncan Phyfe piece of furniture is very valuable today. Phyfe died in 1854, when he was 86 years old.

physical education

Physical education is a course of study that is taught to young men and women in many colleges and universities. Some colleges give degrees in physical education. Some give a degree in the field of education (teaching), and others give the degree of Bachelor of Science.

There are many careers open in the field of physical education. You may become a teacher of physical education, or a coach in some particular sport, or a playground or recreation director in a large organization. During World War II recreation directors did an important job in keeping up the morale of the United States armed forces. Some graduates in physical education work with the American Red Cross or the Y.M.C.A. and Y.W.C.A. or the Boy or Girl Scouts. Still others find jobs in settlement houses for underprivileged children, or in hospitals.

In some schools students of physical education may specialize in *physical therapy*. Physical therapists help doctors in treating some kinds of disability, injury, and disease, as by massage and exercise. Such diseases include infantile paralysis (polio), arthritis, and cerebral palsy.

WHAT THE STUDENTS LEARN

For the first two years of a four-year course in physical education, the student takes general courses, studying English, psychology, philosophy, and history. The student also learns about the human body through courses in physiology, anatomy, nutrition, and hygiene. He learns gymnastics, folk dancing and social dancing, and many forms of recreation. He takes part in sports and games, both individually and on teams, and learns how to teach others to play the games. During the last two years the program of study depends on what career the student has chosen. A student who plans to become a coach in a particular sport studies that sport and other sports, and also learns about safety measures and first-aid and group psychology (the relations between people in a group, such as a team or a class). The student also practices teaching the sport by actually teaching it to children in nearby schools.

If the student wants to become a physical therapist, the course of study stresses biology and anatomy even more. The student learns about how children grow, and about educating a community (group of people) in hygiene.

physics

Physics is the scientific study of matter (anything that has weight and takes up space), its motion, and the changes it undergoes, such as changes in size, shape, and weight, changes from a solid to a liquid, and so on, called physical changes. The term *energy* is used to describe all these changes and motions. Thus it is often said that physics is the study of matter and energy.

People who study and work in physics are called *physicists*. Research physicists use various kinds of equipment, such as cyclotrons and electric generators, to find out by experiment what actually happens. Theoretical physicists think up ideas, often by using complicated mathematical formulas. Their ideas later are tested by research physicists.

Physics is divided into separate branches, each concerned with a different form of energy and how it can be used to produce changes in matter.

Mechanics deals with mechanical energy, the motion of objects.

Electricity and *magnetism* deal with electrical and magnetic energy produced by the motion of tiny bits of matter called electrons.

Electronics and *ionics* deal with the movement of electricity through vacuum (no air) and gas-filled tubes. It includes the study of fluorescent tubes, X-rays, the electron microscope, and other related devices.

Thermodynamics deals with heat energy, which is produced by the motion of tiny bits of matter called molecules.

Acoustics deals with sound energy produced by the vibration or shaking back and forth of air molecules. *Ultrasonics* involves the use of inaudible sounds (sounds that usually cannot be heard by the human ear).

Optics is the study of light or radiant energy caused by the wave motion of particles called *photons*, which travel at a speed of 186,300 miles a second.

Molecular, atomic and *nuclear physics* deal with nuclear energy (also called atomic energy) produced by the high-speed particles inside the tiny particles of matter called atoms.

Engineering physics deals with testing and examining materials such as metals, rubber, plastics and glass to get an understanding of their structure so they can be used more effectively in industry.

Other subjects studied by physicists include *astrophysics,* the study of physics of the planets and stars, and *biophysics,* the use of the ideas of physics in biology.

Many physicists are employed by the government or in defense industries. Some other industries that employ them are the electrical, radio and television, radar, automobile, airplane, petroleum, machinery, rubber, and chemical industries.

physiology

Physiology is the scientific name for the study of how the body works when it is in a normal or healthy condition. If you read the article on ANATOMY you will see that anatomy is the study of the parts of the body but has nothing to do with the working of these parts. Physiology takes up where anatomy leaves off. Physiology is one of the required courses in all medical schools.

Anatomy is probably a very much older science than physiology. Many centuries ago scientists were beginning to study and know about the structure of the human body. They were able to do this because they could dissect or cut up dead bodies and see where various organs were located and what they looked like. But they were not able to observe how all these things operated in the normal living person. Therefore most of what they knew about physiology was guesswork and it was often wrong. For instance, the early Greeks thought that air was carried through the blood vessels instead of blood.

Some early knowledge of physiology came from the great wounds of soldiers on the battlefield. In examining these wounds, doctors saw some organs and parts of the body while they were actually working. Later, when doctors began to perform surgical operations, they were able to observe still more. They also began to experiment with live animals. This type of experiment is called *vivisection,* cutting open a living body. This was done under an anesthetic and the animal suffered no pain.

IMPORTANCE OF PHYSIOLOGY

Physiology is important because it shows doctors how the human body operates when it is healthy. If they did not know this they would hardly know what was wrong with the body or parts of the body when a person is sick. As a simple example, the study of physiology shows that the heart normally beats at a certain pace and normally sends a certain amount of blood at a certain temperature flowing through the body. When the doctor taking a pulse finds the heart beating much too fast, he then knows that there is something wrong.

piano

The piano is a large musical instrument consisting of a number of metal strings that make sounds when they are struck by hammers. The hammers are operated by keys on a keyboard. Any combination of tones can be produced together on the piano. For this reason the piano is the most popular of all musical instruments.

The full name of the piano is *pianoforte,* which is a combination of two Italian words meaning "soft" and "loud." The harder a key is struck, the louder the sound. The length of time the tone continues is controlled by *dampers,* which are pieces of felt that touch the strings. When a key is struck, the damper rises,

permitting the string to vibrate. When the key is released the damper falls on the string and stops its vibration, but there is a foot pedal that can hold the damper up and permit the tone to continue even after the key has been released.

The standard piano has a keyboard of 88 notes, or seven and one-third octaves. There are two principal kinds of piano in use today, the upright (in which the strings run up and down) and the grand (in which the strings lie flat). Until recent years, the upright was a big, ungainly instrument about five feet high. The newest uprights are much smaller. One popular style of small upright piano is called a *spinet*. Grand pianos range in size from the four-foot baby grand to the nine-foot concert grand.

PIANOS IN THE PAST

The piano is descended from two old instruments, the harpsichord and the clavichord. The harpsichord came into use about six hundred years ago. It looked somewhat like the piano, but its strings were plucked instead of struck. The clavichord strings were struck like those of the piano. The first true piano was built in 1709 by Bartolomeo Cristofori.

PLAYER PIANOS

During the 1800s many piano makers worked on the idea of an automatic piano. One such device, called the player piano, came into wide popular use in the early part of this century. This was a regular piano with the addition of machinery to turn a roll of paper. The paper roll was full of holes so placed that when a hole passed over an opening in the mechanism, it caused a stream of air to operate the hammer of a certain key. The device was operated by treadles which the "player" operated with his feet. Later automatic pianos were operated by electricity and could reproduce the playing of the greatest pianists of the day. Perfection of the radio ended the popularity of the player piano.

Picasso, Pablo

Pablo Picasso is the name of a Spanish painter and sculptor. He was one of the originators of a style of painting called *Cubism*. Picasso was born in 1881, the son of a drawing master. When he was 16, he set himself up as an independent artist. After a period in Paris, France, where he painted much and sold very little, Picasso returned for a time to Spain, in 1902. This was the beginning of his Blue Period, so called because his paintings were done almost entirely in various shades of blue.

Then followed the Rose, or Pink, Period, in which he painted in an almost classical style. About this time Picasso became very much impressed with African sculpture, and his Negro Period followed. In the 1920s and 1930s Picasso devoted himself to modern forms, Cubism, and sometimes Surrealism and Symbolism. His work was well received and he became very successful financially.

After World War II Picasso turned to ceramics. In the 1950s he publicly stated that he was a Communist. He designed a "dove of peace" that became a political symbol for the Communists of France and other countries. However, most of Picasso's work is banned in the Soviet Union.

Piccard

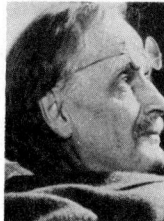

Auguste and Jean Piccard are the names of twin brothers who became famous as explorers of the stratosphere in balloons and of the depths of the sea in a bathyscaphe. They were born in 1884 in Switzerland, and both chose careers in chemistry, engineering, and aeronautics. Auguste made his home in Belgium, and Jean became a citizen of the United States.

Auguste was first to become famous when in the 1930s he invented a balloon with an airtight gondola, or cage, in which a man could survive in the stratosphere, the upper air where there is not enough oxygen to support life. In 1931 he reached a record altitude of 51,775 feet, and the following year he reached 53,152 feet.

In 1934, in the United States, Jean Piccard broke his brother's record by ascending to an altitude of 57,549 feet.

In the 1940s Auguste Piccard became interested in deep-sea exploration and perfected a bathysphere, or diving device, with which he hoped to break William Beebe's record descent of 3,028 feet. With no one in it, this bathysphere reached a depth of 4,500. In 1953, Auguste and his son Jacques built another diving device, a *bathyscaphe*, and descended to 10,330 feet. Auguste died in 1962 and Jean in 1963.

piccolo

The piccolo is a musical insrument of the FLUTE family, about which you can read in a separate article. The piccolo is the smallest of the woodwind instruments. It is a half-sized flute and has a high, shrill tone. It is very important in military bands, and parts have been written for the piccolo in many concert works. See MUSICAL INSTRUMENTS.

pickerel, a small fish that belongs to the pike family: see the article on PIKE.

Among the best known early works of the Spanish artist Pablo Picasso is this oil-on-canvas portrait of Gertrude Stein, done in 1906.

Pickett, George Edward

George Edward Pickett was a general in the Confederate Army during the Civil War. He is famous for leading his cavalry (soldiers mounted on horseback) on a charge up Cemetery Ridge during the Battle of Gettysburg, the most important battle of the Civil War. "Pickett's Charge" failed, he and his men were driven back, and more than 2,500 of his men were killed or taken prisoner by the northern forces.

George Pickett was born in Virginia in 1825. He was a graduate of West Point Academy and served in the United States Army before he resigned his commission to fight on the side of the South. His handsomeness and long, flowing hair made him a romantic figure. He was a friend of Abraham Lincoln, and Lincoln continued to be friendly toward him even when they were on different sides in the war. Pickett died in 1875.

Pickford, Mary

Mary Pickford is the stage name of one of the great stars of the silent motion pictures. She was called "America's Sweetheart," and her face was known to millions through her many films, such as *Tess of the Storm Country, Daddy Long Legs, Rebecca of Sunnybrook Farm,* and *Poor Little Rich Girl.* She also was one of the few stars, and the only woman, who became rich in the motion-picture industry through forming her own producing company.

Mary Pickford was born in 1893 in Toronto, Ontario. Her real name was Gladys Mary Smith. When she was 4 years old, her father died and her mother worked as an actress to support three children. Gladys played her first part in one of her mother's plays when she was 5. At 14 she made her first appearance in New York in a play directed by David Belasco. Two years later she went to work at the Biograph motion-picture studios in New York. She quickly became famous even though the names of players were not given on the screen in the early days of the movies. In 1919 she was one of the organizers of United Artists Corporation.

When talking pictures came in, about 1930, Mary Pickford starred in several, but her interest turned more and more to producing. She was married three times, first to Owen Moore, then to Douglas Fairbanks, and in 1937 to Charles Rogers. She was very active in raising funds for the war effort in both World Wars and in charitable work.

pickle

A pickle is any fruit or vegetable that has been preserved in vinegar or brine (salt water). Usually when we speak of pickles we mean pickled cucumbers, but other vegetables frequently pickled include tomatoes, onions, cauliflower, cabbage, and beets. Among fruits

that are often pickled are peaches, pears, plums, and watermelon rind. Some meats, such as pig's feet, are also pickled.

Most pickling is done by soaking the fruit or vegetable in vinegar and brine: For sweet pickles, sugar is added. Many spices are used in pickling, including dill, cinnamon, cloves, and peppercorns. Dill pickles are cucumbers pickled with dill. Sweet gherkins are small cucumbers, usually pickled whole with sugar. Piccalilli is a mixture of chopped cucumbers, onions, and cauliflower, pickled together. Chow-chow is a mixed pickle with mustard added. Chutney is an East Indian pickle served with curried dishes. It contains various fruits, chiefly mango, and spices.

Picts, one of the ancient Celtic peoples of Scotland: see the section on English History in the article on ENGLAND. The Picts and Scots intermarried and eventually they were all called Scots.

Pied Piper of Hamelin

The Pied Piper is a character who is told about in legends. The story is that almost 700 years ago, in 1284, the people of the town of Hamelin, in Germany, found their town overrun by rats. One day a mysterious stranger, dressed in a beautiful suit of many colors, appeared. He promised to get rid of all the rats if the people would pay him a certain sum of money. They agreed. The Pied Piper played his pipe, and all the rats followed him and left the town. When all the rats were gone, the people refused to pay him. This made the Pied Piper very angry. He returned to Hamelin and began to play his pipes so beautifully that all the children of the town followed him. He led the children to a mountain and they all disappeared into a mountain cave, except one child who was blind and one child who was lame. The children were never seen again.

The English poet Robert Browning wrote a famous poem that is called "The Pied Piper of Hamelin."

Franklin Pierce

Franklin Pierce was the 14th President of the United States. He served from March, 1853 to March, 1857. During his administration the United States purchased fifty thousand square miles of territory from Mexico—the Gadsden Purchase of 1853. Pierce was the youngest man who had ever been elected to the Presidency. He was 48 at the time.

HIS EARLY YEARS

Franklin Pierce was born in Hillsboro, New Hampshire, on November 23, 1804.

His father was a member of the state legislature for several years, and was Governor of New Hampshire at one time. Pierce attended Exeter Academy, and was graduated from Bowdoin College in Brunswick, Maine. He studied law and became a lawyer. He served in the New Hampshire House of Representatives, and in 1833 was elected to Congress. In 1837 he became a United States Senator, but in 1843 he resigned and returned to Concord, New Hampshire, to become Federal District Attorney.

At the start of the war between the United States and Mexico, Pierce joined the army as a volunteer. From private he rose to the rank of brigadier general, and was wounded in battle. After the war was over he returned to his law practice in New Hampshire.

HOW HE BECAME PRESIDENT

At the time of the Democratic Party's nominating convention in 1852, there was a contest between James Buchanan, Stephen A. Douglas, and Lewis Cass, a Senator from Michigan. Franklin Pierce was nominated on the 49th ballot, as a compromise to break the deadlock. It appeared that the supporters of Buchanan, Douglas, and Cass would not vote for any other of the three.

Pierce was opposed to slavery personally, but he was greatly influenced by associates who were in favor of slavery. His Secretary of War was Jefferson Davis, from the slave state of Mississippi, who later became President of the Confederacy. While Pierce was President, Congress was planning to open the Northwest region for settlement. There was great argument over whether or not new territories and states should permit slavery. Pierce thought each should make its own choice. Anti-slavery groups wanted the Federal government to require them all to be "free" states (no slavery permitted). Pierce's attitude antagonized the anti-slavery groups.

Another problem that arose during his administration was the question of acquiring Cuba. Many people favored the idea of taking Cuba by force, since Spain was not willing to sell it. Pierce took a firm stand against this idea.

At about this time a man named William Walker organized a small army and captured Nicaragua, with the intention of having that small country made a part of the United States as a pro-slavery territory. Pierce recognized Walker's conquest, and this too made people angry, especially in the North. Pierce was not nominated for a second term.

HIS LATER YEARS

After his term as President, Pierce returned to Concord, New Hampshire, and spent the remaining twelve years of his life there, except for a three-year period in which he traveled through Europe. He died in Concord on October 8, 1869, a little more than a month before his 65th birthday.

MRS. FRANKLIN PIERCE

Jane Means Appleton Pierce was born in New Hampshire in 1806. She was the daughter of the president of Bowdoin College, where Franklin Pierce was a student. She married Pierce during his

first term in Congress. They had three sons, none of whom lived past childhood. Mrs. Franklin Pierce died in 1863.

Pierre

Pierre is the capital of South Dakota. It is on the east bank of the Missouri River, in an important farming and cattle region. More than ten thousand people live in Pierre. They ship out large quantities of livestock, wheat, and other farm products. Others work in railroad shops, in stockyards, and in plants that make dairy products and beverages. Pierre has a number of fine parks along the Missouri River. There is a United States Indian school there.

Pierre was settled in 1880 and was named after Fort Pierre, a fur-trading post on the opposite bank of the Missouri. After a railroad was built through Pierre it became an important cattle-shipping center. In 1889 it became the capital of South Dakota.

PIERRE, SOUTH DAKOTA. Population (1960 census) 10,088. Capital of South Dakota. County seat of Hughes County. On the Missouri River. Settled, 1880.

pig

The pig is an animal that first lived in many parts of Europe, Asia, and Africa. Scientists have discovered the remains of huge pigs that lived more than a million years ago and they believe that the people of China have raised pigs for many thousands of years. Grown pigs are called *hogs* or *swine*. A female pig is called a *sow* and a male pig is called a *boar*. Wild members of the same family are called *wild boars*.

The pig is not a very pretty animal. It has a large, fat body and short legs. The pig is an "even-toed" animal. This does not mean that a pig has an even number of toes. It means that the pig carries all of its weight on its third and fourth toes. Sometimes a pig has more toes but it does not use them to hold its weight. The pig has a remarkable snout. It looks like a very long, thick nose. The end of the snout is flat, tough, and round. The pig uses its snout to dig and burrow in the ground and to push objects from one place to another. Many pigs have tusks. Pigs have small eyes and a tough skin. Some pigs are white, and other are black with white spots, and others are a reddish-brown color.

The wild pigs that live in Europe and Africa and Asia are fierce animals. Some pigs, such as the giant forest hog of Africa, are almost three feet high and weigh more than 250 pounds. Other pigs, such as the pygmy hog of India, weigh about twelve pounds. Pigs eat fruit and nuts and berries and small animals. The female pig (sow) has from eight to more than twenty babies at a time, two and sometimes three times a year.

Pigs are raised in many parts of the world because they are valuable animals that people use in many ways. The flesh of the pig is a nourishing meat. Bacon and ham and pork and other meats come from parts of the pig's body. (The flesh of the pig is considered unwholesome in the Jewish, Mohammedan and Hindu religions, and followers of these religions are forbidden to eat the flesh of the pig.)

The fat from the pig is used to make

lard. The skin of the pig makes leather used in gloves and belts and pocketbooks and wallets. The hairs of the pig's skin, called *bristles*, are used to make paint brushes.

Farmers have developed new kinds of pigs that grow quickly and are very healthy. The Poland China pig is a popular breed that is raised by many farmers in the United States. It is a black pig with white markings. The Poland China is a large pig. The males (boars) weigh about a thousand pounds, and the females weigh about eight hundred pounds.

Pigs are very greedy animals and they eat great quantities of corn and other crops. Buttermilk and peanuts are good for pigs. Pigs are not very particular about what they eat and will devour almost anything they can find in the garbage

The Hampshire sow has many offspring.

can. For this reason people sometimes say that a greedy person "eats like a pig."

pigeon

The pigeon is a bird that lives in many parts of the world. There are more than 650 different kinds of pigeon. One of the most important members of the pigeon family is the dove.

Pigeons have smooth, plump bodies and small heads. The male pigeon has a wobbly walk and struts around proudly. People like to watch pigeons and feed them in parks. Pigeons that live in cities become very tame and friendly and can learn to eat out of a person's hand.

The pigeon has a soft, sad call that sounds like "coo." Pigeons build crude nests out of straw and sticks. The female pigeon lays two white or light tan eggs. It feeds its babies with pigeon "milk." This is a substance that comes from the bird's body. The pigeon is the only bird that does this. The pigeon is one of the few birds that can drink water without lifting their heads to swallow.

Pigeons are strong fliers, and they have been very useful to man. Homing pigeons (also called carrier pigeons) can carry messages for more than a thousand miles. Many people raise carrier pigeons as a hobby.

Pigeons are very good to eat, and they have been a favorite bird of sportsmen. The passenger pigeon that once lived in the United States was hunted so much that it was wiped out. For the last forty years there have been no passenger pigeons.

Some of the pigeons that live on the tropical islands in the Pacific Ocean are handsome birds. The largest pigeon is called the crowned pigeon. It lives on New Guinea. It is about as large as a chicken, with a dark red body and gray wings. On its head it has a magnificent crown of plumes.

pike

The pike is a fish that lives in the fresh waters of the United States and Canada. The northern pike may grow to be almost five feet long.

The pike is one of the largest fresh-water fish, and is found in many lakes.

The pike is a fierce fish that suddenly darts out of the weeds that grow on the bottom of the lake and pounces on smaller fish. It has many sharp teeth. When these teeth wear out the pike grows new teeth. Pikes eat snakes, frogs, and birds, as well as other fish. Young pikes eat worms and insects.

There are three kinds of small pike that are usually about one foot long. They are called pickerel and they live in the fresh-water rivers and lakes of the United States.

Pike, Zebulon

Zebulon Montgomery Pike was a great American explorer and military leader. He was born in Trenton, New Jersey, in 1779. At the age of 20, he became a lieutenant in the United States Army. When he was 26 years old, Pike was assigned to head a party of explorers who set out to discover the source of the Mississippi River. On another exploration Pike searched for the sources of the Arkansas and Red rivers. The trail led him to Colorado where he saw the huge mountain that was named Pikes Peak in his honor. (You can read about PIKES PEAK in the next article.)

During the War of 1812 against Great Britain, Pike was made a brigadier-general. He was killed when he led an attack against York, which is now the city of Toronto, Ontario. This was in 1813.

Pikes Peak

Pikes Peak is a high mountain in Colorado, about 60 miles from the city of Denver. It is part of the Rocky Mountains. Although other mountains are higher, Pikes Peak is one of the most famous because of the beautiful view of the countryside that can be seen from the top. It is 14,110 feet high. Some visitors ride to the top of Pikes Peak on horseback, while others take the motor highway from Colorado Springs or the nine-mile cog railway. At the top of Pikes Peak is a United States weather station. Pikes Peak was named for Zebulon PIKE, about whom there is a separate article.

Pilate, Pontius, see the article PONTIUS PILATE.

Pilgrims

The Pilgrims were a group of people who in 1620 founded a permanent English colony in what is now Plymouth, Massachusetts. At that time the Church of England was the only church in which English people were allowed to worship.

The Pilgrims did not like this Church and had separated from it. For this reason the Pilgrims were also called Separatists.

The Pilgrims landed at Plymouth on December 21, 1620. Before that they had

Plymouth Chamber of Commerce

Plymouth Rock, now covered by a Doric-columned portico, is traditionally considered the place where the Pilgrims debarked to found their colony at Plymouth.

anchored off the coast of Provincetown, Massachusetts, while they explored the coast for the best place in which to build their settlement. The Pilgrims had intended to land much farther south, in the Virginia colony, and they were not prepared for the hardship of the cold winter they had to endure. Even before they landed, they had suffered a great deal of hardship, for the boat was overcrowded and many of the people were ill. During the first winter nearly half of the Pilgrims died.

Forty-one men and their families sailed to the New World on the ship *Mayflower*. There were 102 people in all. Before the Pilgrims landed, the men in the party signed the Mayflower Compact, an agreement that set up the rules by which the colony would be governed. The signers of the Mayflower Compact are known as the Pilgrim Fathers. They were: John Carver, William Bradford, Edward Winslow, William Brewster, Isaac Allerton, Miles Standish, John Alden, Samuel Fuller, Christopher Martin, William Mullins, William White, Richard Warren, John

In Plymouth you can see a house and fort exactly like the ones the Pilgrims built.

The date of their landing was carved much later in historic Plymouth Rock.

Howland, Stephen Hopkins, Edward Tilley, John Tilley, Francis Cook, Thomas Rogers, Thomas Tinker, John Ridgedale, Edward Fuller, John Turner, Francis Eaton, James Chilton, John Crackston, John Billington, Moses Fletcher, John Goodman, Degory Priest, Thomas Williams, Gilbert Winslow, Edward Margeson, Peter Brown, Richard Britteridge, George Soule, Richard Clarke, Richard Gardiner, John Allerton, Thomas English, Edward Doty, and Edward Lister. The religious leader of the Pilgrims was Elder William Brewster, and the first governor was John Carver.

Many of the Pilgrims have become known to Americans through Henry Wadsworth Longfellow's poem, "The Courtship of Miles Standish." The poem tells of the fiery, red-headed soldier Miles Standish, who got his best friend, young John Alden, to propose to Priscilla Mullins. Although the story told by Longfellow is not historically true, the poem gives a good picture of the kind of life the Pilgrims lived.

Today in Plymouth, Massachusetts, there is a house exactly like the ones that the Pilgrims first built in the New World. There also is the famous Plymouth Rock, around which the Pilgrims are said to have buried the people who died during the first winter.

pillory is an old form of punishment: see STOCKS AND PILLORY.

piloting

Piloting is another name for guiding or steering ships and airplanes. A person who guides ships or boats through the water close to shores, bays, harbors or rivers is called a harbor or river pilot. A person who guides an airplane or airship through the air is called an aircraft pilot.

PILOTING AN AIRPLANE

The article on FLIGHT explains the forces acting on an airplane in flight, and the article on AIRPLANE describes the different parts of a plane and their flight operation.

When an airplane is ready to take off, the pilot switches on the engine to start the propeller turning. Then he *taxis* (drives the plane on the ground) to the end of a runway, a long, smoothly paved stretch of ground in the airfield, 2,000 or more feet long. If there is a wind, he heads the plane in the direction the wind is blowing.

After the engine has warmed up sufficiently, the pilot opens the throttle to increase its speed and starts down the runway. As he does, he moves the control stick forward. This lowers the rear edges of the movable portions of the horizontal tail surface, called the elevators. As a result, the tail is lifted from the ground by the air blast from the propeller.

The plane is guided in a straight line by the action of the left and right rudder pedals, which control the rudder, the movable portion of the upright tail section. When the rudder is straight, the plane will go straight ahead. When the rudder is moved to the left by the action of the left rudder pedal, the plane will swing toward the left. The plane will swing to the right when the right rudder pedal is pressed, moving the rudder to the right.

After the plane has traveled 600 to 1,500 feet along the runway, the lift on the wings will become sufficiently great to raise it off the ground. The pilot then raises the elevators by pulling back on the control stick, causing the plane to climb into the air. In climbing, it is very important not to try to climb too steeply. If the pilot does this, the plane will stall, lose speed, and start to fall.

After the plane has reached a sufficient height, the pilot levels it out by lowering the elevators. He makes sure that he is level by sighting along the nose of the plane. When the nose is in line with the horizon—the line in the distance where the earth and the sky seem to meet—the plane is level. The pilot also checks to see that each wing tip has the same amount of space between it and the ground.

If the plane tends to climb or dive, it may be because it is tail heavy or nose heavy. In such cases, the pilot adjusts the level of the plane by means of a crank called the horizontal stabilizer control. He moves the crank forward when the plane tends to climb, and back when the plane tends to dive. This is called trimming the ship.

BANKING

In making turns in the air, the action of the rudder pedals is often not enough. In many cases, when the nose of the plane has been turned to the left or to the right the plane will continue going straight ahead. This is because the plane has not been *banked*. The effect is similar to the skidding of an automobile while turning a corner. The sharper the turn, the more bank is necessary.

An airplane is banked by the action of the control stick. Moving the stick to the left or right raises and lowers the movable sections of the wing called *ailerons*. Moving the stick to the left raises the left aileron and lowers the right one, causing the plane to bank to the left. Moving the stick to the right raises the right aileron and lowers the left one, causing the plane to bank to the right.

In landing, the pilot heads the plane toward the runway into the wind. The nose is lowered below the horizon and the speed of the engine reduced. The plane glides toward the ground at a steady speed. When the plane is about 20 feet above the ground, the pilot eases back on the stick to level out the plane and further reduce its speed. The plane then touches the runway with both its wheels and tail just as its speed is reduced. This is known as a "three-point" landing. The pilot then pulls the stick all the way back, keeping the rudder straight, until the plane has come to a full stop.

PILOTING A SHIP

When a ship enters a harbor, it often stops to take aboard a skilled helmsman or pilot whose function is to steer the ship through the narrow harbor waters. He uses his knowledge of the tides, currents, depth of water and rocks along the shore to guide the ship safely into port.

In the Pacific Northwest, the pilots must be skilled in guiding ships and boats through waters bordered by large rocks, mountains, and even icebergs. In such cases, the pilot uses the echoes of his shouts to gauge his distance from the shore. Many ships often are equipped with radar for this purpose. There is a separate article on RADAR.

pimiento

The pimiento is a tree of the myrtle family that is found in the West Indies and Central America. The pimiento is an evergreen and grows to a height of 20 to 30 feet. It has shiny green leaves and a small flower that grows into a black berry. This berry, before it becomes ripe, is used as a food flavoring called *allspice,* or Jamaica pepper.

The bright red, sweet pepper called pimiento is the fruit of an entirely different plant, the paprika. *Pimiento* is the Spanish word for "pepper." Both of these kinds of pimiento are sometimes spelled *pimento*.

pine

The pine is a very valuable tree that grows in many parts of the world where the climate is not too hot. There are about a hundred different kinds of pine. They are easy to recognize because they have thin, needlelike leaves. Most pine needles grow in clusters, but a few grow separately. Pine trees are evergreens, which means that they do not lose their leaves in the fall.

Pine tree seeds grow in cones. Many pines grow to be 200 feet high or even higher and have trunks that are 5 or more feet thick. Other pines are short, scrubby

An unusual picture shows a spray from a Ponderosa pine with cones growing in clusters. Its wood is used in furniture.

trees. Pine trees often grow together in huge forests.

There are two large groups of pine trees, the white pines and the yellow pines. The wood of the white pines that are found in the northern parts of the United States and Canada is very valuable. It is a soft wood that is used to make boxes, furniture, and houses. The early settlers in America used white pine wood to build their homes, and some of these houses are still in good condition more than three hundred years later. People have cut down so many of the white pines that there are not many left.

The yellow pines grow in the southeastern part of the United States. The wood of the yellow pine is much harder than white pine wood.

Pine trees contain valuable substances that ooze from the bark of the trees. This substance is made into turpentine and rosin. The nuts of some varieties of pine are good to eat.

pineapple

The pineapple is a sweet fruit that first grew in the northern parts of South America and is now grown in many places where the climate is very warm. The Hawaiian Islands raise more pineapple than any other place in the world.

The pineapple is a perennial plant, which means that it comes up from the same roots every year. It grows to a height of two to four feet. The leaves are prickly. They grow in a kind of cluster and in the center of the leaves the pineapple develops. Most pineapples weigh only about one pound, but there are some that weigh as much as thirty pounds.

Pineapple contains a substance that helps digestion. It is eaten raw, cooked, or as juice. Most pineapple is picked before it is ripe, so most people never eat pineapple at its best, when it has ripened.

The leaves of the pineapple plant are used to weave a cloth that is strong and waterproof. People who live on the Philippine Islands make a fine material called pina cloth from pineapple-leaf fibers.

Ping-pong, see TABLE TENNIS.

pinkeye

When a person has pinkeye his eyes become red and swollen. Pinkeye is an infection that is caused by germs that get into the soft tissues that surround the eyeballs. It is also called *infectious conjunctivitis*. A person with pinkeye may feel sharp pains in his eyeballs when he looks into the light.

Pinkeye is very infectious, which means that a person can easily catch it from someone who has it. A person may get pinkeye if he uses the towel of someone who has it, or he may get it by rubbing his eyes with dirty hands. Anyone who has pinkeye should stay away from others so that the disease will not spread.

pinochle

Pinochle is a card game that is based on German games but was invented in the United States about a hundred years ago. There are several forms of pinochle, and two, three or four may play. The regular pinochle pack of playing cards has 48 cards—two aces, kings, queens, jacks, tens and nines of each suit. Some packs have 64 cards—two eights and sevens of each suit added to the regular pack. "Double pinochle" is played with an 80-card pack—four aces, kings, queens, jacks and tens in each suit. In pinochle the ace is the highest card, then the ten, then the king, queen, jack, nine, eight, seven. The object of the game is to score points by *melding* (announcing) certain cards held in the hand, and by winning cards in the play. One combination of cards, the queen of spades and jack of diamonds, is called ⌐ *pinochle* and scores 40 points.

pinworms

Pinworms are small, round worms about half an inch long. The female pinworm lays its eggs inside the stomach of a human being. The eggs hatch in the stomach and in about five or six weeks the worms are full grown.

A person who is infected with pinworms feels very uncomfortable, with severe itching and pain. Often the person loses weight, feels restless, and is unable to sleep. It is very easy for pinworms to spread from one person to another and great precautions must be taken so that one member of a family will not infect the entire household. Absolute cleanliness is necessary to prevent the pinworms from spreading. People should wash their hands carefully after going to the bathroom and before meals. All towels and sheets and clothing should be boiled. Hot water kills the pinworm eggs. A person who has pinworms must visit a doctor.

pipeline

A pipeline is a method of transporting oil or other petroleum products, natural gas, or water, to a place where it will be shipped or used. The pipe is laid underground, often crossing mountains and swamps and other kinds of difficult territory. Movement of the product through the pipeline is maintained by pumping stations about 40 miles apart.

The first pipeline, only four miles long and made of two-inch pipe, was built in 1865 in Pennsylvania. This was soon after the first oil well had been drilled in the United States. The first long pipeline for natural gas was built in Texas in 1910. In 1931 a 1,000-mile line was laid from Texas to Chicago. During World War II the United States government financed the building of the "Big Inch" and the "Little Big Inch," the longest pipelines ever laid. The Big Inch carried crude oil through a 24-inch pipe more than 1,300 miles from Texas to the Philadelphia area. The Little Big Inch carried gasoline and other petroleum products about 1,475 miles from Texas to the New York area. In 1947 these two pipelines were sold to private firms for the moving of natural gas.

The biggest United States pipeline today, and the longest natural gas pipeline in the world, is a 30-inch pipe which runs 1,840 miles from Texas to New York City. However, pipelines that will eventually be much longer are under construction in both Canada and the Soviet Union.

Pipelines are an important part of the oil industry in many countries.

pipestone

Pipestone is a kind of red clay that got its name because American Indians used it for making the pipes in which they smoked tobacco. They prized it especially for peace pipes, which they called *calumets*. The Indians considered pipestone to be sacred, and even when they were at war they kept the pipestone quarries as neutral ground.

Most kinds of clay are soft enough for you to mold them with your fingers, but pipestone is as hard as stone, and you must grind and carve it as you would stone. You can find it in Pipestone County, Minnesota; in South Dakota; and in a very few other places in the United States. You can also find it along the banks of the Pipestone River in Canada. Henry Wadsworth Longfellow's poem *Hiawatha* begins with these lines:

On the Mountains of the Prairie,
On the great Red Pipe-stone Quarry . . .

This is the pipestone quarry in Minnesota.

The scientists' name for pipestone is *catlinite*. They named it after George Catlin (1796–1872), who was an artist and explorer of America's northwest frontier. He lived among the Indians and was the first to tell about the red clay stone.

piranha

The piranha is the fiercest and most dangerous fish in the world for its size. It is found in South American rivers, especially the Amazon and the Orinoco, and the natives of these regions fear it more than they fear the crocodile. The piranha, also called the cannibal fish, is usually less than a foot long. Its body is slender and has a row of saw-toothed plates along

The piranha has razor-sharp teeth and is greatly feared in South American waters.

the narrow underside. The fish has razor-sharp teeth with which it tears its prey to pieces. Piranhas travel in schools and attack any animal or human being in their waters. It is said that a school of piranhas can tear a carcass down to a skeleton in a matter of minutes.

pirate and privateer

Piracy is the crime of armed robbery on the high seas. A ship that is used for this robbery is called a pirate, and any officer or member of the crew of the ship is also called a pirate.

There have been pirates almost as long as there have been armed ships. In times before most of the world was civilized, nearly every tribe or country attacked and robbed any other tribe or country whenever it was strong enough. The same was true of ships at sea. In modern history, there have been only a few times when there were many pirates.

Some ships became pirates when the crews mutinied against cruel officers and took over the ship. The crews were then outlaws who could not return home, so they would try for riches by attacking weaker ships. Other pirate crews were deliberately assembled by some vicious and greedy captain who was much the same as any master criminal of the land.

The traditional flag of a pirate ship was black, with a picture of a skull and crossbones in white. Pirates in stories always killed the crews of the ships they captured by making the men "walk the plank" (walk off the ship on a plank, and fall in the sea and drown). Actually this was no more common than any other way of putting their victims to death.

During the 1500s and 1600s, when ships were carrying great treasures of gold from America to Europe, there were many pirates in the Caribbean Sea and Atlantic Ocean. During the 1700s there were pirates in the Mediterranean Sea, called the BARBARY PIRATES. The United States had a lot to do with stopping their piracy (see the article about them).

Pirates who are famous in American history include Captain William Kidd, an Englishman, who is supposed to have buried his treasure somewhere on the

American coast or islands; Sir Henry Morgan, also English, who later became prominent in respectable life; and Jean Laffite, a Frenchman, who did great damage to shipping but later helped General Andrew Jackson and the United States Army to win the Battle of New Orleans against the British.

PRIVATEERS

Some ships practiced piracy by permission from their own countries, and so were not actually breaking the law. They were called privateers. The captains of these ships had official papers called *Letters of Marque and Reprisal,* which authorized them to attack and capture ships of an enemy country. This is somewhat like "commerce raiders" in modern warfare, except that the privateers kept any treasure they captured for their personal benefit and not for their countries. Many famous and respectable men, including Sir Francis Drake, were privateers at one time or another. However, the Letters of Marque were supposed to end when the war against the enemy country ended, but many of the privateers kept right on attacking merchant ships. This made them legally pirates, and the warships of their own countries hunted them down.

Pisa

Pisa is a city in central Italy. It is in the region of Tuscany and is on the Arno River. About ninety thousand people live there. They work in factories that make cotton goods, glass, bicycles, and railroad equipment. Others make pottery and beautiful marble statues. Pisa is a very old city and is noted for its beautiful buildings. The most famous is the LEANING TOWER, about which there is a separate article.

PISA, ITALY. Population (in 1959) 90,000. Capital of Pisa Province. On the Arno River.

Pisces

Pisces is the name of a constellation, or group of stars, whose pattern in the sky is supposed to look like the shape of two fishes. Pisces is the Latin word for "fishes." This constellation is very faint. Its brightest star is Alpha Piscium, which is a double, or binary, star—two stars so close together that they appear to be one.

Pisces is the twelfth sign of the ZODIAC, about which there is a separate article. Pisces is often represented by the sign ♓.

pistachio

The pistachio is a small green nut of a tree that grows in warm climates. The tree grows to be about twenty feet high. The fruit is about the size of an olive. Inside the fruit are found two small seeds in a reddish shell. The seeds are bright green. When salted in their shells, they are a popular nut. Pistachio nuts are used to flavor ice cream and candy.

pistol

A pistol is a short-barreled gun that is fired from the hand. It includes such weapons as single-shot pistols, revolvers, semiautomatics, and automatics.

Single-shot pistols are used mostly for target practice and therefore are manufactured in limited quantities. They can fire only one cartridge for each pull of

the trigger, and then another cartridge must be inserted.

A revolver has a single barrel with a cylinder containing five to nine cartridge

The automatic pistol fires bullets held in a clip in the gun's stock. It fires more rapidly than the revolver.

chambers behind it. Each time the revolver is fired the cylinder revolves, bringing a new chamber in line with the barrel. In this way the revolver can fire several cartridges in succession without being reloaded. A six-shooter is a revolver with six cartridge chambers.

In automatic pistols (automatics), the kick (recoil) of the gun on being fired is used to open the breech (rear of the barrel), throwing out the used cartridge shell and at the same time loading a new cartridge into the firing chamber. A fully automatic pistol will continue firing as long as the trigger is held back. A semiautomatic pistol will fire each time the trigger is pulled back.

Pitcher, Molly

Molly Pitcher was a heroine who helped the soldiers fighting for independence in the Revolutionary War. Her real name was Mary Ludwig Hays, but she got the name "Molly Pitcher" because she carried pitchers of water to the wounded and thirsty soldiers during the Battle of Monmouth. Later many legends grew up about Molly Pitcher, the most famous being that she took her husband's place at his cannon when he was killed in this battle. Another legend says that she received a commission in the army from George Washington. Molly Pitcher was born in New Jersey in 1754 and died in 1832. During the last ten years of her life she received a pension from the State of Pennsylvania as a reward for her services during the Revolution.

Pitt, William

William Pitt was the name of two great English statesmen. William Pitt the Elder was born in 1708. When he was 27 years old he became a Member of Parliament. In 1757 he was made prime minister. Pitt was called the "Great Commoner" because he was a member of the House of Commons. Later Pitt accepted the title of Earl of Chatham and became a member of the House of Lords.

Pitt's leadership helped Great Britain defeat the French in India and in America, in the French and Indian Wars. Pitt opposed harsh treatment of the American colonies, but when the Revolutionary War began Pitt felt that the colonies should not be given their independence. In 1778 he made a speech about this in Parliament. When he had finished the

speech he fell to the floor in a faint and died a few days later. Pitt was then 70 years old.

His son, called William Pitt the Younger, was born in 1759. He was a very bright student and amazed his teachers with his abilities. He became prime minister when he was only 24 years old. He never married and for twenty years Pitt devoted almost all his time to the conduct of the British government. Some believed that he was the greatest statesman England ever had.

Pitt the Younger was against the French Revolution and he hated Napoleon. Under his leadership, the British continued to fight Napoleon after everyone else had given up. When Napoleon won his great military victory over the Austrians and the Russians at Austerlitz, in 1805, the news was a terrible blow to Pitt. It was said that this was what killed him. He died in 1806, when he was 47 years old.

Pittsburgh

Pittsburgh is the second-largest city in Pennsylvania and the sixteenth-largest city in the United States. It is on the Allegheny and Monongahela rivers, where they meet to form the Ohio River. Their meeting place, called the "Golden Triangle," is one of the richest and most important business districts in the United States.

Pittsburgh is sometimes called the "Smoky City" because at one time its great steel and iron mills, blast furnaces, and coke plants filled the air with smoke and soot. Chemical controls have changed this, but a person driving through the city at night can see the sky lit up by the flames from the great furnaces and foundries that are at work all night long. The flames can be seen for miles around.

Over 500,000 people live in Pittsburgh. Most of them work in great factories. Pittsburgh is the greatest steel center in the world. Other large factories make electrical equipment, aluminum, glass, petroleum products, and machinery.

Pittsburgh is a hilly city. It is an important railroad center and river port. Although Pittsburgh is a busy industrial city, it also has beautiful residential sections on the hills behind the manufacturing and business districts. There are also fine parks and several important colleges and universities. Among them are:

University of Pittsburgh. Enrollment, 25,260 in 1971 (co-ed).

Carnegie Institute of Technology. Enrollment, 5,100 in 1971 (co-ed).

Duquesne University. Enrollment, 7,123 in 1971 (co-ed).

Chatham College. Enrollment, 650 in 1971 (women only).

The French built a fort more than two hundred years ago where Pittsburgh now stands. They called it Fort Duquesne. It was later captured by the British, who renamed it Fort Pitt, for William Pitt, the British prime minister. The blockhouse of this fort, built in 1764, can still be seen. Settlements grew up around the fort, and after 1784 the town of Pittsburgh grew rapidly. In 1816 it became a city. The rich coal and oil fields near by helped Pittsburgh grow.

PITTSBURGH, PENNSYLVANIA. Population (1970 census) 520,117. On the Allegheny

and Monongahela rivers. Settled, 1764.

Pius, Pope

Twelve popes of the Roman Catholic Church have been named Pius. The first, Pope Pius I, was probably born in Rome, about ninety years after the birth of Jesus. He was Pope from about 140 to 157, and became a saint when he died as a martyr in 157. Several other Popes named Pius have been sainted.

Pope Pius IX was born in Italy in 1792 and became Pope in 1846. He put through many reforms in the Papal States, lands in Italy then ruled by the Pope. He declared that the Pope could make no error when defining doctrines of faith and morals. This is called the doctrine of papal infallibility. He died in 1878.

Pope Pius X was born in Italy in 1835 and became Pope in 1903. He was a very holy man who worked hard to help the poor. He was heartbroken at the approach of World War I, and died in 1914, just after the war began. He was made a saint in 1954.

Pope Pius XI was born in 1857 and became Pope in 1922. His name was Achille Ratti and he came of a poor family in Italy. One of his most important achievements was to reach the agreement with the Italian government that set up Vatican City. He died in 1939.

PIUS XII

Pope Pius XII was born in Italy in 1876 and became Pope in 1939. His name was Eugenio Pacelli. He became a priest in 1899 and was made a cardinal in 1929. He visited many countries as a representative of Pope Pius XI. In 1936 he made a tour of the United States, where he met many thousands of American Catholics. When he became Pope, he was the first Pope who had been in the United States and who had traveled by airplane. He is considered one of the most scholarly Popes in history.

World War II began shortly after the other cardinals chose him as Pope. Frequently throughout the war Pope Pius XII asked everyone to pray for peace, and offered to try to help the heads of the warring nations to settle their differences. In 1942 he made a speech condemning dictatorships and the practice of racial discrimination.

Pope Pius XII declared 1950 a Holy Year of Jubilee, and thousands of Catholics from all over the world went to Rome to receive his blessing. He died in 1958.

Pizarro, Francisco

Francisco Pizarro was an early Spanish adventurer and conqueror in the New World. In 1538 he became the ruler of Peru, a large country in South America. He founded the city of Lima, which is the capital of the modern country of Peru.

Pizarro was born in Spain nearly five hundred years ago, about the year 1471. His parents were very poor, and as a boy he worked as a swineherd. He never learned to read and write. He came to the New World in 1510 and later got permission from the Spanish king to conquer the Inca Indians and become the governor of Peru. Pizarro found a great deal of wealth in Peru. He was cruel and treacherous to the Indians in order to get this wealth.

Pizarro pretended to be friendly to Atahualpa, the Inca king, then took him prisoner. Atahualpa offered millions of dollars' worth of jewels and gold to Pizarro in return for his life. Pizarro took the gold and jewels, but had Atahualpa killed just the same. Later he killed Almagro, another adventurer who had helped him in his conquest. In 1541 Pizarro was killed by Almagro's son.

plague

The plague is a deadly disease. It is caused by germs, or bacteria, that are often carried by fleas. One form of the plague is called *bubonic plague* because it takes the form of buboes (swollen glands). The plague was called the Black Death during the Middle Ages, the period several hundred years ago. When the disease began in any area, it often spread rapidly (became an epidemic) and killed millions. Epidemics of CHOLERA, about which there is a separate article, have also been called the plague.

Another use of the word *plague* occurs in the Bible, in the Book of Exodus. This tells how God sent ten plagues to punish the pharaoh (ruler) of Egypt because he was keeping the Jews captive. The ten plagues were: 1, blood: all water turned to blood. 2, frogs. 3, lice. 4, flies. 5, murrain of beasts (a disease that killed cattle). 6, boils. 7, hail. 8, locusts. 9, darkness. 10, death of the first-born child in every Egyptian home, but God passed over, or spared, the homes of the Jews, and for that reason the Passover is one of the great festivals of the Jewish religion.

Plains Indians

The Plains Indians were the American Indian tribes that lived in the vast region that stretches from the Mississippi to the Rocky Mountains and from Texas to Canada. Many different tribes made their home in this area. Among them were the Cheyenne, the Dakota, the Blackfoot, the Cree, and the Crow. Most of them belonged to the Sioux family of tribes. The Indians of the plains are the Indians we usually see in western movies.

These Indians depended almost entirely on the buffalo for their food, shelter, and clothing.

The Plains Indian lived in a buffalo-skin tent called a *tepee*, which was supported by three or more poles about 8 feet long and tied together at the top. It was a surprisingly warm shelter even in the bitter cold of the western winters. A flap of skin in the front of the tepee acted as a door. Inside, the Indian slept on a pile of buffalo hides. A small fire on the earthen floor was enough to keep the family warm. Smoke from the fire escaped through a small opening at the top where the poles were tied together.

In warm weather the Indian brave wore only a breechclout and moccasins. In the winter he wore a warm buffalo robe that had sleeves and came down as far as his knees. When he wanted to dress up he added a pair of leggings and a skin skirt. The robes were worn with the fur side next to the body. The flesh side or outside was often decorated with designs in very bright colors. Women wore a skin skirt but otherwise dressed like the men. Both sexes liked to paint their faces with bright clay colors. Hair was worn long by both men and women and was usually braided in two pigtails.

The Plains Indian was a magnificent horseman. He rode bareback or sometimes used a blanket. When hunting he would gallop alongside the buffaloes and shoot arrows into them with great accuracy. When the white traders began selling rifles, the Indian began to use it in hunting and in war.

In war the Plains Indian seldom attacked the enemy with a direct charge. Instead he rode around the entrenched soldiers or the white man's covered wagon train in ever narrowing circles, firing at every target he could see. To present as small a target as possible, he hung down on one side of his galloping horse, holding onto the animal with one foot on its back and one arm around its neck. In this position he would fire his rifle from under the horse's head. When an Indian was wounded and fell from his horse, one of his comrades would gallop past him and pick him up off the ground with one hand and swing him up on the horse.

The Plains Indians believed that there was a great buffalo god who ruled over the earth. They prayed to this god to make the buffalo plentiful. They also thought of the sun as a sign of the gods that ruled over men. Their greatest festival was the sun dance, during which the men would thrust sharpened wooden sticks into their flesh and dance until they fell unconscious with pain.

The Plains Indians disliked the white man not only because he took their land but also because he killed off their buffaloes. Many Dakotas and members of other tribes of Plains Indians now live on reservations.

planet

A planet is one of the large heavenly bodies that revolve about the sun in paths called *orbits*. There are nine known planets, one of which is the earth we live on. The planets in order of their distance from the sun are Mercury, Venus, Earth, Mars, Jupiter, Saturn, Uranus, Neptune, and Pluto; there is a separate article about each of them.

So far as astronomers have been able to tell, the planets are all made of the same materials as the earth. Some of them have an atmosphere with clouds, as the earth has. Some have surface temperatures as high as 700 degrees above zero Fahrenheit. Others are hundreds of degrees below freezing.

When seen with the naked eye, the planets appear to be bright stars. However, all their light is reflected sunlight. They have no light of their own.

See the article on the SOLAR SYSTEM.

plankton

Plankton is the mass of tiny, one-celled plants and animals that float in oceans, lakes, and rivers. Most plankton is found in fresh water. The plants and animals that form plankton are so small that most of them cannot be seen except through a microscope. Some plankton masses are a blue-green color and others are red. They often color the water where they float. Plankton is not able to move very much and so it drifts with the currents and tides. Plankton is very useful. Plant plankton is the food that animal plankton eats, and animal plankton is an important part of the diet of fish.

Properly spaced kohlrabi plants almost large enough to harvest. (Kohlrabi is a vegetable related to cabbage.)

plant

All living things are divided into two great groups: *fauna,* or animal life, and *flora,* or plant life. These two groups are sometimes called the *animal kingdom* and the *vegetable kingdom.*

When we think of plants we usually think of such things as trees and bushes and flowers, but the plant kingdom includes many growing things that do not look very much like our idea of plants.

THE DIFFERENCE BETWEEN PLANTS AND ANIMALS

All living things must eat and breathe in order to live. It is by finding out the answers to these questions: *How does it eat?* and *How does it breathe?* that we are able to tell the difference between most plants and most animals.

The biggest difference is that plants can make most of their own food out of air and water, aided by sunlight. Most plants contain the green substance *chlorophyll.* This makes it possible for them to perform *photosynthesis,* the changing of air and water into food. Animals cannot make their own food in this way. Therefore animals must get their food by eating plants, or by eating other animals that get their food by eating plants.

Plants "breathe in" a gas called *carbon dioxide* from the air and "breathe out" the gas called *oxygen.* Animals breathe in oxygen and breathe out carbon dioxide.

Another difference between plants and animals is that plants cannot feel things and cannot move about.

Most plants continue to grow throughout their period of life, while most animals have a definite limit beyond which they do not grow.

There are times when it is hard to tell whether a living thing is a plant or an animal, and some very simple living things are classified as both plant and animal.

HOW PLANTS ARE CLASSIFIED

There are many different kinds of plant on the earth, and often they are related to other types that are very much like them in some ways, but different in others. For instance, among trees there are oaks, elms, birches, chestnuts, and many others. They are of different sizes, and look different in many ways, but they are all trees and belong to the same class.

To make it easier to study plants or to discuss them, botanists (the scientists who study plant life) classify them, or separate them into different groups. There are a number of ways of classifying plants.

Most of these ways are based on certain principal groupings.

The largest group is called a *subkingdom;*

The basic parts of a flowering plant include: sperm or pollen (S), blossom (B), leaf (L), trunk or stalk (T), and roots (R).

Each subkingdom is divided into *phyla,* which is the plural of the word *phylum.*

Each phylum is divided into *classes;*

Each class is divided into *orders;*

Each order is divided into *families,* and many botanists divide some families into *tribes.*

Each family or *tribe* is divided into *genera,* which is the plural of the word *genus,* meaning "kind";

Each genus is divided into *species;*

And a species may have two or more *varieties.*

For example, an oak tree belongs to the subkingdom *Embryophyta,* plants that form embryos or seeds for reproduction;

It is a member of the phylum *Tracheophyta,* plants that have vascular tissues to carry food;

It is of the class *Angiospermae,* the flowering plants, and of the subclass *Dicotyledonae,* plants having a seed with two parts;

It is of the order *Fagales,* which includes two large families;

It is of the family *Fagaceae,* which includes oaks, chestnuts, and others;

It is of the genus *Quercus,* or oak;

It may be one of several species of Quercus, such as red oak, white oak, pin oak, all of which have their own scientific names.

You can read more about classification in the articles on BOTANY and ANIMAL LIFE.

HOW PLANTS ARE FORMED

All living things, whether animals or plants, are made up of tiny particles called CELLS, about which there is a separate article. The cells that form most plants are so small that they can be seen clearly only with the aid of a very strong microscope. It would take from 250 to 2,500 cells of most plants to make an inch. Some plant cells are even smaller, and others are larger. There are cells so small that it would take 50,000 of them to make an inch, and certain cells of plants in the nettle family may be eight inches long. The living substance of the cell is called *protoplasm.*

A plant that has only one cell is called a *unicellular* organism. Sometimes a number of similar one-celled organisms group together but still remain distinct organisms. These groups are called *colonies.* An organism composed of many cells with different structures and functions is called a *multicellular* organism. Most of the higher plants are multicellular organisms. Their cells vary greatly in size, structure, and function. A group of similar cells that perform the same function is called a *tissue.* A major part of a plant, such as a leaf or a stem, is composed of various kinds of tissue.

The responses of plants are partly governed by the growth of plant cells. A plant will bend because the cells on one side grow larger than those on the other.

HOW PLANTS LIVE

The life of a plant is a series of chemical changes that, taken all together, are called *metabolism.* The principal metabolic processes of plants are as follows:

Photosynthesis, the manufacture of food from carbon dioxide and water with the help of sunlight and chlorophyll.

Respiration, a chemical process that releases the energy in foods and makes it available for growth.

Assimilation, the changing of foods into living protoplasm.

Digestion, the changing of complex foods into simpler ones.

Food storage, the changing of food to starch, sugar, proteins, or all three together, which are stored until needed.

Most of the complex plants have roots that grow beneath the surface of the soil. These roots serve to anchor the plant in the soil. They absorb water and minerals from the soil and conduct them upward to the stem and leaves. The root is usually

1249

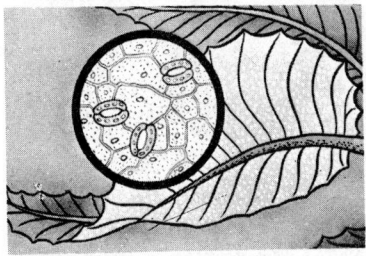

The leaf of the plant takes in carbon dioxide through small holes called *stomata*.

the first part of the plant to grow out of the seed when it germinates. Roots absorb water and minerals that the plant needs for additional growth.

Plants grow by the formation of new cells, a process that is called *cell division*. There are two steps in the process: *mitosis*, in which the nucleus, or central part, of the cell divides in two; and *cell wall formation*, in which the two nuclei are enclosed into two new cells.

HOW PLANTS REPRODUCE

Reproduction is the way in which a living thing creates a new living thing like itself. The higher plants are formed by *sexual reproduction*, in which two sex cells join together to create a new organism. There are two kinds of sexual reproduction: *isogamy*, which is the joining of two sex cells of the same kind; and *heterogamy*, in which two sex cells of different kinds, called the *egg*, or *ovum*, and the *sperm*, or *pollen*, are joined together.

Many plants are formed by *asexual reproduction*, which does not require the joining of sex cells. A part of the plant separates from the parent plant and when placed under the right conditions may grow into a new plant. Plant structures that separate naturally from the parent plant, or may be easily separated from it, are commonly used in growing new plants. Bulbs are an example of the asexual method of starting new plants. Grafting and budding is the way new fruit trees and some flowering shrubs are obtained.

WHERE PLANTS LIVE

There is no part of the earth on which there is not some plant life. Some plants, such as mosses, grasses, and lichens, grow at the North and South Pole where it is always frozen. Many plants live in the water of ponds and oceans.

The surroundings in which a plant lives are called its *environment*. A group of plants that live in the same environment is called a *plant community*.

The growth of plants in an environment is affected by temperature, light, wind, humidity (the amount of moisture in the air), and precipitation (the amount of rain or snow that falls). The temperature and chemical makeup of the soil and the amount of water in it have a great deal to do with the kinds of plant that can grow in it.

The geography of the environment may determine whether a particular plant will spread or die out. *Barriers*, such as oceans, high mountain ranges, and deserts, will prevent the spreading of some plants. *Highways*, such as mountain passes and rivers, will make it easy for plants to spread.

DIFFERENT KINDS OF PLANT

All plant life is divided into two large groups, or subkingdoms: *Thallophyta*, plants that do not form embryos, and *Embryophyta*, plants that do form embryos. An *embryo* is a small beginning of a plant, as contained in a seed.

Thallophyta in general can be called the *lower* plants. They do not have true roots, stems, or leaves. Reproduction is very simple. There are very few kinds of tissues. Thallophyta are chiefly water plants, but those that do grow out of water are mostly *parasites* (plants that live on other plants), or *saprophytes*, which live on decaying matter.

The subkingdom *Thallophyta* is divided into two major kinds of plant, *algae* and *fungi*. Most algae live in water, and most of them reproduce by fission, in which each one-celled plant divides into two new one-celled plants. Some forms, usually called seaweed, reproduce sexually. Almost all algae contain chlorophyll.

The fungi, like the algae, lack true roots, stems, and leaves, and do not form embryos; but they do not contain chlorophyll. Fungi are divided into three phyla: *bacteria*, *slime molds*, and *true fungi*.

Bacteria are the most widely distributed of all living organisms. They are found in air, soil, water, and on and in other living things. They are one-celled organisms and are the smallest of all living things. Bacteria reproduce by fission. They are both useful and harmful to man.

Slime molds have a mixture of plant and animal characteristics. They move, or flow, like an amoeba and take in solid food. They reproduce by spores and by fission.

The *true fungi* are mostly multicellular. Most of them reproduce sexually. Fungi are responsible for many plant diseases. Others are food for man, such as truffles and mushrooms. The yeast used in baking is a fungus.

The second subkingdom of plant life is the *Embryophyta*, plants that form embryos. The Embryophyta are divided into two phyla: *Bryophyta*, the mosses and their relatives; and *Tracheophyta*, which include all of the familiar trees, shrubs, and flowers. A subphylum of this group, *Pteropsida*, is the principal group of plants now growing on earth. The individual plants vary from small herbs to huge trees. Most are land plants, but some live in the water. All have true roots, stems, and leaves. This subphylum is divided into three classes: *ferns*; *conifers* and their relatives; and true *flowering plants*.

The ferns, called *Filicineae*, have roots, stems, and leaves. They reproduce by spores. In the tropics the stems of ferns grow above ground and a plant may reach a height of 30 or 40 feet. In temperate climates the stems of most ferns grow underground and only the leaves can be seen above ground. The ferns that are living today are of little use to man, but the ferns of prehistoric time were of great importance in the formation of coal.

The other two classes of this group are called *seed plants*.

The conifers, called *Gymnospermae*, are woody plants. Most of them are evergreen trees with needles or scalelike leaves. The most familiar conifers include the pines, spruces, firs, cedars, redwoods, and so on. Gymnosperms reproduce by structures called *cones*, which may contain seeds or pollen or both.

The third group of this important subphylum is the true flowering plants, or Angiosperms. These plants reproduce by means of the flower, which contains the pollen in the stamen and the egg in the pistil. They are fertilized by various kinds of pollination—by wind, water, and insects and birds. Angiosperms are the most widely distributed of all green land plants. Some varieties are water plants. The Angiosperms are separated into two groups: *Monocotyledons* and *Dicotyledons*. Every seed contains an embryo, or miniature plant.

In the Monocotyledons, this tiny plant has one leaf. These include such plants as palms, lilies, irises, tulips, bananas, and many others. In the Dicotyledons, the embryo has two leaves. These include such plants as willows, oaks, apples, roses, buttercups, violets, and many others. There are separate articles on FLOWER and most of the best-known plants.

Plantagenet

The Plantagenet family was a royal family of England. Members of this family ruled England for about three hundred years.

The name Plantagenet first belonged to a French nobleman, Count Goeffrey V of Anjou. He usually wore on his helmet a sprig of the broom plant and the French words for this (*plante* and *genet*) became the English name Plantagenet. Geoffrey's son was the first Plantagenet king of England. He was crowned as Henry II and ruled about eight hundred years ago, from 1154 to 1189. His direct descendants ruled for the next two hundred years. They were Richard I, John, Henry III, Edward I, Edward II, Edward III, and Richard II. While Richard was king, members of two related families, called the Lancasters and the Yorks, began to fight over who should be the next king. Their fights are told about in the articles on ENGLAND and WARS OF THE ROSES. Richard II died in the year 1400, and after that there were no more Plantagenet kings of England.

plantain

Plantain is a weedy plant that grows in many parts of the world, especially where the climate is hot. There are about seventy-five different plants of the plantain family. One kind of plantain, a large plant, has a fruit very much like the banana. People cook this fruit or make it into a flour. The kinds of plantain best known in North America are weeds that are bad for lawns.

plasma, the fluid or liquid part of blood: see the article BLOOD.

plaster

Plaster is a material made of sand and gypsum or lime or cement. It is used to give a smooth, airtight finish to the walls and ceilings of houses.

The sand and the cementing material are prepared dry and mixed with water

when ready for use. This makes a thick paste, which is applied with a trowel over a base of wood laths or steel mesh. Usually three coats of plaster are applied. The first, called the scratch coat, is mixed with hair or fiber to give it strength. It is forced well into the plaster base, and the surface is scratched so that it will hold the other coats. The second, called the *brown coat*, contains no hair or fiber, but it is made rough so that the third, or *finishing,* coat will stick to it. The final coat is made of plaster of Paris, slaked lime, and white sand. It provides a smooth, white finish.

When plaster is applied to the outside walls of houses, it is called *stucco.* Most stucco is made of sand and lime or cement. Stucco can be colored. It is applied with a trowel like any plaster, but the surface coat is usually left rough.

Plaster of Paris is a special plaster made of the mineral GYPSUM, about which there is a separate article. When gypsum is heated, a large amount of water is driven off. This leaves a fine white powder. This powder is remixed with a certain amount of water to form a paste that can be molded or cast into any shape. It dries into a hard, rocklike substance. Plaster of Paris is used for making small statues, casts in dental and surgical work, and many other things. I got its name because for many years the world's supply of gypsum came from huge quarries just outside the city of Paris in France.

plastics

A plastic is a material that can be made soft so that it may be molded into useful articles. The plastic, after being softened, must then become hard again so that articles made from it may be put to use. Thousands of different articles are made from plastic materials. Among them are many kinds of toys, automobile steering wheels, television and radio cabinets, drug vials, bottle caps, telephones, photographic film, toothbrush handles

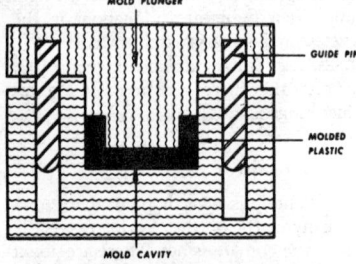

Compression molding is like making a waffle. The plastic is baked in the mold under pressure from top and bottom.

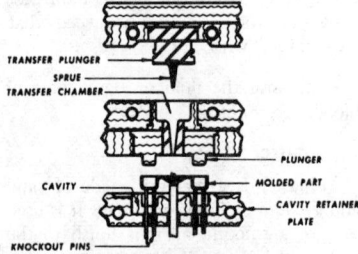

Transfer molding uses pressure to shape "bricks" of previously heated plastic.

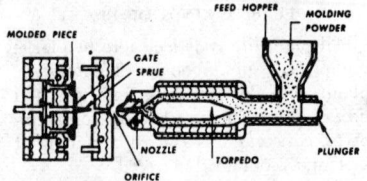

In injection molding, the hot plastic material is fed into an unheated mold and becomes solid as it cools.

and bristles, knife handles, buttons, buckles, pencils and pens, fabrics and many, many others.

THE MAIN KINDS OF PLASTICS

Plastic materials are divided into two main kinds, according to the way in which they harden. One kind of plastic, called *thermoplastic* or *thermolabile,* softens whenever it is heated and hardens whenever it is cooled. The other kind of plastic, called *thermosetting,* softens the first time it is heated but then hardens once and for all, and if it is heated again it will not soften any more.

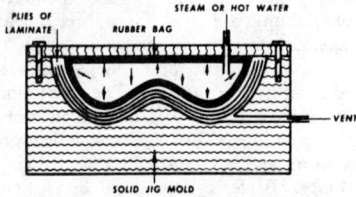

High pressure laminating is like making a layer cake. Layers of plastic and another substance like cloth are glued together under heavy pressure.

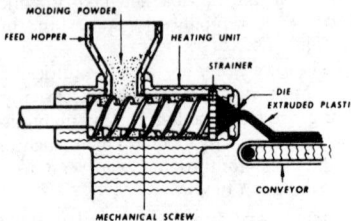

In extrusion molding, tubes, rods or sheets of plastic are squeezed through a mold, as shaving cream is from a tube.

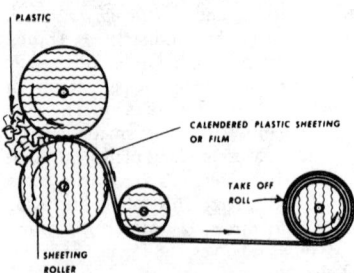

Calendering is used to apply a thermoplastic to a cloth by pressing plastic and cloth together by means of rollers.

MOLDING PLASTICS

There are four ways to mold plastics. These ways have the names *compression, injection, transfer,* and *extrusion.*

Compression molding is done by putting powders of thermosetting plastics into a mold, and then applying pressure and heat in order to shape the plastic and to cause it to harden.

In *injection molding,* a thermoplastic material is melted in a heating chamber, and then a plunger forces it out of the chamber and into molds where it hardens.

Monsanto Co.
Plastic furniture such as this bookshelf is inexpensive, colorful, and washable.

Monsanto Co.
This plastic cup holds seven ounces of hot liquids.

Canadian Information Office
These Canadian Eskimos are carrying a plastic portable igloo.

In *transfer molding,* a thermoplastic material is melted and then is poured into a mold where it cools and becomes hard; or a thermosetting plastic is melted, poured into a mold, and hardened by further heating.

In *extrusion molding,* the plastic material is heated under pressure until it becomes about as soft as molasses taffy; then the soft plastic is pushed by a plunger through a die, a block of steel with a hole through it. The hole has the shape that is wanted for the plastic, and long continuous bars, rods or threads of the plastic material come out through the die-hole. Then they are cut to whatever length is wanted.

WHAT PLASTICS ARE MADE OF

Plastics are made from many kinds of resin, cellulose, or protein. All plastics are organic materials, which means that they all contain the chemical element carbon combined in many different ways with the elements hydrogen and oxygen, and perhaps nitrogen. Dividing plastics according to their chemical make-up gives seven main classes of them. The names of these classes are phenolic, urea,

casein, cellulose, acrylic, polystyrene, and vinyl.

Phenolic plastics are thermosetting. Bakelite is the best-known of this class of plastics. Most of the phenolics are inexpensive. They are tough and are not easily harmed by heat, water, or chemicals. They are not translucent (you cannot see through them) and they can be made only in dark colors.

Urea plastics are made from the chemicals urea and formaldehyde. They are thermosetting. They are glass-clear, may be dyed any color, are odorless and tasteless, and do not scratch easily. When cotton linters (short cotton fibers) and purified wood pulp are added to urea plastics, they can be made to look like ivory.

Casein plastics are made from the solid matter that makes up the curd of milk. They are hornlike in look and feel. They are thermosetting and are hard to mold but easy to stamp or work with tools. Therefore sheets, tubes or rods of casein plastic are extrusion-molded and then are stamped or cut to shape. Casein plastics are cheap, strong, and available in many colors, but they warp in damp weather. They are used mostly for buttons, buckles, and other small objects.

Cellulose plastics include rayon, and also CELLULOID, the first modern plastic, about which there is a separate article. The cellulose plastics can be made to look like pearl, jade, onyx, horn, ivory, or tortoise shell, and in any color.

Acrylic plastics can be made as clear as glass or in any color. They can carry light around a corner, so doctors use acrylic rods to light up the throat or the inside of the nose or other parts inside the body. Mechanics light up hard-to-get-at places in machinery with acrylic rods. Acrylic plastics are very easily formed and are nearly shatterproof. The windows and the transparent "bubbles" on airplanes are made of an acrylic plastic best known by the trade name Plexiglas. Thread made of acrylic materials is called Orlon.

Polystyrene plastics are light in weight and are not harmed by water, alkalis, or acids. They can be made to exact dimensions and will not change size or shape as they grow old. They are clear and available in many colors, so one of their many uses is for costume jewelry.

Vinyl plastics are able to withstand water, acids, alkalis, oils, and other chemicals. They are almost as flexible as rubber. Sheets of vinyl plastics are used to make raincoats and shower curtains. Squeeze-bottles, used to spray perfumes, deodorants, and drugs, are made of vinyl plastics. There are hundreds of other uses.

Two other plastics that are spun into threads are named polyamide, from which Nylon is made; and polyester, from which Dacron is made.

plastic surgery

Plastic surgery is a branch of medicine that can change or replace outside parts of the body. If a part is ugly or deformed, or has not developed properly, or if it has been destroyed by accident or disease, plastic surgery can often make it useful or good-looking again. A plastic surgeon can replace a missing nose, ear, or lower jaw. A plastic surgeon can make a leg longer or shorter by adding or removing a section of bone. He can replace a missing thumb with a toe or finger.

Plastic surgery requires tremendous skill. The plastic surgeon is like a sculptor. Instead of using clay, stone, or wood, he molds living skin and bone. If a person loses a lower jaw, the surgeon may replace it with a long piece of bone from the person's hip. He may take skin from the patient's abdomen and mold the skin around the bone to make a chin. He will attach the new jaw to the face with wires, clamps, and stitches. Slowly the new jaw will attach itself to the tissues of the face.

An operation of this kind may take months or years to complete. It must be done in a number of steps. Each step involes a separate operation and the skin must heal before the next operation can be performed.

Plastic surgery is sometimes used to improve a person's appearance. This is called cosmetic surgery. A person may have a large, crooked nose that makes him feel unhappy. The plastic surgeon can make the person a new nose. Sometimes actresses and other women find it important to look young. They may have their faces "lifted." This is done by pulling the sagging tissues of the face tight so that there will be no wrinkles.

Plata River

The Plata River, or Rio de la Plata, forms the wide mouth of the Parana and Uruguay rivers in South America. It is a large inlet, called an *estuary,* of the Atlantic Ocean. It extends inland for almost 200 miles. Montevideo, the capital of Uruguay, is on its northern shore, and Buenos Aires, the capital of Argentina, is on its southern shore.

platinum

Platinum is a silvery-white metal. It is a chemical element, which means that it is one of the basic substances of which everything in the world is made. Platinum is very useful and there is not much of it, so it is expensive.

Platinum is malleable, which means it can be hammered into whatever shape is wanted. It is extremely ductile, which means it can be drawn out into very thin wire without breaking. It will not tarnish. These properties make platinum a very popular metal for jewelry.

Platinum will not melt until it is heated to 3,225 degrees Fahrenheit. This is a very high melting point; only four or five other metals have a higher one. Because of this high melting temperature, and because it resists acids and other chemicals so well, platinum is very important to chemists, who make it into crucibles, dishes, spoons, and other pieces of laboratory equipment.

Platinum is very heavy. It is twice as heavy as lead. A baseball weighs five ounces, but a baseball made of platinum would weigh ten pounds, or thirty-two times as much.

Platinum is found in the earth in small grains. In these grains, platinum is combined with one or more of the metals palladium, iridium, osmium, and rhodium. To separate platinum from these metals is a difficult and complicated process. The countries that produce the most platinum ore are, in order, Canada, South Africa, the Soviet Union, and the United States.

Plato

Plato was one of the greatest philosophers of all time. He lived in Greece more than two thousand years ago. A philosopher is a student of all forms of human knowledge.

Plato was born about the year 427 B.C. He was the son of noble parents. As a young man he became a pupil of Socrates, another great philosopher and teacher. Socrates taught by simply talking to his disciples, and this was the method that Plato later chose for his own.

Plato spent much of his time listening to Socrates until Socrates' death in 399 B.C. After that he traveled widely. When he was about 40, he settled in Athens and founded the first university, the Academy. Instruction was given in philosophy, mathematics, astronomy, and government. Plato spent his time lecturing there and writing *dialogues,* conversations from which his philosophy can be learned. Socrates is a character in many of these dialogues and much of what we know about Socrates comes from them. In the *Republic* and the *Laws,* Plato discusses problems of government. The *Timaeus* is a general account of how the world was created and what it is like. Plato also wrote many other dialogues.

Plato taught that one should not pay too much attention to physical things, because the whole physical world is only an imperfect copy of a world of ideas or forms. He taught that men should be more interested in these ideas and forms, which are perfect and unchanging. Plato's teachings influenced his pupil, ARISTOTLE, about whom there is a separate article.

Platte River

The Platte River is one of the largest branches of the Missouri River. It is the most important river in Nebraska. It is 310 miles long. It is formed by the North Platte and South Platte rivers in the western part of Nebraska, and from there it flows east and empties into the Missouri at Plattsmouth, near Omaha. The Platte is used for irrigation and hydroelectric power. Although the river is of great use to the farmers, it is quite shallow and ships cannot travel on it.

platypus

The platypus is a strange animal that is found in Australia and Tasmania. It is often called the duckbill platypus, because it has a beak like a duck's bill, only it is not horny but soft and leathery. It uses its bill for nuzzling in mud to find worms and grubs, its favorite food. The platypus is a mammal, which means that it nurses its young, but unlike most mammals its young are not born alive but are hatched from eggs, like a hen's. The female platypus usually lays two eggs, once a year, in an underground nest it has dug in swampy ground. It holds the eggs close to it for about ten days, and then feeds the young on milk. The platypus looks very queer. It is 1½ to 2 feet long and is covered with thick, grayish-brown fur. It has a furry, flattened tail and broad, webbed feet that make it an expert swimmer and diver. The male has horny, hol-

low spurs on its hind feet, which it uses to attack its enemies. The spurs contain a poisonous fluid that is quite dangerous.

play, a kind of entertainment in which a story is told by being acted out by people on a stage: see the articles AC-TORS AND ACTRESSES and DRAMA.

playing cards

Playing cards are small pieces of pasteboard, about 2¼ by 3¼ inches, used for playing games and sometimes for "telling fortunes." The Chinese invented playing cards more than a thousand years ago and Europeans first used playing cards nearly seven hundred years ago.

The pack of cards most used in the United States and other English-speaking countries is called the "standard pack" and came originally from France. It has 52 cards. These are divided into four groups called *suits,* two of them printed in black (spades [♠] and clubs [♣]) and two in red (hearts [♡] and diamonds [♢]). In each suit there are 13 cards, called the ace, king, queen, jack, 10, 9, 8, 7, 6, 5, 4, 3, and 2. The king, queen and jack are called *face cards* or *court cards.*

Sometimes other packs are used. The Spanish pack has 40 cards, the German pack 32 or 36 cards, the Italian pack 56 cards. Each of these packs has four suits, but these may not be the same as the English suits.

See also CARD GAMES.

plebeians, the common people of ancient Rome. See PATRICIANS.

Pleiades

The Pleiades are a group or cluster of bright stars in the constellation Taurus. They are named after the daughters of Atlas, a famous giant in Greek mythology. The Pleiades are also called the "Seven Sisters," because at one time seven bright stars could be seen in that area with the naked eye, but now only six are visible. More than 250 can be seen through a telescope. The Pleiades can be seen most clearly in the early evening during the month of November.

pleurisy

Pleurisy is an infection of the lining that covers the lungs and the inner surface of the chest. When a person has pneumonia, tuberculosis, or influenza, there is a danger that he may develop pleurisy. A person who gets pleurisy usually develops a severe cough and a fever. He has sharp pains in his chest when he takes a deep breath or when he moves. Sometimes pus forms in the chest (a condition called *empyema*), and this may have to be removed by an operation, but usually the antibiotic drugs stop the infection. Pleurisy is not as dangerous as it was before these drugs were discovered.

Pliny

Pliny was the name of two great writers of ancient Rome. Pliny the Elder was born in the year 23. He was a soldier and he was acquainted with most of the important people of his time in Rome. He was a great scholar and wrote many books. The best-known of his

books is called *Natural History,* a kind of encyclopedia that deals with many subjects such as geography, zoölogy, botany, and art. Today we know that many of the things that Pliny wrote are wrong, but his book is valuable because it shows us what the ancient Romans believed to be true. Pliny died in 79.

Pliny the Younger was born in the year 62. He was the nephew and adopted son of Pliny the Elder. When he was only 14 years old he wrote a play in the Greek language. He is most famous for his letters, which tell us much about life in ancient Rome. He died about 114.

Ploesti

Ploesti is a city in Rumania, in a region of rich oil fields. About 115,000 people live there. Many of them work in large oil-refining plants. During World War II, the oil refineries of Ploesti were very valuable to the Germans, who had occupied Rumania. The Allies bombed these plants several times and put most of them out of operation.

plover

The plover is a bird that lives along coasts and in fields and swamps in almost every part of the world. It is sometimes

The plover is found along the coasts of many nations. Its distinctive bill and three-toed feet are easily recognized.

nicknamed the "rain bird," because it makes a loud scolding noise just before rain comes.

There are more than sixty different kinds of plover. All plovers are medium-sized birds with short legs. Some plovers are plain birds and others, such as the golden plover, are handsome black birds with touches of brilliant yellow color on their backs.

The plovers are great fliers. The golden plover spends the summer months in the Arctic regions. When fall comes it travels 2,400 miles to Hawaii for the winter. Thousands of plovers make this journey. They fly at a rate of 40 to 70 miles an hour and they do not stop for food or drink along the way. Another kind of plover spends the summer in Nova Scotia and journeys to South America for the winter months.

plum

The plum is a sweet fruit that grows on a small tree. There are many different kinds of plum.

The plum tree is usually 20 or more feet high. It is deciduous, which means that it loses its leaves in the fall. The tree bears white flowers. The plums grow in clusters. They may be dark blue, green, red, or a yellowish-orange color. They

have smooth skins and one smooth pit or "stone."

People in Europe raise more than nine hundred different kinds of plum. Among the most popular are Damson plums and Green Gage plums. The "sloeberry" is a kind of plum.

A few varieties of plum tree produce a fruit that is sweet and fleshy but not very juicy. This fruit is dried to make prunes. A Japanese plum tree that was brought to California about fifty years ago is now grown by many people.

Plums are eaten fresh or are cooked. They are used to make jams and preserves.

plumbing

Plumbing is the installing and repairing of pipes and fixtures for water, sewage, and gas. A person who works at the plumbing trade is called a journeyman plumber.

As a part of such work, the plumber cuts and makes screw threads in pipe with threading and cutting tools; makes different kinds of joints with lead and solder; and fits and connects fixtures and appliances.

The plumber uses such tools as wrenches, drills, blowtorches, soldering irons, and many different kinds of measuring instruments. The journeyman plumber may have an apprentice or helper working with him.

Most journeyman plumbers work in the construction industry. Others work for gas and electric companies, and in such industries as shipbuilding, aircraft manufacturing, food, paper, chemical, petroleum, iron and steel, and rail, ship, and air transportation.

There are more than 330,000 journeyman plumbers and pipefitters in the United States, and about 8,300 apprentice plumbers. Before a person can become a journeyman plumber he usually works as an apprentice for five years.

Plutarch

Plutarch was a great writer in ancient Greece, nearly two thousand years ago. He was born about the year 46 and received his education in the city of Athens. When he grew up Plutarch visited Rome and gave lectures there. He then returned to Chaeronea, the city where he was born, and spent the rest of his life there.

Plutarch is best known for a book of biographies, the stories of the lives of ancient Greeks and Romans who lived before his time. This book is called *Parallel Lives.* It consists of a series of pairs of biographies, one of a Greek and one of a Roman who occupied a similar position. For example, he pairs the life stories of the great orators Demosthenes and Cicero and of the great conquerors Alexander the Great and Julius Caesar.

When William Shakespeare wrote his plays about Julius Caesar and Mark Antony he took many of his facts from Plutarch.

Plutarch died about the year 120.

Pluto (mythology)

Pluto was a character in Greek mythology, the stories the ancient Greeks told about their gods and goddesses. Pluto was the ruler of the underworld, or Hades, the place where dead souls went if they were not good enough to get into Elysium, or heaven. Pluto married Persephone (whom the Romans called Proserpine), the daughter of the goddess of grain. Each year, Pluto let his wife rejoin her mother for six months, so that the goddess would let the grain grow. This Greek story represents the six months of spring and summer in which plants grow, and the winter months in which they do not.

Pluto (planet)

Pluto is one of the planets that revolve around the sun. Pluto is the farthest planet from the sun. Astronomers (scientists who study the stars) used to think that Pluto was smaller than the earth, but some now think it is larger. It is about 3,670,000,000 miles from the sun, nearly forty times as far as the earth is.

Pluto revolves around the sun about once every 248 years, compared to one year for the earth.

We know less about Pluto than we do about any other planet. One reason is that it is so far away. Another is that Pluto was the last planet to be discovered. It was first discovered in 1930.

plutonium

Plutonium is a chemical substance that is made from uranium. Like uranium, plutonium is a chemical element, one of the basic substances of which everything in the world is made. Plutonium is not found in nature as most other chemicals are. It can be obtained only by smashing the atoms of uranium. Plutonium is a radioactive element, which means that it gives off rays of small particles that travel at high speeds.

To change uranium into plutonium, uranium is put into an "atom smasher" (cyclotron), where for more than two days it is bombarded by atomic particles called deuterons. The United States government makes plutonium in two huge plants, one at Oak Ridge, Tennessee, and one at Hanford, Washington. Plutonium has largely replaced uranium in the atomic bomb because it is more powerful. Plutonium was first made in 1940 by American chemists.

Plymouth

Plymouth is a town in Massachusetts. It is one of the most famous historical spots in the United States because it was there that the Pilgrims landed in their ship, the *Mayflower*, in the year 1620. More than 14,000 people now live in Plymouth. Many people make cord and rope in the oldest and largest cord factory in the United States. Many people visit Plymouth to see Plymouth Rock, the spot where the Pilgrims were said to have landed from the *Mayflower*. At Plymouth there is a house built exactly like the houses of the Pilgrims. It is open to the public. There are also a number of interesting houses that were built during the days of the Plymouth Colony,

about three hundred years ago.

PLYMOUTH, MASSACHUSETTS. Population (1970 census) 18,606. County seat, Plymouth County. On Plymouth Bay (Atlantic Ocean). Settled, 1620.

plywood

Plywood is made by gluing together thin sheets of wood and then pressing them under fifty or more tons of pres-

Plywood is made of several panels of wood glued together. The grain runs along the first panel, across the second, and so on. The face panel is ready for finishing.

sure. This process is called lamination. Plywood usually has three or more layers of wood. The pressure makes it such a solid piece of wood that the separate layers will never come apart. Plywood is usually stronger but lighter in weight than a solid board of the same thickness, and it does not warp as badly. It is used for doors, panels, furniture, trunks, airplanes, and so on. See also LUMBER.

pneumonia

Pneumonia is a sickness in which one or both of a person's lungs become infected. It is caused by bacteria or by a virus, a kind of one-celled plant that is too small even to be seen through a microscope. All people have some of these germs in the nose and throat passages of their bodies. Healthy lungs are made so that they can keep these harmful germs out. When the lungs become weak, the germs enter the lung passages, which become swollen and sometimes filled with pus.

When a person has had a disease such as influenza, measles, or whooping cough, his lungs become weak and there is a possibility that he may develop pneumonia. Heart disease and hardening of the arteries are other diseases that may bring on pneumonia. A person who breathes poisonous fumes or certain chemical powders may weaken his lungs, and a hard blow on the chest can also weaken the lungs.

When a person gets pneumonia he has chills and a high fever. He cannot breathe easily and coughs a great deal. His skin becomes a light bluish color. Until 1940, pneumonia was one of the most serious of all diseases and many persons who got pneumonia died. Then doctors began to use the "wonder drugs" called sulfa drugs and antibiotics. These drugs have made pneumonia much less serious.

When a person has pneumonia he is sometimes given extra oxygen to help him breathe more easily.

Po River

The Po River is the longest river in Italy. It is 420 miles long. It flows through the most fertile region in the country, and the farmers use the Po to irrigate their farms. The valley of the Po is called "the breadbasket of Italy."

The Po begins high up in the Alps, near France. It flows east past important cities, such as Turin, Piacenza, and Cremona, and empties into the Adriatic Sea. At the mouth of the Po is a large delta that has been built up by the deposits of sand, mud, and gravel from the river. This delta continues to grow more than a hundred feet out into the sea each year.

The upper part of the Po River flows swiftly, but the lower part is much slower. The river often overflows its banks and causes severe floods. To prevent these floods, the people have built up the banks of the river at various places. Much of the Po is navigable and is very useful for transportation. Most of the rivers of northern Italy are branches of the Po.

Pocahontas

Pocahontas was the name of a beautiful Indian princess. She saved the life of Captain John Smith, the leader of the Jamestown colony in Virginia, and she married John Rolfe, a young Englishman living in the colony. She was the first Indian in Virginia to become a Christian. She was very pretty and was liked by all the Jamestown settlers. Later she lived in London, where she was treated as royalty. Her son, Thomas Rolfe, became a distinguished man in Virginia, and her descendants are living in Virginia today.

Pocahontas was the daughter of Powhatan, the powerful chief of about thirty tribes of Indians living around Virginia. Captain John Smith was captured by these Indians in 1607. He was brought before Powhatan, who sentenced him to death.

Pocahontas, who was about 16 years old, begged her father to spare Captain Smith's life, but Powhatan refused. Large stones were placed in front of Powhatan, and Captain Smith was forced to place his head on these stones. Indian braves stood above him with huge clubs, ready to beat him to death. At this point Pocahontas broke away from her father's side, put her arms around Captain Smith, and laid her head against his. Again she begged her father to let Captain Smith go free, and this time Powhatan agreed. John Smith was taken back to Jamestown with an escort of Indian warriors.

From that time on, Pocahontas was a friend of the settlers and influenced her father to be friendly, too. Two years later she heard of an Indian plan to destroy the white settlement. On a dark and stormy night she left her father's home and ran through the woods to Jamestown to warn Captain Smith of the plan. Then she hurried back home before dawn so that the Indians would not know she had been away.

After John Smith returned to England, a sea captain captured Pocahontas and held her prisoner to try to force Powhatan to give the settlers food. While she was a prisoner, she met young John Rolfe, who taught her Christianity and who later, in 1613, became her husband. Three years later the Rolfes returned to England, where Pocahontas received as much attention as the daughter of a European king would have received. Pocahontas remained in England for about a year. She was ready to return to America in June, 1617, when she caught smallpox and died. She was then about 26 years old.

Pocahontas was buried in Gravesend, England.

Poe, Edgar Allan

Edgar Allan Poe was an American poet, short-story writer, and literary critic. He was one of the first American writers to be admired by European critics, and he is given credit for establishing the form of the modern short story as well as the modern detective story.

Poe's stories are filled with supernatural and horrifying events. Perhaps the greatest is "The Cask of Amontillado." The best of his detective, or mystery, stories are "The Purloined Letter," "The Murders in the Rue Morgue," and "The Gold Bug." His most famous and most cleverly-constructed poem is "The Raven," and his other well-known poems include "Annabel Lee" and "The Bells."

Poe's life was a very unhappy one. He was born in Boston in 1809, but most of his life was spent in Richmond, Virginia. Poe's parents, who were actors, died when he was a child, and he was brought up by foster parents, Mr. and Mrs. John Allan. Poe was educated in England and at the University of Virginia. Later he served in the American Army and attended the United States Military Academy at West Point. His first book of poems was published when he was only 20 years old.

When Poe was 27 years old he married his cousin, Virginia Clemm, who was only 14 years old at the time. She died eleven years later of tuberculosis, having suffered greatly because Poe was too poor to give her the proper care. Poe was poor all his life, although he was editor of several successful magazines in Richmond, Philadelphia, and New York. He lost many jobs because of quarrels that he had with the men for whom he worked and because he often drank too much. Poe died in Baltimore in 1849.

poet laureate

In ancient times, the Greeks and Romans used to honor poets by giving them wreaths of laurel leaves that they wore on their heads as crowns. In England the government still selects one of the British poets for special honor and calls him the poet laureate. There is only one poet laureate at a time. When he dies, another usually is appointed. The poet laureate is expected to write poems for official occasions, such as the king's or queen's birthday.

The first English poet laureate was John Dryden. Others included William Wordsworth, Robert Southey, and Alfred Tennyson. John Masefield was named poet laureate in 1930.

poetry

Poetry is a form of literature. It is the use of words to make beautiful sounds and at the same time to express beautiful ideas. Poetry is often compared to music because it uses sound to appeal to the human sense of beauty. Poetry is also compared to painting, because fine poetry can make a reader "see," in his imagination, a beautiful picture.

Most poetry uses rhythm and much poetry uses rhyme. Rhythm is a pattern of sounds in which some are louder or longer than others. Rhyme is the use of words that sound the same, such as *hand* and *sand*. But writing is not called poetry simply because it has rhythm or rhyme. Unless it expresses serious ideas, it is called "verse" or "jingles" or "doggerel" or by some such word.

METER

The study of rhythm and rhyme is an old one. It is called *prosody*, but it has nothing to do with prose, which is the other main form of literature. It is also called the science of versification. The pattern of rhythm used in a poem is called the meter. Each line, or verse, is divided into *feet*. There are four principal kinds of foot.

The *iambic* foot is one short syllable followed by one long syllable, as in the word "because." The *trochee* is a foot with one long followed by one short syllable, as in the word "rather." The *anapest* is two short followed by one long, as in the expression "if at all." The *dactyl* is one long followed by two short, as in the word "capable." In English, the syllables called "long" are the stressed, or accented, syllables and the others are unstressed, or unaccented.

A verse is named according to the kind of foot and how many there are. The foot most used in English is the iambic, and most often there are five feet to the line (in which case it is called *iambic pentameter*) or four feet to the line (in which case it is called *iambic tetrameter*). The following line is in iambic pentameter:

> Roll on, thou deep and dark blue ocean; roll!

The following lines are in iambic tetrameter:

> In Xanadu did Kubla Khan
> A stately pleasure-dome decree.

A poem becomes monotonous if the meter never changes, so most poetry mixes different feet in each line and occasionally changes the number of feet in a line.

Not all poetry is written in regular meter, and a great deal of poetry does not use rhyme. Much English poetry has been written in iambic pentameters but without rhymes; this is called *blank verse*. Many great poets, especially since the time of Walt Whitman about a hundred years ago, have avoided using any regular meter.

In some languages, such as Japanese, the best poetry is written without meter or rhyme.

KINDS OF POETRY

Lyric poetry expresses the personal thoughts and feelings of the poet. The words of a song are usually a lyric poem.

Epic poetry tells a story about great heroes or great historical events. The long poems of the ancient Greek poet Homer, the *Iliad* and the *Odyssey*, were epic poems.

Dramatic poetry is written as a play in which the characters speak in poetry. Shakespeare's plays were mostly in poetry.

POETICAL FORMS

Many of the ancient poets were minstrels, or troubadours, who sang their poems. The old ballads were poems that usually followed some strict rules for the number of lines and the places where rhymes would occur.

From this custom developed certain types of poem. The one best known in English poetry is the *sonnet*. A sonnet always has fourteen lines. Different writers have used different methods of using rhyme in these fourteen lines.

Various English poets have also developed special *stanzas* that they used in their poetry. A stanza is a group of lines, from four lines to as many as eleven or more, in which the same rhymes are used. Each new stanza has a different set of rhymes.

See also the article LITERATURE.

Poincaré, Raymond

Raymond Poincaré was President of France during World War I and was three times Premier of France. Poincaré was born in 1860 and became a lawyer. He entered public life at the age of 30, and held various posts in the government. In 1912 he became Premier and in 1913 he was elected President.

After World War I, Poincaré thought Germany should be severely punished. Because he thought the peace treaty signed at Versailles, France, did not punish Germany enough, he resigned as President in 1920. He remained in the French Senate and two years later became Premier again. By this time Germany had fallen behind in paying money to the Allies for damage done in the war, and Poincaré sent troops to occupy the Ruhr, a valuable territory of Germany's. Poincaré retired from office in 1929 and died in 1934.

poinciana

Poinciana is a shrub or small tree that grows where the climate is very warm. It is also grown in some southern states of the United States.

Poinciana shrubs grow to be more than ten feet high. They have large flowers that are bright red and yellow in color. People in California sometimes call the poinciana plant the "bird of paradise."

poinsettia

The poinsettia is an attractive shrub that grows where the climate is very warm. Many people in the United States and Europe raise poinsettia in pots. Grown outdoors, it may reach a height of ten feet. At the top of the plant the leaves form a kind of pinwheel. These leaves are usually bright red, but may be pink or white. Many people think of these bright leaves as the flower, but the real flower of the poinsettia plant is a small cluster of yellow blossoms that grows in the center of the red leaves. The poinsettia is especially popular during the Christmas season.

pointer

A pointer is a kind of hunting dog. When a pointer sees a game bird, such as grouse or woodcock, in a tree or behind a bush, he stops still in his tracks and stands with his nose pointing directly at the bird. Then, when the bird flies out,

The German short-haired pointer is increasingly popular among American hunters.

the dog stands still while the hunter shoots over him.

Pointers have been used in hunting for more than three hundred years. They are sometimes kept as house dogs and pets.

A pointer stands about 23 to 26 inches high at the shoulder, and it is about the same length from the chest to the base of its tail. Its weight is 50 to 70 pounds. It has a long, curving tail, and ears that droop slightly. Its legs are straight and slender, made for swift running. Its coat is smooth, short and sleek, and its color may be white with large brown, yellowish, reddish or black markings. Sometimes it is solid black.

poison

A poison is a substance that causes a person to become ill or to die. There are many different kinds of poison. Some foods, gases and chemicals may cause poisoning. Animals, such as snakes and scorpions, may also cause poisoning. Many plants have poisonous qualities, either when they come in contact with the skin (for example, poison ivy) or when they are taken internally (for example, some mushrooms and the locoweed).

Just how severely a poison will affect a person depends on many things. Of course, the amount of the poison taken is important. The age of a person plays a part too. Babies are affected by some substances that grown-ups can take without harm. The state of health of the person can determine the seriousness of a poison.

TREATMENT FOR POISONING

When a person has swallowed a poison it is important to give him immediate treatment. Call a doctor immediately, and while waiting for him to come give first aid. First aid for poisoning varies with the kind of poison taken. The poison may have to be diluted by giving large amounts of water. The person may have to be made to vomit by giving an emetic such as mustard in water. For some poisons there are *antidotes*, which are substances that counteract the effect of the poison in the body. Stimulants such as strong coffee may have to be given.

THE UNIVERSAL ANTIDOTE

The following antidote may safely be given when the nature of the poison is unknown:

Your Druggist Will Make It From	Or Make It Yourself From
Pulverized Charcoal	Burned Toast
(two parts)	
Magnesium Oxide	Milk of Magnesia
(one part)	
Tannic Acid	Strong Tea
(one part)	

For all poisoning, the patient should be kept warm. The patient must be watched to see that he keeps breathing; if it stops, he must be given ARTIFICIAL RESPIRATION, which is discussed in a separate article.

poison ivy

Poison ivy is a plant that grows in many parts of the United States. It is a vine that creeps along the ground or climbs on fences and trees. It can be recognized by its groups of three green leaves. The plant contains a poisonous oil. A person who touches any part of the poison ivy plant may develop a rash. (Some people are not harmed by poison ivy. They are said to be immune to it.)

A person who gets poison ivy develops small blisters on his skin about twenty-four hours after he has touched the plant. The blisters become crusty, and the rash spreads easily from one part of the body to another. The rash is very itchy and uncomfortable, and can last as long as a month. There are some soothing preparations that ease the irritation of a poison ivy rash, but nothing is known that cures it. Although poison ivy is uncomfortable, it is not dangerous. People try to clear away all poison ivy from their gardens and from parks and picnic grounds, but the plant is hardy and hard to destroy. It is important to be able to recognize the plant and to stay away from it.

poker

Poker is a card game played throughout the world, but it has often been called the national card game of the United States. Poker is played in so many different ways that it would take a book to describe all the ways, but every form of poker is based on a few simple rules.

In poker a "standard pack of cards," with 52 cards, is used. The ace is the highest-ranking card, and the two is the lowest. Each player tries to get the best possible combination of five cards. The players bet on which has the best hand. All the bets are put together in what is called a "pot" and the best hand is entitled to win the entire pot.

The poker hands are:

Straight flush, five cards of the same suit in sequence. For example, 10-9-8-7-6 of spades. The ace is considered the lowest card in A-2-3-4-5 and the highest card in A-K-Q-J-10. A "royal flush" is A-K-Q-J-10 and is the highest possible hand in most games.

Four of a kind, such as four jacks or four sixes.

Full house, three of one kind and two of another.

Flush, five cards of the same suit.

Straight, five cards in sequence but not all of the same suit.

Three of a kind.

Two pairs, such as K-K-5-5-3.

One pair, such as K-K-7-6-3.

No pair, in which the highest card decides how good the hand is.

Two or more players may hold the same kind of combination. In such a case, the winner is determined by the highest card in a straight flush or straight, the highest four of a kind or three of a kind, the highest three of a kind in full houses, the highest pair in two-pair or one-pair hands, and the highest card in other hands. If the highest card is the same, the next-highest determines the winner, and so on. Suits do not count, so if two hands have cards that are all of the same rank they tie.

BETTING

Each player puts a certain number of chips in the pot when his turn comes. He must put in at least as many chips as any player has put in before him (in which case he is said to "call" or "see" the previous bets) or he may put in more (in which case he is said to "raise"). When a player is unwilling to bet as much as each player before him, he gives up his hand and is said to "drop."

When every player has dropped or has called the previous bets, there is a *showdown.* Everyone shows his hand and the player with the highest-ranking hand takes the pot.

FORMS OF POKER

In *draw poker,* each player is dealt five cards. No other player may see his cards before the showdown. There is betting, and when it is completed there is not a showdown but a *draw.* Each player discards some of his cards and the dealer gives him new ones to replace them. Then there is another "round" of betting and a showdown.

In *stud poker,* each player receives one card face down and the rest of his cards are dealt face up. The face-up cards are dealt one at a time, and after each round in which each player receives a face-up card there is a round of betting. At the showdown, each player turns up his face-down card ("hole card").

Poker is played in forms in which certain cards are "wild" (can be made to stand for any other card the holder chooses) and in forms in which a player receives more than five cards in the deal but finally chooses his best five cards to be his poker hand.

Poland

Poland is a country in east central Europe. It is about 120,000 square miles in area, which is more than twice the size of New York State. More than thirty million people live there, nearly twice as many as live in New York State.

Poland is largely a lowland country, but there are some mountains. More than half of the land is good for farming, and there are large forests. The country is rich in coal, oil, and other natural resources, and it has important industries. Its main rivers flow into the Baltic Sea on Poland's northern border, and they are important commercial routes.

The country is surrounded by powerful neighbors, such as Germany, Russia, and formerly Austria and Hungary, and for hundreds of years these nations fought to control it. Poland has not been truly independent for more than a few years in the last 250. After World War II a Communist government was set up, under the domination of Soviet Russia.

THE PEOPLE WHO LIVE THERE

The people of Poland are a Slavic people, related to the people of Russia, Czechoslovakia, Bulgaria, and Yugoslavia. Other peoples such as the Germans, Lithuanians, Finns and Celts have settled in Poland and intermarried with the Slavic people from time to time in

the past, so the modern people called Poles are distinct from any other Slavic stock. They are strong and well-built, mostly blond. Among the world figures who were of Polish birth were the musicians Frederic Chopin and Ignace Jan Paderewski, the astronomer Copernicus, the writer Joseph Conrad, and Marie Curie, the discoverer of radium. Two of the great heroes of the American Revolutionary War, Casimir Pulaski and Tadeusz Kosciuszko, were Poles who left their own country to help the Americans win independence. Later, more than a million Poles settled in the United States.

The Polish language is one of the Slavic, or Slavonic, languages. It is a member of the Indo-European family of languages, and so is related to English, German, French, and most other languages spoken in Europe.

Almost all of the people of Poland belong to the Roman Catholic Church. A few belong to the Eastern Orthodox Church or are Protestants. There were once many Jews, but most of them were killed by the Germans during World War II, and some escaped to other countries.

The schools try to teach children to be Communists. Children of ages from 7 to 14 are required to attend school. There are many nursery schools for children 3 to 7. Poland has 76 universities, technical universities, medical academies, schools of economics, art, music, and other institutions of higher learning. In 1959 there were 119,142 students. The University of Kracow, founded in 1364, is one of the world's oldest and most famous. Other universities are those of Warsaw (almost destroyed in World War II, but since rebuilt), Lodz, Torun, Poznan, and the new Marie Curie Sklodowska Radium Institute at Lublin.

HOW THE PEOPLE LIVE

The Polish people call their country *Polska*, which means "fields" or "plains." About half the people of Poland are farmers. The other two chief industries are mining and manufacturing, especially of textiles (cloth). The chief farm products are rye, potatoes, and sugar beets. Other important crops are oats, wheat, barley, tobacco, and flax. The raising of livestock is a major occupation. Horses, cattle, sheep and poultry are raised, and

Poland is famous for its ham.

Poland's mineral resources are great. It is among the world's leading producers of coal. Other important minerals include iron, lignite, petroleum, natural gas, lead, sulphur, potassium salts, zinc, and uranium.

Under the Communist government, all the mines, heavy industries, banks, railroads and airlines, telegraph and telephone companies, radio and most manufacturing companies are owned and operated by the State. The Communists tried collectivizing the farms, but this failed and most of the 12,500 collective farms were dissolved after 1956. However, the farmer has to give the state a percentage of his crops.

WHAT KIND OF PLACE IT IS

Almost half of Poland is lowland. The country slopes gradually from the low coastline on the Baltic Sea in the north, up to the Carpathian Mountains in the south. The highest point in Poland, almost 8,000 feet, is in the Tatra range of the Carpathians.

Almost all of the rivers of Poland flow into the Baltic Sea. The principal rivers are the Vistula, the Oder-Neisse, and the Bug. Almost half of Poland lies in the valley of the Vistula, and this is the principal agricultural region. The important coal mines are in Polish Silesia, in the eastern part of the country.

Poland's climate is moderate. It ranges from an average of 25 degrees Fahrenheit in the winter to 75 degrees in the summer. The rivers are frozen for two or three months in the winter. Most of the rainfall occurs during the summer months.

The most important industrial transportation in Poland is by river, but there are about 17,000 miles of railroads. Poland's four seaports on the Baltic Sea, Gdansk (Danzig), Gdynia, Kolobrzeg (Kolberg), and Szczecin (Stettin), handle about half of the commercial traffic on the Baltic. Transportation by highway has been hampered by the poor condition of the roads in many areas, but a highway-development program is under way.

CHIEF CITIES OF POLAND

The leading cities of Poland, with populations as estimated in 1973, are:

Warsaw, population 1,283,900, capital of Poland and its largest city. There is a separate article about WARSAW.

Lodz, population 751,300, the second-largest city in central Poland. It is the principal industrial city.

Wroclaw (Breslau), population 514,100, the fourth-largest city. There is a separate article about BRESLAU.

Kracow (Cracow), population 570,700, third-largest city. There is a separate article about CRACOW.

Poznan, population 459,700, the fifth-largest city. There is a separate article about POZNAN.

HOW THE PEOPLE ARE GOVERNED

After World War II the Communists gained control of the Polish government. The country became known as the Polish People's Republic. Its lawmaking body is the Sejm (diet, or parliament). The Sejm is elected by the people for four-year terms. It then elects a president, a Council of State, and a Council of Ministers (cabinet). The head of the government

is the premier, who is appointed by the president but must represent the majority party in the Sejm. In spite of this form of government, the people of Poland are under the complete control of the Communists, since only the Communist party, or parties that agree with their policies and objectives, are permitted.

POLAND IN THE PAST

About 1,100 years ago, a Slavic tribe called the Polani settled in the region that is now Poland. They gained control over the other Slavic tribes that were living there and in the year 960 they made Poland a kingdom. In the legends of the Polish people, the first kings were descended from a hero named Piast. They ruled Poland for more than three hundred years, though they had to fight many wars against their neighbors to keep their independence.

Poland had become a Christian country very early (in 966) and in some of their fights they had received help from the *Teutonic Knights,* a German order of Christians who had gained control of the German land of Prussia. By the 1300s, the Teutonic Knights wanted to rule Poland too. In 1384, a queen named Jadwiga, who also is a favorite heroine in Polish history, came to the throne of Poland and married the Lithuanian ruler, Jagiello. Together they defeated the Teutonic Knights and saved Poland, but they had to give the Teutonic Knights large territories. This region, which later became East Prussia, shut Poland off from the sea. Much of the struggle of Poland for more than five hundred years has been to get or to keep an outlet from its country to the Baltic Sea.

During the 1500s, the Polish kings gradually lost their power. The lesser noblemen (owners of small estates) formed a parliament and ran the country almost as a republic, electing their kings.

By the 1700s, Poland had three powerful neighbors—Russia, Prussia, and Austria—and each wanted to own Poland but could not seize it without risking war against the others. They finally settled this by dividing Poland among themselves, in a series of agreements called the Three Partitions of Poland. The First Partition was in 1772, and each country got a small piece of Poland. The Second Partition, in 1793, gave larger parts to Russia and Prussia. The Third Partition, in 1795, split up the rest of Poland among all three countries. Kosciuszko, the hero who had helped America, started a fight for Polish independence in 1794, but lost. A revolution against Russia in 1830 was put down.

It seemed that Poland had vanished as a separate nation, but the people never lost their patriotism for their own country, language, and customs. At the end of World War I, between 1918 and 1921, Poland was again formed into an independent country with a strip of land called the *Polish Corridor* that ran through Germany and gave Poland an outlet on the Baltic Sea.

In 1926 a Polish war leader, Joseph Pilsudski, made himself the dictator of Poland. From that time on the people did not have much voice in their government. Meanwhile Adolf Hitler and his Nazi Party had come to power in Ger-

many and they wanted to take back the Polish Corridor and other Polish territory that had once been ruled by Germany. In August, 1939, Germany and Russia made an agreement to conquer and divide Poland, and on September 1, 1939, Hitler started World War II by sending his armies into Poland. Two weeks later Russian armies marched in from the east. Poland was beaten in less than a month and was divided about evenly between Germany and Russia.

Poland suffered more than any other country in World War II. Warsaw was almost wholly destroyed. More than three million Polish Jews were massacred or were starved and tortured to death in concentration camps. Other millions of Poles were made to work almost as slaves. It has been charged that the Russians took ten thousand Polish army officers and educated leaders and killed them so that the country would not have leadership for a new uprising.

Poland set up a government-in-exile in London, England, first with General Wladyslaw Sikorski and then with Stanislaw Mikolajczyk (the head of the Peasant Party) as its premier. During the war Poland's three principal allies, the United States, Great Britain, and Russia, after many disputes, set Poland's boundaries at the "Curzon Line," a boundary that had been suggested by Lord Curzon, a British statesman, after World War I.

When World War II was over, Poland became a separate state again. Mikolajczyk returned and headed a new government in Warsaw. The Russians wanted a Communist government and set one up in the city of Lublin. In 1946 the two governments were united, but with Russian support the Communists were much stronger. They drove Mikolajczyk and other opposition leaders out of the country, and Poland has had a Communist government ever since. For about ten years Soviet Russia controlled Poland completely. In 1956 many Poles rebelled against their Russian-dominated government and Russia was forced to give the people more freedom and to restore to power Wladyslaw Gomulka, whom they had put in prison. Since then Poland has been more independent of Russia than the other satellite states.

POLAND. Area, 120,355 square miles. Population (1973 estimate) 32,750,000. Language, Polish. Religion, chiefly Roman Catholic. Government, republic (official name: Polish People's Republic). Monetary unit, the zloty, worth 25 cents (U.S.). Flag, one white and one red stripe.

polarized light

Polarized light is a ray of light whose waves are all traveling in the same direction. A ray of light coming from a light bulb sends out waves in all directions. When such light is polarized, all but one direction is eliminated.

Light can be polarized in several ways. Passing light through certain substances will polarize it. One such substance is tourmaline. Tourmaline is a material that looks very much like glass. If a piece of tourmaline is held in front of a source of light, the light will give off less glare than before. The reason is that the tourmaline absorbs some of the light waves and lets through only those that are trav-

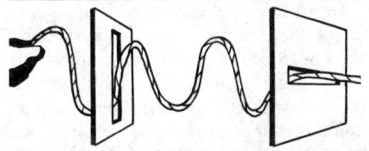

When light is polarized by means of two sheets of tourmaline, much the same thing happens as when a rope is passed through vertical and horizontal slots in pieces of wood, and one end is shaken. The vertical slot stops the rope from moving side to side and the horizontal slot stops the rope from moving up and down.

eling in the same direction.

The plastic known as Polaroid is a material especially manufactured to polarize light. It is used to eliminate glare in sunglasses, automobile headlights, and windshields. Polaroid can be manufactured in large sheets whereas tourmaline is found only in small crystals. Polaroid is made of sulfur and oxygen with some iodine and quinine.

polecat

The polecat is a small animal that lives in many parts of Europe, Asia, and Africa where the climate is not too hot or too cold. The polecat is a member of the weasel family. It is about as large as an alley cat, with soft tannish-gray fur and a bushy tail. In the United States, the name polecat is often used for the SKUNK, about which there is a separate article.

The polecat, like the skunk, has a tiny gland near its tail that can let off an unpleasant odor. The soft fur of the polecat is used to make coats for women. The fur is sometimes called *fitch*.

pole vault

The pole vault is a contest at track and field meets, in which athletes try to jump over a high bar, using a long pole to help them swing high above the ground.

A pole-vaulter uses a pole about 15 feet long, made of bamboo or aluminum. He must be able to run fast, have great strength in his arms and shoulders, and be a good acrobat. A really good pole-vaulter should be tall.

The bar over which the jump is made is placed like a bridge between two high standards. It is placed as high as the athlete is going to try to vault. Beyond these standards is a pit filled with sawdust. After making his jump, the vaulter falls into this pit.

Directly underneath the crossbar, there is a small box in the ground. The vaulter holds his pole at one end. He stands about 50 yards back from the crossbar as he starts his run. He gains great speed and as he reaches the box he jams the bottom of his pole into it and takes off from the ground.

The vaulter uses his arms to pull himself up through the air. At the height of his jump, his feet are high above his head. If he is successful he gets his feet over the bar, pushes the pole away from him so that it falls back and at the same time pushes his body upward so that he clears the bar and falls into the pit. If he touches the bar, he knocks it off the standards and has failed to make the jump.

In the past fifty years the pole-vault record has gone up and up from about 11

feet to well over 16 feet. An American, Cornelius Warmerdam, revolutionized the sport in 1943 by clearing 15 feet 8½ inches, the first time anyone had ever jumped more than 15 feet. But now the record is held by another American, John Pennel. He pole-vaulted 16 feet 8¾ inches in 1963.

police

The police are the group of uniformed men employed by a city, town or state to enforce its laws, protect the people, catch criminals, and keep everything running smoothly. This group is called a police force, or simply "the force." The oldest uniformed police force in the United States, that of New York City, was formed in 1848. Since then city police forces have grown tremendously. In a large modern city the police may number anywhere from 1,000 to 15,000 men—even more in a very big city.

The organization of the police in a big American city is pretty much the same throughout the United States. At the head of the force is usually a Police Commissioner who is appointed by the mayor of the city. In some cities he is called the Director of Public Safety. The highest rank among regular police officers is Chief Inspector. Often there are several Inspectors, or Deputy Inspectors, under him. The next-highest rank is captain, then lieutenant, then sergeant, and finally the ordinary patrolmen (uniformed men) and detectives (plain-clothes men) who make up the bulk of the force.

The higher officials have their offices in a building that is usually known as police headquarters. The city is divided into districts called precincts. There is a building called a station house in each precinct.

The station house is commanded by a captain, who has several lieutenants to assist him. A certain number of patrolmen are assigned to each precinct. Each police station in the city is connected to headquarters by special telephone lines and Teletype machines. (The Teletype is an automatic electric typewriter that prints messages sent over telephone lines.) Headquarters may be connected by Teletype with the Federal Bureau of Investigation in Washington, D.C. and with the headquarters of the police in other large cities nearby.

The police also make great use of radio. Policemen patrol (travel around) the city in radio cars. Police headquarters uses a radio transmitter and receiver to keep in touch with all police cars patrolling the city. Each car has a two-way radio so that the policemen in it can talk to headquarters and receive instructions.

Finally, there is a special telephone network that links every part of the city with its precinct police station. The telephones are in metal boxes attached to lamp posts or buildings. The patrolman reports to his precinct station over one of these telephones at least once an hour. In an emergency, the public may use a police telephone to summon help.

POLICE TRAINING AND WORK

Before a young man can join the police, he must pass a written examination, have a certain amount of education, be in good health, and not be under a certain

height. He must be a person of good character who has never committed a crime or been in prison. Once he is accepted he goes through a stiff training course. He learns all the police regulations, the traffic rules of his city, and a certain amount of law. He is taught how to shoot a police revolver and must practice on the police pistol range until he has learned to hit targets accurately.

He must know first aid, how to subdue a criminal by wrestling tricks or judo, and how to use weapons such as tear-gas shells, riot guns, and submachine guns.

When he has finished his training, he becomes a patrolman. He is assigned to a precinct and puts on the uniform of the city police force. Usually this is a navy-blue cap, shirt, jacket, and trousers, with a silver-colored shield on the front of the cap and another on the left breast of the jacket. On each shield there is a number, assigned to that policeman. The equipment of the ordinary patrolman includes a .38 caliber revolver in a leather holster, a cartridge belt with loops in it for additional bullets, a whistle, a pair of steel handcuffs, and a short wooden club called a nightstick or "billy."

A patrolman usually works about eight hours a day but this may be any of the three 8-hour shifts around the clock. At the beginning of his shift he reports to his precinct station. Then he assembles with the other patrolmen on his shift for inspection by the officer in charge of the station. This officer sees to it that the men are properly dressed and equipped before they go out on duty. He reads instructions to them, telling them about wanted criminals who may be in the district, and about houses, stores and other places to which they must pay particular attention.

Once inspection is over, each patrolman goes to his "beat," which is the part of the city he must patrol. Nearly all patrolling used to be done on foot. Now most of it is done in radio cars.

SPECIAL DUTIES

One special division of the uniformed police is known as the traffic squad. Attached to this division are specially trained police who direct traffic at busy street corners, motorcycle police who watch for motorists who go too fast or violate other traffic rules, and radio patrol cars manned by one or two policemen who not only watch for traffic violators but also patrol a section of the city.

At headquarters there is a huge wall map of the entire city. It shows the beat covered by every radio patrol car. In case of emergency requiring quick action, headquarters can call any car by radio and have it rush to the scene of a crime or accident. When a citizen calls the police for help, in most cases it is a patrol car that arrives first. It seldom takes more than three minutes for the patrol car to get to any place in the city, and often it is much less.

Many cities still have mounted police attached to the traffic squad. These are used to control large crowds at parades and other public gatherings. The horses of the mounted police are wonderfully trained so that they will not become excited or disturbed by the presence of shouting crowds pressing against them or by loud, sudden noises.

In a few cities with very large police forces, helicopters are used to observe parts of the city where traffic is unusually heavy because of parades, public meetings, or week-end driving. The pilot sees traffic from above and tells headquarters, by radio, where extra traffic police are needed. Police helicopters have been used many times to rescue citizens who lose control of small boats and drift helplessly in rivers and bays.

POLICE DETECTIVES

In addition to its uniformed men, every

large police organization has a detective bureau or department whose officers work in ordinary clothes. The duty of the detective is to discover persons who have committed a crime, find them, and arrest them.

Detectives are divided into different squads, each of which is specialized in certain crimes and has developed its own expert methods of catching criminals. In most cases the lieutenant and some of the other detectives in the squad have received some training from the United States government's famous Federal Bu-

A radio-equipped motorcycle officer makes his report following a minor accident. The dispatcher will clear him of his assignment and give him the next one.

Helicopters are used for emergency rescues and for policing the harbor.

reau of Investigation, or FBI.

Some of the squads in the detective bureau are: homicide, burglary, robbery, bunco, auto theft, and missing persons. The homicide squad works on murders. The burglary squad devotes its attention to the work of burglars and knows all about their methods of opening safes and breaking into houses and stores. The robbery detectives go after holdup men. The bunco squad concentrates on swindlers and forgers. The auto theft detectives track down stolen cars. The missing persons bureau tries to find persons who have disappeared and are sought by their relatives.

TECHNICAL POLICE SERVICES

Each squad makes use of the police department's technical specialists whenever necessary. The coroner or medical examiner is a doctor who examines the bodies of the dead in order to tell detectives the cause and probable time of death. In the police laboratory there are chemists who can tell whether a stain on clothing or other objects was caused by paint or blood, whether food or drinks contain poison and if so what kind of poison, whether the ink on a ransom note is the same as that found in a suspect's fountain pen, and so on. Another technical specialist in the police laboratory is the ballistics expert, who often can tell if a bullet used in a crime was fired by a particular gun.

Another specialist is the fingerprint expert. He takes the fingerprints of persons suspected of crimes and compares them with fingerprints found at the scene of the crime or kept on file in the identification division of the police organization. The photograph, fingerprints and record of past arrests and convictions of anybody who has ever committed a crime are kept on file at police headquarters. Even though an arrested person may give a false name to hide his criminal background, the fingerprint expert can often uncover the truth about him by comparing his fingerprints with those on file.

The police also employ photographers to take pictures of arrested persons and of the scenes of crimes. Citizens who have been held up or attacked by bandits or other criminals are usually asked to look through a collection of photographs of criminals to try to identify the criminal. This collection of pictures is called a "rogues' gallery." The photographer also goes to places where crimes have been committed and takes photographs of dead bodies and the contents of the room or place, so that the detectives will have a record of what happened and will not have to rely on their memories.

STATE POLICE

Every state in the United States has its own police force. Like the city police, the state police have uniformed men, often called state troopers, and detectives. Wherever a village or town is too small to have a police force of its own, the state troopers take over. They are organized somewhat like an army and usually have inspectors, captains, lieutenants, sergeants, and troopers. The trooper is like the city patrolman except that he usually rides around in a radio patrol car because of the large distances he must cover on his beat.

The headquarters of the state police is usually a large building, called a barracks, where a number of troopers and officers live and work. It is equipped in the same way as a city police headquarters. Smaller buildings scattered throughout the state are used as local police stations.

The police of the western states who work in farm and forest areas are often expert woodsmen and very skillful in tracking down wanted persons. In many states the state police patrol highways between cities in radio cars or motorcycles.

Nearly every city and state police department uses the services of the FBI, or FEDERAL BUREAU OF INVESTIGATION, about which there is a separate article.

Polk, James K.

James K. Polk was the eleventh President of the United States. He served from 1845 to 1849. During his term in office the United States added many thousands of square miles to its territory. The land that became the states of California, Utah, Nevada, and parts of Arizona and New Mexico was made part of the United States during Polk's administration. Like most people at that time, Polk was determined that the United States should expand its territory as far as possible on the continent. He did not try for a second term as President. He died three months after he left the White House.

HIS EARLY YEARS

James K. Polk was born in Mecklenburg County, North Carolina, on November 2, 1795. His father was a farmer of Irish descent. Young Polk attended the University of North Carolina. He was graduated in 1818 and two years later became a lawyer. He practiced law for a time in Columbia, Tennessee, and began his political career as a member of the Tennessee House of Representatives. In 1825 he was elected to the United States House of Representatives. He served in Congress for fourteen years.

While Polk was in Congress, he was active in his support of Andrew Jackson and Martin Van Buren and he became a leader in Democratic politics in the House. He was elected Speaker of the House in 1835 and held that position for the next four years. He retired from Congress in 1839 to become Governor of Tennessee.

HOW HE BECAME PRESIDENT

In the Democratic National Convention of 1844, the group that supported Martin Van Buren as Presidential candidate realized that it would be impossible to get the necessary two-thirds for his nomination. As a compromise, they chose James Polk, who was a "dark horse," one not so well-known as other candidates. Polk was very popular in the South and had declared himself in favor of annexing Texas and extending the northern border of Oregon.

One of the battle cries of the political campaign that helped to elect Polk was the slogan, "Fifty-four forty or fight." At that time the United States wanted to set the northern border of the Oregon Territory at 54 degrees, 40 minutes latitude. Great Britain refused to accept this. Such a border would have run through what is now the center of the provinces of British Columbia and Alberta, in Canada. After the election, in which Polk defeated Henry Clay, a compromise was made that settled the border where it now stands, at 49 degrees north of the equator. (Distance north and south of the equator is measured in degrees of latitude.)

The Mexican War took place during Polk's administration. When that was concluded in the treaty of 1846, the United States acquired another large area of undeveloped territory. Texas had been annexed in 1845, and at the end of Polk's administration the United States reached from ocean to ocean.

POLK'S EARLY DEATH

President Polk did not seek re-election. In March, 1849, he returned to his home in Nashville, Tennessee, but he did not live to enjoy his retirement. He died three months later, on June 15, 1849.

MRS. JAMES POLK

Mrs. Sarah Childress Polk was born in 1803 near Murfreesboro, Tennessee. She was the daughter of a prosperous planter. She and James Polk were married in 1824. Mrs. Polk was a deeply religious woman. No liquor or dancing were permitted in the White House during the four years the Polks lived there. They had no children. Mrs. Polk died in 1891.

poll, a way of finding out what people think about any given thing: see the article STATISTICS AND SURVEYS.

pollination

Pollination is a part of the process by which certain plants, such as trees, shrubs, and flowering plants, reproduce themselves—that is, cause young plants of the same kind to come into existence. Pollination consists of bringing together the pollen (containing the male cells) and the female cells (contained in the ovules), to form seeds.

In flowering plants, pollination takes place in the flower. The pollen is formed in *stamens,* slender stalks that grow inside the circle of petals. The *ovules,* or undeveloped seeds, are formed in the *ovary,* a hollow base at the bottom of the pistil. The *pistil* is a structure at the center of the flower. At the top of the pistil is a surface called the *stigma,* into which the pollen must be placed.

The pollen is carried to the stigma by wind or water, or by animals such as insects and birds.

Cross-pollination is the transfer of pollen from a stamen to a stigma on another plant.

Self-pollination is the transfer of pollen from a stamen to a stigma on the same plant.

Wind and insects are the most important carriers of pollen. Flowers that are pollinated by insects usually have bright and often scented petals, and sometimes contain nectar (a sweet juice) which attracts insects. The sticky pollen is carried on the legs of the insects from one flower to another. Plants that are pollinated by wind have light, dry pollen that can easily be blown away.

Another large group of plants that reproduce by means of pollination are the conifers, or cone-bearing plants, such as the pine tree. In these plants the pollen and the seed cases (ovules) are in the cones, and the pollen is usually carried to the seed cone by wind.

polo

Polo is a game played on horseback by two teams. Each team tries to hit a hard, wooden ball into the goal of the opposing team.

Polo is said to be the oldest game in the world played with a ball. Travelers who visited Persia and other Eastern countries many hundreds of years ago found the people playing polo. About a hundred years ago, British army officers stationed in India learned the game, and they introduced it into England.

The English developed the modern game. They made each team consist of four men and they decided that the game should be played in periods called *chukkers*, with a short rest between each chukker. A chukker is eight minutes long, and there are seven chukkers in a full game.

Each player has a long-handled mallet, which he uses to hit the ball as he rides over the field. The field may be up to 300 yards long and 200 yards wide. The goals are 24 feet wide.

The horses (called polo ponies) are very important. They are wonderfully trained and know how to follow the ball almost without being guided. They wheel (turn), gallop and stop very quickly. Because of the speed of the game, a polo pony is usually used for one chukker and then rested, and not used again until several chukkers later.

HANDICAPS

The idea of the game is simple. The team that scores the most goals wins. Since some polo players are much better than others, the players are given *handicaps*. In handicapping, each player is judged by his ability and is given a *rating*. The highest rating is ten goals. Players are handicapped from zero to ten goals. When a match is made up between two teams the handicap ratings of the four players on a team are added together and compared to the sum of the handicaps of the four players on the other team. If one team has a handicap total higher than the other, then the lower team receives that many goals' difference at the start of the game. If one team had a total handicap of 30 goals and the other team

27, the second team would have 3 goals given to it at the start of the game.

Polo is most popular in England, India, the United States, Mexico, and Argentina. Before World War II, when cavalry (mounted troops) was important in armies, there was much polo played by cavalry officers. Now mechanized units have replaced cavalry, and there are fewer players and fewer polo teams.

Polo, Marco

Marco Polo was a great Italian traveler. He was born in Venice in 1254. When he was 17 years old, Marco Polo went with his father and uncle on a great journey to China, which was then called Cathay. In those days few men from Europe ever traveled to China. The trip took the Polos about four years.

The emperor of Cathay, Kublai Khan, gave the three members of the Polo family important positions in the government. Marco Polo became governor of an important city for three years. The Polo family was so useful to Kublai Khan that he would not allow them to return home for sixteen years. Finally they did return to Venice and arrived in 1295, after an absence of twenty years. Although Marco Polo and his father and uncle brought with them many rare and precious jewels and other gifts from Kublai Khan, the people of Venice did not believe the story of their adventures.

In a war between Venice and Genoa, Marco Polo became commander of a ship. He was captured and held prisoner. While he was in prison, he dictated the story of his adventures to another prisoner. Even on his deathbed, Marco Polo was urged by his friends to admit that he had made up all of his stories about Cathay. Marco Polo died in 1324. Later, people found that everything he had said was true.

Polynesia

Polynesia is the name given to a large number of islands in the Pacific Ocean. The natives of these islands are called Polynesians.

The principal islands of Polynesia are the Hawaiian Islands, Tonga, Samoa, and many smaller islands such as Pitcairn and Easter. The Maori natives of New Zealand are Polynesians, but New Zealand is not usually considered a part of Polynesia.

Polynesians are a tall, light-skinned people, with straight or wavy black hair. Most scientists believe they came to their islands from various parts of Asia, but a recent theory is that they came from Peru across the Pacific Ocean on rafts. This theory was developed and tested by Thor Heyerdahl, a Norwegian scientist who made this difficult trip by raft in 1947 and wrote the book *Kon-Tiki* about his adventures.

The Polynesians have long had a complicated social and religious culture, with rule by chiefs who inherited their position, and an elaborate mythology of gods and religious rites.

Polynesia includes high volcanic islands and low coral islands, and the natives live very differently in the two kinds of island. Natives of the volcanic islands live by farming many crops and by fishing, but on the coral islands fishing is

much more important than farming. Polynesians are highly skilled in various arts, for instance the stone and wood carvings of the Maoris and the huge statues found on Easter Island. Since ancient times Polynesians have been known as daring and skillful sailors. They have sailed vast distances in their flimsy dugout canoes and guided themselves by the stars long before astronomy was used by European sailors.

There are about twenty Polynesian languages, but they are much alike. They belong to the same family of languages as the Malay languages.

pomegranate

The pomegranate is a fruit that grows in the warm parts of Europe and Asia and to some extent in the United States.

The pomegranate fruit grows on a bush or small tree. The tree bears bright orange or red flowers and is very attractive. The pomegranate is about as large as an orange. It has a hard skin and is slightly pointed at one end. The flesh of the pomegranate is reddish-orange. It is sweet and juicy. Pomegranates are eaten for dessert and the juice is used in drinks. The fruit contains many small seeds with ingredients that are used in certain medicines.

Pomeranian

The Pomeranian is one of the smallest toy dogs. It has a heavy, thick coat of fur that makes it look like a fluffy ball of wool walking around. Its nose is pointed and sharp and its tail is thick and bushy and turns up over its back, lying almost flat against the spine. It stands about 10 inches high at the shoulder, and weighs usually between 6 and 8 pounds. It is a very lively, playful dog. A Pomeranian is called a "pom." Pomerania is a section of Europe that is now mostly in East Germany.

Pompadour, Madame de

Jeanne Antoinette Poisson was a very beautiful and influential French woman. She was born in Paris in 1721. When she was 24 years old, King Louis XV of France saw her at a ball and fell in love with her, even though he was already married. He gave her a palace at Versailles and made her the Marquise de Pompadour.

For twenty years Madame de Pompadour had a great deal to say about how the government of France was run. She insisted that her friends be given important positions in the government, even if they were not suited for the work. She encouraged poets and painters and spent huge sums of money. She was very unpopular with the people, who thought that she influenced the king to do many unwise things.

Madame de Pompadour died in 1764, when she was 43 years old.

pompano

The pompano is a fish found in the southern Atlantic Ocean and the Gulf of Mexico. It is very popular as food. The

average weight of a pompano is about two pounds, and only about a million pounds of pompano are caught each year. The pompano is bluish-green on the back, shading down to a silver shade on the under parts. Its fins are yellowish.

Pompeii

Pompeii was a city of the Roman Empire about two thousand years ago. It was at the foot of the volcano Mount Vesuvius, near the city of Naples in modern Italy. Pompeii was a popular summer resort with beautiful homes. It was also a prosperous trading center. At that time about twenty thousand people lived there. Then in the year 79 Mount Vesuvius erupted. Huge masses of red hot rocks and ashes rained down on Pompeii, setting fires and burying the entire city under more than fifteen feet of cinders, ashes, and stone. More than two thousand people were killed and the rest fled from the city. The great eruption of Vesuvius also buried the cities of Herculaneum and Stabiae near by.

The buried city of Pompeii was forgotten for about 1,600 years. Then in 1748, a farmer, digging on his land, discovered part of a buried wall. The Italian government became interested and sent men to dig out this region. Gradually the buried city of Pompeii came to light. It was found that much of the city had been preserved under the lava. Today people may visit the ruins of Pompeii and see the houses, temples, shops and streets that the people of Pompeii used two thousand years ago.

The city of Pompeii was surrounded by walls. The homes of the rich people were beautifully decorated with wall paintings and sculpture. There were theaters, temples, and a huge stadium that seated five thousand people. The Pompeians had drinking fountains, a sewage system, and roofs with drain pipes. Some of the furniture and household equipment also were quite modern in design. Many inscriptions were found on the walls that showed how the people felt about various subjects such as politics, sports, and love. During World War II, the city of Pompeii was somewhat damaged by bombings but it is still a great point of interest to tourists.

Pompey

Pompey was a great Roman soldier and statesman who lived about two thousand years ago. His full name was Gneius Pompeius Magnus. He was born in the year 106 B.C. When he was only 17 years old he began to prove what an excellent soldier he was. He had many military victories and conquered important territories for Rome. One of Pompey's most famous victories was over Mithridates the Great, king of Pontus, a country in Asia Minor.

In 60 B.C., Pompey joined Julius Caesar and another Roman statesman named Crassus in a triumvirate (three-man government) that ruled Rome until 53 B.C. Then Pompey had Crassus murdered, and by 50 B.C., with Caesar

away at war, Pompey was ruling alone. But in 48 B.C. Caesar led his armies back and defeated Pompey's armies at Epirus, in Greece. Pompey fled to Egypt, where he was killed that same year (48 B.C.), perhaps by agents of Caesar.

Ponce de Leon

Ponce de Leon was a Spanish explorer who discovered Florida more than four hundred years ago. He was in search of a magic "Fountain of Youth." According to legend, any man who bathed in the waters of the Fountain of Youth would become young again. It was described as being surrounded by sweet-smelling flowers and huge trees bearing rich fruit. There were supposed to be beautiful maidens near the Fountain of Youth to pick the fruit for visitors.

Ponce de Leon was born about 1460. He came to America with Christopher Columbus on Columbus's second voyage. Here he heard the legend of the Fountain of Youth. Ponce de Leon was an old man and was very anxious to find the fountain that would make him young again. He explored the islands of the Bahamas, bathing in every waterfall or stream that he came to, but he did not become young again. When he landed in Florida, on Easter Sunday in 1513, the country was so beautiful that he was sure the Fountain must be nearby. He did not find it but he claimed Florida for Spain. Eight years later, in 1521, he returned to Florida to found a colony. Unfriendly Indians fought with him and his followers and drove them back to Cuba, where Ponce de Leon soon died from wounds received in this fighting.

Pontiac

Pontiac was a powerful American Indian leader who was chief of the Ottawa Indians. Pontiac is believed to have been born about 1720. By 1755 he had achieved his great power among his people because of his great courage and his skill as an organizer. During the French and Indian Wars, Pontiac is believed to have helped the French against the British, but after the British won the war Pontiac offered to live in peace with them.

Pontiac soon found that the French had been much more generous in their treatment of the Indians than the British were, and in 1761 he became one of the leaders of an Indian uprising, called Pontiac's Rebellion, against the British. He and his followers planned a surprise attack on the settlement of Detroit, but the English commander was warned in time to prevent it. For several years, battles were fought and many settlers were killed by Indians. At last most of Pontiac's followers made peace with the British, and finally Pontiac too signed a treaty and was pardoned. Pontiac died in 1769, but it is not known just how or where. The city of Pontiac, Michigan, is named for him.

Pontius Pilate

Pontius Pilate was the Roman procurator, or governor, of Judea, a colony of the great Roman Empire nearly two thousand years ago. Judea included the places where Jesus lived and preached. Since Jesus's teaching did not follow the official Jewish religion, Jesus was brought to trial and Pontius Pilate was persuaded

by the high priests to let him be put to death. Pilate did this, though he said that he believed Jesus was innocent. Little else is known about Pontius Pilate, except that he was removed from his post because a group of people called the Samaritans complained against him. The story of the trial of Jesus by Pontius Pilate is told in the Bible, in the Gospels of Matthew, Mark, Luke, and John.

pony

A pony is any horse that is not more than fourteen hands, or four and a half feet, in height. However, certain breeds, or kinds, of horse never grow beyond this height, so they are known as *pony breeds*. All of the pony breeds originated in Britain, so scientists think that they were descended from a different animal than other horses. They call this original animal the *Celtic pony*.

Ponies are used mostly for children. Formerly they were hitched to a small cart called a governess cart, and they were used because they are so gentle and easy to handle. Now they are used more in teaching the young children how to ride.

The two best-known pony breeds are the Shetland pony and the Welsh pony. The Shetland pony was first found in the Shetland Islands, off the coast of Scotland. It is the shortest kind of pony, and is usually from nine to twelve hands (three to four feet) high. It is strong and sturdy in build, with a deep chest and a wide back. Its coat is quite thick and grows quickly. It may be brown or black, streaked with white or gray or tan.

The Shetland pony has been bred in America as a saddle pony (for horseback riding).

The Welsh pony was first found in the mountains of Wales. It is taller and a little lighter in build than the Shetland pony, and its coat is usually a dull brown, black or gray color. The Welsh pony is very useful in mountainous country, because it is very sure-footed. It is a clever animal and is often trained to act in circus and other performances.

The name pony refers also to horses used in herding cattle, which are called cow ponies, and to horses used in the game of polo, which are called polo ponies. Neither of these is a pony breed.

Pony Express

The Pony Express was the first fast mail service in the United States, in the pioneer days of the old West. Although it operated for less than two years, its service forms one of the most colorful and exciting chapters in American history.

In the 1840s and 1850s hundreds of thousands of adventurous Easterners had traveled to the western states and the Pacific coast to make their homes. Transcontinental mail in 1860 was carried by overland stage, but the way was so dangerous because of Indian raids that often the mail never arrived. Most important mail was therefore sent by way of Panama, and this took a month or more. The telegraph line ended at St. Joseph, Missouri.

In 1860 a mail contractor named Ben Holladay and a freight firm undertook to establish the Pony Express. They set up

about 200 stations and bought 500 fast horses. The mail was carried by eighty of the most daring riders they could find. The stations were about 25 miles apart and each rider was expected to ride 75 miles a day, taking a fresh horse at each station. The pony express riders traveled from St. Joseph, Missouri to Sacramento, California, where the mail was then sent by steamship to San Francisco. This usually took eight days, but the fastest trip ever made was 7 days and 17 hours, to deliver Abraham Lincoln's inaugural address. The postage was $5 a half-ounce at first, but later was reduced to $1.

Pony Express riders earned from $100 to $150 a month, which was very good pay in those days. They were armed and rode alone through the wilderness, day and night in all kinds of weather. Their courage and skill in the face of constant Indian attack and ambush gave point to the slogan that "the mail must go through." Some of the great names in the history of the West belonged to Pony Express riders, such as "Buffalo Bill" Cody, "Wild Bill" Hickok, and others. The Pony Express was gradually discontinued after the day in 1861 when the first telegraph line to California was completed.

poodle

Poodles are dogs that are usually clipped in an odd way. To be admitted to dog shows, poodles must follow this style. (Not all poodles are clipped. Those with unclipped hair are called *corded poodles*.)

If a poodle's hair is allowed to grow unchecked, it becomes extremely long and twists into long strands that look like ropes. When it is shorter, it is tightly curled.

Poodles are very intelligent, and are fine pets and house dogs. There are three different sizes. The largest are called standard poodles, the medium-sized dogs are called miniature poodles, and the very smallest are called toy poodles. The only difference between them is in their size. Standard poodles stand about 15 inches or more at the shoulder, miniature poodles stand between 10 and 15 inches high, and any poodle under 10 inches high is a toy. A poodle may be any solid color, but most are black, brown, or white. Puppies' tails are clipped medium-short when they are a few days old.

popcorn

Popcorn is a kind of corn that can be exploded by heat into a fluffy white confection. It is very popular in the United States.

Popcorn plants and ears are smaller than other varieties of corn, and the kernels have a very hard covering. The ears are not picked until they are dry on the stalk. When the popcorn is placed over a very hot fire, moisture inside the kernels turns to steam and the pressure explodes the kernel, which enlarges six or eight times in size.

Popcorn was known to the Indians of South America long before white settlers arrived. In recent years experiments have led to development of a hybrid popcorn that is greatly superior to the older varieties. Most United States popcorn is produced in the midwestern states. It is sold

already popped, and seasoned with butter and salt, in most motion-picture theaters and other places of entertainment.

In the 1950s popcorn began to be marketed unpopped, with salt and butter, in a sealed aluminum foil container that can be placed over a fire. The corn pops and when the container is fully expanded the popcorn is ready to eat.

Pope

The Pope is the religious leader of the Roman Catholic Church. He is also the Bishop of Rome and the ruler of the tiny state of Vatican City, which is in the city of Rome, Italy.

HOW THE POPE IS CHOSEN

After one Pope dies, all the cardinals (the highest-ranking men in the Roman Catholic Church) gather in the Vatican, which is the Pope's palace and headquarters. They go to a closed room, where they pray and ask God for guidance, because they will have to vote for a new Pope. The Pope is almost always chosen from the cardinals, and to be elected he must get more than two-thirds of the votes cast. After a vote is cast, if no one has been elected, the ballots are burned. Straw is added to the fire, and black smoke comes out of the chimney of the Sistine Chapel in the Vatican. Great crowds always gather outside the Vatican on these occasions, and when they see the smoke they know that no one has been chosen yet. When the new Pope has been elected, no straw is added to the fire, and the white smoke that pours from the chimney is a signal for great rejoicing.

The new Pope chooses the name he will use as Pope. Usually it is different from his own name; for example, when Cardinal Montini was elected, in 1963, he chose to be called Pope Paul VI. Then the new Pope puts on the Papal robes, and all the cardinals visit him. His robes are white. He wears red shoes with a cross embroidered on the front, and he wears the beautiful Fisherman's ring of St. Peter, who was the first Bishop of Rome. His crown, which is called the tiara, is worn for official occasions. At these times he also carries a gold cross, which traditionally contains a piece of wood from the cross on which Jesus died.

Catholics feel a deep love for the Pope, and every year thousands come from all over the world to have an audience with him.

HISTORY OF THE POPES

Catholics recognize the Pope as the successor of St. Peter. Jesus is recognized as the invisible head of the Church, and the Pope as his visible representative on earth. St. Peter died about the year 70, and each Bishop of Rome after him was the Pope, but very little is known about some of the early Popes.

As the Catholic Church grew, so did the power of the Pope. Besides leading their Church, the Popes became rulers of their own territories, called the Papal States, which were in Italy. They ruled this territory for more than a thousand years, from about 740 to 1860. During much of this period, the spiritual leadership of the Pope was often more powerful than the armed might of the kings of Europe, and most of the kings recognized

the Pope as the leader of all Europe.

THE GREAT SCHISM

There were many wars in and near Rome during the Middle Ages (which began about 1,500 years ago). In the year 1305, conditions around Rome were so bad that Clement V, a French bishop who had just been elected Pope, chose to make his residence in Avignon, a town in the south of France. For more than a hundred years, Avignon was the seat of the Popes, but during part of this period (from 1378 to 1417) there were parts of the Church that disagreed and elected other Popes in Rome. This condition is called a schism, or division (lack of agreement). The section on *Antipopes*, below, tells more about it.

THE POPE'S RELIGIOUS POWERS

The most important teaching of the Catholic Church about the Pope is that he is the representative of Jesus Christ on earth. Because of this, Catholics believe in the Pope's infallibility in matters of faith and morals. This means that when the Pope speaks *ex cathedra* (with the authority he has as the Pope and not as a man) he cannot make a mistake about what Catholics should believe or do to please God.

The doctrine of infallibility does not mean that the Pope cannot make a mistake as a man, nor that he cannot sin. Catholic historians recognize some Popes as bad rulers, but point out that it is the office and not the man that is important.

ANTIPOPES

An Antipope is someone who claims to be Pope but has not been chosen Pope by the proper authorities. There have been no Antipopes since the Middle Ages, but in those times a king sometimes tried to appoint a Pope who would do what he wished. The best known of these Antipopes was Clement VII. During the time that the Popes lived in Avignon, the Popes were French. After Pope Gregory XI, a Frenchman, moved his court back to Rome, the French were angry. When Gregory died, they claimed the right to make their own Pope at Avignon. This was Antipope Clement VII, who had great power in Avignon. He was never recognized in Rome, where Pope Urban VI was the actual Pope.

Pope, Alexander

Alexander Pope was a great English poet who lived more than two hundred years ago. He is one of the most-quoted English poets, particularly because many of his couplets (two lines of poetry that rhyme) are epigrams. That is, they contain witty and pointed thoughts expressed in a few words. His two most-quoted poems are "Essay on Criticism" and "An Essay on Man." Pope was the first English writer to earn much money from his writing. His translations of the *Iliad* and the *Odyssey*, two great Greek poems, were very popular.

Pope was born in 1688 and died in 1744. He suffered from poor health most of his life.

poplar

The poplar is a large tree that grows in many parts of Europe and the United States. There are about twenty different kinds of poplar tree, including the cottonwood and the aspen.

The poplar grows very rapidly. It is deciduous, which means that it loses its leaves in the fall. The white or silver poplar is about 80 feet high. It gets its name because its dark green leaves are a soft, silvery color underneath. The tree bears flowers that hang in graceful tassels. They appear early in the spring before the first leaves. The wood of the white poplar does not swell or shrink, and it is used to make furniture and toys.

The Lombardy poplar is unusual because though most poplar trees have large spreading branches, the branches of the Lombardy poplar grow straight up towards the sky The tree grows to be more than 100 feet high.

Popocatepetl

Popocatepetl is a volcano in Mexico. It is the second-highest mountain peak in the country, 17,887 feet high. It is so high that the top of it is covered with snow all through the year. A beautiful view of the volcano can be seen from Mexico City. Popocatepetl has not erupted for more than 150 years, but smoke still pours from its mouth at times. The huge crater of Popocatepetl is about half a mile around and more than a thousand feet deep in some places. Inside the crater are large deposits of sulfur, which have been mined at times. The mountain was first climbed more than four hundred years ago, and people now climb Popocatepetl frequently.

poppy

The poppy is a handsome flower that grows in many parts of the world where the climate is warm. There are a number of different kinds of poppy. Some kinds are less than a foot high and others, such as the oriental poppy, grow to be about three feet high. The oriental poppy has large, bright red blossoms. Some poppies have pink, purple, and orange flowers.

The opium poppy first grew in the western parts of Asia. It is raised in India and China and grows wild in many places. It is a handsome plant with white blossoms. The opium poppy contains the drug called opium, which is very dangerous but can also be very useful. The seeds of the opium poppy contain an oil that is used to make soap and paints, in cooking, and in lamps.

population

Population is the number of people who live in a particular place at a particular time. Today, partly through the work of the United Nations, an attempt is made to determine the populations of all countries and the population of the entire earth. Population is best determined by a *census*, a careful count of everyone living in the country in which the census is taken.

Populations do not remain the same year after year. The things that cause them to change are the *birth rate*, the *death rate*, and *migration*.

By birth rate is meant the number of babies born each year for each thousand people. A country with a high birth rate increases its population and a country with a low birth rate remains the same or loses in population. The death rate is the number of people who die each year for each thousand people in the population. The migration figure is the number of people who change their permanent homes from one place to another.

With modern science and medical knowledge, the death rate is going down in most parts of the world. This means that people are living to much older ages. Therefore in most places the population is increasing. This is not true in all countries. The birth rate in many countries is going down. Many people do not care to have the large families that people once had. Wars often keep the population from increasing. Many men are killed who would have been fathers. Their deaths not only increase the death rate but also decrease the birth rate. But the world as a whole increases its population steadily.

PROBLEMS OF POPULATION

Throughout history, one of man's great problems has been finding enough food. As the world population increases, the need for food becomes greater. During this century, the world population has grown from less than two billion people to about two and a half billion people. So far, scientific advancements in food-raising have kept up with the growth of populations. Some experts believe science can continue to do this, even though the world population seems sure to pass three billion before the end of this century. Irrigation can turn some barren land into fertile farm land. Large areas near the North and South Poles can be settled. Jungles can be cleared in South America and Africa. Food can be produced by chemistry and "grown" in factories instead of on farms.

Other experts believe the population will soon be too big for the world, and that the problem must be solved by preventing the population from growing too much. This can be done by keeping the birth rate down. Some people favor "planned parenthood" and urge parents not to have more children than they and their countries can support. Some such methods, including those called "birth control," are opposed by other people for religious reasons.

porcelain, see the articles POTTERY and CHINAWARE.

porcupine

The porcupine is an animal that makes its home in many parts of the world. The American porcupine is about three feet long. It is called a tree porcupine because it is a good climber. It has a black coat, and its back is covered with sharp quills that are about 1½ inches long.

The porcupine is clumsy and is not a fast runner, but it is seldom killed by enemies because of its quills, which it uses as a weapon. When an enemy approaches, the porcupine turns its back and raises its quills. They are sharp and barbed and stick in the flesh of any animal that dares to attack it.

The porcupine is not much of an offensive fighter, but it is a master of defense.

The porcupine eats plants. It builds its den in a hole in the ground. The female porcupine has one baby in the spring. Porcupines are peaceful animals and prefer to climb a tree to escape danger rather than to fight.

The crested porcupine lives in Africa and is the largest of all the porcupines. It is more than three feet long and weighs more than 40 pounds. Its quills are protected by long thin spines. Some of these spines are almost two feet long. The crested porcupine can kill a leopard with its quills.

porgy

Porgy is the name of a group or family of fish that includes more than a hundred different kinds. Most kinds live in warm ocean waters, in shallow waters near the shore. The largest members of the porgy family live in the colder waters around South Africa and southern Australia. One kind, called the *musselcracker*, sometimes weighs as much as a hundred pounds. The porgy is an important food fish in those sections.

On the Atlantic coast, from New England to Virginia, porgies are plentiful and thousands are caught for food every year. These are much smaller than their South African cousins. Their average weight is about one pound.

The eggs of the porgy hatch in less than two days from the time the female deposits them. They must remain in water at least as warm as 72 degrees on the Fahrenheit scale. The newly-hatched porgies are less than an eighth of an inch long, but by the end of their first winter they are three inches long. Porgies eat clams, worms, and smaller fish.

porpoise

The porpoise is an animal that lives in the coastal waters of the Atlantic and Pacific oceans. Some porpoises also live in the fresh-water rivers of Asia. The porpoise looks like a fish, but it is not a fish. It is a mammal and bears its young alive and nurses them with milk. The porpoise is closely related to the dolphin.

A porpoise grows to be about five feet long. It is black in color, and its underside is white. It eats shellfish and small fishes. The female porpoise has one baby at a time. It is usually more than a foot

long when it is born. The mother nurses the baby as she swims through the water.

Porpoises are sociable animals and travel in groups. Sometimes more than a hundred porpoises are seen together.

Sailors sometimes say that when porpoises are seen it means that there is going to be a storm. There are stories that tell how porpoises are friends to man and will push a drowning person close to shore.

Port-au-Prince

Port-au-Prince is the capital city of the Republic of Haiti, on Hispaniola Island in the West Indies. Over 340,000 people live there, making it about the same size as Miami, Florida, or Omaha, Nebraska. Most of the people work around the port, because the city's fine harbor at the head of the Gulf of Gonaives makes it Haiti's chief seaport.

Port-au-Prince was founded more than two hundred years ago, in 1749, by French sugar planters. It became the capital of the French colony of Saint-Domingue in 1770. The city is built in a half-circle around the harbor, with places of business near the waterfront and houses on the hills above. It has been badly damaged by several earthquakes and fires. The University of Haiti is there. PORT-AU-PRINCE, HAITI. Population (1973) 340,175. Capital, Republic of Haiti. On the Gulf of Gonaives. Settled, 1749.

Porter, David

David Porter and his son, David Dixon Porter, were two famous officers in the United States Navy. The father, David Porter, was born in 1780. He was one of the heroes of the War of 1812 and later fought against pirates in the Caribbean Sea. He died in 1843. David Dixon Porter was born in 1813 and was one of the leading naval commanders for the Union during the Civil War. He was the second man in United States history to be given the rank of full admiral. (The first full admiral was David G. Farragut, who was an adopted son of David Porter.) David Dixon Porter later became superintendent of the United States Naval Academy at Annapolis. He died in 1891.

Porter, William Sidney, see the article on HENRY, O.

Portland

Portland is the name of two cities, one in Oregon and one in Maine. Each is the largest city in its state.

Portland, Oregon, is an important port city on the Willamette River. It ships more lumber than any other port in the world.

Almost four hundred thousand people live in Portland. They work in big lumber and flour mills and in factories that make furniture, woolen goods, and chemicals. There are also big shipyards. Portland is famous for its beautiful rose gardens, and every June many people go to see the famous Rose Festival held in the city. There are several colleges and universities in Portland, including the University of Portland. The university had 1,695 students in 1962.

Portland was settled in 1845 and was named for Portland, Maine. It was an important supply point, more than a hundred years ago, for miners who joined the gold rush to California. Fifty years later it supplied miners in the Alaska gold rush. The salmon industry helped the city to grow. Despite two bad fires, which swept the city in 1872 and 1873, it continued to prosper. Portland was badly damaged by floods in 1948.

PORTLAND, OREGON. Population (1970 census) 382,619. County seat of Multnomah County. On the Willamette River. Settled, 1845.

Portland, Maine, is on Casco Bay, on the Atlantic Ocean, and is the chief seaport in the state. More than 65,000 people live there. Many of them work at handling more than 16 million tons of products that are shipped through the harbor yearly. The harbor at Portland is one of the finest on the Atlantic coast. There are also large fisheries, and paper and food-packing plants. Portland has many fine parks and beach resorts and many people go there on their vacations.

Portland was settled in 1632, but it has had many difficult times. About sixty years after it was settled, Indians raided the colony and wiped out all the people. In 1716 a new town called Falmouth Neck was built. The British navy shelled and burned this town in 1775. About ten years later the town was rebuilt and became known as Portland. For a time it was the capital of Maine. In 1866, the city was destroyed by fire. The people courageously rebuilt it and Portland grew into one of the most important ports on the Atlantic coast. During World War II, it served as the base for the North Atlantic Fleet.

PORTLAND, MAINE. Population (1970 census) 65,116. County seat of Cumberland County. Settled, 1632.

Portugal

Portugal is a country in western Europe. It is about the size of the state of Indiana with 35,466 square miles, but more than nine million people live there, which is twice the population of Indiana. Portugal became a nation about eight hundred years ago, but people had lived there since ancient times. Along with Spain, Portugal is on the Iberian Peninsula, an arm of land that stretches into the Mediterranean Sea and Atlantic Ocean. Portugal's capital city, Lisbon, is one of the world's most beautiful cities.

THE PEOPLE OF PORTUGAL

The people of Portugal are almost all descended from several ancient peoples who settled on the Iberian Peninsula. These peoples included the Lusitanians, a warlike tribe that fought against the great Roman empire; the Celts, related to the people of Ireland, Scotland, and Wales; the Phoenicians, Greeks, Carthaginians, and Romans, who had great empires thousands of years ago; the Suevi and the Visigoths, warlike tribes of Germans from northern and central Europe; and the Berbers and the Moors, from Africa. The language of Portugal is PORTUGUESE, about which there is a separate article. Most of the Portuguese today are of the Roman Catholic religion.

HOW THE PEOPLE LIVE

Most of the people of Portugal make their living by farming, but many live in modern cities such as Lisbon, Coimbra, and Oporto. In the country they raise the cork oak, from which cork is taken, and pine trees from which rosin and turpentine are made. They also raise grapes to make such wines as port (named for the city of Oporto) and Madeira (named for the Atlantic island that produces most of it). Fishing is an important occupation, and Portuguese sardines are known the world over. Another important product is olive oil. Some of the people work in mines that produce tungsten, copper, and other ores, and in factories.

Since 1911 children have had to go to school, and since World War I thousands of schools have been built. There are many people in Portugal who have never learned to read and write, but most of them are older people in farming districts. Portugal has four universities and several special colleges.

About four hundred years ago, in the 16th century, Portugal was a very rich country. Its kings sent explorers to Africa and Asia, and these explorers established important colonies in faraway places. Portugal still has many of those colonies. The principal Portuguese possessions are: Portuguese Guinea, Angola

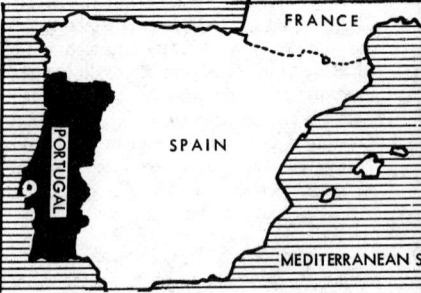

(Portuguese West Africa), and Mozambique (Portuguese East Africa) in Africa; Madeira, the Cape Verde Islands and the Azores, in the Atlantic Ocean; part of Timor, an island in the Pacific Ocean; and part of Macao, an island off China.

WHAT KIND OF PLACE IT IS

Portugal rises from the Atlantic coast to a high, central plain, with several ridges of high mountains. In the central part there are rich valleys. There are mountains, lakes, and a number of rivers, including the Mondego, Tagus, Douro, and Guadiana. The Atlantic beaches are popular resorts.

Portugal's climate is usually mild and pleasant, except in the high mountains. The average annual temperature is about 61 degrees Fahrenheit. There are two seasons, one very dry, from April to September, and the other producing about 40 inches of rainfall.

HOW THE PEOPLE ARE GOVERNED

Portugal is a republic. By its constitution it is governed by a president, elected for a seven-year term; a National Assembly, whose members are elected for four-year terms; and a prime minister, called the president of the Council, who is responsible only to the president. But actually Portugal became a dictatorship in 1932 when Dr. Antonio de Oliveira Salazar became prime minister and achieved

complete power, even controlling the election of the president. The Salazar government, though not democratic, proved to be moderate and Portugal has had a peaceful rule.

PORTUGAL IN THE PAST

Through most of its history Portugal was a kingdom. Late in the Middle Ages, about eight hundred years ago, the different peoples of Portugal united to fight the Moors, a people from Africa who were invading the country. In 1140 Portugal was set up as an independent kingdom under Alfonso I. Portugal reached the height of its power during the 1500s. Earlier its explorers had discovered new lands and had established colonies in America. The most important of these was Brazil, which became an independent nation in 1822. There are separate articles about great Portuguese explorers, including Bartholomeu DIAS, Vasco da GAMA, and Ferdinand MAGELLAN.

About 150 years ago, Portugal was involved in some of the wars that raged in Europe during the time of the French emperor Napoleon. At one point the French invaded Lisbon, and Portugal's capital was moved to Rio de Janeiro in Brazil. Kings of Portugal continued to be emperors of Brazil until 1889, when Brazil became a republic. Portugal became a republic in 1910.

The Portuguese republic had many troubles in its early years. Salazar's rise to power and his support of Antonio Carmona (president from 1928 until his death in 1951) stopped the constant threats of revolution. In 1958 and again in 1965 Americo de Deus Rodriguez Tomaz, Salazar's candidate, was elected president with little or no opposition.

Under the world's oldest treaty, made in 1386, Portugal and Britain have been allied in nearly all wars. In World War II Portugal gave Britain and the U.S. bases in the Azores islands. Portugal became a member of the United Nations in 1955, after years of Soviet opposition.

PORTUGAL. Area, 35,466 square miles. Population (1973 estimate) 8,950,000. Language, Portuguese. Religion, chiefly Roman Catholic. Government, corporative republic. Monetary unit, the escudo, worth about 3.5 cents (U.S.). Flag, green and red, with the coat of arms in center. Capital, Lisbon.

Portuguese Guinea

Portuguese Guinea is an overseas Portuguese province on the western coast of Africa. It is located between Senegal and the Republic of Guinea. The people depend primarily on agriculture for their livelihood. The important crops are peanuts, rice, coconuts, and palm oil kernels. Portuguese Guinea is about the size of Maryland and Connecticut combined. The largest city and capital is Bissau.

PORTUGUESE GUINEA, overseas province of Portugal. Area, 13,948 square miles. Population (1973) 560,000. Capital, Bissau.

Portuguese language

The Portuguese language is spoken in Portugal and its colonies, and in Brazil. Altogether more than 108 million people speak Portuguese.

Portuguese is one of the Romance languages, along with French, Italian, Spanish, and others, which means that it comes chiefly from the Latin language spoken by the ancient Romans. Portuguese is more like Spanish than any of the others, partly because Portugal and Spain are neighboring countries.

Portuguese man-of-war

The Portuguese man-of-war is a strange animal that lives in the Gulf Stream of the Atlantic Ocean off the coast of the United States. It is really a whole colony of little animals that always live together. People in boats sometimes see large purple or pinkish bubbles that look like balloons floating in the water. These are Portuguese men-of-war. The Portuguese man-of-war can blow up the bubble or deflate it just as a person blows up a balloon.

Beneath the balloon of the Portuguese man-of-war there are long, threadlike parts, or tentacles. Some of these tentacles are almost 40 feet long. Others are short. The Portuguese man-of-war can twine these tentacles around objects. Along the tentacles there are cells that sting. If a person touches one of these tentacles he will get a severe, painful sting. The Portuguese man-of-war uses its tentacles to sting fish that it eats.

Portuguese West Africa, another name for Angola, a province of Portugal, located in Africa. See the article on ANGOLA.

Poseidon, the god of the sea, according to the mythology of the ancient Greeks: see the article on NEPTUNE.

Post, Emily

Emily Price Post is the name of an American writer who became famous as  an authority on good manners. She is best known for her book *Etiquette: the Blue Book of Social Usage*, which was first published in 1922. Emily Post was born in 1873 in Baltimore, Maryland. Her first work was writing novels, but after publication of her etiquette book she devoted herself almost exclusively to that field, including appearances on the radio and writing daily for newspapers. She died in 1960.

Post, Wiley

Wiley Post was an American aviator who gained fame as the first man to fly alone around the world. Post was born in 1900 in Grand Plain, Texas. He worked in Oklahoma as an oil driller until he lost an eye in an accident. With $2,000 he was awarded for this injury, Post bought a secondhand airplane and began flying in 1924. Six years later he won the Chicago–Los Angeles Air Derby. In 1931, with Harold Gatty, Post made a record round-the-world flight in 8 days, 15 hours, 51 minutes. His solo flight came two years later, when he circled the globe in 7 days, 18 hours, 49 minutes. Post was killed in 1935 in a plane crash near Point Barrow, Alaska. He was flying with the American humorist Will Rogers, who also died in the crash.

Postal Union

The Universal Postal Union is an international organization that makes rules governing postal service between countries. Today most of the countries of the world belong to it. Its principal body is the Postal Congress, which meets every five years.

The Postal Union was organized in 1875 by 22 nations, including the United States, Egypt, and all the countries of Europe. The International Bureau of the Postal Union has headquarters in Bern, Switzerland.

post and postage stamp

For thousands of years men have found ways to send letters to other men far away, but only in the last two hundred years or less have men had the "mail" or "post" as we know it today. We may take for granted the post office that can be found in every country, city and town throughout the world, but it is one of the principal modern miracles that a man who comes to your house will pick up a letter and another man will deliver it to someone three thousand miles away and the entire service often costs only ten cents and thirteen cents air mail.

The two things that have done most to make this remarkable service possible are the government post office and the postage stamp. When the government supplies a postal service, everyone uses it and the number of letters is so great that it is possible to charge a small price for each of them. It might cost several hundred dollars to send one messenger with one letter from New York to California, but it does not cost much more for the messenger to carry several thousand letters. This means that each letter costs only a few cents. The postage stamp, which proves that the cost of sending the letter has been paid in advance, saves a great deal of time that used to be spent in collecting the postal charges from each individual person.

For hundreds of years, important personages (such as noblemen) would "seal" their letters. That is, they would close the ends of the paper or envelope together with a waxlike substance called sealing wax, and on the sealing wax they would stamp their own private design with a ring called a signet ring or with some other device, called a seal, that was carved with their name or special sign. This showed who sent the letter and also showed that the person sending the letter had paid to have it delivered.

Then the sender of the letter began to sign his name in the upper right-hand corner of the envelope. Usually this meant he had paid to have the letter delivered, but sometimes the person who received the letter had to pay for it when it arrived.

A little more than a hundred years ago, in 1841, Great Britain produced the first postage stamp. It was not beautifully printed in colors as today's stamps are, but it was one of the most popular and most important inventions of all time. Anyone could buy a stamp (for a penny, at that time) and could show by putting the stamp on the envelope that he had paid to have it carried to the person he addressed it to. The postage stamp was such an immediate success that Switzer-

land was issuing postage stamps a little more than a year later and other countries soon followed. The United States first issued postage stamps in 1847. By the 1860s nearly every country was issuing them.

Almost as soon as postage stamps first appeared, people began to collect them. Because postage stamps proved to be so useful and because so many people wanted to build up collections of them, most countries came to issue stamps in many denominations (that is, in many different values, such as 3 cents and 15 cents and so on), and countries also tried to make their stamps beautiful, with fine pictures and colors. See the article on STAMP COLLECTING.

CARRYING THE MAIL

Beginning with the ancient Romans nearly two thousand years ago, and lasting until a hundred or so years ago, letters and other mail were carried by fast horseback riders and sometimes by horse-drawn vehicles such as stagecoaches. When railroads were built, they gradually came to carry most of the mail and they still do. Ships have carried overseas mail for thousands of years. AIRMAIL, about which there is a separate article, has come to be used for letters and packages that must be delivered as soon as possible, whether overland or to overseas countries. Nearly every kind of transportation has been helped by the money governments pay to have mail carried.

The postman, or mailman, or letter carrier, who delivers the mail to the door of a house or office, has been used in most countries for about a hundred years. Until then, a person expecting a letter would have to go to the post office and get it. This is still true in many towns that are quite small, but for places far out in the country there is usually "rural delivery" to mailboxes along the side of the road.

The post office has existed in most countries for almost 200 years. Post offices have come to furnish many services besides carrying the mail. In the United States and other countries, they accept savings. They sell money orders so that money can be safely sent from one person to another. In many countries the post office operates the telegraph and telephone services.

Post Office

Up until 1970, today's Postal Service was called the Post Office Department. On August 12, 1970, President Nixon signed the Postal Reorganization Act, which converted the United States mailing system from a government department to an independent agency under the executive branch. Since the new system could not accurately be called the Post Office Department, the new name Postal Service was given. Authorities believe the reorganization increased the efficiency of the mail service by removing political control of the budget.

The chief purpose of the Postal Service is to collect and deliver mail. Besides this basic function, it also does the following: the making and selling of *postage stamps;* the *registry* of mail, which is keeping a record of a piece of mail by giving a receipt to the sender and

by obtaining one from the receiver; the providing of *money orders,* a safe way to send money; the *special delivery* of mail at anytime; the *parcel post,* which is the mailing and insuring of packages; the *air mail;* the acceptance of *passport* applications; and the sending of *mailgrams,* a combination letter-telegram.

The new Postal service is headed by an eleven-member Board of Governors. Nine of the eleven are appointed by the President with the consent of the Senate. These nine then select a tenth person to be Postmaster General, the head of the entire system. The Postmaster General and the other nine then choose an eleventh member to be Deputy Postmaster General. Under this new system, the Postmaster General is not a member of the President's Cabinet.

The old Post Office Department was established as an executive department in 1872, although it had existed prior to that date. In 1775 under the Continental Congress, Benjamin Franklin was the very first Postmaster General.

Since those early days, the Postal Service of today has grown into an agency with 31,686 post offices in 1973 and 706,400 employees. In 1973, the Postal Service delivered about 87.2 billion pieces of mail. To handle these great amounts, the Postal Service uses a network of trucks, railroads, and airplanes. As the Postal Service continues to update its techniques, everyone hopes for an improving system.

potassium

Potassium is a very soft metal that usually looks like silver. It is a chemical element, which means that it is one of the basic substances of which everything in the world is made. Potassium is so light that it can float on water.

1. This optical zip code reader "knows" the zip codes written on envelopes and sorts the envelopes into the proper bins.

2. From 1837-1970, this seal was used by the former Post Office Department. The seal is believed to have been inspired by Benjamin Franklin.

3. These men are placing letters on conveyors at the post office in Washington, D.C.

4. The new seal of the Postal Service is a bald eagle ready for flight and was adopted on August 12, 1970, the day of the creation of the Postal Service.

The compounds of potassium have hundreds of uses. Potassium nitrate, or saltpeter, is the main ingredient in black gunpowder. It is also used in preserving meats, and it has some use in medicine. Potassium chloride is a very important fertilizer. Potassium hydrogen tartrate, or cream of tartar, is used in baking powder.

Potassium carbonate, or *potash,* used to be made from wood ashes. The ashes were placed in pots and the potassium carbonate was dissolved out of them by adding water to the pots. It is from these pots that potash (pot ash) first got its name. Potash is an excellent fertilizer and is also widely used in the manufacture of glass.

Potassium is obtained from minerals called sylvite, carnallite, and kainite. The biggest supply of these minerals is at Stassfurt, Germany. They are also found at Carlsbad, New Mexico, and Searles Lake, California.

potato

The white potato is one of the most important food plants in the world. It first grew in South and Central America and was introduced into Europe by the Spaniards who returned from the New World over four hundred years ago. Now the potato is raised in almost every part of the world except where the climate is very hot.

Potatoes grow best in cool, damp places. The plant is an annual, which means that a root must be planted every year. It grows to be two or three feet high. It has small white or bluish flowers. The fruit of the potato plant is a small purple or brownish-green berry that is not good to eat. Part of the stem of the potato plant grows underground. It swells to form a tuber, and it is this part that we eat.

Potatoes are hardy and can be stored for long periods in a cool, dark place. Potatoes are a nourishing and healthful food that contains a large amount of starch. Alcohol is made from the potato. Potatoes are an important food for animals as well as human beings.

The SWEET POTATO belongs to a different family of plants. You can read about it in a separate article.

Potomac River

The Potomac River is in the eastern part of the United States. It forms the boundary between Maryland and West Virginia on one side, and between Virginia and Maryland on the other. Washington, D.C., the capital of the United States, is on the Potomac. The Potomac is 450 miles long and is noted for its beauty. Its chief branch is the Shenandoah River. The river begins in the Allegheny Mountains and flows through the Blue Ridge Mountains. At Washington and below it, the river passes Arlington Cemetery and Mount Vernon, the home of George Washington. The Potomac empties into Chesapeake Bay. Large ships can travel on the river up to Washington.

Potsdam

Potsdam is an important city in Germany, on the Havel River. It is about sixteen miles southwest of the city of Berlin, and is considered a suburb of Berlin.

About 115,000 people live in Potsdam. Many of them work in factories that make cloth, locomotives, and scientific instruments, and many others are employed in the motion-picture industry. Potsdam has many parks, monuments, and fine buildings, including a number of palaces that used to be occupied by the royal families of Germany.

Potsdam was founded more than six hundred years ago. It was the capital of Brandenburg province. About two hundred years ago, Frederick II of Prussia (Frederick the Great) made Potsdam his chief residence. He built a great palace and park there and also a military college to train the officers of his armies.

Toward the end of World War II, in 1945, the leaders of the United States, Russia and England held a conference at Potsdam and signed a treaty called the Potsdam Agreement. By this treaty Germany was to be divided into four zones, or sections, which were to be occupied by French, American, Russian and British troops. The city of Potsdam became the headquarters of the Russian occupation forces.

Potter, Beatrix

Beatrix Potter was an English writer and artist. She was born in 1866. When she grew up she began to write stories for children. One of her best-known stories is called *Peter Rabbit.* Beatrix Potter made all of the pictures for *Peter Rabbit* herself. She began the story in letters that she wrote to a little boy who was sick. Beatrix Potter also wrote *The Tale of Benjamin Bunny,* and *Mrs. Tittlemouse,* and many other stories that children have enjoyed. She died in 1943, at the age of 77.

pottery

Pottery is any kind of dishes or other objects that are formed of clay and baked until they are hard. The finest chinaware and the roughest clay pots are both forms of pottery. The science of making pottery is called *ceramics.* Pottery has been called the oldest of all arts. Men were making pottery thousands of years before they discovered metals. In the course of these thousands of years, they have developed hundreds of different ways of making pottery and decorating it so that it can be beautiful as well as useful. The article on HANDCRAFTS in this encyclopedia describes one way in which you can make pottery as a hobby.

THE CLAY USED IN POTTERY

Wet clay can be worked into various shapes because of its doughlike condition. Clay is made up of tiny particles that cling together when wet but are easily separated when dry. If we stir dry clay dust into a dish of water, the small particles will become suspended in the water. Besides, there is always some water in the clay. This, when once dried out by fire, cannot be replaced. Clay once burned never again can be worked or molded.

Clay is found in all stages of purity. It is often combined with sand, iron, or vegetable matter so that it is not fit for use. *Kaolin* is the purest form. *Ball clay* (clay containing more impurities than kaolin) is used in the making of table dishes.

Various means have been used for separating clay from its impurities. Most of these depend upon the principle that the small particles can be suspended in water and thus carried away from other substances that are heavier and will therefore sink.

All clay fired (baked) at a low temperature is porous; that is, it absorbs water. The same clay fired at a higher temperature *vitrifies;* that is, becomes glassy and no longer absorbs water. All clay products can be classified as *porous* or *vitrified.* Tableware may be either porous or vitrified. Porcelain is vitrified.

METHODS OF FORMING

The earliest method of making pottery was probably the hand method of building. Coils of clay are wound around, one on top of the other, and welded together by pressing, the clay first having been worked to a soft or plastic state by mixing with water. The dish is shaped and smoothed by hand.

When vessels of circular form were to be made the *potter's wheel* was formerly used. When this method is used, the lump of clay is placed on a revolving horizontal disk and shaped by the hands of the potter, who keeps his hands moist by dipping them frequently into water. The water keeps his hands from sticking to the revolving lumps of clay. Handles and spouts are stuck onto the clay vessels before firing.

It is probable that the Egyptians invented the potter's wheel. At any rate we know that they were using it at least six thousand years ago. The ancient Greeks used it, and their vases were beautiful in their richness and simplicity of color and shape and the refined quality

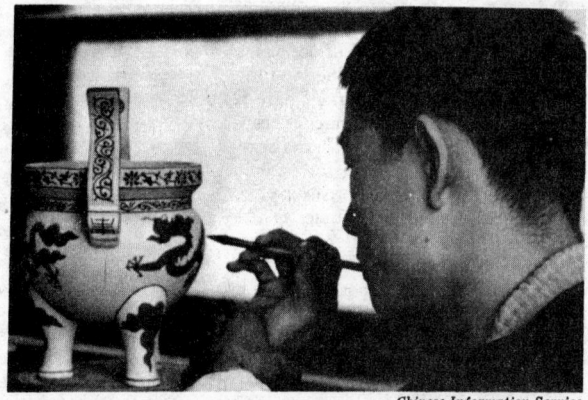

Chinese Information Service

A ceramics artist puts the finishing touches on a piece of Chinese pottery.

of their decorations. The Greek vases usually had handles. Red clay was used almost entirely. In the black-figured ware the natural red surface of the dish served as a background, the figures being painted in black. In the red-figured ware the figures were first sketched in black outline and the background filled in with black. The red on the black background came to be used more and more until the earlier method disappeared entirely.

CASTING

Casting is often used today when pottery of a high quality is desired and when the walls are to be very thin. A mixture of clay and water, called *slip,* is poured into a plaster-of-Paris mold. The plaster of Paris absorbs the water, thus causing a thin coating of clay to be deposited all around the inside of the mold. When the deposit is thick enough to form the walls of the vase, the remaining free slip is poured out, leaving the wet piece of ware on the inside of the form. As this dries it shrinks somewhat and can be removed from the mold. Usually the molds are so constructed that they can be taken apart.

FIRING

When the piece becomes thoroughly dry it is smoothed and prepared for firing. It is placed in a fire-clay box called a *sagger,* which protects the piece from the flames and gases just as an oven protects a loaf of bread. The saggers are placed one on top of the other in a *kiln.* The kiln is a large boxlike structure built of fire brick and surrounded by flues so that the fire may entirely surround the dishes and yet not actually come in contact with them, as smoke would discolor them.

Most dishes are fired twice. The first firing is called the *bisque* firing and the piece of pottery once fired is called a *biscuit* or *bisque piece.*

The temperature for firing bisque chinaware is about 2,262 degrees Fahrenheit. The firing lasts about fifty hours from the time the saggers are placed until the desired heat is reached. The kiln then takes from two to three days to cool. Coal and natural gas are the fuels commonly used.

The bisque ware, when taken from the kiln, is rubbed with pieces of hard wood. In this way the sand and clay adhering to the surface are removed. After it is cleaned, heavy ware (such as is used in restaurants) is placed in a *tumbling mill,* which tumbles the dishes over and over with fragments of broken ware much as clothes are tumbled in a revolving washing machine. This frees the surface of the ware from the bits of clay adhering to it.

The biscuit is now *glazed.* A glaze is a glassy covering placed on wares to beautify them and to make them more serviceable. Glazes usually contain a metal, which gives them their color. Iron gives red; copper, green; cobalt, blue. Glazes contain silica, which is often just fine-ground sand and is the main ingredient used in making glass. Other things used in making glazes are lead oxide, calcium oxide, zinc oxide, and alumina. Clay and feldspar are also used in glazes. The various materials are ground together with water to a fine milky condition. The biscuit is then dipped into this and comes

out covered completely. When fully dry the ware is again placed in the kiln and fired to a heat so high that the glaze mixture fuses (melts and runs together).

If the ware is to be without decoration it is dipped in the glaze at once after firing. If it is to be decorated under the glaze, the design is put on before the ware is dipped.

Colored lines and bands are put on the once-fired ware with a brush. Each dish is spun round on a *whirler* as the decorator applies the color.

Most of the tableware used today is decorated. This decoration is often accomplished by the use of colored glazes (from coloring put into the glaze mix). China may be hand-painted before glazing. Most often, especially with the less expensive dishes, the decoration is put on by the print method or by the use of decalcomanias.

The *print* method of transferring designs to dishes is a simple process by which ceramic colors instead of ink are printed upon a special paper called printer's tissue, and transferred from this paper to the ware. The designs for the prints are engraved by hand on a copper plate. Then they are printed on the printer's tissue just as visiting cards are engraved from the copper plates.

Decals (decalcomania patterns) are usually produced by LITHOGRAPHY (about which there is a separate article). Decals are like the "transfers" that children often use.

Either the print or the decal papers are pressed, color-side down, on the ware. When the paper is washed away the pattern remains. When a single color is wanted the engraved plate or print method is used. When more than one color is wanted the decalcomania method is generally used.

The Chinese have long been masters of the art of making porcelain. The vases were made in China more than 700 years ago.

MODELING

The *modeler* makes the models or patterns from which molds for plates and hollow ware are made. He makes them from clay or from plaster of Paris and sometimes from clay and plaster combined. He also makes the models for handles.

From the modeler's model, a mold-

maker casts a *block mold.* The block mold serves as a form for casting a *case mold.* By means of the case mold the mold maker is able to cast as many working molds as he needs. Many *working molds,* each exactly like the block mold, are needed to turn out dishes in large quantities.

Plates and flat dishes, both round and oval, are formed over a plaster form that whirls. The machine used is called a *jigger.* A lump of clay is thrown on a wet plaster slab, and is flattened. The flat clay disk thus made is called a *bat* and the process of making a bat is called *batting out.* The clay bat is made to whirl, and the workman lets down on the bat a form, called a *templet,* that gives the outside or the back or bottom of the dish or plate a desired shape. Bowls and cups are made, without their handles, on jiggers. The plaster form in this instance shapes the outside of the ware while the templet shapes the inside. For oval jiggering there is a special device on the machine.

Casting is always used for making hollow ware of irregular shape. Handles are either cast or pressed, as are also all small, irregularly shaped flat dishes. In pressing, the plastic clay is pressed into forms made of plaster of Paris.

KINDS OF POTTERY

Stoneware is a pottery made from either light or dark clay. It is glazed on the unburned body either before setting in the kiln or by means of salt during the burning process, and is burned to a dense, hard condition.

Porcelain is a white, vitrified ware. It is translucent, which means that you can see light shine through it. In porcelain, the body and glaze are brought to completion and maturity at one and the same burning, which takes place at a very high temperature.

China is a ware similar to porcelain in appearance, though scarcely as white. It is produced by a double burning in which the body is brought to its density and translucency before glazing. The glaze is added later and fired at a lower temperature.

Bone china is a variety of china in which calcined (burned) bone is used as an ingredient, constituting about forty percent of the mass.

Earthenware is a white or nearly white body. It is produced, like china, by two burnings, but its body remains porous. The glaze is similar to that used for china, but is made from cheaper materials.

Vitreous ware and *semi-porcelain* are "fancy" names applied, often without justification, to the varieties of earthenware as they approach more or less the composition of china. There is no essential difference between these wares and earthenware.

Faïence is fine glazed earthenware used for ornamental and decorative purposes. Usually there is no attempt to produce a white body and the glazes are frequently colored.

Majolica is a kind of faïence. It includes those wares on which the glaze has been made opaque (so that you cannot see through it) by the use of oxide of tin.

poultry

Poultry includes various members of the bird family, called fowl, that men raise for their meat and their eggs. By far the chief kind of poultry is the chicken, but turkeys, ducks and geese are also included. The raising of poultry, or "chicken-farming," has been one of the most important occupations of man for thousands of years. Breeds of fowl have been scientifically developed to produce the most and tenderest meat, or the most and largest eggs. Until fifty years or so ago, millions of families kept a few chickens in their back yards, even if they were not farming families. This custom has largely died out, because the raising of poultry on large farms has become so efficient that people can buy poultry and eggs almost everywhere.

POULTRY-FARMING

Chickens are raised in nearly every part of the United States (and, in fact, in nearly every part of every country on earth). Feed for the chickens is almost always bought from large companies, instead of being raised on the farm as it once was. The feed is very scientifically prepared, with grain mixed with chemicals that help the fowl grow. Sometimes drugs such as the antibiotics are mixed into the feed, to prevent disease in the poultry. There are different mixtures for baby chicks and for older fowl.

A hen lays its eggs in a nest in the chicken house and would naturally sit on the eggs and let them hatch and become baby chicks, but modern farms take the eggs from the nest and put them into incubators to hatch. There are many special hatcheries that are in the business of hatching eggs for farmers. In many cases they send boxes of live baby chicks back to the farmers by mail.

Chickens sold for meat are graded according to their age and weight. A broiler is about 6 to 8 weeks old and weighs up to 2½ pounds. A frier is 9 or 10 weeks old and weighs 2½ to 4 pounds. A spring chicken is about 4 months old and weighs up to 4 pounds. Heavier and older chickens are called roasters, or simply fowl.

There is a separate article on EGGS.

OTHER POULTRY

Ducks are raised chiefly on Long Island and along the coast of New England. The ducks most often eaten are two to three months old. Most of them are called Long Island ducklings. The ducks that are raised for meat are unlike wild ducks that can fly long distances at high speeds. Domestic ducks are poor fliers and do not leave the farms.

Turkeys are important as poultry only in the United States and Canada, but are becoming popular in other countries. They are raised on big turkey farms in many states. For many years turkeys were eaten chiefly at big parties and on special occasions such as Thanksgiving and Christmas, because turkeys are too big for the average family. The rest of the turkey supply was used by restaurants. In recent years farmers have developed turkeys that weigh only seven or eight pounds and they have become more popular for everyday meals. Parts of turkeys can be bought, fresh or frozen, and this too has permitted more people to eat turkey. Turkey-farming has increased because of these developments.

Geese are the least popular kind of poultry raised in the United States. In Great Britain, a goose is the usual fowl for a holiday dinner, as at Christmas.

See the articles on DUCK, GOOSE, and TURKEY.

power, the number of times a certain number is to be multiplied by itself: see the article LOGARITHMS.

power of attorney

A power of attorney is a legal paper in which one person appoints another person to represent him. The person who receives the power of attorney is called an attorney-in-fact. The person who gives the power of attorney is called the principal. The attorney-in-fact can make any kind of agreement for the principal, and the principal has to live up to it just as though he had made it himself.

Powhatan was the father of Pocahontas and the chief of about eight thousand Indians of thirty different tribes living around Jamestown, Virginia, in 1607, when the first colony was founded there. He was a good chief and a good man, and the English settlers lived in peace with the Indians until Powhatan died in 1619. See the article on POCAHONTAS.

Poznań or Posen

Poznań is a province of Poland, in the western part of the country. It is nearly 11,000 square miles in size, about the size of the state of Maryland, and more than two million people live there. Most of them are farmers. The capital of the province is also called Poznań, a city of about 408,000, on the Warta River.

The German and English name for Poznań is *Posen*. More than 160 years ago the most powerful kingdom of Germany, Prussia, took the western part of Poland. The name Posen was often used for the entire section that Prussia took. Poznań remained part of Prussia until the end of World War I, when it again became part of Poland. In World War II Germany again took Poznań, but it was returned to Poland at the end of the war. The city had been badly damaged by bombs.

Prague

Prague is the capital of Czechoslovakia. It is on the Moldau River, in the region called Bohemia, and it is an important industrial city. About a million people live there. There are factories that make railway cars, automobiles, heavy machinery, clothing, furniture, and leather goods, particularly gloves. The Czech name for the city is Praha.

Prague is an old and beautiful city. Along the Moldau River are palaces with high towers and important public buildings. On the right (eastern) bank of the city is the Old Town with its ancient churches and historic monuments. The spires of the famous Tyn Church can be seen from all parts of the city. Surrounding the Old Town is the New Town. This section is more modern and has parks, schools, theaters, and business buildings. On the left (western) bank of the

Prague, capital of Czechoslovakia, has many beautiful buildings hundreds of years old. The one shown above is St. Vitus' Tower.

Moldau is the Little Town. It is connected with the rest of the city by several bridges. The most noted is the Charles Bridge, which is lined with statues on both sides. The Little Town is chiefly a residential section. Behind it rises Hradcany Hill. At the top of the hill is a huge palace where the Bohemian kings once lived. It is now used for government offices.

Prague has been a center of culture and learning for centuries. The most famous school is Charles University. The city has many museums and art galleries, and a stadium which seats 200,000.

Prague was settled over twelve hundred years ago by Germans. Within a century it grew to be the second-largest city in Europe and the capital of Bohemia. For hundreds of years, Prague was ruled by Austria; when Czechoslovakia gained independence in 1918 Prague was made the capital. In 1939, German troops occupied the city. In 1945 it was freed by Russian troops with the help of Czech patriots, and in 1948 the country was taken over by Communists, aided by the Russians who kept control of Czechoslovakia from Moscow. In 1969 the Russians and some of their allies marched into Prague (without much fighting) to show that they would not tolerate the freedoms which the Czechoslovakian government had been allowing.

PRAGUE. Population 999,573 (in 1960). Capital of Czechoslovakia and of Praha Province. On the Moldau River.

prairie dog

The prairie dog is an animal that lives in the western parts of the United States and in some parts of Canada and Mexico. It is not a dog but a kind of squirrel. It is about a foot long. The black-tailed prairie dog has light tan or reddish-brown fur and a black tip on its tail.

Prairie dogs eat leaves, plant stems, and roots. Sometimes they also eat insects. Prairie dogs that live where the

winter is very cold sometimes sleep the whole winter.

The prairie dog is a wonderful builder. Prairie dogs build whole cities 10 or 12 feet underground. These cities consist of many miles of tunnels and dens, and sometimes thousands of prairie dogs make their homes in them.

Many prairie dogs have been killed because they eat crops. Now there are very few prairie dogs in the United States.

Praxiteles

Praxiteles was a great sculptor of ancient Greece. He lived in Athens almost 2,500 years ago. His favorite subjects were young Greek gods and goddesses and he made many beautiful marble statues of them, but the only one that remains is a statue of the god Hermes carrying the boy Dionysus. This statue was discovered in Greece about seventy-five years ago. There are Roman copies of some of the sculptures of Praxiteles.

prayer, asking God to help or bless one: see the article on RELIGION.

premier, the head of the government in many countries. See the article on PARLIAMENT.

preposition

A preposition is a word such as *in, to, after,* and so on. Prepositions are used to show how, where, when, or in what direction. Many prepositions are used in the English language, but there are some languages in which the same job is done by *inflection,* or changes in the form of a word. In Latin, for example, the word *puer* means "boy" and the word *pueri* means "to the boy." The spelling of the word *puer* is changed to show the meaning. In English, the preposition *to* shows the meaning, so the spelling of *boy* does not have to be changed.

Use of a preposition calls for the use of a special form of a pronoun. You would say, "I was given a book," but "A book was given to me." The word *me* is called the object of the preposition *to.*

Prepositions do much the same job that adverbs do. See the article on ADVERBS.

Presbyterian

A Presbyterian is a member of one of the Christian Churches that are governed by *presbyters.* Presbyters do not have to be clergymen, as the governing members of some churches must be. Many presbyters are elders, who are elected by the members of each Presbyterian congregation. The minister and the elders together watch over the spiritual welfare of the congregation.

Most Presbyterians follow the teachings of John CALVIN, about whom there is a separate article. A Presbyterian church is organized on principles laid down by Calvin. In addition to the elders and ministers, there are trustees who take care of money problems, and deacons who help the poor. The congregations are guided by a General Assembly, which is made up of representatives of all the congregations and meets once a year.

There are many branches of Presbyterianism. The first group was that of John Calvin, who founded the Reformed Church in Geneva, Switzerland, about 450 years ago. The Presbyterian Church spread rapidly, especially in Ireland, Scotland, and Wales. Many Presbyterians left the British countries and settled in America in the 1600s, but the greatest number came a hundred years later, when many people from Ireland and Scotland moved to America.

There are more than ten million Presbyterians throughout the world. Of these, 4,320,686 belong to the eleven main Presbyterian groups in the United States. They have 14,690 churches and have missions in every country in the world.

Prescott, William

William Prescott was the American colonel in command at the Battle of Bunker Hill, one of the first battles fought in the Revolutionary War. There is a separate article about the Battle of BUNKER HILL. Prescott was born in 1726 and died in 1795.

Prescott, William H.

William Hickling Prescott was one of the greatest American historians. He was born in Salem, Massachusetts, in 1796. While Prescott was attending Harvard University he received an eye injury that left him nearly blind for the rest of his life. This did not stop him from doing the studying necessary to gather the material for his books. His two best works of history are called the *Conquest of Mexico* and the *Conquest of Peru.* Prescott was the grandson of the Colonel William Prescott who commanded the American army at the Battle of Bunker Hill. He died in 1859.

presidency

Countries that have a republican form of government usually have a President at their head. In most countries the President is the head of the state and another man, often called the Prime Minister, is the head of the government. In such governments the President is not a member of any political party and has little power in the government. He holds a position much like the position held by the King or Queen of England. In the United States, the President is both the head of the state and the head of the government and has much more power than the Presidents of most other republics.

PRESIDENT OF THE UNITED STATES

In the United States the President is the most important man in the government. He is the head of the political party to which he belongs. According to the Constitution, which established the office of President, the President of the United States is the head of the executive branch of the government. The executive branch of the government carries out the laws made by Congress, the legislative branch of the government. (The Supreme Court, which interprets the laws and decides whether they are constitutional, is the third branch of the government.)

The President of the United States must be at least 35 years old. He must have been born in the United States, and he must have resided in the country for at least 14 years. He has the right, with the consent of the Senate, to make treaties with other countries, and the right to appoint officials of the government, but here also he often needs the consent of the Senate. He is commander in chief of the Army and Navy. The President must sign bills that are passed by the Congress before they become laws, though it is possible for the Congress to pass laws that the President does not like.

There have always been disagreements as to exactly what powers the President of the United States does have. Actually

The President of the United States appoints the heads and other employees of all government departments. He appoints the judges of Federal courts. He signs or vetoes laws passed by Congress, and may suggest laws to Congress.

the powers of the President depend upon the conditions existing in the country. In times of war and times of bad business conditions, both Congress and the people have always permitted, and wanted, the President to have special powers. During times of peace and prosperity the Congress and the people have not wanted him to have so much power.

According to the Constitution, everybody who works in any government bureau and anybody who serves in the armed forces is working for the President. This makes the job of President such a big one that no one man could possibly perform all the duties required. During World War II, for example, the President was responsible for 18,000,000 people.

The President gives responsibility for certain jobs to a whole chain of executives working under him, but he is usually blamed for any mistakes these people make.

ELECTION OF THE PRESIDENT

Since 1824 the candidates for President and Vice President have been nominated at national political conventions. Before that time they were nominated by the members of the Congress. The first President, George Washington, was not officially nominated by anybody, since everybody who had any part in forming the new government wanted him to be at the head of it.

Until 1800, the candidate who received the most votes for President became the President, and the candidate who received the next-highest number of votes became the Vice President. This meant that it was possible for the President and the Vice President to belong to two different political parties. The Twelfth Amendment to the Constitution

provided that each party should nominate a man for President and a man for Vice President. Since then the elected President and Vice President have been from the same political party.

The President is not elected by the direct vote of the people but by a group of *electors*. You can read how this system works in the article on the ELECTORAL COLLEGE.

George Washington established the idea that the presidency of the United States should not be held by the same man for more than two terms, or eight years. No President served more than two terms until Franklin D. Roosevelt, who died during his fourth term as President. During the administration of Harry S. Truman, who followed Roosevelt as President, the Twenty-second Amendment to the Constitution was passed. This amendment sets two terms as the most that a President may serve. If a President has served more than two years of another President's term, he may be elected President only once.

If the President dies in office, the Vice President finishes out his term for him. If the Vice President dies, the Speaker of the House of Representatives becomes President. After him comes the President of the Senate, and then the heads of the government departments in the order in which they were formed, beginning with the Secretary of State. This order of succession to the presidency was established by law in 1947.

The President cannot be arrested for any crime. If a President is thought by Congress to have fallen down at his job, he may be impeached by Congress.

Pretoria

Pretoria is the administrative capital of the Republic of South Africa; that is, it is the city where the government has its offices. Pretoria is also the capital of Transvaal Province. The population of Pretoria was estimated at 420,053 in 1962. See the article on the Republic of SOUTH AFRICA.

Priam

Priam was the king of Troy in Homer's great poem, the *Iliad*, written in ancient Greece three thousand years ago. Priam's wife was Hecuba. One of Priam's sons was named Paris. He started a war with Greece by stealing a Greek princess, Helen. The war was called the TROJAN WAR and there is a separate article about it. Another of Priam's sons, Hector, was a great Trojan warrior but was killed by Achilles, the greatest Greek warrior. Priam was killed on the night that the Greeks conquered Troy.

Pribilof Islands

The Pribilof Islands are a group of four islands off the coast of Alaska, in the Bering Sea. They are owned by the United States. They are important for the seals and white foxes that the people of the island hunt for their valuable fur. The people on the Pribilof Islands are known as Aleuts. The islands are hilly and cold, and very little grows there.

The Pribilof Islands were discovered almost two hundred years ago by a Russian navigator named Gerasim Pribilof.

In 1867, the United States got the Pribilof Islands when it bought Alaska from Russia.

price control, a system under which the government fixes the highest prices that may be charged for various goods. See the articles on INFLATION and RATIONING.

prickly heat

Prickly heat is a skin rash that attacks people who live in very warm climates. When a person perspires a great deal and wears clothes so tight that the perspiration cannot evaporate properly, he may develop prickly heat. Babies who are dressed too warmly often get this rash. It is made up of tiny red pimples or blisters that burn and itch uncomfortably.

prickly pear

The prickly pear is a fruit that grows on a variety of cactus plants. It originally grew in the southwestern part of the United States and in Mexico, but spread to many parts of the world, including Europe and Australia.

The prickly pear is sometimes called the Indian fig. It is an oval-shaped fruit that is about the size of an egg, with a prickly skin. It is yellow or purple, and has a pleasant sharp flavor. Some kinds of prickly pear are a favorite food of cattle. Farmers singe off the prickles so that the cattle can eat the fruit more easily.

primate

Primate is the name given to the order of mammals which includes lemurs, apes, monkeys, and man. See separate articles.

prime minister, the head of the government in many countries. See the article on PARLIAMENT.

primrose

The primrose is a flower that grows in many parts of the world where the climate is not too hot or too cold. People in Europe, Asia, and the United States raise primroses in their gardens. Many primroses are grown in greenhouses. Almost all the varieties of primrose are perennials, which means that they grow up from the same roots every year. Some plants are only a few inches high and others grow to be more than two feet high. They have blossoms of many different colors. There are yellow, purple, pink, and white primroses.

Prince Edward Island

Prince Edward Island is the smallest of the provinces of Canada. It is 2,184 square miles in size, about the size of Delaware. In population it ranks tenth in Canada, with about 109,000 people living there. It is in the east, in the Gulf of St. Lawrence, north of Nova Scotia. Prince Edward Island became a province in 1873. The capital is Charlottetown. The province was named for Prince Edward of England.

Most of the people of Prince Edward Island are of English, Irish, and Scottish descent. Some are of French descent. About half the people belong to the Roman Catholic Church. Other important Churches are the United Church of Canada and the Presbyterian, Anglican and Baptist Churches.

Many people on Prince Edward Island are farmers. They raise large crops of potatoes, hay, fruits (especially apples and strawberries), and grains. Many have dairy farms and produce cattle and dairy products.

A large number of people are fishermen. Off the coast of Prince Edward Island they catch lobsters, oysters, clams, and herring. Others raise silver foxes, beavers and minks for their valuable furs. In the cities there are dairy plants that make butter and cheese, fish-canning

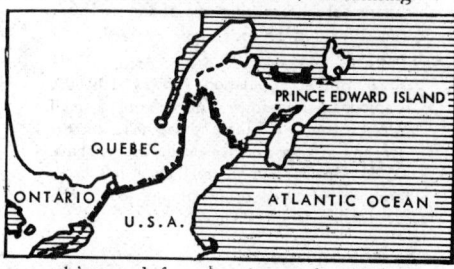

plants and factories that make lumber products.

WHAT THE PROVINCE IS LIKE

Prince Edward Island is low and flat except in the central section, where there are low hills. Along the northern coast are long, sandy beaches, and there are excellent harbors along the eastern and southern coasts. The summers on Prince Edward Island are pleasantly cool, with an average temperature of 65 degrees. The fine beaches, fishing and climate have made the island a popular summer resort. The winters are long and cold, with an average temperature of 15 degrees. There are heavy snowfalls in winter.

The island has a number of short rivers, but none of them is navigable. Trains and roads reach most parts of the island, and there are several airports.

Charlottetown is the provincial capital and the largest city on Prince Edward Island, with a population of over 18,000 in 1967. It is the chief port and commercial center of the island.

THE GOVERNMENT

The head of the government of Prince Edward Island is a lieutenant-governor who is appointed by the British Queen on the recommendation of the Canadian government. The province is actually run by a Premier. He is appointed by the legislature, which is elected by the people. The Premier stays in office as long as he can keep the confidence of the majority of the legislature. The legislature is elected for a five-year term. Half of the members are elected by all the voters and half are elected only by the people who own property. The provincial government is in the capital, Charlottetown.

PRINCE EDWARD ISLAND IN THE PAST

The first white man to enter the region of Prince Edward Island was Jacques Cartier, the French explorer, more than four hundred years ago. More than fifty years later, Samuel de Champlain claimed the land for France, but it was many years before the French actually started settlements on the island. After the French and Indian Wars, about two hundred years ago, Prince Edward Island (which was then called Isle Saint Jean) was given to the British, who made it part of the colony of Nova Scotia. In 1769 it was made

a separate colony.

Many people from the United States settled on the island after the Revolutionary War, and others came from Scotland, but most of the land was owned by Englishmen who never visited the island and simply collected rents from the tenants who lived on their land. This was changed when the government began to buy up this land and sell it to the people who were living in the colony.

Prince Edward Island did not join the other Canadian colonies when they formed the Dominion of Canada in 1867, but joined in 1873.

PRINCE EDWARD ISLAND. Area, 2,184 square miles. Population (1971) 109,000. Capital, Charlottetown. Coat of arms, a small green island with three young oaks on the left and a large oak tree on the right; above it, the British lion in gold on a red background. Admitted to Dominion, 1873. Official abbreviation, P.E.I.

Princeton

Princeton is the name of a town in west New Jersey and of a famous university there. The population of the town of Princeton, in the 1970 census, was 12,311. Many Princeton people work in the nearby city of Trenton. Others work in the educational institutions there, which include the Institute for Advanced Study, St. Joseph's College (a Roman Catholic college for men), Princeton Theological Seminary, and Westminster Choir College, as well as Princeton University. The Institute for Advanced Study has become especially well-known since such famous scholars as Albert Einstein have been connected with it.

The town of Princeton was settled nearly 300 years ago, in 1696. During the Revolutionary War, in 1777, George Washington won a battle against the British there. Several years later, in 1783, the Continental Congress had a session in Nassau Hall, which is now one of the buildings of Princeton University. The town has several monuments and buildings in memory of these and other important historical events.

Princeton University for men was founded more than two hundred years ago, in 1746, as the College of New Jersey. It has schools of liberal arts and sciences, public and international affairs, architecture, and engineering. One of its most famous presidents, Woodrow Wilson, later became President of the United States. In 1962, there were 3,945 students enrolled there.

printing

Printing is a way of making many copies of reading matter or pictures. Because printing has made books and newspapers available to everyone, it has been one of the most important things in the progress of mankind.

There are three main ways of printing. Their technical names are *relief, planographic,* and *intaglio,* but they are usually called *letterpress, offset,* and *engraving* (or *gravure*).

In letterpress printing, raised type is used. (Typewriters and rubber stamps also use raised type.) When ink is rolled on the type and the type is then pressed against paper, the ink comes off on the paper.

In offset printing, a flat plate is used, but the plate is chemically treated so that ink will stick to some places and not to others. The plate is prepared so that ink will stick only where words and pictures are desired. Now ink is rolled onto the plate. This ink will eventually come off the plate and onto paper. To see how this works, write on a piece of paper with pen and ink, then press a blotter against the paper, and then look at the blotter. The blotter will have marks of the ink on it.

In engraving, or gravure printing, the outlines of words or pictures are cut into a metal plate. Ink is rolled over the plate and it enters the places where the plate is cut. The plate is wiped dry, but the ink remains in the cut places. When paper is pressed against the plate, the ink comes out of the cut places and onto the paper.

PRINTING PRESSES

Printing is very simple in principle, but such elaborate machines and processes have been invented for it that it has long been a science that is wholly understood only by professionals. A print-

MDCCXXIX.
THE
Rhode-Island
ALMANACK,
For the Year, 1729.
Being the First after *Leap-Year.*
Carefully fitted, and exactly
calculated to the Meridian of
NEWPORT on *Rhode Island*;
Whose Latitude North is 41 gr.
30 m. Longitude from *London,* 72 grs.
But may without sensible Error serve all Parts
of *NEW-ENGLAND.*

By *Poor* ROBIN.

NEWPORT:
Printed and Sold by *J. Franklin,* at his Printing-House on *Tillinghast's* Wharf. Sold also by *T. Fleet,* in *Pudding-Lane, Boston.* 1729.

N.Y. Public Library.
Yearly "almanacks" were among the first books printed in colonial America.

ing press is so carefully designed that it may use several tons of pressure in pressing the type against the paper, but the type does not press into the paper for more than a thousandth of an inch. Modern printing presses can turn out thousands or even tens of thousands of sheets of paper per hour, fully printed and sometimes even folded to form newspapers or books.

Modern printing began when the German printer Johannes Gutenberg began to print from separate pieces of type, about five hundred years ago. Between the years 1500 and 1800 there was not much change in printing. All printing was by the letterpress process. The flatbed press was used. This kind of press lays the sheet of paper against a flat surface, called the *platen,* and presses the inked type against it.

Shortly after the year 1800 the first *cylinder press* was built. In the cylinder

press a cylinder, or roller, rolls the sheet of paper over the type. The cylinder press is much faster than the flatbed press. Most of the large presses built in the last hundred years have been cylinder presses.

The largest and fastest presses are rotary presses. In most rotary presses, huge rolls of paper are used instead of separate sheets of paper. The printing type is made into curved plates that fit onto cylinders. The paper travels between these plates, which print the paper on both sides. At the end of the press is special machinery that cuts the printed paper into sheets and folds it to form a complete newspaper or a folded section (*signature*) of a book or magazine, as explained in the article on BOOK. Rotary presses will produce 30,000 or more complete newspapers or signatures in an hour. The cylinder press seldom produces more than 1,200 sheets, and usually the output is 800 to 1,000.

During the last century, many other improvements were made in printing presses. One was the automatic feeder. The Dexter feeder, which has remained the most popular, uses an air pump to create suction (as on a vacuum cleaner). Little tubes pick up each sheet of paper by suction and deliver it to the press, where it is printed. The *perfector* press prints both sides of a sheet of paper. Most presses print only one side of the paper. Then the sheet has to be turned and put through the press again to print the other side. Printing the second side is called *perfecting* the sheet.

The most popular small press for a hundred years and more was the *job press.* This press uses the flatbed principle. An operator feeds a sheet of paper into the press, which closes and prints the sheet. Then the press opens and the operator takes out the printed sheet and feeds in another sheet. In the smallest job presses, the operator even pulled a handle to close and open the press. More modern job presses are opened and closed by motors, are fed by automatic feeders, and have ejectors to push out the printed sheet each time the press opens.

OFFSET AND GRAVURE PRESSES

Offset presses are similar in principle to cylinder presses. The printing plate is mounted on a cylinder. This is rolled against ink, then against a rubber cylinder on which the ink comes off. The rubber cylinder is then pressed against the paper (which is on still a third cylinder) and the paper is printed. Offset printing grew out of LITHOGRAPHY, about which there is a separate article. It has become most popular within the last sixty years. Offset printing is better for some kinds of work, especially for books in which there are many photographs. Though there are roll-fed offset presses as well as sheet-fed presses, the fastest offset presses are not as fast as the big rotary presses. The fastest offset presses may produce 7,000 to 10,000 printed sheets an hour, but seldom more.

Gravure presses, on the other hand, are very fast. The biggest roll-fed gravure presses, called *rotogravure* presses, are at least as fast as rotary letterpress presses and in many cases are even faster. It costs more to make the printing plates for gravure presses, so that they are seldom used unless a tremendous number

of copies must be printed. If there are several million copies to be printed, rotogravure is cheaper than other processes. Newspaper magazines such as the *American Weekly, This Week,* and *Parade* are printed by rotogravure.

In letterpress printing, a set of printing plates may last for a million or more copies. In offset printing the plates last for about 125,000 copies, but new plates are inexpensive. In gravure printing the plates last for millions of copies.

STEPS IN PRINTING

All printing begins with the setting of type. (There is a separate article about TYPESETTING.) In letterpress printing, when the type is set it is ready for printing, but if more than a few thousand copies are desired the type is made into plates that have the exact shape of the type but are made of harder metal and will last much longer. In offset or gravure printing, the type is first printed on a very fine, glossy paper, and the printed sheet of glossy paper is called a reproduction proof (or "repro proof"). This repro proof is photographed, and from the photograph the offset or gravure plate is made.

When type or printing plates are used, in the letterpress process, there are two additional steps known as *lock-up* and *makeready.* The type is locked up in *imposition,* which means that each part of the type is put into a place where it will print exactly where desired on the paper. (This is explained more fully in the article BOOK.) Locking up consists of putting the type in place in an iron frame called a *form,* or *chase,* and then tightening metal pieces called *quoins* that press against the type and keep it from slipping. Makeready consists of raising or lowering the type or the platen, depending on whether a heavy impression (much ink) or a light impression (very little ink) is wanted in that particular place.

A good pressman requires years of experience. Sometimes this is obtained through APPRENTICESHIP (about which there is a separate article), and sometimes it is learned in trade schools.

prism

A prism is a particular kind of solid figure, just as a ball (sphere) or a toy block (cube) is. There are many different kinds of prism, but in some ways they are all alike. Every prism has a top and bottom (called its *bases*) and while different prisms may have differently shaped bases, on any particular prism both bases are the same. The sides of the prism are flat, four-sided figures called *parallelograms.*

Prisms are very useful because when light passes through a clear prism it refracts (bends) in certain ways. Some prisms can make light turn sharply to one side or the other. Such prisms are used in binoculars. Other prisms break up light rays into different colors. Such prisms are used in SPECTROSCOPES, about which there is a separate article. Chandeliers hanging from a ceiling often have many little glass prisms on them. These prisms sparkle with the different colors into which they break up the light.

prison

A prison is a place where a person is kept for a certain length of time, as a form of punishment for some crime he has committed. (Persons who have not yet been brought to trial for crimes of which they are accused, and some persons who are needed as witnesses in trials or whose lives have been threatened, may also be kept in prison.)

Most prisons are surrounded by high, strong walls and guarded by armed guards to prevent prisoners from escaping. Inside the prison, the rooms are called cells and the windows and doors of the cells are made of strong iron bars. Persons who are put in prison are called prisoners. Their punishment is that they have little or no personal freedom.

The study of the treatment of prisoners is called *penology.* Scientific ideas of penology have changed a great deal in the last hundred years. At one time, prisons were intended for *retributive punishment,* which means making a person suffer because he has done wrong. Modern penologists believe in *corrective punishment,* or *rehabilitation,* which means treating a prisoner so that he will be anxious and able to lead a good life and be a useful citizen when the time he spends in prison (called his *term,* or his *sentence*) is ended.

A big prison, especially a prison of the United States government or a state institution, is usually called a penitentiary. A small prison is usually called a jail.

A prisoner in any kind of prison sleeps on a bunk with a hard pad or thin mattress, with a blanket in cold weather but no sheets. The prison day begins at 5:30 or 6 o'clock in the morning. All the prisoners in one part of the prison (called a cell block) leave their cells when the guards open the doors, and line up to be counted so that it can be made sure that no one has escaped. Then they march to breakfast. In most prisons, the prisoners are not allowed to talk to one another at meals.

After breakfast, all the prisoners go to the parts of the prison where they work. Prisons have laundries, machine shops, factory rooms where various things are made, libraries, hospitals, and other departments where work is needed. In the best prisons, the prisoners learn a useful trade if they do not already know one. There is time off from work for the midday meal, for some exercise in the prison yard, and at times for sports and entertainments. After supper, the men are marched back to their cells, counted again, and locked up for the night.

About 150 years ago, people could be put in prison and kept there for a long time because they could not pay their debts, or because they were wanderers without jobs or homes, or for various other reasons. In modern countries, a person is not put in prison unless he has been tried in court and convicted of crime. Even so, there is always some criticism of prison conditions—bad food, cruel treatment, and so on—and occasionally the prisoners rebel and start a riot that may lead to the injury or killing of guards or other innocent persons.

prisoner of war

As long as there have been wars, there have been prisoners taken in war. In ancient times prisoners were taken only to make slaves of them (or, in a very few cases, those who had rich families were held for ransom). Other captured men were put to death. In the last five hundred years, as slavery vanished and nations became more civilized, it has become customary to keep captured enemy men in prison camps and perhaps make them work or exchange them for prisoners taken by the enemy. At the end of the war, prisoners are usually released.

The "law" governing the treatment of prisoners of war is an international agreement made in 1899 at Geneva, Switzerland, and called the Geneva Convention. Changes were made in 1929. The important parts of the Geneva Convention are: Prisoners may not be punished merely for having fought against their captives. Enlisted men may be made to work reasonable hours, but must be given some payment and may not be abused. Officers cannot be made to work and must receive the regular pay given to officers of their rank by the country holding them. Prisoners must receive sufficient food and medical care and must be allowed to attend church services. The government holding a prisoner must inform his country that he is being held, must allow him to receive and send mail, and must allow a relief group such as the Red Cross to visit him and give him packages.

HOW THE LAW HAS WORKED

Millions of prisoners were taken in World Wars I and II. Generally the Geneva Convention was observed fairly well, but a country fighting a war is likely to break any law at all to increase its chances of winning. Also, in every war there is usually at least one country that does not have enough food for its own people and armed forces, and such a country seldom gives its prisoners enough to eat. In both World Wars, Germany also had a labor shortage and used its millions of prisoners (chiefly Russians) as forced laborers. In the bitterest fighting of World War II, both Germans and Russians killed many prisoners because they could not spare transportation to carry them to prisons, or men to guard them. Some hundreds of thousands of prisoners taken by the Russians were not released after the war but were kept as forced laborers (called "slave labor") for years afterward. American and Philippine prisoners taken by Japan in the early days of World War II were often treated brutally (as you can read in the article on BATAAN), but prisoners taken later were usually treated properly. United Nations prisoners taken by the North Koreans and Chinese Communists during the Korean fighting were given too little food and medical care, so that many of them died.

The United States has always taken many prisoners who surrender willingly because they know they will be well treated. In the Revolutionary War, General George Washington invited the Hessian troops fighting for the British to desert and become American farmers, and many of them did. In World War I many Germans surrendered to the United States because they were not getting

enough to eat in the German Army. In the Korean fighting, many North Koreans deserted and became prisoners willingly because they had been forced to fight and preferred the South Korean government.

BRAIN-WASHING

The Communists have developed a kind of treatment called "brain-washing" that is a form of torture and yet is not applied to the body. They talk to the prisoner hour after hour, allowing him little or no sleep and hardly any food. The purpose of the talk is to make the prisoner admit that his country is in the wrong and that he and others have committed crimes. Many men break down under this treatment and are willing to admit or do almost anything.

privateer, a private ship, or its commander, that is paid to attack the vessels of a certain country: see the article PIRATE AND PRIVATEER.

privet

The privet is a shrub that is grown for making hedges. It is a member of the olive family. Some privets are evergreens and do not lose all their smooth green leaves in the fall. The privet has small white flowers that have a sweet smell. It has small black berries that stay on the shrub all winter. Sometimes the berries of the privet are yellow, green, or white. They are about as large as peas and have a bitter taste. Birds are fond of the privet berry.

Privy Council

The Privy Council is a group of honorary officials appointed by the king or queen of Great Britain. In the days before the Parliament became powerful in Great Britain, the king or queen ruled the country and the Privy Council was composed of the ruler's principal advisers. The Cabinet was a committee chosen from among the privy councillors. Now the Cabinet controls the government, but Cabinet members are almost always members of the Privy Council.

prize fighting, a contest for money in the sport of boxing: see the article BOXING.

Progressive Party

There have been several political parties in the United States called the Progressive Party. The first of these was formed in 1912, when a group in the Republican Party refused to support President William Howard Taft for a second term. They held their own convention as the Progressive Party and nominated Theodore Roosevelt for President. This split the vote of the Republican Party, and Woodrow Wilson, the Democratic candidate, won the election. When Theodore Roosevelt refused the nomination in 1916, the Progressive Party disbanded.

Another Progressive Party was formed in 1924 by a group under the leadership of Robert M. LaFollette (about whom there is a separate article). LaFollette was nominated for President and he polled almost five million votes. This Progressive Party continued until 1946, when it voted to join the Republican Party.

The name Progressive Party was used by an entirely different party in 1948. Henry A. Wallace was its candidate for the Presidency. The party drew a large vote, but it was widely recognized as being controlled or at least influenced by Communists. For this reason, many voters who approved of many of Wallace's policies refused to vote for him. In 1950 Wallace himself resigned from the Progressive Party because of Communist influence on it.

Prohibition

The evil of alcoholic liquor when it is used to excess has been recognized almost as long as alcohol has been known. Millions of people have felt that the way to overcome this evil was to stop all drinking of alcoholic beverages. Among the most prominent groups to hold this belief have been the Women's Christian Temperance Union and the Anti-Saloon League. For many years they urged the states and Congress to pass laws that would make it illegal to drink alcoholic liquor, but the United States Constitution did not allow this because it would restrict the personal liberty of the people. Then, in 1919, Congress passed the 18th Amendment to the Constitution, forbidding the manufacture, sale and transportation of intoxicating liquors in the United States and all its territories. A law was proposed by Andrew Volstead and passed by Congress, providing for the enforcement of this amendment. The Volstead Act went into effect January 16, 1920.

From the beginning, this act was hard to enforce. Persons called "bootleggers" continued to get and sell liquor and people continued to buy it. A lot of this illegal liquor was bad, and some of it was poisonous. Bootlegging became a big criminal industry, and there were many gang wars in which gangsters and innocent people were killed.

In 1931 President Hoover appointed a group called the Wickersham Commission to look into the whole matter of Prohibition, which he called a "noble experiment." The commission in its report favored keeping Prohibition, but more and more people thought the 18th Amendment should be repealed, or called off. In 1932, when Franklin D. Roosevelt ran for President, one of the policies he said he would follow if he was elected was to stop Prohibition. After he won, Congress and the states did repeal the 18th Amendment, in 1933.

Prokofiev, Serge

Serge Prokofiev was a Russian composer, or writer of music. He is best remembered in the United States for two of his works, *Peter and the Wolf* and the *Classical Symphony*. Prokofiev was born in 1891. His mother was his first music teacher, and by the time he was 6 years old he was writing music. When he was 13 he composed a four-act opera.

Later Prokofiev traveled in Europe. He lived in Paris, France, for some years, and there he wrote an opera, *The Love of Three Oranges,* for the Chicago Opera Company, and the *Classical Symphony*. He returned to Russia in 1934. For a time Prokofiev was in high favor with the Soviet government, and he won the Stalin Prize for one of his piano sonatas. Later

he was accused of writing in "Western style," which the Communists considered bad, but he apologized and promised not to do it again. Prokofiev died in 1953.

Prometheus

Prometheus was a hero in Greek mythology, the stories the ancient Greeks told about their gods and goddesses. Prometheus stole fire from heaven and gave it as a present to mankind. This made the gods very angry. Zeus, the king of all the gods (he is called Jupiter in Roman mythology), chained Prometheus to a rock, as a punishment. Each day a vulture devoured the liver of Prometheus and each night it grew back again.

Prometheus could have brought this terrible fate to an end by telling Zeus certain secrets that Zeus wanted to know, but Prometheus would not do this. For this reason, he has stood for courage and strength and determination. Finally the hero Heracles (Hercules) killed the vulture and set Prometheus free.

One of the best-known plays of the great Greek playwright Aeschylus was called *Prometheus Bound.* The English poet Shelley wrote one of his finest poems about the legend, calling it *Prometheus Unbound.*

pronghorn

The pronghorn is an animal that makes its home in the western part of the United States and in some parts of Canada and Mexico. It looks somewhat like a deer. The male is about three feet high and weighs more than 100 pounds. The female is a little smaller. The pronghorn has a reddish-brown coat of thick hair, and its back part is white. The hairs are hollow and contain a substance that helps to keep the pronghorn warm in very cold weather. The pronghorn gets its name from its horns, which are fork-shaped. It grows new horns every year.

The pronghorn is one of the swiftest animals of the United States. It can run almost a mile a minute. Pronghorns eat grass and roots.

pronoun

A pronoun is a word that stands for a person or thing that has some other name. *I, he, she, it, they,* and other forms of these words are pronouns, because they take the place of other words. For example, *he* might stand for *man* or for *John Smith* and *it* might stand for *table* or *bird.* Pronouns make speech easier and less monotonous. Instead of having to say, "When John Smith arrived, John Smith ate," you can say, "When John Smith arrived, he ate."

A word such as *who* or *which,* in a sentence such as "I saw the man who was walking down the street," is called a *relative* (connecting) pronoun. A word such as *this* or *that,* in a sentence such as "This is my hat," is called a *demonstrative* (pointing out) *pronoun.*

Pronouns are among the few words in the English language that have many *inflections* (changes in form). For example, *me, my* and *mine* are inflected forms of the pronoun *I.*

propaganda

Propaganda is information that a government or organization gives out when it wants the general public to have

certain beliefs or ideas. Usually propaganda is used to give people false ideas, but this is not always so. The famous novel *Uncle Tom's Cabin,* written by Harriet Beecher Stowe about a hundred years ago, was propaganda intended to make people believe that slavery was wrong, and most people believed then and believe now that slavery is wrong. The government of Germany, when it was controlled by the Nazi Party from 1933 to 1945, used propaganda to make the German people believe they had been treated unfairly and should go to war, and these were false ideas.

The professions called public relations and advertising use what are considered respectable forms of propaganda. Every political party uses propaganda before an election. A country at war always uses propaganda to convince its citizens that they are in the right and that the enemy is wrong. Propaganda consists of posters, radio and television shows, motion pictures, and stories in newspapers, magazines, and books. In wartime, a country may send airplanes over enemy country to drop leaflets urging the enemy people not to fight. Radio programs are sent to enemy countries in wartime and to unfriendly countries in peacetime, often to weaken the people's confidence in their own government and try to persuade them to start a revolution. All propaganda tells only one side of the question. See the article on PUBLIC RELATIONS.

propeller

A propeller is a device with blades that can push air or water backward, which causes an airplane or ship to move forward. A propeller is a kind of screw. In fact, a ship's propeller is called a screw and in England the correct name for an airplane propeller is an air screw.

A propeller can be put either in back or in front. When it is in front it is called a *tractor,* and when it is in back it is called a *pusher.* Usually it is found in the front of an airplane and in the back of a ship. However, the first plane to fly under its own power, built by the Wright brothers in 1903, had the propellers behind. Where the propeller is makes no difference in the way it works, as long as it pushes the air or water backward.

A propeller consists of two or more blades with a hub at the center. The hub is turned by the driveshaft of the engine. The size of the circle made by the blades in turning is the *diameter* of the propeller. The *leading edge* of the blade is the one that strikes the air or water first as the propeller turns around. The other edge is the *trailing edge.* The *tip* is the end of the blade away from the hub. The leading edge is usually farther forward than the trailing edge. The way the blade is slanted determines the *angle* of the propeller. The angle is greater near the hub than at the tip because the hub moves more slowly and therefore needs to cut through a greater chunk of air. The blade is also thicker at the hub, because it has to be stronger there.

The angle of the blade determines the *pitch* of the propeller. The pitch is the distance the propeller will advance through the air or water in one complete turn (revolution). The greater the angle of the blades, the greater the pitch. When the blades are almost flat, the propeller is in low pitch; when the blades are at a considerable angle, it is in high pitch. At high pitch the propeller bites off a bigger chunk of air or water and moves a greater distance forward with each revolution.

For a take-off, a fairly low-pitched airplane propeller is desirable. The engine must be able to turn the propeller fast enough so that it can develop its full power. Once the plane is moving faster, a higher pitch is desirable. To accomplish this, the *variable pitch* propeller was developed. The blades are mounted on the hub in such a way that they can be twisted during flight, changing the pitch of the propeller.

Many multi-engine planes have *full-feathering* propellers. This means that the blades can be twisted beyond the ordinary highest pitch, so far that the leading edge is pointing directly forward. In this position the propeller cannot be turned by the moving air stream. A propeller is put in this position in case of trouble with one engine. If the air stream is allowed to turn the propeller when the engine is not running, the engine may be ruined.

Some propellers are designed so that the blades can be adjusted far enough to give *negative pitch*—to try to move the plane backward. These are useful in maneuvering large multi-engine planes on the ground or water, and are used as brakes after landing.

Originally all propellers had two blades and were carved out of wood, usually *laminated,* that is, made up of thin layers of wood glued together, which gives more strength than a solid piece of wood. Light planes still use propellers of this kind. For large engines, most blades now are solid aluminum alloy or hollow steel.

To make a propeller more powerful, three things can be done: the diameter can be increased; the blades can be made wider; or more blades can be used. Two-bladed propellers used to be universal. Now there are at least three blades on all large propellers and four blades on many of them. In a six-blade dual-rotation propeller, there is one three-bladed propeller rotating in one direction. Close in front of this is another three-bladed propeller rotating in the other direction. The driveshaft of the front propeller runs inside the driveshaft of the back one. Both shafts are driven by the engine. Though the propellers turn in different directions, the blades are made so that they drive the air in the same direction.

In a boat, it often is necessary to back up. This is done by reversing the direction in which the propeller turns.

prophet

A prophet is a person who speaks for God or for a deity. (A deity is any of the gods worshiped by people who believe in more than one god.) Sometimes prophets foretell the future, but more often they recommend action for the present, that is, they tell people how to be holy.

In the Old Testament there are many books of prophets. These are the books of Isaiah, Jeremiah, and Ezekiel (the Major Prophets), and of Hosea, Joel, Amos, Obadiah, Jonah, Micah, Nahum, Habakkuk, Zephaniah, Haggai, Zachariah, and Malachi (the Minor Prophets). There are other Old Testament prophets, including Daniel and Elijah.

The writings of the Major and Minor Prophets are mostly concerned with how men act. Amos, who wrote more than eight hundred years before Jesus was born, is a good example. In his brief book, he tells the Jewish rulers that they are leading the people away from God, and that they are unjust to the poor. Then he warns that unless they mend their ways, the Lord will destroy their kingdom.

People also find predictions for the future in reading the works of the prophets. Christians see many predictions about Jesus in the prophetic books of the Old Testament, especially in the Book of Isaiah. Other prophetic books predict political events that may not have happened yet. The Book of Daniel is often read for its political prophecies.

proportional representation

Proportional representation is a system of electing the members of a law-making body. Its purpose is to have as many groups of people as possible represented in the lawmaking body. This can be done if a certain number of votes is needed to elect a member. This number is fixed, so it does not matter if a candidate for election has more votes than his opponent; if he has the required number of votes, he is elected. It is done in the following way. The voter gets a ballot that lists all the candidates. He then puts down which candidate is his first choice, which is his second choice, and so on. As soon as the candidate who was the voter's first choice has the required number of votes, the votes for him are no longer counted. Instead, the vote goes to the candidate who was the voter's second choice, and so on.

Proportional representation is used in all elections in France, Italy, and some other nations. In the United States the system has been tried in New York City, Cincinnati, and other cities, but has not proved popular and most cities that have tried it have given it up.

prose, the writing of a language in the way that it is generally spoken without the rhyme or meter used in poetry: see the article LITERATURE.

proteins

Proteins are the basic substances from which all living matter is made. Proteins are necessary for building body tissues, muscles, bones, cartilage (connecting tissue), and skin. More than one-half of the dry matter of the body is protein (the rest is fats and carbohydrates). A person weighing 100 pounds has about 18 pounds of protein in his body. About 8 pounds of that is in the muscles, 3 pounds in the bones and cartilage, and 2 pounds in the skin. The other 5 pounds are distributed throughout the body in such substances as enzymes, needed for digestion and other chemical changes in the body; hormones, produced by the endocrine glands needed by the tissues; and antibodies of the blood that defend the body against disease.

All proteins contain carbon, hydrogen, oxygen, and nitrogen. Some also contain sulfur and phosphorus. The basic substances of the proteins are the amino acids, of which there are 22 different kinds. Different combinations of these acids produce the different kinds of protein.

The three most important proteins are *myosin,* found in muscles; *collagen,* found in bones and cartilage; and *keratin,* found in skin.

Because the body needs protein to remain healthy, it is wise to eat a serving of some protein-containing food at least twice a day. Chicken, milk, cheese, lean meat, fish, eggs, navy beans and liver are good protein foods.

Protestant

A Protestant belongs to a Christian Church that is not called "Catholic." More than four hundred years ago (in 1529) a German priest named Martin Luther left the Roman Catholic Church because he protested against (objected to) some teachings of the Church. His followers came to be called Protestants (persons who protest). All the Churches that are now called Protestant grew out of that movement.

There are other Christian churches that are separate from the Roman Catholic Church but are not called Protestants. The largest of these is the Eastern Orthodox Church. Its members are often called "Orthodox Catholics." The Church of England was one of the first Protestant Churches (and Protestant Episcopal Churches through the world are allied with it), but many members of the Church of England call themselves Anglo-Catholics.

There are many Protestant groups or denominations. Though each group has some beliefs and practices of its own, the different groups have many beliefs in common. They do not recognize the authority of the Pope, the religious leader of the Roman Catholic Church. Most of them believe that each man must decide for himself what the Bible means.

There are about 217,000,000 Protestants throughout the world. Of these, 64,434,966 live in the United States, where almost six out of ten church members are Protestants. They belong to 228 different denominations. In recent years, many Protestants have felt that there are too many denominations, and in 1938 a group of Protestant Churches organized the World Council of Churches. The council meets to discuss different ways of working together, and ways in which they could unite some or all of the various denominations. Several notable mergers have taken place as a result of their activity.

The period in which Protestantism began is called the Reformation because many early Protestant leaders said their purpose was to reform the Catholic Church.

Proteus

Proteus was a character in Greek mythology, the stories the ancient Greeks told about their gods and goddesses. He was an old man who was the favorite of Poseidon, the god of the sea. (The ancient Romans called this god Neptune.)

Proteus took care of the sea calves that belonged to Poseidon. He had a wonderful gift of prophecy and could see into the future and tell exactly what would happen. But Proteus did not like to do this, and anyone who wanted to know the future had to catch Proteus and hold him fast. This was very difficult because Proteus could change himself into any shape he pleased. He could become a fierce lion or a terrible dragon or a roaring fire. If the person was brave and held Proteus fast, then he would turn into his real shape and foretell the future.

protoplasm

Protoplasm is a jellylike or clear grayish material from which all living things are made. It is made up mostly of proteins and water. Fatty substances and sugars and starches, called carbohydrates, also are contained in protoplasm.

Protoplasm exists in plants and animals in small units called *cells.* Each cell has a round, darker and thicker piece of protoplasm inside it. This is called a *nucleus.*

The protoplasm in plants and animals enables them to live. It takes in food and from that food makes all the chemicals that they need. It also makes more protoplasm from the food. In growing, the protoplasm of the nucleus splits into two parts to form new cells.

Protoplasm is a kind of COLLOID, about which there is a separate article.

protozoa

Protozoa are tiny one-celled animals, so small that they can be seen only with a microscope. They are found mostly in water and in the soil, but some protozoa live in the bodies of other animals. There are about 15,000 different kinds of protozoa. The AMEBA, about which there is a separate article, is one kind. Some protozoa cause diseases such as malaria, Texas fever, and African sleeping sickness.

Many different kinds of protozoa are found in stagnant water. They make such water smell and taste bad.

Proust, Marcel

Marcel Proust was a famous French writer. He is best known for his seven-volume novel, *Remembrance of Things Past,* which took him seventeen years to write. Proust was born in 1871 in Paris, France, the only son of a rich, noble family. He was sickly in his youth, suffering from asthma, so he studied with private tutors. In 1896 he published a book of short stories, *Pleasures and Regrets.* Then, when he was 34 years old, Proust withdrew from all his friends and shut himself up in a room to write. After a few years his work became very successful, and in 1919 he won the Goncourt Prize. Proust died in 1922. In his book he tells the story of his own life and of France during his lifetime. Also, he gives his ideas on art, religion, and philosophy.

Provence

Provence is a region in southwestern France. It is noted for its beauty and for its history and traditions. Provence is on the Mediterranean Sea. In most of the region the soil is very fertile. Grapes,

fruits, olives, flowers, vegetables and mulberry trees (for silkworms) are grown there.

In another part of Provence there are the Maritime Alps, and there the soil is barren.

The chief cities of Provence are Marseilles, Toulon, Cannes and Nice on the coast, and Avignon, Arles, Nîmes and Aix-en-Provence in the interior. Many of them were founded by the Romans almost two thousand years ago.

The language of Provence is called Provencal. It is one of the two main branches of the French language.

The climate of Provence is dry and mild. The coast, or Riviera, is the most famous vacation spot in the world. In fall and winter there is often a cold, dry wind from the north, called the *mistral.*

IN THE PAST

Provence was settled more than 2,000 years ago by the ancient Greeks, who set up colonies along the coast. A few hundred years later the Romans established colonies there, and built many towns and roads. Most of an aqueduct that was built by the Romans near the town of Avignon is still standing. For hundreds of years Provence was divided into sections ruled by various noblemen, but for the last five hundred years it has been part of France.

Proverbs

Proverbs is a book of the Old Testament, in the Bible. It is a collection of short sayings that give advice for acting wisely. Every country has its own proverbs, and some of those in the Book of Proverbs are taken from ones composed in Egypt. The Biblical writer who collected these proverbs says that they were written by Solomon, because the proverbs teach wisdom and Solomon had a reputation as a wise man. The book includes (in chapter 31) a famous poem in praise of a good wife. The collection was probably made about 350 years before Jesus was born, but many of the proverbs are much older.

Providence

Providence is the capital and largest city of Rhode Island. It is on Providence Bay, on the Atlantic Ocean, and is an important port. More than 200,000 people live in Providence. They work in factories that make jewelry, silverware, cloth, petroleum products, and many other things. The city has many old churches and buildings, several of which were built during colonial days. Providence also has a number of fine parks, including Roger Williams Park, named after the founder of the city. It has many historic buildings, libraries, and monuments. There are several universities, including Brown University and Providence College. Adjoining Providence is Pawtucket, also a busy manufacturing city.

Providence was founded by Roger Williams in 1636. He had been forced to leave Massachusetts because of his religious beliefs and, moving south, he obtained a large grant of land from the friendly Indians. He set up a colony where people could have religious freedom. He named it for "God's merciful providence." The little colony grew, but

it did not become a city until 1831. It became important for its metal work and silverware. For a time it was one of the two capitals of Rhode Island (Newport was the other) but in 1900 it became the only capital of the state.

PROVIDENCE, RHODE ISLAND. Population (1970 census) 179,213. Capital of Rhode Island. Settled, 1636.

province

Provinces are the main divisions of Canada and some other countries, as states are in the United States. Canada is divided into ten provinces and two territories. Each province has its own legislature and a Lieutenant Governor who is appointed by the Canadian government. The Lieutenant Governor has a cabinet of ministers headed by a premier, who is the leader of the political party that has a majority in the legislature. This cabinet holds the real executive power of the province. In all the provinces except Quebec, the legislature has only one house, the Assembly, the members of which are elected for four-year terms. In Quebec there is an upper house called the Legislative Council, whose members are appointed for life by the provincial government. The Governor General of Canada may disallow (veto) certain laws passed by a provincial legislature, and the Lieutenant Governor of a province may hold such a law until it has the approval of the Governor General.

proxy

A proxy is a person who casts a vote for another person. It is also the official piece of paper that a person signs when he gives someone else the right to cast his vote. In most big businesses, which are corporations owned by stockholders, each stockholder signs a proxy before the meeting of stockholders and lets someone else vote for him at that meeting. If it were not for the proxy system, the biggest companies could not operate. Many of them have several hundred thousand stockholders and not all could attend the same meeting.

You cannot give someone else a proxy to vote for you in a meeting in which you have personal responsibility. For example, a Congressman cannot give another Congressman a proxy, and a director of a corporation cannot give another director a proxy. You can give a proxy only when it is your property and not your personal duty that gives you the right to vote.

At times there are two or more groups that want to control a big company, and then they have a "proxy fight." Each side publishes advertisements and sends agents to all the stockholders to ask for their proxies. The side that gets the most proxies usually wins the election and controls the company.

A stockholder in a corporation can give proxies to any number of different people. The one he gives last is the one that counts.

prune

The prune is a plum that has been dried in a special way. Plums that have a large amount of sugar are used to make prunes. The plums are picked very carefully and the skin of the fruit is broken to help them dry out. The drying is usually done in the hot sun, but sometimes prunes are dried by fire. When the prunes are dry they are heated in boiling water that is mixed with certain substances to make the skins clean and shiny.

Prussia

Before Germany became one country, in 1871, it was made up of several separate kingdoms. The largest and most powerful of these kingdoms was Prussia, which occupied more than half of all Germany.

In Prussia were most of the principal cities of Germany, including its capital, Berlin, the largest German city, and also Cologne, Breslau, Essen, Frankfurt-on-Main, Düsseldorf, Halle, and Hanover. Prussia was the most important manufacturing section of Germany, though it did not have the biggest steel mills and coal mines. Prussia was also a prosperous farming region.

After World War I, the Polish Corridor, a section given to Poland, cut East Prussia off from the rest of Prussia. After World War II, Prussia (like the rest of Germany) was divided into four zones to be occupied by Allied troops. In 1947 the Allied Control Council, which was then the governing body of Germany, declared that Prussia no longer existed as a separate state.

The early Prussians were a Germanic people from farther north. They were conquered and converted to Christianity by the Teutonic Knights, a German military and religious group, more than seven hundred years ago. More than two hundred years later, Prussia was partly controlled by Poland. After a long time it gradually came under the control of the Elector (king) of Brandenburg, a member of the Hohenzollern family, and about 250 years ago it became independent.

Under Frederick II, who lived about two hundred years ago, Prussia became a strong military state. It conquered or absorbed a number of other provinces and greatly increased its size. In 1871 the King of Prussia, William I, was made the German emperor, largely through the efforts of the Prussian statesman Otto von BISMARCK, about whom there is a separate article. In 1918, at the end of World War I, Prussia became part of the German republic. See the article on GERMANY.

Psalms

The Book of Psalms is a book of the Old Testament, made up of 150 religious songs or hymns. They were written to be sung in the Jewish temple. Some of them were probably written by King David. Because of their great beauty, the Psalms are still sung in Christian churches and in Jewish synagogues. They are also considered to be among the world's most perfect lyric poems.

Psyche, a beautiful maiden in Greek mythology who represented the human soul. See the article on CUPID AND PSYCHE.

psychiatry

A psychiatrist is a doctor who specializes in treating people who are mentally ill or disturbed, and the branch of medicine that he practices is called psychiatry. Until about two hundred years ago psychiatry was not recognized as a branch of medicine, though doctors had been trying to cure mental illnesses for more than two thousand years.

At one time, most people thought that mental disturbances were caused by things outside of the mind, such as the anger of the gods, or the moon. Doctors knew that injury to the brain could cause some mental illnesses, but still they knew very little. They could almost never cure a mental illness. People whose mental conditions made them dangerous were put in "asylums" that were like prisons.

About 150 years ago, a French doctor called Philippe Pinel said it was wrong to treat mental patients as criminals. He made many improvements in mental hospitals in France. At about the same time, in the early 1800s, the Philadelphia doctor Benjamin Rush began to be interested in this problem. Many people call him the father of American psychiatry.

During the next hundred years, more and more doctors studied the causes of mental illness and tried to find ways of treating these illnesses. They found that not only injuries and germ diseases but also disturbing experiences could cause mental illnesses. The greatest advances in psychiatry were made by a doctor named Sigmund Freud, in Vienna, Austria. He showed how a person can be mentally ill from experiences of which he is not even conscious—that he never knew occurred. Freud also developed new methods of treating mentally ill persons. One of them is PSYCHOANALYSIS, about which there is a separate article.

Freud had a great deal of influence on other doctors who studied mental illness. Some of these men were Alfred Adler, Carl Jung, John B. Watson, and William MacDougall.

The treatment of any mental disturbance is called *psychotherapy*. Psychoanalysis is only one of many important methods of treatment. Another is *shock therapy*, in which a patient is made to undergo shock by giving him drugs or by mechanical methods. *Psychosurgery* is operating on the brain to cure bodily causes of mental illness.

See also the articles on MENTAL ILLNESS and PSYCHOLOGY.

psychoanalysis

Psychoanalysis is a way of treating people who are mentally ill or disturbed. Often it is called simply "analysis." It was developed by the psychiatrist Sigmund FREUD, about whom there is a separate article.

In psychoanalysis, the patient is made comfortable (often lying on a couch) and is encouraged to talk about anything that comes into his mind. One idea leads to another, a process called "free association," and soon the patient will talk about things that he remembers from far in the past. The psychoanalyst (the doctor who is giving the treatment) listens carefully but says very little except perhaps to ask a question that will help the patient to go on talking. The patient visits the psychoanalyst regularly, perhaps several times a week, and the treatment may go on for years. If the treatment is

successful, the patient may recall to his conscious mind old experiences that have been troubling him without his knowing it. When he knows and understands these experiences they are likely to stop troubling him and he will be well again.

psychology

Psychology is the study of the human mind and why people think and act as they do. Until about a hundred years ago, psychology was considered a branch of another science (philosophy), but now it is a separate science. In some ways it is related to psychiatry, the medical science that deals with mental illnesses and disturbances.

Psychologists have many jobs today that did not exist until this century. Many schools and colleges have psychologists to help the students solve their problems. Many big companies have psychologists to keep their employees contented and to advise the management on how the public might like certain products, advertising campaigns, selling methods, and so on.

There are several important branches of psychology. *Applied psychology* deals with the attitudes and opinions of people on certain subjects. The *clinical psychologist* tries to help people who have emotional problems. *Child psychology* is an important branch of clinical psychology. *Educational psychology* deals with the guidance or counselling of people and uses intelligence tests and aptitude and achievement tests (see the article on INTELLIGENCE). Experimental psychologists study animals as well as human beings and have made discoveries of great value to psychologists who deal with human beings only. There are numerous other branches of psychology.

ptarmigan

The ptarmigan is a bird that lives in northern countries. It is a member of the grouse family. Like all grouse, it changes its colors with the seasons. In the summer the ptarmigan has black, brown, and white feathers. When the fall comes it changes to white feathers, so that it is well hidden as it scratches in the snow for the seeds and buds that it eats. The ptarmigan also eats fruit and insects.

Most ptarmigans are about the size of chickens. The white-tailed ptarmigan makes its home in the Rocky Mountains in the United States.

PT boat

A PT boat is a small vessel of the United States Navy. Its full name is Patrol Torpedo Craft, and it is also called *mosquito* because of its speed and small size. The PT boat is about 80 feet long and looks somewhat like a speedboat. It carries four torpedoes that are shot underwater through tubes, two 50-caliber machine guns, and sometimes depth bombs.

The PT boat has a speed of 50 to 85 miles an hour. It is manned by one officer and a crew of eight men. The PT boat was used during World War II, but has been largely replaced by vessels of newer design.

pterodactyl

The pterodactyl was a strange flying lizard that lived on the earth millions of years ago. It had a body like a lizard's and wings like a bat's. Some pterodactyls had a wingspread of more than two feet. Others were much smaller. The bones of the pterodactyl were strong and light. Some of the early varieties had strong teeth and long thin tails. Later they lost their tails and teeth and developed long pointed jaws that looked more like a bird's beak. Some pterodactyls were powerful fliers. Others were able to leap and soar through the air as flying squirrels do.

Ptolemy, a famous Egyptian scholar who lived more than 1,800 years ago. Little is known about his life, except that at one time he lived and taught in the city of Alexandria. See the article on ASTRONOMY.

ptomaine poisoning

Ptomaine poisoning, or food poisoning, is an illness that is caused when a person eats food that is spoiled or that contains germs of disease. Bacteria cause food to decay and the food may then become poisonous. Food that is not canned properly may become poisonous.

Some spoiled food tastes or smells bad, but this is not always true. A person may eat food that seems to be all right but actually is spoiled. A human being can die from food poisoning, or he may feel very sick for a short time. A person who thinks he has food poisoning should see a doctor immediately.

An Italian chemist gave the name "ptomaine" to certain substances that are formed when matter decays. That is how people came to call food poisoning "ptomaine poisoning." The name is not used so much now.

public relations

Public-relations work is one of the newest of the important professions. It is also called publicity work, but some experts say there is a great difference between public relations and publicity.

Publicity is anything that is written about a person or company in newspapers or magazines, and anything that is said about a person or company on radio or television or simply by people when they talk. Some people want as much publicity as possible. Actors and actresses, for example, are successful only when a lot of people know about them, and the more their names are mentioned the better-known they will be. Manufacturers of trademarked products want their products to be as well known as possible. Of course, they want good things and not bad things to be said about them or their products. The job of the public-relations man is to try to get "good publicity" for his client, the person or company that hires him.

A few clients of public-relations men want to keep their names out of the newspapers, and not to be very well known. In such a case, the public-relations man does his work by not getting publicity for his client.

Public-relations work is very important in politics. Before any election, each political party has a large staff of men and women working on publicity for its candidates.

The public-relations man works mostly by helping the people who write for newspapers, magazines, radio, television, and other "media" through which his client's name may be mentioned. It pays him to help these writers, because then he can advise them to say good things about his client. Public-relations men also give advice, or counsel, to their clients. If the client is a candidate in an election and is going to make a speech, the public-relations man may warn him against saying things that the public will not like, and suggest things that the public will approve of. If the client is a manufacturer who is putting out a new product, the public-relations man may advise him on how the public will like certain names for it.

For this reason, people in public-relations work are often called public-relations counselors. A man named Ivy Lee was the first public-relations counselor, and he invented the name for the profession in 1916. At that time, John D. Rockefeller had made himself the richest man in the world by controlling the biggest oil companies in the world but he was unpopular with the public. He arranged for Ivy Lee to represent him in his public relations. Lee made the public hear about the many millions of dollars that Rockefeller had spent to advance science and education and for charitable purposes, and after a few years the name Rockefeller was no longer unpopular.

Today, nearly every big company pays some public-relations firm to represent it, and most big companies have public-relations staffs of their own. Political parties, motion-picture studios, and other firms that depend on publicity have departments constantly at work on their public relations. Most advertising agencies have public-relations branches to serve their clients.

Experience as a newspaperman is very useful to a person who wants to make a career of public relations. Work on magazines or in radio or television is also useful. Another way to start is in a minor job in some public-relations office, where you can learn by seeing how the experienced members of the firm handle their work.

public utility

A public utility is a company that furnishes to the public such things as gas and electricity, water, telephone service, and certain kinds of transportation, such as buses. In some cases cities have provided such services for themselves and the city owns and operates the equipment. In most cases the people of the city did not want to put up the money that was necessary, and a private company would put up the money. Then the city would give the company a *franchise,* or license to run the business, and would agree not to give the same franchise to anybody else.

As a result of the franchise system, public utilities grew into a tremendous power in the United States representing companies worth billions of dollars. From time to time there has been a lot of political argument about the rights of these companies. When the United States government formed the Tennessee Valley Authority (the TVA), a government corporation that sells electric power,

some people complained that it violated the rights of private companies. Other people argued that there should be no public utilities, that the government should own them all. But the public utility companies have remained among the richest, most powerful and most efficient companies in the United States.

publishing, the business of putting writing into the form of a book or magazine or newspaper: see the article BOOK.

Puccini, Giacomo

Giacomo Puccini was an Italian composer who wrote some of the most popular operas ever produced. Many of them are performed almost every year, but he is best remembered for *Madame Butterfly, La Bohéme,* and *Tosca.* Puccini was born in 1858 of a family of noted musicians. He became an accomplished pianist and organist. His first opera was produced in 1884 and was well received, but his real fame came with the performance of *Manon Lescaut,* in 1893. Puccini placed the scenes of his operas in many different countries. *Madame Butterfly* takes place in Japan, *La Bohéme* and *Manon Lescaut* in France, and *Tosca* in Italy. The Metropolitan Opera Company commissioned Puccini to write an opera on an American theme, and in 1910 Puccini came to the United States for the first performance of *The Girl of the Golden West.* Puccini's last opera, which he did not finish, was *Turandot,* based on an old Chinese legend. It was not performed until two years after his death in 1924.

Pueblo Indians

When the Spaniards arrived in what is now New Mexico, about the year 1540, they found tribes of Indians living in what looked like six-story apartment houses built of stone or adobe (sun-dried clay). They called these Indians *Pueblo Indians* because the word *pueblo* means "village" in the Spanish language. The Zuni and the Hopi tribes are among the best-known of the Pueblo Indians. The Pueblos live in New Mexico, Arizona, and southern Utah and Colorado.

The Pueblo dwellings were built in little groups around a court. Each floor of the Pueblo building was narrower than the one below it and the apartments on each floor were set back from the front to form a sort of terrace. Ladders, which could be removed in case of an attack by other Indians, were used to get from one floor to another. The buildings were controlled and built by the women.

Although he hunted deer and rabbits, the Pueblo Indian was mostly a farmer and raised corn, beans, squash, and cotton. He knew how to irrigate his field with water from nearby rivers. The Pueblo Indians were fine basketmakers and could also make excellent clay pottery. They raised turkeys and kept eagles for their feathers. They could spin and weave cotton into cloth before the Spaniards came. The Spaniards introduced sheep and wool-weaving became important. The Pueblo men do the weaving.

Each village was ruled by an elected council. Their religion is very complicated and has many priests. Much of their religion concerns the rain god. The Hopi Indians are famous for their snake dance,

which they perform to make their god grant rain for the crops. Live rattlesnakes are sprinkled with corn and carried around by the dancers in their mouths.

There are about 20,000 Pueblo Indians in the United States.

Puerto Rico

Puerto Rico is an island in the West Indies between the Atlantic Ocean and the Caribbean Sea. It became a Territory of the United States more than fifty years ago, but since 1952 it has been largely self-governing. Puerto Rico is 3,435 square miles in size and over two and a half million people live there. For its size, the island is one of the most crowded areas in the world.

THE PEOPLE OF PUERTO RICO

Most of the people of Puerto Rico are of Spanish descent and of mixed Spanish and Negro blood. Many are darker in complexion than most North Americans. There are also many Negroes.

The island does not grow enough crops to feed all its own people, and in the past many Puerto Ricans have been very poor. Poverty caused many of them to leave the island. Most often they settled in New York City. In recent years a large-scale program has greatly improved the people's living conditions. Manufacturing has become the most important source of income. In the new factories the workers make clothing, electrical equipment, and plastic products. Also there are tobacco factories and sugar mills. But most of the people of Puerto Rico are still farmers. They grow sugar cane, tobacco, coffee, and bananas and other fruits.

The language of the people is Spanish, but English is taught in all the schools and many Puerto Ricans can speak some English. Almost all belong to the Roman Catholic Church.

WHAT PUERTO RICO IS LIKE

Puerto Rico is a mountainous island. There are large sugar plantations on the plains along the coast. Coffee and tobacco are grown in the central part of the island. Although Puerto Rico does not have large forests, it has many high palm trees. The palms are used to make many products, such as straw hats, furniture, and baskets. The island is beautiful, has a warm and pleasant tropical climate, and is a popular winter vacation spot. Many fine hotels and resorts have been built for visitors.

Puerto Rico has few large cities. The

most important is San Juan, the capital and largest city, with a population (in 1972) of about 441,000.

Puerto Rico discontinued its railroad, but there are many highways, and airlines and boats connect the island with the rest of the world.

THE GOVERNMENT OF PUERTO RICO

Puerto Rico is called a commonwealth. The governor is elected by the people for a four-year term. The laws of Puerto Rico are made by a Legislature composed of two houses, a Senate and a House of Representatives. The members of both houses are elected for four-year terms. The courts are ruled by United States laws. All Puerto Ricans over 21 years old may vote.

Everyone has to go to school through elementary school at least, but there are not enough schools or teachers and many children get little education.

The most important university is the University of Puerto Rico, at Rio Piedras. In 1972 it had about 43,000 students.

PUERTO RICO IN THE PAST

The island was discovered by Christopher Columbus on his second voyage to

Gov't of Puerto Rico Photo
A Puerto Rican fisherman casts his net. He catches a dozen sardines in a single toss.

the New World, more than 400 years ago. The first settlement was made by Spaniards in 1508. For a time the white settlers got along well with the native Indians, who helped the Spaniards to mine the gold in the mountains. Later

Surfing in Puerto Rico.

Eastern Airlines

the Indians revolted against Spanish rule, but they were put down. Many left Puerto Rico while others intermarried with the Spaniards. Gradually the pure-blooded Indians disappeared from Puerto Rico.

Puerto Rico did not prosper under Spain. The people were backward and the government did little to help them. The island was constantly attacked by disease and hurricanes. More and more the people wanted to rule themselves, and Spain finally gave Puerto Rico some independence early in 1898. Later that year, the Spanish-American War broke out between the United States and Spain. At the end of the war, in 1898, Spain gave Puerto Rico to the United States.

The United States appointed a governor of the island and began to modernize Puerto Rico. Railroads, highways, hospitals and schools were built. In 1917, the United States made the Puerto Ricans citizens with the right to elect their own legislatures. Still, some Puerto Ricans wanted complete independence. The leader of the independence party, Pedro Albigu Campos (born 1891), was convicted of trying to start a revolution in 1937. Some of his followers tried to assassinate President Truman in 1950, and in 1954 they tried to explode a bomb in the U.S. Congress, though Congress had voted in 1952 to make Puerto Rico a commonwealth with almost complete self-government except in matters of defense and foreign relations. Most Puerto Ricans are against complete independence while many U.S. citizens are for it.

PUERTO RICO. Area, 3,435 square miles. Population (1970 census) 2,712,033. Capital, San Juan. Flag, three red and two white horizontal stripes; a white star in a blue triangle at the mast.

puffin

The puffin is a funny-looking bird that makes its home on the lonely coasts of the North Atlantic Ocean in regions where the climate is very cold. The puffin is not much more than a foot long. It has a big black head. Its face and breast are white and it has red legs and a most unusual, bright red and blue bill. Every year it grows a new outer covering for its bill. The puffin waddles in a clumsy way when it walks and it makes a hoarse croaking sound.

Puffins are skillful divers. They plunge deep below the surface of the water to catch the fish that they eat. The puffin digs a hole in the ground to make its nest. It lines the nest with soft grass and feathers. The female bird lays one white egg. The puffins are good parents and both the male and female birds care for the eggs.

pug dog

The pug is a dog that was very popular for many years in both England and North America. It has a black face with deep wrinkles on the forehead and a short, pug nose. The pug's tail is distinctive. It curls tightly into a circle over one hip, and sometimes even curls into a double hoop.

A pug dog is a "toy" size, standing about 10 or 11 inches high at the shoulder and weighing between 12 and 14 pounds. Its ears are soft and silky, like black velvet, and its entire coat is very smooth, fine, and soft. Pugs may be a reddish-tan color, silvery, or black.

Puget Sound

Puget Sound is a large inlet of the Pacific Ocean in the State of Washington. It is about 100 miles long. It is deep enough for large ships and is one of the important shipping centers in the country. Among its chief ports are Seattle, Tacoma, Olympia, and Everett. Many people work in large lumber mills, fisheries and canning plants along the shores of Puget Sound. Puget Sound is connected to the Pacific Ocean through the Juan de Fuca Strait. The northern part of the sound is called Admiralty Inlet, and this branches into Hood Canal. Puget Sound is a beautiful body of water with woods along its shores and many bays and islands, including the San Juan Islands and Whidbey Island, the second-largest in the United States. The region around Puget Sound is the most densely populated in the state of Washington.

Pulaski, Casimir

Count Casimir Pulaski was a Polish nobleman and patriot who helped George Washington and his armies in the Revolutionary War. He was killed in Savannah, Georgia, in 1779, while fighting in the war. Count Pulaski was born in Poland in 1748. He and his father had both fought for Polish independence, but they had been defeated. Pulaski became a brigadier general under Washington and was put in command of cavalry by Congress. He fought bravely in many battles of the Revolution before he was killed. Several monuments have been raised in his honor in the United States, and two great highways, the Pulaski Skyway in New Jersey and the Pulaski Highway in Maryland, were named for him.

Pulitzer, Joseph

Joseph Pulitzer was an American newspaper publisher who is best remembered for the large amount of money he left to give prizes to Americans for outstanding work in various fields. These are now known as Pulitzer Prizes.

Pulitzer was born in Hungary, in 1847, and came to the United States in 1864. He served in the Union forces in the Civil War. Later he settled in St. Louis, Missouri, and became an American citizen, a lawyer, and a newspaper editor. In 1878 Pulitzer founded the St. Louis *Post-Dispatch* by merging two other newspapers, and in 1882 he bought the New York *World.* Pulitzer died in 1911.

In his will Pulitzer left a large sum of money to found the Columbia University School of Journalism, and additional money to establish the Pulitzer Prizes. These prizes, usually $500 or $1,000, are given each year for outstanding achievement by an American in these fields: meritorious public service by an American newspaper; fine newspaper work in various categories, such as local and international reporting, editorial writing, cartooning, and photography; best works of fiction, drama, history, biography, and poetry on American subjects. In 1943 an award in music was added. There are also three traveling scholarships for graduates of the School of Journalism and one for an art student. These scholarships are worth $1,500 each.

The prizes need not be given every year. They are awarded by the trustees of Columbia University, on the recommendations of the Advisory Board on the Pulitzer Prizes.

pulley

A pulley is a small, grooved wheel with a rope running over its rim. It is used to reduce the force needed to lift a load.

In a *fixed pulley,* the wheel is held by a hook and a weight is attached to one end of the rope. Pulling down at the other end of the rope will raise the weight. Such a pulley is used to change the direction of a force, as in pulling a flag to the top of a flag pole. It does not reduce the force required.

In a *movable pulley,* one end of the rope is held fast from above and the rope is run over a pulley below. A weight is attached to a hook on the pulley. Pulling upward on the free end of the rope will raise the weight with a force that is only one-half as much as the weight.

A combination of several pulleys and a rope, called a *block and tackle,* is often used by workmen to lift heavy loads, as lifting a piano or raising a painter's scaffold. There are many different kinds of block-and-tackle arrangements. With some it is possible to raise a load of 500 pounds with a force of only 50 pounds.

Pullman

A sleeping car on an American railroad is usually called a Pullman because the first successful sleeping cars were made by a man named George Mortimer Pullman, about a hundred years ago.

George Pullman was born in 1831 in Brocton, New York. In 1853 he traveled in the only kind of sleeping car then in use, and found it very uncomfortable. It had narrow, hard bunks, in tiers of three. In 1859 Pullman founded his company to make "palace" cars. At first he changed regular railroad coaches into sleeping cars, but in 1865 he built a car that had comfortable seats for daytime riding and comfortable beds for night. The family of President Abraham Lincoln rode to his funeral in this car. Pullman later built the first "chair car" or "parlor car" and the first dining car. He died in 1897, but his company continued to grow.

For many years, Pullman cars were divided into sections, with each section having one lower berth and one upper berth. Usually a car had one private room, a drawing room. Most modern Pullman cars have only private rooms, each with its own toilet and lavatory. Even the smallest and lowest-priced space, the roomette, is a private room. The newest trains have rooms that are like living rooms, with separate comfortable chairs and beds that disappear when they are not in use. A Pullman employee called a conductor is in charge of all the Pullman cars on a train. A Pullman employee called a porter is in charge of each car. He makes the beds and sees to it that the

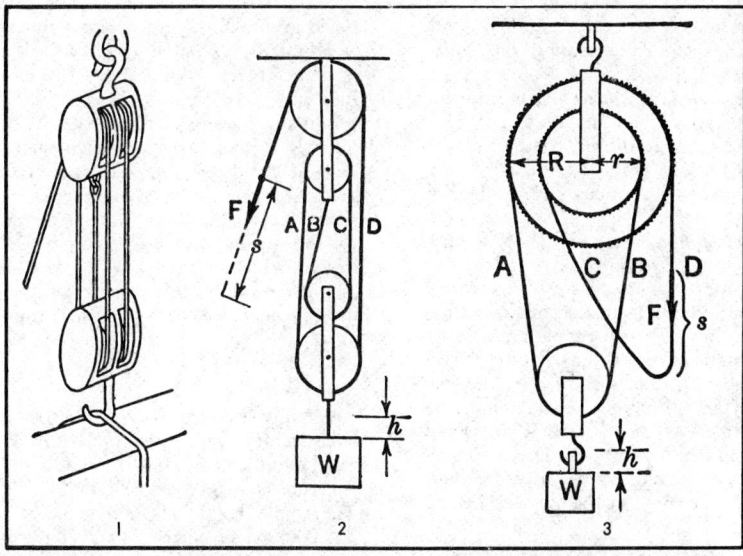

A block and tackle with four pulleys (1) makes lifting easier. The diagram of a block and tackle in 2 shows two ways of finding the help or mechanical advantage it gives: Divide the length of a pull on the rope (s) by the height (h) the weight (W) is lifted. Here, the height is one-fourth the length of pull, and only one-fourth the force (F) is needed to lift the weight that would be needed without pulleys. This mechanical advantage is also found by counting the moving strands (A, B, C, D) connected to the weight. In 3, a differential block and chain is shown. The mechanical advantage is found by dividing s by h. It is also given by dividing twice the radius of the larger pulley ($2R$) by the difference between the radii of the two pulleys (R-r).

passengers are comfortable.

Until 1947, the Pullman Company operated all sleeping cars and nearly all parlor cars on American railroads, collected separate fares from passengers, and paid the railroad companies to include the Pullman cars on trains. In 1947, fifty-nine railroad companies bought the Pullman Company. Today most sleeping cars are owned by separate railroads, but the Pullman Company still services and operates them. Although most people still refer to sleeping cars as "Pullmans," the Pullman Company no longer manufacturers them.

pulse

The pulse is the throbbing or beating of an artery that can be felt at a person's wrist, or in other parts of the body where the artery is close to the surface of the skin. Each time the heart beats, it sends blood through the arteries, which expand and then contract. This motion is called the pulse beat. A person can feel his own pulse if he places two or three fingers on the underside of his wrist. (He should not use his thumb because he has pulse in his thumb and this will make it difficult to feel the pulse beat.)

Doctors can judge a person's condition by counting the number of times his pulse beats in one minute. The number of beats is called the pulse rate. The normal pulse rate for men and women, when they are sitting or lying down, is between 66 and 88 beats in a minute. The pulse rate of a child is faster, from 80 to 140 a minute.

Excitement or exercise makes the heart pump more often and this causes the pulse rate to go up. When a person loses a lot of blood his heart beats more slowly and the pulse rate is lower. A person who is frightened or sick will have a fast pulse beat. If the person's pulse rate is very fast or very slow, the doctor knows something is wrong.

puma, a large, wild cat, also called the mountain lion or cougar: see COUGAR.

pumice

Pumice is a grayish stone that is very light in weight. It looks like solid soap-suds with very fine bubbles. Crushed pumice is used as an abrasive (a polishing, scouring, smoothing material) in hand soaps, tooth powders, and metal polishes.

Lava (melted stone) inside a volcano may contain great amounts of steam and other gases. When the lava flows out of the volcano, the gas tries to escape just as bubbles of gas escape from soda-water, but if the lava cools quickly, some of the bubbles are caught before they can escape. It is these bubbles that make pumice look like foam. Although pumice is two and a half times as heavy as water, a piece of pumice will float on water because it is held up by the gas or air in its bubbles.

The solid part of pumice is natural glass. As found in nature, pumice is called pumice stone. A very fine powder of pumice, called *pounce,* is made into blocks and is used by women to rub the hair off their arms and legs. Hundreds of years ago, natural blocks of pumice were used by men as a way of shaving.

pump

A pump is a device for making a liquid or gas flow through a tube. It does this by increasing the pressure on the liquid or gas. One familiar kind of pump is the bicycle pump and other pumps that work like it. This kind of pump is explained in the article on AIR COMPRESSION. Pumps are used to raise water from wells, to make oil and other fluids flow through pipelines, to discharge fluids (make them flow out) from flooded cellars, ponds, and so on, and for many other purposes

KINDS OF PUMP

One of the simplest pumps is the *lift pump.* The principle is the same as when you sip a drink through a straw. By sucking on the straw, you reduce the air pressure in the straw. Now there is greater air pressure on the drink and it is forced into the straw. A lift pump has a piston that forces air out of a cylinder, or tube. Water from the well then fills the tube and will pour out of a spout at the top of the tube.

Lift pumps cannot be used in wells deeper than 34 feet, because the weight of a column of water 34 feet high is the same as normal atmospheric or air pressure.

A *force pump* is used in some wells deeper than 34 feet. It is similar to a lift pump, except that after water has filled the cylinder a piston presses against the water to make it flow out of the cylinder.

A *centrifugal pump* is used to discharge liquids at high speeds. It is like a fan, with a suction pipe leading into the center of the curved blades. Water enters the pipe and is thrown out toward the

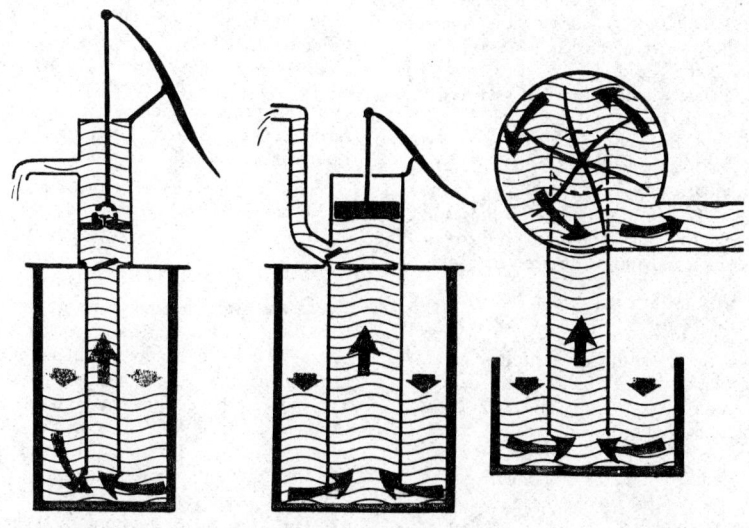

Three types of pump: the common lift pump; the force pump; the centrifugal pump.

edges of the whirling blades. The water flows out through a discharge pipe at high speeds. (See the article on CENTRIFUGAL FORCE.)

A *jet pump* is used to draw water from wells 200 feet deep. A centrifugal pump, driven by a motor at the top of the well, forces water down a pipe, called a pressure pipe, sunk into the water in the well. The bottom end of the pressure pipe is curved like a U. One end of the U sticks up into a larger pipe called the main pipe. Water forced down the pressure pipe shoots up in a jet into the main pipe. The well water in the main pipe is forced to the surface and is discharged into the open.

A *screw pump* is a form of rotary, or turning pump. It has a screwlike attachment, turned by a motor. As the screw turns, it traps water at one end and discharges it at the other end.

Centrifugal and force pumps are used for air compression.

pumpkin

The pumpkin is a fruit that is a member of the gourd family. Gourds are fruits that grow on vines. Pumpkins grow in the United States and in parts of Africa where the climate is warm.

The pumpkin vine often grows to be more than 20 feet long. It has a strong stem and large, rough leaves. The pumpkin rests on the ground. It is a large fruit and may weigh as much as 40 pounds. It has a round shape and is flat at the ends. The pumpkins that are most often grown have thick skins and have a bright orange or yellow color. People cook the pulp and eat it as a vegetable or use it as a filling for pies. It is also used as food for cattle.

The Indians raised pumpkins before any white men came to the United States. The early settlers ate pumpkins, and pumpkin is a traditional food that is served at Thanksgiving. Pumpkins are carved to make jolly faces. These are called jack-o'-lanterns and are especially popular at Hallowe'en.

Punch and Judy

Punch and Judy are characters in a very old puppet show that was first given in Italy about 350 years ago. (You can read about PUPPETS in a separate article.) Different versions of the Punch and Judy show have been given in many parts of the world.

Punch is usually presented as a rather ugly fellow with a large, hooked nose and a hunched back. He is a great coward but boasts about his courage and the marvelous things he can do. Judy is the wife of Punch. He often beats Judy and anyone else in sight with a club. Parts of the Punch and Judy show are very funny.

punctuation

Punctuation is the use of marks to make the meaning of writing clearer. Punctuation marks include the period, the comma, the colon and semicolon, quotation marks, parentheses, and others. Most of these marks show places where you would pause for a moment if you were speaking the words instead of writing or reading them. There are many rules for punctuation, but most people can learn to punctuate properly if they learn only a few of these rules and then think carefully before punctuating what they write.

The *period,* or *full stop,* is used at the end of a sentence. It marks a place where there should be a distinct pause in speaking or reading aloud. The period is also used after abbreviations, such as Dr. or U.S.A.

The *comma* is used to show a very slight pause. A comma never ends a sentence. More commas are used in writing than all other punctuation marks put together, but very few people are able to use commas correctly in all cases. Even when you are not sure of the rule, you can often tell when to use a comma by reading the sentence aloud. If you would not pause at a particular place, a comma does not belong there; if you would pause, a comma probably does belong there.

The *semicolon* marks a longer pause than a comma. It is used, sometimes, when two closely related sentences come together. For example,

He did not go; he saw no reason to.

It would be equally proper to use a period after "go."

The *colon* introduces something that will follow the sentence. It is often used after the word "said" and before spoken words; for example,

He said: "I intend to stay here."

He took the following things: A table, four chairs, dishes and silverware, and napkins.

The *question mark,* or *interrogation point,* is used after any question. For example,

Where are you going?

The *apostrophe* is used to show that one or more letters have been left out, as when you use *can't* for *cannot.* It is also used to show possession, as in *John's hat.*

The *hyphen* is used to connect words that are used together, as in *father-in-law.* It is also used to divide a word at the end of a line.

Parentheses are used to show that a certain part of a sentence could be left out without spoiling the sense. For example,

Seeing that he was beaten, he quickly (though not willingly) resigned.

In many cases, commas can be used instead of parentheses.

Quotation marks show that certain words were spoken. In English, double quotation marks ("and") are usually preferred. Some people prefer single quotation marks. Examples are:

He said: "John told me he would stay."

He said: "John said to me, 'I will stay.'"

Punic Wars

About two thousand years ago there was a city called Carthage, in North Africa, that became a powerful empire with colonies in other countries. About that time Rome became very powerful also. The Romans wanted to control the territories that the Carthaginians considered theirs. The two powers fought three wars from the year 264 B.C. until 146 B.C. They were called the Punic Wars because Punicus was the Latin word for "Carthaginian." The first Punic War lasted twenty-three years and was almost won by HANNIBAL, on whom there is a separate article. He crossed the Alps into Italy and won several big battles, but he was finally defeated in Africa by the Romans. In this war a young Roman named Cato fought. Later Cato became a great statesman, and he used to end every speech he made in the Roman Senate with the words, "Carthage must be destroyed." In the year 149 B.C. Rome started the third Punic War and within three years destroyed Carthage completely.

Punjab

Punjab is a large region in India and Pakistan. In 1947, when India was divided into the two countries of India and Pakistan, each received half of Punjab. The whole region of Punjab is about 110,000 square miles in size, almost as big as Nevada, but more than 35,000,000 people live there, more than one hundred times as many as live in Nevada. Wheat is Punjab's most important crop. Millet, barley, fruits and cotton are other important crops. There are factories where flour and cloth are made, and there are coal and salt mines. Punjab has several important rivers, including the Indus and five small rivers that form the Panjnad. There is not enough rainfall, but the land is irrigated by water from all of these rivers.

The part of Punjab that belongs to Pakistan was merged with the other provinces of West Pakistan in 1955 to form a single administrative unit. Before the merger, it had an area of about 63,000 square miles and about 20,000,000 people lived there. Its capital was Lahore. The Indian state of Punjab is about 47,000 square miles in size, and more than 16,000,000 people live there. In 1956 the former states of Patiala and East Punjab States Union were united with it. Its capital is Chandigarh.

pupa

Pupa is the name for a stage in the development of certain insects. The pupa is usually enclosed in some kind of covering. The pupal stage may last from several weeks to perhaps eight months, over the winter season. At the end of it the insect emerges as a full-grown adult. See also the article on INSECTS.

puppet

A puppet is a doll operated by a human being so that it can move or talk or dance or sing. The puppet show is one of the most ancient forms of entertainment, and it has always delighted children and grownups.

There are several different kinds of puppet. One of the oldest is the *shadow puppet,* a flat figure cut from cardboard or some other stiff material and operated against a lighted screen by wires or rods. The *glove puppet* has a solid head and a loose costume into which the operator puts his hand, with his fingers in the head and arms. The puppets used by Burr Tillstrom on the "Kukla, Fran and Ollie" show are glove puppets. The *marionette* is a puppet worked by strings from above. This is the most complicated and the most realistic form of puppet, since it

can be elaborately jointed and even facial expressions can be changed by the operator. Howdy Doody is a marionette. In 1954 a new kind of puppet, called a Kinemin, was invented and used in the motion picture *Hansel and Gretel*. Kinemins are electronic puppets that are operated by remote control and made to walk and move with great realism.

HOW PUPPETS BEGAN

The origin of puppets is very much of a mystery. Some scholars say that the first puppet shows were held in ancient Egypt and Greece during religious festivals, thousands of years ago. Others believe that puppets may have originated in the Far East, in Burma, China, and the islands of Java and Bali. It is known that the shadow puppets of Java were popular as long as a thousand years ago. Shadow puppets were popular for a while in Europe during the 1700s. In Germany the poet Goethe established his own shadow theater. In England, the playwright Ben Jonson included a five-scene shadow play at the end of one of his real plays.

GLOVE PUPPETS

The glove-puppet operator stands behind a screen and holds his hands either high above him or directly in front of him, where the puppets perform on a stage. The glove-puppet stage may be just a curtained doorway or an overturned table, or it may be a portable theater which fits into a light case and can be carried anywhere. The most famous glove-puppet figures are Punch and Judy, who have probably performed more often than any other actors in the world.

The character of Punch can be traced back to ancient Greek and Roman times, when puppets often had hooked noses and the plays they performed were often slapstick comedies. The Punch we know today, who has changed very little in three hundred years, was born the Italian Pulcinella, a hooknosed, hunchbacked servant who was always getting into and out of trouble. In England he became Mr. Punch; in France he became Polichinelle, except in the city of Lyons, where he was called Guignol and represented a witty weaver. In Germany Punch is called Kasperle, and in Russia he is Petrouchka.

MARIONETTES

The standard marionette has nine strings attached to its body, two each to the head, shoulders, arms, and legs, and one to the back. More intricate marionettes have many more strings, sometimes controlling facial expressions so that the marionette can roll its eyes, blink its eyelids, smile, and talk.

The strings are held together on a wooden rod, which the operator holds in one hand. With the other hand he plucks the strings to control the movements of the marionette. Marionettes are of almost any size. Amateurs usually use figures twelve to eighteen inches high. Professionals have marionettes two to three feet high, and the largest of all, the Japanese marionettes, are three-quarters the height of a human being.

String marionettes were invented by an Italian named Fantochinni, in the 16th century, and in Italy they are still called by his name. The marionette show was at first a street affair, but later the Italian marionettes had a theater of their own in London. France developed its own marionettes. At first the marionettes were silent, and the story was explained by a narrator. Later the operator or an actor spoke directly for the marionettes.

Perhaps the most colorful of all marionette theaters is the Japanese *Ningyoshibai*. Japanese puppeteers devote their whole lives to the art of operating their almost life-size figures. The showmen are visible to the audience. The male figures are operated by four men, and can move even their eyebrows, eyes, and lips. The female figures are less complicated and require only three handlers. Each marionette has its own performer, who sings and acts for it. The marionette theater is such a deep part of Japanese culture that living actors often study their art from marionettes.

Purim

Purim is a Jewish feast day. It is celebrated on the 14th and 15th days of Adar, the sixth month of the Jewish calendar. Pious Jews fast on the day before Purim, but the day itself is one of joyful prayer and merrymaking. This is because it is in memory of the delivery of the Jews in Persia from persecution. The story is told in the Book of Esther, in the Old Testament. Esther, a Jewish woman, married the Persian king, Ahasuerus. When one of the king's ministers, Haman, plotted against the Jews, Esther persuaded Ahasuerus to spare her people. Haman had prepared a gibbet, or gallows, on which to hang Esther's brother, but Ahasuerus had Haman himself hanged on it instead.

Puritan Revolution

The Puritan Revolution took place in England more than three hundred years ago. It was a civil war between the forces that supported Charles I, the king of England, and the forces that supported the Parliament, or lawmaking body of England. It is called the Puritan Revolution because many of the people who supported the Parliament were Puritans, members of a religious group that wanted to change the Church of England, which was the official Church of England at that time. The Puritan Revolution was not fought for religious reasons alone. The political and economic questions were even more important than the religious ones.

CAVALIERS AND ROUNDHEADS

The followers of the king in the Puritan Revolution were called *Cavaliers*. They consisted of most of the nobility, most of the members of the Church of England, and the Catholics. The followers of the Parliament were called *Roundheads*, a name given to them originally to poke fun at their short haircuts, which they wore because they disapproved of the long curls worn by the men in the king's court. The Roundheads were mostly merchants and landowners who were not members of the nobility. The Parliament was also supported by great numbers of Scottish Presbyterians, who disapproved of the Church of England and of the king himself.

The most famous of all the Puritans was Oliver Cromwell, who led the Puritans in battle against the king and became ruler of England when the king was defeated.

The Puritan Revolution broke out in 1642. At first the Cavaliers won most of the battles, but by 1647 they had been defeated by the Roundheads, and the king surrendered to Parliament. The Presbyterians were willing to let Charles remain king, with limited powers, if he would make Presbyterianism the state religion.

The Puritans would not agree to this. Charles again tried to get control of the country, and this time the army led by Oliver Cromwell, a Puritan, defeated him. The Presbyterians were forced out of Parliament, the king was tried for treason and beheaded, and the Puritans made England a republic, called a Commonwealth, with Cromwell at its head. Cromwell paid no more attention to the wishes of the people than King Charles had. He ruled England for ten years, but he never had the support of a majority of the people. After he died, his son, Richard Cromwell, was unable to control the country. In 1660 Charles II, the son of Charles I, was invited by Parliament to become king, with limited powers. This period was known as the Restoration.

Puritans

Puritan was a name first given to a group of people living in England about four hundred years ago. These people wanted to "purify" the English Church. Later these people were also known as "nonconformists" because they did not conform, or agree, to the practices of the church. The strictest of the nonconformists continued to be called Puritans, not only because of their religious beliefs but also because they demanded such strictness, or "purity," in morals and manners.

Some Puritans wanted changes in the ceremonies and rites practiced in the Church of England. Others wanted the church government changed. Still others did not want the Church of England to have any power at all. People from the three groups of Puritans formed many of the early settlements in New England. In England itself the Puritans overthrew the king's government in a Civil War and formed a Commonwealth, or republic, that lasted for ten years, from 1649 until 1659.

In recent times the word Puritan has not been used to describe a person of any particular religious belief, but rather a person who is very strict about manners, morals, or religion.

PURITANS IN AMERICA

One group of Puritans broke away from the other Puritans and came to America in 1620. They were called the Pilgrims.

The largest colony of Puritans was the Massachusetts Bay Colony. By 1630 this colony had a thousand people living in it and had become prosperous.

The Puritans (Pilgrims) living in New England made the laws of Massachusetts according to their religion. The colony of Massachusetts was very intol-

erant of anyone who was not a Puritan. At first, no member of any other religion was allowed to live there. The laws relating to the behavior of the Puritans in early New England were called BLUE LAWS, and there is a separate article about them.

There have been many novels and stories written about Puritanism in America. The best of these is Nathaniel Hawthorne's novel called *The Scarlet Letter*, which tells about the early Puritans living in Salem, Massachusetts, and shows how unjust and cruel many of their laws were.

Pushkin, Alexander

Alexander Pushkin was a Russian poet and writer of stories and plays. He was born in 1799. Pushkin came from a noble family and received a fine education. When he was 18 years old Pushkin received a position in the government. He had many liberal ideas and wrote poems about these ideas. The poems made the czar (emperor) of Russia angry. As a punishment, Pushkin was sent to the south of Russia, but after a few years he again gained the favor of the czar.

Pushkin wrote many poems and stories and some novels. His best-known poem is *Eugene Onegin*, which is a long story in verse. He wrote a play, *Boris Godunoff*, that became a very popular opera with the same title. Pushkin was killed in a duel in 1837, when he was 38 years old.

pussy willow

The pussy willow is a large shrub or small tree that belongs to the willow family. It grows in the eastern part of the United States. Some pussy willows grow to be about 20 feet high. The pussy willow is deciduous, which means that it loses its leaves in the fall.

The pussy willow gets its name because in the spring, before the first leaves appear, the straight branches bear small knobs, covered with a soft fuzz, that are called catkins.

Putnam, Israel

Israel Putnam was an American general in the Revolutionary War. He was born in Salem, Massachusetts, in 1718. He settled in Connecticut and there raised a company of men to fight in the French and Indian Wars. During this war Putnam was captured by an Indian, who tied him to a tree and almost burned him to death. Putnam was saved by a sudden thunderstorm that put out the fire. Later he was rescued by a French officer and taken to Montreal, where he was kept a prisoner.

In April of 1775 Putnam was working in the fields near his home when a messenger arrived with the news that fighting had started between the Americans and the British. Putnam immediately set out for Massachusetts, and got there at sunrise the next day, having ridden the same horse a hundred miles in eighteen hours.

Putnam was one of the American officers at the battle of Bunker Hill. He served in the American army until 1779, when he was forced to retire because he became paralyzed in one side of his body. Putnam died in 1790.

putty

Putty is a material that has long been used to seal window panes into their frames, to fill holes in wood, and for many other purposes. It is made by mixing either powdered chalk or a chemical called oxide of lead with linseed oil. Oxide of lead is also called white lead and it is the same substance that is used in preparing many paints. Linseed oil is the oil pressed from the seeds of the flax plant.

Freshly mixed putty is almost as soft and workable as peanut butter. When it is allowed to dry a little, it becomes about as firm as dough. After it has been exposed to the air longer, it dries to be almost as hard as plaster.

Putty is usually applied with a short, broad knife with a sharp end, called a putty knife. Fresh putty is tan in color, due to the linseed oil used in mixing.

puzzle

A puzzle is a kind of problem that people try to work out for fun and not because it is part of their school or business duties. Nearly every kind of puzzle requires some thought, but there are some puzzles that are worked with the hands and other puzzles that are worked, or solved, only by thinking about them.

Men have amused themselves with puzzles for thousands of years, and there is no way of knowing how long ago the first puzzles were made. The Chinese made puzzles hundreds of years ago that are still being used. Some of these are "ring" puzzles. Two or three rings or other pieces of twisted wire are joined together, and the problem is to take them apart. If you hold them exactly right, they will come apart easily. Sometimes it takes hours to learn the proper way to hold them.

Another old kind of puzzle that is still popular is the jigsaw puzzle. A picture is cut up into small pieces and the problem is to fit the pieces together so that the picture can be seen again. Some jigsaw puzzles are called "three-dimensional." They are blocks of wood or little statues that are cut into pieces. When the pieces are fitted together, you have a solid figure instead of a picture.

WORD GAMES

Some of the most popular puzzles are made of words only. The word puzzle that is best-known is the CROSSWORD PUZZLE, about which there is a separate article. Another kind is called *anagrams*. The letters of a word are rearranged and the puzzle is to put them back into the proper order. The rearrangement might make sense, as when the puzzle is to find the word in *great help* (the answer is *telegraph*), but often the anagram is simply a jumble of letters.

Word golf is a kind of puzzle in which you try to change one word into another by changing one letter at a time. For example, the puzzle might be, "Go from *some* to *many* in five steps." The solution would be:

SOME
SAME
SANE
MANE
MANY

There are hundreds of different puzzles based on words.

MATHEMATICS AND LOGIC

Perhaps the greatest number of puzzles are based on mathematics, especially algebra. One of the most famous puzzles of this kind, invented by a puzzle expert named Sam Loyd, was called "How old is Ann?" The puzzle was: "The combined ages of Mary and Ann are 44 years and Mary is twice as old as Ann was when Mary was half as old as Ann will be when Ann is three times as old as Mary was when Mary was three times as old as Ann. How old is Ann?" The answer is that Ann is 16½ years old, making Mary 27½ years old; but many steps are needed to work this out.

A puzzle of logic, or an elimination puzzle, might go like this:

A banker, a dentist, a doctor, and a lawyer were named Jim, Jack, Joe, and Jerry (but that does not have to be the order of their names). Jim and the dentist were unfriendly with Joe. Jack and the lawyer were good friends. Joe and the doctor lived in the same neighborhood. The banker was friendly with Jerry and the lawyer. Match up the professions with the names of the men.

These puzzles are solved by writing out everything that is known about each man. Gradually, you can figure out which professions and names cannot be matched (for example, Jack cannot be the lawyer, because the puzzle says that Jack and the lawyer were friends). Finally you discover that the banker is Jack, the dentist is Jerry, the doctor is Jim and the lawyer is Joe.

Some puzzles are based on games. One of the most popular is the "knight's tour," based on the game of chess The piece called the knight must be moved over the board in such a way as to touch every square exactly once. The article on CHESS explains how the knight moves. There are many ways to solve this problem, but all are difficult.

There are many books of puzzles, and some puzzles can be found in newspapers and magazines. There is almost no such thing as a "new" puzzle. The ones called new are usually old puzzles that have been changed slightly to make them different or bring them up to date.

Pygmalion

Pygmalion was the king of Cyprus in stories told by the ancient Greeks thousands of years ago. He was a fine sculptor and made a statue of a young woman named Galatea. The statue was so beautiful that he fell in love with it. He gave presents to the statue and dressed it in fine clothes and put precious jewels around its neck. Pygmalion asked the goddess Venus to give him a wife as beautiful as the statue he had made. When he returned home he discovered that his request had been granted, for the lovely statue had come to life. Pygmalion was overjoyed and married the beautiful woman.

Pygmy, a member of one of several Negro tribes found in Africa and in some of the islands of the Pacific Ocean. The Pygmies are a very small people, averaging about four and a half feet tall. See the article on AFRICA.

Pyle, Ernie

Ernest Taylor Pyle was an American newspaperman who became famous for his reporting of World War II and his stories about American soldiers in action. Pyle was born in 1900 in Dana, Indiana. He worked as a newspaperman in Washington, D.C., and in New York City. His fame came from his reports of World War II fighting in Africa, Europe, and the South Pacific. Ernie Pyle, as he was known to thousands of Allied soldiers, tried always to be at the front lines. He lived the life of the men he wrote about. In 1943 Pyle won a Pulitzer Prize for his war reporting. Among his books were *This Is Your War* and *Brave Men.* In 1945 Pyle was killed by Japanese machine-gun fire on an island near Okinawa.

pyramids

The pyramids are the great stone tombs that were built thousands of years ago to hold the bodies of the Egyptian pharaohs (kings). Many pyramids still stand in the desert along the Nile River, about ten miles south of the modern city of Cairo, in Egypt.

The first tombs were covered with piles of stones. As time went by these piles began to assume a definite shape. They were carefully built of fitted blocks of stone. Each king wanted the largest tomb, so the pyramids were built higher and higher. For five thousand years pyramids were the highest structures in the world.

At the base a pyramid is square—each of the four sides is exactly as long as the others. From each side the pyramid slopes up to a point, so that each side is like a triangle.

The biggest of all the Egyptian pyramids is the one built by a pharaoh called Khufu, whom the ancient Greeks knew by the name Cheops. This great pyramid is 756 feet long on each side of its square sides. The point is 450 feet above the ground. Inside the bottom of the pyramid are large rooms that were used as tombs for the royal family. Like those in other pyramids, these rooms contained many splendid objects of gold, precious gems, and wonderfully carved furniture. The Egyptians believed a dead person could take earthly possessions to heaven with him. Artists painted scenes on the walls of the tomb rooms. Because Egyptians believed that the dead soul would travel through space, they enclosed large ships in the tombs.

It is hard to believe that the ancient Egyptians, with nothing like the great cranes and engines that we use in building today, were able to build these marvels. To the ancients the pyramids were one of the Seven Wonders of the World. It is believed that the great pyramid of Khufu took about twenty years to build and that at least 100,000 men labored to complete it. Most of these men were slaves who labored endlessly, hauling the large stones and putting them in place.

People who travel to Egypt can drive out to where the great pyramid and other pyramids stand, and then ride on camels around the pyramids. They can watch the native guides make a sport of climbing the pyramids and then sliding and scrambling from the top to the bottom.

Pyramus and Thisbe

Pyramus was a young man and Thisbe a young woman about whom an old story was told. They lived in the ancient city of Babylon. They loved each other very much, but although they lived next door to each other, their parents would not allow them to meet. So each night the lovers would go to the thick wall that separated their gardens. They had discovered a small crack in the wall and through this crack they whispered and sent notes back and forth.

Once they made a plan to meet beneath a white mulberry tree outside the city. When Thisbe arrived at the spot, a lioness appeared. It had just killed an ox and was covered with blood. Thisbe was frightened and ran away to hide. She dropped her scarf and the lion tore at and covered it with blood. When Pyramus arrived and saw the bloody scarf, he was certain that the lioness had killed his beloved Thisbe. He was so filled with sorrow that he ran a dagger through his heart and his blood stained the white mulberries a bright red color. When Thisbe returned and saw what had happened she no longer wished to live and she too killed herself. It is said that ever since that time the berries of the mulberry tree have been red, in memory of the lovers.

Shakespeare used the story of Pyramus and Thisbe in his play *A Midsummer Night's Dream.*

Pyrenees

The Pyrenees are a chain of mountains between France and Spain. They extend for about 270 miles, from the Mediterranean Sea to the Atlantic Ocean. In the past thirty years, two railroads have been built through the Pyrenees.

The highest peak in the Pyrenees is the Pico de Aneto, 11,168 feet high. The mountains are covered with valuable forests, and there are deposits of iron, zinc, and lead. Many wild animals roam through the Pyrenees, including the bear, wolf, wild boar, and deer.

In the western part of the Pyrenees live the Basque people. (There is a separate article about the BASQUES.) Along the Atlantic shore in France are some famous vacation resorts, including Biarritz and Saint Jean-de-Luz, and the city of Lourdes, which has a famous shrine. Andorra, one of the smallest countries in the world, is in the eastern part of the Pyrenees.

pyrite

Pyrite is a bright yellow mineral that looks like brass. It is made of iron and sulfur. Because of pyrite's shiny yellow color, people finding it have sometimes thought they have found gold, so it is sometimes called "fool's gold." But you can tell pyrite from gold because gold can easily be scratched with a steel knife, while pyrite is hard enough to scratch the knife.

Pyrite is found in Virginia, New York, Massachusetts, California, Colorado, and Arizona. Much pyrite is mined in Spain and Portugal.

Marcasite, or *white pyrites,* is much like ordinary pyrite except that it is a paler yellow and its surface is covered with tiny ridges. It is used in inexpensive jewelry. *Chalcopyrite,* or *copper pyrites,* looks like marcasite but does not have the ridges on the surface and is softer. It is made up of pyrite plus copper. *Arsenopyrite* or *mispickel,* is silvery white. It is pyrite plus arsenic.

Pyrrhus

Pyrrhus was a king of Epirus, a country of ancient Greece. He was born about 318 years before Jesus. Pyrrhus was a brave soldier and gained fame throughout the world of the Mediterranean. The people of Tarentum, a place in the south of Italy, asked Pyrrhus to help them fight the Romans. In the year 280 Pyrrhus went to meet the Romans with many soldiers and twenty elephants. When the Romans saw the elephants they were so frightened that they fled.

The next year he attacked the Romans again and once more defeated them, but he lost so many men that he remarked, "One more such victory, and I am lost." We now call a victory that is won at too great a cost a Pyrrhic victory. In 276, the Romans defeated Pyrrhus at Beneventum. He then invaded Macedonia and became its king. Pyrrhus was killed during a battle in the streets of Argos, in Greece, in 272 B.C., at the age of 46.

Pythagoras

Pythagoras was a Greek philosopher, or student of knowledge, who lived about 2,500 years ago. He worked in the fields of music and geometry, formed a religious society, and wrote a general account of the world.

Very little is known about the life of Pythagoras. He was born on the island of Samos, near Greece. Later he went to live in Crotona, in southern Italy, where he formed a religious brotherhood. Members of this brotherhood had to live according to rules that he laid down. There were many rules that seem quite strange to us, such as one that forbade the eating of beans. The group believed that after men die their souls go into other bodies, sometimes into the bodies of animals.

Pythagoras discovered that if one plucks a stretched string, as on a harp, the longer the string, the lower the tone will be. He worked out a system of numbers, representing the lengths of the strings, that showed when two tones are harmonious (sound well together). Then he decided that number underlies not only music but everything. Sometimes, as in the case of music, his explanations were excellent, but in other cases they were senseless, as when he said that the number 3 represented marriage and the number 4, justice.

Pythagoras also worked in geometry, in which he is best remembered for a principle called the Pythagorean theorem.

Pythias, a partner in one of the most famous friendships of all time: see the article on DAMON AND PYTHIAS.

python

The python is a snake that lives in Asia, Africa, and Australia. One kind of python lives in Mexico. The python is the largest of all snakes. The regal python, which makes its home in Asia, grows to be about 30 feet long and weighs about 200 pounds. Many of the pythons have beautiful diamond-shaped markings on their reddish-brown skin.

Pythons are at home in trees and on the ground. They prefer to live in deep forests where the climate is damp. They eat small animals such as rats and ducks. They squeeze their prey to death.

Many pythons have tiny pits at the sides of their mouths. These pits are special organs that are very sensitive to heat, so a python is able to tell when a warm-blooded animal is near. Pythons hunt for food at night. They see well in the dark. Some pythons in zoos live to be about 30 years old. A python can get along without food for one or even two years, but it must have water.

See also the article on SNAKES.

Canadian Government Travel Bureau

Jacques Cartier Bridge was named for the discoverer of New France, who in 1535 sailed up the St. Lawrence River to what is now Montreal, in the province of Quebec.

Canadian Government Travel Bureau

The Changing of the Guard ceremony is conducted daily at the Citadel, the historic fortifications in the old walled city of Quebec, Canada.

N.F.B.

Quebec City, on the St. Lawrence and St. Charles Rivers, is the capital of the Canadian province of Quebec.

1287

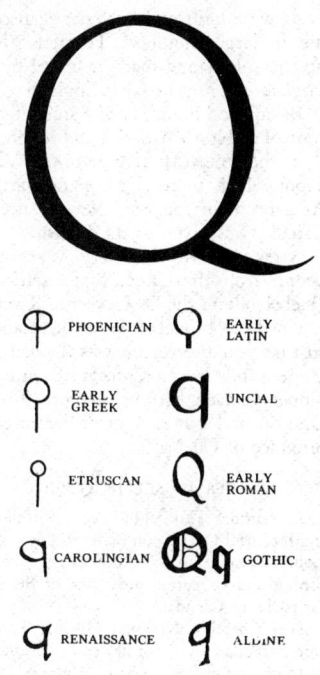

PHOENICIAN EARLY LATIN

EARLY GREEK UNCIAL

ETRUSCAN EARLY ROMAN

CAROLINGIAN GOTHIC

RENAISSANCE ALDINE

Q or q

Q, the seventeenth letter of our alphabet, was perhaps a symbol used by the ancient Egyptians in their hieroglyphics (picture-writing). It probably was a picture of a knot. In Hebrew, the word for knot was *qoph*. The ancient Greeks, calling their form of the q *koppa,* removed that part of the vertical (up-and-down) stroke which was inside the circle. Later forms are seen above.

Read also the article ALPHABET.

Q fever

Q fever is a disease caused by germs that are carried by certain ticks. When a person is bitten by this kind of tick, he may get the disease. It used to make people dangerously sick, but now it can be controlled by antibiotics. The disease is like Rocky Mountain Spotted Fever, except that the person does not get a rash. See the article on TICK.

quail, a game bird that lives in most parts of the world: see the articles on PARTRIDGE and BOBWHITE.

Quaker, a member of the Society of Friends. See the article on FRIENDS.

Quantico

Quantico is a town in northeast Virginia, on the Potomac River. Only about 1,015 people live there, but the town is famous because it is the site of a training camp where officers of the United States Marine Corps are trained. This training camp was established in 1917, during World War I. See the article on the MARINE CORPS.

quantum theory

The quantum theory is an explanation of how rays, such as electrical or light rays, travel through the universe. A German scientist named Max Planck, who was born in 1858, introduced the quantum theory in 1900. His theory was that radiation, or rays, are not continuous streams but are made up of tiny particles.

He called these particles *quanta* (which is the plural of the word *quantum*). Later, the scientist Albert Einstein used Planck's theory in working out some of his own famous theories. The quantum theory led scientists to a better understanding of atomic energy, electric currents, and light. The "electric eye," or photoelectric cell (explained in the article on ELECTRONICS), was one of the inventions that grew out of the quantum theory. Planck received the Nobel Prize in 1918. He died in 1947.

quarantine

Long before people knew what caused most diseases, they knew that a person having a certain disease could pass it on to someone else. To prevent this they made such a person stay in a particular room or house until he was well. This was called putting him in quarantine. Putting people in quarantine used to be a very common practice, but today it is not often considered necessary.

The word quarantine refers also to inspecting ships that are about to enter another country's harbor. This began because people were afraid that someone on the ship might have plague or another dangerous contagious disease that would infect people in the new country. Ships are still inspected for disease, but very few of them have to be stopped because of it. The word quarantine comes from the Latin word meaning "forty," and refers to the number of days a ship had to wait before anyone from it might enter a country.

quarry

A quarry is an open excavation (dug-out place) from which rock is taken for use in building. Marble, granite, sandstone, limestone, slate, and other useful kinds of rock can be found in the earth in huge blocks that may measure thousands of feet. The rock may be cut from the earth by any of three methods —channeling, sawing, or wedging.

In channeling, engine-driven drills cut the rock into slabs that are lifted out, just like slices of layer cake. In sawing, a piece of heavy wire is used as a saw to make the channels.

Rocks that split cleanly along straight lines are quarried by wedging. Rows of holes are drilled into the stone and wooden wedges are put into the holes. The wedges, when struck with a hammer, gently split off a slab of stone.

When very large pieces of a tough rock are wanted, holes are drilled and filled with explosive. The amount of explosive must be carefully calculated so that it splits off a slab of rock but does not shatter it. If engineers want broken stone for cement or for the foundation of railroad tracks, they use enough explosive to shatter the stone.

Quartermaster Corps

The Quartermaster Corps is the branch of the United States Army that feeds and clothes soldiers and provides them with almost all their supplies except their actual guns and ammunition. The head of this service is called the Quartermaster General. See the article on U.S. ARMY.

quartz

Quartz is a kind of rock. It is one of the most common minerals in the earth's crust. Most grains of sand are quartz. Quartz is hard enough to scratch glass, it will give sparks when struck with steel, and it will become electrified when rubbed with cloth.

When it is pure, quartz is colorless, like glass. The best clear quartz is called *rock crystal* and is carved into vases and other artistic objects. Sometimes rock crystal is cut to look like diamond. Clear quartz can be melted and is used to make camera and telescope lenses.

Many kinds of colored quartz are used as semiprecious stones. Of these, the clear ones are: *rose quartz,* pink; *amethyst,* purple or bluish-violet; *cairngorm* or *smoky quartz,* smoky-yellow or brown; *citrine* or *false topaz,* yellow. Colored quartz that is opaque (does not let light pass through it) is called CHALCEDONY, about which there is a separate article.

Flint is another kind of quartz. The first tools and weapons used by mankind were made of flint. The Indians that fought the first white settlers in America used flint for arrowheads and tomahawks. Indians of the Amazon River in South America still use flint for spearheads.

Quebec

Quebec is the largest of the Canadian provinces. It is in the northeast, between Hudson Bay and the St. Lawrence River. Quebec's area is 594,860 square miles, which makes it more than twice as large as Texas. In population it ranks second in Canada, with more than six million people living there. The province was named after the city of Quebec. It became a province in 1867. The capital is Quebec.

THE PEOPLE OF QUEBEC

Most of the people of Quebec are of French descent. Most of them speak Canadian French, though many also speak English, and they have kept many of their French customs. They belong to the Roman Catholic Church. Most of the French Canadians live along the St. Lawrence. Quebec has a number of people of English descent, most of them living in Montreal.

More than half the people of Quebec live in the cities. They work in factories that make paper, lumber products, shoes, clothing, chemicals, and many other things. There are also many farmers living along the Saguenay and St. Lawrence Rivers. They raise grain, cattle and dairy products, potatoes, fruits, and vegetables. A number of people work in the dense forests of Quebec, cutting down the valuable timber for making paper and other wood products. Others work in mines that produce iron, copper and zinc.

WHAT QUEBEC IS LIKE

Most of Quebec is a large plateau, a high, level region, above which rise the Laurentian Mountains. This region has large lakes and rivers but is not very fertile for farming. The mountains are very popular for winter sports. They contain important minerals.

Most of the people live in the St. Lawrence Valley in the southeast. This sec-

tion is very fertile for farming. The large cities are situated along the St. Lawrence River because of the water power it provides. In the southern part of Quebec are the Notre Dame Mountains, which are part of the Appalachians. These mountains rise to a height of more than 3,000 feet in the Gaspé Peninsula that juts out into the Gulf of St. Lawrence.

Among the many rivers of Quebec, the most important is the St. Lawrence. It connects the Great Lakes with the Atlantic Ocean, and large ships can travel on it from the Atlantic for 2,342 miles, to Duluth, at the western end of Lake Superior. The St. Lawrence also furnishes water to make electricity.

The winters in Quebec are very cold. The temperature is about 10 degrees, and often it can drop far below zero. The rivers and lakes are frozen for about five months every year. Heavy snowfalls cover the mountain slopes and make the regions around Quebec and Montreal popular skiing and tobogganing centers. In summer it is cool in most of Quebec, but in the St. Lawrence Valley it can be quite warm. The average temperature in summer is about 70 degrees.

Canadian Pacific Railway Photos

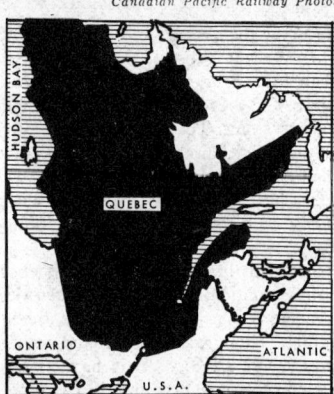

Quebec has many industries, but the visitor is most impressed by its scenery and Old World charm.
1. A French-style gate in the city of Quebec.
2. A map of Quebec, Canada's largest province.
3. The Shrine of the Good Saint Anne at St. Anne de Beaupré, visited by many pilgrims.

There are railroads throughout the southern and eastern sections of Quebec, where most of the people live. The province has many highways. In winter these roads are often closed to automobiles because of heavy snowfalls, but sleighs carry traffic over the roads and frozen rivers. There are airports at the big cities, and planes are often used to fly supplies and equipment to the mining districts in the north.

THE GOVERNMENT OF QUEBEC

The head of the government of Quebec is a Lieutenant Governor, who is appointed by the Canadian government. The province is actually run by a premier. He is appointed by a legislature, which is elected by the people. The premier has a cabinet, just as the President of the United States has. He stays in office as long as he can keep the confidence of the majority of the legislature. The legislature is composed of two houses, the Legislative Council and the Legislative Assembly. The members of the Legislative Council are appointed for life by the provincial government. Quebec is the only province that has a Legislative Council. The members of the Legislative Assembly are elected for a five-year term. Judges are appointed by the Canadian government in Ottawa and hold office permanently. The provincial government is in the capital, Quebec.

Everyone has to go to school until the age of 16. There are separate schools for Catholics and Protestants. Quebec has several important colleges, including McGill University and the University of Montreal, both at Montreal, and Laval University in Quebec.

CHIEF CITIES OF QUEBEC

The leading cities of Quebec, with populations from the 1971 census, are:

MONTREAL. Population 1,214,352, the largest city in Canada. There is a separate article about MONTREAL.

QUEBEC. Population 186,088, the capital and second-largest city. There is a separate article about QUEBEC.

SHERBROOKE. Population 80,711, the third-largest city, hosiery-manufacturing center, in the southern part of the province.

TROIS RIVIERES. Population 55,869, the fourth-largest city, paper-manufacturing center, in the southern part of the province.

QUEBEC IN THE PAST

The first European to visit the region of Quebec was the French explorer Jacques Cartier, more than four hundred years ago. He claimed this large territory for France, which hoped to establish a great empire in the New World. In 1608, Samuel de Champlain founded the colony of New France and the city of Quebec, and settlers began to arrive in 1617. The new colony grew slowly because of many attacks by the Iroquois Indians. When Count Louis de Frontenac was governor he defeated these Indians. Then trading

posts were built and settlers began coming in larger numbers. Frontenac built up the colony and made it feared by the English colonies in New England.

Britain and France both wanted to gain control of North America and fought for it in the FRENCH AND INDIAN WARS, about which there is a separate article. As a result of the war, New France, or Canada, was given to the British.

After the Revolutionary War many people from the United States settled in Quebec, along the St. Lawrence River.

Until 1791 Quebec was called Canada. In that year the region was divided into Upper and Lower Canada. Eventually, Upper Canada became the province of Ontario and Lower Canada became the province of Quebec.

PLACES TO SEE IN QUEBEC

Laurentides Park, 4,000 square miles, in south central Quebec, on State Highway 54A. Contains more than 1,500 lakes; excellent fishing and recreation area; one of the largest parks in Canada.

Fort Chambly National Historic Park, 2 acres, at Chambly, 15 miles east of Montreal, in southern Quebec, on State Highway 1. Site of Fort Chambly, built by the French in 1665; a museum contains relics of several wars.

Fort Lennox National Historic Park, 210 acres, at Ile-aux-Noix, 12 miles south of St. Jean, in southern Quebec, on State Highway 9B. Old French fort fought over by the British and Americans before the Revolutionary War.

Montmorency Falls, near the mouth of the Montmorency River, about 10 miles north of Quebec, in the southern part of the province. Magnificent falls, 275 feet high.

Isle of Orleans, in the St. Lawrence River, 5 miles northeast of Quebec. A charming island where the people live as they did in France in the Middle Ages; farmers use ox-drawn carts and plows and live in houses with thatched roofs.

Percé Rock, just off the coast of Percé on the Gaspé Peninsula, in eastern Quebec, on State Highway 6. A huge rock, 290 feet high and 1,500 feet long, shaped like a ship; a popular tourist attraction; also a bird sanctuary.

Trois Rivières Canoe Races, on the St. Lawrence River, every August. An exciting series of water sports.

Kandahar Ski Run, at the city of Quebec, held each spring. Skiing contests with people from many countries participating.

QUEBEC. Area, 594,860 square miles. Population (1971 census) 6,027,764. Capital, Quebec. Flower, maple leaf. Admitted to Dominion in 1867. Official abbreviation, Que.

Quebec

Quebec is the capital of the Province of Quebec in eastern Canada. It is on the St. Lawrence and St. Charles Rivers. Almost 170,000 people live there. Most of them are of French descent and speak Canadian French, but they also speak English. There are factories that make shoes and clothing and newsprint (paper), and there are breweries. Many of the people of Quebec take care of the tourists who go there each year on their vacations. There are many ski resorts near Quebec.

Quebec has a very old section with narrow, cobblestone streets, as in a French city of the Middle Ages. It also has castles and monasteries. The new part of the city is modern, with wide streets, hotels, and public buildings. Visitors may

obtain a fine view of Quebec from a boat on the St. Lawrence River. The city is built high up on rocks, and in the past this made the city easy to defend. Overlooking the St. Lawrence is the ancient fortress of Quebec, surrounded by big guns. Quebec has a number of excellent schools, including Laval University, and many fine museums and monuments.

Quebec was settled about 350 years ago by the French explorer Samuel de Champlain. The French held the city until 1759, when the British under General James Wolfe stormed the city and captured it from the French General Montcalm, in the Battle of the Plains of Abraham, or Battle of Quebec. See the articles on the Plains of ABRAHAM and the FRENCH AND INDIAN WARS.

QUEBEC. Population (1971 estimate) 170,000. Capital of the Province of Quebec.

Quebec Act

The Quebec Act was a law passed by the British Parliament in 1774. It was hated by the American colonists and was one of the acts that led to the Revolutionary War. The Quebec Act extended the boundaries of the province of Quebec to include a great deal of land that lay north of the Ohio River. This land had already been claimed by many of the American colonies, such as Pennsylvania and Virginia. After the American colonists won the Revolutionary War, the land north of the Ohio became a part of the United States.

Quebec, Battle of

The Battle of Quebec was an important English victory over the French during the French and Indian Wars, about two hundred years ago. A large French force under the Marquis of Montcalm was encamped on a level hill called the Plains of Abraham, high above the St Lawrence River. On the night of September 12, 1759, the English general, James Wolfe, led 4,500 British soldiers to the Plains of Abraham by a narrow path up a cliff on the side of the hill. On the following morning the French were forced to attack. The British waited until the French were forty paces (about 120 feet) away and then defeated them with two great volleys of fire. The city of Quebec fell to the British four days later. See the articles on the Plains of ABRAHAM and the FRENCH AND INDIAN WARS.

Queens

Queens is the largest in area and second-largest in population of the five boroughs of New York City. It is between the East River and the Atlantic Ocean, on the west end of Long Island. Almost two million people live in Queens, and most of them work in the Borough of Manhattan and in Long Island City (which is a section of Queens). They travel to work by subway, train, and automobile. Queens is mostly a borough of homes.

Many people who live in New York visit Queens in the summer to go swimming at Riis Park and Rockaway Beach. One of the most important events each year in Queens is the tennis championship match for the Davis Cup at Forest Hills. People can also see horse races at the Belmont and Aqueduct race tracks.

Queens was settled by the Dutch, more than three hundred years ago. It became a borough of New York City in 1898, but very few people lived there until subways and bridges were built. As Manhattan, Brooklyn, and the Bronx became overcrowded, more and more people went to live in new houses and apartments in Queens. Since 1920 the population of Queens has grown enormously. The New York World's Fair was held in Queens in 1939–1940 and again in 1964.

QUEENS. Borough of New York City. Population (1970 census) 1,973,708. Settled, 1635.

quetzal

The quetzal is the national bird of Guatemala. It is one of the most beautiful birds in the world, and was considered sacred by the Aztecs, the Indians who lived in that region before Columbus discovered America. Today the quetzal is found only in Central America and Mexico. It is brilliantly colored, and the male has a long train of shining green tail feathers. The train is sometimes two feet long by itself. The underside of the bird is a bright scarlet and the head is green.

The quetzal lives on insects and fruit. Its nest is a hole in a tree, and the male bird shares in the work of hatching the two to four eggs, which are white or pale blue-green.

Quezon, Manuel

Manuel Luis Quezon was a lifelong fighter for Philippine independence and became the first President of the Commonwealth of the Philippines when it became an independent country in 1935. Quezon was born in 1878, when Spain ruled the Philippines. He served in the Spanish-American War and fought with Emilio Aguinaldo in the revolution against Spain. Later, he studied law. In 1909, Quezon was appointed Resident Commissioner from the Philippines to the United States. In this office he worked very effectively to persuade Congress to pass a law pledging independence to the Philippines as soon as a stable government had been formed. In 1916, Quezon was elected to the Philippine Senate, and he held this position until 1935, when he was elected as the first President of the Philippine Commonwealth. Quezon kept his country a good friend to the United States. When the Japanese occupied the Philippines in World War II, Quezon returned to Washington and led a government in exile until his death in 1944. He was buried in Arlington National Cemetery in Virginia until after the war, when his body was returned to the Philippines.

Quezon City

Quezon City is the capital of the Republic of the Philippines. It is on the island of Luzon, 10 miles east of Manila, which was formerly capital of the Philippines. About 545,500 people live in Quezon City. For several years before World War II, men began to build the city as an expansion of the capital at Manila. Streets were laid out and many houses were built. During the war, most of the government buildings in Manila were destroyed, and in 1948 the capital was moved to Quezon City. The city was named after Manuel Quezon, the first President of the Philippines.

QUEZON CITY. Population (1973 census) 545,500. Capital of the Republic of the Philippines. On Luzon Island.

quicksand

Quicksand is a thin, mushy mixture of sand and water. Once you get into quicksand it is very hard to get out of it. There are many stories about people who were caught in quicksand. The more they struggled to get out, the deeper they sank, until they were swallowed up by the quicksand and suffocated. These stories are exaggerated. No one is actually known to have died in this fashion. You may sink down for a way in quicksand, but you will eventually come to a level where you can float just as you would float in water. Heavy objects that would sink in water will sink in quicksand. Once, in Colorado, a locomotive fell into quicksand and sank so far that it could not be found, although poles were poked down into the sand to a depth of 50 feet.

The reason quicksand acts as it does is that it has grains of sand that are round. They roll over one another and never lock together as do the sharp grains of most kinds of sand. Under quicksand there is usually a layer of clay that keeps the water from sinking down into the earth and letting the sand dry out.

The only worrisome thing about quicksand is that you cannot tell it from any other kind of sand just by looking at it. If you should accidentally walk into quicksand, try to lie flat on your back with your arms and legs outstretched. Do not struggle. Shout for help. If no help comes, try to roll yourself back to solid ground.

quince

Quince is the name of a tree or shrub that is grown for its beautiful blossoms and its fruit. It belongs to the rose family. Most quince trees are low and crooked. The largest seldom grow higher than 20 feet. There are several small varieties that grow like shrubs. They have red, white or pink blossoms. The fruit cannot be eaten raw, but it is used to make jelly or marmalade. The fruit is shaped like a pear and has seeds inside as pears and apples have.

quinine

Quinine is one of the most important drugs known to doctors, because for many years it was the only remedy for the disease called malaria. Quinine is made from the bark of the cinchona tree, which grows in South America and the Far East. The bark is stripped from the tree and dried and ground to a powder. Quinine is taken in the form of either powder or pills. It has a very bitter taste. In tropical countries, where the danger of getting malaria is very great, many people take a dose of quinine every day. A number of other drugs have been developed for malaria, notably the drug atabrine.

Quirinal

The Quirinal is one of the seven hills on which the ancient city of Rome

was built. According to legend, two brothers named Romulus and Remus founded Rome, and after the death of Romulus the people built a temple to him on top of the hill and worshiped him as Quirinus, the god of war. Almost four hundred years ago a palace was built on Quirinal Hill and used as the summer home for the Popes. In 1870 it became the home of the king of Italy and in 1948 the home of the president of Italy.

Quisling, Vidkun

Vidkun Quisling was a Norwegian who helped Germany to conquer his country in World War II. His name and deeds have given the word *quisling*, meaning "traitor," to the English language. Quisling was born in 1887. He became an army officer, and in 1931 he was appointed minister of defense. Two years later he resigned to form a Norwegian Fascist party. When the Germans invaded Norway in 1940, Quisling helped them and was made premier. After the war, in 1945, Quisling was arrested, tried for high treason, and shot.

Quito

Quito is the capital and the second-largest city of Ecuador in South America. It is in the Andes Mountains. More than 450,000 people live there. There are factories that make cotton and woolen goods, lace, and carpets. Quito is an important educational center, with fine schools, museums, and collections of art. It is a beautiful city, set in a valley 9,350 feet above sea level and surrounded by the snow-capped peaks of the Andes. Part of the city is very old, with narrow streets, old churches, and open market places.

Quito was one of the first cities settled in South America. More than five hundred years ago it was ruled by Inca emperors. Spaniards conquered the city in 1534 after fierce fighting, and kept it under Spanish rule for almost three hundred years. It became the capital of Ecuador in 1830.

QUITO. Population 462,863. Capital of Ecuador. In the Andes Mountains.

quoits, a game played by tossing rings at stakes to try to make the ring go over the stake. See the article on HORSE-SHOES.

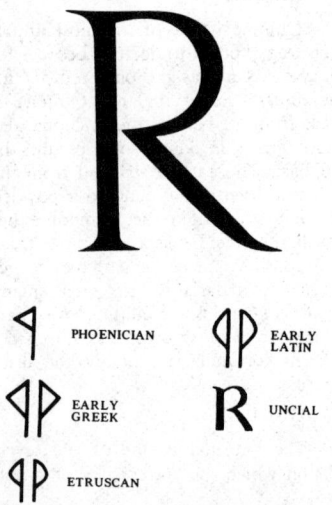

PHOENICIAN

EARLY GREEK

ETRUSCAN

EARLY LATIN

UNCIAL

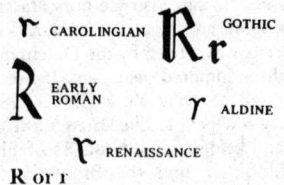

CAROLINGIAN

EARLY ROMAN

RENAISSANCE

GOTHIC

ALDINE

R or r

The letter R, the eighteenth letter of our alphabet, came to us as most of our letters did: First, thousands of years ago, it was perhaps one of the symbols used by the ancient Egyptians in their system of "picture-writing," or hieroglyphics. In this system a picture of something, instead of a letter, finally came to stand for a single sound. Some people believe that the letter R began as a picture of a mouth, but other scholars have come to think that it began as a picture of a head. In the Hebrew language, the word for head was *resh,* and the sign for it was the same as the Phoenician letter shown on this page.

The ancient Greeks adopted this symbol, but they called the letter *rho.* The Hebrews read from right to left, but later the Greeks began to read from left to right as we do today, so they turned the letter around, as shown just below the Phoenician letter. When the Romans borrowed the letter, they added another stroke, making it look like the R in our alphabet. In the illustration above, at the far right is the "German black-letter" (or "Gothic") capital R that is used in many German books.

Read also the article ALPHABET.

rabbit

Rabbits are long-eared, large-eyed, and four-legged mammals found throughout the world. Their hind legs are long and powerful, which enable them to move very quickly in a series of leaps. The term rabbit was first used to refer to the European rabbit of southern and central Europe. Other rabbits include the Angora rabbit, the Dutch rabbit, the cottontails of North America, and the Belgian hare. Despite its name, the Belgian hare is a rabbit. Hares differ from rabbits. See the entry on HARES.

All rabbits are vegetarians, and they use their two long front teeth to gnaw vegetables, shrubs, tree bark etc. Most rabbits weigh from 2 to 4 pounds, except the Flemish Giant rabbit, which can weigh as much as 18 pounds. Usually, rabbits breed from February to September with several litters each year and 3 to 9 rabbits per litter. As a result, rabbits multiply rapidly.

Most rabbits do not group together, but live apart in nests or holes under rocks or logs. The European rabbit, however, prefers to live in large colonies of the underground burrows called *warrens.*

Rabelais, François

François Rabelais was a French writer who lived about 450 years ago. He was born about 1490. He was educated in a monastery and became a member of the Franciscan Order of monks. Later he changed and became a Benedictine monk.

Rabelais studied sci-

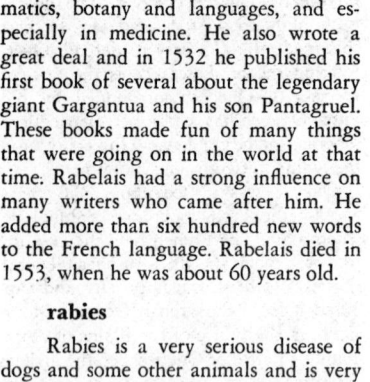

ence and was very learned in mathematics, botany and languages, and especially in medicine. He also wrote a great deal and in 1532 he published his first book of several about the legendary giant Gargantua and his son Pantagruel. These books made fun of many things that were going on in the world at that time. Rabelais had a strong influence on many writers who came after him. He added more than six hundred new words to the French language. Rabelais died in 1553, when he was about 60 years old.

rabies

Rabies is a very serious disease of dogs and some other animals and is very dangerous to a person who has been bitten by a rabid dog (a dog that has the disease). Rabies is also called *hydrophobia.* It is caused by a virus that is so small it cannot be seen even under a microscope. The virus is present in the saliva in the mouth of the diseased animal. There is no cure for rabies, but fortunately the disease is rare in human beings.

Dogs develop two kinds of rabies. The furious type is easier to recognize than the dumb type. A dog that has the furious type of rabies becomes very unsociable and refuses food. It grows nervous and restless and begins to snarl and growl at imaginary objects. Gradually it becomes vicious and chases and bites other animals and human beings. At this stage it is called a "mad dog." Finally the dog becomes paralyzed and dies.

A dog with the dumb type of rabies is quiet. It is unable to swallow and acts as if it were choking on a bone. Gradually its body becomes paralyzed and the dog dies.

A person who has been bitten by a dog should immediately take certain precautions. He should see a doctor at once. If possible the dog should be examined to see if it has rabies. The person should wash the wound thoroughly with strong soap and water. If there is any possibility that the dog has rabies the person must receive a series of 14 injections. These are given each day for two weeks. This is called the Pasteur treatment and it protects the person against rabies. Dogs may receive injections to prevent the disease.

raccoon

The raccoon is a four-legged animal that lives in North America between southern Canada and Mexico, and occasionally farther south. It has valuable fur and it is sometimes kept as a pet. It has a black face, a sharp nose, and small, upstanding ears. The raccoon's large, bushy tail is its most noticeable feature. There are darker rings of color around the tail, and the fur on the entire body is long and thick, usually brownish or yellowish with darker markings.

Raccoons eat fish, frogs, eggs, small birds, insects, and mice, plus nuts, fruits, and berries. Raccoons are fond of ripe corn and often become a nuisance to farmers. The raccoon has an amusing habit of washing its meat carefully before eating it.

Although the raccoon is an excellent tree climber, it spends most of its time on the ground. It is an expert swimmer and usually lives near a brook or lake. Raccoons hibernate during the winter

months. They live in hollow trees or caves. In midwinter they wake up to mate, and the young raccoons are born in April or May. There are four or five in a litter.

races of man

Almost all of the more than three billion human beings on earth can be divided into three main groups called *races* These are usually called the "white" race, or Caucasians; the "black" race, or Negroes; and the "yellow" and "brown" race, or Mongolians.

Certain things about the appearance and form of the body make these races different from one another. The most obvious characteristic is the color of the skin, but skin color does not necessarily place a person in a particular race. Some of the people of India, for example, are darker than most Negroes yet racially they must be grouped with the very blond peoples of Norway and Sweden—that is, in the "white" race.

Anthropologists (scientists who study mankind) prefer to use the words Caucasoid, Negroid, and Mongoloid. The *-oid* at the end of a word means "like," or "resembling." In each of the three main groups, which the anthropologists call racial *stocks*, the members are like one another in certain ways but in other ways they can be quite different. In each stock there may be dozens or even hundreds of different peoples who may not look enough alike to seem related—except to a scientist. Each of the racial stocks is divided into smaller groups called races or subraces, and each of these smaller groups has its own characteristics. For example, among the Caucasoid stock there are the Nordics of northern Europe, who are usually tall and blond; the Alpine people of southern Europe, who are usually short and olive-skinned; the Mediterranean people of North Africa and southwestern Asia, who may be considerably darker (as many Arabs are) but may also be quite light-skinned; and the Hindu or Dravidic people of India, the ones mentioned above, who resemble the "black" race in skin color.

In the same way, the Mongoloid stock has its subdivisions, such as the yellow-skinned Chinese, the brown-skinned Malays, and the red-skinned American Indians; and the Negroid stock has its subdivisions, ranging from the very tall Bantus to the very short Hottentots.

There are many cases in which members of different races have intermarried to form a people who cannot be wholly classed in any race. For example, millions of "American Negroes" are a combination of Negroid and Caucasoid stocks.

The best-known physical characteristics of the three main groups are:

Caucasoid, or "white." Light skin, blond to black hair, brown or blue eyes. Straight to wavy hair. Much body hair. Head form varies greatly. Narrow nose and lips, small teeth.

Negroid, or "black." Very dark brown skin, dark brown or black hair, brown or dark brown eyes. Very curly (frizzled) hair. Little body hair. Long head, broad nose, thick lips, large teeth.

Mongoloid, or "yellow" and "brown." Yellowish to reddish-brown skin, dark brown or black hair, brown eyes. Straight hair. Little body hair. Round head, medium-broad nose and lips, small teeth.

It must be remembered that exceptions to all of these characteristics can be found in every race. Anthropologists judge by many other inherited physical features, such as blood types and the measurements of heads, arms, legs, and other parts of the body.

There is no difference in mental ability or in behavior among the different races. Throughout history certain peoples have boasted that they were racially superior to other peoples, but they were only fooling themselves. There is no scientific knowledge to support such claims.

A few small groups in various parts of the world are not definitely known to belong to any of the three main races. Examples are the Ainus of Japan and the Australian aborigines (the people who were there before the first white men arrived). Most anthropologists place them among the Caucasoid peoples.

The word "race" is often used incorrectly, as when people speak of a Jewish race or an Italian race. A group that has the same religion or the same nationality may have a separate *culture* but is not a separate *race*.

Each of the main groups is considered to have a "home continent": the Mongoloid in Asia, the Negroid in Africa, and the Caucasoid in Europe (and, since the 1500s, in the Americas). Here again there are exceptions in all cases. For example, the Magyars of Hungary and the Finns of Finland are Mongoloid peoples in Europe; the Berbers and Egyptians in Africa are Caucasoid; many Hindu peoples, as well as Arabs, Iranians and others in Asia, are Caucasoid; and the American Indians in North and South America are Mongoloid.

Rachmaninoff, Sergei

Sergei Rachmaninoff was a Russian musician. He was a composer (writer of music), a pianist, and a conductor. Rachmaninoff was born in Russia in 1873. He began his career as a piano teacher, and at the age of 24 became conductor of a private opera company. He was conductor of the Moscow Imperial Theater from 1904 to 1906. He appeared as a pianist and conductor in many cities of Europe and America. In 1918 he came to the United States and lived in New York City until his death, in 1943. Among the many works he composed are several short operas, some symphonies, four piano concertos, and many piano pieces and songs. His most popular piano composition is the *Prelude in C Sharp Minor*.

Racine, Jean

Jean Racine was a French poet and playwright who lived about three hun-

dred years ago. He was born in 1639. He studied to be a priest, then decided to be a writer. When he was 19 years old he went to Paris. He wrote a poem in honor of the marriage of the king and soon became well known.

Racine wrote plays that were very successful. Most of them were based on sub-

jects that the ancient Greek playwrights had used. Racine's best-known play is named *Phèdre*. Many people believe that Racine was the greatest French tragic playwright who ever lived. He died in 1699, when he was 60 years old.

radar

Radar is a way of using radio signals to locate an object, determine its speed, and find its distance from an observer. The name was invented by the United States Navy and is an abbreviation for *RAdio Direction And Range*. During World War II many enemy planes were shot down by anti-aircraft guns controlled by radar, even when the planes could not be seen from the ground. Today, radar is used to guide ships and planes.

Radar operates on the same principles as radio and televsion. A transmitter antenna sends out powerful radio signals (electromagnetic beams) that travel short or long distances, up to hundreds of miles, with the speed of light (186,-300 miles a second). When these signals strike an object such as a ship or an airplane, they are reflected (bounced off). The reflected signals, called echoes, return to the radar unit, where they are picked up by a receiver antenna. To permit the receiver to pick up these signals, the transmitter must be shut off for a fraction of a second. Instead of sending out a continuous signal, the transmitter

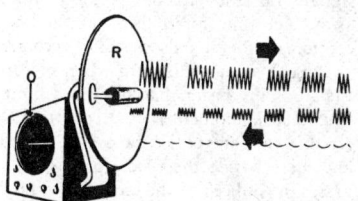

Radar (R) finds objects by means of the reflections of radio waves that hit the object and bounce back to the radar. Distances are measured by timing the return with an oscilloscope (O).

sends out interrupted signals, or pulses, each lasting for about a millionth of a second, called a *microsecond*. When the transmitter is on, the receiver is off, and vice versa.

Both the transmitter and the receiver are connected to an indicator called a cathode-ray oscilloscope, which is like the picture tube of a television set. The oscilloscope changes the signals into a small beam of light that traces a line on a screen. Each time a signal is transmitted or received, a small peak (called a *pip*) is traced on the screen. The distance between a transmitted pip and a received pip shows the time it has taken for the signal to travel out into space, strike an object, and be reflected back to the radar unit. This time tells how far away the object is.

By revolving the receiver antenna it is possible to determine the direction in which the reflected signals are the strongest. In this way the exact location of the object can be found. The object's speed is found by tracking, or following, the object with the radar signals and checking its position at various times. Distance, speed and direction are automatically determined by an electronic calculator ("giant brain") connected to the radar unit.

USES OF RADAR

Various systems using the principles of radar have been developed since the first radar unit was installed on the battleship *New York* in 1938. During World War II a system known as BTO (an abbreviation for *bombing through overcast*) was used in bombing planes to direct bombs accurately on targets in cloudy weather. Another system known as IFF (an abbreviation for *identification, friend or foe*) was used by friendly planes and ships to identify themselves to ground radar units. A friendly plane or ship caught in the signals of a radar unit would respond by sending back special signals in code. A transmitter on the plane or ship would send these signals automatically whenever the radar beam fell on it.

The most important system using radar is the PPI (an abbreviation for *plan-position indicator*). The indicator traces an outline somewhat like the outline of a map. By examining the trace for different shades of light, the operator can tell if an area contains water, land, mountains, valleys, cities, ships, islands, and even storms.

A system known as GCA (an abbreviation for *ground-controlled approach*) is used at airfields to guide airplanes in for landings. Other uses of radar are in aerial photography and in astronomy. In 1946 astronomers were able to reflect radar signals off the moon, 240,000 miles away. The time for transmission and reception of the signals was 2½ seconds.

Police use radar to learn when motorists are going faster than the speed limit. The radar equipment is usually carried in a police car. The police car can be placed anywhere beside the road. As a speeder passes the police car, the radar shows how fast he is going in miles per hour. The men at the radar car then call another police car or a station farther down the road, and a policeman there stops the motorist. The radar record is more accurate evidence of speeding than a policeman's opinion can be.

FOOLING RADAR

Several methods of fooling radar have been developed. The first was developed by the Germans and was nothing but a device that detected the radar signals, telling the operator of a plane or ship that he was being tracked. The operator could then change his course. A much more effective device was a receiver that picked up the radar signals and prevented them from being reflected back to the radar unit. Other methods were developed to send back false echoes to the radar unit, causing incorrect pips to show on the screen.

Several years after the development of radar it was discovered that bats in flight send out high-pitched squeaks, so high that the human ears cannot hear them. The sensitive ears of the bats can pick up the echoes these squeaks make when they strike objects ahead of them. In this way the bats can tell where they are going in much the same way as a radar operator tracks objects.

See also the article on SONAR.

radio

Radio is a method of sending sounds for long distances by the use of electricity but without connecting wires. Radio is a popular means of entertainment throughout the world and is also important to business, industry, and governments. Although television became a more popular form of home entertainment in the United States in the 1950s, almost every home has one or more "radio sets" to receive the sounds, and there are more than 5,000 "broadcasting stations" to send "programs" and messages. Radio is used in business for sending telegraphic messages and telephone calls overseas and for other long distances. It is used by police departments and taxicab operators to keep in touch with their automobiles on the streets. Governments use it for sending messages and to inform the people, as when there is an emergency. And, of course, radio furnishes the sound that goes with the television picture.

Radio really began more than sixty years ago when an Italian inventor named Guglielmo Marconi perfected the wireless telegraph. It had been discovered some years before that electromagnetic waves could be sent through the air. These waves are like light waves but they go out from a wire carrying an electric current instead of from a shining light. Many miles away, these waves are still traveling. Their power is very faint by that time, but Marconi worked out a way by which the weak electromagnetic waves could turn a battery on and off. The battery, in turn, supplied an electrical current strong enough to operate a telegraph set. Marconi's wireless made it possible for messages to be sent to and from ships far out at sea and to other places where there were not or could not be telegraph cables.

The wireless telegraph used a device called an *electronic tube,* which is explained in the article on ELECTRONICS. In 1907 an American inventor, Lee De Forest, produced another kind of tube that would amplify (strengthen) the waves from the air so much that sounds could be heard, as they are on the telephone. These sounds were still too weak to be heard throughout a room, and the early radio receivers could be heard only through earphones, by one person at a time. Improved tubes made possible the *loudspeaker,* which was introduced in the early 1920s. Radio then grew rapidly and by the end of the 1920s nearly every American home had a radio set or was planning to buy one.

HOW RADIO WAVES ARE SENT

Just as a wave in an ocean or lake changes direction constantly, flowing back and forth, so do radio and sound waves go back and forth (or up and down) as they travel through the air. The movement of the waves is like a zigzag line. The changes in direction are called *oscillations.* The *wave length* is the distance the wave travels forward each time it completes a trip back and forth. The *frequency* is the number of times the wave changes direction in a second. The waves always travel at about 186,000 miles per second, so if the wave length is long, the frequency has to be very low.

Radio waves are sent out by a *transmitter.* First, the sound is spoken, sung or played into a microphone. The sound waves make a part of the microphone vibrate (shake). This shaking generates and then sends electromagnetic waves through a wire, and every difference in the sound waves makes a difference in the electromagnetic waves.

Before these electromagnetic waves are actually broadcast (sent through the air), two things are necessary: they must be *modulated* and then *amplified.*

Because the wave oscillates back and forth, it would be a succession of loud and soft tones unless something were done to stop the tone from being uneven all the time. *Modulation* means "making even." In amplitude modulation (AM) radio, the broadcasting station automatically raises and lowers the power so that all the sound corresponds to the original sound. In *frequency modulation* (FM) radio, the frequency of the wave is made to vary with the original sound

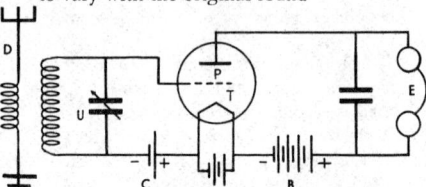

A simple radio works as follows: With the help of the aerial (D), the tuning circuit (U) picks up signals that it sends to the radio tube (T), making the plate (P) vibrate. This produces sound in the earphones (E). A, B and C are batteries.

FM is considered better, because static (waves that were not broadcast, but that travel along with the radio waves) can be heard along with AM radio but not with FM radio. Also, FM radio can carry a wider range of sounds than AM radio. FM radio is used with all television sets.

The electromagnetic waves from the microphone are modulated and additional electric power is used to send them out through the air with great force. This is done by *carrier waves,* which have great power and have the same frequency as the sound-carrying waves. Radio transmitters range from a few hundred watts to 50,000 or more watts in power. The largest licensed stations in the United States are 50,000 watts, though experimental stations up to 500,000 watts have been tried. (A bright light bulb burns about 100 watts.) The higher the wattage, the farther the waves are likely to carry.

WHERE THE WAVES GO

The radio waves are sent out from a tower that is usually built 50 or more feet high and on a hill or on open ground so that they will not strike nearby hills or buildings. The waves travel out in all directions from the transmitter. Some of them travel straight to radio sets in nearby homes. Some strike the ground and bounce back into nearby sets. But most of them travel 100 miles or more into the air and strike a zone of the atmosphere called the *ionosphere.* This is a zone charged with ions, which are particles of electricity. When the radio waves strike the ionosphere they bounce back to earth. This may be hundreds of miles from where they started.

The *amplitude* of a wave is the distance the wave travels from the extreme bottom or top of its zigzag path to the

midway line of that path. This distance ranges from many miles to a few hundred feet. "Standard broadcast" uses medium-length waves, and may be heard for several hundred miles under the best possible conditions. Short-wave radio can sometimes be heard for thousands of miles, but it is not as dependable as the standard wave lengths at short distances because it bounces off the ionosphere more easily.

In the United States, the Federal Communications Commission, an agency of the United States government, makes the rules that broadcasters must follow. It assigns to each station a wave length that no other station may use—unless the other station is too far away to be heard.

RADIO RECEIVERS

A radio receiver is usually called simply a "radio set." One of its parts is an *antenna*, or long wire. The radio wave in the air strikes this wire and is carried by a *lead-in* wire to the *chassis*, or combination of parts, that make the receiver work. A large, outdoor antenna is best, but modern radio receivers are so powerful that a length of wire in the set will give satisfactory reception.

Of course, the air is full of radio waves of different wave lengths, broadcast by different stations. The listener wants to select only one of these wave lengths. For this purpose the receiver has a *tuner*. A tuner has a coil of wire or a set of metal plates through which the current flows, and a *condenser* made of two or more metal plates separated by a material that will not conduct electricity. The coil or the set of metal plates can be moved back and forth along the condenser. (Turning the dial makes it move.) At each position a different frequency will flow into the condenser.

The *detector* is a radio tube that changes alternating current to direct current. (In early radio sets, called "crystal sets," a piece of crystal did this, because a current will flow in only one direction through certain crystals.) The radio waves come through the air on an alternating current carrier, which constantly changes direction. In order to get the sound from the carrier, a *detector* must be used. The detector solves the problem by changing the current to direct current, which always flows in the same direction. The waves flowing through the detector change into sound waves, which will eventually be heard by the ear.

Other radio tubes (or, in many sets, transistors) amplify the sound (make it louder). They add electric power to the weak signal (radio wave) received from the air. In an *heterodyne* receiver, special tubes reduce the frequency of the wave. (Heterodyne means "different force.")

A large radio set may have eleven or more tubes to perform these many tasks. Transistors have replaced tubes for many uses because they are much smaller and last indefinitely.

RADIO BROADCASTING

All entertainment and information broadcast by radio is free in the United States. The broadcasting stations pay the cost of some programs. Advertisers pay for other programs so that they can broadcast an advertising message (called a "commercial") at the same time. The owners of the radio station make a profit by charging fees for the advertising messages. (This is explained in the article on ADVERTISING.) In some countries, radio time is not sold to advertisers but the owner of a radio set pays a tax.

The first broadcasting stations in the United States, established just after World War I (which ended in 1918), were owned by manufacturers of radio sets. They paid the cost of sending music and news over the air, because nobody would have wanted to buy a radio if there were no programs to hear. By the middle 1920s it was clear that the manufacturers could not afford to do this, and the plan of selling advertising time was adopted. Advertisers soon learned that the radio was one of the most effective means of advertising that had ever been discovered, and radio broadcasting became big business.

Broadcasting companies can be individual stations or networks. A network puts on a program in one place but sends it over telephone wires to radio stations throughout a region or all over the country ("coast-to-coast network"). For the cost of putting on one program, the network reaches the audiences of many stations. The advertiser pays a rate based on the number of persons who will probably hear his program.

Radio broadcasting grew until the biggest programs were heard by more than forty million people. The star performers on radio were known to everyone. Advertisers would pay $50,000 to put on a single program. Some of this went to the "talent" (performers on the show), some to the technical staff (producer, director, engineers, stagehands, and so on), some to the network for "time," and some to the advertising agency as a commission.

After World War II, which ended in 1945, television became popular. By 1951, the nighttime shows on television had bigger audiences than radio ever had, and most advertisers stopped paying for expensive shows with famous stars. Radio remained popular in the daytime, when most housewives are working and are able to listen to radio but cannot stop to watch television. Recorded music, news, plays and reports of sporting events were the most popular radio programs. Radio found a new large audience when millions of automobiles came to be equipped with radios.

radioactivity

Radioactivity is the breaking up or explosion of the center (nucleus) of the tiny particle of matter called the atom. When nuclei break up, they radiate (send out) high-speed particles, or rays.

These rays are of three kinds: *alpha*, *beta* and *gamma* rays, named after the first three letters of the Greek alphabet. Some substances give off only one kind. Others, such as radium, give off all three. The alpha rays actually are streams of nuclei of helium atoms. They are charged with positive electricity. Beta rays are streams of electrons, tiny particles of negative electricity. Gamma rays are very similar to X-rays and do not have any electrical charge. Some radioactive substances also release uncharged particles, called neutrons, that are found in the nuclei of all atoms except one form of hydrogen. These particles are very important in the explosion of an atomic bomb and in the creation of atomic energy. X-rays also are sometimes released by radioactive substances.

Particles released by radioactive substances can be detected by a GEIGER COUNTER, about which there is a separate article. They can be detected also by a Wilson cloud chamber, invented by an English scientist, Charles T. R. Wilson, about 1911. It is a container filled with a very moist gas. When the particles are

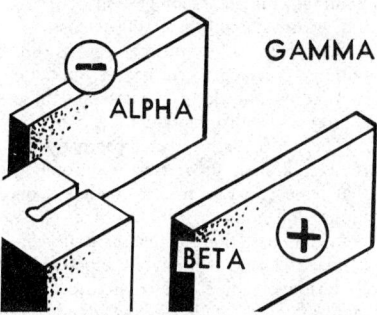

Strong magnets will separate rays from radioactive material. The negative magnet attracts alpha rays, the positive attracts beta rays, and gamma rays escape.

passed through the gas they collide with its atoms, giving them an electrical charge. This causes the moisture to collect on the atoms, showing the track or path along which the particles have gone.

DISCOVERY OF RADIOACTIVITY

Radioactivity was discovered by a French scientist, Antoine Henri Becquerel, in 1896. He was experimenting with different substances to see if they would glow in the dark after being exposed to light. He would expose them to light and then place them on some photographic paper to see if any light came from them after exposure. One day he put some uranium metal, the substance so important in the development of atomic energy, on some photographic paper without having exposed the metal to sunlight. The paper was in a heavy black wrapper to keep out the light. On examining the paper a few days later, Becquerel discovered small white streaks, indicating that the paper had been exposed to light. Since the paper had been kept in a wrapper all this time, the only answer was that radiation of some sort from the uranium metal had passed through the wrapper on to the paper even though the uranium itself had not been exposed to light.

After this discovery, many scientists started to investigate the behavior of uranium. Two scientists, Marie Curie and her husband Pierre, found that the ore from which uranium was made, called pitchblende, gave off even stronger radiation than uranium. This led them to the discovery of radium, a very powerful radioactive substance. Other naturally radioactive substances that have since been discovered are polonium, ionium, radon, and thorium.

RADIOACTIVE ELEMENTS

There are at least sixteen basic substances, or elements, in the earth that are radioactive and gradually break up or disintegrate into new substances. When an atom of radium explodes it breaks up

into two other atoms—a heavy gas called radon and a light gas called helium. Actually only a very small number of radium atoms explode at any instant. It takes about 1,600 years for half of a given quantity of radium to change into radon. We say that the *half-life* of radium is 1,600 years. The half-life of radon is only about 4 days, after which it changes into polonium. The process continues until the final product, lead, is formed. Radium itself is the product of a whole series of breakdowns starting with uranium. It is the fifth such breakdown, beginning with the disintegration of thorium, whose half-life is 70,000 years.

Scientists can tell the age of rocks containing radioactive substances, because they know how long it has taken those substances to disintegrate.

There are artificial radioactive substances, known as radioactive isotopes, that have valuable uses in medicine, biology and industry. Radioactive phosphorus is used in the treatment of leukemia, a cancer of the white blood cells. Radioactive iodine is used in the treatment of cancer of the thyroid gland. Scientists use radioactive materials as "tracers" to probe into the structure of metals and into the hidden processes of plant and human life.

RADIATION SICKNESSES

Radioactivity can be very dangerous. Beta rays, for instance, can penetrate about a third of an inch of human tissue. Neutrons can penetrate several feet of tissue. Radiation can attack and destroy the small particles of matter inside living things. It can damage and kill the cells out of which human muscles, nerves and tissues are formed. Even when radiation does not kill these cells, it prevents them from functioning in a normal way. This was proved by examination of victims of the atomic bomb explosions in Hiroshima and Nagasaki, Japan, during World War II. Many people were made sick by the radiation released by the bombs. They were made sick in the same way as many factory workers were made sick many years ago by swallowing small quantities of radium as they licked their paint brushes containing radium paint for painting clock dials. Many died horrible deaths due to the severe destruction of the body cells.

See also the article on ATOM.

radish

A radish is a vegetable whose fleshy root is usually eaten raw as a relish or in salads. There are red, pink, and white radishes. The roots may be round or long and pointed. The icicle radish has a slender, long, white root. It tastes like the red types but may be slightly stronger. The winter radish, which is planted late in summer, grows to about the size of a small turnip. It may have a black or white skin. It is usually cooked and served like turnips.

Radishes are annual plants, which means that they must be replanted from seed each year. Most varieties grow very quickly and are ready to eat in three to five weeks.

radium

Radium is a white metallic chemical element, which means that it is one of the basic substances of which all things in the world are made. Radium is radioactive—it is continually shooting off from itself X-rays, electrons, and helium atoms. The X-rays can kill cancer cells, so one of radium's first important uses was to fight cancer. A tiny bit of radium will make paint or varnish shine in the dark, so it is used in the luminous dials of watches and clocks.

Radium is obtained from either of two minerals, pitchblende or carnotite. The French scientists Marie and Pierre Curie discovered and named radium in 1898, and in 1910 Madame Curie was able to separate a tiny bit of pure radium.

As radium shoots off radioactive particles, it slowly turns into lead. It takes 1,700 years for half of a new piece of radium to turn into lead, and in not quite 3,400 years all but a very tiny bit of it will have turned into lead.

Radium is very rare. The largest amount of radium ever collected weighed less than two ounces and would not fill a thimble.

raffia

Raffia is a dried fiber made from the long leaves of the raffia palm that grows on the island of Madagascar. It is used to tie plants to stakes in gardens, to hold bunches of vegetables together in markets, and for making trays and baskets.

Raffia usually appears in its natural yellowish color, but it can be dyed many bright colors.

ragweed

Ragweed is a common plant that grows wild in many places. It has a cluster of small blossoms at the end of each stalk. The pollen of the ragweed is blown through the air and makes many people suffer from hay fever and asthma. Serious efforts have been made to eliminate the ragweed, but it still grows in most parts of the United States and spreads widely when it is not controlled.

rail

Rails are birds that usually run swiftly through the grass instead of taking to the air. They are found in all parts of the world, and there are more than 130 different kinds. Rails belong to the group of birds called marsh birds. They usually live in marshes or swamps. Hunters shoot rails, which are delicious to eat.

The rail most common in North America, the clapper rail, is a brown bird about as large as a small pigeon. It builds its nest on the ground of salty marshland.

railroad or railway

A railroad is a method of transportation in which engines on wheels, called locomotives, pull trains of cars over tracks made of smooth steel girders fastened in place. Railroad trains carry passengers and freight.

Railroads began to spread through the civilized world about the year 1830, when the first steam engines were built with enough power to pull heavy loads. Within twenty years railroads had become the most important land transportation in the world and they have remained so ever since, in spite of competition in the present century from motor vehicles and aircraft.

There have been great changes in the history of railroads and even in the last twenty-five years. For more than a hundred years, all trains were pulled by locomotives that got their power from steam. At first they burned wood, and then for many years they burned coal. At first a speed of 30 miles an hour was considered good. The cars were made of wood and shook and rattled as they rolled along. The brakes were not very safe and there were many accidents. Though the railroads were by far the fastest and most comfortable means of travel, passengers choked and were soiled by smoke and soot from the soft coal, sweltered in heat in the summer, and had to sit stiffly upright in seats that were almost straight-backed. An overnight journey, though it may have seemed comfortable then, was far from the comfort of a night in a hotel room with private bath.

The modern passenger train rolls smoothly at average speeds of 60 to 80 miles per hour. The locomotive probably uses a diesel engine that burns oil and is as clean to ride in as an automobile. The cars are made of heavy steel and are protected from accidents by air brakes and a scientific system designed to prevent two trains from being on the same section (called a block) of track. The seats are soft and can be adjusted so that a passenger can sit up or lean back, whichever he wishes. Many cars are air-conditioned so that they are cool in summer and warm in winter. Overnight trips are made in private rooms with private toilets.

There are many people whose hobby is studying old-fashioned trains and riding on them, where they still exist. They especially like the steam locomotives that were used on all trains of the past and are still used on many trains. These are described in the article LOCOMOTIVE, and sleeping cars are described in the article PULLMAN.

RAILROAD CONSTRUCTION

A railroad begins with the *roadbed* and *track*. The more solid the roadbed and the heavier the track, the smoother the ride will be and the heavier the load that the railroad can carry.

The roadbed runs along a *right of way*, a stretch of land that the railroad company must buy or lease before it can begin to lay its track. The right of way should be as straight and as level as it can be. The roadbed is prepared with a foundation of crushed rock called *ballast*. Across this are laid heavy pieces of lum-

ber called *ties*. There are two rails, made of steel in the shape of an upside-down T. Each piece of rail is usually 39 feet long. The rail weighs 100 pounds or more per yard. It is fastened down by big spikes driven into the ties.

In *standard gauge* railways, which are used in most countries of the world, the rails are 56½ inches apart (4 feet 8½ inches). A *narrow gauge* railroad is one whose rails are less than 4 feet 8½ inches apart, while a *broad gauge* railroad is one whose rails are more than that distance apart.

Many railroads have double tracks, so that trains may use different tracks to travel in opposite directions. In places where railroad traffic is very heavy, as between New York and Philadelphia, there may be four or six tracks side by side, so that two or three trains can travel in each direction at the same time. Most railroads have only a single track that they must use for trains traveling in both directions. This means that to pass one another, one of the trains must "go in the hole" (off on a siding) until the other has passed. Some single-track lines are equipped with centralized traffic control (CTC), by which one man in a tower may cause trains to be sidetracked a hundred or more miles away. With the use of CTC and sidetracks, two trains approaching each other on a single track are often able to pass without either train's having to stop.

The movements of passenger trains are published in a printed folder called a *timetable*. This shows when each train is supposed to arrive at each station and leave each station on its journey. Timetables mystify many people who have not learned to read them, but after you learn it is easy. Freight trains run on the same kind of schedules, but the average person does not often see their time tables.

The principal business of a railroad is carrying freight. Most railroads make more money on their freight trains than on their passenger trains, and some railroads actually lose money on their passenger trains and could not continue to operate if it were not for freight. There is a separate article about FREIGHT.

RAILROAD OPERATION

In nearly every country, the industrial (manufacturing) development depends on the railroads. The United States has far more railroads than any other country on earth. It has more than 217,000 miles of tracks. Germany, Great Britain, and France have about as much railroad development as the United States. They have far fewer miles of tracks, but they are smaller countries. Russia and Canada are well served by railroads in the sections where most of their people live and most of their manufacturing is done, but both of them have vast areas of land where few people live and there are no railroads.

Because railroads are so important to the prosperity of a country, most governments have laws that regulate the operation of railroads. In the United States the Interstate Commerce Commission, or ICC, an agency of the United States government, regulates railroads that do business in two or more states. This means nearly every railroad in the United States.

The ICC has to approve the rates charged by railroads for carrying passengers and freight.

The cost of travel on a railroad depends on the distance traveled and the kind of train taken. Many railroads carry passengers from suburbs of a big city into the city, for work or shopping. "Commuters" (people who travel regularly on these trains) can buy tickets, called *commutation tickets*, that are good for many rides and cost less for each ride than a passenger would have to pay for a single trip. A round-trip ticket, which will carry a passenger to a certain city and then back home again, usually costs less for each trip than a one-way ticket.

For long trips, there are special trains that offer a great many extra comforts not found on the average train. These trains are usually streamliners, pulled at high speeds by diesel locomotives. All seats are reserved, so tickets have to be bought in advance. There are fine dining cars, and lounge rooms where passengers can read and play games and listen to the radio. All trains of this kind are air-conditioned.

Extra-fare trains are usually trains on which all the cars are equipped with the latest in modern comforts and conveniences. The fares on extra-fare trains are regular Pullman fares, plus a flat additional charge for each ticket sold. An extra-fare train usually makes the trip from one city to another faster than a regular train. It is given right of way on the tracks; that is, other trains scheduled to use the same track must be sidetracked until the extra-fare train has passed.

Nearly every train that goes a long distance carries a dining car and some Pullman cars.

Railroad Brotherhoods

The Railroad Brotherhoods are a group of the largest and most powerful labor unions in the United States. All of them are made up of workers on railroads. The biggest and most widely known of these unions are: Brotherhood of Locomotive Engineers; Brotherhood of Locomotive Firemen and Enginemen; Brotherhood of Railroad Trainmen; Brotherhood of Railway Carmen of America; and Order of Railway Conductors and Brakemen. The five unions have a total of about 320,000 members.

The Railroad Brotherhoods succeeded more than thirty years in persuading Congress to pass laws that gave their members more protection than any labor union had ever had before. See the article on LABOR.

rainbow

Sometimes when the sun is shining during or just after a rain, we can see a huge curve of many colors in the sky. This curve, called a rainbow, is made up of bands of different colors and is caused by the fact that the light from the sun is bent by the drops of rain or moisture in the air.

Sunlight appears white but actually is composed of several colors. If you have ever seen a wheel that had different colors on it, you have noticed that the faster the wheel spins, the whiter it seems. Bending light breaks it up into its differ-

ent colors. Each color bends differently. Violet light is bent the most, and red light is bent the least. Since the colors bend differently, bending the white light separates them.

A rainbow appears because the drops of water in the air bend the light coming from the sun. See also the article PRISM and SPECTRUM.

rainfall

Rainfall is the amount of rain that falls on a particular place during a certain period of time. Usually rainfall is expressed in a number of inches of rain that falls in a certain locality during a year's time.

Rainfall is measured, usually at weather stations, by allowing the rain to collect in a large open can that has a funnel at the top leading to a tube at the bottom. After a rain has stopped, the amount of rainwater collected in the tube is measured with a ruler. At the end of a year the weathermen add up all the measurements to find the rain that fell at that place for the whole year. After several years they average the amount of rainfall by dividing the total amount that fell during those years by the number of years. If 100 inches of rain fell during a five-year period, then the weathermen divide 100 by 5 and get 20 inches as the average annual rainfall for that place.

The average annual rainfall differs greatly in different places. Some places have rain almost every day. Other places rarely have rain. The great rain forests in the hot tropical parts of South America, Africa, and the East Indies have the greatest average rainfalls in the world, more than 100 inches a year. The deserts of North Africa, Arabia, Central Asia and the southwestern United States have the least average rainfalls, less than 10 inches a year.

Weathermen use the word annual average *precipitation* as a complete measure of all the moisture that falls to the earth, including sleet, hail, and snow.

RAINFALL AND MAN

Rain is of great importance to man. He not only needs water for drinking and washing but his crops could not grow without it and his herds of animals would not be able to live without it. Therefore man rarely lives in the desert areas. Too much rain can be almost as bad, and makes living uncomfortable.

Most of mankind is concentrated in areas where there is a decent amount of rainfall, but not too much—perhaps 20 to 60 inches a year.

The article on WEATHER tells how rain is caused and why it falls.

Rainier, Mount

Mount Rainier is a mountain peak in the state of Washington. It is 14,408 feet high, the highest point in the state and the second-highest in the United States. Mt. Rainier is a volcano and still gives off fumes of sulfur, but it is regarded as extinct because its last eruption took place very long ago. In this eruption a large part of the peak was blown off, leaving a huge cauldron full of lava that eventually cooled and became the snow-covered Columbia Crest. The summit of Mt. Rainier is coated with more than

twenty glaciers, and it is a dangerous but exciting and popular climb. The 100-mile Wonderland Trail encircles the mountain. Mt. Rainier was discovered and named in 1792 by Captain George Vancouver, a British explorer.

An area of about 378 square miles surrounding the peak was established in 1899 as Mt. Rainier National Park. Other mountains in the park are Mt. Fremont, 7,300 feet; Pinnacle Peak, 6,562 feet; Crystal Peak, 6,515 feet; and Lane Peak, 6,000 feet.

Rain-in-the-Face

Rain-in-the-Face was a famous chief of the Sioux Indians of North America. Less than a hundred years ago, the Sioux and other tribes often fought settlers who were moving west and taking land from the Indians. In the 1870s gold was found in the Black Hills, in Montana, and many settlers went there in hopes of making a fortune. The Sioux fought many battles against them. In one of these battles, fought on June 25, 1876, Rain-in-the-Face and another great chief, Sitting Bull, led the Sioux against American soldiers under General George A. Custer and completely wiped out Custer's forces. More troops were sent against the Sioux and conquered them. Chief Rain-in-the-Face died in 1905.

Wash. State. Ad. Comm.
Majestic scenery surrounds a camp site on Lake Klapatcha at Mt. Rainier.

raisin

Raisins are a dried fruit made from some kinds of grapes. Small, sweet grapes without seeds make seedless raisins. Larger sweet grapes with seeds make raisins after the seeds are taken out, which is done by hand and sold in packets labeled "seeded raisins." The ripe, fresh grape is dried by heat and air. This is done by allowing ripe fruit to dry on the vine, or by dipping bunches of ripe grapes into a chemical solution and then letting them dry in the sun. As the grape dries, its skin shrivels.

Raisins contain large quantities of sugar, iron, and vitamins.

Raleigh

Raleigh is the capital and the fourth-largest city of North Carolina. It is in the central part of the state and is an important trading center for the rich farmlands surrounding the city. Raleigh is also an important center for education

and manufacturing. It was named for Sir Walter Raleigh.

About 121,000 people live in Raleigh. Many of them work in plants that process farm products. Other industries are textiles, electronics, concrete products, woodworking, and steel. There are printing and publishing houses and tobacco markets. The city has a city manager form of government, with an elected council.

The site on which Raleigh is built was originally a settlement called Bloomsbury. It was chosen to be the state capital in 1788, and the city was laid out in 1792.

Raleigh is the birthplace of President Andrew Johnson. There are several colleges, including the State College of Agriculture and Engineering of the University of North Carolina, Meredith College for Women, Shaw University, and St. Augustine's College. There are also state schools for the deaf and the blind.

RALEIGH, NORTH CAROLINA. Population (1970 census) 121,577. Capital of North Carolina. County seat of Wake County. Founded, 1792.

Raleigh, Sir Walter

Walter Raleigh was an English soldier, statesman and writer who lived about four hundred years ago. He was born in 1552 of a very old English family.

He grew up to become one of the most brilliant men in England. There are many stories about Raleigh. One of the best-known is about how Raleigh won the favor of Queen Elizabeth. One day the queen went for a walk. When she came to a mud puddle, Raleigh threw his handsome velvet cloak over the puddle so that the queen would not get her feet wet. Raleigh also is credited with introducing tobacco-smoking to England.

The Queen gave Raleigh many important positions. Twice he was sent on colonizing expeditions to America. The colonies, which were in Virginia, were unsuccessful but the explorers brought back the first tobacco and potatoes known to England.

Raleigh married Elizabeth Throckmorton, one of the Queen's ladies-in-waiting. This made the Queen angry and Raleigh was imprisoned in the Tower of London a few months. Finally the Queen forgave Raleigh and he again became important.

When Queen Elizabeth died, James I became king of England and he did not like Raleigh. Raleigh was sent once again to the gloomy Tower of London. He stayed there for thirteen years. While he was there he made chemical experiments, wrote poetry, and began to write a History of the World.

Finally James freed Raleigh from the Tower and sent him on an expedition to South America. Against the king's orders, Raleigh captured a Spanish settlement. When Raleigh landed in England he was arrested, and a few months later James had him executed. This was in 1618, when Raleigh was 66.

It is said that just before Raleigh died he touched the ax that was to end his life and said: "This is sharp medicine but it will cure all diseases." Raleigh, the capital of North Carolina, is named in his honor.

Rameses

There were twelve pharaohs, or kings, of ancient Egypt named Rameses, or Ramses, as it is sometimes spelled. Of these, the most important was Rameses II, who ruled Egypt more than three thousand years ago, from about 1292 to 1225 B.C. He was sometimes called the Great King. He built many magnificent buildings and palaces and tombs. His own tomb was found in 1881. It is believed that Rameses II may have been the pharaoh who oppressed the children of Israel, as told in the Bible (in the Book of Exodus).

ranch

A ranch is a big farm where cattle, and sometimes horses and sheep, are raised. Usually a ranch is not fertile farm land, but is sandy soil on which enough grass grows to feed large numbers of grazing animals. There must also be enough water for the animals to drink.

In the United States, nearly all ranches are in the western states. Some of them are very big, with tens of thousands of acres. Many of the biggest are in Texas.

The work of operating a ranch is called *ranching*. It has always been considered by Americans to be a very interesting kind of work, and many thousands of stories have been written about the cowboys and other workers on cattle ranches. Most of these stories are about times in the years soon after the Civil War, when most of the western territory had not yet become states with regular law-enforcement officers and when there were many outlaws and unfriendly Indians and others against whom the law-abiding people had to protect themselves.

On a ranch there is usually a ranch house where the owners live, and other buildings nearby where the cowboys and other workers live. Until recent years, nearly all ranch workers did their work on horseback, and there were many horses kept for them to ride. There is still much use for horses on a ranch, but in most cases the men can travel around the ranch in Jeeps or other light cars.

The men ride out to work each morning, and since ranches are very large they may have to go quite a distance. They keep the cattle or other livestock together, drive them to new grazing ground or to water, and each year they drive them to a city or other place where there is a railroad and load them into cattle cars for shipment.

In the old days the animals used to be shipped to market, but now they are usually shipped to farms in midwestern and eastern states, where they are fed on grain and other fodder to be fattened for market.

Once each year, ranches in the same neighborhood have a round-up. They drive the cattle together and brand the calves that have been born since the last round-up. Each ranch has a special design called its brand. This is burned into

the thick hide of the animal with a hot iron shaped in the design of the brand. (Horses and sheep are not branded.)

There are many vacation resorts called *dude ranches*. People can go there and learn to ride horseback and live somewhat as the cowboys do. In California and some other states, almost any farm is called a ranch.

Rangers

The Rangers are military troops that are trained for special kinds of combat. They usually operate in small groups or alone, and are used in surprise attacks on enemy troops and to perform difficult and daring military feats.

The first troops called Rangers were a group of men who fought under Colonel Robert Rogers on the side of the British in the French and Indian Wars, two hundred years ago. These Rangers learned to use many methods of the Indians, such as surprise attacks and ambushes in the thick forests.

During World War II the British used specially trained troops called Commandos to get behind enemy lines and capture high officers, destroy headquarters or radio stations, and make other surprise attacks. The United States formed units of the same kind and called them Rangers in honor of the Rogers' Rangers of long ago.

After World War II the United States Army continued to train Rangers, but they were not kept in special Ranger units. Instead, a few Rangers were placed in regular infantry units to teach their methods to regular soldiers.

HOW RANGERS ARE TRAINED

Rangers are trained in an eight-week course. The training is given to officers and enlisted men who volunteer for it. They must be in excellent physical condition and able to swim at least 50 feet.

The first three weeks of the course are given at Fort Benning, Georgia. There the men must pass tests of physical endurance to prove that they are strong enough to continue the course.

The second part of the course is given in the jungles and swamps of northern Florida. There the men take long hikes and learn how to live outdoors with only a compass to guide them. They must find their own food, and they must perform such difficult tasks as blowing up a heavily guarded "enemy" bridge.

The third part of the course takes place in the mountains of northern Georgia. There the men learn how to climb mountains and how to fight on hilly ground.

Before a soldier can graduate and become a Ranger, he must pass several more tests that prove his courage. One of these may be crossing a river by means of a rope bridge more than thirty feet above the water.

Ranger training stresses initiative and teamwork. Initiative means going ahead and doing something without being told or shown how to do it. The trainees are encouraged to solve their own problems. They are taught to work together by a system called the "buddy system." Each man is assigned to one other man, who is called his buddy, and the pair must work together. If a man disobeys a rule and is punished for it, his buddy is also punished.

A Ranger wears a special patch with the word "Ranger" on the left shoulder of his uniform.

Rangoon

Rangoon is the capital city of Burma, in eastern Asia. About 1,717,650 people live there. Rangoon is on the Rangoon River, about twenty miles from the sea. It is an important seaport, handling about three-quarters of Burma's shipping. The city is an important commercial center, connected with all parts of Burma by roads, railroads and waterways. It is one of the world's great rice markets. Other exports are petroleum and teakwood. Rangoon also has rice and lumber mills, oil refineries, and other industrial plants.

Until Burma became an independent country in 1948, Rangoon was a city of many nationalities, only about a third of the population being Burmese. Since that time the number of Burmese has increased to more than half.

Rangoon is carefully laid out, with numbered streets crossing at right angles as in most American cities. Towering over Rangoon is the magnificent Shwe Dagon Pagoda, the largest Buddhist temple in the world. This gilded temple stands on a high hill, and the building itself is 326 feet high. It is visited by thousands of Buddhist pilgrims every year.

The University of Rangoon was founded in 1920. During World War II, Rangoon was occupied by the Japanese for three years. Much of the city was destroyed by bombing.

RANGOON, BURMA. Population (1973 estimate) 1,717,649. Seaport on the Rangoon River. Capital of Burma. Founded, 1755.

Raphael

Raphael Santi (or Sanzio) was an Italian painter of the Renaissance, the time about 450 years ago when artists and sculptors were producing some of the finest works of art ever seen. With Leonardo da Vinci, Michelangelo, and Titian, Raphael is considered among the greatest Italian artists. He was born in 1483. His father, who was a painter, taught him his art.

When Raphael was 25 years old, he was called to Rome as one of the painters to decorate the Vatican. His paintings in the Vatican include the *School of Athens*, which shows the philosophers of ancient Greece.

Raphael remained in Rome the rest of his life, painting pictures for the Church and doing portraits of some of the great men of his day. He was kept very busy at his art, so busy that he had to employ assistants to help him.

Raphael is best known for his religious paintings, particularly those of Mary, the mother of Jesus, and the infant Jesus. These are all known by the title *Madonna and Child*. He painted many of these. The best known is the *Sistine Madonna*, painted for the monks of San Sisto.

When he was only 37 years old, in 1520, Raphael caught a fever and died. The people of Rome gave him a magnificent funeral and he was buried in the Pantheon, a splendid building dating from ancient times, where many great men are buried.

raspberry

The raspberry is a plant that bears sweet berries. The plant spreads widely. Raspberry plants have small spiny thorns all along the stems of the canes and shoots, and even the leaves have stickers on them. This makes picking raspberries unpleasant unless one is very careful.

There are black, red, yellow and purple raspberries. All are used as dessert fruits and for making jams, jellies, and preserves. Each berry is divided into several sections, with a small seed in each. Raspberries look somewhat like blackberries and dewberries, and all these plants are called brambles.

Rasputin

Gregory Efimovich Rasputin was a Russian monk who became one of the most powerful men in the country at the time of World War I. Rasputin was born in Siberia in 1872, of a peasant family. Although he had little or no education, he became a monk. He managed to work his way into the confidence of the czar (emperor) of Russia, Nicholas II, and his family by supposedly curing the crown prince of a serious blood disease. Within a short time, the czar was listening to Rasputin's advice, most of which was bad. When Russia was fighting in World War I, the nobles thought that Rasputin was trying to make a separate peace with Germany. A group of them, led by Prince Yussupov, plotted to get rid of him. First they poisoned him, and when this did not kill him they shot him and dumped his body into the river. This was on December 31, 1916, when Rasputin was 44 years old.

rat

A rat is a rodent, or gnawing animal. There are thousands of different kinds of rat. The most familiar is the house rat, a pest that lives in city dumps, around farms and houses, and wherever else man goes. This is an unpleasant, dirty animal that causes millions of dollars worth of loss and damage every year. Man has never been able to exterminate rats. A rat breeds all year round, with litters of six or seven as often as twelve times a year. The smallest of these rats are about 5 inches long and the large ones may be as long as 12 inches. There are more rats in North America than there are people.

Some kinds of rat are not dirty and are not pests. See the article on the PACK RAT.

ratel

The ratel is an animal like the badger, but it lives in Africa and Asia, while the badger lives in Europe and America. The ratel may be as much as three feet long and weigh about 25 pounds. Its fur is white or light gray on the back and jet black on the underside. Like the skunk, it gives off an unpleasant odor when enemies alarm or attack it.

The ratel lives on rocky hills and plains, and in forests. It eats the larvae (young) of termites, bees, ants, and other insects, but it also eats snakes, small

animals, birds, and occasionally fruit. Its hide is thick and rubbery, and hangs loosely all over its body, so that snake-bites and bee stings do not bother the ratel.

rationing

At certain times, things that everybody needs become very scarce so that there are not enough to go around. For example, there may not be as much meat as everybody wants, or as much coffee, or sugar. This may happen in wartime, or in the years following a war, or in times of famine. When food and needed supplies are scarce, rich people are willing and able to pay very high prices for these things, and if the government did not do something people with ordinary incomes would not be able to buy their share of the scarce goods. So in most countries the government gives each person a *ration,* a certain amount of the scarce things that he is allowed to buy, no matter how much he can pay. Usually the government combines rationing with price controls, setting a ceiling that is the highest price that can be charged for each item.

During World War II, nearly all countries in the war used rationing. In the United States, each person had books of coupons, or stamps, called ration books. Each time he wanted to buy a rationed article, he had to give the dealer a stamp as well as money. Each stamp was worth some number of points, and a person could use a certain number of points each month.

Automobile tires were the first thing to be rationed. Sugar, gasoline and coffee followed soon after. By 1943 the ration list also covered meat, butter, some canned and dried foods, and shoes. Rationing was handled by a government department called the Office of Price Administration. Boards made up of citizens in each community decided if anyone could have extra rations. Items were taken off the ration list even while the war was going on. The last rationed item, sugar, was released early in 1946. In some countries, such as Great Britain, rationing lasted long after the war.

rattan

Rattan is a name used for the flexible stem of certain kinds of palm tree. Some climbing palms have very tough, strong, long stems. These are used to make rope, chair seats, wicker furniture, baskets, and many other products. The heavier stalks of the small, erect palm tree are used to make walking canes. Islands in the South Pacific provide most of the world's rattan. It is usually marketed in large bundles and exported to manufacturers in foreign lands.

rattlesnake

The rattlesnake is a poisonous snake found only in the Americas. Many people think that its rattle is a warning device, used to give notice that the snake is about to strike, but this is not true. If it were used in this manner, the rattler would have great difficulty in catching the small animals that it eats. The rattle is used to frighten an enemy. The rattles on the snake's tail consist of sections of a horn-like substance that clatter slightly when the snake vibrates it tail back and forth. Each time a rattler sheds its skin, it grows a new rattle.

Rattlesnakes vary in length from less than 2 feet to more than 7 feet. The largest kind is the eastern diamondback of the southeast United States. There are more rattlesnakes in the American southwest and in northwestern Mexico than in any other region.

The rattlesnake uses its venom to stun or paralyze the small animals or birds that provide its food. These include rabbits, gophers, ground squirrels, rats, mice, and some lizards. Where winters are cold, rattlesnakes hibernate in underground places such as prairie-dog burrows. The young are born alive, in late summer or fall, litters sometimes have as many as thirty baby snakes. A den of rattlesnakes may have a population as large as two thousand snakes.

Ravel, Maurice

Maurice Ravel was a French composer, or writer of music. He was born in 1875. He and another French composer, Claude Debussy, became the leaders in writing a new kind of music, which was soft and restrained in contrast to the violent, dramatic music written by such composers as Richard Wagner. Among Ravel's works are a string quartet; a piano concerto for the left hand; *Schéhérazade,* a set of songs; *Boléro, L'Heure Espagnole* (The Spanish Hour), and *Daphnis and Chloe,* works for the stage; and the orchestral works *La Valse* (The Waltz) and *Ma Mère L'Oye* (Mother Goose).

Ravel died in Paris in 1937.

raven

The raven is a large black bird of the crow family. Unlike the crow, it usually lives in wild country instead of near people.

The raven is more than two feet long from the tip of its beak to the end of its tail, and it has a wingspread of more than four feet. The raven is a powerful flier. It can be taught to talk if it is captured and made a pet when very young.

Ravens eat almost anything, and they seem able to live in almost any kind of climate, from cold Greenland to the hot deserts of the United States Southwest. Ravens usually live alone or in pairs, instead of in flocks as crows live. They kill large numbers of mice, other rodents, and insects. They nest on rocky ledges or trees.

Pet ravens have been known to live as long as forty years.

The raven has a hoarse, croaking sort of voice. Because of its croak and its black color, the raven has been disliked and wrongly feared as a bringer of misfortune or death. Edgar Allan Poe wrote a gloomy poem called "The Raven."

Rawlings, Marjorie Kinnan

Marjorie Kinnan Rawlings was an American writer of stories and novels about her adopted state of Florida. She was born in 1896 in Washington, D.C., and was graduated from the University of Wisconsin. She worked on newspapers until 1928, when she moved to Florida and began to write. Her first novel, *South Moon Under,* was published in 1933. *The Yearling,* the story of a little boy and a pet deer, won the 1938 Pulitzer Prize for fiction. It was later made into a motion picture. Mrs. Rawlings died in 1953.

ray

The ray is a flat fish that is related to the shark. There are several different kinds of ray, and they vary in size from the giant devil ray (or *manta,* or *devilfish*) of tropical waters, which may weigh more than 3,000 pounds, to small freshwater rays no larger than a pancake.

The sting ray has a barb on its long tail that can inflict a painful wound. It lies on the bottom of the water in seas, bays, or rivers. It is hard to see because it is half buried in the sand, and its color blends with the stone and silt of the bottom. If an unfortunate swimmer happens to step on the fish's back, the tail swings up swiftly, wraps itself around the bather's leg, and stick it with its barb, leaving a painful wound. Dizziness and nausea are often caused by the poison left by the barb.

Rays bear living young, usually one at a time.

rayon

Rayon is a plastic material that is made in the form of thread and is used in making hosiery and clothing and various kinds of cloth. Rayon is a cellulose material, which means that it is made from the walls, or coverings, of the cells that form wood, cotton, and other plants. The wood or cotton fibers are dissolved in chemicals until a thick liquid is formed. This is forced through tiny holes, and as it comes through the holes it dries and forms thread. The first kind of rayon to be used was *viscose rayon,* which is usually made from wood fibers. A better but more expensive kind is called *acetate rayon.* This is made of cotton fibers treated with acetic acid. Rayon is very smooth and silky. It has been much used as a substitute for silk, and is often called "artificial silk," but actually it is an important material of its own kind and need not be considered a substitute for anything.

real estate

Real estate is land and any buildings or other "improvements" on it. The improvements may be wells or mines dug in the ground as well as houses or other buildings built on the land.

For hundreds of years there have been special laws dealing with real estate. It is called *real property,* while other possessions are called *personal property.* A simple difference between them is that real property cannot be moved and personal property can be. Therefore personal property includes the furniture in a house, because it is movable. The house itself is real estate, though there are many cases in which houses are moved from one piece of property to another.

BUYING AND SELLING REAL ESTATE

Ownership of real estate is called *title* to the property. A complete record of everyone who ever owned any particular piece of real estate is kept on file in a government office. In the United States this is usually the county courthouse, which is part of the state government. Often the

record goes back hundreds of years to a grant of land made by a king of England or other European king to an early settler. Also recorded is anything that affects the title. For example, a landowner might sell a piece of land that has a stream running through it, but keep the right to take water from that stream. This would be recorded and the new owner cannot sell the property "free and clear." Any new buyer must continue to let the former owner take water from the stream.

When a person sells real estate, he gives a new owner a document, or legal paper, called a *deed*. The deed must describe the property exactly, and often a surveyor is hired to make a map showing exactly where the boundaries of the property are. The new buyer usually makes a *title search* (a study of all the recorded papers that have been filed before) and buys *title insurance* from an insurance company that agrees to pay him the cost of the property if it turns out later that it is not free and clear. This is important because real estate can be taken away from the present owner if at any time someone can prove he has a better title to it. Thousands of property owners in Arizona were in danger of losing their property during the 1930s when a man claimed ownership through a grant from Spain hundreds of years ago, when that property belonged to Spain.

Money can be borrowed on real estate by means of a MORTGAGE, about which there is a separate article.

Certain rights go with real estate ownership. The owner owns all mineral rights, which means that he can dig down as far as he wishes for mining metals, for oil wells, and so on, and no one else may dig under his land for these things. Waterfront property (on a stream, river, lake, ocean, and so on) carries with it certain *riparian rights*. The owner of property on a stream owns the bed of the stream and the water in the stream halfway across it. On a lake or on the ocean, he has the only right to use the water for swimming, boating, or fishing, for a certain distance from the shore. The distance is usually established by law. There are also certain legal restrictions on land. In some places, certain property cannot be used for business purposes but only for private houses. Riparian rights are often limited by laws that prevent the landowner from taking too much water or from emptying sewage or poisonous materials into the water.

REAL-ESTATE BUSINESS

Real estate is one of the most important occupations in the United States. It has three main branches: the buying and selling of real estate; the renting of buildings such as stores, houses, apartments, and so on; and property management, in which the real-estate firm acts as agent for the owner and collects rents, makes repairs, and does everything else that is necessary.

There is an association of real-estate men who call themselves *Realtors*.

There are certain standard units in which property is sold. Farm land is usually sold by the *acre*. In cities, residential property is usually sold by the *lot*. Different cities have different standard sizes for lots. In New York City, for example, a

lot is usually 20 feet wide and 100 feet deep. In most other cities a lot is wider. Property in a business district is usually sold by the *front foot*. A piece of land 50 feet wide and 50 feet deep would be worth more than a piece of land 25 feet wide and 100 feet deep, though they cover the same area, because the wider piece can be used for bigger store windows to attract passers-by. Property on beaches, also, is often sold by the front foot.

Real-estate firms receive commissions on property they buy, sell, rent, or manage for the owners. Often these commissions are established by state laws.

reaper, a machine for cutting and gathering grain: see FARM MACHINERY.

recall, the method by which a government official can be removed from office by the people: see the article INITIATIVE.

reclamation

Reclamation is any method of making land usable. The two chief methods of reclamation are irrigation of dry land and drainage of wet land. The planting of new forests in cut or burned areas, and the prevention of soil erosion, are also sometimes called reclamation. Reclamation is important in many countries of Europe. For instance, more than half of the Netherlands is land reclaimed from the sea by the building of dikes.

In the United States, reclamation of land first began when the Mormon pioneers arrived on the sun-baked plains of the Salt Lake valley in 1847. The Federal Government extended assistance in the reclamation of land after Congress passed the Reclamation Act of 1902. The Reclamation Service was established in the Department of the Interior and later became the Bureau of Reclamation. By 1959, it had built irrigation facilities in seventeen western states that serve more than seven million acres. Bureau of Reclamation projects also make electric power from water. Other activities include drainage, flood control, supplying cities with water, and building of recreation areas and wildlife refuges.

The Bureau operates such huge dams and power plants as Grand Coulee on the Columbia River in Washington State, which is the largest concrete structure in the world, and Hoover Dam on the Colorado River between Arizona and Nevada, which is the highest dam in the world.

Reconstruction

The Civil War in the United States, fought between the Union (northern) and Confederate (southern) armies from 1860 to 1865, left the southern states badly damaged and disorganized. There had to be a period of reconstruction (rebuilding) before American life could go on normally again. The period in American history from 1865 to 1877 is therefore called the Reconstruction period. It was a slow process and often did more harm than good because the political leaders of the North often used methods that were unwise or dishonest.

President Abraham Lincoln wanted to reinstate the southern states, set up new state governments, and take back into the Union all those who would promise to be good citizens from that time on. President Andrew Johnson, who came after him, wanted to do the same. But many of the leading men in the United States government were bitter about the war and wanted revenge.

RECONSTRUCTION AMENDMENTS

Congress passed, and the northern states ratified, three amendments to the Constitution (the 13th, 14th and 15th Amendments) that are called the Reconstruction Amendments. The 13th Amendment, adopted in 1865, made slavery illegal in the United States. The 14th, adopted in 1866, assured full rights of citizens to the Negroes who had been slaves in the South before the war. The 15th, which was not adopted until 1870, assured to Negroes and former slaves the right to vote.

The white citizens of the southern states would not accept these amendments at first, especially the 14th Amendment. They used all kinds of devices to keep the Negroes from voting, and they formed secret organizations (such as the KU KLUX KLAN, about which there is a separate article) to increase the power of the white people. Congress, which was controlled by northerners, became angry and in 1867 it passed a law called the Reconstruction Act. This law divided the South into five districts, each under a military commander. United States troops were stationed in the southern states to enforce the Reconstruction Act. No southerner who had fought against the Union was allowed to hold office in a state government.

Gradually, the southern states accepted the new Amendments and in 1877 the occupying troops were finally withdrawn. By this time, the governments of the southern states were again totally controlled by the white citizens. The white southerners remained bitter against the Republican Party, which had controlled Congress throughout the Reconstruction period, and it was more than fifty years before any Republican candidate for President could carry a southern state. (Herbert Hoover was the first, in 1928.) The southern states came to be called "the Solid South" because they always voted solidly for the Democratic Party.

Reconstruction Finance Corporation

The Reconstruction Finance Corporation (called the RFC) was a division of the United States government that was created in 1932 to lend money to businesses during the depression. At first the RFC lent money only to financial, agricultural and commercial firms, but later it also financed the building and operation of war plants and made loans to foreign governments. The RFC was supposed to operate for only ten years, but its life was extended over and over again by acts of Congress. On July 30, 1954, the RFC turned over to the Treasury Department its remaining assets of $100,000,000, and went out of existence. During its 22-year lifetime the RFC made about 640,000 loans totaling almost fifty billion dollars.

recorder

The recorder is a musical instru-

ment. It is the ancestor of the modern flute and was called simply the flute until about six hundred years ago. The recorder is blown through a mouthpiece at the end. It has one thumb hole and four to eight finger holes. The recorder fell out of use for several hundred years after the modern flute came into use about 1700, but in the 1940s the recorder became popular in schools and among amateur musicians.

recording

Sounds can be recorded in various ways so that a machine can produce the same sounds at any later time. Anything that the ear can hear—speeches, music, or noises of any kind—can be recorded. There are several different ways to record sound. The phonograph record uses the most familiar method. There are also tape recording, wire recording, the "sound track" of motion pictures, and other methods that are not so well known or so often used.

Recording is less than a hundred years old but has become a very important part of modern life. Besides its use for entertainment (as in phonographs and motion pictures), recording is used for the dictation of letters in offices, for crime detection by police, for sending messages to persons far away, and for making a long-lasting record of a conversation that has some legal or business importance.

In 1878 Thomas A. Edison, the most famous American inventor, patented the first device for recording sound. This turned out to be the invention of the phonograph.

The sounds we hear are waves that travel through the air. These waves are caused by the vibrating, or shaking, of something. Each particular sound is caused by a certain way of vibrating. The sounds we make when we speak or sing are caused by the vibration of a part of the body called the larynx, which is in the throat, as air breathed out from the lungs passes over it.

Edison recorded sound by talking so that the vibrations of his voice would strike a thin, flat piece of the mineral called mica. Such a thin object is called a *diaphragm*. Edison's voice made the diaphragm vibrate. Attached to the diaphragm was a hard, sharp needle. The needle therefore vibrated just as the diaphragm did. The needle was held against moving tinfoil, and because it was sharp it cut a groove in the tinfoil; because it was vibrating it cut the tinfoil in an irregular pattern. Later, Edison ran another needle through the same grooves, and the irregularities in the groove made the needle vibrate just as the first needle had, and send out sound waves that made the same sounds Edison had made when he spoke.

For fifty years, phonograph records and all other sound recordings were made by this method, though it was greatly improved. In the 1920s, "electrical recording" appeared. This introduced part of the method that is used today. The sound of the voice or orchestra goes into a microphone. In the microphone there is a disk or diaphragm placed so that this sound will cause it to vibrate, making sound waves. Through a wire attached to the diaphragm, these sound waves are changed into electromagnetic waves, carried by a current of electricity. The current passes through electronic tubes (which are described in the article on ELECTRONICS). By controlling the amount of electricity passing through the various tubes, an engineer can control the volume (loudness) of the sound and also the tones, treble (high) or bass (low). The electrical recordings proved to be so much better than the previous "mechanical" recordings that there was no comparison.

These are the principal ways in which sound recording is done:

Disk Recording. This is the same as Edison's original method, except that the cutting needle is caused to vibrate by the electrical current that passes from the microphone through the electronic tubes. The needle cuts the recording into a disk made of a plastic material, usually cellulose acetate or vinyl, and sometimes into wax. Phonograph records were first recorded in this way until after World War II, when tape recording became the preferred method.

Magnetic recording. The sound that enters the microphone is changed into magnetic impulses. A thin tape, made of a plastic material and treated with chemicals so that it can be magnetized, runs from one spool to another and passes a magnet on its way. From this magnet, the tape receives an effect that changes according to the sounds entering the microphone. Later the tape is run the other way and the magnetic impulses are turned into the same sounds that caused them in the first place. By passing the tape over an "eraser head" that demagnetizes it, the recording can be removed and the tape can be used for a new recording; but unless the recording is erased, the tape will play the original recording many times—even more times than a phonograph record, which wears out when it has been played a certain number of times. This method is called *tape recording.* In the early days of magnetic recording, wire instead of tape was used. The tape proved more satisfactory, and wire recording is seldom used now.

Sound tracks. The sound for a motion picture is recorded on a narrow strip at the side of the film from which the picture is projected. Usually the sound, like the picture, is a photographic record on this strip of film. As the film runs through the projector, an "electric eye" controlled by the sound track sends out sound waves that match the sound waves that were recorded on the sound track. Running the sound track and the film together makes sure of perfect *synchronization* (which means "same time")—that is, the recorded voice will always be heard at exactly the same time that the picture shows the person speaking.

HOW RECORDS ARE MADE

A phonograph record begins with a recording, usually on tape. This is cut on a disk called a master. The master is used to make dies from which thousands of records can be stamped.

First, the master is plated by electricity with a thin coating of metal. This metal takes the exact form of the irregularities in the grooves. From this metal, a mold is made (as explained in the article on FOUNDRY). A hard metal is cast in the mold, and this results in a piece of metal called a stamper. A "biscuit," or lump of soft plastic, is put in a press and the stamper is brought down on it with great force. This presses the plastic into the form of a disk and presses into this disk the exact grooves that were on the master. This disk is the phonograph record that you buy in a store. When you put it on a phonograph and play it, you will hear the same sounds as if you were playing the master.

Actually, two stampers are put in the press, so that one side of the disk is stamped with one recording and the other side with another.

"Popular" records are usually made of a material such as shellac, which is cheap but will break quite easily. "Unbreakable" records are made with a mixture of plastics and cheaper materials. They can be broken, but are unlikely to break unless you actually try to break them. The best LP records are usually made of a pure plastic material. This is usually one of the vinyl plastics.

Red Cross

The Red Cross is an organization for the relief of suffering in war or in peacetime disaster. The Red Cross movement was begun about a hundred years ago by Jean Henri DUNANT, about whom you can read in a separate article. In 1864 delegates from sixteen nations met in Geneva, Switzerland, and signed the Geneva Convention, which became the basis of Red Cross work throughout the world. The sixteen governments agreed to recognize Red Cross societies of all nations under the emblem of a red cross on a white flag. Men wounded in war and the workers caring for them were to be considered neutral and to be safe from attack. From that beginning, the Red Cross has grown until it has 71 societies throughout the Christian world. Red Cross organizations of the Mohammedan world have as their emblem a red crescent on a white background. Israel uses the red Star of David on a white background.

AMERICAN RED CROSS

The American Red Cross was founded in 1881, with Clara Barton as its first president. (There is a separate article about Clara BARTON.) By 1962 it had 3,654 local chapters. The society is supported by voluntary contributions from the public. In 1961 the Red Cross raised more than $98,000,000 to carry on its work. More than 2,000,000 Americans work as Red Cross volunteers without pay.

During World War II, the Red Cross gave many kinds of service to members of the armed forces at home and abroad. Red Cross staffs served at army posts, naval stations and hospitals in the United States. Field workers were on duty in the front lines and behind them. Clubs for servicemen and women were maintained, with places for those on leave to sleep, eat, and be entertained. Units on wheels brought entertainment and comfort to troops in isolated war fronts, and Red Cross ambulances carried the wounded back to hospital centers. The Red Cross also helped servicemen and women with

personal and family problems, and got word to men on the fighting fronts when there were family emergencies at home. After the war, many devastated countries abroad looked to the American Red Cross for help in rebuilding.

The Red Cross Donor Service was begun during World War II to supply blood and blood plasma to the armed forces. More than thirteen million pints of blood were collected from civilian donors and turned over to the armed forces. This program was so successful that after the war it was continued as a civilian service. In 1961 about 2,508,000 donations of blood were collected and distributed among 4,100 civilian and federal hospitals.

The Disaster Service is always ready in time of need, as when great damage is done by floods and hurricanes. It provides food, clothing, shelter, and medical and nursing care. In 1961 the Red Cross aided 310,700 persons in 339 disasters in 43 states. After an emergency has passed, the Red Cross helps individual families get back to normal by giving money for medical care, rebuilding of homes, and furniture or equipment.

The Red Cross Nursing Service trains nurses and nurse's aides for work in times of disaster and during epidemics. It also gives home nursing instruction. The Food and Nutrition Service helps plan for work in disasters and feeds the hungry when

This photograph of Clara Barton was taken about 1875. Today, her dream has come true: The American Red Cross helps all in their times of greatest need. Whatever and wherever the calamity, the Red Cross is ready to send help and comfort. In times of war, the international Red Cross helps families locate missing relatives and tries to make the lives of prisoners easier.

disaster strikes. The Safety Service works to prevent accidents. It gives instruction to the public in first aid and lifesaving. Special courses are given at all Red Cross chapters.

Volunteers for Red Cross work are trained in a number of different services: Entertainment and Instruction Service, for work in hospitals and other institutions; Production and Supply Service, making clothing and surgical dressings; Gray Lady Service, giving comfort and help to patients in hospitals; Motor Service; Nurse's Aide Service; Canteen Service; Social Welfare Aide Service, assisting social workers; Staff Aide Service, helping institutional staffs; and Arts and Skills Service, teaching handcrafts and other skills.

Another important Red Cross activity

is in civil defense, by training defense workers and the public in first aid and home care of the sick and injured, by preparing to give emergency care to thousands of people in case of attack, and in other ways working with civil defense authorities.

The American Red Cross Youth program, founded in 1917 as Junior Red Cross, gives students from elementary school through college a chance to help others. Young people work with mentally and physically handicapped children as well as with poor, sick, and old people. They serve during disasters which strike their own towns or cities and send friendship boxes to children and adults in tragedies elsewhere.

INTERNATIONAL RED CROSS

There are two international Red Cross organizations. The International Committee of the Red Cross is a committee of Swiss citizens. It acts as a neutral go-between for nations at war and gives aid to prisoners of war. The League of Red Cross Societies is an organization of the national Red Cross groups. It promotes coöperation among them in time of peace.

Red River

Red River is the name of two rivers in the United States.

The larger Red River is the most southerly large tributary branch of the Mississippi River. It rises in Texas near the border of New Mexico, flows east through Texas, and forms the entire southern border of Oklahoma. It then flows through Arkansas and Louisiana and empties into the Mississippi. The river is about 1,500 miles long. It is navigable by small boats for about 350 miles from its mouth.

The Red River of the North rises in Lake Traverse, which lies between South Dakota and Minnesota. It forms the boundary between Minnesota and North Dakota, flows into the Canadian province of Manitoba, and empties into Lake Winnipeg. The river is about 545 miles long. It flows through one of the world's richest wheatlands, but it is little used for shipping.

Red River Rebellion

The Red River Rebellion was a revolt of the settlers of the Red River region against the Canadian government. It took place almost a hundred years ago, in 1869. The Red River region was in what is now the province of Manitoba. The land had been owned by the Hudson's Bay Company, an important fur-trading company, but in 1869 it was sold to the Canadian government. The settlers felt that their land rights were being threatened by the sale. Under the leadership of Louis Riel, a settler of French and Indian parentage, they set up their own government at Fort Garry, where the city of Winnipeg now stands, and made Riel their president. A few months later the fort was captured by Canadian troops under Colonel Garnet Wolseley. Manitoba became a territory of the Dominion of Canada, and more than a million acres of land were granted to the settlers.

See also the article on Louis RIEL.

Red Sea

The Red Sea is a long, narrow body of salt water that separates Arabia from northeastern Africa. At the northern end of the Red Sea are the Gulf of Suez and the Suez Canal, which connect it with the Mediterranean Sea. At the other end is the Gulf of Aden, which opens into the Arabian Sea.

The Red Sea is about 1,400 miles long, and it varies from about 130 to 250 miles in width. Its greatest depth is more than 7,000 feet. There are many islands and coral reefs in it. The water of the Red Sea is very salty. The climate of the lands around it is hot and dry.

The Red Sea was an important commercial route thousands of years ago. The Arabs used it to keep in touch with India, Persia, and East Africa. When the Suez Canal was opened in 1869, making a shorter route from Europe to the countries of the East, the Red Sea became one of the great waterways of the modern world.

The story is told in the Bible about how the waters of the Red Sea parted to let the Israelites cross on dry land when they were escaping from slavery in Egypt.

Modern scholars believe it was the Gulf of Suez that the Israelites really crossed.

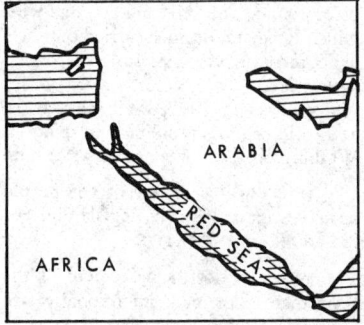

red-winged blackbird

The red-winged blackbird is a bird often seen in the United States. There are several kinds of red-winged blackbird. The male red-winged blackbird is black all over except for a small shoulder patch, which is bright red. It is about 9½ inches long. The female is brownish or grayish, with stripes of a darker color.

Red-winged blackbirds nest in willows along the sides of streams, and sometimes in dry hayfields.

redwood

Redwood is one of the two kinds of sequoia tree. (The other is the BIG TREE, about which there is a separate article.) When a redwood is first cut, the wood is a rich red color. Later it fades, but still retains a reddish tint. The lumber is used in building and it is very resistant to rain and damp weather. For this reason it is often used in the manufacture of porch or other outdoor furniture.

The redwood is the tallest of all trees. Some redwoods are more than 300 feet high. Many are more than a thousand years old. Redwoods are found only in California.

reed

Reeds are tall grasses that usually grow in wet and marshy places. There

are several kinds of reed, and they vary in height from 18 or 20 inches to 6 or 8 feet. Reeds are notable for their tough stems, which can be dried and used for constructing many different things. Reed is used to thatch the roofs of houses and barns in some parts of the world. Chair seats, trays, baskets, screens, and many other things are woven of reed. The largest reeds may be cut to make the mouthpieces of musical instruments such as the saxophone and clarinet.

Reed, Walter

Walter Reed was an American doctor and military officer. He was born in Virginia in 1851. He studied medicine in New York City and when he was 24 years old he became a surgeon in the United States Army. He rose to the rank of major. When the United States Army was in Cuba after the Spanish-American War, many soldiers were dying from yellow fever. Reed led an expedition of scientists who went to Havana in Cuba to study the cause of yellow fever. They discovered that yellow fever is caused by a germ that is carried from one person to another by a particular kind of mosquito. The skill and courage with which Reed and his men carried out their experiments made it possible to control yellow fever.

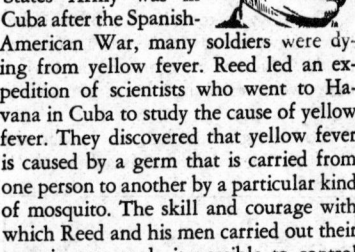

Reed died in 1902, when he was 51 years old. A great military hospital in Washington, D.C. was named after him.

referendum, a vote by the people on a law passed by the legislature. See the article on INITIATIVE.

reflex action, a movement of the body that is not made intentionally: see the article NERVOUS SYSTEM.

Reformation, the name given to the movement in Europe that began about five hundred years ago and out of which grew the Protestant churches of today. See the article on PROTESTANT.

Reform Bill

A reform bill, in English history, is a law passed by Parliament (the British lawmaking body) to change the way members are elected to the House of Commons. Once the English nobility and rich landowners controlled nearly all seats in the House of Commons. The Reform Bills of 1832, 1867, and 1884 made it possible for people living in cities and working in factories, shops, and offices to elect more members of parliament.

Reformed Church

The Reformed Church in America is a Christian Church that follows the teachings of John Calvin. The first Reformed Church in the United States was built on Manhattan Island (New York City) about 350 years ago, by colonists from the Netherlands. It grew rapidly and for a long time kept its original name of Dutch Reformed Church. It took its present name in 1867. In 1972, it had 939 churches and 375,546 members in the United States. On the continent of Europe the term *reformed church* refers to any

church that follows the teaching of John Calvin. In Great Britain and the United States, Calvinist churches are usually called Presbyterian.

reform school

A reform school is a kind of prison for boys and girls who have committed serious crimes. Very few states now use the term "reform school," and very few states now have places that are like old-fashioned reform schools, which were almost exactly like prisons. Modern governments try to train youthful offenders for useful lives in places where they can live comfortably and can learn useful trades. See JUVENILE DELINQUENCY.

refrigeration

Refrigeration means "making cold." In all the food we eat there are tiny living plants and animals (such as bacteria and yeast) that will spoil the food if we permit them to multiply. They multiply very slowly in a temperature of 40 to 45 degrees. The job of a refrigerator is to keep food this cold or colder.

We can cool food by putting it near something that is colder. Heat always travels from a hot body to a colder body. For many years people used refrigerators, or ice boxes, in which the cold object was a block of ice. Heat from the food flowed to the ice, melting the ice and cooling the food. The electric refrigerator has since become more popular.

Here is the principle on which the

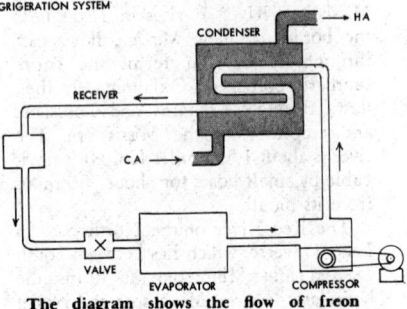

The diagram shows the flow of freon through a refrigerator system. Cold air (CA) and hot air (HA) change the freon from a liquid to a gas. In the evaporator it absorbs heat, and in this way cools the freeze chest.

electric refrigerator works: When a liquid changes into a gas or vapor (moist gas), it absorbs heat and so cools whatever is around it. In an electric refrigerator, tubes full of a liquid extend around the sides and bottom of the freeze chest. In most refrigerators, this liquid (called the *refrigerant*) is the gas called freon. This gas normally boils at about 21 degrees below zero on the Fahrenheit scale. Liquid freon is fed into the freeze chest, where the pressure is low. The freon changes into a gas rapidly; that is, it boils, absorbing heat from inside the refrigerator.

The freon vapor is drawn from the freeze chest by a compressor, a kind of pump, driven by an electric motor. The pump forces the vapor into a condenser, a winding tube. The tube is exposed to the air of the room. As the freon passes through the tube it is cooled by the air in the room. This condenses the freon, changing it back to a liquid again. As a liquid, the freon is fed slowly back into the freeze chest to vaporize. This continues as long as the motor runs.

A mechanical watchman, or thermostat, is placed inside the food compartment. The thermostat automatically starts and stops the motor, keeping the food compartment at the correct temperature. The better the insulation on the refrigerator and the better the condenser and compressor operate, the less the motor has to run.

Too much frost hinders refrigeration. Thick frost on the freeze chest acts as insulation and prevents proper cooling. There an electric refrigerator must often be "defrosted"—the frost is allowed to melt. Many refrigerators do this automatically.

See the articles on ICE and INSULATION.

regeneration

Regeneration is the name given to the ability of a living thing to grow new parts when it has lost part of its body. Some very simple animals can grow whole new parts of their bodies, such as a tail, a leg or a claw, or even a head. More complex animals, including man, cannot grow new parts; they can grow only minor parts (such as new skin tissue) or make repairs to broken bones or muscle.

If a planarian (a kind of flatworm) is cut in half, each half will grow into a whole new worm. The half of the worm that has the head on it will grow a new tail, and the half that has the tail will grow a new head. Lobsters and crabs can grow new claws when they have lost full-grown ones. A newt, a salamander or a lizard can grow a new tail. A starfish can grow a new arm when it has lost one.

In some very simple forms of animal life a very small part of the animal can grow an entirely new animal. This is the case with most animals that are so tiny and simple in structure that they can be seen only under a microscope.

Regina

Regina is the capital city of the province of Saskatchewan in Canada. It is in the central part of the province, about a hundred miles from the United States border. About 140,000 people live there. Regina is the chief market for the entire province. It has grain elevators, flour mills, meat-packing plants, sawmills, tanneries, and oil refineries. *Regina* is the Latin word for "queen," and the city was named for Queen Victoria of England.

Regina was founded in 1882. It was made the capital of the Northwest Territories in 1883 because it was on the route of the new transcontinental railway. In 1905 it became the capital of the new province of Saskatchewan. Regina was also the headquarters of the Royal Northwest Mounted Police, now called the Royal Canadian Mounted Police. Regina is a beautiful and carefully planned city. The provincial parliament building is on Lake Wascana, a man-made lake. Regina is the seat of theological and junior colleges connected with the universities of Saskatchewan, Ottawa, and Montreal.

REGINA, SASKATCHEWAN. Population (1971 census) 139,469. Capital of the province of Saskatchewan. On Wascana Creek. Founded, 1882.

registration

A citizen registers when he goes to his election board and presents himself as a voter who will be permitted to cast a ballot in the next election. This process is called registration.

A person who goes to register must sign his name on the voting books. At the same time several questions are asked of the voter: his age, where he was born, how long he has lived in the state, how long he has lived in the United States, and whether he voted in the last election. If he has never voted before, he must take a *literacy test* to prove he knows how to read and write. Between registration time and the election itself the election officials can examine the registration books to see that everyone who registered has told the truth.

There are two main methods of registration in the United States. The first is a yearly one in which the voter must appear before the election board about one month before each election. This means that he must register year after year. The second method is called *permanent registration,* or PPR. The voter has only to register the first time he is eligible to vote. When the person has reached the age of 21 under PPR, he goes to his election board and registers and from that time on he need not register again but can vote in each year's election. Of course if a voter in this type of registration should move he would then have to register again with the new election board nearest his home.

Reims or Rheims

Reims is a city in northeastern France. It is on the Vesle River in a valley surrounded by vineyard-covered hills. About 215,000 people live there. Reims is the center of the champagne industry of France and also has a large woolen industry. Underground wine cellars extend for miles under the city. Reims is famous as the site of a great cathedral. It is the city where the Germans surrendered in 1945, ending World War II in Europe.

Reims is an ancient city. Two thousand years ago it was the capital of the Remi, a Belgian tribe. In the year 496 Clovis, king of the Franks, was baptized at Reims by St. Remi, and the city became the most important religious center of Europe. Later it became the place where French kings were crowned. In the Cathedral of Reims, Joan of Arc stood beside King Charles VII of France when he was crowned.

During World War I, the Germans bombed Reims until it was almost leveled and the cathedral was in ruins. The city and cathedral were rebuilt after the war with the help of John D. Rockefeller. In World War II the Germans occupied Reims for four years until the liberation of France, but the city was not seriously damaged. Reims has a Fine Arts Museum in an old building that was once the Abbey of St. Denis, and a university that was founded in 1547. It also is the birthplace of St. Jean Baptiste de la Salle, founder of the Christian Brothers.

reindeer

Reindeer are a kind of deer that live in northern countries. They are called the "camels of the frozen north." They are the only type of deer of which both the males and females have antlers. They live farther north than any other hoofed animal except the musk ox. In their wild state, reindeer are called *caribou.* Reindeer can be ridden or hitched to vehicles (usually sleds), and the females are milked as cows are.

relativity, an idea first published by Albert Einstein to explain many things about the world we live in. See the article on EINSTEIN.

religion

Religion is belief in some power that is greater than man and that controls the universe. The word *god* stands for this power. "Nature" cannot replace God in a religion, because the idea of religion is that the supernatural power creates and controls the world intentionally and can cause things to happen at will, while nature cannot.

Men have had religions from the earliest times, long before history was written. Some of men's early religious beliefs are told in the article on GOD. Almost always, religion has been connected with good behavior, and even when men have believed in many gods they have considered the good gods to be more powerful than the evil gods.

For 1,500 years and more, Christianity has been the chief religion of the Western World, which includes the countries of Europe and later of the Americas. Christianity grew out of the Jewish religion, and together they are called the Judaeo-Christian religion. For more than 1,200 years, Islam (Mohammedanism) has been the chief religion of the large region called the Near East and of large parts of Africa and of southwestern Asia. These are the greatest religions of *monotheism,* which means "belief in one God." Other great religions include Buddhism, Hinduism, Confucianism, Taoism, Lamaism, and Shinto. These are religions of southern and eastern Asia. Most of them practice *polytheism,* or belief in many gods. There are separate articles on all these and other religions.

In nearly every religion there are different sects, or denominations. These are groups that believe in the most basic or important parts of the religion but that have special ways of following or practicing the religion. Presbyterians, Methodists, Quakers and Mormons are examples in the Christian religion. These denominations or sects should not be called "religions." In Christianity they are often called Churches, for example, the Presbyterian Church or the Roman Catholic Church.

PRAYER AND SACRIFICE

Prayer and sacrifice have been a part of nearly all religions. In prayer, a person asks God (or, in polytheistic religions, he asks a god or goddess) for help or protection or approval. In sacrifice, a person makes an offering of something valuable. This is a way of showing love or respect for the deity (god). Thousands of years ago men began to kill animals, such as sheep, as a sacrifice. The earliest men may have thought that the god could actually use the slaughtered animal as food. After men stopped believing this, they continued to sacrifice animals because of the meaning of the act.

Religions have many *rites* or *rituals* that are acts intended to show devotion to the deity. These may include dances, music, special clothing worn by priests or other followers of the religion, and many other things.

FREEDOM OF RELIGION

In early times, the king or government of a country would have an official religion that everyone in the country was expected to follow. The priests or other heads of the religion would be as powerful as high officials of the country. Anyone who refused to follow the religion would be breaking the law and might be severely punished.

A few hundred years ago there began to be a strong movement for men's rights to belong to whatever religion they chose. Many early settlers of America left Europe so that they could follow their own religion instead of the official one. In England there was an established (official) Church, and in most European countries the Roman Catholic Church was the official Church. The first words of the Bill of Rights of the United States Constitution forbid Congress to "establish" any religion. France and several other countries have adopted the principles of "separation of Church and State" (so that no particular religion or Church has any more influence on the government than any other) and freedom of worship, so that a person can follow any religion he wishes.

religious education

When children are taught about God and their religion, they are receiving religious education. Much religious education is given at home by parents, but many children also go to schools where they are taught their religion.

The most common kind of organized religious education is the Sunday School, or Sabbath School. This consists of classes in the church, usually before the regular service. In these classes, children and some adults learn about the Bible and about the beliefs of their religion. Many churches use the CATECHISM, about which there is a separate article.

Another kind of religious education is the parochial school. This is a school where all subjects are taught as well as religion. Many Catholic children go to parochial schools, which are paid for by members of their parish. They are usually taught by sisters, women who have dedicated their lives to their religion. There are also many schools supported by other faiths. These include colleges and universities.

In some countries, religious education is given in all schools. Because the Constitution of the United States provides for the separation of church and state, the United States government cannot do any thing that will help one religion more than another. For this reason, religion is not taught in public schools in the United States, though there are often readings from the Bible and sometimes prayers.

Some states have a program called *re-*

leased time. This means that children are let out of school early on one day a week in order to attend classes in religion at their own churches.

Rembrandt

Rembrandt van Rijn was a very great Dutch painter. He was born in Leiden, in the Netherlands, in 1606. His father was a miller, a man whose occupation is grinding grain to make flour. Rembrandt began to study painting when he was about 12 years old. When he grew up he went to Amsterdam, the capital of Holland, where for almost forty years he painted pictures and made etchings (pictures that are drawn on copper plates and then printed). Rembrandt was such a great artist that many young painters wanted to study with him. They sometimes helped him to complete some of his great works. He painted landscapes and religious subjects but he especially liked to paint people. Rembrandt's best-known picture is *The Night Watch*, which hangs in the Rhys-Museum in Amsterdam.

Rembrandt's paintings are made with rich red and gold and brown colors that glow in the dim light of the paintings. He made many pictures of old people. He wanted to show poor and ugly people with dignity and kindness, and he made them look beautiful. When Rembrandt painted Jesus, he made him an ordinary humble man. Rembrandt painted many pictures of his wife Saskia.

Rembrandt had many sorrows in his life. Saskia died after they had been very happily married for only eight years. Although Rembrandt was famous, some people did not understand his work and they made fun of it. He also had many money troubles. Rembrandt died in 1669, when he was 63 years old.

Remington, Frederic

Frederic Remington was an American painter, illustrator, and sculptor. He was best known for his paintings and sculptures of horses, soldiers, cowboys, and Indians, in which the subjects are usually shown in action. Remington also wrote articles for magazines and newspapers. He was a war correspondent during the Spanish-American War. Remington was born in 1861 and died in 1909.

Renaissance

In ancient times in Europe, two thousand and more years ago, there had been great interest in art and literature. Then, as a result of many wars, people found themselves so busy just trying to keep alive that they had no time for such things.

A period came in the world called the Dark Ages, in which almost no great books were written, no great buildings built, no great pictures painted, and so on. The Dark Ages lasted almost a thousand years. Then conditions became more settled and men began once again to think about beautiful things, fine writing, painting, sculpture, and so on. This period is called the *Renaissance*, which means "rebirth." This rebirth of learning and art began about six hundred years ago, and it is usually divided into two periods, early Renaissance and late Renaissance. During this period Leonardo da Vinci, Michelangelo and other great men of art lived and produced some of the greatest paintings and sculptures the world has ever known. Architecture had a rebirth too, a return to the classic Greek and Roman styles that is shown in St. Peter's Church in Rome and in the Louvre in Paris. The Renaissance is usually considered to have lasted from about 1450 to about 1600, with the early Renaissance beginning 75 to 100 years before 1450.

Reno

Reno is a city in western Nevada. It is the largest city in the state. It is on the Truckee River between Pyramid and Tahoe Lakes. Reno is the commercial center of Nevada and a shipping point for lumber products, wool, livestock, mining machinery, and other products.

About 73,000 people live in Reno, but it calls itself "the biggest little city in the world." There are packing houses and lumber mills, and plants that make soap, metal and chemical products, and leather goods. The city is close to important gold, silver, copper and lead mines.

Reno has the city manager form of government, with an elected council. It is the site of the University of Nevada.

Because Nevada law requires very short residence in the state before a person from another state can obtain a divorce, Reno has become famous as a place to which people go to get divorces. It is also a popular vacation spot because of its pleasant climate and many resorts and ranches for tourists. Gambling is legal in Nevada, and Reno has many large gambling houses.

The site on which Reno is built was a settlement called Lake's Crossing beside the Truckee River. In 1868 the name was changed to Reno when the town was made a stop on the Central Pacific Railroad. It was named for Jesse Lee Reno, a general in the Civil War.

RENO, NEVADA. Population (1970 census) 72,863. County seat of Washoe County Founded, 1868.

Renoir, Pierre Auguste

Pierre Auguste Renoir was a famous French painter who was born about a hundred years ago. He was the leader of a group of painters called the impressionists, who tried in their paintings to give a general idea of a subject, without giving much attention to detail.

Renoir was born in 1841. His family was poor, and when he was 13 years old he went to work in a porcelain factory. Later he went to art school, where he met men who were also to become famous painters—Claude Monet and Paul Cézanne.

At first Renoir made a living by painting rich people's portraits, but his reputation grew and then he could paint what he wanted to.

Today, Renoir's paintings are very valuable. He is best known for his pictures of women and children. His most famous works include *The Bathers*, in the Louvre in Paris, France; *Circus Children*, in the Art Institute at Chicago, Illinois; and *Girl Doing Her Hair*, in the Barnes Collection at Philadelphia, Pennsylvania.

Renoir died in 1919.

Representatives, House of, see the article on CONGRESS.

reproduction

Reproduction is the way all living things are created from other living things. A stone cannot reproduce (make another stone), but all living things, plants and animals, can reproduce themselves. All living things are made up of cells. The tiniest living things consist of only one cell, and larger living things consist of billions of cells.

There are two main ways in which living things reproduce themselves. In the simplest living things, a cell divides itself into two or many parts. This is called *asexual* reproduction.

The other kind of reproduction is called *sexual* reproduction. Two different kinds of tiny cells have to unite before a new living thing is created. The two sexual cells are called the male cell and the female cell.

Sometimes these two sexual cells are in the same plant or animal, but in most cases there are two separate animals, one the male or father, and the other the female or mother. The male gives off male cells called sperm cells and the female gives off or manufactures female cells called eggs.

REPRODUCTION BY DIVISION

As a one-celled animal or plant grows, it becomes larger. Finally it splits and two smaller cells are formed. Each is a completely independent living thing.

Some more complicated plants reproduce in an asexual way. If you look at a potato you will notice it has several buds around its surface. These buds, or eyes, can be cut out of a potato and planted in the ground. From these plantings new potato plants will grow. Grafting is really another form of asexual reproduction. If you cut a twig or vine off some plants, and plant the cuttings, new plants will grow.

REPRODUCTION BY JOINING

Sexual reproduction is the joining of a male (sperm) cell and a female (egg) cell. This is called fertilization. In plants what happens when the sperm joins with the egg is the beginning of a seed. The seed grows and soon is ready to leave the flower. In most flowering plants the seed is contained in a case and sometimes this case is called a fruit. The seed contains in it the cells of a new life and also food for them to grow on.

Not all plants have seeds. Mushrooms, ferns and mosses do not have seeds. Neither do molds, such as the kind that we often see growing on bread. These plants have *spores*. Spores are not seeds, but they do the work of seeds. When spores reach the ground they grow new plants, as seeds do.

ANIMALS THAT LAY EGGS

We are all familiar with the eggs that come from hens. From these eggs new chicks can grow, but most of the eggs will never grow into new chickens. Unless they have been fertilized, the female reproductive cells will not grow. When

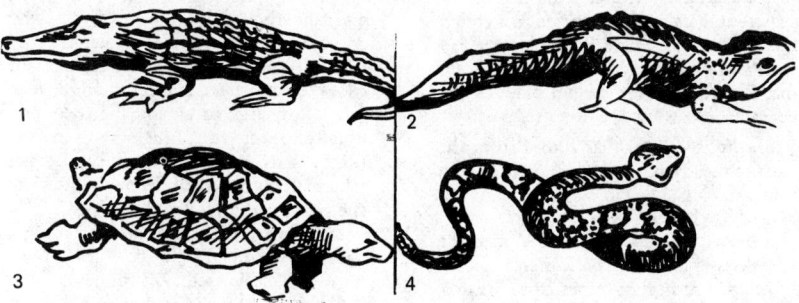

The four main branches of the reptile family are: 1. Crocodile. 2. Lizard. 3. Turtle. 4. Snake. Only the lizard and snake are found in great numbers in the modern world.

a rooster fertilizes the eggs with the male reproductive cell, a new chick will be produced.

There are many animals besides chickens and other birds that lay eggs. Insects do, and amphibians such as frogs and toads, and fish, and most snakes and other reptiles.

A female fish may lay thousands of eggs in the water. A male fish then drops sperm cells over the eggs. The tiny sperm cells actually swim to the eggs and enter the egg cells. When this fertilization has occurred, new fishes are on their way to being developed.

REPRODUCTION IN MAMMALS

Mammals are those animals that nurse their young—the children get milk from their mothers after they have been born. Cats, dogs, squirrels, cows, camels, and horses, as well as human beings, are mammals. Each female mammal produces egg cells. When they are fertilized inside the body by the sperm cells of the male mammal, the young will grow. Mammal mothers do not lay their eggs, but keep the fertilized eggs in their bodies. The young stay there until they have grown enough to live outside the mothers' bodies.

To learn more about human reproduction, read the article on CHILDBIRTH.

reptile

A reptile is any animal belonging to the group that includes alligators, crocodiles, turtles, tortoises, lizards, and snakes. Nearly all reptiles are cold-blooded animals, which means that they do not have any system for heating their bodies from the inside, and a reptile is only as warm as the ground on which it lies or the air around it. The body of a reptile might be compared to a house without a furnace and radiators. If the weather is warm outside, the house is warm too. If the weather is cold, the house becomes cold.

Reptiles live where they can get the proper amount of heat—not too much or too little. Most reptiles that live on land prefer temperatures between 75 and 100 degrees in the summer. They avoid too much heat or cold by finding shelter of some kind, especially holes or openings in the ground. Some reptiles, like the sea turtles, prefer the coolness of the ocean.

REPTILES OF LONG AGO

Reptiles first appeared on the earth about 275,000,000 years ago. Before reptiles existed, there were animals called amphibians that lived first in water and then on land. Frogs are examples of present-day amphibians. They are hatched from soft, shell-less eggs that remain under water. The young amphibians start their lives as tadpoles or polliwogs, which breathe water. They develop lungs for breathing air later, and move to the land.

Unlike amphibians, reptiles hatch from eggs with shells, and the young are very much like tiny copies of their parents from the beginning. Baby reptiles can breathe air immediately.

There were many different reptiles before the time of written history. Scientists have discovered the fossils and skeletons of those prehistoric animals and have learned a great deal about them. Some of the prehistoric reptiles were vegetable-eaters and some were meat-eaters. Among those huge animals were the gigantic DINOSAURS, about which there is a separate article.

GROUPS OF REPTILES TODAY

Reptiles exist today in four distinct forms or groups. The alligators and crocodiles are one type. These are four-legged, egg-laying animals with long, thick tails. They live along the shores of streams and rivers and lay their eggs on the shore. They spend part of their time in the water and part on land.

Turtles and tortoises are reptiles that wear armor to protect themselves. Some are almost always in water; some spend part of their lives on land; and others (tortoises) spend all of their lives on land. Many of these reptiles live for a great many years. The giant sea turtle used for making turtle soup is believed to be more than three hundred years old when caught. Turtle eggs are laid on the sandy shores.

The lizard group of reptiles includes dozens of different kinds. Lizards are like snakes with legs. In fact, snakes developed from lizards. Most lizards live on land.

Snakes are the fourth group. The word "reptile" to most people means snake. The snake is the latest development among reptiles. Snakes have existed on earth only about a hundred million years.

Today there are nearly three thousand different kinds of snakes. They range in size from tiny garter snakes only a few inches long to the immense python and boa constrictor that reach lengths of 25 or 30 feet.

Like other reptiles, snakes lay eggs, but some snakes hatch the eggs in the body of the female so that the young snakes are born alive.

Snakes are very much like lizards except that they have no legs and move about by wriggling along the ground.

republic

Any country that does not have a king or other royal person at the head of its government is called a republic. The United States is a republic, and so are France and all the American countries except Canada, and dozens of other countries. A republic does not have to be a democracy, as explained in the article on DEMOCRACY. Less than fifty years ago, most countries were monarchies (ruled by kings) and republics were very unusual. Now most countries are republics.

The earliest republics known to history were the city-states of ancient Greece and some other lands, about 2,500 years ago. All the free citizens would assemble and select their leaders or decide what the government should do. The ancient Roman people formed a republic at about that time, and the word comes from the Latin language that they spoke. They called their state the *res publica,* or "affair of the people."

The oldest republic in Europe is also the smallest independent country, San Marino. It has been a republic for perhaps a thousand years or even more. Switzerland was the first modern republic in Europe. Parts of it have had a republican form of government for about four hundred years. The United States was the first large country to have a successful republican government.

Republican Party

The Republican Party has been one of the two main political parties in the United States since it was founded more than a hundred years ago, in 1854. At that time most of the southern states allowed people to own slaves, while the northern states did not permit slavery. More land was being added to the United States, and one of the main questions was whether or not slavery would be permitted in the new states. The Republican Party was organized by people who were opposed to slavery, in opposition to the other main political party, the Democratic Party.

In 1856 the Republicans nominated John C. Fremont for President, but he was defeated by the Democratic candidate, James Buchanan. The Republicans grew more powerful, and in 1860 their candidate, Abraham Lincoln, was elected. The Republicans continued to win Presidential elections until 1885, when Grover Cleveland became President. Altogether, the Republican Party has won fifteen Presidential elections since 1860, while the Democratic Party has won only nine. There have been thirteen Republican Presidents and four Democratic ones (because in several cases the same man was re-elected).

The name Republican Party was also used in the earliest days of the United States by a political party headed by Thomas Jefferson. This party was set up in opposition to the Federalist Party headed by Alexander Hamilton. Jefferson's party later became the Democratic Party.

research

Research is the work by which new things are learned in education, manufacturing, medicine, and nearly all scientific fields. During the present century, tens of thousands of career opportunities have become open to research workers. Most of the scientific advances have been due to research. Big companies have their own research laboratories where they study new methods. Many rich men have given money to establish foundations for research. Examples are the Rockefeller Foundation and the Carnegie Institution. The United States government has many agencies for research, including the Office of Scientific Research and Development, the National Science Foundation, agencies specializing in such fields as atomic energy and aviation, and dozens of special research groups attached to the various government departments.

A research worker conducts experiments and keeps a record of the results. These experiments may test new products or methods to make sure they work satisfactorily, or they may seek ways of doing things that have not been done before, such as finding a cure for a particular disease.

The term *researcher* is also used for certain editorial workers on magazines and newspapers. Researchers are usually young women or men who are being trained for higher editorial jobs. They look up facts for the writers, and they check the truth or accuracy of statements in articles that have already been written.

resin

Resins are sticky substances that ooze out of certain trees, usually in the form of yellow or brown tear-shaped lumps. Resins can also be made entirely from chemicals. Such resins are called synthetic (man-made) resins.

Natural resins—those that come from trees—harden in the air. When purified they have no color or taste, and usually no odor. They will not dissolve in water. They are brittle, and when they are heated they first soften, then melt, and finally burn.

KINDS OF NATURAL RESIN

The resins named *rosin* (or *colophony*), *copal*, *lac*, *sandarac* and *dammar* are often dissolved in drying oils and used to make lacquers and varnishes. Rosin is a resin that is obtained from turpentine (which comes from pine trees). It is a clear, yellow solid. It is used in the making of soaps, sealing wax and cements; for preparing certain metals for soldering; and for ointments and plasters. Players of string instruments put rosin on their bows so that the bow will not slip too easily across the strings. Acrobats and athletes put powdered rosin on their hands or shoes to keep them from slipping.

Canada balsam, which comes from balsam fir trees, is used in laboratories to cement glass covers to microscope slides.

Amber, *kauri*, and *copal* are fossil resins, which means that they have come from trees that died millions of years ago and were buried. Glass-clear pieces of this kind of resin are used in jewelry, and amber is used for pipestems, cigarette holders, and small art objects.

The resin called *frankincense* has a very pleasant odor, and is burned as incense; and ever since ancient Egyptian times, it has been used in embalming.

Bdellium, or *dragon's blood*, is a resin that is used to stiffen certain kinds of paper, and also is used as incense.

Mastic is a resin that comes from the mastic tree. From it is made varnish and a mouthwash, and, in the East Indies, it is used as chewing gum.

Storax and *sandarac* are used to make varnishes and also as perfumes.

Jalap, a resin that comes from Mexico, is used in medicines.

respiration, the method of breathing: see the article BREATHING.

restaurant

A restaurant is a kind of store that sells full meals to its customers. In some restaurants, people are served their food by waiters or waitresses. In other restaurants, usually called cafeterias, people serve themselves and carry the food on trays to tables where they eat it.

There have been public eating places for thousands of years, but the early ones were almost always in inns (hotels) where travelers could also spend the night. Restaurants as we know them are only about four hundred years old and probably the first ones were in London, England. Women seldom ate in restaurants until about a hundred years ago.

Restaurants today are of many different kinds. CAFETERIAS are described in a separate article. Lunch counters, and diners (which look like the dining cars of railroad trains) have long counters at which you sit and eat, instead of at a table. The soda fountains in most drug stores have become lunch-counter restaurants. There are also many large restaurants that specialize in national styles of cooking such as Italian, German, Chinese, and others.

THE FRENCH RESTAURANT

Nearly all fine restaurants follow the French style of service and organization, and most of them (including the main dining rooms of hotels) also follow French methods of cooking. The French language is used for many of the foods that are served and for the kinds of service that the guest may select. There are two main kinds of service: One kind is called *table d'hôte*, in which the guest pays one fixed price and receives a full meal with appetizers (*hors d'oeuvres*), soup, *entrée* (the main dish), and dessert. Usually the guest has a choice of several different entrées and the price of the full meal depends on the one he selects. The other kind of service is called *à la carte*. There is a separate price for each dish, and the guest pays for what he orders. If he does not want soup, he does not pay for it. On a table d'hôte meal he pays for the entire meal, even if he does not want part of it.

The restaurant staff is usually divided into two groups, the dining room and the kitchen. The man in charge of the entire restaurant is called the *maître d'hôtel*. In the dining room there are *captains* (head waiters) who greet the guests and take them to their tables and usually take their orders; *waiters* who serve the food; and *bus boys* who assist the waiters, lay the tables, bring the guests water and butter, and sometimes clear the table, but who do not serve food. In the kitchen the *chef* is in full charge. He is assisted by assistant cooks, dishwashers, and other employees. He is in charge of buying the food, and usually spends part of his time in market places selecting the best meats, vegetables, and other foods. In many cases the chef is also the maître d'hôtel.

In many French and Italian families, children are taught the restaurant business from early youth. A young man who is to be trained for the restaurant business almost always starts in the kitchen, because knowledge of cooking and buying food is the most important part of the business. Nearly every great maître d'hôtel was once a chef. After working in the kitchen for a few years, the young man is made a bus boy and then a waiter. He may next become a captain if he has the necessary qualities (a pleasing personality, quick wit, good memory for names and faces); or his talents may make him better suited to return to the kitchen and work his way up to a chef's position.

RUNNING A RESTAURANT

Restaurant management is an excellent career. When a restaurant loses money and goes out of business it is almost always because of bad management. Hundreds of hotels lose money on their restaurants. A man who can run a restaurant efficiently and make a profit can get a big salary or can make a big profit by owning his own restaurant.

A good restaurant manager must know every part of the business. He must know the different kinds of meat and fish, fruits and vegetables, and other food products—how to buy them at the best prices and how to buy just enough so that none will have to be thrown away. He must have a good sense of timing so that the kitchen will have the food ready at exactly the right time and the waiters will serve it when it is at its best.

There are schools that teach restaurant management, but successful restaurant men say that actual experience in different restaurant jobs is also necessary.

Restoration

The Restoration was a time in English history when the country went back to being a kingdom, after a period in which it had no king. About three hundred years ago Charles I was king of England. He thought the king should have supreme power, but Parliament (the British lawmaking body) disagreed with him. There was a civil war, and in the year 1649 Charles I was executed. Then for more than twenty years England did not have a king. A man named Oliver Cromwell became dictator of the country, with the title Lord Protector. Cromwell allowed the people even less freedom than the king had allowed, so pretty soon the people wished they had the king back. Cromwell died in 1658, and in 1660 the people called on Charles II, the son of Charles I, to come back and be king; that is, they restored him to the throne. Parliament's power also was restored, and for these reasons the period is called the Restoration. See the articles on CHARLES and ENGLAND.

retriever

A retriever is a dog that is specially trained for going after game that has been shot and bringing it back. The dog sees the game fall, or scents its location, and runs swiftly to pick it up. The game may be a duck or goose floating in the water, or it may be a land bird shot down over thick woodland or brush. Retrievers are equally at home on land and in the water. They have extra thick, heavy coats with an oily texture that protects them from icy waters. They are large dogs and are not usually kept as house pets but as sporting dogs.

There are several kinds of retrievers. The most important breeds are the Chesapeake Bay, the curly-coated, the flat-coated, the golden, and the Labrador. All are heavy, strong dogs with powerful legs for swimming and running over rough country. They stand 21 to 26 inches high at the shoulder and weigh 50 to 75 pounds. The Labrador retriever is black, the golden is yellow. Others are black and white, dark brown, tan, or liver-colored.

Revere, Paul

Paul Revere was an American patriot in the Revolutionary War, in which the American colonists fought for their independence from Great Britain. He is best remembered by a poem that Henry Wadsworth Longfellow wrote about him. This poem, called "Paul Revere's Ride," tells how Paul Revere rode on horseback, in the middle of the night of April 18, 1775, through the towns of Medford, Lexington, and Concord, in Massachusetts. He went to warn the people that a British army in Boston had been sent out to capture the munitions stored by the patriots at Concord and to arrest Samuel Adams and John Hancock, two Revolutionary leaders, who were staying in Lexington. The next day, April 19, the colonial patriots, called minutemen, fought with the British at Lexington and Concord in the first battles of the Revolutionary War.

Paul Revere was born in Boston in 1735 and died there in 1818. He was a silversmith and copper-plate engraver by profession. He designed the plates from which was printed the "continental money" used by the colonists during the war. Paul Revere was only one of three messengers sent to warn the people at Lexington and Concord, and he was captured before he reached Concord. Later he escaped and during the rest of the war fought for the colonists. He also operated a gunpowder mill near Boston. After the war he founded a copper and silver factory that was very successful.

revolution

A revolution occurs when the people of a country throw out their government and set up a new government. In some cases this is a new form of government, as when a king is replaced by a republic. In other cases, the form of government is not changed but the head of the government is replaced. A revolution is always accomplished by armed force or by the threat of armed force. In 1946 the Italian people voted to change from a monarchy (headed by a king) to a republic, but this was not a revolution because it was done peacefully.

The most famous revolutions were the American Revolution, the French Revolution, and the Russian Revolution. In each case a monarchy was replaced by a republic.

The year 1848 was called the "year of revolutions" in Europe. In that year there were attempted revolutions in Hungary, France, and several German countries. Only the one in France was successful. At that time most of the countries of Europe were controlled by the noblemen, or aristocracy, and the other people had almost no voice in their governments. The revolutions of 1848 were mostly efforts to make the governments more democratic and not necessarily to change to republics, though in France the revolution resulted in a change to a republic.

Another year of many revolutions was 1918, when World War I ended. Germany, Austria-Hungary and Turkey, the defeated nations, changed their forms of government. Other countries of Central and Eastern Europe declared themselves independent of the larger countries that had previously ruled them.

National Park Service

"Mount Vernon" is the home and burial place of Revolutionary War General George Washington. It was built in 1743 near Alexandria, Virginia.

Revolutionary War

The Revolutionary War was the war in which the thirteen British colonies in North America fought for independence from their parent country, Great Britain. As a result of the war the colonies became an independent country, the United States of America. The war is also called the American Revolution or the War for Independence. It was the first great and successful revolt of the colonies of any country. (Colonies are settlements of people who are living away from their home country but are still under its government.)

The Revolutionary War officially began in June 1775, though actual fighting had begun two months earlier and several major victories had already been won by both sides. The peace treaty was signed eight years later, in 1783. The heroes of the Revolutionary War became the leading statesmen of the new nation, and three of them, George Washington, John Adams, and Thomas Jefferson, became its first three Presidents.

HOW THE WAR BEGAN

More than two hundred years ago, in the 1700s, England had thirteen colonies in the territory that is now the eastern United States. They were New Hampshire, Massachusetts, Rhode Island, Connecticut, New York, New Jersey, Pennsylvania, Delaware, Maryland, Virginia, North Carolina, South Carolina, and Georgia. Most of the people who lived in them were of English descent and felt a kinship with the British people. But the British Parliament and the governors sent over by the British king felt that the people of the colonies should not have as many rights as the people who had stayed behind. For fifty years or more there had been quarrels about this between the American colonies and the British officials.

At the end of the French and Indian Wars, in 1763, these quarrels became more bitter. England wanted the colonies to pay back the money it had spent in fighting that war. The money was to be paid back by taxes on certain things, such as tobacco and sugar and tea. One of these taxes was called the Stamp Tax. It required an extra payment on any legal document such as a birth certificate or marriage license or any other official piece of writing. The colonists objected to these taxes.

There were other laws passed that the colonists thought unfair. Officials were allowed to search the house of anyone who was thought to be hiding goods on which he had not paid the required tax. The colonists had to take English soldiers into their homes, and board and feed them without being paid for it.

In 1770, in Boston, Massachusetts, the people turned against the English soldiers, who then fired on the unarmed citizens and wounded and killed some of them. This was called the Boston Massacre. In 1773, also in Boston, the colonists decided to fight the British tax on tea, which they were allowed to buy only from England. Three British ships carrying tea were anchored in Boston Harbor, and some colonists climbed aboard one night and dumped the tea into the harbor. This episode came to be known as the Boston Tea Party.

By 1774, most of the American colonies were resisting the British government. Representatives of all the colonies except Georgia met in Philadelphia, and they established the first Continental Congress. They decided that the colonies would act together against England.

FIGHTING THE WAR

In November, 1774, the Massachusetts colonists set up their own small army to defend themselves in case of trouble. Most of its members were not soldiers, but they agreed to be ready to fight at a minute's notice, and so were called the Minute Men. Other patriotic groups had been formed even earlier. Among them were the Sons of Liberty (led by Samuel Adams, John Hancock, and others) and Ethan Allen's Green Mountain Boys. The articles on Patrick HENRY and Thomas PAINE tell how American patriotism was aroused.

General Thomas Gage, the English governor of Boston, knew that the citizens were arming themselves. In the spring of 1775, he decided to stop their plans for revolt by surprising an army that he knew was gathered at the village of Concord. The American army was warned, but it was defeated at the Battle of Lexington and Concord.

By this time all thirteen colonies were aroused. American soldiers from the other colonies were sent to Boston. Expeditions were sent out to get cannon and powder, which was done by capturing two British forts in New York State, Fort Ticonderoga and Crown Point. In June, 1775, the second Continental Congress met and appointed General George Washington commander-in-chief of the American forces. Before Washington arrived, the colonists near Boston had fought the Battle of Bunker Hill, in which the British had won more ground but had lost many men. In March, 1776, Washington defeated the British general, William Howe, and the British troops were forced out of Boston. Washington then moved his army to New York, but Howe's larger forces defeated the Americans, who in midwinter of 1776 were forced to retreat across New Jersey into Pennsylvania. On Christmas night, however, Washington crossed the Delaware River into New Jersey, took Howe's army by surprise, and won victories at Princeton and Trenton.

Early in 1777 the British hoped to take the Hudson Valley. General John Burgoyne was to come down from Canada and combine his forces with those of Howe. Their meeting never took place, and Burgoyne was forced to surrender to the American General Horatio Gates at Saratoga, New York. In the meantime, Howe's army defeated Washington at the Battle of Brandywine Creek and took the city of Philadelphia. Washington and his men were forced to spend the bitterly cold winter of 1777 and 1778 at Valley Forge, where they suffered great hardships from lack of food, clothing, and fuel.

WHY THE AMERICANS WON

Though the English could send much larger forces against the colonial army, and the Americans were poorly equipped

Causes of the American Revolution

ECONOMIC SUBORDINATION OF COLONIES TO ENGLAND.

LIMITING OF COLONISTS TO RAW MATERIALS PRODUCTION.

CHANNELIZING OF ALL TRADE THROUGH ENGLAND.

APPEARANCE OF MANY SKILLED COLONIAL LEADERS.

STRUGGLE FOR MORE HOME RULE.

war for freedom

A. M. Willard's spirited painting, *The Spirit of '76*, records the determination of the ill-equipped American soldiers.

and not trained for fighting, other reasons account for the colonies' victory. Great Britain was threatened by France, the strongest European country. Though the two countries were not yet at war, their ships were raiding each other and the British government wanted to keep its soldiers at home. It did hire some soldiers from the Duke of Hesse, a country in Germany, to fight against the Americans, but the Hessians had no real quarrel with the Americans and did not fight very hard.

Several important members of the English Parliament, especially Edmund Burke and Charles Fox, sympathized with the American cause. Also, the bravery of the Americans was greatly admired in Europe, and several prominent European officers came to help them. Among them were two Poles, Thaddeus Kosciuszko and Count Casimir Pulaski; the Marquis de Lafayette from France, and Baron Frederick von Steuben from Germany.

Early in the war, in 1776, the Continental Congress decided to declare to the rest of the world that the colonies were independent states. On July 4, 1776, the Declaration of Independence, drafted by Thomas Jefferson, was adopted. The Congress then began working on setting up a government for the new nation. These plans were set forth in 1777 in the Articles of Confederation. The American states sent Benjamin Franklin, John Adams, and other statesmen to France. Franklin especially had great influence on the French, and the brave fighting of the colonies so impressed the French king that in 1778 he decided to become America's ally against England. In a short time Spain and Holland were drawn into the war against England, which was kept busy defending itself against them in Europe.

There were many British successes in America. The British won the support of the Indians, who thought a British victory would stop the colonists from taking more of their land. The British won several victories in the South, capturing Savannah and later Charleston; and in 1780 their greatest leader, General Charles Cornwallis, defeated an American army under General Gates at Camden, South Carolina. At the same time, General Benedict Arnold treacherously plotted to deliver West Point to the British, but his

scheme was discovered before it was carried out.

General Nathanael Greene replaced General Gates in the South, and forced Cornwallis to retreat to Wilmington, Delaware. Then Washington advanced to meet Cornwallis at Yorktown, Virginia. He was aided by French ships that held off a British fleet. The British army had to surrender, on October 19, 1781.

By then England was tired of fighting and proposed peace. This was agreed upon in the Treaty of Paris, signed in 1783, and the United States was recognized as an independent nation.

There are separate articles about many of the important events, battles, and leaders named in this article.

revolver, a kind of pistol in which several cartridges can be fired one by one from a cylinder that turns when the trigger is pulled: see PISTOL.

Reykjavik

Reykjavik is the capital and chief city of Iceland. It is on Faxa Bay (an inlet from the ocean) in southwest Iceland. More than 81,000 people live there. Many of them work in the fisheries nearby. The city has a university. The hot-water supply of the city is taken mostly from natural hot springs rather than from man-made heating systems as in most cities. During World War II, Great Britain and the United States used Reykjavik for military bases. Its name is sometimes spelled Reikjavik.

REYKJAVIK, ICELAND. Population (1973 estimate) 81,288. Capital of Iceland. Chartered in 1786.

Reynolds, Sir Joshua

Joshua Reynolds was an English painter who lived about two hundred years ago. He was born in 1723. His father was a clergyman and a teacher. When Reynolds was a young man he went to London to study painting. Later he traveled in Italy for  three years and studied the great works of art in Rome. When he returned to London, in 1752, he opened a studio as a painter of portraits (pictures of people) and painted portraits of many of the famous men of his day. Reynolds' paintings of children are especially fine.

Reynolds formed a literary club that included Dr. Samuel Johnson and Oliver Goldsmith, two great English writers, and David Garrick, the famous actor.

In 1768 the Royal Academy of Arts was founded in London, and Reynolds became its first president. He gave lectures that were published in a book called *Discourses.* Students of art still find these lectures very valuable. Reynolds died in 1792, when he was 68 years old. He was buried in St. Paul's Cathedral.

rhea

The rhea is a South American bird, closely related to the ostrich. The rhea is about 4 feet high, which is smaller than the African ostrich. Like the ostrich, the rhea cannot fly but can run very swiftly. The long, thin neck of the rhea is black toward the shoulders and gray toward the head. The rhea's body is grayish-white underneath, and the front of the face is unfeathered and black.

Male rheas have several females in the family, and the male takes care of all the eggs laid by his mates. This is usually between 24 and 60 eggs. The male sits on them to keep them warm until the young birds hatch. The eggs are golden yellow to deep green. They hatch after about six weeks. Rheas live on seeds, grasses, roots, and occasional lizards and worms.

Rhee, Syngman

Syngman Rhee is the name of a great Korean statesman. In his early youth he began to work to make Korea an independent country. When Korea became a republic, in 1948, he became its first president.

Rhee was born in 1875. Before he was 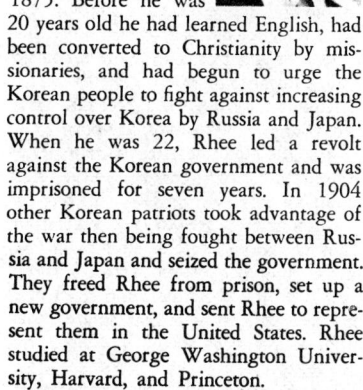 20 years old he had learned English, had been converted to Christianity by missionaries, and had begun to urge the Korean people to fight against increasing control over Korea by Russia and Japan. When he was 22, Rhee led a revolt against the Korean government and was imprisoned for seven years. In 1904 other Korean patriots took advantage of the war then being fought between Russia and Japan and seized the government. They freed Rhee from prison, set up a new government, and sent Rhee to represent them in the United States. Rhee studied at George Washington University, Harvard, and Princeton.

In 1910 Korea came under Japanese control. Rhee returned to his own country and tried to organize a secret movement against the Japanese, but he failed. He escaped to the United States and later to Hawaii, where he founded the Korean Christian Church.

All through World War I, the period between the two world wars, and World War II, Rhee worked to make Korea independent, but no other country would help him. He finally had partial success when Japan was defeated in World War II. Korea was divided into two main zones, with the northern zone under control of Soviet Russia, and the southern zone under the United States. Rhee feared that the Russian and Chinese communists would never give up their half. He asked for a general election in the south, which was held in 1948. The Republic of Korea was set up, and Rhee became its first president at the age of 73. He was re-elected in 1952, 1956, and 1960 even though the president was supposed to be limited to two terms. His increasingly dictatorial methods of governing caused wide-spread riots after the 1960 election and, under pressure, President Rhee resigned. He died in 1965.

rhesus monkey

The rhesus monkey is the playful brown monkey that amuses the public in zoos and with organ grinders. It is about two feet long and has a 13-inch tail. It is common in northern India. The rhesus is a member of the macaque family, and like other macaques it is fully grown when it is 4 or 5 years old.

The rhesus monkey has become well-known because of experiments that determine whether people have "Rh positive" or "Rh negative" blood. Most doctors test women before they have babies, to find out which blood type is present. The "rh" comes from the first letters in "rhesus," because the Rh factor was first discovered in rhesus monkeys.

rhetoric

Rhetoric is a set of rules or principles for the elegant, beautiful or effective use of a language. In ancient Greece, nearly 2,500 years ago, the spoken language was more important than the written language because the important men in the government held their power by making speeches to the public. At that time, rhetoric was fine speaking. Later, rhetoric came to apply even more to fine writing, first in poetry and then in both poetry and prose.

Rhetoric is different from grammar, and the proper use of a language must include both correct rhetoric and correct grammar. Use of the wrong form of a word is an error in grammar, for example saying "I is going" instead of "I am going." Use of incorrect words or of unnecessary words is an error in rhetoric, for example saying "The battle still continues" when "The battle continues" would mean the same thing.

See the article on FIGURE OF SPEECH, which covers one of the branches of rhetoric.

rheumatic fever

Rheumatic fever is a serious disease that often affects the heart. It usually occurs in young people between the ages of 5 and 15 years. When a person develops rheumatic fever, his muscles become inflamed, including the chief muscle, the heart. The disease may damage one or more of the four valves that connect the chambers of the heart. The valve then becomes leaky, and scar tissue may form, which makes it more difficult for the heart to do its work.

Doctors do not know exactly what causes rheumatic fever. They know that the disease begins with a particular kind of sore throat or infection of the tonsils, caused by the streptococcus germ. Not every person who is infected with the streptococcus germ develops rheumatic fever. A person may not develop any serious after-effects from rheumatic fever if he receives good medical care and follows the doctor's instructions carefully. A person who has rheumatic fever must stay in bed for a long time so that the heart can rest and become strong and healthy.

A person who has once had rheumatic fever is likely to get it again. This means more of a strain on the heart. Sometimes when a person has had one attack of rheumatic fever the doctor gives him penicillin to protect him against colds and sore throats that might lead to another attack.

rheumatism

Rheumatism is a kind of disease that causes soreness or stiffness of the joints and muscles. Rheumatism may have any of several causes. It may be caused by an injury, and infection, or a wearing out of

parts that belong to or surround the joints. It can happen to anyone, but most often bothers people who are middle-aged or older.

When there is an injury or a germ infection that hurts the joints, the soft material around the joints swells up. This causes a lot of pain and often causes difficulty in moving the part of the body where the joint is located. Cold, damp, and nervous strain, caused by worry or fear, may also lead to rheumatism.

A very common type of rheumatism, called *rheumatoid arthritis*, bothers three times as many women as it does men. It makes the finger joints swell up and become twisted, and sometimes it so affects the spine that persons who have it become crippled.

Rheumatism may last for a short time, or it may be chronic, which means that it goes on for years and years. Many people are relieved of painful rheumatoid arthritis by drugs called cortisone and ACTH; these are chemicals, called hormones, that are made in the body by glands, but can also be made in laboratories. Other treatments that sometimes relieve rheumatoid arthritis are hot baths, electric pads, ray lamps, and other heat treatments. Some people feel better in hot, dry climates, such as that of Arizona.

Another kind of rheumatic disease in children affects the heart. You can learn more about this type of rheumatism in the article on RHEUMATIC FEVER.

Rhine

The Rhine is the most important river of western Europe. It is about 820 miles long. It begins in central Switzerland and flows northward into the North Sea. It forms part of the border between Switzerland and Austria, flows through Lake Constance (also called the Boden Sea) and then forms part of the border between France and Germany. Farther north it flows through the Netherlands, where it divides into two rivers, the Upper Rhine and the Lower Rhine, that both end in the North Sea.

Ships and barges carry a great quantity of freight over the Rhine and the rivers and canals that connect with it. The main products are coal, iron, wheat, and other grains. Rivers that flow into the Rhine include the Aar River in Switzerland, and the Neckar, Main, Moselle, and Ruhr Rivers in Germany. Important cities along the Rhine include Basel, Switzerland; Strasbourg, France; and Mannheim, Mainz, Wiesbaden, Bonn, Cologne and Düsseldorf, Germany.

The scenery along the Rhine is famous for its beauty, especially between the cities of Mainz and Bonn. There are many vineyards and gardens, and many old castles and fortresses on cliffs along its banks. The wine produced in that area, which is called Rhine wine, is known all over the world.

The Rhine was an important frontier (fortified boundary) in the times of the ancient Romans. France and Germany fought over its control for hundreds of years. One of Germany's most popular patriotic songs was "The Watch on the Rhine."

In 1919, after World War I, an inter-national commission was set up to control navigation on the Rhine. The commission's work was interrupted by World War II, but it began to function again after the war.

rhinoceros

The rhinoceros is one of the world's largest land animals. It lives in the warmer sections of Africa, Asia, and Indonesia. It is a big, clumsy beast with a hide that is one-half to three-quarters of an inch thick. The African black rhino has two large horns on its snout. The front horn is usually larger and longer than the rear horn. This rhinoceros stands about five feet high at the shoulder, and a full-grown male may weigh up to 3,000 pounds. The white rhinoceros is the largest of the family. It lives in a small section of Central Africa. It grows to a height of 6½ feet and may weigh as much as four tons, or 8,000 pounds. Both black and white rhinos are ill-tempered, irritable beasts, but the black is more excitable and dangerous than the white. A rhino is somewhat nearsighted, but when it gets the scent of man it often charges wildly toward the scent.

Rhinos have no fixed breeding time. The young, called calves, are born 17 to 18 months after the parents mate. They are nursed for two years before they start taking care of themselves.

Rhinoceroses are strictly vegetarian. They eat leaves, grasses, and twigs. Although they usually move at a leisurely pace from food to water, and from mud or a dust bath to their grazing area, they often go as fast as 30 miles an hour in a charge.

Indian rhinoceroses have one horn, and their hide is folded into plates that make it look like armor from a distance. Smaller members of the rhino family live in Java, Sumatra, Borneo, and Malaya.

Rhode Island

Rhode Island is one of the New England states in the United States. It was one of thirteen original colonies. Its nickname is "Little Rhody" because it is the smallest state in the country; but, for its size, it has more people living in it than any other state.

Rhode Island is one of the most important manufacturing states and is the place where the textile industry in the United States began. Rhode Island is also famous for its many summer resorts, old churches, and colonial houses. The people of Rhode Island played an important part in the early history of America, and were noted for their independence and love of freedom. Rhode Island was named after the Island of Rhodes in the Mediterranean Sea.

Rhode Island ranks 50th in size among the states, with 1,214 square miles. In population it ranks 39th, with about 950,000 people living there. It became a state in 1790, and was the 13th state admitted to the United States. The capital is Providence.

THE PEOPLE OF RHODE ISLAND

The first settlers in Rhode Island were English settlers from the colonies in Massachusetts. They were seeking religious freedom. Many more came from

Ireland and Scotland, because the colony became known for its laws that allowed people to worship as they pleased. In the past hundred years, since Rhode Island's industries have grown, many people have come from Canada, Italy, Portugal, Poland, and other European countries to work in the factories and mills. Today there are also large groups of Italians and French Canadians. Many of these live in neighborhoods where they speak their own language.

Most of the people in Rhode Island live in the cities. They work in textile mills that make cotton, woolens, nylon, silk, and lace. Others work in jewelry factories that make more jewelry than is made in any other state. Many people make machinery, metal products, electrical supplies, and machine tools. For its size, Rhode Island manufactures more products than any other New England state.

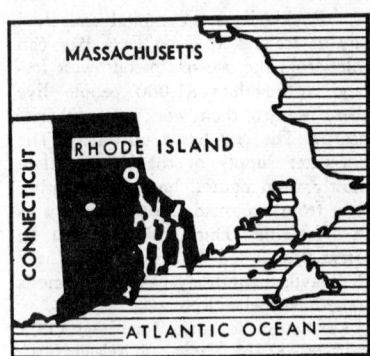

Only a small number of Rhode Island people are farmers, because in most of the state the soil is not very fertile. In sections in the north there are dairying, fruit-growing, and the raising of turkeys and chickens.

Many people work at fishing in Narragansett Bay, which is filled with lobsters, clams, oysters, and many kinds of fish. Rhode Island's clambakes and seafood dinner are famous.

WHAT RHODE ISLAND IS LIKE

The eastern and western parts of Rhode Island are quite different. The western section is rough and hilly. The eastern part is a low, sandy region that is broken up by Narragansett Bay. This large bay extends 28 miles inland from the Atlantic Ocean, and has several large islands in it. The largest are the islands of Rhode Island, Conanicut, and Prudence. On the island of Rhode Island is Newport, which once was America's most fashionable summer resort. Along the coast are many inlets and lagoons where people can swim, fish, and go boating.

The climate of Rhode Island is generally mild because of its location on Narragansett Bay. Its pleasantly cool summers have made it extremely popular with vacationists. The average temperature in July is about 69 degrees, and in winter about 23 degrees.

Rhode Island has a number of short, swift rivers that have waterfalls. These have provided waterpower for mills and factories built along the banks. Railroads and highways reach most parts of the state, and there are airports in the important cities.

THE GOVERNMENT OF RHODE ISLAND

In Rhode Island, as in other states, a governor is at the head of the government. He is elected for a two-year term. A legislature makes the laws. It is composed of two houses, a Senate and a House of Representatives. The members of both houses are elected for a two-year term. Judges are elected by the legislature and hold office permanently. The capital is Providence. There are five counties.

There are about 180,000 students attending public elementary and high schools. Among the principal colleges and universities are:

University of Rhode Island, at Kingston. Enrollment 5,013 in 1971 (co-ed).

Brown University, at Providence. Enrollment, 5,374 in 1971 (co-ed).

Providence College, at Providence. Enrollment, 3,140 in 1971 (men only).

Bryant College, at Providence. Enrollment, 3,231 in 1971 (co-ed).

CHIEF CITIES OF RHODE ISLAND

The leading cities of Rhode Island, with populations from the 1970 census, are:

Providence, population 179,213, the state capital and largest city. There is a separate article about PROVIDENCE.

Pawtucket, population 76,984, the third-largest city, manufacturing center. Pawtucket is so near Providence that they are practically one city.

Warwick, population 83,694, the second-largest city, summer resort on Narragansett Bay.

Cranston, population 73,037, the fourth-largest city, manufacturing center, in the eastern part of the state.

Woonsocket, population 46,820, the fifth-largest city, a textile center, in the northern part of the state.

The Hunter House, built about 1740, is one of the most elegant Colonial mansions.

RHODE ISLAND IN THE PAST

The coast of Rhode Island was first explored by Giovanni da Verrazano, more than four hundred years ago. Fur traders came to the region, but the first permanent settlement was not made until 1636, when Roger Williams founded Providence. He had been forced to leave Massachusetts because of his religious beliefs. Other English colonists started several more settlements, and eight years later the settlements were joined into one colony called the Providence Plantations. In 1663, this became the colony of Rhode Island. The colony was known for its freedom of religion, freedom of the press, and freedom of thought. The colonists were the first to declare their independence from England, and they played an important part in the Revolutionary War. One of the most famous American generals, Nathanael Greene, came from Rhode Island.

The start of the textile (cloth-manufacturing) industry in the United States was made in Rhode Island in 1790, by Samuel Slater, and Rhode Island quickly grew into the leading manufacturing state in the country. Many of the people who had been farmers moved to the cities to work in the new factories. Many people were also in the shipping business, and their ships visited ports in all parts of the world. Later, when railroads were built, Rhode Island's shipping industry became less important.

PLACES TO SEE

Old Stone Mill, at Newport. The oldest structure in the state, believed to have been built before 1677.

Nathanael Greene's House, in East Greenwich, in the central part of the state, on U.S. Route 1.

Touro Synagogue, in Newport. The oldest Jewish synagogue in America, built in 1763. It is now a national historic site.

Block Island, in Narragansett Bay. Often thought to be the hiding place of treasures buried by Captain Kidd; a popular summer vacation spot.

Newport-Bermuda Yacht Race, held in June, every other year, at Newport.

RHODE ISLAND. Area, 1,214 square miles. Population (1970 census) 946,725. Capital, Providence. Nickname, Little Rhody. Motto, Hope. Tree, maple. Flower, violet. Song, "Rhode Island." Admitted to Union, May 29, 1790. Official abbreviation, R.I.

Rhodes

Rhodes is the largest island in the Dodecanese group of islands in the Aegean Sea. These islands belong to Greece.

Rhodes is 542 square miles in size, less than half the size of the state of Rhode Island, the smallest of the United States. About 70,000 people live on Rhodes. Most of them are of Greek descent, but some are Italians. They are farmers and fishermen. Some of them dive for sponges. The chief city is also called Rhodes. It has a population of about 28,000 and is a seaport. The interior of the island is mostly mountainous. The highest peak is Mount Ataito, which is about 4,500 feet high.

The history of Rhodes goes back more than three thousand years. The people who lived there were called Dorians, one of the Greek tribes. They had an independent country for almost five hundred years, when they were conquered by the Persians. Rhodes was a center of learning and culture. A huge bronze statue, called the Colossus of Rhodes, was built in the city's harbor. It was one of the Seven Wonders of the World in ancient times.

Rhodes, Cecil John

Cecil John Rhodes was an English statesman and financier. He was born in

1853. When he was 17 years old he went to Africa and there he made a tremendous fortune in the rich diamond mines. He returned to England to attend Oxford University, but his health failed and he went back to Africa, where he spent the rest of his life. He lived in the Cape Colony and became its prime minister, or head of the government. He obtained control of a large territory that was named Rhodesia in his honor.

Many people in South Africa did not agree with Rhodes' ideas, and he had to resign his position as prime minister. He died in 1902, at the age of 49.

RHODES SCHOLARSHIPS

Rhodes left most of his great fortune for education. He set up the Rhodes scholarships, which have made it possible for many young men to receive a fine education at Oxford University in England. Young men who live in the colonies of Great Britain, in Germany, and in the United States are eligible to win Rhodes scholarships. In the United States thirty-two Rhodes scholarships are awarded each year. Each state may nominate two people for this honor. To receive a scholarship, a young man must be a citizen of the United States and must have an outstanding record.

Rhodesia

Rhodesia is a country in southeast Africa, named after Cecil Rhodes. It declared itself independent of Great Britain in 1965 and a republic in 1970. It used to be called Southern Rhodesia.

The former territory of Rhodesia is divided into two parts by the Zambezi River, which flows eastward through southern Africa into the Indian Ocean. The larger part of this former territory, once called Northern Rhodesia, is now the independent country of ZAMBIA. From 1953 to 1963, all of Rhodesia was combined with NYASALAND and called the Federation of Rhodesia and Nyasaland, but now Nyasaland also has become an independent country, MALAWI.

Rhodesia (former Southern Rhodesia) has an area of about 150,000 square miles and about 4,000,000 people live there. About 175,000 of these are European, or white, people; some are Asians, and most are of African Negroid birth. The capital city, Salisbury, has a population of about 300,000 including its suburbs and nearly 100,000 of these are white settlers.

Rhodesia has been famous for its gold mines for more than 2,000 years, and it has Africa's best mines for chrome and some other minerals, but most of the people work on farms, raising cotton, tobacco, and grain, also cattle. Rhodesia has the spectacular Victoria Falls and also the great Kariba Dam, which produces electricity.

From 1963 to 1966, Rhodesia was a self-governing country in the British Commonwealth. Neither the British nor the majority of the other African nations and of the United Nations favored Rhodesian independence, which would mean about 200,000 white persons governing nearly 4,000,000 Negroes. Ian Smith, the Rho-

desian prime minister, proclaimed independence anyway. The British refused to go to war to prevent this, but with the support of the United Nations they established an embargo designed to stop trade between Rhodesia and other countries.

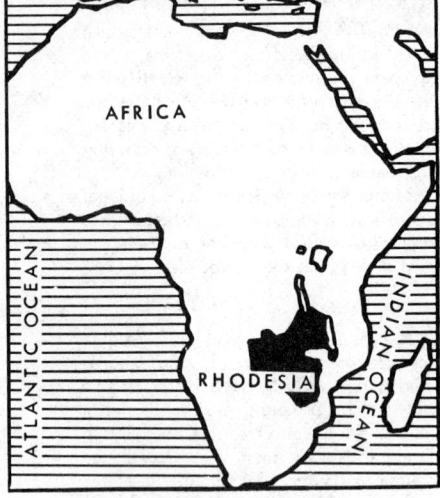

rhododendron

The rhododendron is a decorative evergreen shrub or tree that bears large clusters of brightly colored flowers. There are many different kinds of rhododendron. Some are small bushes that reach a height of only two or three feet when fully grown. Others are more like trees and grow to a height of 12 to 20 feet. There is great variety also in the color of the blossoms. They may be any shade from pale creamy white to a deep purple. Some kinds of rhododendron are hardy and can live in the climate of northern New England, but others require a warmer year-round temperature. The rhododendron is the state flower of the State of Washington.

Rhone

The Rhone is an important river of southern France. It rises from a glacier in Switzerland, flows into Lake Geneva, in Switzerland, and enters France near the city of Lyons. It then flows south into the Mediterranean Sea near the city of Marseilles. The Rhone is more than 500 miles long. Because a number of small rivers flow into the Rhone, it has the largest water flow of any river in France and is able to supply a great deal of electric power. The valley of the Rhone River is very fertile. Vegetables and fruit, especially grapes, are widely grown there, as well as olives and flowers. The valley was settled by the Romans in ancient times, and many ruins of buildings from that period are still standing.

rhubarb

Rhubarb is a garden plant that is used in pies and as a cooked fruit. It is also called *pie plant*. The stalks of rhubarb are pink at the root end and a mixture of pink and green over their entire surface. The leaves are very large and are not good to eat. The leaf stalk is usually cut into small sections and stewed. It is very tart and requires considerable sweetening. Rhubarb is a perennial, which means it grows each year from the same roots, and a patch has been known

to keep reproducing itself for more than fifty years.

rice

Rice is a cereal grain. It is the chief food of about one-half of the people of the world. It is grown in fields called "paddies," and it requires a great deal of water. The seed rice is planted each year in trenches that are flooded. The plants grow to be anywhere from one to six feet high. When the grain (the seed of the plant) is almost ready to pick, the paddy is flooded again.

Rice is picked by hand, by workers who stand in water halfway to their knees. After the grain is dry, it is threshed to remove the seed from the stalks. The white rice that is most often eaten in America was polished after threshing. This means that the hull around each individual seed has been removed. Brown rice is the same kind of rice, but the hull is left intact. Removing the brown hull causes the loss of valuable minerals and vitamins, but many people prefer the flavor of the white, polished rice. Rice is high in starch but low in proteins and fats.

The people of the East, who are the greatest eaters of rice, use it in many forms. It is eaten boiled, or boiled and then fried, and is served with meats, fish, and other foods, much as other people use potatoes. Some people use rice to make liquor. A Japanese liquor called *sake* is made from rice.

Rice is grown in China, India, Burma, and other parts of Asia. In the United States it is grown in South Carolina, Louisiana, Texas, Arkansas, and California.

Wild rice is the seed of a wild water grass that grows in marshy places. It is considered a great table delicacy.

Richard

Richard was the name of three kings of England. Richard I, often called Richard the Lionhearted, was born about eight hundred years ago, in 1157, and began to rule in 1189. He fought in the Third Crusade, in the Holy Land, against the Mohammedan emperor Saladin I. There are many legends about Richard's bravery in battle, and he is known as *Coeur de Lion,* which in French means "the Lionhearted." His army defeated Saladin, and Richard made a treaty with him and set sail for England. On the way he was shipwrecked and had to cross Europe. He was captured and held for ransom by his enemy, the Holy Roman Emperor Henry VI. Meanwhile King Philip of France and Richard's brother John tried to take advantage of Richard's absence and make John the king of England. The English people disliked John and raised a huge sum for Richard's ransom. Richard returned to England in 1194 and regained his throne. In 1199 he was killed in a minor battle and John became king. One story about Richard tells how his minstrel, Blondel, wandered through Europe looking for him, and found him by singing outside his prison window.

Richard II began to rule almost two hundred years later, in 1377, when he was only 10 years old. Because he was so young, his two uncles, the Duke of Lancaster and the Duke of Gloucester, ruled

for him. When Richard was older, he struggled to get control away from his uncles and from other powerful nobles. His cousin, Henry of Bolingbroke, assembled an army and defeated Richard. Parliament imprisoned Richard and made Bolingbroke king as Henry IV. It is believed that Richard was murdered in prison soon afterward, in the year 1400.

Richard III was one of the fiercest, most ruthless kings in English history. He was born in 1452. In trying to get power for himself, he betrayed his most faithful friends and had many people killed, including two kings of England. This was during the Wars of the Roses, about which there is a separate article. Richard helped to dethrone King Henry VI and is said to have murdered Henry's son, the Prince of Wales. Richard's brother, Edward IV, then became king. When Edward died, in 1483, Richard was made guardian of Edward's two sons, Edward V and young Richard. He imprisoned the two children in the Tower of London, had himself crowned king and is said to have had the young princes murdered. But two years later, in 1485, Richard himself was killed in a battle against Henry Tudor, who was then crowned as King Henry VII.

Richardson, Samuel

Samuel Richardson was an English novelist. He was born in 1689. For most of his life Richardson was a successful printer, but when he was about 50 years old someone asked him to prepare a book of original letters. Richardson thought that such a book would be more interesting if all the letters were about the same people. From this idea developed the novel *Pamela,* one of the first great English novels. The book consists of letters written by a young servant girl, Pamela. She has many adventures and in the end she marries her master, whom she loves. The book shows that it pays to be good, that wickedness will be punished, and that virtue will be rewarded. Other popular books by Richardson, also written in letter style, are *Clarissa Harlowe* and *Sir Charles Grandison.* Richardson died in 1761, when he was 72 years old.

Richelieu, Cardinal

Armand Jean Duplessis, Duke of Richelieu, was a great French statesman and cardinal. He was born in 1585 and studied to become a soldier. Richelieu's older brother was a bishop and when he resigned his place Richelieu dropped his idea of becoming a soldier. He studied religion in order to take his brother's position and keep the bishopric in the family.

Richelieu had a brilliant mind. At the age of 37 he became a cardinal and two years later he became chief minister to King Louis XIII of France. For the next eighteen years Richelieu was the most powerful man in France. The king never liked Richelieu but he realized what a clever man he was and followed Richelieu's advice.

Richelieu had three aims. He wanted

to make the king as powerful as possible. He wanted to put down the Huguenots, the Protestants, of France. He wanted to humble the Hapsburgs, who ruled Austria. He succeeded in all of these things. He did many things that seemed cruel and wrong in order to achieve his purposes. He made many enemies. The nobles of France were jealous of Richelieu and there were several plots to kill him, but none succeeded.

Richelieu was interested in art and literature. He founded the great French Academy, about which you can read in the article on ACADEMY. He encouraged many writers and artists and he wrote some plays himself. These plays have been forgotten but Richelieu's *Memoirs*. the story of his life, is still read. Richelieu died in 1642.

Richmond

Richmond is the capital and second largest city of Virginia. It is on the James River, about 125 miles from the Atlantic Ocean. Richmond is an important shipping, financial, and commercial center, and a United States Customs port of entry. It is the principal manufacturing center of Virginia and is one of the greatest tobacco markets in the United States. The city is also noted for its historic landmarks. During the Civil War it was the capital of the Confederate States of America.

Richmond has a city-manager form of government, with a nine-member council elected by the people. About 250,000 people live there. Many of them work in plants that process tobacco or make machinery, paper, and textiles. Six railway lines and several airlines serve the city.

RICHMOND'S HISTORIC PAST

A trading post was established on the site of Richmond in 1637. The town was laid out in 1737 and incorporated in 1742. It was made capital of Virginia in 1779. Richmond was a battleground in several Civil War campaigns, and part of the city was burned in the final days of the war. Some of the battlefields are preserved in Richmond National Battlefield Park.

The state capitol contains a famous statue of George Washington by Jean Houdon and busts of the seven other United States Presidents who were born in Virginia. Other notable buildings are St. John Episcopal Church, where Patrick Henry said "Give me liberty or give me death"; the White House of the Confederacy, which was once the home of Jefferson Davis; and the Edgar Allan Poe shrine, the oldest building in the city. There are several universities in Richmond, including Union Theological Seminary, Virginia Union University, the Medical College of Virginia, the University of Richmond, and a branch of the College of William and Mary.

RICHMOND, VIRGINIA. Population (1970 census) 249,621. Capital of Virginia. County seat of Henrico County. Settled, 1637.

rickets

Rickets is a bone disease that may develop in babies and young children who do not get the proper food. Certain food substances are necessary to build strong, healthy bones. One of these sub-

stances is called vitamin D. It is found in milk, butter, the yolks of eggs, leafy green vegetables such as lettuce and spinach, and fish-liver oils. Vitamin D is also present in sunlight.

Children who live in places where there is not very much sunshine and where vitamin D foods are scarce may not grow properly. Their bones may become soft and unable to carry the weight of the body. The bones then become bent or twisted as the body grows. Children who have rickets may be knock-kneed or bowlegged. Some children have such bad cases of rickets that they cannot walk at all.

Children who have rickets are given medicines and special foods that contain vitamin D and calcium and phosphorus, two minerals that help to build bone.

The disease is also called *rachitis*.

riddle

A riddle is a question with an answer that is very hard to find. Riddles are also called *conundrums*. Some riddles are intended simply to be humorous or amusing; for example, "What is black and white and red all over?" to which the answer is a newspaper, which is read and which is black and white. There are many famous riddles in legend and literature. Examples are "the Riddle of the Sphinx," which you can read in the article SPHINX, and an ancient Greek riddle that is told in the article LOUSE.

Ridgway, Matthew B.

Matthew Bunker Ridgway is a general in the United States Army who has held several of the highest positions possible for an Army officer, including Chief of Staff. He was born in 1895 in Fort Monroe, Virginia, and was graduated from the United States Military Academy at West Point. During World War II he commanded a division in Europe.

In 1950, during the Korean War, Ridgway was sent to command the Eighth Army in Korea, and a year later, in 1951, he replaced General Douglas MacArthur as Allied commander-in-chief in the Far East. He was then made Supreme Commander of the NATO forces in Europe. In 1952 he was recalled to the United States to serve as chief of staff. He retired in June, 1955.

Riel, Louis

Louis Riel was a Canadian who lived about a hundred years ago and who led many of the Canadian and Indian people of northwestern Canada in rebellions against the Canadian government. Riel was born in 1844 in the region that is now the province of Manitoba. His parents were part French, part Irish, and part American Indian. He was sent to school in Montreal and studied to be a priest but never became one. He went back to Manitoba, and when he was only 25 years old he led a rebellion called the Red River Rebellion.

At that time the Hudson's Bay Company, an English company that had controlled vast territories in the Canadian

northwest, had just turned over to the Canadian government its northwestern lands. There were about 10,000 métis (people of mixed French and Indian blood) living in this territory. They were afraid the Canadian government was going to take their land away from them. Riel set up a government, which he called the Republic of the Northwest, and declared this an independent state with himself as president. This government lasted eight months. The Canadian government sent troops into Manitoba to put down Riel's government, but there was no bloodshed and in 1870 Riel and the Canadian government made an agreement that established the province of Manitoba as part of Canada.

In 1884 Riel led another rebellion, called Riel's Rebellion. Again the reason was that metis were afraid the Canadian government was trying to take their land away from them. In this rebellion there were several bloody battles. The ones best remembered are the Battle of Duck Lake, where a force of Canadian Northwest Mounted Police was captured; and the Battle of Frog Lake, when many members of the Mounted Police were killed. The Mounted Police gained complete control and Riel had to flee. He hid in the United States for a few months but then returned to Canada and was captured, sentenced to death, and hanged in 1885.

Riel never lost his popularity with the people of Manitoba, who elected him to the parliament of the Dominion of Canada while he was in exile in the United States. Canadian historians today look on Riel as a well-meaning man who wanted nothing more than freedom for his people but who was so suspicious and hot-headed that he started fights and caused bloodshed when they were not necessary.

Rienzi

Cola di Rienzi was a patriot of the city of Rome and the leader of a revolution, about six hundred years ago. He was born in 1313, of parents who were not noble or wealthy but who gave their son a fine education. He was a good student and became an excellent speaker. At that time Rome was ruled by a group of noblemen who had no regard for the rights of the people. When Rienzi's brother was killed by the nobles, Rienzi determined to rid Rome of the aristocrats and make it a more democratic city.

Rienzi became popular and in 1347 the people of Rome chose him to be tribune, or head of their government. He was very successful for a while, but he became extravagant and too eager for power and this made the Romans angry. Rienzi had to disguise himself as a monk and escape from Rome. Two years later he returned to Rome and won back his power, but many of the people were still dissatisfied and Rienzi was murdered in 1354 while he was making a speech. He was then 41 years old.

rifle

A rifle is a kind of firearm in which spiral (twisting) grooves are cut inside the barrel. This is called a *rifled bore*. The

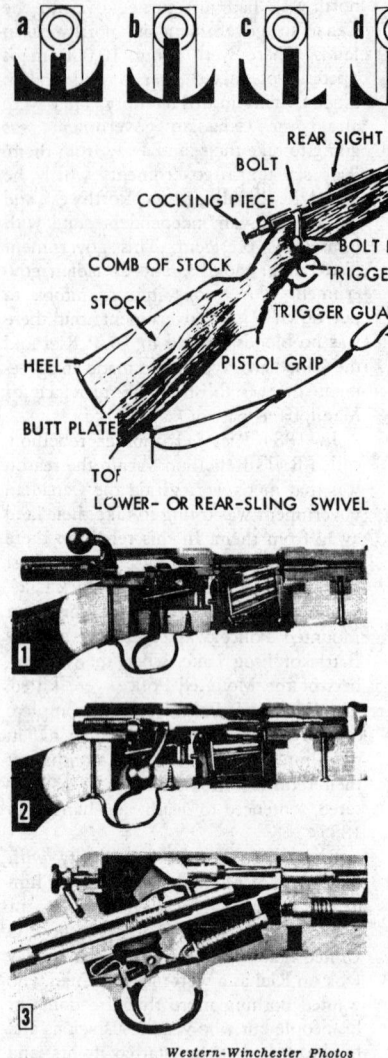

FRONT SIGHT

BARREL

MUZZLE

REAR SIGHT

FORE-END OR FORE-ARM

BOLT

UPPER- OR FRONT-SLING SWIVEL

COCKING PIECE

BOLT HANDLE

KEEPER

COMB OF STOCK

TRIGGER

SLING

STOCK

TRIGGER GUARD

HEEL

PISTOL GRIP

ARM LOOP

BUTT PLATE

TOE

LOWER- OR REAR-SLING SWIVEL

Western-Winchester Photos

1 *and* 2. The clip pushes up a new bullet when the repeating rifle's bolt is opened. When the bolt is closed, the bullet is pushed into place for firing.
3. A self-loading model does this automatically after the rifle is fired.

The parts of a single-shot bolt-action rifle are the basic parts needed for a modern rifle. The inset shows the "picture" seen through the rifle sight when it is aimed too low (A), too high (B), to the right (C), and perfectly (D).

See the articles on CANNON and AMMUNITION.

grooves cause the bullet or shell to spin as it travels through the air, and the spinning makes it follow a much straighter path. Usually the word *rifle* is used for small firearms that are held against the shoulder when they are fired, but most big cannons, such as naval artillery, field guns, and howitzers, also have rifled bores.

Riga

Riga is the capital city of Latvia. It is at the mouth of the Western Dvina River on the Gulf of Riga, which is an arm of the Baltic Sea. Riga is an important seaport and manufacturing city. About 733,000 people live there. Many of them work in factories that make railroad cars, electrical and heavy machinery, telephone and radio equipment, and other products, and in the shipbuilding industry. Riga has a university, an agricultural college, and academies of art and music.

The city of Riga was founded in 1201. It became the seat of Christian bishops, and from Riga Christianity was spread through the Balkan countries by the Livonian Knights, a German religious order. In 1282 Riga joined the Hanseatic League, a powerful organization of merchants. In modern times, Riga has usually been under the control of Russia (see the article on LATVIA).

There are many historic landmarks in Riga. A section called the old Hansa town contains the city's principal buildings, including a cathedral that dates from the 1200s, a castle that was built in 1515, and old churches and guildhalls. A popular beach resort, Rigas Jurmala, is part of the city of Riga.

RIGA, LATVIA. Population (1973 estimate) 633,000. Capital of Latvian Soviet Socialist Republic. On the Western Dvina River and the Gulf of Riga. Founded, 1201.

Riley, James Whitcomb

James Whitcomb Riley was an American poet who wrote poems about the simple farm life of the Midwest. He was born in Greenfield, Indiana and came to be known as the "Hoosier poet." (Indiana is called the "Hoosier state.")

Riley was born about the year 1849. His father was a lawyer but Riley was not interested in that profession. He worked for a while as a sign painter, then traveled with a company of actors, for whom he wrote plays and songs. When he was 20 years old Riley began to work for newspapers. In 1877 he joined the Indianapolis *Journal* and started to write poems for that paper.

Many of Riley's most popular poems were written in dialect, the way the farm people of Indiana actually talked at that time. Some of his poems are funny, some are sad. Many of the best ones are for children. Two of the most popular of Riley's poems are "Little Orphant Annie" and "The Raggedy Man."

Riley received many honors, and the year before he died the people of Indiana began to celebrate his birthday as a state holiday. Riley died in 1916, when he was about 67 years old.

Rimsky-Korsakov

Nicolai Rimsky-Korsakov was a famous Russian composer, or writer of music. He was born in Russia in 1844. He served as an officer in the Russian Navy for several years and then became a music teacher in the city of St. Petersburg (now Leningrad). He was the first Russian composer to write a symphony. He wrote his first symphony at the age of 21. He later wrote important operas, including *The Snow Maiden* and *Le Coq d'Or* ("The Golden Cock"). His *Scheherazade* is still played very often by orchestras. He died in 1908.

Ring operas

The Ring operas are four music dramas written by the German composer Richard Wagner about the legend of the NIBELUNGS, a race of dwarfs, about which there is a separate article. The four operas together are called *Der Ring der Nibelungen,* or The Ring of the Nibelungs. The names of the operas are *Das Rheingold* (the Rhine gold), *Die Walküre* (the Valkyries), *Siegfried,* and *Die Götterdämmerung* (the Twilight of the Gods). Wagner composed the first two operas and most of *Siegfried* between 1853 and 1857. He laid them aside and went on to compose other operas, and more than ten years later he completed *Siegfried* and wrote *Götterdämmerung.* In the town of Bayreuth, in Germany, he built a special theater large enough for the performance of his operas, and in 1876 the entire Ring cycle was first performed there. The Ring operas have been favorites of opera-lovers ever since.

The story of the Ring operas concerns a hoard of gold hidden in the Rhine River and guarded by three Rhine maidens. This gold is magic, and anyone who is willing to give up love and who makes a ring of the gold can gain wealth and power in the world. In *Das Rheingold,* the dwarf Alberich gives up love and takes the gold to the land of his people, the Nibelungs. Alberich makes the magic ring. Now, the great god Wotan had promised a race of giants that he would let them take away the goddess of love, Freya. Wotan persuades the giants to accept the ring and the treasure instead. He tricks Alberich into turning himself into a toad and then steals the treasure. The giant Fafner leaves with the ring, and Alberich puts a terrible curse on it.

In *Die Walküre* (which means the Valkyries, daughters of Wotan), the hero Siegmund comes to a place in the forest where the heroine Sieglinde lives with her husband Hunding, whom she hates. Siegmund learns that he is fated to take a magic sword from a tree and free Sieglinde. He does so, and they flee together, but Hunding follows and is able to kill Siegmund because Wotan has broken Siegmund's sword. Wotan then kills Hunding. One of Wotan's daughters, Brünnhilde, has tried to shield Siegmund in the fight, and as punishment Wotan decrees that she must lie asleep surrounded by magic fire until a brave man comes to rescue her. In this opera the "Ride of the Valkyries" and the Magic Fire music are very famous.

The third opera tells the story of the hero Siegfried. The drama opens in the

cave of the dwarf Mime, one of the Nibelungs. Mime reveals that Siegfried is the son of Siegmund and Sieglinde, and tells the youth that he has been reared by the dwarfs and now must regain the golden ring from the giant Fafner. This can be done only with the sword of Siegfried's father, but the sword is broken and only a man who has never felt fear can forge it together again. Siegfried succeeds in repairing the sword and then kills Fafner, who has changed himself into a fearful dragon. Siegfried also kills Mime, having learned by listening to the birds that Mime intended to betray him and steal the ring. He also learns from the birds where Brünnhilde lies sleeping, and he breaks through the ring of magic fire and awakens her with a kiss.

In *Die Götterdämmerung,* a king named Gunther plots to win both Brünnhilde and the ring from Siegfried. Gunther gets Brünnhilde away by giving Siegfried a magic potion to drink, which destroys his memory of Brünnhilde. Wotan wants the ring returned to the Rhine maidens, in order to thus lift the curse that Alberich has put upon the possessor of the ring and upon Valhalla, the home of the gods. But Siegfried is killed by Hagen, son of the dwarf Alberich. The brokenhearted Brünnhilde builds a funeral pyre for the body of Siegfried and then rides her horse into the fire. The Rhine maidens come and take their ring, and Valhalla burns.

ringworm

Ringworm is a skin disease that can affect the feet, fingernails, scalp, or body of a human being. Dogs and cats also get ringworm. Ringworm is not a worm at all. It is a fungus, a kind of plant. The most common kind of ringworm is the fungus that grows on the feet. It is called *athlete's foot.*

Ringworm is very infectious, which means that a person can easily catch it from someone who has the disease. Many children catch ringworm from playing with infected dogs and cats.

Scalp ringworm causes a patch of hair to break off near the roots, leaving a bald spot on the head. It can be spread by using another person's comb and brush, or even wearing the hat of someone who has the disease. A person might catch scalp ringworm if his barber used scissors that had not been properly sterilized.

Body ringworm occurs usually on a person's face or neck. It makes a small ring of rough, pink skin, with a clear spot in the center.

Nail ringworm is very difficult to cure. The fungus attacks the fingernails and causes them to become brittle, dark, and pitted or grooved.

Rio de Janeiro

Rio de Janeiro is the former capital of Brazil and one of the largest cities in South America. It is on Buanabara Bay of the Atlantic Ocean, and has one of the great harbors of the world. Rio, as it is popularly called, is an important railroad and airline center and is the chief trading center of Brazil. The city exports many products to other countries, including coffee, iron ore, meat, cotton, and hides for leather. More than four million people live in Rio. Many of them work in the city's varied industries, including factories that make glass, cotton goods and clothing, chemials, foods, and many other things.

Rio has a warm climate, and the beauty of the city has made it popular with tourists from all over the world. It rises from the harbor to surrounding low mountains among which lie fine residential districts. Towering over the harbor are Sugar Loaf Mountain and a peak called Corcovado, on which stands a huge, white concrete statue of Christ the Redeemer. This statue is floodlighted at night and can be seen from every part of the city. The beaches of Rio are famous, especially the crescent-shaped Copacabana. The annual Mardi Gras carnival fills the city with visitors every year.

The city and its suburbs are connected by beautiful drives, one of the loveliest of which is the Avenida Beira Mar, running for four miles along the waterfront through handsome residential sections. This avenue, like many others, has a walk of white marble inlaid with brilliantly colored mosaic work. Among the notable buildings in Rio are the municipal theater, one of the largest in the world; the Catete and Guanabara palaces; the Candalaria Church; and the National Museum. Rio has a university and military and naval academies.

Rio de Janeiro was named in 1502 by Portuguese explorers who founded a colony on its site. The name means "river of January"; the explorers arrived in that month and believed that the harbor was the mouth of a great river. In 1576 Rio became the capital of one of the two provinces into which Brazil was then divided. Later it was made the capital of all the Portuguese colonies in South America, and still later it was the capital of the empire of Brazil. In 1889, when Brazil became a republic, Rio remained the capital. However, in 1960 the new city of Brasilia became the capital.

Rio de Janeiro has been the scene of important Pan American conferences.

RIO DE JANEIRO, BRAZIL. Population (1973 estimate) 4,296,782.

Rio Grande

The Rio Grande is a river 1,800 miles long, the fourth-longest in the United States. It rises in southwestern Colorado, flows south through New Mexico, and for its last 1,300 miles forms the international border between the United States and Mexico. It empties into the Gulf of Mexico. Mexicans call the river *Rio Bravo del Norte,* or Brave River of the North.

In Colorado the Rio Grande is a mountain stream. In New Mexico it flows mostly through a series of valleys and canyons. From El Paso, just south of the Texas-New Mexico border, to the Gulf of Mexico the Rio Grande is a winding stream. It is wide and shallow, and during the dry season it almost disappears. Most of the rainfall in this region is in the form of sudden cloudbursts, and for this reason the Rio Grande frequently floods.

The Rio Grande has been used for irrigation of the dry lands around it since Indian times, before the arrival of the first white settlers. There are now many irrigation projects along its length. Elephant Butte Dam in New Mexico is more than three hundred feet high and provides irrigation, power and flood control for a wide area. Caballo Dam, 22 miles downstream, is about 100 feet high. The Texas course of the Rio Grande flows through rich farmland called the Rio Grande Valley. It is irrigated by a series of dikes and floodways and is noted for its citrus fruits, wheat, and garden produce.

Along the Texas course of the Rio Grande there are a number of paired towns, one on each side of the river, where there are international crossing points. Among these are Brownsville, Texas, and Matamoros, Mexico; Laredo, Texas, and Nuevo Laredo, Mexico; El Paso, Texas, and Juarez, Mexico. The river is navigable by small boats for about 450 miles from its mouth, but an agreement between the United States and Mexico forbids navigation. Big Bend National Park, established in 1944, is in the U-shaped bend of the river in southwest Texas. It covers almost 700,000 acres.

river

A river is a large stream of water that flows downhill until it reaches the sea, or another river, or perhaps a lake. A small stream of water is called a brook and a somewhat larger one is called a creek. Rivers are the largest. Some rivers, such as the Nile and the Amazon and the Mississippi, are thousands of miles long.

Rivers have been of great importance in the history of mankind. The earliest civilized communities were built along rivers because the water was needed for farms. Rivers were used for inland transportation thousands of years before railroads were built.

HOW RIVERS ARE FORMED

Most rivers begin in mountains. Some start as springs. Some are formed by rainwater that runs down the slopes or by snow that melts when the warm season comes. A few begin at the ends of glaciers (rivers of ice) as they reach the warmth of lower altitudes.

Water always flows downhill and always follows the easiest (deepest) path. Usually, many tiny streams flow downward until they meet to form one larger stream, and the larger streams flow downward until they meet to form a river. Every rain and melting of snow feeds the river.

As water flows along, it wears away anything in its path, even the hardest rock. Rivers carry along with them bits of earth and tinier bits of any rock that they pass as they flow. In the course of thousands or millions of years, this wearing-away cuts a groove, or valley, in the land through which the river flows. The bottom of this valley is called the river bed. In the Grand Canyon of the Colorado River, in Arizona, the river has cut away so much rock that its valley is more than a mile deep in some places, though the water in its channel is only a few feet deep there. The Hudson River in New York and the Amazon in South America have cut channels into the bottom of the ocean, many miles out.

Since rivers always flow to lower

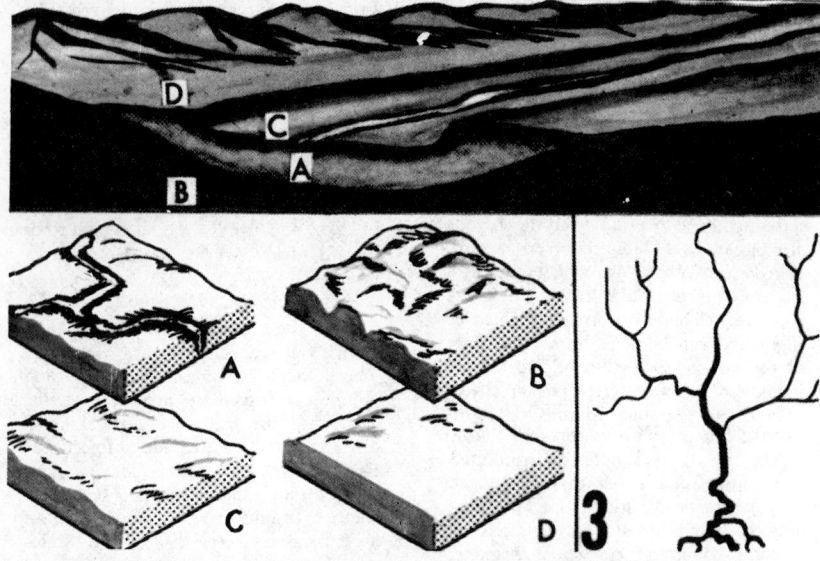

1. The river flows in a bed of soft earth (A), which covers the original bed of rock (B). On either side are its valley (C) and the terraces (D) between river and mountain.

2. Four stages of development as a river acts on a region: A youthful region (A) such as the Grand Canyon is cut with deep "Vs" by the river. An older region (B) like the Alleghenies has rivers that cut sideways, form flat plains, and flood easily. A very old region (C) such as the Mississippi River basin has broad valleys and gentle slopes. The final stage of development (D) shows how its rivers can make a region almost entirely flat.

3. A typical large river system looks like a tree, with small branches entering the main trunk. In time, the system forms a vast, fertile delta where it empties into the sea.

ground, and the land is uneven, river channels are seldom straight. Rivers wind through the land, especially when they cross plains. Sometimes they change course. The Mississippi, which flows through the flat country of the central United States, has often abandoned one channel and cut another.

In springtime, when rains are heavy and the winter snows are melting, rivers are often fed by more water than their channels can carry. This causes FLOODS, about which there is a separate article. Throughout history rivers have done far more good than harm, but their floods are still among the greatest of disasters.

THE RIVER MOUTH

The place where a river flows into the ocean is called the river's mouth. Here the river leaves much of the soil it has carried for many miles, and in the course of the centuries this soil builds a section of land, usually in the shape of a triangle. Such a place is called a DELTA, and there is a separate article about it.

Most rivers widen at their mouths. The mouth of the Amazon is more than 150 miles wide. The Mississippi, Nile and other rivers separate into several rivers when they reach their mouths.

USES OF RIVERS

The principal uses of rivers are:

They bring water and fertile soil to farms along the way.

They carry freight on boats and barges.

They supply water for drinking, washing and other purposes.

They carry away waste products.

They supply fish for food.

They can be damned to provide power that used to run mills and now makes electricity, and at the same time the dams form lakes that are useful for recreation.

PRINCIPAL RIVERS

The longest river in the world is the Nile, in Africa. The Amazon in South America carries more water than any other river, and the Congo in Africa and Yellow (or Hwang) River in China are next to it. These are the longest and largest river systems:

RIVER	LENGTH (MILES)
Nile (Africa)	4,160
Amazon (South America)	3,900
Mississippi-Missouri-Red Rock	3,890
Ob (Siberia)	3,200
Yangtze Kiang (China)	3,100
Amur (China)	2,900
Congo (Africa)	2,900
Lena (Siberia)	2,800
Yenisei (Siberia)	2,800
Missouri-Red Rock	2,714
Hwang Ho (China)	2,700
Niger (Africa)	2,600
MacKenzie (Canada)	2,514
Mékong (Asia)	2,500
Missouri	2,466
Paraná (South America)	2,450
Mississippi	2,348
Murray (Australia)	2,310
Irtish (Siberia)	2,300
Volga (Russia)	2,300
Madeira (South America)	2,000

Many famous rivers are not as long or large but are famous for the part they have played in history. These include the Tiber and Po in Italy, the Thames in England, the Rhine and Danube in central Europe, the Euphrates and Tigris in southwestern Asia, the Ganges in India, the Colorado, Rio Grande and Ohio in the United States, and many others. There are separate articles about these rivers.

Riviera

The Riviera is the most famous resort area in the world. It extends along the coast of Italy and France, on the Mediterranean Sea, for almost 200 miles, from the town of La Spezia, in Italy, to Hyères, in France. The city of Genoa, in Italy, marks the center of the Italian Riviera. The French section of the Riviera is also called the *Cote d'Azur,* or "blue

coast," because the waters of the Mediterranean near the shore are very blue.

The climate along the coast is mild in the winter and pleasant in the summer. Beautiful flowers and trees grow there. In some places flowers are grown for use in perfume.

The famous resort towns along the Riviera include Portofino, Rapallo and San Remo in Italy, Nice and Cannes in France, and Monte Carlo in the little state of Monaco.

roads

A road is a surface prepared so that automobiles, trucks and other vehicles can travel over it. Main roads that connect important places are often called highways, and roads in cities are called streets or avenues or boulevards.

To be strong and prosperous, a country must have good roads. Until the United States built good roads it could not develop its automobile industry, which gives employment to millions of people. In 1960 the United States had 3,545,693 miles of roads, which is far more than any other country has. Of these, about 2,500,000 miles were paved roads. Nevertheless, with 71,503,000 motor vehicles in use, the United States needed more and better roads.

The ancient Romans, two thousand years ago, were the first people to build fine roads. They controlled most of the civilized world and their roads connected all parts of their vast empire. The Roman roads were built of stone blocks, cut so that they were flat and level, and fitted together carefully. They were so good that some parts of them can still be used.

After the time of the Romans, no good roads were built for many hundreds of years. Most roads, even in cities, were "dirt roads" that became muddy when it rained and dusty when it was dry. Cities later paved their streets with stones, but often these were cobblestones, rounded on the top, so that the surface was uneven and gave a very bumpy ride. The best country roads had foundations of stone with sand and gravel on top. Water could drain through these roads and did not form mudholes and ruts as it did on dirt roads.

The first modern advancement came about 150 years ago when a Scottish road-builder named John Loudon MacAdam used a foundation of crushed limestone, bound together and often covered with tar on asphalt. This kind of road, still called a macadam road in honor of the inventor, has enough strength to remain level but enough "give" to keep from breaking when heavy loads pass over it.

REQUIREMENTS OF GOOD ROADS

The three requirements of a good road are long life, safety, and comfort.

Long life depends on the wearing quality of the surface and the resistance to certain natural forces. Most of the problems of today's roadbuilders are far different from the problems of even so short a time as fifty years ago. The wonderful stone roads of the ancient Romans and the fine brick roads of the early 1900s would never stand the traffic of today. Though tires are made of soft rubber, the rubbing of millions of tires would soon wear away

the soft surfaces that were so good for horses. The pounding force of a heavy truck or trailer going 50 or more miles per hour would crumble the best old roads.

Natural forces can destroy the best road if it is not well engineered. The heat of the sun causes a road to expand (become larger) and cold weather makes it contract, or shrink. A road may soak up water, which will freeze, and its expansion when it freezes will crack the strongest materials. Therefore good roads are in sections an inch or two apart, to allow for expansion and contraction, and there is a crown (a high point in the center) so water can drain off.

For comfort a road should have a smooth and level surface and should be as straight as possible. Steep grades and curves cause accidents, partly because the driver cannot see so far ahead. Modern highways must be much wider than they were even thirty years ago. Cars are wider now and there are many more big buses and trucks on the road.

A superhighway, or "limited-access highway," has two one-way roads, separated by at least 20 feet or by a high divider so there can be no head-on collisions, which usually cause death, and with tunnels or bridges for crossroads so that there need be no stoplights to slow down traffic or cross-traffic to cause accidents. The surface of the road should be rough enough so that rain will not make it slippery and cause skidding. Concrete and some forms of macadam have been found best for this. At curves the road should be *banked*, which means that it slopes down from the outside as the sides of a saucer do. The sharper the curve, the more the road should be banked. Highway engineers must calculate this scientifically.

TURNPIKES

Roads called turnpikes or toll roads have been known for thousands of years. Kings or landowners or the farmers of a community used to make a private road and charge every traveler for using it. Often these were poor dirt roads.

In modern times the governments of states own the turnpikes. Pennsylvania began it in 1945 by buying an abandoned railroad that went from Harrisburg, the capital, to Pittsburgh. Along the "right of way" of this railroad, Pennsylvania built a super-highway with two one-way roads, each having two or more lanes, with no sharp curves or steep grades and with tunnels through the high mountains. The speed limit was 70 miles per hour. To use this road, passenger cars paid about one cent per mile. Heavy trucks paid much more but it was worth while because of the saving in time. The success of the Pennsylvania Turnpike caused most other states to build turnpikes. One famous one is the New York Thruway. A chain of state turnpikes runs without a stop from New York City through New Jersey, Pennsylvania, Ohio, Indiana and Illinois to Chicago.

FEDERAL AND INTERSTATE HIGHWAYS

Rapid growth of automobile traffic caused Congress in 1916 to pass the Federal Aid Road Act, under which the United States government pays part of the cost of state highways that connect two or more states. Most roads of those times were simply leveled dirt that was muddy and often impassable when it rained.

Beginning with the Lincoln Highway, which runs 3,284 miles from the Atlantic Coast in New Jersey to the Pacific Coast in California, the U.S. Government has helped build more than 1,000,000 miles of roads. The Bureau of Public Roads has charge of spending the money allowed by Congress and usually pays about one-half the cost. The state pays the rest, and most states use for this purpose the money they receive from taxes on gasoline.

The Interstate Highway System was established after World War II, partly so that military supplies could be moved more quickly in case of an enemy attack. All turnpikes and other superhighways are joined in this system. Many of the superhighways have been built by the government and do not charge tolls. The states take care of the roads but receive Federal money to help them.

Robbia, della

Della Robbia was the name of a family of Italian artists who worked in Florence, Italy, about five hundred years ago. The greatest member of the family was Luca della Robbia. He was born about 1400. When he was a boy Luca became an apprentice to a goldsmith. He grew up to become one of the great sculptors of the world. For a cathedral in Florence he made a bronze door and ten panels of angels and dancing boys, called the *Singing Galleries*. Luca della Robbia is best known for the figures of graceful children and Madonnas that he made out of terra cotta, a kind of clay.

Luca della Robbia trained his nephew Andrea, who grew up to be a famous artist. Andrea was born in 1435. When Luca della Robbia died in 1482, Andrea carried on his work. He died about 1525. Andrea had four sons who became artists. They continued to make terra-cotta figures.

Robespierre

Maximilien Marie Isidore Robespierre was a leader of the French Revolution. He was born in France in 1758. His family was poor but Robespierre received a scholarship from his bishop and was able to complete his education. He studied law. When the troubles  began in France that led to the French Revolution, Robespierre made speeches and wrote articles on the side of the people. When the Revolution got under way, Robespierre, along with two other leaders, Danton and Marat, became the real rulers of France. They helped to set up the Reign of Terror, a period when hundreds of people who did not agree with them were murdered.

Robespierre was a serious man who tried to do what he believed was right, but he was very cruel. He caused the execution of his friend Danton. Finally other leaders of the Revolution resolved to do away with him. Robespierre was arrested and put to death on the guillotine in 1794, when he was 36 years old.

robin

One of the most familiar birds in North America is the robin. It nests as far south as Mexico on the west coast of the United States, and as far north as southern Canada on both east and west coasts. It goes south in winter and returns in early spring. Its nest is strongly built of mud and grass, and may be set on a tree branch, on a window sill, or on a roof. Two or three broods of young are reared by a pair of robins each year. The eggs are the shade of greenish blue that is known as robin's-egg blue.

The robin's chief food is worms and insects, but when cherries are ripe there are always flocks of hungry robins around.

A robin is about ten inches long. Its plumage is dark brownish gray on the back and wings, becoming darker at the back of the head. The under part is a reddish orange, so the bird is often called "robin red-breast."

Robin Hood

Robin Hood was a legendary English outlaw. Some people believe he really lived but most do not. In the legends, Robin Hood lived in Sherwood Forest with his band of merry men. Friar Tuck, Little John and Will Scarlet are the best-known members of Robin Hood's band. They wore green suits and pointed caps, and they were gay and bold. Robin Hood and his men had many exciting adventures. Robin Hood robbed rich people and gave the money to the poor. He traveled around the countryside in many different disguises so that no one knew who he was. Whenever Robin Hood got into trouble he would blow his horn and his men would come to his aid.

The story is that Robin Hood became ill and went to see a nun in order to be bled. (It was thought then that sickness could be cured by letting some of a person's blood out.) The nun let the great hero bleed to death.

Many stories and poems have been written about the daring adventures of Robin Hood and his merry men.

Robinson, Edwin A.

Edwin Arlington Robinson was an American poet who has been called one of the greatest of the 20th century. He was born in Head Tide, Maine, in 1869. He was a shy, quiet boy and was considered odd by his family and friends because all he wanted to do was to write poetry. Robinson began writing while he was in high school. After studying for a year at Harvard, he went to New York and made a living at various poorly paid jobs. He published his first volumes of poems himself and no one even noticed them.

In 1904 some of his poetry came to the attention of President Theodore Roosevelt, who was much impressed by it and wanted to help the young poet. He gave Robinson a job in the New York Customs House, where he worked for five years. But Robinson was an unhappy man and he began to live the life of some of the outcasts he wrote about.

Mrs. Edward MacDowell, the widow of the composer of music, invited Robinson to live at the colony for artists that she had established at Peterboro, New Hampshire, and Robinson had security for the rest of his life.

Beginning in 1916, Robinson brought out a new volume of poems almost every year. He won three Pulitzer prizes, in 1922, 1925, and 1928. Among his best-known works are *The Children of the Night, The Man Against the Sky, The Man Who Died Twice,* and *Tristram.* Robinson died in 1935.

Robinson, Jackie

Jack Roosevelt Robinson is an American baseball player who is known

not only as an athlete but also because he was the first member of the Negro race to become a member of a major-league team. He was born in Cairo, Georgia, in 1919, but his father died when he was 5 years old and his mother took him to California. He attended UCLA (the University of California at Los Angeles) and was a star baseball and football player. He served in World War II and became a lieutenant. After the war he played baseball on teams made up of Negroes. At that time, Negroes were not permitted to play on teams in organized baseball. Branch Rickey, who ran the Brooklyn Dodgers team in the National League, decided to force the other teams to accept Negro players. He selected Robinson as the best Negro player for a test. In 1947, Rickey made Robinson a member of the Brooklyn team. At first there was much opposition to Robinson because he was a Negro, but within a few years Negroes were accepted as regular players on most baseball teams. Robinson proved to be outstanding as a player. In 1949 he led the National League in batting with an average of .342. He usually played second base. He died on October 24, 1972.

robot, a machine that appears to act like a human being. The word robot was first used by a Czech writer named Karel Capek in a play called *R.U.R.,* which was put on in 1920: see the article AUTOMATON.

Rochambeau, Count

Jean Baptiste Donatien de Vimeur, Count of Rochambeau, was a French general who helped George Washington and the American forces in the Revolutionary War, in which the American colonists won their independence from Great Britain. Rochambeau also fought in the French Revolution, during which he was given the rank of marshal, the highest military rank in France. Rochambeau was born in 1725. He entered the army when he was 14 years old. The king of France sent him to help the American colonists in 1780, and he joined Washington's army in New York. Later he helped capture Yorktown, Virginia, where the British general, Lord Cornwallis, was defeated. During the French Revolution Rochambeau had command of the Army of the North and narrowly

escaped being put to death. He died in 1807.

Rochester

Rochester is the third-largest city in New York State. It is on Lake Ontario and on both sides of the Genesee River, in the northwestern part of the state. Rochester is noted for its industries and for its colleges and musical enterprises. About 300,000 people live there. Many of them work in the city's important photographic and optical industries, and in factories that make precision instruments, business machines, chemicals, and many other products. Rochester has large plant nurseries that have won it the name of "Flower City." The Genesee River is spanned by eleven bridges in the city and its course is broken by a number of falls that supply power to industrial plants. The New York State Barge Canal passes just south of the city. The abandoned bed of the Erie Canal is used as the route of a subway line.

Rochester is the home of the Rochester Philharmonic Orchestra and of the Eastman Orchestra and School of Music. George Eastman and his Eastman Kodak Company did a great deal to make the city both a business and a cultural center, and his home has been made a museum of photography and painting. There are several universities, including the University of Rochester and its medical center, Rochester Institute of Technology, Nazareth College, and Colgate-Rochester Divinity School.

Rochester has the city manager form of government.

The site of Rochester was first settled in 1789. The first permanent settlement was established in 1812 by Col. Nathaniel Rochester and was first called Rochesterville. A few years later the name was shortened. Before the Civil War Rochester was a station on the Underground Railway for slaves escaping from southern states.

ROCHESTER, NEW YORK. Population (1970 census) 296,233. County seat of Monroe County. Settled in 1789.

Rockefeller

Rockefeller is the name of one of America's richest and most prominent families. The first famous member of the family was John Davison Rockefeller (usually called John D. Rockefeller), who was born at Richford, New York, in 1839. He was descended from an old American family and his ancestors had fought for American independence in the Revolutionary War. Rockefeller went into the oil business in Cleveland, Ohio, and founded the Standard Oil Company, which at one time owned three-fourths of the oil business of the United States. This made Rockefeller the richest man of his time and one of the richest men of all times. His great wealth caused him to be attacked by many who thought that wealth should be more evenly divided among all the people. In 1896 Rockefeller retired from active business. He had always given all he could to worthy causes and many of his gifts for education and research now amount to millions of dollars. Among the institutions that he founded or helped in this way are the Rockefeller Institute for Medical Re-

John D. Rockefeller Sr. (*left*) and John D. Rockefeller Jr. (*right*).

search, the Rockefeller Foundation, the General Education Board, and the University of Chicago. Before his death in 1937, Rockefeller gave away more than five hundred million dollars.

John D. Rockefeller Jr., his son, was born in 1874. He was graduated from Brown University. Like his father, he has made many gifts for education and other worthy causes. One for which he is best known is the gift of the land on which the United Nations building stands in New York City. The five sons of John D. Rockefeller Jr. have been prominent in business and government work and one of them, Nelson Rockefeller, was elected governor of New York in 1958.

Rockefeller Center

Rockefeller Center is a group of buildings in New York City. It is probably the most famous group of buildings in the world and surveys have shown that it is one of the five biggest tourist attractions in New York (the other four being the subways, the Automat cafeterias, the observation tower of the Empire State Building, and the United Nations building). Rockefeller Center is sometimes called "Radio City," because part of it was originally planned as a center for the radio industry.

John D. Rockefeller Jr. planned and built Rockefeller Center, beginning in 1931 when the United States was suffering from its greatest business depression. The buildings were largely an expression of his faith in the future of the country. Rockefeller rented most of the land from Columbia University, on a long-term lease. Among the first buildings were the 70-story RCA Building (still the largest building) and the Radio City Music Hall, largest and most lavish motion-picture theater in the world.

Among the attractions in Rockefeller Center are beautiful gardens on the ground level and on terraces of the buildings; a giant Christmas tree each year; an outdoor ice-skating pond during the winter; and dozens of restaurants and fine shops.

rocket

A rocket is something that propels or drives itself by means of an explosion or the burning of something. The idea of rockets has been known for hundreds of years, but they have been little used except in fireworks and some weapons of war. During the past fifty years or less, new and far more important uses for rockets have been recognized. Greater speeds can be obtained with rockets than with any other form of driving power, which suggested the use of rockets in

aircraft and self-propelled missiles. Unlike propeller-driven or jet-propelled aircraft, rocket-driven aircraft do not need the oxygen in the earth's atmosphere, so space travel is possible only by the use of rockets.

The principle of the rocket is the same as the principle on which firearms and jet propulsion are based. When something explodes, or burns and produces expanding gases, it creates pressure in all directions at the same time. An explosion in a closed box, if strong enough, will break the box open at its weakest point. Take off one side of the box and the explosion will push the box forward at the closed side while the force of the explosion escapes at the other side.

The familiar rocket used in fireworks burns gunpowder. Gunpowder burns rapidly and produces expanding gases. At the closed tip of the rocket the gases force the cardboard shell of the rocket forward. At the open rear end the gases merely enter the atmosphere.

The V-2 self-propelled missile used by the Germans in closing months of World War II was driven by rockets. It used alcohol, ether and liquid oxygen to produce gases that would expand rapidly.

Designers of space ships use a series of rockets. The first rocket drives the space ship forward and then drops off. Another rocket then gives the space ship additional impetus (forward driving power) and then drops off. When the rocket drops off the ship, it reduces the weight and this increases the speed.

Rocket-powered aircraft are still in the experimental stage, but one of the most famous of these, the X-15, has been flown as high as 67 miles.

JATO, initials standing for jet-assisted take-off, has been much used to help airplanes with heavy loads to get into the air. Actually JATO is not jet propulsion but rocket propulsion. Rockets are attached to the wings of the plane and drive it forward during the take-off. When the plane is in the air, the rockets drop off, reducing the weight. (See also the article on JET PROPULSION.)

Rockets are among the newest developments of the United States and other major nations in their preparations for warfare or defense and for control of space. See the articles on ARTIFICIAL SATELLITES and GUIDED MISSILES.

Rockne, Knute

Knute Rockne was a famous coach of football teams at Notre Dame University in South Bend, Indiana. He was born in Norway, in 1888, but was brought to the United States when he was 5 years old. He became a star football player at Notre Dame, and with another player on the team, Gus Dorais, proved the effectiveness of the forward pass. After his graduation from Notre Dame in 1914 he became assistant coach, and in 1918 he was made head coach. His teams were always among the strongest and several times they were considered the national champions. Rockne was killed in an airplane crash in 1931.

rocks

Rocks are the hard parts of the earth's crust. They are what pebbles,

boulders, ledges and cliffs are made of. Most rocks can be broken by nothing less than a hammer, compressed air drills, or dynamite. All rocks are made by nature.

There are three large families of rocks: igneous, sedimentary, and metamorphic.

IGNEOUS ROCKS

Igneous means fire-made, and igneous rocks are those that have risen red-hot and melted from deep below the earth's crust. When they are deep in the earth, all igneous rocks are in the forms of *magma,* an extremely hot, syrupy mixture of melted minerals. When the magma rises into the earth's crust and cools, it hardens into different kinds of rock. Just what kind of rock will come from any particular batch of magma depends on which minerals are mixed in it and how fast it cools. If the magma pushes up onto the earth's crust but does not reach the surface, it cools slowly and becomes coarse-grained rock such as granite and gabbro. If the magma flows out on the earth's surface, it cools quickly and forms fine-grained rock such as basalt. If the magma is thin and cools very quickly, it becomes natural glass, which has no grain at all. The first rocks in the world were igneous, and all the other kinds of rock come from them.

SEDIMENTARY ROCKS

Weather and running water, working together for millions of years, grind igneous rocks down to grains of sand, gravel, dust, and silt. All these different grains are called sediments. When sediments pile up—layer upon layer—for hundreds of thousands of years, the upper layers push down on the bottom layers with such great weight that the grains of the bottom layers become squeezed together so tightly that they form hard rocks. These rocks are called *sedimentary* rocks. Sand grains become sandstone, clay silt becomes shale, and gravel becomes conglomerate. Another very important sedimentary rock is limestone, which is made up of the shells of animals that live by the billions in shallow seas.

METAMORPHIC ROCKS

The folding of the earth's crust and the pushing into the crust of great masses of fiery magma may change the rocks from igneous or sedimentary to *metamorphic* rocks. Metamorphic means "changed in form." The pressure of the folding of the earth's crust and the great heat of the magma squeeze, stretch, bend and melt igneous and sedimentary rocks. Under this severe treatment new minerals are formed and the rock is hardened. Shale is hardened into slate, limestone becomes marble, and sandstone becomes quartzite, one of the hardest rocks known.

Rocky Mountain goat

The Rocky Mountain goat is a member of a group of animals called "goat antelopes." None of these animals are truly goats or antelopes, but in some ways they are like both. The Rocky Mountain goat is white with black horns and hoofs. Its horns are like curved daggers. A full-grown male Rocky Mountain goat may stand as high as 40 inches at the shoulder and may weigh as much

as 300 pounds. Both males and females have horns and are bearded. The Rocky Mountain goat lives high in the barren, rocky stretches of crags and mountain peaks. It lives on mosses and other plants that it finds growing among the rocks.

Rocky Mountains

The Rocky Mountains, or Rockies, are the biggest chain of mountains in the United States and Canada. They stretch for more than three thousand miles, from New Mexico in the United States up through Colorado, Utah, Wyoming, Idaho, and Montana, and in Canada along the boundary between Alberta and British Columbia, until they end in northern Alaska. In this long stretch of mountains are most of the high peaks in North America. Some of the most majestic scenery in the United States and Canada is in the Rocky Mountain ranges.

Several smaller mountain ranges are included in the Rockies. Among them are the Sacramento Mountains in New Mexico; the Front Range, Sangre de Cristo Mountains, San Juan Mountains and Sawatch Mountains in Colorado; the Wasatch Mountains in Utah; the Wind River range in Wyoming; the Bitterroot range between Idaho and Montana; and the Selkirk range in Canada.

PEOPLE AND ANIMALS

The Rockies have the fewest inhabitants of any part of North America. The mountains are wild and rugged and many of the peaks are always covered with snow. The few people who do live in the Rocky Mountains are mostly miners who dig for gold, silver, lead. copper and other minerals. There are some who herd sheep on the high mountain pastures, and some who work in the forests as lumberjacks.

The Rockies have always had much animal life, except near the very tops of the snow-covered mountains. In the forests on the lower mountain slopes there are bears of many kinds, deer, beavers, muskrats, wolves, coyotes, and mountain lions. High on the peaks of the Rockies there are Rocky Mountain goats and bighorn sheep. These sure-footed animals scamper about on the rocks and jump from rock to rock with ease.

SCENERY

The highest peak in the whole Rocky Mountain system is Mount Elbert in Colorado. It is 14,419 feet high. Some of the great national parks of the United States and Canada are in the Rocky Mountains, including Yellowstone National Park (Montana) in the United States, and Banff National Park and Jasper National Park, in Alberta, Canada. There are many fine streams where trout and other fish may be caught. There are excellent snow-covered slopes for skiing. Many mountain climbers go to the Rockies.

The highest automobile road in the United States winds up the slopes of Pike's Peak in Colorado. Pike's Peak is over 14,000 feet high.

There are thousands of high peaks in the Rockies. In Colorado alone there are more than 1,500 peaks higher than 10,000 feet. Many rivers start in the Rocky Mountains. The melting snows start trickling down the slopes of the mountains and soon form larger streams.

The Rocky Mountains form part of the great CONTINENTAL DIVIDE, about which you can read in another article. There are many pictures of the Rockies with the articles on the states of the United States and the provinces of Canada through which the Rockies go.

Rocky Mountain spotted fever,

a serious disease that may infect a person bitten by a particular kind of tick: see the article on TICK.

rococo

Rococo is a style of art and architecture that is very fancy. It is similar to BAROQUE, about which there is a separate article, but paintings or buildings in the baroque style are bigger and heavier. The rococo style tries to give the appearance of lightness and grace.

The rococo style started in France about 250 years ago and was popular in other European countries for about fifty years. It was used in every branch of art, including painting, music, furniture, architecture, and interiors of houses. Typical rococo designs used for decoration are such things as shells, flowers, scrolls, leaves, and small animals.

rodent

Rodents are gnawing animals. That is, they cut things with their teeth. They are mammals, which means that they bear living young and nurse them. There are thousands of different rodents. Most people think of rats and mice in connection with the word "rodent," but they are only part of one rodent group.

There are three main rodent types. One includes rats, mice, lemmings, and similiar animals. The second group of rodents consists of squirrels, chipmunks, beavers, woodchucks, gophers, and others. The third group includes the porcupine, guinea pig, chinchilla, cavy, agouti, and others.

Two chisel-like cutting teeth in the front of the jaw are present in all rodents. Rabbits and hares have teeth almost like rodents' teeth, but they also have two other teeth directly behind the chisel-like cutting teeth. This puts rabbits and hares out of the rodent classification.

A rodent's teeth keep growing throughout the animal's life. This is necessary, because rodents' teeth are constantly worn down from continued gnawing. If the teeth did not keep growing they would wear down to nothing, and then the animal could not live.

rodeo

A rodeo is a show in which cowboys show their skill and try to win prizes that are given for the best performances. The principal competitions are:

Bronc busting. Riding an unbroken horse. The purpose is to stay on as long as possible.

Bareback riding. Riding a horse without a saddle.

Bulldogging. Throwing a steer to the ground, by holding and twisting its horns.

Steer riding. Riding a steer, bareback, and staying on as long as possible.

Roping. Throwing the lariat (lasso) so as to catch and control a calf or steer.

In addition, the cowboys give exhibitions of skill in riding, whirling the lariat, shooting, and other things.

Rodeos began as games at round-up time on ranches. The games proved so much fun to watch that professional exhibitions were put on and admission charged. Eventually annual rodeos were put on in big cities, for example at Madison Square Garden in New York, and many men and women make a profession of exhibiting their skill at rodeos. Usually music and other forms of entertainment are included.

See also the article COWBOY. The rodeo grew out of "Wild West Shows" that used to be a part of traveling circuses, but the Wild West Shows included mock fights between cowboys and Indians, and other exhibitions that are not a part of the modern rodeo.

Rodgers, Richard

Richard Rodgers is an American composer, or writer of music. He is famous for his many popular musical plays. He was born in New York City, and studied there at Columbia University and the Institute of Musical Art. In 1925 Rodgers and one of his friends, Lorenz Hart, wrote a revue, or musical play,  *Garrick Gaieties.* Hart wrote the words and Rodgers the music. The show was a great success, and they continued to work together on such plays as *A Connecticut Yankee, Babes in Arms,* and *By Jupiter.* Hart died in 1943 and Rodgers began to write with Oscar Hammerstein II. Their musical play *Oklahoma!,* produced in 1943, was the most successful musical play of all time and won a special Pulitzer prize. Beginning with that success, Rodgers and Hammerstein became the most successful theatrical writing team since Gilbert and Sullivan. Hammerstein died in 1960, but Rodgers continued to write the music, as well as the words, to popular songs and musicals.

Rodin, Auguste

Auguste Rodin was a French sculptor. He was born more than a hundred years ago, in 1840, and most of his work was done fifty or more years ago. His work aroused much disagreement during his lifetime. Some thought it beautiful and others abused it as ugly. Rodin tried to make his figures of human being realistic, or true to life, but at the same time he wanted them to express feelings such as love or hate or sadness.

Rodin was born of poor parents. While he was studying art he had to earn his living by working for ornament-makers and architects, first in Paris and later in Brussels, in Belgium. His sculpture called *The Age of Bronze,* a nude male figure, aroused a storm of criticism when it was shown in 1877, because it was so lifelike. Later it was purchased by the French government, which gave Rodin money to continue his work. In 1880 he began to design a huge bronze door for a museum in Paris. Though he never finished it, many of the figures for it were completed and are among his greatest works. They include *Adam and Eve,* now in the Metropolitan Museum in New York City, and *The Thinker,* now in Paris. Rodin died in 1917.

Roebling

Roebling was the name of two famous American engineers, father and son, who are remembered mainly for the bridges they built. John Augustus Roebling was born in Germany in 1806 and came to the United States when he was 25. He was one of the first engineers to build suspension bridges, about which you can read in the article BRIDGE. One of his first famous bridges was the Niagara Falls Suspension Bridge. In 1869 Roebling designed and began to supervise work on the Brooklyn Bridge, in New York City, but he died in that year before the bridge was completed. The work was taken over by his son, Washington Augustus Roebling, who had aided his father with other projects. The bridge was completed in 1883, even though Washington Roebling had become an invalid some years earlier. He was born in 1837 and died in 1926.

Roentgen

Wilhelm Conrad Roentgen was a German scientist. He is best-known for  discovering the X-ray. He was born in 1845 and studied at the University of Zurich, in Switzerland. He then taught physics at several German universities. In 1895 he discovered the short-wave ray, which was was later called the X-ray. (In the German language the spelling of his name is Röntgen, and the short-wave ray is still called the Röntgen ray in his honor.) For his discovery of the short-wave ray, he received the Nobel Prize in physics in 1901. He died in 1923.

Rogers, Will

Will Rogers, whose full name was William Penn Adair Rogers, was an American actor and humorist. He was the most successful and most popular entertainer of his time. He was born in 1879 in what is now Oklahoma, worked for a time as a cowboy, and then began his stage career in vaudeville shows as a cowboy rope-twirler. During the 1920s he was the star of the Ziegfeld Follies and other musical stage shows in New York City, and during the 1930s he starred in many successful motion pictures. In 1926 he began to write a daily paragraph of humorous comment for the New York *Times,* and these articles later appeared in many newspapers each day. Will Rogers was killed in an airplane crash in 1935. He was so popular that more than a million copies of books about him were sold after his death.

Roland

Roland was a legendary French warrior and hero. Most people believe that he did not really live. In the legends, Roland was the nephew of the mighty emperor Charlemagne. There was a great friendship between Roland and Oliver, another hero. Roland is best known as the main character in a great poem called the *Song of Roland*, which was written nearly a thousand years ago. The poem tells about how Roland fought a terrible battle with the Saracens, a people of the Moslem religion who were invading Europe. Roland and his men killed 100,000 Saracens in this bloody fight and only fifty of Roland's men were left. Then another army of 50,000 Saracens attacked Roland. Roland blew his magic horn and Charlemagne heard the sound and came to the aid of Roland, but it was too late to help Roland because he had blown his magic horn so loud that the veins in his neck had burst. He died before Charlemagne arrived with help.

Rolland, Romain

Romain Rolland was a French writer of novels and biographies. He was born in 1866. For a time he taught art, then music. Rolland wrote the biographies of Beethoven, Michelangelo, Tolstoy, and Mahatma Gandhi. He is best known for *Jean Christophe*, a novel in ten volumes about a musical genius. It took Rolland eight years to write this book. Rolland received the Nobel Prize for Literature in 1915. He died in 1944, when he was 78 years old.

Roman Catholic Church

The Roman Catholic Church is the largest of all Christian Churches. About 560,000,000 people in the world have been baptized in the Roman Catholic Church. This means that more than one out of every six persons in the world belongs to the Roman Catholic Church.

Nearly all the people of Italy, Spain, France, Ireland, Poland, Austria, Portugal, and all the Latin American countries, are Roman Catholics. There are large numers of Catholics in other countries of Western Europe and in Canada, and there are about 43,000,000 Catholics in the United States. Missionaries have introduced Roman Catholicism to every part of the world.

CHURCH GOVERNMENT

The church is governed by a *hierarchy*, a word formed from two Greek words meaning "sacred" and "rule." At the head of the hierarchy is the Pope, the leader of the Catholic Church on earth. Under him are the bishops. The Papacy (office of Pope) and Episcopate (office of bishop) are considered to have been set up by Jesus, who appointed the Apostles as the first bishops and St. Peter as the first Pope or head of the Church.

Next to the Pope in dignity are the cardinals, who are related to him in somewhat the same way cabinet officers are to the head of a government. Then there are the archbishops and bishops. A bishop rules over a *diocese*, which includes all the individual churches in a specific area. An archbishop rules over an *archdiocese*, which is larger and more important than a diocese. The archbishop or bishop usually has his headquarters in the largest city in his diocese. The city is called his *see*, and the cathedral, which is the bishop's church, is usually the largest church in the diocese. Many of the cathedrals of Europe are hundreds of years old. They are among the most beautiful buildings in the world. There are other bishops, called *titular bishops,* who assist archbishops and bishops.

After the bishops come the *protonotaries apostolic,* or monsignors. They are priests who are doing special work for the Pope, or priests who have been given the title as a special honor.

In each diocese there are many priests who assist the bishop. Most of them work in individual churches or parishes. Below the priests are deacons and subdeacons, who are usually men studying to become priests.

There are also many religious orders and congregations in the Roman Catholic Church. These are groups of men or women who devote their lives to working for the Church. The heads of orders and congregations, such as abbots and superior-generals, have very important jobs and come next after bishops in dignity.

All Roman Catholic priests take vows (solemn promises) to obey their superiors and to remain unmarried. Priests in religious orders also take a vow of poverty. For some this means owning nothing at all. For others it means not using anything they own without permission of superiors. The orders and some congregations have monks and lay brothers who are not priests but take the same vows. There are also separate societies for men who are called brothers, and for women who are called nuns and sisters. These men and women also take vows.

There are also societies for laymen and laywomen, persons who do not belong to the clergy. Many of these societies help others by giving them food or clothing, or by providing care for them when they are sick. Others are devoted to special prayers, such as the rosary, or to specific persons, often the Virgin Mary.

DOCTRINES AND PRACTICES

The Roman Catholic Church teaches that there are three Divine Persons in one God—God the Father, God the Son, and God the Holy Ghost. God the Father created man and made him good. Man lost this grace (God's favor) and innocence by sinning. God the Son—Jesus—took a human nature from the Virgin Mary and paid for man's sin and won back grace for man by dying on the cross. Within the Church God the Holy Ghost distributes the benefits of the death of Jesus, chiefly through the seven sacraments and the sacrifice of the Mass.

The Roman Catholic Church teaches that those who die in grace go to heaven immediately, or after a time of suffering in purgatory. Those who die without grace go to a place of punishment called hell. At the end of time there will be a resurrection of the body and a general judgment of all men by God.

There are separate articles on many of the subjects discussed in this article. See POPE, CHRISTIANITY, SACRAMENT, MASS, CHURCH, COMMUNION, CANON, and SIN.

Romance languages

About two thousands years ago, when the Roman Empire was the most powerful nation on earth, it controlled many parts of Europe. To these places the Romans sent colonists to develop the land and soldiers to keep order and to drive off invaders. The Roman people spoke the Latin language. The Romance languages are a group of languages that has grown out of the Latin speech of the colonists and soldiers, mixed with the speech of the native people of those countries, and gradually changed as all languages change in the course of centuries.

The principal modern Romance languages are: Spanish, Portuguese, French, Rumanian, and Italian. Linguists (those who make a scientific study of languages) include several other languages that once were spoken but now have partly or wholly disappeared, such as Provençal, the old language of southern France.

There were other countries in which Roman armies were stationed and Roman colonies were built, for example England; but in these countries the early Latin influence was overcome by the later influence of other languages. Nearly all modern languages have some words that came from Latin, and in the English language there are many such words, but none is as closely related to Latin as the Romance languages. See also the article LANGUAGE.

Roman Empire

The Roman Empire, which is also called simply "Rome," was the greatest empire of ancient times. It ruled over more territory and more people than any other empire of early history. At its greatest, the Roman Empire included all the countries around the Mediterranean Sea, all of western Europe, the British Isles, and parts of central Europe. It was called the Roman Empire because its capital was the city of Rome, which is the capital of the modern country of Italy. (There is separate article about the city of ROME.)

The history of the Roman Empire goes back more than 2,700 years, to the time when the ancient city of Rome was first founded.

FOUNDING OF ROME

About 2,700 years ago a tribe of shepherd people came to a point on the Tiber River, in central Italy, and built a small village. The village was on one of the seven hills that overlooked the Tiber. As time went on the village grew until it occupied all seven hills. These early Romans were called Latins and their territory in Italy was called Latium.

There are several old stories or legends that tell how Rome was founded. One of the most famous stories is about Romulus and Remus, who were twin brothers. At the time they were supposed to have lived, more than three thousand years ago, it was said that an ancient king was slain by his brother. The brother, wanting to make sure that the king's sons would not grow up and depose him, ordered that the sons should be killed too. These two sons, Romulus and Remus, were taken by their mother and placed in a basket. The basket was set afloat on the Tiber River. When the basket came to rest on the banks of the river, a she-wolf found the two babies and cared for them. When the boys grew up they de-

cided to start a city. They argued about the name and Romulus won the argument and had the city named for him—Rome.

As the tiny village grew into a city, the people of Rome began to have wars with other villages and tribes in central Italy. They were usually stronger than their enemies and won additional territory. Their most important wars were with their strong neighbors to the north, a people called the Etruscans. The wars with the Etruscans lasted many years and at times Rome was ruled by the Etruscans. From the Etruscans the Romans learned much. They learned how to make things of metal. They learned how to build and make bridges and roads. They also learned something about art.

After the city of Rome became strong it was ruled for many centuries by kings. Under the kings the Romans prospered and conquered more of Italy. But they became dissatisfied with their rulers and finally threw the kings out and established a republic. This was about 500 B.C.

THE ROMAN REPUBLIC

The Roman republic was not exactly like republics today. Not all the people had the same rights as other people. Since the ancient Romans believed that the father was the most important member of the family and that the father must be obeyed, the Romans took their word for father, which is *pater*, and called the important people of Rome the *patricians*. The other people in the ancient republic were called *plebeians*.

The republic was ruled by the Senate, which was made up of the most important patricians in the city of Rome. When the plebeians wanted more power they were allowed to elect two officials called *tribunes*. The tribunes were very powerful and saw to it that the plebeians' rights were upheld. There were other important officials in the Roman republic. Some of these were called *consuls*. As time went by the consuls became more and more powerful. Finally they really ruled the Roman republic. At times the Romans chose a *dictator*, but this dictator was chosen for only a short time, usually during times of war.

The republic grew steadily for hundreds of years. In the Punic Wars, the Romans destroyed the North African city of Carthage, which was the greatest rival of Rome. In other wars the Romans became rulers of Greece, which had been the greatest center of art and learning. Great generals such as Pompey and Julius Caesar added territories in Europe, Africa, and the Near East (the part of Asia that is on the Mediterranean Sea).

By the year 50 B.C. (about fifty years before Jesus was born), Rome was al ready the strongest country in history, and the patrician families were the richest people. They owned vast farms and thousands of slaves, men and women, that the Roman armies had captured in warfare. These slaves did most of the work in the cities and on the farms. Some of the slaves who had been taken in Greece became the teachers of the Romans. In this way the Roman civilization learned much from the old Greek civilization.

At the height of its power, the Roman Empire ruled all the lands on the Mediterranean.

THE BEGINNING OF THE EMPIRE

The spirit of the Roman republic was still strong. The Senate killed Julius Caesar because he was suspected of wanting to become emperor. Then for a while Rome was ruled by a *triumvirate*, which means three men ruling together. One was Caesar's nephew, Octavian. The second was a great general Mark Antony. The third was a Senator named Lepidus. But Octavian defeated Antony in battle, Lepidus died, and Octavian was left as the sole ruler of Rome. In 27 B.C., Octavian became the emperor of Rome and the Roman Empire began.

As emperor, Octavian was called Augustus Caesar. Since that time the word Caesar has come to mean emperor. The Russians later called their emperors *czars*, and the Germans called theirs *Kaisers*.

ROMAN RULE

With the founding of the Roman Empire began the period of strong Roman rule over what was then most of the civilized world. The Romans maintained great armies in the conquered territories. For a long time in the Roman Empire there was hardly any war because the Roman armies were so strong. This condition was called the *Pax Romana*, or "Roman peace."

With Roman rule came Roman law. The Romans had established a good system of laws. They had laws for almost all activities, for business and for trade. They kept the people in an orderly state and in many of the conquered territories they ven allowed the people to have their wn courts and try cases. But even where his was so, governors sent from Rome o the territories were really the powerful rulers of the territories.

The Romans were great builders. During the reign of Augustus the capital city of Rome was almost completely rebuilt. It was said that Augustus found a city of brick and left it a city of marble. Dozens of other cities of the empire were just as beautiful and just as comfortable, with fine houses, temples, baths, coliseums vhere the entertainments were held, and many other great buildings.

LIFE IN ROME

In any great city of ancient Rome tens or hundreds of thousands of people lived and carried on business. The richer people, of course, lived in fine marble homes and the poorer people were crowded in stone tenement buildings. A fine Roman house was built around an open courtyard where the people could sit in the milder weather and enjoy the balmy air and sunshine. The Roman houses were nicely furnished but the furniture was hard and uncomfortable. It was made of wrought iron, hardwood and marble. In Rome and most of the other cities there were excellent libraries, full of manuscripts written on rolls of parchment. There were also many buildings that were used for athletics and sports.

Among the most popular of all public buildings were the great Roman baths. In these great bathhouses the Romans had large pools of hot and cold water. At different times men and women could come to the baths and enjoy them. There were also steam rooms and massage rooms. The water for the baths was carried in lead pipes from the cellar, where great furnaces fed with wood heated the water. The water that supplied the baths and other buildings and homes of Rome was brought from the mountains and carried to the city through great aqueducts, long bridgelike structures.

The Romans were also great road builders. They built long, level stretches of stone roads extending for hundreds of miles. The roads were so well built that some of them are in use today. The Romans built these roads as far away as England. In building the roads the Romans went up mountains and through valleys and across level plains. When they came to rivers, they built stone bridges whose arches still stand in many places. The building of the roads from Rome to many of the conquered territories led to the saying, "All roads lead to Rome."

SPREAD OF CIVILIZATION

During nearly five hundred years, the great Roman civilization was spread throughout the conquered territories. Everything the Romans had learned from the Etruscans and the Greeks they passed on to the conquered people. They

spread reading and writing and the use of the Latin language. With their great system of laws, they brought respect for law and order to all parts of the empire.

Religion was changed very much during the life of the Roman Empire. The old Romans believed in many gods. They allowed peoples in conquered territories to worship their own gods but they made these people worship Roman gods too. Especially they made everyone worship the Roman emperors, who called themselves gods.

At the very beginning of the Roman Empire, during the reign of Augustus Caesar, a very important event occurred in Palestine, which was a Roman province. In a small village called Bethlehem a child named Jesus was born. As Jesus grew up and preached to the people and led them to believe in a newer and greater religion, he attracted many followers. Jesus was arrested and was put to death by the Romans, but the lessons he had preached became the most important religion in the western world. In the year 311—about 311 years after Jesus was born the emperor of Rome was a man named Constantine. He came to believe in Christianity and he decreed that henceforth it would be the religion of the Roman Empire. That began the greatness of Christianity, which continues to this day.

TWO ROMAN EMPIRES

Constantine also was responsible for the establishment of two separate Roman Empires. The Roman Empire at that time was often attacked by tribes of people whom the Romans called barbarians, who lived on the borders of the empire. Constantine decided that it would be necessary to establish a second capital of the empire, to the east. He chose the city called Byzantium, which later was named for him and became Constantinople, and which today bears the name of Istanbul. This eastern city soon became even more important than Rome and during the latter years of the Roman Empire there were two emperors—a western Roman emperor in Rome and an eastern Roman emperor in Constantinople. The East Roman Empire is also called the Byzantine Empire. It lasted almost a thousand years longer than the western empire.

FALL OF THE EMPIRE

The barbarians became stronger and raided deeper into the empire. Among these barbarians were tribes called the Goths, the Vandals, and the Huns. The Romans had become soft and lazy. The Roman Empire also became weaker because of high taxes. The emperor spent so much money and took so much money in taxes from the people that there was great grumbling and discontent. This all made it easy for the barbarians to defeat the Romans.

The barbarians did not conquer the Roman Empire all at once. Sometimes they would defeat the Romans and sometimes the Romans would defeat them. But many raids were made into Roman territory in Italy and gradually the Roman Empire began to fall apart. All Roman soldiers were called back to Rome and no guards were left at the borders of

the empire. There was no one to keep the great hordes of barbaric tribes from moving in. Finally there were not even enough soldiers to protect Rome itself. In the year 476, the Goths, a Germanic people drove the last Roman emperor from his throne in Rome. The West Roman Empire was at an end.

The East Roman Empire continued for many centuries. Not until the year 1453, just a few years before Christopher Columbus discovered America, did the Roman Empire finally fall to the Turks

There are separate articles about most of the men, peoples, and events mentioned in this article. See also the article on ROME.

Romania, another spelling of the name RUMANIA.

Romanov or Romanoff

Romanov is the name of a royal family whose members were czars (emperors) of Russia for more than three hundred years, from 1613 to 1917. The name is sometimes spelled *Romanoff*. The family came from Germany but settled in Russia in the 1300s. More than two hundred years later a daughter of this family married the czar Ivan the Terrible. The first man to use the name Romanov was Ivan's son Theodore. His nephew, Michael Romanov, was chosen czar by the Russian nobles in 1613, and his descendants ruled until 1917, when the Russian Revolution resulted in the execution of Czar Nicholas II and most of his family.

Romans, Epistle to the, a book of the New Testament. See EPISTLE.

Romberg, Sigmund

Sigmund Romberg was a composer of light operas, or operettas, which are humorous plays in which many of the words are sung rather than spoken. He was born in Hungary in 1887 and became a resident of the United States when he was 23 years old. Later he became an American citizen. He played in restaurant orchestras, then organized his own orchestra. His first operetta, *Maytime*, was produced in 1917, and was a great success. Among his most popular operettas are *The Student Prince, Blossom Time*, and *The Desert Song*. He also wrote the music for several motion pictures. Romberg died in 1951.

Rome

Rome is the capital city of Italy. It is a handsome, modern city, with a population of more than 2,656,000. Rome is also one of the great historic cities of the world and for this reason it is called the Eternal City. About two thousand years ago it was the capital of an empire that ruled most of Europe and Great Britain, and parts of Africa and Asia. (There is a separate article on the ROMAN EMPIRE.)

ANCIENT ROME

The beginning of Rome was a tiny village on the Palatine Hill beside the Tiber River. There is an old legend that it was founded by Romulus and Remus, two young men who were supposed to be twin sons of Mars, the Roman god of

war. The village spread out along the banks of the Tiber until it covered seven hills, the Capitoline, Aventine, Quirinal, Viminal, Caelian, Palatine, and Esquiline. It is believed the first settlement was begun about 2,700 years ago.

For about four hundred years Rome was just a town in a small section of Italy called Latium, occupied by a people who spoke Latin. A people called the Etruscans, from the north, controlled Rome. Then the Roman people rose up, overthrew the foreign rulers, joined an organization of tribes called the Latin League, and began a series of victories in warfare that made them masters of the western world.

During the early years of Rome, some of its greatest buildings and monuments were created. The aqueducts that brought water to the city are among the earliest engineering works of which ruins can still be seen. The Appian Way was one of many great highways paved with lava or stone blocks. The Romans learned to use concrete about 200 B.C. Among the beautiful buildings that were built about two thousand years ago are the Pantheon, the temple of Jupiter, the Forum (a great square surrounded by public buildings), and the Colosseum (an amphitheater seating 50,000 people). Ruins of many buildings can be seen in Rome today.

About the year 350 there were invasions of Italy by Germanic and other tribes from the north, the Ostrogoths, Huns, Visigoths, and Vandals. The city itself was attacked, captured, and sacked. In 476 the last Roman emperor was deposed by a barbarian king.

Over the next three hundred years the strength of Christianity was growing, and the Popes of the Roman Catholic Church gained more and more power. Rome became the capital of the Papal States and slowly began a second rise to fame, now as the seat of the Pope and the capital of the Roman Catholic Church. Much of the Renaissance, or rebirth of learning and art, was centered in Rome. In the 1600s and 1700s the city became again a center of literature and the arts and sciences. In 1862 Italy became a kingdom and in 1871 Rome became its capital.

MODERN ROME

The modern city of Rome is a religious, educational and cultural center and a great attraction for tourists because of its historic ruins and monuments. It is a city of many levels, though the seven hills are less noticeable now because many of the marshy valleys have been filled in.

Rome lies on both sides of the Tiber River, about twenty miles from the Tiber's mouth at the Mediterranean Sea. In the center of Rome is Vatican City, an independent state governed by the Pope. Vatican City is about 108 acres in size and has a population of about 1,000.

The Tiber is crossed by ten bridges within the city and is lined with walls to keep it from overflowing during rainy seasons. The plain around the city was once very swampy and was a breeding place for mosquitoes that carried malaria. Most of it has now been drained, and Rome is a healthful city.

The seven hills of Rome divide the city roughly into districts. The Quirinal

Hill is the center of the modern city, and the site of the presidential palace and the principal public buildings. The Capitoline Hill is largely a cultural center. It is the site of the Capitol, where the city government offices are located. Michelangelo designed the present plans of the Capitol buildings, which include two museums containing some of the most ancient art in existence. Most of the ancient ruins of Rome are on the Palatine, Aventine and Caelian Hills. The industry of Rome is largely centered on the Esquiline and Viminal Hills.

Rome is a trading and industrial center. Its industries include the manufacture of textiles, leather products, perfumes, machinery, and also food processing. There is also a thriving motion picture industry there. Rome is one of the railroad and airline centers of Italy. There is a great university, founded in 1303, several academies and research institutes, a number of religious schools, and the Academy of Saint Cecelia, the oldest music school in the world. Many of the World's greatest art treasures are in palaces, museums and churches in Rome. In Vatican City is St. Peter's Church, the largest Christian church in the world.

ROME, ITALY. Population (1973 census) 2,656,104. Capital of Italy.

Romulus and Remus

Romulus and Remus were twin brothers, sons of the war god Mars, according to the legends of the ancient Romans. Their mother was Rhea Silvia, daughter of Numitor, a king. A wicked younger brother of Numitor seized his throne and ordered the twin babies to be thrown into the River Tiber. Fortunately, the babies were saved and a mother wolf fed them until a shepherd found them. He raised Romulus and Remus with his own children.

When they grew up, Romulus and Remus killed their grandfather's wicked younger brother and restored Numitor to the throne. They loved the banks of the Tiber, where they had grown up, and decided to build a city there. They agreed that the gods should decide which of them was to name the great new City. Remus saw six vultures in the sky and Romulus saw twelve vultures. People knew then that the gods had decided that Romulus should name the city. Romulus built the city and named it Rome after himself. This made Remus angry. He jumped over the walls of the city to show that the city was not very well protected. There was a terrible quarrel and Romulus killed his brother. Then Romulus became ruler of Rome.

rook

The rook is a bird that belongs to the crow family. It is a black bird about 18 inches long. It is found in Europe and the British Isles, and occasionally in Greenland. The rook is the most familiar of all birds in England. Rooks nest' in large groups in a grove of trees. They are very suspicious of a man carrying a gun. If they see one, they fly from their nests in great crowds, loudly cawing as they go. The rook is a menace to crops, and each year at nesting time thousands of them are shot in "rook shoots."

Roosevelt, Eleanor

Anna Eleanor Roosevelt is the name of a great American woman who did a great deal to improve conditions for people everywhere. As the wife of President Franklin D. Roosevelt she also was a famous "First Lady."

Mrs. Roosevelt was born in 1884, in New York City. She was the niece of another President, Theodore Roosevelt. She studied in private schools and in 1905 she married her distant cousin, Franklin Delano Roosevelt. When he was crippled by infantile paralysis her courage helped him to continue his work. Mrs. Roosevelt worked in many ways to improve conditions for working people and for those who did not have fair opportunities because of their race or religion. In 1935 she began to write a daily newspaper article, named "My Day," which was published in hundreds of newspapers in the United States. For a time she also conducted her own radio program, and she traveled widely and gave many lectures. In 1945 she was made a United States delegate to the United Nations, and a year later she was appointed to its Commission on Human Rights. She wrote many articles and several books. She died in 1962.

Franklin D. Roosevelt

Franklin Delano Roosevelt was the 32nd President of the United States. He served from March 4, 1933, until his death on April 12, 1945. He was the only man who ever held the office of President for more than two terms. He was elected for a third and then for a fourth term, but had served only three months and twelve days of his fourth term when he died suddenly at Warm Springs, Georgia.

Franklin D. Roosevelt was a hero to millions in Europe and Asia, as well as to the nations of North and South America. Throughout his administration, tremendous problems and terrible struggles beset the world, and at no time while he was in office was there a period of peace, prosperity, and calm. International unrest, financial and business disaster, and finally World War II marked his Presidency. Like George Washington, John Adams, and others who were President in difficult times, Roosevelt was bitterly criticized and by many citizens was hated while he was President, but he was always able to win the votes of the majority of the people.

No President before Roosevelt ever seemed so near to the people. He had a magnetic personality, and with his compelling voice and speech and his naturalness and informality he won the support of the people by talking to them on the radio, especially in regular speeches that he called "Fireside Chats." He was the first President to use the radio in this way.

The people also admired the courage of Franklin Roosevelt, for he had won his way to the highest position though he was crippled by infantile paralysis and could not walk.

People usually referred to Roosevelt as "FDR," an informal, friendly nickname—use of his initials.

HIS EARLY YEARS

Franklin Delano Roosevelt was born on January 30, 1882, at Hyde Park, New York, on a beautiful estate on the Hudson River. (Part of this estate was made

a National Historic Site after his death.) His family was a prominent one (Theodore Roosevelt, the 26th President, was his distant cousin) and also was rich. Roosevelt was sent to Groton, an exclusive boys' school, and was graduated from Harvard College in 1904. He then attended Columbia Law School and became a lawyer in New York State.

In 1905, the year after his graduation from Harvard, he married his sixth cousin, Anna Eleanor ROOSEVELT, about whom there is a separate article.

Roosevelt practiced law for a few years in New York City, but returned to Hyde Park after his father died and left him the family estate.

Roosevelt in 1910 was elected to the New York State Senate as a representative of Dutchess County, in which Hyde Park is located. This was the beginning of his political career.

HIS EARLY POLITICAL CAREER

When Franklin Delano Roosevelt was 30 years old, he was a delegate to the Democratic National Convention that nominated Woodrow Wilson for the Presidency. Roosevelt was active in Democratic politics in his home county and state, and his popularity was already growing. When Wilson was elected, he made young Roosevelt Assistant Secretary of the Navy, and during World War I Roosevelt had the opportunity to prove his ability and his skill as an administrator. Also during this period Roosevelt formed a friendship with Winston Churchill, the head of the British Navy. When this friendship was renewed, many years later, it had a great effect on world history.

As Assistant Secretary, Roosevelt was active in enlarging and developing the naval reserve of the United States, and through his efforts an important small warship, the submarine chaser, was made part of the Navy's equipment. After the war was over, he was placed in charge of disposing of unused naval supplies and equipment that were still in Europe.

During this period, he became well known as a vigorous, active man and a competent organizer. He also made many

friends. Two years after World War I, in the Democratic National Convention of 1920, Roosevelt was nominated for Vice President, when James Cox won the Presidential nomination. The Democratic Party lost the election, and five months later Roosevelt was struck with the dread disease that almost took his life and left him physically handicapped for his remaining years.

HIS FIGHT AGAINST POLIO

On a visit to Campobello, in New Brunswick, in August, 1921, Franklin D. Roosevelt was taken ill with infantile paralysis. Both of his legs were paralyzed. This was an especially great tragedy for him because he had always been fond of sports and was very active physically.

Even while he was helpless and unable to use his legs, he never resigned himself to the thought of living a life of paralysis. He determined to overcome his handicap, and worked hard and patiently to bring life back to the useless muscles. He continued to exercise by swimming. He became able to walk a few steps by using a cane and wearing heavy metal leg braces. One valuable result of his personal tragedy was the establishment of the National Infantile Paralysis Foundation, at Warm Springs, Georgia, where thousands of people stricken with polio have received treatment. Another result was a nationwide campaign against infantile paralysis. The March of Dimes, an annual fund-raising campaign, also was inspired by Franklin D. Roosevelt's handicap, and this campaign led to many valuable discoveries for the prevention and cure of polio. During Roosevelt's years in the White House, an annual Birthday Ball was held throughout the country to raise additional funds for polio research and assistance to those stricken. The ball was held on Roosevelt's birthday, January 30.

ROOSEVELT IN THE 'TWENTIES

In 1924, Roosevelt attempted to make Alfred E. Smith the Democratic Party's nominee for President. He made the nominating speech for Smith, who was then governor of New York, but John W. Davis won the nomination instead, and Roosevelt supported him.

At the Democratic National Convention in 1928, held in Texas, Roosevelt again nominated Alfred E. Smith. He called Smith the "Happy Warrior," a nickname by which Smith is still remembered. This time he succeeded in winning the nomination for Smith. In the same election, Roosevelt himself ran for governor of New York, and although Smith lost in the Presidential campaign, Roosevelt was elected and served for two terms as governor.

Meanwhile the financial crash of 1929 had occurred, and the country was in the midst of a great depression.

HOW HE BECAME PRESIDENT

For twelve years the Republican Party had been in power. It had seen years of prosperity and rising prices, and now, in 1932, it had the depression. Prices fell, business failed, millions were unemployed. The people were unhappy and wanted a change of Presidents.

In the Democratic National Convention of 1932, the name of Franklin Delano Roosevelt seemed to represent everything that the country needed. He had a fine record of efficiency in administration that dated back to World War I. His personal courage was unquestionable. As governor of New York State he had instituted many important reforms. The convention enthusiastically nominated him for the Presidency.

A Democratic victory seemed sure as the campaign progressed. Roosevelt promised to give the country a "New Deal for the Forgotten Man." He promised to do something about the poverty and unemployment. When the returns came in, he had defeated Herbert Hoover, who was running for re-election, with 472 electoral votes to Hoover's 59. Roosevelt and his followers, who became known as the New Deal administration, took power on March 4, 1933.

ROOSEVELT AS PRESIDENT

Franklin D. Roosevelt took over the government at a time of panic. Many people did not have enough to eat. Banks were failing and not even the people's savings were safe. Roosevelt asked for emergency powers, and Congress promptly granted them. He could then issue directives and short-cut the tedious process of passing each small measure through Congress. On the day of his inauguration, Roosevelt closed all the banks for a few days, to prevent more failures. One by one, the New Deal's organizations took shape. There were measures to aid banks, farmers, and individuals. These are described in the article on the NEW DEAL.

Gradually, employment increased, and business improved. When Roosevelt's first term was ending, the Democratic Convention nominated him unanimously for a second term. In the 1936 campaign, Roosevelt's Republican opponent was Alfred M. Landon, governor of Kansas. Roosevelt won by the greatest margin in modern history, 523 electoral votes to Landon's 8. Only the small states of Maine and Vermont voted for Landon.

Roosevelt's second term began in January, 1937. It was the time when war was threatened in Europe, and the international situation was difficult and dangerous. In Germany, Adolf Hitler and his Nazi Party were ruling in a reign of terror. In Italy Benito Mussolini and his Fascists were scarcely better. In Asia, Japan was fighting China and threatening other wars. Roosevelt gave his personal support to the democratic countries, Great Britain and France. He tried to make America realize that there was danger to the United States in the way things were going in Europe and Asia.

When Germany invaded Poland in 1939, beginning World War II, and both Great Britain and France declared war, Roosevelt asked Congress to alter the neutrality law, so that he could help the French and British. Later he proposed, and Congress passed, the Lend-Lease law. This permitted the United States to supply materials to the British (and later to the Russians and other countries fighting Germany) without requiring payment.

At the Democratic Convention of 1940, Franklin D. Roosevelt became the only man in American history to be nominated by his party for a third term as President. In the election, Roosevelt defeated the Republican candidate, Wendell Willkie, with 449 to 82 electoral votes.

Eleven months after Roosevelt's third inauguration, Japan attacked the United States at Pearl Harbor, Hawaii, and the United States was in World War II. Roosevelt was the country's wartime President for the next five years. In meetings with the British Prime Minister, Winston Churchill, and at times with the Russian Premier, Josef Stalin, Roosevelt planned the long-range conduct of the war, which finally resulted in a complete victory for the United States and its Allies.

The President's wartime powers made him more powerful than any President had been before. He was at the head of the United States' military forces, civilian defense forces, labor, industry, and transportation. By the time his third term was ending, Italy had surrendered, Germany was losing, and the Japanese had been driven from many Pacific islands.

With this record of triumph, Roosevelt was nominated for a fourth term and defeated Governor Thomas E. Dewey of New York in the Presidential election. In January, 1945, Roosevelt started his thirteenth year in the White House.

He was destined never to finish that year. In April he visited Warm Springs, Georgia, for a brief rest before attending a conference with United Nations leaders in San Francisco. On April 12, 1945, at the age of 63, Franklin Delano Roosevelt died of a cerebral hemorrhage, leaving his country on the threshold of victory in the first global war in history.

His body was buried in the garden of his family estate at Hyde Park, and his grave is visited each year by thousands of American and European travelers.

Theodore Roosevelt

Theodore Roosevelt was the 26th President of the United States. He was a Republican, and served from September 14, 1901, the day President William McKinley died, until March 4, 1909. He was 42 years old when he took the oath of office as President, the youngest man ever to hold the position. His administration was notable for the start of conservation of natural resources such as forests, minerals, and water power, for the beginning of work on the Panama Canal, and for a serious effort to prevent unfair business methods that hurt the public.

He was a popular and vigorous President. His friendly personality, his spirit of adventure, his active life and his personal honesty made him a hero during his lifetime. He continued to be active in public life until his death in 1919. He was called "Teddy" Roosevelt and "TR."

HIS EARLY YEARS

Theodore Roosevelt was born in New

York City on October 27, 1858. He was a delicate boy, so sickly that he did not attend school during childhood years but was taught at home by private tutors. He was determined to overcome his physical weakness and to strengthen himself for strenuous life. He succeeded so well that his endurance later became almost a legend.

By the time he was 22 he was strong and vigorous. He was graduated from Harvard College and married a Boston girl the same year. He returned to New York City, where he studied law at Columbia. His interest in politics then began. Roosevelt was elected to the New York State Assembly in 1881 at the age of 23. His wife, Alice Hathaway Lee Roosevelt died in 1884, after the birth of their first child, Alice Lee Roosevelt.

After his wife's death, Roosevelt moved to North Dakota. For three years he lived in the Badlands there, working on a ranch and living a rugged outdoor life. He kept his interest in public welfare during these years, and organized a protective organization to combat cattle thieves.

In New York again after his ranch experience, Roosevelt ran for mayor of New York City but was defeated. In 1889 he became a member of the United States Civil Service Commission. His efforts were mainly directed toward correcting the "spoils" system then in effect, by which almost all government appointments went to members of the winning political party. Roosevelt believed in awarding positions on the basis of merit, regardless of politics. After six years with the Civil Service Commission, he became president of the police board of New York City, and here he was more successful in building a merit system of promotions.

ROUGH RIDER TO PRESIDENT

When William McKinley was elected president in 1896 he appointed Theodore Roosevelt as his Secretary of the

Navy. Roosevelt worked to prepare the Navy for war with Spain, which he foresaw. In 1898 the Spanish-American War began. Roosevelt immediately resigned his post as Secretary of the Navy and with a young Army surgeon, Dr. Leonard Wood, he organized the 1st United States Volunteer Cavalry. This outfit later became known as the Rough Riders. Roose-

velt's skill as a commander won him more fame, especially when he led a successful cavalry charge at San Juan Hill in Cuba.

Now Roosevelt was a national hero, and after the war was over he was elected governor of New York. He fought to remove graft and corruption from public office. He opposed the illegal activities of big business combinations, which often tried to destroy small business firms. His work as governor pleased the people. He was chosen the Republican Party's candidate for Vice President when William McKinley was nominated for a second term in 1900.

HIS WORK AS PRESIDENT

McKinley had served just six months and ten days of his second term when he was assassinated. On September 14, 1901, Theodore Roosevelt took the oath of office as President.

Until Roosevelt's time, no attempt had been made to conserve the natural resources of the country. Lumbering firms cut down whole forests, not considering that the growth of many years was destroyed in a single season's operations. Roosevelt realized that unless new trees were planted when the old ones were cut, one day there would no longer be any trees left. During Roosevelt's years in office a complete account was made of the country's natural resources and a program for conserving them was established. This was perhaps his greatest achievement.

Roosevelt also declared that everyone was entitled to a "square deal" (fair treatment) and that laws must control commerce and industry. There were many big business combinations called "trusts," and Roosevelt became an enthusiastic "trust-buster." He was viciously attacked by many businessmen but increased his general popularity.

He was nominated for a second term and was elected in 1904 with the largest majority ever given any Presidential candidate up to that time.

The work of building the Panama Canal started during Roosevelt's last years in office. There was considerable disagreement over building the Canal, and Theodore Roosevelt's comment was, "I took the Canal Zone and let Congress debate; and while the debate goes on, the canal does also." During his second administration he sent the United States battleship fleet around the world to impress other nations with the United States' naval might. He voiced a saying then that has been quoted many times since: "Speak softly, and carry a big stick." He won the 1906 Nobel Peace Prize for his work in ending a war between Russia and Japan.

At the end of his administration he was still popular with the people and remained active in Republican politics. During the four years that followed he went on several big-game hunting expeditions to South America and Africa. These trips provided a great deal of interesting material for articles and books that he wrote later.

ROOSEVELT'S LATER YEARS

When Roosevelt returned to the United States he expressed disapproval of

the way the Republican Party was being led by President William Howard Taft. In an attempt to restore the policies he had followed as President, Roosevelt tried to win for himself the Republican Presidential nomination in 1912. The Republican Party chose Taft anyway, and Roosevelt founded his own party, the Progressive Party, which was called the "Bull Moose" Party at that time. The split in the Republican forces helped elect Woodrow Wilson, a Democrat, as President in 1912.

When Germany invaded Belgium two years later, at the start of World War I, Roosevelt was irritated by the fact that Wilson kept the United States neutral. He thought the invasion was a threat to international law. Wilson wrote a note of protest to Germany, but Roosevelt declared that if he had been President he "should have backed the protest with force." Throughout World War I Roosevelt repeatedly tried to enlist for duty on the battlefield but each time he was rejected. His four sons went overseas and one—Quentin—was shot down in a plane and killed.

Roosevelt was an active letter-writer all his life, and his correspondence has been published in eight large volumes.

There was some talk that Roosevelt might seek the Republican nomination in 1920, but the opportunity never came. Theodore Roosevelt became ill in January, 1919, at his home in Sagamore, Long Island, on the shore of Oyster Bay. He went to bed early on the evening of January 6, and the next morning he was found dead of a heart attack, of the kind called coronary thrombosis. He was 60 years old when he died.

ALICE HATHAWAY LEE ROOSEVELT

Alice Hathaway Lee was born in Massachusetts in 1861. She married Theodore Roosevelt in 1880 and died when their only child, Alice Lee Roosevelt, was born in 1884. Mrs. Roosevelt was 23 years old when she died. Alice Roosevelt married Nicholas Longworth in the White House. At that time she was called "Princess Alice." Longworth became Speaker of the House of Representatives, so Alice Longworth remained prominent in public life.

EDITH KERMIT CAROW ROOSEVELT

Mrs. Edith Kermit Carow Roosevelt was born in Connecticut in 1861. She married Theodore Roosevelt in 1886 and they had five children, four sons and one daughter. The sons were Theodore Jr., Kermit, Archibald Bullock, and Quentin. The daughter was Ethel, who became Mrs. Richard Derby.

root

The word *root* is used in mathematics. It is a number that is multiplied by itself a certain number of times to produce some particular other number. For example, $3 \times 3 \times 3 \times 3 = 81$, and 3 is said to be a root of 81. The *square root* of a number is multiplied by itself only once, so 3 is the square root of 9, since $3 \times 3 = 9$. This is written $\sqrt{9} = 3$. Each number used in multiplying is called a *factor,* so this mathematical sign means that there are two factors and each of them is 3. When there are three or more factors, it

is marked with a small number, like this: $\sqrt[3]{27}$. This also means 3, because $3 \times 3 \times 3 = 27$. When the root is one of three factors, it is called the *cube root,* and we would say the cube root of 27 is 3. Going back to the original example, in which there were four factors, we would write that $\sqrt[4]{81} = 3$. The number that results from multiplying the root by itself is called a *power,* which is explained in the articles on ALGEBRA and LOGARITHMS.

Root, Elihu

Elihu Root was an American statesman who served as a United States Senator and as an ambassador. He was born in Clinton, New York, in 1845, and became a lawyer. President Theodore Roosevelt appointed him Secretary of State in 1905 and he served in that office until 1909. Then he was a Senator from 1909 to 1915. He was one of the American lawyers who helped to set up the Permanent Court of International Justice (about which you can read in the article on the WORLD COURT.) He died in 1937.

Root, George Frederick

George Frederick Root was an American composer, or writer of music, who lived about a hundred years ago. He was born in Sheffield, Massachusetts, in 1820, and taught music for many years. He wrote many religious songs and patriotic ballads. He is remembered mainly for his songs about the Civil War, which include *The Battle Cry of Freedom,* and *Tramp, Tramp, Tramp.* Root died in 1895.

roots

The roots of a plant are the parts by which the plant is attached to the ground, and by which it obtains water and nourishment. Some roots are small, hairlike pieces. Some roots are large, heavy, and hard, and branch out widely in all directions. The roots of some plants, such as carrots, are eaten as food.

Tiny rootlets extend from the main body of the root. They reach into the soil and transfer minute particles of nourishment to the main root. Some plants, such as lilacs and rambler roses, have roots that develop buds, and the buds work their way to the surface and grow into new plants.

Some plants, called "air plants," have no connection with the ground at all, but their roots may be important because they hold the plant to a rock or wall or to another plant on which it grows.

See the article on PLANT LIFE.

rope and twine

Rope and twine are made of strong fibers twisted together. They are called *cordage,* and the fibers used are hemp, sisal, and jute. (Strangely enough, *cord* is made of cotton and is not usually considered cordage.) The thickest ropes are often called cables. Twine is any rope that is less than $\frac{3}{16}$ of an inch in diameter (thickness).

Rope has been made for thousands of years. It has always been of the utmost importance for lifting and hauling things. Before the time of steam power, rope was equally important at sea, for it was used to handle the sails on sailing ships.

There are thousands of different kinds, weights and sizes of rope. For nearly every purpose there is a special kind of rope. Some rope has to be very thin and flexible, but strong. Some rope has to be thick, heavy, and stiff. The whaling ships of a hundred years ago had rope so thin that a mile of it could be carried in a small boat but so strong that it would pull in a whale weighing fifty tons or more.

All rope is made by first twisting the fibers into thin lengths called strands and then twisting several strands together to form the rope. Twine may consist of only two or three strands twisted together.

About half of all rope made in the United States is made of Manila hemp. This is grown in the Philippines and perhaps was first shipped from the Philippine city of Manila. but it is now grown in many places. Russian hemp is somewhat stronger and is used in some cases where strength is very important. About a third of the rope is made of sisal, which is cheaper than hemp. A very few kinds of rope are made of linen, and the common "clothesline" is a rope made of cotton. Rope is often waterproofed, and rope used on ships is treated with tar, to prevent rotting from rain or from sea and river water. This is important also in the rope used in fish nets. A fiber called Widuri, from Indonesia and other East Indian islands, lasts an especially long time in sea water. The latest material to be used for cordage is nylon, which is both strong and light. Nylon is used for the shroud lines of parachutes and has been used for fish nets, but its cost is too great for many uses. Before nylon was produced, silk ropes were often used on parachutes.

Rope is made by machinery that automatically twists the strands together. The fibers are usually treated with oil before they are spun into yarn, especially if a flexible rope is wanted. The advantage of a stiffer rope is that the strands will not easily separate.

The heaviest ropes will lift loads of twenty tons or more. For heavier loads, cables made of twisted wire are used. (Actually, these cables, such as the cables used on elevators, are called "ropes" by those who work with them.)

Worn or broken rope can often be spliced. The tying of knots in rope can be a matter of great skill. In the days of sailing ships, nearly all sailors were expert at tying knots. See the article on KNOTS, HITCHES, and SPLICES. There are also separate articles about FIBER, HEMP, JUTE, and SISAL.

Rosario

Rosario is the second-largest city in Argentina. More than 591,000 people live there. Rosario is on the Paraná River, about 175 miles north of Buenos Aires, the Argentine capital. The river is broad and deep all the way from the ocean, making Rosario a seaport. Rosario is both a shipping and a manufacturing city, but both shipping and manufacturing are chiefly connected with the wheat and other grain and farm products that are grown in the region around Rosario. The city is modern and beautiful, with wide avenues and clean, attractive buildings. There is a large cathedral. The docks along the river are almost three miles long.

ROSARIO, ARGENTINA. Population (1973 estimate) 591,428. In Santa Fé province. On the Paraná River.

rosary

A rosary is a string of beads used in saying a group of prayers. The person saying the prayers uses the beads to help him remember what prayer is to be said.

The Roman Catholic rosary is the best known. The first part of the Catholic rosary is made up of a crucifix, one large bead, three small beads, and a large one. After reciting the Apostles' Creed, the person saying the rosary says the Lord's Prayer at the large beads and the Ave Maria at the small beads.

The rest of the rosary is attached to a medal in a circular chain. This section has five series of ten small beads each. Between each series is a large bead. Each series is called a *decade* of the rosary. A decade consists of ten Ave Marias and one Our Father. Before a decade, the person praying recalls and thinks about an event from the life of Jesus or the Virgin Mary. These are called *mysteries.* There are fifteen mysteries. They may be sorrowful, as the Crucifixion; glorious, as the Resurrection; or joyful, as the Annunciation. Most Catholics say five decades of the rosary at one time. Longer rosaries, which have fifteen decades and include all the mysteries, are also said. The rosary is one of the most popular Catholic prayers. It is said frequently, especially by those devoted to the Virgin Mary, to whom the rosary is dedicated.

OTHER ROSARIES

Moslems (followers of the Mohammedan religion) and Buddhists also use rosaries for saying prayers of their religions.

rose

The rose is one of the most familiar and most popular flowers in the world. It has been known and cultivated since ancient times. Dried roses have been found in Egyptian tombs thousands of years old.

Although there are hundreds of different kinds of rose grown throughout the world, these have all been developed from a few wild varieties. New kinds are produced constantly through the experiments of rose growers.

There are three general classifications of rose: shrubs, bedding roses, and climbers. The bedding roses are grown for

The rose is the most popular flower of America. It is England's national flower.

blossoms that are cut, and this is the type usually seen in a florist's shop. Shrubs are roses that are used for landscaping purposes. They blossom plentifully, but the flowers themselves are usually not cut. Climbers, or ramblers, are roses that grow on vines. They are often planted along a fence or a wall.

Most roses have prickly stems, and the larger stalks have heavy thorns. Most varieties of rose are very fragrant, though a few kinds have almost no scent at all.

Roses may have a single ring of petals, or they may have many tightly rolled layers of petals. Every rose has a fuzzy-looking yellow center, which can be seen when the blossom is open, or full blown.

A rose bush will bear flowers for several years if it is protected from cold weather, and new plants are usually grown by cutting off a stalk and letting it form its own new roots in water or damp sand.

rosemary

Rosemary is an evergreen shrub usually grown for its leaves, which are used as a seasoning in cooking. An oil used in medicine is also made from the leaves. The plant has small, light blue blossoms that appear in April and May. A rosemary plant grows to a height of about six feet. It will live many years if it is protected from freezing winter weather. Dried rosemary leaves can be bought in most food stores.

Rosenkavalier

Rosenkavalier is the name of a grand opera by the German composer Richard Strauss. (In a grand opera, the actors sing all their words instead of speaking them.) This opera was first performed in Dresden, Germany, in 1911. The music is full of charming melodies, many of which (especially the waltzes) are frequently played as separate music for orchestra.

The name *Rosenkavalier* means "knight of the rose." The story is about a young girl, Sophie Faninal, whose father has promised her in marriage to the elderly, ugly and drunken Baron Ochs. They live in Vienna, the capital of Austria. Sophie is very unhappy about this marriage, but she must do as her father wishes. It was the custom in Vienna about two hundred years ago for a suitor to give the girl of his choice a silver rose as a token of his love. Baron Ochs is afraid he will not make a good impression on the lovely Sophie. He asks a relative of his, a beautiful but aging Marschallin (or princess), to have her young and handsome lover Octavian deliver the silver rose to Sophie. Octavian and Sophie fall in love at once, and the rest of the opera is devoted to their tricks and schemes to get Sophie out of her engagement to the Baron so that she and Octavian can be married. At last, with the help of the Marschallin, they expose the Baron as a vulgar schemer, and the young lovers are promised to each other.

Roses, Wars of the

The Wars of the Roses were a series of battles fought about five hundred years ago between the members and supporters of two English royal families, the house of York and the house of Lancaster. Each family wanted its members to be the kings of England. The struggle is called the Wars of the Roses because the Yorkists' badge was a white rose and the Lancastrians' badge was a red rose.

For more than fifty years England had been ruled by kings of the Lancastrian family, Henry IV, Henry V, and Henry VI. Henry VI was very weak, and his queen, Margaret of Anjou, actually had more power in the government than he.

In 1455, Richard, the ambitious duke of York, stirred up people to support his family's claim to the English throne. At that time England was losing in a war with France, and the people were displeased with Henry's government. Richard gathered together an army and attacked the king's forces. A number of battles were fought, and at one point King Henry was captured by two of the most powerful Yorkists, the earls of March and Warwick. It was then agreed that Henry would be allowed to keep the throne but that Richard and his heirs would inherit the throne when he died, rather than Henry's own children.

Queen Margaret would not agree to this, and raised an army that defeated Warwick's forces and rescued King Henry. Then the Yorkists became more powerful. Margaret fled to Scotland, and Henry was captured again.

Richard's brother Edward quarreled with Warwick, who decided to change sides and support Margaret. Margaret returned and with Warwick's help, won another battle and rescued Henry.

A few months later, Edward returned from Holland, where he had fled, and defeated the Lancastrians again. Warwick and Henry's son were killed in battle, and Margaret was imprisoned. Shortly afterward, Henry died, probably by violent means, and a few years later Richard became king as Richard III.

The Wars of the Roses finally ended when Henry Tudor defeated Richard and was crowned Henry VII. The York and Lancaster families were united by Henry VII's marriage to Edward's daughter (and Richard's niece), Elizabeth

Rosetta Stone

The Rosetta Stone is a slab of stone that gave scholars the key to the meaning of Egyptian hieroglyphics, or picture-writing. It was found about 160 years ago, in 1799, near the town of Rosetta, in Egypt, by a French soldier named Boussard. At the time the British and French were fighting each other, and two years later the stone was captured by the British and taken to London, England. On the Rosetta Stone is a piece of writing in hieroglyphics and beside it is a translation of it in the Greek language. The writing is a decree made by ancient Egyptian priests in honor of their ruler, Ptolemy V. It lists the things Ptolemy did for Egypt and says that a statue of him must be placed in every temple and he should be honored as a god. The Rosetta Stone is now in the British Museum, in London.

Rosh Hashanah

Rosh Hashanah is the Jewish New Year's Day. It is celebrated on two days, beginning on the first day of the Jewish month of Tishri. This day usually falls in September or early October. The day is marked by solemn prayers for a happy and prosperous New Year. On this day, according to tradition, the life of every man is judged by the Lord, and written in either the Book of Life or the Book of Death. For this reason it is a Jewish custom on Rosh Hashanah to greet friends with the words, "May you be inscribed for a Happy New Year," that is, recorded in the Book of Life.

The services of Rosh Hashanah open the most important time of the Jewish religious year—the ten-day period leading up to Yom Kippur, the Day of Atonement. During this time pious Jews fast and pray. In preparation, on Rosh Hashanah, a Jew may eat an apple dipped in honey and round, smooth loaves of bread. These stand for the hope for a "sweet, smooth, and prosperous" year. Rosh Hashanah is also called the Feast of Trumpets, because the shofar, a trumpet made of a ram's horn, is blown in the synagogue to call people to prayer.

Ross, Betsy

Betsy Ross was a flagmaker who lived in Philadelphia during the Revolutionary War, in which the American colonists won their independence from Great Britain. For many years American historians said that Betsy Ross designed and made the first American flag, and that she showed George Washington himself how it was possible to cut out the five-pointed stars used in the American flag.

Historians now doubt that Betsy Ross really made the first flag and are sure that she did not design it, though she was making flags at the time the new flag was designed. Members of her family continued to make flags for many years after the United States became a country. Betsy Ross was born in 1752 and died in 1836.

Rossetti

Dante Gabriel Rossetti and Christina Georgina Rossetti were a brother and sister, both of whom were English writers. Dante Gabriel was also a painter. Their father was an Italian who had to flee from Italy.

Dante Gabriel was born in 1828. When he was a young man he studied painting and wrote poetry. He formed the Pre-Raphaelite Society, which was a group of painters and writers who wished to be true to nature in their work, just as they believed the painters before Raphael had been. Christina Rossetti and another brother, William, were members of the Pre-Raphaelite Society, along with many well-known painters and writers of the day.

Dante Gabriel Rossetti painted many fine paintings. He also wrote beautiful poems. When his wife died Rossetti was so unhappy that he buried all of his poems in the grave of his wife, but a few years later, in 1870, he allowed them to be dug up. Although they were published with much success, Rossetti was not happy. He lived a lonely life and died in 1882, when he was 54 years old.

Christina Rossetti was born in 1830. She was a shy person and led a very quiet life. She never married and from about the age of 40 was an invalid. Some of her best poems were written for children.

Christina Rossetti also wrote religious poems and poems about love. She died in 1894, when she was 64 years old.

Rossini, Gioacchino

Gioacchino Rossini was a great Italian composer, or writer of music, who lived about 150 years ago. He is best known for his comic operas, or humorous plays in which many of the words are sung rather than spoken. His opera *The Barber of Seville* is considered by some people to be the greatest comic opera ever written. Rossini was born in Italy in 1792.

When Rossini was only 23 years old, he was made director of two big theaters in the city of Naples. He wrote 39 operas, the most famous of which include *Tancredi, Otello,* and *William Tell.* He also wrote religious music, of which his *Stabat Mater* is considered his greatest work. Rossini died in 1868, when he was 76 years old.

Rostand, Edmond

Edmond Rostand was a French playwright and poet. He was born in 1868. Rostand's most famous play is *Cyrano de Bergerac* (see the article on CYRANO). Rostand was also well known for his poetry. He died in 1918, when he was 50 years old.

Rotary International

Rotary International is a club of businessmen. It was founded in Chicago Illinois, about sixty years ago. Today it has 723,000 members in 15,400 clubs in 149 countries. It was formed to unite men of different nationalities, religious faiths, and occupations, and to help people in the places where they lived. The Rotary clubs raise money for worthy causes and have a Foundation that gives scholarships to young people so that they can study in foreign countries.

rotogravure, a method of printing with etched plates on a rotary printing press: see the article PRINTING.

Rotterdam

Rotterdam is the largest port and the second-largest city of the Netherlands. It is on the New Maas River, near its mouth on the North Sea. The river runs through the city and is crossed by several bridges and a tunnel for automobiles. Rotterdam is an important industrial and commercial city. A canal called the New Waterway connects Rotterdam with Hook of Holland, a port on the North Sea that is part of the city. Ocean-going ships sail up the New Waterway and dock in the heart of Rotterdam. The city is connected by other waterways with cities in the Netherlands and Germany.

Almost 700,000 people live in Rotterdam. Many of them work in shipyards and oil refineries and in factories that make chemicals, machinery, food products, and clothing. Others work in offices of many important shipping and trading companies.

Rotterdam was chartered in 1328, but it began to grow to its present importance after the New Waterway was built in 1866 to 1872. In World War II the Germans captured Rotterdam early in 1940. Several hours after the city had surrendered it was savagely bombed by German planes. Thousands of people were killed and the entire center of the city was destroyed. After the war the Dutch people rebuilt Rotterdam into a handsome, modern city.

ROTTERDAM, THE NETHERLANDS. Population (1973 census) 686,586. Second-largest city of the Netherlands. On the New Maas River. In South Holland Province. Founded in 1328.

Rouault, Georges

Georges Rouault was a French painter and sculptor. His way of painting was quite different from most painters', and some of his oil paintings look somewhat like stained-glass windows. Rouault was born in 1871 and began to paint at an early age. Many of Rouault's favorite subjects are concerned with injustice and human suffering. One of his best-known paintings is called *Le vieux roi,* which means "the old King." He painted many portraits of Jesus. He died in 1958.

roundworm

The roundworm is a kind of tiny worm. Most roundworms are so small that they cannot be seen by the naked eye. There are so many roundworms in the world that their numbers are almost beyond belief.

Some roundworms are parasites (that is, they live in the bodies of other forms of animal life), and these can cause serious diseases. Examples of this kind of roundworm are the hookworm and the trichina worm, about which you can read in the articles HOOKWORM and TRICHINOSIS. Another parasite is the hair worm. It is about as thick as the hair from a horse's tail and is 2 to 4 feet long, but it is so tightly curled up that it seems very small. Hair worms live in water, especially in shallow ponds, and lay millions of eggs in long, hairlike strands. To hatch, the egg must be swallowed by an insect. It then hatches and lives inside the insect's body, tightly curled up, until it is ready to leave and lay its own eggs.

There are more than three thousand kinds of roundworm. They live in water and in soil almost everywhere, even in soil that is too dry for other animal or plant life. It has been said that if every other thing in the world were suddenly removed, the outlines of the earth, vegetation and animals could still be seen because of the roundworms that are on them everywhere.

Rousseau, Henri Julien

Henri Julien Rousseau was a French painter. He was born in 1844 and as a young man he worked as a customs officer and then served for a while with the French Army in Mexico. When he was about 36 years old he decided that what he wanted to do most was to paint pictures. He had no art lessons and his style of painting was very primitive; that is, almost like that of a child. Rousseau was very poor and sometimes he gave lessons on the violin to make enough money to buy food. At first many people made fun of Rousseau's paintings, but now they are very much admired. Rousseau died in 1910.

Rousseau, Jean Jacques

Jean Jacques Rousseau was a French writer whose ideas about freedom had a great influence on the world. He was born in Switzerland in 1712. Rousseau's mother died when he was a baby and he had a difficult time during his early life. He was brought up by relatives and when he was very young he was sent to work to an engraver as an apprentice. This man was cruel and when Rousseau was about 16 years old he ran away. He had many adventures. He later wrote about many of the things that happened to him in a book called *Confessions.*

Rousseau could do many things. Sometimes he made his living by copying music. He wrote an opera and several novels. He won a prize for writing an essay in which he expressed some of his ideas. Rousseau wrote that civilization is bad for people and that simple savages have a better life than more civilized people. He had many ideas about government and about how children should be brought up.

The most important thing Rousseau wrote was called the *Social Contract.* In it he put forth the ideas of liberty, equality, and fraternity. These three words became the war cry of the French Revolution.

Rousseau made many enemies and some people thought he did a great deal of harm with his radical ideas. Others refused to take him seriously at all. Still he was one of the most important influences of his time. Rousseau died in 1788, when he was 66 years old. Some people believe that he took his own life, but this was never proved.

rowing

Rowing is a way of making a boat travel through the water by pushing the water back with oars. Both boats and oars are made in different sizes and shapes, and therefore there are different kinds of rowing. Rowing has been useful through the ages, and was once the principal way of making even the heaviest ships go forward. Rowing is also a popular sport.

The usual rowboat is built to be rowed by one person holding two oars, one in each hand. Each oar is held at the boat's side in a slot called an *oarlock.* Both skill and strength are required to row well. The handles must be pushed forward through the air, at the same level and both together. Then the oars must be dipped into the water together, in such a way that the *blade,* or broad, flat part of the oar, is held straight against the water. Then the handles must be pulled back together, which requires strength. (Sometimes the oar is purposely held so that the sharp edge of the blade, instead of the flat side, is pulled through the water. This is called *feathering* and slows down the boat.)

Ancient ships called galleys had many rowers pulling together, often in two or three tiers, as explained in the article

NAVY. Rowing of this sort is now seen in boat races among boats called *shells*. In these races there are usually eight rowers (who are called "oars"), plus a *coxswain* who does not row but faces the rowers and tells them at what rate of speed to row. In the old galleys, each man pulled only one oar, using both hands on it, and this same system is used in shell races.

Other popular races are between small, one-man boats called *sculls*. The oarsman, or *sculler*, uses two oars.

The paddling of a canoe is a form of rowing but is not usually classed as such since only one oar (called a paddle), held in both hands, is used to direct the canoe.

Ruanda-Urundi: see RWANDA.

rubber

Rubber is an elastic, springy substance that comes from the milky juice of certain plants. It can also be made from chemicals in a factory. Rubber is tough, waterproof, and very resistant to electricity. Gases and liquids cannot pass through it. It has thousands of uses, such as in automobile tires, rubber bands, balls, cushions, raincoats, boots, hoses, floor coverings, adhesives, balloons, materials to make roofs waterproof, and linings for chemical tanks.

Pure rubber is a hydrocarbon, which means that it is made up of the chemical elements hydrogen and carbon.

LATEX

The milky substance that natural rubber comes from is called *latex*, and it is contained in many plants. More than nine-tenths of the world's supply of latex comes from a tree, usually called the rubber tree, which is grown on large plantations in tropical countries. Most of the rest of the latex is taken from a shrubby tree called *guayule*, and from the Siberian dandelion.

To get latex from a rubber tree, a special knife is used to make cuts in the bark, about as high off the ground as a man's chest. The cuts—five or six of them—circle the tree trunk on a slant. A thin shaving of bark is removed between each cut. The latex runs down to the point of the lowest cut and drips into a small cup that has been attached to the tree just below the cuts.

The latex is then taken to collecting stations, where it is poured through strainers into large tanks. A chemical called formic acid is added, and this makes the latex curdle, or coagulate, forming a doughy, white mass. This is rubber.

The liquid part of the latex is drained off in much the same manner as the whey is separated from the curd when milk turns sour. The curdlike rubber is put through rollers that squeeze out the remaining water and form the rubber into sheets. These are dried and exposed to smoke and then are pressed together in bales for shipment to a rubber factory.

Sometimes, the latex is not coagulated at the plantation. It is partly dried by evaporating some of the water and then is shipped in big drums or tanks to a factory for processing into products such as foam rubber.

HISTORY OF RUBBER

Before Columbus discovered the New

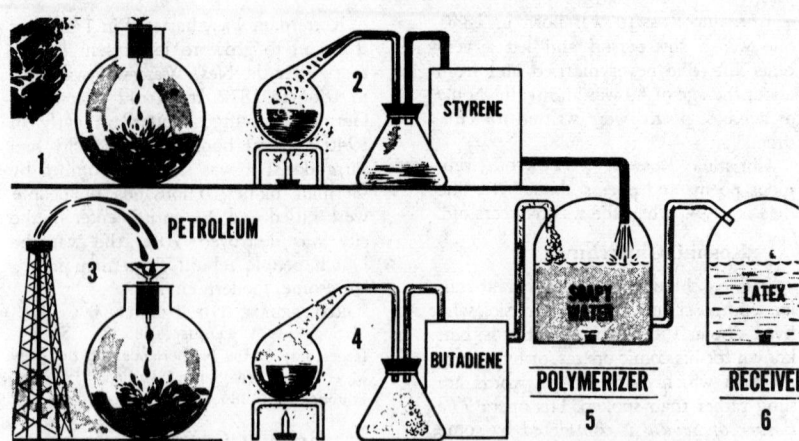

Making synthetic rubber from coal: From coal (1) is made styrene (2). From petroleum (3) is made butadiene (4). Styrene and butadiene are mixed with soapy water to make a mixture of higher molecular weight (5). This yields synthetic rubber latex (6).

World, the Indians of Central and South America were gathering rubber. They used it to waterproof their shoes and capes and to make playing balls. The Indians called the tree from which the gummy substance came *caoutchouc,* meaning "weeping wood," and for a long time Europeans knew rubber by this name.

In 1770, the English chemist Joseph Priestley found that pieces of this substance would rub out pencil marks, and this gave it the name *rubber.* The first rubber factory was established in Vienna, Austria, in 1811. In 1823 a Scotsman, Charles Macintosh, learned to use rubber to waterproof cloth, and certain raincoats still bear his name.

All the articles made of rubber at that time were soft and sticky in hot weather and stiff and brittle in cold weather, and the rubber soon lost its elasticity.

VULCANIZING

In 1839, Charles Goodyear, an American inventor, accidentally dropped a bit of a mixture of sulfur and rubber on his kitchen stove. The lump charred and became tough, and it remained tough and elastic in both heat and cold. This process —the mixture of rubber with sulfur, and the heating of the mixture—was named *vulcanization,* for Vulcan, the Roman god of fire.

Modern vulcanizing includes more than just adding sulfur to rubber. Materials called *softeners* and *plasticizers* are added. These materials make the rubber easier to mold. Fillers, materials that give added strength and wearing qualities to the rubber, are added. Also added are chemicals called *antioxidants,* which greatly slow down the rate at which the finished rubber combines with the oxygen gas of the air. This keeps the finished rubber soft and pliable for years, but all rubber eventually combines with enough oxygen to make it brittle. Pigments may be added in order to color the rubber. Lastly, *accelerators* are added. These are chemicals that hasten the vulcanizing process. Vulcanizing a batch of rubber may take as long as two days, but when a tiny quantity of an accelerator is added the batch can be cured in five minutes.

MAKING RUBBER ARTICLES

Even with the best plasticizers, rubber is difficult to shape. Only simple articles such as rubber heels and hot-water

bottles can be molded easily. Tires, rubber hose, overshoes, and many other articles are built up from sheets of unvulcanized rubber with layers of fabric between the rubber sheets. Other articles are made by spraying liquid latex onto fabric, or by dipping fabric or other materials into liquid latex, and then vulcanizing the resulting foam.

SYNTHETIC RUBBER

Rubber that is made entirely from chemicals in a factory is called *synthetic rubber.* The first synthetic rubber was made at the end of the 19th century, but it was not much good. In World War I, when Germany was unable to receive any latex from rubber plantations because the British Navy had cut off all German shipping, the Germans managed to supply their army with synthetic rubber.

Just before World War II, Germans made a good quality rubber that they called Buna rubber. Other countries developed other kinds of synthetic rubber, and nowadays much synthetic rubber is manufactured to be made into various articles or to be mixed with natural rubber.

The raw materials in synthetic rubber are petroleum, alcohol, turpentine, coal tar, natural gas, or acetylene, or combinations of these. Some kinds of synthetic rubber are resistant to oils and other liquids that harm natural rubber. They are also more resistant to the harmful effects of sunlight, heat, and acids. Synthetic rubber is not as elastic or as adhesive as natural rubber.

rubber plant

The rubber plant is a popular house plant. It is easy to grow and will last for years if given a reasonable amount of care. There are two kinds of rubber plant suitable for keeping in the home. One has long, shiny, oval-shaped leaves that vary in length from three to ten inches. The other has irregularly shaped, cabbagelike leaves. Both kinds grow well in the dry atmosphere and limited sunlight of the living room. They grow to a height of two to six feet.

Rubens, Peter Paul

Peter Paul Rubens was a Flemish painter. He was born in Germany in 1577. His family was from Antwerp, in Flanders (now part of Belgium), but his

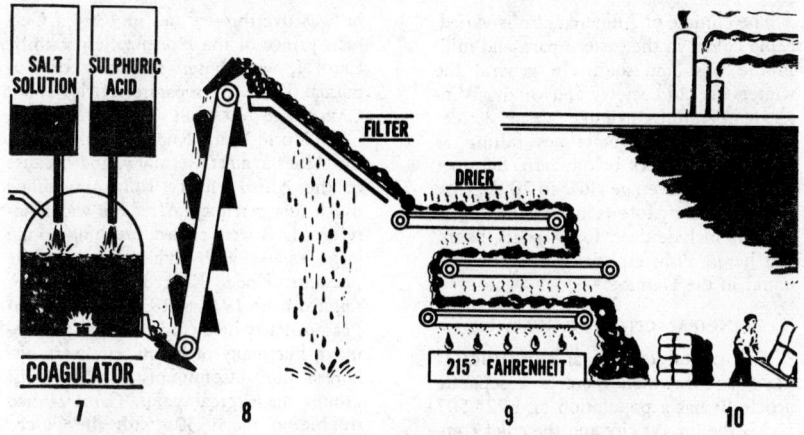

SALT SOLUTION SULPHURIC ACID

FILTER

DRIER

COAGULATOR

215° FAHRENHEIT

7   8   9   10

The latex is coagulated with a mixture of salt and sulfuric acid (7). Rubber is formed in crumbs that look like popcorn. On a moving screen (8), the water is filtered from the rubber crumbs. The damp crumbs are passed through hot air (9) to dry them. The dried rubber is pressed into bales (10) and is ready for use by manufacturers.

father had been banished from that city. When Rubens was 11 years old his father died and the family returned to Antwerp.

Rubens studied painting in Antwerp, and when he was 23 years old he went to Italy, where for eight years he was court painter to the Duke of Mantua. When he returned home he very soon became the leading and busiest painter of Antwerp. Two of his greatest paintings were done at this time, *The Raising of the Cross* and *The Descent from the Cross.* Both have to do with the crucifixion of Jesus.

Many of the pictures that Rubens is supposed to have painted were actually done mostly by his assistants, and all Rubens himself did was to supervise the work and add some finishing touches.

Rubens, who knew many languages, became a diplomatic representative of his country and traveled in Spain and England. Wherever he went he painted pictures, up to the time of his death in 1640.

Rubicon

Rubicon was the name given by the ancient Romans, more than two thousand years ago, to a small stream in northern Italy. The Rubicon was part of the boundary system between Italy and the territory to the north, which at that time was called Gaul, but is now France. About the year 50 B.C., the great Roman general Julius Caesar was in command of the Roman armies in Gaul. The Roman Senate, which was under the control of a general named Pompey, had told Caesar to stay in Gaul. Since the Rubicon was the boundary, if Caesar crossed the stream he would be disobeying the orders of the Senate. Caesar knew that if he led his armies across the Rubicon he would be at war with Pompey and the Roman Senate. After much thought, he decided to make the crossing anyway. He fought and won control of Rome. Today, when someone says he has "crossed the Rubicon" he means he has made a great decision from which he cannot turn back.

Rubinstein, Anton

Anton Rubinstein was a Russian pianist and composer, or writer of music, who lived about a hundred years ago. He was born in Russia in 1830. At the age of 10 he gave his first concert, in Moscow,

and later played in many cities of Europe and the United States. He founded and directed the Conservatory of Music at St. Petersburg (now Leningrad), Russia. His best-known compositions are "Kamenoi-Ostrow" and "Melody in F." Rubinstein spent his last years in Germany. He died in 1894. His brother, Nicholas Rubinstein, was also a noted musician. He founded the Moscow Conservatory of Music. Nicholas Rubinstein was born in 1835 and died in 1881.

Rubinstein, Artur

Artur Rubinstein is the name of a famous pianist. He was born in 1889 in Warsaw, Poland, which then was ruled by Russia. His first performance was a recital for charity, when he was only 6 years old. He has since played many times in the principal cities of every continent on earth. In 1939 he moved to the United States and in 1946 he became an American citizen. He has appeared in motion pictures and on television.

ruby

A ruby is a kind of red precious stone. It is transparent, which means that you can see through it. In star rubies can be seen six lines of light crossing each other to form a six-pointed star. A perfect star ruby is worth more than a diamond of the same size.

In ancient times, rubies were believed to have magical powers. The best rubies are found in Burma, Ceylon, and Thailand, and people in these lands once believed that if you made a gift of rubies to their chief god, Krishna, you would surely be a king or emperor in a future life.

In former times the ruby was the birthstone of December, but modern jewelers have assigned it to July.

A ruby is a kind of corundum, which is made of the chemical elements aluminum and oxygen. Ruby is one of the hardest substances known. Rubies can be made synthetically, which means that they can be made by man from chemicals. Only an expert in gems can tell a synthetic ruby from a natural one.

Rudolf

Rudolf was the name of two emperors of the Holy Roman Empire, which was made up of a group of German kingdoms and was one of the great empires of Europe for more than six hundred years. Rudolf I was the founder of the

HAPSBURG family, about which there is a separate article. He was born about 750 years ago, in the year 1218, and became Holy Roman emperor in 1273. He attacked his enemy Ottokar, King of Bohemia, and took from him much of the land that became the Austrian Empire. This land remained under the rule of the Hapsburg family until the end of World War I in 1918. Rudolf II, also a Hapsburg, was born in 1552 and became emperor in 1576, but he was mentally ill and in 1606 his brother Matthias took control of his possessions. He died in 1612.

rug, a piece of heavy cloth that is used for a floor-covering: see the article CARPETS.

Ruhr

The Ruhr is a great mining and manufacturing section in the western part of West Germany. It gets its name from the Ruhr River, which flows for about 140 miles through that part of Germany, then empties into the Rhine River. The land through which the Ruhr flows is sometimes called the Ruhr Valley or the Ruhr Basin. It has great coal mines in which thousands of men work and many huge steel plants, where for many years German cannons and the weapons and munitions were made, as well as machines and tools for German factories in other parts of the country.

After Germany lost World War I, the French occupied the Ruhr Valley for several years. They gave it back to the Germans in 1925. By World War II the Germans had built up the Ruhr so that it was again producing much heavy machinery and war goods. During World War II, Allied planes continuously dropped thousands of tons of bombs on the Ruhr Valley. The great cities of the Ruhr—Essen, Dortmund, Düsseldorf, and others—were almost in ruins. After the war, under the control of the Allies, the Germans were allowed to clean up the Ruhr and rebuild it. Today, the Ruhr is one of the biggest and most modern industrial centers in the world.

Rumania

Rumania is a country in southeastern Europe. Its name is also spelled *Romania* and sometimes *Roumania.* It is about twice as big as New York State, with more than 90,000 square miles, and about 20,000,000 people live there, which is not many more than live in New York State. Rumania is fairly young as a nation, having been formed in 1859 by the joining of two smaller countries, Wallachia and Moldavia. Rumania fought on the side of the Germans in World War II. Russian armies invaded the country in 1944 and Rumania gradually fell into the power of a Communist government controlled by Soviet Russia.

THE PEOPLE WHO LIVE THERE

The Rumanian people are descendants of a tribe that the ancient Romans called Dacians. Their territory was called Dacia. The Dacians mixed and intermarried with Germanic, Magyar and Slavic peoples to form the nationality now called Rumanian. But many other peoples live

in Rumania today, including Germans, Transylvanians, Magyars, Turks, Jews, Bulgars, Macedonians, and Tatars. Most of the people speak the Rumanian language, which is one of the Romance languages that grew out of the Latin language. The principal religion of Rumania is Christian and the principal Church is the Rumanian Orthodox Church. Some of the people are Roman Catholics. Most Transylvanians are Protestants. Others follow the Jewish and Mohammedan religions.

HOW THE PEOPLE LIVE

More than half of the people who live in Rumania are farmers. They raise chiefly grain—corn, wheat, and some barley and oats. They also grow various fruits, walnuts, and vegetables. Livestock-raising is important, including sheep, cattle, horses, and pigs.

Rumania is rich in natural resources. Large quantities of petroleum and natural gas are produced, as well as coal, salt, lignite, iron, copper, gold, and silver. After World War II, Rumania became heavily industrialized. The chief industries manufacture iron and steel products,

chemicals, and textiles. Other important industries are flour milling and food processing. Almost all Rumanian industry is nationalized, that is, run by the state. Many industries are operated by joint Rumanian-Russian companies. Most of Rumania's trade is with other Communist countries.

WHAT RUMANIA IS LIKE

Rumania is a country of widely varied geography, with mountains, hills, and plains. It is roughly divided into seven regions: the Carpathian Mountains in the northeast; the Transylvanian Alps in the south; the Moldavian plateau, or high plain, east of the Carpathians; the Wallachian hills and plains south and east of the Transylvanian Alps; Dobruja, a hilly region in the southeast; Transylvania, a large area north of the Transylvania Alps; and Banat, a part of the Hungarian Plains.

The Danube is the most important river of Rumania. It forms most of Rumania's border with Bulgaria, then flows north through Rumania to its mouth on the Black Sea. Two other important rivers are tributaries of the Danube: the Prut, which forms most of the border with Russia, and the Siret, which flows south from the Carpathians.

The climate of Rumania also is varied, being colder in the eastern part, and mild in the west and south. In general the winters are cold, snowy and windy. Winter temperatures average about 25 degrees Fahrenheit, sometimes falling as low as 30 degrees below zero. Summer temperatures average close to 70 degrees. There are many forests in Rumania. Wild animals include deer, foxes, goats, boars, and hares. Fish, especially sturgeon, are found in the Danube.

PRINCIPAL CITIES OF RUMANIA

The capital of Rumania is BUCHAREST, about which there is a separate article. It has a population of 1,225,507 and is the largest city and the chief commercial and manufacturing center of Rumania. Other important cities are:

Cluj, population 161,931, commercial center with a large metal industry.

Timisoara, population 146,988, railroad and industrial center

HOW THE PEOPLE ARE GOVERNED

Rumania is a so-called "people's republic" with a constitution similar to that of the Soviet Union. There is an elected National Assembly, a law-making body, but all its members belong to the Workers' (Communist) Party or to parties that follow the Communist line. There is also a State Council, elected by the Assembly, which takes over the law-making functions between sessions. Its president is head of the state, but the real head of the government is the Chairman of the Cabinet, which is called the Council of Ministers.

All children must go to school through the elementary grades. Rumania also has many secondary (high) schools, and four universities, at Bucharest, Iasi, Cluj, and Timisoara.

RUMANIA IN THE PAST

Almost two thousand years ago, the Romans conquered the Dacians, ancestors of the Rumanian people, and made Dacia a Roman province. When the Roman Empire fell, the territory that is now Rumania was invaded and occupied by barbarians of many tribes who mixed with the Dacians and gradually formed the Rumanian nation. About six hundred years ago the two independent states of Wallachia and Moldavia were formed. These states tried hard to keep their independence, but they came more and more under the power of Turkey until by the early 1700s the ruler of Turkey appointed rulers of his own choice to the thrones of Wallachia and Moldavia. These rulers were usually chosen from among the privileged Greek families who lived in Turkey. They were very greedy, and the taxes and tribute they demanded turned the people into starving peasants and wandering shepherds. Gradually Russia gained a good deal of power over the two states, until by 1829 all rulers and political leaders had to be approved by both Turkey and Russia.

In 1859 a Rumanian leader named Alexander Cuza was elected as governor of both states. Two years later the two were officially united as the country of Rumania. Cuza began helping the peasants to have a better life, but in 1866

he was overthrown and in 1881 a German prince of the Hohenzollern family, Carol I, was chosen first king of Rumania. There are separate articles about CAROL and MICHAEL.

In World War I Rumania fought with the Allies against Germany, and because of the Allied victory Rumania gained much new territory. After the war land-reform laws were passed, breaking up the large estates and giving them to the peasants. Under King Ferdinand, who reigned from 1914 to 1927, the National Peasant Party held control of the government, but many of its officials were dishonest and Communist and Fascist groups made great gains. Carol II had trouble in the 1930s with the Fascist Party called the Iron Guard, which was made up of young men who followed the ways of Adolf Hitler's Nazi Party in Germany. The Iron Guard was opposed to democratic government, the Jewish people, Communists, and big business. It operated through terrorism and murder. In 1933 members of the Iron Guard killed the premier, Ion Duca, and the party was banned but it continued to operate secretly.

As World War II came closer, King Carol tried very hard to remain neutral, but Soviet Russia made him give up Bessarabia and other important Rumanian territory. The Rumanian people were so angry about these losses of territory that King Carol had to abdicate (resign as king), giving the throne to his son Michael, who was then 18. General Ion Antonescu was appointed premier in 1940 and became dictator of Rumania. He sided with the Germans. The Iron Guard became powerful again and the country was occupied by German troops. When Germany attacked Russia in 1941, the Rumanians fought beside the Germans and soon regained the territories they had been forced to give up to Russia. By 1944 Germany was losing and Russian armies were nearing Rumania. King Michael overthrew Premier Antonescu and signed an armistice with the Allies, once again giving up Bessarabia to Russia. Rumania then joined the war on the side of the Allies.

After the war Communists took control of Rumania. Antonescu and his leaders were shot as traitors. Leaders of the Peasant Party were put in prison. King Michael was forced to give up the throne and a republic was established under the Communists.

RUMANIA. Area, 91,584 square miles. Population (1973 estimate) 20,470,000. Language, Rumanian. Religion, Rumanian Orthodox. Government, republic. Monetary unit, the leu, worth 17 cents (U.S.). Flag, blue, yellow and red vertical bands with coat of arms in center band. Capital, Bucharest.

ruminants

Ruminants are animals that chew a cud. Cows, goats and deer are examples of ruminants.

The cud consists of food that the animal swallows hastily without stopping to chew it. It passes to a stomachlike compartment called the *rumen,* where it is stored. After a time it is brought back to the animal's mouth, and there it is thoroughly chewed and made ready for digestion.

Ruminants have no teeth at the front of their upper jaws. They have back teeth in both jaws. The cud is chewed for a time on one side and then is transferred to the other side.

Ruminants include all cattle, deer, sheep, giraffes, goats, and antelopes. Another group of animals also chew the cud, but they are not true ruminants because they have front teeth in the upper jaw. These are the camels, dromedaries, llamas, guanacos, alpacas, and vicunas. They are called "primitive ruminants" to distinguish them from those that have no upper front teeth.

rummy

Rummy is the best-known card game played in the United States. It is played in several forms. One of the forms of rummy is CANASTA, about which there is a separate article. Another is gin-rummy, which is the most popular game for two players.

The various forms of rummy are different in some ways but all of them follow certain basic rules, which are described in this article.

The standard pack of 52 playing cards is used. Some forms of rummy use two or more packs, mixed together. There may be two to six (and in some cases even more) players. Usually each player is dealt ten cards when there are only two players and seven cards when there are more than two players. This leaves certain undealt cards, which are called the *stock*. The stock is placed in the center of the table, face down.

The object of the game is to form combinations of cards. These may be *matched sets*, or *groups*, of three or four cards of a kind, such as three or four kings; or they may be *runs*, or *sequences*, which are three or more cards of the same suit in order, such as the eight, nine and ten of spades.

In each turn, a player draws one card and discards one card. The card that he discards is placed face up beside the stock. All the discards form a pile called the *discard pile*. When a player draws, he may take either the top card of the stock or the top card of the discard pile and put it in his hand. Then he may take any card from his hand (including the one he just drew) and discard it.

After he draws and before he discards, a player may put down a group or a run if he has one. This is called a *spread* or *meld*. He does not have to do this, and in some forms of rummy he is not allowed to meld until his complete hand is matched and can be spread.

The play ends when any player has melded (spread) his entire hand, so that after discarding he has no cards left. Usually he wins from each other player the value of the cards that player still has. These values usually are: ace, 1 point; face cards, 10 points each; other cards, as many points as the number on the card. In some forms of rummy a player's own melds count a certain number of points for him.

GIN-RUMMY

Gin-rummy is a two-hand game, so ten cards are dealt to each player. Each player draws and discards as described in this article. A player's matched cards never count against him. When the point value of a player's unmatched cards is 10 points or less, that player may *knock* and end the play. If his opponent's unmatched cards have a higher point value, the knocker wins the difference between the two point values. If the opponent's unmatched cards have the same or a lower point value, the opponent wins the difference plus a bonus, usually 25 points. When a player knocks with all ten of his cards matched, he is said to *go gin* and wins the difference plus 25 points. A player who goes gin cannot lose the hand. The game ends when either player has won 100 points or more. At that time, a player receives an additional bonus for each hand he has won. Usually this bonus also is 25 points. It is called a "line" or "box" bonus.

In gin-rummy, as in many other forms of rummy, a player may "lay off" cards that match an opposing meld. That is, he may add cards from his hand to the opponent's matched sets, and those cards count as matched or melded cards. In many gin-rummy games a player is not allowed to lay off if his opponent has gone gin.

There are many books giving the full rules of the various games of rummy.

Rushmore, Mount

Mount Rushmore is a mountain in the Black Hills of South Dakota. It is 6,200 feet high. Its top is a solid block of granite 1,000 feet long, 450 feet wide, and 300 feet high. On the face of the mountain is the Mount Rushmore Memorial, the four biggest statues in the world. They are the faces of George Washington, Thomas Jefferson, Abraham Lincoln, and Theodore Roosevelt.

From the top of Washington's head to the tip of his chin is a distance of 60 feet. The other statues are just as big. A man could stand upright in the eye of any one of them. If the whole body of each of these former Presidents had been carved and if it were in the same proportions as the face, each man would have been 465 feet tall—tall enough to look into the forty-second story of a skyscraper. You can recognize the faces from about twenty miles away.

Mount Rushmore Memorial includes a park of 1,668 acres of land surrounding the mountain.

The huge faces were carved by Gutzon Borglum, a sculptor who liked to work on large statues. In 1925 he persuaded the Congress of the United States to vote him enough money to pay for carving the faces in the mountain. He began work in 1927, and the park was dedicated in 1929.

Gutzon Borglum chose Mount Rushmore because granite is a rock that lasts a long time. All rocks are harmed by sun, wind, rain, and snow, and some day the Presidents' faces will crumble, but they will probably last several hundred years.

Borglum and his assistants hung down from the top of the cliff on scaffolds and slings. They used compressed-air drills to carve the rock. These drills are the same as the ones workmen use when they dig up part of a street. The sculptors also used picks, chisels, and hammers.

In 1941, just before the great statues were finished, Gutzon Borglum died, but the work was completed by his son, Lincoln Borglum.

Ruskin, John

John Ruskin was an English writer and art critic. He was born in 1819, the son of a prosperous wine merchant. Ruskin had enough money so that he was able to devote his life to study. He wrote many important books on art and architecture and on literature. Ruskin also wrote a fairy story, *The King of the Golden River*, which many children have enjoyed. Ruskin died in 1900.

Russia

Russia is the name generally given to a large country in Europe and Asia. Officially it is now named the Russian Soviet Federated Socialist Republic, or R.S.F.S.R., and it is the principal part of the Union of Soviet Socialist Republics, or Soviet Union. Since the Russian Revolution in 1917 it has been under the control of the Communist Party. Since the Russian part of the Soviet Union is the largest and most important part, and controls all the other parts, the entire Soviet Union is often spoken of as "Russia" or "Soviet Russia."

Until the revolution in 1917, Russia was a vast empire ruled by czars (emperors). The czars and their governments had been greedy for territory for hundreds of years, so the Russian Empire included many lands whose people were not related to the Russians. In the Soviet Union, most of these lands have been made into separate states somewhat like the separate states of the United States.

Russia itself has two main parts, one in Europe and one in Asia. The European part is the largest country in Europe. It covers about 1,700,000 square miles, which is more than half the area of the United States and almost half the area of all Europe. The part in Asia consists mostly of Siberia, which covers about 5,000,000 square miles. The population of Russia is more than 125,000,000 and the population of the whole Soviet Union is least 227,687,000 (1964 UN estimate), which is about forty million more than live in the United States.

The capital of Russia, and also of the Soviet Union, is Moscow, a city of more than 5,000,000 population. The second-biggest city, with a population of about 3,000,000, is Leningrad, which under other names (Petrograd and St. Petersburg) was once the capital of the Russian Empire of the czars.

THE PEOPLE OF RUSSIA

The people of Russia, called Russians, are a Slavic people related to the Poles and the people of Czechoslovakia, Bulgaria, and Yugoslavia. The White Russians, or Byelorussians, and the Ukrainians, or "Little Russians," are closely related peoples who have their own governments in the Soviet Union. There are about 8,000,000 White Russians and about 44,000,000 Ukrainians.

The language of all these people is called Russian. It is one of the important literary languages of the world and is the subject of a separate article, RUSSIAN LANGUAGE AND LITERATURE.

The religion of Russia for a thousand years was Christian and nearly all the people belonged to the Russian Orthodox Church, which grew out of the Greek Orthodox Church. The Communist government is the enemy of all religions, so it is now difficult for people to be church members without risking persecution, but there are still many millions of Christians in Russia.

WHAT THE LAND IS LIKE

Russia in Europe is mostly a plain, level and suitable for farming; but the most fertile portions are in the Ukraine and in White Russia. The R.S.F.S.R. is north of these regions and is very cold in the winter, which makes the farming season shorter than it is in other parts of Europe or in the United States. The Asian part of Russia is described in the article on SIBERIA. Most of it is too cold to support a large population, but there are valuable mines and some important farming districts.

In spite of the long and cold winters, Russia is one of the best-developed countries on earth. It has many big cities in which there are important factories. Highways and railroads connect these cities. In the country are millions of acres of farms. The great rivers, the Volga, Don, and Dnieper, provide transportation, have great dams that furnish electrical power to the factories, and provide fish for food.

RUSSIAN HISTORY

The present form of the Russian government, under the Communists, is described in the article on the UNION OF SOVIET SOCIALIST REPUBLICS.

The former Russian Empire grew out of a country founded about a thousand years ago by a Slavic people under a Norse (Germanic) prince named Rurik. Russian historians have set the year 862 as the date of the founding of Russia. The ancient capital was the city of Kiev, which is now the capital of the Ukraine. This was close to the East Roman, or Byzantine, empire that had its capital in Constantinople and its principal territory in Greece, so early Russia was influenced by Greek and Roman civilization and became Christian as a branch of the Greek Orthodox Church. The Russian Orthodox Church later became independent but was always much like the Greek Church in its organization and customs as well as in its beliefs.

Russia was a wild and warlike country for several hundred years after that. The Russian princes and kings fought against Mongol and Tatar invaders from Asia and from time to time they were ruled by the Asiatic peoples. Many Mongols and Tatars settled in the eastern parts of Russia and intermarried with the Slavs who were already there. The Russians fought many wars against neighboring countries and whenever they were powerful enough they conquered these countries and made them part of Russia. Ever since, the Russian governments have constantly tried to add more territory to their empire.

The first real czar, or emperor, in Russia was Ivan IV, called Ivan the Terrible, who lived from 1530 to 1584. He was called "the Terrible" because he killed all the noblemen (called *boyars*) who op-posed him, and often he tortured them first as a warning to others. Ivan established a principle of absolute rule by the czar, and though there were many weak or foolish czars after him, any czar who wanted to be a supreme ruler was able to do so.

The czar best remembered is Peter I, or Peter the Great, who lived from 1682 to 1725. Russia at that time was far less civilized than other countries of Europe. Peter traveled to other European countries and introduced their ways into Russia.

Gradually Russia added to its territories. It explored and annexed the vast region of Siberia. It fought the Turks and took away some of their possessions. It made deals with other European countries to let it take over parts of Poland, Finland, and the Baltic states of Estonia, Latvia, and Lithuania. Though Russia remained far behind the other large European countries in education, manufacturing, and scientific progress, it grew so large in population and territory that in 1853 Great Britain and France joined Turkey in the Crimean War against Russia, to keep Russia from expanding its territories any father.

Russia retained the system of serfdom longer than any other European country. Serfdom was a kind of slavery whereby many of the farmers belonged to the noblemen who owned their land. Finally, under Czar Alexander II, the serfs were freed in 1861.

In 1904, Japan went to war against Russia to increase Japanese power in eastern Asia. Japan's navy almost destroyed the Russian navy in their first battle, and Russia had to give some of its Siberian territory and make many concessions to Japan when peace was made in 1905.

The Russian Empire ended when Russia was badly beaten by Germany in World War I. Though Germany later lost the war, the Russian disaster made possible the overthrow of the czars and the establishment of the Communist government. For this part of the history, see the article on the UNION OF SOVIET SOCIALIST REPUBLICS. There are separate articles on most of the persons and events in this article.

Russian language and literature

Russian is the language spoken by about 200,000,000 people in Russia and other parts of the Union of Soviet Socialist Republics. It is a member of the INDO-EUROPEAN family of languages, about which there is a separate article, and it is one of the Slavic group of languages, being closely related to Polish, Czech, Bulgarian, and other languages of the Slavic peoples.

Until twenty or thirty years ago, there were few people in western Europe and the Americas who learned Russian. More recently the Russian language has been studied by many more people, especially by scientists and military men who want to read Russian magazines that contain information in their fields.

The Russians use the Cyrillic alphabet, which is different from the English alphabet. The Cyrillic alphabet is named for a Greek bishop named Cyril, who spread Christianity through Russia about 1,100 years ago. Cyril took the letters of the Greek alphabet and added others to fit sounds of the Russian language that were not used in Greek. The alphabet has been simplified since then, but it still has thirty letters.

RUSSIAN LITERATURE

The greatest Russian literature was written in the 1800s, and the most important part of it was fiction (novels and short stories) and plays. English translations of these works are still read by millions.

Leo Tolstoy's novel *War and Peace* has been considered by many critics to be the greatest novel ever written. Fedor Dostoevski's novels *The Brothers Karamazov* and *Crime and Punishment,* and another Tolstoy novel, *Anna Karenina,* are almost as highly ranked and widely read. Alexander Pushkin, who lived from 1799 to 1837, was the outstanding Russian poet, and his long poem *Eugene Onegin* and poetical drama *Boris Godunoff* were made into grand operas. Anton Chekov was one of the greatest short-story writers of all time and even greater as a playwright. *The Cherry Orchard* and several other of his plays are still popular in English-speaking countries.

Among modern writers, Maxim Gorki is best known. Writing before the Russian Revolution of 1917, he expressed the feelings that led to the revolution. When the Communists came to power in Russia they made a hero of him, but it is probable that he was later killed for disagreeing with some of the acts of Josef Stalin, the Communist dictator.

Under Communist control, Russia has placed many restrictions on its writers, for they cannot write anything that might seem to criticize the government. Great literature is seldom produced in such conditions. Nevertheless, translations of several recent Russian novels and other books have been published successfully in the United States and in British countries, especially those dealing with the period of World War II.

rust

Rust is the common name of a disease that attacks many different plants. There are several kinds of rust, but they all are caused by tiny plants, of the kind called *fungi,* that live on other plants. These fungi produce reddish-brown scales that attach themselves to the leaves, stem or root of the plant they live on. Certain plants seem to resist rust, and farmers often use plants that are grown from the seed of those plants. Sometimes chemical sprays are used to fight rust.

Rust is also a name for the reddish-brown scales that form on iron and other metals when they are exposed to moisture. It occurs when the carbon and iron in the metal combine with oxygen in the air. This is called *oxidation* and is described in the article OXYGEN.

rutabaga, a plant like a turnip: see the article on TURNIP.

Ruth

Ruth was a brave and faithful woman whose story is told in the Bible, in the Book of Ruth. The book tells how Elimelech and his wife Naomi leave their

home in Bethlehem because there is a terrible famine in the land. They travel to the land of Moab, where their two sons marry girls named Ruth and Orpah. Then Elimelech and his two sons die. Naomi decides to return to Bethlehem. She tells Orpah and Ruth to stay in Moab and find new husbands. Orpah agrees to do as Naomi says, but Ruth does not want to leave Naomi and she says: "Whither thou goest I will go; and where thou lodgest, I will lodge: thy people shall be my people, and thy God my God." Naomi and Ruth go to Bethlehem and Ruth marries Boaz, one of the powerful leaders of Jerusalem.

Ruth, Babe

George Herman Ruth, who was always called "Babe" Ruth, was the most famous of all baseball players and probably the most famous person in the history of all sports. He was known even to millions of people who had no interest in baseball. His fame came partly from the fact that he was such a great player and partly from the fact that he was such an interesting person.

Babe Ruth was born in Baltimore, Maryland, in 1895. He was hard to discipline as a child and his parents sent him to school at St. Mary's Industrial School in Baltimore, a school noted for correcting "bad" boys. He played on the school's baseball team and the priests recognized him as an outstanding player. Through their recommendation he was given a tryout with the Baltimore baseball team,

"Babe" Ruth was the greatest home-run hitter in the history of baseball.

which was then in the International League. In 1914 he became a member of the Boston Red Sox in the American League, as a pitcher. He appeared certain to become one of the greatest left-handed pitchers of all time, and in the 1916 and 1918 World Series he set a record by pitching 29 scoreless innings in a row, but he was so good as a batter that he was turned into an outfielder so that he could play every day.

In 1919, Boston sold Ruth's contract to the New York Yankees (supposedly for $125,000, the highest price ever paid for a baseball player up to that time). It is as a Yankee that he is remembered. He specialized in hitting home runs. He hit 54 home runs in 1920, then broke his record with 59 in 1921, and later broke this record with 60 in 1927. He was a very big man, 6 feet 2 inches tall and

weighing more than 225 pounds. He had very wide shoulders, a narrow waist, and very thin legs, so that it seemed impossible that his legs could support his great bulk; but he could do everything well in baseball—run, field, throw, and bat. He led the American League in batting with an average of .378 in 1924, and made an even higher average, .393, in a year in which he did not win the batting championship. During his career he hit 714 home runs.

Ruth liked children. He spent much time visiting sick children in hospitals, and sometimes he would stop at a park and play baseball with boys who were having a game there. He was loved by boys and young baseball players everywhere. When he died of cancer, in 1948, millions mourned.

Rutledge, Ann

Ann Rutledge was a friend of Abraham Lincoln. Her father was the innkeeper at the inn in New Salem, Illinois, where Lincoln lived for several years. According to a story told after Lincoln's death by William Herndon, Lincoln's law partner, Ann Rutledge was engaged to be married to Lincoln. Herndon said that Ann Rutledge's early death (when she was only 22) was the greatest sorrow of Lincoln's life. Many who have studied Lincoln's life do not believe this story. Ann Rutledge was engaged to John McNamar, one of Lincoln's friends, and Lincoln probably knew her only as a friend. She was born about 1813 and died in 1835.

Rutledge, John

John Rutledge was an American judge and statesman. He was one of the members of the convention that drew up the Constitution of the United States, and he was a member of the First Continental Congress. Rutledge was both president and governor of South Carolina during the Revolutionary War. He was born in South Carolina in 1739 and studied law in London, England. He became a very successful lawyer while he was still a young man. He was appointed Chief Justice of the United States Supreme Court in 1795, but for political reasons the Senate refused to confirm his appointment. Rutledge died in 1800.

Rwanda

Rwanda, in East Central Africa, is one of the newest nations, having become independent on July 1, 1962. It is about the size of Maryland in area and population. Before World War I, Rwanda was a German colony named Ruanda; then it became part of a United Nations trust territory, administered by Belgium, called Ruanda-Urundi (see BURUNDI).

The people are Negroes belonging to three main tribes, the Watusi (the tallest human beings alive), the Bahutu, and the Batwa (who are pygmies).

Rwanda is chiefly a farming and cattle-raising country. Coffee, tobacco and vegetables are its main crops.

Rwanda is a republic governed by a president, 12 ministers, and a 47-member Assembly elected by the people. The capital is Kigali, a city of about 15,000.

REPUBLIC OF RWANDA. Area, 10,169 square miles. Population (1973 UN estimate) 3,830,000. Languages, Swahili, Banrya-Rwanda, French.

Ryder, Albert P.

Albert Pinkham Ryder was an American painter. He is best known for his paintings of scenery, especially of the sea. He was born in 1847 in New Bedford, Massachusetts. When he was 20 years old his family moved to New York City, where he studied painting. After a time he shut himself up in a small apartment and did little but paint. He died in 1917. His famous paintings include *Death on a Pale Horse, Toilers of the Sea,* and *Moonlight at Sea.*

rye

Rye is a cereal grain that is grown for its seed, and to make straw, and sometimes as a cover crop on farms. (A cover crop is any vegetation planted when the land is not being used for a regular crop, to improve the soil.) Rye is also used as a source of plant food. After farmers have used a field for growing vegetables through the spring and summer, they may sow rye in the early fall and let it remain in the ground, to be plowed under the following spring.

The seed of rye grown for cereal use is ground into flour, and also is used in making alcohol and whiskey. In Europe, rye is fed to cattle. It will thrive in soil that is not rich enough for wheat.

Ryukyu Islands

The Ryukyu Islands, in the western Pacific Ocean, extend in a 400 mile chain from Kyushu Island, Japan to Taiwan. The Ryukyu Islands fall into three subdivisions: in the north, the Amami Islands; in the center, the Okinawa Islands; and in the south, the Sakishima Islands. There are 64 main islands, and the total land area is 1,800 square miles.

The islands are composed of either volcanic material or coral deposits. As a result, the islands formed from volcanic eruptions are rugged and mountainous. In contrast, the islands built from coral are low and flat. The climate is warm and damp and subject to seasonal typhoons.

The Ryukyu people are believed to be descendants of the AINUS, an ancient Japanese people. (See the entry on the subject.) Today, the Ryukyus are farmers of sugar cane, a major source of income. Besides farming, others make a living from fishing and textile manufacture. In 1973, the population figure was about 900,000.

Throughout the history of the Ryukyus, the people have been under the rule of China, Japan, and the U.S. Only in ancient times did they govern themselves. During World War II, the islands were a battleground of fighting between the U.S. and Japan. After the Japanese defeat, the U.S. took control of the islands. In 1953, the Amami Islands were returned to Japan. By 1972, the last of the islands under U.S. control were given back to the Japanese.

Fishermen in many villages of the Ryukyu Islands
participate in an annual Sea God Festival on May 4th
of the lunar calendar.

S

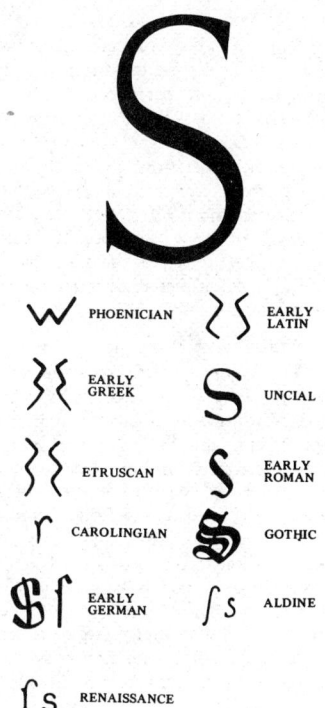

ᗯ PHOENICIAN	≷≷ EARLY LATIN
≥≷ EARLY GREEK	Ϩ UNCIAL
≷≷ ETRUSCAN	Ƨ EARLY ROMAN
ſ CAROLINGIAN	𝕾 GOTHIC
ℰſ EARLY GERMAN	ſ s ALDINE
ſ s RENAISSANCE	

S or s

The letter S, the nineteenth letter of our alphabet, came to us as most of our letters did: First, thousands of years ago, it was perhaps one of the picture-symbols used by the ancient Egyptians in their system of hieroglyphics. In this system a picture of something, instead of a letter, finally came to stand for a single sound. Some people believe that the letter S began as a picture of a flooded garden, but other scholars have come to think it began as a picture of teeth. In the Hebrew language the word for teeth was *shin*, and the sign for it was just like the Phoenician letter shown above, left.

When the ancient Greeks took this letter they turned it on end. At first the ancient Greeks read from right to left, but later they read from left to right as we do today. They then turned the letter around, and called it *sigma*. By the time the Romans came to use it, the top and bottom cross-strokes had been changed from slanting to straight. Then the angles (corners) were rounded, and the letter became the S we use today.

For many years two kinds of letters were used for the small s we use today. One was called the middle s, which is shown at the top of the page to the right of the Greek sigma; the other was called the final s, which is like the small s we use today. About a hundred years ago the use of the middle s was dropped, because the form of the letter looked so much like a small letter f that it confused people. You can still see the old form in many old English books, and also in German books, because the Germans still use it. In the illustration above, the "German black-letter" (or "Gothic") capital S is also shown, at the far right.

Read also the article ALPHABET.

Saar

The Saar is a region in western Europe between France and Germany. It is very small, having an area of only 991 square miles and a population of little more than one million, but France and Germany have both wanted to own the Saar, because it is one of the most important coal-mining regions of the world. At the time of World War I the Saar belonged to Germany, but after the war it was made part of France. However, most of the people living there were Germans, and in 1935 nearly all of them voted to be part of Germany. After World War II the Saar was taken from Germany again and economically attached to France, but in 1956 it was returned to Germany and became a state of the German Federal Republic (West Germany). The chief cities of the Saar are Saarbrücken, its capital, and Neunkirchen. The Saar is a hilly region, with some forests. The main river is the Saar River, which flows north from eastern France to the Moselle River.

Sabbath

The Sabbath is the seventh day of the week. Since ancient times, Jews have celebrated it on Saturday. Some Christians, such as the Seventh Day Adventists, also observed Saturday as the Sabbath, but most Christians observe it on Sunday. The Sabbath is the day set aside for worshiping God. The reason for the Sabbath is found in the Bible. The Old Testament Book of Genesis says that God created the world in six days, and that on the seventh He "rested." One of the Ten Commandments is to "keep holy the Sabbath Day."

As observed by Orthodox Jews, the Sabbath begins at sundown on Friday and lasts till sundown on Saturday. It is a day devoted to strict prayer.

Some places in the United States have "blue laws," which are laws that prohibit almost all amusements on the Sabbath.

saber-tooth tiger

The saber-tooth tiger is an animal that lived on the earth millions of years ago. There are no more saber-tooth tigers, but scientists have studied bones and remains of this animal and they know many things about it. It was usually about as big as a small fox, but some saber-tooth tigers were as large as lions. It had a powerful body and a short tail. It had long, sharp upper teeth that often hung several inches below the animal's lower jaw. These teeth (they are sometimes called fangs) had jagged edges. They were a deadly weapon with which the saber-tooth tiger defended itself against enemies. The saber-tooth tiger was probably not a very fast runner, so it had to eat animals that it could catch without having to chase them.

sable

The sable is a handsome animal that lives in Europe and in parts of Russia and Japan where the climate is cold.

The Russian sable is about 18 inches long. It has a magnificent bushy tail and beautiful fur. The sable's fur is a dark grayish-brown color with underfur that is light gray or yellowish brown. Fine sable fur makes the most valuable fur coats and scarfs.

The sable is a shy and suspicious animal and is not easy to catch. It makes its den in a hollow tree or on the ground. It eats smaller animals and birds and fish.

sabotage

Sabotage is intentional destruction of something valuable, so as to hurt somebody else. The word probably comes from a time when factory workers in France (where *sabot* means "shoe") threw their shoes into machinery to spoil it, because they were angry at the low pay and poor working conditions that were forced on them. Today sabotage is interfering with an enemy's production in wartime, or with an employer's production when there is trouble between labor and management in an industry.

In wartime, sabotage is a very effective weapon and for that reason every country has laws against it and can even put a saboteur to death. During World War I, when the United States and its Allies were fighting against Germany, a munitions plant was blown up at a place called Tom's River, New Jersey, and this explosion (called the Black Tom explosion) was believed to be the work of German saboteurs. During World War II, Germany trained saboteurs to interfere with production in factories making war supplies. They sent some of these saboteurs to the United States, landing them on the Atlantic Coast from submarines. Some of the saboteurs were caught and imprisoned. The Communist government of Russia has trained saboteurs who live in other countries and prepare to commit sabotage if war should come. In the countries that Germany occupied during World War II, there were "underground" movements of native patriots who sabotaged the German plans by blowing up supply trains and doing other things to hurt their enemy.

saccharin, a substitute for sugar. It is made from coal tar and can safely be taken by people who have diabetes and cannot eat sugar.

sacrament

In Christian religions, a sacrament is a religious ceremony, begun by Jesus while he was on earth, for the purpose of giving grace to the person receiving the sacrament. Almost all Christian Churches have two sacraments, baptism and communion. Catholics have five more, some or all of which are part of the practices of other Christian Churches. The other sacraments are: *confirmation*, in which a person is confirmed or strengthened in his faith; *penance*, in which a person confesses his sins in order to have them forgiven; *extreme unction*, in which a dying person is anointed with holy oils; *holy orders*, in which a man is made a priest; and *matrimony*, in which a man and woman marry.

Sacramento

Sacramento is the capital and sixth-largest city of California. It is in the central part of the state, 75 miles northeast of San Francisco. The city is on the Sacramento River where it is joined by the American River. The region is surrounded by mountains. Sacramento is an important trade and shipping center for the farming, lumbering and mining regions of the Sacramento Valley and northern California.

About 254,000 people live in Sacra-

mento. There are huge processing plants for food products, lumber mills, railroad shops, and factories that manufacture metal products. Sacramento is the headquarters for the Central Valley Project, a great irrigation and power development. Nearby are two United States Air Force bases, Mather Field and McClellan Field. The city is governed by a city manager and an elected council.

Sacramento was founded by Captain John A. Sutter in 1839, on a 50,000-acre tract of land granted to him by Mexico. Sutter called his estate New Helvetia. The town was laid out and named Sacramento in 1848, when gold was discovered on Sutter's property and a Gold Rush began. Sacramento served as a supply base for the prospectors and grew rapidly. It became the state capital in 1854. In 1860 it became the western end of the PONY EXPRESS, about which there is a separate article. Among the historic landmarks in Sacramento are Sutter's Fort, now rebuilt as a museum for Indian and pioneer relics, and the Pony Express Museum. The capitol building is among the handsomest in the country. The California State Fair is held in Sacramento.

SACRAMENTO, CALIFORNIA. Population (1970 census) 254,413. Capital of California. County seat of Sacramento County. Founded 1839.

safari

A safari is a hunting party that goes out to shoot big game in Africa. Lions, elephants, rhinoceroses, giraffes, antelopes and other large animals are classed as big game.

Usually a safari is organized for an American or European who enjoys hunting and is willing to pay the cost, which may range from $2,000 to $10,000. The safari lasts three weeks or more, sometimes several months.

A "white hunter" is in charge of the safari. He is an expert at big-game hunting, and receives a fee for managing the safari and protecting the hunters who are paying for it. The rest of the safari are usually African natives, members of the Negro peoples there. One of them is usually a guide and also gives the commands to the other natives. Some of them are skilled hunters and help to find and kill the game. The rest are "bearers" who carry the food, clothing and supplies. Once there were forty, fifty or even more of these bearers, each carrying a heavy package. Everyone in the safari went on foot. Now many safaris go to regions that can be reached by Jeeps and trucks, and bearers are not needed. Sometimes it is possible to have a trailer in which the hunters can live in comfort.

Many safaris are organized for a flat price in which the "white hunter" or some professional organization furnishes all supplies and men and even guarantees that the hunters will kill certain big game, such as a lion or an elephant and other animals.

safety: see the article ACCIDENT.

saffron

Saffron is a dye and seasoning that is made from the crocus flower. The dye, which is a deep orange color, and a pleasant-tasting seasoning are made from part of the blossom. A small pinch of saffron is enough to color an entire bowl of rice a bright shade of yellow and also to improve its flavor. Saffron is also used in the manufacture of some kinds of medicine.

saga

Hundreds of years ago stories were not often written down in books. They were passed on from older to younger people by word of mouth. The stories that were told again and again in the Scandinavian countries (Denmark, Norway, Sweden and Iceland) were called sagas. In Iceland, about seven hundred years ago, many of these stories were written down. The sagas usually told about great events of history of real or imaginary heroes. Among the most famous sagas are the *Njala*, the *Heimskringla*, and the *Grettla*, all of which have been translated from the old Icelandic language into English. The most famous of all the sagas is the *Volsungasaga*, about the hero Siegfried. You can read more about some of the stories taken from it in the article NIBELUNGS.

sage

Sage is a small, shrubby plant. Its grayish-green leaves are used for flavoring and seasoning foods. The leaves are usually dried and then crushed or ground to season sausage meats, poultry stuffing, and other foods. Sage grows in most parts of the world, except where the climate is extremely hot, extremely cold, or extremely dry.

sagebrush

Sagebrush is a North American plant that grows mainly in the dry, near-desert plains and prairies of the western United States, and in northern Mexico. It is an evergreen shrub with a fragrant odor somewhat like that of pine. It requires very little moisture and therefore grows in places where nearly any other plant would die. The flowers grow in clusters. They are usually yellow and sweet-smelling. Sagebrush is the state flower of Nevada.

Sagittarius

Sagittarius is the name of one of the constellations, or groups of stars in the sky. It was given this name thousands of years ago, in ancient Greece. (In the Latin language, *sagittarius* means "archer"—that is, a man shooting with bow and arrow.) The Greeks thought this particular group of stars looked like an archer with his arrow aimed at the heart of another constellation called Scorpion, which looked like a kind of serpent. The sign that stands for the constellation Sagittarius is ♐. Read also the articles CONSTELLATION and ZODIAC.

sago

Sago is a kind of starch made from the soft inner pulp of a tree, the sago palm, that grows in the East Indies and the Philippines. Some sago is made from a few other pulpy plants. The pulp is dried and ground to form sago flour, which is used in cooking and to starch clothes. It can be used wherever cornstarch is used.

saguaro

Saguaro is the name of a giant cactus found in the southwestern United States and in northern Mexico. It has a thick stalk from which heavy arms, or branches, stick out. The saguaro sometimes reaches a height of 60 feet. It bears white flowers. The fruit of the saguaro can be eaten and is often very important to persons crossing stretches of desert country. The saguaro is the state flower of Arizona. For a picture of it, see the article CACTUS.

Saguenay River

The Saguenay River is a river about 110 miles long in south central Quebec province. It flows from Lake St. John and empties into the St. Lawrence River. About halfway down the river's course is an inlet called Ha Ha Bay. Below this point the river becomes wider and is navigable. At some points it flows between banks a thousand feet high. Near its mouth the Saguenay is very deep. The lower course of the river is popular for salmon and trout fishing, canoeing, and steamer excursions. The Saguenay was discovered by Jacques Cartier in 1535.

Sahara Desert

The Sahara Desert is the greatest desert in the world. It is in northern Africa and covers as much territory as the entire United States, having an area of more than 3,000,000 square miles. In Libya and Egypt it is called the Libyan Desert; the strip between the Nile River and the Red Sea is called the Arabian Desert; and in the northern Sudan it is called the Nubian Desert.

The Sahara Desert varies from very low country, below sea level, to mountain ranges with peaks as high as 11,000 feet. Much of the Sahara is the sandy dunes that most people think of as desert, but parts of it are bare rock and other parts are made up largely of gravel.

The Sahara is a region of almost no rain. When rain does fall, it usually comes in torrents. There are areas where no rain falls for years at a stretch. The climate of the Sahara is very hot. Temperatures as high as 140 degrees Fahrenheit have been recorded. Because the air is so dry, it heats and cools rapidly, and there may be a difference of almost 100 degrees between daytime and nighttime temperatures.

The dryness of the Sahara is largely due to winds that arise in the desert itself. These winds also have a great effect on the lands around the Sahara. The *sirocco* and *simoom* are two of the winds that arise in the Sahara.

The only places where plants and animals can thrive in the Sahara are the oases, patches of fertile land watered by underground streams. These are the regions where most of the Sahara's three to four million people live. Date palms grow in the oases, and the people grow cereals, vegetables, and fruit, and raise animals.

The people who live in the Sahara are Berbers, Arabs, and a Negroid tribe called the Tibbus. Most of them are nomads, or wanderers.

The western Sahara is controlled by Algeria, Mauritania, Mali, and Niger. The eastern section is divided among Libya,

Egypt, Chad, and the Sudan. Read also the articles on AFRICA and DESERT.

Saigon

Saigon is the capital of the Republic of South Vietnam (see VIETNAM). It is a beautiful city, often called "the Paris of the East." Though forty miles from the sea, Saigon is an important seaport because big ships can reach it on the Saigon River. During the Viet Cong and other wars, Saigon has suffered only small damage from bombs.

About 2,000,000 people live in Saigon. Most of them are Annamese, but there are also Chinese and French people. Many of them work around the port, and many others work in Saigon's huge rice mills. Most of the city is modern, with large buildings and wide, tree-lined avenues. The old part of the city, the *Ville Indigène,* still has tiny, old houses and stores that sell such delicacies as pickled snakes and glazed pig snouts.

sailfish

The sailfish is a sleek and powerful fish that lives in the Atlantic and Pacific Oceans. Many people who live in Florida and California like to fish for sailfish. It requires great strength and skill to catch a sailfish because it is a strong and courageous fighter. The sailfish got its name because on its back it has a large fin that looks like a sail. The sailfish has a slim, dark blue body and its underparts are a light color. It has a long sharp spear that is really its upper jawbone sticking out in front.

The sailfish that is found in the Atlantic Ocean weighs between 35 and 100 pounds. One of the largest sailfish ever caught in the Atlantic weighed 123 pounds and was more than ten feet long. The Pacific Ocean sailfish is larger than the Atlantic Ocean variety. It usually weighs about 100 pounds.

The female sailfish lays its eggs in the summer. The baby sailfish has spines on its head and does not look at all like its parents.

The sailfish is a good fighter. It is a challenge to the skill of fishermen.

sailing

Sailing is the use of large sheets of canvas, called *sails,* to catch the wind

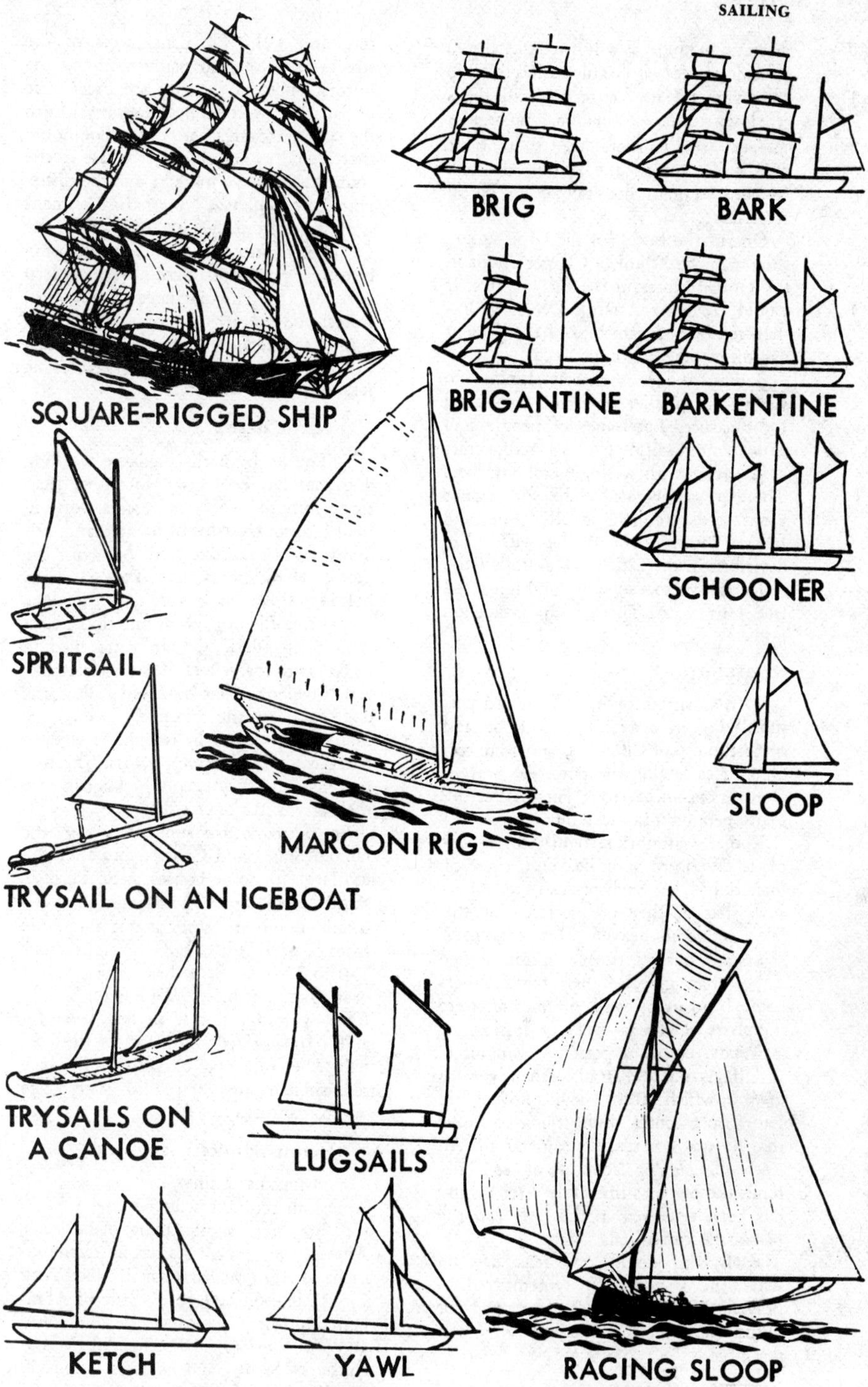

SQUARE-RIGGED SHIP

BRIG

BARK

BRIGANTINE

BARKENTINE

SCHOONER

SPRITSAIL

MARCONI RIG

SLOOP

TRYSAIL ON AN ICEBOAT

TRYSAILS ON A CANOE

LUGSAILS

KETCH

YAWL

RACING SLOOP

There are dozens of different ways to rig a ship (arrange the sails).

and cause a ship to go forward. Until about a hundred years ago, nearly all ships used sails and hundreds of years of study had made sailing a matter of great science and skill. Since steam engines and other engines have been used, sailing has become unimportant except as a sport.

Men have used sails for thousands of years, but the sailing ship did not begin its full development until about a thousand years ago, when men learned to sail into the wind. (That is, they learned to arrange sails in such a way that the ship could go forward even when the wind was blowing in the opposite direction.) After that many different kinds of sailing ship were designed, some of them large enough to carry hundreds of people.

The arrangement of sails on a ship is called the *rigging.* The largest of the old sailing ships used complicated systems of rigging in which dozens of different sails would be used and a large crew was needed to handle them. Smaller ships used fewer sails and required smaller crews.

A sailing ship has one or more masts, upright posts that hold the sails. Across the mast are crosswise pieces, called yards, to which the sails are attached. The yards are hung from the masts so that they can be turned in any direction to catch the wind. A complicated system of ropes permits the sailors to turn the yard; to roll up the sail when the wind is too strong for safety or when that sail should not be used; or to lower the sail to the deck for repairs or to make it safe in a storm.

Sailing against the wind is usually a matter of *tacking,* or sailing a zigzag course. When the wind is made to hit

a sail at an angle, it will drive the ship to the side and forward. This pushes the ship somewhat off its course but still sends it closer to its destination. At regular intervals the sails are fixed so that the ship sails toward the other side, and forward, so that it does not get too far off its course.

One of the fastest of the large sailing ships was the "Yankee Clipper" built in the United States in the early 1800s. It would cross the Atlantic Ocean in less than ten days. Steamships of the present day often take as long.

Sailing today is largely limited to yachts and smaller boats that are sailed for pleasure. Thousands of people find enjoyment in sailing even so small a craft as a canoe with a single sail attached. There are many yacht clubs, and regular yacht races are held in all oceans and lakes. The biggest of the yachts are described in the article AMERICA'S CUP.

Iceboats also use sails for high-speed travel over ice. There is an article on ICEBOAT.

saint

In Christian belief, a saint is a person living in heaven. In Catholic and some Protestant Churches, saints are recognized as having the power to pray to God for specific persons. For this reason, many people "pray to saints."

Roman Catholics recognize some people as certain to be in heaven because of their holy lives. Such persons are *canonized,* that is, they are declared by the Pope to be in heaven. Most canonized saints are martyrs, people who have died rather than give up their faith. Others come from every walk of life and were members of almost every profession.

Today, before a person is canonized, his life is put on "trial." An *advocatus diaboli,* which means "devil's lawyer," in Latin, "prosecutes" him, trying to prove that he was not really a saint at all. An *advocatus Dei,* or "advocate of God," defends the person's life. Only after his life has been reviewed in this way can the person be canonized.

Each saint has his own feast day, on which he is especially remembered in prayers. Many Christians are named for saints whom their parents hope they will resemble.

Saint Augustine

St. Augustine is a city in Florida. It is the oldest city in the United States. St. Augustine is on a narrow point of land where three rivers, the San Sebastian, North, and Matanzas, meet the Atlantic Ocean.

About 13,000 people live in St. Augustine. Many of them are connected with the city's important tourist trade, for St. Augustine is a popular vacation resort. The principal industry is fishing for shrimp, and there are railroad shops, shrimp and vegetable canneries, and factories that make cigars, lumber, boats, and cement.

St. Augustine was founded in 1565 by the Spanish explorer Pedro de Aviles, who sighted the coast on St. Augustine's day. St. Augustine still has a Spanish air about it. The streets are narrow and twisting and the old buildings are in Spanish style, with wrought-iron balconies, pa-

tios, and walled gardens. Most of the streets have Spanish names. Among the historic spots in the city are the Castle of San Marcos, the oldest masonry fort in the United States; an old schoolhouse that is said to be the oldest house in the country; the slave market; and the cathedral. Fort Matanzas National Monument is 15 miles from the city. Since 1937, the Carnegie Institution has been restoring historical points of interest. The modern part of the city includes skyscrapers, stores, and hotels.

ST. AUGUSTINE, FLORIDA. Population (1970 census) 12,352. County seat of St. Johns County. Founded 1565.

Saint Bernard

The St. Bernard is a large working dog that has been used for more than three hundred years in rescue work in the high, snowy Alps of Switzerland. For many years the dogs went out with the monks of the St. Bernard Pass Hospice, helping them look for lost travelers. Sometimes the dogs went out alone, each with a tiny flask of brandy fastened to its collar to revive a chilled or nearly frozen traveler so' that he could follow the dog back to the Hospice. Today the monks are warned by telephone when a party is about to attempt a trip through the Pass, and they keep a lookout in case the party is lost or overdue.

St. Bernards are kept as pets in the United States and Canada, but they are too large for some houses. A St. Bernard stands about 25 to 29 inches high at the shoulder and measures about the same from chest to base of tail. It weighs about 150 to 200 pounds. It has a thick, warm coat of straight hair, and a big, bushy tail. Its eyes droop slightly in the lower lid and a spot of red shows below the eyeball. The color may be white with large reddish markings, or reddish with large white markings.

Saint-Gaudens, Augustus

Augustus Saint-Gaudens was an American sculptor who became famous for his statues of great Americans. Among these noted statues are a monument to Admiral Farragut in New York City's Madison Square, a statue of Abraham Lincoln in Chicago's Lincoln Park, and *The Puritan,* in Springfield, Massachusetts. Saint-Gaudens was born in Dublin, Ireland, and was brought to the United States as an infant. He studied sculpture in New York and in Paris. During his life he was recognized as the greatest American sculptor. Saint-Gaudens died in 1907. His estate in Cornish, New Hampshire, has been made a memorial to him, with plaster and bronze replicas of his works.

Saint Helena

St. Helena is an island in the south Atlantic Ocean, about 1,200 miles off the coast of Africa. It is famous as the place where the French emperor, Napoleon I, was kept in exile after his defeat in the Battle of Waterloo, in 1815. St. Helena is a British crown colony.

The island of St. Helena has an area of 47 square miles, and about 4,700 people live there. It is mountainous country, with deep ravines and rushing brooks. The climate is pleasant, although

the island is in the tropics. The people who live in St. Helena are of mixed European, Asian and African blood. English is the only language spoken. Jamestown is the capital and chief port, and almost half of the population lives there. Most of the people are farmers, and almost all of them grow New Zealand flax. There are mills that make lace, rope, and twine.

St. Helena was first sighted in 1502 by the Portuguese, who found no one living there. Since 1673 it has been British. During World War II it was an important naval base.

Saint John

Saint John is the largest city in the province of New Brunswick, Canada. It is in the southern part of the province, on the Bay of Fundy at the mouth of the St. John River. Saint John is a commercial and manufacturing center, with one of the world's largest drydocks. It is a major Canadian port because it is ice-free the year round, while St. Lawrence ports are closed to sea traffic for several months during the winter.

More than 100,000 people live in Saint John. There are large grain elevators, a shipping industry, factories, and mining industries. The fishing industry is also important; the principal catches are lobsters, sardines, and herring. A main point of interest is the Reversing Falls Rapids of the St. John River, which reverses its flow because of the strong tides in the Bay of Fundy.

Saint John was founded in 1635 as a fort and Indian-trading post. The French held the settlement until 1758, when it was ceded to Great Britain. British Loyalists settled there after the Revolutionary War in the United States. They named their city Parr Town. In 1785 it was joined with Carleton (on the other side of the harbor) as the city of Saint John.

SAINT JOHN, NEW BRUNSWICK. Population (1973 estimate) 106,744. County seat of St. John County. Settled in 1635. On the Bay of Fundy at the mouth of the St. John River.

Saint John's

St. John's is the capital and largest city of the province of Newfoundland, Canada. It is a seaport on the northeast coast of Avalon peninsula on Freshwater Bay, an arm of the Atlantic Ocean. St. John's is an important commercial and industrial city, the center of the great Newfoundland fishing fleet. Close to 131,000 people live there. Many of them work in the fishing industry and in factories that make many cod and herring products. Outside the city there are mink and fox farms, and dairy, poultry and vegetable farms.

The site of St. John's was first visited in 1497 by John Cabot. In 1583, Sir Humphrey Gilbert landed there and took possession of the entire island for England. The first permanent settlement at St. John's was established shortly after 1600, and it is one of the oldest cities in the New World.

St. John's has been the site of important scientific experiments. The first transatlantic wireless message was received by Marconi, in 1911, in Cabot Tower on Signal Hill, overlooking the city. In 1911, the first nonstop transat-

lantic flight took off from St. John's.

During World War II, a United States army and navy base and a Canadian air base were established just north of the city. The principal United States army base in Newfoundland was at Argentia, across the Avalon Peninsula.

ST. JOHN'S, NEWFOUNDLAND. Population (1973 estimate) 131,814. Capital of Newfoundland. Settled about 1600.

St. Laurent, Louis Stephen

Louis Stephen St. Laurent is the name of a Canadian lawyer and statesman who became Prime Minister of Canada. He was born in 1882 in Quebec Province, and when he grew up he became a lawyer and practiced in the city of Quebec. He was very successful, and was president for a time of the Canadian Bar Assocation. In 1941 he was Minister of Justice and Attorney General under Prime Minister Mackenzie King, and later he became Minister of External Affairs (similar to the United States post of Secretary of State). In 1948 he was chosen to succeed Mackenzie King as leader of the Liberal Party and as Prime Minister. He resigned in 1957.

Saint Lawrence River

The St. Lawrence is one of the important rivers of North America. It is the outlet of the Great Lakes to the Atlantic Ocean. It flows from the east end of Lake Ontario for 744 miles to the Gulf of St. Lawrence, which is an arm of the Atlantic Ocean. For 114 miles the St. Lawrence forms the international boundary between the United States and Canada. The rest of the river is in Canadian territory.

In the St. Lawrence, not far from Lake Ontario, are the THOUSAND ISLANDS, about which there is a separate article. Below the islands are the International Rapids, where the river falls sharply for about 25 miles. This section is not navigable and has been by-passed by canals for shipping. In several places the river widens to form lakes. It flows past Montreal, the biggest city on the St. Lawrence, and Quebec. Near Quebec, mountains rise on both sides of the river. At its mouth, the river is 90 miles wide.

The St. Lawrence Valley is an important source of lumber and is the site of big paper mills. The river provides hydroelectric power for these plants. Many great bridges cross the St. Lawrence.

The St. Lawrence was discovered in 1535 by Jacques Cartier. It was an important route for missionaries and fur traders in pioneer days. It has been important for heavy shipping for many years. During much of this time the United States and Canada discussed the construction of a St. Lawrence Seaway that would make the river navigable for ocean-going ships all the way up to and through the Great Lakes. In 1954 the United States Congress agreed to join Canada in construction of the seaway and it was opened in 1959.

Saint Louis

St. Louis, the largest city of Missouri, is on the Mississippi River. St. Louis is a major transportation center, reached

The St. Louis Arch, with the domed Old Courthouse in the background.

by more than twenty railroads, river shipping lines, airlines, and many highways. The city extends for nineteen miles along the Mississippi.

About 750,000 people live in St. Louis—about two million with the suburbs included. The city is one of the world's biggest fur markets and is important in the handling of livestock, grain, wool, and lumber. There are big meatpacking plants, breweries, and distilleries, and factories that make chemicals, drugs, shoes, machinery, airplanes, railroad cars, and many other things.

The city is the seat of St. Louis University, Washington University, Concordia Theological Seminary, two teachers' colleges, and schools of music and pharmacy. The St. Louis Symphony Orchestra is one of the oldest in the United States. Forest Park is the second-largest public park in the United States and is the site of the country's largest municipal theater. Also in Forest Park is a notable art museum and the Jefferson Memorial Building. There are many historic landmarks and buildings.

St. Louis was founded in 1764 as a French fur-trading post. It was named for King Louis IX of France. It was sold to the United States in 1803 as part of the Louisiana Purchase. The period of St. Louis' greatest growth began about 1817 when the first river steamer docked. By 1850 a large number of German immigrants had settled in St. Louis, and in the following ten years the city more than doubled its population. In 1904 the Louisiana Purchase Exposition (which people called the St. Louis World's Fair) drew hundreds of thousands of visitors.

In 1966 St. Louis neared completion of a distinguished rebuilding plan that changed its rundown waterfront district from slums to an assemblage of architectural beauties and parks.

ST. LOUIS, MISSOURI. Population (1970 census) 622,236. On the Mississippi River.

Saint Paul

St. Paul is the capital of Minnesota and the second-largest city of the state. It is in the eastern part of the state, lying on both sides of the Mississippi River. It adjoins Minneapolis, the state's largest city, and together they are called the "Twin Cities." St. Paul is a commercial, industrial and transportation center.

More than 309,000 people live in St. Paul. There are large meat-packing and dairy plants, and factories that make many other products. St. Paul is a distributing center for the agricultural and other products of the entire Northwest.

Among St. Paul's distinctive buildings is the state capitol, with its great dome copied from St. Peter's Church in Rome. There are several colleges. The University of Minnesota is between the Twin Cities and its agricultural college is in St. Paul. Fort Snelling, a pioneer military outpost and now a military training camp, is just outside the city.

The site of St. Paul was bought from the Sioux Indians in 1805 and was settled by hunters and fur traders. In 1841 Father Lucien Galtier built a church called St. Paul's, and the settlement was named for it. It became the capital of the Louisiana Territory in 1849 and state capital in 1858 when Minnesota was admitted to the Union.

ST. PAUL, MINNESOTA. Population (1970 census) 309,980. Capital of Minnesota. County seat of Ramsey County. On the Mississippi River. Settled about 1800.

Saint Pierre and Miquelon

St. Pierre and Miquelon is an island group off the southern coast of the province of Newfoundland, Canada. It consists of the islands of Grande Miquelon, Petite Miquelon, St. Pierre (with the capital city of St. Pierre), and several tiny islands. Together they form a French territory with a total area of 93 square miles. More than 4,000 people live there.

The islands are near the great fishing grounds of the Grand Banks, and the processing of fish is the principal industry. Almost nothing can grow on the rocky islands, so that everything the people need has to be imported. The territory is governed by an administrator assisted by a council. It sends representatives to the French Parliament in Paris, France.

Saint-Saëns, Camille

Charles Camille Saint-Saëns was a French musician and composer, or writer  of original music. He was born in 1835. At the age of 10 he gave his first public piano recital. He also studied the organ, and was for almost twenty years the organist at a famous Paris church, the Madeleine. But by far his greatest fame came from the music he wrote. His best-known compositions include the opera *Samson and Delilah*, his Third Symphony, and such works for orchestra as *The Carnival of the Animals* and *Danse Macabre* (supposed to be a dance of ghosts and goblins). He died in 1921.

Saint Vitus's dance

St. Vitus's dance is a nervous disease of children. It makes a person's body move in jerks, as if he were having a fit. The medical name of the disease is *chorea*. It happens mostly between the ages of 7 and 14, and girls have it much more often than boys. It is often a sign of another very serious sickness called rheumatic fever.

Chorea is caused by damage to a small part of the brain that controls the muscles of the body. This part of the brain has nothing to do with thinking. Children who have chorea can think and do things as well as other children, except when the sickness is troubling them, which is about six to ten weeks a year, usually in the spring. During the sickness the child often has fever and poor appetite and sometimes vomits. His feelings change very quickly, so that he may laugh, cry, and be fretful, all in the space of a few minutes. Sometimes the jerky motions become so wild that he must be held to keep him from getting hurt. Doctors and parents help the sick child by putting him to bed in a quiet room, giving him massages and long warm baths, and doing other things to relax his muscles. He may also be given a medicine to help quiet his nerves. It is important for the child to be treated gently, with friendship, and to keep him away from all noise and excitement. The sickness usually goes away after several seasons.

Sakhalin

Sakhalin is a long, narrow island north of Japan. It belongs to Soviet Russia. The island has an area of almost 30,000 square miles, and about 900,000 people live there. Sakhalin has two mountain ranges along its shores, divided by a valley through which flow the Tym and Poronai rivers. The climate is cold, with an average temperature near freezing. Most of the people are fishermen, and fish is their main food. However, the people grow grains, potatoes, vegetables, and sugar beets. Coal and oil are produced. More than half of Sakhalin is forests, and lumbering is an important industry. The capital and chief city is Alexandrovsk.

Sakhalin was discovered in 1644 by a Russian explorer. In the Russian-Japanese War of 1904, Japan seized the southern part of Sakhalin and renamed it Karafuto. After World War II the entire island returned to Russian control.

Saladin

Saladin was a great warrior and sultan (king) who lived about eight hundred years ago. He is famous as the leader of Mohammedan armies that fought against Christian forces led by King Richard of England, in the Third Crusade for possession of the Holy Land.

Saladin was born in 1138, in Mesopotamia (which is now Iraq). He was a member of a people called Kurds. He lived for a number of years in Damascus, the capital of Syria, where he studied the Mohammedan religion and fought in campaigns against Egypt. The Syrians conquered the Egyptian rulers, and later Saladin ruled as sultan of Egypt and also of Syria. He won many new territories and united all the Mohammedan peoples in a great war against the Christian Crusaders who came to capture the holy city of Jerusalem.

The story of the battles between the Crusaders and the armies of Saladin (called *Saracens* by the Christians) is told in Sir Walter Scott's novel, *The Talisman*. Saladin is said to have been a chivalrous soldier, merciful and just to his enemies. Neither the Saracens nor the Crusaders could win a clear victory, and the Third Crusade ended with Saladin giving the Crusaders a strip of land along the coast of Palestine and free entry to Jerusalem. Saladin died in 1193.

salamander

The salamander is an amphibian, an animal that lives part of its life on land and part in the water. (You can read about AMPHIBIANS in a separate article.) The salamander is not a very attractive animal. It looks somewhat like a lizard except that it has a soft body and a smooth skin, which is moist and slimy. Salamanders are found in almost every part of the world where the climate is not too hot. Salamanders spend their lives in ponds and streams and in underground caves and wells.

The salamander always has a tail. If it loses its tail or one of its legs it can grow a new one. Some salamanders breathe through gills and others breathe with lungs. Some salamanders have neither gills nor lungs and they breathe through their skins. Salamanders eat insects and other tiny creatures that live in damp places or in the water.

There are many different kinds of salamander. The pygmy salamander, which is found in the eastern part of the United States, is only about an inch long, while the giant salamander of China and Japan grows to be about five feet long. The people of China and Japan eat the flesh of this salamander.

Salazar

Antonio de Oliveira Salazar is the name of a Portuguese statesman who became Prime Minister and actual ruler of Portugal. He was born in a Portuguese village named Vimeiro in 1889, and was graduated from the University of Coimbra, where he later became professor of economics. In 1921 he was elected to the Portuguese parliament, but he was so disappointed with political life that he soon returned to teaching. In 1926 he was appointed Minister of Finance in the government of General Carmona, but he resigned when he found that his advice was not followed. Two years later he was recalled, and he returned on the condition that he would be allowed to have his own way.

In 1932, Salazar became Prime Minister and Minister of Finance. He was responsible for having the new Portuguese constitution of 1933 put in effect, and this gave him complete power for 35 more years. In July, 1970 after a severe illness of nearly two years, he died thinking that he was still the Prime Minister. Because of his illness, he was never told that he had been replaced by Marcello Caetano in 1968.

Salem

Salem is the capital of Oregon and the second-largest city of the state. It is in the northwest part of the state, on the Willamette River about 50 miles from Portland. About 70,000 people live in Salem. It is a marketing center for the rich farm land that surrounds it. The region is noted for its long-fiber flax, and Salem's industries include linen and paper mills. Others are canneries, packing houses, ironworks, and sawmills.

Willamette University is in Salem. Other schools include state institutions for the blind and deaf. The state capitol was built in 1939 to replace an earlier building that was destroyed by fire.

Salem was founded in 1834 by Jason Lee, a Methodist missionary. It was made the capital in 1860. The following year the city was largely destroyed by a flood of the Willamette. Salem's rapid growth began in 1871 with the coming of the railroad.

SALEM, OREGON. Population (1970 census) 68,296. Capital of Oregon. County seat of Marion County. On the Willamette River. Founded 1834.

Salem, Massachusetts, is one of the oldest cities in the United States. It was founded in 1626, and some of its oldest buildings are still standing. Salem is on the Atlantic Ocean and for many years was the center of shipbuilding and the home port of trading and fishing ships. Salem is also famous for its trials of women for WITCHCRAFT, about which there is a separate article. The 1970 population of Salem was 40,556.

Salerno

Salerno is a city on the west coast of Italy, at the head of the Gulf of Salerno. It is an industrial and railroad center and a seaport. About 110,000 people live there. Salerno is the seat of a cathedral that was built more than 1,100 years ago. During the Middle Ages, one of the world's great medical schools was in Salerno. During World War II, Salerno was a landing point for Allied troops invading Italy and was the scene of a great battle in which the city was damaged.

salesmanship

Salesmanship is the skillful presenting of something that is for sale to someone who has a reason to buy it. About four and a half million men and women in the United States work as salesmen. They have one of the most useful of all occupations. If there were no salesmen, stores and factories would have to spend billions of dollars more to find the goods and supplies they need. Nearly everything in the world would cost more.

The salesman has many advantages in the business world. He can find a job, or keep his job, when he would be considered too old for many kinds of work. In hundreds of selling jobs, the opportunities are as great for women as for men. Salesmen and sales executives usually make more money than employees in other departments of the same company.

There are two main branches of selling work. One is retail selling. More than two and a half million sales workers in the United States are retail salesmen. Many of them are sales clerks in stores. Others call on customers in their homes or offices. All of them sell to the *consumer*, the person who is actually going to use the merchandise.

Almost two million of the sales workers in the United States are wholesale salesmen. Their customers buy for business purposes. The customers may be stores that are going to resell the merchandise, or factories that are going to use it in making other products.

In either branch of selling, the salesman may be paid by salaries, by commissions, or by a combination of the two. A salaried salesman receives the same pay every week, no matter how much or how little he sells. The commission salesman receives a percentage—some number of cents out of every dollar's worth of goods he sells.

QUALITIES OF A SALESMAN

The first and most important thing that a salesman needs is knowledge of the product he is selling. In some fields, salesmen even need college training in engineering, chemistry, or some other scientific subject. Such salesmen are often called *sales engineers*. In most fields it is not necessary to have technical training of this kind, though salesmen of insurance and of many manufactured products must have a great deal of special information before they can begin to sell. In any kind of selling, the salesman should spend much of his time studying his own products, the products of his competitors (other companies that sell the same kind of thing), and the needs of his customers. He should read the trade journals (publications dealing with his kind of business) and should talk to other salesmen and exchange information with them.

The second thing a salesman needs is willingness to work. A salesman often has a great deal of personal freedom. It is up to him to decide how many hours he should work each day. Successful salesmen work at least as long and as steadily as they would if they were keeping regular hours in an office or factory.

It is a salesman's job to give "good service" to his customers. In wholesale selling this includes following up every order to make sure the merchandise is shipped to the customer and that it arrives and is satisfactory. In retail selling it includes trying to understand what the customer actually needs and will find most useful, and then showing or suggesting that product.

A salesman must do everything possible to be on friendly terms with his customers. This does not mean that the salesman must flatter the customer, but it is good salesmanship as well as good manners to be courteous at all times, whenever possible, and to avoid arguments that might lead to hard feelings.

Salk, Jonas

Dr. Jonas Edward Salk is the name of the American scientist who developed the first vaccine against the disease poliomyelitis (polio). He was born in New York City in 1914 and attended college and medical school there. He developed the anti-polio vaccine in 1953 while he was a research professor at the University of Pittsburg.

salmon

The salmon is one of the most valuable and also one of the most fascinating of all fish. Although scientists have spent much time studying the habits of the salmon, there are still many things they do not know about it. Some salmon live in the Atlantic Ocean off the coasts of Europe, and other kinds of salmon live in the Pacific Ocean. All salmon spend part of their lives in fresh-water rivers, where the females lay their eggs, and some salmon never leave the fresh-water rivers.

The Atlantic salmon weighs about 20 pounds and is dark-red in color when it is full-grown. The young salmon is bluish-gray in color. Salmon are always born in fresh-water rivers; then they begin a long journey to the sea. Once they reach the sea, they feed on fish and shellfish, and soon grow big and fat. Then the full-grown salmon starts its long trip back to the river in which it was born. The salmon is a swift swimmer; its rate of speed is possibly as high as 65 miles in a single day.

Once the salmon reaches fresh water, it usually takes no food, although it may have to travel as long as a year to reach the river in which it was born.

When a female salmon reaches the place where it was born, it is ready to lay its eggs. (This is called *spawning*.) It first builds a nest, which is called a "redd." To do this the female lashes its tail, pushing sand and gravel out where the stream can wash it away. Gradually the nest grows deep. The male watches the female work and fights off other males. When the nest is deep enough (this may take several days) the female lays the eggs. When some of the eggs are laid, the female moves a few feet away and begins to lash around on the bottom again and to dig up sand and gravel and cover the eggs with it. When all of the eggs are covered the female moves upstream and makes another nest and lays some more eggs. The female may make several nests before all the eggs are laid. Most females do not lay eggs more than once in their lives. (Salmon that never leave fresh-water rivers lay eggs more often.)

One kind of salmon that makes its home in the Pacific Ocean is the red, or sockeye, salmon. Fishermen who live on the west coast of the United States and in Alaska catch millions of pounds of salmon every year. Most of it is canned and some of it is eaten fresh.

The sockeye salmon is a green or grayish color when it is young. When it reaches its full size it becomes a deep red color and has a green head. The female of the Pacific salmon always dies after the eggs are laid.

There are not as many salmon as there once were. Millions of young salmon have died because great man-made dams have prevented them from reaching the sea and have made it impossible for the females to return to the spot where they can lay their eggs. Men have built special channels for the salmon but still many have died.

The salmon is such a valuable food fish that men have brought the salmon to many rivers and lakes where none existed. Now there are salmon in Maine and Pennsylvania and other places in the eastern parts of the United States.

Salome

Salome was a girl whose story is told in the Bible. Her mother, Herodias, was the wife of Herod Antipas, king of Galilee, the land where Jesus was born. Herod had imprisoned John the Baptist, the prophet who baptized Jesus. The Gospels of Mark and Matthew tell how Herod promised Salome anything she wished if she would dance for him. Salome danced and then asked for the head of John the Baptist. Herod kept his promise and had the prophet put to death.

The story of Salome was used in a poem by Oscar Wilde, and the poem was made into an opera called *Salome* by Richard Strauss, a German composer. *Salome* was first produced in 1905. At first it was unpopular because of its unpleasant subject and its strange, clashing music. In the opera, Herod is so horrified at what Salome has forced him to do that he has her put to death.

Salomon, Haym

Haym Salomon was an American patriot during the Revolutionary War. He was born in Poland more than two hundred years ago, about 1740, and settled in America just before the war, becoming a merchant in New York City. When the war broke out he worked as a spy for the Americans. He was once captured and condemned to death by the British, but escaped. He handled many of the money arrangements between the American and other governments, mainly the French. This work made it possible for the colonists to go on fighting. After the war he continued to help by lending his own money to the United States government, and also by personally aiding many of its leaders, including Thomas Jefferson and James Madison. Salomon gave and lent so much money to the government and its leaders that when he died in 1785 he had almost none left.

salt

Salt is one of the most important and most useful chemicals in the world. Human beings and other forms of animal life need salt to stay alive. It has hundreds of other uses in manufacturing, chemistry, and various industries.

Blood must contain salt. The blood of human beings and many animals has as much as 3½ parts of salt in every 100 parts of the whole blood. We get this much salt into our blood by the small amounts of salt that are already in the meat that we eat and that cooks add to other food they cook. We also add small amounts of salt to certain foods before we eat them. Some animals, such as cattle and deer and antelopes, which eat only grass and leaves and other vegetable matter, do not get enough salt in their food. Throughout the world where such ani-

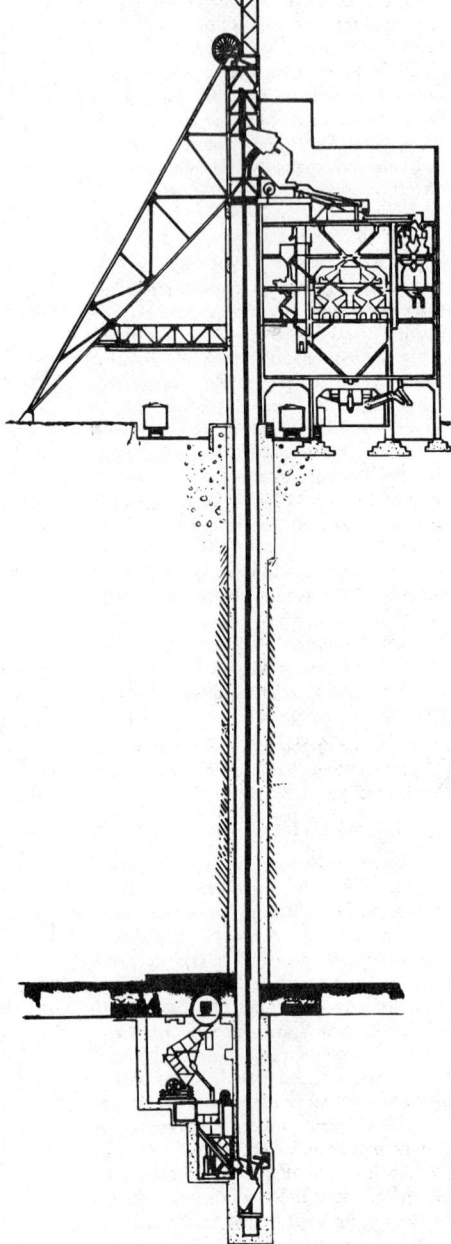

Rock salt is mined like other minerals. The solid salt is cut from the mine in large lumps. These are brought to the head of the shaft, where they are crushed, screened and graded according to use, for anything from seasoning to melting ice.

mals live in a wild state there are "salt licks" where large deposits of salt are exposed by nature and the animals can go now and then to lick the salt and supply what their blood needs. On farms, animals are given large blocks of salt that they can lick when they need it.

When there is less than enough salt in the blood, a person's blood pressure becomes lower. Because of this, doctors often prescribe "salt-free" or "low-salt" diets to patients whose blood pressure is too high or who are overweight. If the salt in the blood becomes much lower than it should be, a person may faint, or lose consciousness. This often happens in a heat stroke, or heat prostration. Perspiration, or sweat, contains, salt, about 1 part in 100. This is much less salt than blood contains, but heavy perspiration caused by heat can still carry off more salt than the body can afford to lose, and a heat stroke may be the result. People in hot and humid climates, or people whose work makes them prespire a lot, such as workers in steel mills or in mines or tunnels, often take "salt tablets." These tablets are about three-quarters salt and one-quarter sugar (to give them more energy). Workers in many British coal mines put salt instead of sugar in their coffee.

Salt will dissolve in water, and water with salt dissolved in it is called brine. More than 25 pounds of salt can be dissolved in 100 pounds of water, but most brine has far less salt than this in it. Sea water, which is "salt water," has only about 2 pounds of salt to 100 pounds of water.

When we drink salt water, the body does not absorb the water and it passes through us, acting as a cathartic. Partly for this reason (but also because of other minerals in it), sea water is not drinkable. Epsom salts and other mineral salts, used as cathartics, are different chemicals from common table salt, however.

The chemical name for table salt is *sodium chloride*. It is made of sodium and chlorine, two of the chemical elements of which all things in the world are made. Salt is a mineral, and mineralogists call it *halite*. Salt always forms in crystals—small pieces with smooth, flat sides or faces. Dissolve salt in water and let the water evaporate, and the crystals can be seen to form again. Under a microscope and even under a strong magnifying glass, the form of the crystals can be seen clearly.

Salt has a taste all its own. It is one of the four "primary tastes," along with sweet, sour, and bitter. That is, we can taste salt even when our noses are stopped up and we cannot "taste" things that we usually taste with our sense of smell. Most foods seem tasteless without some salt in them.

USES OF SALT

Besides its use as food, salt is important in making ice, preserving meat and other foods, making soap, cooling metals, tanning leather, and in many other ways.

In almost all these uses, brine and not solid salt is used. One familiar use of solid salt is in making ice melt (an example of which is in a home ice-cream freezer). Meat that is salted will resist spoiling much longer than unsalted meat. This is

because bacteria that attack the meat are not able to grow where there is salt. Most salted meats, such as ham and corned beef, are soaked in brine, but meats can be preserved in homes by placing them between layers of solid salt. Many pickles are made by soaking them in brine.

The salt used in manufacturing does not have to be as pure as the salt used in food; that is, it may contain more minerals of other kinds. Such minerals are often found in the salt when it is first mined, and are called impurities. For use in food, most of the impurities are removed.

PRODUCTION OF SALT

More than 25,000,000 tons of salt are produced in the United States every year. Salt exists in vast underground deposits in many parts of the United States. Nearly all salt for use is taken from these deposits. In spite of the great supply of salt in sea water, most salt is taken from other sources. The salt in sea water is very impure (contains many other minerals). Salt found underground is usually much more nearly pure.

In many cases, salt is mined just as coal is. Men working in underground mines cut out blocks of salt, which are carried to the surface. Some salt deposits are hundreds of feet thick and cover miles of underground area. A few are so close to the surface of the earth that salt can be dug out like rock from a quarry. Salt that is taken from the earth in solid blocks is called *rock salt*. It is used mostly in manufacturing.

Table salt usually comes from wells that are sunk far into the earth. The well is drilled into the deposit of salt. Water is sent down through the well. The salt is allowed to dissolve in the water, making brine. This brine is pumped up to the surface again and is put in great pans. The water evaporates, leaving the salt. Salt obtained in this way has far fewer impurities than rock salt. This is because most of the other minerals in the salt deposit do not dissolve in the water. More than half the salt produced in the United States— about fifteen million tons each year—is made by the brine process.

Salten, Felix

Felix Salten was a Hungarian writer of stories and plays. He is best-known for some of his books for children, among them *Bambi* and *Bambi's Son*, stories about a deer called Bambi. These stories have been translated into many languages and made into motion pictures. Salten's real name was Felix Salzmann. He was born in 1869 and died in 1945.

Salt Lake City

Salt Lake City is the capital of Utah and the largest city of the state. It is in northern Utah on the Jordan River, which flows into Great Salt Lake about ten miles from the city. Salt Lake City lies on the lower slopes of the Wasatch Mountains, with a view of the Salt Lake Valley below and mountain peaks above. The climate is dry and healthful, with moderate temperatures. The city is a major commercial, transportation and cultural center.

Nearly 200,000 people live in Salt Lake City. There are factories that manufacture iron, steel, and petroleum prod-

ucts, coke and textiles, and many other products. Mines near Salt Lake City produce copper, silver, lead, zinc, coal, and iron, and these minerals are refined in smelters in the city. The surrounding region is rich farm land.

Salt Lake City was founded in 1847 by Mormons under the leadership of Brigham Young. From its founding it was the leading city of Utah, and it became the state capital in 1896. Among the points of interest are the Mormon Tabernacle, the Brigham Young Monument where the founder is buried, and Fort Douglas, one of the nation's oldest

Salt Lake City, capital of Utah, is also the great center of the Mormon religion. The Mormon Temple is a main feature.

military posts, now an Air Force base. The city is the seat of the University of Utah, the College of St. Mary-of-the-Wasatch, and the McCune School of Music and Art.

SALT LAKE CITY, UTAH. Population (1970 census) 175,885. Capital of Utah. County seat of Salt Lake County. On the Jordan River. Founded, 1847.

saltpeter, another name for niter: see the article NITROGEN.

Salvation Army

The Salvation Army is a religious and charitable organization that tries to convert and to help people, especially those who do not belong to any Christian Church. It was founded in 1865 in London, England, by William BOOTH, about whom there is a separate article. At first it was called the Christian Mission, but then its name was changed to Salvation Army and it was organized as an army is, with privates and officers. Members wear uniforms. The head of the organization is called the General. The first American branch was founded in 1880 in Pennsylvania, and other branches were set up all over the world. The Salvation Army operates settlements and homes for the poor, nurseries, and similar projects. In 1972, it had nearly 332,000 members in the United States.

Salween River

The Salween River is one of the great rivers in southeast Asia. It is about 1,750 miles long. The Salween rises in Tibet and flows south through China and Burma, emptying into the Andaman Sea, a branch of the Indian Ocean. The river is navigable for only about 75 miles above its mouth. In its lower course it forms part of the border between Burma and Thailand. The river is very important in irrigation. The upper Salween is crossed by the Burma Road, on which supplies moved to Allied forces in China during World War II.

Samaria

Samaria was a city of ancient Palestine. It was made the capital of the kingdom of Israel nearly three thousand years ago, about 900 B.C. Its people were called the Samaritans, and today we remember them mostly because a Samaritan figured in one of the best-known parables told by Jesus. (You can read the story in the article PARABLE.) Samaria was conquered by the Assyrians, who sent many of its people to be slaves. Because the Samaritans were a conquered people, they were considered inferior by the Hebrews and other peoples. Samaria (renamed *Sebaste*) is now a small village in the country of Jordan.

Samoa

Samoa is a group of islands in the South Pacific Ocean, about 2,500 miles east of Australia. The islands are divided into two groups: American Samoa, an unincorporated territory of the United States since 1900 when William McKinley was President; and the Independent State of Western Samoa, which includes the large islands of Savaii, Upolu,

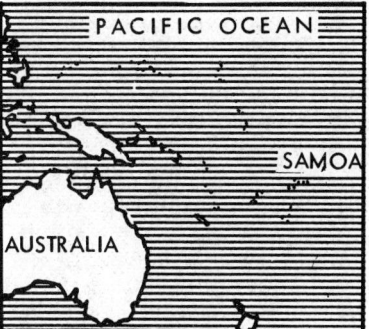

Apolima, Manono, and four uninhabited islets. American Samoa includes Tutuila, Aunuu, the Manua group, Swains Island, and the uninhabited Rose Island.

The Samoan islands are mountainous. The climate is mild, with alternating wet and dry seasons, and hurricanes are frequent. The people of Samoa are POLYNESIANS, about whom there is a separate article. They are tall and light-skinned. They have long been known as great warriors and sailors, and they are highly skilled in handcrafts, especially the manufacture of *tapa,* a cloth made from the bark of the paper mulberry tree. Most Samoans are farmers, raising breadfruit, cacao, pineapples, oranges, bananas, taro and yams. The islands also have rubber, hardwood, and coconut trees, and the chief export is copra from the coconut trees. The islands were discovered in 1722 by Dutch explorers.

American Samoa has an area of 76 square miles and a population of 20,051. Pagopago, on Tutuila Island, is the principal port. For many years it was the headquarters of a United States naval command that governed the American islands. In 1951 American Samoa was put under civilian control.

Western Samoa has an area of 1,133 square miles and a population of 113,500. The chief port is Apia, on the island of Upolu. Western Samoa belonged to Germany until the end of World War I, when it was placed under the control of New Zealand by the League of Nations.

Samson

Samson was a Hebrew hero told about in the Bible. He was the strongest man in the world. Before Samson's birth an angel appeared to his mother and told her never to cut her son's hair because it would give him the strength of many men.

When Samson was grown he married a woman of the Philistine people, in spite of the fact that they were great enemies of the Hebrews. Then Samson went away for a time, and while he was away his wife's father gave her in marriage to another man. When Samson returned he burned the fields of the Philistines in revenge, and later he killed a thousand Philistines with the jawbone of an ass.

After this, Samson fell in love with a woman named Delilah, who had been sent by the Philistines to betray him. She teased him until he told her that the secret of his great strength was in his hair, and one night while he was asleep she had it cut off. Samson was then easily captured by the Philistines, who put out his eyes and chained him and forced him to work turning a grindstone in their city of Gaza. The Philistines showed him off at feasts and mocked and tormented him. But they failed to notice that his hair was growing again, and one day when he was being shown to the people during a Philistine festival, Samson pulled down the pillars of the house. The building collapsed, killing him and more than three thousand Philistines.

The story of Samson was made into an opera, *Samson and Delilah,* by the French composer Camille Saint-Saens. Samson was also the subject of a poetic play, *Samson Agonistes,* by the English poet John Milton.

Samuel

Samuel was a great leader of the Jewish people and the last of the judges. A judge in the Old Testament is a man raised up by God to guide the Jewish people in time of danger.

When Samuel was 12 years old he was dedicated to the Lord. Twenty years later he led the Jewish army to a victory over their greatest enemies, the Philistines. In his old age, Samuel was asked by the people to make someone king, and he appointed Saul, the first king of Israel. Later, when Saul showed that he was unworthy, Samuel made David the king. Saul persecuted David. After Samuel died, Saul had a vision of him and realized that he had been doing wrong.

The two books of Samuel in the Old Testament are named for this great leader, although only the early chapters of the first book tell Samuel's story.

samurai

The samurai were a Japanese warrior class, just as the knights were once the special warrior class of Europe. About a thousand years ago there was a special code of conduct for the samurai warriors.

Like knights, the samurai served one of the great Japanese lords.

A member of the samurai had to be well-trained in the use of weapons. His special weapon was a long, curved sword that was finely engraved. The samurai were very skillful in the use of this sword and also were good shots with a bow and arrow.

A samurai had to be courteous and had to be obedient to his lord. He had to devote his life to his country. A samurai was well taken care of by his lord but was not interested in making money. Above all, a samurai had to have honor and courage. If his honor was stained, even though there might seem good reason for it, a samurai had to take his own life.

The way in which he took his own life, or committed suicide was by HARA-KIRI, about which there is a separate article. Even to this day, hara-kiri has been used by people in Japan as a means of committing suicide.

During World War II the word *samurai* was often used to describe the regular officers in the Japanese army and navy. Some of these men committed hara-kiri rather than be captured. Actually, the samurai code had been almost forgotten in Japan in the last century. Since the end of World War II the meaning of the samurai has once more come to be almost forgotten.

San Antonio

San Antonio is the third-largest city in Texas. It is in the south central part of the state, on the San Antonio River. San Antonio is one of the oldest cities in Texas. It is a manufacturing center and a winter tourist resort, and is the site of the Alamo where heroic Texans were massacred by Mexican forces in 1836. The San Antonio River winds through the center of the city, flowing 15 miles to cover six city blocks. It is spanned by many bridges. One of the largest military installations in the country is at San Antonio, including Fort Sam Houston, Brooke Medical Center, and four Air Force bases—Brooks, Kelly, Lackland and Randolph Fields. The city is a foreign trade zone for commerce with Mexico.

More than six hundred thousand people live in San Antonio. An important business is the shipping and handling of cattle, wool, cotton, farm produce, fruit and nuts from the surrounding region, and oil-refining. San Antonio was founded in 1691 by a Spanish priest.

SAN ANTONIO, TEXAS. Population (1970 census) 654,153. Third-largest city in Texas. County seat of Bexar County. Settled in 1691.

sand, a gritty, yellowish substance made up of rock and silica that have been broken up: see the articles ROCK and SILICA.

sandalwood

The sandalwood is a tree that grows in southern Asia. Its wood has an odor that is displeasing to insects but pleasant to human beings. For this reason, sandalwood is sometimes used to line chests and boxes in which clothing or blankets are stored. The wood is soft and easily carved.

Sandburg, Carl

Carl Sandburg is the name of an American poet and historian. His poems

The San Diego Stadium seats 50,000 people.

celebrate the roughness and the beauty of the young American nation. Sandburg also wrote a biography of Abraham Lincoln for which he was awarded the Pulitzer Prize, and *Abe Lincoln Grows Up* and other books for young readers.

Sandburg was born in 1878 in Galesburg, Illinois. He had little formal education, spending his youth and early manhood working at various jobs on farms and in towns. He fought in the Spanish American War and then used his mustering-out pay to attend Lombard College in Galesburg. In 1912 he moved to Chicago, where his poetry first began to be published.

These first poems, later collected as *Chicago Poems,* shocked many people. Sandburg wrote in the language of the Midwest, in verse without any rhyme. He wrote about hoboes and farmhands and working people. He called Chicago "Hog Butcher for the World." Gradually his poems became popular. In 1951 Sandburg received another Pulitzer Prize for his *Complete Poems.*

Sandburg also wrote books for children, among them the *Rootabaga Stories.* He collected American folk songs which he sang and played on his guitar, and wrote one novel, *Remembrance Rock,* published in 1948. He died in 1967.

San Diego

San Diego is the third-largest city in California. It is on the southern coast of the state, on the San Diego River and San Diego Bay on the Pacific Ocean, about 17 miles north of the Mexican border. The city is a popular winter resort for swimming and game-fishing. It has the most even temperature in the United States. San Diego is an important transportation and industrial center. It has the biggest fleet of tuna-fishing boats in the country, and their catch supports six packing plants in the city.

More than half a million people live in San Diego and its suburbs. There is a big airplane industry in and near the city. San Diego has one of the best natural harbors in the United States. It is the seat of important Navy and Marine bases and training schools.

The first permanent settlement at San Diego was established in 1769. From 1825 to 1830 the city was the capital of Upper and Lower California. In 1850 it was established as a United States city. In 1915 the Panama-California Exposi-

tion was held in Balboa Park to celebrate the opening of the Panama Canal. This park is one of the city's most popular spots, with museums, art galleries, a zoo, and an open-air auditorium.

SAN DIEGO, CALIFORNIA. Population (1970 census) 696,769. County seat of San Diego County. On San Diego Bay. Founded in 1769.

sandpiper

Sandpipers are birds that make their homes in the northern parts of the world, especially in arctic regions where the climate is cold. Sandpipers travel to southern shores during the winter. The sandpiper was given its name because of its piping call and because it spends most of its time on the sandy shores of oceans.

Some sandpipers are small birds no larger than sparrows. Others are about a foot high. They are graceful birds with long, thin legs. They have long bills that are useful when they search for small crabs and insects in shallow water. Sandpipers are usually brown, white, and gray. The sandpiper builds a rather simple nest with soft grass. The female lays four eggs that are pointed at one end.

One of the best known sandpipers in the United States is the woodcock. Unlike most sandpipers, the woodcock does not live along shores.

sandstone, see the article ROCK.

San Francisco

San Francisco is the second-largest city of California and the 13th-largest in the United States. It is on a narrow, hilly peninsula (arm of land) that separates the Pacific Ocean from San Francisco Bay, one of the world's great harbors. To the north of San Francisco is the Golden Gate, the entrance to the bay, which is spanned by the famous Golden Gate Bridge. The city is joined to Oakland (fourth-largest city of the state) by the San Francisco-Oakland Bridge, one of the longest bridges in the world. San Francisco is the center of a group of cities, including Oakland Berkeley, Alameda, Richmond, Vallejo, Sausalito, and many others. It is the financial center of the West and the commercial and distribution center for much of California and the Pacific Coast. It is the site of the Presidio, a large military reservation.

There are a number of islands in San Francisco Bay, among them Yerba Buena,

a United States lighthouse depot; Treasure Island, a man-made island built for the Golden Gate International Exposition, a world's fair held in 1939 (the island was made a naval base during World War II); Alcatraz, once a United States prison for dangerous criminals; and Angel Island, an immigration station.

About 715,600 people live in San Francisco. A large proportion of them were born in countries other than the United States. San Francisco has a large Chinese population. There are many kinds of work for the people of San Francisco. The city is a great importing center and ships come from all over the world. Among the city's industries, the refining of oil is very important. Others are shipbuilding, canning and processing of foods, and the manufacture of many products. The San Francisco Stock Exchange is important and the city is the insurance center of the West.

San Francisco is built on a number of hills. Many of its streets are very steep, and others tunnel through hills. In the main business section of the city is the Civic Center, a group of public buildings that includes the City Hall, Civic Auditorium, courthouses, public library, and the Opera House, home of the only city-owned opera in the United States and of the San Francisco Symphony Orchestra. Chinatown, the largest Chinese settlement in America, is also in San Francisco.

The Embarcadero is a long street of wharves and docks running along the bay front. Telegraph Hill is the site of the "Latin Quarter," home of artists and foreign colonies. Nob Hill was once the home of millionaires. Along the ocean shore are many resorts and beaches and the city's largest park, Golden Gate Park. The park includes museums of art and natural history and an aquarium. Mount Davidson Park is the site of the Easter Cross, a 100-foot cross of concrete and steel, where there is an outdoor Easter sunrise service each year.

San Francisco is the seat of several branches of the University of California, the University of San Francisco, the school of medicine of Stanford University, and San Francisco State College.

San Francisco was founded in 1776. The city belonged to Mexico until 1846, when it was taken by the United States and named San Francisco. In 1848 it was a town of about 800 people. Then gold was discovered in California, and two years later the city had a population of 25,000.

During the Gold Rush days, San Francisco was a lawless and violent city. A section called the Barbary Coast became famous for crime. Vigilante committees were formed and the people took the law into their own hands, hanging many people without trial.

In 1906 an earthquake and fire devastated the city, killing hundreds of people. The Panama-Pacific Exposition celebrated the opening of the Panama Canal in 1915.

The San Francisco–Oakland Bay Bridge was opened in 1936 and the Golden Gate Bridge in 1937. The conference that drafted the charter of the United Nations was held in San Francisco in 1945, and the peace treaty with Japan was signed there in 1951.

SAN FRANCISCO, CALIFORNIA. Population (1970 census) 715,674. Forms San Francisco County. On San Francisco Bay. Founded in 1776.

San Francisco Conference, a meeting held at San Francisco, California, in 1945, where the charter of the United Nations was written: see the article UNITED NATIONS.

Sanhedrin

In the days of the ancient Hebrews, more than two thousand years ago, the Sanhedrin was their court of justice in the city of Jerusalem. It had 71 members and its head was the high priest of Jerusalem. Its members were held in great respect by the people, and the Sanhedrin was very powerful.

sanitation

Sanitation is all the things that are done in a city or community to keep the place clean. Cleanliness is necessary to health in a city just as washing and bathing are necessary to your own health.

In times gone by, there were often plagues and epidemics of disease that might kill half the people of a city. Sometimes this was because people did not know how important it is to keep a city clean. Waste and garbage were not carried away promptly and safely, and these are things in which disease germs gather and breed. Modern sanitation methods make sure that waste and garbage are removed before they can cause damage.

Nearly every city has a Department of Sanitation that is in charge of keeping the city clean. The Department of Sanitation is supported by laws that punish citizens who make the city dirty. In many places there is also a Department of Public Health that works in cooperation with the Department of Sanitation. (See the article on HEALTH.)

Here are ways in which every good citizen must coöperate in keeping the city clean:

Citizens must keep the sidewalks in front of their houses clean of dust and litter, and free of snow and ice in the winter.

All trash (even bits of paper) must be put in cans or containers and not thrown on the streets. Persons who throw trash in the streets are called "litterbugs" and many cities have laws against them.

Garbage must be put in covered containers, in a place where Sanitation workers will collect it and carry it away. If garbage is not covered it attracts flies and other insects, and rats, and these vermin are disease-carriers.

It is against the law to spit on the sidewalks or in any public place, because a sick person might spread his germs by spitting. One should not sneeze or cough in a public place without covering the mouth. It is not only unsanitary, it is bad manners.

A public drinking fountain should be kept clean and a person should not touch his mouth to it when drinking.

THE SANITATION DEPARTMENT

Here are some of the things the Department of Sanitation does to keep the city clean:

It sends trucks to collect trash and garbage and take them to a safe place. There

is a separate article on GARBAGE.

It sends trucks with big brushes through all the streets to sweep away the dust and trash, and it sends tank trucks full of water through the streets to wash them. The tank trucks send powerful sprays of water along the street. The current is so strong that it carries along almost everything in its path, washing it into the sewers.

In the winter, the Department of Sanitation removes snow from the streets. It sends out large crews of men to shovel up the snow and pile it in trucks that carry it away.

The Department of Sanitation is also in charge of the SEWERS, about which there is a separate article. It manages the plants at which trash, garbage, sewage and other waste products are burned or treated with chemicals to make them harmless.

San José

San José is the capital of Costa Rica, in Central America. It is in the central part of Costa Rica, on a high plain. San José is on the Inter-American Highway and is an important industrial and commercial center, with railroad connections with the Pacific Ocean and the Caribbean Sea. It is a modern city, but its buildings are mostly low because of the danger of earthquakes. About 203,000 people live in San José. Many of them work in the marketing of produce from the surrounding agricultural region, such as coffee, cacao, and sugar cane. Others work in plants that make textiles, shoes and leather goods, furniture, and other products. La Sabana, a large, flat area outside the city, is the site of the airport, a national stadium, and a large park.

SAN JOSÉ, COSTA RICA. Population (1973 census) 203,148. Capital of Costa Rica and of Costa Rica Province. Founded, 1738.

San Juan

San Juan is the capital and principal city of the island of Puerto Rico, in the West Indies. The business section of San Juan is on two rocky islets in a fine harbor. They are connected with the mainland of Puerto Rico by bridges. The suburbs and residential districts of San Juan are on the mainland. Railroads, highways and airlines link San Juan to all of Puerto Rico, and it has an international airport. The city is a popular resort.

About 463,000 people live in San Juan. Many of them work in marketing and shipping Puerto Rican products, such as sugar cane, tobacco, coffee, and fruit.

San Juan was founded in 1521 by Ponce de Leon. It was made one of the most strongly fortified Spanish strongholds in the New World, with a huge stone fortress called Morro Castle at the entrance to the harbor and the Fortaleza (now the governor's palace) overlooking the bay. The city was often attacked by British, Dutch and French forces, but it remained in Spanish hands until it was taken by the United States in the Spanish-American War in 1898. Among the historic buildings in San Juan are the Cathedral of San Juan, which contains the tomb of Ponce de Leon, and the Casa Blanca, built in 1523.

SAN JUAN, PUERTO RICO. Population (1970 census) 463,242. Capital of Puerto Rico. Founded, 1521.

San Marino

San Marino is the smallest republic in the world. It is entirely surrounded by Italy, near the coast of the Adriatic Sea. San Marino is 38 square miles in area and has a population of 20,000. Almost all of the people are farmers. They grow corn, grapes, and fruit, and raise cattle and pigs. There are some stone quarries.

San Marino is governed by a Grand Council of 60 members, who are elected by the people. Two regents are chosen by the Grand Council to hold executive power for six-month terms. San Marino uses the courts of Italy. It issues silver coins but no paper money; the paper money of Italy and Vatican City is in general use. Much of San Marino's income is from the sale of postage stamps. New stamps are designed frequently and are in demand among collectors. The capital city is also called San Marino.

San Marino claims to be the oldest state in Europe. According to legend, it was founded by St. Marinus, a Christian who settled there with his followers about

the year 350 to escape religious persecution. The state has been independent throughout most of its history. It remained neutral in both World Wars. After World War II, it was ruled by the Communists for twelve years, but they were overthrown in 1957.

San Martin, José

José de San Martin was a South American patriot who helped to make Argentina, Chile and Peru independent nations. He was born in Argentina in 1778 and was an officer in the Spanish army as a young man, but in 1812 he joined a revolt against Spain in the Argentine. He became commander of an army and led it to victories over Spanish troops in Chile and Peru. In 1821 he became the head of the first independent government of Peru, but he resigned a year later, probably because of a disagreement with Simon Bolivar, another great South American patriot. San Martin lived the rest of his life in France. He died in 1850.

San Salvador

San Salvador is the capital and principal city of El Salvador in Central America. It is in the central part of the country, at the foot of the volcano San Salvador, on the Inter-American Highway. San Salvador is a commercial and

manufacturing center. About 349,000 people live there. Many of them work in factories that make cotton and silk goods, cigars and cigarettes, flour, soap, candles, matches, shoes, and sisal sacks. Other industries are woodworking, distilling, and meat-packing. San Salvador is also a cultural center, with a national library and the National University that includes a school of science and art and an astronomical observatory. San Salvador is subject to earthquakes, and the public buildings are specially designed to withstand shocks.

San Salvador was founded in 1525 on a nearby site. Twenty years later the settlement was moved to its present site. It was the capital of the Central American Union from 1823 to 1839 and became capital of El Salvador in 1841.

Sanskrit

Sanskrit is a language that has been used in India for more than four thousand years. The Vedas, which are the earliest sacred books of the Hindu religion, are written in Sanskrit. Sanskrit was introduced into India by a people called ARYANS, about whom there is a separate article. It is a member of the Indo-European family of languages, and so is related to English and most of the other languages spoken in Europe and the Americas. Sanskrit is no longer a spoken language, but it is still used for some religious writing in India, though the Sanskrit now used has changed a great deal from the old Sanskrit. See the article on INDO-EUROPEAN LANGUAGES.

Santa Anna, Antonio de

Antonio Lopez de Santa Anna was a Mexican leader who helped to free his country from Spanish rule and later became dictator of Mexico. He is best remembered in the United States as general of the army that massacred many Texas soldiers at the Alamo at San Antonio, Texas.

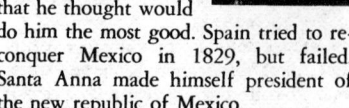

Santa Anna was born in 1794. After Mexico won its independence from Spain in 1821, Santa Anna joined and then deserted several Mexican leaders, always taking the side that he thought would do him the most good. Spain tried to reconquer Mexico in 1829, but failed. Santa Anna made himself president of the new republic of Mexico.

At that time Texas was trying to win its freedom from Mexico, and Santa Anna was defeated by the Texan general Sam Houston. This defeat cost him his power in Mexico, but later he became president and dictator several times. He led the Mexican army in the war with the United States in 1847. At last Santa Anna was permanently driven from power. He was exiled, but two years before his death in 1876 he was permitted to return to Mexico.

Santa Claus

Santa Claus is the spirit of Christmas. Every small child believes that the presents he receives at Christmas are given to him by a wonderful, jolly, gray-bearded fat man in a red suit who travels through the air from somewhere near the

North Pole in a sled drawn by reindeer and comes down the chimney to leave the presents. When children become old enough to read they learn that there really is no Santa Claus and that he is only a part of a young child's imagination. Then, when people grow older they realize that there is some spirit that makes people want to give presents at Christmas, and that Santa Claus is as good a name as any for this spirit.

Santa Claus, though he does not actually bring toys to children at Christmastime, was long ago a person. He was Nicholas, the bishop of a church on the southern coast of Asia Minor, about 1,600 years ago. He was a kindly man and did much to help people. He was especially loved by the sailors who sailed the waters between Cyprus and Rhodes. After his death many people spoke of the miracles he had worked, and the Church made Nicholas a saint. The Dutch, or low German, people called him San Nicholaas; the high German people called him Nikolaus, which name is shortened to Klaus or Claus. Santa Claus is the American and English way of saying Saint Nicholas.

The people in western Europe told their children that San Nikolaus brought them gifts on his saint's day, December 6th. The Dutch and German settlers in America shared this view. Later Saint Nicholas became associated with Christmas in Germany and became popular in America, along with the Christmas tree, through the German immigrants.

Santa Fe

Santa Fe is the capital and second-largest city of New Mexico. It is the second-oldest city in the United States, next to St. Augustine, Florida. About 41,000 people live there. It is a popular health and vacation resort, and its principal business is taking care of tourists and manufacturing and selling souvenirs such as Indian jewelry, blankets, rugs, and so on. Near the city of Santa Fe there are lead, zinc, coal, gold, and silver mines.

Santa Fe was founded in 1609 by the Spanish, on the site of an ancient Indian village, and it has been a seat of government almost ever since. Spanish governors ruled New Mexico from a palace that was built in Santa Fe in 1610 and is still standing. The Pueblo Indians seized the settlement in 1680 and held it for 12 years, destroying much that the Spaniards had built. A Spanish governor retook the city in 1692 and it remained under Spanish rule until Mexico won its independence in 1821. From then on it was a Mexican city until in 1846 it was taken over by American troops.

While Santa Fe was under Spanish control, trade with the United States was forbidden. In 1822 an American trader and explorer named William Becknell learned that New Mexico had come under Mexican rule. He went to Santa Fe with a wagon train of merchandise to sell. He became known as the "father of the Santa Fe Trail." The trail became an important trade route between the Missouri River and Santa Fe. Stagecoaches operated on it until the coming of the Atchison, Topeka and Santa Fe Railway in 1880.

Santiago

Santiago is the capital and largest city of Chile and the fourth-largest city

of South America. It is in the central part of Chile, on a wide plain at the foot of the Andes Mountains, which rise to snow-capped peaks behind the city. Santiago is Chile's most important commercial, industrial and cultural center. The surrounding fertile valley ships its cereals, fruit, vegetables and livestock from Santiago, and the city is headquarters for national and international banks and business firms.

Over two million people live in Santiago. There are many factories and busy importing and exporting businesses.

Santiago is the seat of the University of Chile, which was founded in 1738 as the University of San Felipe; of Catholic University; and of art, military and aviation schools. In the center of the city is the Plaza de Armas, site of the original settlement and of the cathedral, built in 1619. Rising from the heart of the city is Santa Lucia Hill, which is covered with a 100-acre Park. Behind the city is Mt. San Cristobal, which is topped by a huge statue of the Virgin Mary and is reached by a funicular railway. The city was founded in 1541. In that same year it was wiped out by Araucanian Indians, but it was rebuilt. A hundred years later it was leveled by an earthquake. The Mapocho River caused frequent flood damage until it was confined in strong embankments. Santiago played an important part in Chile's wars for independence and it became the capital after Chile won its freedom in 1818.

SANTIAGO, CHILE. Population (1973 estimate) 2,516,421. Capital of Chile. Founded in 1541.

Santo Domingo

Santo Domingo is the capital city of the Dominican Republic. From 1936 to 1961 it was called CIUDAD TRUJILLO (see the separate article).

Santo Domingo is located at the mouth of the Ozama River on the Caribbean Sea. It has a warm, pleasant climate, but there is not enough rainfall for year-round farming without some irrigation. More than 654,000 people live there. Most derive their living from commerce and industry. Sugar cane, the Dominican Republic's most abundant crop, is grown nearby and is exported through the city's port. Many people work at making cement, clothing, hats, wood products, meat products, and rum. There are several fine beaches nearby, and the pleasant climate attracts many visitors from the United States.

Santo Domingo is the oldest community settled by Europeans in the Western Hemisphere. It was founded in 1496 by Bartholomew Columbus, nephew of Christopher Columbus. At that time it was named *Nueva Isabela*. When Christopher Columbus died, he was buried in the Cathedral of Santa Maria la Menor, the oldest cathedral in the Western Hemisphere. In 1930 a hurricane destroyed most of the city and it was rebuilt along modern lines.

In 1965 Santo Domingo was the scene of civil warfare during a revolution by which one group of Dominicans fought to change the men in charge of the government. Many of those who lived in the city were killed. Marine and Army units of the United States were sent in to protect U.S. citizens who were visiting there.

SANTO DOMINGO, Dominican Republic. Population (1973 estimate) 654,757. Capital of the Dominican Republic.

São Paulo

São Paulo is the largest city in Brazil and the largest in South America. It is also one of the world's fastest-growing cities. It is in southeastern Brazil. São Paulo is on the Tietê River, a few miles from the Atlantic Ocean. It is separated from the coast by a high, rocky cliff called Serra do Mar. It is the most important industrial city on the continent and is called "the Chicago of South America." There is a four-lane highway across the Serra do Mar to Santos, São Paulo's coastal port.

Almost six million people live in Sao Paulo. Many of them work in the processing and shipping of coffee and cotton, the two most important products of the state of São Paulo. There are factories that make heavy machinery, textiles, automobiles, pianos, and many other products.

São Paulo is a beautiful city, combining old Spanish and modern architecture. Although it is in the tropics, its climate is invigorating and healthful because of the city's height above sea level. The business center of the city is surrounded by handsome residential suburbs. Among the important buildings are the government palace and the state university; Mackenzie Institute (a Methodist school); Catholic University; the municipal theater, and the stadium, which seats 70,000 persons.

São Paulo was founded in 1554 by Jesuit missionaries. It was made capital of the territory in 1681, but it remained a small frontier community until after 1885, when coffee-growing became a major industry in the state and brought large numbers of settlers from Europe.

SÃO PAULO, BRAZIL. Population (1973 estimate) 5,901,533. Capital of São Paulo State. On the Tietê River. Founded, 1554.

sapodilla

The sapodilla is an American evergreen fruit tree. It grows in the warm climate of Mexico, in parts of the southern United States, and in the West Indies. The tree grows to a height of about 50 feet. Its fruit, when ripe, is brown on the outside and yellow inside. The flesh of the ripe fruit is very soft and sweet.

sapphire

A sapphire is a kind of precious stone. It is transparent, which means that you can see through it. The most valuable sapphires are blue and are as valuable as diamonds, rubies, and emeralds. In *star sapphires,* rays of light can be seen to cross. The best sapphires are found in Ceylon, India, and Thailand. The sapphire is the birthstone for September.

A sapphire is a kind of corundum, which is made of the chemical elements aluminum and oxygen. Sapphire is one of the hardest substances known. Sapphires that are not beautiful enough to be gems are still useful for certain kinds of grinding, as bearings in watches, and as phonograph needles. Industrial sapphires of this kind are found in Montana and other states of the United States. Fine sapphires can be made synthetically, which means they can be made by man from chmicals.

sapsucker

The sapsucker is a bird that is a member of the woodpecker family. It makes its home in many parts of the United States and Canada. The sapsucker drills small holes in trees and sucks the sap from them. That is how it got its name. The sapsucker is especially fond of apple and other fruit trees. This habit does not make the sapsucker a popular bird with farmers. Sapsuckers also eat fruit and insects.

Saracen, a name that was used in the Middle Ages to apply to the Arabs and other Mohammedan peoples who fought against the Christians for the Holy Land: see the article CRUSADES.

Saratoga Springs

Saratoga Springs is a health and vacation resort in New York State, about 30 miles north of Albany. It is sometimes called simply Saratoga. The mineral springs of Saratoga have been known since Indian times. New York State owns and operates a 1,300-acre mineral spa, including baths. The waters of the spa are bottled and sold.

Saratoga Springs is also an important social center, and the site of one of the best-known horse-racing tracks in the United States. Nearly 19,000 people live there.

An important battle that turned out to be a turning point in the Revolutionary War was fought near Saratoga in 1777. The British were trying to take the Hudson Valley, and the British general John Burgoyne was to come down from Canada and combine his forces with those of General Howe. Burgoyne's plans failed because Howe did not get the message. Burgoyne's army of 6,000 men was surrounded at Saratoga and he was forced to surrender to the American general, Horatio Gates.

Sarawak

Sarawak is a former British colony on the island of Borneo in the Pacific Ocean that is now part of the independent Federation of Malaysia. It is a long, narrow strip on the northwest coast of the island, with an area of 47,500 square miles, about the size of the state of New York. The capital is Kuching, a city of about 63,500. The area near the coast is low and swampy, but the land rises to mountains in the interior. Almost 976,000 people live there. Half of them belong to tribes such as the Dyak; the rest are mainly Chinese or Malayans.

Most of the people are farmers. They raise rice, pepper, and rubber. The climate is warm and rainy, and many of the people suffer from malaria. Sarawak was a dependency of Brunei until 1841, when the sultan of Brunei gave it to an Englishman, James Brooke, for his help in putting down a rebellion. Brooke became rajah of the country, which he named Sarawak, and the rulership became hereditary in his family. In 1888 Sarawak became a British protectorate. During World War II the Japanese occupied Sarawak. After the war, in 1946, Sir Charles Brooke, the last rajah, ceded Sarawak to Great Britain. It became part of Malaysia in 1963.

sardine

"Sardine" is the name given to several

different kinds of soft-boned herring which are usually canned in oil or in a flavorful sauce. Sardines are caught mostly in the North Atlantic Ocean and are also known as "Atlantic herring". The center of the sardine industry in the United States is Maine.

Until recently not very much was known about the sardine's habits. Now scientists have discovered some things about the life of the sardine. The female sardine begins to lay its eggs when it is between 2 and 4 years old. It is then about eight inches long. The female lays about 100,000 eggs, which float on the surface of the water. The eggs hatch in two or three days.

The sardine has a sievelike structure near its gills. This is very useful to strain the mud and water from the floating plants and water animals that the sardine eats. Sardines travel in large groups (called *schools*) and make long journeys.

Sardines are a healthful food that contains many rich oils and vitamins. They are usually canned, and are eaten in salads and sandwiches. Some of the best sardines come from the coasts of Norway and Portugal. The sardine is used also as a food for cattle and chickens, and young sardines are used by fishermen as bait to catch other fish. The oil of the sardine is used in many ways.

Sardinia

Sardinia is the second-largest island in the Mediterranean Sea (after Sicily). With several smaller islands, Sardinia forms a self-governing region of Italy. The capital is Cagliari, a city of about 165,000. Sardinia has an area of 9,283 square miles, and about 1,500,000 people live there. Most of the island is mountainous, except for a lowland region called the Campidano in the southwest. There are three principal rivers, the Tirso, Flumini Mannu, and Flumendosa rivers. The climate is hot and dry in the summer and moderate in the winter.

Farming is the most important occupation of Sardinia. Cereals, grapes, olives and citrus fruits are grown. Sardinia leads all of Italy in the production of cork and in the raising of sheep and goats.

The island is also the most important mining region of Italy, producing zinc, lead, manganese, iron, copper, and other metals. Fishing for tuna, sardines and lobsters is an important industry.

Almost nothing is known about the

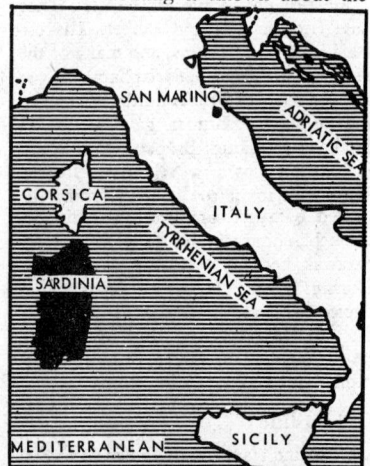

first inhabitants of Sardinia. They were a prehistoric people who built strange towers called *nuraghi*, which are found scattered over most of the island. Sardinia was settled by Phoenicians, then conquered by Carthage and later by Rome. The island was almost independent for many hundreds of years, but was conquered and held by Spain in the early 1700s and was then turned over to the king of Savoy (who called himself king of Sardinia). In 1861 the king of Sardinia became king of Italy.

sardonyx, a kind of onyx, made up of layers of chalcedony and carnelian or sard: see CHALCEDONY and ONYX.

Sargasso Sea

The Sargasso Sea lies in the very center of the Atlantic Ocean, between

the Bahamas and the Azores. It is not really a sea at all, for it is not surrounded by land, but many things make it easy to tell it from the rest of the ocean. The waters of the Sargasso are almost completely motionless. There are no strong winds in this region. The water is warm and very salty.

The Sargasso Sea takes its name from a kind of seaweed, called *sargassum*, that is found floating on the surface of the water. This seaweed is also called gulfweed. It is so thick that many stories have been told of ships being caught in the gulfweed and being unable to proceed. This is not true, but it was difficult for sailing ships to pass through the Sargasso Sea because of the lack of winds and current.

The Sargasso Sea is filled with many kinds of plants, fish, eels, snails and other tiny creatures that are found nowhere else on earth. Scientists often go there to study these unusual kinds of life.

Sargent, John Singer

John Singer Sargent was a famous American painter. He is best-remembered for his portraits of rich and fashionable people.

John Sargent was born in 1856 in Italy, of American parents, and he studied in Italy, France, and Germany. In 1884 he moved to London, England, where he remained for most of his life. King Edward VII offered to reward Sargent by making him a knight (which would have given him the title "Sir"), but Sargent refused because he was an American citizen. Late in life, Sargent stopped painting portraits and worked on water-color landscapes. He died in 1925, at the age of 79. His best-known works include a series of murals (wall-paintings) called *The History of Religion*. in the Boston Public Library.

Saroyan, William

William Saroyan is an American writer of plays and short stories. His parents had come to the United States from Armenia, and when he was 26, one of his most successful short stories, "The Daring Young Man on the Flying Trapeze," was published. In 1939 he wrote a play, *The Time of Your Life*, that won both the New York Drama Critics' Award and the Pulitzer Prize. His novel *The Human Comedy* was made into a motion picture.

sarsaparilla

Sarsaparilla is a plant from which a flavoring is made. It is a climbing vine that grows in Central America, Mexico, and parts of South America. The flavoring is made from the roots of the plant and is used in the manufacture of medicines and in a soft drink that also is called sarsaparilla.

Sarto, Andrea del

Andrea del Sarto was an Italian painter who lived about 450 years ago, in Florence, Italy. He is famous for his frescoes, or wall paintings, and also for smaller pictures. Del Sarto was born in 1486, the son of a tailor. (The Italian word *sarto* means "tailor.") He was apprenticed to a goldsmith, but his talent was noticed by an artist, who gave him lessons in painting. Del Sarto became a member of the painters' guild in 1508, when he was only 22 years old, and soon he was commissioned to paint a series of frescoes in the church of Sant' Annunziata in Florence. These paintings included five scenes from the life of Saint Philip Benizzi, an *Adoration of the Magi,* and *The Birth of the Virgin,* which were so much admired that he was called "the faultless painter." He also painted a series of ten scenes from the life of John the Baptist. His *Last Supper,* which shows a scene just a moment later than Leonardo da Vinci's painting of the same name, is considered by many to be as fine as Leonardo's. Del Sarto died in 1531.

Saskatchewan

Saskatchewan is one of the ten provinces of Canada. It has an area of more than 250,000 square miles, which makes it almost the size of Texas. However, only about 916,000 people live there, which is somewhat less than live in Rhode Island, the smallest of the United States. Saskatchewan became a province in 1905. It was named for the Saskatchewan River, from an Indian word meaning "swiftly running." The capital city is Regina.

THE PEOPLE OF SASKATCHEWAN

Most of the people of Saskatchewan are native-born, of British descent. Others come from families that moved to Canada from countries of Europe, such as Germany, Norway, Sweden, France, and Russia. Most of the people belong to the United Church of Canada or the Roman Catholic Church. Others are Anglicans or Lutherans.

About three-quarters of the people of Saskatchewan are farmers. They grow great quantities of grain such as wheat, oats and barley, and they raise cattle, pigs

and poultry. In the cities there are factories that make food products such as flour, butter, cheese, meat products, and animal feed. Fishing is an important industry. Pike, pickerel and whitefish are caught in Saskatchewan's many lakes. The province is rich in mineral deposits, including gold, copper, zinc, silver, and other metals. Oil and natural gas are produced. One of the greatest uranium fields of North America is in Saskatchewan.

WHAT SASKATCHEWAN IS LIKE

Saskatchewan is one of the three Prairie Provinces of Canada. The others are Alberta and Manitoba. The southern half of Saskatchewan consists of a great plain, where farming is good. Most of the people of the province live in this region. The nor hern part of the province is made up of rocks, lakes, forests, and swamps. Few people live there, but some lumbering is done and wild animals are trapped for their fur.

The principal river of the province is the Saskatchewan River, which has two branches. The North Saskatchewan River rises in the province of Alberta; the South Saskatchewan River rises in Montana. They join at about the center of the province, and the river flows into Lake Winnipeg in Manitoba. The Saskatchewan is about 1,205 miles long. Another large river is the Churchill, which flows across the northern part of the province into Hudson Bay. It is about 1,000 miles long. Saskatchewan has many lakes, the largest being Lake Athabasca (part of which is in Alberta), and Wollaston, Reindeer, La Ronge, and Frobisher lakes.

The climate of Saskatchewan varies sharply from summer to winter. The summers are dry and sunny, with temperatures ranging from 67 degrees to 110 degrees Fahrenheit. The winters are long and very cold, with temperatures falling as low as 50 degrees below zero. Most of the rainfall is in the farming season, from May to September.

Saskatchewan has many railways and a network of good highways.

PRINCIPAL CITIES

The capital of Saskatchewan is REGINA, about which there is a separate article. Other important cities are:

Saskatoon, population 126,449 (1973 estimate), in the south central part, an industrial and distribution center.

Moose Jaw, population 31,285 (1973 estimate), in southern part, center for transportation and food processing.

Prince Albert, population 27,600 (1973 estimate), in the central part, center of a lumbering and fur-trapping region.

GOVERNMENT

The head of the government of Saskatchewan is a Lieutenant Governor, who represents the Canadian government. The province is actually run by a premier. The premier is appointed by a legislature, which is elected by the people. The premier has a cabinet, just as the President of the United States has. He stays in office as long as he can keep the confidence of the majority of the legislature. The members of the legislature assembly are elected for five-year terms. Judges are appointed by the Canadian government and hold office permanently.

All children in Saskatchewan must go to school. The University of Saskatchewan, at Saskatoon, is the principal university.

SASKATCHEWAN IN THE PAST

The territory of Saskatchewan was part of the great lands controlled by the Hudson's Bay Company, which was chartered by the king of England in 1670. In 1870 Canada bought all this territory and called it the Northwest Territories. In 1905 the province of Saskatchewan was formed from the districts of Athabasca, Saskatchewan, and Assiniboia. During the 1920s and 1930s the province had great trouble because of droughts (dry spells).

PLACES TO SEE

Saskatchewan is one of the favorite vacation spots of Canada. Its lakes and streams are popular with fishermen, and its forests are full of game animals such as deer and bears. The province has many interesting places to visit. Among them are:

Prince Albert National Park, 1,868 miles, in the center of the province, with seven large lakes and more than 100 small lakes.

Cypress Hill Park, 18 square miles, in the southern part, a game and forest preserve.

Moose Mountain Park, 192 square miles, on Lake Kenosee, with a hotel, golf course, and camping site, and fine hunting in the forests.

Duck Mountain Park, 81 square miles, in the west central part, containing Madge Lake, which is noted for its beauty and its fishing.

Cumberland House, on the Saskatchewan River, an old Hudson's Bay Company post.

Fort Walsh, in Cypress Hills Park, first headquarters of the Northwest Mounted Police.

SASKATCHEWAN. Population (1973 estimate) 916,000. Area, 251,700 square miles. Religion, Christian (Roman Catholic and United Church of Canada). Capital, Regina. Flower, prairie lily. Admitted to Dominion, 1905. Official abbreviation, Sask.

sassafras

Sassafras is the name of several different trees that grow in North America and parts of Asia. The roots of the sassafras have a spicy flavor. A flavoring made from the bark of these roots is used in medicines, foods, candies, and drinks such as root beer. People often cut off tender twigs of sassafras to chew while walking through the woods. The leaves also are chewed.

One kind of sassafras is a beautiful, large tree that often grows to a height of 60 feet.

Satan

Satan is a name given to the spirit of evil or wickedness in three great religions, Judaism, Islam (Mohammedanism), and Christianity. Satan is usually identified with Lucifer, an angel who tried to rebel against God and so fell from heaven to eternal damnation. He is considered as the ruler of the underworld, or hell, where he has many assistants to aid him in spreading evil throughout the world. His assistants, called devils, were lesser angels who fell with Lucifer. Satan is also called the Devil. In the Bible he is pictured as a serpent and is supposed to have been the serpent that tempted Eve and led to God's making Adam and Eve leave the Garden of Eden. Today he is usually pictured as a man dressed either in red (like the fires of hell) or in black (as a sign of evil).

Satan is an important character in the Bible. Some of the most famous stories about him are in Dante's *Divine Comedy*, Goethe's *Faust*, and Milton's *Paradise Lost*. Satan is also called the Prince of Darkness, Beelzebub, and by many other names.

satellite

A satellite is a small heavenly body that revolves, or moves in a curved path, around a planet. Satellites vary in diameter (greatest thickness) from about 3,200 miles to about 15 miles. Six of the planets have satellites: the earth has one (the moon); Mars has two; Jupiter has twelve; Saturn has ten; Uranus has five; and Neptune has two. Man-made objects which have been put into orbit around the Earth or other planets are also referred to as satellites.

Saturday

Saturday is the seventh day of the week. It is named for the Roman god Saturn. Saturday is observed as the Sabbath, or day of rest, by the Jews and by Seventh-Day Adventists and some other Protestant denominations.

In the United States, Saturday has come to be considered part of the "weekend," and in many businesses it is a holiday or half-holiday.

Saturn

Saturn was the god of agriculture and the sowing of seeds in Roman mythology, the stories the ancient Romans told about their gods and goddesses. Saturn was the husband of Ops, the goddess of plenty. He was the father of Ceres, the goddess of agriculture. Saturn was believed to have ruled the world during a Golden Age of peace and plenty. His feast, called the Saturnalia, began on December 17 and lasted for several days. It was a time of rejoicing and feasting and the giving of gifts. No work was done, and slaves were given many special privileges, such as being served by their masters at dinner. Saturday, the seventh day of the week, is named for Saturn. The Roman Saturn is usually identified with the Greek god Cronus.

Saturn

Saturn is the second-largest planet in the solar system, which consists of the sun and bodies (including the earth) that revolve around the sun. Before the inven-

tion of the telescope, it was thought that Saturn was the planet farthest away from the sun, but now Uranus, Neptune and Pluto are known to be even farther. Saturn is about 886,000,000 miles from the sun, about nine and a half times as far as the earth is. The diameter (greatest thickness) of Saturn is about 72,000 miles, eight times that of the earth.

Saturn revolves around the sun about once every 29½ years. About Saturn itself revolve ten satellites.

One of the most interesting things about Saturn is its system of rings, which was discovered by the astronomer Galileo nearly 350 years ago, in 1610. There are three rings, one inside the other, that revolve around the planet. Their diameter is quite large, the biggest being 171,000 miles, but they are very thin, probably less than 10 miles in thickness. The rings are made up of separate particles, and most scientists believe they are the remains of a satellite that was broken up. The rings are about 5,000 miles apart and each is about 12,000 miles wide.

Because it is so far from the sun, Saturn is very cold (about 250 degrees below zero Fahrenheit).

satyr

A satyr was an imaginary creature described by the Greeks more than two thousand years ago. Satyrs were considered minor gods. They were thought to live in the woods or mountains. A satyr was part man and part beast, with pointed ears, the feet of a goat, and a tail. The older satyrs were shown as ugly, with beards; the younger ones were handsome young men with horns growing from their foreheads. The satyrs were followers and attendants of Dionysus, the Greek god of wine and revelry. The Romans believed in spirits called *fauns,* which were like the satyrs.

Saudi Arabia

Saudi Arabia is a kingdom in southwestern Asia. It occupies most of the Arabian peninsula, having an area of about 870,000 square miles. The kingdom has two capitals: Riyadh, the capital of the former sultanate of Nejd, and Mecca, the capital of the former kingdom of Hejaz. About 7,700,000 people live there (You can read about the people and how they live in the articles on ARAB, ARABIA, and ARABIC LANGUAGE.) Saudi Arabia is primarily an agricultural country. Its principal products are dates, wheat, barley, fruit, hides, and wool. However, Saudi Arabia is also one of the great oil producing countries of the world. Other recently discovered minerals are iron ore, gold, and silver.

The kingdom of Saudi Arabia is fairly new as nations go. For hundreds of years it

was ruled by Turkey, but in the early 1900s a strong Arabian religious group called the Wahabis, under the leadership of Ibn Saud, defeated the Turks in war. By 1913 they had won all of Nejd and the Turkish province of Hasa. During World War I, Ibn Saud helped the British fight the Turks, and after the war they recognized him as ruler of Nejd. Ibn Saud then went on to conquer Hejaz in 1925 and most of Asir in 1926. In 1932 he created the United Kingdom of Saudi Arabia. When Ibn Saud died in 1953, his son Saud became king, and in 1965 another son, Faisal, became king.

SAUDI ARABIA. Area 830,000 square miles. Population (1973 estimate) 7,700,000. Language, Arabic. Religion, Islam. Government, kingdom. Monetary unit, the rial, worth about 22 cents (U.S.). Flag, green with a white sword below a quotation from the Koran in white Arabic characters. Capitals, Riyadh and Mecca.

Saul

Saul was the first king of the ancient Hebrew country of Israel. His story is told in the Bible, in the Books of Samuel. He reigned from about 1025 B.C. to 1010 B.C. Saul was the protector and great friend of David, until they quarreled. In battle against the Philistines, enemies of the Hebrews, Saul took his own life to avoid capture. David became the next king. Saul's son, Jonathan, was David's dearest friend. See the entry on DAVID.

Sault Sainte Marie

The Sault Sainte Marie Canals are two ship canals that go around rapids in the St. Mary's River between Michigan and the Canadian province of Ontario. The river joins Lakes Superior and Huron. The canals are usually called the Soo Canals, and they carry more shipping than the Suez and Panama Canals combined.

The St. Mary's River is one of the world's busiest waterways, but because of its steep rapids (19 feet at one place) canals had to be built so that ships could pass through. There is a canal at each of the twin cities of Sault Sainte Marie (one in Michigan and one in Ontario, with a combined population of about 89,700). The American canal is about a mile and a half long and has two channels, each with two locks. Two of these locks, each

1,350 feet long and 80 feet wide, are among the largest in the world. The Canadian canal is a little less than a mile and a half long and has one lock.

The first canal around the St. Mary's Rapids was built on the Canadian side in 1798 by the Hudson's Bay Company, to take canoes loaded with furs and supplies around the rapids. The new Canadian canal was completed in 1895 and the first American canal in 1881. The newest of the American locks is MacArthur Lock, completed in 1943.

sausage

Sausage is meat that is ground, seasoned with various spices, and stuffed into a casing. The casing is twisted every few inches to make separate lengths that can easily be cut apart. The casings for all sausages used to be the cleaned intestines of the pig, sheep, or cow, and these casings are still used for sausages made at home and for some sausages made in meat-packing plants, but other kinds of casing are now used: plastics, which can be removed before the sausage is sold, and gelatins, which can be eaten or which dissolve when the sausage is cooked. Many kinds of sausage are smoked or cooked before they are sold, but pork sausage is usually sold uncooked. Pork sausage is sometimes sold in its ground form without any casing.

The most popular sausage in the United States is the frankfurter, familiar as the "hot dog." Smaller sausages of the same kind are called "wieners." The frankfurter is supposed to come from Frankfurt, Germany, and the wiener is supposed to come from Vienna, Austria, but in Frankfurt they call this kind of sausage wieners and in Vienna they call them frankfurters.

Savannah

Savannah is the second-largest city of Georgia. It is in the southeastern part of the state, on the Savannah River, 17 miles from the river's mouth on the Atlantic Ocean. Savannah is an industrial and shipping center and is one of the world's biggest markets for naval stores (ship's supplies). About 118,000 people live in Savannah. Savannah has a huge paper mill, a sugar refinery, shipyards, and many other factories. Savannah's pleasant winter climate makes it popular for vacations.

The city was founded in 1733. During the Revolutionary War it was captured and held for four years by the British. From 1782 to 1785 it was the capital of Georgia. The *Savannah,* the first steamship to cross the Atlantic, was named for the city and sailed from its harbor to Liverpool, England, in 1819. During the Civil War, Savannah was the end of General Sherman's famous "march to the sea."

SAVANNAH, GEORGIA. Population (1970 census) 118,349. On the Savannah River. County seat of Chatham County. Founded, 1733.

savings

Savings are sums of money that people put aside for future use or to help them in times of need. A child who does not spend all his allowance but puts some in a piggy bank is saving. So is a person

who receives a salary and does not spend all of it. Whatever is left after all expenses are paid, and is put aside somewhere, is considered savings.

The habit of saving is as old as mankind itself. Before there was money, people saved food and necessities. An ancient farmer was saving if he kept extra grain stored in a bin. Today when we speak of savings we mean only the saving of money.

For hundreds of years, there were no special banks for savings and people hid the money they saved. A few people still do this, but most people know the money is much safer in a savings bank.

SAVINGS BANKS

Savings banks as we know them today are only about 150 years old. The first ones were opened in Scotland in 1810. By 1820, savings banks had been opened in many cities of the world, including Boston, New York, and Philadelphia. Now there are thousands of savings banks.

When a person has extra money and wants to put it in a savings bank, he takes his money to the bank and gives it to one of the bank employees called tellers. He is given a bank book that shows how much money he has deposited in the bank. Each time he puts money in a savings bank the amount of money is entered in the bank book (also called a passbook). Whenever he draws money out of the savings account the amount is put down in the book.

A savings account pays interest. Interest is money that the banks pay the depositor for the use of his money. For every dollar left in the bank for a year, the bank will usually pay 3 cents or more as interest. Therefore savings increase in value when they are in the bank. Savings kept at home, in cash, cannot increase in value.

OTHER FORMS OF SAVINGS

Savings banks are not the only safe places for savings.

There are postal savings accounts. People who have money go to a post office and deposit it there. Instead of a passbook they receive certificates, pieces of paper that show that a certain amount has been deposited with the post office. Whenever they want to get their money back, they turn in the certificates and are given the cash plus any interest it has earned.

Another form of savings is the purchase of bonds. Bonds are certificates that show that someone has lent money to a government or to a company. The bond promises that the money will be paid back in the future. Bonds, like savings accounts, pay interest. The best-known bonds are United States Government war bonds or defense bonds. During World War II millions of Americans bought war bonds. Many of them did this on a regular basis, buying a bond a month out of their salaries. This kind of bond costs $75 and is worth $100 ten years later. The extra $25 is the interest the government pays.

INSURANCE

Another form of savings is insurance. When a person takes out a life insurance policy, part of the money he pays is for protection (the insurance company's promise to pay a large sum of money if he dies), but the rest of what he pays is a kind of savings. The insured person can always get back the cash value of the savings part of his payments, or can borrow this amount from the insurance company.

Another form of savings is the purchase and holding of such things as real estate (land and buildings), jewelry, or stocks (shares of ownership in large companies). A person owning shares of stock in a large company usually gets dividends, which are like interest but are a share of the profits made by the company.

CHRISTMAS CLUBS

Banks have special kinds of savings accounts. The best-known is the Christmas Club. People who belong to Christmas Clubs deposit a certain amount of money in the bank each week, beginning in January. Just before Christmas they take the money they have saved in the Christmas Club and use it to buy Christmas gifts.

Another form of savings is the school savings account. This is familiar to most students in the United States. School savings accounts are run very much like regular bank savings accounts, but they usually handle smaller sums of money.

The United States leads all other countries in the world in the amount of savings by its people, because in the United States people earn more money and have more money to save. Savings in the United States total several billion dollars.

Savonarola

Girolamo Savonarola was a Roman Catholic priest and reformer who lived  about five hundred years ago. He is best remembered for his fiery sermons, in which he berated the wealthy and the sinful, warning them of damnation to come. Savonarola was born in Italy, in 1452. When he was 22 years old he entered the Dominican religious order. In 1481 he went to the city of Florence, where he was admired by Lorenzo de' Medici, ruler of the city, and by the people. Savonarola believed that life at Lorenzo's court and in the city was wicked and irreligious. He preached sermons that led to the ousting of the Medici, and he became the spiritual ruler of the city.

Then he began to make prophecies of things to come, and his sermons became even more violent. Savonarola was ruthless in punishing those he believed guilty of wrongdoing, and he became so outspoken and so powerful that Pope Alexander excommunicated him from the Church in 1497. Savonarola then turned against the Pope, declaring that the Pope had been elected illegally. The people of Florence turned against Savonarola, and in 1498 a mob seized him, forced him to confess to being a false prophet, and put him to death.

sawfish

The sawfish is a big, fierce fish that is found in warm waters of the Atlantic Ocean off the eastern and southern coasts of the United States. A sawfish may be ten to fifteen feet long, though some kinds are smaller. The sawfish lives in shallow waters and sometimes it will swim into fresh-water rivers and streams.

The sawfish gets its name because of its long, flat nose, which has sharp points on the sides. This nose may be three or four feet long. It looks very much like a saw and is a very useful weapon that helps the sawfish defend itself against enemies and catch its food. The sawfish wounds a fish with its saw, takes it to the bottom of the water, and gulps it down. Sometimes the sawfish will go into a large school of fish. It swings from side to side with its sharp saw and many fish are wounded or killed. Baby sawfish are born with soft saws.

sawmill, a factory where wood is cut into boards: see the article LUMBER.

Saxons, an ancient German people: see the articles ANGLES AND ANGLO-SAXONS and SAXONY.

Saxony

Saxony is a region in Germany and a former province of the German Democratic Republic (East Germany). It is in east central Germany, lying almost entirely in the Erzgebirge Mountains and their foothills. Before it was abolished as a political unit in 1952, it had an area of 6,651 square miles, which is a little smaller than the state of New Jersey, and about 5,600,000 people lived there, which is a little less than the number of people who live in New Jersey.

The people of Saxony are Germans, descended from the ancient people called Saxons, some of whom settled in England. The region is the site of many important industries and rich mineral deposits, including coal, iron, lead, silver, and other metals. Saxony has some of the best farm land in Germany.

Saxony is a place of wooded mountains, fertile valleys, and busy cities. Its principal river is the Elbe. Among its important cities are Chemnitz (Karl-Marx-Stadt), Dresden, Zwickau, and Leipzig.

SAXONY IN THE PAST

About 1,700 years ago the name Saxony was given to a great region of northwestern Germany that was occupied by the Saxon people. The region was broken up into small countries and Saxony became a duchy, ruled by dukes. In the 1300s the duke of Saxony was made an elector, which meant that he could vote for the emperor of the Holy Roman Empire. By 1648 the elector of Saxony had become one of the two most powerful princes of Germany, and from 1697 to 1763 the electors of Saxony were also kings of Poland.

In 1871 Saxony became a member of the German empire. After World War I Saxony became a republic, but then it became part of Germany again. After World War II Saxony became a province of East Germany. In 1952 the East German government abolished the provinces as administrative units, and Saxony was divided into three districts.

Lower Saxony is a state in West Germany. Its capital is Hanover.

saxophone

The saxophone is a musical instrument that was invented in 1840 by Adolphe Saxe. It is a cone-shaped, single-reed wind instrument made of brass. There are about twenty keys with which different notes can be produced. The saxophone is made in several sizes, and it has a wide variety of tone, sometimes sounding like a clarinet and sometimes like a cello.

Although the saxophone is most popular in military bands and in jazz and dance bands, much serious music has been written for it. Composers who have written for the saxophone include Debussy and Bizet and several more recent composers.

scabies

Scabies is a skin disease that causes itching. It is caused by tiny insects, called mites, that are about one-fiftieth of an inch long. These mites live on the skin, and the female digs its way under the skin to lay eggs. As more and more mites are born, they spread over the skin, causing tiny blisters, redness, and itching. To get rid of the mites, the person should take baths every day and use medicines against scabies as advised by a doctor. Underclothes and bedclothes should be changed every day until the sickness is gone. Scabies is catching and persons who have it should be very careful about not spreading it to others.

scale

A scale, in music, is a succession of tones, or notes. There are a number of different kinds of scale, but the two principal ones in use are the *major scale* and the *minor scale*. Each of these scales includes five whole tones and two half-tones, and the difference between them is in the order of the whole and half-tones. If you play all the white notes in a piano upward from A to A you will have the natural minor scale. Play all the white notes from C to C and you will have the major scale. The first (lowest) note of a scale is called the *tonic* or *keynote*. The scales are named from the keynote, such as "the key of B flat minor."

There are twelve half-tones in an octave (eight notes) and when all of these are played in succession the scale is called *chromatic*. Tones from the chromatic scale have long been used to add color to music written in traditional keys. Some modern composers such as Arnold Schoenberg have used this scale, without any key, as the entire basis of their music, and have called it the *twelve-tone scale*.

scale, a device that is used to find the weight of objects: see the article BALANCE

scale insect

There are several different kinds of scale insect. They are all very tiny individually, but they live in colonies of many dozens, sometimes entirely covering a small branch or twig. They hurt fruit trees and many plants because they suck the juices of the plant.

A mass of scale insects may look like tiny lumps growing under the bark of the twig or branch, or like tiny heaps of white absorbent cotton with a brown roof over the heap.

The female of the scale insect usually deposits its eggs under its shell in late fall. During the winter the young develop inside the eggs, and the female dies before they emerge. The young later move to another piece of shrubbery and settle down for the rest of their lives.

One very useful kind of scale insect is the LAC insect, about which there is a separate article.

scales

Scales are hard outside coverings produced by the skin of certain animals. The scales on the wings of insects are quite different from the scales of fishes, and these in turn differ from those of reptiles, birds, and mammals. Hair and feathers are forms of scales. The scales of fishes are of two kinds. Most of them overlap like shingles but some fit side by side like paving stones. The scales on reptiles may be small and rounded, flat, or large plates like those on turtles. Most birds have scales on their legs like those of reptiles. Some mammals, such as rats, have scales on their tails and others, such as armadillos, have scales on their bodies. Scales are made of separate pieces but are securely fastened together by tough body tissues, or fibers. The scales can be of almost any color or a combination of colors, some of them very beautiful.

The scales of a fish are of a substance like bone. The scales of a reptile are of a substance like skin, just as are the fingernails and toenails of a human being. A snake uses the scales on the bottom of its body to help it crawl. It does this by moving the separate scales backward and forward.

scallop

The scallop is a small shellfish found in almost all parts of the world. Scallops are plentiful in most seas, and there are more than two hundred different kinds. Many kinds can be eaten.

The scallop is a bivalve, as are oysters and clams. That is, it has two slightly hollowed-out shells joined by a muscle at the back. The shell of a scallop is ribbed and fan-shaped and has scalloped edges. When scallops are young they swim around in the water, but older ones attach themselves permanently to rocks, as oysters do.

Scandinavia

Scandinavia is a name used for the countries of Norway, Sweden, and Denmark, and sometimes Iceland. Sometimes the name is used only to mean Sweden and Norway, the two countries that are on the land called the Scandinavian Peninsula.

The Scandinavian countries are grouped together because their people, their languages and their geography are very much alike. There is a separate article on each of these countries.

Scapa Flow

Scapa Flow is a small area of water, about 15 miles long and about 8 miles wide, off the coast of Scotland, in the Orkney Islands. Since before World War I it has been the place where the main British fleet stays when it is not at sea.

scarab

Scarab is a name for a kind of beetle.

Often the word means a piece of jewelry in the form of a beetle. Thousands of years ago in ancient Egypt the people believed that the scarab brought good luck. Therefore they carved precious stones in the form of beetles, and baked little pieces of clay in the shape of beetles. On the flat underside of the baked or carved beetle the Egyptians scratched hieroglyphic (picture-writing) characters that meant "May good luck come to the wearer," or some other statement that would bring good fortune.

Scarlatti

Scarlatti was the name of two Italian composers, or writers of original music. Alessandro Scarlatti was born in Sicily about 1659. He lived most of his life in Naples, where he had many followers. He is often regarded as the founder of the modern opera (a musical play in which the words are sung rather than spoken). He wrote more than a hundred operas, but they are seldom performed today. He also wrote a great deal of religious music. He died in 1725. His son, Domenico Scarlatti, was born in 1685. He became famous as a harpsichord player and composed many pieces for that instrument. He died in 1757.

scarlet fever

Scarlet fever is a childhood sickness that makes a rash of tiny red spots come out on the neck, chest, back, and other parts of the body. It is started by a germ that first enters the nose and throat and then gets into the blood stream. Sometimes the germ infects the tonsils, sinuses, or mastoids, but does not cause a rash. The first signs of scarlet fever are chills, fever, and sore throat. The child may have headaches and may vomit, but will not seem to be very ill until the rash comes out. The rash feels hot and may be itchy. It usually lasts from two to seven days, followed by scales that look like bran on the neck and chest. Toward the end of the sickness, the dead skin may peel off in large, white patches from the toes, fingers, and buttocks. Sometimes hair is lost, but it grows back later, after the child is well.

A person with scarlet fever is usually kept in bed and given germ-killing medicines, such as sulfa drugs and antibiotics. An icebag for the head, or aspirin, may be used to relieve or bring down the fe-

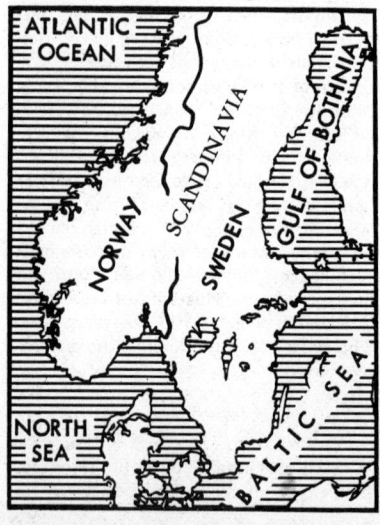

ver. Gargles are used to soothe and clear the swollen throat.

Scarlet fever is very catching. The sick child should be kept away from all other persons. Thirty and forty years ago, many children used to die of scarlet fever. Doctors today know how to cure it most of the time. If it is not taken care of in time, or if it is very bad, scarlet fever can sometimes lead to deafness, nervous fits, or damage to the heart, liver, and other organs.

Schiller, Johann von

Johann von Schiller was a German poet, playwright and historian who lived about two hundred years ago. Next to Goethe, who was his great friend, Schiller was considered the greatest German writer of his time. During a period of great tyranny, Schiller stood for freedom and equality of all men. One of his famous poems, the *Ode to Joy,* so well expressed the ideal of the brotherhood of man that Beethoven set it to music. It is used in the final movement of Beethoven's Ninth, or Choral, Symphony.

Schiller was born in 1759. His father was an army surgeon and forced his son to attend the military school of the Duke of Württemberg and to become an army doctor. Schiller wrote his first play, *The Robbers,* while he was still a student. It was produced in 1782 in another city, but without the author's name. Schiller determined to see it and left the duke's territory without permission. For this he was arrested. He was so angry that after his release he ran away and lived as a fugitive, first at Mannheim and later at Leipzig and Dresden. He wrote many plays, historical works, and essays on art and poetry. He became a professor of history at the University of Jena in 1789, but resigned because of illness four years later. Schiller's last years were spent at Weimar. Some of his plays were translated into English by the poet Samuel Taylor Coleridge. Just before his death in 1804, Schiller finished his most popular play, *William Tell.*

Schleswig-Holstein

Schleswig-Holstein is a state of West Germany. It is in the northwestern part of Germany, on a peninsula just south of Denmark. Schleswig-Holstein has an area of about 6,000 square miles, and about 2,300,000 people live there. On the east it borders the Baltic Sea and has many fine natural harbors. On the west it faces the North Sea, with a low, sandy shore that has to be diked against the rough waves. The state has three principal rivers, the Elbe, Trave, and Eider, and it is crossed from the mouth of the Elbe to the Baltic Sea by the Kiel Canal.

Most of the people of Schleswig-Holstein are farmers and cattle-breeders. The chief crops are wheat, rye, and vegetables. In the cities there are shipbuilding yards and many factories. The capital city is Kiel, which is also the seat of the University of Kiel.

For hundreds of years, Schleswig and Holstein were separate states ruled by dukes. Denmark and German countries were in constant conflict over possession of the states. In 1864 Austria and Prussia defeated Denmark in a war and took them over. Then Prussia won them from Austria in the Austro-Prussian War of 1866. After World War I, part of Schleswig voted to belong to Denmark. After World War II Schleswig-Holstein became a state of the German Federal Republic (West Germany).

schnauzer

The schnauzer is a dog that was developed in Bavaria, a section of Germany, at least five hundred years ago. The schnauzer looked then just about the same as it does now. It was used to herd cattle and sheep.

Since then, careful breeding has developed three distinct sizes of schnauzer. There is the *giant schnauzer,* a very big dog almost as big as a great Dane, but with a body shaped more like that of an oversized wire-haired terrier. There is the *standard schnauzer,* a medium-sized dog (about as big as a boxer) and there is the *miniature schnauzer,* which looks like both the larger schnauzers but is only about as large as a cocker spaniel. All three sizes are the same general shape, and all have about the same kind and color of coat, which has wiry hair and a black-and-white or black-and-tan color. The giant schnauzer is not often seen in the United States and Canada, and it was not known outside of Bavaria until about 1900. During World War I it was found that the giant schnauzer was easily trained for police work, and it has been used in Germany for that purpose ever since. Most giant schnauzers in the United States and Canada are kept as pets and as show dogs. The standard schnauzer is a fine rat-catcher.

Miniature schnauzers are terriers. They are most often kept as pets, but they can become expert at catching mice and they are alert watchdogs.

Schnauzers have their ears and tails clipped when the puppies are a few days old.

school

A school is any place where people go to learn something. Schools include primary (or elementary) schools, secondary (or high) schools, and institutions of higher education (colleges and universities). There are schools that teach special trades, professions, and arts. One special kind of school is the correspondence school, which does not conduct classes but sends out written lessons for people to study at home. The different schools are described in the article on EDUCATION.

In ancient times there were no schools. The sons of rich men were taught by private tutors. The poorer people never learned to read and write. Women seldom learned to read and write.

The first schools were probably those of ancient Greece, about 2,500 years ago. They, too, were only for boys and only for the rich people. The schools did not have buildings. The classes were held outdoors, usually near a playing field where the boys had their exercise. Sometimes classes were held in the house of the teacher. Each school consisted of a single teacher. He taught the students everything they learned.

For hundreds of years, during the period called the Middle Ages (from about the year 500 to the year 1500), the only schools in Europe were the monasteries and convents of the Roman Catholic Church. Sons and daughters of noble families went to these schools and were taught by monks and priests and by nuns and sisters.

After England became a Protestant country, about four hundred years ago, clergymen of the Church of England sometimes opened "public schools." These were not like public schools in the United States. They were what Americans would call private schools, because they charged for tuition and only the sons of upper-class families attended them.

The cities of Europe also began to establish schools about four hundred years ago. In one way they were like today's schools, because they had their own buildings and the pupils (all boys) were taught in classrooms. Little was taught except writing, Latin grammar, and simple arithmetic.

Not for hundreds of years after this were there schools for farm families in the country.

SCHOOLS IN AMERICA

There have been schools in America since the first English colonists came, more than three hundred years ago. The early schools were very simple. The schoolhouse usually had only one room. It was built of wood, and perhaps was a log cabin. All the students sat in the one room and were taught by the one teacher. One age group, or grade, would be taught at a time, while the others studied. There was only one teacher, so no group of students could have much of the teacher's time.

As cities grew, schools of a more modern kind began to be built. For more than a hundred years now, there have been city schools in which each grade could have its own classroom and its own teacher. The school buildings were dark and gloomy and uncomfortable compared to the ones being built today, but they were much better than the "little red schoolhouse" of pioneer times.

In villages and farming districts, the one-room school continued. There were not enough people in the community to have separate grades and classes. Many of the students had to travel many miles to get to school, so the school day had to be short and the school had to shut down in the winter when snow blocked the roads.

All this changed when the motor age arrived. The change began in a big way during the 1920s. Good roads have been built, and buses take the children to school and back home again. An entire district, and even two or three districts, can have a single school building just as big and well-equipped as any big-city school.

That is the system in use throughout the United States today. The schools in small towns and farming areas are likely to be even more modern than the city schools, because they have been built more recently. Often they are bigger than city schools, too, with fleets of as many

as a hundred big buses picking up thousands of students every day and carrying them many miles over concrete superhighways. Schools are light and airy. They have gymnasiums and playgrounds and recreation rooms. They use motion pictures and television and recordings in their classwork. One of the great changes brought about by the modern school is that most of the students enjoy going to school (even though they may like to pretend they don't). In the cold, dirty, cheerless schoolhouses of the past, almost nobody liked going to school.

New schoolhouses have remained one of the greatest needs of the United States and most other countries, but great steps forward have been taken already.

Schopenhauer, Arthur

Arthur Schopenhauer was a German philosopher, or thinker, who lived about 150 years ago. He is known as the philosopher of pessimism, which means that he believed there is no such thing as real happiness, that the pleasures and satisfactions we find in life are just temporary relief from boredom and frustration. Schopenhauer was born in 1788, the son of wealthy parents. He studied much and traveled throughout Europe, but he became a bitter and lonely man. His most important work, *The World as Will and Idea*, was published in 1818 but received very little notice at the time. More than 25 years later a second edition was published and this time the book aroused great discussion. By 1854 Schopenhauer was a famous man. He died in 1860.

Schubert, Franz

Franz Schubert was an Austrian composer who lived to be only 31 years old but gave the world some of the greatest romantic music ever written. He is considered the father of the German *Lied*, or romantic song, of which he wrote more than six hundred. His chamber music and symphonies rank high, and the total number of his musical compositions reached more than 1,200. Nevertheless, Schubert's life was one of poverty and much unhappiness, and his music was not widely appreciated until after his death.

Schubert was born in 1797, the son of a schoolmaster. His father and older brother began teaching him music when he was 5, and the boy early showed remarkable talent. Unfortunately, Schubert never received enough professional training to make him a first-rate performer on any instrument. This made it hard for him to earn a living in later life.

When Schubert was 11 he sang in a choir. He began writing music when he was 14, and by the time he was 18 he had written the first of nine symphonies and many songs. Among the songs was a famous one called the *Erl King*. Schubert and his school friends used to hold musical sessions each week, playing ev-

erything from chamber music to symphonies, and here many of Schubert's works had their first performance. All during this period Schubert was unable to get any of his music published, and he was forced to live on the charity of his friends and admirers, of whom he had many. Finally he achieved some little fame, but never enough to make him financially independent.

Schubert's genius seemed to increase as his life moved toward its early end. In 1821 he wrote the symphony that is called the *Unfinished Symphony* because it consists of only two movements instead of the usual four. Schubert died of typhoid fever in 1828.

Schumann, Robert

Robert Schumann was a German composer and pianist who lived about a hundred years ago. He is perhaps best remembered for his piano pieces and his German *Lieder*, or songs, but his symphonies are very popular.

Schumann was born in 1810. His father was a bookseller and publisher, and young Schumann early learned to know and love literature. He began studying and writing music as a child, but his father died when he was 16 and his mother then insisted that he give up music and study law.

When Schumann was 20, his mother at length gave in and permitted him to go to the city of Leipzig to study piano with Friedrich Wieck. Schumann lived with Wieck and practiced the piano for long hours each day. Trying to gain greater finger strength, he used a stretching device and strained a tendon in his right hand. This put an end to his hopes for a career as a concert pianist.

Schumann then turned in earnest to composing and also founded a publication, the *New Journal of Music*. His articles were largely responsible for bringing attention to Chopin, Berlioz, and Brahms, and added greatly to the growing fame of Mendelssohn and Schubert.

Friedrich Wieck's daughter Clara had been a child when Schumann went to live in their home. She also was a gifted pianist, and she performed many of Schumann's works in concerts. As she became a young woman the two gradually fell in love. Clara's father opposed their marriage for many years, but in 1840 he gave in and they were married. The young couple were very happy. Schumann went with Clara on her concert tours, and she introduced most of his new piano music.

In 1854 Schumann became mentally ill and tried to kill himself by jumping into the Rhine River. He was rescued and taken to a sanitarium, where he spent the last two years of his life. He died in 1856. Clara Schumann lived for forty years more and devoted herself to gaining fame for her husband's music.

Schurz, Carl

Carl Schurz was an American political leader who lived about a hundred years ago. He was born in 1826 in Germany. He took part in a revolution in

Germany in 1848, and in 1851 he was forced to flee. He settled in the United States and became a citizen.

At first, Schurz was a lawyer. He supported Abraham Lincoln in his campaign for the Presidency in 1860, and when Lincoln was elected he made Schurz minister to Spain. Schurz also took part in the Civil War, and was made a major general. Next he wrote for a number of newspapers, and in 1869 he was elected Senator from Missouri. In 1877 President Rutherford B. Hayes appointed Schurz Secretary of the Interior. Schurz later became editor of the New York *Evening Post*. He died in 1906.

Schweitzer, Albert

Albert Schweitzer is the name of a great French physician, missionary, and thinker. He was born in 1875 in Alsace, which then belonged to Germany. He became a Protestant minister, then when he was 30 he decided to study medicine and became a doctor. In 1913 he went to a small village in French Equatorial Africa, where he set up a clinic for the natives. Except for trips to the United States and Europe to raise money for his clinic, he remained there, at the town of Lambaréné. Schweitzer also became a fine organist. He is the author of several books, including an autobiography called *Out of My Life and Thought*. In 1952 he was awarded the Nobel Prize for peace. He died in 1965.

sciatica

One of the great nerves of the human body is called the sciatic nerve. It runs along the back part of the thighs, from the hips downward, and has many branches. When this nerve becomes inflamed, the condition is called sciatica. Sciatica often occurs together with rheumatism and neuritis. It is so much like rheumatic pains that it is sometimes called *sciatic rheumatism*. Sciatica is seldom dangerous but it is very painful. The pain may be brought on by exposure to damp, cold weather, or by diseases in the pelvis (the part of the body that forms the hips and bony middle of the body), or by disease or injury to the lower part of the back. The pain may be in the hip, down the leg, or in the foot. Rest in bed may relieve the pain, and sometimes injections are given. Surgery may be necessary in some cases.

scissors

Scissors are an instrument for cutting. They are made of two blades fastened together, so people usually speak of a *pair of scissors*. Large scissors, or shears, were used by the ancient Egyptians, Greeks and Romans for cutting the wool of sheep, and also for clipping hedges and cutting hair. These scissors were made from a single piece of metal that was bent so that the two blades touched. About two thousand years ago someone invented shears with blades crossing, one above the other, and fastened at the center. They were made of iron and other metals, but they were usually brittle and did not wear well. Then,

some six hundred years ago, the first steel scissors were made in Nuremberg, Germany. They were very expensive until cheaper ways of making steel were found. Today scissors are made in hundreds of sizes and shapes and are inexpensive.

Scone, Stone of

The Stone of Scone is a stone shaped somewhat like a pillow. For hundreds of years it was in the abbey at the village of Scone, in Scotland. Scone was at one time the residence of the kings of Scotland. The stone, according to legend, dates from Biblical times. In 1296 King Edward I of England took the stone to Westminster Abbey, in London, England, where the British kings are crowned. The stone lies under the throne in which the new king or queen sits during the coronation ceremony. In 1950 three young Scottish people stole the Stone of Scone from Westminster Abbey and took it to Scotland. They did this partly as a joke, and partly because they thought it should remain in its historic home. They returned it in time for the coronation of Queen Elizabeth II in 1953.

Scotland

Scotland is a country in the northern part of the island of Great Britain. Along with England, to the south, and Wales, to the southwest, and Northern Ireland on the other British island, Scotland is part of the United Kingdom of Great Britain and Northern Ireland. Scotland is an ancient country with a long history of independence.

Scotland is about 30,000 square miles in area, which is about the size of the state of South Carolina. About five million people live there, which is more than twice as many as live in South Carolina. The capital of Scotland is Edinburgh.

WHAT SCOTLAND IS LIKE

Scotland can be divided into three main parts, the Highlands in the north, the Lowlands in the center, and the Uplands in the south. The coastline is rocky and irregular, indented with many sea lochs (narrow inlets) and firths (wide inlets). The country is dotted with beautiful lakes, also called lochs. Many islands surround Scotland, including the Shetland and the Orkney Islands to the north and the Hebrides to the west.

The Uplands are a region of rolling hills and valleys, with many rivers such as the Tweed, the Clyde, and the Teviot. The Lowlands are the industrial heart of Scotland. Three-quarters of the people live here, although it is only one-tenth of the country. The Lowlands have the best farm land of the country and rich mineral deposits. The Highlands occupy the entire northern half of Scotland and have scenery of breathtaking beauty. In this region is Ben Nevis, 4,406 feet high, the highest point on the island of Great Britain.

There are many beautiful and famous lakes, including Loch Lomond, the largest lake in Scotland. Among the many rivers are the Tay, the Dee, the Don, and the Spey. The summer home of the British royal family, Balmoral Castle, is on the Dee.

The climate of Scotland is mild for a country that lies so far to the north. The summers are cool and the winters are cold except in the Hebrides, where waters from the Gulf Stream of the Atlantic Ocean help to keep the winter weather mild.

THE PEOPLE OF SCOTLAND

Very little is known of the people who first lived in Scotland. At the beginning of history, Scotland was inhabited by a people called Picts. When Roman armies occupied England about 1,900 years ago, the Picts and wandering bands of Gaels from Ireland kept them from entering Scotland. The Romans built a huge barrier called Hadrian's Wall across the island to keep the fierce Picts out of England.

During the Roman occupation of England, St. Ninian and other missionaries introduced Christianity to Scotland. After the Romans had left the island, four separate kingdoms grew up in Scotland: the Picts; a Gaelic tribe from Ireland called Scots (who gave the country its name); the Britons; and the Anglo-Saxons. Later invasions of Norsemen and Danes combined with the early settlers. These people mixed and intermarried to form the Scottish people of today.

For many hundreds of years the Scottish people were organized in family groups called CLANS, about which there is a separate article. The ancient language was Gaelic, but today very few Scots speak Gaelic. The national language is English, but the Scots have their own way of speaking it. Their accent is called a "burr," because they stress the r's in a special way.

Most of the people of Scotland belong to the Church of Scotland, a Presbyterian Church, but there is complete freedom of religion. Some of the people are Roman Catholics and some are members of other Protestant Churches.

HOW THE PEOPLE LIVE

The greatest number of the people of Scotland are coal miners or farmers. The principal crops raised are wheat, barley, oats, flax, potatoes, and vegetables. In the Highlands, sheep- and cattle-raising are important. From this region come Ayrshire and Aberdeen Angus cattle, Shetland ponies, and Clydesdale horses. In the Lowlands there are fine orchards.

Scotland is a great industrial nation. In the cities there are important shipbuilding yards, and factories that make locomotives, heavy machinery, textiles, and Scotch whisky. Scotch woolens are famous the world over, and the town of Paisley has given its name to a beautiful fabric design. Fisheries are an important industry.

HOW THE PEOPLE ARE GOVERNED

Since Scotland became united with England in 1707, it has been represented in the British Parliament in London. Scotland has 16 peers in the House of Lords and 71 members in the House of Commons. The Secretary of State for

Aberdeen, population 185,379, in the northeast, a commercial center and fishing port.

Dundee, population 182,959, in the east central part, an industrial and commercial center.

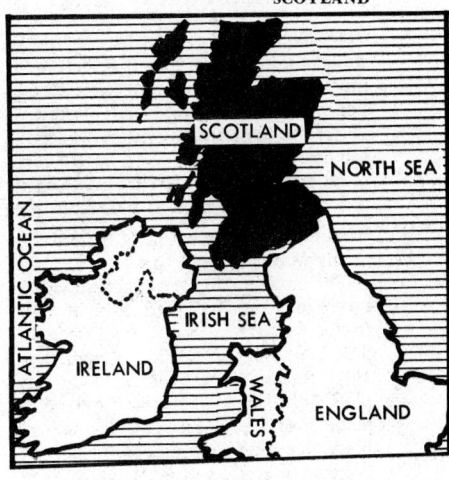

Scotland is a member of the British Prime Minister's Cabinet, and he is responsible for the departments of agriculture, health, education, and home affairs. Local government is by counties, of which there are 33, and by burghs, or cities. The counties and burghs have councils elected by the people to govern local affairs. Scotland has its own courts. The High Court of Justiciary is the chief criminal court, and civil suits are heard in the Court of Sessions.

Scotland has long been a pioneer in education, and it has four of the world's oldest universities, in St. Andrew's, Glasgow, Aberdeen, and Edinburgh. Children from the ages of 5 to 13 must go to school.

PRINCIPAL CITIES

The capital of Scotland is EDINBURGH, about which there is a separate article. Other important cities are:

Glasgow, population 1,054,913, largest city of Scotland, in the west central part, an important industrial port.

SCOTLAND IN THE PAST

Scotland's history as a united nation began almost a thousand years ago when Duncan I proclaimed himself King of Scotland. He was the son of Malcolm II, king of the Picts, who had won control of a large part of Scotland.

Duncan was soon killed by a nobleman named Macbeth, about whom Shakespeare wrote a famous play, but Duncan's son killed Macbeth and became king as Malcolm III. This was in the year 1057. Malcolm III married an English princess named Margaret (who later was declared a saint) and they introduced English ways into Scotland. Their court became a center of culture and Scotland was peaceful and prosperous.

The next five hundred years of Scottish history were marked by wars in which English kings tried to gain control of Scotland and Scottish noble families plotted and fought against one another to win the Scottish throne. In 1174 the English king Henry II captured King William the Lion of Scotland and brought Scotland under English control, but Henry's son, Richard I ("the Lion-Hearted"), sold Scotland its freedom for money that he needed to make a Crusade to the Holy Land. English kings after Richard claimed the Scottish throne several times, but the Scottish patriots William Wallace and then Robert the Bruce (who became King Robert I of Scotland)

were able to win enough battles to discourage the English claims. Robert won the throne in 1314 when he defeated the English at the Battle of Bannockburn, one of the most famous victories in Scottish history. The Baliol and Douglas families were among the Scottish noble families that tried to become kings, but the Bruces and their descendants, the Stuarts, finally won.

The English kings never again made a successful claim for the Scottish throne. In fact, Mary Stuart (Mary Queen of Scots) was put to death in England in 1587 because it was thought she was plotting to become queen of England in place of Queen Elizabeth I. The son of Mary Queen of Scots did become king of England as well as of Scotland, as King James I of England and James VI of Scotland, when Elizabeth died in 1603. This united England and Scotland under the same king, and in 1707 they became officially one country, Great Britain.

Trouble between England and Scotland was not ended. In 1688, the English Parliament overthrew James II, a member of the Stuart family. James became a refugee in France, and after him his son James and his grandson Charles both claimed the English throne. Many of the Scottish people supported these claimants (called *pretenders*) and fought several battles against the English in trying to restore the throne to them. At the last of these battles, the Battle of Culloden in 1746, the English won such a decisive victory that the Stuart pretenders gave up the fight. The English and Scottish nations have been wholly united ever since, though for fifty years more some of the Highland families, who had been supporters of the pretenders, had occasional fights with the Lowland people, most of whom had sided with England.

The remaining history of the Scottish nation is the history of Great Britain. See the article ENGLAND. There are also articles on most of the kings, queens, and events mentioned in this article.

SCOTLAND. Area, 30,405 square miles. Population (1973 census) 5,217,000. Government, part of the United Kingdom of Great Britain and Northern Ireland. Capital, Edinburgh. Language, English. Religion, Presbyterian (Church of Scotland).

Scott, Robert F.

Robert Falcon Scott was a great English explorer and was one of the first men to reach the South Pole. He was born in 1868 and became an officer in the British Navy. He led a party that reached the South Pole on January 18, 1912, but the Norwegian explorer Roald Amundsen had reached it a few weeks before. Scott and his party died tragically on the return trip when they were trapped by bad weather.

Scott, Sir Walter

Walter Scott was a great British writer who lived more than a hundred years ago. His novels of romance and adventure, such as *Ivanhoe, The Talisman,* and dozens of others (called the Waverley novels), and his long poems such as *Marmion* and *The Lady of the Lake,* are still read by children and grownups alike. Scott was born in 1771. He made a great deal of money, bought a famous estate called Abbotsford, and was

made a baronet (giving him the title "Sir") in 1820. But in 1826 he became bankrupt, and though he was not legally required to pay his debts he went to work to do so. His hard work ruined his health and he died in 1832, but the writings published during his lifetime and after his death paid all the debts.

Scottish terrier

The Scottish terrier, or Scottie, is a small terrier that came originally from the county of Aberdeen, Scotland. It is often called an Aberdeen terrier. It is kept mainly as a pet, but it will catch any mice or rats that happen to appear where it lives. Scotties are good pets and are always ready for a brisk run or a game of tag with their owners.

A Scottish terrier is nearly always a very dark gray or black. It has a curved tail and small ears that stand up in V-shaped points. Its front legs seem very short, and its nose looks long and squared-off at the end. A Scottie stands about ten inches high at the shoulders and usually weighs between 18 and 22 pounds.

Sculptor Simon Moselsio chisels a work called "Mother and Child" from granite.

Sculpture

Sculpture is the art of carving or modeling a reproduction of something that has been seen or imagined. Sculpture, like painting, is one of the fine arts. Anything artistic that is solid, such as a statue, is considered sculpture. Also, any kind of carved picture that is raised from a flat surface or cut into a flat surface is a form of sculpture. This kind of sculpture is called *relief.* You often see relief sculpture on the sides of buildings.

The earliest sculptural art that can still be seen is the relief carvings on buildings of the Sumerians who lived more than five thousand years ago in the country now called Iraq. The Assyrians, who came after the Sumerians and lived in the same region, were even finer relief sculptors. They made huge figures of their kings and of their gods and of great animals. Many of these were made from imagination. Some of the animals had the bodies of bulls, the wings of eagles, and the heads of lions.

At about the same time the Egyptians were beginning to express themselves in sculpture. The Egyptians carved ornaments out of precious stones. They built huge temples with great towering carved figures of their kings and their gods. Some of these figures still stand in the deserts of Egypt. The great Sphinx, a huge figure of a lion with a woman's head, still stands in the desert near Cairo, Egypt.

GREEK AND ROMAN SCULPTURE

Of all the ancient peoples, the Greeks were the finest sculptors. The period of the greatest Greek sculpture began about 2,500 years ago. Two of the greatest Greek sculptors were named Phidias and Praxiteles. These two sculptors made some of the finest works of art of all time. They modeled statues of the heroes of Greece and created statues of some of the Greek gods. One of the Seven Wonders of the World was a statue of their chief god, Zeus. The great public buildings and beautiful temples of ancient Greece were covered with relief sculpture and contained many beautiful statues. The Greeks worked almost entirely in stone; they carved or chiseled their statues from marble or granite.

The sculpture of the ancient Romans was a continuation of the great Greek sculpture. The Greeks had a finer eye and feeling for beauty, but the Romans produced many fine pieces of sculpture.

EARLY ORIENTAL SCULPTURE

For thousands of years the people of the East, the Chinese, Indians, and other Asiatics, have been making great sculpture. Some of the work of these Eastern people is very delicate. Many of the carvings are small pieces of ivory or hardwood. Some are in precious stones. Green jade was a favorite stone of the Chinese carvers. The sculptors of Asia used much more imagination than the Greeks, Romans, and others in the West. Throughout Asia there are temples made hundreds of years ago that contain wonderful examples of Oriental sculpture. Many of these statues and relief carvings are highly imaginative ideas of what these people thought their gods looked like. There are figures with several heads or with several arms and legs.

SCULPTURE AND ARCHITECTURE

Sculpture has gone hand in hand with the art of building, called architecture. Most of the ancient temples had sculpture in them or carved on the outside. During the Middle Ages, when great cathedrals were being built in Europe, the sculptor worked closely with the architect. Many of the cathedrals have relief sculpture on their walls. The main doors of the cathedrals are often relief sculptures showing scenes from the Bible. Both inside and outside the cathedrals there are statues placed in niches and arches. Among the most famous exam-

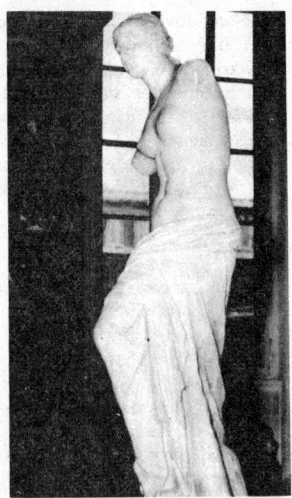

The *Venus de Milo* is another example of the gracefulness of the best Greek sculpture.

A medieval carved-ivory Madonna is less realistic, but has great religious beauty.

French work of the early Renaissance shows a merchant at the balcony of his home.

ples of church sculpture are the carved statues of Biblical persons and saints on the outer walls of the cathedral at Chartres, France, and the hundreds of figures on the Cathedral of Notre Dame in Paris, France.

STATUES AND MONUMENTS

Statues and monuments are among the greatest examples of sculpture. In every large city in every park and public square, there are statues of heroes and patriots. Some of these are carved in stone. Others are cast from bronze.

When a sculptor works with rock, he carves with a chisel and hammer until he has chipped away everything except the figure he wants. For a bronze statue or monument the sculptor first models the figure in clay. When the clay hardens, he pours a coat of plaster over it. When the plaster is hard, he cuts it away carefully and then puts the pieces of plaster together again to form a mold. Into this mold is poured melted bronze or another metal. The finished metal statue looks the same as the original clay model, except that it will last for a much longer time.

Probably the greatest sculptor was MICHELANGELO, about whom you may read in another article. He lived in Italy about four hundred years ago. Many of his statues can still be seen in Italy, particularly in the cities of Rome and Florence, and in museums in other parts of the world. His greatest works are probably his statue of the young David of the Bible and the lawgiver, Moses. Another great Renaissance sculptor about whom there is an article is LEONARDO DA VINCI.

KINDS OF SCULPTURE

There are many different kinds of sculpture. Basically there are the full, rounded sculpture and the relief sculpture already mentioned, but modern sculptors have developed other kinds of sculpture.

Some modern sculptors hammer and fashion pieces out of soft, heated metal. They create very imaginative works of art by twisting, bending and hammering metal strips and plates into various forms. One kind of modern sculpture is called the *mobile*. You may see a mobile hanging from a ceiling in a modern building. A mobile is composed of different pieces of metal or wood or other substances. The pieces are strung together and sway in the slightest current of air.

STUDYING SCULPTURE

There are many schools where sculpture is taught. At these schools the student learns how to work with the various materials of a sculptor and also to draw, sketch and plan the works he will make.

The student learns how to model with soft clay before he begins to carve. The better students progress to stone sculpture, woodcarving, and casting. Many people who go to art school to study sculpture do not expect to become professional sculptors but merely enjoy working with their hands and creating something. To many people sculpture is a hobby. They carve figures out of all kinds of material, including soap.

scurvy

Scurvy is a sickness that is caused by not eating an important food element called *Vitamin C*. Vitamin C is found in fruits, especially oranges, lemons, and grapefruits, and in vegetables. Persons who do not eat these foods may get swollen, infected gums, and their teeth may become loose and even fall out. In children, scurvy may cause the bones to grow crooked. Scurvy is especially dangerous to babies. It makes them have loose bowels and fever, and lose weight. It can also cause loss of blood through the intestines. Scurvy is quickly cured when the sick person or child is given the missing Vitamin C, in drugs or in citrus fruits. Green vegetables such as broccoli, Brussels sprouts, kale, mustard, and turnip greens, and green peppers have a lot of Vitamin C in them, but they lose much of it when they are cooked.

Scylla and Charybdis

Scylla and Charybdis were two fearful sea monsters, in stories told by the Greeks more than two thousand years ago. Scylla had been a beautiful girl, but an enchantress named Circe was jealous and turned her into a monster having six heads with terrible teeth, and twelve feet. Scylla lived in a cave high up on a cliff and each of her heads was on a long neck with which she could reach out and seize sailors on passing ships. Charybdis was supposed to suck in great waves of water, making a whirlpool that engulfed passing ships.

These monsters were believed to live on the sides of the Strait of Messina, a narrow stretch of water between Italy and the island of Sicily.

When we say today that a person is "between Scylla and Charybdis," we mean that he has two choices of action but each is so bad that things cannot go well for him, no matter what he does.

sea, a large body of water, usually salty. A sea may be an arm of an ocean, as the Caribbean Sea is. Sea is often used as another name for the OCEAN.

sea horse

The sea horse is a small sea animal, or fish. It has a head like a horse's, a tail that can grasp things the way a monkey's tail can, a pouch like a kangaroo's, and a scaly outer shell like an insect's. Sea horses live in tropical (warm) and temperate (cool) seas all over the world and usually in shallow water. The largest seldom grow more than one foot in length. These live in the Pacific Ocean, between southern California and northern Peru. The common sea horse of the Atlantic Ocean is usually about four inches long, but the dwarf sea horse of Florida never grows to be more than about two inches long.

In addition to the oddities of its appearance, the sea horse has another unusual feature. It is the male sea horse that carries the eggs about until they are hatched. The female lays eggs in the late spring and early summer, placing them in the pouch on the abdomen of the male. The male carries them for about a month and a half. The common sea horse hatches between 150 and 200 young at a time, but the dwarf sea horse usually has 10 or fewer.

Sea horses live only in sea water and eat only small, live animals called crustaceans.

seal

The seal is a special mark that is put on certain official papers. In early times, a seal was a sort of signature. A person

would have a piece of metal or perhaps a ring (called a signet ring) with a special design carved in it. When he sent a message he would press this design into a melted material called sealing wax, which would harden. This kind of "sealing" could be done over the place where the paper or envelope was folded, and if the seal was not broken it would mean that the letter had not been opened. Some envelopes are sealed in this way even today, and postage stamps were once used to seal envelopes and at the same time pay the postage.

The modern legal seal is a die, a kind of tool, made of metal. It is cut so that it will press words and designs into the paper. Governments, public officials and corporations have seals of this kind.

The first country to use such a seal was England. It was adopted by the English king, Edward the Confessor, more than nine hundred years ago. It is called the Great Seal. Now most countries have such seals.

The Great Seal of the United States was designed by a man named Will Barton, in 1782. Its face shows the motto *E Pluribus Unum* (Latin words meaning, "from many, one"—that is, one nation formed from many states).

seal and sea lion

Seals are animals with flippers in place of legs and feet. They live in the sea, but come ashore to mate and bear their young. They are expert swimmers and can remain under water for several minutes at a time, but they must come to the surface to breathe. They are warm-blooded animals and are mammals—they bear living young and nurse them.

The animals that most people call seals are not true seals but *sea lions*. This group includes the "trained seals" of circuses and the seal that provides the valuable fur for women's coats.

THE TRUE SEALS

There are many different kinds of true seal. None have ears on the outside of the head.

The true seal is covered with short, coarse hair, with no undercoat. (It is the undercoat of the fur seal that is used as fur. The coarse outer hair is removed completely.) The true seal is often called a *hair seal*, because of that coat.

True seals are found in all the oceans of the world, and they have traveled into many large rivers and even to some inland lakes. The *harbor seal* is the most familiar along the northern coasts of the Atlantic Ocean in both Europe and North America. Like other seals, it lives on fish. The full-grown male harbor seal is about five feet long and weighs about 100 pounds.

The ringed seal spends its life in Arctic waters. It does not migrate to warmer waters when its home freezes over, but keeps air holes open in the ice so that it can come up for air when necessary.

Other kinds of seal include the *harp*, or *Greenland*, *seal*; the *gray seal* of Ireland and Scotland; the *bearded seal* of the Arctic; the *elephant seal*, largest of all seals, which sometimes weighs as much as 5,000 pounds; the *monk seal* of the warm Mediterranean, Caribbean, and South Pacific waters; and others.

SEA LIONS

Sea lions have ears and are also called "eared seals." The coat of the sea lion has a dense undercoat and coarse outer hair.

The seal fur that is used to make costly fur garments is made from the skin of the sea lion that is called the *northern fur seal*. The pelt of the *southern fur seal* is also used, but it is of inferior quality.

The largest of the sea lions is the *northern*, or *Steller's*, *sea lion* (named for the German scientist who discovered it). A male of this group may be as long as thirteen feet and weigh as much as 2,000 pounds, but the female reaches less than half that size and weight.

Sea lion bulls (males) spend the mating season battling to assemble a harem of cows (females). The male of the northern fur seal is very jealous, and will fight if any of his wives strays into another bull's herd.

Sealyham

The Sealyham is a small terrier that was bred originally in Wales to catch otters, badgers, and foxes. It has very short legs and can dig its way into a foxhole quickly. Because of its low body, it

The Sealyham is small, but a good fighter.

can catch the fox underground. Most Sealyhams in America are kept as pets, but there are contests every year in the United States to keep up their fox-hunting ability.

A Sealyham is usually white all over. It has a short tail, which is clipped when the puppy is a few days old. Its coat is rough and wiry, and thick underneath to keep the dog warm in the coldest weather. The dog stands about ten inches high at the shoulder and usually weighs about twenty pounds.

Sea Scouts, a branch of the Boy Scouts whose members are trained in sea duties: see the article BOY SCOUTS.

seasickness

Seasickness is a kind of motion sickness, caused by the rocking of a boat. It makes a person feel like vomiting. In a car it is called *carsickness*, in a plane *airsickness*. It is very unpleasant but is not usually serious. Seasickness happens more easily when you are in a hot stuffy cabin, or where there are unpleasant odors. It may also happen from nervous upset or excitement. Persons who get seasick should avoid heavy meals, breathe plenty of fresh air, and relax as much as possible. They should not look at the waves,

as the up-and-down motion will make them feel like vomiting. Weak tea or another warm drink with a dry cracker may help to quiet the stomach. During World War II, a medicine called *Dramamine* was taken before sea voyages to help prevent or control seasickness. Since then other drugs, such as *Benadryl,* have been found to relieve seasickness.

seasons

A season is a particular time of each year. In some parts of the world people speak of a dry season and a rainy season. Children call a time of the year a season by the games they play. There is a sleigh-riding season, a swimming season, a baseball season, a football season, and so on. But usually when we speak of seasons we mean the four seasons of the year: spring, summer, fall or autumn, and winter. These four seasons are not the same all over the world. They are caused by the way the sun shines on the earth, and at any particular time the sun is shining differently on different parts of the earth.

WHAT CAUSES THE SEASONS

The earth is always moving. It moves in two ways. It travels around the sun in a slightly flattened circle called its *orbit*. This trip around the sun takes the earth one year. While the earth is moving around the sun, it is also spinning on its *axis*. The axis of the earth is an imaginary line that goes through the earth from the North Pole to the South Pole. This line is tilted at an angle to the sun.

As it moves around the sun and spins on its tilted axis, the earth receives different amounts of light from the sun at different places. Also, it receives the sun's rays in different ways. If you take a flashlight and direct it against the wall straight ahead you will see that a fairly small round portion of the wall is lighted up. Now tilt your flashlight quite a bit and you will see that you light up a greater portion of the wall but there is less light on each spot. This experiment shows how the rays of the sun fall on the earth. When the direct rays of the sun are striking a particular part of the earth, that part of the earth is having its summer season. It is receiving more light and more heat than when it is tilted away from the sun. When the earth is tilted so that a particular region receives slanting rays, that region is having its winter. Spring and fall are in-between times.

ZONES OF THE EARTH

The earth is divided from the North Pole to the South Pole into several different *zones*. Starting from the top we have the first zone, called the Arctic Circle. Below that we have the North Temperate Zone. Most of the United States and Canada is in this zone. Below the North Temperate Zone is the middle belt of the earth, called the Torrid Zone. Below that is the South Temperate Zone, and finally the Antarctic Circle.

The Torrid Zone, in the middle of the earth, is always hot because no matter where the earth is, in its journey around the sun, this zone receives much sunlight. The Torrid Zone has about a twelve-hour day and a twelve-hour night all through the year.

The North Temperate Zone has the four seasons, spring, summer, fall, and winter. The South Temperate Zone has the same four seasons but at the opposite times. When it is summer in the United States it is winter in South American countries such as Brazil and Argentina. When it is spring in one place it is fall in the other.

The seasons come at almost exactly the same times each year. In the North Temperate Zone, spring comes about March 21, summer about June 21, fall about September 21, and winter about December 21. On each of these dates the earth has completed another quarter its journey around the sun. Winter, for instance, is at that time when the earth is at one end of its orbit with the axis pointed away from the sun. See also the articles on EQUINOX and SOLSTICE.

LIVING THINGS AND SEASONS

All living things on the earth, whether plant or animal life, are affected by the change in seasons. During the spring, plants bud and begin to grow. During the summer they reach their full growth and life. During the fall they start to die, and by winter they are gone. That is why farmers plant in the spring, grow their crops in the summer, harvest in the fall, and let the ground be idle in the winter.

During the cold winters some animals escape the cold by migrating, moving away to warmer climates. Other animals take care of themselves by hibernating, sleeping through the winter. Man is the only living thing that has learned to live the same life, in the same place, in all seasons.

SEATO, a name used for the Southeast Asia Collective Defense Treaty Organization: see SOUTHEAST ASIA TREATY ORGANIZATION.

Seattle

Seattle is the largest city of the state of Washington. It is in the western part, on the shore of Puget Sound, which gives the city an outlet to the Pacific Ocean. Seattle is one of the principal cities of the Pacific Northwest, a commercial, industrial and transportation center. It is the closest United States port to the Far East and is the southern end of the Inside Passage to Alaska. Seattle is set in a scene of great beauty, with the Cascade and Olympic Mountains towering over it. Its location on Puget Sound makes it a popular vacation spot.

More than half a million people live in Seattle. There are large airplane and shipbuilding plants, and factories that make metal products, textiles, and clothing. Food-processing is also important. Seattle is a fur market and is the home port for a large fishing fleet.

Seattle is the seat of the University of Washington, which is noted for its beautiful buildings and campus on the shore of Lake Washington. On its grounds are an art gallery, the Washington State Museum, and the Show Boat Theater on the lake. Also on Lake Washington is the world's largest floating bridge, largely supported by pontoons.

Seattle was founded in 1851 by a group of pioneers led by Arthur Denny. Lumbering was the principal business of the town until the discovery of gold in Alaska in 1897, when it became the supply center and departure point for gold prospectors. Seattle was the site of the Alaska-Yukon-Pacific Exposition in 1909 and the Century 21 Exposition in 1962.

SEATTLE, WASHINGTON. Population (1970 census) 530,831. County seat of King County. On Puget Sound. Founded in 1851.

sea urchin

The sea urchin is a small animal that lives in the ocean. It looks like a tiny porcupine. It has spiny points that stick out all over it, making it look like a pincushion with the pinpoints sticking out instead of in. It is found in oceans all over the world, except in the very coldest Arctic waters.

The common sea urchin of the American Atlantic coast, found from New England to Central America, is a purplish color. It can be found from low-tide mark to water six or seven hundred feet deep. It is round in shape, about 1¾ inches across. Sea urchins are popular as food in Italy and southern France.

seaweed

Seaweed is the name given to a large number of plants that grow in the sea. There are many different kinds. Some merely float in the water, some are fastened to the bottom of the sea or to rocks. Some seaweeds are used for food, some make fertilizers for gardens, some are used in the manufacture of medicines, and there are other uses.

Seaweed is a form of ALGAE, about which there is a separate article.

secession

When a state withdraws from a union with other states, it is said to secede and its act is called secession. Secession has been an important question in American history ever since the United States was formed. At first most states thought they had the right to secede. At various times, Kentucky, Virginia, Maine, Massachusetts and other states threatened to secede. The only time that secession actually occurred was in 1860, when eleven southern states did secede and formed the Confederate States of America. This resulted in the CIVIL WAR, about which there is a separate article.

secretary

A secretary is a person whose job is to write letters and reports for a person or company, or to assist someone of higher rank or importance. The word forms a very high title in governments. The Secretary of State in the United States is the head of one of the most important branches of the government and is the highest-ranking member of the President's cabinet. The heads of the most of the other departments also have the title Secretary, for example the Secretary of the Treasury and the Secretary of Labor. In a corporation (a business firm licensed by a state), the secretary is one of the four principal officers, the others being president, vice-president, and treasurer. The secretary keeps the records of meetings and often represents the company in business dealings just as any other officers would. In a club, there are often two secretaries, the recording secretary, who keeps the records, and the corresponding secretary, who writes official letters for the club. In a business office, a secretary is an assistant to an executive. The title is often used for a stenographer who works for only one executive. See STENOGRAPHY.

secretary bird

The secretary bird is related to the eagle but does not look like an eagle except for its hooked beak. It has very long legs and is about four feet in height. The secretary bird lives in Africa. It seldom flies, though it can fly very well if necessary. It spends most of its time on the ground, catching lizards, large insects, small animals, and snakes. Its long, horny legs protect it from snakebites.

The secretary bird has long, graceful feathers sticking out from the back of its head. They look like old-fashioned quill pens. The birds are slate-gray or black all over.

Secret Service

The United States Secret Service is a division of the Treasury Department. It is one of the main detective services of the United States government, and until the Federal Bureau of Investigation was formed in 1908 it was almost the only one. The principal work of the Secret Service is in preventing the counterfeiting of United States money, postage stamps, and government bonds. It also protects government banking and moneylending branches against any embezzling or cheating by their employees. Detectives of the Secret Service are often called "T-men" (Treasury men).

The best-known work of the Secret Service is done by its White House Detail, whose job is to guard the President. In 1901, after President William McKinley was assassinated, Congress gave the Secret Service the job of guarding every President. The Secret Service worked out scientific ways of doing this, and its methods have been used by the police of nearly every other country. Usually the Secret Service is able to guard the President without disturbing his privacy greatly, but the President has to be carefully guarded whether or not he likes it, because he must obey the laws passed by Congress.

The Secret Service began its work in 1864. During its early years its detectives did some counter-espionage work (to prevent foreign spies from stealing official secrets), but the F.B.I. now has this duty.

In Great Britain, the Secret Service is a branch of the government that does counter-espionage work and also gets information about enemy countries.

Securities and Exchange Commission

The Securities and Exchange Commission, or S.E.C., is an agency of the United States government. Its job is to protect persons who buy and sell securities (stocks and bonds). The S.E.C. was set up in 1934, after millions of people had lost money by buying securities that were dishonestly advertised.

The Commission has five members. They are appointed by the President,

with the approval of the Senate, for five-year terms. They are assisted by a staff of experts in law, engineering, accounting, and other fields. The S.E.C. makes certain regulations (rules) and in most cases a person who wants to sell stocks or bonds must have the S.E.C.'s approval and must follow its rules. One is that anyone who sells a security must give certain information about it to the person buying it. If a corporation has many stockholders throughout the country, there are certain things its management cannot do without the approval of the S.E.C. See also the article on STOCK EXCHANGE.

sedative

A sedative is a chemical or drug that helps persons to sleep or relax, or to feel less pain when they have been hurt. Persons who are very nervous or worried, or who have suffered from a shocking experience, are sometimes given sedatives. Sedatives are also given to relieve nervous fits or spasms, coughing spells, and nausea.

Strong sedatives or "sleeping pills," such as phenobarbital, may be habit-forming. If used carelessly, without the advice of a doctor, they are bad for the health.

Sedatives work by affecting the nerves that control the muscles of the body. When certain chemicals reach these nerves, the muscles become relaxed instead of tense, and a person's feelings and thoughts, which are put together by billions of nerves in the brain, become less active.

seed

A seed is the "egg" of a flowering plant. It contains everything necessary for producing a new plant that will grow to be like the one from which the seed came. Seeds may be so tiny you can hardly see them or as large as three or four inches from end to end. A peach pit is an example of a large seed.

Inside every fertile seed—that is, a seed that can grow into a new plant—there are several necessary parts.

There is always the "germ" of the seed, from which the growth must start. Then there is an important supply of "food" for the germ, also contained within the seed itself. This food supply may be so small that it can be seen only with a microscope, but it is always present. Around the outside of the food section, and covering the germ of the seed as well, there is a protective coating. In the case of a peach pit, it is heavy and hard. In the case of many flower and vegetable seeds, it is thin and delicate. The covering is strong enough to protect the seed but not too tough for the sprouting seed to break through when it is ready to grow.

Nature provides many seeds with special traveling devices, so that they may be carried on air currents or winds to new ground in which to grow. An example is the white feathery substance of a dandelion blossom. There is a seed at the base of each tiny strand of feathery white. A maple tree's seed is carried in a pod. At the end of the pod there is a flat wing that travels on air currents.

See the article on PLANT.

Seeds travel in many ways: The milkweed floats, the lupine explodes, the maple flies, the sandburr sticks to animals, and the hawthorn hitchhikes when birds swallow it whole but do not digest it.

Seeing-Eye dogs

A Seeing-Eye dog is a dog that is specially trained to guide a blind person. The training is given to dogs by an organization at Morristown, New Jersey, called The Seeing Eye. More than a thousand dogs trained by this organization are in use at all times.

The Seeing-Eye dog wears a harness with a handle sticking up from it. The blind person holds this handle when he walks, and the dog guides him safely. Seeing-Eye dogs are trained to avoid holes, anything that a person might trip over, approaching automobiles or other vehicles, and many kinds of danger. There are hundreds of known cases in which Seeing Eye dogs have saved blind persons from accidents or fires.

Not only the dog but also the blind person must have special training. The blind person goes to The Seeing Eye school and is taught how to be guided by the dog.

Nearly all Seeing-Eye dogs are German shepherds, but some other breeds, such as boxers, can be trained to be just as good.

Seine

The Seine is a river in France, 482 miles long. It rises in west central France, flows northwest in a very winding course, and empties into the English Channel at Le Havre. Many French rivers are tributaries of the Seine, including the Marne, Aube, and Oise. The Seine flows through the city of Paris, where it divides around an island, the Ile de la Cité. It is linked by canals to the Meuse, Rhine, Loire and other rivers. The Seine is the principal navigable river of France, and much of the growth of such cities as Paris, Rouen and Le Havre has depended on it.

seismograph

A seismograph is an instrument that tells when an earthquake occurs. Usually it also tells where the earthquake is and how severe it is.

An earthquake sends waves through the earth, just as a stone dropped in a pond sends waves (ripples) through the water. Most seismographs work by means of a pendulum that swings smoothly unless some shaking disturbs the earth. This shaking will affect the swing of the pendulum enough to show irregular lines on a chart, called a *seismogram,* that keeps a record of the swinging pendulum. This chart shows the speed at which the waves travel and the direction from which they come, and from this information experts can calculate the place and time of the earthquake. There is a famous seismograph at Fordham University in New York City and there are others, maintained by governments and by universities, in many parts of the world. See also the article EARTHQUAKE.

Selective Service

Selective Service is a method used in the United States to draft men for the armed forces in times of war or threatened war.

Under the Selective Service System, each man in a certain age group established by Congress must register. (In World War II, the age group extended from 18 to 45 years of age.) Each man is then given a classification. This classification may be 1A in the case of a young man who is physically fit, who has no dependents, and who is not doing a kind of work that is highly important to the war effort; or 3A for a person who has a wife and children to support; or 4F for a person who is not well enough to stand military life or to be useful; or any one of a number of other classifications.

The Selective Service System is under the direction of a government agency, which makes the rules; but in each county a Draft Board is appointed from citizens who live in that county. This Draft Board makes the decisions on how the men of the county should be classified. The idea is that the members of the Draft Board can judge their neighbors much better than government or military officials could.

There are Appeal Boards in all states, and men can apply to them if they think the Draft Board's decision has been unfair.

The Selective Service System was first used when the United States entered World War I in 1917, and was again used in 1940 when World War II was under way. It was continued after World War II because of the continuing wars or threat of war in Korea and Vietnam.

Seljuks

The Seljuks were a tribe who appeared in western Asia and Europe about nine hundred years ago, when they settled in the region that is now Iran. They were a Turkish people. They became Moslems (followers of the religion of Mohammed). Under a leader named Alp Arslan, they conquered much of Asia Minor and the Near East, including the Holy Land.

The Crusades, in which Christian knights tried to recapture the birthplace of Jesus, were fought mostly against the Seljuk Turks.

See also the article TURKS.

semantics

Semantics is a branch of linguistics, the study of languages. Semantics deals with the meanings of words. A word can have two kinds of meaning. One is called its *denotation,* or direct meaning. The other is its *connotation,* which is an idea that the word expresses at the same time. Consider the sentence, "James ran when John wanted to fight." The word "ran" *denotes* only that James moved his legs rapidly in getting from one place to another. It *connotes* that James was afraid. In 1933 a scientist named Alfred Korzybski introduced a branch of psychology (the study of the mind) called *General Semantics,* based on the idea that people's behavior is influenced by the ideas they receive from words.

semaphore

A semaphore is a device for giving signals by the position of arms. It is used chiefly on railroads. The device is placed above the track where the locomotive engineer can see it as his train approaches. Depending on the position of the arms, it tells him that it is safe to go ahead, or that he should stop, or that he should go slowly. There are signal lights, like traffic lights, on the same device. Some semaphores are automatically controlled by electricity.

Semaphore signaling is also done with flags. A person holding the flags can signal the different letters of the alphabet by the position of his arms, and so can spell out a message to someone who can see him but is too far away to hear him. This method of signaling was once much used on ships but now blinker lights are most often used.

Seminole Indians

The Seminoles are a tribe of American Indians in Florida. About 150 years ago the Seminoles made many raids against the white settlers. Also, slaves who had run away found refuge among the Seminoles and became members of the tribe. For both of these reasons, the settlers appealed to the United States government, which sent troops to fight them. Beginning in 1816, there was a

series of small battles known as the Seminole Wars. One of the Seminole chiefs who led the fight against the white men was Osceola. The Seminoles retreated into the great Everglades swamps and for a long time successfully resisted all attack. Actual fighting did not end until 1842, when about four thousand Seminoles were sent to Indian Territory in Oklahoma. About three hundred remained in Florida. The war did not come to an official end until 1934. There are now about six hundred Seminoles in Florida, and most of them live in the Everglades. The Seminoles of Oklahoma number about two thousand.

Semites

The Semites are a group of people who for thousands of years have lived in the lands around the eastern Mediterranean Sea. Their name comes from Shem, one of the sons of Noah, in the Bible. After the great flood, when Noah's ark landed, Shem went forth and started a family. All those peoples who are supposed to have descended from Shem's family are the Semites. They are not a race, but are those people who speak a group of languages that are called Semitic languages. Hebrew and Arabic are the only important Semitic languages that are still spoken. Thousands of years ago there were many others, including Babylonian, Assyrian, Aramaic, and Phoenician.

People often speak of Jews as Semites, because the ancient language of the Jews is Hebrew. The Arabs also are Semites.

senate

A senate is a group of men who make laws. In ancient times, the senate was the counsel of elders, or wise, old men. Usually these men belonged to the richest and most powerful families of the country. The word *senate* comes from a word in the Latin language, used by the ancient Romans, meaning "old man," and the first group of elders called a senate was in ancient Rome. Many states and countries today have two lawmaking bodies, one of which has more rights and powers than the other. The more powerful is often called the upper house, or the senate. In the United States Congress, the Senate is the upper house.

The men who wrote the United States Constitution wanted the Senators to be elected by the state legislatures instead of by all the people, because they did not trust the people to choose the best men. Many states followed this practice until 1913, when the Seventeenth Amendment to the Constitution was passed. This Amendment said that Senators would be elected by all the people, as members of the House of Representatives are. In most states, if a Senator dies the Governor of his state may appoint a Senator to fill out his term.

Seneca

Seneca was a Roman philosopher, or thinker, and playwright. He lived al-

most two thousand years ago. He was a member of the Stoic school, which believed that virtue should be the highest aim in life and that man should avoid the pleasures of the world and think mostly of doing his duty to his fellow man. Seneca was the tutor of young Nero, who became one of the cruelest emperors in the history of Rome. During the first years of Nero's rule, Seneca had great influence over him and persuaded him to be a good emperor. Then Nero surrounded himself with wicked advisers. He accused Seneca of conspiring against him and commanded Seneca to commit suicide. Seneca killed himself in the year 65, by opening his veins in his bath.

Senegal, The Republic of

Senegal, a former territory in French West Africa, achieved its independence on June 20, 1960, joining with Sudan to become the Federation of Mali. However, this union was dissolved a few months later and the Republic of Senegal became a separate nation. Its capital is the important port of Dakar. The Senegalese peoples are mostly Negroes who follow the Mohammedan religion. Farming and livestock-raising are the most important occupations, and peanuts are the chief crop. Senegal is a member of the French Community.

THE REPUBLIC OF SENEGAL. Area, 76,124 square miles. Population (1973 estimate), 4,020,000. Capital, Dakar (300,000).

senility

A person is said to be *senile* when he has lost some of his mental and physical abilities because of old age, and his condition is called *senility.* "Old age" comes to different people at different ages. It may be as early as 60, it may be 70, it may be 80 or even older. However, after a certain age the body, and sometimes the mind, begins to develop various kinds of trouble. The bones become brittle, the hair loses its color, the eyes see less clearly, and the different organs of the body, such as the stomach, heart, kidneys, and bladder, begin to work poorly. In some persons who are senile the mind wanders, they cannot remember things from day to day, or they begin to say and do senseless things. Today doctors can use drugs made from chemicals called *hormones* to help some persons who show the signs of senility.

Sennacherib

Sennacherib was king of the ancient country of Assyria, more than 2,600 years ago. In the Bible the Books of Isaiah and 2 Kings tell about him. He led armies that destroyed the ancient city of Babylon. In the year 701 B.C. he attacked Jerusalem, but was forced to retreat because his armies were suffering from disease. The English poet Lord Byron wrote a famous poem about Sennacherib's attack on Jerusalem. It is called "The Destruction of Sennacherib."

senses

There are five senses, or kinds of feeling, that animals have. They are sight,

hearing, smell, touch, and taste. Man is the only animal in which all five senses are well-developed, but other animals may have one sense that is better-developed than the same sense in man. For example, a dog has a keener sense of smell than that of a man. People sometimes talk of a "sixth sense," by which they mean some unusual ability to foresee the future or to know about something that is happening in a place far away. See also the articles ANIMAL LIFE and NERVOUS SYSTEM.

sensitive plant

The sensitive plant is a member of the pea family. It is a very interesting plant. If any object touches a leaf of the plant, even very lightly, that leaf will curl up and the leaf stalk will droop as if it were withered and about to fall off. Gradually it returns to its normal state. Many people raise the sensitive plant as a curiosity. It can be kept in a flowerpot in the house or grown in outdoor gardens where there is plenty of sunshine and warmth. It bears purple flowers.

sentence

A sentence is a group of words put together so that they express a complete thought. In a sentence, someone (or something) does something or has something done to him. The "someone" is called the *subject*. What is said about him is called the *predicate*.

The subject is usually a NOUN, and the predicate is a VERB. There is an article about each.

The subject and predicate are the basic parts of a sentence, but some sentences are more complicated and have other parts. There are three other parts: *modifiers*, *complements*, and *connectives*.

A modifier is a word or group of words that tells more about the subject or predicate. If the subject is the word "rose," the word "red" may be its modifier. The modifier may also be a *phrase* or a *clause*. A phrase is a group of words that are put together to do the work of a single word. A phrase modifying the word "rose" might be "in the garden." A clause is a group of words that do have a subject and predicate, and are combined to do the work of a single word. A clause modifying "rose" might be "which blooms." The word "which" is the subject, and "blooms" is the predicate.

COMPLEMENTS

Some sentences express a complete thought with only a subject and a verb predicate; for example, "Dogs bark." But the sentence "He is" or "He gives" has a subject and verb predicate yet does not express a complete thought. Such a sentence makes one ask "is what?" or "gives what?"

Two kinds of verb, called *transitive* and *copulative*, require *complements*, or something to complete the thought. There are four kinds of complement.

One kind is the *direct object*, or the thing on which the subject is acting. In the sentence "He said nothing," the word "nothing" is the direct object.

A second kind of complement is the *indirect object*, which is something else that is affected by the subject's action. In the sentence "He told her nothing," the word "her" is the indirect object.

A third kind is the *objective complement*, which gives more information about the direct object. In the sentence "He named his dog Rover," the word "Rover" is the objective complement.

The fourth kind of complement is the *subjective complement*, which tells more about the subject. This kind is always necessary when a copulative verb, such as *is*, *are*, and so on, is used. In the sentence "John is a lawyer," the word "lawyer" is the subjective complement.

CONNECTIVES

A connective is any word, other than a verb, that joins together two or more parts of a sentence. The connectives in the English language are conjunctions, pronouns, adverbs, and prepositions.

A conjunction used as a connective may be either *coördinating* or *subordinating*. In the sentence "The sun is shining and the sky is blue," there are two thoughts and each is equally important. They are joined by the coördinating conjunction *and*. The word "and" works in the same way in these two sentences: "Bob *and* Joy went home." "The crowd shouted *and* sang."

A subordinating conjunction introduces a subordinate clause. A subordinate clause is a clause that depends on the subject or predicate to make sense. For example, in the sentence "He would do so if he could," the clause "if he could" cannot stand alone and still make sense. It is subordinate, and the word "if" that introduces it is a subordinating conjunction.

Relative adverbs and *relative pronouns* also are connectives. They introduce subordinate clauses. In the sentence "This is a house that was built by Jack," the word "that" is a relative pronoun. In the sentence "Jack lived in a town where we also lived," the word "where" is a relative adverb.

A preposition is a connective that joins a substantive (a word that means something by itself) and some other word. The substantive is called the object of the proposition. In the sentence "The tree grows in the shade," the word "in" is the preposition and its object is "shade."

SENTENCE STRUCTURE

A sentence may be *simple*, *compound*, or *complex*, depending on how it is put together. This is called its structure.

A simple sentence has only one subject and one predicate; for example, "The flowers bloomed." The subject and predicate may each be compounded, that is, be more than single; for example, "The roses and daffodils budded and bloomed."

A sentence that has two or more clauses of equal importance is called compound. An example of this is, "Jack built one house, and soon he built a second one."

A sentence that has a subordinate clause is called a complex sentence. An example of this is, "We will go away now, since you want to."

A compound sentence that also has a subordinate clause is sometimes called a compound-complex sentence. An example of this is: "It was morning, and the robins, which were building their nests, were singing." The subordinate clause is "which were building their nests." The coördinate clauses are "It was morning" and "the robins were singing."

PARSING

Parsing is breaking up a sentence into its separate parts. It is also called "diagramming sentences," because it is usually done by drawing a diagram. The subject, verb and direct object are all written on one line, and the parts of the sentence that modify them are written on lines below the part they modify. A diagram of the sentence "The robins, which were building their nests, were singing loudly this morning," would look like this:

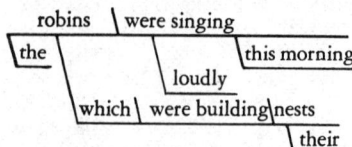

Seoul

Seoul is the largest city of Korea. It is the traditional capital of the country, and since the Korean War it has been the capital of the Republic of Korea (South Korea). Seoul is in the central part of the country, on the Han River. It lies in a broad valley, surrounded by granite hills. Almost 4,000,000 people live in Seoul. The city is a business and cultural center. There are cotton and textile mills, railroad workshops, flour mills, and breweries, but most of the people are small shopkeepers and tradesmen. The city is the seat of the University of Seoul, a medical school, and several religious schools. In the early 1900s Seoul was built up into a handsome modern city, but much of it was damaged or destroyed during the Korean fighting from 1950 to 1953.

Seoul was founded in 1392 as the capital of Korea. There are three old palaces in the city, one of which was built in the 1300s. There is also a Roman Catholic cathedral. In 1910 Japan seized control of Korea and made Seoul the headquarters of the governor general, who represented the Japanese emperor. After World War II, Seoul became the headquarters of the United States occupation forces.

SEOUL, KOREA. Population (1973 estimate) 3,794,959. Capital of the Republic of South Korea. On the Han River.

September

September is the ninth month of the year. It has thirty days. In ancient Roman times the year began with March, and September was the seventh month. It was called *Septembris*, which means seventh in the Latin language. About two thousand years ago the Romans began to use the calendar that we know now, and September became the ninth month. People who were born in September have the sapphire, a blue stone, as their birthstone. The flower of the month of September is the aster.

Serbia

Serbia is one of six republics that form the country of Yugoslavia, and it was formerly an independent country. Serbia has an area of about 35,000 square miles, making it about the size of Indiana. About seven and a half million peo-

pie live there, which is many more than live in Indiana. Northern Serbia is a great plain and the rest of the land is made up of mountains divided by deep valleys. The Danube and Sava rivers form Serbia's northern border and the Drina River forms the western border. The ancient capital, Belgrade, is now the capital of Yugoslavia.

The people of Serbia are called Serbs. They are Slavs, like most of the people of eastern Europe. The principal Church is Serb Orthodox, a Christian Church similar to the Greek Orthodox, but some of the people are Roman Catholics, Greek Catholics, Protestants, or Moslems. More than three-quarters of the people are farmers. In the cities there are factories that make paper, glass, textiles, shoes, chemicals, and food products. Serbia is rich in mineral deposits, including coal, copper, and gold. The region is noted for its health resorts.

Serbs settled the region of Serbia about 1,300 years ago. It was ruled by Turkey for hundreds of years but in 1882 it became an independent kingdom. An Austrian attack on Serbia began World War I. After that war, Serbia became part of Yugoslavia. See also the article on BALKAN WARS.

serenade

The serenade was originally a piece of music to be sung or played by a young man under the window of a girl he was courting. The word later came to be used for any love song or piece of music. There are serenades in several operas, for example Mozart's *Don Giovanni.* Serenades are still used in Spain and in Spanish-speaking countries. Sometimes a lover hires musicians to serenade his lady.

Sermon on the Mount

The Sermon on the Mount is a series of lessons given by Jesus to his Disciples and to a great multitude of people. It may be read in the Bible, in the 5th to 7th chapters of Matthew. Jesus gave the sermon on a mountaintop. The first part of the Sermon is called the BEATITUDES, about which there is a separate article. In the next part, Jesus told his Disciples to go out in the world and teach others what they had learned from him. Then Jesus told them more about how they should behave: they should put God first and their own wishes second; they should not try to judge other men but leave judgment to God; they should beware of false teachings. He promised that all who followed his teachings would be blessed by God and would enter the kingdom of heaven. In the course of the sermon Jesus gave the Lord's Prayer, which all Christians use.

serpent, another word for a snake. In the Bible, the snake that tempted Eve in the Garden of Eden is called a serpent, and Satan (the Devil, or the Evil Spirit) is called a serpent. See the article SNAKE.

serum

Serum is the clear liquid part of the blood that is left after the red cells and other substances have been removed from the blood. When human or animal blood is placed in a glass and left standing, after several hours it separates. The red cells sink to the bottom and form a jellylike clot covered by a clear yellowish liquid. This liquid is the serum.

Serum is mainly water but contains other chemicals that are important to the body. Some of these chemicals help you to stay well by fighting the germs that cause disease. They are tiny particles, called *antibodies,* and you can learn more about them in the article on IMMUNITY. The blood serum of certain persons and animals may have antibodies against particular germs, such as the germs of scarlet fever or measles. Doctors can inject these serums into other persons who do not have these sicknesses. This is called *inoculation.* It usually protects a person against catching that particular disease.

Serum is also used after bad burns and serious accidents to overcome *shock.* When shock happens serum leaks out from the blood vessels and unless serum is put back to make up for this loss, the person may die. Usually it is put back in the form of plasma, which is the serum plus some other chemicals of the blood. See the section on blood transfusions in the article on BLOOD.

Service, Robert W.

Robert William Service was a Canadian writer of novels and poetry. He was born in England in 1874 and studied at the University of Glasgow, in Scotland. When he was 20 years old, Service went to Canada and settled on Vancouver Island, in British Columbia. Later he moved to South Africa, where he died in 1958. Service is better-known for his verse than for his novels. One of his most popular poems is "The Shooting of Dan McGrew." Like many of his poems, it is about the Yukon Territory of Canada at the time of the Gold Rush in the late 1890s.

sesame

Sesame is a plant grown in India and other countries of the East. It produces small seeds that are used in cooking and are a source of sesame oil. In the *Arabian Nights* story of "Ali Baba and the Forty Thieves," the word *sesame* is a magic word that opens a secret cave.

Sesame seed is used in the United States and Canada as a spice and flavoring in rolls, cookies, and other food. The oil that is pressed from the seed is used both as a flavoring and in the manufacture of some kinds of soap.

Set

Set is the name of a god that was worshiped by the ancient Egyptians. He was the god of evil and of darkness, the god of the desert and of the countries that were Egypt's enemies. Set was thought to be the brother of Osiris, the god of goodness. According to some of the stories, Set tried to spoil Osiris's plans to spread goodness and light in the world, and when he failed in this he killed his brother. Later, Set was punished for this by Horus, the son of Osiris.

Seton, Ernest Thompson

Ernest Thompson Seton was an American writer and artist. He was born

in England in 1860 and came to America when he was 22 years old. First he lived for some years in the backwoods of Canada, and then he lived on the western plains of the United States and became an American citizen. Originally his name was Ernest Seton Thompson. He is best-known for his nature stories for boys and girls, many of which he illustrated himself. Some of them are *Wild Animals I Have Known* and *The Biography of a Grizzly.* He died in 1946.

setter

A setter is a hunting dog. It is trained to find game birds (birds that are shot by hunters). The setter locates the spot where a bird is perched or standing. Then the setter stands perfectly still with its nose pointing toward that spot. When the hunter has shot the bird, the setter goes and brings it back for him. Many people call setters "bird dogs."

The most familiar kind of setter is probably the *English setter.* It has markings of black and white, or tan and white, or sometimes black, tan, and white. It stands about 25 inches high at the shoulders and is about 30 inches from the chest to the base of its feathery-looking tail. It weighs 50 to 75 pounds.

The *Irish setter* is a beautiful red color. Irish setters are usually more slender, and a trifle smaller, than English setters.

The *Gordon setter* is seldom seen in the United States and Canada, but is very popular in the Scandinavian countries. Its color is always black and tan. It is the largest and heaviest of the setters.

All setters are usually gentle and affectionate. They are good pets and house dogs.

Seven Wonders of the World

In the centuries before the coming of Christ people talked about seven wonders of the world. They thought chiefly of the most marvelous works of architecture or sculpture. They were: 1, the Egyptian pyramids. 2, the Hanging Gardens of ancient Babylon. 3, the mausoleum (burying place) of King Mausolus at Halicarnassus. 4, the temple to the Greek goddess Artemis (called Diana by the Romans) at Ephesus. 5, the Colossus (a huge statue) at the harbor of Rhodes. 6, the Olympian *Zeus,* a great work of art by the Greek sculptor Phidias. 7, the lighthouse on the island of Pharos, near Alexandria, Egypt.

The largest pyramids in Egypt are found near Cairo at Giza. The pyramids are one of the seven wonders of the Ancient World.

Seven Years' War

The Seven Years' War was a war that was fought about two hundred years ago. It lasted seven years and was fought in many parts of the world. Austria, Spain, France, Russia, Saxony (a German kingdom) and Sweden were fighting against the German kingdoms of Prussia and Hanover, and Great Britain. The French and British were fighting over colonies in North America and India. The part of the war that was fought in North America was called the FRENCH AND INDIAN WAR, and there is a separate article about it.

The European fighting began in 1757, and by 1763 all the nations were tired of the war and made treaties of peace. The main results were that Prussia became a leading European power, which it had not been before, and that Great Britain had more and richer colonies than any other nation.

Sevier, John

John Sevier was an American soldier and explorer, and the first governor of the state of Tennessee. He was born more than two hundred years ago, in 1745, in Virginia. When he was 24 years old he went to Tennessee with an exploring party and built a fort there. He fought the Indians who were attacking white settlers on the frontier. When the Revolutionary War began, Sevier fought with the other colonists against the British, and in 1780 he led a force to victory at King's Mountain. After the war he served in the House of Representatives and as governor of Tennessee. In 1815 he died during a campaign against the Creek Indians, who were raiding border settlements.

Sévigny, Marie

Marie de Rabutin-Chantal, the Marquise of Sévigny, was a French writer who lived about three hundred years ago. She wrote many letters that were so gay, witty, and charming that they are still read today. Madame de Sévigny was born in 1626. When she was 18 she married the Marquis de Sévigny, who lived only seven years after the marriage. Madame de Sévigny devoted the rest of her life to her daughter, to whom most of her 1,500 letters were written. The letters give a vivid picture of French life of the day.

Seville

Seville is the third-largest city of Spain. It is in the southwest part, on the Guadalquivir River, which makes it an inland port. The city is noted for its great cultural and historical traditions. It is also the commercial and industrial center of the region of Andalusia. Seville is beautifully set in a wide plain and is surrounded by beautiful gardens. Its pleasant climate, historic landmarks and gay fiestas make it one of Spain's most popular tourist attractions. It has the second-largest bull ring in Spain.

About 503,400 people live in Seville. There are factories that make ammunition, metal products, cigars and other tobacco products, china and earthenware, and other things. Seville is a shipping point for the produce of all Andalusia. It is Spain's biggest cork market.

The city of Seville covers a wide area. It has narrow, winding streets with whitewashed houses that have patios (open-air courts) and wrought-iron balconies. Among the points of historic interest is the cathedral, which was begun in 1402 and took more than a hundred years to build. In the cathedral are many great paintings and also a monument to Christopher Columbus, who is believed to be buried there. There is an alcazar (castle) built by the Mohammedan people who ruled Seville a thousand years ago.

SEVILLE, SPAIN. Population (1973 estimate) 503,490. Capital of Seville province.

Seward, William Henry

William Henry Seward was an American statesman of about a hundred years ago. He is remembered chiefly for his opposition to slavery during the time when Negroes were slaves in the southern states, for his work in Lincoln's cabinet during the Civil War, and for the purchase of Alaska in 1867, then called "Seward's folly."

Seward was born in 1801 in Orange County, New York. When he grew up he became a lawyer and began to practice law at Auburn, New York. He became a leader of the Whig Party, the political party that was opposed to President Andrew Jackson. In 1838, when he was 37 years old, Seward became governor of New York, and in 1848 he was elected United States Senator from New York.

Lincoln appointed Seward Secretary of State in 1861, and he served eight years in that office. He was in charge of the relations between the United States and foreign countries during the difficult period of the Civil War. When Lincoln was assassinated, in 1865, someone tried to murder Seward too but the attempt failed. Seward retired from office in 1869 and died three years later, in 1872.

sewers

Sewers are large pipes or tunnels under the streets of a city. Streams of water flow constantly through these sewers. Drainpipes from houses empty into the sewers, carrying away waste from bathrooms and kitchens.

Sewers have been very important in the history of the world. Long ago, men did not know how important it is to keep a city clean. Great cities would arise with no sewers. Women would empty their dishwater and other waste into the streets. Germs breed in filth, and sometimes there would be great epidemics of disease. In some cases, the greatness of modern cities is credited partly to the fact that they had good sewers. Paris, France, is a famous example. For hundreds of years it has had huge sewers, so big that men could walk through them. Often Paris escaped from diseases that killed millions in other parts of Europe.

Every modern city has sewers on almost every street. Many cities also have sewage-disposal plants. Sewers used to carry the waste into rivers, lakes, or (in the case of a coastal city) into the ocean. This contaminated the water. In a river, it would make the water impure for cities downstream. In a river, lake or the ocean it would make swimming unsafe. In a sewage-disposal plant, the water from the sewers runs through a series of tanks. In these tanks it is treated with chemicals that purify it, and the solids in the water are allowed to settle. The water is then safe and can be emptied anywhere. The solids are often useful as fertilizers or to make new land by filling in swamps.

Sewers are usually built by city governments. Sometimes the city pays the cost, but more often there is an assessment against owners of property along each street where the sewer goes. The assessment is an amount of money the property-owner must pay as his share of the cost. After that, there is often a sewer tax each year. The money from this tax is used to keep the sewers operating properly. The city's Department of Sanitation is in charge of the sewers. See the article on SANITATION.

sewing

Sewing is a way of fastening things together by drawing thread or any other thin strip through them. Sewing is most often used to hold pieces of cloth together and it is almost always done with a needle and thread.

For countless thousands of years, human beings have known how to sew. The first needles were probably made of bone or thorns and the first "thread" was sinews or strips of hide taken from animals that were killed for food. Thread made as it is made today—by twisting together the fibers of certain plants—was probably made at least 25,000 years ago.

Until very recent times, sewing was the chief occupation of women. The men worked in the fields or hunted to find food and the women stayed at home and made the clothes for the family. In the course of time, women became artists at fancy sewing—embroidery, the making of lace, and fine dressmaking. In cities, women came to be employed in sewing shirts, handkerchiefs, and other garments called "linens," which were sold in shops. This work was badly underpaid.

When sewing for themselves and their families, however, most women found sewing very enjoyable. They formed social clubs called "sewing circles" and met at the members' homes to talk while they worked. At fairs they displayed their best needlework to win prizes.

Fine needlework is still practiced by millions of women, but in other ways sewing changed greatly after the sewing machine was invented and made a practical machine, about a hundred years ago. This made possible the garment factory in which ready-made clothes could be made so inexpensively that even a poor housewife did not have to make homemade clothes. Rich women had employed dressmakers, or seamstresses, who made their clothes by hand; now the dressmakers and their customers alike used sewing machines or bought readymade clothes.

THE SEWING MACHINE

Several attempts to invent sewing machines had been made before a Frenchman named Barthélmy Thimonnier invented the first successful one in 1830. His machine was operated by a wheel turned by hand. It made a kind of stitch called the *chain-stitch*. It used a single thread, carried through the cloth by a needle. Each time the needle went through the cloth, it made a loop, throw-

ing each loop through the one before. The stitches on one side of the cloth formed a chain. Chain-stitch machines are still used for some kinds of sewing, especially for making decorative effects.

A new machine was invented in the United States in the 1830s by Walter Hunt of New York City. It was a lock-stitch machine. It used two threads, one in a curved, eye-pointed needle and the other in a shuttle. The machine operated so that the threads locked tightly together in the middle of the work. But Hunt was told that his machine would throw many seamstresses out of work, and so he abandoned his invention.

In 1846 Elias Howe Jr. of Cambridge, Massachusetts, obtained a patent for another lock-stitch machine. His machine also used an eye-pointed needle and shuttle. It could sew straight seams (a straight line of stitches) a few inches at a time. The cloth to be sewed was fastened to a small metal plate a few inches long, and was fed into the machine vertically (up-and-down). This made sewing somewhat difficult. When the stitching needed was longer than the plate, the material had to be moved and fastened again.

A more practical machine was invented about 1850 by Isaac M. Singer of Boston. In Singer's machine the cloth rested on a flat table and passed under a straight needle that worked up-and-down. This machine could sew endlessly any kind of seam, straight or circular or bent, and was operated by a foot treadle instead of a hand-turned wheel. Later an electric motor replaced the treadle. Special machines are designed for the home and the factory. Factory machines can be driven so as to make five thousand or more stitches a minute. Machines for home use come with several special attachments for hemming, binding, and so on. You can read more about these in the article DRESSMAKING.

sex, the division of some plants and animals into two kinds, male and female, which together can produce offspring: see the article REPRODUCTION.

Seychelles

Seychelles is a small nation consisting of about 86 islands in the Indian Ocean, north of the Malagasy Republic, near Africa's east coast. The islands have an estimated total area of about 107 square miles, and a population of about 58,000 in 1975. The capital city of Victoria, with about 14,000 inhabitants, is on the main island of Mahe, which is about 57 square miles in area.

In the mid-18th century the French colonized the islands and established spice plantations. In 1794 the islands were captured by the English; in 1814 they became a dependency of Mauritius, and a separate colony in 1903. Independence was granted in June, 1976, and the following September Seychelles became the 145th member of the United Nations.

The two most important products are copra (dried coconut meat) and cinnamon bark. The two largest industries are a brewery and a tobacco factory, and some frozen fish is exported. Tourism

has become important to the economy, especially since the opening of the international airport and four new hotels.

shad

The shad is a popular food fish of the Atlantic Ocean. Shad roe (the eggs of the female shad) is considered even better as food than the fish itself.

Shad, like salmon, swim up rivers to spawn, or lay their eggs. During the spring months (when the shad are said to be "running") both male and female shad swim up the rivers of the Atlantic Coast to their spawning grounds. There the female lays about thirty thousand tiny, pale pink or amber-colored eggs, which hatch in six to ten days. The young fish remain in the fresh water of the river for a few months, then in the fall they start their swim back to the ocean they have never seen.

Male shad are called "buck shad," female shad are called "roe shad." A male usually weighs two to six pounds, and the female weighs three to eight pounds.

Fishermen set nets to catch the fish on their trip upstream. They used to catch so many that there was danger that shad would disappear from the ocean. Now the catch is limited and the spawning grounds are protected by law.

In 1871 the shad was introduced into the Pacific Ocean and is now found from southern California to Alaska.

Shakers

The Shakers are a religious group that was founded in England about two hundred years ago. Some of the members of another group, the Society of Friends, or Quakers, decided that they believed in different things and founded their own Church. They were called Shaking Quakers, or Shakers, because they danced and marched and moved their bodies while they worshiped.

The Shakers believe that Jesus was the male form of God come to earth, and that one of their early leaders, a woman called Ann Lee, was the female form of God on earth. Ann Lee and some of her followers came to America and in 1776 they founded a colony at what is now Watervliet, New York. Groups of Shakers soon settled in other parts of the country. They lived in settlements apart from other people. The Shakers believe that men and women should not marry and have children. In their settlements the men and women members live and work apart. Most of the Shaker communities were in farming areas. The Shakers are noted for the fine clothing and furniture they make. The Shakers believe in simple dress, and their costume is somewhat like that of the early Quakers. The women wear old-fashioned bonnets and ankle-length dresses, and the men wear old-fashioned breeches and hats. Today there are fewer than fifty Shakers in the United States, though 150 years ago they had about five thousand members.

Shakespeare, William

William Shakespeare is generally considered the greatest of all writers in the English language, and some have called him the greatest writer in any lan-

guage, throughout history. He wrote plays and poetry. He lived 350 years ago, but his plays are still performed more than the plays of any other person and his poems are still read more than the poems of any other person. Translated into German, his plays are the most popular plays of Germany; translated into French, they are among the most popular plays of France; and they are performed in several other languages.

Very little is known of Shakespeare's life. Because of his fame as a writer, scholars for hundreds of years have made a fascinating detective game of trying to learn or guess the details of his life, and many books have been written about him. There are groups who believe that Shakespeare did not actually write the plays and poems that are credited to him, but that someone else wrote them and put Shakespeare's name on them. The largest group of these people believes that Sir Francis Bacon, a great English writer and scientist, or Edward de Vere, Earl of Oxford, a poet and playwright, was the real author of Shakespeare's works. A smaller group believes it was Christopher Marlowe, an English playwright and poet who was thought to be dead before Shakespeare's plays began to appear.

WHAT IS KNOWN

The little that is known about Shakespeare's life is this: He was born, probably on April 23, in the year 1564, in the English town of Stratford-on-Avon. His father was a glove-maker and a respected citizen of the town. He went to school in Stratford, but there is no record of how long he went to school or whether he went to a university afterward. He probably did not, because when he was 18 years old he married a girl named Anne Hathaway. They had three children, two girls and a boy.

Some years after this, Shakespeare's name appeared in London. He had become a successful actor and playwright. In 1596 his father was given a coat of arms, which made him officially a "gentleman." In 1599 he became one of the owners of the Globe Theatre, which is still remembered because of him.

All this happened during the reign of Queen Elizabeth I. She died in 1603 and James I became king. He made Shakespeare's company of actors "the king's players," or official actors to the king, which was the highest honor a group of actors could have. Shakespeare died in 1616, on his birthday, April 23. A few of his plays and most of his poems had already been published, but the bulk of his plays were published in 1623, seven years after his death, in what is called the "First Folio Edition" of Shakespeare's plays. (*Folio* means it was a large-size book, about as big as a modern tabloid newspaper.)

SHAKESPEARE'S WORKS

Thirty-seven or thirty-eight plays are supposed to have been written by Shakespeare. In some of them it seems probable that he had a collaborator, or co-author, with whom he wrote. In some cases it is

possible that the plays were not written by Shakespeare at all but were added to the First Folio Edition by the publisher, simply because the author was unknown and Shakespeare's famous name would help the sales.

The plays are divided into three groups: the tragedies, the histories, and the comedies.

The tragedies, which have unhappy endings, are the most famous group. They include *Hamlet*, the most successful play ever written; *Macbeth*, which contains Shakespeare's greatest writing; *Romeo and Juliet*, which contains the best part Shakespeare wrote for a woman; *Julius Caesar*, *Othello*, and *King Lear*.

The histories tell the stories of kings of England. They include *Henry IV*, *Henry V*, and *Richard III*, which have remained popular.

The comedies have happy endings. *The Merchant of Venice*, *As You Like It*, *A Midsummer Night's Dream*, *The Taming of the Shrew* and *Twelfth Night* are the most popular.

Nearly every one of history's most famous actors who has performed in the English-speaking countries, has developed his reputation as a result of his ability to act in Shakespearian plays.

Shakespeare's most important poems were his series of 154 *Sonnets*. A sonnet is a poem of fourteen lines. Shakespeare's sonnets are partly addressed to a man whom Shakespeare loves and admires. Partly they tell of his own unhappy experiences and his love for a woman who has come to be called "the Dark Lady of the Sonnets." The first published edition of the *Sonnets* included a dedication to a "Mr. W. H." whose initials have caused much detective work and many arguments among students of Shakespeare. No one is sure who the man might be.

THEORIES ABOUT SHAKESPEARE

Those who say Shakespeare did not actually write "Shakespeare's Works" have one main argument: Shakespeare could not possibly have written them, because he did not have enough education. Shakespeare used more words in his writings than any other early English writer. His "vocabulary" (the number of words he could use) has been set at 40,000 words. Shakespeare showed a knowledge of the Latin and Greek classical authors, a complete understanding of English life in many trades and professions, and a familiarity with the latest scientific discoveries.

Others maintain that for such a genius this should not be unexpected. Ben Jonson, a great English writer who lived at the same time as Shakespeare, and John Milton, generally considered the second-greatest English poet, who lived soon after Shakespeare, both wrote poems in honor of Shakespeare and acknowledged him as the greatest writer.

Shakespeare is buried in Stratford. He is thought to have written the verse for his own tombstone. It is:

Good frend, for Jesus sake forbeare
To digg the dust enclosed heare
Bleste be the man that spares thes stones
And curst be he that moves my bones

Most great English poets are buried in Westminster Abbey, but no one has wanted to risk Shakespeare's curse by moving him. Spelling followed no regular rules in those days, and Shakespeare spelled his own name Shakspere. The traditional picture of him comes from the First Folio Edition of his plays.

shamrock

The shamrock is a low-growing plant with three-parted leaves. It looks like the field clover of the United States and Canada. It has been the symbol of Ireland for hundreds of years. An Irish legend about the shamrock in Ireland dates back to the time of St. Patrick. He is said to have used the shamrock and its three-leaved form to illustrate the story of the Holy Trinity, which is one of the principles of Christianity.

Shamrocks are used throughout the Christian world in the celebration of St. Patrick's Day. They are usually a clear, bright shade of green. Shamrocks will grow in most parts of the United States and the warmer sections of Canada, and they can be raised indoors in flower pots.

Shanghai

Shanghai is the largest city of China and the largest city on the continent of Asia. It is in east central China, on the Whangpoo River, a narrow stream opening into the Yangtze River near the China Sea.

The Yangtze Valley is one of the richest regions of China, and Shanghai is the natural commercial and shipping center for its products. It is also the industrial heart of the country. Before World War II, Shanghai was the headquarters of most of the British, American, French and other foreign businesses in China.

Almost 7,000,000 people live in Shanghai. Many of them work in the cotton mills that make up half of China's great cotton industry, and in factories that make silk, cigarettes, machinery, and many other things. Others work in plants that process foods and in shipbuilding yards. Printing and publishing are also important. The banks of the Whangpoo are lined with docks. Before World War II these handled half of China's overseas trade, including exports of raw silk, hog bristles, hides, tea, and vegetable oils.

The business section of Shanghai is the former International Settlement. There are big office and apartment buildings, department stores, hotels, and foreign-language newspapers. Many of these are on a famous street called the Bund, which runs along the river. Before World War II, Shanghai was a glamorous and mysterious city, with drug peddlers and gunmen, spies and adventurers of many countries.

There has been a town of Shanghai (which means "above the river") for almost a thousand years, but for most of that time it was an unimportant fishing village. In 1842 Great Britain forced China to open its ports to trade, and Shanghai was one of the first to be opened. The British established a base in the city, and the United States soon did the same. These two included most of the city and were called the International Settlement. This was governed by a Municipal Council, which was always dominated by British members. The French later established its own section. During the war between China and Japan, the Japanese occupied the Chinese sections of Shanghai from 1937 to 1945. In 1943 Great Britain and the United States returned their settlement to the government of China. In 1949 the Chinese Communists took Shanghai and the city ceased to be a great metropolis open to Western trade.

SHANGHAI, CHINA. Population (1973 estimate) 6,900,000. On the Whangpoo River.

shark

A shark is a kind of fish. There are many different kinds of shark. Some are extremely dangerous to man, and some are quite harmless. Their size varies a great deal. Some are only about two feet long, while others reach lengths up to 50 feet. Some small sharks lay eggs, but the larger ones bear living young. Sharks live in all the oceans of the world except the extremely cold seas of the Arctic and Antarctic regions. These are some of the sharks:

GREAT WHITE SHARK

The great white shark is a vicious and dangerous fish. It attacks small boats, swimmers, bathers, and any other object it may see in the water. It eats anything —even other sharks, giant sea turtles, tuna, seals, and sea lions. The great white shark lives in temperate and tropical oceans and frequently swims close to shore. It is about 16 feet long when full-grown. The female bears living young.

NURSE SHARK

The nurse shark lives in the tropical parts of the Atlantic Ocean. It is a slow-moving, sluggish fish. It lies on the bottom of the ocean. The nurse shark is usually about 5 feet long. Its hide is the best for making sharkskin leather. The female nurse shark bears twenty to twenty-five young at a time.

WHALE SHARK

The whale shark is the largest living fish. It grows to a length of 45 feet, and sometimes longer, so it may be bigger than many real whales. It usually lives in tropical seas, but occasionally is seen farther north. To get its food, the whale shark swims through a school of smaller fish with its mouth wide open and scoops up enormous numbers of fish in passing.

HAMMERHEAD SHARK

One of the strangest-looking members of the shark family is the hammerhead shark. There is a hammer-shaped arm on each side of its head, and the fish's eyes and nostrils are placed on the ends of the hammers. The hammerhead shark provides excellent hide for leather, and its liver oil contains large quantities of Vitamin A. The hammerhead has thirty to thirty-five young in a litter, about 18 inches long at birth. Adults are about 13 feet long.

SAND SHARK

The sand shark has never been known to injure people. It is one of the most common kinds of shark on the Atlantic coast. The largest known sand shark was 11 feet long, and it is usually only about 4 or 5 feet in length. The sand shark is a light brown or sand color. It lives on smaller fish. The female sand shark bears living young, one at a time.

SOUP-FIN SHARK

There is actually a "shark's fin soup," made from the fins of the soup-fin shark. This is a delicacy that has been known to the Chinese people for hundreds of years. About twenty years ago it was discovered that the soup-fin shark's liver is rich in Vitamin A. This made many people start fishing for this kind of shark, and so many were caught that the number of soup-fin sharks along the California coast was greatly reduced. The soup-fin shark is usually about 6 feet long. The female has huge litters of about thirty-five young.

TIGER SHARK

One of the most dangerous and vicious kinds of shark is the tiger shark. It is striped all over like a tiger, and it is as savage as any tiger in the jungle. It attacks and eats every living thing it sees in the water. The tiger shark's hide is valuable for leather, and its liver is rich in Vitamin A. The tiger shark grows to about 15 feet, but the young are only about 18 inches long at birth. Any number from ten to seventy-five are born in a litter. The tiger shark usually remains in tropical waters.

Shasta Dam

Shasta Dam is the twelfth-highest dam in the world and one of the largest. It is on the Sacramento River, near Redding, California. Shasta Dam is 602 feet high and 3,500 feet long. Just downstream is the Keswick Dam. Shasta Lake, the reservoir formed by the dam, is about 35 miles long. The Shasta system is part of the Central Valley Project to regulate distribution of water and to control floods and improve navigation on the Sacramento and San Joaquin rivers.

Other dams in the project include the Friant Dam on the San Joaquin River and Folsom Dam on the American River.

Shasta, Mount

Mt. Shasta is a peak at the south end of the Cascade Range in northern California. It is 14,161 feet high and its base is 17 miles in diameter. Mt. Shasta is an extinct volcano. Its summit is covered by five glaciers, the largest of which is Hotlum Glacier, more than two miles long. There is a second peak, called Shastina, more than 12,000 feet high. Shasta was discovered in 1827 and was first climbed in 1854 by E. D. Pearce. At its base is the town of Mt. Shasta.

shaving

Shaving is the removal of hair from the body, and particularly it means the removal of hair from a man's face. If allowed to grow, this facial hair would form a BEARD, about which there is a separate article. Men have shaved their faces for thousands of years, but in many ages a beard has been considered a mark of manly beauty and at those times there has been less shaving. Until hard steel was developed, there was no way of shaving comfortably but men used sharpened stones, then bronze knives, then iron knives.

About 1,500 years ago, the razor was developed. It is simply a very sharp knife but for hundreds of years razors have been hollow-ground, which means that the original piece of steel is hollowed out on each side to make it thinner and allow it to be given a sharper edge. This edge is *honed,* which means it is rubbed against a fine-grained stone, or hone, to sharpen it; and then it is *stropped,* or rubbed back and forth against a leather strap, called a *strop,* which makes the edge even thinner and smooths out any tiny rough spots that remain after the honing. The face is covered with a thick lather of soap, which is rubbed in. Actually the water in the lather, and not the soap, does most to soften the hairs and make shaving easier; but the lather holds the water on the face. The razor (called a straight razor) is scraped over the face and cuts off the whiskers. This method of shaving was used for hundreds of years and is still used in most barber shops.

During the 1890s, King C. Gillette and some other inventors introduced *safety razors.* They were of different designs but all had the same principle. A razor blade, a small piece of sharpened steel, was held in a metal frame and used for shaving. When the blade became dull it could be thrown away and a new blade put in. The small blade could be made sharper by machine than a straight razor usually was. The frame exposed only a small part of the blade, so a person could not cut himself badly. Safety razors did not become popular quickly, but by the 1920s nearly every man in the United States was using a safety razor.

In the middle 1930s, the electric shaver was introduced. The electric shaver follows the same principle as the clippers that barbers had used for many years in cutting hair. The hairs enter openings in the shaver, and blades cut them off by the same kind of action as when a pair of scissors closes. Electric shavers were gradually improved until they gave a clean shave, and by the 1950s millions of men were using them.

Usually a boy finds it necessary to shave occasionally by the time he is 14 or 15 years old, but it is not unusual for facial hairs to grow on boys who are 13 or 12 or even younger. Some boys try to encourage their facial hair to grow, considering it a sign of manliness, just as their ancestors did; but there is no known way to make the hair grow sooner. It is often said that shaving makes the hair grow faster, but this is not so. Hair does grow more rapidly in summer (that is, in hot weather) than in winter or cold weather. Many women shave hair off their legs and from under their arms. Most of them use safety razors.

Shaw, George Bernard

George Bernard Shaw was a British playwright, or writer of plays, and many people consider him the greatest playwright of the 20th century. Most of his plays are comedies, in which he makes fun of certain habits and ideas and at the same time presents his own ideas on government, marriage, history, and many other subjects.

Shaw was born in 1856 in Dublin, Ireland. His family was poor, and when

he was only 14 years old he left school and went to work. His mother and sister moved to London, and when Shaw was 20 years old he joined them there. During the next nine years he wrote five novels, and articles for various newspapers, but he made very little money. In 1888 he became music critic for the London *Star,* and his reviews helped to interest many people in the work of a new German composer, Richard Wagner. In 1895 he became drama critic for the *Saturday Review,* and in this position he did a great deal to make the plays of the Norwegian writer, Henrik Ibsen, very popular. About this time, too, he became actively interested in systems of government. He was one of the founders of the Fabian Society, or group of socialists.

Throughout this time Shaw had been writing plays, and in 1904 he had his first success, *John Bull's Other Island.* In the same year a play he had written earlier, *Candida,* was put on in New York City and was a great hit. From that time on he devoted himself to writing plays, and even those who disagreed with his ideas liked his wit and humor.

Shaw lived to be very old. In his later years he was known for his biting remarks and for some of his strange habits. He drank no alcoholic liquors and he was a vegetarian (would eat no meat). In 1925 he was offered the Nobel Prize in literature, but he refused the money that went with the prize. Shaw died in 1950, at the age of 94.

Among Shaw's most popular plays are *Caesar and Cleopatra* and *Saint Joan,* which are historical plays; and *Man and Superman, The Doctor's Dilemma, Pygmalion,* and *Major Barbara.* Several have been made into motion pictures.

Shays' Rebellion

After the United States won its independence in the Revolutionary War, the new government began to collect taxes as all governments do. In the state of Massachusetts there were many farmers who were poor, and whose land had been damaged badly by the fighting there. They objected strongly to the taxes. Some of these people gathered together under the leadership of a man called Daniel Shays, and in 1786 they captured the town of Worcester, Massachusetts, to prevent the state's Supreme Court from meeting. Shays had been a brave soldier in the Revolutionary War and had distinguished himself in many battles. He and his group then tried to take the city of Springfield, but their rebellion was soon suppressed by the state militia and they were forced to retreat. Many of them fled to other states, mainly to New Hampshire. The government pardoned all but a few of the leaders. Shays was pardoned later.

Sheba

Sheba was an ancient country on the southwestern tip of Arabia, where Yemen and Aden are now. Almost three thousand years ago, when Solomon was

king of Israel, Sheba was a prosperous and important country. The people who lived there were called Sabaeans. Their capital was a city called Mariba. The Queen of Sheba paid a visit to King Solomon that is told about in the Bible, in the first book of Kings (the third book of Kings, in Catholic Bibles). She took very rich gifts to Solomon and received very rich gifts from him. The present emperors of Ethiopia trace their descent from the Queen of Sheba.

sheep

Sheep are cud-chewing animals with hollow horns. They have been raised for their meat and fleece (wool) for many thousands of years. Sheep were kept by man even earlier than cattle. Today there are both wild and domestic (tamed) sheep. The main difference between wild and domestic sheep is in their tails and coats. The wild sheep have short tails and stiff, hairy coats, while domestic sheep have long tails and woolly coats. There are several different kinds of both types.

DOMESTIC SHEEP

Lamb and mutton, the meat of young or older sheep, make up the chief meat food of many people in Asia. Sheep rather than cattle are raised for meat because sheep need less grazing land and can live in drier climates than cattle. The fleece of the sheep also provides the wool for clothing and blankets, and often for the tents in which the people live.

Of all the sheep raised in various parts of the world, the Merino sheep has the finest and thickest wool. It grows so long that it covers the sheep's eyes. Merino sheep came from Spain originally, but they have been taken to many other lands, and are now raised all over the world. The meat of the Merino is not as good as that of other breeds of sheep, but its wool is very valuable. Often the whole skin is dyed and used as a fur, called mouton.

Another kind of sheep that is famous for its coat is the KARAKUL sheep, about which there is a separate article. Persian lamb fur is made from baby karakul lambs.

Some sheep are raised especially for fine meat, and some, such as the Corriedale sheep, are called "dual-purpose" good for both meat and wool.

Millions of sheep are grown every year in the United States, Canada, Australia, and Great Britain.

WILD SHEEP

There are several kinds of wild sheep throughout the world. The largest is the ammon or argali wild sheep of central Asia. This sheep has long curving horns that form almost a complete circle, and it reaches a height of 4 feet at the shoulder. The argali often weighs as much as 350 pounds. Other wild sheep live in Siberia and along the west coast of North America.

The Rocky Mountain bighorn sheep is the chief wild sheep in North America. See the article BIGHORN.

Sheffield

Sheffield is a city on the Don River in north central England. It is the principal steel center in Great Britain. More than six hundred years ago Sheffield was a great cutlery-manufacturing city. The Sheffield process of plating copper tableware with silver was invented there in 1742. Henry Bessemer opened a plant using his new steel-making process in Sheffield in 1858, and stainless steel was invented there in 1914.

Almost 532,000 people live in Sheffield. Most of them work in the great steel foundries, rolling mills, and machine shops. There are also factories that make armorplate, rails, weapons, and cutlery.

The University of Sheffield was established in 1905. It has a medical school and technical college. The city also has a museum, an observatory, art galleries, and the Church of St. Peter's, nearly six hundred years old, which was seriously damaged by bombs in World War II. Mary Queen of Scots was held prisoner in Sheffield from 1569 to 1584.

SHEFFIELD, ENGLAND. Population (1973 census) 531,800. On the Don River.

shell

Shells are hard, protective coverings that surround the soft, boneless bodies of certain animals called MOLLUSCS, about which there is a separate article. This group of animals includes oysters, clams, mussels, and snails. The hard covering of an egg is also called a shell. Lobsters, armadillos, turtles, and some other animals are enclosed in hard coverings also called "shells," but the word is properly applied only to molluscs. Many of their shells can be found on beaches, especially after a storm.

The animal's shell is not only its protection but also its home. A mollusc manufactures the shell as a liquid in its body and deposits it, bit by bit, around itself. The liquid hardens and becomes the shell. On the inside this shell is smooth, like glass, to protect the soft body of the mollusc. The outside becomes rough from the action of water and sand.

Shells come in all sizes and shapes and in many colors. Some shells are as beautiful as gems, and jewelry is made from them. Pearls are a kind of shell substance.

Some molluscs, such as the oyster and clam, have two shells. These shells are hinged at one point so that they can open and close. Other molluscs, such as snails, have one shell into which they can retreat for safety. They can close a tiny trap door at the opening. Some shells are in graceful spiral or scalloped shapes.

COLLECTING SHELLS

Many people collect shells. They go about the beaches looking for different kinds and some have thousands of different ones in their collections. Many peoples have used shells as money. American Indian money, called wampum, consisted of bits of colored shells, usually strung together in beadlike fashion.

Shells are used to manufacture buttons, beads, and other things. Buttons are cut mostly from clam shells. The inner, smooth part of some sea shells is called mother-of-pearl.

shellac

Shellac is a clear, sticky liquid that hardens quickly and then covers surfaces with a tough, smooth film that protects them from hard wear. Shellac can be molded and is used to make phonograph records. It is also used in making certain kinds of varnish. Shellac comes from a thick, sticky liquid produced by the lac insect, which lives on the twigs of certain trees. As the insect eats the tree sap, it secretes a thick liquid which hardens and forms a tough protective covering over the insect. This substance, called stick-lac, is taken from the trees, crushed, washed, melted, squeezed through cloth, and dried in sheets. It can be dissolved in denatured alcohol to make a kind of varnish. Most of the world's shellac is made in India and Burma. It takes about 150,000 insects almost six months to secrete enough liquid to make a pound of shellac.

Shelley, Percy Bysshe

Percy Bysshe Shelley was an English poet who lived about 150 years ago. He believed very strongly in the equality of men and in personal freedom, and he expressed his beliefs in many of his poems. He was born in 1792. While still in college, he eloped with a 16-year-old girl, Harriet Westbrook. After three  years Shelley left his wife. He fell in love with a girl named Mary Wollstonecraft Godwin. Shelley and Mary Godwin married after Harriet committed suicide in 1816 and went to live in Italy, where they became close friends of Byron. During this period Shelley wrote most of the poetry for which he is remembered today. In 1822 Shelley was sailing on the Mediterranean Sea when his boat overturned in a storm and he was drowned.

Among Shelley's greatest works are the poetic drama Prometheus Unbound, in which he dreamed of the freeing of mankind from tyranny; Adonais, written in grief at the death of John Keats; and delicate and lovely shorter poems such as "Ode to the West Wind," "The Cloud," and "Ode to a Skylark."

Shepard, Alan

Alan Bartlett Shepard, Jr., a Commander in the United States Navy, was the first American astronaut. He achieved this distinction on May 5, 1961 by riding a Mercury capsule named Freedom 7 into space. With millions watching on television and following the flight by radio, the capsule, with Shepard at the controls, rose to a height of 115 miles and reached a maximum speed of 5,160 miles per hour. It landed safely 302 miles out at sea just 15 minutes later. This feat earned Shepard the plaudits of a grateful nation that was

concerned lest we were falling behind in the space race with Russia. He was also awarded the civilian Distinguished Service Medal of the National Aeronautics and Space Administration by President Kennedy. Shepard, a former test pilot and a graduate of the U.S. Naval Academy, was born in East Derry, New Hampshire, on November 18, 1923. He graduated from the Naval War College in 1958.

Sheraton, Thomas

Thomas Sheraton was a great English furniture designer who lived about two hundred years ago. He was born in 1751. As a boy he was apprenticed to a cabinetmaker. Later he went to London and wrote several books on furniture design. These books were largely responsible for his fame. Sheraton was a very religious man, and he also wrote religious books and preached. He made very little furniture himself, and he was poor all his life. He died in 1806. The Sheraton style is noted for its grace and sturdiness. It uses beautiful woods designed in sweeping curves, and elaborate ornamentation.

Sheridan, Philip

Philip Henry Sheridan was one of the great generals of the Union forces during the American Civil War. He was

born in 1831 at Albany, New York, and when he was 22 years old he was graduated from the United States Military Academy at West Point. By 1862 he had risen to brigadier general. He distinguished himself in many of the major battles of the Civil War and early in 1864 he was appointed commander of the cavalry of the Army of the Potomac. His greatest campaigns were carried out in that year, in the Shenandoah Valley in northwestern Virginia.

Sheridan figured in one of the most famous incidents of the Civil War. Early one morning, a Union army had been attacked at Cedar Creek, Virginia, and was retreating. Sheridan was twenty miles away at the time, and he rode swiftly to the battlefield. The Union soldiers were so cheered by his arrival that they turned around and defeated the Confederate forces. This incident came to be called "Sheridan's Ride," and a poem was written about it by Thomas Buchanan Read.

After the war, Sheridan continued his army life. In 1883 he was made commander-in-chief of the United States Army, and later he was made General of the Army. He died in 1888.

Sheridan, Richard

Richard Brinsley Sheridan was a British playwright who lived about two hundred years ago. He is best remembered for two comedies, *The Rivals* and *The School for Scandal,* which are still performed. Sheridan was born in 1751 in Dublin, Ireland. When he was 19 he moved with his family to Bath, England, where he met and fell in love with a 16-year-old concert singer, Elizabeth Linley. The girl had been promised by her father to another man, and she was also being pursued by an older married man. To rescue her, Sheridan eloped with her to

France, but her father brought them back and separated them. Sheridan fought two duels with Elizabeth's married suitor, and at last was permitted to remarry his bride.

After that, Sheridan and his father-in-law, a composer of music, worked together in many theatrical ventures. Sheridan wrote a comic opera, *The Duenna,* for which Linley wrote the music. Sheridan and Linley bought a share in the Drury Lane Theater, and Sheridan managed it for many years.

At the height of his career in the theater, Sheridan dropped it almost completely and entered politics. He was elected to Parliament in 1780 and won new fame as a speaker. In 1809 the Drury Lane Theater burned, and Sheridan lost all his money. His political party went out of power, and Sheridan was put in jail for debt. In 1816 he died in poverty. Friends who had forgotten him in his times of trouble gave him a big funeral, and he was buried in Westminster Abbey among many of the great men of England.

Sherman, William Tecumseh

William Tecumseh Sherman was a general in the Union forces in the Civil War and was one of the most famous

military leaders in American history. He was born in Lancaster, Ohio, in 1820 and was graduated from the United States Military Academy at West Point, but after serving as an officer for a few years he resigned and became a businessman and a lawyer.

After the Civil War began he reentered the army in 1861 as a colonel. By 1862 he had distinguished himself in several battles and was a major general. In 1864 he was put in command of a Union Army to invade Georgia.

Sherman's greatest fame came from this campaign. After much fighting he captured Atlanta, then led his army on a "march to the sea," crossing Georgia from Atlanta to Savannah on the Atlantic coast. This cut the Confederate (southern) territory in two parts and hastened the end of the war. A song called "Marching through Georgia" became very popular in the North. In the South, and especially in Georgia, Sherman was a hated man for many years because of the burning and destruction done by his army on this march.

After the war, Sherman rose to General of the Army and commander in chief of the United States Army. He was so popular that he was offered the nomination for the Presidency of the United States, and he could easily have been elected, but he refused in a famous message in which he said, "If nominated, I will not accept; if elected, I will not serve." Sherman is also remembered for having said, "All war is hell."

Sherman resigned from the Army in 1884 and died in 1891.

Shetland Islands

The Shetland Islands are a group of several hundred islands in the Atlantic

Ocean, north of Scotland. They form the Scottish county of Shetland, which is 550 square miles in area and had a population of 17,809 in the 1961 census. Only 24 of the islands are inhabited. The largest island, Mainland, covers three-quarters of the entire area. The capital is Lerwick, on Mainland.

The islands have rocky coastlines. The land is poor and there are few trees. Most of the people make their living by fishing or by weaving and knitting woolens. Some of the people are farmers. Among the animals raised are the famous Shetland ponies.

The first settlers of the islands were Norsemen, and the people of the Shetland Islands are mostly of Norwegian descent.

shingles

Shingles is a skin disease that occurs mostly in grownups, especially after the age of 50. The name doctors use for shingles is *herpes zoster.* It forms a bunch of blisters about the size of a matchhead, with red behind them. These blisters form a wide line, usually on one side of the chest or back, following the line of a nerve underneath. They are caused by a *virus* or germ that infects the nerve.

Shingles may also happen after some kinds of poisoning or after some serious illnesses.

Shingles is sometimes very painful. The blisters may last for several weeks, and the pain may go on for months after the blisters are gone. The pain can be relieved by some medicines. The disease cannot be cured but goes away by itself. Usually it is not serious.

Shinto

Shinto is the ancient, native religion of Japan. It has about 51,000,000 followers. *Shinto* means "the way of the gods." The ancient Japanese believed in many gods, some good and some bad. The good gods were called *kami,* which means "superior," and were worshiped with offerings and prayers.

More than 1,300 years ago, Chinese people came to Japan and brought with them another religion, Buddhism. Shinto and Buddhism were combined in a religion called Ryobu-Shinto. The native gods of the Shinto religion were now considered as different representations, or parts, of the god Buddha. The Shinto priests became either Buddhist priests or fortune-tellers and magicians.

Then in the 18th century, about two hundred years ago, a movement began in Japan that attacked all foreign influences, including the Chinese and their religion. Certain scholars tried to revive the ancient Shinto. They taught that the most important thing was to obey nature and the Japanese emperor. A hundred years later, about 1865, Shinto was made the official religion of Japan.

In the course of time, the worship of many gods came to be a less important part of the Shinto religion. Shinto became more a code of ceremonies and rites at the emperor's court, and also came to mean patriotism and loyalty to the emperor, who was considered divine (a god).

SHINTO SINCE WORLD WAR II

At the end of World War II Shinto became less important. The emperor, Hirohito, announced that he was not divine, and General Douglas MacArthur, in command of the American forces occupying Japan, said that Japanese government money could no longer support Shinto as an official religion. Japanese officials had used Shinto to persuade some of the people that Japan should go to war.

ship

A ship is a big boat that travels on oceans. Modern ships are built of steel and are driven by steam, diesel oil, or nuclear power. They may be warships, liners that carry passengers, freighters that carry freight (called *cargo*), or tankers that carry oil or other liquids. The biggest liners (the *Queen Elizabeth* and *Queen Mary* of the British Cunard Line) would be as high as the Empire State Building if stood on end and carry more than 3,000 persons—2,000 or more passengers and 1,200 or more in the crew. The fastest liner (the *United States* of the United States Lines) crosses the Atlantic Ocean, a distance of about 3,000 miles, in about three and a half days.

Ships have developed gradually over the course of three thousand years or even more, and every age has brought its advancements. The first big ships were driven by many oarsmen, who later were assisted by sails. Then the use of sails was perfected and ships were driven by sails only. The biggest ships were warships, and some of them could carry several hundred fighting men and crewmen, but they were still tiny compared to the ships of today. The *Queen Elizabeth*, which displaces more than 80,000 tons of water, is about a thousand times as big as the ships with which Columbus crossed the Atlantic to discover America in 1492.

Until about a hundred years ago, all big ships were sailing ships. In 1838 the first steamship to cross the Atlantic, the *Great Western*, made the trip in 13½ days. In the 1860s, during the American Civil War, the warships *Monitor* and *Merrimac* proved that it was practical to make ships of iron. Before that, all ships had been made of wood, which rotted and was eaten away by small sea animals. The *Scotia*, a Cunard liner built of iron in 1862, was the largest ship in the world at 3,871 tons, and the first steel liner, the *Servia* of 1881, was again the largest at 7,392 tons.

OCEAN LINERS

The sailing ships that crossed the ocean before the days of steam were called "mail" ships because one of their important duties was to carry the mail. They also carried passengers, and it was not altogether a pleasant voyage. It often took weeks to make the crossing. There was little fresh water or fresh food. Usually there was no provision for bathing, except with sea water put in an open tub on the deck. The ships were small and did much rolling and rocking. Only the few most important passengers could have private rooms. Others slept in bunks in one large, badly ventilated room.

The deluxe liners of the 1880s introduced many comforts: private staterooms for two or perhaps four persons; bathrooms; refrigeration to keep food fresh; and many other conveniences. This, however, applied only to first-class passengers. Ships were adopting the system of three classes. First class was quite comfortable. Second class was not much worse. But third class, called *steerage,* gave passengers about the same accommodations that cattle would have on a freighter today. Steerage passengers had wooden bunks or none at all, no privacy, no provisions for washing except at occasional hours, and little or no food. Many thousands of immigrants to the United States crossed from Europe in the steerage of ocean liners.

The modern ocean liner has existed more or less unchanged for about fifty years, except that the ships have become larger, faster, more beautiful, and more comfortable. There are still three classes on most liners, though many of the smaller liners are "one class" or "cabin class" ships. First-class passengers have staterooms with private baths and often private decks. There are luxurious lounges, motion-picture theaters, swimming pools, fine shops, and often a night club or cabaret where passengers can see a floor show with their dinner. The food is the finest served anywhere. Every kind of entertainment is provided for the passengers who want it. Second class is not so fine, but has almost the same conveniences, always has its own motion-picture theater, and on the finest liners has its own swimming pool. Third class, or "tourist" class, is better than first class once was. There are no private baths, and the staterooms or cabins usually hold four passengers, but here again there is a motion-picture theater and often there are special times when the passengers may use the swimming pool.

The largest liners make the Atlantic run between New York City and the channel ports of England and France, but equally fine liners are used on the Pacific Ocean between San Francisco and the Hawaiian and Asiatic ports, and between the United States or Europe and South America, Italy and other Mediterranean countries, and many other parts of the world.

In the winter, when other passenger traffic is light, the best ships are often used for "cruises," pleasure voyages for ten or more days of travel and sightseeing in foreign countries. The longest cruises take several months and go around the world.

In wartime, the great liners are turned into troop transports and used to carry soldiers to overseas battle areas.

SHIPBUILDING

The general shape of a ship has changed little in the course of the ages, and the general plan of shipbuilding changed little until the constant doubling and redoubling of the size of ships, and the change of materials from wood to iron and then to steel, revolutionized the shipbuilding industry.

Ships today, as for ages, are built in shipyards. These are actually yards. They have shops and even big factories in them, but the ships are built in the open.

The old wooden ships began with the laying of a *keel,* a long timber that formed the bottom center line of the ship from bow to stern (front to back). At one time a single tree trunk, carefully selected for strength and straightness, could serve as the keel. Bigger ships required stronger and straighter keels, made of separate pieces of wood tightly braced and joined.

The keel was placed between wooden tracks called *ways,* where the ship would rest until it was almost finished. Stretching upward from each side of the keel was built a framework of *ribs*. These were timbers that had been steamed until they were soft enough to bend into a curved shape. They were strongly braced. Wood planks were put on the outsides of the ribs, forming the sides of the ships, and across the inside braces, forming the decks. The planking was sealed, or *caulked,* with packing materials and binders such as tar. In sailing days, masts went in before the decks, for they ran all the way from the keel through the decks and far above the sides of the ship.

Though the basic construction plan is simple, the wooden ship represented the finest carpentry of all time, for it had to be able to withstand the stresses of ocean storms and the constant pounding of the seas and action of the waters on the wood.

When the ship was complete except for some interior work and the rigging of sails, it was *launched*—allowed to slide down the ways, which always led to the water's edge, and into the water. This was always a joyous occasion, accompanied by ceremonies, music, and cheering.

Except for the masts and the one-piece keel, the steel ship follows the same

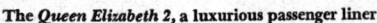

The *Queen Elizabeth 2,* a luxurious passenger liner.

pattern. Frameworks of heavy steel girders are put together in factories and conveyed to the ways by giant cranes that lower them into position on the ways. Steel plates instead of planks are fastened to the framework to form the sides. Since each section of a modern ship weighs many tons, the shipyard today needs huge equipment to do these jobs.

For many years, the parts of steel ships were riveted together. This process used bolts that were heated and hammered tightly into place so that they became almost a part of the solid metal pieces that they joined together. In recent years, welding has become the usual method of fastening the parts of ships together. After World War I, Germany as a defeated nation had to agree not to build large warships. German naval engineers adopted welding instead of riveting because the welding process saves weight. In welding, the edges of two pieces of metal are melted and allowed to flow together and harden, which causes them to join almost as though they were the same piece of metal. The Germans built two warships, called "pocket battleships," that were bigger and more powerful than other warships because of the weight saved by the use of welding.

In World War II, when the United States needed more freighters than ever before to replace losses to submarines and to supply fighting forces 12,000 miles apart, methods were developed to assemble ships from prefabricated parts. The chief pioneer in this work was Henry J. Kaiser, but other shipbuilders made great contributions. Whole sections of ships were made complete in separate factories, taken to the shipyard, and put together. This method cut more than half off the time required to make a ship. It is not used for warships, which are much heavier and must be much more carefully built than cargo ships.

SHIPPING

All the freight-carrying ships of a nation, considered together, are called its merchant fleet. Some of these ships belong to big shipping lines. Some belong to individual owners. The lines usually have regularly scheduled voyages for their freighters. Some ships are called *tramps.* They do not follow regular schedules but will take on any particular load that a shipper wants transported.

Shipping is usually a profitable business, but big countries often subsidize their freight lines just as they do their passenger lines, because shipping is so important to the prosperity of the country's business and industry and because the freighters are needed in time of war. The subsidies may be in the form of payment for carrying the mails, government money paid to the shipbuilder as part of the cost of construction, and free engineering and other services supplied by government experts.

U.S. MARITIME ADMINISTRATION

In the United States, the Maritime Administration is in charge of helping the country's merchant fleet (also called the merchant marine). It is a branch of the Department of Commerce. Before 1950 it was called the United States Maritime Commission.

Another branch of the Department of Commerce, called the Federal Maritime Board, regulates the shipping business in the United States. It controls the rates that can be charged by merchant ships and the services they must perform.

The Maritime Administration maintains reserve fleets of government-owned ships, so that they will be available in time of war. The Administration can hire government-owned ships to private firms, for use in shipping during peacetime.

The Maritime Commission also decides what kind of shipping services and what kind of ships can best promote United States foreign trade. When it thinks a certain amount of government money should be given to shipowners for the building of more ships or special kinds of ship, it makes a recommendation to the Federal Maritime Board and the Board makes the final decision. As in all government spending, the money to be spent must be authorized by Congress.

REGISTRY

Every merchant ship must be registered as being a ship of a certain country, and must fly the flag of that country and carry official papers from that country.

Each country has its own rules governing registry. A merchant ship must pass certain inspections, pay its sailors a certain rate and provide certain conveniences for them, and pay certain fees. Sometimes a shipowner prefers not to follow one or more of the rules of his own country and will register his ship in another country. For example, a large number of ships owned by United States citizens are registered with Panama or Greece.

For many years the world's largest merchant fleet belonged to Great Britain, but during World War II the United States built so many ships that it became first and Great Britain second. Norway is third. The countries with the biggest merchant fleets in 1962 were:

COUNTRY	NO. OF SHIPS	TONNAGE
United States	2,733	23,273,000
Great Britain	2,363	21,658,000
Norway	1,360	12,511,000
Liberia	811	10,393,000
Japan	1,133	7,084,000
Greece	726	6,537,419
Italy	646	4,932,000

Most of the ships of Liberian registry are owned by citizens of other countries, chiefly the United States. France, Netherlands, West Germany, and Soviet Russia also have large merchant fleets.

FREIGHTERS

Freighters are never as big as the biggest passenger liners. The passenger ships may range from 20,000 to more than 80,000 tons displacement. Freighters seldom go over 20,000 tons and average about 10,000 tons.

During World War I, when German submarines were sinking hundreds of Allied ships, the United States necessarily became the greatest builder of freighters in the world. During World War II again, the United States built freighters to replace the losses of the Allied countries and to carry an amount of freight that was far greater than anything history had known before. Many of the American freighters were of a size and type

known as "Liberty ships," displacing about 10,000 tons each. Hundreds of these are still in service.

Some freighters carry a few passengers as well as the freight and crew. A few freighters are built especially for this purpose and offer almost as fine rooms and services as the de luxe liners.

See also the articles NAVY and SAILING.

shock

When a person has had a serious accident or surgical operation, he often suffers from a condition called shock. This condition is physical, though people also speak of being "shocked" when they are surprised or have received bad news.

In a person suffering from shock, the blood flows more slowly throughout the body. As a result, the person's body temperature falls below normal and he becomes pale. He may have difficulty in breathing and will have chills. He will also feel very thirsty. If nothing is done for him, he will suffer nausea and vomiting and he may faint and lose consciousness. Though he suffers no pain, shock can make any other injury worse, because it weakens the body.

The doctor should be sent for at once. In the meantime the patient should lie down, with his head lower than his body. He should be covered with blankets and kept absolutely still. If he is unconscious, dampen a cloth with aromatic spirits of ammonia and hold it to his nose. If he is conscious, the aromatic spirits of ammonia may still help, and he may also be given a little black coffee.

SHOCK THERAPY

Persons suffering from mental illness are sometimes given "shock treatment." Electricity or certain drugs will send a person into a state of shock. This is done intentionally, because sometimes when the person recovers consciousness his mental condition is improved. An overdose of insulin was once used in shock therapy (treatment), but other drugs have been developed that are better.

shoe

A shoe is worn to cover and protect the foot. Usually we use the word only for footwear made of leather and covering the whole foot and perhaps part of the ankle. If it covers little except the sole we call it a sandal; if it goes above the ankle we call it a boot. If it is not firm enough or tough enough for outdoor wear it is a slipper.

Children still go barefoot at times, and the human foot can become so tough that it can carry a person almost anywhere, but still men made foot-coverings for themselves long before they became civilized in other ways. They wrapped animal skins around their feet, and these became moccasins; they tied pieces of tough leather to the soles of their feet and these became sandals. The ancient Greeks and Romans, 2,500 years ago, wore sandals. There had been shoes of various kinds for thousands of years before then.

The shoemaker, called a *cobbler,* was already a skilled craftsman in the time of Jesus. He did not greatly increase his skill for two thousand years. As late as the early 1800s, most people were having their shoes made by hand by cobblers who

Shoes have been made since ancient times. The most comfortable styles are often also the oldest. *Row 1:* An Egyptian sandal of 2500 B.C. An Egyptian shoe of the same period. An Assyrian design. A Greek laced boot of 500 B.C. *Row 2:* A Roman sandal. An ornate medieval shoe. A medieval *sabot,* still worn by many peasants. *Row 3:* A riding boot of 1650. An early "wedgie" for women. A 17th-century woman's dress shoe. A military riding boot. *Row 4:* A woman's house slipper. Her street slipper, designed to lift her above muddy streets. A high laced boot from before the Civil War. A modern woman's shoe. *Row 5:* A casual shoe, similar in design for both men and women. A woman's shoe for evening wear. *Row 6:* The man's shoe for the same occasion. A Japanese peasant's *geta.* A Chinese slipper. A Mongolian boot.

had small shops in the towns or traveled from town to town making shoes for whoever needed them.

The cobbler worked at a bench, with a knife, an awl (a sharp-pointed drilling or punching tool), a hammer, wooden pegs, tacks, rubbing sticks to smooth and polish the leather, and a few other simple tools.

Shoes then, as they do now, had three main parts: the upper of soft leather that covers the top of the foot; the sole, a stiffer leather on which to walk; and the heel, which keeps the foot in the most comfortable position for walking. The cobbler would put the sole leather on a flat stone (called a lapstone) and pound it with a hammer to make it tough. He would cut several pieces of soft leather with his knife and sew them together by hand to make the upper. He would fit these parts on a foot-shaped block of wood called a *last* and tack them together. Then he would place several pieces of leather together at the back and tack them on to form the heel. With his sharp knife he would trim the edges, and with his rubbing sticks he would smooth them.

About a hundred years ago there were several important inventions that changed shoemaking completely, replacing the cobbler with the shoe factory. The first, in 1845, was a rolling machine that removed the necessity for beating the leather to smooth it. The second was Elias Howe's sewing machine, which helped the shoemaker as much as it did the garment manufacturer and housewife. The third was a machine for sewing the soles of shoes. This was invented in 1858 by a Massachusetts man named Lyman Blake, but was bought from him by a man named Gordon McKay. A process that grew out of this machine is still in use and is called the McKay process. A few years later Charles Goodyear Jr., son of the man who began the modern rubber industry, invented another shoemaking method, which is still used and is called the Goodyear process.

All of these inventors were Americans, and the modern shoe industry began in the United States. The operating plan of the industry was a very unusual one. Machines for making shoes were not sold to the factories where shoes are made. The machinery manufacturers (principally the United Shoe Machinery Company) built and owned most of the machines and rented them to the factories. This system is still being used in the case of a great deal of machinery with which shoes are made and repaired.

The rental system helped the shoe industry to grow very fast, because a person could start a factory even if he could not afford to buy expensive machinery.

SHOE MANUFACTURING

About 600,000,000 pairs of shoes, including slippers, sandals, boots, tennis shoes, baseball shoes, and others, are made and sold in the United States each year. Women buy more new shoes than men. The shoes are sold in about 25,000 shoe stores and in other stores, such as department stores, that sell shoes and other things too.

Shoes are made in thousands of different styles and sizes. The length of a shoe is shown by a number, such as 6 or 9½. The width of a shoe is shown by a letter, from A (narrow) to E (wide). The letter is repeated to show very wide or very narrow sizes, so that AAA is very narrow and EEE is very wide.

Though there are so many different styles in shoes, and sixteen or more standard ways of making shoes, the general method of manufacture is much the same in all cases.

Every shoe is made on a last, the same kind of wooden foot-shaped form that the old-fashioned cobbler used. Lasts are made in special factories. They are made in two parts, the toe and the heel, which are fastened together by a hinge so that the last can easily be taken out of the shoe when it is finished.

The *upper* of the shoe is made of several pieces. These are cut from the leather with dies that work on the same principle as the biscuit-cutter a housewife uses in her kitchen; except, of course, that the dies are made of the finest steel.

For each part of the upper there is a *lining,* which is cloth or softer leather. The uppers and linings are sewed together.

At the front of the shoe there is a stiff strip called a *box toe* and at the back there is a stiff strip called a *counter.* These keep the toe and heel of the shoe from collapsing.

When the upper and linings are sewed together they are put on the last. An *insole* is sewed or glued to them. This is the sole that the foot actually touches. Then an *outsole* is sewed to the insole and uppers. The outsole and insole are often fastened together with staples (small, U-shaped nails), in addition to being sewed. The outsole is the thick, tough leather that you walk on.

Leather is not the only material for shoes. The uppers may be made of plastic-coated cloth or of woven fabrics. The outsoles are often made of rubber or plastic materials.

Finally the heel goes on. The heel on a man's shoe usually has a rounded piece of thick leather as a *heel base.* On top of that may go other pieces of leather to make a leather heel, or a piece of rubber to make a rubber heel. A woman's shoe with low heels may be made the same way, but a woman's high heels are usually made of a block of wood. This is wrapped with the same leather that is used to make the upper, or it may be wrapped with a piece of a plastic material. (On low-priced shoes and slippers the wooden heel may be painted.) At the bottom of the wood heel a small piece of leather or rubber is tacked on. This is called the *lift.*

Every stage of this process of shoe manufacture is done with many special steps that have been scientifically developed, and with special materials and machinery. Making shoes is more complicated than it sounds.

STYLES IN SHOES

Styles in shoes have often changed because new ways have been found to make shoes more comfortable, or longer-lasting; but styles have changed just as often because people were tired of the appearance of the old shoes and wanted something new and different. Hundreds of men and women work constantly designing shoes that may satisfy the public idea of beauty.

In ancient times it was sometimes thought that the toe of a shoe should curl up to a little point. Such shoes can be seen in old drawings. Our great-grandparents wore "high shoes." Both men and women wore shoes that came above the ankles. These were often fastened with buttons. A shoe-buttoner was used to put them on —a hook that drew the button through the buttonhole

Gradually the buttons gave way to shoelaces. In the 1920s, low shoes came to replace the high shoes. Women began to wear chiefly a shoe with no buttons or shoestrings or straps needed to hold the shoe on the foot. Men's low shoes were usually called Oxfords, and women's low shoes were usually called slippers or pumps, because they were different from the high shoes that were then called simply "shoes." Now when we speak of a pair of shoes we mean the low shoes that everyone wears.

shooting star, another name for a meteor: see the article METEOR.

shore patrol, the police force of the United States Navy, which maintains order, enforces naval regulations, and makes sure sailors on leave return safely to base: see the article MILITARY POLICE.

shorthand

Shorthand is any system of writing without fully spelling any of the words. Some systems of shorthand use letters of the alphabet, so they are somewhat like handwriting in which nothing but

abbreviations is used. Most systems of shorthand use symbols (special marks) to stand for the sounds of words.

There are three main uses of shorthand today. By far the greatest use is by stenographers, who take notes as their employers dictate (speak) the words of a letter or something else that is to be written. The stenographer then "reads back" the notes and types out the words on a typewriter. A second use is by court reporters, who take down all the words that are spoken in a trial in a court of law. The third use is by businessmen and others who use shorthand to save time.

The two most popular methods of shorthand are called Pitman and Gregg. In both methods, little marks and dots are made to stand for the sounds. They are written in a stenographer's notebook, which has lines on it like the lines on a school tablet. It makes a difference whether the mark is on the line, above the line, or below the line. The Pitman system was invented by Sir Isaac Pitman, an Englishman, who lived from 1813 to 1897. He called his system *phonography* (the writing of sounds). The word *stenology* has also been used for it. The Gregg system was invented by John Robert Gregg, who was born in Ireland in 1867. He developed his system to simplify the Pitman system.

Shorthand is taught as part of a course in STENOGRAPHY, about which there is a

From top to bottom, the three samples of shorthand read: "This is a sample of Gregg shorthand." "This is a sample of Pitman shorthand." "This is a sample of Speedwriting."

separate article. It is taught in high schools and also in business schools that high-school graduates may attend for one or two years after graduating. A method known as *Speedwriting* is taught in shorter courses. It uses regular letters of the alphabet to represent the sounds.

The average stenographer can take down 100 to 125 words per minute. A court reporter must be much faster, able to take 250 or more words per minute.

A machine called the Stenotype takes down words in shorthand. It has a small keyboard that can be operated with one hand. Like a typewriter, it prints letters (standing for sounds) on paper; but it is almost completely silent and the letters are printed on a narrow roll of paper. A skillful Stenotype operator can take down more words per minute on his machine than anyone can take by hand.

Systems of shorthand have been used for at least two thousand years. The most famous use of shorthand was by an Englishman named Samuel Pepys, who lived almost three hundred years ago. He kept a diary in a system of shorthand he invented himself. After he died, scholars finally figured out his system and his diary was published.

Shoshone Indians

The Shoshone tribes are the Indians of the Far Western plains and the eastern Rocky Mountains. They included the Comanche, the Banock, the Paiute, the Panamint, the Ute, and the Shoshone tribes.

The western Shoshone were a poor people who lived a hard life. They hunted deer and small game but had to live mostly on roots, nuts, and wild vegetables. The eastern group rode horses, hunted buffalo, and lived very much like the Sioux. The Shoshones remained friendly to the whites, and under their great leader, Chief Washakie, they joined the United States in its wars against the Plains Indians.

One of the most famous Indian women in American history was a Shoshone named Sacajawea, or Bird Woman. She became the chief guide of the great Lewis and Clark expedition that explored the land west of the Mississippi in 1803. Sacajawea successfully guided the expedition to the Pacific Coast.

shotgun

A shotgun is a gun that shoots a mass of tiny pellets called *shot,* as explained in the article AMMUNITION. The shotgun is held at the shoulder when fired. It looks like a rifle but its bore (inside of the barrel) is smooth, not rifled (grooved). Shotguns are used mostly for hunting birds and small animals such as rabbits. Shotguns are used also in the sport of trapshooting.

A shotgun usually weighs seven to ten pounds. Most shotguns are *double-barreled.* That is, they have two barrels side by side with a trigger for each. A shell may be loaded in each barrel and the hunter can fire a second shot without pausing to reload if he misses the first shot. The size of the barrel, and of the shell it will take, is called its *gauge.* A 10-gauge shotgun is the largest in general use. Smaller sizes are 12-gauge, 14-gauge, and sometimes 16-gauge. (The higher the number, the smaller the gauge.) Usually only a strong man can handle a 10-gauge shotgun.

The *sawed-off shotgun* is a weapon that has been used by vicious criminals. The barrels are sawed off to shorten them. From the short barrel the shot from the shell spreads very quickly and will kill at a distance of a few feet, even if careful aim is not taken. The principal reason for sawing off the barrels is to make the gun small enough to conceal under the clothing or in a suitcase or small bag. Most states have laws against sawed-off shotguns.

shotput

The shotput is a weight-throwing contest. It is one of the events in track and field athletics.

The shot is an iron ball that may weigh 8, 12 or 16 pounds. The weight depends upon the age and strength of the competitors. An 8-pound shot is used for younger high school boys or in events in which women compete. The 16-pound shot is the championship weight used by fully grown men.

The shotputter stands in a circle marked on the ground. He places one foot on the back of the circle. At the front edge of the circle there is a marker over which he must not step. The shotputter holds the ball in his right hand (unless he is left-handed) with his fingers wrapped around the shot and, with his palm supporting the weight of the shot. His hand is held next to his neck and resting on his shoulder. His other arm is extended in front of him. As the athlete prepares to "put" the shot, he dips back several times to get rhythm. Then he kicks his left leg into the air, he whirls around, and as he turns toward the front marker he puts all his weight behind the hand and arm holding the shot. As he reaches the front marker he pushes or heaves the iron ball out and away from him. The speed of his turn has much to do with the distances he can throw the iron ball.

The distance from the shotput has increased over a number of years. About fifty years ago it was considered good if a shotputter could reach 40 feet. Sixty feet was at one time considered an impossible distance, but an American athlete named Parry O'Brien reached that distance in 1954. In 1967 another American, Randy Matson, set a record of 71 ft. 5½ in.

shrapnel

Shrapnel is a kind of shell fired from a cannon. The shell is hollow and is filled with bullets and an explosive. Just before the shell reaches its target, the explosive causes it to burst. The bullets and the pieces of the shell fly off in all directions. This kind of shell was invented in 1784 and named for a British major named Shrapnel, who died more than a hundred years ago (in 1842). It was used in World War II, but modern ammunition based on the same idea is not usually called shrapnel.

shrew

The shrew is a small animal that very few people ever see. It lives in all parts of the temperate and tropical zones of the world except in Australia. Some shrews are swimmers and live near the edges of ponds or streams, and some live in burrows just below the surface of the ground. Shrews are the smallest mammals in the world. The largest is about the size of a house rat, and the smallest is only about half an inch long and weighs less than a dime.

Shrews are extremely nervous, excitable animals, and their lives are short. They are quarrelsome and fight each other constantly. Their eating habits are remarkable. A shrew must eat constantly, or it will starve to death. It eats almost its own weight in insects or vegetable matter every three hours, twenty-four hours a day. It sleeps very little, and if it goes without eating for more than three hours it dies of starvation.

Shrews have two or three litters of young a year. Adults are like tiny mice in appearance. Some kinds have bright red teeth, others have white teeth. Their fur is brown above and gray on the underside.

shrike

The shrike is a small bird of prey, about the size of a robin. There are

shrikes in North America, Europe, Asia, and Africa. All of them live on insects, mice, and other small animals, swooping down on their victims as a hawk does. Shrikes often kill more than they need to eat at the moment, and store their catch by hanging it on a thorn or sharp twig. For this reason they are called *butcher-birds*.

The shrike has pale grayish feathers, with darker wavy markings on the breast and black patches on the face. The female builds a nest in a tree or shrub and lays four or five gray, spotted eggs each spring.

shrimp

The shrimp is a sea animal, a small relative of the lobster. It is a crustacean, which means that its entire body is covered with a jointed shell. It breathes water through gills. It is a sandy or muddy color.

Shrimps are found in coast waters from North Carolina to Texas, and are plentiful in the Gulf of Mexico. They are usually about one to two inches long, but occasionally they grow an inch or two larger. They swim backwards, unlike most other sea animals. Most shrimp are good to eat, and the shrimp-fishing business is an important one. The *prawn* is a kind of large shrimp.

Shrove Tuesday, the Tuesday before Ash Wednesday. See the articles on TUESDAY and MARDI GRAS.

shrub

Shrubs are plants with woody stems that grow in groups of two or more, instead of in a single trunk. Because of the several stems, each with its leaves and branches, shrubs usually have a tendency to be bushy and to spread out. Gardeners plant shrubbery in gardens, on lawns, around houses and other buildings, and in places where the ground seems bare or where the soil may wear away if there are no plant roots to hold it in place.

There are hundreds of different kinds of shrub. They may be as high as some trees or less than a foot in height. Some are evergreen, keeping their leaves all year round, and some shed their leaves in the fall.

Many shrubs bear flowers. Low-growing shrubs are often used for hedges. They are clipped to keep them from growing shaggy and untidy looking. Barberry and privet hedges are popular in most parts of the United States and Canada, but many other kinds can be used.

shuffleboard

Shuffleboard is a game that is popular on shipboard and in many resorts. The object of the game is to shove a wooden disk toward a diagram marked on a floor or deck and make the disk stop at certain places within the diagram. Each player has a long stick with an end shaped somewhat like the end of a shovel. The disk is a round piece of wood about one inch thick and six inches across. The diagram is in the form of a triangle (a three-sided shape) and is marked into sections. Each time the disk stops in the triangle it

scores a certain number of points, depending on the section in which it stops.

Originally shuffleboard was played on a table, with coins instead of disks, and was called *shovel-board*. It is very much like the game of CURLING, about which there is a separate article. Shuffleboard may have grown out of curling, or curling out of shuffleboard. Both are very old games, more than four hundred years old.

Siam, a former name for THAILAND.

Sibelius, Jean

Jean Sibelius is the name of a Finnish composer, or writer of music. He was born in 1865. He studied music as a child, but when he was 20 he entered the University of Helsinki to become a lawyer. He soon gave this up and studied music again.

After several of his compositions had been performed successfully, Sibelius came to worldwide attention in 1899 with *Finlandia*, a short work that has become a kind of unofficial national anthem. Besides this and other music about Finland, Sibelius wrote seven symphonies, a violin concerto, and the popular *Valse Triste*. He settled in a small town near Helsinki, but toured Europe in 1900 and made a brief trip to the United States in 1914. He wrote much less music after 1925. He died in 1957.

Sibelius is considered one of the major modern composers. On his eightieth birthday, in 1945, his music was given special performances in many countries, including the United States, Great Britain, and Russia. The Finnish government issued a postage stamp bearing his picture. Sibelius' birthday each year is observed with special honors in Finland.

Siberia

Siberia is a vast region that covers all the northern part of Asia. Its area is about 5,000,000 square miles, which makes it much larger than the United States, and it is about one-third of Asia, the largest continent on earth. Siberia extends from the Ural Mountains in the west, where Europe ends and Asia begins, to the Pacific Ocean in the east, a distance of more than 4,000 miles.

Only about 25,000,000 people live in Siberia, because the region is so far north that it is very cold and because very little of it has good farm land. Even this number of people is far more than lived there until the last thirty years.

For about three hundred years, Siberia has belonged to Russia. During most of that time, the Russian government of the czars (emperors) did little to develop Siberia. Convicted criminals and political prisoners (those who had opposed the czars' governments) were sent to prison camps in Siberia. Most of them were made to work in mines. In the 1890s, Russia began to build the Trans-Siberian Railroad from European Russia to the the city of Vladivostok on the Pacific coast of Siberia. The railroad, the longest in the world, was completed in 1905 and some cities grew up along it.

In recent decades, the Soviet government has made great efforts to develop

the resources and agriculture of Siberia. Some of the richest mineral deposits in the world are in Siberia, including gold, uranium, and a few metals that are scarce in all other parts of the world. There are also valuable oil fields. The Communist government under Stalin had its big prison camps in Siberia. It sent millions of prisoners, including prisoners of war, to work there. Life was so hard that many of these prisoners died. Today many of these camps have been closed.

WHAT THE LAND IS LIKE

Most of Siberia is a flat plain. In the far north, this is mostly the kind of land called tundra. It is marshy and is frozen most of the year, and very little vegetation will grow there except mosses and lichens (similar to moss). There are several high mountain ranges. The plains are cut by big rivers, the chief ones being the Ob, Yenisei, Lena, and Amur. There are many lakes, including Lake Baikal, the largest in Asia.

Northern Siberia is in the arctic regions. It is dry and it is very cold. In the south it is warmer and there are many valuable forests.

The original people of Siberia belonged to the Mongolian race. In the northeast they were peoples closely related to the Aleuts, Eskimos, and various American Indians. Today most of the people are Russians and other Slavic peoples. Besides mining, there are farming and cattle-grazing in the southern parts and fur-trapping in the northeast.

The main cities are Omsk, Tomsk, Tobolsk, Stalinsk, Irkutsk, Komsomolsk, Yakutsk, Novosibirsk, and Vladivostok. In the cities there are some factories.

sibyl

A sibyl was a woman who could foretell the future, according to the beliefs of the ancient Greeks and Romans more than two thousand years ago. Sibyls were supposed to be inspired by the god Apollo or by other gods. The most famous sibyl lived in a cave at Cumae, near Naples in Italy. She was called the Cumaean sibyl, and she had nine books of prophecies about the future of the city of Rome. According to one story, she offered to sell these books at a high price to Tarquin, one of the first kings of Rome. Tarquin refused to buy the books, so the sibyl burned three of them and then offered the remaining six to Tarquin at the same price. He again refused to buy, so she burned three more and offered the remaining three at the same price. Finally Tarquin paid the price and the books were placed in the temple on the Capitoline Hill in Rome. They were consulted by the rulers of Rome in times of emergency until the temple burned and the books were destroyed. Read also the article on ORACLE.

Sicily

Sicily is the largest island in the Mediterranean Sea. It lies just off the toe of Italy, and with some neighboring islands it forms a self-governing region that is part of Italy. Sicily has an area of about 10,000 square miles. It is separated from Italy by the Strait of Messina, which is 2 to 10 miles wide.

The island is a continuation of the Apennine Mountains of Italy, and it is

largely mountainous, rising in the northeast to the peak of Mt. Etna, 10,742 feet. Mt. Etna is the highest active volcano in Europe, and the area surrounding it is subject to frequent earthquakes.

The only lowland in Sicily is the Plain of Catania in the south. Sicily has a few rivers, including the Simeto, Salso, and Platani, and there are many mountain streams that are rushing torrents during

the winter rains and dry in summer. The climate is mild and rainfall is light. During the summer the island is frequently swept by the sirocco, a hot, dry wind from Africa.

Almost five million people live in Sicily. Their principal occupations are farming and the raising of livestock. The chief crops are grain, grapes, olives, and citrus fruits, in which Sicily leads all of Italy. About one-quarter of Italy's fishing boats are from Sicily, and large quantities of tuna are caught. There is some mining, chiefly of sulphur, asphalt, and salt. Sicily has few factories.

The capital of Sicily is Palermo, a city of 652,380 population in 1973. It is a seaport on the Gulf of Palermo, in the northeast. Other important cities include Catania, population 407,941, in the east, at the foot of Mt. Etna; and Messina, population 269,757, on the Strait of Messina.

HISTORY OF SICILY

The earliest inhabitants of Sicily were two tribes called the Siculi (who gave their name to the island) and the Sicani. The island was settled by Phoenicians, Carthaginians, and Greeks hundreds of years before the birth of Jesus. The Greek cities, such as Syracuse and Agrigentum, were among the world's centers of civilization. The island became a part of the Roman Empire in 210 B.C. Later it was under Arab rule for several hundred years until it was conquered by the Normans in the 11th century. With Naples in Italy, the island became part of the Kingdom of the Two Sicilies. In the 1500s, the Two Sicilies came under Spanish rule, which continued until 1861 when they became part of the kingdom of Italy. The island of Sicily was important during World War II. The Allies bombed its naval bases and airfields, and in 1943 British and American forces invaded and conquered the island.

SICILY. Area, 9,926 square miles. Population (1973 estimate) 4,721,000. Region of Italy, with nine provinces. Capital, Palermo.

Sidney, Sir Philip

Sir Philip Sidney was an English soldier and writer who lived about four hundred years ago. He was a favorite of Queen Elizabeth I and of all the English people. He was born in 1554, of a noble English family. As a young man he was given several important missions abroad by the Queen. Later Elizabeth became angry with him because he warned her not to marry the Duke of Anjou, which he thought she was about to do. Sidney left the court for a few months, but Elizabeth relented and called him back.

Sidney was a great enemy of Spain and wanted to command a warship, but Elizabeth was afraid of losing "the jewel of her dominions." Nevertheless, in 1586 he was fatally wounded in a land battle against a Spanish army. He was only 32 when he died, and his death caused great unhappiness in England. He was considered the ideal of a knight, kind, gracious, witty, and charming. His writings were not published until after his death. His most notable work was *Astrophel and Stella,* a group of love poems.

siege

A siege is a method used in warfare to conquer a city or a strong fortress of the enemy. Instead of attacking the city or fortress, an army simply camps around it, prevents any food or supplies from being taken in, and waits. Sooner or later the people inside run out of food and surrender. The army outside is said to *besiege,* or *beleaguer,* the place.

Sieges have been used in warfare for thousands of years. The most famous siege of modern times was the siege of Paris, France, during the Franco-Prussian War, a war between France and the German kingdom of Prussia in 1870 and 1871. Food became very scarce in Paris, and after four and a half months the city surrendered to the Prussian army.

Airplanes have made sieges less effective, but airplanes still cannot supply a large city or army for a very long time.

Siegfried, a hero in Germanic legends: see NIBELUNG and RING OPERAS.

Sierra Leone

Sierra Leone, a republic in Africa on the northwest coast between Guinea and Liberia, was a British protectorate until it became independent in 1961. In area, Sierra Leone is about the same size as the state of West Virginia. Some of the people, called Creoles, are descendants of freed former slaves; they live in Freetown, the capital. Others are members of African Negro tribes. The principal products are diamonds, iron ore, bauxite, and palm kernels. Sierra Leone is governed by a parliament and its prime minister. It is a member of the (British) Commonwealth.

SIERRA LEONE. Area, 27,925 square miles. Population (1973 estimate) 2,600,-000. Capital, Freetown (178,600).

Sierra Nevada

The Sierra Nevada is a great range of mountains in eastern California, extending into western Nevada. It forms a wall between the Central Valley of California and the Great Basin, which covers most of Nevada and parts of neighboring states. The Sierra Nevada range is 430 miles long. The mountains are chiefly of granite. The east face is steep and barren. On the west there is a more gradual slope into foothills along Central Valley. The Sierra Nevada has many peaks of more than 14,000 feet, including Mt. Whitney (14,495 feet), the highest peak outside of Alaska in the United States. Others are Mt. Williamson (14,375 feet) and North Palisade (14,242 feet).

On the western slope of the Sierra Nevada there is a belt of gold-bearing ore called the Mother Lode, which was the source of the California Gold Rush in 1849. Many passes for automobiles and railroads cross the range, including the Donner, Truckee, Carson, and Sonora passes.

Much of the magnificent scenery of the Sierra Nevada is now set aside in national parks such as Yosemite, Kings Canyon, and Sequoia. In these parks there are gorges and waterfalls, towering peaks, forests of giant redwood trees, and beautiful mountain lakes.

Sikhs

The Sikhs are a sect, or special religious group, in Hinduism, the principal religion of India. There are over seven and a half million Sikhs. Their religion was founded about five hundred years ago by a Hindu teacher called Nanak. He taught that there is only one God and that people of different religions all worship the same God. He was opposed to the caste system. He had many followers, and the city of Amritsar became the Sikhs' sacred city. About two hundred years later, the Sikhs had a new leader, Govind Singh. He introduced certain customs of Sikh men, such as wearing a turban, carrying a dagger, and never cutting the hair or beard. He made the Sikhs a warlike group and they began to conquer much territory.

Until about 100 years ago, the Sikhs fought bitterly against British control of India, but the British won. In 1947, when India and Pakistan became independent, the Sikhs' territory was split between them. In 1966, after many uprisings, India created a separate state for the Sikhs and made their language, Punjabi, one of the official languages.

silhouette

A silhouette is the shadow outline of something. When we speak of something being silhouetted, we mean that it stands out as a dark shadow against the light.

Silhouettes are easy to make. A person sits between a strong light and a wall, so that his profile shows as a shadow on a piece of paper attached to the wall. The artist traces the profile on the paper. The tracing is then cut out. It may be colored with black ink or paint, or a piece of black paper may be cut into the same shape. Some artists are able to look at a person silhouetted against a strong light, and cut the silhouette out of black paper

with scissors. These black paper outlines are then pasted on white paper.

silicon

Silicon is a chemical element, one of the basic substances of which everything in the world is made. We know silicon best in the form called *silica* (for example, the sand we see on a beach). There is more silicon in the earth's crust than any other element except oxygen.

When made pure in a laboratory, silicon is a brown or gray powder, but it is never found pure in nature. It is always combined with other elements.

SILICA

Almost all rocks contain silicon combined with oxygen and other elements. Silicon and oxygen alone form silica. Silica is usually found in the form of crystals, and is called quartz. There is much silica in the "earth," or soil. Sea sand, gravel, pebbles, flint and sandstone are all made of silica. Amethyst, agate, jasper, carnelian, opal and chalcedony are forms of silica that are valued as gems. Tiny animals called diatoms, which live in the oceans in countless billions, make their skeletons of silicon dissolved in the sea water. Dead diatoms are ground up to make a fine kind of sand. Sponges are made of silica.

SILICATES

Silica combined with a metallic chemical element forms a substance called a *silicate*. All clays are silicates. Ordinary window or bottle glass is a silicate. Asbestos is a silicate in the form of fibers, and mica is a silicate in the form of thin, glasslike sheets. "Water glass," is a liquid silicate. Eggs dipped in water glass will not spoil for a long time.

ABRASIVES

Silica is a fairly hard substance; it cannot be scratched with a steel knife. When silicon is combined with the chemical element carbon, by means of heating the two in an electric furnace, there is made one of the hardest substances known. Its chemical name is silicon carbide, and its best-known trade name is Carborundum. Carborundum is used as an abrasive, or grinding and polishing material. It will cut and polish hard steel and many gems.

SILICONES

Modern chemistry has discovered a new family of compounds of silicon, which it has named silicones. Silicones may be liquids, solids, rubbery materials, or greasy substances. They are used to put a long-lasting glaze on metals (such as pots and pans), to polish glass, and to give machine parts a smooth surface. They resist heat and chemicals so well that they are used in bad weather conditions and in factories where ordinary oils, greases, enamels, or rubber would be destroyed.

silicosis

Silicosis is a disease that is caused by breathing in too much dust that contains a large amount of silica (sand). This disease attacks persons who work in mines, tunnels, quarries, and other places where there is much sandy dust in the air. Breathing in silica injures the delicate tissues of the lungs so that eventually the air passages are blocked and the patient cannot breathe. This condition almost always results in death.

There is no real cure for silicosis, so workers wear masks to protect themselves. There used to be many deaths from silicosis but now there are very few.

silk

Silk is the fine thread spun by certain insects that make cocoons, coverings in which they develop into moths. Silk is also the fine thread of a spider's web.

One insect makes the strongest and the finest of all silk when it spins its cocoon. This is the silk that has long been used by man to weave fine fabrics that we call silk. The insect that spins this silk is a small worm called the silkworm. The silkworm is really the larva, or very young stage, of a moth. The larva of an insect looks like a worm.

The first people to use silk, about five thousand years ago, were the Chinese. They found out how to treat the cocoons of the silkworm and to weave the silk cloth.

From China the art of raising silkworms spread to other places in Asia, including Japan and India. From Asia the silk was carried to European lands. At the time of the Roman civilization, nearly two thousand years ago, silk was worth its weight in gold. For hundreds of years the most important product traded between Europe and Asia was silk. It is still very valuable, though nylon and other man-made fibers have replaced it for some of its former uses.

China and Japan are the most important silk producing countries. Italy, southern France, Bulgaria, Iran, and parts of Russia and Asia are also important places. Many attempts have been made to raise silkworms in the United States. but they have all failed.

SILKWORMS

Silkworms hatch from the tiny eggs laid by the female of a particular kind of moth. The tiny silkworms grow as they feed on leaves of a kind of mulberry tree. Silkworms can be raised only where this mulberry tree will grow.

The worms are carefully hatched in heated rooms or incubators. They are fed chopped pieces of mulberry leaves and later whole mulberry leaves. It takes about six weeks for a silkworm to reach full growth.

When the silkworm has reached its full growth it is ready to spin its cocoon. From a tiny opening near its mouth it gives off a jellylike substance, which hardens when it meets the air. This is the silk.

As the worm spins its cocoon it waves its head back and forth. The silk comes out at a rate of about six inches a minute. It takes a silkworm about three days to finish its cocoon. At the end of that time the worm is snugly enclosed in the tightly woven cocoon. A cocoon is made up of a continuous length of very fine silk about a thousand feet long.

MAKING SILK THREAD

The silkworm is allowed to remain in the cocoon for about eight days. If allowed to remain longer, it will change into a moth, which will break its way out of the cocoon. This would destroy the silk thread. Therefore the people who run the silkworm farms must do something to the cocoon before the moth breaks out and destroys it.

At the end of about eight days the farmers take the cocoons and run hot steam or very hot air over them. This kills the worm inside. The cocoons are then spread out to dry. They are also sorted so that all the finest cocoons are kept together. Even those that have been badly damaged or have been broken out of by the moth are kept. They are used to form a cheaper kind of silk.

The good cocoons are taken to a place where the silk threads will be unwound from them. Mostly women work at this job. The cocoons are placed in almost boiling water to loosen them because the thread is held to the cocoon by a gummy substance. Then the cocoons are brushed lightly so that the silk thread is loosened from them. The women then take the thread from each of several cocoons and nimbly wind the threads together. Usually two to six cocoon threads are woven into a single stronger thread. The thread is wound onto reels and is given several twists to make it firmer and stronger. The threads from several reels are then wound together. Thus a final silk thread may be wound and twisted from the threads of more than twenty cocoons. This thread is still very fine and thin but it is strong enough to be used. The threads are next wound into long hanks, or skeins, and are shipped to silk-weaving plants where it usually remains before the silk is woven. This is called throwing, which means twisting. Several more twists are given to the thread to join it with other threads that make an even stronger thread. After throwing, the silk yarn is ready for weaving.

MAKING SILK FABRICS

Weaving silk is not much different from weaving other fibers, such as cotton and wool. Silk can be woven into several different kinds of fabric. *Taffeta* has a crisp, strong feel. *Satin* has a very glossy finish and a smooth feel. *Crepe* is made of highly twisted silk yarns and has a rougher feel than other silk fabrics. Some silk fabrics are very thin and light. Others such as velvet, are heavy.

Sometimes silk is *weighted*. Weighting is dipping the silk fabric in certain dissolved chemicals including tin or lead compounds. The silk fibers soak up the weighting solution and when they dry out the cloth is heavier.

Silk fabrics can be dyed in any color and can be printed as cotton fabrics are.

IMPORTANCE OF SILK

Silk has always been valuable because of its beauty but also it has been important because of its fineness and strength. It has been used in fine screens to sift powder, and where a combination of lightness and strength is necessary, as in parachutes and in the bags that hold gunpowder used for big guns (cannons). In some of these uses (for example, in women's fine stockings and in parachutes) nylon and other man-made materials have replaced silk.

silo

A silo is a farm building in which hay, grasses, and the whole plants of corn and other grains eaten by farm animals are stored. Usually the silo is a tall, round building, but in ancient times a cave or pit in the ground was often used. Fodder (food for livestock) that has been stored in a silo is called *silage* or *ensilage*. The

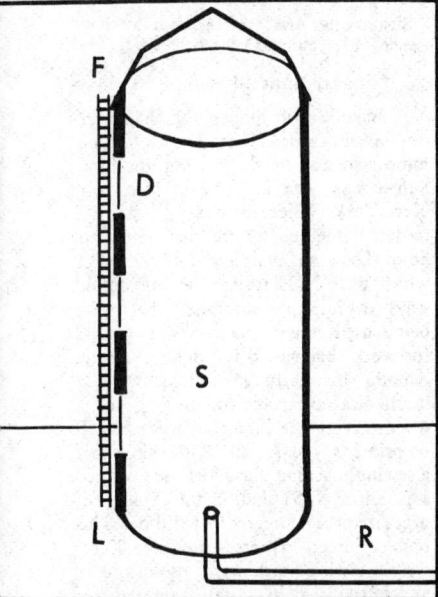

The silo is filled through a door at the top (F). It is emptied through doors in the side (D), the silage (S) always being removed from top to bottom. The ladder (L) is used to reach the doors, and the drain (R) takes off excess moisture.

silo should be airtight inside. The plants are put in at the top and are sometimes pressed down with weights. Salt and some water may be added. In the silo the plants ferment slightly, which makes them more nourishing. The ensilage is taken out from the sides of the silo and fresh plants are constantly added at the top.

silver

Silver is a shiny white metal. It is soft enough to be scratched by a penny, but it lasts a long time and is so useful that it is classed as one of the "precious" metals. It is a chemical element, which means that it is one of the more than one hundred basic substances of which everything in the world is made.

Silver was known in ancient times, thousands of years ago. It was highly prized and was used in the manufacture of coins, jewelry, and drinking and eating vessels. Two thousand years ago, when Rome was the most powerful nation, much silver was mined in Spain. Most silver now comes from American countries.

USES OF SILVER

Silver is very malleable, which means that it can easily be beaten into whatever shape is wanted. A piece of silver can be beaten into foil so thin that light can be seen through it; a pile of ten thousand sheets would measure only an inch. Silver is also very ductile, which means that it can easily be drawn to thin wires. Silver is surpassed only by gold in these properties. Silver is the best conductor of electricity, and is second only to gold as a conductor of heat. It is one of the heavier metals, being ten times as heavy as water. The air causes it to tarnish (become black) but it will not crumble from rust as iron does.

SILVER ALLOYS

Silver forms alloys with mercury, lead, copper, zinc, and other metals. In the United States, silver coins are made of an alloy that is nine parts silver and one part copper. British coin silver is 9¼ parts silver and ¾ part copper. This alloy is also called *sterling silver*. Jewelry or silverware that carries the stamp "sterling" is supposed to be made of the same alloy as British coins, but actually it contains much more copper and less silver. An alloy of silver and mercury is called an *amalgam.* When first made it is soft, but later it hardens. Silver amalgam is used by dentists for filling cavities in teeth.

Silver can be plated onto other metals, which means that they can be covered by a thin layer of silver. This gives the plated metals a very long-lasting luster and pro-

1.

3.

5.

tection from corrosion. Much table silverware and jewelry is plated. Glass can be plated with silver to make mirrors.

SILVER IN PHOTOGRAPHY

Silver combined with the chemical element bromine makes the compound called silver bromide; combined with iodine it makes silver iodide. These compounds have the special property of undergoing chemical change when struck by light. Either of them can be mixed with gelatin and coated on glass or transparent plastic to make photographic film.

SILVERWARE

Silver is no longer used nearly as much as it once was to make drinking cups, teapots, and other large pieces, but it is the favorite metal for eating utensils—knives, forks, spoons, and serving pieces.

Less expensive "silverware" is plated silver. The piece is stamped out of "white metal," which is an inexpensive alloy (mixture of metals) made with iron and

2.

4.

6.

1. A United States 1858 Silver Dollar.

2. A United States 1795 Half Dollar.

3. King George II appears on this coin from Great Britain, issued in 1746. The word *LIMA* at the bottom of the coin indicates it was made from silver found in a Spanish ship captured by Admiral Lord Anson in 1743.

4. This coin from Bohemia, issued between 1519 and 1536 by the Counts Schlick, was called a *Joachimstaler.*

The word *dollar* was derived from the name of this coin.

5. This coin, called a *Shekel*, was used in the ancient Phoenician city of Tyre. (The present city of Sur in Lebanon was the site of Tyre.) The coin is considered to have been of the type described in the Bible as "The Thirty Pieces of Silver."

6. The most famous coin of the Ancient Greek world was called a *Tetradachm.* It was circulated in Athens about 400 B. C.

other metals. A thin silver coating is put on by electroplating, which is explained in the article on ELECTROLYSIS. Plated silver can be treated chemically to resist tarnish, but of course when the thin plating wears off the cheaper metal shows through. A somewhat more expensive silverplate is called *inlaid*. Experience has shown where forks and spoons wear fastest, and at these places small blocks of solid silver are placed before the pieces are plated.

The best silverware is sterling silver, and it has become increasingly popular. Six times as much sterling silver was sold in the United States in the 1950s as was sold before World War II.

WHERE SILVER COMES FROM

Silver is a mineral and is mined. Some pure silver is found in jagged-shaped bunches, or in thin branched threads in quartz. The minerals called argentite and cerargyrite (horn silver) are the chief silver ores. Silver is also found in lead and copper ores, which are the most important sources of silver. Four-fifths of the world's supply of silver comes from North and South America. Mexico, the United States, Canada and Peru are the chief producers, in that order.

German silver is not real silver. It is an alloy of copper, zinc, and nickel.

simoom

The simoom is a strong, dry wind over the deserts of North Africa and Arabia. It carries along with it clouds of sand and dust. Experts believe that the simoom spreads dust for hundreds of miles, into parts of Europe. See the article HURRICANE.

sin

A sin is the breaking of a law of God. In the early Christian Church, a sin consisted of breaking one of the Ten Commandments or other laws that are set forth in the Bible, or of disobeying the laws of the Church. About a thousand years ago, during the Middle Ages, there were seven sins that were classed as the worst possible kinds of sin. These sins were called "the seven deadly sins." They were pride, covetousness or greed, wrath or anger, envy, gluttony or greediness in eating, sloth or laziness, and lechery or unfaithfulness. Most people think there are more serious crimes, such as murder, and the "deadly" sins seem to be bad personal habits.

The Roman Catholic Church makes a distinction between two kinds of sin, called mortal sin and venial sin. Less serious crimes, or faults, are considered venial sins. A venial sin might be stealing something that has very little value. Lying, blaspheming (taking the Name of God in vain) and murder are mortal sins.

Sinai, Mount

Mount Sinai is a mountain in Egypt that is mentioned many times in the Bible. The Book of Exodus tells how Moses went to the top of Mount Sinai and there received the Ten Commandments from God. Mount Sinai is part of a chain of mountains on the Sinai peninsula (arm of land), which stretches into the Mediterranean Sea. Experts are not certain as to which of the mountains is the Mount Sinai told about in the Bible, but most of them believe that it is the mountain that the Arabs call Jebel Musa, which in their language means "mount of Moses."

Sinclair, Upton

Upton Beall Sinclair was an American writer noted for his novels exposing poor working conditions and anti-democratic forces. Born in 1878 in Baltimore, he was a Socialist who ran for the House of Representatives, the Senate, and the Governorship of California at various times, but always lost. His first novel, *The Jungle,* exposed the unsanitary conditions in the Chicago meat-packing industry and led to the passage of the first Food and Drug Act. For 10 years starting in 1939, he wrote 11 books about an imaginary hero, Lanny Budd, through whose adventures the author retold world history from 1913 to 1949. *Dragon's Teeth,* a Lanny Budd novel about the rise of Hitlerism in Germany, won the Pulitzer Prize in 1943.

Before his death in 1968 at the age of 90, Upton Sinclair had written an astounding total of 90 books—one for each year of his life. His works have been translated into 40 languages.

Singapore

Singapore is an island plus other isles and territory at the southern tip of the Malay Peninsula, long part of the British Empire and from 1963 to 1965 part of Malaysia, but since 1965 an independent nation. The area of Singapore is only 224 square miles (217 of them on the main island), but about two million people live there, more than three-quarters of them Chinese and the others Indian, Malayan, and European.

The city of Singapore, capital of the nation, is one of the great cities and seaports of southeast Asia, with a population of about a million. Until World War II it was the seat of the greatest British naval base in Asia. It is considered one of the world's most glamorous cities and many adventure stories have been set there. Two rivers run through the city, the Singapore and the Rochore, filled with colorful native boats. In the European section there are fine buildings and streets, a Botanical Garden, two universities, a school of medicine, and a Polytechnic Institute. The Chinese section of the city is very colorful with its narrow streets and many open shops. There is also a Malay section, where the houses are built on stilts. There are Protestant, Roman Catholic, Moslem, and Buddhist places of worship.

Much of Singapore's prosperity is built on trade, but the state also has large industries. There are tin smelters, saw mills, food processing plants, and factories producing rubber goods, soap, concrete, and many other goods. Many of the people are farmers. They grow vegetables, coconuts, tobacco, pineapples, and rubber trees. The climate of the island is hot and damp, with little change from one season to another.

Singapore is believed to have been a prosperous trading center seven hundred years ago, but the first British traders who arrived in the early 1800s found only a small fishing village and miles of jungle. In 1824 the entire island came under British control and began a period of remarkable growth and prosperity as part of the Straits Settlements colony.

Singapore was occupied by the Japanese during World War II, but it was returned to the British and became a separate Crown colony in 1946 and self-governing in 1958, before it joined Malaysia and then, in 1965, became independent.

SINGAPORE. Area, 224 square miles. Population (1973 estimate) 2,110,000.

Singer, Isaac M.

Isaac Merritt Singer was an American inventor. He is best known for his improvements on the sewing machine. Singer was born in 1811 in Pittstown, New York. When he was 12 years old he left home and for the next ten years he worked at many different jobs, most of which were in factories. He soon found ways to improve machines that were being used and to make new machines for work that was being done by hand. Among his early inventions were a mechanical excavator for digging and a wood-carving machine that made wooden printer's type. About 1850 he invented a sewing machine, for which he obtained a patent in 1851 and, in the same year, organized the company that still bears his name. Singer invented the first lightweight sewing machine for use in homes and introduced the installment plan for selling it. He died in 1875, when he was 63 years old.

Sinn Fein

The Sinn Fein was a group of Irish patriots who wanted their country to be independent from England. It was started by Arthur Griffith in 1899. The words *Sinn Fein* mean "we, ourselves" in Gaelic (the Irish language). The group was small and disorganized until the outbreak of World War I. In 1916 it supported an uprising against the English that was called the Easter Rebellion, but the revolt was put down by British troops and the Sinn Fein leaders were exiled or executed. The Sinn Fein was reorganized under the leadership of Eamon de Valera. In 1918 it formed its own Irish lawmaking body, called the Dail Eireann. The main aim of the Sinn Fein was accomplished when the Irish Free State was established in 1921. See also IRELAND.

sinus

The sinuses are the air spaces in the bones of the face and head. These air spaces are connected with the nose by small openings, and the lining of the nose and the lining of the sinuses are connected. Sinusitis is an infection of the lining of the sinuses.

When a person has measles, scarlet fever, or whooping cough, his sinuses may become infected. Colds, sore throats and coughs sometimes bring sinus infections. If a person blows his nose too hard he may force infections into the sinuses. People who often swim under water are likely to develop sinus trouble. People

who work in warm crowded rooms are more likely to get sinus infections than people who work out of doors.

The pressure of the infected sinus causes pains in the head, above the eyes, or in the cheek. Sometimes when a person has sinus trouble his upper teeth pain him. Usually the pain of sinus infection is more severe in the morning and grows less as the day continues.

Sinus is not a very serious infection, but it is often very uncomfortable. It is important for a person who thinks he has sinus infection to visit a doctor because the infection can lead to more serious ailments, such as bronchitis and arthritis. Doctors have many medicines that can help cure sinus infections, but sometimes an operation may be necessary or the person may be advised to live in a different climate. The antibiotic drugs have made sinus infections much less common than they once were.

Sioux

The Sioux Indians were a group of American Indian tribes that lived in the northern part of the plains between the Mississippi River and the Rocky Mountains. They were PLAINS INDIANS, about whom there is a separate article. Among the Sioux were such tribes as the Dakotas, the Tetons, the Winnebagoes, the Kansas, and the Omahas. The Sioux were often involved in wars, either with neighboring peoples or with white men. The most famous fight between the white men and the Sioux was the massacre of General George A. Custer and his men at Little Big Horn. Some of the famous Sioux chiefs were Sitting Bull, Crazy Horse, and Rain-in-the-Face. The Sioux and the white men agreed to peace in 1891.

There are now about 35,000 Sioux Indians in the United States, which is slightly more than at the height of their power. Many of the Sioux live on reservations in North and South Dakota, Minnesota, Nebraska, and Montana.

Sioux City

Sioux City is the second-largest city of Iowa. It is in the western part of the state, where the Big Sioux and Floyd Rivers flow into the Missouri River. Two bridges across the Missouri join the city to South Sioux City, Nebraska. Sioux City is a livestock, grain and produce market and is the meat-packing center for the surrounding region. About 90,000 people live there. Many of them work in the large stockyards. Others work in plants that make dairy products, heavy machinery, tools, brick and tile, and many other things. The city is the seat of Morningside College and Briar Cliff College and has a symphony orchestra. A livestock show is held there every year. Sioux City was founded in 1848 as a trading and military post.

SIOUX CITY, IOWA. Population (1970 census) 85,925. County seat of Woodbury County. On the Missouri River. Founded, 1848.

Sioux Falls

Sioux Falls is the largest city in South Dakota. It is in the southeastern part of the state, on the Big Sioux River. The waterfalls from which the city gets its name furnish electric power to the city's industries. Sioux Falls is a marketing center for a large farming region. More than 72,000 people live there. Many of them work in a great meat-packing plant, which is the city's largest industry. Others work in factories that process foods, make paint, cement blocks, silos, and other products. Sioux Falls has two cathedrals. It is the seat of Sioux Falls and Augustana colleges and a state school for the deaf.

Sioux Falls was founded in 1857, but was abandoned five years later because of raids by Sioux Indians. In 1865 an army post, Fort Dakota, was built nearby and the city was again settled.

SIOUX FALLS, SOUTH DAKOTA. Population (1970 census) 72,488. County seat of Minnehaha County. Founded, 1857.

siphon

A siphon is a bent pipe or tube through which a liquid can be made to flow over the top of one container and into another container. A siphon is often used to draw gasoline out of the gasoline tank of an automobile into a can or bucket. One end of the siphon is put into the liquid. A person sucks on the other end until air pressure makes the liquid flow through the tube—the same thing that happens when you sip a drink through a straw. Once the liquid is flowing, the air pressure will keep it flowing as long as the empty container is lower than the full container. On large siphons, a vacuum pump is used to start the flow.

siren

A siren is a device for making a sound that can be heard for a long distance. It is used chiefly for warnings. Ambulances and police cars use sirens to warn other cars to get out of their way. The largest sirens are used by cities in wartime to warn the people that enemy bombers are approaching; this is called an *alert* and when it is sounded the people are supposed to go to air-raid shelters. When the enemy bombers have left, the siren sounds an *all-clear* signal to tell people that the danger is over. Sirens are sometimes used as foghorns by ships and as whistles by railroad locomotives.

Sirens can be operated by compressed air or by steam. A siren is usually a disk (a round, flat piece of metal) with a circle of holes drilled in it. This disk is made to revolve rapidly. As each hole passes over the air or steam outlet, a sound is caused. While the speed of the revolving disk is increasing, the tone becomes higher. Therefore, at the start the tone of the siren rises until it becomes very shrill. When the siren is shut off, the tone will become lower as the speed decreases.

Sirens

The Sirens were three sea nymphs in Greek mythology, the stories the ancient Greeks told about their gods and heroes. The Sirens lived on an island and sang so beautifully that sailors who heard them were lured to the island and their ships were wrecked on the rocks. Jason and the Argonauts, who sailed to find the Golden Fleece, were saved from the Sirens by listening instead to the music of Orpheus' lyre. In Homer's *Odyssey*, Odysseus safely passed the island of the Sirens by stuffing the ears of his sailors with wax and having himself tied to the mast so that he could hear the Sirens' song without danger.

Sirius

Sirius is the name of the brightest star we can see in the sky. It is 8.6 light years, or more than 51 trillion miles away from the earth, but this is actually quite near compared to other stars. Sirius is part of the constellation (group of stars) called Canis Major, which means "big dog," so Sirius is sometimes called "the Dog Star." Sirius is a double star. That is, there are actually two stars where we see Sirius. The star we see is thirty times as bright as the sun. The other is a faint star that revolves around it once every fifty years.

sirocco

The sirocco is a very warm wind that rises in the Sahara Desert, in North Africa, and blows across the Mediterranean Sea to Italy, southern France, Greece, and Yugoslavia. The sirocco carries some sand and dust from the desert and picks up a great deal of moisture as it crosses the sea. This makes it very unpleasant.

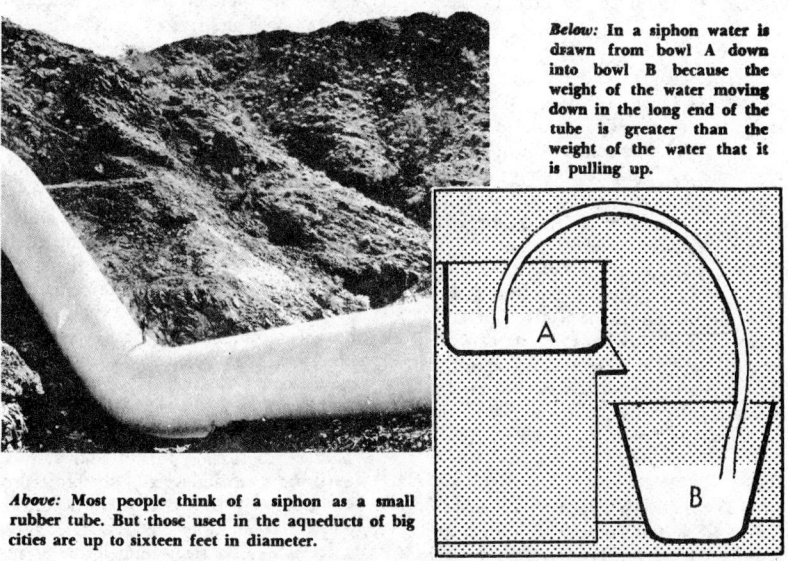

Below: In a siphon water is drawn from bowl A down into bowl B because the weight of the water moving down in the long end of the tube is greater than the weight of the water that it is pulling up.

Above: Most people think of a siphon as a small rubber tube. But those used in the aqueducts of big cities are up to sixteen feet in diameter.

sisal

Sisal is a plant that grows in Java, East Africa, the West Indies, and Mexico. Its leaves have strong fibers that are dried and twisted into ropes, twine, and cord. The dried fibers are white, and before twisting they are usually about three or four feet long, which is about the length of the plant's leaves. Sisal bushes grow wild in a warm, damp climate. The harvesting of the leaves for their fibers is an important industry. Sisal rope is often used to make cowboys' lariats, or lassos, because of its strength and durability. It does not wear out as quickly as cotton rope. Sisal is also twisted into fine cord, dyed, and used to make fiber rugs.

sisters, women who belong to religious orders and take simple vows not to marry, to obey their superiors, and not to make use of property they own for their own profit. See the article on NUNS AND SISTERS.

Sistine Chapel, a chapel in the Vatican: see the article VATICAN.

Sitting Bull

Sitting Bull was a famous Indian chief who lived about a hundred years

ago. He was the head of the Sioux tribe's war council, and led his tribe in many raids on white settlements. He was one of the chief leaders at the battle of the Little Bighorn, in 1876, when General Custer and his American troops were all slain. Later he and the other Sioux warriors were forced to retreat, and in 1881 they surrendered to the United States Army. He toured the world with Buffalo Bill's Wild West Show. A few years later he again tried to rouse the Indians against the white settlers, but he failed and was arrested. He was shot by his guards and died in 1890.

Six-Day War

The Six-Day War was one of the shortest wars in history. It was fought in 1967, when ISRAEL defeated the Arab countries of EGYPT, JORDAN, and SYRIA. See the entries on these countries.

Skagerrak

The Skagerrak is an arm of the North Sea between Norway and Denmark. It is about 150 miles long and 80 to 90 miles wide. It is continued by the Kattegat into the Baltic Sea. Along the Danish shore the Skagerrak is very shallow, with many sandbars. On the Norwegian side it is as much as 2,000 feet deep. The Skagerrak is a dangerous place for ships because of frequent violent storms. Because shipping from the principal ports of Germany and Russia passes through the Kattegat and the Skagerrak to reach the Atlantic Ocean, both waterways were favorite hunting grounds for submarines in World Wars I and II.

skate

The skate is a flat, triangular-shaped fish with a long, thin tail. It is found mainly in the ocean, but skates often swim upstream to inland river sections. They live on the bottom of the water, eating crabs, shrimps, worms, and small fish. The skate's mouth is on the bottom of its body and its eyes and gills are on top. There are many different kinds of skate. Some are as long as eight feet, but usually skates are only about a foot long.

In the late spring skates lay eggs in small brownish-black rectangular cases that look like leather, and they hatch several months later. The cases are sometimes found on beaches. Children call them "mermaid's purses."

skating

Skating is either gliding on ice on small blades attached to the shoes or rolling over a smooth, hard floor on small wheels attached to the shoes. The two

Ice hockey players.

ways are called *ice skating* and *roller skating.*

Ice skating began many hundreds of years ago among the Norsemen, who lived in what is now Norway, Sweden and Denmark. They tied smooth bones to the bottoms of their boots. On these bones they could glide over the surface of the ice. Other people learned to skate too. For runners (the pieces attached to the shoes), bones were later replaced by hard wood and finallly by metal. Today ice skating is a popular sport in nearly every country where the winters are cold enough to freeze ponds and rivers.

MODERN ICE SKATING

The runners are now always made of metal, usually steel, and ice-skating shoes usually come complete with ice skates attached. There are several different kinds of ice skate. On *speed skates,* the metal blades are held tightly in a tube of aluminum. The aluminum tube is screwed to the bottom of the shoe. Speed skates are about 18 inches long and can be dangerous if they are not used expertly. The blades are quite thin and sharpened to a knifelike edge. Skates somewhat like speed skates are called hockey skates. They are about six inches shorter. Hockey players cannot use the longer speed skates because they cannot turn and stop as easily on them and because the projecting front edges of the speed skates would be dangerous to other players. The *figure skate* is a solid steel runner that is not quite as thin as a speed or hockey skate. It is not set in an aluminum tube but is screwed onto the bottom of the shoe. The front edge of the figure skate is curved toward the toe of the shoe and on the curve there are several saw teeth. These are used for standing on the toes, for spinning, and also for quick stops.

SKATING COMPETITIONS

Skating races are held in many places and are an event of the Olympic Games every four years. Figure skating is much like ballet dancing on ice. Figure skaters must learn to skate with grace and ease. In a figure-skating competition each skater must first do a set of *compulsory figures.* An example is the "figure 8," which looks like an 8 traced on the ice by the skates. There are several others. The second part of a figure-skating competition is called *free figures.* In this part each skater can do whatever he pleases so long as it shows his skill. Figure-skating competitions include events for men, women, and mixed couples. The mixed couples do dances together.

There are many skating rinks in the United States and Canada. Some of these rinks are outdoors and the ice is frozen naturally in cold weather. Others, either indoors or outdoors, are artificial rinks where the ice is frozen by ice-making machinery.

ROLLER SKATING

Roller skating is not nearly as old as ice skating. It began just a few hundred years ago when someone made small wooden wheels to attach to the shoes. Since then these have been changed to metal wheels with ball bearings inside. These bearings, tiny little metal balls, make the skates roll more easily. Almost all children learn to roller-skate.

Wooden-wheeled roller skates are used in indoor roller-skating rinks. These wooden rollers do not hurt the hardwood floors as metal skates would.

Many people become very expert on roller skates. They can perform many acrobatic feats and fancy dances.

skeleton

The skeleton is all the bones of an animal body. Both vertebrates (animals with backbones) and invertebrates (animals without backbones) have skeletons. The human skeleton is generally considered to have 206 bones though not all experts agree on what should be counted as bones. The teeth are never numbered among the bones of the skeleton. Most mammals (animals that bear living young and nurse them, such as dogs and cats), and also birds and some reptiles, for example lizards, have skeletons somewhat like the human skeleton.

The skeleton in the human body is an *endoskeleton* (meaning "inside skeleton"). Some members of the animal world have their skeletons outside the body. Such a skeleton is called an *exoskeleton* (outside skeleton). The spider's outer covering is an exoskeleton. There is a difference between the exoskeleton of a spider and the shell of an oyster or other shellfish, though the oyster's shell is considered to be one form of exoskeleton.

The horny outer covering of the ar-

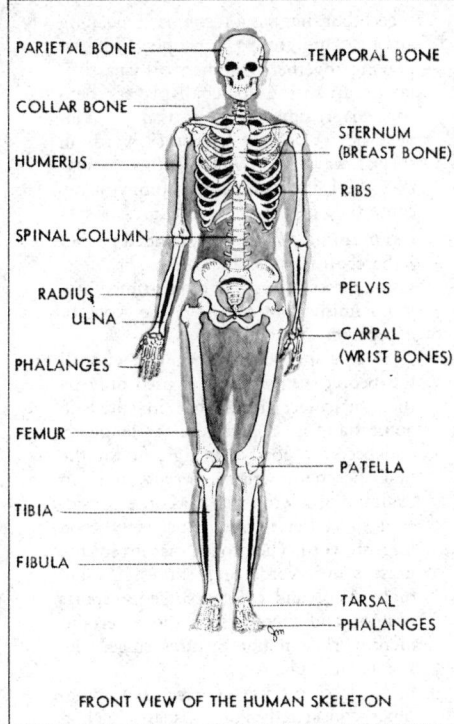

FRONT VIEW OF THE HUMAN SKELETON

PARIETAL BONE — TEMPORAL BONE
COLLAR BONE
STERNUM (BREAST BONE)
HUMERUS
RIBS
SPINAL COLUMN
RADIUS
ULNA
PELVIS
PHALANGES
CARPAL (WRIST BONES)
FEMUR
PATELLA
TIBIA
FIBULA
TARSAL
PHALANGES

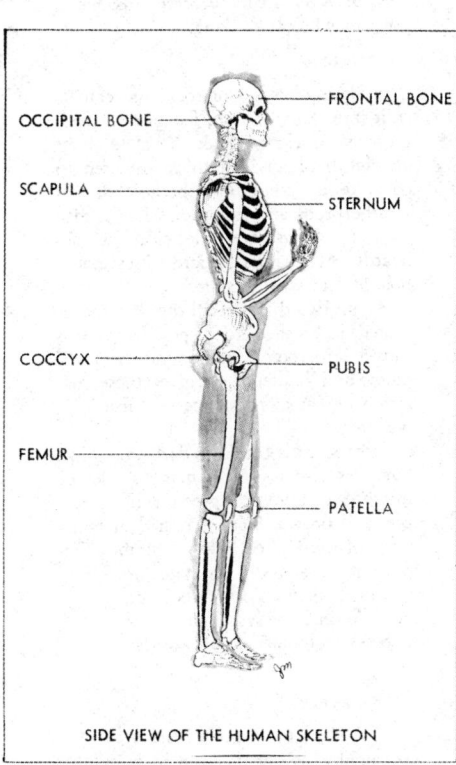

SIDE VIEW OF THE HUMAN SKELETON

OCCIPITAL BONE — FRONTAL BONE
SCAPULA
STERNUM
COCCYX
PUBIS
FEMUR
PATELLA

madillo and similar animals is also considered to be a kind of exoskeleton, so that such an animal has both kinds of skeleton. The fingernails and toenails of a human being, the claws of a dog or cat, the feathers of a bird and the scales of a fish are also called "exoskeleton" parts, but they are not made of bone and so are not true skeletons.

The human skeleton grows gradually in the unborn baby. The bones of the spine, or backbone, have begun to take form by the end of about the fifth week. At the end of the third month the principal bones of the arms and legs are growing, but they are separated from one an-

other by several inches and grow toward one another gradually until finally they join.

skiing

A ski is a long strip of wood that is used for gliding over the snow. Skis may be from five to ten feet long. One is attached to each foot, at about the center of the length. The ski should be about an inch wider than the user's shoe. Below the foot the ski may be as much as an inch thick, but it tapers to about ¼ inch at each end. The bottom of the ski is polished and waxed so that it will slide easily.

Skiing is a fascinating sport that millions of people have adopted as a hobby. It has been used for many hundreds of years—perhaps for thousands of years—in countries such as Norway and Sweden, and in mountains such as the Alps, where the ground is covered with deep snow for several months each year.

A skier carries in each hand a pole with a disk (round, flat piece) at the end to keep it from sinking into the snow. With these ski poles he can push himself along when he is going uphill. He also uses the ski poles to steady himself.

Expert skiers can go downhill at very fast rates, 60 miles per hour or even more, and they can change direction or stop very fast. When they are at the top of a rise in the snow they often jump to the next level place, where they land and keep going. There are many contests in skiing each year, and it is one of the sports in the Winter Olympic Games. There are contests in jumping (in which the experts often jump more than 300 feet), in speed downhill, and in speed in a *slalom*, or zigzag and uneven course. There are many *ski runs* in the United States, Canada, and other countries. At these there are usually *ski tows*, on which skiers can ride to the top of the hill.

skin

Skin is the outer protective covering of many animals. It has so many different forms that it is sometimes hard to think of all of them as skin. The tough leather of cowhide, the scales of a snake or crocodile, the horns of a moose or the horny covering of an armadillo, all are skin. Skin may be covered with feathers, as on a bird, or with hair or fur, as on so many animals.

Human skin is a covering that does many protective jobs. It is waterproof and does not permit water to either enter the body or vital fluids to leave the body. It is elastic and stretches with the movements of the body. It acts as the heat regulator and air conditioner for the body.

Skin is actually composed of several layers. The two main layers are called the *epidermis* and the *dermis*. The epidermis is the outer layer of the skin and the dermis is the inner layer.

EPIDERMIS

The epidermis is itself composed of separate layers. The outer or horny layer is transparent. Through it we can see the color in the layer beneath it, which contains the pigment or cells that give color to the skin. The very outside of the epidermis is actually made up of cells that

are dead or dying. These cells are constantly being sluffed or scraped off, and new live cells replace them. On the surface of the epidermis there are pores, openings in the skin. We send out perspiration through some of these pores, and hair grows from others. The epidermis is sensitive to heat and cold, pain, and pressure. Much of our sense of touch lies in our skin. This is because there are sensitive nerve endings that lie just below the epidermis.

DERMIS

The dermis, or underlayer of the skin, contains several things that are important. There are sensitive nerve-endings, which give the skin the ability to feel differences in temperature and in pressure. There are sweat glands, which lead through tiny spiral tubes to the pores or openings in the epidermis. The dermis contains the tiny cells from which hairs

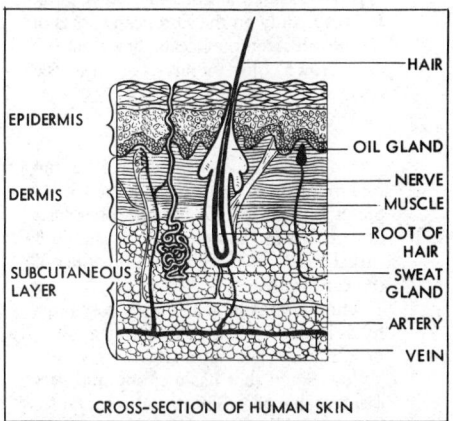

CROSS-SECTION OF HUMAN SKIN

EPIDERMIS
DERMIS
SUBCUTANEOUS LAYER
HAIR
OIL GLAND
NERVE
MUSCLE
ROOT OF HAIR
SWEAT GLAND
ARTERY
VEIN

grow. These are called *follicles,* and they too lead to openings in the epidermis. The dermis contains many tiny blood vessels.

The sweat glands and blood vessels make the skin the air conditioner of the body. When the body gives off sweat from the skin it helps to cool itself. The presence of the many tiny blood vessels also helps to control the body temperature. When it is cold outside, the blood vessels contract (become smaller), thus giving off less heat through the skin to the air outside. When it is hot the blood vessels expand (become larger) and through the larger surface give off more heat to keep the body cool.

CARE OF THE SKIN

The skin is the body's first line of defense against disease. At all times there are tiny germs on the surface of the skin. The skin is able to fight off most of these germs and prevent them from entering the body. But the more dirt there is on the skin, the more germs there are too. If too much dirt is allowed to accumulate on the skin, the germs will grow so rapidly that they well penetrate the skin and cause infection and disease. Therefore it is most important to keep the skin clean by bathing and washing with soap and hot water.

If the skin should be bruised or cut so that blood appears, something should be done quickly to clean the wound. An antiseptic (a chemical that kills germs) should be used, and then the break or wound should be covered with a bandage.

The skin itself may become diseased. Usually a skin disease appears as a rash, a breaking out in red splotches or spots.

Usually there is itching. If the rash remains after several days, a doctor should be consulted. Some skin rashes are indications of other diseases in the body. Chicken pox and measles are first shown through rashes on the skin.

Some skin diseases are not infectious—they cannot be given to other people. Others are highly infectious and you can catch them by touching someone who has the disease, or by wearing clothing or using a towel of such a person. Most skin diseases are easily cured by using the proper medication. Almost all skin diseases can be avoided by keeping the skin in a clean, healthy condition.

skua

The skua is a bird of the same family as the gull. Its other name is *jaeger,* which is German for "hunter." The skua is a hawklike bird, with a hooked beak. It preys on small animals and other birds. It lives mainly on the European shores of the North Atlantic Ocean. The skua is a dark brown color and about as large as a barnyard rooster.

skunk

The skunk is an unusual little animal that lives in many parts of the United States and Canada and in some other parts of the world. Sometimes the skunk is called a *polecat,* but it is not a member of the cat family.

The skunk is famous for the way it defends itself. When the skunk is frightened or angry it sends out a stream of a thick yellow liquid that has a strong and very disagreeable odor. This liquid is contained in two small glands at the base of the skunk's tail. If the liquid gets on a person's clothes the odor will remain for several days. If it gets on the skin it will smart and burn. The skunk is a peaceable animal and uses this defense only when it is disturbed. Even when it is angry or frightened it will first raise its tail as a warning before it discharges the liquid. Most animals and human beings learn to stay away from a skunk.

The skunk has black fur with two bright white stripes on its back and one white stripe between its eyes. It is about 18 inches long and weighs four to ten pounds.

The skunk usually sleeps during the day and comes out at night to hunt for food. It eats frogs and snakes, and fruit and seeds. It lives in a den in a hollow log or in a burrow in the ground. During the very cold weather the skunk stays in its cozy nest. The female has four to eight babies in the early spring.

The skunk's fur is used to make coats for women. This fur is sometimes called "Alaska sable." A strange fact is that the bad-smelling fluid of the skunk is used in making perfume. Sometimes skunks are captured and their glands are removed. They then make affectionate and playful pets.

sky, a name for the upper atmosphere: see the article ATMOSPHERE.

Skye terrier

The Skye terrier is a small dog with long, bluish-gray or tan hair. Its eyes are almost entirely hidden under hair that hangs down from its forehead. It is only about nine inches high at the shoulder, but it is much longer than it is tall, measuring about 23½ inches from the chest to the base of the tail. It was used for years to catch small animals such as foxes, weasels, and badgers. Today it is kept mainly as a pet, but if there are any mice or rats in its home it will catch them quickly.

skywriting

Skywriting is a way of advertising a product or sending some other message by spelling out the words in thick smoke in the sky. The smoke is heated paraffin oil and other chemicals. It is let out by an airplane that has a special machine for the purpose. The airplane flies at a height of 10,000 to 17,000 feet, and the letters spelled out by its movements are usually about a mile high and a mile wide. Skywriting can be done only on a clear day when the wind is not too strong. The message must be short or the first letters will be blurred before the last letters are completed.

Skywriting was first used in 1922 in England. It was developed by an English aviator named J. C. Savage, who wrote the name of a newspaper in the sky over Epsom Downs, a place near London. It soon became popular in France, the United States, and other countries.

In 1949 a new kind of skywriting, called *skytyping,* was developed in the United States. Its main advantage is that the message can be written more quickly, so that its beginning and end are clear at the same time. Skytyping uses several airplanes, usually five to seven. They fly in the same direction, at equal distances from each other. The planes are hooked together by radios connected to their smoke devices. One plane, called the lead plane, has a copy of the message set up in a pattern of electric switches inside a control box. When the planes have been set up in proper formation, the pilot of the lead plane throws the main switch on the control box. This sets the contacts revolving, so that each switch closes and sends an electric current to the radio in the other planes. This current forces into each plane's exhaust a certain amount of "smoke," which makes one dot in the formation of a letter. The message is in large block (capital) letters that are made up of separate dots of smoke. Each plane has a 70-gallon tank that holds enough smoke for twenty to thirty-five messages. Skytyping was invented and patented by S. S. Pike of New York City. Seven planes, flying at about 180 miles per hour, 10,000 to 15,000 feet high, can print a 21-letter message, which is 15 miles long, across the sky in five minutes. Each letter, about a mile long and half a mile wide, is made in ten seconds. Instead of doing complicated and dangerous flying maneuvers, the planes fly in a straight line.

There are other kinds of advertising messages in the sky. Sometimes a huge sign is hung between two airplanes or trailed by one plane. A lighted sign may be hung on the wing of a plane or the side of a blimp that flies at night.

slang

Slang is a word or phrase, or group of words and phrases, that is not considered good enough for careful writing and speech but that has a recognized meaning among some groups of people. Children playing together, members of a particular group such as baseball players, dentists, advertising men, and so on, often invent new words or use other words in special ways. They may do this because they think the word sounds funny or because they need a word to express a special meaning. When a left-handed pitcher in baseball is called a *southpaw,* or a television director says that a well-timed program finished *on the nose,* the word or expression is slang.

Some slang becomes popular with all the people. Other slang is used only by the particular group that invented it. Some slang is adopted into the language and becomes good language, fit for the best speech or writing; *strenuous* is an example of a word that was once considered slang but is now a perfectly good English word. The groups that invent the most slang words and expressions are high-school and college students, sports writers, and members of the entertainment world (motion pictures, stage, television, and radio).

An incorrect use of a word is sometimes considered slang. Usually such a use is an exaggeration. If someone says he is *horribly* tired or *terribly* anxious to go, it may be called slang.

slate

Slate is a kind of rock that can be split into slabs, or thin, flat pieces, of almost any thickness. Sheets of slate about an eighth of an inch thick are used to cover roofs of buildings, because slate is weatherproof and fireproof. Slate is also used for flagstones, electrical switchboards, grave vaults, billiard tables, blackboards, and writing slates.

About two-thirds of all the slate that is mined is crushed to a powder and is mixed into roofing compounds, asphalt, paint, and linoleum. It gives these materials greater resistance to fire and weather.

Most slate is black or dark gray-blue, but it is also found in many shades or mixtures of blue, red, green, yellow, purple, and brown. Slate is mined in many parts of the United States. The most important slate-producing states are Pennsylvania, New York, Vermont, Maryland, Maine, and Virginia.

See also the article on ROCKS.

slavery

A slave is a human being treated as personal property that can be bought or sold. An owner of a slave can treat him as he would a machine or a tree or a horse, using him as long as he is useful and then killing him or letting him die. This system is called slavery.

Slavery in one form or another has existed as long as written history has existed and probably long before. In ancient times, thousands of years ago, prisoners captured in wars were often made slaves.

In many of the countries of Asia and Africa, most of the women were slaves because they were not as strong as the men. Often an entire people or racial group was made slaves, in which case their children were born slaves and belonged to the owner of the parents.

During the Middle Ages in Europe, beginning about 1,500 years ago and lasting for about a thousand years, there were no slaves by that name but the system was about the same. Farmers called *serfs* belonged to the land they worked on. They could not be bought and sold, but if their land was sold they had to work for the new owner of the land. They could not leave the land. Serfdom lasted in several European countries until less than two hundred years ago and in Russia it lasted until less than a hundred years ago.

There was slavery in the United States until the Civil War ended in 1865. It began in the early days with persons called *bond servants.* These were persons convicted of minor crimes or of inability to pay their debts. They would be transported from England to America and sold to someone for a certain period of time, such as five or ten years. After working without pay for that period of time, they would become free.

During the 1600s, ships began to buy or capture Negro men and women in Africa, carry them to America, and sell them as slaves. They were sold mostly in the southern colonies or states and in the islands of the Caribbean Sea, such as Cuba, Haiti, and Puerto Rico. The landowners in these places wanted cheap laborers to work on their big farms (called *plantations*). By the middle 1800s, there were more than three million Negro slaves in the southern states of the United States.

The evils of slavery had been recognized by wise statesmen long before that. Thomas Jefferson, though he came from the southern state of Virginia and was a slave-owner himself, proposed laws that would end the bringing of more slaves into the United States. The Constitution of the United States, adopted in 1789, gave Congress the right to prohibit the bringing in of slaves after twenty years. Georgia, though it was a slave state, passed a law ending slave trade with foreign countries in 1798.

Nevertheless, the southern states bitterly opposed efforts to end slavery, because much of the wealth of those states was invested in slaves. Because the southern states were afraid President Abraham Lincoln and the Republican Party would pass laws against slavery, they seceded (withdrew) from the United States when Lincoln was elected, and they fought the Civil War in their effort to continue slavery. When they lost the war, slavery in the United States was ended.

The League of Nations, formed in 1920, and after it the United Nations, formed in 1945, outlawed slavery. In Ethiopia, Saudi Arabia, and a few other countries there were still slaves, and Ethiopia had to agree to end slavery before it could join the United Nations.

"Slave labor" is the use of convicts or prisoners in work that they cannot leave or refuse to do without suffering torture or death. Germany used many captured Russians and Poles as slave laborers during World War II. The Communist government of Russia has continued to use prisoners of war and citizens convicted of crimes or of opposition to the government as slave laborers.

PEONAGE, about which there is a separate article, is another method of slavery.

It has been much used in countries of South and Central America.

Slavs

The Slavs are a people who have lived in Europe and western Asia for many hundreds of years. The Slavs who settled in western Europe include the Poles of Poland, the Czechs and Slovaks of Czechoslovakia, and the Wends of eastern Germany. The Slavs who settled in southern Europe include the Serbs, Slovenes and Croats of Yugoslavia, the Bulgarians of Bulgaria, and the Macedonians of northern Greece. The Slavs who settled in eastern Europe and in Asia are the largest group. They include the Great Russians, the White Russians, and the Ukrainians, all of whom live in what is now the Soviet Union.

It is not certain where the Slavs lived originally, but most people think it was between the Oder and Dnieper rivers, in Russia. About 1,800 years ago they began to move from their homes, probably in search of better farm lands. Their wanderings were stopped in the west by Germanic peoples and in the south by the Turks.

Each Slavic group has its own language and its own customs, and many times the Slavic peoples have fought among themselves, but the languages are much alike and the Slavs feel a strong kinship with one another.

The languages of the Slavs, which are called Slavic or Slavonic, are members of the INDO-EUROPEAN family of languages about which there is a separate article.

sled and sleigh

A sled is a vehicle that has runners instead of wheels. It is used to travel over snow and ice. It usually consists of a piece of wood placed on two long, sharp strips of wood or metal, called runners. The runners are usually turned up in front. A sleigh is a large sled that is drawn by horses, dogs, or other animals. Sleds are used by children for winter sports in almost all places where there is snow. Sleighs are still a common means of transportation in the arctic regions. They are usually pulled by dogs or reindeer. See also the articles BOBSLED and TOBOGGAN.

sleep

Sleep is a period in which the body rests almost completely. It is as much a part of living as wakefulness. During most of our day we are active, exercising and working. During the rest of the day we sleep and restore the energy that our bodies have used in our exercise and work.

At different stages of our lives we need different amounts of sleep. The tiny baby sleeps most of its day. A child needs at least twelve hours of sleep. A student in the upper grades of elementary or high school usually gets about eight hours of sleep.

Scientists are still trying to understand exactly what happens when we sleep, and why we sleep. They know many things about sleep but they still have much to find out. Perhaps some day they will know so much about sleep that they will be able to find a substitute for it. The substitute might be some pill that will be taken to do everything for the body that sleep does.

WHY WE MUST SLEEP

Scientists do know that sleep is necessary to restore energy to the body after a day's work or exercise, and even when we have been inactive but awake. Something happens after we have used our energy for a number of hours. Perhaps we do not have enough oxygen in our muscle tissues. Perhaps the blood supply to our muscles becomes less than it normally should be. Our body tissues, particularly our muscles, accumulate waste products. Some scientists believe that the brain has become tired from sending out the many messages that direct the activity of the body. Whatever the reason, the brain begins to relax and refuses to do its complete job. Then we are sleepy.

WHAT IS SLEEP

Sleep is a state of unconsciousness. All our important body activities are being carried on—our hearts beat, we breathe, our digestive system continues to work—but we are not aware of what is going on around us. We do not consciously hear things and we may not even respond to light. It depends how deeply asleep we are.

During a normal night's sleep, we are not always in the same deep sleep. When we first fall asleep we do it gradually. After the first hour we are usually in the deepest part of our sleep. At this point we are unlikely to be disturbed even by loud sounds. Depth of sleep is measured by the loudness of a sound that is needed to awaken a sleeper.

While we are asleep, our hearts beat slower than they do when we are awake. We breathe more deeply than when we are awake. Every body activity is slowed down. The brain, in particular, slows down to a point at which it is just able to do the necessary work of keeping our body alive. During sleep our muscles relax; they lose their tension and get rid of some of the waste products and poisons they have accumulated during the day. They also build up their supply of energy that comes from the oxygen in the bloodstream.

During sleep the millions of body cells do their greatest repair work. Worn or damaged cells build themselves up much more during sleep than during waking hours. After a night's sleep the body is repaired and refreshed and ready to do a day's work again.

PREPARING FOR SLEEP

The best preparation for sleep is to form the habit of going to bed at the same time each night. A normally healthy person, especially a child, will usually become so sleepy by a certain time that it is no job at all to fall asleep quickly. Some people have more trouble falling asleep. They toss and turn, and their minds remain active.

Inability to fall asleep easily is called *insomnia.* There is no real cure for this, but there are some things that help people fall asleep. The most important thing is to relax. Some people exercise moderately before going to bed, to loosen their muscles. Others read something that is not exciting or listen to soft music to relax their minds. Some people eat something, often with a glass of warm milk or some other warm beverage.

After getting into bed a person may do other things to bring about sleep. One of the best things is to start breathing deeply and slowly. It is important to find a comfortable position in bed. It does not matter whether a person sleeps on his side, his back, or his stomach, as long as he feels comfortable and relaxed.

Sleeping conditions are important. The room should be dark and as quiet as possible. The bed should be firm, not so soft that it gives no support to the resting body. The blankets should not be tucked in too tightly.

There is an old saying that "one hour's sleep before midnight is worth two after midnight." This is good advice for children. If you go to bed too late you are probably overtired and it takes your body longer to relax.

sleeping sickness

Sleeping sickness is the name for a group of illnesses in which the brain and spinal cord become inflamed or feverish. It is sometimes known as "brain fever." An illness of this kind is called sleeping sickness because persons who get it sometimes stay drowsy or become unconscious, as though they are asleep, for long periods of time.

Sometimes sleeping sickness is caused by germs or viruses that are carried by animals, birds, and insects. African sleeping sickness is gotten mostly in the tropics from the bite of the tsetse fly, which carries a germ. Other kinds of sleeping sickness happen during or after other diseases that may hurt the brain. Infantile paralysis is considered to be a kind of sleeping sickness.

In most kinds of sleeping sickness, because the brain is hurt, the muscles that are controlled by the brain act in a strange way. Sometimes they jerk wildly in a fit or *convulsion;* at other times they are stiff and do not move—in other words, they are paralyzed.

Doctors sometimes can make the sick person feel better, but they have not found a cure for sleeping sickness.

sleepwalking

Sleepwalking, also called somnambulism, is a condition in which a person can walk around and do complicated things while he is asleep. When he wakes up, he has no memory of what he has done. He may also talk, but what he says is related to what he is dreaming, rather than to the actual circumstances, as a sleepwalker is not conscious of his real surroundings. The condition is more common in children than in adults, and is not necessarily serious. Many children simply outgrow it. In adults, however, it may be caused by serious emotional disturbances which need the help of a doctor or a psychologist.

sleet

Sleet is frozen raindrops. Sleet is caused when falling rain passes through a current of cold air (with a temperature below 32 degrees Fahrenheit, the freezing point of water). Since the cold air is moving, sleet is usually driven by the wind as it falls. Sleet is formed of smaller bits of ice than hail, which is also frozen rain. See the article on WEATHER.

slide fastener, a device with which two edges of a dress, handbag, brief case, and so on, can be rapidly fastened together or unfastened: see the article ZIPPER.

slime

Slime molds are a very low form of vegetable life. They grow in damp ground and on decaying vegetable matter. A slime mold grows from spores, which are cells that reproduce themselves without seeds. The individual cells of slime mold creep along the surface of the substance on which they grow. They are a kind of FUNGUS, about which there is a separate article.

A few kinds of slime mold damage crops. One kind injures cabbage plants, and another kind causes a potato disease. Most slime molds are not harmful to plants.

sling

A sling is a kind of weapon that was used in ancient times to throw a stone at an enemy in warfare or at an animal in hunting. The sling has a leather pocket in which the stone is put. Two strings are attached to the leather pocket. A person holds the ends of both strings in his hand and whirls the stone around his head. When he lets go of one string, the stone will fly off at great speed. (This is explained in the article on CENTRIFUGAL FORCE.) Accuracy in aiming the sling depends on the exact moment that the string is let go. Warriors of ancient times were remarkably good marksmen. The Bible tells how David killed the giant Goliath, a Philistine warrior, by hitting him on the head with a stone from a sling.

A *slingshot* is a different kind of device. It is made of a fork-shaped piece of wood (usually from the branch of a tree) with a rubber band attached to the two ends of the fork. A stone or other hard object is held in the center of the rubber band and pulled back. When the band is let go, the stone flies forward. Strong slingshots have been used in hunting small game.

sloe

The sloe or blackthorn tree is a member of the plum family. It is a small tree that bears white blossoms in spring and small, dark purple, plumlike fruit near the end of the summer. The fruit is very sour. It is used to flavor an alcoholic beverage called sloe gin. The tree is thorny, and its wood is tough when it is cut and dried. It is not suitable for general use as lumber but it is often cut into short lengths to make walking sticks or canes.

sloth

The sloth is a clumsy, slow-moving animal that lives in the warm parts of Central and South America. It is one of the laziest of animals. It sleeps about eighteen hours out of every twenty-four, and the few hours when it is awake, it spends hanging upside-down in trees and eating the leaves. It goes to sleep hanging in the crotch of a tree.

There are two kinds of sloth. The three-toed sloth is about two feet long, with thick coarse hair that is brown or gray with patches of white. The male sloth has a bright yellow spot on its back where the fur is softer and shinier. One kind of three-toed sloth is called the *ai.* The two-toed sloth is larger than the three-toed kind. It may be three or four feet long.

A female sloth has one young sloth during the summer, and the baby sloth learns to hang head-down from birth. It clings to its mother's stomach until it is about five weeks old.

Sloths are called *edentate* (which means "toothless") animals, but actually they have some teeth.

slot machine, a kind of vending machine: see VENDING MACHINE.

Slovakia

Slovakia is part of the country of Czechoslovakia. Its area, about 19,000 square miles, makes it about half as big as Virginia, but its population of 4,100,000 is about the same. Slovakia is very mountainous, with fine farm and pasture lands in the valleys. The people who live there are called Slovaks. For hundreds of years the Slovaks were ruled by the Magyars of Hungary. About the beginning of the 1800s the people began to fight for freedom, and in 1918 Czech and Slovak leaders agreed to join their lands in a single country. You can read more about the Slovaks and their land in the article on CZECHOSLOVAKIA.

slug

Slugs are snails without shells. Some slugs live on land and others in the water. The yellow sea slug can sometimes be found under rocks or stones on beaches at low tide along the New England coast. It is about an inch and a half long, and it has bright yellow "feelers" on its head and back. The underskin is tan or brownish. Another kind of sea slug is pale red with light tan spots, or sometimes white spots. This slug is about three and a half inches long, and its back is covered with branching arms or "feelers" that give it a rather startling appearance. Sea slugs may also be seen in orange and green.

Land slugs are usually brownish or tannish yellow. The land slug is somewhat larger than the sea slug, and may be as long as three and a half inches when fully grown. One type, which is gray, grows to six inches or more. Some land slugs have become a pest in gardens, feeding on young and tender leafy plants such as lettuce. More often, slugs live on d   moldy leaves and grasses.

smallpox

Smallpox is a very serious disease that used to cause the death of thousands of people, made others blind, and left still others with terrible scars. It has been a very rare disease since Dr. Edward Jenner introduced vaccination, in the year 1796. (There are separate articles about JENNER and VACCINATION.) Almost all babies in the United States are vaccinated before they are one year old, and in some states the law requires that every child must be vaccinated every five years.

Smallpox is caused by a virus, the kind of germ that is too small to be seen even

under a microscope. The disease is very contagious, which means that it spreads rapidly. If one person in a community gets smallpox, many others in the community will get it unless they have been vaccinated.

When a person gets smallpox he feels aches and pains in various parts of his body and he usually has a fever. A few days later a rash appears. The rash forms crusty scabs that leave deep scars. The rash may last as long as five weeks and may spread into the mouth, nose, and eyes.

Anyone who has been exposed to smallpox must receive vaccination immediately. No one who has been vaccinated for smallpox within five years needs to worry about getting the disease. In 1947, a man who had just arrived from a foreign country died of smallpox in a New York City hotel. About two million people in New York were vaccinated within the next few weeks, and the disease did not spread.

smelt

The smelt is a food fish that lives in most of the northern oceans and in lakes and rivers. It is usually six to eight inches long. The smelt goes to fresh water to lay its eggs. There are about twelve different kinds of smelt.

Smelts are caught for sale in markets. They are found in the Great Lakes, in the St. Lawrence River, and along the Atlantic coast from Labrador to New York.

smelting, a furnace method used in preparing ores, especially iron and steel, for manufacture: see the articles METAL and IRON AND STEEL.

Smetana, Bedrich

Bedrich Smetana was a Czech composer, or writer of original music. He is  best remembered for his music based on folk melodies of his native land. He was born in 1824. He became a teacher of music in Prague, the capital of Bohemia (now part of Czechoslovakia). Smetana was popular as a pianist and made concert tours throughout Europe. He wrote eight operas, one of which, *The Bartered Bride,* has been successful in other countries. Smetana became completely deaf when he was 50. Later he suffered a mental breakdown and died in 1884 in a mental hospital.

smilax

Smilax is the name of a group of climbing vines that grow in many parts of the world. There are several different kinds.

One kind of smilax is popular as a decoration in the winter because it has bright red berries and shiny green leaves. Another kind is known as *catbrier,* because it has sharp, heavy thorns.

Florists use some of the true smilax in their work, but the plant that is usually called "smilax" in a florist's shop is a kind of asparagus and not a smilax. It is a long, trailing vine of rich green that remains fresh and crisp-looking for days after cutting.

Smilax is popular for use in stage scenery where an outdoor garden effect is wanted, and it is often used as party decoration in homes.

Smith, Adam

Adam Smith was a Scottish writer who has been called the founder of the  science of economics, which is the study of the production and distribution of wealth. Smith lived about two hundred years ago, having been born in 1723. His best-known work is a book called *An Inquiry into the Nature and Causes of the Wealth of Nations.* This long title is usually shortened to *The Wealth of Nations.* In this book he said that wealth grows from man's labor, and not from land or money. He was strongly opposed to government restriction on business. Smith died in 1790. For most of his life he was a teacher, but he served also as commissioner of customs in Scotland and as lord rector of the University of Glasgow.

Smith, Alfred E.

Alfred Emanuel Smith was governor of New York State for four terms and was a candidate for the Presidency of the United States in 1928. He was one of the most popular public figures of his time.

Smith was born in 1873 in New York City. His family was poor, and at an early age he had to go to work. He worked as a truckman's helper, fish peddler, and shipping clerk. When he was 22 he joined Tammany Hall, the Democratic political organization in New York City, and began his public life. In 1903 he was elected to the New York State Assembly, where he served for twelve years. After that he served as sheriff of New York County (Manhattan) and as president of the New York City board of aldermen. He was elected governor in 1918, 1922, 1924, and 1926.

In 1928, with the help of Franklin Delano Roosevelt, Smith won the Democratic nomination for the Presidency, but he was defeated by Herbert Hoover. He tried to win the nomination again in 1932, but was defeated by Roosevelt. Smith then served for two years as editor of the magazine *New Outlook,* and took part in several business enterprises. He was the first president of the company that built the Empire State Building, the highest building in the world. Smith was a leader of a group of prominent Democrats who were against President Roosevelt.

Alfred E. Smith was noted for his liberal ideas, and he was responsible for many laws that helped working people. He made much of the fact that he came from a poor, "lower east-side" section of New York City. He deliberately used a manner of speech that people consider typical of New Yorkers. His symbol was a brown derby hat of a kind formerly worn in New York City, and his campaign song was "The Sidewalks of New York." Roosevelt, in nominating him for the Presidency in 1928, called him "the Happy Warrior."

Alfred E. Smith died in 1944.

Smith, John

Captain John Smith was an English soldier and explorer who founded the first English colony in North America, at Jamestown, Virginia, in 1607. Smith was born in 1579 and became a soldier in early youth. He was persuaded by an English merchant, Bartholomew Gosnold, to found a colony in Virginia, and he set sail for America with 105 colonists. He tried to land at Cape Henry, Virginia, but the Indians there were unfriendly, so he sailed to the mouth of the James River and the settlement was made there.

At one time Smith was captured by the Indian chief Powhatan. He was condemned to death but, according to Smith, his life was saved by Pocahontas, daughter of the Indian chief Powhatan. Smith returned to England in 1609. Later he led other exploring expeditions up the New England coast, but he never returned to Virginia. He wrote several books about his adventures. He died in 1631.

Smith, Joseph

Joseph Smith was the founder of the Church of Jesus Christ of Latter Day Saints (Mormons). He was born in 1805, in Vermont. When he was only 11 years old he told of a vision in which God told him to found a new Church. In 1830 he did found the Church, as you can read in the article MORMONS. Joseph Smith died in 1844.

Smith College

Smith College is a college for women in Northampton, Massachusetts. It was founded about one hundred years ago, in 1871. It has the largest library of any women's college in the United States and also has a fine collection of paintings. There are divisions of arts and sciences, education, social work, and architecture. In 1976 there were 2,518 women enrolled in Smith College.

Smithsonian Institution

The Smithsonian Institution is a center for study and research in Washington, D.C. It is an agency of the United States Government and is partially supported by government funds. It was named for James Smithson, an English scientist who died in 1829 and left a large fortune to be used for founding such an institution. The institution is governed by a board of regents, among whom are the Vice President of the United States, the Chief Justice of the United States, and several Congressmen and prominent citizens. The Institution carries out research projects, especially in scientific fields, and publishes its findings, which are distributed without charge all over the world. It has a library containing about a million books. Branches of the Smithsonian include the United States National Museum; the National Air Museum; three art galleries,

including the great National Gallery of Art; the National Zoölogical Park, a 175-acre park that has 2,500 animals; the Astrophysical Observatory; the Bureau of American Ethnology, which studies the American Indian; and the new Museum of History and Technology, which opened in 1963.

smoke

Smoke is made of tiny solid particles carried upward in the hot air and other gases that rise from materials that are on fire but are not burning completely. For instance, when damp wood is afire some parts become tiny particles of carbon that are charred but not completely burned. These are carried upward by currents of hot gases rising from the wood, making a dark smoke. When white phosphorus is set on fire, the completely burned portion of it produces a thick white smoke that is used for smoke screens.

In places where there are many factories that burn coal, the great amount of smoke from their chimneys may make a cloud so thick it cuts out most of the sunlight beneath it. Smoke dirties houses and other buildings. It may kill all trees and plants for miles around a factory.

In smoky towns a large number of people have diseases of the lungs and suffer from sinus trouble.

Because smoke is such a nuisance, many efforts are made to get rid of it. One way of doing this is to force a blast of air into the furnace where the burning material is. The extra air helps the material to burn almost completely, so there is very little smoke. Another way is based on the fact that the solid particles in the smoke have electric charges. Highly electrified metal plates are placed in the smokestack. As the smoke passes them, each smoke particle is drawn to one of the plates. This process is called the Cottrell process because it was invented by an American chemist named Frederick Gardner Cottrell.

SMOG

Some cities that are often foggy and also have many factories suffer from *smog,* which is air carrying a great deal of smoke and the particles of moisture that makes clouds. Los Angeles, California, is the best-known city that suffers from smog. Usually smoke is soon carried away from a city by the hot air, which continues to rise; but the fog may hold the smoke over the city for many hours. This is harmful in several ways. Both smoke and fog make the air less healthful to breathe, and the smog shuts out the sunlight that people need. The principal cure for smog is to remove the smoke. This has been done in many places. Pittsburgh, Pennsylvania, has so many coal-burning factories that it used to be called the Smoky City, but it has done so much smoke-prevention work that many manufacturing cities now have much more smoke than it has.

Smollett, Tobias

Tobias George Smollett was a Scottish novelist who lived about two hundred years ago. He was born in 1721. He went to London as a young man and joined the British Navy as a surgeon's mate. From this experience he wrote a lively and exciting story of the sea, *The Adventures of Roderick Random.* Smollett had begun to practice as a surgeon, but when his early books were successful he gave up medicine and worked as a publisher and editor. One of his next works was *The Adventures of Sir Lancelot Greaves,* which was an imitation of *Don Quixote.* It was the first English novel to be published in installments in a magazine. Smollett's best book, *The Expedition of Humphry Clinker,* was written in the year of his death, in 1771.

Smuts, Jan Christiaan

Jan Christiaan Smuts was a South African statesman and soldier. He was one of the chief leaders of the Boers (the Dutch settlers) in their war against Great Britain about fifty years ago, as told in the article about the BOER WAR, but later he became friendly toward the British. Smuts was born in Cape Province, South Africa, in 1870. When he grew up he became a lawyer. Smuts had been born in the Cape Colony and had been educated in England, but when the Boers and British began to quarrel he gave up his British citizenship and sided with the Boers. In the Boer War he was a commander of guerrilla forces.

The Boers lost the war, and Smuts became convinced that only through co-operation between the two nations could anything be settled. In 1910, he was prominent in forming the Union of South Africa. During World War I, Smuts helped organize his country's forces on the side of the British, though many of the Boers protested. He commanded British troops against the Germans in East Africa.

In 1919 Smuts became Prime Minister of the Union of South Africa. He lost this position in 1924, but regained it in 1939, at the start of World War II. In 1941 Smuts was made a field marshal, the highest military rank. After the war he was active in organizing the United Nations. He died in 1950.

Smyrna

Smyrna is the English name of Izmir, a city in western Turkey, on the Gulf of Smyrna in the Aegean Sea. It has a fine harbor and is the principal port of Turkey in Asia. About 400,000 people live there. Smyrna is famous for its figs. It also produces soap, dyes, hides, cotton and leather goods, and many other things.

Smyrna was one of the great cities of the ancient world. Hundreds of years before the birth of Jesus, it was a Greek colony. It was destroyed by invaders and rebuilt three hundred years later. The Romans conquered Smyrna and it became Christian, the seat of one of the "seven churches of Asia" mentioned in the Bible. It was controlled by several different countries until, in 1924, it was taken by the Turks. In 1919, after Turkey was defeated in World War I, Greek and Turkish forces fought for Smyrna. The following year Greece and Turkey signed a treaty returning Smyrna to Turkey, and most of the Greeks left Turkey. Many of the best craftsmen and workers of Smyrna were Greek, and the city declined as a trade center. Severe earthquakes did great damage in 1928 and again in 1939. With the growth of Turkey as a modern nation, Smyrna has again become an important port.

SMYRNA (IZMIR), TURKEY. Population (1973 estimate) 411,626. On the Aegean Sea. Capital of Smyrna province.

snail

Snails are small animals that are found in almost every part of the world. There are thousands of different kinds. It is usually easy to recognize a snail because most of them live in cone-shaped or spiral-shaped shells.

Snails are members of the mollusc family. They have soft bodies without any backbone. Some snails live in ponds and fresh-water rivers and lakes, and others live on land.

Many snails are less than an inch long, but some, which live in tropical climates, grow to be about four or five inches long. These often have beautiful red shells.

The snail that makes its home near ponds in many parts of Europe is about an inch and a half long. It has a yellowish shell with broad bands of brown color on it. People in Europe raise this snail, which feeds on lettuce and other types of leafy vegetation. When the snails are fat they are sent to market. They are considered a great delicacy when they are fried or cooked in other ways.

Many kinds of snail live in the sea. The largest snail that is found off the coast of the United States in the Atlantic Ocean is called the giant conch snail. It often grows to be about ten inches long and weighs about four pounds. The shell of the giant conch snail is quite beautiful, and is used to make cameos and other types of jewelry, or as an ornament. This snail is made into a chowder, or fish soup.

snake

Snakes are long, slender animals that have backbones and ribs and scales on the outside of their bodies. They are reptiles, crawling animals. They make their homes in trees and under bushes, in holes in the ground, in crevices of rocks in high mountains, and in hot deserts. Some snakes live in the sea and are fine swimmers. There are very few places in the world where there are no snakes.

The snake has no legs (though the boa has tiny hind legs that are of no use in walking). The snake crawls along the ground on its belly. It has rough scales on its underside and these help it to drag its body along. Snakes can move very fast.

Some snakes grow to be only about six inches long, while others, such as the giant pythons and boas, often grow to be more than 25 feet long.

All snakes have fine skins, some beautifully marked. They make a fine leather used for shoes, handbags, belts, and other articles. Snakes often shed their skins and get new ones. They also grow new teeth when they have lost their old teeth. Snakes always have their eyelids closed,

but the eyelids are transparent and the snake can see through them.

The snake's mouth is unusual. The jaws are held together very loosely, so that a snake can stretch its mouth very wide open from side to side, or up and down. This makes it possible for a snake to swallow an animal much larger than itself. The snake has a thin forked tongue. It uses its tongue to touch things, the way human beings use their fingers. The snake's tongue may be red or yellow or black or green.

Snakes eat frogs, toads and insects, rats, mice and birds, rabbits, fish and eggs. Some snakes eat other snakes. A snake may swallow another animal alive or it may kill it first.

Many female snakes lay eggs. Often female snake will lay as many as fifty eggs at a time. It usually does not care for the eggs but leaves them to hatch by themselves. Some snakes hatch the eggs in the body of the female so that the young snakes are born alive.

Although people are often afraid of snakes, many snakes are harmless and are very useful to farmers, because they kill rats and mice and insects that destroy crops. These helpful snakes should not be killed.

Some snakes are poisonous. Rattlesnakes, coral snakes and copperheads are poisonous snakes that live in the United States. Poisonous snakes have two long, hollow teeth called fangs, through which they eject a poison, called venom. If such a snake pierces a person's skin with its fangs, the bite can be very dangerous.

Even a poisonous snake will not bite a person unless it becomes frightened or angry.

SNAKEBITE

No person should ever tease a snake or handle it. No one should ever put his hand into bushes or holes where a snake may be resting. Once a snake becomes frightened there is no time to move away. The snake can move more quickly than any human being. It usually raises its body into a curbed position that looks like the letter "S," and then strikes.

When a person is bitten by a poisonous snake he feels a sharp burning pain. The skin around the place where the fangs have pierced becomes swollen and changes color.

When a person has been bitten by a snake he must be given first aid at once. He should be taken to a doctor as soon as possible. The doctor will give him injections called "antivenom injections."

Before the person who has been bitten is taken to the doctor he must be treated on the spot.

FIRST AID FOR SNAKEBITE

If a person has been bitten on the arm, someone must tie a bandage around his arm just above where the fangs have entered the skin. (A necktie or shoestring can be used.) Then cuts must be made through the fang marks to open the wound. These cuts can be made with a razor blade or a sharp knife that has been held in a flame to kill all germs on it.

The venom (poison) must then be drawn out of the wound. People who go on trips to the country can buy first-aid kits for snakebite. These kits contain a small pump that can pump out the

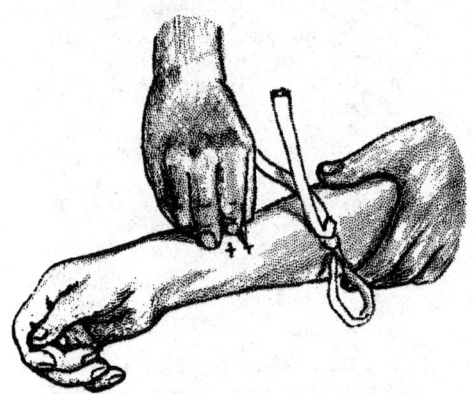
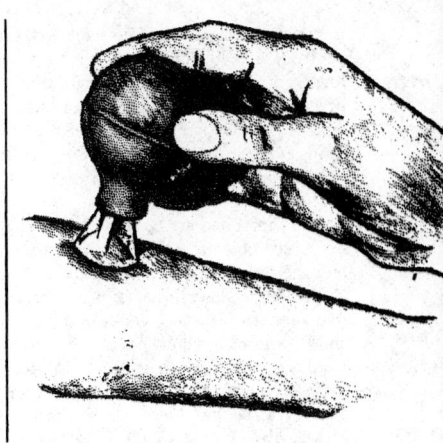

If a person is bitten by a poisonous snake, a band should be tied just above the bite. Then a cross cut one-fourth of an inch deep should be made across the fang marks. If a suction cup is at hand, it may be used to draw out the poison. The victim should remain quiet.

venom from a snakebite. If a person has no first-aid kit he must suck out the poison with his mouth. This poison will not hurt the person unless he has cuts or sores in his mouth. He should of course spit out all of the poison.

The process of sucking out the venom takes at least a half hour. Then the patient must be taken to the doctor. If possible he should avoid walking, because exercise makes the blood circulate and this might spread the poison to other parts of the body. If the patient has to walk, he should walk slowly so that the blood will not circulate too much.

snakebird

The snakebird is a funny-looking bird that gets its name from its long, thin neck. Snakebirds are found near swamps and ponds in Europe and the United States. People in the United States often call this bird a *water turkey* or *darter*. When the snakebird swims in the water only its head rises above the surface and it looks very much like a water snake. It uses its long neck as a weapon to spear the fish that it eats.

There are several different kinds of snakebird. The type that makes its home in the United States is about three feet tall. It has shiny greenish black feathers with silvery markings. In the summertime the male grows a handsome plumage of gray feathers. The female is brown and has a reddish band on its breast. The snakebird has webbed feet.

The snakebird builds a crude nest of clay and twigs and grass.

Snake River

The Snake River is a river 1,038 miles long in the northwestern part of the United States. It is the principal tributary of the Columbia River. The Snake River rises in Yellowstone National Park in Wyoming. It flows south through Jackson Hole National Park, then west into Idaho and across the southern part of the state through a region called the Snake River Plain. The river then turns north and forms a large part of the Idaho-Oregon border and part of the Idaho-Washington border. It turns into Washington and flows into the Columbia in the southeastern part of the state. It is navigable from the Columbia to Lewiston, near the Washington border.

The Snake River flows through many deep gorges, one of which is the Grand Canyon of the Snake River, one of the deepest in the world. It has a number of waterfalls, of which the best known are the Shoshone Falls in Idaho. Other falls along its course have been dammed for irrigation purposes.

snapdragon

Snapdragon is a flowering plant that is grown in many gardens and greenhouses. It is a perennial and will grow year after year without replanting, but most people plant new seed each spring. The blossoms are usually bigger and more attractive if this is done.

Some snapdragons are only about six inches high and some grow to be as high as three feet. The flowers are unusual. A light pressure on the sides of a single blossom will cause it to open its two sections, which look like jaws. When the pressure is released the "jaws" will close again. Snapdragons grow in many colors.

snapper

The snapper is a fish that lives in the waters off the coasts of Florida and Mexico and Central and South America. It is a strong, fast fish and a powerful fighter. It gets its name because it snaps up other fish very suddenly. It has large jaws and sharp teeth.

The gray snapper weighs about five pounds. Scientists have used the gray snapper to make many important experiments. The gray snapper can learn to avoid unpleasant tastes and odors and can be taught to recognize the colors and patterns of the different kinds of fish that it likes to eat.

The red snapper is a handsome fish that is found in warm waters off the coast of Mexico. It often weighs more than 70 pounds. Snappers are such powerful and fierce fighters that fishermen find it fine sport to catch them. The red snapper is a popular food fish.

A kind of turtle is called a snapper. See the article TURTLE.

sneezing

Sneezing is a sudden, usually uncontrollable explosion of breath from the nose or mouth. It is usually caused by an

irritation in the nose. The irritation can be from a cold, an allergy such as hay fever, or a dust or chemical that is breathed in and tickles the nose passages. The muscles move to throw out the irritating matter by a *reflex action,* which is explained in the article on NERVOUS SYSTEM.

It is not good to hold back a sneeze by force, but the sneeze should always be covered so germs cannot be blown in other people's faces. It was once believed that sneezing was very good for a person, and people would sniff powdered tobacco (called snuff) up their noses to make themselves sneeze. This is no longer done, but an occasional sneeze is not harmful and can be of help by cleaning out passages through which we breathe. When a person sneezes almost constantly for long periods of time, he should see a doctor.

snipe

The snipe is a bird that lives in many parts of Europe and the United States. The snipe that is found in marshes and fields in the United States is called Wilson's snipe. It grows to be about one foot long. It has brown and black and light tan feathers. The feathers that grow on the snipe's tail are stiff and thin. When the bird flies, the air rushes through these tail feathers and makes a loud sound. In the spring the male courts the female by flying in circles around it. The snipe is a strong flier. It builds its nest on the ground and the female lays four large eggs. The snipe is popular as food and good game for hunters.

snoring

Snoring is noisy breathing during sleep. The sounds made by a person when he talks come from a part of the throat called the larynx, which vibrates (shakes) and makes sound waves when air passes through it. While we are awake, we keep the larynx from making any sounds we do not want to make. When we sleep, we stop controlling the larynx and air passing over it makes rattling noises that are called snores.

Some people snore because they do not sleep in the right position. Sometimes a person will snore when he is sleeping on his back and not when he is sleeping on his side. A cold, or adenoids, or anything that blocks the breathing passages, can make a person snore. There is nothing dangerous about snoring, and it is not a sign of bad health, but a person who snores is wise to ask a doctor to examine him and see if there is anything wrong.

snow

Snow is frozen moisture (tiny particles of water) that falls to earth. It is in the form of snowflakes, which are crystals that appear in many strange and beautiful shapes. There is very little water in a snowflake, even when it seems large; and it falls slowly because the resistance of the air holds it up, much as it does a feather. Unlike hail and sleet, which are also frozen water, snow almost never falls in any season except winter. In any other season it would be almost sure to pass through air warm enough to melt it before it could reach the earth.

In regions near the North and South Poles, and on high mountaintops where it is very cold, there may be snow on the ground all year. Great quantities of snow may form ice and become glaciers (rivers or seas of ice).

Snow is not clear as water and ice are. It is white. This is because it is formed of crystals. The crystals break up the light inside themselves, as explained in the articles on CRYSTAL and PRISM. Snow crystals combine the colors of the light that strikes them, and this gives them a white color. See also the article on WEATHER.

snowball

The snowball is a shrub raised for its clusters of attractive white blossoms. It is also called the *European cranberry bush.* It reaches a height of 11 or 12 feet when fully grown. Its leaves turn bright orange and crimson in the fall, and after the blossoms disappear it produces bright red berries, but these are not the cranberries sold in American markets, and are not good to eat.

snowbird, another name for the junco, a bird that makes its home in many parts of the United States: see the article on JUNCO.

snowdrop

The snowdrop is a flower that blooms in the very early spring, sometimes even before the snow has completely melted away. It grows from bulbs that can be planted in the fall. It can stand extremely cold winters without harm. The blossoms are bell-shaped. They are white with thin green lines on the back of the petals. The stem is usually about 10 or 12 inches long.

snowshoe

A snowshoe is not really a "shoe." It is something that a person attaches to his shoes for walking over snow. Most snowshoes are wooden or metal frames about three feet long and one foot wide. Inside the frame is woven cane or some other light material, as on the cane seat of a chair. The snowshoe may also be a solid piece of light wood. When a person tries to walk in deep snow, his feet usually sink far down and it is almost impossible to walk. The snowshoe covers so much surface that the person does not sink into the snow. Walking on snowshoes is slow and tiring.

snuff

Snuff is powdered tobacco. About two hundred years ago it was very fashionable for a man to take a little snuff between his thumb and forefinger, hold it to his nose, and sniff it up. This made him sneeze, and sneezing was thought to be very good for one. Men had little metal boxes, beautifully made and decorated, to carry their snuff in. These were called snuffboxes and looked like women's very fine compacts, except that they were smaller.

Some people still use snuff, but it is not considered at all refined to use it. Such people are sometimes said to "dip snuff." They smear the snuff on their gums, in their mouths, with a stick called a snuff stick. They like the taste of it, just as some people like to chew tobacco.

soap

Soap is a material that cleans things. It is the oldest of all the cleaning materials made by man, being almost three thousand years old. Soaps are made of fatty oils treated with one of the chemical substances known as alkalis. The alkali is usually potash or lye or caustic soda.

No one knows exactly how the ancient peoples made soap. About 1,200 years ago the first men to follow soap-making as a trade appeared in Spain and in France. Soap as we know it was invented about the year 1800, by a French scientist. He found that soda, an alkali, could be made from table salt, which was very inexpensive. Soap then began to be made and used extensively.

Soap is used for other things besides washing. It is a good lubricant, or material that keeps other things from sticking together. It can be used to ease a stuck drawer or window, and factories use it for the same purpose on the molds and rollers used in making tires and other rubber products, aluminum and tin and lead foil, wire, and many other things. Soap is used as a polish in making jewelry. It softens leather, scours grease from wool, holds together the coating materials on glossy paper, and holds together rust-preventing substances in anti-freeze liquids. Soap is used to make coal dustless.

HOW SOAP IS MADE

In colonial days soap was made in the home, from fat drippings and wood ashes. Hot water was poured through the wood ashes to obtain potash. Then the potash was boiled together with the fat, producing a harsh, strong soap.

The modern way of making soap uses the same principles, but ways have been found to make soap gentler on the hands and on the materials it cleans. Fats, oils, and lye are boiled together for several days in huge steel kettles, each as high as a two-and-a-half story house and holding 150 tons at a time. This produces glycerin as well as salt. Tons of salt are dumped into the kettle to separate the soap from the glycerin. The glycerin-and-water mixture is heavier than the soap and settles to the bottom, where it is drawn off.

After the glycerin has been removed the soap is again boiled with soda. Then it is washed with salt water and the soap settles in two layers. On top is the pure soap, from which the finished flakes, granules and bars are made.

A faster method of making soap includes the use of a hydrolyzer, a huge stainless-steel tube as big around as a barrel and as high as an eight-story building. Soap fats and water are pumped through the hydrolyzer under very high pressures and at very high temperatures. Fats go in at the bottom and rise through the scalding water pumped in at the top. The glycerin is drawn off at the bottom and the fatty acids for soap-making are taken off at the top.

The soap comes out as a liquid. To make bars, it is poured into large iron boxes mounted on wheels. Each box, called a frame, holds about 900 pounds

of soap. The soap is allowed to harden for several days and then is cut by wires to form bars. The bars of soap are dried by moving air and then machines stamp a name or design on the bars and wrap them.

Soap flakes are made by pouring liquid soap between two steel rolls, one hot and one icy cold, that act like a giant clothes-wringer. The warm soap sticks to the cold roll in a thin film. This filmy sheet of soap is cut into ribbons that are scraped off by a cutting blade.

Soap powder, or granulated soap, is made in an eight-story blowing tower. The liquid soap is pumped to the top and is sprayed through heavy steel nozzles. It falls as a fine mist to the bottom of the tower, where gusts of hot air dry it. The bits of soap that form the mist dry as grains or granules.

DETERGENTS

Any substance that cleans is a detergent. Soap is a detergent. But in recent years the word *detergent* has come to have a special meaning—a substance that cleans but is not soap.

Modern detergents are chemical compounds made from oils, as soap is, but chemically more like alcohol than like soap. The most important job of most cleaning materials is to wash away oils and greases, and the new detergents do this even better than most soaps. In hard water and sea water, in which soap dissolves very slowly, detergents are as effective as they are in soft fresh water. These chemical compounds are also called *wetting agents,* because they break down oils that water will not dissolve and let the water wash them away.

The first detergents of the modern kind were used for washing clothes and dishes. Next came a shampoo sold under the name Drene. By the 1950s, detergents were outselling soap powders and soap flakes for household uses, but soap was still used almost exclusively for bathing and washing the face and hands.

The cleaning action of a detergent is just the same whether or not it makes suds, but manufacturers discovered that people do not think clothes or dishes are being washed if there are no suds, so special chemicals are added to many detergents to make suds.

Soap Box Derby

The All-American Soap Box Derby is a race of motorless cars that are designed, built and driven by boys 11 to 15 years old. The race is held each year, in cities in the United States, Canada, and some foreign countries. More than fifty thousand boys enter it, and about three million people watch the races. Each city has its own race, then the city champions, about 150 of them, go to Akron, Ohio, for the finals, which are run on a course called Derby Downs.

Each of the city winners receives a wrist watch and a diploma. The boys who finish in the first five places in the finals receive scholarships—$7,500 for first place, $5,000 for second place, and so on, down to $2,000 for fifth place. The champions have their expenses paid when they go to the finals. In Akron they live at a YMCA camp on a lake shore. After the finals they attend a banquet in Goodyear Hall, and prizes are awarded.

The first Soap Box Derby was held in 1933 in Dayton, Ohio. A newspaper photographer named Myron E. Scott, of Dayton, began it. The next year the Chevrolet Motor Company decided to run the Soap Box Derby and to give the prizes. Newspapers in the various cities coöperate with Chevrolet. To enter, a boy goes to the Chevrolet dealer's place in his city and registers. At least one of his parents must be with him.

Derby Downs, where the finals are held, is a concrete course about 975 feet long. The stands hold about 65,000 people. They pay for their seats and the money they pay goes to charity. The course has electric-eye and photo-finish equipment. The racers average about 26 miles per hour in 27 seconds of racing. Each of the boys races five "heats," or separate races.

Three days before the race, drawings are held to determine the heat and the lane in which the champions will race in their first round. During later eliminations, lanes are determined by lot between rounds. Three, and occasionally two, cars race in each heat.

At the starting line near Topside, cars are lined up with noses against metal baffle plates. These plates are attached to a metal shaft. When the starting lever is released, the baffle plates drop even with the track and the cars are away to a perfect start.

There are special prizes for the best cars in design, construction, and other features, as well as for the fastest cars.

soapstone, another name for the mineral talc: see TALC.

soccer

Soccer is a form of football. In British countries and in most of the countries of Europe it is the most popular outdoor game, as popular as baseball and football are in the United States. Crowds of 100,000 watch the games in the big cities. Soccer is played in many schools and colleges in the United States and Canada, especially in the eastern parts. The British people call the game Association Football.

In soccer there is no carrying or throwing of the ball as there is in American football or in the Rugby football played in England. A player kicks the ball, or may hit it with his knee or shoulder or even butt it with his head, but he may not touch it with his hands. The ball is almost always kicked.

The ball used in soccer is round, being much more like a basketball than like the football used in American football. The game is played on a field that is 100 to 130 yards long and 50 to 100 yards wide. There are eleven men on each team. At each end of the field there are goalposts, as on an American football field, but the object of the players is to kick the ball through the opponents' goal, not over a crossbar. One player on each team is a goalkeeper, stationed at his team's goal to guard it. He is the only player who is permitted to use his hands, to keep the ball from going through the goal. Penalties in soccer are usually free kicks at the opposing goal.

Soccer is one of the fastest and most interesting of all games. There are many professional players, and there are also amateur teams that play international matches, including contests connected with the Olympic Games.

socialism

Socialism is a form of government in which all the people together own all property that can be used to make a profit. This includes not only land and factories but also machines, tools, and everything else that can be called a means of production. Socialism is opposed to *capitalism,* which is the system used in most countries today. Under capitalism, a person can own a factory and machines. He can hire workers to run the machines. He can sell the goods made by these workers and make a profit on them. The socialistic system would not allow him to make a profit on the use of the property or on the work of others. In socialism, a person can make money, he can save it, he can spend it as he pleases, he can give it away or leave it to his family when he dies, but he cannot use it to make a profit. He cannot buy stocks or bonds, he cannot charge interest if he lends money, and he cannot earn interest by keeping his money in a bank.

Originally, the system that is now called communism was called socialism. The Communist Party that rules Russia and other countries grew out of the Socialist Parties of European countries. Today socialism and communism are different. Socialists usually favor a democratic kind of government in which the people can elect their officials, while the Communists have a dictatorship in which the government controls the people instead of the people controlling the government.

HOW SOCIALISM BEGAN

Socialism as a proposed political system is not very old. It was not much more than a hundred years ago that a group of writers began to propose seriously that there might be socialist governments. In those times, great landowners and factory-owners were very rich while the people who worked for them were hardly paid enough to eat on and lived in the most horrible slums. Some men, such as Robert Owen in England and Pierre Proudhon in France, wrote that this was wrong and that the land and factories should belong to all the people.

The German writers Karl Marx and Friedrich Engels are sometimes called the founders of socialism. Their ideas are explained in the article COMMUNISM. Marx and Engels wrote that if the workers of the world would unite, they could rule the world. This was a different approach from most of the earlier writers. Proudhon and others believed there should be socialism because it is wrong for one man to profit from another man's work; that is *idealistic* socialism. Marx and Engels said the working people should seize power not because it was right to do so but simply because they were strong enough to do so; that is *materialistic* socialism.

After Marx and Engels had published several things, Socialist Parties were organized in most of the countries of Europe and in America, but they never became powerful until the Russian Revolution of

1917 put the Communist Party in power, and then the socialists did not see at all the kind of socialism they had expected. Instead they saw a cruel dictatorship.

SOCIALIST PARTIES

During the 1880s a group of British "intellectuals" (writers, artists, and others) formed the Fabian Society and called themselves Fabian Socialists. They thought the world should have socialism but was not yet ready for it, and they planned to educate the people so that eventually they would be ready. The Fabians took their name from an ancient Roman general called Fabius the delayer, who won victories by just waiting.

The Fabians never accomplished much, but the British Labour Party, a Socialist Party founded chiefly by labor union leaders, became very powerful and controlled the government of Great Britain for periods in the 1920s and after World War II. In the late 1940s the Labour Party introduced several socialist measures in England. The government took over ownership of the railroads and other important industries, and put into effect "socialized medicine" in which the government pays for all medical care.

In the United States, the Socialist Party's most prominent leader for more than twenty years was Norman THOMAS, about whom there is a separate article. The party profited from the fact that Thomas was greatly respected, but still it was never successful politically, except in electing mayors of a few cities.

Several United States governments have been accused of "socialism" when they have permitted the government to own profit-making enterprises that compete with privately owned businesses. This is described in the article on GOVERNMENT OWNERSHIP.

The idea of socialism still appeals to many people, especially while they are young. The difficulty is that socialized enterprises have seldom been anywhere near as efficient as enterprises under private management, and after giving socialism a trial the voters usually want to return to the capitalistic system. See the articles on CAPITALISM and LABOUR PARTY.

Social Security

Social Security is a name given to a kind of government insurance plan that pays a monthly income to nearly everyone who retires from work because of old age. The workers and their employers pay for the plan, but the government holds the money and makes the monthly payments.

The Social Security Act in the United States was passed by Congress in 1935. At first each employed person paid one percent of his earnings and his employer had to pay an additional one percent. These payments were gradually increased until by 1963 they were 3⅝ percent of the first $4,800 earned each year. Plans called for them to be increased to 4⅝ percent by 1968.

A person can retire at 62 or 65 and begin to collect monthly payments. The amount of the payments depends on several things besides retirement age. A man with a family to support receives more than a man with no dependents. The amount depends partly on how much the

person has earned and paid into the Social Security fund. Each person has a Social Security number, and all payments by himself and his employer are credited to his account on records kept by the government. If the head of a family dies before reaching retirement age, the Social Security plan pays an income to a wife and children who were dependent on him.

Every employer must keep Social Security records, collect the money due from the employee, add the employer's share, and send the money to the government every three months.

For almost fifteen years, workers of some kinds were not covered by Social Security. Now almost anyone who earns money can have the benefit of Social Security. A "self-employed" person, who has no employer, adds his Social Security payment to his income tax each year. Employers and employees who are not in business, such as housewives and houseworkers, can get information at any post office.

Society for the Prevention of Cruelty to Animals

The Society for the Prevention of Cruelty to Animals, or S.P.C.A., is an organization that works to prevent the mistreatment of animals, to take care of sick animals, and to teach people how to take care of their pets. It was founded in England more than a hundred years ago, in 1824, and an American society, the A.S.P.C.A., was founded in 1866 by a man called Henry Bergh. The society has many activities. It runs hospitals where sick animals are treated, and if their owners are poor the treatment is free of charge. It helps owners find pets that they have lost. It has classes where people learn how to train their pets. It takes care of animals that no one wants and coöperates with the United States government in protecting wild animals from hunters and trappers. It advises farmers on how to care for their livestock. In some places it provides water for dray horses (horses used to pull carts and other vehicles).

Society for the Prevention of Cruelty to Children

The Society for the Prevention of Cruelty to Children, or S.P.C.C., is an organization that works to protect children from neglect and mistreatment. It was founded in 1875 in New York City by Elbridge T. Gerry. At that time there were many cases in which children were badly beaten and otherwise mistreated by their parents.

The S.P.C.C. takes care of children who have been abused or neglected. In some cases it brings the parents to court and has new guardians appointed for the child. It helps children who have committed crimes. It also works in cases where grownups have committed crimes against children. Often the help it gives consists of obtaining medical and mental care for children who need it.

Society Islands

The Society Islands are two groups of islands belonging to France, in the South Pacific Ocean. They have a total area of about 650 square miles, and about 70,000 people live on them. One of the

groups is called the Windward Islands, which include TAHITI (about which there is a separate article). The other group is the Leeward Islands. The islands produce copra, sugar, rum, and mother-of-pearl. They were discovered in 1767 by British explorers. Two years later they were visited by Captain Cook and members of the Royal Society of London, for which they were named.

Society of Jesus, a Roman Catholic religious order: see the article on JESUIT.

sociology

Sociology is the study of how human beings live together in various kinds of groups. It is an important science because civilization and progress depend on the coöperation of people living together in groups. In spite of the wars and cruel acts that are described in history, most of the time men have helped one another and life has therefore become better in many ways.

The student of sociology learns from the way different groups of people (sometimes called *societies*) have lived in the past and are living now in all parts of the world. In the study of the group life of man, sociology is related to ethics (what men consider right and wrong), criminology (what crime is and why people commit crimes), psychology (the study of the human mind and how people think), political organization (the study of the state and how people govern themselves), and other aspects of human group behavior. Students of sociology often use their training and knowledge to help people who are unfortunate or who need help in getting along with others. There are many branches of sociology. It is closely related to ANTHROPOLOGY, the general study of man, about which there is a separate article.

Socrates

Socrates was one of the first and greatest philosophers (thinkers). He lived in ancient Greece, about 2,300 years ago. About that time some men were be-ginning to wonder about the reasons for everything that goes on in the world—why fire is hot and water is wet, how plants and animals grow, and why men think and act as they do. These men called themselves philosophers, which means "lovers of wisdom." Socrates, unlike most of the Greek philosophers, said that the most important thing he knew was how little he knew. He taught that only by knowledge could man be virtuous and that no man intentionally does wrong, and he spent his life trying to make men study and think.

Socrates was born in 469 B.C. He did not write books, and most of what we know about his life and teachings has come down to us in the writings of his most famous pupil, Plato. Socrates spent his time where people gathered, in the market place and the gymnasiums, talking about virtue, justice, and other good qualities of man. In order to make the people realize how little they knew and

how diligently they must study, he would explain that he was very ignorant on some subject. When his companion would begin to explain the matter to him, Socrates would ask such searching questions that the person would be unable to answer them and would end up with the realization that he did not really know.

This method of teaching irritated many of the people of Athens. They began to accuse Socrates of corrupting the youth of the city, and although Socrates denied their charges, he was condemned to kill himself by drinking hemlock, a poison.

Two of Plato's writings tell the story of Socrates' trial and his reasons for being willing to die. Socrates drank the fatal hemlock in 399 B.C. His wife, Xanthippe, whom he always pictures as a shrewish (scolding or ill-natured) woman figures in many stories about Socrates.

soda is a name used for some chemicals, made from SODIUM, about which there is a separate article.

soda water

Soda water is water that is full of bubbles of carbon-dioxide gas. It is used for making ice-cream sodas and soft drinks such as ginger ale and soda pop. It is called soda water because when it was first invented the chemical compound called bicarbonate of soda, or baking soda, was used in making the carbon-dioxide gas. Nowadays the carbon dioxide is either manufactured from coal or is gotten from natural gas wells. It is put into steel bottles and the bottles are delivered to soda fountains. Here the gas is piped into tanks of water. The water comes out of a spigot at the fountain. Soda water is also called carbonated water, fizz water, sparkling water, or Vichy.

sodium

Sodium is a soft, silvery-white metal. It is a chemical element, which means that it is one of the basic substances of which everything in the world is made. Sodium is never found pure in nature, but is always combined with other elements. All salt contains sodium. Chemical compounds of sodium are very important in industry, medicine, chemistry, and photography.

Pure sodium is as soft as putty and is so light that it will float on water; but if it is put on water it will combine with the oxygen of the water so fast that the hydrogen in the water will catch on fire. It will also react with the oxygen in the air, so sodium must be stored in some liquid that has no oxygen in it, for example kerosene.

USES OF SODIUM

Pure sodium is used in sodium-vapor lamps, the yellow, glareless lights that are used on many highways. The best-known sodium compound is sodium chloride, or common table salt. There is enough sodium chloride in the oceans to cover the earth's land surface to a depth of 400 feet. Sodium carbonate, or washing soda, is composed of the chemical elements sodium, carbon, and oxygen. It is used in making glass and soap, in oil refining, in paper-making, and to soften water. A very similar compound, sodium bicarbon-

ate, is called baking soda. Sodium hydroxide, or lye, is used in the manufacture of many articles, among them soap and glycerin. Sodium nitrate, or Chile saltpeter, is an important fertilizer. The "hypo" that all photographers use in developing their films is a compound of sodium. There are hundreds of other useful sodium compounds.

Sodium is obtained from the very large beds of salt that are found in all parts of the world.

Sodom and Gomorrah

Sodom and Gomorrah were two ancient cities in Palestine, near the Dead Sea. In the Bible the two cities are almost always mentioned together, and are also called two of the five "cities of the plain." According to the Book of Genesis, the people of Sodom and Gomorrah were so wicked that God destroyed them and the two cities by a rain of brimstone. The only one who escaped was LOT, about whom there is a separate article.

Sofia

Sofia is the capital and largest city of Bulgaria. It is in the western part of the country. Sofia is a transportation and industrial center and is also the cultural center of Bulgaria. More than 850,000 people live there. There are factories that make machinery, weapons, and textile, rubber and food products.

Sofia has a university and schools of science, art, music, and military sciences. There are an opera house, theaters, a national library, an observatory, and many museums. Among the noted buildings are the chapel of St. George, which was an ancient Roman bath, the Church of St. Sophia, almost 1,400 years old, and several mosques, or Mohammedan places of worship.

Sofia was a military camp of the Romans almost two thousand years ago. It was captured and ruled by several countries after that, and for hundreds of years it was controlled by Turkey. In 1878 it was captured from the Turks by Russia and turned over to Bulgaria.

SOFIA, BULGARIA. Population (1973 estimate) 858,140. Capital of Bulgaria.

softball

Softball is a form of the game of baseball. It is much like baseball in many respects, but the ball used is bigger and softer, the bats are much thinner, the distance between the bases is different, and some of the rules of play are slightly different.

The ball used in softball is about three inches greater in circumference (around the outside) than a baseball. It weighs about an ounce more than a baseball. While it is not really soft, it is not nearly as hard as a regulation baseball. Nevertheless, it is hard enough so that gloves are used by the fielders in a softball game.

The distance between the bases in a softball game is 60 feet, as compared with 90 feet in official baseball. There are nine men on a softball team, just as there are on a baseball team. A regulation softball game is seven innings, while a baseball game is nine innings.

In softball the pitcher stands 43 feet away from the home plate in a man's game, and 35 feet in a women's game.

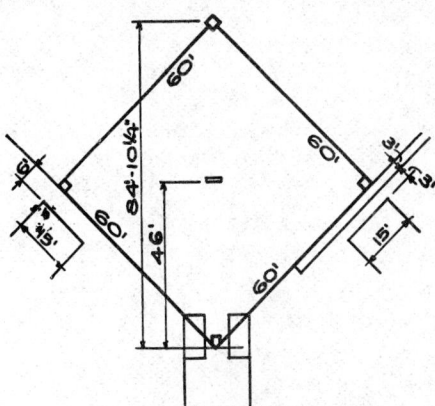

The diagram shows the size of a regulation softball diamond. The fence should be two hundred feet from home plate.

Instead of pitching overhand as in baseball, a softball pitcher throws the ball to the plate with a sweeping underhand motion.

Some softball pitchers acquire great speed, and it is not unusual for them to strike out more than half of the batters who oppose them during a game.

SOFTBALL LEAGUES

During the last forty years softball has become a very popular game in the United States and parts of Canada. There are many leagues of club teams, business teams, church teams, and town teams. There are also some professional softball leagues in which the players receive pay. Softball is played during the same seasons of the year as baseball.

Softball grew out of a game almost exactly like it, called indoor baseball, that is still played in gymnasiums during the winter.

soil

Soil is the soft layer that covers most of the land areas of the earth, and in which plants with roots can grow. Soil is made up mainly of three things: rock that has weathered to a powder; humus, which is the decayed remains of dead plants and animals; and vast numbers of bacteria.

The upper part of the soil, the part that has the most humus and bacteria, is called the *topsoil*. Lower layers of soil, which are usually full of larger grains of rock and of pebbles, are called the *subsoil*. In the United States, topsoils average one to five feet in depth. Scientists who study the soil have distinguished thousands of different kinds of soil, but all of them can be divided into three large groups: sandy, clayey, and loamy. Usually a black or dark soil is more fertile than lighter-colored soil, because it contains more humus, but this is not always so.

SOIL CONSERVATION

Not only does soil support the growth of plants, but plants hold soil together and help to keep rainwater from washing it into streams and rivers that carry it to the ocean. The method used in keeping the soil from washing and blowing away is called soil conservation. The washing-away process is called EROSION and there is a separate article about it.

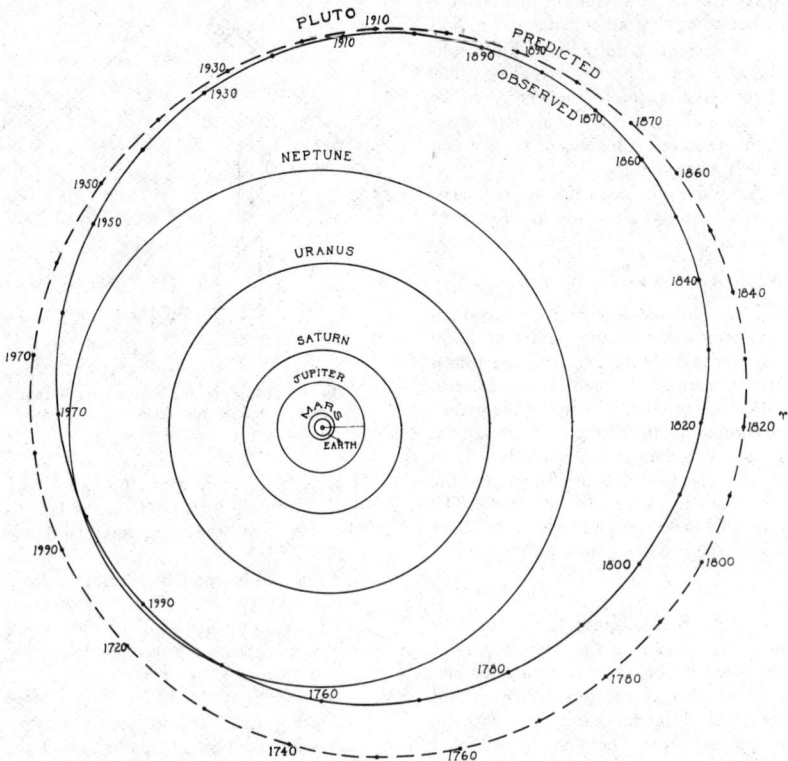

The diagram shows the planets of the solar system and how their distances from the sun compare. Pluto is the planet that was discovered last. The dotted line shows where it was predicted that Pluto would be (or had been) in certain years. The "observed" dates, made after larger telescopes were made, show how close the predictions were.

solar system

Solar system means "system of the sun." It is made up of the sun and all the heavenly bodies that revolve around it and shine by reflecting the sunlight. These heavenly bodies are planets, satellites, asteroids, comets, and meteorites. A few are large but most of them are very small. There are thousands of them, many millions, counting the meteorites.

Each of these bodies is attracted by the gravity of the sun, so that it does not fly off into space. The larger bodies, such as the earth and the other planets, have such strong gravitational attraction that they have satellites (such as the moon) revolving around them while they revolve around the sun.

The farthest extent of the solar system is about eight billion miles. The entire solar system is part of the galaxy (body of stars) called the Milky Way.

solder

Solder is an alloy, or combination of metals. Because solder is easily melted, it is used as a cement to hold two metal surfaces together. Plumbers use solder to join pipes together, electricians to join wires, tinsmiths to join metal sheets, and so on.

There are many kinds of solder, each with a different melting point. Soft, or common, solder is half lead and half tin. Plumbers' solder is one-third tin and two-thirds lead. Hard solders, or brazes, are made of copper and zinc, and are used for soldering iron, copper, or brass. Jewelers' solder is made of silver, copper, and zinc.

When two pieces of metal are to be soldered together, the surfaces to be joined are first cleaned of dirt and grease. Then they are placed so that they touch each other in the position that is wanted. A solder whose melting point is close to that of the metals to be joined is placed upon them where they touch. A tool called a soldering iron is heated and placed on the solder to melt it. A blowtorch is used for solder with a very high melting point. The melted solder fills the crack between the two pieces of metal. Sometimes it also partly melts the metal surfaces and combines with them. When the solder cools, it forms a strong metal joint.

Modern solder is sometimes made in the form of long thin tubes that look like macaroni. The inside of the tube is filled with a material called *flux*, which dissolves certain impurities that might weaken the joint.

sole

The sole is a fish that lives in oceans, where the water is not too hot or too cold. It is one of the FLATFISH, about which there is a separate article.

The sole that is found in the waters of Europe is usually caught for market when it is about 8 inches long. It is called English sole. Filet of sole is considered a great delicacy. Fish eaten as sole in the United States is usually flounder.

solitaire

Solitaire is a game of cards played by one person alone. It is also called Patience. There are hundreds of different ways of playing solitaire. In some of them the player's object is to get the cards arranged in a particular pattern; in others

it is to find some legal play for every card; and other forms of the game have their own special rules. The game selected is a matter of personal preference, but by far the majority of solitaire players play a game that is usually called Canfield.

RULES OF CANFIELD

Use one regular pack of 52 cards. Deal a card face up at the left, then a row of six cards, face down, to the right. Put a face-up card on the second card, then a second face-down card on each of the five cards to its right. Put a face-up card on the third pile, then a face-down card on each pile to its right. Continue until there are seven "piles"—one card in the first, two in the second, and so on, up to seven cards in the last pile, with the top card of each pile face up.

Each ace, as it shows up, will be placed in a row beyond these piles. An ace starts a *foundation* pile. The foundations are built up in order in the suit of the ace— the two on the ace, the three on the two, and so up, ending with jack, queen, king. The object is to get all four aces out and built up all the way to the king.

There is also building on the piles of the original layout (the cards first dealt). In this building, a card that is next-lower in rank and different in color may be played. That is, any red three can go on any black four. Any black queen can go on any red king. If there are several face-up cards on a pile (due to previous building) all must be moved at once. For example, if a pile has seven of hearts, six of spades, five of diamonds on it, they may be moved to a black eight.

If a pile in the layout is all played, a king may be put in the space that is left. The undealt cards are called the *stock*. The player turns up the cards one at a time. He may play this card either on a foundation pile or on the layout. If he cannot play it, he leaves it face up in a *discard pile* in front of him, and turns another card. The top card of the discard pile may be played if the next card of the stock has not yet been turned.

Strict rules are that you may go through three times, turning over the discard pile each time to form a new stock. Some turn up the cards three at a time. In this case, only the top card of the three turned up may be played, but if it is played the next may be played, and so on. Even if you go through the stock an unlimited number of times, you will seldom get all the cards played to the foundations.

Canfield takes its name from Richard Canfield, a famous gambler in New York City more than fifty years ago. A more correct name for the game is Klondike.

Solomon

Solomon was a king of ancient Israel, almost three thousand years ago. He was one of the greatest kings of all time. Most of what we know about him is found in the Bible, in the Books of Samuel, Kings, and Chronicles. Solomon was noted most for his great wisdom. He was the son of Bathsheba and DAVID, about whom there is a separate article.

When Solomon became king he divided Israel into twelve parts, to make it easier to rule such a huge land. At that time, Israel extended from the River Euphrates to the border of Egypt. Solomon was very religious, and he built a splendid

Temple at Jerusalem. There are many stories about Solomon's wisdom. The Book of Kings tells how God offered to give Solomon anything he wanted, and Solomon asked for wisdom.

The writing of certain books of the Bible, including Ecclesiastes, Proverbs, and the Song of Solomon, has been credited to Solomon.

A favorite story about King Solomon tells of a time when two women appeared before him, each claiming to be the mother of the same baby. Solomon said that the baby should be cut in half and one half given to each woman. The real mother said at once that the other woman could have the whole baby; so Solomon knew which was the real mother.

Solomon is considered a great prophet by followers of the Mohammedan religion. See also the article SHEBA.

Solomon Islands

The Solomon Islands are a group of islands in the South Pacific Ocean. There are twelve large islands and many small ones, including atolls. The islands have an area of about 16,000 square miles, and about 170,000 people live there. Most of the natives are Melanesian. The largest island is Bougainville, which with Buka and 600 lesser islands is administered by Australia under a United Nations trusteeship, as part of the Trust Territory of New Guinea. To the east are the islands of the British Protectorate, including Choiseul, New Georgia, Santa Isabel, Guadalcanal, Malaita, San Cristobal, and the Santa Cruz and Shortland Islands. The administrative center of the group is the town of Honiara on Guadalcanal.

The larger islands are of volcanic origin, with high, forested mountains. Many of the smaller islands are low-lying coral atolls. The land is very fertile. Copra is the most important crop. Fishing is very important. Almost the only animals found in the islands are the wild pig and wild dog.

The Solomon Islands were discovered in 1568. They were believed to have rich deposits of gold, and so were named for King Solomon, who was very rich. Japan seized the islands, early in 1942, and built naval bases and airfields. Some of

the greatest battles of the Pacific were fought in and near the Solomons. On August 7, 1942, United States Marines landed on GUADALCANAL, about which there is a separate article, and heavy fighting took place there. Read also the article CORAL SEA.

Solon

Solon was one of ancient Greece's greatest statesmen. He lived more than 2,500 years ago, in the city-state of Athens. He was one of the archons, or chief officers of the state. Solon wrote a new constitution that gave even the poor people a voice in the government. He wrote many wise laws. The most important was called the *Seisachtheia,* which means "shaking off of burdens." This law stopped the system of putting people in prison when they could not pay their debts. Solon's laws were considered so great that he was known as one of the Seven Sages, or Wise Men. Lawmakers are often called "solons" today. Solon was born about 639 B.C. and died about 559 B.C.

solstice

Solstice means "sun standing still." There are two points in the earth's journey around the sun that are called solstices. The summer solstice comes on June 21 and is the longest day of the year. The winter solstice comes on December 22 and is the shortest day in the year.

Ancient peoples thought that the sun moves around the earth. From day to day it seems to change its position in the heavens, sometimes moving toward the equator and sometimes moving away from the equator. On the solstices it seems to change direction and begin moving toward the equator. The two days of the years when the sun is directly over the equator are called EQUINOXES, and there is a separate article about them, with a picture.

In the Southern Hemisphere—for example, in Argentina and Brazil and other South American countries—the winter solstice comes on June 21 and the summer solstice on December 22.

solution

A solution is made of at least two substances—solids, liquids, or gases—that combine so completely that one substance seems to disappear into the other. This substance is said to *dissolve* in the other. For example, if salt is put into water and the water is stirred, the salt grains disappear as they dissolve in the water.

The substance that does the dissolving is called the *solvent.* The substance that dissolves in the other is called the *solute.* Usually there is more of the solvent than of the solute.

KINDS OF SOLUTION

There are three kinds of solution:

Gaseous solutions, in which a gas is dissolved in a gas. Air is a solution. It is oxygen and other gases dissolved in nitrogen gas.

Liquid solutions, in which the solvent is a liquid. The solute may be a gas, a solid, or another liquid. Air, sugar and alcohol can all dissolve in water to form liquid solutions.

Solid solutions, in which a solid or a gas is dissolved in a solid. The chemical element palladium can dissolve hydrogen gas. Very hot iron will dissolve the solid chemical element carbon. Many kinds of rock are solid solutions.

HOW TO KNOW A SOLUTION

How can you tell whether a solid, liquid or gas is really a solution, and not a chemical.

There are two main properties that identify a solution, and both must be seen

together. First, a solution is *homogeneous,* which means that a sample taken from any part of a solution will have exactly the same amounts of solvent and solute as a sample taken from any other part. In this way a solution is different from a mixture, because different parts of a mixture may contain different amounts of the substances that make it up. Second, up to a certain point, or limit, the amounts of solvent and solute may be varied at will. For example, you can dissolve sugar in any amount between a fraction of a grain and several teaspoonfuls in a cup of tea. In this way a solution is different from a chemical compound, because the substances that make up a chemical compound cannot be varied at all.

When a solvent has reached the limit of the amount of solute it will dissolve, we say that the solution is *saturated.*

SUSPENSIONS AND EMULSIONS

If very fine grains of a solid substance are thoroughly mixed in a liquid, the result may look like a solution because all parts seem to have the same composition, but in time the separate grains will settle out. Such a thorough mixture is called a *suspension.* Whitewash is a suspension of lime in water.

When a suspension is made of two liquids that do not dissolve in each other, it is called an *emulsion.* Milk is largely an emulsion of fatty oils in water. In time the fats separate out as cream. No suspension or emulsion is a true solution.

Somalia

Somalia is one of the newest of the African states. It was formed by the union of two former colonies, British Somaliland and Italian Somaliland, and achieved its independence on July 1, 1960. The government is that of a republic, with a National Assembly, a president, and a premier. Aden Abdullah Osman was elected its first president.

In area, Somalia is about the size of Texas. It is located on the spur of east Africa, along the coast that runs from the Gulf of Aden to the Indian Ocean. The land there is very dry and stony, and there is almost no rainfall. Almost the only plant growth is a coarse grass, and livestock grazing is the principal occupation of the nomadic (wandering) people. The country is very poor, with

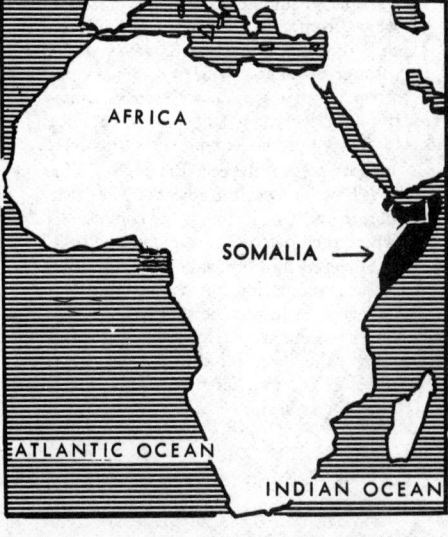

almost no natural resources. Bananas, hides and skins are its principal exports.

SOMALIA. Area, 246,202 square miles. Population (1973 estimate) 2,860,000. Capital, Mogadishu (172,677). Language, Somali. Religion, Moslem. Monetary unit, Somalo.

Somaliland, French. See FRENCH SOMALILAND.

Somervell, Brehon Burke

General Brehon Burke Somervell was commander of the Services of Supply of the United States Army during World War II. Occasionally criticized for his methods, he was nevertheless very successful in keeping our army supplied.

He was born in Little Rock, Arkansas, in 1892, graduated from West Point in 1914, and spent his early years in the Army Corps of Engineers. From 1936 to 1940 he was director of the Works Progress Administration in New York City. Recalled to active duty, he directed the army's program of construction then took over the supply division. He retired after World War II and died in 1955.

Somme

The Somme is a river 150 miles long in northern France. It empties into the English Channel. A ship canal has been built beside the Somme from its mouth to Saint-Quentin. Amiens is the principal city on the Somme.

Important battles of World Wars I and II were fought along the banks of the Somme. The Germans attacked often but did not succeed in capturing the city of Amiens. Early in World War II, in 1940, the Germans won the "battle of France" in the Somme valley, defeating the French armies and forcing France to surrender.

sonar

Sonar is a device that is used to detect the presence and location of enemy submarines, in time of war. Sonar also has peacetime uses.

The principle of sonar is the same as the principle of RADAR, which is described in a separate article. A wave is sent out, and if it strikes anything it sends back an echo. Sonar uses sound waves, while radar uses electrical waves. The electrical waves can be used at a far greater distance, but they cannot be used under water and so they could not detect a submarine that is entirely submerged.

Sonar equipment sends out sound waves from an underwater location on a ship or submarine. Sound waves travel through water at a speed of 4,708 feet per second. If the sound waves strike something under water, they echo (bounce back). The sonar equipment shows how long it takes for the echo to be heard. This tells how far away the object is. The direction from which the echo comes tells where the object is. (See picture below.)

Sonar works both ways in wartime, because a submarine can use it to find an enemy ship, just as the ship can use it to find the submarine. However, it is much more valuable to the ship, because when the ship knows a submarine is nearby it can protect itself.

somnambulism, another name for SLEEPWALKING.

sonata, a musical composition: see the article on MUSIC.

Sons of Liberty

The Sons of Liberty were a secret organization of American patriots in the years before the Revolutionary war. They were against British rule of the American colonies. They took their name from a speech that had been made by Isaac Barré, a British statesman and member of Parliament, in 1765. In this speech Barré called Americans "sons of liberty." The main leaders of the Sons of Liberty were John Lamb and Alexander McDougall in New York and Paul Revere and Samuel Adams in New England. Each colony had its own Sons of Liberty group.

Sophocles

Sophocles was one of three great writers of plays who lived in ancient Greece nearly 2,500 years ago. The other two were Aeschylus, who was older, and Euripides, who was younger. These three wrote great tragedies, or sad plays in which the hero usually dies. Sophocles was born in 496 B.C. As a youth he was famous as a singer and athlete. In Sophocles' time it was the custom for playwrights to compete with one another, and Sophocles won his first great victory over Aeschylus. From that time he was considered the greatest of Greek writers. During his long career, he wrote more than a hundred plays, winning the competition twenty times and never finishing lower than second place. Only seven of his plays have come down to us complete. The most famous of them are *Antigone, Oedipus the King,* and *Electra.*

Sophocles made many contributions to the art of the play. He was the first great playwright to make his characters like real human beings who had to suffer because of their own sins and mistakes. Sophocles became noted for his use of irony: he gave an actor lines to speak that were understood in one sense by the other characters and in an entirely different sense by the audience. Sophocles died in 406 B.C. After his death he was worshiped almost as a god, and a shrine was built to him.

Sorbonne

The Sorbonne is a university in Paris, France. It is one of the oldest and greatest universities of the world. It was founded by a priest named Robert de Sorbon, about seven hundred years ago (probably in the year 1257). For about four hundred years it was a center for the study of religion, but it also had a college for the arts and sciences. After the French Revolution in 1789 (when the French people overthrew their king and set up a republic), the Sorbonne became best known as a college of arts and sciences. Today it is a branch of the University of Paris, which also has schools of medicine, pharmacy, and law.

sorghum

Sorghum is a grasslike plant that is grown in many parts of the world. A sweet juice is taken from it, and its stalks are used as fodder for cattle. There are several varieties of sorghum. A variety grown in the southern United States is the source of sorghum syrup, which many people use as sweetener instead of cane or maple sugars.

sorrel

Sorrel is a leafy plant that is used in salads and as a flavoring in cooking. It is a perennial, which means that it will grow year after year in the same spot without replanting. Sorrel is grown mainly in California and some of the southern states.

There is also a common weed known as sorrel. It bears brownish-red, flat seeds on spiky stalks. This weed is also called *sorrel dock,* or *sheep sorrel.*

sound

The air around us is a gas. The sound that we hear is waves that make the air move and strike our ears. Sound waves are caused by the vibration, or shaking, of something. The voice is caused by vibration of a part of the throat called the larynx; a drumbeat is caused by the vibration of a drumhead stretched over a frame; a musical tone from a piano is caused by the vibration of a string in the piano when it is struck by a hammer.

There is a difference between a sound wave in the air and a movement of air

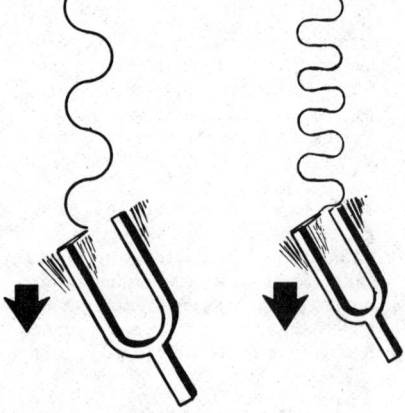

An experiment that shows how sound waves travel: Cover two pieces of glass with soot (by holding a burning match or stick under them). Take two tuning forks of different pitch, and attach a pin to a tine of each fork. Strike one fork and draw the pin across one piece of glass, then do the same with the other fork and the other piece of glass. The fork of lower pitch and frequency will trace fewer waves (a) than will the other fork (b).

such as the wind. When the wind blows, quantities of air actually change their location from one place to another. A sound wave moves through the air but leaves the air where it was.

Sound waves do not move through the air in a straight line. They *oscillate,* or go back and forth in a zigzag. The waves travel through the air at about 1,087 feet per second, but there can be a great difference in the number of changes in direction, or oscillations, they make in the process. The sound that we hear depends largely on this number, which is called the *frequency* of the sound wave. Low frequency (very few vibrations per second) usually produces a low sound and high frequency (many vibrations) a high sound. The human ear can usually hear as few as 40 vibrations per second and as

many as 18,000 or even 20,000 vibrations per second. "Hi-fi" (high-fidelity) recordings and record-players are those that give the greatest possible range of these sounds that we are capable of hearing. (Some members of the animal kingdom can hear sounds that human beings cannot. There are dog whistles of such high frequency that to the human ear they sound noiseless but they bring the dog running.)

DIFFERENCES IN SOUND

The different frequencies produce differences in *pitch*. These differences are what make one musical note different from another. But there is also a difference between a note played on a violin, the same note played on a piano, the same note played on a trumpet, and so on. These are differences in the *quality*, or *timbre*, of the sound.

The reason for these differences is that very few sounds come to us as sound waves all of the same frequency. In addition to the main sound waves, there are others that have a higher frequency. These are called *overtones*. We seldom realize that we hear these overtones, but they are strong enough to make the difference in what we hear.

There is also a great difference in the loudness, or *intensity*, of the sounds we hear. This is a question of the *amplitude* of the sound wave—the distance it travels each time it zigs or zags in its course. The amplitude is measured from the midway line to the point at which it changes direction. The loudness of a tone is expressed in units called *decibels*. The more decibels, the louder the sound we hear.

ACOUSTICS

Acoustics is the name for the science of sound; it is also a word generally used for the "listening qualities" of a particular room or place. More about sound is explained in the article on ACOUSTICS.

Sousa, John Philip

John Philip Sousa was a famous bandleader and the composer of some of

America's most popular military marches. He wrote about a hundred marches. Among them are such favorites as *Semper Fidelis*, *The Washington Post March*, *The Stars and Stripes Forever*, and *Hands Across the Sea*. He was called "The March King."

Sousa was born in 1854 in Washington, D.C. His father was a member of the United States Marine Band and Sousa studied as an apprentice to the band. He conducted theater orchestras, then served as leader of the Marine Band for twelve years. In 1892 he formed his own band with which he toured the United States, Canada, and later the world. Sousa also wrote several comic operas. He died in 1932.

sousaphone, a large brass band instrument. See MUSICAL INSTRUMENTS.

South African Tourist Corporation
A Bantu drummer of South Africa.

South Africa

The Republic of South Africa is one of the independent nations of Africa and is the oldest settled outpost of Western civilization on the continent. It is at the southern tip of Africa, with coasts on the Atlantic and Indian oceans. The country has an area of almost 500,000 square miles, about ten times the size of the state of New York, but only about nineteen million people live there, slightly more than live in New York State. It is the most highly-developed country of Africa, both in manufacturing and in the development of its great natural resources, and has better communications than any other part of Africa.

The Republic of South Africa, until 1961, was a self-governing member of the British Commonwealth of Nations. The country left the Commonwealth after the white population, in a referendum held in 1960, voted for proclaiming South Africa a republic. This was done largely because of the opposition of the other Commonwealth nations to South Africa's racial policies, which maintain the strict separation of the races and keep the white people in control of the government. The name of the country, which had been Union of South Africa, was then changed.

The lovely blossom of the protea bush is the national flower of South Africa.

THE PEOPLE OF SOUTH AFRICA

Four main groups of people live in the Republic of South Africa. The largest group, making up about two-thirds of the entire population, are the native Africans, most of whom are members of the Bantu section of the Negro race. There are more than twelve million of them.

The second-largest group are the Whites, descendants of the settlers who came to Africa from many countries (not necessarily European ones). Most of them are of Dutch and English descent. The Dutch outnumber the English about three to two. Together they represent more than three million people, about one-fifth of the entire population.

The third-largest group is made up of people called "Colored." They are of mixed descent as a result of marriages between Whites and Bantus or other dark-skinned people. There are nearly two million "Colored" people.

The fourth-largest group is the Asiatic or Indian group, numbering about 561,000. It includes descendants of Indians and Malays who were brought to Africa as slaves during the 1800s. The Malays are also known as "Cape Malays."

The first settlement was made by the Dutch in 1652, about three hundred years ago. The earliest settlers had no contact with the Bantu tribes. The only natives they met were Bushmen and Hottentots, nomadic (wandering) peoples, most of whom were later killed in wars with the Bantu tribes. About 150 years later the colonists pushed farther north and the Bantu came farther south. Though they fought each other at first, after a short time they lived in peace, with the Bantu living in outlying regions and the Europeans in the settled areas.

Since most of the White settlers were Dutch and English, the country today has two official languages, Afrikaans and English. There is a separate article about AFRIKAANS. It is much like the Dutch language, but over the years the Dutch settlers have changed it somewhat and have added many new words. The native tribes have their own languages, but almost everyone in the country speaks one of the official languages, and many people speak both.

In the past there has been some conflict between the White and native groups. The present government is following a policy called *apartheid*, which means about the same thing that *segregation* means in the United States. The white and native people are kept apart in almost every way. The Whites have the control over the country.

The people follow several different religions. Most of the Whites are Protestant,

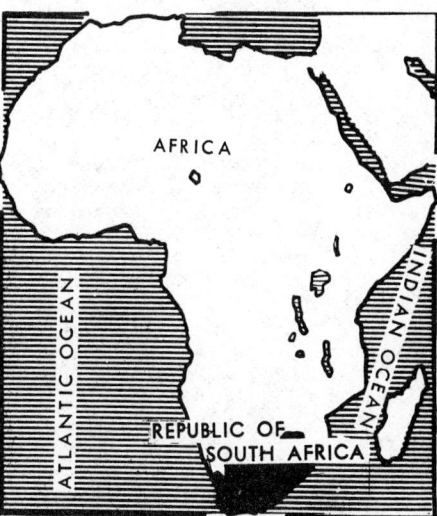

AFRICA

ATLANTIC OCEAN

INDIAN OCEAN

REPUBLIC OF SOUTH AFRICA

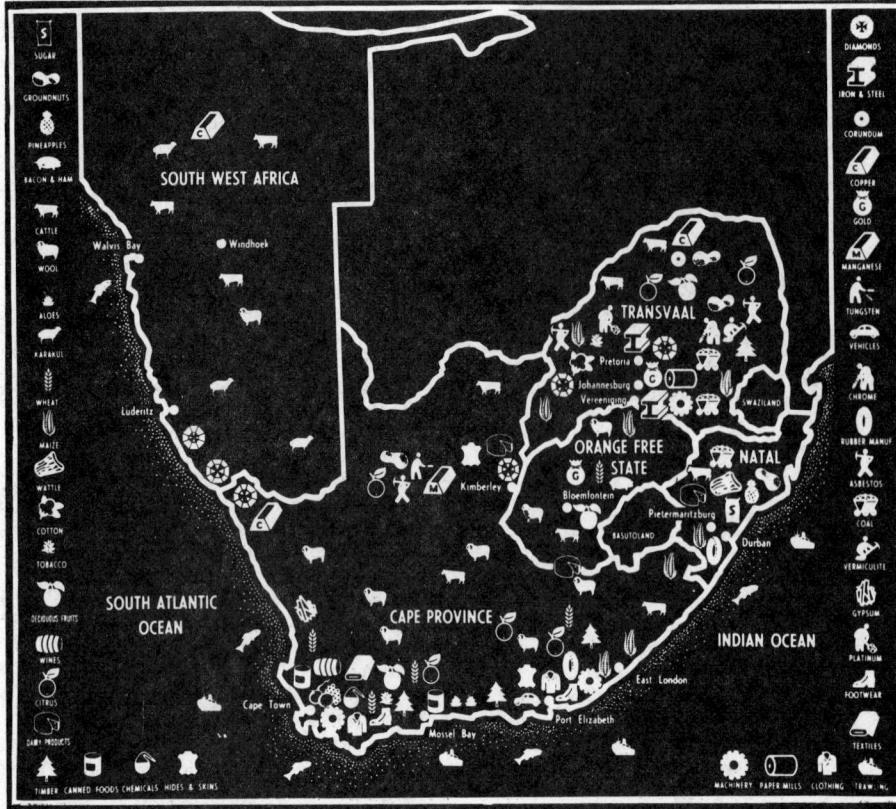

as are the people of mixed descent. The Malays and Indians are chiefly Hindus or Moslem (followers of the religion of Mohammed). The Bantu and other native peoples follow their ancient tribal religions, though many of them have been converted to Christianity.

HOW THE PEOPLE LIVE

More than half of the Whites live in large cities such as Johannesburg and Cape Town, but most of the other people, including the Bantus, live in the country and make their livings by farming. The principal crops are maize (corn), wheat, groundnuts (peanuts), potatoes, sugar cane, fruit, and tobacco.

Most of the fertile farm land is near the coasts, and the interior has plains and prairies well-suited for grazing. Large numbers of sheep are raised and their wool is an important product.

The country is rich in minerals, especially gold, uranium, and diamonds. Gold was first found in 1886, and today nearly eight hundred million dollars' worth is produced each year. Most of the country's forty-five big gold mines are near Johannesburg, in a section called the Witwatersrand (meaning "ridge of white waters"). This is the busiest industrial and commercial area.

Diamonds were first discovered in 1871, in the famous Kimberley mines, and are still a great source of wealth. Today the country has a special laboratory in which scientists are finding new uses for diamonds (other than in jewelry). The first uranium plant was opened in 1952, and many more have been established since then. There is a large supply of coal, large enough to serve the country's need for hundreds of years. A new industry that employs many people is refining oil from coal, to make gasoline. The steel industry also is very important.

During the past fifty years much has been done to make South Africa a modern industrial nation, but there are still native peoples who follow the ways of their ancestors, about which you can read in the article on AFRICA. Some of the Bantus work in nearby mines and cities for six months of each year, and return to their homes for the remaining six months.

Much of the development of the country has been achieved through education. The central government is in charge of universities and colleges and the governments of the four provinces control elementary and high schools. All children of White parents must go to school between the ages of 7 and 16. Both English and Afrikaans are taught. There are 11 universities in the Republic of South Africa, and several trade and technical colleges. The University of Witwatersrand specializes in mining; Stellenbosch and Pretoria in agriculture; and Cape Town in fine arts. Average enrollment in these universities exceeds 30,000 students. There are separate schools and colleges for non-whites. Primary education is free.

WHAT THE LAND IS LIKE

Most people think of Africa as being hot, moist jungle, but the Republic of South Africa has none at all. Most of the country is a plateau (high, level land) more than 3,000 feet high. There are three general regions. Along the coast the land is fertile and flat. This coastal belt is separated from the interior by high mountain ranges, including the Drakenberg, Langeberg, and Swartberg ranges, with the two highest peaks almost 11,000 feet high.

Beyond the mountains lie the large central plateaus. The innermost and high-est plateau is called the Northern Karoo, or Highveld, with an average height of 4,000 to 6,000 feet. Most of this plateau is dry prairie.

Farther north is the low Veld, where many people hunt for lions and other wild game, and the eastern coastal region of the province of Natal.

There are no large rivers. The Orange River rises in the east and flows west across the central plateau to the Atlantic Ocean. On it are the Aughrabies Falls, which are more than twice as high as Niagara Falls.

Kruger National Park is the main wildlife area. It is about the size of the state of Massachusetts, with an area of about 8,000 square miles. Most of it is flat bush prairie, called *veld*, with some hills and high rocky places called *kopjes*. Here roam the big game of Africa—lions, leopards, giraffes, elephants, black rhinoceroses, and buffaloes. There are also hyenas, jackals, civets, baboons, monkeys, zebras, and many kinds of antelope. The streams in the park are a home for the hippopotamus and crocodile. There are strict game laws that visitors must obey, so that the animals are protected for all of the year. The park also has many interesting birds.

Lumber is scarce in the Republic of South Africa. There are some natural forests near the southern coast. The trees are stinkwood, yellow-wood, sneeze-wood, wagon-wood, ironwood, and Assegaiwood (from which the natives make spears). All of these trees grow very slowly and reach a great height, some being more than a thousand years old and almost 300 feet high. To make up for the lack of forests, about eighty years ago the government started a big program of tree planting, and there are now about 3,000,000 acres of forest reserves, of which more than half are state-owned.

The climate is dry and temperate. The average yearly rainfall is about 17½ inches, but many areas receive less than 10 inches a year. It rarely snows, nor does it get very hot.

HOW THE PEOPLE ARE GOVERNED

The Republic of South Africa has four provinces, but they are not federated as are the provinces of Canada or the states of the United States. This means that the central government has more power than any of the provincial governments. The provinces are Cape Province, Transvaal, Orange Free State, and Natal. In addition, the Republic of South Africa administers South-West Africa, a former German colony which was surrendered to South Africa during World War I. (The capital of South-West Africa is Windhoek.) After the war, South Africa administered it as a League of Nations mandate and continued to administer it after the League was dissolved. In 1966 the United Nations General Assembly declared that the mandate was ended, and it established a United Nations Council to administer South-West Africa until it could become independent. In 1968 the United Nations General Assembly proclaimed that South-West Africa should be renamed Namibia. South Africa, however, would not recognize the United Nations as the legal successor to the League of Nations, declared that the removal of the mandate was an

All of the following animals are found wild in South Africa

HIPPOPOTAMUSES

LION

HYENA

CHEETAH

LEOPARD WITH DEAD MONKEY

GEMSBOK

WILDEBEEST

province in the Parliament. In addition each one has an administrator, who is appointed by the State President, and a four-member executive committee. All members of the provincial governments are elected for five-year terms.

There are three capitals. Pretoria, the administrative capital, is headquarters of the President, Prime Minister, and Executive Council. Capetown, the legislative capital, is where the Parliament meets. Bloemfontein, the judicial capital, is where the courts of final appeal are located.

CHIEF CITIES OF SOUTH AFRICA

The leading cities of the Republic of South Africa, with populations from the 1973 estimate, are:

Bloemfontein, population 145,273, judicial capital of the country, provincial capital of Orange Free State.

Cape Town or Capetown, population 691,296, legislative capital of the country, capital of Cape Province, second-largest city.

Durban, population 721,265, third-largest city, important seaport and commercial center.

East London, population 116,056, commercial center for rich farming region and major seaport.

Johannesburg, population 1,432,643, largest city in the country and principal commercial center. There is a separate article about JOHANNESBURG.

Port Elizabeth, population 290,693, industrial center and seaport.

Pretoria, population 561,703, administrative capital of the country, capital of Transvaal, seat of government offices and educational institutions.

SOUTH AFRICA IN THE PAST

The first European settlement in South Africa was made more than three hundred years ago, in 1652, when the Dutch East India Company established a post for company ships at the Cape of Good Hope. During the next two hundred years many Dutch colonists went there to make their homes. The first English settlement was made in 1806, and more were made during the next few years. They joined the Dutch in fighting the natives. However, the Dutch were soon dissatisfied with English policies, and moved farther inland. So many moved north that this came to be called the Great Trek. Though many settlers were killed in wars with unfriendly natives, they did establish the communities that later became the provinces of the Orange Free State and the Transvaal. In 1843 the British claimed another state, Natal (in addition to Cape Province), and soon afterward the Transvaal and Orange Free State were recognized as Dutch republics.

There were some quarrels between the Dutch and English, but on the whole relations were friendly until 1867, when diamonds were discovered in the Orange Free State. This led to a boundary dispute between it and the British Cape Colony. In 1877 the British government claimed control of the Transvaal. This caused an uprising, and four years later it again became a free republic. More problems were created by the discovery of gold in the Transvaal in 1886. The quarrels grew more heated until, in 1899, war broke out. This war, the Boer War, is described in the article BOER.

"illegal act", and continues to administer the area. In 1969, 40 members of the United Nations requested a meeting to examine the whole situation, which at present is still in dispute.

The laws of South Africa are made by a Parliament consisting of two branches, the Senate and the House of Assembly. Both houses elect the State President, who serves for a term of seven years and has the power to convene and dissolve the Parliament. The Senate consists of 54 members, 43 of whom are elected from the provinces and from South-West Africa. The remaining 11 senators are nominated by the State President. The House

of Assembly is the more important of the two houses, since it proposes most laws and controls all the finances. Its 170 members are elected from the four provinces and South-West Africa. Only white people can become members of the Parliament.

The Prime Minister is the leader of the party that has the most members in the House of Assembly. He appoints a cabinet and an Executive Council, each of whose members has charge of one of the government departments.

Each province has a lawmaking body called the Provincial Council, which has about as many members as represent the

The treaty that ended the Boer War made the Boers accept British rule for the time being, with the hope of becoming self-governing very soon. In 1906 both the Transvaal and Orange Free State became independent, but the colonies soon wanted to unite and in 1910 the Union of South Africa was set up as a dominion of the British Commonwealth.

In World Wars I and II, South Africa took part on the side of Great Britain. After the war, in 1945, it became a charter member of the United Nations. In the Korean War it contributed a fighter squadron to the United Nations forces in Korea.

You can read more about the country's history in articles about some of its famous men, Paul KRUGER, Louis BOTHA, and Jan SMUTS.

REPUBLIC OF SOUTH AFRICA. Area 472,359 square miles. Population (1973 estimate) 22,090,000. Language, Afrikaans, English, native languages. Religion, chiefly Protestant. Government, republic. Capitals, Pretoria, Cape Town, and Bloemfontein. Monetary unit, the Rand, worth $1.40 (U.S.). Flag, three horizontal bands, orange, white, and blue; Union Jack, Orange Free State flag and Transvaal *Vierkleur* in center of white band.

South America

South America is the fourth-largest continent in the world. It is in the southern part of the Western Hemisphere and is between the Atlantic and Pacific Oceans. At the north it is joined to Central and North America by the narrow strip of land known as the Isthmus of Panama. At the south it ends at the tiny island of Cape Horn.

South America has an area of about 6,800,000 square miles. It is a little smaller than North America. There are more than 160,000,000 people living in South America.

South America was discovered a few years before North America. Before the arrival of the Spaniards and Portuguese about four hundred years ago, only Indians lived there. When people in Europe started moving to the Americas, they called them the "New World."

COUNTRIES OF SOUTH AMERICA

There are ten independent republics in South America, and three colonies of European countries. The republics are Argentina, Bolivia, Brazil, Chile, Colombia, Ecuador, Paraguay, Peru, Uruguay, and Venezuela. The colonies are British Guiana, Dutch Guiana (Surinam), and French Guiana.

Some parts of South America are very thickly populated, and in other parts there are almost no people at all. The jungles of the lowlands are so dense that it is almost impossible to get through them. Parts of the great mountains are unfit for human life, but some of the continent's most important centers of population are high in the Andes Mountains.

THE PEOPLE OF SOUTH AMERICA

The Indians who lived in South America before the coming of the white man had their own great civilizations. There were two principal groups of Indians, the Incas of Peru and the Chibchas of Colom-

bia. The Spanish and Portuguese settlers gradually intermarried and mixed with the Indians, and the great majority of South American peoples today are partly or wholly Indian descent. A small number of Negroes from Africa were brought as slaves to South America. Among modern South Americans of mixed stocks there are *mestizos,* who are part white and part Indian, and *zambos,* who are part Indian and part Negro.

In recent years millions of Europeans have emigrated to South America, including Italians, Spaniards, Portuguese, and Germans. There are also Japanese and other peoples from the Far East.

South America in general is a land of the very rich and the very poor. Much of the wealth is owned by foreign business firms and by a small "upper class," most of whom are of European descent. The mestizos, zambos and Indians are poor.

Spanish is the official language of all the South American republics except Brazil, where Portuguese is spoken.

WHAT THE CONTINENT IS LIKE

The land of South America is extremely varied. The Andes Mountains extend for 4,000 miles down the entire west coast. They are the second-longest mountain chain in the world and contain the highest peaks in the Western Hemisphere, including Aconcagua, which rises to 23,081 feet. Also in the Andes is the world's highest lake Titicaca, at an altitude of 12,507 feet. In the east is the great plateau (high but level region) of Brazil, which contains most of South America's mineral wealth and much of its best agricultural lands. To the south, Argentina has the greatest unbroken stretches of fertile farm land in the world. Between the Andes and the plateau are vast lowlands that are almost uninhabited and have not even been fully explored.

South America has great rivers. The Amazon system with its many tributaries is one of the largest in the world. Others are the Orinoco and the Plata. The basin of the Amazon river system has one of the world's greatest expanses of forests, which produce rubber, Brazil nuts, and cinchona, from which quinine is

made. The pampas, or plain, of Argentina is one of the greatest grain- and cattle-raising regions. Most of the people of the continent are farmers or livestock raisers. The continent produces great quantities of coffee, grain, meat, and timber. There are great mineral deposits, which are being only partly exploited. Much petroleum is produced and refined, especially in Venezuela. Iron, manganese, diamonds, copper, asphalt, tin and many other minerals are mined.

South America has great variations in climate, although three-quarters of it lies in the tropics. In the lowlands it is hot throughout the year, but in the uplands and the mountains it is always cool. The people are often grouped more by the climate of their region than by their race, as hot-country or cold-country people. The seasons are the opposite of those in North America. The summer months are from December to February and the winter months are from June to August. The greatest rainfall is in the Amazon River basin, where the forests are constantly drenched, and in southern Chile. There is a strip of desert land on the west coast running from northern Chile into southern Ecuador.

The animal life of South America is notable for its birds, insects, and reptiles. The jungles are full of brilliantly colored birds such as flamingoes, toucans, and parrots, and of huge and beautiful butterflies. There are alligators, boa constrictors, and turtles. Among the wild animals the most dangerous is the jaguar. The llama and the alpaca, which are related to the camel, are the only native South American animals that have been put to domestic use. There were no horses, cattle, or sheep in South America when the first Europeans came nearly 500 years ago, but now there are many.

South Carolina

South Carolina is one of the South Atlantic states in the United States. It was one of the thirteen original sates. Its nickname is the "Palmetto State" because of the many palmetto trees found there. Carolina was named after King Charles I of England.

In area, South Carolina is one of the smaller states, ranking 40th with 31,055 square miles. In population it ranks 26th, with more than two million people living there. South Carolina became a state in 1776, and was the eighth of the thirteen original states to ratify the United States Constitution. The capital is Columbia.

THE PEOPLE OF SOUTH CAROLINA

Spanish and French people founded the first colonies in South Carolina, but they were unsuccessful. The first permanent colony, at Charleston, was established by the English. Later many German, Swiss, Scotch-Irish and Welsh people settled there. About 830,000 Negroes now live in South Carolina. Before World War II, they made up almost half of the population, but since that time many of them have moved to northern cities.

Three-quarters of the people of South Carolina live in country areas, and most of them are farmers. The state ranks fourth in the production of tobacco. Other im-

Wax
Petroleum
Rubber
Mining
Cotton
Coffee
Sheep
Cattle

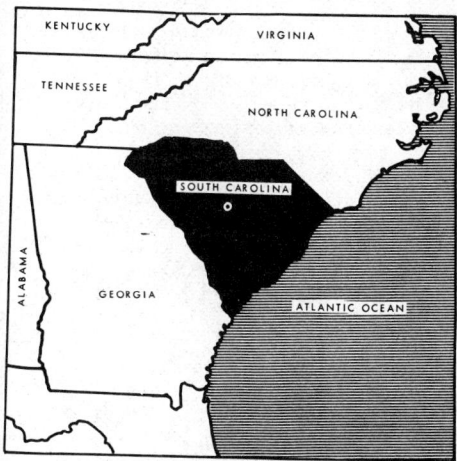

portant crops are corn, cotton, peaches, grains, and peanuts. Many of the farmers raise cattle, hogs, and poultry. Forests cover more than half of South Carolina, and lumber industries rank second only to cotton milling. Other important industries are food-processing, mining, and the making of metal products. There is a great United States atomic-energy plant on the Savannah River in the west.

The largest religious group in South Carolina is the Baptists. Other large groups are Methodists and Presbyterians.

WHAT SOUTH CAROLINA IS LIKE

The eastern two-thirds of South Carolina is a coastal plain, about half of which is forest. There is a belt of swampland along the coast, and offshore there is a series of islands that were built up over the centuries by silt carried out to sea by the rivers. These are called the Sea Islands, and they extend all the way down the coast to northern Florida.

The land rises gradually to the piedmont region in the northwest and to the Blue Ridge Mountains in the northwest corner of the state. A piedmont is high land at the base of mountains.

There are three principal rivers in South Carolina, the Pee Dee, Santee, and Savannah.

All of these rivers rise in the Blue Ridge Mountains and empty into the Atlantic Ocean. Through the piedmont region the rivers are swift and they have been dammed to provide hydroelectric power.

Several lakes, including Lakes Murray, Moultrie, and Wateree Pond, have been formed by the dams.

The climate of South Carolina is warm and humid, with long, hot summers and short, mild winters. Snow falls only in the upper piedmont and mountain regions. Rainfall is evenly distributed. The state's average temperature in winter is about 48 degrees and in summer about 80 degrees.

THE GOVERNMENT

South Carolina, like most states, has a Governor at the head of the government and a Legislature that makes the laws. The Governor is elected for a four-year term, and may not serve two terms in succession. The Legislature is composed of two houses, a Senate and a House of Representatives. The members of both houses are elected for two-year terms. Supreme Court judges are elected for ten-year terms. There are 46 counties.

The total enrollment in the public schools is about 648,000 students. Among the principal colleges and universities are:

University of South Carolina, at Columbia. Enrollment, 14,931 in 1971 (co-ed).

Clemson Agricultural College, at Clemson. Enrollment, 6,835 in 1971 (co-ed).

Bob Jones University, at Greenville. Enrollment, 3,545 in 1971 (co-ed).

South Carolina State College, at Orangeburg. Enrollment, 2,436 in 1971 (co-ed).

Medical College of South Carolina, at Charleston. Enrollment, 1,021 in 1971 (co-ed).

Winthrop College, at Rock Hill. Enrollment, 3,263 in 1971 (women only).

The Citadel—The Military College of South Carolina, at Charleston. Enrollment, 2,550 in 1971 (men only).

CHIEF CITIES OF SOUTH CAROLINA

The leading cities of South Carolina, with populations from the 1970 census, are:

Columbia, population 113,542, the state capital and largest city. There is a separate article about COLUMBIA.

Greenville, population 61,208, the third-largest city, manufacturing center, in the northwestern part of the state.

Charleston, population 66,945, second-largest city. There is a separate article about CHARLESTON.

Spartanburg, population 44,546, fourth-largest city, a textile center, in the northwestern part of the state.

SOUTH CAROLINA IN THE PAST

The first white men to visit the region of South Carolina, more than four hundred years ago, were Spaniards. They founded a colony, and so did a group of French Huguenots, but neither group stayed. The first permanent settlement was in 1670, when an Englishman named William Sayle and 200 colonists founded Charleston. By 1729 South Carolina had become a crown colony of Great Britain.

The South Carolina settlements were prosperous from the first. Rice and indigo were grown and the farms developed so rapidly that Negro slaves were imported until they outnumbered the whites 4 to 3. As the Revolutionary War neared, the people of South Carolina at first remained loyal to the British king, because much of their prosperity came from exports to England and most of the people were rich and aristocratic. Finally, dissatisfaction with the heavy taxes brought South Carolina into the war against Great Britain. In the Revolutionary War South Carolina contributed such great military leaders as Francis Marion and Andrew Pickens.

In 1860, South Carolina was the first state to secede from the Union and join the Confederacy, and the first shots of the Civil War were fired at Fort Sumter in Charleston harbor. General Sherman led his army across South Carolina in his famous "march to the sea," and left ruined lands behind him. After the war was over, South Carolina refused to adopt the Fourteenth Amendment to the Constitution, which established the citizenship of Negroes, and for twelve years the state had a military government. Finally the state was readmitted to the Union. Its agriculture was almost ruined by the Civil War, but after South Carolina turned more to industry it began to prosper again.

PLACES TO SEE IN SOUTH CAROLINA

Kings Mountain National Military Park, 4,012 acres, 40 miles northwest of Spartanburg, on U.S. Route 321. Site of an important Colonial victory in the Revolutionary War.

Cowpens National Battlefield, 1 acre, 8 miles northwest of Spartanburg, on U.S. alternate Route 29. Site of Revolutionary War battle.

Castle Pinckney National Monument, 4 acres, on an island in Charleston harbor, near U.S. Route 17. Confederate stronghold in Civil War.

Fort Sumter, 2 acres, on a sandbar in Charleston harbor, near U.S. Route 17. Site of the first shots of the Civil War.

Cheraw State Park, 7,361 acres, on a lake near Cheraw in the northeast, on U.S. Route 1.

Gardens famous for their beauty, near Charleston (on U.S. Route 1), and Georgetown on Winyah Bay (on U.S. Route 17).

SOUTH CAROLINA. Area, 31,055 square miles. Population (1970 census) 2,590,516. Capital, Columbia. Nickname, Palmetto State. Motto, *Dum Spiro Spero* (While I Breathe, I Hope). Flower, yellow jasmine. Bird, Carolina wren. Song, "Carolina." Admitted to Union, May 23, 1788. Official abbreviation, S.C.

South Dakota

South Dakota is a state in the great plains of the United States. Its nickname is the "Coyote State." It is also called the "Sunshine State." The state is named for the Dakota Indians who used to live in the region.

In area, South Dakota ranks 16th among the states, with 77,047 square miles. In population it ranks 45th, with about 666,000 people living there. It became a state in 1889 and was the 40th state admitted to the United States. The capital is Pierre.

THE PEOPLE OF SOUTH DAKOTA

The first white settlers in the region of South Dakota were French fur trappers and traders. The first farming settlements were made in the 1850s by people from Minnesota and Iowa, from the Scandinavian countries, and from France, Germany, Russia, and the Netherlands. In 1960 South Dakota had the sixth-largest Indian population in the United States, with more than 25,000 Indians living there. Most of them are Sioux. There are five Indian reservations in the state.

About half the people of South Dakota are farmers. They have large farms and use modern, power-driven machinery. South Dakota is one of the leading states in the growing of rye, wheat, corn, oats, barley, and in raising cattle. Corn, oats and hay are grown for animal feed. There are many dairy farms, and sheep and hogs are also raised.

In the cities, the most important factories are meat-packing plants, plants that make butter and other dairy products, and large flour mills. There are also factories that make farm tools and equipment, and wood products.

South Dakota is rich in mineral resources, most of them lying in the Black

Mount Rushmore, the largest work of art in the world.

Hills. The state leads the United States in the production of gold. Other minerals mined are precious stones, silver, feldspar, manganese, and lithium.

WHAT SOUTH DAKOTA IS LIKE

The eastern part of South Dakota is a rolling plain, with few trees but with very fertile soil. It is one of the most important farming regions in the United States. At the western edge of the plain, South Dakota is cut in half by the Missouri River. On the west side of the river is high land that includes the famous Badlands, a region of strange rock towers and columns. In the southwest are the Black Hills, which are heavily forested and supply much lumber.

Many wild animals live in the forests of the Black Hills, including elk and deer, beaver, porcupine, squirrel, raccoon, and bobcat. In the eastern section are found the badger, weasel, skunk, muskrat, and gopher. There are still many coyotes in the western part of the state. Pheasant hunting in the eastern part of the state attracts many vacationists.

South Dakota has long, cold winters with heavy snow and blizzards. The summers are short but hot. The air is very dry and summer days are long and sunny. The temperature goes as high as 115 degrees in summer and as low as 43 degrees below zero in winter, but it is seldom so cold.

GOVERNMENT OF SOUTH DAKOTA

South Dakota, like other states, has a governor to head the government and a Legislature that makes the laws. The Governor is elected for a two-year term and may not serve more than two terms in succession. The Legislature is composed of two houses, a Senate and a House of Representatives. The members of both houses are elected for six-year terms. The capital is Pierre. There are 67 counties.

There are about 166,000 pupils attending public elementary and high schools. Among the principal colleges and universities of South Dakota are:

University of South Dakota, at Vermillion. Enrollment, 5,072 in 1971 (co-ed).

South Dakota State College of Agriculture and Mechanic Arts, at Brookings. Enrollment, 5,528 in 1971 (co-ed).

South Dakota School of Mines and Technology, at Rapid City. Enrollment, 1,599 in 1971 (co-ed).

Dakota Wesleyan University, at Mitchell. Enrollment, 785 in 1971 (co-ed).

CHIEF CITIES OF SOUTH DAKOTA

The leading cities of South Dakota, with populations from the 1970 census, are:

Sioux Falls, population 72,488, the largest city in the state. There is a separate article about SIOUX FALLS.

Rapid City, population 43,836, second-largest city, a resort and trade center, in the west.

Aberdeen, population 26,476, third-largest city, a rail and distribution center, in the northeast.

Huron, population 14,299, fourth-largest city, a trade and shipping center, in the east central part.

Pierre, population 9,699, the capital of the state. There is a separate article about PIERRE.

SOUTH DAKOTA IN THE PAST

The first white man to explore the Dakota region, more than two hundred years ago, was a French-Canadian named Pierre de la Vérendrye. Fur-traders set up trading posts, one of which was named Fort Pierre. In 1803 the United States acquired the territory as part of the Louisiana Purchase. The first permanent farming settlement was established at Sioux Falls around 1857, but settlers came slowly because of Indian raids, droughts, and insect plagues. The Gold Rush began in the 1870s, and the towns of Deadwood and Lead grew up as gold-mining centers. There were constant wars with the Sioux Indians, during one of which General George Custer was killed in the Battle of the Little Bighorn.

Until 1889 there was only one Dakota territory. Then Congress passed an act permitting the territory to divide into two states, and North and South Dakota were admitted to the Union in 1889.

Heavy droughts and dust storms in the 1920s and 1930s caused great suffering for the farmers. It was also a time of very low prices. Many farmers gave up their lands and went to other states. In more recent years, irrigation and soil conservation have helped the farmers.

PLACES TO SEE IN SOUTH DAKOTA

Badlands National Monument, 192 square miles, 64 miles east of Rapid City, on U.S. alternate Route 16. Strange rock formations and many animal fossils.

Custer State Park, 128,000 acres, 30 miles southwest of Rapid City, on U.S. Route 16. One of the largest state parks in the United States, with beautiful Black Hills scenery.

Mount Rushmore National Memorial, 1,220 acres, in Black Hills 17 miles southwest of Rapid City, near U.S. Route 16. Giant sculptures of Presidents Washington, Jefferson, Lincoln, and Theodore Roosevelt.

Wind Cave National Park, 41 square miles, 10 miles north of Hot Springs, on U.S. alternate Route 75. Limestone cavern and buffalo preserve.

Deadwood, old gold-mining town, in the west, on U.S. Route 85. The place where the famous "Wild West" figures Wild Bill Hickok, Calamity Jane and Deadwood Dick are buried.

Homestake Gold Mine, at Lead in the west, near U.S. Route 85. Largest gold mine in the Americas.

SOUTH DAKOTA. Area, 77,047 square miles. Population (1970 census) 665,507. Capital, Pierre. Nickname, the Coyote State. Motto, Under God, the people rule. Flower, pasqueflower. Bird, ring-necked pheasant. Song, "Hail, South Dakota." Admitted to Union, November 2, 1889. Abbreviation, S. Dak.

Southeast Asia Treaty Organization

The Southeast Asia Collective Defense Treaty Organization, often called SEATO, is a group of countries that have territories or business in eastern Asia and that agreed in 1954 to coöperate if the Communist countries, China or Soviet Russia, should attack any one of them. The organization was modeled on NATO, the North Atlantic Treaty Organization, in Europe. The first meeting of the SEATO nations was in Manila, the capital of the Philippines, in 1954. Thailand, the United States, Great Britain, France, Pakistan, Australia, New Zealand and the Philippine Republic became members. In 1955 they met at Bangkok, the capital of Thailand, and set up a permanent headquarters there.

Southern Cross

The Southern Cross is a constellation, or group of stars. It cannot be seen in most parts of North America, but throughout the Southern Hemisphere it is bright and easily seen. Navigators have found it valuable for many years, because the line between two of the bright stars points toward the South Pole. The con-

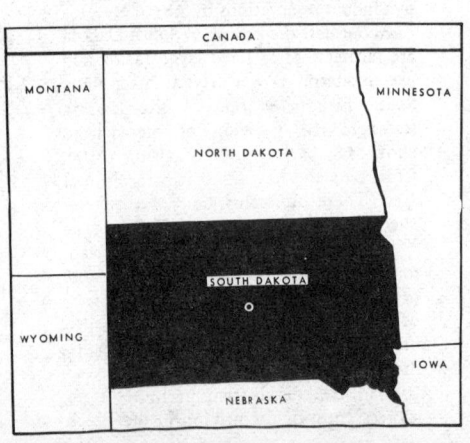

stellation is also called Crux, which means "cross" in Latin.

Southey, Robert

Robert Southey was an English poet and historian who lived about 200 years ago. Millions of students in schools have read his short poems "The Battle of Blenheim" and "Inchcape Rock." Southey was born in 1774. During his college years he was considered a radical in politics and he sympathized with the aims of the French Revolution. Later he became more conservative and joined the Tory Party. This caused other poets to criticize him, but the king rewarded him by appointing him poet laureate (in 1813). Southey's historical works and his long epic poems are seldom read, but his biographies of Nelson and Wesley are considered very fine. Southey died in 1843. He, William Wordsworth and Samuel Taylor Coleridge are called the Lake poets because they lived in a part of England where there are many lakes.

South Pole

The South Pole is the southern end of the earth's axis, the imaginary "line" on which it turns around. It lies at the point opposite to the North Pole on the earth's surface. At the South Pole the speed at which the earth turns is zero (at the equator it is about 1,000 miles per hour), and every direction is north. The South Pole is inland on the vast ice-covered continent of Antarctica. It is on a plateau (a high, level region) 10,000 feet above sea level. It was first reached by Roald Amundsen in 1911. See the article ANTARCTICA.

South West Africa

South West Africa, which was renamed Namibia by the United Nations in 1968, is a territory on the southwestern coast of Africa. In size, the area is about twice as large as California. Currently, the territory is under the control of the Republic of South Africa, but their right to rule has been challenged by the United Nations. Important economic activities of the country include diamond mining, fishing, and sheep raising. See the entry on SOUTH AFRICA.

SOUTH WEST AFRICA, territory ruled by the Republic of South Africa. Area, 317,836 square miles. Population (1973 estimate) 650,000. Capital, Windhoek.

Soviet

A soviet, in Russia, is a council or lawmaking body. For hundreds of years the citizens of Russian towns and farming communities met in soviets, which were very much like the town meetings of New England villages in the United States. They talked over community problems and made rules for everyone to follow.

In the big cities, the workers in the factories had their soviets, or group meetings, which were much like the meetings of members of labor unions in the United States. These workers' soviets were the first supporters of the revolutionary Bol-

sheviks (now called Communists) who won control of Russia in 1917. The Communists called their official assemblies soviets, and later they divided the vast Russian Empire into states called Soviet Socialist Republics.

Now the official name for the entire Communist nation of Russian and other countries is Union of Soviet Socialist Republics, and most people speak of the whole country as the Soviet Union, or Soviet Russia.

Each division of the Soviet Union has its own soviet. Each of these soviets sends delegates, or representatives, to a higher soviet. The principal soviet, which meets in the capital city of Moscow, is called the Supreme Soviet. Actually the members of the soviets have no power to pass laws or to make decisions unless they are instructed or permitted to do so by the heads of the Communist Party. See UNION OF SOVIET SOCIALIST REPUBLICS.

soybean

Soybean is a plant that came originally from eastern Asia and is now an important source of food and industrial material in all parts of the world. It is grown in the United States for cattle feed and as a cover crop, which means that it is planted to nourish the soil and keep it in place between plantings of other crops. Soybean plants often grow as high as six feet. Soybean pods are brown and hairy-looking.

Soybeans contain a larger percentage of protein than most other vegetables, so soy beans are sometimes eaten as a substitute for meat. Some people cook soybeans as a vegetable like peas or lima beans. The dried beans can be ground into meal and used to make loaves or patties that are baked or fried and served in place of meat loaves or ground-beef patties. Still other uses of soybeans as food include roasted, salted appetizers of soybeans instead of peanuts or popcorn, and shredded soybeans in some dry cereals for added flavor and extra protein.

People who have eaten in Chinese restaurants are familiar with the dark brown, salty liquid that is usually on the table, to be used for seasoning. This is soy sauce, another product of the soybean.

space, the largely unknown, vast region beyond the earth's atmosphere. See the article SPACE TRAVEL, following this, and also ARTIFICIAL SATELLITE.

space travel

To a person living on earth, "space" is the vast region in which one is so far from any heavenly body—the sun, the earth, or any planet or moon—that he is not affected by the gravitational pull of these big bodies and does not have to overcome the resistance of an atmosphere. (See GRAVITATION and ATMOSPHERE.)

In space there is nothing solid, not even the particles that make up the air we breathe and the gas we burn in our stoves. These particles are so tiny we cannot see them, but they are so real that airplanes weighing hundreds of tons can "ride" on them, and friction with them can create so much heat that meteors entering the earth's atmosphere at high speeds usually burn up long before they can reach the earth. When there is no friction and no effective gravitational pull, an object traveling in space can keep going almost forever, at speeds so great they can approach the speed of light. (See FRICTION and INERTIA.)

Space travel is the voyaging of vehicles to the moon, the planets, and conceivably even the stars. Space travel is not the same as the journeys made by vehicles orbiting the earth, such as artificial satellites. An artificial satellite has escaped from the friction of the atmosphere but not from the gravitational pull. For space travel, a vehicle must escape from both.

For nearly 2,000 years men have dreamed of traveling to the moon, planets, and stars. From the scientific point of view, it has been known for well over a hundred years that travel through space, to the moon or to other planets, is theoretically possible. In July 1969, the Apollo 11 team proved that man can reach the moon. (See DISCOVERY AND EXPLORATION for a description of the mission.)

It was necessary to find or invent, by scientific knowledge and experimentation, the following:

1. Rocket engines with enough power to carry the vehicle into space.

2. Fuels that are powerful enough for the rockets, but light enough to be lifted along with the vehicle. Several fuels, both liquid and solid ones, were found.

3. Metals or other materials that can withstand the great heat caused by friction with the atmosphere at such speeds. This problem was solved partly by developing new alloys and partly by controlling the spacecraft's speed where the atmosphere is dense and the friction is

A lunar explorer collects rock samples, while another astronaut stays in LEM (the Lunar Exploration Module at right in illustration). The earth, reflecting the light of the sun, shines bright in the airless space.

greatest, then increasing the speed at heights at which the atmosphere is rare and offers less resistance.

4. A way of guiding the vehicle to its destination. This requires mathematical calculations that our ancestors could never have attempted, but electronic computing machines, plus radio and radar, provided the answer.

5. Protection of the astronauts, or persons in the spacecraft. This required years of experiments (in space medicine and other fields), but it was solved.

By 1963 it was known that the dream could become a reality. The question then was, Is it worth the cost?

POWER FOR A SPACECRAFT

To launch a spacecraft, controlled thrust of great magnitude is needed. Thrust, like horsepower, is a word to describe a force, but thrust is a force to drive a vehicle in one direction. Rockets are the only engines that can provide the needed thrust for spacecraft. A rocket used for the first lifting of a spacecraft off the earth, against the downward pull of gravity and the resistance offered by the atmosphere, is called a *booster* rocket. A typical booster is the American Titan II rocket, whose 430,000 pounds of thrust can lift either a nuclear warhead or a spacecraft above the atmosphere. Rockets with four to eighteen times this thrust (more than 7,500,000 pounds, the Saturn V) were being developed in 1966.

Any vehicle launched into space to travel to the moon or beyond must be given a velocity that enables it to overcome the earth's gravity. This is called *escape velocity*. At or near the earth's surface, escape velocity is a little more than 7 miles per second or 25,000 miles per hour. Given this velocity, a spacecraft will escape from the earth's gravity. When a spacecraft has "escaped," the earth's gravity cannot slow it enough to overcome the force of the craft's forward motion. Therefore gravity can never return the craft to the earth.

A big booster rocket gives the spacecraft its initial velocity as it pushes through the resistance of the very dense lower atmosphere. Then smaller rockets renew the velocity of the craft with the firing of each rocket. The smaller rockets lift as much as the first big booster because they work where the atmosphere is not so dense and offers little resistance, and where gravity is less powerful. At 500 miles from the earth, escape velocity goes down from 25,120 to 23,500 miles per hour. At 5,000 miles, it is only 16,630 miles per hour.

Chemical rockets, those that burn liquid or solid fuel, are necessary for launching a space vehicle against the pull of the earth's gravity. However, chemical rockets are not desirable for long space journeys because their bulky fuel would have to be transported great distances through space. Other propulsion systems have been devised for use in airless space, away from the strong pull of a planet's gravity.

Nuclear Fission or Fusion. In this system, a nuclear reactor heats ammonia, hydrogen or helium in liquid form. The resulting gas vents at high velocity through the exhaust nozzles of a rocket. The fusion system, producing heat mil-

lions of degrees higher, is the more efficient. But this heat, plus the heavy screens that might be required to ward off deadly radiation, have made nuclear power only a hope for the future.

Ion Power. In this system, ions (atoms unbalanced electrically by the loss of one or more electrons) form the rocket jet. Strong electrical fields produce the ions from a chosen gas. The ions are propelled through the rocket's exhaust nozzle by another part of the electrical field. The ions leave the nozzle at very high velocities. However, the exhaust stream is quite small, and ion engines produce weak thrust. They are to be used after chemical or nuclear rockets have provided the tremendous shove needed to accelerate a spacecraft to escape velocity.

Photon Engine. Light exerts pressure. The pressure comes from the extremely small and lightweight particles, called photons, that make up a beam of light. A sufficiently intense beam of light might provide enough thrust to drive a spacecraft in airless, weightless space.

Solar Sail. A huge circular sail, two or three miles in diameter, made of thin plastic sheeting covered with a reflecting coating of aluminum, could gather up enough light-pressure from the sun to drive a small spacecraft. The pressure of the sunlight would be like the pressure of wind on the sail of a boat. This form of space propulsion requires no fuel at all.

PROCESS OF SPACE TRAVEL

The following are essential steps in space travel. There are tens of thousands of details, and each of them is so expensive that even the shortest manned space flight requires a series of tests of several rockets and space capsules, and costs billions of dollars spent over the course of a number of years.

Launching the spacecraft. Though much larger, a spacecraft is launched like any artificial satellite or ballistic missile. The whole assembly is perhaps hundreds of feet high, including the first booster rocket, the other rockets that go off in series, and the nose or actual spacecraft that holds the astronauts and the hundreds of instruments. When each rocket has expended its fuel it drops off, so by the time the rocket is in space it is much lighter than when it left the earth; but it must still carry the unused rockets the astronauts will need to maneuver it in space and to bring it back to earth. Before a spacecraft (or any other space vehicle) can take off, tens of thousands of delicate parts in engines, instruments, computers, and cameras, as well as the materials, the complete sealing of the spacecraft and its rockets to prevent the leakage of oxygen or fuel, and the fuel supply itself, must be checked. Spacemen jokingly refer to "Murphy's law": Anything that *can* go wrong *will* go wrong. This is very far from true, but it is true that even a slight failure may result in the loss of human lives and billions of dollars. When all checking has been completed, the "countdown" begins: a counting of the number of seconds that remain before the spacecraft will be launched. When the count (10 . . . 9 . . . 8 . . . 7, etc.) reaches zero, the first booster rocket is fired and the spacecraft is on its way.

All of the problems of launching, or

of proving new and bigger launchings possible, were solved by the hundreds of artificial satellites and unmanned spacecraft sent out by the U.S.S.R. and the U.S. between 1957 and 1961.

Space station or space platform. This is an artificial satellite that will carry supplies and new rocket engines to be picked up by the spacecraft before it resumes its journey into space. This will reduce the weight the spacecraft must carry when it makes its first escape from the earth's gravitational pull. The space station is planned as a wheel-shaped vehicle that rotates, creating centrifugal force that will act almost the same as gravity on human beings inside it (see CENTRIFUGAL FORCE). A trip to the moon is possible without use of a space station, but the most effective trips must depend on it. One problem is for the spacecraft to find and attach itself to the space station. This was proved possible in 1966 when two American astronauts reached and coupled with an artificial satellite that had previously been put into orbit.

Aiming the spacecraft. When the distance to be traveled is measured in millions of miles, the slightest miscalculation can cause the ship to miss its target by many thousands of miles. Electronic computers solved this problem, as proved when the U.S.S.R. series of Luniks (1959-1965) and the American series of Rangers (1961-65) got close enough to the moon to photograph it and then actually landed on the moon, sending back television pictures. American spacecraft also got within 4,700 miles of Venus (1961) and Mars (1965) to send back by radio information on the nature of these planets.

Making a soft landing. Until 1966, spacecraft that reached the moon crashed on it. This would not be acceptable for a manned flight, for the astronauts would be killed. In 1966 a U.S.S.R. spacecraft succeeded in landing on the moon at a low speed, so that the vehicle was not destroyed and presumably passengers in the vehicle would not have been injured. In 1969, the United States orbited three astronauts around the moon. Two of the astronauts descended to the lunar surface in a *lunar module* while the third remained in the orbiting *command ship.* The smaller lunar module later rejoined the larger command ship and returned safely to earth.

Bringing the astronauts back safely (and also the spacecraft with the valuable data recorded on its instruments). From the start, both the U.S. and U.S.S.R. safely brought back the astronauts who were in their artificial satellites. The American astronauts, who always made their landings at sea, seldom came down far from the designated place and were promptly picked up by U.S. Navy ships and helicopters waiting there for them.

A take-off from the moon or a planet is not a great problem. Escape velocity depends on the size of the heavenly body; while 7 miles per second is required on earth, it takes only 1½ miles per second from the moon and only 3 miles per second from Mars.

NAVIGATION OF SPACE VEHICLES

Navigation in space is far more complex than navigation on earth. Ships and airplanes use ports and airfields whose

locations and distances remain fixed in relation to each other. A spacecraft travels between astronomical bodies that are continually in motion. A space navigator may have to aim his spacecraft at a point in space which is empty at the time but where, months later, the astronomical body that is his destination will be.

Space travel takes place at such high speeds that short-range corrections are practically impossible, while long-range corrections carry great possibility of error. If a space vehicle launched on a voyage to Venus were to miss by more than six inches per second its calculated velocity of 37,000 feet per second, the rocket would completely miss Venus, which has a diameter of 7,750 miles. To achieve an accuracy of less than six inches per second is not possible because of the many uncontrolled factors present in the launching of any large rocket. Hence, for a spacecraft to reach its destination corrective guidance must be applied to the craft during its journey.

THE GUIDANCE OF SPACECRAFT

The guidance of manned spacecraft is, in one way, similar to the guidance of a ship or airplane. The pilot makes observations to determine where his craft is, then changes his direction to keep it most accurately on the course the navigator planned. Here the similarity ends. No matter how skillful the pilot may be, the human brain and muscles cannot make accurate corrections in a spacecraft's course when it is traveling so many thousands of miles per hour. The controls must be directly actuated by signals from electronic computers. The astronaut feeds the results of his observations into the computer, which makes the calculations and then signals the controls.

There are other methods of guidance. They can be used by both manned and unmanned spacecraft.

Inertial guidance. Because of inertia, the moving spacecraft resists changes in speed and direction—changes that would take the spacecraft off course. Sensing devices convert these changes to electrical impulses; the impulses cause mechanisms to correct the craft's controls. The course that the craft should travel is set into the guidance mechanism before the craft is launched.

Radio-inertial guidance. The computers on board spacecraft are not large enough to have the accuracy needed in space navigation. The errors are small, but several small errors will send the spacecraft off its course. With radio-inertial guidance, the sensing devices, instead of actuating the controls, send radio messages to large computers on earth. The large computers send directions by radio back to the spacecraft.

Stellar-inertial guidance. The spacecraft may be so far away that it will not receive radio signals very well. A form of onboard correction of guidance errors is needed. This can be provided by placing two telescopes in the spacecraft's guidance mechanism. The telescopes are pointed at a pair of stars and remain pointed at them as long as the craft is on course. If the spacecraft deviates from its course, the telescopes no longer point at the chosen stars. This actuates a mechanism that moves the controls of the space-

craft so as to keep the telescopes pointed at the stars, which brings the spacecraft back on course.

Homing guidance. When a spacecraft approaches its destination—a planet or natural satellite—radar aboard the spacecraft may broadcast impulses toward the astronomical body being approached. The radar waves reflected back to the spacecraft can be used to control steering and landing controls.

ASTRONAUT

An astronaut is anyone who pilots a spacecraft, or orbits in an artificial satellite, or is a member of the crew of either. The word means "sailor of the stars." The Russians use the term *cosmonaut,* which means "sailor of the universe."

From the time an astronaut climbs aboard a spacecraft atop a launching rocket, to the time he climbs out of the craft after its flight and touchdown on the earth or some other astronomical body, he is called upon to display a high degree of skill, courage, and resistance to both kinds of stress, mental and physical. Choosing men and women with these characteristics requires special standards of selection. In the United States, the standards set by the National Aeronautics and Space Administration (NASA), in choosing the first American astronauts in October 1958, proved successful. To qualify, each astronaut had to be an airplane test pilot and a jet pilot with at least 1,500 hours of flight time. He had to have a degree in engineering or its equivalent. He had to be under 40, stand no taller than 5 feet 11 inches, and weigh no more than 180 pounds.

More than 100 men who met the preliminary requirements volunteered. NASA interviewed 69 and chose 32 for final physical and mental tests. Six finally made space flights. All of these came from the armed services.

The names of America's first astronauts and the order in which they made the space flights of the first space program—Project Mercury—are:

Alan Bartlett Shepard, Jr., born 1923, a lieutenant commander in the U.S. Navy. He was the first American in space, on May 5, 1961.

Virgil Ivan Grissom, born 1926, a captain in the U.S. Air Force. He made his flight on July 21, 1961.

John Herschel Glenn, Jr., born 1921, a lieutenant colonel in the U.S. Marine Corps. Glenn piloted the first space flight by an American to orbit the earth, February 20, 1962.

Malcolm Scott Carpenter, born 1925, a lieutenant commander in the U.S. Navy. Carpenter orbited the earth three times on May 24, 1962.

Walter M. Schirra, Jr., born 1923, a lieutenant commander in the U.S. Navy. Schirra made a six-orbit flight on October 3, 1962.

L. Gordon Cooper, Jr., born 1927, a major in the U.S. Air Force. Cooper made a 22-orbit flight lasting 34 hours, beginning on May 15, 1963.

Little is officially known about the selection and training of the cosmonauts of the U.S.S.R., but there must have been the same problems. The first ones were:

Yuri Alekseyevich Gagarin, born 1934, a major in the Soviet Air Force, became, on April 12, 1961, the first human being in space and the first to orbit the earth. He orbited the earth once in the spacecraft *Vostok I.*

Gherman Stepanovich Titov, born 1935, also a Soviet Air Force major, spent 25 hours

in space, August 6-7, 1961, orbiting the earth 17 times.

Adrian Grigoryevich Nikolayev, born 1929, another major in the Soviet Air Force, was the first human being to travel a million miles in space, between August 11 and 15, 1962.

In 1964, the Russians sent Junior Lieutenant Valentina Tereshkova on a one-day space flight, demonstrating that women can be competent cosmonauts.

LIVING AND WORKING IN SPACE

Space travelers on long voyages may have to live and work in space for months. The environment of space is so different from the one in which man lives on earth that it poses many serious problems.

First, in space there is no air, and man must have oxygen to sustain life. On short flights, those as far as the moon, a spacecraft can carry enough oxygen in tanks, but for longer voyages the tanks would have to be too numerous or too bulky; but nature can do the job as it does on earth, producing pure oxygen from green plants in the process of photosynthesis. In a spacecraft, the plants will be kept in tanks of water and will be fertilized by waste matter produced by the human beings aboard. The oxygen-carbon dioxide cycle can be kept going as long as the plants can be kept growing. An added advantage of this system is that new plants grown during the process furnish fresh food for the people aboard.

Another problem is weightlessness. In "free fall," far from the noticeable pull of gravity, unsupported objects do not fall to the floor of a spacecraft; they hang in midair and must be deliberately placed on table or floor. Dust does not settle. Spilled liquids remain suspended in midair. A special effort must be made to get food into one's mouth. The effort needed on earth to rise from a chair propels a weightless man to the ceiling.

During space journeys within the solar system, spacemen will be exposed to intense radiation from the sun and from space outside the solar system. This radiation can be deadly. Shielding of lead or concrete can keep the radiation out, but the craft would be too heavy to launch. Special plastic, glass and light metal materials have been developed in the effort to solve this problem.

ASTRONAUTS' TRAINING

Astronauts are subjected to as rigorous training as has ever been devised for man.

They are put into deserts and forests and at sea with no more clothes and equipment than they would have if a space capsule made an unscheduled landing far from the waiting rescue teams. They must show that they can survive for days under the harsh conditions of desert, forest, and sea.

They must fly regularly in the fastest jet planes to maintain their flight proficiency and reflex actions.

They must practice escaping from space capsules under every condition that might possibly arise.

They learn star identification and how to navigate by the stars.

For the Gemini (two-man craft) and Apollo programs, new astronaut trainees were selected. Because the Gemini and Apollo programs were more complex

than the original Mercury program, the new astronauts faced training even beyond that given earlier.

Some of the later astronaut trainees were qualified scientists who were not members of the armed forces.

SPACE MEDICINE

Space outside the earth's atmosphere is a very harsh environment. It is cold—459° below zero Fahrenheit; it is airless, and it lacks atmospheric pressure. Sudden exit of a lightly-clothed astronaut from a spacecraft would kill him.

To protect astronauts who leave their spacecraft, a space suit was developed. Besides protecting the astronaut, the suit had to be light and flexible so that it would not hamper the astronaut's movements.

The space suit that met these requirements was made of 17 alternating layers of Mylar plastic and Dacron fabric. A plastic helmet with a transparent visor fitted tightly to the neck of the suit. Two hoses, one for pumping in an oxygen mixture and the other for pumping out the astronaut's exhaled carbon dioxide, give the astronaut air for breathing and also maintain the required pressure.

During the launching period, an astronaut is subjected to acceleration that produces the equivalent of increased gravity acting upon him. This artificial force of gravity, or "g" force, increases the astronaut's weight by several times and subjects him to disagreeable and sometimes harmful crushing forces. Similar g forces are encountered when a spacecraft suddenly decelerates to reënter the atmosphere without burning up from friction with the air. Part of the training of astronauts includes being placed in a large centrifuge that whirls them around, subjecting them to acceleration equal to as much as 16-g forces. In a spacecraft, each astronaut has his own foam-rubber couch, which has been molded to fit the contours of his body. This helps him to absorb the stress of g forces.

Aerospace doctors have found that weightlessness has adverse effects on the astronaut. His rate of heartbeat is greatly lowered. An extra amount of blood collects in the blood vessels of his legs and causes swelling. Changes take place in his bone structure. In training flights, astronauts have been kept weightless as if in space, for weeks. No permanent bad effects resulted, but aerospace medical authorities are not satisfied that man can withstand very long periods of weightlessness.

Another problem of weightlessness is disorientation. On the surface of the earth, we know which direction is up, and which is down. An astronaut in space, with no pull felt from the floor under his feet, cannot tell up from down. Space outside his spacecraft does not help; it all looks the same, above, below, and to the sides. He may temporarily lose his orientation, a condition that could cause him to pilot his spacecraft in the wrong direction. Therefore an astronaut in training is placed in a large machine that moves him in a manner that disorients him. He is then taught how to regain his sense of direction and to manipulate the controls of a spacecraft while making his recovery.

Space medicine is a new study and not fully explored, but experience gained in the early years of man's venture into space

has shown that the medical problems of space travel are not as serious as expected. Man survives quite well in space if he prepares for it.

Spain

Spain is a country in Europe, the fourth-largest country in area (which is about 195,000 square miles, making it somewhat larger than the state of California). About thirty million people live in Spain. Spain occupies most of the Iberian Peninsula, the part of southwestern Europe that extends into the Atlantic Ocean and Mediterranean Sea. Spain owns the Canary Islands in the Atlantic, the Balearic Islands in the Mediterranean, and enclaves (small areas) on the coasts of Morocco and Spanish Sahara on the continent of Africa.

At one time Spain was the most powerful country in Europe and controlled most of the New World (all of South and Central America and parts of North America). Wars and revolutions over a period of hundreds of years weakened Spain, so that today it is the poorest of the large nations of Europe. However, in recent years the Spanish government has made great efforts to expand industries, to increase and modernize production, and to expand trade with other countries.

THE PEOPLE OF SPAIN

The Spaniard of today is descended from many different peoples of ancient times. There were Celts, Phoenicians, Greeks and Romans from times before the Christian era, and Germanic peoples who invaded Spain about 1,500 years ago, and Arabs and Moors who came from North Africa about a thousand years ago. Generally, the Spanish people are of the "Mediterranean" type—dark, and short or of medium height.

About half the people of Spain earn their living by farming. The main crops are wheat, barley, and other grains, and fruits and vegetables. Oranges, grapes, almonds, wines, and olives and olive oil from Spain are sent to countries all over the world. Spain produces more olive oil than any other country, about half of all the olive oil used in the world, and more oranges than any other country except the United States and Brazil. Spain is noted for its fine bulls. About one-fifth of these are raised for bullfights, which are Spain's favorite entertainment. Also famous are Spain's Merino sheep and fine horses. Fishing is an important industry, and Spanish sardines are shipped all over the world. In the forests there are many

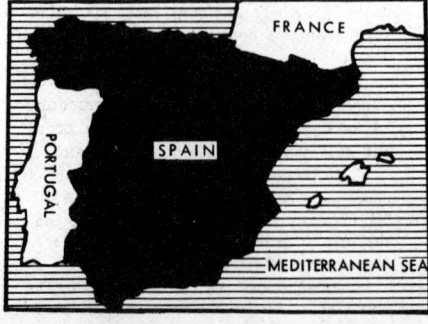

cork oaks, and cork is an important product.

Spain is rich in minerals and coal. It is a leading producer of mercury. Its other important minerals include iron, copper, lead, zinc, tungsten, and silver.

About three of every ten people live in big cities such as the capital city, Madrid, the ports of Barcelona and Valencia, and Seville, Málaga, Saragossa, and others. There are important textile (cloth) factories. Other factories produce chemicals and sugar. A large tobacco industry has been developed since the 1930s.

Though there are many schools in Spain, in 1960 about one of every ten persons of school age or older did not know how to read and write.

There are twelve colleges and universities. In most of the schools boys and girls study separately, but in some they study together.

REGIONS AND PROVINCES

Spain can be divided into fourteen historic regions, most of which were separate kingdoms at some time in the past. Officially there are fifty provinces. The old regions were Valencia, Murcia, Estremadura, León, New Castile, Old Castile, Catalonia, Andalusia, Aragon, Galicia, Asturias, and Navarre. The Balearic Islands and the Canary Islands are also considered as separate regions.

The official language is Spanish, but there are many different dialects (ways of speaking the language). Some differ so greatly that people speaking one cannot understand people speaking another. The literary language of the country is the form of Spanish called Castilian. The official religion is Roman Catholic.

WHAT SPAIN IS LIKE

The mainland of Spain is almost an island. It has nearly 1,900 miles of coast line and only about 400 miles of land border that separates it from the rest of Europe. That border consists of the Pyrenees Mountains, whose highest peak, Pico de Aneto, towers more than 11,000 feet. Spain's highest peak, Mulhacén, is in the Sierra Nevada range in the southeast, and rises to 11,420 feet. Most of Spain is made up of a plateau (high, level land) surrounded by even higher mountains. The many mountain ranges cause great extremes of climate. The average winter temperature is 26 degrees on the Fahrenheit scale, but it is much colder in the mountains. The average summer temperature is 73 degrees, but in many places it is much warmer.

There are several important rivers, and their valleys are the most fertile region for farming. Along the east coast and in the central part are the Ebro, Tagus, Guadiana and Guadalquivir Rivers. Others include the Miño, Duero, Segura, and Júcar. On many of these rivers there are powerful waterfalls that provide hydroelectric power. Spain has the highest waterfalls and most powerful hydroelectric plants in Europe.

HOW SPAIN IS GOVERNED

Since 1939, the government of Spain has been a dictatorship under Francisco Franco. There is only one political party, called the Falange. All other parties are outlawed. The party is ruled by a Na-

tional Council of 100 members. The head of the government is Franco, who is chief of the state, commander-in-chief of the armed forces, prime minister, and head of the Falangists. He is assisted by sixteen ministers (heads of departments) and by a number of councils that include the members of the Supreme Court of Justice, the presidents of the State Council, the mayors of the capitals of Spain's fifty provinces, the heads of the universities, and others. In 1947 a new law made Spain a kingdom but provided that Franco would remain head of the government for the rest of his life and was to choose his successor.

The people of Spain have little to say about their government. The government controls public utilities, railroads and other transportation. Workers are represented by unions but the unions are subject to government control. Each province has a governor who is appointed by the central government.

CHIEF CITIES IN SPAIN

The leading cities in Spain, with populations from the 1973 estimate are:

Madrid, population 2,939,175, the capital, largest city in the country.

Barcelona, population 1,827,838, second-largest city, commercial center and leading seaport, in the northeast, on the Mediterranean Sea.

Seville, population 503,489, third-largest city, in the southwest.

Valencia, population 498,159, fourth-largest city, commercial center and seaport, in the east central part, on the Mediterranean Sea.

There are separate articles about all these cities, and about the historic Spanish cities of CADIZ, TOLEDO, BURGOS, and GRANADA.

SPAIN IN THE PAST

Spain has been inhabited for many thousands of years. In northern Spain is found the Altamira Cave, whose walls have paintings that experts believe were made as far back as twenty to thirty thousand years ago.

The recorded history of the country dates back more than three thousand years, when Phoenician traders settled on the south coast, near Cadiz, and the ancient Greeks established colonies along the east coast. In the interior lived the Iberians, the people who were already there, but no one knows where they came from originally. At some point their lands had been invaded by Celts from the north, who intermarried with the Iberians. The Phoenicians could not conquer the Iberians, so they asked for help from the city of Carthage, in North Africa. The Carthaginians defeated the tribes, and so Spain came under the rule of Carthage.

More than two thousand years ago, in 201 B.C., Carthage lost its lands to Rome, and the Romans ruled there for about six hundred years. Then the Roman Empire fell apart and Spain was invaded by Vandals and Goths, Germanic peoples from the north.

In 711, Spain was invaded and conquered by Mohammedan peoples of North Africa. For nearly eight hundred years after that, much of Spain had Mohammedan rulers. The north consisted of three Christian kingdoms, Asturias, Navarre, and Catalonia. The greatest progress was made under King Alfonso VI. In time the Christian rulers won more territory back from the Mohammedan rulers, and other separate kingdoms were formed.

Spain was finally united in 1492 through the marriage of Ferdinand II of Aragon and Isabella of Castile. In the same year Granada, the last stronghold of the Moors (Mohammedans), was conquered.

Then began the greatest period in Spain's history. When Columbus discovered America he did so for Spain. Throughout the 1500s and 1600s, wealth from the New World and from other lands made Spain the richest and most powerful nation in Europe. At one time or another, Spain controlled all of South and Central America, large parts of the southern and western parts of what is now the United States, many islands in the Pacific Ocean including the Philippines, much of North Africa, and the Netherlands, Luxembourg, and parts of Italy on the continent of Europe. Spain had a great navy to protect its overseas possessions and to carry its wealth back to Spain.

Gradually a series of wars and revolutions cost Spain its power and most of its possessions. The process began in 1588 when King Philip II of Spain tried to conquer England and lost his greatest fleet, the Armada, in the attempt. In the 1600s, England took some of Spain's colonies and the Netherlands and Luxembourg won their independence. The Seven Years' War in the middle 1700s and the Napoleonic Wars, fought in the early 1800s while Napoleon I was the French emperor, cost Spain more territory. Also in the early 1800s, the South American countries revolted and won independence under the leadership of Simón Bolívar, José de San Martín, and others.

By this time Spain was in a state of unrest and confusion. There was a revolution in 1846 that resulted in the overthrow of the king and nobles and the establishment of a republic in Spain. This soon gave way to a military dictatorship, and finally, in 1876, a new constitution made Spain a kingdom again, with Alfonso XII on the throne.

In 1898 Spain lost the SPANISH-AMERICAN WAR, about which there is a separate article. This cost still more lands, the most important of which were Cuba and the Philippines.

Spain remained neutral during World War I. During the 1920s it again had a military dictatorship under General Primo de Rivera. After Rivera's death in 1930, there were riots and uprisings among the people. In 1931 King Alfonso XIII abdicated (gave up the throne) and left the country. In that year a republic was set up. Its government was democratic, but still the people were not satisfied. The peasants wanted more land. Others wanted more political power. Unrest grew until in 1936 there began the SPANISH CIVIL WAR, about which there is a separate article. By the end of the war a military dictatorship was in power.

During World War II Spain again was neutral, but it coöperated with the fascist governments of Germany and Italy and was unfriendly toward the Allies. After the war the United States and Spain became more friendly. In the 1950s the United States and Spain signed an agreement whereby the United States could set up military bases in Spain. Spain did not become a member of the United Nations until 1955.

SPAIN. Area, 195,504 square miles. Population (1973 estimate) 34,130,000. Capital, Madrid. Government, monarchy, governed by dictator. Religion, Roman Catholic. Monetary unit, the *peseta,* worth about 1.67 cents (U.S.). Flag, two red horizontal bars separated by wider yellow band on which is coat of arms.

spaniel

A spaniel is a dog that was developed more than a hundred years ago, for hunting. All spaniels are fond of the water, and are excellent swimmers. They are gentle, affectionate dogs and usually get along well with children.

Cocker spaniels are the smallest of the spaniels. An American cocker spaniel stands about 12 inches high at the shoulder and is about 15 inches from the chest to the base of the tail. It has long, drooping ears, and a gentle, friendly expression on its face. The tail is clipped when puppies are a few days old. Cocker spaniels may be solid black, reddish brown, cream color, tan, or a mixture of colors.

English cocker spaniels are somewhat larger than American cockers.

The *springer spaniel* is a larger dog, and is mainly a hunting dog.

There are two kinds of *water spaniel* that are fairly common in the United States and Canada. They are the Irish water spaniel, and the other is the American water spaniel. These dogs are expert swimmers and love the water. The Irish water spaniel has a curly tuft of very long hair on its head, between the eyes, and the hair on its ears is long and curly. Its tail is long and thin. The tail of the American water spaniel is flat, and acts like a rudder to help steer the dog in swimming.

The Irish water spaniel stands about 21 to 24 inches high at the shoulder, and the American water spaniel about 15 to 18 inches. Both dogs are brown, and both have curly hair that is thick and water-repellent.

Spanish-American War

The Spanish-American War was a very short war that took place about sixty years ago. It lasted from April to August, 1898. There was not much fighting and not many men were killed, but the war was very important for the United States, which won an easy victory, gained some valuable possessions, and was recognized as a leading world power for the first time.

HOW THE WAR BEGAN

Spain had owned the island of Cuba, in the West Indies, for about four hundred years. In 1895 the Cubans started a revolt against Spain. Most people in America were very sympathetic to the Cubans, especially because the Spanish rulers were very harsh in putting down the revolt. The United States newspapers exaggerated the stories of Spanish bru-

tality, and soon a lot of people wanted to throw the Spaniards out of Cuba.

On February 15, 1898, the United States battleship *Maine* blew up in the harbor of Havana, Cuba, and 260 sailors were killed. Most people then believed the Spaniards had done it, but to this day nobody really knows what caused the disaster. But people in America were so angry at Spain that they wanted to fight first and ask questions afterwards. Even though the Spanish government promised to give Cuba partial independence, Congress declared war on Spain on April 25, 1898.

THE WAR

Another possession of Spain was the Philippine Islands in the Pacific. When the war began, an American fleet under Commodore George Dewey sailed to the Philippines and on May 1 defeated a Spanish fleet there in the Battle of Manila Bay. An American army landed in the Philippines a few months later.

The United States Army was very small when the war began, and it was about two months before a fighting force could be assembled and sent to Cuba. Meanwhile the main Spanish fleet, under Admiral Pascual Cervera, sailed into the harbor of Santiago, in the southeastern part of Cuba. There an American fleet commanded by William Sampson bottled it up.

In June, 1898, an American expeditionary force of about 18,000 men, under Major General William Shafter, landed at Daiquiri, a few miles from Santiago. The idea was to capture the city of Santiago and force the Spanish fleet either to surrender or to sail out where the United States Navy could fight it. But Santiago was protected by San Juan Hill, which was very steep. The Americans attacked on July 1. The Spanish soldiers fought very well at first, firing from trenches that they had dug, but they finally were forced to retreat. One of the regiments that charged up San Juan Hill was the First Volunteer Cavalry (they had actually left their horses at home and they fought on foot), which was called the Rough Riders. This regiment had been organized by Colonel Theodore Roosevelt and Colonel Leonard Wood. Roosevelt led the famous charge, and this made him a great hero. Later he became President and Wood became the top general in the Army.

On the same day, another American force beat the Spanish near Santiago in the Battle of El Caney. Admiral Cervera saw that Santiago would probably be captured now, and on July 3, 1898, he sailed his fleet out of the harbor. It was completely destroyed by gunfire from the American ships. With both of their two fleets beaten, the Spanish asked for surrender terms. Meanwhile an American army landed on the island of Puerto Rico and captured it in a few days.

THE PEACE

The fighting stopped in August, and in December a peace treaty with Spain was signed in Paris. Spain had to give the United States Puerto Rico, Guam (in the Pacific Ocean), and the Philippines. Cuba became an independent country. In return for the Philippines, the United States gave Spain twenty million dollars. The natives of the Philippines had thought they would be allowed to run their own government, and they soon started a revolt against the United States. This was called the Philippine Insurrection. (See the article on the PHILIPPINES.)

During the war the United States Army had about 275,000 men, but fewer than half of them went overseas. About 5,500 Americans died in the war, but fewer than 400 of these were actually killed in battle. Most of the others died of disease. One important result of the war was that it led to the finding of ways to control yellow fever and other diseases.

Spanish Civil War

The Spanish Civil War was a war fought in Spain from July, 1936, to March, 1939. When the war began, Spain had been a republic for five years, since King Alfonso XIII had been forced to abdicate (resign as king) in 1931. At first the new government was a democracy, with free elections; but the Socialists who controlled the government were unable to give the people employment or good living conditions, and Communists kept the workers stirred up. The people voted the Socialists out of power, but the Communists caused even more trouble for the new government. Finally the officers of the Spanish Army, who had supported the republican government for several years, began a revolution to change the government. The elected government opposed them with forces that remained loyal to it, and the fighting began.

The Army officers and their supporters were called the Nationalists, or Insurgents. They were led by General Francisco Franco, who later became head of the Spanish government. The government group was called the Loyalists. They included almost all of the Socialists (chiefly poor farmers and laborers), the Communists, who were a small group, and many "intellectuals" (teachers, writers, scientists, and so on).

During the first months of fighting, the Loyalists held the eastern and most of the southern parts of Spain securely. The Nationalists were strong in the north and set up a government in the northern city of Burgos. They besieged the capital city of Madrid, and the Loyalists had to move their government to Valencia, on the east coast. The fighting during this period was very bitter, with much unnecessary killing by each side.

The fascist nations of Europe, Italy and Germany, were preparing to start a war at this time and saw a great opportunity to test their weapons and train some of their officers; besides, they were bitter enemies of Communism. Therefore they sent weapons, munitions and men to help the Nationalists. The Communist government of Russia, for much the same reasons, helped the Loyalists. This policy was called *intervention*. Great Britain and France, though they favored the Loyalists because they did not want Germany and Italy to get a new ally, adopted a policy called *nonintervention*, and were more or less neutral. Thousands of young men from the United States and other countries went to Spain to fight for the Loyalists. Some of them were Communists, but most of them went because they thought they would be fighting for democracy and were anxious to fight against fascism.

The Nationalists received much greater support from their allies than the Loyalists did from Russia. Within a few months the Nationalists controlled the air. One by one the cities and territories of Spain fell to them, and though the Loyalists won some victories there was little doubt that the Nationalists would eventually win. Nevertheless the Loyalists kept on fighting, even after it seemed hopeless.

Early in 1939, the Loyalist premier Juan Negrin, and the president, Manuel Azaña, had to flee to France. Madrid held out against the siege until March 28, then surrendered. Franco set up a dictatorial government and joined Germany, Italy, and Japan in an agreement to oppose Communism. Great Britain, France and the United States recognized Franco's government at once. See the article on SPAIN.

Spanish language and literature

Spanish is one of the great languages of the world. It is spoken by the people of Spain, by nearly all the people of South America (except in Brazil), and in Central America, Mexico, most of the islands in the Caribbean Sea, and other former or present Spanish colonies. More than 150,000,000 people speak Spanish.

Spanish is a Romance language, which means it grew out of the Latin spoken by the ancient Romans. In Spain it was influenced by the speech of Germanic peoples, of Mohammedan peoples who spoke Arabic, and of the Basques, who may have been the earliest inhabitants of Spain, and in the American countries it was influenced by the speech of the Indians.

The "literary" language of Spain is Castilian. This is considered the purest form of Spanish. There are many dialects, or other forms of Spanish, spoken in Spain and in the Spanish-speaking countries overseas.

A knowledge of Spanish has become more and more important in the United States because of the great amount of business that United States firms do with Spanish-speaking American countries. Spanish is taught in nearly all high schools in the United States.

SPANISH LITERATURE

Spain has an old and a great literature. Hundreds of years ago the Spanish troubadours (wandering poets and musicians) wrote ballads that set a pattern for poets in other European countries. One of the early Spanish epics (a long poem, telling a story) was about the CID, about whom there is a separate article. The masterpiece of Spanish literature is *Don Quixote,* written nearly four hundred years ago by Miguel CERVANTES, about whom there is a separate article. The most popular Spanish writer of recent times, in the United States, was Blasco Ibáñez, whose novels were translated into English and widely read. South American countries have produced several great writers in the Spanish language.

Spanish Main

"Spanish Main" is an old name for

the Caribbean Sea, because hundreds of years ago Spain owned all the American territory around it. This was rich gold-mining land, and pirates used to sail the Spanish Main to attack ships carrying gold back to Spain.

Spanish moss

Spanish moss is not a true moss like the mosses that grows on trees and rocks. Spanish moss is a member of the pineapple family. It grows in long, trailing streamers, and has no roots in the ground. It is an *epiphyte*, or air plant, and gets its nourishment from the air. The long stems of the Spanish moss are covered with very small leaves and tiny flowers, so close together that a mosslike appearance is created. Spanish moss clings to trees and climbs through the branches.

The dried fibers of Spanish moss are used as a packing material in the shipment of breakable articles.

Spanish Sahara

Spanish Sahara, often called Rio de Oro, is a Spanish province in northwest Africa. It is about the size of the state of Colorado. The land is largely desert, and many of the people are nomads, who make a living by raising cattle, sheep, goats, and camels. Since the country is located on the Atlantic Ocean, fishing is another important source of income. Where water is available, vegetables and grains can be grown.

SPANISH SAHARA, Spanish province. Area, 102,703 square miles. Population (1973 est.) 60,000. Capital, El Aaiún.

sparrow

The sparrow is a little bird that is found in many parts of Europe and the United States. Some sparrows are friendly, useful birds with lovely songs. Others are noisy, quarrelsome pests.

The best-known sparrow in the United States is the *song sparrow*. The song sparrow is about six inches long. It has brown feathers and a white breast that is streaked with brown. It builds a nest of grass and twigs that is usually placed on the ground. The female lays several white or blue eggs that are speckled with red and brown colors. It usually lays eggs twice each year. The song sparrow is one of the first birds to return from its winter home in the spring.

The sparrow that is best known in Europe is called the *house sparrow*. It often drives away more attractive gentle birds. During the mating season the male chirps and scolds and makes a great commotion. The house sparrow was brought to the United States, where farmers find it a pest because it eats grain and fruit. Other sparrows are useful to the farmer because they eat the seeds of weed plants and insects that destroy crops.

sparrow hawk

The sparrow hawk is a handsome bird that lives in many parts of the United States. In spite of its name, the sparrow hawk does not kill many sparrows. The sparrow hawk grows to be about one foot long, which is smaller than most members of the hawk family. It has reddish-brown feathers and black markings on its face. It is a good hunter. It swoops down on mice and insects without warning. It

also eats some small birds. It has a cry that sounds like "killy, killy." The sparrow hawk builds a rather crude nest in the hollow of a tree or on the side of a building. The female lays between three and seven light tan eggs.

SPARS, a name by which women in the United States Coast Guard were called. The Women's Reserve branch of the U.S. Coast Guard Reserve was created by an act of Congress in 1942. SPARS served in Coast Guard stations in the United 'States and its possessions. They were dissolved in 1946. See the article COAST GUARD.

Sparta

About 2,500 years ago, Greece was made up of several independent countries called city-states. Sparta was one of the two most powerful city-states. The other was ATHENS, about which there is a separate article.

Sparta had about 400,000 people. It was the chief city of a region called Laconia or Lacedaemonia. Sparta was in the Peloponnesus, a peninsula (arm of land) extending from the mainland of Greece into the Aegean Sea. The Spartans had invaded the Peloponnesus and conquered the people who were living there, the Mycenaeans. The conquest was not an easy one, and the Spartans had established a military way of life. They made slaves of the conquered people, and were always afraid that the slaves might rise up against them. They cut themselves off from Athens and the other city-states and discouraged trade and travel. Boys had to begin their military training when they were 7 years old. They had to pass difficult tests of physical strength and endurance. Girls, too, had to undergo physical training. The country was run almost like an army camp.

In 431 B.C. war broke out between Sparta and Athens. Sparta, with the help of a powerful ally, Corinth, conquered Athens after about 27 years of fighting, and ruled Greece for about thirty years. Then it was defeated by another state, Thebes, and began to lessen in power and importance. In the end, it fell to the Romans, along with the rest of Greece. In the 19th century a modern city called Sparta was built, a little to the south of the ancient city. About 10,000 people live there.

Spartacus

Spartacus was a slave of ancient Thrace who led some of the other slaves in a revolt against their conquerors, the Romans, about two thousand years ago. Spartacus was a gladiator, one of the men who were forced to fight other men with swords, in arenas, to entertain the Romans. He broke out of prison and raised an army of slaves, which he led as far as southern Italy. For almost two years his army was successful, but in 71 B.C. it was conquered by a Roman army under a general named Crassus and Spartacus was killed in battle. The revolt of Spartacus is also called the Servile War.

spasms and fits

A spasm is a sudden, uncontrollable twitching, jerking or pulling of a muscle. A fit, which doctors call a convulsion, is a much more severe attack of the same

kind. Each is a kind of *paroxysm*, or series of bodily movements that a person cannot control.

These attacks come when nerves are overexcited or damaged in some way. The twitching of a muscle in the face or in another part of the body is called a *tic* and may become a habit that begins in the mind and can be cured only by a psychiatrist, a doctor who specializes in mental illnesses. Other attacks may be caused by epilepsy, St. Vitus' dance, infantile paralysis or other forms of paralysis, cerebral palsy, and other diseases.

An occasional twitching of a muscle is nothing to worry about, but if the pain is great or the attack is repeated many times a doctor should be consulted.

Speaker, Tris

Tris Speaker was one of the greatest baseball players of all time. He was born in Hubbard City, Texas, in 1883. He played for the Boston team of the American League from 1905 to 1915, and for Cleveland from 1916 to 1926. His lifetime batting average was .344. But Tris Speaker is primarily known for his fielding skill. He played center field. Because he was so quick and so fast, and because his hair turned gray so early, he was known as the "gray eagle." He died in 1958.

spearmint

Spearmint is a plant of the mint family. It is used as a flavoring for candies, chewing gum, beverages, and foods. Spearmint grows in all parts of the world where it is reasonably warm and moist. It is a perennial and will grow for many years without replanting. It can be grown easily in flowerpots indoors.

spectrum

The spectrum is a series of bright-colored lines that appear when a ray of light passes through a prism or some other substance that breaks up the light. A rainbow is lines of the spectrum produced by sunlight passing through particles of water.

A *continuous spectrum* is an unbroken band of colors shading into one another. In some conditions, light produces separate bright lines or bands.

Every chemical element has its own pattern of lines. This fact has been very useful to scientists, and especially to astronomers (scientists who study the stars and other heavenly bodies). They break up the light from any shining object, using an instrument called a *spectroscope*, which separates light into the lines or bands of the spectrum. From this spectrum, the scientists can tell whether certain elements are present or absent in a substance or in a star. They have found also that the appearance of the spectrum depends partly on the temperature of the star. This permits them to find out how hot any particular star is. It also permits them to find out how bright the star is, and once they know how bright it is they can tell how far away it is and how big it is.

The spectrum that we can see is only a small part of the whole spectrum. We see the rays that we call red, yellow, green, and blue. We do not see x-rays, for example, or heat rays, but these are all parts of the spectrum.

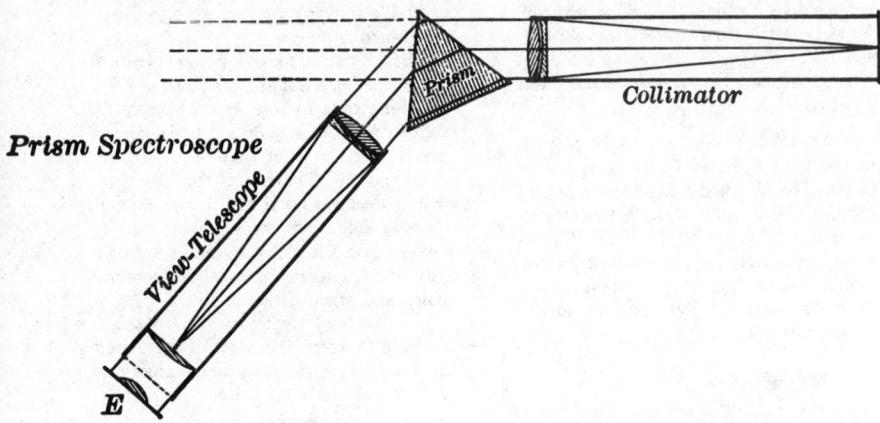

Prism Spectroscope

Prism

Collimator

View-Telescope

S

E

THE SPECTROSCOPE

The spectroscope has a telescope that collects light and makes it fall on a prism. (There is a separate article about the PRISM.) The light passing through the prism is broken up into its pattern of lines, or spectrum. This pattern falls on a mirror or lens, which the observer sees through an eyepiece. Often the pattern is photographed so that it can be studied later.

Spectroscopy (the scientific use of the spectroscope) requires much study, for the scientist must be able to recognize most of the patterns.

The study of the spectrum as an aid to astronomy began with a German scientist named Joseph von Fraunhofer, who lived about 150 years ago. In the year 1814 he announced a study of more than six hundred lines in the spectrum of the sun. These lines are still called Fraunhofer lines. The German scientist BUNSEN proved and demonstrated the accuracy of the spectroscope. Today's scientists have found more than twenty thousand lines in the spectrum of the sun.

spelling

Spelling is the proper arrangement of letters so that they can be read and understood to mean a particular word. Most people take it for granted that there is a "right" way to spell every word, but it was not so long ago that nearly every writer made up his spelling as he went along. Spelling in English did not begin to be "standardized" until Dr. Samuel Johnson, a great English scholar, published his Dictionary about two hundred years ago (in 1755). At that time there were several ways to spell most English words. Dr. Johnson chose the way he thought was best, and his reputation was so great that most people followed his advice.

The first important American lexicographer (writer of dictionaries), Noah Webster, started out with a "spelling book." This was in 1784.

A great many people say they are simply "bad spellers" and cannot learn to spell. It may comfort them to know that at one time the best-educated men disagreed on spelling, and in many cases one way to spell a word is about as good as another. Nevertheless, everyone should try to learn to spell and should make it a habit to look a word up in a dictionary if he is not sure. People are judged by their spelling, just as they are judged by their manners, and a person who spells badly can be thought ignorant.

SPELLING BEES

The "spelling bee" has long been a good way to learn spelling and it is fun besides. The contestants are given words to spell. Whenever one misspells a word, he drops out. The speller who has not missed at the end is the winner.

Spellman, Cardinal

Francis Joseph Spellman was a Roman Catholic priest who rose to the position of cardinal. (In the Roman Catholic Church, cardinal is the highest position, except for Pope).

Francis Spellman was born in Whitman, Massachusetts, in 1889. He went to school at Fordham University in New York City and then in Rome, Italy. Shortly after his 27th birthday, he was made a priest. For several years, he worked at Vatican City, the state in Italy ruled by the Pope. There he became a friend of Cardinal Pacelli, who later was elected Pope Pius XII. In 1939, Francis Spellman, who was then a bishop, was made Archbishop of New York. He was appointed cardinal in 1946.

Cardinal Spellman was known for his kindness and his ability to manage the business affairs of the Church. During World War II and the Korean War, he visited American servicemen around the world in his capacity as Military Vicar. He died on December 2, 1967 at the age of 78.

Spencer, Herbert

Herbert Spencer was an English philosopher, or thinker, of about a hundred years ago. He was born in 1820. He studied engineering and for some years devoted his time to inventing mechanical devices such as candle-extinguishers and salt shakers. At the same time he became interested in social and psychological problems and in the theories of evolution that were new at that time (about 1850). He wrote books on these subjects for the rest of his long life, including a nine-volume book called *System of Synthetic Philosophy*. He died in 1903. Spencer was considered one of the most important philosophers of his time.

Spenser, Edmund

Edmund Spenser was a great English poet who lived about four hundred years ago. He is best known for his long unfinished poem, *The Faerie Queene*. This poem is allegorical, that is, the characters in it represent ideas such as virtue, evil, and truth. The poem has to do with the reign of the great English queen, Elizabeth I.

Many other great English poets, such as Byron, Keats, and Shelley, learned much from studying Spenser's poems. Spenser also introduced the stanza used in *The Faerie Queene*, called the Spenserian stanza. It has nine lines, the last of which is longer than the other eight.

Edmund Spenser was born in London in 1552. He studied at Cambridge University. One of his first poems, "The Shepheardes Calendar," was very popular and interested many of the important writers and noblemen of his time, including Sir Philip Sidney and Sir Walter Raleigh.

When Spenser was 28 years old, these friends helped him to become secretary to Lord Grey, who was governor of Ireland. From that time on Spenser spent most of his life in Ireland, where he held jobs that gave him time to continue writing his poetry. In 1594, to honor his own marriage to Elizabeth Boyle, Spenser wrote "Epithalamion," considered the greatest poem of its kind in the English language. An *epithalamium*, in Latin, is a poem celebrating a marriage.

Spenser died in London in 1599 and was buried in Westminster Abbey, where many great English poets are buried.

Sphinx

The Sphinx was a monster in Greek mythology, the stories the ancient Greeks told about their heroes and gods. The Sphinx was supposed to have the head of a woman, the body of a lion, the wings of a bird, and the tail of a serpent.

According to the stories, the Sphinx lived on a high rock near the city of

Various elements can be "fingerprinted" by means of their spectra. The spectrum lines of iodine vapor, for example, are easily distinguished from those of solar helium.

Thebes, in Greece, and asked a riddle (a trick question) of all who passed by. All those who could not answer the riddle were killed. The riddle was: "What has four feet, three feet, and two feet, and is weakest when it has the most feet?" The Greek hero Oedipus answered the riddle: "Man, for he has four feet when he is a baby and crawls, two feet when he is a man, and three feet when he is old and must use a staff to lean on, and he is weakest when he is a baby." The Sphinx then killed itself. Oedipus later became king of Thebes.

There were many statues of the Sphinx. The most famous one is the Great Sphinx of Giza, in Egypt. (See the picture on page 1767.) It was put among the pyramids, and was made out of rock. It is about 175 feet long, and the head alone is about 30 feet long. About 150 years ago, in 1816, it was discovered that a small temple is built into the Sphinx.

spice

A spice is a flavoring for foods. Spices are made by drying some part of a plant and grinding it to a powder. Pepper is by far the most popular spice, and in the United States mustard is the only other spice that is used a great deal. There are separate articles about these spices. Other popular spices are paprika, allspice, and chili, which are like pepper, and cloves, nutmegs, and cinnamon, which are sweet spices. In all there are hundreds of different spices.

Spices were highly valued in the Middle Ages, hundreds of years ago, when refrigeration had not been developed. Spices helped to keep food from spoiling and improved its flavor when it was near to spoiling. The great navigators of five hundred years ago made discoveries because they were trying to reach the south of Asia and the "Spice Islands" near it, where most spices are grown. Columbus discovered America while seeking a short way to the sources of spices.

The bird spider lives in South America.

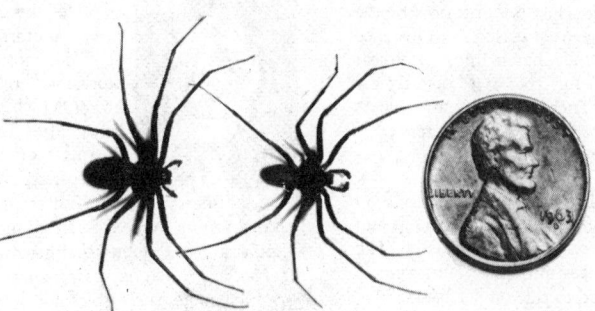

Two poisonous Brown Spiders photographed next to a penny to indicate their sizes.

spider

Spiders are air-breathing, egg-laying animals. They are usually thought of as insects, but they actually belong to a different group of animals, called *arachnids*. Spiders have four pairs of legs. A spider's body is divided into two main sections, with a tiny "waist" between the front and rear. The front section contains the head and the poison fangs used to paralyze the insects on which the spider lives. All four pairs of legs are attached to the front section. The rear section contains glands with which the spider spins "silk" for making the web in which it lives. The web traps insects that fly or crawl into it.

There are thousands of different kinds of spider. The smallest is less than a sixteenth of an inch across when it is fully grown, and the largest measures about seven inches.

Most spiders are very useful to man. They catch and eat harmful insects. Spiders catch flies, locusts, grasshoppers, plant lice, aphids, and many other insects that are bad for gardens and plants.

A spider bite is usually not dangerous. Once in a while there is a report of some one who has been bitten by a "black widow" spider. Unless the person bitten was very weak, or ill from some other cause, very old, or very young, the bite usually results in painful illness for about two weeks, but rarely causes death. The tarantula is another spider that many people believe to be extremely dangerous to human life. Its bite is painful, but here again it is most unusual for a tarantula bite to cause death.

HOW SPIDERS EAT

Spiders have very small mouths. At each side of the mouth are two sharp fangs. There are small holes at the ends of these fangs, and poison from inside the spider's head comes out through the holes. This is the weapon that is used to paralyze the insects that the spider wishes to eat. A spider also has a pair of "arms" beside its head. It uses these to hold an insect after it has been paralyzed. These extra arms (which are really legs) are not used for walking, but just for moving things around.

After a spider has killed an insect and is ready to eat it, its "arms" hold the insect so that the spider can reach it with the small mouth. The spider has no real jaws, so it cannot chew its food. All its food must be soft enough so that it can be swallowed without chewing. Only the soft parts of the insect's body are eaten by the

spider. The hard outer shell is thrown away.

If a spider catches more insects than the spider wants at the time, the spider will spin a covering over the other insects, wrapping them neatly for some future time when it may be hungry.

Spiders often catch insects larger than spiders. When this happens, the paralyzing effect of the poison in the spider's fangs makes the larger insect quiet so that the spider can spin a net around it and keep it captive. Several more bites from the poison fangs will usually kill the larger insect.

Spiders use the silk also as a casing for the eggs that will eventually hatch into young spiders. Each casing may hold about five hundred eggs.

HOW SPIDERS GROW

When the spider eggs hatch, a tiny animal just like the adult comes out of the little shell. Spider eggs look like tiny white pearls, until the young spider breaks the shell. The newly hatched spider can spin silk immediately, and in the case of most spiders, it starts to take care of itself at once.

There is one kind of spider that behaves differently. The young of the wolf spider stay near their mother for a time after they are hatched. In fact, they even ride around on their mother's back, instead of walking on their own eight legs.

Most other baby spiders start spinning immediately. The first silk they spin is not used for trapping insects, however. It is simply a means of transportation. A baby spider will spin a strand of silk, and then another, and then another, but it does not attempt to do anything with them. It simply spins and leaves the strands attached to its body. Then, when a current of air or a light breeze comes along, the strands of silk drift into the air. The baby spider is so tiny, and so light, that it drifts into the air with them, and it is carried away on the current of air. This is called "spider ballooning," and spiders have been known to float many miles before coming to earth.

When the baby spider finds itself settling to the ground, it prepares to start catching its food. It is so small it can catch only very small insects at first, but it knows how to do this without being taught.

The spider has a hard shell, and the shell does not grow. As the spider becomes larger, it grows too big for its shell, and it must get rid of the old shell. This

is called *molting*. A spider molts several times before it is full-grown.

If baby spiders do not drift on a breeze far from home, or at least a short distance from where they hatch, they often eat each other. Adult spiders frequently eat young ones. There are so many spiders this does not make any difference. A single female may lay more than a thousand eggs.

The female spider usually dies soon after she has finished laying her eggs and placing them where they will hatch. The wolf spider lives until the young spiders no longer need to ride on her back.

SOME DIFFERENCES IN SPIDERS

Not all spiders weave nets in which they hope to trap their insect food. Some do not spin webs at all. The tarantula, for example, does not spin webs. It hides in cracks in a tree, or under a stone or a piece of wood, and comes out at night to find food.

The trap-door spider makes a nest in the ground, and lines it with its own silk. It makes a top, or door, out of silk combined with dirt and leaves. It sits in the opening of the nest, peeking out through the slightly opened trap-door top, and when it sees an insect passing by it pounces on it.

The wolf spider is another one that does not catch its food in webs. The wolf spider runs after insects, and catches them. A wolf spider does not make a web for a home, but lives in holes or burrows in the ground.

The jumping spider has very strong legs and can jump in any direction. A jumping spider lies in wait, motionless, until a fly or mosquito or some other insect is within reach. Then it gives a great leap and pounces on its victim.

The black widow. Note the telltale hourglass on the black widow's underside.

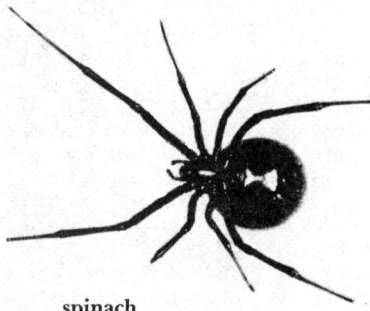

spinach

Spinach is a leafy green vegetable that came originally from southwestern Asia and is now grown in most parts of the world. Its leaves, which are broad and smooth and about ten inches long, make one of the most popular of cooked leafy vegetables. Spinach is a rich source of Vitamins A and C in the diet.

spine, or **backbone,** the chain of bones running along the back of human beings and other animals called *vertebrates*: see the articles NERVOUS SYSTEM and SKELETON.

spinning, a method of making thread to be used in the manufacture of textiles (cloth): see the article TEXTILES.

Spinoza

Baruch Spinoza, who is also known  as Benedict Spinoza, was a great Dutch philosopher, or thinker. He lived about three hundred years ago. His most famous work is his book *Ethics,* which was published after his death. In this work Spinoza wrote that everything that exists is a part of God and that God is everything that exists. In all his writing Spinoza urged men to think for themselves and to fight against any law that would make such thinking impossible. Spinoza's philosophy influenced many later philosophers.

Spinoza was born in Amsterdam, Holland, in 1632. He was by religion a Jew, and his parents had lived in Spain but had gone to Holland to find religious freedom. Spinoza became a very fine lensmaker, and made a living at this trade while he wrote and studied. In 1656 he was excommunicated, or expelled, from the synagogue, because the Jewish religious leaders did not agree with his ideas.

Spinoza wrote many letters to famous men of his time, and these letters were later published. Spinoza died of tuberculosis in 1677, when he was only 45 years old.

spiraea

Spiraea is the name of a large group of shrubs. They range in height from a few inches to over six feet. They are perennials, which means that the shrub remains year after year in the same place, blossoming each year at about the same time. Some varieties bloom early in the spring and some in the late summer and early fall. All the spring-blossoming bushes have white flowers. The others may be pink, rose, purple, or blue.

There are many popular names for the different kinds of spiraea. Examples are "bridal wreath," "meadowsweet," and "steeple bush."

spiritual

A spiritual is a kind of hymn that was made up and sung by Negroes in the southern states of the United States in times when they were slaves there. The composers of most of the spirituals will never be known, for slaves were unable to write them down or have them published. Spirituals are Christian songs. The music for them is like folk music but was influenced by the African music that the Negroes remembered from their native land and that they used also in "blues" songs. Examples of spirituals are "Steal Away to Jesus" and "Swing Low, Sweet Chariot."

THE JUBILEE SINGERS

One of the first of the universities for the newly freed Negroes, Fisk University in Nashville, Tennessee, wanted to raise money in the 1870s and sent a Negro chorus called the Fisk Jubilee Singers on a tour of American and European cities. The Jubilee Singers were a sensational success with the spirituals they sang, and Fisk University still has a group of Jubilee Singers each year. William C. Handy, a noted Negro composer and author of songs, has published many spirituals remembered from his youth in the South but never before written down.

spiritualism

Spiritualism is a kind of religion. Followers of it believe that the souls or spirits of dead persons can communicate with living persons—that is, can send messages to living persons. The spirits are supposed to be able to do this through a living person who is called a medium (which means a "go-between"). Usually spiritualists assemble in a meeting called a séance. The medium goes into a trance, or deep sleep. During this trance, the spirit of the dead person supposedly enters the medium's body and talks to living persons, or gives signs by knocking on tables or in some other way.

Many people honestly believe in spiritualism. Unfortunately, there have been many professional magicians and others who used trickery to make themselves appear to be mediums. Because of this, anyone who says he is a medium is likely to be suspected of dishonesty, and various states and cities have laws against the practice of spiritualism. Sir Arthur Conan Doyle, the English writer who wrote the "Sherlock Holmes" detective stories, believed in spiritualism. An organization called the Society for Psychical Research investigates reports of possible spirit appearances, to find out if any are true. Harry Houdini, the most famous American professional magician, distrusted spiritualism so thoroughly that he spent a great deal of time trying to prove that it could not be true.

Spitsbergen

Spitsbergen is a group of islands belonging to Norway. The islands are in the Arctic Ocean, about 400 miles north of Norway. The chief islands are West Spitsbergen, Northeast Land, Edge Island, Barents Island, and Prince Charles Foreland. There are also many smaller islands. About 3,500 people live on the islands. The chief settlements are on West Spitsbergen.

The islands are cold and have no trees, but arctic plants grow along the coasts. Arctic birds are found on the coasts, and seals, whales and fish are caught nearby. Glaciers move down the sides of the many mountains, and icebergs form in the bays. In winter, the islands are mostly covered with ice and snow, which make them a brilliant white. The chief reason people live in this barren land is the great quantity of coal mined there. There are also deposits of asbestos, copper, and iron. In World War II, when Norway fell to the Germans, British and Norwegian troops destroyed the mines so that they could not be used by the Germans. Since World War II, coal mining has been carried on by Norwegians and Russians.

Spitsbergen has been a base for arctic expeditions by Roald Amundsen and Richard E. Byrd, and others.

spleen

The spleen is a small organ in the body. Worn out red blood corpuscles go to the spleen, where they are destroyed. The iron taken from the old corpuscles is used by the spleen to make new red blood cells.

The spleen is in the abdomen, the in-

side of the body between the hips and the chest. It is bean-shaped and about the size of your fist. It is spongy and when full of blood can be considerably larger than normal.

The spleen also acts as a storehouse for blood. At times when the body is not very active, the spleen swells up and stores extra blood much as a reservoir holds water. When you exercise and need extra blood to supply your muscles with energy, the spleen discharges its reserve blood supply into the main bloodstream.

spoils system

The spoils system is a system by which a political party that controls a government gives all the good government jobs to its own members, even if members of other parties could do the jobs better. The name came from a speech made in the United States Senate in 1832 by a Senator from New York State named William Learned Marcy. He was a supporter of Andrew Jackson, who had just been elected President, and he said, "To the victors belong the spoils." (*Spoils* means plunder, or something valuable that is taken by force.) Because of this speech, the spoils system is generally believed to have begun with the administration of President Jackson; but actually the same system had been followed in all countries for thousands of years and Jackson was opposed to it. More than fifty years later, the spoils system was partly ended by the CIVIL SERVICE, about which there is a separate article; but the most important government jobs still go to members of the political party that won the last election.

Spokane

Spokane is a city in Washington. It is in the eastern part of the state, on the falls of the Spokane River. About 180,000 people live in Spokane. Spokane is called the capital of the "Inland Empire," the great lumbering and fruit-growing region of the northwestern United States. Most of the food products of the Inland Empire are shipped out of Spokane by railroad. The city has two large airports, and one is an international airport serving airplanes from other nations. Many of the people who live in Spokane make their living by working in plants that smelt and roll aluminum and make aluminum products. There are important food-processing plants, sawmills, and furniture factories. Gonzaga University is in Spokane.

Spokane is young compared to many big cities. Fur traders and missionaries visited the region 150 years ago, but Spokane was not settled as a town until 1872. Nine years later it became a city with the name Spokane Falls. It grew rapidly in the 1930s after the building of GRAND COULEE DAM about which there is a separate article. The dam provides cheap electric power for manufacturing in plants and factories.

SPOKANE, WASHINGTON. Population (1970 census) 170,516. County seat, Spokane County.

sponge

The sponge is an odd, plantlike animal that lives in salt water. It lives on still smaller animals and on plants. It usually lives in groups that fuse themselves together and look very much like plants or small, many-branched trees. The young sponge can swim about, but soon attaches itself to a rock or shell because when it is fully grown it cannot move. Sponges have no tentacles or legs, no muscles, and no organs for breathing or feeling.

Sponges are usually tube-shaped or cone-shaped and have hundreds of tiny holes, called pores, in their bodies. Through these pores they breathe and absorb food. There are about three thousand different kinds of sponge, including a few fresh-water kinds.

The sponge that is used by man is actually the skeleton of a dead sponge. The most useful thing about sponges is that they will absorb (take in) and hold water, which then can be squeezed out again.

Sponges are used for cleaning furniture and many other things, for washing cars, for putting on shoe polish, and even for putting on beauty preparations, such as face cream. Artificial sponges, made out of rubber or plastics, are stronger and wear longer than natural sponges. Fishing for sponges is both a trade and a sport in many parts of the world where the water is warm, such as off the Florida coast in the Gulf of Mexico.

spontaneous combustion

Spontaneous combustion means "catching on fire by itself." Sometimes a pile of hay or rags, or the gases rising from a swamp, will begin to burn where there has been no flame or spark to set them afire. This is because certain processes, such as decay, make heat. If the heat becomes great enough, the material may begin to burn. There are some other fires that are said to be caused by spontaneous combustion, meaning simply that no person or animal caused the fire. For example, an accidental spark from an electric wire may cause a fire. This is not actually spontaneous combustion.

spoonbill

The spoonbill is an unusual bird that lives in many parts of the world where the climate is warm. It makes its home near ponds and marshes. There is only one type of spoonbill in the United States. It is called the *roseate spoonbill.* It gets its name because it has white feathers with delicate shades of pink. Its head and long neck are yellowish brown and are usually almost bare. Its long, thin legs are a bright red color. It is a large bird, almost three feet long.

The spoonbill is named for its unusual bill. The bill is about a foot long. It is narrow in the middle and widens out at the end, like a spoon. The bill is very handy for scooping up tiny insects and snails that live in the muddy water. The spoonbill wades slowly back and forth, scooping up its food in its bill. It has a special strainer in its bill so that it can strain out the mud and water.

Spoonbills are sociable birds that nest in large colonies. They build crude nests on the branch of a tree. The female lays three white eggs that are spotted with brown. There are very few spoonbills left in the United States. Most of them are found along the coast of the state of Texas.

spore, a plant cell from which a new plant will grow as it would from a seed: see PLANT LIFE.

sprain

A sprain is an injury to a joint. It happens most often when you twist an ankle or wrist. This pulls the ligament or cord that supports the joint. In a bad sprain the ligament is stretched or torn, and there may be a lot of pain. Sometimes the sprained part is black and blue and usually it becomes swollen. A sprain can be helped by putting the hurt arm or leg in a position so that the injured part rests on a pillow or in a sling. The pain can often be eased by icebags or cold wet cloths. Hot compresses, or soaking the sprain in a bath of hot Epsom salts, can also help. A doctor should always be consulted.

sprat

The sprat is a small fish that is a member of the herring family. It makes its home in the northern parts of the Atlantic Ocean, especially off the coast of England.

The sprat grows to be about six inches long. Fishermen catch great numbers of sprats. They are dried and salted and make a nourishing food that is not very expensive. There are no true sprats in the waters off the coast of the United States, although some varieties of sardine are called sprats.

spring

A spring is a place where water flows out to the surface of the earth from underground. If the water seeps out, as if it were leaking, it is called seepage. When the water flows out with some force, it is called a spring.

HOT AND COLD SPRINGS

Springs are formed in two ways, and are called either hot springs or cold springs. A hot spring is formed from water that comes from hot igneous rock underground or has been heated by igneous rock. The water in such springs often contains minerals that may be valuable in treating certain bone and muscle diseases. Some of them are therefore called mineral springs. Cold springs come from rain water that has soaked into the ground and then has come out again at some point where the earth surface is lower than where it soaked in. Cold springs are an important source of drinking water. Many are found in mountainous regions.

springbok

The springbok is a graceful animal that is named for its habit of suddenly leaping into the air. It is a kind of ANTELOPE, about which there is a separate article. It stands about 30 inches high at the shoulder and weighs 70 to 80 pounds. It is brown in color. The springbok has an unusual fold of skin on its back. When it is alarmed the fold turns inside out, showing a row of white hairs. The springbok has two evenly curved horns. Springboks used to live in large herds on

the plains of South Africa, but they have been hunted so much that very few are left.

Springfield

Springfield is the name of several cities in the United States.

Springfield, Illinois, is the capital of Illinois. It is in the central part of the state, on the Sangamon River. About 83,000 people live in Springfield. Springfield is a business center for a coal-mining and wheat-growing region. There are factories that make bread and other wheat products, and machines. Concordia Theological Seminary and Lincoln College of Law are in Springfield.

Springfield was first settled about 1820. In 1837 the town was made the capital of Illinois, partly through the efforts of Abraham Lincoln, who was then a member of the Illinois Legislature. Lincoln moved to Springfield in 1837.

Many tourists visit Springfield to see such places as the only house Lincoln ever owned, the monument and tomb where he and his wife are buried, and the many historical items relating to Lincoln's life that are in the state museum at the Centennial Building. Other places to see are the State Capitol, completed in 1887, and the Archives Building, where state documents are kept in filtered air so that the papers will not crumble with age.

SPRINGFIELD, ILLINOIS. Population (1970 census) 91,753. Capital of Illinois. County seat, Sangamon County.

Springfield, Massachusetts, is the largest city of western Massachusetts. The population in 1970 was 163,905. It is on the Connecticut River and is on important railroads and highways that lead to the large resort area in northwest Massachusetts. A famous United States arsenal (factory where firearms are manufactured) is in Springfield. Two of the most famous colleges for women, Smith and Mount Holyoke, are in suburbs of Springfield. The city was settled in 1636.

SPRINGFIELD, MASSACHUSETTS. Population (1970 census) 163,905. County seat, Hampden County.

Other important cities named Springfield are Springfield, Ohio (1970 population, 81,926) and Springfield, Missouri (1970 population, 120,096).

spruce

The spruce is an evergreen tree that is found in many parts of the world. It is a member of the pine family and has cones and needles.

A spruce that is often seen in the United States and Canada is the Norway spruce. This tree may reach a height of a hundred and fifty feet.

There are smaller varieties of Norway spruce that are used around houses and in gardens. The blue spruce is popular as a Christmas tree.

The needles of the spruce are shiny and may be dark green, green and white, bluish green, or yellowish green. All spruce cones hang down from the branch on which they grow. (On fir trees, the cones stand upright on the branch.)

"Spruce gum," a sticky substance that oozes from the bark of a spruce tree, is gathered by the people in some sections of the country and used as a kind of natural chewing gum.

spy, a person assigned to get secret information: see the article ESPIONAGE.

Spyri, Johanna

Johanna Spyri was the author of many children's books. She was born near Zurich, Switzerland, in 1827. Her greatest work is *Heidi,* a book that tells the adventures of a little girl who lived in the mountains of Switzerland with her old grandfather. Johanna Spyri wrote her books in German, but they have been translated into many languages. She died in 1901.

square dance

A square dance is a kind of folk dance. It is danced by a group of people, usually ten or more, half men and half women. Most "barn dances" popular in country districts are square dances, and square dancing has become very popular in cities.

The most popular instruments for the music for square dancing are the violin and accordion. There is a *caller* who directs the dancers. Square dances have been danced for hundreds of years. The quadrille and the reel are examples of old square dances. See the article on FOLK DANCING.

squash

Squash is a vine that grows along the ground. Its fruit is pulpy and is popular. There are two kinds of squash: "summer" squash, which is picked and eaten as soon as the fruit is large enough to be useful; and "winter" squash, which is cooked after it is fully grown and the rind has hardened. Both pulp and skin of summer squash are eaten, but only the pulp of winter squash.

The "summer" squashes include yellow crooked-necked squash, vegetable marrow or white squash, and zucchini. The "winter" squashes include Hubbard, acorn, and butternut. Hubbard squash is the largest of these. It is a dark green in color, and its meat (pulp) is frequently used in making squash pies. Acorn squash is usually much smaller. It is unusual to find an acorn squash more than seven inches long from tip to tip, but a Hubbard squash is often a foot or more in length. Butternut squash is a pale tan color. Zucchini look like large cucumbers. Vegetable marrow, or white squash, is pie-shaped, with scalloped edges.

squatter

A squatter is a person who has settled on land that has not yet been organized into a state or other official division of a government. In the early history of the United States, most of the pioneers who settled in the West were squatters. About a hundred years ago the question of "squatter sovereignty" became important politically.

Sovereignty means the right to govern, and squatter sovereignty meant the right of people in unorganized areas to govern themselves. At that time new states and territories were being added to the United States, and the question was whether or not slavery should be permitted in them.

People who were in favor of squatter sovereignty said the new states should decide this for themselves; people against it said the Federal government should decide this before admitting them. In a series of "compromises," sometimes the government decided and sometimes the people were allowed to decide.

squid

The squid is a strange-looking sea animal that lives in the warm oceans of the world. It is a member of the mollusc family, animals that have soft bodies and do not have any backbones. The squid is sometimes given the nickname "sea arrow," because it looks very much like a thick arrow or a long sausage. It is about eight inches long and two inches around. It has a pointed tail with two fins. On its head the squid has ten feelers, or arms, with tiny suction cups at the tips. These suction cups help the squid to capture its food. The squid has a sac of inky fluid. When it is frightened it will discharge this fluid and can escape from its enemies in a black cloud. The squid is dark gray and has red spots.

Squids usually travel in large groups (schools), which makes it easy for fishermen to catch them. Cod and other fish are fond of squid and it is often used by fishermen for bait. People in Europe and China sometimes eat the flesh.

The giant squid is the largest of all the molluscs. It lives in the open sea. Very few people have ever seen one of these huge creatures alive. Sometimes dead giant squid are washed up on beaches and people tell stories of having seen great sea monsters. The giant squid grows to be about 19 feet long and its great arms stretch about 35 feet in front of it.

squirrel

The squirrel is an animal that makes its home in many parts of the world. Some squirrels live in trees and others live on the ground. There are squirrels that swim and others that "fly." Squirrels are *rodents,* or gnawing animals, related to rats and beavers.

The squirrel that lives in trees is usually a small animal, about one foot long. It has a big, bushy tail. The tail helps the squirrel keep its balance as it leaps from branch to branch high above the ground. The tree squirrel is a busy little animal. It spends its days hunting for fruit and nuts and seeds. It hides its food in holes in trees or under logs or in the ground. In climates where the winters are very cold the squirrel often sleeps for several months. It makes its den in a hollow tree and does not come out until the weather is mild. The baby squirrels are born in this den, in the spring. When the babies are large enough to move about the squirrel family moves to a summer home, a nest of dried leaves and twigs, high in a tree.

The gray squirrel that lives in the eastern parts of the United States and Canada is a friendly, curious little animal.

Some of the squirrels that live in Central and South America have bright red or yellow coats. Others are black and white. The largest squirrel is the Oriental giant squirrel, which lives in Asia. It is often more than three feet long. It can leap about 20 feet through the branches. It becomes quite tame and can be taught to take food from a person's hand. At one

time people hunted this squirrel for food. The gray squirrel's fur is used to make coats and other fur garments.

The smallest of all squirrels makes it home on islands in the South Pacific Ocean. It is only about three inches long, including its tail.

Many squirrels live on the ground. These include the marmot, woodchuck, and prairie dog.

Sri Lanka, see CEYLON.

stadium

A stadium is a place that is built so that thousands of people can sit and watch athletic games. Stadiums were built by the ancient Greeks more than 2,500 years ago. Their most famous stadium was at a place called Olympia. Every four years the Greeks held the Olympic Games there. The ancient Romans built stadiums throughout their empire. The most famous was the COLOSSEUM, about which there is a separate article.

Today there are big stadiums in many cities of the world. Some stadiums completely surround the field and are shaped like bowls. Others are shaped like horseshoes, with one end open. Stadiums are usually built of steel and concrete and have row upon row of seats slanting up from the playing field. In the United States, the Los Angeles Stadium, Soldiers' Field in Chicago and the Municipal Stadium in Philadelphia will each hold more than 100,000 people.

Almost all stadiums are used for outdoor sports. A few that are completely roofed are used in rainy or cold weather. These are smaller than outdoor stadiums, but the Chicago Stadium will hold 20,000 people. Madison Square Garden in New York City is almost as large and became the most famous indoor stadium through the many big sports events held there.

stage, a platform or other area that is used to put on plays or other performances: see the articles DRAMA and THEATER.

stagecoach

A stagecoach was a big horsedrawn carriage that was used to carry passengers over long distances before the time of railroads. Usually a stagecoach was drawn by four or six horses. Six or perhaps eight passengers would ride inside the carriage, and often four or more passengers would ride on outside seats on top of the carriage. In England and European countries, men passengers would often sit in the "box," or driver's seat, and drive the horses. In the United States it was more usual for an employee of the stagecoach company always to drive. On lonely roads there were often bandits, so the driver had an armed guard beside him. Highwaymen (robbers) were often encountered in England and Europe also, and most of the men passengers were armed with pistols.

A stagecoach made about a hundred miles a day, in regions where the roads were fairly good. (Even the best roads in those days, more than a hundred years ago, were pretty bad, and a stagecoach ride was a rough ride.) Every forty or fifty miles along the road there would be an inn where fresh horses were hitched to the coach and where the passengers could rest, wash, and eat.

stained glass

Stained-glass windows are used in many churches. Pieces of differently colored glass are put together so as to make a picture, usually of a Bible scene, or Biblical character, or saint. The light shines through the colored glass and creates a beautiful effect inside the church.

Churches have used stained glass for a thousand years. Great artists have designed stained-glass windows and still do. Some stained-glass windows are made of pieces of colored glass, cut to fit the artist's design and joined together with strips of lead. In some cases the artist paints his colors on the glass, which is then glazed so that the colors will not wash or wear away.

A little less than a hundred years ago, stained-glass windows became popular in private houses. This was a "Victorian" style of decoration that is no longer used.

stalactite and **stalagmite,** formations seen in caves: see CAVE.

Stalin, Josef

Josef Stalin was the dictator, or absolute ruler, of Russia and the other countries of the Soviet Union for nearly thirty years. He started as an unimportant young revolutionary and made himself at least as powerful as any emperor in history. Probably he was the most powerful ruler who ever lived, for he not only had power of life and death over all the 200,000,000 people of Russia's territory but his wishes and ideas were blindly followed by hundreds of thousands of Communists in other countries. Toward the end of his life he insisted on being treated with adoration, almost as a god. Cities were named for him, his pictures and statues appeared everywhere, everything good that happened in his country was credited to him, and his name appeared dozens or even hundreds of times in the official newspapers each day.

Stalin was born in 1879 near the city of Tiflis, in Georgia, a Russian possession in the Near East. His real name was Iosif Vissarionovich Dzhugashvili; he later took the name Stalin, meaning "steel," because revolutionaries had to have false names. His father was a shoemaker and he studied for the priesthood, but he was thrown out of school because he liked the revolutionary ideas of Karl Marx, the founder of communism.

In Stalin's youth, revolutions were constantly being plotted and tried in Russia, where the people suffered under the selfish rule of the czar (emperor) and noblemen. For his part in several plots, Stalin was exiled (sent out of the country) to Siberia. He was there nine years.

In 1917, the czar was overthrown in a revolution and Stalin was released. He joined the Bolshevik Party headed by Nikolai Lenin. This is the party that became today's Communist Party. Stalin became secretary of the party and was wise enough to build up the party's power instead of trying to advance himself personally, which might have been dangerous. Lenin died in 1924. He had warned the other leading Communists against Stalin, but it was too late. Though

Leon Trotsky was thought to be the most powerful Communist next to Lenin, the party itself had become more powerful and Stalin controlled the party. He soon made Trotsky leave Russia. After about 1927 Stalin was a complete dictator.

Stalin proved to be one of the most ruthless rulers of all time. When the Russian farmers opposed his plans to combine their farms into large "collective" farms, Stalin shut off their food supply so that millions of farmers starved to death. Many more were sent to prison camps in Siberia. Stalin had some of the most famous of the old Bolsheviks put to death because they opposed him. No one who criticized him in any way was safe. Between 1936 and 1938 he had hundreds of high-ranking army officers and government leaders executed because they seemed to be growing too powerful.

Stalin was a small man, a little over five feet four inches. To become very important in the government, a man had to be shorter than Stalin. Stalin selected men who would agree with him and flatter him. He worked at unusual hours, usually in the middle of the night, and every government official had to be at his desk late into the night in case Stalin might want to talk to him. Stalin had Russian history and all the encyclopedias rewritten to make it appear that he had been Lenin's chief associate. The books were also rewritten to take out the names of those who had offended Stalin and had been executed.

In August, 1939, Stalin made a deal with the dictator of Germany, Adolf Hitler, who had been his worst enemy. By this agreement, Germany and Russia became "friends." Russia agreed to let Germany start World War II and to help with food and supplies. In return, Russia was permitted to seize the independent countries of Lithuania, Latvia, and Estonia, and parts of Poland, Finland, and Rumania.

During the first two years of World War II, Communists in all countries did things to help the Germans. In June, 1941, the Germans broke their word and invaded Russia, and after that Stalin was an ally of Great Britian and the United States. He had several famous meetings with the British Prime Minister, Winston Churchill, and President Franklin D. Roosevelt, and the three men got along well and made many agreements, but after World War II was won Stalin made Russia an unfriendly country again and broke nearly all the agreements.

During most of his time as dictator, Stalin did not have a high title in the Russian government, though he was its ruler. In 1939 he made himself premier, or official head of the government, and in 1943 he made himself a marshal, the highest title in the Russian army.

DEATH OF STALIN

As Stalin entered his seventies he became more and more insistent on being treated like a kind of god, and conditions in Russia became more difficult for the other important men in the government. Stalin died suddenly in 1953, and since he was almost 74 years old it might have been a natural death, but there were rumors that he was planning another "purge" in which many government of-

ficials would lose their lives, and he may have been murdered to prevent this. Almost immediately after he died, his name almost disappeared from the Russian newspapers. By 1956 the new Communist leaders had admitted that Stalin was guilty of unspeakably great crimes.

Stalingrad (Volgograd)

Stanlingrad is the name by which a city in the Soviet Union, now called Volgograd, will probably be remembered in history.

The city is on the Volga River near where it empties into the Caspian Sea. About 818,000 people live there. It is a river port and has important factories, making steel and tractors. There are also sawmills, furniture factories, and oil refineries. There are colleges, and universities of medicine, agriculture, and engineering.

Long ago the city was called Tsaritsyn, and it became an important shipping point for goods moved between the Don and Volga Rivers. In the Russian Revolution it was held by Communist troops under Joseph Stalin, so in 1925 it was renamed for Stalin. Then Stalin was discredited in Russia and in 1961 the name was changed again to Volgograd.

Historically the name Stalingrad is immortal because of the Battle of Stalingrad in early 1943. By many students of military history this is considered the turning point of World War II. Stalingrad was important to both German and Russian supply lines. The Germans, advancing into eastern Russia, sent 600,000 men to take Stalingrad. The Russians defended the city with fewer men. In sixty-six days of fighting the Germans lost 330,000 men. The shelling, bombing and house-to-house fighting almost totally destroyed the city. On February 2, 1943, the remnants of the German army surrendered. That day marks the time when the Russian armies ceased to be on the defensive and took the offensive.

STALINGRAD (VOLGOGRAD), SOVIET UNION. Population (1973 est.) 818,000.

stammering and stuttering

Stammering and stuttering are two words for the same speech defect, or condition in which a person cannot speak properly. A stammerer may hesitate before he can make the sound he wants, or repeat it when he has already made it. When a young child does this without knowing it, it is called *primary stuttering*. The treatment is to leave the child pretty much alone. *Secondary stuttering* occurs when the stutterer knows of his speech defect, feels a fear of it, and tries to avoid it.

Stuttering may be caused by a nervous condition or lack of confidence. The former treatment, by breathing exercises, is not often used now. Instead, the stutterer is encouraged to feel more confident and is taught to control his emotion as well as his speech.

stamp

A stamp is a small piece of paper that is stuck on something to show that a certain amount of money has been paid. The greatest use of stamps is to show that postage has been paid, but governments for many years have used stamps to show that certain taxes have been paid.

In the United States, the Treasury Department collects a tax on all alcoholic drinks and on cigarettes and other tobacco products by means of a stamp that is put on each package or bottle. Some states and cities collect a further tax by having their own stamps put on these products.

State governments usually collect taxes when stocks and bonds are sold. Tax stamps issued by the state must be put in the book in which the sale is recorded. Stamps are also used to collect taxes on the sale of real estate.

See the articles POST AND POSTAGE STAMP and STAMP ACT.

Stamp Act

The Stamp Act was a law passed by the British Parliament in 1765, before the American colonies of Great Britain won their independence in the Revolutionary War.

The Stamp Act said that every legal document (official written papers) or other printed matter in America would have to have a tax stamp on every page. The stamps were to cost threepence (six cents) to two pounds (about ten dollars), depending on the kind of document. The money was to go to Great Britain.

The Americans protested bitterly against this tax. They called it "taxation without representation," meaning that they were expected to pay a tax passed by Parliament when they were not allowed to elect any members of Parliament. Committees to protest against the Stamp Tax were formed in many American cities. A secret society called the SONS OF LIBERTY (about which there is a separate article) was formed to oppose it. Prominent men from the American colonies met in a "Stamp Act Congress" in 1765 and sent a message to England saying that the colonies would not pay any tax that their own lawmaking bodies had not approved. Because the law was so unpopular, Parliament called it off the next year; but the damage had been done, and the Stamp Act was one of the important causes of the Revolutionary War.

stamp collecting

Stamp collecting is a hobby that began almost as soon as the first postage stamp was printed (in England, in 1840) and has interested many millions of people ever since. A stamp collector tries to get many different stamps of a particular kind. So many stamps have been issued that it would hardly be possible for anyone ever to collect all of them, so collectors usually "specialize." That is, they try to get all the stamps of a particular country or of a particular kind.

The value of a stamp depends on how scarce it is and on its condition. If there are only a few stamps of a certain kind in the world, each of them may be worth thousands of dollars. In many cases a *canceled* stamp (one that has actually been used to send a letter through the mail) is worth more than a *mint* stamp (one that is just as new and clean as when it was printed). Some stamp collections are worth hundreds of thousands of dollars. King George VI of Great Britain and President Franklin D. Roosevelt of the United States had stamp collections that were famous. But a person does not need a lot of money to build up an interesting stamp collection. Many boys and girls do it on small allowances. Small packages of a dozen or more stamps can be bought for ten to twenty-five cents. When collectors know one another they can do a lot of trading, each giving up a stamp that he does not need and the other does.

The original equipment of a stamp collector is not expensive. It consists of one or more albums, looseleaf books in which the stamps are kept; gummed hinges to hold the stamps in place (they are never pasted into the album); tweezers to handle the stamps; and usually a magnifying glass for use in examining them closely. Other special equipment can be added from time to time.

WHAT COLLECTORS COLLECT

Most collectors begin by collecting all the stamps of different values or issues from a single country. It is not often possible to make a complete collection, because nearly every country has one or more rare stamps that are very expensive

This stamp was issued by the United Nations. Designed by Leonard Mitchell of New Zealand, it depicts man in his fight against cancer (symbolized by a giant crab). United Nations' stamps can be used on letters destined anywhere in the world, but those letters must be mailed at a United Nations postal station.

100TH ANNIVERSARY
UNITED STATES POSTAGE STAMPS

1

2

3

4

5

6

So many stamps are issued throughout the world that most serious stamp collectors specialize in particular kinds of stamp, such as airmail stamps, French stamps, or the like.
1. Some collect stamps issued for special occasions. (Uncanceled United States stamps must have a line drawn through them when reproduced.) 2. Some collect stamps honoring great men, such as Louis Braille. 3. Stamps may be valuable when the original value has been changed by overprinting on the faces of the stamps. 4. Similarly, a new inscription overprinted on the stamp interests many collectors. 5. Collectors may like oddities, such as the two separate Australian stamps printed together. They must be saved in pairs. 6. Many collectors specialize in stamps printed purposely with one upside down. When this occurs through an accident, a pair of such stamps becomes very valuable.

or even impossible to get. For example, United States airmail stamps include one issue in which an airplane was printed upside down, and since there are only 100 of these stamps they are expensive.

The little holes at the edges of stamps are called *perforations*. Sheets of stamps without these holes are called *imperfo-*

rates and some people collect them. A *block* of stamps is four stamps that have not been separated, and some people collect blocks. Others collect *sheets*, usually a hundred stamps that have not been separated. *Covers* are stamped envelopes that have been sent through the mail. A *first-day cover* is an envelope postmarked

on the first day the stamp was issued. A few people collect the postmarks themselves, rather than the stamps.

There are many catalogs listing stamps for sale and giving the *catalog values* of stamps (the prices for which the stamps ought to sell). Many magazines are published for stamp collectors. In big cities there are stamp shops at which stamps and collectors' equipment are sold. The proprietors of these shops will give advice to inexperienced collectors.

It has been figured that if a person had bought every postage stamp ever issued by the United States, he would have made a greater profit on his investment than he could have made in any other way ever known. At no time would he ever have been in danger of losing even a penny of what he had spent in the purchase of his collection.

Standish, Miles

Miles Standish was one of the Pilgrim Fathers, or English colonists who came to America on the ship *Mayflower* in 1620. He was appointed captain of the colony and handled its dealings with the Indians and with the British government. He served on the governing council of the colony for about thirty years. With his friend John Alden, Standish founded another colony at Duxbury, Massachusetts, where he lived until his death. The American poet Henry Wadsworth Longfellow wrote a famous poem called "The Courtship of Miles Standish." This poem is described in the article on John ALDEN. It tells how Standish loved a girl named Priscilla Mullens but was too shy to propose to her and asked Alden to do it for him. Probably it is just a story and never actually happened.

Standish was born about 1584 and died in 1656.

Stanley, Henry Morton

Sir Henry Morton Stanley was an explorer of Africa and also a famous newspaperman. He lived about a hundred years ago. He was born in Wales in 1841 and his real name was John Rowlands, but when he was 18 years old he moved to the United States and changed his name.

Stanley fought in the Confederate (southern) Army in the Civil War, then became a writer for the New York *Herald*. In 1871, the famous editor of the *Herald*, James Gordon Bennett, sent Stanley to find Dr. David Livingstone, who had been lost in the wilds of Africa for two years. Stanley spent months looking for Livingstone and finally found him. The words with which he greeted Livingstone, "Dr. Livingstone, I presume," have been quoted ever since.

Stanley had become so interested in Africa that he spent most of his remaining years exploring it. His discoveries made it possible for both Great Britain and Belgium to claim large territories there. He wrote several books and articles on his explorations. In 1895 he became a member of the British Parliament and in 1899 he was made a knight, which gave him the title Sir. He died in 1904.

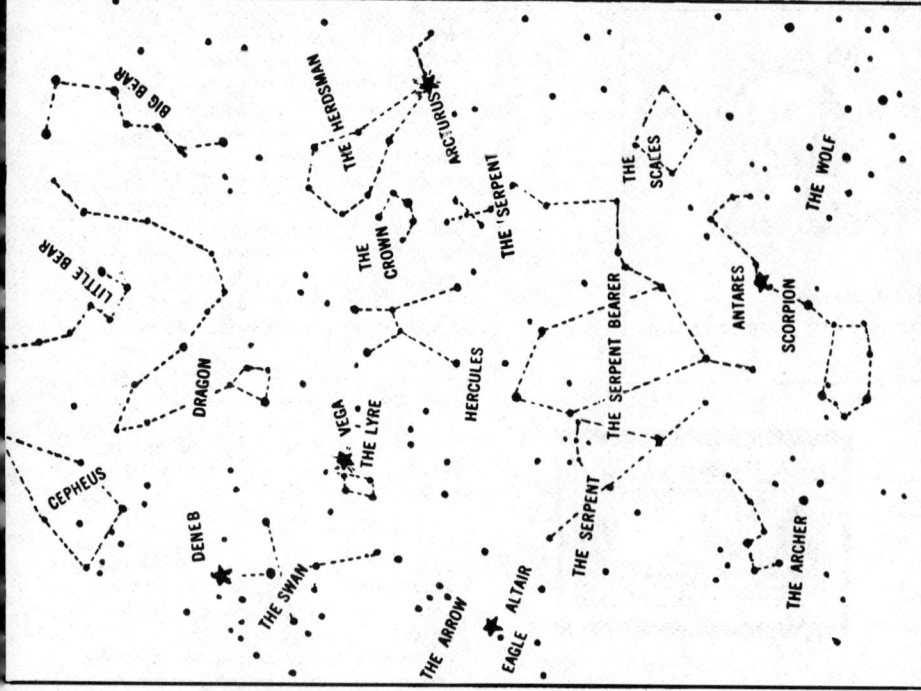

The skies in the summer, as seen in the Northern Hemisphere.

star

Stars are huge masses of gas that shine by their own light in the heavens. There are so many billions of stars that they cannot be counted. The sun is an average star. It is one of about a hundred billion stars in the galaxy, or group of stars, called the Milky Way. This is only one of billions of galaxies in the universe. Some stars are much larger than the sun, but some are smaller; some are hotter, and some are not as hot.

The heat and light from a star is produced by the changing of the nature of the atoms of which the star is made. The article ATOM explains how these particles of matter are built. A star uses hydrogen as fuel and produces helium. Both of these are gases and are chemical elements; that is, they are among the basic substances of which everything is made. The life of a star depends on its supply of hydrogen. The sun or a star like it should shine for at least thirty-five billion years. (The sun has now been shining for about five billion years.)

Stars are much hotter in their centers than at their surfaces. The surface temperature of a star may range from as high as 50,000 degrees to as low as 3,000 degrees on the Centigrade scale. (By the Fahrenheit scale that we use in discussing "the weather," there would be almost twice as many degrees.) The sun has a surface temperature of about 6,000 degrees on the Centigrade scale, or 11,000 degrees on the Fahrenheit scale. The temperatures of the centers of stars are millions of degrees.

Stars are separated by immense distances. Each star is usually three of four light-years from the nearest star. A light-year is the distance light will travel in a year, going at the rate of 186,000 miles per second. These are distances almost too great to imagine. Some stars are thousands or millions of light-years apart.

The brightness of a star is called its *magnitude.* The brightest stars are called stars of the first magnitude. The faintest stars that can be seen without a telescope are stars of the sixth magnitude. There are about six thousand stars that we can see with the naked eye and twenty of them are stars of the first magnitude.

Some stars change their brightness from time to time. These are called *variable stars.* The most important variable stars are the ones called *Cepheids.* They change from their brightest stage to their faintest stage very regularly, perhaps every few hours and perhaps over a period of as many as forty days.

Binary stars are two stars that revolve around each other. Often they are so close together that they appear as one star to the eye or even to the telescope.

A *nova* is a star that suddenly explodes and becomes very bright, then sinks to faintness again. The nova stars may be almost out of hydrogen. When a star runs almost out of hydrogen it becomes a *white dwarf* star. About 125 white dwarf stars are known. All of them are smaller than the sun. They have shrunk so that the elements in them are pressed very tightly together. A pint of the material from one of these stars would weigh 40 or 50 tons.

See also the articles on the SUN, UNIVERSE, and SPECTROSCOPE.

starch

Starch is one of the most important foods for plants and animals. Chemists know it as one of the CARBOHYDRATES, about which there is a separate article. Starch is the chief reserve food for green plants.

The most important sources of starch are the cereal grains, such as corn, rice and wheat, and the underground root plants, such as the potato, but starch is found in other vegetables and in nuts.

Starch is used not only for food but in many industries. It is used in making cloth, to strengthen the fibers and glue the loose ends together. It also gives a smooth, shiny finish to cloth. It is used to thicken colors, and also in mixing other substances to make paper, medicines, toilet powders, china clay, and many other things. It is also used in laundering clothes, to stiffen them. The plants that furnish most of the industrial starch are root, and sago.

Cornstarch is used more than any other starch in the United States. It is also a source of glucose, a kind of sugar that all starch contains.

In European countries the starch most used is potato starch. It is used mainly in making cloth, and also as a source of sugars and alcohol.

starfish

The starfish is a sea animal that lives

The skies in the spring, as seen in the Northern Hemisphere.

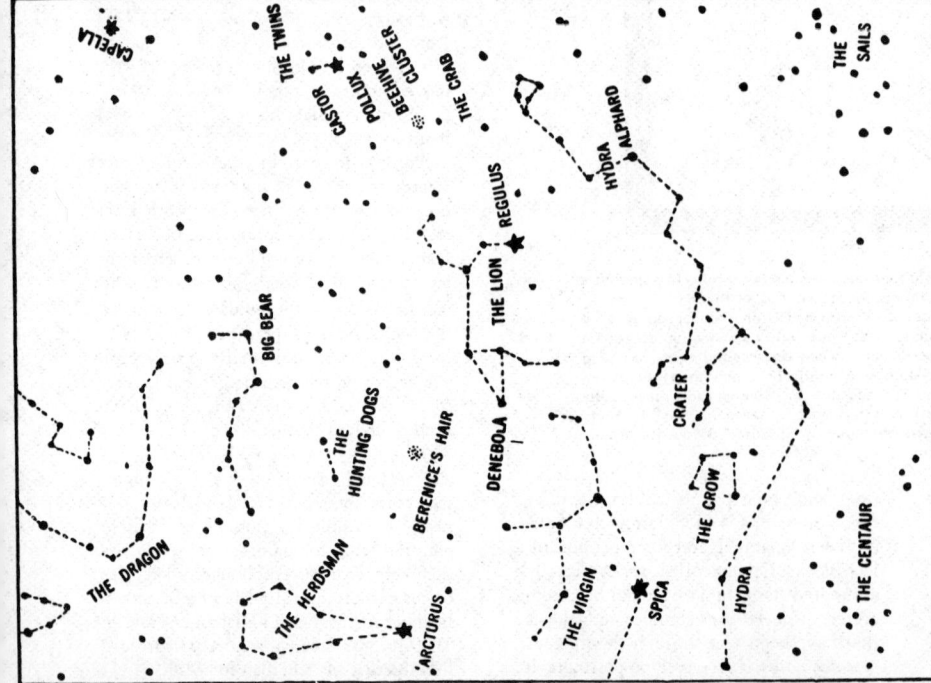

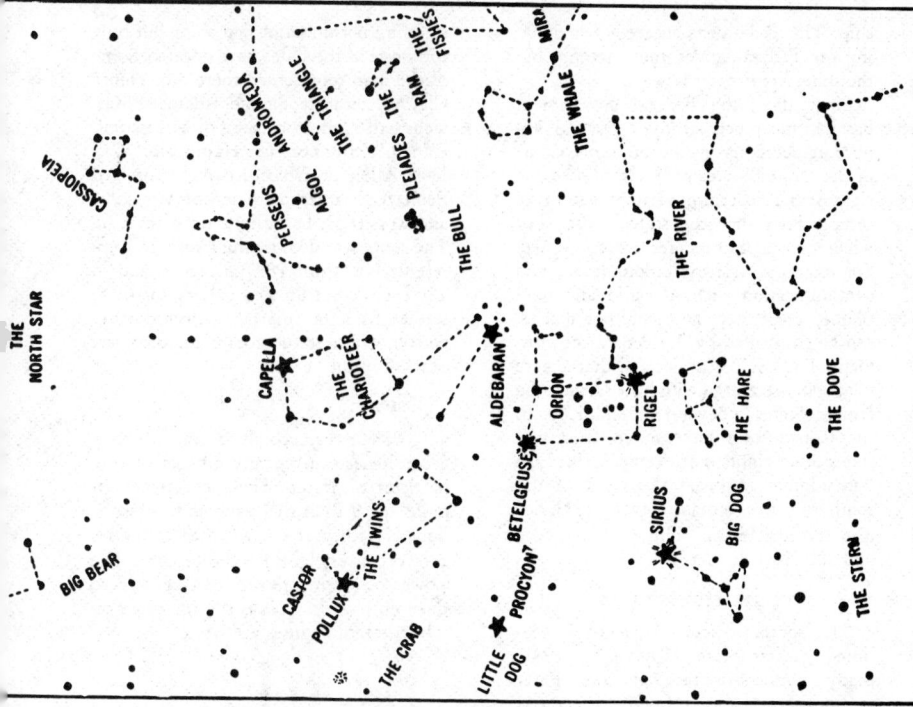

The skies in the winter, as seen in the Northern Hemisphere.

The skies in the fall, as seen in the Northern Hemisphere.

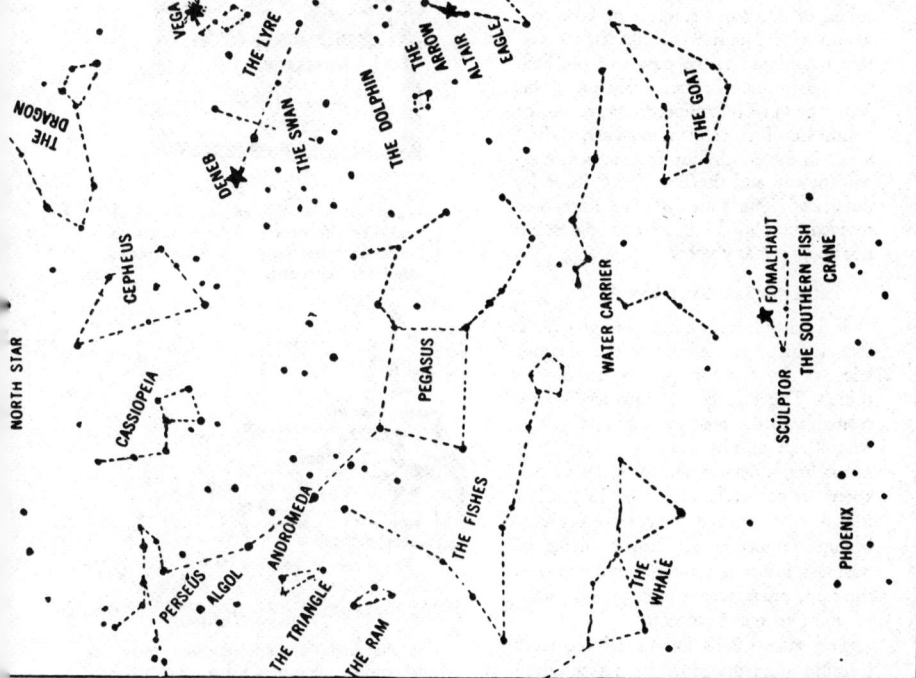

in the warm waters of the world. It is not really a fish.

People who live on the coasts of the southern United States and Europe sometimes find starfish on beaches, where they have been washed up by the tides. Most starfish have bodies that are made up of five points or arms. (A few starfish have six or even more arms.) The upper surface of the starfish's body is rough. Some starfish are about a foot across their bodies, while others are only about three inches across. Starfish are usually bright red or purple, but some kinds are green.

It is a remarkable sight to see a starfish taking a walk along the beach. It raises one of its points (arms), curls it up, and then thrusts it out and pulls itself along

the ground. The starfish can move in any direction without turning around. It simply leads with the arm that happens to point in the direction it wants to go. The starfish sometimes stands on its pointed arms and looks as if it were doing a dance. It can squeeze its body through very narrow openings.

The starfish's mouth is on the underside. It eats small shellfish and after it has digested its food it spits out the hard shells. Starfish are especially fond of mussels and oysters. If a starfish loses some part of its body it can grow back the missing part.

Brittle starfish are a special kind of starfish. They are found in all the warm waters of the world. One kind of brittle

starfish, often see along the Atlantic coast of the United States, is a greenish-brown color. Brittle starfish have longer, thinner arms than other starfish.

starling

The starling is a bird of Europe and the United States. It is a handsome bird, about nine inches long, with shiny black feathers and a bright yellow bill. It eats many harmful insects that destroy valuable crops, but has a loud, harsh voice and a bad habit of killing other birds so that it can take over their nests. When necessary the starling will build its own nest. This is a careless construction of twigs and rags and pieces of paper or whatever other materials may be handy. The female starling lays seven or eight shiny white or pale blue eggs.

The talking mynah is a member of the starling family that makes its home in India. It can learn to talk as well as a parrot or a crow.

Star-Spangled Banner

"The Star-Spangled Banner" is the national anthem of the United States. In 1814, the words were written by Frances Scott Key during the War of 1812. Key, a lawyer, went to a British ship in behalf of his client held prisoner. The British made Key remain on board, in case he had overheard their plans to fire on Fort McHenry near Baltimore, Maryland. While Key watched, the British fired on the American fort. Finally at daybreak, the firing stopped and Key saw the American flag flying over the fort. Inspired by the sight, he wrote the words.

The tune of the anthem had been popular in America for some years. It had been called "To Anacreon in Heaven" and was written for the Anacreontic Society of London, England, about 1775. For some reason it has been called an "old drinking song," but probably it never was. "The Star-Spangled Banner" was treated as a national anthem for nearly a hundred years before it was officially adopted by Congress in 1931.

state

Any independent country or nation is often called a state, but in the United States the word *state* has a special meaning. The states are the main divisions of the United States. When the United States came into existence, in 1788, the thirteen original states were called *sovereign states,* which meant that each was completely independent and the sole judge of its own affairs. Once the United States was formed, this was no longer true because each state gave up part of its independence (or sovereignty) to the national government. Ever since that time, there have been arguments between states and the national, or federal government as to how much power the states have. The Civil War, fought from 1860 to 1865, established the fact that a state does not have the right to withdraw from the United States.

The Constitution of the United States gives the federal government certain rights. All other rights belong to the states. The state government has complete authority over anything that happens in its own territory and does not concern any other state. As the United States has grown, fewer and fewer things

can happen without affecting more than one state, and whenever anything affects two or more states the federal government has certain rights. For example, any businessman who does business with people in another state can be considered subject to federal laws.

The government of nearly every state is set up in the same way. The head of the state government is called the Governor. The laws of the state are made by a legislature, which has two separate houses, or branches, in every state but Nebraska, where there is only one legislative house. Each state elects its own judges and runs its own courts of law in any way it thinks best. Each state decides which of its citizens may vote in its elections—how old they must be, whether they must own property, whether they must pay special taxes, and so on. There are some restrictions a state may not place on voting, because of the United States Constitution. For example, they may not refuse the vote to people merely because they are Negroes or because they are women.

State, Department of

The Department of State is one of the main divisions of the United States government. It is headed by the Secretary of State, who is appointed by the President and is the highest-ranking member of his Cabinet. The Department of State handles all the relations between the United States and the other countries of the world. Though some of the most important questions are decided by the President or by Congress, the Department of State carries on nearly all the dealings with other nations. Its members represent the United States in foreign countries and in the United Nations.

The Department of State has many branches, because it is concerned with so many different things. One important branch issues passports and visas to people who want to enter the United States from other countries. Separate branches deal with countries in different parts of the world—the Western Hemisphere, South Asia and Africa and the Near East, Europe, and the Far East. There is another branch for the United Nations.

Another of the most important branches is the Foreign Service. Its members serve in the United States consulates and embassies and legations all over the world. They protect the rights of American citizens in foreign countries.

Altogether, about 39,000 people work for the Department of State. The United States government is represented by about 100 embassies, several legations, and several hundred consulates and consular agencies throughout the world.

States' Rights

States' Rights has been an important issue in the United States ever since the Revolutionary War was won and the Constitution was written. The question was which should have more power, the state governments or the Federal (national) government. Alexander Hamilton and his party, the Federalist Party, believed the Federal government should be stronger. Thomas Jefferson and the anti-Federalists feared that strong Federal government might lead to a dictatorship. The Federalists succeeded in making the Federal government strong, but the states kept many powers.

Since then, the Federal government has become much stronger. Several important decisions by the Supreme Court of the United States have established the right of the Federal government to make certain laws that the states must obey when two or more states are concerned. For example, transportation, trade, and communication such as radio and telephone, when they cross state boundaries, can be controlled by the Federal government. The Civil War decided that a state may not secede (withdraw from the United States). Several amendments to the Constitution have taken from the states other rights. For example, the 13th Amendment removed the right of the southern states to make slavery legal. See also the articles on John C. CALHOUN and SECESSION.

STATES' RIGHTS PARTY

The southern states have always favored greater States' Rights. In 1948, many members of the Democratic Party in southern states refused to support President Harry S. Truman for re-election and set up a new party called the States' Rights Party. Members of this party were called "Dixiecrats." They objected to Truman's support of laws that would give Negroes greater rights and that would add to the power of the Federal government. Their candidate was James Strom Thurmond, the governor of South Carolina. Thurmond carried four states in the South, but Truman was elected anyway and the States' Rights Party disbanded. The States' Rights Party was revived in 1960, but its candidates did not receive many votes.

statistics and surveys

Statistics are numbers that give facts, such as the populations of cities and countries, or how many people do certain things. The science of statistics is concerned with the best ways of finding out what these numbers are and what they mean, and a person who is skilled in this science is called a *statistician*. In the last fifty or one hundred years, statistics have become important in many branches of business, insurance, and government, and the study offers great career opportunities to young men and women.

The statistician's job usually requires training in advanced mathematics. Often his information comes from a *poll*, or *survey*, in which questions are asked of a few hundred or a few thousand persons. If the survey is carefully planned, these persons will be selected from groups in various parts of the country and with different incomes, jobs, and so on. From this information, the statistician will learn what is true of millions of people. The statistician also uses records of what happened in past years, and from such records he can often learn what is likely to happen in the future.

Statuary Hall

Statuary Hall is a large room in the Capitol building in Washington, D.C. In it are the statues of forty-one famous Americans. Each state may select one outstanding person from that state, but only forty-one of the states have done so. Some of the men represented there are: Henry Clay of Kentucky; Samuel Adams of Massachusetts; Jefferson Davis of Mississippi; Daniel Webster of New Hampshire; William Allen of Ohio; Robert Fulton of Pennsylvania; Ethan Allen of Vermont; and Robert M. La Follette of Wisconsin. The room was used by the House of Representatives from 1807 to 1857, and in 1864 it was set up as a gallery for these statues. Each state may also select a second person, whose statue goes in another part of the Capitol.

steam

When water boils it changes to a gas called steam. Steam consists of tiny particles of water. These occupy much more space than the water did before it boiled. If they are in a closed container they press very hard in all directions. The power of steam pressure can be used to do useful work. This is the principle on which steam engines are based.

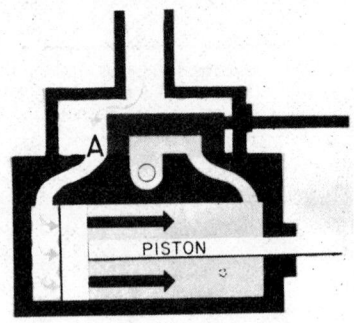

In a steam engine, steam under high pressure enters the cylinder through the open port (A), and pushes the piston (here, to the right).

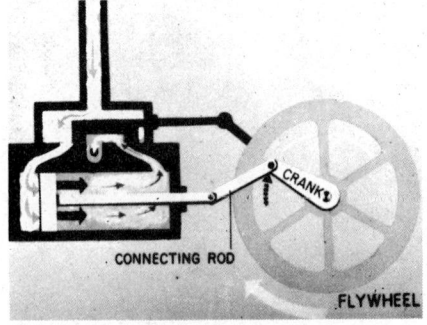

As the engine's connecting rod turns the crank, the piston's back-and-forth motion is changed into the rotary motion of the flywheel.

There is an interesting story that tells how James Watt, an English scientist who made the first successful steam engine, got his idea by watching steam blow the top off a teakettle. It is only a story, of course, because men had known for thousands of years that the power of expanding steam might be made to run an engine, and several engines had been built to make use of steam. Watt simply improved on ideas that had been tried before. His engine made the steam drive a piston, a solid piece of metal tightly enclosed in a cylinder, or tube. The piston pushed a rod and the rod turned a wheel. Watt finished his first successful engine about the year 1768. His work was used

by Robert Fulton to make an engine for a steamboat and by George Stephenson to make an engine for a locomotive. Since that time, steam has been used to run engines for factories, ships, railroads, and many kinds of machinery, including the steam shovel used in moving earth and the steamroller used to smooth roads. A better steam engine was developed a hundred years after Watt's time. It was the TURBINE, about which there is a separate article.

Some of the early automobiles used steam for power, but they lost popularity because it took too long to "get the steam up."

steel, one of the most important metals: see the article IRON AND STEEL.

Stefansson, Vilhjalmur

Vilhjalmur Stefansson is the name of a famous Arctic explorer who led many expeditions in northern Canada, Alaska, and other regions near the North Pole. He was born in 1879, in Manitoba. His parents had gone to Canada from Iceland. Stefansson studied at several universities in the United States, including Harvard. In 1904 he led an important expedition to Iceland. He was one of the first Arctic explorers to adopt the Eskimos' way of life, because he believed that people who lived in the North knew best how to survive the cold. He continued to explore northern Canadian and Alaskan regions and wrote several books about them, including *My Life with the Eskimo, Hunters of the Great North,* and *The Friendly Arctic.* He died in 1962.

Stein, Gertrude

Gertrude Stein was an American writer who lived in France for most of her life and who became known for her experiments with writing and with words. She was born in 1874 in Allegheny, Pennsylvania, and studied at Radcliffe College and at Johns Hopkins University. She traveled a great deal, and in 1903 settled in Paris, France. She wrote several books, in which she tried to use words in new ways. One of her most famous sayings is, "Rose is a rose is a rose is a rose." She meant by repeating the word "rose" to change its meaning each time, but many people thought that she was just trying to make her works difficult to understand. She died in 1946. Her works include *Three Lives, The Making of Americans, The Autobiography of Alice B. Toklas,* and two operas for which Virgil Thomson composed the music, *The Mother of Us All* and *Four Saints in Three Acts.*

Steinbeck, John

John Ernst Steinbeck was an American novelist. He was born in 1902 in Salinas, California and studied at Stanford University. Though he had written several earlier books, his first great success was *Tortilla Flat* in 1935. His best-known works are *Of Mice and Men* (about ranch workers) and *The Grapes of Wrath* (about dust-bowl migrants) which won the Pulitzer Prize in 1940. Steinbeck received the Nobel Prize in 1962. He died of a heart attack in 1968.

Steinmetz, Charles

Charles Proteus Steinmetz was an American inventor who made a large number of useful inventions in the field of electricity. He was born in Germany (in 1865) and became a college professor there, but when he was 23 years old he had to leave the country be-cause he had fought against the government. He settled in the United States, became an American citizen, and rose to be head of the research department of General Electric Corporation in Schenectady, New York. He also served as professor of physics at Union College in Schenectady. Many modern developments in radio, television and other electrical equipment are based on inventions that Steinmetz made or supervised. He died in 1923. Steinmetz was a small, crippled man, but his brilliance was so obvious that he was always able to persuade capitalists to support his inventions.

stenographer

A stenographer is a person who has the necessary skill for taking notes in shorthand and transcribing them (writing or typing them on a typewriter). Nearly all stenographers are women. In 1970 there were nearly two and a half million women working as stenographers in the United States and only about one hundred twenty five thousand men.

The things a stenographer must learn are: SHORTHAND, about which there is a separate article; typing by the "touch system" (which permits typing without looking at the keys of the typewriter); English grammar, spelling, and punctuation; and general knowledge of how a business office works. These subjects are taught in most high schools, and there are also business schools, or business colleges, attended by high-school graduates.

A stenographer who works for one executive of a company and who keeps a record of his appointments, answers the telephone or makes telephone calls for him, and does certain personal work for him not connected with the business, is called a *secretary.* A secretary usually receives higher pay than a stenographer who does not do these extra jobs. Many stenographers learn particular kinds of work: for example, a legal stenographer, who is experienced at the legal papers needed by lawyers; or a stenographer who knows two or more languages or can take technical dictation from chemists, engineers, doctors, and so on.

Stenography is actually another word for shorthand, but there are now many persons who do the same work as a stenographer except that they do not know or use shorthand. They do their typing from dictation that is put on a dictating machine. See the articles SHORTHAND, SECRETARY, and DICTATING MACHINE.

Stephen, Saint

St. Stephen was the first king of Hungary and established Christianity in that country almost a thousand years ago. He came of a noble family of Magyars, a people from Asia who settled in Hungary. Originally Stephen's name was Vajk, but he was converted to Christianity and baptized Stephen when he was 25 years old, which was in the year 994. He worked so hard to convert his people to the Christian faith that Pope Sylvester II crowned him king. His crown, the Crown of St. Stephen, became the national symbol of Hungary and was used in crowning its kings for eight hundred years until Hungary became a republic in 1918. Stephen died in 1038 and was canonized (declared a saint) about fifty years later, in 1087. Hungarians celebrate August 20 as a national holiday in honor of St. Stephen.

Another St. Stephen was the first Christian martyr. The seventh chapter of the Acts of the Apostles, in the New Testament, tells how he was stoned to death, a few years after the time of Jesus.

Stephens, Alexander

Alexander Hamilton Stephens was an American statesman of about a hundred years ago. He was one of the leaders of the southern states that broke away from the United States and formed the Confederate States of America. Stephens was born in 1812 in Taliaferro County, Georgia. He became a lawyer, served in Georgia's legislature and senate, and then was a member of Congress from 1843 to 1859. Though Stephens was against the secession (withdrawal) of the southern states from the Union, he remained loyal to his state in 1861 when it voted to secede. He was made Vice President of the Confederacy. Toward the end of the Civil War, in 1865, he was captured by Union forces and was imprisoned in Boston for several months, but was released. After the war he again became a member of the House of Representatives. In 1883 he was elected Governor of Georgia, but he died the same year.

Stephenson, George

George Stephenson was an English inventor who built the first successful steam locomotive. He was born in 1781 and as a boy he went to work as a coal miner. In 1814 he built an engine that was used with great success to haul coal from the mines, and the following year he built his first locomotive. He then directed the building of an eight-mile railway and began to build other railways all over England and in other countries of Europe. He also invented a safety lamp for miners about the same time Sir Humphry Davy did, but Davy's was used in-stead. Stephenson died in 1848. His son, Robert Stephenson, and his nephew, George Robert Stephenson, also became noted engineers.

sterilization, a method of making things free from germs: see the article ANTISEPTIC.

Sterne, Laurence

Laurence Sterne was a British writer who lived about two hundred years ago. He wrote one of the first English novels, *The Life and Opinions of Tristram Shandy,* published in 1760. Sterne's style, or way of writing, was humorous

and sentimental. Many later writers have been influenced by Sterne.

Sterne was born in Ireland in 1713, of an English father and an Irish mother. After attending Cambridge University he became a minister in the Church of England. He wrote many volumes of sermons, as well as a humorous account of his travels called *A Sentimental Journey Through France and Italy*. Laurence Sterne died in 1768.

Steuben, Baron von

Baron Friedrich von Steuben was a German nobleman and soldier who aided the Americans in the Revolutionary War. He was born in the German kingdom of Prussia in 1730. When he grew up he became a military officer and fought for Prussia in many campaigns. He so admired the bravery of the Americans in their fight for independence that in 1777 he came to America and joined the army under General George Washington at Valley Forge. He was made a major general, and he taught the untrained colonists much about warfare and military discipline. He was so strict that he was nicknamed "the drillmaster." He served in many important campaigns, among them the great Battle of Yorktown in 1781. At the end of the war the states of New York and New Jersey both gave him land and the United States government gave him a pension. He became an American citizen, retired to his home in New York State at a town that was later named Steubenville in his honor, and wrote a number of books about military tactics. He died in 1794.

Stevenson, Adlai E.

Adlai Ewing Stevenson is the name of two American statesmen, grandfather and grandson. The first Adlai Ewing Stevenson was born in 1835 in Christian County, Kentucky. He became a lawyer in Bloomington, Illinois, and later served in Congress and as Vice President under President Grover Cleveland from 1893 to 1897. He died in 1914.

His grandson, Adlai Ewing Stevenson,

was born (in 1900) in California but always was a resident of Illinois. He too became a lawyer and practiced in Chicago, Illinois. During World War II Stevenson was made assistant to the Secretary of the Navy and later to the Secretary of State. He was adviser during the San Francisco Conference in 1945, when the United Nations was formed, and later was a member of the United States delegation to the United Nations. In 1948 he was elected Governor of Illinois and in 1952 and 1956 he was the Democratic Party's candidate for President of the United States, but lost both times. In 1961 he became the U.S. Ambassador to the United Nations. He died in 1965.

Stevenson, Robert Louis

Robert Louis Stevenson was a Scot-

tish writer of novels, essays, and poems. He was born more than a hundred years ago. He is best remembered for his stories of adventure, such as *Treasure Island* and *Kidnapped*, and for his book of poems for young children, *A Child's Garden of Verses*.

Stevenson was born in 1850. His father was a lighthouse engineer and Stevenson wanted to follow the same profession, but a serious illness at the age of 8 left him too weak for such active work. Stevenson then studied law, but instead of working as a lawyer he turned to writing.

When Stevenson was 26 years old he met an American woman, Mrs. Fanny Osbourne. He fell in love with her and followed her to America, and in 1880 they were married. He returned with her to Scotland, but the climate was bad for him and he began to travel to health resorts. From 1880 to 1886, Stevenson published most of the books that made him famous, including *The Strange Case of Dr. Jekyll and Mr. Hyde*.

In 1887 Stevenson and his family sailed for America, and he never saw Europe again. He lived in New York for a time, but in 1888 he hired a ship and sailed for the South Pacific. The last years of Stevenson's life were spent on the island of Samoa, where he became a good friend to the natives and helped them fight against the injustices of some of the British governors.

Robert Louis Stevenson died in Samoa in 1894. He was only 44 years old and had been in bad health nearly all his life.

Stewart, another spelling of the name STUART.

Stilwell, Joseph W.

Joseph Warren Stilwell was an American general who served the United States in World Wars I and II. He was born in 1883 in Palatka, Florida and was graduated from the United States Military Academy at West Point. He served in France in World War I and then was sta-

tioned in China from 1920 to 1939. In 1942 he was made a lieutenant general and was placed in charge of all American forces in China, Burma, and India. He helped train the Chinese forces. Stilwell planned a road through the jungles that has since been named Stilwell Road in his honor. In 1944 he was recalled to the United States because he had disagreed with the Chinese leader, Generalissimo Chiang Kai-shek. He was promoted to full general and made commander of the Army Ground Forces. In 1945 he was made commander of the Tenth Army in the Pacific. He died in 1946.

sting ray

The sting ray is a strange fish that lives in oceans and rivers where the climate is not too cold. The sting ray is very flat. It hides on the bottom of the ocean or river. It has a long tail with a sharp

spine on it, and it uses this tail as a weapon. If a person steps on a sting ray it will lash out with its tail. The sharp spine wounds the leg and injects poison into the person's body. A wound from a sting ray can be painful and dangerous.

The largest sting ray is a huge fish that is found in the waters of Australia. The sting ray that lives in fresh-water rivers is only about the size of a pancake. Scientists believe that female sting rays have live young.

stock exchange

Most of the big business companies of the world have thousands of owners. Each of these owners has a number of shares of stock in the company. These shares entitle him to a part of the profits made by the company. For example, if a company has 100,000 shares of stock owned by various persons, and makes a profit of $300,000, each share earns $3; and if a person owns 10 shares of the stock of that company, he has earned $3 for each share, or $30 altogether.

A stock exchange is a place where people can buy and sell shares of stock in certain companies. A stock exchange is a kind of club, with members. A member can go on the "floor" of the stock exchange and buy or sell stocks. Others cannot do this. So members of a stock exchange usually act as representatives, called *brokers*, for other people who want to buy or sell stocks. The broker does the buying and selling for the other person and charges a fee for doing so. His fee is based on the number of shares he buys or sells and on the price at which those shares are bought or sold.

There are stock exchanges in most of the big cities of the world. A company must have its stock *listed* by a stock exchange before that stock can be traded (bought or sold) by the members of that stock exchange. To have its stock listed, a company must obey certain rules and meet certain requirements of the stock exchange. These are some of the requirements of the New York Stock Exchange, which is the biggest in the world:

The company must have substantial assets (things it owns) and must have shown that it has an earning power of at least a million dollars a year.

It must be owned by at least 1,500 stockholders and must have at least 300,000 shares of stock in the possession of its stockholders.

It must agree to send one full financial report each year to its stockholders and to publish statements of its earnings once every three months.

There are many stock exchanges that will list the stocks of smaller companies. A company never lists its stock with more than one stock exchange in any city, and usually a company lists its stock with only one stock exchange in the world.

A stock exchange keeps a record of every transaction (buying or selling of shares) and the price at which the shares were bought and sold. These prices go out over an automatic telegraphic device called a *stock ticker*. The ticker prints the name of the stock, the number of shares and the price on a narrow paper tape.

"Ticker tape" rolls out of the machine almost constantly. Nearly every stock has a special symbol shown on the ticker tape; for example, Canadian Pa-

cific is CP, and the American Telephone and Telegraph Company is merely T.

Millions of people, and thousands of firms make their livings on the buying and selling of stocks and other securities (such as bonds). Very complete records are kept of sales and prices, and these are published in newspapers and books. Since 1935 stock exchanges in the United States have been under certain rules of the SECURITIES AND EXCHANGE COMMISSION, about which there is a separate article.

A stock exchange is an interesting place, well worth visiting, and most stock exchanges welcome visitors. The largest ones are in New York (sometimes called "Wall Street"); in London ("the 'Change"); and in Paris (the "Bourse").

The New York Stock Exchange, or N.Y.S.E., is at 20 Broad Street, near Wall Street. It has a special visitors' gallery, guides who explain the workings of the exchange, and exhibits by companies whose stocks are listed on the Exchange. It is to the advantage of the Exchange and brokers to have stocks owned by as many persons as possible, and they carry on an "educational" program to induce people to "buy shares in America." In 1970 almost thirty-one million people in the United States owned stocks.

The "floor" of the N.Y.S.E. is huge, and more than a thousand members are on their feet there every day from 10 in the morning to 3:30 in the afternoon. On the front wall are two huge illuminated ticker tapes, one showing price changes of stocks on the "Big Board" (N.Y.S.E.), the other for stocks of the American Exchange, the second-largest New York Exchange, formerly called the "curb." On one side is a tremendous blackboard on which numbers flash; these numbers "page" floor members, telling them to go to their posts or to answer their telephones. The members seem to wander around, making signs with their fingers to other members, and jotting down things on bits of paper or in notebooks.

On the "floor" are eighteen trading posts. Each handles about eighty stocks, or a smaller number of the very important stocks. A number of traders do business at each post. Some are "specialists" in a particular stock.

HOW STOCKS ARE TRADED

This is the way stocks are bought and sold: Suppose a man in Los Angeles wants to buy 100 shares of General Motors Corporation, whose symbol is GM, at a definite price, $96 a share. He goes to a local broker, whose main office is in New York. The broker sends a flash by Teletype to his New York Office: "Buy 100 GM at 96." The New York office telephones the order, by private wire, to its floor member. The floor member goes to the GM trading post and sees if anyone wants to sell 100 shares at $96. If the price has meanwhile risen higher than $96, the order cannot be put through at once. If the order was to buy "at the market," the member pays whatever is being asked and the order is quickly filled.

When the stock is bought, the floor members jot down the deal and the price. There is no legal contract to be signed and no witnesses are necessary. Everything is by word-of-mouth. Just a few words are needed to arrange a deal that may run into millions of dollars. After a deal has been completed, it will appear on the Big Board ticker, not only in New York but in brokerage offices all over the country, as follows: "GM 96." The stock certificate for the 100 shares of GM would, at the N.Y.S.E., be delivered about four days later. Delivery takes longer at some exchanges. The 100 shares in this case might be kept by the New York brokerage office, as the buyer might want to sell them later on at a profit. If he has bought them for a long-time investment, they would be put in his own name and sent to him.

The unit of trading in stocks is 100 shares. But many people cannot afford 100 shares; they may want to buy one or two or seven shares. Less than 100 shares is called an "odd lot." Buying an odd lot is slightly more expensive than buying a unit; the broker charges one-eighth of a point (that is, 12½ cents) as well as his regular fee. For example, if a man bought one share of GM for $96 he would have to pay $96 plus one-eighth, or $96.125, plus fee. The broker would get the 12½ cents. There are a few brokers that deal only in odd lots. They simply collect all small orders for a stock until 100 is reached, then the deal is made.

MEMBERSHIPS

Memberships or "seats" on the N.Y.S.E. are bought for cash, usually by brokerage firms for their members. The price of a seat depends partly on how much can be made in fees by a broker using it. The highest price, in 1929, was $625,000; in 1961 the price of a seat on the Exchange ranged from a low of $147,000 to a high of $225,000. The N.Y.S.E. in 1961 had 1,366 members, representing 678 firms. There were 1,541 stocks listed, totaling more than 7 billion shares worth almost 400 billion dollars.

BULLS AND BEARS

Stock-exchange people, and those who often trade in stocks, have a special language all their own. Those who think stock prices will go higher, and want them to go higher, are called "bulls" (as though they might toss the stocks up on their horns). People who want prices to go lower, and who think they will go lower, are called "bears" (as though they might "growl" the stocks down). The "bulls" usually own stocks; the "bears" want prices to drop so they can buy stocks more cheaply. Of course, a man who is a "bull" today might sell his stocks and then become a "bear," hoping prices will go lower so he can buy them again. Such a man is also called a "sold-out bull."

The "bears" also include people who have "sold short" a number of stocks. This means that they believed a certain stock would go down in price, and so they sold that stock even though they did not own it. If the price *does* go down, the seller can buy the stock at a cheaper price and thus make money. If the stock goes up instead, he will still have to buy it sooner or later to make delivery and so will lose money.

Many of the ordinary stocks of large corporations have nicknames that are used by brokers and customers. For example, the Bethlehem Steel Corporation, whose abbreviation or symbol on the ticker is BS, is known as "Bessie." The United States Steel Corporation, called X on the ticker, is called simply "Steel" or "Big Steel."

THE CRASH OF 1929

There have been several "crashes" of the stock markets, which have been usually followed by business depressions. The worst and best-known was the 1929 crash.

In the late 1920s prices of stocks rose steadily and rapidly until they reached heights that seem fantastic today. It was easy to borrow money then, too easy, and many people who could not afford to speculate borrowed money and "played the market," that is, bought stocks "on margin" by putting up only 10 percent of the stocks purchased. This means that if a person had about $100 he could buy stocks worth $1,000. The broker charged him interest on the rest of the stock's price, the $900. But if the price of the stock went down, the owner would have to provide more margin. (In 1962, in contrast, the margin required was at least 50 percent).

More and more people of moderate means bought stocks, owing more and more money, until the banks and brokers had lent so much money that actually they and not the people had bought the stocks at those fantastically high prices. In October, 1929, stock prices began to drop rapidly, and people who did not have money for more margin had to sell stocks at a loss. In late October came the big crash, when 16 million shares were sold in a single day. There were few buyers, so prices kept on dropping and many people lost huge "fortunes" they thought they owned. A financial panic followed, banks and businesses failed, and millions of people lost their jobs. Many of those who were ruined committed suicide.

Then came the Great Depression, which was felt around the world. It lasted several years. Things began to improve, slowly, after 1933. The Securities and Exchange Commission was formed, and speculation in stocks was better regulated.

See also the article COMMODITY EXCHANGE.

Stockholm

Stockholm is the capital and largest city in Sweden. It is in the eastern part of the country, on Lake Malar, where it joins the Baltic Sea. More than 745,000 people live in Stockholm. Stockholm is an important seaport and is also Sweden's chief manufacturing city. There are big shipbuilding yards, factories that make rubber and chemical products, and mills that make textiles and paper.

Stockholm is one of the most beautiful cities in the world. It includes thirteen islands along the coast. One of these, the Old City, is the oldest part of Stockholm. It has many buildings built hundreds of years ago and also the Royal Palace where the Swedish king lives. Bridges join it to the mainland part of the city. Many bays and inlets of the Baltic and Lake Malar cut into the mainland, and have given Stockholm the name "Venice of the North," but Stockholm's modern buildings and its cold climate really make it very unlike Venice.

There are many interesting places to visit in Stockholm. Among them are the Royal Dramatic Theater, where Nobel

Prizes are given; the very modern City Hall; the great stadium built for the 1912 Olympic games; and the Riddarholms Kyrna, where many of the kings and great men of Sweden are buried.

Stockholm was founded about seven hundred years ago, when a nobleman built a castle to guard Lake Malar against pirates. The city grew rapidly as a business center under the German merchants of the HANSEATIC LEAGUE, about which there is a separate article.

In 1520, Stockholm was the scene of the "Stockholm Blood Bath." Christian II, King of Denmark, invaded Sweden after the Swedes had revolted against his rule. He promised not to take revenge if the Swedes would surrender Stockholm to him, but during his coronation as king of Sweden he had eighty-two of his former enemies seized and executed.

STOCKHOLM, SWEDEN. Population (1973 estimate) 745,000. Capital and largest city of Sweden. Seaport and industrial city on the Baltic Sea.

stocks and pillory

The stocks and the pillory were forms of punishment that once were used for persons who had committed very minor crimes. They were first used late in the Middle Ages, about six hundred years ago. About three hundred years ago they were used in the American colonies. The stocks were a wooden frame that held the prisoner, sitting down, with his hands and feet locked in the frame. The pillory was a frame that held him standing, with his head and hands locked in the frame. The frames were usually set up in a public square, so that the prisoners might be jeered at and pelted with stones by the townspeople. Sometimes he was also whipped. In the colonies this punishment was used for people who told malicious lies about their neighbors or committed similar misdemeanors. The pillory was legal in the state of Delaware as late as 1905.

Stoics

The Stoics were a group of philosophers (thinkers) who lived in the city of Athens, in ancient Greece, more than two thousand years ago. The group was founded by a philosopher named Zeno. The Stoics believed that the most important thing was for men to be happy in this world, and not to hope for a better world (or heaven) after death. Since there were many things to make man unhappy, such as pain or disease, they taught that man should resign himself to these things and not try to fight them. The Stoics taught that men should be understanding of each other's differences, and that all men were brothers under one God. They were opposed to slavery and war.

There were many fine writers who were Stoics. Among them were Epictetus, who was a Greek slave in Rome, and the Roman emperor Marcus Aurelius.

Today when a man calmly accepts the bad things that have happened to him, or seems to take them for granted, he is said to be "stoical."

stomach

The stomach is one of the most im-

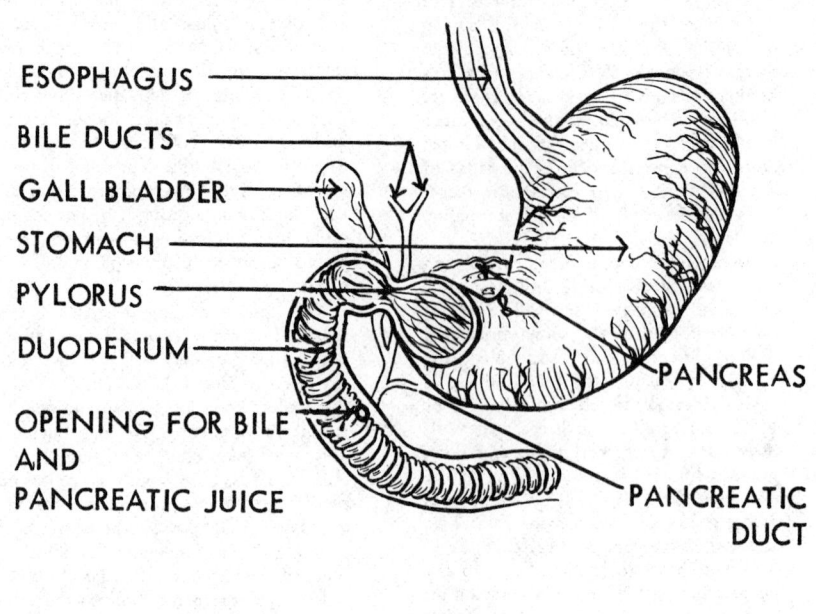

ESOPHAGUS
BILE DUCTS
GALL BLADDER
STOMACH
PYLORUS
DUODENUM
OPENING FOR BILE AND PANCREATIC JUICE
PANCREAS
PANCREATIC DUCT

STOMACH

portant organs of the body. It is in the abdomen, the inside of the body between the hips and the chest. People often speak of this entire section as the stomach, but the stomach actually occupies only a small part of it.

The stomach is a pear-shaped, ballon-like organ. It lies just to the left of the center of the body below the ribs. When full, it is about a foot long and about five inches across and can hold about two quarts of food.

The article on DIGESTION tells how food passes from the mouth down through the tube called the esophagus into the stomach. Before the food enters the stomach it has been chewed and partly broken up by the teeth, and the saliva in the mouth has begun to work on it chemically. In the stomach the food is again worked on chemically and is given a good shaking-up.

The stomach is lined with mucous membrane. It is the same sort of lining that the mouth has, but the mucous membrane in the stomach is very wrinkled, giving it a greater surface. In the mucous membrane there are many small glands that manufacture liquids, or gastric juices, that work on food in the stomach. One is called *rennin*. This is the chemical that curdles milk and makes it into a cheesy substance. The second liquid is called *pepsin*. This helps to break down protein foods such as meat into slightly different substances. The third liquid is *hydrochloric acid*. This helps to dissolve the food (turn it into a liquid).

While the food in the stomach is being treated by the liquid chemicals it also receives a churning or mixing. The outer wall of the stomach is made of strong muscles that send rippling waves from the top of the stomach to the bottom and then back again. These waves press the stomach wall in and out.

Food remains in the stomach about four hours after a meal. During this time it is changed into a pasty substance about as thick as pea soup. This is released through a small opening, called the *pyloric valve*, at the bottom of the stomach. The valve is kept closed by an elastic ring of muscle until the pressure at the bottom, and the acid condition of the digested food, causes the muscles to relax and open the valve. The food then passes from the stomach into the small intestine.

Stone Age, a period in the early life of man when he had not learned to use metals and made all his tools of stone: see AGE and ARCHAEOLOGY.

Stonehenge

Stonehenge is the name of a group of stones that stand on Salisbury Plain, a meadow in Wiltshire, England. Experts used to think that Stonehenge was an ancient temple for worshiping a sun god, but now they believe it was really a primitive astronomy laboratory, built more than 3,500 years ago! The stones are set up in two circles, one inside the other, with a long block of stone in the center. Certain stones point to areas in the sky where the sun rises, the sun sets, the moon rises, the moon sets, and where various stars are seen. This was how some ancient people were able to learn and predict facts about the universe.

Stone Mountain

Stone Mountain, in Georgia, is a huge granite dome, two miles long and seven miles around. It rises 648 feet above the ground. It is fifteen miles east of Atlanta. On this mountain, Gutzon Borglum, under the sponsorship of the United Daughters of the Confederacy, began in 1916 to carve giant statues of Confederate heroes of the Civil War. Henry Augustus Lukeman continued his work later. Before the work was abandoned for lack

of money, the statues of Generals Robert E. Lee and Stonewall Jackson, and President Jefferson Davis of the Confederate States of America, were completed. The statues are similar to those on Mt. RUSHMORE, about which there is a separate article.

stork

The stork is one of the most popular of all birds. It makes its home in many parts of the world where the climate is not too hot or too cold. The best-known stork lives in Europe and parts of Asia. It is a large, attractive bird, about 3½ feet long. It has white feathers and its wings are touched with black. It has a long red bill and red legs.

The stork is a powerful, graceful flier. The storks of Europe make long journeys to South Africa for the winter. When spring comes they return to their nesting places. Storks build large nests on the roofs of buildings or chimney tops or in trees. The female lays three or four white eggs. The baby storks are born with almost no feathers. Even when they are about two feet tall they are quite helpless and must be cared for by their parents.

The stork does not make any sound with its mouth. It can bend its long neck back until its bill almost touches its tail, then it claps its bill and seems to enjoy the noise. Storks eat frogs and other small animals that live in swamps and marshy places.

The only true stork native to the United States is the *wood stork,* once misleadingly called the *wood ibis,* though it is not an ibis at all. It lives in the southern states. About 3½ feet tall, it has a white body with black tail and wing feathers. Its head is bare, which explains its nicknames of "leatherhead" and "flinthead." At one time there were over 100,000 wood storks in Florida alone, but by 1957 there were only about 8,000 in the entire country. Sanctuaries have been provided for them in southern Florida, but they are still listed as an endangered species.

storm

A storm is a disturbance in the weather. There are different names for different kinds of storm, but nearly every storm is accompanied by a very high wind. A snowfall is not called a storm, but if a strong wind blows the snow it becomes a storm of the kind called a *blizzard.*

The worst storms are called HURRICANES and TORNADOES, about which there are separate articles. (There are other names for the same kind of storm.) Almost the only kind of storm that need not be windy is the *thunderstorm,* which usually occurs on a hot summer day. This is lightning and thunder followed by a heavy rain. Sometimes a thunderstorm is accompanied by a high wind. See the article on WEATHER.

Stormalong, Alfred B.

Alfred B. Stormalong was not a real person. He was a legendary figure created by the storytellers in New England in the days of the great sailing ships, more than a hundred years ago. He was an enormous giant who stood as tall as the tallest mast on a sailing ship. The stories about him are many and wonderful and tell of

his great exploits at sea and his ability to do the work of many ordinary sailors. He could hoist and lower great sails as easily as if they were window blinds. He could steer a large ship in the roughest seas and the most howling windstorms. For all his great size and strength he was a kind man and would help people whenever he could. Some stories tell how he even went inland at times and helped farmers do their heavy work.

Stowe, Harriet Beecher

Harriet Beecher Stowe was an American writer and one of the most famous abolitionists (persons who worked to have slavery outlawed in the United States). She was born in 1811 in Litchfield, Connecticut. Her father, Lyman Beecher, was a famous Congregational minister. When Harriet grew up she became a teacher, and in 1836 she married Professor Calvin Ellis Stowe, a professor at Bowdoin College in Brunswick, Maine.

Mrs. Stowe had been much impressed by the hard life of slaves in the southern states, and in 1851 she began the publication of a novel, *Uncle Tom's Cabin,* in an abolitionist newspaper. The novel was later published as a book and became the biggest-selling novel of its century. More than 300,000 copies were sold during the first year. *Uncle Tom's Cabin* was then put into the form of a play and was performed more often than any other play in history. As late as the 1900s, "Tom shows" were still touring the United States, putting on performances of the play.

The novel *Uncle Tom's Cabin* did much to arouse hatred of slavery in the northern states. It was one of the factors that led to the Civil War. Mrs. Stowe wrote another anti-slavery novel, called *Dred,* and several other novels. She also wrote a book of religious poems. She died in 1896.

strabismus

Strabismus is a trouble of the eyes. It is usually called "cross-eyes" or "cockeyes" and it is usually caused by a weakness of the muscles that move the eyeballs from side to side, so that one muscle pulls the eye harder than another. The result is that both eyes do not look at the same thing at the same time. This would make most people see double, but a cross-eyed person does not because he manages to see with only one eye and neglects the other. The unused eye therefore becomes weaker and weaker.

A great many of the children who have cross-eyes inherit it from their families, but there may also be other causes. It can be helped by wearing glasses that improve the vision of the weaker eye and sometimes by special exercises to make the eye muscles stronger. The usual way to cure strabismus is by an operation on one or both eyes, to shorten or lengthen the muscles so that they balance. This brings the eyes back to normal position. Sometimes a child may outgrow crosseyes, but this seldom happens, and a doctor should always be consulted.

Stradivari

Stradivari was the name of a family of violin makers who lived in Cremona, Italy, about three hundred years ago. The greatest violin makers of all time lived in Cremona during the same period. The most famous member of the Stradivari family was Antonio, who was born in 1644. He was a pupil of Nicolo AMATI, about whom there is a separate article. The violins made by Antonio Stradivari (whose name is also spelled *Stradivarius*) are generally considered the finest ever made. Some of them have actually sold at prices about $50,000 (and newspapers have reported sales as high as $100,000, though it is doubtful that any such price was ever paid). Stradivari also made many violas and cellos. Other members of his family who made fine violins included his sons, Francesco and Omobono.

Straits Settlements, a former name for British possessions in southeast Asia: see MALAYA.

Stratford-on-Avon

Stratford-on-Avon is a city in Warwickshire, England, that is famous as the birthplace of the great English writer, William Shakespeare. It is on the Avon River, northwest of London. About 15,000 people live there. In the town are the house that is thought to be Shakespeare's birthplace, a school that he may have attended, and his burial place in the Church of the Holy Trinity, which also contains a memorial to him. A theater dedicated to Shakespeare burned in 1926 but was rebuilt and Shakespeare's plays are presented there.

Strathcona, Lord

Donald Alexander Smith, Lord Strathcona, was a Canadian fur-trader and statesman. He was born in 1820 in Scotland and settled in Canada when he was 18 years old. He got a job with Canada's most important fur-trading company, the Hudson's Bay Company, and soon rose to a high position in the company. Later he served in the Canadian Parliament and became prominent in the building of railroads. He completed the greater part of the Great Northern Railway and the Canadian Pacific Railway. In 1896 he was made high commissioner for Canada in England. There he was rewarded by being made first Baron of Strathcona and Mount Royal, which gave him the right to use the title "Lord" before his name. He died in 1914.

Strauss, Johann

Johann Strauss was the name of two Austrian composers (writers of music) who made the Viennese waltz famous. They were father and son. The elder was called "father of the waltz," and the younger was called "king of the waltz."

Johann Strauss, the Elder, was born in Vienna in 1804. For five years he played the viola in Viennese orchestras, and in 1824 he organized an orchestra of his own. With this group he gave the world some 150 waltzes, including *The Lorelei* and *The Victoria Waltz.* He died in 1849.

Johann Strauss, the Younger, was born in 1825 and became far more famous than his father. The elder Strauss op-

posed his son's wish to become a musician, but the younger man studied music secretly and became conductor of an orchestra. Among the most popular of five hundred waltzes he wrote are *The Blue Danube*, *Tales from the Vienna Woods*, the *Emperor Waltz*, and *Artist's Life*.

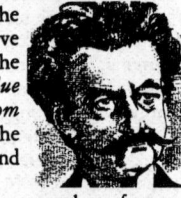

Strauss also wrote a number of operettas, or gay musical plays, the most popular of which are *Die Fledermaus* (The Bat), *Gypsy Baron*, and *One Night in Venice*. Johann Strauss, the Younger, died in 1899. His two brothers, Josef and Eduard Strauss, were also orchestra conductors.

Strauss, Richard

Richard Strauss was a German composer, or writer of music. He is famous for his opera *Der Rosenkavalier* (the Knight of the Rose), and his compositions for symphony orchestras.

Strauss was born in 1864. He could play the piano at the age of 4 and he wrote his first music when he was 6. At the age of 21 he became conductor of an orchestra in the city of Meiningen. There he became interested in the new idea that music should express feelings in whatever way the composer felt them, rather than be held to rigid rules. Among his most successful operas, in addition to *Der Rosenkavalier*, are *Elektra* and *Salome*. His compositions for symphony orchestra include *Death and Transfiguration*, *Don Juan*, *A Hero's Life*, *Don Quixote*, and *Till Eulenspiegel*. He also wrote many beautiful songs. Strauss made concert tours all over the world, including the United States. He died in 1949.

Stravinsky, Igor

Igor Stravinsky was one of the greatest composers of music of all time, and probably the finest composer of the Twentieth Century.

He was born in Russia in 1882 and later lived in Paris, France. Although his first compositions were for orchestra, he became famous overnight for the production in 1910 of a ballet called *The Firebird*. The music for this ballet was so strange and full of dissonances (harsh sounds) that it created a riot in the Paris theater where it was performed. Two other Stravinsky ballets which are often performed are *Petrouchka* and *The Rite of Spring*. He also wrote symphonies, chamber music, piano concertos, and other pieces.

In 1940, Stravinsky settled in the United States and, in 1945, composed *Ballet Scenes* upon becoming an American citizen. He conducted the world premiere of his opera, *The Rake's Progress*, in 1951. Stravinsky died in New York City in 1971.

straw

Straw is the hollow stem of grain plants after the grain has been threshed out. There are as many different kinds of straw as there are cereal grains. Straw is used for many different purposes. It forms both bedding and fodder (food) for cattle and other animals. It is used for padding and packing breakable articles for shipping. Some kinds of straw are woven into material to make straw hats and ladies' handbags, and some are used to weave rugs and table mats. For many years people slept on mattresses filled with straw, and in some parts of the world straw mats are used for beds even today.

strawberry

The strawberry is the sweet fruit of a vine that grows wild and is also cultivated in gardens in many parts of the world. Technically it is not a true berry, but is an aggregate fruit. The little seedlike parts on the outside of the strawberry are actually small individual fruits, each having a seed covered with a thin, pulpy skin. The part eaten is a fleshy receptacle for the individual fruits.

Strawberries are perennial plants that grow close to the ground, with trailing runners that grow out from the main crown of the plant. At certain places on the runner, called nodes, new plants are formed and those closest to the mother plant may bear fruit the same year they are formed. The younger plants toward the ends of the runners may not bear fruit until the following year.

Wild strawberries are much smaller, but they are often sweeter than the cultivated strawberries.

streamlining

Streamlining is designing something so that it can move through the air without too much resistance from the air. The air is a gas, and though it does not seem to hold us back when we move slowly it can greatly slow down an object moving at high speed, such as an airplane, automobile, or bomb. To overcome the resistance of a solid substance, a sharp point or edge is best, as on a knife, wedge, icepick, or nail; but this is not so with the air. The best streamlined shape, the shape that meets the least air resistance, is that of a teardrop—rounded at the front and tapering to a point at the rear. The air flows smoothly around this shape. In the early days of automobiles and airplanes, little thought was given to streamlining. Now almost all moving bodies are streamlined.

streetcar, a kind of electric railway car: see the article ELECTRIC RAILWAY.

streptomycin, one of the antibiotic drugs: see the article ANTIBIOTICS.

strike, a refusal of workers to work unless they receive more pay or different working conditions: see the article LABOR.

Stritch, Cardinal

Samuel Stritch was a Roman Catholic priest who became an archbishop and a cardinal. Cardinals are called princes of the Church.

Samuel Stritch was born in Nashville, Tennessee, in 1887, and went to school in Rome, Italy. He was such a good student that he finished his studies when he was 22 years old and had to get special permission to be made a priest because he was so young. In 1930 he was made Archbishop of Milwaukee. While in Milwaukee he did much to help people who were out of work. In 1940 he was made Archbishop of Chicago, and six years later he was appointed a cardinal. During and after World War II he worked very hard to help people in Europe and Asia who had lost all their goods in the war. Cardinal Stritch died in Rome in 1958 while he was there to undertake important new duties.

strychnine

Strychnine is a dangerous poison. It is used in rat biscuits and other poisons that are used to kill animal pests. It comes from the seed of a tree, called the *nux vomica*, that grows in India. Very tiny amounts of strychnine are used in medicines to stimulate the nerves. If someone has been poisoned by strychnine a doctor should be called at once. The person should be given strong tea and a tablespoon of powdered charcoal in a pint of water. He should be kept in a dark room, away from all noise. The signs of strychnine poisoning are stiff neck, locked jaws, twitches, and convulsions.

Stuart or Stewart

Stuart was the name of a royal family of Scotland and England. The first notable member of the family was Walter Fitzalan, a Norman-English nobleman who lived about eight hundred years ago and became steward (chief official) of Scotland under the Scottish king David I. King David made the stewardship hereditary (so it would pass from father to son in the Fitzalan family) and Fitzalan's descendants changed their name to Steward or Stewart. In 1371 one of them became Robert II, king of Scotland, and after him his descendants ruled Scotland. In 1603 one of them, James VI, became also king of England, where he was called James I. He changed the family name to Stuart. Six of his descendants then ruled both England and Scotland, from 1625 to 1714. They were James I, Charles I, Charles II, James II, Mary II (who ruled with her husband William), and Anne, the last of the Stuarts. You can read more about the Stuarts in the articles on these persons and on ENGLAND and SCOTLAND.

Stuart, Gilbert

Gilbert Stuart was the most popular American portrait painter of his time, which was about 150 years ago. He is famous particularly for his portraits of George Washington. Stuart was born in North Kingstown, Rhode Island, in 1755. He began to study drawing at an early age, and when he was about 15 years old he went to Scotland to continue his study. He returned to the United States for a few years, but he had little success. He then went to London, where he became the pupil of Benjamin West, another great American painter. In 1782, Stuart's *Portrait of a Gentleman Skating* made him famous. He returned to the United States ten years later and painted portraits of many great Americans, including Presidents Jefferson, Madison, and Monroe, and many portraits of George Washington. The most famous is the *Athenaeum Head*, a portrait that Stuart had not finished when he died in 1828. It has been copied many times. Most of Stuart's paintings hang in museums in Boston, New York, and Philadelphia.

Stuart, J. E. B.

James Ewell Brown Stuart was an American soldier who became a famous cavalry general in the Confederate Army during the Civil War. He was born in 1833 in Patrick County, Virginia, and attended the United States Military Academy at West Point. After graduation he fought against Indians who were attacking white settlers on the frontier. When the Civil War broke out in 1861, Stuart resigned from the United States Army and joined the Confederate (southern) army.

By 1862, Stuart was a major general. The main activity of his cavalry was scouting, finding out where the enemy troops were and then riding back swiftly to inform the main army. Stuart took part in almost all the major battles of the war. On May 10, 1864, his forces were defeated by Union cavalry troops under General Philip H. Sheridan at the Battle of Yellow Tavern, near Richmond, Virginia, and Stuart was killed in action. He is considered one of the most colorful soldiers in American history.

study

Studying is reading and thinking in order to learn something. There is no more important part of education than studying. Many students are "bright" and find that they can get by in class and pass examinations without much study, but they may throw away most of their opportunities. The student who does not learn quite as fast, and who spends more time in study, often learns things more thoroughly. In the struggle of life, the slower student who studies is likely to get much farther than the bright student who does not study. The only advantage the bright student has is in time. Usually there is time to think things over carefully, and then the businessman who has studied the question thoroughly may do better than the businessman who thought he understood it at a glance and did not have to study.

There is a great deal of difference between studying and memorizing. The first object of studying is to understand the lesson or problem being studied. Most people find that once they understand something thoroughly, they can remember it more easily. You can read more about this in the article on MEMORY.

RULES FOR STUDY

Three rules can help you to study better and to get more from your studying:

1. *Be comfortable.* A good place to sit, good light, good equipment (paper, pencils, ruler, compasses, and so on) that you can reach easily, help study because you can do all your thinking about the problem and not have to think about finding what you need at the moment.

2. *Give yourself plenty of time.* You cannot study well if you have to worry about getting through in time for a date or a show you want to see.

3. *Do not be discouraged.* If you find that you cannot understand at first, even if you feel bewildered, stop thinking about the thing that puzzled you and start all over. Everyone has had the experience of being puzzled and then suddenly having a clear understanding come to him

like a burst of light. This will usually happen if you continue to study.

sturgeon

The sturgeon is a fish that lives in the Atlantic Ocean off the coasts of Europe and the United States. It is also found in the Pacific Ocean and in fresh-water rivers. The Atlantic sturgeon is about eight feet long. Its body is covered with bony plates instead of scales. It has a long, flat nose or snout with four feelers at the end of it. This snout is not very pretty but it is very useful. With it, the sturgeon digs up sand and mud from the bottom of the water, and finds the small fish and molluscs that it eats.

The female sturgeon travels to fresh-water rivers and streams before it lays its eggs. The female lays more than a million eggs. The eggs (roe) are salted and eaten. They are called caviar and are considered a great delicacy. The flesh of sturgeon is very tasty, especially when it is smoked.

The *white sturgeon* is found in the Pacific Ocean and in the rivers of the western part of the United States. It is usually much larger than the Atlantic variety. It often weighs about 18 pounds.

The largest fresh-water fish in the world is a sturgeon. It is called *beluga*. It lives in the Caspian and Black Seas and in the fresh-water rivers of Russia. One beluga weighed more than 3,000 pounds. It is reported that a female beluga laid more than 320 pounds of eggs in a season. Other fresh-water sturgeon are found in the Great Lakes. They are not as large as the beluga but may weigh several hundred pounds.

Sturgeon are becoming scarce because many have been caught and great dams make it impossible for others to reach the rivers where they lay their eggs.

Stuyvesant, Peter

Peter Stuyvesant was the last Dutch governor of New York, more than three hundred years ago. He was born in 1592 in Holland, which he served as a soldier and as an official in its colonies. In 1647, when he was 55 years old, he was appointed governor of New Netherland, which was then the name of the present state of New York. He was a very strict governor and was greatly feared. As a soldier he had lost one leg, and he wore a wooden leg. He soon became a dictator, and the colonists so hated him that when the English tried to take New Netherland from the Dutch, the Dutch colonists went over to their side. Stuyvesant was forced to surrender to the English in 1664. He went back to Holland, but returned to New Netherland the following year. He died in New York City in 1672.

sty

A sty is an infection or sore on the eyelid. It happens very often among children. It is caused when a germ gets into one of the tiny glands around the eyelashes. It starts as a small red area on the edge of the lid. The lid hurts and becomes swollen. After a few days the sty develops a yellow center that may burst and run pus. A doctor can help to soothe the pain and can also prescribe an ointment or medicine that will prevent the infection from spreading to other parts of the eye.

Styx

The Styx was a river told about by the ancient Greeks, thousands of years ago. It was supposed to be the most important river of the underworld, or Hades, to which people went after they died. The souls of the dead were carried across the river by a ferryman named Charon.

In northern Greece there was a waterfall, which also was called the Styx, and it was believed by the ancient Greeks that behind this waterfall was the entrance to Hades.

submarine

A submarine is a warship that can operate under water. It can travel under water or lie on the bottom of the ocean (if it is not too deep) and wait. Submarines have been among the most important ships in warfare since the beginning of World War I, in 1914. Many scientific devices have been perfected to protect ships against submarines, but at the same time the submarine has been improved to make it more and more deadly.

Inventors for thousands of years had tried to build vessels that could fight under water. The first submarine in history was built in England by a man named Cornelius van Drebbel in 1623. During the Revolutionary War an American, David Bushnell of Connecticut, made a little submarine with which he tried to sink a British warship in New York Harbor. The attack was not successful, but it did prove that a submarine could approach and attack unseen.

In 1888 the United States Navy began a competition for inventors of submarines. The first naval submarine was ordered from John P. Holland of New Jersey, who had already built four submarines for private concerns. Simon Lake was another New Jersey inventor who entered the competition. He later built several submarines for the Navy. The first submarine for the United States Navy, accepted in 1900, was built by the Electric Boat Company of New Jersey— now of Connecticut—and was named the *Holland* for its inventor. The same company delivered the first atomic submarines to the U.S. Navy: the *Nautilus* in 1954, the *Seawolf* in 1955, and the *Skate* in 1958.

HOW THE SUBMARINE WORKS

The principle on which the submarine works is very simple. On the surface, the submarine is like any other ship, except that it has tanks built around its hull. When the submarine wants to submerge (go under water) water is allowed to fill these tanks, adding weight enough to the boat to sink it. When the submarine wants to surface (rise to the top of the water) water is pumped out of the tanks, making the ship light enough to rise.

On the surface, the early submarines most careful study has gone into making the men comfortable. Oxygen tanks supply air when the submarine is submerged. The food is excellent. The men are volunteers who enjoy the excitement of the life and are proud of their assignment.

A submarine used to be very dangerous because if the ship could not rise the

men would be trapped under the water. At great depths, the pressure of the water will kill a person or make him seriously ill. Ways have since been perfected to allow the men to rise to the surface gradually and become used to the lessening pressure before they reach the surface.

EFFECTIVENESS OF THE SUBMARINE

During World War I and again during World War II, German submarines sank so many British and Allied merchant ships that they almost won the war alone. Great Britain was running out of food and war supplies, and if the United States had not built thousands of new ships the British might have lost.

After World War II, Russia built the greatest fleet of submarines in the world, but did not claim any atomic-powered submarines. The atomic submarines of the U.S. broke all existing records for speed (an Atlantic crossing in 8 days, 11 hours, by the *Skate*) and for submerged travel (more than 60 days for the *Seawolf*), and the *Nautilus* and then the *Skate* crossed the North Pole under water. All these records were made in 1958. Also in 1958 the United States launched two more atomic submarines (*Seadragon* and *Triton*) and began building a new, larger series of atomic submarines, including some (*Polaris*) that can launch guided atomic missiles.

DEFENSE AGAINST SUBMARINES

Though some submarines have been destroyed in battles against other submarines, and some have been sunk by gunfire when they are on the surface, the principal weapon against the submarine is the *depth bomb* (also called an "ash can"). This is a bomb that can be dropped from a ship or plane and will explode when it reaches the depth at which the submarine is submerged. Warships locate submarines by sonar, and patrol planes and blimps sight them from the skies, and drop depth bombs to destroy them.

In wartime, unarmed merchant ships usually travel in *convoys,* large groups of ships guarded by warships.

subway

A subway is an underground tube or tunnel through which an electric railway runs. Subways are used in very big cities where people have to travel long distances from their homes to their work and where the street traffic does not allow fast transportation by buses or streetcars.

London had the first subway (called the "underground," or "tube"). It was opened in 1863, before the time of electric railways. The cars were pulled by horses. When electric railways became a practical matter, late in the 1890s, London adopted electricity for its subways and Paris, France, and the American cities of Boston, New York and Philadelphia planned or began to build subway lines for electric cars. In Paris the subway is called the *Metropole.*

Most subways use trains of cars that are like railroad cars. They take their power from a third rail. Trains of ten or more cars, each holding 100 to 200 passengers, travel from station to station. In some cities, as in Boston and Philadelphia, some of the cars are trolley cars (getting their power from overhead wires). They travel on the surface of the streets in the residential districts where there is not much traffic and enter the tunnel when they approach the business district. Most of the subways in the United States date from the early 1900s.

Chicago and Moscow (in Russia) opened subways late, during the 1930s. Both are models of efficiency, and the Moscow subways are decorated with mosaics (pictures made of differently colored tiles) that are works of art. Several cities, including New York and Boston, have extended their subways for many additional miles since the 1930s.

The fares charged on subways have been a political issue in most cities. In London and Paris, passengers pay as they would on railroads. They buy tickets from the station they enter to their destination, and the greater the distance, the more they pay. On American subways, passengers pay a single fare on entering any

subway station and may then ride as far as they want to. In New York City, the fare was only 5 cents until 1948. The subway operators lost millions of dollars, since the 5 cents entitled a person to a ride as long as 27 miles, which on a railroad would cost more than 50 cents; but no political party was willing to raise the fare because of the risk of losing the next election. Eventually New York's subway fare was increased to 10 cents and then to 15 cents. In 1976 New York's subway fare rose to 50 cents.

Building a subway is much the same as building any TUNNEL, about which there is a separate article. For the early subways it was much simpler. A big ditch was dug in the street, tracks were laid, and a street was laid over the tracks. Now underground tunnels must carry many things—telephone and electric wires, sewers, gas and water mains, and often two or three subways that cross one another at different levels under the street. In many cities, subway tubes run under rivers or harbors. Therefore the building of a subway has become as difficult a job as building any other kind of tunnel.

Subway trains in big cities carry passengers from station to station at average speeds of 20 to 30 miles per hour, which is much faster than automobiles can travel over the same streets. The stations are usually about one-half mile apart. On many subways there are four tracks, one pair of tracks carrying "local" trains that stop at every station and the other pair of tracks carrying "express" trains that stop only at important stations two or more miles apart. Express trains on long runs often go as fast as 45 miles per hour.

In 1946 a survey showed that the things visitors to New York City want most to do are: ride in the subway; eat at an Automat (a restaurant operated by slot machines); see Rockefeller Center and the show at the Radio City Music Hall, the world's largest theater; and see the view from the top of the Empire State Building. A visit to the United Nations buildings, built since then, has probably joined the list; but at the time, the ride in the subway came first.

sucker

The sucker is a fish that is found in the lakes and rivers of northern Canada and in many parts of the United States. It grows to be about two feet long. It has a slender body and a short, blunt snout that covers its mouth. The sucker uses its snout to search for food at the bottom of lakes and rivers. It is particularly fond of the eggs of other fish.

During the mating season the male gets a black band along its side, just above a rose-colored band.

White suckers travel to small, swift-moving streams in the spring. There the female lays many small, light-yellow eggs. The eggs are heavier than water and sink to the bottom of the stream, where they remain until they are ready to hatch, any time from one week to three weeks later. A female sucker often lays as many as 100,000 eggs. The flesh of the sucker is used for food and small suckers are often used for bait. Some people raise suckers in fish hatcheries and sell them to fishermen for bait.

SECTION THROUGH 33rd STREET AT SIXTH AVENUE AND BROADWAY.

In New York City, and other major cities of the world, subways form a honeycomb beneath the pavement. The drawing includes an elevated line now torn down.

Sudan

The name Sudan was applied for many years to a vast region of north central Africa (see map), south of the Sahara Desert. *Sudan* in the Arabic language means "black," and the region got its name from the many Negroes who lived there. Parts of French Equatorial Africa, the Anglo-Egyptian Sudan and French West Africa were in this region.

Today the area is composed mostly of free nations, including the Republic of the Sudan—see the next article.

Sudan, Republic of the

The Republic of the Sudan, formerly the Anglo-Egyptian Sudan, is the eastern part of the region once called the Sudan and extends eastward to the Red Sea. It has been independent since 1956. It covers a very large area, nearly a million square miles, and its population is about 13,000,000. The capital is KHARTOUM, about which there is a separate article.

The Sudan consists mostly of a great plain surrounded by mountains. In the north there is almost no rainfall and the plant life is the low grass of semi-desert regions. In the south rainfall is heavy and there are some tropical forests. The Nile River system runs through the country, providing irrigation and transportation. Most of the people are nomads (wanderers), who graze livestock. There is some mining of gold and salt. Long-staple cotton is raised in the north and in narrow strips along the Nile and is the leading export.

The people of the northern region are mostly Arabs and Nubians, descendants of the ancient kingdom of Nubia. They are Moslems (followers of the religion of Mohammed). Negro tribes, such as the Dinkas, Nuers, and Shilluks, live in the southern region. They are either Christians or followers of tribal religions. In 1963 the southern provinces revolted against the control of the north. Warfare continued into 1966 and left the country weakened.

The Egyptians had much influence in northern Sudan for thousands of years, and in the early 1800s took control of the Sudan. In 1881 a revolt against Egyptian rule was begun by a group of Sudanese led by a Mahdi, or religious leader. The Mahdis were finally defeated by British and Egyptian forces in 1898, when the British General Kitchener captured Khartoum, and Great Britain and Egypt agreed to rule the territory together. They did so until they granted Sudan its independence in 1956.

SUDAN, REPUBLIC OF THE. Area, 967,500 square miles. Population (1964 estimate) 13,180,000. Capital, Khartoum. Government, republic. Monetary unit, Sudanese pound, worth $2.87 (U.S.). Flag, three horizontal bars, blue, yellow and green.

Suez Canal

The Suez Canal is a waterway across the Isthmus of Suez, a stretch of land that lies between the Red Sea and the Mediterranean Sea. The canal runs through two lakes along its course, Bitter Lakes and Lake Timsah. The canal is about 100 miles long and it takes a ship about 13 hours to pass through it. Because the canal is at sea level, no locks are needed to raise and lower ships. In 1958 more than 17,000 ships used the canal.

The Suez Canal is important as a short route for shipping from Europe to the Far East. Until July 1956 the canal was operated by the Universal Company of the Suez Canal, with headquarters in Paris, France, with international agreements providing for it to be open to ships of all countries. Since 1875 Great Britain and France had controlled the Suez Canal Company, with an agreement that in 1968 Egypt would obtain sole control; but in 1956 Egypt seized control of the canal. President Nasser of Egypt stated that his purpose was to increase Egypt's income so as to build a new Aswan Dam (see the article on the NILE).

A canal from the Red Sea to the Mediterranean was built about two thousand years before Jesus was born, but about a thousand years ago it was abandoned. In 1854 a French diplomat named Ferdinand de Lesseps persuaded Egypt to authorize a new canal, which was opened in 1869. Benjamin Disraeli, British Prime Minister, bought control of it for his country in 1875. Until 1954 British troops guarded the canal; then they withdrew and left Egypt in control.

Egypt caused an international crisis by seizing the canal in 1956. Britain and France attacked Egypt, and Egypt blocked the canal by sinking ships in it. The United Nations took control and the issue was settled in 1958. After the Six-Day War of 1967, the canal was again closed due to the presence of sunken ships in it. The chief ports on the Canal are Port Said, a city of 283,000, at the Mediterranean end, and Suez, a city of 264,000 at the Red Sea end.

suffrage

Suffrage means the right to vote. In countries where the government, or some of the officials, were elected by the people, formerly only men who owned land or came from noble families were allowed to vote. In most countries today, all men and women who have reached a certain age, usually 21, and who know how to read and write, are permitted to vote. Until 1920, women were not allowed to vote in the United States. Woman Suffrage, or "Votes for Women," was an important political issue in the United States for about fifty years. Each state makes its own laws on who may vote, but the Nineteenth Amendment to the Constitution, which went into effect in 1920, says that a state may not deny the right to vote "on account of sex." Another word for suffrage is FRANCHISE, about which there is a separate article.

sugar

Sugar is one of the most important foods for plants and animals. It supplies much of the energy needed for the process of living. Sugar is a carbohydrate, which means it is made up of carbon, hydrogen, and oxygen. It can be dissolved in water. When dry, it forms small crystals, pieces with regular and not rough shapes. Other carbohydrates, such as starch, must first be broken down into sugar by chemical substances in plants and animals before they can be used.

Sugar is made by green plants, from air and water and sunlight. This process is called PHOTOSYNTHESIS and there is a separate article about it. The sugar that plants do not use is stored in their roots, stems, and leaves, either as sugar, or more usually as starch. This stored sugar is the source of all the sugar used by man.

The SUGAR BEET and SUGAR CANE plants provide most of the sugar that is used as table sugar. There is a separate article about each. This kind of sugar is called *sucrose*.

Other kinds of sugar are made from other plants. Maple sugar is made from the sugar maple tree. Glucose, also called dextrose or grape sugar, is made from corn and other cereal plants, and from fruits. Fructose, or fruit sugar, is made from fruits, and also from a chemical that is found in the tubers (thick roots) of the dahlia, Jerusalem artichoke, and other plants. Honey, which is largely glucose and levulose, is made by bees from the nectar (sweet liquid) of certain flowers, among them alfalfa, clover, and buckwheat. In some of the tropical regions of the world, sugar is made from certain kinds of palm tree.

In the United States about a hundred pounds of sugar are eaten by each person every year. This sugar usually is not in foods that are called sweets, such as candy or cake. It is mostly in other foods. Sugar is used in making many foods, for example bread.

Some sugar is produced in the United States, but most of it is imported. The leading sugar-producing areas of the world are India, Pakistan, Cuba, Japan, Formosa, the Philippines, Hawaii, Puerto Rico, and Brazil.

The most important use of sugar other than in food is in making ethyl alcohol. Sugar is used in jams and jellies not only to sweeten them but also because it helps to keep them from spoiling.

A healthy human body must have a certain amount of sugar in the blood. The sugar that is eaten is broken down into glucose, by chemicals in the body, and then passes into the bloodstream. The amount of sugar in the blood is controlled by a chemical substance called insulin, which is produced in the part of the body called the pancreas. If a person has too much sugar in his bloodstream, he is suffering from a disease called DIABETES, about which there is a separate article. If he has too little sugar in his bloodstream, he goes into a state of shock and may die.

sugar beet

The sugar beet is a vegetable that is grown for the sake of the sugar in its white root. It is shaped more like a carrot than like the familiar round, red beet, and grows with an extremely long, cord-like taproot that may extend as far as three and a half feet down into the earth.

Sugar beets contain a large percentage of sugar, which can be refined and purified until it has exactly the same quality and flavor as refined cane sugar and can be used for the same purposes. Three-quarters of the white sugar produced in the United States is beet sugar, and almost a quarter of the white sugar used is beet sugar.

Sugar beets are biennial plants, which means that they do not bear flowers and go to seed during their first year. The beet root forms in the first year after seeds are planted, and leaves grow above the ground. Most sugar beets are harvested the first year, to make sugar, but some are left to produce seed the second year.

To make beet sugar, the tops of the roots are cut off, sliced and put in water. The water dissolves the sugar, forming a sirup. This sirup is filtered and treated with chemicals to remove impurities. Then it is boiled to remove the water and leave the crystals of sugar. The full process is a complex one and is done in great factories using scientific methods and equipments.

sugar cane

Sugar cane is a grassy plant that is grown in warm and tropical sections of the world for the sugar that is contained in its stalks. Most of the white sugar and much of the sirup used in the United States and Canada is produced from sugar cane, but beet sugar has become increasingly important in the last fifty years.

Sugar cane is a perennial plant, which means that it grows year after year in the same place without replanting. The stalks of the plant are cut once each year. They are crushed and pressed to remove the sweet juices inside them. These raw juices are then processed several times, to reduce them to the crystals that eventually reach the table.

During the first process of refinement, when the juice is filtered and treated with chemicals to remove impurities, molasses remains after the crude sugar has been removed. The crude sugar then goes through several more refining processes, gradually becoming lighter in color. The first stage is a dark brown, moist sugar. It becomes both lighter and dried in each stage, until finally it is in fine-grained, pure white crystals.

suite, a group of short musical compositions put together to form one longer composition. About four hundred years ago, the short pieces were different dances. Johann Sebastian Bach wrote suites of this kind. More modern examples are Tschaikovsky's *Nutcracker Suite* and Grieg's *Peer Gynt Suite*. See the article on MUSIC.

Suleiman

Suleiman was the name of three sultans, or rulers, of Turkey. The most famous of them was Suleiman I, who lived more than four hundred years ago. He was born about 1496 and became sultan in 1520. Suleiman led his armies in a great invasion of central Europe, and after the year 1529 he controlled nearly all of Europe south and east of Budapest, Hungary. He then turned east and conquered much of Mesopotamia (now Iraq), Arabia, and what is now southern Russia. He was called "Suleiman the Magnificent." His might and splendor frightened and dazzled the nations of Europe. He built many beautiful buildings and encouraged the arts. He also set up a code of law, and for this reason Moslems (followers of the Mohammedan religion) remember him as Suleiman the Lawgiver. He died in 1566. The name is another spelling of Solomon.

sulfa drugs

Sulfa drugs are a group of chemicals that kill the bacteria, or germs, that cause certain diseases, such as tonsilitis, blood poisoning, scarlet fever, and pneumonia. Sulfa drugs are also called *sulfonamides.* They were the first of the many chemicals called *wonder drugs* that now save thousands of people who not many years ago would have died because there was no medicine to cure them. The first sulfa drug was named *sulfanilamide.* Many others have been developed—*sulfadiazine, sulfapyridine, sulfathiazole,* and others. Each is most effective against certain kinds of germ.

The first use of a sulfa drug as a medicine came almost by accident. Chemicals of this kind were being used as dyes but not as medicines. About forty years ago a little German girl pricked her finger. A germ known as the *streptococcus* got into her blood through the injury and she became dangerously sick. No medicine

could help and it looked as though she was sure to die. Her father was a chemist for a German dye company, and he had a chemical that was used for dyeing cloth brick-red. He had found that this chemical killed certain germs in mice. When there seemed to be no hope left, he gave his daughter some of the powder. The chemical brought her fever down, and after a few days she was well. After that, sulfa chemicals of different kinds were made in laboratories and became a leading medicine. In World War II they saved thousands of lives. Sometimes sulfa drugs are used together with the ANTIBIOTICS, about which there is a separate article. Millions of pounds of sulfa drugs are produced each year, more than almost any other medicine except aspirin. However, sulfa has become less important as other new drugs have been developed.

sulfur or sulphur

Sulfur is a soft brittle bright-yellow substance that has many uses in industry and chemistry. It is a chemical element, which means that it is one of the hundred basic substances of which everything in the world is made. Sulfur has been known since ancient times. In the Bible it is called *brimstone.* It is often spelled *sulphur.*

Sulfur exists in three different forms: 1, thick crystals that look like two pyramids set together, base to base; 2, thin, needlelike crystals; 3, a brown, rubbery mass.

MINING SULFUR

Sulfur makes up only a trace of the earth's crust, but in almost all parts of the world there are enormous beds of sulfur below the ground. The world's largest deposits of pure sulfur are found in Louisiana and Texas.

Mining sulfur used to be difficult, because the sulfur beds are usually far below the ground and deep shafts had to be dug down to them. In those times the sulfur was dug out with picks and shovels. In modern sulfur mining, the Frasch process is used. This process was invented about 1900 by Herman Frasch, a chemist, who was born in Germany but became an American citizen. In the Frasch process four pipes, of four different sizes, are placed one within the other and are poked down through a hole drilled to a bed of sulfur. The four pipes have three separate spaces between them. Down the outer space is pumped very hot water. This melts the sulfur. Down the center pipe is pumped compressed air. This mixes the melted sulfur and water to a froth, which is forced to the surface through the middle space in the pipes. At the surface, the melted sulfur cools and the water flows away. This leaves a huge block of solid sulfur, which may be three or four stories high and hundreds of feet long. Needed supplies of sulfur are blasted from the block.

SULFURIC ACID

The most important chemical made from sulfur is sulfuric acid. Sulfur burns in air to form a gas called sulfur dioxide. This gas, combined with water and oxygen, gives sulfuric acid. Sulfuric acid is used in the treatment of the mineral called phosphate rock to make fertilizer. It is also used in the refining of petroleum;

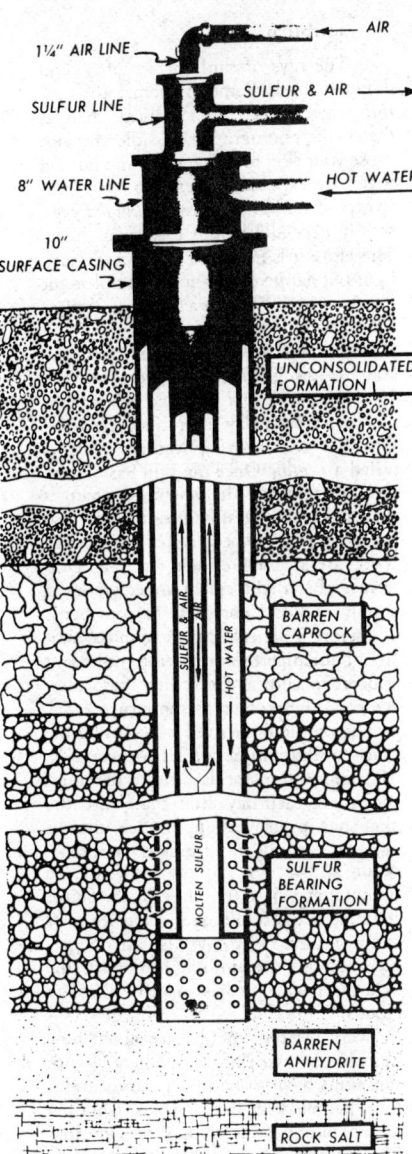

1¼" AIR LINE — AIR
SULFUR LINE — SULFUR & AIR →
8" WATER LINE — HOT WATER
10" SURFACE CASING
UNCONSOLIDATED FORMATION
BARREN CAPROCK
SULFUR & AIR — HOT WATER
MOLTEN SULFUR
SULFUR BEARING FORMATION
BARREN ANHYDRITE
ROCK SALT

The diagram shows the superheated-water method of mining sulfur. The well is sunk down into the sulfur-bearing formation. Hot water pumped through the side tubes enters the formation, melting the sulfur. The melted sulfur enters through the holes at the bottom of the pipe, and is pushed up into the center tube. The small pipe in the center tube introduces great air pressure, which forces the sulfur to the surface, where pipelines carry it off.

in the cleaning, or "pickling," of iron and steel; and in the manufacture of explosives. A list of all the uses of sulfuric acid would be a catalog of the industries of the world.

OTHER USES OF SULFUR

Many dyes are sulfur compounds. Many insect-killing sprays contain sulfur. Sulfur is one of the three elements of old-fashioned black gunpowder. Sulfur is an important ingredient of match-heads. Sulfur is used in the vulcanizing of rubber, by which rubber is made springy and soft instead of sticky and brittle.

Sullivan, Sir Arthur

Sir Arthur Sullivan was an English composer, or writer of original music. He is best known for writing the music of the GILBERT AND SULLIVAN comic operas, about which you can read in a separate article. He was born more than a hundred years ago, in 1842, and began to write music at a very early age. In 1871 he began to work together with William Gilbert. In spite of the success of their comic operas, Sullivan felt that his best work was the more serious music that he also composed. He wrote a number of oratorios (religious stories that are sung but not acted out), an opera called *Ivanhoe*, and many songs and music for hymns. His most famous hymn is "Onward, Christian Soldiers," which is often sung today. Another famous song he wrote is "The Lost Chord." Sullivan was made a knight by Queen Victoria in 1882. He died in 1900.

For a picture of Sullivan, see the article GILBERT AND SULLIVAN.

Sullivan, John L.

John Lawrence Sullivan was one of the great heavyweight champions in boxing history. He was born in Boston, Massachusetts, in 1858. When Sullivan first began to fight, boxing gloves were not used. In 1880 Sullivan was called the champion because he had defeated all the other heavyweight fighters in long and bloody battles with bare fists. In 1889, when modern rules and boxing gloves were adopted, Sullivan became the first modern champion of the world. He held the title until 1891, when he was defeated by James J. Corbett. Corbett was not as big and strong as Sullivan but he was a faster and better boxer. Sullivan was a big man, weighing well over 200 pounds. He was called the "Boston strong boy." With his black handlebar mustache, he was a fearsome looking man. He liked to walk into a room and shout, "My name is John L. Sullivan and I can lick any man in the house." Later in life he became an actor and a lecturer for temperance in drinking. He died in 1918.

Sullivan Trophy

The James E. Sullivan Memorial Trophy is given each year to the outstanding amateur athlete in the United States. Winners have included:

1930—Bobby Jones, golf.
1931—Barney Berlinger, track.
1932—Jim Bausch, track.
1933—Glenn Cunningham, track.
1934—Bill Bonthron, track.
1935—Lawson Little, golf.
1936—Glenn Morris, track.
1937—Don Budge, tennis.
1938—Don Lash, track.
1939—Joe Burk, rowing.
1940—Greg Rice, track.
1941—Les MacMitchell, track.
1942—Cornelius Warmerdam, track.
1943—Gil Dodds, track.
1944—Ann Curtis, swimming.
1945—Felix Blanchard, football.
1946—Arnold Tucker, football.
1947—Jack Kelly Jr., rowing.
1948—Bob Mathias, track.
1949—Richard Button, figure skating.
1950—Fred Wilt, track.
1951—Robert Richards, track.
1952—Horace Ashenfelter, track.
1953—Sammy Lee, diving.
1954—Mal Whitfield, track.
1955—Harrison Dillard, track.
1956—Patricia McCormick, diving.
1957—Bobby Joe Morrow, track.
1958—Glenn Davis, track.
1959—Parry O'Brien, track.
1960—Rafer Johnson, track.
1961—Wilma Rudolph Ward, track.
1962—James T. Beatty, track.
1963—John T. Pennel, track.
1964—Don Schollander, swimming.
1965—Bill Bradley, basketball.
1966—Jim Ryun, track.
1967—Randy Matson, track.
1968—Debbie Meyer, swimming.
1969—Bill Toomey, track.
1970—John Kinsella, swimming.
1971—Mark Spitz, swimming.
1972—Frank Shorter, track.

sulphur, see SULFUR.

Sulu Sea

The Sulu Sea is a large area of the west Pacific Ocean, between the Philippines and Borneo. It covers about 150,000 square miles. On the eastern side of the sea is the chain of Philippine islands called the Sulu Archipelago. There are a number of other islands and many reefs (very shallow places) in the Sulu Sea. Its greatest depth is about 16,000 feet.

sumac

Sumac is the name of a group of shrubs and trees. Some sumac plants are decorative for gardens and some, including "poison ivy," are harmful. Another variety is sometimes called poison sumac, or poison elder. This kind is a shrub or tree that may grow as high as 20 feet. Its leaves turn a bright red color and it bears greenish-white flowers. It is even more poisonous than poison ivy.

Other kinds of sumac are totally harmless. One kind, which grows wild in many places, is called red sumac. It gets its name from leaves that turn bright red in the fall.

Sumatra

Sumatra is the second-largest of the islands of Indonesia, which is a country made up of many islands between the Pacific and Indian Oceans. Sumatra has an area of 163,145 square miles, making it about the size of California. In 1973 it was estimated that 19,300,000 people live there. Along the entire west coast is a chain of mountains, the Barisan Mountains, which rise to 12,487 feet in Mt. Kerinchi, the highest peak. The east coast is largely swampy. Off the southern tip of Sumatra is the island of Krakatoa, on which is an active volcano. The island has a number of rivers and lakes. The climate is hot and humid, with heavy rainfall. Much of the mountain area is covered with forests so thick that they are impassable. There are many wild animals, including elephants, panthers, rhinoceroses, tigers, and snakes.

The people of Sumatra include Malays, Chinese, Arabs, and Indians. Most of the people follow the Mohammedan religion. Lumbering and agriculture are the chief occupations. Tobacco, tea, coffee, sugar and pepper are grown. Rubber, copra,

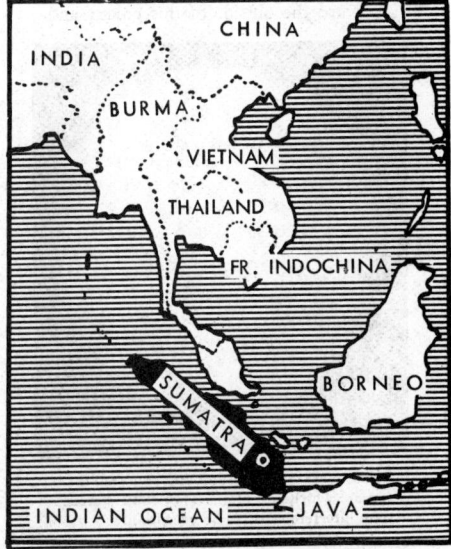

CHINA
INDIA
BURMA
VIETNAM
THAILAND
FR. INDOCHINA
SUMATRA
BORNEO
INDIAN OCEAN
JAVA

palm oil and resin are produced from the forests. The mineral resources include oil and coal, gold, and silver. The principal city is Palembang, with a population of about 474,971.

The Dutch controlled Sumatra as part of the Netherlands East Indies until World War II. In 1945 most of the island was included in the first Republic of Indonesia. In 1950 all Sumatra was made part of INDONESIA, about which there is a separate article.

Sumerians

The Sumerians were an ancient people who built a great nation in the Near East about six thousands years ago. Experts think that they came originally from central Asia or from India. They settled where Iraq now is. Their territory came to be called BABYLONIA, about which there is a separate article. The Sumerians were chiefly farmers, but they were also skilled in making things of gold, copper, and silver. Their greatest achievement was the invention of CUNEIFORM writing, about which there is a separate article. Their chief cities were Ur, Kish, and Erech.

At the same time Semitic people also lived in that area. In time they became stronger, and about 2600 B.C. they became the chief power. The Sumerians continued to rule in southern Babylonia for another three hundred years, until they were conquered by the ancient nation of Elam.

sun

The sun is the star around which the earth and other planets revolve in the solar system. The sun provides the earth with most of its warmth, light, and power. It controls the motion of the planets. The sun is about 93,000,000 miles from the earth, but the next-closest star is 275,000 times as far away.

Much of the nature of the sun—how it produces light and heat—is told in the article on STARS. The sun is a fairly small star. It is ball-shaped, 864,000 miles in diameter (across), and made of gas. It is 332,000 times as heavy as the earth. It is almost one and a half times as dense as water. It sends out energy at the rate of 70,000 horsepower per square yard.

The sun is part of the galaxy, or huge group of stars, called the Milky Way. It is toward the outside of this galaxy and

is revolving around the center of the galaxy at the rate of about 170 miles per second, carrying the earth and all the other planets and bodies of the solar system with it. It will take the sun about 220,000,000 years to make the complete revolution around the galaxy.

Sixty-six of the chemical elements (basic substances) known on the earth are known to be present in the sun, and the others are probably there also.

Dark regions called sunspots are often seen on the sun. The smallest spots are as small as 450 miles across and the biggest about 125,000 miles across. The sunspots have strong magnetic attractions. On earth they can interfere with radio and television reception.

With their telescopes, astronomers can see scarlet-colored flames called *prominences* shooting out from the sun. All around the sun is a vast circle of pale light called the *corona*. It can be seen only when there is an ECLIPSE, about which there is a separate article.

HOW THE SUN HEATS THE EARTH

Though it seems hot in the sun, especially in the summertime, it is not the direct rays from the sun that make the air warm. The rays pass through the atmosphere and are absorbed by the soil and by the oceans, lakes, and other bodies of water. The heat then rises in waves from the soil and water, heating the air. That is why it remains almost as warm at night, after the sun goes down, as it is in the daytime.

The sun's rays reaching the earth carry with them enough energy to do every necessary job on earth. This energy is chiefly in the form of heat. It has never been necessary for man to make use of the billions of "horsepower" that could be taken from sunlight, but experiments have shown how it can be done. A simple experiment with a magnifying glass will show how the sun's rays, concentrated at a point on a sheet of paper, will set the paper on fire. Great mirrors in open fields, to catch the sunlight and concentrate it as the magnifying glass does, can produce enough heat to boil water, make steam, and run a factory. Some houses are heated through the winter by solar heat, as described in the article on HEATING.

The great use of solar energy is by plants, which use the sunlight to make their food. Without this use of solar energy, no one could live. It is explained in the article on PHOTOSYNTHESIS.

sunburn

The rays of sunlight are of several different kinds. Some of them, called *actinic* rays, cause the chemical changes that make photography possible and also cause your skin to become red and burned if you are exposed to them too long. Other rays of sunlight, called *ultraviolet* rays, supply needed Vitamin D to your body. Therefore it is healthful to be in the sunlight but dangerous or at least unpleasant if overexposure to the actinic rays causes the condition known as sunburn.

The problem is solved by exposing the body to sunlight gradually; for example, 15 minutes the first day, and a few minutes more each day after that, until the skin has a brown appearance that is called a *suntan*. Once the skin has a thortinic rays, cause the chemical changes that make photography possible and also cause your skin to become red and burned if you are exposed to them too long. Other rays of sunlight, called *ultraviolet* rays, supply needed Vitamin D to your body. Therefore it is healthful to be in the sunlight but dangerous or at least unpleasant if overexposure to the actinic rays causes the condition known as sunburn.

The problem is solved by exposing the body to sunlight gradually; for example, 15 minutes the first day, and a few minutes more each day after that, until the skin has a brown appearance that is called a *suntan*. Once the skin has a thoroccur at beaches and on snow-covered mountains, where the glare of the sun is reflected back from the sand and water or snow and ice. Hazy days also are dangerous, because the sunlight can burn the skin even when it has to come through clouds.

Every person should learn about how quickly his own skin burns. People with fair skins have to be much more careful than people with darker skins. Children and babies have very tender skin that burns easily.

If a person does get a sunburn he should stay out of the sun. A soothing dressing, applied to the burned skin, may help to relieve the pain.

Sunday

Sunday is the first day of the week. It is observed as the Sabbath, a day of rest and worship, by most Christian peoples. It is named for the ancient sun god; and the day was a holiday even in ancient times before the birth of Jesus. When the Christian religion began, Sunday was

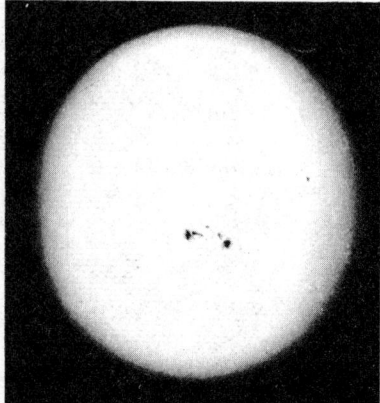

Black markings, or sunspots, seen on the sun are whirlpools of gas. They cause storms that interfere with radio reception.

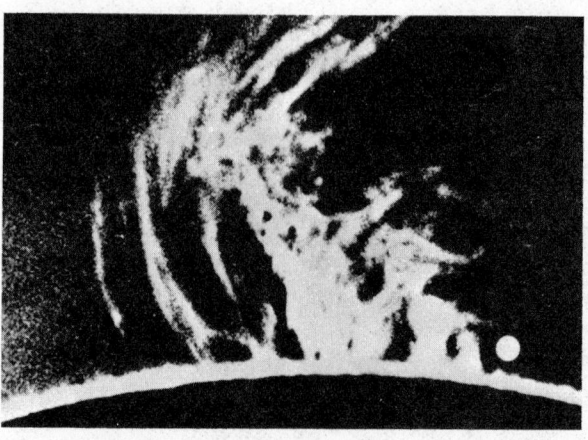

This photograph of the sun's *prominences*, was taken by a motion picture camera. A filter was used to remove the light of all colors but one. A photograph of the sun taken in this way is called a *spectroheliokinematograph!* The white dot at the right, near the sun's surface, was put in later; it represents the earth as it would look if placed next to the sun's surface.

made a day of special worship in celebration of Jesus' Resurrection, or rising from the dead.

There have been laws against certain kinds of work on Sunday from ancient times. The Roman emperor Constantine, who was the first emperor to become a Christian, passed a law that "magistrates, city people, and artisans" were to rest on the day of the sun.

In England and Scotland the "Dissenters," people who left the Church of England and founded the Congregational and Presbyterian Churches, observed Sunday as a day of rest. The Puritans and Scotch-Irish people brought this idea to the New World with their Sunday laws, often called Blue Laws. These laws were very strict in prohibiting many forms of work and almost all forms of entertainment. Some American cities still have such laws, as, for instance, laws forbidding baseball games and motion pictures on Sunday, but few of them are strictly enforced. All banks and most businesses are closed on Sunday. See also the article SABBATH.

Sunday School, classes that meet in a church once a week, in which boys, girls, and some grownups are taught about their religion: see the article RELIGIOUS EDUCATION. In Christian Churches that observe the Sabbath on Saturday, the same thing is called Sabbath School.

sundial

The sundial is an instrument that was used by many ancient peoples for telling the time of day. It was made of a circular, flat stone, or dial, on which sections were marked off as hours and minutes are marked on the face of a clock. A pole or bar called a *gnomon* was so placed that when the sun shone, it would cast a shadow against the line on the dial that showed the time. As the sun moved, the shadow moved from line to line.

The earliest sundial known was found in Egypt and is thought to date back about 3,500 years. Later sundials were made very accurate. Though clocks and watches came into use during the 18th century, sundials were also in use and clocks were set by them. The largest sundial in the world was made almost 250 years ago in India. It covers almost an acre and its gnomon is more than 100 feet high.

The sundial needs no winding and no electric outlet, but unfortunately it "runs down" at night and on cloudy days.

sunfish

Sunfish are a large group of fish that live in rivers and streams in many parts of Europe, Canada, and the United States. Sunfish are also found in warm ocean waters.

One of the best-known of the sunfish is called the *bluegill*. It is a small fish, usually weighing less than a pound. Like most sunfish, the male bluegill builds a nest at the bottom of the water. It does this by vigorously moving its tail about until it makes a hollowed-out place. It works only in the sunlight, which is probably how it got its name. The female sunfish lays thousands of eggs. The bluegill is popular as food.

The ocean sunfish is a strange fish that can often be seen floating lazily on the waves in the warm oceans of the world. It has a flat, egg-shaped body that often grows to be about 11 feet long. It is not unusual to find ocean sunfish that weigh one ton. The ocean sunfish's skin is often more than two inches thick. Its bones are soft and can easily be cut with a knife. The flesh is too tough to be good to eat.

sunflower

The sunflower is a tall plant that is grown mostly for its seeds. It looks somewhat like an oversized daisy, with large yellow petals and a round center that is sometimes yellow and sometimes dark brown, purple, or black. The flowering heads of sunflowers may be a foot across, but there are smaller kinds. The most common varieties reach a height of twelve to fifteen feet. Some farmers plant sunflowers for beans to climb, instead of using wooden poles.

KIDC (Kansas) Photo
The blossom of the sunflower may be as much as a foot across.

Many birds eat sunflower seeds. People sometimes eat sunflower seeds as appetizers or between-meal snacks, as they do salted peanuts or popcorn. The tough outside shell is removed and the meat inside is tender and sweet.

Sunflowers are grown in parts of Europe and in Asia for the oil that can be pressed from the seed. The oil can be used in cooking and also makes oil cakes to feed to farm animals.

The sunflower is the state flower of Kansas.

sunstroke

Sunstroke is a serious illness that occurs when a person remains too long in the hot sun. The sun causes the body to perspire and large amounts of salt and water that the body requires are lost. This helps to bring about sunstroke.

A person who has sunstroke develops a severe headache. Everything looks red to him and he may become unconscious. He develops a fever that may go as high as 110 degrees. If this continues the person may die.

Sunstroke can be avoided. No person should exercise too vigorously in hot weather just before or after eating. It is sensible to eat light meals in hot weather and to wear loose clothing. A person should always wear a hat in the hot sun.

When a person has suffered from a sunstroke he must be cooled with cold compresses. Nothing should be done for a person who has collapsed until a doctor comes. The collapse might not be due to sunstroke and treatment might do more harm than good.

Sun Yat-sen

Sun Yat-sen was a Chinese statesman and revolutionary leader. He is called the "father of the Revolution" in which the Chinese people overthrew their emperor and set up a republic.

Sun Yat-sen was born in 1866 near Canton. When he grew up he studied medicine and became a doctor. At that time China was badly ruled by an emperor and empress. Sun took part in several secret movements against them. For a time he had to flee from China, and he traveled all over the world, studying and trying to interest other countries in the cause of the Chinese people. In 1911 the revolution succeeded and the people made Sun Yat-sen the first president of their new republic. He soon resigned in favor of another leader called Yuan Shih-k'ai, though he later disagreed with his ideas.

Sun Yat-sen founded a political party called the Kuomintang. China was in a state of great confusion. The leaders of the new republic could not agree on different questions. For a time Sun Yat-sen was president of a new government set up at Canton, but he was overpowered by other forces. He also began to coöperate with Communist officials of Soviet Russia, hoping that they would help him conquer the rest of China. But he never succeeded. He died in 1925. The Kuomintang controlled China until 1949, when it lost to a Communist government. Sun Yat-sen remains a great national hero.

Superior, Lake

Lake Superior is the largest of the Great Lakes and the largest body of fresh water in the world. It has an area of 31,820 square miles, which is about the size of the state of South Carolina. About two-thirds of the lake is in the United States and the rest is in Canada. It is bordered by the states of Minnesota, Wisconsin, and Michigan, and the province of Ontario. Lake Superior is connected with Lake Huron by St. Marys River and the Sault Ste. Marie Canals. Shipping on the lake carries grain, and iron and other minerals from the rich surrounding region. Duluth and Two Harbors, in Min-

nesota, are the principal United States cities on the lake. On the Canadian side are Port Arthur and Fort William. Most of the lake is frozen for three to four months in the winter.

superstition

A person is said to be superstitious when he believes that certain acts or things can bring "good luck" or "bad luck," but does not have a clear idea of why he thinks so. Examples of superstition are the belief that breaking a mirror can cause seven years of bad luck, the belief that the number 13 is unlucky and the number 7 is lucky, and so on. Pagan religions have been called examples of superstition, because people worshiped little statues or animals or trees, but their beliefs were not real superstition. They believed the statues or animals or trees were gods or spirits that could help or hurt them. A superstitious person has no idea of why he thinks things are lucky or unlucky.

Some superstitions have sensible origins. For example, it is said to be unlucky to walk under a ladder, and it is true that when a person walks under a ladder it may fall on him or a bucket of paint may fall on his head. Most superstitions cannot be explained so easily.

Probably more than half of all the people in the world are superstitious in some ways. Many hotels number their thirteenth floors "14" because so many of their guests do not want rooms on the thirteenth floor. Office and apartment buildings often do the same.

These are some of the best-known superstitions:

It is unlucky to spill salt unless you immediately throw a pinch of it over your shoulder.

13 is an unlucky number, 7 is a lucky number.

A rabbit's foot, a horseshoe or a four-leaf clover brings good luck.

It is unlucky for a bridegroom to see the bride on the day of the wedding, until they meet at church. It is lucky for the bride to wear "something old, something new, something borrowed, and something blue." It is lucky for the bridegroom to carry the bride over the threshold (doorway) of their new home.

It is unlucky to predict any good fortune, but immediately knocking on wood will keep it from being unlucky.

It is unlucky if a black cat crosses your path, if you walk under a ladder, if you throw your hat on a bed, if a bird flies in the window, or if you break a mirror, and there are many other things thought to be unlucky.

Many of these superstitions may have come from ancient times when men believed in omens (signs that showed whether the gods were for or against some plan).

See also the article on AUGURS.

Supreme Court

The Supreme Court is the highest court of law in the United States. It can overrule the decisions of other courts, but no court can overrule its decisions. In certain ways, the Supreme Court of the United States is more powerful than the President or the Congress, for the President must enforce the laws made by Congress and the Supreme Court can make

those laws unenforceable if it rules that they are unconstitutional (not permitted by the Constitution of the United States).

There are nine members of the Supreme Court. One, the head of the court, is called the Chief Justice of the United States. The other eight are Associate Justices. When the nine justices do not agree on a decision, the majority decides. That is, five or more of the justices who agree can make the decision. Usually one of these justices writes a statement of the "opinion" of the court, telling what the decision is and why the majority of the justices think it is the right decision. Any justice who disagrees may write a "dissenting opinion," telling why he thinks the decision is wrong. Usually there is not more than one majority opinion and one dissenting opinion; for example, if six justices decide one way and the other three decide the other way, one of the six will write the majority opinion for all six and one of the three will write the dissenting opinion for all three. In other cases, justices may decide the same way but for different reasons. In such a case, any justice may write an opinion giving his reasons.

Almost all the cases that come to the Supreme Court are appeals—cases in which a lower court has already made a ruling and the Supreme Court is asked to overrule it. If the Supreme Court agrees with the lower court, it may simply refuse to rule on the case.

The Supreme Court meets in its own building in Washington, D. C. The nine justices sit side by side along a bench. Lawyers must have special permission to argue cases before the Supreme Court. There is a gallery for those who want to hear the case argued.

The Supreme Court rules only on questions of law, never on questions where there is a dispute about the facts, so there is never a jury.

The most famous Chief Justice was a man named John Marshall, who lived about 150 years ago and was Chief Justice from 1801 to 1835, in the early years of the United States. Marshall was the man who decided that the Supreme Court could nullify (cancel) a law passed by Congress, by calling it unconstitutional. This decision established the United States Constitution as the highest law of the land and the Supreme Court as the highest authority on the law.

Congress and Presidents at various times have questioned the decisions of the Supreme Court, but its rulings have always been obeyed. In 1937 President Franklin D. Roosevelt became dissatisfied with the Supreme Court because it had declared several laws unconstitutional. He asked Congress to pass laws permitting him to appoint more Justices, but Congress would not do it. The President appoints all the Justices and needs the consent of the Senate for any appointment he makes, but once the appointment is made and approved the President and Senate have no power over the Justice.

In 1969, when Chief Justice Earl Warren retired, President Nixon appointed Warren E. Burger to be the 15th Chief Justice of the Supreme Court.

See also the article on COURTS.

surface tension

Surface tension is a way that liquids

have of clinging together and forming drops instead of flying off in all directions as a gas would. If you fill a glass to the brim with water and then slowly add more water, a little at a time, the level of the water will rise above the level of the glass instead of overflowing. It is surface tension that holds the water together. Eventually you will add enough water so that the gravity pulling the water downward is greater than the surface tension. Then the top of the water will break and the water will flow over the sides of the glass. In many liquids, for example oils, the surface tension is lower than it is in water; in a few liquids it is greater.

surgery

Surgery is a way of treating sickness by opening the body with a knife or other sharp instrument. This kind of treatment is known as an *operation*. The word surgery also applies to the fixing of fractures (broken bones), even when this is done without cutting into the body. Doctors who do operations and set broken bones are called *surgeons*. Surgery is used to help the body get rid of germs, as when the doctor cuts open a boil to let the pus out. It is often done to remove an infected organ, such as the appendix or the tonsils, from inside the body. Surgery that cuts off an infected or badly injured outer organ, such as an arm, leg, or finger, is called an *amputation*. Much dental work is a form of surgery. Another kind of surgery is used to improve the shape of a crooked part of the body or to put back a missing feature, such as a nose or ear, by borrowing and modeling skin and soft bone from other parts of the body. This is called *plastic surgery*.

In big operations, called *major surgery*, the doctor puts you to sleep so that you know and feel nothing and wake up when it is all over. In small operations, or *minor surgery*, he may inject you with a chemical or spray a drug on the sick place so that part of your body becomes numb (without feeling) although your mind is awake. The chemicals that put you to sleep or kill pain are called *anesthetics*. Before anesthetics were discovered, about a hundred years ago, persons often suffered terrible pain during surgery and had to be tied down or held down by force. Now all operations are painless.

OPERATIONS

When a surgeon makes a large cut into some part of the body, he stops the bleeding by tying off the ends of the cut arteries and veins. As the wound of the operation heals, other blood vessels grow and branch out through the flesh to circulate the blood that was carried by the tied-off blood vessels. In major surgery, where there is a lot of bleeding, the lost blood is replaced by a blood transfusion (explained in the article on BLOOD). A surgeon finishes a major operation by sewing the flesh, skin, and other soft tissues together with fine silk thread, catgut thread, or other kind of thread. Some types of surgical stitching have to be taken out after the wound has healed; others can be left inside the body, where they later dissolve. Fractured bones are sometimes held together by stainless steel wires or rustproof screws that can stay in the body for life.

When a surgeon operates he makes sure that everything is very clean so that no germs get into the operation to cause an infection. He scrubs his hands and arms thoroughly, wears rubber gloves, and sees to it that everything else—the cutting instruments, bandages, surgical thread, and the clothes of everyone in the room—are *sterile*, which means free from germs. Except in very minor surgery, the surgeon and nurses all wear masks, so that they cannot breathe germs into the open wound.

The importance of keeping operations free of all outside germs was first shown by an English surgeon, Joseph Lister, about eighty-five years ago. He had learned from the French scientist, Louis Pasteur, that infection and many kinds of sickness are caused by tiny germs, called *bacteria*, that can be seen only under a microscope. Before the time of Lister and Pasteur operations were dangerous and many persons died from them because germs got into the body and caused infection and blood poisoning.

MODERN DEVELOPMENTS

Surgeons today can do operations that take as long as eight or ten hours with perfect safety. They know how to remove a whole organ, such as a lung, a kidney, and even the stomach, without endangering their patients. Surgeons can cut into the heart to sew up leaks or to open passages that have been blocked. They can operate on the human brain. In some serious sicknesses, such as cancer, they have been able to remove almost half of the brain to save the patient's life.

Surinam

Surinam is a land in South America that is part of the Netherlands. It is in the northeast, on the Atlantic Ocean. It is sometimes called Dutch Guiana. Surinam has an area of about 55,000 square miles, and more than 300,000 people live there. Its capital is Paramaribo.

Surinam's coastline on the Atlantic is a fertile plain, but the land rises into mountains where there are hardwood trees such as teak and mahogany.

The people of Surinam are descendants of the Dutch colonists and of Negroes, Chinese and Javanese who were brought in to work on the sugar plantations. After World War II, many European refugees settled in Surinam as farmers.

The British were the first to establish settlements in the region of Surinam, more than two hundred years ago. In 1667 it was given to the Dutch in exchange for New Netherlands (now New York).

SURINAM. Area, 55,400 square miles. Population (1968 estimate) 377,000. Capital, Parmaribo, population about 110,000.

surveying

Surveying is a method of finding exact directions and measuring distances on the surface of the earth. Surveying is used to fix boundaries between pieces of property, states, countries, or other divisions of the earth. Maps are usually based on surveys. It is also used to give necessary information to engineers when roads, railroads, and other public works are to be built. A surveyor needs training in the special work of surveying and also in mathematics, drafting, and other kinds of knowledge or skill.

Usually two or three men must work on a surveying job. One uses a telescope mounted on a tripod (three-legged stand). The telescope has a device that will make it exactly level, for which reason it is called a *level*. Another similar instrument called a transit has an attached direction-measuring device as well as a leveling device. The surveyor sights through the telescope and his assistants make a mark at a distant point that the surveyor chooses. From this the surveyor can learn both the exact direction and the exact distance, which are marked on a map or chart. Often the measuring is done with a 100-foot steel tape which is carefully made to show exact distances between two points. The surveyor calculates the area of the land he surveys by dividing it into sections marked by straight lines and curves.

George Washington was a surveyor in his youth. Probably the two most famous surveyors in American history were Mason and Dixon, who surveyed the boundary between Maryland and Pennsylvania. "Mason and Dixon's line" came to be considered the dividing line between the northern states and the southern states.

Susquehanna River

The Susquehanna is a river 444 miles long in the northeastern United States. It rises in Otsego Lake, New York, and flows south through Pennsylvania to empty into Chesapeake Bay at Havre de Grace, Maryland. There is not much navigation on the river, but it supplies important water power. The West Branch of the Susquehanna rises in central Pennsylvania and flows 230 miles to join the main stream at Northumberland. The principal cities on the Susquehanna are Binghamton, New York, and Wilkes-Barre and Harrisburg, Pennsylvania.

Suwanee River

The Suwanee is a river 250 miles long, in Georgia and Florida. It rises in the Okefenokee Swamp in southeastern Georgia and flows across northern Florida to empty into the Gulf of Mexico. The river is navigable to White Springs in Florida. It is full of bass, perch, catfish, and bream, and has a few alligators. Stephen Foster used the river's name, but misspelled it, in his song "Old Folks at Home," or "Swanee River."

swallow

Swallows are among the most graceful and attractive of all birds. There are a great many different kinds of swallow and they are found in many parts of the United States.

One of the best-known kinds is the *barn swallow*. It makes its nest on ledges or beams of barns and is a great friend to the farmer because it eats many harmful insects.

The barn swallow is about seven inches long. It has bluish-black feathers on its back and a reddish colored breast. It has a graceful, long, forked tail with white spots on it. The barn swallow builds its nest of mud and lines it with soft feathers that it often borrows from chickens. The female lays four or five pretty white eggs that have reddish-brown spots on them. The barn swallow has a sweet song and is generally a very popular bird.

The *cliff swallow* is sometimes called the "eave" swallow because it builds its mud nest under the eaves of buildings. Some cliff swallows that built their nests under the eaves of the Mission of San Capistrano in California, and return there each year, became famous because a song was written about them. The name of the song is "When the Swallows Come Back to Capistrano."

As soon as the first cold weather comes, the swallows gather in large flocks and begin a long journey to warmer climates. When spring comes they return to their nesting places. Sometimes they are fooled by a short spell of warm weather very early in spring. Because of this there is a saying, "One swallow does not make a summer."

swamp

A swamp is a piece of land that is covered with shallow water, seldom more than a few feet deep. Reeds and tall grasses, shrubs and trees grow in the swamp, rooted in the wet ground below the water. The water that covers a swamp sometimes comes from springs in the ground and sometimes from river or sea water that has backed up or has overflowed from tides. Usually the word *marsh* is used for the same kind of wet land, but sometimes marshes and swamps are considered to be two different things. In many parts of the world swamps and marshes have been drained of their water and have become valuable farm land. See also the article BOG.

Famous swamps and marshes include OKEFENOKEE (about which there is a separate article), in Georgia and in Florida; the Pripet Marshes of Russia, a region along nearly 500 miles of the Pripet River, which once covered an area greater than the entire state of Indiana but now has been largely drained; and the Back Bay of Boston, a former sea swamp that was filled and became the city's finest residential section.

swan

The swan is one of the most graceful and stately of all birds. Since ancient times people have made up many stories and legends about the swan. It was the bird of Apollo, the god of the sun, according to the mythology of the ancient Greeks. Some legends say that Apollo was turned into a swan.

There are many different kinds of swan. Most of them are large birds, some being five feet long. They have slender, curving necks and lovely white feathers. They move quietly and smoothly, but are swift fliers and swimmers.

The two best-known varieties of wild swans are the *whistling swan* and the *trumpeter swan*. The whistling swan gets its name because in flight it makes a loud, clear, whistling sound. The whistling swan makes its home in the Arctic regions. It builds a large clumsy nest on swampy ground. The female lays from two to seven pure white eggs. Some male and female swans are very affectionate and faithful and stay together for life.

The trumpeter swan looks very much like the whistling swan but is larger. In

The trumpeter swan has a strong trumpet-like call. It is now rather rare.

flight it gives a deep, clear call that sounds like a trumpet's note. At one time there were many trumpeter swans in the United States and Canada, but many of them were shot, or killed by wolves and other enemies. Now there are only a few trumpeter swans left.

There are stories that say that before a swan dies it sings a beautiful song. This is not true, but because of the story an artist's last great work is called his "swan song." The great ballet dancer Pavlova was best known for a dance called "The Dying Swan."

Swanee River, a misspelling of the name of the SUWANEE RIVER.

Swaziland

Swaziland is a small independent kingdom in southeast Africa. It is almost completely surrounded by the Republic of South Africa, except its eastern border adjoins Mozambique. Its area is 6,705 square miles or about the size of Connecticut and Delaware combined. The capital city is Mbabane in the western part of the country.

Swaziland is located on a plateau of grasslands and forests, which is divided into 3 geographic regions—a highland, a middleland, and a lowland. The highland has an altitude of 3,500 feet, the middleland is about 2,000 feet, and the lowland is about 1,000 feet. Compared to many African countries, Swaziland has a good water supply in its rivers and streams. The climate is hot and humid with the rainfall ranging from less than 30 inches to over 70 inches in certain areas.

The Swazi, an African tribe, settled in this country in the early 1800's and gave the country its name. In 1894 the Boers, descendants of Dutch settlers, took control of the country. In the Boer War (1899-1901) the British fought the Boers and won Swaziland from them. After being under British control for many years, Swaziland became independent on September 8, 1968.

The country's economy is based on agriculture and mining. The chief crops are sugar, corn, cotton, and rice. Asbestos, iron ore, and coal are major mining products.

SWAZILAND. Area, 6,705 square miles, Population (U.N. est. 1973) 420,000. Language, English and Swazi. Religion, Christian and traditional African beliefs. Government, constitutional monarchy. Capital, Mbabane. Monetary Unit, Rand.

Sweden

Sweden is a country in northern Europe. It is one of the Scandinavian countries, on the Baltic Sea, connected with the North Sea and the Atlantic Ocean by two waterways called the Kattegat and the Skagerrak. Sweden is on the east side of the Scandinavian Peninsula, and covers most of the peninsula. About one-tenth of Sweden lies in the cold Arctic Circle, a region known as the "Land of the Midnight Sun" because from May to July the sun never entirely sets there.

Sweden is about 173,000 square miles in area, which is a little larger than the state of California, and about 8,129,000 people live there, which is less than half as many as live in California. The northern part of Sweden is cold and barren, so nine out of ten of the people live in the southern half of the country.

THE PEOPLE OF SWEDEN

The Swedish people belong to one of the purest ancient races in the world. The Swedes are descendants of Germanic tribes that lived in Scandinavia in prehistoric times. Except for about 30,000 Finns in the northeast, and about 10,000 Lapps, all of the people of Sweden are Swedes. The Swedes are a friendly and polite people, with an intense love for their native land. They have made their country a "land of light," in which even the cities are bright and open, and the smallest cottage has its little patch of flower garden. The Swedes are a sports-loving nation; one out of every four Swedes belongs to a sports club, and the national game is soccer. They are famous for their skill in skiing and ice-skating. Although the people are up-to-date, they keep alive many of their old customs and colorful costumes in national festivals and celebrations each year.

Sweden is a very democratic country. About half the people belong to coöperatives, in which they act together to get the things they need more cheaply than they could buy them as individuals.

The language of Sweden is Swedish, which closely resembles the languages used in Norway and Denmark. It is a North Germanic language, a member of the Indo-European family of languages. The Lutheran religion is the state religion, but everyone may belong to the church of his choice and many of the people belong to other Protestant denominations.

HOW THE PEOPLE LIVE

Almost half of the people of Sweden earn their living in industry. About a quarter of the people are farmers or fishermen, and the rest work in business, transportation, and other occupations.

More than half of the land of Sweden is covered with forests, and many people work in the lumber and woodworking industries and in paper mills. Swedish stainless steel cutlery, glassware and furniture are known the world over. Sweden is very rich in mineral resources. Iron is the chief mineral product; others are copper, zinc, and manganese. The Swedish steel industry is famous, and there are great steel smelters and mills, and factories that make machinery, locomotives,

The hippopotamus lives in the waters of Swaziland.

turbines, and generators. One of the important armament factories of Europe is in Sweden. Other industries include shipbuilding and the making of textiles, shoes, and matches.

Only about ten per cent of Sweden is used for farming, but modern methods are used. The crops include grains, flax, potatoes, and sugar beets. Livestock is raised, and there are important dairy farms.

The Swedish people have a very high standard of living. About two-thirds of them live in cities, but the cities are mostly small and open, with many parks. They are very clean because of the wide use of electricity instead of coal.

Everyone has to go to school between the ages of 7 and 14, and a law was passed in 1950 to extend this period to the age of 16. There are many excellent, modern elementary schools and high schools. There are two very old universities at Uppsala and Lund, and two newer ones in Stockholm and Göteborg. Almost everybody in Sweden can read and write.

WHAT THE COUNTRY IS LIKE

Sweden is a land of mountains and rolling plains, with many beautiful lakes. The mountains are in the west along the Norwegian border, and the highest point is Mt. Kebnekaise in the north, almost 7,000 feet. In the center of the country is a hilly plateau, or high plain. Along the east coast and in the south is a low, fertile plain. Most of the lakes are in the southern plain.

Sweden has a number of great rivers, which are especially important in the huge lumbering industry. They are frozen in the winter, and huge quantities of logs are hauled to the nearest river and unloaded on the ice. In the spring the logs are automatically carried to the coast when the ice melts. In southern Sweden is the Gota River, which supplies power to many parts of the country.

The climate of Sweden is moderate, in spite of its being so far north. The Gulf Stream brings warm winds, so that even north of the Arctic Circle the average summer temperature is 54 degrees. In the southern part of Sweden the average summer temperature is about 63 degrees and the average winter temperature is about 26 degrees.

CHIEF CITIES OF SWEDEN

The leading cities of Sweden, with populations from the 1973 census, are:

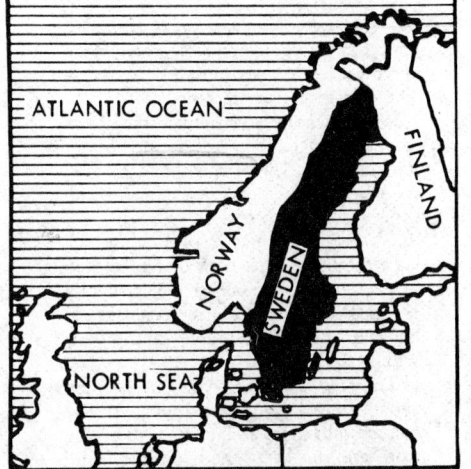

Stockholm, population 1,350,999, the capital and largest city. There is a separate article about STOCKHOLM.

Göteborg, population 676,105, the second-largest city and principal seaport, in southwest Sweden, on the Kattegat.

Malmö, population 445,653, the third-largest city, a seaport and transportation center, in southern Sweden.

Norrköping, population 92,600, fourth-largest city and chief textile center, in the southeast, on the Motala River.

HOW THE PEOPLE ARE GOVERNED

Sweden is a constitutional monarchy, which means that it has a king, a parliament that makes the laws, and a written constitution that protects the rights of the people. The king of Sweden is Gustaf (or Gustavus) VI Adolph.

The parliament, called the Riksdag, is composed of 350 members. The Riksdag formerly had two houses of equal rank and power, but in 1971 it changed over to a unicameral (one-house) system. All members of the Riksdag are directly elected for three-year terms. Although there is a king, the real chief executive is the prime minister. Elections are by proportional representation, a system in which each political party wins a number of seats in proportion to the votes cast for it. Everybody 21 years old or older is permitted to vote. The capital is Stockholm.

Sweden is one of the most advanced nations in laws for public welfare. Laws provide for old-age, disability and maternity benefits, workmen's compensation insurance, cash allowances to the family for each child under the age of 16, and compulsory health insurance. The state owns many of the public utilities, including railroads, telephones, iron mines, and electric power plants.

Every man over 19 years old must receive military training, and all men are subject to military service until the age of 47.

SWEDEN IN THE PAST

In ancient times, Sweden was divided into two regions: Gotaland in the south was the home of the people known as Goths, while Svealand in the north was the home of the Svear people. They were always at war, and by the 6th century the Svear had conquered and mixed with the Goths. Christianity was brought to Sweden in the 9th century, but three hundred years passed before paganism disappeared completely. The ancient Swedish kings were not very strong, and gradually the real power of the country came into the hands of the church and the noblemen. German merchants of the Hanseatic League founded cities in Sweden, and these cities began to want their independence.

In 1397 Queen Margaret of Norway and Denmark, which were then ruled as one country, became ruler of Sweden too. But the Swedish people did not like being ruled from Denmark, and in 1521 Gustaf I led an uprising that put him on the throne of Sweden.

For several hundred years after Gustaf's death in 1560, Sweden was involved in wars with Denmark, Russia, and Poland. Sweden gained much land, and by 1630 was the most powerful Protestant country of Europe. From 1611 to 1718 Sweden fought great wars under three kings, Gustaf II, Charles X, and Charles

XII, and at various times controlled Finland and large Russian, Prussian and Polish territories. After Charles XII was killed in battle in 1718, Sweden became weak and lost most of its great territories in Europe.

King Charles XIII, who was king from 1809 to 1818, had no children. He adopted as his heir a French officer, Jean-Baptiste Bernadotte, who later became Charles XIV and founded the present line of Swedish kings.

In 1813, Sweden fought against Emperor Napoleon of France, on the side of England and Russia. When Napoleon was defeated in 1814, Norway was united with Sweden, but in 1905 Norway became independent again.

The war with Napoleon was Sweden's last war. During the 1800s Sweden made great progress in industry and government.

Sweden remained neutral in World Wars I and II. In 1946 it joined the United Nations and it is a member of the Nordic Council, of which Denmark, Norway and Iceland also are members.

SWEDEN. Area, 173,378 square miles. Population (1973 estimate) 8,129,000. Language, Swedish. Religion, Lutheran. Government, constitutional monarchy. Monetary unit, the krona, worth 19 cents (U.S.). Flag, yellow cross on blue field.

Swedenborg, Emanuel

Emanuel Swedenborg was a Swedish philosopher, or thinker, and a scientist and religious leader. He lived about 250 years ago. Many people believed in his teachings, and after his death they founded a Church based on what he had taught.

Swedenborg was born in 1688 at Stockholm, Sweden. He studied at the University of Uppsala, in Sweden, and then spent several years traveling through Europe. He then turned to science, especially mechanics and engineering, invented a number of useful things, and wrote books on mathematics and minerals and other subjects. He had always been interested in philosophical questions, such as the relation of man's body to his soul, and he hoped to answer many such questions by studying biology, the science of all living things. In 1747, when he was 59 years old, he turned from the study of nature to the study of religion. He said that God had told him to do this, and had appeared to him directly, and so he devoted the rest of his life to religion.

Swedenborg taught that God is love, that He is the cause of all things in the world, and that men should love God so that they might understand themselves and the world they live in. Swedenborg died in London, England, in 1772. His followers, called Swedenborgians, organized the Church of the New Jerusalem, also called the New Church. Its first public services were held in London in 1788. The first congregation in the United States was founded in 1792 in Baltimore, Maryland. Swedenborgians teach that Christ, or God, appeared to Swedenborg, which they call the Second Coming. In 1953 there were 5,896 Swedenborgians in the United States. The headquarters is

in Boston, but the Church is strong in Ohio.

sweet gum

The sweet gum is a tree that grows mainly in the southeastern part of the United States. Until 1937 its wood was the most important wood for making veneer (an outer coating for things made of wood), but today the wood of the Douglas fir is used even more. Sweet gum wood is still used to make boxes, crates, and furniture, and sometimes for railroad ties. Sweet gum trees grow to be 80 to 120 feet high and are from 1½ to 3 feet around the trunk. The wood is reddish-brown and can be polished until it shines. The bark of the sweet gum contains a sticky brownish-yellow substance called *storax*, which is used to make perfumes and certain medicines. Sweet gum is known also as *red gum*, *star-leaved gum*, or simply *gum*.

sweet pea

Sweet peas are sweet-smelling flowers that are grown in beds and on walls or trellises. There are both climbing and bed varieties. Both are annuals, which means that seeds for them must be planted every year.

Sweet peas have a multitude of colors, ranging from pure white to deep red and purple, and including many that combine two colors, such as pink and white, and some that are striped or mottled. The entire blossom is seldom more than an inch and a quarter from top to stem.

When sweet peas are allowed to go to seed, they form pods that look somewhat like the pods of ordinary garden peas, and their seeds when dried look very much like dried peas.

sweet potato

The sweet potato is a vine that grows in tropical and warm climates. It bears lavender flowers. It is not related to the white potato but is a close relative of the morning glory. Sweet potatoes have much-thickened, oblong roots that are cooked and eaten as a vegetable. The roots are starchy and somewhat sweet in flavor, with a texture that is somewhat like that of pumpkin or squash.

There are many varieties of sweet potato, and a variety may have a white, a purple, or a golden skin color. The flesh of the root may be white or a deep orange color inside. The moist-meated varieties are commonly called "yams," and are preferred over the starchy ones for eating. The true yam is an entirely different plant.

sweet William

Sweet William is a popular garden flower that is a member of the same family as garden pinks. The blossoms are borne in large, nearly flat clusters. Sweet William occurs in many different colors, and some of the clusters have a combination of shades in the blossoms. There are many flowers on a single plant. Another name for sweet William is *dianthus*. The plants are about eighteen inches high.

swift

The swift is a little bird that makes its home in almost every part of the world. There are many different kinds of swift.

They get their name because they are very fast fliers. The larger swifts are said to be the fastest fliers of all birds. Most swifts are only about five inches long. They have greenish-black or dark brown feathers.

Unlike most birds, swifts have very weak legs. They cannot perch on branches or telephone wires because their legs cannot hold the weight of their bodies. The swift has to catch the insects that it eats while it flies through the air. Its large mouth helps it to do this. It must gather the material to build its nest as it flies past leaves and twigs.

The swift has sharp claws and it can cling to the side of a tree. The *chimney swift* builds its nest on the inside of a chimney. It uses leaves and twigs and sticks them together with a special sticky substance that is produced in its body. The female swift lays pretty oval-shaped white eggs.

The *cave swiftlets* of China build nests that the Chinese people eat as a great delicacy in "bird's-nest soup." The nest is somewhat like gelatin.

Swift, Jonathan

Jonathan Swift was an English writer who lived more than two hundred years ago. He was famous as a writer of satire. Satire is a kind of writing in which human beings and their actions are criticized by being made to look ridiculous. Swift's most famous satire is *Gulliver's Travels*, a book that tells of the 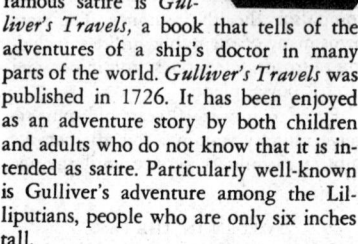 adventures of a ship's doctor in many parts of the world. *Gulliver's Travels* was published in 1726. It has been enjoyed as an adventure story by both children and adults who do not know that it is intended as satire. Particularly well-known is Gulliver's adventure among the Lilliputians, people who are only six inches tall.

Jonathan Swift was born in Dublin, Ireland, in 1667. His father was very poor but his uncle helped him get an education. After Swift graduated from Trinity College in Dublin, he became a priest in the Church of England. In 1713 he became Dean of St. Patrick's Cathedral in Dublin, and for this reason he is often called Dean Swift.

Many of Swift's satires are concerned with political questions and leading political figures of his day. Although Swift often portrayed human beings as stupid and cruel, he has been much admired for the clearness and the cleverness of his writing. For the last few years of his life Swift was insane.

Jonathan Swift died in 1745.

swimming and diving

Swimming—the ability to move through the water without sinking—is one of the most useful things a person can learn. It is always an enjoyable sport and exercise, and it can be a protection against death or a way of saving the life of another person.

The human body, held motionless, will ordinarily sink if it is upright but will float when a person is lying on his back or stomach. In this is found the explanation of why nearly every animal can swim quite naturally, without being taught, for its natural positon is with its body stretched out and the same movement of its legs that it used when running will push the water back and send it forward.

Learning to swim is largely a matter of learning not to be afraid of the water. Once a person finds out that he can easily keep afloat, he will be able to swim for the rest of his life. After that, swimming is a matter of learning the best "strokes," or methods of swimming.

THE STROKES

The idea of all strokes is to push the water back. Usually this is done with the arms. At the same time the legs "kick," pushing the water downward so that they will not sink. Otherwise the legs, which do not have the advantage of air-filled lungs to hold them up, will sink unless they are held stiff, and this is too much effort to keep up for a long time.

The *crawl* is one of the most popular strokes in swimming. It is fast but not very tiring. Often it is called the Australian crawl, because probably it was first used in Australia, about sixty or seventy years ago.

The body is face downward in the water. Each arm in turn, pointed straight ahead, dips into the water and pulls backward. Then the arm is lifted up out of the water and returned forward while the other arm dips into the water. The legs, bent at the knees, kick up and down at the same times as the arms move back and forth, but two or three times as often. With each stroke, the face turns from one side to the other, and the swimmer breathes in under the arm that is being returned.

The *breast stroke* begins with the arms bent in and the hands together at the chest. Both arms are thrust forward at the same time, and make a sweeping movement forward and then back. When they have gone all the way back they are returned to the chest for the next stroke. The legs are pulled up under the body and are then thrust backward together, held as though they were "froglegs."

The *backstroke* is performed while the swimmer is on his back. It is done somewhat like the crawl, one arm at a time. The arm is thrust backward into the water, then pulled to the thigh. The legs are pulled up to the body and thrust away from it, which helps send the body through the water.

The *sidestroke* is slow but restful. The body lies on its side and the arm on the downward side does most of the work. The legs kick from the hip.

Expert swimmers learn many variations on these strokes. They can swim without moving their legs, or without moving their arms. Only experience and confidence teaches such tricks.

Floating is a matter of holding the body straight on its back and breathing slowly so that the air is never wholly emptied from the lungs. The natural buoyancy (floating ability) of the body will do the rest.

Treading water is a way of keeping afloat while in a upright position. The feet are moved up and down as in a "dog trot," and this keeps the body from sinking.

Underwater swimming is a matter of experience and practice. After trying it a few times, a swimmer finds it easy to open his eyes under water.

USEFUL THINGS TO KNOW

There are certain important things to observe in any form of swimming. They include: balance; exhaling and inhaling; easy power; no tightening.

There are several facts that apply to all strokes.

First, it is known that if there is air in the lungs, the body will float.

To swim well, the body should be in a good position to move through the water.

A human being must have air—must breathe in and out—whether swimming or walking.

Any sudden, jerky motion tightens the muscles and makes the swimmer tired. A good thing to know is that if the lower jaw is relaxed, the whole body seems to stay loose, which will help in swimming.

There are many styles of swimming, all of which are good. For racing the four styles generally used are: freestyle, backstroke, breast stroke, and butterfly. Under the heading freestyle may be any form of swimming.

Balance in the water is determined mainly by the position of the head. If it is held too high, the legs and hips sink. If too low, it is difficult to pull the hand on the dipped shoulder side fully through the water. Therefore a balance somewhat like the dead man's float should be maintained.

TECHNIQUE OF THE CRAWL

The crawl stroke produces the speediest swimmers in the world. It requires much practice and supervision, for it is hard for the swimmer to know exactly how the stroke is being executed.

The swimmer lies on the water, face down. The legs and arms are stretched out full length in the position of a dead man's float. The legs start their motions at the hips and develop a rhythmic up-and-down motion. Each leg in turn is driven down with a slightly bent knee, the motion starting at the hip and ending at the toes. Each joint of the leg and foot presses down in turn. Each leg then starts an up-drive, again starting at the hip, moving the thigh, then the calf, and lastly the sole of the foot. The heel should break the water slightly, which will induce the sole of the foot to come right to the surface of the water. There are three complete kicks to each pull.

The arms propel alternately in a ratio of three kicks to each arm pull. The arms are extended in front of the shoulder with a very slight break at the elbow. The hand is then pulled firmly through the water, about on a line with the shoulder, until it approaches the thigh. Then the wrist is thrown away from the thigh and the arm recovers and repeats the entire motion of entering, pulling, and recovering, while the strokes and kicks are made. The head is turned to inhale so that it swivels loosely. This means that the neck turns while the shoulders stay nearly parallel to the water. It is commonly good practice to exhale while the face is in the water.

TECHNIQUE OF THE BREAST STROKE

The body lies face down on the water, with the legs and arms fully extended and the toes pointed. The legs are drawn up towards the body. The knees bend and separate while the feet sweep out. Then the knees drive together, with the legs and feet coming together in the original position. From the extended dead man's float position, turn the palms of the hand slightly outward and pull out and slightly down in a heart shape. Care must be taken not to pull far past the shoulders, or the hands will not be able to recover.

As the hands go past the shoulder line, the palms are rotated on the wrists in an inward motion so that when the hands come under the chest they are palms down and ready to reach out again to the original position at arm's length in front of the face.

Breathing is done by slightly lifting the head when the hands have been pulled almost to the shoulder line. Exhale under water.

TECHNIQUE OF THE BACKSTROKE

The position of the swimmer on this stroke is, as the name suggests, on the back. Again the legs and arms are stretched out but the swimmer can breathe at will. The stroke is commenced by the legs pressing down alternately, starting at the hip and ending with the soles of the feet pressing down. The ankle is fixed. As each leg reaches its lowest point it starts upward. Again the first impulse is at the hips, not the knee. Then the knee is raised very slightly, followed by the shin, and lastly the foot flips up so that the toes break the water. It is important that the ankles be flexed and the knees be below water.

The hands, from their extended position in back of the head and about in a line with the shoulder joint, are pulled firmly through the water. The elbows bend very slightly and the arms move through an arc that is usually not more than fifteen inches under the surface of the water. At the end of the pull, do not allow the hand to stop at the thigh. Keep the hand moving. The overall motion is up and down with the legs, and sidewise with the arms. Three complete leg kicks are made to each single arm pull. Inhale with one arm pull, and exhale with the other.

THE BUTTERFLY

This was originally swum under the classification for the breast stroke. The main difference is in form of recovery of the arms. In the breast stroke, the hands finish under water and go to the point of catch under water. In the butterfly, the hands pull as in a two-handed crawl stroke and recover by moving over water from the finish to the catch.

The kick is executed by moving the legs as in the breast stroke, but usually it is shorter and more up-and-down. It differs from the kick in the crawl mainly because both legs must move in the same pattern at the same time. The butterfly stroke is comparatively new.

SWIMMING CHAMPIONSHIPS

The important swimming contests are at distances measured in meters. A meter is slightly more than a yard. There are separate contests for men and women. The important championships include:

100-meter freestyle
200-meter freestyle
400-meter freestyle
1,500-meter freestyle
100-meter breast stroke
200-meter breast stroke
100-meter backstroke
200-meter backstroke
100-meter butterfly

There are also relay races for teams of swimmers, and many special events, at swimming meets.

SWIMMING THE CHANNEL

Long-distance swimming has been a challenge to swimmers for many years, but for some reason the English Channel has been the swim they are proudest to make. Usually swimmers try to swim across the Channel at its narrowest point, which is about 21 miles, between Dover in England and Cape Griz Nez in France. Some swimmers try to swim it in one direction, some in another; a few have swum it in both directions (at different times). The water is cold and stormy. The swimmer is usually coated with heavy grease, which is a protection against the cold and at the same time makes it easier to travel through the water. A boat travels beside the swimmer to take him (or her) out of the water if necessary.

The first woman to swim the Channel was Gertrude Ederle, an American girl from New York City, in 1926. The first woman to swim the Channel in both directions was another American girl, Florence Chadwick, who did it in 1950 and 1951. More than 100 persons have swum across the Channel. The record time, 10 hours and 23 minutes, was established by a Canadian swimmer, Helge Jensen, in 1960. Most swimmers have taken from twelve to fourteen hours or more.

DIVING

The practical value of diving is not likely to be as great as the practical value of swimming, unless a person finds himself with an emergency need to enter the water from a great height. Otherwise diving is a skill that adds pleasure to the sport of swimming.

Competitive, or fancy, diving is done in exhibitions and is among the contests in the Olympic Games and between school and club teams. Diving is almost always done from a springboard. At diving contests, judges decide which contestant has shown the best form. Points are awarded for good performance, and the contestant with the most points wins.

Swimming contests are mostly to determine the fastest swimmer at various distances, using various strokes. The principal races are "free style" (any stroke the swimmer wants to use).

See also the article DIVING.

Swinburne, Algernon Charles

Algernon Charles Swinburne was an English poet. He is remembered chiefly for his skillful use of words and rhythm. He was born in 1837 in London, and began to write poetry as a schoolboy. He was a fine scholar, especially of French literature and the works of the Middle Ages and of ancient Greece and Rome. He was a close friend of many of the great poets of his time. Swinburne wrote a great many poems and also wrote essays about other books. His chief poetical works include *Atalanta in Calydon*,

A Song of Italy, Songs before Sunrise, Poems and Ballads, and Tristram of Lyonesse. He died in 1909.

swine, a name for the pig family: see the article PIG.

Swiss chard

Swiss chard is a vegetable of the beet family. It is grown for its leaves and thick, pulpy stalks. The stalks are cooked and eaten like asparagus, and the leaves are treated like spinach or kale. Like the leaves of spinach, Swiss chard greens are rich in iron. It is a good leaf vegetble to grow in very small gardens, because as the heavier outer leaves are cut off and used, new leaves grow from the stem. One plant can be harvested repeatedly from the middle of summer until frost time. Another name for Swiss chard is "leaf beet."

Swithin, Saint

St. Swithin was an English clergyman who lived more than a thousand years ago. He was bishop of Winchester. Swithin died in the year 862. He had wished to be buried just outside his church at Winchester, so that people passing by might see his grave, and if it rained, raindrops from the eaves of the church's roof would water his grave. About a hundred years later the Roman Catholic Church declared Swithin was a saint, and at that time his body was moved to be buried inside the church. This was to be done on July 15, but on that day it rained so hard that the body could not be moved, and it continued to rain for forty days. From this story came the belief that if it rained on July 15 it will go on raining for forty days. There is an old poem about this story:

St. Swithin's day if thou dost rain
For forty days it will remain;
St. Swithin's day if thou be fair,
For forty days 'twill rain nae mair.

Switzerland

Switzerland is a country in central Europe. It is a landlocked nation; that is, it has no seacoast. Switzerland is called the "playground of Europe," but it is also an important industrial and cultural nation.

Switzerland is about 16,000 square miles in area, which is more than twice the size of New Jersey. About six million people live there, which is a little less than the population of New Jersey.

THE SWISS PEOPLE

The people of Switzerland, called the Swiss, are mostly of Germanic descent, but some are more closely related to the Italians and some to the French. There are four official languages: *Schwyzertütsch,* or Swiss-German, a German dialect that can hardly be understood by persons who speak true German; French and Italian dialects; and Romansh, a language derived from ancient Latin. Almost three-quarters of the people speak Swiss-German, and the people of only one canton (or department) speak Romansh. The laws and official publications of Switzerland are issued in German, Italian, and French.

The predominant religion in Switzerland is Christianity. Slightly more than half of the people are Protestant, and the rest are Roman Catholic.

HOW THE PEOPLE LIVE

Switzerland is a prosperous nation. It exports many manufactured products to other countries, and this and its great tourist trade bring in much money. Almost half of the people work in industry or trade. Many of them work in the great watch and clock industry. There are factories that make chemicals and dyes, metal products, textiles and embroidery, foods, paper, and books. Banking and insurance are important. About one-quarter of the people are farmers. They raise grains, potatoes, grapes and other fruit, and vegetables, but the most important farming is dairy farming. Swiss cheese and other dairy products are world-famous. Switzerland does not raise enough food for its people or its livestock, and must import large quantities.

Switzerland has very few mineral resources. Some asphalt, salt, iron, and manganese are mined.

The Swiss people live well. Their living standard is the highest in Europe. Switzerland is one of the most democratic nations on earth, and it has remained at peace and prosperous during many European wars.

Everyone has to go through elementary school. There are many fine elementary schools and high schools. Switzerland has seven well-known universities, at Zurich, Basel, Bern, Geneva, Lausanne, Neuchâtel, and Fribourg, and a number of technical schools. Almost everyone can read and write.

WHAT THE COUNTRY IS LIKE

Switzerland is a mountainous country of great beauty. The great mountain chain of the ALPS (about which there is a separate article) runs east and west through the southern part of the country. In the central part is the Swiss plateau, a high region of plains and rolling hills, which covers about 20 per cent of Switzerland. North of the plateau is the Jura range of mountains on the border between Switzerland and France.

Some of the highest peaks of the Alps are in Switzerland, including the Dufourspitze (15,203 feet), Matterhorn (14,-

701 feet), Finsteraarhorn (14,032 feet), and Jungfrau (13,635 feet). In the Engadine Valley of the Alps are many world-famous summer and winter resorts. The valley is about 5,000 feet above sea level and contains many mountain lakes. Among the best-known resorts are Saint Moritz, Sils, Silvaplana, Davos, and Pontresina.

Switzerland is famous for its lakes, most of which are on the plateau. Among them are Lakes Constance, Zurich, Lucerne, Neuchâtel, and Geneva. The Rhine and the Rhone rivers rise in Switzerland, as does the Inn River, which flows into the Danube. Most of the rivers supply hydroelectric power for Swiss industry.

The climate of Switzerland varies according to the region, but mostly it is moderate. In the Alpine section the winters are very cold and snowfall is heavy. The summers in the Alps are pleasantly cool.

In the lowlands the average winter temperatures are 34 to 41 degrees and the average summer temperatures are 55 to 63 degrees. Switzerland has two unusual winds: the *foehn,* a warm, dry wind that comes down from the Alps; and the *bise,* a cold north wind.

CHIEF CITIES

The leading cities of Switzerland, with populations from 1973 estimates, are:

Zurich, population 674,000, the largest city and an international banking center. See article about ZURICH.

Basel, population 370,700, the second-largest city.

Geneva, population 314,900, the third-largest city.

Bern, population 260,600, the capital and fourth-largest city.

Lausanne, population 217,700, the fifth-largest city, a year-round resort in the west, on Lake Geneva.

HOW THE PEOPLE ARE GOVERNED

Switzerland is a republic with a government somewhat like that of the United States. The country is divided into 22 cantons. These are similar to the states of the United States. Switzerland has a president, a parliament that makes the laws, and a written constitution that protects the rights of the people.

The parliament is called the Federal Assembly. It has two houses. The Council of States (*Ständerat*) has 44 members, two for each canton. The National Council (*Nationalrat*) has 200 representatives, one for each 24,000 inhabitants. The National Council members are elected by the people for four-year terms. The members of the Council of State are elected according to rules made by each canton individually.

The highest governing body of Switzerland is the Federal Council of seven members, who are elected by the Federal Assembly for four-year terms. Each year the Federal Council elects one of its members to be president. All men 20 years old or over have the right to vote. Women can vote only in federal elections.

Switzerland has no standing army. Every man from the age of 20 to 60 years must serve in the militia. After a first term of service of 118 to 132 days, each man spends brief periods each year in training.

Switzerland is known as the country of the beautiful Alps, with their many health and winter resorts. On the Bernina Pass on the Swiss-Italian border, countless flowers brighten the shore of a quiet lake.

SWITZERLAND IN THE PAST

The first known inhabitants of the region of Switzerland were Celtic tribes whom the Romans called Rhaetians and Helvetians. The region was conquered by Julius Caesar about two thousand years ago and was ruled by Rome for several hundred years. When the Roman Empire began to decline, about 1,500 years ago, Germanic tribes gradually occupied Swiss territory. Christianity was brought to Switzerland in the 6th century by Irish monks, who founded many churches and monasteries.

The beginnings of unity among the Swiss cantons came in 1291, when three free cantons became disturbed because the Hapsburg family, kings of Austria, had so much power in the region. The cantons joined together and won an important victory against Leopold of Austria. They were joined by other cantons, and by 1388 the Austrians were completely defeated. Switzerland became an important military power, and other cantons joined the federation until in 1513 there were 13 of them.

In the 1500s a civil war was fought in Switzerland between Catholics and the new and growing forces of Protestantism. Peace was finally made, with each canton being free to follow the religion of its choice.

In 1798 French armies invaded Switzerland. They were commanded by Napoleon, who later became the French emperor. Napoleon set up a new republic, called the Helvetic Republic, to take the place of the loose confederation of cantons. This republic was unpopular with the cantons, and after Napoleon lost power in 1814 the country again became a federation, which the powers of Europe agreed should be neutral in all wars.

In 1847 Switzerland had another civil war, again over religion. Seven Roman Catholic cantons decided to form a separate league, called the Sonderbund. The Protestant cantons defeated them in three weeks of fighting. A new constitution was established, for the first time setting up a federal government and legislature. This constitution was revised in 1874.

Switzerland has remained neutral in every modern war. The Red Cross was founded in Switzerland, and the League of Nations headquarters was in Switzerland. Because of its insistence on neutrality, Switzerland did not join the United Nations, but it is a member of various bodies of the U.N., such as the International Labor Organization and the World Health Organization.

SWITZERLAND. Area, 15,944 square miles. Population (1973 estimate) 6,300,000. Languages, dialects of German, French, and Italian; and Romansh. Religion, Protestant and Roman Catholic. Government, republic. Monetary unit, the franc, worth 23 cents (U.S.). Flag, white cross on red ground.

sword, a weapon that has a long, sharp cutting blade: see the articles FENCING, CAVALRY and KNIGHTHOOD.

swordfish

The swordfish is a large, powerful fish that lives in the warm oceans of the world. It is easy to recognize a swordfish because of its long "sword," which is actually its upper jaw sticking several feet out in front of the rest of its body. The sword is usually about one-third as long as the body of the fish. The whole fish is six or seven feet long.

The swordfish has no teeth, but its sword is a powerful weapon. When a swordfish swims into a school of mackerel or other fish it begins to swing about with its sword and many fish are killed or wounded.

Grown swordfish often weigh 600 pounds or even more. They are considered one of the best food fish. Fishermen often catch the swordfish with a harpoon, but sportsmen like to use a hook and line.

sycamore

The sycamore is a large shade tree that is planted in many streets and parks in the United States and Canada. It is also called the *plane tree.*

The sycamore's bark seems to have bare or bald spots all over the trunk and larger branches. The seed pods of the sycamore form rough, lumpy-looking round balls, with the seeds themselves on the outside. Each seed is attached to a small, fluffy parachute, like the fluff of a dried dandelion. This enables the wind to carry the seeds to new ground when the pod breaks open.

Sydney

Sydney is the oldest and largest city in Australia. It is the capital of the state of New South Wales and is on Port Jackson, an arm of the Pacific Ocean. About two million people live in Sydney. It has one of the finest harbors in the world. Railroads bring goods to Sydney from many parts of Australia. Sydney has textile (cloth-manufacturing) mills, automobile factories, metal foundries, and chemical plants.

Sydney is the chief educational center of Australia. Its colleges and universities include the University of Sydney, and New South Wales University of Technology. The National Art Gallery in Sydney has a fine collection of paintings and sculpture. Sydney-Harbor Bridge, which joins the central part of the city with its suburbs, is the largest arch bridge in the world.

The old sections of Sydney have picturesque narrow streets that twist and turn just as they did when they were horse and cattle paths.

Sydney was founded in 1788 as a penal (prison) colony, but grew rapidly along with Australia. During World War II it was an important Allied naval base.

SYDNEY, AUSTRALIA. Population (1971

The majestic Matterhorn dominates the scene above the Swiss resort at Zermatt.

estimate) 2,500,000. Capital of New South Wales. On Pacific Ocean. Founded, 1788.

symphony, a long musical composition for a large orchestra: see MUSIC.

synagogue

A synagogue is a house of worship, like a church, in the Jewish religion. Synagogues were built by the ancient Jews more than two thousand years ago. At that time a building called a temple was the actual place of worship, and the Jews met in the synagogue for both religious and other purposes. Then the Jews were forced to move from Palestine and scatter throughout other lands. The synagogues kept alive their ancient traditions as well as their religion.

The religious service in the synagogue was simpler than that in the temple. There was no special priest to conduct it, and the leader was the *chazan,* the official reader of the sacred writings. Religious music was sung by the official singer, the *cantor.* The synagogue was also a place of study for both young and old.

The first American synagogue was built in 1763, at Newport, Rhode Island.

Syracuse

Syracuse is a large city in the northern part of New York State. It is on the beautiful south shore of Onondaga Lake, a salt-water lake. More than 200,000 people live in Syracuse. There are factories that make air-conditioning machinery, air-cooled engines, jet engines, automobile parts, and many other things. Syracuse University is a large and important university. The enrollment in 1971 was 22,667 (both men and women). Le Moyne College is also in Syracuse.

The region around Syracuse was first settled about 1788, but only five hundred people lived there when it became a village in 1825. The first industry was the making of salt from Onondaga Lake, but the salt industry has been unimportant for more than fifty years. Syracuse grew rapidly after the Erie Canal was built, and the New York State Barge Canal is still an important means of shipping heavy goods from Syracuse.

A great city of ancient times, on Sicily, was named Syracuse: see SICILY.

SYRACUSE, NEW YORK. Population (1970 census) 197,208. Industrial city in central New York. County seat of Onondaga County.

Syria

Syria is a country in the part of Asia that is called the Near East, on the east coast of the Mediterranean Sea. It has an area of more than 72,000 square miles, which makes it about the size of North Dakota. More than six million people live there. Most of central and eastern Syria is covered by the Syrian Desert, and the greatest numbers of people live in the western part of the country, nearer the sea. This is a region of low mountains, hills, and plains. In the northeast, the valley of the Euphrates River creates a fertile region in the desert. The climate of Syria is mild on the coast, but in the desert summers are very hot and winters are fairly cold. There is very little rainfall, except in the west.

THE PEOPLE OF SYRIA

Most of the people of Syria belong to the Arab family of peoples. They speak the Arabic language, and about three-quarters of them follow the Mohammedan religion. The rest are Syrian Christians or Jews. In the south live the Druses, a separate Moslem sect. The desert has several Bedouin tribes. Very few Syrians can read and write.

Most of the people of Syria are farmers. They raise livestock, including sheep, goats, cattle, and camels, and they grow wheat, barley, corn, figs, olives, and citrus fruits. In recent years cotton and tobacco have become important. Most of their crops require irrigation. There is very little industry, and there are few mineral resources, except for oil.

The Syrian people have a very low standard of living. Farming is done by ancient methods and therefore many of the people are very poor. In recent years western methods have begun to come into use, especially in the larger cities, and many schools have been built.

From 1958 to 1961, Syria was united with Egypt in a federation called the United Arab Republic. Gamal Abdel Nasser of Egypt was the president. Some Syrians felt the UAR was dominated by Egypt. This led to a revolution in 1961, and the federation was dissolved. Syria is now governed by a president, a parliament, called the National Assembly, and a cabinet, headed by a Prime Minister. The capital is Damascus.

CHIEF CITIES OF SYRIA

The leading cities of Syria, with populations as estimated in 1973, are:

Damascus, population 835,000, the capital. There is a separate article on DAMASCUS.

Allepo, population 639,000, a commercial and industrial center in the northwest.

Hama, population 216,000, and Homs, population 331,408, business centers.

Lattakia, population 121,570, an important seaport.

SYRIA IN THE PAST

Syria was settled in ancient times, thousands of years before the birth of Jesus. The name Syria was long used for the present region plus Lebanon, most of Israel and Jordan, and part of northern Arabia. Its first importance was as a trade and military route between Egypt and Mesopotamia. Through most of its history, Syria has been ruled by foreign powers, including the Egyptians, Babylonians, Hittites, Assyrians, and Persians. It was conquered by Alexander the Great and later by the Romans. Christianity came early to Syria; it was on the road to Damascus that St. Paul was converted.

In the 7th century Syria was conquered by the Arabs, and soon it was converted to the Mohammedan religion. Syria was a battleground in fighting between Turks who had conquered much of the land and the Christian Crusaders from Europe. By the early 1500s the Turkish empire controlled all of Syria and held it until World War I.

After Turkey was defeated in World War I, present Syria and Lebanon were placed under French protection. The Syr-

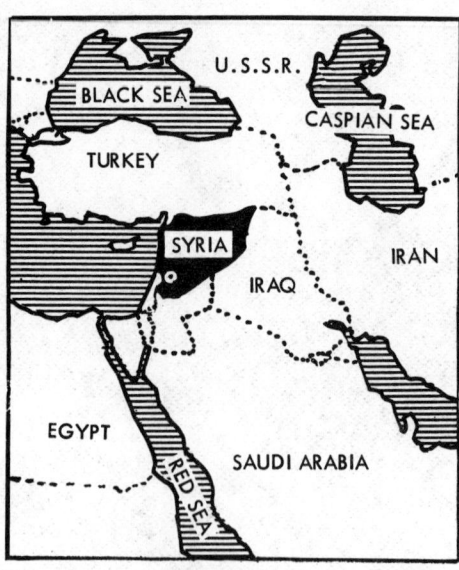

ian people did not like French rule, and in 1936, after many disorders, Syria and France agreed that Syria would become an independent state in 1939. Then World War II broke out and France retained control over Syria and stationed many troops there. Great Britain and the Fighting French forces of General de Gaulle discovered that German planes were using Syria, so they invaded the country and this permitted the Syrian people to proclaim themselves an independent republic in 1941. Syria was one of the original members of the United Nations.

The history of free Syria has been one of violence and military coups. In 1949 a military government took control, headed by General Adib Shishekly. It was Syria's 16th change of government since 1946. Shishekly tried to bring order and reforms, but he governed as a dictator, without a constitution. In 1952 Syria returned to constitutional government, and Shishekly was elected President in 1953. But he was overthrown only a year later, in 1954.

Syria was one of the countries that most strongly supported the Arab League and fought in 1948 and 1949 to prevent Israel from becoming an independent country. Even after the fighting ended and Israel established its independence, in 1949, there continued to be frequent clashes between Israeli and Syrian troops along the border between the two countries.

The Syrian people strongly favored President Nasser of Egypt and his efforts to unite all Arab peoples and to resume war against Israel. When Nasser proposed uniting Egypt and Syria, in 1958, the Syrian people voted overwhelmingly in favor of the union. After growing dissatisfaction and a revolution in 1961, Syria dissolved the union again. In 1967, Syria and other Arab nations were defeated in a six-day war with Israel in which the Israelis captured parts of Syria. In 1973 the Arab countries attacked Israel on Yom Kippur, the Jew's holiest day. See the article on ISRAEL.

SYRIA. Area, 72,234 square miles. Population (1973 estimate) 6,450,000. Capital, Damascus. Language, Arabic. Religion, Mohammedan. Government, republic. Monetary unit, the Syrian pound, worth about 26 cents (U.S.). Flag, three horizontal bars, green, white, and black, with three red stars.

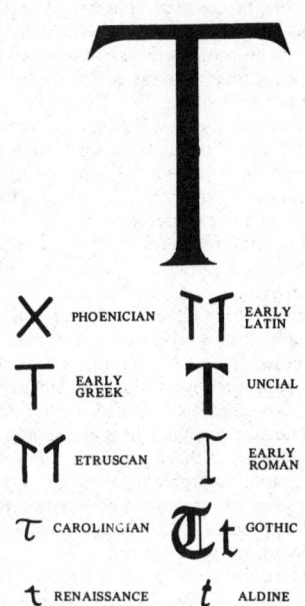

✕ PHOENICIAN		ᴛ EARLY LATIN	
T EARLY GREEK		T UNCIAL	
ꓕ ETRUSCAN		T EARLY ROMAN	
τ CAROLINGIAN		𝕿t GOTHIC	
t RENAISSANCE		t ALDINE	

T or t

The letter T, the twentieth letter of our alphabet, came to us as most of our letters did: First, thousands of years ago, it was perhaps one of the picture-symbols used by the ancient Egyptians in their system of hieroglyphics. In this system a picture of something, instead of a letter, finally came to stand for a single sound. Most scholars believe that the letter T began as a picture of a mark, or sign. In the Hebrew language the word for mark was *taw*. The Hebrews had different ways of writing the letter taw. One of the ways resembled a plus sign (+), like the Phoenician letter above, tipped up.

The ancient Greeks took this letter, which they called tau, and moved the cross-bar up to the top. The Romans used the same letter, which is exactly like the letter T in our alphabet.

In the illustration above, at the far right is the "German black-letter" (or "Gothic") capital T, which is used in many German books.

Read also the article ALPHABET.

tabernacle

The tabernacle is a temporary place of worship that the Jews set up in the wilderness, on their journey out of Egypt to the Promised Land. The Bible tells us about it, in the book of Exodus. A clearing was made in the wilderness and in this clearing a tentlike temple was erected. The tent was divided into two equal parts. The front was called the holy place and the back part was called the holy of holies. In this back part were placed the two stone tablets containing the Ten Commandments that Moses received from God. In the holy place stood a table with incense burning on it and a seven-branched candlestick.

Some places of worship are still called tabernacles. The best known is the Mormon Tabernacle in Salt Lake City, Utah.

There is a Feast of the Tabernacles in the Jewish religion. It begins five days after Yom Kippur (the Jewish Day of Atonement), and lasts for seven days. During the Feast of the Tabernacles the Jews built booths made of branches and reeds in their gardens or back yards. This is because the Israelites lived in such booths in their journey through the wilderness.

table tennis

Table tennis is an indoor game played somewhat like the game of tennis. It is played on a large table with a net across the center. The players bat a small ball back and forth over the net, using wooden paddles. Table tennis is often called Ping Pong, which is a trade name used by a manufacturer of the equipment.

The official table is 9 feet long, 5 feet wide, and 30 inches high. It is usually green or some other dark color with white stripes along the borders and a white stripe down the center of the table. The net across the center of the table is 6 inches high.

The paddles usually have a rough, hard rubber surface on each side. The ball is made of a thin plastic material and is hollow.

Table tennis can be played by two or four players. Two play "singles" and four play "doubles," with two on each side. Each player in turn is the server. He hits the ball with his paddle so that it first bounces on his side of the net, then over the net and bounces on his opponent's side. The object then is to hit the ball on the first bounce so as to make it go over the net and hit the table on the other side. The ball is hit back and forth until one player misses it or hits it off the table or into the net. A point is scored each time this happens.

A server serves until 5 points are scored, then the next person serves for 5 points. A game is won when a player makes 21 points. If both players or both sides should have 20 points, a game cannot be won until one has scored 2 more points than the opponent. Thus a game could end with the score 22–20, or 23–21, and so on.

There is an International Table Tennis Federation that controls matches between teams representing about thirty countries.

Many homes have table tennis tables in their basements or game rooms.

taboo or tabu

A taboo is a strict law against saying or doing something. Many savage or uncivilized peoples have taboos as part of their religions. Usually there seems to be no reason why a particular taboo was adopted. Some tribe may have a religious law that says no one may eat meat when there is a full moon, or that a married man may never enter the same house as his mother-in-law. In a few cases it is possible to guess a reason why a taboo was adopted, but most often this is not possible. The people who live on the islands in the Pacific Ocean had many taboos before European explorers arrived there, and some of the taboos are still observed there. The word *taboo* (which is also spelled *tabu*) comes from the language of the Polynesian people who live on some of the Pacific islands, for example the Hawaiian Islands. The tribes of Africa and other lands have taboos that are much like those of the Pacific.

Table tennis is a fast-action game that can be played indoors on rainy days.

Tacoma

Tacoma is an important seaport and the third-largest city in the state of Washington. It is on Commencement Bay in Puget Sound about 150 miles from the Pacific Ocean. To the southwest of the city lies Mt. Rainier, the highest peak of the Cascade Mountains, and Tacoma is the gateway to Mt. Rainier National Park. The city was named after the Indian name for Mt. Rainier, which was either Tacoma or Tahoma.

About 150,000 people live in Tacoma. Many of them work in the lumber industry, manufacturing plywood, furniture, and pulp and paper. Shipbuilding is also an important industry. Tacoma is a seaport and also a terminal for four transcontinental railroads. The city has the city-manager form of government, with an elected council.

The site on which Tacoma now stands was first explored by Captain George Vancouver, an Englishman, in 1792. It was incorporated under its present name in 1864 and grew in importance after the Northwestern Pacific Railway arrived there in 1873. The Washington State Historical Society Museum is in Tacoma, and also the world's largest totem pole and the Tacoma Narrows Bridge, the third-longest bridge in the United States. The College of Puget Sound and the Pacific Lutheran College are in Tacoma.

TACOMA, WASHINGTON. Population (1970 census) 154,581. County seat of Pierce County. Founded, 1864.

tadpole

A tadpole, also called a polliwog, is a young frog or toad. Most frogs and toads lay their eggs under water, where they remain until they hatch. When the eggs hatch, tiny wriggling creatures come out. They look like small black lumps of flesh with long, thin tails. These are tadpoles. They have no lungs, but breathe water through gills as fish do. As a tadpole grows, it develops lungs, its tail becomes smaller and finally disappears, and legs appear. Eventually the tadpole becomes a frog or toad and can breathe air and live on land. The tail is absorbed into the young frog's or toad's body. It does not fall off.

Some tadpoles become toads within

three or four months, while the giant bullfrog may remain in the tadpole stage for as long as three years. See the article on FROGS AND TOADS.

Taft

Taft is the name of an American family that is prominent in American history. Foremost among them was William Howard Taft, the 27th President of the United States, about whom there is a separate article.

Alphonso Taft was the first famous member of the family. He was born in 1810 in Townshend, Vermont, became a lawyer, and settled in Cincinnati, Ohio. He served as Secretary of War, Attorney General, and ambassador. He died in 1891. William Howard Taft was his son, and he had three other sons who became famous: Charles Phelps Taft, born in 1843, became editor and chief owner of the Cincinnati *Times-Star*. He worked there until his death in 1929. Henry Waters Taft, born in 1859, became a lawyer and wrote many books on law. He died in 1945. Horace Dutton Taft became an educator, and founded the Taft School in Watertown, Connecticut. He was born in 1861 and died in 1943.

ROBERT A. TAFT

Robert Alphonso Taft was the grandson of Alphonso Taft and the son of William Howard Taft. He was born in 1889, became a lawyer, and practiced law in Cincinnati. He became active in the Republican Party in Ohio, and in 1938 he was elected to the United States Senate, where he served until his death. In every Republican Convention from 1940 through 1952 he was proposed as a nominee for President. In 1947 he sponsored the Taft-Hartley Act, a labor law that was passed in spite of the fact that it was vetoed by President Harry Truman. He died in 1953.

Taft, Lorado

Lorado Taft was an American sculptor. He was born in 1860 in Elmwood, Illinois, and studied at the University of Illinois and in Paris, France. When he was 26 years old he began to teach in the Art Institute of Chicago, and through his teaching and writing and lecturing about art he gained many followers among the young artists of the Midwest. His own work consisted mainly of large groups of figures and of military monuments and memorials. He died in 1936. His works include the statue *Black Hawk*, in Oregon, Illinois; *Columbus Memorial Fountain*, in Washington, D.C.; and *Ferguson Fountain of the Great Lakes* and *Fountain of Time*, in Chicago, Illinois.

William H. Taft

William Howard Taft was the twenty-seventh President of the United States. He served from March 4, 1909 until March 4, 1913. During his administration the first complete national budget in United States history was prepared. Taft established models for treaties to settle international arguments by means of peaceful negotiation and discussion between the countries concerned.

William Howard Taft was a large,

heavy man with a white mustache and a deep, booming voice. He was good-humored and slow-moving. After being President he served his country as Chief Justice of the United States Supreme Court.

HIS EARLY YEARS

William Howard Taft was born in Cincinnati, Ohio, on September 15, 1857. He was a member of a prominent family and became familiar with national politics in his early teens, when his father was appointed Attorney General under President Ulysses S. Grant. Young Taft attended Yale University and was graduated with honors in 1878. He attended the law school of the University of Cincinnati and became a lawyer when he was not quite 23. He practiced law in Cincinnati.

Public service drew Taft from the start, and within a year of his graduation from law school he became assistant prosecuting attorney. It was the start of a lifelong political career.

HIS POLITICAL CAREER

Taft advanced rapidly in the legal profession. From the position of assistant prosecuting attorney he rose to assistant county solicitor. He became a judge of the Superior Court of Ohio in 1887, when he was only 30 years old. In 1890 he was appointed United States solicitor general, and after serving for two years in this position he became a judge of the Federal Circuit Court.

The Spanish-American War, which ended in December 1898, gave the United States possession of the Philippine Islands, and William Howard Taft was appointed by President William McKinley to serve as president of the Philippine Commission. In 1901 he became governor-general of the islands, and his service there did a great deal to cement friendly relations between the Philippine and American people.

President Theodore Roosevelt recognized Taft's ability by making him Secretary of War in 1904. Due to Taft's efforts, the government of Cuba was straightened out of the confused state in which the Spanish-American War had left it. Taft then served for a time as provisional governor of Cuba.

As Secretary of War, Taft in 1907 selected Colonel George W. Goethals to take charge of the building of the Panama Canal. Goethals was the third man to attempt the task, and he succeeded where others had given up. Taft's choice of Goethals was one of his important contributions to American history.

HOW HE BECAME PRESIDENT

Theodore Roosevelt decided not to try for another term as President in the 1908 election, and his choice of a successor was William Howard Taft. In November, 1908, Taft defeated his opponent, William Jennings Bryan, and was inaugurated as President in March 1909.

Taft called an extra session of Congress to revise the tariff laws. Congress passed a law that placed high duties (taxes) on many products that were being brought in from foreign countries at low prices and were sold at much higher prices by manufacturers in the United States. This was known as the Payne-Aldrich bill and

was one of the first protective tariff laws enacted in the country. It pleased American manufacturers but since it raised the prices of many things it did not please the general public.

Taft was the first President to present a complete budget showing how much money he expected the government to spend during the next year. This let Congress know exactly how much money would have to be collected in taxes.

Taft was responsible for many other improvements in the running of the country, although most of them did not go into effect until his term was over. He proposed the postal savings system that has been used by millions of Americans. He also negotiated treaties with France and Great Britain in which all three countries agreed to meet peaceably and settle international problems through discussion and arbitration. The treaties that Taft proposed have been models for many others since his time.

Toward the end of Taft's Presidential term, the Republican Party was split into two groups. One group favored nominating Taft for a second term. When the nomination went to Taft at the Republican Convention of 1912, Roosevelt's supporters broke away and formed the Progressive Party, with Roosevelt as its candidate. In the 1912 election the Republican vote was split, which resulted in a Democratic victory.

After his single term as President was over, William Howard Taft became a professor of law at Yale University, where he served for eight years. In 1921, President Warren G. Harding appointed him Chief Justice of the United States Supreme Court, and Taft remained in that post until in 1930 his health compelled him to resign. William Howard Taft died in Washington, D.C. on March 8, 1930, at the age of 72. He was buried in Arlington National Cemetery.

MRS. WILLIAM HOWARD TAFT

Helen Herron Taft was born in Cincinnati in 1862. Her father was the law partner of Rutherford B. Hayes, who became President of the United States. Mrs. Taft was a musician and was one of the founders of the Cincinnati Symphony Orchestra. The Tafts were married in 1886 and had three children—two sons and one daughter. Both sons were prominent in public life; see the article TAFT. Mrs.

William Howard Taft died in 1943, at the age of 81.

Tagalog, a Malayan language which, since 1946, has been the official national language of the Republic of the Philippines. English and Spanish are used for government and commercial purposes. See the entry on the Republic of the PHILIPPINES.

Tagore

Sir Rabindranath Tagore was an Indian poet. He was born in 1861 in Calcutta, India, and for a time he studied law in England. He returned to India and started an international university called Visva-Bharati. Tagore was one of those who wanted India to be independent from British rule, and he first began to write poems and songs about the cause of the Indian nationalists. Most of his writings were in the Bengali language, but Tagore himself translated many of them into English. He traveled all over the world and became very famous. In 1913 he won the Nobel Prize in literature, the greatest honor a writer can have, and in 1915, he was knighted by the British king, which meant that he could use the title "Sir" before his name. Tagore died in 1941, at the age of 80. His books of poetry include *The Gardener, The Crescent Moon,* and *Fireflies.* He also wrote novels, including *The Home and the World,* and plays, including *Red Oleander* and *Sacrifice.*

Tagus River

The Tagus River is a long river that rises in east central Spain and flows for more than 560 miles through Spain and Portugal until it empties into the Atlantic ocean near Lisbon, the capital of Portugal. Toledo, Spain, is built on its banks. In Spain the river is difficult to navigate because of its many rapids, but it is important for irrigation for the farm lands through which it passes. In Portugal, the river becomes much wider and is very important for transportation for the last 75 miles, from Abrantes to Lisbon. The Tagus is called Tajo in Spain and Tejo in Portugal.

Tahiti

Tahiti is the largest and most important of the Society Islands in the South Pacific Ocean. It is about 2,500 miles south of Hawaii and more than 3,000 miles southwest of San Francisco. The Society Islands belong to France. All French islands in the Pacific are called a part of Oceania and are ruled by a French governor. Papeete, the chief city and capital of Tahiti, is also capital of Oceania.

Tahiti is mountainous and beautiful. It is about 30 miles long and has an area

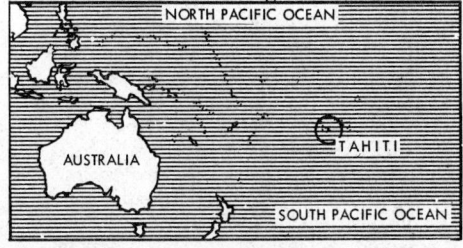

of about 400 square miles. About 45,000 people live in Tahiti. The native people are Polynesians and they had a high culture long before Europeans discovered their island about three hundred years ago. In recent years many foreigners have settled in Tahiti, particularly Chinese and French. Tahiti is important as a stopping place for many ships in the South Pacific, and also for its exports of rum, vanilla, sugar, and copra. There are pearl fisheries along the coast.

The French painter, Paul Gauguin, lived on Tahiti, and some of his greatest paintings are of Tahitian people and landscapes.

Taipei

Taipei is the capital and largest city of the Chinese island of Taiwan, or Formosa. It is near the northern coast of the island, where there are rich mining lands. Over 1,712,000 people live in Taipei. It is an industrial city, with factories that prepare rice, tea, sugar, and pineapples.

Taipei is a city with modern buildings, beautiful parks, and a university. It was built up by the Japanese, who controlled the island from 1895 until the end of World War II. Taipei was heavily bombed by Allied planes during the war. Since 1949 it has been the headquarters of the Chinese Nationalist government headed by Chiang Kai-shek.

TAIPEI, TAIWAN (FORMOSA). Population (1973 estimate) 1,712,108. Capital of Formosa. Headquarters of the Chinese Nationalist government.

Taiwan, Chinese name of the island FORMOSA.

Taj Mahal

The Taj Mahal is one of the most beautiful buildings in the world and a fine example of Mohammedan architecture. It was built in Agra, India, more than three hundred years ago. The emperor Shah Jehan built it as a burial place for him and his wife. The Taj Mahal is built entirely of white marble. It stands on a marble platform that is more than 300 feet square, and the building is about 130 feet square and has a domed roof that is more than 80 feet high. The inside of the building is decorated with mosaics of precious stones. Around the Taj Mahal is a walled garden in which there are marble walks and a pool that reflects the building.

talc

Talc is a kind of mineral. It is ground fine and used in face powder, tooth powder, soap, lubricants, linoleum, oilcloth, fireproof roofing, electrical insulation, and pottery. It is used to fill the pores in the making of smooth-surface paper. It withstands heat well, and is used to line furnaces.

Talc is usually white but may appear in shades through gray and dull green to red. Some varieties are translucent, which means that light can pass through them. Talc has a greasy, soapy feel. It is very soft and can easily be scratched by a fingernail. It is mined in the United States in New York, Vermont, California, Geor-

gia, Maryland, Pennsylvania, New Jersey, and North Carolina. It is also mined in Canada, Austria, Italy, Germany, and France.

Talc is also called *soapstone* or *steatite.*

Tallahassee

Tallahassee is the capital and tenth-largest city of Florida. It is in the north central part of the state, about halfway between the Atlantic Ocean and the western border. Tallahassee is chiefly important as an educational and governmental center. Tallahassee is an Indian word meaning "old town."

About 71,897 people live in Tallahassee. There is little industry in the city, and many of the people make a living from the tourist trade. Florida State College and the Florida Agricultural and Mechanical College for Negroes are in Tallahassee, and many people work in these schools and in the government offices.

The Indians had a settlement on the site of Tallahassee when Hernando de Soto reached the area in 1539. In 1824, Tallahassee was chosen as capital of the Florida Territory, and it became a city the next year. The State capitol, completed more than a hundred years ago, and the Governor's mansion are interesting places to visit in Tallahassee.

TALLAHASSEE, FLORIDA. Population (1970 census) 71,897. Capital of Florida. County seat of Leon County.

Talleyrand

Charles Maurice de Talleyrand-Périgord was a French nobleman who lived over 200 years ago. He was one of the cleverest statesmen of all time. He was born in 1754 in Paris, the oldest son of an army officer. When he was still an infant an accident lamed him, and he remained crippled for the rest of his life. He became a priest when he was 21 years old, and fourteen years later he was made bishop of Autun. At that time (1790) the French people were rebelling against their king and his government. Their revolt (the French Revolution) succeeded, but though Talleyrand was a nobleman he soon became an important official in the new government.

Talleyrand served as French Minister of Foreign Affairs for ten years, first under the revolutionary government and then under the Emperor Napoleon. After a time Talleyrand quarreled with Napoleon and retired from his job. Napoleon's conquests were beginning to rouse all the other European countries against him, and Talleyrand was the leader of this opposition in France. By the time Napoleon fell, in 1814, Talleyrand had arranged for the members of the Bourbon family to be restored to the throne of France.

Talleyrand represented France at the Congress of Vienna, in 1815, when the chief nations of Europe met to decide what to do with the lands Napoleon had taken. He gained a great deal for France, and persuaded Austria and Great Britain secretly to ally themselves with France against Russia and Prussia. However, Napoleon suddenly returned from exile and this spoiled Talleyrand's plans. He re-

tired from politics for the next fifteen years, then served as his ambassador to England for four years. He died in 1838, at the age of 74. Many of his witty sayings and clever plots are told about in his *Memoirs,* a sort of diary that was published after his death.

Tallinn

Tallinn is an important seaport and the capital of Estonia, which is now called the Estonian Soviet Socialist Republic. It is on the southwest coast of the Gulf of Finland, a part of the Baltic Sea. About 363,000 people live in Tallinn, and each year many tourists go there to enjoy its beaches and visit its old buildings. Tallinn is important for its harbor, which is usually free of ice the year round and is used for shipping most of the goods in and out of Estonia.

Tallinn was founded more than seven hundred years ago. It has belonged in turn to Denmark, to Sweden, and to Russia. During World War II Tallinn was captured first by the Russians and then by the Germans, who did a great deal of damage to the city. At the end of the war Tallinn was again captured by the Russians.

TALLINN, ESTONIA. Population (1959 census) 280,000. Capital of Estonian S.S.R. On the Gulf of Finland in the Baltic Sea.

Talmud

The Talmud is the name given to a set of books dealing with the religious laws of Judaism, or the Jewish religion. There are sixty-three separate books of the Talmud. They include laws that were passed on by word of mouth by the ancient rabbis, or Jewish teachers, and later were written down. The basic laws, written in the Hebrew language, are contained in the part of the Talmud called the *Mishna.* These laws are discussed, interpreted and illustrated in a second part, called *Gemara.* The Gemara also contains countless beautiful parables, or stories. The Talmud was completed in the year 499 A.D.

tambourine

The tambourine is a kind of musical instrument. It is a small wooden hoop, over one side of which a parchment has been stretched. Small metal plates called "jingles," which hang loosely in pairs, are put inside and all around the hoop. The tambourine can be played in any of three ways: 1, the player holds it in one hand and strikes the head (the stretched parchment) with the other hand; 2, the player holds it up and shakes it, making the jingles ring; 3, the player rubs his thumb in circles near the rim of the head, making the jingles ring.

Tamerlane

Tamerlane was a great conqueror who lived in Asia about six hundred years ago. His real name was Timur, but he was called Timur the Lame because he limped from an old wound. He conquered and ruled all of central and southwestern Asia and parts of Europe, including much of Russia.

Tamerlane belonged to a Tartar tribe, a people related to the Turks. He was born about the year 1336, in northern Afghanistan. At that time descendants of Genghis Khan, who had been the greatest Asiatic conqueror before Tamerlane,

ruled most of Asia. Tamerlane led some small revolts against them and finally assembled a powerful army. By the time he was about 30 he had made himself master of Samarkand, the great city that was the capital of central Asia. For the rest of his life he led his armies and increased his territories.

Europeans told of Tamerlane as a cruel barbarian, because they feared him so, but actually he was less cruel and more cultivated than most of the Europeans who fought against him. He encouraged arts and learning and had beautiful cities built. Human life was cheap in Tamerlane's time, and twice when cities defied him he slaughtered their people and built piles of their skulls, but usually he was a generous victor. He was a follower of the Mohammedan religion but one of his greatest enemies was the sultan (king) of Turkey, Bajazet.

Tamerlane wanted to conquer China, as Genghis Khan had, and when he was almost 70 he started a campaign against China, but he died on the way, in 1405. Tamerlane never called himself an emperor but his descendants became emperors (called Moguls) in India.

Tammany Hall

Tammany Hall is the name of the headquarters of the Democratic Party in the Borough of Manhattan, a part of New York City. Tammany Hall was organized just after the Revolutionary War was won. Its first name was the Sons of St. Tammany. Tammany was an Indian chieftain and these early politicians took his name to show that they believed in something American rather than in something British, since Americans and British were then unfriendly.

In its early days it was merely a patriotic society, but soon the Tammany organization became powerful in the politics of New York City. The name Tammany Hall came from the building they used as their headquarters. During much of New York City's history Tammany Hall has been so powerful that it ruled the city and often the state government too. A famous cartoonist named Thomas Nast pictured Tammany Hall as a tiger, and people often call the organization "the Tammany Tiger."

The leader of Tammany Hall is given the title Grand Sachem, which is an Indian title. Some of the leaders of Tammany Hall, particularly a man named William M. Tweed, were very dishonest and made personal fortunes of millions of dollars by their corrupt rule of the city. "Boss" Tweed was finally sent to jail. After him there were some other Tammany leaders who were dishonest. Tammany Hall began to lose its importance because of its bad reputation and also because the other boroughs of New York City were growing in population and becoming more important. During the administrations of President Franklin D. Roosevelt, when the Democrats were in control of the Federal government, the control of Democratic politics in New York city went to a man named Edward Flynn, who was a political leader in Bronx County. During the twelve years when Fiorello LaGuardia, who was not a Democrat, was mayor of New York City, Tammany Hall lost much of its power because it could not place its members in

government jobs. The power of a political organization rests on its ability to give government jobs to its supporters. Tammany Hall is still powerful but it no longer has control of New York City.

Much of the power that Tammany Hall once had came from its influence with the many immigrants arriving in New York City from other countries. Tammany politicians helped these new citizens to find jobs and to get used to American ways. Such small things as an occasional basket of food or a pail of coal were much appreciated by the poor and made them believe that Tammany Hall was interested in their welfare. When election time came they would vote the way Tammany told them to.

Tampa

Tampa is the third-largest city of Florida. It is in west central Florida, on the northeastern shore of Tampa Bay in the Gulf of Mexico. Tampa serves as a shipping point for a large part of the state. Its name was given to it by the Seminole Indians, who made the first settlement there. The name means "split wood for quick fires" and referred to the driftwood that was plentiful along the shores.

More than 250,000 people live in Tampa. There are factories that manufacture paint, cigars, and tin cans. The waters around Tampa are famous for shrimp fishing, and shrimp packing is a major industry in the city.

The site on which Tampa now stands was discovered by Panfilo de Narvaez, a Spanish explorer, in 1528, but a permanent settlement was not made until about 150 years later. Tampa was incorporated in 1855. The University of Tampa and Florida Christian College are in Tampa.

TAMPA, FLORIDA. Population (1970 census) 277,767. County seat of Hillsborough County, Incorporated, 1855.

tanager

A tanager is a member of a large group of birds. The most familiar of the tanager family in North America is the brilliantly colored scarlet tanager, a bright red bird with black wings and tail. The male tanager wears the gay and vivid plumage. The female is a dull greenish color. The male is bright scarlet during the mating season in early summer. Later, when the young are hatched and the family is ready to start for South America to spend the winter in a warm climate, the male is the same dull green as his mate.

The tanager's nest is built of grass and twigs on a branch of a tree. Four or five eggs are deposited. The male helps to feed the young when they arrive.

Tanganyika

Tanganyika, a region in eastern Africa on the Indian Ocean, is part of the United Republic of TANZANIA. It was a British Trust Territory, became independent in 1961, and joined with Zanzibar in 1964. About 13 million people live there. Dar-es-Salaam, a city of 343,-911, is the capital (also of Tanzania). The land rises from a low coastal strip to a plateau, or high plain, which covers most of the territory. In the northeast, rising sharply from the level plateau, is 19,565-foot Mt. Kilimanjaro, the highest peak in

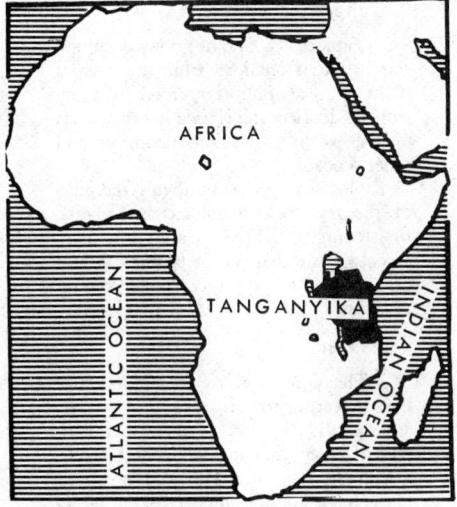

AFRICA

ATLANTIC OCEAN

TANGANYIKA

INDIAN OCEAN

Africa. There are other mountains in the south. Tanganyika shares three great lakes with other territories: Lake Victoria in the north; Lake Nyasa in the south; and Lake Tanganyika in the west. Lake Tanganyika is the longest and deepest and the second-largest lake in Africa. All of its 400-mile length is navigable.

The native peoples of Tanganyika are mostly of Bantu tribes, but there are also Bushmen, Swahilis, and Masais. The non-native peoples include Europeans, Indians and Arabs. The climate of Tanganyika is hot, and two-thirds of the land is too dry for people to live in. Farming is the principal occupation and sisal fiber the main crop. Mineral deposits are rich, including diamonds, gold, tin, salt, iron, copper, and many others.

TANGANYIKA. Area, 362,688 square miles. Population (1973 estimate) 13,000,000. Government, federal republic; with Zanzibar it forms the United Republic of Tanzania. Capital, Dar-es-Salaam (population 150,000).

tangerine

A tangerine, or *mandarin orange,* is a kind of small orange. It has a thin rind that is easy to peel off. Tangerines are usually very sweet. They are not ordinarily used for orange juice but are simply peeled and eaten. The tangerine came originally from China. It is grown in warm sections of the United States and other countries where citrus fruits are grown.

Tangier

Tangier is a seaport and city in the kingdom of Morocco, in northern Africa, across the Strait of Gibraltar from Spain. It had a population, in 1960, of 142,000. The location of Tangier at the crossroads of Europe and Africa has made it an important port and commercial center. Most of the people work in the harbor district in importing and exporting firms. There are three official languages, French, Spanish, and Arabic.

The city of Tangier is a mixture of the old and the new. The native part of the city, called the *casbah,* is walled and has white houses and narrow winding streets. The European section is modern and luxurious.

Tangier is an ancient city. For many years it was a base for bandits and pirates, and in the early 1700s a native Berber chief captured several Europeans and

held them for ransom. These incidents, and the fact that several European nations wanted power in Morocco, led to the establishment of Tangier and its surrounding area as an international zone by agreement among England, France, and Spain in 1923. Tangier was absorbed into the Kingdom of Morocco in 1956 when that nation gained its independence. But with the loss of its special status, Tangier lost much of its trade. To save the economy of the city, Tangier was made a free port in 1962.

Tanglewood

Tanglewood is the name of a country estate near the town of Lenox, Massachusetts. A famous music festival called the Berkshire Symphonic Festival, is held there every summer. It is attended by musicians and others from all over the United States and even from other countries. About a hundred years ago the American writer Nathaniel Hawthorne used to spend some time in a small cottage on the estate. He named one of his books *Tanglewood Tales.* It was a sequel to a book called *A Wonder Book.* Both books tell the mythology of ancient Greece in story form for children.

tank

A tank is an armed vehicle of modern mechanized warfare. It carries heavy guns and travels on metal tracks that keep turning and push it forward at high speeds. The metal tracks are like the ones used on big tractors. They are belts of metal plates. Wheels called *bogeys* run along the insides of the tracks and make them move. The covering of a tank is strong, thick steel that is hard to penetrate except by powerful artillery shells or bombs.

Tanks as used in modern warfare are not very old. They were first built during World War I. Since that time they have become highly developed. World War I tanks were not capable of going more than five miles an hour and could not operate on rough ground. They ran out of gasoline quite quickly and they did not have the strong steel armorplating that modern tanks have.

TANK WARFARE

The tanks of World War I were used to clear the way for foot soldiers, or infantrymen. Tanks could roll over enemy trenches and destroy machine-gun nests. The infantrymen would follow directly behind the tank or, more often, would advance soon after the tanks had cleared the way. Tanks were also used to knock down barbed wire entanglements and trees that stood in the way of advancing soldiers.

In World War II, with greater speed from better engines, tanks were used differently. Sometime they engaged in battle without any infantry soldiers behind them. They were used much as battleships are used at sea, to invade deeply into enemy territory. Many battles of World War II were fought between opposing groups of tanks. The tanks that had the thickest armor and heaviest guns usually won out. During the early part of World War II the Germans had the most powerful tanks and in most battles were able to knock out the enemy tanks. As the

war progressed the Allies (Americans, British, and Russians) developed larger, faster and better-armored tanks.

In modern warfare armored tanks are part of armored divisions, which include also heavy artillery and soldiers carried in armored cars or trucks. All these units together are called "armor." In the early part of World War II, the German armored divisions, called *Panzer* divisions, were given much of the credit for the German victory over France. Their tanks were many miles ahead of their armies as they penetrated deeply and swiftly into enemy territory.

TANK SOLDIERS

The men who operate tanks have different jobs. In each tank there are the driver, the radioman, and usually several gunners.

There are different sizes of tanks, light, medium, and heavy. The weights of tanks vary between about 10 and 70 tons. At first it was thought that tanks of 70 or more tons would be almost unbeatable, but when it was found that these tanks were too heavy to cross bridges, they were no longer made. The best fighting tanks weigh 30 to 40 tons. They can maneuver rapidly and the crews keep in touch with each other by radio and with the headquarters of the division and even of the whole army. The gunners fire their heavy guns from the turret of the tank. Many tanks also have machine guns mounted on them, each one fired by a gunner.

When a tank is hit by a heavy shell or bomb, it may be so severely damaged that it can no longer run. The easiest way to knock a tank out is to hit it in the tractor treads or wheels. Men who fight in tanks are well protected by the tank's armor, but should something happen such as a direct hit or a flash of fire from an exploding shell or bomb, the men are practically trapped in the tank and have only seconds to get out in safety. Should a tank be hit, its escape hatch or cover may become jammed and the soldiers inside have no chance of escaping.

TANK DESTROYERS

The rise in importance of tanks led to many attempts to make the tank less effective. Great artillery guns were fired at them, but these guns were usually placed firmly and could not be moved to follow the path of the rapidly running tanks. The vehicle that was developed to fight tanks was really nothing much but a sort of tank itself, except that it sometimes had no top covering. It was the bottom part of a tank with its tractor treads and wheels and a large platform to mount an artillery gun. These *tank destroyers* were just as fast and maneuverable as tanks. Because they were stripped of the top weight of tanks and carried less equipment, they were able to mount larger and heavier guns than the tanks. Tanks can also be attacked by airplanes flying above, heavy artillery fired behind enemy lines, and foot soldiers who come up them with bombs. The Russians in World War II fought German tanks with a fire bomb called "the Molotov cocktail," which spread fire over the tank and made it unbearably hot for the men inside.

Tannhäuser

Tannhäuser is an opera by the Ger-

man composer of music, Richard Wagner. Wagner wrote both the words and the music of the opera, which was first produced in 1845 in Dresden.

The story of the opera is taken from an ancient legend about a German hero named Tannhäuser. The scene of the story is a castle in Germany about seven hundred years ago. Near the castle is a mountain called the Venusberg, which is the home of Venus, the goddess of love, and her court of beautiful sirens. Tannhäuser has lived there with Venus for a year. When he returns to the world of mortal men, he realizes that he has committed a great sin and he decides to join a pilgrimage to Rome to ask forgiveness from the Pope. The beautiful Elizabeth, who has loved him for many years, promises to wait for him. When the pilgrims return and Tannhäuser seems not to be with them, Elizabeth dies of a broken heart. Tannhäuser has returned, but the Pope told him he would not be forgiven until the dead stick he carried sprouted leaves. He was dressed in rags and was unrecognizable. Tannhäuser's friend Wolfram takes him to where Elizabeth lies dead. Tannhäuser falls in sorrow on her body and dies, and the dry stick immediately sprouts leaves.

Tanzania

The United Republic of Tanzania was formed in 1964; it consists of Tanganyika on the east coast of Africa, and the nearby island of Zanzibar. The government is a federal republic, both states having kept separate governments for local affairs. The federal capital is at Dar-es-Salaam in Tanganyika. See TANGANYIKA and ZANZIBAR.

TANZANIA. Area, 363,328 square miles. Population (1973 estimate) 13,630,000.

Taoism

Taoism is a religion that is followed by millions of people in China and other parts of east Asia. The religion is based on a book written more than two thousand years ago by LAO-TSE, about whom there is a separate article. The book is called the *Tao-teh-king*, which might mean *The Book of Reason and Virtue*. It teaches that Tao is the beginning of all things in the world and must be followed by people who want to live a good life. But it never explains just what Tao is, and so many people have called it many different things. Some say it means the Way or the Path, others call it Reason, still others the Word, and same say it means God. The book says that if we do not know what Tao is, we cannot learn it.

Some of the ideas taught in the *Tao* are very much like those in the Bible. For example, it says that a truly good man loves all men, even those who do not love him, and hates no one. But because the *Tao-teh-king* is very mysterious, many people came to believe that it taught magic. One of these people, a man called Chang Tao-ling who lived about five hundred years after the *Tao-teh-king* was written, was said to have discovered a drink that would make people live forever. The followers of Taoism, called Taoists, began to worship him. The Taoists also worship many idols, including dragons, rats, weasels, and snakes; and they believe in many evil spirits, such as devils, gnomes, vampires, and goblins.

They think they can keep evil spirits from harming them by singing special songs, or by building crooked halls in their houses so that an evil spirit rushing into a house would dash against the wall and be killed.

tapestry

A tapestry is a kind of cloth that is woven by hand. A design of threads going in one direction (for example, up-and-down), is threaded by the fingers into threads going in the opposite direction (crosswise). The design is the same on both sides of the cloth, except for loose thread ends on the "wrong" side.

Tapestries were made by different peoples long before the loom was invented. Examples of primitive tapestry that are still made today include the Oriental rug, Navaho blanket, and Mexican serape (shawl). In the Middle Ages, about a thousand years ago, very complicated tapestries using many-colored pictures as designs became popular in Europe, especially in Flanders and Germany. They were used chiefly to decorate the walls of churches. They showed scenes from the Bible and from ancient legends. They were very large and took many years to make. The threads used were of wool, linen, silk, and precious metals, such as silver and gold.

The most famous old tapestries are often named for the places where they were made. Some of them are: Aubusson (France); Arras (Flanders); Gobelin (a factory founded by members of the Gobelin family in Paris, France); and Beauvais (France).

The art of tapestry-making spread to other countries. In Italy beautiful tapestries were designed by some of the most famous artists. The most famous of these is the tapestry designed by Raphael in the Sistine Chapel in Rome. Some tapestry has been made in the United States. The best collections of tapestry in the United States are those of the Metropolitan Museum of Art in New York City and the Museum of Fine Arts in Boston, Massachusetts. The famous BAYEUX tapestry is not a real tapestry. There is a separate article about it.

tapeworm

The tapeworm is a parasite, a tiny animal that lives on other animals. It is a flat, ribbonlike worm. Its body is made up of segments that contain eggs. The segments separate and form new segments. The tapeworm has suckers on its head and uses them to attach itself to the intestines of cattle, fish, or human beings.

There are three main kinds of tapeworms. The beef tapeworm grows to be about 25 feet long. A person who eats beef or pork that is raw or not well cooked can get a beef tapeworm, though this is not likely if the beef has been properly inspected. Fish tapeworms grow to be about 30 feet long. Dwarf tapeworms are only about an inch long. They may live in the intestines of a human being.

Doctors have many ways to treat a person who has tapeworm. The United States Government and the health departments of cities and states carefully inspect all meat and fish to make sure that no tapeworms are present.

tapioca

Tapioca is a kind of grainy or lumpy starch that is obtained from the cassava plant. It is an important food in many tropical districts and is used in other parts of the world to thicken puddings and other foods.

Tapioca is made by removing the pulp of the rootstocks from cassava plants, moistening it, and then heating it to form a sticky paste that can be spread out and dried. When it is dry it can be broken up into small lumps.

tapir

The tapir is a strange animal that lives in warm parts of Asia and in Central and South America. It is a mammal, which means that it bears living young and nurses its young. The tapir is related to the horse and the rhinoceros, but tapirs have four toes on their hind hoofs, and three toes on their front hoofs. The tapir is a heavy thickset animal with short legs, tiny tail, and a strangely lengthened nose and upper lip that form a small "trunk." The tapir hides during the day and hunts for food at night.

tar, a black sticky substance taken from coal and wood: see COAL.

Taranto, Gulf of

The Gulf of Taranto is a large body of water at the southern tip of Italy. It lies between the "toe" and "heel" of Italy and is part of the Mediterranean Sea. It is about seventy miles long and eighty-five miles wide. The important Italian naval base of Taranto is located on the northeast coast of the Gulf of Taranto.

tarantula

Tarantula is a name that has been generally applied to many different kinds of spider. At one time it was believed in Italy that a person bitten by the spider called the "tarantula" would die if he did not do a wild dance to a certain kind of music. Usually, a bite from a tarantula is not dangerous but can be very painful.

Today there are several different spiders that are called tarantulas. Each one has a different scientific name. One is about two inches long in the body and its legs spread out to four or five inches. This gives it a terrifying appearance, but it is quite peaceable and will not even attempt to bite unless it is badly frightened by rough treatment. Another kind of "tarantula" is often kept as a pet and may live from ten to fifteen years in captivity. This tarantula is found only in the warm sections of the southwestern United States.

Tarawa

Tarawa is one of the two largest of the Gilbert Islands, in the western Pacific Ocean, but it is a very tiny island, with an area of about eight square miles. About 3,500 people live there. Tarawa is a commercial center and has various government stations. During World War II, in 1941, the Japanese captured the island. Two years later, in 1943, it was taken by United States Marines in one of the bloodiest battles of the war.

Tarbell, Ida M.

Ida Minerva Tarbell was a popular American historian. She was prominent in the "muckraking" movement at the beginning of this century and did much to expose dishonesty and the lack of ethics in government and business. One of her most important books was called the *History of the Standard Oil Company*. Her work led to important reforms. She was born in Pennsylvania in 1857 and died in 1944.

tariff

A tariff is a tax on goods that are imported (brought into a country) from a foreign country. Since earliest times governments have charged some sort of fee to merchants and traders coming across their borders. Modern tariffs are complicated systems using long lists of the many different articles that may come into a country from other countries and the amount of money charged on each.

Tariffs, which are also called *duties,* or *customs,* are collected at borders or at places where goods may first come into a country; for example, at airports, docks, and boundaries crossed by roads and railroads. Some things may be brought in at a small cost and others at a high cost. Some things are allowed to come in duty-free, which means that nothing must be paid to bring them in.

There are two reasons for tariffs. The first reason is to provide money for a government. The second reason is to protect the business men and manufacturers of a country. An American manufacturer may be selling an article for one dollar when an imported article, from a country where labor is paid less, could be sold for fifty cents. The government can put a fifty-cent duty on that article so that it cannot be sold for less than the American article.

TARIFFS IN THE UNITED STATES

In the United States, Congress decides what the tariffs should be. The very first law passed by the United States Congress was a tariff law.

In the history of the United States there have been periods of high tariffs and of low tariffs. The important political parties have had different ideas about tariffs. The Republican Party has become known as a "high tariff" party and the Democratic Party as a "low tariff" party. Depending on which party has been in power, tariffs may have been high or low.

Manufacturers are usually in favor of high tariffs. Farmers and workers are usually against high tariffs because they raise the prices of articles. But manufacturers say that low tariffs cause unemployment, because factories have to shut down if they cannot meet foreign prices.

Among the best-known tariffs passed by Congress were the McKinley tariff of 1890, which set very high duties on hundreds of different articles, such as wool, machinery, and many other things, and the Payne-Aldrich Tariff Act of 1910, which raised duties even higher. When Woodrow Wilson, a Democrat, became President in 1913, Congress passed a tariff act that lowered duties on almost everything. After World War I, when the Republican Warren G. Harding was elected

to the Presidency, the Republicans again passed a high tariff act.

RECIPROCAL TRADE TREATIES

In the Democratic administration of Franklin D. Roosevelt, from 1933 to 1945, the tariffs were lowered on most things through a series of *reciprocal* trade treaties signed with many other countries. Reciprocal means "back and forth." Most of the reciprocal trade treaties were continued during the administration of the Republican President, Dwight D. Eisenhower, though Congress passed some higher tariffs. Finally, when the Democratic candidate, John F. Kennedy, was elected President in 1960, he called for freer trade between nations. Congress, as a result, passed the Trade Expansion Act in 1962. This replaced the Reciprocal Trade Agreements Act and allowed the President to cut all tariffs up to 50% and even to eliminate the tariff altogether on some products.

Tarkington, Booth

Newton Booth Tarkington was an American author. He wrote plays, short stories, and novels, but was best known for his novels. He was born in 1869 in Indianapolis, Indiana, and studied at Purdue and Princeton Universities. In 1919 his novel *The Magnificent Ambersons* won the Pulitzer Prize. He is remembered chiefly for his books about young people, including *Penrod* and *Seventeen.* Another novel, *Alice Adams,* and his best-known short story, *Monsieur Beaucaire,* were made into motion pictures. He died in 1946.

tarpon

The tarpon is a large fish that lives in the warm waters of the Atlantic Ocean near Florida, the coasts of the Gulf of Mexico, and as far south as Brazil. Tarpons are large, silvery fishes with great leaping ability. They can leap high out of the water, and often use this power to escape from fishermen's lines. Tarpons are not valuable as a food, because their flesh is tough and has a bitter taste, but sportsmen like to fish for tarpon because of the fierce fight the fish will make when it is caught.

A mature tarpon may be as large as eight feet long and may weigh up to 300 pounds. It does not reach such a size until it is about seven years old.

The tarpon must come to the surface for air occasionally. It has gills, as other fish have, but it also needs a supply of dry air, which it stores in a special air bladder. This is a sac in the fish's body, and it must be refilled with fresh air from the atmosphere at frequent intervals.

Tarshish or Tartessus

Tarshish was a very important city in the ancient world, about three thousand years ago. It is mentioned several times in the Bible, in the Old Testament. Tarshish was in southern Spain. It was probably founded by people from Carthage. It was the major source of tin,

which was very important for hundreds of years because it was needed to make bronze, the chief metal of those times.

The Romans called this city Tartessus, and it was probably destroyed by them when they defeated and destroyed Carthage in the Punic Wars, about 2,200 years ago. Tarshish was destroyed so completely that no traces of it have been found. Most people think it was on the Guadalquivir River, perhaps near the present city of Seville.

Tartar, or **Tatar,** an ancient people of Asia. See the article TATAR.

task force

A task force is a group organized in warfare to do a special job. In the article on AMPHIBIOUS WARFARE you can read how groups of ships, soldiers and equipment are assembled to make a landing on an enemy shore. A group of warships is most often called a task force. It usually includes one or more aircraft carriers, big-gun ships and destroyers to guard it, and supply ships to supply it. A group of army men or forces sent on a particular mission is usually called a *detachment.*

Tasmania

Tasmania is an island 150 miles south of Australia, between the Tasman Sea and Indian Ocean. With several smaller islands, it forms a state of Australia. The state has an area of 26,215 square miles, and in the 1961 census the population was 350,332. The capital is Hobart, a city of 115,887.

Parts of the southwest of Tasmania have never been explored. The climate of Tasmania is mild but can be changeable. In Hobart, the hottest month is February, with an average temperature of 63 degrees, and the coldest in July, with an average temperature of 46 degrees.

The first European settlers in Tasmania found a very primitive people living on the island. The Tasmanian aborigines are now extinct, the last of them dying in 1870. On the island scientists have found two unusual animals, which are marsupials, called the Tasmanian wolf and the Tasmanian devil.

Tasso

Torquato Tasso was a famous Italian poet who lived about four hundred years ago. He was born in 1544 and was educated by the Jesuits, a Roman Catholic religious group, at Naples. His father, Bernardo Tasso, was also a poet, and Tarquato Tasso became interested in writing at an early age. He studied at a number of universities and then a Roman Catholic cardinal named Luigi d'Este was impressed by his work and decided to support him. Tasso taught for a time at the University of Ferrara, then he became mentally ill and was confined for seven years in an institution. He died in 1595, at the age of 51. Tasso's most famous work is *Jerusalem Delivered,* a poem about the Third Crusade.

taste

Taste is the ability to recognize the flavor of different substances and to be able to tell the difference between them. It is one of the senses of the body, like

touch, smell, hearing, and sight. The sense of taste is located in the mouth. There are many sensitive nerve endings in the mouth that make it possible for us to taste things. Most of these nerve endings are located in the tongue. The rough surface of the tongue contains many tiny nerve endings called taste buds. They lie just below the surface and are scattered over the tongue.

Not all the taste buds respond to different kinds of taste. The "primary tastes" are sweet, sour, salt, and bitter. We taste sweet and salty things at the tip of our tongues, sour at the sides, and bitter at the back.

We do not taste anything until it begins to dissolve. The sense of taste is also tied up with the sense of smell. There are some things that we cannot taste unless we can smell them. Onions are in this class. If you have a cold and your nose is stopped up so that you cannot smell, you cannot taste an onion. This is because onions, like most other things we eat, give off a gas that affects the nerve endings of smell in the nose. When these nerve endings are affected and we smell the gas from an onion, we also are able to taste it.

Experience is very important to taste. A baby cannot distinguish easily between the tastes of different things. As we grow older and become used to tasting things, we can distinguish between different kinds of taste. We also learn to connect certain tastes with certain "feels"—and so on. Usually if the things we eat are too hot or too cold, we cannot taste them very well. When we eat food containing different tastes we have trouble picking out each individual taste.

Not all people taste things in the same way. For example, some people have taste buds that respond especially to sweet, or to sour. There are people who have a very poor sense of taste, or who cannot distinguish some particular taste, just as there are people who are color-blind and cannot distinguish some particular color.

Tatars or Tartars

The Tatars, or Tartars, were an ancient people of Asia. They came from northern Manchuria and northeastern Mongolia. Very little is known about the Tatars, largely because they did not know how to write. About a thousand years ago they hired foreign secretaries to write for them, but the written language was different from the spoken one. The Tatars were conquered by another people, the Mongols, about the year 1200. From that time on they married Mongols, and their descendants joined with the Mongol armies that later conquered most of Asia and went as far west as Europe. The first European travelers, who reached eastern Asia, early in the 13th century, called all the people they found Tatars, and called their lands Tartary. Later the name Tatars came to be used for all Asiatic peoples who came from the east to the Near East and the Mediterranean countries.

tattooing

Tattooing is the art of decorating the skin with pictures in any color. It is a very ancient practice. Many Indian tribes

and people of the Pacific islands of Asia and Africa have practiced tattooing. Tattooing is not merely drawing or painting a picture on the skin. It is permanent and cannot be washed off or even worn away.

A picture is tattooed by puncturing the skin with tiny holes and putting bits of color into the holes. In its primitive form it is quite painful, but modern tatooing is done with an electric needle and is practically painless.

Sailors have themselves tattooed more than any other people do.

The usual place for a tattooed picture is on the arm or on the chest. Some people have had almost their entire bodies covered with tattoos. Usually a circus has a tattooed man or woman who is completely covered with pictures.

Tattoos probably began as good luck charms that were supposed to protect a person against evil spirits.

Taurus

Taurus is the name of a constellation, or group of stars. It was given this name thousands of years ago, in ancient lands. In the Latin language, taurus means "bull." The Greeks thought this particular constellation looked somewhat like a bull. The star that is where the bull's eye should be is called Aldebaran, and is one of the twenty brightest stars in the heavens. On the "bull's shoulder" is a group of stars called the Pleiades, or the Seven Sisters. The sign of the zodiac that stands for the constellation Taurus is ♉, which looks like a bull's head and horns. Read also the articles CONSTELLATION and ZODIAC.

tax

A tax is money that a person pays to help run the government of his country. The method by which a government collects this money is called taxation, and throughout history it has been almost the only way for a government to get the money it needs.

HISTORY OF TAXATION

In former ages, conquerors used to make conquered people pay tribute to them. That was a form of tax. One of the oldest taxes, and still one of the chief ways in which people are taxed, is to collect money for the use of land. During the Middle Ages, about a thousand years ago, noblemen protected farmers against attack and in return the farmers gave the noblemen part of the crops they raised each year.

There are many kinds of tax, but every tax should follow at least three principles:

1. There should be no favoritism; whatever tax one person has to pay, everyone else in the same position should have to pay.

2. The tax should be something the people can afford.

3. Representatives elected by the people should decide what taxes the people have to pay. The Revolutionary War, in which the United States won its independence, was fought chiefly because the British Parliament wanted to collect taxes and the American people had no representatives in the British Parliament. The Constitution of the United States says that only the House of Representa-

tives can introduce laws calling for taxation. Only the House of Representatives is elected directly by the people. Senators usually are, but they can be appointed by state legislatures (lawmaking bodies) or by state governors when there is a vacancy to fill.

KINDS OF TAX

The main kinds of tax are: Real estate taxes, which owners of land and buildings pay; customs, duties, or tariff, paid on merchandise imported into a country from a foreign country; personal taxes on income or personal wealth; excise and sales taxes, based on the value of merchandise manufactured or bought; and head taxes, a set amount collected from every person. Head taxes are usually quite small and have become unusual. In the United States some states introduced poll taxes, a kind of head tax in which a person must pay some small amount such as two dollars before he has the right to vote; but these taxes were never expected to bring in much money and most states have dropped them.

In the United States there are Federal taxes, collected by the government of the United States, and state or local taxes, collected by states and cities. The biggest Federal tax is the income tax, but customs and excise taxes are also collect. Every state collects real estate taxes and most states also have sales taxes and personal taxes (based on a person's income or personal wealth).

REAL ESTATE TAXES

In a state or city that collects real estate taxes, a board of assessors is appointed. The assessors fix a value on each piece of real estate. The value depends partly on the land and partly on the buildings on the land.

When the assessors have placed a value, or assessment, on every piece of real estate, all the assessments are added up. Then the state or city government fixes a tax rate. Suppose the assessors figure that all the real estate is worth $2,000,000 and the government needs $80,000 during the year. The government will fix a tax rate of $4, which means that everyone must pay $4 for every $100 that the assessors say his property is worth. If he has a house assessed at $10,000, he must pay $400 in taxes. It is the custom to make the assessments less than the property is actually worth and make the tax rate high, because experience has shown that people object less when it is done that way.

SALES TAXES

Most states and many cities collect sales taxes. Every time a person spends a dollar, he has to pay two or three cents as a tax. The Federal government and state governments both collect taxes on certain things, such as gasoline.

Many people say that sales taxes are unfair because poor people have to pay as much as rich people. Even if this is true, sales taxes usually cause less criticism than other forms of taxation because people hardly notice the few pennies that they spend. Usually there is no sales tax on food and on necessary drugs.

PERSONAL TAXES

The Federal government collects in-

come taxes, about which there is a separate article. Some state governments collect income taxes and some collect taxes on "intangibles" (investments such as stocks and bonds) or on personal property such as furniture, jewelry, and other possessions.

Income and other personal taxes are a way of dealing with INFLATION, about which there is a separate article. Inflation exists when people are making a lot of money but there is not much merchandise for sale in the stores. High income taxes return some of the people's money to the government so that they cannot spend it foolishly by paying more for things than they are worth.

One form of personal tax is called the *capital levy*. Each person must give the government a certain portion of what he is worth. For example, if his property altogether is worth $10,000 he must pay the government $250 and if his property altogether is worth $100,000 he must pay the government $2,500. Capital levies have seldom been used because no one has figured out a good way to collect them without forcing people to sell things to raise cash.

There are separate articles about CUSTOMS, TARIFF, INCOME TAX, INHERITANCE TAX, REAL ESTATE, and STAMP TAX.

Taxco

Taxco is known officially as *Taxco De Alarcón*. It is located in southwestern Mexico, about 60 miles (100 km.) southwest of Mexico City. About 15,000 people live in Taxco which occupies a magnificent site on the southern slope of the central plateau. The city is now actually a national monument, a resort in a mining area. The famous silver mines in Taxco were developed after the arrival of the French miner Joseph le Borde (better known in Spanish as José de la Borda) in the early 18th century. The Mexican government helps preserve the picturesque town's colonial appearance.

Tax Court of the U.S.

The Tax Court of the United States is an independent executive agency and was created by the Revenue Act of 1924. Until the year of 1942, it was known as the Board of Tax Appeals. The Tax Court of the United States has the authority to try and then help solve the many problems that arise when people or companies somehow have overpayed or underpayed their taxes. The government calls this *deficiencies,* (underpayments) and *overpayments,* and often includes income, excess profits, estate, gift, and personal-holding-company taxes. This court also has the authority to judge the amount of excessive profits made from contracts that involve the purchase of war material.

The Tax Court of the United States has 16 judges, and practically all of the court's decisions are subject to review by the U. S. Court of Appeals and later by the U. S. Supreme Court.

taxicab

A taxicab, or taxi, is an automobile that anyone can hire to ride a short dis-

tance. Taxicabs are very familiar sights on the streets of all big cities. They are usually brightly colored and have special lights so that they can be recognized quickly at night. A taxicab may be owned by the driver but most taxis are owned by companies that hire drivers. In big cities taxicabs often "cruise"—drive around the streets until someone hails them. In other places, a person phones a cab office and has one sent to where he is. Many taxis have meters in them which record the distance the cab has traveled and how much the ride will cost. The driver starts the meter as soon as a passenger enters the cab, and stops it when the cab reaches its destination.

Taxicabs are regulated by law. The owner of each cab must pay a license fee and must charge what the law determines is the proper pay for a ride. The cost of the ride is shown on a taximeter next to the driver. The driver calls this a "clock," because it usually measures the time spent as well as the distance traveled. It is something like a cash register and shows on its face how much money one must pay for the ride. Usually there is a beginning fee of 25 to 40 cents for the first part of the ride (a quarter or fifth of a mile) and 5 or 10 cents for each additional part of a mile. When the ride begins the driver pulls down an arm on the meter and sets the meter in operation. This is called the "flag throw" because there is a metal flag on the arm. If a policeman sees a driver carrying a passenger without having thrown the flag, the driver may lose his license. In many places, taxis do not have meters and passengers pay a flat fee for each ride, whether it is long or short.

Before the days of automobiles, cabs were small carriages pulled by horses. The most popular kind of cab was called a hansom cab. It carried two passengers. Another kind of horsedrawn cab was called a hackney. It usually carried four passengers. Taxicab drivers still call themselves "cabbies" or "hackies" and speak of their work as "hacking."

taxidermy

Taxidermy is the art of skinning a dead animal, preserving the skin, and then filling it with something to make the model appear lifelike. In the old days the skin was stuffed with straw, sawdust, or some other substance. Modern taxidermists do the job differently. Instead of stuffing the skin, they stretch it over a model of the animal's body.

A visit to a museum of natural history will give one a fine idea of the art of taxidermy. All the animal models in such a museum are created by taxidermists. A taxidermist must be a highly trained and skillful person. In most museums animals have been made to look as they do in the places in which they live.

PREPARING THE SKIN

When a taxidermist starts to work on a dead animal he carefully studies the appearance of the skin—the fur, hair or feathers, and colorings. He then slits the skin and peels it off the animal's body. He prepares the skin in much the same way as leather is tanned. He dips the skin in chemicals that keep it from rotting and falling apart.

In removing the skin the taxidermist must be sure to remove all bits of flesh and muscle and to make sure that the skin neither stretches or shrinks as he works. He is very careful not to tear or cut the skin any more than he must in order to remove it from the body.

PREPARING THE MODEL

When working with birds or mammals that have legs, wings, and a movable skeleton, the taxidermist usually first makes a wire framework that is somewhat like the skeleton of the animal. He covers this with clay, molding it carefully so that it is like the original body. Sometimes a plaster mold or cast is then made from the clay model. At other times a papier mâché or burlap composition cast is made. The hardened cast is then covered with the preserved skin. If necessary the taxidermist recolors parts of the skin, fur, hair, scales, or feathers. He finishes the job by putting in glass eyes.

Such a model lasts for many years if it is kept clean and free from moths and other destructive insects.

Taylor, Maxwell D.

Maxwell D. Taylor, as a general in the United States Army with a great war record, was appointed Army Chief of Staff in 1955 and Chairman of the Joint-Chiefs of Staff. After he retired, he was made ambassador to South Vietnam in 1964.

Zachary Taylor

Zachary Taylor was the twelfth President of the United States. He served from March 1849 to July 9, 1850—a period of just sixteen months—and died in office, leaving the Presidency to Millard Fillmore, the Vice President.

Zachary Taylor was one of several Army generals that a grateful country has rewarded with the Presidency. "Old Rough and Ready," as Zachary Taylor's soldiers called him, was a general during the War of 1812 and afterward became the hero of the Mexican War, which gave him great personal popularity and resulted in his nomination for the Presidency on the Whig Party ticket.

There is an interesting sidelight on the history of Zachary Taylor's family. In 1835 one of his five daughters became the wife of Jefferson Davis, who was later elected President of the Confederate States of America, the southern states that fought against the North in the Civil War. Sarah Taylor Davis died shortly after marriage.

HIS EARLY YEARS

Zachary Taylor was born on November 24, 1784, in Orange County, Virginia, but before he was a year old his family moved to Kentucky. They lived in frontier country, and there were no schools for miles. A private tutor was hired by young Taylor's father, to instruct the children of the family.

Zachary Taylor was given a commission as first lieutenant in the Army when he was 24 years old, and he remained in military service for the next forty years. As a career soldier, he served well in the

War of 1812, and was sent to campaign against the Indians in the Northwest, after which he went to Florida to put down Spanish-Indian revolts in that territory.

When trouble developed over territory claimed by both Texas and Mexico, President James Polk ordered General Taylor to take over the section under dispute. The general obeyed and the war with Mexico followed. Taylor earned the nickname of "Old Rough and Ready" during these campaigns. His troops won a series of victories, making him a military hero.

HOW HE BECAME PRESIDENT

When it was time to nominate a Presidential candidate in 1848, the Whig Party felt that it needed someone who had great personal popularity. The Whigs had been badly beaten in the previous election, when Polk defeated the Whig candidate, Henry Clay.

Taylor was the choice of the Whig Party partly because of his popularity as a military hero and partly because he was a Southerner and could be expected to attract votes from the slave states of the South. He had never run for any political office before that time, but in spite of his inexperience in political matters Zachary Taylor was elected President of the United States in November, 1848. He was inaugurated in March, 1849.

After Taylor became President, he tried to speed the organization of the newly acquired territories of California and New Mexico. He was in favor of admitting California as a state immediately, but there were too many arguments about whether California should permit slavery or be a "free" state. Before Taylor had an opportunity to carry out any of his hopes or plans, he became ill with typhus fever on July 4, 1850, and after a five-day illness he died, on July 9, 1850, at the age of 65.

MRS. ZACHARY TAYLOR

Margaret Smith Taylor was born in Maryland in 1788. She married Zachary Taylor in 1810, and they had six children, five daughters and one son. The son, Richard Taylor, became a general in the Confederate Army in the Civil War. Mrs. Zachary Taylor died in 1852, at the age of 64.

tea

Tea is one of the world's most popu-

lar drinks. It is made from the leaves of the tea plant, which is an evergreen shrub or tree that grows in very warm countries. The leaves are dried and then are steeped (put in boiling water and allowed to stand for a few minutes). This makes a hot drink with a reddish-brown color and a pleasant flavor.

Tea has been drunk for hundreds of years. It is the national drink of China, Japan, Russia, the British Isles, New Zealand, and Australia. Other important tea-drinking countries are Canada, South Africa, Morocco, and the Netherlands. Though tea did not become very popular in Europe until about three hundred years ago, Great Britain today is the chief buyer of tea, and London, England, is the great tea market of the world. People living in England use an average of ten pounds each every year. This would make 1,500 to 2,000 cups of tea for each person. Most of the world's tea is grown in India, Ceylon, Japan, and Indonesia, but it is grown in several other countries.

THE TEA PLANT

The wild tea plant can grow up to 30 feet high, but growers of tea usually cultivate smaller plants, 2 to 6 feet high. The plant has many branches, with grayish-green leaves that are 3 to 5 inches long. Once a year the plant blooms with small, fragrant, white flowers. The tea plant has deep taproots that extend several feet underground. It can grow high on rocky mountainsides, because the deep roots slip down between rocks and boulders.

The tea leaves are picked by hand or cut off with scissors. In China, where the plants do not grow during the winter, the leaves can be picked only three or four times a year. In warmer areas, such as Ceylon, growth continues throughout the year and the leaves may be picked from 25 to 30 times a year.

KINDS OF TEA

The grade or variety of tea depends on the soil in which it is grown, the age of the leaves at the time of picking, and what kind of care is given to the plants. In *golden tips* only the youngest buds are used; in *orange pekoe,* the smallest leaf; in *pekoe,* the second leaf; in *pekoe-souchong,* the third leaf; in *souchong,* the fourth leaf; and in *congou,* the fifth and largest leaf.

The flavor of tea depends on how it is prepared. Usually the freshly picked leaves are first exposed to the sun or are heated in shallow trays until they become soft. They are then rolled, by hand or machine, until the leaves are curled and some of the sap (juice) is removed. The curled and twisted leaves are then completely dried in the sun, or over a fire, or in hot-air currents. The final product is called *green tea.* The leaves are dull-green in color and are quite smooth.

Black tea is made by fermenting the leaves after they have been rolled. The leaves are covered and kept warm. This causes them to lose their green color and changes their flavor. After being fermented, the leaves are dried in the same way as those for green tea.

Oolong tea is made by partially fermenting the leaves. The leaves have the dark, almost black color of black tea and

a flavor almost exactly like that of green tea.

Scented teas are made by drying the leaves together with fragrant flowers, such as jasmine. The blossoms are later sifted out.

The names of teas refer to many different things. They may refer to the place where it was grown, such as Darjeeling or Lapsang. More often the name refers to the kind of leaf, the flowers with which it was scented, and how it was prepared. The tea leaf contains a substance called *theine,* which is almost exactly like caffeine in coffee and has a stimulating effect on the heart and brain. Tea also contains *tannin,* a slightly poisonous substance. Because of these substances tea is not considered a good drink for children, but it is harmless for grownups if they do not drink too much of it. The tannin in tea increases when the leaves are allowed to steep in water for too long a time (the usual time is five minutes).

Tea was first used as a medicine, and then people in China and Japan began to drink it. They usually drink it plain. In Ireland and England people brew their tea very strong and dark, and add sugar and milk or cream. In Russia people drink tea with sugar and lemon, out of glasses instead of cups. In other areas, such as Tibet and the countries of central Asia, people often add salt or rancid butter. In the United States, people often use the *tea bag,* a small bag holding an individual portion of tea that is placed in a cup of hot water. Americans also introduced iced tea, usually drunk with lemon and sugar, which has become a popular summertime beverage.

teaching

A teacher tells one person or group what other persons have learned by experience. This is called *teaching,* and more than anything else it is responsible for man's progress. Each generation, or new group of human beings born on earth, can start off with all the knowledge of the billions of human beings who lived before him.

Almost everybody, at one time or another, has taught another person to do something or to know something, but usually we use the word *teacher* to mean someone whose lifework is teaching others. Teachers may do their work almost any place, but most often they work in schools.

Teaching is one of the oldest human activities. The first teachers were probably the priests of the primitive religions and the only persons they would teach were young men who were learning to be priests. Later there were men called scribes, who knew how to read and write and who kept accounts and records for kings and nobles. These scribes taught young men to become scribes.

The first teachers to have schools were probably the scholars of ancient Greece. They taught the Greek boys to know something about the Greek language and history, about music and poetry, and about the proper forms of exercise for the body. From that time on, teaching follows the history of education, about which you can read in the articles EDUCATION and SCHOOLS.

BECOMING A TEACHER

The teacher of today should have a full college education and usually must also have special training in a school of education or a college. (These are sometimes called *normal schools,* which means "a college where rules are learned.") These special colleges or schools of education teach how to teach. In many states, a teacher must pass a state examination.

Each kind of teaching work usually requires some special training; for example to teach the very young in kindergarten and the first grades; to teach in the later elementary schools; to teach in junior and senior high schools; and to teach in colleges and universities. Teachers of special subjects, such as languages or science, also receive special training.

A good teacher must like to teach. He must like the subject he teaches. He must know that teaching is as important as any other job in the world. He must like to work with children or with the students of the age group he teaches. A good teacher cannot expect to earn a very high salary, though he must spend much time and money to prepare for his work and must continue to study as long as he remains a teacher.

MODERN TEACHING

Once it was believed that a good teacher had to show or tell his pupils everything he expected them to learn. Now many educators believe that a good teacher is the one who gives the student a chance to learn things for himself. The modern teacher gets the students interested in what they are doing, and then lets them work out problems for themselves. The teacher is there to answer questions and give advice. Students today usually enjoy school, because they are interested. Most students used to dislike going to school. The modern teacher is more of a specialist than teachers used to be. There is too much knowledge in today's world for one person to understand all of it and pass it on to others. Therefore there are specialists who teach science, social studies, languages, mathematics, and so on; and within these special groups there may be teachers who teach just one part of one subject.

teak

The teak is a tall timber tree that grows in southeastern Asia and the East Indies. It has large flat leaves of a pointed oval shape. The leaves are used in making red dye. The wood of the teak is a yellowish brown in color. It contains a sweet-smelling oil that makes it extremely resistant to water. For this reason teak was important in shipbuilding for many years, while ships were made of wood. The wood is strong and durable and needs no painting to protect it from weather. Many ships' deck plankings are still made of teak. The wood is useful also in building outdoor furniture, where weather resistance is essential.

tears

Tears are the watery substance that is always in the eyes. Tears come from tiny glands lying near the outer part of the eye sockets, behind the eyeballs. These spongy glands, about the size of an almond, manufacture a fluid that constantly bathes the eyeballs. We seldom think of this except when crying produces a large quantity of tears. The rest of the time just a thin film of moisture, or tears, is spread over each eyeball by two tiny openings, one in each lid of an eye. The openings lead from the glands called the lachrymal glands.

The job of tears is to make the eyeball move easily and to wash away all harmful substances. When something irritating gets into the eye, tears flow much more than usual, to wash away the irritating substances. Other eyewashes are sometimes necessary to wash away something such as a speck of dirt, but tears are usually the only eyewash we need, and the best.

Tecumseh

Tecumseh was a famous American Indian chief of the Shawnee tribe. He led a war against the white settlers of the United States about a hundred years ago. Tecumseh was born about 1768, probably in Ohio, and soon became known as a good military leader. Early in the 1800s the United States government began to buy Indian lands from the particular tribes living on the land. Tecumseh thought such land belonged not to one tribe but to all the American Indians, and tried to unite the western Indians against the white settlers. The plan failed when his brother, known as "the Prophet," was defeated at the Battle of TIPPECANOE, about which there is a separate article. Soon after this the War of 1812 broke out between the United States and Great Britain. Tecumseh and his followers joined the British, and Tecumseh was killed in action at the Battle of the Thames, in Canada, in 1813.

teeth

Teeth are important tools given by nature to man and many animals. They are bonelike structures that are embedded in the jawbone, and they are used to cut, tear and grind food. Without teeth, man and other animals would find it hard to get enough nourishment. Many animals use teeth also as weapons, and the teeth of some can do as much damage as claws, talons, or horns. In man the teeth are used chiefly to break down food into small pieces, which can then be swallowed, digested, and used by the body. Man's teeth also help him to talk, and they influence the shape and appearance of his face.

THE STRUCTURE OF TEETH

If you looked at a tooth cut through the middle, you would see four different sections. The outer section is called the *enamel* and is the hardest part of the tooth. Inside it is a layer called the *dentine.* It also is hard but not as hard as the enamel. Inside the dentine is a sort of hollow tube that contains tiny bits of flesh, blood vessels, and nerves. The blood keeps the tooth alive, and the nerves are responsible for feeling pain in a tooth. Pain can be felt only if there is an opening in the enamel through which germs or very hot or cold substances can get through to the dentine. The dentine rots, or decays, easily. The decay or hole is called a *cavity.*

The fourth section is the *root,* which also is made of dentine. It anchors the tooth in the mouth. It may consist of one, two or three roots. It is embedded in the gums and jawbone and is covered by a kind of bone called the *cementum.*

Both the enamel and the dentine are made up almost entirely of calcium, the same substance that makes bones hard. One of the best ways of keeping teeth healthy is eating foods such as milk and cheese, which contain large amounts of calcium.

THE TWO SETS OF TEETH

Every person has two different sets of teeth during his lifetime. The first set contains twenty teeth, which are called the "milk" or "baby" teeth. The second set, which replaces the first, is the permanent set and contains thirty-two teeth.

The newborn baby has no teeth. When a baby is about six months old the first teeth begin to grow through the gums of the mouth from tiny buds in the jawbone. By the time a child is 30 months (2½ years) old he usually has all twenty baby teeth. Between the ages of 5 and 6 the baby teeth begin to loosen and fall out one by one. By this time there are new tooth buds in the gums beneath them, and from them grow the permanent teeth.

SHAPES AND USES OF TEETH

Both baby and permanent teeth have several different shapes and sizes, but the teeth in the front of the mouth are sharp, for cutting and tearing, and the teeth in the back of the mouth are broad, for chewing and grinding. There are exactly as many upper teeth (in the upper jaw) and lower teeth (in the lower jaw) and each upper tooth is directly above the same kind of tooth below. The kinds of tooth are:

Incisors, or front teeth. They have edges, like dull knife blades, and are used for cutting food. There are four in each jaw.

Cuspids, next to the incisors on each side. They are also called *canines* (because they are like the long teeth of a dog) or *eyeteeth* (because their roots point directly to the eye). Each cuspid has a long, sharp point, or cusp, used for tearing food. There are two in each jaw.

Bicuspids, next to the cuspids. Each of them has two cusps. They are used for grinding food. There are four bicuspids in each jaw.

Molars, or grinding teeth. They are the

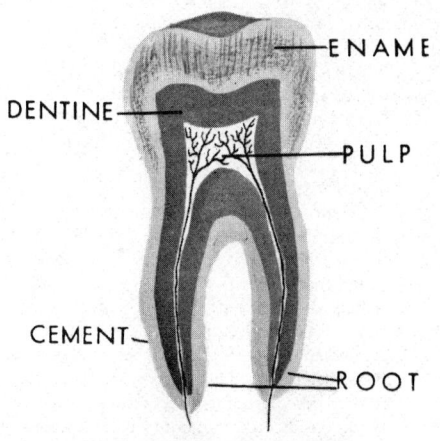

The parts that make up a tooth.

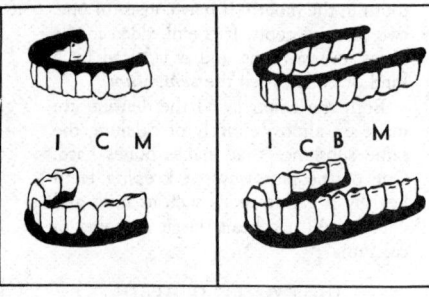

Baby teeth (*left*) and permanent teeth (*right*) both have incisors (I), cuspids (C), and molars (M). The permanent teeth also include bicuspids (B), and other molars.

largest teeth and are farthest back. They are used for chewing and grinding. The baby teeth include only four molars in each jaw, two on each side. The permanent teeth include six molars in each jaw, three on each side. First come four "six-year molars," one on each side, upper and lower, when a child is about 6; then four "twelve-year molars," at about the age of 12; and finally, at any time after the age of 16, four more molars called "wisdom teeth" (because at this age a person is expected to have gained some wisdom). Often there is too little room in the jaw for the wisdom teeth and they cannot grow out properly. They may grow sideways instead of straight up or down. This condition is called *impacted wisdom tooth*. Because they often become infected, and can push aside other teeth, the dentist often pulls them out.

The shape of the teeth varies in different persons. There are three general shapes: square, ovoid (egg-shaped), and tapering (triangle-shaped). The color of the teeth varies not only in different persons but within one person's mouth and even within one tooth. Most teeth are lightest near the biting edge and become darker (yellowish) near the gum line. The cuspids usually are darker than the other teeth. Fair-skinned, blue-eyed persons tend to have lighter teeth than do dark-skinned, dark-eyed persons.

TOOTH DECAY

By the age of 15 years, nearly everyone in the United States has had an average of seven decayed teeth. Tooth decay is one of the most common diseases, and scientists have not yet found a complete explanation for it. Decay usually begins either in the tiny grooves on the chewing surfaces of teeth or just below the point where one tooth touches another. It is caused by the action of germs that lodge on the less exposed parts of the teeth. These germs act on bits of food, especially sweet foods, to form acids that soften and destroy the tooth structure.

Scientists do not know how decay can be prevented entirely, but they have found that certain things will help. They have found that a chemical called fluoride will reduce decay when it is applied to the teeth. Fluoride treatments should be begun when a child is about 3 years old and should be repeated once every 3 or 4 years until all the permanent teeth are in place. If there is a certain amount of fluoride in the community's drinking water it is also helpful. However, the most important

way of preventing decay is through proper care of the teeth.

CARE OF THE TEETH

Eating the proper foods will help keep your teeth healthy. This means eating foods that contain enough calcium and not eating too many sweet foods. Chewing food well gives the teeth, gums and jaws the exercise they need. Even so, tiny bits of food can accumulate between the teeth and eventually cause decay. Therefore the teeth should be brushed after each meal. They should be brushed the way they grow—up on the lowers and down on the uppers. This permits the bristles of the toothbrush to remove the food between the teeth without carrying pieces of it under the gums. Crosswise brushing may wear away the enamel.

Regular visits to the dentist, twice each year, are also important. See the article DENTISTRY.

Teheran

Teheran, or Tehran, is the capital and largest city of Iran. It is in the northern part of the country and is connected by railroads to ports on the Caspian Sea in the north and the Persian Gulf in the south. More than 2,719,000 people live in Teheran. There are factories that make ammunition and metal products, cotton and leather goods, matches, glass, and food and lumber products.

Teheran has a modern university, beautiful mosques (Mohammedan churches), and several museums. Parts of the city are old, with narrow, winding streets, but there is a handsome modern section that has wide avenues, electric lights, theaters, schools, and hospitals. The city was built about eight hundred years ago but it was

unimportant until the 1600s, when it became the residence of some of the Persian kings. It became the permanent capital of Iran in 1788. In the 1900s the ancient walls were torn down and the city was enlarged and modernized.

In 1943 during World War II, the Teheran Conference was held by President Franklin D. Roosevelt, Prime Minister Winston Churchill, and the Russian dictator, Josef Stalin. They made plans for the final defeat of Germany.

TEHERAN, IRAN. Population (1974 estimate) 2,719,730. Capital and largest city of Iran.

Tel Aviv

Tel Aviv is the largest city of Israel. It is a seaport in the western part of the country. It is next to the city of Jaffa and was built in 1906 as an all-Jewish suburb of Jaffa, which was then controlled by Mohammedans. Now Tel Aviv is much larger than Jaffa. The two cities are usually grouped as Tel Aviv-Jaffa, and have a combined population of about 800,000.

Tel Aviv is a beautiful, modern city, with broad, tree-lined avenues and with many beaches. It has become the business and manufacturing center of Israel. There are factories that make textiles and knitted goods, metal and wood products, chemicals, drugs, machine tools, and many other things. Tel Aviv has a university, theaters, museums, zoological gardens, and many parks.

In 1948, when there was fighting between Jews and Arabs after the United Nations divided Palestine between the two peoples, Tel Aviv-Jaffa saw much violence and was bombed several times.

TEL AVIV-JAFFA, ISRAEL. Population (1974 estimate) 838,000 including suburbs.

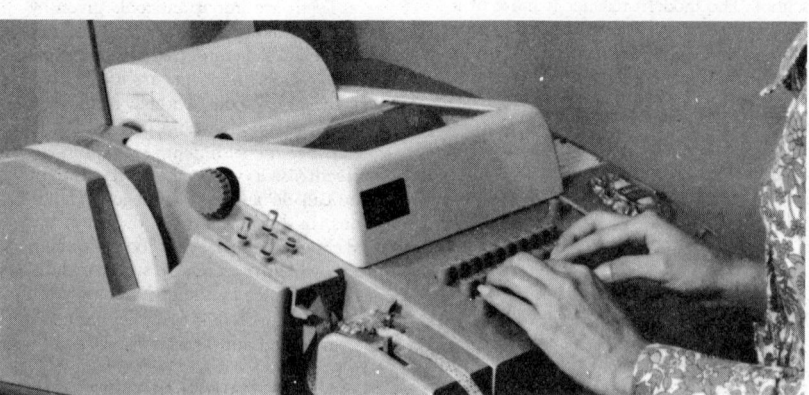

telegraph

The telegraph is an instrument that can send messages over long distances, by electricity. It was the first great invention in modern communications. It led to the marvels of wireless radio and television.

Not much more than a hundred years ago there was no good way of sending messages quickly. The American Indians used smoke signals, which were good only as far as the eye could see. Jungle tribes in Africa sent messages by beating loud drums. In Europe there were attempts to send messages across such spaces as the English Channel by flashing lights on and off. Just before the invention of the tele-

graph the fastest way of sending a message in the United States was by the pony express. It took several days for a letter to cross the country. With the invention of the telegraph this could be done almost instantaneously.

The telegraph was not only the first improvement in communication, it was the first practical use of electricity. Electricity had been known to man for hundreds of years but not much had been done about it. In 1831 an American, Joseph Henry, found that if he wound a coil around a piece of iron and then sent electricity through the wire, the piece of iron would act as a magnet. When the electricity ran through the wire this electric magnet

These men are installing a microwave (radio-beam) antenna. Microwave is the most advanced method of sending messages because it is capable of handling telegraph, voice, data, facsimile, and even television pictures.

would attract a piece of metal to it. Henry made an electric magnet with a bar swinging freely next to it. This bar was called an armature. When the electricity was turned on, one end of the armature was pulled toward the electric magnet and the other end would swing around to hit a bell. All house bells that work by electricity, even the telephone bell, work on that principle.

THE INVENTION OF THE TELEGRAPH

An American named Samuel F. B. Morse, who was best known as a painter, was returning from Europe on a ship when he heard about Henry's invention of the electric magnet. He had been wondering how messages could be sent by electricity, and the electromagnet gave him an idea. When he arrived in the United States, he began work on his invention. At the same time two men in England had gotten somewhat the same idea, but the credit for the invention of the telegraph usually goes to Morse.

This is a "facsimile device". The message is typed on a piece of paper and the paper is wrapped around the drum on the machine. When a button is pressed, the message is automatically copied onto another piece of paper on another machine in a central telegraph office. Even drawings and pictures can be sent by this speedy, modern method.

Morse's idea was simple. He sent a current of electricity through a wire and when it reached the other end it magnetized a piece of iron that had been wound around with wire. The electric magnet attracted a swinging armature, which made a clicking noise as it hit another piece of metal. Morse also tried having the free end of the armature move a pencil. As the pencil moved it made marks on a piece of rolling paper under it.

Opening and closing an electrical circuit controlled the messages sent over the wire. Electricity travels through the wire when the circuit is closed. No electricity goes through the wire when the circuit is open. The operator uses a key to open and close the circuit. The longer he keeps the key pressed down, the longer the click will be. A very short click is called a "dot" and a longer click is called a "dash," because on paper they are represented by a • and a – These dot-and-dash signals were used in different combinations to make a kind of alphabet called the Morse code, with which any words can be sent. Other codes have been developed, using the same dots and dashes in other arrangements.

THE FIRST TELEGRAPH

Morse attempted to interest rich men in his invention but few were interested and many thought it was a crazy idea. Morse also tried to persuade the United States government to furnish the money to build a telegraph line between Washington, D.C., and Baltimore, Maryland. After many discouragements, Congress gave Morse the money to construct his line. This was in 1843. He first laid an underground wire between Washington and Baltimore, but this did not work because the wire was not properly covered. Morse then strung an overhead wire between Washington and Baltimore using poles to hold the wire. Finally, on May 24, 1844, he succeeded in sending a clear message. The first message read, "What Hath God Wrought."

At that time one of Morse's assistants explained how a message is sent by telegraph with these words: "Suppose you stretch a dog from Washington to Baltimore. If you step on the dog's tail in Washington, he will yelp in Baltimore. Well, the telegraph responds in Baltimore to something done to it in Washington. However, it's a lot easier to lay a telegraph wire than it is to stretch a dog."

MODERN TELEGRAPHY

The greatness of Morse's invention soon was recognized. Many improvements were made. Within a few years there were telegraph wires connecting the principal cities of most nations. For many years messages sent with electricity had to be sent over wires. Then came wireless telegraphy and then radio, which permit the sending of messages by electricity through the air without any wires at all. You can read about these in the article RADIO.

The same code system invented by Morse is still used, though not as much as it once was. At first, attempts were made to have the dot or dash written on a piece of paper in some way, but soon it was learned that when the dot or dash sound is loud enough an operator can

hear and understand it. Telegraph operators became so well trained in the use of the Morse code that they could listen to dots and dashes very easily and write down the meaning in letters and words.

It was also learned that the electrical impulse that carries messages over the wire was not strong enough to be useful over a distance of more than twenty miles. Something had to be done if the messages were to be carried over a longer distance. Morse established a *relay system* along the electric wire that carried the message. At a distance of twenty miles from the sending set, and each twenty miles thereafter,

MORSE CODES

	I	II		I	II
A	•–	•–	N	–•	–•
B	–•••	–•••	O	–––	• •
C	–•–•	•• •	P	•––•	•••••
D	–••	–••	Q	––•–	••–•
E	•	•	R	•–•	• ••
F	••–•	•–•	S	•••	•••
G	––•	––•	T	–	–
H	••••	••••	U	••–	••–
I	••	••	V	•••–	•••–
J	•–––	–•–•	W	•––	•––
K	–•–	–•–	X	–••–	•–••
L	•–••	⸺	Y	–•––	•• ••
M	––	––	Z	––••	••• •

I. *International Morse Code*
II. *American Morse Code*

he placed a device that would strengthen the electric impulse. It is much like a relay race. The first runner, when he begins to tire, passes the stick to the next runner, who carries it until he tires, then passes it to a third runner, and so on. In the electric relay system new current is fed to the telegraph wire every twenty miles to strengthen the signal.

The Teletype, and not the wireless, radio, or telephone, has largely replaced dot-and-dash messages. Today if you walk into a Western Union office you will see a boxlike machine with a keyboard like a typewriter's. An operator types out the message and in so doing makes a kind of electric typewriter, or *teleprinter,* operate the keys at the other end of the system. The teleprinter prints the message on a tape or roll of paper. Companies that have offices in several cities often have teletypewriters in each office.

The telegraph wires on land are strung on poles covered or carried by cables underground. There are also great submarine cables, laid along the bottom of the oceans, for sending telegraphic messages between continents. There is a separate article on CABLE.

telepathy

Telepathy is a process in which a thought, feeling, or movement is said to be transmitted from one person to another without personal contact or other communication between them. An example of telepathy might be that one man in New York City "knows" that his friend in California is feeling pain at a particular moment. Telepathy and clairvoyance (special ability to know things) are the two main subjects of a field called *extrasensory perception,* which means knowing or feeling something that has not come to a person through sight or hearing or any of the other senses.

Almost all claims of clairvoyance or telepathic powers can be readily proved to be false, but a few scientists have at-

tempted to clarify the problem through carefully controlled experiments. Such experiments have, for example, been carried on for some years by psychologists at Duke University in Durham, North Carolina, and at other places. These experiments have not convinced many scientists that telepathy is actually possible.

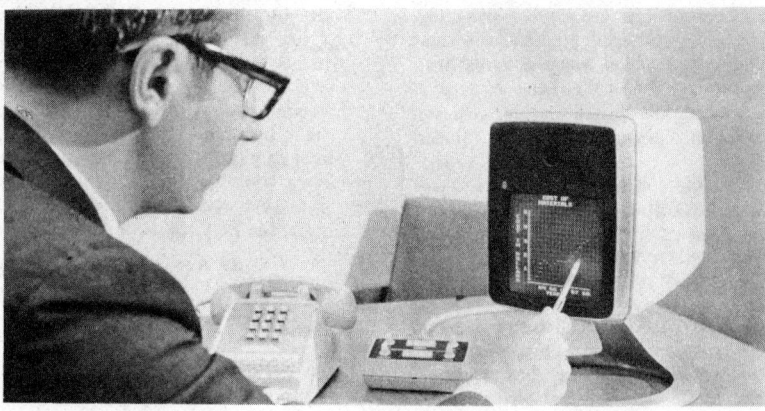

This Picturephone enables you to see the person to whom you are talking. It can also be connected to a computer to obtain special information, as seen in this photograph.

telephone

The telephone is a device that changes sound into electricity and back again, so that words spoken by one person can be carried by electrical wires to be heard by another person far away. We take the telephone for granted today, but it is less than a hundred years since the first telephone was invented. Only for sixty years or so has the telephone been a commonplace convenience that almost everyone uses.

Alexander Graham Bell, who invented the telephone in 1875, could hardly have imagined the complicated electronic instrument that now carries voices over continents and oceans. The first telephones were not usable at distances of more than a few miles and you had to shout to make yourself heard. But Bell's first simple principle is still the basis of the most modern equipment. Furthermore, somewhere in the world every kind of telephone made in the last fifty years and more is still being used—not as a curiosity but as a practical, working convenience. In 1961 there were an estimated 141,700,000 telephones in use throughout the world, half in North America.

THE FIRST TELEPHONE

Bell had studied sound because he was interested in the problems of deaf people. He knew how sound is carried by waves caused by vibrations, or shaking. At first he did not know a great deal about electricity, but he understood the telegraph and he knew that an electric current can be *induced* (brought about) by moving a magnet in a coil of wire.

In Bell's first telephone there were a *transmitter,* or sending part, and a *receiver,* or listening part, just as there are today.

The transmitter had a *diaphragm,* a thin metal disk that would vibrate as sound waves from the voice reached it. Behind the diaphragm was an electromagnet, which is a piece of soft iron with wire wound around it. This coil of wire was connected to the receiving apparatus in another room or house.

When Bell talked to the transmitter, the diaphragm vibrated back and forth exactly as his voice vibrated. In vibrating, the diaphragm moved first toward the magnet and then away from it. The movement of the magnet inside the wire made an electrical current flow to the receiver, where there was another coil of wire, another magnet, and another diaphragm. As the transmitter's diaphragm vibrated, the receiver's magnet pulled the diaphragm back and forth and made it vibrate in exactly the same way. Since it vibrated in exactly the same way, it produced the same sound waves, and Bell's voice could be heard at the receiving end.

Bell's first telephone did not even need a battery. The vibrations of the voice were the only "power" used. The shaking of the diaphragm moved the magnet enough to induce an electrical current that would carry the voice for several miles.

HOW THE TELEPHONE COMPANY BEGAN

Alexander Graham Bell married soon after he invented the telephone, and he gave the patent rights to his wife as a present. A company was set up with his wife's father in charge. This company offered to rent telephones at $20 a year for "dwelling-houses" and $40 a year for business offices. The first offer was made in May, 1877, in Boston, Massachusetts. The New England Telephone Company was the first of the telephone companies.

The earliest telephones did not have bells that would ring to summon a person to answer. Two telephones were always connected and were always open. If a person on one end wanted to talk to the person on the other end, he simply went to his telephone and shouted. "Any voice within ordinary hearing distance can hear the voice calling through the Telephone," the company explained.

Once Bell's invention had been announced, other inventors went to work on it. Some of them made improvements that Bell's company bought. Others tried to set up their own companies without making any payment to Bell for his original invention, and there were many lawsuits.

Among the earliest improvements were the telephone bell and the central exchange, or switchboard. The bell would call a person to the telephone even when he happened to be out of the room and could not hear the voice calling him. To work the telephone bell, a person simply turned a crank at his telephone set. This turned a magneto, a simple kind of electric generator, and the magneto would produce enough electricity to ring the bell at a faraway place. The vibrations of the voice could not produce anywhere near enough power for that. Thousands of telephones still have bells that must be worked by cranking magnetos.

The central exchange permitted a person to talk to many different telephones and not merely to one other telephone. The first exchange was set up in New Haven, Connecticut, in 1878. A "subscriber" with a telephone first called the operator at the exchange and told her that he wanted to speak with "Mr. Smith," or "the ice company," or whomever he wanted. She took the wire connected with his telephone and connected it with the wire that led to the telephone he wanted. This system too, with many refinements but with little basic change, is still in use throughout the world. It was the only system in use for more than fifty years, until dial telephones were developed.

The convenience of the telephone was so apparent that there were many subscribers and telephone companies had to be set up in all the principal cities. These were separate companies, but one larger company was formed to link them all together with "long distance" lines. A line between Boston and New York was opened in 1884, a line between New York and Chicago in 1892, and the first coast-to-coast line, New York to San Francisco, in 1915.

The parent telephone company grew into the American Telephone and Telegraph Company. Each city or section still has its own telephone company, which handles service in its territory. The national company connects the different companies with its long distance lines, does the research and development to continue improvements, and manufactures the telephone equipment (by owning Western Electric Company, which actually operates the factories). For many years there were sometimes two or even more telephone companies in a single city, and people could talk only to others who were subscribers of the same company. This has gradually been changed, but there are still more than five thousand telephone companies that are not owned by the "Bell System," though many of them have connections with Bell System lines.

The Federal Communications Commission is the United States government agency that regulates the use of telephones. There is a separate article about it.

THE MODERN TELEPHONE

The great developments in electronics have made possible many improvements in the telephone. The principal ones are the more sensitive instruments, the carrier lines that make it possible to have millions of telephones connected together, and the dial system that makes the use of the telephone automatic and much faster. The present telephone transmitter is

like the delicate microphones used in broadcasting and sound-recording. It no longer takes tremendous lung power to make the diaphragm vibrate. Fastened to the back of the diaphragm is a chamber filled with an exactly measured quantity of carbon granules, which are grains of roasted coal. Through this carbon chamber and the connecting wires a battery sends an electric current. This means that electrons, tiny particles of electricity, are constantly moving through the carbon granules. The slightest movement of the diaphragm, which can be caused by a whisper, changes the pressure on the carbon granules and affects the flow of electrons. This in turn affects the action on the telephone receiver far away.

The carrier lines are lines that carry electric power whether or not someone is speaking on the telephone. The current actually induced by the sound waves is weak and will not travel far, so it is connected to the carrier line, which carries it along. At certain places along the way, every fifty or more miles, the current is amplified. Vacuum tubes (as described in the article on ELECTRONICS) are used to amplify the electrical waves, to make them stronger so that they will carry over greater distances.

With so many millions of telephones, there would be an impossible number of wires if every connection between telephones required a separate private wire. This is not necessary because different conversations are carried at different frequencies (that is, by different wave lengths) along the same wires. One connection can carry as many as sixteen different telephone conversations at once. The vacuum tube is used to separate the current into its different frequencies.

THE COAXIAL CABLE

The coaxial cable is another means of carrying many conversations without the use of separate wires. The coaxial unit is a copper tube that is not much thicker than a pencil. In its center it has a wire about as thick as a pencil lead. The wire and copper tube will carry several dozen frequencies. Two coaxial units are used together, one to carry the current in each direction. The coaxial cable is a larger tube carrying perhaps eight coaxial units. One coaxial cable can carry several hundred telephone messages at once. Along the line, about every eight miles, the currents are amplified.

THE TELEPHONE AND RADIO

It is not generally realized that network radio, which permits one program to be broadcast in all parts of the country, was accomplished largely by means of the telephone. A single broadcasting station reaches only a limited area, but the program is carried over telephone wires to other broadcasting stations, and each broadcasts the program in its territory.

The same is true of television. For the first few years of television there was a limited number of network programs, solely because the telephone company did not have enough coaxial cables to carry all the programs from city to city. Network television increased when more coaxial cables were laid from place to place.

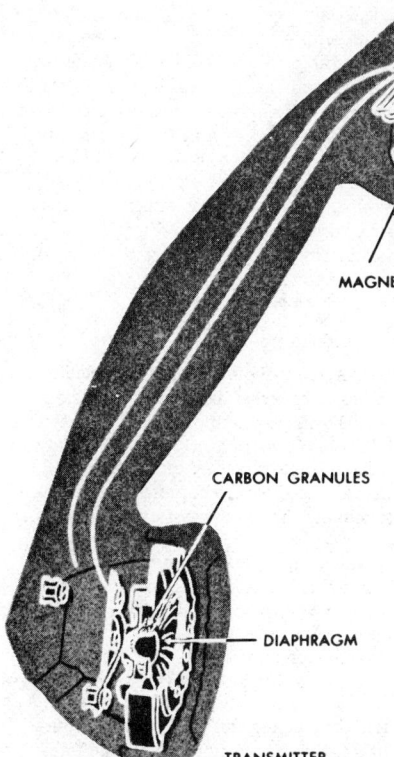

Bell Telephone Laboratories

A cut-away view of the handle of a telephone, showing the main parts of the transmitter and receiver. Speech causes vibrations in the diaphragm. The vibration activates the carbons, and sends the message over the wire. The sound that comes through the receiver is caused by vibrations in the diaphragm at that end. Speech through another telephone connected to this one sends electrons through the wire coils, making the magnet pull with greater and lesser force against the iron diaphragm, which vibrates, producing speech.

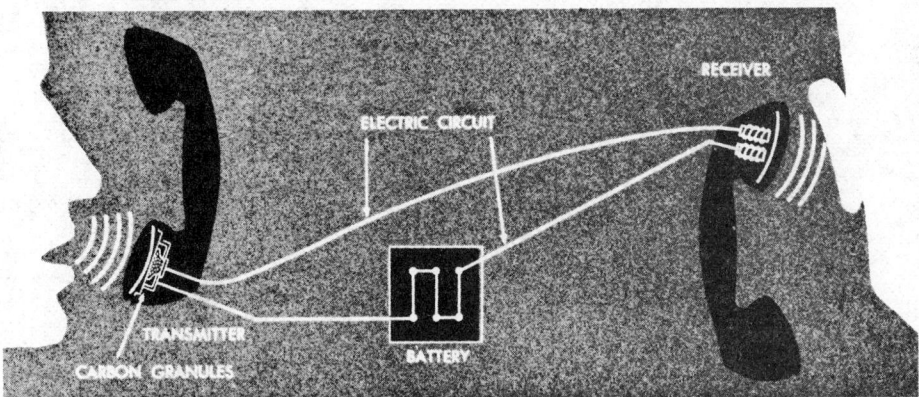

This chart shows a simple telephone circuit with a battery introduced to cause billions of electrons to march in procession around the telephone circuit.

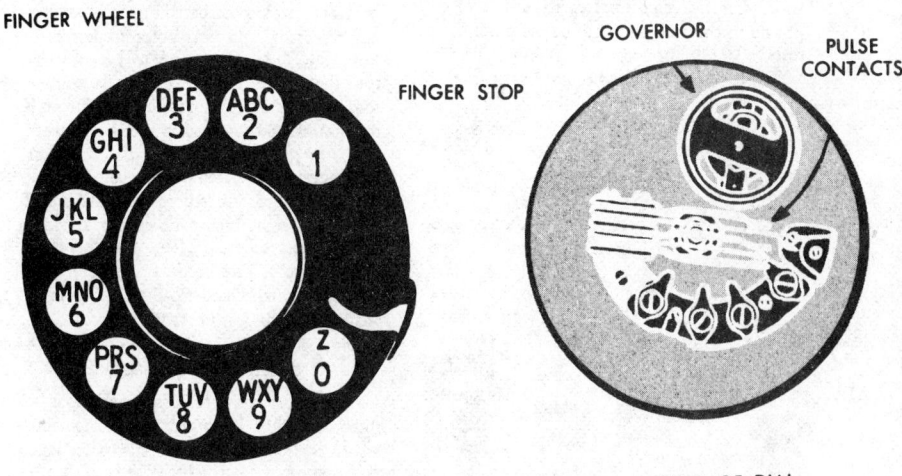

Every click of the telephone dial, as it spins back to its starting position, sends a pulse of current through an electromagnet in the dial equipment in the central office.

DIAL TELEPHONES

The dial system uses automatic machinery to connect two telephones, just as the operator connects them by taking a wire and pushing it into an opening ("plugging it in") on her switchboard. The most important part of the dial equipment is the electromagnet. The electromagnet is set to push another piece of equipment a certain distance each time a current is sent through its wires. Every click of a telephone dial supplies that amount of current and causes the electromagnet to move the equipment another step.

When you pick up a dial telephone and hear the buzz called the "dial tone," it means that an electromagnet has detected your line as being open and has made connection with you. Now you begin to dial, and each set of clicks causes another electromagnet to find a certain hole having that number. When you have dialed all the numbers, it completes a combination and you are connected with the telephone you want, which will at once begin to ring. Another device on the dial telephone times your call and automatically charges you for it. Today you can dial any telephone in the country and be connected automatically. In 1962 the first push-button telephone went into commercial use.

SPECIAL TELEPHONE SERVICES

Overseas telephones are usually a form of radio rather than telephone. The message is carried by telephone wire to a radio transmitting station, then by radio to a receiving station near the overseas point, and then by wire again through regular telephone exchanges. Calls from the United States to Europe or South America usually go through New York City, and calls from the United States across the Pacific Ocean go through Oakland, California. In 1955 undersea cable was laid to carry some telephone calls to Europe.

Mobile service provides telephone service to and from an automobile or train. It too is a combination of radio and telephone. A telephone in an automobile or train can be connected with any telephone in the Bell System, just as a home or office telephone can be.

To call someone who has a mobile

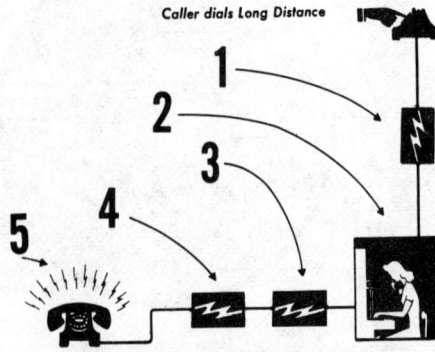

Caller dials Long Distance

When long distance is called: 1. The call is switched to toll office by local dial equipment. 2. The operator takes the call and dials the wanted telephone in distant city. 3. Toll dial equipment switches the call to distant city. 4. Dial equipment in distant city switches the call. 5. The called telephone rings.

telephone, you call long distance and get the mobile service operator. You give the number of the mobile telephone. If the car with mobile telephone is in the same city, it is called by the telephone company's radio transmitter in that city and the connection is made almost at once. If the car with the mobile telephone is in some distant place, you must know about where it is and usally it must be within thirty miles or so of a principal city where there is a radio transmitter used for mobile service.

telescope

A telescope is a device for making things seem nearer than they are and larger than they appear to the naked eye. When we speak of a telescope we usually mean a single tube that you look through with one eye only. The same kind of instrument with eyepieces for both eyes is called a *binocular*. The word *telescope*, however, covers many instruments, large and small, some for use with one eye, some with two, and some used chiefly for taking photographs.

There are two chief kinds of telescope. One is the *refracting* telescope. *Refracting* means "bending," and the refracting telescope bends rays of light so that they make things appear larger. The other kind of telescope is the *reflecting* telescope. It uses mirrors that collect light and magnify it to make things seem larger. The biggest telescopes are reflecting telescopes.

Telescopes have many uses. Navigators, forest rangers and many other people use them to see things far away. Hunters use telescopic sights, small telescopes attached to the tops of rifles, to help them aim at far-off things. Surveyors use the same kind of small telescope in measuring distances. Thousands of amateur astronomers use telescopes to study the heavens, and professional astronomers, in great observatories, use the world's largest telescopes.

FIRST USE OF THE TELESCOPE

The first use of the telescope was in astronomy. The invention of the telescope, according to an old story, was an accident. About 350 years ago a Dutch spectacle-maker named Hans Lippershey happened to hold two different lenses in a straight line. He found to his surprise that the top of the village steeple seemed much larger when he looked at it through the lenses. He wrote about his discovery and the great Italian scientist, Galileo, read about it. Galileo made a telescope of the same kind and studied the stars and planets wth it. He made important discoveries that opened a new field of study in astronomy. The kind of telescope used by Galileo, which is the simplest kind, is still called the Galilean telescope.

THE GALILEAN TELESCOPE

In the Galilean telescope, there is a large lens that is convex (bulging outward) on both surfaces and a smaller lens that is concave (curved inward) on both surfaces. The larger lens is pointed toward an object and the smaller one is placed against the eye. Light enters the large, or *objective,* lens and is magnified just as it is through a magnifying glass (which also is a lens that is convex on both surfaces).

However, this lens distorts the picture (twists it out of shape). To be seen clearly, the light must travel from the convex lens through the concave lens, or eyepiece, which bends it back to a form that is clear to the eye.

For the picture to be clear, the objective lens and the eyepiece must be a proper distance apart. This distance depends on how far away the object (the thing you are looking at) is. Therefore the two lenses are put at the ends of a tube made in sections. The sections can be slid in and out to make the telescope longer or shorter. When you use a telescope you lengthen or shorten it until the picture is clear. It is then *in focus,* which means that the light rays meet at the proper point inside the telescope.

Children usually like to look through a telescope "the wrong way," putting the large lens to the eye. This makes nearby things seem very tiny, because of the way the light is bent when it first enters the concave lens.

Telescopes are described by their *power,* which is the number of times they will magnify something. A 30-power telescope will make things look thirty times as big as they would appear to the eye.

Dozens of improvements have been made in refracting telescopes since Galileo's time. Some of these improvements have been made to increase the magnifying power of the telescope, but most of them have been made to prevent *aberration,* or distortion of the picture. Scientists in the field of optics have found many ways to combine different kinds of lens to improve the telescope, but there is a limit to the size of refracting telescopes and for the biggest jobs a reflecting telescope must be used.

THE REFLECTING TELESCOPE

The reflecting telescope is a big mirror that is concave (curved inward) on its surface. Light falls on this mirror. The mirror magnifies it and reflects it onto a flat or slightly convex mirror. The person using the telescope looks at this second mirror through an eyepiece, or a photograph can be taken from the second mirror through a lens that is like the lens of the eyepiece.

The biggest reflecting telescope, and the biggest telescope of any kind, is on Mount Palomar, in California. Its mirror is 200 inches in diameter (across). The moon, which is more than 235,000 miles away from the earth, appears to be only 40 miles away in the Mt. Palomar telescope. The mountain is 5,568 feet high (about one mile), and the telescope is placed on a mountain not so much to bring it nearer to the heavens as to put it where the air is purer and clearer and the noises and vibrations of cities are avoided.

The next-biggest reflecting telescope, and the biggest before the Palomar telescope was built, is also on a mountain in California, Mt. Wilson. Its mirror is 100 inches across. The Palomar telescope is much more effective in many ways, and shortly after it was put into use in 1952 the astronomers discovered that all the stars are actually twice as far away as they had previously been thought to be.

Telescopes used by astronomers are automatically turned by clocks of great accuracy so that they will follow the stars through the heavens.

The making of the reflecting mirror requires extreme skill and care and is very expensive. The metal of the mirror is aluminum. The glass is cast, that is, melted and poured into place. One section is cast at a time. The casting must be done so that there are no air bubbles or impurities in the glass.

television

Television, called TV (or "telly" in England), is the most popular form of entertainment in the home. In 1949 it took that position ahead of radio. By 1965 there were 65,000,000 television sets in the United States, at least one in each of 50,000,000 houses. In other countries television is similarly popular though fewer families have TV sets. By 1965 both color television and transcontinental telecasting (see the article on ARTIFICIAL SATELLITES) had become a reality.

With television, you see a talking motion picture in the home. The "talking" or sound part of the show, called the *audio*, is simply FM radio that is broadcast at the same time and from the same place as the picture. The picture is taken by a camera that changes light waves into electrical energy that can be sent through the air. A "picture tube" in the television receiving set, in the home, changes this back into light waves that can be seen on the screen of the set as a picture.

Television was invented early in the 1920s and there were several satisfactory experimental TV broadcasts in the late 1920s and early 1930s, but it took almost twenty years to make it possible for everyone to enjoy TV. There were several reasons for this.

First, such a complicated piece of machinery as a television set must be sold at a very high price unless a great many can be made. Some manufacturing difficulties had to be worked out before most people could afford television. It also takes a great deal of money and time to build a television broadcasting station. Until enough stations were built, people did not have much choice of programs and it was hardly worth while for them to buy TV sets. Advertisers pay the cost of nearly all television programs, and it was not worth while for them to spend the money until millions of people could watch the programs and see their advertising. Because of all these things, television grew gradually instead of spreading over the country all at once.

There is another reason why television had a slow start. The electrical (electromagnetic) waves that carry the television picture go straight out from the transmitting (broadcasting) station. Radio waves can carry sound for thousands of miles; TV waves for only 40 or 50 miles.

Therefore TV networks had to lease *coaxial cables* (explained in the article TELEPHONE) to carry their broadcasts from city to city, or to relay stations, so they could be rebroadcast, and for several years there were not enough of these coaxial cables to do the work.

For a few years the relay stations were a great help. These stations are spaced about 40 miles apart. The broadcast travels from the first transmitting station to a relay station, which amplifies it (makes it stronger) and passes it along to the next station, and so on across the country. But it took time to build the high towers that made up the chain of relay stations.

Finally the problem was solved, in 1965, with communication satellites. These are artificial satellites that go around the earth hundreds of miles up. TV waves from the earth hit the satellite and bounce back to be received thousands of miles away. Instead of needing wires to cross a continent, broadcasters can now cross the widest oceans.

HOW TELEVISION WORKS

The two chief inventions that made television possible were the *iconoscope* and the *kinescope*. The inconoscope is the important part of the camera that takes the picture at the television sudio. The kinescope, or picture tube, is the important part of the receiving set on which you see the picture in your home.

The iconoscope uses the principle of the electric eye, which is explained in the article on ELECTRONICS. Certain substances will give off electrons, or particles of electricity, when light falls on them. First, the TV camera takes a picture just as any camera does. This picture falls on a plate that changes the light into streams of electrons. There are millions of separate streams of electrons, each one depending on whether that part of the picture is light, or dark, or shaded somewhere in between. The plate is made up of thousands of small squares of material. Each small square acts like an electric eye. This plate is called a mosaic. (A real mosaic is a picture made up of many pieces of tile, glass, or stone, in different colors.

The next step is *scanning* the picture. A stream of electrons called the *cathode beam,* scans the mosaic plate by sweeping back and forth over it, picking up each stream of electrons, and sending them to the transmitter where they are sent out through the air just as the radio waves are sent (as explained in the article on the RADIO). In the receiving set in your home, the kinescope or picture tube has another cathode beam that receives the streams of electrons, turns them back into light rays, and casts them on the screen where you can see them as a picture.

The picture is actually transmitted and received not as one whole picture but as a moving series of light or dark dots traveling across the screen, back and forth, all the time. At any particular instant, only one of these incredibly tiny dots is actually

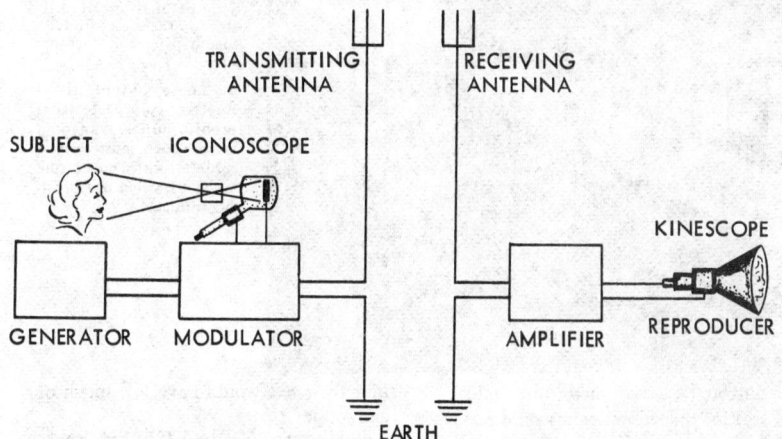

How television works: The iconoscope receives the image of the subject, the amount of light passing through the modulator from the generator being determined by the amount of light reflected by the different parts of the image. The radio waves sent out from the transmitting antenna are picked up by the receiving antenna. They are amplified, and changed back into light in the kinescope, producing a picture on the screen.

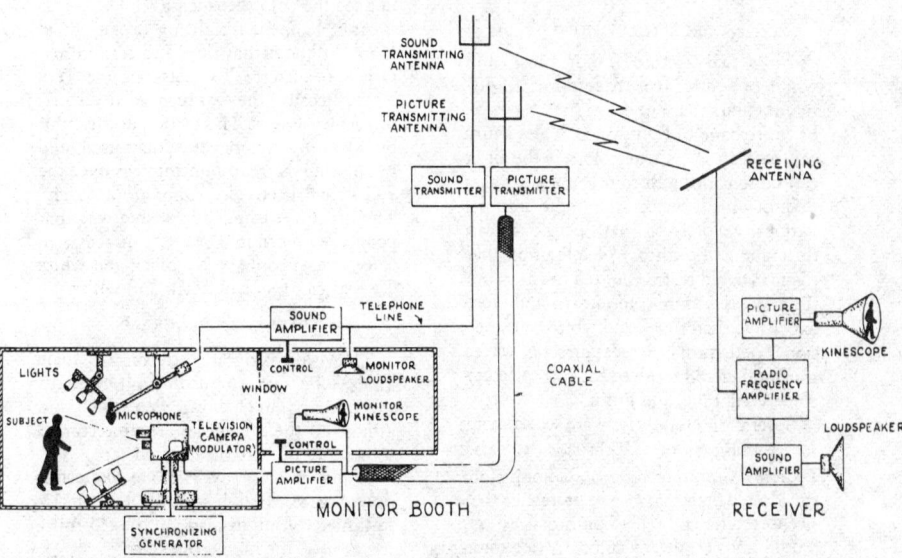

Diagram of the steps in the simultaneous television transmission of sight and sound.

1. Ernie (on the left) and Bert are two of the puppets seen by millions of children on the successful television program, "Sesame Street".

2. These 40-foot ultra-modern color television mobile units transport crews which must televise subjects located outside the usual television broadcasting studios.

appearing on the screen, and if time could stand still for that instant you would not see any picture at all. But electricity travels so fast—about 186,000 miles per second—that your eyes cannot tell you that you are seeing only one dot at a time. It all happens so fast that it looks like one complete picture.

COLOR TELEVISION

An actual picture is not black and white, of course. It is made up of all different colors that appear in the *spectrum,* or entire band of light waves. The picture can be seen in its true colors if the light can be sent through something such as a prism, which breaks the light into its various colors. It has been known throughout the history of television that pictures could be transmitted in color, but the process is more complicated and more expensive than black-and-white transmission. There must be a separate set of waves transmitted and received for each primary color (red, blue, and green).

Several different ways were worked out for sending color TV broadcasts. The Federal Communications Commission, the United States government agency that licenses radio and television broadcasting, would not permit any color TV for some years. It did this to protect the public. The people owned millions of TV sets, and if the best programs had begun to appear in color their sets would have lost much of their value.

Finally, in 1950, the F.C.C. did license color broadcasting, but the system of color broadcasting that it licensed was of the kind called *incompatible.* That means that a person with a regular set, made to receive black-and-white broadcasts, could not see the color broadcast.

As it happened, fighting broke out in Korea at about that time and certain materials needed in TV sets became very scarce because they were needed also by the armed forces. The incompatible color broadcasting was never widely used, and by the time Korean fighting was over the F.C.C. had licensed a *compatible* system. The broadcast is made in such a way that people with color TV sets can see it in color and people with black-and-white TV sets can see it in black and white.

TELEVISION PROGRAMS

Television programs are of two main kinds, *live* and *prerecorded.* Originally the most popular shows were live; now almost all the big shows are prerecorded, sometimes on film, usually on tape.

A filmed TV show is made like a motion picture, though usually it is on 16-millimeter film instead of the 35-millimeter used for movie theaters.

Tape recordings are used much more often. The TV tape recorder is like the familiar one that records only sound, but it is larger and more complicated because it must record not only sound but pictures, sometimes in color.

The most expensive television shows are "variety" shows, with comedians, singers, dancers, big orchestras, and other attractions. All big shows are paid for by advertisers and an advertiser may pay as much as $500,000 to "sponsor" one show or more than $5,000,000 a year for a series of shows. The value of the advertising is great, because thirty million people may watch the show and see the advertiser's message, but even so the cost is more than most advertisers are willing or able to pay, so an expensive show may have two, four, or even more sponsors who divide the cost.

The next most popular, and most expensive, shows are dramatic (like movies but shorter). They cost $30,000 to $100,000 for a 30-minute show, but the first sponsor does not pay all of this. The producer of the show loses money on the first run and gets his profit from re-runs, with new sponsors, on smaller TV stations or on the big networks at less desirable times. "Prime time" is at night between 7 and 11 o'clock and on Sunday afternoons. An advertiser pays less for re-runs but after two or at most three showings the producer of the show makes a profit.

KINESCOPES

In the early years of television, when most shows were live, films were made for re-runs by making a movie of the show as it appeared on the TV screen. This was called a *kinescope,* or *kine-recording,* or simply a "kinny." The method is still used, but not so often. The kinny is not as clear as a movie, but often it takes an expert to tell the difference.

Some TV shows are filmed, or taped, for use by local advertisers on small stations. This is called *syndication.*

TV networks usually try to have "balanced programming," which means that every day part of their time will be devoted to fun programs—music and comedy—but part to news, part to serious or artistic programs, and part to education. The Federal Communications Commission (FCC), which gives the licenses that all broadcasters need, favors this.

Many motion pictures that were made to be shown in theaters can now be seen on television. When television was new, the motion-picture industry feared that TV would put it out of business, and movie producers would not sell their good pictures to TV stations. Even so, thousands of movie theaters had to close because people were staying at home to watch television.

Then the motion-picture producers found in television the biggest profits they had ever made. Some of the big Hollywood studios have sold the rights to show their old movies on TV for as much as $50,000,000—ten times as much as they could have gotten without TV. Also, TV is used to advertise new movies that cannot be shown immediately on TV because they cost millions and no advertiser can afford to pay so much for one show.

PAY TV

Several companies have tried to find a system by which people can pay a reasonable amount to see a show—such as a new, expensive motion picture—that no advertiser or network can afford to put on the air free.

Every method would require some special attachment or connection on the television set. One method would be a direct wire from the telephone company. A person's bill for special shows would appear on his next telephone bill. It might be about one dollar a month. Other methods have been tested. For example, a meter might be put on a TV set and then the meter would be read, and people would pay their bills, just as they do for gas and electricity. People seem to like pay TV, but in 1964 the California legislature passed a law against pay TV and, temporarily at least, put the biggest pay-TV company out of business and discouraged other companies that were experimenting with it.

Pay TV might make it possible to show expensive movies just on TV. Since several million television sets might be paying to see a single motion picture, the price might be reduced to twenty-five cents or even less and still the motion-picture companies could afford to show the costliest pictures on television.

HOW A TELEVISION SHOW IS PRODUCED

Usually a television show is produced as a "package." That means it is produced by a person or a company, called the producer, that pays all the expenses and sells the full show to the sponsor or broadcasting company. The producer is also called the *packager*. The producer, or packager, hires the "talent" (actors, actresses, and other performers), rents or provides the studio, pays the cameramen and electricians and stagehands and the director and writers and others who work on the show, and makes a selling price that will leave a profit. For example, all the expenses may come to $28,000 and the selling price to the sponsor may be $35,000, in which case the producer makes a profit of $7,000. In some cases the broadcasting company owns half of the package and the producer owns the other half; in some cases it is an advertising agency or the sponsors that own a share along with the producer.

Usually the broadcasting company owns or rents the studio and hires the stagehands, electricians, engineers, cameramen, announcers, musicians, and perhaps even the director, producer and performers, on a weekly salary. It sells the services of all these people plus the rent of the studio to the packager for a price that will give the broadcasting company a profit.

The work of the producer is the work of any "boss" in a company. He is responsible for the entire show and hires the people connected with it. The director is responsible for having everything happen at the correct time and in the right way. Time is especially important in television, because the sponsor buys time from the broadcasting company and when the sponsor's time is over another show comes on, even if the sponsor's show is not quite finished. The engineers sit in a *control booth* and work numerous controls that make the picture and sound go out over the air in the right way. Each of the other people connected with the show has his own particular duty.

Every television show must be timed so as to leave time for the *commercials*, or advertising messages, for the commercials pay the cost of the show. Usually the principal commercial comes in the middle of a show. The sponsor also has commercials at the beginning and end of each show. In addition the broadcasting company sells time between shows. Usually this time occupies twenty to thirty seconds, just long enough for an advertiser to give a brief message to the audience. Such a short message between shows is called a *spot*. A commercial before a show is called a *cowcatcher;* one after is a *hitchhiker.* See also the article on CATV.

Tell, William

William Tell is a hero in a Swiss legend. The story told about him dates back more than six hundred years. In it, William Tell is a very skillful marksman with the bow and arrow. He lived in the town of Altdorf. In 1307 an Austrian official named Gessler commands everyone in Altdorf to pay homage to Austria. Tell refuses to do so and is condemned to death; but it is agreed that he will be freed if he shoots an apple from the head of his young son, whom he loves. Tell passes the test but then says that if he had killed his son he would also have killed Gessler. For this he is put in chains and put on a boat that will take him to prison. During the voyage a storm arises, and Tell is released from his chains so that he can help to save the boat. He then leaps to the shore and kills Gessler.

The story then tells of a revolt in which Tell later takes part, and in which certain provinces of Switzerland, called the Forest Cantons, win their independence from Austria. The story of William Tell became the subject of a play by the German poet Schiller and an opera by the Italian composer Rossini. Both are called *William Tell.*

telstar, a communications satellite designed to make intercontinental television possible. See the article ARTIFICIAL SATELLITE.

temperature

Temperature is a measurement of hotness or coldness. We can measure the temperature of the air, or a piece of metal, or the human body, or any other substance. There is a great deal of difference between the temperature of something and the amount of heat in something. A big piece of metal that is barely warm may have much more heat in it than a small piece of metal that is very hot. An iceberg weighing thousands of tons has much more heat in it than a piece of red-hot metal.

Heat always flows from a substance that is hotter into a substance that is colder. We say that the hotter substance has a higher temperature than the colder substance. The question of how much hotter it is can be answered with the measuring device called the thermometer, which measures temperature in degrees just as a speedometer measures speed in miles per hour. An automobile going 10 miles per hour will get to the same place as an automobile going 60 miles per hour, but it will take longer. Cold water in a pan will evaporate (pass into the air as vapor) just as very hot water in a pan will boil (pass into the air as steam), and just about as much heat is needed in either case, but the cold water will take much longer because its temperature is lower.

The temperatures we measure most often are air temperature, which shows how hot or cold the weather is, and body temperature, which shows whether we are sick or well. We usually measure these by the Fahrenheit scale, in which the freezing point of water is 32 degrees and the boiling point of water is 212 degrees.

The "normal" temperature of the human body is generally set at 98.6 degrees, but many people have normal temperatures somewhat above or below this. When a person's temperature rises much over 99 degrees, it is usually a sign of illness and the person is said to have "a temperature" or "a fever." High body temperature is a sign that the body is fighting against germs that cause disease. Many germs are killed by high temperatures.

In considering the climate of a place, the average (or *mean*) annual temperature is often important, but it can be misleading. For example, a place where the temperature is as high as 100 degrees in the summer and as low as zero in the winter may have an average temperature 50 degrees, but so might a place where it is never hotter than 70 in the summer or colder than 40 in the winter. The place where there is less change between the seasons would be said to have a more *temperate* climate.

See also the articles on HEAT and THERMOMETER.

Temple

A temple is a building set aside for religious worship in certain religions. The most famous temple was the Temple of Solomon. It was a Jewish house of worship that was built nearly three thousand years ago by King SOLOMON, about whom there is a separate article. It took seven years to build, from about 990 B.C. to 983 B.C., and the story of its building is told in the Bible, in the books of 1 Kings and 2 Chronicles. The Temple was about 100 feet long and about 65 feet wide. It was built by skilled workers from the city of Tyre, and it used cedars and firs from Lebanon. The Temple was destroyed by the king of Babylonia, Nebuchadnezzar, in 586 B.C., but was rebuilt in the same century. The rebuilt Temple was the building from which Jesus threw out the money-changers, as told in the Gospel of St. Matthew. It was destroyed about two thousand years ago, in the year 70, by Titus, a Roman prince who later became emperor of Rome. After the year 70, the Jewish people were scattered all over the world, and for nearly two thousand years the date of the destruction of the temple was considered also as the date when the Jewish nation ended.

Ten Commandments

The Ten Commandments are ten rules that for thousands of years have controlled Jewish and Christian ideas of right and wrong. In the Bible, the Book of Exodus tells how God gave the Commandments to Moses on Mount Sinai. They were written on tables (tablets) of stone. They are listed in chapter 20 of the Book of Exodus and also in chapter 5 of the Book of Deuteronomy. The Ten Commandments are sometimes called the *Decalogue,* a name that comes from Greek words meaning "ten" and "speech."

tendon

A tendon is the cord that attaches a muscle to a bone. All the muscles that cause the various parts of the body to move are made up of bundles of fibers. Each fiber has a covering of strong body tissue. The tissues that cover the fibers are joined together to form tendons at the end of the muscle. The other end grows into the bones. A tendon is not hard like bone but is wiry and pliable. You can feel one of the important tendons at the back of your heel. This tendon attaches the calf muscle to the bones of your foot. Tendons are not easily damaged but a severe blow or wrench can sprain them. A sprained tendon is painful and makes it hard to move the bone or joint to which it is attached. The best cure for a sprained tendon is rest.

Tennessee

Tennessee is a state in the east south central part of the United States. Its nickname is the "Volunteer State" because of the great number of Tennessee men who volunteered to fight in the Mexican War. Tennessee is a Cherokee Indian word and was the name of an early settlement in this area.

For many years Tennessee was important for its farming, but in the last fifty years it has become more important for its industry. Tennessee is the largest mineral-producing state in the south, and the largest income of the state is from mining of coal.

The first important atomic-energy headquarters was built in Oak Ridge, Tennessee. Industry has been helped greatly by the power supplied by dams and lakes built by the TENNESSEE VALLEY AUTHORITY, about which there is a separate article. Two presidents of the United States, Andrew Jackson and Andrew Johnson, came from Tennessee.

Tennessee ranks thirty-fourth in size among the states, with 42,244 square miles. In population it ranks seventeenth, with a little less than four million people living there. It became a state in 1796, the sixteenth state admitted to the United States. The capital is Nashville.

THE PEOPLE OF TENNESSEE

The earliest white settlers in Tennessee were the French, who built several forts near where the cities of Nashville and Memphis now stand. The state was permanently settled by colonists of Scotch-Irish, English and French origin, who went to Tennessee from Virginia and North Carolina about two hundred years ago. Most of the people who live in Tennessee are descendants of these early settlers. About 631,696 Negroes live in Tennessee.

The leading industries in the state are chemical and textile (cloth and hosiery) manufacturing. Lumbering is also a major industry. The principal crops are corn, cotton, and tobacco. Tennessee has rich deposits of coal, zinc, limestone, phosphate rocks, and clay. Tennessee marble is famous all over the United States.

The people of Tennessee belong to many religions. The largest number of them are Baptists and Methodists, but there are also many Presbyterians, Roman Catholics, and Episcopalians.

WHAT TENNESSEE IS LIKE

Tennessee divides naturally into three regions. In eastern Tennessee are two ranges of mountains, the Great Smoky Mountains, which are part of the Appalachian Mountain chain, and the Cumberland Mountains to the west of them. Between these two mountain ranges is the Valley of Eastern Tennessee. Mostly it is the valley of the Tennessee River, and rivers that flow into it. The big mining and lumber industry of Tennessee is in this eastern region. Farmers in the valley grow corn, tobacco, and fruit.

Central Tennessee is a high but level region surrounded by highlands and cut by many rivers, the largest of which are the Cumberland and the Tennessee. There are good farm lands in the south and rich phosphate deposits in the north.

Western Tennessee is part of the plain drained by the Mississippi River. It is low and flat, like the land of states farther south. The soil is not good for many crops, but much cotton is grown.

Except in the mountains, Tennessee has very hot, long summers and mild winters, with little or no snow. The average temperature for the state is 38 degrees in winter and 76 degrees in summer.

Railroads and highways reach most parts of the state, and there are airports in all the important cities.

GOVERNMENT OF TENNESSEE

Tennessee, like most states, has a governor at the head of the government and an Assembly that makes the laws. The governor is elected for a four-year term. The Assembly is made up of two houses, a Senate and a House of Representatives. The members of both houses are elected for a two-year term. Judges are elected for an eight-year term. The capital is Nashville. There are 95 counties.

There are about 891,000 students attending public elementary and high schools. Among the principal colleges and universities are:

University of Tennessee, at Knoxville. Enrollment, 35,993 men and women in 1971.

Tennessee Agricultural and Industrial State University, at Nashville. Enrollment, 4,750 men and women in 1971.

Tennessee Polytechnic Institute, at Cookeville. Enrollment, 6,044 men and women in 1971.

Memphis State University, at Memphis. Enrollment, 15,542 men and women in 1971.

Vanderbilt University, at Nashville. Enrollment, 5,722 men and women in 1971.

University of Chattanooga, at Chattanooga. Enrollment, 3,447 men and women in 1971.

University of the South, at Sewanee. Enrollment, 906 men in 1971.

East Tennessee State College, at Johnson City. Enrollment, 9,181 men and women in 1971.

Fisk University, at Nashville. Enrollment, 1,140 men and women in 1971.

CHIEF CITIES OF TENNESSEE

The leading cities of Tennessee, with populations from the 1970 census, are:

Memphis, population 623,530. The largest city in the state, a river port and cotton-trading center, on the Mississippi River.

Nashville, population 447,877, the capital and second-largest city, on the Cumberland River, in the center of the state.

Chattanooga, population 119,082, the fourth-largest city, on the Tennessee River, in the southeast.

Knoxville, population 174,587, the third-largest city, livestock and tobacco market, on the Tennessee River, in the east.

TENNESSEE IN THE PAST

The first white man to visit the region of Tennessee, more than four hundred years ago, was Hernando De Soto, a Spanish explorer. In 1769 the first permanent white settlement in the area was founded by William Beane. Several years before that the region had been visited by Daniel Boone, the famous wilderness scout.

During the Revolutionary War, the settlers in Tennessee fought on the American side. They won the important battle of King's Mountain. In 1777 the Tennessee settlements became part of the state of North Carolina. Later North Carolina gave all its western lands to the new United States government. The settlers in this land (Tennessee) called the territory the state of Franklin. In 1789 North Carolina again claimed the land, but the region was finally admitted to the Union in 1796 as the state of Tennessee.

During the War of 1812 soldiers from Tennessee fought under the leadership of Andrew Jackson, who later became the President of the United States. At the beginning of the war the United States government asked for 2,800 men from the state of Tennessee. More than 30,000 men volunteered to fight, and Tennessee got its nickname of the "Volunteer State."

During the Civil War, Tennessee was the last of the southern states to leave the Union, and it was the first to be readmitted to the Union after the war. Many of the war's bloodiest battles were fought in Tennessee, including the battles of Shiloh, Murfreesboro, and Lookout Mountain.

A reproduction of the Parthenon stands in beautiful Centennial Park in Nashville, Tennessee's second-largest city.

Throughout the war many people in Tennessee favored the North rather than the South. One of these was Andrew Johnson, who later became President. Most of East Tennessee favored the North.

Tennessee remained an agricultural state for many years after the Civil War. Since the 1930s, when the United States Government organized the Tennessee Valley Authority, Tennessee has become more of an industrial state.

PLACES TO SEE IN TENNESSEE

Great Smoky Mountains National Park, 231,415 acres in Tennessee, 229,-588 acres in North Carolina, in the southeast. Headquarters at Gatlinburg, 25 miles southeast of Knoxville, on State Highway 71. Resort area, with lakes and scenic mountains.

Reelfoot Lake, 20 miles long, near the Kentucky border and the Mississippi River, in the northwest, on State Highway 78. Formed by earthquakes in 1811–12.

Lookout Mountain, 2,126 feet high, about 10 miles southwest of Chattanooga, in the southeast, on U.S. Route 41. Cable railway to the top of the mountain. Caves and interesting rock formations.

Chickamauga and Chattanooga National Military Park, 1,849 acres in Tennessee, 6,277 acres in Georgia, southeast of Chattanooga, on U. S. Route 11. Civil War Memorial.

Shiloh National Military Park, 3,729 acres, near Savannah, in the south, near U. S. Route 64. Scene of one of the first battles of the Civil War.

The Hermitage, home of Andrew Jackson, near Nashville, in the central part, on U.S. Highway 70N. Formal gardens and excellent example of a Tennessee planter's home.

Cumberland Gap, at the border of Kentucky, Virginia, and Tennessee, in the northeast, on U.S. Route 25E. Natural opening in the mountains through which settlers from the east made their way west.

TENNESSEE. Area, 42,244 square miles. Population (1970 census) 3,923,561. Capital, Nashville. Nickname, the Volunteer State. Motto, Agriculture, Commerce. Flower, iris. Bird, mockingbird. Song, "My Homeland, Tennessee." Admitted to Union, June 1, 1796. Official abbreviation, Tenn.

Tennessee River

The Tennessee River is the most important river that flows into the Ohio River. It is 650 miles long. It is formed by the Holston and French Broad Rivers in northeastern Tennessee, near Knoxville. It flows southwest through eastern Tennessee, across northern Alabama, then north through Tennessee and Kentucky. It empties into the Ohio at Paducah, Kentucky. The Tennessee River drains a basin of more than 40,000 square miles and is an important source of power for several southern states.

For many years the Tennessee was an important transportation route, especially during the Civil War, when the Union army used it for the invasion of the South. Many of that war's important battles were fought along its banks. Since the 1930s the Tennesse Valley Authority has built a series of dams and lakes along the Tennessee, and it has become an open waterway through which steamers pass easily. The most important cities on the Tennessee River are Knoxville and Chattanooga, Tennessee; Decatur, Alabama; and Paducah, Kentucky. Read also the article on the TENNESSEE VALLEY AUTHORITY.

Tennessee Valley Authority

The Tennessee Valley Authority, or TVA, is an agency of the United States government. It was formed in 1933 to develop the natural resources of the Tennessee River and the region through which it flows, called the Tennessee Valley. This valley has an area of almost 41,000 square miles, making it about the size of the state of Ohio, and parts of it lie in seven states—Tennessee, Alabama, Georgia, North Carolina, Kentucky, Virginia, and Mississippi.

The main work of the TVA has been building and managing dams to control floods, aid navigation, and produce power. The TVA has built more than twenty such dams on the Tennessee River and on its main tributaries (small rivers flowing into it). The TVA has bought five other dams that had already been built.

These dams save many millions of dollars each year by preventing floods that used to cause much damage, and by providing new deep-water channels through which larger boats can pass and carry on shipping. At the dams there are great hydro-electric plants, which use water power to make electricity, and the TVA has also built many large coal-burning steam plants to make electricity, so that its total output is about twelve million kilowatts. This has changed many places along the Tennessee from poor farming communities to manufacturing centers.

TVA has developed several other projects. It operates a 25,000 kilowatt experimental nuclear reactor at Oak Ridge. Its chemical plants at Muscle Shoals, Alabama, carry on research in finding better fertilizers for farmers. It has begun work in growing new trees where forests have been cut down for timber. The dams have created new lakes, which have become one of the greatest recreation and vacation areas in the United States. TVA has a program to control malaria.

TVA was first supported by money from the government, but now by selling power it makes enough to support itself. It is governed by a Board of Directors with three members. The chairman and members are chosen by the President of the United States and serve nine-year terms. In 1961, about 17,000 people worked for the TVA, most of them at Knoxville, Chattanooga, and Muscle Shoals.

Tenniel, Sir John

Sir John Tenniel was an English artist who is best-remembered for his illustrations for Lewis Carroll's book *Alice in Wonderland*. He was an illustrator for the famous English humor magazine, *Punch*, for which he worked for fifty years. Tenniel also illustrated Carroll's *Through the Looking-Glass* and many other books. He was born in 1820 and died in 1914.

tennis

Tennis is a game of hitting a ball with a kind of bat called a racket (or racquet). Tennis is popular in most parts of the world. It is played by men, women, and children. Compared to many games, tennis is not very old. It was first invented about seventy-five years ago by an Englishman, Major Walter Wingfield. He called the game lawn tennis. He laid out a court and made rules almost exactly like those used today.

The idea of tennis has been used by different peoples for thousands of years. Among the games played by the ancient Egyptians was one that had to do with hitting a ball with a paddle or racket.

THE COURT

Tennis can be played on almost any kind of smooth, level surface. It can be played indoors or outdoors, in daylight or at night under strong lights. Tennis is played on grass that is smooth and closely cropped, or on sand, clay, cement, wood, or a special composition of finely ground material that is closely packed and rolled. Composition courts are good because they dry out quickly after rain.

A tennis court is 78 feet long and 27 feet wide. A net 3 feet high is stretched across the middle of the length of the court. A line called the *service line* stretches across each half of the court 21 feet behind the net. Another line is drawn halfway between each sideline and stretches from one service line to the other. These lines form four *service courts,* two on each side of the net. This court is for "singles," a game of tennis in which two players oppose each other. For "doubles," in which there are two players on each side, an *alley* 4½ feet wide is added on each side of the tennis court.

The lines of a tennis court are marked with powdered chalk or lime, or are painted on surfaces such as cement, or are marked by white tapes tacked to the court.

THE EQUIPMENT

Tennis balls are 2½ to 2¾ inches in diameter (through the middle). A new tennis ball has lots of bounce, but after some playing the cover becomes worn and smooth and lighter, and the ball is harder to control. In tournaments, new balls are frequently put into play. A tennis racket is a wooden frame in which lamb's gut or nylon cord is crisscrossed tightly.

Most people play tennis wearing sneakers (rubber-soled shoes), but on lawn or

grass courts players often wear half shoes with tiny spikes on the soles.

RULES

An organization called the International Lawn Tennis Federation makes up the rules of tennis. Nearly every country has a national tennis association that is a member of the Federation; in the United States, the association is the U.S. Lawn Tennis Association.

The most important rule in tennis is that the ball must be hit in the air or after one bounce. When a player hits the ball, he must hit it back over the net and into the court. If he hits it into the net or past the sidelines or backlines, he loses the point. If a player does not hit the ball before it has taken a second bounce, he loses the point.

In tennis the play begins when one player *serves* the ball. This player tosses the ball into the air and hits it with his racket. It must go over the net and land in the service court across from where the server is standing. The server stands at his own base line.

The server has two chances on each service. If he does not hit the first ball into the service court, but hits the second ball in, he has made a proper service. If he hits neither ball in, it is a *double fault*, and he loses the point. If he steps over the base line as he serves he has committed a *foot fault* and the service is no good. If the served ball hits the net and drops over it into the service court it is called a *let ball* and does not count.

In a singles match each player serves a game and then the next player serves. In doubles each player serves in turn, a member of one side and then a member of the other side. In doubles also each member of a team must receive service alternately. An important rule in doubles is that if one member of a team has touched the ball with his racket the other may not then hit it.

SCORING

The object in tennis is to win points, games, sets, and matches. Each time the opposing player or side fails to return a ball properly, you score a point. The first point a player or side scores in a game counts 15, the second point 15, and the third point 10. A score of zero, or nothing, is always called "love." This method of scoring dates from long ago and its is simpler to count each point as 1. It takes at least 4 points to win a game, and every game must be won by at least 2 points. If a player leads his opponent by a score of 40-30 (3 points to 2), he wins the game if he wins the next point. If he loses the next point, the score is 40-40, or 3 points each, which in tennis is called *deuce*. After that, the game is won by whichever player or side gets 2 points ahead. When a game ends, the service (right to serve) changes to the other side.

A set is won by the first player or side that wins six games, but a set must be won by at least two games. A set may be won by a score of 6-0 (called "six-love"), 6–1, 6–2, 6–3, or 6–4; but once the score is 5–5 (called "five-all"), the set is not won until one player or side is two games ahead. Games are sometimes won by scores of 19–17 or 23–21 or some other high score.

A match is two of three sets or three sets out of five in men's plays and must be two sets out of three in women's play, and two of three sets in boys' and girls' and junior play.

STROKES

Most tennis players hold the racket in their right hands (except those who are naturally left-handed). The various ways of hitting a tennis ball are called *strokes*. The *forehand* stroke is used when the ball bounces to the side of the body on which the racket is held. The *backhand* stroke is used when the ball bounces on the other side of the body and the racket must be held across the body so as to hit the ball. The *volley* is a stroke used to hit the ball when it is still in the air, before it lands and bounces. The *smash* is a hard stroke used to hit the ball almost straight down so that it will bounce very high when it lands. The *lob* is a stroke that sends the ball in a slow, high loop to the back of the opponents court. It is mostly used when the opponent is close to the net and may not have time to reach the ball after it falls and bounces.

Good players learn to hold the racket at an angle so that it gives the ball a spin and makes it bounce crazily when it lands.

ORGANIZED TENNIS

In the United States and other countries there are many tennis clubs and tournaments. Play is held for men and women in both singles and doubles, for mixed doubles (one man and one woman on each side), for seniors (older men and women), for younger people, and for boys and girls. Each year there are national championship matches. In the United States the singles championships on grass courts are held at the West Side Tennis Club in Forest Hills, Long Island. In England, these matches are held at Wimbledon. Players from foreign countries may enter most national championships. The most important tennis championships are played on grass courts. There are also local and national tournaments played on clay courts, hard courts, and indoors on board floors.

The most important tennis matches are the Davis Cup matches. Each country has a team of several players that play in four singles and one doubles matches in Davis Cup competition. The team that holds the Davis Cup finally plays the team that has won all its matches against all other countries. An American ambassador named Dwight F. Davis gave the Davis Cup in 1900. Only four nations, the United States, England, Australia, and France, have ever won the cup.

Most tennis players are amateurs, which means that they cannot accept cash prizes for winning tournaments or fees for teaching or playing tennis. The Davis Cup and all the national championships are played for by amateurs. There are also professional tennis players. Many of them are teachers who instruct others. Others receive payment for playing matches in stadiums where people pay to watch. The top professionals have usually won amateur championships.

Tennyson, Alfred

Alfred, Lord Tennyson, was a famous English poet of the 19th century who lived about a hundred years ago. During much of his life he was the most popular poet, and for forty-two years he was Poet Laureate, the highest honor for an English poet. Tennyson was born in 1809 and began to write poetry when he was a boy. His first book of poems was published when he was 18 years old. It was called *Poems by Two Brothers*, but it included the work of Tennyson and two of his brothers, Charles and Frederick. Tennyson then went to Trinity College, at Cambridge University. One of his closest friends was a man named Arthur Henry Hallam, who was engaged to be married to Tennyson's sister, Emily. Hallam went to Europe and died there quite suddenly. His death was a great shock to Tennyson, who wrote one of his greatest poems, *In Memoriam,* in memory of Hallam. It took Tennyson seventeen years to finish the poem.

In 1842, when Tennyson was 31 years old, he finished a volume of poems that brought him great fame. It included "Break, Break, Break," "Morte d'Artur," and "Ulysses," as well as some of the poems that had appeared in his earlier books.

TENNYSON AS POET LAUREATE

In 1850 the Poet Laureate, William Wordsworth, died and Tennyson was appointed in his place. Nine years later was published one of his most popular works, *Idylls of the King,* which consisted of poems about King Arthur and his Knights of the Round Table. He dedicated the book to Queen Victoria's husband, Prince Albert, and several years later Victoria honored Tennyson by giving him the title of baron, which made him Lord Tennyson.

During his last years Tennyson wrote more poetry and several plays. He died in 1892, at the age of 81.

tent

A tent is a temporary home or shelter made of a heavy cloth, such as canvas, or of animal skins. A tent may be easily put up and taken down and may be carried from one place to another, though some tents are put up to stand for long periods of time, as in army camps.

Tents are among the earliest homes built by man. Early man usually constructed a rough framework of twigs and stretched animal skins over this. Later, when man learned to weave, he often used cloth instead.

Tents have long been the homes of nomadic peoples, those who wander in search of grazing lands for their flocks and herds. Even today there are parts of the world, such as the deserts of North Africa and Asia, where nomads live in tents. When they move on, they take down their tents, fold the coverings, and carry them to the next place, where the tents are put up again. Some of the tents used by the Arabs are made of very fine woven materials, including silks, and the chiefs (sheikhs) have rich rugs covering the ground inside.

TEPEES AND WIGWAMS

The American Indians were among the best-known users of tents. The Indian tents were called tepees or wigwams. They were almost all covered with the skins of animals such as buffalo and deer, but thin bark was also used. The Indian tent was shaped like an upside-down ice-cream cone. It was made on a framework of long poles joined together at the top. The skins were often decorated with Indian signs and pictures.

ARMY TENTS

Tents have always been associated with armies. Soldiers in campaigns are always on the move and need shelters that can be put up and taken down easily and quickly. In army camps today there are usually wooden or stone barracks for the men, but in addition there are often tents that hold four or five soldiers each.

The best-known army tent is the pyramid tent. It has four triangular (three-cornered) sides that come to a point at the top. Below each triangular side is a flap that drapes to the ground. A pyramid tent is erected with a set of poles from which the canvas hangs. The four corners of the tent are firmly tied to stakes driven into the ground. Ropes attached to the sides and corners of the tent are tied to pegs in the ground and stretched to make the tent hold its shape. The flaps may be rolled up in good weather to give the tent more light and air, and they may be dropped and tied securely during cold or rainy weather. Some pyramid tents are built over board flooring.

PUP TENTS

When an army is on the march or in battle, soldiers usually carry "shelter halves." Each soldier carries a rectangular (four-sided) piece of canvas that folds up into a small bundle. Each soldier's shelter half can be buttoned to another soldier's shelter half to form what is called a "pup tent." This kind of tent is very small but has room for two soldiers to stretch out on the ground to sleep. Two small poles, one at each end of the tent, hold up the buttoned shelter halves. Short ropes are attached to pegs in the ground to hold the tent securely. Boy Scouts and others who go on overnight hikes use pup tents.

LARGE TENTS

Tents range in size from the small pup tents to the great circus tents that cover an area large enough to hold several thousand people at one time. These tents are made of a very strong canvas called duck. Almost as much fun as watching the circus itself is watching the workers put up and take down the circus tents. They are hung from tall poles that must be firmly anchored in the ground and held by chains stretching in several directions. Then great spreads of canvas are pulled up to the tops of the poles, where they are attached by chains. The men then spread the canvas in all directions. Stakes are pounded into the ground and ropes are tied from the edges of the canvas to the stakes. The largest tent carried by a circus is called "the big top." Often there are smaller tents for sideshows, refreshment booths, and temporary living quarters. Perhaps the most important thing

about a tent is that it be waterproofed. No tent would be any good if at the first rain the people inside got wet. Closely woven canvas ducks can hold water out indefinitely. Only when small tears occur does a good duck tent begin to leak. With the invention of materials such as nylon, tents have been made that are lighter but more waterproof.

termite

Termites are insects that look like ants. They are social insects, as ants and bees are. That is, they live in groups or colonies and each member of the colony has its own particular duties to perform.

Termites are often called "white ants," but they are a separate group of insects and their bodily form is quite different from that of the true ant. True ants have bodies in three distinct sections, whereas a termite has a body made up of a series of rings.

Termites cause a lot of damage. They burrow through hard, dry wood, eating as they go but never touching the outside layer. Finally the wood is a hollow, thin shell that can easily be crushed. Entire buildings have collapsed because termites had hollowed out the beams of the foundation without being detected.

In forests, termites are useful because they hollow out the bases of dead, dried trees. They cause the trees to fall down, where the moisture of the ground and the work of other insects can make the wood disintegrate and return to the soil. This process enriches the earth of the forest and helps other plants to grow.

A colony of termites lives in much the same fashion as a colony of ants. There is a queen, which lays the eggs and which is cared for by worker termites. Soldier termites guard the nest. The life of the termite is very much like the life of a colony of ants, as described in the article on ANT.

Termites in tropical regions often build large, high hills that are the skyscrapers of the insect world. Some have been found that were as much as twenty feet high and covered several square feet at the base. These strange buildings are built with grains of sand, carried one at a time by the workers and cemented together by the insects' saliva, which has a gluelike quality. When this "cement" dries and hardens it often becomes so strong that even a pickaxe can scarcely break it down. A termite house is called a *termitary*.

Some tropical natives eat termites. This seems strange to some Americans, but dried and roasted termites are considered both nourishing and delicious in many parts of the tropics. There are some tribes that eat the insects raw.

tern

The tern is a bird related to the gull. It lives on seashores and eats fish from the ocean. The most remarkable tern is the Arctic tern, which is the champion long-distance migrator of all the birds. It spends the summer at breeding grounds near the North Pole and travels 22,000 miles to the Antarctic to spend the winter.

Terns usually nest in colonies. That is, many of them make nests on the same sandy beach. The nests are merely shallow holes in the sand. Terns dive under

the surface of the ocean water to catch the small fish that are their main food.

One kind of tern makes no nest at all, but deposits its single egg on a tree branch, where it balances until it is hatched.

terra cotta

Terra cotta is baked clay, made the way pottery is made and used chiefly for sculpture (such as statues and ornamented panels and vases) instead of for dishes. Terra cotta is also used for tiles. It is usually red in color, which comes from the iron in the clay that is used. Many fine works of art were made of terra cotta in prehistoric times, before men carved statues from marble or molded them of metals. The artist would mold his statue or pictured panel in the clay while it was soft and then it would be "fired" (baked). As with other pottery, terra cotta will last for a very long time, many thousands of years. You can read more about how it is made in the article on POTTERY.

terramycin
one of the antibiotic drugs, first announced in 1950 and since used with great success to treat pneumonia and other diseases: see ANTIBIOTICS.

terrapin

A terrapin is a kind of turtle that lives in the sea. Usually the name means the diamond-back terrapin that is found in the shallow coastal waters of the Atlantic Ocean off the coast of the United States. This terrapin is considered very fine as food but usually is very expensive. See the article on TURTLE.

territory

A territory is a division of the United States. It is like a state but does not have many rights and powers that a state has. Most of the states of the United States were territories before they became states. In 1912, Congress made states of all the regions that were still territories, except for Alaska and Hawaii. Puerto Rico was later made a territory.

A territory is headed by a governor, but usually he is appointed by the President of the United States and not elected by the people of the territory. The people do elect their own legislature, or law-making body, which makes the local laws for the territory. They do not have the right to vote for President of the United States. A territory may send one delegate, or representative, to the House of Representatives in Washington, and he may speak on matters that concern the territory, but he may not vote. A territory does not have any representative in the United States Senate. The affairs of territories are controlled by the Office of Territories, a branch of the Department of the Interior.

tetanus

Tetanus is a serious disease that is caused by a tiny germ. The germ lives in the intestines of horses, cattle, and other animals that eat grass. If a person gets a deep wound from stepping on a rusty nail, the wound may become infected with tetanus germs that were on the nail.

When a person gets tetanus he de-

velops painful spasms of the jaw muscles. For this reason the disease is sometimes called "lockjaw." Muscle spasms may occur in other parts of the body and often the disease is so serious that the person dies. Fortunately, a person can be inoculated with a substance that protects him against getting tetanus. Any person who gets a deep wound should go to a doctor, who can decide whether he should have an injection. Most babies receive injections that protect them against tetanus.

Texas

Texas is a state in the southwest of the United States. Its nickname is the "Lone Star State" because its state flag has one star in it. It gets its name from an Indian word, *tejas,* which means "friend."

Texas leads the nation in petroleum (oil) output. It is second only to California in the value of its farm products and leads the nation in the production of cotton, beef, and wool.

Until Alaska became a state in 1959, Texas had been the largest state in area for more than a hundred years; its 267,·339 square miles make it bigger than most of the world's independent countries. It is more than 750 miles from north to south and 800 miles from east to west. Now it ranks second in area among the states. In population it ranks fourth, with about eleven million people living there. It became a state in 1845, and was the twenty-eighth state admitted to the United States. For nine years before that it had been recognized as an independent republic. Texas still has the right to divide itself into five states if its people want to. The capital is Austin.

THE PEOPLE OF TEXAS

The earliest settlers in Texas were Spaniards. In the 1800s, English-speaking people from the southern states began to settle in Texas, and about a hundred years ago many immigrants from Ireland, Germany, France, and other European countries settled there. The foreign-born population is made up mostly of Mexicans, with some Italians, Germans, and Russians. There are about one million Negroes in Texas.

Most of the people in Texas live in and around the big cities, where there are huge petroleum-refining plants, meat-packing plants, and factories making many things. Texas has huge ranches and is first in the number of beef and dairy cattle raised. It is also first in sheep raising and wool production, and it ranks among the leading states in the growing of cotton, grain, fruits, vegetables, and rice.

Many Texans work in mines and oil fields. Texas leads all other states in the value of its minerals, especially oil, sulfur, asphalt, and magnesium. It has about 50% of the nation's crude oil and natural gas reserves.

The people of Texas belong to many different Churches. The largest are the Baptists, Methodists, and Presbyterians. Many of the people who live near the Mexican border are Roman Catholics.

WHAT TEXAS IS LIKE

Texas is so large that it includes many different kinds of land and climate. There are mountains, fertile plains, desert lands, rolling hills, and sandy beaches. Eastern Texas, along the shore of the Gulf of Mexico, is part prairie and part forest. Some of the oilfields and many coal mines are in this region.

Central Texas is part of the Great Plains. Cotton, wheat and livestock are grown here. The northern part of central Texas is the most heavily populated and has the most oil wells.

Southwestern Texas is a high, flat region in which there are some foothills of the Rocky Mountains. There are many large ranches in this area, and irrigation has made the growing of cotton and some grains possible. Northwest Texas is the most barren part of the state, but there are valuable mineral deposits in the mountains.

The climate in Texas is almost tropical in the southwest and is moderate in the northerly sections. The best climate is found along the Gulf of Mexico, where the sandy beaches have become favorite vacation spots. Northern Texas often has severe winters, with much snow, while southern Texas is always warm. The average temperature in Texas in the summer is about 83 degrees and in the winter about 48 degrees.

Texas has several important rivers. The most famous is the Rio Grande, which forms part of the border between the United States and Mexico. Others are the Red, the Brazos, and the Colorado (which is not the same as the Colorado River farther west). Most of these rivers flow east into the Gulf of Mexico. Texas has more miles of railroad than any other state in the country, yet there are some sections that are not touched by railroads. There are almost 200,000 miles of highways and there are airports in all the major cities and many of the more remote areas.

Texas has few natural seaports, but it has built many excellent harbors, including those at Houston and Galveston.

THE GOVERNMENT OF TEXAS

Texas, like other states, has a governor at the head of the government. He is elected for a two-year term. The laws are made by a legislature composed of two houses, a Senate and a House of Representatives. The members of the Senate are elected for four-year terms, the members of the House for two-year terms. Judges are elected for six-year terms. The capital is Austin. There are 254 counties.

There are almost three million pupils enrolled in the public elementary and high schools. Among the leading colleges, universities, and other schools of higher learning are:

University of Texas, at Austin. Enrollment, 62,275 men and women in 1971.

Agricultural and Mechanical College of Texas (Texas A. & M.), at College Station. Enrollment, 12,778 men in 1971.

Arlington State College, at Arlington. Enrollment, 13,869 men and women in 1971.

Texas Southern University, at Houston. Enrollment, 4,306 men and women in 1971.

North Texas State University, at Denton. Enrollment, 14,397 men and women in 1971.

Texas Technological College, at Lubbock. Enrollment, 18,500 men and women in 1971.

Texas Woman's University, at Denton. Enrollment, 4,901 women in 1971.

Texas Western College (a division of University of Texas), at El Paso. Enrollment, 10,485 men and women in 1971.

Among the leading private colleges and universities are:

Southern Methodist University, at Dallas. Enrollment, 9,360 men and women in 1971.

Rice University, at Houston. Enrollment, 3,123 men and women in 1971.

Texas Christian University, at Fort Worth. Enrollment, 6,080 men and women in 1971.

Hardin-Simmons University, at Abilene. Enrollment, 1,617 men and women in 1971.

Baylor University, at Waco. Enrollment, 6,704 men and women in 1971.

University of Houston, at Houston. Enrollment, 23,186 men and women in 1971.

CHIEF CITIES IN TEXAS

The leading cities of Texas, with populations from the 1970 census, are:

Houston, population 1,232,802, the largest city in the state. There is a separate article on HOUSTON.

Dallas, population 844,401, the second-largest city. There is a separate article on DALLAS.

San Antonio, population 654,153, the third-largest city. There is a separate article on SAN ANTONIO.

Fort Worth, population 393,476, the fourth-largest city. There is a separate article on FORT WORTH.

El Paso, population 322,261, the fifth-largest city, transportation and trade center, on the Mexican border, at the extreme western point of the state.

Austin, population 251,808, the capital and sixth-largest city. There is a separate article on AUSTIN.

Corpus Christi, population 204,525, seventh-largest city, naval air-training base and oil-refining center, on southeastern coast.

Amarillo, population 127,010, ninth-largest city, in northern Panhandle region, center of wheat and oil-producing area.

Lubbock, population 149,101, eighth-largest city, in Great Plains area of west Texas, center of agricultural and oil-producing region.

Beaumont, population 115,919, tenth-largest city, an oil-refining center and an inland port near the Gulf of Mexico.

TEXAS IN THE PAST

Spanish explorers traveled along the coast of Texas for the first time almost 450 years ago. In 1685 the French explorer La Salle founded a small settlement in eastern Texas. Soon after that the Spaniards founded several settlements, the most important of which is now San Antonio.

In the early 1800s the United States and Spain argued about the boundary between their possessions, and the Sabine

River was agreed upon. In 1821 Mexico won its independence from Spain and Texas became a state in the new Mexican Republic. Increasing numbers of people from the United States settled in Texas until Mexico passed laws that tried to stop them from coming in.

In 1835 the Texans, led by men such as Stephen Austin and Sam Houston, began to fight for their independence from Mexico. In 1836 Texas won its independence and set up its own republic, with the Lone Star flag and with Sam Houston as the first president.

Texas remained a republic for nine years and then, in 1845, was annexed by the United States.

In 1846 the United States went to war with Mexico because of continued troubles about the boundary of Texas. In 1848, after the Mexicans had been defeated, the boundary was set at the Rio Grande, and the United States received additional territory from Mexico that later became part of several other western states.

The question of slavery was long an important issue in Texas. Many of the northern states did not want Texas to become part of the Union, because it permitted slavery. In the Civil War Texas fought on the side of the South and furnished many supplies to the Southern troops. Texas was readmitted to the Union in 1870.

Since the Civil War, Texas has grown rapidly. Its size and the richness of its soil and natural resources have made it one of the most prosperous states in the nation. Its most rapid growth came after the discovery of oil in 1901.

PLACES TO SEE IN TEXAS

The Alamo, in San Antonio, in the southeast, on U.S. Route 81. The "Cradle of Texas Liberty."

Big Bend National Park, 691,978 acres, 50 miles south of Marathon, in the southwestern part, on State Highway 227. Desert and mountain scenery. Indian relics.

San Jacinto Battlefield Monument and

"Remember the Alamo" carried Texans to victory at San Jacinto 46 days later. The monument is 22 miles southeast of Houston.

Museum State Park, 10 miles east of Houston, in the southeast, on State Highway 134. A 570-foot monument and historic battlefield.

King Ranch, nearly 1,000,000 acres, around Kingsville, in southeastern part, on U.S. Route 77. Largest ranch in the world.

Southwestern Exposition and Fat Stock Show (each year in March), at Fort Worth, in east central part, on U.S. Route 377. World championship riding and roping contests. Cattle exhibition.

Texas State Fair (each year in October), at Dallas, in east central part, on U.S. Route 67. Rodeos and livestock exhibitions.

TEXAS. Area, 267,339 square miles. Population (1970 census) 11,196,730. Capital Austin. Nickname, The Lone Star State. Motto, Friendship. Flower, bluebonnet. Bird, mockingbird. Song, "Texas, Our Texas." Admitted to Union, December 29, 1845. Official abbreviation, Tex.

textiles

All kinds of cloth and other materials woven from threads and fibers are called textiles. The textile industry is one of the world's oldest. The ancient Assyrians and Babylonians used much cotton, as did the Greeks and Romans. The Greeks also kept herds or flocks of sheep and from the wool of these animals they made woolen cloth. Thousands of years ago the Chinese were making fine silk cloth from the fibers spun by silkworms.

The art of making textiles or weaving cloth did not originate in any one place. In many different parts of the world people learned to make cloth without knowing that other people were also doing it. The need for clothing, and for textiles for other uses, made it necessary for people to learn to make these things.

KINDS OF TEXTILES

Textiles are generally classified by the kind of fiber they are made from. The best-known are wool, cotton, linen, and silk. In recent years, plastic fibers such as rayon and nylon have become almost as important as natural fibers. Often the fibers are combined. The Americans in colonial times wove a textile called linsey-woolsey, which was made of both linen and wool. There are combinations of silk and wool, cotton and wool, silk and rayon, wool and nylon, and so on.

Textiles are divided according to weave. There are fine, thin weaves and heavy, thick weaves. There are open and tight weaves. There are smooth weaves and rough weaves. There are plain weaves and fancy weaves. The kind of weave does not depend on the kind of fiber used. We usually think of wool as a rough, heavy material, but wool can be woven into very thin cloth. The weave depends on the fineness (thinness) of the thread and the number of threads to the inch.

Not all textiles are made by weaving. One other way is by knitting. Still another way is by felting. (Felt is made by matting the fibers together.)

DYEING AND PRINTING

Textiles may be bought in many colors and patterns. After a thread has been spun and cleaned it may be bleached to make

it white or dyed to make it any color. Sometimes threads of one color are used to weave a solid-colored textile, and sometimes threads of different colors are mixed to weave a pattern.

Other textiles are given their color and design by printing. The printing of cloth is almost the same as the printing of paper. Ink rollers cover a plate that has the pattern or design on it, and the ink is transferred to the textile. There are other ways of transferring patterns or designs to textiles. One way is described in the article BATIK.

TEXTILE CENTERS

The manufacture of textiles has grown up in some places much more than in others. In some cases crops such as cotton or flax were grown near these places and furnished an abundance of fibers. In other cases there was easy transportation from the cotton markets (as in Liverpool and Manchester in England) or cheap water power from rivers and streams, as in many New England towns.

Over the years the English became famous for fine woolens, the Belgians for linens, the French and Italians for their fine silks, and the Chinese also for silk fabrics. In modern times there is not much difference between the quality of textiles manufactured in one place and another.

TEXTILE STANDARDS

Textiles that look good to the average person may not actually be strong, fine, and useful. Therefore governments have set up standards by which textiles are graded. The standards state how strong a textile must be, how it must resist fading and shrinkage, and how long it should last. Government laboratories and manufacturers constantly test textiles to see that they meet all the standards.

There are separate articles on COTTON, SILK, WOOL, LINEN, WEAVING, BATIK and other subjects connected with textiles.

Thackeray, W. M.

William Makepeace Thackeray was an English writer who lived about a hundred dred years ago. Next to Charles Dickens, he was considered the greatest English novelist of his time. He was born in 1811 in Calcutta, India, of English parents, and studied at Trinity College

of Cambridge University. He traveled in Europe, then studied law for a time, but soon turned to writing for various London magazines. He continued as a writer for the rest of his life. He died in 1863. His novels *Vanity Fair* and *Henry Esmond* are among the greatest in English literature. Other famous novels by Thackeray are *Pendennis, The Newcomes,* and *The Virginians* (a sequel to *Henry Esmond*).

Thailand

Thailand is a kingdom in southeast Asia on the Indochinese and Malay peninsulas. Through most of its history Thailand was called Siam. The people call

call themselves *Thai*, which in their language means "the free people." In 1949 the Thai government changed the name of the country to Thailand.

Thailand has an area of about 200,148 square miles, which is not quite as large as Texas. Its population is thirty-five million. When compared to other Asian countries, Thailand's population is quite low.

THE PEOPLE OF THAILAND

The People of Thailand belong to the Mongoloid race, which includes Asian and Japanese people. Mongoloids often have straight black hair, light brown or yellow skin, and brown eyes. The first Thais came from southwestern China and reached Thailand in the 6th century. Besides these original settlers, Chinese, Malays, Cambodians, Indians, and several tribal groups live in Thailand.

Thailanders are an independent and courageous people, and there are no caste divisions in Thailand. All the people, including the women, have equal rights. Thailand is a very musical country, although its music sometimes sounds strange to American ears, and the people are fine dancers.

Thailanders are also noted for their artistic abilities, ranging from the making of jewelry to the architecture of the beautiful Buddhist temples. There are many religious festivals in Thailand, with colorful costumes and ceremonies.

The people speak the Siamese language, which is a member of the Indochinese family of languages. Most of the people follow the Buddhist religion, but there are some Moslems, Christians, and Hindus.

HOW THE PEOPLE LIVE

Thailand is largely a nation of farmers, fishermen, and lumbermen. The principal foods of the people are rice and fish. Nearly all of the farm land is planted in rice. In addition to the large quantities eaten by the people, Thailand exports surplus rice to Asian countries. Other Three-fifths of Thailand is covered with forests from which come the country's famous teakwood, as well as bamboo, ebony,

rosewood, boxwood, and palmyra palm. The forests also provide lac, a resin deposited on trees by the lac insect, rubber, oils, and dyes.

Thailand's most important mineral resource is tin. Thailand helps to supply the world with tin. Other useful minerals include iron, tungsten, gold, lignite, and gypsum, but these have not been found in large amounts. Industry in Thailand is limited. Thailand hopes that the Yanhee Dam, built in 1964, will encourage industry by supplying it with cheap electrical power.

WHAT THAILAND IS LIKE

Thailand can be divided into four geographical regions. In the north are mountain ranges and deep valleys in which are the sources of Thailand's principal river, the Chao Phraya. The mountains are covered with forests of teak and evergreens. In central Thailand is the plain of the Chao Phraya. This is the most densely populated region, and it has the best farm land. In the east is the Khorat Plateau, a high, stony plain, where cattle, hogs, buffaloes and horses are raised. The fourth region of Thailand is the part that lies on the Malay Peninsula, which is mountainous and contains the principal tin and other mineral deposits.

The climate of Thailand is tropical. It is governed largely by the monsoon, a wind that blows from the southwest from May to November, bringing a warm, rainy season, and from the northeast from November to March, bringing a dry and cooler season. The months of April and May, between the monsoon seasons, are the hottest of the year.

Thailand has many wild and strange animals, including more than a thousand varieties of brightly colored birds. It is famous for the elephant, which is the national symbol of the country and is protected by law. The so-called white elephant (which is really a lighter shade of gray) is considered sacred. A favorite animal from Thailand is the Siamese cat.

The largest city and capital is Bangkok. A modern city located 25 miles inland from the ocean at the delta of the Menam River, Bangkok is the financial, cultural, and social center. International airlines, linking Asia with the entire world, stop at Don Muang airport in Bangkok. See BANGKOK.

THE GOVERNMENT

In 1932 Thailand's absolute monarchy was changed. The government was set up to be a constitutional monarchy, which greatly limited the king's power. The prime minister and his cabinet were to have the real authority, and the people were to elect officials to represent them. But military leaders, rather than the people, gained control. After several changes in military rule, this constitution was suspended. A new constitution, providing for an appointed Senate, an elected House, and a prime minister, was written in 1968. In 1971 another military group governed. After students demonstrated for a return to constitutional government, this military group resigned in 1973. Thailand's King Bhumibol named a non-military person to be prime minister. The country is divided into changwats or provinces. Each changwat is governed by an appointed official.

Everyone between the ages of 7 and 15 must go to school. Thailand has elementary and high school level schools. Thailand also has 9 universities, 31 teacher colleges, many training schools, and military, naval, and police academies. About 70 percent of the people can read and write.

THAILAND IN THE PAST

In ancient times Thailand was a land of independent city-states. These were usually at war with the Mongols and the Burmese. The greatest of the city-states was Ayutthaya, which became strong in the 1300s and won much territory from neighboring states. Marco Polo visited Ayutthaya, and many other Europeans came to trade with the Siamese, including Dutch, English, and French. After four hundred years of prosperity, Ayutthaya was invaded and conquered by the Burmese, in 1767.

Another city-state arose at Thonburi, and in 1782 a Thai king arose who was the founder of the present Thailand dynasty, or family of kings. He was Rama I, and he established Bangkok as his capital. During the 1800s European nations were establishing claims to territories all around Thailand. The king was forced to give up Laos and Cambodia to France, and parts of the Malay Peninsula to Great Britain, but Thailand never gave up its independence.

RECENT HISTORY

In 1932, in a bloodless revolution, the king was forced to grant the people a constitution. In World War II, Thailand sided with Japan and retook parts of Laos and Cambodia, but lost these territories again after the war.

Modern ways have been introduced into Thailand, but the ancient customs still persist, so that an up-to-date airport may be reached by a road that runs between farms worked by buffaloes.

Thailand joined the United Nations in 1946. In 1955 Bangkok became the headquarters of the SOUTHEAST ASIA TREATY ORGANIZATION, about which there is a separate article. It bound Thailand, the Philippines, Pakistan and other countries in an alliance to block Communist aggression.

THAILAND. Area, 200,148 square miles. Population (1974 estimate) 35,340,000. Capital, Bangkok (population 1,608,305). Language, Siamese. Religion, Buddhist. Government, constitutional monarchy. Monetary unit, the baht or tical, worth about 5 cents (U.S.). Flag, horizontal stripes of red, white, blue, white, and red, the blue stripes being twice as wide as the others.

Thames

The Thames is the chief river of England. It is 210 miles long. It begins as four streams—the Thames or Isis, the Churn, the Coln, and the Leach. All rise in the Cotswold Hills. They join, and the Thames flows east and south across central England, through London, and empties into the North Sea. Before it reaches London, the Thames flows through a farming region that was the first part of England to be settled.

The Thames is one of the busiest rivers in the world. Barges carry goods along

CHINA

BURMA

LAOS

N. VIETNAM

CAMBODIA

S. VIETNAM

MALAYSIA

much of its length. Canals join the Thames with other rivers, making a great network of waterways that covers much of England.

The city of London is on both sides of the Thames. Ships from all over the world sail up the Thames to dock at London. Fifteen bridges cross the Thames at London. Famous ones are London Bridge, Westminster Bridge, Waterloo Bridge, and Tower Bridge. Some of London's most famous buildings and finest mansions are on the banks of the Thames.

In Connecticut there is a Thames River that empties into Long Island Sound at the city of New London. Boat races are held there each summer. In Ontario there is a Thames River that flows past London, Ontario, and empties into Lake St. Clair (between Lakes Huron and Erie). During the War of 1812, General William Henry Harrison and an American army won a victory over the British on the banks of this Thames River. The battle was fought on October 5, 1813, and lasted only about fifteen minutes. Harrison had about 8,000 men, the British about 2,000 including 1,200 Indians. Harrison captured 600 men and routed the rest.

Thanksgiving

Thanksgiving Day is one of the best-loved holidays observed in the United States. It was begun more than three hundred years ago by the Pilgrims who had come in the Mayflower to Massachusetts in 1620. When they harvested their first crops and saw that the earth of their new home had been good to them, they prepared a feast and gave thanks to God for what they had received. This Thanksgiving Day in 1621 was the first in America.

From time to time after that, the colonists would set aside a day for giving thanks in much the same way. The first officially proclaimed Thanksgiving Day was in Massachusetts in 1631. President Abraham Lincoln was the first President to proclaim Thanksgiving Day. He named the last Thursday in November as Thanksgiving Day, and so did each President after him, and the governors of the states, until 1939, when President Franklin D. Roosevelt proclaimed the fourth Thursday in November as Thanksgiving Day. He did this to give retail stores a longer "Christmas buying season." At first some states continued to observe the last Thursday, but in 1941 Congress passed a law declaring the fourth Thursday in November as the national holiday. Canada observes Thanksgiving on the second Monday in October.

theater

A theater is any place (usually a building) used for the presentation of plays and other types of dramatic or entertaining performances. These performances are presented before a gathering of viewers or listeners called an audience. The article on DRAMA tells about the kinds of entertainment in theaters.

The kind of theater building used today has been in use for only four or five hundred years, though other kinds of theater date back more than 2,500 years. Even during the past fifty years theaters have changed a great deal, largely due to the development of modern equipment.

The important parts of a theater are the stage on which the performance is given; the dressing rooms "backstage" (usually to the side of the stage and behind it); the curtains that separate the stage from the audience; the seating arrangement for the audience, usually on several different levels; the theater lobby, into which the main entrance from the street leads; the box-office, usually a small room in the lobby in which tickets are sold; and various lighting and sound equipment throughout the theater building. The modern theater has borrowed different things from the theaters of the past.

THEATERS OF THE PAST

The earliest theaters in the Western World were those of the ancient Greeks, about 2,500 years ago. At first their plays, dances and religious celebrations were presented outdoors, in places somewhat like a modern football stadium. The audience sat on a hillside, and the performance took place at the bottom of the hill, which came to be called the dancing-circle, or orchestra. Later the Greeks added a hut, or small building, in which the performers put on their masks or costumes. In time this building came to serve also as background scenery for the play, and finally a raised platform was built, so that the performers no longer worked at ground level.

The ancient Romans made this kind of theater more elaborate. The platform was raised even more. The most important officials were now seated in the orchestra and were separated from the platform by a curtain. The hut grew into a large building, usually decorated with high columns. This was the theater of two thousand years ago.

During the next thousand years the Christian Church became very powerful, and it discouraged any performances that did not deal with religion. Therefore religious plays and entertainments became popular, and they were suitable for presentation in a church. The altar area at the front of the church served as the stage. Later the performances became longer and more elaborate, so they were given on a simple platform stage on the church porch or in the church courtyard.

About six hundred years ago, plays on nonreligious subjects began to be written again. The stage was moved from the churchyard to the marketplace in the center of town. Actors began to form companies that traveled in wagons and used one of the large wagons as a stage.

The next permanent theaters were built in Italy in the early 1500s. They had stages that were separated from the audience by an arch called the proscenium. Large painted pictures were used for backgrounds, and later a few mechanical devices were used to show thunder, lightning, and other effects.

The theaters in England were much simpler. Plays were put on in the courtyards of public inns, and the first permanent theater was not built until 1576. The most famous English theater of this time was the GLOBE THEATER, about which there is a separate article. The most famous designer of theaters was a man called Inigo Jones, who lived about 1600. He introduced movable scenery and a curtain that rose and fell instead of being drawn to the sides.

The modern organization of a theater dates from the early 1800s. There is a director, who is in charge of the actors and actresses; a producer, who provides the money needed to put on the play and is in charge of the theater and everyone connected with the play; a stage manager, who is in charge of costumes, properties (such as furniture), scenery, lighting, and sound; stagehands, who put the stage in order; a set designer, who designs the scenery; and specialists in makeup, costumes, lighting, and all the other things that the actors need.

The first theaters in the United States were built in the 1760s in New York City and Philadelphia, Pennsylvania. New York City soon became the country's theatrical center.

As early as 1812 a theater was built in London, England, that could seat an audience of more than 3,000 persons, but today the average theater in the United States seats about 1,000 to 1,500 persons.

THE STAGE OF TODAY

In most theaters today the stage is a platform shaped like a rectangle and raised about five feet above the floor where the first row of the audience is seated. Between the stage and the audience is the proscenium arch, which is somewhat like a picture frame. The parts of the stage at each end of the proscenium are called *wings*. Above the proscenium is an area called the *fly gallery*, where scenery and lighting equipment are raised and lowered by wires or ropes.

A person standing in the center of the stage and facing the audience can move in any of four directions: *upstage*, or away from the audience; *downstage*, or toward the audience; *right*, which is to his right (and the audience's left); or *left*, to his left (the audience's right). He may leave the stage through either wing, or through the back.

STAGECRAFT

Stagecraft is a term that refers to the arts of designing scenery and of stage lighting. Until about fifty years ago, scenery consisted of a painted background called a *backdrop*. This showed a village street or a mountain scene or some other background.

The backdrops, which are also called *flats*, were too flat to look real. At first, scenery was made to look more realistic by painting in perspective (the sense of distance). Then furnishings exactly like those in a house, or realistic models of outdoor scenery, were put on the stage. The beauty of the "sets" came to be almost as great an attraction as the play.

In the old outdoor theaters, performances were usually given during the day. The early indoor performances were lighted by candles, and later by oil or gas lamps. Some of these were overhead lights, but there was always a row of bright *footlights* around the front of the stage. When electric lighting was invented, the same overhead lights and footlights were used, plus *spotlights*, lights that shine on certain actors or parts of the stage to stress their importance.

The lighting of the stage has changed greatly in recent years. Lighting is more indirect. Different colors and angles are used for different effects. Lighting can contribute a great deal to the audience's understanding of the performance.

PRODUCING A PLAY

After a producer has selected a play he must get enough money to put it on. He does this by inviting people interested in the theater to invest money. These investors are called "backers" or "angels" and there may be from ten to thirty of them for one show. This money will pay for renting a theater, supplying the scenery, paying the actors and backstage crew, advertising the production, and other things. Much of this work will be handled by the business manager.

Then contracts for a theater must be signed. Arrangements must be made for tryout performances out-of-town. The scenic designer's plans must be accepted and scenery-building begin. Various unions must approve the arrangements. Equipment must be obtained and hauled to the theater.

Then the producer, director and playwright select the cast and rehearsals begin.

ACTING GROUPS

There have always been groups of actors working together in companies. During the past fifty years several kinds have developed in the United States.

The *summer-stock* company sets itself up in a place near a popular summer vacation resort. It puts on a certain number of plays throughout the summer. It hires one or two big stars each season to attract a large audience, and also hires many inexperienced young actors. Many stars got their early training in summer stock.

The *repertory* company specializes in certain plays, often plays of historical or literary interest. The plays it presents are its *repertory*.

Another kind of group is the *little theater group*. It specializes in putting on plays that interest a relatively small number of people and therefore are not produced on Broadway. Some of the little theater groups, such as the Provincetown Players of New York City, are also summer-stock companies.

Though many Americans are interested in drama, the United States is one of the few countries that does not have a national theater, that is, a government-supported theater. Several groups of actors have tried to begin a national theater. The most important of these is the American National Theater Association, called ANTA.

ANTA was created by an Act of Congress in 1935. It is supported not by government funds but by money paid for its own performances and by its 2,000 paying members. It was set up mainly to encourage the building of theaters outside New York City, to found a theater school, and to train young people who are interested in the theater. It has sponsored several series of plays in New York City. It also serves as a center of information on the theater, for both the United States and other countries.

Thebes

Thebes was the name of two famous cities of the ancient world, one in Egypt and the other in Greece.

Thebes in Egypt was on the banks of the Nile River. It became one of the most important cities of the world about four thousand years ago, when it was made the capital of Egypt. For several hundred years it was the home of the Egyptian pharaohs (kings) and was more splendid and beautiful than any other city. Thebes was the center of worship for the Egyptian god Amon-Rā and had many fine temples, statues, and tombs. The modern villages of Luxor and Karnak, in Egypt, lie in the area of the old city. The greatest temple was the temple of Pharaoh Amenophis III, built at Karnak, more than 1,500 years before the birth of Jesus. The famous tomb of the king Tut-ankh-amen was also near Thebes, in the great valley of the Tombs of the Kings. The great age of Egypt ended more than 2,500 years ago. Thebes was captured in turn by Nubians, Assyrians, Persians, and Romans, and finally ceased to exist.

THEBES IN GREECE

The city of Thebes in Greece still exists. It is near Athens. About 12,500 people live there. In ancient days it was the capital of Boeotia, an ancient region in central Greece. In the 7th century B.C., Thebes became head of the Boeotian League, a group of cities in Boeotia that were allies in war. Thebes was long an enemy of Athens. It was conquered by King Philip of Macedon in 338. Two years later it rebelled against Philip's son, Alexander the Great, who had become king. As a warning to other Greek cities not to rebel against him, Alexander destroyed Thebes completely.

Thebes is mentioned in many of the legends about ancient Greece, and in the play *Seven Against Thebes* by Sophocles.

Themistocles

Themistocles was a great Greek statesman and general in the ancient city-state of Athens, more than 2,500 years ago. He was born about the year 525 B.C. Themistocles became the leader of the democratic party in Athens. He defeated his political rival, Aristides, and became the most powerful citizen of Athens. At that time Athens was fighting Persia. Themistocles led the Athenian navy to victory over the Persians at Salamis, in 480 B.C. Ten years later he lost his power and was exiled (forced to leave the country). He went to Persia, where he was honored by the Persian King Artaxerxes. He died about 460 B.C.

Theocritus

Theocritus was a poet of ancient Greece. He lived about 2,300 years ago. Very little is known about his life, but he is considered as the first poet to write pastoral poetry, poems about people in the country and their way of life. His style and form of writing were later imitated by such great writers as the Latin poet Virgil and the English poet Edmund Spenser.

thermometer

A thermometer is an instrument for measuring the temperature of something —that is, how hot or cold it is. A thermometer does not measure the amount of heat in anything. As explained in the articles on HEAT and TEMPERATURE, there is a lot of difference between the two. A big piece of metal that is barely warm may have much more heat in it than a small piece of metal that is red hot, but the red-hot piece has a much higher temperature. The thermometer measures this temperature in units called degrees, just as a ruler measures distance in units called inches.

The principle of a thermometer is quite simple. As substances become hotter, they expand (grow larger); as they become colder they contract (become smaller). The most familiar thermometer is a glass tube with a liquid, usually colored alcohol or mercury, inside. Heat makes the liquid expand and fill more of the tube. The glass is marked to show degrees, just as a ruler is marked to show inches. Other thermometers use the expansion of a piece of metal to show temperature. All-metal thermometers are usually used where high temperatures must be shown—for example, on the oven doors of a stove. Alcohol boils at too low a temperature for such a use, and mercury would require a tube too long to be convenient.

The marking of the thermometer depends on the system, or *scale*, being used. The Fahrenheit scale is most often used in the United States and other English-speaking countries. On this scale, 32 degrees is the temperature at which ice melts and 212 degrees is the temperature at which water boils (at sea level). Scientists use the Centigrade scale, on which zero marks the melting point of ice and 100 the boiling point of water.

You can change Centigrade temperatures to Fahrenheit temperatures in this way: Multiply the Centigrade temperature by 9; then divide the result by 5; then add 32. For example, you read that the temperature in a foreign city is 15 degrees Centigrade. Is it hot or cold? You multiply 15 by 9, which gives you 135; you divide 135 by 5, which gives you 27; and you add 27 and 32, which gives you 59. The Fahrenheit temperature would be 59, a cool day, neither hot nor cold.

There was a third popular thermometer, the Réaumur, which was used in Russia and some other European countries until about fifty years ago. On the Réaumur scale, the melting point of ice was zero and the boiling point or water was 80 degrees. Most of the countries that used the Réaumur scale now use the Centigrade scale.

A *clinical* thermometer is used to take the temperature of the human body. Clinical thermometers used in homes usually are marked with the Fahrenheit scale, starting at about 94 and ranging to about 108 degrees, and clinical thermometers used in hospitals usually are marked with the Centigrade scale, at about the same range above and below 37 degrees (which is the same as 98.6 degrees Fahrenheit). Clinical thermometers are glass tubes with mercury in them. The thermometer is put into the mouth or rectum for about two minutes. Rectal temperature is usually almost one degree higher than mouth temperature. The

mercury will expand to show the temperature. The inside of the glass is roughened to hold the mercury at this point even when the thermometer is removed. To make the mercury fall, the thermometer must be shaken.

See also the articles FAHRENHEIT, TEMPERATURE, and HEAT.

Thermopylae

Thermopylae is a mountain pass in the eastern part of Greece. In ancient times it was the only short way to go from southern Greece to northern Greece. At one end, the pass was so narrow that only one carriage could pass through at a time.

Nearly 2,500 years ago—in 480 B.C. —a famous battle was fought at Thermopylae. The Persians under King Xerxes had invaded Greece and were advancing to attack the Greek cities of Athens and Sparta. A few Greek soldiers (some say there were 300, but others say 1,000) met the Persians at Thermopylae, between the mountains and the sea. Under the Spartan general Leonidas, the few Greeks fought a Persian army of many thousand men. Finally, some of the Persians crossed over the mountains and attacked the Greeks from the rear, killing every one of them. The Persians did capture Athens, but they were defeated the next year and were forced to leave Greece. The defense of the pass by Leonidas and his men is still used as an example of great bravery.

thermostat

A thermostat is an automatic device for turning heating or cooling equipment on or off, depending on changes in the temperature. The word *thermostat* comes from Greek words that mean "heating standing still." You set a thermostat at the temperature you want a room to be, for example 75 degrees. When the temperature reaches 75 degrees, the thermostat automatically shuts off the heat. When the temperature drops below 75 degrees, the thermostat automatically turns the heat on and keeps it on until the temperature reaches 75 again.

Thermostats are used chiefly in connection with furnaces. They can be used with furnaces that burn any fuel—coal, oil, or gas. Sometimes thermostats are used on air-conditioning machines, and they are used on stoves and ovens. In manufacturing, thermostats are of great importance to many machines.

The thermostat is a simple combination of a therometer and an electric switch. When the thermometer shows that the temperature has reached the desired level, the electric switch operates the furnace or other machine. The working of a thermostat is explained in the article on EXPANSION.

Some thermostats have clocks attached to them. You can set them to turn the heat on automatically at a certain hour, for example six o'clock in the morning, or to turn it off at a certain hour.

A sprinkler system, which is used for fire protection in factories, stores, and other business places, is worked by a kind of thermostat. Pipes carry water all along the ceilings of such places. Every few feet there is a nozzle sealed with a metal that melts at a fairly low temperature. If a fire should start, the heat of the fire melts the metal and lets water out of the pipes to sprinkle the fire and put it out. The soft metal cap on the nozzle is called a thermostat because it is controlled by heat.

Theseus

Theseus was a hero in Greek mythology, the stories the ancient Greeks told about their gods and goddesses. He was the son of Aegeus, the king of Athens, and had to prove his strength and courage so that he would be recognized as his father's successor. Theseus had many adventures. The most famous was his killing the Minotaur.

Each year the people of Athens had to send seven youths and seven maidens to the island of Crete to be eaten by the Minotaur. The Minotaur was a monster with the head of a bull and the body of a man. It lay in wait for its victims in a complicated garden called a labyrinth. Theseus was sent there but Ariadne, the daughter of King Minos of Crete, fell in love with him and promised to save him. She gave him a sword, and one end of a long thread, while she held onto the other end. Theseus then killed the Minotaur with the sword, and found his way out of the labyrinth by following the thread.

Ariadne hoped Theseus would marry her, but he left her and sailed on to Athens and to his father Aegéus. A plan had been made to show Aegeus the outcome of Theseus' adventure. If he had succeeded, he was to show a white sail on his ship. But Theseus forgot to do this. Aegeus thought his son had been killed, and in his sorrow he killed himself before the ship arrived. Therefore Theseus became the new king of Athens.

He then had several other adventures. He took part in a fight against the AMAZONS, about whom there is a separate article. Finally Theseus was killed by King Lycomedes of Scyros.

Stories about Theseus have been used by several famous writers, including the Austrian playwright Hugo von Hofmannsthal and the French novelist André Gide.

Thessalonians, a people of the city of Thessalonica, in ancient Greece, who founded a Christian Church about 1,900 years ago. St. Paul wrote two Epistles to the Thessalonians, which are books of the Bible: see the articles EPISTLE and BIBLE.

Thessaly

Thessaly was the largest division of ancient Greece. Today it is a division of modern Greece. About 700,000 people live there, and it is 8,000 square miles in size, which is about the size of Massachusetts. It is on the Aegean Sea. Most of the region is a flat plain surrounded by high mountains. The plain is fertile and much of the wheat supply of Greece is grown there.

thirst

Thirst is the way our bodies indicate that they need water. The human body is about two-thirds water. Since it is constantly losing water in such ways as perspiration, it must get water frequently to replace what it loses. A healthy person should drink at least a quart of water a day. This need not be plain water. It may be any liquid or food that contains a high amount of water. A child that drinks plenty of milk will not need much extra water.

The first feeling of thirst is usually an unpleasant dryness in the mouth. When the body does not have enough water, some parts of it begin taking water from other parts. Blood is the most important fluid in the body and it always maintains its high percentage of water even when it has to borrow from other parts of the body. When the saliva in the mouth and throat begins to dry up, we say we are thirsty and drink some liquid. In deserts, where there is not enough water, people often pass the stage where the mouth is merely dry. They begin to feel pain and distress as the tissues of the mouth and throat become almost leathery and begin to crack. Since there is no more moisture in the throat passages the air that enters the lungs is too dry and the lungs hurt. Extreme thirst can cause death, and many people who have been stranded in deserts without water have died in a few days.

When we have eaten things that are salty or spicy, we often feel thirst even though our bodies may not need water. After heavy exercise or play in which the body has passed off much water in perspiration, we feel very thirsty. One should be very careful not to drink too much water at these times, and it is not good to drink iced or very cold water when the body is overheated.

Thirty Years' War

The Thirty Years' War was a war fought in Germany more than three hundred years ago. It lasted from 1618 until 1648. It started out as a religious war between Catholics and Protestants, but finally the nations were fighting for power and land. The Thirty Years' War was one of the worst wars in history, and some historians think that it did more damage to Germany than all the bombing of World War II.

The Holy Roman (German) Emperor Ferdinand II was a Catholic, but he ruled over many Protestants. In 1618 the Protestants in the city of Prague, which was the capital of Bohemia (it is now part of Czechoslovakia), revolted against Ferdinand's rule and threw the two German governors of Prague out of the windows of their palace. (This event is called the Defenestration of Prague.) Ferdinand's army invaded Bohemia and put down the rebellion, but some other Protestant parts of Germany began fighting the emperor. They made an alliance with the Protestant king of Denmark. The Catholic armies of the Emperor, commanded by two famous generals, Count Tilly and Albert of Wallenstein, completely defeated the Protestants.

It looked as if the Protestants had lost the war, but in 1630 King Gustavus Adolphus of Sweden, a Protestant, led his army into Germany. Gustavus was the best general in the war, and his army was the best army the world had seen for a long time. It was the first army with cannon that had wheels and could be pulled into battle by horses. The soldiers fought bravely for their king, who paid them well and took care of them.

In 1631 Gustavus beat the Germans in

the Battle of Breitenfeld, and the next year he won the Battle of Lützen but was killed there. In 1634 the Germans beat the Swedes in the Battle of Nördlingen. There were not many big battles after this, but the armies went around the countryside stealing food, burning buildings, and terrifying the people.

In 1635 France entered the war. France was a Catholic country, but it wanted some of the German land. The French, together with the Swedes and the German Protestants, invaded Bavaria, a Catholic part of Germany. The German emperor then asked for peace. Peace talks went on for many years, but in 1648 the Treaty of Westphalia was signed, which ended the war. Both Sweden and France took some German territory, and Germany was divided into about three hundred little countries, some Catholic and some Protestant. France became the most powerful country in Europe.

Some of the foot soldiers in the Thirty Years' War fought with muskets. These were not very accurate and took a long time to load. While the musketeers loaded their guns, other soldiers with long pikes protected them from the enemy cavalry, who fought with spears and with heavy pistols.

thistle

Thistle is the name of a group of flowering plants with spiny, prickly leaves and stems. There are several varieties. The blossoms may be purple, white, reddish-rose, or yellow. The most familiar thistle is the tall, purple thistle that is the national flower of Scotland. This type of thistle grows wild in many places throughout the world. It often reaches a height of nine feet. Other thistles are low-growing plants, and are used in rock gardens, or as part of a border planting for lawns or flower beds.

Most thistles are biennial; they go to seed every second year. If undisturbed, the plants will spread widely and reappear year after year. The seed is carried by wind and air currents on tiny parachutes of down, as the seeds of the dandelion are.

Thomas, Dylan

Dylan Thomas was one of the great poets of modern times. He was Welsh, which means he was born in Wales, a part of Great Britain, and of course he wrote in the English language. He was born in 1914 and his first book of poems was published before he was 21 years old. Thomas gave many lectures and readings of his poems in the United States. He died in 1954, when he was only 40 years old and might still have written even greater poetry.

Thomas, Norman

Norman Mattoon Thomas is the name of an American politician who was the Socialist Party's candidate for President six successive times. He was born in 1884 in Marion, Ohio, and when he grew up he became a Presbyterian minister. While he was a pastor in New York City he became interested in working with underprivileged people. In 1918 he founded a magazine called *The World Tomorrow* and then for a time was editor of another magazine, *The Nation*. In the meantime he had become active in the Socialist Party and twice was their candi-

date for mayor of New York City, and in 1924 for governor of New York State. In 1928 the Socialists made him their candidate for the Presidency, as they did also in 1932, 1936, 1940, 1944, and 1948. He then lost the leadership of the party to Darlington Hoopes, but continued to remain active in reform movements through writings and speeches. He had been against the United States' entering both World Wars. In 1968, Norman Thomas died at the age of 84.

Thomas à Kempis

Thomas à Kempis was a German priest and religious writer who lived about 550 years ago. He was born about 1380 in the town of Kempen, and his real name was Thomas Hemerken. At an early age he entered the Roman Catholic order of the Augustinians (a group of monks who took the name of Saint Augustine) and spent the rest of his life in religious studies. He died in 1471. He is best-remembered as the author of the book *Imitation of Christ*, which is still read.

Thomas Aquinas, Saint

Saint Thomas Aquinas was a great Italian scholar. He is generally considered to be the foremost philosopher of the Roman Catholic Church. He lived about seven hundred years ago, but his works are still studied.

Thomas Aquinas was born about 1225 and studied under Benedictine monks (a Roman Catholic religious order) and later at the University of Naples, in Italy. His father was a wealthy noble, but in spite of his family's objections Thomas entered the Dominican order when he was 22 years old. He studied for several years with one of the greatest teachers of the time, Albertus Magnus. He then founded a school for religious study at Cologne, Germany, and taught there for a time. In 1261 he returned to Italy, where he lived until his death in 1274.

About fifty years later, in 1323, Pope John XXII canonized him (declared him a saint), and his feast day is March 7. Later the Roman Catholic Church proclaimed him a doctor of the church, and, still later the patron of Catholic schools.

St. Thomas wrote several books. Probably the greatest was his *Summary of Theology*. (Theology is the study of religion.) In this book he presented a system of philosophy (thought) that came to be called Thomism. St. Thomas says that man is born good and has the power to choose a good way of life and to avoid an evil one but cannot make the right choice without the help of God, and God's representative in the world is the Church.

Saint Thomas was the greatest of a group of thinkers called the Scholastics.

Thomas More, Saint, see Sir Thomas MORE.

Thompson, Sir John

John Sparrow David Thompson was a Canadian statesman and Prime Minister. He was born in 1844 in Halifax, Nova Scotia, and when he grew up he became a lawyer. In 1885 he became Minister of Justice of Canada, and in this position he defended the decision to hang

the leader of a rebellion, Louis RIEL, about whom there is a separate article. He supported coöperation between his country and the United States, and helped set up treaties by which the two countries shared fishing rights. In 1892 Thompson became Prime Minister. He died two years later, in 1894, at the age of 50.

Thor

Thor was the god of thunder in Scandinavian mythology, the stories the ancient Scandinavian and Germanic peoples told about their gods and heroes. Thor was the oldest and strongest son of Odin, the chief god. Thor was also the god of war and military strength. He had a magic hammer, which returned by itself when it was thrown. He was always at war with the giants, and his magic hammer terrified them. A day of the week, Thursday, was named for Thor. See also the article MYTHOLOGY.

Thoreau, Henry David

Henry David Thoreau was an American writer who lived about a hundred years ago. He is remembered chiefly for his beliefs that men should live very simply and be close to nature. Thoreau was born in 1817 in Concord, Massachusetts, and studied at Harvard. He taught school in Concord for two years, then lived in the home of his friend, the great writer Ralph Waldo Emerson. There he came to know some of the leading writers and thinkers of the time, including Bronson Alcott and Margaret Fuller. Then Thoreau moved to a small hut beside a pond called Walden Pond, near Concord, and for two years he devoted himself to writing and nature study. His best-known book, *Walden*, tells of his experiences during this time. He then returned to Concord and remained there until his death, in 1862.

Thorpe, Jim

Jim Thorpe has been called the greatest of all American athletes and perhaps the greatest athlete who ever lived. He was an American Indian of the Sac and Fox tribe and was born on an Indian reservation near Prague, Oklahoma, in 1888. He went to the famous Carlisle Indian School, a college in Pennsylvania. At Carlisle, Thorpe made the All-American football team in 1911 and 1912, was a great baseball player, and was practically a one-man track and field team. He could run, jump, hurdle, and throw the weights. In 1912 in the Olympic Games at Stockholm, Sweden, Thorpe won the greatest of all Olympic competitions, the decathlon. He won many trophies and the King of Sweden said to him, "You, sir, are the greatest athlete in the world." But the next year the Olympic officials found that he had once accepted a small amount of money for playing baseball. This made him a professional athlete, and he had to give back the medals and trophies.

After leaving college, Thorpe became a great professional football player. He played mostly with the Canton Bulldogs. He was also good enough at baseball to

be a major-league player with the New York Giants baseball team. In 1950 a large group of newspapermen chose the great athletes of the first fifty years of the twentieth century, and Jim Thorpe's name led all the rest. He died in 1954.

Thousand Islands

The Thousand Islands are a group of more than 1,500 small islands in the St. Lawrence River. The islands are on both sides of the border between the United States and Canada, which runs through the St. Lawrence River. Some are part of New York State and others are part of Ontario. Most of the islands are very small, but they are very beautiful and many people spend their summer vacations in the Thousand Islands. Some people own entire islands.

Thrace

Thrace was an ancient region of southeastern Europe. It included what is now Bulgaria and parts of Greece and Turkey. Most of the region is very mountainous. Between the mountain ranges are low plains.

The earliest people of Thrace were not civilized, but the Greeks founded many colonies in Thrace along the shores of the Black Sea and Aegean Sea. In later times Thrace was held by the Romans and then by the Turks. Today the name Thrace is used for a much smaller province in northeastern Greece.

thrasher

The thrasher is a medium-sized bird that lives in thick shrubbery and bushes. It sings beautifully during its mating season. When it is about to sing it perches on top of a tall bush or tree.

The brown thrasher is the only member of this bird group found in the east of the United States. It is reddish brown in color with white under parts, and has a long tail. There are other thrashers in the deserts of the Southwest. These are sand-colored and have long bills with which they dig in the soft dirt for worms and insects.

thread and yarn

Thread and yarn are long, thin strands of fibers that have been spun (drawn out and twisted). The strands that are used to make cloth by knitting or weaving is usually called yarn. The tightly twisted yarn that is used in sewing is usually called thread.

Two or more single strands of fibers, twisted together, form *ply yarns,* known as two-ply, three-ply, and so on, depending on the number of strands used. Ply yarns are stronger than single ones. Yarns of high twist (with many twists per inch) usually are very strong. Sometimes single yarns of two different fibers, such as cotton and wool, are twisted together.

SPINNING

Both yarn and thread are made by *spinning,* which is the process of drawing out and twisting the fibers into a continuous strand. At first spinning was done by hand. It involved drawing out the fibers from a bundle tied to a stick, known as the *distaff.* Then the strand was twisted between the fingers, and finally it was wound on a notched stick called a *spindle.*

More than a thousand years ago, during the Middle Ages, this process was made easier by the use of a spinning wheel. The strand was wound around the wheel, which was turned by hand. Spinning is still done by hand in many parts of Asia, and in the mountains of Peru.

Almost two hundred years ago, in the second half of the 18th century, came three inventions that revolutionized spinning. They were the spinning jenny, by James Hargreaves in 1764; the water frame, by Richard Arkwright in 1768; and the spinning mule, by Samuel Crompton in 1779. These were the forerunners of the modern spinning mule.

Today, all cotton spinning and much woolen and worsted spinning in the United States are done on a machine known as a ring spinning frame. It was invented by a man named Thorpe in the early 1800s in Massachusetts. In cotton spinning, bobbins of soft-twisted strands of fibers, called roving, are placed in a rack or creel of the ring spinning frame. The roving is drawn out to a finer size by passing it between pairs of rollers. The yarn is actually spun by a spindle that revolves very rapidly, sometimes as much as ten thousand revolutions a minute. The strand of fibers coming down from the rollers passes through a small piece of steel, about the size and shape of the letter D and called a traveller. This traveller rides around a steel ring almost as fast as the spindle that turns in the center of the ring. In this way, the twist is put into the yarn, giving it strength. At the same time, the yarn is wound onto a wooden bobbin that fits down over the spindle.

There are about 20,000,000 spindles in the United States.

KINDS OF YARN

Yarns can be spun in such a way that cloth made from it will have a rough surface. This is done by various methods. *Flake yarns* are made by enlarging the size of a single yarn so as to make lumps at certain places. *Loop yarns,* which give a twisted effect, are made by winding the yarn differently.

Chenille yarn is made by a weaving process. It is used for drapery and carpeting.

Carded yarns are yarns of cotton or wool that has been cleaned and disentangled, arranged in fairly even rows, and drawn out. *Combed yarns,* either cotton or wool, have been both carded and combed. Combing is much like carding, but the combination of the two processes makes the yarn smoother and stronger.

Knitting yarns are spun especially for knitting. They are softer than those used for weaving.

SEWING THREAD

Sewing thread is generally made from Egyptian or Sea Island cotton fibers, which are long. The fibers are spun as for yarn. Next the strands are doubled and twisted. They may be made in two-, three-, four- or six-cord construction. For six-cord thread, three strands of the two-ply yarn are twisted together in opposite directions. In three-cord thread, three single yarns are twisted together. The threads are bleached and dyed and then are wound on large bobbins, from

which the thread is rewound onto the spools you use in a sewing basket.

Darning and embroidery threads are softly twisted threads. Cotton threads may be *mercerized,* which means they are put through a chemical process that gives them a high luster, or sheen.

White cotton thread is made in sizes numbering from 8, the coarsest (thickest) kind, to 200, the finest. Black thread ranges from 8 to 100 and other colors from 50 to 80. Mercerized cotton is made only in sizes 50 and 60. For general sewing, 50 or 60 thread is used.

Three Wise Men, the three Eastern kings who took presents to the infant Jesus: see the article on MAGI.

throat

The throat is the open space at the back of the mouth. It acts as a kind of crossroads or traffic circle. From the throat there are seven openings or passages to other parts of the body. First, the mouth opens into the throat. Then there are two openings at the top of the throat that lead to the nostrils of the nose. From each side of the throat there is an opening called the Eustachian tube that leads to each ear. At the bottom of the throat there are two openings, one to the esophagus, the tube going down to the stomach, and the other to the windpipe, which carries air to the lungs.

The throat is covered with the same type of skin, called mucous membrane, that covers the inside of the mouth. In a healthy state this membrane is pink and moist. Doctors call the throat the *pharynx.* When they speak of a sore throat or some illness of the throat they call it *pharyngitis.*

The throat acts as a trap to keep germs from entering the body. At the back of the throat there are two small, spongy glands called *tonsils.* The tonsils act as strainers. They collect germs and keep them from going down into the body. When the tonsils collect too many germs and become infected or inflamed, we have the disease called *tonsilitis.*

One of the most remarkable things in the throat is a small flap, or trapdoor, at the bottom. This is called the *epiglottis.* When we breathe, the epiglottis is in the up position, leaving the opening to the windpipe free. When we swallow food, the epiglottis drops over the top of the windpipe and prevents food from entering it. Sometimes we say "food went down the wrong way." On these rare occasions the epiglottis did not fall into place quickly enough and some particle of food entered the windpipe. When this happens we cough violently as the windpipe attempts to get rid of the substance in it.

thrush

The thrush family of birds includes many different kinds. Thrushes live in all parts of the world, except in extremely cold or extremely hot and dry places. Many thrushes have remarkably beautiful songs.

In the United States and Canada, the most familiar members of the thrush family are the robin, bluebird, wood thrush, and Townsend solitaire (also known as

the Rocky Mountain thrush). Most members of the thrush family migrate to warmer climates when the northern winter is approaching.

Some kinds of thrush are as large as nine or ten inches long, others as small as five and six inches long.

Thucydides

Thucydides was a Greek writer of history who lived in the city-state of Athens almost 2,500 years ago. He was, perhaps, the greatest writer of ancient history, and he was certainly the first writer to deal with history in such a way as to understand and interpret it. His great work was the *History of the Peloponnesian War,* an account of a war between Sparta and Athens. He was born about 470 B.C. and died about 404 B.C.

thunder, the loud noise that follows a flash of lightning: see LIGHTNING and WEATHER.

Thurber, James

James Grover Thurber is the name of an American humorous writer and cartoonist. He was born in 1894 in Columbus, Ohio, and studied at Ohio State University. He wrote for several newspapers, then at the age of 31 he joined the staff of *The New Yorker,* a weekly magazine in New York City. Thurber's drawings and articles soon became very popular. In them he pokes fun at people and the things they do, and at himself. Many of them have been collected and published in books, among which are *The Owl in the Attic, My Life and Hard Times,* and *The Thurber Carnival.* With Elliott Nugent he wrote a play, *The Male Animal. The Thirteen Clocks* was a book for children. Thurber died in 1961.

Thursday

Thursday is the fifth day of the week. The name means "Thor's day," in honor of the ancient Germanic god of thunder. In the United States, the President always sets a Thursday in November as Thanksgiving Day. Holy Thursday, the day before Good Friday, is called Maundy Thursday in England.

thyme

Thyme is an attractive, evergreen herb that is grown in rock gardens and flower garden borders in temperate regions of the world. It is often grown in the home, planted in flower pots. It has small blossoms that may be lavender, pink, white, red, or purple, depending on the kind grown. The dried leaves are used in seasoning meats, poultry stuffing, soup, and other dishes.

thyroid, one of the important glands of the body: see GLAND and GOITER.

Tiber

The Tiber is a river in central Italy. It is one of the world's most famous rivers because the city of Rome was built on its shores. The Tiber is 251 miles long. It rises on the southern slopes of the Apennine Mountains and flows southwest to the Tyrrhenian Sea, an arm of the Mediterranean. It follows a zigzag course. The Tiber passes through Rome about 21 miles above the point where it empties

into the Tyrrhenian Sea. It is often called "the yellow Tiber."

Tibet

Tibet is a country in central Asia. It is usually considered as part of China. Tibet lies in the midst of the Himalayas and other great mountain ranges and is the highest country in the world. It is cut off from the outside world by the mountains, which almost surround it.

About six million people live in Tibet. Its area of 470,000 square miles makes it almost twice the size of Texas. The capital is LHASA, about which there is a separate article.

WHAT THE PEOPLE ARE LIKE

The people of Tibet are members of the Mongoloid race and are akin to the Chinese. They are pleasant but do not often encourage foreign visitors. Many of the people are nomads (wanderers) who move from place to place with their flocks of yaks (cattle), goats, and horses. Yaks are the chief domestic animal because they do not mind the high altitude or the severe cold. Farmers in Tibet grow small quantities of grains and fruits. Handcrafts include the making of carpets, fabrics, and jewelry.

The people of Tibet speak the Tibetan language, which is somewhat like Chinese. Almost all of them follow the Lama branch of Buddhism. About one man in six is a Lama monk and never marries.

WHAT KIND OF PLACE IT IS

Tibet is a plateau (high but level region) surrounded by mountains. In most places it is more than 13,000 feet above sea level and some peaks are more than 20,000 feet high. Tibet is the source of several important rivers that flow through India and China. The Brahmaputra is the largest of these rivers. There are many lakes, some of which contain salt water.

The climate of Tibet is very dry. The air loses most of its moisture before it has crossed the mountains into Tibet. Because of the dryness, and because it is very cold, plants do not grow well during six months of the year. There are regions of gravelly desert in Tibet. Tibet has deposits of salt and gold, and also some radioactive ores, but the difficulties of transportation across the mountains have prevented these minerals from being mined in great quantity.

HOW THE PEOPLE ARE GOVERNED

Since 1950, Tibet has been controlled by the Chinese Communists. The country has little central government. The Dalai

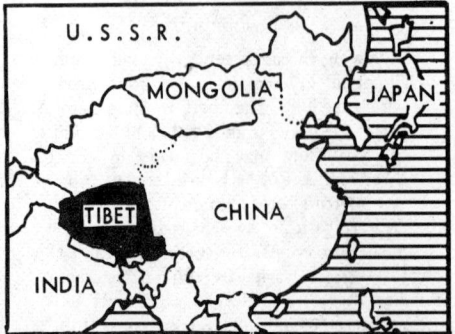

Lama, who is the head of the national religion, also was head of the government until in 1959 he fled from the Communists and took refuge in India. Since then, Tibet has been fully under Chinese Communist control, with the Panchen Lama the supposed head of the government but actually subject to orders from China. (See the article on LAMAISM.)

TIBET IN THE PAST

Little is known of the history of Tibet before the people were converted to the Buddhist religion about 1,200 years ago. The people have had little contact even with their close neighbors, and few Europeans have entered the country. China took control of Tibet in 1720, but actually the Tibetans continued to run their own affairs. In 1904 the British began to trade with Tibet, and nine years later Tibet declared itself independent of China. China did not recognize Tibetan independence. In 1950, the Chinese Communists sent troops into Tibet and took possession without firing a shot. In 1959 many of the Tibetan people revolted but Chinese troops put down the revolution. See DALAI LAMA.

TIBET. Population 6,000,000. Area, 470,000 square miles. In central Asia. Highest country in the world.

tick

A tick is a small air-breathing animal related to spiders. It differs from insects in having all of its body parts joined together in one piece. A tick passes through four stages in its life. The egg (the first stage) hatches into a larva that sucks blood from some animal or man, then drops to the ground. The larva molts and becomes a nymph, which finds another animal and gets another blood meal, after which it drops to the ground. The nymph molts and changes to an adult. The adults must also get blood meals. The female usually stays on an animal longer than the male, while her eggs develop. She lays thousands of eggs.

If an animal has a disease when the tick is sucking blood, the tick may get some of the disease germs and give them to the next animal or person that it bites. In this way, a tick may spread tick fever, tularemia, plague, and other diseases.

When a tick bites a person, the head burrows into the skin and feeds there. It can be removed by applying a drop of alcohol or the hot end of a match. This makes the tick pull out its head, and it can be removed.

TICK FEVER

Ticks in the skin usually cause unpleasant itching and irritation, but one kind of tick causes a dangerous disease called tick fever. One form of it is called Rocky Mountain spotted fever, because this kind of tick was first found in the Rocky Mountain area. The disease is caused by a germ that is carried by the ticks. Tick fever begins with a red rash on the hands and wrists. This is followed by headache and mental confusion and a high fever. A severe case lasts about three weeks. Another form of tick fever is called Q FEVER. There is a separate article about it. Tick fever used to cause death, but the new antibiotic drugs can cure it.

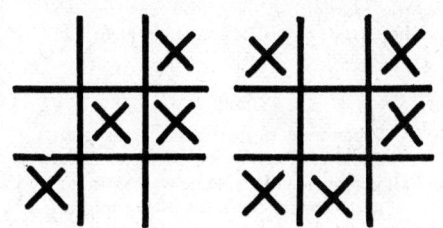

If two skilled players play tick-tack-toe, the game usually ends as a tie (*right*) instead of with a winner (*left*).

tick-tack-toe

Tick-tack-toe is a very old game, sometimes called *noughts and crosses* or *tit-tat-toe*. Lines are drawn, crossing one another as shown in the picture. One player puts a cross in any section he chooses, then the other player puts a circle in any other section, and so on. If a player gets three of his marks in a row he wins the game. When the game is carefully played this seldom happens and every game ends in a tie. To be sure of a tie, if your opponent plays first and puts his mark anywhere except in the center, you must take the center; if he starts in the center, you must take one of the corners.

tides

Tides are the regular flow of ocean waters onto the beaches and shores of the land and out from them. Tides come at regular intervals during the day, sometimes flowing high on to the beaches and at other times flowing back and leaving the beaches uncovered by water.

Tides are caused by gravity, the same kind of force that holds everything on the surface of the earth, that keeps us from flying out into space, and that makes us fall from high places to the earth. The tides are not caused by the gravity of the earth itself but by the gravity pull of the moon and sun upon the earth. The sun is much bigger than the moon, but it is also much farther away from the earth. The shorter distance makes the gravity pull of the moon greater.

Most of the earth is solid material and cannot easily be moved by the pull of gravity. Since the seas and oceans are composed of water, which flows freely, they are the things that are most affected by gravity. The pull is greatest on the part of the ocean nearest the moon (or sun). The pull is smallest on the opposite side of the earth. Water moves towards both these parts of the ocean from other parts where the pull is not extra large or extra small. Water rises on the shores closest to the moon and on shores on the opposite side of the earth farthest from the moon. Other shores have low tide. As the earth turns, different shores experience high tide and low tide. The irregular shape of the oceans causes many changes in this simplified picture. See the article on GRAVITATION.

Tides change about every six hours in most places. High tide is reached, then six hours later low tide is reached. In some places the water at high tide may be as much as fifty feet higher than it is at low tide. This can happen in a bay or inlet. Since bays and inlets are usually narrow channels, the force of the incoming tide raises the water level higher in these places than on open beaches. Twice a month—near the first quarter and also near the last quarter of the moon—there is not much difference between high tides and low tides. The tides at these periods are called neap tides.

Tides also flow into the mouths of rivers that flow into the sea. Usually ships coming or going in river ports must move when the tide is high. At low tide many of these river ports have not enough water to float great ships. In harbor cities and many coastal places, newspapers and weather bureaus give the exact times at which the tide will be high and low.

Tientsin

Tientsin is the third-largest city of China. It is a Yellow Sea port in the northeastern part of the country. Its name means "Heavenly Stream" in the Chinese language. Tientsin is the chief railroad center and manufacturing city of northern China. It is on the Pai River at its joining with several other navigable rivers and the Grand Canal, and it is 30 miles from the coast.

More than 3,000,000 people live in Tientsin. There are factories that make cotton and leather goods, camel's hair fabrics, iron and steel products, and other things. Tientsin exports many products from the surrounding region, including hog bristles, furs and hides, wool, and vegetable oils. There are two universities in Tientsin and several technical colleges.

Tientsin was not of much importance until the middle 1800s, when European countries became interested in trade with China. Trading rights were granted in 1860 to Great Britain and later to many European countries. In the early 1900s the old city wall was torn down and Tientsin was rebuilt into a modern city. The Japanese captured Tientsin in 1937 and occupied it until 1945. In 1949 the Chinese Communists took the city.

TIENTSIN, CHINA. Population (1957 estimate) 3,220,000. On the Pai River.

Tierra del Fuego

Tierra del Fuego is a group of islands off the southern tip of South America. They are separated from the mainland by the Strait of Magellan, named in honor of the Portuguese explorer who discovered the islands in 1520. The group consists of one large island, called Great Island or simply Tierra del Fuego, and many small islands and islets. The southernmost island is Horn Island, on which is Cape Horn. Tierra del Fuego has an area of about 28,000 square miles, and about 10,000 people live there.

Great Island is divided about equally between Chile and Argentina. The eastern part of this island, plus the many small islands offshore, form the Argentine territory of Tierra del Fuego. The western part of Great Island, plus the smaller islands to the south and west, are part of the Chilean territory of Magallanes. The name Tierra del Fuego means "land of fire."

Most of the people live on Great Island and make their livings by farming, livestock-raising, and mining. The climate is cool, with frequent storms and much rainfall.

tiger

A tiger is a wild, fierce cat. Some tigers are the biggest of all cats, even bigger than lions. Tigers live in all parts of Asia, from India to Siberia, but they are not found in Africa.

Tigers are more savage and bloodthirsty than lions. They do not form groups as lions often do, but usually travel alone. They live by killing and eating other animals, anything from a rabbit to a cow or a sheep.

Tigers are expert climbers and jumpers. A jump of fifteen feet in a single bound is not unusual. Tigers swim well, and seem to have no hesitancy about leaping into the water to escape hunters or to reach prey they can see across a stream.

THE TIGER'S KITTENS

A female tiger is a devoted mother. Kittens may be born at any time of the year. They weigh about two or three pounds, and they are born blind, as domestic kittens are. Two to four is the usual size of a litter. The kittens start learning to hunt with the mother when they are about six weeks old.

Young tigers often kill for the sake of killing, while an older tiger will kill only when it is hungry.

Tigers in different sections of Asia vary slightly in size and markings. An Indian or Bengal tiger is a yellowish tan with long, narrow, black stripes all over its body and legs. An adult male averages a weight of four hundred pounds, and including the tail may be nine feet long.

The Caucasian tiger has stripes of brown. The Siberian tiger, largest of all tigers, has fur of a lighter shade than the others, and its coat is softer and thicker. A Siberian tiger is about thirteen feet long and may weigh about six hundred pounds. Tigers in captivity have lived as long as twenty-five years.

THE TIGER'S BAD REPUTATION

For many years, the people of India have feared and dreaded the presence of a tiger near their villages. The "man-eating tiger" is not common, even in India, but occasionally a tiger develops a taste for human flesh. These tigers are usually old or weak, and they find man easier to strike down than other animals.

Tigers are hunted not only as a defense against loss of life but also as a sport. Tiger-hunts from the backs of elephants are popular in Asia. Hunters have killed so many tigers that there are not many left, and the government of India has opened game reservations to save them.

tiger lily

The tiger lily is a flower with petals of a reddish-orange color with dark purple or black dots on them. The petals curl backward, away from the center of the blossom. Several flowers bloom on a single stem. The plants grow in most sections of the United States and southern Canada, and once a bed has become well established it will produce blossoms every year. Like most lilies, the tiger lily grows from bulbs. These are usually planted in the autumn. Plants are three to four feet high when in flower.

The tiger lily was so named because its petals resemble the fur of a tiger.

Tigris

The Tigris is a river, one of the most important rivers in history. It rises in eastern Turkey, flows southeast and forms the border between Turkey and Syria, then enters Iraq. In Iraq it flows more or less parallel with the Euphrates River, and then joins it to form the Shatt al Arab, which empties into the Persian Gulf. The Tigris flows through a territory that is called "cradle of civilization" because five thousand and more years ago men built some of their first great cities there. The great cities along the Tigris were Nineveh and Seleucia. On its bank is the supposed site of the Garden of Eden. Baghdad is now the biggest city on the Tigris.

Tilden, Samuel J.

Samuel Jones Tilden was an American statesman who almost became President. In 1876 he ran for President against Rutherford B. Hayes and received more votes than Hayes, but there was a mix-up in counting the votes of some states and as a result Tilden lost the election.

Tilden was born in 1814 in New Lebanon, New York. He became a lawyer and practiced in New York City, where he became a leader in the Democratic Party. After the Civil War, Tilden became state chairman of the Democrats and helped to break up a group of dishonest politicians called the Tweed Ring. In 1874 Tilden was elected governor of New York, and in 1876 the Democrats made him their candidate for President. He won more electoral votes than the Republican candidate, Hayes, but a commission decided that Hayes had won the election by one vote. (This is covered in the article on Rutherford B. HAYES.) Tilden claimed their decision was unjust, but he gave in to it. Most people today think he should have won the election. Tilden then retired from public life. He died in 1886, and left a large sum of money for setting up a free public library in New York City.

Tilden, William

William Tatem Tilden II was one of the greatest tennis players who ever lived, and many consider him the greatest. He was born in Philadelphia, Pennsylvania, in 1893, and attended the University of Pennsylvania. Unlike most athletes, he did not become great until he was 27 years old. He won his first national singles championship in 1920. Then he

was champion every year through 1925, and again in 1929. He also won the championships of other countries, including England and France, and he was the great star of the United States Davis Cup team. Tilden was a tall, wiry man. He could use more strokes than any other player. When he was long past the age when most players are able to compete, he was still good enough to play against the best. In the latter years of life he was a professional, playing and teaching for money, and he won the professional championship several times. Tilden died in 1953.

Timbuktu

Timbuktu is a town in the Republic of Mali, in West Africa. It is on the Niger River and is a center of caravan trade on the route across the Sahara to Algeria and Morocco. About 7,000 people live there. Five hundred years ago, Timbuktu was a cultural center of the Sudan. It became famous in Europe as a slave and gold market. Timbuktu was captured by Moroccans in 1591 and lost most of its importance. It was in ruins when the French took it in 1893 and rebuilt it.

time

Time is the way man knows when a thing happened in the past and when a thing is due to happen in the future, so that he can remember things in the past and prepare for things in the future. All methods of telling time since the days of prehistoric man have been based on some occurrence in nature, such as the rising and setting of the sun and moon, and the changing of the seasons. The length of time it takes the earth to revolve around the sun (about 365 days) is called the year. The length of time it takes the earth to rotate on its axis (about 24 hours) is called the day.

There are two principal methods of keeping the time of day. Sidereal time is measured by the position of the earth in relation to the stars. Only astronomers use it. Solar time is measured by the position of the earth in relation to the sun. The clocks and watches in our homes, and offices, and schools keep time by the sun. Time of day is measured by the position of the sun. It is noon when the sun is on the meridian (due south for people in the United States). One o'clock in the afternoon would mean that one hour ago the sun was on the meridian. Ten o'clock in

the morning would mean that in two hours the sun will be on the meridian, and due south.

STANDARD TIME

When modern methods of transportation and communication began to make all people neighbors, some way was needed to make time mean the same things to people in different parts of the world. Depending on where you are on the earth, 12 o'clock noon will be at different times. Because the earth is constantly turning, the farther west you go the later noon comes. For example, it is noon in New York City about an hour earlier than it is in St. Louis, Missouri, so that noon in New York is only 11 o'clock in St. Louis.

In 1884 a large group of nations held a conference in Washington, D.C., and established Standard Time, which was based on solar time as figured at the Royal Observatory of Greenwich, England. Then the earth was divided into 24 time zones, beginning at Greenwich. All places in a zone keep the same time. In the United States there are four of these time zones, in which time is called Eastern Standard Time, Central Standard Time, Mountain Standard Time, and Pacific Standard Time. When it is 12 o'clock by Eastern time it is 11 o'clock by Central time, 10 o'clock by Mountain time, and 9 o'clock by Pacific time.

In the summertime people like to have more hours of daylight to enjoy, and so many countries set their clocks ahead an hour in DAYLIGHT SAVING TIME, about which there is a separate article. See also the article on the INTERNATIONAL DATE LINE.

Timor

Timor is an island northwest of Australia, between the Savu and Banda Seas in the north and the Timor Sea in the south. It is the largest of the Lesser Sunda Islands, and it belongs partly to Indonesia and partly to Portugal. Timor has an area of 13,132 square miles, and about 800,000 people live there. The island is mountainous and the plant life is scanty. There are some forests that provide sandalwood, coffee, and copra. The people of Timor are a mixture of Malay, Papuan, and Polynesian. Some are fishermen and others raise cattle and ponies.

Portuguese Timor occupies the eastern half of the island, some offshore islands, and a small section called Oe-Cusse that is surrounded by Indonesian territory. The

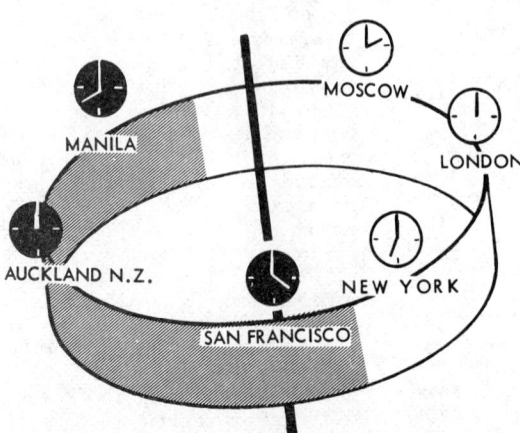

What time is it? That depends on where you are when you ask the question. The earth is like a belt that makes a full turn every 24 hours. In the shaded part of the belt it is night; in the white part it is day. It is twelve o'clock in both London and Auckland, but in London it is noon and in Auckland it is midnight. The world is divided into time zones, with the time advancing an hour for every 15 degrees east of Greenwich.

capital is Dili. The region became an independent colony in 1926. Indonesian Timor occupies the western half of the island. Its capital is Kupang.

Timor was settled by the Portuguese in the early 1500s. A hundred years later Dutch settlers arrived and soon took over the western part of the island. The boundary was disputed for almost a hundred years but the argument was settled in 1914.

During World War II the Japanese occupied much of the island. The Indonesian section was called Netherlands Timor until 1950, when it became part of Indonesia.

timothy

Timothy is a grass that farmers plant for hay. It is a perennial, which means that it grows year after year in the same fields, without replanting. Timothy grows four or five feet high and has a rough spike on a coarse stem. Timothy hay is excellent feed for livestock.

Timothy, Saint

St. Timothy was the founder of one of the earliest Christian churches, about 1,900 years ago. He was a friend of St. Paul, who gave Timothy advice on how to run his church. St. Paul wrote two letters, or Epistles, to Timothy that became books of the New Testament. Timothy became the first bishop of Ephesus. He was killed there by people who opposed the Christian religion. He was made a saint and his feast day is January 24.

tin

Tin is a soft silvery-white metal. Its chief use is the coating of the thin sheets of iron from which containers called cans, or "tin cans," are made. Tin is a chemical element, which means that it is one of the basic substances of which everything in the world is made.

Tin has been used since very ancient times, thousands of years ago. At first it was thought to be the same metal as lead. Men then learned to mix one-tenth tin and nine-tenths copper and make bronze. This was the hardest metal that had been made at that time and it revolutionized manufacturing and warfare. The greatest tin mines were in Spain and at Cornwall, in Wales. The Indians of South America were using tin when they were discovered by Europeans.

THE PROPERTIES OF TIN

Tin is softer than gold but harder than lead. It can be scratched by a fingernail. Tin has the lowest melting point of any common metal except mercury. Tin is very malleable, which means that it can be hammered into any shape that is wanted, but when it is heated almost to the melting point it becomes brittle. When it is exposed to very cold weather, it crumbles to a gray powder. This action is called *tin pest.* Tin will not tarnish in air; even when the air is moist, tin retains its luster indefinitely. When a bar of pure tin is bent, it makes a creaking sound.

USES OF TIN

More than one-third of the tin that is produced is used to plate sheets of iron and steel to keep them from rusting. The sheets of iron or steel may be plated by simply dipping them into melted tin. This is called a "hot tin dip." A more even coating can be gotten by electroplating, which is explained in the article on ELECTROLYSIS.

Pure tin, which is called *block tin,* resists the corroding action of water, so it is used to make pipes for carrying distilled water, soda water, and beer. About one-fifth of the tin produced is used to make the alloy (mixture of metals) called solder. Tin is used in many important alloys; among them are bronze, pewter, type metal (for printing type), bell metal, and Babbitt metal.

Chemical compounds of tin are used to make fabrics waterproof, to make the dyeing of fabrics permanent, to make silk seem heavier than it is, and to imitate gold in the gilding process. Paper-thin sheets of tin are called tin foil. They are used to wrap foods and other things so that dampness will not get to them and spoil them.

HOW TIN IS FOUND AND REFINED

There is about an ounce and a third to the ton of earth in the earth's crust, so tin is not a very rare metal, but there are not many places where it can be mined. The chief ore of tin is called *cassiterite,* or tinstone. Malaya, Bolivia, Indonesia, the Congo, Thailand, parts of the Soviet Union, and Nigeria, in this order, are the chief producers of tin ore. No tin ore is mined in the United States, but about half the world's production of tin is used in the United States.

After the ore is crushed and concentrated, it is roasted. Then it is treated with acids that remove everything but the *tin dioxide,* which is composed of tin and oxygen. Pure tin is then gotten from the tin dioxide by the process of electrolysis.

Tintoretto

Tintoretto was a great Italian painter who lived in Venice about four hundred years ago. His real name was Jacopo Robusti and he was son of a dyer. The Italian word for dyer is *tintore,* and from this Jacopo came to be called *Il Tintoretto,* or "the little dyer." When he was a boy he began to study painting under one of the great masters of the time, Titian. After a time Tintoretto moved to his own studio. He continued to paint in Venice for the rest of his life. He was born in 1518 and died in 1594. His most important works are paintings of religious subjects and portraits (pictures of one or more persons). Among the religious paintings are *Circumcision, Last Judgment,* and *Crucifixion,* all of them in churches in Venice.

Tippecanoe, Battle of

The Battle of Tippecanoe was a battle fought in 1811 between United States troops under General William Henry Harrison and a much larger force of Indians, on the Tippecanoe River in what is now Indiana. The United States government had been acquiring more and more Indian territory, and the Indians were urged to rebel by the Shawnee chief TECUMSEH, about whom there is a separate article. Tecumseh's brother, known as "the Prophet," led the Indian forces. The Indians attacked Harrison's camp but were badly beaten in a fight that lasted only a few hours. As a result Harrison became a popular hero. When Harrison ran for President twenty-nine years later, with John Tyler as candidate for Vice President, one of their campaign slogans was "Tippecanoe and Tyler too."

Tipperary

Tipperary is a county in Ireland, in Munster Province. Its area is about 1,640 square miles and in 1961 there were 123,779 people living there. Most of the country is low plains, including good farm land. Cattle-raising is the chief occupation. The county seat is the town of Clonmel. Tipperary became a familiar name in the United States through a song that was popular during World War I, "It's a Long Way to Tipperary."

Tirana

Tirana is the capital and largest city of Albania. It is in the central part of the country, about 20 miles from the port of Durazzo on the Adriatic Sea. About 170,000 people live in Tirana. Most of them work in industries that process agricultural products of the surrounding fertile farmlands. There are factories that make cotton goods, cigarettes, flour, and dairy products. Tirana is a modern city, with a university and technical colleges, music and art schools.

Tirana was founded in the 1600s by a Turkish general and was named in honor of a Turkish victory at Teheran in Persia. It was made capital of Albania in 1920, and it then began to grow into a modern city.

TIRANA, ALBANIA. Population (1974 estimate) 169,300. Capital of Albania.

tire

A tire is any kind of band that goes around the outside of a wheel on an automobile or other vehicle. In the early days of wagons and carriages, tires were hoops of iron or steel. They protected the wheel against damage from the road, but they did not add to the comfort of the passenger. When ways were found to make soft rubber, tires of solid rubber were used. They made riding only a little more comfortable. The greatest improvement came with the development of the pneumatic (air-filled) tire. It was invented more than a hundred years ago, in 1845, for use on carriages, but was not widely used until bicycling became popular, about 1890. Pneumatic tires were then adopted for automobiles and are still the only kind used, though many changes and improvements have been made in them.

Automobile tires for fifty years required two parts. One was the actual tire, called the *shoe* or *casing,* on which the car rode. The other was the inner tube, a tube of soft rubber that was put inside the tire and pumped full of air. With pneumatic tires, a car actually rides on air, compressed until it will hold heavy weights.

In the early 1950s the tubeless tire was introduced. The tire itself holds the air and no inner tube is necessary. By 1955 many of the new automobiles were using tubeless tires.

EARLY TIRES

The iron or steel tire was put on the wheel by use of the fact that heat makes

things expand (grow larger). The tire would be made about the same size as the rim of the wheel. Then it would be heated until it was large enough to be fitted tightly onto the wheel. When it cooled it would return to its smaller size and grip the wheel tightly. Usually it was fastened with bolts also.

Solid rubber tires were fastened to the wheel with both bolts and adhesives (glue). A solid rubber tire was simply a thick band of rubber. Sometimes it had a groove cut between the tire and the wheel, or holes drilled through the rubber, to make it springier. Solid rubber was all right as long as cars and trucks traveled at low speeds. At one time most big trucks used solid rubber because pneumatic tires were not considered strong enough. Today a heavy truck with solid rubber tires would pound a road to pieces, and such tires are banned by law in most places.

The pneumatic tires used on bicycles did not (and do not) need inner tubes. When air is pumped into the tire, the air pressure holds the soft rubber tightly against the rim of the wheel. The load carried is not heavy enough to make the air escape. It was soon found that automobiles were too heavy and too fast for such tires (though they were much lighter and slower than they are today). The jouncing would force the tire away from the rim just enough to let the air escape gradually. This problem was not solved until modern tubeless tires were developed, and in the meantime the inner tube had to be used.

The first automobile tires were "high-pressure" tires. They carried perhaps 60 or more pounds of air pressure, and they were quite narrow compared to modern tires. They were much easier to ride on than solid rubber, but with the high air pressure they were still pretty hard and automobiles bounced about quite a lot. High air pressure also created a kind of danger. If a tire was cut, the air would rush out at a tremendous rate, causing a "blow-out" and perhaps sending the car off the road.

In the early 1920s the balloon tire was introduced. This was the same kind of tire except that it was much wider and required much less air pressure, perhaps 30 pounds. It made riding more comfortable and reduced the danger of blow-outs.

From almost the earliest days of the automobile, tires have had *treads,* or coverings of soft rubber molded in a pattern that makes it grip the road and resist skidding, even on wet roads. Special treads called *snow treads* can be used in the winter. They have treads cut very deeply so that they grip even in deep snow.

HOW A MODERN TIRE IS MADE

A tire has an *outer casing* and a *lining.* The foundation of the outer casing is hoops made of strong steel wire. The hoops of wire are wrapped with many layers of a fabric made of nylon, rayon, or cotton. This fabric has been dipped in liquid rubber. More than a mile of cord and thread goes into the making of an ordinary automobile tire. Layers of fabric and rubber, one after another, are built up. They are joined together by high pressure. The ordinary tire is usually a *four-*

ply tire (having four layers). Tires that must be stronger are six-ply or more.

The last layer is the extra amount of rubber put on the tire where it is to be in contact with the road. This layer is the tread. Often a tire is still good when the tread is worn down, and such a tire can be *retreaded*—have a new top layer of rubber put on.

After these operations the tire is vulcanized (treated with heat to soften it, as explained in the article on RUBBER). It is then ready for use.

This process makes tires that are strong enough for automobiles, heavy trucks and buses, airplanes, tractors, gun carriages, and other heavy loads. A tire on a passenger automobile often lasts for 100,000 miles. Huge tires on giant bombers are as much as ten feet high. Tires on some earthmoving machinery are eight feet high and almost three feet wide, weigh more than a ton, and can carry a load of more than twenty tons with as little as 45 pounds of air pressure in them.

USE OF SYNTHETIC RUBBER

Natural rubber was used for all tires made in the United States until World War II. Then a shortage of rubber made it necessary to try synthetic (man-made) rubber. It proved satisfactory and modern tires use some synthetic rubber mixed with natural rubber.

TUBELESS TIRES

Automobile drivers today seldom have tire trouble. In the early days of automobiling, it was unusual to make a trip as long as 40 miles without having to change a tire at least once. Nails would cut into tires and cause *punctures,* letting air escape and causing a "flat tire." Occasionally a whole section of a tire would burst, causing a blow-out.

In years of research, the rubber industry developed heavier and stronger tires and also designed a number of different safety tires and tubes. Some of these were self-sealing, which means that if a nail or other sharp object cut through the tire the rubber would close around it and prevent air from escaping.

These developments made possible the tubeless tire. The rubber sides of this tube will cling to the rim of the wheel so tightly that air will not escape. A nail hole or small injury can be repaired by filling the hole with a liquid rubber preparation. This hardens and makes a permanent repair.

tissue, any substance of which the body is made: see the articles on CELL and on HUMAN BODY.

Titanic

The *Titanic* was a British ocean liner that crashed into an iceberg and sank on its first voyage, on April 15, 1912. Its sinking caused a loss of more than 1,500 lives and was probably the greatest sea disaster in history. The *Titanic* was the most modern, most luxurious and most expensive ship ever built, and was called "unsinkable." It was trying to break a speed record on its first trip, from England to New York. It struck the iceberg about five hundred miles south of Newfoundland. The people aboard thought the ship could not sink, and the few life-

boats it carried were not lowered until some time after it struck the iceberg. This disaster led to setting up a North Atlantic Iceberg Patrol, which warns ships about icebergs, and new regulations about the number, kind and handling of lifeboats carried on passenger ships.

titanium

Titanium is a silvery-white metal, about as hard as iron. It is a chemical element, which means that it is one of the basic substances of which everything in the world is made. It is usually brittle, but when absolutely pure it can be forged and hammered to shape and drawn into wire.

When titanium is added to steel it makes alloys that increase the hardness and strength of the steel. An alloy of nickel, chromium, and titanium can withstand great heat, and is used for the combustion chambers of jet engines. Titanium and ammonia make the bright white smoke that is used for smokescreens and skywriting. Combined with oxygen, titanium forms a brilliant white powder that is used to color white paints. Added to oxygen in another way, it forms the mineral called rutile. Rutile will bend rays of light more than any other substance, and can be cut into gems that sparkle more brilliantly than diamonds.

Titanium is also used to add whiteness to paper, face powder, shoe whitening, enamels, glazes, and artificial pearls.

Titans

The Titans were six giants and six giantesses in Greek mythology, the stories the ancient Greeks told about their gods and goddesses. They were the sons and daughters of Uranus (Heaven) and Gaea (Earth) and at first lived in heaven. One of them, Cronos, rose up against his father and then ruled in his place. Then he married his sister Rhea, and they had many children. Cronos feared that one day one of his children might kill him, as he had killed his father, so to protect himself he swallowed them. Only one of his sons, Zeus, escaped. When Zeus grew up he made war on Cronos, and eventually with the help of other gods Zeus conquered the Titans and became king of Heaven.

Titian

Titian was one of the greatest Italian painters during the Renaissance, or rebirth of learning and the arts, more than four hundred years ago. His full name was Tiziano Vecelli, and he was born in 1477 in a small town in Venice, which at that time was one of the separate kingdoms in Italy. He began to study painting when he was a boy, working with one of the great masters of the time, Giovanni Bellini. Bellini was the official state painter of Venice, and in time Titian succeeded him in this position.

When Titian was 55 years old, he became an official painter at the court of Charles V, the Holy Roman Emperor. After the death of Charles he served Charles' son, Philip II of Spain, for the rest of his life. Titian died in 1576, at the age of 99. He had been one of the few great painters whose greatness was recognized throughout his lifetime.

Titian painted hundreds of paintings and used many different subjects. One of his favorite subjects was his daughter, Lavinia, who had beautiful red hair, and that particular shade of red has come to be called titian. Many of his works show scenes from mythology, the stories ancient peoples used to tell about their gods and goddesses. During the last years of his life Titian used chiefly religious subjects.

Titicaca, Lake

Lake Titicaca is the largest lake in South America and one of the highest lakes in the world.

The lake is partly in southeastern Peru and partly in western Bolivia and is an important transportation route between the two countries. Lake Titicaca has an area of about 3,200 square miles. It is 110 miles long, 35 miles wide, and about 700 feet deep. The lake has two sections, Lake Chucuito and Lake Uñamarca, which are connected by the Strait of Tiquina. Several rivers flow into Lake Titicaca, and its outlet is the Desaguadero River. In the lake are the islands of Titicaca and Coati, on which have been found ruins of the civilization of the Incas, the Indian people that lived in Peru hundreds of years ago.

titmouse

The titmouse is a bird, a member of the same family as the chickadee. Titmice are found in the warmer parts of Europe, North America, and Africa. They live on small insects, insect eggs, and occasional seeds.

The bush tit of the southwestern United States and Mexico makes a long sacklike nest that hangs in the desert brush. Some African titmice are expert weavers, and their bag-shaped nests are so skillfully woven that they look like heavy felt. Titmice usually live in small flocks, but some pair off at the breeding season to raise their families.

Tito, Marshal

Marshal Tito is the name used by the dictator of Yugoslavia. During World War II he was the military leader of the Yugoslav forces fighting the Germans, and after the war he set up a Communist government with himself at the head. Under him Yugoslavia became the only Communist country in Europe that was independent of Soviet Russia.

Almost all the Communist revolutionary leaders took names that were different from their real names. Tito's real name was Josip Broz. He was born about 1890 in Croatia, which was then a province of Austria but is now part of Yugoslavia. When he grew up he became a locksmith and worked in a factory in the city of Zagreb, the Croatian capital. There he became interested in the problems of the workers and tried to organize them into labor unions. In World War I he served in the Austrian army, was captured by Russian troops, and was forced to serve for a time in the Russian army. In Russia he became a Communist. After the war

he returned to Yugoslavia and tried to promote communism there.

In World War II, when Yugoslavia was occupied by German troops, Tito joined the underground forces led by General Draza Mikhailovich. He disagreed with Mikhailovich's political ideas, so he formed a different fighting force called the Partisans, which fought not only the German's but also anyone opposed to communism. The Partisans soon became very strong. Tito held the highest rank, marshal, in their army, which was called the People's Army.

During the war Peter, the king of Yugoslavia, and his government were in exile (out of the country). Tito and the Partisans formed a new government, and when Yugoslavia was liberated from the Germans he set up his government in opposition to that of the king. It was recognized as the official government by the chief Allied countries (United States, Great Britain, and Russia).

Tito put in practice many ideas of communism, such as government ownership of industries, and of some land. His government was not friendly toward capitalist nations, such as the United States, and was very friendly toward Soviet Russia. Then, in 1948, he said that Soviet Russia was trying to control Yugoslavia for its own benefit. He became unfriendly toward Russia, and the term Titoist came to mean any Communist who wanted his own country to be independent of Soviet Russia. After this Tito became more friendly toward capitalist countries and made agreements with several of them, including the United States, which lent Yugoslavia money. In 1955 the new Soviet leaders tried to make friends again with Tito, and in the following years, after some renewed quarreling, both countries gradually developed better relations, though Tito did not give up his insistence on independent policies for his country. See YUGOSLAVIA.

Titus

Titus Flavius Sabinus Vespasianus was emperor of Rome about 1,900 years ago. He was born about the year 40, received military training, and then served under his father, the emperor Vespasian, in many campaigns. He was put in charge of the Roman armies in Judea (most of which is now Israel), and in the year 70 he captured the city of Jerusalem and destroyed the great Jewish Temple there. On the death of his father, in the year 79, Titus became emperor, but he died two years later, in the year 81.

Tlingit Indians

The Tlingit are a group of Indian tribes that live along the Pacific Coast of Canada and Alaska. The Tlingit are famous for their carved totem poles made from big tree trunks. A totem pole may be twelve feet or more high and has many strange faces and animal heads carved into it, one above the other. Each face or head is the sign of a clan or family group in the tribe. The clans are named after various wild animals, such as the beaver, eagle, raven, bear, whale, wolf, and owl. A child born in any clan can marry only a person of certain other clans. Each Tlingit Indian family once had

a totem pole standing at the door of its house and carved on this pole were the different signs of the clans to which it belonged by ancestry and marriage. It was a kind of family tree or history.

The Tlingit lived in villages made up of rows of houses near the shore, facing the sea. Their houses were made of cedar planks and were quite large, up to 60 feet long. Not only the immediate family but a great many relatives lived together in these long houses. The Tlingit ate fish that they caught in the ocean. They also hunted seal and sea otter.

The Tlingit people were divided into slaves, common people, and aristocrats. Slaves did not have to work very hard and were just as well fed as the common people but were sold or bought like animals. When a new house was built, a slave was killed and buried underneath one of the posts in the belief that this would make it last a long time.

One of the strange customs of the Tlingit Indians was the potlatch. This was a feast given after the death of a relative. At the feast slaves and all kinds of property were given away to the guests. All near relatives of the dead person were expected to contribute property to be given away. The more generous a Tlingit was in giving away his possessions during this feast, the more he was respected. A rich Indian might become very poor after a potlatch, but a big potlatch increased his importance and usually he became rich again. The Tlingit still live along the Alaskan coast but most of their old customs are dying out.

toad, a froglike amphibian animal: see the articles on FROGS AND TOADS and AMPHIBIANS.

toadstool

Toadstool is a name often used for a kind of mushroom that grows in many fields and woods. Usually people think of toadstools as a poisonous kind of mushroom. Often these mushrooms are quite harmless, but some of them are so poisonous that it is dangerous for anyone but an expert to judge whether they should be eaten. See the article MUSHROOM.

tobacco

Tobacco is a name used for several different plants. All are members of the Nicotiana family of plants, named for a Frenchman, Jean Nicot, who first grew tobacco in France. Some of these plants have beautiful, sweet-smelling blossoms, and grow as high as thirty feet.

The best-known tobacco plant is grown so that its leaves can be dried and made into cigarettes, cigars, smoking tobacco for pipes, and other products. This is not the same plant as the flowering varieties, but it is a member of the same Nicotiana family. The leaves contain nicotine, which in its pure form is a poison, but which in very small quantities (as in the tobacco used for smoking) increases the blood pressure and may calm a person's nerves.

Tobacco is the principal crop that man grows to furnish not a necessity but to provide for a habit. Scientists have long argued about the harmful effects of tobacco, but people (including the scien-

tists) have gone right on using it.

When Columbus and other early explorers reached America they found Indians smoking tobacco through hollow tubes, probably made of cane or bark. They took tobacco back to Europe and Europeans were soon smoking. Now tobacco is a worldwide crop. Much of it is still grown in the Americas, but large quantities are produced in Turkey, India, China, and other places.

THE PLANT

The tobacco plant grows to a height of 4 to 6 feet and has large, broad leaves that sometimes are more than 3 feet long. Some special plants, including those grown in Turkey, are much smaller and the leaves are only a few inches long. Tobacco grows best in places with warm climates and sandy soil where the water drains off quickly.

In the United States, North Carolina is far ahead of all other states in the production of tobacco; next comes Kentucky and then Tennessee. The other important states in tobacco production are Virginia, South Carolina, and Georgia. Several other states grow tobacco but not in as large quantities.

CURING

After tobacco is grown, the leaves must be cured, or prepared for use. Some of this curing is done by tying up bundles of leaves and hanging them up in sheds that have open sides. The air circulates through the sheds and cures and dries the tobacco. In some places the tobacco is dried in the sun.

Two-thirds of all the tobacco used in cigarettes is cured by the flue-curing method. The tobacco is dried by intense heat conducted through flues (pipes). Flue curing is not done to cure the tobacco more quickly, but to make it sweeter, lighter, and more flavorful.

The cured leaves are then either sold directly to buyers or sent to warehouses where buyers bid for them in auction sales. Most tobacco is bought by large companies that manufacture cigarettes. Special crops are grown for cigar tobacco. Smoking and chewing tobaccos are usually made from the same tobaccos that are used in cigarettes, but they are graded, cut, and flavored differently. Of every ten pounds of tobacco used in the United States, about eight pounds are used in cigarettes, one pound in cigars, and one pound in pipe and chewing tobacco.

CIGARETTES

The cured tobacco bought for cigarettes is taken to factories where it is shredded by machines, treated with flavorings such as molasses, and put into machines that automatically roll it in paper and pack the finished cigarettes in packages and cartons. About four hundred billion cigarettes are bought in the United States every year—more than a hundred packs for every man, woman, and child.

During the 1950s, repeated medical reports indicated that smoking—especially the smoking of cigarettes—increases the likelihood that a person will have cancer of the lungs. The tars and nicotine in cigarettes were thought to be the principal carcinogens (causes of cancer). This news did not stop most people from

smoking, and in fact cigarette-smoking increased in the United States; but millions of smokers changed to "filter cigarettes," which have tips composed of filters that remove some of the tars and nicotine from the smoke.

Until about sixty years ago, cigarettes were not very popular. Most men smoked cigars or pipes, and respectable women never smoked. Cigarette-smoking has increased more than a hundred and fifty times since the year 1905, while the smoking of cigars and pipes has gone down. Today, in the United States, people smoke more than 500 billion cigarettes each year and about seven billion cigars.

Cigars are made by rolling the dried tobacco leaves and pressing them together to form a kind of tube. The tube of tobacco is then wrapped around several times with a kind of special tobacco leaf called *wrapper*. The wrapper keeps the cigar from drying out too quickly and also gives it a special flavor. The finest leaf for cigar-making comes from Cuba and is called Havana, but good wrapper tobacco is grown in the United States and other places.

OTHER USES OF TOBACCO

Pipe tobacco is usually shredded, but not as finely as cigarette tobacco. Usually pipe tobaccos are composed of a mixture of different kinds of leaf. Thus, a particular brand of pipe tobacco may include a tobacco called burley that grows in Kentucky, a kind of tobacco that grows in Turkey, and another kind that grows in Syria.

Many different kinds of pipe are made for smoking tobacco. Among the most familiar are the briar pipes, which are carved out of the roots of certain briar plants that grow in Greece and other parts of the Middle East. Other well-known pipe materials are clay, corncob, cherry wood, porcelain, and a mineral called meerschaum. An interesting pipe, called a *hookah*, is used in Turkey. The hookah consists of a bowl in which the tobacco is burned, a tube leading from the bowl into a jar of water, and a tube leading from the top of the jar of water to the smoker's mouth. When the smoker draws (sucks) on the mouthpiece, the smoke from the burning bowl passes through the water and into the tube to the smoker's mouth. This is said to "purify" the smoke and cool it.

CHEWING TOBACCO AND SNUFF

Chewing tobacco is flavored with molasses and other flavorings. It is sometimes packed in shredded form in bags, and sometimes it is compressed into little cakes called plugs. Tobacco-chewing is a habit that is becoming more and more rare, especially since it is not considered refined to chew tobacco.

Tobacco used for snuff is ground almost to a powder. There is a separate article about SNUFF.

Whether or not the use of tobacco in any form is harmful to grownups, all agree that young people should not smoke until they are at least 18 years old.

toboggan

A toboggan is a flat sled without

runners. It is usually made of strips of wood joined together. Some toboggans are made of aluminum or other light metal. A toboggan is curved at the front end. It is used mostly on snow-covered slopes or on special chutes, or sledding courses, on mountainsides. A toboggan cannot be used on sharp curves, or where it might have to be guided around rough spots, because unlike most sleds it has no steering gear. Some toboggans are made for one person and others for two or more.

A modern kind of toboggan is much like a great plate or saucer. In one of these "flying saucers" a person whirls and spins as he slides down a slope.

Tobago, an island in the Caribbean Sea: see the article TRINIDAD AND TOBAGO.

Togo

Togo is a country in western Africa which became independent in 1960. Before that, it was called French Togoland. Togo is about 22,000 square miles in size, making it a little smaller than West Virginia. It is bounded by Upper Volta, Dahomey, the Atlantic, and Ghana. The people are Negro and speak various tribal languages, although the official language is French. These people make their living by farming. The chief exports are coffee, cacao, palm kernels, palm oil, cotton, and copra. Togo is a republic which is governed by a president and his council of ministers. The capital is Lomé, a city of about 95,000.

TOGO. Area, 21,800 square miles. Population (1975 estimate) 2,197,900.

Tojo, Hideki

Hideki Tojo was a Japanese general who was head of the Japanese government during World War II. He was born in 1885 in Tokyo, received military training, and became an officer in the Japanese Army. After rising to the rank of general and then serving as Minister of War in the Japanese government, in October 1941 he became premier, or head of the government. Therefore it was by his order that the Japanese Navy bombed Pearl Harbor on December 7, 1941. In 1944 the Japanese forces suffered heavy losses in the war against the United States, and Tojo resigned. In 1945 he was tried as a war criminal and found guilty. He was hanged in 1948.

Tokyo

Tokyo is the capital and largest city of Japan. It is on the east coast of the principal Japanese island, Honshu, and is a seaport on Tokyo Bay. It is a financial, industrial and cultural center. There are large automobile, chemical and textile plants. Estimates of 1974 gave Tokyo a larger population than either New York or London, making Tokyo the world's biggest city with a population of about 8,840,950, (11,454,000 with suburbs); but the relative sizes of big cities depend on how many of the suburbs they include.

Most of Tokyo is very modern. The city is divided by the Sumida River, and there are many other rivers and canals. The streets are wide and there are streetcars, motor buses, and subways. Among the places of interest are the Imperial

Palace where the Japanese emperor lives, the Diet (parliament) building, St. Luke's Hospital (one of the best equipped in the world), astronomical observatories, and the "earthquake-proof" Imperial Hotel built by the American architect Frank Lloyd Wright. Tokyo has more than twenty universities, the largest being Tokyo University, Waseda University, and St. Paul's University. There are many beautiful parks and more than a thousand temples and shrines.

Tokyo was founded about eight hundred years ago as a village called Yedo, meaning "gate to the gulf." In 1868 Yedo was made capital of all Japan, in place of Kyoto, and it was renamed Tokyo, which in Japanese means "eastern capital." This was to distinguish it from Saikyo (meaning "western capital"), which was another name for Kyoto.

In 1923 half of Tokyo was destroyed by earthquake and fire. In the following years the city was rebuilt in more modern style, but the buildings were limited to eight stories as a safeguard against other earthquakes. In World War II much of Tokyo was damaged by United States bombers. When Japan was defeated, and was occupied by United States forces in 1945, Tokyo became the capital of the occupation forces. In 1952 a peace treaty made Japan independent again, with Tokyo as its capital.

TOKYO, JAPAN. Population (1970 census) 9,013,000. Capital of Japan.

Toledo, Ohio

Toledo is a large city in northwestern Ohio. It is on Lake Erie, near the place where the Maumee River empties into the lake. Toledo has an excellent natural harbor and is the second-largest port on the Great Lakes.

More than 380,000 people live in Toledo. It is a manufacturing city and its factories make many things, but the most famous product is glass. Toledo has been called the "glass capital of the world." In Toledo are the University of Toledo, a fine museum of art, and other cultural institutions.

Toledo was founded in 1833 when the villages of Port Lawrence and Vistula joined and took the name Toledo. Toledo grew as a lake port during the 1840s, after the building of the Wabash and Erie Canal and the Miami and Erie Canal. The first railroad reached Toledo in 1836. Since then it has become one of the largest railroad centers in the United States.

An interesting incident from Toledo history is the Toledo War, which took place in 1835–1836. Michigan and Ohio had a dispute over some territory and declared war on each other, but Congress awarded the territory to Ohio.

TOLEDO, OHIO. Population (1970 census) 383,818. County seat of Lucas County. On Lake Erie. Founded, 1833.

Toledo, Spain

Toledo is a city in central Spain. It is built on the slopes of a granite mountain, and the Tagus River flows in a curve around the bottom of the mountain. Over 40,000 people live in Toledo. Toledo is famous because of its history. It is not an important manufacturing or business city today, but its craftsmen still make fine sword blades, for which the city has been famous since the Middle Ages, and fine silk and wool fabrics are produced.

Toledo is an old city, with houses and buildings that were built more than a thousand years ago. Narrow streets follow a zig-zag path up the steep hill. In the cathedral of Toledo there are paintings by the artist El Greco, who lived in Toledo.

Toledo was an important city of the ancient Roman Empire and was the capital of Spain until the year 712, when it was taken by the Moors, a Mohammedan people who invaded and conquered Spain at that time. Spanish forces recaptured Toledo about 375 years later and it again became the Spanish capital. In 1560, Madrid became the capital of Spain and Toledo became less important. Toledo was the scene of fierce fighting during the War of the Spanish Succession and the Spanish Civil War.

TOLEDO, SPAIN. Population (1974 estimate) 43,955.

Tolstoy, Leo

Count Leo Tolstoy was a famous Russian novelist. Many people regard his novel *War and Peace* as the greatest ever written. He was born in 1828 on his father's big estate at Yasnaya Polyana. When he grew up he became a soldier and fought against the Turks in the Crimean War. After the war he retired to his country estate to devote himself to writing and thinking.

His first writings were about his experience in the army, and won him immediate success. Among them were *The Cossacks* and *Two Hussars.* When Tolstoy was about 49 years old he became interested in religion. He withdrew from the Russian Orthodox Church and founded his own religion. He thought people ought to live simply and close to nature. He was opposed to war and any other kind of violence, and he thought people should not try to resist when they were attacked or mistreated but should patiently bear these evils. He wrote many books about his beliefs, which he tried to apply to social questions, art, and many other things. He died in 1910 at the age of 82.

PRINCIPAL WORKS

Most of Tolstoy's greatest works were written before he became interested in his new religion. The most famous are *War and Peace*, which is a very long novel about Russia in the days of the French emperor Napoleon, and *Anna Karenina.*

Toltecs

The Toltecs were a people who lived in Mexico a thousand years before it was discovered by Europeans. Their civilization was much older than that of the AZTECS, about whom there is a separate article. What little is known about the Toltecs was discovered by scientists who have dug in the ruins of some of their cities. Their economy was based on farming, and they seem to have known a great deal about growing crops.

The Toltecs were fine artists in metals, pottery, and stone carving and they wove beautiful cloth. Their priests were the leaders of the culture and knew how to use hieroglyphics (picture writing). They also had developed a mathematical system and had an accurate 365-day calendar. They built great pyramids in ceremonial centers, and on the pyramids they built their temples and palaces.

About eight hundred years ago the culture of the Toltecs collapsed, and after several hundred years of warfare, the Aztec culture became dominant.

tomato

The tomato is an annual plant that is grown in many parts of the world for its fruit. The plant grows best when the air and soil are warm. It requires a warm growing season of four to five months for commercial production. In cooler sections of the world the seed is not planted directly in the garden but in hotbeds or greenhouses where the young plants are grown until they can be planted in the garden.

A tomato fruit may be as small as a cherry, or as large as a grapefruit, depending on the variety. The color of kinds grown commercially is red or reddish-yellow. There are a few yellow-skinned varieties. The different varieties have somewhat different flavors but in general they are tart to the taste. The juice is more acid than the flesh.

Tomatoes are used in many different ways. They may be eaten raw as a salad or served cooked. The juice of tomatoes is a very popular drink. They are also canned and preserved and made into a paste and catchup. Tomato soup is one of the most popular of all soups sold in grocery stores. The Vitamin C content of tomatoes is preserved after cooking, which is not the case in many other vegetables.

At one time tomatoes were called "love apples" and people thought eating them was harmful. Now it is known that tomatoes are one of the most healthful of all foods.

Tonga Islands

The Tonga Islands are a group of about 150 islands in the South Pacific Ocean. There are three main groups of islands: Tongatabu, Vavau, and Haabai. They form an independent kingdom in the British Commonwealth. The islands have an area of about 270 square miles, and about 80,000 people live there. The capital is Nukualofa, on the largest island, Tongatabu. Some of the islands are volcanic; others are built of coral. The people are mostly Polynesians who fish and farm for their livings.

The Tonga Islands were discovered in 1643 by a Dutch explorer, Abel Tasman, who also discovered Tasmania. In 1773, Captain Cook visited the region and named it the Friendly Islands. The British took over in 1900, but local government was controlled by Queen Salote who died in 1965. Her son, Prince Tongi, became King Taufa'ahau when she died. Tonga became independent in 1970.

tongue

The tongue is a small but important

part of the human or other animal body. It is a well-developed muscle with a special covering. Because it is a muscle, it can move in many ways and help the body to do many things. Its special covering on top, which looks like rough, moist velvet, contains the sensitive nerve endings that give us our sense of taste.

The tongue helps the body in three important ways. One is the sense of taste. A second is as an aid in speaking. The movement of the tongue inside the mouth permits us to make different sounds and form different words as the tongue rises and lowers in the mouth and touches or leaves the teeth. The third way is in chewing. Here the tongue acts as a mixer to move the food around inside the mouth.

The tongue in human beings and many other animals is attached at the back of the lower part of the mouth. It sometimes indicates by its coating whether or not a person is healthy or ill. When the tongue is coated with a thick, white substance, a doctor can often tell that something is wrong in the stomach or in another part of the body.

Tonkin or Tongking

Tonkin is a region in Indo-China, in the northern part of Viet Nam. It is about 45,000 square miles in size, about the size of the state of Louisiana. About ten million people live there, three times as many as live in Louisiana. Most of the people are Annamese, about whom you can read in the article on ANNAM. Farming is the chief occupation. The chief crop is rice, and cotton, sugar, tobacco, coffee and jute are also raised. The capital is Hanoi. In 1946 Tonkin became a province of the Republic of Viet Nam, and in 1954 it was yielded to a Communist government after much fighting. See the article VIET NAM.

tonsils

The tonsils are two masses of tissue at the back of the throat. There is one tonsil on each side of the throat. They are like little sponges that act as filters and traps for germs that might infect the body.

Sometimes the tonsils collect too many germs and become infected. This condition is called *tonsilitis*. Very young children often have cases of tonsilitis. The doctor usually first tries to clear the infection in the tonsils. He may paint them with an antiseptic, a drug to kill the germs. If a child 4 or 5 years old, or older, continues to have frequent attacks of tonsilitis, the doctor usually removes the tonsils in a simple operation. After diseased tonsils are removed the patient recovers quickly and almost always enjoys better health. If diseased tonsils are allowed to remain in the throat they can cause more serious infections in other parts of the body.

topaz

Topaz is the name of a semiprecious stone. It gets its name from the name of an island in the Red Sea, where it used to be found in great quantities. Topaz is a kind of mineral. It is usually a clear crystal that is yellow in color. It is often used in rings and other kinds of jewelry, and is used as a birthstone for November. Some topaz is found in the United States,

but more stones come from Russia, Siberia, the British Isles, Brazil, Australia, and Mexico

Topeka

Topeka is the capital and third-largest city of Kansas. It is in the northeastern part of the state, on the Kansas River. More than 125,000 people live in Topeka. The headquarters and shops of the Atchison, Topeka and Santa Fe Railroad are there, and also there are factories that make metal products, tires, tents, and awnings, and flour-milling and meatpacking plants. Topeka is the seat of the Menninger Foundation, a hospital for mental diseases, and of the Washburn University of Topeka. The city has an art museum, the state library, and the museum of the Kansas Historical Society.

Topeka was founded in 1854 on the Oregon Trail by Cyrus K. Holliday, who later organized the Santa Fe Railroad. The early settlers were mostly New Englanders who were opposed to slavery. They drew up the Topeka Constitution, which made the territory a "Free State," but their government was soon overthrown by Federal troops. In 1861 Topeka became the state capital when Kansas was admitted to the Union. The city's greatest growth came after the Santa Fe Railroad was completed through Topeka in 1872.

TOPEKA, KANSAS. Population (1970 census) 125,011. Capital of Kansas. County seat of Shawnee County. On the Kansas River. Founded, 1854.

Torah, Hebrew name for the first five books of the Bible: see the articles BIBLE and MOSES.

tornado, a violent windstorm that can do great damage: see the article on HURRICANE.

Toronto

Toronto is the capital and largest city of Ontario, and the second-largest city of Canada. It is on Lake Ontario, at the mouth of the Humber River. Toronto is a commercial, financial and industrial center, and one of the best ports on Lake Ontario. Its harbor receives shipping of agricultural products and minerals from much of Canada.

Over two million people live in Toronto and its suburbs. The city has large industries, including shipbuilding yards, railroad shops, and plants that make automobiles and farm machinery. There are livestock markets and meatpacking plants. Toronto is Canada's largest book-publishing center.

Toronto is the seat of Toronto University, which includes an observatory; the Royal Ontario Museum; Toronto General Hospital; schools of music and architecture; and the Toronto Symphony Orchestra. There are many parks, beaches and other places of amusement. The yearly Canadian National Exhibition is held in Toronto. The city has two cathedrals, one Anglican and one Roman Catholic.

HISTORY OF TORONTO

Toronto was the site of a fur-trading post as early as 1656. In 1749 the French built a fort there called Fort Rouillé, but

ten years later they burned it to prevent the English from taking it. The English rebuilt the site and in 1793 the town was made the capital of Upper Canada and was renamed York. During the War of 1812 the town was twice captured by the Americans. In 1834 it was given its present name, Toronto, which is an Indian word meaning "a place of meeting." In 1867 it became the capital of Ontario.

TORONTO, CANADA. Population (1973 estimate) 712,786 (2,628,043 with suburbs). Capital of Ontario. Founded, 1749.

torpedo

A torpedo is the most dangerous weapon that can be used to sink a ship. It is a long, cigar-shaped steel case filled with explosives. Torpedoes are fired from metal tubes that submarines and other warships carry. They can also be dropped from airplanes. Like little submarines, they have their own motors, which drive them along under the water so that they can hit ships near their bottoms, where they are weakest.

The torpedo was invented in 1866 by a Scotsman named Robert Whitehead. During World War I and II, German submarines sank so many British ships with torpedoes that they almost won the wars alone by cutting off the food and supplies that the British people had to have to go on fighting.

HOW A TORPEDO WORKS

A torpedo is usually about two feet thick and about twenty feet long. In its nose (front end) it carries about 600 pounds of explosives. When the torpedo hits the side of a ship, a device in the nose works a trigger that sets off the explosive. A torpedo may have an electrical device in its nose that makes it blow up when it even gets near a ship. These are called magnetic torpedoes, and they do not have to be as accurate as other torpedoes.

At the back of the torpedo tubes is a small amount of explosive. When this is set off, the torpedo shoots out of the tube and plunges into the water. Some torpedoes can be fired by compressing air and letting it out suddenly. When the torpedo is "fired," a switch automatically turns on, starting the torpedo's motor. A torpedo may have an electrical motor that turns two little propellers, or it may be driven by a mixture of alcohol, compressed air, and water. When a spark touches this mixture, steam is formed. The steam turns the wheel of a turbine motor that turns the propellers.

Some torpedoes go about 50 miles an hour. Unless they hit something, they will keep going for about ten miles, then sink to the bottom of the sea.

It is not easy to make a torpedo hit the ship it is aimed at, especially if the ship is moving. Much training is required before a person is an expert at aiming one.

Each torpedo has two rudders in its tail, one to keep it from going too far up or down and the other to keep it from going from side to side. The rudders of a torpedo look somewhat like the tail of an airplane.

Torpedoes travel about 25 feet below the surface of the sea, so that they will hit a ship almost at its bottom. The torpedo has a device called a hydrostatic valve,

which keeps it at the right depth. The hydrostatic valve measures the pressure of the water. The deeper it goes, the more pressure there is, and when the pressure gets too great, the valve makes the up-and-down rudder move, raising the level of the torpedo. The torpedo also has a spinning gyroscope, which keeps it steady (see the article on the GYROSCOPE).

torque converter

A torque converter is a kind of transmission used on automobiles. The transmission transmits (sends) power from the engine to the rear wheels, which drive the car. Torque is twisting power. While an automobile engine is running, it is turning at high speed and delivering great twisting power, but the driver cannot control this. The torque converter changes it to power that he can control, making it greater or less as he pleases.

Until the time of World War II, all automobiles used transmissions in which the driver could select his speed by the use of a clutch and gears. With the clutch he could connect the engine to the rear wheels or disconnect it; with the gears he could change speeds or directions. (This is explained with pictures in the article on GEAR.) Torque converters came into use after World War II. They make the clutch unnecessary and replace the kind of transmission that uses gears.

When a torque converter is used, the automobile engine is made to run a pump. The pump makes a heavy oil flow rapidly around a kind of wheel that is cut so that the moving oil will turn it. When the pump is not running fast enough to turn the wheel, the oil flows harmlessly past it. By speeding up the engine, the driver makes the oil flow fast enough to turn the wheel. If something goes wrong and the wheel cannot be turned, the oil flows past it. In gear transmissions, the power of the engine sometimes broke the gears in such cases.

Torquemada, a Spanish monk, one of the leaders of the Inquisition in Spain. His full name was Tomás de Torquemada, and he was born about 1420 and died in 1498. See the article INQUISITION.

Torrid Zone, the regions of the earth that are closest to the equator: see the articles TROPICS and ZONES.

tortoise, an animal of the turtle family: see the articles TURTLE and REPTILE.

Tory

Tory was the name of one of the two main political parties of Great Britain for about two hundred years. The term Tory was first used about 1680. The other main party was called Whig, and this name was later used for an American political party. In general, the Tories supported the king and the Church of England. The Whigs favored reforms that would make the government more democratic, though in the 1700s the members of the Whig Party were mostly landowners and noblemen. The Whig and Tory parties lasted until about 1832. The Tories were later succeeded by the Conservative Party and the Whigs by the Liberal Party.

Toscanini, Arturo

Arturo Toscanini is the name of a great Italian conductor, or orchestra leader. Many people regard him as the greatest conductor of all time.

Toscanini was born in 1867 in Parma, Italy, the son of a poor tailor. At the age of 18 he graduated from the Parma Conservatory (music school) with high honors. He played the cello in several orchestras, and then got a job as cellist with an opera company that was going to tour South America. Then, before a performance in Rio de Janeiro, Brazil, the Brazilian conductor quarreled with the Italian singers and refused to conduct. Toscanini took over in his place, and his conducting met with great success. He was 21 years old at the time.

In the next few years Toscanini was invited to conduct at several European opera houses. He conducted the first performances of several operas that have since become famous, among them Verdi's *Otello,* Leoncavallo's *I Pagliacci,* and Puccini's *La Bohème.* He became the most important conductor of Italy's most famous opera house, La Scala in Milan. From 1908 to 1915 he was conductor at New York City's Metropolitan Opera. In 1925 he became director of New York's Philharmonic Symphony Orchestra, a position he held for eleven years.

Toscanini, 69 years old, then thought of retiring, but the National Broadcasting Company assembled a symphony orchestra especially for him and he conducted their concerts until he retired, in 1954, at the age of 88. He died in 1957.

Toscanini was called by the title *Maestro,* which in Italian means "master."

totem

A totem is a sign of a special god or spirit that is supposed to belong to a particular person, family, or tribe. Among some primitive peoples, including some tribes of American Indians, there was a division of the tribe into different groups and each group was represented by some animal or plant. This animal or plant was its totem, the spirit or minor god of that group.

The group usually painted pictures of the totem on its house or tent, and a few carved totem poles with pictures of the spirit. Totem poles are described in the article on the TLINGIT Indians. Sometimes the family worshiped the totem, but usually it did not.

Totems that belonged to a particular person acted as the guardian spirit and helper of that individual. A common way to acquire a personal totem was for a young man or woman to dream of an animal or plant during special ceremonies.

It is not known when or why totemism began, but it is known throughout the world. Some scientists believe its purpose was to prevent too many marriages within a family or group. The rule would be that each young man and woman would have to marry someone from a different totem group.

toucan

The toucan is a tropical bird that lives in the Americas from Mexico to Argentina. It is a brilliantly colored bird, but its most distinctive feature is its extremely large, thick bill. The bill of a toucan is more than twice as long as its head, and it is as thick at the base as the height of the head. The bird itself is about the size of a crow. The call of the toucan is a harsh shriek.

A toucan's plumage may be a mixture of many colors, including a brilliant scarlet combined with blue and black, or a yellow, red, black and green combination, or vivid blues, yellows, and reds with black touches. The toucan's beak is almost as brightly colored as its plumage.

Toucans live on fruits, seeds, young birds, eggs, and insects. They nest in holes scooped out of high tree branches.

Toulouse

Toulouse is a city in southwest France. It is on the Garonne River and on canals that connect it with the Mediterranean Sea and with Bordeaux on the Atlantic Ocean.

Over 380,000 people live in Toulouse. It is a manufacturing city, with many factories. Toulouse is a very old city, and some of its ancient buildings are still standing. It is the site of the Church of St. Sernin, where St. Thomas Aquinas is buried. The University of Toulouse, founded in 1230, is the second-oldest in France.

Toulouse was an important city as early as the days of the ancient Romans. In 1271 it became part of the kingdom of France, but it remained almost independent under its powerful counts for hundreds of years. In World War II Toulouse was a center of French underground resistance against the Germans, and it was badly damaged by bombs.

TOULOUSE, FRANCE. Population (1974 estimate) 380,340. Capital of Haute-Garonne department. On the Garonne River.

Toulouse-Lautrec, Henri

Henri Toulouse-Lautrec was a famous French artist who is best-remembered for his paintings, sketches and posters of life in Paris and of popular entertainers. He was born in 1864 and was a sickly child. As a boy he broke both his legs, which did not heal properly, and he  had a deformed appearance for the rest of his life. He studied art under several fine masters of the time. The most popular nightclub entertainers of his time were Yvette Guilbert, Jane Avril, and La Goulue, and he made many lithographs (a kind of print) as posters for them. His work was not considered particularly good at the time, but in recent years it has become very valuable. Toulouse-Lautrec lived a very wild life. While young he began to suffer from mental disturbances.

Toulouse-Lautrec died in 1901, at the age of 37.

tourmaline

Tourmaline is a semiprecious stone. It is usually black in color, but some kinds are blue, red, green, brown, or colorless. It is often used in rings and other kinds of jewelry, and is one of the birthstones for October. Tourmaline is found in the United States, the islands of Madagascar and Elba, Russia, Siberia, and Mexico.

tournament

A tournament was a kind of contest and military practice that knights in armor engaged in five hundred and more years ago, throughout Europe and in England. They fought on horseback, using spears and swords. This kind of fighting was called jousting, and the tournament was sometimes called a joust. It is described in the article on KNIGHTHOOD. The word *tournament* is used today for contests in various games, such as bowling, billiards, chess, and contract bridge.

Toussaint L'Ouverture, Pierre

Pierre Dominique Toussaint L'Ouverture was a Negro general who led the natives of Haiti in a rebellion against their European rulers, which resulted in the forming of the Republic of Haiti. He was born in 1743 in San Domingo (now the Dominican Republic). At that time Haiti was ruled by the British, French and English, and many of the Europeans living there made slaves of the natives. Toussaint became superintendent of slaves on a plantation where he himself was a slave. In 1791 the slaves rebelled, and two years later they were freed and the French slavery abolished.

Toussaint then helped the French against the British, with whom they were quarreling, and eventually the British had to leave the island. A few years later Toussaint led a rebellion against the French and in 1801 he became master of the entire island, having defeated several rivals. The French emperor Napoleon then tried to re-establish slavery and sent troops to enforce this. The Haitians resisted successfully, but Toussaint was captured. He was freed, but was later sent to prison in France, where he died in 1803.

township

A township is a division of land that is used for dividing a state or county into smaller parts. Usually the township is square in shape and is six miles long on each side, making it 36 square miles in area. In some states a township can be other shapes and sizes.

TOWN MEETINGS

Usually the citizens of a township run their local affairs while the county government is a branch of the state government and takes care of the courthouse, the county records, the policing of the county, and so on.

The citizens of a township make their decisions in a gathering called the *town meeting*. The first American town meetings were held in the New England states. Every citizen can take part in the meeting, discussing any question that comes up and making any suggestions or complaints he wants to. The town meet-

ing has been called the most democratic of all forms of government. Usually a town meeting elects a board of selectmen, which makes decisions for the township between meetings. Some townships also elect other officers.

toxins, poisons produced in our bodies by germs or bacteria that cause certain kinds of disease: see the article ANTITOXIN.

toy

A toy is a plaything, or something that someone plays with to amuse himself. Toys have been used by children in all countries since ancient times. There are many different kinds of toy, ranging from a simple ball or set of blocks to a mechanical doll that may cost $300 or more. The leading maker of toys in the United States makes about five thousand different kinds each year. Almost always a toy is an imitation of something that grownups use, and is used by children who are pretending they are grownups. Many toys are educational. That is, they are made so that children can learn something by playing with them. For example, a child can learn how to spell words by playing with blocks that are marked with the letters of the alphabet. Probably the most popular kind of toy is the doll, and there is a separate article DOLLS.

Children in the United States have more and fancier toys than children in any other country. While the children of other countries may have to play soldiers with pieces of wood, and pretend that each piece is a soldier, American children usually can get whole sets of toy soldiers. There are several reasons for this. People in the United States have a high standard of living, which means that many persons can afford to buy things that are not necessary as food and clothing are. Americans also tend to be very good to their children and to give them the things they want. Another reason is that toys are sold not only in toy shops and department stores, but also in clothing, drug, stationery and other stores. In the two months before Christmas, when people buy 70 percent of all the toys bought in one year, toys are sold in more kinds of store than any other single product.

Until the 1920s most of the toys bought in the United States were made in foreign countries, especially in Germany and Japan. During the two World Wars people could not get toys from these countries, but they still wanted to buy toys. The American toy industry, which had been small before, quickly grew to be a billion-dollar business.

Toy manufacturers often increase their business by making their toys like products that are widely advertised or characters that are already well known. For example, a toy company makes a doll that s named for and looks like a character n a comic strip or a popular radio or television show. The comic strip or show s a kind of free advertising for the doll. A toy that looks like an advertised product benefits from the advertising of that product. By this method toy companies get hundreds of million dollars' worth of free advertising every year.

About fifty companies make half of all the toys sold in the United States. The

center of the toy industry is New York City, where nearly three-fourths of the country's toy manufacturers are. Each year they hold a Toy Fair, where the new toys of the year are shown to buyers of toys from all over the country. The second-largest toy-making center is Chicago, Illinois. Dallas, Atlanta, Boston, San Francisco and Los Angeles are also important toy-producing cities.

track and field

Track and field sports are those forms of athletics that include running races, jumping contests, and weight-throwing contests. Along with boxing and wrestling, they are the oldest forms of organized athletics. More than 2,500 years ago the Greeks had track and field contests, and every four years held their most important meets at the Olympic Games. Everywhere in the world, in almost every age, running and jumping and throwing have been important in athletics.

Track and field meets are held for schools, colleges, clubs, and even countries (in the Olympic Games). They are held outdoors whenever the weather is good. Sometimes they are held in large indoor halls.

At each meet, records are kept of the times and distances made by the winners of various events. In addition to trying to win an event, each competitor wants to set a new record; that is, to beat the best performance of previous years. The best performance ever made anywhere is called a world record. World records are sometimes set in college meets, in club meets, and in national championship meets, but most often in the Olympic Games. There the finest athletes in the world compete.

TRACK EVENTS

Track events consist of running races. They are run on a track, which is usually a wide, oval-shaped path, paved with cinders, and a quarter of a mile around. The standard track events are the 100-yard dash, the 220-yard dash, the 440-yard dash, the half-mile run, the mile run, the two-mile run, and the three-mile run. These distances are used in the United States, Canada, British countries, and a few other places where the foot, yard, and mile are used in measuring. In the rest of the world the distances are measured by the metric system. A meter is equal to about three feet, four inches.

These races are called *flat races*. Other track events are the *hurdles*. There are 120-yard high-hurdle races and the 220- and 440-yard low-hurdle races. Hurdles are small fences put up in the running lane. The high hurdles are 3 feet, 6 inches high, and the low hurdles 2 feet 6 inches high. Each runner in a hurdle race must jump over, or hurdle, these little fences as he comes to them.

Relay races are another kind of track event. A relay team is usually four men, who race against other teams. The first man runs his distance, then passes a baton (stick) to the second man on his team. The second man runs his distance and passes the baton to the third man, and so on, until the fourth man finishes the race. Members of a relay team must not only be fast runners but must be skillful—

trained in passing the batons so that they do not waste time. This takes much practice.

Other races are held at various distances. Short sprints of 40, 60 or 70 yards are usually held at indoor meets. Longer runs, such as 10 miles, are called *cross-country races*. These and marathon races (26 miles, 385 yards) are usually run separately and are seldom part of track meets. They are usually run on roads or over country that is slightly hilly.

FIELD EVENTS

The field events are of two kinds; the jumping and vaulting contests, and the weight-throwing contests. The standard jumping events are the broad jump, the high jump, the hop-skip-and-jump, and the pole vault. The standard weight-throwing events are the shotput, the discus, the javelin, and the hammer throw. At some track meets there are also heavier weight-throwing events, such as throwing the 35-pound weight.

The broad jump consists of jumping from a mark to see how long a jump can be made. At one time this event was called the long jump. Sometimes, particularly in meets among younger people, there is a standing broad jump. In the regular broad jump, there is a starting run up to the mark.

The high jump is a jump over a bar held between two supports. Here too there is sometimes a standing high jump, but usually the event permits a starting run.

The hop-skip-and-jump is made up of a starting run, then a hop on one foot, then another hop on the other foot, and then a jump to land on both feet.

The pole vault is a high jump with the aid of a long pole. There is a separate article on the POLE VAULT.

The weight-throwing events usually call for heavier, stronger athletes. There are separate articles on the DISCUS, JAVELIN, and SHOTPUT. These weight-throwing events call for speed and coördination as well as strength.

In the hammer throw, the athlete whirls a 16-pound steel ball attached to a wire about three feet long, with a handle at the other end of the wire. The competitor takes the handle in both hands and whirls the iron ball around and around, finally releasing it. The 35-pound weight is a large iron ball with a triangular handle attached to it. This is thrown much in the same way as the hammer except that it does not gain as much distance because of its heavier weight and because it does not have the long wire attached to it.

SCORING

Most track and field meets are held between teams. If there are only two teams, it is a *dual meet*. If there are more teams it is a championship, usually held by some amateur athletic organization or by a university.

In most meets, each event is run off to find a winner and the second, third, fourth, and perhaps fifth and sixth places. Usually the winner receives 10 points, the second 5, the third 4, the fourth 3, the fifth 2, and the sixth 1. After the meet, the points are added up and the team

with the most points is declared the champion for that year.

WOMEN'S MEETS

Track and field meets are held for women as well as for men. The women have running, jumping, and weight-throwing events but the distances differ in the running races, usually being shorter than the men's. The longest race for women is usually the 220-yard dash. The women do not throw the hammer or 35-pound weight, and in their competitions an 8-pound shotput and a light discus are used. In many women's meets there are additional events such as throwing a basketball and throwing a baseball for distance.

TRAINING

All track and field athletes, whether men, women, or children, must be well trained. Training is necessary not only to win or set records, but also so that a competitor will not hurt himself. In running and jumping and throwing weights, strains are put on the body and a sudden demand is made on the lungs for more oxygen. If an untrained person were to compete in these events, he might very likely injure himself. A well-trained athlete is seldom injured.

tractor

A tractor is a motor vehicle that is used to pull or push a load. In this way it is different from a truck, which carries a load. Tractors are among the most important of all machines. They are used on farms, to pull farm machinery; in construction and roadbuilding work, to pull or push earthmoving machinery; in factories, railroad stations, and other places to pull loaded trucks short distances; and for many other jobs.

There are two main kinds of tractor. One kind runs on wheels as an automobile does, but the wheels and tires are bigger and broader. The other kind is the crawler tractor, which runs on a moving belt or track. This type of tractor is often called a "Caterpillar" tractor because Caterpillar is the best-known trade-name under which such tractors are sold, and a track tractor is often called a "cat."

The tractors with wheels are used for lighter jobs and for any kind of job on paved or hard surfaces. The crawler tracks, which cover more area and so are less likely to sink down into soft ground, are used for heavy outdoor work. Tractors use both gasoline engines, as do automobiles, and diesel engines. The diesel engine is used in the big tractors. Both these engines are described in the article on INTERNAL COMBUSTION ENGINES.

The first crawler tractors were made in 1905 by the company that is now the Caterpillar Tractor Company. During World War I the crawler tracks were used on the first tanks and they are still used on all tanks and on the heavy military trucks called "half-tracks," which have wheels in front for steering and are driven by crawler tracks behind.

All tractors do heavy work, compared to automobiles and to trucks of the same sizes; but tractor engines do not always have horsepower ratings that seem high compared to automobile engines. Tractors run at low speeds but must be care-

fully built because they have to last a long time. A tractor engine must still be running when nine or ten automobile engines would have worn out.

The engine drives a series of wheels inside the crawler tracks. These keep the tracks turning. They will climb hills and go through mud and rough territory where a truck could not go. The tracks can be turned just enough to steer the tractor, but it cannot change direction very fast.

The truck chassis that pulls a trailer or semi-trailer over roads is also called a tractor. It is usually the same in construction as a truck that carries loads.

trade-mark

A trade-mark is a name or design that is used on a product to show that it is made by some particular person or firm. Anyone who uses a trade-mark may register it with the United States Patent Office in Washington, D.C., and then no one else may use the same trade-mark.

Certain names for products may not be registered as trade-marks. If the name is simply a word that describes the product, the Patent Office will not accept it. For example, if a manufacturer makes rulers out of steel he may not trade-mark the name Steel Rulers. Sometimes a manufacturer changes the spelling of a word so that it will be a trade-mark and not merely a description. For example, the maker of a pen that writes cleanly might call it the Klene-Rite pen. A person may trade-mark his own signature or picture to mark his product. Many words that began as trade-marks have become popular words in the English language. Examples are *aspirin* and *cellophane*.

trailer

A trailer is a small house on wheels that is pulled by an automobile. (Trailers are also used to carry loads, but that kind of trailer is described in the article on TRUCKS.) A trailer that is at least 29 feet long and weighs over 4,500 pounds is called a mobile home. It has facilities for sleeping and cooking. A trailer that is smaller than a mobile home is called a travel trailer.

Trailers were first manufactured and sold commercially in 1929. They became popular, and the trailer business grew. In 1970 trailer manufacturers shipped over 400,000 mobile homes to fill the demand. Some people own trailers and use them only on their vacations; some people who travel nearly all the time, such as musicians, acting troupes, lecturers, and some salesmen, live in trailers while they are traveling; and some people fix up their trailers as stores, driving from city to city and from street to street and opening up the store wherever they park.

LIFE IN A TRAILER

It is possible to live quite comfortably in a trailer. There is room for a small bedroom, a kitchen with a stove that uses bottled gas and an electric refrigerator, and some living-room furniture. Everything is carefully planned to make use of all the space in the trailer.

The front end of the trailer is attached to the back of the automobile. Usually

the trailer has wheels only in the rear and the front end is supported by the automobile. As the trailer rolls along, the turning of its wheels can be used to run a generator, which makes electricity for lights and for the refrigerator, radio or television, and so on. Some trailers have bathrooms with showers. They carry a water tank and an air compressor (which also is run by the turning of the trailer's wheels) which produces running water for the kitchen and bath. A trailer can even have a mobile telephone, as explained in the article on the TELEPHONE.

TRAILER CAMPS

Many people buy trailers when they retire, so that they can travel and see the country while living in their own house. Near every city there is at least one trailer camp. The trailer parks there, connects to the city electric line, and has running water nearby. The automobile can easily be uncoupled and used for trips into the nearby city or town, for shopping or to go to the theater.

There are also trailer camps that have bath houses and usually restaurants and recreation rooms for the use of all who stay there.

There are many cases in which owners of trailers do not travel, or travel very seldom. They use their trailers for almost permanent homes. Many trailer-owners stay in one place throughout an entire season, for example in Florida during the winter or near a beach in the summer. They plant gardens outside their trailers and settle down.

During World War II, when there were not enough places to live in many parts of the country, the United States government set up communities in which all the people lived in trailers that were permanently parked.

Trajan

Trajan was emperor of Rome about 1,900 years ago. His full name was Marcus Ulpius Trajanus and he was born about the year 52. He served in the Roman armies all over Europe and the Near East. In the year 98 Trajan was elected emperor by the Roman senate. He made many improvements in Rome, especially the building of roads, bridges, and public buildings. The most famous of these is known as Trajan's Forum. A monument called Trajan's Column commemorates his victories in warfare. He died in the year 117.

transfusion, a method of replacing blood lost through wounds, disease, or surgery: see the article BLOOD.

transistor

The transistor is a device that can be used instead of a vacuum tube to amplify an electric current and for other uses. The article on ELECTRONICS explains how the vacuum tube made the radio loudspeaker possible by increasing the strength of the electric waves received from the air. The transistor does the same job and has several advantages over the tube. A transistor can be made almost as small as the eraser on a pencil, making good "vest-pocket" radios possible. A transistor needs only the current from the tiniest of batteries yet can amplify elec-

tric signals many thousands of times. A transistor does not have to "warm up." And a transistor never wears out.

Instead of a heated filament inside a tube, which gives off a flow of electrons in a vacuum tube, the transistor uses a small piece of a substance that gives off streams of electrons. Silicon and Germanium are the substances most often used in transistors. Both are chemical elements, being among the basic substances of which everything in the world is made.

Transvaal

The Transvaal is a province in the northeastern part of the Republic of South Africa. It has an area of 110,450 square miles and a population (in 1960) of 6,225,052. Its capital is Pretoria, which is also one of the capitals of the Republic. The Transvaal consists mostly of high grasslands called *veld,* rising in the south to the rocky ridge called the Witwatersrand (which means "white water ridge" in the Afrikaans language). The principal rivers are the Vaal, the Limpopo, and the Crocodile. (Transvaal means "across the Vaal River.") The native peoples are mostly Bantus. The Europeans are mostly of Dutch and British descent.

Gold-mining is the principal industry of the Transvaal, most of it being done in the Witwatersrand, which produces much of the world's gold. Other minerals mined are diamonds, coal, and iron. Many of the people are ranchers who raise sheep and cattle. Others are farmers who grow wheat, corn, fruits, tobacco, and vegetables. The principal city is Johannesburg, the largest city of the Republic of South Africa.

The Transvaal was settled by Boers (Dutch settlers) about 1835. In 1853 it became an independent republic, called the South African Republic. Twenty years later Great Britain tried to gain control of the Transvaal, but the people there resisted so bitterly that self-government was restored. The Transvaal fought against Great Britain in the BOER WAR, about which there is a separate article. After the war, Transvaal became one of the provinces of SOUTH AFRICA.

trapping

For thousands of years man has trapped animals for their meat and their fur. In modern times, there is little trapping for food except among primitive tribes, but trapping animals for fur is still an occupation for thousands of people. Much of the United States and Canada was first explored by fur-trappers.

There are three chief kinds of equipment for trapping: traps, snares, and pitfalls. Usually food is put nearby to lure the animal to the trap.

A trap is usually made of metal. It has two jaws, connected by a spring that pulls them together with great speed and force. The jaws are propped open, but if an animal steps on a trigger in the center it will release the spring and the jaws will close on the animal's leg so that it cannot get away. The size of the trap and the strength of the spring must be selected for the particular animal. A small trap, for example, will not hold a bear, while a trap heavy enough for a bear, if it should close on a skunk, will cut off the

skunk's leg and cause pain without accomplishing anything. Trappers place their traps where they find traces of the animal they want, so they usually can set the proper trap for that particular animal.

A snare is a noose attached to a flexible pole or young tree that has been bent over across a trail. When the wild animal puts its head through the noose (perhaps to take food that has been placed beyond it), the cord attached to the noose will release the catch that holds the pole or tree down. The pole or tree springs upright to its normal position, tightening the noose around the animal's neck and killing it. Snares are used chiefly by primitive peoples that do not have manufactured traps available, but many modern trappers use them for some animals that cannot be caught with steel traps.

The pitfall is perhaps the oldest form of trap that is still in use. It is simply a hole dug in the ground and covered over with light branches and grass. An animal that steps on the covering will fall into the pit and cannot get out. Men who hunt animals for circuses, zoos, or scientific study often use pitfalls because they want to capture the animals alive and unharmed.

All traps, snares and pitfalls are disguised so that the animal cannot see them. This was probably the earliest form of man-made camouflage. Even so, many animals are smart enough to avoid traps. Chiefly they are warned away by the scent of the men who set the traps.

Many of the methods of catching fish are forms of trapping. Lobsters and eels are among the sea animals for which special traps are set, and fishnets are a kind of trap. See the article on FISHERIES.

Trappists

The Trappists are monks who are members of a religious order in the Roman Catholic Church. The order was founded about three hundred years ago, in France, by a priest named Jean le Bouthiller de Rancé. It took its name from the abbey at La Trappe, France, where de Rancé was abbot. The order of the Trappists is very strict. The monks must live completely away from the rest of the world and must promise to keep the vow of silence. They spend their time in prayer, study, and work. There is no recreation, and unless a monk is ill he may eat no meat. There are four Trappist monasteries in the United States. In 1949 an American writer named Thomas Merton wrote a best-selling book about his life at the Trappist monastery at Gethsemane, Kentucky. The name of the book was *The Seven-Storey Mountain.*

trapshooting

Trapshooting is a sport of shooting at disks made out of clay and called "clay pigeons." Shotguns are used.

Originally, trapshooters shot at live pigeons. The pigeons were put into boxes called traps. When a string was pulled, the top of the box came off and the sides fell away and the pigeon would fly into the air. The trapshooter would try to hit it in the air.

About a hundred years ago, the clay disks began to be used. They are shot into the air by a spring in a device somewhat like a catapult. This device also is called

a trap, because it replaced the actual traps in which the live pigeons were kept. Usually one hundred disks are released, one after the other, and the object is to hit as many as possible. Experts usually score in the 90s, and perfect scores (100) are not unusual.

A popular form of trapshooting is called *skeet shooting*. Contests are held in which each contestant must shoot from eight different "stations," each a different distance and direction from the trap.

There are large trapshooting and skeet-shooting contests each year, with dozens of contests for men, women, and juniors.

Travelers Aid

The National Travelers Aid Association is an American organization that helps persons who are away from home and are having trouble of any kind. It was founded in 1917 by a number of separate societies that wanted to have a central organization. Today it is represented in 3,000 places in the United States and is made up of more than a hundred local societies. Its services include helping physically handicapped travelers, children traveling alone, and persons from foreign countries. It helps people whose money has been lost or stolen during their journey. During World War II it coöperated with the United Service Organizations (USO) in helping traveling servicemen.

treason

A person commits the crime of treason when he goes to war against his own country, or when he helps his country's enemies in time of war. In former times it was the crime of fighting against the king or trying to overthrow him, and this is still treason in countries where there are kings, for example in Great Britain. Even threatening the king was once called treason. When Patrick Henry made his famous speech in 1775, in which he urged Virginia to fight in the Revolutionary War, it seemed that he was going to say that King George III of England ought to be killed. Some of the men shouted, "Treason!" and Henry answered, "If this be treason, make the most of it."

CASES OF TREASON

After the Civil War in the United States, some people in the North wanted to bring the heads of the Confederate (southern) government to trial for treason, but President Andrew Johnson prevented it. During World War II, a British subject named William Joyce, who was nicknamed "Lord Haw Haw" by the British people, helped the Germans by broadcasting for them. After the war he was tried for treason and in 1946 he was hanged. The United States did not put anyone to death for treason during World War II, though several United States citizens made radio broadcasts for Japan and other enemies of the United States. Several Communists have been convicted of plotting to overthrow the United States government and have been put in jail.

Treasury, Department of the

The Department of the Treasury is one of the main divisions of the United States government. Its principal job is to handle the government's money. The Treasury pays out money authorized by Congress, collects Federal taxes, and controls the printing and coining of money. It was formed in 1789, and its head is the Secretary of the Treasury, one of the government's most important officials and a member of the President's Cabinet. The first Secretary was Alexander Hamilton. The Secretary is appointed by the President after approval from Congress. The Secretary advises the President on monetary problems, gives Congress a financial report each year, and manages the public debt.

The Department of the Treasury is divided into twelve big sections. There are separate articles about two of them—the United States COAST GUARD and the SECRET SERVICE. Others are the Bureau of Customs, which collects taxes on goods coming into the country; the Bureau of Engraving and Printing, which is in charge of printing all paper money, stamps, and other official government papers; the Internal Revenue Service, which collects the taxes; the Bureau of the Mint, which handles the coining of money; and the Bureau of Narcotics, which is in charge of enforcing laws that concern narcotic drugs. Another bureau is in charge of accounting for all of the government's money. A division promotes the sale of government Savings Bonds. See also the articles MONEY and TAX.

treaty, a written agreement between two independent nations: see the article on INTERNATIONAL LAW.

tree

A tree is a plant that has one main, woody stem, called the *trunk,* growing above the ground. There is little difference between some trees and some woody-stemmed plants called shrubs; but most shrubs have several woody stems instead of only one. Also, in most shrubs the leaves and flowers grow from all the stems, while in trees they grow from the branches and twigs and not from the trunk.

There are many different kinds of tree. Some grow only three or four feet high and others grow several hundred feet high. All trees are seed-plants, which are described in the article PLANT. They have roots that grow underground, stems that grow above the ground, leaves or needles that grow from the stems, and cones or flowers that bear the seeds from which young trees grow.

The kinds of tree that produce needles instead of leaves, and cones instead of flowers, are called *conifers.* Among the conifers are the pine, hemlock, spruce, fir, and cedar.

Most trees are *deciduous,* which means they drop their leaves every autumn and grow new ones every spring. Some trees are *nondeciduous,* or *evergreen;* they keep their leaves for a longer time, usually from three to four years. Conifers are usually evergreen.

Trees are among the plants that are most useful to man, to whom their fruits and, especially, their wood are very important. Trees supply almost all the foods known as fruit—apples, pears, cherries, oranges, and so on. Besides wood, their stems supply sap, a sticky liquid that is used to make cork and many other things.

THE WOODY STEM

If you looked at a cross-section of a large branch or tree trunk, you would see several rings inside one another, and the outside ring would look quite different from the ones inside. The outermost ring is the bark and the inside rings are the wood, which botanists (scientists who study plants) call the *xylem.* Between the bark and xylem is another ring that cannot be seen without a magnifying glass or microscope. This ring is the *cambium,* a layer of cells that cause the wood and bark to grow. In the outer part of the bark is another layer of cells called the cork cambium, which forms cork cells in the outer bark. The cambium forms wood

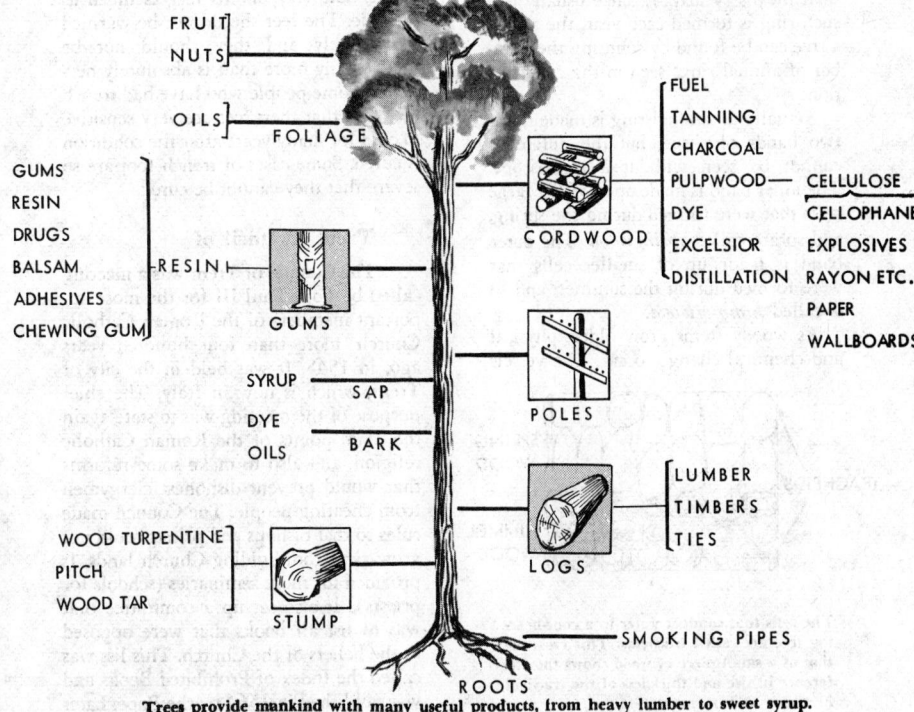

FRUIT
NUTS
OILS
FOLIAGE

GUMS
RESIN
DRUGS
BALSAM
ADHESIVES
CHEWING GUM
RESIN
GUMS

SYRUP
DYE
OILS
SAP
BARK

WOOD TURPENTINE
PITCH
WOOD TAR
STUMP

FUEL
TANNING
CHARCOAL
PULPWOOD — CELLULOSE
DYE
EXCELSIOR — CELLOPHANE
DISTILLATION — EXPLOSIVES
CORDWOOD — RAYON ETC.
PAPER
WALLBOARDS

POLES

LUMBER
TIMBERS
TIES
LOGS

SMOKING PIPES

ROOTS

Trees provide mankind with many useful products, from heavy lumber to sweet syrup.

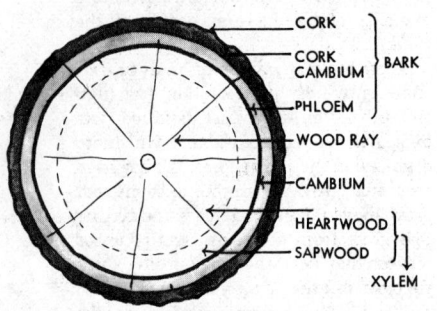 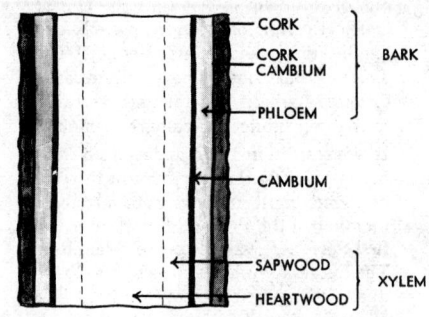

The diagrams show a cross section (*left*) and a long section (*right*) of a tree trunk.

much more quickly than it forms bark, so that as a stem grows older it has much more wood than bark.

In the center of some kinds of stem there is a third small ring, called the *pith*, which consists of a spongy, soft material.

In most trees, the wood is made up mainly of two substances, cellulose and lignin. It also contains water, dyes, minerals, oils, starch, gums, and other materials. These substances form different kinds of tissue called fiber, vessels, tracheids, and parenchyma, and each has a different job to perform. The *fibers* strengthen and support the other tissues. The *vessels* and *tracheids* send food and water throughout the stem. The *parenchyma* stores food and other substances.

Not all trees have all of these tissues. The wood of most conifers has no vessels or fibers. For this reason it is weaker and so is called *softwood*, while the wood of other trees is called *hardwood*.

THE ANNUAL RINGS

In the parts of the world where there are two main seasons, warm and cold (as in most of North America and Europe), trees and other plants grow during the warm season and stop growing during the cold season. Since the wood that grows during each year looks a little different from the wood grown the year before, it is said to form an *annual ring* (annual means "yearly"). Since usually one such ring is formed each year, the age of a tree can be found by counting the number of annual rings seen in the cross section.

Actually an annual ring is made up of two bands of tissue, but the difference cannot be seen without a microscope. The inner band is made up of rather large cells that were formed during the spring, and so are called *springwood*. The outer band is made up of smaller cells that were formed during the summer, and so is called *summerwood*.

As woody stems grow older, physical and chemical changes occur. The vessels

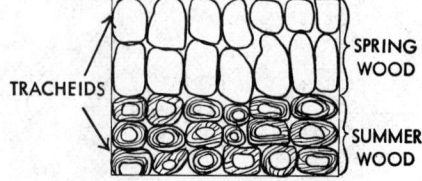

The cells that conduct water in a cone-bearing tree are called *tracheids*. This cross-section of a small piece of wood shows the difference in size and thickness of the tracheid in spring and in summer.

sometimes become blocked by other cells. Also, there is usually an increase in the amount of the chemical substances known as tannins (bitter substances), resins, gums, and dyes. The younger, outer layers of the wood do not undergo these changes, but the inner ones do. Therefore the young wood is called *sapwood* and the old wood is called *heartwood*. Heartwood is usually darker in color than sapwood. Materials such as water cannot pass through its blocked tissues, and the tannins and other chemicals are poisonous to termites and other organisms that cause wood to rot. For these reasons heartwood is more valuable for outdoor construction work.

There is other information about trees in the articles PLANT, WOOD, LUMBER, and FOREST.

trench foot

Trench foot is a condition that is caused when the feet are exposed to cold and dampness for long periods of time. In war, soldiers often have to spend long hours in trenches and foxholes and they are likely to get trench foot. When a person has trench foot his blood does not circulate properly in his feet and the skin may be damaged and other infections may develop.

When a person has trench foot his feet first feel numb. Later they swell and become very painful. A person with trench foot should stay off his feet as much as possible. The feet should not be warmed too quickly and they should not be touched any more than is absolutely necessary. Some people who have had trench foot find that their feet are very sensitive to cold for many years after the condition is cured. Some cases of trench foot are so severe that they cannot be cured.

Trent, Council of

The Council of Trent was a meeting called by Pope Paul III for the most important members of the Roman Catholic Church, more than four hundred years ago, in 1545. It was held in the city of Trent, which is now in Italy. The chief purpose of the meeting was to state again the main points of the Roman Catholic religion, and also to make some reforms that would prevent dishonest clergymen from cheating people. The Council made rules so that bishops and priests could not grow rich from holding Church lands. It provided for more seminaries (schools for priests). It also set up a committee that was to list all books that were opposed to the beliefs of the Church. This list was called the Index of Prohibited Books and was published in 1564 by the Pope. Later

a permanent committee was set up to revise this list from time to time, and the Index is still used by the Catholic Church.

Trent Affair

The Trent Affair was an incident that almost caused war between the United States and Great Britain in 1861. At that time the United States was engaged in the Civil War, and eleven southern states had formed a new government called the Confederate States, or Confederacy. The Confederacy sent two men, John Slidell and James M. Mason, to represent this new government in England and France. The two were traveling on a British steamer, the *Trent*. On November 8, 1861, Captain Charles Wilkes, in command of the United States ship *San Jacinto*, stopped the *Trent* and took the two men as prisoners. This was a serious violation of international law. The government of Great Britain sent a note to the United States government in which it threatened war unless the two men were released. President Abraham Lincoln and Secretary of State William Seward agreed that the act had been wrong and returned the men with an apology.

Trenton

Trenton is the capital and fifth-largest city of New Jersey. It is on the Delaware River and is an important manufacturing and railroad center.

About 105,000 people live in Trenton. There are factories that make pottery, hardware, rubber goods, machinery, and many other things. The city is governed by a City Commission, which consists of five elected Commissioners, one of whom is elected by the others to serve as mayor.

FOUNDING OF TRENTON

The site on which Trenton now stands was first settled in 1679 by Mahlon Stacy, an Englishman who had been given a large land grant along the Delaware River. In 1714, Colonel William Trent bought some of this land and built a mill and a home there. The city was named for him. The Trent home is the oldest building in modern Trenton. The settlement grew and became important because of its position between the large cities of New York and Philadelphia.

Trenton became the state capital in 1790 and was incorporated as a city two years later.

BATTLE OF TRENTON

One of the most important battles of the Revolutionary War was fought at Trenton. In December of 1776, General George Washington and his American troops were across the Delaware River a few miles above Trenton, which was held by the British. On Christmas night Washington and his men crossed the Delaware, in spite of strong currents and floating pieces of ice. They attacked the British at dawn, and the Battle of Trenton ended in a great victory for the Americans. The old barracks in which the soldiers once stayed is now a museum.

TRENTON, NEW JERSEY. Population (1970 census) 104,638. Capital of New Jersey. County seat of Mercer County. On the Delaware River. Founded, 1679.

trichinosis

Trichinosis is a disease caused by a tiny worm called a trichina. This worm is a parasite that lives in hogs and human beings. Heat kills the trichina worm, but if pork, ham, or sausage meat comes from an animal that had trichina worms in it, and if the meat has not been cooked well, these worms may enter the body of a person who eats it.

The trichina worm travels to the intestines of a human being. The female lays hundreds of eggs and the baby worms travel through the blood stream to the muscles.

A person who has trichinosis may have many different symptoms. He may suffer from headache, from difficulty in breathing, or from other uncomfortable feelings. Few people die from trichinosis but it is an unpleasant disease and can last a long time. Drugs do not kill the worm. Doctors can seldom tell whether or not a person has trichinosis without certain tests that always detect the disease.

Fortunately no person need ever get trichinosis if he makes certain that any pork he eats is well cooked. The United States Government inspects all pork products and marks all meat that is free from the trichina worm. This makes it safe for people to eat certain kinds of ham and sausage without cooking them.

Trieste

Trieste is an important city and seaport at the head of the Adriatic Sea, a branch of the Mediterranean Sea. Since October 1954 it has been under the control of Italy. It is the most important city of the Territory of Trieste, which is controlled by Yugoslavia and Italy. About 300,000 people live in the city. Though the city's port is controlled by Italy, it is a free, or international, port and is open to all nations for trading purposes.

Trade is Trieste's biggest business. The waterfront is more than eight miles long, and ships from all over the world go there. Another important industry is shipbuilding. There is also much manufacturing, especially of parts to be used in building ships.

For hundreds of years the nations around the Adriatic Sea have fought for the control of Trieste. Because of its location it has always been very important as a shipping and transportation center between that part of Europe and the rest of the world. More than a thousand years ago, Trieste was part of the Roman Empire. For hundreds of years it was controlled by Austria. From the end of World War I until the end of World War II, Trieste was an Italian city.

At the end of World War II Trieste was claimed by both Italy and Yugoslavia. From 1947 to 1954, while the question was being decided, Trieste was ruled by the Security Council of the United Nations and was occupied by British, United States and Yugoslav troops. In the meantime Yugoslavia and Italy continue to argue about it. In October 1954 the territory was divided so that one part, including the city, came under the control of Italy and the other under the control of Yugoslavia.

TRIESTE. Population (1974 estimate)

298,192. International port controlled by Italy. On the Adriatic Sea.

trigonometry

Trigonometry is a branch of mathematics in which triangles are studied. A triangle has three straight sides that join and form three angles. When a triangle is drawn on a plane surface it is called a plane triangle. A plane surface that has length and breadth but no thickness. The surface of a table is a plane, but the whole board or piece of wood that makes the table top is not a plane because it has thickness.

Triangles are used to solve many problems in which the length of a line or the size of an angle are required. For example, if you know two of the sides of a triangle and the angle between them, or two of the angles and any one of the sides, or all three sides, the triangle is determined; that is, the information is sufficient to figure out what the missing sides or angles are. Surveyors use trigonometry to find out distances that they cannot actually measure, and ancient astronomers used it to estimate the distances to the stars.

Trigonometry is usually studied in college or in the last year of high school, although introductions to it are often included in ninth- and tenth-grade mathematics.

See also the article on GEOMETRY.

Trinidad and Tobago

Trinidad and Tobago are islands in the West Indies. They became an independent nation within the British Commonwealth in 1962. Trinidad, a large island 16 miles east of Venezuela, has an area of 1,864 square miles. Tobago, a much smaller island just north of Trinidad, has an area of 116 square miles. About a million people live on the two islands. Most are English-speaking West Indian Negroes. About a third of the population is East Indian, and there are also many people of European descent.

Trinidad is low and flat except for three ranges of hills. Tobago is mountainous and has thick hardwood forests. Most of the people of the colony are farmers. They grow sugar, coffee, and citrus fruits.

Trinidad is noted for its asphalt production. Lake Trinidad is a lake of asphalt, the largest in the world. Trinidad also produces much oil.

The capital and largest city is Port of Spain. Although English is the official language, many of the people speak French and Spanish. Many tourists visit both Trinidad and Tobago during the late winter and early spring. Trinidad is the site of several United States air and naval bases.

Trinidad-Tobago is governed by a Prime Minister and a legislature consisting of a 24-member Senate and a 30-member House of Representatives.

TRINIDAD-TOBAGO. Area, 1,980 square miles. Population (1974 estimate) 1,030,000. Independent nation, British Commonwealth.

Trinity

Trinity means "three." The doctrine of the Trinity is a belief held by members of most Christian Churches, including the Roman Catholic Church. It means

that God is in three persons: the Father, the Son (Jesus Christ), and the Holy Ghost, or Holy Spirit. Each of these is equally divine.

About 1,600 years ago, in the early days of Christianity, not all Christians agreed with this view of God. Some thought that Jesus had been wholly a human being. In the year 325 the Church held a meeting called the Council of Nicaea, where it was declared that the Trinity was an official part of the Christian religion. Today most Christian churches uphold the idea of the Trinity, but a few, such as the Unitarians, do not. See also the article CHRISTIANITY.

Tripoli

Tripoli is an important city in Libya (see LIBYA for picture). Tripoli is on the Mediterranean Sea and is a very old city. Almost 250,000 people live there. It is noted for its excellent harbor and for its manufacture of tobacco and carpets, and it is a shipping point for Libyan oil.

Tripoli was founded thousands of years ago by the Phoenicians, a great people of the ancient world. They called the city Oea. There are many interesting ruins to be seen in the city, including a wall and a triumphal arch dating from the time when the city was part of the Roman Empire, about 1,800 years ago. There are also many beautiful mosques (Mohammedan churches). At one time the people of Tripoli were very powerful and controlled the waters of the Mediterranean. You can read more about this in the article on BARBARY PIRATES.

During World War II Tripoli was an important supply base for Germany until it was captured by the British in 1943.

TRIPOLI. Population (1965 estimate) 250,000. Capital of Libya, in North Africa. Capital of the region of Tripolitania. On the Mediterranean Sea.

Tristram

Tristram was a character in old English and European legends. He was a brave knight of King Arthur's court, and the story of his love for the Irish princess Iseult is one of the great love stories of all time. The story was the subject of a grand opera, *Tristan and Isolde,* by Richard Wagner. (An opera is a play in which all the conversation is sung, not spoken.) Wagner finished the opera in 1859, but it was not performed until six years later, in 1865, in Munich, Germany. It is still performed regularly, throughout the world.

THE STORY OF THE OPERA

Tristan has told his uncle, King Mark of Cornwall, of the beauty of the Irish princess Isolde, and is sent to bring her by ship to Cornwall to marry the king. Isolde hates Tristan, who long ago killed her lover in battle, and on the journey she instructs her maid Brangane to poison him. Instead Brangane prepares a magic potion, and when Tristan and Isolde drink it they fall in love. They arrive at Cornwall but King Mark is away hunting. The lovers meet secretly, but when the king returns a traitor named Melot tells him about them. Tristan fights Melot and is badly wounded. He is taken to his own castle in Brittany, where he lies dying. His faithful friend Kurwenal sends

for Isolde, but she arrives too late. Tristan dies, and at his side Isolde dies of grief. King Mark, who has followed the pair to give them his blessing, prays beside their bodies.

This opera has some beautiful music that is often played and sung in concerts. The most famous song is the "Liebestod" (love's death), which Tristan and Isolde sing just before they die.

Triton

Triton was a god of the sea in Greek mythology, the stories the ancient Greeks told about their gods and heroes. He was the son of the chief god of the sea, Poseidon, and the goddess Amphitrite, and he lived in a golden palace at the bottom of the sea. Artists and writers often speak of Triton blowing his horn, a seashell, to soothe the sea. Later they pictured not one Triton but a whole race of men called tritons, who had the bodies of men above the waist and the bodies of fish below the waist.

Trojan War

The Trojan War is told about in legends of the ancient Greeks. The legends are more than 3,000 years old. They tell about a war between the ancient Greeks and the people who lived in the city of Troy. The most famous story of the war is in a long poem by the Greek poet Homer. The poem is called the *Iliad,* because the Greek name for Troy was Ilium.

The Trojan war started because Paris, son of King Priam of Troy, stole Helen, the wife of a Greek prince named Menelaus. Helen was the most beautiful woman in the world. Paris took Helen to Troy with him. Menelaus, helped by his brother Agamemnon, who was a Greek king, and other great Greek warriors, including Achilles and Ulysses, raised an army and set out in more than a thousand ships to bring her back from Troy. There are separate articles about most of these people.

For ten years the Greeks and the Trojans fought outside the walls of the city of Troy. There were many famous battles, some of which you can read about in the article on the ILIAD.

The Greeks could not break through the walls of Troy, but they finally won by tricking the Trojans. They pretended to give up trying. First they built a huge wooden horse; then they got into their boats and sailed away. The Trojans thought the horse was a god, for in those days people believed that such objects could have supernatural powers. They grew curious about the horse and dragged it inside the city. Secretly, the Greeks had hidden soldiers inside the horse, which was hollow. That night the Greek soldiers crept out of the wooden horse, surprised the Trojans, and destroyed the city. Almost all the people of Troy were killed.

There probably was some sort of war between Greeks and Trojans, but no one knows if any of the stories told about the war are true.

Trollope, Anthony

Anthony Trollope was an English writer who lived about a hundred years ago. He is best-remembered for his novels about life in an imaginary English county called Barsetshire. Trollope was born in London in 1815. When he grew up he worked for the English Post Office, which later sent him on missions to Ireland, the West Indies, Egypt, the United States, Australia, and South Africa. On these journeys Trollope gathered a great deal of material for his books. He wrote about fifty novels. Among them are the novels about Barsetshire, which include *The Warden* and *Barchester Towers,* and a series of novels about politics, which include *The Prime Minister, Phineas Finn,* and *The Eustace Diamonds.* Trollope died in 1882.

trombone

The trombone is a brass wind instrument. It consists of a long, bent brass tube that is in two sections so that one section can be slid in and out of the other. The pitch, or note, played by wind instruments depends largely on the length of the tube. In the trombone this change of pitch is achieved by lengthening or shortening the tube by means of the sliding section. See also the article on MUSICAL INSTRUMENTS.

tropics

The tropics are two imaginary lines that run around the earth, parallel to the middle line called the equator. The northern tropic is called the Tropic of Cancer. It extends 23½ degrees north of the equator. The southern line, called the Tropic of Capricorn, extends 23½ degrees south of the equator.

Between these two lines lies the earth's *torrid zone,* which is usually called the tropics. The torrid zone or the tropics always have about twelve hours of sunshine every day. They are always warm, because the sun always shines almost straight down on this part of the earth. The hot jungles of South America, Africa, and Asia are in this zone.

Many of these jungle spots are very wet and have heavy rains. The combination of much rain and sunshine makes plant life grow rapidly. The people who live in the tropics need little clothing and simple housing, since it is always warm.

Trotsky, Leon

Leon Trotsky was one of the two principal leaders of the Bolsheviks, the revolutionary group that became the Communist Party of Soviet Russia. The other principal leader was Vladimir Lenin, and when he died in 1924 most people thought that Trotsky would succeed him. However, Josef Stalin, the secretary of the Communist Party, had become very powerful by that time. He succeeded Lenin, and later had Trotsky thrown out of Russia.

Most of the early revolutionists changed their names. Trotsky's real name was Lev Davidovich Bronstein. He was born in 1877, in the Ukraine region of Russia, and studied at the University of Odessa. He soon became a revolutionist and was imprisoned and exiled (sent out of the country) several times.

After the Russian czar (emperor) was overthrown early in 1917, Trotsky returned to Russia and with Lenin helped the Communists to win control of the government. He became commissar for foreign affairs (similar to the Secretary of State in the United States) and head of the Russian Army. He was the second most important man in the Russian Communist government, which was headed by Lenin. When Stalin replaced Lenin, Trotsky was given an unimportant government job and then, in 1927, he was accused of working against the Communist Party. He was sent out of Russia and finally was allowed to make a home in Mexico. Many people who believed in Communism still supported Trotsky, and the term Trotskyite came to mean any Communist who opposed Stalin.

In 1940 Trotsky was murdered in Mexico by a man named Jacques Mornard, and many people think Mornard had been paid by the Russian Communist government. Trotsky had written a number of books, including a long *History of the Russian Revolution.*

troubadour, a poet and musician of the Middle Ages: see the article MINSTREL.

trout

The trout is a member of the same fish family as the salmon. Like salmon, trout spawn (lay their eggs) in fresh water. Many varieties of trout remain in fresh water all their lives, but some travel to salt water and spend some time there before returning to a river to spawn.

Of the many varieties of trout, the most familiar to most people are the rainbow trout, brown trout, brook trout, cutthroat trout, and lake trout.

The largest variety is the lake trout, which sometimes reaches a weight of seventy-five pounds.

Rainbow trout, another variety, have been introduced to many parts of the world. The eggs of the rainbow trout can be carried for long distances from their original home to new lands and will still hatch upon arrival.

Troy

Troy was one of the most famous cities in the legends of the ancient Greeks, three thousand years ago. Many of these legends tell about the wars between Greece and Troy, which are described in the article TROJAN WAR. Until nearly a hundred years ago most people were not sure that such a city had actually existed. Then in 1871 there were discovered the ruins of Troy near the coast of the Mediterranean Sea, in what is now part of Turkey. Another name for Troy was Ilium, and the Greek poet Homer's story about the Trojan War is called the *Iliad.*

Trucial States

The Trucial States are a group of eight sheikdoms on the eastern Arabian Peninsula. (A sheikdom is an area ruled by an Arab leader called a sheik.) In the 19th century this region was inhabited by pirates who threatened Oman (formerly called MUSCAT AND OMAN) to the south. Great Britain intervened and, in 1853, declared a permanent truce. This is where

the name Trucial States comes from. They are British Protected States and have a treaty giving Britain responsibility for their foreign relations.

Most of the 32,278 square miles of land is desert, and the population is about 180,000. The boundaries between the various sheikdoms are vague and often disputed. The northern coast borders the Persian Gulf, with the Sultanate of Oman to the south and Saudi Arabia to the west.

trucks

A truck is a motor vehicle that carries goods or freight, rather than passengers. There are about twelve million trucks in the United States. Most of them are used only by their owners, such as farmers, stores that use trucks to make deliveries, factories that use trucks to make shipments, and so on. The rest of the trucks are *common carriers* that carry freight for others and charge for carrying it. The trucking industry has become one of the most important in the United States and is a rival of the railroads, but we could not do without either one.

Trucks are rated by the loads they are built to carry. The smallest trucks are half-ton trucks, built to carry 1,000 pounds. The biggest trucks may be rated as high as ten tons, or even more, but few trucks are now made so big. For the biggest loads, a truck-tractor is used to pull a trailer, and the load is in the trailer.

All trucks will easily carry more than they are rated to carry. For example, a two-ton truck will easily carry three or four tons. State laws usually make it dangerous to overload a truck. License fees are based on the gross weight of truck and load. For example, if the unloaded truck weighs 5,000 pounds, and it is rated to carry a *payload* of 4,000 pounds, its gross weight is 9,000 pounds and the license fee is based on that. Most states have weighing stations beside highways, and at these stations trucks are stopped and are weighed. If a truck's gross load is more than its license permits, the owner of the truck must pay a big fine. Of course, the owner can license a truck for any load he wants to—he may license a two-ton truck for an 8,000-pound payload instead of a 4,000-pound payload—and then he will be safe against the fine, but his license will cost more.

TRUCK BODIES AND EQUIPMENT

The manufacturer of a truck often sells only the chassis and cab; that is, the part of the truck that does the running plus the cab that the driver sits in. The body is made or sold separately because there are dozens of special body types designed for different kinds of work. Some of the truck bodies most often used are:

Pick-up. An uncovered body with low sides, used on light trucks.

Panel. A closed body, used chiefly by stores to make deliveries. On a panel truck, the driver's seat is part of the body and not in a separate cab.

Platform. A large platform, or kind of floor, mounted behind the cab, usually on medium-sized trucks. Often the sides have a framework around them, to keep things from falling off. A medium-sized framework makes it a *stake* truck, and a higher framework makes it a *rack* truck.

Van. A very large closed body, used

for carrying furniture or other bulky loads that have to be protected against the weather. Van bodies can be put on medium-sized or very large trucks. Often a van has a *bulkhead,* or section that reaches far out over the top of the driver's seat. Freight can be carried in the bulkhead or it can have a bunk in which the driver can sleep.

Dump. A dump truck is an open body, made of heavy metal. It can be used to carry earth, coal, or some other loose load. The truck engine is attached to a device that will tilt the body to the rear or to the side. To unload, the driver tilts the body and the load slides out.

Tank. A tank truck has a big container to carry liquids such as gasoline, chemicals, milk, and so on.

There are special types of truck body for many different businesses: for example, to carry pies, or chickens, or racehorses, or long logs, or almost anything you can name.

TRAILERS

The heavy trucking business was revolutionized by the development of the semi-trailer in the late 1920s. A truck can pull a much bigger load than it can carry. The semi-trailer is a big truck body with rear wheels but no front wheels. The front of the semi-trailer is attached to the rear of the truck. The truck in this case is called a truck-tractor or simply a tractor. It has a cab but no body. Behind the cab there is mounted a round metal plate called a *fifth wheel.* At the front of the semi-trailer is a round metal plate that fits onto the fifth wheel.

The semi-trailer is tilted to the rear so that most of its weight is carried by its wheels and not by the rear wheels of the truck-tractor. The two metal plates turn freely, so that when the truck-tractor turns a corner the semi-trailer follows after it.

Truckmen soon learned that a three-ton truck could handle as much as a ten-ton load in a semi-trailer. Since light trucks are cheaper than heavy trucks, this was a great economy. Most hauling of heavy freight has been done by semi-trailers since the 1930s. Semi-trailers are often giants forty feet long or longer and holding twenty or more tons.

Trudeau, Pierre Elliott

Pierre Elliott Trudeau became the fifteenth Prime Minister of Canada when Lester B. Pearson retired in 1968. Mr.

Trudeau was born in Montreal in 1919. He graduated from Jean-de-Brebeuf College and obtained a law degree from the University of Montreal. He also received a master of arts degree in political economy from Harvard University and did postgraduate work in law, economics, and political science at the University of Paris and the London School of Economics.

Pierre Trudeau later practiced law in the Province of Quebec. In 1961, he was appointed Associate Professor of Law at the University of Montreal.

Mr. Trudeau was elected to the House of Commons in 1965 and became the

Parliamentary Secretary to the Prime Minister in 1966. In 1967, he was appointed Minister of Justice and Attorney General of Canada. These are the positions he held until he was sworn in as Prime Minister.

truffle

Truffles are underground plants that can be eaten. They are plants of the FUNGUS kind, about which there is a separate article. The truffle has an underground tuber (rootlike part) and seed pods, and both can be eaten. The seed pods are properly called "spore sacs," because a fungus grows from spores and not from a seed. The spore sac of a truffle is a reddish-black, lumpy object, shaped rather like a potato. Truffles are considered a delicious food, and are very costly. The finest truffles grow in France and Italy. Both dogs and pigs are trained to scent and dig up truffles.

Trujillo, Rafael

Trujillo was the dictator, the absolute ruler, of the Dominican Republic for nearly thirty years, from soon after 1930 until his death in 1961. His full name was Rafael Leonidas Trujillo Molina, Molina being his mother's family name. He was born in 1891. He became Dominican president in 1930 by winning a revolution against the previous president and within three years he had made himself dictator by persecuting, exiling and even killing his political enemies. Trujillo took millions of dollars from Dominican taxpayers to make himself and his family rich and he had thousands of his enemies killed. He glorified himself with statues and pictures throughout the country and even changed the name of the capital city to Ciudad Trujillo (Trujillo City). In 1961 one of Trujillo's political enemies killed him with a bomb that exploded under his automobile, and at once there was a new Dominican government that threw out all Trujillo supporters who had held power.

Harry S. Truman

Harry S. Truman was the thirty-third President of the United States. He served from April 12, 1945, until January 4, 1953. He was Vice President during Franklin D. Roosevelt's fourth term as President, and became President when Roosevelt died. He was re-elected in November, 1948. In 1952 he refused to run for another term.

President Truman was in office at the conclusion of World War II. He was the first man to authorize the use of the atomic bomb in warfare.

After his term in office, Harry Truman retired to his home in Independence, Missouri, to write his memoirs, his own story of his political career during one of the most troubled and eventful periods of United States history.

HIS EARLY YEARS

Harry Truman was born in Lamar, Missouri, a town of about 3,000 in the southwestern corner of the state, on May 8, 1884. His middle name caused a family problem: Should it be Shippe, for one grandfather, or Solomon, for the other? They decided to use only a middle initial,

to stand for both names. Harry's father was a farmer. While Harry was a boy, he moved to a farm at Grandview, Missouri, near the larger town of Independence and only a few miles from the big city of Kansas City.

Harry Truman attended schools in Independence. It was in high school there that he met his future wife, Elizabeth Virginia Wallace, although they were not married until about twenty years later.

After he finished high school, Truman had several different jobs. He worked for the Kansas City *Star,* then as a railroad timekeeper, and then as a helper in a Kansas City bank. He tried to obtain an appointment to West Point, but his poor eyesight caused him to be rejected. When he was 21, he joined the National Guard.

From 1906 to 1917, Truman ran the family farm at Grandview, Missouri, and by then the United States was at war with which Harry Truman belonged was called into service, and he went to Fort Sill, Oklahoma to train with the field artillery. He became a first lieutenant and went to France with his unit. He was a competent officer, and won the respect and affection of his men. In recognition of his services, he was given two promotions and at the end of the war held the rank of major. After World War I was over, and Harry Truman was discharged from the Army, he entered the Field Artillery Reserve, where he eventually rose to the rank of colonel.

HOW HE BECAME PRESIDENT

In 1918 Harry Truman and a friend from his Army days opened a haberdashery shop in Kansas City, but it was not successful and they were forced to close in 1921. Truman's first election to any public office occurred in 1922, when he was elected a county judge in Jackson County, Missouri. He attended the Kansas City School of Law from 1923 to 1925, continuing to serve as judge during most of this period.

He was defeated in his campaign for re-election to the judgeship in 1924, but won the election of 1926 and became presiding judge. He remained in this position for eight years. In 1934 he was elected to the United States Senate on the Democratic ticket, and in 1940 he was re-elected.

As a Senator Truman won national fame as head of the Senate Committee to Investigate the National Defense Program. His committee was largely responsible for saving the taxpayers of the country many millions of dollars, by finding where wasteful and inefficient methods were hindering the war effort. Because of this success, in 1944 Truman was chosen by the Democratic Party as its candidate for Vice President. Franklin Delano Roosevelt was seeking his fourth term as President in that election. Roosevelt and Truman were elected.

Three months and eight days after the Presidential inauguration, Roosevelt died and this made Harry Truman President of the United States.

TRUMAN'S PRESIDENTIAL CAREER

To become President of a large and important country while it is engaged in war is a tremendous responsibility. Nearly every one thought Truman would not be equal to this enormous task and would be a weak President, but he proved to be a very strong one. Less than a month after he took office, the German forces surrendered in Europe (on May 8, 1945). Two months later Harry Truman was confronted with a decision that might affect the future of the whole world. He authorized the dropping of the first atomic bomb on the Japanese city of Hiroshima and another, a few days later, on the Japanese city of Nagasaki. Japan quickly accepted the Allies' surrender terms, and World War II came to an end.

Truman found himself beset by new and serious problems when the war ended. In Europe, the Communists of Russia, (who had been friendly as long as they needed help to win the war) at once became unfriendly toward the United States and also caused international fear by seizing control of several small countries of eastern Europe and threatening other countries such as Turkey and Greece. In 1947, Truman sent American aid to Greece and said that the United States would help any country to save itself from communism. This became known as the Truman Doctrine. Truman made George C. Marshall, the highest-ranking American general, his Secretary of State and one of the high points of the Truman administration was the Marshall Plan, which promised to help European and other countries with large sums of money if they also would help themselves to recover from the effects of the war. This led to the European Recovery Program, which was accepted by nearly all countries in Europe except those under Communist control.

In the United States, Truman had equally serious problems. Congress disagreed with many of the things he proposed. He vetoed the Taft-Hartley Labor Act, and Congress passed it over his veto. Businessmen grumbled at his veto, but Truman fearlessly defied the powerful railroad unions to end a strike that was hurting the country. The head of the railroad unions called Truman an enemy of labor and said that labor would not support him in the next election.

Political observers agreed, as the time came for the Presidential election of 1948, that Harry Truman's popularity had fallen. The Republicans nominated for President the popular governor of New York, Thomas E. Dewey. The Democrats nominated Truman after many powerful members of the Democratic Party had tried to find another candidate. As soon as Truman was nominated, the Democrats in several southern states (the states that have long been the greatest strength of the Democratic Party) withdrew their support from Truman because he favored laws called the F.E.P.C. (Federal Employment Practices Commission) laws, to protect blacks in certain jobs. These southern Democrats formed a new party called the States Rights Party, or "Dixiecrats," to oppose Truman.

Newspapers, radio commentators, public-opinion polls, and nearly everyone else predicted that Truman would lose the election. Truman answered with a vigorous campaign. He traveled through the United States, making speeches, telling the people his reasons for doing as he did. He stumbled over some words and made some mistakes in grammar, but the people did not mind that. They were more interested in what he had to say. The Presidential election of November, 1948, was one of the closest in American history. It was easily the greatest upset, or surprise, in American history. When all the returns were in, Truman had beaten Dewey and was President of the United States for another term.

THE KOREAN WAR

The United States and the rest of the world were just beginning to get adjusted after World War II in June, 1950—and then the Communist forces of North Korea suddenly invaded South Korea in an effort to control the whole country. Truman immediately told Douglas MacArthur, the Supreme Commander in the Pacific, to send United States forces to help South Korea. The United Nations backed the United States and the Korean War was fought in their name. But Truman was a storm center again in 1951 when he suddenly took MacArthur's command away from him, replacing him with General Matthew Ridgway. Many Americans disagreed with this act.

In March, 1952, Truman announced that he would not be a candidate for the Presidency again. Dwight D. Eisenhower was elected President, and on January 20, 1953, Harry Truman retired to his home in Independence, Missouri, to write his memoirs. These were published as a set of books. President Truman continued to be influential as a member of the Democratic Party and received great honors when he visited Europe in 1956. In Independence a library was built to hold his Presidential papers, records, and souvenirs, and in 1959 the house in Lamar in which he was born was made a public shrine and museum. He died December 26, 1972.

MRS. HARRY TRUMAN

Elizabeth Virginia Wallace Truman ("Bess" Truman) was born in Independence, Missouri, on February 13, 1885. She attended the same high school as Harry Truman, and they were graduated together in the class of 1901. Eighteen years later, when Harry Truman returned from his service in World War I, they were married. The Trumans had one daughter, Mary Margaret Truman. As Margaret Truman she became famous as a concert singer and television and stage actress. She was born in 1924.

trumpet

The trumpet is a brass wind instrument. It consists of a curved brass tube with a mouthpiece at one end and a bell-shaped opening at the other end. The pitch, or note, played by a wind instrument depends largely on the length of the tube. In the trumpet this change of pitch is achieved by three valves inside the tube. The player can open or close these valves, to lengthen or shorten the tube, by pressing buttons. The modern trumpet was developed from the CORNET, about which there is a separate article (and a picture). See also the article on MUSICAL INSTRUMENTS.

trust, a method of organizing a business: see the article MONOPOLY.

trustee

A trustee is a person who keeps and manages money or property that belongs to someone else. In recent years (since the United Nations was formed in 1945) a nation can also be a trustee.

A person who is a trustee is expected to keep or manage the other person's property carefully. He may charge a fee for his services but he may not borrow any money entrusted to him or use any money or property for his own benefit. If he does such things, he may be put in jail as though he had stolen the money. The property he manages is called the *trust estate* and the trustee is sometimes called a *fiduciary.*

A nation that is a trustee has some territory put under its control. This is a territory that the Security Council of the United Nations thinks is not quite ready to govern itself but soon may be. The trustee nation and the United Nations sign a written agreement saying what should be done with the trust territory. In some cases the trustee nation must agree to let the trust territory set up its own government within a certain number of years. The United States is trustee for some islands in the Pacific Ocean that belonged to Japan before World War II.

Certain business organizations are called trusts. You can read about some of these in the article on MONOPOLY.

Tschaikowsky

Peter Ilyitch Tschaikowsky was a great Russian composer, or writer of original music, who lived about a hundred years ago. He was born in 1840. He studied law, entered the government service, and did not take up music seriously until he was 22 years old. Then he entered the newly founded Petersburg Conservatory, or music school, in the capital of Russia, then called St. Petersburg. He graduated with honors, then returned to teach there for eleven years. He devoted the rest of his life to composing music and lived in and visited many foreign countries. In 1891 he visited New York City for the dedication of Carnegie Music Hall, where he conducted some of his own work. He died two years later, in 1893.

His chief works include six symphonies, of which the best-known is the sixth, the famous *Pathétique;* many other pieces for orchestra, among them *Romeo and Juliet* and the *Nutcracker Suite;* eleven operas, including *Eugène Onégin* and *Pique Dame;* and many songs and other pieces.

tsetse fly

The tsetse fly is an insect that lives in central and southern Africa. Its bite is dangerous, not because it is poisonous but because the tsetse fly carries a tiny parasite that causes sleeping sickness in human beings and a serious disease called nagana that affects cattle, horses, and goats. One kind of tsetse fly carries the parasite that causes sleeping sickness, and another kind of tsetse fly carries the parasite that causes nagana. The parasites go from the flies to the people or animals they bite.

In several sections of Africa there have been campaigns to wipe out known breeding grounds of the tsetse fly. These campaigns have succeeded in reducing the number of cases of sleeping sickness, but the fly is still dangerous to people and animals in many places.

tuba

The tuba is a brass wind instrument. It is the largest and deepest in tone of the brass instruments. The tuba consists of a coiled brass tube with a mouthpiece at one end and a bell-shaped opening at the other end. The pitch, or note, played by wind instruments depends largely on the length of the tube. In the tuba there are valves inside the tube that the player can open or close, by pressing keys, to lengthen or shorten the tube. In an orchestra the tuba usually supplies the bass accompaniment to the higher-pitched instruments, but sometimes it carries a melody of its own. See also the article on MUSICAL INSTRUMENTS.

tuberculosis

Tuberculosis is a disease that is caused by a germ. This germ may attack various parts of the body, such as the kidneys, the bones, or the skin, but most often it attacks the lungs. Because several members of one family often got tuberculosis, it was formerly believed that people inherited the disease from their parents. Now we know that this is untrue. People who live together get the disease because it is very infectious, which means that it easily spreads from one person to another. Sneezing and coughing spreads the germs. People of any age may get tuberculosis.

One hundred years ago tuberculosis was one of the most serious of all diseases and many people died from it. Now doctors can treat it with new "miracle" drugs. In the ten years following World War II the death rate from tuberculosis dropped 80 percent.

Many people do not know that they have tuberculosis until the germs have already done a great deal of harm. For this reason health departments in many states and large businesses often provide free X-ray examinations, which show when a person has tuberculosis.

A person with tuberculosis begins to have pains in his chest, a fever, or a cough, and perhaps begins to cough up blood. When these symptoms appear the disease is already serious.

Many people have tuberculosis germs in their bodies and never get the disease. This is because the body can sometimes defend itself against the tuberculosis germs. The body covers the germs that are present in the lungs with scar tissue so that they cannot do any harm.

When a person becomes ill with tuberculosis he must receive medical care immediately. People used to think that a dry mountain climate was good for patients who were ill with tuberculosis. Now doctors do not believe that climate is important. A person with tuberculosis goes to the hospital and receives drugs and other necessary treatment.

tuberose

The tuberose is a flowering plant with a very sweet, heavy fragrance. It grows in Mexico and in other places where the climate is very warm. The eastern part of North Carolina is the tuberose-growing center of the United States.

Tuberoses grow from bulbs. They are not really roses. The tuberose has a single stalk that bears white, waxy-looking flowers that are somewhat trumpet-shaped. Tuberoses are not thorny.

Tudor

Tudor was the name of an English royal family whose members ruled England from 1485 to 1603. The family was founded by a minor Welsh nobleman named Owen Tudor, who married Catherine, the widow of King Henry V of England. The Tudor monarchs were Henry VII, Henry VIII, Edward VI, Mary I, and Elizabeth I. See the articles on HENRY, KING OF ENGLAND; LANCASTER; YORK; and the Wars of the ROSES.

Tuesday

Tuesday is the third day of the week. Its ancient name was "Tiu's day," or "Tiw's day," in honor of the Anglo-Saxon god of war. In the United States, Election Day is the Tuesday after the first Monday in November. Shrove Tuesday is the day before Ash Wednesday, which is the first day of Lent. *Shrove* means "pardoned," and the day is so called because it was a special day in the church for confessions, and because the priest shrove the penitents, or gave them absolution. In France and in old New Orleans this day is the last day of the carnival that comes before Lent. It is called *Mardi Gras,* which in French means "fat Tuesday."

tulip

The tulip is a flower that is grown in temperate zones. It was introduced to Europe from Turkey, about 1550, and has had a romantic and interesting history. Thousands of varieties have been developed, and at one time there was intense rivalry among the tulip-growers of Holland in the production of new and more beautiful strains. Many people gambled large fortunes on their tulips. There were nationwide contests sponsored by royalty, with big prizes for the finest new tulip varieties.

Growing tulips to sell as bulbs or for their flowers is still a big business. The bulbs are shipped to nearly all parts of the world for planting in gardens or to be grown in greenhouses.

Most tulips are bell-shaped, or cup-shaped flowers with six colorful petals and long broad, shiny green leaves. The color may be any shade from pure white to a deep purplish black, with the exception of the shades of blue. Some flowers are of mixed colors or shades. Bulbs are planted in the fall, for blossoms early in the following spring or summer.

Tulsa

Tulsa is the second-largest city in Oklahoma. It is in the northeastern part of the state, on the Arkansas River. About 330,000 people live there. Tulsa is in one of the richest oil regions in the United States, and it has been called the "oil capital of the world." Many of the great oil companies have headquarters in Tulsa, and the business and industry of the city are centered around oil. There are huge refineries and factories that make oil-field equipment, but there are also factories that make many other things. The surrounding region is rich farm land. One of Tulsa's suburbs is the industrial village of Sand Springs, seven miles west of the city.

Tulsa is the seat of the University of Tulsa, which has an important school of petroleum engineering. Every two years the International Petroleum Exposition is held in Tulsa.

The site of Tulsa was a mail post in the Indian Territory in 1879. Several years later the town became a railroad terminal and white settlers began to arrive. It was first called Tulsey Town, the white man's way of saying Tallahassee, which was the Alabama home of the Creek Indians before they moved to Oklahoma. When oil was discovered in the area in 1901, the city had a period of great and fast growth. Tulsa became a city in 1902.

TULSA, OKLAHOMA. Population (1970 census) 331,638. On the Arkansas River. County seat of Tulsa County.

tumor

A tumor is a lump that grows in the body. It is an unnatural swelling or enlargement that is not needed in the workings of the body and should not be expected to grow in a healthy body.

A tumor may be *benign*, or harmless, or it may be *malignant*, in which case it is called a cancer. Benign tumors include warts, corns, and lumps of various kinds called cysts, or moles. Each benign tumor has a capsule, that is, it has a thin wall of some kind surrounding it so that it cannot grow in more than one spot or spread its growth through the body. Doctors seldom remove benign tumors unless they suddenly becoming too large or show signs of breaking through their walls and becoming malignant. Usually benign tumors grow to a certain size and then stop growing. The article on CANCER tells how a cancerous tumor spreads throughout the body and finally can destroy life itself.

Doctors can usually recognize benign tumors on the surface of the body and distinguish them from cancers. When the tumor is inside the body, it is not so easy to tell. Sometimes the doctor needs a *biopsy*, which is an examination of the tissue of the tumor. The doctor cuts into the tumor, scrapes off a small part of it, and examines this under a microscope. He can tell from this whether the tumor is benign or malignant.

tuna

The tuna, or tuna fish, is an important food fish. It is found in ocean waters throughout the world, except where it is very cold.

Tuna fishing is an important industry in many parts of the world. The tuna is also a popular fish for sport, because it is so hard to hook and land. The tuna is never still in its entire lifetime. The tuna goes as fast as 40 miles an hour. When hooked, it fights gamely to get away, so it is quite a victory for a fisherman to catch one.

There have been records of tuna fish that were more than nine feet long and weighed more than a thousand pounds.

The tuna lays small eggs that float about on the surface of the water and hatch after two or three days. A young tuna usually weighs about thirty pounds when it is three years old. A tuna can live to an age of about 15 years.

tundra, a marshy, treeless plain of regions in the north: see the article ARCTIC REGIONS.

tungsten

Tungsten is a heavy, gray metal. In September 1949, chemists from all parts of the world meeting in Amsterdam, Holland, decided that this metal, which had been called *tungsten* in some countries and *wolfram* in others, should be officially called wolfram in all countries. You can read about it in the article WOLFRAM.

Tunis

Tunis is the capital and largest city of Tunisia. It is on the Lake of Tunis, an inlet of the Mediterranean Sea. The inlet is very narrow and between it and the city is a salt flat that blocks it. A channel allows ships to pass through, so Tunis is an important port. About 469,000 people live in Tunis. The main occupations are working at the port, through which wine, iron ore and phosphates are shipped all over the world, and fishing.

Tunis is a very old city, but many modern buildings have been built there. There are several beautiful old mosques (Mohammedan churches), and parts of the walls built a thousand years ago still stand. When the French began to rule Tunisia, in 1881, they built a modern section, which includes a university and national museum. Most of the Europeans live in the modern part, while the native Arabs live in the old sections, with narrow crooked streets and dark, covered passageways.

Tunis has been the capital of Tunisia for about 700 years. It was a base for the Barbary pirates, who attacked and plundered ships sailing the Mediterranean.

During World War II Tunis was held by the Axis (Germans and Italians) from November 1942 to May 1943. Their troops made their last stand in Africa there, and it was the scene of heavy fighting until it was taken by the Allies.

TUNIS. Population (1974 estimate), 468,997. Capital of Tunisia.

Tunisia

Tunisia is a country in North Africa, on the Mediterranean Sea across from Italy. In its long history it has been controlled by many different peoples and countries, but since 1956 it has been independent and since 1957 it has been a republic. Before 1957 Tunisia had a king (called a *bey*) and before 1956 Tunisia had been controlled by France for nearly seventy-five years.

Tunisia is about 63,378 square miles in size, which is a little larger than the state of Georgia. Over five million people live in Tunisia or about as many as live in Indiana. During World War II, Tunisia was the scene of great battles between the Germans and the Allies.

THE PEOPLE OF TUNISIA

Most of the people in Tunisia are Berbers, who have lived there longer than any other race of people. They speak their own language, which has in it many words taken from the languages of other peoples who settled in Tunisia. One of these peoples were the Arabs, who speak Arabic. Most of the people who live in the cities also speak French.

About 280,000 Europeans, mostly French, live in the cities of Tunisia. There are also about 85,000 Jews. Most of the people of Tunisia, except the Europeans and Jews, are Moslems (follow the Mohammedan religion).

Most Tunisians are farmers. They raise olives, dates, wheat, grapes and citrus fruits, almonds, henna, and cork. Some breed sheep and goats, and there are some fishermen and many miners. Oil may become the most valuable mineral wealth, but Tunisia is noted for its phosphates and iron ore, lead, lignite and zinc are also mined. In the cities are some factories, chiefly making carpets, leather gods, and copperware.

Some Tunisians live and dress like city dwellers in the United States and Canada, but many of them still wear their native dress, with the Mohammedan women wearing veils over the lower part

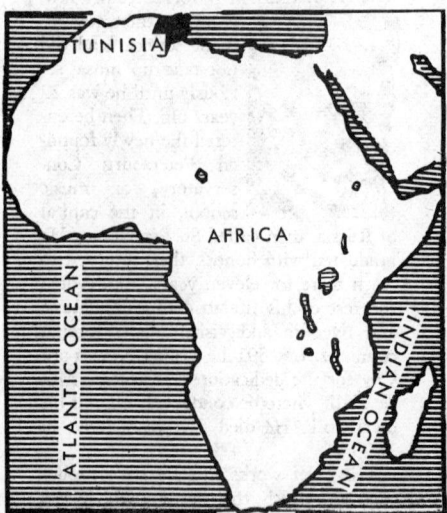

of their faces. Few of the poorer people can read or write.

WHAT KIND OF PLACE IT IS

The southern part of Tunisia lies in the great Sahara Desert. North of this is a dry plateau (high, flat land), with several shallow salt lakes. Between the plateau and the coast is a range of mountains called the Tell Atlas. The land near the coast is more fertile. The chief river is the Medjerda, which rises in the mountains and flows north to the Gulf of Tunis. Along the east coast are marshy lakes.

The climate of Tunisia is dry and warm. In January, the coldest month, the average temperature is about 55 degrees, while during the hot summer months it is about 80 degrees.

The cities of Tunisia are interesting to visitors. TUNIS is the capital and largest city, and there is a separate article about it. Sfax, the second-largest city, is an important seaport on the Gulf of Gabes, and the region around it is known for its fine olive groves. Sousse is another important port and commercial center, and Kairouan (or Kairwan) is a religious center for Moslems. Bizerte is an important seaport and former French naval base on the Mediterranean.

HOW THE PEOPLE ARE GOVERNED

Tunisia has a president who is the head of the government and an Assembly, like the United States Congress, that makes the laws. The first president elected, in 1957, was Habib Bourguiba, who had been premier before under the rule of the bey and the French governor. The president is assisted by a cabinet.

TUNISIA IN THE PAST

Tunisia was settled about 3,000 years ago by the ancient Phoenicians. It became a part of Carthage, a powerful city of ancient times, which was very near the site of modern Tunis. The Romans destroyed Carthage about 150 B.C. and Tunis became a province in the Roman Empire. Later the country was conquered by different peoples, and finally by Arabs, who brought the Mohammedan religion.

More than 200 years ago the coast of Tunisia was part of the famous Barbary Coast. Fierce Mohammedan pirates used to attack ships and capture Christians to be held for ransom or sold as slaves. This went on until the early 1800s.

European countries became interested in Tunisia about a hundred years ago, especially France and Italy. Finally it became a French protectorate, in 1881.

During World War II Tunisia supported the Vichy government, the government of France that was controlled by the Germans from 1940 to 1944. In 1942 Tunisia was the scene of heavy fighting between the Germans and the Allies. The Tunisian people were so determined to win independence that the French government had to grant it, in 1956. Tunisia then joined the United Nations. Algeria, in its struggle for independence from France, had the support of the Tunisian people and government, but Tunisia remained friendly toward the democratic countries of Europe and America and did not ally itself with the Egyptian leader, Nasser.

TUNISIA. Area, 48,332 square miles. Population (1974 estimate) 5,100,000. Government, republic. Capital, Tunis. Religion, Mohammedan. Monetary unit, the dinar, worth about $1.92 (U.S.).

tunnel

A tunnel is a big tube built under the ground. Most tunnels are built for railroad trains or for automobiles and other vehicles. Such a tunnel may be as much as 40 feet wide and 20 feet high inside, but many are much smaller. Still smaller tunnels are built for carrying water, for electric lines, for conveyors that carry packages, and for many other purposes. Many mines are great underground networks of tunnels through which the miners reach the coal or ores that they dig. Often these tunnels were originally filled with ore or coal.

The longest tunnel in the world is the Simplon Tunnel, which runs through the Alps mountains from Italy to Switzerland. It is more than twelve miles long. In the United States, the Moffat Tunnel through the Rocky Mountains in Colorado is more than six miles long.

Men have built tunnels for thousands of years, and some of their early tunnels showed great engineering skill. More than four thousand years ago the ancient Egyptians built a tunnel under their great river, the Nile. They did this by cutting a channel to turn the river from its regular course, then building a watertight passage across the dry bed. When they closed off the channel and let the river follow its regular course again, they had a tunnel.

Some of the early tunnels went through solid rock, as many modern tunnels do, but the rock had to be chipped away slowly with metal tools and even a short tunnel required that many men work for years. When gunpowder was invented, tunneling became much easier.

A little more than a hundred years ago, railroads began to be built and tunnels became far more important than they had ever been before. Locomotives then were not nearly as powerful as they are today, and they could not pull heavy loads over high mountains. Even today it would be very costly for the railroads and uncomfortable for the passengers if there were no tunnels. Tunnels help the trains to follow straight and level courses. For example, the Moffat Tunnel through the Rockies makes it possible to shorten the course of a train by 176 miles.

Later came the automobile age, and tunnels were found to solve many traffic problems. A tunnel through which automobiles and other vehicles can go is called a vehicular tunnel. The most famous vehicular tunnels are the Holland and Lincoln Tunnels, through which automobiles and trucks drive under the Hudson River between New Jersey and New York City. Before these tunnels were built, vehicles crossed the Hudson on ferryboats. Nearly every big city now has vehicular tunnels, and many big cities have subways, which are tunnels under the streets. The longest vehicular tunnel in the world runs for 7¼ miles under Mont Blanc in the Swiss Alps between France and Italy.

HOW TUNNELS ARE BUILT

When a tunnel is built through dry ground, the job of digging is usually quite simple and the big problem is to prevent a cave-in that would bury the workmen while they are building the tunnel or the people who use the tunnel after it is built. As the workmen dig their way into the solid ground, they protect themselves by *shoring,* which is the use of heavy wooden timbers to hold up the sides of the tunnel and planks laid across the shores to keep the top from falling in. This is only temporary protection. To make the tunnel permanent, stone or bricks or steel are used. For thousands of years, the favored construction has been the ARCH, about which there is a separate article.

Besides the danger of a collapse, or cave-in, there is often the problem of water. Men digging a long tunnel will usually come across underground springs or streams in many places. This water may flood the tunnel, making it impossible for them to work, and after they have built the permanent tunnel the water will still be pressing against the lining of the tunnel, weakening it and shortening its life. The stone or steel lining of the tunnel must be sealed against this water, and even so you will often see water seeping through the ceiling and sides of a tunnel.

Long tunnels must usually be bored through solid rock for part or all of the distance. Dynamite and other explosives are used to blast the rock away. Even though the rock is "solid," shoring must be used to prevent loosened rock from falling. A metal, stone or concrete lining is then built to keep the sides and top of the tunnel in place. Workmen are also exposed to the danger of rock dust and often must wear masks.

Tunnels built through mud, as is the case with nearly all tunnels built under rivers, are built by the method described in the article CAISSON. An open chamber called a *shield* is moved slowly through the soft ground. Compressed air holds back water and mud while the workers, called "sandhogs," dig the tunnel.

Long tunnels are usually started from both ends at once. This cuts in half the time needed to build the tunnel. Engineers can calculate the direction of the tunneling so accurately that when the two sections of the tunnel come together they will not be more than a fraction of an inch apart. The first tunnel built in this way was the Hoosac Tunnel, one of the early railroad tunnels. In 1851 work started on this tunnel, to run five miles through the Hoosac Mountain in western Massachusetts. Crews of workmen started on both sides of the mountain at once. They were the first tunnel builders to use power drills, and also the first to use nitroglycerine as an explosive. Even so, the work took more than twenty years.

One of the big problems of long tunnels is ventilation. The early railroad tunnels were not ventilated. Since the locomotives burned coal, which made large amounts of smoke, a trip through a tunnel would leave the passengers choking from the smoke and blackened with soot. Ventilation of vehicular tunnels is even more important, because the exhaust gases from automobile engines are deadly. Modern tunnels have huge air-pumping stations that circulate filtered air through all parts of the tunnel.

Tunney, Gene

Gene Tunney was heavyweight boxing champion of the world from 1926 to 1928. He retired undefeated, because he did not want to risk the damage that professional fighters sometimes suffer in the course of many fights. Tunney's real name was James Joseph Tooney. He was born in New York City in 1897. During World War I he served in the United States Marines and won the light-heavyweight championship of the American armed forces. As a professional, he became light-heavyweight champion before winning the heavyweight championship from Jack Dempsey in 1926. He was never defeated, and until a return bout against Dempsey, in 1927, he was never knocked down. This knockdown resulted in a "long count" (described in the article on DEMPSEY) that is still talked about, but Tunney won the fight. After retiring, he became a successful businessman. He was considered a most unusual prizefighter because of his interest in literature and his ability in business. During World War II he served as a naval officer in charge of physical training programs.

Tupper, Charles

Charles Tupper was a Canadian statesman who became Prime Minister of Canada. He was born in 1821 in Amherst, Nova Scotia, and was graduated as a doctor of medicine from Edinburgh University in Scotland. He practiced medicine for twelve years, then was elected to the Legislative Assembly of Nova Scotia. At that time Canada consisted of provinces that were separate and sometimes not friendly with one another. Tupper was one of the men who thought the provinces should join to form one nation. In 1867 the different parts of Canada did join together, and Tupper served the new government in several important offices. He was Canada's first Minister of Railways, and in this job he played an important part in having the Canadian Pacific Railway completed. In 1896 he became Prime Minister but served for only two months. He retired from public life in 1900 and lived in England until his death in 1915. He had been made a baronet, which meant he could use the title "Sir" before his name. His son, Sir Charles Hibbert Tupper, who was born in Nova Scotia in 1855 and died in Vancouver, British Columbia, in 1927, also held several high offices in the Canadian government.

turban

A turban is a headdress worn by men in parts of Asia and North Africa. It is made by winding a long strip of cloth around and around the head. Many Arabs and other peoples who follow the Mohammedan religion wear turbans. The greatest use of the turban is in India, where it is a Hindu religious observance. The turban is wound according to the beliefs and social position of the wearer. The kind of cloth used also depends on the religion and social position of the wearer. The upper classes use silk or other fine materials for their turbans. The poor people use cotton cloth.

turbine

A turbine is an engine shaped like a wheel. It is turned by outside force, such as water, steam, or gas. It works somewhat like a windmill, which has blades that catch the air, or a water wheel, which is turned by the weight of falling water striking paddles on the wheel. But windmills and water wheels are wasteful. They do not use all of the air or water that strikes them. A turbine is enclosed in a case or shell so that it uses almost all the power of the force that is turning it.

The first real turbine was invented about 1880 by an English engineer named Sir Charles Parsons. The steam engines that were used at that time wasted nine-tenths of the power that was used to run them. Parsons built a machine that looked like a series of windmill blades mounted around a central shaft or axle. He enclosed his bladed wheel in a shell, and fed steam into the shell at high pressure. The steam was directed against the faces of the blades and exerted so much force that the wheel spun very rapidly. Parsons' turbine was six times as efficient as the other steam engines of the time. It used more than half of the steam power that entered it. Soon steam turbines were in wide use to run factories and to turn electric generators. They are still widely used. Coal is the fuel most often burned to boil the water and turn it to steam.

HYDROELECTRIC PLANTS

Water turbines are very important in the production of electric power. They are located in huge dams, or at natural waterfalls such as Niagara Falls. The water is allowed to drop from a great height through long tubes or pipes. It drops through these tubes with great speed against the blades of large turbines. The shafts of the turbines whirl rapidly, turning generators that manufacture the electricity. Plants where water power is used to make electricity are called hydroelectric plants. (*Hydro-* means "water.")

GAS TURBINES

Steam is just a gas formed by boiling water. Any other gas released with great force can be used to turn a turbine. Inventors found that gases released by burning gasoline or oil have greater force than steam. Gas turbines are built for many purposes and do much of the world's work. Small gas turbines have been used in automobiles to turn the driveshaft; they are simpler (have fewer working parts) than the usual internal-combustion engine and are cheaper to run.

In turbo-jet airplanes, a gas turbine is turned by the gas from the burning jet fuel. The turbine runs an air compressor and then releases the gas to supply jet power. This is explained in the article on JET ENGINES.

turbot, a kind of flatfish that lives in temperate and tropical seas and has eyes on the left side of its head: see the article on FLATFISH.

Turin

Turin is the fourth-largest city of Italy. It is in the northwestern part of Italy, on the Po River. Its Italian name is Torino.

Turin is one of Italy's most important industrial and transportation centers. Almost one million people live there. There are factories that make automobiles (such as the Fiat and Lancia), clothing, leather goods, airplane motors, and many other things. Electric power for industry is supplied by hydroelectric plants on the swift rivers flowing down from the mountains to the west. The city is the seat of the University of Turin, founded in 1400, and of a polytechnical school. There are many old and beautiful churches, but many of Turin's historic buildings were destroyed by bombing in World War II.

TURIN IN THE PAST

In ancient times Turin was the capital of the Taurini, a Celtic tribe. It became a city of the Roman Empire, and then in the Middle Ages (about seven hundred years ago) it was ruled by the Counts of Savoy, whose family later became the kings of Italy. Turin was the capital of Sardinia until 1860, and the capital of Italy until 1865.

TURIN, ITALY. Population (1974 census) 1,142,210. Capital of Piedmont and Torino province. On the Po River.

turkey

The turkey is a large member of the bird family that chickens, pheasants and peacocks belong to. A full-grown male turkey, called a "gobbler," is about three feet high with an average weight of about twenty pounds. Some turkeys weigh far more.

Turkeys are the favorite food at big dinners in the United States, especially on Thanksgiving Day and Christmas Day, and restaurants use many turkeys, but the average family seldom wants so big a bird. Therefore small turkeys, weighing about seven pounds, have been developed. See the article on POULTRY.

Turkey

Turkey is a country that is partly in Asia and partly in Europe. Most of it is in Asia, occupying the section of southwestern Asia called Asia Minor. A small part of it is in Europe, a section called "Turkey in Europe." For hundreds of years, from the early 1500s almost to the year 1900, Turkey was one of the largest and most powerful empires in the world. Then it became weak and was called "the sick man of Europe." Now Turkey is simply a medium-sized, independent republic; but it still has unusual importance because of the geographical importance of its territory.

The northern part of Turkey is nearly all a coast of the Black Sea. The western and southern parts are on the Mediterranean Sea. The only sea route between the Mediterranean and Black Seas—a narrow strait called the Dardanelles and the Bosporus, and a larger body of water called the Sea of Marmara—lie entirely within Turkish territory. By an agreement called the Montreux Convention, this sea route must be kept open to warships and merchant vessels of all countries in time of peace. In time of war, Turkey has the right to deny passage to the warships of any country against which it may be at war. Soviet Russia has objected to having the route controlled by

a single country. Turkey maintains close and friendly relations with the western powers and is a member of the North Atlantic Treaty Organization.

At one time, the Turkish Empire included most of southeastern Europe, the best part of southwestern Asia, and an important section of North Africa, including Egypt. Now Turkey is a country of only 296,500 square miles, somewhat larger than the state of Texas. The population is about thirty million.

WHAT THE PEOPLE ARE LIKE

The Turkish people came originally from central Asia. (There is a separate article about the TURKS.) For more than a thousand years they have been followers of the Mohammedan religion. Their language, Turkish, came from Asia but was influenced by the Arabic language in which the Koran, the Mohammedan holy book, was written.

In the cities, the Turks dress much as they do in American cities. In the country, the changeover to modern ways of life has been slower. The people use oxen and carts instead of tractors and trucks, and many women still wear clothes of a kind that are seldom seen in cities.

HOW THE PEOPLE LIVE

Two out of three Turks are farmers. Turkish wheat, which is the largest crop, is known for its high quality. Barley, cotton, citrus fruits (especially oranges) and bananas are grown in the south. Figs and raisins produced near Smyrna are considered to be the best in the world. Tobacco is an important product of the north. Though most of the soil is fertile, only one-fourth of the available land is used for farming. On much of the rest farmers raise sheep, Angora goats, cattle, horses, and donkeys.

There are coal, chrome, iron, and copper mines. Turkey is one of the largest producers of chrome in the world. Oil fields discovered in the southeast produce petroleum.

Factories have been built in Turkey only in recent years. The most important factories manufacture textiles (cloth), paper, leather, and shoes. There are some iron and steel mills and chemical plants. The Turkish silk and carpet industries, which are very old, are still important.

One of the most interesting things about Turkey is the change in the lives of women during the last fifty years. Like the women of many other Asiatic countries, Turkish women used to receive little education. Their parents often married them to men they had never even spoken to, and they wore long robes and veils designed to hide the face and body from view. Today, all women may wear comfortable styles of dress and all may

choose their own husbands. Women in Turkey now have the same rights and educational opportunities as men.

Everyone in Turkey has to go to school between the ages of 7 and 14. From elementary school through college and university, education is provided by the state free of charge. The best-known universities are in Istanbul, the largest city, and Ankara, the capital.

WHAT KIND OF PLACE IT IS

The coasts of Turkey are mostly a fertile plain. Behind the coastal plain are high mountain ranges. In the south are the Taurus Mountains and in the north are the Kure Mountains. Turkey has twenty mountain peaks that are over 10,000 feet high. The most famous is Mount ARARAT, about which there is a separate article.

Inland, the country is dry in summer and is often covered with snow in winter. There are many rivers but none are deep enough for any but very small boats.

The climate of Turkey differs from place to place. The Istanbul region has a climate like that of New England. In the central region the winters are severe and the summers are hot. In the region along the Mediterranean Sea, the climate is like that of Florida.

HOW THE PEOPLE ARE GOVERNED

Turkey is a constitutional republic, which means that it has a president, a legislative body, or assembly, that makes the laws, and a written constitution.

The people elect the members of Parliament, who elect a President from among themselves. He serves for a seven-year term. The President appoints a Prime Minister, or Premier, who is the leader of the majority party in Parliament. He appoints the cabinet. The lawmaking body is called the Grand National Assembly and has two houses: the National Assembly and the Senate.

CHIEF CITIES IN TURKEY

The leading cities of Turkey, with populations from the 1974 estimates, are:

Istanbul, population 1,742,980, the largest city and former capital. There is a separate article about ISTANBUL.

Ankara, population 905,660, the capital and second-largest city. There is a separate article about ANKARA.

Adana, population 289,920, the third-largest city, a business center for a farm district, producing textiles and farm machines, in the south part of the country.

Smyrna, population 263,520, the fourth-largest city. There is a separate article about SMYRNA, which is the English name for the Turkish city of Ismir.

Bursa, population 211,645, the fifth-largest city, a port on the Sea of Marmara, in the northwest part of the country.

TURKEY IN THE PAST

The history of modern Turkey begins with the fall of the Byzantine Empire in 1453 before the invading Osman, or Ottoman, Turks. The new Turkish Empire became known as the Ottoman Empire. It grew rapidly. In 1520, the great sultan Suleiman the Magnificent came to power. Before he died in 1566, the Ottomans had overrun Hungary, some of Austria, the Balkan countries (now Albania, Yugoslavia, Bulgaria, and Greece), Persia (now Iran), Palestine, much of Arabia, Egypt, Algiers, Tunisia, and Tripoli. The Ottoman Empire was the greatest military power in Europe and had an area as large as that of the United States. It was ruled by sultans (emperors) who had complete power over millions of people.

But the empire began to decay. Hungary was lost in 1699. Russia gradually took pieces of Turkish territory in its efforts to win an outlet to the Mediterranean through the Dardanelles. The Ottoman Empire continued to exist, with a great deal of land but little real power. In 1821, Greece declared its independence from Turkey. Soon many of its African holdings were lost. Algeria and Tunis were lost to France, Egypt was lost to Great Britain, and Tripoli was lost to Italy.

The losses in war made Turkey poor. The sultans who ruled the dying empire grew cruel and harsh. In 1908 a group of young men formed the Young Turks, a revolutionary party to reform the government. They led a successful revolt in 1909 and gained power in the government of Turkey. But they were more interested in regaining lost land than in making needed reforms. They led Turkey into war in the BALKANS, about which there is a separate article. The war ended with Turkish defeat and complete loss of territory there. In World War I, Turkey fought on the side of the Germans and was once again defeated, with more loss of territory.

After World War I, Turkey formed a new government under KEMAL, about whom there is a separate article. Under him, Turkey became a republic in 1923. Kemal introduced many reforms to make Turkey a modern, industrial country. He is called Ataturk, or "Father of Turkey."

In World War II Turkey was neutral until 1945, when it entered the war on the side of the Allies (including the United States, Great Britain, and Russia.) After the war, Soviet Russia demanded rights in the Dardanelles, but Turkey refused.

Turkey is a member of the United Nations. The United States has given military and economic aid to Turkey. The Turkish Army sent troops to fight for the United Nations during the Korean War. In 1951 Turkey joined the North Atlantic Treaty Organization (NATO).

In 1961 a constitutional government with a bicameral legislature was established. The President is elected by Parliament for a seven-year term and the leading political party chooses the premier.

In 1971 martial law was imposed and Communism was outlawed. By 1973, the condition of martial law was lifted.

The long entangled conflict with Greece over the island of Cyprus flared again on July 20, 1974 when Turkey invaded Cyprus. Turkey sought to install a new government in Cyprus designed to provide separate zones for Greek Cypriots and Turkish Cypriots respectively. In response to Turkey's intervention in Cyprus, the United States Congress stopped military support to Turkey in 1975.

TURKEY. Area, 301,380 square miles. Population (1976 estimate) 36,300,000. Language, Turkish. Religion, Moslem. Government, constitutional republic. Monetary unit, Turkish lira (of 100 piastres), worth 11 cents (U.S.). Flag, white crescent and white five-pointed star on red field.

Turks

The Turks are a people whose original home was somewhere in central Asia. There are many groups of Turks, and not all of them are closely related, but their languages are much alike.

About two thousand years ago some of the Turks began to move westward through Asia to the shores of the Mediterranean Sea. They married people from Europe, and today very few of the original Turks have remained the same race. Most of the Turks became Moslems, followers of the religion of Mohammed.

SELJUK AND OTTOMAN TURKS

About nine hundred years ago a group of Turks became very powerful. They were called the SELJUKS, and there is a separate article about them. Two hundred years later, during the 1200s, another group called the Ottoman Turks, or Osmans, became powerful. They were not related to the Seljuks but were wandering tribesmen descended from the ruling groups. They conquered almost all eastern Europe, and their lands were called the Ottoman Empire.

The descendants of the Ottoman Turks are the principal group of people who live in Turkey today. See also the article TURKEY.

Turner, Joseph

Joseph Mallord William Turner was an English painter who lived about 150 years ago. He is best remembered for his water-color pictures of landscapes. He was born in 1775, began to draw when he was a boy, and studied art under several famous masters. He used both oils and water colors. When he was 70 years old his eyes and mind began to fail, and in 1851, at the age of 76, he died.

turnip

The turnip is a root vegetable that grows in many parts of the world. There are several different varieties of turnip, but all have about the same shape and flavor.

Some turnips have a white pulp, some a pale yellow, and some a deep orange. The rutabaga is a kind of turnip. It is sometimes lumpy in shape. White turnips are about the size of medium or large onions and usually have a purple tint at the top where the leaves grow out of the root. Yellow turnips are about the same shape as the white ones but are usually larger.

Turnip greens (the leaves of young turnips) are cut and cooked as a vegetable like spinach. Some turnips do not have large roots and are grown for their leaves.

turpentine

Turpentine is a colorless, transparent, oily liquid with a sharp odor. It is mixed with paints and varnishes to cause them to dry more quickly. It is also mixed with paints to make them thinner. Turpentine is made from a thick, pale-yellow or brown, sticky substance that comes from the wood of evergreen trees, especially pine and fir.

turquoise

Turquoise is a semiprecious stone. It is usually blue, bluish-green or greenish-gray in color and becomes very shiny when polished. It is often used in rings and other kinds of jewelry and is one of the birthstones for December. A great deal of turquoise is found in the United States, especially in the Southwest, but the finest stones come from Turkey, the Ural Mountains, and Siberia.

turtle

Turtles have been on the earth for more than 200 million years. They are egg-laying, air-breathing reptiles. There are a few more than fifty different kinds of turtle including the desert tortoises and the giant sea turtles.

All turtles have certain things in common. All lay their eggs on land. All have shells but some have leathery shells and some have bony shells. All turtles are slow-moving on land. Under water, turtles can swim with moderate speed but not as fast as most fish.

The turtle lives longer than any other of the animals that have backbones. A desert tortoise has been known to reach the age of 152, and ages of 100 to 125 years are quite usual.

THE GREAT SEA TURTLES

Enormous turtles live in the warm oceans of the world. These turtles have flippers instead of feet, and they spend most of their lives in deep water, but they must leave the water to lay their eggs. Hundreds of female turtles are caught each year while they are plodding slowly back toward the ocean, after depositing their eggs in a sandy nest where the young turtles will hatch several months later.

The most familiar of the giant ocean turtles is the green turtle, from which green turtle soup is made. A green turtle often weighs 200 to 300 pounds.

The leatherback, whose shell is a thick, leathery substance, is even larger than the green turtle. It may weigh as much as 1,500 pounds and be 6 to 8 feet long.

The diamondback terrapin is a smaller kind of sea turtle. Its meat is considered the most desirable. Its shell has diamond-shaped markings all over its back.

TORTOISES

Unlike the sea turtles, a tortoise will never voluntarily enter the water. It lives entirely on land. In the desert sections of southwestern United States and Mexico there are many land tortoises. Some are about 1½ feet long. When it is very hot or very cold, tortoises burrow into the sand and remain there until the temperature is more moderate.

On the Galápagos Islands in the Pacific Ocean, off the coast of Ecuador, the world's largest tortoises are found. They weigh about 500 pounds. Like other land turtles, they eat grasses, and when the season is extremely dry they manage to survive on a diet of spiny cactus, of which they eat the blossoms, stems, and spiny leaves. There were once thousands of Galápagos tortoises, but the invasion of these islands by man has reduced their number greatly. Today they are protected by law.

BOX TURTLES

The greatest numbers of turtles in America spend part of their time on land and part in the water. The box turtle is common from New England to Central America. It can pull its head, tail and legs into its shell, then fold shell flaps over them all to make a completely closed box. It does this when it seems to be in danger.

The female lays its eggs in the summer. It selects a spot where there is plenty of sunlight and digs a hole with its back feet. It lays four to eight eggs, one at a time, and then covers each one with loose dirt. Then the turtle replaces the dislodged soil and treads back and forth over the closed nest, pressing the earth down smoothly to conceal the nest.

The eggs will start to hatch in late September, and some of the young will not emerge from their shells until November. Young box turtles are about an inch and a quarter long when they hatch. They grow about an inch a year for five years.

Box turtles eat almost anything—mushrooms, slugs, snails, worms, caterpillars, berries, leaves, and sometimes garden vegetables such as tomatoes.

THE TURTLES IN PET SHOPS

The small turtles that are sold in pet shops are *sliders*. These are fresh-water turtles that must come out into the air to breathe. They breed in tremendous numbers in the southern United States and in the Mississippi valley.

When these young turtles are kept as pets, they should be given a spot where they can come out of the water and bask in the sunlight occasionally. They should be fed small bits of meat and tender fresh vegetables. If they have been painted or decorated on their backs, the paint should be removed.

THE FEROCIOUS SNAPPERS

Snapping turtles, or snappers, are the only members of their family with a means of defense other than the armor-like shell. Snapping turtles can inflict painful wounds, and a large one could remove the tip of a finger with little difficulty. Snapping turtles usually live in ponds and lakes and come out of the water to bask in the sunlight from time to time. If a snapper senses danger, or sees something ahead of it that may be a threat of danger, it lunges forward with a ferocious snap of its powerful jaws. It sometimes gives such a powerful lunge that its entire body leaves the ground as it snaps.

Snapping turtles are disagreeable by nature. Anyone who sees a turtle beside a pond or a lake, or even near the edge of a stream, should test first with a long stick before attempting to pick up the turtle. If it is a box turtle it will pull its head into the shell quickly. A painted turtle—very like a box turtle but with bright colors on its shell—will pull its head and limbs in as far as possible. A slider will scuttle toward the water as fast as possible. A snapper will immediately attack the end of the stick.

The alligator snapper is the largest and most vicious of the snapping turtles. It lives mainly in Florida. It grows to a length of about two feet and weighs up to thirty pounds. Alligator snappers spend most of their time at the bottom of ponds and streams.

Tuscany

Tuscany is a region of central Italy, on the west coast, on the Ligurian and Tyrrhenian seas. It includes nine Italian provinces and the Tuscan Islands, of which Elba is the largest. Tuscany has an area of about 9,000 square miles, and about three million people live there. Most of Tuscany is mountainous, except for a narrow plain along the coast and several river valleys. The most important valley is that of the Arno River, where wheat, olives, grapes and mushrooms are grown in the fertile soil. Tuscany is rich in minerals. It produces 90 per cent of Italy's iron, most of its mercury, and large quantities of copper, manganese, and other ores. The Carrara marble quarried in its mountains is famous.

Tuscany has several important manufacturing cities, such as Florence, Leghorn (Livorno), and Piombino. It has long been recognized as a region important in the arts and culture. The Tuscan form of the Italian language is considered the purest form.

Tuskegee Institute

Tuskegee Institute is the oldest college for blacks in the United States. It is in Tuskegee, Alabama. It was founded in 1881 by the first great black educator, Booker T. Washington, as a vocational school and training school for teachers. Soon it was teaching many skills and trades. Today it has schools of agriculture, home economics and commercial dietetics, education, mechanical industries, nursing, and veterinary medicine, and departments of physical education and music. It also has a museum and library. It specializes in research on southern farm products, rural housing, and social problems.

The faculty has included many eminent educators; the most famous, after Washington, was George W. Carver. In 1976 Tuskegee had 3,196 students, both men and women, and a faculty of 353.

Tut-ankh-amen

Tut-ankh-amen was pharaoh (king) of Egypt more than three thousand years ago. He married the daughter of King Ikhnaton, who had made Aton the official god of the Egyptian religion. Tut-ankh-amen made Amon the official god, and that is how Amon or Amen became part of his name. He also changed the capital of Egypt from Ikhnaton's city back to Thebes. Little was known about this time in Egypt's history until 1922, when some explorers, who were digging in the Valley of the Tombs of the Kings near Thebes found Tut-ankh-amen's tomb. This was a very great discovery, for while the tombs of many pharaohs are known, they were all opened and emptied out by tomb-robbers in ancient times. "King Tut's" tomb contained all the valuable furniture and equipment that was supposed to be at his disposal in the life beyond.

Twain, Mark, the pen name of Samuel Clemens. see the article Samuel CLEMENS.

Tweed Ring

The Tweed Ring was a group of dishonest politicians who became very powerful in New York about a hundred years ago. The group was named for its principal leader, William Marcy Tweed (called "Boss" Tweed). As powerful members of Tammany Hall, the Democratic Party's organization in New York City, Tweed and his friends were able to use public funds for their personal gain. The group became very strong and very rich, and often bribed other public officials to do what it wanted. In 1865 the Tweed Ring's candidate for mayor of New York City was elected, and three years later its candidate for governor of the state also won and the state legislature was under its control.

In 1871 the New York *Times* ran a series of articles that told people about the Tweed Ring's dishonest activities. This led to an investigation by a committee headed by Samuel J. TILDEN, about whom there is a separate article. Many of the leaders, including William Tweed, were tried in courts of law and were put in jail, and the ring was broken up.

twilight

Twilight is the light from the sky between sunset and full night. The same light shows between full night and sunrise, but is usually called dawn.

The sky at twilight usually looks purplish-blue and remains that color for one and a half to two and a half hours. In the extreme northern and southern parts of the world, twilight lasts much longer, sometimes for several months. Twilight is caused by dust particles in the air. They reflect the light of the sun after it has set (and before it rises), filling the sky with sunlight even when the sun cannot be seen. The dust particles are denser at the horizon, where more air lies between the seer and the sun. They absorb a great deal of the blue color of the sun's light, and so turn objects that are low in the sky to a reddish color.

John Tyler

John Tyler was the tenth President of the United States. He was Vice President under William Henry Harrison, and was the first Vice President in American history to succeed to office after the death of the President. Tyler served from April, 1841, to March, 1845. The Democratic Party nominated him for re-election, but he withdrew from the contest and the nomination went to James Polk.

The most important event that occurred during John Tyler's term in office was the negotiations that led to adding the state of Texas to the Union. His administration was somewhat troubled, because Tyler was a man of extreme independence and did not hesitate to antagonize either political party.

HIS EARLY YEARS

John Tyler was born in Charles City County, Virginia, on March 29, 1790. His

father, also named John Tyler, became Governor of Virginia when young John was 18. John attended William and Mary College in Virginia, and became a lawyer after his graduation.

He entered politics and was elected to Congress, as a member of the House of Representatives, in 1816. At the age of 35 he was elected Governor of Virginia and later he became a United States Senator. He was a member of the Whig Party, but belonged to a branch of the party that sided with the Democrats on certain aspects of the States' Rights question, believing that the states should have many rights that were claimed by the Federal government.

HOW HE BECAME PRESIDENT

When William Henry Harrison was nominated for the Presidency in 1840, John Tyler was the Vice-Presidential nominee. The campaign slogan was "Tippecanoe and Tyler too." (Harrison was famous for having won the Battle of Tippecanoe.)

The Whigs won the election, but Harrison died of pneumonia one month after the inauguration and Tyler succeeded him in office. As President he sometimes sided with the Whigs and sometimes with the Democrats, which irritated both.

In spite of the fact that Tyler was not very popular, the Democrats thought that his work in admitting Texas to the United States was a strong enough point to win his re-election. They nominated him, although he was officially a member of the Whigs, but Tyler decided not to run.

HIS LATER YEARS

After Tyler had finished his term as President, he went back to Virginia and retired temporarily from political life. When the Civil War started in 1860, he became a member of the Peace Commission that attempted to stop the fighting. Then it became apparent that no compromise could be reached and Tyler recommended the secession of Virginia. He accepted membership in the provisional Congress of the Confederate States of America, but before the Congress met he became ill with bronchitis and died on January 18, 1862.

THE FIRST MRS. TYLER

Letitia Christian Tyler was born in Cedar Grove, Virginia, in 1790. She was the daughter of a planter (rich farmer). She married John Tyler in 1813, when each of them was 23 years old. The first Mrs. Tyler became an invalid. She died in the White House in 1842. John and Letitia Tyler had nine children, of whom three sons and four daughters lived past infancy.

THE SECOND MRS. TYLER

Julia Gardiner Tyler was born in New York in 1820. She married John Tyler in 1844, when she was 24 and he was 54. She died in 1889. There were seven children of this marriage, five sons and two daughters.

Tyler, Wat

Wat Tyler was an Englishman who lived about six hundred years ago. In 1381 he led some poor English farmers in a rebellion against the government and king. At that time the English government had passed laws that made the farmers pay heavy taxes in order to vote. Tyler roused the people in southern and eastern England to rebel against the government. He gathered together an army and they marched on London, where they were joined by the poor city people. They also wrote a petition (a list of requests) that was presented to King Richard II. The king granted all their requests, but after the rebels had peacefully left London and returned to their homes, the king's soldiers followed them, killed their leaders (including Tyler) and severely punished others with beatings and torture. This was wholly dishonorable behavior on the part of the king and the English noblemen, but according to their beliefs in those times there was no reason for them to act honorably toward the lower classes. "Wat Tyler's Rebellion" is remembered partly by a rhyme that the rebels used as a kind of motto: "When Adam delved and Evé span/Who was then the gentleman?"

Tyndale, William

William Tyndale was an English religious reformer and translator of the Bible. He was born around 1492 and became a Catholic priest in 1521. Tyndale is remembered for his translations of the New Testament and parts of the Old Testament. The Bible of the Roman Catholic Church was written only in Latin. Tyndale translated it into English, so more people could read it. Tyndale's translations and religious views were disliked by the religious authorities. Possibly because of the efforts of King Henry VIII, Tyndale was imprisoned, convicted of heresy, and burned at the stake in 1536. Today his translations are the foundation of the King James Version of the Bible. See the entry on BIBLE.

typesetting

Type, or printer's type, is pieces of metal with raised letters on them. When they are inked and pressed against paper, they produce printing. A rubber stamp or a typewriter works on the same principle of raised surfaces. The arranging, or setting, of type to be used in printing is called *typesetting,* or *composition.*

Typesetting began nearly five hundred years ago, when Johannes Gutenberg first used "movable type." At first, each letter was carved on a piece of wood. Soon printers were making type by casting metal into molds. This method was the only one used for nearly four hundred years, and cast type (called *foundry type*) is still much used. In the 1880s ways were found to set type by machine, and nearly all printing is now done with machine-set type. Late in the 1940s, machines were developed that would prepare a printing plate by a photographic

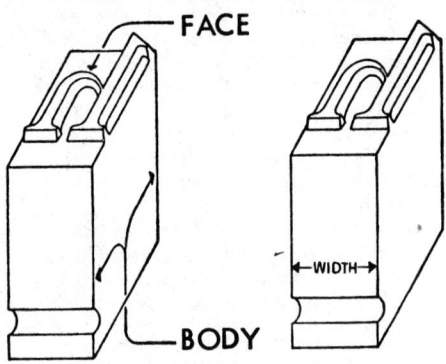

A block of type has a body and a face that is raised above the body. The width depends on the width of the letter.

process, and for the first time in history it became possible to make a printed book without first going through the process of typesetting.

HAND COMPOSITION

Until typesetting machines came along, type was set by skilled *compositors* who worked by hand. The compositor had a tray called a *case* that was divided into about eighty small compartments. Each compartment held a handful of pieces of type that would print a particular capital letter, small letter, numeral, punctuation mark, and so on. In his hand the compositor held a small metal tray called a *stick.* He set the type letter by letter, reaching into the case for the piece of type and putting it in place in the stick. Compositors learned to know the case so well that their hands worked with remarkable speed.

As the stick became full, the type was transferred to a long metal tray called a *galley.* When the galley was full, a *proof* was taken. Ink was rolled on the face of the type, paper was laid over it, and a heavy roller was passed over the paper. This produced a *galley proof.* A proofreader would read it, mark mistakes with a special system of marks, and send it back to the compositor, who would make the corrections by changing the type standing in the galley. This system of proofreading and correction is still in use.

Compositors developed their own system of measuring, their own special names for kinds and sizes of type, and many methods that were worked out in the days of hand-set type are still used in these days of automatic machines. Usually they are puzzling to almost everyone except a printer.

Type is not measured by inches, as nearly all other things are. The typesetter uses a measuring system based on the *point* and the *pica.* There are 12 points in each pica, and 6 picas, or 72 points,

measure just about one inch. The width of a line of type is called the *measure.* The space occupied by a piece of type is called the *body.*

There are special names for "type faces" of different appearances. Regular type, such as this, is called roman. Slanted type is called *italic.* "Old style" type uses a fairly heavy line in all parts of each letter, while "modern" type uses both thin and heavy lines, as in the letter M, where the upright line on the left is thin and the one on the right is heavy. The little cross-strokes at the tops and bottoms of the letters are called *serifs.* Type that does not have any serifs is called *Gothic,* or *sans serif.*

Type can be designed in many different ways. Styles of type are often named after great type-designers who first designed them, for example Bodoni and Garamond, who lived hundreds of years ago. Each style of type is made in several different sizes, for example 6-point, 8-point, and so on, up to 72-point or more (and sometimes down as low as 3-point). The number of points shows how far it is from the top of a capital letter (or from the top of an *ascender* on such a letter as b or h) to the bottom of the *descender* on such a letter as p or q. The most readable type sizes are generally considered to range from 8-point to 12-point. English typesetters first used names instead of points to show the size of a type, and some of the old names are still used: *agate* for 5½-point, *nonpareil* for 6-point, and *pica* for 12-point.

The capital M, in most type faces, is a square letter. That is, the width of the letter is exactly the same as the depth or body. For that reason the typesetter uses an "em" as a unit for measuring the space occupied by any particular size of type. Usually each paragraph is indented (set in) one em. With 6-point type, this means an indentation of 6 points, with 10-point type an indentation of 10 points, and so on. A small n is about half as wide as the M, so an "en" is another unit for measuring.

TYPESETTING MACHINES

When a hand compositor sets a line of type, he *justifies* it. That is, he puts between the words just enough space so that each line will be the same width. The problem of early designers of typesetting machines was to make the machines justify lines automatically.

The first practical system for this was worked out by a German-born American inventor named Ottmar Mergenthaler. He produced his first perfected typesetting machine in 1886. This machine, called the Linotype, is still the one most used. The same principle is used in a machine called the Intertype.

In the Linotype machine, the operator uses a keyboard like a typewriter keyboard but having many more keys. Every

The basic faces used in typesetting are (*left to right*): text, roman, italic, and script. Roman is the most common.

time he presses a key, a small mold called a *matrix* drops from a container, or *magazine,* into place on a line. Between words the machine puts a wedge-shaped space. When the operator has set enough words to fill a line, he moves a lever. This forces the wedge-shaped spaces up between the words, and this produces even spacing between all the words. The machine then pours melted lead into the molds, casting one solid piece of metal for each line of type. This piece of metal is called a *slug.* If there is a mistake in any line, the entire line is reset and the entire slug is replaced in the galleys.

Linotype machines not only made typesetting much faster and more accurate but also made the handling and arrangement (make-up) of the type faster and easier, because it is so much easier to handle one large, solid slug of type than many tiny individual pieces. Nevertheless, another kind of typesetting machine, which automatically sets individual pieces of type, is extremely valuable for certain jobs. This is called the Monotype machine.

The Monotype was invented by Tolbert Lanston, of Washington, D.C., and was finally made practical during the 1890s. A Monotype operator works with a keyboard, just as a Linotype operator does; but his keyboard cuts holes in a paper tape. This tape is then fed into a separate typecasting machine. The matrixes are kept in a frame called a *mat case.* Compressed air blown through the holes in the tape causes little arms to lift the desired mat, melted lead is poured into the mat, and a piece of type is cast. These pieces of type come out of the machine in properly justified lines, ready to go into a galley and have a proof taken. A correction can be made by replacing a single piece of type, without having to set the entire line again.

There is a third popular kind of typesetting machine. It was first made by Washington I. Ludlow, in 1906, and is called the Ludlow machine. The Ludlow system combines hand composition with machine casting. The compositor sets the mats in place by hand, then puts them in a machine that casts a solid slug like the one cast by the Linotype. The Ludlow machine can be used for larger type sizes than the Linotype and Monotype.

PHOTOGRAPHIC TYPESETTING

The photographic method does not really set "type." It sets into place tiny photographic negatives, each representing one letter or symbol. The Intertype Photosetter works just as the Intertype (or Linotype) hot metal typesetting machine does, except that the "mats" are these photographic negatives. When a line is complete, light is directed through the negatives and a photographic print of the line is made. This photographic print is ideal for offset or gravure printing, about which you can read in the article on PRINTING. It saves the steps in which type is cast, proofs are taken, and then the type is thrown away.

One other method is to write the desired material on special typewriters that can justify the lines; and then either make line cuts (as explained in the article on PHOTOENGRAVING) or make plates for use in offset printing.

ELECTRONIC TAPE

Since the 1950s Linotype and Intertype machines, as well as Monotype machines, have used a punched tape (much like the sound track for a motion picture) that controls the casting of type by electricity. When the keyboard operator touches a key, the mat does not drop from the magazine; instead, certain holes are punched in the tape. Later the tape is fed into an automatic type-casting machine, which may set either solid slugs or separate letters.

typewriter

A typewriter is a machine that prints letters of the alphabet, and numerals and other marks, when you press keys on a keyboard. It is such a familiar machine, with millions of typewriters in use throughout the world, that it seems hard to believe that the typewriter was invented less than 100 years ago and has been widely used for only about 50 years.

Most typewriters work by the force of the fingers striking the keys. This moves arms that make type bars strike a ribbon that has been impregnated (soaked) with ink. On a piece of paper behind the inked ribbon, the mark of that particular type bar shows up, making the letter the typist wants. The advantages of the typewriter are that it is faster and less tiring than handwriting and makes writing that is neater and more legible (easier to read).

For about thirty years electric typewriters have been popular. Pressing each key connects a little electric motor to the type bar. The motor, not the force of the fingers, makes the type bar strike. When the electric typewriter is properly adjusted, each key strikes the ribbon with exactly the same force, making an evener and better-looking printing. The electric typewriter also reduces the amount of work that the typist has to do. Because the keys do not have to be struck so hard, the work is less tiring.

The first practical typewriter was invented in 1867 by a Milwaukee printer named C. Latham Sholes. It was put on the market in the 1870s. At first typewriters were too expensive to sell in great quantities. Gradually typewriters became popular and by 1909 there were eighty-nine typewriter manufacturers in the United States. Since then, many of these companies have combined or have gone out of business.

In the early typewriters the paper was placed in such a position that you could not see what you were writing. You had to write a few lines, then lift up the top part of the typewriter and look. About 1908, manufacturers began to bring out the "visible" typewriter, on which you could see what you were writing as you went along. Since about 1915, all typewriters have been "visibles."

Some of the early typewriters did not use the inked ribbon. Instead, a little ink-soaked roller was used. As the type bar moved toward the paper, it brushed against this roller and picked up enough ink to print on the paper. The cloth ribbon soon replaced this. Now many electric typewriters use a carbon ribbon. This is a paper ribbon coated as carbon paper is coated. Each section of the ribbon is used only once and it is thrown away as it comes off the machine. The carbon makes blacker writing than the cloth ribbon, and it does not become fainter as

the ink is used up or dries out of the ribbon.

Every typewriter now has one "shift key" with which the typist can change from small letters to capital letters, but many early typewriters had two shift keys and the typist used one shift key to change from small to capital letters and the other to change to numerals and certain punctuation marks.

THE STANDARD KEYBOARD

One of the most important things about a typewriter is the arrangement of the letters on the keyboard. A typist becomes used to a certain arrangement, and if different machines had different arrangements it would be hard to use more than one particular make of machine. Yet in the early days there were many different arrangements. Gradually these came down to two popular ones, called the "universal" and the "standard." Finally the "standard" keyboard was adopted by all manufacturers.

The standard keyboard arrangement is:

```
2 3 4 5 6 7 8 9 0
Q W E R T Y U I O P
A S D F G H J K L
Z X C V B N M , .
```

There are other keys, but they are not always the same.

The problem in designing a typewriter keyboard is this: Some letters of the English language are used more often than others, and some combinations of letters are used more often than others. The keyboard should place the most-used letters where they are easiest to reach with the fingers, but it should separate the letters of the most-used combinations. For example, the combination TH is used a great deal (in such words as *the, that, than, this, thing,* and so on) while the combination TQ is never used. If the T key and the H key were too close together, the type bar for H would always be striking the type bar for T.

Sholes, the inventor, worked out the standard keyboard. It prevents most clashes between type bars, but in other ways it is very poor. The forefinger and middle finger of the hand are the ones we can use best, and the most-used letters should be where these fingers can reach them most easily, but on the standard keyboard many of the most-used letters are at the sides where they are within easy reach of the little finger but not of the middle fingers.

Many people have worked out better keyboard arrangements, but so many millions of people have learned the standard keyboard that it would cause them a great deal of trouble if the arrangement were changed.

TYPING SYSTEMS

High schools and business schools teach what is called the "touch system" of typing. It actually has nothing to do with the sense of touch. It simply means that the typist memorizes the keyboard so thoroughly that she can type without looking at it, and that she learns to use all of her fingers, each finger on a particular group of keys. Untrained typists use what is called the "hunt and peck" system. Usu-

ally they use only their two forefingers or at most their four best fingers, the forefinger and middle fingers. Actually these typists can learn the keyboard just as well and go just about as fast, but very fast typing is more tiring for them than for the touch typist because the hands have to leap all around the keyboard to reach all the keys with only two or four fingers.

There are speed-typing contests in which the champions get to speeds greater than 200 words a minute, but an acceptable typist in an office is expected only to write about 60 words a minute with only occasional mistakes, and 90 to 100 words a minute is a very fast speed for any ordinary work.

Though typewriters are all the same, each has its own peculiarities in appearance—special marks on the letters, and a special line-up of the letters—that can be seen through a microscope. In court trials, experts are often called upon to prove that a particular typewriter produced a particular typewritten page.

typhoid fever

Typhoid fever is a serious disease. It is caused by a germ that is found in shellfish and other foods, and in some milk and water. Typhoid fever once caused the death of many people. Now doctors, scientists and public-health officials inspect food, supervise the supply of water and disposal of sewage, and make sure that milk is pasteurized. Because of these precautions, in the United States, Canada, and other modern countries few people now get typhoid fever.

Typhoid fever begins with a headache and a slight fever. Then, three days to a month after the person becomes ill, he breaks out in a rash of rose-colored spots. Doctors make tests of the blood and urine so that they can tell immediately whether a person has the disease. Typhoid fever is very infectious, which means that it is easy to catch from someone else. For this reason a person having the disease is best treated in a special hospital.

Some people have typhoid germs but do not become ill. They are called "carriers," and they can give the disease to others. One woman who lived about fifty years ago became well known as "Typhoid Mary," because although she herself was never ill she gave the disease to many other people. Some states in the United States have laws that require every person who is known to be a typhoid carrier to register with the health department of the state. These people are taught how to care for themselves and protect others from the disease.

Typhoid fever is still common in places where living conditions are simple and unsanitary. People who travel to such places should receive injections that can help protect them against the disease.

typhoon, another name for a HURRICANE.

typhus

Typhus is a serious infectious disease caused by a germ that is carried by the rat flea and the body louse. For this reason it usually occurs in slums and other areas where living conditions are crowded and dirty. Thousands of people used to die in typhus epidemics. Good sanitation and hygiene now prevent typhus from breaking out, and modern drugs, especially the antibiotic drugs, can often cure it.

Typhus may not be noticed until two weeks after a person has become infected. He then has pains in the head, back, and limbs, and a fever that rises to 104 or 105 degrees. After four or five days a rash of rose-colored spots breaks out all over the body. The high fever does not go down until the tenth day, and often not until the fourteenth. During this time, the patient is in danger of falling into a coma and dying.

tyrannosaurus

The tyrannosaurus was one of the largest and most fearful of the dinosaurs, the great reptiles that lived 100,000,000 years ago. Scientists have dug up and reconstructed the bones of tyrannosauri and they can be seen in several museums. The tyrannosaurus was almost 50 feet from the tip of its tail to its great, ugly head. It stood 20 feet high on its large hind legs. It looked somewhat like a huge ugly kangaroo, with its great lashing tail that it used for balance, its small front legs, and its powerful hind legs. The head of the tyrannosaurus was more than four feet long and its jaws were filled with sharp, jagged teeth, each six inches long.

The tyrannosaurus was one of the few dinosaurs that ate flesh. Most dinosaurs fed on plants and grasses. The tyrannosaurus, like all the dinosaurs, vanished from the earth millions of years ago.

tyrant

A tyrant is a cruel and unjust ruler. In the days of the ancient Greeks, almost three thousand years ago, the word *tyrant* meant any ruler who won the throne by warfare or by the support of the people and not by inheritance from a father who was a king, or by election. Tyrant then meant much the same as *dictator* does now. Adolf Hitler and Josef Stalin, called dictators in modern times, would have been called tyrants then. Because it was hard for a man to get power and keep it, most tyrants have been cruel rulers.

When Sparta won a war against Athens, about 2,500 years ago, it set up a body of rulers over Athens who were called the Thirty Tyrants. They were extremely unjust and were soon overthrown. The most famous tyrants of history were Miltiades of Thrace and Dionysius of Syracuse (a city of Sicily) at about that same time.

Tyre

Tyre was the most important city of ancient Phoenicia, more than three thousand years ago. It lay on the shores of the Mediterranean, about fifty miles south of the modern city of Beirut, Lebanon. It was the most important commercial center of Phoenicia. It was noted for producing beautiful silks and a dye used by the ancient Phoenicians was called Tyrian purple.

Phoenicia had very close links with Egypt in the early times, but after Egypt became weak the Phoenicians began to do much trading and colonizing in the Mediterranean. Carthage (which means "the new city" in Phoenician) was founded by the Tyrians. King Hiram of Tyre, who reigned during the time of the Israelite kings David and Solomon, provided them with cedar wood from Lebanon for their palace and Temple and also with skilled craftsmen.

Tyre lay on an island and so was hard to conquer. Alexander the Great conquered Tyre by building a mole (pier) from the mainland to the island. Drifting sand has piled up against the mole, which now forms an isthmus. Alexander destroyed Tyre, but it was rebuilt and soon was rich again.

About 1,300 years ago Tyre was conquered by Moslems, followers of the religion of Mohammed. In 1124 it was taken from them by the Christian Crusaders and became the chief city of the kingdom of Jerusalem. Today the town of Sur, with a population of about 6,000, stands on the site of ancient Tyre.

Tyrol

The Tyrol is a region in southern Austria and northern Italy, lying entirely within the Alps. It is a land of great beauty, with many health and pleasure resorts. Almost half of the Tyrol is covered with forests. Its two principal rivers are the Inn and the Adige, and in their valleys the land is fertile and farming is done. Most of the people of the Tyrol speak German, even in the Italian part, and almost all of them are Roman Catholics. The Tyrol is a favorite winter playground for skiers and other sport lovers.

The Austrian Tyrol is the smaller of the two parts of the region, having an area of about 4,900 square miles. More than 450,000 people live there. The most important city of the Austrian Tyrol is Innsbruck, which is both an industrial city and a popular resort.

The Italian Tyrol covers an area about the size of the administrative region of Trentino-Alto Adige, about 5,250 square miles, and has a population of almost 800,000. Its most important city is Trento. The Italian Tyrol is famous for its vineyards and fruit orchards. The famous Brenner Pass is located at the border between Austria and Italy.

Austrian Consulate
A young girl wearing Tyrolean costume greets visitors to an Alpine inn.

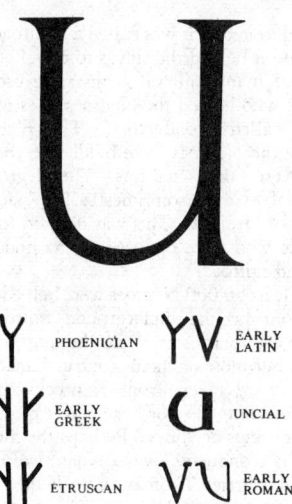

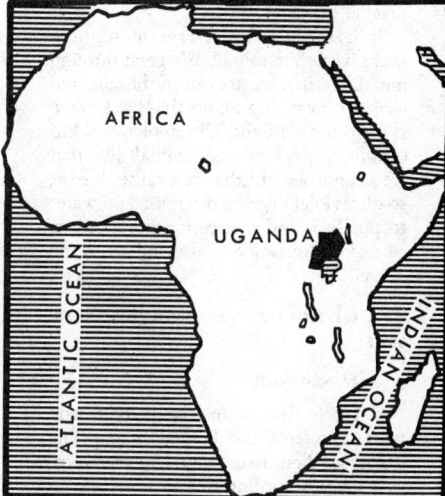

The letter U, the twenty-first letter of our alphabet, came to us as most of our letters did. Thousands of years ago it may have been one of the picture-symbols used by the ancient Egyptians in their system of writing called *hieroglyphics*. In this system a picture of something, instead of a letter, came to stand for a single sound. Some people believe that the letter U began as a picture of a horned serpent, but other scholars have come to think it began as a picture of a hook. In the Hebrew and Phoenician languages, the word for hook was *waw*, and the sign for it was the one shown at the top of this page, at the far left.

The ancient Greeks took the Hebrew letter, which they called *upsilon*, and used three different signs for it. Two of these signs are shown at the top of the page, to the right of the Phoenician *waw*. When the Romans came to use the letter U, they removed the bottom stroke so that the up-and-down lines met in a point at the bottom, just as in the letter V in our alphabet. For many centuries this letter stood for the sound of "u" and "v" or "w". The bottom of the V was also sometimes rounded. Until about three hundred years ago, there was no difference between the letter U and the letter V in the English alphabet. Then U began to be used for the *u* sound and V began to be used for the sound "v."

In the illustration above, the "German black-letter" capital U, which is used in many German books, is shown at the far right.

Read also the articles V and ALPHA-BET.

Ubangi River

The Ubangi is a river about 660 miles long in central Africa. It is one of the biggest rivers that flow into the Congo River. The Ubangi flows west and south, forming part of the northern and western border of the Republic of Congo (Kinshasa). The upper Ubangi is navigable for about a hundred miles, and it is navi-gable for about 375 miles from its mouth at the Congo. In its middle course there are steep rapids.

Ubangi-Shari, former name of the CENTRAL AFRICAN REPUBLIC.

Uganda

Uganda is a country in Africa. It is in the central part, near the equator. It became independent in 1962. Until then it had been a British protectorate. The area of Uganda is 93,981 square miles, which is about the size of Oregon. About ten million people live there.

Uganda is a land of mountains, lakes, and plains. Parts of Lake Victoria, Lake Albert and Lake Edward are in Uganda. Mount Ruwenzori is in a mountain range with peaks above 16,700 feet. The chief rivers are the Victoria Nile and Albert Nile, branches of the great Nile river.

The climate is usually very hot. The many wild animals include the elephant, buffalo, hippopotamus, and crocodile.

Almost all the people of Uganda are African Negroes of various tribes. The Bugandas are most powerful and their language, Luganda, is semi-official, but there are more Bantus. The people who live in the north form another group. Nearly everyone understands the Swahili language.

Most of the people are farmers. There are some wandering tribes that raise livestock, workers in the few factories, and miners. Important crops are coffee, tea, cotton, oil seeds, sugar, sisal, maize, and peanuts. The rich minerals deposits are not mined, except tin and apatite.

Uganda, is a republic and a member of the (British) Commonwealth. It has a National Assembly, a prime minister, and a president. But since independence there has been much political trouble, which has been caused by sectional and tribal rivalries.

UGANDA. Area, 93,981 square miles. Population (1974 estimate) 10,130,000. Government, republic. Capital, Kampala (population 50,000). Monetary unit, East African pound. Languages, English (official); Luganda, Bantu, Swahili.

Ukraine

The Ukraine is a large territory in Europe. Its official name is the Ukrainian Soviet Republic. It is part of the Soviet Union and a member of the United Nations.

The Ukraine has an area of more than 200,000 square miles, which makes it almost as big as the state of Texas, and more than 45,000,000 people live there, which is about four times as many as live in Texas.

The people of the Ukraine belong to a Slavic group called Ukrainians. They are closed related to the Russians, and the Ukraine was once called "Little Russia." There are also some Russians and Poles. Most of the people belong to the Orthodox Church, but the Ukraine is controlled by Communists and all religions are discouraged.

Except for the narrow strip of the Carpathian Mountains in the west, all of the Ukraine consists of the great plain called the *steppes*. The land is famous for its fertile soil. Long ago it was called "Europe's granary," or grain-raising region, but under Communist control the Ukraine's wheat and other farm products are used almost entirely by the Soviet Union. Other crops are grains, potatoes, tobacco, sugar beets, and fruits. Dairy farming is also important.

The Ukraine has several important rivers, including the Dnieper, the Bug, and the Donets. Russia's biggest dam and hydroelectric power station is on the Dnieper. During World War II, when the Germans overcame and occupied the Ukraine, the Russians themselves destroyed the dam. After the war it was rebuilt.

The climate of the Ukraine is moderate. The winters are very cold and stormy.

The Ukraine has some of the richest mineral deposits in the Soviet Union, including iron, coal, manganese, and many others. Some of Russia's most important cities are in the Ukraine, such as Kiev, Kharkov, Odessa, and Dnepropetrovsk.

The first state to be called Russian was established more than a thousand years ago at Kiev, the capital of the present Ukraine. Christianity was brought from Constantinople, the seat of the Greek Othodox Church. Several hundred years later, the state was conquered and partly destroyed by invading Tartars. Much of the region later fell under the control of Lithuania and later of Poland.

Meanwhile Moscow became the center of a strong Russian state, and Turkey took over the southern region of the Ukraine. The word *Ukraine* means "borderland" in Russian, and it was a borderland fought over by four nations. The Ukrainian people began to develop as a separate group, and they were constantly at war, being invaded and trying to defend their land. A group of Ukrainians called Cossacks formed a state that was almost independent, and they fought fiercely against the Poles and others until in 1654 they agreed to join the Moscow state because they felt closer to the Russians in race and religion than to any other of the peoples occupying Ukrainian territory. In 1667 Poland gave up the northeast Ukraine, and in 1783 Russia conquered the region called the Crimea and won control of all of the Ukraine.

In the late 1800s, the Ukrainian people wanted very much to become independent of Russia. After World War I, an independent Ukraine was established, but the new Communist government of

Russia did not permit it and the Ukraine became one of the first republics of the Union of Soviet Socialist Republics. During World War II the Ukraine was the greatest battleground of the German and Russian troops. Millions of Ukrainians were killed and millions of others were captured. In 1945 the Ukraine was admitted to the United Nations as a separate state, but it is still completely controlled by the Soviet Union.

UKRAINE. or Ukrainian Soviet Socialist Republic. Area, 232,046 square miles. Population (1964 estimate) 44,868,000. Capital, Kicv.

ukulele or ukelele

The ukulele is a small stringed instrument with a sounding box and a long neck. Its four strings are tuned to the notes A, D, F♯, and B. Along the neck of the ukelele are little metal bars called *frets*. With the fingers of one hand the player holds down the strings at various fret points; with the fingers of the other hand he strums all four strings with a sweeping motion. *Ukulele* is a Hawaiian word, and the ukulele was introduced into the United States from the Hawaiian Islands. It became very popular among young people in the United States.

ulcer

An ulcer, or a *peptic ulcer,* is a sore on the inner wall of the stomach or the intestines. It causes pain after one has eaten. The ulcers that occur in the stomach are called *gastric ulcers.* Those that occur in the part of the intestine known as the duodenum are called *duodenal ulcers.* Most ulcers are of the duodenal type.

The ulcer (sore) is formed when the juices that help the body digest food begin to hurt the lining of the intestine or the stomach. Doctors do no know just why this happens. Normal stomach and intestine linings are not hurt by these strong juices, but when the lining becomes weak and the juices begin to attack it, an ulcer is formed. When a person with an ulcer has no food in his stomach the juices will begin to digest the lining of the stomach, as if it were food. Doctors believe that when a person is nervous and worries a great deal, ulcers may form.

There are many medicines that relieve the pain of ulcers. A person with an ulcer has to be on a special diet and eat mild foods that will not irritate the ulcer. Usually the ulcer will clear up in a few weeks. Doctors try to find out what causes the person to be upset and try to calm him, so that he will not get another ulcer. Ulcers are not unusual, and it has been estimated that three out of every thousand people have them.

ultraviolet rays

Ultraviolet rays are rays of light that we cannot ordinarily see. If you look at the spectrum, which is light broken up into different colors (as in a rainbow), you will see how the colors range from red at one side of the spectrum to blue at the other side. Just beyond the light rays that you see as blue are the ultraviolet rays that you cannot see.

The article on FLUORESCENCE tells how these ultraviolet rays can make certain substances glow. Special lamps, which are often called "black light" lamps, send out ultraviolet rays, and while these cannot be seen coming from the lamp they can be used to light up materials that have been specially treated. Sometimes in a stage show you may see all the lights go out, leaving the stage dark, but the costumes of dancers or other performers on the stage will continue to glow brightly. These performers are wearing costumes that have been chemically treated so that they will glow with ultraviolet rays, and special lamps are shining the ultraviolet rays on the stage.

It is the ultraviolet rays in sunlight that give us Vitamin D. We get it through our skin when we are out in the sun, and we get it by eating plants that have taken it from the sunlight. Ultraviolet rays kill certain tiny plant and animal life that we cannot see but that can cause disease, so ultraviolet rays are often used on water to purify it and in treating our skins to cure skin diseases. See also the article on X-RAYS.

Ulysses, another name for ODYSSEUS.

Uncle Sam

Uncle Sam is an imaginary person who represents the United States. The name was first used about 150 years ago, as a joke. According to one story, a man named Samuel Wilson, who was usually called "Uncle Sam," was a government inspector of meat at Troy, New York, in 1812. A man named Elbert Anderson bought a large number of barrels of meat, and they were marked with his initials, E.A., and also with the initials, U.S. (United States) to show that the meat had been inspected. One day one of the workmen asked what the initials stood for, and someone answered jokingly, "I don't know, unless they mean 'Uncle Sam.'" The joke spread, and soon the initials of the United States were regarded as "Uncle Sam." This story may be true, but most stories of this kind are not true.

The custom of picturing Uncle Sam as a tall, thin, graybearded man with a tall hat and suit striped in red, white, and blue, grew out of a cartoon that showed a "Yankee peddler" in this costume. The cartoon appeared in 1829 in a newspaper, the *Courier,* in Portland, Maine, and that may have been the first time. Later a famous minstrel named Dan Rice wore this costume on the stage and it became well known.

underground railroad

The underground railroad was not a real railroad. It was a system by which people helped Negro slaves escape from the southern states about a hundred years ago, before the Civil War in the United States.

In 1850, Congress passed a law called the Fugitive Slave Act. This law said that any Negro who had run away, no matter how long he had been free and no matter where he was, could be seized and shipped back to the person who had "owned" him.

This law angered many northerners, most of whom were against slavery. They determined to help Negro slaves escape. That is how the underground railroad came into existence. It was called "underground" because of the secrecy attached to it, and it was called a "railroad" because it helped the slaves to travel and because many railroad terms were used. Those who helped the Negroes to escape were called "conductors." The places where the Negroes were hidden on their way were called "stations." The Negroes themselves were somtimes called "packages" or "freight." This was done to fool people who were opposed to the underground railroad.

At least 50,000 Negroes were helped to freedom by the underground railroad. Some of them stayed in the northern states but most of them went to Canada. They were taken from Kentucky and Virginia into the northern states by different routes or "lines." Perhaps the most famous "conductor" was a Negro woman named Harriet Tubman, who helped at least three hundred of her fellow people to freedom. She was sometimes called "Moses" because, like the ancient leader of the Hebrews, she was leading her people to the "Promised Land."

Undset, Sigrid

Sigrid Undset was a Norwegian writer of novels. She is best-remembered for her long novel *Kristin Lavransdatter.* She was born in 1882 in Denmark, and when she was 2 years old her family moved to Oslo, Norway. She studied at the university there until her father died, and then she became a secretary. Four years later, when she was 20 years old, she wrote her first novel. It was not published, but she continued to write and in 1928 she was awarded the Nobel Prize, the highest honor a writer can receive. She died in 1949, at the age of 67. Her works include *Ida Elisabeth* and *The Master of Hestviken.*

undulant fever

Undulant fever is a disease that is caused by bacteria, one-celled plants so tiny that you cannot see them without a microscope. The bacteria that cause the fever are called *brucella,* and the scientific name for the disease is *brucellosis.* People do not catch this disease from one another, but from animals. Goats and cattle and hogs have brucella germs. A person who drinks goat's milk or cow's milk that has not been pasteurized may catch the disease. Farmers and others who come in contact with animals, and butchers and cooks who handle meat, sometimes become infected.

When a person gets undulant fever he has pain in his muscles and joints, and attacks of fever followed by chills. These attacks come in undulations (waves). Usually there are several attacks and they make a person very weak. At one time undulant fever was quite common on some islands of the Mediterranean Sea, including the island of Malta, and it was known as "Malta fever."

unemployment

Unemployment is the condition of a person when he wants a job and does not have one. Usually a country is prosperous when it has little unemployment; that is, when most of the people who want to work can find jobs. A country is said to be undergoing a depression when it has a great deal of unemployment.

Early in the 1930s the United States

U.S.S.R.

was in the midst of the worst depression in its history, with many millions of people unemployed. This caused great hardship. To prevent such hardships for unemployed people in the future, the United States government and the state governments set up a kind of insurance called *unemployment insurance*. The insurance is paid for partly by the employer and partly by the employee. When an employee loses his job and is unable to find another, he is entitled to receive a certain amount of money per week for a certain number of weeks, until he has found work.

Most states have also set up employment agencies, which try to find jobs for people free of charge. If such an agency can find a suitable job for the person and he is unwilling to take it, he can no longer claim unemployment insurance.

Another way in which governments sometimes try to keep down unemployment is by creating jobs. During the depression of the 1930s, the United States government set up the Works Progress Administration (WPA) and other government agencies that provided work for many people. Some of the persons who got jobs in this way were called "boondogglers," which meant that the work they were doing was not important, but a great deal of useful work was done.

ungulates

Ungulates are animals that have hoofs. There are many different kinds of animals included in this group, but they all have hoofs instead of claws or fingers or talons. Some of them, for example, the horse, have solid hoofs. Others, for example the cow, have split or cloven hoofs.

Scientists usually divide ungulates into two main groups, even-toed and odd-toed. The hoof may seem solid, but it merely covers the toe bones that lie inside. Actually an ungulate walks on its tiptoes, for the hoof is similar to the nails we grow on our fingers and toes. The horse and the zebra are odd-toed ungulates because imbedded in their hoofs are the bones of three toes. Pigs, llamas, camels, deer, cattle, sheep, goats, antelopes, and other animals are even-toed ungulates. Their hoofs cover four toes. Elephants are also grouped with the ungulates, but their padded hoofs have toenails growing on the front edges. Except for the pig family, all ungulates are herbivorous animals, eating only plants.

unicorn

The unicorn was an imaginary animal that people told about in songs and stories for hundreds of years. *Unicorn* means "one horn." Since there never actually was a unicorn, different people described it in different ways, but all agreed that it had one large horn growing from the center of its forehead. The horn was the source of all the unicorn's strength, according to the old fables. Some told how when a unicorn was trapped on top of a high cliff it could jump through the air and land on its horn without being hurt. The horn was also supposed to have magic powers. It could work against poison and purify things. Some ancient pictures show animals gathered around a pool of poisoned water waiting while a unicorn stirred it with its horn and purified the

water. The most famous picture of a unicorn appears on the coat of arms of the English kings. This unicorn is simply a horse with a horn on its forehead.

union, an organization of working men and women: see the article on LABOR AND LABOR UNIONS.

U.S.S.R.

The Union of Soviet Socialist Republics, or U.S.S.R., is the official name of the country that is usually called the Soviet Union and sometimes Soviet Russia because Russia is the controlling part of the union. The U.S.S.R. is by far the largest of all countries in area, covering about one-sixth of all the land on earth; its 8,649,821 square miles make it almost three times as big as any other country. About 245,070,000 people live in the U.S.S.R. The U.S.S.R. is considered to rank second only to the United States in manufacturing capacity, mine production, and military strength.

The government of the U.S.S.R. is Communist. It was the first Communist country and is still the most powerful. Because it is a Communist country, it is a dictatorship in which people have little personal liberty. All other countries of the world are more interested in the U.S.S.R. than in any other country and watch it more carefully than they do any other country, because Communists in all countries want to overthrow the present governments and put in Communist governments, and the U.S.S.R. is the leader of communism throughout the world. Most Communists in other countries are loyal to the U.S.S.R. rather than to their own countries.

The name "Union of Soviet Socialist Republics" means that the U.S.S.R. is made up of different divisions that partly govern themselves, just as the United States is made up of different states that partly govern themselves. Each of these divisions of the U.S.S.R. is called a "Soviet Socialist Republic." The *Soviet* in the name means that there is a lawmaking body of the soviet type (see SOVIET). The *socialist* in the name means that all the property is owned by the government and not by individuals as it is in most countries. The word *republic* is used to show that the division is a separate country.

EUROPEAN RUSSIA

U.S.S.R

CHINA

Actually, since the U.S.S.R. is a dictatorship, the separate republics do not have quite as much power as the states do in the United States, since the government of the entire U.S.S.R., which is in

the capital city of Moscow, can control all the elections and all the laws passed in the separate republics. The United States government in Washington does not have this power over the states. But in some other ways, the republics of the U.S.S.R. are much more separate and self-governing divisions than the states of the United States are. Two of the republics—the Ukraine and Byelorussia—are members of the United Nations as though they were independent countries.

THE REPUBLICS

There are fifteen Soviet Socialist Republics that make up the U.S.S.R. Perhaps the greatest difference between them and the states of the United States is that the fifteen republics are made up of different peoples, having different languages in many cases and having different national backgrounds. In most cases the peoples of these republics are unfriendly toward some or all of the peoples of the other republics. Nearly all of the present territory of the U.S.S.R. was the Russian Empire before 1917, when the Russian Revolution gave the Communists control of the country. The Russian Empire had many parts that had been conquered and forced into the empire, and the people of those parts did not feel friendly toward the Russians.

The fifteen Soviet Socialist Republics are:

RUSSIAN SOVIET FEDERATED SOCIALIST REPUBLIC, by far the largest in area and population. It covers two-thirds of the area and has more than half the population of the entire U.S.S.R. Most of the people are of the Slavic people called "Great Russians." You can read more about this in the article on RUSSIA. In 1956 the Karelo-Finnish S.S.R. was incorporated into the Russian S.F.S.R., reducing the federation from 16 to 15 republics. This is territory that was formerly called Karelia. It lies between Russia and Finland, and the people are akin to the Finns rather than to the Russians. It belonged to the old Russian Empire, but Finland had part of it after World War I.

UKRAINIAN S.S.R., the next-largest republic in population, having about 47,136,000 people or one-fifth of all the people in the U.S.S.R. These are a Slavic people called "Little Russians." There is a separate article on the UKRAINE.

BYELORUSSIAN S.S.R., a small, thickly settled area with about 9,003,000 people, who are called "White Russians."

ESTONIAN S.S.R., LATVIAN S.S.R., and LITHUANIAN S.S.R. These were independent countries at one time, but the U.S.S.R. seized them in 1940 and by armed force made them become part of the U.S.S.R. Each has its own people, language, and customs. There are separate articles about them.

MOLDAVIAN S.S.R. This is a small territory south of the Ukraine. Most of it is usually spoken of as BESSARABIA, about which there is a separate article. The people are mostly Moldavians, related to the Russians. This territory has been fought over for years. The U.S.S.R. last took it from Rumania, during and after World War II.

ARMENIAN S.S.R. This is part of the larger region once called ARMENIA, about which there is a separate article. Its inhabitants have lived there for a long time and are a distinct people with their own language.

AZERBAIJAN S.S.R. This is next to the country of Iran, in which there is a region also called Azerbaijan. The people are mostly of the Mongoloid race, originally from farther east in Asia and related to the Turks.

They follow the Mohammedan religion. From time to time the U.S.S.R. has encouraged the people of Iranian Azerbaijan to rebel and become part of the U.S.S.R., but these efforts have not succeeded.

GEORGIAN S.S.R. This is the old region of Georgia, about which there is a separate article. It has been part of Russia for more than 150 years, but the people still speak their own language in addition to Russian. Josef Stalin, long the dictator of the U.S.S.R., and many other men important in the government have come from Georgia.

KAZAKH S.S.R. This is a large region in central Asia. The people are of the Mongoloid race and the Mohammedan religion. They have never been friendly toward the Russians and during World War II they gave the U.S.S.R. very little support. Large numbers of them tried to break away and become independent. After World War II, Russian armies were sent to bring them back under control.

KIRGHIZ S.S.R., TADZHIK S.S.R., TURKMEN S.S.R., and UZBEK S.S.R. These are smaller regions south of Kazakh, with people related to those of Kazakh and also following the Mohammedan religion.

THE GOVERNMENT

The idea of the U.S.S.R. government is fairly simple. If it worked as it is supposed to, it would be somewhat like the government of the United States.

Within each of the fifteen republics, which are called *constituent republics,* there are large subdivisions called *autonomous republics* (which means that they have some self-government) and smaller subdivisions such as regions and cities. Each of these subdivisions has its own assembly, or soviet.

Each of the constituent republics has a Supreme Soviet, like a state legislature in the United States. Some members of these Supreme Soviets are elected by the smaller soviets and some are elected directly by the people. The Supreme Soviet of the republic makes the laws for that republic.

The highest body is the Supreme Soviet of the U.S.S.R., which meets in Moscow. Like the United States Congress, this has two "houses." Members of one house are elected by the Supreme Soviets of the republics and by other soviets. Members of the other house are elected directly by the people. The Supreme Soviet of the U.S.S.R. appoints the men to head the government and make laws that apply to the whole country.

Actually it does not work this way at all. The people cannot really elect their representatives, because they must vote for the candidates selected by the rulers of the country. The soviets must pass the laws their rulers tell them to pass and no other laws, and they must appoint men their rulers tell them to appoint.

As in any country in which the people have no power to govern themselves, in the U.S.S.R. the real power lies with the men who can control the greatest actual armed force. There are two such forces, the Soviet Army, called the Red Army, and the police. Under Stalin there was also a large, powerful secret police system which was hated and feared by all people. The secret police arrested people, often during the night, and imprisoned or executed them without trial, in many cases for political reasons.

Only one political party is allowed in Russia, the Communist Party. The Party controls the police, so whoever controls the Party has great power. While Josef Stalin was alive and the dictator, he controlled both the Party and the Army, so he could rule alone. When it seemed that the Army was becoming too strong, he had the principal generals arrested, tried for various crimes, and put to death.

After the death of Stalin in 1953, the men who control the Party and the men who control the Army shared power for a few years; then Nikita Khrushchev, who controlled the Party, also controlled the entire country until in 1964 he was replaced by Aleksei Kosygin as Premier and Leonid Brezhnev as head of the Party.

The controlling body of the Communist Party, which was also the controlling men in the government, was called the Politburo (political committee) for many years. It usually had twelve members. Then its name was changed to the Presidium (presiding, or controlling, body), but it was about the same group of men with the same powers.

The head of the government is the Premier. The heads of the chief government departments are commissars. They are like members of the cabinet in other countries. They are the men who have the actual power in the government. These men in Moscow not only control the government throughout the U.S.S.R. but also control nearly all the other countries that have Communist governments, including Bulgaria, Czechoslovakia, Hungary, Rumania and East Germany in Europe, and North Korea in Asia. Only Yugoslavia, Albania, and China, among the Communist countries of the world, are not under their direct power.

POLICIES OF THE U.S.S.R.

Throughout the U.S.S.R. and the countries it controls, there is no individual liberty. Newspapers and magazines, broadcasts and plays and even music and art, must say what the government wants them to. No one may criticize the government without its consent.

Official government policy is against all religions. No member of a church can become important in the government or the Communist Party. For some time, the government persecuted the churches and people had to worship secretly. In more recent years, the people in most parts of the U.S.S.R. have been permitted to attend their churches.

The constitution of the U.S.S.R., which was adopted in 1936, said that the country belongs to "the workers and the peasants," meaning chiefly the factory workers and the farmers. Actually, the government has always favored the factory workers (who first put the Communist Party into power) and has always been against the farmers, because the farmers have tried to hold on to their ownership of property. Millions of farmers in the U.S.S.R. have been killed or imprisoned for disobeying the government's orders.

Under Stalin, prisoners were treated as "slave labor." They were sent to huge prison camps near mines and factories, where they had to do the hardest and most unpleasant work. They were fed so badly and treated so cruelly that many did not survive. Even after Stalin, a person considered dangerous to the government was called an "enemy of the people" and was often sentenced to long prison terms. Members of his family, in many cases, suffered with him. They were not able to get jobs and lived in great poverty. However, in recent years the government has been more lenient.

THE LAND AND DEVELOPMENT

The U.S.S.R. is partly in Europe and partly in Asia. The European part is considered to end at the Ural Mountains in the east and at the Caucasus Mountains in the south. It is less than a third of the total area but is the best land and more than three-quarters of the people live there. The Asiatic part is mostly SIBERIA, about which there is a separate article, and Kazakh. Sakhalin Island off the eastern coast of Siberia, and many islands in the Arctic waters north of Europe and Asia, are part of the U.S.S.R.

In so vast a land, there are all kinds of climates and regions. There are many great mountain chains and long rivers. Most of the good farmlands are in Europe, especially in the Ukraine. Most of Siberia is too cold to support farming. In Kazakh and the other lands in central Asia, there are some good farm lands but mostly the land is good only for grazing livestock.

The mountains of the U.S.S.R. supply a wealth of minerals, and since the present government came into control these have been developed more and more. The building of factories, the damming of rivers to supply electric power, and the building of railroads and roads has also been carried on at a rapid rate except for the World War II years. Most of the time, the government of the U.S.S.R. has devoted most of its effort to building up "heavy industry" such as steel mills and automotive works, because these increase its power to make war and also can supply farm equipment and factory machinery that will improve the standard of living, which is very low for most of the people.

The U.S.S.R. still has very few railroads and roads compared to the United States, and very few factories turn out "consumer goods" such as clothing and household conveniences, but in heavy industry the country has become the second-greatest power.

PRINCIPAL CITIES

The U.S.S.R. has many big cities. The most important are industrial cities—manufacturing centers. There are separate articles about MOSCOW, the capital of the U.S.S.R., and also about the following important cities:

Baku	Leningrad
Kaunas	Odessa
Kiev	Riga
Kharkov	Volgograd

Others include:

Gorki, population 1,170,000, in Russia, on the Volga River.

Tashkent, population 1,385,000, capital of the Uzbek S.S.R.

Dniepropetrovsk, population 863,000, in the Ukraine, on the Dnieper River.

Rostov, population 789,000, in Russia, on the Don River.

Minsk, population 907,000, capital of the Byelorussian S.S.R.

Vladivostok, population 442,000, in Siberia, principal port on the Pacific Ocean.

Some other cities, such as Talinn, the capital of Estonia, and Yerevan, the capital of Armenia, are described in the

articles on the different parts of the U.S.S.R.

HISTORY OF THE U.S.S.R.

The history of the U.S.S.R. begins with the Russian Revolution of 1917. Until then, Russia had been a country hundreds of years behind most big European countries. It was ruled by czars (emperors) and rich noblemen. The people were poor, they could not read or write, and they had few human rights.

In 1917, the czar was overthrown, as told in the article on RUSSIA. For a while there was a democratic, republican government under Alexander Kerensky, but the Communists plotted to seize control of the government. The capital was then in Petrograd (the present city of Leningrad), and in that city the Communists won the support of the workers in the factories and of the sailors and some of the soldiers in the Russian armed forces.

These Communists were led by Vladimir Lenin. They called themselves the Bolsheviks, which means "the majority." Between November 7 and November 16, 1917, they seized control of the city and the Russian lawmaking body by force, refusing to permit other members of the body into its meetings. Kerensky and his government were forced to flee. Lenin became dictator.

At that time, Russia was still at war with Germany in World War I. Leon Trotsky, the second-ranking Bolshevik next to Lenin, was put in charge of the armed forces. He made peace with Germany, in a treaty signed at the city of Brest-Litovsk, in Byelorussia, early in 1918. Russia had to give up large territories to Germany and make many other sacrifices, but it ended the necessity for fighting the Germans and left the Bolsheviks free to win control inside Russia.

A civil war then broke out in Russia. The Bolsheviks, who used a red flag and called their fighting forces the Red Army, were attacked by anti-Communist Russians, who were called the White Army. The White Army was helped by Poles and by some British, French and American forces. But the workers and peasants believed the Bolsheviks' promises of freedom and socialism, and they supported the Bolsheviks. Fighting went on for several years, but by 1922 the Bolsheviks were in complete control and Lenin was master of Russia.

Lenin died in 1924, and it was expected that Trotsky would take his place; but a young Communist named Josef Stalin, who was Secretary of the Communist Party, had made himself so powerful that within three years he had taken away all of Trotsky's power and had made him leave Russia permanently.

As the new ruler of Russia (which by that time had become the U.S.S.R.), Stalin set out to do three things: First, to get rid of everyone in the government who was against him or was strong enough to threaten his control. Second, to make Russia an industrial nation, strong enough to protect itself against all enemies. Third, to increase Russia's power throughout the world by building up Communist Parties in other countries.

Using the government's secret police, which were then called the Ogpu, Stalin arrested and executed hundreds of important men who opposed his plans. Throughout his dictatorship, which lasted for nearly thirty years, he continued to have his enemies killed or imprisoned without mercy or fairness.

To build up Russia as an industrial power, Stalin began a Five-Year Plan. It was the first of several such plans. Factories were to be built; farms were to be *collectivized* (small farms united into big ones) so that farmers could share the limited number of tractors and other farm machines; dams and railroads and roads were to be built. There was a quota, or goal, for every part of the plan. The quotas were never made in any of the Five-Year Plans, but the Plans did turn the U.S.S.R. into an industrial nation in a remarkably small number of years.

To promote communism throughout the world, Stalin used the Comintern (Communist International), an organization that was already operating. The Communist Parties of most countries today grew out of the work done then by the Comintern.

Stalin pushed his plans through ruthlessly. When farmers opposed the collective farms, he let three or four million of them starve to death and killed and imprisoned millions more. Workers were punished when they were absent from work; managers were put in prison if anything went wrong in their factories.

During the 1930s, Stalin began to fear some of the old Bolsheviks, who were horrified by his methods, and also some of the important men in the Red Army. At that time Adolf Hitler and the Nazi Party had come to power in Germany, and they were threatening to attack Russia and seize some of its territory. Stalin had hundreds of government and army leaders arrested and tried in a series of trials called a "Purge." Somehow Stalin's secret police made these men appear at the trials and confess to all kinds of crimes they could not possibly have committed. Most of the trials took place between 1935 and 1937. The prosecutor, a man named Andrei Vishinsky, became famous in these trials.

Stalin continued to concentrate on making Russia a strong military power, for protection against Germany. The U.S.S.R. tried to make alliances with Great Britain and France to oppose Germany, but the British and French were too suspicious and were unwilling to risk war. Therefore Stalin came to terms with his principal enemy, Hitler. In August, 1939, Germany and the U.S.S.R. made a treaty, or agreement, to help each other. The next month, Germany started World War II. The U.S.S.R. seized several territories, including part of Poland, the independent countries of Latvia, Lithuania and Estonia, and part of Rumania. In the winter of 1939 the U.S.S.R. started a war against its neighbor, Finland, and took some Finnish territory. Throughout the world, Communists supported Germany against the democratic countries.

Then in June, 1941, Germany suddenly broke its word and invaded Russia. The U.S.S.R. at once became an ally of Great Britain and later of the United States. For two years the Germans won great territories in Russia, but then the Allied armies began to win. Early in 1945, the Red Army invaded Germany and captured the capital, Berlin. Peace was made and the U.S.S.R. gained control over nearly all the countries of eastern Europe. After World War II, the U.S.S.R. again became unfriendly toward the United States and other democratic countries. Other countries reduced their armies and military power, but the U.S.S.R. continued to increase all branches of its armed forces and the rest of the world became fearful that the U.S.S.R. was planning a new series of wars to conquer the world.

Stalin died suddenly in 1953. It seemed then that the two most powerful men in the U.S.S.R. were Georgi Malenkov and Lavrenti Beria. Beria, who controlled the secret police, seemed to have the best chance, but Malenkov got the support of the army and had Beria arrested and put to death. Malenkov became the premier, but in 1955 he was forced to resign by Nikita Khrushchev, who had become most powerful in the Communist party, and Georgi Zhukov, who had become most powerful in the Red Army. Nikolai Bulganin became the new premier. But Zhukov (in 1957) and Bulganin (in 1958) were dismissed from their positions and Khrushchev became premier in 1958, apparently with as much power as Stalin had. However, he denounced the "cult of personality" rule of Stalin and his ruthless oppression of the people, and he abolished much of the terror and secret police methods of Stalin's day. While acting alternately belligerent and conciliatory toward the western democracies, Khrushchev talked much about "peaceful coexistence." This became increasingly so in the 1960s as disagreements between Russia and its major ally, Communist China, led to a split in 1963.

Under Khrushchev the U.S.S.R. made great progress, especially in science (for example, in space exploration). But other government officials did not like Khrushchev's "hasty decisions and actions, and bragging." In October 1964 Khrushchev was replaced as Premier by Aleksei Kosygin and as Party Secretary by Leonid Brezhnev.

Unitarian Universalists

Unitarian Universalists are members of a liberal religious group in the Christian-Judaeo tradition who believe that God is one (or single) rather than a Trinity (threefold). They believe also that God should be worshiped without elaborate ceremony, and that each person is privileged to seek God in his own way and arrive at his own beliefs without the necessity for accepting dogma (old beliefs). They believe Jesus was not divine, but a human being, though better than other men.

The first Unitarian Church in the United States was started in 1796 in Philadelphia, Pennsylvania, by Joseph Priestley. One of the greatest Unitarian leaders was William Ellery CHANNING, about whom there is a separate article.

The first Universalist Church in the United States was established in New Jersey in 1770 by an English preacher, John Murray. It took its name from the fact that its members believed in universal salvation, that is that all mankind will be saved.

In 1961 the American Unitarian Association and the Universalist Church in

America were merged to form the Unitarian Universalist Association. It has 222,776 members in 1,025 churches and fellowships in the U.S. and Canada.

United Arab Republic; former name of the Arab Republic of Egypt. See EGYPT.

United Churches

The United Church of Canada is a Protestant Church that was formed in 1925 when four other Protestant Churches decided to join together. They were the Methodist Church, the Presbyterian Church, the Congregational Churches of Canada, and the Local Union Churches in Western Canada. They have a combined membership of more than three million.

The United Church of Christ was formed in 1961 by the merger of the Congregational Christian Churches and the Evangelical and Reformed Church. It has a membership of 2,056,000.

United Kingdom

The United Kingdom of Great Britain and Northern Ireland is the official name of the nation made up of England, Scotland, Wales, and Northern Ireland. This nation is on the islands called the British Isles, which include two big islands and many very small ones. The biggest island is called Great Britain, and England, Scotland and Wales are on it. The other big island is Ireland, and most of it is an independent country but the northern part, called Northern Ireland, is joined with the countries of Great Britain.

Except in official matters, this country is almost never called the United Kingdom. People speak of it as "Great Britain," or just "Britain." Some people even call the whole country England, although that is incorrect.

The official name United Kingdom was adopted in the year 1800. In 1927, when most of Ireland became self-governing, the present name was adopted.

See also the article on the BRITISH COMMONWEALTH OF NATIONS.

United Nations

The United Nations is an organization of independent countries. The purpose of the organization is to maintain international peace and to help nations to coöperate in various ways for the good of all people. Its headquarters is the United Nations Building in New York City, but some of its branches have their headquarters in other places. The United Nations is often called the U.N.

The United Nations was first planned in 1944 at a conference at Dumbarton Oaks, an estate near Washington, D.C. It was formally set up in a Conference at San Francisco, California, in 1945 and it began to operate in January, 1946. At first it was called the United Nations Organization and known as the UNO, then it became the U.N. The first UNO headquarters was at Lake Success, a part of New York City, but in 1950 John D. Rockefeller, Jr. gave the U.N. a section of land on Manhattan in New York City, on the East River, and the United States government lent the U.N. $65,000,000 to build the buildings it needed. The U.N. Headquarters is not legally part of New York City but has extraterritoriality—that is, it is treated as if it were an independent country.

The term "United Nations" was devised by President Franklin D. Roosevelt and was first used in a "Declaration by United Nations" in January, 1942, when representatives of twenty-six countries pledged their governments to continue fighting against Germany and Italy in World War II. At the San Francisco Conference the Charter (constitution) of the United Nations was drawn up by the representatives of fifty countries.

MEMBERS OF THE UNITED NATIONS

Any peace-loving nation may join the United Nations if it accepts the provisions of the Charter and if none of the most important members votes against it for any reason. It must promise to settle any quarrels with other nations peacefully, and it must promise to coöperate with the other members in preventing war between nations. In 1975 the United Nations had 144 member countries, as follows:

Afghanistan	Dominican Rep.	Kuwait	Romania
Albania	Ecuador	Laos	Rwanda
Algeria	El Salvador	Lebanon	Saudi Arabia
Arab Republic of Egypt	Equatorial Guinea	Lesotho	Senegal
Argentina	Ethiopia	Liberia	Seychelles
Australia	Fiji	Libya	Sierra Leone
Austria	Finland	Luxembourg	Singapore
Bahamas	France	Madagascar	Somalia
Bahrain	Gabon	Malawi	South Africa
Barbados	Gambia	Malaysia	Southern Yemen
Belgium	Germany (East)	Maldive Islands	Spain
Bhutan	Germany (West)	Mali	Sri Lanka
Bolivia	Ghana	Malta	Sudan
Botswana	Greece	Mauritania	Swaziland
Brazil	Guatemala	Mauritius	Sweden
Bulgaria	Guinea	Mexico	Syria
Burma	Guyana	Mongolia	Tanzania
Burundi	Haiti	Morocco	Thailand
Byelorussia	Honduras	Nepal	Togo
Cambodia	Hungary	Netherlands	Trinidad and Tobago
Cameroon	Iceland	New Zealand	Tunisia
Canada	India	Nicaragua	Turkey
Central African Rep.	Indonesia	Niger	Uganda
Chad	Iran	Nigeria	Ukraine
Chile	Iraq	Norway	United Arab Emirates
China	Ireland	Oman	United Kingdom
Colombia	Israel	Pakistan	United States
Congo (Brazzaville)	Italy	Panama	Upper Volta
Costa Rica	Ivory Coast	Paraguay	Uruguay
Cuba	Jamaica	Peru	U.S.S.R.
Cyprus	Japan	Philippines	Venezuela
Czechoslovakia	Java	Poland	Yemen
Dahomey	Jordan	Portugal	Yugoslavia
Denmark	Kenya	Qatar	Zaire (Kinshasa)
			Zambia

NOTES: China's seat in the United Nations was held by the Nationalist government, based on Taiwan, until October, 1971 when the Nationalists were expelled and Communist China, which controls the mainland, was installed in its place. Indonesia, a member since 1950, resigned in 1965 and was readmitted in 1966. North and South Korea are not members because the right to govern the entire country is disputed. Switzerland is not a member because it wishes to maintain strict neutrality.

Unations

The United Nations headquarters in New York City overlooks the East River.

THE UNITED NATIONS AND RELATED AGENCIES

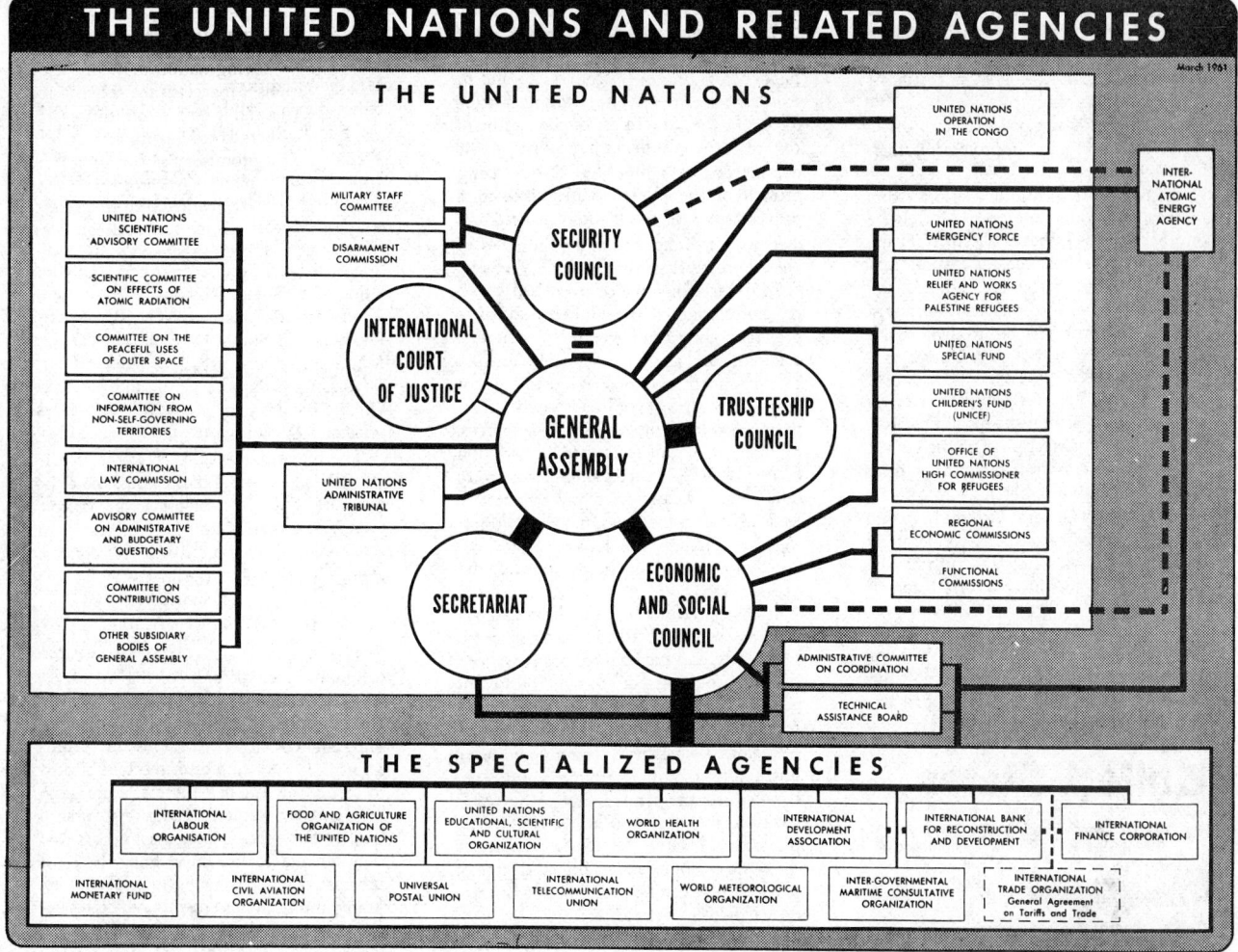

March 1963

THE UNITED NATIONS

THE SPECIALIZED AGENCIES

MAIN BODIES OF THE U.N.

There are six main bodies of the United Nations. Officially they are equal, but the Security Council has the greatest actual power and the General Assembly is next most powerful.

Security Council. This has fifteen members. Five are permanent members: United States, United Kingdom (Great Britain), Union of Soviet Socialist Republics (Soviet Union), France, and China. The other ten members serve two-year terms. They are elected by the General Assembly (which is composed of all the member nations). The Security Council cannot make an important decision if any of the permanent members votes against it, so each permanent member is said to have "veto power." The principal duty of the Security Council is to keep peace throughout the world, but it also has rights and powers that are far greater than those of any of the other main bodies.

General Assembly. Each member nation has one vote in the General Assembly. The General Assembly can discuss all matters. In many cases it can investigate matters on which it wants to have more information. In some cases it can make recommendations to the Security Council, but in other cases it is not permitted to make recommendations—for example, when the Security Council is already dealing with the case. The General Assembly appoints various committees to do parts of its work. New members of

the U.N., and members of most of the main bodies of the U.N., are elected by the General Assembly, but in many cases they must be recommended or approved by the Security Council. The General Assembly has great influence.

Economic and Social Council. This has twenty-seven members, serving three-year terms. They are elected by the General Assembly. It works to make living conditions better, and human rights greater, throughout the world. It sets up committees to study special questions, such as slavery. It works with various agencies, or groups, that are partly independent. Examples of these are the World Health Organization and the Universal Postal Union.

Trusteeship Council. This group is in charge of the system for dealing with Trust Territories—regions of the world that are not yet independent and are controlled by independent nations that are U.N. members. Each member that is in charge of a Trust area, plus the Soviet Union and China (because they are permanent members of the Security Council) are members of the Trusteeship Council. Some Trust Territories do not come under the Trusteeship Council. These are territories that are called "strategic areas," meaning that they may have unusual value in warfare. The Security Council is in charge of strategic areas. See also the article TRUSTEE.

International Court of Justice. This has fifteen judges. Each is selected for a nine-year term and may be re-elected. The

judges are elected by the General Assembly and the Security Council. All nations, even those that are not members of the U.N., may ask the International Court of Justice to settle their disputes. The permanent offices of the International Court of Justice are in The Hague, in the Netherlands. See also WORLD COURT.

Secretariat. This is the administrative body. That is, it carries out certain work that other main bodies decide should be done. It prepares reports, keeps records, is in charge of United Nations buildings and other property, and does similar work. The Secretariat has three to four thousand employees, depending on the amount of work it has to do. At the head of the Secretariat is a Secretary-General. The first Secretary-General was Trygve Lie of Norway, who served from 1946 to 1952. In 1953, Dag Hammarskjold of Sweden was elected Secretary-General. After his death in a plane crash in the Congo in 1961, U Thant of Burma became Secretary-General. U Thant was succeeded by Kurt Waldheim of Austria on January 1, 1972. The Secretary-General is elected by the General Assembly, but the General Assembly cannot elect a person unless he has been recommended by the Security Council. Most of the employees of the Secretariat work at the U.N. headquarters in New York City.

WHAT THE U.N. HAS DONE

Although the United Nations was hampered almost from the start by clashes in which the democratic nations (such as

the United States, Great Britain, and France) were opposed by the Communist nations (the Soviet Union and the countries it controls), the U.N. nevertheless succeeded in accomplishing valuable work in keeping the peace, in improving living conditions, and in promoting international coöperation.

Before 1950, recommendations from the Security Council helped to settle wars or other armed clashes between Israel and Arab countries, between India and Pakistan, and between the Netherlands and Indonesia. In 1950, when Communist forces of North Korea invaded South Korea (a member of the United Nations), the Security Council decided to have a United Nations armed force to resist the North Koreans. This United Nations force, mostly supplied by the United States, prevented the Communists from conquering and ruling South Korea.

In 1956 the General Assembly passed strongly-worded resolutions condemning the Soviet Union's part in crushing the people's uprising in Hungary, and it moved swiftly to prevent full-scale war between Israel, France, Britain, and Egypt over the Suez Canal. The United Nations maintained peace in Lebanon in 1958 and in the Congo in 1960, and it helped settle a dispute over Cuba in 1962.

United States of America

Orville Andrews

The Statue of Liberty.

The United States of America is the most prosperous and most powerful country in the world. Its people, who number about 203,000,000 have the highest standard of living in the world and enjoy the greatest amount of personal freedom. Its territory on the continent of North America is the richest with which any people were ever blessed, with fertile fields, dense forests, great mineral resources, and many rivers and lakes for irrigation and transportation, plus long seacoasts for foreign trade.

The government of the United States of America is a federal republic. That is, the country is composed of separate states that govern themselves in certain ways but are federated (united) in one strong national government. The country is usually called simply the United States and often is called America, though that is not correct because all the countries of the Western Hemisphere are American and all their people are Americans. The United States was the first big country of

modern times to have a republican form of government, and it is the youngest of the great nations of the earth, its independence dating only from 1776 and its existence as one nation dating only from 1788. At that time most of the people of the earth thought that a big country could not succeed as a republic. The amazing growth of the United States since then proved that a republic could succeed and did much to influence other countries to become republics instead of kingdoms.

In its brief history of over 200 years, the population of the United States has grown to sixty times greater than it was originally and its area to ten times greater. In every form of industrial development —manufacturing, railroads and highways, development of water resources, production of minerals, and distribution of goods—the United States leads every other country, and in many of these it leads all other countries of the world put together, though the United States has only one-sixteenth of the people and land of the earth

The people of the United States have been assembled of all races and from all continents, and the country has long been called a "melting pot" in which different peoples are mixed together. In other countries made up of different origins, the result has always been separate and often unfriendly national groups within the country. In the United States the result has been just the opposite—a single people with the same language, very nearly the same customs, and as high a degree of patriotism as can be found in any country on earth.

UNITED STATES. Area, 3,615,211 square miles; with territories and possessions, 3,628,150. Population (1970) 203,184,772; with territories and possessions, 206,056,488. Government, federal republic. Language, English. Religion, Christian (about 60% Protestant, 35% Roman Catholic, 4% Jewish). Flag, 13 horizontal stripes (7 red and 6 white, alternating), with 50 five-pointed white stars on a blue field. National anthem, Star Spangled Banner. Symbol, bald eagle. Abbreviation, U.S.A., or U.S.

MAIN DIVISIONS OF THE U.S.

The "continental United States" consists of about 3,600,000 square miles on the continent of North America, including Alaska, the largest state, which is separated from the other states by a stretch of Canadian territory. In the Pacific Ocean are numerous islands, including the state of Hawaii. In the Caribbean Sea are Puerto Rico and the Virgin Islands. In Central America is the Panama Canal Zone, a narrow strip of territory that includes the Panama Canal.

The "conterminous United States" (excluding Alaska and Hawaii) is divided into forty-eight states, plus the District of Columbia, in which is the city of Washington, capital of the United States.

For convenience these forty-eight states are usually grouped in broad regional areas. These regions are best known as New England, the Middle Atlantic area, the South, the Southwest, the Midwest, the Rocky Mountain states, and the Pacific Coast, though geographers have different technical names for some of them.

The New England states are Maine, Vermont, New Hampshire, Massachusetts, Connecticut, and Rhode Island. The Middle Atlantic states are New York, New Jersey, and Pennsylvania. The South includes Maryland, Delaware, West Virginia, Virginia, Kentucky, Tennessee, North Carolina, South Carolina, Georgia, Alabama, Mississippi, Florida, Louisiana, and Arkansas. In the Southwest are Texas, Oklahoma, New Mexico, and Arizona. States of the Midwest are Ohio, Indiana, Illinois, Michigan, Wisconsin, Minnesota, Iowa, Missouri, Kansas, Nebraska, North Dakota, and South Dakota. The Rocky Mountain states are Montana, Idaho, Wyoming, Colorado, Utah, and Nevada. On the Pacific Coast are California, Oregon, and Washington.

The biggest state is Alaska; the smallest is Rhode Island. New York is the richest state, but California has the largest population, more than 19,953,000.

There is a separate article about every state, territory, and possession.

THE PEOPLE OF THE U.S.

The people of the United States came originally from all parts of the world. At no other time in history had so many people come to a new land from so many different countries. Millions of immigrants left their homes in the Old World to seek a new life in America. Some came because they wanted freedom to worship God as they chose. Others came because they wanted to live in a land where all men are equal and have the right to vote. Many immigrated to the United States because it is "the land of opportunity," where even a poor man can make a good living for himself and his family and become rich if he works hard.

English-speaking people from England and Scotland, with a smaller number of Dutch and German people, were the first settlers along the Atlantic Coast of the United States. They lived in colonies that belonged to England, and these colonies became the original states of the United States, so the country has always had English as its language and has followed the English (often called the Anglo-Saxon) traditions.

At the same time, and in some cases even earlier, Spanish people and a smaller number of French people were forming settlements in the states along the Gulf of Mexico and in the Southwest. The Spaniards did much intermarrying with the American Indians who were already there, so that Spanish, French and Indian blood became mixed into the American melting pot.

More than three hundred years ago, great numbers of black men and women were brought from Africa and sold into slavery in the United States. When slavery was abolished they became citizens of the United States and their descendants now are more than 11% of the people of the United States.

After the United States became an independent country, immigrants came in even greater numbers. Through the 1850s, most of these came from Ireland and from Germany.

After 1865 most of the immigrants came from southern and central European countries. Hundreds of thousands of

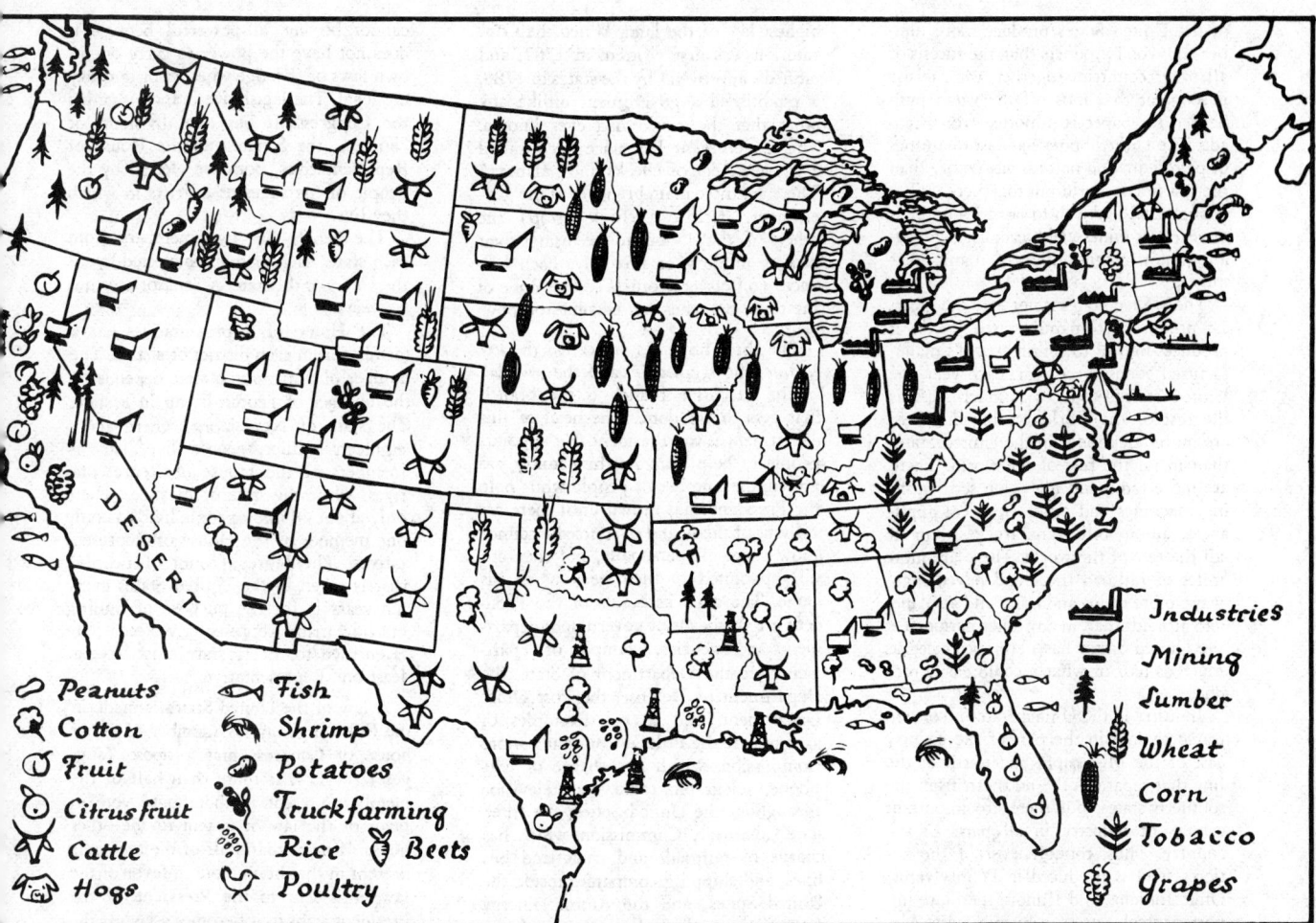

Legend:
- Peanuts
- Cotton
- Fruit
- Citrus fruit
- Cattle
- Hogs
- Fish
- Shrimp
- Potatoes
- Truck farming
- Rice
- Beets
- Poultry
- Industries
- Mining
- Lumber
- Wheat
- Corn
- Tobacco
- Grapes

DESERT

Czechs, Serbs, Slovenes, Italians, Austrians, Hungarians, Poles, Bulgarians, Rumanians, Russians and others came to work in America's mines, mills, factories, fields, and forests. Smaller numbers of Chinese and Japanese settled in the Pacific Coast states. Spanish-speaking people from Mexico moved into the regions that are now California, New Mexico, Arizona, and Texas. Finally there are the American Indians, the original people of America. In the long struggle against the invading white man, which lasted from colonial times to as late as 1890, it seemed as if the Indians might be wiped out completely by war, sickness, and hunger. But the Indian survived, and in 1973 there were about 800,000 Indians and their numbers are increasing.

THE WONDERFUL LAND

On the entire surface of the earth, only Europe can compare to the United States in its wealth of farm lands, forests, mineral deposits, and rivers. In most parts of the earth, there are only scattered areas in which human beings can support themselves in large numbers. Most of the land is too poor to yield enough food. In the United States, nearly every part of the land is suitable for farming and also supplies the other necessities of comfortable living.

Geographically, America presents a picture of tremendous variety. Along the east coast there is a long coastal plain that stretches from Maine in the north to Florida in the south. Beyond these plains to the west is the great Appalachian range of mountains, broad but not very high, which extends roughly north and

south from Maine to Alabama. West of the Appalachians are the vast central plains, which stretch from the Canadian border to the Gulf of Mexico and westward to the Rocky Mountains. Through these plains the Mississippi River flows, fed by other great rivers such as the Missouri and the Ohio, which in turn are fed by hundreds of rivers, large and small.

Other great rivers of America are the Rio Grande, which forms part of the boundary between Mexico and the United States; the Colorado River, which flows through the famous Grand Canyon and passes through the states of Colorado, Utah, Nevada, Arizona, and California; and the Columbia River, which flows through the states of Washington and Oregon. The eastern and western rivers are divided by the Continental Divide, in the Rocky Mountains.

The Rocky Mountains are North America's greatest mountains. They run north and south, and in the United States they stretch from Montana to New Mexico. Between the Rockies and the Sierra Nevada Mountains, which lie west of the Rockies and follow the Pacific Coast, there is a vast valley known as the Great Basin. This basin includes most of Nevada, the western part of Utah, and southeastern California.

The lowest spot in America is in the Great Basin, in the desert of Southern California. This is Death Valley, which lies 278 feet below sea level. Not far from America's lowest spot, and also in California, is one of the highest points, Mt. Whitney, a mountain peak that soars to 14,501 feet. Mount McKinley in Alaska is North America's highest spot.

The northern continuation of the Sierra Nevadas are the Cascade Mountains of northern California, Oregon and Washington. Closer to the Pacific coast are other chains of mountains, called coastal ranges, and between these mountains and the Pacific Ocean is a stretch of lowlands.

One of the most valuable geographic features of the United States is the Great Lakes, which form part of the border between Canada and the United States. These lakes, named Superior, Michigan, Huron, Erie, and Ontario, are the greatest body of fresh water in the world. They are important to transportation and they produce great numbers of fish to feed the people.

PRODUCTS OF THE UNITED STATES

The United States is the greatest producer of agricultural products in the world. It raises more corn and as much cotton as the rest of the world together. It is among the biggest producers of wheat and other cereal crops such as oats, barley, and rice. It grows enormous quantities of alfalfa, hay and other grasses for its livestock. Its great herds of sheep, cattle, hogs, chickens, ducks, and turkeys provide more meat and dairy products than its people can eat. Vegetables and fruits are grown in vast abundance and no other nation in the world can equal the nation's production of citrus fruits, such as oranges, lemons, and grapefruit. Much more of all these products could be produced if there were use for them. Great surpluses pile up and must be given away or allowed to rot.

The mineral and forest resources of the nation are also very great. The forests

of the United States produce more lumber and wood products than the forests of all other countries together, yet the use is so great that most of the wood pulp needed for paper is imported from Canada. The United States has vast quantities of petroleum and natural gas (more than the rest of the world put together). It has enough coal and iron to last for hundreds of years. Its mines yield lead, zinc, copper, aluminum, magnesium, and many other minerals.

The United States is not only the greatest producer of manufactured goods, it produces half of the entire world's manufactured goods every year. Each year, the United States produces as much steel as the rest of the world combined. There are more telephones in the United States than in all the rest of the world. There are more radio and television sets, washing machines and other electrical appliances, automobiles and trucks, than in all the rest of the world. There are more miles of railroad track and paved highways, more trains and buses and airplanes and airfields than in any other nation. Yet the United States has never produced as much as half of what it could easily produce.

Industry in the United States is concentrated mainly in the part of the country east of the Mississippi and north of the line that separates the northern from the southern states, but there are important centers of industry in all parts of the country. Thus, though most of the nation's steel is produced in Pennsylvania, Ohio, Indiana, and Illinois, there are important steel centers in Birmingham, Alabama, and in new plants in the Far West. Though New York City is the center of the nation's clothing industry, other big cities and the state of California also produce a variety of clothing.

The South, which was once largely a farming region, has become important in manufacturing also, producing chemicals and textiles (such as cloth) and metal products. Many states that were mostly agricultural before World War II now have numerous centers of industry in the midst of their farm lands.

HOW THE PEOPLE ARE GOVERNED

The government of the United States is based on the Constitution, which is the highest law of the land. When the Constitution was first written, in 1787, and ratified (approved) by the states in 1788, it established a government unlike any other that the world had ever known. This government has since been called a "government of checks and balances." There are three main branches of the government. Each can check (stop) the others if they seem to be using their powers unfairly or unwisely. Each balances (offsets) the others so that none of the three branches can become too powerful.

The three branches are called the *executive,* the *legislative,* and the *judicial.*

The executive branch is the branch that gets things done. The head of this department is the President. He appoints people to help him. As the country has grown, the number of people who "help the President" has grown until there are millions of them, and of course he cannot know them all personally, but they are still appointed to their positons in his name. The chief assistants of the President are the heads of government departments and agencies. Examples of departments are the Department of State, the Department of Defense, the Post Office Department, and so on. Examples of agencies are the Federal Communications Commission, which has charge of telephone, telegraph, radio and television throughout the United States; the Interstate Commerce Commission, which has charge of railroads and truck and bus lines, and shipping companies inside the United States; and the Atomic Energy Commission, which has charge of the use of atomic power. There are many other agencies. The President, every department and every agency must carry out the laws passed by Congress and may not do anything the law does not say they may do.

The executive branch includes a Vice President, who becomes President if the President dies. The President and Vice President are elected together for a four-year term. A person may not be elected more than twice.

The legislative branch is the branch that makes the law that the President and his assistants must carry out. Thus it can "check" the executive branch (the President) by refusing to pass laws; but it cannot become all-powerful because it does not have the power to carry out its own laws or to judge whether or not they are legal. The legislative branch is called the Congress. It has two divisions, or "houses," the Senate and the House of Representatives. Both are elected by the people of the states or districts in which they live.

The Senate has two members from each state. Each of them is elected by all the voters of the state. A Senator's term is six years.

The House of Representatives has a member from each district of a state. The number of districts in a state depends on the number of people living in a state. The state of New York, where about eighteen million people live, has 39 members of the House of Representatives, while the state of Nevada, where only about 488,000 people live, has only one member of the House of Representatives. The census (count of people) that is taken in the United States every ten years is for the purpose of finding out how many Representatives each state is entitled to. Every state must have at least one Representative.

A law of the United States is made in the following way: A member of either house of Congress may propose (suggest) the law. If more than half of the members present in that house vote in favor of the law, it is sent to the other house. If more than half of the members present in that house vote in favor of the law, it is sent to the President. If the President signs it, it becomes a law. If the President refuses to sign it, he is said to "veto" it and it will not become a law unless two-thirds of each house then votes for it again.

The third branch of the government, the judicial branch, is the branch that decides whether a law should be carried out. The judicial branch includes all the courts of law, the highest being the Supreme Court of the United States. If the Supreme Court decides that a law is unconstitutional (not permitted by the Constitution of the United States) the law cannot be enforced. Therefore the judicial branch can check and balance both the other branches.

See also the articles on CONGRESS, the CONSTITUTION, the SUPREME COURT and the PRESIDENCY.

STATE AND LOCAL GOVERNMENTS

The Constitution of the United States says that unless it gives rights to the federal government, those rights belong to the states or to the people. Each state has its own government and its own constitution. The constitution of a state cannot disagree with the United States Constitution.

The government of a state keeps the peace within the state. It can collect taxes. It can pass laws that do not conflict with the laws passed by Congress.

A city or town also has its own government. This government too can keep the peace, collect taxes, and pass laws, but only within the town or city.

One of the rights of a state is to decide who in that state may vote—even who shall vote for officers of the federal gov-

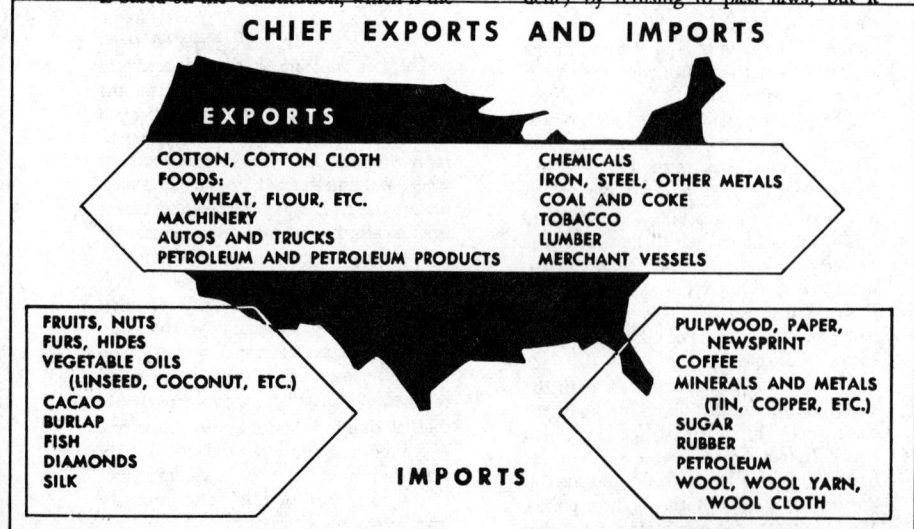

CHIEF EXPORTS AND IMPORTS

EXPORTS

COTTON, COTTON CLOTH
FOODS:
  WHEAT, FLOUR, ETC.
MACHINERY
AUTOS AND TRUCKS
PETROLEUM AND PETROLEUM PRODUCTS

CHEMICALS
IRON, STEEL, OTHER METALS
COAL AND COKE
TOBACCO
LUMBER
MERCHANT VESSELS

FRUITS, NUTS
FURS, HIDES
VEGETABLE OILS
  (LINSEED, COCONUT, ETC.)
CACAO
BURLAP
FISH
DIAMONDS
SILK

IMPORTS

PULPWOOD, PAPER,
  NEWSPRINT
COFFEE
MINERALS AND METALS
  (TIN, COPPER, ETC.)
SUGAR
RUBBER
PETROLEUM
WOOL, WOOL YARN,
  WOOL CLOTH

Graphics Institute for Laidlaw Brothers

THE NATIONAL GOVERNMENT

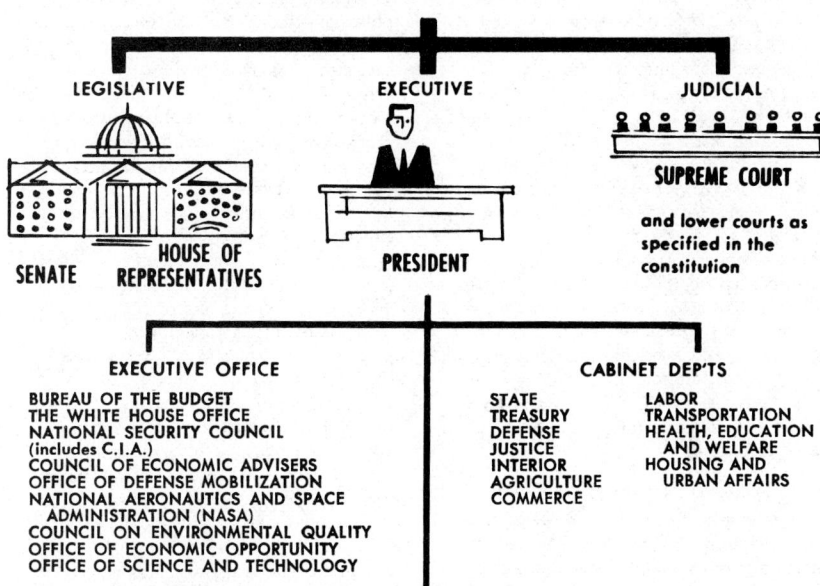

CONSTITUTION

LEGISLATIVE

SENATE · HOUSE OF REPRESENTATIVES

EXECUTIVE

PRESIDENT

JUDICIAL

SUPREME COURT

and lower courts as specified in the constitution

EXECUTIVE OFFICE

BUREAU OF THE BUDGET
THE WHITE HOUSE OFFICE
NATIONAL SECURITY COUNCIL
(includes C.I.A.)
COUNCIL OF ECONOMIC ADVISERS
OFFICE OF DEFENSE MOBILIZATION
NATIONAL AERONAUTICS AND SPACE
ADMINISTRATION (NASA)
COUNCIL ON ENVIRONMENTAL QUALITY
OFFICE OF ECONOMIC OPPORTUNITY
OFFICE OF SCIENCE AND TECHNOLOGY

CABINET DEP'TS

STATE
TREASURY
DEFENSE
JUSTICE
INTERIOR
AGRICULTURE
COMMERCE

LABOR
TRANSPORTATION
HEALTH, EDUCATION
AND WELFARE
HOUSING AND
URBAN AFFAIRS

SOME INDEPENDENT OFFICES, DEPARTMENTS AND COMMISSIONS*

*These show less than half of the total. They illustrate the many varied activities in all branches of national life in which the Executive is active. The President's appointments to these agencies must have the consent of the Senate

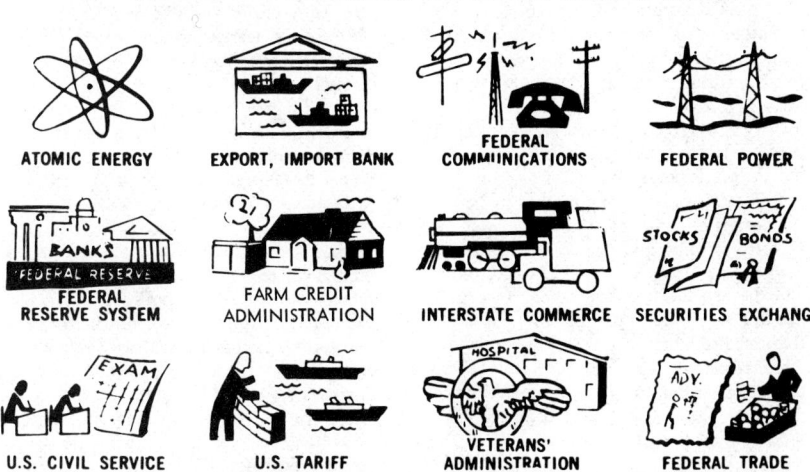

ATOMIC ENERGY · EXPORT, IMPORT BANK · FEDERAL COMMUNICATIONS · FEDERAL POWER

FEDERAL RESERVE SYSTEM · FARM CREDIT ADMINISTRATION · INTERSTATE COMMERCE · SECURITIES EXCHANGE

U.S. CIVIL SERVICE · U.S. TARIFF · VETERANS' ADMINISTRATION · FEDERAL TRADE

TENNESSEE VALLEY AUTHORITY · CIVIL DEFENSE · GENERAL SERVICES · SELECTIVE SERVICE

ernment, such as the President, Vice President, Senators, and Congressmen.

Therefore a citizen of the United States is subject to several governments, each of which has power in a different way. The Federal government governs the citizen's dealings with citizens of other states and other countries. The state government governs his activities within his own state. The local government governs his activities in his own city or town. But every one of these governments is limited by a constitutional law that says they may not take away any of the citizen's personal rights unless he has broken a law and is convicted in a fair trial.

THE CHIEF CITIES OF THE UNITED STATES

The capital of the United States is

Washington, D.C., and the largest city is New York City. There are many other big cities. There are separate articles about them and they are listed among the chief cities of their states, which may be found in the articles on the states.

AMERICAN HISTORY

The history of the United States is usually called "American history," because it goes back to a period long before the United States was officially formed. There are separate articles throughout this encyclopedia on the principal events and the important men and women of American history.

The first people known to have lived in any part of America were the people called American Indians. Originally these American Indians were members of

one of the Mongoloid races of Asia, but at least twenty thousand years ago and perhaps fifty thousand years ago the first of them came to America. Some of them undoubtedly crossed over the narrow stretch of water called the Bering Strait that separates Asia from Alaska. This is frozen solid in winter months and they could have walked over it. Others probably came by water, crossing the narrow water of the north or drifting far across the Pacific Ocean in the south. By the time the first white men reached North America there were Indians living in all parts of the continent. They were to play an important part in American history.

It is possible that several different groups of explorers had landed on North America hundreds of years before Christopher Columbus discovered the New World in 1492, but the modern history of America begins with Columbus's discovery. Within the next fifty years, several European nations had sent explorers and claimed territory in what is now the United States. The Spaniards were first. Ponce de Leon landed in Florida in 1513, and that territory was claimed for the King of Spain in 1528. The French explorers came as early as 1524, and Jacques Cartier explored the Atlantic Coast territories in the 1530s.

In 1585 the first group of English colonists set out, and in 1586 they formed the first English colony, in North Carolina. This colony did not last, but by the early 1600s the English had colonies in New England and Virginia. Later they added colonies in Pennsylvania and the Carolinas.

The Dutch settled in what is now New York as early as 1614, but fifty years later they lost their colony in a war with England. The Swedes began a colony at what is now Wilmington, Delaware, but it too became English. The French had colonies in Canada. The Spaniards were settled in St. Augustine, Florida, and Santa Fe, New Mexico.

HOW THE ENGLISH COLONIES GREW

During the early 1700s, the English colonies became the only strong and well developed ones in North America. There were thirteen in what is now the United States. They were Massachusetts, New Hampshire, Rhode Island, Connecticut, New York, New Jersey, Pennsylvania, Maryland, Delaware, Virginia, North Carolina, South Carolina, and Georgia. All the colonies together had a population of about 1,350,000 in the year 1750. About 200,000 of them were slaves in the southern states and about 100,000 had come from Germany, Holland, or other European countries, but at least a million were British in descent or had been in America long enough to be English-speaking.

In each of these colonies, except Connecticut and Rhode Island, there was a governor appointed by the British Crown (that is, by the king or his government). The colonies had their own lawmaking bodies, but the governor could set aside their laws. Even in Connecticut and Rhode Island, the people obeyed British laws. The British governors usually treated the American people scornfully and so were greatly disliked, but nearly all the American people were loyal to the

king and proud to consider themselves an outpost of England or Great Britain.

During the 1750s, the British fought against the French for control of Canada, in the series of battles called the French and Indian War. The British sent some soldiers, but most of the British force was recruited from the colonies. The American forces were commanded by British officers, and these officers treated the Americans so rudely that they too were hated. George Washington, then a young American officer, resigned in protest. Yet the Americans supplied the necessary troops, and armed and fed them.

When the war ended, the colonies had lost thirty thousand men in the fighting and most of them were in debt or had spent most of their money. It was not a good time for the British governors or the Parliament (the British lawmaking body) in London to try to tax the colonies, but that is what the governors and the Parliament tried to do.

In 1765, Parliament passed the Stamp Act, requiring the colonies to pay taxes by buying stamps to put on all official papers. There were riots in Boston and protests in all the colonies. Men from several colonies met in a "congress" in New York City and wrote a paper called a "Declaration of the Rights and Grievances of the Colonists in America," which they sent to the British government in London. In this paper they said that the Americans had the same rights as other Englishmen and if they could not elect members of Parliament, Parliament could not tax them—a principle called "no taxation without representation." In Virginia, a young man named Patrick Henry persuaded the Assembly to declare that it was the only group that had a right to tax the people of Virginia. A secret society called the Sons of Liberty and groups of prominent men called Committees of Correspondence were organized to oppose the tax.

The Stamp Tax was so unpopular that Parliament repealed it (called it off) within two years, but in the early 1770s even more trouble was caused by a British tax on tea. The colonists refused to buy tea. In Boston, two patriots named Samuel Adams and John Hancock led a group of men disguised as Indians who went on board British ships in the harbor and dumped all the tea overboard. This was called the "Boston Tea Party." It happened at the end of 1773.

REVOLUTION AND INDEPENDENCE

In 1774, representatives of the colonies met in Philadelphia in the first Continental Congress. The most prominent men of nearly all the colonies were there. Only a few of them wanted to form an independent country then, but they formed themselves into a body that could take action if it was necessary.

That action became necessary in April, 1775. On April 19, British troops left Boston to capture Samuel Adams and John Hancock, who were to be arrested as rebels. Paul Revere and other Americans had warned the people living in Lexington and Concord that the British were coming. The farmers armed themselves and met the British, and the first battle of the Revolutionary War was fought.

The second Continental Congress met less than a month later, and after a month's argument they decided to form an American army and put George Washington in charge of it. A year later, on July 4, 1776, the Congress signed a "Declaration of the thirteen United States of America," saying that they were free and independent. This paper, the Declaration of Independence, is considered the beginning of the United States.

The Revolutionary War went on for six years. The Americans did not win many great victories, but the British were not able to break down their resistance. France, which was fighting the British in Europe, helped the Americans. In 1781, the last battle of the war was fought at Yorktown, Virginia, and the British commander, Lord Cornwallis, surrendered to George Washington. In 1783, in Paris, the capital of France, the Treaty of Paris was signed, making the United States independent.

FORMATION OF THE UNION

There still was no United States as a single country. Every colony had become an independent state. The Continental Congress continued to meet, but the states had trouble agreeing on how a federal (united) country could be formed. The small states were afraid the big states would have too much power. Finally, in 1787, a Constitutional Convention met in Philadelphia and wrote a Constitution that satisfied all of them. Supporters of this Constitution, chiefly Alexander Hamilton of New York and James Madison of Virginia, wrote a series of papers called the Federalist Papers in which they urged the people to accept the Constitution. It took almost a year after that, but by September, 1788, all but two of the states (North Carolina and Rhode Island) had ratified, or accepted, the Constitution, and the first elections were held. George Washington was unanimously elected the first President. The first Senators and Representatives were elected. In 1889, the Congress met for the first time. Within a year North Carolina and Rhode Island ratified the Constitution.

THE EARLY YEARS

The first census of the United States was taken in 1790. The country had 3,170,000 citizens and there were about 750,000 slaves in the southern states. In addition, there were large settlements in Vermont and Kentucky, and a growing one in Tennessee, and all three were soon admitted as states.

From the earliest years of the United States, there were two great arguments. One was the question of States' Rights. One party, called the Federalists, thought the national government should be strong. The other party, the anti-Federalists, wanted the states to be strong and the national government to have very little power. The Federalists were more successful, but the question is still being argued.

The other great question was slavery. In the southern states, Negroes were slaves. In the northern states they were free. For more than seventy years, the slave states tried to make sure that every new "free" state admitted to the union was balanced by a new slave state, so that

the free states would not get too much power in Congress.

The earliest big problem of the United States was caused by the wars that were going on in Europe (called the Napoleonic Wars). Because Great Britain was fighting France, British warships caused great trouble for American ships at sea. This led to the War of 1812, the second and last war fought between the Americans and the British. It was not a very big war and neither side actually won it. When the European wars ended, in 1815, the American war was simply called off.

By 1823 the United States and Great Britain were friendly. That year the United States issued the most important statement of its history, and the British supported it (and had even offered to join the United States in making it). This statement is called the Monroe Doctrine. It was made by President James Monroe and was written chiefly by John Quincy Adams, who was Secretary of State at that time. The Monroe Doctrine said that the United States would not permit any European country to conquer and rule any part of the Americas. This is still the most important part of the policy of the United States in its dealings with other countries of the world.

In its first sixty or more years, the United States was chiefly busy growing. Americans were settling new lands in the west. New states were entering the Union. New territories were being bought and opened by settlers.

The biggest purchase by far was the Louisiana Purchase of 1803, when President Thomas Jefferson bought almost the entire central part of the continent— the valley of the Mississippi River—from France. In 1821, the United States bought Florida from Spain, and in 1848 the United States won some southwestern territories in the Mexican War and paid Mexico $10,000,000 for much of the present territory of New Mexico and Arizona.

After the early political battles between the Federalists and the anti-Federalists had been settled, the two chief parties became the Whigs and the Democrats. The leaders in public affairs, year after year while Presidents came and went, were three Senators—Daniel Webster of New Hampshire, Henry Clay of Kentucky, and John C. Calhoun of South Carolina. Webster was against slavery and for a strong Union. Calhoun was for slavery and for greater States' Rights. Clay, being from a "border state" (between the North and the South), proposed compromises that would be acceptable to both sides of the argument.

After Andrew Jackson, a strong and courageous President, served two terms from 1829 to 1837, no President was re-elected for a second term for nearly thirty years. It was too difficult to please the people in the strong arguments that were raging. The principal argument was over slavery.

SECESSION AND CIVIL WAR

In 1860, there were thirty-one states. Sixteen of them were free states. Fifteen were slave states.

In that year a new political party, the Republican Party, was formed, and it

elected its first candidate for President, Abraham Lincoln of Illinois. Lincoln was known to be against slavery. He was no sooner inaugurated than South Carolina voted to secede (withdraw) from the United States and become an independent country. Other southern states did the same thing until eleven of them had seceded. They met and formed a new federal government, which they called the Confederate States of America.

President Lincoln said they did not have the right to do this. He called for 75,000 volunteers to join the Union army and force the southern states to remain in the Union. Most of the people in the South felt more patriotism for their states than they did for the United States. Armies of the South and the North fought bitterly for four years. It was one of the biggest wars of all time. It is now usually called the Civil War, though for a long time people in the South said it should be called the War between the States, or the War for Southern Independence.

The North was much stronger than the South in the resources needed to win a war, such as factories and iron mines and ships. The South lost the war, and many people in the North wanted to punish the South. Lincoln knew this was wrong, but he was assassinated before he could use his power to protect the South. Andrew Johnson, who was Vice President and so became the new President, tried to carry out Lincoln's plans but he was suspected of favoring the South because he came from a southern state, Tennessee. The period was one of much quarreling and has been called "the age of hate."

The result of the Civil War was three amendments to the Constitution that made Negroes citizens and gave them the right to vote. During about ten years, called the Reconstruction Period, the United States was gradually made into one nation again; but there are parts of the United States in which people have not yet forgotten all the disagreements of the Civil War.

RAILROADS, FACTORIES, AUTOMOBILES

The fifty years following the Civil War saw the United States grow to be the greatest manufacturing country the world has ever known. It happened so fast that the rest of the world could not believe it and did not actually believe it for almost another fifty years, until World War II in the 1940s.

During these fifty years, railroads were built from coast to coast and in a close network throughout the country. Seventeen more states were admitted to the union. Electric lights and electric power were introduced. The custom arose of forming giant corporations to make steel and heavy machinery and ships and all the things needed in a giant industrial nation. The automobile was perfected and the motor industry grew up. The telephone and the airplane and other inventions changed the nature of life throughout the country and affected all the world.

Business was bold and ruthless during the growing period. Great fortunes were made, but the men who made them bribed lawmakers; raised money by selling stocks to the public but taking the profits for themselves; imported laboring men from foreign countries and made them work in unsafe conditions and live in filthy slums; hired thugs to beat and even kill working men who tried to form labor unions and protect their rights; and did almost anything that was dishonest and unfair. Yet out of these violent and unscrupulous practices grew the richest country with the highest standard of living in the world.

The first President elected after the Civil War was Ulysses S. Grant. He had been commander of the Union armies in the war and was the greatest hero of the North. Though he was an honest man, he did not interfere with businessmen. Neither did most of the Presidents who came after him until Theodore Roosevelt, who became President in 1901, started a campaign to end some of the worst business practices. By that time, the most rapid growth was over and American business was becoming settled and respectable anyway.

The United States fought one war during this period. It was the Spanish-American War, fought in 1898. The war was easily won by the United States Navy and small Army forces fighting only in Cuba. This war added to the reputation of the United States as a powerful nation and it added also to the wealth of the country, because the United States gained control over the Philippines and some other quite small islands in the Pacific Ocean. The people of the Philippines rebelled briefly against American control, so there was some more fighting called the Philippine Insurrection, but this was stopped and the United States promised that the Philippines would eventually have independence, a promise that was kept in 1935.

THE END OF ISOLATION

From the earliest days, it had been a policy of the United States to stay out of the quarrels of European countries and to have no allies.

In 1914, World War I broke out in Europe. Great Britain, France and Russia were on one side against Germany and Austria-Hungary on the other side. Most of the people of the United States were on the side of Great Britain because they had the same language and general ideas. Also they liked France because of the help France had given them in the Revolutionary War.

Woodrow Wilson, the President of the United States, kept the country neutral for the first three years of the war. But part of the German campaign was to sink all merchant ships that might be carrying supplies to the British, and several United States ships were sunk. President Wilson warned Germany, but they continued to sink American ships. In April 1917, the United States entered the war against Germany.

The United States had continued to grow in manufacturing capacity and general wealth. In 1914 the United States had completed the building of the Panama Canal, joining the Atlantic and Pacific Oceans. The automobile industry had begun to be an important one. The population had grown until there were 120,000,000 people in the United States.

During World War I, the United States showed some of its power by building more ships than had ever been built before, equipping an army of four million men in a little more than a year, and sending vast supplies of food and various materials to its allies, but the war ended before the United States actually got into full production.

After World War I, every big nation on earth except the United States was poor. The principal nations of Europe had been badly damaged by the war. President Wilson wanted the United States to join the newly formed League of Nations and work with other countries to prevent future wars, but the Senate preferred the former policy of isolation —forming no alliances with other countries. However, the United States sent food, clothing and other supplies in great quantities to help the people of Europe.

During the 1920s, when other countries were poor, the United States seemed to grow richer and richer. Then, late in 1929, a big depression, or period of bad business conditions, began. Through most of the 1930s the people of the United States also were poor. During this period a government called the New Deal, under President Franklin D. Roosevelt, passed many laws of a kind the country had not had before. They included laws to create jobs by spending government money, and laws to pay regular incomes to people more than 65 years old and to people who are unemployed.

During the depression, some new governments appeared in Europe. They were called Fascist in Italy and Nazi in Germany. These were dictatorships in which the citizens of the countries had no personal freedom. These governments were also willing to start wars whenever they thought they could profit from them. In Asia, Japan was another country that started wars in order to grab territory from neighboring lands.

The practices of these governments led to World War II in 1939. The United States stayed out of the war but helped Great Britain and other countries that fought against the dictatorships. In 1941 the Japanese, who were afraid the United States would stop their plans to seize more lands in Asia, made a surprise attack on United States ships and planes in Hawaii. Two days later, Germany and Italy declared war on the United States.

During World War II, the United States made the greatest war effort in history, fighting two wars at the same time, more than twelve thousand miles apart, and winning both of them. Factories in the United States were able to support twelve million American fighting men and at the same time supply their principal allies, Great Britain and Russia, with much of the war equipment, food and supplies they needed. At the end of the war the United States used the first atomic bombs in history, dropping them on two cities of Japan, and they led Japan to surrender quickly.

After World War II, the United States joined the United Nations and abandoned the old policy of isolation. The policy of the United States, under President Harry Truman, was to help other countries with loans of money and even with armed as-

U.S. STATES, TERRITORIES, AND POSSESSIONS

STATES

NAME	AREA (square miles)	POPULATION (1970 census)
Alabama	51,609	3,444,165
Alaska	586,400	302,173
Arizona	113,909	1,772,482
Arkansas	53,104	1,923,295
California	158,693	19,953,134
Colorado	104,247	2,207,259
Connecticut	5,009	3,032,217
Delaware	2,057	548,104
Florida	58,560	6,789,443
Georgia	58,876	4,589,575
Hawaii	6,424	769,913
Idaho	83,557	713,008
Illinois	56,400	11,113,976
Indiana	36,291	5,193,669
Iowa	56,290	2,825,041
Kansas	82,276	2,249,071
Kentucky	40,395	3,219,311
Louisiana	48,523	3,643,180
Maine	33,215	993,663
Maryland	10,577	3,922,399
Massachusetts	8,257	5,689,170
Michigan	58,216	8,875,083
Minnesota	84,068	3,805,069
Mississippi	47,716	2,216,912
Missouri	69,674	4,677,399
Montana	147,138	694,409
Nebraska	77,227	1,483,791
Nevada	110,540	488,738
New Hampshire	9,304	737,681
New Jersey	7,836	7,168,164
New Mexico	121,666	1,016,000
New York	49,576	18,190,740
North Carolina	52,712	5,082,059
North Dakota	70,665	617,761
Ohio	41,222	10,652,017
Oklahoma	69,919	2,559,253
Oregon	96,981	2,091,385
Pennsylvania	45,333	11,793,909
Rhode Island	1,214	949,723
South Carolina	31,055	2,590,516
South Dakota	77,047	666,257
Tennessee	42,244	3,924,164
Texas	267,339	11,196,730
Utah	84,916	1,059,273
Vermont	9,609	444,732
Virginia	40,815	4,648,494
Washington	68,192	3,409,169
West Virginia	24,181	1,744,237
Wisconsin	56,154	4,417,933
Wyoming	97,914	332,416
District of Columbia	69	756,510
TOTAL OF UNITED STATES	**3,615,211**	**203,184,772**

TERRITORIES AND POSSESSIONS

NAME	AREA	POPULATION
American Samoa	76	27,769
Canton & Enderbury Islands	27	Not available
Guam	212	86,926
Midway Islands	2	2,220
Puerto Rico	3,435	2,689,932
Swan Islands	1	22
Virgin Islands	133	63,200
Wake Island	3	1,647
Others	5	Not available
GRAND TOTAL	**3,628,150**	**206,056,488**

U.S. PRESIDENTS AND VICE PRESIDENTS

YEARS	PRESIDENT	VICE PRESIDENT
1789–1797	1. George Washington	John Adams
1797–1801	2. John Adams	Thomas Jefferson
1801–1809	3. Thomas Jefferson	Aaron Burr
		George Clinton
1809–1817	4. James Madison	George Clinton
		Elbridge Gerry
1817–1825	5. James Monroe	Daniel D. Tompkins
1825–1829	6. John Quincy Adams	John C. Calhoun
1829–1837	7. Andrew Jackson	John C. Calhoun
		Martin Van Buren
1837–1841	8. Martin Van Buren	Richard M. Johnson
1841	9. William Henry Harrison	John Tyler
1841–1845	10. John Tyler	
1845–1849	11. James Knox Polk	George M. Dallas
1849–1850	12. Zachary Taylor	Millard Fillmore
1850–1853	13. Millard Fillmore	
1853–1857	14. Franklin Pierce	William R. King
1857–1861	15. James Buchanan	John C. Breckinridge
1861–1865	16. Abraham Lincoln	Hannibal Hamlin
		Andrew Johnson
1865–1869	17. Andrew Johnson	
1869–1877	18. Ulysses Simpson Grant	Schuyler Colfax
		Henry Wilson
1877–1881	19. Rutherford B. Hayes	William A. Wheeler
1881	20. James A. Garfield	Chester A. Arthur
1881–1885	21. Chester A. Arthur	
1885–1889	22. Grover Cleveland	Thomas A. Hendricks
1889–1893	23. Benjamin Harrison	Levi P. Morton
1893–1897	24. Grover Cleveland	Adlai E. Stevenson
1897–1901	25. William McKinley	Garrett A. Hobart
		Theodore Roosevelt
1901–1909	26. Theodore Roosevelt	Charles W. Fairbanks
1909–1913	27. William Howard Taft	James S. Sherman
1913–1921	28. Woodrow Wilson	Thomas R. Marshall
1921–1923	29. Warren Gamaliel Harding	Calvin Coolidge
1923–1929	30. Calvin Coolidge	Charles G. Dawes
1929–1933	31. Herbert Clark Hoover	Charles Curtis
1933–1945	32. Franklin Delano Roosevelt	John N. Garner
		Henry A. Wallace
		Harry S. Truman
1945–1953	33. Harry S. Truman	Alben S. Barkley
1953–1961	34. Dwight D. Eisenhower	Richard M. Nixon
1961–1963	35. John F. Kennedy	Lyndon B. Johnson
1963–1969	36. Lyndon B. Johnson	Hubert H. Humphrey
1969–1974	37. Richard M. Nixon	Spiro T. Agnew
		Gerald R. Ford
1974-1977	38. Gerald R. Ford	Nelson A. Rockefeller
1977-	39. Jimmy Carter	Walter F. Mondale

sistance so that they could prevent Communists from getting control of their countries. This was called the Truman Doctrine. Another policy was called the Marshall Plan, because it was proposed by Secretary of State George C. Marshall. The Marshall Plan was a way by which other nations could get loans from the United States to help build up their countries so that they could be self-supporting again. Another way in which the United States abandoned isolation was in joining the North Atlantic Treaty Organization and keeping armed forces in Europe to guard against Communist invasions of the democratic countries of Europe. In Asia, the United States twice sent large forces to oppose Communist aggression — in Korea in 1950 and in Vietnam in 1962.

Every President since Truman has continued to use the influence of the United States in world affairs. The country continued to grow more prosperous and great gains were made in civil rights and in the exploration of space.

Universal Military Training

Universal Military Training, or UMT, is the name given to a system requiring every young man in the United States to receive military training in one of the branches of the armed services. The purpose is to train men in peacetime so that they will be ready if the nation goes to war. The deaths of many Americans in World Wars I and II have been blamed on the fact that most of the fighting men had to be hastily trained after the war began. Often they entered battles without knowing how to protect themselves. Congress discussed UMT several times after the Korean War began, but many members always opposed it.

The UMT plan would require every 18-year-old boy to receive six months' active training in one of the branches of the armed forces. He could choose the branch. After the six months' basic training, he would be considered part of the reserves and could be called up at a moment's notice to serve in the armed forces. Probably he would also be called upon to take several weeks' training each year for the first few years of his reserve duty. Those who were in high school at 18 would be allowed to finish high school, and those who were in college would be allowed to finish the college year.

Those who are against UMT think that taking boys out of civilian life, particularly when they are finishing their education, is not good. Some say that UMT

should be a part of their regular education, with some military training while they are in school and training camps during the summer.

Universal Military Training was used by nearly every European country before World War I. France, Russia, and later Italy and Germany, continued it after World War I. Switzerland, where there has not been a war for many years, still makes every healthy young man receive military training. But Great Britain and the United States have traditionally been against Universal Military Training for hundreds of years, except when there was a war or threat of war.

universe

The universe is everything that exists. It is so huge that the mind of man cannot quite understand it. Distances in the universe are measured in light years, and a light year is the distance that light can travel in a year, going at the rate of 186,000 miles per second; but most of the universe is so far away that it would take a big book just to write down the number of light years you would have to travel to get to a distant part of it.

The earth we live on is tiny compared to the sun; but the sun is only one of a billion or more stars that make up a single galaxy, or group of stars, called the Milky Way, and the Milky Way is only one galaxy out of a number that probably reaches a million galaxies and may be a countless number.

ORIGIN OF THE UNIVERSE

The study of how the universe began, and how it is developing, is called *cosmogony*. Through the ages there have been many theories to explain the way the universe was formed and how it reached its present form and condition.

According to the theory of the *expanding universe*, for about four billion years the stars have been traveling away from the center of the universe, at speeds up to 38,000 miles per second. Our sun, for example, is moving at a rate of about 170 miles per second and is carrying the earth and all the other planets along with it.

The most popular theory to account for the origin of the universe is the "Dust Cloud" theory of a scientist named Fred L. Whipple. He supposes that the present stars and other things in the universe were originally a giant cloud of dust and gas. Sections of this cloud condensed (came together and became solid) to form stars such as the sun. He calculates that it would take about a billion years for a portion of the dust cloud to condense enough to make the sun. Parts of this dust cloud would fly off, just as bits of water fly off from a waterfall and form spray, and these bits would become planets such as the earth.

A huge mass of gas in space is called a NEBULA, and there is a separate article about it. See also the articles on ASTRONOMY, GALAXY, and MILKY WAY.

university, a school made up of two or more colleges, where you can obtain both an undergraduate and a graduate degree. See COLLEGES AND UNIVERSITIES.

Upper Volta, Republic of the

The Republic of the Upper Volta, a new African nation, became independent in 1960. It had been part of the French Community.

Upper Volta is in northwest Africa. Once it was called the Mossi Empire. France made it a protectorate in 1897 and a colony in 1919. The region was divided in 1919 between the Ivory Coast, Sudan and Niger but was reëstablished in 1947. In area it is about twice as big as North Carolina, but they are about the same in population.

Most of the people are Negroes of the Mossi and Bobo tribes and are farmers, raising cotton, peanuts and cattle and producing animal products.

As a new republic, Upper Volta had a president and an Assembly of 75 members, elected for five-year terms. In 1966 the Army overthrew the government and took over control.

THE REPUBLIC OF THE UPPER VOLTA. Area, 105,839 square miles. Population (1974), 3,490,000. Capital, Ouagadougou (150,000). Languages, French and African.

Ur

Ur, or Ur of the Chaldees, was an ancient city on the Euphrates River, in the southeastern part of the land that is now Iraq. Thousands of years ago this region was called Sumer; later it was known as Chaldea. Ur was the chief center of the SUMERIANS, an ancient people about whom there is a separate article. The city had a great tower, like the more famous one of Babel, and the ruins of it still are impressive. In the Bible, Ur is named as the place from which Abraham, the ancestor of the Hebrews, emigrated. The city was abandoned, probably after the Euphrates changed its course and the city was left out in the desert. It was covered by desert sands and was forgotten until 1854, when explorers dug up a few tablets there that proved its identity. Since World War I great excavations have been conducted there and many important finds were made which show how the Sumerian people lived four or five thousand years ago.

Ural Mountains

The Ural Mountains are a long but fairly low range of mountains in Russia. They are considered to form the boundary between Europe and Asia. They extend about 1,300 miles, from the Arctic Ocean in the north to the Ural River in the south. The highest point in the mountains is about 6,000 feet.

The Urals are covered with dense forests. They are one of the chief sources of minerals in the Soviet Union, containing great quantities of coal, iron, manganese, nickel, chrome, copper, platinum and gold, precious stones, and petroleum. The Urals have become a great manufacturing region of the Soviet Union. Several railroads cross the mountains and run north and south on both sides of the range.

uranium

Uranium is a heavy, white, hard metal whose chief use is in the production of atomic energy for weapons and for making power. Uranium has been known since 1789, when it was discovered by a German chemist named Martin Heinrich Klaproth. The first pure uranium was made about fifty years later by a French chemist, Eugène-Melchior Peligot. He named it for the planet Uranus.

A Canadian uranium mine worker. *N.F.B.*

SOME USES OF URANIUM

Before the production of atomic energy was worked out in 1939, uranium was not very important. Its chief use was in making steel alloys (mixtures of metals). Uranium increases the hardness, elasticity and strength of the steel without making it brittle. It was used also to make yellow-green and red fluorescent glass, a velvety-black glaze for pottery, and brown stains to color leather and wood. It was used in medicine to make a germ-killing solution, and in chemical processes in the manufacture of nitrogen and rubber.

Since 1939, uranium has rarely been used for anything but the making of atomic energy.

URANIUM ORES

Uranium ore is the most sought-after mineral in the world. The chief ores are called *pitchblende, carnotite,* and *uraninite.* Uranium ore is found in Colorado and Utah, and in the Belgian Congo, the Union of South Africa, Canada, Austria, and Russia and other parts of the Soviet Union. The ore is treated with chlorine and then heated in an electric furnace, along with carbon, to get pure uranium.

ATOMIC ENERGY FROM URANIUM

The articles on the ATOM and ATOMIC ENERGY explain that all matter is made of *atoms.* Atoms are tiny particles, so small that they cannot be seen even with the most powerful microscope. About 250,000,000 atoms set side by side would make a line only one inch long. But atoms, small as they are, are made up of smaller particles. The names of these smaller particles are *electrons, protons,* and *neutrons.* The protons and neutrons are packed into the center, or *nucleus,* of the atom. The electrons are arranged around the nucleus in rings.

The total number of neutrons and protons in the nucleus is called the *atomic weight* of the atom. (The electrons are so light that they hardly count.)

When coal burns or dynamite explodes, or when any other chemical change takes place in matter, the atoms change their positions and may move from one element to another but the nuclei of the atoms remain unchanged.

THE TWO KINDS OF URANIUM ATOM

There are two kinds of uranium atom. One kind has 92 protons and 146 neutrons, so its atomic weight is 238. The other kind has 92 protons and 143 neutrons, so its atomic weight is 235. The first kind, which makes up 99⅓ percent of all uranium atoms, is called U-238; the second kind, which makes up only ⅔ of 1 percent of all atoms, is called U-235. U-235 is the kind from which atomic energy is gotten; U-238 must be changed to another element called *plutonium* before it can be used.

The nucleus of either kind of uranium atom has its protons and neutrons so tightly packed together that if you could collect a quart milk bottle full of these nuclei, it would weigh 200 billion tons.

Uranium and many other chemical elements are constantly undergoing changes that eventually will change them to lead. The elements change by sending out streams, or rays, of particles of the atoms of which they are made. The process of change is called RADIOACTIVITY, and there is a separate article about it.

NUCLEAR FISSION

Radioactive changes within the uranium atom may shake loose neutrons from the nucleus. The neutrons leave the nucleus at speeds that range from one mile a second to 12,000 miles a second. When one of these speeding neutrons strikes the nucleus of a neighboring atom, it may cause the whole atom to fly apart.

The two largest fragments of the nucleus will re-form to make atoms of other elements of lower atomic weight. Krypton and barium are two elements frequently formed when uranium is split. Several neutrons will fly free of the smashed uranium nucleus. The splitting of the nucleus releases a vast amount of energy in the form of heat, light, and X-rays. The splitting apart of the nucleus of the atom is called *nuclear fission*, and the energy that is released is *atomic energy*.

When the neutrons fly out of a splitting atom, some of them may hit another nucleus, if one is nearby. Another nuclear fission will take place, more energy will be released and more neutrons will be set free to hit and split apart still more atoms. This can go on until most of the nuclei in a piece of uranium have split. This process is called a *chain reaction*.

IMPORTANCE OF URANIUM

Uranium is the main source from which scientists can obtain *fissionable* elements that can produce a chain reaction. The chain reaction is necessary to the atomic bomb. Therefore it is necessary to the still deadlier hydrogen bomb, because only the great heat of an atomic bomb can set off a hydrogen bomb.

For this reason, uranium has become the most valuable metal in the world. Thousands of scientists and untrained "prospectors" are looking for uranium ores. In some parts of the world it is like the "gold rushes" that took place fifty to a hundred years ago when gold was just being discovered in out-of-the-way places. One man found a uranium deposit and was ten million dollars richer overnight.

The peaceful uses of uranium are very great, both for useful power and in medicine and science. The articles on ATOMIC ENERGY and RADIOACTIVITY explains these uses.

Uranus

Uranus is a planet in the solar system, which consists of the bodies (including the earth) that revolve around the sun. Uranus was the first planet that was discovered after the invention of the telescope. It was first seen in 1781 by an English astronomer named William Herschel.

Uranus takes 84 years to travel around the sun, compared to one year for the earth, and is nineteen times as far from the sun as the earth is. That is, Uranus is almost two billion miles from the sun. Uranus takes about 11 hours to make one complete turn on its axis, while the earth makes one complete turn in 24 hours. Therefore Uranus turns at a much greater speed.

Uranus is about four times as large as the earth and weighs about 15 times as much as the earth. It can be seen with the naked eye, but then appears to be a distant star. Because of its great distance from the sun, Uranus receives very weak sunlight and is very cold. Its temperature is about 300 degrees below our coldest winter temperature. Because of the extreme cold it is doubtful that anything lives on Uranus.

Uranus has five satellites, or moons, that revolve around it. They are held near Uranus by gravity. Even though Uranus is much larger than the earth, the pull of gravity is a little weaker than on the earth. If you weigh 100 pounds on the earth, you would weigh only 90 pounds on Uranus.

The planet Uranus is named for a character in Greek mythology, the stories the ancient Greeks told about their gods and goddesses. Uranus was the chief of the giants called Titans. He married Earth, and their descendants were the chief gods. See the article on the TITANS.

Uruguay

Uruguay is the smallest country in South America. It is in the southeastern part, between Brazil and Argentina, and has a seacoast on the Atlantic Ocean. Uruguay is one of the most advanced of all South American countries. Its area is 72,172 square miles, which is about the size of North Dakota. More than 2,900,000 people live there, which is about four times as many as live in North Dakota. Uruguay is the most densely populated country in South America.

THE PEOPLE OF URUGUAY

Most of the people in Uruguay are of European descent, particularly Spanish and Portuguese. There are very few of the native Indian people living there. The language of the country is Spanish. Most of the people belong to the Roman Catholic Church, but there is complete religious freedom for everyone.

Some of the people are farmers, but one out of every three people lives in the area around Montevideo, the capital, which is one of the largest cities in South America.

The farmers raise livestock, especially sheep and cattle, and grow corn, wheat, rice, and fruits. Most of the farms are small, but there are large ranches in parts of the country where there are few people.

In the cities there are meat-packing plants and factories that manufacture textiles, leather goods, and other things. Uruguay buys most of its raw materials for these manufactures from other countries. It buys a great deal from the United States. In return the United States buys most of Uruguay's meat products.

There is free education in Uruguay, including college education. Primary education is required of all children, and most of the people in the country know how to read and write. There is a university at Montevideo.

WHAT URUGUAY IS LIKE

Uruguay is surrounded on three sides by water. The Atlantic Ocean is on its east coast. Here there are sandy beaches where tourists, many from other South American countries, come for vacations. On the west, forming the boundary between Uruguay and Argentina, is the Uruguay River, which is very important for irrigation and for watering the rich farmlands and grazing fields. To the south of Uruguay is the Plata River, or Rio de la Plata, which is a wide inlet of the Atlantic Ocean. It is nearly 140 miles wide at its mouth. Montevideo is on the Plata River, at a point where it is more than 50 miles wide.

The northern part of Uruguay is a land of low mountain ranges and wide valleys. The southern part of the country is a low, flat, grassy region. This is watered by streams that branch off from the Uruguay River, making it suitable both for grazing cattle and for farming.

In the mountains are deposits of many minerals, but few have been mined. Uruguay does sell some flagstone, limestone and other building stone to other countries of South America and to the United States.

Many tropical trees and shrubs grow in Uruguay, particularly in the valleys and along the northern edge of the plains area. Many of the shrubs are purple and often the whole countryside has a purplish color to it. For this reason, Uruguay has been called the Purple Land.

Many of the wild animals that once

lived in Uruguay have disappeared. There are herds of wild horses and hogs in the interior sections, where few people live. There are also foxes, deer, and many dangerous snakes and insects. Many brightly colored tropical birds including the parakeet, are found in Uruguay.

The climate of Uruguay is subtropical, which means that it is much like the climate of Florida, and in most sections it is mild and pleasant most of the year. In summer, which is when it is winter in North America, the heavily populated districts have an average temperature of about 75 degrees, but there are parts of the country that have temperatures of 100 degrees or more. In the winter the average temperature is about 50 degrees.

The best transportation in Uruguay is by its rivers. There are about 1,500 miles of railroads in the country, modern highways near the big cities, and a few airports.

HOW THE PEOPLE ARE GOVERNED

Uruguay is a republic with an elected president at its head. It has a constitution that protects the rights of the people and a legislature that makes its laws. The legislature consists of a Senate and a Chamber of Representatives. Every citizen in Uruguay has the right to vote. Montevideo is the largest city and the capital. There is a separate article about MONTEVIDEO.

URUGUAY IN THE PAST

The first colony in Uruguay was founded by Spaniards in 1624. Later the Portuguese also founded colonies in the same area. The Portuguese and the Spanish fought for control of the area, and the Spanish won. The land that is now Uruguay became a possession of Spain. It was called the Spanish Viceroyalty of Rio de la Plata.

In 1810 the people of Uruguay fought for their independence from Spain, and four years later they became independent.

Later Uruguay was taken over by Brazil, a larger and more powerful country. Again the people fought for their independence. In 1830 a constitution was written and an independent republic was set up. Since that time Uruguay has been friendly with Brazil, and also with Argentina, the other powerful bordering country. In the last hundred years there have been several revolutions or civil wars within Uruguay, when leaders have tried to take the rights of the people away from them.

The present constitution has been in effect since 1966. Uruguay has prospered under it, and is one of the most progressive countries in South America. Until 1952 there was a president at the head of the government, but the constitution was revised in 1951, giving the leadership of the country to the nine council members.

During World War II Uruguay helped the United States and its allies. Afterwards it joined the United Nations.

URUGUAY. Area, 72,172 square miles. Population (1974 estimate) 2,920,000. Capital, Montevideo. Language, Spanish. Religion, Roman Catholic. Government, republic. Monetary unit, the peso, worth about 2/5 of a cent (U.S.). Flag, horizontal bars, four blue and five white, with a picture of the sun in the upper left corner.

Utah Travel Council (Hal Rumel)
Bonneville Salt Flats in Utah, where automobile speed records are periodically set and broken.

Utah

Utah is a state in the western part of the United States, in the Rocky Mountain group of states. Its nickname is the "Beehive State," because it was first called Deseret, a name (from the Book of Mormon) meaning "honey bee." The state is named for a tribe of Indians called Utes who originally lived in this region.

Utah is one of the most important mineral-producing states in the United States. It is the chief coal-producing state of the west. It has large uranium deposits, and ranks second in the United States in the amount of copper, gold and silver taken from its mines each year.

In area, Utah ranks 11th among the states, with an area of 84,916 square miles. In population it ranks 36th, with about a million people living there. It became a state in 1896, and was the 45th state admitted to the United States. The capital is Salt Lake City.

THE PEOPLE OF UTAH

The first permanent settlement in Utah was made only about a hundred years ago, in 1847, by the Mormons, a religious group. (You can read more about the MORMONS in a separate article.) Many other Mormons followed the original settlers, and later Mormons from England, Scotland and other European countries went to Utah. Today three out of every four persons in the state are Mormons and most of them are descendents of the early settlers. There are very few people in the state who are not American-born.

When gold was discovered in California, in 1849, many easterners went west. Some of them settled in Utah. There are only about 7,000 Indians living in the state, and about 6,000 Negroes.

Most of the people in Utah live in and around the big cities. These cities are mostly in the north central part of the state, around Great Salt Lake. In this region there are several plants where iron and lead are smelted and many food-processing plants.

Utah's most valuable natural resource is its minerals, and a great many of the people work in copper, lead, silver, zinc and gold mines. Recently, more and more people are working in oil fields in the northeastern part of the state.

Agriculture has become almost as important as mining in recent years. The farmers grow sugar beets, fruits, alfalfa, and wheat. Many farmers also raise dairy cattle, and there are large sheep ranches in the state.

WHAT UTAH IS LIKE

The Great Salt Lake is in the northwest part of Utah and is the largest salt lake in the United States. It is more than 75 miles long and about 50 miles wide at its widest point. It was here that the Mormons first settled, and it is in this section that most of the people live.

The Wasatch Mountains run throuugh the central part of the state from north to south. To the east of the mountains is a plateau (a high, level region) that is bordered on the north by the Uinta Mountains, where there is grazing land for sheep and cattle. In this eastern plateau there are mines of uranium, coal, and potash.

The western part of the state is a part of the Great Basin, which extends over other western states. The northern part of this Great Basin is desert land. It was once a large inland lake, of which only the Great Salt Lake remains. Here in the northwest are the Bonneville Salt Flats, a beachlike stretch of salt instead of sand, where famous automobile races are held.

The rivers and lakes in Utah are very important for irrigating the crops. Many of the farmers would be unable to make a living from the land if they did not irrigate it. The principal rivers are the Colorado, the Bear, and the Green. The scenic beauty of the state consists of large canyons made by the passage of these and other rivers through the mountain ranges.

Most of the people live on the plateaus or in the valleys, where the climate is cool and mild. The average temperature for these regions is about 27 degrees in winter and about 71 degrees in summer.

Many of the important transcontinental railroads run across Utah. There are many miles of highways, though parts of the state do not have any highways at all. Roads through the mountains are difficult and expensive to build, and their chief value is for the tourists who like to visit the national parks and monuments. There are airports in a few of the larger cities, and Salt Lake City is an important terminal for several airlines.

GOVERNMENT OF UTAH

Utah, like other states, has a governor at the head of the government and a legislature that makes the laws. The governor is elected for a four-year term. The legislature is composed of two houses, a Senate and a House of Representatives. The members of the senate are elected for four-year terms, and the members of the House for two-year terms. Judges are

elected for a ten-year term. The capital is Salt Lake City. There are 29 counties.

Everyone has to go to school between the ages of 6 and 18. There are about 302,000 pupils enrolled in the public schools. Among the colleges, universities and other schools of higher learning are:

University of Utah, at Salt Lake City. Enrollment, 20,763 men and women in 1971.

Utah State University of Agriculture and Applied Science, at Logan. Enrollment, 8,500 men and women in 1971.

Brigham Young University, at Provo. Enrollment, 25,021 men and women in 1971.

College of Southern Utah, at Cedar City. Enrollment, 1,603 men and women in 1971.

CHIEF CITIES OF UTAH

The leading cities of Utah, with populations from the 1970 census, are:

Salt Lake City, population 175,885, the capital and largest city in the state. There is a separate article about SALT LAKE CITY.

Ogden, population 69,478, the second-largest city, a railroad center, in the northern part.

Provo, population 53,131, the third-largest city, steel producing center, in the central part.

Logan, population 22,333, the fourth-largest city, food processing center, in the north.

UTAH IN THE PAST

In 1540 a Spanish explorer, Cardenas, discovered the Grand Canyon and probably traveled north from it into what is now the state of Utah. In 1776, two missionaries trying to find a way to the Pacific explored parts of the region and discovered Utah Lake. The Great Salt Lake was discovered in 1824, although many explorers had heard about it from the Indians long before that time. A few years later, travelers going west used a route that went across the southern part of Utah.

Until 1847, when the Mormons reached Utah, there were no white settlers living there. The Mormons went to Utah so that they could practice their religion without interference. At that time the United States did not own this region, but the Mormons claimed it for the United States. The Mormons settled in the valleys around the Great Salt Lake and began to build up communities that were self-supporting.

After the Mexican War in 1848, the Utah region became United States territory. For many years, the citizens there tried unsuccessfully to become a state. The United States would not give the Mormon people statehood because they practiced polygamy, which means that a man was allowed to have more than one wife. Utah remained a territory, with the great Mormon leader, Brigham Young, as

its governor. In 1890 the Mormon church agreed to stop polygamy, and in 1896 Utah was admitted to the United States.

The Mormons were hard-working, and they managed to build successful farming communities even where the soil was poor and there was little rainfall. For many years they did not make use of the rich mineral deposits, for it was against their policy to take minerals from the earth before they developed farms and cities, but by the 1940s Utah had become one of the five leading mineral-producing states in the United States. Since that time industry in the state has grown greatly. After the invention of the atomic bomb, Utah became important for its uranium deposits.

PLACES TO SEE IN UTAH

Bryce Canyon National Park, 36,010 acres, 50 miles south of Junction, in the southwest, on State Highway 12. Large, bright-colored natural rock formations.

Dinosaur National Monument, 190,798 acres, partly in Colorado, near Vernal, in the northeast, on U.S. Route 40. Fossil quarries, relics of an ancient people.

Great Salt Lake, at Salt Lake City, in the north central part, on U.S. Route 40 Largest inland salt lake in the United States, Mormon Temple and Tabernacle.

Bonneville Salt Flats, near Wendover, in the northwestern part, on U.S. Route 40. Famous motor speedway.

UTAH. Area, 84,916 square miles. Population (1970 census) 1,059,273. Capital, Salt Lake City. Nickname, the Beehive State. Motto, Industry. Flower, sego lily. Bird, seagull. Song, "Utah, We Love Thee." Admitted to Union, January 4, 1896. Official abbreviation, UT.

Utica

Utica is the seventh-largest city in the state of New York. It is in the central part of the state, on the Mohawk River and the New York Barge Canal. About 91,000 people live there. More cotton textiles and knitwear are manufactured in Utica than in any other city in the United States. There are huge factories where sheets and pillowcases are made.

Utica was founded about two hundred years ago by settlers from along the Atlantic Coast.

UTICA, NEW YORK. Population (1970 census) 91,611. County seat of Oneida County. Incorporated, 1832.

Utopia

Utopia is a name used for any imaginary country where everything is perfect —where people live together in perfect harmony and have everything they need, and happiness rules. The name comes from a book written more than four hundred years ago by an Englishman, Sir Thomas More. He described a perfect country and named it Utopia. Many writers have written about such places, under different names. The Garden of Eden might be called a Utopia. The Greek philosopher Plato described an ideal government in his book, *The Republic.* Within recent times a writer named James Hilton, in a book called *Lost Horizon,* described a place called Shangri-La where no one grows old for many years and everyone lives a life of simple contentment.

Utrecht

Utrecht is a city in the Netherlands and the capital of a province that is also called Utrecht. About 250,000 people live in the city. It is on the Merwede Canal, about 21 miles southeast of the Netherlands' capital, Amsterdam. It is an important railroad center and also has factories that produce steel, aluminum, machinery, wood products, asphalt, and radios. It also has the national mint, where the Netherlands' coins are made.

Utrecht was founded about 1,200 years ago, in the year 695. It has a famous old university, founded in 1636, that is attended by students from all over the world. Among its fine old buildings is a cathedral that was built six hundred years ago. Utrecht has been a center of commerce since the Middle Ages, about a thousand years ago.

In the 1500s the Netherlands was ruled by Spain, and in 1566 its people revolted against the Spanish rulers. Utrecht was the center of this rebellion, which succeeded and resulted in the union of most of the Netherlands provinces. In 1713 a treaty was signed there, called the Peace of Utrecht. It ended the War of the Spanish Succession, which was fought between England and the German countries on one side and France and Spain on the other.

Utrillo, Maurice

Maurice Utrillo is the name of a French painter who is best known for his many paintings of street and village scenes around the city of Paris. He was born in 1883 and his mother taught him to paint when he was a boy. Among his many pictures of Paris is *Rue Ordener, Paris,* which is now in the Art Institute of Chicago, Illinois. He died in 1955.

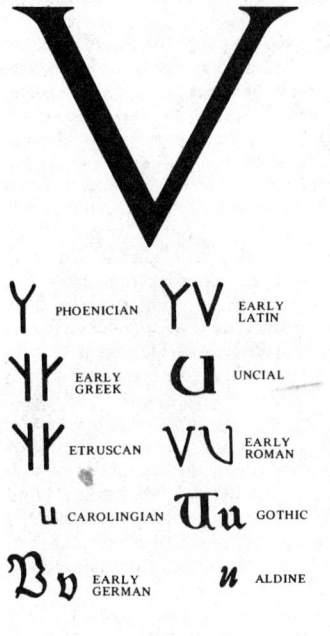

V or v

The letter V, the twenty-second letter of our alphabet, came to us in exactly the same way as the letter U, about which there is a separate article. There was no difference between the letters V and U

until about three hundred years ago. For the ancient Hebrews, Greeks, and Romans, a single sign stood for the two different sounds. The pictures on the opposite page show that the V and the U developed in the same way, the only difference being in the early German V, which is not like the Early German U. The "German blackletter" (or "Gothic") is used in many Germany books.

Read also the articles on the letter U and on the ALPHABET.

vaccination

Vaccination is a way in which the human body can be protected against certain diseases. The best-known and most common vaccination is that used to prevent smallpox. Smallpox used to be a dreadful disease that killed many thousands of people each year. About 150 years ago an English doctor named Edward Jenner discovered vaccination was a way to prevent smallpox. Since then, vaccination has almost wiped out the disease of smallpox.

Vaccination is a form of INOCULATION, about which you can read in a separate article. First a vaccine is prepared. It is a liquid composed of weakened or dead germs of a disease called *cowpox*, which is like smallpox but much less dangerous. A small drop of the vaccine is placed on the skin of a person and the doctor, using a sharp needle, scratches the skin at that point so that the vaccine enters the body. Usually a small scar or lump is formed at the point of vaccination to show that the vaccine has taken effect.

The vaccine in the body stimulates the body to build up stances called antitoxins. In the article on ANTITOXINS you may read how these substances fight the poisons of the disease, which are called *toxins*. In this way the body develops immunity to that particular disease.

In the case of smallpox, the vaccine makes it possible for the body to build up enough antitoxin so that if a person is exposed to the disease, the antitoxin will prevent his getting sick from it. A vaccination is effective for five to seven years, so it should be renewed at least once. Af-

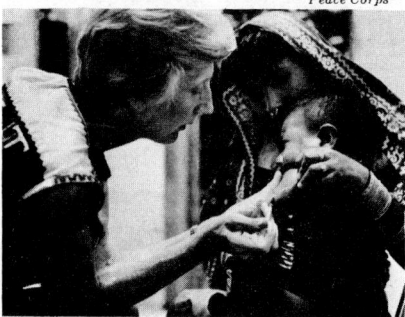

A Peace Corps volunteer innoculating a Cuna Indian child against tuberculosis on the Island of Aligandi, off the coast of Panama.
Peace Corps

ter two vaccinations, some people develop a lifetime immunity to smallpox; but if they should be exposed to it again, doctors consider it necessary to give them another vaccination.

vacuum

A vacuum is an enclosed space from which all or most of the air has been taken out. In a perfect vacuum there is no air

and no gas of any kind. In practice, only a partial vacuum is possible.

When you sip a soda through a straw, you first suck the air out of the straw. This creates a partial vacuum, and the soda rises through the straw. The reason for this is that the air is exerting pressure on the soda in the glass, while there is no pressure in the straw. The air pressure therefore forces the soda up into the straw. It is said that "nature abhors a vacuum." This means that wherever there is a vacuum, the forces of nature try to fill it.

For more than 350 years, scientists have understood the vacuum and have been trying to devise ways of creating a vacuum. The first experiment was conducted by a German scientist, who filled a container with water and then pumped out the water. After the water was pumped out there was very little air left in the container and a partial vacuum had been created. It was only a partial vacuum because the container was not airtight and air leaked in in several places. Since then scientists have made better pumps and better containers, so that almost complete vacuums can now be created.

When a vacuum is created in a container, the air pressure on the outside of the container is great and the pressure inside hardly anything at all. Unless the walls of the container are strong, they may collapse inward. A well-known experiment consists of fitting two halves of a hollow metal ball together so that they fit perfectly without any cracks or openings. The air is then pumped out of the hollow metal ball, creating a vacuum. The pressure of the outside air then holds the two halves of the ball together so firmly that a team of horses cannot pull them apart.

USES OF VACUUM

The principle of the vacuum is used by scientists in many important ways. The kind of tube used in a radio or television set is a vacuum tube. The electrons, which make it possible for radio and television to work, are able to travel more easily through space in the vacuum tube because there is no air to offer resistance.

Food-packing uses the vacuum principle. Many foods are packed in cans from which the air is taken out. The air carries bacteria and other tiny bits of plant life, such as yeast, that make food spoil. In vacuum cans the food is not spoiled by the injurious effects of bacteria in the air.

Many engines work because vacuums are created in them to help the engine function. In a gasoline engine, for instance, the gasoline is forced into the cylinders, where it explodes and does work, because a vacuum has been created to suck the gasoline into the cylinder. Pumps also operate because vacuums are created in them. When water is pumped out of a place, the machine doing the pumping creates a vacuum into which the water is sucked. This is much like what happens when you drink a soda through a straw.

Most thermometers and barometers work because vacuums have been created

in the glass tubes in which the mercury or other liquids rise. These liquids are able to rise to the top of the tube because there is a vacuum in the closed top.

COFFEE-MAKERS

Many people use vacuum coffee-makers. This kind of coffee-maker has two parts. Water is boiled in the lower part. It rises through a tube into the upper part, in which finely ground coffee is placed. After the water has boiled for a minute or two, most of it has risen to the upper part and has carried with it most of the air in the lower part, creating a partial vacuum. When the heat is turned off and the water stops boiling, the vacuum sucks all the water from the top to the bottom. The vacuum pulls the water through the filter in a matter of seconds, when it would take many minutes for the water to drip through.

VACUUM BOTTLES

Vacuum makes an excellent insulator against heat and cold, as you can read in the article on INSULATION. This makes possible the popular vacuum bottle, which is sold under the trade name Thermos and other names. A glass bottle is put in a container and surrounded by a space from which the air has been pumped out. Springs hold the inside bottle in place so that it will not be broken by shocks (for the vacuum chamber gives it no support). Hot drinks put in the bottle stay hot; cold things stay cold.

The next article deals with the VACUUM CLEANER.

vacuum cleaner

The vacuum cleaner is a machine that cleans rugs, floors, upholstery, cushions, walls, and other things. It draws dust and dirt out of such things by creating a vacuum, as described in the article before this one. The vacuum cleaner was invented and named by a man named H. C. Booth, in 1901. Since then many improvements have been made in the vacuum cleaner, and many new kinds have been made, but all vacuum cleaners are based on the same principle: When a vacuum is created by an air pump, air rushes in to fill the vacuum and carries with it any dust or dirt in its path. An electric motor turns a pump. The pump sucks the air out of the cleaner. This creates the suction that draws substances into the cleaner.

One type of vacuum cleaner looks like a carpet-sweeper. It has a base that rolls on the floor. Attached to the base is a long handle. Strung to the handle is a large, strong bag. A vacuum pump sucks air out of the bag, causing air from the room to rush into the bag, carrying dust with it.

Improved models of the same kind are still used by many people, but most modern vacuum cleaners are of the "tank type." Instead of a large canvas bag, the tank-type cleaner has a small bag inside it. This bag can be emptied, or it can be thrown away and a new bag inserted. Rubberized metal tubes can be attached to the tank and will reach high walls and even ceilings, as well as floors, chairs, shelves, and so on. A great variety of nozzles, or ends for the hose or tube,

makes possible cleaning in hard-to-get-at places.

Modern vacuum cleaners may also be reversed so that they blow air instead of sucking it. The tube can be attached to a jar or other receptacle containing some kind of fluid and the fluid can be sprayed. Paint can be sprayed by a vacuum cleaner, and fluids that kill moths and their eggs can be sprayed into closets to protect clothing.

Valencia

Valencia is the fourth-largest city of Spain. It is the capital of a province that also is named Valencia. The city is in the eastern part of Spain, on the Turia River, and its seaport on the Mediterranean is Grao, two miles away at the mouth of the Turia. About 500,000 people live in Valencia.

The city is a market and export center for the many agricultural products of the rich surrounding plain. It is also a busy commercial city, with shipyards, railroad and machinery factories, oil refineries, and textile mills. Other plants process food products such as vegetable oils, rice, and meat.

Valencia has an old section with white buildings, domes of colored tile, and narrow streets, such as were built by the Moors, a Mohammedan people that once ruled most of Spain. The modern section has spacious streets and fine buildings. Valencia is noted for its parks and gardens. It has many old churches, museums, and art galleries. The University of Valencia was founded in 1411.

The city of Valencia has been known since Roman times. In the 8th century it was the capital of an independent kingdom under the Moors. During the Spanish Civil War it served for some time as the headquarters of the Loyalist government. It was taken by Francisco Franco's forces in 1939.

There is also an important city in Venezuela named Valencia.

VALENCIA, SPAIN. Population (1974 estimate) 498,150. Capital of Valencia province. On the Turia River.

Valentine

On Valentine's Day, which is celebrated on February 14 each year, people send cards expressing love and affection to each other. The day is named after two different saints named Valentine. Both of them lived many hundreds of years ago in Rome, Italy. No one knows why these saints are associated with the custom of sending messages of love. The name of these saints is used because February 14 is the feast day on which they are honored and celebrated.

The custom of sending greetings on St. Valentine's Day has grown through the years, and now millions of people in the United States, and many other countries, send greeting cards or Valentines. Some of them are sent by lovers. These are beautifully decorated with hearts and Cupids and other symbols of love. Some people send "comic Valentines." A few of these are clever, but most of them are not really comic and can even be unkind or cruel.

Candy and flowers also are often sent on Valentine's Day.

Valhalla

Valhalla is the name the Germanic peoples gave to the palace of their chief god, Odin, in their mythology (stories of gods and goddesses) of many years ago. These peoples, who lived in Germany, Norway, Denmark, and other parts of northern Europe, told of a place "over the rainbow" where the gods dwelt. The chief god, Odin, lived in the palace called Valhalla. All heroes who had fallen bravely in battle went there to live with Odin. Those who died a peaceful death were not permitted to dwell in Valhalla. The Norse peoples considered it glorious to die in battle, so that life ever after could be spent in the wonderful palace of Valhalla, feasting with Odin and watching entertainment and amusing themselves with fighting and hunting. See the article on MYTHOLOGY.

Valkyries

The Valkyries were nine maidens in Scandinavian mythology, the stories the ancient Germanic peoples told about their gods and goddesses. The Valkyries were the attendants of Odin, the chief of the gods. They rode through the air on horses. They delivered Odin's orders during battles, which concerned who was to win and who was to die. The Valkyries were also thought to represent storm clouds. They wore robes made of feathers, and whoever could get hold of their robes was supposed to be able to control them. In some of the stories the daughter of Odin, Brünnhilde, was also one of the Valkyries. An opera by the German composer Richard Wagner is called *Die Walküre* (German for *The Valkyries*). It is one of the RING OPERAS, about which there is a separate article.

Valley Forge

Valley Forge is one of the most honored spots in the United States. It is about twenty miles from Philadelphia, Pennsylvania. At Valley Forge the soldier of the Continental army, who fought for American freedom in the Revolutionary War, weathered a terrible winter and lived to fight successfully against England. This was in the winter of 1777 and 1778. General George Washington commanded the American troops and spent the winter at Valley Forge with them.

In the fall of 1777 the British forces defeated the Americans at Philadelphia and occupied that city. General Washington withdrew his troops to Valley Forge for the winter. They made camp in log huts. When the severe winter weather set in, the huts offered little protection against the cold and snow. There was not enough food, and many of the men had no shoes and walked on the icy ground with bleeding feet.

General Washington set such an example of courage to his men that most of them stuck it out. Only a few deserted.

When spring came, the Americans were ready to fight again. In the spring of 1778, Valley Forge became the first military training camp in United States history. Here the German general, Baron von Steuben, became the "drill-master" of the American army. Day after day he trained the troops for the battles ahead.

He took a ragged, untrained force and made it a well-disciplined army.

There are many stories of the courage and endurance shown by George Washington and his men at Valley Forge.

Valley Forge is now maintained as a historic site by the state of Pennsylvania. Visitors may now see some of the log cabins and the headquarters of General Washington. There are also markers that indicate where the troops of each of the original thirteen colonies were quartered.

Valparaiso

Valparaiso is the second-largest city of Chile. It is the most important port on the Pacific coast of South America and is the home port of a big fishing and whaling fleet. A railroad across the Andes Mountains connects it with Argentina.

Valparaiso is in a beautiful natural setting on the wide Valparaiso Bay. The city is in three sections: the port, with old buildings and narrow, crowded streets; the Almendral, the commercial section, which also is on the waterfront; and Los Cerros, the residential district, high up in the hills behind the coastal strip. Elevators and funicular railroads carry passengers to Los Cerros. Valparaiso has a mild climate and is a popular tourist resort, especially the suburb of Viña del Mar, four miles from the city, where there are many beautiful beaches.

About 290,000 people live in Valparaiso. There are factories that manufacture metal and petroleum products, sugar, chemicals, paint, textiles, and many other things. The city is the seat of the Catholic University, the law school of the University of Chile, and technical, mining and art schools.

Valparaiso was founded about 1536 by the Spanish governor of Chile. It was raided many times by Dutch and English pirates during its early years. The city has suffered severely from earthquakes; it was almost destroyed in 1906 and many lives were lost in 1965. Each time the city has rapidly been rebuilt.

VALPARAISO, CHILE. Population (1974 census) 289,456. Seaport on the Pacific Ocean. Founded 1536.

vampire

A vampire is an imaginary creature that people used to fear, much as they feared witches and ghosts. A vampire was supposed to be a corpse (the body of a person who had died) that rose from its grave at night and sucked the blood of living men. It appeared either in human form or in the form of some animal, such as a dog or cat or toad. A vampire could be killed only by driving a wooden stake through its heart or by chopping off its head with a gravedigger's shovel, but it could be driven away by a sight of the Cross (of Jesus) or by the smell of garlic. The most famous story about vampires is a book called *Dracula*, by an English writer named Bram Stoker. A kind of bat that sucks the blood of other animals is called the vampire bat.

Martin Van Buren

Martin Van Buren was the eighth President of the United States. He served from March, 1837, to March, 1841. He was the first President who was born in the United States after it declared its in-

dependence from England. His administration was troubled by a financial panic, and he was blamed for it at the time, but later historians decided that it was caused by the mistakes of Andrew Jackson's administration and Martin Van Buren was given credit for his sound and courageous action. As President, Van Buren established the Treasury of the United States.

Van Buren was a pleasant man and popular personality, but he had a reputation for extreme cautiousness. One story about him tells of his being in a railroad train (which was a new thing in those times) when the train passed a flock of sheep. "Fine-looking sheep, aren't they, Mr. President?" asked the man beside him. "Well," Van Buren replied, "they look all right from *this* side." The story probably is not true, but it was told to give an idea of what the President was like.

HIS EARLY YEARS

Martin Van Buren was born in Kinderhook, New York, on December 5, 1782. His father was a farmer and tavern-keeper, and young Martin attended only local schools. Later he worked as a clerk in a law office and became a lawyer in 1803. He practiced law in New York City for the next twenty-five years.

HOW HE BECAME PRESIDENT

Martin Van Buren became interested in politics early in his career. He served in the United States Senate from 1821 until 1828. His first term ended in 1827, and though he was re-elected for a second term, he resigned in 1828 when he was elected governor of New York. He was 46 years old at the time.

Van Buren did not finish his term as governor. He resigned to accept from President Andrew Jackson an appointment as Secretary of State. He served in that position from 1829 to 1831, and a year later he was elected Vice President under Andrew Jackson, for Jackson's second term.

In the Democratic convention of 1836, Martin Van Buren was nominated to run for President against William Henry Harrison, a Whig. Van Buren won the election, but served only one term. He was nominated again in 1840 but was defeated by the same man he had beaten four years before, William Henry Harrison.

Van Buren's administration suffered from financial problems brought on by Jackson's term. Van Buren angered many people by the measures he took to

straighten out the government's financial problems. Years later, most experts agreed that he had been wise in most of his decisions. They agreed also that in founding the Treasury of the United States he had made an important and constructive move. Before that, the government had been forced to keep its money in private banks owned and operated by private firms and individuals, and the people as a whole could lose if one of these banks failed.

Another thing that helped to cause Van Buren's defeat for re-election in 1840 was his opposition to taking Texas into the United States. Most of the people in the country were in favor of accepting Texas as a state. One reason they elected William Henry Harrison was that he had announced himself in favor of admitting Texas.

History shows that Van Buren made a serious mistake in this opinion, and the great land area of Texas became a state in 1845.

HIS LATER YEARS

After his term as President was over, Martin Van Buren remained active in politics. He worked for a time with anti-slavery Democrats and was part of a group that formed a new party, the Free-Soil Party. He ran for President in 1848 on the Free-Soil Party ticket, but he was defeated by Zachary Taylor. Later he returned to the Democratic Party.

Van Buren did not think the southern states had a right to secede (withdraw from the United States) in 1860 and 1861. Though he was a Democrat, he supported the Republican President, Abraham Lincoln, on the secession issue.

Van Buren lived to see the start of the Civil War, but not its end in 1865. He died in the town where he had been born, Kinderhook, New York, on July 24, 1862, at the age of 80.

MRS. MARTIN VAN BUREN

Hannah Hoes Van Buren was born in 1783 in the same part of New York state as the future President. She and Van Buren were classmates in school and were married in 1807. They had four sons.

Mrs. Van Buren died in 1819, at the age of 36.

Vancouver

Vancouver is a seaport in British Columbia. It is the third-largest city of Canada and is the most important Canadian port on the Pacific coast. Vancouver is in southwest British Columbia, near the border of the state of Washington. It has a fine harbor on Burrard Inlet, an arm of the Straight of Georgia between Vancouver Island and the mainland.

About 426,256 people live in Vancouver. Many of them work in the shipping industry, on the docks or in the exporting of grain, lumber, fish, metals, and minerals. There are the huge grain elevators, shipbuilding and lumbering plants, and factories where steel products, furniture and other things are made. Vancouver is the seat of the University of British Columbia. An outstanding feature of the city is Stanley Park, 900 acres of recreation area almost entirely surrounded by water. It contains a zoo, gar-

dens, and a memorial to the friendship between the United States and Canada.

The site of Vancouver was settled as the town of Granville in 1875. Eleven years later it was renamed in honor of Captain George Vancouver, who had explored the region in 1792.

VANCOUVER, BRITISH COLUMBIA. Population (1973) 426,256. Seaport on the Pacific Ocean. Founded, 1875.

Vancouver Island

Vancouver Island is a part of British Columbia, Canada. It is the largest island off the west coast of North America, with an area of about 12,408 square miles. More than 325,000 people live there. The city of Victoria, capital of British Columbia, is on Vancouver Island.

Most of Vancouver Island is mountainous, being a continuation of the Coast Mountains of British Columbia and the Olympic Mountains of Washington. The mountains are covered with thick forests, and lumbering is one of the island's most important industries. Some of the people are miners, who dig coal, gold, and copper. Dairy farming and fishing are important occupations.

The island was first visited by Captain James Cook in 1778, and a few years later it was surveyed by Captain George Vancouver, for whom it is named.

Vandals

The Vandals were a tribe of warlike people who first became known about two thousand years ago. They probably originated in what is now northern Germany, but soon began to spread south and west to what is now France. They grew more powerful and more numerous, and about 1,500 years ago they crossed the Pyrenees Mountains between France and Spain and conquered much of what is now Spain. The section of Spain called Andalusia comes from the earlier name Vandalusia, which was the headquarters of the Vandals.

From Spain the Vandals crossed the Strait of Gibraltar and conquered most of the Roman possessions in North Africa. They later established fleets of pirate ships and menaced all the peoples of the Mediterranean area. They attacked Rome and robbed and pillaged so much that ever since that time any destructive robbers are given the name "vandals."

About 1,400 years ago the soldiers of the Eastern Roman Empire, which had its capital at Constantinople (now Istanbul, Turkey), set forth to conquer the Vandals in North Africa. These troops of Emperor Justinian I finally succeeded in defeating the Vandals. Since that time the Vandals as a separate people have disappeared from history.

Vanderbilt

Vanderbilt is the name of a family that has been prominent in American business and social life for more than a hundred years. The family is best known in connection with the building and management of railroads.

The first member of the family to become nationally known was Cornelius Vanderbilt, who was usually called Commodore Vanderbilt. He was born in 1794

on Staten Island, New York, which is now a part of New York City. At first he was in the shipping business, running a ferry line between Staten Island and Manhattan and then a line of ships on the Hudson River. In 1858 he sold his ships and entered the railroad business. He formed the New York Central Railroad, which became one of the two biggest in the United States, and he built the first railroad from New York City to Chicago. He was 83 years old when he died, in 1877. He made very big gifts to the United States government during the Civil War and to charitable and educational causes.

The Commodore's son, William Henry Vanderbilt, doubled the Vanderbilt fortune and and made it the largest in the United States. He was born in 1821 and died in 1885. He and his sons, William Kissam Vanderbilt and Cornelius Vanderbilt II, did almost as much as the Commodore in extending the network of railroads through the northeastern United States. After them, Harold Stirling Vanderbilt was a leader in railroad management, and also invented contract bridge, the world's most popular card game, and in yachting won the AMERICA'S CUP (about which there is a separate article) three times.

Other prominent members of the family include George Washington Vanderbilt, who built a famous estate called Biltmore (now part of a national park) in western North Carolina; Consuelo Vanderbilt, for many years Duchess of Marlborough, who wrote her memoirs in a book called The Glitter and the Gold; and Alfred Gwynne Vanderbilt, who assembled a famous stable of race horses.

VANDERBILT UNIVERSITY

Soon after the close of the Civil War, the original Commodore Cornelius Vanderbilt, a northerner, gave a million dollars to found Vanderbilt University in the southern city of Nashville, Tennessee. He explained that he did this "to strengthen the ties which should exist between all sections of our country." Several of his descendants have since made large gifts to Vanderbilt University. It is now one of the principal American universities, with an enrollment of 3,585 men and women in the spring of 1962.

Van Dyck, Anthony

Sir Anthony Van Dyck was a Flemish painter who lived about three hundred years ago. He is best known for his portraits, or pictures of one person or a group of persons. He was born in 1599 in the city of Antwerp, which was then part of the Spanish Netherlands and is now a part of Belgium. Van Dyck began to study painting at the age of 10, and his work soon came to the attention of the greatest painter of the time, Peter Paul Rubens. He worked with Rubens until, in 1620, he was invited to England. There he was made court painter under King Charles I, who also made him a knight (which gave him the right to use the title "Sir" before his name). He remained in England for the rest of his life, except for some trips to other countries. He died in 1641. His name is sometimes spelled Vandyke. His work includes many religious paintings, among them Elevation of the Cross, but he is best-known for his many portraits of King Charles I, members of the British royal family, and English nobles.

van Eyck, Jan and Hubert

Two of the most important painters in the history of art are Jan van Eyck and his brother, Hubert. They lived in Flanders, which is now part of Belgium. They were the founders of what is called the Flemish school of painting. (Flemish means "of Flanders.") This school, or kind of painting, used dark and rich colors, and the pictures look almost like color photographs.

Very little is known about Hubert van Eyck. He may have been born in 1366, but historians are not sure. It is certain that he died in 1426.

Jan van Eyck was probably born about 1386. He became a famous painter and also traveled on private political journeys for Philip the Good, ruler of Burgundy, who was his patron. When he did travel he had to sleep in the stable with the horses, because artists in those days were considered servants. Jan van Eyck painted many pictures before he died in 1440. Most of them are in Europe, in private homes and museums. In the Metropolitan Museum in New York City you can see The Annunciation by Jan and Crucifixion and Last Judgment by Hubert.

vanilla

Vanilla is a popular flavoring that is made from the seeds that grow inside the long pods of the vanilla orchid plant. The plant is a tropical air plant, which means that it grows without having any roots in the ground. A vanilla plant grown in the West Indies has large seed pods from which both liquid vanilla extract and grated or powdered vanilla are made.

A garden plant in the southern United States, called Carolina vanilla, is a different kind of plant entirely. It has roots that grow in the ground and lacks the seed pods of the West Indian variety. The leaves smell something like vanilla when they are bruised or crushed.

Vargas, Getulio

Getulio Dornelles Vargas was a Brazilian political leader who became president of Brazil. He was born in 1883 and when he grew up he became a lawyer. He became active in politics and in 1930 he led a revolution against the president of Brazil, Washington Luiz Pereira. The revolution succeeded and Vargas served as president for fifteen years, until 1945. During this time he put through a new constitution that put him in the position of dictator of his country. In 1945 the Brazilian Army forced Vargas out of office, but a year later he was elected to the senate, and in 1950 he again became president. In 1954 he lost the presidency again and committed suicide.

varicose veins

Varicose veins is a condition in which the veins bulge. Most often the veins of the legs are affected. The condition is caused because the blood does not flow freely through the body. Doctors are not certain why this occurs. Some doctors believe that a person can inherit varicose veins from his parents. Others think that varicose veins are caused by pressure on the back or abdomen. (A tumor or a chest inflammation causes pressure and may prevent the blood from circulating properly.) People who must stand on their feet a great deal, and those who lift heavy weights, are likely to get varicose veins. Tight clothing that prevents good blood circulation can help bring about varicose veins.

When a person has varicose veins in in his legs, his legs have a heavy feeling and he loses energy. Sometimes his legs burn or ache and have cramps. Doctors know many things that can help this condition and it can usually be cleared up.

varnish, a clear paint made of a resin: see the article on PAINT.

Vassar College

Vassar College is a college for women in Poughkeepsie, New York. It was founded in 1861 by a businessman named Matthew Vassar. The students there can work for a Bachelor of Arts or Master of Arts degree. In 1972 there were 2,041 students. During World War II a few men were allowed to attend Vassar

The campus of Vassar is beautiful and is quite large, so that nearly every student and many teachers use a bicycle to go from place to place. Vassar is the woman's college closest to the United States Military Academy at West Point, which is across the Hudson River, and the Vassar students and West Point cadets often meet at dances and parties.

Vatican City

Vatican City is the world headquarters of the Roman Catholic Church and is located in Rome, Italy. It is an independent state ruled by the Pope. Vatican City covers over 108 acres and includes the Vatican Palace, which is the Pope's residence, the Vatican Library, gardens, museums, offices, and even a radio and television station.

Vatican City is an independent state. By a treaty called the Lateran Treaty, made with the Italian government in 1929, the Roman Catholic Church was permitted to govern the Vatican City as a separate country. The Italian laws and government have no power over Vatican City.

There are about a thousand people living in Vatican City. Most of them are priests and religious students. The Pope's palace is near St. Peter's Church, which stands at the entrance to Vatican City.

The museums of the Vatican hold many of the finest paintings, sculpture and other art objects in the world. Here some of the finest Italian artists painted great religious works. In the Sistine Chapel the great painter and sculptor Michelangelo painted some of his most famous works of art, scenes from the Bible, on the walls and ceiling of the chapel.

The famous Swiss Guards guard Vatican City. They are dressed in colorful costumes designed in the style of hundreds of years ago.

Vatican City has some of the finest and most beautiful gardens in the world. It has its own radio station, observatory, and newspaper (*L'Osservatore Romano,* which in Italian means "The Roman Observer"), and it also has one of the world's greatest libraries.

Veda and Vedanta

The Vedas are four sacred books in an early Aryan religion in India, and the Vedanta is the system of philosophy, or ideas, that was developed from them.

The four Vedas are the Rig-veda, Yajur-veda, Sama-veda and Atharva-veda. All of them contain religious poems of different kinds, written in the Sanskrit language. It is not known exactly when these poems were first written, but the ideas of the earliest Veda, the Rig-veda, are thought to date back about 3,500 years.

The Rig-veda contains chiefly hymns that were addressed to the various gods of the Aryan religion. The Yajur-veda contains poems about the different ways of worshiping the gods, such as sacrificing animals. The Sama-veda has poems of worship to be said during the services. The Atharva-veda contains many prayers for long life and special charms against devils and disease.

The Vedanta is a system of ideas that was developed from the Vedas and other ancient religious writings. The most important part of the Vedanta is called the Upanishads. Religious Hindus are supposed to follow the teachings of the Vedanta, which are described in the article HINDU.

vegetables

When people speak of vegetable life they mean all forms of plant life. But when they speak of vegetables it is hard to tell exactly what they mean. Vegetables are among those plants that we eat, but we eat many forms of plant life or parts of plants that we do not call vegetables. We do not call grains and cereals vegetables, nor fruit and nuts, yet they are all forms or parts of plant life.

Some say that vegetables are any form of plant life that we cook before we eat; but this is not completely true because we also cook some fruits, and some vegetables are not cooked but are eaten raw.

It is perhaps best to say that vegetables are plants or parts of plants having a high water content that are most often eaten cooked or raw with the main course of a meal. Grains or cereals then cannot be classified as vegetables, since they have a low water content before cooking, and they are usually processed before cooking.

KINDS OF VEGETABLE

There are many kinds of vegetable. Some are the roots of plants, such as beets and carrots. Some are the stalks of plants, as asparagus, and some are the leaves of plants, such as celery, spinach, and cabbage. Some are from the blossoms as the seed corn, beans, and peas; but to be vegetable the seed must be eaten while immature. Other fruit-vegetables are tomatoes, peppers, cucumbers, and squash.

Vegetables are among the most healthful of all foods. They contain many needed vitamins and minerals that help the body to grow and gain energy. Man

has been growing vegetables for thousands of years and has learned how to grow them better all the time. Today most vegetables are grown on large farms, usually called *truck farms.* Others are sometimes grown out of their regular season in large hothouses, or greenhouses. The rapid increase in transportation, with the railroad and automobile and finally the airplane, permits farmers in warm states such as California and Florida to grow great crops of many vegetables and ship them quickly to markets in northern cities far away.

PROCESSING VEGETABLES

Fresh vegetables are the best, but after a short time many vegetables lost their freshness. Therefore great quantities of vegetables are cooked and canned almost immediately after they are picked. More and more vegetables are being quick-frozen at or close to the farms where they are grown. Quick-freezing keeps the vegetables fresh and permits them to retain their vitamins and minerals. After being thawed out at home, they must be quickly cooked and eaten.

Vegetables may be considered to include salad greens such as lettuce, cucumbers, radishes, endive, and others, plus onions, and other things. Many vegetables are pickled. The most popular are cucumbers, tomatoes, and peppers. Cabbage that has been pickled is called *sauerkraut.*

vegetarianism

Vegetarianism is a belief that animals should not be used for food. No vegetarian will eat meat or fish, but some strict vegetarians will not even take milk or cheese, because they come from animals.

Vegetarians eat vegetables, fruits, nuts, and cereals. They believe for several reasons that it is wrong to eat anything else. Some think they will be healthier if they eat only plant life, because they feel that animal life probably contains germs that could make them ill. Others believe that it is wrong for man to keep herds of animals, or to kill animals or fish for their meat. Some people are vegetarians because they believe a vegetable diet is more nourishing and will make them stronger and healthier. A few feel that it is cheaper to be a vegetarian; that meats and other foods are too expensive.

Most doctors and scientists do not argue with vegetarians, but most of them say that meat, eggs, milk and cheese contain rich body-building elements.

vein

A vein is a blood vessel or tube that carries blood from all parts of the body back to the heart. In the articles on HEART and BLOOD you can read how the blood in the body is pumped by the heart and circulates through the body in miles and miles of tubes that are called blood vessels. Arteries are blood vessels that carry fresh blood, full of oxygen, from the heart to the many parts of the body. Veins are blood vessels that carry the used blood back to the heart, to receive more oxygen.

Veins, like arteries, are somewhat like macaroni in form—thin, hollow tubes. Unlike arteries, they do not have a strong

muscular wall. An artery will not collapse when cut, but a vein will.

Because the veins have to carry blood back to the heart from the lower parts of the body, so that the blood in veins must flow uphill, something must happen to prevent the blood from falling back. Therefore there are valves located in the veins. These valves are like small trapdoors. Each time the heart beats, the blood in the veins is forced upward to the heart. As the blood pushes upward it opens the small slats or valves in the veins and flows through them. When the heart pauses in its beating, the blood is no longer being pushed and has a tendency to fall back in the veins. At this moment the flaps close, keeping the blood where it is.

If you let your arm hang down and clench your fist several times you will see little bumps in the veins of your arms. These bumps are the valves.

There are two important veins in the body. One is called the *pulmonary* vein. It carries fresh blood, rich with oxygen, from the lungs to the heart. It is the only vein in the body that has bright red blood, which gets its color from the high amount of oxygen. All other veins have darker red blood, since they are carrying blood that has given its oxygen to the cells of the body.

The second important vein is called the *portal vein.* This vein leads from the intestines, where the blood picks up food that has been digested. The portal vein carries this blood to the liver, where it leaves some of the digested food to be stored for future use.

See also the article on VARICOSE VEINS.

Velásquez, Diego

Diego Rodríguez de Silva y Velásquez was a Spanish painter who lived about three hundred years ago. He is considered one of the great painters of all time. He was born in Seville in 1599 and when he was 13 years old he began to study painting with some of the masters of his time. Ten years later, in 1622, he went to live in Spain's capital city, Madrid, and soon afterward he became the official court painter at the court of King Philip IV. Except for some years spent in Italy, Velásquez spent the rest of his life in Spain. He died in 1660, at the age of 61.

Velásquez's paintings are very realistic, which means his subjects look very true-to-life. He painted many portraits (pictures of one or more persons), and also used many subjects from the Bible, ancient legends, and history. Among his most famous paintings are *Water Carrier of Seville, Boar Hunt, Aesop, Adoration of the Magi, Crucifixion,* and portraits of King Philip IV, his brother Don Carlos, and other members of the royal and noble families of Spain.

vellum, a fine grade of parchment. See the article on PARCHMENT.

vending machine

Vending means selling; a vending machine is a machine that sells something.

Vending machines are also called coin machines or slot machines, because they are operated by the dropping of a coin into a slot, or narrow pening. The coin causes the machine to open and deliver the merchandise.

Vending machines have been known for hundreds of years. For more than fifty years they have been used in many public places to sell candy, chewing gum, drinks, and various foods, and the same kind of device has been used in telephone "pay stations." Some "player pianos" (automatic pianos) and other music-making instruments were operated by coins, and in some big cities gas meters were operated by coins, as explained in the article on the GAS METER. Even so, the number of vending machines was almost nothing compared to what it is today, when there are more than three million vending machines in the United States alone and they make more than twenty billion sales every year

The modern age of the vending machine is supposed to have begun in the middle 1920s when William H. Rowe of Los Angeles founded a company to make cigarette machines and install them in public places. During the 1930s, the soft-drink machine and the "juke box," or coin-operated phonograph, spread throughout the country, and nearly every big office and factory began to have cigarette machines, soft-drink machines, and other machines that sold candy, sandwiches, hot coffee, and other things, for the benefit of its employees. The electric refrigerator and various electronic inventions helped to make it possible for vending machines to sell many more kinds of merchandise.

The success of the vending machines encouraged their use for nearly every imaginable product. Silk or nylon stockings, books and greeting cards, handkerchiefs, medicines, and about five hundred other products are sold through vending machines. The same kind of coin-in-the-slot device is used on games of various kinds, turnstiles through which people pass into streetcars, buses, or subways, and even change-making machines that will accept a quarter and deliver five nickels or make change in other ways. At airline and railroad stations a person can buy insurance, or send someone a gift or a message, by dropping a coin in a slot.

HOW VENDING MACHINES WORK

The basic principle of the vending machine has not changed greatly in hundreds of years, though modern coin-operated machines are far different in many ways from the ones that were used only twenty or thirty years ago.

In the simplest device, the coin drops from the slot onto one end of a balanced bar that is hinged in the center. The weight of the coin pushes down the end on which it falls. This pushes the other end up and causes it to release a lock or a spring and open a door that lets the customer take his merchandise. Meanwhile, the coin has tilted the bar downward at its end, so the coin slides off the bar into a drawer below. A spring then returns the bar to its level position, ready for the next sale. Every now and then the owner of the machine takes out the

drawer and empties it of the coins that have been taken in.

The great problem of vending-machine manufacturers for many years was that dishonest people often used "slugs," pieces of worthless metal shaped like coins. Many devices have been invented to keep people from using slugs. Usually the precious metals, from which genuine coins are made, are heavier than the cheaper metals. Therefore, in some machines the bar would be balanced so that a light metal would not push it down far enough to make the machine work. However, some cheap metals (such as lead) are even heavier than the copper, nickel and silver in coins. Therefore other devices had to be tried. Some machines were made to take only coin-shaped tokens that had a special pattern of holes cut through them. The customer could buy these tokens for use in the machines they fitted. Inside these machines, the token would stop at a point where a key-like device would press against it. If it was a genuine token, it would fall the rest of the way and operate the machine; if it was a worthless slug, it would be pushed aside and drop out of the machine into a "coin return."

Use of new electronic devices, including the "electric eye," have made it much easier to detect worthless slugs in vending machines, so that tokens are seldom used and it is even safe for the machine to return change when the customer wants to make a purchase that costs ten or fifteen cents but does not have the exact coins required. Some machines will sound an alarm when someone tries to use a slug. The use of slugs is counterfeiting and can be severely punished.

The mechanisms on the most modern vending machines are much different from those on the old-fashioned machines. Instead of moving a bar, the coin operates an electric switch that causes the machine to deliver the merchandise. On some machines, the customer moves a dial to select the particular kind of merchandise he wants the machine to deliver. The most elaborate of these devices are found on the juke boxes, where the customer may select any one of a hundred different "sides," and may select five or more sides to be played in order, and the machine will select and play the desired records.

THE VENDING-MACHINE BUSINESS

Vending machines are usually owned by "operators" who buy them from the manufacturers and place them in "locations" at which people buy from them.

The center of manufacturing vending machines is Chicago, though many are made in other cities. The manufacturers sell the machines to operating companies in various cities. A few of the manufacturers rent the machines instead of selling them.

The operating company may own anywhere from five or ten machines to thousands of machines of different kinds. The operating company buys all the merchandise needed to stock the machines. A representative of the operating company approaches a store or restaurant or office or other "location" and suggests that his company install a machine there. If

the owner of the location agrees, the operating company puts in the machine at its own expense. Every few days (or every day, in the case of some machines that sell food or drinks), a service man from the operating company visits the location, fills the machine with merchandise to replace what has been sold, and takes out the money that the machine has taken in. Modern machines have counting mechanisms that make a record of how much the machine has taken in. Part of this money goes to the operating company, to pay for the use of the machine and for the merchandise and the service; part of it goes to the owner of the location.

Though the vending-machine business makes its profits only in pennies and fractions of pennies, it has become a very big business. During the 1950s, about ten billion dollars worth of merchandise was sold in the United States each year through vending machines.

veneer

A veneer is a thin slice or sheet of wood that is glued on the outside surfaces of furniture and other wooden things to strengthen and beautify them. Veneer is used chiefly to save valuable wood. A veneer of a fine, expensive wood can be used to cover an inferior, cheap wood.

Veneers have been used for more than two thousand years. At first they were used only in furniture and cabinetwork to cover up less beautiful woods, and they were made from mahogany, walnut, and other woods with a beautiful color and grain. Today many other kinds of wood are used, and veneers are put on boxes, baskets, door panels, and many other things. Good veneers for these purposes are made of wood from the red gum tree. The wood of the yellow pine is used for less expensive veneers. Other kinds of wood used are maple, tulip, cottonwood, oak, fir, birch, spruce, walnut, and cedar.

Veneers can be cut as thin as 1/200 of an inch thick. First, logs or pieces of wood are boiled. Then they are cut with a knife. They may be cut by the rotary process, in which a log is turned on a lathe and held against a stationary knife. They may also be cut by the slicing process, in which the logs are first quartered (cut in four) and then are sliced with a rotating knife.

Veneers are applied also to the outside surfaces of plywood. See the article LUMBER.

Venezuela

Venezuela is the northernmost country in South America. It is on the Caribbean Sea and is bordered by Colombia to the west, Brazil to the south, and Guyana to the east. Venezuela is the world's third-ranking oil-producing nation, after the United States and the Soviet Union. It has an area of 352,148 square miles and is the sixth-largest country in South America. Venezuela is more than twice as large as California. Over ten million people live there.

The word *Venezuela* means "little Venice" in Spanish, and the name is said to have been given it by explorers who thought of Venice when they saw the

native huts perched on poles along the shores of Lake Maracaibo.

THE PEOPLE OF VENEZUELA

Most of the people of Venezuela are *mestizos,* or mixtures of Spanish and Indian blood. The few other Venezuelans are mostly of Spanish descent. There are a few tribes of pure Indians, some of whom are still very primitive and fierce, and a few people of Negro descent. After World War II, many Europeans emigrated to Venezuela, most of them skilled workers from Italy, Austria, Germany, and Portugal. Within ten years, more than 350,000 of these people had settled in Venezuela. About 30,000 United States citizens live and work there.

The principal language of Venezuela is Spanish, and most of the people belong to the Roman Catholic religion. Everyone must go to school from the age of 7 to 14, but this is difficult for children who live in country regions far from schools. All education, including college, is free. In 1958 about 40 per cent of the people could not read or write. By 1965 this figure had been reduced to 20 per cent.

HOW THE PEOPLE LIVE

The people of Venezuela were for hundreds of years divided into two groups, the wealthy white people and the very poor mestizos and Indians. Under the government's tremendous building program the standard of living of all the people has been greatly improved. New schools and hospitals are being built in all regions, the death rate has been sharply cut, and malaria has been almost wiped out. New highways and roads make it easier for farmers to market their products.

Although most of the petroleum and other industries of Venezuela are owned by foreign businessmen, Venezuela has a law that three-quarters of the employees of all businesses must be citizens of Venezuela. Many of the people work in the oil fields and in industries that process petroleum. Construction is a major industry, and there are many workers in the building trades. There are important iron deposits, which has led the government to build a steel industry. Other min-

erals mined are gold, diamonds, coal, copper, asbestos, and manganese.

About one-fifth of the people of Venezuela are farmers, and coffee is the most important crop. Others are sugar cane, rice, cotton, tobacco, wheat, and potatoes.

Venezuela was once an important cattle-raising country, but this occupation has declined in recent years. Pearl fishing is done off the Venezuelan islands in the Caribbean Sea, especially the island of Margarita.

WHAT VENEZUELA IS LIKE

Venezuela has four principal geographic regions. In the northwest, on each side of Lake Maracaibo and running across the Caribbean coastline, there are mountain ranges divided by deep valleys. In these mountains are most of the principal cities and most of the agriculture and industry.

Between the mountain ranges of the northwest is that hot lowland region around Lake Maracaibo, which is the center of the great petroleum industry. The city of Maracaibo, at the entrance to the lake, is the center for the shipping of oil. Venezuela is the world's largest exporter of petroleum products.

South of the coastal mountains is the vast Orinoco basin, the valley of the Orinoco River. This region includes the plains called the *llanos,* where for hundreds of years great herds of cattle were grazed by the *llaneros,* Venezuela's cowboys, who are similar to the *gauchos* of Argentina. The *llanos* are called the "Wild West" of Venezuela, but the government has built roads and encouraged new settlers so that farming is gradually taking the place of cattle-raising.

Near the mouth of the Orinoco is a region of dense tropical jungles. South of the Orinoco the land rises into the Guiana Highlands, which extend into British Guiana and Brazil. The Highlands make up more than half of Venezuela. They are densely forested and still largely unexplored. Some of the mountains rise to more than 9,000 feet, and swift rivers rush down into the valleys, forming magnificent waterfalls. Angel Fall, on the Caroni River in the southeast, is the highest uninterrupted drop in the world, falling more than 3,000 feet. The Highlands have much of Venezuela's mineral wealth. Gold, diamonds and iron are mined there.

Venezuela has more than a thousand rivers, the greatest of which is the Orinoco, navigable for about a thousand miles across the country to the Colombia border. The principal lake is Lake Maracaibo, which is connected with the Gulf of Venezuela and the Caribbean Sea through a channel about 30 miles long.

The climate of Venezuela is tropical, with dry and rainy seasons. The weather becomes cooler on the mountain slopes and is cold above 6,000 feet.

Many wild animals live in Venezuela. In the forests there are monkeys, jaguars and other members of the cat family, and deer. Brilliantly colored birds are found, including the egret, whose feathers used to be gathered for plumes, and parrots, macaws, pelicans, flamingos, and many different kinds of eagle. In the valleys are found sloths and anteaters. There are many reptiles, including big snakes such

as the anaconda, boa constrictor, coral snake, and bushmaster.

HOW THE PEOPLE ARE GOVERNED

Venezuela is a republic. It has a president, a parliament that makes the laws, and a constitution that protects the rights of the people. The parliament has two houses, a Senate and a Chamber of Deputies. The President is elected for a five-year term. Everyone between the ages of 21 and 65 is required to vote.

PRINCIPAL CITIES

The leading cities of Venezuela, with populations from the 1961 census, are:

Caracas, population 1,371,875, the capital and largest city. There is a separate article on CARACAS.

Maracaibo, population 456,000, the second-largest city, a great oil center in northwest.

Barquisimeto, population 203,000, the third-largest city, an industrial and agricultural center in the northwest on the Pan American Highway.

Valencia, population 161,443, the fourth-largest city, a trading and manufacturing center in the north, near Lake Valencia.

Ciudad Guayana, a new city in the southeast, started by the government in 1960. The area was undeveloped but was rich in mineral resources. By 1965 the city's population was 100,000.

VENEZUELA IN THE PAST

The coast of Venezuela was first seen by Christopher Columbus on his third voyage to America in 1498. In 1520 the first permanent European settlement in South America was made by Spaniards at Cumana, on the Caribbean Sea. The region was governed by Spain until the 1800s. Venezuela was the first South American colony to fight for its independence. In 1810 the citizens of Caracas overthrew the Spanish governor. Simon BOLIVAR led a revolutionary movement that drew up a formal declaration of independence. The Spanish government brought in more troops and Bolívar was forced to flee to Haiti, but he returned in 1817 and set up a government that elected him president of Colombia, which at that time included Venezuela and Ecuador as well as the present land of Colombia. In 1830 Venezuela withdrew and formed an independent republic.

For many years Great Britain and Venezuela carried on a dispute over the boundary between Venezuela and British Guiana. This dispute was settled in 1899 by a commission established by the United States. This was one of the most important occasions on which the Monroe Doctrine was invoked, under which the United States asserted its right to keep peace in the Americas.

In 1908 Venezuela came under the control of Juan Vicente Gomez, who ruled as dictator for 27 years. The country made great progress during this period, largely because oil was discovered and Gomez called in foreign experts to exploit it. The government became very prosperous, but Gomez was ruthless and cruel in his management of internal affairs and he put to death or imprisoned anyone who thought the people should have greater freedom. After the death of Gomez, Venezuela had a succession of presidents. Like most South American countries, it has had many revolutions and changes of government, but Venezuela has made great prog-

ress toward democracy. In the early 1950s the country began its greatest period of prosperity and peaceful growth.

VENEZUELA. Area, 352,150 square miles. Population (1964 estimate) 8,459,000. Capital, Caracas. Language, Spanish. Religion, Roman Catholic. Government, republic. Monetary unit, the bolivar, worth 22 cents (U.S.). Flag, horizontal bars of yellow, blue, and red; arc of seven white stars in blue portion.

Venice

Venice is a city in Italy at the north end of the Adriatic Sea. It is one of the most famous cities in the world because of its unusual construction. Venice is built on 118 small islands in a lagoon, or river-like arm of the Gulf of Venice. Instead of streets the city has canals, and all traffic is by means of boats called gondolas and other boats. Through the center of the city curves the Grand Canal, and there are more than 150 other canals, crossed by about 400 bridges. A causeway, or road built through water, connects Venice with the main land.

The Grand Canal is the principal "street" of Venice. Along its banks are some of the city's famous churches and palaces. At one end are the Doge's Palace, which has a magnificent collection of paintings, and the Church of St. Mark, where St. Mark is believed to be buried. This church has a noted campanile, or bell tower. A famous bridge across one of the canals is the Bridge of Sighs, which connects the Doge's Palace with an old prison. At the other end of the canal is the Rialto Bridge, which is lined with shops. Most of Venice's beautiful churches and palaces are full of art treasures by great Venetian painters of the past, including Titian, Tintoretto, Bellini, Fra Bartolomeo, and others.

About 367,000 people live in Venice. The city has a famous glass-making industry and manufactures jewelry and art objects. There is also some shipbuilding, and textiles and laces are made.

The first inhabitants of Venice were an ancient tribe called Veneti, who gave the city its name. They established a number of separate communities on the islands. As early as 1,250 years ago these had joined together into a state under a *doge,* or magistrate. Venice became one of the strongest states of Europe, with many territories and colonies. About four hundred years ago, Venice lost much of its power. Venice became part of the kingdom of Italy in 1866.

VENICE, ITALY. Population (1974 census) 367,323. Capital of Veneto and Venezia province. On the Gulf of Venice.

Venizelos, Eleutherios

Eleutherios Venizelos was a Greek statesman and premier of Greece (head of the Greek government). He was most prominent about the time of World War I. Venizelos was born in 1864 on the island of Crete, which then was ruled by Turkey. He studied in Greece and at the age of 22 he became a lawyer. He returned to Crete to practice law, and soon became active in the government. In the 1890s Crete rebelled against Turkish rule, because it wanted to become a part of Greece. The rebellion finally succeeded, with the help of Greece, and in 1899 Venizelos was appointed Crete's Minister of Justice and set about organizing a new code of laws for the island.

In 1909 Venizelos was called to the Greek capital, Athens, as a political adviser and a year later he was appointed Premier of Greece. During the time Venizelos held this position Greece became involved in the Balkan Wars, which are described in a section of the article on the BALKANS. In 1914 World War I broke out. Venizelos wanted Greece to join the Allies, while the King of Greece favored neutrality. In 1917 the king, Constantin, had to abdicate (resign as king) and Venizelos took Greece into the war against Germany.

Venezelos helped the Greek people to form a republic in 1924. In 1933 he organized a revolt against Panages Tsaldares, who was then premier, but the revolt did not succeed and Venizelos was forced to flee the country. Two years later the Greek government changed back to a monarchy, headed by King George II. The king pardoned Venizelos, who died a year later, in 1936, at the age of 72.

ventriloquism

Ventriloquism is the art of using the voice so that it seems to be coming from someplace else, or from a dummy. The word *ventriloquism* means "speaking from the stomach," but a ventriloquist does not actually speak from his stomach. He controls his voice by tightening the muscles of his chest and neck, and by letting the air escape slowly from his lungs through his larynx, the part of the throat where voice sounds are created. A good ventriloquist can keep his mouth almost completely closed and his lips almost perfectly still while speaking. He keeps his tongue back from his teeth and does not move it as much as a person does in ordinary speaking. By long practice and training, a ventriloquist can imitate almost any number of voices and make it appear that they are not coming from his mouth.

A ventriloquist does not "throw his voice," but he creates an illusion of doing so. The illusion (making something seem what it really is not) is created by distracting the attention of the people who are listening to him. He does this by turning his eyes in a certain direction and making them think the sound is coming from that direction, or by making some other motion to deceive the listener.

A ventriloquist usually works with a dummy, a large doll that can be manipulated easily. The ventriloquist sticks one hand through the back of the dummy and works levers that control the movements of the dummy's mouth, eyes, and body. When the ventriloquist wants to seem to speak through the dummy's mouth, he makes the dummy's lips move, and the dummy seems to be speaking.

For nearly a hundred years it has been traditional in show business that a ventriloquist's dummy should have an Irish name. Sometimes the dummy becomes as famous as the ventriloquist, or even more so. An example is "Charlie McCarthy," the name given to the dummy used by the ventriloquist Edgar Bergen.

Venus

Venus was worshiped as the goddess of love by the ancient Romans. The Greeks called her Aphrodite. Many stories are told about Venus. One of the best-known is about her love for the boy Adonis, which is told in the article ADONIS. Venus was often opposed to Mars, the god of war, because she loved all men and did not want them to be killed in battle. Her son, Cupid (also called Amor, and known as Eros to the Greeks), was the god of love. Venus was also the goddess of spring and growth, and the month of April was set aside as her month.

Many temples were built to Venus, including a great one built in Rome by the emperor Hadrian in the year 135. Venus has been used as a subject by the greatest artists of all time. Perhaps the world's most famous statue is the *Venus de Milo,* by an unknown artist. It was found on the Greek island of Melos, or Milo, in 1820. Among the great artists who have shown Venus are the Greek sculptor Praxiteles and the painters Botticelli, Giorgione, and Watteau. William Shakespeare wrote a poem about *Venus and Adonis.* See also the article on APHRODITE.

Venus

Venus is the second planet from the sun and nearest to earth of all the planets. It is 67 million miles from the sun, and about 26 million miles from earth at its closest. Because it is about the same size as earth and weighs about four-fifths as much, it is sometimes called our twin planet. After the sun and moon, Venus is the brightest object in the sky, and can easily be seen with the naked eye. It appears in the east just before sunrise and in the west just after sunset, and therefore is often called the "morning star" or the "evening star." It is, of course, not a star at all. Because Venus passes between the sun and earth, it has phases of light and dark as our moon does. The Babylonians recorded the movements of Venus 4,000 years ago. After the telescope was invented, astronomers lost interest in Venus, a planet that was always hidden by clouds, had no moons, no rings like Saturns, nor markings such as Mars has. However, in the 1950's and 1960's, the Russian *Venera* and American *Mariner* series of space explorations discovered a great deal about Venus. Its surface temperature averages about 900° F. and may reach 1,300° F. where the sun's rays hit directly. The dark side of Venus is nearly as hot due to the thick layer of clouds that prevents cooling. It was found that Venus rotates on its axis in the opposite direction from other planets, and its "day" is about 243 earth-days long. Its orbit around the sun (its "year") takes about 225 earth-days. Venus seems not to have a magnetic field, a radiation belt, nor any changing seasons. Life as we know it would be impossible on Venus.

Venus's flytrap

Venus's flytrap is a plant that catches and digests insects. Plants that do this are called *insectivorous.* Venus's flytrap grows wild only in the swamps of North and South Carolina. Its white flowers are about an inch across, with stems about a foot tall.

It is the leaves that catch insects. Each leaf is in two sections covered with very sensitive hairs. When an insect touches the hairs, the leaf immediately closes up

and traps the insect. The plant absorbs the juices from the dead insect's body.

verb

A verb is a word that tells what someone or something does, or what is done to something or someone. If you say, "I sing," the word "sing" is a verb that tells what you do. A verb is one of the parts of speech. A part of speech is a word that has a particular duty when you say it or write it. The duty of a verb is to show action. Every group of words that makes a sentence must have a verb in it.

A verb has different forms, depending on who did something and when it was done. Often these different forms are shown by changes in the spelling of the verb. At other times they are shown by using two verbs together.

PERSON, NUMBER, AND TENSE

The "who" is shown by the *person* and *number* of the verb. The "when" is shown by the *tense* of the verb.

Person. You say "I have" but you say "He has." *Have* and *has* are different forms of the same verb, because they are used for different persons. The person speaking is called *first person,* the person spoken to is called *second person,* and the person spoken about is called *third person.* Hundreds of years ago, a different form of the verb was used for each person. The English language has been simplified since then, but there are still cases in which the change is made. You say "I am" (first person), "You are" (second person), and "He is" (third person). You say "I walk" but "He walks."

Number. The number of a verb shows whether the action is done by one person or thing, or by more than one. A verb that shows action by one is called *singular* and a verb that shows action by more than one is called *plural.* You say "The boy walks" (singular) but "The boys walk" (plural). In modern English there are not many changes of spelling to show number.

Usually the same form of the verb is used for both singular and plural.

Tense. Tense means "time." Nearly all verbs must be changed in form (spelling) to show the tense, or when the action takes place. There are six tenses:

Present tense (The boy walks)
Past tense (The boy walked)
Perfect tense (The boy has walked)
Future tense (The boy will walk)
Past perfect tense (The boy had walked)
Future perfect tense (The boy will have walked)

In every tense except the present and perfect tense, two or more verbs must be used to show the time of the action. The added verbs are *have* in its various forms to show action that has already happened and *will* or *shall* in their various forms to show action that is going to happen. These added verbs are said to "help" the main verb.

REGULAR AND IRREGULAR VERBS

The forms of a verb can be *regular* or *irregular.* All regular verbs change their forms in the same way. The verb "walk" shown in the example above is a regular verb. The form used in the past and per-

fect tenses was made by adding *ed.* Every regular verb is changed by adding *ed* in the same cases. The forms of irregular verbs are formed in different ways. They are always different from the regular verbs and usually they are different from one another. The irregular verb "sing" changes to "sang" and "sung," not to "singed." The irregular verb "take" changes to "took" and "taken," which is different not only from the regular form but also from the irregular forms of the verb "sing."

The form of a verb that shows the perfect tenses is called the *past participle.* When you say "I have walked," "I have sung" or "I have taken," you are using the past participle of the verb along with the verb "have."

Each verb also has a *present participle.* This is formed by adding *ing.* The present participle is used to show the same kind of action that the verb itself shows. For example, "I am walking" (which is called the *present progressive*) or "I was walking" (which is called the *past progressive*). The present participle can also be used as a noun, as when you say "Walking is fun," and it can be used as an adjective, as when you say "The walking man turned the corner." There are separate articles about these other parts of speech, NOUN and ADJECTIVE.

The simple form of a verb, such as "walk" or "have," is called the INFINITIVE and there is a separate article about it.

MOOD AND VOICE

The *mood* of a verb helps to show the full meaning or intention of the person who uses it. There are three moods. The *indicative* mood is used to make a simple statement or ask a simple question, as when you say "I see the boy" or "Do you see the boy?" The *subjunctive* mood is used to show that something is not certain or is not so. You do not say, "If I am you, I will not go." You say, "If I were you, I would not go." The "were" and "would" are in the subjunctive mood and show that the speaker knows "I" am not "you." Most often, the subjunctive is used after "if." Until about fifty years ago, careful speakers and writers of English made various changes in the form of a verb to show that they were using the subjunctive mood. This is seldom done now, but we still use "were" and "should," "would," and "could," to show the subjunctive mood.

The third mood is the *imperative.* This is used to give a command, as when you say, "Go and open the door."

The *voice* of a verb shows whether the action is performed by someone or something, or to someone or something. If you say "I hit the ball," you are using the *active* voice, which shows that you do or did something. If you say "I was hit by the ball," the "was hit" is a *passive* voice of the verb, showing that something was done to you. The passive voice is formed by using the verb "to be" in its various forms with the past participle of the main verb.

TRANSITIVE AND INTRANSITIVE VERBS

A verb is either *transitive* or *intransitive.* A transitive verb shows that something is done to something. In the sen-

tence "I fixed the lamp," the verb "fix" is transitive; it shows that something was done to the lamp. A transitive verb is said to take a *direct object.* In this case, "lamp" is the direct object. An intransitive verb does not take a direct object. It simply shows that something was done. When you say "I breathe" you are using an intransitive verb.

Some verbs are always transitive verbs and some verbs are always intransitive verbs, but many verbs can be used either way. When you say "Now I will sing," you are using "sing" as an intransitive verb. If you said "Now I will sing a song," you would be using "sing" as a transitive verb, taking the direct object "song."

verbena

Verbena is a name given to any plant of a group of flowering plants that are used in gardens to provide attractive colored blooms from early summer to autumn. Verbena blossoms may be white, lavender, or red, and they grow in flat clusters on low, spreading plants. Lemon verbena is familiar as a house plant. Its leaves have a pleasant, lemon scent. It is usually grown indoors in pots or in window boxes, but can be placed outdoors through the warm summer weather.

Verdi, Giuseppe

Giuseppe Verdi was an Italian composer, or writer of original music, who lived about a hundred years ago. He is best known for his operas, which are plays in which the words are sung rather than spoken. Today more of Verdi's operas than those of any other composer are performed in the chief opera houses of the world.

Verdi was born in 1813 in an Italian town named Roncole. At the age of 7 he learned to play the organ. He wanted to go to the conservatory (school of music) in Milan, but the director there said Verdi lacked ability and would not let him study. Instead Verdi studied with the director of Milan's great opera house, La Scala. In 1839 his first opera was produced. It was called *Oberto,* and was fairly successful. He continued to write operas and also religious music for the rest of his life. He died in 1901.

The operas of Verdi that are most popular today include *Macbeth, Rigoletto, Il Trovatore, La Traviata, Un Ballo in Maschera, La Forza del Destino, Don Carlos, Aida, Otello,* and *Falstaff.* Among his other works are the *Manzoni Requiem Mass,* two symphonies, and six piano concertos.

Verdun

Verdun is a town in France that was the scene of the longest and bloodiest battle of World War I. The town lies close to the border between France and Germany, and the French had built forts to protect it. For more than two years the Germany Army made one attack after another on Verdun, at times using forces of several hundred thousand men and the heaviest artillery bombardments of the entire war. The French adopted the slo-

gan "They shall not pass," and defended Verdun so desperately that the Germans never did take it. General Henri Philippe Petain, who commanded the French forces during the period of the heaviest fighting, became a national hero by turning the Germans back. The battles at Verdun are often used as an example of the way generals in World War I wasted human life. About a million men were killed or wounded there, yet neither side ever gained more than a few miles. The bitterest fighting took place in 1916 and 1917.

See the article on WORLD WAR I.

Vermeer, Jan

Jan Vermeer was a Dutch painter who lived about three hundred years ago. He was born in 1632 in Delft, where he spent the rest of his life. He began to paint when he was a boy, but worked slowly and did not paint many pictures. Most of his paintings are portraits, or pictures of people. He died in 1675. Among his best-known works are *Diana at Her Toilet*, *The Lace Maker*, and *The Painter in his Study*. Vermeer was also called Jan van der Meer van Delft.

Vermont

Vermont is one of the New England states, in the eastern part of the United States. It was the fourteenth state to be admitted to the United States, the first to join the Union after the original thirteen colonies. Its nickname is the "Green Mountain State," which is the English meaning of the French words *vert mont*, from which the state gets its name The principal mountains of Vermont are the Green Mountains.

In area, Vermont ranks 43rd among the states, with 9,609 square miles. In population it ranks 49th, with about 444,000 people living there. It became a state in 1791. The capital is Montpelier.

THE PEOPLE OF VERMONT

More than three hundred years ago the first permanent settlements were made in Vermont by colonists from Connecticut and Massachusetts. These colonists were for the most part of English and Scottish descent. About a hundred years ago immigrants came into Vermont from Canada and from Italy, Russia, Czechoslovakia, Poland, and other European countries. About 30,000 people in Vermont are foreign-born, and the greatest number of these are French Canadians. There are very few Negroes and Indians in the state.

The people of Vermont are called typical Yankees. They are independent and conservative. They are characterized as being hard-working people who have little time for talking. Most of the people in the state are Republicans.

Vermont is an agricultural state. Many of the people live in rural areas and make their living by farming. In Vermont the farms are apt to be small and owned by individual farmers. Dairy farming is the most important kind, but many farmers raise poultry, particularly turkeys. The chief crops grown are corn, hay, oats, and apples.

Since World War II, more and more people have moved into the large cities, where there are factories that make machines, wood products and paper, and other things. Lumbering has always been important to the state.

Vermont has rich deposits of stone and mineral ores. Many of the people work in the mines. Others make a living by tapping the maple trees for sap, which they boil down and make into maple syrup, sugar, and candy. Most of the maple-sugar products sold in the United States come from Vermont.

In recent years, many of the people of Vermont have made their living taking care of the tourists who flock into the state both summer and winter.

The original settlers were Congregationalists, but today the leading Churches are Roman Catholic, Methodist, and Baptist.

WHAT VERMONT IS LIKE

Vermont, as its name states, is a region of tree-covered mountains. The Green Mountains, the most important, go through the state from north to south in the central part. The highest peak is Mount Mansfield, 4,393 feet high. In the southwest are the Taconic Mountains, which form part of the western boundary between Vermont and Massachusetts. In the western part of the state, along Lake Champlain, are the Red Sandrock Hills. Between these mountains lies a fertile valley. Just east of the Green Mountains are the Granite Hills, which start in the central part of the state and extend into Canada. Here valuable mineral deposits are found. There are other, smaller mountains within the state.

There are many lakes and rivers in Vermont. The largest lake is Lake Champlain, more than 100 miles long. It lies between Vermont, New York, and Quebec. This lake on the west and the Connecticut River, which forms the eastern boundary of the state, are the two principal waterways. Several rivers cross the state, cutting canyons through the Green Mountains.

More than a third of Vermont is covered with forests. The land along the Connecticut River is a fertile plain.

Hunters find many animals in the woods of Vermont, particularly deer. Trappers find many muskrats, minks, and raccoons. The rivers and lakes are well supplied with bass, pike, and trout, and game birds, such as partridge and woodcock, are plentiful.

Vermont is cool in the summer, with an average temperature of about 70 degrees, and cold in the winter, with an average temperature of about 24 degrees. Vermont has railroads that go to most parts of the state, and many miles of paved highways. There are also many miles of unpaved highway, but almost all parts of the state can be reached by public roads. There are airports in the major cities.

THE GOVERNMENT OF VERMONT

Vermont, like other states, has a governor and a legislature. The governor is elected for a two-year term. The legislature is composed of a Senate and a House of Representatives. The members of both houses are elected for a two-year term. Judges are elected by the legislature for a two-year term. The capital is Montpelier. There are 14 counties.

There are about 99,000 pupils attending public elementary and high schools. Among the principal colleges and universities are:

University of Vermont and State Agricultural College, at Burlington. Enrollment, 3,-6,221 men and women in 1971.

Middlebury College, at Middlebury. Enrollment, 1,595 men and women in 1971.

Bennington College (for women), at Bennington. Enrollment, 550 in 1971.

Norwich University (for men), at Northfield. Enrollment, 1,098 in 1971.

St. Michaels College (for men), at Winooski. Enrollment, 1,148 in 1971.

Trinity College (for women), at Burlington. Enrollment, 442 in 1971.

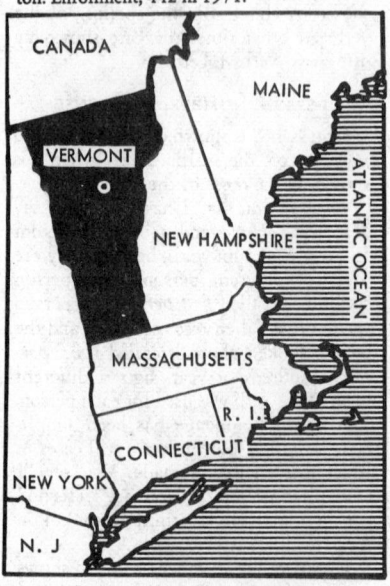

CHIEF CITIES OF VERMONT

The leading cities of Vermont, with populations taken from the 1970 census, are:

Burlington, population 38,633, the largest city in the state, industrial and education center, in the northwest.

Rutland, population 19,293, the second-largest city, marble quarrying and manufacturing center, in the west central part of the state.

Bennington, population 14,586, the third-largest city, textile and paper manufacturing center, in the southwest.

Brattleboro, population 12,239, the fourth-largest city, textile and printing center, in the southeastern part, on the Connecticut River.

Barre, population 10,209, the fifth-largest city, granite and industrial center, in the east central part of the state.

Montpelier, population 8,609, capital of the state. There is a separate article about MONTPELIER.

VERMONT IN THE PAST

Vermont was first explored by Samuel de Champlain, the great French explorer, in 1609. Champlain went up along the course of the lake that is now named for him. In 1724 the first permanent settlement was made at Fort Dummer, near the present city of Brattleboro, by settlers from New Hampshire. Other settlements were made in the area by the English and French.

At the end of the French and Indian Wars, the territory was claimed by England and the region became part of the New Hampshire colony. Later it was claimed by New York.

During the Revolutionary War the settlers in Vermont fought on the side of the colonists. They called themselves the Green Mountain Boys and were led by Ethan Allen, a famous Vermonter. In 1777 the colonists in Vermont declared their independence. They called their colony New Connecticut but soon changed its name to Vermont. The colony remained independent until 1791, when it was admitted to the United States as the fourteenth state.

There were fewer than 100,000 people living in Vermont when it became a state, but soon people from other New England colonies and from Canada came there to live.

The people of Vermont were strongly against slavery from the beginning; their first constitution had prohibited the keeping of slaves in the colony. When the Civil War broke out, thousands of Vermonters volunteered to fight on the side of the Union.

Two presidents of the United States, Chester Alan Arthur and Calvin Coolidge, were Vermonters. Coolidge, who took his oath of office at his father's farm in Vermont, is thought by many to typify the Vermont native.

The state is economically important chiefly for its agriculture and its attraction for tourists.

PLACES TO SEE IN VERMONT

Shelburne Museum, near Burlington, 40 acres, with 30 colonial and early American buildings.

Green Mountains National Forest, 580,520 acres, in the southern part of the state, on U.S. Route 7. Scenic beauty; beginning of Long Trail, hikers' 250-mile.

Calvin Coolidge's birthplace, at Plymouth, about 25 miles southwest of White River Junction, in the south central part, near U.S. Route 4.

Granite quarries at Barre, in the east central part, on U.S. Route 2. Cutting and polishing of granite.

Mount Mansfield State Forest, 20,944 acres, about 20 miles east of Burlington, in the northwest, on State Highway 15. Highest mountain peak in the state; 100 miles of ski runs and trails.

VERMONT. Area, 9,609 square miles. Population (1970 census) 444,330. Capital, Montpelier. Nickname, the Green Mountain State. Motto, Freedom and Unity. Flower, red clover. Bird, hermit thrush. Song, "Hail, Vermont." Admitted to Union, March 4, 1791. Official abbreviation, Vt.

Verne, Jules

Jules Verne was a French writer who wrote many popular novels of the kind that are called "science fiction" today. In these novels he imagined inventions and developments that seemed scientifically possible but had not yet been worked out, and he wrote about them as though they actually existed. For example, in one of his most popular books, called *Twenty Thousand Leagues Under the Sea*, he wrote about a submarine that could do many things that submarines actually can do today; but he wrote the book in 1869, more than twenty years before the modern submarine had been developed.

Verne was born in 1825. He studied to be a lawyer, but he preferred to write and his first book was so successful that he never had to do anything else. In various books he wrote about a trip to the center of the earth, a trip to the moon, a balloon somewhat like the airships that were developed years later, and similar subjects. His most popular book was *Around the World in Eighty Days*. A New York newspaper sent one of its reporters, a young woman named Nellie Bly, to see if she could get around the world in eighty days. She made it in even less time. Verne wrote so many books that some of them have not been published yet. He died in 1905.

Veronese, Paolo

Paolo Veronese was a great Italian painter who lived about four hundred years ago. He became one of the chief masters of the Venetian school of painting, a style of painting that was developed in Venice. He is sometimes called the "painter of pageants," because he often painted pictures of feasts and other celebrations.

Veronese's real name was Paolo Cagliari. He was born in 1528 at Verona, Italy, where he began as a boy to paint. He then went to Venice and remained there for the rest of his life, except for some short trips to other cities. He was often asked to decorate churches and other buildings with his frescoes, which are wall paintings done on wet plaster. Among these are a series of banquet scenes he did in a number of monasteries. The most famous of these is *The Marriage at Cana*, which is now in the Louvre, in Paris, France. Veronese died in 1588 at the age of 60. Among his frescoes are those in the Library of St. Mark's Cathedral in Venice, and his paintings include *The Raising of Lazarus, Holy Family,* and *Mars and Venus.*

Veronica, Saint

The Gospel of St. Luke, in the Bible, tells how Jesus carried his cross to Calvary and was followed by a crowd of women. Later a story was told about a woman who wiped Jesus' face with her veil and a miracle occurred: A picture of Jesus' face was left on that veil. This picture was called "Veronica," from the Latin words *vera* and *icon,* meaning "true image." Later the woman herself was called Saint Veronica.

Verrazzano, Giovanni da

Giovanni da Verrazzano (also spelled Verrazano) was an Italian who explored for France in the 16th century. In 1524, he sailed into New York Bay and became the first white man known to see the Hudson River. He was probably born in Florence in 1485 and may have been killed by Brazilian Indians in 1528. The Verrazano-Narrows Bridge, in New York City, is named for him.

Versailles

Versailles is a famous suburb of Paris, France. About 85,000 people live there. Versailles is most famous for the Palace of Versailles, which stands at the center of the city and was the residence of French kings for more than a hundred years. This magnificent palace was built for King Louis XIV of France, nearly two hundred years ago, at such enormous cost that the people of France were very indignant. It contains apartments for the royal family, a gallery of mirrors, and corridors lined with paintings by famous artists. The palace is surrounded by beautiful gardens containing fountains, statues, and pools. There are two smaller palaces on the grounds, the Grand Trianon, built by Louis XIV; and the Petit Trianon, which was built by Louis XV and later given to Marie Antoinette by Louis XVI.

Many historic events have taken place

French Press & Inform. Serv.

The palace built at Versailles by King Louis XIV more than 325 years ago remains one of the world's most imposing buildings. The Treaty of Paris, which ended the Revolutionary War, and the Treaty of Versailles, which ended World War I, were among those signed here.

in the Palace of Versailles. The treaty between France and Great Britain that recognized the independence of the United States was signed there in 1783. In 1789 citizens of Paris marched on the Palace and seized the king, at the beginning of the French Revolution. The establishment of the German Empire was proclaimed there in 1871. The Peace Congress that ended World War I was held in the Gallery of Mirrors, and the Treaty of Versailles was signed there in 1919.

Versailles, Treaty of

The Treaty of Versailles was an agreement that ended World War I. It was made in Versailles, France, in 1919, about six months after the actual fighting ended. The treaty forced Germany, which had lost the war, to give up many possessions and rights to the Allied nations, which had won.

At the conference that led to the treaty, the "Big Four" were Georges Clemenceau, Premier of France; David Lloyd George, Prime Minister of Great Britain; Woodrow Wilson, President of the United States; and Vittorio Orlando, Premier of Italy. Japan and other countries that had joined the Allies, but had not done as much of the heavy fighting, were also represented.

Germany was forbidden to have more than a small navy and army. Germany had to agree to pay a large amount of money (called *reparations*) to the Allied nations. The amount was later fixed at about $33,000,000,000. In addition, France got the provinces of Alsace and Lorraine, which the Germans had previously won from France in war; Great Britain got various African and island colonies that had belonged to Germany; Italy got some of the territory of Germany's ally, Austria-Hungary; and smaller German possessions were given to Belgium, Denmark, and Japan.

President Wilson wanted nothing for the United States except the assurance of peace. He insisted that the Germans and their allies give up important possessions, but they were to go to Poland and other new independent countries and not to the United States. Wilson was heartbroken when the other countries proved to be interested only in increasing their territories and their military power and not in assuring peace. In his list of FOURTEEN POINTS, about which there is a separate article, Wilson had said what he thought the peace treaty should be. The Treaty of Versailles was not the kind of treaty he had wanted, except that it did lead to the formation of new countries that gave some of the European peoples the independence they had long wanted. These countries were Yugoslavia, Czechoslovakia, Poland, Latvia, Lithuania, and Estonia.

The Treaty of Versailles also set up the League of Nations, which Wilson had wanted; but it did not give the League enough power to prevent future wars.

The United States never accepted the Treaty of Versailles. No treaty can be made without the consent of the Senate, and the Senate objected chiefly to joining the League of Nations.

The German government protested that the treaty was unfair. Germany accepted the treaty because it had to, but later it refused to live up to the treaty. Historians agree that the treaty was hard on Germany, but point out the fact that when Germany had conquered Russia, earlier in the war, the Germans made the Russians sign a much harsher treaty (called the Treaty of Brest-Litovsk).

See also the articles on WORLD WAR I, the SAAR, and Woodrow WILSON.

vertebrate, any animal that has a bony skeleton with a backbone: see the article on ANIMAL LIFE.

Vespucci, Amerigo

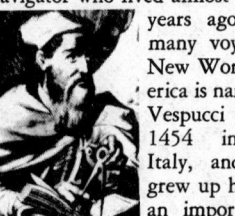

Amerigo Vespucci was an Italian navigator who lived almost five hundred years ago. He made many voyages to the New World, and America is named for him. Vespucci was born in 1454 in Florence, Italy, and when he grew up he worked in an important trading house there. He then went to Seville, Spain, where he worked for a business that supplied ships that sailed to the West Indies. Vespucci soon became interested in the New World, and in 1497 he began his first voyage. It took him eighteen months, and he sailed a great distance along the coast of South America. In the following years he made several other voyages that he later wrote about. His writings were read throughout Europe and caused mapmakers to use his name for the New World. Vespucci died in 1512.

Vesta

Vesta was the Roman name of the goddess of the hearth fire in the mythology of the ancient Romans and Greeks, the stories they told about their gods and goddesses. The Greeks called their goddess of the hearth Hestia. The Greek hero Aeneas was supposed to have taken Vesta with him from Troy, along with images of the Penates, or household gods. In the ancient Roman home, the hearth was the central part of the house and the members of the family sat around it for their main meal of the day. Before eating this meal they would make a sacrifice to Vesta and to the Penates.

Rome had one large temple to Vesta, who was represented not by a statue but by a fire burning on an altar. This fire was kept burning continuously by priestesses known as the vestal virgins. There were six vestal virgins, all of them young unmarried women, and each of them served for thirty years. They had certain special rights and were greatly respected by all the people. However, if they broke their vow of chastity (for example, by marrying secretly) they were punished by being buried alive. Vestal virgins were chosen from girls between the ages of 6 and 10 whose parents were free Roman citizens (that is, not slaves).

Vesuvius, Mount

Mt. Vesuvius is a volcano in southern Italy, eight miles from Naples. It is the only active volcano on the mainland of Europe. Vesuvius began as a submarine volcano, and its eruptions gradually built up earth and lava into a 4,000-foot mountain. The shape of the summit changes with each eruption, and the sides are scarred from many rivers of boiling lava. On the west slope is an observatory from which studies of the volcano's activity are made. Mt. Vesuvius has been erupting at intervals since the year 79, when it destroyed the ancient cities of Pompeii, Herculaneum, and Stabiae. The next violent eruption was in 1631, when several villages were destroyed. During the following centuries the volcano became more active, and severe eruptions occurred in 1779, 1794, 1822, 1872, 1906, and 1929.

The most recent eruption was in 1944, during World War II. At that time a group of United States Army Air Force planes was stationed on a field near the mountain. The eruption of Vesuvius covered the planes with hot ash and damaged most of them so severely that they could not be used again. Several towns in the vicinity were destroyed by the flow of hot lava.

A scenic railroad for tourists runs around the base of Mt. Vesuvius, and a funicular railway carries visitors to the edge of the crater, which is more than two thousand feet across. On the lower slopes of the mountain the soil is extremely fertile. The villagers grow grapes, citrus fruits, and vegetables. They live in constant danger of another eruption.

Veterans' Administration

The Veterans' Administration is an agency of the United States government. A veteran is anyone who has been a member of one of the armed services of the United States. Congress has passed laws that call for certain benefits to veterans, and the Veterans' Administration carries out these laws.

The Veterans' Administration keeps a record of all veterans. There are more than 22,000,000 names on its lists. To some of these it pays pensions, and in many cases pensions are paid to the widows and children of veterans who have died. The Veterans' Administration has hospitals in all parts of the United States, and at these "VA hospitals" veterans can receive free medical treatment for any trouble connected with their military service. In some cases veterans can receive money for schooling, receive incomes when they cannot find work, or borrow money. The Veterans' Administration operates its own "insurance company," the largest in the world, in which veterans can buy limited amounts of life insurance at low cost. At Veterans' Administration offices in many cities veterans are given information and advice as to how to get these benefits.

Veterans of Foreign Wars

Veterans of Foreign Wars of the United States, called the V.F.W., is an organization of veterans, or former soldiers, who have served in United States forces overseas. The organization was founded in 1899 to help soldiers who served in the Spanish-American War, the Philippine Insurrection, and the China Relief Expedition. Today the organization has about 1,300,000 members, including veterans of both World Wars and of the Korean War.

One of the most important early activities of the V.F.W. was working to have Congress pass laws that would grant pensions, hospitalization, and other benefits to veterans of World War I. It also helped to have the G.I. Bill of Rights passed for World War II and Korean veterans.

Another important activity is its National Rehabilitation Service, which helps veterans obtain pensions, hospitalization, vocational training, education, and other benefits provided by law. It also assists their families when they are entitled to such benefits.

Since 1925 the V.F.W. has had a National Home at Eaton Rapids, Michigan, for children whose fathers were disabled or died during overseas service. In addition it coöperates with other agencies in community services, such as providing better recreation and educational facilities for everyone.

Members are male officers, enlisted men, and men who were honorably discharged, who served in any United States armed service during any foreign war, insurrection or expedition for which the government issued a campaign badge. There are about ten thousand units, or "Posts," in places in the United States and its territories and possessions. Each Post is a separate club, running its own affairs. There is also a Ladies' Auxiliary, which the mothers, wives, widows, sisters and daughters of veterans may join.

veterinary medicine

If you own a pet dog or cat that becomes sick, you take it to a doctor who specializes in the diseases of animals. This doctor is a doctor of veterinary medicine, also called a veterinary surgeon or a veterinarian. Veterinary medicine is the science of treating the sicknesses of animals, especially domesticated animals such as cats, dogs, cows, sheep, pigs and horses.

A veterinarian must go to college to learn his profession. Before entering a veterinary school or college, a student is required to take a pre-veterinary medical program consisting of studies of language, literature, and the basic sciences. After entering veterinary college a stu-

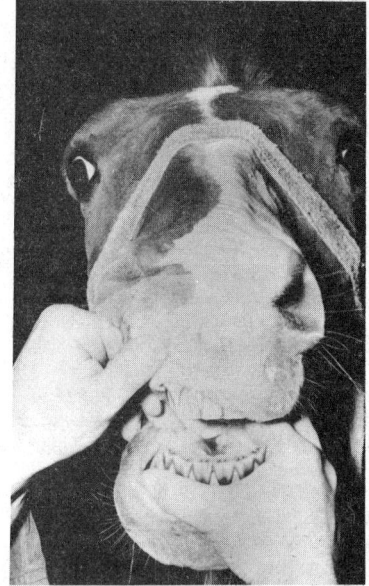

A veterinarian examining a horse's mouth.

dent studies four more years learning all about the different parts of the animal body and what each part does and how disease interferes with the various parts. After graduation, some veterinarians set up city offices and treat pets. Others work in rural areas doing what they can to help farm animals. Many veterinarians work for state and national governments, some of them as inspectors.

IMPORTANCE OF VETERINARIANS

Veterinarians are very important to the health of all of us. The animals that work for us and that give us food are subject to diseases, and can pass these diseases along to human beings. The veterinarian keeps these animals healthy. Veterinarians have many ways of testing animals such as cows, sheep, and pigs, and fowl such as chickens, ducks, and turkeys, to make sure they are healthy and that their flesh does not bear germs that can infect human beings. Just as regular doctors now have more and better ways of curing human disease, so veterinarians have progressed in their knowledge of treating animals. Diseases that once were dangerous and widespread among animals are now under control or entirely eliminated.

The skill of modern veterinarians also insures the happiness and health of our pets. If you have a pet that does not seem to be acting properly, does not eat well, or seems to have difficulty moving about, a veterinarian will probably be able to cure him.

Though most veterinarians treat domesticated animals, some specialize in wild animals in zoos and circuses.

veto

The power of veto is the power to turn down a law passed by a legislature, or lawmaking body. The President of the United States has the power of veto over laws passed by Congress, and the governors of states of the United States have the power of veto over laws passed by their states. The heads of many governments have power of veto.

The Constitution of the United States says that a law passed by Congress does not become effective until the President signs it. When the President returns a law to Congress without having signed it, he is said to have vetoed that law. Usually he sends a message, called a veto message, telling Congress why he was not willing to sign the law. Congress still has the power to pass the law "over the President's veto," if two-thirds of the members of the Senate and two-thirds of the members of the House of Representatives vote for the law after the President has vetoed it. This happens occasionally but not very often.

In state governments, the governor can veto a law and the legislature can pass it over his veto in much the same way.

THE POCKET VETO

The President can wait ten days before he returns a law to Congress, with or without his signature. If he has not returned the law within that time, it becomes effective even if he has not signed it. One exception comes when Congress adjourns (ends its session) before the ten-day period is ended. In that case, the law

cannot become effective without the President's signature.

Sometimes, when Congress is due to adjourn within ten days or less, the President can veto a law by doing nothing about it. He simply fails to sign it and waits until Congress adjourns. This is called a "pocket veto" because the President does the same thing as putting the law in his pocket and leaving it there until it is too late.

VETO IN THE UNITED NATIONS

In the Security Council of the United Nations, important acts cannot be taken unless all five of the permanent members vote in favor of it. The five permanent members are the United States, the United Kingdom (Great Britain), the Soviet Union, France, and China. When one of those nations votes against an important question, it is said to exercise its "veto power." The Soviet Union has used this power many times, and other permanent members have used it occasionally. It is not the same kind of veto as the veto in the United States and state governments.

viaduct, a bridge that crosses dry land: see the article on BRIDGE.

Vice Presidency

The Vice President of the United States can become the most important man in the country if the President dies, but otherwise the duties assigned to him by the Constitution are very few and his powers are even fewer. He is the presiding officer of the Senate, but the only time he can cast a vote is when there is a tie, which seldom happens. The first man ever to be Vice President was John Adams, who was elected in 1788, when George Washington was first elected President. Adams was not pleased with the office. He wrote to his wife, "My country has in its wisdom contrived for me the most insignificant office that ever the invention of man contrived or his imagination conceived."

During the first few years of the United States, the candidate who got the most votes for President was elected and the candidate who was second became Vice President. The result was that the President and Vice President belonged to different political parties. After there had been four elections under this system, the Constitution was amended so that candidates for President and Vice President run as a team (called "running mates") and win or lose the election together.

In recent years, the President has usually given the Vice President more powers and duties than the Constitution calls for, so that the Vice President has become an important member of the government.

Vichy

Vichy is a city in central France. It was the headquarters of the French government from 1940 to 1944, when German troops occupied northern France during World War II. About 30,000 people live in Vichy. It has long been one of Europe's leading health resorts, because of mineral springs nearby. The water from these springs, called Vichy water, is bottled and sent all over the world. Any kind of sparkling or carbonated water is

often called "vichy," but real Vichy water is not a sparkling water.

Vichy has many hotels and mineral baths. It was founded about two thousand years ago by the Romans, who called it Aquae Calidae (place of hot waters).

THE VICHY GOVERNMENT

In 1940, the Germans invaded France and the French government surrendered. Another French government was set up, with Marshal Henri Philippe Petain the head of it and Pierre Laval the premier. It was called the Vichy government because Vichy was made its capital. Petain and Laval favored the Germans, rather than their former allies, Great Britain and the United States. The former government of France, the Third Republic, was voted out of existence, and a new constitution was written. In the meantime General Charles de Gaulle had set up another French government abroad, and this was recognized by the Allies as the official French government.

The Vichy government was controlled by such men as Jean François Darlan and Jacques Doriot, besides Laval. Laval especially was regarded as a traitor to France. Petain gave him dictatorial powers, which enabled him to send Frenchmen to Germany to work for the Nazis and to set up a rigid police system within France.

In 1944 the Allies invaded France and Laval moved the Vichy government to Germany, where it later fell apart. Laval himself surrendered to the Allies and was executed as a war criminal.

Vicksburg

Vicksburg is a city in Mississippi. It is the state's chief river port on the Mississippi River. Vicksburg is built on a bluff above the river, where the Yazoo River flows into the Mississippi.

About 25,000 people live in Vicksburg. It is both a market and transportation center for the cotton, cattle and lumber produced in the surrounding region. There are factories that process these products and other factories that make house trailers, metal products, clothing, and chemicals.

The first settlement on the site of Vicksburg was a French fort called St. Pierre, which was built in 1715 and wiped out by the Yazoo Indians in a massacre fifteen years later. In 1791, Spaniards built Fort Nogales on the same site. The fort came into the possession of the United States in 1798 and its name was changed to Fort McHenry. The town of Vicksburg was founded by the Rev. Newitt Vick in 1814, and it was named for him.

BATTLE AND SIEGE OF VICKSBURG

Vicksburg was the center of important fighting during the Civil War, in 1862 and 1863. It was a very important city because the Union forces needed it to control the Mississippi and cut off the western Confederate States from the eastern ones. General Ulysses S. Grant commanded Union forces that won a victory over Confederate forces commanded by General John C. Pemberton. On May 22, 1863, Grant's army besieged Vicksburg (surrounded the city so that no food could be taken in), and on July 3 the city

was threatened with starvation and had to surrender.

VICKSBURG, MISSISSIPPI. Population (1970 census) 25,478. On the Mississippi and Yazoo Rivers. County seat of Warren County.

Victor Emmanuel

Victor Emmanuel was the name of three kings of Italy.

Victor Emmanuel I became the king of 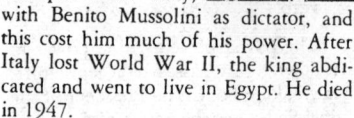 Sardinia, a part of Italy that was then a separate kingdom, in 1802. In 1821, France forced him to abdicate (resign as king). He was born in 1759 and died in 1824.

Victor Emmanuel II was the first king of united Italy. Until 1848 Italy consisted of several separate kingdoms and states, and most of them were controlled by Austria. Victor Emmanuel II became king of Sardinia in 1849 and king of united Italy in 1861. He was a very good king. He set up a democratic government, and insisted on freedom of religion. He was born in 1820 and died in 1878.

Victor Emmanuel III, the grandson of Victor Emmanuel II, was king of Italy through both World Wars. He was born in Naples in 1869 and became king at the age of 31, in 1900. In 1922 he allowed the Fascist Party to take dictatorial power in Italy, with Benito Mussolini as dictator, and this cost him much of his power. After Italy lost World War II, the king abdicated and went to live in Egypt. He died in 1947.

Victoria

Victoria is the capital and second-largest city of the province of British Columbia in Canada. It is at the southern tip of VANCOUVER ISLAND, about which there is a separate article. Victoria is important as a shipping point for the products of Vancouver Island. About 195,000 people live there, and the city is principally a residential one, with a very British air about it. It is a popular tourist center. Victoria's industries include fish-canning and the manufacture of paper, furniture, and woodworking and mining equipment. It is the home port of a deep-sea fishing fleet.

Victoria was founded in 1843 by the Hudson's Bay Company, as a fur-trading post. It became the capital of Vancouver Island in 1859 and the capital of British Columbia in 1866. A suburb of Victoria is Esquimalt, the site of an important naval base, west of the city.

VICTORIA, CANADA. Population (1974 estimate) 195,800. Capital, province of British Columbia.

Victoria, Queen

Victoria was Queen of England (and other British countries) for sixty-four years, longer than any other British sovereign had ever reigned. During this period, which began a little more than a

hundred years ago, Great Britain became the strongest and richest nation of the world.  From the time Victoria became queen, in 1837, to the time of her death, in 1901, Great Britain's rule was extended over an area five times the size of all Europe, with colonies in almost every part of the world. England became a great industrial nation, and its people moved from the country to the city, from farms to factories. England's government became more democratic, for laws were passed that gave the people more voice in their government. The time of her reign became known as "the Victorian Age" and stood for peace and prosperity.

THE QUEEN

Victoria was born in 1819. She was a granddaughter of King George III. Her father died a year after her birth, and when her uncle, King William IV, died without leaving sons who might inherit the throne, Victoria became Queen of England. Her mother, Princess Louise-Victoria of Saxe-Coburg, and her governess, Louise Lehzen, were both German, and Victoria spoke German before she spoke English and better than she spoke English.

When Victoria began to reign in 1837, she was only 18 years old. Many Englishmen feared that she might be swayed by foreign advisers, but she took as her principal adviser William Lamb, Lord Melbourne, who was Prime Minister and leader of the Whig political party in Parliament.

When Victoria was 20 she fell in love with her first cousin, Prince Albert of Saxe-Coburg-Gotha, a small German country. She married him in 1840. Victoria had to propose marriage to Albert, because her high rank prevented him from proposing to her. He remained her principal adviser as long as he lived, and was a very wise one.

They lived a respectable married life that became a model for people throughout Europe and America, and they had nine children. When Prince Albert died, in 1861, Victoria was so grieved that she retired from public life.

Victoria was brought back to public life by her friendship with Benjamin Disraeli, the leader of the Tory (later the Conservative) Party. He was her trusted adviser from 1868 until his death in 1881. Under Disraeli's guidance Victoria took more interest in setting up British colonies abroad. Her friendship with Disraeli led her into conflicts with Disraeli's rival, William Ewart Gladstone, leader of the Liberal Party, but Gladstone too was a great minister for her. Disraeli obtained a new title for Victoria in 1876, Empress of India.

In 1887 Victoria celebrated her golden jubilee, or fiftieth year as queen, and in 1897 her diamond jubilee, or sixtieth year. Hundreds of thousands celebrated these occasions with her. When she died in 1901, at the age of 82, three kings and an emperor marched in her funeral procession, together with members of every royal family of Europe. She was succeeded by her eldest son, Edward VII.

THE VICTORIAN AGE

Because Victoria was so greatly admired, people throughout the world tried to live as she did. Victoria had certain set ideas; she was opposed to women marrying again after the death of their first husbands. She never remarried after Albert's death, but honored his memory by erecting statues of him all over Great Britain. She believed in freedom of religion, but favored the Church of England over other religions. She believed in womanly modesty, and often criticized Queen Elizabeth I for lack of it. These ideas, which have come to be known as "Victorian morality," in turn influenced the literature, art and even the furniture of the time. The heroes and heroines in Victorian novels are sedate and prim, and Victorian poetry is often didactic (teaches a lesson). Victorian art, architecture (buildings) and interior decoration show a desire for large size and fancy designs that would glorify the hugeness and wealth of the British Empire.

Victoria Falls

Victoria Falls is one of the great waterfalls of the world. It is on the Zambezi River in south central Africa. The falls are more than a mile wide. They are separated into several sections by tiny islets at the edge of the precipice. The waters plunge into a chasm that is only 400 feet wide. The chasm has a narrow opening called the "Boiling Pot," through which the water rushes out of the chasm and back into the river's course.

The highest point of Victoria Falls is about 350 feet. The water crashes into the chasm, sending a cloud of spray as high as 5,000 feet into the air with a roar that can be heard for miles. Just below the falls, the Zambezi River is spanned by a bridge. Victoria Falls was discovered in 1855 by David Livingstone and was named for Queen Victoria of England.

Victoria, Lake

Lake Victoria is the largest lake in Africa and the second-largest fresh-water lake in the world. Only Lake Superior is larger. Lake Victoria, which is also called Victoria Nyanza, is 26,828 square miles in area and about 250 feet deep. Its area is divided between Uganda and Tanganyika, with a small portion lying in the territory of Kenya. Lake Victoria is considered the first source of the Nile River. The Kagera River, which is called the headstream of the Nile, flows into the lake and the Victoria Nile flows out of it. Lake Victoria was discovered in 1858 by J. H. Speke, for whom a gulf at the southeast end of the lake is named. It was explored by Henry Morton Stanley in 1875 and was named for Queen Victoria of England.

vicuña

The vicuña is a South American hoofed animal that is raised for its fine, soft hair. It has been said that a human hair looks like coarse wire when compared with the delicate hair of the vicuña. For many years, only royalty was permitted to have clothes made of vicuña wool in Peru. Anyone who injured or captured a vicuña was subject to severe penalties. The animals were wild for hundreds of years, but today they are raised commercially. Vicuña wool is the finest of the wools borne by hoofed animals.

Vicuñas are relatives of the llama, and so are members of the camel family. Wild vicuñas live high in the Andes Mountains and usually travel in herds of ten or twelve females with one male, and their young. A full-grown male stands less than three feet at the shoulder. It is a tan color with white markings.

Vienna

Vienna is the capital of Austria. For centuries it has been one of the cultural capitals of the world, a city of gaiety and beauty and a center of science, music, and literature. It was once the seat of great empires and was one of the richest cities in Europe. But after World War I, Austria was reduced to a small country, and Vienna, a city of two million people, lost much of the banking and trading business that had made it rich. Then in 1938 the German dictator, Adolf Hitler, seized Vienna along with the rest of Austria and the next year he plunged them into World War II. When Germany lost the war, Vienna was poorer than ever.

After World War II, Vienna was divided into four parts, called zones, each occupied by one of the four principal Allied powers, the United States, Great Britain, France, and Soviet Russia. Because Russia refused to make a fair peace treaty with Austria, the occupation continued long after the war.

Meanwhile the Viennese have worked to make their city prosperous again. The parts of the city that were damaged by Allied bombs during World War II have been rebuilt, the opera and the theaters again play to packed houses, the stores are full of fine clothing, jewelry, and food, and Vienna's famous restaurants and coffee houses are thriving as if there had been no war.

Vienna's industry has been restored since the war and its great factories again produce machinery, textiles (cloth), chemicals, and food products. The city is also a center for the manufacture of luxury and fashion goods such as jewelry, leather goods, clothing, and art objects.

The population of Vienna is less than it was before the war, partly because it had many Jewish people and they were killed or driven out by Austrian and German Nazis, but nearly two million people still live and work in Vienna.

Vienna is built on the Danube River, in northeastern Austria. A branch of the river, called the Danube Canal, runs through the center of the city. The center of Vienna is called the Inner City. It was once walled, but is now surrounded by the Ringstrasse, the most famous street of the city, on which are many historic buildings. Among them is the Cathedral of St. Stephen and the former palace of the Austrian emperors. Also along the Ringstrasse are the Museums of Art and Natural History, the old Rathaus or Town Hall, the modern Parliament buildings, and Vienna University, founded in 1365 and noted especially for its medical school.

VIENNA IN THE PAST

Vienna is the English spelling of the Austrian *Wien*. The site of Vienna was an old settlement the Romans named Vindobona and made an important trade center in the Roman Empire, about two thousand years ago. In 1251 Vienna became the seat of the Hapsburg rulers of Austria. In the 1600s and 1700s Vienna was besieged by the Turks and by the French, but never fell.

About two hundred years ago Vienna rose to its position of a great capital. Many of its most beautiful buildings were built then. It was the home of great composers such as Haydn, Mozart, and Beethoven. Later it was the home of Johann Strauss, famous composer of Viennese waltzes, and of Brahms, Mahler, and other great composers. Medicine and science flourished.

In 1921, after World War I had broken up the Austrian empire, Vienna became a self-governing province of Austria. For some years it made great improvements in social welfare and public housing. Since the end of the occupation of Austria by the Allies after World War II, Vienna has again become a great cultural capital.

VIENNA, AUSTRIA. Population (1974 estimate) 1,644,976. Capital of Austria. On the Danube River.

Viet Nam or Vietnam

Vietnam is a region in Southeast Asia where war has been going on for more than twenty years, a war in which the United States became more and more involved from 1960 on. The region is divided into two independent countries of about equal size and population: The Republic of South Vietnam, and the Democratic Republic of Vietnam (usually called North Vietnam).

Most of the people of Vietnam, both North and South, are farmers or fishermen and are quite poor; see the articles on ANNAM and FRENCH INDO-CHINA. After being governed by France for nearly 100 years, then occupied by Japanese forces during World War II, they wanted independence and fought for it against soldiers sent by France to keep control of the country. The Vietnamese armies were called the Viet Minh and were helped by Soviet Russia and later by Communist

China. In 1949 France agreed that Vietnam should be a republic with a former king of Annam, named Bao Dai, as president.

The Viet Minh, led by the Communist leader Ho Chi Minh, did not agree and kept on fighting. France supported the new republic with large armies, but after the Viet Minh won a big victory at a place called Dien Bien Phu in 1954, the French people became tired of having a war so far away. In a conference of fourteen nations at Geneva, Switzerland, in 1954, it was agreed to form the present separate countries of South and North Vietnam. Ho Chi Minh headed the new Communist government of North Vietnam.

The Communists continued to plot for control of the entire country. North Vietnam helped organize a revolutionary army called the Viet Cong in South Vietnam, supplying it with materials and later with soldiers. Many South Vietnamese were glad to fight for the Viet Cong. They were poor and did not like their government, partly because most South Vietnamese are Buddhists but the government was controlled by Christians.

In 1960 President Eisenhower sent a few hundred American "advisers" to train and help the South Vietnamese military forces, and the United States supplied South Vietnam with arms. President Kennedy increased this help in 1961. In 1964 President Johnson sent American forces into actual battle against the Viet Cong, and American planes bombed supply lines and depots in North Vietnam. By the end of 1967, over 455,000 Americans were fighting the Viet Cong and the North Vietnamese. Australia, New Zealand, the Philippines, and South Korea sent men to help South Vietnam.

The war in Vietnam became a political issue in the United States. Many Americans thought the United States should take no part in the war, yet there were also many people who agreed with President Johnson and his military advisers that the United States should fight until the independence of South Vietnam was assured.

On May 13, 1968, the United States and South Vietnam entered into negotiations with North Vietnam in order to try to end the war peaceably. Even though there had been very little agreement at these Paris talks, President Nixon decided to continue them when he took office in January, 1969. In June, 1969, he announced the new Administration's program for American withdrawal from Vietnam. The United States would gradually remove its troops from Indo-China and, at the same time, prepare the South Vietnamese Army to carry the full burden of the war after American men had left. This procedure was known as the Vietnamization of the war.

On April 30, 1970, the American and South Vietnamese forces attacked Viet Cong sanctuaries in Cambodia, a country that borders South Vietnam. President Nixon said the purpose of these attacks was to capture enemy ammunition and supplies and then withdraw by July 1, 1970. Even though he called this operation a success, there was much disagreement about it in the United States.

The Paris Peace talks continued as the number of American forces gradually diminished.

Finally, on January 27, 1973, American involvement in the Indochina conflict ended. A cease-fire agreement was signed in Paris which provided for the return of all American prisoners, and by April 1, 1973, more than 590 prisoners of war returned home. Throughout the remainder of the year, many violations of the cease-fire agreement were reported with especially intense fighting in the Mekong Delta.

War continued in Vietnam, without the Americans, during the months of 1974. Then in the spring of 1975, the North Vietnamese initiated another strong offensive. By April 30, Da Nang, Phan Rang and Saigon fell to Viet Cong forces. President Thieu resigned on April 21 and the South Vietnamese government was led briefly by Vice-President Tran Van Huong. On April 27, he was in turn replaced by General Duong Van Minh, a man characterized by neutrality and an understanding with the Communists. General Minh surrendered the capital city of Saigon on April 30, 1975, to the Communists.

Then began the evacuation of the remaining American officials and their families (about 7,000 people). The evacuation additionally included some 1,400 South Vietnamese orphans. United States transport ships effected "Operation Air-Lift." One tragedy occurred which in particular reminds us of the horrors of war: On April 4, 1975, 100 innocent and orphaned children died when a defective latch on a C-58 jet plane caused a door to blow out, resulting in a devastating crash. The whole world mourned this disaster. Despite this tragedy, the evacuation flights continued until refugees, numbering in the thousands, had been flown to Guam and the American shores.

On May 16, 1975 Congress appropriated $405 million for resettlement of the refugees. Many orphaned Vietnamese children were welcomed and adopted by American families.

SOUTH VIETNAM (Republic of Vietnam). Area, about 66,000 square miles. Population, about 20,000,000. Language, Annamese (akin to Chinese), plus dialects like Thai and Lao. Monetary unit, the piastre, worth about 1 2/3 cents (U.S.). Flag, yellow with three horizontal red stripes. Capital, SAIGON.

NORTH Vietnam (democratic Republic of Vietnam). Area, about 63,000 square miles. Population, about 23,787,000. Language, Vietnamese (akin to Chinese). Monetary unit, the dong. Flag, red with a gold star in the center. Capital, HANOI.

Vikings

The Vikings were a group of warlike peoples who lived in what is now Norway and parts of Denmark, more than a thousand years ago. They were a Germanic people, ancestors of the Scandinavian peoples of today. They were among the greatest sailors of their time and they traveled in their seagoing boats from their homeland to many places in Europe, and fought and won many battles.

The long, slim boats of the Vikings were pointed at both ends. The front end had a carved figure of a snake or dragon on it. A Viking boat was moved either by a large, square sail in the center, which was used when the wind was right, or by many men pulling long oars. At least twenty men sat at the oars of a Viking boat. While they were rowing, other men were resting. By this method the Vikings could make long journeys over water.

At the height of their power the Vikings controlled Norway and most of Denmark, and made successful raids on England, Scotland, Ireland, and parts of Germany, Holland, and northern France. They were greatly feared by other peoples in northern Europe.

The Vikings are perhaps best known for the fact that they were the first Europeans to reach the land that is now called America. Although Columbus is given credit for discovering America, a Viking leader named Leif Ericsson took some of his men to the shores of America almost five hundred years before Columbus reached it. This was about the year 1000. See the article BOAT for a picture.

Villa, Francisco

Villa was a Mexican bandit who became very influential in the government of his country. He was born about 1877 and his real name was Doroteo Arrango, but after he became a bandit he was called Pancho Villa. In 1911 he led a group of farmers in support of the revolution against President Porfirio Diaz; then he supported Venustiano Carranza and helped him become president in 1914. Villa became complete master of northern Mexico, though the Mexican Army sent several expeditions against him and his large bandit force; but in 1916, after Villa had made several raids across the border in United States territory, President Woodrow Wilson ordered the U.S. Army to pursue and capture him. The U.S. Army did not capture Villa but did stop his raids into the United States. In 1923 Villa was assassinated by a political enemy.

Villon, François

Francois Villon was a great French poet who lived about five hundred years ago. He is remembered not only for his poems but also for the wild and criminal life he led. Villon was born about 1431, of a very poor family. Probably his real name was François de Montcorbier, but he was adopted by a clergyman, Guillaume de Villon, whose name he took. François attended the great university of Paris, studying to be a priest, but in 1455, when he was 24 years old, he became involved in a quarrel with a priest and killed him. He fled from Paris, but was later pardoned and allowed to return. Later, Villon was arrested as a thief and for brawling and was sentenced to death. The sentence was changed to banishment from Paris. Little is known about his life from that time on.

Villon's chief works are *The Little Testament* and *The Great Testament*. In these and his other works he used an old form of poem called the *ballade*. It usually consists of three stanzas of eight or ten lines each, plus a shorter stanza, called the *envoy,* in which the poet addresses the person to whom the poem is written. One of Villon's best ballades was translated by the English poet Rossetti as "Where Are the Snows of Yesteryear?" Many English

poets, including Swinburne and Henley, have translated Villon's poems.

Vilna

Vilna (officially Vilnius) is a capital of Lithuania (Lithuanian Soviet Socialist Republic). It is in the southeast, on the Viliya River. About 293,000 people live there. Vilna has many factories. They make farm machinery, electrical goods, and many other products. The surrounding region has fine forests and farm lands, and Vilna is a trade center for their products. Vilna is the seat of a university, teachers' colleges, schools of music and art, and many churches.

Vilna was founded about a thousand years ago. In the 1300s it became the capital of the grand duchy (small kingdom) of Lithuania. Lithuania and Poland were joined in 1569 and Vilna became a Polish city in character. In 1795 it was made part of Russia.

After World War I, Vilna was fought over by Lithuanians, Poles, and Russian Communist troops. Poland won the city in 1922, but when the Russians took eastern Poland in 1939 they gave Vilna back to Lithuania. The following year the Soviets seized all of Lithuania, including Vilna. The city was occupied by the Germans for three years during World War II, and the Russians retook the city in 1944.

VILNA, LITHUANIA. Population (1974 estimate) 271,000. Capital of Lithuanian Soviet Socialist Republic. On the Viliya River.

Vinci, Leonardo da: see the article on LEONARDO DA VINCI.

vinegar

Vinegar is a sour liquid that is used to season and preserve food, and, in cooking, to soften vegetables that have tough fibers. It is composed of water and acetic acid.

Vinegar is made when a certain kind of bacteria (tiny plant cells) get into wine, beer, cider, or fruit juices and cause them to turn sour. The souring of these beverages is actually brought about when the alcohol in them is turned into acetic acid by the bacteria.

In ancient times, vinegar was obtained when the souring took place accidentally in the process of brewing or aging, but about three hundred years ago the manufacture of vinegar was begun as a separate industry. Vinegar is made in large quantities by exposing alcohol to bacteria that turn it into acetic acid. Homemade vinegar is made from apple cider in most parts of the United States, but in California and some other states it is made from grape wine. In Great Britain it is made from malt beer and in Europe it is made from grape wine.

viola, a musical instrument of the violin family: see the article VIOLIN.

violet

The violet is one of the most popular of all flowers. It is a member of the same flower family as the pansy. There are many kinds of violets, and they may have purple, blue, white or yellow flowers. They are perennials, which means that they grow year after year in the same place without replanting.

One of the most common and familiar violets is the purple violet. It grows both wild and in gardens. It has one very interesting characteristic: if violets are growing wild in grass that is about three or four inches high, the stems of the violets will grow long enough for the purple blossoms to reach the light above the top of the grass. When violets grow in very short grass, the flower stems will be just barely long enough for the blossoms to peep out above the top of the grass.

White and yellow violets can often be found in woodlands and meadows in later spring. The sweet-scented violet is grown in greenhouses and cultivated in gardens. It sometimes grows wild, but the wild blooms are usually scentless.

The plant called dog-tooth violet, which has yellow flowers, is really not a violet, but belongs to the lily family.

violin

There is a group, or family of musical instruments called the "violin family." The instruments of the violin family are the violin, the viola, the cello (or violoncello), and the bass viol (usually called the double bass or simply the bass). These instruments look much alike, except in size. They are called stringed and bowed instruments. Each of them has four strings. The strings are stretched down a long part called the *neck* and over a hollow box. An upright piece called a *bridge* holds the strings tight. The instrument is played with a *bow,* a stick about thirty inches long with strands of horsehair stretched between its ends. When the bow is drawn across the strings it makes them vibrate, producing the musical tones. The strings may also be played by plucking them.

The violin is the smallest member of the violin family. The viola is slightly larger than the violin, and it produces somewhat lower notes. Both the violin and the viola are held by the chin, with the box resting against the shoulder. The strings are fingered, or controlled, by one hand, while the other hand uses the bow. The cello is the next-largest instrument. The cellist (player of a cello) sits in a chair and stands the cello on the floor, holding it between his knees as he plays it. The bass is the largest instrument of the violin family. It is about as tall as a man, and it too must be rested on the floor when it is played. The player stands or rests against a tall stool as he plays it.

There are separate articles about the greatest violin-makers of history, named STRADIVARI, GUARNIERI, and AMATI. See also the article on MUSICAL INSTRUMENTS.

viper

Viper is the name of a group of poisonous snakes. All vipers are poisonous, but not all poisonous snakes are vipers.

True vipers live only in Europe, Africa, and Asia. There are many different kinds. Some kinds are as slender as an ordinary pencil and grow to a length of about one foot. Others may be more than five feet long. The color and markings of different vipers also vary widely.

The main characteristic of all vipers is the fangs. All snakes in this group have the same method of attacking their victims and discharging their venom into the bite. A viper's fangs can be folded within its mouth when it is not attacking its prey. The venom is forced out through the hollow fangs in the same way in all kinds of viper.

Little is known about the breeding habits of vipers in general, but scientists believe that most vipers bring forth fully formed young. They do not lay eggs, as some other snakes do. The eggs are there but are developed inside the female's body.

Virgil

Virgil was a Roman poet who lived about two thousand years ago. Scholars consider him the greatest of all the Roman poets and one of the three or four greatest poets of all time. He was born in the year 70 B.C., and his full name was Publius Vergilius Maro. He studied in Rome, where he became a friend of another great poet, Horace. He soon found rich men who offered to support him while he devoted himself to poetry. One of them was the Roman emperor Augustus. Except for some trips, Virgil remained in Rome until his death, in the year 19 B.C. His name is sometimes spelled *Vergil.*

Virgil's chief works are the *Eclogues* (or *Bucolics*), the *Georgics,* and the *Aeneid.* All of his work was written in the Latin language, in the form called classical, in which there were many more rules than in the Latin that the ancient Romans actually spoke. The *Bucolics* contain poems about life in the country, and later became the model used by poets of England and other countries who wrote about similar subjects. The *Georgics* were poems that glorified the simple life led by the peasants, or simple farmers. These poems told how farms should be managed and how different things on a farm should be done. The *Aeneid* is one of the greatest epics, or long story poems, ever written. It tells of AENEAS, a Greek whose ancestors are said to have founded Rome.

Virginia

Virginia is one of the South Atlantic states in the United States. It was one of the thirteen original colonies. The first permanent colony in the United States was founded at Jamestown, Virginia, in 1607.

The state's nickname is "Old Dominion" because its charter originally gave it a large territory, or dominion, that included all the lands that lay between South Carolina and Pennsylvania, from the Atlantic to the Pacific. Virginia was named for Queen Elizabeth I of England, who was called the Virgin Queen.

Virginia is famous for its early colonial culture and its great statesmen. Many of the leaders of the Revolutionary War and the founders of the United States came from Virginia. Eight presidents—George Washington, Thomas Jefferson, James Madison, James Monroe, William Henry Harrison, John Tyler, Zachary Taylor, and Woodrow Wilson—were born in Virginia. The state has been called "the mother of presidents."

In area, Virginia ranks 36th among the states with 40,815 square miles. In population it ranks 14th, with more than 4,000,000 people living there. It became a state in 1788, and was the tenth of the thirteen original states. The capital is Richmond.

THE PEOPLE OF VIRGINIA

The earliest settlements in Virginia were made by the English. Today many of the people living in the state are descendants of these early settlers, and most of the people in the state are American-born. More than 800,000 Negroes live in Virginia.

Most of the people in Virginia once worked on the farms and lived in rural areas away from the big cities. In recent years more and more people have moved to the cities, where there are large tobacco and textile factories. Some of the people make furniture, paper, and leather products, while others work in shipyards.

The farms in Virginia are small, though at one time there were many large plantations. The farmers raise grain, tobacco, peanuts, and apples. They grow some cotton, but this is no longer a very important crop. Many farmers grow vegetables, which they sell to nearby northern cities. These vegetables include potatoes, sweet potatoes, beans, peas, and tomatoes. Other farmers in Virginia raise poultry and livestock, particularly beef cattle.

Virginia has coal, zinc and lead mines and many forests. The fishing along the coast is good, and Virginia fishermen sell large quantities of oysters and crabs and shad and other fish.

At one time nearly all the people living in Virginia belonged to the Episcopal church. Today the largest church in the state is the Baptist. There are also many Methodists, Presbyterians, and Episcopalians.

WHAT VIRGINIA IS LIKE

The eastern part of Virginia is a broad coastal plain that is known as the Tidewater region. Here the farmers grow tobacco and vegetables. In this area were the large plantations. The Tidewater section has some of the most important cities of the state, including Norfolk, Richmond, Portsmouth, and Newport News, one of the largest shipbuilding centers in the United States. Near Norfolk is Virginia Beach, one of the most popular resort areas in the state.

The central part of the state is a plateau, or high plain, where there are good grazing lands and dairy farms. Tobacco and corn are grown in the southern section.

Western Virginia has two mountain chains, the Blue Ridge Mountains and the Allegheny Mountains. The Blue Ridge Mountains extend through the west central part of the state and follow a course that runs northeast to southwest. The Allegheny Mountains form the western border of the state. Between the two ranges is the broad, fertile Valley of Virginia, where much fruit is grown. Most of Virginia's minerals are found in this western section.

The climate of Virginia is warm and humid most of the year. The Tidewater region has the most pleasant climate. Virginia's average temperature in winter is about 35 degrees and in summer about 75 degrees.

There are several important rivers. Four of them flow from the central part of the state into the Atlantic Ocean and form three peninsulas that make up most of the Tidewater region. From north to south, these rivers are the Potomac, the Rappahannock, the York, and the James. They are all important for transportation and for the seaports that have grown up at their mouths. Railroads and highways reach almost all parts of the state. There are airports in all the major cities.

THE GOVERNMENT OF VIRGINIA

Virginia calls itself a "Commonwealth" and not a state, but, like other states, it has a governor at the head of the government and a legislature that makes the laws. The governor is elected for a four-year term. The legislature is composed of two houses, a Senate and a House of Delegates. Senators are elected for four-year terms, delegates for two-year terms. Judges are elected by the legislature for twelve-year terms. The capital is Richmond. There are 98 counties and 32 independent cities.

There are about 1,076,000 pupils attending public elementary and high schools. Among the principal colleges and universities maintained by the state are:

College of William and Mary, at Williamsburg. Enrollment, 7,271 men and women in 1971.
University of Virginia, at Charlottesville. Enrollment, 9,670 men and women in 1971.
Virginia Polytechnic Institute, at Blacksburg. Enrollment, 9,568 men and women in 1971.

The Tomb of the Unknown Soldier at Arlington National Cemetery in north Virginia, across the Potomac from Washington, D.C., honors all the men who died in both World Wars.

Virginia State College, at Petersburg (mainly for Negroes). Enrollment, 2,579 men and women in 1971.

Among the leading private colleges and universities are:

Washington and Lee University, at Lexington. Enrollment, 1,450 men in 1971.
Hampton Institute, at Hampton (mainly for Negroes). Enrollment, 2,544 men and women in 1971.
Randolph-Macon College, at Ashland. Enrollment 760 men in 1971.
Randolph-Macon Women's College, at Lynchburg. Enrollment, 799 in 1971.
University of Richmond, at Richmond. Enrollment, 4,149 men and women in 1971.

CHIEF CITIES OF VIRGINIA

The leading cities of Virginia, with populations taken from the 1970 census, are:

Norfolk, population 307,951, the largest city in the state. There is a separate article about NORFOLK.
Richmond, population 249,621, the capital and second-largest city in the state. There is a separate article about RICHMOND.
Portsmouth, population 110,963, the fourth-largest city, naval shipyard and trade center, in the southeast.
Newport News, population 138,177, the third-largest city, port and shipbuilding center, in the southeast.
Alexandria, population 110,938, the fifth-largest city, railroad center and residential suburb of Washington, D.C.

VIRGINIA IN THE PAST

The first permanent settlement in North America was made at Jamestown, Virginia, in 1607, by the London Company, a group of Englishmen. The London Company had been granted a charter by Queen Elizabeth I. This charter gave the company the right to settle a great section of the New World.

Va. Chamber of Commerce

The Victory Monument at Yorktown in southeastern Virginia honors the victory of 1781 that ended the Revolutionary War.

The early days in Virginia were hard ones, but under leaders such as Captain John Smith, the Jamestown settlement prospered. By 1619 there were a dozen

settlements near Jamestown. One of the things that helped the growth of the colony was the introduction of tobacco cultivation. The early Virginia colonies began to grow tobacco for the rest of the world. In 1619 Negroes from Africa were brought to Virginia as slaves, and there came to be many planters, or owners of large plantations on which the slaves did the work. Within a hundred years eastern Virginia became a very prosperous region, with a way of life much like that of the rich and noble families of England.

Even when settlements were made in the western part of Virginia, the state was controlled by eastern planters. Many statesmen from Virginia were among the leaders in the fight for American independence and in the setting up of the government of the United States. In the Virginia House of Delegates, Patrick Henry made one of the most famous speeches in American history, urging the people of Virginia to break away from England. George Washington, a Virginian, commanded the American armies during the Revolutionary War and later became the first President of the country. Thomas Jefferson wrote the Declaration of Independence, and James Madison, with the help of other statesmen, wrote the Constitution. These men too were Virginians.

After the Revolutionary War, Virginia continued to be influential in politics but the state's wealth began to decline. The land, once so fertile, began to wear out, for the plantation owners had not planted their crops wisely.

During the early 1800s, Virginia and other southern states began to be criticized by the northern states for permitting slavery. The plantation owners in Virginia did not want to give up the slave labor, and at the beginning of the Civil War the state seceded (withdrew) from the United States and joined the Confederacy. At this time the farmers in the western part of Virginia, who had small farms and very few slaves, broke away from the state of Virginia fought on the side of the Union in the Civil War.

Just as many battles of the Revolutionary War were fought in Virginia, so were many of the important battles of the Civil War, including Bull Run, Chancellorsville, and Fredericksburg. Richmond, the capital of Virginia, was also the Confederate capital. The surrender of the Confederate Army took place at Appomattox Court House, Virginia.

After the Civil War industry in Virginia increased greatly.

PLACES TO SEE IN VIRGINIA

Virginia is visited each year by thousands of tourists, who are attracted by the beautiful scenery and the many historic landmarks. The principal attraction is probably Williamsburg, a town in the Tidewater area, and the old colonial capital has been restored to its original beauty, mainly by gifts from John D. Rockefeller, Jr. Other attractions are:

Shenandoah National Park, 193,472 acres, near Waynesboro, in the central part, near U.S. Route 250. Scenic Skyline Drive north through the Blue Ridge Mountains, 107 miles long.

Colonial National Historic Park, 7,129 acres, most of the peninsula between the York and the James Rivers, in the southeast, on Colonial Parkway.

Arlington National Cemetery, 420 acres, just south of Washington, D.C., off Route 1. Tomb of the Unknown Soldier.

Mount Vernon, near Alexandria and Washington, D.C., off Route 1. George Washington's home and tomb.

Monticello, home of Thomas Jefferson, 5 miles southeast of Charlottesville, in the central part, near U.S. Route 29.

Appomattox Court House National Monument, 968 acres, 25 miles east of Lynchburg, in the central part, on U.S. Route 460. Site of surrender of Confederate Army at the end of the Civil War.

Natural Bridge, about 35 miles north of Roanoke, in the central part, on Route 11. Limestone arch 215 feet high, over Cedar Creek.

VIRGINIA. Area, 40,815 square miles. Population (1970 census) 4,648,494. Capital, Richmond. Nickname, the Old Dominion State. Motto, Sic Semper Tyrannis (Thus Always to Tyrants). Flower, American dogwood. Bird, cardinal. Song, "Carry Me Back To Old Virginia." Admitted to the Union, June 26, 1788. Official abbreviation, Va.

Virgin Islands

The Virgin Islands are a group of about 100 small islands in the West Indies, about 40 miles east of Puerto Rico. They make up part of the Lesser Antilles. Some of them belong to the United States and others to Great Britain. The climate is tropical but pleasant, and the islands have become a very popular winter resort.

The Virgin Islands of the United States are a territory, with an area of about 130 square miles. About 80,000 people live there. The group includes St. Croix (the largest island), St. Thomas, St. John, and about sixty uninhabited islets. The capital is Charlotte Amalie, a town of about 30,800, on the island of St. Thomas. Most of the people are Negroes, some are of mixed descent, and a few are white. Farming is the principal occupation, and the chief crops are sugar cane, cotton, vegetables, and tropical fruits. Some of the people are dairy farmers. The only important manufactures are rum, bay rum, and alcohol.

The British Virgin Islands are a division of the Leeward Islands colony. They have an area of 67 square miles, and about 7,000 people live there. The largest island is Tortola, on which is the capital, Road Town; others are Anegada, Virgin Gorda, Jost Van Dyke, Peter Island, Salt Island, and a number of uninhabited islets. Most of the people raise cattle. Others grow sugar cane, cotton, tobacco, limes, and other crops. Fishing is an important occupation.

HISTORY OF THE ISLANDS

The islands were discovered by Christopher Columbus on his second voyage in 1493. They were first settled by the Dutch. The British islands have belonged to Great Britain since 1666. The American group belonged to Denmark for many years, and were valuable because of the sugar plantations. Slavery was abolished in the 1800s. The United States bought the islands for $25,000,000 in 1916. In 1927 Congress passed a law making the people of the islands citizens of the United States.

Virgo

Virgo is the name for one of the constellations, or groups of stars in the sky. It is one of the most ancient constellations, and has always been known as the "Wheat-bearing Maiden" in every age and race. The ancient peoples thought this particular group of stars looked somewhat like a maiden holding a palm branch in her right hand and a sheaf of wheat in her left.

Virgo is the Latin name for the constellation, and means "virgin." The sign of the zodiac that stands for the constellation is ♍.

Read also the articles on CONSTELLATION and ZODIAC.

virus

A virus is a particle of matter so tiny that it cannot be seen with an ordinary microscope. It can be seen only if it is magnified about 50,000 times under a special device called an electron microscope.

Although the electron microscope was not invented until 1931, viruses were suspected, long before that, of causing such diseases as chicken pox, measles, and influenza (flu). Viruses are now known definitely to cause not only these diseases but many others, including the common cold, polio, and, in certain animals, cancer.

When viruses were seen for the first time, scientists were amazed to find that, in some respects, viruses behave like living things while, in other ways, they act like non-living things. Viruses seem "alive" only when they are in the cells of a living body. When they are removed from living cells, they show no life whatsoever and some look more like crystals of salt or sugar than like living cells.

Viruses are made of a protein coat on the outside and a substance called a nucleic acid on the inside. The virus attaches its protein coat to a living cell and then injects its nucleic acid into the living cell. This nucleic acid then causes the living cell to use its own chemicals to manufacture more viruses.

In 1967, scientists announced that they had been able to make an artificial form of the nucleic acid found in viruses. When this artificial nucleic acid was injected into a living cell, the cell used its own chemicals to manufacture more viruses. Some people thought that this meant that scientists had created life in the laboratory. However, whether or not you think life was created depends upon your definition of "life".

Vishnu, one of the forms taken by the Hindu god Brahma: see the article BRAHMA.

visual education

Visual education is a way of teaching by showing pictures, models, and specimens. Students can learn by reading or by listening to a teacher talk, but usually they learn more easily if the book has pictures in it or if the teacher uses pictures to illustrate the lesson. Visual education includes much more than the use of pictures in a book or pictures to illustrate a lecture. It includes motion pictures, slides, film strips, models, graphs

and charts, sand-table modeling, and even television. Sometimes the term "audio-visual education" is used. This means "ear and eye education." It includes not only things that are seen but also things that are heard, including radio and recordings.

FIELD TRIPS

School children are often taken on "field trips," to factories and other places where they can learn things, but not every class can go on field trips and not every subject can be studied through field trips. Only a few big cities have the necessary museums and other displays. Audio-visual education can also be used to show what life was like in ancient times, how people live in different parts of the world, how things are manufactured, and the wonders of nature.

Audio-visual aids are not a substitute for teachers. A good teacher can make the best of such aids.

We profit from audio-visual education in the home as we watch television and listen on radio. Travel is a form of audio-visual education, because as we go from place to place we understand better about people and about the various aspects of nature.

vitamins

Vitamins are chemical substances that are found in small quantities in foods that we eat. Without vitamins we could not live, and without a proper amount of each of the different vitamins we cannot be healthy. Yet these powerful and important substances come in such small quantities that we cannot see them. A single drop of a vitamin may be enough to furnish us with the necessary health-giving qualities for weeks or even months.

DEFICIENCY DISEASES

Vitamins have been known to man for less than a hundred years. Before that, it was known that people who had to live without certain foods would be sick, but no one knew why. Sailors who went on long voyages often got a disease called scurvy, which caused them to grow weaker and finally die. They had no fresh foods. In the Far East people got a disease called beri-beri, which also caused weakness. They ate only white rice. There were many other diseases for which there was no apparent cause except the food the people ate. These diseases could be helped by a change of diet. Such diseases are called *deficiency diseases,* because they come from a deficiency, or lack of something.

About seventy years ago, scientists began to think that there was something in food besides the proteins, fats, minerals, sugars, and other things that give energy to the body. The scientists studied the different things that happened when certain foods were included or left out of the diet. They finally began to understand that the presence of certain foods caused good health, and the absence of certain foods caused certain illnesses.

VITAMIN C

The first discovery was made by an English sea doctor named Lind. He was on a voyage on which many sailors grew

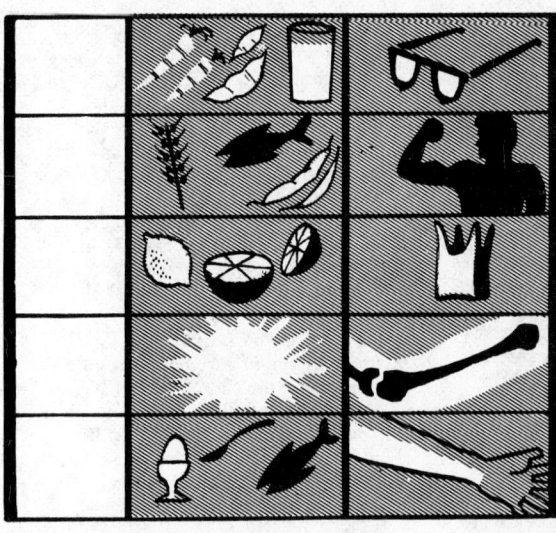

Vitamin A, which is present in carrots and orange juice, improves ability to see at night.

Vitamin B, which is in wheat, fish, and green vegetables, helps the body grow healthier and stronger.

Vitamin C, which is found in the citrus fruits, helps the teeth and gums to remain healthy.

Vitamin D, which is absorbed from the sun's rays, is necessary for well-formed bones and teeth.

Vitamin K, which is found in egg yolks and liver, helps blood flowing from a wound to form a scab.

sick with scurvy. Doctor Lind decided to experiment with these sailors. He gave some of them pepper and oil, others cider, others the juice of oranges or limes, and some nothing at all. In a few days the sailors who had drunk the juices of the fruits recovered, while the others remained just as sick. The sailors who recovered did so because they had received Vitamin C from the citrus fruit.

Doctor Lind did not know that he had made one of the great discoveries in science. He had never heard of vitamins and it was many years before the vitamin he had given these sailors was named Vitamin C. Today we know that Vitamin C, sometimes called *ascorbic acid,* is present in many fruits and vegetables. Cooking and drying these fruits and vegetables usually destroys the Vitamin C they contain. Therefore it is important that you eat enough fresh fruits and vegetables.

VITAMIN B1

In much the same way that Doctor Lind was responsible for the first use of Vitamin C to cure scurvy, a Japanese naval doctor was responsible for the first use of Vitamin B1 to cure beri-beri. This doctor, whose name was Takari, wondered why so many sailors got this weakening disease. He thought it might have something to do with the rice they were eating. He saw that they were eating white, or polished, rice which did not have the husk (outer rough covering) of the rice kernel. He gave some of the sailors rice that was not hulled and he noticed that these men did not get beri-beri while the men who had only white rice did get the disease.

Dr. Takari's work was the beginning of the work done by many scientists in discovering and understanding Vitamin B1, which is now called *thiamin.* Vitamin B1 helps digestion and prevents many nervous diseases in addition to beri-beri. Meat, particularly liver, and milk, oysters, whole-grain cereals, eggs, peas and beans, and nuts are rich in Vitamin B1.

VITAMIN B2

Less than fifty years ago Dr. Joseph Goldberger, a member of the United States Health Service, was asked to study a disease that was affecting people in the southern states. Dr. Goldberger found that these people were getting almost no

milk, eggs, or green vegetables, and very little meat. They were suffering from a disease called pellagra. After many experiments Dr. Goldberger found that the disease was caused by a lack of foods containing a vitamin called B2, or riboflavin. By having the sick people eat the foods they had not been getting, he was able to cure the disease.

Vitamin B2, or riboflavin, helps growth.

OTHER VITAMINS

Now we know about many vitamins and what they mean to our diet and health. An important vitamin is Vitamin A, which helps to prevent colds and is necessary for good eyesight, and also makes it possible for us to see at night. Carrots are the best single source of Vitamin A, but milk, butter and cheese, egg yolk, liver, green and yellow vegetables, and fruit are also rich in it.

Vitamin D is necessary for strong bones. Most of the milk we now buy has been *irradiated,* or placed under a certain kind of light whose rays produce Vitamin D. The greatest source of Vitamin D for all of us is sunlight. Those who have been exposed to the sun absorb much Vitamin D through their skins.

Vitamin K, which is present in green, leafy vegetables, helps our blood to clot. Without this vitamin our blood would flow from open wounds. Doctors often give patients large doses of Vitamin K before operations, so that they will not lose too much blood.

The best source of all vitamins is the foods we eat. However, many people who for some reason or other do not eat the exact foods they need, take vitamins in pill form or in capsules or drops of liquid that are rich in vitamins.

Vladivostok

Vladivostok is a city on the eastern coast of Siberia, which is part of the Russian Soviet Federated Socialist Republic (Soviet Russia). It is on the peninsula near the border of Manchuria. It is the chief Russian port on the Pacific Ocean, lying on Peter the Great Bay, which is an arm of the Sea of Japan. The city includes Russian Island and several others in the bay.

Vladivostok is a great manufacturing and shipping center. About 442,000 people live there. There are shipbuilding and airplane factories and meat, fish and other

food-processing plants. The port is the home base of fishing and whaling fleets. It handles the export of coal, lumber, fish, furs, and grain. Icebreakers keep the port open in winter.

There are popular summer resorts near Vladivostok. The city is the seat of a university, the Pacific Institute of Fisheries and Oceanography, and other technical schools. The site of Vladivostok was settled by Russians in 1860. The city grew rapidly after the Trans-Siberian railroad was completed in the 1890s. It was a supply port in World War I and a shipping point for lend-lease supplies during World War II.

VLADIVOSTOK, RUSSIAN S.F.S.R. Population (1974 census) 442,000. On the Sea of Japan. Capital of Maritime Territory.

voice

The human voice is the most remarkable sound-producing instrument ever created. No musical instrument can equal it. Other animals have the ability to produce voice sounds, but only man can make the voice sounds that have such complete range and variety.

A tiny "voice box" called the larynx is the place where the human voice originates. In the larynx are two small elastic membranes, or skinlike cords, called vocal cords. Air breathed out from the lungs passes by these vocal cords and causes them to vibrate. Vibration in anything produces sound waves. If you take a rubber band and stretch it and then pluck it, you will hear sound produced by the vibration of the rubber band. The vibration of the vocal cords produces sound in much the same way. The sound it produces is the human voice.

No two human voices make exactly the same sounds. There are several ways in which the voices are different.

The first difference is in *pitch*. This is the highness or lowness of the voice. It is the same as pitch in musical notes. The faster the vocal cords vibrate, the higher the pitch. Men have lower-pitched voices than women because their vocal cords do not vibrate as rapidly as women's.

The second difference is in *intensity*. This is the loudness or softness of a speaking or singing tone. Intensity can be controlled by the amount of force that we use to send the air past the vocal cords. When we whisper or speak softly, we are not using much force; when we shout, we are using a great deal.

The third important difference is in *quality*. Some voices are husky, some are soft and mellow, some are harsh, and so on. The size and shape of the vocal cords, and the way they vibrate in a particular person, and also the size and shape of the passages through which the air is expelled from the lungs, affect the quality of voice. A saxophone may play the same notes or sound the same pitch as a trumpet, but we can easily tell the difference between the two sounds because of their differences in quality. Another name for quality is *timbre*.

Another thing that affects the quality of a voice is *resonance*. If you stretch a rubber band, as explained before, but this time pluck it over a box or other hollow space, you will notice that the sound is made louder and fuller than when the rubber band was twanged in the open.

This is because the box or hollow space vibrates with the elastic band. Resonance in the human voice comes from the cavities or spaces in the head, including the mouth, throat, nose, and other cavities around the throat and nose called sinuses. If your nose is stopped up, you will notice that your voice has a different quality than when the nasal passages are open.

A fourth difference is that of *duration*, or *time*. This means the length of time it takes to make each sound in speech or note in music. The rests or pauses between sounds are also important. One person may speak slowly and another rapidly, and their voices will be different for that reason.

KINDS OF VOICE

There are several kinds of human voice. Among women there are three main kinds of singing voice. They are the *soprano*, the highest; the *contralto*, the lowest; and the *mezzo*, or *middle*, *soprano*. Men also have three main kinds of voice; *tenor*, the highest; *baritone*, the middle range; and *bass*, the lowest. A person with a particular kind of voice can usually speak or sing in another voice but will be most comfortable in the voice that is normally his. Singers must have pleasant voices to start with, but they must practice to develop the power of the voice, sweetness, ability to produce musical tones on pitch, and many other things.

IMPORTANCE OF THE HUMAN VOICE

Many scientists believe that the human voice has contributed as much or more than any other thing to the progress of man. With the human voice, man can express an unlimited number of words, and with these words he can pass along knowledge to the men who live after him, so that each group of men has the advantage of everything that has been learned by men before then. The human voice allows men to express feelings and emotions—fear, anger, love, doubt, and so on. Our entire written language, which stores knowledge forever, came originally from the sounds made possible by the human voice.

volcano

A volcano is a hole in the earth's surface through which hot, molten (melted) rock flows. The crust of the earth, below the soil, is a thick layer of hard rock. Underneath this thick crust there are boiling masses of molten rock, called *magma*. The great bubbling mass of magma constantly seeks to come through the crust of the earth to the surface. When it finds a weak spot in the rocky crust, it breaks through. This weak spot becomes the hole we call a volcano. It is like a tall chimney leading down to the inner masses of magma.

Usually when we speak of a volcano we mean a mountain that has a hole (called a *crater*) in its top, through which lava once flowed or still flows. Actually the mountain was built by the action of the volcano. Volcanoes do not start by breaking through the tops of high mountains. They form the mountains. The volcanic mountains are made up of either ashes and cinders or lava or a combination of both.

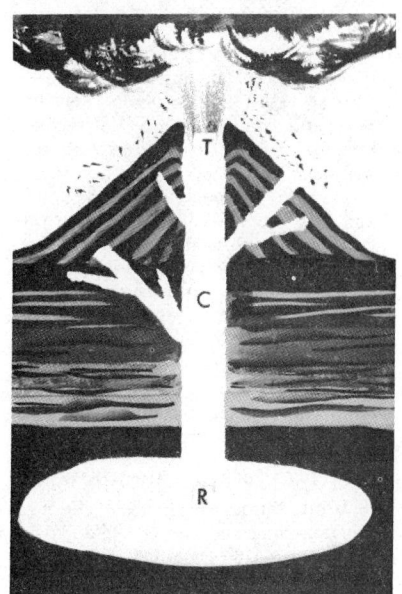

A volcanic mountain is made up of layers of lava and ash. The mountain is hollow, with a conduit (C) going down to a reservoir (R) miles below the surface. Inside the reservoir is hot *magma*. Gas from the magma rises, causing pressure against matter clogging the throat (T) of the volcano. Finally the matter is blasted upward and the volcano erupts.

FORMING A VOLCANO

Most volcanoes in the world are no more than a few million years old, which is a short time in the history of the earth. When the earth was much younger there were many active volcanoes. Today there are very few. Some of the best-known are Vesuvius in Italy, Etna in Sicily, Krakatua Island in the Pacific Ocean, Popocatepetl in Mexico, Mount Pelee on the island of Martinique in the West Indies, and Mauna Loa in the Hawaiian Islands.

All of these volcanoes were formed long ago, but there is one active volcano that was formed only a few years ago, beginning in 1943. One day a Mexican farmer stood in his field hoeing his corn. Suddenly the ground around him began to shake. He heard strange rumbling noises. He saw the earth cracking and clouds of steam pouring out of cracks in the earth. The farmer ran to tell his neighbors. When they returned to the field, hot rocks and ashes were spouting out of the hole. Rocks and ashes fell to the ground and started to form a cone around the hole. The hole grew and grew, and the sloping sides of a hill began to take shape.

The volcano kept erupting. By the end of the week the hill had grown to 500 feet. After several months it was 1,000 feet high. By now it is more than 2,500 feet high and is still growing as the ashes and rocks pour out of the crater. The lava continues to flow down the mountain and spread over vast amounts of territory. It has traveled for many miles and destroyed many villages. Heaps of ashes from the new volcano, sometimes ten feet deep, have covered much of the countryside.

The new volcano is called Parícutin. It is named after one of the villages nearby. Scientists have traveled from all over the world to Parícutin to study how the volcano started and how it keeps growing. They have learned much about volcanoes from this newest one.

ERUPTIONS

Many volcanoes continue to pour out streams of lava and hot steam and smoke. They are called "active volcanoes" but are not particularly dangerous unless they erupt or explode. This happens when the hot, liquid rock under the earth's surface cannot get out through the volcano easily, and finally a tremendous explosion occurs, as the earth suddenly gives way. Exploding volcanoes have sometimes made such a terrible roar that the sound could be heard hundreds of miles away. At the same time terrible masses of hot rocks, ashes, gases and great flowing streams of lava have shot forth. Cities and villages near volcanoes are always in danger of being destroyed by eruptions.

VOLCANOES HELP THE EARTH

While volcanoes are terrible things and cause much destruction and are to be greatly feared, they also do some good for the earth. A volcano is like a safety valve on a steam boiler. If the steam in a boiler is under too much pressure, the whole boiler will explode unless there is a safety valve on it. The safety valve opens at the right time, allowing the steam to escape and reducing the dangerous pressure. A volcano acts in much the same way in the earth. If there were no volcanoes or weak spots on the earth's surface, the great mass of fiery magma under the surface might build up so much pressure that it would blow away much of the earth's surface.

Volcanoes are also helpful in another way. The ashes they spread finally become part of the rich soil that is good for growing things. Much of the soil of the states of California and Washington is rich because it is covered by volcanic matter that long ago flowed from volcanoes in that area, such as Mt. Shasta and Mt. Rainier, now inactive.

Most of the time, active volcanoes produce small amounts of lava, steam, and smoke. Unless they violently erupt, they are not too dangerous. Volcanic eruptions can cause disasters. In 1963, Mt. Agung on the island of Bali erupted and caused the death of 1,500 persons and great property damage. A serious volcanic eruption occurs when molten rock cannot find a way out of the volcano. The pressure builds until the volcano explodes and sends out lava, rock, pumice, ash, and gas. The sound of an exploding volcano can often be heard hundreds of miles away.

vole, a mouselike animal: see the article on MOUSE.

Volga River

The Volga is the largest river of Europe. It is in Russia and is the principal navigable river of the Soviet Union. The Volga is 2,290 miles long and is navigable for 2,200 miles. It rises in the Valdai Hills in the north, flows east to the city of Kazan, and then south to empty into the Caspian Sea. The two largest rivers that flow into the Volga are the Oka and Kama Rivers. The Volga is dammed for hydroelectric power at various places along its course.

The Volga connects the agricultural region of southeast Russia with the central industrial region and the Ural Mountains. With other rivers and canals it gives the inland city of Moscow an outlet to the Caspian Sea and joins the Caspian with the Baltic and White Seas. At the great city of Volgograd near its mouth, the Volga is connected by canal with the Don River, which empties into the Sea of Azov. The Volga has been an important trade route for more than a thousand years. The Russian people have a great feeling for the river, and it plays an important part in their literature.

Volgograd, the former city of Stalingrad, on Volga River. See STALINGRAD.

volley ball

Volley ball is a fast and interesting team game played in gymnasiums and on outdoor courts. It is based on the rules of tennis, having a net stretched across the middle of the court over which balls must be hit; but the ball is like a basketball and the game of volley ball is a team game, usually played with six persons on each side.

The game was invented in 1895 by an instructor named William C. Morgan at the Holyoke, Massachusetts, Y.M.C.A. The standard court for outdoor volley ball games is 80 feet long by 40 feet wide. Smaller courts may be used indoors or for women's and children's games. Whatever the size of the court, a net three feet high is stretched across the center of the court. The top of the net should be eight feet above the ground.

The game starts with a player on one team serving. He hits the ball with his palm or fist so that it goes over the net and into the opposing team's court. If he hits it short and it does not clear the net, or if he hits it so far that it goes over the opposing team's back line, he gets another serve. If he hits the ball out of bounds or over the sidelines of the opposing team's court, he loses his serve. He also loses his serve if the opposing team bats the ball back and his team fails to get it back over the net again. Points are scored only by the team having service. The team that first scores 15 points wins the game. If both teams should have fourteen points, then one team must score 2 points on service before it wins the game.

In volley ball the ball must be kept in the air. If a team allows it to drop to the floor in its court, it either loses a point (if the opposite team is serving) or it loses its service.

Members of a team may hit the ball to one another as many as three times before getting it over the net, as long as it does not touch the floor, but one man may not hit the ball twice in succession. While the ball is in play, it may be hit only with the palms of the hands. It may not be punched, kicked, or held.

The idea of the game is to work the ball toward the men close to the net, so that one of them may try on the third hit to get the ball over the net into the opposing team's side where they cannot hit it back.

The players on each side move from position to position. As one man finishes his service he moves to the left-hand front row at the net. When the next man has finished his service the first man moves to the center position at the net. He finally works into the backline and into the service position. Thus each player gets a chance at each position, either in the front line or in the backline. There are three players at all times in the front line near the net and three in the back court.

Volley ball is great exercise, fast and safe to play. Anyone, no matter what age, may enjoy it.

Voltaire

Voltaire was the pen name of a famous French writer who lived about 250 years ago. He is remembered chiefly as a champion of individual liberty, but he made many enemies at the time because he was against all organized religions or Churches, and he thought that a government's main duty is to guard every man's right to personal liberty, property, and protection by law.

Voltaire's real name was François Marie Arouet. He was called *Arouet le jeune,* meaning "Arouet Jr.," and he rearranged the letters of this name to spell Voltaire. (In the French language of his time, the letter "u" was the same as the letter "v" and the letter "j" was the same as the letter "i.")

Voltaire was born in 1694 near Paris, France, and studied with Jesuit priests. He began to write at an early age, and almost at once he began to get in trouble because his writings poked fun at serious things. When he was 21 years old he was put in prison for a year. There he finished his first play, *Oedipus.* A few years later he was again put in prison but was soon released on the condition that he would leave France. He went to England, where he lived for three years. He was much impressed by English thinking and social conditions, which he described in a book called *Letters Concerning the English Nation.* Its publication caused another scandal, because the book criticized France and its conditions.

In 1750 Frederick the Great, king of Prussia, invited Voltaire to his court in Berlin, and Voltaire stayed there for three years, until he quarreled with Frederick. During this time he wrote a historical work called *The Time of Louis XIV.* Voltaire then went to Geneva, Switzerland, where he lived for the rest of his life. He died there in 1778, at the age of 84. Voltaire's ideas had much to do with causing the French Revolution, which began eleven years after his death.

Voltaire's writings include plays, histories, essays, several short novels, and his *Philosophical Dictionary.* Among his most popular works are the novels *Candide* and *Zadig,* the plays *Brutus, Zaïre,* and *Mérope,* and such historical works as *Charles XII* and *Essay on Manners.*

voodoo

Voodoo is a name for certain religious practices among some Negro peoples of the West Indies and the southern United States. In voodoo there is an all-powerful spirit that is represented by a snake. It communicates with the worshipers through a priest and a priestess. The snake is usually worshiped at night, and the rites include wild dances. Voo-

dooists (people believing in voodoo) believe in charms and spells, which are described in the article MAGIC. They believe that when someone kills an animal any powers the animal had are transferred to that person. For example, when a man kills a strong animal he himself becomes very strong. They also believe that some persons can control certain other persons and can make them do what they wish. The people so controlled are called *zombies* and are said to behave as if they were walking in their sleep. Today voodooism is practiced mainly in Haiti and a few other islands of the West Indies.

voting: see the articles on ELECTION and BALLOT.

vowel

A vowel is a kind of sound you make in speaking. Most of the vowel sounds used in English are shown by the letters a, e, i, o, and u. In English, vowel sounds are made when the air coming out of the lungs makes the vocal cords vibrate and then passes out of the mouth without being stopped or hindered. (When the other kind of sound, called a *consonant*, is made, the tongue, teeth, or other parts of the mouth interfere with the escaping air.)

If the flap at the back of the mouth is down and some of the air goes through the nose, the vowel is *nasalized* (has some of the sound of an *n*). Some people regularly speak with a nasal twang. Many languages have some vowels that are said only through the mouth and others that are said partly through the nose. Vowels also change according to the position of the lips. We round our lips to say *who* but not to say *hat*. The position of the tongue gives us such differences as in the word *bit* (with the tongue close to the roof of the mouth and far front), *bet* (with the tongue still forward but lower),

bat (with the tongue still lower), *but* (with the tongue about as high as for *bet* but farther back in the mouth). When the doctor wants to look at your throat he makes you say "ah" because for that vowel the tongue is very low down in the mouth.

English uses eight or nine vowels and we often have to spell several different vowels with the same letter. For example, *u* has to stand for different sounds in *but* and *put*. The words *pit, pet, pat, cut, pot, put, horse, law* give you eight different vowels. These are called *simple vowels.* English also has combinations of these vowels with y and w, for example the *ey* of *obey*, the *oy* of *boy*, and the *ow* of *low*. The combinations are called *diphthongs*. Like the simple vowels, diphthongs may have several different spellings in English. The *ey* of *obey* is most often spelled with *a* followed by a consonant and *e*, as in *late*, and it may be spelled with *ai* as in *maid*, *eigh* as in *eight*, *ay* as in *lay*, and in other ways. Another diphthong is the sound of *y* in *by*. This is the *a* of *father* followed by a *y* sound. It, too, is spelled in various ways, such as *igh* in *night*, *ye* in *rye*, and *i* followed by *e* (*kite, die*).

The names of the English letters a, e, i, and o are all diphthongs; the name of *u* is just like the word *you*, which is *y* followed by the diphthong *oo* of *moo*. In English these diphthongs are often called "long" vowels, but ordinarily a long vowel is one that sounds like a short vowel but takes longer to say; the sound "ah" is this kind of long vowel. In some parts of the United States the letter *r* after a vowel makes the vowel longer.

Vulcan

Vulcan was the god of fire in Roman mythology, the stories the ancient Romans told about their gods and goddesses. The Greeks called their god of fire Hephaestus.

Vulcan was the son of Jupiter and Juno, who were the king and queen of all the gods. He was born deformed, so Juno threw him from the mountain where the gods lived, down into the sea. Vulcan was also the god of the forge, and in some places he was the god of artisans, or craftsmen, especially of metal workers. Vulcan had a great workshop on the mountain. The word *volcano* (fire mountain) comes from his name, and also *vulcanizing*, the process of treating rubber with heat.

vulcanizing, a process used in the manufacture of rubber: see the articles Charles GOODYEAR and RUBBER.

vulture

Vultures are birds that live by eating dead animals. They are related to hawks and eagles, but they do not attack and kill living animals as hawks and eagles do. Vultures are important in nature because they dispose of dead animals that otherwise would pollute fields and forests.

Vultures live in Africa, southern Europe, Asia, and the Americas. There are different kinds in different parts of the world. Their size ranges from the Central American black vulture, which is about twenty-seven inches long, to the great condor of California and South America, which has a wingspread of ten feet.

The turkey buzzard is the best-known American vulture. It is an ugly-looking bird with a featherless red head and a savage-looking hooked beak. It has extraordinary skill at locating the bodies of dead animals, and seems to appear out of nowhere when an animal dies.

Vultures build crude nests or none at all. Sometimes a hole in a tree or a crack between rocks is used for a nest. There are seldom more than one or two eggs at a time. The young vulture is helpless until it is nearly fully grown, and its parents feed it.

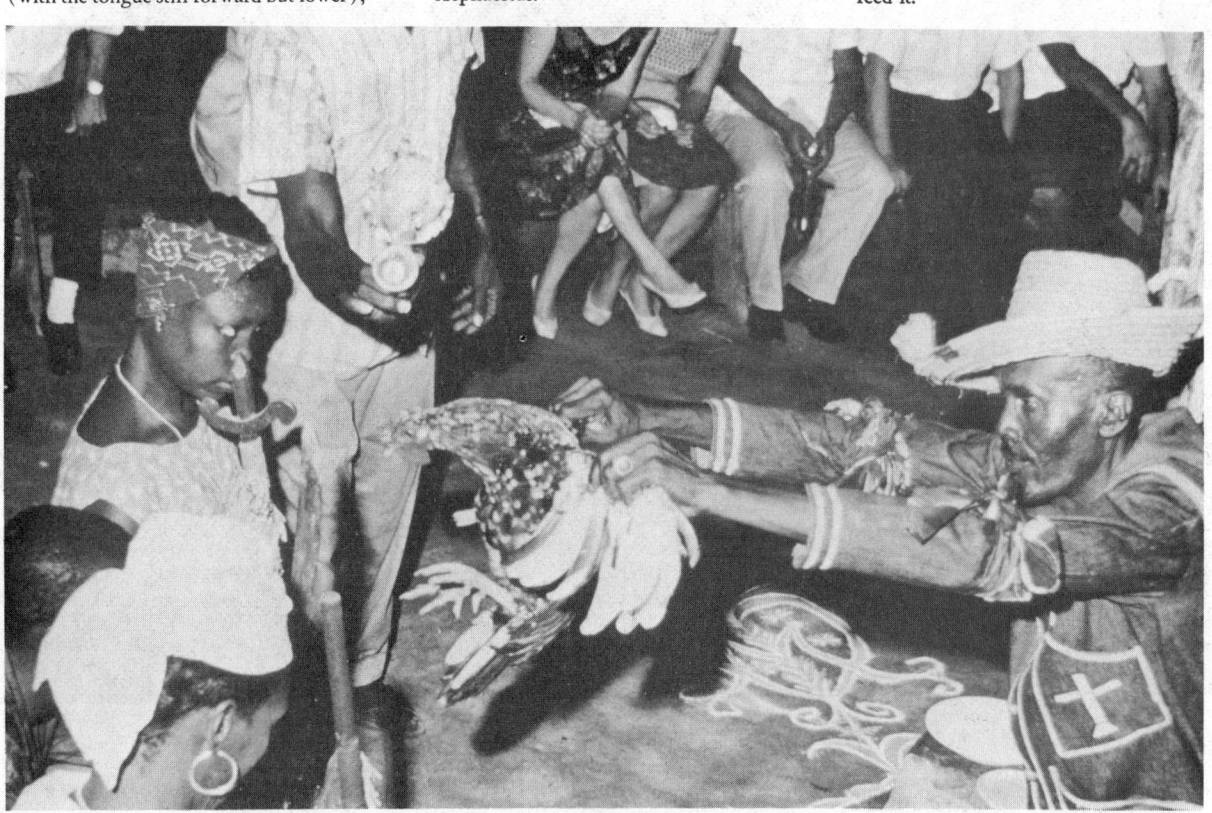

Richard Wagner

W w EARLY GERMAN

W w GOTHIC

W or w

The letter W, the twenty-third letter of our alphabet, came to us in exactly the same way as the letters U and V. Until about three hundred years ago, there was no difference between the letters V and U, though the same sign stood for two different sounds. When V and U became two different letters, each used for one of the sounds, a third letter was made by doubling the V. We still call it "double-U" because the letters V and U were once so closely related.

The illustration above shows three forms of the letter W. At the far left is the "German black-letter" (or "Gothic") capital W, used in many German books.

Read also the articles on the letters U and V, and on the ALPHABET.

Wabash River

The Wabash is a river 475 miles long in the midwestern United States, mainly in Indiana and Illinois. It rises in Grand Lake, in western Ohio, flows northwest into Indiana, then west and south to form the Illinois-Indiana border for about 200 miles, and empties into the Ohio River at the southwest tip of Indiana.

The White, Little Wabash, Embarrass, Tippecanoe and Vermilion Rivers flow into the Wabash.

The chief cities on the Wabash are Logansport, Lafayette, Terre Haute, and Vincennes, all in the state of Indiana.

WAC, an abbreviation for Women's Army Corps: see the article on WOMEN IN THE ARMED FORCES.

WAF, an abbreviation for Women in the Air Force: see the article on WOMEN IN THE ARMED FORCES.

wages and hours

There have been many times when jobs have been scarce and people have been willing to do almost anything to get or keep a job. At such times, some greedy employers have made their employees work for very long hours at very low wages. Since 1938 there have been United States laws to prevent this. The principal law is officially the Fair Labor Standards Act, but it is usually called the "wages and hours law."

In 1963 this law raised the minimum a person can be paid for each hour he works from $1.15 to $1.25, and in 1976 to $2.30. If a person works more than forty hours in a week, he must be given extra pay, called *overtime*. According to

the law, each hour of overtime must be paid at one and a half times the regular rate (called "time and a half"). So if a person works 40 hours, his pay must be at least $102, and if he works 44 hours he receives $13.80 for the extra four hours, making his pay for that week $115.80. Actually, most workers in the United States get much higher pay.

Many labor unions have contracts under which their employers pay "double time" or "triple time" for overtime work on certain days, such as Sundays and holidays.

The Federal wages and hours laws apply only to employees of companies that do business in more than one state, so many local jobs pay less than the national minimum.

Wagner, Hans

Hans Wagner was one of the great baseball players of all time. Nearly all experts consider him to have been the finest shortstop. He was born in Carnegie, Pennsylvania, in 1874. His real name was John Peter Wagner, but as a baseball player he was called either "Honus" or Hans. He started his baseball career in Louisville, Kentucky in 1897. From 1900 to 1917 he played for Pittsburgh in the National League. He led the league in hitting in eight different years. He also led the league in stolen bases five different times. He played more games, 2,785, than any other player in National League history. He made 3,430 hits during his career, which was the highest in National League history. He also made more runs and stole more bases than any one in National League history, and he included among his hits more singles, doubles, and triples. When the baseball Hall of Fame was created in 1936, Hans Wagner was among the first group to be elected members. A bronze plaque with his record engraved on it is in the Baseball Hall of Fame building in Cooperstown, New York.

Wagner, Richard

Richard Wagner was a German composer, or writer of original music, who lived about a hundred years ago. He is considered among the greatest composers of operas, which are serious plays in which all of the conversation is sung, not spoken as in other plays.

Wagner was born in 1813 in Leipzig, which was then one of the chief cities of the German kingdom of Prussia. He did not study music at first, but he was a brilliant student and by the time he was 14 he had translated 12 books of Homer's great poem, the *Odyssey*, from Greek into German. He then became interested in music and at the age of 21 he became conductor of an orchestra in the city of Magdeburg, where he remained for two years. In the following years he conducted at several other towns.

In 1840 and 1841 Wagner's first two operas, *Rienzi* and *The Flying Dutchman,* were produced with great success. Wagner then went to Dresden, in Saxony, where he conducted at the king's court. In 1849 Wagner was accused of taking

part in an uprising against the king, called the May Day Rebellion, and was forced to flee from Germany. For the next twelve years he lived in Zurich, Switzerland, but also conducted in other cities, notably in London, England. In 1861 he and others who had been accused were pardoned, and he returned to Germany. He settled in Bayreuth, where a special theater was founded to produce his operas. He finally lived in Italy, where he died, in Venice, in 1883.

Wagner wrote several books on music, some poems, and many musical compositions. His operas, however, were his greatest works, and most of them are performed today in the leading opera houses of the world. Wagner is credited with making an opera a real play, in which the story is as important as the music. He also developed the technique of the *leit-motiv*. This meant that a certain melody was associated with a certain character in an opera, and whenever that character was about to appear "his" melody was played, announcing him to the audience.

Among the Wagnerian operas that are most often performed today are the *Ring of the Nibelung,* a cycle (group) of four operas; *The Meistersinger, Parsifal, Tristan and Isolde, Tannhäuser, Lohengrin,* and *The Flying Dutchman.* There are separate articles about most of these.

Wake Island

Wake Island is a coral atoll in the Pacific Ocean, about 2,500 miles west of Hawaii. It is best known as the second United States territory attacked by Japan in World War II and the scene of heroic defense by American forces. Wake Island was discovered in 1796 by British sailors and was named Halcyon Island, but because it stands alone in a vast ocean area it was many years before its existence was verified by an American expedition and claimed for the United States. It was renamed Wake Island for the British explorer who had discovered it. In 1899 the United States took possession of the island, and in 1935 it became a base and stop-over point for airplanes flying across the Pacific.

In 1941 Wake Island was made a national defense area. About 400 Marines were stationed there and a thousand American workmen were brought in to build an air base. On December 8, 1941, the day after the attack on Pearl Harbor and the Philippines, Japanese planes began to bomb Wake Island, destroying eight of the garrison's twelve planes. Three days later the Japanese attempted a landing, but the gallant Americans drove them off and managed to destroy four Japanese naval vessels. Several more landing attempts were made, until by December 23 the garrison was almost helpless and was forced to surrender.

The captured Marines and civilians were held prisoner in Japan for the remainder of the war. United States forces frequently bombed the Japanese installations on Wake Island but no attempt was made to retake it. The Japanese garrison surrendered in 1945, and the island again became a military and civilian air base.

Waldenses

The Waldenses were a Christian religious group that became popular about

eight hundred years ago, in the 12th century. They took their name from a man named Peter Waldo, of Lyon, France. His followers were known as the Poor Men of Lyon. They believed everyone should follow the command of Jesus to a certain young man to give all he had to the poor, as told in the Bible in the Book of Matthew. They asked the church to recognize them as a separate order, but the church refused. Most of them fled to Piedmont, a region between Italy and France. When the Reformation began, they became a Protestant group. In 1848, they were officially granted liberty to worship as they pleased. Today there are Waldensian Churches in various parts of the world, but they are very small, with only a few thousand members in all. To their own membership they are known as the *Vaudois*.

Wales

Wales is a region in the southwestern part of the island of Great Britain. Along with England to the east and Scotland, to the north, and Northern Ireland on the other British island, Wales is part of the United Kingdom of Great Britain and Northern Ireland. It is a political division of England, with which it has been united since 1536.

Wales is about 8,000 square miles in area, which is about the size of the state of Massachusetts. More than 2,500,000 people live there, which is about half as many as live in Massachusetts.

Wales is a land of wild and rugged beauty. Its coastline is deeply indented with bays and off the northwest coast is the island of Anglesey, which forms a county of Wales. Most of the region consists of highlands, with mountains rising in the northwest and southeast. There is a coastal plain around three sides. Most of the people live on the coastal plain.

The principal river of Wales is the Severn. Others are the Taff, the Usk, the Wye, and the Dee. There are two important lakes: Lake Bala in the north, which is the source of the Dee; and Lake Vyrnwy.

In the western part of Wales the climate is cool in summer and mild in winter; in the eastern part the summers are warm and the winters cold. Rainfall is heavy throughout the region.

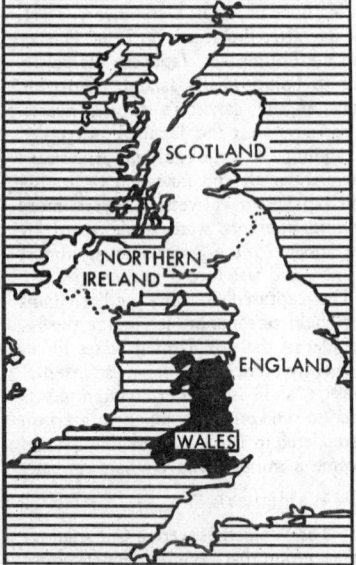

THE WELSH PEOPLE

The Welsh people (people of Wales) are descended from the earliest known inhabitants of the region and from the Celts who invaded the British Isles about 2,500 years ago. Most Welsh people have dark hair and eyes.

Most of the people belong to Protestant Churches. Until 1920 the Church of England was the state Church of Wales. The ancient Welsh language, a member of the Celtic group of languages, is still spoken, though in the 1500s English was made the official language. Almost all of the people speak English, and about a third of them can speak both Welsh and English.

The great Welsh national festival is the Eisteddfod, a music festival that has been held almost every year for some five hundred years. Welsh poets, composers and musicians take part in this yearly festival, and in recent years it has become an international event with musicians invited from countries all over the world.

Mining and manufacturing are the major occupations of the people of Wales. The country is rich in minerals, especially coal and iron, and a great many of the people work in the mines. The industries of Wales are mostly connected with the mine products. There are great iron and steel mills and tin-plating factories. In the interior of the country most of the people are dairy farmers or raise cattle and sheep. The chief cities of Wales are Cardiff, Swansea, Rhondda, and Merthyr Tydfil.

WALES IN THE PAST

In ancient times the Romans conquered Wales, but they made little impression on the people except to bring them Christianity.

After the Romans left, the Anglo-Saxons invaded England and gradually hemmed the Welsh people into the region that now forms the Welsh peninsula. The Welsh tribes became a nation under one king and began to build their own tradition of folklore, music, and literature.

After the Norman French began to rule England in 1066, the English began to put pressure on the Welsh. Little by little the Welsh chieftains came to adopt some English ways and to take part in English affairs. By 1282 Wales completely conquered by England. To please the Welsh, Edward I of England had his son (later Edward II) proclaimed Prince of Wales, and the eldest son of the British king has usually held this title ever since.

For several hundred years there was considerable unrest in Wales, and the English kings tried to quiet it by making Wales as English as possible. Welsh ways and laws were dropped in favor of English ones. In 1536, during the reign of Henry VIII, the Act of Union was passed making English the legal language and abolishing all remaining Welsh laws. The further history of Wales is that of England, about which you can read in a separate article.

WALES. Area, 8,016 square miles. Population (1961 census) 2,640,632. Government, part of the United Kingdom of Great Britain and Northern Ireland. Languages, English and Welsh. Religion, Protestant Christian.

Wales, Prince of

The eldest son of the king or queen of England becomes the Prince of Wales. In most kingdoms, he would be called the crown prince. The title of Prince of Wales does not automatically belong to the eldest son. The king (or queen) does not have to give him that title, but it has usually been done for more than six hundred years. Probably the most famous holders of the title were Edward the Black Prince, who lived from 1330 to 1376 and never became king; the son of George III, who was the regent, or actual ruler of England, for several years because his father was mentally ill, and who later became George IV; and the Prince of Wales who later became Edward VIII and then gave up the throne and became the Duke of Windsor.

The Prince of Wales has no real position in Wales. The title is purely honorary. However, the Welsh people usually have a particular fondness for the Prince, because of his title. The Prince of Wales inherits the additional title of Duke of Cornwall; when he is old enough he becomes a member of the House of Lords.

walkie-talkie

Walkie-talkie is the nickname for a small radio set that can both receive and send messages. A walkie-talkie is a radio in a small box about the size of a shoe box. It was carried by soldiers in World War II. A long metal rod attached to the box served as the antenna. The soldier carrying the walkie-talkie could talk into a small microphone in the box and carry on a conversation with headquarters or with another soldier carrying a walkie-talkie. By holding the set close to his ear he could hear the messages coming in. The walkie-talkie could operate up to a distance of about a mile. More modern

British Inform. Services

The Welsh language has many long words. The full name of Llanfair in northwest Wales on the Isle of Anglesey is given on its railroad station. The name means: "The church place of St. Mary by the pool of the white hazel by the rapid whirlpool of the church of St. Sillogog of the red cave." The name is almost as long as the tiny town itself.

walkie-talkies have extended the operating distance. Walkie-talkies operate on batteries.

Wallace, Henry A.

Henry Agard Wallace is the name of an American political leader who held several high offices in the United States government, was Vice President of the United States under President Franklin D. Roosevelt, and was a candidate for President in 1948. Wallace was born in 1888 in Adair County, Iowa. He was graduated from Iowa State College and first worked as editor of his family's magazine, *Wallace's Farmer*.

Wallace was successful in experimenting with new strains of plants, and he developed several varieties of hybrid corn that soon were widely used by farmers in the Midwest. In 1933 he was appointed Secretary of Agriculture by President Roosevelt. He did a great deal to reorganize the Department of Agriculture and to develop the Agricultural Adjustment Administration, a government agency organized during the depression to help farmers. In 1940 Wallace was elected Vice President. Under President Truman he was appointed Secretary of Commerce in 1945, but the following year he resigned.

In 1948 Wallace became a leader of a new political party called the Progressive Party, and he was its candidate for the Presidency, but most people did not vote for him because they believed his party was controlled by Communists. Wallace himself resigned from the Progressive Party in 1950. He retired but wrote several books on modern methods of farming and on political affairs. Wallace died in 1965.

Wallenstein, Albrecht von

Albrecht Eusebius Wenzel von Wallenstein was an Austrian general of about 450 years ago. He is remembered chiefly for his prominence in the THIRTY YEARS' WAR, about which there is a separate article. Wallenstein was born in 1583, of a noble family. He entered the Austrian Army and served in many campaigns. He later quarreled with Ferdinand II, the Holy Roman Emperor (then also Austrian Emperor) and was removed from command of his armies. He was assassinated in 1634.

Walloons

The Walloons are a French-speaking people who live in the southern part of Belgium. For the most part they work in the mines and in manufacturing. They have a very different background and culture from the Flemings, the people who live in northern Belgium. The word Walloon originally referred to a French dialect. Protestant Walloons, along with Huguenots, or French Protestants, were among the first settlers in New Amsterdam, which is now New York. The Dutch people living there called all these settlers Walloons.

wallpaper

Wallpaper is used to cover walls with an attractive design or pattern. It was invented about five hundred years ago, in Europe, to replace the costly silk hangings and tapestries that people had

been using to cover the walls of castles and palaces.

Probably the Chinese had been using wallpaper long before the Europeans. Old Chinese wallpaper was hand-painted and was very beautiful but very expensive. European wallpaper was invented after the invention of the printing press and cost much less.

Wallpaper is a thick, heavy paper that will last a long time. There are many different designs. Some are simple patterns and some are pictures. Wallpapers come in many different price ranges. Some are very inexpensive and can be used by people everywhere. Others are so expensive that the wallpaper in one house can cost thousands of dollars.

HANGING WALLPAPER

Wallpaper is put on a wall with paste. The process is called *paperhanging*. A good paperhanger is as much a craftsman as any other skilled workman.

Wallpaper comes in rolls that are usually about two feet wide and 50 to 100 feet long. The paperhanger unrolls the paper and may cut it into lengths. Each length of paper must be slightly longer than the height of the wall to which the paper is to be applied. The paperhanger then puts a paste on the back of the wallpaper with a large brush. The paste is somewhat like the homemade paste that is made from a mixture of flour and water.

After the paste is thoroughly applied, the paperhanger folds the paper so that the pasted side is put together at the ends. He then folds it again several times, being careful to keep the edges together. He then takes a sharp knife and trims the edges of the paper. Then he takes the folded paper, goes up his ladder, and unfolds the paper. He applies the paper to the wall with a little bit extending over the top. He then smooths the whole length of the paper on the wall, using a roller and a wide, soft brush. At the bottom of the wall there is another overhang of paper, which he trims off evenly.

He then takes the next length of paper and applies it to the wall next to the first length. He brings the edges together so carefully that it can hardly be seen where they join. If the paper has a large, overall pattern, such as leaves and flowers, the paperhanger must very carefully place one length of paper next to another so that the patterns match. This is not necessary if the paper is a plain color or design. The most difficult paper to hang is that which has a picture on it.

There are papers on the market today that are made so that almost anyone can but them up. These are usually pretrimmed and prepared, so that all the home paperhanger has to do is wet them, stick them on the wall, trim them at the top and bottom, and smooth them down.

Wallpaper can be used to decorate many things, not only walls. It can be used on screens, wastepaper baskets, furniture, and many other things.

Some wallpapers are waterproofed or treated so that they can be washed. There is also a preparation that can be sprayed on wallpapers to protect them from dust and dirt and make it possible to clean them by wiping them off with a damp cloth.

walnut

Walnut is a name given to any number of a group of trees, some of which are grown for their lumber, some for decorative or shade purposes, and some for their nuts. Most kinds of walnut trees are graceful and attractive in shape. There are varieties that can be raised in most parts of the world. Walnuts are deciduous trees, which means that they lose their leaves in the fall and grow new leaves in the spring.

The black walnut is the largest kind of walnut tree. It is a wide-spreading tree that affords excellent shade. The English, or Persian, walnut tree is smaller. It is the source of the walnut most often used as food, but the black walnut is very popular as a nut. In California the English walnut is grafted to the California walnut and grown in large orchards.

Walpole, Sir Robert

Robert Walpole was an English statesman who lived more than two hundred years ago. He is considered the man who introduced the custom of having a Prime Minister in the British government.

Walpole was born in 1676. He was elected a Member of Parliament when he was 25, and he soon rose to hold such offices as Secretary for War and Treasurer of the Navy. When King George I took the throne in 1714 Walpole quickly became the most important man in the government. He spoke for King George because the king was German by birth and did not speak English well. Walpole was head of the cabinet, which ran the country, so he was really the Prime Minister of Great Britain, though the title had not then been created officially.

Walpole held power for 21 years. He made Great Britain stronger and richer than it had been, but in 1739 he took England into a war that was very unpopular with the people and in 1742 he was forced to resign. He was made Earl of Orford and remained a powerful political leader until his death in 1745.

walrus

The walrus is an animal that lives partly on land and partly in the sea in the northern Atlantic and Pacific Oceans, in the icy stretches of the Arctic Ocean. It is related to the seal and sea lion but has big tusks. Both males and females have tusks. Valuable ivory is taken from walrus tusks, but it is not as fine as the ivory from elephants' tusks.

The walrus is a mammal, which means that the young are born alive and the mother nurses them. A large male walrus may be ten or eleven feet long and may weigh between 2,000 to 3,000 pounds. A herd, or large group, of walruses will often sleep on huge ice floes in closely packed rows. At the first hint of danger to the herd, the bellowing of the bulls can be heard for miles. The walrus has the loudest and most powerful voice of any of the Arctic animals.

The walrus gets food by diving to the

bottom of the ocean and scraping up shellfish with its powerful tusks. Young walruses must live on their mothers' milk until they are about two years old.

Walton, Izaak

Izaak Walton was a writer who lived in England almost four hundred years ago. He wrote *The Compleat Angler.* one of the best-known and best-loved books in the English language. *The Compleat Angler* is about the sport of fishing. It is also full of descriptions of a peaceful way of life that have appealed to many people who cared little about knowing how to fish. The book was first published in 1653. Walton added material to later editions.

Izaak Walton was born in 1593 in Stafford, England. He was by profession an ironmonger, and he had little formal schooling. He also wrote biographies of several important men of the time, most of whom were his friends. He died in 1683.

wampum, shells and other colored materials often used by American Indians for money: see the articles on MONEY and SHELLS.

wapiti, a kind of elk: see ELK.

war

War is fighting between nations. Ever since men first formed themselves into groups to live together, there has been fighting between the groups. As the small groups became tribes, and then cities, and finally nations, wars have become bigger and bigger. The two World Wars fought in the present century were by far the biggest of all time.

In warfare, almost everything that is a crime in peacetime is legally done against the enemy—killing, robbing, destruction of property, kidnapping, and almost any crime you can think of.

There are various reasons why wars are fought, but usually they begin with the greed of some men who have power in a country. The country that begins a war is called an *aggressor nation.* Thousands of years ago, one tribe would make war on another tribe so as to steal its possessions and make slaves of its people. Modern wars are often fought because two countries are competing with each other in business and trade, or because one country wants territory that another country controls.

Wars are often caused by fear and suspicion. Each of two countries thinks the other is planning to attack it. One of the countries finally reasons, "If we have to fight sooner or later, we may as well attack first and have the advantage of surprise." Then the war begins. It may be that the other country was not planning to attack.

One war has a way of causing another war. The victor in a war takes territory from the loser. The loser wants revenge and may start a war later to get its territory back. There are some territories that have changed hands several times. Every nation that ever owned it is likely to claim it, saying, "Once it belonged to us and it was taken away from us." The nation is likely to forget it too once won the territory in warfare.

CHANGE IN METHODS

The earliest warfare was hand-to-hand fighting. Gradually weapons and machines of war were developed, but until the present century most of the fighting was still done by men on foot or on horseback, fighting against each other with swords or guns. For thousands of years, many young men were thrilled by war. They were willing to risk their lives for the excitement of battle and the chance of winning glory.

In those days, war was more like a sporting encounter in many ways. There were "rules" that fighting men obeyed. Often the "champion" (best fighter) or perhaps the king or leader of one army would fight against the champion or leader of the other army. All the other fighting men would stand and watch but would not interfere. If one of the leaders was defeated, his whole army would surrender.

Now warfare has changed. Most of the damage is done by bombing planes miles high and by artillery that fires shells for distances of twenty or more miles. People have learned that war helps no one and hurts millions.

EFFORTS TO OUTLAW WAR

In all ages there have been wise men who knew that war is stupid. They have tried many ways to end wars. So far they have not been successful.

From time to time, there have been long periods of peace in some parts of the world because one nation became so strong that it could force other nations to keep the peace. Nearly two thousand years ago the Roman Empire kept peace in most of Europe and the lands around the Mediterranean Sea. This period of peace was called the *Pax Romana,* or Roman peace. Some great emperors in Asia have kept the peace in the same way. Sooner or later, other nations would become strong enough to attack the great empire and the peace would end.

There has never been a time when there has been peace all over the world for more than a few years. In modern times, there have been three principal ways in which countries have tried to bring peace to the world. One way is disarmament, another is by treaties or agreements between nations, and the third is by setting up an international organization such as the United Nations.

The idea of disarmament is that wars often begin because nations fear one another. Because of this fear, each nation makes its own armed forces as big and strong as possible. This creates more fear. An "armaments race" begins, and usually ends in war. There have been several Disarmament Conferences at which the big countries have been asked to reduce their armed forces so much that no other nation will fear them. But always there has been at least one other country that insisted on remaining very strong, and as long as one nation does this every other nation does the same thing for self-protection.

Treaties to end war are usually called "nonaggression" treaties. Two or more nations agree not to attack each other. The most famous modern treaty was the Locarno Pact (agreement), signed at Locarno, Switzerland, in 1925. Germany, France, Great Britain, Italy and Belgium agreed not to start a war. But Germany's government changed, and the new government (the Nazis) went back on the promises of the former government and started World War II.

The Kellogg-Briand Peace Pact was signed by Frank Kellogg, the United States Secretary of State, and Aristide Briand, the Premier of France, in 1928. Nearly fifty nations agreed not to use war as a way of settling arguments. This did not work either, because some of the nations broke their promises again.

The League of Nations, formed in 1920, and the United Nations, formed in 1945, are examples of international organizations that are formed chiefly to end wars.

There are separate articles on DISARMAMENT, the LEAGUE OF NATIONS, and the UNITED NATIONS.

COST AND FINANCING OF U. S. WARS

WORLD WAR II $251.7 BILLION

TAX RECEIPTS VS. COST OF WAR
126%
100%
54%   45%
40%
CIVIL   SPAN.   W.W.   W.W
AMER.   I   II

CIVIL WAR $3.4 BILLION

Graphics Institute for "American National Government" by Swisher; Houghton Mifflin Co.

In the years between the Civil War and World War II the cost of war was multiplied by seventy. In no major war has the country been able to pay for the cost of war out of tax receipts. The rest of the money needed had to be borrowed.

War, U.S. Department of

The United States Department of War was a department of the United States government that was in charge of the army. It was established in 1789 and was one of the first departments in the government. The head of the Department of War was the Secretary of War. He was a member of the President's cabinet. In 1947 the department's name was changed to Department of the Army, which became a part of the Department of Defense. The head of the Department of the Army is called the Secretary of the Army, but he is not a member of the President's cabinet.

Warm Springs Foundation

The Georgia Warm Springs Foundation is an organization that treats people who suffer from infantile paralysis. It was founded in 1927 by Franklin D. Roosevelt, who had been treated there after he was stricken with the disease.

The city of Warm Springs, Georgia, has long been a health resort. The springs, which flow from the side of Pine Mountain, have a never-changing tem-

perature of 88 degrees. The Indians used to visit them when wounded or sick. For many years Warm Springs was a popular health resort that rich southern people enjoyed.

Roosevelt bought a farm at Warm Springs. Later he gave it to the Foundation, but he kept his cottage there, which was known as the "Little White House" after he became President. He died in the cottage, which was later made a national shrine.

Today, the Foundation has many buildings where the patients can live while receiving care. There is a swimming pool fed by the springs where hydrotherapy is given. (Hydrotherapy is a way of developing muscles by massage and exercise in warm water.)

Many of the people treated at Warm Springs cannot pay for their care. Their expenses are paid by the National Foundation for Infantile Paralysis, which raises money through the yearly March of Dimes. See the article on INFANTILE PARALYSIS.

War of 1812

The War of 1812 was a war between the United States and Great Britain. It began in 1812 and the fighting went on until 1815. It cannot be said that either side won the war, because the situation was about the same at the end as it was at the beginning, but it did have one important result. After the War of 1812 the countries of Europe had more respect for the United States.

HOW THE WAR BEGAN

In 1812 Great Britain and France were at war against each other. Great Britain did not have enough sailors for its navy, and British warships would often stop American ships at sea and take off sailors who had been born in British countries. The British said these men were subject to their laws and had to fight in the British navy. Many of these sailors were really Americans, and the United States protested against this custom.

The British also tried to stop American ships from trading with France, and there were other causes for the war. At that time American frontier settlers were pouring into the area that is now the states of Illinois, Michigan, and Indiana. They had many fights with the Indians. The British in Canada helped the Indians to fight against the Americans, so some people in the United States wanted to invade Canada and take it away from the British. Finally, on June 18, 1812, Congress declared war on Britain.

THE FIGHTING

At the beginning of the war there were several battles in the Atlantic Ocean between American and British warships. Perhaps the most famous of these battles was the one in which the *Constitution,* an American warship, beat the British *Guerriere.* But though the Americans won most of the sea battles, Britain still controlled the seas and was able to stop most of the American trade with Europe.

When the war began, the Americans decided to attack Canada. This attack failed and the British were then able to invade the United States and take Detroit. The Indian friends of England killed many Americans on the frontier. But in 1813 an American fleet under Commodore Oliver Hazard Perry defeated the British in the Battle of Lake Erie, and another American fleet beat the British in the Battle of Plattsburg, which was fought on Lake Champlain in New York State, and an American army under General William Henry Harrison beat a British and Indian army at the Thames River in Canada.

About 400,000 Americans volunteered to fight the British, but they were mostly untrained men, and very few of them actually did any fighting. In August, 1814, a British force landed near Washington, D.C., and captured the nation's capital. President James Madison and his wife, Dolly Madison, had to flee from the city. The British burned down the White House and several other buildings before they left. Then they sailed up Chesapeake Bay to attack Baltimore. On the night of September 13, 1814, the British ships bombarded Fort McHenry, which guarded Baltimore. A man named Francis Scott Key watched the attack and described it in "The Star Spangled Banner," which was put to music and became the national anthem of the United States.

END OF THE WAR

In December, 1814, a British army landed near the city of New Orleans, but the next month it was beaten by the Americans under General Andrew Jackson in the Battle of New Orleans. This was a great American victory, but it did not make any difference, because a peace treaty had already been signed with England at the town of Ghent in Belgium. The armies at New Orleans did not know about this, because it took about a month for the news to be brought across the Atlantic.

The Treaty of Ghent did not decide much, except to stop the fighting. Since the war between England and France was now over, the trouble that had started the War of 1812 had almost all disappeared. A committee was appointed to decide what would be the exact boundary line between the United States and Canada. These two countries have been at peace with each other ever since.

Warren, Earl

Earl Warren served as the 14th Chief Justice of the United States, from 1953 (when he was appointed by President Eisenhower) to 1969 (when he was succeeded by Judge Warren Earl Burger).

He was born in 1891 in Los Angeles, California and, in 1914, was graduated from the University of California Law School at Berkeley.

After serving in the United States Army in World War I, Warren was elected Governor of California in 1942, serving for three successive terms. In 1948, he became the Republican candidate for Vice President—but the Republicans lost.

Under Warren, the Supreme Court made several notable decisions in the areas of civil rights, criminal justice, and legislative reapportionment.

In 1963, Warren was appointed by President Johnson to head a special commission to investigate the assassination of President Kennedy. After an exhaustive study of all the facts, the commission published the *Warren Report* in 1964, in which it was concluded that there was no evidence of any conspiracy (agreement among several people to do evil) to kill President Kennedy.

Warsaw

Warsaw is the capital and largest city of Poland. It is in the east central part of the country, on both banks of the Vistula River. The residential section of the city, called Praga, is on the east bank of the river. Warsaw is the cultural and industrial center of Poland. More than one million people live there. Many of them work in the great metal industry and in factories that make electrical equipment, machine tools, precision instruments, chemicals, and textiles. Railroad lines link Warsaw with the great cities of Europe and the Soviet Union.

Warsaw arose as a city about six hundred years ago, as the residence and capital of the dukes of Masovia. After Poland's capital city of Cracow was destroyed by fire in 1595, Warsaw was made the capital. The city was occupied in turn by Sweden, Russia, Prussia, and then Russia again. After World War I, Warsaw again became the capital of an independent Poland.

During World War II, Warsaw was the first city to fall to the Germans, though it put up a strong resistance. About a third of the people were Jews, and the Germans killed almost all of them in brutal massacres. During the war almost nine-tenths of Warsaw was destroyed, including most of its beautiful old churches and palaces and almost half of the suburb of Praga. After the war Warsaw became the capital of Communist, Soviet-dominated Poland. It was rebuilt rapidly along modern lines. The university was reopened, new schools, theaters and other buildings were built, and some of the famous landmarks were reconstructed.

WARSAW, POLAND. Population (1974 census) 1,283,900. Capital of Poland. On the Vistula River.

warship, a ship equipped for fighting at sea: see the articles on NAVY, AIRCRAFT CARRIER, BATTLESHIP, CRUISER, DESTROYER, and SUBMARINE.

Wars of the Roses: see ROSES, WARS OF THE.

wart

A wart is a small, rough growth on the skin. Warts appear most often on the hands but may grow on any part of the skin. A wart is colorless, painless, and harmless unless it is torn. For this reason a wart should never be picked at, nor should a person try to remove it. A doctor is the only one who should remove warts. Doctors have several simple ways of doing this. They can prevent the wart from growing again and becoming harmful.

Warts are caused either by a virus infecting a small part of the skin, or by constant rubbing or friction. Sometimes a person will get a wart on a part of a finger that is constantly rubbed by a pen or pencil. The most painful wart is called a plantar wart, that is, a wart on the sole of the foot. As soon as a plantar wart is noticed a doctor should be consulted.

There are many old stories and superstitions about warts. People used to believe such nonsense as that warts were caused by handling toads. They also had many magic cures for warts.

wart hog

The wart hog is a member of the same family as pigs, peccaries, and hippopotamuses, and is the ugliest-looking animal in the entire group. In fact, many people declare that the wart hog is the ugliest creature in the world. Its head is oversized for its body, its eyes are tiny and deeply sunken in its face, and it has ugly lumps or warts on both sides of its face, which is flat and hollowed-out. Its nose is a dull-shovel-shaped snout with tusks that curve upward, and it is covered with ugly lumps and bumps of gristle.

The wart hog lives in the grassy plains of northeastern and central Africa. It digs up roots for food, and sometimes it grazes on plants growing above the ground.

A large boar may be about two and a half feet high at the shoulder and weigh about two hundred pounds. The female usually raises two litters of young a year, with six to eight in a litter.

Washington

Washington is a state in the northwestern corner of the United States. It is on the Pacific Ocean. Its nickname is the "Evergreen State," because of the many pine, fir, and other evergreen trees that grow in its forests. The state is named for George Washington.

In area, Washington ranks 20th among the states, with 68,192 square miles. In population it ranks 22nd, with about three million people living there. It became a state in 1889, and was the 42nd state admitted to the United States. The capital is Olympia.

THE PEOPLE OF WASHINGTON

The earliest permanent settlements in Washington were made about a hundred years ago by American, French and British fur-traders. The early settlers of the region came from states that had been settled earlier, and from Canada. Later, Chinese workers came north from California and immigrants came from Sweden, Norway, England, and other European countries. There are about 50,000 Negroes in the state and about 20,000 Indians. Many of the Indians live on government reservations.

About half the people in Washington live in and around the big cities. Many work in lumber mills, where they make wood pulp, shingles, and furniture, and in aluminum plants, aircraft factories, and shipyards. There are also large factories where fish, vegetables and fruits are packed.

The people who live on farms and in rural areas of Washington grow vegetables and grain, particularly wheat, and fruits. More apples are grown in Washington than in any other state.

Many farmers raise large numbers of cattle and sheep, for there are excellent grazing lands in the state. The raising of horses and goats has also become important in recent years. In the western part of the state there are many dairy farms, as well as huge plants where dairy products are prepared.

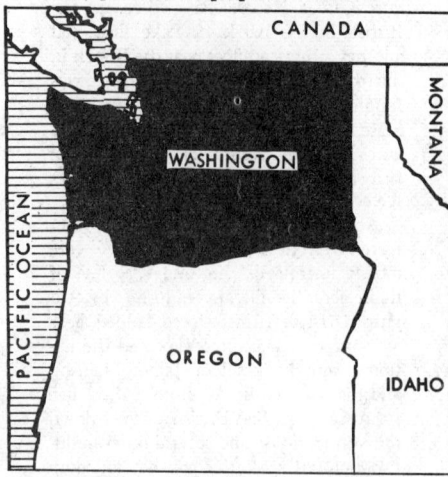

Washington has rich deposits of coal, clay, building stones, gold, silver, and copper, and many of the people work in the mines. The fishing is excellent along the coast and in rivers. Many of the fishermen go as far north as Alaska for their catches of salmon and halibut.

The largest religious groups are the Roman Catholics, the Methodists, and the Presbyterians.

WHAT WASHINGTON IS LIKE

Washington is divided into two parts by the Cascade Mountains, which run from north to south toward the western half of the state. In these mountains are some of the highest peaks in the country, including Mount Rainier (14,408 feet) and Mount Baker (10,750 feet). Near the center of the state are a series of passes through the mountains. Most of the minerals in the state are found in the Cascade Mountains.

East of the Cascade Mountains is a large plain, where there are very few trees. Here the Spokane, Columbia and Snake Rivers provide water for the growing of wheat and other crops. This land was once almost all pasture land, but the building of the GRAND COULEE DAM, about which there is a separate article, turned this plain into rich farm land.

West of the Cascade Mountains is a low valley, bordered on the northwest by the Olympic Mountains. The valley is cut in two by Puget Sound, an arm of the Pacific Ocean, which is more than 100 miles long. There are two main branches to the sound, Hood Canal on the west and Admiralty Bay on the east. There are many islands in the sound, of which the largest is Whidby Island, more than 50 miles long. In this part of the state are most of the large cities.

Washington has a cool climate. The average temperature in winter is 30 degrees, and in summer is 65 degrees.

There are many wild animals in the mountains, including the elk, deer, and bear. The state is famous for its game fish, particularly its salmon, which come up the rivers to spawn.

Puget Sound has made northwestern Washington very important. Seattle, on the sound, is the principal seaport of the northwest, and, along with other cities, serves as a center of world trade. There are many miles of railroads in the state. Scenic highways, along which thousands of tourists drive each year, reach most parts of the state. There are airports in all the major cities.

THE GOVERNMENT OF WASHINGTON

Washington, like other states, has a governor at the head of its government and a legislature that makes its laws. The legislature is made up of a Senate and a House of Representatives. The governor is elected for a four-year term, the Senators for four-year terms, and the members of the House for two-year terms. Judges are elected for six-year terms. The capital is Olympia. There are 39 counties.

Everyone has to go to school between the ages of 8 and 16. There are about 820,000 pupils attending public elementary and high schools. Among the colleges and universities are:

University of Washington, at Seattle. Enrollment, 31,009 men and women in 1971.
Washington State University, at Pullman. Enrollment, 12,714 men and women in 1971.
Gonzaga University, at Spokane. Enrollment, 2,598 men and women in 1971.
Whitman College, at Walla Walla. Enrollment, about 1,063 men and women in 1971.
Walla Walla College, at College Place. Enrollment, 1,564 men and women in 1971.

CHIEF CITIES OF WASHINGTON

The leading cities of Washington, with population from the 1970 census, are:

Seattle, population 530,831, the largest city in the state. There is a separate article about SEATTLE.
Spokane, population 170,516, the second-largest city. There is a separate article about SPOKANE.
Tacoma, population 154,581, the third-largest city. There is a separate article about TACOMA.
Yakima, population 45,588, the fourth-largest city, apple growing center, in the south central part.
Everett, population 53,622, the fifth-largest city, port and center of commerce and of lumber-processing industry, on Puget Sound.
There is a separate article about the capital, OLYMPIA.

WASHINGTON IN THE PAST

For many years Washington was part of what was called the Oregon Territory. This territory included, besides the present state of Washington, all of Oregon and Idaho and parts of Montana, Wyoming, and the Canadian province of British Columbia.

The part of this territory that is now the state of Washington was probably first explored by the Englishman, Sir Francis Drake, in 1578. In 1592 Juan de Fuca, a Greek exploring for the Spanish, discovered the strait that leads into Puget Sound. This strait is named for him. These explorers were followed by others, among them Captain Cook, MacKenzie, Lewis and Clark, and Vancouver. In 1834 Methodist missionaries founded the first permanent settlements.

The Oregon territory was first claimed by Spain and later by both Great Britain and the United States. In 1846 the boundaries of the region were finally agreed upon, after a bitter argument that almost led to war. (See the article on FIFTY-FOUR FORTY OR FIGHT.)

The state of Washington received its present boundaries only after Oregon

and Idaho had been admitted as states, in 1859 and 1863.

Until about a hundred years ago, there were only about 4,000 people living in Washington. When it became a state in 1889, there were only 300,000 people living there. Many of these settlers came to Washington along the OREGON TRAIL, about which there is a separate article. Since the building of the Grand Coulee Dam and the Bonneville Dam, industry and agriculture have increased greatly. During World War II Washington became important for its plutonium plant at Hanford, near the city of Richland, and for its production of aluminum.

PLACES TO SEE

Mount Rainier National Park, 241,-524 acres, about 50 miles southeast of Tacoma, in the west central part, on U.S. Route 410. Mount Rainier, highest peak in the state. Mountain trails and beautiful scenery.

Olympic National Park, 846,765 acres, south of Port Angeles, in the northwest, on U.S. Route 101. Rain forests and glaciers.

Grand Coulee Dam, 4,300 feet long and 550 feet high, about 80 miles northwest of Spokane, in the central part, on U.S. Route State Highway 10A. Roosevelt Lake, 151 miles long, a recreation center, is formed by the dam.

Tulalip Indian Reservation, near Everett, in the northwest on Puget Sound, on U.S. Route 99.

WASHINGTON. Area, 68,192 miles. Population (1970 census) 3,409,169. Capital, Olympia. Nickname, Evergreen State. Motto, Alki (By and By). Flower, rhododendron. Bird, willow goldfinch. Song, "Washington Beloved." Admitted to Union, November 11, 1889. Official Abbreviation, Wash. or WA.

Washington, D.C.

Washington is the capital of the United States of America. It is the ninth-largest city in the country, and about 760,000 people live there. It is on the Potomac River.

The city of Washington is not in any state. It is in a separate district called the District of Columbia. The District of Columbia has an area of 69 square miles, and the city covers the entire area.

Until 1895, Georgetown was a separate city in the District of Columbia, but at that time it became part of the city of Washington.

Most of the business of the United States government is carried on in Washington. Here, too, the embassies and legations of foreign countries have their own buildings.

There are more than 200,000 people who work for the government in Washington. Some of these people live in the city, but many of them live in nearby cities such as Alexandria, Virginia, and in residential suburbs in Virginia and Maryland. Nearly three-fourths of the people who live in Washington are Negroes.

Washington has some factories and many business offices not connected with the government. Each year millions of people visit Washington.

WHAT WASHINGTON IS LIKE

Washington is one of the most beautiful capital cities in the world. Its original

The United States Congress holds session at the Capitol in Washington, D.C.

design was made by Pierre Charles L'Enfant, a French architect. He was helped by George Washington. Later, other architects changed his plan somewhat.

L'Enfant wanted the city laid out so that the most important building, the Capitol itself, would be at the center of the city and would be visible from all parts of the city. He thought of the city as being surrounded by a series of parks. Although the parks have not all been finished yet, much of the original plan for the city has been followed. The Capitol is on Capitol Hill, a flat topped hill that is higher than the land surrounding it. From the hill, the city is divided into four equal sections by three streets running east, north, and south, and by Washington Mall. The Mall runs to the west and is an area of walks, gardens, and memorials, including the Lincoln Memorial at one end and the Washington Monument in the middle.

Washington then can be thought of as a large circle that has been divided into four sections. The dividing streets are called East Capitol Street, North Capitol Street, and South Capitol Street. The four sections are called Northeast, Northwest, Southeast, and Southwest. These sections are usually written N.E., N.W., S.E., and S.W.

Other streets run north-south and east-west in even squares. The streets running north and south have numbers, and the streets going east and west have letters.

The streets are cut diagonally by twenty-one broad avenues named for states in the United States. Pennsylvania, New York and Massachusetts Avenues run through the business district. Pennsylvania Avenue is the best known because the White House, the President's mansion, is on it. Every President rides from the Capitol down Pennsylvania Avenue to the White House in the Inaugural Parade on the day he takes his Oath of Office.

Many of the important government buildings, including the Library of Congress, the Department of Labor Building, the Department of Justice Building, and the Department of Agriculture Building,

are on Constitution and Independence Avenues.

Most of the buildings in Washington are of classical (ancient Greek) design and are made of white stone. There are no skyscrapers. The city has many parks, museums, libraries, and churches. The Library of Congress and the Smithsonian Institution are particularly famous. The National Gallery of Art has some of the greatest art treasures in the world, and the Washington Cathedral, as yet unfinished, attracts visitors of all religions. The most famous memorials are the Lincoln Memorial, the Jefferson Memorial, and the Washington Monument.

GOVERNMENT

The present form of government of the District of Columbia was adopted in 1967. The government is headed by one commissioner, one deputy (assistant) commissioner, and a nine-man city council, all appointed by the President. In the performance of their duties they are responsible to the President, to Congress, and to the Bureau of the Budget. Their duties are to pass ordinances, determine tax rates, and review the budget. The commissioner can veto the decisions of the council, but in turn they may override his veto with a three-fourths vote. From 1874 until 1967 Washington was administered by three commissioners with Congress acting as city council.

Until recently, residents of the District of Columbia could vote in neither national nor city elections. In 1960, the XXIII Amendment gave them the vote in presidential elections; the amendment was ratified in 1961.

There are many colleges, universities, and other schools of higher learning in Washington. Among them are:

American University. Enrollment, 15,000 men and women in 1971.

Catholic University of America. Enrollment, 6,161 men and women in 1971.

Georgetown University. Enrollment, 7,942 men and women in 1971.

Howard University. Enrollment, 8,200 men and women in 1971.

George Washington University. Enrollment, 13,638 men and women in 1971.

Washington's average winter temperature is about 34 degrees, and the average summer temperature is 77 degrees. The summers are unpleasantly hot and humid.

WASHINGTON IN THE PAST

The site for the capital of the United States was chosen when George Washington was president. In 1788 and 1789 the states of Virginia and Maryland each gave territory to the Federal Government. The territory included the cities of Georgetown and Alexandria and lay on either side of the Potomac River. In 1846, Virginia's share of land was returned, so the capital is on land that was once part of Maryland.

By 1800 the Capitol building had been nearly completed, and Congress held its first session there in 1800. John Adams was the first President to use the White House. Thomas Jefferson was the first President to be inaugurated in Washington. When he came to the city, in 1801, it was a very small, ugly community with only about 3,000 people living there.

During the War of 1812 parts of Washington were burned by the British. For many years, even after the Civil War, the city remained unfinished and unattractive. In 1901 the building of parks was begun, in accordance with the original plans, but most of the beautiful buildings, memorials and parks have been built since the end of World War I.

During World War II Washington became one of the most crowded cities in the world, and even after the war the government found there was not room in the city for all the offices it needed. Today many government offices are outside the city, even as far away as New York and Chicago.

WASHINGTON, D.C. Area, 69 square miles. Population (1970 census) 756,510. Capital, United States of America. Center of world diplomacy.

Washington, Booker T.

Booker Taliaferro Washington was a great American educator. His mother was a black slave and when he was born, which was in Virginia about a hundred years ago, that made him a slave too. There are no records to make the year of his birth certain, but it was probably 1858. In 1865, when he was about 7 years old, the Civil War ended and all slaves became legally free.

Washington and his mother were very poor. He began to work soon after the Civil War. His first jobs were in salt furnaces and coal mines in West Virginia. Though it seemed impossible for anyone who was so poor, young Booker T. Washington wanted an education. Finally he was admitted to Hampton Institute, in Hampton, Virginia, a college that missionaries had set up for freed black slaves. During his three years there he worked as a janitor to support himself. He graduated from Hampton Institute in 1875, and became a teacher.

In 1881, Booker T. Washington was asked to start a school for blacks in Tuskegee, Alabama, to train them for trades and professions. He served for many years as the principal of Tuskegee Insti-

tute. The school opened with thirty students in an old church. By the time Booker T. Washington died, in 1915, Tuskegee had grown into a school with more than a hundred buildings, a faculty of 225, and a student body of 3,001.

George Washington

George Washington was the first President of the United States. He was the greatest hero of the country in its earliest days, the commanding general of the armies that won American independence, and the only President who was ever elected unanimously (without a single vote against him). He served two terms, from April 30, 1789 until March 4, 1797. He refused to run for a third term, although he could have been reelected if he had wanted to be. By this act he established the "no third term" tradition that the United States observed until the election of 1940, when Franklin Delano Roosevelt was elected for the third time.

Organizing the new country's government was an enormously difficult and complicated task. It fell to George Washington, as the first Chief Executive, to oversee the thousands of details that required attention. By the end of his second term, the country was well started on its way toward becoming a great power.

Washington was a great general, a wise and courageous President, and a patriotic American. He had a stern sense of duty to his country. Throughout his life, his duty came before everything else.

He was a handsome, distinguished-looking man, tall, erect, and dignified. His bearing and manners were courtly and gracious, though he had an appearance of sternness and severity that discouraged familiarity. In his private life he could be gay, witty, and friendly. The tight-lipped expression about his mouth in the familiar photographs and paintings of this great American was caused by badly fitted artificial teeth. He suffered almost constant discomfort because of this misfortune.

When Washington died, at the age of 67, he was mourned at home and abroad as one of the great men of his day, and later historians have regarded George

Washington as one of the great men of all time.

HIS EARLY YEARS

George Washington was born on February 22, 1732, in a house called Wakefield, in Westmoreland County, Virginia. His father, Augustine Washington, was a rich planter and a member of an aristocratic family. His mother's name before she was married was Mary Ball.

The family moved to a farm near Fredericksburg when young George was six years old, and five years later Augustine Washington died.

At this time the family had large holdings of rich farm land in Virginia, and Washington learned to value good land when he was still very young. At the time of his death he owned more than a hundred thousand acres in all—land that he either inherited or bought, combined with land that had belonged to the woman he married, Martha Dandridge Custis, a rich widow.

Washington had considerable ability in mathematics, and he studied surveying. When he was 16 he went to live with his half-brother, Lawrence. They spent some time on the island of Barbados, in the West Indies, and while there Washington contracted smallpox. He recovered, but his features were badly scarred from the disease for the rest of his life.

After returning from Barbados, Lawrence Washington died, and George inherited his acres of land in Virginia, including Mount Vernon, the mansion and estate in which he lived after that. The mansion had been rebuilt after the original building was destroyed by fire. It is now preserved as a memorial to George Washington and thousands of visitors see it every year.

HIS MILITARY CAREER

George Washington's military career began when he was 21 years old, in 1753. Governor Dinwiddie of Virginia appointed him lieutenant colonel of militia, to serve in the French and Indian War. He was an aide to General Braddock in the historic battle of Fort Duquesne in 1758, about which you can read in the article on William BRADDOCK.

A year later, in 1759, Washington married Martha Dandridge Custis, the widow of a rich Virginia planter. When Washington first met her, she was introduced as the "prettiest and richest widow in Virginia." He married her a year after they met and they settled down at Mount Vernon, where Washington raised fine horses and cattle.

Martha Custis was very wealthy, and her property, combined with what Washington himself already owned, made them one of the richest families in Virginia.

For the next six years Washington's life was quiet, but in 1765 the Stamp Act, in which Great Britain tried to tax the American colonies, opened the agitation that eventually led to the Revolutionary War and marked the end of Washington's peaceful life as a farmer.

The people of Virginia protested against the British taxes. Washington was on the side of the Virginians. At first he was not in favor of demanding American

independence, but merely wanted fair treatment of the colonies. Soon he realized that the colonies must seek their freedom, and he returned to the service of his country as a soldier. At first he commanded the troops of Virginia, and in June of 1775, two months after the Battle of Lexington and Concord had begun the Revolutionary War, the Continental Congress appointed him commander-in-chief of the American forces. He took command before the date of the Declaration of Independence.

During that year and the five bitter years of war that followed, Washington took ragged, untrained, ill-equipped men and made them into an effective fighting force. It was his leadership that made them a powerful fighting force, but he had the ability to choose skillful generals and assistants, to win their loyalty, and to let them make their own decisions. Washington's personal bravery, his skillful use of Indian fighting methods, and his unwillingness to stop fighting in the face of defeats, eventually wore down the British strength and spirit.

On October 19, 1781, the British general, Lord Cornwallis, surrendered to George Washington at Yorktown, Virginia. It proved to be the last battle of the war. The American colonies were free and independent at last.

HOW HE BECAME PRESIDENT

After the war was over, Washington returned to Mount Vernon and private life, but he was not to remain there for long.

The separate states found it hard to agree on what kind of government they wanted. The Constitution was completed only after long arguments, and even after it was finished it had to go to the various states for ratification, or approval. The country itself, in fact, did not have its first President for almost eight years.

Washington's sense of duty made him return to public life in this difficult time. He became chairman of the Constitutional Convention and did a great deal to persuade the states to ratify the Constitution and make the United States of America possible.

When it became time for the country to select its first President, Washington was unanimously chosen. The capital was New York City at that time, and on April 30, 1789, George Washington was inaugurated as the first President of the United States. The ceremony took place on the balcony of Federal Hall at Broad and Wall Streets, New York City.

The capital was moved temporarily to Philadelphia in 1790; however, plans for the permanent capital at Washington were already under way. The city was named in honor of the country's first President, and in 1793 George Washington himself laid the cornerstone of the north wing of the Capitol building, but the city of Washington was not used as the seat of government until 1800, a year after Washington's death.

WASHINGTON AS PRESIDENT

Washington believed in a strong central government and in a united country. The new nation had many problems, and with his usual thoroughness Washington approached each of them courageously and sensibly.

The first problem was to make the other nations of the world recognize the United States as an important country. Washington chose the members of his cabinet carefully, selecting the ablest, most respected men of the country. Among these cabinet members were Thomas JEFFERSON and Alexander HAMILTON, about whom there are separate articles.

By the end of Washington's first term, the Constitution had been ratified by all thirteen of the original states, and two new states, Vermont and Kentucky, had been admitted to the Union. During Washington's second term, to which he was unanimously re-elected, Tennessee was admitted to the Union.

Although he was urged to remain in office for a third term, he refused and declared that the country needed a change of administration after eight years. He delivered a noteworthy "Farewell Address" to Congress. In this speech he warned the country against the danger of foreign entanglements and against placing party politics ahead of the welfare of the country and government as a whole. Washington's Farewell Address has influenced the policy of the United States ever since.

HIS FINAL YEARS

Washington lived only two years after the end of his second term as President. He retired to his estate at Mount Vernon, and once again devoted his time to its management. On a cold, snowy day early in December, 1799, he rode his horse around the grounds at Mount Vernon and caught a severe cold. It developed into pneumonia, and George Washington died at Mount Vernon on December 14, 1799, at the age of 67.

His body was buried in a vault on the estate, and he was mourned by people of America and Europe alike, as a great leader and a great man.

MRS. GEORGE WASHINGTON

Martha Dandridge Custis Washington was born in New Kent County, Virginia, on June 2, 1732, so she was less than four months younger than George Washington. When she was 17 years old she married a rich Virginia planter, Daniel Parke Custis, and had four children in the next eight years. Two died in infancy, but a son and daughter were still living when she married George Washington in 1759.

During the Revolutionary War, Mrs. Washington often visited her husband at army posts. She was admired as a gracious and charming hostess. She died in 1802 and was buried at Mount Vernon.

wasp

Most wasps, like bees and ants, are social insects. That is, they live in groups or colonies where each individual has its particular job to do and does that job throughout its life. There are a few kinds of wasp that live alone.

Every wasp has four wings, as a bee does, and every female wasp can inflict a painful sting. Wasps use their sting to paralyze or kill insects which their larvae, or young, feed on.

Wasps build nests in various places: underground, in trees and bushes, in deserted buildings, under the eaves of roofs, and sometimes inside the attics of houses. The wasps called *mud daubers* make nests of clay that look as if they were pressed into tubes by machinery. In the tubes the female wasp puts the paralyzed insect. When the tubes are well stocked with food for the larvae that will inhabit them the female deposits eggs on top of the paralyzed insects and closes up the tubes with mud. When the eggs hatch, the larvae have enough food to live on until they are grown.

HORNETS

The hornet is a kind of wasp that builds a large, bag-shaped nest made of a kind of paper. The hornets make the paper by chewing wood pulp until it is thin and pastelike. In that condition it can be spread and shaped easily by the worker wasps. It dries almost instantly, because it is so thin, and soon the cells inside the bag are ready to receive the insects that will nourish the larvae.

The entire hive of hornets, except the queen, dies in the fall at the first severe frost. The queen hibernates (sleeps through the winter) and founds a new colony when spring comes.

YELLOW JACKETS

Yellow jackets are another kind of wasp. They build nests underground. They steal the burrow of a field mouse or take over any suitable hollow in the earth, and line it with paper like that which makes the hornet's bag-shaped nest. Yellow jackets are among the most unfriendly of all wasps. Most wasps will leave people and animals alone unless they or their nests are threatened, but yellow jackets will sting anyone who merely happens to be around.

Many of the habits of wasps are similar to those of bees, but wasps do not make honey or wax. See the article on BEE.

watch, a timekeeping instrument small enough to be worn or carried: see the article on CLOCKS AND WATCHES.

water

Water is a substance that exists everywhere on, in and around the earth. It is necessary to life, without it there would be no life. All living things, both plant and animal, must have water. The human body is composed of two-thirds water. Blood and other fluids in our bodies are composed mostly of water. To maintain this high level of water in our bodies, we drink so much water that if the amount we drink each year were weighed it would amount to about a ton.

The earth itself is more than two-thirds water. Much of the earth's surface is covered by oceans and seas. In other parts there are rivers, lakes, streams, and ponds.

Water is a chemical compound because it is made up of two different elements, or basic substances. The elements are both gases, hydrogen and oxygen, but when they are together in the proper quantity, two atoms of hydrogen to every atom of oxygen, they make water. The chemical name, or formula, for water is H_2O.

Water exists in three forms. The first is in the familiar liquid that we call water. The second is a solid form, which we call ice. The third is in an invisible gas in the

air, which we call vapor. If you boil a kettle of water, the steam that comes from the spout goes into the air as vapor. When you dry clothes on a line, the water that leaves the wet clothes by evaporation goes into the air in the form of vapor.

THE WATER CYCLE

Water is constantly changing in form from the liquid state to the vapor state and back again. Evaporation is taking place all the time, chiefly from the surfaces of the oceans and other large bodies of water but also from everything that contains water. When vapor changes back to water, it is said to *condense*. The water vapor going up into the air is eventually condensed to form liquid water.

Condensation usually occurs because warm air can hold more water than cold air. Warm air rises from the earth with much water vapor in it. It reaches the colder upper atmosphere, where the water vapor forms larger particles. The condensed water vapor in the upper air forms clouds. From the clouds it may fall back to the earth in the form of rain or it may freeze in the air and form sleet, hail or snowflakes, which fall back to earth. Over a long period of time, just as much water condenses and falls back to earth as evaporates from the surface originally. The endless process of evaporation and condensation is called the *water cycle*.

The water that condenses in the upper air does not always fall on the places from which it evaporates. Water may evaporate from the Atlantic Ocean and be carried by the winds over the land and fall as rain in Europe. Water that evaporates from the farms in the midwestern United States may be carried in the form of water vapor and finally as rain in New England.

The water cycle is the reason why the rivers flow constantly. The rivers are fed chiefly by water vapor that condenses over mountains and other high places and falls as rain or snow. The rain or snow (when it melts) trickles down in small streams into larger streams and finally into great rivers. Water constantly flows downhill. That is why it is possible for great rivers to form and finally carry the water into the oceans.

WATER IN THE EARTH

Much of the water in liquid form flows in streams and rivers or is contained in oceans, lakes, and ponds. But not all the rain that falls on the earth finds its way into these streams and larger bodies of water. Much of it soaks into the ground. The soil has spaces in it, between the grains of earth and sand, through which the water trickles downward. Even some rocks can absorb water.

Deep in the ground there are always places where there is water. The upper level of the water in the ground is called the *water table*. Sometimes the water table lies far below the surface. At other times it is close to the surface of the earth. The level of the water table depends on the amount of rain. When there is a great deal of rain, the water table rises.

It is because there is water in the ground that men can dig wells and bring the water to the surface, where it can be used. In a separate article you can read about WELLS.

WATER DISSOLVES THINGS

Water is seldom pure. It usually contains other things that are dissolved in it. Many chemicals and substances seem to disappear when we place them in water. If you place a spoonful of sugar or salt in a glassful of water and stir it, the water will become clear again and the salt or sugar will seem to have disappeared. This is because these substances dissolve in water. They are still present in the water but they have been changed so that they cannot be seen. If you allow the water in the glass to evaporate, the salt or sugar will be left at the bottom of the glass, showing that it has been present in the water all the time.

Because many things dissolve in water, water contains a great number of substances. Ocean water is called "salt water," and it does contain salt, but many other minerals are dissolved in it. Ocean water is unfit for drinking.

As water flows and trickles over the surface of the earth it gathers much soil and other material. If the water is allowed to stand, as it does sometimes in lakes, the soil or mud and other substances sink to the bottom. When water flows rapidly, as it does in rivers, the soil keeps the water looking muddy, because it has not had a chance to settle to the bottom. Water also contains many germs, which at times make it unfit for drinking purposes.

USES OF WATER

Not only do we need water in our bodies, we use it in many other ways. It helps us to clean and wash things. It is used to carry away wastes (sewage, wastes from industrial plants, and so on). It helps us to move our goods, as the waters of the world serve as highways for our ships. It helps us to stay clean when we use it for washing and bathing purposes, and it gives us great pleasure when we swim as a sport. Water as ice helps us to keep cool in the summer.

WATER SUPPLY

A constant supply of water is necessary wherever man makes his home. If he lives on a farm, he must be close to a spring where water bubbles from the ground, or he must dig a well to reach the water table below the surface of the earth.

When men come together to live in large towns and cities, their first problem is getting enough water. Man has solved this problem in various ways. In the article on AQUEDUCT you may read how ancient peoples built long channels to carry pipes or streams of water from high mountains to cities. In modern cities the same thing is frequently done. Drinking water for Los Angeles, California, is brought 250 miles. Much of the water used in New York comes from the Catskill Mountains, more than a hundred miles away. Huge reservoirs have been built to provide water for cities. These reservoirs may be natural lakes or may be created by building dams across rivers, to hold back the water and store it. The water brought into the city is carried in pipes called *water mains* until it reaches the houses and buildings in the city. Here it is carried in pipes to the rooms where water is used. Usually the reservoir must

be higher than the town, because water flows downhill. If the reservoir is not high enough, the water pressure is helped by pumps.

PURIFYING WATER

Much of the water that is carried into towns and cities is not fit to drink. It contains harmful minerals or germs that may carry disease. Therefore the city's Water Department must purify the water before it is used.

The main ways of treating water so that it will be fit for drinking purposes are by filtration, aeration, and chemical treatment.

Filtration is allowing the water to seep through fine sandy soil. The sand removes some of the impurities and some of the minerals from the water.

Aeration is spraying the water into the air. This is done at stations along the path of the water flowing from the reservoirs to the city. Sunlight and air kill germs that cause disease, but sunlight and air cannot reach far below the surface of water. That is why the water is sprayed in a fine mist into the air. This aerated water is then piped into homes.

The third way of treating water is with chemicals that kill germs. The chemical most often used is chlorine. In tiny quantities it is harmless to human beings, but it kills germs. About a pound of chlorine put into a million pounds of water is enough to purify it.

Sea water can now be made fit for drinking purposes. In a famous poem, *The Rime of the Ancient Mariner,* by the English poet Samuel Taylor Coleridge, the story is told of a ship that is drifting in the middle of the ocean. The fresh water on the ship is used up and the men are dying of thirst. The lines "Water, water everywhere / Nor any drop to drink" means that with all the sea water around there was nothing fit for drinking. Now scientists have been able to distill sea water so that the harmful minerals and bad taste are taken out. Distillation is a process in which water is boiled and the steam or water vapor is then condensed to form new water. Ocean liners have salt-water distillers as a constant source of fresh water.

HARD AND SOFT WATER

Some cities have water that is called hard water. Other cities have soft water. Hard water contains more of certain types of minerals than soft water. These minerals do not make water unfit for drinking, but they do make it difficult for soap to make suds. People who live in places where there is a hard-water supply find it difficult to wash clothes (or even to wash themselves).

Hard water can be turned into soft water with the proper use of filters or by distilling the water. Since this is often a very costly process, many cities do nothing about hard water. Some people have tanks in their homes to change the hard water to soft water.

water buffalo, a kind of cattle used in Asia. In the wild state it is savage and can be very dangerous. Domesticated water buffalo are mild and gentle and can be tended safely by children. See the article on BUFFALO.

Waterbury

Waterbury is the fourth-largest city in Connecticut. It is in the south central part of the state, on the Naugatuck River. More than 100,000 people live there. Waterbury was first settled about three hundred years ago. Waterbury produces watches, clocks, and brass.

WATERBURY, CONNECTICUT. Population (1974) 108,033. County seat of New Haven County.

water color, see PAINTING.

waterfall

A waterfall occurs when a stream or river drops suddenly from a high to a low level. A series of low waterfalls is called rapids. The world's most remarkable falls include: Angel Falls, Venezuela, which is 3,212 feet high; Victoria Falls, Rhodesia, which is one mile wide; and Niagara Falls in the U.S. and Canada, which flows at the rate of more than 230,000 feet per second.

Watergate

The 1972 Presidential campaign between President Nixon and Senator George McGovern was shaken by a political scandal. On June 17, 1972, five men were arrested for breaking into the Democratic National Headquarters in the Watergate building in Washington, D.C. and for wiring it with recording devices. This incident and the many related events have become known as Watergate.

The five men found in the Democratic Headquarters were acting under the orders of Gordon Liddy, counsel to the Committee for the Re-election of the President; James McCord, security chief for the Committee; and Howard Hunt, White House consultant. After President Nixon's re-election, the Watergate scandal was discovered to include more people of high authority. John Mitchell, head of the Committee for the Re-election of the President, had resigned two weeks after the Watergate break-in. The Senate Select Committee on Presidential Campaign Activities investigated Watergate and other campaign activities. Nixon received resignations from his staff including H. R. Haldeman, White House Chief of staff, John Ehrlichman, chief domestic affairs advisor, Attorney General Richard Kleindienst, and John Dean, chief legal counsel. The Watergate scandal and the many related crimes which were later uncovered captured headlines daily. The American people were horrified at the levels to which corruption in the government had spread. On May 17, 1973 hearings by the Senate Select Committee on Presidential Activities into the Watergate scandal commenced, headed by Senator Sam J. Ervin of North Carolina. These hearings were televised in an attempt to allow the American public to witness this historic investigation.

After months of testimony before the Committee, as well as additional court battles and judicial investigations, it became clear to many Americans that the President, himself, probably had approved of some of the questionable activities which had occurred. At last, after impeachment proceedings had begun against him and unbearable pressure had been placed on him from government leaders and others (including members of his own Republican Party) to leave office, Richard M. Nixon resigned on August 8, 1974. Vice President Gerald R. Ford was sworn in the following day as the 38th President.

On September 6, 1974, ex-president Richard Nixon was unconditionally pardoned by President Ford for any and all crimes he "committed or may have committed" while holding the office of President. (See NIXON).

water lily

A water lily is a fragrant flower with roots that grow in the soil at the bottom of a lake or pond and with leaves and blossoms on the water's surface. A water lily can be one of over fifty varieties, which differ in size, color, climate, etc. See WATER PLANTS.

Grace Lines

Most water lilies have delicate blossoms.

Waterloo

Waterloo is a village in Belgium, a few miles south of the Belgian capital, Brussels. One of the most famous battles in history was fought near Waterloo in 1815. It was the last battle of the NAPOLEONIC WARS, about which there is a separate article.

For more than fifteen years, the French emperor, Napoleon, had ruled France and had been the most powerful man in Europe. In 1814 his enemies, headed by Great Britain, had finally defeated him and imprisoned him on the island of Elba in the Mediterranean Sea. In 1815 Napoleon escaped, returned to France, and raised a powerful army. The British and their allies, who were chiefly German countries, raised a large force to fight him. The British had about 75,000 men commanded by the Duke of Wellington. The combined German force was about 125,000 men commanded by Marshal Gebhard von Blucher. Napoleon had more than 100,000 men.

Portions of these armies fought small battles in the early days of June, 1815, and then on June 18 Napoleon's main army met Wellington's British army at Waterloo. Blucher was marching his army toward Waterloo to help Wellington. During the day Napoleon had the best of the fighting and most armies in Wellington's place would have retreated, but Wellington stubbornly kept on fighting, though once late in the afternoon he said, "Night or Blucher!" meaning that only darkness or the arrival of Blucher's army could save him from defeat. Just as it was beginning to grow dark, Blucher's army arrived. The French were now hopelessly outnumbered and their victory was turned into a bad defeat in which they lost 30,000 men. Napoleon was again exiled, this time on the island of St. Helena in the Atlantic Ocean, where he spent the rest of his life.

watermelon

The watermelon is a plant that grew originally in Africa but is now grown in the United States and other countries. It is a low, spreading vine that bears large, green-skinned fruit. In some varieties the fruit is green striped with gray or mottled with gray and black.

The most familiar watermelon has juicy, sweet, red pulp, which is a favorite dessert in the summer. A few kinds have pulp of a pale golden color, or pink, or almost white. All watermelons need a warm climate, and grow best in sections where the temperature remains high for about four and a half to five months. They are annuals, which means that they must be planted from seeds each year.

water plants

Water plants grow in water or in very moist, wet places on the ground. They are also called *aquatic plants*. Some of these plants grow entirely under water, and some grow partly under water. Some aquatic plants grow in sea water, and some grow in fresh water.

There are thousands of different kinds. Some have flowers and some do not. All plants that grow entirely under water are flowerless. Only those plants that grow partly out of the water may have flowers. If you read the article on ALGAE you will learn about one type of water plant. Most of the plants that grow in sea water are algae. These algae are almost always some form of seaweed.

All green plants must have oxygen and must have sunlight. We get oxygen from the air we breathe, and water plants get it from the air in the water. They absorb the oxygen through tiny holes in their leaves. The holes are called *stomata*. Most water plants have very long, narrow leaves so that they can have enough leaf surface to absorb oxygen from the water. Water plants do not grow deeper than 300 feet below the surface of the water. This is because sunlight does not penetrate any deeper into the water.

A well-known kind of water plant is the water lily. Its roots are in the mud at the bottom of a pond, and it has long stems that grow up to the surface of the water. On the surface, the water lily has very large leaves and beautiful flowers. The leaves are called lily pads.

The water hyacinth is another freshwater plant. Like the water lily it has flowers and leaves on the surface of the water, but its roots do not go down to the mud. The water hyacinth has roots that float in the water, and therefore the plant is a floating plant. In some southern states of the United States, the water hyacinth grows so thickly and rapidly that it has clogged streams and rivers. Boats often have difficulty passing through the thick plant growth. The water hyacinth is called the "million dollar weed" in the South, because it would

cost that much to keep it under control in the waterways.

Some water plants have their roots in water or in very watery soil. These are the plants that grow in swamps and marshes.

Fish and other water animals feed on water plants. In water where there are no plants, there can be no fish or other animal life.

water polo

Water polo is the sport of polo played in the water. (There is a separate article on POLO.) It is played by two opposing teams of swimmers, each of which tries to get the ball into the other team's goal. Water polo is a fast, exciting game, and the players must be expert swimmers. It is very popular in Europe and in the western United States, and is on the program of the international Olympic Games.

Water polo is played in deep water, in an area at least 60 feet long and 20 feet wide. At each end of the "field" is a net-cage goal that is ten feet wide. It is somewhat like the cage used in hockey. It has an upper crossbar, which must be three feet above the water.

There are seven men on each team. One man, called the goalie, stays in his team's goal. At the beginning of the game the remaining six players on each team line up at their team's goal line. The referee tosses the ball into the center of the "field" and the players swim out to get the ball. A player may not touch the ball with two hands at the same time. He may not carry the ball underwater, nor may he touch any player of the opposing team unless that player has the ball.

The game is played in two periods of ten minutes each. A goal is scored as one point, and the team that has scored the greatest number of goals wins.

water power

Water, in streams and rivers, is constantly flowing over the surface of the earth. It moves because water always flows downhill. Most streams and rivers start in mountain places and as the water rushes from the heights it gains great speed. Moving water has great force or power. It can move things and can be made to do work.

Long ago man learned how to make water work for him. He saw how swift water could move rocks and even knock down trees. After he had invented the wheel, he saw that flowing water could turn a wheel. When special buckets or paddles were put in the outside rim of the wheel, the water would turn it more efficiently.

The early Greeks were among the first to use water power in this way. They placed a water wheel in the bottom of a stream bed and ran a shaft from the center of the wheel up into a small hut built over the stream. The shaft had a millstone connected at its top. As the water flowing in the streams turned the wheels in the stream bed, the shaft turned the millstone and the millstone ground wheat.

WATER WHEELS

The water wheel was later improved by turning it on its side and taking all but the bottom of it out of the flowing stream. The stream flowing past the bottom of the wheel turned it easily. This type of wheel was called an *undershot* wheel, because the water flowed under the wheel. Another kind of water wheel was the *overshot* wheel. The water flowed from above the wheel and dropped with force on the buckets, causing the wheel to turn. Some wheels were a combination of the undershot and overshot. These wheels were placed close to a little waterfall so that the falling water would hit the edge buckets of the wheel, then after falling the water would flow past the under-buckets of the wheel and move them. Hundreds of "mill towns" had factories run by water wheels.

In modern times water power is used almost entirely to turn generators that make electricity. In the article on the TURBINE you may read how water held back by huge dams or pouring over waterfalls is used to turn great water wheels called turbines. All large rivers are sources of water power when dams are built. Electric power made from water power is called hydroelectric power because *hydro* is from the Greek word for water.

water sports, games or exercises in the water: see the articles on AQUAPLANING, DIVING, SWIMMING, and WATER POLO.

waterspout

A waterspout is a kind of windstorm over the ocean or a lake. The wind whirls as it does in a hurricane or tornado. The whirling wind is filled with a spray of water. It looks like a funnel or tube rising from the water. Like the whirling column of air in a HURRICANE (which is described in a separate article), the waterspout moves over the water, sometimes at great speeds.

There are two kinds of waterspout, the *tornado-waterspout* and the *fair-weather waterspout*.

TORNADO WATERSPOUT

The tornado waterspout begins with a big cloud over the water. The whirling air carries the moisture of the cloud down toward the water. At the surface of the water, the whirling air picks up more spray from the body of water, and carries this spray upward to the cloud. A tornado waterspout may begin as a hurricane on the land. If it moves from the land onto water, it may change to a waterspout, with spray instead of dust and debris (bits of trash and other material) in the moving column. In other cases the tornado waterspout begins over the water, then moves onto the land, picks up dust and debris, and looks like any other tornado. There is always the dark cloud on top. Tornado waterspouts can become very dangerous.

FAIR-WEATHER WATERSPOUTS

The fair-weather waterspout is seldom dangerous. It begins over water, often when the sky is clear and there are no threatening clouds to be seen. The whirling air at the surface of the water turns the water into spray and carries it upward in a column. If this column later moves from the water onto land, it usually dies down. The spray that has been carried up may then form itself into a cloud and float away harmlessly.

Watt, James

James Watt was the inventor of the modern steam engine. He was born in Scotland in 1736. As a boy he was sickly and had to spend much time at home instead of going to school. He loved mechanical devices and spent much of his time building model machines. He also read widely to educate himself.

As a young man Watt became an instrument-maker at the University of Glasgow. The university had a Newcomen engine, which was one of the first steam engines. The Newcomen engine used the power of steam to move a piston inside a hollow cylinder (such as a pipe, or tube). When blasts of steam were shot into the cylinder, the piston moved back and forth powerfully, operating pumps and other machines. The trouble was that the piston moved much too slowly. Watt made a machine that shot steam into both ends of the cylinder, causing the piston to whiz back and forth at a furious rate of speed. This steam engine changed our whole way of life, since it could operate huge machines and was later used (by a man named George Stephenson) to drive a railroad locomotive. The century following Watt's invention is often called the Age of Steam.

Watt spent all his time and almost all his money to improve the steam engine. He almost had to give up for lack of money, but finally a manufacturer came to his aid. Watt later worked on many other inventions, such as a screw propeller for boats and a machine for reproducing statues. He received many honors before his death in 1819. The watt, a unit of power, was named for him.

Watteau, Antoine

Antoine Watteau was a French painter who lived more than two hundred years ago. He was born in 1684, in northern France. He was very poor as a boy but began to paint pictures when he was quite young and earned a poor living in a "picture factory" that employed artists to turn out cheap pictures. Soon his talent was recognized and he became successful as a painter of the fashionable people of Paris. His best-known paintings include small canvasses showing shepherds and shepherdesses. He died in 1721, when he was only 37 years old.

waves, see RADIO, ELECTRONICS, and SOUND.

WAVES, women serving in the United States Navy (abbreviation for Women Appointed for Voluntary Emergency Service): see the article on WOMEN IN THE ARMED FORCES.

wax

Wax is a soft, solid material that looks much like fat but is usually harder and always less greasy. It is used for making candles, shoe and floor polishes, crayons, carbon paper, and many other useful things. It is also used to seal packages, to

soften leather, and to strengthen shoe-makers' thread.

Insect waxes are secreted from the bodies of insects. *Beeswax,* from which bees make honeycombs, is given off by the abdomen of bees. It is used in medicine for ointments. *Chinese wax* and *shellac wax* are two other kinds that come from insects.

Animal waxes are made by the bodies of animals. The wax called *spermaceti* comes from the blubber of whales and dolphins. *Woolwax,* or *lanolin,* which is much used in ointments and creams, comes from sheeps' wool.

Vegetable wax comes from the nuts or berries of trees and plants. *Carnauba wax* comes from the nuts of a palm tree that grows in Brazil; *cocoa wax* from cocoa beans; *candelilla wax* from berries of a Mexican plant; and bayberry wax from the berries of the wax myrtle tree.

Mineral waxes come from petroleum or from bitumens (such as coal), both of which are gotten out of the ground like minerals. Mineral waxes include *paraffin,* which is used to seal jars of jam, jelly, and other preserves; *ozocerite,* from which is made high-grade candles, colored-lead pencils, and electrical insulation; and *montan,* which is used in making phonograph records.

Sealing wax is not really a kind of wax. It is a resin.

Wayne, Anthony

Anthony Wayne was an American general in the Revolutionary War. He won many battles for the colonists. The greatest of his victories was at Stony Point, New York. Wayne was a very clever general. He was so brave and daring that he came to be called "Mad Anthony."

Wayne was born in Pennsylvania in 1745. Before the Revolutionary War he was a farmer and a surveyor in Pennsylvania. He became a general in 1777, early in the war. He was wounded three times, and for his brave deeds he received a gold medal from Congress. After the war he led a successful campaign against the Indians in the Northwest Territory. Fort Wayne, Indiana, where he had a camp, is named for him. In 1792 he was appointed general-in-chief of the United States Army. He died in 1796.

weasel

The weasel is a member of the same animal family as the ermine, the mink, the skunk, and the badger. Weasels are the smallest of the flesh-eating mammals, but they are ferocious fighters and often kill when they do not need food. Northern weasels are often confused with ermine because both animals have white coats in winter, when the snow is on the ground, and tan or brownish coats the rest of the year. Weasels that live in more southerly regions do not change color in the winter but remain a dark reddish-brown color all year round.

Weasels are short-legged, slender animals. They can slip through small holes in fences, or into the burrow of rats and rabbits, with very little trouble. They can also climb trees and swim.

A weasel usually mates in July or August, and the young are born the following March or April. There are between six and twelve in a litter. The male remains to help in feeding the young weasels, which are born blind and are helpless for more than a month. A baby weasel weighs only about half an ounce at birth. It remains under its parents' care until late summer.

Weasels are useful because they destroy thousands of mice, rats, and rabbits. They eat birds and their eggs occasionally, and can be a nuisance by killing poultry and stealing eggs.

ERMINE

The ermine is one of the best-known members of the weasel family, because of the beautiful white coat it wears in winter, which is popular as fur. The ermine lives in cold northern countries. After the first snow it begins to shed its summer coat of brown and grows a new coat of pure white. This helps it to avoid its many enemies, such as hawks and owls, which cannot see it against the snow. In the spring the ermine molts (sheds its coat) again and grows a new brown coat.

weather

Weather is the condition of the air around the earth. The air may be hot or cold, wet or dry, calm or stormy. It may change from day to day, and even hour to hour. Everyone is concerned about the weather. All the things we do and plan to do are affected by the kind of weather we have.

The weather depends on several things. The most important thing is the sun that shines down on the earth. Another thing that affects the weather is the fact that the air is constantly moving. A third important thing is the presence of water on the earth's surface.

THE SUN AS WEATHERMAKER

The sun, located about 93,000,000 miles from the earth, is a great, hot ball of fire. Rays from this fiery mass shine down on the earth's surface. These rays warm the earth. As the earth becomes warm it gives off heat to the air above. Sometimes, on a hot summer day, you can even see heat waves rising from the earth's surface. The more the sun shines the more the earth is heated and the more it gives off this heat to the air above it.

During the night, when the sun is not shining on a particular place on the earth's surface, that place is not being heated by the sun's rays; but it can still be very hot, because the earth still gives off the heat it has absorbed.

The sun shines on most places for more hours during the summertime than it does during the wintertime, and its rays strike the earth more directly in the summertime. A few simple experiments will show how much difference this makes in the weather.

AN EXPERIMENT WITH SUNLIGHT

Take two pieces of black paper. Place one in the direct sunlight for about one minute. Place the other in the sunlight for five minutes. You will find that the piece that has been in the sunlight longer feels hotter to the touch.

Now take one of the pieces and put it in the sunlight so that the sun's rays are striking it directly. Place the other piece so that the sun's rays are striking it at an angle. You will see that the piece receiving direct sunlight becomes hotter than the piece receiving the angled, or indirect, rays of the sun.

These two facts, the sun shining directly and the sun shining a longer period, make summers warmer than winters. It makes a difference whether the sun shines on land or on water. Most people have learned that it is cooler at the beach in the summertime than it is further inland. This is because water takes longer to heat than soil. If you place a bowl of water and a bowl of dirt in the sunlight for about ten minutes, you will notice that the soil feels hotter than the water. Not only soil but also rock and all the building materials that go into city streets and buildings absorb heat faster than water does.

Though soil heats more quickly than water, it also loses its heat more quickly. In the desert the days may be very hot because of this fact, but not long after sundown the soil has lost its heat and the air is cold. This is not so at the beach. The evenings are not much cooler than the days because the water continues to give off heat for many hours.

This fact affects the winter weather in many places. Portland, Maine, is just as far north as Pierre, South Dakota, but the winters in Portland are not as cold. Portland, being on the sea coast, benefits from the fact that the Atlantic Ocean is giving off some heat that it has stored up during the hot summer. This heat helps warm the air above Portland. Pierre, being far inland and not near any large body of water, has very severe and cold winters because the soil has soon lost the heat of the summer sun.

AIR IN ACTION

The air around the earth is constantly moving in many directions and at different speeds. The movement of the air is caused chiefly by heat. Warm or hot air weighs less than cold air. This causes warm air to rise and cold air to fall. The

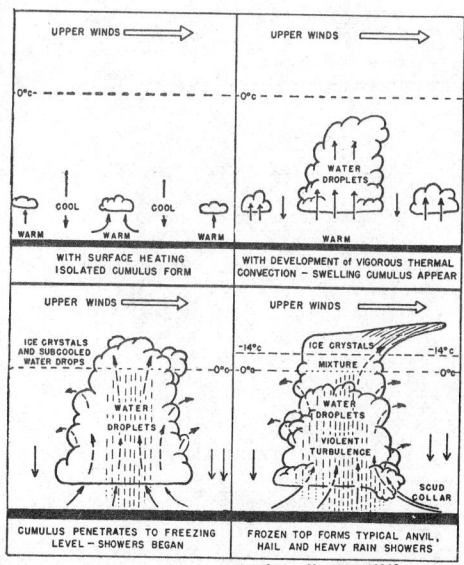

Aerology—Navpers 10362

The development of a thunderstorm.

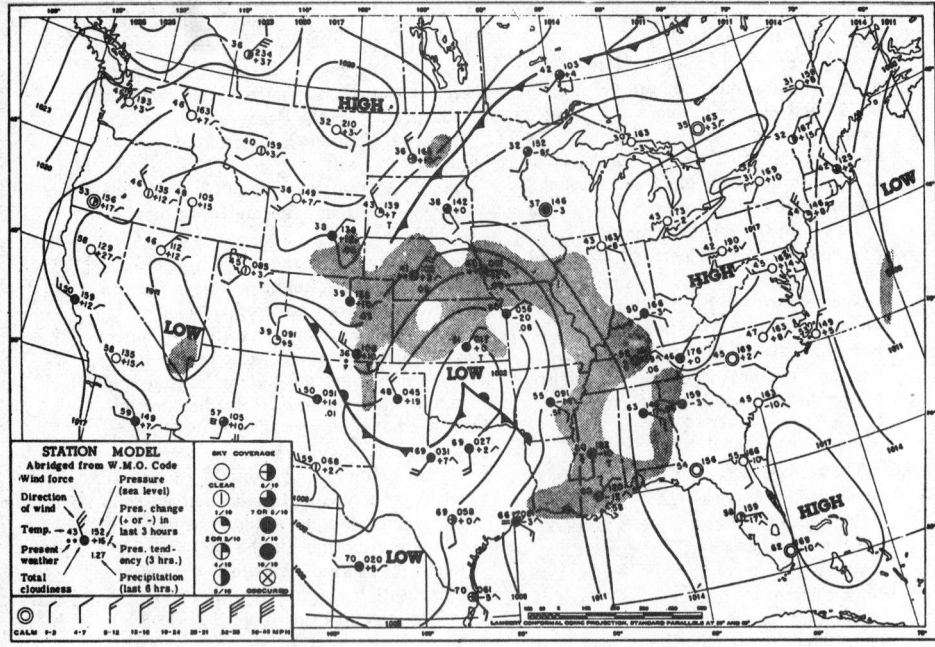

Every day the U.S. Weather Bureau prepares a weather map of the United States. It shows precipitation, isobars, high and low centers, and direction of wind.

The weather map shows the average world temperatures for July. The wavy lines, called isotherms, connect places that have approximately the same temperature.

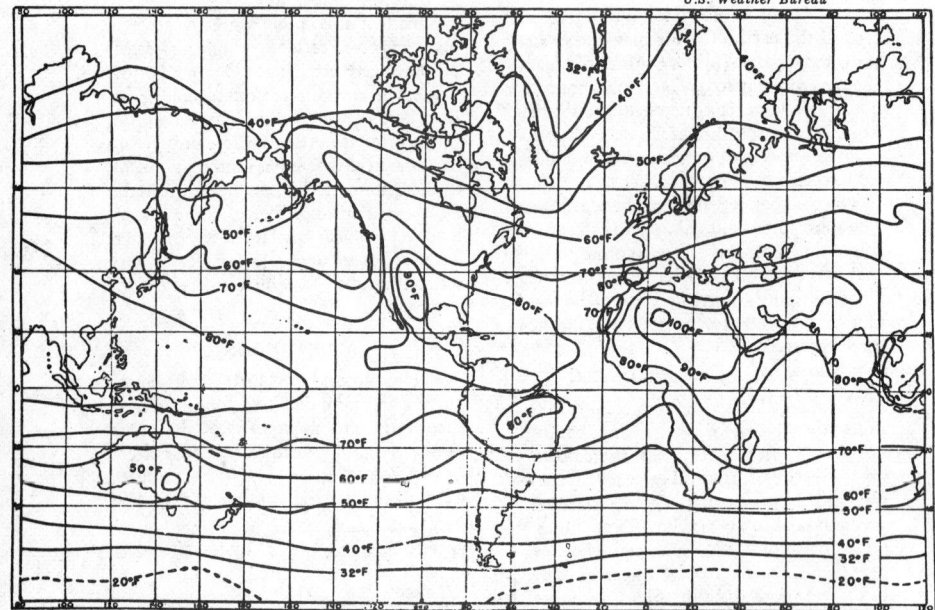

cold air moves into places where warm air has risen from the surface of the earth. This movement makes breezes and winds.

If you are at the beach in the summertime you will notice that the breeze during the day is coming from the water toward the land. This is because the sun heats the sand and soil on the land much more quickly than it heats the water. The hot air rises from the land. The cooler air above the water flows in to replace the hot air rising from the land. This causes what we call a sea breeze.

At night the opposite is true. The sand and soil quickly lose their heat. The water has retained much of its heat and continues to give off heat to the air above it. This warmed air rises, and soon the cooler air from the land rushes out to take its place. In this way a land breeze has been created.

Local breezes are caused by cool air moving from place to place, as from the shady side of a street to a sunny side.

PREVAILING WINDS

Since the sun shines directly and for longer periods of time at the middle of the earth (the equator), the air at the equator is constantly being heated and rising. Since the sun shines less directly and for shorter periods of time at the poles of the earth, the air above these places receives less heat. This makes two mass movements of air. The heated air rising from the equator starts streaming toward the poles. The cold air at the poles starts moving toward the equator.

The rotation, or spinning, of the earth affects these movements of air. The earth is also spinning at speeds up to 1,000 miles per hour. The air masses affected by the rotation of the earth create the major

earth winds. In the United States the major wind or air movement is from west to east generally. This is called the *prevailing westerlies*. Because of the prevailing westerlies, an airplane travelling from San Francisco to New York, or from any place west to east, usually flies faster than an airplane going from east to west. The prevailing westerlies help blow the plane along in one direction but blow against the plane flying in the other direction.

Air moves at different speeds and names have been given to describe the winds at these different speeds. A *breeze* blows from about 5 to 35 miles an hour; a *gale* blows from about 40 to 60 miles an hour; a wind of 75 miles an hour or more is said to blow at a *hurricane* speed. (See the article on WIND.)

WATER IN WEATHER

The third most important factor in making weather is water. We have already seen how the sun heats water differently than it does the soil, but there is another thing about water that makes it important in weather. Water evaporates, which means that it passes off into the air. Water is always present in the air, in the form called water vapor, which is usually invisible.

Warm air holds more water vapor than cold air. Water vapor is constantly passing into the air from the surfaces of oceans, rivers, lakes, and from such things as drying streets and wet clothes on a line. What happens to this water vapor in the air has much to do with the kind of weather we have.

Since warm air can hold more water vapor than cold air, something happens when warm air rises high above the earth. You have noticed that on a cold winter day your breath may look like steam in the outside air. This is because your warm breath contains water vapor. When the warm breath hits the cold air, the water vapor *condenses,* which means that it forms into larger, more visible particles of water. This is because the cold air can hold less water vapor.

As warm air, containing much water vapor, rises high above the earth it is cooled. Its tiny, invisible particles of water condense (usually around bits of dust) and form larger particles of water. When this happens a cloud is formed, much as little "clouds" are formed when you breathe your warm breath into the cold air. All the clouds in the sky have been formed by the cooling of warm air.

As the water vapor continues to condense, the clouds become full of larger drops of water. When these drops become large enough, they fall to earth as rain. Since the air is moving, the rain seldom falls on the part of the earth from which the water vapor originally rose.

RAINMAKERS

Places where there is not enough natural rainfall, or that are suffering from drought (a very dry spell), sometimes employ "rainmakers" who try to make rain artificially. Artificial rainmaking is a matter of cooling the air above the earth, to condense the water rapidly and make it fall as rain.

Rainmaking is done from airplanes. They fly above the place that needs rain, and they scatter something such as silver

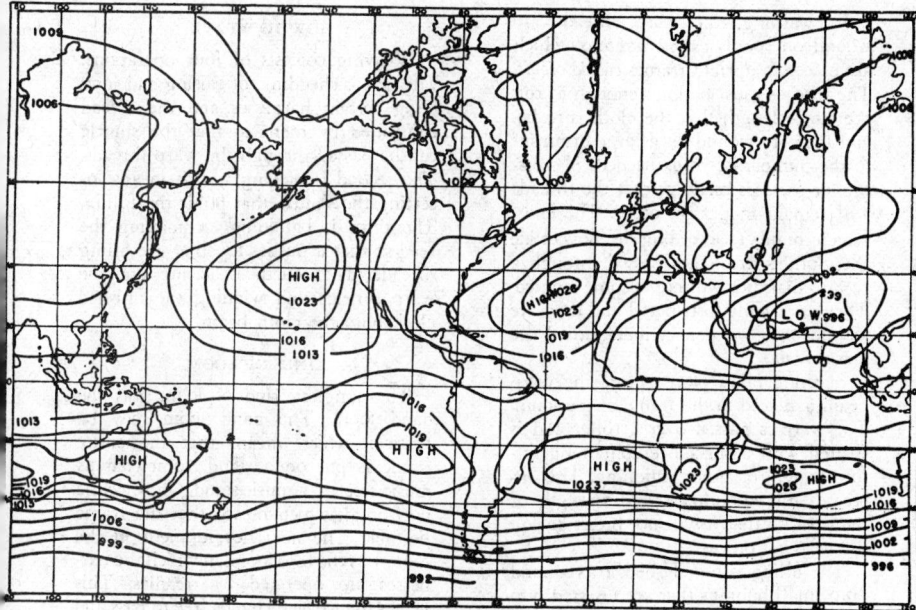

The weather map shows the average world atmospheric pressures for July. The wavy lines, called isobars, connect places that have approximately the same pressure.

iodide or frozen carbon-dioxide gas (like the "Dry Ice" often used to pack ice cream). This scattering of coldness is called "seeding." Sometimes it works and sometimes it cannot work because there simply is not enough moisture, or water vapor, in the air to make raindrops.

SLEET, HAIL, SNOW, AND DEW

Sometimes rain falling through very cold air freezes and comes down in the form of *sleet*, or frozen raindrops. *Hail* is rain frozen in another way. Strong upward currents of air carry raindrops to very cold heights, where they freeze into ice.

The small, frozen drops, called *hailstones*, fall to lower air and pick up more water. These wet hailstones are again blown high into the air, and now the water on their surfaces freezes, making the hailstones larger. Finally they become too heavy to be blown upward again and they fall to earth.

If you cut a hailstone through the middle you will find it has several rings or layers. By counting these rings you can tell how many up-and-down trips the hailstone took before it fell to earth. Hailstones may be as small as tiny pebbles or as large as a baseball.

When a cloud is cooled very quickly below the freezing point of water, the water vapor in the cloud may almost instantly form into ice. When this happens the ice formed is called crystal ice. More simply we know it as snow. It is the same kind of ice crystal that forms on the coils of a refrigerator. All snow crystals have six sides or six points. They are very beautiful and no two are exactly alike.

The dew you often see on the ground in the early morning is caused by water vapor in the air condensing on the cold surface of the ground.

STORMS

Storms are caused by the action of large, rapidly moving air masses in which, very often, heated air containing large amounts of water vapor meets cold air.

A thunderstorm is the most dramatic and exciting of all storms. Thunderstorms occur usually in the summertime when the sun has been heating the air for long hours. The heated air, full of water vapor, rises and begins to cool and form clouds. The typical thundercloud is a high, thick, mountainous pile with a flat bottom and a peak at the top. Fliers have a saying that a pilot flies into a thundercloud only once in his life. By this they mean that if he is lucky enough to get out, he will never want to fly into such a cloud again. The air currents in a thundercloud rush about violently, carrying condensed water vapor. The clashing of the masses of water vapor against each other causes electricity to be formed. When enough of this electricity has been formed it jumps from one part of a cloud to another, or from one cloud to another, or from the cloud to the ground. This is *lightning*. As the lightning flashes, it heats the air around it, causing it to vibrate. This makes the noise we call *thunder*. We see lightning before we hear thunder because light travels faster than sound. At the height of a thunderstorm, with the lightning flashes and the thunder booming, the rain comes down in torrents.

Never stay in water during a thunderstorm, because water conducts the electricity in lightning. Never stand under a large tree or near a wire fence during a thunderstorm; stay in the open away from anything. You will be wetter, but safer.

Weather Bureau, United States

The United States Weather Bureau is a branch of the Department of Commerce. Its job is to issue storm warnings and provide other information about the weather. In 1870 the United States government set up a weather service, and twenty years later, in 1890, this service was named the Weather Bureau.

Today the Weather Bureau has many different jobs. Besides distributing storm and flood warnings, it supplies daily weather forecasts over radio and television stations and through newspapers. It works with weather stations all over the world, exchanging information about climate (average weather) and weather (the condition of the atmosphere at a certain time). It conducts research on weather and climate, to find out more about the causes and effects of different conditions so that it can make its weather forecasts more accurate. It has special services for fruit- and vegetable-growers, whose crops are immediately affected by changes in weather; for airlines and pilots; and for shipping lines. It publishes its findings in daily, weekly and monthly magazines and newspapers.

The Weather Bureau has about 300 local offices, in cities and at airports throughout the United States and Puerto Rico, and on some of the islands of the Pacific Ocean. In addition it has more than 10,000 coöperative or part-time stations. About 350 of these are part of its Aviation Weather Service; 6,300 keep climate records; about 2,400 work in the river and flood warning service; and about 1,000 provide general weather service. These offices are assisted by thousands of voluntary observers who report different conditions, such as rising rivers, to the local stations.

WEATHER OBSERVATIONS AND FORECASTS

Daily weather observations describe the temperature, air pressure, wind and other conditions that exist at certain points throughout the United States. At frequent intervals each day these reports from more than six hundred places are transmitted by teleprinter circuits so that all Weather Bureau offices can use them. Weather maps are prepared from the reports, and these maps are the main means of making weather forecasts, or predicting what the weather in a given place will be for the next day or two.

In addition to these reports, information is needed about conditions several miles above the earth's surface. This information is obtained through the use of special instruments called *radiosondes* or *rawinsondes*, which are carried up in balloons and are equipped with devices to send radio signals. Twice a day about 45 Weather Bureau stations in the United States make these observations about winds, pressures and temperatures above the earth. Measurements of wind speed and direction are obtained by balloons sent from about 125 stations four times a day.

Radar is now used at many places to get information about the weather within an area of about a hundred miles. Radar reports of a storm show where the heavy rains, high winds or hail are likely to move.

There are many special studies being made to improve weather forecasting. Some deal with predicting the amount of rainfall, and others with predicting the highest and lowest temperatures for the next few days. Scientists are trying to find out more about how clouds form and grow, how electricity affects rain and snow, and whether rainfall can be increased by new ways of rainmaking, which are described in the article WEATHER. Scientists are trying also to make forecasts for a month in advance and even for an entire season in advance.

Weather forecasts are published in newspapers and broadcast by radio and television. In some large cities the telephone company has installed automatic answering devices on which the weather forecast is given. This service is listed in the telephone directory under "Weather Bureau."

Twice each week the Weather Bureau issues a forecast of the weather expected during the following five days. Twice each month, on or about the 1st and 15th, an "outlook" is published. This gives the average conditions of temperature and rainfall expected during the next thirty days.

The study and forecasting of the weather is part of the science of METEOROLOGY, about which there is a separate article.

weaving

Weaving is the process of making cloth on a loom, by interlacing two sets of threads. The simplest kind of loom is a frame across which the threads are stretched. One set of threads, running lengthwise and parallel to each other, is placed on the loom first, stretched between two beams. This set is called the *warp*. The other set, called the *filling* (or *weft*, or *pick*), is interlaced at right angles (running crosswise) with the stretched warps.

Weaving is one of the most ancient crafts, dating back at least four thousand years. It was practiced by almost all the peoples of the world. About 1,500 years ago, at the beginning of the Middle Ages, weaving underwent great development in Europe and the Near East. The East Roman, or Byzantine, Empire was the earliest center of silk weaving, which soon spread to Greece, Italy, and Spain. In Flanders wool weaving was developed. It was soon introduced into other countries, especially England. Tapestry weaving became an important art in France. In the American colonies, weaving was done in most homes.

About two hundred years ago there were several inventions that improved weaving. The invention of the power loom, run by an engine instead of by hand, made weaving a factory industry. However, some of the finest kinds of cloth are still woven on hand looms.

Woven cloth has several advantages over cloth made by looping or twisting threads, as in knitting. Cloth is firmer and does not pull apart easily. Also, woven cloth can be made from many different kinds of yarn in many designs, textures, and weights. It can be as light and sheer as chiffon, or as heavy as carpeting. Different kinds of fabric are woven on different looms. These include carpet, narrow fabric, blanket, velvet, double cloth, plain cotton, silk and worsted looms. For making complicated designs, special attachments are used with the loom.

Weaving involves preparing the threads, threading the loom, and the actual weaving.

PREPARING THE THREADS

The first step is preparing the warp threads, which are usually stronger than the filling and are prepared in operations called *warping* and *slashing*.

In warping, the warp threads are wound on spools called *bobbins*, which are placed in upright frames called *creels*. The threads must be long enough to run the entire length that the cloth is to be, and they are wound on a large drum into the number of yards needed. A crossing, or *lease*, is made so that the threads will remain in perfect order. The ends, which number according to how wide the cloth is to be, are passed through a reed so that they will not become tangled. They are evenly distributed and then wound on a wooden cylinder called the *warp beam*.

Slashing takes place before the warp beam is placed in the frame of the loom. The warp is passed over a roller and is treated with a substance containing tallow, starch, or other stiffening. This increases the smoothness and strength of the yarn, so that it will not break during the weaving process.

The filling is not slashed. It is wound onto small bobbins that are inserted into a boat-shaped device called the *shuttle*. The shuttle carries the filling back and forth through the warp.

THREADING THE LOOM

Threading the loom is a slow process that requires a great deal of skill. In the center of the loom, between the warp beam at the back and the cloth beam at the front, on which the woven cloth will be wound, are three special parts. They are the *harnesses*, the *heddles*, and the *reed*.

A loom may have from two to twenty harnesses, depending on how complicated the pattern is to be. Each harness is made up of a metal frame to which are attached, at the top and bottom, a certain number of fine metal strips, or heddles. Each heddle has an opening, or eye, in the center. Every warp thread must pass through the eye of one of the heddles on one of the harnesses, and they must be arranged in the order that the pattern requires. In the power loom, each harness is lifted and lowered by automatic controls, and during each operation it carries up or down the threads passing through the eyes in its heddles. These threads form a shed with the other warp threads, in the harnesses that have not been moved.

A few inches in front of and parallel to the harnesses (running in the same direction as the harnesses) is a reed that stretches across the loom. The reed is a narrow rectangle-shaped frame that holds a large number of fine up-and-down wires. They are set close together, the exact distance depending on the distance desired between the warp threads. In the spaces, or dents, of the reed are passed one or two warps on their way to the cloth beam (at the front of the loom). The reed moves back and forth, while the harnesses move up and down. The reed helps control the width of the cloth, keeps the warps in line as they come from the heddles, and battens (presses together) the filling threads after they have been inserted in the shed. When the warp ends are finally fastened to the cloth beam at the proper tension (that is, when they are stretched exactly enough, and not too much), weaving can begin.

HOW TO WEAVE

Weaving consists of four operations. The first is shedding, or raising and lowering certain harnesses and the thread controlled by them so that the shuttle can be passed through the warp threads. The second is picking, which means inserting the shuttle that holds the filling. The third is battening, or moving the reed so that it pushes together the filling threads. The fourth is letting out the warp threads and winding the finished cloth onto the cloth beam.

KINDS OF LOOM

The simplest kind of loom was the hand loom. The hand loom may be vertical, which means that the entire frame is put on a stand, somewhat as music rests on a music stand. Or it may be horizontal, which means that the frame lies flat. The next development in the loom was the foot loom, in which the harnesses are operated by treadles. This leaves the weaver's hands free to pass and catch the shuttle. In 1733 an Englishman named John Kay invented an automatic fly shuttle.

In 1785 Edmund Cartwright invented the power loom. With various new improvements this loom is the one in use today.

KINDS OF WEAVE

The weave is the pattern in which the cloth is to be woven. There are three main kinds of weave—the plain weave, the twill weave, and the satin weave.

In the plain weave the filling thread goes under and over every second warp thread. If the threads are woven closely, and are battened with some force, the cloth will be stronger, thicker, and heavier. If they are woven loosely, the cloth will be porous and lighter in weight. Among the fabrics woven in plain weave are taffeta, chambray, seersucker, poplin, organdy, and flat crepe.

In the twill weave the weft thread goes over one or more warp threads and under a different number of warp threads. It may go over one and then under the next three warp threads. There are many variations, depending on the different combinations of numbers. The cloth surface then looks like a series of diagonal (slanting) lines. Serge, covert, foulard, tweed, flannel and gabardine use the twill weave.

The satin weave is actually a variation of the twill weave, but no diagonal lines are seen on the surface of the cloth. Threads pass over single threads at certain intervals and under groups of other threads. There is no diagonal effect because the points where the threads cross are not in diagonal lines. The smooth surface is due to the fact that the face of the cloth is made up almost entirely of threads running in one direction only, while in the plain and twill weaves threads running in both directions can be seen.

Weber, Carl Maria von

Carl Maria von Weber was a German composer of operas. He lived about 150 years ago. He is best remembered for the operas *Der Freischütz* (The Freeshooter) and *Oberon*, and for the piano

piece *Invitation to the Dance.* Weber was born in 1786, of a musical family. At the age of 13 he performed in public as a pianist, and he began writing music at about the same time. He became a conductor in the great opera

houses of Germany, and he gained world fame with *Der Freischütz,* which was first presented in 1821. In 1826 Weber went to England to conduct his new opera, *Oberon,* but he became ill and died in London at the age of 40. Weber's other music includes songs and religious works.

Webster, Daniel

Daniel Webster was one of the principal American statesmen more than a

hundred years ago. He was best known as a United States Senator and as one of the Senate's best public speakers. He favored a strong Federal government, against John C. Calhoun of South Carolina, who was for States' Rights, and Henry Clay of Kentucky, who favored compromises in which each side gave up something. Webster was called the "Defender of the Constitution."

Daniel Webster was born in Franklin, New Hampshire, in 1782. He attended Dartmouth College and then became a lawyer. In 1812 he was elected to the House of Representatives, where he opposed the War of 1812 against Great Britain. In 1817 he left public life and became a lawyer in Boston.

Webster returned to politics in 1822 as a Representative, and five years later he was elected to the United States Senate. In the Senate, in 1830, he made his most famous speech. It was a reply to Robert Y. Hayne, a Senator from South Carolina, who argued that states had the right to set aside Federal laws. Webster's "Reply to Hayne" was a brilliant speech in which he said that the United States must remain a single nation. It ended with the words, "Liberty and Union, now and forever, one and inseparable!"

In 1841, President William Henry Harrison appointed Webster Secretary of State. He negotiated the northeast boundary of the United States with Great Britain. In 1843 he resigned from office and two years later he returned to the Senate. He devoted most of his talents to strengthening the Union and trying to prevent slavery from being allowed in new states. He was again Secretary of State in 1850–1852, but he lost much of his popularity in the North because of his willingness to compromise on the slavery question for the sake of the Union. He tried to obtain the nomination for the Presidency in 1852, but had little support. He died in the same year.

Webster's ability as an orator, or public speaker, became a legend. The American writer Stephen Vincent Benét, wrote a famous short story, "The Devil and Daniel Webster," that tells how a farmer sold his soul to the Devil, then hired Webster as his lawyer and was saved by

an eloquent speech that Webster made to a jury of demons.

Webster, Noah

Noah Webster was the author of the first important dictionary written in the United States. It was the *American Diction-ary of the English Lan-guage,* better known as *Webster's Dictionary,* and it is still famous, though Webster died more than a hundred years ago.

Webster was born in 1758 in West Hartford, Connecticut. He studied at Yale University and then fought for American independence in the Revolutionary War.

After the Revolution, Webster became a teacher and also wrote several books on grammar and spelling. His *Elementary Spelling Book,* or "Blue-backed Speller," was used throughout the United States. It was so popular that in 1850, seven years after Webster died, a million copies of it were sold. And at that time only 23,000,-000 people lived in the country.

Webster's schoolbooks made him a rich man. He gave up teaching and set out to write a complete dictionary for Americans. He finished a short dictionary in 1806, then worked for twenty-two more years on the big *Webster's Dic-tionary.* The dictionary has been revised many times since then, and Webster's name has remained so famous that many other dictionaries use the title "Webster's." Noah Webster died in 1843.

wedge

The wedge is one of the simple machines told about in the article on MACHINE and is a form of the INCLINED PLANE, about which also there is a separate article. A wedge is usually made of metal and is thick at one end, tapering to a thin blade at the other end, somewhat as an axhead does. A wedge is used to split wood. When you hammer on the thick end, the other end gradually enters the wood and forces it apart. It takes less force to hammer on the wedge than it would take to pull the pieces of the wood apart, so the wedge gives you a mechanical advantage. Wedges are also used in machinery to lift heavy working parts in the machine.

Wedgwood, Josiah

Josiah Wedgwood was one of the greatest pottery makers of all time. He lived about two hundred years ago in England, where he was born in 1730. When he was nine years old, he began working at a pottery plant that belonged to his brother. Later he started his own business, and in 1769 he built a village called Etruria around his pottery factory. His work is called "Wedgwood" or "Etruria" ware.

Wedgwood made many experiments and produced many new types of pottery and dishes. One of the first was a cream-colored earthenware called "Queen's ware," in honor of Queen Charlotte, the wife of King George II. He also developed a black ware called "basalt," which was used for beautiful vases. His greatest achievement was "jasper," an earthenware. Jasper is especially beautiful when colored blue and some of Wedgwood's

best pottery is jasper with raised white figures on a background of blue. Many of the artistic designs used by Wedgwood are taken from Greek and Roman myths, or stories of gods, goddesses, and heroes. Wedgwood died in 1795.

Wednesday

Wednesday is the fourth day of the week. It is named for the god Odin, who was the chief god and the giver of all wisdom in the ancient Norse and Germanic religion. The Germanic tribes called this god Woden. ASH WEDNES-DAY, about which there is a separate article. marks the beginning of the Lenten season.

weed

A weed is any plant that grows where it is not wanted. There are only a very few plants that might be called weeds by everyone. Plants that are called "wildflowers" in fields and forests are called weeds in vegetable gardens. A potato is an important crop when grown in the vegetable garden, but it is a weed when found growing in a flower bed.

Generally speaking, weeds are not useful as food or admired for their beauty. They may grow anywhere and need no special care. They spread their seeds very easily. Weeds often grow even better than plants which have been cultivated by man.

Weeds must be killed or they may choke out flowers or crops that have been planted for man's use. The best way to get rid of weeds in small areas is to pull them out by hand. Hoeing them into the ground, burning them out, or using some chemical that destroys the weeds but does not harm the planted crops, are other methods used to destroy them.

week

The week is a period of seven days, used as a division of time in the calendar. It is the only part of the calendar that is not based on nature. (The day is the length of time it takes the earth to rotate completely, and the year is the length of time that it takes the earth to travel around the sun.) There have been various explanations of how the week became part of the calendar. In Christian countries an explanation could be the account of the creation of the world, in the Bible, where God made the world in six days and rested on the seventh day; but the week was used by ancient peoples who did not know about the Bible. See also the article on CALENDAR.

weevil

A weevil is a special kind of beetle with a beak. All weevils live solely on vegetable matter. Some weevils are pests. Some are useful in reducing plant matter to a form that permits it to return to the earth and enrich the soil. See also the article on BOLL WEEVIL.

weight

Weight is the force with which something is pulled by gravity. On earth, for example, a person's weight is a measure of the force with which gravity is pulling him toward the center of the

earth. The weight of a substance depends partly on its density and partly on how much of the substance there is. All substances are made up of tiny particles called molecules, and DENSITY (about which there is a separate article) depends on how tightly these molecules are packed together. Iron is denser than wood, so a piece of iron weighs more than a piece of wood of the same size; but a big piece of wood might weigh much more than a small piece of iron. The less the pull of gravity is, the less an object's weight is. On the moon, where the pull of gravity is much less than it is on earth, you could lift weights that on earth you could never budge. Your own weight would be much less too, but your strength would be just as great.

weights and measures

In the United States, Canada, and British countries, things are weighed and measured by different units from those used in nearly all other countries. The English-speaking people, except scientists, weigh things in ounces and pounds, measure distance by the foot, yard, and mile, and measure liquids in pints, quarts, gallons, and so on. Other countries use the METRIC SYSTEM, about which there is a separate article.

Special systems of weights or measures are used by certain professional and businessmen, such as druggists, surveyors, and jewelers.

The following tables gives the weights and measures that are most in use.

LINEAR (LENGTH) MEASURE

1 foot = 12 inches
1 yard = 3 feet, or
36 inches
1 rod = 5½ yards, or
16½ feet
1 furlong = 40 rods, or
220 yards, or
660 feet
1 mile = 8 furlongs, or
320 rods, or
1,760 yards, or
5,280 feet

OTHER UNITS OF LENGTH

1 hand = 4 inches
1 link (Gunter's) = 7.92 inches
1 chain (Gunter's) = 4 rods, or
22 yards or
66 feet, or
100 links
1 span = 9 inches
1 fathom = 6 feet, or
8 spans
1 league = 3 miles, or
24 furlongs, or
960 rods, or
5,280 yards, or
15,840 feet
1 sea mile = } 6,080.20 feet
1 geographical mile =
1 nautical mile
(international) = 6,076.10 feet

The hand is a unit used in measuring the height of horses. The chain is a unit of measure used by surveyors. It is so called because surveyors use an actual chain, and the link is the length of an actual link in the chain. The fathom is used for measuring rope, and depths of water at sea.

SQUARE OR LAND MEASURE

1 square foot = 144 square inches
1 square yard = 9 square feet, or
1,296 square inches
1 square rod = 30¼ square yards, or
272¼ square feet, or
39,204 square inches
1 rood = 40 square rods
1 acre = 4 roods, or
160 square rods, or
4,840 square yards, or
43,560 square feet, or
6,272,640 square
inches
1 square mile = 640 acres, or
102,400 square rods, or
3,097,600 square
yards, or
27,878,400 square
feet, or
4,014,489,600 square
inches
1 square chain = 16 square rods, or
4,356 square feet, or
627,264 square inches

DRY MEASURE

1 quart = 2 pints
1 gallon = 4 quarts, or
8 pints
1 peck = 2 gallons, or
8 quarts, or
16 pints
1 bushel = 4 pecks, or
8 gallons, or
32 quarts, or
64 pints

LIQUID MEASURE

1 gill = 4 ounces
1 pint = 4 gills, or
16 ounces
1 quart = 2 pints, or
8 gills, or
32 ounces
1 gallon = 4 quarts, or
8 pints, or
32 gills, or
128 ounces

AVOIRDUPOIS WEIGHT

1 dram = 27.34375 grains
1 ounce = 16 drams
1 pound = 16 ounces, or
256 drams
1 stone = 14 pounds
1 quarter = 28 pounds
1 hundredweight = 4 quarters, or
100 pounds, or
1,600 ounces
1 short ton = 20 hundredweights, or
2,000 pounds, or
32,000 ounces
1 long ton = 1.12 short tons, or
22.4 hundredweights,
or
2,240 pounds, or
35,840 ounces

The long ton is used principally for weighing coal and minerals in the United States. The standard United States ton is the short ton. The short ton is the only ton weight used in Great Britain.

TROY WEIGHT

1 pennyweight = 24 grains
1 ounce = 20 pennyweight, or
480 grains
1 pound = 12 ounces, or
240 pennyweight, or
5,780 grains
1 carat = 3.0865 grains

Troy weight is used only for weighing gold, silver and all jewels except pearls

and diamonds. These two jewels are weighed by carats.

APOTHECARIES' WEIGHT

1 scruple = 20 grains
1 dram = 3 scruples, or
60 grains
1 ounce = 8 drams, or
24 scruples, or
480 grains
1 pound = 12 ounces, or
96 drams, or
288 scruples, or
5,760 grains

APOTHECARIES' FLUID MEASURE

1 dram = 60 minims
1 ounce = 8 drams, or
480 minims
1 pint = 16 ounces, or
128 drams, or
7,680 minims
1 gallon = 8 pints, or
128 ounces, or
1,024 drams, or
61,440 minims

A convenient way of estimating apothecaries' fluid measure is: 1 minim = 1 drop; 1 dram = 1 teaspoonful; 1 ounce = 2 tablespoonfuls.

VOLUME MEASURE

1 cubic foot = 1,728 cubic inches
1 cubic yard = 27 cubic feet, or
46,656 cubic inches
1 cord = 128 cubic feet

The cord is a unit used only for measuring firewood.

Weimar

Weimar is a city in East Germany. After World War I, when the former German emperor had to abdicate (resign), Germany became a republic for the first time in its history and Weimar was its capital for a very short time. For this reason the German republic, which lasted from 1919 to 1933, was often called "the Weimar republic."

Before World War I, Weimar was the capital of the grand duchy of Saxe-Weimar, a small state ruled by a grand duke, which was part of the German Empire. No small city in Europe was more famous in the arts and literature. Two of Germany's most famous poets, Goethe and Schiller, are buried there. There are many beautiful buildings and works of art in Weimar. It is now under Communist control, like the rest of East Germany. The population is about 50,000.

Weimaraner

The Weimaraner is a hunting dog that was developed in Germany. For many years only members of the grand duke's court in Weimar were allowed to own Weimaraners.

The nobles of the court wanted a powerful, fast, intelligent dog that could hunt the wild boar, and the Weimaraner was bred to fit this requirement. It was also used to hunt wolves, deer, bears, and other animals, and its keen sense of smell, its courage and its intelligence made it very valuable to sportsmen in Europe many years ago. Today the Weimaraner is kept as a bird dog and a pet in both

Europe and America. It is a good family dog, and a loyal, trustworthy pet.

The Weimaraner stands 22 to 26 inches high at the shoulder and is about 23 to 27 inches long from its chest to the base of its tail. It usually weighs 55 to 85 pounds. The color of the Weimaraner's eyes is unusual. They are always blue, gray, or amber-colored. Its coat is smooth and short-haired, and a light grayish-tan in color.

Weizmann, Chaim

Chaim Weizmann was the first President of the modern Republic of Israel. Before Israel became an independent state, he had devoted most of his life to getting an independent homeland for the Jewish people. He was among the founders and most outstanding leaders of Zionism, the movement for establishing a modern Jewish nation in Israel, the ancient country of the Jews, which the Romans called Palestine.

Weizmann was born in Russia in 1874. He studied chemistry in Germany, then taught at universities in Switzerland and England. During World War I, he devised an improved method of making acetone, which is used in explosives.

At the end of World War I, the British Foreign Secretary, Arthur Balfour, issued a statement (called the Balfour Declaration) that promised the support of the British government to the Zionists. Many thought this was a reward for Weizmann's work.

The promise of a Jewish homeland was not soon fulfilled. During the following years, Weizmann divided his time between the laboratory and his work for Zionism. During World War II, Weizmann spent some time in the United States where he helped in the production of synthetic rubber which was of great importance in winning the war. In 1948, the new nation of Israel was finally formed and Weizmann was elected its first president. He governed wisely and worked hard to make Israel a modern state in the Middle East. He died in office in 1952. In a book called *Trial and Error*, published in 1949, Weizmann told the story of his life.

welding

Welding is a way of joining two pieces of metal together. The pieces of metal are heated to such a high temperature that they melt and flow into each other. When the heated metals cool they are joined in a seam that is usually as strong as any part of the pieces of metal themselves.

There are two main kinds of welding. The first is done by passing an electric current through the metals at the edges that are to be joined. The electric current heats the metals so that they grow white-hot and finally melt together. The second main method of welding is done with a torch that burns acetylene gas mixed with oxygen. The flame from this torch is hot enough to melt most metals. When they melt they flow together.

With both methods of welding, a welding material is sometimes used. This is usually a rod of metal that is melted by the heat at the point at which the other two metals are being joined. The welding-rod metal mixes with the melted metal of the pieces being joined, and helps to form a strong seam.

Sometimes, where two pieces of metal do not have to be joined in a continuous seam, they are *spot welded*. Spot welding is much like buttoning a shirt. The spots occur at frequent intervals but they do not cover the entire joint. Spot welding is all right when a joint does not have to be airtight or watertight, or where two pieces of metal merely have to be held firmly together.

In all kinds of welding, the high degree of heat and the melting of the metal may cause great sparks to fly. The sparks and the intense brightness of the white-hot metals make it necessary for a welder to wear a safety mask. The mask has a dark glass-covered opening through which the welder can watch the work. In small jobs, usually done with an acetylene torch, the welder usually wears only dark goggles (eyeglasses).

Welding is used in making automobiles, ships, airplanes, boilers, tanks, pipelines and nearly all heavy machines.

Welensky, Sir Roy

Sir Roy Welensky was born at Salisbury, Southern Rhodesia, in 1907. He was a locomotive fireman and engineer and a trade union official before he became a political leader in 1938. He helped form the Federation of Rhodesia and Nyasaland in 1953 and was its Prime Minister from 1956 to 1963, when the Federation ended. Welensky strongly supported the policy that the few white residents of the country should rule over the many Negroes. See the article on RHODESIA.

well

A well is a hole that has been dug or drilled into the earth. Nearly everyone who does not live in a city has to depend on a well for water. Some wells are only about 20 feet deep, and some are more than 200 feet deep. The much deeper wells are called ARTESIAN WELLS. You can read about these in a separate article.

WATER TABLES

Rain water soaking into the earth often reaches a point where the soil holds as much water as it possibly can. In this case the soil is said to be *saturated*. At other times rain water collects between layers of rock. It is held, almost in the form of a pool, in a porous layer of earth or rock.

In any case where there is a collection of water underground, it may be reached by digging a well down to the top level of the water. The level of water underground is called a *water table*. If the water table in a particular place is 20 feet below the surface of the earth, a well must be dug 20 feet deep to reach water.

Usually wells are dug deeper than the surface of the water table. During very dry spells the water table drops, and if the well were not deeper than the usual water table the well would run dry.

Most wells are lined with brick or stones after they have been dug, to keep loose earth and dirt from falling and closing the well again. Ordinary wells, which do not go down very deep, are called shallow wells or ground wells. Another kind of well is called a driven well. A driven well is made by forcing a large, pointed metal tube or pipe into the ground. When the point strikes the water table, the well flows. Still another kind of well is drilled to the water table, and the hole is then filled with pipe which has a screen at the bottom.

Wells that are near old farmhouses usually have a bucket to bring the water up from the bottom of the well. The bucket is raised and lowered on a rope or is connected with a crank that makes it easier to bring up a bucket of water. There are also hand pumps in wells. A person using a hand pump works the handle up and down to bring water up through a pipe reaching down through the well. Modern wells have motors connected to the pumps. The motors may run by electricity or gasoline. They pump water from the well to a tank. When the water in the tank reaches a certain level, the pump is automatically shut off by electricity. When the water drops below this level, the pump is automatically turned on.

Welland Ship Canal

The Welland Ship Canal is a Canadian water route between Lake Ontario and Lake Erie. It carries shipping around the Niagara River, which is not navigable because of the falls, and is an important link in the St. Lawrence Seaway. The canal is 27 miles long and has eight locks. At the Lake Ontario terminal is the town of Port Weller and at the Lake Erie terminal are the towns of Port Colborne and Humberstone. Lakes Ontario and Erie were first connected by a canal in 1833. The present canal was opened in 1932.

Wellesley College

Wellesley College is a college for women in Wellesley, Massachusetts, a town near Boston. It was founded in 1870. There are about 1,700 students at Wellesley and about 187 teachers. The college offers bachelors' degrees in the liberal arts and in education. There is a museum with a fine collection of modern painting, and the science departments have particularly good equipment.

Wellington

Wellington is the capital city and principal port of New Zealand. It is on North Island, at the head of Wellington Harbor, which was formerly called Port Nicholson Harbor. About 134,000 people live in Wellington. There are many factories, including an automobile assembly plant. The city exports dairy products, wool, meat, and hides.

Wellington is the seat of the Governor General's offices, the Houses of Parliament of New Zealand, the University of New Zealand, and Victoria University College. The National Museum has a fine collection of art by the Maoris, the original inhabitants of New Zealand.

The first white settlement of New Zealand was at Wellington in 1840. The capital was transferred from Aukland to Wellington in 1865.

WELLINGTON, NEW ZEALAND. Population (1974 census) 134,400. Capital of New Zealand. Seaport. Founded, 1840.

Wellington, Duke of

Arthur Wellesley, 1st Duke of Wellington, was a British statesman and one of Great Britain's greatest soldiers. He is best remembered for his defeat of Napoleon, the French emperor, at the Battle of Waterloo.

Wellington was born in 1769 in Dublin, Ireland. He joined the British Army in 1787, at the age of 18. His brother, Richard Wellesley, was a Member of Parliament and with his help Wellington quickly rose to high rank in the army. In 1796 he went with his regiment to India, where he made a name for himself by defeating local rulers in several wars. He received the official thanks of Parliament and was made a knight.

Wellington returned to England in 1805 and served as a Member of Parliament, but in 1808 he was sent to help Portugal, which was resisting an attack by Napoleon, who had controlled it from France. Napoleon was the greatest enemy of Great Britain. In this campaign, called the Peninsular War, Wellington's forces often had to fight greatly superior armies. The British Parliament was not altogether in favor of the war, and Wellington was hampered by lack of supplies and men. He commanded British, Portuguese and Spanish forces, and by 1813 he had driven the French out of Spain and Portugal. He pushed into France in 1814 and had captured the French city of Bordeaux when news reached him that Napoleon had abdicated (resigned as emperor) and the war was over. For his great success he received many honors and was made Duke of Wellington.

In 1815 Wellington was representing Great Britain at the Congress of Vienna, which had met to reorganize the countries and boundaries of Europe, when word reached the Congress that Napoleon had returned to France and had raised an army to resume the war. Wellington was put in command of the allied forces and in June he defeated Napoleon at Waterloo. This was the final defeat of Napoleon.

Wellington became a member of the British cabinet and was sent on missions to foreign countries. He was a rich man and a member of the upper classes, and he did not believe in democracy. This made him very unpopular with the people for a time, and in 1828 when he became Prime Minister he was often in disagreement with the members of his Cabinet.

At that time, there was a movement to reform, or change, the system of electing members of Parliament. The system in force was very unfair to many of the British people. Wellington spoke against the Reform Bill, and the people were so angry that his house was stormed by a mob and he was jeered at in the streets.

Gradually Wellington became popular again. Only his military victories were remembered. His prestige became so great that his word was seldom questioned and every suggestion he made was acted upon, even if it was only an offhand opinion. He was made commander-in-chief of the army for life and became the idol of the people. When he died in 1852 he was buried with a great state funeral at St. Paul's Cathedral.

Wells, H. G.

Herbert George Wells was an English writer who was born in 1866 and died in 1946 and who turned out an astonishing number of books and stories during his long lifetime. At different times in his career he was most popular for different kinds of writing. In his early days he wrote science fiction, and he predicted several inventions and scientific marvels that later were worked out, including a bomb very much like the hydrogen bomb. He wrote a very successful novel, *Tono-Bungay,* in 1909 and another, *Mr. Britling Sees It Through,* during World War I. In 1920 he wrote his most successful work, *The Outline of History,* in which he put together the work of many other historians to make a brief, readable story of the history of the world through all ages.

Two stories by Wells caused great discussion in the United States. One was *The War of the Worlds,* in which he imagined that men from Mars invaded the earth. A radio broadcast was based on this in 1938 and caused a panic because people thought they were listening to a news broadcast and that the world actually had been invaded. The other was called *The Shape of Things to Come,* which was made into a motion picture. In this story, which Wells wrote in 1933, he predicted that World War II would come and would cause even greater destruction than it actually did.

Welsh terrier

The Welsh terrier is a small dog that looks almost exactly like a miniature Airedale. It stands about fifteen inches high at the shoulder and is almost as long as it is tall. Its weight is about twenty pounds. The coat is always black and tan, like an Airedale's colors. Its tail is clipped when the puppy is a few days old.

Wends

The Wends (or Sorbs) are a people who live in eastern Germany, chiefly in Saxony but also in an adjoining part of Prussia. They are a Slavic people, related to the Czechs, Poles, and other Slavs. Their old Wendish language is like Polish and Bohemian (Czech). It contains a number of German words, since the Wends are surrounded by German-speaking people and are only a small national group. Most of the Wends are farmers. The region of Germany in which they live is called Lusatia.

werewolf

According to an old superstition, a werewolf is a man who from time to time changes into a wolf. The change is usually said to occur when the moon is full. Many people used to believe in the werewolves, but few do today. There are many legends about werewolves. In the Middle Ages, people thought that the werewolf roamed about at night, attacking and eating humans. They believed that if a werewolf were injured, the injury would still show the next day when the werewolf had changed back into a man.

Wesley, Charles and John

Charles and John Wesley were two English religious reformers who lived about two hundred years ago. John Wesley founded the Protestant faith of Methodism, and Charles was one of his chief followers. (There is a separate article about the METHODIST Church.)

John Wesley was born in Lincolnshire, England, in 1703. He was a gay youth who loved a good time. He studied at Oxford University and was ordained a priest of the Church of England in 1728. During his studies he had become deeply religious. At Oxford he became the leader of the Holy Club, a group of young men who lived a strict religious life. Other students made fun of the methodical lives of this group, calling them "methodists." Wesley and his group adopted this name.

In 1735, John and his brother Charles went to Georgia with James Oglethorpe. On the trip they met some Moravians, whose simple faith impressed them deeply. When John returned to London in 1738 he attended a Moravian meeting, and this proved to be the turning point of his life. There he became certain that men could be saved only through Jesus. He experienced a great desire to spread this message.

Soon after the meeting, John Wesley began to preach. Clergymen of the day disapproved of Wesley and his followers and would not let them use the churches, so they preached in the open air. Lay preachers (men who were not priests) were appointed, and they traveled over the countryside, starting new groups of Methodists. During this time Wesley worked constantly, preaching, writing pamphlets about Methodism, and organizing the movement. He had thousands of followers before he died in 1791.

Charles Wesley was born in 1707. Like his brother John, he was first a priest in the Church of England. He worked with his brother throughout his life. He is best known as the writer of several thousand hymns. Two of these are "Hark! the Herald Angels Sing" and "Jesus, Lover of My Soul." He died in 1788, three years before his brother.

West, Benjamin

Benjamin West was an American painter who lived more than 150 years ago. He was one of the first painters to present historical scenes realistically, with the people in proper costume, and he influenced other historical painters to paint realistically. Among his best known works are *Christ Healing the Sick* and *Death of General Wolfe.* West was born in Pennsylvania in 1738. He spent much of his life in Europe, and during his later years he lived in London, where he became president of the Royal Academy.

Benjamin West died in 1820.

Western European Union

The Western European Union (or W.E.U.) is a group of nations that made an agreement to protect one another if

Soviet Russia should try to conquer and control the nations of western Europe, as it did the nations of eastern Europe after World War II. The treaty (agreement) that set up the Western European Union was made in 1954 and was approved by the nations early in 1955.

One important thing about the W.E.U. agreement is that it permits West Germany to join and have an army. Under a treaty made after World War II, Germany was not permitted to have armed forces.

Another important thing about the W.E.U. agreement is that it set "ceilings" (limits) on the armed forces and armaments that member nations were to contribute to NATO (the NORTH ATLANTIC TREATY ORGANIZATION, about which there is a separate article). The German army was limited to 500,000 men by the treaty. The limits were to remain unchanged unless all the nations of the W.E.U. voted to change them.

The original members of the W.E.U. were Great Britain, France, Italy, Belgium, the Netherlands, Luxembourg, and West Germany.

Western Reserve

The Western Reserve was a name given to a large tract of land that is now part of northeast Ohio. Before the Revolutionary War this land was part of large western territories belonging to the state of Connecticut. When the United States was first organized, Connecticut gave most of its western land to the federal government but held in reserve the part that came to be called the Western Reserve. Farmlands in the Western Reserve were given to people of Connecticut whose homes were burned during the Revolutionary War. This part of the Western Reserves was known as the "Fire Lands." The rest of the territory was sold to the Connecticut Land Company in 1795 and was settled by New Englanders. All this territory became part of the state of Ohio.

WESTERN RESERVE UNIVERSITY

Western Reserve University is in Cleveland, Ohio, which is in the territory that was once part of the Western Reserve. In 1962 Western Reserve University had an enrollment of 8,350 men and women.

West Indies

The West Indies is an archipelago, or group of islands, that stretches from the southern tip of Florida in the United States almost to the coast of Venezuela in South America. It separates the Caribbean Sea and the Gulf of Mexico from the Atlantic Ocean. There are three main chains of islands, the Bahamas and the Greater and the Lesser Antilles.

In the Greater Antilles, independent countries are Cuba, Haiti and the Dominican Republic on the island of Hispaniola, and Jamaica (including the smaller Turks and Caicos Islands) which is a member of the British Commonwealth with dominion status like Canada's. Puerto Rico is a territory of the United States.

The Lesser Antilles include Trinidad and Tobago, a dominion within the British Commonwealth; Barbados, which has a British governor but makes its own laws; the Windward Islands (most of them British), and the Leeward Islands (including the Virgin Islands), all very small and allied with Great Britain, France, the Netherlands, or the U.S. (which owns some of the Virgin Islands).

The Bahamas are a separate chain, with a British governor but the right of self-government. They are near the eastern and southern coasts of Florida.

The islands that belong to France are all in the Leeward group: Martinique, and Guadeloupe and its dependencies. The Netherlands own Curaçao and five other islands in the Lesser Antilles.

There are separate articles on most of the islands or island groups of the West Indies.

Westinghouse, George

Gale Research Co.

George Westinghouse was an American inventor and businessman. He is most famous for his invention of the air brake and for the introduction of the use of alternating current for electric power in the United States. He was the head of the Westinghouse Electric Company and the owner of many factories in the United States and Europe. He is considered one of the men most responsible for making the United States the leading industrial nation in the world.

George Westinghouse was born in Central Bridge, New York, in 1846. His father manufactured agricultural machinery, and Westinghouse showed his inventiveness even as a boy working in his father's factory. During the Civil War he fought with the Union forces. Later he attended Union College, but left without graduating in order to spend more time with his inventions. He became particularly interested in making railroads safer, and, in addition to the air brake, invented a railway frog (a device that enabled tracks to cross each other) and several signaling devices. For his work in engineering George Westinghouse received awards from governments all over the world. He died in 1914.

Westminster Abbey

Westminster Abbey in London is the most famous church in Great Britain. The kings and queens of England are crowned there, and many rulers and famous men of England are buried there. The church is built in the shape of a cross, in the style of architecture called Gothic. There are a number of chapels in Westminster Abbey, of which the most notable is the Chapel of Henry VII. There are nearly 100 statuettes in the Chapel of Henry VII, and in it are buried Mary Queen of Scots, William and Mary, Queen Elizabeth I, and other kings, queens, and members of the royal family. The Poet's Corner contains the tombs of Chaucer, Spenser, Browning, Tennyson, and many other famous writers and poets.

The first church on the site of Westminster Abbey was built in 616, but the present building was begun about seven hundred years ago. Further building was done over several hundred years. The building of two of the Abbey's towers was begun in 1732. Westminster Abbey was hit by bombs during World War II, but it was not seriously damaged and the damage has been repaired.

West Point

West Point is a town on the Hudson River, about fifty miles north of New York City. About eight thousand people live there. West Point has become famous because it is the site of the United States MILITARY ACADEMY, about which there is a separate article. The Academy is usually called West Point.

West Virginia

West Virginia is one of the South Atlantic States in the United States. It is the only state in this group that has no seacoast.

Until the time of the Civil War, West Virginia was a part of the state of Virginia. Its nickname is the "Panhandle State," because it is shaped like a two-handled pan. One panhandle area is in the north and the other in the east. West Virginia is also called the "Mountain State," because of its mountainous regions.

In area, West Virginia ranks 41st among the states, with 24,181 square miles. In population it ranks 34th, with a little less than two million people living there.

It became a state in 1863, and was the 35th state admitted to the Union. The capital is Charleston.

THE PEOPLE OF WEST VIRGINIA

The earliest white settlers came to the region that is now West Virginia more than two hundred years ago. Many of them were Scotch-Irish settlers from Pennsylvania, Maryland, and New York. Later many German, Irish and Welsh immigrants came to build the railroads or work in the mines. There are over 73,900 Negroes living in West Virginia.

Many of the people in West Virginia work in the mines or in the industries supported by the mines. The state has large deposits of soft coal. It mines more soft coal than any other state in the United States. There are also deposits of petroleum and natural gas. There are large iron and steel plants.

West Virginia has thousands of acres of forests, and many people also work at lumber production. In the mountainous areas there is good grazing land for sheep and cattle, and in the fertile valleys the farmers grow corn, oats, wheat, potatoes, and many kinds of fruit. Tobacco is grown in the western part of the state.

WHAT WEST VIRGINIA IS LIKE

West Virginia is separated from Virginia by the Allegheny Mountains, which run from the northeast to the south central part of the state. In the eastern panhandle region is a fertile plain drained by the Potomac River, which forms part of the northern boundary of the state. Many of the coal mines are found in the mountains.

The central part of West Virginia is part of the Appalachian Plateau, which

was once a high, level region, but is now a region of high hills and deep valleys. There are deposits of coal and natural gas in this region, and it is here that several of the larger cities, including the capital, Charleston, are located.

The northwestern part of the state, which includes the northern panhandle, is a lowland drained by the Ohio River, which forms part of the western boundary of West Virginia. The best farm lands and several of the cities are in this section of the state.

In most parts of the state, the winters are mild and the summers warm. The average temperature in winter is about 35 degrees and in summer about 75 degrees.

The Ohio River provides a route to the Mississippi River and to the Gulf of Mexico. The Monongahela River is important as a transportation route to industrial cities in the north. Other rivers provide the water power that has made it possible for West Virginia to become an important industrial state.

Railroads reach to most parts of the state, and there are many miles of good highways, though it has been difficult in many instances to build roads through the mountains. There are airports in the largest cities.

THE GOVERNMENT OF WEST VIRGINIA

West Virginia, like other states, has a governor at the head of the government and a legislature that makes the laws. The governor is elected for a four-year term. The legislature is composed of two houses, a Senate and a House of Delegates. Members of the Senate are elected for four-year terms and members of the House of Delegates for two-year terms. Judges are elected for twelve-year terms. The capital is Charleston. There are 55 counties.

There are about 400,000 pupils attending public elementary and high schools.

Among the principal colleges and universities are:

West Virginia University, at Morgantown. Enrollment, 15,921 men and women in 1971.

West Virginia State College, at Institute. Enrollment, 3,314 men and women in 1971.

Marshall University, at Huntington. Enrollment, 8,442 men and women in 1971.

Davis and Elkins College, at Elkins. Enrollment, 733 men and women in 1971.

Bethany College, at Bethany. Enrollment, 937 men and women in 1971.

CHIEF CITIES

The leading cities of West Virginia, with 1970 census populations, are:

Charleston, population 71,505, the capital and second-largest city. There is a separate article about CHARLESTON.

Huntington, population 74,315. The largest city in the state, industrial center and port on the Ohio River, in the west.

Wheeling, population 48,188, the third-largest city, in the panhandle region. There is a separate article about WHEELING.

Parkersburg, population 44,208, fourth-largest city, industrial center, in the northwestern part of the state.

Clarksburg, population 24,864, fifth-largest city, industrial center, in the north central part of the state.

WEST VIRGINIA IN THE PAST

The region that is now West Virginia was first explored nearly three hundred years ago, but the first settlement was not made until 1719. About two hundred years ago, settlers came to West Virginia from Maryland and Pennsylvania. The settlements were small at first and the people had to fight many battles with the Indians.

During the Revolutionary War the settlers in West Virginia fought the British and also the Indians who were on the side of the British.

The settlers in western Virginia were for the most part farmers. They built small farms which they worked themselves. Few of them had slaves. During the early 1800s they complained that the government of Virginia was being run by and for the eastern Virginians and that they did not have a full share of the government. When the Civil War started in 1861, Virginia joined the Confederate (southern) States, but the counties in the western part of the state refused to join, and broke away from the state entirely. In 1863 these counties were admitted to the Union as the state of West Virginia.

West Virginia has become more and more of an industrial state as its natural resources have been developed. It has always been a popular vacation spot.

PLACES TO SEE

Watogo State Park, 10,048 acres, 10 miles east of Hillsboro, in the east, near U.S. Route 219. Wildlife preserve and largest of the state parks.

Harpers Ferry, in the northeast, where Virginia, West Virginia, and Maryland meet, on U.S. 340. Scene of John Brown's historic raid.

White Sulphur Springs, in the southeast, on U.S. Route 60. World-famous health resort.

Moundsville, in north panhandle region, on U.S. Route 250. Largest Indian burial mound in the United States.

Blennerhasset's Island, 5 miles south of Parkersburg, in the Ohio River, near U.S. Route 50. Mansion in which Aaron Burr conspired to overthrow the United States government.

WEST VIRGINIA. Area, 24,181 square miles. Population (1970 census) 1,744,237. Capital Charleston. Nickname, the Panhandle State or the Mountain State. Motto, *Montani Semper Liberi* (Mountaineers Always Free). Flower, rhododendron. Bird, cardinal. Song (one of the official), "West Virginia My Home Sweet Home." Admitted to Union, June 20, 1863. Abbreviation, W. Va.

whale and whaling

Whales are the largest of all animals. There are some whales that are only 5 feet long, but most of them are more than 50 feet long. The largest whales, the blue whales, grow to 100 feet in length and can weigh almost 300,000 pounds.

Whales live in water. Most of them inhabit the oceans, but a few swim in the large rivers of the earth. The kinds that live in rivers have almost died out.

Whales are not fish. They are mammals, just as cows, horses, dogs, and human beings are. They give birth to live young, instead of laying eggs, and the mother whales nurse their young by giving them milk from their breasts. Like all mammals, whales have lungs and breathe the air, instead of having gills to get oxygen from water as fish do.

A whale does not have a nose, but has two blowholes at the top of its head, or in some cases one blowhole. A whale comes to the surface of the water, breathes in air through the blowholes, and then goes back down in the water. A whale usually breathes about once every five minutes, but it can remain in the water for more than thirty minutes without taking another breath. When the whale comes back to the surface, it exhales through the blowhole. It does this with great force and appears to be spouting water into the air. This is not so, but it seems so because the heated breath expelled by the whale contains water vapor, which condenses when it meets the colder outer air.

Whales can descend about half a mile beneath the ocean's surface. They are able to do this because about half of their bodies is made of *blubber,* which is very much like fat. The blubber may be more than a foot thick below the skin of the whale and it protects the whale from extreme cold at the ocean depths to which it descends. The whale's tail also helps it to go down very deep. The tail is a large fin, shaped like a triangle (three-sided), and horizontal, or flat, instead of upright as a fish's tail usually is. By using this tail with great strength, the whale can push itself up from the depths of the ocean.

WHALE CALVES

A bull (male) whale often has a whole harem of cows (female). A cow gives birth to a single calf. Very rarely twins are born. Whale calves can swim immediately at birth. The mother nurses her calf for about six months, and she will protect it until it is weaned (begins to take other food).

The newborn calf of the sperm whale is about fourteen feet long at birth, which is as large as some whales are when they are fully grown.

WHALEBONE AND TEETH

There are two main groups of whales. One group has teeth and the other group has a substance called whalebone or *baleen.* The whalebone grows from the top of certain whales' mouths in long, thin, whiplike form. The large mouth of a whale that has this baleen seems to have a great curtain of these long strips of whalebone, almost completely filling the mouth. When the mouth is open, the many hundreds of whalebone strips hang

down as the whale swims through the water.

The whalebone is covered with smaller fuzzy or hairlike projections. It almost looks as though the whale had an enormous doormat hanging from the roof of its mouth.

Whales that have baleen in their mouths get their food by swimming in water and straining tiny particles of animal and plant life, called plankton, through the baleen. When the whale has taken in a mouthful of food, it closes its mouth. The baleen is pushed upward and back by the whale's tongue. The water is strained out of the mouth through the sides, and the food drops down into the whale's throat. Whales that have whalebone instead of teeth live mostly in the cold polar oceans where they can find much of the plankton on which they feed.

The whales that have teeth live mostly on molluscs and fish. The best-known toothed whale is the sperm whale. This whale feeds mostly on cuttlefish. Strangely enough, the largest whales are not the toothed whales, which can feed on large fish, but the whalebone whales, which feed on tiny plankton. The largest of these, besides the blue whale, are the right whale, the Greenland whale, and the thin whale. Among the toothed whales, in addition to the sperm whale, are the bottlenosed whale and the killer whale. The killer whale is ferocious and will attack and eat larger whales. It has not been known to attack man.

WHALING

For hundreds of years man has been hunting and killing whales. At one time there were many whales in the ocean waters, but they have been hunted and killed for so many centuries that there are not many whales left in the world today. Because of this, there is now an international commission which regulates whaling and does not permit more than a certain number to be killed each year. Each nation that has whaling ships must report to the international commission and tell how many whales have been killed. In the old days there was no regulation and men could hunt and kill as many whales as they could find.

Whaling was once an important seagoing industry. In the United States the chief whaling port was New Bedford, Massachusetts, and there were other important ones along the New England coast. Many of the men who lived there went to sea and stayed for long periods of time on their whaling expeditions. It was not unusual for a ship to be away from port for two or three years. During this time the men on the ships sailed to the far oceans in search of whales.

One habit of whales that has made it easy for man to hunt them is their way of traveling in groups called schools, or *gams.* If whales lived alone it would be more difficult for whaling crews to catch many. Because they stick together in schools, whalers can often catch many at one time.

WHALING SHIPS

Until about 75 years ago, the whaling ships had sails and could not go very fast. A man up on the mast, in a little cage called the "crow's nest," would look out over the ocean to spot whales spouting.

When he saw one, he would shout, "Thar she blows!" The sailors would then go out in rowboats called dories, or whaleboats. The men in these small boats hurled iron spears called harpoons when they came close to a whale. The harpoons had hooks on the end so that when they entered the whale's body they would hold fast. A rope was attached to the other end of the harpoon so that the whale could be pulled in. However, before the whale could be pulled in it often thrashed about for hours. Sometimes it upset the dory and the men were drowned. Finally, after the whale grew weak and died, it was towed to the ship. Here it was cut up and the pieces of blubber were boiled down in large vats and made into oil. An even finer oil was made from the *spermaceti,* a fat found in the head of the sperm whale but not other whales. The oil was the most valuable part of the whale and the main reason it was hunted and killed. Whale oil was considered the best oil for oil lamps and was used for fine candles and as a lubricant for the most delicate machinery, such as watches. The flesh of the whale could be eaten, but there was more than was needed. Most of the rest of the whale was thrown away.

A very famous book called *Moby Dick,* by an American writer named Herman Melville, tells about the oldtime whalers.

FACTORY SHIPS

Modern whaling is much different. Now large steel ships called *factory ships* sail into the polar seas. Most of the factory ships come from Norway, Japan, England, and Russia. Other small ships sail along with the factory ships. They are powerful little ships called *catchers,* about the size of tugboats. Very often the factory ship has an airplane that it can catapult out over the ocean. The pilot of the plane can easily spot a whale in the ocean below, even under the surface, by its dark shape.

No longer do men go out in dories. Now the harpoonist stands on a platform in front of the catcher ship. He does not throw the harpoon, but fires it from a gun. The end of the harpoon has a charge of explosive powder. When the harpoon strikes the whale and enters its body, the powder explodes and kills the whale. When the catcher ship has harpooned a whale, it usually pumps air into the whale's body so that it will float on the surface. A flag is stuck in the body so that the factory ship will spot it and pull up to take the body aboard.

The back end of the factory ship opens up so that a long ramp leads from the surface of the water to the deck of the ship. The huge body of the whale is pulled up this ramp by a chain attached to a motor. As soon as the whale's body is on deck, the men begin to cut it up. They have sharp knives attached to long poles with which they can easily cut into the blubber and other parts of the whale. After the blubber has been taken out and melted into oil, the rest of the whale's body is used. The meat is packed away in refrigerators.

Whale meat has been eaten by people of many countries, particularly since World War II, when other meats were scarce. Whale meat looks and tastes much like beef, except that it is tougher

and has a slight fishy flavor. Even the bones of the whale are now ground into fertilizer on board the factory ship.

Whalers prefer to catch sperm whale, because of the spermaceti, or very fine oil, in its huge snout. Sometimes as much as 500 gallons of oil is obtained from the head of a sperm whale.

In a separate article you may read about AMBERGRIS, which is a substance given off by sick whales. It is very valuable and is used in making perfumes.

See also the articles on the DOLPHIN, NARWHAL, and PORPOISE, which are smaller members of the whale family. All members of this family are called *cetaceans.*

Wharton, Edith

Edith Wharton was an American novelist. Most of her novels tell of the changing ways of life among the rich and fashionable people of New York City between the Civil War and World War II. Among her best books are *The Age of Innocence,* for which she won a Pulitzer Prize in 1921; *The Old Maid, Ethan Frome,* and *The House of Mirth.* Several of her novels have been made into plays and motion pictures.

Edith Wharton was born Edith Newbold Jones, in New York in 1862. She belonged to a rich and prominent family and she wrote of the people she knew best. She was educated at home by private tutors and spent much of her youth traveling in Europe. In 1885 she married Edward Wharton. Her first book was not published until 1899, and she wrote more than 50 books before her death in 1937.

For the last thirty years of her life Edith Wharton lived in Paris. She was influenced by Henry James, another great American novelist, with whom she was friendly.

wheat

Wheat is one of the most important of the world's food crops. It is a cereal grain, which means it is a kind of grass whose seeds are used for food. Wheat is more widely used than any other grain except rice. The greatest part of the world's wheat is grown in North America, Australia, and Europe. The people of the world consume millions of tons of wheat each year, in many forms. Most wheat is ground into flour for bread and for macaroni and spaghetti products. The coarser, rough parts of wheat are used as cattle feed. Wheat is usually grown in large fields, and is known as a "field crop."

Wheat has been a basic food of the human race for thousands of years. It has been cultivated so long that it is difficult for scientists to know where it first grew.

A spike of wheat may be "bearded" or "beardless." Bearded wheat has threadlike tendrils growing upward between the grains on the head of the stalk.

The grains are removed from the stalks by *threshing,* a beating process that removes the husks, or outer coverings. The coating of dried skin over the grains is removed at the same time. This is called the *chaff.*

Both graham (whole-wheat) flour and bran meals are wheat products. Graham or whole-wheat flour is ground from the grain kernel with the outer shell left

DISTRIBUTION OF WHEAT IN THE UNITED STATES

1. White wheat
2. Hard red spring
3. Hard red winter
4. Soft red winter

Each dot represents 5,000 acres

U. S. DEPARTMENT OF AGRICULTURE

BUREAU OF AGRICULTURAL ECONOMICS

on, and bran is the shell itself. The most valuable nourishment comes from the bran, which contains most of the vitamins in wheat, so whole wheat is better for you than white flour, but white flour is more popular. (See the article on FLOUR.)

Whole wheat is slightly less starchy than corn and contains more protein, the substance that builds body tissues.

Wheat is the most important crop in most big countries, and in the United States it is one of the two most important crops, along with corn. It is grown on huge farms and is cultivated and harvested by automatic machines, as explained in the article on FARM MACHINES. Other machines thresh the grain and separate the kernels from the stalks, and giant conveyors carry the threshed grain to grain elevators, or storage sheds.

wheel and axle

The wheel and axle is one of the simple machines told about in the article on MACHINE. It makes it easier to do certain kinds of work, such as lifting weights. This is because it is much farther around the wheel than around the axle. Suppose it is 100 inches around the wheel and only 10 inches around the axle. You want to lift a weight of 500 pounds, but it is too heavy to lift. You attach the weight to a rope around the axle. Then you turn the wheel. Every time you turn the wheel around, which is 100 inches, you turn the axle 10 inches, and that lifts the weight 10 inches. To turn the wheel you need only as much force as it would take to lift a weight of 50 pounds. Therefore the 500-pound weight is no longer too heavy for you to lift. A crank is an example of the wheel-and-axle principle. It is much easier to turn the crank than it would be to turn the axle, but you have to turn the crank farther.

The wheel that is used on vehicles such as the wagon and automobile is considered one of the most important inventions ever made by man. Heavy loads that could never be pulled over the ground can be pulled easily if they are on wheels. The reason for this is that only a small part of the wheel rests on the ground at one time. This reduces the friction, or rubbing together of two surfaces. The less friction there is, the easier it is to slide the load along. Men have used the wheel for thousands of years.

Wheeling

Wheeling is an important city in West Virginia. Almost fifty thousand people live in the city, and it is the center of a large group of cities in which about 300,000 people live. Wheeling is on the Ohio River. It has factories that make steel, cans, electrical equipment, and many other products. For a few years, from 1875 to 1885, Wheeling was the capital of West Virginia. In the 1970 census its population was 48,188.

Whig

There have been two important political parties called Whig, one in England and one in the United States.

The Whig Party in England was one of the two powerful parties in the Parliament (English lawmaking body) for more than 150 years, from about 1680 to about 1835. The other important party was the Tories. The Whigs believed the Parliament should have most of the power, and the Tories believed the king should have it. The Whigs later became the Liberal Party and the Tories became the Conservative Party. There are separate articles on these parties.

The Whig Party in the United States was one of the two most important parties from about 1828 to about 1856. The most prominent Whig was Henry Clay of Kentucky, and the only Presidents the Whigs ever elected were William Henry Harrison and John Tyler in 1840 and Zachary Taylor and Millard Fillmore in 1848. The other big political party at that time was the Democrats. When the Republican Party became powerful, in 1860, the Whigs ceased to be a party.

whippet, a fast-running dog, like the greyhound but smaller: see the article on GREYHOUND.

whippoorwill

The whippoorwill is a bird seldom seen except as a vague shadow in the early evening as it flies low over fields, trapping insects in its enormous mouth. It lives on night-flying insects, and a single bird can devour several hundred insects in a night. The whip-poor-will grows to be nine or ten inches long. It has mottled brown and black feathers which blend into its surroundings as the bird hides and rests during the day. Whip-poor-wills have very small feet and weak legs, and cannot walk very well. They live in most parts of the United States and southern Canada; a western cousin, the poor-will, is the only bird known to hibernate. Whip-poor-wills do not build nests, but lay their two white or gray spotted eggs among leaves or on a gravel-covered spot where the color of the ground makes the eggs almost invisible.

whiskey or whisky

Whiskey is a drink that contains a large amount of alcohol. It is made from grains such as corn, wheat, rye, and barley. First the grain is mixed with water in a *mash* and allowed to ferment, or turn sour. The mash is then heated, and the steam that rises from it is condensed (turned back to a liquid). Since alcohol boils at a lower temperature than water, most of the liquid that condenses is alcohol (see DISTILLATION).

The alcohol must be aged before it can be called whiskey. It is put in casks (barrels), usually made of oak and charred (burned) inside. The alcohol is white at first, but after two or more years in the cask it turns to a color between yellow and red. Since it costs money to store whiskey long enough to age it, cheap whiskeys are sometimes made to change color faster. One way to do this is to put pieces of uncharred oak into the cask.

When aged, the alcohol can be used as whiskey; but it is much too strong to drink. It is mixed with water, and usually half or more of each bottle of whiskey is water that was added after the whiskey was aged. The flavor of the whiskey depends on the grain used and the water used. Bourbon, for example, is a whiskey made from corn and finally mixed with water that comes from Kentucky or other regions where there is a limestone taste to the water. Scotch whiskey is made from wheat, barley, and malt, mixed with water from peat bogs found in Scotland and parts of Ireland. Rye whiskey is made from rye and waters that are found in various parts of the United States and Canada.

BONDED, STRAIGHT, AND BLENDED

The *proof* of a whiskey or other alcoholic drink is a number that shows how much alcohol there is in it. The proof number is the number of parts of alcohol in 200 parts. Whiskey that is 100 proof has 100 parts of alcohol out of 200 parts, so it is exactly half alcohol. Whiskey that is 90 proof is slightly less than half alcohol.

Straight whiskey is aged whiskey that

has not been mixed with any other whiskey or alcohol. Many whiskeys made in the United States say "Bottled in Bond" on their labels, and are often called "bonded whiskey." The law says that a bonded whiskey must be straight whiskey, must be aged at least four years, and must be at least 100 proof.

Some straight whiskeys are not bonded because people prefer to have them a little weaker than 100 proof. There are also blends of straight whiskeys—two or more straight whiskeys mixed together, to make a different flavor. Nearly all Scotch whiskeys are blended in this way. However, the term blended whiskey usually means a whiskey that is made by mixing part neutral spirits (alcohol that has not been aged) and part whiskey. The whiskey gives it a desired flavor.

The drink called gin is usually neutral spirits flavored with juniper berries.

EFFECTS OF WHISKEY

Except in small quantities, whiskey can be very harmful. Organizations have worked for many years to have whiskey made illegal, and at one time the United States had PROHIBITION, about which you can read in a separate article. In some states, the law forbids whiskey to be sold.

The effects of whiskey are due to the alcohol it contains. As a drug, alcohol is a *depressant,* which means that it makes the body slower to obey the commands of the brain. A person who has taken too much alcohol cannot drive an automobile as well. Usually he cannot think quite as clearly and so does not do his work as well. If a person drinks a great deal of an alcoholic drink, he becomes intoxicated, or drunk. He may be helpless, unable to do anything but sleep. The next day he may have a headache and be unable to think or work well, a condition called a *hangover.* In small quantities, alcohol may reduce the blood pressure somewhat and cause a person to relax. See also the article on ALCOHOL.

Whiskey Rebellion

The Whiskey Rebellion was a rebellion against the government of the United States in 1794, only a few years after the United States was founded. It happened in western Pennsylvania, when the farmers there refused to pay a Federal tax on whiskey. At that time, when governments were first being set up in the frontier regions, people were not used to paying any taxes at all.

United States marshals were sent into the region to collect the tax and to arrest the farmers who would not pay it. The farmers took up arms and fought bitterly. Buildings were burned, the mails were robbed, and government officers were insulted and abused. The rebellion spread into Virginia. George Washington, who was President then, saw with alarm that there was danger of a revolution. He ordered the rebels to lay down their arms, but they refused. He then raised an army of 15,000 men, whom he prepared to send into Pennsylvania. Washington's prompt action frightened the rebels. There was still opposition to the tax, but the men returned to their homes. Two of their leaders were convicted of treason, but President Washington later pardoned them.

This was an important event in American history because it proved the power of the President's office, and established the right of the Federal government to enforce Federal law within a state.

Whist

Whist is a card game that has been played for more than four hundred years. It was probably first played in England. Contract Bridge, which is one of the most popular card games today, was developed from Whist.

There are four players in a Whist game, two playing as partners against the other two. A standard pack of cards, which is 52 cards, is used. They are dealt out one at a time until each player has thirteen cards, except that the dealer turns the last card face up and shows it. This card is called the trump card, and its suit (spades, hearts, diamonds, or clubs) becomes the trump suit.

The object of the game is to win tricks. The player at the dealer's left plays a card. This is called a lead. Each other player must play a card, in turn. A player must follow suit (play a card of the suit led) if he can, but if he has no card of the suit led he may play any card he has in his hand. Four cards, one from each player, make a trick. If there is no trump card in a trick, the highest card of the suit led wins the trick. If a trick contains a trump, the highest trump wins the trick. The winner of a trick leads to the next trick. When all the cards have been played, the side that won more than six tricks scores one point for every trick over six.

Whist is seldom played now, except in a few parts of the United States and other countries.

Whistler, James A. McNeil

James Abbott McNeil Whistler was an American painter and etcher who lived and worked in England most of his life. His most famous work is a portrait of his mother, which now hangs in the Louvre known as "Whistler's Mother," the painting was entitled "Arrangement in Grey and Black No. 1" by the artist.

Whistler was born in Lowell, Massachusetts, in 1834. He spent much of his boyhood in Russia, where his father was a railroad engineer for the United States Army. Whistler attended the Military Academy at West Point for a time and then became a map engraver. In 1855 he went to Paris to study painting. His first success was in 1863, when his painting called "Little White Girl" was shown.

For most of the time after 1863, Whistler lived in London. He disagreed with art critics and with other painters about his work, and he became known in London as an interesting and colorful person long before he achieved success as an artist. He wrote several popular essays and became popular as a lecturer.

Whistler painted both portraits and landscapes. He signed each work with a sketch of a butterfly. He was an even better etcher than he was a painter. He died in 1903.

whitefish

The whitefish is a fish that is found in the salt waters of northern seas and in the lakes of Europe and North America. There are more than thirty-five kinds of whitefish.

The lake whitefish is one of the most valuable food fishes in North America. It is found particularly in the Great Lakes. It is an oval-shaped fish with a light green back and silver-colored sides and underside. It may weigh as little as an ounce or as much as 25 pounds. The whitefish spawns in the fall, laying its eggs in shallow water. It feeds on insects, molluscs, and other fish.

White House

The White House is the home of the President of the United States, in Washington, D.C. It is a large, stately mansion surrounded by spacious lawns and gardens. It was designed in 1792 by an architect named James Hoban. The building was finished in 1799, and John Adams was the first President to live in the house. Sometimes it is called the Executive Mansion, because the President is the Chief Executive of the United States. The address of the White House, 1600 Pennsylvania Avenue, is famous throughout the world.

The White House was originally built with walls of gray Virginia stone. In 1814, during the War of 1812 between the United States and Great Britain, the White House was captured and burned by the British Army. Only the outside stone walls were left standing. The mansion was rebuilt and was painted white to hide the marks of fire on the stone walls. It has been known as the White House ever since.

To add office space for the President and his staff to work in, two wings, containing offices, have been added to the original building. While Franklin D. Roosevelt was President a swimming pool was built in the west wing.

During President Truman's administration the White House was found to be unsafe to live in. Engineers and architects found that some of the floors and walls were in danger of collapsing. President Truman and his family moved to Blair House, a government-owned mansion across the street, where they lived for several months. Blair House is usually used to entertain important visitors from other countries. While President Truman lived in Blair House, workers repaired most of the interior of the White House. The outside appearance was hardly changed at all and the inside was rebuilt so that it differs very little from its former arrangement. It was modernized and the bathrooms and kitchens were made modern.

The White House is the scene of many important state dinners and entertainments given by the President and his wife. There are several famous rooms in this beautiful old mansion. Some of them are the Oval Room, the Blue Room, the state dining room, and the President's study. The President receives all his guests in the White House and makes most of his radio and television speeches from his study. Each Easter many children come there to join the President and

his wife in an egg-rolling contest on the lawn.

Whiteman, Paul

Paul Whiteman is the name of an American orchestra conductor who became famous as the "king of jazz." He was born in 1891 in Denver, Colorado, and began his musical career as a violinist with symphony orchestras. After World War I Whiteman's interest turned to jazz music and he organized a large orchestra and played jazz in serious concerts. In 1924 he gave the first performance of George Gershwin's *Rhapsody in Blue*, a serious composition with jazz rhythms and melodies. Whiteman is chiefly notable for bringing jazz musicians to popularity and for making the whole field of jazz a respectable form of music. His orchestra included at various times many of the all-time greats of the world of jazz. Later Whiteman became a vice-president and musical director of the American Broadcasting Company. He died in 1968.

White Mountains

The White Mountains are a group of mountains in northern New Hampshire and western Maine. They are part of the Appalachian system and they contain the highest peaks in the New England states.

The White Mountains are divided into two groups by a pass called Crawford Notch. The group east of the notch is called the Presidential Range. It contains the highest peaks of the White Mountains. These peaks are named after Presidents of the United States, including Mt. Washington (6,288 feet, the highest peak of the White Mountains), Mt. Madison (5,363 feet), Mt. Adams (5,805 feet), Mt. Jefferson (5,785 feet), and Mt. Monroe (5,390 feet). West of the notch is the Franconia Range. The highest peak of the Franconia group is Mt. Lafayette (5,785 feet).

The White Mountains are noted as a summer resort. There are many hiking and skiing trails. The oldest cog railway in the world (opened in 1869) takes people to the top of Mt. Washington, from which there is a famous view. There are many swift streams and beautiful waterfalls. Profile Mountain is famous for its rock formation, which makes a natural sculpture called the "Old Man of the Mountain."

White Sea

The White Sea is a great gulf of the Arctic Ocean. It is surrounded by territory of the Soviet Union, including the Karelo-Finnish Soviet Socialist Republic, and the Archangel and Murmansk Regions. The White Sea has an area of about 37,000 square miles. The chief rivers that flow into it are the Dvina, the Mezen, and the Onega. The chief port is Archangel. The sea is frozen for about six months of the year, but icebreakers can usually keep the harbor of Archangel open. The White Sea is connected with the Caspian and Black Seas by the Dvina River, which is linked by canals with the Volga and the Dnieper rivers.

White, Walter

Walter Francis White was a leader of the American Negro people. He was born in Atlanta, Georgia, in 1893, attended Atlanta University, and became a writer. His novel, *Flight*, which was published in 1926, was popular.

White was white-skinned and had no Negroid racial characteristics, so that most people refused to believe he was a Negro; probably he had many more white than Negro ancestors. White voluntarily adopted the Negro race as his own and in 1931 he became secretary of the National Association for the Advancement of Colored People (NAACP), an organization devoted to helping the Negro. He soon was regarded as a spokesman for the American Negro. He fought against lynching (the killing of accused persons when they have not been sentenced to death in a fair trial) and also against discrimination (unfair treatment) because of race. He never advised Negroes to oppose these practices with violence.

Before White died, he saw many of the things he believed in come about through peaceful, democratic means. In *A Man Called White*, published in 1948, he told the story of his life. He died in 1955.

Whitman, Marcus

Marcus Whitman was an American missionary who lived more than a hundred years ago. He was one of the first settlers in the northwestern part of the United States. Whitman was born in New York in 1802. He studied and became a doctor of medicine before becoming a missionary. In 1836 he and his wife and three other missionaries took the first wagon across the Rocky Mountains. They established a mission near what is now Walla Walla, Washington. In the next few years other missions were set up in the territory. In 1847 Whitman, his wife, and 12 other people were killed by Indians.

Whitman, Walt

Walt Whitman was an American poet who lived about a hundred years ago. He is recognized as one of the greatest poets ever born in the United States. His best-known work is *Leaves of Grass*, his first book of poetry, which was published in 1855. Whitman was a great admirer of Abraham Lincoln, and two of his best-loved poems, "O Captain! My Captain!" and "When Lilacs Last in the Dooryard Bloom'd," are in memory of Lincoln.

Walt Whitman was born in New York in 1819. He lived most of his early years in Brooklyn, New York, where he later worked on a newspaper. During the Civil War, Whitman's brother was wounded, and Whitman went to Washington to nurse him. He remained there throughout the rest of the war, nursing other wounded men. After the war, Whitman served as a government clerk, but in 1873 he had a stroke and was partly paralyzed. He lived the rest of his life in Camden, New Jersey, where he died in 1892. His home in Camden is now a museum.

Whitman has become known as the poet of democracy because he stated in his poems that all men are brothers and must work together. He stated his ideas in a long preface to his first edition of *Leaves of Grass*. For many years, however, few people appreciated his poetry. It had no rhyme and no set rhythm. Many people considered it immoral and unfit to be read. It was only in the late years of his life that he became well known, but his reputation has grown steadily since his death. He is often called the Good Gray Poet.

Whitney, Eli

Eli Whitney was an American inventor who lived about 150 years ago. He is famous for inventing the cotton gin, but he also made great contributions to modern mass-production methods.

Whitney was born in 1765 in Westboro, Massachusetts. His father was a farmer and had a shop where he made and repaired his own farm equipment, and where Eli learned to use tools as a boy. Eli worked his way through Yale and then went to Georgia as a teacher. There he met the widow of General Nathanael Greene, who befriended him and encouraged him to invent a machine to help the cotton farmers speed up their production. In about ten days Whitney invented the gin that made cotton the South's most important and profitable crop. Whitney himself made almost nothing out of his invention. Although he obtained a patent on it, other manufacturers stole the plans and made their own machines. Whitney brought suit and won his right to the patent, but all the money he got back went to pay the costs of the legal battle. When his patent expired, Congress refused to renew it because of all the conflicting claims.

Later Whitney opened a firearms factory near New Haven, Connecticut. He was given a government contract to make a large quantity of muskets. He decided to make all the parts of them separately, and then have unskilled workmen put them together. To do this Whitney had to make special tools and this took a long time. A government inspector who came to his factory was dismayed to see that not a single musket had been completed, but Whitney convinced him that he would be able to meet the delivery date. When the tools were ready, workmen could turn out muskets a hundred times faster than ever before. This was the first use of interchangeable parts. Whitney's factory became very successful. He died in 1825.

Whitney, Mount

Mt. Whitney is among the highest mountain peaks in the United States. Only Alaska has higher. Mt. Whitney is 14,495 feet high, and is a peak of the Sierra Nevada in Eastern California. Its steep slopes are difficult to climb. Its summit is a nearly level field and is covered by snow except during the summer.

Mt. Whitney is named for Professor Josiah D. Whitney, head of an expedition that explored the surrounding highlands

in 1864 but failed to reach the summit. The summit was first reached in 1873.

Whittier, John Greenleaf

John Greenleaf Whittier was a popular American poet and newspaper editor who lived about a hundred years ago. He is chiefly remembered for his poems about New England and for his fight against slavery, which was practiced in the southern states at that time. Whittier's poetry is not considered great, but it is simple and sincere and has always appealed to the people for whom he wrote.

Whittier was born on a farm near Haverhill, Massachusetts, in 1807. His parents were Quakers. They were poor farmers, and Whittier had to work hard as a boy. He received very little schooling. His early poems attracted some attention and got him the position as editor of the *American Manufacturer,* a Boston magazine. Later he became the editor of several newspapers, all of which were against slavery. Many of his poems and editorials were against slavery.

Whittier suffered from bad health most of his life, and when he was still a young man he had to give up his job and return to the farm. He lived there quietly for the rest of his life, writing poems and a few works in prose. The longest and best-known of his poems is *Snowbound,* which tells of his memories of winters of his childhood. Other poems are "The Barefoot Boy," "Maud Muller," and "Skipper Ireson's Ride." Whittier never married. He died in 1892, at the age of 85.

Whittington, Dick

Richard Whittington, better known by his nickname "Dick," is today remembered chiefly because of legends about him. He was born in England about six hundred years ago. He went to London, where he made a fortune buying and selling fabrics. He became Lord Mayor of London, and he lent large sums of money to the king. He died in 1423, leaving all his money to charity.

According to the stories, Dick Whittington was a poor orphan who went to London to seek his fortune because he had heard that its streets were paved with gold. In London he found a job helping the cook of a rich merchant. The merchant was sending a vessel full of goods to Barbary (North Africa) and he told his employees that each of them could send one thing in the ship to be sold along with the merchant's goods. The only thing Dick Whittington owned was a cat, so he sent the cat.

Meanwhile, he was badly treated by the cook and he decided to leave London. As he was walking away from London, on his way back home, he heard the Bow Bells of Newgate ringing and they seemed to say to him,

Turn again, Whittington,
Lord Mayor of London.

Dick turned and went back. Soon the ship returned, and Dick learned that his cat had been sold for a great price because Barbary was full of rats and needed cats to kill them. This started Dick on the road to wealth.

whooping cough

Whooping cough is a disease that gets its name because a person who has it makes a whooping sound when he coughs. The scientific name for the disease is *pertussis.* Whooping cough is caused by a germ. It is an infectious disease, which means that it is easy to catch it from another person. The disease is most infectious before the bad coughing begins.

Whooping cough begins like a cold. The person has a running nose and a slight cough. About a week later the whooping begins. This may last a month or longer, and it usually takes another two or three weeks for the cough to disappear completely. A person may not feel very sick when he has whooping cough, and he can sometimes even go outside if the weather is fine, but he must be careful because he might catch other diseases, such as pneumonia.

Any person may get whooping cough, but babies and young children are especially likely to get it. Babies are usually inoculated (given injections) against whooping cough before they are six months old. Many children get another inoculation before they begin school.

whooping crane

The whooping crane is the tallest bird native to North America. It is five feet tall, white with black markings on its face, and a red patch of bare skin on top of its head. The species is almost extinct; in 1970 there were only seventy-nine, of which twenty-three were in captivity. Their only known nesting spot is a refuge in Alberta, Canada, from where they fly to another refuge in Texas for the winter. Also see the article CRANE.

Wichita

Wichita is the largest city in Kansas. It is in the southern part of the state, where the Arkansas River and the Little Arkansas River meet. More than 276,000 people live in Wichita. It is the chief manufacturing city of southern Kansas. There are flour mills, meat-packing plants, oil refineries, and airplane factories.

Wichita was first settled about a hundred years ago as a trading post for people who were going west. Later it became the starting point on the Chisholm Trail, a route on which many people traveled west. It soon became important as a trading center for the farmers and ranchers who lived near it. Wichita has many beautiful public buildings, including an art museum. Friends University and the Municipal University of Wichita are in Wichita.

WICHITA, KANSAS. Population (1970 census) 276,554. County seat of Sedgwick County. Incorporated, 1871.

wildcat, any of various small, fierce cats, especially the bobcat and lynx: see the articles on CAT, BOBCAT, and LYNX.

Wilde, Oscar

Oscar Wilde was a British playwright and poet. During his lifetime he

became famous for his witty remarks and unconventional behavior. He is remembered as much for his personality as for his writing. His most popular play was *The Importance of Being Earnest,* a farce that is still popular. Other plays include *Lady Windermere's Fan* and *The Ideal Husband.* His most popular poem is "The Ballad of Reading Gaol." He also wrote a short novel called *The Picture of Dorian Gray.*

Oscar Wilde was born in Dublin, Ireland, in 1856. He attended Trinity College in Dublin and Oxford University in England. He became known in both places for his wit and for his peculiar dress and manners. In 1882 he visited the United States on a lecture tour. He dressed in silk knee pants and elaborate hats and made insulting and witty remarks about the country that both annoyed and delighted the people who came to hear him lecture. In 1884 Wilde married and began to write the plays and poems that established his reputation. In 1895 he was sent to prison for immoral behavior. When he was released, he went to France and lived under an assumed name. He died there in disgrace and poverty in 1900, when he was only 44 years old.

wildlife

The wildlife of a country is the animals that live wild on its land and the fish that live in its lakes and rivers. Usually we think of wildlife as being only the animals that hunters like to hunt for sport and that photographers and nature-lovers like to photograph and watch or study, and the fish that give pleasure to fishermen, but other forms of wildlife are also important.

For example, some animals may be too small to appeal to hunters but are valuable as food for the larger animals. More fish are caught for sale as food than for sport, and many wild animals are trapped or hunted for their valuable furs. Nearly every living thing has a use in the plan of nature, to help keep other living things alive, or to reduce the numbers of harmful animals and insects. Even the insects themselves can be important in many ways.

The United States was once the home of countless millions of wild animals and birds. Bison (American buffaloes), deer, and antelopes and bears roamed the land in hundreds of millions. Wild ducks and geese flew overhead in such flocks that they darkened the skies. The forests were full of squirrels, and muskrats, minks and beavers lived along the streams, all valuable for their fur. These were only a few of the wild animals. There were thousands of other kinds. Together they were an important part of the natural wealth of the United States.

Most of the wildlife of the United States is now gone, partly because the clearing of the land for farms and cities left the animals no place to live but chiefly because of the wastefulness and stupidity of men. Millions of bison were killed "just for fun." If men had killed

only as many as they needed for meat and leather, there would still be great herds of bison. Wild birds were killed by the billions, partly for food, partly for feathers in women's hats, but chiefly for no reason at all. After a hundred years of this kind of killing, much of the wildlife was in danger of dying out completely.

Fish were greatly reduced in numbers when cities and factories poured waste products and chemicals into the rivers, making the water impure. The reduction in numbers of fish hurt not only those who go fishing for pleasure but also the millions who depend on fish for enjoyable and inexpensive food.

In many cases, men learned too late how much damage can be done by destroying wildlife. For example, farmers in Pennsylvania killed most of the hawks, because hawks often killed chickens. Then the farmers learned that their crops were being ruined by field mice, because there were not enough hawks to keep the numbers of field mice down.

THE FISH AND WILDLIFE SERVICE

Nearly a hundred years ago, the United States Congress began to see the damage that was being done by the destruction of wildlife.

The Fish and Wildlife Service of the Department of the Interior now does most of the work of protecting American wildlife. Its scientists study animals and fish and learn the best ways to save kinds that are dying out and to help others to live. The Service has about a hundred hatcheries for fish, and it stocks lakes and rivers with fish and tries to keep the water in condition for them to live and grow. The Service also has about two hundred refuges where wild birds can live, and nearly a hundred preserves for land animals, places where they can live without being hunted.

At the same time, the Fish and Wildlife Service works out ways to reduce the numbers of animals that are harmful to farmers, or that spread disease, or that kill desirable wildlife.

The State Department has a special officer that represents the United States in coöperating with other countries to protect fish and wildlife in the oceans and throughout the world. Many birds of the United States, for example, may spend the summers in Canada and the winters in Latin American countries.

See also the article on CONSERVATION.

Wilhelmina

Wilhelmina was Queen of the Netherlands for more than half a century, from 1890 to 1948. She was born in 1880, the daughter of King William III of the Netherlands. She became queen when she was 10 years old, but did not reign actively until she was 18. Wilhelmina's good judgment and her popularity among the people gave her great influence in the Dutch (Netherlands) government. During World War II, when the Germans overran the Netherlands, the Queen and her government moved to England and the Queen spent some time in Canada and visited the United States. In 1948, she abdicated in favor of her daughter, JULIANA, about whom there is a separate article. She died in 1962.

Wilkins, Sir George Hubert

Sir George Hubert Wilkins was one of the first men to explore the polar regions from the air. He was born in Australia in 1888. Because he wanted to travel, he became a photographer and accompanied expeditions to the polar regions as their official photographer.

In 1928, Wilkins flew 2,200 miles across the Arctic. In that year he was made a knight, which gave him the title *Sir*. Soon after, he explored the Antarctic regions by plane. In 1931 he led an expedition that sailed under the Arctic ice in a submarine. He came within a few hundred miles of the North Pole before he had to turn back. His book *Under the North Pole*, published in 1931, describes this adventure.

will

A will is an official paper that a person signs to tell what he wants done with his money and property after he dies. To make a will, a person must be mentally healthy. That is, he must know clearly what he wants done with his property. He must sign the will when two other people are present, and then these two people must sign their names as witnesses and give their addresses. A person is not supposed to be a witness if the will says he is to receive anything.

When a person dies without having made a will, he is said to be *intestate*. If he has made a will, he is *testate* and the will can be entered for *probate;* that is, it can be recorded in a court and the court will see to it that the testator's wishes are carried out. A will usually names a person to be the executor, or administrator, who will be in charge of carrying out the instructions of the will.

CONTESTING A WILL

Sometimes people contest a will. They go to court and say that the person who made the will was not mentally well enough to know what he wanted, or that someone influenced him to make an unfair will. The court can change the instructions of the will in such cases.

In many cases a will is not in the exact form that the law requires but the court will usually follow the will anyway if it is clear what the decedent (person who died) wanted to have done.

Willard, Emma

Emma Hart Willard was an American educator who lived about 150 years ago. She was born in 1787 in Berlin, Connecticut. When she grew up she became a schoolteacher, and then she married Dr. John Willard. At that time there were no colleges or universities for women, and women were not permitted to attend schools for men. After several years of teaching Emma Willard opened a school in her home and taught college subjects to women students. Later she founded a school in Troy, New York, where women teachers taught these subjects to women students. She also tried to persuade the New York State legislature to let women attend public schools of higher education. Emma Willard died in 1870. She was elected to the Hall of Fame in 1905.

Willard, Frances Elizabeth

Frances Elizabeth Willard was an American woman who became noted for her work in education and in trying to end the evils that result from drinking too much alcohol. She was born more than a hundred years ago, in the year 1839, in Churchville, New York. She became a teacher in colleges and then president of Ladies' College in Evanston, Illinois. In 1874 she became president of the WOMAN'S CHRISTIAN TEMPERANCE UNION, about which there is a separate article, and she remained president until she died in 1898. She was a noted speaker and writer and was the author of many books and articles.

William, King of England

There were four kings of England named William. William I was known as William the Conqueror, and he is considered the first king of modern England. He ruled from 1066 to 1087. About nine hundred years ago the English king called Edward the Confessor died. Two men claimed the right to be the next king of England. One was a Saxon, Harold; the other was William, duke of the French territory of Normandy. In 1066 William invaded England with a Norman army and defeated Harold at the Battle of Hastings. His victory is called the Norman Conquest. William made great changes in English life. Before his time the land was ruled by earls, and most of the working people were little more than slaves. William made the king the real ruler of the country and brought order and peaceful government to England.

William II was the son of William the Conqueror. He was called William Rufus (which means William the Red) because of his ruddy complexion. He was born about 1056. William Rufus fought constant wars to increase his territories. In 1100 he was killed by an arrow while hunting.

WILLIAM AND MARY

William III was born a prince of the Dutch country of Orange in 1650. At this time England had become a Protestant country but its king, James II, had remained a Catholic. William had married James II's daughter Mary, who was a Protestant. Some leading English noblemen offered to help William take the throne from James. William invaded England in 1688 and James fled to France. William and Mary were made king and queen. William's reign increased the power of Parliament because he had to accept laws that limited his power.

James went to Ireland and raised an army to try to retake the English throne, but William defeated him at the Battle of the Boyne and gradually brought Ireland completely under English rule. Most of William's later efforts were devoted to trying to keep France from becoming a greater power in Europe. Queen Mary died in 1694 without any child. William

reigned alone until 1702, when he was killed in a fall from his horse.

William IV ruled from 1830 to 1837. He was the third son of George III, and did not become king until he was 65 years old. He had spent many years in the British Navy and was called the "sailor king." His only notable act as king was to support his ministers in the dispute over the Reform Bill, which was a law to change the election districts of Members of Parliament. For many hundreds of years seats in the House of Commons had been divided so that they were controlled by the big landowners. The House of Commons passed the Reform Bill, but the House of Lords voted it down. The king of England has one special privilege: he can appoint new peers, who are members of the House of Lords. William IV sent a message to the House of Lords that if they did not pass the bill he would appoint enough new lords to pass it. The House of Lords gave in and passed the bill. William IV died in 1837 and was succeeded by his niece, Victoria.

William, German emperor

There were two German emperors named William (in German, Wilhelm). They were members of the HOHENZOLLERN family, about which there is a separate article.

William I was the first German emperor. He was born in 1797 and became king of Prussia in 1861. He appointed the skillful statesman Otto von Bismarck as chancellor (head of the Prussian government). At that time Germany was made up of several small kingdoms, Prussia being the largest and most powerful. By leading Prussia into several wars and winning them all easily, Bismarck was able to unite the northern German kingdoms into one empire, called Germany, with William I as the emperor. William died in 1888, at the age of 91, and his son Frederick III, the second emperor, died three months after him.

WILLIAM II

William II, the son of Frederick III, was the third German emperor. He was a grandson of Queen Victoria of England. He was emperor during World War I, and usually when anyone in an English-speaking country speaks of "the Kaiser" he means William II. (*Kaiser* means "emperor" in German.)

William II was born in 1859 and became emperor in 1888. Bismarck was still chancellor, but the Kaiser wanted to run things himself and forced Bismarck to resign in 1890. William II was so determined to make Germany the greatest and richest power in the world that he set out to build an even greater navy than the British Navy and to compete with Great Britain for foreign colonies and trade.

William was a very impulsive man, and often he said thoughtless things that made enemies for him and his country. He had a withered left arm, about which he was sensitive, and this may have caused him to be unusually aggressive.

The Kaiser did not actually start World War I or take an active part in running it, but the people in the Allied countries blamed him for it. In 1918, when the Germans were beaten and asked for peace, President Wilson of the United States said that the Kaiser must abdicate (resign as emperor) before Germany could have peace. The German people were very tired of the war and when the Kaiser did not abdicate they started riots. The Kaiser gave in and fled to the Netherlands. Two weeks later he abdicated for himself and his family, and Germany became a republic. The peace treaty said that the Kaiser must be tried for starting the war, but the government of the Netherlands refused to turn him over to the Allies. William II spent the rest of his life in the town of Doorn, in Holland. He died in 1941, the last German emperor.

Williams, Roger

Roger Williams was the founder of the state of Rhode Island. He was born in Wales in 1599, studied religion in London, and went to the Massachusetts Bay Colony in 1630 because he did not want to follow the teachings of the Church of England. He became a Puritan minister in Salem and Plymouth.

Williams found that the Massachusetts colony, though founded by people who wanted freedom to worship God as they pleased, did not allow others to have freedom of religion. Because Roger Williams preached that each man should be free to worship as he chose, the leaders of the colony banished him, in 1635.

The next spring Williams, with his family and a few friends, formed a settlement at Providence, which is now the capital of Rhode Island. In his colony Williams guaranteed religious freedom, and many other settlers came from Massachusetts and from England. In 1644, they formed the colony of Rhode Island. By that time there were settlements at Portsmouth and Newport as well as a large settlement at Providence.

Roger Williams was a trusted friend of the Indians. He bought the land on which Providence was founded, because he did not believe white men should simply take the land from the Indians. Later he persuaded the Narragansett Indians to help the settlers fight the unfriendly Pequot Indians. He also wrote a key to the languages of the New England Indians. Roger Williams died in 1683. Although he was admired and respected in his colony and in England, his banishment from the Massachusetts colony was never withdrawn.

Williams, Ted

Ted Williams became famous as one of America's great baseball players. He was born in San Diego, California, in 1918. His full name is Theodore Samuel Williams. He joined the Boston Red Sox team of the American League in 1939 and soon became one of the best

hitters in baseball. He played with the Boston Red Sox every year after that except for two periods in which he was a flier for the Marine Corps, first during World War II and again during the Korean War. Williams led the American League in batting several times, and also hit more home runs in each of several years than any other American League player. In 1941 Ted hit .406, becoming one of the few players who have hit over .400 in any one season.

Williamsburg

Williamsburg is a city in Virginia, on the peninsula between the James and York rivers, about 50 miles from Richmond. About nine thousand people live there. Williamsburg is famous for its part in early American history and as the seat of the College of William and Mary.

The site of Williamsburg was first settled in 1633. It was called Middle Plantation, and was an outpost of Jamestown, the capital. When the statehouse at Jamestown burned down in 1699, Middle Plantation was renamed Williamsburg in honor of King William III of England and was made the capital of the colony. For almost a hundred years Williamsburg was the most important city of Virginia. In 1780 the capital was moved to Richmond.

Because of its historic interest, John D. Rockefeller, Jr., gave millions of dollars to restore Williamsburg to what it was in colonial days. The project involved the razing of hundreds of modern buildings and the building of more than three hundred houses and buildings to be just as they were in the days of the city's importance. Among the buildings that have been restored are: the capitol; the Governor's Palace, where Patrick Henry and Thomas Jefferson lived as governors; Bruton Parish Church, said to be the oldest American church in continuous use; the Wren Building of the College of William and Mary, designed by the English architect Sir Christopher Wren; the Wythe house, which was headquarters for George Washington before the siege of Yorktown; and the Raleigh Tavern, where the honor fraternity Phi Beta Kappa was founded by students of William and Mary.

The College of William and Mary was founded in 1693, and is the second-oldest in the United States. George Washington was one of the first chancellors, and Presidents Thomas Jefferson, James Monroe and John Tyler attended the college. William and Mary became a state college of Virginia in 1906 and became co-educational in 1918. There is a division of William and Mary at Norfolk, and at Richmond is the Professional Institute of the college.

WILLIAMSBURG, VIRGINIA. Population (1970 census) 9,069. County seat of James City County. Founded, 1633.

Willkie, Wendell

Wendell Willkie was an American industrial and political leader. He was born in 1892 in Elwood, Indiana. He received his law degree from Indiana University in 1916 and then became very successful in business, as the head of public utilities companies.

Willkie had never been a candidate for political office until 1940, when the Republican Party nominated him to run for the Presidency against Franklin D. Roosevelt. He lost the election but gained the esteem of many people. In 1941 and 1942 President Roosevelt made Willkie his personal representative and asked him to visit many countries of the world. When he returned, Willkie wrote a book, *One World,* that was one of the best-selling books of the century. In this book he told the American people that they must give up isolationism (the political policy that is against having the United States make alliances with other countries). Willkie died suddenly in 1944, when he was only 52 years old.

will-o'-the-wisp

A will-o'-the-wisp is a strange flickering light that is sometimes seen at night over swampy or marshy lands. It is usually blue in color and seems to move about. There is no proved scientific explanation for the light, but it is probably caused by a combination of gases rising from the damp earth. Many superstitions have grown up about the will-o'-the-wisp, especially among the people who live in areas where it is commonly seen. Some people have said it is an evil spirit that leads travelers to their deaths. Often a person who is flighty is said to be a will-o'-the-wisp.

The will-o'-the-wisp is sometimes called *ignis fatuus* (Latin words meaning "foolish light"), and sometimes Jack-o'-Lantern.

willow

Willow is the name of a family of trees. There are several different kinds. Some are large trees, growing as high as 75 feet, and some are mere shrubs.

The most familiar willow of the United States and Canada is probably the weeping willow. Its branches hang in graceful, drooping curves, with long, slender leaves that create a lacy effect.

Not all willow trees follow the pattern of the weeping willow. The white willow is an erect, handsome tree.

Most willows have catkins, or tassels, before the leaves come out in spring or at the same time as the leaves. The commonest willow of this kind is the pussy willow. The pussy willow's catkins are silver-colored and of satiny texture. Other catkins, on other kinds of willow, may be gray, brown, reddish, or tan.

Willows grow fast, and are easy to raise in most places.

Willow Run

Willow Run is the name of a huge factory that was built by the United States government for the manufacture of airplanes during World War II. It is in the town of Willow Run, near Detroit, Michigan. The Willow Run plant had the biggest bomber assembly line in the world, but it was something of a disappointment because it did not reach full production until the war was almost over. After the war the plant was turned into an automobile factory. The airport adjoining it, which had been used to test bombers, was converted into a civilian field and became the chief commercial airport of Detroit.

Wilmington

Wilmington is the largest city of Delaware. It is in the northern part of the state, on the Delaware River. About 100,000 people live there, which is about a fourth of all the people who live in the state. Wilmington is the chief commercial and industrial city of Delaware. It is the headquarters for many of the largest corporations of the United States, including the three biggest chemical companies in the world. Many of the people of Wilmington work in the plants and laboratories of these great companies, in railroad shops and shipyards, and in factories that make iron and steel products, textiles, paper, leather and lumber products, and processed foods. The city is the seat of the Delaware Academy of Medicine and several theological schools. Among the features of interest in Old Swedes Church, one of the oldest in the country.

Wilmington is the site of the first settlement in Delaware. In 1638 a group of Swedish colonists settled there and founded Fort Christina, named in honor of the Swedish princess Christina. In 1654, Dutch forces led by Peter Stuyvesant captured Fort Christina and the surrounding Swedish settlements, and in 1664 the town came under British control along with the rest of New Netherlands. The name of the city was changed to Wilmington in 1745, in honor of the English Earl of Wilmington. Before the Civil War Wilmington was strongly against slavery, and it was a station on the Underground Railway by which Negro slaves were helped to escape from the southern states.

WILMINGTON, DELAWARE. Population (1970 census) 80,386. County seat of New Castle County. On the Delaware River. Founded, 1638.

Wilson, Harold

Harold Wilson was the Prime Minister of Great Britain (the highest office in the British government) from 1964 to 1970, and then from 1974 to 1976. The election of 1964 was so close that his Labour Party had a majority of only four votes in Parliament, but Wilson used his position to advance all the policies of his party (see the article on SOCIALISM).

Wilson was born in 1916, became a prominent member of the Labour Party after World War II, and helped Hugh Gaitskell to become party leader over left-winger, Aneurin Bevan. When Gaitskell died, Wilson became party leader. In the 1970 election, Conservative Edward Heath surprised most observers by defeating Prime Minister Wilson. However in 1974, Prime Minister Wilson defeated Heath. James Callaghan then became Prime Minister in 1976.

Woodrow Wilson

Thomas Woodrow Wilson was the twenty-eighth President of the United States. He served two terms, from 1913 to 1921, and was President during World War I, which the United States entered just one month and two days after the start of his second term, in 1917. A year and a half later the Armistice was signed, ending the war with the United States on the winning side. President Wilson went to France to take part in the Peace Conference, determined to set up a League of Nations that would prevent war forever after. He was the first President ever to leave the United States while in office. In England and France he was received as the world's greatest hero, but he could not persuade people to make a genuine effort toward peace.

Woodrow Wilson seldom used his first name, Thomas, and many people think that Woodrow was his only given name.

He was tall, clean-shaven, a handsome man, with a serious, thoughtful manner

and expression. He was an intellectual with high ideals, as great a scholar as ever held the Presidency, and a man of great integrity (honesty).

Even after he had set up a League of Nations, he could not persuade the people of the United States to join it. This was a bitter disappointment to him. He had worked so hard that he had undermined his health, and serious illness forced him to give up his fight.

Wilson is remembered as an expert organizer, as the author of the famous Fourteen Points on which the peace following World War I was supposed to be based, as a great leader during a critical period of history, and as a man who devoted himself completely and unselfishly to the tasks he believed to be his duty. Eventually that devotion to duty was the indirect cause of his death, and history has recorded his greatness—a greatness not fully appreciated during his lifetime and perhaps not even yet.

HIS EARLY YEARS

Thomas Woodrow Wilson was born in Staunton, Virginia, on December 28, 1856. His father and his mother's father were both Presbyterian ministers. The family was of Scotch-Irish descent.

During the years young Woodrow was growing up, the family moved frequently. They lived in Augusta, Georgia; Columbia, South Carolina; and in Wilmington, North Carolina. In 1873 Wilson entered Davidson College in South Carolina, but did not finish his college course there. Instead he transferred to Princeton, where he was graduated in 1879. Three years later he obtained his master's degree from Princeton. Meanwhile he had studied law at the University of Virginia, and he became a lawyer in Atlanta, Georgia, in 1882. He found he preferred teaching, and in 1885 he became a professor of history and political economy at Bryn Mawr

College for women, at Bryn Mawr, Pennsylvania.

He continued to study, and in 1886 he received the degree of Doctor of Philosophy (Ph.D.) at Johns Hopkins University in Baltimore, Maryland. To earn this degree he wrote a book called *Congressional Government*.

After leaving Bryn Mawr, Wilson taught for a time at Wesleyan University in Middletown, Connecticut. Then he went to Princeton as a professor of jurisprudence and political economy. After he had been there for twelve years, he was made president of Princeton, a position he held for eight years.

HOW HE BECAME PRESIDENT

In 1910 Woodrow Wilson was asked to run for governor of New Jersey as the candidate of the Democratic Party. He accepted the nomination and was elected by a substantial majority. As governor, in 1911 and 1912, he made many improvements in the government of the state. He accomplished so much in his single term as governor that he became nationally known.

Professional politicians had been controlling the state's government. Wilson fought against their methods. He succeeded in having laws passed to make employers responsible for accidents to workers in their plants, and another law that required primary elections, so that the voters could name their own candidates instead of having to accept the candidates of the political bosses. Today it seems quite natural that such laws should be in effect almost everywhere, but it was the work of men like Woodrow Wilson that caused them to be passed in the first place.

The news of what he had accomplished became known throughout the country. When the Democratic Presidential Convention was held in the summer of 1912, Wilson had strong support from a large group of delegates. It was a very hotly contested convention, but on the forty-sixth ballot Woodrow Wilson won the nomination.

The election in November was an overwhelming victory for the Democratic Party, and for Woodrow Wilson. The Republican vote was split because two prominent Republicans were candidates, William Howard Taft and Theodore Roosevelt. Together they had more votes than Wilson, but neither of them had enough votes to beat him.

The world was on the verge of war at this time. Wilson was inaugurated in March of 1913, and little more than a year later World War I had broken out in Europe. The United States began losing ships and American lives as Germany sent submarines to attack shipping in the waters of the Atlantic.

Most people in the United States wanted to stay out of "Europe's war." Wilson tried earnestly to keep his country neutral, but there were repeated sinkings of American ships. Wilson sent several warnings to Germany, but the sinkings continued. In 1916 Wilson sent a final warning to Germany and secured a promise from that country not to sink merchant ships without warning, and to rescue passengers aboard any sinking ship in any case. His threat was so strong that

Germany left neutral shipping alone for a time, and the people of the United States were greatly encouraged. In the Presidential election of 1916, Wilson re-elected on the slogan, "He kept us out of war."

Shortly afterward, however, Germany started again to sink American ships, with no regard for the promise made to Wilson a few months before. Thousands of people lost their lives, and the situation became impossible. Wilson asked Congress for a declaration of war in April, 1917.

The United States was stronger than Europe had realized, and World War I was won before the end of 1918. Wilson was deeply concerned with insuring future peace, in addition to the actual winning of the war itself. He believed that the United States was not fighting merely in self-defense but for the sake of civilization, humanity, and free government. His phrase was that the United States was fighting to "make the world safe for democracy." In a famous speech in January, 1918, he named FOURTEEN POINTS, or conditions, for a lasting peace. There is a separate article about them. Ten months later, when Germany agreed to give up, it was on the basis of Wilson's Fourteen Points.

Now Wilson was hopeful that the countries of the world would agree to a firm understanding and an organization to insure peace. After the Armistice of 1918 he went to France to attend the Peace Conference, in the sincere belief that treaties could and would be drawn that would prevent another war. But the statesmen of the European countries did not want to give up the chance to take new territories from their defeated enemies. When the treaty of peace was finally written, it did not guarantee the fair settlement and lasting peace that Wilson had hoped for. Still, it was agreed that a League of Nations would be set up, and Wilson returned to the United States with great hopes that his dream of peace would come true.

Unfortunately, though Wilson was a brilliant man he was inclined to be impatient and even intolerant of those who did not understand his ideas or who disagreed with the ideas. When he went to Paris for the Peace Conference he did not take with him any members of the Republican Party because that party had opposed so many laws he wanted. Now the Republicans in the United States Senate, led by Senator Henry Cabot Lodge, refused to support Wilson's plan to have the United States join the League of Nations. A long and bitter struggle began.

HIS FINAL YEARS

Wilson traveled throughout the United States, writing, lecturing, and arguing for the League. He worked so hard that he undermined his health. At Pueblo, Colorado, in September, 1919, Woodrow Wilson broke down. A few days later he suffered a stroke, and for the rest of his life he was an invalid.

When the Senate finally voted on the treaty that might have made the United States a member of the League of Nations, the vote was 49 to 35 against it. This was in March, 1920. Wilson had been given the Nobel Peace prize in

1919, but his own Congress refused to accept the treaty that he believed would insure peace.

A sick and weary man, Woodrow Wilson made a public appearance at the inauguration of the new Republican President, Warren G. Harding, in March, 1921; but he was unable to remain active in either politics or his legal profession.

Two years and eleven months later, Woodrow Wilson died, on February 3, 1924, in Washington, at the age of 68. He was buried there.

THE FIRST MRS. WOODROW WILSON

Ellen Axson Wilson was born in 1860 in Rome, Georgia. Her father, like Wilson's, was a minister. She and Woodrow Wilson were married in 1885, and they had three daughters. Mrs. Wilson died in the White House in 1914.

THE SECOND MRS. WOODROW WILSON

Edith Bolling Galt Wilson was born in 1872 in Wytheville, Virginia. She was a widow when she met Woodrow Wilson. They were married in December, 1915, while Wilson was President. After his death she continued to live in Washington until her death in 1961.

wind

A wind is a movement of air. It is caused by the fact that hot air rises and cold air moves into the space that it occupied. (This is explained in the article WEATHER.) Meteorologists, or scientists who study weather, rate winds according to the speed at which they travel. This is measured by a method called the Beaufort scale, which was worked out by an English admiral named Francis Beaufort. The scale, as it is used by the United States Weather Bureau, uses numbers from 0 to 12:

0 Calm (less than 1 mile per hour)
1 Light air (1 to 3 miles per hour)
2 Slight breeze (4 to 7 miles per hour)
3 Gentle breeze (8 to 12 miles per hour)
4 Moderate breeze (13 to 18 miles per hour)
5 Fresh breeze (19 to 24 miles per hour)
6 Strong breeze (25 to 31 miles per hour)
7 Moderate gale (32 to 38 miles per hour)
8 Fresh gale (39 to 46 miles per hour)
9 Strong gale (47 to 54 miles per hour)
10 Whole gale (55 to 63 miles per hour)
11 Storm (64 to 75 miles per hour)
12 Hurricane (more than 75 miles per hour)

windmill

A windmill is a device that uses the force of the wind to perform some kind of work. Man has used windmills for at least a thousand years. He always knew how to use sails on a boat or ship. Now he attached the sails to a large wheel. As the wind blew against the sails, the wheel turned. This turned a pole or axle to which the wheel was attached. A turning wheel or axle can always be used to do useful work. The first windmills were probably used to turn grindstones to grind grain into flour.

Later, in the Netherlands, where large sections are below sea level and constantly threatened with a flood of water, windmills were used to work pumps that

pumped water out of the fields and into canals, which carried the water back to the sea. The Dutch also used windmills for grinding grain. There are still thousands of windmills in the Netherlands, though much of the pumping is now done by steam or electricity.

The early sails of a windmill were made of heavy canvas and were quite large. Modern windmills have metal sails or blades. There are many more blades on these windmills, and the wheel can be much smaller and lighter because there are more blades to catch the wind. In the United States and other countries many farmers use metal-bladed windmills to pump water from wells or to turn a generator that produces electricity.

Windmills are constructed so that the wheel can turn freely and always catch the wind, no matter which way the wind blows.

Any toy "pinwheel" can give you an idea of how the windmill works. When you blow on the wheel, it spins.

Windsor Castle

Windsor Castle is one of the residences of the kings and queens of England. It stands on a hill near the Thames River, in the municipal borough (city) of Windsor, about 20 miles from London. The buildings of Windsor Castle cover about twelve acres of land. The castle has three sections: the Lower Ward, which includes St. George's Chapel and the Albert Memorial Chapel; the Middle Ward, consisting of the Round Tower where the royal flag is flown when the sovereign is present; and the Upper Ward, containing the living quarters of the royal family and the state apartments (reception and meeting rooms).

THE CASTLE'S HISTORY

St. George's Chapel was begun nearly five hundred years ago, in 1478. It contains the tombs of many English kings, including Henry VI, Edward IV, and Henry VIII and one of his wives, Jane Seymour. The state apartments include the magnificent St. George's Hall, where meetings of the Order of the Garter are held. All the state apartments are hung with priceless works of art. The castle is surrounded by beautiful parks, and beyond these is Windsor Forest.

Windsor has been the home of kings since the days of the Saxons, a thousand years ago. William the Conqueror chose the site of Windsor Castle because he believed that on that hill King Arthur had had his Round Table of knights. The castle has been rebuilt and expanded by other British kings.

Windsor, House of

The royal family of Great Britain calls itself the House (family) of Windsor. George V, who was the king during World War I, was actually a member of the House of Saxe-Coburg-Gotha, but that is a German name, and when Germany and Great Britain became enemies he changed the family name. He selected Windsor because Windsor Castle is a famous old seat of the British kings. In 1936, when King Edward VIII gave up the British throne so that he could marry as he pleased, he was given the title Duke of Windsor.

Windsor, Wallis Warfield

Wallis Warfield was the maiden name of an American woman who became Duchess of Windsor in one of the most romantic stories of all time. She was born in Baltimore, Maryland, in 1894, and her full name was Bessie Wallis Warfield. She was married and divorced twice. In 1916 she married Earl Spencer, a lieutenant in the United States Navy, and they were divorced in 1927. The next year she married Ernest Simpson, an American businessman. They lived in London, England, and there she met the Prince of Wales, who became King Edward VIII. They fell in love, but the British government would not let the king marry a woman who had been divorced. In 1936 the Simpsons were divorced, the king abdicated (resigned as king) and was given the title Duke of Windsor, and the Duke and Duchess of Windsor were married in France. The duchess became famous also as one of the best-dressed women in the world. See also the article on Edward VIII, under EDWARD, KING OF ENGLAND.

wind tunnel

A wind tunnel is a place where airplanes are tested to see what will happen to them in flight. There are two kinds of wind tunnel. One is quite small and is built to test small models of planes. The other is very large and can be used to test actual airplanes.

A wind tunnel is like a box or barrel through which air is blown by fans. When an airplane flies, its engines pull it through the air at varying rates of speed. In a wind tunnel the airplane is mounted on a platform and held rigid. The fans blow the air past the model of the airplane, or past the airplane itself, at varying rates of speed. The faster the fan spins, the faster the air blows past the standing airplane. The effect is the same as if the airplane itself were moving at great speed through the air.

The purpose of wind tunnels is to test airplanes before they are flown. Any defect in the airplane can be found when it meets the high-speed winds in the wind tunnel. For instance, if the wings are so constructed that they would weaken at high speeds, this fact can be discovered in the wind tunnel, saving many lives and millions of dollars.

In a wind tunnel scientists also find how different plane models will act at different speeds. They find such things as how the air drives by the wing surfaces; how slowly a plane can fly before it stalls or starts to drop; how fast it can climb; and many other things.

Windward Islands

The Windward Islands are a group of islands in the Caribbean Sea, north of Venezuela. They are part of the West Indies. With the Leeward Islands to the north, they form an island chain called the Lesser Antilles. Among the Windward Islands are Trinidad and Tobago, which form an independent nation; Barbados, Dominica, St. Lucia, St. Vincent, Grenada and the Grenadines, which are possessions of Great Britain; Martinique, which is a possession of France; and Curaçao and five smaller islands, which are possessions

of the Netherlands. There are separate articles on the more important islands of the Windward Islands.

wine

Wine is a drink made from grapes. Beverages called wines are also made from other fruits, such as elderberries and blackberries, but wine usually means only the beverage made from grapes.

Wine is fermented, and this changes some of the sugars of the grapes to alcohol. For this reason many people are opposed to drinking wine, because they are opposed to all alcoholic drinks, but throughout most parts of southern and western Europe wine is drunk by all the family at nearly all meals, just as Americans drink water, milk, or coffee.

HOW WINE IS MADE

The making of wine really begins with the growing of the grapes. The vines must be carefully tended to be sure that the grapes will be of the finest quality. The grapes must be picked at the perfect moment of ripeness so that they will have the greatest possible amount of sugar. The grapes are picked and sorted, and unripe or bruised grapes are removed. The remaining grapes are then "mashed."

While the grapes are ripening on the vine, a special kind of yeast settles on their skins. When the grapes are mashed this yeast begins to ferment, changing the grape sugar to carbon dioxide and alcohol. If a red wine is being made, the entire mash is allowed to ferment, so that it takes on some of the color of the skins. If a white wine is being made, the juice of the grapes is pressed out and then fermented without the skins.

The first fermentation usually takes several weeks. After this period the wine is fairly clear. It is drained off to remove the sediment, or solids, and then is placed in casks for further fermentation. During this time the wine acquires its *bouquet*, or special aroma, and it changes color. White wines become darker; red wines usually become lighter because still more solids settle to the bottom. Fine wines are usually stored for two years before they are considered ready for bottling.

KINDS OF WINE

There are a number of special terms used to describe wines. In general, wines are divided into red and white wines; dry and sweet wines; light and heavy wines; and still and sparkling wines.

Wines are red or white according to the way they are made. Red wines are made by including the skins in the fermenting process. White wines are made by fermenting only the juice of the grapes. Red wines are usually fuller (have more "body") than white; that is, they have more solids in them.

Wines are called *dry* when they are completely fermented so that almost no sugar remains; they are called *sweet* when fermentation is stopped before all the sugars have been changed. Wines are called *light* when there is fairly little alcohol in them, and *heavy* when there is a good deal of alcohol. *Still* wines are made by allowing all the carbon dioxide to escape before bottling. *Sparkling* wines are bottled while there is still some of the carbon dioxide in them, so that they bubble like carbonated water.

HOW WINES ARE SERVED

Certain wines are considered best with certain foods. Generally, light, dry wines are served with light foods such as fish, eggs, and white meats; red wines are served with red meats and heavy foods. Sparkling wines are served with fruits and desserts. Usually sweet wines are not served with food.

White and dry wines are generally served chilled, and most other wines are served at room temperature.

SOME FAMOUS WINES

Wines are called by the region where the grapes are grown. The soil of the vineyard makes so much difference in the taste of the grapes that an expert can often taste a wine and tell within a few miles where the grapes were grown. Many castles and monasteries in Europe became famous for their wines.

The wines of France include some of the world's most famous kinds. The region of Bordeaux produces red wines called claret, and various white wines. These are all dry wines, except the white wine called sauterne, which is sweet. Each of them is named for the vineyard where the grapes are grown, but all of them are sometimes called simply Bordeaux.

Other famous red and white French wines are called Burgundy wines, for the region where they are made. The white wines of the Burgundy region are often called Chablis.

The sparkling white wine called champagne is made in the Champagne region of France.

Germany makes many wines in the regions of the Rhine and Moselle rivers. Most of these are light, dry, white wines. They are called Rhine or Moselle wines.

Most Italian wines are named for the grape rather than for the district. One of the most famous Italian wines is Chianti, a dry wine that may be either red or white. From the island of Sicily, which belongs to Italy, comes a sweet dessert wine called Marsala.

The special wine of Spain is sherry It is named for the city of Jerez, near which the grapes are grown. Sherry wine is made heavy by the addition of brandy after fermentation. There are many famous kinds of sherry, such as Amontillado and manzanilla. Some of them are dry, some are sweet, and some are very sweet. The color may range from pale amber to dark golden brown. Sherry is widely used in cooking.

Portugal is famous for port, a sweet, heavy wine that is named for the city of Oporto. Port also varies in color and heaviness, from a light golden brown wine called tawny port to a deep ruby red variety. Port is called a "dessert wine." It is often drunk after dinner.

Other countries have wines for which they are famous. Hungary's most famous wine is tokay, a sweet dessert wine. Another famous dessert wine is called Madeira, because it comes from the Portuguese island of Madeira in the Atlantic Ocean. South America and North Africa are great wine-producing regions.

Some wines are prepared by adding extra alcohol and flavorings such as herbs, spices, and roots. The best known of these is vermouth, which is used as an appetizer before dinner and in the preparation of the mixed drinks called cocktails. French vermouth is light colored and fairly dry. Italian vermouth is sweeter and darker in color.

Grape wines are not widely used in the countries of Asia. A Japanese drink called sake, made from rice, is often called a "rice wine" but it is more like beer. Fermented beverages are also made from rice in China and other countries of the Far East.

AMERICAN WINES

Most of the principal kinds of wine are also made in the United States. Grapes from the great European wine making regions have been brought to the United States and planted in areas where the soil is especially good for vineyards, such as California, New York State, and northern Ohio. Most of these wines are called by the name of the region from which the grapes were originally brought, just as the European wines are. World opinion is that some of the American wines are among the finest in the world.

Winnipeg

Winnipeg is the capital and largest city of the province of Manitoba, Canada. It is the eighth-largest city in Canada. Because it is the principal city of midwestern Canada, it is sometimes called "the gateway to the West." Winnipeg is located at the joining of the Assiniboine and Red Rivers, about 60 miles from the United States boundary. About 246,000 people live in Winnipeg. Its grain market is the largest in the world, and it has important livestock and fur markets. Winnipeg is the shipping center for the agricultural products of the rich surrounding farm lands.

Winnipeg's important industries include meat-packing plants, flour and paper mills, creameries where dairy products are made, and factories that make iron and steel products, railroad cars, mining equipment, clothing, and food products. There are also railroad shops and an automobile assembly plant. The University of Manitoba is at Winnipeg.

The site of Winnipeg was first settled in 1822, as a Hudson's Bay Company trading post. It was called Fort Garry, and as the settlement grew it was renamed Winnipeg after Lake Winnipeg, which is nearby. The name comes from Indian words meaning "murky water." Winnipeg became the capital of Manitoba when the province was admitted to Canada in 1870.

WINNIPEG, CANADA. Population (1974 estimate) 246,246. Capital, province of Manitoba.

wintergreen

Wintergreen is an evergreen plant of North America. It bears small, white, bell-shaped blossoms, and later it has spicy red berries. Another name for wintergreen is *checkerberry*. The leaves contain an oil with a distinctive flavor and odor. The oil is used in medicine and as a flavoring in candy and chewing gum.

Winthrop, John

John Winthrop was one of the founders of the Massachusetts Bay Colony, one of the first English settlements in America, which was founded in 1629. He was the first governor of the colony and probably its most important man in its first years. His journal, which was published many years after his death, tells of the life in the colony and is a very important reference work for historians. John Winthrop was born in England in 1588. He was a founder of the Massachusetts Bay Company, which started the colony, and in 1630 he went to Boston and became its governor. He served as governor most of the time from then until his death in 1649.

wire

Wire is any long, thin strand of metal that can be coiled or twisted. Many kinds of metal are used to make wire, including iron, steel, copper, brass, gold, silver, and platinum. Wire has been known to man for about four thousand years. The earliest wire was probably made of copper and was hammered from solid pieces of metal until it became long and thin enough to be used. For many hundreds of years, hammering hot metal was the only known way to make wire. It took a long time to make wire in this way, and the wire was not as even as the wire we know today.

Wire is now made by a process called *drawing*. A thin bar of metal is forced through a small hole in a piece of hard metal called a *draw plate*. It is grasped and drawn through the hole, so of course it cannot be thicker than the size of the hole.

Several hundred years ago a man would attach the front end of the wire to a belt he wore around his waist, and then would pull backwards with all his force to draw the wire slowly through the draw plate. Machines now do the work much more quickly and efficiently.

Some kinds of wire are drawn by what is called the dry method, and other kinds by what is called the wet method. In the dry method, a thin bar or rod of metal, which has been rolled out on giant presses, passes through a box containing dry powdered soap and then goes into the hole in the draw plate. On the other side of the draw plate there is a large spool that revolves, pulling the attached wire through the draw plate. The wet method is much the same except that the rod of metal passes first through a soapy liquid solution.

Another way of drawing wire, mostly used for hard metals such as steel, is to heat the rod of metal until it becomes soft.

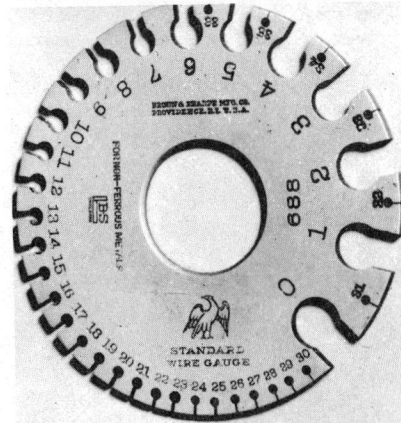

Brown & Sharp Mfg. Co.

Wire is measured according to its thickness. The circular wire gauge is designed to measure all standard sizes.

The softened metal is then drawn through the hole in the draw plate and wire is made from it.

Wire comes in many different thicknesses. The thickness of wire is shown by the gauge. Number 1 gauge wire is about a third of an inch thick. The higher the number of the gauge, the thinner the wire. Thus, number 5 gauge is about a fifth of an inch thick, number 12 gauge is about a tenth of an inch thick, and so on.

Wire is used in many ways. It is an excellent conductor of electricity and is used in lighting, radio, television, and all sorts of electrical machines and appliances. Wire is also used for fencing, for fastening things, to make stiff brushes, and for a variety of other uses. Gold, silver and platinum wire are used in making jewelry and also for such things as braces for teeth. Wire is twisted to make cables, and sometimes small cables are twisted together to make large ones.

wireless, a telegraph in which the signal is sent through the air (as in radio) instead of through wires: see the articles TELEGRAPH and RADIO.

Wisconsin

Wisconsin is a state in the East North Central group of states. It is on Lakes Michigan and Superior and the Mississippi River. Its nickname is the "Badger State," because the holes dug in the hillsides by early lead miners looked like the holes made by badgers.

The name of the state comes from an Indian word meaning "gathering of the waters."

In area, Wisconsin ranks 26th among the states, with 56,154 square miles. In population it ranks 16th, with four million people living there. It became a state in 1848, and was the 30th state admitted to the United States. The capital is Madison.

THE PEOPLE OF WISCONSIN

The first white men to explore Wisconsin were French fur traders and missionaries, who made several settlements in the region about three hundred years ago. Many of the people living in Wisconsin today are of French ancestry. Later Wisconsin was settled by people coming from the colonies in the east. About a hundred years ago many immigrants from Germany, Switzerland, and Scandinavian countries settled in Wisconsin. There are about 14,000 Indians living in Wisconsin, most of them on government reservations.

About a third of the people in Wisconsin live in farm areas, and many of them have large dairy farms. Wisconsin leads all other states in the production of milk and milk products. It is one of the principal cheese-making regions of the world. Wisconsin farmers grow more hay than the farmers in any other state, and great quantities of corn, oats, beets, peas, and fruits.

In the big cities there are many factories, and all kinds of manufacturing are done. The leading industry is the manufacture of automobile parts, but textiles, machinery and paper are also important

products, and beer is important in several cities, especially Milwaukee.

There are few mineral deposits in Wisconsin. There is some building and monument stone, and there are a few zinc and lead mines in the southern part of the state. For many years, Wisconsin led the world in lumber production, but too many trees were cut down and now the industry is less important.

Wisconsin has thousands of lakes and streams and it has become a favorite vacation spot for tourists.

The largest religious groups are the Roman Catholics, the Lutherans, and the Methodists.

WHAT WISCONSIN IS LIKE

Wisconsin lies in the northern part of the Great Plains area. Thousands of years ago, glaciers (great sheets of ice) cut the land into valleys and lakes and hills. At one time most of the state was under water, and there are still large areas of swampland, particularly in the western part of the state. Along Lake Superior there are forested highlands and thousands of lakes. Along Lake Michigan there are forested lowlands and sandy beaches. Both areas attract many tourists. Throughout the central part of the state is a plains area with much swampland. In the southwest is an upland area of hills and plains.

Rivers in the eastern part of Wisconsin provide water power for industrial use, and it is here that most of the people live. The largest cities are in this part of the state, including Milwaukee and Racine, both on Lake Michigan.

Wisconsin is surrounded on three sides by water. The Mississippi River and the St. Croix River form all but a few miles of the western boundary of the state, and Lake Superior and Lake Michigan border on the north and east. All these bodies of water are important transportation routes, and many of the cities of Wisconsin are important ports.

Wisconsin has long, cold winters and short, warm summers. The best climate is found along the shores of Lake Michigan. The average winter temperature for the state is 15 degrees and the average summer temperature is 70 degrees.

Wisconsin has many thousands of miles of railroads and highways. There are airports in all the larger cities.

GOVERNMENT OF WISCONSIN

Wisconsin, like other states, has a governor at the head of the government and

a legislature that makes the laws. The governor is elected for a two-year term. The legislature is composed of two houses, a Senate and an Assembly. Members of the Senate are elected for four-year terms, and members of the Assembly for two-year terms. Judges are elected for ten-year terms. The capital is Madison. There are 71 counties.

Everyone has to go to school between the ages of 7 and 16. There are about 5,500 elementary schools, 500 high schools, and 59 colleges, universities, and other schools of higher learning. Among the principal colleges and universities are:

University of Wisconsin, at Madison. Enrollment, 29,327 men and women in 1962.

Marquette University, at Milwaukee. Enrollment, 10,654 men and women in 1962.

Ripon College, at Ripon. Enrollment, 682 men and women in 1962.

Beloit College, at Beloit. Enrollment, 989 men and women in 1962.

CHIEF CITIES OF WISCONSIN

The leading cities of Wisconsin, with populations from the 1960 census, are:

Milwaukee, population 741,324, the largest city in the state. There is a separate article about MILWAUKEE.

Madison, population 126,706, the capital and second-largest city. There is a separate article about MADISON.

Racine, population 89,144, the third-largest city, a Lake Michigan port and machinery manufacturing center, in the southeast.

West Allis, population 68,157, fourth-largest city, suburb of Milwaukee.

Kenosha, population 67,899, fifth-largest city, automobile and machinery manufacturing, in the southeast, on Lake Michigan.

Green Bay, population 62,888, sixth-largest city, harbor, cheese-processing center, in the east, on Green Bay, inlet of Lake Michigan.

WISCONSIN IN THE PAST

Wisconsin was first visited in 1634 by a French explorer, Jean Nicolet. French missionaries and fur traders went to the region in the years following, building forts at La Croix and Green Bay. In 1671 the whole area that is now Wisconsin became a part of France. In 1763, at the end of the French and Indian Wars, the French gave the land to the British, who developed a prosperous fur trade in the region. At the end of the Revolutionary War the land became part of the United States.

Wisconsin was part of the land known as the NORTHWEST TERRITORY, about which there is a separate article. It was first permanently settled by homesteaders who moved into the territory shortly after the Revolutionary War. The boundaries of the Wisconsin territory were at one time much larger than those of the present state, including part of Iowa, Minnesota, and the Dakotas. Wisconsin became a state, with its present boundaries, in 1848.

In the early part of the 1900s, under the leadership of Robert La Follette and other progressive men, Wisconsin led the United States in the introduction of social legislation that has since been adopted by many other states. Wisconsin was the first to provide unemployment compensation, teachers' pensions, child labor laws, and aid to dependent mothers.

First Capitol Park, 2 acres, near Belmont, in the southwest, on U.S. Route 151. Site of first capitol of Wisconsin, where the territory was created in 1836.

Devils Lake Park, 2,465 acres, 5 miles southeast of Baraboo, in south central part, on State Highway 113. Interesting rock formations and historic Indian mounds.

Little Norway, 5 miles north of Blue Mounds, in the south central part, near U.S. Route 18. A typical Norwegian village, imported and reconstructed.

Great Northern Elevator, at Superior, in the northwest corner of the state, on U.S. Route 53. Largest grain elevator in the world.

WISCONSIN. Area, 56,154 square miles. Population (1974 estimate) 4,417,933. Capital, Madison. Nickname, the Badger State. Motto, Forward. Flower, violet. Bird, robin. No official song. Admitted to Union, May 29, 1848. Official abbreviation, Wis.

wisteria

Wisteria is a flowering, climbing vine that is used as a decoration for gardens, houses, and fences. It bears large clusters of lavender, purplish or white flowers that have a sweet smell and remain in bloom for several weeks during the late spring or early summer. Wisteria can be trained to grow over trellises or arches, and it usually lives for many years. If allowed to grow naturally it will twine around any convenient tree or post. It is best to give the vines something to climb on, rather than let them trail at random over the ground. They spread very rapidly.

witchcraft

A witch, in old stories, was supposed to be a person who could summon spirits and make them do evil things. Usually the word *witch* is used for a woman. The ideas of people who believed in witchcraft are explained in the article on MAGIC.

Only a few hundred years ago most people believed in witches and magic. In Salem, Massachusetts, about 250 years ago, several women were burned at the stake because their neighbors accused them of summoning evil spirits to do mischief. We know now that there were false beliefs and that there is no witchcraft.

witch hazel

Witch hazel is the common name of a group of small trees and shrubs that grow in Asia and America. Witch hazel blossoms are yellow, and they have a pleasant fragrance. The common witch hazel of eastern North America blooms late in the autumn, after the plant has lost its leaves. Most of the other varieties of witch hazel, however, flower in late winter or early spring.

The bark of the witch hazel is used in alcohol to make a lotion or liniment. It has an odor that is somewhat like the scent of the witch-hazel blossoms.

Witherspoon, John

John Witherspoon was a Presbyterian minister and an American patriot. He was the only clergyman among the signers of the Declaration of Independence. At that time he was president of Princeton College in New Jersey.

Witherspoon was born in Scotland in 1723. He studied for the ministry and served in several churches before coming to America. In 1768 he became president of Princeton and remained there until he died in 1794. He wrote several books, some of which are valuable to historians because they tell of the customs and language of Americans in colonial times.

Woden, or Wotan, the Germanic form of the name of the god the Norse called Odin: see the article on ODIN.

wolf

The wolf is a furred, four-legged meat-eating animal. It belongs to the dog family but is wild, though its reputation for fierceness is considerably exaggerated. Wolves do not make a practice of attacking people, and they do not kill for the sake of killing.

Wolves run in packs (groups). When a wolf pack sets out on a hunt, it is in search of food. Most wolf packs are composed of members of the same family—male and female parents, their offspring, and perhaps some other adult wolf relatives. Tales have been told of hundreds of wolves hunting in packs, attacking campers, killing men, and stealing children, but these stories are made up by adventure-story writers.

The gray wolf, or timber wolf, is the most important kind of wolf in North America. It is found from the Arctic regions to Mexico, on the west coast, but its numbers are growing less every year.

Wolves usually mate for life, and they are good parents. The pups are born about two months after mating, and both parents take care of the young. A litter usually has six to eight, but there may be as few as four or as many as twelve. The mother never leaves her pups until they are able to go about by themselves, and she depends on her mate to provide her food during this period. A young male wolf is fully mature when it is two years old. A female is mature at a year and a half.

Full-grown wolves are about four feet long, not counting the twenty-inch tail. Their average weight is about 150 pounds.

Wolfe, James

James Wolfe was a British general in the French and Indian Wars, about two hundred years ago. These were wars that Great Britain fought against France for control of territories in North America.

Wolfe was born in 1727. He was sent to America in 1758, to be second in command to General Jeffrey Amherst, and led the British troops in their victory over the French at Louisburg, a fort in Nova Scotia. In 1759, because of his heroism at Louisburg, he was put in charge of a British force sent to capture the French city of Quebec, in Canada. Quebec was defended by a French army under the Marquis de Montcalm. Montcalm threw back all the attacks against Quebec until Wolfe and five thousand British soldiers climbed a steep cliff to the Plains of Abraham, a field near Quebec. They forced Montcalm into a battle, which they won. This victory gave the British control of North America. Wolfe was wounded in the battle and died, a few hours before Montcalm, who had also been wounded. See the article on the Plains of ABRAHAM and the FRENCH AND INDIAN WAR.

wolfram

Wolfram is a heavy gray metal that is used chiefly for making very tough steel alloys (mixtures of steel with other metals) and electric light bulb filaments. Another name for it is *tungsten*. It is a chemical element, which means that it is one of the basic substances of which everything in the world is made.

Wolfram is very hard. It can be compressed (squeezed) less than any other metal. Because of its hardness, it is used for phonograph needles. It is very ductile, which means that it can be drawn out into thin wires. The melting point of wolfram is above 6,000 degrees Fahrenheit. That is why it is a good material for filaments for electric light bulbs, contact points of spark plugs, and electron targets in X-ray tubes.

Wolfram has great tensile strength, which means that it can stand a very strong pull before breaking. A wolfram wire one inch thick can stand a pull of more than half a million pounds. Wolfram is not corroded by water, air, or even pure oxygen; and it is very resistant to chemicals, even to the powerful mixture of nitric and hydrochloric acids called *aqua regia*. Because of this, wolfram wire gauze is used to filter chemical liquids that would corrode, or burn, most substances.

When wolfram is combined with the chemical element carbon, the compound *wolfram carbide* is formed. This compound is one of the hardest materials known. It is used to make grinding wheels and edges for high-speed cutting tools.

WOLFRAM STEEL

Alloys of wolfram and steel keep their hardness and toughness even at high temperatures. Wolfram steel cutting tools are able to keep their sharp cutting edges even when the high speed at which they work makes them red-hot. Nine-tenths of the world's supply of wolfram is used to make wolfram steel.

WOLFRAM ORE

The two chief wolfram ores are called *schaelite* and *wolframite*. The leading producers of wolfram ore are the United States, China, Korea, Burma, Bolivia, Brazil, and Portugal.

Pure wolfram is gotten from the ore either by the process of ELECTROLYSIS (about which there is a separate article) or by mixing the crushed ore with carbon, heating the mixture until it is red-hot, and then passing hydrogen gas over it.

Wolsey, Cardinal

Thomas, Cardinal Wolsey was an English clergyman and statesman who lived about 450 years ago. As the chief adviser to King Henry VIII he was at one time the most powerful man in England, next to the king.

Thomas Wolsey was born about 1475. He studied at Oxford University and was ordained a Roman Catholic priest. He rose to a position of importance in the

court and in 1514 he was made Archbishop of York. A year later he was appointed cardinal.

Cardinal Wolsey was most important in foreign affairs. He allied England first with France against the Holy Roman Empire; then abandoned France and made England an ally of the Holy Roman Empire against France; and then, in 1528, when the Holy Roman Empire seemed to be becoming too strong, he again allied England with France. In this way he tried to preserve the balance of power in Europe and force other nations to seek England's favor.

Cardinal Wolsey lived extravagantly and he made many enemies. When Henry VIII wanted to get out of his marriage to Catharine of Aragon, so that he could marry Anne Boleyn, he ordered Cardinal Wolsey to seek the Pope's approval. Cardinal Wolsey was unsuccessful, and the king was persuaded that he had not tried. Henry had him arrested, but Cardinal Wolsey died, in 1530, before he could be brought to trial.

wolverine

The wolverine is the largest member of the weasel family and is by far the most vicious and dangerous member of the family. It is not a wolf, in spite of its name, and its nature and disposition are more vicious than those of any wolf. Wolverines live in the far northern parts of America, Europe, and Asia. They stalk and kill any animal within range. They are apparently totally without fear and have been known to attack and kill large bears and deer.

Wolverines are solitary animals except during mating season in the early spring. After it is over males and females go their own ways. There are usually only two or three young in a wolverine litter. The mother takes care of them until early fall, and by winter they are on their own.

A full-grown wolverine usually weighs 30 to 35 pounds, but some may reach 50 pounds. The thick, shaggy fur is dark brown all over except for two light tan stripes on each side, running from front to back.

wombat

The wombat is an animal that lives in Australia. It is a marsupial, which means that the female carries the young in a pouch until they can take care of themselves. The wombat looks like a small bear, but its burrowing and digging habits are more like those of the badger. A wombat digs itself a tunnel with a living chamber at one end. The tunnel is usually about 15 feet long, but wombats have been known to dig tunnels as long as 100 feet.

The wombat has strong, sharp claws and sturdy, short legs, well suited for digging and burrowing. It is almost tail-less, and its color varies from a light tan or gray to a deep gray that is almost black. The wombat lives on grasses, roots, and the inner bark of trees. For this diet it needs strong teeth, and nature has provided it with teeth that continue to grow throughout the animal's life, as fast as its strenuous chewing wears them down.

Most of the year, wombats live alone. There is a mating season from April to June, and males and females separate before the young wombat is born. Usually only one young wombat is born at a time See the article on MARSUPIALS.

Women in the Armed Forces

Only in recent years have women been active members of the armed forces of any country of the world. In the early days of the United States, in the defense of the frontier, women loaded guns for the men. Before World War I the Army and Navy Nurse Corps were formed, and nurses served in the front lines. During World War I the Navy recruited a few thousand women, who were called *Yeomanettes,* and the Marine Corps had a few hundred women, who were called *Marinettes.* In World War II, Russia and Yugoslavia had women who fought and marched with the men.

Also during World War II, both Great Britain and the United States had a great shortage of manpower. They decided to enlist women to do many jobs that women do as well as men or better than men. This freed men for actual fighting and for jobs that public opinion would not permit women to do. The special women's branches that were formed at that time were:

Women's Army Corps. This service began in 1942 as the Women's Army Auxiliary Corps (WAAC). In 1943 it was made a regular part of the Army as the Women's Army Corps, or WAC. In World War II there were 150,000 WACs, doing more than 200 different Army and Air Force tasks all over the world. During the invasion of France, WACs landed 38 days after D-Day. For a time, like the soldiers, they lived in tents, waded and slept in mud, and washed themselves in helmets. In the Pacific area some of the vital jobs of the WACs were in postal and censorship work.

Sixteen WACs received the Purple Heart for wounds, more than six hundred were awarded decorations for meritorious service, and ten got the Soldier's Medal, which is given only for heroism at the risk of life.

In peacetime, WACs get eight weeks' basic training, after which they are sent to one of the many Army specialist schools, for training in such fields as medical technician, communications expert, engineering draftsman, stenographer, machine accountant, recruiter, postal operator, and many others. The three fields in which the greatest number are serving are administrative (office work), medical, and communications. About a third of the WACs are on duty in Europe, the Far East, and the Caribbean.

Women in the Navy. These servicewomen are usually called WAVES. In World War II about 86,000 WAVES served in the United States and in Hawaii. In the Navy mail service and in Radio Washington, the heart of the Navy communications system, three out of four of the workers were WAVES. About a third of the WAVES were in naval aviation. They repaired planes, packed parachutes, handled weather information, and did other important work.

In peacetime, WAVE recruits are trained at the Naval Training Station at Bainbridge, Maryland. Twenty-eight ratings are open to enlisted women. The five fields in which the majority serve are general administration (office work), avia-tion, supply, hospital work, and communications. WAVES now can serve in many parts of the world.

Women Marines. In World War II the Marines had 18,000 enlisted women and 800 officers, filling more than 200 jobs. In peacetime, Women Marine recruits get eight weeks' training at Parris Island, South Carolina. They are assigned in about 180 special jobs in 44 fields. Most of them are filling jobs in personnel and administration, supply, accounting, and communications.

Women in the Air Force, usually called the WAF. This branch came into being in 1948. After training at the Air Force Base at San Antonio, Texas, many of the WAF recruits go to Air Force technical schools. The Air Force has found that women are suitable for four out of five of all its job classifications. Some of the fields open to women in the WAFs are photomapping, parachute rigging, air traffic control and warning, radio, radar, and aircraft maintenance.

Coast Guard Women's Reserve, usually called SPAR. This name was made up of the initial letters of the Coast Guard's Latin motto and its English translation: *Semper Paratus*—Always Ready. By the end of World War II, about 10,000 enlisted women and 1,000 officers were on duty as SPARS. They were trained at the U.S. Coast Guard Academy, making them the only women in service trained at one of the Armed Forces academies.

NURSE CORPS

The Army, the Navy and the Air Force each has its own Nurse Corps. The Army and Navy Nurse Corps are the oldest women's services in the armed forces. The Army Nurse Corps was established in 1901 and the Navy Nurse Corps in 1907.

In World War II there were 57,000 Army nurses. They served in every combat theater. Sixty-six nurses were captured by the Japanese in the Philippines. One out of every forty nurses who served was decorated for outstanding service.

As in the other military nursing services, an Army nurse must be a graduate of a recognized nursing school and must be properly registered. All nurses are officers. Before being assigned to an Army hospital, the Army nurse is given several weeks' training at the Medical Field Service School at Fort Sam Houston, Texas. Besides all the fields of nursing, supervisory and administrative jobs are open to Army nurses.

The Navy Nurse Corps had more than 11,000 nurses serving in World War II. Eleven of them, captured in the Philippines, spent three years in Japanese prison camps. They carried on heroically, caring for sick and wounded prisoners under great difficulties.

In addition to nursing duties, Navy nurses take advanced study, do research, and teach. Navy nurses are responsible for the training of hospital and medical corpsmen of the Navy. They serve in all parts of the world.

The Air Force Nurse Corps was not organized until after World War II. The qualifications for Air Force nurses are the same as those for the Army and Navy Nurse Corps. Most of them work in Air Force hospitals in many parts of the

world. A small number serve as flight nurses. They are trained for flight nursing at the School of Aviation Medicine at Montgomery, Alabama, which also trains Navy and Royal Canadian Air Force flight nurses.

A flight nurse is always assigned to the planes carrying the sick and wounded from combat areas. Other flight nurses serve on the planes that carry wounded men from overseas areas to hospitals in the United States, from one hospital in the United States to another nearer their homes, or to hospitals where they can receive additional treatment.

Women's Medical Specialist Corps. Both the Army and the Air Force have branches of this service. All the women in these Corps are officers. Each of the Corps has three types of specialist: dietitians, physical therapists, and occupational therapists. The Navy also commissions women in these specialties, but they are in the regular Medical Service Corps and not in a separate women's corps.

Dietitians are assigned to Army and Air Force hospitals throughout the United States and at overseas bases to plan meals for wounded and sick servicemen. The dietitians also carry on research in foods; suggest, design and test new equipment and methods; and train others in their work.

The physical therapist teaches men to live useful lives when they have lost the use of an arm or leg. She prepares them to use prosthetic appliances (artificial limbs). No matter what a man's disability, the physical therapist plays an important part in helping him back to normal activity and independence.

The occupational therapist helps the wounded soldier learn to do things that interest him and are within his abilities and interests. By developing skills that are suited to the patient's needs, she helps the patient to recover faster. She instructs him in arts and crafts, which may include woodworking, printing, ceramics, leather work, and so on.

Women's Christian Temperance Union

The National Women's Christian Temperance Union, which is usually called the WCTU, is an organization of several hundred thousand women which publishes books and produces films to teach children not to drink beverages containing alcohol. The WCTU was started by a group of churchwomen in Cleveland, Ohio, in 1874. A world WCTU was organized in 1883, and now has groups in 63 countries.

The chief purpose of the WCTU is to teach boys and girls the effects of alcohol on the mind and body and to get laws passed which will prevent the drinking which causes crime and so many traffic accidents. National WCTU Headquarters and Rest Cottage Museum are in Evanston, Illinois.

Women's Clubs

The General Federation of Women's Clubs is an organization that was founded in 1890 to unite the work of women's clubs throughout the world. In 1963 there were about 15,000 clubs and 11,000,000 members of the Federation in the United States and many foreign countries. Through the Federation, the women's clubs work in such fields as government, citizenship, child welfare, juvenile delinquency, public health, and education. The Federation played an important part in bringing about the establishment of the United States Public Health Service, and the Children's Bureau and Women's Bureau in the United States government. The Federation has headquarters in Washington, D.C. It publishes a monthly magazine, the *General Federation Clubwoman.*

wood

Wood is a material that is produced chiefly in the trunks and stems of trees. The structure of wood and how it is formed are described in the article TREE. How wood is prepared for use is described in the article LUMBER. For thousands of years wood has been one of the raw materials most valuable to man.

Long before history was written down, men were using wood to build shelters and also to make canoes and rafts, tools, and utensils. Even when men learned how to use metal, wood remained important. Until about a hundred years ago all ships were made of wood. Today we think of wood mainly as it is used to make furniture, floors, houses, boxes, and so on. Actually wood has many other uses, in the manufacture of paper, rayon and plastics, and many other things.

Wood has many advantages over other materials. It is easily available, and with proper care the supply of timber (trees that yield wood) should last forever. Wood is lighter, and easier to work with tools and fasten together, than any metal can be. Wooden structures can be altered, moved, or rebuilt. Wood is very strong for its weight. It is a good insulator against heat, electricity, and moisture. It does not rust. It can also be used in thin sheets, as veneers and in plywood.

Wood also has some disadvantages. It can decay in damp places, where the action of tiny plants called fungi destroy it. Several kinds of insect, among them the termite, attack wood by eating it. To prevent decay, paint and certain preservatives are used to protect wood against moisture. Insects can be destroyed by poisons that do not damage the wood itself.

PRINCIPAL USES OF WOOD

Nearly half of all the wood produced in the United States is used for lumber. By far the most important use of lumber is in building and construction work, which uses up two-thirds of a year's lumber supply. More than one-fourth of the lumber is used for boxes and crating and for manufacturing purposes. The most important wood manufactures are furniture, flooring, containers, and millwork. Other uses of lumber are in railroad and bridge building.

Though coal, oil and other materials seem to be the most important fuels used, almost as large an amount of the year's wood is used for fuel as is used for lumber. A relatively small amount, about 3 percent, is used for pulpwood, from which not only paper and paperboard but rayon and many plastics are made. Wood is also used for materials used in the tanning and dyeing industries. From wood are made certain products that are used in still other industries—wood alcohol, acetate of lime, charcoal, wood tar, and wood gas.

About half of the world's wood is used in North America, and most of it in the United States. In 1960 about 35 billion board feet were produced for lumber alone. The leading lumber-producing state is Oregon, which produces about 20 percent. Washington and California produce about 10 percent each. Other leading states are Alabama, Georgia, and North Carolina.

Wood is either hard or soft depending on its structure, and to some extent where it grows. The most important kinds of softwood used are Southern pine and Douglas fir; the most important hardwood is oak.

See also the articles on LUMBER, PAPER, TREE, and FOREST.

Wood, Grant

Grant Wood was an American artist who became famous for the realistic pictures he painted of rural people and landscapes. He is called a regional painter, because his subjects are all of the region in which he grew up. Grant Wood was born in Iowa in 1892. His parents were farmers. He had little formal training in art, although he studied for short times at the Chicago Art Institute and in France. He worked as an art teacher, as a house painter, and as a metal worker. His most famous paintings are *American Gothic,* which won a prize in 1930, and a series of murals at Iowa State College. He died in 1942.

woodchuck, a groundhog or marmot: see the article on MARMOT.

woodcock

The woodcock is a member of the same family of birds as the sandpiper, but the woodcock does not live at the seashore. It inhabits muddy or marshy land where it may find a good supply of earthworms, which are its main food. The woodcock's long, slender bill can pierce far under the surface of the mud to find worms. The bill has an unusual characteristic. The upper half is flexible, and the end can be curled or curved slightly open, like a pair of tweezers, to grasp worms under the ground.

Woodcocks are American birds and are a favorite game bird of hunters. A woodcock is about twelve inches long, with a plump, short-tailed body.

The woodcock mates in spring. The nest is just a grassy or sandy hollow in the earth, where the female deposits four rather large eggs. By fall the young are ready to take care of themselves.

woodcut, a kind of engraving block for printing: see articles on BLOCK PRINTING and ENGRAVING.

woodpecker

Woodpeckers are birds with exceptionally strong, chisel-like bills, well-suited for boring holes in trees or telegraph poles in search of the insects that are the woodpecker's chief foods. The neck muscles of woodpeckers are also exceptionally strong, and the pecking of the bird's bill is so fast the eye can hardly follow it. The sound seems to roll in a

continuous drumming rumble. It is so fast that the individual taps cannot be distinguished.

Another distinctive feature of woodpeckers is their feet. Perching birds have three toes in front, and one in back, to grasp the limbs and twigs on which they perch. Woodpeckers are climbing birds, and their toes are arranged as talons that can grasp the bark of a tree. There are two toes in front and two in back. The woodpecker's tail is also designed to help the bird in tree climbing. The tail feathers are stiff and straight-edged at the bottom, so that they can act as a prop against the side of the tree while the bird is at work. The woodpecker literally leans on its tail.

There are more than two hundred kinds of woodpecker in the world, but only a few are common in the United States and Canada. Of these, the most familiar are the downy woodpecker, the flicker, the redheaded woodpecker, and the pileated or crested woodpecker. The downy woodpecker is the size of a sparrow; the flicker is slightly larger than a robin; the pileated woodpecker is almost as large as a crow; and the redheaded woodpecker is between the flicker and pileated woodpecker in size.

Most woodpeckers build their nests in hollows in trees. They may use a natural hollow that is already present, or they may hollow out a new space with their powerful bills. A female woodpecker lays between four to eight shiny white eggs. Often the male does the major part of the baby-tending, while the female loses interest in the hatchlings even before they leave the nest.

woodwinds, musical wind instruments that are, or originally were, made of wood: see the article on MUSICAL INSTRUMENTS.

wool

Wool is the soft, curly hair of a sheep, which is used to make cloth. Wool is much softer and fluffier than most other animal hair. Some animals, such as the camel, vicuña, alpaca and cashmere goat, also have fine soft hair that is used to make cloth, but the hair of these animals is not properly called wool.

Man has been raising sheep for thousands of years and shearing their wool. Woolen cloth is one of the oldest kinds of cloth woven by man.

KINDS OF WOOL

There are many different kinds of wool, depending on the breed of sheep, where the sheep graze, and the age of the sheep. Countries that are important in sheepraising, and therefore in the woolen industry, are Great Britain, Australia, the United States, Russia, Argentina, New Zealand, and South Africa. Spain produces a very high quality of wool from the Merino sheep. Other breeds of sheep that produce fine wool are Shetland, Lincoln, Cheviot and South Dall. Shetland wool is very soft. It is the wool most used for knitting. The Cheviot sheep, which grazes in Scotland, produces a hard, strong wool that is fine for weaving rough, long-lasting cloths.

The softest, longest and finest wool grows during the first year of the sheep's life. Wool sheared during the first year is called lambs' wool and is finer than the wool of older sheep.

The sheep are clipped and sheared each year. When the sheep is just one year old, its wool is much longer than it is in later years, after it has grown in again after each shearing.

Sheep used to be sheared by hand, with a pair of clippers very much like the kind used to trim hedges. An expert shearer could clip only a few sheep in one day. Automatic shears, run by electricity, now make it possible for one man to shear from 100 to 200 sheep a day. A good shearer is able to clip all the wool from an animal so that it stays in one piece. The animal is not harmed by shearing.

CLEANING WOOL

As sheep roam and graze, their woolly coats become dirty, full of burrs, and very greasy. Before wool can be used for knitting and weaving it must be cleaned. The first step is cleaning it while the animal still has it on its back. The sheep are run through strains or channels of water where they are thoroughly soaped and rinsed off.

The wool must be further cleaned after it has been sheared from the animal. Special machines scour and scrub the wool thoroughly and help to untangle it.

After the wool has been scoured and cleaned it must be carefully dried. The wool is spread out over a wire netting and dry, hot air is blown through it. There are also machines that tumble the wool about in a large drum or barrel and pass hot air through it to dry it.

After the wool is dried it must be completely untangled and the separate fibers straightened out. Sometimes burrs or bits of grass still cling to the wool and these must be combed out. The completely clean wool is then *carded,* passed between wire brushes that completely untangle and separate the wool fibers. The next step is to spin the wool into yarn or thread. You can read about this in the article on THREAD AND YARN.

WOOLENS AND WORSTEDS

There are two basic types of wool cloth: woolen cloth and worsted cloth. Woolen cloth is woven from short fibers and worsted cloth is woven from much longer fibers. Woolen cloth is usually softer than worsted, because the short fibers do not become twisted together as much. Most worsted cloth is strong and long-wearing but has a harder finish than woolen cloth. A blanket is a good example of a woolen, and a man's serge suit a good example of a worsted.

woolly bear, a kind of caterpillar: see the article on BUTTERFLIES AND MOTHS.

Worcester

Worcester is the second-largest city in Massachusetts. It is on the Blackstone River, in the central part of the state, about 40 miles west of Boston. Worcester is an important manufacturing city. About 177,000 people live there. There are factories that make machinery and machine tools, clothing and leather goods, airplane and automobile parts, firearms, paper, and many other things. Six large insurance companies have their headquarters in Worcester. The city is the seat of Clark University, Holy Cross College, Worcester Polytechnic Institute, Assumption College, a teachers college, and other schools. Since shortly after the Civil War the Worcester Music Festival has been held each year.

The first settlement on the site of Worcester was made in 1674, but it was abandoned the following year. The first permanent settlement was made in 1713. A stagecoach line to Boston was begun in 1783. Worcester was a manufacturing center even in early times, using water power from the small streams nearby.

WORCESTER, MASSACHUSETTS. Population (1970 census) 176,572. County seat of Worcester County. On the Blackstone River. Founded, 1713.

Wordsworth, William

William Wordsworth was a great English poet who lived about 150 years ago. He is best remembered for his poems about nature and rural life. Wordsworth believed that poetry should be written in simple language about things in everyday life. For many years he lived in the Lake Country of England, and he is known as one of the Lake Poets.

Wordsworth was born in 1770. He attended Cambridge University. Wordsworth believed strongly that all men should be free, and for several years after graduating he lived in France, where he took an active part in the French Revolution. He returned to England in 1793 and began to write poetry. He had little success until 1798, when he and Samuel Taylor Coleridge, another great poet, published a book of their poems called *Lyrical Ballads.* This was an important book in the history of English literature, because in the preface Wordsworth gave his ideas on poetry.

Soon after this, Wordsworth and his sister Dorothy moved to the Lake Country. In the following thirty years he wrote his greatest poetry. In 1802 he married Mary Hutchinson. He held a minor civil job that gave him a living and permitted him to go on writing his poetry. Although he lived until 1850, he wrote his best poetry before 1820.

Perhaps Wordsworth's most admired poem is "Ode on Intimations of Immortality." Many of his short poems are among the most-quoted poems in the English language. Wordsworth's fame reached its height during his lifetime, and in 1843 he was appointed Poet Laureate.

workmen's compensation

Workmen's compensation is payment that an employer must make to an employee who is injured while he is working on a job for the employer. The employer must also pay if the employee becomes sick because of something he had to do when he was working. For example, if a worker's job requires him to be outside in very cold weather, and as a result he gets pneumonia, his employer has to pay his medical expenses.

Every state requires employers to pay workmen's compensation, and nearly every state requires employers to carry

insurance so that if workmen's compensation is due the insurance company will pay it. The law usually says that the worker must not only have his medical expenses paid but must receive some regular payment in place of the wages he would have earned if he had not been injured. Large payments are required if the worker dies or suffers a permanent injury such as the loss of an arm, leg, eye, or general health.

world, see the articles on EARTH and UNIVERSE.

World Court

A World Court is a place to which nations can go to have problems settled by judges. It is different from courts of law in states and countries, because it has no power to enforce its decisions. If a person is sued by another person, he must appear in court, and if he does not the police make him appear. If he is sentenced to thirty days in prison, the police make him go to prison. However, if one country is "sued" by another, a World Court has no police to make it appear before the court, and if a country is told to pay a certain amount of money, the court has no way of making it pay that amount.

A kind of World Court was set up in the Hague, one of the capitals of the Netherlands, more than fifty years ago. It was called the Hague Tribunal, and was set up by an agreement that was made by several nations in 1899. When two nations had disagreed and wanted the Tribunal to settle their quarrel, they selected members from a panel of legal experts and agreed to abide by their decision.

After World War I, the organization called the League of Nations was set up. It set up a World Court, also at the Hague, which was made up of judges selected by the League. The official name of this court was the Permanent Court of International Justice. It was to settle cases submitted to it by nations. Though the United States was not a member of the League of Nations (which many Americans opposed), it supported the World Court and most Americans were in favor of it. Such prominent Americans as Frank Kellogg and John Bassett Moore were elected to serve as judges.

After World War II, the United Nations, which replaced the League of Nations, set up another World Court, again at the Hague. Its official name is the International Court of Justice and it is made up of fifteen judges, each from a different country. The judges are elected by both the General Assembly and the Security Council. They serve for a nine-year term, and they may be re-elected. Any member of the United Nations may refer a dispute to this court, and other countries may also do so under certain conditions laid down by the Security Council and General Assembly. Decisions are made by a majority of the judges present, and in the event of a tie the President of the Court has the deciding vote.

World Government

A World Government would be a government that would have some power over everybody in the world, just as the United States government has some power over everybody in the United States. At present there are nearly a hundred national governments for the different lands and peoples of the world, and at times in the past there have been many more national governments than that. The people of a nation do not have to obey any laws except the ones made by their own government. If a national government wants to start a war or commit any other kind of crime, there is no higher government to prevent it.

For hundreds of years, there have been men who dreamed of a World Government and made plans for one. The principal purpose of a World Government would be to prevent wars between nations, but a World Government might also be able to protect the human rights of people everywhere.

No plan for World Government has ever succeeded, and there are so many problems in the way of World Government that many men believe there can never be one.

HOW A GOVERNMENT RULES

The work of a government is to make laws, to have courts that judge whether or not people have broken the laws, and to have executive officers who carry out and enforce the laws.

No government can rule unless it has *police power.* That is the power to force people to obey its laws and to punish them if they break laws. A legislature may pass a law that forbids robbery, and a court may decide that a person is guilty of robbery and sentence him to five years in prison, but it is very unlikely that the robber would go to prison and spend five years if there were no police to make him go.

Every national government claims what is called *sovereignty,* or the right to make all laws and decisions concerning the people of its nation. If there were some police power that could force a national government to obey other laws, the government would lose its sovereignty. No nation has ever been willing to give up its sovereignty.

METHODS OF WORLD GOVERNMENT

A World Government cannot be an organization such as the United Nations, for the United Nations is an organization of sovereign nations. None of these nations is willing for any other government to have police power over it.

From time to time in the past, great conquerors have dreamed of conquering all the world and ruling it. If one of them had ever succeeded, his government would have been a World Government, but it would have been the worst kind of government. Most of its people would have come under the government because they were conquered and forced to, and not because they wanted to. There would have been constant rebellions and before long the World Government would have been wrecked anyway. Wise men have long known that a lasting World Government cannot be created by force.

Even if all the peoples of the world were willing to form one worldwide government to replace their national governments, no expert believes that would work any better. The people of a country such as France or England can have a single government, because they are the same kind of people, living the same kind of lives, speaking the same language, following the same customs. In the world as a whole there are so many hundreds of different groups, with different customs, languages, religions, and problems, that laws that were right for one group might seem entirely wrong to another group.

Therefore, nearly all experts on world government have favored a federal form of government. In this form of government, each nation would keep some of its powers but would give up certain other powers to the World Government.

The United States has a federal form of government. Each state has certain powers, and the national government cannot interfere with those powers (unless the Constitution is amended, and this can be done only by the states themselves). But the federal, or national, government also has certain powers and the states cannot refuse to obey the federal government when it exercises those powers. Two states could not go to war against each other, for the federal government would have the right and the strength (the United States Army and other armed forces) to stop the fighting promptly. A state government cannot collect customs (taxes on imported goods) on products made in another state unless the same tax is being collected on the same products made in its own state. A state government cannot take away certain rights of the people: It cannot have slavery, or refuse to let women vote when men can, or favor one religion or church over another, or refuse to let people express their opinions, or do a number of other things that would reduce the rights of the people.

Plans for a World Government are usually based on the same principles. Each nation would give up part of its sovereignty. It would give the World Government the right and the power to prevent war, and according to some plans it would protect some of the rights of all people in all parts of the world, but it would leave every nation free to choose its own form of government and to rule itself in all other matters.

Nearly every plan for world government depends on having the nations join the federation willingly. Since some of the nations may not want to join, at least until they find out whether or not the government will be successful, all the plans are based on beginning with a World Government that does not include all the nations. Other nations may join later, and the planners hope that in time the World Government will be truly worldwide.

PLANS FOR WORLD GOVERNMENT

During the 1930s, when it became clear that the dictatorships of Italy, Germany, and Russia might begin wars, several groups proposed plans for international governments that could prevent wars and eventually end the causes of war. Other groups have proposed such plans during and since World War II. Among the best-known groups are:

Federal Union, a movement begun by a former newspaperman named Clarence Streit. It is often called the "Union Now" movement, because Streit's first proposal

An artist's view of the world's fair that opened in New York City during 1964.

was for immediate union of the United States, Great Britain and the British countries in one federal government. Later he proposed that France and all other democratic countries be members of the union. One of his principal plans was to eliminate tariffs throughout the world.

Citizens' Committee for United Nations Reform, begun by Ely Culbertson. This plan proposes that each nation have a "quota" for its armed forces, giving it enough power to protect itself but not enough to attack any other nation. Each member of the United Nations would keep its sovereignty except that it would not have the power to start a war. The United Nations would have control of heavy weapons (such as atomic weapons) and would have an international armed force whose members would come from the smaller nations. Most of the organization of the United Nations would remain unchanged. Among members of Congress and other high United States officials, this plan has received more support than any other.

United World Federalists, and other groups under the names *World Federalists, World Federation,* and similar names, have proposed federal governments uniting all the nations of the world, or as many of them as possible, under plans similar to the ones described in this article.

See also the articles on the LEAGUE OF NATIONS and the UNITED NATIONS.

World Health Organization, an agency of the United Nations that works to fight disease and promote good health in all the countries of the world: see the article UNITED NATIONS.

World Series, a series of championship baseball games played each year: see the article on BASEBALL.

World's Fair

A World's Fair is a place where different nations of the world exhibit their products and the work of their artists and craftsmen. At a World's Fair there are usually many fine and beautiful buildings to house these exhibits and to show other exhibits in science, industry, and the arts. Usually there is also an amusement section, like a big carnival, where there are rides and shows and other entertainments.

Fairs have been held in most countries of the world for hundreds of years, but World's Fairs are not much more than a hundred years old. The first was held in 1851 in England. Since then there have been many held in the great cities of the world, such as Paris, Vienna, Brussels, Chicago, St. Louis, Philadelphia, Seattle and New York City.

Often a World's Fair celebrates some anniversary. For example, the Columbian Exposition, held in Chicago in 1893, celebrated the 400th anniversary of the discovery of America by Columbus. The Philadelphia Sesquicentennial Exposition of 1926 celebrated the 150th anniversary of the Declaration of Independence. The word *Exposition* is often part of the official name, but most people call them World's Fairs anyway.

Before a World's Fair is held, men of many nations meet to plan for it. Architects design the special buildings. Usually each nation has its own building to exhibit its wares. Most World's Fairs last for one year, but some last two. New York City had two-year World's Fairs in 1939-40 and 1964-65. Most of the buildings are torn down after the fair is over, but there are exceptions: The Eiffel Tower in Paris, France, was built for a World's Fair held there in 1889, and it still stands as the most famous landmark in that city.

Awards are made at these World's Fairs for the finest products exhibited. On many products you will see pictures of gold medals won at various World's Fairs.

Millions of people attend each World's Fair to see the many exhibits and to learn of the new things being developed in the world, and also to enjoy themselves. People can spend many full days at a World's Fair and still not come close to seeing all of it. Visitors return day after day to see the interesting exhibits and to eat at the many fine restaurants.

World War I

World War I was one of the most terrible wars of all time. More than eight and a half million men were killed or died from wounds that they suffered in it. The war lasted more than four years, from 1914 to 1918.

The two sides were called the Allies and the Central Powers. The Allies originally included Great Britain, France, Russia, and Serbia. Later Italy, Rumania, Greece, Japan, the United States and other countries joined the Allies. Great Britain was joined by Australia and New Zealand, Canada, and the Union of South Africa. The Central Powers were Germany, Austria-Hungary (which was then a large empire), Turkey, and Bulgaria.

The principal fighting was done in France and Belgium, along their borders with Germany. This was called the Western Front. In the early years of the war there was also heavy fighting on the Eastern Front, along the border between Russia and the Central Powers. The war at sea was very important. It was fought mostly between Germany and Great Britain.

The Allies won the war. For the first three years the Germans were winning, but when the United States entered the war, bringing into it more wealth and power than the world had ever before known, the Germans could not hold out. It has been widely said, however, that though the Allies won the war they "lost the peace." Germany was helpless at the end of World War I in 1918, but twenty years later it had become the strongest nation in Europe and was threatening war again.

HOW THE WAR STARTED

During the years before 1914 the important countries of Europe were engaged in a rivalry for trade and power and had become more and more suspicious of one another. They had divided into two groups, which were called the Triple Entente (England, France, and Russia) and the Triple Alliance (Germany, Austria, and Italy). Because each group was afraid that the other would start a war, every nation desperately made munitions and built up armed forces. Several times before 1914 there had almost been a war, but the diplomats got together each time and settled the argument —at least for a time.

In 1914 there were several places in the world where two or more of the great countries came into conflict. One of these was in the Balkans, in the southeastern part of Europe. The people of the little country of Serbia (now part of Yugoslavia) were Slavic and were against Austria

because Austria ruled many Slavic territories. Serbia was too weak to fight Austria, but expected the great Slavic country of Russia to give support. Germany, the most powerful European country, was unfriendly with France and wanted Austria as an ally. Great Britain was afraid of Germany because Germany was building a great fleet of warships that might threaten British control of the seas.

On June 28, 1914, Archduke (Prince) Franz Ferdinand, the nephew of the Austrian emperor, went to the town of Sarajevo, near the border of Serbia. While he was driving through the streets, he and his wife were shot and killed by a young Serbian. The Austrians were furious, and they told the Serbians that they would declare war unless Serbia met a very hard set of conditions. When Serbia refused to meet all the conditions, Austria declared war. Russia then mobilized (called up its army). Germany had warned Russia that "mobilization means war." At the beginning of August, 1914, Germany declared war on Russia and France and the German army marched through the small, neutral country of Belgium to invade France. Great Britain had promised to protect Belgium and so declared war on Germany and Austria. Italy broke its alliance with Germany and a year later joined England and France in the war.

THE EARLY YEARS

Germany really had to fight two wars —against France in the west and Russia in the east. The German plan was to defeat France quickly and then turn around and beat Russia. German armies swept through Belgium in less than a month. A British army quickly went to France, but even with this help the French could not stop the Germans at first. By the beginning of September, 1914, the Germans had reached the River Marne, only about thirty miles from Paris, the French capital. There the French got together an army and stopped the German advance in the first Battle of the Marne, one of history's greatest battles. Meanwhile, the British, who held the left side of the Allied line, to the north of the French, stopped the Germans at the town of Ypres in Belgium.

TRENCH WARFARE

For the next four years, the war was fought pretty much along the same line that had been reached in September, 1914. Both armies dug trenches to protect themselves from enemy bullets and explosive shells, until there were two continuous lines of trenches running from the coast of the North Sea in the north to Switzerland in the south. In front of the trenches they placed barbed wire to stop the enemy.

This does not mean that nothing happened during the long years. Both armies tried very hard to win the war. The only way they knew how was to get out of their trenches and charge the enemy trenches. First there would be "artillery preparation," a great bombardment of the enemy trenches with artillery shells; then the infantry would charge.

This kind of fighting had worked in previous wars, when weapons were not very accurate or powerful, but now the defenders had machine guns, and a few

men armed with machine guns could kill hundreds of charging soldiers in a few minutes. If they could not stop the attack at first, they would fall back to a second line of trenches and stop it from there.

There were many of these attacks. They all failed and millions of lives were sacrificed for no purpose. In February, 1915, the French General Joseph Joffre tried an offensive in the province of Champagne, east of Paris. A few months later, the British under Field Marshal Douglas Haig tried one at Ypres. In February, 1916, the Germans under General Erich von Falkenhayn started an offensive near the town of Verdun. The French stopped them, and their commander, General Henri Petain, became a great hero. In July, 1916, the British attacked along the River Somme, and in four months of fighting lost almost half a million men and pushed the Germans back only about seven miles. A year later the British attacked again, this time near the town of Passchendaele, and the result was about the same.

NEW METHODS

The generals and scientists on both sides tried to invent new ways of winning the war. Although these methods killed many men, they were not really successful, because the war went on. In 1915 the Germans started using poison gas, which is described in the article on CHEMICAL WARFARE. Soon the British and French were using it too. The next year the British used tanks for the first time in an attack. At first this seemed to be the answer, because they burst right through the German lines, but there were not enough tanks to prevent the Germans from halting the attack. For the first time in a great war, airplanes were used, but they were very small and could do little damage.

Mostly, the war was fought by foot soldiers who used rifles or machine guns. They wore khaki uniforms and steel helmets, and they lived a terrible life in the mud of the trenches, never knowing when the enemy would bombard them with artillery shells or when they would be ordered to make an attack.

THE OTHER FRONTS

The war was going on in many other places besides the Western Front. In 1914, a Russian army attacked Austria and won a victory in the Battle of Lemberg (in Poland). But the Germans, under Generals Paul von Hindenberg and Erich von Ludendorff, beat the Russians in the Battle of Tannenberg (in East Prussia). The Germans then pushed the Russians back, and the two armies began fighting trench warfare in Poland.

In Serbia. where the war had started, the Austrians attacked in 1914, but the Serbian army stopped them. The next year, Bulgaria joined the war on the German side, and Bulgarian, Austrian, and German armies easily conquered Serbia. A British and French army went to the north of Greece, but it did not start an attack until the war was almost over.

Turkey and Russia had always been enemies, and Turkey entered the war on the side of Germany at the end of 1914, but there was not much fighting between Turkey and Russia. The British tried in

March 1915 to land an army at Gallipoli, a piece of Turkish land on the shore of the strait called the Dardanelles, but the attack was handled very badly and the Turks killed many British troops. Finally those that were still alive got back to their ships and left. The British did persuade many Arab peoples ruled by Turkey to rebel, and this helped the Allied cause.

SUBMARINES AND THE WAR AT SEA

Britain's best weapon was its powerful navy. With it Britain planned to stop any food and supplies from reaching Germany. When a ship of a neutral country approached Germany, a British warship would stop it and British sailors would search it. This made many neutral countries, including the United States, very angry. But the Germans made them even more angry.

Germany's navy was strong, but not as strong as Britain's. So most of the time Germany's big ships stayed in port, and German submarines were sent out to sink Allied and neutral ships that were carrying supplies to England. On May 7, 1915, a German submarine without warning sank the British liner Lusitania, and 1,100 people, many of them Americans, were drowned. This made the Germans and their Kaiser (emperor) Wilhelm II, very unpopular in America, and for a while the Germans stopped sinking neutral ships.

On May 31, 1916, the main British and German navies finally met in the Battle of Jutland on the North Sea. The British lost the most ships, but the Germans never again dared to use their main fleet. Instead they built more submarines and again began sinking neutral ships. This way they hoped to prevent England from getting any food, and so Germany would win the war.

The Germans were correct in one way. If the British had continued to lose so many ships, they would have had to quit. But when several more American ships were sunk the Americans became more and more angry. Finally, on April 6, 1917, the United States declared war on Germany and her allies.

Now United States warships guarded ships crossing the Atlantic carrying food, war supplies, and men. United States shipyards began to make more new ships than had ever been made before. This lessened the danger of the submarines.

A huge American army was sent to France under the command of General John J. Pershing, but the American army did not get into battle until 1918.

THE LAST GERMAN OFFENSIVE

Even though America was in the war, things did not look bright for the Allies in 1917. Russia had a big army, but it did not have enough ammunition or even enough shoes and clothing for the soldiers. The Russians lost many battles against the Germans, and in February, 1917, a revolution overthrew the Russian government. The new government, which was more democratic, ordered the Russian troops to keep on fighting, but in August, 1917, they were again defeated. Two months later the Communists took over in Russia, and they made peace with Germany. Now the Germans could use all their troops in the west.

WAR! SAYS WILSON; BIG ARMY WANTED

FIRST OF U.S.ARMED SHIPS IS 'U' VICTIM

LATEST EARLY MORNING NEWS

Billboards Help Thugs in Robbery

500,000 MEN NEEDED AT ONCE; AID TO ALLIES WITHOUT LIMIT

President Calls on Congress to Throw All Nation's Resources Against German Autocracy

Promise Given of Safety to Passenger Ships and Due Warning to Others

Here Is American Congress War Declaration Resolution

CONGRESS RALLIES TO STIRRING PLEA OF NATION'S CHIEF

Amid Scenes of Wild Enthusiasm President Advises 'State of War' Declaration and Men, Ships and Money to Crush 'Foe of Liberty'

On April 6, 1917, three days after a resolution declaring war on Germany had been introduced in Congress, the United States entered World War I as a member of the Allies.

They decided to beat Italy first. The Austrians had been fighting the Italians in the northeastern part of Italy since 1915, but neither side had really gained anything. Now the Germans sent some of their best troops there, and in October, 1917, they completely defeated the Italian army near the village of Caporetto. The Italians lost more than half a million men, but they finally stopped the Germans and Austrians not far from the city of Venice. Italy stayed in the war but was no longer of much value in the fighting.

On the Western Front, the German army was now commanded by Ludendorff, while the French were commanded by Petain and the British by Haig. In March, 1918, Ludendorff started an offensive that he hoped would win the war. Instead of having his soldiers charge right into the guns of the Allies, he had them first find a weak spot in the lines, then pour through it and spread out in all directions.

At first the Germans were very successful. They pushed the British back about twelve miles and captured many of their soldiers. In May, Ludendorff's men attacked the French east of Paris, and just as in 1914, they drove to the Marne.

VICTORY FOR THE ALLIES

But this was the last gasp of the German army. After four years of war, the German soldiers were tired of fighting and the German people at home were not getting enough to eat. The Allies were growing stronger and more united. When the German attacks began, Marshal Ferdinand Foch, a French officer, was made commander-in-chief of all the Allied armies. In addition to the British and French, there were more than a million fresh, eager American soldiers in France, and 300,000 more were arriving every month.

On July 15, 1918, the Germans attacked at the French town of Chateau-Thierry, but this time they were beaten back by American troops. Three days later the French and Americans defeated the Germans in the second Battle of the Marne. The British, who were fighting in the north, joined the attack on August 8, and the whole German army began to retreat. In September, the Americans defeated the Germans at St. Mihiel, and the next month they opened a great offensive in the Argonne Forest, where they were helped by bombing planes.

The end of the war was now in sight. The Allied army in Greece made the Bulgarians surrender on September 29, 1918. Turkey gave up on September 30. The Italians, who had built up a new army, defeated the Austrians, who surrendered on November 4. It still seemed that the Germans might go on fighting, but in October a revolution broke out in Germany. The people had had enough of war, and the Allies continued to advance toward the German border. Finally, on November 6, the German government sent a group of men to France to surrender. At eleven o'clock in the morning of November 11, 1918, they signed an armistice (agreement to stop fighting) in a railroad car that Foch used as his headquarters, and World War I came to an end.

The peace treaty that was made after the war is described in the article on the Treaty of VERSAILLES. There are also separate articles on most of the important men and places that are mentioned in this article.

World War II

World War II was the biggest and most terrible war that has ever been fought. Nearly thirty million people were killed in it. About half of them were civilians, while the other half were soldiers, sailors, and airmen. More than 400,000 of these were Americans.

The war was fought all over the world, but the most important battles took place in Europe and on islands in the Pacific Ocean. The two sides were called the Axis and the Allies. The war lasted from 1939 to 1945, when the Allies beat the Axis powers. The chief countries of the Allies were the United States, Great Britain, Russia, France, and China. The Axis countries were Germany, Italy, and Japan.

HOW THE WAR BEGAN

World War I, which ended in 1918, caused a great amount of destruction and left many countries very poor. The democratic countries, the United States, Great Britain, and France, were tired of war, but Germany and Italy were poor countries, and they were willing to risk another war if there was a chance that they would win it and become rich.

In 1922 a man named Benito Mussolini, leader of the Fascist party in Italy, became dictator of Italy. In 1933 a man named Adolf Hitler became dictator of Germany. Hitler was the leader of the Nazi Party, whose leaders were a group of men who wanted to conquer the world.

Soon Hitler began building a big army and air force, but the democracies did nothing to stop him. In March, 1938, Germany took over Austria by force. A few months later Hitler said he wanted to take part of the little country called Czechoslovakia. Hitler and Mussolini met the heads of the governments of Great Britain and France in the German city of Munich to talk it over, and Hitler was allowed to have exactly what he wanted. The democracies thought they could prevent a war by just giving in. This policy is called appeasement. It did not work.

In 1939 Hitler took the rest of Czechoslovakia, which was too small and weak to resist by itself, and he threatened war against Poland. Mussolini conquered Albania, a country near Greece in the southeastern part of Europe. Many people hoped that Russia would help to stop Hitler, but in August, 1939, Hitler made an alliance with Russia's dictator, Joseph Stalin, and did not have to fear Russia as an enemy.

On September 1, 1939, the German army attacked Poland from the west. This was the start of World War II. Great Britain and France saw that appeasement would not work, and two days later they declared war on Germany.

THE WAR IN EUROPE, 1939–41

The Germans used a bold way of making war, which they called the *Blitzkrieg* (a German word that means "lightning war"). They used many tanks, which burst through the Polish lines. The infantry, or foot soldiers, many of whom actually rode in trucks, followed through the gaps that had been made by the tanks. Airplanes bombed the Polish troops and scared and killed peaceful civilians by bombing the cities. Poland did not have many tanks or planes and was beaten in less than a month.

Now Hitler offered peace to Great Britain, but the British had agreed to fight for Poland and could not accept. Through the winter of 1939–40, neither side did anything. People joked about the war and called it the "Sitzkrieg." But all the time Germany was planning its biggest attacks.

In April 1940, Germany attacked Norway and Denmark in northern Europe. There was no justification for this for both were peaceful, neutral nations, but the Germans seemed not to care. The attacks were successful in a matter of days. Great Britain sent an army to help Norway, but it was defeated.

A month later, in May, Hitler's troops invaded Holland, Belgium, and Luxembourg. They surrendered after a few days.

The French still thought they could stop the Germans with the Maginot Line, which was a system of concrete forts that stretched along the border between France and Germany. But the German tanks went right through the line, and airplanes bombed the forts. A British force was in northern France, but the Germans cut it off from the French army. It seemed as if the British would all be killed or made prisoners, but a fleet of small boats from England rescued most of the soldiers from the beach at Dunkerque, a French town on the English Channel, and took them back to England.

Many of the French leaders did not really want to fight Germany, since they did not believe in democracy, and the French Army did not put up much of a fight. On June 14, 1940, the Germans entered Paris, the capital of France, and three days later the French government surrendered. For the next four years the French were really ruled by the Germans, though they had their own government (called the Vichy government). Some patriotic Frenchmen escaped from France and fought with the Allied armies against Germany. Millions more, who stayed in France, fought the Germans in any way they could, killing German soldiers at night, blowing up railroads, and doing whatever would hurt the Germans. They called themselves the Resistance.

In 1940 the situation looked very bad for democracy. Great Britain was fighting the Nazis. The United States sent guns, planes and supplies to help the British, but was not in the war. When Germany attacked France, Italy entered the war on Germany's side. An Italian army went to North Africa to fight the British who were in Egypt, but the British beat them and also captured Italy's colonies in East Africa. Soon Mussolini had to ask Hitler for help. (See the article on the AFRICAN CAMPAIGN).

When he had beaten France, Hitler wanted to conquer Great Britain. He could not invade England, because the British Navy controlled the seas, but he hoped that the German air force, called the *Luftwaffe,* could bomb England so badly that the British government would have to give in. Winston Churchill, who became Prime Minister of England in May 1940, told the Germans that England would never surrender. All through that year German planes bombed the cities of England, killing thousands of people, but the British people became more determined than ever to win the war. The Royal Air Force shot down many German planes, until Hitler had to admit that he could not beat the British that way. This was known as the Battle of Britain, and it was really the first Allied victory of the war.

In the spring of 1941, the Germans conquered Yugoslavia and Greece in southeastern Europe, and they took the island of Crete in the Mediterranean Sea. Thousands of German soldiers were dropped onto the island by parachute and defeated the small force of English and Greeks who were there.

On June 22, 1941, the Germans suddenly attacked Russia, even though they had a friendly treaty with that country. At first the German army did very well, capturing and killing many Russian soldiers and coming very close to the Russian cities of Moscow and Leningrad. Then the terrible Russian winter began, the German advance was stopped, and the Russians were able to win back some of the ground they had lost.

Great Britain immediately accepted Russia as an ally, and the United States started sending war supplies to Russia.

HOW THE U.S. GOT INTO THE WAR

On the other side of the world, Japan had also begun a program of conquest. In 1931 a Japanese army invaded and seized Manchuria, in the north of China. In 1937 a Japanese army attacked the main part of China, whose government was headed by Chiang Kai-shek. In 1940, Japan, Germany and Italy became allies. The Japanese war leaders hoped to divide the world with Germany. In 1941 the Japanese invaded part of French Indo-China in southeastern Asia and threatened to take the Dutch East Indies. The United States warned the Japanese that if they tried to make any more conquests it would mean war.

PEARL HARBOR

The Japanese thought they could beat the United States, which was unprepared for war, and on December 7, 1941, without any warning, Japanese planes attacked the American naval base at Pearl Harbor in the Hawaiian Islands. By this attack Japan nearly destroyed the whole United States fleet that was anchored at Pearl Harbor. Everyone in the United States became determined to fight until Japan was beaten. The next day, December 8, President Franklin D. Roosevelt asked Congress to declare war on Japan, and this was done. Three days later Germany and Italy declared war on the United States.

In 1941 the United States Army and Air Force were very small, compared with those of Germany and Japan. Because of this, some people had thought that the United States could be beaten. But American industry, the greatest in the world, quickly stopped making automobiles and refrigerators and other peacetime products and started making guns, planes tanks, ships, and other things needed to fight a war. One of the most important reasons why the Allies won the war was that the United States could produce far more weapons than all other countries.

At first the war did not go well for the American forces. The Japanese quickly landed on the Philippine Islands. The Americans, under General Douglas MacArthur, defended themselves heroically for four months on a little piece of land, jutting into the sea, called Bataan, but there were too many Japanese soldiers and the Americans finally had to surrender. MacArthur went to Australia, promising to return to the Philippines.

Within a few months, the Japanese took the Dutch East Indies (now Indonesia), the British territories in Malaya, including a famous British naval base at Singapore, most of the other islands of the western Pacific, and the American islands of Guam and Wake. A United States army under General Joseph Stilwell went to Burma, where, together with British and Chinese troops, it fought the Japanese in the jungle.

THE WAR IN EUROPE, 1942–45

In Europe too, the Axis went on winning victories. In Russia the Germans started to advance again. They got as far as Stalingrad, a big city in the southeast of Russia, a thousand miles from Germany. In North Africa the German forces went almost to the Suez Canal before they were stopped. In the Atlantic Ocean, German submarines sank so many Allied ships that the British nearly ran out of war supplies and food.

Then the tide turned. At Stalingrad the Russians stopped the German army and captured a large part of it. In North Africa the British won a great victory in October 1942 and began driving the German forces westward across North Africa. The German and Italian forces were pushed into the country called Tunisia, where they surrendered in May 1943. Then the Allies landed on the island of Sicily and captured it, and in September 1943 the Americans and British invaded Italy. That country agreed to surrender, but the German army stayed in Italy and fought the Allies there until the end of the war. (See the article ITALIAN CAMPAIGN.)

Meanwhile thousands of American troops were arriving in England, and American and British planes began bombing German cities and factories. The Germans began to get a taste of their own medicine. The Russians were winning back all the territory they had lost to Germany. The British and United States navies protected the ships going across the Atlantic with troops and supplies and prevented the German submarines from sinking many more of them.

THE ALLIED VICTORY IN EUROPE

On June 6, 1944 (known as D-Day), a force of more than 200,000 Allied troops landed on the coast of Normandy in northern France. It was the most amazing military operation the world had ever seen. The Allies arrived at the beaches in hundreds of boats called landing craft, which were built especially for that purpose. Other soldiers were dropped by parachute. Allied planes bombed all the roads and bridges nearby to prevent the Germans from bringing fresh troops to stop the landing. In the middle of August another American army landed in the south of France and drove northward. At the end of August the Allies entered Paris, where the people were so happy they danced in the streets.

The war was not over yet. The Germans had invented a flying bomb, called the V-1, which they launched across the English Channel. It caused great damage in London and other English towns. Then the Germans started using an even deadlier weapon, the V-2, which was a rocket that flew faster than the speed of sound.

The V-2 could not be shot down, and when it hit the ground it exploded. Once again the British seemed to be threatened with defeat. Fortunately, the Germans did not have many of these V-bombs.

By December 1944, the Allied armies were on the borders of Germany. Then Hitler got together all the good troops he had left and attacked the Americans in the Ardennes Forest of Belgium. In this battle, which was called the Battle of the Bulge, the Germans did very well at first, but the Americans stopped them by the end of December 1944 and in January 1945 the Germans were retreating again.

By this time the cities and factories of Germany had all been badly damaged or destroyed by bombing attacks. Russian forces had entered Germany from the east. The Americans crossed the Rhine River into the heart of Germany in March 1945, and the next month they met the Russian army, which was coming from the other direction. In Italy the German forces held out through the winter, but then they too collapsed. Mussolini was killed by patriotic Italians in Milan on April 28, 1945, and Hitler killed himself in his bomb shelter in Berlin two days later. On May 7, 1945, a day called V-E Day (Victory in Europe), Germany surrendered, and the Nazi dream of conquest came to an end.

THE WAR IN THE PACIFIC, 1942–45

In May 1942, Japan had control over all of the western part of the Pacific Ocean and most of the eastern part of Asia. Many people thought Japan could capture Australia, India, and Hawaii. But that month the Allies won an important victory over Japan when a strong Japanese fleet was beaten by American planes from aircraft carriers in the Battle of the Coral Sea, not far from Australia. In June 1942, a Japanese fleet that was sailing toward Hawaii was defeated in the Battle of Midway.

In August 1942, American troops landed on the island of Guadalcanal in the South Pacific, and started on the long road that led to Japan itself and victory. For three years, Americans captured one island after another, always getting closer to Japan. It was a terribly hard campaign, because each island was a new battle and the Japanese were tough, fanatical fighters. They would not give up until almost all of them had been killed. Most of the islands were covered by jungle, and it was easy for the Japanese to hide and then creep up on the American soldiers without being seen.

The United States Navy, whose Pacific forces were under the command of Admirals Chester Nimitz and William Halsey, played a very big part in the Pacific campaign. The Navy carried the soldiers to the islands that were to be invaded. Warships bombarded the islands before the attack. Naval planes from aircraft carriers supported the Marines or soldiers who landed.

In March 1943, a Japanese fleet was destroyed by American carrier planes in the Battle of the Bismarck Sea. In November 1943, the Americans invaded the Gilbert Islands. On one of these islands, called Tarawa, the Japanese killed or wounded nearly 4,000 American Marines. Three months later American troops captured the Marshall Islands. Fighting in New Guinea went on from 1942 until 1944, when the Japanese there were finally beaten. In June 1944, the island of Saipan was captured.

Then, in October 1944, American forces under General MacArthur landed on the island of Leyte in the Philippines. The Japanese Navy tried to stop the invasion, but it was completely beaten in the Battle of Leyte Gulf.

As islands close to Japan were captured, air bases were built on them and American planes started bombing the cities of Japan. In June 1944 new planes called B-29 Superfortresses, which were the biggest bombers ever seen up to that time, starting dropping thousands of tons of bombs on Japan. In February 1945, Manila, the capital city of the Philippines, was taken by Americans, and the same month American troops landed on the island of Iwo Jima, where a terrible battle took place. It ended after a month, with a victory for the Americans, though nearly 20,000 of them were killed or wounded. On April 1, U.S. troops landed on Okinawa, only a few hundred miles from Japan itself. This was another hard fight, and it was nearly three months before the island was finally captured. It was the last big battle of the war.

By the end of July 1945, Japan had lost nearly all of the islands in the Pacific that it had captured, and its navy and air force had been beaten. But there was still a big army in Japan waiting to fight the Americans if they invaded. It looked as if many more Americans might be killed before Japan was beaten.

The war came to an end suddenly and unexpectedly. On August 6, 1945, the first atomic bomb was dropped by an American plane on the Japanese city of Hiroshima, and it killed more than 70,000 people. The next day, Russia, which wanted people to think that it had helped beat Japan, declared war on Japan. On August 9, an American plane dropped another atomic bomb on the city of Nagasaki. Japan immediately offered to surrender, and on September 2, 1945 (called V-J Day), the Japanese leaders signed the surrender papers on board the United States battleship *Missouri* (nicknamed the "Big Mo"), which was anchored in Tokyo Bay, Japan.

worm

Worms are slender, soft-bodied animals, usually without any leglike appendages. There are thousands of kinds of worm, but they can be separated into three main groups:

The *segmented worms* are formed of ringlike pieces (segments) that are attached end-to-end in a series. These worms have a head and a digestive tract. The best-known of these segmented worms is the earthworm, often used as fishing bait. The earthworm helps nature by burrowing and plowing up the soil.

The *roundworms* are very simple, long, slender animals. Some of these worms cause diseases in plants, animals, and man, such as the hookworm and the trichina, which causes the disease called trichinosis.

Flatworms are usually flat, not round, in shape. Some flatworms live in water; others are parasites of animals and man, such as the tapeworms.

See also the separate articles on EARTHWORM, ROUNDWORM, and TAPEWORM.

wormwood

Wormwood is any plant of a group whose scientific name is *Artemisia*. The group includes many different plants. One kind is planted as a decorative, flowering shrub in gardens. It ranges in height from six to twelve inches, and bears yellow blossoms in August and September. It is a perennial, which means that it grows year after year in the same place without being replanted.

Some kinds of wormwood are grown for their medicinal value, and one kind is the source of an alcoholic drink called absinthe.

The sagebrush of the western United States is a member of the wormwood, or Artemis, plants, and so is tarragon, which is used for seasoning foods.

Wotan, a name used by the German composer Richard Wagner for a character in his music drama-cycle, "The Ring of the Nibelungs," who is patterned after the Germanic god Woden, who was called Odin by the Norse people. See the article on ODIN.

wren

The wren is a small, lively bird that is related to the thrasher and the thrush. The house wren is common throughout the United States and Canada. It is a small, gray bird with a pert-looking tail that stands up almost straight. The female wren is quiet, but the male has a pleasant, bubbling song.

Wrens will usually make their home in a birdhouse if one is convenient and will spend the summer raising two or three broods of young. If no birdhouse is available, house wrens build clumsy nests of twigs in the hollow of a tree stub.

Winter wrens make a ball-shaped nest of moss. They live in more northerly regions than the house wren, and are also found in Europe. Cactus wrens are larger than house or winter wrens. They live in the deserts of the southwestern United States. Their nests are globes of twigs and grasses, often placed high on a cactus where it is protected from enemies.

Wren, Sir Christopher

Sir Christopher Wren was a great English architect who lived about three hundred years ago. He was born in 1632. He studied mathematics and astronomy and in his own day was best known as a scientist, but today he is remembered as an architect.

In 1666 the city of London, England, was almost destroyed by fire. Wren designed many of the buildings that replaced the ones that had been burned. The best-known of these is St. Paul's Cathedral. During his life he designed more than fifty churches, some of which can still be seen in England. He also built many fine homes in an elegant style. He died in 1723 and is buried at St. Paul's Cathedral.

Wrens

The Wrens were British women who were enlisted in the British navy

during World War II. They were one of the first uniformed, organized group of women in an armed service of a modern nation. They did many kinds of work on land, freeing men for sea duty.

"Wren" was a nickname, standing for Women's Royal Naval Service.

wrestling

Wrestling is one of the oldest of all sports. It is a contest between two persons, each of whom tries to throw the other to the ground and pin him down. Throughout the ages, men have tried many different kinds of wrestling and have made many different rules. Ancient statuettes and pieces of carved stone show that the Egyptians and other peoples wrestled more than five thousand years ago.

In most forms of wrestling, no blows are permitted. A man may not hit or strike his opponent. In modern professional wrestling, however, a man is allowed to hit his opponent so long as he does not do it with a clenched fist.

A good wrestler does not always have to have great strength, but he must be able to move very quickly and he must be trained in a large number of *holds*. A hold is any kind of grip on the opponent with which a wrestler can throw the opponent or place him in an uncomfortable or painful position. Examples of well-known holds are the nelson, in which a wrestler holds his opponent from behind and presses his neck down, and the hammerlock, in which an opponent's arm is held behind his back and pushed up toward his neck. Some damaging holds are barred by the rules because the opponent might be seriously hurt.

NATIONAL STYLES

Each country has its own style of wrestling and its own special rules. For instance, in Japan, where wrestling is a very honored sport, the wrestlers face each other in a 12-foot circle. If one of the wrestlers touches the ground with any part of his body except his feet, he is beaten. He also loses if he is forced out of the circle by his opponent. Japanese wrestlers often weigh more than 300 pounds, but they are very quick on their feet.

The most familiar form of wrestling is called *catch-as-catch-can*. In this style, the wrestlers start standing up, facing each other. At a signal from the referee, each of them reaches out and attempts to gain some kind of hold. If one man throws another to the ground, the match is not over; he must pin his opponent—hold his shoulders squarely on the ground. Much wrestling in the catch-as-catch-can style is therefore down on the ground or on a mat placed on the floor. This is the kind of wrestling conducted in schools and colleges. Unfortunately, it is not always interesting to watch. The wrestlers are often locked in holds and nothing seems to happen for long periods of time. Usually in these matches a time limit is set, and if a wrestler has his opponent in a hold for a certain period of time, he is given points.

PROFESSIONAL WRESTLING

Professional wrestling, in which the wrestlers are paid to perform before thousands of spectators, differs greatly from amateur wrestling.

A professional wrestling match is held in a ring, as a boxing match is. There is a great deal of acting. To entertain the spectators, the wrestlers often shriek, groan, pound the mat, and appear to be beating each other horribly. They are allowed to strike any kind of blow, provided they do not use their fists. They are allowed to kick and jump on a fallen opponent, and they throw each other through the air, even out of the ring.

Most people believe that professional bouts are not contests to prove who is the better man, but merely exhibitions to entertain people who like to see what appears to be horrible torture and also skillful tumbling and jumping about. At one time there were real contests among professional wrestlers, as there are among boxers. As in boxing, there were weight classes, ranging from the 118-pound class through the unlimited or heavyweight class, which included anyone weighing 191 pounds or more.

Some of the best-known professional heavyweight wrestlers were Frank Gotch, Ed "Strangler" Lewis, and Joe Stecher, all of whom were Americans; Stanislaus Zbyszko of Poland; George Hackenschmidt of Germany; the "Terrible Turk," from Turkey; and many others.

Wright, Frank Lloyd

Frank Lloyd Wright, an American architect who ranks as one of the greatest architects of this century, was born in 1869 in Richland Center, Wisconsin. He attended the University of Wisconsin. He became an architect in 1893 and soon attracted much attention because of the new styles of building he designed. He designed a series of "prairie" houses, which were long and low. Modern ranch-type houses are based on them. Wright built the Imperial Hotel in Tokyo, Japan, which he designed as "earthquakeproof," and it was one of the few buildings not destroyed by the Japanese earthquake of 1923. He designed many famous buildings, including the Johnson's Wax Company's laboratory at Racine, Wisconsin. He founded the Taliesin fellowship (named for his home, Taliesin, at Spring Green, Wisconsin), to help the study of the arts. He died in 1959.

Wright, Orville and Wilbur

Orville and Wilbur Wright were two brothers who built the first successful airplane. On December 17, 1903, at Kitty Hawk, North Carolina, they made the first successful flights in an airplane. They designed and built both the plane and its motor.

Wilbur Wright was born in 1867 and died in 1912. Orville Wright was born in 1871 and died in 1948. The brothers grew up in Dayton, Ohio, where as young men they ran a small bicycle shop. They were both expert mechanics and since childhood had been interested in the possibility of man's being able to fly. They read all they could about aviation and about 1898 they began to experiment with kites and gliders. They built the first wind tunnel so that they could test their inventions, several of which were used on the plane they flew at Kitty Hawk.

A few years after the Wright's first flight, the United States Army accepted the plane they invented and their achievements had become known throughout the world. In 1909 they formed their own company and began manufacturing airplanes.

writing

In one sense, writing is simply making marks that other people can understand. Such writing is treated in the articles ALPHABET, HANDWRITING, PEN, PENCIL, and others. In another sense, writing is a combination of a profession (like that of doctor or lawyer) and an art (like that of a painter or sculptor).

Professional writing appeals to many people, but only a few of those who try it find that they can make good livings at it. So many people want to write that most of them cannot get their writings published.

A professional writer may either be a salaried employee or a "free lance" (which means that he works for himself and sells his writings to whoever will publish them). Usually a person must start as an employee, so that he can earn a salary while he is learning.

The principal fields in which a writer can work for a salary are: journalism (newspapers and magazines); advertising, either in an advertising agency or in the advertising department of a business firm; public relations, or publicity; and, to a small extent, book publishing. There are other opportunities as secretaries, researchers or assistants to established professional writers.

Writers who are not employed, but who live by selling their writings, may specialize in any of several kinds of writing: fiction (novels and short stories); nonfiction (articles in magazines, or features in newspapers, or books of various kinds); playwriting, which includes motion-picture, television and radio scripts; and poetry.

Novelists and playwrights can make the most money. This is principally because of high prices paid to use stories in motion pictures and on television, but the author of a best-selling novel also receives large sums in royalties, which may be anywhere from 30 cents to 75 cents on every copy sold. The author of a successful play also receives large royalties. But very few novels are best-sellers and very few plays are hits. Short stories bring high prices from the big magazines (perhaps $750 or more).

Writers of articles for magazines are paid higher prices than the same magazines pay for short stories, but in this case also there are few who ever succeed in selling articles regularly to the magazines that pay the high prices. Though an article can be sold for a higher price than a story, there are almost never any later earnings for motion-picture or other dramatic rights, as there are with stories.

Almost no poets can make a living by writing poetry. Most of them must teach or lecture for a living.

Some writers of nonfiction books, es-

pecially textbooks used in schools or useful books such as cookbooks, earn as much or more than novelists; but most nonfiction books earn only moderate amounts.

The best training for a writer is to read a great deal, especially the classics written in former times, and to write a great deal, even if for a long time nothing is sold. Practice means much more to a writer than most people suppose.

Wycliffe, John

John Wycliffe was an English religious reformer who lived about six hundred years ago. He was the chief forerunner of the Protestant faith in England. He was the moving force behind the "Wycliffe Bible," an early translation of the Bible into English.

John Wycliffe was born in 1328. He became a Roman Catholic priest, but sided with those Englishmen who opposed the political power of the Pope. He taught that the Bible was the basis of religious faith. Because of this, he wanted to translate the Bible into English so that it could be understood by the common people. He probably did not do much of the actual translation, which was chiefly the work of his followers. The translation was published in 1388.

Wycliffe gained many followers, who were called "poor priests," though they were not ordained to the priesthood. They went from village to village preaching to the people. Wycliffe was condemned twice by the Catholic Church before he died in retirement in 1384.

Wyoming

Wyoming is a state in the Rocky Mountain region of the United States. Its nickname is the "Equality State," because it was the first state to give women the right to vote. The state gets its name from the Wyoming Valley in Pennsylvania, and the word Wyoming comes from an Indian word meaning "upon the great plain" or "mountains and valleys alternating."

In area, Wyoming ranks ninth among the states, with 97,914 square miles. In population its ranks forty-ninth with about 332,000 people living there. Alaska is the only state that has a smaller population than Wyoming, and many cities in the United States have more people than the whole of Wyoming. Wyoming became a state in 1890, and was the 44th state to be admitted to the United States. Its capital is Cheyenne.

THE PEOPLE OF WYOMING

The first white settlers were fur-traders. They advertised in other, more settled regions for men to trap fur animals in the wilderness of Wyoming. Men came from many parts of the United States and from some foreign countries to open up the rugged new land. South pass, a way through the Rocky Mountains in Wyoming, was an important link of the Oregon Trail. Thousands of pioneers passed on their way to California during the Gold Rush, and some of them stayed to settle in Wyoming. There are about 4,000 Indians of the Shoshone and Arapaho tribes in Wyoming. They live on the Wind River Reservation.

Wyoming Travel Commission
The Rocky Mountains of Wyoming.

HOW THE PEOPLE LIVE

Sheep and cattle raising is the main occupation of the people of Wyoming. The state is second only to Texas in the amount of wool and mutton it produces. Many of the people raise horses, and in places where the land is irrigated there is some dairy farming. Many of the people of Wyoming are farmers, but they can grow good crops only with the help of irrigation, and most of the crops they grow, such as hay, alfalfa, and oats, are used for animal feed. Wheat is grown in the eastern part of the state, and other crops are corn, potatoes, sugar beets, and beans.

The mineral resources of Wyoming provide work for many of the people, but these resources are not yet fully developed. Wyoming has richer coal deposits than any other state, and they provide much of the state's income from mining. Petroleum, natural gas and natural gasoline are also important. There is some mining of iron, copper, and other metals, and uranium fields have been found.

The cities of Wyoming are all small. There are few important manufactures. There are smelters and refineries where the state's mineral products are processed, and sawmills where lumber is prepared for shipment. Cheyenne has airplane and railway workshops.

Because of the great beauty and pleasant climate of Wyoming, it is popular with tourists. There are many hotels, resorts and dude ranches for visitors.

The largest religious group in Wyoming is the Roman Catholics, with the Mormons second. Several Protestant Churches also have large memberships in Wyoming.

WHAT WYOMING IS LIKE

The eastern part of Wyoming lies in the upland region of the Great Plains, where there are great expanses of grass-

land for grazing cattle and sheep. Running from the northwest corner to the south central border of the state is part of the Continental Divide, the great ridge of the Rocky Mountains that marks the dividing line between rivers that flow east and rivers that flow west. The chief ranges of the Rockies in Wyoming are the Absaroka Range and the Big Horn Mountains in the north, and the Gros Ventre, Teton and Salt River ranges in the west. The Wind River Range, in the west central part, contains Gannett Peak (13,-785 feet), the highest point in the state. In the southeast are the Laramie and Medicine Bow Mountains, which surround the Laramie Plains.

The chief rivers west of the Continental Divide are the Snake River, which flows into the Columbia River; and the Green River, which flows into the Colorado River.

The chief rivers that flow east from the Divide are the Yellowstone, which rises in Yellowstone National Park and flows into the Missouri River; and the Powder and Big Horn rivers, which flow into the Yellowstone. The North Platte also flows east from the Divide, later joining the Platte River.

Three-quarters of Wyoming is included in the great Missouri River reclamation project, a program of building about twenty big dams and power plants and doubling the area of land that is under irrigation.

Wyoming has a dry, cool climate. The winters are very cold and the summers are pleasant. There is a great deal of sunshine all year round.

About 48% of the land of Wyoming belongs to the United States government, and much of it is devoted to national parks and wildlife preserves. There are legal hunting seasons, and many sportsmen go to Wyoming to hunt deer, bear, and many kinds of game bird including pheasant, duck, and grouse. Fishing is very good in Wyoming, and the government operates fish hatcheries to keep the streams well supplied with trout and other kinds of fish.

THE GOVERNMENT OF WYOMING

Wyoming, like other states, has a governor at the head of its government and a legislature that makes its laws. The governor is elected for a four-year term. The legislature is composed of two houses, a Senate and a House of Representatives. The 27 members of the Senate

are elected for four-year terms, and the 56 members of the House of Representatives are elected for two-year terms. Judges of the Supreme Court are elected for eight years and district judges are elected for six-year terms. There are 23 counties.

There are about 86,000 pupils attending public elementary and high schools. The University of Wyoming at Laramie had an enrollment of 7,735 men and women in 1971.

CHIEF CITIES OF WYOMING

The leading cities of Wyoming, with populations from the 1970 census, are:

Cheyenne, population 40,914, the capital and largest city. There is a separate article on CHEYENNE.

Casper, population 39,361, the second-largest city, a distribution center for an oil and livestock region, in central Wyoming.

Laramie, population 23,143, the third-largest city, an industrial center, in the southeast.

Sheridan, population 10,856, the fourth-largest city, a railroad center, in the north.

WYOMING IN THE PAST

The first white man to explore the region of Wyoming was probably John Colter, a member of the Lewis and Clark expedition, in 1807. He was a fur-trapper, and fur-trading soon became widespread and profitable and many trading posts were established. The first permanent ones were Fort Laramie, built in 1834, and Fort Bridger, built in 1843. When South Pass through the Rocky Mountains was discovered, many pioneers and settlers passed through or stayed in Wyoming, and with the coming of the Pony Express, and later the railroad and the telegraph, Wyoming began to develop rapidly. The Indians fiercely resisted the white man's invasion and for a period of about twenty years there were bitter battles. By 1880 all the Indian tribes except the Shoshones and Arapahoes had been driven from the territory, and those two tribes were established on reservations.

Cheyenne was founded in 1867, and two years later it was made capital of the new Wyoming Territory. Sheep- and cattle-ranchers flocked to the region, and there was a period of feuds and fighting between them. In 1890 Wyoming was admitted to the United States. In 1912, oil and other mineral resources were discovered, and a boom of prosperity followed.

In 1869 when Wyoming became a territory it was the first in the United States to give women the right to vote, and in 1925 the state elected the first woman governor in the United States, Mrs. Nellie Tayloe Ross.

PLACES TO SEE IN WYOMING

Yellowstone National Park, 3,458 square miles, in the northwest, on U.S. Routes 14 and 20. There is a separate article on YELLOWSTONE NATIONAL PARK.

Grand Teton National Park, 465 square miles, in the northwest, on U.S. Routes 89 and 187. A region of mountains, glaciers and lakes, finest scenery of the Teton Range.

Devils Tower National Monument, 1,-193 acres, in the northeast, about 115 miles east of Sheridan, near U.S. Route 14. Great tower of volcanic rock, the first national monument in the United States.

Shoshone Cavern National Monument, 212 acres, in the northwest, about 5 miles from Cody, near U.S. Routes 14 and 20. Underground caverns with strange crystal formations.

Thermopolis, a town in the north central part of the state, about 110 miles northwest of Casper, on U.S. Route 20. Site of mineral springs at Hot Springs State Park.

Fort Laramie National Monument, 214 acres, in the southeast, near U.S. Routes 30 and 287. Buildings of the fur-trading post and stockade of Oregon Trail days.

WYOMING. Area, 97,914 square miles. Population (1970 census) 332,416. Capital, Cheyenne. Nickname, the Equality State. Motto, *Cedant Arma Togae* (Let Arms Yield to the Gown). Flower, Indian paint brush. Bird, meadowlark. Song (unofficial), "Wyoming." Admitted to Union, July 10, 1890. Official abbreviation, Wyo.

Wyoming Valley Massacre

Wyoming Valley is one of the most beautiful spots in Pennsylvania. (The state of Wyoming is named for it.) During the Revolutionary War most of the people in the Wyoming Valley were on the American side. They forced the Tories (the people who were loyal to Great Britain) to leave the valley. Some of the Tories joined groups of Tories and Indians who were fighting for the British. In July, 1788, a group of Tories and Indians attacked the valley. The people of the American side retreated to Forty Fort, near the present city of Wilkes Barre. They were outnumbered by almost three to one. They met in a bloody battle that saw 225 of the defenders killed and many tortured. The survivors fled from the fort, but many died on the way to their homes or to the homes of settlers who lived near by. Wyoming Monument near Wilkes Barre honors those who died in the fight.

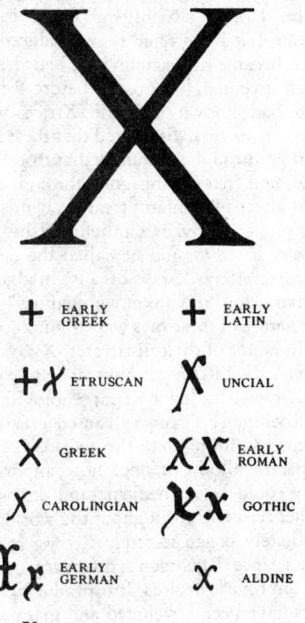

X or x

The letter X, the twenty-fourth letter of our alphabet, came to us as most of our letters did: First, thousands of years ago, it was one of the picture-symbols used by the ancient Egyptians in their system of hieroglyphics. In this system a picture of something, instead of a letter, stood for a single sound. Some people believe that the letter X began as a picture of a chair back, but other scholars have come to think it began as a picture of a post, or prop. The Phoenician symbol for this letter was called *sameth,* and it resembled a cross with three horizontal bars. The Greeks simply dropped the up-and-down bar, leaving only the three horizontal bars. They called this letter *xi,* and gave it the sound of "ks". The form of this letter underwent many changes, and no one is quite sure how all the changes came about. The form that was adopted by the Romans was actually another Greek letter called *chi,* which looked exactly like the X in our alphabet.

In the illustration below, at the far right, is the "German black-letter" (or "Gothic") X, which is used in many German books.

The X as an abbreviation often stands for the words Christ and Christian (from its Greek name, *chi,* the first letter in the name *Christos,* or Christ.) X also stands for number 10 in Roman numerals.

Read also the article ALPHABET.

Xavier, St. Francis, see the article on FRANCIS.

Xenophon

Xenophon was a Greek historian who lived about 2,400 years ago. He was born in 430 B.C. As a young man he fell from his horse in a battle, and his life was saved by the great Greek philosopher, or thinker, Socrates. He then became a pupil of Socrates at Athens. He left Socrates to serve in a Greek army in Persia, and he became a general in this army and led it on an adventurous march back to Greece. He wrote the story of this march in a famous book the ANABASIS, about which there is a separate article. Xenophon lived for many years after that and wrote several historical works, including some on Socrates.

Xenophon died in 355 B.C.

Xerography

Xerography is a method of duplicating anything written, typed, photographed, or printed. It was invented by Chester Carlson, American physicist and lawyer, who called his process "electrophotography." Some methods of xerography require special coated paper on which the image is formed, then developed and fused. The "transfer" method (used only by the Xerox Corporation) employs ordinary bond paper. The document to be copied is illuminated and the light reflected by a lens onto the surface of either a plate or a rotating drum that is coated with a photoconductor—a chemical which can hold a charge of static electricity as long as it is kept in darkness. When light strikes this chemical, the electrical charge leaks away from that part of the plate or drum, but the dark parts are not affected. The result, therefore, is an invisible image formed by electrical charge patterns that conform to the light and dark parts of the original document. To make the image visible, powdered ink called "toner",

which is also charged, is sifted over the plate or drum. These particles stick to the charged part of the plate or drum, bringing out the pattern. The image is then transferred to paper when an electrical charge is delivered to the back of the paper, which is in contact with the drum or plate. This charge attracts the particles away from the drum to the paper. The image is then permanently fused into the paper by means of heat.

In 1950 manually-operated Xerox flat-plate equipment was put on the market. It is still used to make plates for offset printing and to make electronic circuits. The first fully automatic xerographic copier was put on the market in 1960. About the size of a desk, it made seven copies a minute. One of the most recent Xerox machines can make 60 copies a minute, either the same size as the original or in one of several smaller sizes. For further information, see the entries on DUPLICATING MACHINE and PHOTOSTAT.

Xerxes

Xerxes was the name of a king of ancient Persia, who lived about 2,400 years ago.

Xerxes, called Xerxes the Great, was king from 485 B.C. until his death in 465 B.C. He conquered Egypt and then determined to take Greece as well. He raised a great army and built a bridge of boats across the Hellespont (Dardanelles). The army crossed into Greece on this bridge and advanced to Athens, which his army plundered. However, the Greeks crippled his navy in a great sea battle, and Xerxes had to retreat to Asia. He was killed in 465 B.C. by one of his bodyguards. In the Book of Esther in the Old Testament he is referred to as Ahasuerus.

X-rays or x-rays

X-rays are rays that are like light rays, except that we cannot see them and they can go through some substances that the visible light rays (the ones we *can* see) cannot go through. X-rays are very important to doctors and dentists, both to find out what is going on inside a person and also to treat certain illnesses. X-rays are also used in other sciences and in manufacturing, to inspect the insides of manufactured products.

X-rays, like light rays and radio waves, travel in waves. A wave is a movement inside something that does not itself move. If you flick one of your fingernails against one of your teeth, you will feel the shock travel through the tooth though the tooth has not moved. What you feel is a shock wave traveling through the tooth. In much the same manner, sound waves can travel through air that is not moving, and when they strike your ear they cause you to hear; and X-rays can travel through your body when it is not moving.

X-rays are caused by streams of the tiny particles of electricity called *electrons*. Electrons are almost too small to imagine. There are electrons in every atom, but small though the atom is, it is vastly larger than an electron.

The article on ELECTRONICS tells how vacuum tubes and other devices can release streams of electrons. These streams of electrons send out certain electromagnetic waves. Each kind of electromagnetic wave has a certain wave length

—the distance the wave travels back and forth as it travels. Some radio waves have a wave length of many miles. X-rays have a very short wave length, a tiny fraction of an inch. It may be this short wave length that permits an X-ray to find its way through the atomic structure of a substance that would stop ordinary light rays, which have a longer wave length than X-rays.

PENETRATING POWER

The X-ray's power to penetrate, or go through, a solid substance depends on two things. One is the density, or solidness, of the substance. The other is the speed at which the electrons are traveling.

Even though you cannot see X-rays, they will affect a photographic film just as light rays do. When X-rays go through a body and reach a photographic film, they cause a "picture" (called a radiograph) to appear on the film. Where the body is most dense (for example, where there is bone), fewer X-rays get through and the photographic film shows more or less white. Where the body is not very dense (where there is flesh), many more X-rays get through and make the film dark. A physician, dentist, or other scientist, looking at the film, can see where there is bone and where there is flesh; where the bone is sound and where it is broken; where the flesh is firm and solid and where it is eaten away by disease.

The greater the voltage (electrical force) used to release the electrons, the greater will be the penetrating power of the X-rays. For medical and dental examinations, when it is necessary only to penetrate soft flesh and relatively soft bone, 100,000 volts or less are enough. For some forms of medical treatment, a million volts are used, and to examine dense substances such as steel several million volts may be needed.

DEVELOPMENT OF THE X-RAY

X-rays were discovered in the year 1895 by a German scientist named Wilhelm Konrad Roentgen. There is no doubt that X-rays had been produced before, because the vacuum tube had already been invented, but no one before Roentgen had known that the X-rays were there. Roentgen discovered that these rays will go through substances that stop light rays, and that having gone through they will affect glass plates treated chemically for photography. He announced his discovery in 1896, and he called the newly discovered rays X-rays because in algebra *x* stands for "the unknown quantity" and the nature of these rays was still unknown.

In honor of their discoverer, X-rays are often called Roentgen rays, and an expert in X-rays is called a Roentgenologist.

Roentgen's discovery caused great excitement throughout the world. It was apparent almost at once how important they could be in medicine and dentistry. Other scientists throughout the world immediately began to study X-rays. In the years since Roentgen's discovery, greatly improved devices for producing X-rays have been developed and many uses for X-rays have been found. For more than thirty years, nearly all dental and bone-setting work, a great deal of other surgery, the diagnosis or investigation of disease, and in some cases the treatment

of disease, has been based on the use of X-rays.

MEDICAL AND DENTAL USES

A dentist puts a small photographic film behind the teeth and then directs an X-ray machine so that the X-rays pass through the teeth and onto the film. The film is coated with a substance that shuts out light rays, so that only the X-rays will affect it. When the film is developed, it will show where part of a tooth is eaten by decay; it will show cavities between the teeth, when the dentist cannot see them by looking at the teeth; it will show when a nerve has died. If you have ever seen an X-ray picture of teeth, you may have seen how a metal filling in a tooth shows up as a solid mass where the X-rays could not penetrate.

Quite early in the use of X-ray it was discovered that the tissue of a lung diseased by tuberculosis looks different from a healthy lung. The use of X-ray has saved many lives that would previously have been lost, by showing up tuberculosis in its early stages and giving the doctor time to treat and cure it.

X-ray locates gallstones, kidney stones, and bladder stones. It discovers ulcers (infected sores inside the body) and tumors. It causes diseased par s to show up in many parts of the body, not only in the lungs.

For some examinations, the patient swallows a dye or a chalky substance that will pass through certain organs of the body and permit a better X-ray picture of them.

X-rays show where a bone is broken, or whether a bone is dislocated. It shows whether a broken bone has been properly set and whether it is healing properly.

The X-ray effect can be used to show the organs of the body actually working. This is done by the FLUOROSCOPE, about which there is a separate article.

X-RAY IN TREATMENT

X-rays in too great quantity can be damaging, because they destroy certain cells of the body. Because of this, X-ray technicians are careful not to expose themselves too much to X-rays. Lead and certain other substances will block out X-rays almost entirely. These substances are used to shield parts of the patient's body where the X-rays are not needed, and Roentgenologists and others who are exposed to X-rays wear gloves, masks and other coverings to prevent the X-rays from reaching their bodies.

In many cases the destructive power of X-rays has been very valuable in treating animals. For example, some skin ailments are caused by tiny forms of plant life such as the fungus. X-rays kill such forms of plant life and so can be used to cure skin diseases.

X-ray has been much used to treat cancer. Cancer is a disease caused by cells that grow too fast. X-rays directed at cancers can kill many of the cells and prevent them from growing too rapidly and destroying the body. For treatment of cancer, the most powerful X-ray machines—million-volt machines—are used.

USE OF X-RAY IN INDUSTRY

Another use of million-volt machines is in factories, chiefly for testing metal

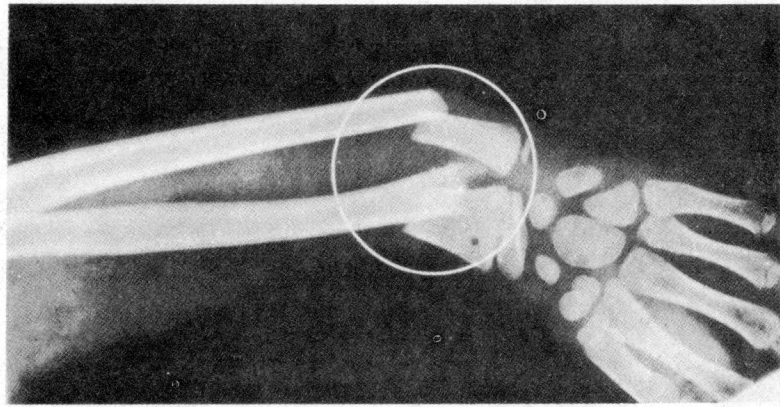

Eastman Kodak Co.

The X-ray picture shows that an injured boy has broken his wrist. It will help the doctor to set the fracture correctly, and later X-rays will show whether the fracture has knit well.

tools and parts of machines. Especially when these metal parts are castings, they may have weak spots inside that do not show on the surface. In use, such a part would give out too soon and might cause great loss in manufacturing time or even serious damage in industry. X-rays show up the weak parts inside the metal, so that faulty parts can be replaced by good ones.

Some metals, after long use, suffer from "fatigue," a gradual weakening that does not show. X-ray machines are used to show when a metal is weakening in this way.

The food industry makes great use of X-rays to inspect foods. X-rays show a difference between healthy plant tissue and decayed plant tissue, just as they show such differences in body tissue. Oranges, lemons and other citrus fruits can be inspected for spoilage or frost damage. Other foods can be inspected for impurities. Usually the foods are carried on a conveyor past a screen that shows an X-ray picture of each object that goes by. An inspector, trained to know what imperfections look like on the screen, watches the screen and removes any imperfect product as it passes by.

xylophone

The xylophone is a musical instrument in which wooden bars are struck with mallets. The bars are tuned to different pitches, and they produce a high, sharp tone.

The marimba is an instrument much like the xylophone except that it is usually longer, that is, there are more notes possible on it from the lowest to the highest, and under each wooden bar there is a metal tube or cylinder that acts as a resonator and gives each note struck a richer tone.

Xylophones and marimbas are used in dance bands, and have been included in the scores of some classical compositions.

XYZ Affair, a case in American history when the United States was asked to pay to have its ocean-going ships spared by armed French ships and adopted the slogan, "Millions for defense but not one cent for tribute": see the article on JOHN ADAMS.

General Electric X-Ray Corp.

The dentist uses X-rays to find cavities. He will place the square of film behind the tooth, then "snap" the picture through the cheek.

Westinghouse Electric Corp.

X-ray pictures of the chest catch tuberculosis early. X-rays of the chest are part of the routine of many physical examinations.

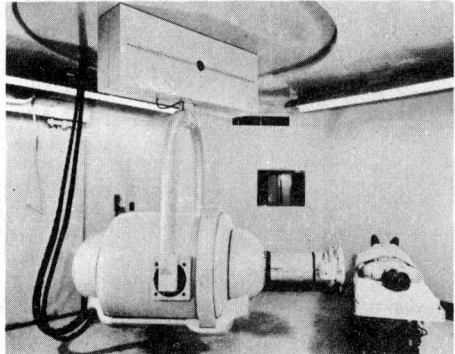

General Electric X-Ray Corp.

A patient suffering from a tumor receives an X-ray treatment. The million-volt X-ray unit sends rays deep into the patient's body.

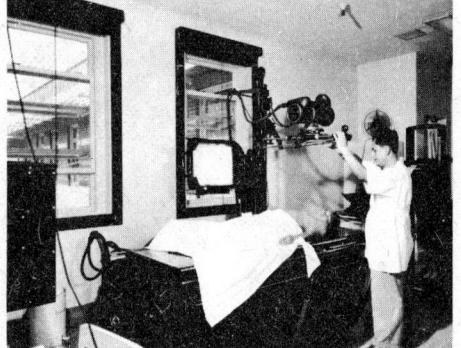

Standard Oil Co.

The patient was in an automobile accident. The X-ray will reveal whether his injuries were minor or he broke a collarbone.

Yale University

Y

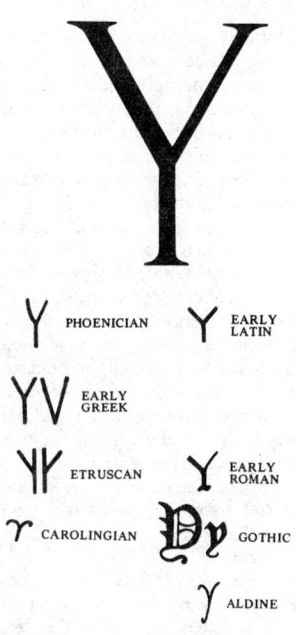

Y PHOENICIAN — Y EARLY LATIN

YV EARLY GREEK

YⱯ ETRUSCAN — Y EARLY ROMAN

ϒ CAROLINGIAN — Ðy GOTHIC

ɣ ALDINE

Y or y

The letter Y, the twenty-fifth letter of our alphabet, was developed long after the other letters. It was used by the ancient Romans in certain words they borrowed from the ancient Greeks. It stood for a sound for which the Greeks had a sign they called *upsilon*. Before that, the Romans had made another letter from the upsilon. This was the letter for which we now have the letters U, V, and W in our alphabet. The Y was also borrowed by the Romans from the Greek *upsilon*, which came from the Phoenician *vau*, seen above. At the right is the "German black-letter" (or "Gothic") Y, which is used in many German books. See also the articles on the letter U and on the ALPHABET.

yachting, the sport of sailing in small ships or boats: see SAILING.

yak

The yak is a member of a family of cattle related to the buffalo and zebu. It is sometimes called the grunting ox, because of a grunting noise it makes when it pulls a heavy load. Wild yaks live on the high plains of Tibet, but some have been domesticated for hundreds of years. Tibetans use yaks to pull carts and carry pack loads over rough mountain trails. The yak's strength and surefootedness are unequalled by any other animal in that part of the world. The milk of the yak is also used.

The yak is a big animal. It has long, trailing fur that hangs down over the sides of its body, almost completely concealing its feet. It has long, curving horns. Yak hair is brown, and Tibetans twist it into long ropes for many uses. The animals are often harnessed with ropes made of their own hair.

In the winter, a male yak acquires a harem of five or six cows. Ten months later, in the autumn, the calves are born. A full-grown yak bull stands about six feet high and weighs about 1,200 pounds.

Yale University

Yale University is the third-oldest university in the United States, after Harvard and the College of William and Mary. It was founded in New Haven, Connecticut, in 1701, by a group of Congregational Ministers. Today Yale University has about 8,200 students and about 2,000 teachers. Several hundred of the students are women, who are studying for advanced degrees. There are no women among the students that make up the undergraduate college. Yale has many graduate schools for students who wish to do graduate work in special subjects, including schools of law, medicine, architecture, religion, music, forestry, and nursing.

Yale University was first called "Collegiate School," and was renamed in 1718 for Elihu Yale, a merchant who gave a large gift to the school. The library at Yale has more than four million volumes and is the third-largest university library in the United States. The two main branches of the college for undergraduates is Yale College for liberal arts students and science students, and the Yale School of Engineering for engineering students.

Yalta Conference

Yalta is a Russian winter resort in the Crimea, a peninsula (arm of land) on the Black Sea. In February, 1945, near the end of World War II, the leaders of the chief Allied nations met there to make decisions about how to end the war and what to do after it had been ended. The leaders were President Franklin D. Roosevelt of the United States, Prime Minister Winston Churchill of Great Britain, and Premier Josef Stalin of Soviet Russia. The decisions they made have been argued about ever since. Winston Churchill wrote of what happened at Yalta, and in March, 1955, the United States State Department issued some important statements on the conference.

They discussed forming the United Nations; dividing Germany into four zones to be occupied by the United States, Great Britain, France, and Russia; making Germany pay for damage done during the war; and setting up a government in liberated Poland. Soviet Russia secretly promised to declare war on Japan after Germany's surrender. In return Soviet Russia was to be given control over certain Japanese possessions and certain rights in Manchuria, which belonged to China, one of the Allies. China later protested because it had not been informed of this decision. Soviet Russia did not live up to most of the promises it made at Yalta, such as the promise of free elections for Poland.

yam

The yam is a twining vine that grows in warm climates. It produces edible tubers (pulpy roots) that are sometimes confused with sweet potatoes, but the yam is an entirely different plant. Yams are cooked and eaten like sweet potatoes.

Some yams grow enormously large, and a single tuber may weigh as much as a hundred pounds. These are not as desirable for food as the smaller yams, which weigh only three or four pounds. Yams are raised commercially in Florida in the United States, where they grow readily. They are not numerous enough to be shipped in any quantity to other parts of the country, and they will grow only in a very warm climate.

Yangtze River

The Yangtze River is the longest river in China and one of the longest rivers in Asia. It rises in the mountains of southwest China and flows into the East China Sea. It is more than 3,000 miles long.

Many of China's largest cities are on the Yangtze—Chungking. Nanking, Wuchang, Hanyang, and Hankow. Shanghai is on a river that flows into the Yangtze. Ocean liners can go up the Yangtze River for about 500 miles, to Hankow, and smaller boats can go about 300 miles farther, to Ichang. Beyond that the river is filled with deep gorges and in many places is so rough that it cannot be used for navigation.

The Yangtze drains most of central China, and its water irrigates the valleys and plains along its banks. The delta of the Yangtze River is one of the principal rice-growing regions of China.

Yankee

Yankee is a slang name used principally in the United States to mean a citizen of the New England states. The typical Yankee is thought of as a man of few words, independent, shrewd, thrifty, and hardworking. During the Civil War, the people of the South came to call all Northerners "Yankees" as a kind of insult. Many Southerners still do this, but the term has lost its insulting meaning. Yankee is also used by people in Great Britain to mean any United States citizen.

No one knows how the word Yankee began. In Colonial days it was a common term of contempt among the British for the American settlers, but when the Revolutionary War began the American soldiers used it proudly and the song "Yankee Doodle" became their favorite marching song. No one knows who wrote the song, but the tune is believed to have been used before for an old English nursery rhyme. Some of the verses of "Yankee Doodle" may have been written by a British Army surgeon to make fun of the American soldiers in the camp at Albany. Others were probably written by Americans.

yarn, see THREAD AND YARN.

year, the period of time (about 365 days) that it takes the earth to travel all the way around the sun: see the articles CALENDAR and TIME.

yeast

Yeast is a kind of very simple plant. It is a FUNGUS, about which you can read in a separate article. A yeast plant consists of only one cell and is so tiny that it cannot be seen without a powerful microscope. Young yeast plants are formed by a process called budding. Part of the cell grows outward, forming a new area that looks somewhat like a bud on a plant stem. After a time the new bud breaks off and becomes a separate yeast plant.

There are several different kinds of yeast, and the air contains many kinds. Some kinds of yeast are used in baking bread. Others are often responsible for the spoilage of food. Another kind secretes a chemical called *zymase*, which

changes glucose (a kind of sugar) to alcohol. This kind of yeast is very important in the brewing industry. Brewers have found ways to keep this kind of yeast separate from all the other kinds. They use it to make beer and other alcoholic beverages.

Yeats, William Butler

William Butler Yeats was an Irish poet and writer of plays. He has been called Ireland's greatest lyric poet and one of the finest English-writing poets of his time. His poems are very musical and beautiful. He was interested in the legends of Ireland and wrote about them in his poetry. He wanted Ireland to be an independent country, and he worked through his writings to urge the people to fight for their freedom.

Yeats was born in Dublin in 1865. He was the son of a painter, and for several years he also studied painting. Then he turned to the theater and to poetry. He fell in love with Maud Gonne, an Irish patriot, and she influenced him to work for Irish independence. With other writers, Yeats formed the Irish National Theatre Society in 1902. A few years later the group was given the use of the Abbey Theatre in Dublin, the capital of Ireland. The experimental plays they put on there made them world famous. From 1922 until 1928 Yeats was a member of the Irish Senate. In 1923 he received the Nobel Prize for Literature. He died in 1939. Yeats' best-known plays include *Deirdre, The Hour Glass, and Cathleen ni Houlihan.* Many of his best poems are in his book *Last Poems,* which was published the year after his death.

yellow fever

Yellow fever is a disease that once infected many persons living in the tropical and warm parts of the world. It is now under control and very few people get it.

Those who have yellow fever first become very hot and their temperature is very high. Their nostrils, lips and tongues become very red. After two or three days the temperature goes down and the patient's skin becomes cold and very yellow in color. Most yellow-fever patients vomit frequently. If the vomit is dark it shows that the patient is bleeding internally. Most of those who bleed internally die.

The article on Walter REED tells how yellow fever was conquered. Reed was an American doctor. He and the men who worked with him risked their own lives to learn about yellow fever. They found that it was carried by a mosquito with the scientific name of *Aëdes aegypti.* This mosquito would bite a person who had the disease, and suck up his infected blood; then it would give the disease to the next person it bit.

Once it was known that this mosquito carried the disease, it was possible to control the disease by killing all the *Aëdes aegypti* mosquitoes and covering all the bodies of water where they laid their eggs. Covering the water with oil killed the eggs before they hatched. Fish such as minnows were put in pools of water and they ate the eggs, or the larvae that hatch from the eggs.

A virus, too tiny to be seen under an ordinary microscope, is the cause of yellow fever. Since this fact was discovered, even more has been done to wipe out the disease. There are vaccinations and inoculations that make people immune (safe against the disease). There are also drugs for treating people who have become infected.

yellow jacket, a kind of wasp: see the article on WASP.

Yellow River, the English name for the river Hwang Ho in China: see HWANG HO.

Yellow Sea

The Yellow Sea is a large section of the North Pacific Ocean. It lies between China and Korea. In area it is about 100,000 square miles. It is not a deep body of water, being about 300 feet deep at the most. It gets its name from its color, which is yellowish from the deposits of mud carried down by the rivers that empty into it. Dairen, China, and Inchon, Korea, are among the most important cities along its shores.

Yellowstone National Park

Yellowstone National Park is the largest and oldest national park in the United States. It was established in 1872. Most of Yellowstone National Park is in Wyoming. Other sections are in Montana and Idaho. The park has an area of 3,458 square miles, most of which is a plateau (high but level region) surrounded by mountain ranges. There are about 3,000 geysers and hot springs in Yellowstone Park, more than there are in all the rest of the world. The most famous geyser is Old Faithful, which spouts a fountain of water 150 feet into the air every 65 minutes. The largest lake in the park is Yellowstone Lake, out of which flows the Yellowstone River. The Grand Canyon of the Yellowstone River runs through the northern half of the park. Its walls show every color of the rainbow and there is a 300-foot waterfall at the upper end. The park is an animal preserve and has great herds of deer, bears, and bison, and hundreds of kinds of birds. The park has great forests. Some of these are petrified, or fossil, forests (in which the trees have turned to stone). They have been covered through the centuries with mineral deposits from the geysers and springs.

Yellowstone River

The Yellowstone is a river 671 miles long in Wyoming, Montana, and North Dakota. It rises in the Absaroka Range in northwestern Wyoming. It flows northwest through Yellowstone National Park, where it for. s Yellowstone Lake, and through the Grand Canyon of the Yellowstone. It then enters Montana and flows northeast across the North Dakota border, where it empties into the Missouri River. The chief rivers that flow into the Yellowstone are the Bighorn, Tongue and Powder Rivers. There are important irrigation projects on the Yellowstone, and it is included in the great Missouri Basin irrigation and power project of the United States Bureau of Reclamation.

Yemen

Yemen is a small country on the southwestern tip of the Arabian peninsula. For many years most of us knew Yemen only as the home of the Queen of Sheba, about whom the Bible tells, but a revolution in 1962, then years of civil war, put Yemen back into the news.

Yemen once ruled large parts of Arabia and Africa. It was also important as an overland route between East and West. Yemen now has an area of 75,000 square miles, which is about the size of Nebraska. About 5,000,000 people live there, which is about four times as many people as live in Nebraska.

Most of the people who live in Yemen are Arabs and follow the Mohammedan religion. There are some people of African descent and some Jews. The people are mostly farmers and grow coffee, citrus fruits, and grains. They also raise many sheep and goats. The people manufacture clothing and shoes for themselves, and sell some coffee, herbs and precious stones to other countries.

The western part of Yemen, which lies along the Red Sea, is very dry and in some parts is actually a desert. The rest of the country is mountainous. Most of the people live on the high plains of these mountains. The principal Red Sea ports are Hodeida, Mocha, and Loheiya. The capital and largest city is Sana, an inland city of about 60,000.

YEMEN IN THE PAST

In the ruins of many Yemeni cities can be seen remains of the country's ancient culture. Yemen lost importance and its civilization decayed. The people still live as they did thousands of years ago. There are no railroads or paved highways, and little is known about modern methods of farming and manufacturing.

For many years Yemen was part of the Turkish Empire but had its own kings, called imams. After World War I, Yemen became an independent kingdom. In 1947 it joined the United Nations and in 1958 it joined Egypt and Syria in the United Arab States, but that union ended in 1961.

In 1962, Yemeni military leaders tried to establish a republic. Tribesmen of the deserts and mountains supported the king, and civil war began. Egypt sent soldiers to help the republicans while Saudi Arabia did the same for the king. Late in 1965 Egypt and Saudi Arabia agreed to stop the war and let the people vote to decide their government.

YEMEN. Area, about 75,000 square miles. Population (1974 estimate), 5,900,000. Language, Arabic. Religion, Islam. Type of government, republic. Monetary unit, the rial, worth about 32 cents (U.S.). Flag, red, with sword and five white stars. Capital, Sana.

Yenisei River

The Yenisei River in Siberia, Soviet Russia, is one of the longest rivers in the world. It rises in the Sayan Mountains of southern Siberia, and flows west and north for 2,364 miles, emptying into the Arctic Ocean. It is four miles wide in the lower part of its course and much wider where it meets the ocean. The Yenisei is important for transportation. Ocean-going vessels can go up it for 400 miles to the port of Igarka during the months from June to October when the river is free of ice. Barges carrying heavy goods like timber, construction materials, and coal graphite, can navigate about 1,700 miles of its length. The Ob-Yenisei Canal joins the Yenesei and Ob Rivers. The Yenesei

flows through a fairly dry region of more than a million square miles in Siberia.

yew

The yew is an evergreen shrub or tree that grows in a variety of shapes and sizes. It is often planted as a lawn decoration because it will remain healthy and strong even though it is clipped repeatedly. It is often used for hedges. Some yew trees reach a height of 60 feet if allowed to grow unchecked, while others remain dwarflike in size no matter what their age. The needles of a yew tree are somewhat wider than those of a fir or a spruce tree, and their dark green color changes little during the year. In the fall, yew trees bear bright red fruits, about the size of small cherries.

Yew wood is springy and has been much used for bows.

yoga

Yoga is a way of thinking and acting practiced by many followers of the Hindu religion. The purpose of yoga is to free the soul from things of the world and finally to achieve union with God. A person who practices yoga is called a *yogi*, and he is supposed to achieve supernatural powers when he has reached the state of union with God, such as the ability to change in size and weight, to be instantly transported to any place, and to understand the language of animals and the thoughts of human beings. There are a number of branches of yoga that emphasize different methods of accomplishing the perfect state. Among these are *hatha yoga*, which is bringing the body under absolute control by physical and mental exercises; *bhakti yoga*, which is a system of prayers; and *karma yoga*, a way of life for persons who cannot retire from the world and live purely religious lives.

yogurt

Yogurt is a food made from the milk of cows, goats, or other cud-chewing animals. The milk is boiled until it loses much of the water in it. Then it is allowed to ferment (become sour). This makes it about as thick as whipped cream.

Yogurt is eaten by many people in Iran, Turkey, Armenia, and the Balkan countries. It is also popular in the United States. It is often eaten with a sweet fruit, such as strawberries.

Yokohama

Yokohama is the fifth-largest city in Japan and a great seaport. It is on Tokyo Bay. Over two million people live there. Besides the big shipping business there are shipyards and factories that produce steel, chemicals, automobiles, and silk.

A hundred years ago, Yokohama was a tiny fishing village. When Japan became a great trading country, Yokohama grew rapidly. In 1923, one of the greatest earthquakes that ever occurred almost destroyed Yokohama. The city was rebuilt with fine parks, broad streets, and modern buildings. During World War II, United States planes bombed the city, destroying many buildings and clogging the harbor with sunken ships.

YOKOHAMA, JAPAN. Population (1972 estimate) 2,050,000. Seaport on Tokyo Bay (Pacific Ocean).

Yom Kippur

Yom Kippur is the most important holy day in the Jewish religion. It falls at the end of September or beginning of October, on the tenth day of Tishri, the seventh month in the Jewish calendar. *Yom Kippur* means "Day of Atonement" in the Hebrew language. It is marked by twenty-four hours of prayer and fasting (going without food and drink). During this time the worshiper prays for forgiveness for all the sins of all men—pride, greed, jealousy, vanity, lust, and so on. The prayer runs: "Father, we have sinned before Thee." The word "we" is used instead of the word "I."

Yom Kippur is the last of the Ten Days of Penitence. As the sun begins to set the night before Yom Kippur, the family gathers for a festival meal. Candles are lit, and members of the family ask each other's forgiveness for the wrongs they have committed, so that they may begin the holy day with a clean slate. Then they go to the synagogue, the Jewish house of worship, to pray. White, which stands for purity, is the color used for the altar cloths and covers of the Torah (part of the Jewish Bible). The synagogue officials wear white robes, and sometimes all the men of the congregation wear white skull caps. Though the spirit of Yom Kippur is solemn, it is also joyous, for the worshipers believe that God will forgive their sins.

See also the article JEWS AND JUDAISM.

Yom Kippur War, see the articles on ISRAEL, SYRIA and EGYPT.

Yonkers

Yonkers is the fifth-largest city in the state of New York. It is on the Hudson River, a few miles north of New York City. About 200,000 people live in Yonkers, and many of them work in New York City. There are important factories in Yonkers. The Otis Elevator Company was founded in Yonkers about a hundred years ago, and Yonkers became the center of the elevator industry.

The site of Yonkers was settled more than three hundred years ago by Dutch people, who also founded the city of New York.

YONKERS, NEW YORK. Population (1970 census) 204,370. Incorporated, 1855.

York, House of

York was the name of a famous English house, or family, about five hundred years ago. The House of York began in 1385 when Edward III gave the title Duke of York to his fifth son, Edmund. Three members of the York family were kings of England. The first was Edward IV, who won the throne in 1461 by defeating the forces of Henry VI, a member of the House of Lancaster. This was the beginning of the Wars of the Roses, in which the Lancasters and the Yorks fought for the English throne.

Edward IV was succeeded in 1483 by his son, Edward V, who was only 13 years old. The duke of Gloucester, uncle of Edward V, had Edward and his brother Robert put in the Tower of London, where they died. Most people believe that they were murdered by their uncle, who had made himself king as Richard III, the third king of the house of York.

Richard was very unpopular with the people. In 1485 he lost the throne to Henry Tudor, who founded the royal house of Tudor. See the articles LANCASTER and Wars of the ROSES.

For almost two hundred years the title Duke of York has been the traditional title of the second-oldest son of the king or the eldest son of the Prince of Wales.

Yorkshire

Yorkshire, or York, is a county in the north of England. It is the largest English county in area, with about 6,000 square miles, and nearly five million people live there. The biggest city is Leeds, a city of about 500,000. Yorkshire is considered as being divided into regions called North Riding, East Riding, and West Riding, but these are unofficial. Yorkshire is famous for many products, but especially for its manufacture of woolen cloths and fine cutlery and other steel products, and for its coal and iron mines. It is also an important farming district.

The Yorkshireman in England is a subject of the same kind of legends as those used for the "New England Yankee" in the United States. He is noted for his distinctive accent, his shrewdness in trading, his taciturnity (unwillingness to do any talking that is not necessary) but also for his "tall tales," and his suspicious attitude toward strangers.

Yorkshire terrier

The Yorkshire terrier is a small terrier that came originally from Yorkshire, England. It is kept mainly as a pet and in size is a "toy" dog. For many years the Yorkshire terrier was kept by the fashionable ladies of England, as it was so small they could carry it around to parties and when they were out paying calls on friends. There are not a great many Yorkshire terriers in America, in comparison to other breeds.

Yorkshire terriers have very long, silky hair that hangs down almost to the ground and falls over the dog's eyes and face. It is so long and thick that it falls into a natural part from the tip of the tail to the nose and looks as if someone had combed it in that position. A puppy's tail is clipped when it is a few days old. All puppies are born black but later change to a golden tan color with a dark stripe down the back.

A Yorkshire terrier stands only 6 to 8 inches high at the shoulder and usually is 11 to 13 inches long from the chest to the base of the tail. It weighs 3 to 6 pounds.

Yorktown

Yorktown is a small town in southeastern Virginia, on the James River. It is now part of Colonial Historic National Park. It was settled in 1631 and so is one of the oldest towns in the United States. Only about 400 people live in Yorktown. The final battles of the Revolutionary War were fought in and around Yorktown. On October 19, 1781, Lord Cornwallis surrendered there to General George Washington, thus ending the Revolutionary War. Moore House, where the surrender terms were signed, and other historic landmarks have been restored and are visited by many tourists each year. The Yorktown Monument is

in memory of the victory. Yorktown was also the scene of fierce fighting during the Civil War.

Yosemite National Park

Yosemite National Park is a great scenic region in east central California. It has an area of 1,182 square miles, with mountain peaks and deep canyons, waterfalls and lakes. Its most remarkable feature is Yosemite Valley, which was cut by the Merced River. The valley is seven miles long, a mile across, and 3,000 to 4,000 feet deep, with steep walls that rise to mountain peaks. High above Yosemite Valley are other valleys with small streams running through them. As these streams drop into Yosemite Valley they form magnificent waterfalls, including the spectacular Upper Yosemite Falls with a drop of 1,430 feet. The Yosemite Park is notable also for its three groves of giant sequoias, or redwood trees. In the Mariposa Grove is a tree called the Grizzly Giant that is 209 feet high and 94 feet thick and is believed to be 3,800 years old. Another famous tree is the Wawona, through which an automobile highway has been cut.

Young, Brigham

Brigham Young was a leader of the Mormons, the religious group that settled the state of Utah. He was born in 1801 in Whitingham, Vermont. While working as a painter he was attracted to the Mormon faith and he joined the church in 1832.

Three years later, Young became a member of the Council of Twelve, the ruling body of the Mormon Church. In 1847, after the death of Joseph Smith, founder of Mormonism, Young was elected head of the church. The Mormons were persecuted by their neighbors in Illinois and Missouri, and Young led them on a long westward journey to found a new community. When they reached the present site of Salt Lake City, Utah, Young elected it as their new home. He called it Deseret.

Young's organizing skill, combined with the hard work of the Mormon people, caused the community to grow and prosper. Young was the first governor of the Territory of Utah.

Brigham Young practiced what was then a principle of the Mormon faith, the doctrine of polygamy (the teaching that a man may take several wives). Young himself had more than twenty wives during his lifetime, and this was part of the reason why he was removed as governor of Utah in 1857.

In 1871 Young was tried but not convicted on charges of polygamy. Today he is recognized as a deeply religious man and a great leader. He died in 1877, survived by seventeen wives and fifty-six children.

Young, Cy

Cy Young was one of the great pitchers in baseball history. His real name was Denton True Young and he was born in 1867 in Gilmore, Ohio. He was a major-league pitcher from 1890 to 1911. He won 511 games out of 906 that he pitched in, the most games that anyone ever pitched, and the most that anyone ever won. He also pitched three no-hit games, and one of them was a "perfect game" (in which no batter reached first base). Cy Young also pitched 23 innings in a row without letting any batter get a hit. He was one of the first men elected to the Baseball Hall of Fame, in 1937. He died in 1955.

Young Men's Christian Association

The Young Men's Christian Association, or Y.M.C.A., is an organization that tries to improve the conditions and opportunities of young men. The first Y.M.C.A. was started in London, England, in 1844 by Sir George Williams. Other associations throughout Great Britain were formed and united with it. In 1851 the movement began in America, in Montreal, Canada, and Boston, Massachusetts. Soon other cities followed their lead, and in 1854 they held a convention at Buffalo, New York, and founded an international committee to serve and advise the associations of Canada and the United States. A year later a world conference was held in Paris, France, with delegates from seven countries.

In 1962 the Y.M.C.A. had about three million members in the United States alone, about two-thirds of them under the age of 17. It had more than 1,800 branches in the United States, with facilities and equipment valued at more than $500,000,000, and spent $167,000,000 for activities and services.

The Y.M.C.A.'s activities cover many different fields. Many of its branches emphasize religious study. The Y.M.C.A. provides libraries and reading rooms, classes, lectures, and clubs. It provides housing for young men in large cities, summer camps for children, and clubs for boys and girls in grade and high schools. It provides swimming pools and equipment so that its members can receive physical training and take part in many sports.

The Y.M.C.A. works with college students, veterans, and employees of various industries. In World War II it combined with other welfare agencies to form the United Service Organizations (U.S.O.) to provide recreation and guidance for American service men.

The Y.M.C.A. coöperates with similar movements in twenty-eight other countries, and has performed special services such as aiding refugees from World War II and the Korean War.

Young Men's and Young Women's Hebrew Association

The Young Men's and Young Women's Hebrew Association, or YM-YWHA, is an organization that works for better conditions and opportunities for young men and women of the Jewish religion. The YM-YWHA, the Jewish Community Centers, and some other agencies are part of a large national organization, the National Jewish Welfare Board.

The YM-YWHA and the Jewish Community Centers give guidance and technical assistance to communities in providing leisure time, informal education, group work and cultural program opportunities for children, youth and adults. Ranging from nursery schools to services for the aged, their programs include clubs, special activities such as arts and crafts, dramatics and physical education, forums and musical programs, and camping and general recreation activities.

Youngstown

Youngstown is a city in northeastern Ohio, on the Mahoning River, about 65 miles southeast of Cleveland. It is a manufacturing city, one of the largest pig-iron and steel-making centers of the United States. It is also the center of a group of steel-milling cities. About 140,-000 people live in Youngstown, and many of them work in the steel mills. There are also important factories that make steel and other metal products, electrical equipment, tires and other rubber products, furniture, chemicals, and cement. There are limestone quarries outside the city. Youngstown is the seat of the Butler Art Institute and of Youngstown University. The city was founded in 1797 by John Young, for whom it was named.

YOUNGSTOWN, OHIO. Population (1970 census) 139,788. Iron and steel center. On the Mahoning River. County seat of Mahoning County. Founded, 1797.

Young Women's Christian Association

The Young Women's Christian Association, or Y.W.C.A., is an organization that works to improve the conditions and opportunities of young women. It was founded in England through the joining of two groups that had been founded in 1855—Emma Robart's Prayer Union and Mrs. Arthur Kinnaird's General Female Training Institute. In 1858 a similar group was formed in New York City. Today the Y.W.C.A. operates in 70 countries. In the United States alone there are more than 1,600 groups, with a membership of more than three million girls and women.

The activities of the Y.W.C.A. cover many fields. Its main purpose is to promote the physical, spiritual and mental health of young women, and much of its work involves religious study and activities. In addition it provides housing in large cities, clubs, classes, employment bureaus, courses, lectures, social activities such as dancing and group singing, and gymnasiums and swimming pools where physical training is given and girls can take part in many sports.

The Y.W.C.A. works to promote coöperation and understanding among peoples of different countries and races. It sends representatives to foreign countries and has organized schools of social work in New Delhi, India; in Montevideo, Uruguay; and in Athens, Greece. It coöperates with other welfare agencies in community, national and international projects.

youth hostels

Youth hostels are places where hikers or other vacation travelers can spend the night for very small fees. In the United States an organization called American Youth Hostels has approved hundreds of hostels where young people may stay overnight when they are on hiking, biking, canoeing, skiing and horseback trips. Most of the hostels are connected with farm homes. They are run by "house

parents," ordinary people who open up their houses, guest houses, summer places or barns for a small overnight fee such as 50 or 75 cents. The hostels provide separate sleeping quarters and washrooms for boys and girls, a kitchen where members can cook their own meals, and usually some extra space for recreation, such as square dances. The hostels supply bunks, blankets, cooking utensils, and cleaning equipment, but all the work is done by the hostelers. Hostelers must take along their own sleeping-sacks and eating utensils.

American Youth Hostels is connected with the International Youth Hostels Association, and a membership pass makes anyone eligible to stay at hostels in 25 countries of the world. This pass costs one to four dollars a year. The American Youth Hostels also plan trips under the direction of trained leaders. Some of these trips lead across the United States and Canada, and others go to Europe, Africa, Mexico, Alaska, and Hawaii. They last from four to eleven weeks. Local councils plan shorter trips, lasting from one day to four weeks. Detailed information may be obtained from the American Youth Hostels, Inc., 14 West 8th Street, New York 11, N.Y.

The youth hostel movement started in Germany in 1910 and was begun in America in 1934.

Yucatan Peninsula

Yucatan Peninsula is a neck of land on the east coast of Central America, between the Gulf of Mexico and the Caribbean Sea. It is made up of British Honduras, part of Guatemala, and part of Mexico. It has about 70,000 square miles —about the size of Oklahoma.

Yucatan Peninsula is low and flat. It is made up of limestone covered by a thin layer of soil. There are only a few rivers, and in the northern part, where rainfall is very light, water is obtained from underground pools and rivers. The region is hot and dry except during a rainy season from August to September. Jungles cover much of the peninsula.

The Mexican part of Yucatan Peninsula takes up most of the region. The state of Campeche on the western part of the Peninsula produces mahogany and other valuable woods. The state of Yucatan in the northern part produces wood dyes and henequin (a paint fiber), which is the most valuable crop. The rest is the territory of Quintana Roo, which has few inhabitants and is mostly wild jungle.

Most of the people of the Yucatan Peninsula are Mayan Indians, who still live in many ways as their ancestors did more than three hundred years ago. There are many remains of the ancient Mayan civilization.

yucca

The yucca is a flowering plant that is related to the lily but is much larger. It grows mostly in the southwestern part of the United States and in Mexico. The largest kind of yucca fiber is taken from the leaves of the yucca and is used to make mats and baskets, and the fruit and buds of the tree may be cooked and eaten.

Cal. Mission Trails Assn.
A yucca blooming in southern California.

Yugoslavia

Yugoslavia is a country in southeastern Europe. Most of it is on the Balkan Peninsula. Yugoslavia is mountainous, and the people are mostly farmers who work hard to make a living from the soil. After being under the influence of Soviet Russia for several years, Yugoslavia broke away in 1948.

Yugoslavia is 98,766 square miles in size, which is about twice the size of New York State. More than twenty million people live there, which is somewhat more than live in New York.

WHAT THE PEOPLE ARE LIKE

Yugoslavia means "land of the southern Slavs." The people belong to Slavic groups, related to Russians, Poles, and other Slavic peoples. The two largest groups are Serbs and Croatians. They are independent and warlike peoples. They fought for their independence for years, against Turks, Germans, and Hungarians. During World War II, when their country was overrun by the Axis forces of Germany and Italy, many hardy Yugoslavs formed bands of guerrillas and fought courageously against the occupiers.

The people speak the Slovene, Macedonian and Serbo-Croat languages, depending on what part of Yugoslavia they live in. Most of them speak Serbo-Croat, even if it is not their traditional language. Serbians most often use an alphabet called Cyrillic, but also use Roman letters like those in this book. All the languages belong to the Slavic language family.

Almost half the people belong to the Greek Orthodox religion. About one-third are Roman Catholics. The rest are Mohammedans or Protestants.

HOW THE PEOPLE LIVE

Six out of ten Yugoslavs are farm-

ers. Most of them have small farms. Others work on "collective farms." Those on collective farms have houses and small gardens but also work on a larger farm under a manager selected by the government. There are also "state farms," sometimes called land factories, which are owned entirely by the government. The Communist government has tried to create many collective and state farms, but the peasants prefer to have their own land, and nine-tenths of the farm land is owned and operated by individuals.

Farms in Yugoslavia produce wheat, maize (Indian corn), hemp, flax, cotton, and tobacco. Sheep, goats, pigs and cattle are raised. Slovenians breed fine horses.

Other people in Yugoslavia work in mines. Yugoslavia produces more bauxite (the ore of aluminum), antimony and lead than any other European country. It is second in production of mercury, zinc, and copper. There are also iron and coal mines.

Before World War II, Yugoslavia had very few large plants and factories. Since then plants for processing copper and lead and for making steel have been built. Steel production is twice what it was in 1939. Most of the new factories are in Slovenia, in the northwest part of the country. There are also factories for making machinery, especially farm machines, and for manufacturing textiles and clothing and processing food products.

WHAT KIND OF PLACE IT IS

The mountains of Yugoslavia make it one of the highest countries of Europe. Most parts of the country are more than 1,500 feet above the level of the sea. The country is divided into three parts: the plains of the north; the eastern end of the Alps, Europe's greatest mountain chain; and the very irregular western coast along the Adriatic Sea.

Most of the people live in the great north-central plain of Yugoslavia. It is part of a great valley between two sections of the Alps. (The valley includes Hungary and part of Rumania.) Serbia, the largest of the Yugoslav states, is in this valley. The Danube and other rivers make it very fertile.

The Dinaric Alps in Yugoslavia are covered with heavy forests. Sheep and goats are grazed in this region. The mountains drop down to a rugged coast with many bays but few good harbors. There are many islands along the coast.

Among the rivers of Yugoslavia are the Sava, Drava and Morava Rivers, all of which empty into the Danube. They are a source of electric power and river boats are an important means of transportation. Yugoslavia's mountains make

travel difficult and most of its railroads were destroyed or damaged during World War II. Since World War II there has been much rebuilding and new construction of railroads and highways.

The climate of Yugoslavia varies. In the north-central plain the temperature in winter is about 27 degrees and in summer about 75 degrees. This is a climate typical of continental Europe. The coast is warm and sunny, with temperatures ranging between 50 and 75 degrees.

The chief cities of Yugoslavia, with populations from the 1974 estimate, are:

Belgrade, population 697,000, the capital and largest city in Yugoslavia. There is a separate article about BELGRADE.

Zagreb, population 503,000, capital of Croatia and second-largest city. There is a separate article about ZAGREB.

Skoplje, population 228,000, capital and industrial center of Macedonia. Three-fourths destroyed by earthquake in July 1963. Before that, the third-largest city.

Sarajevo, population 227,000, capital of Bosnia-Herzegovina and fourth-largest city. Manufactures carpets, oriental jewelry.

Ljubljana, population 182,000, capital of Slovenia and fifth-largest city. Manufactures machinery, chemicals, and tobacco products.

HOW THE PEOPLE ARE GOVERNED

Yugoslavia is a federal republic. Its constitution provides for a legislature of two houses. They are a Federal Council, elected by the people, and a Council of Producers, representing various industries and occupations. The President is elected by the two houses. However, under the Communist government the candidates are either Communists or men approved by the Communists, and the people have no real voice in the government. The legislature approves the laws requested by the Communist leaders, so it too is without power. The actual government is a dictatorship with Tito as dictator. There is a separate article about TITO.

All children must go to school for at least seven years, and they cannot leave school until they are 14. Yugoslavia also has many secondary (high) schools, and there are universities at Belgrade, Zagreb, Ljubljana, and Subotica.

The country is divided into separate "republics" that are like states in the United States, governing their local affairs.

There are separate articles about SERBIA, CROATIA, BOSNIA-HERZEGOVINA, MONTENEGRO, and the SLOVENES.

YUGOSLAVIA IN THE PAST

Yugoslavia did not exist before World War I. Serbia and Montenegro were independent states, and the rest of the country belonged to Austria-Hungary, which was a great empire at that time. These regions had long sought independence, and at the end of the war the "Kingdom of Serbs, Croats, and Slovenes" was created. In 1921 a constitution was adopted, providing for a king as head of the government and a parliament or legislature elected by the people. The previous royal house of Serbia, the Karageorgevitch family, became kings of Yugoslavia.

The new nation had many difficulties. To protect itself from bigger nations it joined Czechoslovakia and Rumania in an alliance called the Little Entente (discussed in the article on ENTENTE). There were arguments with Italy over control of the Adriatic seaport of Fiume. Inside the country, the Croats and some of the other people felt that the Serbs had too much power in the government. In 1929, after a Croat leader was shot, the king (Alexander II) did away with the constitution and made himself a dictator. In the 1930s the government became somewhat more democratic, but the different peoples in Yugoslavia still quarreled with one another.

In 1940, after the start of World War II, Italy invaded Yugoslavia's neighbor, Greece. Germany demanded the right to send troops across Yugoslavia to help the Italians in Greece. The government of Yugoslavia yielded in 1941, but the people of Yugoslavia were so angered by this that a new government took over the country and refused to be Germany's ally. Germany invaded Yugoslavia, conquered it easily, and controlled it throughout the war.

The rugged mountain people of Yugoslavia would not give in. They formed guerrilla groups (unofficial bands of fighting men and women). These made frequent raids on the Axis occupiers and never gave them a moment's rest. The first guerrillas, called the Chetniks, were commanded by a general named Mikhailovitch. A Communist-led group of guerrillas, called the Partisans, broke away and formed their own army under the leadership of Tito.

The Russians and Yugoslavia threw the Germans out of Belgrade in 1944, and Tito set up his Communist dictatorship.

After World War II, Yugoslavia's government was very friendly to that of Soviet Russia, and unfriendly toward the United States. Then, in 1948, Tito broke away from the Soviet Union, saying that the Russians were trying to run Yugoslavia for their own benefit. Though Tito remained a Communist dictator, Yugoslavia received loans from the United States and in 1953 signed a mutual-

Yugoslav Inform. Office

Yugoslavs enjoy skiing in the Julian Alps in the northwest part of their country.

defense treaty with Greece and Turkey. In the 1960s Yugoslavia resumed friendship with the Soviet Union while pursuing an independent foreign policy. There is a separate article about TRIESTE, over which Yugoslavia and Italy had a long dispute.

YUGOSLAVIA. Area, 98,766 square miles. Population (1974 UN estimate) 20,550,000. Language, Serbo-Croat. Religion, Greek Orthodox, Roman Catholic, and Moslem. Government, federal republic. Monetary unit, the dinar, worth 8½ cents (U.S.). Flag, three horizontal bars, blue-white-red, with red star.

Yukon

Yukon is a territory in the northwestern corner of Canada. It is shaped like a triangle, with its upper point north of the Arctic Circle. It is 207,076 square miles in size, which is bigger than any state of the United States except Alaska and Texas, but only 19,000 people live there. Most of the people work in mines at the towns of White Horse and Dawson. Silver, lead, copper, gold and zinc are produced in the mines. Fur-trapping is also important.

White Horse, which has a population of 5,031, is the capital.

Yukon is mountainous and cold. In the east are the northern hills of the Rocky Mountains. Vast forests cover much of this region, but lumbering is carried on only in the south. West of the Rockies are the high Cordillera Mountains, which cover most of the territory. Mt. Logan, near the Alaskan border in the southwest, is 19,850 feet high. It is the highest peak in Canada. Fertile valleys and plains are between the mountains. The Yukon and Lewes rivers are the largest rivers.

In the summer, the temperature in Yukon seldom rises above 60 degrees. In the winter it is usually below zero, and it has gone as low as 70 degrees below zero.

Travel in Yukon is chiefly by airplane or river boat, or along the Alaska Highway, which cuts across the southwest of the territory. There are fewer than a hundred miles of railroad. The government of Yukon is headed by a Commissioner appointed by the Canadian government. His offices are at White Horse. The Royal Canadian Mounted Police maintain law and order in the region.

Robert Campbell, a British fur trader, first explored Yukon, about 120 years ago. In 1897 gold was discovered and many prospectors went to the region (see the article on GOLD RUSH). Mining was been the chief industry ever since. The population of Yukon used to include many Eskimos, but during the 1930s most of them moved to the Northwest Territories. The Canadian government gave them herds of reindeer and caribou.

YUKON. Area, 207,076 square miles. Population (1974 estimate) 19,000. Territory of Canada.

Yukon River

The Yukon River is the fifth-longest river in North America. It is 1,979 miles long. It is formed by the meeting of the Pelly and Lewes rivers in the central part of the Yukon territory, and flows in a great curve through Yukon and Alaska before it empties into the Bering Sea.

The Yukon River is the most important "highway" of the northwest. Wood-burning river steamers travel from its mouth to Dawson, former capital of Yukon territory, during the summer months when the river is free of ice. The boats often pass herds of caribou, which swim in the river. Salmon go far upstream, and the fishing is good.

The Tanana River is the Yukon's chief branch. It joins the Yukon in central Alaska. At its mouth the Yukon forms a great delta, covering about 9,000 square miles.

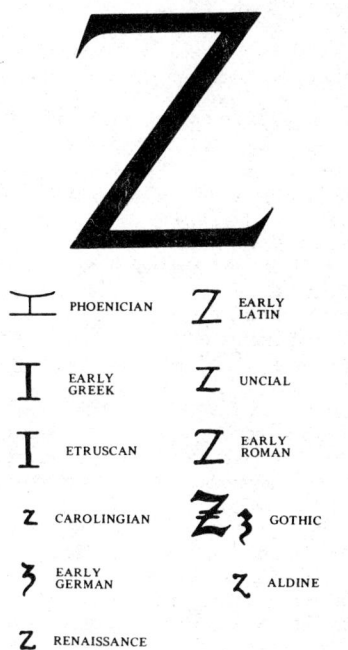

Z or z

The letter Z, the twenty-sixth and last letter of our alphabet, came to us as most of our letters did: First, thousands of years ago, it may have been one of the picture-symbols used by the ancient Egyptians in their system of hieroglyphics. In this system a picture of something, instead of a letter, stood for a single sound. Scholars are not sure what the letter Z began as a picture of. In the Hebrew language, it became the letter called *zayin,* and the sign for it was something like the Phoenician letter, above at the far left.

When the Greeks took this letter, which they called *zeta,* they first changed it so that it looked like the letter I in our alphabet, but later they made the up-and-down stroke a slanting one. In this form the letter was taken over by the Romans and came to our own alphabet.

In the illustration above, you can see that the form has changed very little. At the far right is the "German black-letter" (or "Gothic") Z, which is used in many German books.

Read also the article ALPHABET.

Zagreb

Zagreb is an important manufacturing city in northwestern Yugoslavia and is the capital of Croatia, a republic of Yugoslavia. The city produces machinery, paper, textiles, and leather goods. Zagreb is the center of the oldest university in Croatia and has many fine buildings such as the National Theater. See CROATIA.

ZAGREB, YUGOSLAVIA. Population (1972 census) 430,802. Capital of Peoples Republic of Croatia. On the Sava River.

Zaire

Formerly called the Belgian Congo and the Republic of Congo, this African country has been renamed Zaire. See BELGIAN CONGO.

Zambezi River

The Zambezi is a river about 1,600 miles long, one of the great rivers of Africa. It rises in central Africa and flows south through eastern Angola and the western part of Northern Rhodesia. It then turns east and forms VICTORIA FALLS, about which there is a separate article.

Beyond Victoria Falls, the Zambezi forms the entire border between Northern and Southern Rhodesia, and then flows through Mozambique to empty into the Mozambique Channel, an arm of the Indian Ocean. The river has several mouths, of which the Chinde delta is used for shipping. In its upper course above Victoria Falls, the Zambezi receives a number of other rivers and is broken by rapids and waterfalls. The lower course of the river lies in a broad valley and during dry seasons it is sometimes divided into several streams. Lake Nyasa drains into this portion of the Zambezi, through the Shiré River. The Zambezi is navigable to a point just below Victoria Falls. It is navigable for barges in its upper course between rapids and waterfalls.

Zambia

The Republic of Zambia, in Africa, became an independent nation in 1964 and joined the United Nations. Before then, it was called Northern Rhodesia and was part of the Federation of Rhodesia and Nyasaland. See the article on RHODESIA.

With an area of 287,640 square miles, Zambia is slightly larger than Texas but the population, about 3,600,000, is much less than that of Texas. The country is governed by a parliament, cabinet, and prime minister, under a constitution adopted in 1963. The capital is Lusaka, a city of about 110,000. Zambia took its name from the Zambezi River.

Zambia is very rich in copper and many of the people are miners but many more are farmers. Nearly all Zambians are Bantus, an African Negro people, but about 75,000 are "Europeans," or white, and they have most of the wealth.

Zanzibar

Zanzibar is a small island (only 640 square miles, with a population of about 335,000) in the Indian Ocean, off the east coast of Africa, near Tanganyika.

In 1964 Zanzibar joined with Tanganyika to form the United Republic of TANZANIA, about which there is a separate article.

Most of the people of Zanzibar are Africans of Bantu tribes. There are also Arabs and Indians. Most of the people are Moslems and speak the Swahili language. The soil, made of coral limestone, is very fertile. Cloves, coconuts, fruits and tobacco are grown.

Zanzibar, with Pemba and other nearby isles, has been known since ancient times. About 1,200 years ago, Persians and Arabs settled there. The principal city, also named Zanzibar (population about 60,000), was once a center for trade in slaves, ivory, and cloth. Before becoming independent Zanzibar was controlled by Portuguese, then Arabs, then the British.

zebra

The zebra, a member of the horse family, lives in eastern and southern Africa. It is partly white with dark stripes over its entire body. Its ears are larger than the ears of a horse and its feet are more slender. It is about the size of a pony, being on the average about 4 to 4½ feet high at the shoulder, and it weighs 500 to 700 pounds.

Zebras graze on leaves and grass, as horses and asses do. They usually remain within five miles of water. Their deadliest enemy is the lion, which is always found in sections where herds of zebra live. Other animals are inclined to leave the zebra alone, because it has fast, powerful legs and a blow from a zebra's hoof can kill a wild dog that ventures too close. It also uses its teeth to defend itself.

zebu

The zebu or humped cattle of India is considered sacred by some religious groups in that country. The Brahmins especially respect the zebu, and in most other countries the zebu is often called Brahmin cattle. It has a hump on the shoulder.

The breed has been introduced into the southwestern part of the United States and has been interbred with beef cattle, because it is able to resist Texas fever, a disease of cattle in that part of the country. The zebu is also kept in China, East Africa, and the East Indies. It is used for milk, for meat, and as a beast of burden.

Zenger, John Peter

John Peter Zenger was an American newspaperman who lived more than two hundred years ago and is still remembered because his courage helped to establish freedom of the press in America. Zenger was born in Germany, in 1697, but his parents settled in New York when he was a boy. He learned the printing trade and when he was a young man he started a newspaper, the *New York Weekly Journal.*

At that time, New York and the other American states were colonies of Great Britain and most of them had governors who were sent from England and who had great power. In 1735, Zenger's newspaper criticized the English governor of New York. The governor had Zenger arrested and put in prison. A man named Andrew Hamilton, a prominent lawyer in Philadelphia, defended Zenger in his trial.

Zenger was tried before a jury, as the English law required. Hamilton argued that Zenger could not be punished for criticizing the governor and government, because what Zenger had written had been true. The jury agreed with Hamilton and decided that Zenger was not guilty.

Ever since then, American newspapers have had the freedom to attack the government, as long as they publish the truth. Zenger died in 1746.

Zeno

Zeno was a Greek philosopher, or thinker, who lived about 2,300 years ago. He was born about 336 B.C.

Zeno founded the STOICS, about whom there is a separate article. He was so highly regarded by the people of Athens that they let him hold the keys to the city fortress, which meant that he was the most trusted man in the city. He was sickly all his life, and when he became convinced that he was incurably ill he committed suicide, probably in 264 B.C.

Zeppelin, Count

Count Ferdinand von Zeppelin was a German nobleman and soldier who built the first rigid-type airship, and this kind of airship was called a Zeppelin in his honor. Count Zeppelin was born in 1838. He rose to the rank of general in the German army. He built his first successful airship the *Zeppelin* in 1900 and was active in building airships until he died in 1917.

See also the articles on BALLOON and AVIATION.

zero

Zero means "nothing" in the system of numbers we use, but it does more than any other number to make our counting and our figuring in arithmetic quicker and easier. The symbol for zero is 0. It is also called the *naught*, or the *cipher*, but it should be known as zero.

We use the *decimal system*, which means a system of counting by tens, and in this system the zero means "times 10." Write a zero after 1 and you have 10, which means "1 times 10"; write a zero after 10 and you have 100, which means "10 times 10"; and so on. The zero would be just as valuable if we counted by some other number, such as 8 (the *octonary system*) or 12 (the *duodecimal system*), though it would take us quite a while to get used to the change, once we had learned the decimal system. In the octonary system, the numbers would run 1, 2, 3, 4, 5, 6, 7, 10, 11, 12, 13, 14, 15, 16, 17, 20, and so on. The number ten would then mean 1 times 8, and the 20 would mean 2 times 8, and 100 would mean 8 times 8. Some mathematicians believe it is unfortunate that we do not use the duodecimal system, because 12 can be divided by more numbers than 10 can, which would often make counting and figuring more convenient.

The zero was used in counting at least two thousand years ago in some countries, but it was not known in Europe until after the time of Christ. The Arabs are usually given credit for introducing it to Europeans, but not for inventing it.

Zeus

Zeus was the king of the gods in the mythology (stories of gods and goddesses) of the ancient Greeks, thousands of years ago. The Romans had a god that they called Jupiter, who was almost the same as Zeus.

Zeus was the son of Cronus, a Titan. (The Titans were giants who ruled the universe.) Zeus and his brothers revolted against their father and divided his possessions: Poseidon (the Roman Neptune) ruled the sea, Hades (the Roman Pluto) ruled the underworld, and Zeus ruled the heavens and earth. Zeus was more powerful than his brothers.

Zeus married Hera (the Roman Juno). Ares (the Roman Mars), Hephaestus (the Roman Vulcan) and Hebe were their children. Pallas Athena, or Athena, the daughter of Zeus, sprang fully grown and armed from the forehead of Zeus.

From the heights of Mt. Olympus, Zeus ruled gods and men. He protected the family and state. He punished criminals and controlled the fate of each man. As god of the heavens, he used thunder and lightning as his weapons. Occasionally he came to earth disguised as a man or animal. He turned himself into a swan to woo a Greek princess named Leda. There are many other stories told about Zeus. One may say just the opposite of what another says. This is because Greek ideas about him changed with the times. See also the article on JUPITER.

Zhukov, Georgi

Georgi Konstantinovich Zhukov was a Russian soldier and political leader and Commander of the Russian armies that captured Berlin at the end of World War II. He was born in 1896 and became an officer in the Communist army that was established after the Russian Revolution in 1917, when the Communists gained control of Russia. In 1943 he was made a marshal, highest rank in the Red (Soviet Russian) army.

Zhukov became so popular with the Russian people during World War II that the dictator, Josef Stalin, apparently became jealous or afraid of him and gave him unimportant jobs. When Stalin died in 1953, Zhukov became prominent in government again. By 1955, Zhukov was considered one of the two most powerful men in Russia. The other was Nikita Khrushchev, head of the Communist Party in Soviet Russia. Together they made Georgi Malenkov resign as premier (head of the government). But then Khrushchev became as powerful as Stalin had been and once again Zhukov was removed from his position of power and given unimportant jobs.

Ziegfeld, Florenz

Florenz Ziegfeld was a great producer of musical comedies. He was born in Chicago in 1867. In 1907 he produced his first revue, or musical show, calling it *The Follies of 1907*. The revue was made up of songs, dances by women in elaborate costumes, and humorous skits, many of which made fun of the customs of the day. He began then to produce a new *Follies* almost every year. They became known as *The Ziegfeld Follies*. He married Billie Burke, one of the most beautiful and successful actresses of her time. Ziegfeld produced many shows besides the *Follies*. He died in 1932.

zinc

Zinc is a blue-white, very shiny metal. It is a chemical element, which means that it is one of the basic substances of which everything in the world is made. Zinc is very useful in the metalworking and paint industries. It has been used since ancient times in the making of brass, which is copper and zinc mixed.

Zinc is a little lighter than iron and is soft enough to be scratched by a copper coin. When cold, zinc is brittle. If a lump of it is hit with a hammer, it will break. But if you heat zinc to any temperature between 220 and 300 degrees on the Fahrenheit scale, you can easily hammer or bend it to any shape you want, or you can draw it out into wires. Above 300 degrees it becomes brittle again.

Because it will not corrode, zinc is used to coat sheets of iron and steel to prevent them from rusting. This process is called *galvanizing*. Galvanizing is done in several ways: by dipping the metal to be coated into melted zinc; by spraying melted zinc onto the metal; by covering the metal with powdered zinc and then baking the powder on in a furnace; or by plating the metal sheets with zinc, a process described in the article on ELECTROLYSIS.

There are many important alloys (mixtures of metals) made with zinc. Among them are brass, Muntz metal, German silver, certain kinds of bronze, and certain kinds of solder.

When zinc and certain other metals are connected by a wire, an electric current flows between them. For this reason, the cans that form the outer covering of dry-cell batteries are made of zinc.

When zinc is burned in air, it forms a white powder that is called *zinc oxide*. This white powder has many uses; as a coloring for white paints; as a glass polish; as a dental cement; and in medical ointments. Zinc and sulfur make *zinc sulfide*, which shines in the dark when it is mixed with a tiny bit of radium. It is used to paint the numbers and hands that shine on clocks and watches that have luminous (glowing) dials.

ZINC ORES

Zinc always occurs in nature combined with one or more other chemical elements. The chief zinc ore is called *zinc blende*, or *sphalerite*. *Smithsonite*, or *calamine*, is the next most abundant ore, and *zincite*, *willemite* and *franklinite* are the names of other zinc ores. The leading producers of zinc ore are the United States, Canada, Belgium, Germany, and the Soviet Union. The region around Joplin, Missouri, is the world's largest producer of zinc ore.

Zinc ore is ground to a powder and is mixed with powdered coal. The mixture is heated in furnaces called retorts. The impurities in the ore go up the flue of the retort as waste gases, and nearly pure zinc metal, called *spelter*, is left in the retort. The zinc may be made even purer by means of electrolysis.

zinnia

Zinnias are flowers that are native to Mexico, but grown in gardens throughout North and South America. They grow in three distinct heights, tall,

medium, and dwarf. Each size may bear blossoms of any size, but zinnias are best known for very large, showy flowers. Zinnias grow in an almost limitless variety of colors and types. Some have several layers of petals, some have curled petals, some appear almost fringed, and some have tiny pom-poms of blooms. The color may be anything from white to the deepest reds and purples. They are especially satisfactory as cut flowers because a plant will continue to bear new blooms as the opened blossoms are cut off. They are easy to grow, and require very little special care. The zinnia is the state flower of Indiana.

Zion and Zionism

Zion was an ancient Hebrew city that is often mentioned in the Bible. In the Book of Samuel it is called the City of David. In other places it is spoken of as the hill of Zion, which was probably one of the hills surrounding Jerusalem. To Christians the name Zion has come to mean "heaven," and to Jews it means "the Promised Land." For hundreds of years the Jewish people wanted to restore their ancient homeland and establish a nation of their own, and the movement to found such a nation was called Zionism. There were many Zionist organizations that worked for this aim, though there were also groups of Jews called anti-Zionist, who were opposed to the idea of a Jewish nation. The aim of the Zionists was achieved in 1948, when the Republic of Israel officially became the Jewish nation. Most of the Zionist organizations then devoted their time to helping the new nation.

Zipper

A Zipper is a device for fastening together the edges of clothing, handbags, carrying cases, and other things made out of cloth or a flexible material. The correct name for this device is *slide fastener,* and Zipper is the name of a brand of shoes or overshoes that are closed with slide fasteners, but the trade-marked name became better known than the real name.

The slide fastener is made of rows of small metal teeth attached to pieces of tape. Each tooth ends in a kind of dome shape, somewhat like a tiny spoon. This fits the end of one of the pieces attached to the other piece of tape.

The slide is pulled one way to close the fastener and the other way to open it. In the slide are two bent channels. The top channel will hold the teeth in such a position that they will fit together perfectly. The channel at the bottom of the slide changes this position so that the teeth separate.

The secret of the slide fastener is to make the teeth so accurately that they fit together perfectly. No tooth differs from any other tooth by more than one-thousandth of an inch. They are made on automatic machinery and can be made quite inexpensively.

zirconium and zircon

Zirconium is a fairly light metal. It is a chemical element, which means that it is one of the 103 basic substances of which everything in the world is made. Pure zirconium is either a black powder or gray crystals. Zirconium is used to make glass tough and in the making of some kinds of steel. It is used in enamels (a kind of paint) to make them opaque so that light can not shine through them. It is used with copper and nickel to make alloys (mixtures of metals). Zirconium and oxygen combined form a substance called *zirconium oxide,* or *zirconia.* This material can withstand very high degrees of heat and is used as a lining for furnaces in factories.

The chief ore of zirconium is made up of zirconium plus the chemical elements silicon and oxygen, and is called *zircon.* Large, clear zircon crystals, which may be yellow, orange, red, green, brown, or clear as a diamond, are very attractive stones and are used in jewelry. These stones are also called *hyacinth,* or *jacinth,* or *matara diamond.*

zither

The zither is a stringed instrument. It consists of a shallow sounding box over which are stretched 30 to 45 strings. Some of the strings are plucked with a plectrum, or pick, to form the melody. The others are plucked with the fingers in chords to form the accompaniment. The zither has been known since ancient times in China and other countries of Asia and has long been popular in Switzerland and Bavaria. In 1950 the zither became popular in the United States after it was used in the musical accompaniment to the motion picture *The Third Man.*

zodiac

The zodiac is a name given to an imaginary circle in the heavens above the earth. The sun and moon and some of the other planets are seen at different times of the year in different parts of the heavens within this circle. The ancient peoples first used the zodiac to tell what time of the year it was.

In the circle of the zodiac there are various constellations or groups of stars that were given names by the ancients. They divided the zodiac into twelve parts, or "houses." Each of the twelve parts bore the name of the main constellation, or group of stars, seen in that part of the zodiac. The names of the constellations are as follows:

Aries, The Ram
Taurus, The Bull
Gemini, The Twins
Cancer, The Crab
Leo, The Lion
Virgo, The Virgin
Libra, The Balance
Scorpio, The Scorpion
Sagittarius, The Archer
Capricornus, The Goat
Aquarius, The Water-Bearer
Pisces, The Fishes

The circle of the zodiac is often drawn as a circle of twelve sections. In each there is a special sign, representing the constellations in that section. People who study astrology (which is a belief that the positions of the stars can be "read" to foretell events on earth) use the zodiac. See the article on ASTROLOGY.

Zola, Émile

Émile Zola was a famous French novelist. He was the leader of a literary

movement known as naturalism. Naturalistic writers write of life as it really is but they put an emphasis on detailed descriptions of things as they actually are. Zola's most famous novel, published in 1880, was *Nana.* In 1901 Zola became a hero to the people when he published a pamphlet called "I Accuse." In this pamphlet he accused the French government of acting unfairly, and because of it Zola was put in prison. You can read more about this pamphlet in the article on Alfred DREYFUS.

Zola was born in Paris in 1840. When he was 22 he began writing for newspapers. His first book was published in 1864, but he gained little fame until he published *L'Assommoir* in 1878. After that he became the most famous French writer of his time, and he influenced many writers to write as he did. He shocked many readers by describing situations that no writer before him would have dared or cared to write about. Zola died in 1902. Most of his novels have been translated into other languages.

zone

The earth is divided into zones, or "belts" around the surface of the earth, according to the climate in each zone. The *torrid zone* is the region all around the earth that is nearest to the equator. In this zone it is warm or hot all year round. The *temperate zones* are regions in which it is warm in summer and cold in winter, but usually not very hot or very cold. There are two temperate zones, one in the Northern Hemisphere (northern half of the earth) and one in the Southern Hemisphere. The United States is in the temperate zone of the Northern Hemisphere and Argentina and Brazil and the Union of South Africa are in the temperate zone of the Southern Hemisphere. The *frigid zone* is the region around either of the poles. In the frigid zones it is always cold. There are two frigid zones, the Arctic region (around the North Pole) in the Northern Hemisphere and the Antarctic region (around the South Pole) in the Southern Hemisphere.

These zones are divided by imaginary lines around the earth called *Tropics.* The Tropic of Cancer is the dividing line between the torrid and temperate zones in the Northern Hemisphere and the Tropic of Capricorn is the dividing line between the torrid and temperate zones in the Southern Hemisphere. The same kind of imaginary lines divide the temperate from the frigid zones, the Arctic Circle in the Northern Hemisphere and the Antarctic Circle in the Southern Hemisphere.

The earth is also considered to be divided into *time zones.* See TIME.

zoo

A zoo is a place where living animals are kept. The word "zoo" is short for zoölogical garden. Most zoos are used by zoölogists, scientists who study animal life. All zoos are open to the public so that people can see the animals.

Nearly all the animals in zoos are wild

animals. They do not have such ordinary domestic animals as horses, cows, and dogs. Zoos do have many animals that are domestic animals in far-off lands. For example, a zoo in the United States will have camels, llamas, and yaks, which are strange to people in North America, but are domestic animals in their native countries, just as cows are domestic animals in American countries and in Europe.

The animals shown at zoos are of many kinds. There are many mammals, which are furry or hairy animals that bear living young and nurse them. There are reptiles —snakes, turtles, lizards, and so on. In large zoos there are birds of many strange kinds. Fishes and other forms of water-breathing animal life are kept in an aquarium, which may be part of a zoo but in some places is a separate exhibition.

The most popular animals in most zoos are the big "cats" (lions, tigers, panthers, and other wild members of the cat family); the monkeys, which are usually kept in a big separate cage called the "monkey house," and which do many amusing things that people like to watch; and the bears, which also are usually amusing to watch. Other popular animals, because they are so big and so strange, are elephants, hippopotamuses, and rhinoceroses.

HOW THE ANIMALS ARE KEPT

For many years, nearly all animals in zoos were kept in cages. People could see them only through the bars. Some fierce animals still have to be kept behind bars, but many big-city zoos now keep some of their animals in the open where people can see them living somewhat as they would in their native habitat (living place). The place where the animals live is surrounded by a deep moat (ditch) so that the animals cannot escape. People who go to the zoo can stand at the edge of the moat and watch the animals.

This method of keeping animals at a zoo was first used by the Hagenbeck family, a German family that became famous more than a hundred years ago for showing wild animals in circuses and in zoos. The Hagenbecks first took some of their animals out of cages more than fifty years ago. Gradually other zoos adopted their methods.

The animals to be kept in the open must be carefully selected by zoölogists who are experts on their habits. Animals that fight and eat one another cannot be kept in the same place. That is why the big cats and the bears, which are carnivorous (meat-eating) animals and will kill other big animals for food, are kept separate.

PEOPLE WHO WORK IN ZOOS

Among the people who work in zoos are keepers, zoölogists, and veterinarians.

The keepers watch the animals, give them their food, keep them from fighting or hurting one another or themselves, and try to keep them clean and healthy. The keepers protect the animals against people who come to watch them (and who often would tease the animals, or give them food that would make them sick. The keepers also protect the people against the animals, for some people are foolish enough to get very close to the

bars and are in danger of being clawed or bitten by fierce animals.

The zoölogists study the animals, and based on their scientific knowledge they give instructions as to how the animals are to be fed and cared for. Usually the director or head of a zoo is a zoölogist.

Veterinarians treat and cure diseases of animals. When an animal needs an operation, through illness or injury, a veterinary surgeon performs the operation.

All the people around a zoo learn the habits of the animals and when it is safe to go near them. A keeper will walk fearlessly into a cage with wild animals but anyone else who tried might do it at the wrong time or in the wrong way and might be hurt.

A wild animal is most dangerous when it is frightened or in pain, because then it may attack anything. When a fierce, large animal such as a lion is in pain and needs treatment from a veterinarian, it is usually controlled by means of a "squeeze box."

First, the animal is transferred to another cage in which there is a panel or row of bars that can be slid from one end of the cage to the other. This panel is gradually slid across the cage until it holds the animal too tightly for the animal to move. The veterinarian can then safely treat the animal and make it well.

Many animals do not live in captivity, and even when they can stay alive they will not breed (have young) in captivity. The zoölogists study and test many ways to keep the animals alive and healthy and to help them to breed. Animals that cannot stand hot weather (such as polar bears) are kept in shady places with plenty of cool, flowing water to help them through the summer; animals that cannot stand cold weather are kept in heated rooms through the winter. Air conditioning is used for some animals.

FEEDING THE ANIMALS

Food is one of the biggest problems of a zoo. With some animals, such as the big cats that need huge chunks of raw meat or the elephant that needs hundreds of pounds of hay each day, it is a matter of expense. With other animals it is even more difficult than that. At times it has been necessary to fly in fresh leaves from trees thousands of miles away until the zoölogists could find some substitute food that would keep the animals alive.

HOW THE ANIMALS ARE CAPTURED

Many of the animals in zoos must be trapped in Africa and Asia. It is usually much harder to trap animals than to shoot them, but of course they are of no value to a zoo if they are dead. There are men and companies in Africa and Asia that make a business of trapping animals and selling them to zoos. A zoo wants the finest examples of all animals, so it may be necessary to trap many animals before one is found that can be sold to a zoo for a big price. Circuses as well as zoos buy live animals from the trappers. Usually the animals are trapped in pits or cages so that they will not be hurt.

Zoölogists from zoos and museums often make expeditions to find and capture rare animals. At times, a farmer or other outdoor worker will accidentally come across and capture a rare animal that a zoo

wants. A giant panda was found in this way in China and was shown in American zoos.

FAMOUS ZOOS OF THE WORLD

Until about a hundred years ago, there were very few zoos. Now there are zoos in large cities all over the world.

One of the oldest and most famous zoos is the London Zoo. The famous stories about "Winnie the Pooh," by the English writer A. A. Milne, are based on a bear in the London Zoo.

The largest zoo in the world is the Bronx Park Zoo in New York City. Its official name is the New York Zoölogical Garden. Besides thousands of land animals, it has a famous aviary (enclosure where birds are kept) and an equally famous aquarium. The Bronx Park Zoo is on the outskirts of New York City, and there are smaller zoos in Central Park, near the center of Manhattan, and in Prospect Park, in Brooklyn.

The famous Hagenbeck Zoo is near Hamburg, in West Germany. During World War II, many of the most dangerous animals in this zoo (and also in the London and Paris zoos) were sent to other countries or were put to death, for fear that bombing raids might destroy their cages or enclosures and set them loose to attack people. The Hagenbeck Zoo has slowly been rebuilt.

Famous zoos in the United States include those in Philadelphia, Washington, D.C., Chicago, Cincinnati, and St. Louis, but there are many others.

In many countries there are game preserves where wild animals can live without being killed by hunters or driven out by settlers. In some of these (for example, in Yellowstone National Park) people can watch the animals as easily as they can in zoos. See the article on WILDLIFE.

zoölogy

Zoölogy is the scientific study of animals. As you can read in the article on ANIMAL LIFE, there are countless different forms of animal life, ranging in size from the giant elephant or whale down to tiny water creatures that can be seen only under a microscope. Zoölogists study everything about these creatures—where they came from, how they are formed, where and how they live, and everything else about them.

Zoölogy is one of the main branches of the science of biology. The other main branch is botany, which is the study of plant life.

Because there are so many different kinds of animal life, no zoölogist can be an expert on all of them. Therefore zoölogists specialize in some particular study connected with animals. For example, *ichthyology* is the branch of zoölogy that deals with fishes; *ornithology* is the branch that deals with birds; and *entomology* is the branch that deals with insects. These are only a few of the many branches of zoölogy, and each of the branches is itself divided into many other branches.

FOSSIL ANIMALS

There are tens of thousands of known animals that once lived on earth but no

longer do. Some of these animals lived many millions of years ago. They are known by their fossils, which are marks of their forms or skeletons that have hardened into rock in the course of the ages.

To the zoölogist, fossil animals are as important for study as living animals. The special branch of zoölogy that deals with fossil animals is called *paleontology*.

WORK OF A ZOÖLOGIST

All zoölogists are trained in special college courses. After graduation, many of them work in museums of natural history and in zoölogical gardens (zoos). The United States government and other governments employ many zoölogists to study animal life for the benefit of farmers, fishermen, businessmen, in such fields a the fur and food industries, and many others to whom animal life can be important. Some zoölogists teach, and continue their studies while they are teaching.

Field trips are important in zoölogy. Zoölogists study living animals in forests and fields. Sometimes they make expeditions to far-off lands to study the animal life of those lands or to work with geologists (scientists who study the formation of the earth) in seeking fossil remains of extinct animals.

Zoroaster

Zoroaster or Zarathustra was a prophet of ancient Iran who probably lived about 2,500 years ago. He founded the religion called Zoroastrianism. The sacred writings of the religion are called the Avesta, and in it are found the so-called Gathas, hymns attributed to Zoroaster himself. For hundreds of years, until the year 637, Zoroastrianism was the national religion of Persia. Then Islam conquered the country and everybody had to become a Mohammedan. Those loyal to Zoroastrianism fled to India and constituted themselves as the sect of the Parsees.

The exact time when Zoroaster lived is not definitely established. He spent many years in the wilderness, then began to preach to the people when he was about 30 years old. Zoroaster believed that in the world of nature and of history there was a tug of war going on between two gods—a good god Ormuzd and an evil god Ahriman. He stated that he had been sent to lead people to salvation. He taught that there is a life after death, in which the good people will be rewarded and the bad people punished. Zoroaster converted a prince to his religion, and the prince helped him spread it. The prince's name was Vishtasha. If he was the father of Darius I of Persia (521–485) a 6th century date for Zoroaster would be assured. But this is still uncertain. Zoroaster was supposedly killed in a religious war when he was about 77 years old.

Through the centuries the religion of Zoroaster spread through the countries of the Middle East. Gradually the belief grew up that the world would end three thousand years after Zoroaster's death. Friedrich Nietzsche, a German writer, wrote a book called *Thus Spake Zarathustra*, using the figure of this Aryan prophet to preach his own philosophy. Richard Strauss, a German composer, wrote a musical composition based on Nietzsche's work and gave it the same title (in German, *Also Sprach Zarathustra*).

Zuider Zee

The Zuider Zee, which in the Dutch language means "Southern Sea," was once a gulf of the North Sea, partly cut off from the North Sea by the Frisian Islands, which stretch around its mouth. The Zuider Zee cut into the north central part of the Netherlands. It was more than 85 miles long and about 45 miles wide at its widest point, and it covered an area of more than 2,000 square miles. Amsterdam, one of the capitals of the Netherlands, was a port on the Zuider Zee.

The water of the Zuider Zee was too shallow for large ships, and for many years the Netherlands government planned to drain parts of it and use the land for farming. In 1932 a 20-mile-long dam was completed across the northern part of the Zuider Zee, cutting it off completely from the sea. This dam is 44 feet high and at water level it stretches over a distance of 285 miles. There is a roadway on top of the dam that has become important for transportation. The building of the dam created an artificial lake that is called IJsselmeer. Half of the dammed-up area has been drained, adding more than 900 square miles of farmlands to the Netherlands. The drained areas are called *polders*.

Zulus

The Zulus are a people of the Negro race who live in South Africa, mostly in Zululand, the Orange Free State, and Transvaal. They are a Bantu people and speak the Bantu language. These people are well-built and strong, and of medium height. They have brown skins and black curly hair. The rules of their society are very old and have changed very little in the past centuries. Most of the Zulus are farmers, and they raise a great many cattle. They live in clans, or small communities, and build hive-shaped huts around a circular area in which the cattle are kept.

In the 1800s the Zulus were very warlike. They conquered many of the other Negro tribes in the region, fought the Europeans who tried to subdue them, and even fought among themselves. They have remained the most powerful of the African tribes in South Africa and have resisted most European influences.

Zurich

Zurich is the largest city in Switzerland. It is in northern Switzerland, on the Limmat River at the northern end of the Lake of Zurich. About 432,000 people live in Zurich, and many other people visit the city each year to study at the universities and to enjoy the beautiful scenery.

Zurich was ruled by the Romans more than two thousand years ago. Through the centuries it was controlled by other rulers until, in 1218, it became a free city. It became a part of Switzerland about six hundred years ago. Part of the city is new, with modern buildings and beautiful homes, and part is very old and has museums and churches that have been there for hundreds of years. The two most famous churches are the Grossmünster, built about seven hundred years ago, and the Fraumünster, built about five hundred years ago.

In the 1500s Zurich became the center of the Reformation movement in which the first Protestant Churches were formed. In modern times the city has become an important scientific and educational center, as well as the most important manufacturing city in Switzerland for machinery and textiles and the center of the Swiss printing and publishing business. The University of Zurich and the Federal Polytechnic School are in Zurich.

ZURICH, SWITZERLAND. Population (1974 census) 432,400. Capital of the canton of Zurich in Switzerland.

Zwingli, Huldrech

Huldrech Zwingli was a Swiss religious reformer who lived about 450 years ago. His first name is also spelled Ulrich. He was first a priest of the Roman Catholic Church but left the Catholic Church with many of his followers to start a Protestant group in Switzerland.

Zwingli was born in Switzerland in 1484. He studied at universities at Vienna and Basel, and in 1506 he was ordained a priest. He became a forceful preacher. He opposed many Catholic practices, such as fasting during Lent and the custom of not allowing priests to marry. He also preached against the political power of the Pope. He taught that the Bible should be the chief guide of religious faith.

Many people disliked Zwingli's ideas and he was forced to leave the church where he was pastor, but in 1519 he was asked to become "priest of the people" at Zurich. In this position he was heard by many people. Zwingli supported Martin Luther, the German Protestant leader, and in 1523 he broke with the Catholic Church.

Switzerland was soon divided between Catholics and followers of Zwingli. In 1529 and 1531 there were battles between the Catholics and Protestants. Zwingli fought with his followers, and was killed in 1531. Zwingli's work was the foundation on which John Calvin later built the Calvinist religion, which became the Protestant faith of most Swiss and grew into the Presbyterian Church in other countries.

Zworykin, Vladimir

Vladimir Kosma Zworykin is an electrical engineer and physicist, often called the "father of television" because he invented two of its most important parts, the iconoscope and the kinescope. He was born in Russia in 1889. When he was 30 years old he came to the United States. He developed the iconoscope (the transmitting tube in the television camera) in 1923, and a year later he developed the kinescope, or "picture tube" in the television receiving set. Later he invented a device with which infrared light rays can be seen, and this was used in the "snooperscope" with which soldiers in World War II could see a target in the dark. He also invented an early form of the "electric eye" and helped to develop the electron microscope.

GUIDE TO PRONUNCIATION

In the following pages are listed, in alphabetical order, the names and words used in the Encyclopedia that the reader may have difficulty in pronouncing correctly.

The pronunciation of each name or word is shown in two ways. The first way follows the distinctive method of diacritical marks ("accents") used by the National Lexicographic Board in all its dictionaries and other reference books. *This is by far the more accurate way* and the reader is urged to take the time to learn the pronunciation marks and follow that method. But each name or word is also spelled in such a way as to indicate pronunciation to those who have not learned the method of diacritical marks. In the second respelling of each name or word, each syllable or word should be read in the way in which it is usually pronounced. Each stressed syllable is spelled in capital letters. Whenever possible, a syllable is shown as a common word, for example EYE to mean *i* as in *light*.

GUIDE TO PRONUNCIATION

a	as in fat	**û**	as in pull	**ngg**	as in finger
ā	as in fate	**ə**	as in comma,	**nk**	as in ink (pro-
ä	as in far		label,		nounced
â	as in fall		pupil,		*ingk*)
à	as in ask		censor,	**p**	as in pen
ã	as in dare		focus	**r**	as in rat
e	as in met	**b**	as in but	**s**	as in sit, this
ē	as in mete	**ch**	as in chair	**sh**	as in she
ẽ	as in her	**d**	as in day	**t**	as in to
ė	as in maybe	**f**	as in fill	**th**	as in thin
i	as in pin	**g**	as in go	***th***	as in then
ī	as in pine	**h**	as in hat	**v**	as in van
o	as in not	**hw**	as in when	**w**	as in win
ō	as in note	**j**	as in joke	**y**	as in yet
oo	as in spoon	**k**	as in keep	**z**	as in zone, quiz
ô	as in or	**kt**	as in act	**zh**	as in azure
oi	as in oil	**l**	as in late	**ö**	as in Ger. *schön*
ow	as in owl	**m**	as in man	**ü**	as in Fr. *tu*
u	as in tub	**n**	as in nod	**ṅ**	as in Fr. *bon*
ū	as in mute	**ng**	as in sing	**kh**	as in blockhouse

The symbol ə (an upside-down e, called a schwa) is used for any unaccented vowel sound. In the second respelling, this sound is represented by *uh*.

Aa (ä) AH
Aachen (ä'kən) AH'kun
Aalsmeer (äls'mer) AHLCE-mare
Aar (är) AHR
Aaron (âr'ən) AIR-un
Abaco (ab'ə-kō") AB-uh-ko
Abadan (ab"ə-dan') ab-uh-DAN
Abbeville (äb"vē'ə) ob-VEE-uh
Abbey (ab'ė) AB-ee
Abd-el-Krim (ab'dəl-krim') AB-dul-KRIM
Abdul Kadir (ab'dəl kə-dir') AB-dul kuh-DEER
Abednego (ə-bed'ni-gō") uh-BED-nih-goh
Abel (ā'bəl) A-bul
Abelard (ab'ə-lärd") AB-uh-lard
Aberdeen (ab'ər-dēn") AB-er-deen
Abilene (ab'ə-lēn") AB-uh-leen
Abnaki (ab-nä'kė) ab-NAH-kee
Aboukir (ab"û-kir') ab-uh-KEER
Abraham (ā'brə-ham") A-bruh-ham
Abrantes (ə-bran'tėz) uh-BRAN-teez
Absalom (ab'sə-ləm) AB-suh-lum
Absaroka (ab"sə-rō'kə) ab-suh-RO-kuh
Absecon (ab-sē'kən) ab-SEE-kun
Abu Bakr (ə-boo' bak'ər) uh-BOO BACK-er
Abydos (ə-bī'dəs) uh-BY-dus
Abyssinia (ab"ə-sin'ė-ə) ab-uh-SIN-ee-uh
Academus (ak"ə-dē'məs) ack-uh-DEE-mus
Acadia (ə-kā'dė-ə) uh-KAY-dee-uh
Accra (ə-krä'; ak'rə) uh-KRAH *or* ACK-ruh
Aceldama (ə-sel'də-mə) uh-SELL-duh-muh
Achaea (ə-kē'ə) uh-KEE-uh
Acheron (ak'ər-on") ACK-uh-ron
Achilles (ə-kil'ėz) uh-KILL-eez
Aconcagua (ak"ən-käg'wə) ack-un-KAHG-wuh
Acre (ā'kər *or* ä'kər) A-ker *or* AH-ker
Acrisius (ə-kris'ė-əs) uh-KRISS-ee-us
Actium (ak'shė-əm) ACK-shee-um
Adam (ad'əm) AD-um
Adams (ad'əmz) AD-umz
Adana (ä'dä-nä) AH-dah-nah
Addams (ad'əmz) AD-umz
Addis Ababa (ad'is-ab'ə-bə) AD-is AB-uh-buh
Addison (ad'i-sən) AD-uh-sun
Ade (ād) AID
Adelaide (ad'ə-lād") AD-uh-layd
Aden (ā'dən; ä'dən) AY-dun *or* AH-dun
Adenaur (äd'ə-now"ər) AHD-uh-now-er
Adige (ä'dė-je) AH-dee-jeh
Adirondacks (ad"i-ron'daks) AD-ih-RAHN-dacks
Adler (od'lər; ad'lər) ODD-ler *or* AD-ler
Admiralty (ad'mi-rəl-tė) AD-mih-rul-tee
Adonai (ad"ə-nā'ė) ad-uh-NAY-ee
Adonis (ə-dōn'is) uh-DOHN-iss
Adrianople (ā"drė-ə-nō'pəl) ay-dree-uh-NO-pul
Adriatic (ā"drė-at'ik) ay-dree-AT-ik
Adventists (ad-ven'tists) ad-VEN-tists
Aegean (i-jē'ən) ih-JEE-uhn
Aegeus (ė'jəs) EE-jus
Aegisthus (i-jis'thəs) ih-JIS-thus
Aegyptus (ė-jip'təs) ee-JIP-tus
Aeneas (i-nē'əs) ih-NEE-us
Aeneid (i-nē'id) ih-NEE-id
Aeolian (ė-ō'lė-ən) ee-OH-lee-un
Aeolic (ė-ō'lik) ee-OH-lick
Aeolus (ē'ə-ləs) EE-uh-lus
Aeschylus (es'kə-ləs) ESK-uh-lus
Aeson (ē'sən) EE-sun
Aesculapius (es"kū-lā'pė-əs) ess-kyoo-LAY-pee-us
Aesop (ē'sop) EE-sop
Aesthetics (es-thet'iks) es-THET-icks
Aetius (ā-ē'shəs) ay-EE-shus
Afghan (af'gan) AF-gan
Afghanistan (af-gan'i-stan) af-GAN-ih-stan
Africa (af'ri-kə) AF-rih-kuh
Afrikaaner (af"ri-kan'ər) af-rih-KAN-er
Afrikaans (af'ri-känz) AF-rih-kahnz
Aga Khan (ä'gə-kän') AH-guh-KAHN
Agamemnon (ag"ə-mem'non) ag-uh-MEM-non
Agaña (ä-gä'nyä) ah-GAH-nyah
Agassiz (ag'ə-sė) AG-uh-see
Agincourt (à'zhan-koor) AH-zhan-koor
Agis (ā'jis) AY-jis
Aglaia (ə-glā'ə) uh-GLAY-uh
Agra (ag'rə *or* äg'rə) AG-ruh *or* OG-ruh
Agricola (ä-grē'kə-lä) ah-GREE-koh-lah
Agrigentum (ag"ri-jen'təm) ag-rih-JEN-tum
Agrippa (ə-grip'ə) uh-GRIP-uh
Agrippina (ag"ri-pī'nə) ag-rih-PINE-uh
Aguinaldo (ä"gė-näl'dō) ah-ghee-NAHL-doh
Agusan (ä-goo'sän) ah-GOO-sahn
Ahab (ā'hab) AY-hab
Ahasuerus (ə-haz"yû-er'əs) uh-haz-yoo-AIR-us
Ahriman (ä'ri-mən) AH-rih-mun
Aida (ä-ē'də) ah-EE-duh
Aidan (ī'dan) EYE-dan
Ain (aṅ) AN
Ainu (ī'noo) EYE-noo
Aire (er) AIR
Airedale (er'dāl") AIR-dayl
Aisne (ān) ANE
Aix-les-Bains (eks"lā-baṅ') ecks-lay-BAN
Aix-en-Provence (eks'än-prō-voṅs') ECKS-ahn-proh-VAHNCE
Aix-la-Chapelle (eks"lä-shä-pel') ecks-lah-shah-PEL
Ajaccio (ä-yät'chə) ah-YAHT-chuh
Ajax (ā'jaks) A-jacks
Akkad (ak'ad) AK-ad
Alamo (al'ə-mō) AL-uh-moh
Aland (ō'län) OH'lahn
Alarcón (ä-lär-kōn') ah-lahr-KOHN
Alaric (al'ə-rik) AL-uh-rick
Alava (ä'lä-vä) AH-lah-vah
Albania (al-bān'yə) al-BANE-yuh
Albany (âl'bə-nė) AWL-buh-nee
Albéniz (äl-bā'nith) ahl-BAY-nith
Alberich (äl'bə-rikh) AHL-buh-rik
Albemarle (al'bə-märl") AL-buh-marl
Alberta (al-bẽr'tə) al-BERT-tuh
Albertus Magnus (al-bẽr'təs mag'nəs) al-BER-tus MAG-nus
Albion (al'bė-ən) AL-bee-un
Albuquerque (al'bə-kẽr"kė) AL-buh-KER-kee
Alcatraz (al'kə-traz") AL-kuh-traz
Alcibiades (al"si-bī'ə-dėz) al-sih-BY-uh-deez
Alcmene (alk-mē'nė) alck-MEE-nee
Alcock (âl'kok) AWL-kock
Alcott (âl'kot) AWL-kot
Aldebaran (al-deb'ə-rən) al-DEB-uh-run
Alden (âl'dən) AWL-dun
Alderney (âl'dər-nė) AWL-der-nee
Aldershot (âl'dər-shot") AWL-der-shot
Aldrich (âl'drich) AWL-dritch
Alemanni (al-i-man'ė) al-ih-MAN-ee
Aleppo (ə-lep'ō) uh-LEP-oh
Aleutians (ə-lū'shənz) uh-LOO-shunz
Aleuts (al'ė-ootz) AL-ee-ootz
Alexander (al"ig-zan'dər) al-ig-ZAN-der
Alexandria (al"ig-zan'drė-ə) al-ig-ZAN-dree-uh
Alexandrovsk (al"ik-san'drofsk) al-ick-SAN-drofsk
Alfara (äl-fä'rō) ahl-FAH-roh
Alfonso (âl-fon'sō) al-FON-soh
Alger (al'jər) AL-jer
Algeria (al-jir'ė-ə) al-JEER-ee-uh
Algiers (al-jirz') al-JEERS
Algonkin (al-gon'kin) al-GAHN-kin
Algonquin (al-gon'kin *or* al-gon'kwin) al-GAHN-kin *or* al-GAHN-kwin
Alhambra (al-ham'brə) al-HAM-bruh
Ali Baba (al'i-bab'ə) AL-ih-BAB-uh
Alki (äl'kė) AHL-kee
Allah (al'ə *or* äl'ə) AL-uh *or* AHL-uh
Allahabad (al"ə-hə-bad') al-uh-huh-BAD
Allegheny (al"ə-gā'nė) al-uh-GAY-nee
Allerton (al'ər-tən) AL-er-tun
Alliance (ə-lī'əns) uh-LY-uns
Allston (âl'stən) AWL-stun
Almagest (al'mə-jest") AL-muh-jest
Almagro (äl-mä'grō) ahl-MAH-groh
Almendral (äl-mən-dräl') ahl-mun-DRAHL
Almeria (äl-mə-rē'ə) ahl-muh-REE-uh
Aloha Oe (ä-lō'hä ō'ā) ah-LOH-hah OH-ay
Alp Arslan (älp ärs-län') AHLP ahrs-LAHN
Alpha Centauri (al'fə sen-tôr'ī) AL-fuh sen-TORE-eye
Alpha Cephei (al'fə sef'ė-ī) AL-fuh SEF-ee-eye
Alpha Piscium (al'fə pis'ė-əm) AL-fuh PIH-see-um
Alps (alps) ALPS
Alsace Lorraine (al'sas lə-rān') AL-sass luh-RAIN
Alsatians (al-sā'shənz) al-SAY-shunz
Alster (âl'stər) AWL-ster
Alt (ält) AHLT
Altai (al-tī') al-TY
Altamaha (âl"tə-mə-hâ') awl-tuh-muh-HAW
Altamira (äl"tä-mē'rä) awl-tah-MEE-rah
Altdorf (ält'dôrf) AHLT-dorf
Althing (äl'thing) AHL-thing
Altiplano (äl"ti-plän'ō) ahl-tih-PLAHN-oh
Alton (âl'tən) AWL-tun
Alvarado (äl"və-rä'*th*ō) ahl-vuh-RAH-though
Amager (am'ə-gər) AM-uh-ger
Amalekites (ə-mal'i-kits) uh-MAL-uh-kites
Amami-Gunto (ä-mä'mė goon'tō) ah-MAH-mee GOON-toh
Amanullah (ä"mən-ul'ə) ah-mun-UL-uh
Amargosa (am"är-gō'sə) am-ahr-GOH-suh
Amati (ä-mä'tė) ah-MAH-tee
Amazon (am'ə-zon) AM-uh-zahn
Amboina (am-boi'nə) am-BOY-nuh
Amenhotep (ä"men-hō'tep) ah-muhn-HOH-tep
Amenophis (am"ə-nō'fis) am-uh-NOH-fiss
Amerigo Vespucci (am"ə-rē'gō ves-poo'chė) am-uh-REE-goh ves-POO-chee
Ames (āmz) AIMS
Amharic (am-här'ik) am-HAIR-ick
Amherst (am'hẽrst) AM-herst
Amiens (ä-myaṅ') ah-MYAN
Amish (am'ish *or* ä'mish) AM-ish *or* AH-mish
Amman (äm'män) AHM-mahn
Ammon (am'ən) AM-un
Amon-Ra (ä'mən-rä') AH-mun-RAH
Amontillado (ə-mon"ti-yä'dō) uh-mahn-tih-YAH-doh
Amor (ā'môr) A-more
Amorites (am'ə-rits) AM-uh-rites
Amos (ā'məs) A-mus
Amoskeag (am-əs-keg') am-us-KEG
Amoy (ə-moi') uh-MOY
Ampère (äṅ-per') ahn-PAIR
Amphion (am-fī'ən) am-FY-uhn
Amphitrite (am"fi-trī'tė) am-fih-TRY-tee
Amritsar (əm-rit'sər) um-RIT-ser
Amstel (äm'stəl) AHM-stul
Amsterdam (am'stər-dam) AM-ster-dam
Amu Darya (ä'moo-där'yə) AH-moo-DAHR-yuh
Amundsen, (ä'mən-sən) AH-mun-sun
Amur (ä-moor') ah-MOOR
Anabasis (ə-nab'ə-sis) uh-NAB-uh-sis
Anacreon (ə-nak'rė-ən) uh-NACK-ree-un
Anak (ā'nak) AY-nack
Ananias (an"ə-nī'əs) an-uh-NY-us
Anatolia (an"ə-tōl'yə) an-uh-TOLE-yuh
Anchises (an-kī'sėz) an-KY-seez
Anchorage (ang'kə-rij) ANG-kuh-rij
Andalusia (an"də-loo'zha) an-duh-LOO-zhuh
Andersen (an'dər-sən) AN-der-sun
Anderson (an'dər-sən) AN-der-sun
Andes (an'dėz) AN-deez
Andorra (an-dôr'ə) an-DORE-uh
André (än'drā) AHN-dray
Andrew (an'droo) AN-droo
Androcles (an'drə-klėz) AN-druh-kleez
Andromeda (an-drom'i-də) an-DROM-ih-duh
Andros (an'drəs) AN-drus
Anegada (an"i-gä'də) AN-ih-GAH-duh
Angelico, Fra (an-jel'i-kō, frä) an-JEL-ih-koh, frah
Angelus (an'jə-ləs) AN-juh-lus
Angkor Wat (ang'kôr wät) ANG-kohr waht
Angles (ang'gəlz) ANG-gulz
Anglesey (ang'gəl-sė) ANG-gul-see
Anglican Church (ang'gli-kən) ANG-glih-kun
Angola (ang-gō'lə) ang-GOH-luh
Angora (ang-gôr'ə) ang-GORE-uh
Ankara (ang'kə-rə) ANG-kuh-ruh
Annam (an-nam') an-NAM
Annamese (an"ə-mēz') an-uh-MEEZ
Annapolis (ə-nap'ə-lis) uh-NAP-uh-liss
Annapurna (ä"nə-pûr'nə) ah-nuh-POOR-nuh
Annas (an'as) AN-ass
Anne Arundel (an'ə-run'dəl) AN-uh-RUN-dul
Annie Laurie (an'ė lôr'ė) AN-ee LORE-ee
Annunciation (ə-nun"sė-ā'shən) uh-nun-see-AY-shun
Anrac (an'rak) AN-rack
Anschluss (än'schlûs) AHN-schlus
Antalya (än-täl'yä) ahn-TAHL-yah
Antarctica (ant-ärk'ti-kə) ant-ARK-tih-kuh
Anthony (an'thə-nė) AN-thuh-nee
Antichrist (an'ti-krist") AN-TIH-CHRIST
Antietam (an-tē'təm) an-TEE-tum
Antigua (än-tē'gwä) ahn-TEE-gwah
Antilles (an-til'ėz) an-TIL-eez
Antinomian (an"ti-nō'mė-ən) an-tih-NOH-mee-un
Antioch (an'tė-ok") AN-tee-ock
Antiochus (an-tī'ə-kəs) an-TY-uh-kus
Antipope (an'ti-pōp") AN-tih-POPE
Antonescu (an"tə-nes'kū) an-tuh-NES-kyoo
Antony (an'tə-nė) AN-tuh-nee
Antsirabe (än"tsi-rä'bė) ahnt-sih-RAH-bee
Antwerp (ant'wərp) ANT-werp
Anzac (an'zak) AN-zack
Anzio (än'tsi-ō) AHNT-see-oh
Apache (ə-pach'ė) uh-PATCH-ee
Apalachee (ap"ə-lach'ė) ap-uh-LATCH-ee
Apennines (ap'ə-nīnz) AP-uh-nines
Aphrodite (af"rə-dī'tė) AF-ruh-DY-tee
Apia (ə-pī'ə) uh-PY-uh
Apo (ä'pō) AH-poh
Apocrypha (ə-pok'ri-fə) uh-POCK-rih-fuh
Apolima (ä"pə-lē'mä) ah-puh-LEE-mah
Apollo (ə-pol'ō) uh-POL-oh
Apostle (ə-pos'əl) uh-POS-ul
Appalachian (ap"ə-lā'chan) ap-uh-LAY-chun
Appassionata (ə-päs"ė-ə-nä'tə) uh-pahs-ee-uh-NAH-tuh
Apperson (ap'ər-sən) AP-er-sun
Appert (à-per') ah-PAIR
Appian (ap'ė-ən) AP-ee-un
Appius (ap'ė-əs) AP-ee-us
Appleby (ap'əl-bė) AP-ul-bee
Appomattox (ap"ə-mat'əks) ap-uh-MAT-ucks
Apra (ä'prä) AH-prah
Apsheron (up-shir-ân') up-sheer-AWN
Aquae Calidae (ak'wė kal'i-dė) ACK-wee KAL-uh-dee
Aquarius (ə-kwâr'ė-əs) uh-KWAIR-ee-us
Aquitaine (ak'wi-tān") AK-wih-tane
Arabia (ə-rā'bė-ə) uh-RAY-bee-uh
Arabic (ar'ə-bik) AR-uh-bick
Arab (ar'əb) AR-ub
Aragon (ar'ə-gon) AR-uh-gon
Aral (ar'əl *or* ä-räl') AR-ul *or* ah-RAHL
Aramaic (ar"ə-mā'ik) AR-uh-MAY-ick
Arapaho (ə-rap'ə-hō) uh-RAP-uh-hoh
Ararat (ar'ə-rat) AR-uh-rat
Araucanian (ar"ə-kā'nė-ən) ar-uh-KAY-nee-un
Arawak (är'ə-wäk) AHR-uh-wock
Arbuthnot (är-buth'nət) ahr-BUTH-nut
Arcadia (är-kā'dė-ə) ahr-KAY-dee-uh
Archaeozoic (är"kė-ə-zō'ik) ahr-kee-uh-ZOH-ick
Archangel (ärk-ān'jəl) ark-ANE-jul
Archimedes (är"kə-mē'dėz) ahr-kuh-MEE-deez
Arctica (ärk'ti-kə) ARK-tih-kuh
Arctic (ärk'tik) ARK-tick
Ardennes (är-den') ahr-DEN
Arequipa (ä-rə-kē'pä) ah-ruh-KEE-pah
Ares (ā'rėz) A-reez
Arethusa (ar-ə-thū'sə) ar-uh-THYOO-suh
Argentia (är-jen'shə) ahr-JEN-shuh
Argentina (är"jən-tē'nə) ahr-jun-TEE-nuh
Argo (är'gō) AHR-go
Argonaut (är'gə-nât) AHR-guh-nawt
Argonne (är-gon') ahr-GAHN
Argyll (är-gil') ahr-GUILE
Ariadne (ar-ė-ad'nė) ar-ee-AD-nee
Arians (ar'ė-ənz) AR-ee-unz
Aries (ā'rė-ėz) A-ree-eez
Ariosto (är"ė-os'tō) ahr-ee-OS-toh
Aristides (ar"əs-tī'dėz) ar-us-TY-deez
Aristophanes (ar"is-tof'ə-nėz) ar-iss-TAHF-uh-neez
Aristotle (ar'is-tot"əl) AR-iss-tot-ul
Arius (ə-rī'əs) uh-RY-us
Arkwright (ärk'rīt) ARK-rite
Arlanzón (är-län-thōn') ahr-lon-THONE
Arles (ärlz) ahrlz
Arlington (är'ling-tən) AHR-ling-tun
Armada (är-mä'də) ahr-MAH-duh
Armageddon (är"mə-ged'ən) ahr-muh-GED-un
Armagnac (är-män-yäk') ahr-mahn-YAHK
Armato (är-mät'ō) ahr-MAHT-oh
Armenia (är-mē'nė-ə) ahr-MEE-nee-uh
Arminius (är-min'ė-əs) ahr-MIN-ee-us
Armour (är'mər) AHR-mer
Arnold (ärn'əld) AHRN-uld
Arno (är'nō) AHR-no
Aroostock (ə-roos'tûk) uh-ROOS-took
Arouet (à-rwe') ahr-WEH
Arpad (är'päd) AHR-pahd
Arras (âr'əs *or* ä-räs') AIR-us *or* ah-RAHSS
Artaxerxes (är"təg-zẽrk'sėz) ahr-tug-ZERK-seez
Artedi (är-tā'dė) ahr-TAY-dee
Artemis (är'tə-mis) AHR-tuh-miss
Artemisia (är"tə-mish'yə) ahr-tuh-MISH-yuh
Arthurian (är-thyûr'ė-ən) ahr-THYUR-ee-un
Artibonite (är-tē'bō-net') ahr-TEE-boh-NET
Aruba (ä-roo'bä) ah-ROO-bah
Arunta (ə-run'tə) uh-RUN-tuh
Aruru (ä-roo'roo) ah-ROO-roo
Aryan (ar'ė-ən) AR-ee-un
Asbury (az'ber-ė) AS-behr-ee
Asclepiades (as"klė-pī'ə-dėz) as-klee-PY-uh-deez
Asclepius (es-klē'pė-əs) es-KLEE-pee-us
Asgard (as'gärd) AS-gard
Ashenfelter (ash"ən-fel'tər) ASH-un-FELL-ter
Asheville (ash'vil) ASH-vil
Ashland (ash'lənd) ASH-lund
Ashley (ash'lė) ASH-lee
Ashmolean (ash-mōl'ė-ən) ash-MOH-lee-un
Ashokan (ə-shō'kən) uh-SHOH-kun
Asia (ā'zhə) A-zhuh
Asmara (äs-mä'rä) ahs-MAH-rah
Aspasia (as-pā'zhė-ə) ass-PAY-zhee-uh
Aspdin (asp'din) ASP-din
Aspen (as'pən) ASS-pun
Assam (as-sam') as-SAM
Assiniboin, Assiniboine (ə-sin'i-boin") uh-SIN-ih-boyn
Assisi (ä-sē'sė) ah-SEE-see
Assmannshausen (äs-mäns-how'zən) oss-monce-HOW-zun
Assouan, Assuan (äs-swän') ahs-SWAHN
Assumption (ə-sump'shən) uh-SUMP-shun
Assur (as'soor) AS-soor
Assyria (ə-sir'ė-ə) uh-SIH-ree-uh
Astley (ast'lė) AST-lee
Aston (as'tən) AS-tun
Astor (as'tər) AS-ter
Astoria (as-tôr'ė-ə) as-TORE-ee-uh
Astrakhan (as'trə-khən) AS-truh-kun
Asturias (äs-tûr'ė-əs) ahs-TOOR-ee-us
Asunción (ä-soon-syon') ah-soonce-YON
Aswan (äs-wän') ahs-WAHN
Atahualpa (ä"tä-wäl'pä) ah-tah-WAHL-pah
Atalanta (at"ə-lan'tə) at-uh-LAN-tuh
Atger (at'gər) AT-ger
Athabaska (ath"ə-bas'kə) ath-uh-BAS-kuh
Athanasian (ath"ə-nā'zhən) ath-uh-NAY-zhun
Athapascan (ath"ə-pas'kən) ath-uh-PASS-kun
Atharva-Veda (at-här"vä-vā'də) at-HAHR-vuh-VAY-duh
Athena (ə-thē'nə) uh-THEE-nuh
Athenaeum (ath"ə-nē'əm) ath-uh-NEE-um
Athenian (ə-thē'nė-ən) uh-THEE-nee-un
Athens (ath'ənz) ATH-unz
Atherton (ath'ər-tən) ATH-er-tun
Athos (ath'os) ATH-os
Atitlán (ä"tė-tlän') ah-teet LAHN
Atlanta (at-lan'tə) at-LAN-tuh
Atlantic (at-lan'tik) at-LAN-tick
Atlantis (at-lan'tis) at-LAN-tis
Atlas (at'ləs) AT-lus
Atropos (at'rō-pos) AT-roh-poss
Attic (at'ik) AT-ick
Attica (at'i-kə) AT-ih-kuh
Attila (at'i-lə) AT-ih-luh
Attlee (at'lė) AT-lee
Attu (at'too') AT-TOO
Atuona (ä-twō'nə) ah-TWOH-nuh
Aubusson (ō"bû"säṅ') oh-buh-SAWN
Auchinleck (ʼkhin-lek") AW-kin-leck
Auckland (âk'lənd) AWK-lund
Audubon (âd'yû-bən) AWD-yoo-bun
Augean (â'jė-ən *or* â-jē'ən) AW-jee-un *or* aw-JEE-un
Augeus (â'jė-əs *or* â-jē'əs) AW-jee-us *or* aw-JEE-us
Aughrabies (ō-grä'bėz) oh-GRAH-beez
Augsburg (ogz'bẽrg) OGZ-berg
Augusta (ə-gus'tə) uh-GUS-tuh
Auguste (ow-goos'te) ow-GOOSE-teh
Augustine (â'gus-tēn) AW-gus-teen
Augustus (ə-gus'təs) uh-GUS-tus
Aulanko (ow'läng-kō) OW-lahng-koh
Aunuu (ow-noo'oo) ow-NOO-oo
Aurora (ə-rôr'ə) uh-RORE-uh
Auschwitz (owsh'vitz) OWSH-vitz
Austen (âs'tən) AWS-tun
Austerlitz (âs'tər-litz *or* ows'tər-litz) AWS-ter-litz *or* OWS-ter-litz
Austin (âs'tən) AWS-tun
Australia (âs-trā'lyə) aws-TRAIL-yuh
Australoid (âs'trə-loid") AWS-truh-loyd
Austria (âs'trė-ə) AWS-tree-uh
Avallaneda (ä"vel-yä-ne'dä) ah-vel-yah-NEH-dah
Avalon (av"ə-lon) AV-uh-lon
Aventine (av'ən-tin) AV-un-tin
Avery (ā'və-rė) AY-vuh-ree
Avignon (ä-vė-nyoṅ') ah-veen-YON
Avila (ə-vē'lä) uh-VEEL-ah
Aviles (ä-vē'les) ah-VEE-less
Avogadro (ä"vō-gäd'rō) ah-voh-GAHD-roh
Avon (ā'vən) A-vun
Axminster (aks'min-stər) ACKS-min-ster
Axson (ak'sən) ACK-sun
Ayers (erz) AIRZ
Aymara (ī"mä-rä') eye-mah-RAH
Ayutthaya (ə-yût'tə-yä) uh-YOOT-tuh-yah
Azalea (ə-zāl'yə) uh-ZAYL-yuh
Azaña (ä-thä'nyä) ah-THAHN-yah
Azerbaijan (ä-zər-bī-jän') ah-zer-by-JAHN
Azhar (ä-zhär') (ah-ZHAR)
Azores (ə-zôrz') uh-ZORZE
Azov (ä-zof') ah-ZOFF
Aztec (az'tek) AZ-teck

Baal (bā'əl) BAY-ul
Baalbek (bäl'bek) BAHL-beck
Babbitt (bab'it) BAB-it
Babcock (bab'kok) BAB-kock
Babel (bā'bəl) BAY-bul
Babylon (bab'ə-lon") BAB-uh-lahn
Babylonia (bab"ə-lō'nė-ə) bab-uh-LOH nee-uh
Bacchanales (bak"ə-nā'lėz) back-uh-NAY-leez
Bacchus (bak'əs) BACK-us

Bach (bäkh) BAHK
Baden-Baden (bä'dən-bä·dən) BAH-dun-bah-dun
Baden-Powell (bā'dən pō'əl) BAY-dun POH-ul
Baedeker (bā'də·kər) BAY-duh-ker
Baekeland (bāk'lənd) BAKE-lund
Baffin (baf'in) BAF-in
Baghdad (bag'dad) BAG-dad
Baguio (bag'ē·ō') BAG-ee-oh
Baguli (bä'gûl·ē) BAH-guh-lee
Baha (ba·hä') ba-HAH
Bahaism (bə·hä'iz·əm) buh-HAH-iz-um
Baha Ullah (bä·hä' ûl·lä') bah-HAH ul-LAH
Bahá'i (bə·hä'ē) buh-HAH-ee
Bahamas (bə·hā·məz *or* bə·hä'məz) buh-HAY-muhz *or* buh-HAH-muhz
Bahrein (bä'rān') BAH-RAIN
Baikal (bī·käl') by-KAHL
Bailey (bā'lē) BAY-lee
Baja (bä'hä) BAH-hah
Bajazet (baj·ə·zet') baj-uh-ZET
Baku (bä·koo') bah-KOO
Bala (bä'lä) BAH-lah
Balaam (bā'ləm) BAY-lum
Balaclava (bä"lə·klä'və) bah-luh-KLAH-vuh
Balaton (bä'lə·ton) BAH-luh-ton
Balboa (bal·bō'ə) bal-BOH-uh
Balder (bâl'dər) BAWL-der
Baldwin (bâl'dwin) BALD-win
Balearic (bal"ē·ar'ik) bal-ee-AR-ik
Balfour (bal'fûr) BAL-foor
Bali (bä'lē) BAH-lee
Balkan (bâl'kən) BAWL-kun
Balkash (bäl·käsh') bahl-KAHSH
Balliol (bal'ē·əl) BAL-ee-ul
Balmoral Castle (bal·mor'əl) bal-MAHR-ul
Balsam (bâl'səm) BAWL-sum
Balsamo (bäl'sä·mō) BAHL-sah-moh
Balthasar (bal·thā'zər) bal-THAY-zer
Baltic (bâl'tik) BAWL-tick
Baltimore (bâl'ti·môr) BAWL-tih-more
Baluchi (bə·loo'chē) buh-LOO-chee
Baluchistan (bə·loo'chi·stän") buh-LOO-chih-stahn
Balzac (bäl·zäk') bol-ZAHK
Bamberg (bam'bērg) BAM-berg
Bambi (bam'bē) BAM-bee
Banat (bä·nät') bah-NAHT
Bancroft (ban'kroft) BAN-kroft
Banda (bän'dä) BAHN-dah
Banditanz (bän'dəl·tänts) BAHN-dul-tahnts
Bandung (bän'dûng) BAHN-doong
Banff (banf) BANF
Bangkok (bang'kok) BANG-kock
Bangor (ban'gôr) BAN-gore
Baniyas (bä·nē·as') bah-nee-ASS
Bankhead (bank'hed) BANK-hed
Bannister (ban'i·stər) BAN-ih-ster
Bannockburn (ban'ək·bərn) BAN-uk-bern
Banock (ban'ək) BAN-uk
Bantu (ban'too) BAN-too
Bao Dai (bow·dī') bow-DIE
Baptist (bap'tist) BAP-tist
Barabbas (bə·rab'əs) buh-RAB-us
Barada (bä·rä'dä) bah-RAH-dah
Baranoff (bar'ə·nof *or* bä·rä'nof) BAR-uh-nof *or* bah-RAH-nof
Barba (bär'vä) BAR-vah
Barbados (bär·bā'dōz) bahr-BAY-doze
Barbarossa (bär"bə·ros'ə) bar-buh-ROSS-uh
Barbary (bär'bə·rē) BAR-buh-ree
Barbier (bär·bē·ā') bar-bee-A
Barbizon (bär'bi·zon") BAR-bih-zon
Barcelona (bär"si·lō'nə) bar-sih-LOH-nuh
Barents (bar'əntz *or* bä·rentz') BA-rentz *or* bah-RENTZ
Barisan (bä·rē·sän') bah-ree-SAHN
Barkley (bärk'lē) BARK-lee
Barlow (bär'lō) BAR-loh
Barnabas (bär'nə·bəs) BAR-nuh-bus
Barnard (bär'nərd) BAR-nerd
Barnato (bär·nä'tō) bar-NAH-toh
Barnum (bär'nəm) BAR-num
Barquisimeto (bär"kē·sē·mā'tō) bar-kee-see-MAY-toh
Barranquilla (bär"rän·kē'yä) bar-rahn-KEE-yah
Barras (bä·räs') bah-RAHSS
Barre (ber'ē) BARE-ee
Barré (bä·rā') bah-RAY
Barre des Ecrins (bär·dā·zā·krē') bar-day-zay-KREE
Barrett (bar'it) BA-rit
Barrie (bar'ē) BA-ree
Barrios (bä'rē·ōs) BAH-ree-ohce
Barron (bar'ən) BA-run
Barrowdale (bar'ō·dāl") BA-roe-dale
Barrow (bar'ō) BA-roh
Barry (bar'ē) BA-ree
Barrymore (bar'i·mōr) BA-rih-more
Bartholdi (bär·tol·dē') bar-tahl-DEE
Bartholomew (bär·thol'ə·mū) bahr-THOL-uh-myoo
Bartolommeo (bär"tə·lə·mā'ō) bar-tuh-luh-MAY-oh
Barton (bär'tən) BAR-tun
Baruch—prophet (bär'ook) BAR-ook
Baruch, Bernard (bə·rûk) buh-ROOK
Bascio (bä'shə) BAH-shuh
Basel (bä'zəl) BAH-zul
Basque (bask) BASK *or* BOSK
Basra (baz'rə) BAZ-ruh
Bas-Rhin (bä·ran') bah-RAN
Bass (bas) BASS
Basse-Terre (bäs·ter') bahs-TEHR
Bastille (bas·tēl') bass-TEEL
Bataan (bä·tän') bah-TAHN
Batavia (bə·tā'vē·ə) buh-TAY-vee-uh
Bates (bātz) BAYTZ
Bath (bäth) BATH
Bathsheba (bath·shē'bə) bath-SHEE-buh
Bathurst (bath'ərst) BATH-erst
Batista (bä·tēs'tə) bah-TEES-tuh
Baton Rouge (bat"ən·rooj') BAT-un-ROOJ
Batum (bä·toom') bah-TOOM
Baudelaire (bōd·lār') bohd-LEHR
Baudouin (bō·dwan') boh-DWAN
Baum (bowm) BOWM
Bausch (bowsh) BOWSH
Bavaria (bə·vār'ē·ə) buh-VEHR-ee-uh
Bayard (bä·yär') ba-YAHR
Bayer (bī'ēr) BY-er
Bayeux (bä·yü') bah-YOO
Baylor (bā'lər) BAY-ler
Bayonne (bā'yōn) BAY-yohn
Bayreuth (bī·roit') by-ROYT
Beacon (bē'kən) BEE-kun
Beaconsfield (bē'kənz·fēld") BEE-kunz-feeld
Beagle (bē'gəl) BEE-gul
Beatitudes (bē·at'i·toodz) bee-AT-ih-toodz
Beatrice (bā"ä·trē'che) bay-ah-TREE-cheh
Beatriz, Doña (bā"ä·trēs', dō'nyə) bay-ah-TREECE, DOHN-yuh
Beatty (bē'tē) BEE-tee
Beauchamp (bō'shän) BOH-shahn
Beaufort (bō'fərt *or* byoo'fərt) BOH-fert *or* BYOO-fert
Beauharnais (bō·här·nā') boh-hahr-NAY
Beaumarchais (bō·mär·shā') boh-mahr-SHAY
Beaumont (bō'mont) BOH-mahnt (in French, boh-MAWN)
Beauregard (bō·re·gär') boh-reh-GAHR
Beauvais (bō·ve') boh-VEH
Bechet (be·shā') beh-SHAY
Bechuanaland (bech"û·ä'nə·land) BETCH-yoo-AH-nuh-land
Becket (bek'et) BECK-et
Becquerel (bek·rel') beck-REL
Bede (bēd) BEED
Bedivere (bed'i·vir) BED-ih-vihr
Bedlington (bed'ling·tən) BED-ling-tun
Bedloe (bed'lō) BED-loh
Bedouin (bed'oo·in) BED-oo-in
Beebe (bē'bē) BEE-bee
Beecher (bē'chər) BEE-cher
Beelzebub (bē·el'za·bub) bee-EL-zuh-bub
Beeman (bē'mən) BEE-mun
Beersheba (bir·shē'bə) bihr-SHEE-buh
Beethoven (bā'tō·ven) BAY-toh-ven
Beghards (beg'ərdz *or* bə·gärdz') BEG-erdz *or* buh-GAHRDZ
Behaim (bā'hīm) BAY-hime
Behistun (bā·his·toon') bah-his-TOON
Beiderbecke (bī'dər·bek) BY-der-beck
Beirut (bā"root') bay-ROOT
Bel (bel) BEL
Belasco (bə·las'kō) buh-LASS-koh
Belfast (bel'fäst) BEL-fast
Belgian (bel'jən) BEL-jun
Belgium (bel'jəm) BEL-jum
Belgrade (bel'grād) BEL-grade
Belisarius (bel"i·sā'rē·əs) bel-ih-SAY-ree-us
Belize (be·lēz') beh-LEEZ
Bellacoola (bel"ə·koo'lə) bel-uh-KOO-luh
Bellerophon (bə·ler'ə·fon") buh-LEHR-uh-fon
Bellevue (bel'vū) BEL-view
Bellini (bel·lē'nē) bel-LEE-nee
Bellows (bel'ōz) BEL-ohz
Beloit (bə·loit') buh-LOYT
Belsen (bel'zən) BEL-zun
Belshazzar (bel·shaz'ər) bel-SHAZ-er
Benadryl (ben'ə·dril) BEN-uh-dril
Benares (bə·nä'rəs) buh-NAH-rus
Benedict (ben'ə·dikt) BEN-uh-dickt
Benedictines (ben"ə·dik'tēnz) ben-uh-DICK-teenz
Benelux (ben'ə·luks) BEN-uh-lucks
Benes (be'nesh) BEH-nesh
Benét (be·nā') beh-NAY
Bengal (ben·gäl') ben-GAHL
Bengali (ben·gâ·lē') ben-gaw-LEE
Bengasi (ben·gä'zē) ben-GAH-zee
Beni-Israel (bā'nē·iz'rā·el) BAY-nee-IZ-ray-el
Benjamin (ben'jə·min) BEN-juh-min
Bennett (ben'ət) BEN-ut
Ben Kevis (ben kev'is) ben KEV-iss
Bennington (ben'ing·tən) BEN-ing-tun
Benton (ben'tən) BEN-tun
Benue (bān·wä') bayn-WAH
Benz (bentz) BENTZ
Beowulf (bā'ə·wûlf) BAY-uh-wolf
Berbers (bēr'bərz) BER-berz
Berbera (ber'bə·rä) BEHR-buh-rah
Berchtesgaden (berkh'təs·gädən) BEHRK-tus-GAH-dun
Berea (bə·rē'ə) buh-REE-uh
Berezina (be·re·zē·nä') beh-reh-zee-NAH
Bergen (bēr'gən *or* ber'gən) BER-gun *or* BEHR-gun
Berger (bēr'gər) BER-ger
Bergh (bērg) BERG
Beria (be'rē·yä) BEH-ree-yah
Bering (bā'rəng) BAY-rung
Berka (ber'kä) BEHR-kah
Berkeley (bērk'lē) BERK-lee
Berkshire (bērk'shir) BERK-sheer
Berlin (bər·lin') ber-LIN
Berlioz (ber·lyōz') behr-LYOHZ
Bermuda (bər·mū'də) ber-MYOO-duh
Bern (bērn *or* bern) BERN *or* BEHRN
Bernadette (ber"nə·det') BEHR-nuh-DET
Bernadotte (ber"nə·dot') BEHR-nuh-DOT
Bernhard (bern'härt) BERN-hart
Bernhardt (bērn'härt) BERN-hart
Bernina (ber·nē'nä) behr-NEE-nah
Bertillon (bēr'ti·lon) BER-tih-lon
Beskid (be'skid) BEH-skid
Bessarabia (bes"ə·rā'byə) BES-uh-RAY-byuh
Bessemer (bes'ə·mər) BESS-uh-mer
Bethany (beth'ə·nē) BETH-uh-nee
Bethe (bā'tē) BAY-tee
Bethesda (bə·thez'də) buh-THEZ-duh
Bethlehem (beth'li·hem) BETH-lih-hem
Beverly (bev'ər·lē) BEV-er-lee
Bevin (bev'in) BEV-in
Beyrouth see *Beirut.*
Bhagavad-Gita (bha"gə·vad·gē'tä) BHA-guh-vad-GEE-tah
Bhima (bē'mä) BEE-mah
Bhutan (boo'tän') BOO-TAN
Biarritz (bē'ə·ritz *or* byä·rētz') BEE-uh-ritz *or* byah-REETZ
Bibliothèque Nationale (bib"lē·ə·tek' nä'sē·ə·näl') BIB-lee-uh-TECK NAH-see-uh-NAHL
Binet (bə·nā') buh-NAY
Bigelow (big'ə·lō") BIG-uh-LOH
Bikini (bē·kē'nē) bee-KEE-nee
Bilbao (bil·bow' *or* bēl·bä'ō) bil-BOW *or* beel-BAH-oh
Billings (bil'ingz) BIL-ingz
Billington (bil'ing·tən) BIL-ing-tun
Biloxi (bi·luk'sē) bih-LUCK-see
Bimini (bim'i·nē) BIM-ih-nee
Binghamton (bing'həm·tən) BING-hum-tun
Birchard (bēr'chard) BER-churd
Birdseye (bērdz'ī) BERDZ-eye
Birmingham [England] (bēr'ming·əm) BER-ming·um
[Alabama] (bēr'ming·ham) BER-ming-ham
Biscay (bis'kā) BIS-kay
Biscayne (bis·kān') bis-KANE
Bismarck, Otto (bis'märk) BIS-mark
Bismarck [city] (biz'mark) BIZ-mark
Bissell (bis'əl) BIS-ul
Bithynia (bi·thin'ē·ə) bih-THIN-ee-uh
Bitterroot (bit'ər·root) BIT-er-root
Bizet (bē·ze') bee-ZEH
Blarney (blär'ne) BLAHR-nee
Bled (bled) BLED
Blenheim (blen'əm) BLEN-um
Blennerhasset (blen'ər·has"ət) BLEN-er-HASS-ut
Blériot (blā'ryō) BLAY-ree-oh
Bligh (blī) BLY
Blondel (blän·del') blawn-DEL
Blücher (blü'khər *or* bloo'kər) BLoo-ker
Bly (blī) BLY
Blythe (blīth) BLYTHE
B'nai B'rith (bə·nā' bə·rēth') buh-NAY buh-REETH
Boadicea (bō"ad·i·sē'ə) BOH-ad-ih-SEE-uh
Boaz (bō'az) BOH-az
Boccaccio (bok·kä'chō) bock-KAH-choh
Boden See (bō'dən·zā") BOH-dun-ZAY
Bodleian (bod·lē'ən) bod-LEE-un
Bodley (bod'lē) BOD-lee
Bodmin (bod'min) BOD-min
Bodoni (bə·dō'nē) buh-DOH-nee
Boehm (bōm) BOME
Boeotia (bē·ō'shə) bee-OH-shuh
Boer (bôr) BORE
Bogotá (bō"gə·tä') boh-guh-TAH
Bohème (bō·em') boh-EM
Bohemia (bō·hē'mē·ə) boh-HEE-mee-uh
Bohr (bôr) BORE
Boise (boi'zē) BOY-zee
Boissevan (bwä·sə·van') bwah-suh-VAN
Bok (bok) BOCK
Bolan (bə·län') buh-LAHN
Boleyn (bûl'in) BULL-in
Bolingbroke (bol'ing·brûk) BOL-ing-brook
Bolivar (bō·lē'vär) boh-LEE-vahr
Bolivia (bə·liv'ē·ə) buh-LIV-ee-uh
Bologna (bə·lōn'yə) buh-LONE-yuh
Bolshevik (bol'shə·vik) BOL-shuh-vick
Bolzano (bəl·tsä'nō) bul-TSAH-noh
Bombay (bom·bā') bom-BAY
Bonaire (bâ·nār') baw-NAIR
Bonaparte (bō'nə·pärt") BOH-nuh-part
Bonaventura (bō"nə·ven·too'rə) BOH-nuh-ven-TOO-ruh
Bone (bōn) BONE
Bonheur (bo·nēr') bah-NER
Bohomme (bo·nom') bah-NOM
Boniface (bon'i·fās) BON-ih-face
Bonn (bân) BON
Bonneville (bon'vil) BON-vil
Bonney (bon'ē) BON-ee
Bonnivard (bâ·nē·vär') baw-nee-VAHR
Bonthron (bon'thrən) BON-thrun
Boone (boon) BOON
Boothia (boo'thē·ə) BOO-thee-uh
Bordeaux (bôr·dō') bore-DOH
Borden (bôr'dən) BORE-dun
Borgia (bôr'jä) BORE-jah
Borglum (bôr'gləm) BORE-glum
Boring (bō'ring) BOH-ring
Boris Godunoff (bôr'is goo·də·nof") BORE-iss goo-duh-NAWF
Borneo (bôr'nē·ō) BORE-nee-oh
Borobudur (bō"rə·boo·dûr') BOH-ruh-boo-DURE
Borodin (bə·rə·dēn') buh-ruh DEEN
Bosch (bos) BOS
Bosnia (boz'nē·ə) BOZ-nee-uh
Bosporus (bos'pə·rəs) BOSS-puh-rus
Boston (bôs'tən) BAWS-tun
Boswell (boz'wel) BOZ-well
Bothnia (both'nē·ə) BAHTH-nee-uh
Bothwell (both'wel) BAHTH-wel
Botticelli (bot'ē·chel'ē) bot-uh-CHEL-ee
Bounty (bown'tē) BOWN-tee
Bourbon (bûr'bən) BOOR-bun
Bourges (boorzh) BOORZH
Bourse (bûrs) BOORCE
Boussard (bû·sär') boo-SAR
Bow River (bō) BOH
Bowdoin (bō'dən) BOH-dun
Bowie (bō'ē) BOH-ee
Boycott (boi'kot) BOY-kot
Boyle (boil) BOYL
Boyne (boin) BOYN
Boz (bōz) BOZE
Bozzaris (bot'sä·rēs *or* bə·zär'is) BOT-sah-reese *or* buh-ZAR-us
Brabançon (brä"bän"son') brah-bon-SAHN
Brabant (brä'bänt) BRAH-bahnt
Braddock (brad'ək) BRAD-uck
Bradford (brad'fərd) BRAD-ferd
Bradley (brad'lē) BRAD-lee
Brady (brā'dē) BRAY-dee
Bragg (brag) BRAG
Brahe (brä'e) BRAH-eh
Brahma (brä'mə) BRAH-muh
Brahman (brä'mən) BRAH-mun
Brahmanas (brä'mən·əz) BRAH-mun-uz
Brahmaputra (brä"ma·poo'tra) BRAH-muh-POO-truh
Brahms (brämz) BRAHMZ
Braille (brāl) BRAYL
Bramante (brä·män'te) brah-MAHN-teh
Brandeis (bran'dīs) BRAN-dice
Brandenburg (bran'dən·bērg) BRAN-dun-berg
Brandon (bran'dən) BRAN-dun
Brandt (bränt) BRAHNT
Brangwyn (brang'win) BRANG-win
Brant (brant) BRANT
Brantford (brant'fərd) BRANT-ferd
Braque (bräk) BRACK
Bras d'Or (brä·dôr') brah-DORE
Bratislava (brä'ti·slä·vä) BRAH-tih-slah-vah
Brattleboro (brat'əl·bēr·ə) BRAT-ul-ber-uh
Brazil (brə·zil') bruh-ZIL
Brazos (braz'əs) BRAZ-us
Brazza (brä·zä') brah-ZAH
Brazzaville (brä·zä·vēl') brah-zah-VEEL
Breckinridge (brek'ən·rij) BRECK-un-ridge
Breda (brā·dä') bray-DAH
Breitenfeld (brī'tən·felt) BRY-tun-felt
Bremen (brā'mən) BRAY-mun
Bremerhaven (brā'mər·hä"fən) BRAY-mer-HAH-fun
Brenner (bren'ər) BREN-er
Breslau (bres'low) BRES-low [as in *allow*]
Brest (brest) BREST
Brest-Litovsk (brest'li·tofsk') BREST-lih-TOFSK
Bretagne (brə·tän'yə) bruh-TAHN-yuh
Breton (bret'ən) BRET-un
Breughel (broo'gəl) BROO-gul
Brewster (broo'stər) BROO-ster
Brian Boru (brī'ən·bə·roo') BRY-un-buh-ROO
Briant (brē·än') bree-AHN
Bridgman (brij'mən) BRIDGE-mun
Bridger (brij'ər) BRIDGE-er
Brie (brē) BREE
Brinell (bri·nel') brih-NEL
Brisbane (briz'bān) BRIZ-bayn
Bristol (bris'təl) BRIS-tul
Britain (brit'ən) BRIT-un
Briton (brit'ən) BRIT-un
Brittany (brit'ə·nē) BRIT-uh-nee
Brno (bēr'nâ) BER-naw
Brock (brok) BROCK
Brodie (brō'dē) BROH-dee
Bromfield (brom'fēld) BROM-feeld
Bronck (bronk) BRONCK
Bronstein (brun·shtīn') brun-SHTYNE
Brontë (bron'tē) BRON-tee
Bronx (bronks) BRONCKS
Brooke (brûk) BROOK
Brooklyn (brûk'lin) BROOK lin
Broughton (brâ'tən) BRAW-tun
Brownian (brown'e·ən) BROWN-ee-un
Browning (brow'ning) BROW-ning
Broz (brōz) BROHZ
Bruch (brûkh) BROOK
Bruges (broozh) BROOZH
Brulé (brü·lā') broo-LAY
Brummel (brum'əl) BRUM-ul
Brunei (broo·nā') broo-NAY
Brunn (brün) BROON
Brünnhilde (broon'hild) BROON-hild
Bruno (broo'nō) BROO-noh
Brunswick (brunz'wik) BRUNZ-wick
Brussels (brus'əlz) BRUSS-ulz
Brutus (broo'təs) BROO-tus
Bryan (brī'ən) BRY-un
Bryant (brī'ənt) BRY-unt
Bryce (brīs) BRICE
Bryn Mawr (brin·mâr') brin-MAWR
Bryophyta (brī·of'ə·tə) bry-AHF-uh-tuh
Bubastis (bū·bas'təs) byoo-BAS-tus
Bucephalus (bū·sef'ə·ləs) byoo-SEF-uh-lus
Buchan (buk'ən) BUCK-un
Buchanan (bû·kan'ən) boo-KAN-un
Bucharest (boo'kə·rest) BOO-kuh-rest
Buchenwald (boo'khən·vält") BOO-kun-vahlt
Buckingham (buk'ing·əm) BUCK-ing-um
Bucknell (buk·nel') buck-NELL
Buckner (buk'nər) BUCK-ner
Budapest (boo'də·pest") BOO-duh-pest
Budd (bud) BUD
Buddha (bûd'ə) BOOD-uh
Buddhism (bûd'iz·əm) BOOD-iz-um
Budva (bood'vä) BOOD-vah
Buea (boo·ā'ə) boo-A-uh
Buena Vista (bwā'nə·vis'tə) BWAY-nuh-VIS-tuh
Buenos Aires (bwe'nəs·ī'rəs) BWEH-nus-EYE-rus
Bug River (bûg *or* boog) BOOG
Bugandas (boo·gän'də) boo-GAHN-duh
Bulfinch (bûl'finch) BULL-finch
Bulganin (bûl·gä'nin) bull-GAH-nin
Bulgaria (bul·gar'ē·ə) bul-GAR-ee-uh
Bülow (bü'lō) BYOO-lo
Bulwer (bûl'wər) BOOL-wer
Bunche (bunch) BUNCH
Bunsen (bun'sən) BUN-sun
Bunyan (bun'yən) BUN-yun
Buonaparte (bwâ"nä·pär'tə) BWAW-nah-PAHR-tuh
Buonarotti (bwâ"nä·râ'tē) BWAW-nah-RAW-tee
Buprestis (bū·pres'tis) byoo-PRES-tis
Burbage (bēr'bij) BER-bidge
Burbank (bēr'bank) BER-bank
Burgas (bûr·gäs') boor-GAHSS
Burgeo (bēr'jē·ō) BER-jee-oh
Burgess (bēr'jis) BER-jis
Burgos (boor'gəs) BOOR-gus
Burgoyne (bēr·goin') ber-GOYN
Burgundy (bēr'gən·dē) BER-gun-dee
Burk (bērk) BERK
Burke (bērk) BERK
Burlington (bēr'ling·tən) BER-ling-tun
Burma (bēr'mə) BER-muh
Burmese (bēr·mēz') ber-MEEZ
Burnett (bēr·net') ber-NET
Burns (bērnz) BERNZ
Burnside (bērn'sīd") BERN-side
Burroughs (bēr'ōz) BER-oze
Bursa (bûr·sä') boor-SAH
Burton (bēr'tən) BER-tun
Busento (boo·zen'tə) boo-ZEN-tuh
Bushnell (bûsh'nel) BUSH-nel
Busoni (boo·zō'nē) boo-ZOH-nee
Bute (būt) BYOOT
Butler (but'lər) BUT-ler
Butte (būt) BYOOT
Byelorussia (bye"lə·rush'ə) BYEH-luh-RUSH-uh
Bygdoy (büg'döē) BIG-dewy
Byng (bing) BING
Byrd (bērd) BERD
Byron (bī'rən) BY-run
Byzantine (bi·zan'tin) bi-ZAN-tin
Byzantium (bi·zan'shē·əm) bi-ZAN-shee-um

Caballo (kə·bä'yō) kuh-BAH-yoh
Cabell (kab'əl) KAB-ul
Cabot (kab'ət) KAB-ut
Cabral (kə·bräl') kuh-BRAHL
Cabrillo (kä·brēl'yō) kah-BREEL-yoh
Cabrini (kä·brē'nē) kah-BREE-nee
Cadillac (kad'ə·lak) KAD-uh-lack
Cadiz (kā'diz, kə·diz', *or* [Sp.] kä'dēth) KAY-diz, kuh-DIZ, *or*, in Spanish, KAH-deeth
Cadman (kad'mən) KAD-mun
Cadmus (kad'məs) KAD-mus
Caduceus (kə·dū'sē·əs) kuh-DYOO-see-us
Caedmon (kad'mən) KAD-mun
Caelian (sē'lē·ən) SEE-lee-un
Caen (kän) KAHN
Caernarvon (kär·när'vən) kar-NAR-vun
Caesar (sē'zər) SEE-zer
Caesarea (sez·ə·rē'ə) sez-uh-REE-uh
Caesarean (sə·zār'ē·ən) suh-ZAIR-ee-un
Cagayan (kä·gä·yän') kah-gah-YAHN
Cagliari (kä'lyä·rē) KAH-lyah-ree
Cagliostro (kä·lyōs'trō) kahl-YOSE-troh
Cagney (kag'nē) KAG-nee
Caiaphas (kā'yə·fəs) KAY-yuh-fus
Cain (kān) KANE
Cairn (kārn) KEHRN
Cairo (kī'rō) KY-roh
Cajamarca (kä"hə·mär'kə) KAH-huh-MAR-kuh
Cajun (kā'jən) KAY-jun
Calais (kal'ā *or* kä·le') KAL-ay *or* kah-LEH
Calcutta (kal·kut'ə) kal-KUT-uh
Caldwell (kâld'wel) KAWLD-wel
Calgary (kal'gə·rē) KAL-guh-ree
Calhoun (kal'hoon) KAL-hoon
Calicut (kal'i·kut) KAL-ih-kut
Caligula (kə·lig'yə·lə) kuh-LIG-yuh-luh
Calixtus (kə·liks'təs) kuh-LICKS-tus
Callao (kä'lye) KAHL-yeh
Calliope (kə·lī'ō·pē) kuh-LY-oh-pee
Calumet (kal'ū·met) KAL-yoo-met
Calvary (kal'və·rē) KAL-vuh-ree
Calvert (kal'vērt) KAL-vert
Calvin (kal'vin) KAL-vin
Calypso (kə·lip'sō) kuh-LIP-soh
Camacho (kä·mä'chə) kah-MAH-chuh
Cambodia (kam·bō'dē·ə) kam-BOH-dee-uh
Cambridge (kām'brij) KAME-bridge
Camden (kam'dən) KAM'dun
Cam (kän) KAHN
Camelot (kam'ə·lot) KAM-uh-lot
Camembert (kam'əm·bār) KAM-um-bare
Cameroons (kam"ə·roonz') kam-uh-ROONZ
Camille (kä·mēl') kah-MEEL
Campbell (kam'bəl *or* kam'əl) KAM-bul *or* KAM-ul
Campbellite (kam'əl·īt) KAM-ul-ite
Campeche (kam·pē'chē) kam-PEE-chee
Campobello (kam"pə·bel'ō) kam-puh-BEL-oh
Camp (kamp) KAMP
Canaan (kā'nən) KAY-nun
Canada (kan'ə·də) KAN-uh-duh
Canandaigua (kan"ən·dā'gwə) kan-un-DAY-gwuh
Canberra (kan'ber·ə) KAN-behr-uh
Cancer (kan'sər) KAN-ser
Candide (kän·dēd') kahn-DEED
Candlemas (kan'dəl·məs) KAN-dul-mus
Canea (kä·nē'ə) kah-NEE-uh
Canfield (kan'fēld) KAN-feeld
Cango (käng'gō) KAHNG-goh
Canis (kān'is) KANE-is
Cannae (kan'ē) KAN-ee
Cannes (kan) KAN
Canossa (kä·nos'ə) kah-NAHCE-uh
Canso (kan'sō) KAN-soh
Canterbury (kan'tər·ber·ē) KAN-ter-bare-ee
Canton, China (kan'ton) KAN-ton
Canton, Ohio (kant'ən) KANT-un
Canute (kə·nūt') kuh-NYOOT
Canyon de Chelly (kan'yən de shā') KAN-yun-deh-SHAY
Capac (kä'päk) KAH-pahk
Cape Gris Nez (käp·grē·nā') kahp-gree-NAY
Capernaum (kə·pēr'nā·əm) kuh-PER-nay-um
Capet (kā'pet *or* kä·pā') KAY-pet *or* kah-PAY
Cape Verde (kāp·vērd') kape-VERD
Cap-Haïtien (käp·ä·ē·syan') kalp-ah-ee-SYAN
Capitoline (kap'i·tə·līn") KAP-ih-tuh-LINE
Caporetto (kap"ə·ret'ō) KAP-uh-RET-oh
Capricornus (kap"ri·kôrn'əs) kap-rih-KORN-us
Capua (kap'yoo·ə) KAP-yoo-uh
Capuchins (kap'ū·chinz) KAP-yoo-chinz
Caraballo (kä·rä·bä'yō) kah-rah-BAH-yoh
Caracalla (kar·ə·kal'ə) kar-uh-KAL-uh
Caracas (kä·rä'käs) kah-RAH-kahss
Carboniferous (kär·bə·nif'ər·əs) kahr-buh-NIF-er-us
Cardiff (kär'dif) KAR-dif
Cardenas (kär'de·näs) KAR-deh-nahce
Carey (kar'ē) KA-ree
Caribbean (kar'i·bē·ən) KAR-ih-bee-un
Carinthia (kə·rin'thē·ə) kuh-RIN-thee-uh
Carlotta (kär·lot'ə) kar-LOT-uh
Carlovingians (kär"lō·vin'jē·ənz) KAR-loh-VIN-jee-unz
Carlow (kär'lō) KAR-loh
Carlsbad (kärlz'bad) KARLZ-bad
Carlson (kärl'sən) KARL-sun
Carlyle (kär·līl') kar-LILE
Carmack (kär'mak) KAR-mack
Carmelite (kär'mel·īt) KAR-mel-ite
Carmel (kär'mel) KAR-mel
Carmen (kär'mən) KAR-mun
Carmona (kər·mō'nä) ker-MOH-nah
Carnegie (kär·nā'gē) kar-NAY-gee
Carnivora (kär·niv'ə·rə) kar-NIV-uh-ruh
Carolina (kar"ə·lī'nə) KA-ruh-LY-nuh
Caroline (kar'ə·lin) KA-ruh-lin
Carolingian (kar"ə·lin'jē·ən) KA-ruh-LIN-jee-un
Carol (kar'əl) KA-rul
Caron (kä·rân') kah-RAWN
Carothers (kə·ruth'ərz) kuh-RUH-therz
Carpathian (kär·pā'thē·ən) kar-PAY-thee-un
Carpenisi (kär"pə·nyē'sē) kar-pun-YEE-see
Carpini (kär·pē'nē) kar-PEE-nee
Carrantuohill (kar"ən·too'əl) ka-run-TOO-ul
Carrara (kä·rä'rä) kah-RAH-rah
Carrasco (kä·räs'kə) kah-RAHS-kuh
Carrel (ka·rel' *or* kar'el) ka-REL *or* KA-rel
Carré (ka·rā') ka-RAY
Carroll (kar'əl) KA-rul
Carson (kär'sən) KAR-sun
Cartagena (kär"tə·jē'nə) kar-tuh-JEE-nuh
Carteret (kär'tər·et) KAR-ter-et
Cartesian (kär·tē'zhən) kar-TEE-zhun
Carthage (kär'thij) KAR-thidge
Carthaginian (kär"thə·jin'ē·ən) KAR-thuh-JIN-ee-un
Carthusian (kär·thū'zhən) kar-THYOO-zhun
Cartier (kär·tyā') kar-TYAY
Cartwright (kärt'rīt) KART-rite
Caruso (kə·roo'sō) kuh-ROO-soh
Carville (kär'vil) KAR-vil
Casa (kä'sä) KAH-sah
Casablanca (kas"ə·blank'ə) kas-uh-BLANK-uh
Casa Grande (kas'ə·gran'dē) kas-uh-GRAN-dee
Casanova (kas"ə·nō'və) kas-uh-NOH-vuh
Casa Rosada (rō·sä'thə) roe-SAH-thuh
Casbah (käs'bä) KAHS-bah
Cascade (kas·kād') kas-KAYD
Casino (kə·sē'nō) kuh-SEE-noh
Casper (kas'pər) KAS-per
Caspian (kas'pē·ən) KAS-pee-un
Cassandra (kə·san'drə) kuh-SAN-druh
Cassino (ka·sē'nō) ka-SEE-noh
Cassius (kash'ē·əs) KASH-ee-us
Castile (kas·tēl') kas-TEEL
Castle Pinckney (pink'nē) PINK-nee
Castor (kas'tər) KAS-ter
Castriota (kas"trē·ō'tə) kas-tree-OH-tuh
Castro (käs'trō) KAHCE-troh
Catalina (kat"ə·lē'nə) kat-uh-LEE-nuh
Catalonia (kat"ə·lō'nyə) kat-uh-LONE-yuh
Catania (kä·tän'yä) kah-TAHN-yah
Catechumens (kat"ə·kū'mənz) kat-uh-KYOO-munz
Cathay (ka·thā') ka-THAY
Catherine (kath'ə·rin) KATH-uh-rin
Catherine de' Medici (də·med'ə·chē) duh-MED-uh-chee
Cather (kath'ər) KATH-er
Catlin (kat'lin) KAT-lin
Cato (kā'tō) KAY-toh
Catskill (kats'kil) KATS-kil
Catullus (kat'yə·ləs) KAT-yuh-lus
Caucasia (kâ·kā'zhə) kaw-KAY-zhuh
Caucasoid (kâ'kə·soid) KAW-kuh-soid
Caucasus (kâ'kə·səs) KAW-kuh-sus
Cavalla (kə·val'ə) kuh-VAL-uh
Cavan (kav'ən) KAV-un
Cavell (kav'əl) KAV-ul
Cavour (kä·voor') kah-VOOR
Caxton (kaks'tən) KACKS-tun
Cayapa (kä·yä'pä) kah-YAH-pah
Cayley (kā'lē) KAY-lee
Cayuga (kə·yoo'gə) kuh-YOO-guh
Cecilia (sə·sēl'yə) suh-SEEL-yuh
Celebes (sel'ə·bēz) SEL-uh-beez
Celestine (sel'əs·tīn) SEL-us-tine
Cellini (chə·lē'nē) chuh-LEE-nee
Celotex (sel'ō·teks) SEL-oh-tecks
Celtic (sel'tik) SEL-tik
Cenozoic (sē"nə·zō'ik *or* sen"ə·zō'ik) see-nuh-ZOH-ick *or* sen-uh-ZOH-ick
Cephalonia (sef"ə·lō'nē·ə) SEF-uh-LOH-nee-uh
Cephas (sē'fəs) SEE-fus
Cerberus (ser'bə·rəs) SAIR-buh-rus
Ceres (sē'rēz) SEE-reez
Cervantes (sər·van'tēz) ser-VAN-teez
Cervera (ther·vā'rä) thair-VAY-rah
Cévennes (sā·ven') say-VEN
Ceylon (si·lon') sih-LON
Cézanne (sā·zan') say-ZAN
Chablis (shä·blē') shah-BLEE
Chaco (chä'kō) CHAH-koh
Chad (chad) CHAD
Chadwick (chad'wik) CHAD-wick
Chaeronea (ker·ə·nē'ə) kare-uh-NEE-uh
Chaga (chä'gä) CHAH-gah
Chagall (shə·gäl') shuh-GAHL
Chaldea (kal·dē'ə) kal-DEE-uh
Chaliapin (shə·lyä'pyin) shuh-LYAH-pyin
Chalons (shä·lân') shah-LAWN
Chamberlain (chām'bər·lin) CHAYM-ber-lin
Chamorros (chä·mōr'ō) chah-MORE-oh
Champagne (sham·pān') sham-PANE
Champlain (sham·plān') sham-PLANE
Champollion (sham·pol'ē·ən) sham-PAHL-ee-un
Champs Elysées (shän'zā·lē·zā') SHAHN-zay-lee-ZAY
Chantilly (shän·tē·yē' *or* shan·til'ē) shahn-tee-YEE *or* shan-TIL-ee
Chanukah (khä'noo·kä) KAH-noo-kah
Chao Phraya (chow'prä·yä') CHOW-prah-YAH
Chapultepec (chä·pool'te·pek) chah-POOL-teh-peck
Chares (kā'rēz) KAY-reez
Charlemagne (chär'le·mān) CHAR-leh-mane
Charleston (chärlz'tən) CHARLES-tun
Charlotte (shär'lət) SHAR-lut

Charlotte Amalie (shär'lət ə·mäl'yə) SHAR-lut-uh-MAHL-yuh
Charon (kā'rən) KAY-run
Chartres (shär'trə) SHAR-truh
Chartreuse (shär·trûz') shar-TROOZ
Charybdis (kə·rib'dis) kuh-RIB-dis
Chatauqua (shə·tâ'kwə) shuh-TAW-kwuh
Chateau-Thierry (shä·tō"tye·rē') shah-TOH-tyeh-REE
Chatham (chat'əm) CHAT-um
Chattahoochee (chat"ə·hoo'chė) CHAT-uh-HOO-chee
Chattanooga (chat"ə·nûg'ə) CHAT-uh-NOOG-uh
Chaucer (châ'sər) CHAW-ser
Chavannes (shȧ·vȧn') sha-VAN
Cheaha (chē'hâ) CHEE-haw
Chekhov (chā'khâf) CHAY-kawf
Chéliff (shā'lēf) SHAY-leef
Chelsea (chel'sė) CHEL-see
Cheltenham (chelt'nəm) CHELT-num
Chemnitz (kem'nitz) KEM-nitz
Cheops (kē'ops) KEE-ops
Cheraw (shə·râ') shuh-RAW
Cherbourg (sher'bûrg) SHARE-boorg
Cherokee (cher·ə·kē') chair-uh-KEE
Chesapeake (ches'ə·pēk") CHES-uh-peek
Chetnik (chet'nik) CHET-nick
Cheviot (shev'ė·ət) SHEV-ee-ut
Cheyenne (shī·en') shy-EN
Chiang Kai-shek (jyäng·kī·shek) jee-AHNG-kye-sheck
Chianti (kyän'tė) KYAHN-tee
Chibcha (chēb'chä) CHEEB-chah
Chicago (shi·kä'gō) shih-KAH-go
Chickamauga (chik"ə·mâ'gä) CHICK-uh-MAW-gah
Chihuahua (chė·wä'wä) chee-WAH-wah
Chile (chil'ė) CHIL-ee
Chillon (shė·yâṅ') shee-YAWN
Chimborazo •(chim·bō·rä'zō) chim-boh-RAH-zoh
Chimera (chī·mir'ə) chy-MIR-uh
China (chī'nə) CHY-nuh
Chinde (chin'dė) CHIN-dee
Chinese (chī·nēz') chy-NEEZ
Ch'ing (ching) CHING
Chinkiang (chin·kyang') chin-KYANG
Chinook (shi·nook' *or* chi·nook') shih-NOOK *or* chih-NOOK
Chins (jinz) JINZ
Chios (kī'os *or* [Gr.] hē'os) KY-os *or* HEE-os
Chippendale (chip'ən·dāl) CHIP-un-dayl
Chippewa (chip'ə·wä) CHIP-uh-wah
Chiricahua (chė·rė·kä'wä) chee-ree-KAH-wah
Chiron (kī'ron) KY-ron
Chisholm (chiz'əm) CHIZ-um
Chittagong (chit·ə·gong') chit-uh-GONG
Chlamydomonas (klam"ė·dom'ə·nəs) klam-e-DOM-uh-nuss
Choctaw (chok'tâ) CHOCK-taw
Choiseul (shwä·zûl') shwah-ZUL
Chopin (shō·paṅ') shoh-PAN
Chosen (chō'sen) CHOH-sen
Chou En-lai (jō·en·lī) joe-en-lie
Christchurch (kris'chērch) KRYS-cherch
Christophe (krės·tâf') krees-TAWF
Christopher (kris'tə·fər) KRIS-tuh-fer
Chronicles (kron'i·kəlz) KRON-ih-kulz
Chrysler (kris'lər) KRYS-ler
Chucuito (choo·kwē'tō) choo-KWEE-toh
Chugach (choo'gak) CHOO-gack
Chukchis (chûk'chėz) CHUCK-cheez
Chungking (chûng·king) chung-king
Churchill (chērch'il) CHERCH-il
Cicero (sis'ə·rō) SIS-uh-roh
Ciconians (sī·kō'nė·ənz) sy-KOH-nee-unz
Cid (sid) SID
Cierva (thyer'vä) THYEHR-vah
Cimabue (chē"mä·boo'ə) chee-mah-BOO-uh
Cimbri (sim'brė) SIM-bree
Cimone (chē'mə·nə) CHEE-muh-nuh
Cincinnati (sin"sə·nat'ė) SIN-suh-NAT-ee
Cincinnatus (sin·si·nā'təs) sin-sih-NAY-tus
Cinderella (sin·də·rel'ə) sin-duh-REL-uh
Cinemascope (sin'ə·mə·skōp") SIN-uh-muh-SKOPE
Cinerama (sin"ə·rȧ'mə) SIN-uh-RAH-mə
Circe (sir'sė) SER-see
Cistercians (sis·tēr'shənz) sis-TER-shunz
Ciudad Trujillo (syoo·däd' troo·hē'yə) syoo-DAHD troo-HEE-yuh
Ciudad Vieja (syoo·däd' vye'hä) syoo-DAHD VYEH-hah
Clairvaux (klär·vō') klehr-VOH
Claudius (klâ'dė·əs) KLAW-dee-us
Clearchus (klė·är'kəs) klee-AHR-kus
Cleaveland (klēv'lənd) KLEEV-lund
Clemençeau, Georges (kle·mäṅ·sō', zhôrzh) kleh-mahn-SOH, ZHORZH
Clemens (klem'ənz) KLEM-unz
Clement (klem'ənt) KLEM-unt
Cleopatra (klē"ō·pā'trə) KLEE-oh-PAY-trun
Clermont (kler'mont) KLARE-mont
Clervaux (kler·vō') klair-VOH
Cleveland (klēv'lənd) KLEEV-lund
Clio (klē'ō) KLEE-oh
Clive (klīv) KLYV
Clonmel (klon·mel') klon-MEL
Clontarf (klon·tärf') klon-TAHRF
Clotho (klō'thō) KLOH-thoh
Clovis (klō'vis) KLOH-vis
Clytemnestra (klī"təm·nes'trə) kly-tum-NES-truh
Cnossus (nō'səs) NOH-sus
Coahuila (kō"ä·wē'lä) koh-ah-WEE-lan
Cobh (kōb) KOHB
Cochin (kō'chin) KOH-chin
Cochise (kə·chēs') kuh-CHEECE
Cochrane (kok'rən) KOCK-run
Cody (kō'dė) KOH-dee
Coeur d'Alene (kôr'dəl·ān') KOHR-dul-AYN
Cognac (kō'nyak) KOH-nyack
Conan (kō·han') koh-HAN
Coimbra (kwēm'brə) KWEEM-bruh
Colchester (kōl'ches·tər) KOHL-ches-ter
Coleridge (kōl'rij) KOHL-ridge
Coligny (kə·lē·nyē') kuh-lee-NYEE
Colin (kol'in) KAHL-in
Coln (kûln) KUHLN
Cologne (kə·lōn') kuh-LOHN
Colombia (kə·lum'bė·ə) kuh-LUM-bee-uh
Colombine (kol'əm·bīn") KAHL-um-bine
Colombo (kə·lum'bō) kuh-LUM-boh
Colón (kə·lōn' *or* kə·lân') kuh-LOHN *or* kuh-LAWN
Colosseum (kol·ə·sē'əm) kol-uh-SEE-um
Columbia (kə·lum'bė·ə) kuh-LUM-bee-uh
Columbus (kə·lum'bəs) kuh-LUM-bus
Comanche (kō·man'chė) koh-MAN-chee
Comenius (kə·mē'nė·əs) kuh-MEE-nee-us
Cominform (kom'in·fôrm) KOM-in-form
Comintern (kom'in·tērn) KOM-in-tern
Como, Lake (kō'mō) KOH-moh
Compiègne (kȯṅ·pyen'yə) kon-PYEN-yuh
Compton (komp'tən) KOMP-tun
Comstock (kom'stock) KOM-stock
Comus (kō'məs) KOH-mus
Conan Doyle (kō'nən·doil') KOH-nun-DOIL
Conanicut (kə·nan'i·kut) kuh-NAN-ih-kut
Conant (kō'nənt) KOH-nunt
Concepción (kon·sep·syon') kon-sep-SYON
Conchobar (kon·chō'bär) kon-CHOH-bahr
Concord (kon'kərd) KON-kerd
Conecuh (kə·nā'kə) kuh-NAY-kuh
Conemaugh (kon'ə·mâ) KON-uh-maw
Conestoga (kon"əs·tō'gə) kon-us-TOH-guh
Coney Island (kō'nė) KOH-nee
Confucius (kən·fū'shəs) kun-FYOO-shus
Congaree (kon'gə·rė) KON-guh-ree
Congo (kong'gō) KONG-goh
Connaught (kon'ət) KON-ut
Constantine (kon'stən·tėn) KON-stun-teen
Constantinople (kon"stan·ti·nō'pəl) KON-stan-tih-NO-pul
Conté (kȧṅ·tā') kawn-TAY
Coosa (koo'sə) KOO-suh
Copenhagen (kō·pən·hā'gən) koh-pun-HAY-gun
Copernicus (kə·pēr'ni·kəs) kuh-PER-nih-kus
Cophetua (kō·fet'ū·ä) koh-FET-yoo-ah
Copts (koptz) KOPTZ
Corbett (kôr'bət) KOHR-but
Corcovado (kôr"kə·vä'dō) kohr-kuh-VAH-doh
Corday (kôr·dā') kohr-DAY
Cordilleras (kôr·dil·yā'räz) kohr-dil-YAY-rahz
Cordoba (kôr'də·bä) KOHR-duh-bah
Cordova (kôr'də·və) KOHR-duh-vuh
Corinth (kor'inth) KOR-inth
Corinto (kə·rēn'tə) k-uh-REEN-tuh
Corneille (kôr·nā'yə) kohr-NAY-yuh
Cornelia (kôr·nēl'yə) kohr-NEEL-yuh
Cornell (kôr·nel') kohr-NEL
Corno (kôr'nō) KOHR-noh
Cornwallis (kôrn·wol'is) korn-WOL-is
Coronado (kôr·ə·nä'dō) kohr-uh-NAH-doh
Corot (kȧ·rō') kaw-ROE
Corpus Christi (kôr'pəs·kris'tė) KOHR-pus-KRIS-tee
Corregidor (kə·reg'i·dôr) kuh-REG-ih-dohr
Corsica (kôr'si·kə) KOHR-sih-kuh
Cortes *or* **Cortez** (kôr'tez) KOHR-tez
Corvo (kôr'vō) KOHR-voh
Cossacks (kos'aks) KOS-acks
Costa Rica (kos"tə·rē'kə) KOS-tuh-REE-kuh
Costello (kos·tel'ō) kos-TELL-oh
Coster (kos'tər) KOS-ter
Cote d'Azur (kōt·dä·zür') kote-dah-ZOOR
Cotentin (kȧ·täṅ·taṅ') kaw-tahn-TAN
Cotobato (kō·tä·bä'tō) koh-tah-BAH-toe
Cotopaxi (kō"tə·pak'sė *or* [Span.] kō"tə·pä'hė)
Cotswold (kotz'wōld) KOTS-wohld
Cottrell (kot'rəl) KOT-rul
Coubertin (koo·ber·taṅ') koo-ber-TAN
Coulee (koo'lė) KOO-lee
Courtois (koor·twȧ') koor-TWAH
Coventry (kuv'ən·trė) KUV-un-tree
Covington (kuv'ing·tən) KUV-ing-tun
Cowpens (kow'penz *or* kup'ənz) KOW-penz *or* KUP-unz
Cowper (koo'pər) KOO-per
Coxey (kok'sė) KOCK-see
Cracow (krak'ow) KRACK-ow
Crécy (kre'sė) KREH-see
Cree (krē) KREE
Crémazie (krā·mȧ·zē') kray-mah-ZEE
Cremona (kre·mō'nä) kreh-MOH-nah
Creole (krē'ōl) KREE-ohl
Crerar (krē'rär) KREE-rahr
Crete (krēt) KREET
Creusa (krė·ū'sä) kree-YOO-sah
Crimea (krī·mē'ə) kry-MEE-uh
Cristobal (kris·tō'bəl) kris-TOH-bul
Cristofori (kris·tâ'fə·re) kris-TAW-fuh-ree
Crittenden (krit'ən·dən) KRIT-un-dun
Croatia (krō·ā'shə) kroh-AY-shuh
Croat (krō'at) KROH-at
Croesus (krē'səs) KREE-sus
Cro-Magnon (krō·mag'nən) kroh-MAG-nun
Cronos (krō'nəs) KROH-nus
Cronstedt (kroon'stet) KROON-stet
Croton (krō'tən) KROH-tun
Crouse (krows) KROWCE
Cruikshank (krûk'shank) KROOK-shank
Crux (kruks) KRUCKS
Cuba (kū'bə) KYOO-buh
Culbertson (kul'bərt·sən) KUL-bert-sun
Cullinan (kul'i·nan) KUL-ih-nan
Culloden (kə·lō'dən) kuh-LOH-dun
Cumae (kū'mė) KYOO-mee
Cumana (koo·mä·nä') koo-mah-NAH
Cunard (kə·närd') kuh-NAHRD
Cunaxa (kū·nak'sä) kyoo-NACK-sah
Curaçao (kyûr'ə·sō) KYOOR-uh-soh
Curie (kü·rē') kuh-REE
Curran (kēr'ən) KER-un
Currie (kēr'ė) KER-ee
Currier (kēr'ė·ər) KER-ee-er
Curzon (kēr'zən) KER-zun
Cuza (koo'zä) KOO-zah
Cuzco (koos'kə) KOOS-kah
Cyclades (sik'lə·dėz) SICK-luh-deez
Cyclops (sī'klops) SY-klops
Cynic (sin'ik) SIN-ick
Cyprian (sip'rė·ən) SIP-ree-un
Cyprus (sī'prəs) SY-prus
Cyrano de Bergerac (sir'ə·nō də·bēr'zhə·rak) SIH-ruh-no duh-BER-zhuh-rack
Cyrenaica (sir"ə·nā'ə·kə) SIHR-uh-NAY-uh-kuh
Cyrene (sī·rē'nė) sy-REE-nee
Cyrillic (si·ril'ik) sih-RIL-ick
Cyrus (sī'rəs) SY-rus
Czechoslovakia (chek"ō·slō·väk'yə) CHECK-oh-sloh-VAHK-yuh
Czolgosz (châl'gâsh) CHAWL-gawsh

Dacca (dak'ə) DACK-uh
Dacian (dā'shən) DAY-shun
Dadaism (dä'də·iz·am) DAH-duh-iz-um
Daedalus (dē'də·ləs *or* ded'ə·ləs) DEE-duh-lus *or* DED-uh-lus
Dafoe (də·fō') duh-FOH
Daguerre (də·gār') duh-GAIR
Dahomey (də·hō'mė) duh-HOH-mee
Dail Eireann (dâl·ā'ron) dawl-AY-ron
Daimler (dīm'lər) DIME-ler
Daiquiri (dī·kė·rē' *or* dī'kə·rė) dy-kee-REE *or* DY-kuh-ree
Dakar (dä·kär') dah-KAHR
Dakota (də·kō'tə) duh-KOH-tuh
Dalai Lama (dä·lī' lä'mä) dah-LIE LAH-mah
Dalcroze (dȧl·krōz') dal-KROZE
d'Alembert (dal"əm·ber') dal-um-BARE
Dalhousie (dal·how'zė *or* dal·hoo'zė) dal-HOW-zee *or* dal-HOO-zee
Dali (dä'lė) DAH-lee
Dallas (dal'əs) DAL-us
Dalmatia (dal·mā'shə) dal-MAY-shuh
Dalton (dâl'tən) DAWL-tun
Damascus (də·mas'kəs) duh-MAS-kus
Dambovita (dim"bə·vē'tsä) dim-buh-VEE-tsah
Damien (dȧ·myaṅ') dom-YAN
Damocles (dam'ə·klėz) DAM-uh-kleez
Damon (dā'mən) DAY-mun
Damrosch (dam'rosh) DAM-rosh
Dana (dā'nə) DAY-nuh
Danae (dān'ā·ė) DAY-nay-ee
Danaides (də·nā'ə·dėz) duh-NAY-uh-deez
Danaus (dan'ā·əs) DAN-ay-us
Danelaw (dān'lâ) DAYN-law
Daniel (dan'yəl) DAN-yul
D'Annunzio (dän·noon'tsyō) dah-NOONTS-yo
Dante (dan'tė *or* dän'tā) DAN-tee *or* DAHN-tay
Danton (dän·tāṅ') don-TAWN
Danube River (dan'ūb) DAN-yoob
Danzig (dan'sig *or* [Ger.] dän'tsikh) DAN-sig *or* DAHNT-sick
Daphne (daf'nė) DAF-nee
Daphnis (daf'nis) DAF-nis
Da Ponte (dä·pōn'tə) dah-POHN-tuh
Darazi (da·ra·zē') da-ra-ZEE
D'Arcy (där'sė) DAR-see
Dardenelles (där"də·nelz') dahr-duh-NELZ
Dar-es-Salaam (där"es·sə·läm') DAHR-es-suh-LAHM
Darius (də·rī'əs) duh-RY-us
Darjeeling (där·jē'ling) dahr-JEE-ling
Darlan (där·läṅ') dahr-LAHN
d'Arsonval (där"säṅ"väl') dar-sawn-VAHL
Daudet (dō·de') doh-DEH
Dauphiné (dō·fė·nā') doh-fee-NAY
Davao (dä·vow' *or* dä'vow) dah-VOW *or* DAH-vow
Davos (dä·vōs') dah-VOHCE
Dawes (dâz) DAWZ
Daytona (dā·tō'nə) day-TOH-nuh
Debrecen (de'bre·tsen) DEH-bret-sen
Debussy (də·bü·sē') duh-byoo-SEE
Decameron (de·kam'ə·rən) deh-KAM-uh-run
Decatur (də·kā'tər) duh-KAY-ter
Deccan (dek'ən) DECK-un
Decorah (də·kôr'ə) duh-KOHR-uh
Defoe (də·fō') duh-FOH
De Forest (də·fôr'ist) duh-FOR-ist
Degas (de·gä') deh-GAH
de Gaulle (de·gōl') deh-GOHL
De Grasse (de·gräs') deh-GRAHCE
Deirdre (dir'drė) DEER-dree
Deimos (dī'mos) DY-mos
Deland (de·land') deh-LAND
de la Roche (de·lə·râsh') deh-luh-RAWSH
de la Warr (del'ə·wēr) DEL-uh-were
Delhi (del'ė) DEL-ee
Delilah (də·lī'lə) duh-LY-luh
Delmarva (del·mär'və) del-MAHR-vuh
Delphi (del'fī) DEL-fy
Demerara (dem"ə·rār'ə) dem-uh-RARE-uh
Demeter (də·mē'tər) duh-MEE-ter
De Mille (də·mil') duh-MIL
Democritus (dė·mok'ri·təs) dee-MOCK-rih-tus
Demosthenes (dė·mos'thə·nėz) dee-MOS-thuh-neez
Denis (den'is *or* [Fr.] de·nē') DEN-is *or* deh-NEE
Denmark (den'märk) DEN-mark
de Noyelle (də·nwä"yel') duh-nwah-YELL
Derby Downs (där'bė) DAHR-bee
de Sade (de·sȧd') deh-SAHD
Desaguadero (dās"ä·gwä·*th*ā'rə) DACE-ah-gwah-THEY-ruh
Descartes (dā·kärt') day-KAHRT
Deschutes (dā·shoot') day-SHOOT
Deseret (dez·ə·ret') dez-uh-RET
Desio (dezh'yō) DEZH-voh
Des Moines (di·moin') dih-MOYN
De Soto (dā·sō'tō) day-SOH-toh
Dessalines (de·sä·lēn') deh-sah-LEEN
Detroit (di·troit') dih-TROYT
Deucalion (dū·kā'lė·ən) dyoo-KAY-lee-un
Deuteronomy (dū"tə·ron'ə·mė) dyoo-tuh-RON-uh-mee
Deutsch (doich) DOITCH
Deutschland (doich'lənd) DOITCH-lund
Deutz (doits) DOITS
de Valera (dev·ə·lär'ə) dev-uh-LAIR-uh
Devereux (dev'ə·roo) DEV-uh-roo
Deville (də·vēl') duh-VEEL
Devon (dev'ən) DEV-un
Devonshire (dev'ən·shir") DEV-un-SHEER
Dewar (dū'ər) DYOO-er
Dewey (dū'ė) DYOO-ee
Dey (dā) DAY
Diana (dī·an'ə) dy-AN-uh
Diaspora (dī·as'pə·rə) die-ASS-puh-ruh
Dias (dē'əsh) DEE-ush
Diaz (dē'äs) DEE-ahs
Diderot (dē·drō') dee-DROH
Dido (dī'dō) DY-doh
Dien-bien-phu (dyen·byen·foo') dyen-byen-FOO
Dieppe (dė·ep') dee-EP
Diesel (dē'zəl) DEE-zul
Dijon (dė·zhâṅ') dee-ZHAWN
Dili (dil'ė) DIL-ee
Dimaggio (di·mȧ'zhō) dih-MAH-zho
Dinaric (di·nar'ik) dih-NAR-ick
Dinka (din'kä) DIN-kah
Diocletian (dī"ə·klē'shən) dy-uh-KLEE-shun
Diogenes (dī·oj'ə·nėz) dy-ODGE-uh-neez
Diomedes (dī·ō·mē'dėz) dy-oh-MEE-deez
Dionne (dė·on') dee-AHN
Dionysia (dī·ō·nis'ė·ə) dy-oh-NIS-ee-uh
Dionysius (dī·ō·nish'ė·əs) dy-oh-NISH-ee-us
Dionysus (dī·ō·nī'səs) dy-oh-NY-sus
Dior (dė·ôr') dee-ORE
Dioscorides (dī"əs·kor'ə·dėz) DY-us-KOR-uh-deez
Discobolus (dis·kob'ə·ləs) dis-KOB-uh-lus
Disraeli (diz·rā'lė) diz-RAY-lee
Djakarta (jə·kär'tə) juh-KAHR-tuh
Djemila (je·mė·lä') jeh-mee-LAH
Djibouti (jė·boo'tė) jee-BOO-tee
Djokjakarta (jog"yä·kär'tä) JOG-yah-KAHR-tah
Dnieper (nē'pər) NEE-per
Dnepropetrovsk (dne"prə·pe·trofsk') DNEH-pruh-peh-TROFSK
Dneprostroy (dne"prə·stroi') DNEH-pruh-STROY
Dniester River (nē'stər) NEE-ster
Dobruja (dō·broo'jə) doh-BROO-juh
Dodabetta (dō'də·bet·tə) DOH-duh-bet-tuh
Dodecanese (dō·dek'ə·nėz) doh-DECK-uh-neez
Dollfuss (dâl'foos) DAWL-foos
Dolomite (dō'lō·mīt) DOH-loh-mite
Domesday (doomz'dā *or* dōmz'dā) DOOMZ-day *or* DOHMZ-day
Dominic (dom'ə·nik) DOM-uh-nick
Dominican (də·min'i·kən) duh-MIN-ih-kun
Domrémy (dâṅ·rā·mē') daw-ray-ME
Donatello (don·ə·tel'ō *or* dō"nä·tel'lə) don-uh-TEL-oh *or* DOH-nah-TEL-luh
Dondero (don·der'ō) don-DARE-oh
Donegal (don'ə·gâl) DON-uh-gawl
Donets (do·nets') dah-NETS
Doorn (dôrn) DORN
Dordogne River (dôr·dân'yə) dor-DAWN-yuh
Doré (dō·rā') doh-RAY
Dorian (dō'rė·ən) DOH-ree-un
Doric (dor'ik) DOR-ick
Doriot (dôr'ė·ō) DORE-e-oh
Dortmund (dôrt'mənd) DORT-mund
Dos Passos (dəs·pas'əs) dus-PASS-us
Dostoevski (dos·tə·yev'skė) dos-tuh-YEV-skee
Douala (dwä'lä) DWAH-lah
Douay (doo·ā') doo-AY
Doud (dowd) DOWD
Dougherty (dâ'ēr·te) DAW-er-tee
Douro (dō'rə) DOH-ruh
Dowlah, Surajah (dow'lə, sə·rä'jə) DOW-luh, suh-RAH-juh
D'Oyly Carte (doi'lė·kärt') DOY-lee-KAHRT
Draco (drā'kō) DRAY-koh
Drakensberg (drä'kəns·berkh) DRAH-kuns-bairk
Drava River (drä'vä) DRAH-vah
Dravidian (dra·vid'ė·ən) dra-VID-ee-un
Dravidic (dra·vid'ik) dra-VID-ick
Dreiser (drī'sər) DRY-ser
Drexel (drek'səl) DRECK-sul
Dreyfus (drā'fəs *or* drī'fəs) DRAY-fus *or* DRY-fus
Drin (drēn) DREEN
Druids (droo'idz) DROO-idz
Druse (drooz) DROOZ
Dryad (drī'ad) DRY-ad
Dryden (drī'dən) DRY-dun
Duarte (dwär'te) DWAHR-teh
du Barry (dü·bä·rē') doo-bah-REE
Dubois (də·bwä') duh-BWAH
Duce, Il (ēl doo'che) eel DOO-cheh
Ducos (dü·kō') doo-KO
Duero (dwe'rō) DWEH-roh
Dufourspitze (doo·fûr'shpit"sə) doo-FOOR-shpit-suh
Dufy (dü·fē') doo-FEE
Dukas (dü·kȧ') doo-KAH
Dukhobors (dū'kə·bôrz) DYOO-kuh-borz
Duluth (də·looth') duh-LOOTH
Dumas (doo·mä') doo-MAH
du Maurier (də·mâ'rė·ā) duh-MAW-ree-ay
Dumbarton (dum·bär'tən) dum-BAR-tun
Dunant (dü·nän') doo-NAHN
Dunbar (dun'bär) DUN-bar
Duncan (dung'kən) DUNK-un
Dundee (dun·dē') dun-DEE
Dunedin (dun·ē'din) dun-EE-din
Dunkerque, Dunkirk (dun'kērk) DUN-kerk
Dupin (dü·paṅ') doo-PAN
Duplessis (dü·ple·sē') doo-pleh-SEE
Duquesne (də·kān') duh-KANE
Durani (doo·rä'nė) doo-RAH-nee
Durazzo (doo·rät'sə) doo-RAHT-suh
Durban (dēr'bən) DUR-bun
Durer (dü'rer) DURE-er
Durham (dēr'əm) DER-um
Duroc (dū'rok) DOO-rock
Durres (dûr'əs) DURE-us
Duryea (dûr'yā) DURE-yay
Duse (doo'zə) DOO-zuh
Düsseldorf (düs'əl·dôrf") DISS-ul-dorf
Dvina (dvi·nä') dvi-NAH
Dvorák (dvôr'zhäk) duh-VORE-shock
Dwyfor (dwi'vōr) DWIH-vore
Dyak (dī'ak) DIE-ack
Dzhugashvili (joo"gə·shvē'lė) JOO-gush-VEE-lee

Eads (ēdz) EEDZ
Eakins (ā'kənz) A-kinz
Earhart (ār'härt) AIR-hart
Eastre (ā'os·tre) A-os-treh
Eau de Cologne (ō"də·kə·lōn') OH-duh-kuh-LONE
Ebro (ē'brō) EE-broh
Eclogue (ek'log) ECK-log
Ecuador (ek'wə·dôr) ECK-wuh-dore
Edam (ē'dam) EE-dam
Edda (ed'ə) ED-uh
Ederle (ed'ər·lė) ED-er-lee
Edessa (e'de·sä) EH-dess-uh
Edinburgh (ed'in·bûr"ə) ED-in-ber-uh
Edirne (e·dir'ne) eh-DEER-neh
Edmonton (ed'mən·tən) ED-mun-tun
Eduskunta (ā"dûs·kûn'tə) A-dus-KUHN-tuh
Efate (e·fä'tė) eh-FAH-tee
Eggleston (eg'əlz·tən) EGG-ulz-tun
Egypt (ē'jipt) EE-jipt
Eider (ī'dər) EYE-der
Eiffel (ī'fəl *or* [Fr.] e·fel') EYE-fel, *or, in French,* eh-FELL
Eildon (ēl'dən) EEL-dun
Einstein (īn'stīn) INE-stine
Einthoven (īnt'hō"vən) EYNT-hoe-vun
Eire (er'ə *or* ā'rə) AIR-uh *or* A-ruh
El Alamein (el·ä·lä·mān') el-AH-luh-MANE
Elba (el'bə) EL-buh
Elbe (el'bə) EL-buh
Elbrus (el'brəs) EL-brus
Elburz (el'bûrz) EL-boorz
El Dorado (el"dō·rä'dō) el-doe-RAH-doe
Eleazar (el"ė·ā'zär) EL-ee-A-zahr
Eleuthera (e·loo'the·rä) eh-LOO-thuh-rah
Elia (ē'lė·ə) EE-lee-uh
Eli, Eli (ā'lė, ā'lė) A-lee-A-lee
Elijah (i·lī'jə) ih-LIE-juh
Elimelech (e·lim'ə·lek) eh-LIM-uh-leck
Elisha (i·lī'shə) ih-LIE-shuh
Elisheba (i·lish'ə·bä) ih-LISH-uh-bah
Ellesmere (elz'mir) ELZ-mere
El Morro (el·môr'ō) el-MORE-oh
El-Oued (el·oo·ed') el-oo-ED
El Paso (el·pas'ō) el-PASS-oh
El Petén (el·pe·ten') el-peh-TEN
El Salvador (el·sal'və·dôr) el-SAL-vuh-dore
Elsinore (el·si·nôr') el-sih-NORE
Elysian (ė·lizh'ən) e-LIZH-un
Emmaus (e·mā'əs) eh-MAY-us
Emmenthal (em'ən·täl) EM-un-tahl
Endymion (en·dim'ė·ən) en-DIM-e-un
Engadine (en·gä·dēn') en-gah-DEEN
Engl:r (eng'lər) ENG-ler
Enid (ē'nid) EE-nid
Eniwetok (en·i·wē'tok) en-ih-WE-tock
Enoch (ē'nək) EE-nuck
Entebbe (en·teb'ə) en-TEB-uh
Eos (ē'os) EE-ahce
Epaphus (ep'ə·fəs) EP-uh-fuss
Épernay (ā"pər·nā') A-per-NAY
Ephesus (e1'ə·səs) EF-uh-suss
Ephraim (ē'frə·im) EE-fruh-im
Epictetus (ep·ik·tē'təs) ep-ick-TEE-tuss
Epimetheus (ep·i·mē'thəs) ep-ih-ME-thuss
Epiphany (i·pif'ə·nė) ih-PIF-uh-nee
Epirus (ė·pī'rəs) e-PIE-russ
Erasistratus (er·ə·sis'trə·təs) air-uh-SISS-truh-tus
Erasmus (e·raz'məs) eh-RAZZ-muss
Erato (er'ə·tō) AIR-uh-toe
Erebus (er'ə·bəs) AIR-uh-buss
Erech (ē'rek) EE-reck
Erechtheum (ė·rek·thē'əm) e-reck-THEE-um
Erewhon (er'ə·whon") air-uh-WHAHN
Ericsson (er'ik·sən) AIR-ick-sun
Erinyes (e·rin'ə·ėz) eh-RIN-uh-eez
Eris (er'is) AIR-iss
Eritrea (er"ə·trē'ə) AIR-uh-TREE-uh
Er:van (er·i·vän') air-ih-VAHN
Erne (ērn) ERN
Eroica (e·rō'i·kə) eh-ROE-ih-kuh
Eros (ē'ros) EE-rahce
Erytheia (er·ə·thē'ə) air-uh-THEE-uh
Esau (ē'sâ) EE-saw
Esch-Alzette (esh"äl·zet') ESH-ahl-ZET
Escorial (es·kôr'ė·əl) es-KORE-e-ul
Esdras (ez'drəs) EZ-druss
Esmeralda (ez"mər·äl'də) ez-mer-AHL-duh
Esopus (ə·sō'pəs) uh-SO-pus
Espanola (es·pän·yō'lə) es-pahn-YOH-luh
Esperanto (es"pə·rán'tō) es-puh-RAHN-toe
Esquiline (es'kwə·līn) ESS-kwuh-line
Esquimalt (es'ki·mält) ESS-kih-mahlt
Essen (es'ən) ESS-un
Essenes (ə·sēnz') eh-SEENZ
Este (äs'tė) ACE-teh
Esterhazy (äs'tər·hä·zė) ACE-ter-hah-zee
Estonia (es·tō'nė·ə) es-TOE-nee-uh
Estoril (ish·tə·rēl') ish-tuh-REEL
Estremadura (esh"tri·mə·dûr'ə) ESH-trih-muh-DURE-uh
Ethiopia (ē"thė·ō'pė·ə) ee-thee-OH-pe-uh
Etna (et'nə) ET-nuh
Étoile (ā·twäl') ay-TWAWL
Eton (ē'tən) EE-tun
Etruscan (ė·trus'kən) e-TRUSS-kun
Eucharist (ū'kə·rist) U-kuh-rist
Euclid (ū'klid) U-klid
Eulenspiegel (oi'lən·shpē"gəl) OI-lun-shpee-gul
Eumenides (ū·men'ə·dėz) u-MEN-uh-deez
Euphrates (ū·frā'tėz) u-FRAY-teez
Euphrosyne (ū·fros'ə·nė) u-FRAHCE-uh-nee
Eurasia (yû·rā'zhə) u-RAY-zhuh
Eureka (yû·rē'kə) u-REE-kuh
Euripides (yû·rip'ə·dėz) u-RIP-uh-deez
Europa (yû·rō'pə) u-ROE-puh
Euryale (ū·rī'ə·lė) u-RYE-uh-lee
Eurylochus (yû·ril'ə·kəs) u-RIL-uh-kus
Eurynome (yû·rin'ə·mė) u-RIN-uh-me
Eutaw (ū'tâ) U-taw
Euterpe (ū·tēr'pė) u-TER-pee
Evangeline (i·van'jə·lėn) ih-VAN-juh-leen
Everest (ev'ər·əst) EV-uh-rest
Exeter (eks'ə·tər) EX-uh-ter
Ezekiel (i·zē'kė·əl) ih-ZEE-kee-ul
Ezra (ez'rə) EZ-ruh

Faber (fā'bər) FAY-ber
Fabian (fā'bė·ən) FAY-be-un
Fabre (fȧ'brə) FAH-bruh
Faenza (fä·en'zə) fah-EN-zuh
Faerish (fār'ish) FARE-ish
Faeroe (fār'ō) FARE-oh
Faisal (fā'səl) FAY-sul
Fal (fal) FAL
Falaise (fä·lez') fah-LEZ
Falange (fā'lanj) FAY-lanje
Falkenhayn (fäl'kən·hīn) FAHL-kun-hine
Falkland (fâk'lənd) FAWK-lund
Falla (fä'lyä) FAHL-yah
Falloden (fal'ō·dən) FAL-oh-dun
Falmouth (fal'məth) FAL-muth
Falstaff (fâl'staf) FALL-staff
Faneuil (fan'ū·əl *or* fan'əl) FAN-yoo-ul *or* FAN-ul
Faraday (far'ə·dā) FA-ruh-day
Farouk (fä·rook') fah-ROOKE
Farragut (far'ə·gət) FA-ruh-gut
Fata Morgana (fä'tə·môr·gä'nə) FAH-tuh more-GAH-nuh
Fatima (fä'tė·mä) FAH-tih-mah
Fatimites (fat'i·mīt) FAT-ih-mite
Fauchard (fō"shär') foe-SHAR
Faulkner (fâk'nər) FAWK-ner
Faust (fowst) FOWST
Fawkes (fâks) FAWKS
Faxa (fäk'sä) FAHX-ah
Fayal (fī·äl') fie-AL
Fenian (fen'ė·ən) FEN-e-un
Fermi (fār'mė) FARE-me
Fernandina (fēr·nan·dē'nə) fer-nan-DEE-nuh
Ferrara (fer·rä'rä) feh-RAH-rah
Ferrer (fe·rer') feh-RARE
Ferriere (fer·ė·er') fair-e-AIR
Figaro (fė·gä·rō') fee-gah-ROE
Fiji (fē'jė) FEE-jee
Filipino (fel"ə·pē'nō) fil-uh-PEE-no
Fingal (fing'gəl) FING-gul
Finsteraahorn (fin'stər·är·hôrn) FIN-ster-ar-horn
Firenze (fė·ren'dze) fee-REN-zeh
Fitzalan (fitz·al'ən) fitz-AL-un
Fiume (fū'me) FEW-meh
Flaubert (flō"bār') flow-BARE
Fledermaus (fle'dər·mows") FLED-er-mouse
Flores (flō'res) FLOW-ress
Foch (fâsh) FAWSH
Foerster (fēr'stər) FER-ster
Foggia (fâd'jə) FAW-juh
Fogo (fō'goo) FOE-goo
Folkestone (fōk'stən) FOKE-stun
Folsom (fōl'səm) FOLE-sum
Fond du Lac (fon'də·lak) FON-duh-lack
Fontainebleau (fon'tən·blō") FON-tun-blow
Fontana (fon·tan'ə) fon-TAN-uh
Foochow (foo'chow) FOO-chow
Formosa (fôr·mō'sə) for-MOE-suh
Fortaleza (fôr"tə·lā'zə) for-tuh-LAY-zuh
Fort-de-France (fôr"də·fraṅs') for-duh-FRAHCE
Fort Nogales (nō·gal'əs) no-GAL-us
Fort Rouillé (rooē·yā') roo-ee-YAY
Fouché (foo·shā') foo-SHAY
Fourdrinier (fûr·drin'ė·ər) foor-DRIN-e-er
Fowey (foi) FOI
Fragonard (frȧ·gə·när') frah-guh-NAR
Francesca da Rimini (frän·chās'kə dä rē'mə·nė) frahn-CHASE-kuh dah REE-muh-nee
Frank (fränk) FRAHNK
Franco (frang'kō) FRANG-ko
Franconia (fran·kō'nė·ə) fran-KO-nee-uh
Frasch (fräsh) FRAHSH
Fraunhofer (frown'hō"fər) FROWN-hoe-fer
Fraumünster (frow'mün·stər) FROW-min-ster
Fraunces (frân'səs) FRAWN-sus
Freischütz (frī'shütz) FRY-shutz
Freud (froid) FROID
Frey (frī) FRY
Freya (frī'ə) FRY-uh
Friant (frē'ənt) FREE-unt
Fribourg (frė·boor') free-BOOR
Frietchie (frich'ė) FRITCH-e
Friml (frim'əl) FRIM-ul
Frisian (friz'ė·ən) FRIZ-e-un
Frobisher (frō'bish·ər) FROH-bish-er
Froebel (frû'bəl) FRUH-bul
Frome (froom) FROOM
Frontenac (fron'tə·nak) FRAHN-tuh-nack
Fuad (foo·ad') foo-AD
Fuca (foo'kə) FOO-kuh
Fuegian (fū·ē'jė·ən) few-EE-jee-un
Fuerteventura (fwer"tə·ven·too'rä) fware-tuh-ven-TOO-rah
Fujiyama (foo"jė·yä'mä) FOO-jee-YAH-mah
Fukien (foo·kyen') foo-KYEN
Fulani (fû·lä'nė) foo-LAH-nee
Fulbert (ful·bär') full-BARE
Funchal (foon·shäl') foon-SHAHL

Gaboriau (gȧ·bôr·yō') gah-bore-YO
Gabun (gä·bâṅ') gah-BAWN
Gaea (jē'ä) JEE-ah
Gael (gāl) GALE
Galápagos (gä·lä'pə·gâs) gah-LAH-puh-gawce
Galatea (gal·ə·tē'ə) gal-uh-TEE-uh
Galen (gā'lən) GAY-lun
Galena (gə·lē'nə) guh-LEE-nuh
Galicia (gə·lish'ə) guh-LISH-uh
Galilee (gal'ə·lė) GAL-uh-lee
Galileo (gal·ə·lē'ō) gal-uh-LEE-oh
Gallatin (gal'ə·tin) GAL-uh-tin
Gallaudet (gal·ə·det') gal-uh-DET
Galli-Curci (gäl'i·koor'chė) GAHL-e-KOOR-chee
Gallieni (gȧ·lyā·nē') gahl-yay-NEE
Gallipoli (gə·lip'ə·lė) guh-LIP-uh-lee
Galvani (gäl·vä'nė) gahl-VAH-nee

Galvez (gäl'väs) GAHL-vayce
Galway (gâl'wā) GAWL-way
Gamaliel (gə-mā'lē-əl) guh-MAY-lee-ul
Gama (gam'ə) GAM-uh
Gambetta (gam-bet'-ə) gam-BET-uh
Gambia (gam'bē-ə) GAM-be-uh
Gambrinus (gam-brī'nəs) gam-BRY-nuss
Gamelin (gäm-laṅ') gom-LAN
Gandhi (gän'dē) GAHN-dee
Ganges (gan'jēz) GAN-jeez
Ganymede (gan'ə-mēd) GAN-uh-meed
Garamond (gar'ə-mond) GA-ruh-mond
Garand (gar'ənd) GA-rund
Garcia (gär-sē'ə *or* gär'shə) gar-SEE-uh *or* GAR-shuh
Gargantua (gär-gan'tyû-ə) gar-GANT-yoo-uh
Garibaldi (gär-ə-bäl'dē) gar-uh-BALL-dee
Garonne (gä-rōn') gah-RONE
Gascoigne (gas'koin) gas-KOIN
Gascony (gas'kə-nē) GAS-kuh-nee
Gaspar (gas'pär) GAS-par
Gaspé (gas-pā') gas-PAY
Gastineau (gas'ti-nō) GAS-tih-no
Gatun (gä-toon') gah-TOON
Gauguin (gō-gaṅ') go-GAN
Gaul (gâl) GAWL
Gaulle, de (də-gōl') duh-GOLE
Gawain (gə-wān') guh-WANE
Gay-Lussac (gā″lü-sak') GAY-loo-SACK
Gaza (gā'zə) GAY-zuh
Gedrosia (jə-drō'zhə) juh-DROH-zhuh
Geheime-Staats-Polizei (ge-hī'mə shtäts pō-li-tsā) geh-HIGH-muh SHTAHTZ po-lit-SAY
Gehenna (gē-hen'ə) ghee-HEN-uh
Gehrig (ger'ig) GEH-rig
Gemara (gē-mä'rä) ghee-MAH-rah
Gemini (jem'i-nī) JEM-ih-nye
Genet (zhe-nā') zheh-NAY
Geneva (jə-nē'və) juh-NEE-vuh
Genghis Khan (jeng'gis-kän' *or* kan) JENG-giss-KAHN *or* KAN
Genoa (jen'ə-wə) JEN-uh-wuh
Genseric (jen'sə-rik) JEN-suh-rick
Gerona (he-rō'nə) he-ROE-nuh
Geronimo (je-ron'i-mō) jeh-RON-ih-mo
Gerry (ger'ē) GEH-ree
Geryon (jē'rē-ən) JEE-ree-un
Gessler (ges'lər) GUESS-ler
Gestapo (ges-tä'pō) guess-TAH-po
Gethsemane (geth-sem'ə-nə) geth-SEM-uh-nee
Ghats (gâts *or* gäts) GAWTZ *or* GAHTZ
Ghengis, see Genghis
Ghent (gent) GENT
Ghibelline (gib'ə-lēn) GIB-uh-leen
Ghiberti (gə-ber'tē) guh-BARE-tee
Ghilzais (gēl'ziz) GEEL-ziz
Ghirlandaio (gir″län-dä'yō) gear-lahn-DAH-yo
Gibraltar (ji-brâl'tər) jih-BRAWL-ter
Gide (zhēd) ZHEED
Giffard (jif'ərd) JIFF-erd
Gila (hē'lə) HE-luh
Gilead (gil'ē-əd) GIL-e-ud
Gilgamesh (gil'gə-mesh) GIL-guh-mesh
Gioconda (zhē-ō-kon'də) zhee-oh-KAHN-duh
Giorgione (jôr-jō'ne) jore-JOE-neh
Giotto (jot'ə) JOT-uh
Girard (ji-rärd') jih-RARD
Giraud (zhē-rō') zhee-ROE
Girondin (ji-ron'din) jih-RAHN-din
Girty (gĕr'tē) GUR-tee
Giza (gē'zə) GHEE-zuh
Gjoa (gyō'ə) GYOH-uh
Glasgow (glås'go *or* glås'kō) GLASS-go
Glauber (glow'bər) GLOW-ber
Glomma (glâm'mä) GLAW-mah
Gloucester (glos'tər) GLAHCE-ter
Gluck (glûk) GLOOK
Gneius Pompeius (gnā'əs pom-pā'əs) GNAY-us pom-PAY-us
Goajira (gō-ə-hē'rə) go-uh-HE-ruh
Gobelin (gob'ə-lin) GOB-uh-lin
Gobi (gō'bē) GO-be
Godhavn (gâth'hown) GAWTH-hown
Godiva (gə-dī'və) guh-DIE-vuh
Godey (gō'dē) GO-dee
Godthaab (gât'hōb) GAWT-hobe
Goebbels (gö'bəlz) GEHR-belz
Goering (gö'ring) GEH-ring
Goethals (gō'thəlz) GO-thulz
Goethe (gö'tə) GUR-tuh
Gogh (gokh *or* gō) GAHK *or* GO
Gogol (gō'gəl) GO-gull
Gola (gō'lə) GO-luh
Golgotha (gol-gō'thə) gol-GO-thuh
Goliath (gō-lī'əth) go-LIE-uth
Gomera (gō-mā'rä) go-MAY-rah
Gomez (gō'mās) GO-mace
Gomorrah (gə-môr'ə) guh-MORE-uh
Gonaïves (gâ-nə-ēv') gaw-nuh-EVE
Goncourt (gâṅ-koor') gawn-KOOR
Gonne (gon) GAHN
Gonzaga (gən-dzä'gə) gund-ZAH-guh
Gorboduc (gôr'bə-duk) GORE-buh-duck
Gorgas (gôr'gəs) GORE-gus
Gorgon (gôr'gən) GORE-gun
Gorgonzola (gôr″gən-zō'lə) GORE-gun-ZOH-luh
Gorki (gôr'kē) GORE-kee
Gorrie (gor'ē) GAH-ree
Goshen (gō'shən) GO-shun
Gosnold (goz'nōld) GAHZ-nolde
Gotama (gō'tə- ə) GO-tuh-muh
Gota (yö'tä) YO-tah
Goteborg (yö'tə-bôr″yə) yo-tuh-BORE-yuh
Gotha (gō'tä) GO-tah
Gotland (got'lənd) GOT-lund
Götterdämmerung (göt″tər-dem'me-roong) GET-er-DEM-eh-roong
Gottwald (gōt'vält) GOTE-vahlt
Gouda (khow'dä) COW-dah
Gould (goold) GOOLD
Goulet (goo'lā) GOO-lay
Gounod (goo-nō') goo-NO
Govind Singh (gō-vind' siṅ'hə) go-VIND SIN-huh
Goya (gō'yä) GO-yah
Gracchi (grak'ī) GRACK-eye
Gracchus (grak'əs) GRACK-us
Graciosa (grä-thē-ō'sō) grah-thee-OH-so
Graffir (graf'ər) GRAF-er
Granada (grə-nä'də) gruh-NAH-duh
Granados (grä-nä'dōs) grah-NAH-dose
Gran Chaco (grän-chäk'ō) grahn-CHAH-ko
Grand Manan (mə-nan') muh-NAN
Grand Pré (gran-prā') gran-PRAY
Grand-Terre (grand-târ') grand-TARE
Grand Trianon (trē-ə-nân') tree-uh-NAWN
Gran Paradiso (grän-pä-rə-dē'zə) grahn-pah-ruh-DEE-zuh
Grao (gräṅ) GRAHN
Grasse (gräs) GRAHCE
Gravenhage, 's- (skhrä'vən-hä″khə) SKRAH-vun-hah-kuh
Greco, El (grā'kō *or* grek'ō) GRAY-ko *or* GRECK-o
Greenwich Village (gren'ich) GREN-itch
Grieg (grig) GRIG
Grinnell (gri-nel') grih-NELL
Groningen (grō'ning-ən) GROW-ning-un
Grossglockner (gros'glok-nər) GRAHCE-glock-ner
Grossmünster (grōs-mün'stər) groce-MIN-ster
Gros Ventre (grō-ven'tər) grow-VEN-ter
Grotius (grō'shē-əs) GROW-she-us
Groton (grō'tən) GROW-ton
Gruenther (grun'thər) GRUN-ther
Guadalajara (gwä″də-lə-hä'rə) GWAH-duh-luh-HAH-ruh
Guadalcanal (gwä″dəl-kə-näl') GWAH-dul-kuh-NAL
Guadaloupe (gwä-də-loop') gwah-duh-LOOP
Guadalquivir (gwä-dəl-kē-vir') gwah-dull-kee-VEER
Guadeloupe (gâ-də-loop') gaw-duh-LOOP
Guadiana (gwä-thyä'nə) gwath-YAH-nuh
Guam (gwäm) GWAHM
Guanabara (gwə-nə-bär'ə) gwah-nuh-BAH-ruh
Guanacaste (gwä-nä-kä'stā) gwah-nah-KAH-stay
Guanches (gwän'chiz) GWAHN-chiz
Guarani (gwä-rä-nē') gwah-rah-NEE
Guardi (gwär'dē) GWAR-dee
Guarnieri (gwär-nā'rē) gwar-NAY-ree
Guatemala (gwä-tə-mä'lə) gwah-tuh-MAH-luh
Guayaquil (gwī-ə-kēl') GWY-uh-KEEL
Guayas (gwī'äs) GWY-ahce
Guelph (gwelf) GWELF
Guernica (gwer'ni-kə) GWARE-nih-kuh
Guernsey (gĕrn'zē) GERN-zee
Guerrière (gär-yär') gare-YARE
Guiana (gē-än'ə) ghee-AHN-uh
Guignol (gē-nyol') ghee-NYAHL
Guilbert (gēl-bär') gheel-BARE
Guillotin (gē-yō-taṅ') ghee-yo-TAN
Guinea (gin'ē) GHIN-e
Guipuzcoa (gē-pooth'kwä) ghee-POOTH-kwah
Guiteau (gi-tō') gih-TOE
Gujerati (goo-jə-rä'tē) goo-juh-RAH-tee
Gulick (gū'lik) GYOO-lick
Gurkha (gûr'kə) GHER-kuh
Gustavus (gus-täv'əs) gus-TAHV-us
Gutenberg (goo'tən-berkh) GOO-tun-berk
Guthrum (gûth'rəm) GOOTH-rum
Gwinnett (gwi-net') gwih-NET
Gwoza (gō-zä') go-ZAH

Haabai (hä'pī) HAH-pye
Haakon (hâ'kən) HAW-kun
Haarlem (här'ləm) HAR-lum
Habakkuk (hə-bak'ək) huh-BACK-uk
Haber (hä'bər) HAH-ber
Hadassah (hə-dä'sə) huh-DAH-suh
Hades (hā'dēz) HAY-deez
Hadrian (hā'drē-ən) HAY-dree-un
Haeckel (hek'əl) HECK-ul
Hafiz (hä-fēz') hah-FEEZ
Hagar (hā'gär) HAY-gar
Hagen (hä'gən) HAH-gun
Hagenbeck (hä'gən-bek) HAH-gun-beck
Hague (äg) AHG
Haida (hī'də) HYE-duh
Haifa (hī'fə) HYE-fuh
Haile Selassie (hī″lē-si-lä'sē) HYE-lee-sih-LAH-see
Haiti (hā'te) HAY-teh
Halévy (ha-lā-vē') ha-lay-VEE
Hallam (hal'əm) HAL-um
Halleck (hal'ək) HAL-uk
Hallidie (hal'i-dē) HAL-ih-dee
Hals (häls) HAHLCE
Halsey (hâl'sē) HAWL-see
Haltia (häl'tē-ə) HAHL-tee-uh
Halys (hā'lis) HAY-liss
Haman (hā'mən) HAY-mun
Hamelin (ham'ə-lin) HAM-uh-lin
Hammerskjold (håm'ər-shûld) HAM-er-shuld
Hammurabi (håm″û-rä'bē) HAHM-yuh-RAH-be
Hamsun (häm'sûn) HAHM-suhn
Han (hän) HAHN
Handel (han'dəl) HAN-dul
Hangchow (hang'chow) HANG-chow
Hankow (han'kow) HAN-cow
Hannibal (han'i-bəl) HAN-ih-bul
Hanoi (han'oi) HAN-oy
Hanover (han'ə-vər) HAN-uh-ver
Hanseatic (han″sē-at'ik) han-see-AT-ick
Hanska (hon'skə) HAHN-skuh
Hanukkah (hän'û-khä) HAHN-uh-kah
Hanun (hā'nən) HAY-nun
Hanyang (hän'yäng) HAHN-yahng
Harar (hä'rər) HAH-rer
Hargeisa (här-gā'sə) har-GAY-suh
Hargreaves (här'grēvz) HAR-greevz
Harlequin (här'lə-kwin) HAR-luh-kwin
Haroun-al-Rashid (hä-roon' ar″ ə-shēd') hah-ROON AR-uh-SHEED
Hashemite (hash'i-mit) HASH-ih-mite
Hathaway (hath'ə-wā) HATH-uh-way
Hatshepsut (hät-shep'sət) haht-SHEP-sut
Hatteras (hat'ə-rəs) HAT-uh-russ
Hauptmann (howpt'män) HOWPT-mahn
Haushofer (hows'hō-fər) HOUSE-hoe-fer
Haut-Rhin (ō-raṅ') o-RAN
Haüy (à-ü-ē') ah-oo-EE
Havre de Grace (Md.) (hav'ər-də-gras' *or* grās') HAVE-er-duh-GRASS *or* GRACE
Hawaii (hä-wī'ē) hah-WYE-e
Haydn (hī'dən) HYE-dun
Hayne (hān) HANE
Hazar (hā'zär) HAY-zar
Hearst (hĕrst) HERST
Hebe (hē'bē) HE-be
Hebrides (heb'ri-dēz) HEB-rih-deez
Hecate (hek'ə-tē) HECK-uh-tee
Hecuba (hek'yû-bə) HECK-yuh-buh
Heidelberg (hī'dəl-bĕrg) HYE-dul-berg
Heifetz (hī'fitz) HYE-fitz
Heine (hī'ne) HYE-neh
Hejaz (hē-jaz') he-JAZZ
Hela (hel'ä) HEL-ah
Helena (hel'ə-nə) HEL-uh-nuh
Heliopolis (hē″lē-op'ō-lis) HE-lee-OP-oh-liss
Helios (hē'lē-əs) HE-lee-us
Hellas (hel'əs) HEL-us
Hellespont (hel'əs-pont) HEL-us-pont
Helmand River (hel'mənd) HEL-mund
Heloise (ā-lō-ēz') A-lo-EEZ
Helsingfors (hel'sing-fôrz) HEL-sing-forze
Helsingor (hel'sing-ər) HEL-sing-er
Helsinki (hel'sing-kē) HEL-sing-kee
Helvetian (hel-vē'shən) hel-VEE-shun
Helvetic (hel-vet'ik) hel-VET-ick
Hemans (hem'ənz) HEM-unz
Hemiptera (hə-mip'tə-rə) huh-MIP-tuh-ruh
Henares (ā-nä'rəs) a-NAH-russ
Henlein (hen'līn) HEN-line
Hennepin (hen'ə-pin) HEN-uh-pin
Hephaestus (he-fes'təs) heh-FESS-tus
Hera (hē'rä) HE-rah
Heracles (her'ə-klēz) HARE-uh-kleez
Herculaneum (hĕr″kyû-lā'nē-əm) HER-kyoo-LAY-nee-um
Hercules (hĕr'kyû-lēz) HER-kyoo-leez
Hermes (hĕr'mēz) HER-meez
Hernani (er-nä'nē) air-NAH-nee
Herod (her'əd) HARE-ud
Herodias (he-rō'dē-əs) heh-ROE-dee-us
Herodotus (he-rod'ə-təs) heh-ROD-uh-tuss
Héroult (ā-roo') a-ROO
Herrick (her'ik) HARE-ick
Herzegovina (her″tsi-gō-vē'nə) hurt-sih-go-VEE-nuh
Herzlia (hert-slē'ä) hurt-SLEE-ah
Herzog (her'tzokh) HURT-zock
Hesperia (hes-pē'rē-ə) hess-PEE-ree-uh
Hesperides (hes-per'ə-dez) hess-PARE-uh-deez
Hesse (hes) HESS
Hestia (hes'tē-ə) HESS-tee-uh
Heyerdahl (hī'ər-däl″) HYE-er-dahl
Hiawatha (hī″ə-wä'thə) HYE-uh-WAH-thuh
Hidalgo (ə-thäl'gō) uh-THAHL-go
Hierro (ye'rō) YEH-roe
Hilary (hil'ə-rē) HILL-uh-ree
Hildebrand (hil'də-brand) HILL-duh-brand
Hillaby (hil'ə-bē) HILL-uh-be
Hillel (hil'əl) HILL-ul
Himalaya (hi-mä'lə-yə *or* him″ə-lā'yə) hih-MAH-luh-yuh *or* HIM-uh-LAY-uh
Himmler (him'lər) HIM-ler
Hindenburg (hin'dən-bĕrg) HIN-dun-berg
Hindu Kush (hin'doo-kûsh') HIN-doo-KUSH
Hindustan (hin'doo-stän) HIN-doo-stahn
Hinnom (hin'əm) HIN-um
Hippocrates (hi-pok'rə-tēz) hih-POCK-ruh-teez
Hippocratic (hip″ō-krat'ik) HIP-oh-KRAT-ick
Hippocrene (hip'ō-krēn) HIP-oh-kreen
Hippolyta (hi-pol'i-tə) hih-PAHL-ih-tuh
Hirohito (hē″rō-hē'tō) HE-roe-HE-toe
Hiroshima (hē″rō-shē'mə) HE-roe-SHE-muh
Hispaniola (his-pan″ē-ō'lə) hiss-PAN-e-OH-luh
Hittite (hit'īt) HIT-ite
Hiva Oa (hē'vä-ō'ä) HE-vah-OH-ah
Hoban (hō'bən) HOE-bun
Hobart (hō'bərt) HOE-bert
Hochelaga (hō″shə-lag'ə) HOE-shuh-LAG-uh
Ho Chi Minh (hō'chē-min') HOE-chee-MIN
Hodeida (hō-dā'də *or* hō-dī'də) hoe-DAY-duh *or* hoe-DYE-duh
Hofmannsthal (hōf'mans-täl) HOFE-mance-tahl
Hofmeister (hōf'mis-tər) HOFE-mice-ter
Hogarth (hō'gärth) HOE-garth
Hohenzollern (hō'ən-tsol-ərn) HOE-unt-ZAHL-ern
Hokkaido (hōk-kī'dō) hoe-KYE-doe
Holbein (hōl'bīn) HOLE-bine
Holborn (hō'bərn) HOE-bern
Hollandia (ho-lan'dē-ə) hah-LAN-dee-uh
Hollenberg (hol'ən-bĕrg) HAHL-un-berg
Holofernes (hō″lō-fĕr'nēz) hoe-lo-FER-neez
Holston (hōl'stən) HOLE-stun
Holyrood (hōl'ē-rood) HOE-lee-rude
Homma (hom-mä') HAH-mah
Homs (hâmz) HAWMZ
Honduras (hon-dûr'əs) hahn-DURE-us
Hong Kong (hong'kong') HAHNG-KAHNG
Honiara (hō″nē-ä'rä) hoe-nee-AH-rah
Honiton (hun'i-tən) HUN-ih-tun
Honolulu (hon″ə-loo'loo) hahn-uh-LOO-loo
Honshu (hon'shoo) HAHN-shoo
Hooghly (hoog'lē) HOOG-lee
Hoosac (hoo'sək) HOO-sack
Hoosier (hoo'zhər) HOO-zher
Hopi (hō'pī) HOE-pye
Horae (hō'rē) HOE-ree
Horatius (hō-rā'shəs) hoe-RAY-shus
Horowitz (hôr'ə-vitz) HORE-uh-vitz
Horthy (hôr'tē) HORE-tee
Hosea (hō-zē'ə) hoe-ZEE-uh
Houdin (oo-daṅ') oo-DAN
Houdini (hoo-dē'nē) hoo-DEE-nee
Houdon (oo-dâṅ') oo-DAWN
Housatonic (hoo″sə-ton'ik) hoo-suh-TAHN-ick
Housman (hows'mən) HOUSE-mun
Houston (hūs'tən) HUE-stun
Hoxha (hoy'ä) HOY-ah
Hradcany (hrät'chä-nē) HRAHT-chah-nee
Hsinking (shin'jing) SHIN-jing
Hudibras (hū'di-bras) HUE-dih-brahce
Huelva (wel'və) WELL-vuh
Huesca (we'skä) WEH-skah
Huguenot (hū'gə-not) HUE-guh-not
Huitzilopochtli (wēt-zēl-ō-poch'tlē) weet-zeel-oh-POTCHT-lee
Hukbalahap (huk″bä-lä-häp') HUCK-bah-lah-HAHP
Humboldt (hum'bōlt) HUM-bolt
Humperdinck (hum'pər-dink) HUM-per-dink
Humphrey (hum'frē) HUM-free
Hungary (hung'gə-rē) HUNG-guh-ree
Huron (hyûr'ən) HYOUR-un
Huss (hus) HUSS
Hussain (hû-sān') hoo-SANE
Huygens (hoi'gənz) HOY-gunz
Hvar (hvär) HVAR
Hwang Ho (hwäng-hō') hwahng-HOE
Hyatt (hī'ət) HYE-ut
Hyderabad (hī-drə-båd') hye-druh-BAHD
Hydra (hī'drə) HYE-druh
Hygeia (hī″jə-e'ə) hye-juh-EE-uh

Ibáñez (ē-bä'nyāth) e-BAHN-yayth
Iberia (ī-bir'ē-ə) eye-BEER-e-uh
Iberville (ē-ber-vēl') e-ber-VEEL
Ibn Saud (ib'ən-sû-ood') IB-un soo-OOD
Ibsen (ib'sən) IB-sun
Icarus (ik'ə-rəs) ICK-uh-russ
Ichang (yē″jäng') ye-JAHNG
Idar-Oberstein (ē″där-ō'bər-shtīn) EE-dar-OH-ber-shtine
Idris (i-dris') ih-DRISS
Ignatius (ig-nā'shəs) ig-NAY-shus
Igorot (ig″ə-rōt') ig-uh-ROTE
Iguassu (ēg-wä-soo') eeg-wah-SOO
IJsselmeer (ī'səl-mār) EYE-sul-mare
Ikhnaton (ik-nä'tən) ick-NAH-tun
Ilex (ī'leks) EYE-lex
Ilium (il'e-əm) ILL-e-um
Illampu (ē-yäm-poo') ee-yom-POO
Illyria (i-lir'ē-ə) ih-LEER-e-uh
Indus (in'dəs) IN-duss
Inness (in'əs) IN-us
Innsbruck (inz'brûk) INZ-brook
Innuit (in'ū-it) IN-u-it
Invalides (an″vä-lēd') an-vah-LEED
Io (ī'ō) EYE-oh
Ioannina (yō-ä'nē-nä *or* yä'nē-nä) yo-AH-nee-nah *or* YAH-nee-nah
Iolani (yō-lä'nē) yo-LAH-nee
Ionia (ī-ō'nē-ə) eye-OH-nee-uh
Iphigenia (if″ə-jē-nī'ə) IF-uh-jee-NYE-uh
Iquitos (ē-kē'tos) e-KEE-tahce
Iran (i-ran') ih-RAN
Iraq (ē-räk') e-ROCK
Irazú (ē-rä-soo') e-rah-SOO
Irkutsk (ir-kootsk') ear-KOOTSK
Irrawaddy (ir-ə-wod'ē) ear-uh-WAD-e
Irtysh (ir-tish') ear-TISH
Irwell (ĕr'wel) ER-well
Isaiah (ī-zā'ə) eye-ZAY-uh
Isar (ē'zär) EE-zar
Iseult (i-soolt') ih-SOOLT
Ishmael (ish'mā-el) ISH-may-el
Ishtar (ish'tär) ISH-tar
Isis (ī'sis) EYE-sis
Islam (is'ləm) ISS-lum
Ismaili (is-mä-ē'lē) iss-mah-EE-lee
Israel (iz'rā-el) IZ-ray-el
Istanbul (is-tan-bool') iss-tan-BOOL
Istria (is'trē-ə) ISS-tree-uh
Italia (ē-täl'yä) e-TAHL-yah
Itaska (ī-tas'kə) eye-TASS-kuh
Ithaca (ith'ə-kə) ITH-uh-kuh
Iviza (ē-vē'thä) e-VEE-thah
Iwo Jima (ē'wō-jē'mə) EE-woe-JEE-muh
Ixtaccihuatl (es″tä-sē'wät-əl) ess-tah-SEE-wat-ul
Izabal (ē-sä-bäl') e-sah-BAHL
Izalco (ē-säl'kō) e-SAHL-ko
Izmir (iz'mir) IZ-mere

Jacobean (jak″ə-bē'ən) jack-uh-BEE-un
Jacobin (jak'ō-bin) JACK-oh-bin
Jacobite (jak'ō-bīt) JACK-oh-bite
Jacquard (jà-kärd') jah-KARD
Jadwiga (yäd-vē'gä) yahd-VEE-gah
Jaen (hä-en') hah-EN
Jaffa (jaf'ə) JAFF-uh
Jagganath (jug'ə-nät) JUG-uh-naht
Jagiello (yä-gyel'ō) yahg-YELL-oh
Jain (jīn) JINE
Jakarta (jə-kär'tə) juh-KAR-tuh
Jalna (jal'nə) JAL-nuh
Jamaica (jə-mā'kə) juh-MAY-kuh
Jammu (jum'oo) JUM-oo
Janizary (jan'i-zer-ē) JAN-ih-zeh-ree
Janus (jā'nəs) JAY-nus
Java (jä'və) JAH-vah
Jebel Druze (jeb'əl drûz) JEB-ul DRUHZ
Jebel Musa (jeb'əl moo'sə) MOO-suh
Jehol (re-hû') reh-HER
Jelgava (yel'gä-vä) YELL-gah-vah
Jellicoe (jel'i-kō) JELL-ih-ko
Jena (yā'nä) YAY-nah
Jerez (hā'rāth) HAY-rayth
Jesuit (jez'oo-it) JEZ-oo-it
Jezebel (jez'ə-bel) JEZ-uh-bel
Jinnah (jin'ə) JIN-uh
Jivaros (hē-vä'rōs) he-VAH-rohce
Job (jōb) JOHB
Jocasta (jō-kås'tə) jo-KAS-tuh
Jochebed (jok'ə-bed) JOCK-uh-bed
Joffre (zhâ'frə) ZHAW-fruh
Johannesburg (jō-han'is-bĕrg) joe-HAN-is-berg
Jokjakarta (jog″yä-kär'tə) jog-yah-KAR-tuh
Jokkmokk (yâk'mâk″) YAWK-mawk
Joliet (jō-lē-et') joe-lee-ET
Joliot-Curie (jâ-lyō'kü-rē') jawl-YO-kyu-REE
Jolson (jōl'sən) JOLE-sun
Jonkers (yong'kərz) YONG-kerz
Josephus (jō-sē'fəs) joe-SEE-fuss
Joshua (josh'ū-ə) JOSH-u-uh
Jost Van Dyke (yōst-van-dīk') yohst-van-DIKE
Jostedalsbre (yōs'tə-däls-brā) YOHCE-tuh-dahlce-bray
Jotunheim (yō'tûn-hām) YO-tuhn-hame
Joule (jowl) JOWL
Juan de Fuca (wän″də-fûk'ə) WAHN-duh-FOOK-uh
Juan Fernandez (wän″fer-nän'des) fair-NAHN-dess
Juarez (hwä'rās) HWAH-race
Juba (joo'bä) JOO-bah
Jubal (joo'bəl) JOO-bul
Júcar (hoo'kär) HOO-kar
Judah (joo'də) JOO-duh
Judas Iscariot (joo'dəs is-kar'ē-ət) JOO-duss iss-KA-ree-ut
Judas Maccabaeus (joo'dəs mak″ə-bē'əs) mack-uh-BEE-us
Jude (jood) JOOD
Judea (joo-dē'ə) joo-DEE-uh
Juggernaut (jug'ər-nât) JUG-er-nawt
Jullundur (jə-lun'dər) juh-LUN-der
Jumna (jûm'nə) JUHM-nuh
Juneau (joo'nō) JOO-no
Jung (yûng) YUHNG
Jungfrau (yûng'frow) YUNG-frow
Juno (joo'nō) JOO-no
Jura (jûr'ə) JURE-uh
Jurgen (jĕr'gən) JER-gun
Justinian (jus-tin'ē-ən) juss-TIN-e-un
Juventas (joo-ven'təs) joo-VEN-tuss

Kaaba (kä'bä) KAH-bah
Kabuki (kä-boo-kē') kah-boo-KEE
Kabul (kä'bûl) KAH-bull
Kachin (kə-chin') kuh-CHIN
Kaddish (käd'ish) KAHD-ish
Kadesh (kā'desh) KAY-desh
Kadota (kə-dō'tə) kuh-DOE-tuh
Kaffir (kaf'ər) KAFF-er
Kailas (kī-läs') kye-LAHCE
Kairouan (ker-wäṅ') ker-WAHN
Kakabeka (kak″ə-bek'ə) KACK-uh-BECK-uh
Kalahari (kä-lä-hä'rē) kah-lah-HAH-ree
Kalapana (kä-lä-pä'nä) kah-lah-PAH-nah
Kalgan (käl-gän') kahl-GAHN
Kali Besar (kä'lē-be-sär') KAH-lee-beh-SAR
Kaliningrad (kä-lēn'in-grät) kah-LEEN-in-graht
Kalmuck (kal'muk) KAL-muck
Kama (kä'mə) KAH-muh
Kamchatka (kam-chat'kə) kam-CHAT-kuh
Kamehameha (kä-mā'ə-mā'ə) kah-MAY-uh-MAY-uh
Kanawha (kə-nâ'wə) kuh-NAW-wuh
Kanchenjunga (kun″chən-jung'gə) kun-chun-JUNG-guh
Kano (kä'nō) KAH-no
Kant (känt) KAHNT
Kaph (käf) KAHF
Kapital (käp″i-täl') kop-ih-TAHL
Kaprun (kä'prûn) KAH-pruhn
Karachi (kə-rä'chē) kuh-RAH-chee
Karafuto (kä-rä'foo-tə) kah-RAH-foo-tuh
Karageorgevitch (kar″ə-jôr'jə-vich) KA-ruh-GEORGE-uh-vitch
Karakorum (kar″ə-kôr'əm) ka-ruh-KORE-um
Karelia (kə-rēl'yə) kuh-REEL-yuh
Karnak (kär'nak) KAR-nack
Kashmir (kash'mir) CASH-mere
Kaskaskia (kas-kas'kē-ə) kass-KASS-kee-uh
Kasperle (käs'pər-le) KAHCE-per-leh
Katahdin (kə-tä'din) kuh-TAH-din
Katana (kä-tä'nə) kah-TAH-nuh
Katanga (kä-täng'gə) kah-TAHNG-guh
Katmai (kat'mī) KAT-mye
Katmandu (kät-män-doo') kot-mon-DOO
Kattegat (kat'i-gat) KAT-ih-gat
Kauai (kow-ī') cow-EYE
Kaunas (kow'näs) COW-nahce
Kazakh (kä-zäk') kah-ZAHK
Kazan (kə-zan') kuh-ZAN
Keble (kē'bəl) KEE-bul
Kebnekaise (keb″nə-kī'sə) keb-nuh-KYE-suh
Kecskemét (kech'kə-māt) KETCH-kuh-mate
Kemal Ataturk (ke-mäl'ä'tä-tĕrk) keh-MAHL-AH-tah-terk
Kemi (ke'mē) KEH-me
Keministiquia (kem″in-i-stik'wē-ə) kem-in-ih-STICK-we-uh
Kenduskeag (ken-dus'kēg) ken-DUSS-keeg
Kenesaw (ken'i-sâ) KEN-ih-saw
Kennebec (ken'i-bek) KEN-ih-beck
Kenosha (ki-nō'shə) kih-NO-shuh
Kenya (ken'yə) KEN-yuh
Kerensky (ke-ren'skē) keh-REN-skee
Kerinchi (kə-rin'chē) kuh-RIN-chee
Khadijah (käh-dē'jä) kah-DEE-jah
Khan (kän *or* kan) KAHN *or* CAN
Kharkov (kär'kof) KAR-kahf
Khartoum (kär-toom') kar-TOOM
Khedive (kə-dēv') kuh-DEEV
Khelat (ke-lat') keh-LAT
Khios (kī'əs) KYE-us
Khitai (khi-tī') kih-TYE
Khmer (khmer) KMARE
Khorat (khō-rät') ko-RAHT
Khrushchev (krû'shōf″) KRUH-shofe
Khufu (koo'foo) KOO-foo
Khyber (kī'bər) KYE-ber
Kialing (jyä'ling″) JYAH-ling
Kibo (kē'bō) KEE-bo
Kiddush (kid'ûsh) KID-oosh
Kiel (kēl) KEEL
Kiernan (kir'nən) KEER-nun
Kiev (kē'yef) KEE-yef
Kija (kē'jä) KEE-jah
Kikuyu (kē-koo'yoo) kee-KOO-yoo
Kilauea (kē″lä-wä'ə) KEE-lah-WAY-uh
Kilimanjaro (ki″lə-mən-jä'rō) kih-luh-mun-JAH-roe
Killarney (ki-lär'nē) kih-LAR-nee
Kind (kint) KINT
Kinnaird (ki-närd') kih-NAIRD
Kiowa (kī'ō-wə) KYE-oh-wuh
Kirghiz (kir-gēz') keer-GHEEZ
Kiruna (kē'rə-nä) KEE-ruh-nah
Kishinev (ki-shi-nyef') kih-shih-NYEF
Kismet (kiz'mət) KIZ-mut
Kitimat (kit'i-mat) KIT-ih-mat
Kittatinny (kit'ə-tin″ē) KIT-uh-tin-e
Kiva (kē'vä) KEE-vah
Kiwanis (ki-wän'əs) kih-WAHN-us
Kjellen (kyā'lən) KYAY-lun
Klaipeda (klī'pe-dä) KLYE-peh-dah
Klaproth (kläp'rōt) KLOP-rote
Kleinforth (klīn'fôrth″) KLINE-forth
Knesset (knes'it) KNESS-it
Knox (noks) NOCKS
Kobe (kō'be) KOH-beh
Koch (kokh) cock
Kodiak (kō'dē-ak) KOH-dee-ack
Koerner (kĕr'nər) KER-ner
Koh-i-noor (kō'ē-noor) KOH-ee-noor
Koh-i-Nuh (kō'ē-nû) KOH-ee-nuh
Kohler (kō'lər) KOH-ler
Kölln (kûln) KUHLN
Komodo (kō-mō'dō) koh-MOE-doh
Komsomolsk (kum'sə-mâlsk) KUM-suh-mawlsk
Königsberg (kö'niks-berk) KER-nix-behrk
Kon-Tiki (kon-tē'kē) kahn-TEE-kee
Konya (kân'yä) KAWN-yah
Kootinai (koo'ti-nā) KOO-tih-nay
Koran (kō'rən *or* kō-rän') KOH-run *or* koe-RAHN
Korea (kō-rē'ə) koh-REE-uh
Koritsa (kə-rit'sə *or* kō-rē-tsä') kuh-RIT-suh *or* koe-reet-SAH
Koryak (kər-yäk') ker-YOCK
Korzeniowski (kâ-zhə-nyâf'skē) kaw-zhun-YAWF-skee
Korzybski (kôr-zip'skē) kore-ZIP-skee
Kosciusko (kos″ē-us'kō) kahce-e-US-koe
Kossuth (kos″sooth') kah-SOOTH
Koto (kō'tō) KOE-toe
Kotor (kō'tôr) KOE-tore
Kovno (kâv'nə) KAWV-nuh
Kowloon (kow-loon') cow-LOON
Krakatoa (krak″ə-tō'ə) KRACK-uh-TOE-uh
Kreisler (krīs'lər) KRICE-ler
Kremer (krā'mər) KRAY-mer
Krientz (krēns) KREENCE
Kronstadt (kron-shtät') krahn-SHTAHT
Kru (kroo) KROO
Kruger (kroo'gər) KROO-ger
Krupp (krûp) KRUHP
Kuala Lumpur (kwä'lə-lûm-pûr') KWAH-luh-luhm-POOR
Kublai (koob'lī) KOOB-lie
Kukri (kûk'rē) COOK-ree
Kun (kûn) KUHN
Kuomintang (kwō-min-tang') kwoh-min-TANG
Kupang (koo'pang) KOO-pang
Kura (koo-rä') koo-RAH
Kurdistan (koor-dis-tän') koor-dis-TAHN
Kure (koo'rā) KOO-ray
Kurile (koo-rēl') koo-REEL
Kusaie (koo-sī'ə) koo-SIGH-uh
Kutuzov (kû-too'zâf) kuh-TOO-zawf
Kuwait (kû-wāt') kuh-WAIT
Kwajalein (kwä'jä-lān) KWAH-jah-lane
Kwakiutl (kwä″kē-oo'təl) KWAH-kee-OO-tul
Kwangtung (kwang'tûng) KWANG-toong
Kyi Chu (chē' choo') CHEE-CHOO
Kyoto (kyō'tō) KYOH-toe
Kyushu (kyoo'shoo') KYOO-SHOO

Laban (lā'bən) LAY-bun
Lacedaemonia (las″ə-dē-mō'nē-ə) LASS-uh-dee-MOH-nee-uh
Lachesis (lak'ə-sis) LACK-uh-sis
Lachine (lə-shēn') luh-SHEEN
Laconia (lə-kō'nē-ə) luk-KOH-nee-uh
Ladino (lä-dē'nō) lah-DEE-no
Ladoga (lä'də-gə) LAH-duh-guh
La Farge (là-färj') lah-FARGE
Lafayette (lä-fē-et') lah-fee-ET
Lafitte (là-fēt') lah-FEET
La Follette (là-fol'it) lah-FAHL-it
La Fontaine (là-fâṅ-ten') lah-fawn-TEN
Lagerlöf (lä'gər-lüf) LAH-ger-lif
Lagos (lä'gâs) LAH-gawce
Lagting (läg'ting) LAHG-ting
LaGuardia (lä-gwär'dyə) lah-GWARD-yuh
Lahore (lə-hôr') luh-HORE
l'Aiglon (läg-lâṅ') lay-GLAWN
Laius (lā'yəs) LAY-us
Lamar (lə-mär') luh-MAR
Lambaréné (läm-bä-re-nā') lom-bah-reh-NAY
Lammas (lam'əs) LAM-us
Lanai (lə-nī') luh-NYE
Lancashire (lang'kə-shir) LANG-kuh-sheer
Lancaster (lang'kə-stər) LANG-kuh-ster
Landseer (lan'sir) LAN-sere
Langeberg (läng'ə-berkh) LAHNG-uh-behrk
Languedoc (läṅ-gə-dâk') lahn-guh-DAWK
Lanier (lə-nir') luh-NEAR
Lanzarote (län″thä-rō'tā) lahn-thah-ROE-tay
Lao (läō) LAH-oh
Laocoön (lā-ok'ō-ən) lay-OCK-oh-un
Laoighis (lā'ish *or* lāks) LAY-ish *or* LAKES
Laos (lā'os) LAY-oss
Lao-Tse (low-dzu') loud-ZUH
La Paz (lə-päz') luh-PAHZ
La Plata (lä-plä'tä) lah-PLAH-tah
Lar (lär) LAR
Laramie (lar'ə-mē) LA-ruh-me
La Salle (là-sàl') lah-SAHL
La Scala (lä scä'lə) lah-SKAH-luh
Las Casas (läs-kä'säs) lahce-KAH-sahce
Las Palmas (läs-päl'mäs) lahce-PAHL-mahce
Lassen (las'ən) LASS-un
Las Vegas (läs-vā'gəs) lahce-VAY-gus
Latinus (lə-tī'nəs) luh-TIE-nus
Latium (lā'shē-əm) LAY-she-um
La Trappe (lä-träp') lah-TRAHP
Latvia (lat'vē-ə) LAT-vee-uh
Lauder (lâ'dər) LAWD-er

Laurentian (lä-ren'shan) law-REN-shun
Laurier (lô'rē-ā) LAW-ree-ay
Lausanne (lō-zän') lo-ZAHN
Laval (lá-vál') lah-VAHL
La Vallière (là-vá-lyer') lah-vahl-YARE
Lavoisier (là-vwä-zyā') lah-vwah-ZYAY
Lazard (lá-zärd') lah-ZARD
Lazarus (laz'a-rəs) LAZ-uh-russ
Leahy (lā'hē) LAY-he
Leander (lē-an'dər) lee-AN-der
Lebanon (leb'a-nən) LEB-uh-nun
Lech (lekh) LECK
Leclerc (lə-klâr') luh-KLARE
Le Corbusier (lə-kôr-bü-zyā') luh-kore-byoo-ZYAY
Leeuwenhoek (lā'vun-hook) LAY-vun-hook
Léger (lā-zhā') lay-ZHAY
Le Havre (lə-hävr') luh-HAHV-ruh
Lehzen (lā'zən) LAY-zun
Leibnitz, Leibniz (līp'nĭts) LIPE-nitz
Leicester (les'tər) LES-ter
Leiden (lī'dən) LYE-dun
Leine (lī'na) LYE-nuh
Leinster (len'stər) LEN-ster
Leipsic (līp'sĭk) LIPE-sick
Leipzig (līp'sĭg) LIPE-sig
Leitrim (lē'trĭm) LEE-trim
Leman (lə-män') leh-MAHN
Lemberg (lem'berk) LEM-behrk
Lempa (lem'pä) LEM-pah
Lenin (lyā'nyĭn) LYAY-nyin
Leningrad (len'in-grad) LEN-in-grad
Leofric (lā'ô-rēk or le-of'rĭk) lee-AHF-rik
León (lā-ōn') lay-OHN
Leonardo da Vinci (lā'a-när'dō dä vēn'chē) LAY-uh-NAR-doh dah VEEN-chee
Leonidas (lē-on'i-dəs) lee-AHN-ih-dus
Lepidus (lep'i-dəs) LEP-ih-dus
Lérida (lā're-thä) LARE-e-thah
Lerna (lẽr'nə) LER-nuh
Lerwick (lẽr'wĭk) LER-wick
Lesbos (lez'bəs) LEZ-bus
Lescaze (les-käz') less-KAZE
Lesseps (le-seps') leh-SEPS
Lethe (lē'thē) LEE-thee
Leto (lē'tō) LEE-toe
Letzburgesch (lēts'berg-ish) LETS-berg-ish
Leverrier (lə-ve-ryā') leh-ver-YAY
Levi (lē'vī) LEE-vie
Lewes (lū'is) LOO-iss
Leyte (lā'te) LAY-teh
Lhasa (lä'sə) LAH-suh
Liberia (lī-bir'ē-ə) lie-BEER-e-uh
Libra (lī'brə) LIE-bruh
Libya (lĭb'ē-ə) LIB-e-uh
Lichnowsky (likh-nôf'skē) lick-NOFE-skee
Lie, Trygve (lē, trĭg'və) LEE, TRIG-vee
Liechtenstein (likh'tən-shtīn) LICK-tun-shtine
Lied (lēt) LEET
Lieder (lē'dər) LEE-der
Liège (lyezh) lee-EZH
Ligurian (lĭ-gyŏŏr'ē-ən) lih-GYOOR-e-un
Lilienthal (lil'yən-thäl) LIL-yun-thawl
Liliuokalani (lē'lē-wō-kä-lä'nē) LEE-lee-woh-kah-LAH-nee
Lille (lēl) LEEL
Lima (lē'mä) LEE-muh
Limburg (lĭm'bẽrg) LIM-berg
Limmat (lĭm'ät) LIH-mot
Limoges (lē-mōzh') lee-MOHZH
Limon (lē-mōn') lee-MAWN
Limpopo (lĭm-pō'pō) lim-PO-po
Linde (lĭn'də) LIN-duh
Lingayen (ling-gä'yen) ling-GAH-yen
Linnaeus (lĭ-nē'əs) lih-NEE-us
Linné (lĭ-nā') lih-NAY
Lippershey (lĭp'ərs-hī) LIP-erce-high
Lippi (lēp'ē) LEEP-e
Lisboa (lesh-bō'a) lesh-BOH-uh
Lisbon (lĭz'bən) LIZ-bun
Lisburne (lĭz'bẽrn) LIZ-bern
Lisle (līl) LILE or LEEL
Liszt (lĭst) LIST
Lithuania (lĭth-ū-ā'nē-ə) lith-oo-A-nee-uh
Lityerses (lĭt'ē-ẽr'sēz) lit-e-ER-seez
Li Urh (lē'ẽr') LEE-OOR
Livorno (lē-vôr'nō) lee-VORE-no
Livy (lĭv'ē) LIV-e
Ljubljana (lyōō'blyä-nä) LYOO-blyah-nah
Llanquihue (lyän-kē'we) lyahn-KEE-weh
Llullaillaco (yōō'yī-yä'kō) YOO-yi-YAH-ko
Locarno (lō-kär'nō) loh-KAR-no
Loch Lomond (lokh-lō'mənd) lock-LOH-mund
Lodz (lŭdzh) LUDGE
Lofoten (lō-fō'tən) lo-FOE-tun
Loheiya (lō-hä'yə) lo-HAY-yuh
Lohengrin (lō'hen-grĭn) LO-hen-grin
Loire (lwär) LWAHR
Loki (lō'kē) LO-kee
Lombardy (lom'bär-dē) LAHM-ber-dee
Londinium (lon-dĭn'ē-əm) lon-DIN-e-um
Lopes (lō'pəs) LO-pis
Lorelei (lō're-lī) LO-reh-lie
Loreto (lō-rā'tō) lo-RAY-toe
Lorimer (lor'ə-mər) LAHR-ih-mer
Lorraine (lə-rān') luh-RAIN
Los Alamos (lōs-ä'lä-mōs) lohce-AH-lah-mohce
Losantiville (lō-san'tĭ-vĭl) lo-SAN-tih-vil
Lough Neagh (läkh-nā') lawk-NAY
Lourdes (lŏŏrdz) LOORDZ
Lourenço Marques (lō-ren'sō mär'kes) law-REN-so MAR-kess
Louth (louth) LOWTH
Louvain (loo-veń') loo-VEN
Louvre (loov'rə) LOOVE-ruh
Loyola (loi-ō'lə) loy-OH-luh
Luanda (loo-än'da) loo-AHN-duh
Luang Prabang (loo-äng' prä-bäng') loo-AHNG prah-BANG
Lubbock (lŭb'ək) LUB-uck
Lübeck (loo'bek) LOO-beck
Lublin (lyoo'blĭn) LYOO-blin
Luce (loos) LOOSE
Lucerne (loo-sẽrn') loo-SERN
Lucifer (loo'sĭ-fər) LOO-sih-fer
Ludendorff (loo'dən-dôrf) LOO-dun-dorf
Luftwaffe (lŏŏft'wof'ə) LUHFT-wahf-uh
Luini (loo-ē'nē) loo-EE-nee
Luiz (lwēz) LWEECE
Lully (lü-lē') lih-LEE
Lupescu (loo-pes'ku) loo-PESS-kuh
Lusaka (loo-sä'kä) loo-SAH-kah
Lusatia (loo-sā'shə) loo-SAY-shuh
Lusitania (loo-sĭ-tā'nē-ə) loo-sih-TAY-nee-uh
Luther (loo'thər) LOO-ther
Lutzen (lüt'sən) LIT-sun
Luxembourg (luk'səm-bẽrg) LUX-um-berg
Luxor (lŭk'sər) LOOK-ser
Luzon (loo-zon') loo-ZAHN
Lycabettus (lĭk'a-bet'us) LICK-uh-BET-us
Lycidas (lĭs'a-dəs) LISS-uh-duss
Lycomedes (lī-kə-mē'dēz) lie-kuh-MEE-deez
Lyell (lī'əl) LIE-ul
Lyon (lē-ōn') lee-OHN
Lysenko (lĭ-seng'kō) lih-SENG-ko
Lysistrata (lī-sis'tru-tə) lie-SIS-truh-tuh

Maas (mäs) MAHCE
Macassar (ma-kas'ar) muh-KASS-er
Macaulay (ma-kô'lē) muh-KAW-lee
Macbeth (mak-beth') mack-BETH
Maccabees (mak'a-bēz) MACK-uh-beez
MacCumhal (ma-koom'al) muh-KUM-ul
Macedon (mas'a-don) MASS-uh-dahn
Macedonia (mas-a-dō'nē-a) mass-uh-DOH-nee-uh
McGuigan (ma-gē'gon) muh-GHEE-gun
Mach (mäkh) MOCK
Machado (ma-shä'thoo) mah-SHAH-thoo
Machiavelli (mä'kyä-vel'ē) mock-yah-VEL-e
Machu Picchu (mä'choo-pēk'choo) MAH-choo-PECK-choo
Mackinac (mak'i-nä or mak'i-nak) MACK-ih-naw or MACK-ih-nack
Macomb (ma-kōm') muh-COMB
Macon (mā'kon) MAY-kun
Madagascar (mad'a-gas'kar) mad-uh-GAS-ker
Madeira (ma-dir'a) muh-DEER-uh
Madras (ma-dräs') muh-DRAHCE
Madrid (ma-drĭd') muh-DRID
Maecenas (mē-sē'nəs) mee-SEE-nuss
Maeterlinck (mā'tər-lĭnk) MAY-ter-link
Mafia (mä'fē-ä) MAH-fee-ah
Magdalen (mag'də-lĭn) MAG-duh-lin... muh-JELL-un
Magi (mā'jī) MAY-jie
Maginot (mazh'i-nō) MA-zhi-noh
Magog (mā'gog) MAY-gahg
Magyar (mod'yär) MAHD-yer
Mahan (ma-han') muh-HAN
Mahdi (mä'dē) MAH-dee
Mahican (ma-hē'kən) muh-HE-kun
Mahratta (ma-rät'a) ma-RAT-e
Mahrata (ma-rät'a) muh-RAT-uh
Maintenon (mańt-nâń') mant-NAWN

Mainz (mĭntz) MYNTZ
Majlis (maj-lis') madge-LISS
Majorca (ma-jôr'ka) muh-JORE-kuh
Majunga (mə-jung'gə) muh-JUNG-gah
Makah (mä-kä') mah-KAH
Makere (mä-kā're) mah-KAY-reh
Makin (mä'kĭn) MAY-kin
Malachi (mal'a-kī) MAL-uh-kye
Malaga (mal'ə-gə or mä'lä-gä) MAL-uh-guh or MAH-lah-gah
Malagasy (mal'a-gas'e) mal-uh-GAS-e
Malaita (mä-let'a) mah-LET-uh
Malar (mä'lär) MEH-lar
Malaspina (mal'as-pē'na) mal-us-PEE-nuh
Malay (mä'lā) MAY-lay
Malaya (ma-lā'a) muh-LAY-uh
Malenkov (mä-len'kof) mah-LEN-kahf
Mali Hka (mä'lē hkä) MAH-lee kah
Mallet (ma-le') mah-LEH
Malmo (mäl'mō) MAL-mo
Malory (mal'ə-rē) MAL-uh-ree
Malpighi (mäl-pē'gē) mahl-PEE-guh
Malta (môl'ta) MAWL-tuh
Malthus (mal'thəs) MAL-thus
Mameluke (mam'a-look) MAM-uh-luke
Managua (mä-nä'gwä) mah-NAHG-wah
Manassas (ma-nas'əs) muh-NASS-us
Manasseh (ma-nas'e) muh-NASS-uh
Mancala (mang-kä'lä) mang-KAH-luh
Manche (mänsh) mahnsh
Manchu (man-choo') man-CHOO
Manchukuo (man-choo'kwō) man-CHOO-kwoh
Manchuria (man-chŏŏr'ē-ə) man-CHOOR-e-uh
Mandalay (man'də-lā) MAN-duh-lay
Mandingo (män-dēng'gō) mahn-DEENG-go
Maness (mä'nes) MAY-ness
Manet (ma-ne') mah-NEH
Manila (ma-nĭl'a) muh-NILL-uh
Manitoba (man-i-tō'ba) man-ih-TOE-buh
Manitou (man'i-too) MAN-ih-too
Mannerheim (män'ər-hām) MAHN-er-hame
Manon Lescaut (ma'nôn les-kō') mah-NAWN les-KOH
Manono (mä-nō'nō) mah-NO-no
Manta (män'tä) MAHN-tah
Mantua (man'tyoo-a) MAN-tyoo-uh
Manua (mä-noo'ä) mah-NOO-uh
Manutius (ma-noo'shē-əs) muh-NOO-she-us
Manzailla (män-sä-nēy'ō) mahn-sah-NEE-yo
Manzanares (män-thä-nä'res) mahn-thah-NAHR-es
Manzoni (män-dzō'nē) mahnd-ZOH-nee
Maori (mow'rē or mä'ō-rē) MAH-oh-ree
Mao Tse-tung (mä'ō-dzu-dŏŏng') MAH-oh-dzuh-DUHNG
Mapuche (mä-poo'cha) mah-POO-chuh
Maracaibo (mä-rä-kī'bō) mah-rah-KYE-bo
Maracay (mä-rä-kī') mah-rah-KYE
Marañón (mä-rä-nyōn') mah-rah-nyONE
Marat (mä-rä') mah-RAH
Marciano (mär-sē-ä'nō) mar-see-AH-no
Marconi (mär-kō'nē) mar-KO-nee
Marcy (mär'sē) MAR-see
Mardi Gras (mär'dĭ-grä') MAR-dih-grah
Margate (mär'gāt) MAR-gate
Maria d'Aquino (mä-rē'ä dä-kwē'no) mah-REE-ah dä-KWEE-no
Marianas (mä-rē-ä'nəs) mah-ree-AHN-us
Marib (mä'rĭb) MA-rib
Mariehamm (mä-rē'a-hamm) mah-REE-uh-hahm
Mariposa (mar-i-pō'zə) mar-ih-PO-zuh
Marives (mä-rē-vē'lās) mah-ree-vee-VAY-lace
Marmara (mär'ma-ra) MAR-muh-ruh
Marmolado (mär-mō-lä'dä) mar-mo-LAH-dah
Marne (märn) MARN
Maro (mä'rō) MAY-roh
Marquesas (mär-kā'səs) mar-KAY-suss
Marquette (mär-ket') mar-KET
Marrakesh (mä-rä'kesh) mah-RAH-kesh
Marsala (mär-sä'lä) mar-SAH-lah
Marseilles (mär-sā'yə) mar-SEH-yuh
Martinique (mär-tə-nēk') mar-tuh-NEEK
Marx (märks) MARKS
Marxen (märk'sən) MARK-sun
Masaryk (mä'sä-rĭk) mah-SAH-rick
Masaya (mä-sä'yä) mah-SAH-yah
Maseru (mä'sə-roo) MA-suh-roo
Masefield (mās'fēld) MACE-field
Masham (mas'am) MASH-um
Masis Leusar (mä-sēs' loo-sär') mah-SEECE loo-SAR
Maskelyne (mas'ka-līn) MASS-kuh-line
Masorah (ma-sō'ra) muh-SO-ruh
Masovia (ma-sō've-a) muh-SO-vee-uh
Massasoit (mas'a-soit) MASS-uh-soit
Massey (mas'ē) MASS-e
Massilia (ma-sĭl'ē-ə) ma-SILL-e-uh
Matanuska (mat'a-noo'ska) mat-uh-NOO-skuh
Matanzas (ma-tan'zas) muh-TAN-zuss
Mather (mā'thər) MA-ther
Mathias (ma-thī'əs) muh-THIGH-us
Matisse (ma-tēs') mah-TEECE
Matthias (mat'a-thī'əs) MAT-uh-THIGH-us
Mattatuk (mat'a-tuk) MAT-uh-tuck
Matthias (ma-thī'as) ma-THIGH-us
Maugham (môm) MAWM
Maui (mow'ē) MA-oo-e
Mauldin (môl'dĭn) MAWL-din
Mau Mau (mow'mow') MA-oo-MA-oo
Maumee (mô-mē') maw-MEE
Mauna Loa (mow'nä-lō'ä) MAH-oo-nah LO-ah
Maupassant (mō-pa-sähń') mo-puh-SAHN
Mauritania (môr'i-tā'nē-ə) more-ih-TAY-nee-uh
Mauritius (ma-rĭsh'əs) muh-RISH-us
Maury (mä-rē') maw-REE
Mawenzi (mä-wen'zē) mah-WEN-zee
Maxim (mak'sim) MACK-sim
Maximilian (mak-si-mĭl'e-an) mack-sih-MILL-e-un
Maya (mī'yä or mä'yä) MY-uh or MAY-yuh
Mayan (mī'ən) MY-un
Mayer (mā'ər) MAY-er
Mayo (mā'ō) MAY-oh
Mazama (ma-zä'mä) muh-ZAH-muh
Mazarin (maz'a-rĭn) MAZ-uh-rin
Mazzini (mät-sē'nē) mot-SEE-nee
Mecca (mek'a) MECK-uh
Mecklenburg (mek'lən-bẽrg) MECK-lun-berg
Medea (mē-dē'a) me-DEE-uh
Medellín (me-de-yēn') meh-deh-YEEN
Mede (mēd) MEED
Medici (med'ə-chē) MEH-dih-chee
Medina (me-dē'na) meh-DEE-nuh
Medusa (me-doo'sä) meh-DOO-sah
Mège-Mouries (mezh'moo'rē) MAYZH-muh-REE
Mehemet Ali (me-met'ä-lē') meh-MET-ah-LEE
Meighen (mē'an) ME-un
Meiji (mā'jē) MAY-jee
Meilhac (me-yäk') me-YOCK
Mei-ling Soong (mā'lĭng soong') MAY-ling SUHNG
Meissen (mī'sən) MY-sun
Meistersinger (mīs'tər-sĭng'ər) MY-ster-SING-er
Meitner (mīt'nər) MITE-ner
Mejerda (me-yer'dä) meh-jher-DAH
Meknes (mek-nes') meck-NESS
Mekong (mā'kong') MAY-kahng
Melanchthon (ma-lank'thon) muh-LANK-thun
Melanesia (mel-a-nē'zha) mel-uh-NEE-zhuh
Melbourne (mel'bərn) MEL-bern
Melchior (mel'kē-ər) MEL-kee-er
Melos (mē'lōs) MEE-lahce
Melpomene (mel-pom'a-nē) mel-POM-uh-nee
Memel (mā'məl) MAY-mul
Memnon (mem'non) MEM-non
Memphis (mem'fis) MEM-fiss
Menam (ma-näm') ma-NAHM
Mencken (meng'kən) MENG-kun
Mendel (men'dəl) MEN-dul
Mendelssohn (men'dəl-sōn) MEN-dul-zone
Mendenhall (men'dən-hôl) MEN-dun-hall
Mendoza (men-dō'sä) men-DOH-sah
Menelaus (men-a-lā'əs) men-uh-LAY-us
Menelik (men'ə-lĭk) MEN-uh-lick
Menes (mē'nēz) ME-neez
Menninger (men'ĭng-ər) MEN-ing-er
Menomini (me-nom'a-nē) muh-NAW-mee-nee
Menotti (ma-not'ē) muh-NAW-tee
Menshevik (men'sha-vĭk) MEN-shuh-vick
Mephistopheles (mef'is-tof'a-lēz) mef-iss-TAHF-uh-leez
Mercator (mẽr-kā'tər) mer-KAY-ter
Mercedes-Benz (mer-sā'dēz bentz) mare-SAY-dez BENTZ
Merced (mẽr-sed') mer-SED
Mercia (mẽr'sha) MER-shuh
Mergenthaler (mẽr'gən-tä'lər) MER-gun-TAH-ler
Mérimée (mā-rē-mā') may-ree-MAY
Merino (ma-rē'nō) muh-REE-no
Merlin (mẽr'lĭn) MER-lin
Merovingian (mer'ō-vĭn'jən) meh-ro-VIN-junz
Merrimac, Merrimack (mer'i-mak) MEH-rih-mack
Mers-el-Kebir (mers-el-kā-bēr') merce-el-kuh-BEER

Mersey (mẽr'zē) MER-zee
Merthyr Tydfil (mẽr'thar-tĭd'vĭl) MER-ther-TID-vil
Merwede (mer'vā-də) MER-vay-duh
Mesabi (ma-sä'bē) muh-SAH-be
Mesa Verde (mā'sa-vẽrd') MAY-suh-VERD
Meshach (mē'shak) ME-shack
Meshed (mesh'ed) MESH-ed
Mesopotamia (mes'o-pa-tā'mē-a) mess-uh-po-TAY-me-uh
Mesozoic (mes'a-zō'ĭk) mess-uh-ZOH-ick
Messalina (mes'a-lī'na) mess-uh-LINE-uh
Messiah (ma-sī'a) muh-SIGH-uh
Messina (me-sē'nä) meh-SEE-nuh
Mestrovic (mesh'tra-vĭch) mesh-truh-VEET-ch
Methuselah (ma-thoo'za-la) muh-THOO-suh-luh
Metlakatla (met'la-kat'la) MET-luh-KAT-luh
Métro (mā'trō) MAY-troh
Metternich (met'ər-nikh) MET-er-nick
Metz (mets) METZ
Meuse (mūz) MUSE
Mexicali (mek-sa-kä'lē) meck-suh-KAH-lee
Mexico (mek'si-kō) MECK-sih-ko
Mexitli (mä-hē-tlē) MAY-heet-lee
Mezen (myev'zĭn-ya) MYEH-zin-yuh
Mézières (mā-zyär') maze-YARE
Miami (mī-am'ē) my-AM-e
Micah (mī'kə) MY-kuh
Michelangelo (mī'kel-an'jə-lō) MY-kul-AN-juh-lo
Michiewicz (mēts-kye'vich) meets-KYEH-vitch
Micmac (mĭk'mak) MICK-mack
Micronesian (mī'kra-nē'zhan) my-kruh-NEE-zhun
Midas (mī'das) MY-duss
Midgard (mĭd'gärd) MID-gard
Midianite (mĭd'ē-an-īt) MID-e-un-ite
Mihai (mē-hī') mi-HIGH
Mikado (mĭ-kä'dō) mih-KAH-do
Mikhailovich (mĭ-hī'la-vich) mih-HIGH-luh-vitch
Mikolajczyk (mĭ'kō-lī'chĭk) mih-ko-LIE-chick
Milan (mĭ-lan') mih-LAN
Millay (mĭ-lā') mih-LAY
Millet (mĭ-lā') mih-LAY
Milne (mĭln) MILN
Miltiades (mĭl-tī'a-dēz) mil-TIE-uh-deez
Mindanao (mĭn-da-now') min-duh-NAH-oh
Minerva (mĭ-nẽr'va) mih-NER-vuh
Minnehaha (mĭn'e-hä'hä) min-e-HAH-hah
Minnesinger (mĭn'ē-sĭng'ər) MIN-e-SING-er
Miño (mēn'yō) MEEN-yo
Minoan (mĭ-nō'an) mih-NO-un
Minorca (mĭ-nôr'ka) mih-NOR-kuh
Minos (mī'nəs) MY-nuss
Minot (mī'nət) MY-nut
Minotaur (mĭn'a-tôr) MIN-uh-tore
Minuit (mĭn'ū-ĭt) MIN-u-it
Miquelon (mĭk'a-lon) MICK-uh-lon
Mirabeau (mĭr'a-bō) meer-uh-BO
Miraflores (mĭr'a-flō're) meer-uh-FLORE-iss
Mishna (mĭsh'na) MISH-nuh
Miskito (mĭs-kī'tō) miss-KIT-oh
Miskolc (mĭsh'kälts) MISH-kawltz
Mithridates (mĭth-ra-dā'tēz) mith-ruh-DAY-teez
Mitkof (mĭt'kaf) MITT-kawf
Moab (mō'ab) MO-ab
Mobile (mō-bēl') mo-BEEL
Modena (mä-dē'na) mah-DEE-nuh
Modoc (mō'dok) MO-dock
Modred (mō'drad) MO-dred
Mogadishu (mä-ga-dē'shoo) maw-guh-DEE-shoo
Mogollon (mə-gō-yōn') muh-ghee-YONE
Mohammed (ma-ham'id) mo-HAM-id
Mohawk (mō'hak) MO-hawk
Mohegan (mō-hē'gan) mo-HE-gun
Mohenjo-daro (mō-hen'jō-dä'rō) ma-HEN-jo-DAH-ro
Mohican (mō-hē'kən) muh-HE-kun
Mojave (mō-hä'vē) mo-HAH-vee
Moley, de (mō-lā') dee-muh-LAY
Moldau (môl'dou) MAWL-dow
Moldavia (mōl-dā've-a) mole-DAH-vee-uh
Molière (mō-lyär') mawl-YARE
Molokai (mō'lō-kī') mo-lo-KYE
Molotov (mō'la-tôf) MAW-luh-tahf
Molucca (mō-luk'a) mo-LUCK-uh
Monaco (mon'a-kō) MAH-nuh-ko
Monaghan (mon'a-gan) MON-uh-gun
Mona Lisa (mō'na-lē'sa) mo-nuh-LEE-suh
Mondego (mōn-dā'goo) mawn-DAY-goo
Monet (mō-nā') maw-NAY
Moneta (mō-nē'ta) mo-NEE-tuh
Mongolia (mon-gō'lē-a) mon-GO-lee-uh
Mongoloid (mong'ga-loid) MAHNG-guh-loid
Mongol (mong'gal) MAHNG-gul
Mongngheia (mō-non'ga-hē'la) mo-NON-guh-HE-luh
Monrovia (mən-rō've-a) mun-RO-vee-uh
Montaigne (män-ten'ya) mawn-TEN-yuh
Montalvo (män-täl'vō) mawn-TAHL-vo
Mont Blanc (mōn' blänk') mawn-BLAHNK
Montcalm (mänt-käm') mawn-KAHM
Montcorbier (män'kôr'byā') mawn-korb-YAY
Monte Carlo (mon'tē-kär'lō) MON-tee-KAR-lo
Monte Cassino (män'te kä-sē'nō) MAWN-teh kah-SEE-no
Montenegro (mon'tē-nā'grō) mon-tih-NEE-grow
Monterrey (mon-ta-rā') mon-tuh-RAY
Montespan (män-te-späń') mawn-teh-SPAHN
Montessori (mon-tes-sō'rē) mon-teh-SO-ree
Montevideo (mon'tī-vi-dā'ō) mon-tih-vih-DAY-oh
Montezuma (mon-tī-zoo'ma) mon-tih-ZOO-muh
Montfort (mänt'fart) MAHNT-fert
Montgenèvre (mōn'ja-nev'ra) mawn-juh-NEV-ruh
Montgolfier (mŏN'gäl'fyā') mawn-gawlf-YAY
Montgomery (mont-gum'a-rē) munt-GUM-er-e
Monticello (mon-ti-sel'ō) mon-tih-SELL-oh
Montijo (mon-tē'ō) mon-TEE-oh
Montmartre (mänt-mär'tra) mawn-MAR-truh
Montpelier (mont-pēl'yar) mont-PEEL-yer
Montreal (mon-trē-äl') mon-tree-AWL
Montreux (mōn-trẽ') mawn-TRE
Morava (mä-rä'vä) MAH-rah-vuh
Moravia (ma-rā'vē-a) muh-RAY-vee-uh
Mordecai (môr'də-kī) MORE-duh-kye
Moresque (mə-resk') muh-RESK
Moreno (mô-rā'nō) mo-RAY-no
Morisco (mō-rĭs'kō) mo-RISS-ko
Mornard (môr-när') more-NAR
Morocco (ma-rok'ō) muh-ROCK-oh
Moro (mō'rō) MO-ro
Moscow (mos'kō) MAHCE-ko
Moselle (ma-zel') maze-ZEL
Mosen (mō'zĭn) MOH-sin
Moskva (mos-kvä') maws-KVAH
Mosaddegh (mä-sä-dek') maw-sah-DECK
Mosul (mō'sul) MO-sull
Motagua (mō-tä'gwä) mo-TAHG-wah
Moulouya (moo-loo-yä') moo-loo-YAH
Moultrie (mool'trē) MOOL-tree
Mountbatten (mownt-bat'an) mount-BAT-un
Mourne (môrn) MORN
Moussorgsky (moo-sôrg'skē) muh-SORG-skee
Mozambique (mō-zam-bēk') mo-zuhm-BEEK
Mozart (mō'tsärt) MOTE-sart
Muhlenburg (mū'lən-bẽrg) MYOO-lun-berg
Muir (myŏŏr) MYOUR
Mukden (mŭk'dən) MOOK-dun
Mulhacén (moo-lä-then') moo-lah-THANE
Multnomah (mult-nō'ma) mult-NO-muh
Mumba (mŭm'bä) MUM-buh
Münchhausen (münkh'how-zən) MINCH-how-sun
Muncie (mun'sē) MUN-see
Mundelein (mun'da-līn) MUN-duh-line
Munich (mū'nĭk) MYOO-nick
Munster (mun'stər) MUN-ster
Murcia (mẽr'sha) MER-shuh
Murger (mẽr-zhā') mer-ZHAY
Murillo (moo-rē'lyo or ma-rĭl'ō) moo-REEL-yuh or muh-RILL-oh
Muscatine (mus-ka-tēn') muss-kuh-TEEN
Muscovite (mus'ka-vīt) MUSS-kuh-vite
Muskegon (mus-kē'gan) muss-KO-ghee-un
Musorgski (moo-sôrg'skē) muh-SORG-skee
Mussolini (moos-sə-lē'nē) MOOSE-uh-LEE-nee
Mustafa Kemal (moos'tä-fä kĭ-mäl') MUSS-tah-fah kih-MAHL
Mycenae (mī-sē'nē) my-SEE-nee

Nadir Shah (nä'dər-shä') NAH-der-SHAH
Naga (nä'gə) NAH-guh
Nagasaki (nag'a-sak'ē) nag-uh-SACK-e
Nagoya (nə-goi'ə) NAH-go-yah
Naha (nä'hä) NAH-hah
Nairobi (nī-rō'bē) nye-RO-be
Naismith (nā'smith) NAY-smith

Nakhonratchasima (nä-kä'rät-cha-sē'mä) nah-KAW-rotch-uh-SEE-mah
Nanak (nä'nak) NAH-nack
Nanking (nan'king') NAN-king
Nansemond (nan'sə-mənd) NAN-sih-mund
Nantes (nants) NANTS
Naoise (na-wks) nuh-WAHZ
Napier (nā'pē-ər) NAY-pee-er
Naples (nā'pəlz) NAY-pels
Napoleon (na-pō'lē-ən) nuh-PO-lee-un
Narragansett (nar-a-gan'sət) na-ruh-GAN-set
Narvaez (när-vä'keth) NAR-vah-ayth
Nashua (nash'oo-a) NASH-yoo-uh
Nassau (nas'ô) NASS-aw
Nasser (nä'sər) NASS-er
Natal (na-tal') nuh-TAL
Natchez (nach'iz) NATCH-is
Natoma (na-tō'ma) nuh-TOE-muh
Naugatuck (nä'ga-tuk) NAW-guh-tuck
Nautilus (nô'ti-ləs) NAW-tih-luss
Nauvoo (nä-voo') naw-VOO
Navaho, Navajo (nav'a-hō) NAV-uh-ho
Nazarene (naz'a-rēn') NAZ-uh-reen
Nazareth (naz'a-rēth) NAZ-uh-reth
Ndebele (ən-da-bē'le) un-duh-BEE-lee
Neanderthal (nē-än'dər-täl') nee-AHN-der-TAHL
Nebuchadnezzar (neb'a-kad-nez'ar) NEB-uh-kud-NEZ-er
Neckar (nek'är) NECK-ar
Nefertiti (nef'er-tē'tē) nef-er-TEE-tee
Negev (neg'ev) NEG-ev
Negrin (neg-grēn') neh-GREEN
Negus (nē'gus) NEE-gus
Nehemiah (nē'a-mī'a) NEE-uh-MY-uh
Nehru (ne'roo) NEH-roo
Nejd (nejd) NEDGD
Nemea (nē'mē-a) NEE-me-ah
Nemesis (nem'a-sĭs) NEM-uh-siss
Nemiskan (na-mis'kan) nuh-MISS-kun
Nemunas (nye'moo-näs) NYEH-muh-nahce
Neolithic (nē'ō-lĭth'ĭk) nee-oh-LITH-ick
Nepal (na-pôl') nuh-PAWL
Nepenthe (na-pen'thē) nuh-PEN-thee
Neptune (nep'tūn) NEP-tune
Nereid (nĭr'ē-ĭd) NEE-ree-id
Neri (nā'rē) NAY-ree
Nero (nĭr'ō) NEE-ro
Nervion (nervyōn') nerve-YONE
Neskapi (nes'ka-pē') nes-kuh-PEE
Neufchâtel (nū-shä-tel') nur-shah-TELL
Neunkirchen (noin-kĭr'kun) noin-KEER-kun
Neva (nā'va) NEE-vuh
Newark (noo'ark) NOO-erk
New Zealand (zē'land) ZEE-lund
Ney (nā) NAY
Nez Percé (ne-per-sā') neh-per-SEH
Niagara (nī-ag'ra) nye-AG-ruh
Nibelung (nē'ba-loong) NEE-buh-loong
Nicaragua (nĭk'a-rä'gwa) nick-uh-RAHG-wuh
Nice (nēs) NEECE
Nicolay (nĭ-kō'lā') nick-uh-LAY
Nicolet (nĭ-kā-le') nee-kaw-LEH
Nicomedia (nĭk-ō-mē'dē-a) nick-oh-ME-dee-uh
Nicosia (nĭk'ō-sē'a) nee-ko-ZEE-uh
Nicot (nē-kō') nee-KO
Nielsen (nēl'sən) NEEL-sun
Niemen (nē'mən) NEE-mun
Niépce (nyeps) NYEPCE
Nietzsche (nē'che) NEE-cheh
Niger (nī'jər) NYE-jer
Nigeria (nī-jĭr'ē-a) nih-JEER-e-uh
Nihon (nē'hon) nee-HON
Nihau (nē'hä-oo) nee-HAH-oo
Nijinsky (ni-jin'skē) nih-JIN-skee
Nike (nī'kē) NYE-kee
Nimai Kha (nē-mī' kä) nee-MAH-e KAH
Nîmes (nēmz) NEEMZ
Nimitz (nĭm'ĭts) NIM-itz
Nimrod (nĭm'rod) NIM-rod
Nineveh (nĭn'a-vu) NIN-uh-vuh
Ningyoshebai (nĭng'yō-sha-bī') NING-yo-shah-BYE
Niobe (nī-ō'bē) nye-OH-be
Nipigon (nip'i-gon) NIP-ih-gon
Nipissing (nip'i-sĭng) NIP-ih-sing
Nippon (nip'on) NIP-ahn
Nirvana (nĭr-vä'na) near-VAH-nah
Nitaka (nē-tä'kä) nee-TAH-kah
Nizam (ni-zäm') nih-ZAHM
Nizhni Novgorod (nizh'nē nov'ga-rod) NIZH-nee-NOV-guh-rod
No (drama) (nō) NO
Noah (nō'a) NO-uh
Nobel (nō-bel') no-BELL
Nobile (nō'ba-le) NAW-buh-leh
Nogales (nō-gä'les) naw-GAH-less
Nolan (nō'lan) NO-lun
Nome (nōm) NOME
Nootka (noot'ka) NOOT-kuh
Nordenskjold (nôr'dən-shõld) NUHR-dun-shoold
Nordhoff (nôrd'hof) NORD-huff
Nördlingen (nort'ling-an) NOORT-ling-un
Norfolk (nôr'fak) NOR-fock
Norge (nôr'ge) NORGE
Norkay (nôr'kā) nor-KYE
Nor'Loch (nôr'lokh) nor-LOCK
Normandy (nôr'man-dē) NOR-mun-dee
Norn (nôrn) NORN
Norodom Sihanouk (nä-rä-däm' sē-ä-nook') naw-raw-DAWM see-ah-NOOK
Norrköping (nôr'chə-ping) NOR-chuh-ping
Northern Karoo (ka-roo') kuh-ROO
Northumbria (nôr-thum'brē-a) nor-THUMB-bree-uh
Norway (nôr'wā) NOR-way
Norwegian (nôr-wē'jan) nor-WEE-jun
Norwich (nôr'ĭch or nor'ĭj) NOR-itch or NAHR-idge
Notre Dame (cathedral) (nä'tra-däm') naw-truh-DAHM
Notre Dame (university) (nō'tra-dām') no-truh-DAME
Nova Scotia (nō-va-skō'sha) NO-vuh SKO-shuh
Novgorod (nov'ga-rod) NOV-guh-rod
Novosibirsk (na-va-sē-birsk') nah-vuh-see-BEERSK
Noyes (nois) NOISE
Nubia (noo'bē-a) NYOO-be-uh
Nuer (noo'ər) NWARE
Nugent (noo'jant) NOO-junt
Nukualofa (noo-koo-ä-lō'fa) NOO-koo-ah-LO-fuh
Nuku Hiva (noo'koo-hē'vä) NOO-koo HE-vah
Nuia (noo'lä) NOO-lah
Numitor (noo'mi-tôr) NYOO-mih-tore
Nuremberg (nyŭr'am-bẽrg) NYOOR-um-berg
Nurmi (nŭr'mē) NOOR-me
Nyasa (nī-as'a) nye-ASS-uh

Oahu (ō-ä'hoo) oh-AH-hoo
Ob (äp) AWP
Obadiah (ō'ba-dī'a) oh-buh-DIE-uh
Oberammergau (ō'bar-ä'mər-gow) oh-ber-AH-mer-gow
Oberon (ō'ba-ron) OH-ber-un
Oberto (ō-ber'tō) oh-BARE-toe
Obi (ō'bē) OH-be
Ocala (ō-ka'la) oh-KAL-uh
Ocasset (ō-kas'it) oh-KASS-it
Oceania (ō-shē-an'ē-a) oh-she-AN-e-uh
Ocmulgee (ōk-mul'gē) ok-MUL-ghee
Ocracoke (ō'kra-kōk) OK-ruh-koke
Octavia (ok-tā'vē-a) ock-TAY-vee-uh
Odelsting (ō'dalz-ting) OH-delz-ting
Oder River (ō'dar) OH-der
Oder-Neisse (ō'dar-nī'sa) OH-der NYE-suh
Odessa (ō-des'a) oh-DESS-uh
Odin (ō'din) OH-din
Odysseus (ō-dĭs'ū-us) oh-DISS-use
Odyssey (od'i-sē) ODD-uh-see
Oea (ē'a) EE-uh
Oe-Cusse (ō-koo'se) oh-KOO-see
Oedipus (ed'i-pas) ED-ih-pus
Oersted (ẽr'sted) ER-sted
Oesterreich (ẽs'tar-rīkh) ES-ter-rike
Offenbach (ô'fan-bäkh) AW-fun-bock
Oglala (ō-glä'la) oh-GLAH-lah
Ohara (ō'hä-rä) OH-hah-rah
Ojibwa, Ojibway (ō-jĭb'wā) oh-JIB-way
Oka (ō-kä') uh-KAH
Okeechobee (ō'kē-chō'bē) oh-kee-CHO-be
Okefenokee (ō'ka-fa-nō'kē) oh-kuh-fuh-NO-kee
Okhotsk (ō-kotsk') oh-KOTSK
Okinawa (ō'kĭ-nä'wä) O-kee-nah-wah
Old Sturbridge (stẽr'brĭj) STER-bridge
Olisipo (a-lis'i-po) uh-LISS-ih-po

Olympus (ō-lim'pəs) oh-LIM-pus
Omaha (ō'mə-hä) OH-muh-hah
Oman (ā-män') aw-MAHN
Omar Khayyam (ō'mär-kī-yam') OH-mar-kye-YAM
Omphalos (om'fə-los) OM-fuh-lahce
Omsk (âmsk) AWMSK
Oñate (ə-nyä'tā) uh-NYAH-tay
Onega (ō-nē'gə) oh-NEE-guh
Oneida (ō-nī'də) oh-NYE-duh
Onondaga (on-ən-dâ'gə) ahn-un-DAH-guh
Ontario (on-târ'ē-ō) ahn-TARE-e-oh
Oporto (ō-pōr'tō) oh-PORE-toe
Ops (ops) OPS
Oran (ō'ran') oh-RAN
Ordu (ôr-doo') or-DOO
Orestes (ō-res'tēz) oh-RESS-teez
Oriente (ôr-yen'tā) or-YEN-tay
Orinoco (ō-rə-nō'kō) oh-ruh-NO-ko
Orion (ō-rī'ən) oh-RYE-un
Orlando (ôr-lan'dō) or-LAN-doe
Orléans (ôr-lā-äṅ') or-lay-AWN
Ormuzd (ôr'muzd) OR-muzd
Orozco (ə-rōs'kō) uh-ROHCE-ko
Orpheus (ôr'fūs) OR-fyooce
Osage (ō'sāj) OH-sage
Osaka (ō'sä-kä) OH-sah-kah
Osawatomie (os'ə-wät'ə-mē) ahce-uh-WAT-uh-me
Osceola (os-ē-ō'lə) ahce-e-OH-luh
Osiris (ō-sī'ris) oh-SIGH-riss
Oslo (oz'lō or os'lō) OZ-lo or OSS-lo
Osman (os-män') oss-MAHN
Ostend (os-tend') oss-TEND
Ostrava (â'strä-vä) AW-strah-vah
Ostrogoth (ost'rō-goth) AHCE-tro-gahth
Othello (ō-thel'ō) oh-THEL-oh
Othman (oth-män') ahth-MAHN
Otsego (ot-sē'gō) ott-SEE-go
Ottawa (ot'ä-wä) OTT-ah-wah
Ottokar (ot'ō-kär) OTT-oh-kar
Ouachita (wä'chī-tâ) WAW-chih-taw
Oudot (oo'dō') oo-DOE
Oudtshoorn (owts'hūrn) OUTS-hoorn
Oulu (ō'loo) OH-loo
Ouragan (ūr'ä-gäṅ') OOR-ah-gon
Ourthe (oort) OORT
Outcault (owt'kâlt) OUT-kalwt
Ovid (ov'id) AH-vid
Owasco (ō-wäs'kō) oh-WAHCE-ko
Ozama (ō-sä'mä) oh-SAH-mah
Ozark (ō'zärk) OH-zark

Pacelli (pä-chel'ē) pah-CHELL-e
Pactolus (pak-tō'ləs) pack-TOE-lus
Paderewski (pad-ə-ref'skē) pah-duh-REFF-skee
Padua (pad'ū-ə) PAD-yoo-uh
Paducah (pə-doo'kə) puh-DOO-kuh
Paganini (pä-gä-nē'nē) pah-gah-NEE-nee
Pagliacci (pä-lyä'chē) pahl-YAH-chee
Pago Pago (pang'gō-pang'gō) PANG-go PANG-go
Pahlevi (pa'lə-vē) PAL-uh-vee
Paijanne (pī'ya-nä) PYE-ya-nay
Pai (bī) BYE
Paiute (pī'ūt) PYE-yoot
Pakistan (pak'is-tan) PACK-iss-tan
Palatine (pal'ə-tīn) PAL-uh-tine
Palau (pä-low') pah-LOW (as in allow)
Palembang (pä-lem-bäng') pah-lum-BAHNG
Palermo (pə-ler'mō) pah-LARE-mo
Palestine (pal'əs-tīn) PAL-us-tine
Palestrina (pä'lə-strē'nə) PAHL-us-TREE-nuh
Palio (päl'yō) PAHL-yo
Pallas Athena (pal'əs ə-thē'nə) PAL-us uh-THEE-nuh
Pall Mall (pel'mel') PELL MELL
Palma (päl'mä) PAHL-mah
Palomar (pal'ō-mär) PAL-oh-mar
Panama (pan'ə-mä) PAN-uh-mah
Panamint (pan'ə-mint) PAN-uh-mint
Panay (pä-nī') pah-NYE
Pandora (pan-dôr'ə) pan-DORE-uh
Pantagruel (pan-tag'roo-el) pan-TAG-roo-ul
Pantaleon (pan'tə-lon) PAN-tuh-lon
Pantalone (pän-tä-lō'nē) pon-tah-LO-nee
Pantaloon (pan-tə-loon') pan-tuh-LOON
Panzer (pon'tsər) PAHNT-ser
Paos (pä'ō) PAH-oh
Paotow (bow'tō) BOW-toe
Papago (pä'pä-gō) PAH-pah-go
Papeete (pä-pēt'ē or pä'pe-ā'te) pah-PEET-e or PAH-peh-A-teh
Papuan (pä'poo-ən) PAH-poo-un
Paracelsus (par-ə-sel'səs) pa-ruh-SELL-suss
Paraguay (par'ə-gwā) PA-ruh-gway
Paramaribo (pa'rə-mar'i-bō) pa-ruh-MA-rih-bo
Paraná (pä-rə-nä') pah-ruh-NAH
Paricutin (pä-rē-koo-tēn') pah-ree-koo-TEEN
Panjnad (punj'nud) PUNGE-nud
Paris (par'is or [Fr.] pä-rē') PA-riss or (in French) pah-REE
Parma (pär'mä) PAR-mah
Parnassus (pär-nas'əs) par-NASS-us
Parnell (pär-nel') par-NELL
Paros (pā'ros) PAY-rahce
Parsee (pär'sē) PAR-see
Parsifal (par'sē-fäl) PAR-sih-fahl
Parthenon (par'thə-non) PAR-thuh-non
Pasadena (pas'ə-dē'nə) pass-uh-DEE-nuh
Pascal (pas-kal') pass-KAL
Passaic (pə-sā'ik) puh-SAY-ick
Passchendaele (päs'ən-dä-lə) PAHCE-un-dah-luh
Passy (pa-sē') pa-SEE
Pasta (päs'tä) PAHCE-tah
Pasteur (pä-stėr') pah-STER
Patagonia (pat'ə-gō'nē-ə) pat-uh-GO-nee-uh
Patapsco (pə-tap'skō) puh-TAP-skoh
Pathan (pə-thän') puh-THAN
Patiala (put'ē-ä'lə) puh-tee-AH-luh
Patroclus (pə-trō'kləs) puh-TROH-kluss
Patton (pat'ən) PAT-un
Patuxent (pə-tuks'ənt) puh-TUX-unt
Pátzcuaro (päts'kwä-rō) POTS-kwah-ro
Pauncefote (pâns'fūt) PAWNCE-foot
Pavlova (pav'vlä-və) PAHVE-law-vuh
Pawtucket (pə-tuk'it) paw-TUCK-it
Payens (pä-en') pye-EN
Peary (pir'ē) PEER-e
Pecos (pā'kəs) PAY-kuss
Pegasus (peg'ə-səs) PEG-uh-suss
Peiping (bā'ping) BAY-ping
Pekin (pē'kin) PEE-kin
Pekinese, Pekingese (pē'kə-nēz') pee-kuh-NEEZ
Peking (pē'king) PEE-king
Pelée (pe-lā') peh-LAY
Pelias (pē'lē-əs) PEE-lee-us
Peligot (pē-lih-gō') peh-lih-GO
Pelleas (pel'ē-əs) PELL-e-us
Pelly (pel'ē) PELL-e
Peloponnesus (pel'ō-pə-nē'səs) pel-oh-puh-NEE-suss
Pemba (pem'bä) PEM-bah
Pembina (pem'bi-nə) PEM-bih-nuh
Penang (pē'nang) PEE-nang
Penates (pē-nā'tēz) pee-NAY-teez
Pend Oreille (pon'dā-rā') PON-daw-RAY
Penelophon (pə-nel'ə-fon) puh-NELL-uh-fon
Penobscot (pe-nob'skot) peh-NOB-skot
Pentateuch (pen'tə-tūk) PEN-tuh-TYUKE
Penzance (pen-zans') pen-ZANCE
Peoria (pē-ōr'ē-ə) pee-OR-e-uh
Pepin (pep'in) PEP-in
Pepys (pēps or peps) PEEPS or PEPS
Pequot (pē'kwot) PEE-kwot
Percé (per-sā') pare-SAY
Percheron (per'chə-ron) PER-chuh-ron
Perekop (per-i-kâp') pare-ih-KAWP
Pericles (per'i-klēz) PARE-ih-kleez
Perón (pe-rōn') peh-RAWN
Perrault (pe-rō') peh-ROE
Perry (per'ē) PARE-e
Persephone (pėr-sef'ə-nē) per-SEFF-uh-nee
Perseus (pėr'sūs) PER-syooce
Peru (pə-roo') puh-ROO
Peshawar (pə-show'ər) puh-SHOW-er (as in *shower*)
Peshkov (pesh'kâf) PESH-kawf
Petain (pā-tañ') pay-TAN
Petén-Itza (pā-ten'ēt-sä') pay-TEN-eet-SAH
Petrarch (pē'trärk) PEE-trark
Petrograd (pet'rō-grad) PET-ro-grad
Petropavlovsk (pye'trə-päv-lofsk') pyeh-truh-pahv-LAHFSK
Petrouchka (pə-troo'shkə) puh-TROOSH-kuh
Petrozavodsk (pye'trə-zə-votsk') pyeh-truh-zuh-VAHTSK
Phaeton (fā'ə-tən) FAY-uh-tun
Pharisee (far'ə-sē) FA-ruh-see
Pharnaces (fär'nə-sēz) FAR-nuh-seez
Pharos (fā'ros) FAY-rahce
Pheidippides (fā-dip'ə-dēz) fay-DIP-uh-deez
Phidias (fid'ē-əs) FID-e-us
Philippi (fi-lip'ī) fih-LIP-eye
Philippines (fil'ə-pēnz) FIL-uh-peenz
Philistine (fi-lis'tin) fih-LISS-tin
Phobos (fō'bos) FOE-bahce
Phoenicia (fi-nē'shə) fih-NEE-shuh
Phoenix (fē'niks) FEE-nix
Phrygia (frij'ē-ə) FRIDGE-e-uh
Phyfe (fīf) FIFE
Picasso (pə-kās'ō) puh-KAH-so
Piccard (pē-kär') pee-KAR
Pico de Aneto (pē'kō-thā-ä-nā'tō) PEE-ko-they-ah-NAY-toe
Pico de Teide (tā'dā) TAY-day
Pico Turquino (tūr-kē'nō) tour-KEE-no
Piedmont (pēd'mont) PEED-mont
Pierre, city (pir) PEER
Pierrot (pē'ər-ō or pye-rō') PEE-er-oh- or pyeh-ROE
Pima (pē'mä) PEE-muh
Pimlico (pim'li-kō) PIM-lih-ko
Pinakothek (pin'ə-kō-thek) PIN-uh-ko-theck
Pindar (pin'där) PIN-dar
Pinel (pē-nel') pee-NELL
Pinilla (pē-nē'yä) pee-NEE-yah
Pinocchio (pi-nō'kē-ō) pih-NO-kee-oh
Pinos (pē'nōs) PEE-nohce
Pinta (pēn'tä) PEEN-tah
Piombino (pē'om-bē'nō) pee-om-BE-no
Piraeus (pi-rē'əs) pye-REE-us
Pirandello (pē'rän-del'ō) PEE-rahn-DELL-oh
Pisa (pē'zä) PEE-zah
Pisces (pis'ēz) PIS-eez
Pitot (pē-tō') pee-TOE
Pitti (pēt'ē or pit'ē) PEET-e or PIT-e
Pius (pī'əs) PYE-us
Pizzaro (pi-zä'rō) pih-ZAH-ro
Planck (plänk) PLONK
Plantagenet (plan-taj'ə-net) plan-TADGE-uh-net
Plata (plä'tä) PLAH-tah
Platani (plä'tä-nē) PLAH-tah-nee
Plato (plā'tō) PLAY-toe
Platte (plat) PLAT
Plautus (plâ'təs) PLAW-tuss
Pleiades (plī'ə-dēz) PLY-uh-deez
Pliny (plin'ē) PLIN-e
Ploesti (plâ-yesht') plaw-YESHT
Plovdiv (plâv'dif) PLAWVE-diff
Plutarch (ploo'tärk) PLOO-tark
Pluto (ploo'tō) PLOO-toe
Plymouth (plim'əth) PLIM-uth
Pnompenh (nom-pem') nom-PEM
Pnyx (niks) NIX
Po (pō) PO
Poas (pwäs) PWAHCE
Pocahontas (pō'kə-hon'təs) po-kuh-HAHN-tuss
Pocatello (pō'kə-tel'ō) po-kuh-TELL-oh
Podgoritza (pâd'gə-rit'zə) pawd-guh-RIT-zuh
Poictesme (pwä-tez'mə) pwah-TEZ-muh
Poincaré (pwañ-kä-rā') pwan-kah-RAY
Poisson (pwä-sâñ') pwah-SAWN
Poitiers (pwä-tyā') pwot-YAY
Pola (pō'lä) PO-lah
Polack (pō'lok) PO-lock
Poland (pō'lənd) PO-lund
Polanie (pō-lä'nē) po-LAH-nee
Polaris (pō-lā'ris) po-LAY-riss
Polaroid (pō'lə-roid) PO-luh-roid
Polichelle (pä-li-shel') paw-lih-SHELL
Politburo (pə-lit'byūr'ō) puh-LIT-byuh-ro
Polk (pōk) POKE
Polska (pâl'skä) PAWL-skah
Polyhymnia (pol-ə-him'nē-ə) pahl-uh-HIM-nee-uh
Polynesia (pol-ə-nē'zhə) pahl-uh-NEE-zhuh
Pomerania (pom'ə-rā'nē-ə) pom-uh-RAY-nee-uh
Pompadour (pom'pə-door') POM-puh-dure
Pompeii (pom-pā') pom-PAY
Pompey (pom'pē) POM-pee
Ponape (pon'ə-pā) PON-uh-pay
Ponce de Leon (pän'thə-thə-lā-än') PAWN-thay-thuh-lay-AWN
Pons (päns) PAWNCE
Ponselle (pon-sel') pon-SELL
Ponta Delgada (pân'tə-del-gä'də) PAWN-tuh-del-GAH-duh
Ponte Vecchio (pon'te vek'ē-ō) PON-teh VECK-e-oh
Pontiac (pon'tē-ak) PON-tee-ack
Pontius Pilate (pon'shəs pī'lət) PON-shuss PYE-lut
Pontresina (pân'trə-sē'nə) PAWN-truh-SEE-nuh
Pontus (pon'təs) PON-tuss
Poona (poo'nə) POO-nuh
Poppaea (pə-pē'ə) puh-PEE-uh
Popocatepetl (pō'pə-kat'ə-pet-əl) po-puh-KAT-uh-pet-ul
Poquelin (pâ-klañ') paw-KLAN
Pori (pō'rē) POE-ree
Poronai (pə-rə-nī') puh-ruh-NYE
Port-au-Prince (pōrt-ō-prins') port-oh-PRINCE
Port Colborne (kōl'bərn) KOLE-bern
Port Said (sä-ēd') sah-EED
Porta (pôr'tä) PORE-tah
Portinari (pôr'tə-nä'rē) pore-tuh-NAH-ree
Portofino (pôr'tə-fē'nō) pore-tuh-FEE-no
Porto Rico (pôr'tə-rē'kō) pore-tuh-REE-ko
Porto Santo (sän'tə) SAHN-tuh
Portugal (pôr'chə-gəl) PORE-chuh-gul
Poseidon (pō-sī'dən) po-SIGH-dun
Posen (pō'zən) POE-zun
Potawatomi (pot'ə-wät'ə-mē) pot-uh-WAHT-uh-me
Pothinus (pə-thī'nəs) puh-THIGH-nuss
Potiphar (pot'i-fər) POT-ih-fer
Potomac (pə-tō'mək) puh-TOE-muck
Potsdam (pots'dam) POTS-dam
Poughkeepsie (pə-kip'sē) puh-KIP-see
Powhatan (pow-hə-tan') pow-huh-TAN
Poznań (pâz'nän-yə) PAUSE-nahn-yuh
Prado (prä'thō) PRAH-tho
Praga (prä'gä) PRAH-gah
Prague (präg) PRAHG
Praha (prä'hä) PRAH-hah
Praxiteles (praks-it'ə-lēz) prax-IT-uh-leez
Prescott (pres'kət) PRESS-kut
Presidio (prə-sid'ē-ō) pruh-SID-e-oh
Pretoria (pri-tōr'ē-ə) prih-TORE-e-uh
Priam (prī'əm) PRY-um
Pribilof (prib'ə-lâf) PRIB-uh-lawf
Primo de Rivera (prē'mō-thā-ri-vā'rä) PREE-mo-they-rih-VAY-rah
Princip (prēn'tsēp) PREENT-seep
Pripet (prip'ət) PRIP-ut
Prokofiev (prə-kâf'yef) pruh-KAWF-yef
Prometheus (prə-mē'thē-əs) pruh-ME-thee-us
Proserpine (pros'ər-pīn) PRAHCE-er-pine
Proteus (prō'tē-əs) PRO-tee-us
Proudhon (proo-dôñ') proo-DAWN
Proust (proost) PROOST
Provençal (prov-ən-säl') prah-vun-SAHL
Provence (prə-väñs') praw-VAHNCE
Prussia (prush'ə) PRUSH-uh
Prut (proot) PROOT
Psyche (sī'kē) SIGH-kee
Ptolemy (tol'ə-mē) TAHL-uh-me
Puccini (poo-chē'nē) poo-CHEE-nee
Puebla (pwe'blä) PWEH-blah
Pueblo (pwe'blō) PWEH-blow
Puerto Barrios (pwer'tō bär'yōs) PWARE-toe BAR-yohce
Puerto Montt (mänt) MAWNT
Puerto Rico (rē'kō) REE-ko
Puget (pū'jet) PYOO-jut
Pula (poo'lä) POO-lah
Pulaski (pə-las'kē) puh-LASS-kee
Pulcinella (pool'chē-nel'ə) pool-cheh-NELL-uh
Pulitzer (pūl'it-sər) PULL-it-ser
Punic (pū'nik) PYOO-nick
Punjab (pun-jäb') pun-JOB
Punjabi (pun-jä'bē) pun-JAH-be
Punt (pūnt) PUHNT
Punta Arenas (poon'tä ä-rā'näs) POON-tah ah-RAY-nahce
Purcell (pėr'səl) PER-sul
Purdue (pėr-doo') per-DOO
Purim (poo'rim) POO-rim
Pusan (poo-sän') poo-SAHN
Pusey (pū'zē) PYOO-zee
Pushtu (push'too) PUSH-too (as in *mush*)
Pygmalion (pig-mā'lē-ən) pig-MAY-lee-un
Pygmy (pig'mē) PIG-me
Pylades (pil'ə-dēz) PILL-uh-deez
Pyle (pīl) PILE
Pyongyang (pyung'yäng') PYUNG-YAHNG
Pyramus (pir'ə-məs) PEER-uh-muss
Pyrenees (pir'ə-nēz) PEER-uh-neez
Pyrrhic (pir'ik) PEER-ick
Pyrrha (pir'ä) PEER-ah
Pyrrhus (pir'əs) PEER-us
Pythagoras (pi-thag'ə-rəs) pih-THAG-uh-russ
Pythias (pith'ē-əs) PITH-e-us

Qatif (kä-tēf') kah-TEEF
Quaker (kwā'kər) KWAY-ker
Quantico (kwon'ti-kō) KWON-tih-ko
Quapaw (kwä'pä) KWAH-paw
Quebec (kwi-bek') kwih-BECK
Quechua (kech'wä) KETCH-wah
Quesada (kə-sä'thä) kuh-SAH-thuh
Quezaltenango (kə-säl'tə-näng'gō) kuh-SAHL-tuh-NAHNG-go
Quezon (kā'zon') KAY-ZAHN
Quintana Roo (kēn-tä'nə-rō') keen-TAH-nuh-ROE
Quintilis (kwin'ti-lis) KWIN-tih-liss
Quirinal (kwir'ə-nəl) QUEER-uh-nul
Quirinus (kwi-rē'nəs) kwih-REE-nuss
Quisling (kwiz'ling) KWIZ-ling
Quito (kē'tō) KEE-toe
Quitus (kē'tōos) KEE-tooce
Qum (kūm) KUHM

Rabat (rä-bät') rah-BAHT
Rabban (rab'ən or ra-bän') RAB-un or ra-BAHN
Rabelais (rab'ə-lā) RAB-uh-lay
Rachmaninoff (rukh-mä'nyi-nof) ruck-MAHN-yih-nahf
Racine (rə-sēn') ruh-SEEN
Rainier (rə-nēr') ruh-NEAR
Rais (räs) RACE
Raleigh (rol'ē) RAH-lee
Rama (rä'mä) RAH-mah
Ramapo (ram'ə-pō) RAM-uh-po
Rameses (ram'ə-sēz) RAM-uh-seez
Ramleh (räm'le) RAHM-leh
Ramsay (ram'zē) RAM-zee
Ramses (ram'sēz) RAM-seez
Rancé (räñ-sā') rahn-SAY
Ranco (rang'kō) RANG-ko
Rangoon (rang-goon') rang-GOON
Rapallo (rä-pâl'ä) rah-PAHL-aw
Raphael (rä'fā-el) RAY-fay-el
Rapido (rä'pē-dä) RAH-pee-daw
Rappahannock (rap'ə-han'ək) rap-uh-HAN-uck
Rashid (rä-shēd') rah-SHEED
Rasputin (ras-poo'tyin) russ-POOT-yin
Rathaus (rät'hows) RAHT-house
Ratti (rät'tē) RAH-tee
Ravaillac (rä-vä-yäk') rah-vah-YAHK
Ravel (rä-vel') rah-VEL
Ravenna (rə-ven'ə) ruh-VEN-uh
Read (rēd) REED
Reading (red'ing) RED-ing
Réaumur (rā-ō-mūr') ray-oh-MOOR
Rebekah (ri-bek'ə) ree-BECK-uh
Rebmann (räp'män) RAPE-mahn
Rébuffat (re'bū-fä') reh-buh-FAH
Recife (re-sē'fē) reh-SEE-fee
Regensburg (rā'gənz-bėrg) RAY-gunz-berg
Reggio (red'jä) RED-jaw
Regina (rə-jī'nə) ruh-JYE-nuh
Regulus (reg'yū-ləs) REGG-yuh-luss
Rehoboth (ri-hō'bəth) rih-HO-buth
Reichstag (rīks'täg) RIKES-tahg
Reikjavik (rā'kyə-vēk) RAKE-yuh-veek
Reims (rēmz or [Fr.] rañs) REEMS or (in French) RANCE
Rembrandt (rem'bränt) REM-bront
Remus (rē'məs) REE-muss
Reno (rē'nō) REE-no
Renoir (rə-nwär') ren-WAHR
Reuther (rooth'ər) ROOTH-er
Reykjavik (rā'kyə-vēk) RAKE-yuh-veek
Reynaud (rā-nō') ray-NO
Reynolds (ren'əldz) REN-uldz
Rhadames (rə-däm'əs) ruh-DAHM-us
Rhaetia (rē'shē-ə) REE-she-uh
Rhee, Singhman (rē, sŭng'män) REE, SUHNG-mon
Rheims, see Reims
Rheingold (rin'gold) RINE-gold
Rhine (rīn) RINE
Rhodes (rōdz) ROADS
Rhodesia (rō-dē'zhə) ro-DEE-zhuh
Rhodope (rod'ə-pē) ROD-uh-pee
Rhondda (rân'də) RAWN-duh
Rhone (rōn) RONE
Rhumel (rū-mel') rih-MELL
Rialto (rē-äl'tō) ree-AHL-toe
Richelieu (rish'ə-loo) RISH-uh-loo
Rideau (rē-dō') ree-DOE
Riebeeck (rē'bāk) REE-bake
Riel (ryel) REEL-EL
Riemann (rē'män) REE-mahn
Rienzi (ryen'tsə) ree-ENT-suh
Riesener (rē'zə-nər) REE-zuh-ner
Riga (rē'gə) REE-guh
Rig-veda (rēg-vā'də) reeg-VAY-dah
Rijeka (ri-ye'kä) rih-YEH-kah
Riksdag (riks'däg) RICKS-dahg
Rimac (rē'mäk) REE-mock
Rimsky-Korsakov (rim'skē-kôr'sə-kof) RIM-skee KORE-suh-kahf
Ringstrasse (ring'shträ'sə) RING-shtrah-suh
Rio Cauto (rē'ō-kow'tō) REE-oh COW-toe
Rio de Janeiro (rē'ō-də-jə-ner'ō) REE-oh-duh-juh-NARE-oh
Rio Grande (rē'ō-grand' or gran'dē) REE-oh-GRAND or GRAN-dee
Rio Negro (nā'grō) NAY-groh
Rio Piedras (pyā'dräs) PYAY-drahce
Rion (rē-än') ree-AWN
Riyadh (ri-yäd') rih-YAHD
Rizal (rē-säl') ree-SAHL
Rizzo (rēt'tsə) REET-zuh
Robbia (rōb'byä) ROBE-yah
Robespierre (rō'bes-pyâr' or rōbz'pir) raw-bess-PYARE or ROBES-peer
Robusti (rə-boos'tē) ruh-BOOCE-teh
Rochambeau (rä-shäñ-bō') raw-shom-BO
Rockne (rok'nē) ROCK-nee
Roda (rō'thä) RO-thah
Rodin (rä-dañ') raw-DAN
Roebling (rōb'ling) ROBE-ling
Roentgen, Röntgen (rönt'gən) RENT-gun
Rokko (rō'kō) ROCK-oh
Rolfe (rolf) RAHLF
Rolland (râ-läñ') raw-LAHN
Romanche (râ-mänsh') raw-MAHNSH
Romanov, Romanoff (rō'mə-nof) ruh-MAH-nahf
Romansh (rə-mänsh') ruh-MAHNSH
Romany (rom'ə-nē) ROM-uh-nee
Romania (rō-mā'nē-ə) ro-MAY-nee-uh
Romberg (rom'bėrg) ROM-berg
Rome (rōm) ROAM
Romeo (rō'mē-ō) RO-me-oh
Rommel (rom'əl) ROM-ul
Romulus (rom'yə-ləs) ROM-yuh-luss
Roquefort (rōk'fərt) ROKE-furt
Roraima (rə-rī'mə) ruh-RYE-muh
Rosario (rō-sär'yō) ro-SAR-yo
Rosas (rä'säs) RAW-sahce
Roscommon (ros-kom'ən) rahce-KAHM-un
Rosh Hashanah (rōsh hä-shä'nä) ROHSH hah-SHAH-nah
Rossetti (rō-set'ē) ro-SET-e
Rossini (rō-sē'nē) ro-SEE-nee
Rostand (râs-täñ') ross-TAHN
Rostov (rə-stâf') ross-TAWF
Rotterdam (rot'ər-dam) ROT-er-dom
Rouault (rə-wō) ruh-WOE
Rouen (rwäñ) roo-AWN
Rouillé (rwē-yā') roo-ee-YAY
Rousseau (roo-sō') roo-SO
Rowan (rō'ən) ROE-un
Rowe (rō) ROE
Rowlands (rō'ləndz) ROE-lundz
Roxanne (rok-san') rock-SAN
Rozier (rä-zhā') raw-ZHAY
Rubaiyat (roo-bī-yät') roo-bye-YAHT
Rubens (roo'bənz) ROO-bunz
Rubicon (roo'bi-kon) ROO-bih-kon
Rubinstein (roo'bin-stīn) ROO-bin-stine
Rubruquis (rū-brū-kē') rih-brih-KEE
Rue de la Paix (rū'də-lä-pāē') ROO-duh-lah-PYE
Ruhr (rūr) ROOR
Rumania, Roumania (roo-mā'nē-ə) roo-MAY-nee-uh
Rurik (roo'rik) ROO-rick
Russia (rush'ə) RUSH-uh
Ruthenia (roo-thē'nē-ə) roo-THEE-nee-uh
Ruysdael (rois'däl) ROYCE-dahl
Ruyter (roi'tər) ROY-ter
Ryan (rī'ən) RYE-un
Ryder (rī'dər) RYE-der
Ryobu-Shinto (rī'ə-bə shin'tō) RYE-uh-buh SHIN-toe
Ryks (riks) RICKS
Ryswick (riz'wik) RIZZ-wick
Ryukyu (rū'kū) RYOO-kyoo

Saar (zär or sär) ZAR or SAR
Saarbrücken (zär'brü'kən) ZAR-bruk-un
Saarinen (zär'in-ən) ZAR-in-un
Sabaean (sə-bē'ən) say-BE-un
Sabaki (sə-bä'kē) suh-BAH-kee
Sabine (sā'bēn) sa-BEAN
Sacajawea (sak'ə-jə-wē'ə) SACK-uh-juh-WE-uh
Sac (säk) SACK
Sacramento (sak'rə-men'tō) sack-ruh-MEN-toe
Sacré Coeur (sä'krā-kėr') SAH-kray-KER
Sagres (sä'grish) SAH-grish
Saguaro (sə-gwä'rō) suh-GWAH-ro
Saguenay (sag'ə-nā) SAG-uh-nay
Sahara (sə-hä'rə) suh-HAH-ruh
Sakishima (sä'ki-shi-mä') SAH-kih-shih-MAH
Saigon (sī-gon') sigh-GAHN
Saikyo (sī-kē'ō) sigh-KEE-oh
Saimaa (sī'mä) SIGH-mah
St. Anne de Beaupré (də-bō-prē') duh-bo-PREH
St. Croix (sənt-kroi') sunt-KROY
Saint-Gaudens (sənt-gâ'dənz) sunt-GAW-dunz
St. Jago (sant ē-ä'gō) sant-ee-AH-go
St. Jean-de-Luz (señ-zhäñ'dū-lūz') sen-ZHAHN-doo-LUHZ
St. Laurent (señ-lō-räñ') sen-lo-RAHN
St. Marinus (san mə-rē'nəs) san muh-REE-nuss
St. Mihiel (señ-mē-yel') sen-me-YELL
St. Nazaire (señ-nä-zâr') sen-nah-ZARE
Saint Pierre, Miquelon (sânt-pē-âr', mik'ə-lon) pee-AIR, MICK-uh-lon
Saint-Saens (sañ-säñs') san-SANCE
Sakhalin (sä-kä-lēn') sah-kah-LEEN
Saladin (sal'ə-din) SAL-uh-din
Salamis (sal'ə-mis) SAL-uh-miss
Salazar (sə-lə-zär') suh-luh-ZAR
Salerno (sä-ler'nō) sah-LARE-naw
Salina (sə-lī'nə) suh-LINE-uh
Salisbury (sâlz'brē) SAWLZ-bree
Salk (sâk) SAWK
Salome (sə-lō'mē) suh-LO-me
Salomon (sal'ə-mən) SAL-uh-mun
Salonika (sä-lə-nē'kä) sah-luh-NEE-kuh
Salso (säl'sō) SAHL-so
Salten (zäl'tən) ZAHL-tun
Salvador (säl-vä-dôr') sahl-vah-DORE
Salve Regina (sal'vē re-jī'nə) SAL-vee reh-JYE-nuh
Salween River (säl'wēn') sahl-WEEN
Salzburg (sâlz'bėrg) SAWLZ-berg
Samaria (sə-mar'ē-ə) suh-MA-ree-uh
Samarkand (sam'ər-kand') SAM-er-KAND
Sama-veda (sä-mə-vā'də) sah-muh-VAY-duh
Samoa (sä-mō'ə) sah-MO-uh
Samos (sā'mos) SAY-moss
Samoyed (sam'ə-yed') SAM-uh-YED
Sana (sä-nä') sah-NAH
San Andreas (san-an'drās) san-AN-drace
San Antonio (san-an-tō'nyō) san-an-TONE-yo
San Augustin (san-â-gəs-tēn') san-au-gus-TEEN
Sancho Panza (sän'chō-pän'thä) SAHN-cho-PAHN-thah
San Cristobal (sän-krē-stō'bäl) sahn-kree-STO-bahl
San Diego (san-dē-ā'gō) san-dee-A-go
Sangre de Cristo (sang'grē-də-kris'tō) SANG-greh-duh-KRIS-toe
Sanhedrin (san'hə-drin) SAN-huh-drin
San Jacinto (san-hä-sēn'tō) san-hah-SEEN-toe
San Joaquin (san-wä-kēn') san-wah-KEEN
San José (san-hō-sā') san-hoe-SAY
San Juan (san-hwän') san-WAHN
Sanjuro (sän-hūr'ō) sahn-HOOR-oh
San Marcello (sän-mär-chel'ə) sahn-mar-CHELL-oh
San Marcos (sän-mär'kōs) sahn-MAR-kohce
San Marino (sän-mə-rē'nō) sahn-muh-REE-no
San Martin (sän-mär-tēn') sahn-mar-TEEN
San Remo (sän-rā'mō) sahn-RAY-mo
Sanskrit (san'skrit) SAN-skrit
Sans-Souci (säñ-soo-sē') sahn-soo-SEE
Santa Anna (sän'tä ä'nä) SAHN-tah AH-nah
Santa Cruz (sän'tä-kroos') sahn-tah-KROOCE
Santa Fe (san'tə-fā') san-tuh-FAY
Santa Isabel (sän'tä-ē-sä-bel') SAHN-tah e-sah-BELL
Santa Maria (sän'tä-mä-rē'ə) SAHN-tah mah-REE-uh
Santee (san-tē') san-TEE
Santiago (san-tē-ä'gō or sänt-yä'gō) san-tee-A-go or sahnt-YAH-go
Santo Domingo (san'tə-də-ming'gō) SAN-tuh-duh-MING-go
Santos (sän'tōs) SAHN-tohce
San Vicente (sän-vē-sen'tā) sahn-vee-SEN-tay
Saone (sōn) SONE
São Paulo (säñ-pow'lū) sahn-POW-luh
Sapphira (sə-fī'rə) suh-FYE-ruh
Sappho (saf'ō) SAFF-oh
Saracen (sar'ə-sən) SA-ruh-sun
Saragossa (sar'ə-gos'ə) SA-ruh-GAHCE-uh
Sarajevo (sä-rä'ye-vä) sah-RAH-yeh-vaw
Sarawak (sə-rä'wäk) suh-RAH-wock
Sardinia (sär-din'ē-ə) sar-DIN-e-uh
Sargasso (sär-gas'ō) sar-GAS-oh
Sargent (sär'jənt) SAR-junt
Sargon (sär'gon) SAR-gon
Sarki (sär'kē) SAR-kee
Saronic (sə-ron'ik) suh-RON-ick
Saroyan (sə-rō'yən) suh-ROY-ahn
Sarto (sär'tō) SAR-toe
Saskatchewan (sas-katch'ə-wən) sass-KATCH-uh-wun
Saskatoon (sas-kə-toon') sass-kuh-TOON
Saturn (sat'ərn) SAT-urn
Saudi Arabia (sä-oo'dē) sah-OO-dee
Sauer (sow'ər or zow'ər) SOUR or ZOW-er
Sauk (sâk) SAWK
Sault Sainte Marie (soo'sānt-mə-rē') SOO-saint-muh-REE
Sauria (sôr'ē-ə) SORE-e-uh
Sava (sä'vä) SAH-vah
Savaii (sä-vī'ē) sah-VYE-ee
Savoia (sə-vwä') sahve-WAY
Savonarola (sä'və-nä-rā'lə) sah-vah-nah-RAW-luh
Savoy (sə-voi') sa-VOY
Savoyard (sə-voi'ərd) suh-VOY-erd
Savu (sä'voo) SAH-voo
Sawatch (sə-woch') suh-WATCH
Sax (säks) SOX
Saxe-Coburg-Gotha (säks-kō'bėrg-gō'thə) sox-KO-berg-GO-thuh
Saxe-Weimar (säks-vī'mär) sox-VYE-mar
Saxon (sak'sən) SACK-sun
Saxony (sak'sə-nē) SACK-sun-e
Sayan (sə-yän') suh-YAHN
Saylor (sā'lər) SAY-ler
Scala (skä'lä) SKAH-lah
Scandinavia (skan'dī-nā'vē-ə) skan-dih-NAY-vee-uh
Scaramouche (skar'ə-moosh) SKA-ruh-moosh
Scarlatti (skär-lät'ē) skar-LAHT-e
Schalmey (shäl'mi) SHAHL-my
Schatz (shäts) SHAHTZ
Scheele (shā'lē) SHAY-lee
Scheer (shär) SHARE
Scheherazade (shə-her'ə-zäd) shuh-HARE-uh-zahd
Scheldt (skelt) SKELT
Schellenberg (shel'ən-berk) SHELL-un-behrk
Schickelgruber (shik'əl-groo-bər) SHICK-ul-groo-ber
Schiller (shil'ər) SHILL-er
Schlegel (shlā'gəl) SHLAY-gul
Schleiden (shlī'dən) SHLYE-dun
Schleswig-Holstein (shlez'wig-hōl'stīn) SHLEZ-wig HOLE-stine
Schleyer (shlī'ər) SHLYE-er
Schliemann (shlē'män) SHLEE-mahn
Schmeling (shmā'ling) SHMAY-ling
Schoharie (skə-har'ē) skuh-HARE-e
Schönbrunn (shön'brūn) SHERN-brun
Schopenhauer (shō'pən-how'ər) SHO-pun-HOW-er
Schouten (skow'tən) SKOW-tun
Schubert (shoo'bərt) SHOO-bert
Schumann (shoo'män) SHOO-mahn
Schurz (shūrtz) SHOORTZ
Schuschnigg (shūsh'nik) SHUHSH-nick
Schwann (shvän) SHVON
Schweitzer (shvī'tsər) SHVITE-ser
Scioto (sī-ō'tə) sigh-OH-tuh
Scorpio (skôr'pē-ō) SKORE-pee-oh
Scotia (skō'shə) SKO-shuh
Scotland (skot'lənd) SKOT-lund
Scutari (skoo'tə-rē) SKOO-tuh-ree
Scylla (sil'ä) SILL-uh
Scyros (sī'ros) SIGH-rahce
Sdot-Yam (sə-dōt'yəm) suh-DOTE-yom
Sealyham (sē'lē-əm) SEE-lee-um
Searles (sėrlz) SERLZ
Sears (sirz) SEERZ
Sebaste (sə-bas'tē) suh-BASS-tee
Seder (sā'dər) SAY-der
Segura (si-goo'rə) sih-GOO-ruh
Seine (sān or sen) SANE or SEN
Sejm (säm) SAME
Selangor (sə-lang'gôr)
Seleucia (sə-lū'shə) suh-LOO-shuh
Selene (sə-lēn'ē) suh-LEEN-e
Selig (sē'lig) SEE-lig
Seljuk (sel-jook') sel-JOOK
Selkirk (sel'kėrk) SELL-kerk
Semarang (sə-mə-räng') suh-muh-RAHNG
Semele (sem'ə-lē) SEM-uh-lee
Semite (sem'īt) SEM-ite
Seneca (sen'ə-kə) SEN-uh-kuh

Senefelder (zä′nə-fel′dər) ZAY-nuh-fell-der

Senegal (sen″ə-gâl′) sen-uh-GAWL

Sennacherib (sə-nak′ə-rib) suh-NACK-uh-rib

Senne (zen′ə) ZEN-uh

Seoul (sōl) SOLE

Sepoy (sē′poi) SEE-poy

Sequoia (sə-kwoi′ə) suh-KWOY-uh

Serapis (sə-rā′pis) suh-RAY-pis

Serbia (sĕr′bė-ə) SER-be-uh

Serb (sĕrb) SERB

Sernin (ser-nēn′) sare-NEEN

Serra do Mar (ser′ä dâ-mär′) SARE-ah daw-MAR

Sestos (ses′tos) SESS-tahce

Sevastopol (sə-vas′tə-pōl) suh-VASS-tuh-pole

Severn (sev′ərn) SEV-ern

Sevier (sə-vir′) suh-VEER

Sévigny (sā-vė-nyā′) say-veen-YAY

Seville (sə-vil′) suh-VILL

Sèvres (sev′rə) SEV-ruh

Seward (sū′ərd) SYOO-erd

Seymour (sē′môr) SEE-more

Sfax (sfäks) SFOX

Shadrach (shad′rak) SHAD-rack

Shafter (shäf′tər) SHAHF-ter

Shah Jehan (shä′jə-hän′) SHAH-juh-HAHN

Shakespeare (shāks′pir) SHAKES-peer

Shanghai (shang′hī) SHANG-high

Shangri-La (shang″grė-lä′) shang-gree-LAH

Shannon (shan′ən) SHAN-un

Shan (shan) SHAN

Shantok (shan′tok) SHAN-tock

Shapley (shap′lė) SHAP-lee

Sharaff (sha′raf) SHA-raff

Shari (shä′rė) SHAH-ree

Shatt al Arab (shät″äl-ä-räb′) shot-ahl-ah-RAHB

Shaughnessy (shâ′nə-sė) SHAW-nuh-see

Shawnee (shâ-nē′) shaw-NEE

Shearer (shir′ər) SHEER-er

Sheba (shē′bə) SHE-buh

Shechem (shē′kəm) SHE-kum

Sheen (shēn) SHEEN

Sheffield (shef′ėld) SHEF-eeld

Sheil (shēl) SHEEL

Shelley (shel′ė) SHELL-e

Shenandoah (shen″ən-dō′ə) shen-un-DOE-uh

Shenyang (shun-yäng′) shun-YAHNG

Shephard (shep′ərd) SHEP-erd

Sheraton (sher′ə-tən) SHARE-uh-tun

Sherbourne (shĕr′bərn) SHER-burn

Sheridan (sher′ə-dən) SHARE-uh-dun

Sherpa (sher′pə) SHER-puh

Shevuoth (shä-voo′ōth) shah-VOO-oath

Shiah (shē′ä) SHE-ah

Shih Huang-Ti (shir′hwäng′tē′) SHEER-WHONG-TEE

Shikoku (shė-kō′koo) she-KO-koo

Shilluk (shēl′look) SHEEL-look

Shiloh (shī′lō) SHY-lo

Shinto (shin′tō) SHIN-toe

Shiraz (shė-räz′) she-RAHZ

Shiré (shē′rā) SHE-ray

Shiva (shē′və) SHE-vuh

Shivah (shiv′ä) SHIV-ah

Shwe Dagon (shwē′ dä′gon) SHWEE DAH-gon

Shkumbi (shkoom′bė) SHKOOM-be

Sholes (shōlz) SHOLES

Shoshone (shō-shō′nė) sho-SHO-nee

Shulchan Aruch (shûl-khän′ ä-rook′) shuhl-KAHN ah-RUKE

Siam (sī-am′) sigh-AM

Sibelius (si-bā′lė-əs) sih-BAY-lee-us

Siberia (sī-bir′ė-ə) sigh-BEER-e-uh

Sicani (si-kā′ni) sih-KAY-nye

Sicily (sis′ə-lė) SIS-uh-lee

Siculi (sik′ə-lī) SICK-uh-lye

Siddons (sid′ənz) SID-unz

Sidon (sī′dən) SIGH-duu

Siegfried (sēg′frēd) SEEG-freed

Sieglinde (sēg′lind) SEEG-lind

Siena (sė-ā′nä) see-A-nah

Sierra de Guadarrama (sė-er′ə dā-gwä-*th*ä-rä′mə) see-AIR-uh day-gwah-thah-RAH-muh

Sierra Leone (lė-on′ə *or* lė-ōn′) lee-AHN-uh *or* lee-OHN

Sierra Madre (mä′*th*rā) MAH-thray

Sieyès (syā-yes′) syay-YES

Sigiriya (sig′i-ri-yə) SIG-ih-rih-yuh

Sikh (sēk) SEEK

Sikkim (sik′im) SICK-im

Sikorski, Sikorsky (si-kôr′ski) sih-KORE-skee

Silesia (sī-lē′zhə) sigh-LEE-zhah

Sils (zils) ZILCE

Silvaplana (sēl″vä-plä′nä) SEEL-vah-PLAH-nah

Simenon (sēm-nân′) seem-NAWN

Simeto (sė-mā′tâ) see-MAY-taw

Simla (sim′lə) SIM-luh

Simplon (sim′plon) SIM-plon

Sinai (sī′nī) SIGH-nye

Sind (sind) SIND

Sindhi (sin′dė) SIN-dee

Singapore (sing″gə-pôr) SING-guh-pore

Singaradja (sing″ə-rä′jə) SING-uh-RAH-juh

Singhalese (sing-gə-lēz′) sing-guh-LEEZ

Sinn Fein (shin-fān′) shin-FANE

Sioux (soo) SOO

Siret (sē′ret) SEE-ret

Sirius (sir′ė-əs) SEER-e-us

Sistine (sis′tin) SIS-tin

Sitka (sit′kə) SIT-kuh

Siva (sē′vä) SEE-vah

Sjaelland (she′län) SHE-lahn

Skaggerak (skag′ə-rak) SKAG-uh-rack

Sklodowska (sklə-dâv′skə) skluh-DAWF-skuh

Skouras (skûr′əs) SKOOR-us

Skriabim (skrė-ä′bim) skree-AH-bim

Skuld (skûld) SKUHLD

Skye (skī) SKY

Slav (slâv) SLAHV *or* SLAV

Slavonic (slə-von′ik) sluh-VAHN-ick

Slidell (slī′dəl) SLY-dell

Sligo (slī′gō) SLY-go

Slovakia (slō-väk′ė-ə) slow-VAHK-e-uh

Slovak (slō′vak) SLOW-vack

Slovene (slō-vēn′) slow-VEEN

Smeaton (smē′tən) SMEE-tun

Smetana (sme′tə-nə) SMEH-tuh-nuh

Smuts (smuts) SMUTZ

Smyrna (smĕr′nə) SMER-nuh

Snead (snēd) SNEED

Snoqualmie (snō-kwäl′mė) snow-KWAHL-me

Socrates (sok′rə-tėz) SOCK-ruh-teez

Sodom (sod′əm) SOD-um

Soekarno (soo-kär′nō) soo-KAR-no

Sofia (sō′fė-ə) SO-fee-uh

Solis (sə-lēs′) suh-LEECE

Solon (sō′lən) SO-lun

Somaliland (sō-mä′li-land) so-MAH-lih-land

Somers (sum′ərz) SUM-erz

Somme (sâm) SAWM

Sonderbund (zon′dər-boond) ZON-der-boond

Sonoma (sə-nō′mə) suh-NO-muh

Sonora (sə-nôr′ə) suh-NOR-uh

Soo (soo) SOO

Sophocles (sof′ō-klėz) SAHF-oh-kleez

Sorbon (sôr-bâṅ′) sore-BAWN

Sorbonne (sôr-bon′) sore-BAHN

Sorb (sôrb) SORB

Sorrento (sə-ren′tō) suh-REN-toe

Sosignes (sō-sij′ə-nėz) so-SIDGE-uh-neez

Soto (sō′tō) SO-toe

Soubirous (soo-bė-roo′) soo-be-ROO

Souchong (soo′shâng) SOO-shawng

Soule (sōl) SOLE

Sousa (soo′sə) SOO-suh

Southey (su*th*′ė) SUH-the

Southwark (su*th*′ərk) SUH-therk

Soviet (sō-vė-et′) so-vee-ET

Spaatz (späts) SPOTS

Spain (spān) SPANE

Spallanzani (späl″län-tsä′nė) spah-lahnt-SAH-nee

Spandau (shpän′dow) SHPON-dow

Sparta (spär′tə) SPAR-tuh

Spartacus (spär′tə-kəs) SPAR-tuh-kus

Speke (spēk) SPEAK

Sperry (sper′ė) SPER-e

Sphinx (sfinx) SFINX

Spinoza (spi-nō′zə) spih-NO-zuh

Spitsbergen (spits′bĕr-gən) SPITS-ber-gun

Split (split *or* splēt) SPLIT *or* SPLEET

Spode (spōd) SPODE

Spree (shprā) SHPRAY

Spuyten Duyvil (spī′tən-dī″vəl) SPY-tun-DYE-vul

Spyri (shpē′rė) SHPEE-ree

Srinagar (srė-nug′ər) sree-NUG-er

Stabat Mater Dolorosa (stā′bat mā′tər dō-lə-rō′sə) STAY-bat MAY-ter doe-luh-ROE-suh

Stabiae (stā′bė-ė) STAY-be-e

Stacy (stā′sė) STAY-see

Stalin (stä′lin) STAH-lin

Stalingrad (stä′lin-grad) STAH-lin-grad

Stalinsk (stä′lyinsk) STAHL-yinsk

Stassfurt (shtäs′fûrt) SHTAHCE-foort

Staunton (stan′tən) STAN-tun

Stavanger (stä-vän′gər) stah-VAHN-gur

Stecher (stek′ər) STECK-er

Steele (stēl) STEEL

Stefansson (ste′fän-sən) STEH-fahn-sun

Stein (stīn) STINE

Steinbeck (stīn′bek) STINE-beck

Steinmetz (stīn′metz) STINE-metz

Stellenbosch (stel′ən-bûsh) STELL-un-bush

Stendhal (staṅ-däl′) stan-DAHL

Steuben (shtoi′bən) SHTOY-bun

Steunenberg (stoi′nən-bərg) STOY-nun-berg

Stheno (sthē′nō) STHEE-no

Stilocho (stil′ə-chō″) STILL-uh-cho

Stockholm (stok′hōm) STOCK-home

Stoic (stō′ik) STOH-ick

Storrs (stôrz) STORES

Storting (stôr′ting) STORE-ting

Stowe (stō) STOH

Stradivari (strä″də-vä′rė) strah-duh-VAH-ree

Stradivarius (strad″i-vâr′ė-əs) strad-ih-VARE-e-us

Strasbourg (sträs′bĕrg) STRAHCE-berg

Strassman (shträs′män) SHTRAHCE-mahn

Strathcona (strath-kō′nə) strath-KO-nuh

Strauss (shtrows) SHTROWCE

Stravinsky (strə-vin′skė) struh-VIN-skee

Stritch (strich) STRITCH

Stuart (stū′ərt) STYOO-ert

Stuyvesant (stī′və-sənt) STY-vuh-sunt

Stymphalus (stim-fā′ləs) stim-FAY-lus

Styx (stiks) STICKS

Subotica (soo′bâ-ti-tsä) SOO-baw-tit-sah

Sucre (soo′krā) SOO-kray

Sudan (soo-dan′) soo-DAN

Sudetenland (soo-dā′tən-lond) soo-DAY-tun-lond

Sudra (soo′drə) SOO-druh

Suevi (swē′vī) SWEE-vye

Suez (soo-ez′) soo-EZ

Suleiman (sū-lā-män′) suh-lay-MAHN

Sulu (soo′loo) SOO-loo

Sumatra (sû-mä′trə) suh-MAH-truh

Sumer (soo′mər) SOO-mer

Sumerian (sū-mir′ė-ən) syoo-MEER-e-un

Sumida (sûm′ə-dä) SUHM-uh-dah

Sundarbans (soon′där-bənz) SOON-dar-bunz

Sunwapta (sən-wäp′tə) sun-WAHP-tuh

Sun Yat-sen (sûn yät-sen′) SUHN yant-SEN

Surabaja (soo-rä-bä′yä) soo-rah-BAH-yah

Surakarta (soo-rä-kär′tä) soo-rah-KAR-tah

Surinam (sûr-i-näm′) suhr-ih-NAHM

Susquehanna (sus″kwė-han′ə) suss-kwee-HAN-uh

Sussex (sus′iks) SUSS-ix

Susten (zûs′tən) ZOOS-tun

Susu (soo′soo) SOO-soo

Sutter (soo′tər) SOO-ter

Suva (soo′vä) SOO-vah

Suwanee (sə-wâ′nė *or* swä′nė) suh-WAW-nee *or* SWAH-nee

Svealand (svā′ə-land) SVAY-uh-land

Swahili (swä-hē′lė) swah-HE-lee

Swanee (swä′nė) SWAH-nee

Swansea (swon′zė) SWAHN-zee

Swartberg (svärt′berkh) SVART-behrk

Swazi (swä′zė) SWAH-zee

Sweden (swē′dən) SWEE-dun

Swedenborg (swē′dən-bôrg) SWEE-den-borg

Swinburne (swin′bĕrn) SWIN-bern

Swithin (swi*th*′ən) SWITH-un

Sydney (sid′nė) SID-nee

Sylvania (sil-vā′nė-ə) sil-VAY-nee-uh

Symington (sīm′ing-tən) SIME-ing-tun

Symmes (simz) SIMZ

Syracuse (sir′ə-kūs) SERE-uh-kyooce

Syria (sir′e-ə) SERE-e-uh

Szechwan (se′chwän) seh-CHWAHN

Szeged (se′ged) seh-GED

Tabriz (tä-brēz′) tah-BREEZE

Tacitus (tas′i-təs) TASS-ih-tuss

Tacoma (tə-kō′mə) tuh-KO-muh

Taconic (tə-kon′ik) tuh-KON-ick

Tadzhik (tä-jik′) tah-JICK

Tafir (taf′ər) TAFF-er

Tagalog (tä-gä′log) tah-GAH-log

Tagore (tä′gôr) TAH-gore

Tagus (tā′gəs) TAY-gus

Tahiti (tä-hē′tė) tah-HE-tee

Tahoe (tä′hō) TAH-ho

Taikowa (tī′kə-wə) TYE-kuh-wuh

Taipeh, Taipei (tī-pe′) tye-PEH

Taiwan (tī-wän′) tye-WAHN

Taj Mahal (tazh″mə-häl′) TAZH muh-HAHL

Tajo (tä′hō) TAH-ho

Taku River (tä′koo) TAH-koo

Talamanca (tä-lä-mäng′kä) tah-lah-MAHNG-kah

Taliesin (tal′i-sən) TAL-ih-sun

Tallahassee (tal″ə-has′ė) tal-uh-HASS-e

Talleyrand (ta-lā-räṅ′) ta-lay-RAHN

Tallinn (tä′lin) TAH-lin

Tallulah (tə-loo′lə) tuh-LOO-luh

Talmud (tal′mud) TAL-mud

Talos (tā′los) TAY-lahce

Tamar (tā′mər) TAY-mer

Tamatave (tä-mä-täv′) tah-mah-TAHVE

Tamerlane (tam′ər-lān) TAM-er-lane

Tamil (tam′il) TAM-ill

Tammany (tam′ə-nė) TAM-uh-nee

Tampa (tam′pə) TAM-puh

Tana (tä′nä) TAH-nah

Tananarive (tä-nä-nä-rēv′) tah-nah-nah-REEVE

Tanana (tan′ə-nâ) TAN-uh-naw

Tanganyika (tan-gan-yē′kə) tan-gan-YEE-kuh

Tangier (tan-jir′) tan-JEER

Tan′gun (täng′gun″) TAHNG-gun

Tannenberg (tan′ən-bĕrg) TAN-un-berg

Tannhäuser (tän′hoi-zər) TAHN-hoy-zer

Taoism (dow′iz-əm) DOW-iz-um

Taos (tä′os) TAY-oss

Tao-Teh-King (dow′de″jing′) DOW-deh-JING

Tappan (ta-pan′) ta-PAN

Tara (tar′ə) TAR-uh

Tarawa (tä-rä-wä′) tah-rah-WAH

Tarentum (tə-ren′təm) tuh-REN-tum

Tarquin (tär′kwin) TAR-kwin

Tarragona (tar″ə-gō′nə) ta-ruh-GO-nuh

Tarshish (tär′shish) TAR-shish

Tarsus (tär′səs) TAR-suss

Tartaglia (tär-täl′yä) tar-TAHL-yah

Tartar (tär′tär) TAR-tar

Tartessus (tär-tes′əs) tar-TESS-us

Tasman (täs′män) TAHCE-mahn

Tasmania (taz-mā′nė-ə) taz-MAY-nee-uh

Tasso (täs′sō) TASS-oh

Tatar (tä′tär) TAH-tar

Tatra (tä′trə) TAH-truh

Taurini (tâ-rī′nī) taw-RYE-nye

Taurus (tâ′rəs) TAW-russ

Tbilisi (ət-bil-yē′sė) ut-bil-YEE-see

Tchaikowsky (chī-kâf′skė) chye-KAWF-skee

Tecumseh (ti-kum′sə) tih-KUM-suh

Tecum Uman (tē′kəm oo′mon) TEE-kum OO-mon

Tefnut (tef′nût) TEFF-nuht

Tegucigalpa (te-goo′sė-gäl′pä) teh-GOO-see-GAHL-pah

Teheran (te-hrän′) teh-huh-RAHN

Tehuelche (tə-wel′chə) tuh-WELL-chuh

Tejo (tā′zhoo) TAY-zhoo

Tel Aviv (tel″ä-vēv′) tell-ah-VEEV

Tempelhof (tem′pəl-hōf) TEM-pel-hofe

Tenerife (ten-ə-rēf′) ten-uh-REEF

Tenniel (ten′yəl) TEN-yell

Tennyson (ten′ə-sən) TEN-uh-sun

Tenochtitlan (tā-nō-chet-län′) tay-no-chet-LAHN

Terceira (ter-sā′rə) tare-SAY-ruh

Terek (tye′rik) TYEH-rick

Terhune (tĕr-hūn′) ter-HEWN

Terman (tĕr′mən) TER-mun

Terminus (tĕr′mi-nəs) TER-mih-nuss

Terpsichore (tĕrp-sik′ə-rė) terp-SICK-uh-ree

Terre Haute (ter-ə-hōt′) tare-uh-HOTE

Teton (tē′ton) TEE-tahn

Tetrazzini (tā″trä-tsē′nė) TAY-trot-SEE-nee

Teuton (tū′ton) TYOO-tahn

Teviot (tēv′yət) TEEV-yut

Thackeray (thak′ə-rė) THACK-uh-ree

Thaddeus (tha-dē′əs) tha-DEE-us

Thai (tī) TY

Thailand (tī′land) TY-land

Thales (thā′lėz) THAY-leez

Thalia (thā-lī′ə) thay-LYE-uh

Thallophyta (thə-lof′i-tə) thuh-LAHF-ih-tuh

Thames (temz) TEMZ

Thayendanegea (thə-yen″də-nā′gė-ə) thuh-YEN-duh-NAY-gee-uh

Thayer (thâr) THAIR

Thebes (thēbz) THEEBZ

Themistocles (thə-mis′tə-klėz) thuh-MISS-tuh-kleez

Theocritus (thė-ok′ri-təs) thee-OCK-rih-tuss

Theodoric (thė-od′ə-rik) thee-ODD-uh-rick

Theophrastus (thē″ō-fras′təs) THEE-oh-FRASS-tuss

Thermopolis (thĕr-mop′ə-lis) ther-MOP-uh-liss

Thermopylae (thĕr-mop′ə-lī) ther-MOP-uh-lye

Theseus (thē′sūs *or* thē′sė-əs) THEE-syooce *or* THEE-see-us

Thessalonica (the″sä-lä-nē′kə) theh-sah-lah-NEE-kuh

Thessaly (thes′ə-lė) THESS-uh-lee

Thetis (thē′tis) THEE-tiss

Thibault (tē′bō″) TEE-bo

Thiminnier (tė-mâ-nyā′) tee-mawn-YAY

Thisbe (thiz′bė) THIZZ-be

Thomism (tō′miz-əm) TOE-miz-um

Thonburi (tân″bû-rē′) tawn-buh-REE

Thor (thôr) THORE

Thoreau (thôr′ō) THORE-oh

Thorvaldsen (tûr′val-sən) TOUR-val-sun

Thrace (thrās) THRACE

Thuban (thoo-bän′) thoo-BAHN

Thucydides (thū-sid′ə-dėz) thoo-SID-uh-deez

Thule (thū′lė) THYOO-lee

Thurber (thĕr′bər) THER-ber

Thurston (thĕr′stən) THER-stun

Tibbus (tēb′boos) TEE-booce

Tiber (tī′bər) TYE-ber

Tiberias (tī-ber′ė-əs) tye-BARE-e-us

Tibet (ti-bet′) tih-BET

Ticinus Mena (ti-sī′nəs mē′nə) tih-SIGH-nuss ME-nuh

Ticonderoga (tī-kon″də-rō′gə) tye-KON-duh-ROE-guh

Tiel (tēl) TEEL

Tientsin (tin-sin′) tin-SIN

Tiergarten (tir′gär″tən) TEER-gar-tun

Tierra del Fuego (tye′rə-del-fwā′gō) TYEH-ruh-del-FWAY-go

Tietê (tyi-tā′) tyih-TAY

Tiflis (tif′lis) TIFF-liss

Tigris (tī′gris) TYE-griss

Tilden (til′dən) TILL-dun

Tilghman (til′mən) TILL-mun

Timaeus (tī-mē′əs) tye-ME-us

Timbuktu (tim-buk′too) tim-BUCK-too

Timor (tē′môr) TEE-more

Timsah (tim′sə) TIM-suh

Timur (tė-moor′) tee-MOOR

Tinicum (tin′i-kəm) TIN-ih-kum

Tintoretto (tin″tə-ret′ō) tin-tuh-RET-oh

Tioga (tī-ō′gə) tye-OH-guh

Tippecanoe (tip″ə-kə-noo′) tip-uh-kuh-NOO

Tiquina (tė-kē′nə) tee-KEE-nuh

Tirana (tė-rä′nə) tee-RAH-nuh

Tirnovo (tĕr′nə-və) TER-nuh-vuh

Tishri (tish′rė) TISH-ree

Tissaphernes (tis″ə-fĕr′nėz) tiss-uh-FER-neez

Tisza (tis′ə) TISS-uh

Titan (tī′tən) TYE-tun

Tithonus (ti-thō′nəs) tih-THO-nus

Titian (tish′ən) TISH-un

Titicaca (tit″ə-kä′kə) tit-uh-KAH-kuh

Tito (tē′tō) TEE-toe

Titus (tī′təs) TYE-tus

Tiu (tē′oo) TEE-oo

Tjiliwong (chē′lē-wong) CHEE-lee-wong

Tlingit (tling′git) TLING-git

Tobago (tə-bā′gō) tuh-BAY-go

Tobit (tō′bit) TOE-bit

Tobolsk (tō-bōlsk′) toe-BOHLSK

Tobruk (tō-brûk′) toe-BROOK

Tocorpuri (tō″kôr-poo′rė) toe-kore-POO-ree

Tojo Hideki (tâ′jâ hė-də-kē′) TAW-jaw he-duh-KEE

Tokyo (tō′kyō) TOKE-yo

Toledo (tə-lē′dō) tuh-LEE-doh

Tolstoy (tol′stoi) TAHL-stoy

Toltec (tol′tek) TAHL-teck

Tomsk (tâmsk) TAWMSK

Tonga (tong′gə) TAHNG-guh

Tongass (tong′gəs) TAHNG-gus

Tongatabu (tâng″gä-tä′boo) TAWNG-gah-TAH-boo

Tongkin, Tongking, Tonkin (ton′kin) TAHN-kin

Topeka (tə-pē′kə) tuh-PEE-kuh

Tophet (tō′fət) TOE-fet

Torah (tō′rä) TOE-rah

Torino (tâ-rē′nâ) taw-REE-naw

Toronto (tə-ron′tō) tuh-RAHN-toe

Torquemada (tôr″kə-mä′*th*ä) tore-kuh-MAH-thah

Torrens (tôr′enz) TORE-unz

Torricelli (tôr″ə-chel′ė) tore-uh-CHELL-e

Tortola (tôr-tō′lə) tore-TOE-luh

Tortosa (tôr-tō′sə) tore-TOE-suh

Tortuga (tôr-too′gə) tore-TOO-guh

Toscanini (tos″kə-nē′nė) tahce-kuh-NEE-nee

Toulon (too-lâṅ′) too-LAWN

Toulouse (too-looz′) too-LOOZE

Toulouse-Lautrec (lō-trek′) low-TRECK

Tours (toorz) TOURS

Toussaint L'Ouverture (too-saṅ′ loo-ver-tür′) too-SAN loo-vare-TOUR

Toynbee (toin′bė) TOYN-be

Trafalgar (trə-fal′gər) truh-FAL-gur

Trajan (trā′jən) TRAY-jun

Transvaal (trans-väl′) tranz-VAHL

Transylvania (tran″sil-vā′nyə) tran-sil-VANE-yuh

Trapezus (tra-pē′zəs) tra-PEE-zus

Trebizond (treb′i-zond) TREB-ih-zond

Trento (tren′tâ) TREN-taw

Trenton (tren′tən) TREN-tun

Trevi (trā′vė) TRAY-vee

Trieste (trė-est′) tree-EST

Trinidad (trin′ə-dad) TRIN-uh-dad

Tripoli (trip′ə-lė) TRIP-uh-lee

Tristan (tris′tən) TRIS-tan

Tristram (tris′trəm) TRIS-trum

Triton (trī′tən) TRY-tun

Trois Rivières (trwä″rė-vyâr′) TRWAH-reeve-YARE

Trojan (trō′jən) TROH-jun

Trollope (trol′əp) TRAHL-up

Trondheim (trân′hām) TRAWN-hame

Trotsky (trot′skė) TROT-skee

Trovatore (trō-vä-tō′re) troh-vah-TOE-reh

Troy (troi) TROY

Truckee (truk′ė) TRUCK-e

Trujillo (troo-hē′yâ) troo-HE-yaw

Truk (trûk *or* truk) TROOK *or* TRUCK

Trygve Lie see Lie

Tsaldares (tsäl-*th*ä′res) tsahl-THAH-ress

Tsaritsyn (tsär-it-sin′) tsar-it-SIN

Tschaikowsky (chi-kâf′skė) chye-KAWF-skee

Tsingling (chin′ling) CHIN-ling

Tuareg (twä′reg) TWAH-reg

Tucson (too′son) TOO-sahn

Tucumán (too-koo-män′) too-koo-MAHN

Tudor (too′dər) TOO-der

Tuileries (twē′lə-rėz) TWEE-luh-reez

Tula (too′lə) TOO-luh

Tulalip (too-lā′lip) too-LAY-lip

Tulare (too-lär′ *or* too-lä′rā) too-LAR *or* too-LAH-reh

Tulsa (tul′sə) TUL-suh

Tumacacori (too-mə-kak′ə-rė) too-muh-KACK-uh-ree

Tungus (tûn-gûz′) tuhn-GUHZ

Tunis (tyoo′nis) TYOO-niss

Tunisia (tyoo-nish′ə) tyoo-NISH-uh

Tunney (tun′ė) TUN-e

Tupungato (too-poong-gä′tō) too-poong-GAH-toe

Turia (too′ryä) TOUR-yah

Turin (tyoo′rin) TYOO-rin

Turkey (tĕr′kė) TER-kee

Turku (tûr′koo) TOOR-koo

Turnus (tĕr′nəs) TER-nus

Turrialba (tûr-yäl′vä) tour-YAHL-vah

Tuscan (tus′kən) TUS-kun

Tuscany (tus′kə-nė) TUS-kuh-nee

Tuscarora (tus″kə-rôr′ə) TUS-kuh-RORE-uh

Tuskegee (tus-kē′gė) tus-KEE-ghee

Tut-ankh-amen (toot″onk-ä′mən) TOOT-ahnk-AH-mun

Tutuila (too″tə-ē′lä) TOO-tuh-EE-lah

Tuzigoot (too′zi-goot) TOO-zih-goot

Twain (twān) TWANE

Tweedsmuir (twēdz′mūr″) TWEEDS-myoor

Twillingate (twil′ing-gət) TWILL-ing-gut

Tyler (tī′lər) TY-ler

Tym (tim) TIM

Tyndale (tin′dəl) TIN-dull

Tyre (tīr) TIRE

Tyrian (tir′ė-ən) TEER-e-un

Tyrol (tī′rōl *or* ti-rōl′) TY-role *or* tih-ROLE

Tyrrhenian (ti-rē′nė-ən) tih-REE-nee-un

Tyrvää (tĕr′vä) TER-vah

Ubangi (oo-bang′gė) oo-BANG-ghee

Ubangi-Shari (shä′rė) SHAH-ree

Ubon Rat-thani (oo′bân-rät-thä′nė) OO-bawn-raht-THAH-nee

Ucayali River (oo″kä-yä′lė) OO-kah-YAH-lee

Udall (ū′dəl) YOO-dul

Uffizi (oo-fēt′sė) oo-FEET-see

Uganda (oo-gän′də) oo-GAHN-duh

Uinta (ū-in′tə) yoo-IN-tuh

Ukraine (ū-krān′) yoo-KRANE

Ulan Bator (oo′län-bä′tôr) OO-lahn-BAH-tore

Ulan-Ude (oo-län′oo-de′) oo-LAHN-oo-DEH

Ulio (ū′lė-ō) YOO-lee-oh

Ulster (ul′stər) ULL-ster

Ulua River (oo-loo′ä) oo-LOO-ah

Ulyanov (ûl-yä′nof) ool-YAH-noff

Ulysses (yû-lis′ėz) yoo-LISS-eez

Umpqua (ump′kwä) UMP-kwah

Unaka Mts. (ū-nā′kə) yoo-NAY-kuh

Undset (ûn′set) UHN-set

Upanishad (û-pan′i-shad″) uh-PAN-ih-shad

Upolu (oo-pō′loo) oo-POE-loo

Uppsala (up′sä″lə) UP-sah-luh

Ur (ĕr) ER

Ural (yûr′əl *or* oo-räl′) YOUR-ul *or* oo-RAHL

Urania (ū-rā′nė-ə) yoo-RAY-nee-uh

Uranus (yûr′ə-nəs) YOUR-uh-nuss

Urbana (ər-ban′ə) er-BAN-uh

Urd (ûrd) OORD

Urdu (ûr′doo) OOR-doo

Urgel (ûr-hel′) oor-HELL

Uriah (yû-rī′ə) yoo-RYE-uh

Uruguay (yûr′ə-gwī″) YOUR-uh-gwye

Usk (usk) USK

Ute (yoot) YOOT

Uther Pendragon (ū′thər pen-drag′ən) YOO-ther pen-DRAG-un

Utica (ū′ti-kə) YOO-tih-kuh

Utopia (ū-tō′pė-ə) yoo-TOE-pee-uh

Utrecht (ū′trekt) YOO-trekt

Utrillo (oo-trē′lō) oo-TREE-lo

Uzbek (ûz′bek) UHZ-beck

Vaal (väl) VAHL

Vaduz (vä-doots′) vah-DOOTS

Vail (vāl) VALE

Vaisya (vīsh′yə) VYSH-yuh

Valdai (vul-dī′) vul-DIE

Valdivia (väl-dē′vyä) vahl-DEEVE-yah

Valencia (və-len′shė-ə) vuh-LEN-she-uh

Valenciennes (vä-laṅ-syen′) vah-lance-YEN

Valhalla (val-hal′ə) val-HAL-uh

Valkyrie (val′ki-rė) VAL-kih-ree

Vallejo (və-lā′hō) vuh-LAY-ho

Valletta (və-let′ə) vuh-LET-uh

Valois (väl-wä′) vahl-WAH

Valparaiso (val-pä-rī′zō) val-pah-RYE-zo

Van Alstyne (van-âl′stīn) van-ALL-stine

Van Buren (van-byûr′ən) van-BYOUR-un

Vancouver (van-koo′vər) van-KOO-ver

Vandalusia (van-də-loo′zhə) van-duh-LOO-zhuh

Van de Graaf (van′də-graf″) VAN-duh-graf

Van Dyck (van-dīk′) van-DIKE

van Eyck (van-īk′) van-IKE

Vargas (vär′gəs) VAR-gus

Varhegy (vär-hed′yə) var-HED-yuh

Varus (vâr′əs) VARE-us

Vasa (vä′sä) VAH-sah

Vassar (vas′ər) VASS-er

Vatican (vat′i-kən) VAT-ih-kun

Vaudois (vō-dwä′) vo-DWAH

Vavau (vä-vow′) vah-VOW

Vecelli (ve′chel′ė) veh-CHELL-e

Vedanta (ve-dän′tä) veh-DAHN-tah

Veda (vā′də) *or* vē′də) VAY-duh- *or* VEE-duh

Velásquez (ve-läth′keth) veh-LAHTH-keth

Vence (väṅs) VAHNCE

Veneti (ven′i-tī″) VEN-ih-tie

Venezuela (ven″ə-zwā′lə) ven-uh-ZWAY-luh

Venice (ven′is) VEN-iss

Venizelos (vā″nye-zā′los) vane-yeh-ZAY-lahce

Venus (vē′nəs) VEE-nuss

Vera Cruz (ver″ə-krooz′) vare-uh-KROOZ

Verdi (ver′dė) VARE-dee

Verdun (ver-dun′) vare-DUN

Verdundi (vĕr′*th*ən-dė) VER-thun-dee

Veregin (ver″ə-gēn′) veh-ruh-GEEN

Verendrye (ver′ən-drī″) VARE-un-dry

Vergil (vĕr′gəl) VER-jul

Vergine (ver-zhē′ne) vare-ZHEE-neh

Vermeer (vər-mār′) ver-MARE

Verne (vĕrn) VERN

Veronese (ver-ə-nā′se) vare-uh-NAY-seh

Verrazano (ver″ət-sä′nō) vare-ut-SAH-no

Versailles (ver-sī′yə) vare-SIGH-yuh

Vesalius (və-sā′lė-əs) vuh-SAY-lee-us

Vespasian (ves-pā′zhən) vess-PAY-zhun

Vespucci (ves-pū′chė) vess-PEW-chee

Vesta (ves′tə) VESS-tuh

Vesteraalen (ves″tər-â′lən) vest-er-AW-lun

Vesuvius (ve-soo′vė-əs) veh-SOO-vee-us

Vettore (ve-tôr′ė) veh-TORE-ee

Vichy (vish′ė) VISH-e

Victoria (vik-tôr′ė-ə) vick-TORE-e-uh

Vienna (vė-en′ə) vee-EN-uh

Vientiane (vyaṅ-tyäṅ′) vyan-TYAHN

Viet Minh (vē′ət min′) VEE-ut MIN

Viet Nam (vē′ət-nom″) VEE-ut-NOM

Vijosë (vė-yō′sė) vee-YO-see

Viking (vē′king) VEE-king

Vila (vē′lä) VEE-lah

Vilija (vē′lė-yä) VEE-lee-yah

Villanova (vil″ə-nō′və) vil-uh-NO-vuh

Villarrica (bē″yä-rē′kä) bee-yah-REE-kah

Villefranche (vē″yə-fräṅsh′) veel-FRAHNSH

Villeneuve (vē″yə-nüv′) veel-NERVE

Villon (vė-yân′) vee-YAWN

Vilna (vil′nə) VIL-nuh

Viminal (vim′i-nəl) VIM-ih-nul

Vincennes (vin-senz′) vin-SENZ

Virgil (vĕr′jəl) VER-jul

Virgin Gorda (vĕr′jin-gôr′də) VER-jin GORE-duh

Virgo (vĕr′gō) VER-go

Vishinsky (vi-shin′skė) vih-SHIN-skee

Vishnu (vish′noo) VISH-noo

Visigoth (viz′i-goth″) VIZ-ih-gahth

Vistula (vis′chə-lə) VISS-chuh-luh

Viti Levu (vē′tė le-voo′) VEE-tee leh-VOO

Vizcaya (bith-kä′yä) bith-KAH-yah

Vladivostok (vlad″i-vos-tok′) VLAD-ih-vahce-TOCK

Vlona (vlō′nə) VLOH-nuh

Volga (vol′gə) VAHL-guh

Volstead (vol′sted) VAHL-sted

Volsunga saga (vol-sûng′gə sä′gə) vol-SOONG-guh SAH-guh

Volta (vâl′tä) VAWL-tah

Voltaire (vol′târ′) vahl-TARE

Vosges (vōzh) VOHZH

Vuelta-Abajo (bwel′tä-ä-bä′hō) BWEL-tah-ah-BAH-hoh

Vyrnwy (vĕr′noo-ė) VER-noo-ee

Waal (väl) VAHL

Waco (wā′kō) WAY-ko

Wahabi (wä-hä′bė) wah-HAH-be

Waiblingen (vīp′ling-ən) VIPE-ling-un

Waikiki (wī′ki-kē′) WYE-kih-KEE

Wakatipu (wä′kə-tip) WAH-kuh-tip

Waksman (waks′mən) WAX-mun

Walden (wâl′dən) WALL-dun

Walkure (väl′kü-re) VAHL-kih-reh

Wallachia (wâ-lā′kė-ə) waw-LAKE-e-uh

Walla Walla (wol′ə wol′ə) WAH-luh WAH-luh

Wallenstein (wol′ən-stīn″) WAHL-un-stine

Walloon (wä-loon′) wah-LOON

Walpole (wâl′pōl″) WALL-pole

Wampanoag (wom″pə-nō′əg) wahm-puh-NO-ug

Warmerdam (wär′mər-dam) WAR-mer-dam

Warsaw (wôr′sâ) WORE-saw

Warta (vär′tä) VAR-tah

Warwick (wâ′rik) WAW-rick

Wasatch (wâ′sach) WAW-satch

Washakie (wäsh′ä-kė) WAHSH-ah-kee

Wateree (wä′tə-rė) WAH-ter-e

Watogo (wä-tō′gə) wah-TOE-guh

Watteau (wâ-tō′) waw-TOE

Watusi, Watussi (wä-too′sė) wah-TOO-see

Waugh (wâ) WAW

Wavell (wā′vəl) WAY-vul

Weber (vā′bər) VAY-ber

Webi Shebeli (we′be-she-bel′lė) WEH-beh-sheh-BELL-ee

Wegner (weg′nər) WEG-ner

Weimar (vī′mär) VYE-mar

Weimaraner (vī′mə-rä″nər) VYE-muh-rah-ner

Weizmann (vīts′män) VITES-mahn

Wellesley (welz′lė) WELLS-lee

Wenceslas (wen′ses-los″) WEN-sess-lahce

Werfel (ver′fəl) VARE-fel

Weser (vā′zər) VAY-zer

Westphalia (west-fāl′yə) west-FAIL-yuh

Weygand (vā-gäṅ′) vay-GAHN

Wharton (hwôr′tən) WHAR-tun

Whitsunday (hwit′sun″dė) WHIT-sun-dee

Whittier (hwit′ė-ər) WHIT-e-er

Wichita (wich′ə-tâ″) WITCH-uh-taw

Wickersham (wik′ər-sham) WICK-er-sham

Wicklow (wik′lō) WICK-low

Wien (vē′ən) VEE-un

Wieprecht (vē′presht) VEE-presht

Wiggin (wig′in) WIG-in

Wilde (wīld) WILD

Wildspitze (vilt'shpit"sə) VILT-shpit-suh
Wilkes-Barre (wilks'bar-è) WILKS-ba-ree
Willamette (wi-lam'ət) wih-LAM-ut
Willemstad (vil'əm-stät') VILL-um-stot
Wimbleton (wim'bəl-tən) WIM-bel-tun
Winnebago (win"ə-bā'gō) win-uh-BAY-go
Winnepesaukee (win"i-pə-sâ'kē) win-ih-puh-SAW-kee
Winnipeg (win'i-peg') WIN-ih-peg
Winnipegosis (win"ē-pe-gō'sis) WIN-e-peh-GO-sis
Winooski (wi-noo'skē) wih-NOO-skee
Winyah (win'yä) WIN-yah
Wittelsbach (vit'əls-bäkh") VIT-ulce-bahk
Wittenberg (wit'ən-bərg) WIT-un-herg
Witwatersrand (wit-wä'tərz-rand) wit-WAW-terz-rand
Wodin (wō'dən) WOE-dun
Wöhler (völ'ər) vuhl-er
Wolfram (wŭlf'rəm) WOLF-rum
Wollaston (wŭl'əs-tən) WOOL-us-tun
Wollstonecraft (wŭl'stən-kräft) WOOL-stun-krahft
Wolsey (wŭl'zē) WOOL-zee
Woonsocket (woon-sok'it) woon-SOCK-it
Worcester (wŏos'tər) WUHCE-ter
Wotan (wō'tän) WOE-tahn
Wrangell (rang'gəl) RANG-gul
Wroclaw (vrât'släf) VRAWT-slahf

Wuchang (woo-chong') woo-CHONG
Wupatki (wŏ-pat'kē) woo-PAT-kee
Wycliffe (wik'lif) WICK-liff
Wye (wī) WYE-uth
Wyeth (wī'əth) WYE-uth
Xantippe (zan-tip'pē) zan-TIP-e
Xavier (zā'vē-ər) ZAY-vee-er
Xenophon (zen'ə-fən) ZEN-uh-fun
Xerxes (zėrk'sēz) ZERK-seez
Xylem (zī'ləm) ZY-lem

Yahweh (yä'we) YAH-weh
Yajur-veda (yuj'ŭr-vā'də) YUDGE-oor-VAY-duh
Yakima (yak'i-mä) YACK-ih-maw
Yakutsk (ya-kootsk) yuh-KOOTSK
Yalta (yäl'tə) YAWL-tuh
Yangtze (yang'sē") YANG-see
Yaoundé (yä"oon-dā') yah-oon-DAY
Yapok (ya-pok') yuh-POCK
Yarmuk (yär-mook') yar-MOOK
Yarra (yar'ə) YA-ruh
Yasnaya Polyana (yä'snī-ə-pəl-yä'nə) YAH-sny-uh-puhl-YAH-nuh
Yazoo (yaz'oo) YAZ-oo
Yeager (yä'gər) YAY-gur
Yeats (yäts) YATES

Yemen (yem'ən) YEM-un
Yenisei (yen-i-sā') yen-ih-SAY
Yerba Buena (yėr'bə bwä'nə) YER-buh BWAY-nuh
Yerevan (ye-re-vän') yeh-reh-VAHN
Yerkes (yėr'kēz) YER-keez
Yoho (yō'hō) YO-ho
Yokohoma (yō"kə-hä'mə) YO-kuh-HAH-muh
Yom Kippur (yōm kip'ər) YOME KIP-er
Yonkers (yong'kərz) YAHNG-kerz
Yonne (yon) YON
Yosemite (yō-sem'i-tē) yo-SEM-ih-tee
Ypres (ēpr) EE-pruh
Yucatan (yŏ-ka-tan') yoo-kuh-TAN
Yucca (yŭk'ə) YUHK-uh
Yugoslavia (yoo"gō-slä'vē-ə) yoo-go-SLAH-vee-uh
Yukon (yoo'kon) YOO-kon
Yuman (yoo'mən) YOO-mun

Zachariah (zak'ə-rī'ə) ZACK-uh-RYE-uh
Zacharias (zak'ə-rī'əs) ZACK-uh-RYE-us
Zagreb (zä'greb) ZAH-greb
Zaharias (zä-har'ē-əs) zah-HA-ree-us
Zambesi (zam-bē'zē) zam-BEE-zee
Zamenhof (zä'myen-häf) ZAH-myen-hawf
Zane (zän) ZANE

Zanzibar (zan'zə-bär") ZAN-zuh-bar
Zarathustra (zär-rä-thŏs'trə) zah-rah-THUCE-truh
Zbyszko (zbis'kō) ZBISS-ko
Zenger (zeng'gər) ZENG-ger
Zeno (zē'nō) ZEE-no
Zephaniah (zef-ə-nī'əh) zef-uh-NYE-uh
Zeppelin (zep'ə-lin or [Ger.] tsep'ə-lēn') ZEP-uh-lin or (in German) TSEP-uh-LEEN
Zeus (zoos) ZOOCE
Zhukov (zhoo'kof) ZHOO-kahf
Ziegfeld (zēg'felt) ZEEG-felt
Zobeide (zō-bī'də) zo-BYE-duh
Zog (zôg) ZOGUE
Zogu (zō'lä) ZO-zuh
Zola (zō'lä) ZO-lah
Zoroaster (zō-rō-as'tər) zo-ro-ASS-ter
Zsynthos (zə-sin'thos) zuh-SIN-thos
Zugspitze (tsŭk'shpit"zə) TSUHK-shpit-zuh
Zuider Zee (zī'dər-zā') ZYE-der-ZAY
Zulu (zoo'loo) ZOO-loo
Zuni (zoo'nyē) ZOON-ye
Zuppke (zup'kē) ZUP-kee
Zurich (zŏr'ik) ZOOR-ick
Zwickau (tsvik'ow) TSVICK-ow
Zwingli (tsving'lē) TSVING-lee
Zworykin (zwôr'i-kin) ZWORE-ih-kin

ATLAS
the world in maps

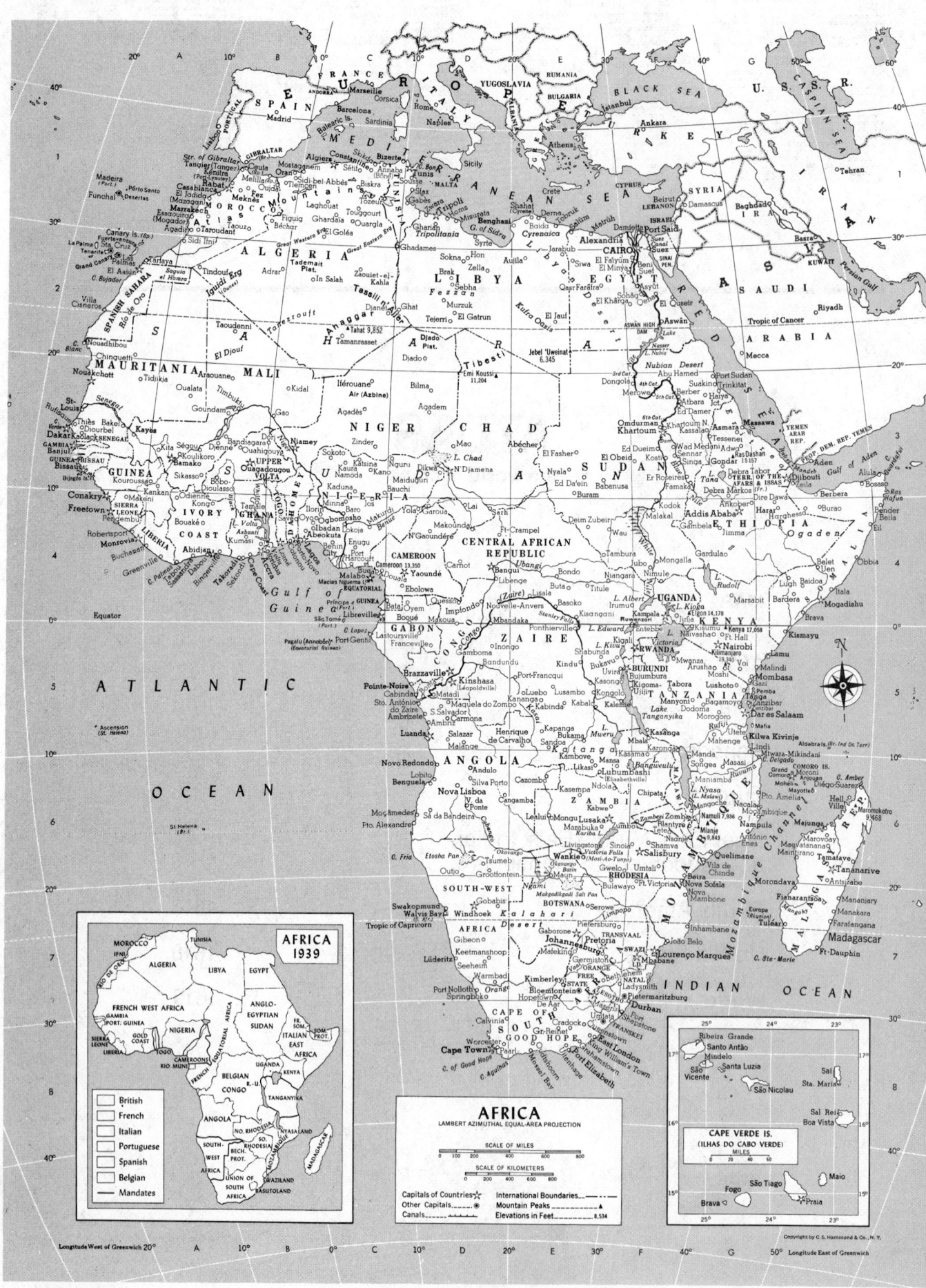

AFRICA 1939

British
French
Italian
Portuguese
Spanish
Belgian
Mandates

AFRICA
LAMBERT AZIMUTHAL EQUAL-AREA PROJECTION

SCALE OF MILES
0   100   200   400   600   800

SCALE OF KILOMETERS
0   200   400   600   800

Capitals of Countries ☆   International Boundaries
Other Capitals ⦿   Mountain Peaks ▲
Canals   Elevations in Feet   8,534

CAPE VERDE IS.
(ILHAS DO CABO VERDE)
MILES
0   20   40   60

Longitude West of Greenwich 20°

Copyright by C. S. Hammond & Co., N.Y.

Longitude East of Greenwich

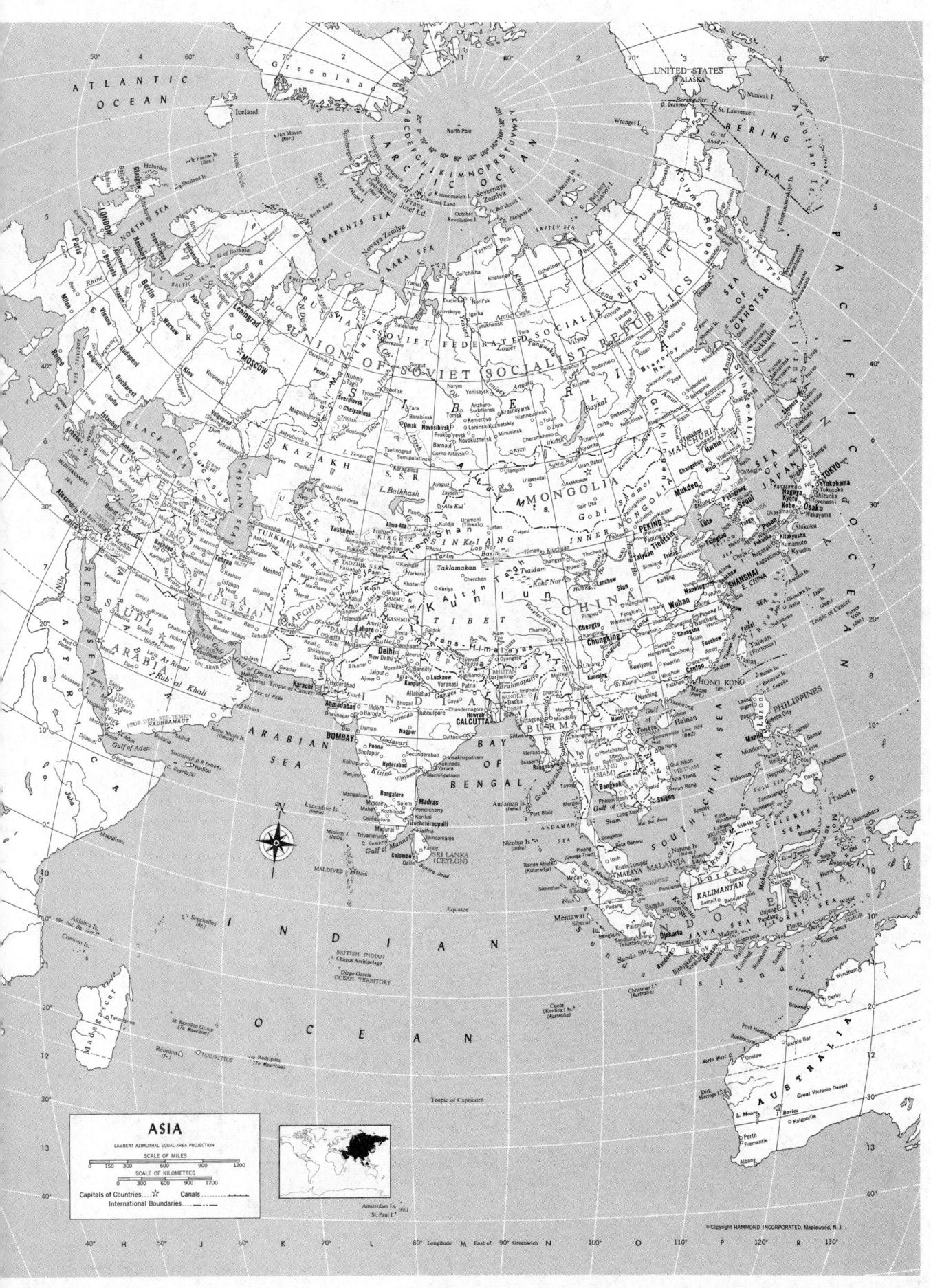

ASIA

LAMBERT AZIMUTHAL EQUAL-AREA PROJECTION

SCALE OF MILES

0   150   300   600   900   1200

SCALE OF KILOMETRES

0   300   600   900   1200

Capitals of Countries....☆   Canals ....
International Boundaries.........

© Copyright HAMMOND INCORPORATED, Maplewood, N.J.

CANADA

CONIC PROJECTION

SCALE OF MILES

SCALE OF KILOMETRES

Capitals of Countries
Provincial & Territorial Capitals
International Boundaries
Provincial Boundaries

Copyright by C.S. HAMMOND & Co., N.Y.

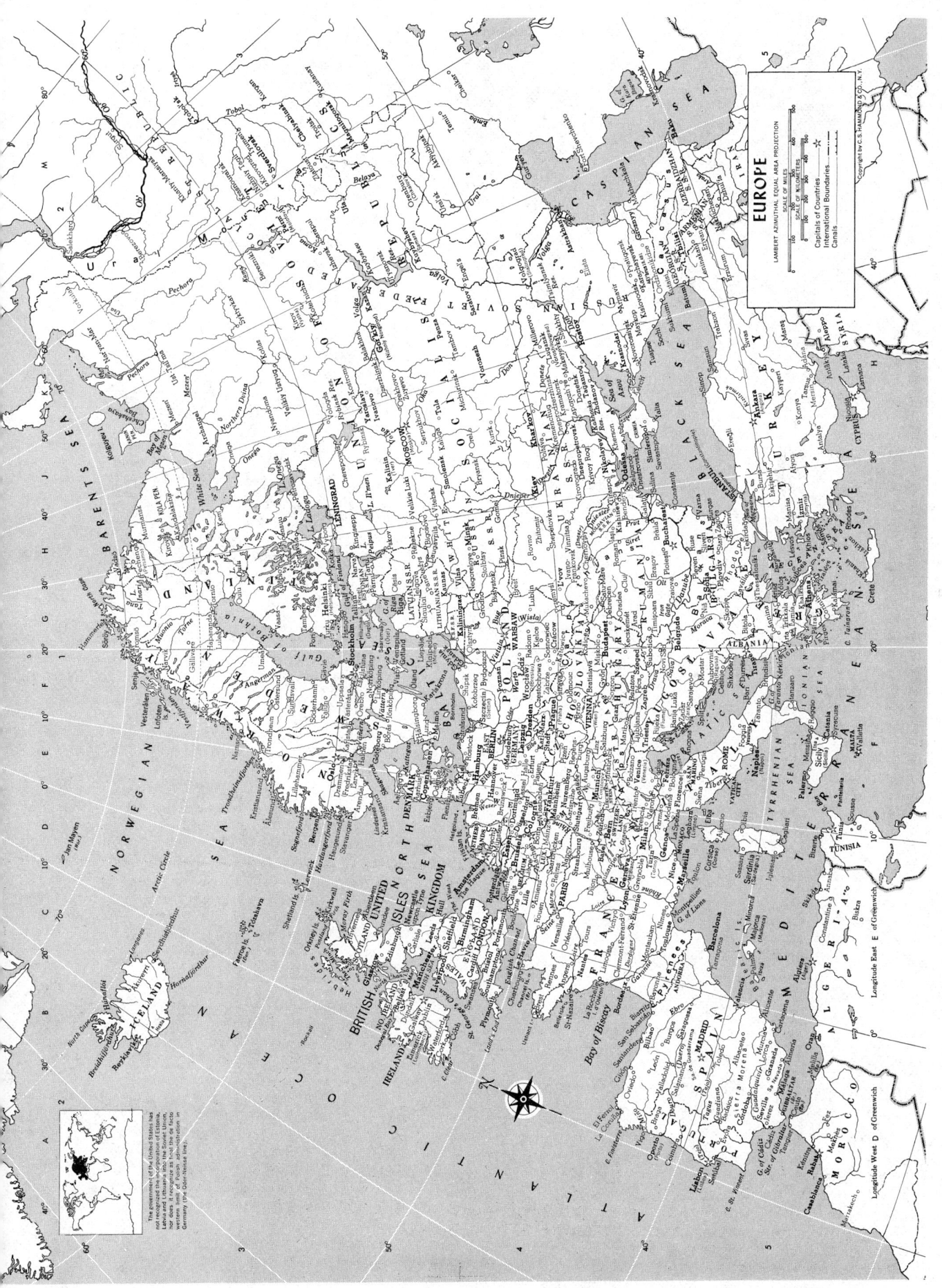

EUROPE

LAMBERT AZIMUTHAL EQUAL AREA PROJECTION

SCALE OF MILES

SCALE OF KILOMETERS

Capitals of Countries
International Boundaries
Canals

Copyright by C. S. HAMMOND & CO., N.Y.

The government of the United States has
not recognized the incorporation of Estonia,
Latvia and Lithuania into the Soviet Union,
nor does it recognize as final the de facto
western limit of Polish administration in
Germany (the Oder-Neisse line).

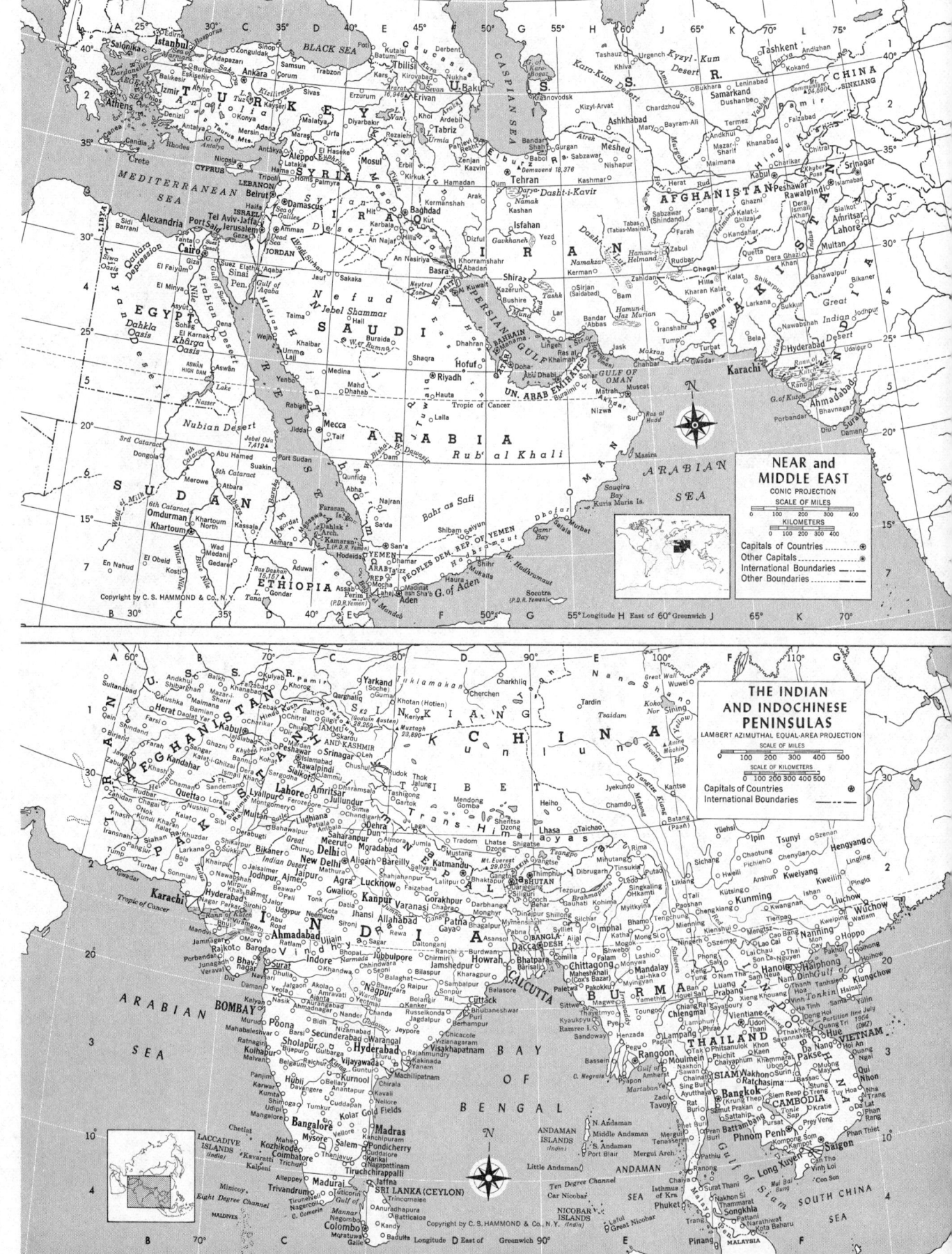

NEAR and MIDDLE EAST
CONIC PROJECTION
SCALE OF MILES
0 100 200 300 400
KILOMETERS
0 100 200 300 400
Capitals of Countries ⊛
Other Capitals ⊛
International Boundaries
Other Boundaries

THE INDIAN AND INDOCHINESE PENINSULAS
LAMBERT AZIMUTHAL EQUAL-AREA PROJECTION
SCALE OF MILES
100 200 300 400 500
SCALE OF KILOMETERS
0 100 200 300 400 500
Capitals of Countries ⊛
International Boundaries

Copyright by C. S. HAMMOND & Co., N. Y.

SOUTH AMERICA

LAMBERT AZIMUTHAL EQUAL-AREA PROJECTION

SCALE OF MILES

0   100   200   400   600

SCALE OF KILOMETERS

0 100 200   400   600

Capitals of Countries .... ☆
International Boundaries ...... – · – · –
Canals .... ┉┉┉┉

Copyright by C.S. HAMMOND & CO., N.Y.

GALÁPAGOS ISLANDS
(ARCHIPIÉLAGO DE COLON)
(To Ecuador)

SCALE OF MILES

PACIFIC OCEAN

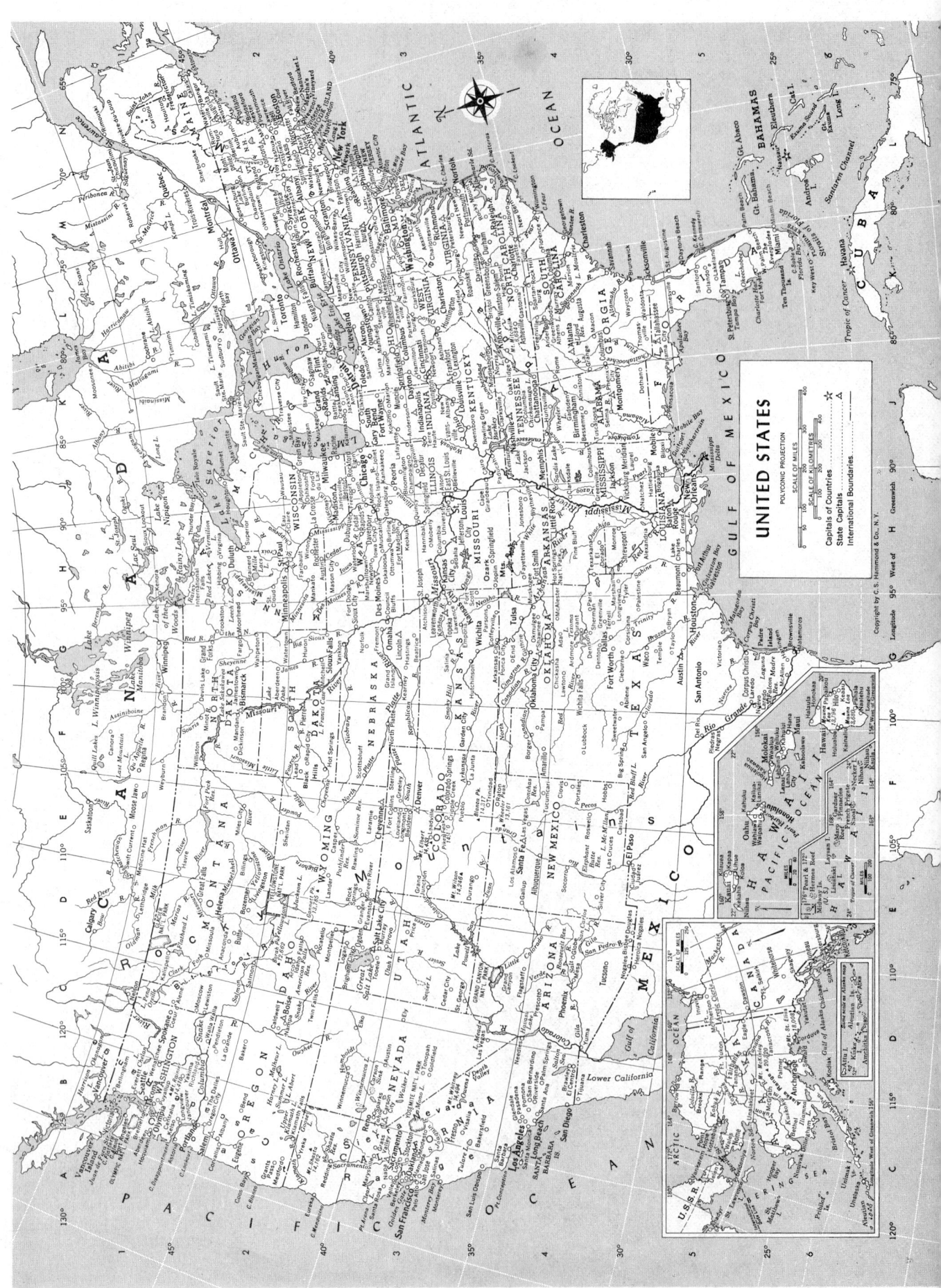

UNITED STATES

POLYCONIC PROJECTION

SCALE OF MILES

SCALE OF KILOMETRES

Capitals of Countries
State Capitals
International Boundaries

Copyright by C.S. Hammond & Co., N.Y.

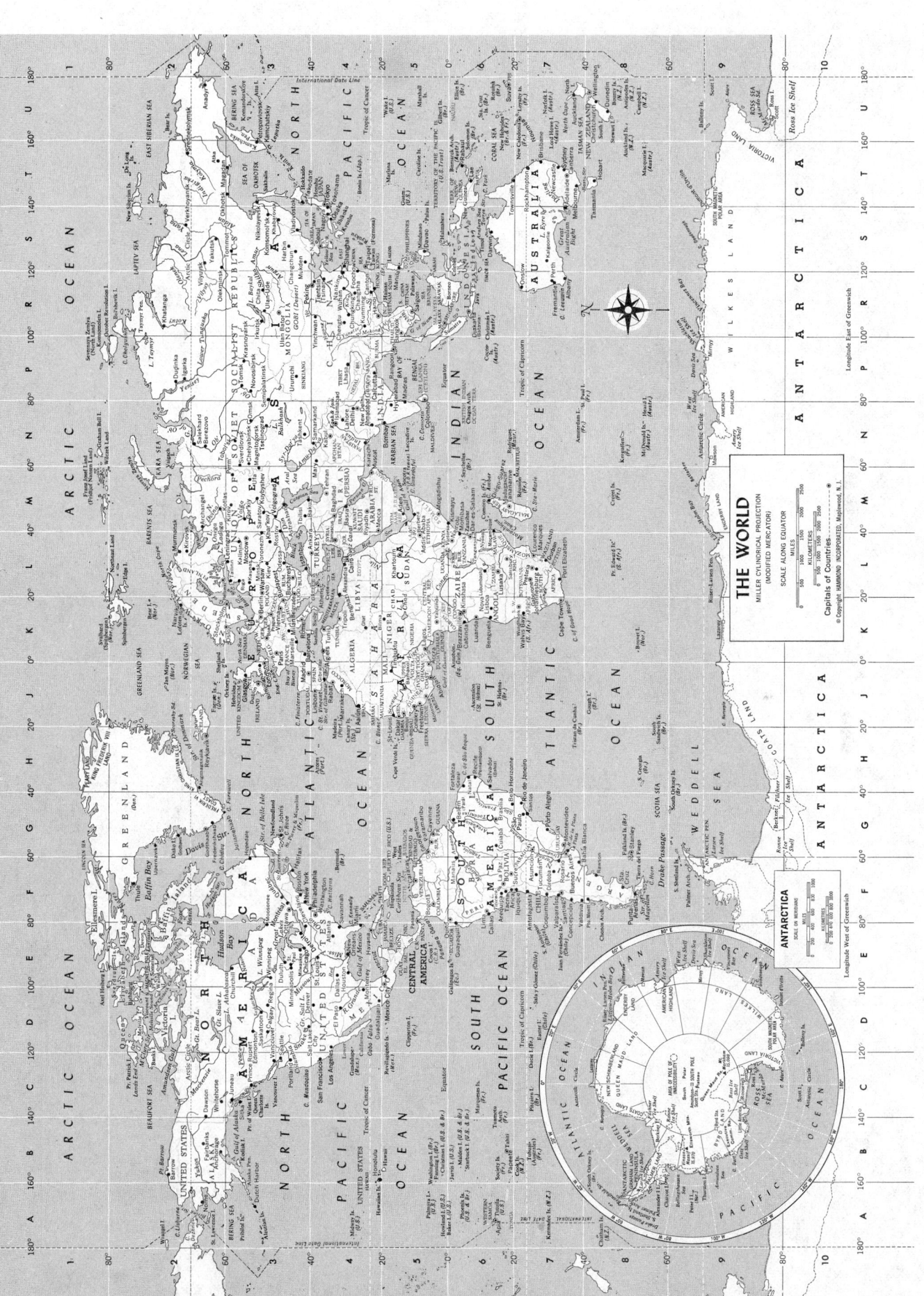